HUTCHINSON'S
NEW
20TH CENTURY
ENCYCLOPEDIA

Editor's Preface

A fuller text, more richly illustrated and widened in scope, is here presented in contemporary and attractive form and entirely brought up to date – especially in developments in technology and science – so that *Hutchinson's New 20th Century Encyclopedia* is more than ever the ideal one-volume reference work, indispensable in the schoolroom desk, on the office shelf, or beneath the television set in the family sitting-room. Aiming at comprehensiveness, we have not forgotten that facts, figures and abbreviations in close array tend to be indigestible – and un-consulted. In contrast, we have tried to stimulate rather than jade the appetite for knowledge and have made the encyclopedia selective, read-able, companionable, browseable, and even – on the appropriate occa-sion – amusing, so that it might not be classed either by younger or older readers among the dull reference tomes condemned by Charles Lamb as 'Things in book's clothing'.

Maps

COLOUR ATLAS
(following page 1118)

Note to the Reader

Pronunciation is indicated approximately by the following simple system:

VOWEL SOUNDS

a as in rack	eh as in Fr. née	oi as in boil
ā as in rake	i as in rick	oo as in book
ah as in father	ī as in mite	$\overline{oo}$ as in boot
āɼ as in mare	o as in rock	ow as in cow
aw as in raw	ō as in so	u as in but
e as in wreck	ö as in Fr. jeune	ü as in Fr. dune
ē as in mete	oh as in Fr. eau	ū as in mute

CONSONANT SOUNDS

b, d, f, h, j, k, l, m, n, p, r, t, v, w, z, present no difficulty; c, q, x, are not used in this key.

ch as in chip	ks for x	ngg as in finger
dh is soft as in this	kw as in quick	s is hard as in set
g is hard as in get	ṅ is nasal as in Fr. bon	th is hard as in think
kh as ch in Scots loch	ng as in singer	y is consonantal as in yet
		zh as in treasure (trezhur)

Abbreviations follow the standard forms and are included in the appendix, page 1113, an exception being the adoption of F.W.W. and S.W.W. to indicate the First and Second World Wars. In any article the title word (or words) may be represented by its initial letter (or letters), e.g. in the article AACHEN the letter A stands for Aachen.

A table of Customary Forms of Address follows on p. 1117.

A The first letter in nearly all the alphabets. The English *a* is derived from the Etruscan *a* through the Lat. alphabet, which is the parent of the West-European alphabets. The Greeks called the first letter *alpha*; the Semites *aleph* or *alph*, which meant 'ox', but more probably because the word began with this letter – a simple mnemonic device – than because the letter was formed as the rough outline of an ox-head, as some scholars have claimed.

AACHEN (ah'khen). German cathedral city and spa in the *Land* of North Rhine-Westphalia, about 5 m. E. of the frontier of Dutch Limburg and 45 m. W.S.W. of Cologne. It is a thriving industrial centre and one of Germany's principal railway junctions. A. was the Roman Aquisgranum, and from the time of Charlemagne until 1531 the German emperors were crowned there. Charlemagne was b. and buried in A., and he founded the cathedral in 796. The 14th cent. town hall, containing the hall of the emperors, is built on the site of Charlemagne's palace. During the S.W.W. A. was the first important German town captured by the Allies (U.S. 1st Army); it was severely damaged by bombing and 7 days' street fighting. Pop. (1969) 176,726.

AALBORG (awl'-). Danish port about 20 m. inland from the Kattegat, on the S. shore of the Limfjord. One of the oldest towns in Denmark, it has a castle and the fine Budolfi church. Pop. (1965) 85,632.

AALST. Flemish form of Alost.

AALTONEN (ahl'-), **Wäinö** (1894–1966). Finnish artist. At first a painter, he later turned to sculpture, and was a pioneer in the revival of carving directly from the stone, his favourite medium being granite. His works incl. portrait busts, notably one of Sibelius, and statues for the Finnish Parliament House and the Univ. of Helsinki.

AACHEN. Ancient bust of Charlemagne in gold and enamel preserved at Aachen, it was made as a reliquary in the 14th century.

AARDVARK (ahrd'-). Afrikaans name for the antbear (*Orycteropus afer*) found in central and southern

ABACUS. An illustration from Reisch's *Margarita Philosophica* (1503) showing Boetius using the Arabic and Pythagoras the abacus system: reproduced from J. M. Pullan, *The History of the Abacus*.

ABADAN. A general view from Braim Creek to Abadan town with the Bahmashire river in the background.
Courtesy of Iranian Oil Participants.

Africa. A timid, defenceless animal about the size of a pig, it has a long head, pig-like snout, and large asinine ears. It feeds at night on termites, which it licks up with its long, sticky tongue.

AARDWOLF (*Proteles cristatus*). One of the Carnivora, resembling a small striped hyena. It is found in E. and S. Africa, usually in the burrows of the aardvark, and feeds on termites.

AARHUS (awr'hoos). Second city of Denmark, on the E. coast overlooking the Kattegat. It is the cap. of A. co. in Jutland, and a shipping and commercial centre with a univ. Pop. (1965) 117,748.

AARON (ā'ron). In the Bible, the elder brother of Moses and leader with him of the Israelites in their march from Egypt to the Promised Land of Canaan.

AASEN (aw'sen), **Ivar Andreas** (1813–96). Norwegian philologist, poet and playwright. Through a study of rural dialects he evolved by 1853 a native 'country language', which he called *Landsmaal*, to take the place of literary Dano-Norwegian.

A'BACUS. Method of calculating with a handful of stones on 'a flat surface' (Lat. *abacus*), familiar to the Greeks and Romans, and used by earlier peoples, possibly even in ancient Babylon, and which still survives in the E. in the more sophisticated bead frame form of the Russian *schoty* and the Japanese *soroban*. In the West arithmetic with written Arabic figures, the so-called 'pen-reckoning', replaced 'countercasting' for some 200 years, but is today being replaced by adding machines and electric calculators, themselves based on the principle of the A. The metal reckoning counters or jettons of the 13th–18th cents. are often very attractive. *See* CAPITAL.

ABADA'N. Persian is. on the E. side of the Shatt-al-Arab. The Nat. Iranian Oil Co. maintains an inst. of technology and A. is the chief refinery and shipping centre for Persia's oil industry, nationalised 1951, when disputes with the Anglo-Persian Oil Co. interrupted production at A. until 1954. A Consortium, Brit. Petroleum holding 40% of the shares, then took over production.

ABAKA'N. Town of the R.S.F.S.R., cap. of Khakass autonomous region, Krasnoyarsk territory, E. Siberia. It lies just N. of the junction of the A. and Yenisei rivers. Pop. (1967) 78,000.

ABALONE (abalōn'i). Marine, snail-like animal (family Haliotidae), also known from its shape as the ear shell. It provides a bluish mother-of-pearl much used in ornamental work, and the animal itself is edible. California has several valuable species, and As. are eaten there, as well as in China and Japan.

ABBAS the Great (c. 1557–1628). Shah of Persia from 1586, he defeated the Uzbegs near Herat in 1597 and also the Turks. Bandar-Abbas is named after him. At his death his dominions reached from the Tigris to the Indus.

ABBAS II, Hilmi (1874–1944). Last khedive of Egypt, 1892–1914. On the outbreak of war between Britain and Turkey in 1914, he sided with Turkey and was deposed following the establishment of a British protectorate over Egypt.

ABBASIDS. Dynasty of the Mohammedan empire who reigned as caliphs in Baghdad 750–1258. They were descended from Abbas, Mohammed's uncle, and some of them, e.g. Harun-al-Rashid (786–809) and Mamun (813–33), were outstanding patrons of cultural development. Later their power dwindled, and in 1258 Baghdad was burnt by the Tartars. Thence until 1517 they were caliphs of Egypt.

ABBAYE (ahbā′). Group of French writers, artists, and musicians, who in 1906 estab. a self-supporting community in an old house at Créteil, near Paris. They included Georges Duhamel, the poets René Arcos and Charles Vildrac, and the cubist painter André Gleizes, and published La Vie Unanime, written by Jules Romains as the manifesto of the new doctrines of brotherhood inspiring the movement, which became known as Unanimisme. The community broke up after 14 months, but the movement continued.

ABBEVILLE (ahbvēl′). Town in N. France in the Somme dept., 12 m. inland from the mouth of the Somme. During the F.W.W. it was an important base for the British armies. Pop. (1962) 22,816.

ABBEY, Edwin Austin (1852–1911). American artist. He painted historical subjects, and was official painter at the coronation of Edward VII.

ABBEY. In the Christian church, a monastery of monks or a nunnery or convent of nuns, all vowed to a life of celibacy and religious seclusion, governed by an abbot or abbess respectively. Sometimes the word is applied to a religious edifice which was once the church of an A., e.g. Westminster A., or to a building or society that has long since been secularized, e.g. Battle Abbey. The first As. as established in Syria or Egypt were mere collections of huts, but in course of time there were built massive and extensive buildings. St. Benedict's A. at Monte Cassino in Italy – so strongly built that for weeks in 1944 it defied blasting by bomb and shell – set the pattern, and soon every country of Christendom could boast a number of noble As. England, esp. the north, is rich in A. ruins.

ABBEY. Among modern foundations is Buckfast Abbey in Devon where the Benedictine community excels in the arts and crafts. At work on a stained glass window are designer Father Charles Norris (right) and Father Paulinus Angold (left): the glass, specially imported from France, is an inch thick and will be set in concrete.   Photo: Associated Press.

ABBEY THEATRE. Playhouse in Dublin associated with the Irish literary revival of the early 1900s that owed its origin to the co-operation of the writers George Russell (Æ) and W. B. Yeats, with the actors W. G. and Frank Fay. The theatre was opened in 1904, and provided a stage for the works of a number of brilliant dramatists, including Lady Gregory, Yeats, J. M. Synge, Lennox Robinson, Padraic Colum, Conal O'Riordan, St. John Ervine, Seumas O'Kelly, and Sean O'Casey. Burned out in 1951, the A. T. was rebuilt 1966.

ABD EL-KRIM, el-Khettabi (1881–1963). Moroccan Arab chief known as the 'Wolf of Riff'. With his brother Mohammed, he led the Riff revolt, inflicting disastrous defeat on the Spanish at Anual in 1921, but surrendering to a large French army under Pétain in 1926. Banished to the isl. of Réunion, he was released in 1947 and d. in voluntary exile in Cairo.

ABDICATION. Renunciation of an office or dignity, usually the throne, by a ruler or sovereign. See the table on page 3.

ABDUL-HAMID II (1842–1918). Last sultan of Turkey 1876–1909. In 1908 the Young Turks under Enver Bey forced A.-H. to restore the constitution of 1876, and in 1909 insisted on his deposition. He d. in confinement. For his part in the brutal suppression of the Armenian revolt of 1894 he was known as the Great Assassin.

ABDULLAH, Sheikh Mohammed (1905–). Kashmiri leader, known as the 'Lion of Kashmir'. He headed the struggle for constitutional government against the Maharajah of Kashmir, and in 1947 became P.M. He agreed to the accession of the state to India to halt tribal infiltration, but was imprisoned from 1953 (with brief intervals) until 1968, when he re-affirmed the right of the people of K. 'to decide the future of the State by their free will'.

ABDULLAH ibn Hussein (1882–1951). King of Jordan. The son of Hussein ibn Ali and brother of Feisal I of Iraq (qq.v.), he worked with Lawrence in the Arab revolt of the F.W.W. From 1921 he was Emir of Transjordan, and assumed the title of King in 1946 when the country – until then a British mandate – became independent. He incorporated Arab Palestine into his kingdom, which then became the Hashemite Kingdom of Jordan, following the 1948–9 Arab-Israeli war. He was assassinated by an Arab fanatic.

ABEL (ā′bel). In Genesis, 2nd son of Adam and Eve. He was a shepherd, and his burnt offerings were more acceptable to the Lord than were the fruits of Cain, his brother. Filled with jealousy, Cain killed A.

ABEL, Sir Frederick Augustus (1827–1902). British scientist. Chemist to the War Dept., he introduced a new method of making gun-cotton, was joint inventor with Dewar of cordite, and invented the Abel close-test instrument for determining the flash point of petroleum.

A′BELARD, Peter (1079–1142). French scholastic philosopher. B. near Nantes, he became canon of Notre Dame in Paris, and master of the cathedral school in 1115. When his seduction of, and secret marriage to, his pupil Héloïse became known, she took the veil and he was castrated by ruffians at the instigation of her uncle, Canon Fulbert, and became a monk. Resuming teaching a year later, he was cited for heresy and became a hermit at Nogent, where he built the oratory of the Paraclete, and later abbot of a monastery in Brittany. His autobiographical Historia Calamitatum drew from Héloïse the famous love letters. He d. at Châlon-sur-Saône, on his way to defend himself against a new charge of heresy. Héloïse was buried beside him at the Paraclete in 1164, their remains being taken to Père Lachaise, Paris, in 1817. A. has a great place in medieval thought as a 'conceptualist', for whom 'universals' have only a mental existence.

ABEOKUTA (abē-ōkoo'tah). Town in Nigeria, West Africa, on the Ogun river, 64 m. N. of Lagos. Pop (1968) 84,000.

ABERBROTHOCK. Another name for ARBROATH.

ABERCROMBIE (ab'ercrumbi), **Sir Patrick** (1897–1957). British authority on town and country planning. As prof. of Civic Design at Liverpool 1915–35, he attained an international reputation, and produced plans for Dublin, Haifa, Plymouth, and Greater London (1944). His brother LASCELLES A. (1881–1938) was a distinguished poet and critic.

ABERCROMBY, Sir Ralph (1734–1801). Scots soldier who in 1801 commanded an expedition to the Mediterranean, charged with the liquidation of the French forces left behind by Napoleon in Egypt. He decisively defeated the French at Aboukir Bay, but was mortally wounded in the action.

FAMOUS ABDICATIONS

Sulla, Roman dictator 79 B.C.	**Constantine** of Greece 1917 and 1922
Diocletian, Roman emperor A.D. 305	**Ferdinand I** of Bulgaria 1918
Edward II of Eng. 1327	**Wilhelm II** of Germany 1918
Richard II of Eng. 1399	**Charles (Karl)** of Austria-Hungary 1918
Charles V, Holy Roman emperor 1555	**George II** of Greece 1923
Mary Queen of Scots 1567	**Edward VIII** of United Kingdom 11 Dec. 1936
Christina of Sweden 1654	**Carol II** of Rumania 1940
Napoleon I 1814 and 1815	**Victor Emmanuel III** of Italy 1946
Louis Philippe of France 1848	**Umberto II** of Italy 1946
Isabella II of Spain 1870	**Michael** of Rumania 1947
Abdul Hamid II of Turkey 1909	**Wilhelmina** of the Netherlands 1948
Manoel II of Portugal 1910	**Leopold III** of the Belgians 1951
Pu-Yi of China 1912	**Farouk** of Egypt 1952
Nicholas II of Russia 1917	

ABERDARE. Town (U.D.) in Glam., Wales. It has a 12th cent. church. Coalfields discovered locally in the early 19th cent. produce first-rate steam coal. Pop. (1961) 39,044.

ABERDEEN, George Hamilton Gordon, 4th earl of (1784–1860). British statesman. B. in Edinburgh, he succeeded his grandfather as earl in 1801, and was a prominent diplomat. In 1828 he was Foreign Secretary under Wellington, and again in 1841. Although a Tory, he supported Catholic emancipation and followed Peel in his conversion to Free Trade. In 1852 he became P.M. in a govt. of Peelites and Whigs or Liberals, but resigned in 1855 because of the hostile criticism aroused by the miseries and mismanagement of the Crimean War.

ABERDEEN. Royal burgh, city, seaport and holiday resort on the E. coast of Scotland, co. town of Aberdeenshire. It is Scotland's third largest city, and is rich in historical interest and fine buildings, including the Municipal Buildings (1867); King's College (1494) and Marischal College (founded 1593; housed in one of the largest granite buildings in the world, 1836) which together form Aberdeen University; St. Machar Cathedral (1378), and the Auld Brig o' Balgownie (1320). The 2 rivers which flank it, the Dee and the Don, are famous in history and the 2 miles of promenade and the sandy beach attract many holiday visitors. Industries include the manufacture of agricultural machinery, paper and textiles; fishing, shipbuilding, granite-quarrying, and engineering. The civic leader is the Lord Provost. Pop. (1961) 185,379.

ABERDEENSHIRE. County in the E. of Scotland, with an area of 1,971 sq. m. In the W. it is mountainous, the peaks of the Cairngorm constituting some of the most impressive scenery to be found in Britain. Here are the sources of the rivers Don and Dee. Eastern A. is mixed farming land with many cattle. The coast is rocky; Buchan Ness is the most easterly point of Scotland. Chief towns are Aberdeen, the co. town; Peterhead, Fraserburgh, Inverurie, Ballater, and Huntly. A. is mainly an agricultural county; important fishing industry is centred at Aberdeen, Fraserburgh, and Peterhead. Pop. (1961) 298,503. See also ANGUS.

ABERFAN (abervan'). Mining village of Glamorgan, Wales, nr. Merthyr Tydfil. An avalanche of coalmine waste overwhelmed a school and houses in 1966: 144 d. incl. 116 children.

ABERHART, William (1878–1943). Canadian politician. He was a schoolmaster before organizing in Alberta a Social Credit (q.v.) party. He was premier of Alberta from 1935 until his death, but his Social Credit proposals were disallowed by higher authority.

ABERNETHY, John (1764–1831). British surgeon. B. in London, he was a surgeon at St. Bartholomew's hospital, 1815–27, and soon became famous for his lectures and eccentric personality.

ABERRATION. Astronomical term for the apparent displacement of a star resulting from the combined effects of the speed of light, 186,271 m. per sec., and the speed of the earth as it moves in its orbit round the sun, about $18\frac{1}{2}$ m. per sec. The *constant of A.* is 20.47 sec. *Chromatic A.* appears as coloured fringes when objects are illuminated and seen through simple lenses.

ABERYSTWYTH. Holiday resort and university town, also a borough, in Cardiganshire, Wales, at the mouth of the Ystwyth river. The town developed round the fortress rebuilt by Edward I in 1277. The Univ. Coll. of Wales was founded in A. in 1872, and maintains the Welsh Plant Breeding Station. On the outskirts of A. is the National Library of Wales. Tanning is an industry. Pop. (1961) 10,418.

ABIDJAN. Town in W. Africa, cap. of the Ivory Coast rep. It is an important port dealing in palm kernels, cocoa, coffee, etc. Pop. (1965) 250,000 (incl. 7,500 Europeans).

ABILENE (ab'ilēn). Town of Kansas, U.S.A., on the Smoky Hill river. A western railway terminus, A. was a shipping point for cattle in the 1860s, and was a wild city until tamed by Marshal Wild Bill Hickok in 1871. President Eisenhower lived here as a boy and is buried here, and there is an Eisenhower Memorial Museum. Pop. (1960) 6,746.

ABINGDON. Ancient market town (bor.) in Berks, England, where the Ock joins the Thames, 6 m. S. of Oxford. There are remains of the 7th cent. abbey around which it was built. The 15th cent. bridge over the Thames was rebuilt in 1929. The grammar school was founded in 1563. Pop. (1961) 14,283.

ABNER. In the O.T. Saul's cousin and chief captain. After his master's death he went over to David, only to be treacherously murdered by Joab.

ÅBO (aw'boh). Port in Finland, now Turku, q.v.

ABOMEY. Town and port of the Rep. of Dahomey, W. Africa, once cap. of the kingdom of Dahomey. The old town was defended by a mud wall 6 m. in circumference. Pop. (1965) 23,000.

ABOMINABLE SNOWMAN. Man-like creature, with long arms and a thick-set body covered with reddish-grey hair. Travellers and climbers have said that it exists in the Himalayas, where it is locally known as the Yeti.

ABORIGINES. The intelligence which enables these hunters with their spears to survive, even in the 'dead heart' of Central Australia, is finding new outlets through the Federal Government's educational scheme.
Courtesy of Australian News and Information Bureau.

ABORIGINES (aborī'jinēz). Those inhabitants of a country who are believed to have been there from time immemorial (Lat. *ab origine*, from the beginning). The word now more particularly refers to the native peoples of those lands which have become the scene of European settlement, e.g. the As. of Australia.

ABORTION. In law, the expulsion of the contents of the pregnant womb at any time before full term; in medicine, the expulsion before the foetus is capable of living—before the 6th month. Expulsion after that is called miscarriage or premature labour. A. may be spontaneous, therapeutic, or criminal. In many countries A. is a recognized method of birth control, and in 1968 it was legalized in certain circumstances in England and Wales.

ABOUKIR (abooker') **BAY, Battle of.** Also known as the Battle of the Nile: Nelson defeated Napoleon's fleet at the Egyptian seaport of A. on 1 Aug. 1798.

ABRAHAM (fl. *c.* 2300 B.C.). Founder of the Jewish nation. B. at Ur, Abram was the son of Terah, and migrated to Haran, N. Mesopotamia, with his father, his wife Sarah, and his nephew Lot. Proceeding to Canaan, he received Jehovah's promise of the land to his descendants, and after sojourning in Egypt during a famine, separated from Lot at Bethel before settling in Hebron. On re-naming him Abraham 'father of many nations', Jehovah promised him a legitimate heir, and then tested him by a command to slay the boy Isaac in sacrifice. By his 2nd wife, Keturah, A. had 6 sons. He was buried in Machpelah cave, Hebron.

ABRAHAM, Edward Penley (1913–). British biochemist. Professor of chemical pathology at Oxford from 1964, he succeeded (with his group) in isolating the antibiotic cephalosporin (q.v.), capable of destroying penicillin-resistant bacteria.

ABRAHAM, Plains (or **Heights**) **of.** Plateau near Quebec, Canada, where on 13 Sept. 1759 the French under Montcalm were defeated by Wolfe, whereby Canada was won for the British Empire. It is now the National Battlefield Park.

ABRASIVES. Substances used for cutting and polishing or for removing small amounts of the surface of hard materials. They are divided into *natural* As., e.g. quartz, sandstone, pumice, diamond, corundum, and emery; and *artificial*, e.g. bath brick, rouge, whiting, and carborundum. They are usually referred to Mohs' Scale of Hardness, a list of 10 minerals ranging from diamond as the hardest and number 10, to talc as the softest and number 1.

ABBRUZZI (ahbroots'ī). Mountainous area of south central Italy, culminating in the Gran Sasso d'Italia (9,560 ft.), highest point of the Apennines.

ABSALOM. In the O.T., the 3rd and favourite son of King David. He headed a revolt against his father, was defeated in battle, and as he fled on a mule, his long hair caught in an overhanging branch. In this predicament he was slain by Joab, David's captain.

A'BSINTH. Strong alcoholic drink containing from 60 to 80 per cent of alcohol, which owes its toxic qualities to the oil of wormwood which gives its characteristic flavour. It attacks the nervous system and causes acute symptoms of narcotic poisoning.

ABSOLUTE ZERO. The lowest temperature which could possibly exist, equivalent to −273·16°C. when molecules would have no energy. Near this temperature the physical properties of materials change substantially, e.g. some metals lose their electrical resistance.

ABSTRACT ART. Abstract works of art may be classified as (1) *semi-abstract* – i.e. those works which are based on nature, though they bear little resemblance to natural forms; and (2) *pure abstract* – i.e. those works which have no relation to nature, but consist of shapes and colours of the artist's own invention. In (1) we may group Cubism, Futurism, Vorticism, and the work of certain artists, such as Henry Moore and Archipenko, who have evolved their own individualistic styles. In (2) we may include Constructivism, Suprematism, and Neo-Plasticism. There are other movements, such as Expressionism, which defy classification. In Expressionist paintings forms are created instinctively, according to the promptings of the artist's emotions, but such works usually consist of lines and shapes, and can therefore be considered as abstract. Surrealist works are also executed in a similar way – they are the expressions of a dream-world – but since their chief interest lies in their subject-matter they cannot, strictly speaking, be classed as A.A. For definitions of the different movements *see* ACTION PAINTING, CUBISM, CONSTRUCTIVISM, FUTURISM, etc.

ABSURD, Theatre of the. *See* ALBEE, E.; BECKETT, S.; IONESCO, E.; and SIMPSON, N. F.

ABU (ah'boo). An isolated granite peak of the Aravalli range in Rajasthan, India. It is 5,650 ft. in height, and one of the most sacred centres of Jain worship.

ABU-BEKR (573–634). Mohammed's father-in-law and the first caliph. B. at Mecca and originally named Abd-el-Ka'ba, he was one of the first notable converts to Mohammed's teaching, accompanied the Prophet on his flight to Medina, and took the name Abu-Bekr, 'Father of the Virgin', when Mohammed married his daughter Ayesha (*c.* 618). As Mohammed's successor (632) he proved a vigorous ruler, adding Mesopotamia to the Moslem world.

ABU DHABI. The largest of the Trucial States on

the Persian Gulf. Its borders are ill-defined and there has been dispute with Muscat and Saudi Arabia over ownership of the villages of the Buraimi Oasis. Its oil resources (production began 1962) are said to rival Kuwait. The cap. is Abu Dhabi on an island in the Gulf. Pop. (est. 1962) 20,000.

ABYDOS (abī′dos). Ancient city of upper Egypt, 7 m. W. of the Nile, about 100 m. above Asyut. The Great Temple built here by Seti I (*c.* 1300 B.C.), is one of the most imposing Egyptian temples.

ABYSSINIA. Another name for ETHIOPIA.

ACACIA (akā′sha). Genus of trees and shrubs of the family Leguminosae. Most of the 400 species flourish in the tropics of Africa and Australia. *See* WATTLE and MIMOSA.

ABSTRACT ART. 'Still Life' a typical example of the work of French artist Georges Braque (q.v.). Dated 1936, it is in the decorative style of Cubism, and falls into the semi-abstract group.

ACADEMY (Gk. *akadēmeia*). Name given to the Platonic school of philosophy, which met in the gardens of Academe, in the N.-W. of Athens. Here among the olive groves Plato and his successors taught their disciples, until in A.D. 529 Justinian closed all the pagan schools.

First of the As., in the modern sense of a recognized society estab. for the promotion of one or more of the arts and sciences, was the Museum of Alexandria, founded by Ptolemy Soter in the 3rd cent. B.C.

The *Académie française* originated as a literary society in 1629, and was granted letters patent by Louis XIII in 1635. Since 1639 its membership has been restricted to 40 at a time, the '40 Immortals'. It is conservatively influential, and is the guardian of the purity of the French tongue, of which it prepared the first standard dictionary 1639–94.

The Soviet *A. of Sciences* was originally estab. by Catherine I in 1725 as the Académie Impériale des sciences de Saint-Petersbourg. Responsible for such achievements as the *Sputnik*, the A. formerly admin. many of the country's 3,000 scientific establishments, but in 1961 was reorganized to concentrate on the most promising lines of theoretical research. The practical side of scientific research work was entrusted to the newly-created State Committee of the Council of Ministers for the Co-ordination of Scientific Research Work.

In Britain an 'academy' generally means a society dealing with the arts, such as the Royal Academy, those dealing with the sciences and with historical and philosophical studies being known as 'societies'. The British Association comes within this category.

ACADIA, or **ACADIE** (ahkahdē′). Name given to Nova Scotia by the original French settlers in 1604. France renounced her claim to the colony in 1713. Many of its inhabitants migrated to New England and

Louisiana: some 4,000 others were expelled in 1755.

ACA′NTHUS. Genus of herbaceous plants, family Acanthaceae, of the Mediterranean region. The A. was frequently used as a motif in classical architec-

ture, the Greeks preferring the species *A. spinosus* (natural leaf and stylized form as illus.) and the Romans *A. mollis*. The latter, often grown as an ornamental plant and also called bear's breach, grows some three feet high. The spineless, hairy leaves are shiny, and the flowers form handsome white or pinkish spikes.

ACAPULCO (ak′apoō′lkō). Mexican holiday resort, famed for its beauty and deep-sea fishing, set in an almost land-locked bay 190 m. S.W. of Mexico City. Pop. (1963) 35,000.

A′CCAD. Ancient town on the left bank of the Euphrates from which a Semitic people of N. Babylonia took their name – Accadians. It was the chief city of the empire of Sargon I.

ACCELERATION. The rate of increase in the velocity of a moving body, usually expressed in feet or centimetres per second per second. The acceleration due to gravity is the A. shown by a body falling freely under the influence of gravity, either in a vacuum or after allowing for the retardation due to air resistance; it varies slightly at different latitudes, but is equivalent to *c.* 32.16 ft per sec per sec. Retardation is actually A. in the reverse direction, e.g. a rising rocket is actually being accelerated towards the centre of the earth.

ACCESSARY. In Eng. law, an *accessary before the fact* is one who instigates another person to commit a felony which that person then commits. If he is present when the crime is committed, he is not an A. but an *abettor* or principal in the second degree. An *A. after the fact* is one who assists a person whom he knows has committed a felony.

A′CCOLĀDE. Gentle blow on the shoulders with the flat of the sword given by the Sovereign, or a representative in conferring a knighthood. The word comes from the French for an embrace or clasping about the neck, and in earlier times the knightly ritual included such an embrace and sometimes a kiss.

ACCOMPLICE. One who is associated with another in the commission of a crime. In law, the word is applied not only to persons who played a minor part in the crime, but also to the principal offenders.

ACCORDION. Portable musical instrument invented by Damian of Vienna in 1829. Box-like in form, it comprises a pair of bellows with many folds and a keyboard of up to 50 keys. On these

ACAPULCO. Though the town is now famous as a swimming and boating centre for the tourist, some of the picturesqueness of the fishing village remains and dried squid are still bought to be hung above the house doors as a charm against evil spirits.
Photo: Barnaby's Picture Library.

being pressed and the bellows worked, wind is admitted to metal reeds, whose length and thickness determines the notes they emit.

ACCOUNTANCY. The art or practice of an accountant. The accountant today enjoys professional status and is entrusted not only with the control of the book-keeping functions and the preparation of Trading and Profit and Loss Accounts and Balance Sheets, but with numerous other duties in connection with the financial affairs of an organization. The auditing of accounts is the work of professional accountants who may also be required to serve as liquidators of companies, receivers for debenture holders, etc.

In the British Isles there are Inst. of Chartered Accountants for England and Wales, Scotland, and Ireland and other professional organizations; the American Inst. of Accountants dates from 1887.

ACCRA'. Capital and port of Ghana, W. Africa. It is an important commercial and industrial centre with good road, rail, and air communications. The Univ. of Ghana (1961) is at nearby Legon, with its medical school in A. itself. Pop. of the Greater A. region (created 1964) 491,820.

ACETALDEHYDE (CH_3CHO). In chemistry, one of the chief members of the group of organic compounds known as aldehydes. It is a mobile inflammable liquid boiling at 20·8°C. (69·6°F.).

ACE'TIC ACID (CH_3COOH). One of the simplest members of a series of organic acids called the fatty acids. In the pure state it is a mobile colourless liquid with an unpleasant pungent odour; it solidifies to an ice-like mass of crystals at 16·7°C., and hence is often called glacial acetic acid. *See* VINEGAR.

ACETONE (CH_3COCH_3). A colourless mobile inflammable liquid used extensively as a solvent. It boils at 56·5°C., is miscible with water in all proportions, and has a pleasant and characteristic odour. Very large quantities are used in the manufacture of nitrocellulose lacquers and aeroplane dope.

ACE'TYLENE (C_2H_2). A colourless inflammable gas produced by the action of water on calcium carbide. It was discovered by Edmund Davy in 1836 by the action of water on some impure by-products of the preparation of potassium.

The most important modern development in the use of A. is its conversion into artificial rubbers. Since the combustion of A. provides more heat relatively than almost any other fuel known – its calorific power is 1,500 Btu ft³ as compared with about 500 for coal gas and 300 for hydrogen – the gas is of great value in obtaining an intensely hot flame, e.g. in oxyacetylene welding and cutting.

ACHAEA (akē'a). Ancient name for Greece. The name Achaeans was originally used for the fair-haired invaders from the N. who swept over the whole of Greece some time before 1100 B.C., submerging the ancient Aegean civilization of Mycenae, and who then captured Troy, as told in the Iliad.

The Achaean League of 275 B.C. united most of the cities of the northern Peloponnesus, and achieved victory over Sparta, but it was worsted by the Romans in 146 B.C.

ACHAEMENIDS (akimen'ids). Dynasty ruling the Persian Empire 550-330 B.C., and named after Achaemenes, ancestor of Cyrus the Great, founder of the Empire. His successors incl. Cambyses, Darius I, Xerxes I and Darius III, who, as the last Achaemenid ruler was killed after defeat in battle against Alexander the Great in 330 B.C.

ACHERON (a'keron). In Greek mythology, one of the rivers of the lower world. The name was taken from a river in S. Epirus which flowed through a deep gorge into the Ionian Sea.

ACHESON, Dean Gooderham (1893–1971). American statesman and lawyer. He was Under-Secretary of State 1945-7, and was closely associated with George C. Marshall in the preparation of the

'Marshall Plan'. He succeeded him as Sec. of State from 1949 till the end of the Truman régime in 1953. In 1961 he was appointed by Kennedy to head a group studying U.S. policy *vis-à-vis* the N.A.T.O. alliance.

ACHILL (ak'il). Largest of the Irish islands, lying off the coast of Mayo. The scenery is wild and mountainous, and on the N. and W. are cliffs reaching 900 ft. Area, 57 sq. m.; pop. *c.* 5,000.

ACHILLES (akil'ēz). Greek hero, the central figure of Homer's Iliad. He was the son of Peleus, king of the Myrmidons in Thessaly. His mother Thetis dipped him into the r. Styx and thereby made him invulnerable except for the heel by which she held him. Bravest and handsomest of all the Greeks, he took part in the Trojan War, and in a mighty combat killed Hector. In the end he was himself slain by Paris, whose poisoned arrow wounded him in the heel.

ACCRA. Christianborg Castle was one of the 3 forts (British Dutch and Danish) which formed the nucleus of the settlement, and was named after Christian V (1646–99) of Denmark. Ceded to Britain in 1850, the castle was later used as Government House, and on Ghana's independence was extended to house the President's Office.
Courtesy of Ghana Information Services.

ACID (Lat. *acidus* acid, sour). In chemistry, a substance which in solution in an ionizing solvent (usually water) gives rise to hydrogen ions. The more obvious properties of As. are their sharp taste, and their ability to turn litmus red, to neutralize alkalis to form well-defined salts, and act as solvents. The first known A. was vinegar. Inorganic As. include boracic, carbonic, hydrochloric, nitric, phosphoric, sulphuric, and sulphuretted hydrogen; and among organic acids are acetic, benzoic, citric, formic, lactic, oxalic, and salicylic. As. combine with bases (alkalis are soluble bases) to form salts. 'Strength' of an acid is measured by its hydrogen-ion concentration, indicated by pH value and expressed on a scale of numbers from 0 = extremely acid, through 7 = neutral, to 14 = extremely alkaline.

ACLAND, Sir Richard (1906–). British politician. The son of a prominent Liberal, he developed left-wing views and in 1942, in association with J. B. Priestley, became founder and leader of Common Wealth. In 1943 he gave the A. family estates at Killerton to the National Trust. He was a Labour M.P. 1947-55.

ACNE (ak'-). A skin eruption due to inflammation of the sebaceous glands that secret an oily substance called sebum, the natural lubricant of the skin. Sometimes their openings become stopped and they swell; the contents decompose and pimples form.

ACONCA'GUA. An extinct volcano (22,834 ft.) in the Andes on the W. border of Argentina. The highest peak in the Americas, it was first climbed in 1897 by Vines and Zurbriggen (FitzGerald Expedition).

A'CONITE. Genus of poisonous plants of the Ranunculaceae family. Of some 60 species, *Aconitum*

napellus, or Monkshood, is the common European species; also known as *A. lycoctonum,* wolf's bane. The roots yield aconitine.

Ā′CORN. Fruit or seed of the oak tree. It is a nut, based in a shallow cup or cupule. The sea-acorn or acorn-shell (*Balanus*) is a genus of Cirripedia, allied to the barnacles.

ACOUSTICS (akoo′- or akow′-). In general, the experimental and theoretical science of sound; but more specially, that branch of the science that has to do with the phenomena of sound in space, e.g. public buildings, concert halls, cinemas, etc. Acoustical engineering is concerned with the technical control of sound, and the subject also enters into architecture and building, with the necessity for the control of vibration, for sound-proofing and the elimination of noise; it also includes all forms of sound recording and reinforcement, and hearing-aids. *See* Sound.

ACQUAVIVA (ahkwah-), **Claudius** (1543–1615). A Neapolitan, he was General of the Jesuits from 1581 and one of their ablest organizers and educators.

ACQUITTAL. In law, the clearing or setting free of a person charged with a crime or accusation. In an English court this follows on a verdict of 'not guilty', but in a Scottish court the verdict may be either 'non-proven' or 'not guilty'. A. by the jury must be confirmed by the judge.

Ā′CRE. City and port of Israel, on a promontory at the northern extremity of the Bay of A. It has played an important part in history, owing to its strategic position. In 1517 it became part of the Turkish empire. Napoleon besieged it in 1799, but was withstood by the Turkish Jezzar Pasha, supported by a British fleet under Sir Sidney Smith. During the F.W.W., General Allenby captured it from the Turks (1918): the Israelis captured it in 1948. A. has lost importance owing to the growth of Haifa, 9 m. S. but exports olive oil, corn, and wool. There is a Naval Officers' School. Pop. *c.* 10,000.

Ā′CRE. English land measure, comprising 4,840 sq. yds. Originally the word meant a field, and it was of a size that a yoke of oxen could plough in a day. But as early as Edward I's reign a statute limited it to a plot 40 poles (220 yards or 1 furlong) long by 4 poles (22 yds.) wide = 4,840 sq. yds., or 4 roods or 160 sq. rods, poles, or perches. A present-day allotment usually consists of 10 rods, i.e., 1/16th of an acre. The Scottish acre is $6,150 \cdot 4$ sq. yds., and the Irish is 7,840 sq. yds. Leicestershire, Cheshire, and Westmorland have their own local acres.

Ā′CRIDĪNE ($C_{13}H_9N$). An organic compound which occurs in crude anthracene oil, from which it may be extracted by dilute acids. It is also obtained synthetically. It gives rise to many dye-stuffs and some valuable drugs.

ACROME′GALY. A disease distinguished by an unsightly enlargement of the prominent parts of the body (Gk. *akra,* high parts), e.g. the hands and feet, and the lips, nose, tongue, and jaws. It is due to an excessive output of growth hormone by the front lobe of the pituitary gland.

ACRO′POLIS. The citadel of an ancient Greek town. Best known is the A. at Athens, famous for the ruins of the beautiful temples built there during

ACONITE

ACRE. The strong walls guarding the seaward side of the city reflect its troubled history, but, though pitted by shot, still stand firm. *Courtesy of the Israel Government Tourist Office.*

the great days of the Athenian empire. *See* illus. pp. 8 and 491.

ACROSTIC. A verse or set of verses whose initial letters form a word, phrase, or sentence; the term comes from the Gk. for 'at the end of a line or row'. Sometimes the end letters form the same (or different) words as the initial ones, and sometimes, too, the letters run down the middle of the verse like a seam. Thus we have single, double, and triple As.

ACTAEON (aktē′on). Greek mythical hero. The son of Aristaeus and Cadmus' daughter Autonoë, he was a famous hunter. He accidentally spied upon Artemis as she was bathing, and the goddess changed him into a stag, whereupon he was torn to pieces by his own hounds.

ACTINIDES. Those chemical elements with nos. 89–103, all radioactive and man-made above uranium, no. 92. They are grouped because of their chemical similarities, and also by analogies with the rare-earth elements (lanthanides). *See* Table p. 244.

ACTI′NIUM. Rare radioactive element, at. no. 89, at. wt. 227, the first of the actinides, a weak emitter of high-energy alpha-rays. Made in quantity by bombarding radium with neutrons.

ACTION. One of the proceedings whereby a person enforces his civil rights in a court of justice. The best-known proceedings not commenced by action but by petition are bankruptcy and divorce.

ACTION PAINTING. Abstract, expressionist style of painting developed in New York in the 1950s. The word was first used by critic Harold Rosenberg, who wrote that the painter's canvas seemed to these artists 'an arena in which to act'. The paint was applied often by violent methods: *see* Pollock, Jackson. Franz Kline and Mark Rothko are also of this school.

A′CTIUM. Ancient name of a promontory in western Greece on the gulf of Arta, where the fleets of Antony and Cleopatra were defeated by Octavian in 31 B.C.

ACROPOLIS. The earliest city was comprised within the bounds of the Acropolis, 1,000 ft. long from east to west. Now modern Athens, glimpsed through the Ionic columns of the north porch of the temple of Erechtheus, legendary founder of the city, stretches far into the distance.
Courtesy of the National Tourist Organization of Greece.

ACT OF CONGRESS. In U.S.A. a bill or resolution that has been passed by the Senate and the House of Representatives and has received the President's assent. If he vetoes it, it may become an A. of C. if it is returned to Congress again and passed by a majority of two-thirds in each House.

ACT OF GOD. Legal term meaning some direct, violent, sudden, and irresistible act of nature which could not reasonably have been foreseen, e.g. extraordinary storms, snow, or frost.

ACT OF INDEMNITY. An Act of Parliament passed to relieve some person from the consequences of some action or omission which, at the time the action or omission took place, was illegal, or of which the legality was doubtful.

ACT OF PARLIAMENT. A parliamentary statute; a decree of the sovereign legislature having the force of law. Acts of P. are of two kinds, public and private, but there is no distinction as to their force, only as to their application; i.e. public Acts of P. have a general effect, while private Acts deal with matters of purely local interest.

Acts are known not only by the year of the reign, but by a short title, e.g. that of 22 Geo. 5 c. 4. is commonly referred to as the Statute of Westminster, 1931.

The body of English statute law comprises all the Acts passed by Parliament, and the existing list opens with the Statute of Merton, passed in 1235. An Act (unless it is stated to be for a definite period and then to come to an end) remains on the statute book until it is repealed.

ACTON, John Emerich Edward Dalberg-Acton, 1st baron A. (1834–1902). British historian. B. at Naples, of old English R.C. stock, he was elected a Liberal M.P. in 1859 and became a friend and admirer of Gladstone. As leader of the Liberal R.Cs. he opposed the promulgation in 1870 of the doctrine of papal infallibility. Appointed prof. of modern history at Cambridge in 1895, he planned and edited the Cambridge Modern History, but d. when only the first 2 vols. were completed.

A'CTUARY. An official of a government department, insurance co., or friendly soc., whose task it is to make the calculations concerning human longevity, etc., on which the tables of mortality, sickness, accident, etc., and hence the premiums or charges, are based. Professional bodies are the Inst. of Actuaries (England, 1848), Faculty of Actuaries (Scotland, 1856) and Society of Actuaries (U.S., 1949, by a merger of 2 earlier bodies).

ACUPUNCTURE (ak'ū-). Method of healing involving the insertion of gold needles into the body (Lat. *acu* with a needle) at points determined according to a system which in China, where A. originated, requires a decade of study. There is a British College of A. at Leamington.

ADAM. Four brothers – Robert, John, James, and William – distinguished Scottish architects and interior decorators.

Robert A. (1728–92), was b. at Kirkcaldy, travelled in Italy and Dalmatia, and was appointed Architect to the King in 1762. With the assistance of his brothers, he designed the district of London between Charing Cross and the Thames, which was named after them the Adelphi (from the Gk. for brothers). The area was largely rebuilt in 1936. The A. brothers were responsible for a great improvement in architectural taste, and developed a style which was decidedly their own. Robert A. also earned a considerable reputation as a furniture designer.

James A. studied in Rome, and succeeded Robert as Architect to the King in 1768; **William A.** is described as an architect and a banker; and **John A.** succeeded his father as an architect in Edinburgh.

ADAM (ahdoñ'), **Adolphe Charles** (1803–56). French composer of light operas. Some 50 of his works were staged; he is best known for the classic ballet *Giselle*.

ADAM (or Adan) DE LA HALLE (c.1235/40–87). French troubadour, known as the 'Hunchback of Arras'. His *Jeu de Robin et Marion* is the earliest French comic opera, and *Le jeu Adan* or *Le jeu de la Feuillée* a precursor of the modern revue.

ADAM and EVE. In the Bible, the first parents of the human race. According to Gen. ii, 7–iii, 24, Jehovah (Yahweh) formed man from the dust, breathed into his nostrils the breath of life, and put him in the Garden of Eden, where the fruit of the Tree of Knowledge of Good and Evil was forbidden him. God formed a woman from a rib of the man while he slept. The woman was tempted by the serpent to eat the forbidden fruit, persuaded A. also to eat, and they were expelled from Eden.

ADAMOV, Arthur (1908–). Russian-born French playwright. He has pub. translations of Gorki, Chekhov, and Gogol and their influence is noticeable in his plays: *La Parodie*, *Le Ping-Pong*, *En Fiacre* and *Spring '71*.

ADAMS, Henry Brooks (1838–1918). American author. A grandson of President John Q. A., his best-known works are the studies of the 13th cent. *Mont-Saint-Michel and Chartres* (1904), and of the contrasting complexities of the 20th, *Education of H.A.* (1907).

ADAMS, James Truslow (1878–1949). American historian, author of *The Epic of America* (1931), and many other works.

ADAMS, John (1735–1826). 2nd President of the U.S.A. B. at Quincy, Mass., he was a member of the Continental Congress, 1774–8, and signed the Declaration of Independence. In 1779 he went to France and negotiated the treaties that closed the

ADAM AND EVE. A scene from Michelangelo's world-famous Biblical frescoes on the vaulting of the Sistine Chapel at Rome. In the centre is the Tree of Knowledge of Good and Evil, round which is coiled the tempting serpent. On the left our first parents are plucking 'the fruit' (in Milton's words) 'of that forbidden tree, whose mortal taste brought death into the world, and all our woe, with loss of Eden'. Adam and Eve are driven from Paradise (right), and go out naked into a cold and hostile world.

War of American Independence. In 1785 he became the first American ambassador in London. Returning home, he was Vice-President (1789–97), and President 1797–1801.

ADAMS, John Couch (1819–92). British astronomer. B. in Cornwall, he deduced the existence of the planet Neptune in 1845, and in 1858 became professor of astronomy at Cambridge.

ADAMS, John Quincy (1767–1848). 6th President of the U.S.A. Eldest son of President John Adams, he was b. at Quincy, and became U.S. minister in turn at The Hague, Berlin, St. Petersburg, and (1815) London. In 1817 Monroe made him Secretary of State, and 1825–9 he was President.

ADAMS, Léonie (1899–). American poet. B. in N.Y., she became instructor in writing at Columbia Univ. in 1947, and is noted for her romantic, metaphysical lyrics, as in *Those Not Elect* (1925) and *This Measure* (1933).

ADAM. Osterley Park, Isleworth, was remodelled by Robert Adam from the Elizabethan mansion built in 1557 for Sir Thomas Gresham. Here is the Eating-Room, with paintings by Antonio Zucchi, which is among the best examples of his decorative work. *Photo: Victoria and Albert Museum.*

ADAMS, Samuel (1722–1803). American statesman. B. in Boston, he was a 2nd cousin of President John Adams, and was a leader of the revolutionary party in Massachusetts. He sat in the Continental Congress 1774–81, and signed the Declaration of Independence. In 1776 he anticipated Napoleon in calling the English a nation of shopkeepers.

ADAMS, Sherman (1899–). American statesman. A New Englander, he is descended from the 8th son of an English West Country immigrant: the 7th son founded the line which produced the 2nd and 6th American presidents. He was gov. of New Hampshire from 1949 until his appointment as assistant to President Eisenhower in 1953: during the President's illnesses great power devolved on him. He resigned in 1958 after it was revealed that he had accepted valuable gifts from a Boston manufacturer, but he emphatically denied influencing the decisions of Government agencies in return. In 1961 he pub. an account of the Eisenhower administration, *First-Hand Report*.

ADANA (ahdah'nah). Town in Turkey-in-Asia, cap. of the il of Seyhan, on the r. Seyhan. It has cotton, tobacco, and agricultural machinery factories. Pop. (1960) 230,024.

ADDAMS, Jane (1860–1935). American sociologist and feminist. A founder and head of the social settlement of Hull House, Chicago, she was active in the peace movement: co-winner Nobel prize 1931.

ADDER. *See* VIPER.

ADDINGTON, Henry (1757–1844). British Tory statesman, Prime Minister of U.K., 1801–4. In 1805 he was created Viscount Sidmouth.

ADDINSELL, Richard (1904–). British composer. B. in London, he studied at the Royal College of Music and abroad, and wrote music for many theatrical productions and films, e.g. *Dangerous Moonlight*, which includes the 'Warsaw Concerto'.

ADDIS ABABA (Amharic, meaning new flower). Cap. of Ethiopia, and of Shoa prov., founded 1887 by Menelik, then chief of Shoa, at the request of his wife Taitu who found the climate of his existing cap. Entotto, lying farther north, too severe. The region chosen for the new cap. formerly uninhabited, lies at 8,000 ft. a.s.l., but is protected by the surrounding

Shoa highlands, and includes hot springs. Eucalyptus woods were planted nearby by Menelik who, when he ascended the throne of Ethiopia in 1889, made A.A. cap. of the whole country. A.A., which is linked by a railway completed 1917 with Djibouti on the coast of the Terr. of the Afars and the Issas, was cap. of Italian East Africa 1936–41. Of the four royal palaces in the city, one was presented by Haile Selassie to Ethiopia's first university, inaugurated by him in 1961; in the grounds of another is a compound of lions, symbolic of the Emperor's role as Lion of Judah. Pop. (1965) 637,831.

ADDISON, Christopher, 1st visct. (1869–1951). British politician. As a Liberal M.P. 1910–22, he was one of the most prominent of Lloyd George's lieutenants in the struggle to secure National Health Insurance, and was the first Minister of Health in 1919–21. He joined the Labour Party in 1922, and his posts under Attlee included that of Dominions Sec. 1945–7, and Lord Privy Seal 1947–51. He was created a baron in 1937, and a visct. in 1945.

ADDISON, Joseph (1672–1719). British essayist and poet, b. in Wilts. In 1699 he was granted a pension to enable him to qualify for the diplomatic service by foreign travel, and in 1704 celebrated Marlborough's victory at Blenheim in his poem 'The Campaign'. In 1706 he became Under-Sec. of State, and in 1708 secretary to the Lord-Lieutenant of Ireland, and an M.P. In 1709 he began to contribute to the *Tatler*, just started by his friend Steele; and in 1711 the two together estab. the *Spectator*, to which A. contributed the 'Coverley Papers'. In 1713 his successful tragedy *Cato* was performed, and he contributed to Steele's *Guardian* and in 1714 to the revived *Spectator*. In 1716 he was appointed a commissioner for trade, and in 1717 a Sec. of State, but failing health led to his withdrawal from public life in 1718.

Kit-Cat Club Portrait by G. Kneller.   *Photo: N.P.G.*

ADDISON, Thomas (1793–1860). Physician. B. nr. Newcastle, he became physician to Guy's Hospital, London, in 1837. He was the first to recognize the condition known as *Addison's disease* – a disease of the suprarenal capsules.

ADELAIDE (1792–1849). Queen of William IV. Daughter of the duke of Saxe-Meiningen, she m. William, then duke of Clarence, in 1818. No children of the marriage survived infancy.

ADELAIDE. Capital of South Australia. Founded in 1836, and named after William IV's queen, it stands on high ground overlooking Holdfast Bay and sheltered on the S. and E. by hills of which the highest peak is Mt. Lofty (2,334 ft.). It is a noteworthy example of town-planning. The residential districts are separated from the commercial by the r. Torrens, dammed to form a lake. The most impressive streets are King William St. and North Terrace. A.'s fine buildings include Parliament House (built of marble), Government House, the Anglican cathedral of St. Peter, the R.C. cathedral, the University, the State observatory, museum and art gallery. Pop. (1961) 587,656. *See* illus. p. 12.

ADÉLIE LAND. *See* ANTARCTICA.

ADELSBERG. German name of Postojna. *See* CARNIOLA.

ADE'MOLA, Sir Adetokunbo (1906–   ). Nigerian judge. The son of Sir Ladapo A., Alake of Abokuta, he became in 1958 chief Justice of the Federal Supreme Court.

A'DEN. Twin peninsulas of barren volcanic rock, A. and Little A., linked by a coastal strip and commanding the southern entrance to the Red Sea, at the S.W. corner of Arabia: from 1967 part of the People's Rep. of Southern Yemen. A. was annexed by Britain in 1839; the harbour was strongly fortified, and after the opening of the Suez Canal, A. developed rapidly as a fuelling and transhipment station. Chief towns are Crater, Sheikh Othman, Tawahi, Maalla, and Khormaksar: there is a large oil refinery in Little A. completed 1954. Created a colony in 1937, A. became in 1963 a state of the Federation of S. Arabia. Area 75 sq. m.; pop. (1966) 250,000.

The protectorates of Western A. and Eastern A. were known from 1963 as the South Arabia Protectorate: area 112,000 sq. m.; pop. (est. 1966) 1,000,000. In 1959 six amirates of the Western A. Protectorate founded the Federation of South Arabia, which other states as well as A. itself later joined: this was intended as the basis of an eventually independent new state. However, from 1964 there was intensive terrorist activity by the Front for the Liberation of Occupied South Yemen (FLOSY), supported by Egypt and also engaged in internecine warfare with the National Liberation Front (N.L.F.). Following Egypt's withdrawal from neighbouring Yemen in 1967, the Fed. of S. Arabia, incl. Aden, became independent. See People's Democratic Rep. of Yemen.

ADENAUER (ah'denower), **Konrad** (1876–1967). German statesman. He was Lord Mayor of his native city of Cologne from 1917 until his imprisonment in 1933 by Hitler for opposition to the Nazi régime. After the war he headed the Christian Democratic Union, and in 1949 became Chancellor of the Federal Republic, being re-elected in 1953 and 1957. A strong supporter of all measures designed to strengthen the Western bloc in Europe, e.g. his support of Britain's entry into the Common Market, he regarded the re-unification of Germany as the primary element in world tension. He retired in 1963.

ADENOIDS. Popular word for the glandular tissue on the back of the upper part of the throat, into which the nose opens. This is apt to overgrow in children as a result of infection, and to cause chronic blocking of the nose and mouth-breathing. The open mouth makes the child's expression look vacant, and the voice has a dull twang. The child is subject to constant colds, is in danger of middle-ear disease and deafness, and often suffers from chronic tonsillitis. The treatment is the removal by surgery of the tonsils and overgrown adenoid tissue.

ADER (ahdār'), **Clement** (1841–1925). French pioneer airman. B. at Muret, he completed in 1890 his first full-scale flying-machine, the *Éole*, the wings of which were bat-shaped when extended in flight, and folded when on the ground. A. claimed to have made a first flight on 9 Oct. 1890, but the machine crashed. In 1897 he built the *Avion*, somewhat larger; but a trial flight before military witnesses was inconclusive.

ADIABA'TIC. The A. expansion or contraction of a gas is one in which a change takes place in the pressure or volume of the gas, although no heat is allowed to enter or leave.

ADIGE (ah'dējeh). Next to the Po, the longest river in Italy, it rises in the lakes of the Resia Pass, traverses the Lombardy Plain, and enters the Adriatic a few miles N. of the Po delta. It is about 254 m. long.

ADI GRANTH or GRANTH SAHIB. The holy book of the Sikhism (q.v.).

ADIRO'NDACKS. Mountainous area in the N.E. of New York State, U.S.A., famous for its scenery and sport facilities. In Mt. Marcy it reaches 5,345 ft.

ADLER (ahd'ler), **Alfred** (1870–1937). Austrian psychologist, founder of the school of Individual Psychology. B. in Vienna, he was a general practitioner and nerve specialist there 1897–1927, serving as an army doctor in F.W.W. He joined the circle of Freudian doctors in Vienna about 1900, but did not accept the more dogmatic Freudian theories of infantile sexuality. After 10 years of collaboration, he parted company with Freud to develop his own distinctive line of thought. His books incl. *Organic Inferiority and Psychic Compensation* (1907) and *Understanding Human Nature* (1927).

ADLER, Felix (1851–1933). Jewish scholar and ethical leader. B. in Germany, the son of a rabbi who emigrated to U.S.A. in 1857, he became prof. of Hebrew at Cornell, and founded the Society for Ethical Culture, New York.

ADMINISTRATIVE LAW. The laws made and the judicial decisions arrived at by the Executive under powers delegated to them by the Legislature; such legislative powers have been vastly extended in the 20th cent. in many countries and have been attacked by lawyers. In the U.S. the Administrative Procedure Act (1946) was an attempt to cope with the problem.

In Great Britain the very many new powers delegated to Ministers of the Crown are so wide as frequently to enable the Ministers to make regulations which amend or override Acts of Parliament, and in some cases they further take away from the courts of law the power they have hitherto exercised of confining the legislative activities of the Executive within the limits of the authority delegated to them by Parliament by declaring any regulation that exceeds these limits to be *ultra vires*, and so of no effect.

ADENAUER. Together in Bonn in 1961 Chancellor Adenauer and President de Gaulle symbolize the Franco-German friendship which was one of the most striking developments of the years following the Second World War.
Courtesy of the German Embassy.

ADMIRAL. Naval officer of the highest rank: in the R.N. (in ascending order) rear-admirals, vice-admirals, and admirals of the fleet; in the U.S.N. there are 4 corresponding grades.

ADMIRALTY. From the reign of Henry VIII until 1964, the **Board of A.** was the dept. of State charged with the provision, control and maintenance of the Royal Navy; its functions—apart from that of management—then passed to the new unified Min. of Defence (q.v.). The 600-year-old office of Lord High Admiral, in commission in the A., then reverted to the Sovereign, to prevent its extinction.

ADŌ′NIS. In classical mythology, a beautiful youth beloved by Aphrodite. While hunting a boar he was gored to death; from his blood sprang the anemone. He was permitted to return each year from the underworld to his mistress for six months. He was worshipped as Adon by the Phoenicians, and earlier still the cult is found in Babylonia and Assyria.

ADOPTION. The legal acquisition of the rights and duties as to the custody and maintenance of a child not one's own legitimate offspring. In antiquity – as in Greece and Rome – emphasis tended to be on the acquisition of an heir, and, as in India, might have religious significance. A. was legalized in England only in 1926, and the modern emphasis is on the welfare of the child and its complete acceptance as if lawfully born to the adopter, e.g. by the Act of 1958 an adopted child inherits on an intestacy as if it were the child of the adopter, and closer restrictions were placed on A. societies. In the U.S. there is a particularly high rate of A., conditions being regulated by the laws of the various states. Stress on care of the child is illustrated by international As., e.g. those of Korean refugee children adopted in the U.K. through the International Social Service of Great Britain.

ADOWA. Alternative form of ADUWA.

ADRENAL GLANDS. A pair of glands situated on the upper poles of the kidneys and known also as 'suprarenal' glands. They are soft and yellow, and consist of 2 parts. The cortex (outer part) secretes various hormones (steroids) related to sex hormones, controls salt and water metabolism, and other processes. The medulla (inner part) secretes **adrenalin**, whose nature was discovered by Oliver and Schäfer in 1894, and which constricts the blood vessels of the belly, lungs, and skin so that more blood is available for the heart, lungs and voluntary muscles – an emergency preparation for 'fight or flight' causes a large output of adrenalin.

A′DRIAN IV. Pope, 1154–9; Nicholas Breakspear, the only Englishman to sit in the papal chair. He was b. at Abbots Langley, became a monk in France, and in 1137 abbot of St. Rufus, near Arles. Elected pope at the end of 1154, he secured the execution of Arnold of Brescia, crowned Frederick I Barbarossa as German emperor; refused Henry II's request that Ireland should be granted to the English crown in absolute ownership; and was at the height of a quarrel with the emperor when he d. at Anagni.

ADRIAN, Edgar, 1st baron (1889–). British physiologist. He received the Nobel Prize for medicine in 1932, for his work with Sherrington in the field of nerve impulses, and was prof. of physiology at Cambridge 1937–51, and Master of Trinity Coll. 1951–65. His books incl. *The Basis of Sensation* (1928) and *The Physical Basis of Perception* (1947) Awarded the O.M. in 1942, he was created a baron in 1955.

ADRIANOPLE. Older name of EDIRNE, after the Emperor Hadrian. who rebuilt it c. A.D. 125.

ADRIA′TIC SEA. Large arm of the Mediterranean Sea, lying N.W. to S.E. between the Italian and the Balkan peninsulas. The western shore is Italian; the eastern Yugoslav and Albanian. The sea is about 500 m. long, and its area is 52,220 sq. m., of which 1,290 are islands. Its greatest depth is 850 fathoms off Durres: average depth 130 fathoms.

ADSHEAD, Stanley Davenport (1868–1946). British pioneer of town planning. He was professor of civic design at Liverpool 1909–14, and of architecture at London 1914–35. His dau. **Mary A.** (1904–) is a mural painter.

ADULTERY. Extra-marital act while married. The Commission of A. by the respondent is one of the facts considered as demonstrating an 'irretrievable breakdown' of marriage in suits for judicial separation or divorce in Britain. It is almost universally recognised as ground for divorce in U.S.A., and in some states is theoretically punishable by fine or prison.

ADUWA (ad′u-wa). Chief town of the prov. of Tigré, Ethiopia, about 110 m. S.S.W. of Massawa at an altitude of 6,270 ft. It was formerly the cap. of Ethiopia, and it was here that the Ethiopians defeated the Italians in 1896.

ADVENT (Lat. *adventus*, approach, arrival). That season in the Christian calendar which is celebrated as a preparation for the festival of Christmas. It includes the four Sundays before Christmas, beginning with the Sunday which falls nearest (before or after) to St. Andrew's Day (30 Nov.).

ADELAIDE. Among the most beautiful of Australia's cities, it has been called the 'Athens of the South', and owes much of its charm to the river Torrens, which is dammed to form a lake The railway station, seen here to the left, is the terminus of all country and interstate passenger lines in S. Australia.
Courtesy of Agent General for South Australia.

ADVENTISTS. Those who hold the view that Christ will return to make a second appearance on the earth. Expectation of the Second Coming of Christ is found in N.T. writings generally. Adventist views are held in particular by the Seventh Day Adventists, Christadelphians, Jehovah's Witnesses, and the Four Square Gospel Alliance.

ADVOCATE (Lat. *advocatus*, one summoned to one's aid, esp. in a court of justice). A professional pleader in a court of justice. The English term is barrister or counsel, but A. is retained in Scotland and in other countries, e.g. France, where the Roman law is still retained. The *Lord Advocate* is the principal law-officer of the Crown in Scotland, a political member of the ministry of the day, retiring with the government by whom he was appointed. A *Judge-Advocate* manages the prosecution in courts-martial, the *Judge-Advocate-General* being the chief of the legal department of the respective Service. The term A. has no special significance in the U.S.

ADVOCATES, Faculty of. Scottish legal body, incorporated in 1532 under James V. Members closely resemble in their powers English barristers.

AEGEAN (ējē'an) **SEA.** Branch of the Mediterranean between Greece and Turkey. The Dardanelles connect it with the Sea of Marmara. The numerous islands in the A. Sea incl. Crete, the Cyclades, the Sporades, and the Dodecanese.

AEGINA (ējī'na). Greek island in the Gulf of A. about 20 m. S.W. of Piraeus. In 1811 remarkable sculptures were recovered from a Doric temple in the N.E. (restored by Thorwaldsen) and taken to Munich.

AEGIR (īgir). In Scandinavian mythology, the god of the sea.

AEGIS (ē'jis). In Gk. mythology, the shield of Zeus, symbolic of the storm cloud associated with him. In representations of deities it is commonly shown as a protective animal skin.

AELFRIC (c. 955–1020). Old-English prose writer. He became a priest and taught at Cernel monastery (now Cerne Abbas) in Dorset, and was abbot of Eynsham in 1005. He is celebrated for his writings in the vernacular, particularly for his two collections of homilies and the *Lives of the Saints.*

AENEAS (ēnē'as). In classical legend, a Trojan prince who became the ancestral hero of the Romans. According to Homer, he was the son of Anchises and the goddess Aphrodite. During the Trojan war he several times owed his life to the intervention of the gods. The legend on which Virgil's *Aeneid* is based describes his escape from Troy and eventual settlement in Latium. The Latins accorded him divine honours, and the house of Julius claimed to be descended from him.

AEOLIAN ISLANDS. Another name for the LIPARI ISLANDS.

AE′OLUS. In Gk. mythology, god of the winds, ruler of the Aeolian islands, where he kept the winds imprisoned in a cavern.

AERONAUTICS. The science of aerial locomotion within the earth's atmosphere, including aerial navigation, aerodynamics, aircraft structures, and jet and rocket propulsion. It should not be confused with *Astronautics,* which is the science of travel through space; *Astronavigation* is, however, used in aircraft as in ships and is a part of A. **Aerodynamics** comprises the study of the airflow around bodies moving through it, and speeds in excess of the speed of sound (760 m.p.h. at sea level) have made subdivision necessary. Subsonic A. has been known in the past under the general term and the aerodynamic forces have increased as the square of the speed, and were thus simply calculated. Streamlining has been all-important. Transonic A. covers the speed range from just below to just above the speed of sound, where shock waves are experienced. Ordinary sound waves move at 760 m.p.h., and air in front of an aircraft moving slower than this is warned by the waves so that it can move aside. But as the flying speed approaches that of the sound waves, the warning is too late for the air to escape and the aircraft pushes it aside by brute force, creating shock waves which absorb much power and largely unpredictable forces. Supersonic A. concerns speeds well above the speed of sound and is a much older study than A. itself, since as ballistics (q.v.), the study of the flight of bullets was undertaken soon after the introduction of firearms, has been applied to aeroplanes and is now better understood than Transonics. Hypersonics is the study of airflows and forces at speeds about five times that of sound and is used for such vehicles as the V.2 rocket. Superaerodynamics is the science of very high speeds in rarefied air such as is found at very high altitudes of between ·50 and 150 miles.

AEROPLANE. A heavier-than-air craft supported in flight by fixed wings (*aerofoils*) when propelled by the reaction from air accelerated rearwards by air-screw(s) or jet(s) to overcome the air resistance (*drag*). Drag depends on frontal area (e.g. large, airliner; small, fighter) and shape (*drag coefficient*); it equals *thrust* in straight, level flight. (Power = thrust × speed. 1 lb. thrust at 375 m.p.h. = 1 THP; at 750 m.p.h. = 2 THP). *See* JET PROPULSION. Less drag (*streamlining*) means increased speed and lower fuel consumption from given power; less fuel need be carried for a given distance (*range*) and the A.'s weight is reduced.

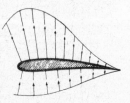

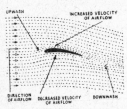

Accelerated airflow over wing resulting in reduced pressure above it.

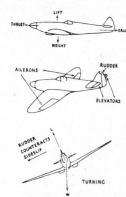

Here we see (above) how in level flight engine thrust overcomes drag, providing speed which creates lift to support the weight of the aeroplane, in this case a Spitfire; the position of the control surfaces (centre); and the aircraft turning (below).

Aerofoils are so shaped and cambered that air passing above them is speeded up, reducing pressure below atmospheric, while that below is slowed. This produces a vertical force (*lift*) to support the A.'s weight. (Lift = weight in level flight.) Minimum weight is thus essential to an efficient A., requiring a smaller wing which has less drag. Very strong but light aluminium alloys are used, and also for the body (*fuselage*) and where possible for controls and in engines. The thin *skin* (outer) panels, with *ribs* and *stringers* at intervals to prevent buckling, support all flight stresses with no separate structure (semi-monocoque construction). The *payload* (crew, passengers, bombs, etc.) may be up to one-third all-up weight.

Control. Aerofoils are unstable and a horizontal *tailplane* is installed behind to overcome this, with hinged flaps (*elevators*) to control pitch (*attitude*). Raising the elevator depresses the tail and the aerofoil is inclined (*angle of attack* increased), which further speeds up the airflow above it until lift exceeds weight, when the A. climbs; the steeper attitude increases drag and more power is needed to maintain speed. Descent results from reducing the angle of attack, when speed builds up rapidly (*diving*) if the engine is not throttled back. Descent without power is *gliding*. Turning (changing direction) is effected not by the rudder (hinged to the vertical *tail-fin*) but by banking A. (*rolling*) so that the lift force inclines inwards to provide a centripetal component as well as supporting the A.'s weight; to do so it must exceed that for level flight, and the angle of attack is increased by raising the elevators. The A. is banked by applying *ailerons* (inter-connected hinged flaps at the rear (*trailing edge*) of the wings, working oppositely). The 'outer' aileron is depressed to increase effectively the camber and therefore the lift, and vice versa. The more aileron applied, the more the A. banks and the quicker it turns, until the wings are nearly vertical. Rudders are fitted only as balance controls, and 'top' rudder (i.e. opposite to the direction of bank) is applied to prevent side-slip inwards when turning, or to fly straight on one engine in a two-engined A.

Flaps are fitted to the rear of wings to increase camber and lift for shorter take-off and landing, To land, the angle of attack is increased until the airflow over the wing breaks down and lift is lost (*stalling*). On the ground, the A. rests on wheels (floats, on water) attached to the *air-frame* by struts; the landing gear (*under-carriage*) is retractable in flight to reduce drag.

These principles apply to all A. types, e.g. biplanes (2 super-imposed wings – now obsolescent), monoplanes, seaplanes, flying boats, airliners, freighters, fighters, bombers, trainers, whether propelled by airscrews, driven by piston engines or by turbines, or by turbo-jets or rocket motors. *Helicopters* (rotating wing aircraft) and *Rockets* are not As.

See FLIGHT, HISTORY OF.

AEGEAN SEA. Seen through the restored columns of the temple of Lindia Athena on the heights of the ancient acropolis of Camiros, on the island of Rhodes. St. Paul once landed in the small port below.
Courtesy of the National Tourist Organisation of Greece.

AEROSOL (ā′rōsol). A colloidal system, e.g. mist or fog, in which air is the dispersion medium; and popularly a form of packaging in which gas under pressure, or a liquefied gas with a pressure greater than atmospheric at ordinary temperatures, is used to spray a very fine mist of liquid droplets from a nozzle; it is generally actuated by a press-button device. As. are used for germicides, insecticides, fire extinguishers, paints, hair lacquers, perfumes, paints, etc.

AESCHINES (ē′skinēz) (4th cent. B.C.). Orator of ancient Athens. Best known of his speeches are those 'Against Timarchus' (345), 'On the Embassy', and 'Against Ctesiphon'.

AESCHYLUS (ē′skilus) (c. 525–456 B.C.), Greek dramatist. B. near Athens, he came of a noble family; fought against the Persians at Marathon (490 B.C.), and wrote nearly 90 plays between 499 and 458 B.C. He twice visited the court of Hiero, king of Syracuse, and d. at Gela in Sicily.

The earliest of his 7 surviving plays is *The Suppliant Women*, performed about 490. There followed *The Persians* (472), *Seven against Thebes* (467) and *Prometheus Bound* (c. 460). Then came the trilogy of the *Oresteia* which won the first prize at the festival of Dionysus in 458; the 3 plays – *Agamemnon, Choephori*, and *Eumenides* – deal with the curse on the house of Agamemnon which was eventually resolved by the action and suffering of Orestes.

A. became famous for the majesty of his language,

ADRIATIC. No exception to the famed beauty of the many islands of the Adriatic is the Isle of Lopud off the Yugoslav coast near Dubrovnik.
Courtesy of Yugoslav National Tourist Office.

the boldness of his speculation upon problems of religion and human destiny, and the grandeur and simplicity of his plots and characters.

AESCULAPIUS. Lat. form of Asklepios, god of medicine in Gk. mythology. His attribute was a staff with a snake coiled about it (now the badge of the R.A.M.C.), because the snake, since it sloughs its skin, was supposed to renew its youth. Sacred snakes were kept in the sanctuaries of A. at Epidaurus and elsewhere. The customary offering to A. was a cock.

AESOP (ē'-). Fabulist of antiquity. Herodotus says he lived in the reign of Amasis of Egypt (mid-6th cent. B.C.). B. a slave, and represented in later art as deformed, he received his freedom and visited Lydia and Greece. No writings by him have survived, and some at least of the fables attributed to him were current in Egypt many centuries earlier.

AESTHETIC MOVEMENT. Artistic movement of the late 19th cent. in England, the chief doctrine of which was Art for Art's sake. It owed much to Pater and Wilde, and found expression in the *Yellow Book*. It was exemplified by painters such as Whistler, draughtsmen like Aubrey Beardsley, poets such as Lionel Johnson and Ernest Dowson, and among critics by J. A. Symonds.

AFGHANISTAN. Her climate has infinite variety—perpetual summer in the south-west, a soft mildness in the central Kabul plains which produces two harvests a year, and winter ice for nine months of the year in the north.
Courtesy of the Afghan Publicity Bureau, Kabul, Afghanistan.

AETOLIA (ētō'-). District of anc. Greece on the N.W. of the gulf of Corinth. The AETOLIAN LEAGUE was a confederation of the cities of A. which, following the death of Alexander the Great, was the chief rival of the Macedonian power and the Achaean League.

AFARS AND THE ISSAS, Fr. Terr. of the. *See* SOMALILAND, FRENCH.

AFFINITY (in law). The relationship which exists between a man and his wife's blood relations, or between a woman and her husband's blood relations. It is distinguished from consanguinity or blood relationship. Many relationships by A. prevent marriage, e.g. a man cannot marry his step-daughter.

AFFIRMATION (in law). A solemn declaration made instead of taking the oath by a person who has no religious belief or objects to taking an oath on religious grounds (Oaths Act, 1888).

AFGHANISTAN. Kingdom to the N.W. of Pakistan. The country is almost entirely mountainous, the Hindu Kush to the N.E. rising in places to 24,000 ft. The chief rivers are Amu Darya (Oxus), Kabul, and Helmand. By irrigation of the small areas of level land crops of wheat and other cereals, sugar cane and sugar beet, fruits, tobacco, rice and cotton are grown in the N. and E. The river pastures are grazed by cattle, and fat-tailed sheep and yaks are raised in the mountains. Minerals, for the most part undeveloped, incl. iron, coal, copper, gold and silver, gypsum, asbestos and various gems. Natural gas is piped to Russia, and other exports incl. karakul lamb skins, carpets, fruit and tobacco. Hydro-electric schemes are helping the growth of industry, and there has been a large road-building programme since the 1950s, though there are no railways and few navigable rivers. Air transport has also been developed. The Khyber, Peiwar, Gomal and Bolan passes link A. with Pakistan, but the Durand Line (1893) marking the border is disputed and A. claims Pakhtunistan. The cap. is Kabul; other towns incl. Kandahar, Herat, and Mazar-i-Sharif.

A. is a constitutional monarchy, with an elected House of the People, and a House of Elders – one-third nominated by the King. Area *c.* 250,000 sq. m.; pop. (est.) 11–12,000,000, the majority being Mohammedans, principally of the Sunni sect.

AFGHANISTAN. Of ancient renown as warriors, Afghan soldiers find no difficulty in incorporating new-style rifles in the routine of an age-old war dance.
Courtesy of the Royal Afghan Embassy.

History. Once part of Aryana, a region of the ancient Persian Empire, A., occupied by many peoples during its early history, first became an independent amirate in 1747. During the 19th cent. Russian influence in the country threatened British India, and in 1838 A. was invaded by a British force, which secured control of the country; but in 1842 the garrison of Kabul was wiped out and the British evacuated A. A second Afghan War followed in 1878, during which General Roberts captured Kabul and, in 1880, marched to Kandahar. A third Afghan War, in which the Afghans invaded India, lasted only a few months in 1919, and subsequent relations with Britain (since 1947 with Pakistan) have been governed by the Treaty of 1921. The ruler adopted the title King in 1926.

AFINOGENOV (ahfēnogā'nov), **Alexei** (1904–41). Soviet dramatist, author of several plays embodying the spirit of the new era, including *Distant Point*. A. was killed in an air-raid on Moscow.

AFRICA. Third largest of the continents of the world; with an area of 11,500,000 sq. m., it is smaller than Asia or America, but two-and-a-half times the size of Europe. In population it takes 4th place.

Geography and Resources. The proportion of desert to cultivated land is unusually high: the Sahara covers 2½ million sq. m. while other large desert tracts occur in Egypt, Somaliland, Kenya, S. and S.W. Africa. There are few fertile alluvial plains to compensate for the deserts, the continent being composed of a great plateau rising sharply from the sea. The rivers cut their way from the plateau to sea-level by cataracts and are therefore generally not suitable for navigation. The Nile receives no tributaries in its lower reaches, and without artificial irrigation would water only a narrow strip of land: the Congo and Niger basins are masked by dense tropical forests. The coastline has

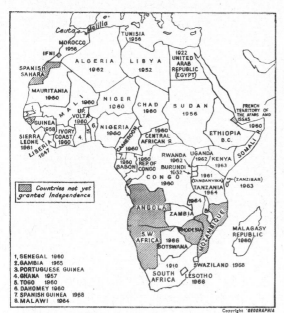

Countries not yet
granted Independence

1. SENEGAL 1960
2. GAMBIA 1965
3. PORTUGUESE GUINEA
4. GHANA 1957
5. TOGO 1960
6. DAHOMEY 1960
7. SPANISH GUINEA 1968
8. MALAWI 1964

Copyright 'GEOGRAPHIA

AFRICA. The growth of independence: Ifni was transferred to Morocco in 1969.

few good harbours, and none at all throughout most of its western length. A wide strip of central A., on either side of the equator, experiences a wet tropical climate; the coast lands of W. Africa are hot, damp, and were long extremely unhealthy for white men, while on the E., though drier, it is even hotter. Great tracts between the tropical regions and the deserts of N. and S. Africa are covered by tropical grassland and bush country. Only the northern and southern extremities and the highlands of the interior are suitable for Europeans to live in comfort.

In some mineral resources A. is poor as compared with other continents, e.g. coal and petroleum, but there are rich reserves of gold in southern A., copper in central A. (Congo Republic and also Zambia), diamonds (S. Africa, Congo Republic, S.W. Africa), manganese (Ghana, S. Africa), phosphate (N. Africa), uranium (Congo Republic, S. Africa), tin (Uganda, Congo Republic), etc., and further discoveries are being made. *See* SAHARA.

Large areas of the continent are unsuited to arable agriculture, and in other areas the tse-tse fly prevents stock raising; but chemical and other scientific aids, artificial irrigation, and development of hydroelectric power are increasing A.'s agricultural and industrial production. Important crops include cocoa (Ghana, Nigeria), cotton (Uganda, Egypt), coffee (Kenya), sisal (E. Africa), tobacco (E. Africa); wine is produced in Algeria and S. Africa.

Population. Numbering altogether some 200,000,000, the pop. of A. is composed of Bushmen and Hottentots living in the Kalahari region, S.W. Africa and Botswana; Negritos or Pygmies in the Republic of Congo; Negroes in W. Africa; Hamites in Egypt, the Republic of Sudan, Ethiopia, Somaliland, N. Africa and parts of the Sahara; various mixed peoples such as the Hamiticized Negroes or Bantus and the Nilotics of the Republic of Sudan; Semites, including the Arabs in N. and E. Africa; recent immigrants of European and Indian origin in E. and S. Africa, Kenya, and other recently developed territories.

AFRICAN NEGRO ART. The chief centres of Negro art are in Nigeria, the Rep. of Congo, Ghana, the Ivory Coast, and the Rep. of Cameroon. In S. Nigeria the most notable works were produced by the Negro peoples of Benin and of ancient Ife. The Beni used the *cire-perdue* process – as used in Italy during the Renaissance – in executing their bronze relief work. In the Belgian Congo the Bakuba and Baluba tribes are famous for their wonderful decorative works such as ornamental spoons, bobbins, and head rests. The artists of the Bushango kingdom (15th–16th cents.) produced wood-carvings of singular beauty, and also practised the art of portraiture. The wooden statues of their early kings are most remarkable. Among the most interesting products of the Gold Coast are the brass weights from Ashanti. These are used for measuring gold-dust, and are made in the form of tiny figures which are said to illustrate local legends. The most skilful artists of the Ivory Coast belong to the Baoulé tribe, who are closely related to the Ashanti peoples. Wood-carvings, drinking cups, basketry, statues, and masks are among the artistic products of the Rep. of Cameroon. The masks of the Cross River are particularly famous for their realistic quality. *See* illus. p. 16.

The Negro art of W. Africa, remarkable for its beauty of form and intense vitality, has had a profound influence on the work of many of the leading European artists, e.g. Picasso, Matisse, Brancusi, Modigliani, and Epstein.

AFRIKAANS. One official language of S. Africa, the other being English. Spoken by the Afrikaners, mainly descendants of the original Dutch colonists, it is a development of the Dutch language, modified by the influence of German, French, and other immigrant and native tongues. Reaching its modern form in the middle of the 18th cent., it did not become a written language until *c.* 1875, and real literature did not appear until *c.* 1900, when the South African war provided a stimulus. Notable writers in A. are the brothers Hobson and C. H. Kuhn; the poets J. D. du Toit ('Totius'), J. F. E. Celliers, E. N. Marais, C. J. Langenhoven, A. G. Visser and, more

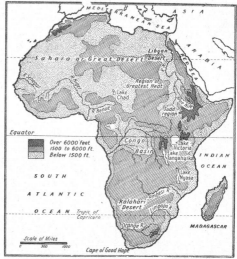

AFRICA. Physical characteristics of the continent.

AFRICAN NEGRO ART. One of a series of 25 typical bronze plaques from Benin, this specimen is 20 inches high and shows one of the rulers or Obas of Benin with attendants.
Photo: British Museum.

recently, N. P. van Wyk Louw, E. Eybers, W. E. G. Louw, and Uys Krige. C. M. van den Heever and T. J. Haarhoff write in prose and verse. A. A. Pienaar's *Adventures of a Lion Family* is famous beyond S. Africa, as are the popular stories of C. J. Langenhoven. Other prose-writers are J. van Bruggen, J. H. H. de Waal, and Leon Maré.

AFRIKA KORPS. Name of the German army in the Western (Libyan) Desert in the S.W.W. They first came into contact with British troops at El Agheila on 24 March 1941, and were finally driven out of N. Africa in May 1943.

AFYON' KARA'HISAR'. Town of an il of the same name in Asiatic Turkey, about 200 m. E. of Izmir. A railway junction, it is a centre for opium. Pop. (1950) 29,881.

AFZELIUS (ahftseh'li-oos), **Arvid August** (1785–1871). Swedish writer. Parish priest of Enköping, he collaborated with the historian Geijer in a collection of folk-songs, translated the Elder Edda and the Herwara Saga, and was also a poet and dramatist.

AGA. Title of nobility, probably of Tartar derivation. The Turks applied it to military commanders, and, in general, to men of high station.

AGADIR (-dēr'). Most southern seaport in Morocco, near the mouth of the Sus. When Fez was occupied by the French in July 1911, the Panther, a German gunboat, appeared off A., and the Emperor William II of Germany made a claim for territorial concessions. On 1 March 1960, the town was virtually destroyed by an earthquake, about a third of its 30,000 inhabitants being killed. A new town was built on solid rock nearby. Pop. (1970) c. 50,000.

AGA KHAN (ah'ga kahn) **III, Aga Sultan Sir Mahomed Shah** (1877–1957). Indian statesman, spiritual head of the Ismaili Moslem sect from 1885. He was knighted in 1902, and in recognition of his loyal services during the F.W.W. was granted the status of a first-class prince. On several occasions he led the Indian delegation at the League of Nations, and strove for Hindu-Moslem agreement within India.

TERRITORIAL DIVISIONS OF AFRICA

Territory	Area in 1,000 sq. m.	Pop. est. in 1,000s	Capital
Algeria	840	10,453	Algiers
Burundi	11	3,000	Kitega
Cameroon, Republic of ...	183	5,200	Yaoundé
Congo Republic ...	905	15,627	Kinshasa
Dahomey	45	2,370	Porto Novo
Egypt (United Arab Republic) ...	386	30,083	Cairo
Ethiopia	395	22,590	Addis Ababa
Guinea, Republic of	95	3,500	Conakry
Ivory Coast ...	124	3,840	Abidjan
Liberia	43	1,016	Monrovia
Libya	679	1,564	Benghazi & Tripoli*
Mali	465	4,700	Bamako
Morocco	174	13,320	Rabat
Niger Republic	486	3,330	Niamey
Ruanda	10	3,300	Kigali
Somali Republic ...	246	2,500	Mogadishu
South Africa, Republic of ...	473	18,298	Capetown & Pretoria
S.W. Africa ...	318	526	Windhoek
Sudan, Republic of ...	968	13,011	Khartoum
Togo, Republic of ...	19	1,650	Lomé
Tunisia	48	4,457	Tunis
Voltaic Republic ...	106	5,000	Ouagadougou
In the British Commonwealth			
Ghana, Republic of...	92	7,945	Accra
Malawi	46	4,042	Zomba
Nigeria, Federation of ...	339	55,653	Lagos
Rhodesia	150	4,530	Salisbury
Zambia	290	3,700	Lusaka
West Africa:			
Gambia... ...	4	320	Bathurst
Sierra Leone ...	28	2,183	Freetown
East Africa:			
Lesotho	12	967	Maseru
Botswana ...	222	543	Gaborone
Kenya	225	9,370	Nairobi
Mauritius ...	·72	773	Port Louis
Tanzania ...	363·02	12,231	Dar-es-Salaam
Swaziland ...	6·70	389	Mbabane
Uganda... ...	94	7,750	Kampala
In the French Community			
Afars and Issas ...	9	108	Djibouti
Central African Republic	238	1,466	Bangui
Chad	496	3,400	Fort Lamy
Congo Republic ...	132	870	Brazzaville
Gabon	103	470	Libreville
Madagascar (Malagasy Republic)	228	6,335	Antananarivo
Mauritania	419	1,100	Nouakchott
Senegal	76	3,500	Dakar
Portuguese Overseas Provinces			
Angola	481	5,000	São Paulo de Luanda
Mozambique ...	298	6,578	Lourenço Marques
Guinea	14	519	Bissau
Spanish Provinces			
Sahara (Rio de Oro)	103	23	Villa Cisneros
Ifni**	74	51	Sidi Ifni
Equatorial Guinea***	10		
Rio Muni ...	·8	183	} Santa Isabel
Fernando Po		62	
	11,499·98	309,396	

*Pending construction of new cap. Beida in Cyrenaica.
**Transferred to Morocco 1969. ***Independent 1968

Prominent on the Turf, he won the Derby in 1930, 1935, 1936, 1948, and 1952.

Aga Khan IV, Shah Karim (1937–) succeeded his grandfather, by whom he had been nominated, on the latter's death in 1957.

AGAME'MNON. Greek hero. The son of Atreus, king of Mycenae he m. Clytemnestra, and became by her the father of three daughters – Iphigenia, Chrysothemis, and Laodice (Electra) – and a son, Orestes. The most powerful of the Greek princes, he was their leader in the Trojan war. When Troy was captured, A. received Cassandra, daughter of King Priam, as his prize, and sailed for home, where he was murdered by Clytemnestra and Aegisthus.

AGAR-AGAR. Organic substance, usually met with as a straw-coloured powder or as pale strips which dissolve in hot water to give a solution which sets to a jelly on cooling. It is obtained from the *Gelidium* species of red algae, and is useful in bacteriology for growing bacteria at blood temperature.

AGA'RICUS or A'GARIC. Genus of fungi of the class Basidiomycetes. It includes the common mushroom (*Agaricus campestris*) and the horsemushroom (*A. arvensis*): closely allied is the genus Amanita (q.v.) with many poisonous species.

AGASSIZ (ahghahsē), **Jean Louis Rodolphe** (1807–73), Swiss-American naturalist. He became professor of natural history at Neuchâtel in 1832, pub. *Researches on Fossil Fishes* and *Freshwater Fishes of Europe*, studied the Alpine glaciers, and in 1848 was appointed professor of geology and zoology at Harvard.

AGATE (ag'āt). Banded or cloudy kind of silica, used to form ornamental stones and objects of art. A. stones are used to burnish and polish gold deposited on glass and ceramics.

AGA'THOCLES (361–289 B.C.). Tyrant of Syracuse in Sicily from 317 B.C. He was defeated by the Carthaginians at Himera in 310, but later invaded their homeland in N. Africa.

AGAVE (agā'vē). Genus of plants of the family Amaryllidaceae. All the species are found in the warmer parts of the New World, especially Mexico. Their leaves are stiff and spiny and the flowers are borne on an upright scape, which sometimes reaches a height of over 30 ft. *A. americana*, the best-known species, was introduced into Europe during the 16th cent.

A'GINCOURT. French village, 40 m. S.E. of Calais, famous for the victory of the English under Henry V over superior French forces on 25 Oct., St. Crispin's Day, 1415. Pop. *c.* 300.

AGNI. In Hindu mythology, the god of fire, the protector of men against the powers of darkness, the guardian of their homes.

AGNON, Shmuel Yosef (1888–1970). Israeli novelist. B. in Buczacz, Galicia (now in U.S.S.R.) setting of his most famous book *A Guest for the Night*, he wrote in Hebrew and shared a Nobel prize 1966.

AGNOSTIC. Word coined by T. H. Huxley in 1869: person believing that in the nature of things we cannot know anything of what lies behind or beyond the world of natural phenomena. It would seem he had in mind the Greek words *Agnosto theo* (To an unknown God) which St. Paul found inscribed on an altar in Athens.

An atheist denies the existence of gods or God; an agnostic asserts that God or a First Cause is one of those concepts – others are the Absolute, Infinity, Eternity, Immortality, etc. – which lie beyond the reach of human intelligence.

AGOULT (ahgoo'), **Marie Catherine Sophie de Flavigny,** Comtesse d' (1805–76). French writer. Daughter of a French officer, she was b. at Frankfurtam-Main, m. the Count d'Agoult in 1827, and left him to become the mistress of Franz Liszt, by whom she had 3 children. She held a famous literary and artistic *salon* in Paris, and wrote under the pseudonym of Daniel Stern a novel *Nélida* (1854) picturing her relations with Liszt.

AGRA (ah'grah). City of Uttar Pradesh, Republic of India, on the Jumna, about 100 m. S.S.E. of Delhi.

Baber, the first great Mogul ruler, made it his capital in 1527. His grandson Akbar rebuilt the Red Fort of Salim Shah (1566), and is buried outside the city in the splendid tomb at Sigandra. In the 17th cent. the buildings of Shah Jehan made A. one of the most beautiful cities in the world. The Taj Mahal, completed 1650, and erected as a tomb for the emperor's wife Mumtaz Mahal, took more than 20 years to build. A.'s political importance dwindled from 1658 when Aurangzeb moved the capital back to Delhi. It was taken from the Mahrattas by Lord Lake in 1803. Pop. (1961) 509,108.

AGRAM. German name of ZAGREB.

AGRI'COLA, Georg (1490–1555). German metallurgist, known as the 'father of mineralogy'.

AGRI'COLA, Gnaeus Julius (A.D. 37–93). Roman general and statesman. B. in Provence, he became consul in A.D. 77, and next year was made Governor of Britain. He advanced the Roman power as far north as the Firth of Forth, defeated the Caledonians at the battle of Mons Graupius (Grampian hills), and built a chain of forts. His fleet sailed round the N. of Scotland, thus proving for the first time that Britain was an island. He was recalled to Rome in A.D. 85. His daughter m. in A.D. 78 the historian Tacitus, who wrote a biography of A.

AGRICULTURE. All the processes of farming in its widest sense. With some peoples A. has still not reached the stage of soil cultivation, e.g. the Australian aborigines and the nomadic pastoralists of Africa, whereas in ancient Egypt there were extensive estates with very varied produce. The settler-farmer was typical of early Greece and Rome, but later huge estates run by slave labour were common. The medieval economy rested on the manorial system which broke down under the enclosure movement: *see* ENCLOSURES. Modern A. first developed principally in Britain: *see* JETHRO TULL, ROBERT BAKEWELL, ARTHUR YOUNG. In the U.S. stress was on the individual working his own land, e.g. the Homestead Act (1862) passed by Lincoln, and using every mechanical device for greater productivity and efficiency, so that American practice is greatly influential in the mechanization now overtaking under-developed countries. The International Institute of A. (1905) was absorbed

AGRICULTURE. Invaluable in modern farming, the combine harvester not only harvests the crop, but also threshes the grain and bales the straw. Key: 1, Reel; 2, Reel adjusters; 3, Driving platform and controls; 4, Threshing drum speed adjusting levers; 5, Steering column and wheel; 6, Driver's seat; 7, Grain tank; 8, Radiator air intake; 9, Top elevator for grain tank; 10, Air intake pipe for engine; 11, Tool box; 12, Side and top panels over shakers; 13, Engine exhaust pipe and silencer; 14, Rear hood; 15, Canvas cover for rear hood; 16, Rear wheels (used for steering); 17, Tailings elevator trunking; 18, Oil bath air cleaner for engine air; 19, Main chassis; 20, Diesel engine (behind main wheel); 21, Main or driving wheel; 22, Front elevator; 23, Feed table and cutter bar; 24, Crop dividers. *Courtesy of Ransomes, Sims and Jefferies.*

by the Food and A. Organization estab. in 1945, also with its H.Q. at Rome: the International Federation of Agricultural Producers (1943) has its H.Q. at Washington.

Agricultural Chemicals. General term for (a) *Herbicides*, mainly selective weedkillers of the 'growth regulating' or 'hormone' type which are used chiefly in cereal crops, e.g. MCPA (4–D Dichlorophenoxy-acetic Acid). This is quickly absorbed by the leaves of broad-leaved plants, passes to the stem and root and affects the growing points, causing malformation and eventual death: 4 ozs per acre will kill practically every charlock plant in a cereal crop. (b) *Insecticides* which defeat soil pests (wireworms, cutworms), root feeding larvae (carrot fly, onion fly, cabbage-root fly), and foliage feeding caterpillars and beetles (flea beetles), e.g. DDT and other direct contact insecticides. Aphids (greenfly and blackfly) which rely on suction of the plant sap and often escape under foliage can be combated by systemic insecticides (organo-phosphorus compounds—use restricted in U.K. from 1964) which enter the plant tissues and render the leaves poisonous to them. (c) *Fungicides*, used as seed dressings (cereals and peas) or, in the case of potato blight, on the growing plant. Bordeaux mixture, or other copper fungicides, are a common choice for this last. From 1900 to 1940 only comparatively few were in use, but today a full range is available and their choice and application calls for advanced technological knowledge.

AGRIGENTO (ahgrējen'toh). City in Sicily, Italy. The Roman Agrigentum, it was long called Girgenti until renamed Agrigento under the Fascist regime. There are fine remains of Greek temples. Pop. (1961) 47,094.

A'GRIMONY. Species of plants (*Agrimonia eupatoria*) of the family Rosaceae, growing in hedge-banks, dry sunny banks, and fields. The flowers are small and pale yellow, and are borne on a slender spike.

AGRI'PPA, Marcus Vipsanius (63–12 B.C.). Roman general. Commander of the fleet at Actium (q.v.), he m. Augustus' daughter, Julia.

AGRIPPA von NETTESHEIM, Heinrich Cornelius (1486–1535). German philosopher, physician, and cabbalist. B. at Cologne, he served the emperor Maximilian, and wrote *De incertitudine et vanitate scientiarum*.

AGUASCALIENTES (ah'gwahskahlē-ān'tes). Industrial city in central Mexico. Pop. (1967) 157,000.

AGULHAS (ahgoo'lyahs), **Cape** (Port., the needles). Most southerly point of Africa, about 110 m. E.S.E. of the Cape of Good Hope.

AGUTI (agoo'ti) (*Dasyprocta*). Mammal of the order Rodentia, related to the porcupines but not armed with spines, the coat consisting mostly of short speckled hairs. Swift-running and about the size of a rabbit, As. live in forested parts of South America and the Antilles.

AHAB. King of Israel, c. 875–854 B.C. His empire included the suzerainty of Moab, and Judah was his subordinate ally; but his kingdom was weakened by constant wars with Syria. By his marriage with Jezebel, princess of Sidon, A. was led to introduce into Israel the worship of the Phoenician god Baal, thus provoking the hostility of Elijah and the prophets. A. d. in battle against the Syrians at Ramoth Gilead.

AHA'GGAR. Plateau of the central Sahara whose highest point, Tahat, 9,850 ft., lies between Algiers and the mouth of the Niger. It is the home of the nomadic Tuaregs.

AHASUE'RUS. Latinized Hebrew form of the Persian Khshayarsha (Gk. Xerxes). Name given to several Persian kings in the Bible, notably to the

AGRICULTURE. A selective weedkiller acts by reducing the weeds to a few strands (centre), leaving the crops unaffected on either side. *Courtesy of Fisons Pest Control Ltd.*

husband of Esther. Traditionally it was also the name of the Wandering Jew.

AH'MADI. Town of Kuwait, the residential and local admin. centre of the Kuwait Oil Co. Some 22 m. S. of Kuwait town, it is *c.* 6 miles both from the oil port of Mina-al-Ahmadi and from the oilfields at Burgan and Magwa. It was created by the co. amid barren desert and is a model city. Pop. *c.* 8,000.

AHMA'DIYYA. Islamic religious movement inaugurated by Mirza Ghulam Ahmad (1835–1908) of Qadian, Punjab, India, who in 1879 claimed to be the Mahdi and the Promised Messiah. In 1914 there was a split, rival Khalifas establishing themselves at Qadian and Lahore. Many regular missions in foreign countries are run under the auspices of the former. There is an A. mosque at Southfields, London.

AHMAD SHAH (1724–73). First ruler of Afghanistan. Elected king in 1747, he had made himself master of the Punjab by 1751. He defeated the Mahrattas at Panipat in 1761, and then the Sikhs.

AHMEDABA'D or **AHMADABA'D.** City of India, on the Sabarmati, provisional cap. of Gujerat state. It was founded in the reign of Ahmad Shah in 1412, and came under the control of the East India Co. in 1818. It has many edifices of the Hindu, Mohammedan and Jain faiths. Pop. (1961) 1,149,852.

AHMEDNA'GAR or **AHMADNA'GAR.** City of India in Maharashtra state, 120 m. E. of Bombay, on the left bank of the Sina. It is a centre of cotton trade and manufacture. Pop. (1961) 118,266.

AH'RIMAN. Name given to the evil principle in the Zoroastrian religion (Parseeism). He is the lord of darkness and death, and wages eternal war with Ahura Mazda (Ormuzd).

AHU'RA MA'ZDA or **ORMUZD.** Name given to the supreme good principle in Zoroastrianism. He is the god of life and light, and will finally prevail over his enemy, Ahriman.

AHVENANMAA. Finnish name of ÅLAND ISLANDS.

AHWA'Z. Town of Persia at the head of navigation on the Karun, 46 m. S. of Shushtar. Pop. (1968) 145,000.

AICARD (ākahr'), **Jean François Victor** (1848–1921). French writer. B. at Toulon, he was widely acclaimed for the purity and glow of his verse. Two of his vols. were crowned by the *Académie*, and he also wrote plays, of which *Le Père Lebonnard* (1890) was most successful, and many novels, of which *Maurin des Maures* and *L'Illustre Maurin* were translated into English.

AIDAN, St. (d. 651). Monk of Iona; first bishop of Lindisfarne. He christianized Northumbria, settled on Lindisfarne, erected churches and monasteries, and founded a school. He d. at Bamburgh.

AIGUN (ī'goon). Port and railway town on the Amur, Heilungkiang prov., China, Here in 1857 China ceded the left bank of the Amur to Russia. Pop. (1952) 42,800.

AIKEN (āk'en), **Conrad Potter** (1889–   ). American poet and novelist. B. in Georgia, he long lived in Sussex. His 1st vol. *Earth Triumphant* (1914) was -written under the influence of the realist school. He then became associated with the Imagist movement, and all his work shows a lyric facility: *Collected Poems* (1953). Among his novels the most remarkable are *Great Circle* (1933), reflecting events of his own life – when he was a boy his father committed suicide after killing A.'s mother—*Conversation* (1940), and *Ushant* (1952).

AILSA CRAIG (āl'sa crāg). Rocky islet in the Firth of Clyde, Scotland, about 10 m. off the Ayrshire coast, opposite Girvan.

AIN (aṅ). French river giving its name to a dept.; it is a right-bank tributary of the Rhône.

AINSWORTH, William Harrison (1805–82). British historical novelist. B. at Manchester, the son of a solicitor, he had a great success with his first novel, *Rookwood* (1834), which had Dick Turpin as its hero. He produced in all some 40 novels, of which the best-known are *Jack Sheppard* (1839), *The Tower of London* (1840), *Old St. Paul's* (1841), *Windsor Castle* (1843), and *The Lancashire Witches* (1848).

AIN TAB. Syrian name of GAZIANTEP.

AINTREE. Racecourse outside Liverpool, Lancs., where, in addition to flat racing, the Grand National, the premier event of the steeplechase season, was estab. 1839. *See* HORSE-RACING.

AINU (ī'noo). Caucasoid race of hunters and fishermen, fair-skinned, blue-eyed and hairy. Until driven out in the 4th cent. A.D. by the Yamato (ancestors of the modern Japanese), they were the dominant race in Japan, but today only a few thousands survive on Hokkaido, where an Institute of A. Studies at the univ. works to prevent their extinction. Possibly originating in Scandinavia, they have tended to intermarry with the 'oriental' population, and to decline with the eradication of their culture, which may go back to 7 or 8,000 B.C. Their language may be one of the world's oldest, having few links with any other, and their religion is a complex animalism, one of its features being a communal bear's festival. A blue tattoo of face and lips is practised, especially by the women.

AIRCRAFT CARRIER. A sea-going aerodrome. The germ of the modern A.C. of large dimensions was inherent in the 22-knot Cunard liner *Campania*, converted into a carrier in 1915 –6, but her flight deck was small and she mainly carried only seaplanes.

The first genuine A.Cs. were the *Argus* and *Furious* which served in the last year of the F.W.W. and throughout the S.W.W. H.M.S. *Hermes* (completed 1924, sunk off Ceylon) was the 1st A.C. specially designed as such. Most famous of the A.Cs. of the S.W.W. was the

AIRCRAFT CARRIER. H.M.S. *Victorious* leaves Singapore for Hong Kong.
Crown Copyright.

Ark Royal (completed 1938, torpedoed off Gibraltar and foundered in tow Nov. 1941) which the enemy repeatedly claimed to have sunk. Typical features of modern A.Cs. are fully-angled flight decks, launching catapults, and arrester gear, to prevent over-running on landing. *See* WARSHIP.

AIRD, Ian (1905–62). British surgeon. Professor of surgery at London Univ. from 1946, he was also head of the Hammersmith postgraduate medical school research unit, and celebrated for his studies of hole-in-the-heart operations and the separation of Siamese twins.

AIRDRIE (ār'drē). Scottish industrial town (burgh) in Lanarkshire, 10 m. E. of Glasgow. Coal and ironstone are mined. Chief industries are engineering, brass-founding, and paper-making. Pop. (1961) 33,620.

AIREDALE TERRIER. British breed of dog. It originated about 1850 in the Aire and Wharfedale districts of Yorks, as a cross of the otter hound and Irish and Welsh terriers.

AIR FORCE. At the anniversary ceremonies of the Allied Nations of AIRCENT (Supreme Command of the Allied Air Forces Central Europe) a star formation of jetfighters. From the top (clockwise) a Gloster Javelin (R.A.F.), F-105 Thunderchief (U.S.A.F.), CF-104 Super Starfighter (R.C.A.F.), F-104 G. Starfighter (Belgian Air Force), Mirage III-C (French Air Force) and F-104 G Starfighter (Netherlands Air Force).
Courtesy of United Press International News Agency.

AIR FORCE. A nation's fighting aircraft, and the organization to maintain them. The emergence of the aeroplane at first brought only limited recognition of its potential value as a means of waging war; like the balloon, used from the American Civil War, it was considered a way of extending the vision of surface forces. The need for a unified A.F. – foreseen in the U.K. in 1911 – was realized with the formation of the R.A.F. in 1918 by merging the Royal Naval Air Service and the Royal Flying Corps. During the inter-war period, unity of air control was achieved by Italy (1923), France (1928), Germany (1935, after repudiating the arms limitations of the Versailles treaty), and by the U.S.A. in 1947. While the main specialized groupings formed during the F.W.W. – combat, bombing, reconnaissance, transport, etc. – were adapted and modified in the S.W.W., activity was extended, with self-contained tactical A.Fs. to meet the needs of surface commanders in the main theatres of land operations; and for the attack and defence of shipping over narrow seas.

In 1945–60 the piston engine was superseded by the jet engine which propelled its craft at supersonic speeds; exquisitely precise electronic guidance systems lessened the difference between missile and aircraft; and flights of unlimited duration became a reality by means of air-to-air refuelling. Together with Polaris-armed submarines, the 24 hr.-a-day patrol of the U.S. strategic air command's bombers, armed with

AIR FORCE. Here seen flying over the East Anglian coast, the Avro Vulcan B. Mk. 2 – the world's first four-jet delta wing bomber – is the spearhead of Royal Air Force, Bomber Command. This aircraft, equipped with the Avro-designed and manufactured stand-off bomb, Blue Steel, forms the frontline of Britain's nuclear deterrent force. *Courtesy of A. V. Roe & Co.*

thermo-nuclear weapons, constitute the West's main deterrents. In the progress towards 'push button' warfare, even the pilot may become obsolete.

AIR RAID CASUALTIES. During the F.W.W. (1914–8) the total number of air raid casualties in Great Britain was 1,316 killed and 3,000 wounded. In the S.W.W. (1939–45) civilian casualties in Great Britain amounted to 60,584 killed and 86,159 seriously injured. The total number in the London area was 29,890 killed and 50,497 seriously injured.

AIRSHIP. Essentially a power-driven balloon. Lift derived from the gas is known as static lift, but in addition As. have a dynamic lift due to their movement through the air. All As. have streamline envelopes or hulls, which contain the inflation gas. There are 3 main types: non-rigid, semi-rigid, and rigid.

The Zeppelin Co. pioneered the rigid type, and were the most successful in operating them, but British and American designers also played an important part. The first British rigid A. to fly was R9, of 889,310 c.f., on 27 Nov. 1916. She was followed by the R23, 27, and 31 classes during the F.W.W., and R36 and 80, R100 and R101 (destroyed by fire 1930), after. The building of As. then virtually ceased.

AIRY, Sir George Biddell (1801–92). British astronomer, Plumian prof. of astronomy at Cambridge from 1828, and Astronomer Royal 1835–81. He did remarkable work in planetary and lunar theory, and in determining the mean density of the earth.

AISNE (ān). River of N. France, giving its name to a dept. For the Battles of the Aisne, *see* FIRST and SECOND WORLD WARS.

AITKEN, Sir Max (1910–). British newspaper proprietor. Already director and chairman of Beaverbrook Newspapers Ltd., he succeeded his father in the baronetcy in 1964, but renounced the barony. *See* BEAVERBROOK.

AITKEN, Robert Grant (1864–1951). American astronomer. B. in California, he was attached to Lick Observatory from 1895, and was director 1930–5. He discovered some 3,000 double stars.

AIX-EN-PROVENCE (āks-). Town in the dept. of Bouches-du-Rhône, France, 18 m. N. of Marseilles. The former capital of Provence, it is the see of an archbishopric, and has a fine Gothic cathedral. Pop. (1968) 89,566.

AIX-LA-CHAPELLE. French name of AACHEN.

AIX-LES-BAINS (āks-lā-ban'). Spa in the dept. of Savoie, France, near Lake Bourget, 8 m. N. of Chambéry. There are sulphurous hot springs and the climate is healthy. Pop (1962) 18,270.

AJACCIO (ajas'siō). Cap. of the French island of Corsica. Situated on the W. coast, on the northern shore of the Gulf of A., it has been French since 1768. It was the birthplace of Napoleon. Pop. (1968) 44,659.

AJA'NTA. Village in Maharashtra state, India, famous for its Buddhist cave temples, dating from 200 B.C. to 7th cent. A.D., and discovered in 1817 and first described by J. Ferguson in 1843.

A'JAX. Homeric hero. Son of Telamon, king of Salamis, he was second only to Achilles among the Greek heroes in the Trojan War. When Agamemnon awarded the armour of the dead Achilles to Odysseus, A. is said to have died of rage, or to have killed himself.

AJMER (ahjmēr'). Town of Rajasthan state, Rep. of India. Situated in a deep valley in the Aravalli mountains, it has many ancient remains, notably a Jain temple. It was formerly the cap. of the small state of A., which was merged with Rajasthan in 1956. Pop. (1961) 230,999.

AKABA. Alternative transliteration of AQABA.

AKASHI. Japanese town in the W. part of Honshu, 12½ m. W. of Kobe. On its meridian 135, Japanese standard time is based. Pop. (1950) 65,642.

A'KBAR, Jellaladin Mohammed (1542–1605). Greatest of the Mogul emperors of India. He succeeded his father in 1556, and gradually established his rule throughout the whole of India N. of the Deccan. The firmness and wisdom of his rule won him the title 'Guardian of Mankind'. Though reared as a Mohammedan, he showed remarkable religious tolerance.

À KEMPIS, Thomas. *See* THOMAS À KEMPIS.

A'KENSIDE, Mark (1721–70). British poet and physician, author of *The Pleasures of Imagination* (1744).

AKHETA'TON (modern Tell-el Amarna). New cap. estab. by Ikhnaton (q.v.) to replace Thebes and its associations with the old religion – when he promulgated his monetheistic cult of Aten, the sun's disc. The name means 'horizon of the sun's disc'.

AK'HNATON. *See* IKHNATON.

A'KINS, Zoe (1886–1958). American writer. B. in Missouri, she wrote poems, literary criticism, and plays, of which the best-known is *The Greeks Had a Word for It* (1930).

AKKAIA. *See* ACHAEA.

AKO. Israeli name for ACRE.

AKO'LA. Town in Maharashtra state, India, near the Purna r. It is an important centre for the cotton and grain trade. Pop. (1961) 115,820.

AK'RON. City of Ohio, U.S.A., on the Cuyahoga, first settled in 1807. Dr. B. F. Goodrich estab. a rubber factory there in 1870, and its rubber factories grew immensely with the rising demand for motor car tyres from c. 1910. A. has a univ. founded 1870. Pop. met. area (1970) 673,485.

AKSA'KOV, Sergei Timofeyevich (1791–1859). Russian writer. B. at Ufa, in the Urals, he became a civil servant, entered the censorship, and, under the influence of Gogol, wrote autobiographical novels, including *Chronicles of a Russian Family*, *Years of Childhood*, etc.

AKSU'. Chinese town (pop. c. 20,000), once the capital of a khanate, and oasis (pop. c. 90,000) in Sinkiang-Uighur near the base of the Tien-Shan mts.

A'KSUM. Ancient city of ruins in the province of Tigré, Ethiopia, 12 m. W.N.W. of Aduwa.

ALABAMA (alabah'ma). State of U.S.A., known as the 'cotton state'; it is in the 'Deep South', with an outlet to the Gulf of Mexico. Through this corridor flows the main waterway, the river A. The state comprises the Cumberland Plateau in the N.; the Black Belt, or Canebrake, excellent cotton-growing country, in the centre; and S. of this the coastal plain, or Piny Woods.

A. was settled by the French in the early 18th cent., and passed to Britain in 1763. At the close of the

18th cent. nearly the whole of A. was included in U.S.A., and in 1819 it became a state. It is mainly agricultural. Cotton, sugar, tobacco, rice, and fruits are grown. Some oil is worked. The capital is Montgomery, and Mobile is the only port. The largest town is Birmingham. The state univ. is at Tuscaloosa, and at Tuskegee is an institute founded for Negroes by Booker Washington. Area 51,609 sq. m. Pop. (1970) 3,444,165.

AJANTA. Some thirty in number, the caves once formed a Buddhist 'monastery' and the frescoes and carvings decorating their walls are a priceless record of pre-Hindu art. Mara's attack, illustrated above, is from Cave 26 and dates from the 7th cent. *Courtesy of High Commissioner for India.*

ALABAMA. Cruiser (1,040 tons) belonging to the Confederate States in the American Civil War. Built at Birkenhead, she was allowed to slip out by the British authorities, and sank many U.S. merchant vessels before being herself sunk by a U.S. man-of-war in 1864. In 1871 a court of arbitration at Geneva decided in favour of the U.S.A., and Britain had to pay damages amounting to $15,500,000.

A'LABASTER. Naturally-occurring form of gypsum which, chemically, is hydrated calcium sulphate, $CaSO_4.2H_2O$. It is a soft material, used for carvings.

ALAIN-FOURNIER (ahlaṅ′ foornyeh′). Pseudonym of Henri Fournier (1886–1914), French novelist, who was killed in action on the Meuse in the F.W.W. His reputation rests on *Le Grand Meaulnes* (1913), an autobiographical fantasy of romantic adventure, a search for *The Lost Domain*, as the book is titled in English. His life is intimately recorded in his correspondence with his brother-in-law Jacques Rivière.

ALAMEIN (alamān′). One of the decisive battles of history, fought 23 Oct.–4 Nov. 1942, during the S.W.W., when the British 8th Army, under Montgomery, completely routed the Axis (German and Italian) forces in the Western Desert of North Africa. A memorial was unveiled there in 1954.

A'LAMŌ. Mission-fortress in San Antonio, Texas. It was besieged 23 Feb.–6 March. 1836 by 4,000 Mexicans under Santa Anna, and the garrison of *c.* 150 incl. Davy Crockett (q.v.) was massacred.

ALANBROOKE, Alan Francis Brooke, 1st viscount

A. (1883–1963). British soldier. Son of Sir Victor Brooke, Bart., of Co. Fermanagh, he served in the artillery, received the D.S.O. in the F.W.W., and afterwards held important military posts. In the S.W.W he commanded the 2nd Corps of the B.E.F. (1939–40) and was C.-in-C. of the Home Forces (1940–1). He became Chief of the Imperial General Staff (1941-6), and a Field Marshal in 1944. He was created a baron in 1945 and a viscount in 1946. Sir Arthur Bryant's *The Turn of the Tide* (1957) based on A.'s war diaries caused much controversy.

ÅLAND (aw′land) **ISLANDS.** Group of some 300 islands, belonging to Finland, in the Baltic Sea, at the S. extremity of the Gulf of Bothnia. Only 80 are inhabited; the island of Å. is the largest and contains a small town, Marienhamn. Area 572 sq. m.; pop. (1960) 20,981.

ALARCON (ahlahrkōn′), **Juan Ruiz de** (*c.* 1580–1639). Spanish dramatist. B. in Mexico, he was ed. in Spain and settled there. His best-known plays are the comedy *La Verdad sospechosa*, and the drama *El Tejedor de Segovia*.

ALARCON, Pedro Antonio de (1833–91). Spanish journalist and poet, b. at Guadix. Out of his experiences as a soldier in Morocco he produced a *Diario* which was acclaimed as a masterpiece. Among his outstanding works were *El sombrero de tres picos* (The Three-cornered Hat, 1874) and *Cuentos amatorios.*

A'LARIC (*c.* 370–410). King of the Visigoths. In 396 he invaded Greece and retired with much booty to Illyria. In 400 and 408 he invaded Italy, and in 410 captured and sacked Rome, but d. the same year on his way to invade Sicily, and was buried in the r. Busento.

ALA'SKA. Detached state of the U.S.A., at the N.W. extremity of N. America. It was discovered in 1741 by Behring, and a settlement was made in 1744 by Russia, from whom it was bought in 1867 by the U.S.A. at a cost of 7,200,000 dollars (a penny an acre). Much of A. is mountainous and includes, besides other lofty peaks, Mt. McKinley (20,464 ft.), the highest peak in N. America, surrounded by a national park of nearly 2 million acres. Reindeer thrive in the Arctic tundra and elsewhere there are extensive forests. Agriculture is rendered difficult by the short summers and the variation of climate from great heat to extreme cold. There are numerous rivers, the largest being the Yukon. The coast is rocky and deeply indented, fringed with many islands; one of these, Little Diomede, is only 24 m. from Big Diomede (or

ALABAMA. Cotton-picking used to be done laboriously by hand, but the machine is taking over. To facilitate the gathering of the crop the leaves of the plant are withered chemically after the ripening of the boll.
Courtesy of the Cotton Board, Manchester

Ratmanov Is.) in the U.S.S.R. The capital is Juneau.

Oil and natural gas, exploited from the 1960s especially in the Prudhoe Bay area 150 m. S.E. of Point Barrow, are the most valuable mineral resources. Gold was discovered in 1880; other minerals incl. coal, sand and gravel. There is an important fur trade. Salmon fisheries and canneries, and lumbering are thriving industries. Reindeer provide food for the Eskimoes and hides. The chief railway runs from Seward to Fairbanks, which is linked by motor road (via Canada) with Seattle. Air services are frequent. Near Fairbanks is the Univ. of Alaska. Area 586,400 sq. m.; pop (1970) 302,173.

ALASKA HIGHWAY. Road which runs from Fort St. John, British Columbia, to Fairbanks, Alaska (1,523 m.). It was built in 1942 during the S.W.W., primarily as a defence measure in the event of a Japanese attack on Alaska.

ALBACETE (ahlbahtheh′teh). City in S.E. Spain, cap. of a province of the same name. Once famous for its cutlery and notably for daggers, it is a market town. Pop. (1960) 74,417.

A′LBACORE. Name loosely applied to several sorts of fish found in the Atlantic, in particular to a large tunny and to several species of mackerel.

ALBAN, St. (d. A.D. 303). First Christian martyr in England. According to tradition, he was b. at Verulamium, served in the Roman army, became a convert to Christianity after giving shelter to a priest, and on openly professing his belief, was beheaded. In 793 King Offa founded a monastery on the site of A.'s martyrdom, and round this the city of St. Albans grew up.

ALBANI (ahlbah′nē). Stage-name adopted by Emma Lajeunesse (1852–1930), Canadian soprano. B. in Chambly, Quebec, she had remarkable vocal flexibility. From her Italian début in 1870 in *La Sonnambula*, she was an established success and was created D.B.E. in 1925.

ALBA′NIA (Alban. Shqiperia). Republic forming part of the Balkan peninsula. The Dinaric Alps extend over the greater part, with thickly forested slopes which are the haunt of wild boars and wolves. Swift streams descend to the alluvial lowland, which fringes the coast. The lowland soil is fertile, but primitive methods are still in use and industry scarcely exists. Roads link the principal towns, and Durres is connected by rail with Tirana and Elbasan. Foreign trade is limited.

The capital is Tirana, Durres is the only port. Other towns are Shkoder, Korrce, Gjinokaster, Elbasan, and Vlone. Politically linked with China, A. broke off relations with the U.S.S.R. in 1961. *See* HOXHA, ENVER.

After forming part of the East Roman empire, A. was overrun by the Turks in 1467 and remained part of the Turkish empire until 1912, when it became a principality under Prince William of Wied. Civil war followed, in which Italy intervened. A. became a republic in 1925, and in 1928 its president, Ahmed Beg Zogu, was proclaimed king and remained on the throne until 1939, when the country was invaded by the Italians. In 1940 the Greeks almost succeeded in expelling the Italians, but were forced to surrender in 1941 to the Germans. These in turn were expelled in 1944, and in 1946 A. became again a republic with a Communist form of govt. There is no state religion, and though two-thirds of the people are traditionally Moslem and the rest Orthodox Christians and R.C., many mosques and churches were closed in 1967 and the govt. claimed A. as the world's first atheist state. Area, 10,629 sq. m.; pop. (1960) 1,625,000.

ALBANY (awl′bani), **Dukes of.** Scottish title created in 1398 for Robert Stewart, earl of Fife, brother of King Robert III. It repeatedly died out and was revived. In 1881 LEOPOLD GEORGE DUNCAN ALBERT (1853–84), youngest son of Queen Victoria, received

the title. His posthumous son, CHARLES EDWARD (1884–1954), succeeded him. In 1900 he became duke of Saxe-Coburg, fought for Germany 1914–8, and was deprived of his title as duke of A. in 1917.

ALBANY, Louise Maximilienne Caroline, Countess of (1752–1824). B. at Mons, the daughter of Prince Gustavus Adolphus of Stolberg, she was m. to Prince Charles Edward Stuart, the 'Young Pretender' (self-styled Count of Albany), in 1772, but left him in 1780 to live with the Italian poet Alfieri.

ALBANY. Capital of New York State, one of the oldest towns in U.S.A., on the Hudson, about 140 m. N. of New York City. With Schenectady and Troy it forms a met. area: pop. (1970) 710,714.

A′LBATROSS. Genus of oceanic birds (*Diomedea*) closely related to the petrels, and belonging to the order Procellariiformes. The best-known species is

D. exulans of the Pacific, which breeds on Tristan da Cunha and other oceanic islands and is the largest sea-bird, having a wingspan of 10 ft. or more.

ALBEE, Edward (1928–). American playwright. B. in Washington, D.C., he was adopted as an infant into a N.Y. family with theatrical links, but did not begin writing until he was 30. His plays belong to the drama of the Absurd and incl. *The Zoo Story* (1961), *The American Dream,* and *Who's Afraid of Virginia Woolf* (1962), and *Little Alice* (1966).

ALBÉNIZ (al-bā-neeth), **Isaac** (1860–1909). Spanish composer and pianist, b. in Catalonia. He composed the suite *Iberia* and other impressive piano pieces, making use of traditional Spanish tunes.

ALBERONI (ahlbehrō′nē), **Giulio** (1664–1752). Spanish-Italian cardinal and statesman. B. in Parma, he became a priest. Philip V made him in 1715 Prime Minister of Spain. In 1717 he became a cardinal. He introduced many reforms, but was forced to flee to Italy in 1719.

ALBERT (1819–61). Prince Consort of the U.K. The second son of Ernest, Duke of Saxe-Coburg-Gotha, he was ed. privately and at the Univ. of Bonn, showing great aptitude in natural science and the arts. His union with Queen Victoria, his first cousin, was the cherished plan of their uncle, King Leopold I of Belgium, and the marriage took place in 1840.

Albert planned the Great Exhibition of 1851, and the surplus profits of £150,000 went to estab. the Victoria and Albert Museum in South Kensington. He d. at Windsor of typhoid, and was buried at Frogmore. Though hard-working and conscientious, he was regarded by the British people with groundless suspicion because of his German connections.

ALBERT I (1875–1934). King of the Belgians. The younger son of Philip, Count of Flanders – the brother of Leopold II – he m. in 1900 the Duchess Elisabeth of Bavaria. He became king in 1909, and in the F.W.W. commanded the Allied army that conquered the Belgian coast in 1918, re-entering Brussels in triumph on 22 Nov. He was killed while mountaineering.

ALBERT (Victor Christian Edward) (1864–92). Duke of Clarence and Avondale and Earl of Athlone. B. at Frogmore Lodge, Windsor, he was the eldest son of Edward, Prince of Wales, afterwards Edward VII, and his consort Alexandra. In 1891 he was bethrothed to Princess Victoria Mary of Teck, afterwards Queen Mary, but before the marriage could take place he d. at Sandringham after a short illness.

ALBERT (ahlbär'), or **Alexandre Martin** (1815–95). French Socialist. He was a member of the Provisional Republican Government in 1848, and was the first factory-hand to hold a government position. An ardent disciple of Louis Blanc, he was deported for 10 years on political grounds, and took part in the Paris Commune of 1871.

ALBERT. French town in Somme dept., 17 m. N.E. of Amiens. During the F.W.W. a statue precariously balanced from Oct. 1914 to March 1918, when it fell on the tower of a shattered church, became known as 'the hanging Virgin'. Pop. (1962) 10,423.

ALBERT, Lake. Lake in Central Africa. Occupying an area of about 1,650 sq. m., some 80 m. N.W. of Lake Victoria, it lies in the Great Rift Valley. It was discovered by Sir Samuel Baker in 1864 and named after the Prince Consort.

ALBERTA. Prov. of Canada, created in 1905 out of part of the North-western Territory. It lies between Saskatchewan and the Rocky Mountains, many of whose highest peaks it includes; and most of it is arable. In the centre and S. is the dry, treeless prairie; towards the N. this merges into a zone of poplar, then mixed forest. The valley of the Peace River is the most northerly farming land in Canada (except Eskimo pastures), and there are good grazing lands in the foothills of the Rockies.

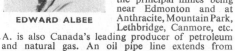

A. is pre-eminently agricultural, millions of acres being devoted to wheat, barley, and oats. Sugarbeet is grown in the S. More than a million head of cattle are fed on the natural pastures E. of the Rockies.

A. has the most extensive coal resources in Canada, the principal mines being near Edmonton and at Anthracite, Mountain Park, Lethbridge, Canmore, etc.

EDWARD ALBEE

A. is also Canada's leading producer of petroleum and natural gas. An oil pipe line extends from Edmonton to L. Superior. The McMurray district has large deposits of bituminous sand. Lumbering is important.

The cities are Edmonton, the capital; Calgary, Lethbridge, Medicine Hat, Wetaskiwin, Red Deer, and Drumheller. A. is represented in the Canadian Legislature by 6 senators and 17 members in the House of Commons. The provincial government is vested in a Lieut.-Governor and a Legislative Assembly of 61 members. The theories of Social Credit have attracted much support in A. and a Social Credit government has been in power since 1935. Area, 255,285 sq. m.; pop.(1966) 1,463,203.

ALBERT CANAL. Designed as part of Belgium's frontier defences; also links the industrial basin of Liége with the port of Antwerp. Built 1930–9, it was named after King Albert I.

ALBÉRTI, Rafael (1902–). Spanish poet, and friend of Lorca. A fine technician, he published such volumes as *Sobre los ángeles* (1928), politico-surrealist impressions of angels; *Retornos de lo vivo lejano* (1952) written in exile in the Argentine – he was on the losing side in the Spanish Civil War; and *Ora Maritima* (1953) in praise of his birthplace, Cadiz.

ALBERTUS MAGNUS (Albert the Great) (1193 or 1206–80). Scholastic philosopher. B. in Swabia, he studied at Bologna and Padua, and entered the Dominican order in 1223. He taught at Cologne and lectured from 1245 in Paris university. St. Thomas Aquinas was his pupil there, and followed him to Cologne in 1248. In 1254 he became provincial of the Dominicans in Germany, and was made bishop of Ratisbon in 1260. Two years later he resigned and eventually retired to his convent at Cologne. He was a man of vast learning on a variety of subjects – theology and philosophy (especially Aristotle), but also the natural sciences, chemistry, physics, etc. He figures as the *doctor universalis* among the Schoolmen, and as a magician in popular legend. He wrote numerous works and was canonized in 1932.

ALBI (ahlbë'). Chief town in the dept. of Tarn, S. France, on the Tarn, 45 m. N.E. of Toulouse. It was the centre of the Albigensian heresy and has a 13th cent. cathedral. Pop. (1962) 41,268.

ALBIGE'NSES or **CATHARISTS.** Heretical sect of Christians who flourished in S. France near Albi and Toulouse during the 11th to 13th cent. They adopted the Manichean belief in the duality of good and evil and pictured Jesus as being a rebel against the cruelty of an omnipotent God. They showed a consistently anti-Catholic attitude with distinctive sacraments, especially the *consolamentum*, or baptism of the spirit. In 1209 Pope Innocent III ordered a crusade against the As. Their lands were invaded by armies under Simon de Montfort, and thousands perished before peace was restored by the treaty of Paris (1229).

AL'BINISM. Absence or great deficiency in the body of the dark pigment melanin. As a result the hair is very light or white, the skin is white, and the eyes pink, yellow, or pale blue. It probably occurs sporadically among most races of mankind; it has been observed in most domestic and many wild animals, and also among plants. Poor daylight vision in albinos, formerly only ameliorated by dark glasses, may be overcome even in infants by fitting coloured contact lenses (q.v.).

A'LBION. Ancient name of Britain, mentioned by Pytheas of Massilia (4th cent. B.C.). It is probably of Celtic origin; but the Romans, having in mind the white cliffs of Dover, assumed it to be derived from *albus* (white). The kindred name of Albany was given to the Scottish highlands in the 10th cent.

A'LBOIN (reigned c. A.D. 561–73). King of the Lombards, who were at that time settled N. of the Alps. Early in his reign he attacked the Gepidae in Rumania, killing their king and taking his dau.

ALBERTA. Surrounded on all sides by landscaped parks, the new city hall at Edmonton typifies in its size and modernity the rapid development and forward outlook of the province.
Courtesy of the Alberta Government.

Rosamund to wife. About 568 he invaded Italy, conquering the country as far as Rome. He was murdered at the instigation of his wife, whom he had forced to drink from a wine-cup made from her father's skull.

ALBUERA (ahlboo-eh'rah). Spanish village, 13 m. S.E. of Badajoz, where on **16 May 1811,** during the Peninsular War, the French under Soult were defeated by Beresford.

ALBU'MIN. A class of proteins which occur in most animal fluids and tissues, and also in the seeds of plants. The most common are: *leucosin*, in the seeds of wheat, rye, and barley; *legumelin*, in the seeds of pea, lentil, soya-bean, etc., *egg-a.*, from the white of hens' eggs; and *serum-a.*, from blood serum.

ALBUQUERQUE (ahlbookār'ke), **Alfonso** de (1453–1515). Viceroy of the Portuguese Indies from 1508. He conquered Goa, Ceylon, Malacca, and Ormuz, and d. at sea on his way home.

ALBUQUERQUE (al'bakerki). Largest city of New Mexico, U.S.A., situated E. of the Rio Grande, in the Pueblo district. Here is the Univ. of New Mexico, founded 1889. Pop. (1960) 201,189.

ALCHEMY. A wood engraving attributed to Holbein, from the German translation of Boethius' *De Consolatione Philosophiae* (Augsburg, 1537).
Photo: Radio Times Hulton Picture Library

A'LBURY-WODONGA. Town in N.S.W., Australia, on the r. Murray, commercial centre of the Riverina. Pop. (1966) 32,019.

ALCAEUS (alsē'us) (*c.* 611–*c.* 580 B.C.). Greek lyric poet. B. at Mytilene in Lesbos, he was a member of the aristocratic party and went into exile when the popular party triumphed. He wrote odes, and the Alcaic stanza is named after him.

ALCALA' ZAMORA Y TORRES, Niceto (1877–1949). Spanish Republican statesman. He was Premier following the revolution of 1931 and Pres. of the Spanish rep. 1931–6. After the Civil War he went abroad.

ALCANTARA (ahlkahn'tahrah). Spanish town on the Tagus in the province of Caceres. It takes its name (Arabic for 'the bridge') from the bridge built by Trajan about A.D. 105. Pop. *c.* 4,000.

A'LCATRAZ. Small island in San Francisco Bay, Calif., U.S.A. Its fortress was a military prison 1886–1934, and then a famous federal penitentiary until closed in 1963. The dangerous currents meant few successful escapes. American Indian 'nationalists' took over the island in 1970 as a symbol of their lost heritage.

ALCAZAR (ahlkah'thahr). Name of Moorish palaces in Spain. There were 5 in Toledo, of which one, defended by Nationalist troops, held out for 71 days against the Republicans during the Spanish Civil War in 1936.

ALCHEMY. The supposed art of transmuting base metals, such as lead and mercury, into silver and gold. A certain field of A. constituted the chemistry of the Middle Ages. More broadly, however, A. was a system of philosophy which dealt alike with the mystery of life and formation of inanimate substances. A. was a complex and indefinite conglomeration of chemistry, astrology, occultism, and magic, blended with obscure and complex ideas derived from various religious systems and other sources.

ALCIBIADES (alsibi'adēz) (*c.* 450–404 B.C.). Athenian general and politician. In 422 he became leader of the war party in Athens during the Peloponnesian War, and in 415 he was appointed one of the 3 commanders of the expeditionary force to Sicily. Shortly before its departure the pillars of the god Hermes in the streets of Athens were mutilated, and the sacrilege was attributed to A. who was recalled to stand his trial. He escaped to Sparta, and was condemned to death in his absence. In 411 the Athenians recalled him, and under his leadership they gained a number of victories. But in 407 he was superseded, and retired to the Chersonese. After the fall of Athens in 404 he took refuge in Phrygia, and was there murdered.

ALCMAEONIDAE (alkmē'-o'-nidē). A noble family of anc. Athens; its members include Pericles and Alcibiades.

ALCOCK, Sir John William (1892–1919). British airman. B. at Manchester, he was apprenticed to a motor-works. In 1912 he took his air pilot's certificate. During the F.W.W. he served in the Royal Naval Air Service. On 14 June 1919, he and Lt. Whitten-Brown made the first crossing of the Atlantic in an aeroplane, a Vickers-Vimy machine, Both were given the K.B.E. A. was killed in a flying accident near Rouen.

ALCOFORADO (ahlkohfohrah'doh), **Marianna** (1640–1723). Portuguese nun. She entered a Franciscan nunnery at Beja at the age of 16, and in 1665–7 had a passionate love affair with Noel Bouton, afterwards Marquis de Chamilly, who abandoned her when their relations were discovered. Five of her letters to him were pub. anonymously in French (1669), and translated by Sir Roger L'Estrange appeared in 1678 as the *Letters of a Portuguese Nun*.

ALCOHOLIC LIQUORS. Alcohol, or, more properly, ethyl alcohol, is the basis of all the common intoxicants. These fall into 3 groups: (1) Wines, ciders, perry, and other drinks in which the alcohol is produced by direct fermentation of their sugars by yeasts; (2) Malt liquors (beers and stouts): the starch of grain is converted into sugar by malting, and the sugar is then fermented into alcohol by the action of yeasts; (3) Spirits, distilled from malted liquors or wines.

Elsewhere in Europe the strength of spirits is measured as a percentage of pure A., but in Britain 'proof spirit' has 57·1 per cent, and in the U.S.A. 50 per cent of A. by volume. In an average person, a concentration of alcohol in the blood of 0·15 per cent causes mild intoxication, 0·3 per cent causes definite drunkenness and partial loss of consciousness, and 0·6 per cent endangers life. Periodic bouts of acute alcoholism are called *dipsomania*.

ALCOHOLS. In chemistry, a group of organic compounds characterized by the presence of one or more OH-groups in the molecule. They may be liquids or solids, according to the size and complexity of the molecule.

The 5 best-known As. form a series in which the carbon and hydrogen atoms increase progressively, i.e. each of the series differs from its predecessors by the presence of an extra CH_2–(methylene) group in the molecule, viz. methyl alcohol or wood spirit (CH_3OH); ethyl A. or spirit of wine (C_2H_5OH), known also as ethanol or simply as A.; propyl A. (C_3H_7OH); butyl A. (C_4H_9OH); and amyl A. ($C_5H_{11}OH$). The lower spirits are liquids miscible with water. The higher members such as amyl A. are oily liquids not miscible with water, and the highest are waxy solids, e.g. cetyl A. ($C_{16}H_{33}OH$) and melissyl A. ($C_{30}H_{61}OH$) which occur in spermaceti and beeswax respectively.

The main uses of A. are: in alcoholic liquors; as a solvent for gums, resins, etc., in the lacquer and varnish industry, and also in the making of dyes; for essential oils in perfumery; and for medical substances in pharmacy. It is also used as a raw material in the manufacture of chloroform, ether, chloral, iodoform, etc. Certain brands of motor spirit contain A., where it is claimed to give increased power to the engine. A. is also used as a fuel.

ALCOTT, Louisa May (1832–88). American writer for girls. B. near Philadelphia, she was the dau. of Amos B. Alcott (1799–1888), a poet and transcendentalist philosopher. Her *Little Women* (1868), the most popular of all American books for girls, had *Good Wives* among its sequels.

A'LCUIN (735–804). English scholar. B. at York, he went to Rome in 780, and in 782 took up his residence at Charlemagne's court in Aachen. From 796 he was abbot of Tours. Though not a profound scholar like Bede, he disseminated the achievements of Anglo-Saxon scholarship, organized education and learning in the Frankish empire, gave a strong impulse to the Carolingian Renaissance, and was a prominent member of Charlemagne's academy.

ALDABRA (ahldah'brah). High limestone is. some 260 m. N.W. of Madagascar, and incl. in the Brit. Indian Ocean Terr. (q.v.). Uninhabited, A. is remarkable for rare animal and plant life, being the last home of the giant land tortoise. Plans for a military staging post aroused controversy 1967, but were abandoned because of modified defence plans.

ALDANOV (ahldah'nov), **Mark Alexandrovitch** (1889–1957). Pseudonym of the Russian novelist Mark Landau. B. in Kiev, he strongly opposed the Bolshevist Revolution, emigrated in 1919, and spent the rest of his life in exile, mainly in France. His novels incl. *The Ninth Thermidor* (1923) and 3 sequels, dealing with the French Revolution, and *The Fifth Seal* (1939), scathingly satirical of the Soviet Union.

ALDEHYDES (al'dēhīdz). In chemistry, a group of organic compounds prepared by oxidation of primary alcohols. The name is made up from *alcohol dehydrogenatum*, i.e. alcohol from which hydrogen has been removed. As. are usually liquids and include acetaldehyde, formaldehyde, benzaldehyde, and citral.

ALDER. Genus of trees and shrubs (*Alnus*) of the family Betulaceae, allied to the birch. The common or Black A. (*A. glutinosa*) is found throughout the temperate zone of the northern hemisphere.

ALDER. The tree, with leaves and catkins.

ALDERMAN (awl'-, Old Eng. *ealdorman*, older man). Senior member of a borough or county council in England and Wales, or of a municipal corporation in certain towns in the U.S.A.

In England Aldermen on borough and county councils (qq.v.) are elected by the councillors: abolition of the office was recommended by the Maud Committee 1967. *See also* LONDON, CITY OF.

ALDERMASTON. Village of Berks., England, site of an atomic weapons research establishment. In 1958 nuclear disarmament campaigners made it the goal of a great Easter protest march from London, and until 1964 marches were made in the reverse direction.

ALDERNEY (awl'-). Third largest of the Channel Islands. It is 3½ m. long, and 1 m. wide, with an area of 1,962 acres. The soil is fertile and well suited for grazing the famous A. cattle. The only settlement of importance is St. Anne (the capital) with an airport.

It suffered severely under the German occupation 1940–5 Pop. (1961) 1,449.

ALDERSHOT (awl'-). English town (bor.) in Hants, 35 m. S.W. of London, H.Q. of A. and Hants Military District of Southern Command. Its military camp and barracks were estab. in 1854. Before the S.W.W. the annual 'Tattoo', or military parade with massed bands, attracted huge crowds. Pop. (1961) 31,260.

ALDHELM (*c.* 640–709). English saint, prelate, and scholar. He was abbot of Malmesbury from 673 and bishop of Sherborne from 705. Of his poems and treatises in Latin, some survive, notably his Riddles in hexameters, but his English verse has perished. He was also a skilled architect.

ALDINGTON, Richard (1892–1962). English writer and poet. B. in Hants, he pub. vols. of Imagist verse, working with Hilda Doolittle (q.v.), to whom he was m. 1913–37. His novels incl. *Death of a Hero* (1929) and *All Men Are Enemies* (1933); his biographical studies of D. H. Lawrence *Portrait of a Genius, but . . .* (1950) and *Lawrence of Arabia* (1955) were controversial.

ALE'GRIA, Ciro (1900–67). Peruvian novelist. He became a reporter on a Trujillo newspaper and worked with a road construction firm. Later he was imprisoned for his associations with the Popular Revolutionary Alliance. Released by the revolutionaries he left for Chile, where he remained as an exile. Of his books, the most widely read is *Broad and Alien is the World*.

ALEMÁN (ahlehmahn'), **Mateo** (1547–*c.* 1610). Spanish novelist, b. at Seville, author of the picaresque novel *Guzmán de Alfarache* (1599).

ALEMBERT (ahlonbār'), **Jean Le Rond d'** (1717–83). French mathematician and encyclopaedist. B. in Paris, he was a foundling, ed. by the Jansenists, and studied law and medicine before devoting himself to mathematics. He made substantial contributions to contemporary mathematical science. He was associated with Diderot in planning the great *Dictionnaire Encyclopédique*, for which he wrote the *Discours préliminaire*.

ALENÇON (ahlonson). French town, cap. of Orne dept., in a rich agricultural plain, 55 m. S.S.E. of Caen. It is famed for its lace, now a declining industry. Pop. (1962) 27,024.

ALEPPO. City of N. Syria, cap. of the mohafazet of Aleppo, situated in the fertile valley of the Kuwaib. A beautiful city, A. was once the trade centre between Europe and Asia, and is still an important market. It dates from *c.* 2,000 B.C. Pop. (1960) 425,467.

ALESSANDRIA (ahlessahn'drēah). City and episcopal see in N. Italy, on the Tanaro, 56 m. E.S.E. of Turin. Pop. (1961) 92,291.

ALETSCH (ah'lech). Most extensive glacier in Europe, stretching for 10 m. along the southern slope of the Jungfrau in the Bernese Alps.

ALEUTIANS (ale-ōō'shi-anz). Chain of islands in the N. Pacific, stretching from Alaska for 1,200 m. W.S.W. They comprise 14 large and more than a hundred small islands, and many rocks and islets. Politically they are part of Alaska, U.S.A. They are ice-free all the year round, but are often wrapped in fog. The is. are mountainous and volcanic, treeless, but with grass and sedge.

The Aleuts are a branch of the Eskimos. Very few are full-blooded today. Most of them belong to the Greek Orthodox Church, speak a language related to Eskimo, and live by hunting and fishing. Pop. 5,520.

ALEXANDER III. Pope 1159–81. Leader of the papal opposition to the emperor Frederick Barbarossa. Shortly after his election he was compelled to flee to France but in 1178 returned to Rome and received the emperor's homage. He supported Henry II of England in his invasion of Ireland, but humbled him after the murder of Thomas à Becket. He held the 3rd Lateran council in Rome in 1179.

ALEXANDER VI. Pope 1492–1503. The infamous

Borgia pope. B. in Spain in 1431, he was speedily advanced in the church by his uncle Pope Calixtus III (1455–8). He secured his own election as pope by bribery, and his papacy became noted for nepotism, immorality, treachery, and ostentatious extravagance. But, himself a man of great gifts, he was a patron of art. When Savonarola in Florence preached against his corrupt practices, A. secured his execution. A. died of poison which he is said to have prepared for his cardinals. He was the father of Cesare and Lucrezia Borgia.

ALEXANDER I (1777–1825). Tsar of Russia. Son of Paul I, he came to the throne in 1801 on his father's assassination, joined the coalition against Napoleon in 1805, and was present at Austerlitz, where his forces were defeated. Defeat at Eylau and Friedland led A. to seek peace, and a treaty was concluded at Tilsit (1807). For a time A. seems to have fallen under the spell of Napoleon's personality, but admiration turned to detestation, and he broke with Napoleon's economic policy and opened his ports to British goods and ships. In 1812 Napoleon invaded Russia, where the determined resistance of the Tsar and his people, the Russian winter and the vastness of the country, proved his undoing. A. led the Russian hosts from Moscow to Paris, and was recognized as the greatest of European potentates. He gave a constitution to Poland, but was also the prime mover in the Holy Alliance which endeavoured to make reaction permanent. His last years were clouded by fear of the liberal movements.

ALEXANDER II (1818–81). Tsar of Russia. Eldest son of Nicholas I, he succeeded him in 1855, when Russia was fighting the Crimean War against Britain, France, and Turkey. The war was concluded in 1856 by the treaty of Paris. In 1863–4 a Polish insurrection was sternly repressed, and in 1877–8 there was war again with Turkey, in which the Russians were successful. Although the serfs were emancipated in 1861, A. became increasingly autocratic and reactionary, and he was assassinated by Nihilists.

ALEXANDER III (1845–94). Tsar of Russia. Son of Alexander II, he succeeded on the assassination of his father in 1881. He m. Dagmar (1847–1928), dau. of Christian IX of Denmark and sister of Queen Alexandra of the U.K., in 1866. Essentially a reactionary, he ruled the empire with a firm hand. The Jews were persecuted, and the subject peoples were relentlessly Russified.

ALEXANDER THE GREAT (356–323 B.C.). King of Macedonia and conqueror of the Persian empire. The son of Philip, king of Macedonia, and Olympias, he was ed. by the philosopher Aristotle. He first saw fighting in 340, and at the battle of Chaeronea (338) contributed to the victory by a cavalry charge. When his father was murdered in 336, the Macedonian throne and army passed into his hands. He first secured his northern frontier, suppressed an attempted rising in Greece by his capture of Thebes, and in 334 crossed the Dardanelles for the campaign against the vast Persian empire. A. marched with 20,000 foot and 5,000 horse, and at the r. Granicus near the Dardanelles won his first success. In 333 he routed the Pers. king Darius at Issus, and then set out for Egypt, where he was greeted as Pharaoh, son of the god Ra, and hailed as son of Zeus. He founded Alexandria, the future centre of Hellenistic civilization. Meanwhile, Darius collected half-a-million men, with scythed chariots and elephants, for a final battle, but at Arbela on the Tigris in 331 A. with 47,000 men drove the Persians in headlong retreat.

After the victory he stayed a month in Babylon, then marched to Susa and Persepolis, and in 330 to Ecbatana. Soon after he learned that Darius was dead. In Afghanistan he founded colonies at Herat and Kandahar, and in 328 reached the plains of Sogdiana,

A posthumous coin-portrait.

where he m. Roxana, dau. of King Oxyartes. India now lay before him, and he pressed on to the Indus. Near the Hydaspes he fought one of his fiercest battles against the rajah Porus. At the r. Hyphasis his men refused to go farther, and reluctantly he turned back down the Indus and along the coast. They reached Susa in 324, here A. took Darius' daughter for his 2nd wife. He d. at Babylon of a malarial fever.

A. left no successor, and his empire broke up into independent kingdoms. But his personality left deep impressions on East and West; peoples of the East all had their traditions of him, whilst medieval romances made him a hero of the type of Arthur and Charlemagne.

ALEXANDER. Name of three kings of Scotland. ALEXANDER I (c. 1078–1124), known as 'the Fierce', reigned from 1107. ALEXANDER II (1198–1249), the son of William the Lion, succeeded his father in 1214, and supported the English barons in their struggle with King John after Magna Charta. By the treaty of Newcastle in 1244 A. acknowledged Henry III of England as his liege lord. His son ALEXANDER III (1241–85) reigned from 1249. In 1263 he extended his authority over the Western Isles which had been dependent on Norway, and strengthened the power of the central Scottish government. He d. as the result of a fall from his horse at Kinghorn, leaving as heiress his granddau. Margaret, the Maid of Norway.

ALEXANDER (OBRENOVICH) (1876–1903). King of Serbia from 1889 while still a minor, upon the abdication of his father King Milan. He took power into his own hands in 1893, and in 1900 m. a widow, Mme Draga Mashin. In 1903 A. and his queen were murdered, and Peter Karageorgevich was placed on the throne.

ALEXANDER I (KARAGEORGEVICH) (1888–1934). King of Yugoslavia, 2nd son of Peter Karageorgevich, King of Serbia, he was declared regent for his father in 1912, and in 1921, on his father's death, became king of the state of South Slavs – Yugoslavia – which had come into being in 1918. Rivalries of neighbouring powers and of the Croats, Serbs and Slovenes within the country led A. to estab. a personal dictatorship in 1929. He was assassinated on a state visit to France, and Mussolini's govt. was later declared to have instigated the crime.

ALEXANDER, Albert Victor, 1st earl A. of Hillsborough (1885–1965). British Labour politician. The son of an artisan engineer, he was Co-operative M.P. for Hillsborough 1922–31 and 1935–50, when he was created a visct. He was 1st Lord of the Admiralty 1929–31, and in Churchill's National Govt. 1940–5, and was again re-appointed under Attlee 1945–6. He was Min. of Defence 1947–50 and Chancellor of the Duchy of Lancaster 1950–1. In 1963 he was created an earl.

ALEXANDER, Frederick Matthias (1869–1955). Australian founder and teacher of the psychophysical method named after him. At one time a professional reciter, he developed throat and voice trouble, and his experiments in curing himself led him to work out the system of mental and bodily control described in his *Use of the Self*.

ALEXANDER, Sir George (1858–1918). British actor, the typical actor-manager of his period. From 1891 he produced at the St. James's Theatre a number of plays by H. A. Jones, Pinero, and Wilde, and was knighted in 1911.

ALEXANDER, Harold Rupert Leofric George, 1st earl A. of Tunis (1891–1969). British soldier. 3rd s.

of the 4th earl of Caledon, he was ed. at Harrow and Sandhurst and commissioned in the Irish Guards. After distinguished service during the F.W.W., he held various staff appointments until 1938 when he commanded the 1st Division taking it to France in 1939. As lieut.-general he commanded the 1st Corps and organized the last phases of defence and final evacuation from Dunkirk. He was then G.O.C.-in-C. Southern Command until he became G.O.C.-in-C. in Burma in March 1942, where he fought a delaying action for 5 months against vastly superior Japanese forces. In Aug. 1942 he went to N. Africa, and in 1943 became deputy to Eisenhower in charge of the Allied forces in Tunisia. When the Axis forces in N. Africa surrendered, A. became deputy C.-in-C. of the Mediterranean Combined Operations and was promoted G.O.C., then Supreme Allied Commander in the Mediterranean and, in 1944, field marshal. Appointed Gov.-Gen. of Canada in 1946, he was created earl A. of Tunis in 1952, and was Min. of Defence 1952–4. In 1959 he was awarded the O.M.

LORD ALEXANDER OF TUNIS

ALEXANDER, Samuel (1859–1938). Australian philosopher, prof. at Manchester 1893–1924, and originator of the theory of Emergent Evolution. According to this, matter is supposed to have emerged from the original space-time matrix, and life to have similarly evolved from matter, which in its turn has given birth to mind; finally God is supposed to emerge from mind. His books incl. *Space, Time and Deity* (1920), and he received the O.M. in 1930.

ALEXANDER NEVSKI (1220–63). Russian hero and saint. Son of the grand-duke of Novgorod, he was a great warrior and in 1240 defeated the Swedes on the banks of the Neva, thus acquiring the name of Nevski. Two years later he won a victory on Lake Peipus against the Knights of the Teutonic Order.

ALEXANDER OF HALES (c. 1175–1245). English scholar and theologian. B. in Glos, he held the chair of theology in Paris, and attempted to combine the thought of Aristotle and the Arabians with the prevailing Augustinianism of his day.

ALEXANDER SEVE′RUS (A.D. 208–35). Roman emperor. B. in Palestine, he succeeded his cousin Heliogabalus in 222. His campaign against the Persians in 232 achieved some success, but in 235 when proceeding to defend Gaul against German invaders he was killed in a mutiny.

ALEXA′NDRA (1844–1925). Queen Consort of Edward VII of the United Kingdom. Eldest dau. of Christian IX of Denmark, she m. Albert Edward, Prince of Wales, in 1863; 3 sons and 3 daus. were born of the marriage. She founded Queen A.'s Imperial Nursing Service in 1902; and in 1912, to mark the 50th anniversary of her coming to England, she instituted A. Rose Day in aid of the hospitals. Widowed in 1910, she spent her closing years at Sandringham.

ALEXANDRA (1872–1918). Last tsarina of Russia. Dau. of Louis IV, grand duke of Hesse, and Princess Alice, dau. of Queen Victoria. She m. in 1894 Tsar Nicholas II. In 1907 she fell under the spell of Rasputin, a dissolute monk who had been brought to the palace to help cure the young Tsarevitch, who was a victim of haemophilia. Rasputin was murdered in Dec. 1916, and on 15 March 1917 the tsar was compelled to abdicate. With her husband, their son

ALEXANDRIA. The beaches of the city are among the finest in the world, and here at Stanley Bay there is every holiday attraction, so that its importance as a port is rivalled by its value as a tourist centre.
Courtesy of the Egyptian State Tourist Administration.

and daus. A. was sent to Siberia by the Bolsheviks; and on 16 July 1918, in a cellar at Ekaterinburg (Sverdlovsk), the whole royal family were murdered.

ALEXANDRA PARK. Public recreation ground in N. London, containing A. Palace (1875), originally a place of popular entertainment. Britain's 1st television station was established here, and it is now the B.B.C. centre for experiments in colour TV.

ALEXANDRETTA. See ISKENDERUN.

ALEXANDRIA. City in the United Arab Republic and chief port of Egypt, situated between the Mediterranean and Lake Maryut. It was founded in 331 B.C. by Alexander the Great, and for over 1,000 years was the capital of Egypt and the principal centre of Hellenistic culture. Since the 4th cent. A.D. it has been the seat of a Christian patriarch. In 641 it was captured by the Mohammedan Arabs, and after the opening of the Cape route its trade rapidly declined. Early in the 19th cent. it began to recover its prosperity, and its growth was encouraged by its being the main British naval base in the Mediterranean during both the World Wars: the Egyptian cotton trade passes through the port and there is an oil refinery.

Few relics of antiquity remain. The Pharos, the first lighthouse and one of the Seven Wonders of the ancient world, has long since disappeared. The world-famous Alexandrian Library was finally destroyed by the Arabs in 641. 'Pompey's Pillar' is a column erected, as a landmark from the sea, by Diocletian. Two obelisks that once stood before the Caesareum temple are now in London ('Cleopatra's Needle') and New York respectively. A univ. was founded in 1942. Pop. (1960) 1,513,000.

ALEXANDRIAN SCHOOL. Name given to the writers and scholars of Alexandria who from about 331 B.C. to A.D. 642 made the city the chief centre of culture in the Western World. They include the poets Callimachus, Apollonius Rhodius, and Theocritus; Euclid, father of geometry; Eratosthenes, the geographer; Hipparchus, who developed a system of trigonometry; Ptolemy, who gave his name to the Ptolemaic system of astronomy that endured for over 1,000 years; and Philo, the Jewish philosopher. The Gnostics and Neo-Platonists also flourished in Alexandria.

ALEXANDROPOL. First name of LENINAKAN.

ALEXANDROVSK. Older name of ZAPOROZHE.

ALE′XEI (SERGEI VLADIMIROVICH SIMANSKY) (1877–1970). Russian churchman. He became a priest in 1903, and in 1943 was appointed metropolitan of Leningrad and Novgorod. In 1945 he became patriarch, and secured some measure of understanding with the Soviet govt. *See* p. 28.

ALFA′LFA. Spanish name for a kind of lucerne or medic (*Medicago sativa*) of great importance as a

B

ALEXEI
Courtesy of C. de Grunwald.

fodder-plant. It is grown in many parts of the Old World, and extensively cultivated in the Canadian prairies.

ALFIERI (ahlfē-ā′rē), **Vittorio,** count (1749–1803). Italian dramatist. B. at Asti in Piedmont, he inherited a large fortune at the age of 14, and travelled abroad 1766–72. In 1775 his tragedy *Cleopatra* was successfully performed. In 1777 he met the Countess of Albany, the separated wife of the 'Young Pretender', in Florence, following her to Rome, Colmar, and Paris. On the outbreak of the Revolution, they fled to Florence, where they resided until A.'s death. His whole output betrays an ardent love for freedom and a glowing hatred of tyranny. The masterpieces among his 28 plays, tragedies most of them, are *Saul* and *Mirra.*

ALFONSO V. King of Aragon, 1416–58. Named 'the Magnanimous', he was one of the most notable figures of the Renaissance period, a patron of letters and a Latin scholar. He inherited the crown of Sicily and acquired the crown of Naples.

ALFONSO VIII. King of Castile, 1158–1214. He formed the alliance of Christian powers which inflicted disastrous defeat upon the Moors at the Navas de Tolosa in 1212; and m. Leonora, dau. of Henry II of England.

ALFONSO X (1221–84). King of Leon and Castile 1252–84. Known as 'the Wise', he is a most important figure in early Spanish literature. At his instigation many great literary projects were undertaken, and he assembled 50 of the greatest astronomers of his time at Toledo to improve the Ptolemaic planetary charts (Alfonsine Tables, 1252).

ALFONSO XIII (1886–1941). King of Spain, 1886–1931. The posthumous son of Alfonso XII, he assumed power in 1906, following the regency of his mother, and in the same year m. Princess Ena of Battenburg, granddau. of Queen Victoria. The wedding was marred by one of several attempts at assassination. Popular discontent, aided by economic depression, led to the proclamation of a republic in 1931, and A. settled in Rome, where he d.

ALFORD, Henry (1810–71). C. of E. divine and hymn-writer. He was appointed dean of Canterbury in 1857, was the 1st editor of the *Contemporary Review,* and composed many hymns, including 'Come, ye thankful people, come'.

ALFRED THE GREAT (*c.* 848–*c.* 900). English king. B. at Wantage, Berks, the youngest son of Ethelwulf, King of the West Saxons, he gained a brilliant victory over the Danes at Ashdown in 871, and succeeded his brother Ethelred after a series of defeats later in the same year. Five years of uneasy peace followed until the Danes attacked once more in 876, and in 878 A. was forced to retire to the stronghold of Athelney, whence he finally emerged to win the victory of Edington, Wilts. By the Peace of Wedmore in 878 the Danish leader Guthrum agreed to withdraw from Wessex and from Mercia W. of Watling Street. A new landing in Kent encouraged a revolt of the East Anglian Danes, which was suppressed (884–6) and after the final foreign invasion under Hasten was defeated (892–6), A. strengthened the navy to prevent fresh incursions.

In the peace that followed, A. extended and consolidated the shire system of local government, and supervised finance, the administration of justice, and the codification of the law. He also revived learning

by establishing a school at his court, to which he invited scholars such as Asser of S. Wales and John the Saxon, and encouraged writing in the vernacular. He himself translated Pope Gregory's *Pastoral Care,* Orosius' *Universal History* (to which he made many additions from his own knowledge), Bede's *Ecclesiastical History,* and Boethius' *Consolation of Philosophy,* and fostered the Anglo-Saxon Chronicle. A. was buried at Winchester. *See* ATHELNEY, ISLE OF.

ALFRETON (al′ferton). English town (U.D.) in Derbyshire, the market centre for a densely populated area and traditionally founded by Alfred the Great. Pop. (1961) 22,998.

ALGAE (al′jē; Lat. seaweeds). Subdivision of plants belonging to the Thallophyta or lower plants distinguished from the more advanced classes by their simplicity of structure, in which there is no distinction of stem, root and leaf; and from the fungi, the other main division of the Thallophyta, by the presence of green colouring-matter (chlorophyll), and in the majority of cases by their aquatic habit. They show great variety of form, the lowest

ALGAE. I, Chondrus crispus; 2, Alavia esculenta; 3, Fucus vesiculosus; 4, Halidrys siliquosa; 5, Phyllophora rubens; 6, Corallina officinalis; 7, Himanthalia loria.

types consisting of only a single cell, while some of the higher seaweeds attain to considerable size and complexity of structure.

They are divisible into 7 groups, largely to be distinguished by their pigmentation, viz. the *Chlorophyta,* green and incl. the Chlorophyceae, the simplest forms, found mostly in fresh water or damp earth and the Charophyceae or stoneworts; *Euglenophyta,* mostly green and freshwater; *Pyrrophyta,* yellow to brown; *Chrysophyta,* yellow-green to yellow-brown, mostly freshwater; *Phaeophyta* or brown seaweeds, ranging from Ectocarpus to the kelps, Laminaria and its allies, the largest of all algae; *Rhodophyta* or red seaweeds, amongst the most specialized A. and mainly marine; and *Cyanophyta,* blue-green of simple cell structure, in which reproduction is never sexual, mostly freshwater or terrestrial. *See* CHLORELLA and SEAWEED.

ALGEBRA. That department of mathematics that deals with calculations in which quantities are designated by symbols.

In ancient times it was developed in connection with certain learned professions, such as astronomy, notably in Babylon, Egypt, and India. This knowledge was preserved by the Arabs and later transmitted to Europe. The word is derived from *Al-jebr w'almuqabalah,* the title of one of the works of Mohammed ibn Musa (*c.* A.D. 820). A. received its modern form in the 16th and 17th cents. in Europe. Descartes connected A. with geometry in 1637. Applications of algebra were found in preparing tables for navigation, in the design of gears for clocks, in scientific investigations, in shipbuilding, in military matters, etc. On this foundation of elementary A. mathematicians have built various types of higher mathematics. The function of higher mathematics is to interpret and classify, to investigate what problems can be solved by what methods, and why.

ALGECIRAS (aljesēr'as). Port in Spain, province of Cadiz, 6 m. W. of Gibraltar across the Bay of A. Founded by the Moors in 713, A. was taken from them by Alfonso XI of Castile in 1344; virtually destroyed in a fresh attack by the Moors, it was re-founded 1704 by Spanish refugees from Gibraltar when that place was bombarded and captured by the British. Pop. (est.) 22,000.

ALGE'RIA. Republic in N. Africa, cap. Algiers. *Northern A.* consists of the Atlas area, and resembles S. Europe in scenery, climate, and products. Its coast is rather inhospitable, but it has a number of ports: Algiers, Oran, Bougie, Philippeville, Mostaganem, etc. S. of the wall of mountain that borders the desert lie the vast territories of *Southern A.*, a region of stony desert and sand dunes, dotted with oases supporting a small nomadic population. The economic value of the desert has been transformed by the discovery since the S.W.W. of oil (Edjélé, Hassi Messaoud, El Gassi) and natural gas (Djebel Berga, Hassi R'Mel), and pipelines to the coast have been constructed.

Other mineral products of A. are iron, antimony, zinc, silver, phosphates, marble, coal, kaolin, and salt. Agriculture is the chief source of livelihood, products including wheat, barley, tobacco, oranges, dates, esparto grass. Sheep, goats, and other livestock are reared. Wine making is an important industry, others being distilling, flour-milling; there are factories making perfume and cement and treating tobacco. There are over 2,700 m. of railway, the road system is good, and there are a number of airfields. Area 840,000 sq. m.; pop. (1963) 10,453,000, the great majority of Arab or Berber blood and Islamic religion.

History. A. formed part of the Roman Empire, but was Islamized and subjugated by the Arabs in the 7th cent. A.D. In the 16th cent. it was overrun by the Turks, but the Sultan's rule was often nominal, and in the 18th cent. A. became a pirate state dominated by *deys*, who preyed on Mediterranean shipping. European intervention became inevitable, and in 1816 an Anglo-Dutch force bombarded Algiers. In 1830 a French army landed and seized Algiers; by 1847 the N. had been brought under control, and in 1848 was formed into the depts. of Algiers, Oran, and Constantine. Many French colonists settled in these depts. which in 1881 were made part of Metropolitan France. The mountainous region inland inhabited by the Kabyles, occupied 1850–70, and the Sahara region, subdued 1900–9, remained under military rule.

After the defeat of France in 1940, A. came under the control of the Vichy government until the Allies landed in N. Africa in 1942. Algiers was the H.Q. of the French Committee of National Liberation from 1943 until it was able to move to a liberated France as the provisional govt. Post-war hopes in France of integrating A. more closely with France were frustrated by opposition in A. from those of both French and non-French origin; and long-drawn-out fighting, violence, and terrorism among various groups did not come to an end until 1962 when A., after referendums in France and in A., was recognized by France as an independent republic. More than 15,000 French military personnel died in the struggle, as well as an uncounted number of civilians of French blood and of Moslem Algerians.

ALGIERS (aljērz'). Cap. of Algeria, N. Africa, situated on the narrow coastal plain between the Atlas mts. and the Mediterranean. Founded by the Arabs A.D. 935, A. was taken by the Turks in 1518, and by the French in 1830. The old town is dominated by the Kasbah, the palace and prison of the Turkish rulers. The new town, constructed under French rule, is in European style. Pop. (1967) 943,000.

ALGÕ'A BAY. Broad and shallow inlet in South Africa, Cape Province, where Diaz landed after rounding the Cape in 1488.

ALGREN, Nelson (1909–). American novelist, whose books deal with the 'little' people of Chicago, the social fringe of gamblers, drug addicts and petty criminals, e.g. *A Walk on the Wild Side* (1956) and *The Man with the Golden Arm* (1949).

ALHA'MBRA. Fortified palace at Granada, Spain, built by Moorish kings mainly between 1248 and 1354. It stands on a rocky hill and remains the finest example of Moorish architecture.

ALI (ah'lē) (*c.* 600–61). 4th Caliph. B. at Mecca, he was the son of Abu Talib, uncle to Mohammed, who gave him his dau. Fatima in marriage. On Mohammed's death in 632, A. had a claim to succeed him, but this was not conceded until 656. After a stormy reign, he was assassinated. Around A.'s name has raged the controversy of the Sunnites and the Shiites, the former denying his right to the caliphate and the latter supporting it.

ALI (Ali Pasha) (1741–1822). Turkish statesman, known as Arslan (the lion). An Albanian, he was appointed pasha of Janina in 1788, and there he maintained a semi-barbarous court, visited by Byron. He was murdered by the Sultan's order.

ALI, Muhammad (1942–). Name adopted by American Negro boxer Cassius Marcellus Clay on joining the Black Muslim movement. He became world heavyweight champion 1964, but in 1967 resisted drafting under the Selective Service System and was prevented from defence of his title.

ALIBI (al'ibī; Lat., elsewhere). In law, a defence to a charge of crime that the person accused was, at the time the crime was committed, at some place other than the scene of the crime and so could not be guilty of it.

ALICANTE (ahlēkan'teh). Leading seaport of Spain on the S.E. coast, 46 m. N.E. of Murcia, and cap. of the prov. of A. Pop. (1960) 122,200.

ALICE SPRINGS. Australian town, originally a telegraph station, in Northern Terr., on Todd r., at 2,000 ft. a.s.l. Terminus of the railway from Adelaide, cap. of S. Australia, it was named after the wife of Sir Charles Todd who directed the construction of the S.–N. transcontinental telegraph line. A strategic highway, completed 1941 along an old trail, connects A.S. with Birdum, terminus of the railway from Darwin. A.S. is a tourist centre, only town in an area producing livestock and opals, and H.Q. of the 'flying doctor' service. Pop. (1961) 4,668.

ALICE SPRINGS. Founded in 1860, almost in the centre of the continent, this remote cattle and mining town is backed by rugged mountain ranges. The scale of the cattle holdings in the surrounding country is vast – the Victoria River Downs station is 5,495 sq. m. in extent.
Courtesy of Australia News and Information Bureau.

WASHINGTON ALLSTON. Imaginatively beautiful scenes such as this 'Moonlit Landscape' in the Museum of Fine Arts at Boston are typical of America's earliest romantic painter, who greatly influenced his generation.

ĀLIEN. Person owing allegiance to a foreign state. Under the Immigration Act (1971) aliens and Commonwealth citizens were placed under a single system of immigration control. Only those Commonwealth citizens known as 'patrials' have a 'right of abode' free of immigration control, i.e. people born in Britain, or who are citizens by adoption, registration or naturalisation; citizens of the U.K. or Colonies who enter from overseas and have been continuously settled in the U.K. for five years; and Commonwealth citizens with a parent or grandparent born in the U.K. Citizens of the Republic of Ireland have reciprocal rights, and are not regarded as aliens. British women marrying aliens lose their citizenship only if they renounce it formally, and alien women marrying British subjects may apply for registration themselves, but do not acquire citizenship automatically.

In the U.S. all As. are subject on arrival to scrutiny by the Immigration and Naturalization Service and for permanent residence must have an immigrant visa from a U.S. consul located abroad. American women marrying As. only lose their citizenship if they formally renounce it. Certain classes are excluded, e.g. the insane, narcotic drug addicts, and members of 'subversive' organisations.

ALIGARH (ahlēgahr'). City of Uttar Pradesh, India. The Moslem Univ. here, constituted in 1920, was opened to non-Muslims in 1956. Pop. (1961) 183,753.

A'LIMONY. In law, a money allowance which a court may order a husband to pay for the support of his wife during the marriage. In Britain, permanent A. ordered after a decree of judicial separation, is usually about a third of the joint incomes of husband and wife. Guilty women often get nothing.

ALIPHATIC (alifa'tik) COMPOUNDS. Chemical term for a group of organic substances of which the most typical are fats. They also include carbohydrates (starch, sugar, etc.), alcohols, and paraffins.

AL ITTIHAD. Town a few m. inland from Aden, founded in 1959 as the cap. of the Federation of South Arabia. In 1967 it became, as **Madinet al-Shaab**, the cap. of Southern Yemen.

A'LKALI. In chemistry a base that is soluble in water. As. neutralize acids, turn red litmus to blue, and are soapy to the touch. The word comes from the Arabic al-qalīy, 'ashes', since soda and potash were derived from the ashes of plants. The hydroxides of metals are As., those of sodium (caustic soda) and of potassium (caustic potash) being chemically powerful.

ALKALOIDS. Physiologically active and frequently poisonous substances contained in certain plants. The As. or vegetable As. are usually bases, i.e. they form salts with acids and, when soluble, give alkaline solutions. But substances are included in the group rather by custom than by scientific rules. Examples of As. are morphine and cocaine, quinine, strychnine, nicotine, and atropine.

ALKEN, Henry Thomas (1784–1851). British sporting artist. Fox-hunting and steeplechasing were the subjects that most frequently occupied him, but the whole range of field sports was covered in his *National Sports of Great Britain* (1821).

ALKMAAR (ahlkmahr'). Town in N. Holland, 20 m. N.N.W. of Amsterdam, on the North Holland canal. It is a centre for cheese export. Pop. (1967) 49,451.

AL'LAH (Arabic *al*, the; *ilāh*, God). The name given to the One True God by the Mohammedans.

ALLAHABA'D. Indian city, in the state of Uttar Pradesh, at the junction of the Ganges and Jumna. A univ. town, it is a centre of culture, commerce, and communication. In the grounds of the fort is one of the surviving pillars bearing an edict of Asoka (d. *c.* 228 B.C.). Remains of a palace built by Akbar are nearby. A. is regarded as a Holy City by Hindus, and is the scene of yearly pilgrimages. Pop. (1961) 431,007.

ALLAN, David (1744–96). Scottish historical painter. He studied in Rome and, after a period in London, he became in 1786 director of the Academy of Arts in Edinburgh. A vein of humour appears in his 'Scotch Wedding', etc.

ALLAN, Sir William (1782–1850). Scottish historical painter, b. at Edinburgh. He spent several years in Russia and neighbouring countries, returned to Edinburgh in 1814, was elected R.A. in 1835, President of the Royal Scottish Academy in 1838, and was knighted in 1842. His paintings include scenes from the Waverley novels.

ALLBUTT, Sir Thomas Clifford (1836–1925). British physician, inventor of the short clinical thermometer. He specialized in nervous pathology, and was Regius prof. of physic at Cambridge from 1892.

ALLEGHENY MOUNTAINS. Range more than 500 m. long extending from Pennsylvania to Virginia, rising to more than 4,800 ft. with an average elevation of 2,500 ft. In places very beautiful, but wild and difficult, they proved for many years an effective barrier to western migration, the first settlement to the W. being Marietta in 1788.

ALLEGIANCE. The duty of obedience owed by a subject to a Sovereign, who in return gives protection. An *Oath of A.* must be taken by aliens on naturalization, by M.P.s, by certain ministers of the Crown, etc. Aliens becoming U.S. citizens swear A. to the 'Constitution and laws of the U.S.A.'

A'LLEGORY. Figure of speech; the description or illustration of one thing in terms of another, it is equivalent to an extended metaphor or parable, and it makes use of obviously fictitious figures. A well-known A. is Bunyan's *Pilgrim's Progress*.

ALLEGRI (ahlleh'grē), Gregorio (1582–1652). Italian composer. B. at Rome, he became a priest, and entered the Sistine chapel choir in 1629. His *Miserere* for 9 voices was treasured at the Sistine.

ALLEN, Hervey (1889–1949). American novelist, best known for his mammoth historical novel *Anthony Adverse* (1933) set in the Napoleonic era. He was a high school teacher at Charleston, S.C., and later lectured at Columbia Univ., and included among his other works vols. of poetry and *Israfel* (1926), a biography of Poe.

ALLEN, William (1532–94). English cardinal. Principal of St. Mary's Hall, Oxford, under Queen

Mary, he refused to take the oath of supremacy on the accession of Elizabeth. In 1568 he founded a theological seminary at Douai, and moved it in 1578 to Rheims, where his followers commenced the Douai version of the Eng. Bible. On being made a cardinal in 1587, he encouraged the Eng. Catholics to rise against Elizabeth, but after the failure of the Armada his influence diminished.

ALLEN. Lough or lake in Co. Leitrim, Rep. of Ireland, on the upper course of the Shannon. It is 7 m. long and 3 m. broad.

ALLEN, Bog of. Morasses E. of the Shannon in Rep. of Ireland, comprising about 240,000 acres of Offaly, Leix, and Kildare.

ALLENBY, Sir Edmund Henry Hynman, 1st visct. A. (1861–1936). British field marshal. He saw much service in S. Africa, and in the F.W.W. was with the B.E.F. in France before taking command in 1917–9 of the British Forces in the Near East. He proceeded to crush the Turks in Palestine, the crowning victory being at Megiddo in Sept. 1918, which was followed almost at once by the capitulation of Turkey. He was created a visct. and promoted to field marshal, and in 1919–25 was British High Commissioner in Egypt.

ALLENSTEIN (ahl'lenstīn). Town in former E. Prussia, placed under Polish admin. 1945, 60 m. S. of Kaliningrad. It was H.Q. of the Grand Master of the Teutonic Knights from medieval times to 1945. Polish form of the name is Olsztyn.

A'LLERGY. A special sensitiveness of the body which makes it react abnormally to the introduction of a foreign substance, proteins (organic substances containing nitrogen). The person subject to hay-fever in summer is allergic to one or more kinds of pollen. Many asthmatics are allergic to certain kinds of dust; some cannot sleep on a feather pillow or go near a horse. Others come out in nettle-rash, or are violently sick if they eat shellfish or egg.

ALLEYN (al'en), **Edward** (1566–1626). English actor. B. in London, the son of an innkeeper, he joined the earl of Worcester's players, was associated with Philip Henslowe, and became proprietor of several playhouses. He founded Dulwich College.

ALLIER (ahlyeh'). River in central France, tributary of the Loire; it is 350 m. long, and gives its name to a dept. Vichy is the chief town on it.

A'LLIGATOR. Genus of reptiles, of which there are 2 species – *A. mississippiensis* in the southern states of U.S.A., and *A. sinensis* of the Yangtze-Kiang in China. The former grows to 12 ft. but the latter is smaller. The genus *Caiman* of Central and South America is closely allied.

As. closely resemble crocodiles in their general habits, swimming well with the assistance of lashing movements of the tail, and feeding on fish and mammals, though seldom attacking man. The eggs are laid in sand. The skin is of value for fancy leather, and A. farms have been established in U.S.A.

ALLINGHAM (al'-), **Margery Louise** (1904–66). British writer of detective fiction, e.g. *Death of a Ghost, Flowers for the Judge, The Case of the Late Pig,* and *More Work for the Undertaker.*

A'LLIUM. Genus of plants belonging to the Lily family (Liliaceae). They are usually acrid in their properties, but form bulbs in which sugar is stored. Cultivated species incl. onion, garlic, chives, leek, etc.

ALLOA (al'ōa). Co. town (burgh) of Clackmannanshire, Scotland, on the Forth. Industries include

brewing and whisky-distilling, and the manufacture of agricultural implements. Pop. (1961) 13,895.

ALLO'PATHY. The treatment of disease of one kind by exciting a disease process of another kind or in another part; commonly used as a name for orthodox medicine, in distinction from homoeopathy (q.v.), which means treatment with minute doses of drugs which induce the same ailment.

ALLOY. A blending together of a metal with one or more metallic (or non-metallic) substances. Some As. have been known to mankind for many thousands of years, e.g. bronze. Most are made by liquefying one metal (usually that with the higher melting point) and adding the others, usually in solid form. As. may be several times stronger than any of the metals used in their manufacture, have generally lower melting points than some of their constituents. Duralumin As. were specially developed for strength and resistance to corrosion, copper with a small proportion of beryllium for toughness, and combinations of iron, nickel, titanium, manganese for a wide range of permanent and non-permanent magnets.

ALL SAINTS' DAY. 1 Nov. Also known as All-Hallows or Hallowmass. The festival for all saints and martyrs, for whom the Church calendar does not provide a separate day.

ALL SOULS' DAY. Festival in the Catholic Church, held on 2 Nov., following All Saints' Day. It was instituted in 993, and its observation is based on the doctrine of the Communion of Saints and the belief that the faithful on earth are able, by prayers and self-denial, to hasten the deliverance of souls expiating their sins in purgatory.

ALLSPICE. Spice prepared from the dried berries of the A. tree or pimento (*Eugenia pimenta*), cultivated chiefly in Jamaica.

ALLSTON, Washington (1779–1843). American artist and writer; he painted chiefly religious subjects, and for the richness of his colours was called 'the American Titian'.

ALMA. River in Ukraine S.S.R. flowing across the S.W. of the Crimean peninsula; it gives its name to a battle fought on 20 Sept. 1854, when the Russians were defeated by the Franco-British armies.

ALMA ATA (ah'ta). Cap. of Kazakh S.S.R., U.S.S.R., at the foot of the Ala-Tau mts. It is an industrial centre with a univ. and a link in the Turkestan-Siberian railway. Pop. (1969) 684,000.

ALMADÉN. Span. town in Ciudad Real province, noted for deposits of quicksilver. Pop. *c.* 12,500.

ALMA MATER (mah'ter; Lat., bounteous mother). Title given by the Romans to the goddess Ceres, and now applied to universities and schools, which are considered as the 'foster-mothers' of their pupils.

ALMANSA (ahlmahn'zah). Spanish town in Albacete, about 50 m. N.W. of Alicante, where on 25 April 1707 British and allied forces were defeated by the French under the Duke of Berwick. Pop. *c.* 14,500.

ALMA-TADEMA (ah'lma-tah'dema), **Sir Laurence** (1836–1912). Anglo-Dutch painter. B. at Dronrijp, Holland, he settled in England in 1873. Some of his best-known paintings depict scenes from Greek and Roman life. He was knighted in 1899.

ALMEDI'NGEN, E(dith) M(artha) (1898 1971). British author. Great-great-granddau. of Peter Khlebnikov, a Moscow seed and corn merchant who was ennobled by Catherine the Great for his services to literature, she also traced her descent through an English grandmother from Edmund Spenser and Robert Southey. She was b. in St. Petersburg, but settled in England in 1923. Besides poetry and novels, she was noted for the living authenticity of her portrayal of Russian history in such biographies as *The Empress Alexandra* and *Catherine the Great.*

ALMEIDA (ahlmā'ēdah), **Francisco de** (*c.* 1450–1510). 1st viceroy of Portuguese India 1505–8. He was killed in a skirmish with the Hottentots at Table Bay, S. Africa, and was buried where Cape Town now stands.

ALMERÍA (ahlmãrē´ah). Spanish city, chief town of a prov. of the same name on the Mediterranean. The prov. is famous for its white grapes and in the Sierra Nevada are rich mineral deposits. Pop. (1960) 86,808.

ALMOND. Fruit of the A. tree (*Prunus amygdalus*), which is closely related to the peach and the apricot. Originally a native of N. Africa and the Near East, it has for a long time been introduced into Europe, and its fruit will ripen in southern England.

ALPS. The ascent of the Matterhorn by Whymper's party in 1865 was a landmark in mountaineering, but four of the seven members of the team were killed on the descent. Seen here from the Mettelhorn, on the Swiss side, the mountain appears an isolated peak, but actually forms the end of a ridge.
Courtesy of the Swiss National Tourist Office.

ALMQVIST (ahlm´kvist), **Karl Jonas Ludwig** (1793–1866). Swedish writer. B. at Stockholm, he won fame by a series of novels, *The Book of the Thorn Tree* (1832–5) and wrote lyrics, dramas, novels, and philosophic studies.

ALOE (al´ō). Genus of African plants of the family Liliaceae, distinguished by their long fleshy leaves. From the juice of the leaves of several species is prepared the drug aloes, a powerful cathartic.

ALOST (ah´lŏst). Town in East Flanders, Belgium, on the Dender. The chief industry is linen bleaching. Pop. (1966) 45,900.

ALOYSIUS (alō-is´i-us), **St.** (1568–91). Patron saint of youth. B. Luigi Gonzaga at Castiglione in N. Italy, he joined the Jesuits at Rome, and d. while nursing victims of the plague. He was canonized in 1726.

ALPA´CA. S. American mammal, a domesticated variety of the guanaco (*Llama huanaco*), found in Chile, Peru, and Bolivia, and herded at high elevations in the Andes. Its flesh is eaten, but it is mainly valued for its wool.

ALPHA and Ō´MEGA (A and Ω). The first and last letters of the Greek alphabet; hence the beginning and the ending, or the sum total of anything.

ALPHA (al´fa) **PARTICLE.** Positively charged particle ejected with very great velocity from a nucleus. It is one of the products of the spontaneous disintegration of radioactive substances such as radium and thorium and is identical with the nucleus of a helium atom, i.e. it consists of 2 protons and 2 neutrons.

ALPHABET (from *alpha* and *beta*, the first two Greek letters). A set of conventional symbols called letters, each denoting a given sound or sounds. It represents the last stage in the long history of writing (q.v.).

Attempts have been made to trace the A. to the cuneiform of Sumer, Babylon, and Assyria; the syllabic writing of Cyprus; and the Hittite hieroglyphics, etc. However, the many attempts at alphabetic systems discovered in the area of Palestine and Syria make it certain that this was the cradle of our A.

HISTORICAL EVOLUTION. The *South Semitic* A. either like the North Semitic a descendant of a Proto-Semitic A., or derived from the N. Semitic A. itself, has produced only one modern offshoot, the Amharic script of Ethiopia.

The *North Semitic* A., however, in use from the 13th cent. B.C. and consisting of 22 letters which, at first, expressed only consonants, developed into all the main alphabetic scripts of today. *See* UGARIT. The principal branches are:

(i) The *Early Hebrew* A. (11th–5th cents. B.C.), with the Moabite and Ammonite As. as its closest relations;

(ii) the *Phoenician* A., employed in Phoenicia (4th–2nd cents. B.C.), Cyprus, and the Carthaginian dependencies; its offshoots are the Numidian, original of the mod. Tifinagh script of the Tuaregs, and the Iberian As.;

(iii) the *Aramaic* A., first known from the 9th–7th cents. B.C., producing numerous eastern As., such as the Nabataean, Arabic, Square Hebrew, Palmyrene, Syriac (with its chief variant Estrangelo), Mandaean, Manichaean As. It also fathered the As. of many non-Semitic languages of Central, S., and S.E. Asia, including the Pehlevi, Sogdian, Mongolian (written downwards), Armenian (*c.* A.D. 400), Brahmi (parent of the *c.* 200 Indian As. and offshoots all over the Far East) and others;

(iv) the *Classical* As. of which (a) the *Greek* A. was adopted from Semitic sources about the 9th cent. B.C.; from the Gk. derived local As. of Asia Minor, the Coptic (1st or 2nd cent. A.D.), Etruscan (9th cent. B.C.), and Italic (Umbrian, Oscan, and Faliscan from Etruscan; Messapian direct from Gk.) As. (b) the *Latin* A., created in the 7th cent. B.C. from 21 letters of the Early Etruscan A., changing some of their values and adding the two last letters of the Gk. A. Medieval additions were J, U and W.

From the Gk. uncial script derive the Gothic A. (4th cent. A.D., with Lat. additions), and the Cyrillic A., which is the parent of the Russian, Bulgarian, Serbian, Ukrainian, Early Rumanian, Siryen (Finns of N. Russia), and Ossetic (Caucasus) As. From the Gk. cursive descend the Glagolitic A., now used for liturgical purposes, and local Albanian scripts. The Runic As. (Common Teutonic, Anglo-Saxon, Scandinavian) show peculiarities of Lat. and N. Etruscan descent, and the cryptic Ogham script of S. Ireland and Wales (5th–6th cents. A.D.), is based on the Runes. The Latin A. through the European peoples became the script of the greater part of the world, and was adapted to many different languages, e.g. English, French, Italian, German, Spanish, Polish, Czech, Croatian, Hungarian, Finnish, Turkish, etc.

ALPHEGE (al´fej), **St.** (954–1012). Anglo-Saxon churchman, bishop of Winchester from 984, archbishop of Canterbury from 1006. When the Danes attacked Canterbury he tried to protect the city, was thrown into prison, and, refusing to deliver the treasures of his cathedral, was stoned and beheaded at Greenwich on 19 April, his feast-day.

ALPS. The mountain-chain which forms the northern barrier to Italy and extends in the form of a crescent from the Mediterranean on the W. to the Adriatic on the E.: 3 depts. of France (Alpes-Maritimes, Basses-Alpes, Hautes-Alpes) take their name from these mts. Among the most famous peaks are Mont Blanc (15,781 ft.), the Matterhorn (14,782 ft.), Monte Rosa (Dufourspitze, 15,217 ft.), Finsteraarhorn (14,026 ft.), and the Eiger (13,000 ft.), remarkable for its almost vertical rock wall (7,730 ft.) on the north face, first scaled in 1938. (*See* HEINRICH HARRER.)

Many of the streams and rivers have been harnessed to provide electricity for small iron and textile industries, railways and lighting. 'The Alps' is used by the alpine people to describe the high summer pastures which are of immense importance for agriculture. Cattle are grazed on the lower parts in June, gradually working upwards as summer advances. The economic conditions of the Alpine peoples have been revolutionized in the last two cents., mainly owing to tourist and winter sports traffic. The chief sports resorts and spas incl. St. Moritz, Davos, Baden, and Tarasp-Schuls-Vulpera in Switzerland, Garmisch-Partenkirchen in Bavaria and Kitzbuhel in Austria. The A. are pierced by rail and road tunnels (Mont Blanc, Gt. St. Bernard, San Bernadino, and the projected St. Gotthard).

ALSACE-LORRAINE (ahlzahs´-lorän). Alsace and Lorraine were formerly provs. of N.E. France. Bismarck introduced the term Elsass-Lothringen (Ger. for Alsace-Lorraine) in 1871 for the territory annexed by Germany, i.e. Alsace, and the N.E. part of Lorraine, an area of 5,605 sq. m., and comprising the present French depts. of Moselle, Bas-Rhin, and Haut-Rhin. Lorraine, rich in coal and iron, is highly industrialized; Alsace produces textiles and is agriculturally important.

Forming part of Celtic Gaul in Caesar's time, the A.-L. area was invaded by the Alemanni and other Germanic tribes in the 4th cent., remaining part of the German Empire till the 17th cent. In 1648, part of the territory was ceded to France; in 1681, Louis XIV seized Strasbourg. The few remaining districts were seized by the French after the Revolution, but A.-L. was conquered by the Germans 1870–1, and declared 'Imperial Territory' (*Reichsland*). France did not regain possession of A.-L. until 1919. In 1940 the country was again annexed by the Germans until liberated in 1944 by the Allied armies.

ALSÃ´TIA. The old name for Alsace. In 17th cent.

ALTDORFER. Thought to be the earliest European landscape painting – c. 1518–20 – 'Landscape with a Footbridge' was acquired by the National Gallery in 1963. The only other purely landscape picture by this artist is in the Alte Pinakothek, Munich.   *Photo: Courtesy of the National Gallery.*

London this name was given to the district of Whitefriars between Fleet St. and the Thames. It afforded sanctuary to debtors and other lawless characters, a privilege derived from the convent of Carmelites, estab. there in 1241. In 1697 this privilege was withdrawn.

ALSATIAN. Breed of dog introduced from Germany into Britain as the Alsatian Wolfdog after the F.W.W. It has a wolf-like appearance, a beautiful coat with many varieties of colouring, and distinctive gait. As war dogs and as guide dogs for the blind, the tractability of the breed has been recognized.

ALTAI (ahltī´) **MTS.** Mountain system of W. Siberia and Mongolia. It is divided into 2 parts, the Russian A., which includes the highest peak, Mount Belukha (15,157 ft.), and the Mongolian or Great A. A territory of the R.S.F.S.R. takes its name from the range.

ALTAMIRA (ahltahmē´rah). Cave near the Spanish village of Santillana del Mar in Santander prov. where in 1879 remarkable palaeolithic wall-paintings were discovered.

ALTAMURA (ahltahmōō´rah). Town of Apulia, S. Italy, 25 m. S.S.W. of Bari. It has Romanesque cathedral built in 1232. Pop. *c.* 50,000.

ALTDORF (ahlt´dorf). Mountain-encircled cap. of the Swiss canton Uri at the head of Lake Lucerne. It is the scene of the legendary exploits of William Tell. Pop. (1950) 6,583.

ALTDORFER, Albrecht (*c.* 1480–1538). German artist. Probably the 1st European painter of a finished picture excluding the human figure, his work breaks with the medieval tradition of 'story-telling'. Few of his pictures survive. He was b. at Regensburg, where he worked as an architect.

ALTENBERG, Peter. Pseudonym of the Austrian poet Richard Engländer (1859–1919). He was the typical representative of Viennese Bohemianism, and pub. many collections of sketches, such as *Wie ich es sehe* (1896).

ALTERNATING CURRENT. Electric current which flows for an interval of time in one direction and then in the opposite direction, i.e. a current which flows in alternately reversed directions through or round a circuit. A.C. power is the usual form in which electric energy is generated in a power station, and A.Cs. may be used for both power and lighting. The value of A.C. over direct current (as from a battery) is that its voltage can be raised or lowered economically by a transformer, high voltage for generation and transmission, and low voltage for utilization and safety, e.g. railways, factories, and domestic appliances.

ALTGELD, John Peter (1847–1902). American political and social reformer. B. in Prussia, he was taken in infancy to U.S.A. During the Civil War he served in the Union Army. He was a judge of the supreme court in Chicago 1886–91, and as Governor of Illinois 1893–7 was champion of the worker against the government-backed power of Big Business.

ALTHING. The parliament of Iceland, created *c.* 930, the oldest parliamentary assembly in the world.

ALTMARK INCIDENT (1940). The *Altmark*, a German auxiliary cruiser, was intercepted on 15 Feb. 1940, by H.M. destroyer *Intrepid* off the coast of Norway. She was carrying the captured crews of Allied merchantmen sunk by the German battleship *Admiral Graf Spee* in the S. Atlantic, and took refuge in Jösing fjord. There she was cornered by H.M.S. *Cossack*, under Capt. Vian, and ran aground. Vian's men released 299 British sailors.

ALTRINCHAM. Town (bor.) of Cheshire, 8 m. S.W. of Manchester. Its first charter dates from 1290. Pop. (1961) 41,104.

ALUM. A white crystalline powder readily soluble in water. It is a double sulphate of potassium and aluminium. Its chemical formula is K_2SO_4, $Al_2(SO_4)_3$ $24H_2O$, and it is the commonest member of a group of double sulphates called As., all of which have similar formulae, the same crystalline form, and the same number of molecules of water of crystallization.

ALU′MINA (Al_2O_3), Oxide of aluminium which occurs widely distributed over the surface of the earth in clays, slaty rocks, and shales. It is formed by the decomposition of the feldspars in granite. Typically it is a white powder, soluble in most strong acids or caustic alkalis, but not in water, and is used extensively in the manufacture of clay articles such as pipes and of various paints.

ALUMI′NIUM. The most abundant metal, valuable for its light weight, having at. no. 13, at. wt. 26·98, and chemical symbol A1. Nearly one-twelfth of the substance of the earth's crust is composed of A. compounds, but A. in its pure state was not readily obtained until the middle of the 19th cent., for it oxidizes rapidly, and much energy is needed to separate the metal from chemical combination. Pure A. is a soft white metal. It is one of the lightest of metals, its specific gravity being 2·70, and for this reason is widely used in shipbuilding and aircraft. In the pure state it is a weak metal, but when alloyed with other elements such as copper, silicon, or magnesium, alloys of great strength are obtained. Commercially, A. is obtained from bauxite (q.v.) and requires large supplies of electric power, as at Kitimat in Western Canada. A. is much used in steel-cored aluminium overhead cables and for canning uranium slugs for reactors. A. is an essential constituent in the Alcomax series of magnetic materials; and as a good conductor of electricity is used in the form of foil in electrical capacitors. In the U.S.A. the original name suggested by Sir Humphry Davy ALUMINUM (alōō′-) is retained.

ALVA, or **ALBA, Ferdinand Alvarez de Toledo,** duke of (1508–82). Spanish statesman and general. He commanded the Spanish armies of Charles V and Philip II, and in 1567 was appointed Governor of the Netherlands, where he set up a reign of terror to suppress the revolt against the Spanish tyranny and the Inquisition. In 1573 he retired, and returned to Spain.

ALVARA′DO, Pedro de (c. 1485–1541). Spanish conquistador. In 1519 he accompanied Hernando Cortez, and distinguished himself in the conquest of Mexico. In 1523–4, he conquered Guatemala.

ALVAREZ (ahl′vahreth), **Don Jos** (1768–1827). Spanish sculptor. His works incl. groups and portrait busts (Ferdinand VII and Rossini).

ALVAREZ, Luis Walter (1911–). American physicist. Ed. at the Univ. of Chicago, he became prof. of physics at the Univ. of California in 1945, being also Assoc. Director of the Lawrence Radiation Laboratory 1954–9, he headed the research team which in 1959 discovered the Xi-zero atomic particle. He was awarded a Nobel prize in 1968.

ALWAR (ul′war). City in Rajasthan, India, chief town of the district (formerly princely state) of the same name. It has fine palaces, temples and tombs. Pop. (1961) 72,724.

ALWYN, William (1905–). British composer. Prof. of composition at the R.A.M. 1926–55, he is well known as a writer of film music (*Desert Victory*, *The Way Ahead*), and has also composed symphonies and chamber music.

AMADE′US (1845–90). King of Spain. As duke of Aosta, the 2nd son of Victor Emmanuel of Italy, he was elected to the Spanish throne in 1870, but had to abdicate in 1873, and returned to Italy.

A′MALEKĪTES. Ancient Semitic tribe of S.W. Palestine and the Sinai peninsula. According to Exodus xvii they harried the rear of the Israelites after their crossing of the Red Sea, were defeated by Saul and David, and finally crushed in the reign of Hezekiah.

AMA′LFI. Port of Italy at the foot of Monte Cerrato, on the Gulf of Salerno, 24 m. S.E. of Naples. For 7 cents. it was an independent republic. It is an ancient archiepiscopal see, and has a fine Romanesque cathedral. Pop. (1951) 6,117.

AMA′LIA, Anna (1739–1807). Duchess of Saxe-Weimar-Eisenach. As widow of Duke Ernest, from 1758 until her son Karl August succeeded her in 1775, she reigned with admirable prudence and skill, making the court of Weimar a literary centre of Germany. She was a friend of Wieland, Goethe, and Herder.

AMANI′TA. Genus of fungi, closely allied to *Agaricus* (q.v.) and often treated merely as a sub-genus. It is distinguished by having a ring, or *volva*, round the stem, and warty patches on the cap, and by the clear white colour of the gills. Many of the species are brightly coloured and highly poisonous. Fly agaric (*A. muscaria*), with bright red cap and white warty patches, is dangerous, and the Death's Cap (*A. phalloides*) is deadly: both are found in Britain.

AMANUL′LAH KHAN (1892–1960). Emir of Afghanistan, 3rd son of Habibullah Khan. On his father's assassination in 1919 he seized the throne and concluded a treaty

ALUMINIUM. A crucible of molten metal.
Courtesy of Aluminium Co. of Canada, Ltd.

with the British, but his policy of westernization led to rebellion in 1928. A. had to flee, abdicated in 1929, and settled in Rome.

AMA′RNA TABLETS. Collection of clay tablets with cuneiform inscriptions, found in the ruins at Tell el Amarna (the ancient Akhetaton), about 190 m. S. of Cairo on the E. bank of the Nile. The majority of the tablets, which comprise royal archives and letters of 1411–1375 B.C., are in the British Museum. They possibly represent the 'waste-paper basket' of officials who discarded inessential documents when the city was abandoned.

AMARYLLIDACEAE (amarilidā′sē-ē). Family of monocotyledonous flowering plants allied to the Liliaceae, but distinguished by the ovary being inferior. Its European species include the narcissus, daffodil, and snowdrop.

AMA′TERA′SU. In Japanese mythology, the sun-goddess, grandmother of Jimmu Tenno, first ruler of Japan, from whom the emperor claimed to be descended.

AMATI (ahmah′tē). Italian family of violin-makers, fl. in Cremona, c. 1550–1692.

A′MATOL. An explosive consisting of ammonium nitrate (A/N) and T.N.T. in almost any proportions.

A′MAZON. South American river. The largest river in the world as regards volume, and the third longest; its main head-streams, the Marañon and the Ucayali, rise in Central Peru and unite to flow eastward across Brazil for some 2,500 m. The total network is 30,000 m. of navigable waterways, draining an area of 2¾ million sq. m., nearly half of the S. American land-mass. The A. reaches the Atlantic on the Equator, its estuary is 50 m. wide and discharges a volume of water so immense that 40 m. out to sea fresh water remains at the surface. The name A. is probably derived from Indian *Amossona*, 'destroyer of boats'. Navigation is difficult, owing to floods, rapids, and tidal waves.

A′MAZONS. Legendary nation o female warriors, whom the ancients believed lived in Pontus, near the Black Sea. They were governed by a queen, made warlike excursions into the adjoining lands, and cut off their right breasts so as to be able to use the bow.

AMBA ALAGI (alah´gē). Mt. in Ethiopia, 10,000 ft., 80 m. N. of Magdala. During the S.W.W. this was the last stronghold of Italian resistance in East Africa, the Duke of Aosta and his forces formally surrendering on 16 May 1941.

AMBALA. Other form of UMBALLA.

AMBASSADOR. Officer of the highest rank in the diplomatic service, who represents the head of one Sovereign State at the court or cap. of another. As personal representatives of the Heads of their States, they enjoy many privileges and powers, which extend also to their families and households.

A´MBEDKAR, Bhimrao Ramji (1893–1956). Indian champion of the Depressed Classes. Himself an Untouchable, the son of a soldier, he studied in Britain and the U.S.A., and was called to the English Bar in 1923. On the attainment of Indian independence, he was Law Minister 1947–51, resigning because he felt that later developments had not sufficiently safeguarded the full rights of his people. In 1948 he m. a Brahmin. Just before his death he and many of his followers embraced Buddhism.

AMBER. Fossilized gum which exuded from coniferous trees of Middle Tertiary age. A light substance, usually yellow or brown in colour, it is found chiefly on coasts such as the Baltic and in Sicily, having been washed up by the sea. It is mined in E. Prussia. Amber has been used as an ornament since prehistoric times.

AMBERGRIS (-grēs). Fatty substance, resembling wax, found in the stomach and intestines of the sperm whale, and used in perfumery as a fixative. Basically intestinal matter, A. is not the result of disease, but probably the pathological product of an otherwise normal intestine.

AMBLER, Eric (1909–   ). British novelist. B. in London, he makes brilliant use of Balkan/Levant settings in the thrillers *The Mask of Dimitrios* (1939) and *Journey into Fear* (1940).

AMBOI´NA. Small island in the Moluccas, Republic of Indonesia. The town of A., formerly an historic centre of Dutch influence, has shipyards. Pop. *c.* 51,000.

AMBON. Other form of AMBOINA.

A´MBROSE, St. (*c.* 340–397). A Father of the Christian Church. B. at Trèves, in S. Gaul, the son of a Roman prefect, A. became governor of N. Italy. In 374 he was chosen bishop of Milan, although he was not yet a member of the Christian Church. But he was baptized forthwith, and was consecrated as bishop 8 days later, on 7 Dec. (St. Ambrose's day). His writings on theological subjects earned him a prominent place among the Latin fathers of the Church; he also wrote many hymns, and devised the arrangement of church music known as the *Ambrosian Chant*.

AMBRŌ´SIA. In Greek mythology, the food of the gods (from the Gk. *ambrotos*, 'immortal'), which was said to confer immortality upon all who ate it.

AMEN. Hebrew word signifying affirmation ('so be it'), commonly used at the close of a prayer or hymn. As used by Jesus Christ in the N.T. it is usually translated 'verily'.

AMENHŌ´TEP III. Pharaoh of Egypt, *c.* 1400 B.C. He erected many famous buildings, especially the great monuments at Thebes. His 2 portrait-statues were known to the Greeks as the Colossi of Memnon.

AMERICA. The western hemisphere of the globe, containing the continents of N. America and S. America, with Cent. America in between. This great landmass extends from the Arctic to the Antarctic, from beyond 75° N. lat. to past 55° S. lat. The area is nearly 16 million sq. m.; and the U.N. est. the pop. in 1960 at some 405 million.

The name A. is derived from Amerigo Vespucci, the Florentine navigator who was falsely supposed to have been the first to discover the American mainland in 1497.

AMERICAN CIVIL WAR. *See* UNITED STATES OF AMERICA.

AMERICAN FEDERATION OF LABOR AND CONGRESS OF INDUSTRIAL ORGANIZATIONS (AFL-CIO). Federation of trade unions in U.S.A. The A.F.L. was founded at Pittsburgh in 1881 by Samuel Gompers, pres. till his death in 1924; pres. 1924–52 William Green; and from 1952 George Meany. Its general outlook is conservative and non-political. In 1935 several unions, objecting to its policy of catering only for craft unions of skilled workers, broke away to form the C.I.O. on a basis of industrial unionism. A merger re-united them in 1955, George Meany remaining pres.: membership *c.* 15½ million.

AMERICAN INDEPENDENCE, WAR OF (1775–83). The revolt of the British colonies in N. America, which resulted in the establishment of the U.S.A. The struggle originated in the resentment of the colonists against such measures as the Navigation Acts, which subordinated American to British commercial and industrial interests. When the British government imposed a stamp tax (1765) and later a tea tax on the colonists, they were bitterly opposed, and measures of repression provoked the colonists to arm. The first shots were fired at Lexington (19 April 1775), where troops sent to seize illegal military stores were attacked by the local militia, and the first battle fought at Bunker Hill, near Charlestown (17 June). Soon after, the Continental Congress appointed George Washington to command its ill-armed and undisciplined forces, and on 4 July 1776 it issued the Declaration of Independence.

An American assault on Quebec (Dec. 1775) was bloodily repulsed. Washington occupied Boston and later New York, but after his defeat at Long Island (27 Aug. 1776), had to retire to Pennsylvania, although he won 2 successes at Trenton (26 Dec.) and Princeton (3 Jan. 1777). The British government planned a junction between Sir William Howe, advancing from New York, and General Burgoyne from Canada; Howe was not given precise instructions, however, and Burgoyne was compelled to surrender at Saratoga (17 Oct.). Meanwhile, Howe invaded Pennsylvania, defeated Washington at Brandywine (11 Sept.) and Germantown (4 Oct.), and occupied Philadelphia. During the winter of 1777–8, which he spent at Valley Forge, Washington had great difficulty in keeping his troops together.

In the summer of 1778 France and Spain entered the war as America's allies; a French fleet was sent to American waters, and a small force under Rochambeau went to Washington's assistance. Howe's successor, Clinton, withdrew from Philadelphia to New York, with an indecisive battle at Monmouth (28 June). The British now carried the war into the south, where loyalists were most numerous; Savannah was captured (29 Dec. 1778), followed by Charleston (12 May 1780), and victories were won at Camden (16 Aug. 1780) and Guilford Court House (15 March 1781). Nevertheless, the British attempt to enforce conscription, and certain excesses of the Loyalists, alienated support from them. It had been planned that Cornwallis, having conquered the south, should march north to join Clinton in New York, but the prolonged struggle in S. Carolina delayed him. Entering Virginia, he withdrew to Yorktown, where he was besieged by Washington and Rochambeau and blockaded by a French fleet. His surrender on 19 Oct. 1781 virtually ended the land fighting.

At sea the Americans built up a strong force of privateers, their best-known commander being John Paul Jones. The entry of France and Spain into the war initiated a hard struggle for naval supremacy, which ended with Rodney's victory off Martinique on 12 April 1782. After Yorktown the other southern ports fell, until only New York remained in British hands. Peace negotiations opened in 1782, and on 3 Sept. 1783 the Treaty of Paris recognized American independence.

AMERICAN INDIANS. *See* INDIANS, AMERICAN.

AMERICAN LEGION. Organization in U.S.A. of ex-servicemen of the F.W.W., founded in 1919. Veterans of the S.W.W. were made eligible to join in 1942. Unlike the British Legion, the A.L. has from time to time engaged in political activity to advance its objects. Its membership in 1968 was 2,553,782.

AMERICAN LITERATURE. *See* UNITED STATES OF AMERICA.

AMERICA'S CUP. International yacht-racing trophy. Won from the Royal Yacht Squadron in 1851 by the schooner-yacht *America*, owned by J. C. Stephens, in a race round the Isle of Wight, the silver cup was presented to the New York Yacht Club in 1857 to be held and competed for internationally: New York still retains it. Originally the yachts were often very large, as they had to sail to wherever the races were held, but since the S.W.W. this rule no longer applies. Although only 12-metres now compete, they cost several hundred thousand pounds and only syndicates are able to finance them.

AMERICA'S CUP
Weatherley, winner in 1962.
Courtesy of H. D. Mercer.

AMERI'CIUM. Man-made transuranic element produced from plutonium. At. no. 95, its isotope of mass 243 has half-life of 480 years. Possible source for radiographic diagnosis because of suitable gamma-emission.

AMERSFOORT (ah'mersfoh'rt). Ancient town of the Netherlands, 12 m. E.N.E. of Utrecht. Pop. (1961) 70,620.

A'MERY, Leopold Stennett (1873–1955). British Cons. statesman. B. in India, he was ed. at Harrow and Oxford, and was on the staff of *The Times* 1899–1909. For 34 years from 1911 he was Unionist M.P. for S. Birmingham, and was a foremost advocate of a united and fully-developed Commonwealth and Empire. He was Colonial and Dominions Sec. 1924–9, and Sec. of State for India and Burma 1940–5. His most famous speech was made in May 1940 when he addressed to Neville Chamberlain the words once used by Cromwell – 'In the name of God, go!' His books incl. *Empire and Prosperity* (1930), *India and Freedom* (1942), and *My Political Life* (1953–5). His son **Julian** (1919–) was Cons. Min for Aviation 1960–4, and Public Building and Works from 1970.

A'METHYST. A kind of quartz coloured violet by the presence of small quantities of manganese, and used as a semi-precious stone. As. are found chiefly in Russia, India the U.S.A., and Brazil.

AMIEL (ahmē-el'), **Henri Frédéric** (1821–81). Swiss philosopher and writer. B. at Geneva, he became professor of philosophy at the university there. His fame rests on his *Journal intime*, pub. 1882–4.

AMIENS (ahmē-añ'). Ancient city of N.E. France at the confluence of Somme and Avre; capital of Somme dept. It has a magnificent Gothic cathedral with a spire 370 ft. high, and gave its name to the battles of Aug. 1918, when Haig launched his victorious offensive. Pop. (1968) 117,888.

AMINES (am'inz) and **AMINO COMPOUNDS.** Nitrogenous substances, usually basic, i.e. they will form salts with acids. The parent substance of most is ammonia, NH_3, to which they are related by the substitution of one or more of the hydrogen atoms by the radicals or groups of atoms. The *simple As.*

are divided into primary, secondary, or tertiary according to whether 1, 2, or 3 hydrogen atoms of the ammonia molecule are replaced. The *methyl As.* have rather unpleasant ammonia odours and occur in decomposing fish. They are all gases at ordinary temperature. *A. acids* are compounds of which the basic and acidic groups exist in the same molecule. The simplest is glycine. Of the *aromatic A. compounds* the most important is aniline. Other interesting A. compounds are the metal amides and the acid amides.

A'MIS, Kingsley (1922–). British author. Ed. at Oxford, he lectured in English at Swansea Univ. Coll. 1949–61, and was fellow of Peterhouse, Cambridge, 1961–3. *Lucky Jim* (1954) is a novel humorously symbolic of 'red-brick' provincial university life as a factor in modern England.

AMMA'N. Capital and chief industrial centre of Jordan, on the site of the ancient Rabbath-Ammon (Philadelphia). The Univ. of Jordan was estab. here 1962, and A. is the centre of a road network and on the Cairo–Baghdad air route. Pop. (1966) 321,000.

A'MMETER. An instrument which measures electric current in amperes. The most common types are moving magnet, moving iron and moving coil, in which the passage of current through the instrument causes movement of a magnet, a piece of soft iron or of a coil. This is balanced by a restoring force (e.g. from a hair spring or the earth's magnetic field) in the opposite direction, and a pointer moving over a scale indicates the amount of current flowing through the instrument.

AMMON. Egyptian deity, identified by the Greeks with Zeus and by the Romans with Jupiter. In art he is represented as a ram, as a man with ram's head, or as a man crowned with feathers.

AMMONIA (NH_3). A colourless, pungent-smelling gas of about two-thirds the density of air, and soluble in water, forming ammonium hydroxide, NH_4OH. The solution is strongly alkaline, and forms crystalline salts on neutralization with acids.

Appreciable amounts of ammonium carbonate are found in the guano deposits of S. America, and in the mineral deposits at Stassfurt. It is also produced

AMIENS. Seen from the town belfry the cathedral, begun in 1220 and reputed the finest Gothic building in France, lives up to Viollet-le-Duc's description of it as 'the Parthenon of Gothic architecture.'

synthetically in gas works, being a product of the destructive distillation of coal, and by the Haber and Cyanamide processes.

AMMONITES. Ancient Semitic people living to the N.W. of the Dead Sea on the edge of the Syrian desert. Worshippers of Moloch, to whom they offered human sacrifices, they were frequently at war with the Israelites.

AMMAN. The Roman theatre, the city's most dramatic monument, dates to the 2nd or 3rd century A.D., and restoration has been undertaken. The three tiers of seats accommodate 6,000 spectators.   *Courtesy of the Jordan Embassy.*

AMMONITES. Extinct cephalopod molluscs akin to the modern Nautilus. The shell is curled in a plane spiral and made up of numerous chambers, only the outermost of which is inhabited by the animal. As. flourished in the Mesozoic times.

AMOEBA (amē′ba). One of the simplest living animals, consisting of a single cell and belonging to the group Protozoa, found in fresh water. The body, which is just visible to the naked eye, consists of colourless protoplasm. The chief organ within the body is the nucleus which largely controls the A's activities. The A. feeds by flowing round and enclosing organic debris, etc., which it encounters. It has no eyes or other sense organs, and no sexual reproduction.

AMOEBA. The nucleus is the large dark spot (right).

AMORITES. Ancient people of Semitic or Indo-European origin, who were among the inhabitants of Canaan at the time of the Israelite invasion.

Ā′MOS. First of the Hebrew O.T. prophets whose utterances were preserved in literary form (*c.* 760 B.C.). A sheep-farmer of Tekoah, he was roused by the increased moral laxity and corruption of Israel under Jeroboam II.

AMOY. Chinese port, on Amoy Is. in Amoy Bay, Fukien Province. One of the original 5 treaty ports, 1842–1943, it has a fine harbour; chief exports are sugar, tobacco, bamboo, paper. Pop. *c.* 150,000.

AMPERE (onpār′), **André Marie** (1775–1836). Fr. physicist and mathematician, prof. at the Collège de France in Paris. The instrument for measuring current, the *ammeter*, is named after him, as is the *ampere*, the unit of electric current, which is defined as the current required to deposit 0·00118 g silver on the cathode of a silver voltameter in 1 sec.

AMPHIBIA. Class of vertebrates standing in zoological classification between the fishes and the reptiles. The A. were the first four-legged animals to inhabit the earth, and our knowledge of them goes back to the Carboniferous age. The modern A. are

divided into 3 orders: *Apoda* or *Gymnophiona* (the Caecilians, limbless and with very short tail); *Caudata* or *Urodela* (salamanders and newts, with limbs and tail); *Salientia* or *Anura* (frogs and toads, with 4 limbs and no tail).

The A. are cold-blooded vertebrates, with the body covered with skin instead of scales and passing the first part of their life in a larval or tadpole state. The majority spend their adult lives on land, generally near water, and salt water except in great dilution is fatal to them.

AMPHINEU′RA. Class of mollusca, including the coat-of-mail shells. They are sluggish animals found in salt water, adhering to rocks, and distinguished from the other mollusca by their double ventral nervous system.

AMPHITHEATRE. Large oval or circular building used by the Romans for the exhibition of gladiatorial contests, fights of wild beasts, and other similar spectacles; the arena of an A. is completely surrounded by the seats of the spectators, hence the name (Gk. *amphi*, around). The Romans built many As., the best-known being the Colosseum at Rome, completed in A.D. 80, and holding 87,000 spectators.

AMPHITRITE (amfitri′tē). Greek sea-maiden, daughter of Nereus and wife of Poseidon.

AMPHORA (amf-). Large earthenware vessel in common use among the ancient Greeks and Romans, having a handle on both sides of the neck and a pointed lower end that was thrust into the ground.

AMPULLA. Small vessel with a round body and narrow neck, used for holding oil, perfumes, etc., used by the Greeks and Romans for toilet purposes. At British coronations the oil is contained in an eagle-shaped A.

AMRI′TSAR. City in the Punjab, India, founded 1577. It is the religious centre of the Sikhs and contains the Golden Temple and a college of the Univ. of Punjab. Pop. (1961) 375,542.

At A. on 13 April 1919, 5,000 unarmed Indian demonstrators were fired on by British troops at the order of Brig.-Gen. Dyer, 379 being killed, 1,200 injured.

AMSTERDAM. Capital, largest city, commercial and intellectual centre of the Netherlands, on the Amstel where it joins the Ij, an inlet of the Ijsselmeer (remnant of the Zuider Zee). A. became important on the decline of Antwerp in the 16th cent. When vessels became too large to navigate the Zuider Zee the port lost some of its importance, but regained it with the opening of the North Holland Canal to Helder in 1825. In 1876 the 15 m. long North Sea Canal to Ijmuiden was opened; this has been repeatedly enlarged and deepened, so that the largest ocean-going ships can now reach A. Various industries are carried on, and A. is the chief diamond market of the world, and has long been famous for its cutting industry. A. has many docks and quays, and is intersected by many canals. Most of the heavy transport is water-borne. Notable buildings are the Royal Palace (1655); the Nieuwe Kerk (1408); the Oude Kerk (14th cent.); the St. Antonieswaag, an old weighhouse, used to house the city's archives, and the Rijksmuseum. There are 2 universities. Pop. (1967) 866,421. *See* illus. p. 38.

AMU DARYA (ahmoo dah′ryah). River in Soviet Central Asia, rising in the Pamirs and flowing through a wide delta into the Aral Sea. It was anciently known as the Oxus and is 1,490 m. long.

AMU DARYA. *See* ARAL.

AMUNDSEN (ah′moondsen), **Roald** (1872–1928). Norwegian explorer. B. in Borge, he was the first to navigate the N.W. Passage in 1906. In 1910 he set sail in the *Fram* to discover the North Pole, but on hearing that he had been forestalled by Peary, he raced Scott to the South Pole instead (1911). In 1918 he made an unsuccessful attempt to drift across the

North Pole in the *Maud*, and in 1925 essayed a flight from Spitzbergen to the Pole by aeroplane. This too failed, but the following year he and Ellsworth joined the Italian General Nobile in his dirigible the *Norge*, which circled the pole twice and landed in Alaska, having journeyed 2,700 m. in 71 hours. A. lost his life when searching by plane for Nobile and his airship *Italia*.

AMUR (ahmoor'). River in the Far East of Asia. Formed by the Argun and the Shilka, the A. enters the sea of Okhotsk. At its mouth at Nikolaevsk it is 10 m. wide. For a large part of its total course of over 2,700 m. it forms the boundary between the R.S.F.S.R. and China. It gives its name to two regions of the R.S.F.S.R., Amur and Lower Amur.

AMYL (a'mil) **ALCOHOL** ($C_5H_{11}OH$). A clear colourless oily liquid, usually having a characteristic rather choking odour.

ANACO'NDA. World's greatest copper plant in Montana, U.S.A. The city founded as Copperopolis 1883, by the Anaconda Copper Mining Co., was incorporated as A. in 1888. A. is 5,300 ft. above the sea, and 26 m. N.W. of Butte. Pop. (1960) 12,054.

ANACONDA. South American snake, allied to the boa-constrictor; one of the largest snakes, it reaches 30 ft. and more.

ANAEMIA (anē'mia). A disease condition in which the patient has too little blood, too few red blood cells or too little haemoglobin. Deficiency in quantity or quality may be due to excessive bleeding, faulty nourishment, or failure to use the food properly. Blood may be destroyed by chemical poisons or infections, and may be impaired by certain diseases of the blood or the lymphatic system. A patient with chronic A. tires quickly on exertion and becomes faint and breathless through lack of oxygen in the tissues. The remedy is proper nutrition and iron.

Pernicious or Addison's A. is a disease due to the failure of the stomach to secrete a certain substance which is necessary to produce blood from the food. It can be rectified by the administration of liver or its extract. Acute A. is also caused by a large whole-body dose of nuclear radiation.

ANAESTHESIA (anesthē'sia). Absence of sensation (Gk. *an-*, not; *aisthēsis*, sensation). A. of a part of the skin, so that the patient is insensitive to a pin-prick or other stimulus, is a sign of nerve disorder, but the more common meaning of A. is a loss of sensation or consciousness produced by an anaesthetic drug.

The beginning of modern A. was the discovery by Thomas Beddoes in 1776 of nitrous oxide. Sir Humphry Davy, inventor of the miner's lamp, did much of the experimental work and first suggested its application to surgery. Horace Wells, a New England, U.S.A., dentist, had a tooth extracted under nitrous oxide (laughing gas) for the first time in 1844. Ether was successfully used by Dr. Crawford Long of Georgia in 1842 for the removal of a tumour of the neck. The credit for the discovery of A. is, however, given to W. T. G. Morton, another dentist, of Boston, Mass., who in 1846 anaesthetized a patient with ether for the removal of a skin tumour at the Massachusetts General Hospital. Prof. James Simpson of Edinburgh used it soon afterwards on women in childbirth, and met great opposition from religious persons. Meanwhile chloroform had been known in France since 1831, and Simpson began to use it in preference to ether. Its use by Queen Victoria at the birth of Prince Leopold in 1853 settled the religious controversy. In 1868 Andrews of Chicago, and after him many American surgeons, developed the use of a mixture of nitrous oxide and oxygen, which is used to this day. The many later developments in anaesthetics incl. ethyl chloride (1847); cyclopropane (1933) espec. useful in chest surgery; the alkaloid d-Tubocurarine (1935) obtained from curare (q.v.) and producing a light plane of anaesthesia useful in

AMSTERDAM. Its growth through the centuries is marked by the 4 great canals, each following the line of a former city wall or moat, and numerous others make a criss-cross pattern. This little bridge is on Prince's Island.
Courtesy of Netherlands National Tourist Office.

abdominal operations; trichloroethylene (1941) an alternative to nitrous oxide in childbirth; and bromochlorotrifluoroethane (1956) which avoids the inflammability of cyclopropane.

Local A. came into use about the beginning of the 20th cent. Cocaine was used as long ago as 1847, but is too poisonous and too likely to lead to addiction to be generally useful. The relatively harmless synthetic substance novocaine, invented about 1905, marked the beginning of the general use of local A. Large areas of the body can be anaesthetized by injecting As. into nerve junctions.

ANALGESICS (-je'siks). Medicines that give freedom from pain, e.g. cocaine and novocaine for local application; opium and its derivatives, antipyrine, aspirin, and certain barbiturate drugs, for internal use.

ANALOG COMPUTER. *See* COMPUTER.

ANANDA (fl. 5th cent. B,C.). Favourite disciple of the Buddha. At his plea, a separate order was established for women.

ANARCHISM. A term in political theory derived from the Gk. *anarkhos*, 'without ruler'. It does not mean 'without order'; most theories of A. imply an order of a very strict and symmetrical kind, but they maintain that such order can be achieved by co-operation, and they claim that other methods of achieving order, which rely on authority, are both morally reprehensible and politically unstable. A. must not be confused with nihilism, a purely negative and destructive activity directed against society as such, it is essentially a pacifist movement.

The religious type of A., claimed by many anarchists to be exemplified in the early organization of the Christian church, has found expression in modern times in the social philosophy of Tolstoy and Gandhi. The growth of political A. may be traced through William Godwin, Shelley, and P. J. Proudhon to Bakunin (q.v.) who had a strong following in Latin Europe, especially France and Spain, until the suppressive dictatorships of Mussolini and Franco. The theory of A. is best expressed in the works of Kropotkin (q.v.).

ANASTA'SIA (1901–1918). Russian Grand Duchess, youngest dau. of Nicholas II (q.v.). She was murdered with her parents, but it has been alleged that A. escaped, and of those who claimed her identity the most famous is Anna Anderson. Alleged by some to be a Pole, Franziska Schanzkowski, she was rescued from a Berlin canal in 1920: the German Federal Supreme Court rejected her claim 1970.

ANATOLIA. Alternative name for TURKEY – in Asia.

ANATOMY (Gk., cutting up, dissection). The study of the structure of the parts of the body, as distinguished from physiology, which is the study of their functions.

Herophilus of Chalcedon (fl. c. 300 B.C.) and Erasistratus of Chios are regarded as the fathers respectively of anatomy and physiology. In the 2nd cent. A.D. Galen of Pergamum produced an account of A. which was the only source of anatomical knowledge until the period of the Renaissance, in particular until the appearance in 1543 of On the Working of the Human Body by the Belgian, Andreas Vesalius (1514–64). In 1628 William Harvey pub. his demonstration of the circulation of the blood. A. was immensely advanced by the invention of the microscope, and the Italian Malpighi (1628–94) and the Hollander Leeuwenhoek (1632–1723) laid the foundations of the study of minute anatomy, or histology. In 1747 B. Albinus (1697–1770), with the help of the artist J. Wandelaar (1691–1759), produced the most beautiful and exact account of the bones and muscles, and in 1757–65 the Swiss Albrecht von Haller (1708–77) gave the most complete and exact description of the organs that had yet appeared. The A. of the nervous system was advanced by the Frenchman Vicq d'Azyr (1748–94), comparative A. by G. Cuvier (1769–1832), whilst in England J. Hunter (1728–93) developed an anatomical museum.

Among the most notable anatomical writers of the early 19th cent. are the London surgeon Sir Ch. Bell (1774–1842), Jonas Quain (1796–1865), and Henry Gray (1825–61). Later in the century came the inventions of staining tissues by dyes for microscopic examination, and the method of mechanically cutting very thin sections of stained tissues. Radiographic A. has been one of the triumphs of the 20th cent. which has also been marked by immense activity in embryological investigation, See HUMAN BODY.

ANAXAGORAS (c. 500–428 B.C.). Greek natural philosopher. B. near Smyrna, he lived in Athens, where he was a friend of Pericles, who saved him from death when A. was charged with impiety and treason.

ANCESTOR WORSHIP. Religious attitude adopted by many primitive peoples towards the deceased of the tribe or family. Thus the Zulus used to invoke the spirits of the great warriors of their race before engaging in battle. The Greeks deified their early heroes, and the ancient Romans held in reverential honour the manes or departed spirits of their forbears. Particularly prevalent in old China, A.W. gives way under Communist teaching.

ANCHOVY. A fish (Engraulis encrasicholus) of the herring family (Clupeidae). It breeds abundantly in the Mediterranean, and is also found on the Atlantic coast of Europe. It is distinguished by its projecting snout and deep cleft to the mouth, grows to a length of 7 or 8 in., and is dark green, with a broad silvery band on the sides.

ANCIEN RÉGIME (oṅsiaṅ′ rāzhēm′). (Fr., old order of things). The system of government under the French monarchy, which was swept away by the Revolution of 1789.

ANCIENT LIGHTS. In Britain the right of an owner of a building, arising through long use, to receive an uninterrupted flow of light at one or more of the windows of the building. The right may be acquired in various ways, but usually under the Prescription Act, 1832, by the enjoyment of the right for 20 years without interruption.

ANCONA. Italian town and naval base on the Adriatic Sea, capital of A. province. It has a Romanesque cathedral and a former palace of the popes. Pop. (1961) 99,678.

ANDALUSIA. Ancient prov. of S. Spain, in 1833 divided into the 8 provs. of Seville, Cadiz, Malaga, Cordoba, Jaén, Granada, Almería, and Huelva. A. forms an extensive and mostly fertile plain, ringed by mountains, producing copper, manganese, molybdenum, etc., and is watered by the Guadalquivir and many other rivers. The principal towns are Seville, Malaga, Granada, and Córdoba. Area c. 33,700 sq. m.; pop. (1960) 5,900,000.

ANDAMANS. Group of islands in the Bay of Bengal, between India and Burma. There are 5 principal islands (forming the Great Andaman), the Little Andaman, and about 204 islets. The A. were formerly used as a penal settlement, abolished 1945, and were occupied by the Japanese 1942–5. Area 2,508 sq. m.; pop. (est.) 40,000. With the Nicobars (q.v.), they form a territory of the Rep. of India.

The aboriginal pop. number only a few hundred; they are pygmies, probably the remnants of a race once spread over S.E. Asia.

ANDERS, Wladyslaw (1892–1970). Polish general. On the German invasion of the Soviet Union in the S.W.W., he was appointed to command the Polish forces being formed in Russia, and in 1944 commanded the 2nd Polish Corps in Italy under Alexander. In 1945 he was C.-in-C. of all Polish armed forces outside Poland. He later settled in England.

ANDERSEN, Hans Christian (1805–75). Danish writer. The son of a shoemaker, he was b. at Odense in Fünen. His first book was pub. when he was only 17, but it was not until 1829 that he attracted notice. In 1835 his novel The Improvisatore brought him popularity, and he began to compose the immortal fairy tales which have been translated into all languages. A.'s other works include romances and a genial autobiography.

ANDERSEN-NEXÖ (ahn′dersen-neks′ö), **Martin** (1869–1954). Danish novelist. Of humble birth and trained as a shoemaker, he ed. himself and took up teaching. His finest work is the great epic on the life of the Danish proletariat, Ditte, Child of Man.

ANDERSON, Carl David (1905–). American physicist. B. in New York, he became prof. at the California Institute of Technology in 1939. Engaged on gamma and cosmic ray research from 1930, he in 1932 discovered the positive electron, or positron, and for this was a 'joint' Nobel prizewinner in 1936.

ANDERSON, Elizabeth Garrett (1836–1917). British pioneer woman doctor, née Garrett. She began to study medicine in 1860, and in 1865 was granted a licence to practise by the Society of Apothecaries. She held hospital posts in London, 1866–1903, and m. in 1871 J. G. S. Anderson, shipowner. In 1908 she became mayor of Aldeburgh, the first woman mayor in England.

ANDERSON, Sir John. See WAVERLEY.

ANDERSON, Dame Judith (1898–). Australian actress. B. in Adelaide, she excels in strongly dramatic roles, e.g. Lavinia Mannon in Mourning Becomes Electra, Gertrude in Hamlet and Lady Macbeth. She was awarded the D.B.E. in 1960.

ANDERSON, Marian (1902–). American contralto singer. B. in Philadelphia, she made her début in 1924, her voice being of remarkable richness. In 1955 she appeared as Ulrica in Verdi's The Masked Ball at the Metropolitan Opera, N.Y., the 1st Negress to appear there, and achieved outstanding success.

ANDERSON, Maxwell (1888–1959). American dramatist. Son of a Baptist minister, he spent some time in journalism, among other very varied occupations, before making his name in collaboration with Laurence Stallings with What Price Glory?, a trenchant war play. His other works range from blank verse historical dramas (i.e. Elizabeth the Queen and Mary of

Scotland) to one-act plays and a musical comedy, *Knickerbocker Holiday*.

ANDERSON, Sherwood (1876–1941). American short-story writer. B. in Ohio, he became manager of a paint factory but abandoned commerce to join the literary circles of Chicago. He estab. a reputation with *Winesburg, Ohio* (1919), with its relish of small-town life and another short story vol. *The Triumph of the Egg* (1921). He deals with the frustration of instinct in modern industrialized society: his novels incl. *Windy McPherson's Son* (1916) and *Dark Laughter* (1925).

ANDES (an′děz). The great mountain system or cordillera that forms the western fringe of S. America, extending through some 67° of latitude and the republics of Colombia, Venezuela, Ecuador, Peru, Bolivia, Chile, and Argentina. For about half of their length of over 4,000 m. the mts. exceed 12,000 ft. in altitude. Geologically speaking, they are new mountains, having attained their present height by vertical upheaval of the entire strip of the earth's crust as recently as the latter part of the Tertiary era and the Quaternary. But they have been greatly affected by weathering. Rivers have cut profound gorges, and glaciers have produced characteristic valleys. The majority of the individual mountains are volcanic, some are still active volcanoes.

The whole system may be divided into two almost parallel ranges. The southernmost extremity is Cape Horn, but the range extends into the sea and forms islands. Among the highest peaks are Cotopaxi and Chimborazo in Ecuador, Cerro de Pasco and Misti in Peru, Illampu and Illimani in Bolivia, Aconcagua in Argentina, and Ojos del Salado in Chile, at least 23,290 ft., the highest mt. in the New World.

The A. are rich in minerals, and the extraction of silver and gold has never ceased. The ores which are of present-day world importance are tin, tungsten, and bismuth in Bolivia, and vanadium, copper, and lead in Peru. Difficult communications make mining expensive. Transport was for long chiefly by pack animals, but air transport has greatly reduced difficulties of communications. Three railways cross the A. from Valparaiso to Buenos Aires, Antofagasta to Salta, and Antofagasta via Uyuni to Asuncion. New roads are being built, incl. the Pan-American Highway from Alaska to Cape Horn.

The population is sparse on the whole. The majority are dependent upon agriculture, the nature and products of which vary with the natural environment.

ANDHRA PRADESH. State of the Rep. of India, created 1953 from the Telugu-speaking areas of Madras (q.v.), and enlarged 1956 from the former Hyderabad state. Rice and sugar cane are grown, there are textile and paper mills, and Vishakhapatnam has an oil refinery and shipyards. Area 106,286 sq.m.; pop. (1961) 35,980,000.

ANDO′RRA. Small European republic in the eastern Pyrenees between France and Spain, consisting of gorges and narrow valleys surrounded by high mountains. Traditionally it received its independence from Charlemagne, and in 1278 it was placed under the joint suzerainty of the count of Foix in France and the bishop of Urgel in Spain. The former's rights are now vested in the President of the French Republic, but the bishop still retains his prerogatives. Bi-annual dues of 960 francs are paid to France and 460 pesetas to the bishop. There is an elected Council General, of 24 members, while the executive power is wielded by a First Syndic. There are no railways but a road links the French and Spanish frontiers via the cap., Andorra la Vella, pop. *c.* 800. The people speak Catalan and are R.C. Area, 191 sq. m.; pop. (1968) 15,500 (5,500 citizens, the rest Spanish).

A′NDOVER. English market town (bor.) of Hants, 14 m. N.W. of Winchester, on the Anton. Its corn and cattle markets, and its November sheep-fair, have been held for centuries. Pop. (1961) 16,974.

ANDRADE (andrād′), **Edward Neville da Costa** (1887–1971). British physicist. B. in London, he was Quain prof. of physics at the Univ. of London 1928–50, and Director of the Davy-Faraday Research Laboratory at the Royal Institution 1950–2. His books incl. *The Structure of the Atom* and a study of Isaac Newton.

ANDRÉ (an′drā), **John** (1751–80). British soldier. B. in London, the son of a merchant from Geneva, he served with the British army in America from 1774, and when Arnold offered to betray West Point to the British, Major A. was chosen to negotiate the surrender. Captured by the Americans, he was hanged as a spy. A monument to A. was set up in Westminster Abbey.

ANDREA (ahndrā′ah) **DEL SARTO** (1486–1531). Italian painter, b. at Florence. His name was Andrea d'Agnolo; he was called Del Sarto because he was the son of a tailor. He was apprenticed to a goldsmith, later studied under Giovanni Barile and Piero di Cosimo, but he owed more to his study of Masaccio, Michelangelo, and others. In 1516 he m. Lucrezia del Fede, a beautiful woman who appears in many of his pictures. In 1518 he went to Paris at the invitation of Francis I, and for him painted the 'Charity' now in the Louvre. In 1519 he returned to Florence, and with the money Francis had entrusted to him for the purchase of works of art built a house for himself. In 1525 he painted the 'Madonna del Sacco', a fresco, usually considered his masterpiece. He d. of the plague.

ANDRÉE (oṅdreh′), **Salomon August** (1854–97). Swedish balloonist. In July 1897 he ascended from Danes Island, Spitzbergen, and nothing more was heard of him and his 2 companions until 6 Aug. 1930 when their last camp and their bodies and diaries, etc., were discovered on White Island (Kvito) by a party of Norwegian scientists. From the diaries it transpired that they had remained in the air for 3 days, reaching long. 83° 4′ N. before the balloon was forced down, and that they perished in Oct. 1897.

FRA ANGELICO. A detail from the central panel of the predella or altar-piece 'Christ Glorified in the Court of Heaven' in the National Gallery. Angels, saints, and Dominican *beati* unite in a chorus of praise.   *Photo: National Gallery.*

A'NDREW, St. (d. *c.* A.D. 70). Apostle. A native of Bethsaida, he was Simon Peter's brother. With Peter, James, and John, who worked with him as fishermen at Capernaum, he formed the inner circle of the 12 disciples. According to tradition he went with John to Ephesus, preached in Scythia, and was crucified at Patras on an X-shaped cross (St. Andrew's cross). His feast is held on 30 Nov. He is the patron saint of Scotland.

ANDREWES, Lancelot (1555–1626), C. of E., divine. B. in London, he went to Cambridge, and took holy orders in 1580, becoming bishop successively of Chichester (1605), Ely (1609), and Winchester (1618). He took part in preparing the text of the A.V., and was remarkable for his fine preaching.

ANDREWS, Roy Chapman (1884–1960). American naturalist-explorer. B. in Wisconsin, he entered the American museum of Natural History in 1906, retiring as Director in 1942. Until 1914 his main interest was in whales, but he led 3 Asiatic expeditions 1916–32 and discovered great fields of fossils and the first-known dinosaur eggs, also mapping large areas of the Gobi desert.

ANDREYEV (andrä'yev), **Leonid Nicolaievich** (1871–1919). Russian author. B. at Orel, he achieved success with a collection of stories in 1901. Later works, obsessed with death and madness, incl. the symbolic drama *Life of Man* (1907), the melodrama *He Who Gets Slapped* (1915); and novels *Red Laugh* (1904), *Seven that were Hanged* (1908), and *S.O.S.* (1919) pub. in Finland, where he had fled from the Revolution.

ANDRIC (andrēch), **Ivo** (1892–   ). Yugoslav novelist. A former member of the nationalist Young Bosnia organization, another member of which shot Francis Ferdinand (q.v.), he began writing while a political prisoner in Austria. He later became a diplomat and then entered the Yugoslav Parliament. A.'s most outstanding work is the trilogy which incl. *The Bridge on the Drina*. He was awarded a Nobel Prize in 1961.

ANDROCLES (and'roklēz) (fl. 1st cent. A.D.). Roman slave. He is said to have fled from a cruel master to a cave in Africa, where he drew a thorn from the foot of a suffering lion. When A. was recaptured and sentenced to fight a lion, he encountered the same animal who repaid his kindness by greeting him as a friend. The emperor Tiberius pardoned A. who was set free, together with the lion.

ANDROMACHE (androm'akē). Heroine of Homer's Iliad; the wife of Hector, who was killed in combat with Achilles, and mother of the boy Astyanax, who was flung from the battlements by the conquerors. After the fall of Troy she was awarded to Neoptolemus, Achilles's son.

ANDRO'MEDA. In Gk. mythology, a beautiful Ethiopian princess who was chained to a rock and exposed to a sea-monster. Perseus slew the latter and married her. When she d. the gods placed her among the stars.

ANE'MONE. Genus of plants of the crowfoot family Ranunculaceae. The wood A. (*A. nemorosa*) or wind-flower is a familiar plant in the shady woods, flowering in spring. *A. pulsatilla*, the Pasque flower, and *A. pratensis* are powerful emetics. *A. hepatica* is common in the Alps. The garden A. (*A. coronaria*) is among the florists' flowers.

ANEROID. See BAROMETER.

WOOD ANEMONE

ANGKOR. Built in the 12th cent. by Suryavarman II the great temple of Angkor Vat was dedicated to Siva, and represents the height of Khmer classical art. Above the gallery roof rise the turrets of one of the two libraries. Constructed in variouscoloured sandstones, no cement being used, it is profusely decorated with scenes from legend and subsidiary floral motifs.
Courtesy of the National Tourist Office of Cambodia.

ANEURIN (anī'rin) (fl. *c.* A.D. 600). Welsh poet. A Strathclyde Briton and member of the Gododdin tribe, he wrote the greater part of the poem 'Gododdin', telling of a disastrous military expedition against the Saxons of which A. is said to have been the only survivor.

ANGEL (Gk., messenger). In Christian, Mohammedan, and Jewish belief a class of supernatural beings, intermediate in status between God and man, whose function is to praise and serve the former, and act as the mediators to man. Later Christian belief evolved a celestial hierarchy of 9 orders: the Seraphim, Cherubim, and Thrones, who contemplate God and reflect his glory; Dominations, Virtues, and Powers, who regulate the stars and universe; and Principalities, Archangels, and Angels, who minister to humanity. In R.C. belief each human soul has a Guardian A, to protect and watch over it.

ANGELFISH, or **Monk Fish** (*Squatina squatina*). A fish related to the sharks, found in warm waters, including the Mediterranean. So called from its winglike pectoral fins. It may be 5 ft. long.

ANGE'LICA. Genus of umbelliferous plants. *A. sylvestris*, the species found in Britain, is a tall perennial herb, with wedge-shaped leaves and clusters of white, pale violet, or pinkish flowers.

ANGELICO (ahnjel'ēkoh), **Fra** (1387–1455). Italian painter, whose real name was Guido di Pietro. B. in Tuscany, he entered the Dominican order. For 10 years from 1436 he lived in the monastery of S. Marco in Florence where he executed some fine frescoes. In 1446 he moved to Rome at the summons of the Pope. Among his outstanding pictures are 'The Coronation of the Virgin' in the Louvre, and a Christ with 265 saints, in the National Gallery, London. He was a mystic, and his saintly character is revealed in all his works. The name *Angelico* was given him because of the angelic beauty of his character.

ANGELL (än'jel), **Sir Norman** (1872–1967). British writer on politics and economics. In 1910 he acquired an international reputation with his book *The Great Illusion*, in which he maintained that any war must prove ruinous to the victors as well as to the vanquished, and in 1933 was awarded a Nobel peace prize. He was a Labour M.P. 1929–31, and in 1931 was knighted.

ANGELLIER (oṅzhelyeh'), **Auguste Jean** (1848–1911). French poet and critic, author of an acute study of Robert Burns and of *A l'Amie perdue*, a series of sonnets addressed to a former love.

ANGERS (oṅzhä'). Ancient French town, cap. of Maine-et-Loire dept., on the r. Maine. It has a 12-13th cent. cathedral and castle, and was formerly the cap. of the duchy and prov. of Anjou whose people are called Angevins—a name also applied by the English to the Plantagenet kings. Pop. (1968) 128,533.

ANGINA, (anji′na). Sore throat, an agonizing spasmodic pain. *A. pectoris* is a sudden agonizing pain in the chest, sometimes extending to the left shoulder and down the arm, associated with a terror of immediate death; it is due to spasm of the coronary arteries which supply blood to the heart muscle, or to an aneurysm of the aorta.

A′NGIOSPERMS. One of the 2 great divisions of flowering plants (Phanerogamia). In contrast to the gymnosperms ('naked seeds')—which comprise only the conifers and cycads—the As. have their seeds enclosed in a fruit, and show a generally higher and more advanced organization.

A′NGKOR. Name applied to the ruins in and around the ancient ruined cap. of the Khmers in Cambodia, S.E. Asia. The remains date mainly from the 10–12th cent. A.D., and comprise temples originally dedicated to the Hindu gods, shrines associated with Hinayana Buddhism, royal palaces, etc. Many are grouped within the great enclosure called Angkor Thom, but the great temple of Angkor Vat (early 12th cent.), one of the most imposing edifices in the world, lies some little distance outside. A. was abandoned in the 15th cent., and the ruins were not adequately described until 1863. *See* illus. p. 41.

ANGLER. A fish (*Lophius piscatorius*) of the order Pediculati, inhabiting the waters of the N. Atlantic, and found off British shores. It has an enormous flattened head and a wide mouth with sharp teeth, and may reach 5 ft. in length. Other names for it are sea devil, frog fish, and goose fish.

ANGLESEY, Henry William Paget, 1st marquess of (1768–1854). British cavalry leader during the Napoleonic wars. He led a great charge at Waterloo, in which he lost a leg, and was made a marquess for his conspicuous services. He was twice Lord-Lieutenant of Ireland, and succeeded his father as earl of Uxbridge in 1812.

ANGLESEY. Welsh island and co., separated from the mainland (Caernarvonshire) by the Menai Straits, which are crossed by the Britannia tubular railway bridge and Telford's suspension bridge, built 1819–26 but since rebuilt. Nature-lovers visit A. for its fauna (especially bird-life) and flora, and antiquarians for its many buildings and relics of historic interest; it is also a popular holiday resort. The ancient granary of Wales, A. now has growing industries, e.g. toy-making, electrical goods, and bromine extraction from the sea. Holyhead is the principal town and port; but Beaumaris is the county town. Area 276 sq. m.; pop. (1961) 51,700.

ANGLICAN COMMUNION, The. Family of churches incl. the Church of England and those holding the same essential doctrines, i.e. the Lambeth Quadrilateral (1888) – Holy Scripture as the basis of all doctrine, the Nicene and Apostles' Creeds, Holy Baptism and Holy Communion, and the historic episcopate.

The Church of England originated during the Roman occupation c. 2nd cent., and, after a period of decline, was estab. as part of the Catholic Church by the mission of St. Augustine who became first Abp. of Canterbury in 597. At the Reformation the chief change was political, the Sovereign (Henry VIII) replaced the Pope and assumed the right to appoint abps. and bps. The Book of Common Prayer (q.v.), the basis of worship throughout the A.C., dates from Edward VI's reign; the Thirty-Nine Articles, the Church's doctrinal basis, were drawn up under Elizabeth I; and the canons of ecclesiastical discipline are essentially those framed under James I, who also authorized the version of the English Bible still generally used.

The Church was early carried by colonizers and explorers to N. America (where 3 American bps. were

ANGUS. The black, polled Aberdeen Angus cattle which are mainly bred for beef originated here and have reached a high standard in both Britain and the U.S., where they were introduced in 1873. Lindertis Evulse, the 13 month-old bull seen here, was bred in Angus and sold to a U.S. breeder for a record price of £63,000 in 1963.   *Photo: Alex C. Cowper.*

consecrated after the War of Independence, whose successors still lead the Episcopal Church in the U.S.A.), Australia and New Zealand, and by traders to India. The main missionary effort, however, came in the 19th cent., especially in Africa, and in the 20th cent. work has been extended to S. America.

In England the 2 abps. head the provs. of Canterbury and York (qq.v.), divided respectively into 29 and 14 bishoprics. *See* PARLIAMENT. The Church Assembly (1919) was replaced in 1970 by a General Synod with 3 houses (bps., other clergy, and laity) to regulate Church matters, subject to parliament and the royal assent. A decennial Lambeth Conference (first held 1867) attended by some 340 bps. from all parts of the A.C. is presided over in London by the Abp. of Canterbury: it is not legislative but its decisions are often put into practice. The Church Commissioners for England (1948) estab. by an amalgamation of the Ecclesiastical Commissioners (1836) and Queen Anne's Bounty (1704) manage the estates of the Church and endowment of livings.

The 3 main parties, all products of the 19th cent., are: the Evangelical or Low Church, which maintains the Church's Protestant character; the Anglo-Catholic or High Church, which stresses continuity with the pre-Reformation Church (*see* KEBLE, FROUDE, NEWMAN, PUSEY) and is marked by ritualistic practices, the use of confession, maintenance of religious communities of both sexes, etc.; and the Liberal or Modernist, concerned with the reconciliation of the Church with modern thought (*see* J. A. T. ROBINSON, M. STOCKWOOD). Steps in the 20th cent. towards reunion with other churches incl. the Anglican-Methodist Unity Commission (1965, which issued details in 1968 of a proposed Anglican-Methodist Reconciliation Act) and the R.C.-Anglican Preparatory Theological Commission (1967).

ANGLING. The art of fishing by means of rod and line as opposed to the use of nets. It has been practised from the earliest times, and the best-known work on the subject is Izaak Walton's *Compleat Angler* (1653). The principal equipment of an angler is rod, reel, line, and hook, with some lure or bait to attract the fish. Trout and salmon are the freshwater fish most highly prized by anglers. Trout are angled for by many methods, of which the artificial fly is the most common. Salmon are caught on artificial flies of gaudy patterns or by spinning lures. Other freshwater fish caught incl. roach, perch, pike, barbel, carp, tench, chub, grayling, dace and gudgeon. Equally popular is sea A., including 'big-game' fishing for tunny, etc., and the recently developed underwater fishing with specialized 'frogman' equipment.

PHYLA OF THE ANIMAL KINGDOM

1. PORIFERA or PARAZOA	Sponges.
2. COELENTERATA	Jelly-fish, sea-anemones, corals, sea-pen.
3. PLATYHELMINTHES	Flat worms, including tapeworms and flukes.
4. NEMERTINEA	No popular name, but Nemertine worms.
5. ROTIFERA or ROTATORIA	Wheel-animalcules.
6. NEMATODA	Round or thread worms.
7. ANNELIDA	Leeches, earthworms, lugworm, sea-mouse.
8. ARTHROPODA	Barnacles, crabs, woodlice, spiders, ticks, scorpions, centipedes, millipedes, insects.
9. MOLLUSCA	Mussels, oysters, limpets, snails, cuttlefishes, squids, nautilus, ammonites.
10. POLYZOA	Moss-polyps, sea-mat.
11. BRACHIOPODA	Lamp-shells.
12. CHAETOGNATHA	Arrow-worms.
13. PHORONIDEA or PODAXONIA	No popular name.
14. ECHINODERMATA	Starfishes, sea-urchins, sea-cucumbers, stone-lilies.
15. CHORDATA	Sea-squirts, lancelet, vertebrates, including fishes, frogs, reptiles, birds, and mammals with man.

ANGLO-EGYPTIAN SUDAN. See SUDAN, Republic of.

ANGLO-SAXONS. The Teutonic invaders who conquered Britain between the 5th and 7th cents. According to Bede they consisted of the Angles, who settled in E. Anglia, Mercia, and Northumbria; the Saxons, in Essex, Sussex, and Wessex; and the Jutes, in Kent and S. Hampshire. The Jutes probably came from the Rhineland and not, as was formerly believed, from Jutland. The Angles and Saxons came from Schleswig-Holstein, and may have united before the invasion. There must have been a good deal of intermarriage with the Romanized Celts, although the latter's language and civilization almost disappeared. After the conquest a number of kingdoms were set up, commonly referred to as the Heptarchy; these were united in the early 9th cent. under the overlordship of Wessex. The English-speaking peoples of Britain, the Commonwealth, and the U.S.A. are often referred to today as A.-Ss., but the term is completely unscientific, as the Welsh, Scots, and Irish are mainly of Celtic descent, and only 35 per cent of Americans are of British stock.

ANGO'LA. Portuguese overseas prov. in W. Africa, lying between the Congo Rep. and S.W. Africa. With a coastline of some 1,300 m. it has an area of 481,000 sq. m. divided into 13 districts. The cap. is São Paulo de Luanda: other towns are Huambo, Benguela, Mossâmedes, and Lobito.

The coastal area is flat, unproductive, and unhealthy, but behind a mountainous edge stretches a vast area of plateau, comparatively healthy and fertile. The principal rivers are the Congo, upper reaches of the Zambesi, Kwanza, Kubango, and Kunene. The staple industry is agriculture—coffee, maize, sugar, and palm kernels and oil are exported: there are also diamonds, and oil was discovered 1967. Benguela is linked by rail with Mozambique. Nationalist guerilla activity has been continuous from 1961. Pop. (1968) 5,000,000, incl. 300,000 Europeans.

ANGORA. Alternative form of ANKARA.

ANGOSTURA. Name 1824–49 of CIUDAD BOLIVAR, Venezuela.

ANGOULÊME (aṅgoolām'). French town, cap. of the dept. of Charente, on the Charente, with a fine cathedral and a castle and papermills dating from the 16th cent. Pop. (1968) 47,822.

ANGRY YOUNG MEN. Group of British writers who emerged after the creative hiatus which followed the S.W.W. They included Kingsley Amis, John Wain, John Osborne (qq.v.), Colin Wilson, Bill Hopkins, Stuart Holroyd. Also linked with the group were Iris Murdoch, Ken Tynan, Lindsay Anderson.

ÅNGSTRÖM (awng'-), **Anders Jonas** (1814–74). Swedish physicist, who did notable work in spectroscopy and solar physics. After him is named the *Angstrom unit*, used to express the wavelength of electro-magnetic radiations (light, radiant heat, X-rays). One A. or A.U. is equal to 10^{-8} cm. (one ten-millionth of a millimetre).

ANGUS. County on the E. coast of Scotland. Part of the Grampians, the 'Braes of Angus', occupies the N.; in the S. are the Sidlaw hills, while in the centre is the Vale of Strathmore. Chief among the rivers are the North and South Esk, the Isla, Tay, Mark, Tarf, Dean, and Prosen. The co. was known as Forfarshire from the 16th cent. until 1928.

The chief industries are jute and linen manufacture, farming and fishing. Dundee is the largest centre of population. Other towns are Arbroath, Montrose, Forfar (county town), Kirriemuir and Brechin. Though native to the county, the A. breed of cattle is not now usually reared there, but rather in Aberdeenshire. Area 873 sq. m.; pop. (1961) 278,370.

ANGUILLA. See under LEEWARD ISLANDS.

ANHUI. Other form of Anhwei, prov. of China.

A'NILINE (Aminobenzene, $C_6H_5NH_2$). The simplest aromatic base known, originally prepared by the dry distillation of indigo, whence its name (Port. *anil*, indigo). When pure it is a colourless oily liquid; it has a characteristic odour, and turns black in contact with air. It occurs in coal tar, and was discovered in 1826. It is highly poisonous.

ANIMALS. One of the two 'kingdoms' of living things, the science of which is zoology, the other being the vegetable kingdom or plants, the science of which is botany.

As. and plants are fundamentally similar in microscopical structure, being composed of a substance, protoplasm, and the tissues in the more elaborately organized examples of the two kingdoms alike consist primarily of minute particles of protoplasm known as cells. But the macroscopical structure of all the familiar As. and plants is so different that there is no difficulty in distinguishing one from the other, and there is also the important physiological difference that As. are capable of living and developing only by the nutritive assimilation of the protoplasmic tissues of other living organisms, plant or A. As. are dependent on plants, and must have succeeded them in the evolution of living things. But these differences, both anatomical and physiological, between the more complex and familiar As. and plants break down in the simplest, most primitive forms of As., the Protozoa, which are so distinct from other As. that they are given the rank of a sub-kingdom, the rest being assigned to the sub-kingdom Metazoa. Owing to the dying out of formerly existing links, the Metazoa can be classified into a number of primary, definable groups, each of which is known as a phylum, meaning a stock or line of descent; and the classification, or taxonomy, of As. is based on the conception that fundamental structural resemblances indicate kinship, not superficial resemblances such as exist between a whale and a shark, and have been acquired as adaptations to a similar mode of life.

The views of zoologists differ to a certain extent regarding the number of phyla of Metazoa that may be admitted, but on p. 43 is a list widely adopted, together with the names of some familiar animals included in each phylum.

Some of these phyla, e.g. Chaetognatha and the Phoronidea, are comparatively unimportant, and the chief interest of the Brachiopoda is geological. On the other hand, the Arthropoda, Mollusca, and Chordata contain a vast number of widely different living forms, quite apart from those known only from their fossil remains.

All the more extensive phyla, including the Protozoa, are subdivided into numerous groups of subordinate status, bearing names of Greek or Latin derivation, the principal subdivisions commonly admitted and arranged according to rank, being sub-phyla, classes, sub-classes, orders, suborders, tribes, families, sub-families, genera, species, and sub-species.

ANKARA. Chosen as his capital by Atatürk, A. is a focal point of communications in Anatolia and since 1925 has developed with astonishing rapidity. The Youth Park offers beauty as well as recreational facilities.   *Courtesy of the Turkish Embassy.*

ANIMAL WORSHIP. A common feature of many primitive religions, arising from animism, totemism, belief in the transmigration of souls under animal forms, or from a desire to propitiate the dangerous or encourage the useful animal. Every variety of A. is eligible, although a preference may be shown for particular types, e.g. the widespread cult of the serpent. Among the animals reverenced are the ancient Egyptian bull, cat, jackal, hawk, ibis, and hippopotamus; the Israelite golden calf; the Hindu cow, monkey, and elephant; and the N. American Indian beaver, buffalo, and deer.

ANIMISM (Lat. *anima*, soul). In psychology and physiology, the view of human personality which rejects materialistic mechanism as a valid explanation of man. In religious theory, the primitive conception of a spiritual reality behind the material one: e.g. the native beliefs in the soul as a shadowy duplicate of the body capable of independent activity, both in life and death. Linked with this is the worship of natural objects such as stones and trees, thought to harbour spirits (naturism), fetishism, and ancestor worship.

ANJOU (oṅzhoo′). An old countship and former prov. in the N. of France: cap. Angers. In 1154 the count of A. became King of England as Henry II, but the territory was lost by John in 1204. In 1480 the countship was annexed to the French crown. The dept. of Maine-et-Loire and part of Indre-et-Loire, Mayenne, and Sarthe cover the area.

AN′KARA. Cap. of Turkey, standing on the Anatolian plateau of Asia Minor and having Roman and earlier relics. In 1415 it became permanently Turkish. Constantinople (Istanbul) being in Allied occupation 1918–23, after the F.W.W., in 1923 Mustafa Kemal (Atatürk) declared A. the cap. of the Turkish rep., and proceeded to turn the small provincial town into a 20th cent. city. The President's palace, the palace of the Grand National Assembly, and Atatürks mausoleum are among the chief buildings. There are 3 univs., the technical univ. serving all the Middle East. Pop. (1965) 905,700.

ANNABA. Arabic form of Bône (q.v.).

ANNAM. Country of S.E. Asia, incorporated in Vietnam (q.v.) in 1946 as Central Vietnam. A flourishing Bronze Age civilization was in existence in the area when Chinese conquerors penetrated it and held it for centuries. Mongolization was not complete and the people remained basically Indonesian. The Chinese named their conquest An-Nam, 'peaceful south'. Their rule ended in 968 when the 1st native dynasty was estab. In 1884 A. became a French protectorate, and the kings were virtually vassals. The Japanese occupied A. during the S.W.W.

ANNAPOLIS. Seaport of the U.S.A., cap. of Maryland, situated 2 m. from Chesapeake Bay on the Severn r. It was founded c. 1648 as Providence, renamed Anne Arundel, and, in 1695, Annapolis. While Congress met here, Nov. 1783–June 1784, it received Washington's resignation of his commission as C.-in-C. (1783) and ratified the peace treaty (1784) of the War of American Independence. The U.S. Naval Academy (1845) is at A.; John Paul Jones (q.v.) is buried in the chapel crypt and there is a museum with relics of U.S. naval history. Pop (1960) 23,385.

ANNAPUR′NA. Mountain (26,502 ft.) in the Himalayas, Nepal. The N. face was climbed by a Fr. expedition 1950 and the S. by a British 1970.

ANNE (1665–1714). Queen of Great Britain and Ireland. The 2nd daughter of James, duke of York, who became James II, and Anne Hyde, she received a Protestant upbringing, and in 1683 m. Prince George of Denmark. Of their 17 children only one survived infancy, William, duke of Gloucester, who d. at the age of 12. For the greater part of her life A. was dominated by her friend, Sarah Churchill, wife of John Churchill, afterwards duke of Marlborough; the Churchills' influence led her to desert her father for her brother-in-law, William of Orange, during the revolution of 1688, and later to engage in Jacobite intrigues. She succeeded William on the throne in 1702. Her devotion to the Church of England led her at first to sympathize with the Tories, but she later acquiesced in the establishment of a Whig government, again under the Marlboroughs' influence. The outstanding events of her reign were the War of the Spanish Succession (1702–13), Marlborough's victories at Blenheim, Ramillies, Oudenarde, and Malplaquet, and the union of the English and Scottish parliaments in 1707. A. finally broke with the Marlboroughs in 1710, when Mrs. Masham succeeded the duchess as her favourite, and supported the Tory government of the same year.

ANNE (1950–). Princess of the U.K. She was b. at Clarence House, London, on 15 Aug. 1950, and is the 2nd child of Queen Elizabeth II and the Duke of Edinburgh. Her education was undertaken privately, and from 1963–8 at Benenden School, Kent.

After leaving school she undertook a full share of the royal duties, and in 1970 accompanied the Queen on visits to Australasia and Canada, and briefly visited Washington together with Prince Charles.

ANNE OF AUSTRIA (1601–66). Queen of France. Daughter of Philip III of Spain, she m. Louis XIII of France in 1615, and on his death in 1643 became regent for her son, Louis XIV. She was much under the influence of Mazarin, to whom she was supposed to be secretly married.

ANSERMET. His earlier experience as a prof. of mathematics at Lausanne made him a skilled interpreter of the most complex scores, attentive – as in this moment at the Royal Festival Hall, London – to the slightest nuance.
Photo: Godfrey MacDomnic.

ANNE OF CLEVES (1515–57). 4th wife of Henry VIII of England. Daughter of John, duke of Cleves, she was recommended to Henry by Thomas Cromwell, who desired an alliance with German Protestantism against the emperor. She proved to be so plain and stolid that Henry had the marriage declared null and void, A. receiving a comfortable pension.

ANNE OF DENMARK (1574–1619). Queen consort of Great Britain. Daughter of Frederick II of Denmark and Norway, she m. in 1589 James VI of Scotland, who became James I of Great Britain in 1603. A. was suspected of Catholic leanings, and was notably extravagant.

ANNECY (ahnse′). Capital of the dept. of Haute-Savoie, France, at the northern end of A. Lake. A beautiful town, it has some light industry. Pop. (1968) 58,484.

ANNE′LIDA. Phylum of animals, including the segmented worms. They are distinguished from the Arthropoda by the absence of jointed appendages, and by the presence of a cavity, part of the coelom, surrounding the alimentary canal. There is a distinct head, and the body is divided into a number of similar segments, which are shut off from one another internally by membraneous partitions. The A. are divided into 3 principal classes, the *Polychaeta* (or many-bristled worms), *Oligochaeta* (or few-bristled worms) – these two together forming the *Chaetopoda* – and the *Hirudinea* (or leeches), which are entirely destitute of bristles.

ANNIGO′NI, Pietro (1910–). Italian artist. He is noted for the etherealized Renaissance style of his portraits, e.g. Elizabeth II in 1955: other sitters incl. the Duke of Edinburgh and Princess Margaret.

ANNO DO′MINI (Lat., in the year of our Lord). In the Christian chronological system, dates since the birth of Christ, denoted by the letters A.D. Earlier years are denoted by the letters B.C. (Before Christ). There is no year 0, so A.D. 1 follows immediately after the year B.C. 1. The system is based on the calculations made in A.D. 525 by Dionysius Exiguus, a Scythian monk, but the birth of Christ should more correctly be placed in 3 B.C. or 4 B.C. It became the standard reckoning when adopted by Bede in the 8th cent.

ANNUNCIATION. The tidings brought to Mary by the angel Gabriel concerning the Incarnation (Luke i, 26–38). The Feast of the A. is kept on 25 March, known as Lady Day.

ANOA. *See* BUFFALO.

A′NODE. The electrode at which positive current enters a device. It is the positively charged electrode of an electrolytic cell, the electrode on which the primary stream of electrons impinges in a vacuum tube and the negative terminal of a battery.

ANOPHELES. *See* GNAT.

ANOUILH (anōōiy′), **Jean** (1910–). French playwright and film writer. Though b. in Bordeaux, he grew up in Paris and became a law student and advertising agency man before finding his true bent in the theatre. Constantly concerned with the antithesis of innocence and experience, his plays have frequently been staged in English versions *L'invitation au Château* (1947: Ring Round the Moon), *Colombe* (1950), and *Becket, ou l'honneur de Dieu* (1959), concerned with Becket and Henry II.

ANSCHLUSS (ahn′shloos: Ger., joining). Term used for the union of Austria with Germany, accomplished by Hitler on 12 March 1938.

ANSELM, St. (1033?–1109). Churchman, b. near Aosta, in Piedmont. Educated at the abbey of Bec in Normandy, which as an abbot (from 1078) he made the greatest centre of scholarship in Europe, he was appointed abp. of Canterbury by William II in 1093, but was later forced into exile. He was recalled by Henry I, with whom he bitterly disagreed on the investiture of the clergy; a final agreement gave the king the right of temporal investiture and the clergy that of spiritual investiture. A. was canonized in 1494. He holds an important place in the development of scholasticism. In his *Proslogion* he developed the ontological proof of theism, which infers God's existence from our capacity to conceive of a perfect Being. His most important work, *Cur deus homo*, deals with the Atonement.

ANSERMET (onsärmeh′), **Ernest** (1883–1969). Swiss conductor and composer. As permanent conductor for Diaghilev's Russian Ballet (1915), he conducted at the premières of several Stravinsky ballets, and afterwards toured the world.

AN′SHAN. Chinese city and iron and steel centre, in Liaoning prov., 55 m. S.S.E. of Shenyang (Mukden). Started here in 1918, expanded by the Japanese, dismantled by the Russians, the iron works were restored by the Communist govt. of China: production 1·5 million tons of pig iron annually. Pop. c. 600,000.

ANSON, George, baron (1697–1762). British admiral. B. in Staffs, he entered the navy at the age of 15. In 1740, during the war with Spain, he commanded a squadron of 6 ships with which he attacked Spanish colonies and shipping in S. America. After circumnavigating the globe, he returned to England in 1744 with only a single ship, but bringing back £500,000 of Spanish treasure. In 1747 he routed a French convoy off Cape Finisterre, and was created Baron A. of Soberton. His *Voyage Round the World* (1748) is a maritime classic.

ANT. Insect of the family Formicoidea of the order Hymenoptera, to which also belong the wasps and the bees.

About 3,500 different species of As. are known. All are social in habit, and live in nests of various kinds. Each A. society or community consists of a number of sterile wingless females, termed workers, and a smaller number of fertile females and males, which are usually winged. The male is smaller and more slender than the female. At certain times of the year the winged males and females leave the parental nest in large numbers on their nuptial flight.

Mating takes place in the air, after which the males soon perish, while the fertilized females (or queens, as they are now called), lose their wings and settle down to colony founding. In some As. the workers are all alike, but in others large-headed 'soldiers' may be distinguished from the small-headed workers.

The most primitive As. are carnivorous and hunt other insects. The tribal As. of the tropics lead a wandering nomadic life. Others are pastoralists, feeding chiefly upon saccharin matter obtained from the extra-floral nectaries of various plants, but more especially on honey dew, discharged by aphids and related insects. The As. induce the aphids to void this substance by stroking them with the antennae; some As. even keep and protect them. Honey As. use certain of their own workers or soldiers as receptacles for storing collected honey dew; when hungry, they stroke these 'repletes' and receive from them regurgitated honey dew. Harvesting As. collect, husk, and store plant seeds in special chambers or granaries. The robber As. (*Formica sanguinea*) raid nests of other As., in particular those of *F. fusca*, and carry off Fusca pupae to their own nests, where they are destined to live as slaves, tending the brood of their captors. The so-called white As. or termites (q.v.) belong to a very different group of insects.

ANTANANARIVO (ahntahnahnahrē'vo). Cap. of the rep. of Madagascar, situated on a hill in the centre of the island. Pop. (1965) 321,654.

ANTARCTICA. Continent surrounding the South Pole, having an area of about 5,300,000 sq. m., and the ice-covered sea surrounding it. In a broad sense the term covers all land and sea S. of about latitude 60° S. There are no inhabitants on the land. The continent is a vast faulted plateau of very ancient rocks with flanking Tertiary deposits showing affinity with geological occurrences in New Zealand and S. America. In places isolated peaks break through the icy surface, or ranges of mountains stand up from the plateau. The great ice sheet which covers the

RED ANT. I, Male; 2, worker; 3, female; 4, larva; 5, nymph; 6, cocoon.

ANTARCTICA. Paradise Bay in the Antarctic, looking towards Le Mare Island.   *Courtesy of Anglo-Chilean Society.*

continent reaches a thickness of about 2,000 ft. The Ross or Great Ice Barrier is a great shelf of ice formed by several glaciers coalescing in the Ross Sea. The coasts are backed by huge walls of ice. The internat. Antarctic Treaty (1959) reserved A. for peaceful purposes of research and recognised existing claims to territorial sovereignty.

A number of islands, all barren and windswept, lie off the continent: these include the Shetlands, the S. Orkneys, the S. Sandwich islands, and Peter 1st Is.

CLIMATE, VEGETATION. Winter is almost continuous in A., no month being free from frost, and even the summer mean temperature is below freezing-point. Winter temperatures are often below zero F. Southerly winds of great velocity are common. Rain never falls. There is very little soil cover. Lichens and mosses encrust the rock faces; there are no trees, and few other plants. Whales, seals, and penguins visit the seas and shore, and many sea birds nest there in summer.

POLITICAL CLAIMS. Claims to sovereignty in A. began when whaling expeditions in the 20th cent. revealed the region's possibilities. There is no part unclaimed, the claims being made in sectors reaching to the Pole. British areas are the Falkland Islands Dependency (1908), the Ross Dependency of New Zealand (1923), and Australian Antarctic Territory (1936). Peter 1st Is. was placed under Norway 1933. There are also Adélie Land (French, 1938) and Norwegian Antarctic Dependency (1939). Marie Byrd Land and Ellsworth Highland are unofficially claimed by U.S.A.; both Argentina and Chile claim the Falkland Islands Dependencies.

Exploration. The first to sail in Antarctic seas was James Cook in 1773–4, and early in the 19th cent. discoveries were made to the south of S. America (E. Bransfield, J. Biscoe, Bellinghausen, and J. Weddell) and Australia (D. d'Urville and C. Wilkes). In 1841–2 James Ross found great land areas in S. Victoria Land and sighted the Great Ice Barrier. The *Challenger* crossed the Antarctic Circle in 1872 and de Gerlache wintered in A. in 1897–9. Scott's initial attempt to reach the S. Pole in 1902–4 (82° 17′ S.) was followed by a number of others, e.g. Shackleton 1908–9; Amundsen succeeded on 16 Dec. 1911, and Scott himself on 18 Jan. 1912. In 1957–8 Vivian Fuchs made the 1st overland journey across the continent via the Pole.

The first aerial flights were made in 1928 by H. Wilkins over Graham Land, and in 1929 R. E. Byrd flew to the Pole and back from the Ross Ice Barrier in 19 hours. In 1935

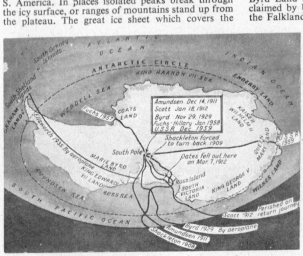

Amundsen Dec 14, 1911
Scott Jan 18, 1912
Byrd Nov 29, 1929
Fuchs-Hillary Jan 1958
U.S.S.R. Dec 1959

Shackleton forced to turn back 1909

Dates fell out here on Mar. 7, 1912

Perished on return journey

ANTARCTICA. Routes of the most famous expeditions.

L. Ellsworth flew 2,300 m. across unknown territory. The largest expedition ever attempted was that under Byrd in 1946, which consisted of 4,000 men, 13 ships, 29 land-based planes, and 35 seaplanes from tenders.

ANTEATER. Name given to several mammals that live wholly or mainly on ants, for which diet they are structurally adapted with toothless jaws, extensile tongue, and powerful fore-paws for breaking up the ant-hills. The Great A. or Ant Bear (*Myrmecophaga jubata*), is common in Brazil, and stands about 2 ft. high. The name is also applied to the aardvark, the echidna, and the pangolins (qq.v.).

A'NTELOPE. Popular name for a number of distinct kinds of hoofed animals of the family Bovidae of the order Artiodactyla. A few medium-sized genera are found in Asia, notably the chiru of Tibet; the saiga of Tartary; several sorts of gazelles that inhabit the deserts of Persia and Arabia spread into India, to which the blackbuck, the four-horned A., and the nilgai are restricted. But most As. are known from

ANTELOPE (Eland)

Africa where they range from the extreme N. to the Cape Province; some of the duikers do not surpass a cat in height, whereas the eland is as bulky as large cattle. Other important species are the kudu, oryx or gemsbok (q.v.), sable A., gnu or wildebeest (q.v.), hartebeest, waterbuck, impala, and springbok (q.v.). There are no true As. in the Americas, although the prongbuck passes under that name in the U.S.A.

ANTHEIL (ahn'tîl), **George** (1900–59). American composer, the son of a Polish political exile. He was at one time a concert pianist, but was best known for his *Ballet Mécanique*, scored for anvils, aeroplane propellers, electric bells, automobile horns, and 16 player pianos.

ANTHONY (an'toni), **St.** (*c* 250–350). Founder of Christian monasticism. B. in Egypt, he renounced at the age of 20 all his possessions and lived in a tomb, and at 35 sought yet further solitude on a mountain in the desert. In 305 he founded the first cenobitic Order, or community of Christians following a rule of life under a superior. When he was about a hundred, A. went to Alexandria and preached against the Arians. A.'s temptations in the desert were a popular subject in art.

ANTHONY OF PADUA, St. (1195–1231). B. at Lisbon, the son of a nobleman, he became an Augustinian monk, but in 1220 joined the Franciscans. He opposed the relaxations introduced into the Order. Like St. Francis, he is said to have preached to animals. He d. at Padua and was canonized in 1232.

ANTHOZO'A (Gk., flower-animals) or **Actinozoa.** Class of animals of the phylum Coelenterata, including sea-anemones, corals, etc. They are sedentary polyps, and never pass through a medusa stage. The most important divisions are the Alcyonaria, Actiniaria, and Madreporaria.

A'NTHRACENE ($C_{14}H_{10}$). White glistening crystalline hydrocarbon with a faint blue fluorescence when pure. Its melting-point is about 216° C., and its boiling point 351° C. It occurs in the high boiling fractions of coal tar, where it was discovered in 1832 by Laurent and Dumas.

A'NTHRACITE (Gk. *anthrakos*, coal). A hard, dense glossy variety of coal, containing over 90 per cent of fixed carbon, and a low percentage of ash and of volatilizable matter, which causes it to burn without flame, smoke, or smell. It gives an intense heat, but is slow-burning and slow to catch alight, and is therefore unsuitable for use in open fires. Its characteristic

composition is thought to be due to the action of bacteria in disintegrating the coal-forming material when it was laid down in the carboniferous age. Amongst the chief sources of A. coal are S. Wales, Pennsylvania, the Donbas (q.v.), and the Shansi province of China.

A'NTHRAX. A disease caused by the anthrax bacillus; woolsorters' disease. It is principally a disease of animals, especially cattle and sheep, and is caught by man from infected hides and fleeces. Consequently, most countries have strict laws regulating the importation of these articles. The disease is so deadly to animals and so dangerous to man that to guard against its spread every animal exposed to it must be slaughtered and burnt. The first sign is a boil on the part of the body exposed to contact; after a few days this grows into a large red area with a dark scab surrounded by clear blisters.

A'NTHROPOID APES (from Gk. for 'resembling man'). A group of the Primates comprising fossil and extinct species, and also living species (gorilla, chimpanzee, orang-utan, and gibbon, qq.v.), referred to as the family Simiidae, which is associated with the Hominidae (Man) in the section Anthropomorpha.

ANTHROPOID APES. So called because of their resemblance to man, which can be seen especially in the shapes of the spine, breastbone, and pelvis. In this drawing after T. H. Huxley their skeletons are compared: a, gibbon; b, orang-utan; c, chimpanzee; d, gorilla; e, man.

ANTHROPO'LOGY (Gk. *anthropos*, man; *logos*, science). The natural history of Man. The term was first used by Otto Casmann in 1594, but A. did not develop as a science until the general adoption of evolutionary theory in the 2nd half of the 19th cent. It deals with man's development from non-human stocks (Physical A.), the races of mankind as they are today (ethnology), social, political and economic organization (Cultural A.), the purposes that cultures are intended to serve (Functional A.), etc. In encouraging the development of colonial peoples the British govt. has made considerable use of applied A. in this century (Social Science Research Council for the Colonies, estab. 1944) and in the U.S. research is co-ordinated by the Society for Applied A. (estab. 1941) and has been particularly active in extending the field of A. to advanced cultures and western societies.

ANTHROPO'METRY. The science that deals with the measurement of the human body, particularly stature, body-weight, cranial capacity, length of limb, etc., in the two sexes and the different living and extinct races of mankind. Anthropology in general is descriptive; anthropometry brings to its study numerical and graphical modes of expression. The founder of A. was Quetelet, the Belgian statistician, whose *L'Anthropométrie* was pub. in 1871. Francis Galton, Karl Pearson, and A. Hrdlička made valuable contributions.

ANTHROPOMOR'PHISM. The attribution of human characteristics to beings above or below humanity in the order of the universe. Plants, animals, and even inanimate objects or forces such as stones or the winds are sometimes given human qualities, but A. is generally limited to the conception of gods in human form. Seen in its fullest development in the mythologies of Scandinavia and Greece, it tends in more advanced religions such as Christianity to be reduced to metaphor.

ANTHROPO'SOPHY. System of mystical philosophy developed by Rudolf Steiner (q.v.), who claimed to possess a power of intuition giving him access to knowledge not attainable by scientific means. The Anthroposophical Society was founded in 1913.

ANTIBES (oñtĕb'). Port and pleasure-resort on the French Riviera, dept. Alpes-Maritimes. Pop. (1962) 35,976.

ANTIBIO'TIC. A chemical substance produced by living micro-organisms such as moulds and bacteria, which is capable of destroying or preventing the growth of other micro-organisms. Under some conditions a disease-causing organism, originally susceptible, may become resistant to the effect of an A., hence 2 or more As. are often used in combination with other drugs. Since the introduction of the first A., penicillin (q.v.) in the 1940s, they have greatly contributed to the decline of tuberculosis, venereal diseases, pneumonia, etc.

ANTICHRIST. The great opponent of Christ, by whom he is finally to be conquered. Although the term first occurs in Christian writings, the idea of conflict between Light and Darkness is present in Persian, Babylonian, and Jewish literature, and influenced early Christian thought. A. may be a fake Messiah, or be connected with false teaching, or be identified with an individual, e.g. Nero at the time of the persecution, and the Pope and Napoleon in later Christian history.

A'NTICLINE. Geological term for a fold in the earth's crust in which the beds dip on each side of a central axis, thus forming a sort of arch, which, however, is seldom preserved intact. The fold may be undulating or sharply curved. Should one side of an anticlinal fold be compressed until it is nearly vertical, it forms a monocline. A SYNCLINE is the geological term for the converse – the structure produced when beds are folded so that they dip towards a central axis, giving rise to a trough or basin.

A — anticline
S — syncline

ANTI-COM'INTERN PACT (Anti-Communist Pact). Agreement signed between Germany and Japan on 25 Nov. 1936, opposing Communism as a menace to peace and order. The pact received the adhesion of Italy in 1937 and of Hungary, Spain, and Manchukuo in 1939. It became a dead letter in 1945.

ANTI-COSMOS. *See* MOHOLE.

ANTICYCLONE and **CYCLONE** (sī'klōn). Terms referring to conditions of atmospheric pressure. A cyclone is an area of low pressure, an anticyclone one of high pressure. *Anticyclones* are caused by descending air, which becomes warm and dry. From a calm centre winds radiate, taking a clockwise direction in the N. hemisphere, and anticlockwise in the S. hemisphere. They are associated with clear weather and are distinguished by the absence of rain and violent winds. In summer they bring hot, sunny days, and in winter fine, frosty spells, though fog and low cloud are not uncommon in winter anticyclonic weather. *Cyclones* are formed by the mixture of cold, dry polar air with warm, moist equatorial air. These masses of air meet in temperate latitudes; the warm air rises over the cold, resulting in rain. Winds blow in towards the centre in an anticlockwise direction in the N. hemisphere, clockwise in the S. hemisphere; the systems are characterized by variable weather, and are common over the British Isles. They bring rain or snow, winds up to gale force, low cloud, and sometimes fog. Tropical cyclones are a great danger to shipping. The tornado is a rapidly moving cyclone.

ANTI'GONE. In Greek legend, a daughter of Jocasta, by her son Oedipus (q.v.).

ANTI'GONUS (382–301 B.C.). A general of Alexander the Great, after whose death in 323 he made himself master of Asia Minor. He was defeated and slain by Seleucus at the battle of Ipsus.

ANTIGUA (ahntĕ'gwah). Largest of the Leeward Islands, an assoc. state of the U.K. from 1967. Discovered in 1493 by Columbus and not inhabited until English settlers occupied it in 1632. There are fine harbours at St. John's the cap., and English Harbour. Sugar is the chief export. Area 171 sq. m.; pop. (1960) 54,354, incl. the dependent islands of Barbuda and (uninhabited) Redonda.

ANTI'LLES. Name sometimes used to describe the whole group of West Indian Islands, which are divided into Greater A. (Jamaica, Cuba, Puerto Rico, and Haiti-Dominican Rep.), and Lesser A.

A'NTIMONY. A metallic element, symbol Sb, at. no. 51, at. wt. 121·76. In the ordinary form it is a silver-white metal, brittle, and readily powdered. It occurs chiefly as stibnite, and is used in a number of alloys and as a photosensitor, with response in blue and blue-green.

A'NTIOCH (-ok). Ancient capital of the Greek kingdom of Syria, founded 300 B.C. by Seleucus Nicator in memory of his father Antiochus, and for long famed for its splendour and luxury. Under the Romans it was an early centre of Christianity. The site is occupied by the Turkish town of Antakiyah; pop. *c.* 33,000.

ANTI'OCHUS (-ok). Name of 13 kings of Syria of the Seleucid dynasty. A. I (b. 324; reigned 281–261 B.C.), son of Seleucus, one of the generals of Alexander the Great, earned the title of A. Soter or Saviour by his defeat of the Gauls in Galatia (278 B.C.). His son A. II (b. 286; reigned 261–246 B.C.), was known as A. Theos, the Divine. During his reign the eastern provinces broke away from the Graeco-Macedonian rule, and set up native princes. A. III the Great (b. *c.* 241; king 223–187 B.C.), grandson of A. II, secured a loose suzerainty over Armenia and Parthia (209), overcame Bactria, received the homage of the Indian king of the Kabul valley, and returned by way of the Persian Gulf (204 B.C.). He took possession of Palestine, entering Jerusalem in 198 B.C. He crossed into N.W. Greece, but was decisively defeated by the Romans at Thermopylae in 191 and at Magnesia in 190 B.C. He had to abandon his domains in Asia Minor, and perished at the hands of the people of Elymais. A. IV (king 175–164 B.C.), 2nd son of A. III, was known as A. Epiphanes, the Illustrious; he occupied Jerusalem about 170 B.C., seizing much of the Temple treasure, and instituted worship of the Greek type in the Temple. This produced the revolt of the Jewish people under the Maccabees, and A. died before he could suppress it.

A. VII Sidetes (king 138–129 B.C.), the last strong ruler of the dynasty, took Jerusalem in 134 B.C., reducing the Maccabees to subjection, and fought successfully against the Parthians. Under A. XIII Asiaticus (reigned 69–65 B.C.), the last of the dynasty, Syria was converted into a province by Pompey.

ANTI'PODES (Gk. *anti*, opposite; *podes*, feet). Places exactly opposite one another on the globe. In Britain, Australia and New Zealand are sometimes so called. The Antipodes islands S.E. of New Zealand are approx. the A. of London.

ANTIRRHINUM (antirīn'um) or **Snapdragon.** Genus of plants belonging to the same group as the foxglove and toad flax (Scrophulariaceae). *A. majus*, a native of central and southern Europe, is a familiar garden flower.

ANTI-SEMITISM. Opposition to the Jews. A. first appeared soon after Christianity had been adopted as

ANTIBES. In 'Cap d'Antibes' with its solitary windswept pine, bold against the sea and sky, Claude Monet captures the essence of this part of the Mediterranean coast.
Courtauld Institute Galleries, London.
© *S.P.A.D.E.M., Paris, 1964*

the official religion of the Roman Empire, and was fanned into activity by the religious enthusiasm of the Crusades. During the 12th and 13th cents. Jews were persecuted in, and expelled from, England, France, and Germany, while they were finally expelled from Spain, where they had flourished under the Moorish domination, in 1492. These persecutions caused an emigration eastwards, and were the beginning of the large Jewish communities in Poland and Russia. Their causes were partly religious and partly economic. Forbidden to own land, excluded from the craft guilds, the Jew was forced to become a middleman. Since usury was forbidden by the Church, Christians who needed money borrowed from the Jews, who became hated as usurers

In the early 19th cent. the Jews attained their emancipation, shared the commercial prosperity of the bourgeoisie, and won considerable influence; nevertheless, they remained a convenient scapegoat in hard times. During the economic crisis in Germany following the Franco-Prussian War a court chaplain, Stöcker, who called himself a Christian Socialist, led an anti-Semitic agitation and preached racial doctrines derived from Hegel. In Austria, where as in Germany, finance was largely Jewish-controlled, A. arose about the same time, and lasted much longer. In Russia the Tsarist government, fearful of revolution, deliberately diverted the anger of the miserable peasantry against the Jewish traders and money-lenders; pogroms began in 1881, and continued sporadically up to the F.W.W. In France the clericals and other opponents of the republic exploited the economic crises and financial scandals of the late 19th cent. to stir up an anti-Semitic campaign which culminated in the Dreyfus case. Even in Britain the influx of Jewish refugees from Russia and Poland aroused some popular feeling, which caused the passing of the Aliens Act (1905).

The persecution begun by Hitler in 1933 was made possible by the economic crisis of 1929, which brought ruin to Germany. The workers and middle classes were assured that Jewish finance was responsible for their sufferings, while the propertied classes were told that Hitler was their champion against Jewish Bolshevism, and the constant repetition of these contradictory assertions achieved a large measure of popular approval for the elimination of the Jews from Germany's industrial, political, and cultural life. The same phrases were taken over by Fascist movements in many other countries, including Britain and the U.S.A., and won particularly strong support in Austria, Hungary, and Rumania. This outburst of A., the worst in history, reached its climax during the S.W.W. in the extermination of millions of German, Polish, Dutch, and French Jews in German concentration camps. In the post-war period there have been sporadic revivals, and not least in the Communist world, as in the mid-1960s, when attacks were supposedly limited to those on 'Pro-Zionists'.

ANTISE'PTICS. Substances which hinder the growth of microbes or prevent their action; substances which *kill* microbes are called disinfectants or germicides. As. began to be evolved almost as soon as Pasteur's discoveries made medical men familiar with the properties of microbes about the middle of the 19th cent. Lord Lister revolutionized surgery by operating in a spray of carbolic acid, but 'antiseptic' has now been almost entirely replaced by 'aseptic' surgery. The number of different As. in use today is very large.

ANTI-VIVISECTION. Movement for the abolition of vivisection, i.e. experiments upon living animals. Vivisection is defended on the grounds that it results, or may result, in discoveries of great importance to medical science. It is attacked on the grounds that it is immoral to inflict pain on helpless creatures, even for the best of motives, that it is unjust that animals should suffer in order that men may benefit, that it is unscientific in that results achieved with animals may not be paralleled with human beings, and that vivisection has not added to man's power over disease. Anti-vivisectionists demand the repeal of legislation permitting experiments on animals by licensed scientific workers.

ANT LION. Larval form of the family of winged insects Myrmeleonidae common in Europe (not Britain) and the U.S. The common A.L. (*Myrmeleon formicarius*) has at this stage a large head and big toothed mandibles. It snares its prey by making, and lying concealed at the bottom of, a pit of loose sandy soil which sends unwary passing insects slipping down into its waiting jaws.

ANTOFAGA'STA. Chilean town on the Pacific coast, about 650 m. N. of Valparaiso. Its port and smelting works serve the silver-mining districts of S.W. Bolivia. Pop. (1967) 75,000.

ANTONE'SCU, Ion (1882–1946). Rumanian marshal and politician. Leader of the fascist Iron Guard, he became Prime Minister in 1940, abolished the constitution, and on the abdication of King Carol and the succession of Michael, assumed the royal powers. In October, German troops occupied the country, and in June 1941 Rumania joined Germany in attacking the Soviet Union. When the Red Army entered Rumania in Aug. 1944 A. was arrested; in May 1946 he was tried as a war criminal and shot.

ANTONINE'S WALL. Line of fortifications built by the Romans across central Scotland from the Clyde to the Forth in A.D. 142, during the reign of the emperor Antoninus Pius. By 200 it was abandoned in favour of Hadrian's Wall.

ANTONI'NUS PI'US (A.D. 86–161). Roman emperor. The son of a consul, he was adopted as heir by the emperor Hadrian early in 138, and became emperor a few months later, on Hadrian's death. His long reign was peaceful and prosperous, and he made various legal reforms.

ANTO'NIO. Stage-name of A. Ruiz Soler (1921–), Spanish dancer. B. at Seville, he began his career while a child, and has achieved a world-wide reputation for his fiery interpretation of national dance.

ANTÓNIO'NI, Michelangelo (1912–). Italian film director, famous for his subtle analysis of neuroses and personal relationships among the leisured classes of society, e.g. *L'Avventura* (1960), *La Notte* (1961), and *Blow-Up* (1967).

ANTONY, Mark, *See* MARK ANTONY.

ANTRIM, N.E. county of Northern Ireland, separated from Scotland by the 20 m. wide North Channel. The coastal districts are hilly, and on the

N.W. coast is the remarkable structure of the Giant's Causeway. The boggy lowlands of the interior produce peat. The pop. is mainly Protestant and of Scottish descent. Industries, of which the chief is linen manufacture, are located in and near Belfast. Including Belfast, the area is 1,122 sq. m.; pop. (1966) 712,954.

ANTUNG. Chinese port in Liaoning province, near the mouth of the Yalu and the Korean border; it is a silk and timber centre. Pop. *c.* 300,000.

A'NTWERP (Antwerpen). City and chief commercial centre of Belgium, one of the principal ports of N.W. Europe; it is situated on the Escaut (Scheldt), 55 m. from the North Sea, and its trade passes down the estuary of the Scheldt, which lies in Dutch territory.

It was not until the 15th cent. that A. rose to prosperity; from 1500 to 1560 it was the richest port in N. Europe. After this A. was distracted by religious troubles and the Netherlands revolt against Spain. In 1648 the treaty of Westphalia gave both shores of the Scheldt estuary to the United Provinces, which closed it to Antwerp trade. The treaty of Paris, 1814, opened the estuary to all nations on payment of a small toll to the Dutch, abandoned 1863. During the F.W.W. A. was in German hands from Oct. 1914 to Nov. 1918; during the S.W.W. from May 1940 to Sept. 1944.

Architecturally the city is well laid out. The Gothic cathedral was begun in the 14th cent., but finished only in 1518; also noteworthy are the Bourse (1872), the house of the 16th cent. printer Plantin, and the Museum. Besides the extensive merchant business, A. has a considerable industry in ship-repairing and ship-building, diamond-cutting, oil-refining, and manufacture of silk, cotton, and woollen goods. Pop. (1960) 256,219.

ANU'BIS. Egyptian god of the tomb, usually shown with the head of a jackal. He is often identified with the Greek Hermes.

ANURADHAPU'RA or **Anuradha.** Cap. of North Central province, Ceylon, 80 m. N. of Kandy. It possesses what is left of the famous Bo-tree, said to be a cutting from that under which Gautama was transformed into Buddha. A. is a great Buddhist pilgrimage centre. Pop. *c.* 13,000.

ANVERS. French form of ANTWERP.

ANYANG (anyahng'). Archaeological site in N. of Honan province, China, where in 1934 an archaeological expedition discovered royal tombs of *c.* 1350 B.C., the first remains of the Shang dynasty to be found *in situ*. The evidence revolutionized conceptions of early Chinese history.

ANZENGRUBER (ahn'tsengröö'ber), **Ludwig** (1839–89). Austrian dramatist. B. at Vienna, he became a bookseller, an actor, and from 1866 held a position in the Viennese police department. In 1870 his play *Der Pfarrer von Kirchfeld*, a flaming protest against intolerance and tyranny of the clergy, made him famous. Nearly all his 14 plays, the best of which deal with the tragic or comic side of peasant life, express an ethical tendency. He also wrote novels and short stories.

ANZHERO-SUDENSK (ahnzhe'ro soojensk'). Coalmining town in W. Siberia, R.S.F.S.R., 50 m. N. of Kemerovo. Pop. (1969) 114,000.

ANZIO (ahn'tsē-oh). Seaport on the W. coast of Italy, 33 m. S.S.E. of Rome, the site of the Roman town of Antium. The battle of A. beachhead (22 Jan.–23 May 1944), was one of the most famous and bitterly contested operations of the S.W.W.

ANZUS. Word coined from the initial letters of the countries of the Pacific Pact (1951): *A*ustralia, *N*ew *Z*ealand, and *U*nited *S*tates. They are pledged to mutual aid in the event of a member being subject to armed attack, and the Pacific Council, consisting of the 3 Foreign Ministers, meets annually for the better co-ordination of security arrangements. Britain was excluded, but the need for some more compre-

hensive agreement to maintain collective security in the area according to U.N. principles was met by S.E.A.T.O. (q.v.).

AO'MŌRI. Port at the head of Mutsu Bay, on the N. coast of Honshu Island, Japan, 25 m. N.E. of Hirosaki. The port handles a large local trade. Pop. (1965) 224,000.

ANTWERP. A storehouse of Flemish art the Mayer van den Bergh Museum, a reconstructed house with a Gothic frontage, contains not only pictures but furniture, embroidery, lace, china, sculpture and ivory of the 9th to 14th cents.
Courtesy of Belgian National Tourist Office.

AOSTA (ah-os'tah), **Amadeo Umberto**, 2nd duke of A. (1898–1942). Italian soldier. He succeeded Graziani as viceroy of Abyssinia in 1937, and on Italy's entry into the S.W.W. became C.-in-C. in East Africa. He was taken prisoner in 1941 and d. in Nairobi.

AOSTA. Italian city, cap. of Valle d'Aosta (French-speaking) autonomous region, 49 m. N.N.W. of Turin. It has extensive Roman remains. Pop. (1961) 30,127.

APACHES (apach'ēs). A group of N. American Indian tribes, formerly inhabiting Arizona and New Mexico, U.S.A. They were reputedly treacherous and savage, and were not subdued until 1886. Only a few thousand survive, living in reservations. The name A. (pron. apash') has also been given to the Parisian gangster type.

APARTHEID. *See* RACIAL DISCRIMINATION.

APE. Originally a synonym of monkey, and still applied to some species of the latter, such as the Barbary ape of Gibraltar, and the black ape of Celebes; zoologically the term usually signifies the 4 man-like or anthropoid apes (q.v.).

A'PENNINES. Chain of mountains stretching the length of the Italian peninsula. A continuation of the Maritime Alps, from Genoa it swings across the peninsula to Ancona on the E. coast, and then back to the W. coast and into the 'toe' of Italy. The system is continued over the Strait of Messina along the N. Sicilian coast, then across the Mediterranean sea in a series of islands to the Atlas mountains of N. Africa.

APE'RIENT. *See* PURGATIVES.

APHIDES (a'fidēz). Family of insects of the sub-order Homoptera, commonly known as green fly or plant lice; the singular is *aphis*. They are small, greenish or brownish insects, and live in colonies on the leaves and stems of certain plants, whose sap they suck. Several As. are of commercial importance, e.g. the phylloxera (q.v.) of the vine. *See* ANT.

APHRODISIAC (from *Aphrodite*, the Greek goddess of love.) Anything arousing or increasing sexual desire. Sexual activity can be stimulated in men and animals by drugs affecting the pituitary gland, for clinical and commercial farming purposes, but preparations commonly sold as As. are valueless, e.g. powdered rhinoceros horn in the East, or dangerous, e.g. cantharidin. Indian hemp and alcohol, both popularly considered A., lessen inhibition, but are directly likely to be the reverse of A.

APHRODI'TE. Greek goddess of love and wedlock, identified with the Roman Venus, the Syrian Astarte, and the Babylonian Ishtar. According to Homer, A. was the daughter of Zeus and Dione, but Hesiod says she sprang from the foam of the sea. She was the wife of Hephaestus (Vulcan), and the mother of Eros, and received the prize of beauty from Paris. Cyprus, Cythera, Corinth, and Eryx in Sicily were centres of her worship. The Greeks distinguished between A. Urania (goddess of the sky) and A. Pandemos (goddess of all the people, i.e. of marriage and family life), and in the course of time the-former became goddess of the higher, purer type of love, while the latter represented sensual lust.

APIA (ah'pē-ah). Port on N. coast of Upolu island, in Samoa, W. Pacific. Chief export copra. It is the cap. of the republic of (W.) Samoa. Robert Louis Stevenson made it his home 1889–94. Pop. (est.) 16,000.

A'PIS. Sacred bull, worshipped by the anc. Egyptians as a god, chiefly at Memphis.

APO'CALYPSE. Form of religious writing which emerged during the Jewish Hellenistic period. The earliest example is the O.T. book of Daniel; during the 19th cent. many later apocalyptic books were discovered. In the N.T. the book of Revelation is frequently referred to specifically as the A. All As. share a common purpose of stimulating faith in God in times of distress by graphic portrayal of the future in terms of triumph and deliverance. They also emphasize that the victory of God at the end of the world will be preceded by evil times.

APOCALYPSE. Movement among writers which developed from Surrealism in 1938, and included G. S. Fraser, Henry Treece, J. F. Hendry, Nicholas Moore, and Tom Scott. Largely influenced by the work of Dylan Thomas, it favours Biblical symbolism and thrusts aside the extremes of political theory and the pressures of a mechanized age in an attempt to obtain integrated expression of the self. Apocalyptic writers have also been active in America under the name of the International Workshop.

APOLLINAIRE (ahpollĕnār'), **Guillaume.** Abbreviated name of Guillaume Apollinaire de Kostrowitsky (1880–1918), French poet. Of aristocratic Polish descent, although of illegitimate birth, he was b. in Rome and ed. in Monaco, but in 1898 went to Paris. There he was a leader of the *avant garde* in literary and artistic circles. His lyrics (*Alcools* and *Calligrammes*), his novel *Le Poète Assassiné*, and play *Les Mamelles de Tirésias* show him as a representative of the cubist and futurist manner, and his work greatly influenced younger French writers, such as Aragon.

APO'LLO. Greek god, son of Zeus and Leto, and twin brother of Artemis. A. was the leader of the Muses, the god of music,

ANUBIS by the bier of the dead.

song, and poetry, of agriculture and the pastoral life. He was supposed to have been born on the island of Delos, and he features in a great number of the Greek myths and legends. The chief centres of his cult were Delphi, Delos, and Didyma in Asia Minor. From Delphi his worship spread to Italy, where he was recognized as the god of healing, oracles, and prophecy. Ancient statues show A. as the embodiment of the Greek ideal of male beauty.

Apollo Belvedere (4th cent.) in the Vatican Museum.

APOLLO'NIUS OF RHODES (fl. 220–180 B.C.). Greek poet and grammarian, whose epic poem, the *Argonautica*, is amongst the most famous examples of the poetry of the Alexandrian school.

APOLLONIUS OF TY'ANA (fl. A.D. 50). Greek ascetic philosopher of the Neo-Pythagorean school. He travelled in Babylonia and India, where he acquired a wide knowledge of oriental religions and philosophies, and taught at Ephesus. He was credited with many miraculous powers.

APOLLO OF RHODES. Huge bronze figure, one of the 7 wonders of the ancient world, said to have been erected by the Rhodians about 280 B.C. Its height was 105 ft., and it took 12 years to construct. In 226 B.C. it was overthrown by an earthquake, and in A.D. 653 the Saracens sold the statue as scrap metal.

APOLOGE'TICS (Gk. *apologeisthai*, to speak in defence). Refutation of attacks on the Christian faith. Famous apologists include Justin Martyr, Origen, St. Augustine, Thomas Aquinas, Blaise Pascal, and Joseph Butler. The questions raised by modern scientific and historical discoveries have widened the field of A. Principal topics are: the claim that religion is merely a projection of the group mind or a psychological illusion; the denial of the existence of God as a Creative Mind in the light of evolutionary theory; the nature of Revelation: the historical truth of the gospel story; and the basis of Christian ethic, first assailed in modern times by Nietzsche.

A'POPLEXY. Sudden loss of consciousness and paralysis caused by the breaking of a blood-vessel in the brain, or the blocking of one of the arteries of the brain by a blood-clot; a stroke, an apoplectic fit. The cause of the rupture of the blood vessel is usually a combination of high blood pressure with hardening of the arteries through age or disease, or through chronic poisoning by alcohol or lead.

APO'STLE (Gk., envoy). In the N.T., the missionaries sent out by Jesus, esp. the Twelve Disciples. In the earliest days of Christianity the term was extended to include some who had never known Jesus in the flesh, notably St. Paul; the *Apostolic Age* in Church history is the period during which the affairs of the infant church were directed by men who either had personal knowledge of Jesus or had received their knowledge and their commission to instruct and preach from members of the Twelve or St. Paul.

APOSTOLIC SUCCESSION. The doctrine in the Christian Church that certain spiritual powers and supernatural grace were received by the first Apostles direct from Christ Himself, and have been handed down in the ceremony of 'laying on of hands' from generation to generation by those who are the only true representatives of the Faith originally entrusted to the Saints.

APO'THECARY. An early name for a person who mixed and dispensed medicines, a pharmacist. The word retains its original meaning in U.S.A. and other countries, but in England an A. became a licensed medical practitioner. The Society of Apothecaries (constituted by Royal Charter in 1617) was by Act of Parliament (1815) given the legal right to grant licences to practise medicine in England and Wales.

APPALA'CHIANS. Mountain system of eastern N. America, stretching nearly 1,500 m. from Alabama in the S.W. to Quebec prov. in the N.E., composed of very ancient rocks, much worn down. They consist of 4 zones: the Allegheny and Cumberland plateaus; the great A. valley; the Blue Ridge, containing the highest peaks, Mt. Mitchell (6,684 ft.) and the Black Brothers (6,690 ft. and 6,620 ft.); and the Piedmont plateau. The E. edge is marked by a fall line, where Philadelphia, Baltimore, Washington, and other large cities stand. The A. are generally forested; coal is mined in the E. The *A. Trail*, a 2,000 m. scenic foot trail crossing 14 eastern states and running from Mt. Katahdin, Maine to Springer Mt., Georgia, was among the first to be designated (1967) in a bill to estab. a series of nat. trails.

APPEASEMENT. Name given to the generally conciliatory policy adopted by the British government, particularly under Neville Chamberlain, towards the Nazi-Fascist dictators. It was strongly opposed by Winston Churchill, but the Munich Pact of 1938 was almost universally hailed as its justification. When Czechoslovakia was occupied by the Germans in March 1939, A. was definitely abandoned.

APPENDICITIS (-sī'tis). Inflammation of the vermiform *appendix*, a small blind extension of the bowel about the size of a little finger, leading off the bottom of the caecum or blind gut, which forms the first part of the large bowel and lies low on the right-hand side of the abdomen. The appendix is very liable to inflammation, because it is narrow, can easily become twisted and kinked, and is a blind alley, so that faecal matter is easily trapped in it and decomposes, and the bacteria which swarm in the bowel multiply to a harmful extent. Sometimes a foreign body sets up inflammation. In acute A. the festering contents suddenly break through into the peritoneum, and the infection spreads rapidly through the abdomen. Often the attack comes on suddenly, usually in the night, with a sharp stabbing pain low down in the right side of the belly, making the patient vomit. He has a high temperature and quick pulse and breathing. The belly is very tender and hard. The usual treatment is operation at the earliest moment: the abdomen is cut open and the appendix is removed. The appendix is not necessary to healthy life.

A'PPERLEY, Charles James (1777–1843). British sportsman and sporting writer, known as 'Nimrod'. Among his books are *The Chase, The Turf and the Road* (1837) and *Hunting Reminiscences* (1843).

APPERT (ahpär'), **Nicolas** (1750–1841). French pioneer of food preservation by canning; author of *L'art de conserver les substances animales et végétales*.

APPLE. Fruit of *Pyrus malus*, a tree of the family Rosaceae. It has been an important food-plant in Europe from the earliest times, all the cultivated varieties being probably derived from the wild crab-apple. There are several thousand varieties of cultivated As., which may be divided into eating, cooking, and cider apples. They grow best in temperate countries with a cool climate and plenty of rain during the winter. The continent of Europe and N. America (both the U.S.A. and Canada) are the main sources of supply, but As. are also produced in Australia, New Zealand, South Africa, and some parts of Asia. As. may be produced from seeds, or by budding and grafting.

APPLETON, Sir Edward Victor (1892–1965). British physicist. B. in Bradford, Yorks, the son of a millhand, he won scholarships to Cambridge, and from 1920 worked under Rutherford in Cambridge. A.'s researches found the Kennelly-Heaviside (E)

APPOMATOX COURT HOUSE. The courthouse building in April 1865, as Grant saw it when he rode up on his great black horse 'Cincinnati', asked a group of Union officers whether Lee was present, and was directed on to the McLean House.   *Courtesy of the Signal Corps, U.S. Army.*

layer at 60 km. and the Appleton (F) layer, with branches, between 100–200 km., with diurnal and seasonal variations affecting radio. A. was prof. of physics at London, 1924–36, and prof. of natural philosophy at Cambridge, 1936–9. Sec. of the Dept. of Scientific and Industrial Research 1939–49, he was knighted in 1941. He was closely associated with the initial work in England on the atom bomb. In 1947 he received a Nobel Prize. He became principal of the univ. of Edinburgh in 1949.

APPOMATOX COURT HOUSE. Village in Virginia, U.S.A., 3 m. from the modern village of A. and scene of the surrender on 9 April, 1865 of the Confederate Army under General Robert E. Lee to the Federals under General Ulysses S. Grant – the end of the Civil War. In 1954 a National Historical Park was estab. incl. A.C.H. which is being restored to its appearance in 1865.

APPONYI (op'pōnyĕ), **Albert**, count (1846–1933). Hungarian statesman. B. at Pest, he was a liberal Catholic, and entered parliament in 1872, subsequently becoming leader of a conservative group. In 1919 he headed the Hungarian peace delegation to Paris, and was a League of Nations delegate, 1924–5.

APPROVED SCHOOL. In Britain a school approved by the Home Secretary under the Children and Young Persons Act; 1933. A child or young person may be sent to an A.S. by a court if he has committed any crime or is in need of care and protection or is refractory.

A'PRICOT. Fruit of *Prunus armeniaca*, a tree closely related to the almond, peach, plum, and cherry. A native of the Far East, it has long been cultivated in Armenia, whence it has been introduced into Europe and U.S.A.

APRIL FOOL'S DAY. The first of April, when it is customary in W. Europe to expose somebody to ridicule by causing him to believe some falsehood or to go on a fruitless errand. When he falls into the trap he is known in England as an April Fool; in Scotland as a gowk (cuckoo or fool); and in France as a *poisson d'avril* (April fish).

APSLEY HOUSE. London mansion at Hyde Park Corner, the residence of the dukes of Wellington since the 1st duke acquired it in 1820. In 1947 it was presented to the nation by the 7th duke, and part of it was opened as a Wellington Museum in 1952.

APULEIUS (apūlē'us), **Lucius** (fl. A.D. 160). Roman author and philosopher, who travelled in the eastern parts of the Roman empire, where he became initiated into mystery religions, practised as an advocate at Rome, and retired to N. Africa, giving the rest of his life to literature. In his *Golden Ass* the hero undergoes many romantic adventures. In this work are preserved a number of anc. legends, notably the story of Cupid and Psyche.

APULIA. Region of ITALY.

AQABA (a'kaba), **Gulf of.** Extending for 100 m. between the Negev and the Red Sea, its coastline is uninhabited except where at its head the frontiers of Israel, Egypt, Jordan, and Saudi Arabia converge. Here are the 2 ports Eilat or Elath (Israeli) and A. (Jordanian, and the country's only port).

AQUAE SULIS. Roman name of BATH.

AQUARIUM. Institution for the study and display of living aquatic plants and animals. These have been common since Roman times, but the 1st modern public A. was opened in Regent's Park, London, in 1853. A recent development is the Oceanarium (q.v.).

AQUATINT (a'kwa-). A process of etching in tone. It deals with broad masses in various gradations of tone, and thus differs from the usual type of etching, in which lines are bitten into a metal plate. J. B. le Prince (1734–81) is credited with its invention, and Goya is the most famous exponent of A.

AQUAVIVA (ahkwahvě'vah), **Claudio** (1543–1615). 5th general of the Society of Jesus. B. at Naples, of noble family, he entered the order in 1567, and became its head in 1581. Under his rule the Society greatly increased in numbers, and the revolt of the Spanish Jesuits was put down. He pub. a treatise on education.

AQUEDUCT (a'kwi-). Artificial channel or conduit for the conveyance of water, commonly an elevated structure of stone, wood, or iron built for conducting water across a valley. Greek As. were marvels of engineering skill, and many of those built by the Romans are still standing, e.g. the A. at Nîmes in S. France, built about A.D. 18, and the A. at Segovia, in Spain, built about A.D. 100, consisting of 109 arches made of rough-hewn granite stones cleverly held together without mortar or rivets. The first modern A. in Britain was that carrying the Bridgewater Canal over the Irwell at Barton, built 1759–72.

AQUI'NAS, Thomas (Thomas of Aquino) (*c.* 1226–74). Christian theologian and philosopher, most famous of the Schoolmen of the Middle Ages, and known as *Doctor Angelicus*. Of noble descent, he was b. at the castle of Roccasecca, prov. of Naples, S. Italy, and ed. at Monte Cassino. From 1239 he studied at the univ. of Naples, and in 1244 joined the Dominicans. Under Albertus Magnus he studied at

AQUEDUCT. The Pont du Gard at Nîmes in southern France is a magnificent Roman example dating from c. A.D. 18. The three tiers of arches reach a height of 160 feet. It was built by Agrippa, responsible also for aqueducts supplying Rome, the Virgo and Julia.

Paris and Cologne. In 1256 he became licentiate in theology at Paris, and soon was remarked for his profound knowledge and dialectical ability. Nine years of teaching, chiefly in Rome (1259–68), were followed by another 4 in Paris. In 1272 he accepted a professorial chair at Naples; he refused the archbishopric, and summoned to the General Council at Lyons by Gregory X, he d. at Fossa Nuova on the way there. In 1323 he was canonized, and in 1567 Pius V ranked him officially with the great Latin fathers of the Church.

A.'s earliest writings were commentaries on the Scriptures, Boethius, and Aristotle. In 1259–64 he wrote the *Summa contra gentiles*, showing that reason and faith are complementary and not antagonistic. In 1265 he began to work on the *Summa theologica*, which consists of 3 parts, concerned respectively with the existence and nature of God, the rules of morality, and the life and work of Christ. This last part was not completed. The complete works of A. were pub. in 1787; a modern ed. was launched in 1882 by Leo XIII, who in 1879 directed that A.'s teaching should be the basis of the theology of the Catholic Church.

AQUITAINE. Ancient province of France, bounded on the S. by the Pyrenees, on the E. and N.E. by the Central Plateau, and on the W. by the Bay of Biscay. A. roughly coincided with the Roman province of Aquitania. It was an English possession 1154–1452.

ARAB EMIRATES, Fed. of. Federation to be formed 1971, following Britain's decision in 1968 to withdraw her forces from the Persian Gulf, by Bahrein, Qatar, and the Trucial States (qq.v.).

ARABIA. Large peninsula, for the most part desert, in the extreme S.W. of Asia, separated from Africa by the Sinai peninsula, Red Sea, and Gulf of Aden. On the E. it is bounded by the Gulf of Oman and the Persian Gulf, on the S. by the Arabian Sea, and on the northern (landward) side by Jordan and Iraq. Arabia proper comprises the independent states of Saudi Arabia, Yemen and Southern Yemen; the independent sultanate of Muscat and Oman; the Fed. of Arab Emirates, and the sheikdom of Kuwait.

A sandy coastal plain of varying width borders the Red Sea, behind which a high mountain chain rises abruptly to 7,000–8,000 ft. Behind this range is the extensive plateau of Nejd, averaging 3,500 ft., with subsidiary ridges superimposed upon it. The land becomes gradually lower towards the E. coast. The interior is occupied by a vast sandy desert. The rainfall is scanty, and day temperatures are high. The total pop. is *c.* 12 millions.

The Beduin tribes of the interior lead a nomadic life, their number indeterminate. On the Oman coast there are a number of Negroes.

Camel and sheep rearing is carried on, but the formerly renowned horses and pearls of A. are no longer in great demand. Most important among the considerable mineral wealth is petroleum, discovered in 1933 and obtained in increasing quantity from Bahrein, Saudi Arabia, Kuwait and Qatar. Mecca and Medina rely largely on the profitable pilgrim traffic: other towns incl. Riyadh, Jidda, Hail, Dhahran (petroleum centre) and the Persian Gulf port of Ras Tanura (oil refineries). There are some roads, but desert transport is still largely by camel caravan: a railway, 350 m. long, linking Dhahran with Riyadh, was opened 1951.

History. The Arabian civilization was revived by Mohammed during the 7th cent. A.D. from the political chaos which existed. In the new empire which was subsequently created A. itself became merely a subordinate state, and its cities were eclipsed by Damascus, Baghdad, and Cairo. Until the 20th cent. the interior was unknown and unexplored, though the outer rim had become fully known. The exploration of the interior deserts and oases was due to the efforts of notable travellers – Gertrude Bell, Harold Ingrams,

ARAB COUNTRIES

	Area in 1,000 sq. m.	Pop. in 1,000s	Capital
*Algeria	840	10,453	Algiers
Arab Emirates, Federation of			
Bahrein	·23	182	Manama
Qatar	4	75	Doha
Trucial States ...	32	110	—
*Egypt (U.A.R.) ...	386	30,083	Cairo
*Iraq	172	8,261	Baghdad
*Jordan	37	2,10u	Amman
*Kuwait	6	468	Kuwait
*Lebanon	3·4	1,750	Beirut
*Libya	679	1,564	Benghazi and Tripoli
*Morocco	174	13,320	Rabat
Muscat and Oman ...	82	750	Muscat
*Saudi Arabia ...	800	6,000	Mecca and Riyadh
*Sudan, Rep. of ...	968	13,011	Khartoum
*Syria	72	4,565	Damascus
*Tunisia	48	4,457	Tunis
*Yemen	75	4,500	San'a and Ta'iz
Yemen, Rep. of ...	112	1,500	Madinet al-Shaab
	4,490·63	103,149	

*Members of the Arab League

T. E. Lawrence, H. St. John Philby, Freya Stark, C. Doughty, etc. See SAUDI ARABIA, etc.

ARABIAN NIGHTS, or The Thousand and One Nights. Collection of tales dealing with scenes in Persia. They had been current for many centuries before being introduced to the West by the French orientalist, A. Galland, in 1704. Collections of stories had existed orally since the 10th cent., some being Arabian.

A'RABIC. The main representative of the southern branch of the Semitic languages. Classical Arabic emerged in Cent. Arabia in the 6th cent. A.D. out of the many dialects spoken throughout the peninsula; as the literary language of Islam, with the Koran as its perfect and inimitable ideal, it spread along with the faith of the Prophet to Syria, Palestine, and Mesopotamia; to Egypt, N. Africa, the Sudan, Nigeria, and several more southerly districts; and today, in various distinct dialects, it is the *lingua franca* over a wide area of the Near East and Africa. It has long lost its footholds in Spain (Mozarabic), Sicily, and elsewhere in the Mediterranean, but the Maltese still speak an A. dialect. The A. vocabulary influenced the Persian, Turkish, Hindustani, and Malay languages; it also left traces in Spanish, and other European languages took up terms of astronomy, chemistry, etc., such as *alchemy, alcohol, alkali, alkahest, algebra,* and many more. A. calligraphy was a highly developed art, and ornamental inscriptions play an important part in interior architecture of Islamic countries. The complexity of the script, requiring the printer to use 300 to 1,000 separate characters has been an important factor in maintaining a low level of literacy in Arab countries. However, in 1961 Nasri Khattar, a Lebanese, perfected a 'unified' Arabic alphabet of 30 letters which is being widely adopted.

ARABIC LITERATURE. The literature of the Arabic-speaking peoples began with poetry which is a developed art, even in the earliest examples. Only the ode is used, varying in length from 30 to 100 lines with a single rhyme throughout. Most A. poems have been composed since A.D. 550, but some may be a hundred years earlier. The works of Pre-Islamic poets have come down to us in the form of *diwans,* consisting of the collected works of an individual poet, and anthologies. The most famous early Islamic poets were Farazdak, Jarīr, and Akhtal. The first love-lyrics were composed by 'Umar ibn abi Rabī'a. Under the Abbasid caliphs, the poets gave up writing about Beduin life, and drew their inspiration from the life of the towns. Typical of this period were Abū Nuwās (d. 810) and Bashshār ibn Burd (d. 783) whose poems deal with wine, women, and song, but the most outstanding poet was Mutanabbi (d. 965). A great deal of literature was of a practical nature, such as works on political and economic geography: handbooks for civil servants; and dictionaries, the first of these being by Khalīl ibn Ahmad (d. 791). Rhymed prose was used for the introduction of books and in a monarch's letters. The Arab is very fond of sitting about and talking, and this custom was exploited in literature in works which consisted of short talks or sketches, such as those by Hamadhāni (d. 1007) and Harīri (d. 1122). The oldest Arabic grammar extant is one by a Persian, Sībawaih (d. c. 795). Among the most famous theological works are the commentary on the Koran by Tabari; the *Kashshāf* by Zamakhshari (d. 1143) which was later abridged by Baidāwi (d. 1286); a commentary by Rāzi (d. 1209); and an 'Introduction' to the study of the Koran by Suyūti.

Modern A.L. shows western, esp. French, influences. Among the most famous literary personalities are the poets Shawki and Hāfiz Ibrāhīm in Egypt, and Zahāwi in Iraq; Jurji Zaydān, a writer of popular historical novels; and the Egyptian essayists Manfalūti and 'Abbād.

ARABIC NUMERALS. The signs 0 1 2 3 4 5 6 7 8 9 which were in use amongst the Arabs before they were taken over by the peoples of Europe during the Middle Ages in place of the Roman numerals. They appear to have originated in India, and reached Europe by way of Spain.

ARAB LEAGUE. League formed at Cairo on 22 March 1945, by Egypt, Syria, Iraq, Lebanon, Transjordan (Jordan, 1949), Saudi Arabia, and Yemen. Its object was to promote unity among the Arab states. Those members bordering Israel (q.v.) fought the Israelis in 1948, but during 1949 made armistices though refusing to recognize Israel. Libya was admitted 1953, Rep. of Sudan 1956, Morocco and Tunisia 1958, Kuwait 1961, Algeria 1962. An Arab Common Market, open to League members, was estab. in 1965. In 1967 Iraq, Jordan, Lebanon and Syria were engaged in further hostilities with Israel (q.v.), and sporadic incidents continued.

ARACHNE (arak'-nē). In Greek mythology, a Lydian girl who was so skilful a weaver that she challenged the goddess Athena to a contest. Athena tore A.'s beautiful tapestries to pieces, whereupon A. hanged herself in despair and was transformed into a spider and her weaving became a cobweb. A. in Greek means 'spider'.

ARACHNIDA. A class of animals of the phylum Arthropoda, distinguished by the single pair of preoral appendages being modified as jaws, typically composed of 2 or 3 segments and commonly pincer-like or chelate. They are classified according to certain external characters and breathing organs, which in marine forms are gills and in land forms either lung-books or fine tubes (tracheae) permeating the tissues, into the following 12 orders: *Xiphosura* (king crabs), *Gigantostraca* (extinct form of marine swimming species), *Scorpiones* (scorpions), *Pedipalpi* (whip-scorpions), *Palpigradi* (minute degenerate pedipalpi), *Araneae* (spiders), *Solifugae* (false spiders), *Pseudoscorpiones* (false scorpions), *Podogona* (obscure isolated order surviving unchanged from the Carboniferous period, living in the forests of Brazil and W. Africa), *Opiliones* (harvest spiders), *Acari* (ticks, mites and gall mites), and *Pycnogonida* (small aberrant and isolated order, including the British species *Pycnogonum littorale*). See SPIDER, etc.

ARABIA. An old-style fort at Saiwun in the Wadhi Hadramaut, Kathiri State, S. Arabia Protectorate. In the foreground a modern truck loaded with a 1,000 gallon rubber-nylon fabric collapsible container used for gas, petroleum vapour, and a variety of fluids. *Courtesy of Dunlop Rubber Co. Ltd.*

ARAD (or'od). Rumanian town on the Mures, 100 m. N.E. of Belgrade; an important route centre with many industries. Pop. (1966) 126,005.

ARAGON (ahrahgoñ'), **Louis** (1897–). French poet and novelist. Beginning as a Dadaist, he became one of the leaders of Surrealism, pub. vols. of verse and in 1930 joined the Communist party. Taken prisoner in the S.W.W., he escaped to join the underground, experiences reflected in the poetry of *Le Crève-Cœur* (1942), *Les Yeux d'Elsa* (1944), and the short stories *Servitude et grandeur des Français* (1945). *La Semaine Sainte* (1958, *Holy Week*) is a novel.

A'RAGON. Ancient kingdom of N.E. Spain with the cap. Saragossa. It was a Roman province until taken by the Visigoths, who lost it to the Moors in the 8th cent. In 1035 it became a kingdom; it was united to Catalonia in 1137, and to Castile in 1479.

ARAKA'N. A natural division of Burma, some 400 m. long, forming a tapering strip of territory on the Bay of Bengal coast which narrows from 90 m. wide in the N. to 15 m. in the S. The coast is strewn with islands, and the chief town is Akyab. The ancient kingdom of A. with the cap. Myohaung, now in ruins, was conquered by the Burmese in 1782, and passed to the British in 1826. The majority of Arakanese are Buddhists. Pop. c. 1,150,000.

A'RAL. Inland sea or lake in western Asia, U.S.S.R. Lying about 200 m. E. of the Caspian Sea, it is 235 m. long, and 180 m. wide. Its area (c. 24,000 sq. m.) is decreasing through evaporation. It is fed by the Sir Darya and the Amu Darya.

ARAM, Eugene (1704–59). British murderer. B. in the West Riding, he was a schoolmaster at Knaresborough, and in 1745 was tried and acquitted on a charge of being concerned in the disappearance of a local shoemaker. After achieving some distinction as a philologist, he was arrested at Lynn in Norfolk, following the discovery of a skeleton in a cave at Knaresborough. He was tried at York, confessed to the murder after his conviction, and was hanged. He is the subject of works by Lytton, Hood, etc.

ARAMAIC. A Semitic language in the Near East, the vernacular of Jesus Christ and the Apostles, and probably the one in which the Gospels were first written. The Aramaeans were nomads who set up states in Mesopotamia in the 13th cent. B.C., and flowed over into N. Syria in 12th and 11th cents. B.C. Damascus, Aleppo, and Carchemish were among their chief centres, but all were subjugated by Assyria by the end of the 8th cent. By the end of the 7th cent. Syria and Mesopotamia had become thoroughly Aramaized. A. was the *lingua franca* of the day, and under the Achaemenides it became one of the official languages of the Persian empire. In some isolated villages A. dialects are still spoken by native Christians.

A'RAN. Group of 3 rocky islands (Inishmore, Inishmaan, Inisheer) across the mouth of Galway Bay, Rep. of Ireland, forming a natural breakwater. The inhabitants are Irish-speaking fisherfolk. Area 18 sq. m.; pop. c. 2,600.

ARANJUEZ (ahrahn-hweth'). Spanish town on the Tagus, 25 m. S.S.E. of Madrid. The palace was for centuries a royal residence. Pop. c. 22,000.

ARANY (or'ony), **János** (1817–82). Hungarian writer, b. at Nagyszalonta (now in Rumania). His comic epic *The Lost Constitution* (1846) was followed in 1847 by *Toldi*, one of the finest products of the popular national school. In 1860 he settled in Pest as editor of literary reviews. In 1864 appeared his epic masterpiece *The Death of King Buda*. During the last years of his life A. produced the remainder of the *Toldi*-trilogy, and his most personal lyrics.

A'RARAT. Mountain mass in Turkey, near the borders of Armenia S.S.R. and Persia, consisting of Great A., 17,000 ft., and Little A., 12,900 ft. Tradition ascribes to A. the resting-place of the Ark after the deluge, and the U.S.-sponsored Archaeological Research Foundation sought to estab. that wood fragments found in 1955 and 1958 were part of its timbers.

ARAUCANIAN INDIANS (arōkān'ian). Original inhabitants of central Chile, comprising various tribes. An agricultural and hunting people, they lived in small villages, and were excellent warriors, defeating the Incas and opposing the Spanish forces for 200 years. Some 120,000 still survive living in reserves.

ARAUCA'RIA. Genus of coniferous trees allied to the firs, natives of the southern hemisphere, and often attaining a gigantic size. They include the monkey-puzzle tree (*A. imbricata*), the Bunya-Bunya pine (*A. bidwilúi*) of Australia, and the Norfolk Island pine (*A. excelsa*).

ARBITRATION. The procedure whereby two nations refer their differences for settlement to a selected person or persons. In the 19th cent. the head of a friendly state or an international commission was usually selected as arbitrator; the 20th cent. has seen 3 attempts to establish permanent machinery for the settlement of disputes – the Hague Court, the League of Nations, and the United Nations.

Proposals for a permanent court were put forward in the 18th cent. by the Abbé de St. Pierre and Jeremy Bentham, but the practice of referring disputes to A. did not come into general use until the 19th cent. A well-known example is the dispute between the British and U.S. govts. over the *Alabama* during the American Civil War.

The Hague Peace Conference of 1899 led to the setting up of a permanent court of A., and after the F.W.W. the Hague Court was maintained, and a Permanent Court of International Justice also set up to deal with disputes of a legal nature. A number of disputes, mainly frontier problems arising from the peace settlement, were successfully settled between 1920 and 1925. By the Locarno Pact of 1925 France and Germany, and by the Kellogg Pact of 1928 fifty-nine states, agreed to renounce war as an instrument of policy and to refer all differences to A.

Under the Charter drawn up at San Francisco (June 1945), the United Nations pledge themselves to seek a solution to all disputes by negotiation, arbitration, or other peaceful means. If these fail, the parties are to refer the matter to the Security Council. Legal disputes should normally be referred to the International Court of Justice.

ARBOR DAY. Day set apart in U.S.A. for the planting of trees along the highways, in parks, etc. It is also observed in S. Australia and New Zealand.

ARBROATH (arbrōth´). Scottish fishing town (burgh) on the coast of Angus. Pop. (1961) 19,533.

ARBUTHNOT, John (1667–1735). British physician and author. B. in Kincardineshire, he practised medicine in London, and was physician to Queen Anne 1705–14. He was the friend of Pope, Gay, and Swift, and was the chief author of the satiric *Memoirs of Martinus Scriblerus*. He also developed the national character of John Bull in his *History of John Bull* (1712).

ARBU´TUS, or strawberry tree (*Arbutus unedo*). Plant of the family Ericaceae, familiar in cultivated state as an ornamental garden tree. It produces handsome white flowers and bright red fruit.

ARCACHON (ahrkahshoń´). Coastal town and fashionable holiday resort in Gironde dept., S.W. France. Pop. (1962) 15,820.

ARCADIA. Central plateau district of Peloponnesus, S. Greece; area 2,020 sq. m., pop. (1961) 135,042. In antiquity it was inhabited by shepherds and hunters, whose mode of life has been idealized in literature as carefree and idyllic, e.g. by Sidney.

ARC DE TRIOMPHE (ahrk´-de-trēoń´). Triumphal arch in the Place de l'Étoile, Paris, begun by Napoleon and completed in 1836 to commemorate his victories of 1805–6. Beneath it rests France's 'Unknown Soldier'.

ARCH, Joseph (1826–1919). British Radical politician and trade unionist. B. at Barford, Warks, the son of an agricultural labourer, he worked in the fields from boyhood. Entirely self-taught, he became a Methodist local preacher, founded the National Agricultural Union (the first of its kind) in 1872, and was Liberal-Labour M.P. for N.W. Norfolk.

ARCH. A curved structure consisting of several wedge-shaped stones or other hard blocks which are supported by their mutual pressure. The term is also applied to any curved structure which is an A. in form only, but not in function.

ARCH. S – springs;
K – key-stone.

ARCHAEAN (arkē´an). In geology, the earliest system of rocks. Underlying rocks of the Cambrian System, they may be composed of igneous, metamorphic, or stratified rocks, and often contain valuable minerals. 'Azoic' and 'Eozoic' are synonymous with A.

ARCHAEOLOGY. The study of the material products of the past, providing in the case of prehistoric man, or of peoples who had no written records, our only source of knowledge, but also supplementing our information on the historic and recorded peoples. The oldest man-made implements found are *c*. 1,820,000 yrs. old, and the written documents of Egypt and Mesopotamia go back *c*. 5,000 yrs.

Systematic classification began when J. C. Thomson placed the specimens in the Danish Nat. Museum *c*. 1818 according to 3 periods, which he called the Stone, Bronze, and Iron Ages. Effective recording of excavation and conservation of objects was practised *c*. 1840 by the early marine salvage workers, the brothers Charles and John Deane, and Gen. Sir Charles Pasley, who had meticulous watercolours made of their finds, complete with encrustations, and pioneers on land were Pitt-Rivers and Petrie (qq.v.), *see* also Schliemann, Evans, Rawlinson, Layard, Ventris, Wheeler, Emery, and Leakey.

During the 20th cent. there has been a widening of scope, for example, to medieval and industrial A., and use of scientific 'tools', e.g. carbon-14 dating (*see* CARBON); chemical methods of conservation, as

with the Swedish warship *Vasa* (*see* illus. p. 1002); and location of sites by aerial photography and sonar, e.g. Alexander McKee's search for Henry VIII's battleship *Mary Rose* off Portsmouth in 1967–8.

ARCHAEOPTERYX (arkēop´teriks). The earliest known bird, remarkable for its reptilian features. Two fossil specimens have been dug out of the Jurassic limestone of Bavaria.

ARCHAEOPTERYX

ARCHANGEL. Seaport in N. Europe in R.S.F.S.R. on the N. Dvina river, at the head of the Gulf of A. It is blocked by ice for some 6 months of the year, but is nevertheless the chief timber-exporting port of the U.S.S.R. Pop. (1967) 308,000.

A. was colonized by Norsemen under Othere in the 10th cent. Chancellor in 1553 built an Eng. factory there. Boris Godunov made it an open port, and it was of prime importance until Peter the Great built St. Petersburg. It was a centre for the interventionist armies after the Revolution of 1917, and during the S.W.W. was a receiving station for Anglo-American supplies.

A. gives its name to a region, area 230,000 sq. m., pop. *c*. 1,050,000, of which the chief industry is lumbering.

ARCHBISHOP. In the Christian Church, a bishop of superior rank, who has authority over other bishops in his jurisdiction. Very often an A. is also a metropolitan, i.e. the head of an ecclesiastical province. In the Church of England there are two As., both of them metropolitans – the A. of Canterbury ('Primate of All England') and the A. of York ('Primate of England').

ARCHDEACON. Originally an ordained dignitary of the Christian Church charged with the supervision of the deacons attached to a cathedral. Today in the R.C. Church the office is purely titular; in the C. of E. an A. has still many duties of a business character, e.g. the periodic inspection of the churches.

ARCHER, Frederick James (1857–86). British jockey. B. at Cheltenham, he won 2,748 of the 8,084 races in which he rode, incl. 5 Derbys (1877, 1880, 1881, 1885, 1886), 4 Oaks, 6 St. Legers, and 5 Two Thousand Guineas. His record of 246 winners in one season was not beaten till 1933 (*see* RICHARDS, GORDON). He shot himself while ill with typhoid fever.

ARCHERY. The use of the bow and arrow in war and the chase. Flint arrowheads have been found in very ancient archaeological deposits, and bowmen are depicted in the sculptures of Assyria and Egypt and indeed all the nations of antiquity. Until the introduction of gunpowder in the 14th cent., bands of archers were to be found in every European army. The English archers distinguished themselves in the French wars of the later Middle Ages; and to this day the Queen's bodyguard in Scotland is known as the Royal Company of Archers. The Honourable Artillery Company was originally a body of archers.

Up to the time of Charles II the practice of A. was fostered and encouraged by English rulers. Henry VIII in particular loved the sport, and it was in his reign that Ascham wrote his *Toxophilus*. By the mid-17th cent. A. was no longer important in warfare and interest waned until the 1780s, although in the N. of England shooting for the Scorton Arrow has been carried on, with few breaks, from 1673. Organizations incl. the European Fédération Internationale du Tir à l'Arc (1931); the British Grand National A. Soc. (1961); and in the U.S. the National A. Assocn. (1879) and, for actual hunting with the bow, the National Field A. Assocn. (1940).

ARCHIMÉ'DES (-k-) (*c.* 287–212 B.C.). Greek mathematician. B. at Syracuse in Sicily, he spent most of his life there. Many of his writings have survived, and he made discoveries in geometry, hydrostatics and mechanics of permanent importance. He is also credited with the invention of the *Archimedean Screw*, a cylindrical device for raising water, still in use in the Nile delta. He invented engines of war for the defence of Syracuse against the Romans, but was slain when Syracuse was captured. *See* BUOY-ANCY.

ARCHIPE'NKO (ahkhipyen'ko), **Alexander** (1887–1964). Russo - American sculptor and draughtsman, b. at Kiev. He produced his first Cubist sculpture in 1911, went to New York in 1923, and has experimented with carved plastic.

ARCHITECTURE. The first of the plastic arts – those concerned with modelling or moulding materials into various forms – the combination of function and beauty in the art of building. From earliest times until the mid-19th cent. all permanent building was governed by 3 structural principles: the post and lintel, the wooden truss and the masonry arch. Latterly the steel skeleton and reinforced concrete have revolutionized A., being the first entirely new principles evolved since Roman times, thus liberating it from limitations imposed by the weight of stone and brick at each floor level, allowing great flexibility in design and buildings of immense height. Further developments have entirely removed the need for structural walls and roofs as separate entities, e.g. the geodesic dome of Buckminster Fuller (q.v.). The basic problem of the A. has always been how best to enclose space to fulfil the varied needs of human occupation, and, in so doing, the trends of contemporary life must be considered, and will be reflected in the shape of buildings. The earliest permanent buildings, dating from *c.* 4,000 B.C. in Egypt, reflect the grandeur of the ruling classes and their system of worship. Progressive changes tended to embrace more varied and specialized structures to suit the needs of a greater proportion of the population. In the 19th cent. the acceptance of the division of A. into ecclesiastical (churches, etc.), civil (houses and public buildings), military and naval, illustrates the rigidity which had overtaken the subject, so that the A. had become merely the creator of academic styles. In the 20th cent. men such as Le Corbusier, Gropius, and Mies van der Rohe broke free from these shackles, and contemporary As., such as Doxiadis (q.v.), widen their scope beyond the individual building or group of buildings to the whole city and its environs, adapting themselves to new synthetic materials and factory-made components, and also to the necessity of making their work capable of change and growth to meet the expansion of a city or the alteration of individual housing requirements as families first increase and then dwindle when children leave home. *See* EKISTICS.

Architects throughout the world are linked through the International Union of Architects 1948): important national organizations are the Royal Inst. of British Architects (1835) and the American Inst. of Architects (1857). *See* GOTHIC A. and sections under individual countries, also illus. p. 58.

ARCHIVES. Historically valuable records and papers which may belong to public bodies, institutions, families, individuals, etc. In 1945 the National Register of Archives was estab. in London to record details of local and private collections and contains over 11,000 reports. The records of the courts of law and govt. depts. since the Norman Conquest are housed at the Record Office (q.v.). In the U.S. the Declaration of Independence, the Constitution of the U.S., and the Bill of Rights are exhibited at the National A. Hall, Washington. The National A. and Records Service is responsible for the permanent preservation of federal records and administers the presidential libraries: the Franklin D. Roosevelt at Hyde Park, N.Y.; Harry S. Truman at Independence, Missouri (q.v.), and Dwight D. Eisenhower at Abilene, Kansas.

ARCOT. Chief city of the district of N. Arcot on the Palar, 65 m. W.S.W. of Madras, India. It is famous for Clive's defence in 1751, when with only 80 Europeans and 150 Sepoys able to carry out their duties he held it for 50 days against 10,000. Pop. *c.* 20,000.

ARCTIC. Regions lying around the N. Pole, comprising those areas of land and water in which typically polar conditions prevail, or those N. of the line of tree growth. Most of this area is taken up by the Arctic Ocean (area 5,440,000 sq. m.), divided into a number of seas. These seas have a low salinity, and freeze readily, the whole ocean being generally impassable to vessels. Some of the pack ice is carried by currents beyond the Arctic Ocean, the main current being a rotary one, which sweeps down the Greenland coast to meet the warm Atlantic drifts, fogs being frequent where the two meet. Often breaks appear in the ice, but the water is never clear for long; the pack ice renders unnavigable the channels of the N.W. Passage, and hinders shipping in the N.E. Passage and N.W. areas of the N. Atlantic.

CLIMATE, VEGETATION, FAUNA. The A. regions have a cold winter and a brief, warm summer lasting up to 2 months. Temperatures fall below zero F. for the winter months, but the A. is not as cold as N.E. Siberia or the Antarctic. There is a slight summer rainfall, replaced by snow in winter, amounting to an annual precipitation of 10–12 in. Vegetation is scattered, occurring in small patches with moss and Alpine plants. In summer brightly-coloured wild flowers occur. There are some bushes but no trees. On the scanty growth of moss, reindeer and musk-oxen

ARCHITECTURE. The American Embassy (1962) in Grosvenor Square is the focal point of 'Little America' in London's Mayfair. Eero Saarinen's design is an example of modern styling planned to harmonize with an existing architectural setting, and blends excellently with the older buildings surrounding the square.
Courtesy of the United States Information Service.

flourish; hares, lemming, foxes, and wolves also dwell on land, while polar bears, seals, and the walrus live on sea products. Birds are rarely seen except in summer.

POPULATION. The only native inhabitants are the dwindling Eskimos of the Canadian Arctic and Greenland. Temporary visitors include fur traders, miners, and trappers, while some of the islands serve as meteorological bases.

Exploration. The desire to find trade routes to the E. was the main incentive to early exploration in the N. of America and Asia. First in the long quest for the N.W. Passage was John Cabot in 1497; M. Frobisher in 1576 discovered the Frobisher and Hudson Straits; H. Willoughby and R. Chancellor began the search for the N.E. Passage in 1553. W. Barents (1596) and H. Hudson (1607) tried to cross the Arctic Ocean, Barents discovering Spitsbergen. Franklin discovered the N.W. Passage, but perished in the attempt. The 1st to sail through it was Amundsen in 1903–5. The N.E. Passage was navigated by A. E. Nordenskjöld in 1878–9. Attention was then turned to the N. Pole. W. E. Parry had made an attempt from Spitsbergen and there were many more attempts before R. E. Peary reached the Pole on 6 April 1909. Aerial exploration began in 1897 when S. A. Andrée made a disastrous balloon flight. Airships were tried by W. Wellman in 1907 and 1910, and hydroplanes by Amundsen in 1925; R. E. Byrd claimed to have flown over the Pole in a monoplane in 1926, but doubt has been cast on the possibility that he could have covered the distance in the time he took; Nobile accompanied by Amundsen crossed the Pole in an airship in 1926; and C. F. Blair made the 1st solo flight in 1951. In 1958 the U.S. submarine *Nautilus* crossed the Pole beneath the ice.

Scandinavian Air Lines began the first commercial service on a 'great circle' route over the Pole in 1954, and from 1960 a Russian nuclear-powered ice-breaker has kept open for 150 days a year a 2,500 m. Asia-Europe passage along the N. coast of Siberia. A number of weather stations are maintained.

ARDEBIL (ahrdebēl'). Persian town, near the Russian frontier. An important road centre, it also has an airfield. A. exports dried fruits, carpets, and rugs. Pop. (1966) 76,780.

ARDÈCHE (ahrdāsh'). River of S.E. France, a

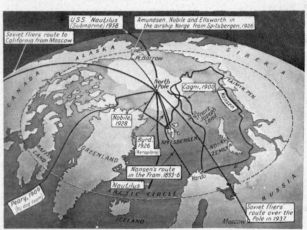

ARCTIC. Routes of famous flights and expeditions.

tributary of the Rhône. Near Vallon it flows under the Pont d'Arc, a natural bridge. It gives its name to a dept.

ARDENNES. A wooded plateau extending from N. France through S.E. Belgium to N. Luxembourg. It has an area of 2,020 sq. m. and is cut through by the Meuse and other rivers in wooded gorges. Towns incl. Sedan, Mézières, Malmédy, Dinant, and Spa. A dept. of France is called A.

Early in the F.W.W., the A. was the scene of fierce fighting, while in the S.W.W. the Germans thrust through it in 1940 to separate the British from the French forces. The A. was retaken in 1944, but in Dec. of that year Rundstedt made a last desperate bid to break through once more to Dinant and Liège. This was defeated and the Allied line restored, 31 Jan. 1945. Nearly 77,000 Americans were killed, missing or wounded in this battle.

ARDIZZONE (ahrditzō'ni), **Edward Jeffrey Irving** (1900–). British artist. An official war artist 1940–6, he is also a book illustrator of individuality, both for adults and children.

A'RECA. Genus of palms, native to tropical Asia. The seeds, known as A. nuts, have purgative properties, and *A. catechu* provides the betel-nut.

AREQUIPA (ahrākē'pa). City of Peru at the base of the volcano El Misti. Founded by Pizarro in 1540, it is the cultural focus of S. Peru, and a busy commercial centre. Pop. (1965) 160,836.

ARES (ā'rēz). Greek god of war, identified by the Romans with Mars. The son of Zeus and Hera, he was worshipped chiefly in Thrace.

ARETHU'SA. In Greek mythology, a Nereid and nymph of the fountain and spring of A. in the island of Ortygia near Syracuse.

ARETINO (ahrātē'noh), **Pietro** (1492–1557). Italian poet and satirist. B. at Arezzo in Tuscany, he was banished for a satirical sonnet on indulgences, but found favour with Leo X at Rome. After he pub. the obscene *Sonetti Lussuriosi*, he removed to the Medicean court at Florence, and later settled in Venice. He is said to have killed himself accidentally by falling off a stool while laughing at an amusing story. His works include sonnets, comedies, a tragedy, and devotional books.

AREZZO (ahret'sō). Italian town in the valley of the Upper Arno, 40 m. S.E. of Florence; it has a Gothic cathedral and a citadel. Pop. (1961) 74,245.

ARGALI (ahr'gali) or **Arkal** The huge Wild Sheep (*Ovis ammon*) of the Altai and other parts of

ARCHITECTURE. Britain is celebrated for her schools. Breaking away from the stiff conventional lines, Tuxford County Secondary in Nottinghamshire has the aspect of a pleasant residential close.   *Photo: Architectural Review.*

Central Asia, where it is represented by many local races. The ram may stand from 3½ to 4 ft. at the shoulder, and has massive, spirally twisted horns.

ARGENTEUIL (ahrzhoṅtöy). French town on the Seine, 5 m. W.N.W. of Paris, in Seine-et-Oise dept. Pop. (1962) 82,458.

ARGENTINA. S. American rep. stretching from within the tropics to the tip of the S. American mainland and including the E. part of the island of Tierra del Fuego; area 1,073,000 sq. m., the 2nd largest country in S. America. The Falkland Is., a British group off the S.E. coast, are claimed by A., as are the Falkland Is. Dependencies in the Antarctic.

The western part of A. is occupied by the high Andes, and includes Aconcagua (23,000 ft.), long thought to be the highest peak of the Americas, displaced 1956 by Ojos del Salados. Chile, 23,293 ft. The long gentle eastward slopes lead down to the rolling plains of central A.; rainfall is sparse, so much is semi-desert, particularly in the Patagonian steppes. Further N. crops can be grown with irrigation, while in the Gran Chaco region of the extreme N. the surface is covered with forest, savannah, and swamp. In the E., between the Parana and Colorado rivers, lie the pampas, a rich pastureland which supports the bulk of A.'s cattle. The country is drained N.W. to S.E. by the Uruguay and the Parana with its tributary the Salado (which enter jointly the estuary of the Plate), the Colorado, the Negro, and lesser ones.

Population. In 1965 the est. pop. was 22,520,000, the great majority being of European origin, particularly Italians and Spaniards. Indians, descended from the original natives, number only 20,000. Immigration on a large scale began during the late 19th cent., when European settlers from the Latin countries poured in. Roman Catholicism is the religion of the majority, and is supported by the State.

Economic Development. Agriculture provides the basis of economy. Livestock are reared extensively on the rolling pampas. High-quality beef cattle are reared on specially grown grasses and fodder crops; millions of acres of poorer land are under alfalfa. Much meat is chilled or frozen for export, a great deal is canned into corned beef. Sheep-rearing, in which A. formerly ranked second to Australia, has greatly declined. Wool, frozen beef, mutton and lamb, and wheat, which is the leading cereal crop, are exported. Mineral wealth, almost untapped, includes oil and gas deposits, gold, silver, iron, copper, etc. Industrial development has been hampered by the lack of hard coal and iron, but industries based on local raw materials have grown up in some cases employing hydro-electric power.

Towns and Communications. The Federal cap. is Buenos Aires. Rosario, Parana, Córdoba, La Plata, Tucumán, Mendoza and Sante Fé are other large cities. The main centres are linked by rail, the system centring on Buenos Aires. There is a network of national roads, and a system of air services.

History. The early exploration and colonization of the area which became A. was carried out by Spaniards in the 16th cent. The belief that rich mineral resources occurred in the interior led to settlement during the 17th and 18th cents.; early in the 19th cent. the states of S. America overthrew their Spanish rulers, and in 1816 the United Provinces of the River Plate (Argentina, Uruguay and Paraguay) declared their independence. A long struggle with Spain ensued, and aid was given to other S. American countries also striving for independence.

The federal republican constitution adopted 1853 endured until Gen. Juan Perón, pres. 1946–55, abandoned his initial apparent liberalism and made himself dictator. He was overthrown by a military coup, but Peronista activities revived and to counteract them Lt.-Gen. Juan Carlos Onganía became pres. in 1966 after a bloodless coup. The National Congress

(Senate and House of Deputies) was abolished, the pres. combining executive and legislative functions: for local administration A. is divided into 22 provs. and a federal district.

ARGENTINITA. Spanish dancer, her real name being Encarnación Lopez (1898–1945). B. in Buenos Aires, she soon achieved fame in Spain. With Garcia Lorca, she started in 1932 the Madrid ballet.

A'RGON. Chemically inert gaseous element, at. wt. 39·944, symbol A., at. no. 18. Discovered in air by Rayleigh and Ramsay after all oxygen and nitrogen was removed chemically, it is used in electric discharge lamps.

A'RGONAUT, or **Paper Nautilus.** Genus of dibranchiate cephalopods (*Argonauta*) belonging to the division Octopoda. *A. argo* inhabits the Mediterranean, and was well known to the ancient Greeks.

ARGONAUTS. In Greek legend the band of heroes who accompanied Jason when he set out in the ship

ARGONAUT

Argo to fetch the Golden Fleece. *See* JASON.

ARGONNE (ahrgon'). Wooded plateau in N.E. France, separating Lorraine and Champagne. It was the scene of fierce fighting in the F.W.W.

A'RGOS. Ancient Greek city in the N.E. Peloponnese, near the head of the gulf of Nauplia. In the Homeric age it was one of the chief cities of Greece, and the name Argives was sometimes used instead of Greeks. The modern town is a rly. junction. Pop. *c.* 15,000.

A'RGUS. In Greek mythology, a giant with 100 eyes, set by the jealous Hera to watch over Io, the beloved of Zeus, who had been turned into a cow. Hermes charmed A. to sleep with his flute, cut off his head, and Hera transplanted his eyes to the tail of her favourite bird, the peacock.

ARGYLL (argīl'), **Earls and Dukes of.** Line of Scottish peers who trace their descent to the Campbells of Lochow. The earldom dates from 1457. **Archibald,** the 8th earl (1607–61), led the Covenanting party during the Civil Wars, crowned Charles II in 1651, submitted to Cromwell in 1652, and was beheaded after the Restoration. **Archibald,** 9th earl (1629–85), was executed for leading a rebellion in co-operation with Monmouth's rising. **Archibald,** 10th earl (1651–1703), received a dukedom in 1701. John, 2nd duke (1678–1743), became a peer of the U.K. for helping to promote the Union.

George Douglas, 8th duke (1823–1900), was Secretary for India 1868–74, and opposed Irish home rule. In his writings he attempted to reconcile Christianity with scientific discovery. **John Douglas Sutherland,** 9th duke (1845–1914), m. Princess Louise, dau. of Queen Victoria, in 1871, and was Gov.-Gen. of Canada, 1878–83.

ARGYLLSHIRE. Second largest co. of Scotland, on the W. coast and including many of the Western Isles. It is mountainous, with a deeply indented coastline. The sea lochs include Moidart, Linnhe, Etive, Fyne, and Long, while Loch Awe is the largest of the fresh-water lochs. The climate is wet and bleak. The farms are run mainly by crofters, and much of A. is moorland. Inveraray is the county seat; other towns include Campbeltown and Lochgilphead, Dunoon, Oban, and Ballachulish. Area 3,124 sq. m.; pop. (1961) 59,345.

ARIA·DNE. In Greek legend, the dau. of Minos king of Crete. When Theseus came from Athens as on of the victims offered to the Minotaur, she fell in love with him and gave him the ball of thread by means of which he was able to find his way out of the labyrinth

A'RIANISM. A system of Christian theology

c

founded about A.D. 310 by Arius (q.v.), and condemned as heretical at the Council of Nicaea in 325. Certain 17th and 18th cent. theologians held Arian views akin to those of modern Unitarianism.

ARID ZONES. Infertile areas with a small, infrequent rainfall that rapidly evaporates because of high temperatures, and which form a serious problem in Morocco, Pakistan, Australia, America, etc. The problem involved is not merely finding new sources of water, although constant research goes on to discover, for example, cheaper methods of distilling sea water, but the conservation of existing sources by avoiding evaporation (e.g. the artificial recharging of natural groundwater reservoirs) and the eradication of salt in irrigation supplies from underground sources or as a surface soil deposit in poorly drained areas.

ARIÈGE (ahrē-āzh'). River in S. France, a tributary of the Garonne. It gives its name to a dept.

ARIOSTO (ahrē-ost'ō), **Ludovico** (1474–1533). Italian poet, b. at Reggio. He wrote Latin poems and comedies on classical lines, joined the household of Cardinal Ippolito d'Este in 1503, was frequently engaged in embassies and diplomacy, and pub. the *Orlando Furioso* at Ferrara in 1516. This is a romantic epic, dealing with the wars of Charlemagne against the Saracens, and the love of Orlando (Roland) for Angelica, a princess of Cathay. The perfection of its style and its unflagging narrative interest place A. among the great Italian poets. In 1521 A. became governor of a province in the Apennines, and after 3 years retired to Ferrara, where he d.

ARISTARCHUS (-ark-) (*c.* 220–143 B.C.). Greek grammarian and critic. B. at Samothrace, he became head of the Alexandrian library about 180 B.C. He carefully revised the poems of Homer.

ARISTARCHUS OF SAMOS (*c.* 310–264 B.C.). Greek astronomer, famed as being the first to maintain that the earth revolves round the sun.

ARISTĬDĒS (*c.* 530–468 B.C.). Athenian statesman. He was one of the 10 Athenian generals at Marathon in 490 B.C., and was elected chief archon. Later he came into conflict with the democratic leader Themistocles, and was exiled *c.* 483 B.C. He returned to fight against the Persians at Salamis in 480 B.C., and next year commanded the Athenians at Plataea. His popular title 'the Just' was probably derived from his just assessment of the contribution to be paid by the Greek states who entered the Delian league against the Persians.

ARISTĬPPUS (*c.* 435–356 B.C.). Greek philosopher, founder of the Cyrenaic or Hedonist school. A pupil of Socrates, he developed the doctrine that pleasure is the only good in life. He lived at the court of Dionysius of Syracuse, and later with his mistress Laïs, the courtesan, at Corinth.

ARISTŎPHANĒS (*c.* 448–380 B.C.). Comic dramatist of ancient Athens. His early comedies are remarkable for the violence of the satire with which he ridiculed the democratic war leaders. In 425 he produced the *Acharnians*, a plea for peace with Sparta. The *Knights* (424) shows the figure of the 'Demos' or 'democracy' beguiled by Cleon. The *Clouds* (423) pours ridicule on the new learning of Socrates. The *Wasps* (422) is a satire on the Athenian love of litigation. The *Peace* (421) was written when negotiations for peace with Sparta were far advanced. In the *Birds* (414), written after the renewed outbreak of the Peloponnesian War, A. tells how two Athenians persuade the birds to build a kingdom in the air known as 'Cloud-cuckoo-land'. In the *Lysistrata* (411) the women, tired of the war, deny conjugal relations to their husbands until they have made peace with Sparta. The *Thesmophoriazusae* (Priestesses of Demeter) (411) satirizes Euripides and the women of Athens. The *Frogs* (405) tells how the god Dionysus was sent to the lower world to bring back Aeschylus to Athens. The *Ecclesiazusae* or *Women in Parliament* (393) describes what happened when the women seized the Athenian parliament. In *Plutus* or *Wealth* (388) the abolition of poverty results in a series of comic episodes. Besides the 11 extant plays A. is known to have written about 40 comedies which are now lost.

A'RISTOTLE (384–322 B.C.). Greek philosopher. B. at Stagira in Thrace, he studied at Athens under

ARMAGH. The Protestant cathedral (left) is the oldest in Ireland, having been founded by St. Patrick in 445, though the building itself dates from the 6th to 12th centuries and was restored in the 19th. On the facing hill, to the far right, is St. Patrick's Roman Catholic cathedral built 1840–73, following Catholic Emancipation.
Courtesy of the Northern Ireland Tourist Board.

Plato, became tutor to Alexander the Great, and in 335 opened a school at Athens. When Alexander d. he was forced to flee to Chalcis, where he d.

Of A.'s works some 22 treatises survive, dealing with logic; metaphysics; physics, astronomy, and meteorology; biology; psychology; ethics and politics; and literary criticism.

A. maintained that sense-experience is our only source of knowledge, and that by reasoning we can discover the essences of things, i.e. their distinguishing qualities. The essence of a thing he regards as real, but not as capable of existing apart from it. He conceives of all being as potentiality and actuality, in the physical order represented by matter and form; God alone is all actuality. Change consists in bringing the potentiality of a substance into actuality. All change is caused, the Supreme Cause being God.

A. held that all matter consisted of a single 'prime matter', which was always determined by some form. The simplest kinds of matter were the 4 elements, earth, water, air, and fire, which in varying proportions constituted all the things we know. A. saw nature as always striving to perfect itself, and first classified organisms into species and genera to show how they subserve this purpose.

The principle of life he terms a soul, which he regards as the form of the living creature, not as a substance separable from it. The intellect can discover in sense-impressions the universal, and as the soul thus transcends matter, it must be immortal. In his works on ethics and politics A. suggests that man's happiness consists in living in conformity with nature, according to reason and moderation. He derives his political theory from the recognition that mutual aid is natural to man, and refuses to set up any one constitution as universally ideal. Art embodies nature, but in a more perfect fashion, its end being the purifying and ennobling of the affections. The essence of beauty is order and symmetry.

In the Middle Ages A.'s philosophy became the

foundation of Islamic philosophy, and was incorporated into Christian theology.

ARITA (ahrē'tah). Japanese town, on the A. river, N. of Nagasaki on Kyushu. High-quality white clay abounds in this area, and for 350 yrs. (since the introduction of potters who had been captured in warfare in Korea) it has been the producing centre of *Akae* porcelain which is predominantly red in colour. Each May a chinaware fair is held.

ARITHMETIC. The branch of mathematics that deals with all questions into which numbers enter, such as counting, measuring, weighing.

Simple A. existed already in prehistoric times. In China, Egypt, Babylon, and early civilizations generally A. was used for commercial purposes and for records of taxation as well as for astronomy. During the Dark Ages in Europe, knowledge of A. was preserved in India and later among the Arabs. European mathematics revived as conditions became more settled, with the development of trade and overseas exploration. The Arabic numerals replaced Roman numerals and allowed calculations to be made in writing, instead of by the abacus (q.v.) method. With the invention of logarithms in 1614, and of the slide rule in 1620–30, A. reached its modern form. The chief development since then has been the growing use of calculating-machines and ready-reckoners.

The basic operation in A. is counting. Most questions in A. could be answered by counting alone, though with great labour and expenditure of time. The object of formal calculations is to achieve the same result more quickly. The fundamental operations are addition and subtraction, and multiplication and division. Fractions arise naturally in the process of measurement. Decimals are a form of fractions.

Powers, i.e. repeated multiplications of the same number, are represented by an index, e.g. $2^5 = $ '2 to the 5th' $= 2 \times 2 \times 2 \times 2 \times 2$. Roots are the reverse of powers: If we ask, 'What number multiplied by itself five times gives 32?' the answer is called the 5th root of 32, i.e. 2, since $2 \times 2 \times 2 \times 2 \times 2 = 32$. *See* also LOGARITHMS.

A′RIUS (c. A.D. 256–336). Founder of Arianism, a Christian heresy which denied the complete divinity of Christ. B. in Libya, he became a priest of Alexandria in 311. In 318 he was excommunicated and fled to Palestine, but his heresy spread to such an extent that the emperor Constantine called a council at Nicaea, where Athanasius confuted the Arian doctrines and persuaded the bishops to draw up a creed in which the dogma of the Trinity was categorically affirmed. A. and his adherents were banished, though later he was allowed to return.

ARIZO′NA. A south-western state (the 'Grand Canyon' state) of the U.S.A. Its main waterway is the Colorado, which flows through the famous Grand Canyon – one of the most impressive natural features of the world. To the E. of the Colorado is a vast barren area called the Painted Desert. In the N.E. lies the Colorado Plateau, another barren region. The Gila desert occupies the S.W. of the state. The deserts of A. are arid, and have the highest temperatures in the U.S.A.

A. is believed to derive its name from the Spanish *arida-zona* (dry belt). The first Spaniard to visit A. was the Franciscan Marcos de Niza in 1539. By 1715 A. was part of New Spain; in 1824 it became part of the United Mexican States. After the Mexican War it passed to U.S.A. in 1848, became a territory in 1863, and developed rapidly as a result of the gold-rush in neighbouring California. In 1912 it was admitted as a state of the Union. Irrigation has been carried out

on a colossal scale, e.g. the Roosevelt dam on Salt river, and Hoover Dam on the Colorado between A. and Nevada, provide the state with both hydro-electric power and irrigation water. At the end of the 19th cent. rich copper deposits were found in A. and there exist deposits of many other minerals. Phoenix is the capital. Area 113,909 sq. m.; pop. (1970) 1,772,482 (c. 85,000 Indians).

ARKANSAS (ahr'kansaw). South-central state of the U.S.A., called the 'wonder state' because of its remarkable natural features.

The Mississippi runs along the eastern boundary; and from the eastern plains the land gradually rises to the Ouachita and Boston mountain ranges, lying S. and N. of the A. river, which runs across the state from W. to E. The climate is warm and healthy. The chief towns are Little Rock, the cap.; Fort Smith, Hot Springs, and Pine Bluff.

A. is primarily an agricultural state, famous for its fruits. Cotton is grown extensively, A. in 1966 being 4th in output in the U.S.A. and 3rd in rice. Natural gas was discovered in 1888, petroleum in 1901; and there are refineries near El Dorado. Bauxite and diamonds are other mineral products.

The first white man to explore the area was the Spaniard Hernando de Soto in 1541. The first European settlement was Arkansas Post by some of the companions of the French explorer La Salle in 1686 who began trading with the local Indians. In 1803 it formed part of the Louisiana purchase by the U.S.A. There followed a wave of immigration and in 1836 A. was constituted a state of the Union, seceded 1861, readmitted 1868.

Area 53,102 sq. m.; pop. (1970) 1,923,295; of whom about 25 per cent were Negroes.

ARKWRIGHT, Sir Richard (1732–92). British inventor and manufacturing pioneer. B. at Preston, Lancs, he experimented in machine-designing with a watchmaker, John Kay of Warrington, and in 1768, with Kay and John Smalley, he set up his celebrated 'spinning-frame' at Preston. He shortly removed to Nottingham to escape the fury of the spinners who feared that their handicraft would be dispensed with. In 1771 he went into partnership with Jedediah Strutt, a Derby man who had improved the stocking-frame, and Samuel Need, and built a water-powered factory at Cromford in Derbyshire. In 1790 he installed steam-power in his Nottingham works. His business prospered and he was knighted in 1786.

A′RLEN, Michael (1895–1956). British novelist. B. at Ruschuk, Bulgaria, of Armenian parents, he changed his name from Dikran Kuyumjian when he became a naturalized British subject in 1922. His greatest success was the cynically smart *The Green Hat* (1924), story of a *femme fatale*. He d. in New York.

ARLES (ahrl). Ancient city in Bouches-du-Rhône dept., S.E. France on the left bank of the Rhône, in a great fruit- and vine-growing district. Roman relics include an amphitheatre for 25,000 spectators. The cathedral of St. Trophime is the finest Romanesque structure in Provence. Pop. (1962) 42,353.

ARLINGTON. Name of the National Cemetery of the U.S.A., on the banks of the Potomac, in Virginia, facing Washington. The mansion was Robert E. Lee's, and the grounds were first used as a military cemetery in 1864 during the American Civil War. Up to 1966, 136,567 military, naval, and civilian persons from every war in which the U.S.A. has been engaged have been buried here, incl. one Unknown Soldier of the F.W.W., one of the S.W.W., and one of the Korean War. Pres. J. F. Kennedy and his brother Robert Kennedy are buried here.

ARMADA. *See* SPANISH ARMADA.

ARMADI′LLO. A mammal of the family Dasypodidae, provided with a protective armour of bony plates, joined in such a way that the body can be rolled up like a hedgehog's. The family ranges from

ARMADILLO

Texas to Patagonia, and contains many species. The largest, the Giant A. (*Priodon gigas*) of Brazil and Guiana, is 3 ft. long. *See* illus. p. 61.

ARMAGH (ahrmah'). Smallest of the 6 cos. of N. Ireland. In the N. it is flat, and there are extensive bogs. The better drained parts are under crops, especially flax. The chief rivers are the Bann and Blackwater, flowing into Lough Neagh, and the Callan tributary of the Blackwater. Chief towns are A., the cap., Lurgan, Portadown, and Keady. Area, 489 sq. m.; pop. (1966) 123,051. *See* illus. p. 60.

ARMED MERCHANT CRUISERS. During both World Wars, a number of merchant ships were converted into cruisers as an emergency measure.

Two deserve special mention. The *Rawalpindi* (Capt. E. C. Kennedy, R.N.) fought on 23 Nov. 1939, S.E. of Iceland, a most gallant action with the German battleships *Scharnhorst* and *Gneisenau*, and went down with her flag flying. On 5 Nov. 1940 the *Jervis Bay* (Capt. E. S. Fogarty Fegen, R.N.) was similarly sunk by the pocket battleship *Admiral Scheer*, while escorting the ships in her convoy. Fegen was awarded a posthumous V.C. During the F.W.W., 17 armed merchant cruisers were lost by enemy action, and 15 during the S.W.W.

ARMENIA. A mountainous region in S.E. Europe and S.W. Asia, divided between U.S.S.R., Turkey, and Persia, and situated between the Black Sea, the Little Caucasus, and the plateaux of Persia and Asia Minor. In legend, it is the site of the Garden of Eden, and the Ark, after the Flood, came to rest on the 'Mountains of Ararat', the highest part of the plateau. In the last cents. of the 2nd millenium B.C. the country was occupied by a people called Urartu, Ararat, Vannic, or Khaldian. Their kingdom flourished in the 9th–7th cents. B.C., and was overrun by an Indo-European people from the W. or N., the two peoples amalgamating and representing the ancestors of the modern Armenian. A. owed allegiance in turn to Assyria, Persia, the Romans, the Byzantine Empire (7th cent.), the Seljuks and Mongols, and in the 16th cent. was divided between Persians and Turks, Russia obtaining a portion during the 19th cent.

The *Armenian Question* arose in 1878 when promised reforms never materialized; unrest broke out and there were massacres by Turkish troops in 1895. Again in 1909 and 1915, the Turks massacred altogether more than a million Armenians, and deported others into the N. Syrian desert where they died of starvation; those who could fled to Russia or Persia, and only some 100,000 were left in Turkish Armenia.

After the Russian revolution of 1917, Russian Armenia in 1920 proclaimed itself a republic; it was one of the reps. of the Transcaucasian S.F.S.R. (the others being Georgia and Azerbaijan) from 1922 until it became a constituent republic of the U.S.S.R. in 1936.

ARMENIAN CHURCH. A. adopted Christianity in the 3rd cent., and about 295 Gregory the Illuminator (*c*. 257–332) was made exarch of the Armenian church, which has developed along national lines. The Seven Sacraments, or Mysteries, are administered, baptism being immediately followed by confirmation. The Catholicos or exarch is the supreme head, and Echmiadzin, 7 m. W. of Yerevan, is his traditional seat.

ARMOUR

ARMY. Key man of the modern army, a section leader with the latest-type bayonet-machine-gun, goes ahead of his men. The khaki uniform, designed for maximum ease of movement, is a striking contrast with the ceremonial uniform of his regiment – the celebrated Black Watch.
Photo: Crown copyright.

LANGUAGE. The Armenian language constitutes one of the main divisions of Indo-European. Old Armenian, the classic literary language, is still used in the liturgy of the Church. Armenian was not written down until the 5th cent. A.D., when an alphabet of 36 (now 38) letters was evolved. Literature flourished in the 4th–14th cents., revived in the 18th; contemporary Armenian, with modified grammar and enriched with words from other languages, is used by a group of 20th cent. writers.

PEOPLE. The total number of Armenian-speakers in the world has been estimated at 4,000,000; about 1,500,000 live in Soviet A., 50,000 in Turkey, 210,000 in Syria and Lebanon, and others in Persia, Iraq, India, etc. Some 100,000 have emigrated to the U.S.A.

ARMENIAN S.S.R. Constituent Rep. of the U.S.S.R., situated in the S. of Transcaucasia and mainly mountainous and wooded. Livestock are raised in the mountains round Yerevan, the cap., and in the Aras valley cotten, tobacco, fruits are grown with the help of artificial irrigation. Area 11,500 sq. m.; pop. (1967) 2,253,000 (*c*. 88% Armenians).

ARMENTIÈRES (ahrmontē-ār'). French manufacturing town in Nord dept., on the Lys, 10 m. N.W. of Lille. The song 'Mademoiselle from A.' originated in the F.W.W. when the town was held by the British. Pop. (1962) 27,254.

ARMI'NIUS (17 B.C.–A.D. 21). German chieftain, whose annihilation of a Roman army led by Varus in the Teutoburger Wald in A.D. 9 led to the Roman withdrawal to the Rhine frontier.

ARMI'NIUS, Jacobus. Latinized form of Jakob Harmensen (1560–1609), the Dutch Protestant divine who founded Arminianism, a school of theology opposed to Calvinism. B. in S. Holland, he was ordained at Amsterdam in 1588, and from 1603 lived as professor of theology at Leyden. A's views were developed and systematized after his death by his follower, Episcopius. A. opposed Calvin's doctrine of predestination, and asserted that forgiveness and eternal life are bestowed on all who repent of their sins and unfeignedly believe in Jesus Christ. In England Arminianism was adopted as the theology of Wesleyan Methodism, in opposition to the Calvinist views of the followers of Whitefield.

ARMISTICE DAY. *See* REMEMBRANCE, NATIONAL DAY OF.

ARMOUR. Protective covering in warfare. The

ARMY. I. Uniforms, introduced in the late 17th century with the growth of national armies, reached in the late 18th and early 19th centuries the height of elaboration and discomfort: (left to right) Austrian (1809), French (1779), and Russian (1812) standard bearers.

though mercenaries were also employed. The superiority of the mounted knight was ended by the longbow (Crécy, Poitiers, Agincourt), and firearms and cannon favoured centralization in the hands of professionals and the development of sustained campaigns and strategy. In Tudor England small standing bodies of troops were employed for external and internal defence, but the defects of raw levies, noble amateurs and mercenaries led to Cromwell's creation of the New Model Army for the larger campaigns of the Civil War. After the Restoration Charles II estab. a small standing army, the beginning of the modern British army, which was expanded under James II and William III. Under George III it failed to subdue the American colonists, showing the superiority of the citizen, or people's army, dramatically illustrated in Europe by the forces of the French Revolution. Conscription was 1st adopted in Prussia to counter Napoleon's imperial ambitions. The British A. under Wellington which eventually broke Napoleon was one of the best ever put into the field, but it afterwards decreased in numbers and efficiency. Its weaknesses were patent in the Crimean War and, despite reforms by Cardwell and Wolseley, in the South African War.

use of body A. is very ancient and is frequently depicted in Greek and Roman art. In the Middle Ages chain mail was extensively developed, and in the 14–16th cents. came the growth of plate A. which eventually encased the whole body and represented a superb degree of craftsmanship. The invention of gunpowder led, though only by degrees, to the virtual abandonment of A. until in the F.W.W. the helmet reappeared as a defence against shrapnel. The pre-requisites of practical modern A., lightness and flexibility, were not met until the development of the nylon and fibre-glass A. which began to come into use in the S.W.W. and the Korean War. A. is also used on tanks, aircraft, ships, and cars.

2. The splendour of British cavalrymen in the Napoleonic period: (left to right) Royal Horse Guards officer, Life Guards trooper, Life Guards officer, Dragoon officer and Royal Horse Guards trooper.

Models such as those illustrated on this page are hand-made and painted, accurate even to the last detail of complexion, and are used in adult 'war games' which reconstruct and sometimes throw fresh light on battles of the past.
Photos: Norman Newton Ltd., London.

R. B. Haldane (on the advice of Roberts) organized an expeditionary force, and for home defence a territorial force, though these were still inadequate. In the 19th cent. there had been immense development of rapidly-produced missile weapons, use of railways (the American Civil War has been called the 'railway war'), etc. The F.W.W. was one of trench warfare in which enormous As. were bogged down, e.g. the British A. expanded from 750,000 to 5½ million men. In the inter-war period As. were greatly reduced until the rise of the Italo-German forces led to reluctant increases: Britain was in many respects less prepared

ARMSTRONG, Anthony. Pen-name of A. A. Willis (1897–). British author of humorous novels and ingenious thriller play *Ten-Minute Alibi*.

ARMSTRONG, Louis (1900–71). American jazz musician, nicknamed Satchmo. A trumpet-player of virtuoso ability, he was b. in New Orleans, joined Kid Ory's band in 1917, and formed his own 7 yrs. later. His reputation is as worldwide as the distribution of his records, and his films incl. *High Society*.

ARMSTRONG, Thomas (1899–). British novelist. B. in the W. Riding, he entered the wool trade and estab. his name with *The Crowthers of Bankdam* (1940), dealing with a family in the trade in the 19th cent.

ARMY. An organized military force: these were common to all ancient civilizations: Sumeria, Babylonia, Egypt, Assyria, China, India, Persia, Greece, Carthage and – above all – Rome. In Britain the Anglo-Saxon *fyrd*, or local militia, saved the country from being wholly overrun by the Danes, but the 1st body of standing troops was raised by Canute. After the Norman Conquest military organization was based on the feudal system common to all Europe, whereby vassals supplied their overlords with a certain number of men for so many days a year, with its obvious drawbacks for continuous campaigning,

3. Still dashing, but tending to the more functional and loose-fitting, uniforms of Confederate troops of the American Civil War: (left to right) soldier of the 1st Virginia Cavalry (with saddle), an infantryman, a cavalry standard bearer, and a Zouave (q.v.) who reflects the French influence in some Southern states.

in 1939 than 1914. The As. of the S.W.W. were remarkable for mobility and the enormous distances they covered, notably Allied forces in the Pacific area, and also for close co-ordination of land, sea and air forces. Nuclear weapons development after the S.W.W. led to a reduction of conventional As. – announced by the U.S. in 1955, followed by the gradual ending of conscription in Britain from 1957, and drastic reductions by the Soviet Union in 1960.

ARNAULD (ahrnoh´). Name of a French family closely associated with the Jansenist movement in the 17th cent. ANTOINE A. (1560–1619) was a Paris advocate, strongly critical of the Jesuits. Many of his 20 children were associated with the abbey of Port Royal, a convent of Cistercian nuns near Versailles, that became the centre of Jansenism: the 2nd daughter, ANGÉLIQUE (1591–1661), became abbess through her father's instrumentality at the age of 8. Later she served as prioress under her sister AGNES (1593–1671), and her niece, LA MÈRE ANGÉLIQUE (1624–84), succeeded to both positions. A.'s youngest child, ANTOINE (1612–94), the 'great Arnauld', was religious director of the nuns at Port Royal. With Pascal, Nicole, and others, he produced not only Jansenist pamphlets, but works on logic, grammar, and geometry. For years he had to live in hiding, and the last 16 years of his life were spent in Brussels. *See* JANSENISM; PORT ROYAL, etc.

ARNE, Thomas Augustine (1710–78). British composer. B. in London, he composed operas and oratorios, as well as much music for the theatre, but is best remembered for his songs, which include 'Where the bee sucks' and 'Rule, Britannia'.

ARNHEM (arn´hem). Cap. of Gelderland prov. of the Netherlands, on the right bank of the Rhine, 35 m. E.S.E. of Utrecht. Sir Philip Sidney died there in 1586. Pop (1967) 134,921. In the S.W.W. it was the scene of a great airborne operation and battle (17–27 Sept. 1944) when 10,095 British troops under Major R. E. Urquhart were dropped in the region of A. with the object of securing a bridgehead over the N. Rhine and facilitating an Allied drive into the heart of Germany. Forces also landed by air at Nijmegen were unable to fight their way along the road to Arnhem, and after a fierce struggle the survivors in that town had to be withdrawn; 7,605 were lost, killed, wounded, or missing.

ARNIM, Ludwig Achim von (1781–1831). German Romantic poet and novelist. B. in Berlin, he wrote short stories, a romance, *Gräfin Dolores* (1810), and plays, but left his finest work, the historical novel *Die Kronenwächter* (1817), unfinished. With Clemens Brentano he collected the Ger. folk-songs in *Des Knaben Wunderhorn* (1805–8). In 1811 he m. Brentano's sister, BETTINA (1785–1859), who as a girl had an intimate friendship with Goethe. In 1835 she pub. her correspondence with the poet.

ARNIM, Mary Annette von (1866–1941). Novelist B. in Sydney (née Beauchamp), she m. H. von A. (1856–1910), and in 1898 became famous with *Elizabeth and her German Garden*. Other books characterized by the same light but effective humour followed. Her later works, like *The Enchanted April* (1923), maintained her reputation. In 1916 she m. the 2nd earl Russell. Her books appeared under the pseudonym 'Elizabeth von A.'.

ARNO. Italian river, 150 m. long, rising in the Apennines, and flowing westward to the Mediterranean. Florence and Pisa stand on its banks.

ARNOLD (d. 1155). Italian religious reformer, known as Arnold of Brescia. B. probably at Brescia, he studied in Paris and became an Augustinian monk. Leading a highly ascetic life himself, he strongly condemned the prevailing laxity in the Church, and opposed the temporal power of the papacy. Banished from Italy by Innocent II in 1139, he returned in 1145, and played a part in the short-lived Roman republic. In 1155 he was forced to flee, but was taken, condemned to death, and hanged. His followers were probably merged in the Waldenses.

ARNOLD, Benedict (1741–1801). American soldier, chiefly remembered for an act of treason to the American side in the War of American Independence. A merchant in Newhaven, Conn., he joined the Colonial forces, but in 1780 plotted to betray the strategic post at West Point to the British. Major André was sent by the British to discuss terms with him, but was caught and hanged as a spy. A. escaped to the British, who gave him an army command.

ARNOLD, Sir Edwin (1832–1904). British scholar and poet. After leaving Oxford, he was a schoolmaster and principal of a college at Poona. In 1861 he joined the staff of the *Daily Telegraph*. He is famed for his *Light of Asia* (1879), a rendering of the life and teaching of the Buddha in blank verse. *The Light of the World* (1891) is a less successful attempt to re-tell the life of Christ.

ARNOLD, Henry H. (1886–1950). American general. Head of U.S. Air Force, 1943–6. B. at Gladwyne, Penn., he was trained at the U.S. Military Academy, and during and after the F.W.W. held commands at various U.S. air fields. In 1940 he was made Deputy Chief of Air Staff, and during the S.W.W. was largely responsible for the efficiency and numbers of the U.S. Air Force.

ARNOLD, Malcolm (1921–). British composer. Principal trumpet in the London Philharmonic Orchestra 1941–4 and 1945–8, he has composed symphonies and film music for *The Bridge on the River Kwai*.

ARNOLD, Matthew (1822–88). British poet. B. at Laleham, he was the son of Dr. A., headmaster of Rugby, and after a short period as assistant master at Rugby was one of H.M. inspectors of schools (1851–86). His first vols. of poetry, *The Strayed Reveller* (1849) and *Empedocles on Etna* (1852), were unsuccessful and anonymous, but 2 further publications under his own name in 1853 and 1855 caused him to be elected professor of poetry at Oxford (1857–67). A classical tragedy, *Merope* (1858) and *New Poems* (1867) followed, and much literary criticism is contained in *Essays in Criticism* (1865 and 1888), and other vols. He also pub. studies in education, *Literature and Dogma* (1873), and a masterly indictment of 19th cent. Philistinism, *Culture and Anarchy* (1869). As a poet and as critic A. held steadfastly to the standard set by classical unity, and demanded 'high seriousness' and 'a criticism of life'.

ARNOLD, Thomas (1795–1842). British schoolmaster. Ordained in the C. of E. in 1818, he was headmaster of Rugby School 1828–42, and his rule there has been graphically described in Thomas Hughes's *Tom Brown's Schooldays*. His emphasis was on training of character, and his influence on public school education was profound.

ARNOULD (ahrnoo´), **Madeleine Sophie** (1740–1802). French actress and opera-singer, immensely popular from her début in 1757 to her retirement in 1778. She was also renowned for beauty and vivacious wit.

ARP, Hans or **Jean** (1887–1966). French painter and sculptor. B. at Strasbourg, he was one of the founders of Dadaism in Zurich *c.* 1917, and was later a member of the Surrealist and Abstract-Creation groups. His

MATTHEW ARNOLD
G. F. Watts
Photo: N.P.G

early painting is fluid, and when he turned to sculpture it was notable for its boneless curves; also remarkable are his *papiers déchirés*, torn paper designs pasted on a white ground.

ARRAN. Large island in the Firth of Clyde, Scotland, part of Buteshire. It is 20 m. by 10 m.: has an area of 165 sq. m., and a pop. (1961) 3,705.

ARRAS (ahrahs'). French town, cap. of Pas-de-Calais dept., on the Scarpe, 100 m. N. by E. of Paris. Formerly it was famed for its tapestry. Pop. (1962) 45,643.

It gave its name to five battles of the F.W.W., when it was almost destroyed. The fiercest was fought April 1917, with losses on either side in killed, wounded, and missing of 145,000. A. was captured in the German advance on Dunkirk in 1940.

ARRAU (ara'ow), **Claudio** (1903–). Chilean pianist. A concert performer since the age of 5, he excels in Bach and Beethoven.

ARREBOE (ahrebō'), **Anders-Kristensen** (1587–1637). Danish poet. B. in the island of Aeroe, he became bp. of Trondhjem in 1618. In 1622 he was deprived of his bishopric for misconduct, but afterwards he reformed and was appointed priest at Vordingborg. His best-known work is the *Hexae-meron rhythmico-danicum* (1641 and 1661), a poem on the Creation.

HANS ARP. 'L'araignée' – the spider – in bronze. *Photo: Galerie Denise René.*

ARREST. Deprivation of personal liberty with a view to detention. In Britain, since the abolition of imprisonment for debt (1869), an A. in civil proceedings now takes place only on a court order, usually for contempt of court. In criminal proceedings an A. may be made on a magistrate's warrant, but a police constable is empowered to arrest without warrant in all cases where he has reasonable ground for thinking a felony has been committed. Private persons may, and are indeed bound to, arrest anyone committing a felony or breach of the peace in their presence. In the U.S. peace officers and private persons have similar rights and duties.

ARRHENIUS (ahrrä'nē-oos), **Svante August** (1859–1927). Swedish scientist, the founder of physical chemistry. B. near Uppsala, he became a professor at Stockholm in 1895, and made a special study of electrolysis. He wrote *Worlds in the Making, Destinies of the Stars*, etc., and in 1903 received the Nobel prize for chemistry.

ARROL, Sir William (1839–1913). British civil engineer. B. in Renfrewshire, he set up as a boiler-maker in 1868, later started the Dalmarnock iron-works, and his firm (Wm. Arrol & Co.) built many bridges, including the Tay, the Forth, and Tower Bridges.

ARROMANCHES (ahromoṅsh'). Bathing resort and fishing village in Normandy on the Channel coast, where a prefabricated port was assembled for the British armies to assault the German 'Atlantic Wall' on D-day, 6 June 1944. Pop. (1962) 298.

ARROWROOT. Starchy substance derived from the roots and tubers of various plants. The true A. (*Maranta arundinacea*) was used by the Indians of South America as an antidote against the effects of poisoned arrows. The W. Indian island of St. Vincent is the main source of supply today.

ARSENIC. Greyish white semi-metallic crystalline element, symbol As, at. wt. 74·91, at. no. 33. It occurs in many ores, and is widely distributed, being present in minute quantities in the soil, the sea, and the human body. The chief source of A. compounds is as a by-product from metallurgical pro-cesses. A. is used in insecticides and medicine; as it is a cumulative poison, its presence in food and drugs is very dangerous. The symptoms of A. poisoning are vomiting, diarrhoea, tingling in the limbs and possibly numbness, and collapse.

Arsenious oxide (As_4O_6), or white A., is an important inorganic compound of A. Arsine (AsH_3) has been made as a war gas. Of the organic arsenicals the best known is Salvarsan (q.v.).

ARSON. At common law, the malicious burning of the house of another. In England the Malicious Damage Act, 1861 laid down heavy penalties for specific offences incl. setting fire to places of worship, ships, and growing crops. *See also* CAPITAL PUNISH-MENT. Setting fire to one s own house, and unintentionally damaging another's in the process is A., and such an act with intent to defraud an insurance co. is also a serious offence. In Scotland A. is termed fire-raising.

ART. The creation of something aesthetically satisfying. The *fine* As. incl. painting, sculpture, engraving, and the *useful* As. such activities as weaving, metal work and furniture-making which combine beauty and practical purposes: in modern usage, however, the distinction becomes increasingly blurred.

In the Middle Ages the term was used, chiefly in the plural, to signify a branch of learning which was regarded as an instrument of knowledge; the seven *Liberal Arts* consisted of the *trivium*, i.e. grammar, logic, and rhetoric, and the *quadrivium*, i.e. arithmetic, music, geometry, and astronomy.

ARTEL. Association of owner-producers in Russia. Formed for the development of agriculture and industry, it has been organized, on the one hand, into collective farming, and on the other hand, into industrial co-operative societies (incops). There are also groupings of intellectual and artistic workers, which may be described as As.

ARTEMIS (ahr'tēmis). Greek goddess, identified with the Roman Diana. She was the goddess of chastity, the virgin huntress, who presided over childbirth and the young. Ephesus was a chief centre of her cult.

ARTERY. One of the vessels which convey blood from the heart. The largest is the aorta, which leads from the left ventricle up over the heart and downwards through the diaphragm into the belly. As. are flexible, elastic tubes consisting of 3 coats. The cutting of an A. of any size is a dangerous injury. With middle and old age the As. normally lose their elasticity; the walls degenerate, and often also become impregnated with lime – arteriosclerosis, hardening of the As.

CLAUDIO ARRAU *Photo: Godfrey MacDomnic.*

ARTESIAN WELLS. Artificial borings made through impermeable rock to water-containing beds, when the water rises to the surface by hydrostatic pressure or is pumped up. The name comes from Artois, the French province where they were first adopted in Europe.

ARTHRITIS. Inflammation of a joint or joints. A joint is lined by a layer of cartilage covered by a thin and very smooth 'synovial' membrane, which provides a lubricated surface for smooth action. This membrane may become infected by various organisms such as rheumatism, gonorrhoea, or tuberculosis, or as a result of injury, such as a sprain or dislocation. The infection may enter through an injury or be carried to the joint in the blood.

In osteo-arthritis, a degenerative condition of the knee and hip joints in older people, artificial joints may replace the natural, and for rheumatoid A., an artificial synovial fluid was under development in 1971. *See* CORTISONE.

ARTHRO'PODA. A main branch or phylum of the animal kingdom. They have the body bilaterally symmetrical and composed primitively of a series of similar segments, and are distinguished essentially by having one or more pairs of limbs near the mouth modified to act as jaws. The integument also, although sometimes thin, is not slimy, but horny, or chitinous.

The A. are divided into the following classes, sometimes given the rank of sub-phyla, essentially distinguished by the number, structure, and function of the appendages in front of the mouth (preoral), and of those behind the mouth (postoral), concerned with mastication. The position of the generative orifices and the nature of the breathing organs, which may be air-tubes (*tracheae*) for land forms, or gills (*branchiae*), for water forms, also supply valuable characters for classification, which is as follows: *Prototracheata*, or Onychophora (a solitary primitive member, Peripatus). *Arachnida* (king crabs, scorpions, spiders, ticks, etc.). *Trilobita* (an extinct marine palaeozoic group, Trilobites). *Crustacea* (crabs, shrimps, woodlice, barnacles, etc.). *Chilopoda* (centipedes). *Insecta*, sometimes called Hexapoda (insects). *Diplopoda* (millipedes). *Pauropoda* (minute forms without popular names). *Symphyla* (minute forms somewhat resembling centipedes).

ARTHUR. Legendary early British king and hero. He is supposed to have been b. at the end of the 5th cent., and to have led the armies of the kings of Britain against the pagan Saxon invaders. Nennius (fl. 796), says he was a Christian warrior in Kent, and fought 12 battles. The story of the Round Table first appears in 1155. Geoffrey of Monmouth (1147) introduces a mythical element, and the interment of A. at Glastonbury (q.v.) is first mentioned in 1195.

ARTHUR (1187–1203). English prince, nephew of King John, who is supposed to have had him murdered on 3 April 1203 because he was a possible rival to the English throne. The story of John's order to blind A. is a famous scene in Shakespeare's *King John*.

ARTHUR, Chester Alan (1830–86). 21st President of U.S.A. Son of a Baptist minister, he was b. in Vermont, and became a lawyer and eloquent Republican spokesman. In 1880 he was elected vice-president; and when Garfield was assassinated in the following year, succeeded him as president, holding office until 1885.

ARTHUR'S SEAT. Hill of volcanic origin standing in King's Park, to the E. of Edinburgh, Scotland. It is 822 ft. high, and provides magnificent views.

ARTICHOKE. Two plants of the family Compositae, both familiar as table-vegetables. The true A. (*Cynara scolymus*) is tall, with purplish blue flowers; the bracts of the unopened flower are eaten. The Jerusalem A. (*Helianthus tuberosus*) has edible tubers; it is a native of N. America, and its name is a corruption of the It. *girasole*, sunflower.

ARTIFICIAL RESPIRATION. The process of maintaining breathing in a helpless person, unconscious persons who have suffered electric shock or are apparently drowned; also in cases of infantile paralysis (anterior poliomyelitis) in which the mechanism of breathing is affected. In cases of electric shock or apparent drowning the first choice is the expired air method (kiss of life), by means of mouth-to-mouth breathing, since it gives greater ventilation than other methods, such as the Holger Nielsen or Silvester Brosch. In cases of paralysis 'iron lungs' are used.

ARTILLERY. One of the 2 main divisions of firearms (q.v.). In general use in Western Europe from the mid-14th cent., A. consisted of very small guns, made of cast iron or bronze, smooth bored; and firing lead, iron or stone balls at low velocities. The barrel, closed at one end (the breech), was filled with a charge of gunpowder, tamped down with a soft 'wad', and the ball placed on top. A tiny 'touch' hole in the breech was filled with powder and lit, forming a 'train' through the barrel to explode the charge. Edward III used guns in his Scottish campaign of 1327, and in the English fleet at the battle of Sluys, 1340. In the 15th cent. attemps were made to eliminate the difficulties involved in obtaining sound metal castings for the bigger guns by fabricating barrels from rods, beaten and welded together lengthwise, and reinforced by iron rings. With the inadequate techniques of the period, this highly unsound method was responsible for many accidents, including the death of James II of Scotland in 1460. With the advent of improved methods, casting prevailed from the 16th cent., but in spite of considerable warfare little progress was made in the next 300 years, except that cannon grew bigger: there had already been a passing fashion in the late 14th cent. for giant cannon, e.g. 'Duille Grete' made in Ghent *c.* 1382, which weighed 15 tons and fired a 600 lb. stone ball. The period 1845–85 saw the evolution of the rifled barrel, permitting greater accuracy, and a return to built-up steel construction. Higher velocities and elongated missiles added considerably to penetrating power, diminishing the need for 'big' guns.

AR'TIODA'CTYLA. The 'cloven-hoofed' mammals; more scientifically, those animals distinguished by the structure of their feet, in which the median axis passes between the enlarged, symmetrically-paired 3rd and 4th digits, constituting the main hoof. The 2nd and 5th digits are also commonly represented by a pair of small hoofs, which seldom reach the ground. By the structure of their teeth and stomach the A. are divided into the *Suina* (pig-like animals), comprising the Suidae (pigs and peccaries) and Hippopotamidae (hippopotami); and the *Ruminantia* (ruminant-like animals), including the Tylopoda (camels), the Tragulina (chevrotains), and the Pecora (true ruminants: deer, giraffes, antelopes, goats, sheep, oxen, etc.).

ARTOIS (ahrtwah'). Old prov. of N. France, bounded by Flanders and Picardy, and almost corresponding with the modern dept. of Pas-de-Calais. Its cap. was Arras.

ARTS COUNCIL OF GREAT BRITAIN. Semi-official organization for the advancement of cultural activities among the people as a whole. It originated in 1940 as a committee of the Pilgrim Trust to encourage the arts in wartime. It was at first known as the Council for the Encouragement of Music and the Arts (C.E.M.A.), but in 1945 it was incorporated under its present name. It is assisted by Committees for Scotland and Wales, and specialist panels for music, drama, and the visual arts.

ARTSYBA'SHEV, Mikhail Petrovich (1878–1927). Russian novelist and dramatist. Impregnated with disenchanted sex, such novels as *Sanin* (1907) and *Breaking-Point* (1912), and the plays *Jealousy* and *The Law of the Savage*, created a sensation. Exiled as a counter-revolutionary in 1921, he settled in Warsaw.

A'RUM. Genus of plants of the family Araceae. The typical species (*A. maculatum*), known as cuckoo-

ARUM or 'cuckoo-pint'.

pint or lords-and-ladies, is a common British hedge-row plant. The A. or trumpet lily (*Zantedeschia aethiopica*), a well-known ornamental plant, is a native of Africa.

ARUNDEL, Thomas (1353–1413). English church-man: 3rd son of the earl of A., he was in turn bishop of Ely, archbishop of York, and (1396) archbishop of Canterbury. He was five times Lord Chancellor. The Lollards suffered severely under his rule.

ARUNDEL, Thomas Howard, 2nd earl of A. (1586–1646). English statesman and patron of the arts. The A. Marbles, part of his collection of Italian sculptures, were given to Oxford university in 1667 by his grandson.

ARUNDEL. Town (bor.) in Sussex, England, 6 m. up the r. Arun, 10 m. E. of Chichester. Situated in a gap in the S. Downs, it has a magnificent castle, the seat for centuries of the earls of A. and dukes of Norfolk. The parish church of St. Nicolas dates from the 14th cent.; the R.C. church of St. Philip Neri was built by the 15th duke in 1873. Pop. (1961) 2,614.

ARUNDEL. Overlooking the River Arun — unseen in the foreground — Arundel castle began as an earthwork built by Alfred against the Danes. Important in the Civil War, it was restored to its present splendour by Charles, 11th Duke of Norfolk, in the 18th cent. *Photo: Aerofilms Ltd.*

A'RVAL BRETHREN (Lat. *Fratres Arvales*, brothers of the field). Body of priests in ancient Rome who offered annual sacrifices to the *Lares* or divinities of the fields in order to ensure a good harvest. They formed a college of 12 priests, and their chief festival fell in May.

ARVI'DA. Industrial town in Quebec prov., Canada, on Saguenay r., site of a huge smelter which produces up to 350,000 tons of aluminium a year. Pop. (1961) 14,460.

ARYAN (ār'ian or ah'rian). Name given to a broad division of the human race, who are supposed to have inhabited the great stretch of country from Central Asia to Eastern Europe, and to have reached India about 3000 B.C. German theorists conceived of the As. as a white-skinned master race, identifiable with the 'Nordic' or Teutonic race, but there is little or no evidence for such a view. With more reason A. is applied to a division of the Indo-European family of languages, comprising Sanskrit and Iranian, but it ought not to be used as synonymous with Indo-European.

ARYANA. Ancient name of AFGHANISTAN.

ARYA SAMAJ (ah'rya sahmahj'). Hindu religious sect founded by Dayanand Saraswati (1825–88), about 1875. He was a Brahman who renounced idol-worship, and urged a return to the purer principles of the Rig Veda.

ASBESTOS. Name given to several related min-erals of fibrous structure which offer great resistance to heat through their non-inflammability and poor conductivity. They are silicates of iron, calcium, and magnesium. Commercial A. is made from chrysotile, a kind of serpentine which comes chiefly from Quebec and Rhodesia, or from tremolite and actinolite and other less common minerals of the hornblende group. The uses of A. incl. brake linings, suits for spacemen and firemen, insulation of electric wires in furnaces and when subjected to heavy neutron bombardment in reactors, and (blended with cement) A. cement sheets and pressure pipes for the building industry. Exposure to A. is a recognized cause of industrial cancer (mesothelioma).

ASBURY, Francis (1745–1816). First bishop of the Methodist Episcopal Church to be consecrated in U.S.A. B. in Staffs, the son of a farmer, he was a domestic servant and blacksmith's apprentice. From 1768 he was a disciple of Wesley, who chose him in 1771 for missionary work in the Eng. colonies in America. There he was consecrated bishop in 1784, and in his 45 years' work travelled over 275,000 m., mostly on horseback.

A'SCARIS. Genus of thread-worms of the class Nematoda. *A. lumbricoides*, the round worm, inhabits the human intestines, and may reach a length of 14 in.

ASCE'NSION. British island of volcanic origin in the S. Atlantic, 700 m. N.W. of St. Helena. Area 34

sq. m. Most of the pop. (336 in 1961) live in George-town, the cap. Discovered on Ascension Day, 1501, by a Portuguese navigator, A. was uninhabited till 1815, when occupied by a British R.N. garrison: attached to the colony of St. Helena in 1922. There are British and U.S. space stations.

ASCENSION DAY. In the Christian calendar, the feast day commemorating Christ's ascension into heaven. Known sometimes as Holy Thursday, it is the 40th day after Easter.

ASCETICISM (aset'isism). The renunciation of the physical pleasures, e.g. in eating and drinking, or the exercise of sexual instincts; and the courting of discomfort, or pain. It ranges from the primitive tabu to the self-denial of the great religions.

ASCH (ahsh), **Sholem** (1880–1957). Polish writer of Jewish descent. He lived for many years in the U.S. and was the last of the great classic writers of Yiddish literature. He produced a great cycle of biblical novels.

ASCHAM (as'kam), **Roger** (*c.* 1515–68). English classical scholar, educationist, and writer. B. in Yorks, he became 1st Regius prof. of Greek at Cambridge in 1540. His prose treatise on archery, *Toxophilus* (1545), recommended him to Henry VIII, so that in 1548 he became tutor to the Princess Elizabeth. From 1550 to 1553 he was sec. to Sir Richard Morrison, ambassador to the court of the emperor Charles V, then, in spite of his Protestant views, became Queen Mary's Latin sec. and subsequently was Queen Elizabeth's sec. and tutor. His original views on education are put down in the *Scholemaster* (1570).

ASCO'RBIC ACID or Vitamin C. A relatively simple organic acid found in fresh fruits and veget-ables. It prevents scurvy.

A'SCOT. Village in Berks, 6 m. S.W. of Windsor. The racecourse, on Ascot Heath, was laid down in 1711 by order of Queen Anne, who presented a piece of plate as a trophy. The circular course is 1⅝ m. long. The Royal A. meeting in June is one of the chief events of the London 'season'. Pop. *c.* 6,500.

ASDIC. *See* SONAR.

ASE'PSIS. Freedom from bacteria, particularly in surgery. Modern surgery rests on a meticulously careful technique of A., by which germs are not ever allowed to reach a surgical wound, and are removed from an accidental wound by cutting out damaged tissues and careful cleansing. Similar precautions are used in childbirth and accidents. *See* illus. p. 68.

ASEXUAL ('without sex'). Biological term applied to those plants and animals which reproduce by division. Unlike sexual reproduction, this does not involve the fusion of two cells, and never needs two parents. Examples are bacteria, amoeba, yeast, strawberry plants, shallots, and apple trees.

ASH. Group of trees of the genus Fraxinus, belonging to the order Oleales. *F. excelsior* is the common species. The timber is of importance. The mountain A. or rowan (*Sorbus aucuparia*) belongs to the Rosaceae.

ASHANTI. Region of Ghana, W. Africa; area 9,700 sq. m.; pop. (1960) 1,108,548. Kumasi is the cap. Crops are cocoa and other tropical products. A. art, notably brass figures, gold work, and drums, provides fine examples of African craftsmanship.

For more than 200 years forming an independent kingdom, during the 19th cent. the warlike Ashanti people came into conflict with the British on the Gold Coast who sent 4 expeditions against them, and in 1901 formally annexed their country. Otomfuo Sir Osei Agyeman, nephew of the then deposed king, Prempeh I, was made head of the re-established A. confederation in 1935 as Prempeh II, and the Golden Stool, symbol of the A. peoples since the 17th cent., was returned to Kumasi. From 1954 A. was represented in the Gold Coast cabinet, and when the Gold Coast attained dominion status as Ghana in 1957, A. became one of its regions.

A S H B Y - D E - L A - Z O U C H (ash′bi-de-la-zoosh′)· Market town (U.D.) in Leicestershire, England, 17 m. N.W. of Leicester. Coal is mined in the vicinity, and there are ruins of a 15th cent. castle. Pop. (1961) 7,425.

ASHCROFT, Dame Peggy (1907–). British actress. B. in Croydon (q.v.), she made her 1st stage appearance with the Birmingham repertory in 1926. Her many parts incl. such Shakespearian roles as Desdemona, Juliet, and Rosalind, and the subtle modernity of Miss Madrigal in *The Chalk Garden*. She was created D.B.E. in 1956.

A′SHDOD. Deep sea port of Israel, on the Mediterranean 20 m. S. of Tel-Aviv, which it superseded 1965. Planned to be second only to Haifa, it stands on the site of the ancient Philistine stronghold of Askalon. Pop. of the completed city will be c. 150,000.

ASHES, The. Cricket trophy, theoretically held by the winning team in any series of Test Matches between England and Australia. A humorous obituary notice of 'English cricket', pub. in the *Sporting Times* in 1882, stated that the 'body' would be cremated and the ashes taken to Australia. During the winter of 1882–3, Ivo Bligh, captain of a successful English

ASIA. Physical features of the great land mass.

eam visiting Australia, was presented by Melbourne ladies with an urn containing the ashes of the stumps and bails used in the match. The urn is in the keeping of the M.C.C. at Lords.

ASHFORD. Town (U.D.) and railway junction on the Stour in Kent, England, 14 m. S.W. of Canterbury. It has large locomotive shops, brickworks, etc. Pop. (1961) 27,962.

ASHKENA′ZY, Vladimir (1937–). Russian pianist. He has a technique rather differing from

ASH, with leaves, flowers, and fruit.

standard Western practice and in 1962 was joint winner of the Tchaikovsky competition with John Ogdon. He excels in Rachmaninov, Prokofiev and Liszt.

ASHKHABA′D. Cap. of the Turkmen S.S.R. in a region on the fringe of the Kara-Kum desert, but well watered by irrigation canals. Founded in 1881, it has textile mills, a large glass factory, etc., and is the business and cultural centre of the Republic. Pop. (1967) 238,000.

A′SHMOLE, Elias (1617–92). British antiquary. B. at Lichfield, he became a lawyer, served with the Royal forces during the Civil War, and after the Restoration held posts in the excise and other offices. He wrote books on alchemy, and on antiquarian

ASEPSIS. Modern drug manufacture. The production of sterile grade material under aseptic conditions: the setting suggests space fiction rather than the factory.
Courtesy of Pfizer Ltd.

subjects, amassed a fine library, and a collection of curiosities, both of which he presented to Oxford Univ. His collection was housed in the 'Old Ashmolean' (built 1679–83), and forms the basis of the present Ashmolean Museum, erected in 1897.

ASHMORE AND CARTIER ISLANDS. Territory transferred to the authority of the Commonwealth of Australia by Britain in 1931, and comprising Middle, East and West Is. (the Ashmores) and Cartier Is., in the Indian Ocean *c.* 200 m. off the N.W. coast of Australia. They are admin. as part of the Northern Territory and are uninhabited, although W. Ashmore has an automatic weather station.

A'SHRAM. An Indian community, the members of which lead a simple life of discipline and self-denial, and devote themselves to social service, e.g. that of Mahatma Gandhi at Wardha, and the poet Sir Rabindranath Tagore's at Santiniketan.

ASHRIDGE. The former seat of the earls Brownlow near Berkhamsted, Herts, England, which in 1928 was bought and endowed as a college of citizenship on conservative and constitutional lines as a memorial to Bonar Law. After various changes, it was in 1959 converted into a management training centre with the backing of major British industries.

ASHTON, Sir Frederick (1906–). British dancer and choreographer. B. in Ecuador, he was trained under Massine and Marie Rambert, subsequently producing and dancing for the Rambert and Camargo ballets. Joining the Vic-Wells in 1935, he was knighted in 1963 and succeeded De Valois as director of the Royal Ballet. Later ballets incl. *Marguerite and Armand* (1963) based on Dumas and *The Dream* (1964) on Shakespeare.

ASHTON UNDER LYNE. Market and manufacturing town (bor.) of Lancs, England, 6½ m. E. of Manchester, on the Tame. Coal-mining and cotton are the chief industries. Pop. (1961) 50,165.

ASH WEDNESDAY. The first day of Lent, so called from the use of ashes as a symbol of penance. In the Catholic Church, members of the congregation are marked on the forehead with a cross in ash, obtained by burning the palms from Palm Sunday of the previous year. The ceremony was abandoned in the C. of E. in the 17th cent., the service of Commination taking its place.

ASIA. The largest of the continents, forming the larger eastern part of Eurasia and the main land-mass of the old world. It occupies ⅓ of the total land surface of the globe, stretching from within the Arctic Circle almost to the Equator, the most northerly point being Cape Chelyuskin, 78° N., the most southerly Cape Romania, at the tip of the Malayan peninsula, 1° N. The E. Indian islands extend to 10° S. of the Equator. The continent, which has an area of about 17,000,000 sq. m., is surrounded by the Arctic, Pacific, and Indian Oceans on the N., E., and S., and adjoins Europe along the Urals, and the shores of the Caspian, Black, and Mediterranean Seas. The isthmus of Suez, cut in two by the Suez canal, joins A. to Africa, while Bering Strait in the N.E., at its narrowest 45 m. wide, separates it from America.

Geography. There are 5 main geographical divisions: (1) The central triangular mountain mass, composed of a number of huge ranges diverging from the Pamir region, and including the Himalayas with the highest mountains in the world. N. of the Himalayas is the great Tibetan plateau, bounded on the N. by the Kunlun Mountains. To the N. of the plateau lie a series of ranges and enclosed basins, most notable of which is the Tarim basin. The Gobi (desert) occupies a vast plateau of central A. (2) The S.W. plateaux and ranges, which form the complicated relief of Afghanistan, Baluchistan, and Persia. (3) The northern lowlands, stretching from the central mountainous mass to the Arctic Ocean, and drained by several huge rivers, e.g. Ob, Yenisei, Lena, which are frozen over for much

TERRITORIAL DIVISIONS OF ASIA

Territory	Area in 1,000 sq. m.	Pop. in 1,000s	Capital
Afghanistan	250	11,000	Kabul
Arab Emirates, Fed. of			
Bahrein	·23	182	Manama
Qatar	4	75	Doha
Trucial States ...	32	110	—
Bhutan	18	700	Thimphu
*Brunei	2·26	127	Brunei
Burma	262	25,800	Rangoon
Cambodia ...	70	6,260	Phnôm-penh
*Ceylon	25	11,504	Colombo
Chinese Republic	3,363	706,000	Peking
Formosa ...	14	12,993	Taipeh
Tibet	470	1,300	Lhasa
*Cyprus	3·57	614	Nicosia
*Hong Kong ...	·39	3,834	Victoria
*India	1,174	500,000	Delhi
*Sikkim ...	2·7	162	Gangtok
Indonesia, Rep. o	895	112,300	Djakarta
Iraq	172	8,261	Baghdad
Israel	8	2,657	Jerusalem
*Jammu & Kashmir	86	3,584	Srinagar
Japan	142	98,281	Tokyo
Jordan	37	2,100	Amman
Korea:			
North	47	12,500	Pyongyang
South	38	29,207	Seoul
Kuwait	6	468	Kuwait
Laos	91	2,300	Luang Prabang and Vientiane
Lebanon ...	3·4	1,750	Beirut
*Malaysia, Fed. of:			Kuala Lumpur
E. Malaysia ...	77	1,440	
W. Malaysia ...	51	8,415	
Maldive Islands...	·115	96	Malé
Mongolian Republic	600	1,120	Ulan Bator
Muscat and Oman	82	750	Muscat
Nepal	54	9,500	Katmandu
*Pakistan ...	365	93,720	Islamabad
Persia (Iran) ...	633	25,781	Tehran
Philippine Rep.	116	27,087	Manila (Quezon)
Portuguese Overseas Provinces			
Macao (China)	·006	200	Macao
Timor ...	7·33	517	Dili
Saudi Arabia ...	·800	6,000	Mecca and Riyadh
*Singapore ...	·224	1,955	Singapore
Syria	72	4,565	Damascus
Thailand ...	198	32,000	Bangkok
Turkey-in-Asia ...	285	31,391	Ankara
U.S.S.R. (Asiatic)			
Kazakh S.S.R.	1,062	12,410	
Kirghiz S.S.R.	76	2,700	
R.S.F.S.R. in Asia	4,923	32,000	
Tadzhik S.S.R.	55	2,654	
Turkmen S.S.R.	187	1,971	
Uzbek S.S.R....	157	10,890	
Vietnam:			
North	63	17,800	Hanoi
South	66	15,100	Saigon
Yemen	75	4,500	San'a and Ta'iz
Yemen, Rep. of	112	1,500	Madinet al-Shaab
	17,333·305	1,890,131	

*Within the British Commonwealth

of their course for some 6 months of the year. Great floods occur in spring when the rivers are full and their mouths still frozen. (4) The eastern margin and the islands, where a large part of the pop. is concentrated. The lowlands are crossed by large rivers, e.g. Menam, Mekong, Si-Kiang, Yangtze Kiang, and Hwang Ho. Off the E. coast of A. lie the islands of Sakhalin, the Kuriles, Japan, Formosa, etc., while off the S.E. coasts lies the great group of the E. Indian islands, with Sumatra, Java, Borneo, the Philippines, and hundreds of others. Other small groups lie off India and Burma. (5) The southern plateaux and river plains which include the ancient masses of Arabia, the Deccan, and the alluvial plains of the Euphrates and Tigris, Indus, Ganges, and Irrawaddy.

Climate. Climatically, A. experiences great extremes and contrasts, the heart of the continent becoming bitterly cold in winter and greatly heated in summer. It is this fact, with the resulting pressure and wind systems, that is basically responsible for the Asiatic monsoons, which bring heavy rain to all S.E. Asia, China, and Japan, between May and October, with a more or less dry season the other half year. The most southerly latitudes have an equatorial climate, while the far N. is arctic.

Vegetation and Agriculture. The vegetational cover varies with the climate, from tropical rain forest, through temperate grassland, to semi-desert scrub. In the wet tropical parts the main crop is rice, the staple food crop of Asiatic peoples. Where rainfall or temperature is unsuited to rice, millet, maize, wheat, or soya bean takes its place. Cotton, jute, tea, rubber, dates and other fruits, olives, and tobacco are grown and silk is reared where the climate is suitable. Timber is an important product from the coniferous woods of Siberia, the hardwood forests of China, and the tropical zones, where teak is found.

ASIA, Soviet Central. Formerly Russian Turkestan, it consists of the Kazakh, Uzbek, Tadzhik and Kirghiz S.S.Rs. Unsatisfactory agricultural production, due in part to nationalist sentiments among the population, led in 1962 to the establishment of a Central Asian Bureau directly responsible to the Party Praesidium, in order to strengthen control from Moscow.

ASIA MINOR. Historic name for a part of W. Asia virtually contiguous with TURKEY-IN-ASIA.

ASIENTO (ahsē-en'tō; Span., 'contract'). Name given to the treaty of 1713, whereby British traders were permitted by Spain to introduce 144,000 Negro slaves into the Spanish-American colonies in the course of the next 30 years. In 1750 the right was bought out by the Spanish government for £100,000.

ASKHABAD. Another transliteration of ASHKHABAD.

ASMARA (asmah'ra). Town in Ethiopia, N.E. Africa, cap. of Eritrea. About 40 m. S.W. of Massawa on the Red Sea, it is a communications centre, with an airfield and is a growing industrial centre. Pop. (1965) 137,700.

ASNIÈRES (ahnē-ār') N.W. suburb of Paris, France, on the left bank of the Seine; a boating centre and pleasure resort.

ASŌ'KA (reigned 264–228 B.C.). Indian king, who made Buddhism the state religion. The grandson of Chandragupta, founder of the Maurya dynasty, he reigned over the ancient kingdom of Magadha, became converted to Buddhism, issued edicts enjoining the adoption of the leading tenets of the new faith, and had these carved on pillars (many of which have survived), and on the walls of caves, rocks, etc.

ASP, or Aspic. Name applied to several species of poisonous snakes. The A. of S. Europe (*Vipera aspis*) is a species of viper closely allied to the adder. The Egyptian horned A. (*Cerastes cornutus*) is supposed to have been the one with which Cleopatra ended her life. The African A. (*Naja haje*) is related to the cobras.

ASPA'RAGUS. Genus of plants of the lily family (Liliaceae). *A. officinalis* is cultivated, and the young shoots are eaten as a vegetable.

ASPA'SIA (fl. 440 B.C.). Mistress of Pericles, the Athenian statesman; since she was b. in Miletus their marriage was not recognized by Athenian law, but their son, Pericles, was subsequently legitimized. Her salon was a famous meeting-place for the celebrities of Athens.

ASPEN. Species (*Populus tremula*) of poplar (q.v.).

A'SPHALT. A mixture of different hydrocarbons forming a kind of semi-solid, brown or black bitumen. Considerable natural deposits occur round the Dead Sea and in the Philippines, Cuba, Venezuela, and in the pitch lake of Trinidad. Bituminous limestone occurs at Neufchâtel. A. is mixed with rock chips to form paving material, and the purer kinds are used for insulating material and for waterproofing masonry.

A'SPHODEL. Genus of plants (*Asphodelus*) belonging to the Liliaceae. *A. albus*, the white A. or king's spear, is found in Italy and Greece, sometimes covering large areas, and providing grazing for sheep. *A. luteus* is the yellow A. These beautiful plants were connected by the Greeks with the dead, and were supposed to grow in the Elysian fields.

ASPIDI'STRA. Small genus of Asiatic Liliaceae. The broad-leaved Japanese A. (*A. elatior*) survives much ill-treatment as an indoor plant, and was popular in Britain in the Victorian parlour.

A'SPIRIN. Name of drug given by the firm of Bayer, Meister & Lucius to a synthetic acety.salicylic acid which they invented in the early years of the 20th cent., and which soon became immensely popular as a household remedy for headaches and minor pains.

ASPLE'NIUM. Genus of ferns of the family Polypodiaceae, and generally known as spleenworts.

ASQUITH, Herbert Henry, 1st earl of Oxford and Asquith (1852–1928). British Liberal statesman. B. in Yorks, he was ed. at the City of London School and Balliol Coll., Oxford, and was called to the Bar in 1876. Elected M.P. in 1886, he was Home Sec. in Gladstone's 1892–5 govt. and in 1905 he became Chancellor of the Exchequer in Campbell-Bannerman's govt.; he introduced the 1st provision for old age pensions, and on the P.M.'s death he succeeded him.

The rejection by the Lords of Lloyd George's budget in 1909 produced a political crisis. In 2 general elections in 1910 the Liberals were returned to power with reduced majorities; the budget was passed, and the Parliament Act (1911) limited the Lords' right to veto legislation. The Home Rule Bill (1912) met with even fiercer opposition, until the outbreak of the F.W.W. temporarily united the nation.

A coalition govt. formed in May 1915 lasted till the reverses suffered by the Allies forced A. to resign in Dec. 1916, when he was succeeded by Lloyd George. At the 1918 election A. and his followers were heavily defeated, he himself losing the seat he had held for 32 years. He returned to the House in 1920.

After the collapse of the coalition in 1923 an alliance was formed between the followers of A. and Lloyd George. The Liberals held the balance of power in the next parliament, and it was A.'s support which enabled the Labour Party to take office. Defeated in the 1924 general election, he was raised to the peerage in 1925, and remained leader of the Liberal Party until 1926, when he resigned following dissensions over the general strike.

His eldest son Raymond A. (1878–1916) was killed in action in the F.W.W.; his 2nd son Herbert A. (1881–1947), barrister, poet and novelist, m. Lady Cynthia Charteris (1887–1960), dau. of the 11th earl of Wemyss, who wrote reminiscences and a diary. Most famous of his children are, Lady Asquith of Yarnbury (1887–1969) who, as Lady Violet Bonham-Carter (she m. in 1915 Sir Maurice Bonham-Carter, who d. 1960), was an active Liberal, being pres. of the Party Organization 1945–7: *see* GRIMOND. In 1964 she was created a life peeress, taking the title Lady A. Anthony A. (1902–68), director of such films as *Quiet Wedding, The Winslow Boy* and *The Millionairess*; and Elizabeth (1897–1945) who m. Prince Antoine Bibesco and wrote short stories, novels and poems. Both the last-named were his children by his 2nd wife, Margot Tennant (1868–1945), daughter of a Glasgow ironmaster, whom he m. in 1894 and

FAMOUS ASSASSINATIONS

B.C.		A.D.	
Sennacherib of Assyria	681	Humbert I of Italy	1900
Hipparchus, tyrant of Athens	514	W. McKinley	1901
Philip II of Macedon	336	Alexander and Draga of Serbia	1903
Julius Caesar	44	Carlos of Portugal	1908
		George I of Greece	1913
A.D.		Archduke Francis Ferdinand	1914
Caligula, Roman emperor	41	Field Marshal Sir H. H. Wilson	1922
Domitian	96	Paul Doumer	1932
Thomas à Becket	1170	Dr. Dollfuss	1934
James I of Scotland	1437	Alexander of Yugoslavia	1934
James III of Scotland	1488	Leon Trotsky	1940
William the Silent	1584	Reinhard Heydrich	1942
Henry III of France	1589	Lord Moyne	1944
Henry IV of France	1610	Mahatma Gandhi	1948
Duke of Buckingham	1628	Count Bernadotte	1948
Prince Wallenstein	1634	Abdullah of Jordan	1951
J. P. Marat	1793	Liaquat Ali Khan	1951
Paul I of Russia	1801	Feisal II	1958
Spencer Perceval	1812	J. F. Kennedy	1963
Abraham Lincoln	1865	Tafawa-Balewa	1966
J. A. Garfield	1881	H. F. Verwoerd	1966
Alexander II of Russia	1881	M. Luther King	1968
Lord F. Cavendish	1882	R. F. Kennedy	1968
M. F. Carnot	1894		

who was a celebrated wit. Her vols. of memoirs offended many by their lack of reticence.

ASS. A mammal (*Asinus*), related to the horse, zebra, and quagga, and with them constituting the family Equidae. The typical form is the African A., which is the source of our domestic breeds. Apart from its familiar 'braying roar', it differs from the horse (*Equus*) chiefly in its smaller size, much larger ears, tufted tail, characteristic fur and markings, narrower hoofs adapted for sure-footed traversing of rocky hillsides. The colour is usually grey.

ASS (Nubian)

ASSAM. Indian state lying between E. Pakistan and Burma, consisting mainly of the valleys of the Surma and Brahmaputra and a surrounding fringe of jungle-clad mountains. The cap. is temporarily Shillong: shared with Meghalaya 1968–70, when it was agreed a new cap. should be built for A. Area, 38,388 sq. m.; pop. (1961) 11,860,059.

Part of British India from 1826, A. in 1874 was made a separate prov. and in 1947 was included in the Dominion of India, save for most of the district of Silhet, which went to Pakistan. Tea is the principal industry, and 3/5ths of Indian tea comes from A. Oil has been worked since 1888, and the Digboi field is important. Rice, coal, and timber are produced.

The Garo, Khasi, and Jaintia tribal hill areas formed an autonomous state within A. 1968–70, which as Meghalaya became a full state of the Union in 1970. Area 8,706 sq. m.; pop. (1970) 900,000, its cap. being Shillong.

ASSASSINATION. Treacherous and violent murder, especially of royal or public personages. Some of the famous As. in history are given in the Table.

ASSAYING. The determination of the quantity of a given chemical substance present in a given amount of a sample to be tested. Usually it refers to determining the purity of the precious metals. The assay may be carried out by 'wet' methods, when the sample is wholly or partially dissolved in some suitable reagent (often an acid), or by 'dry' or 'fire' methods, in which fusion techniques are used.

ASSENT, Royal. Formal consent given by a British sovereign to the passage of a bill through parliament, after which it becomes an Act of Parliament. The last instance of a royal refusal was the rejection of the Scottish Militia Bill of 1702 by Queen Anne. The ceremony in the House of Lords, with representatives of the House of Commons being summoned, and commissioners usually acting on behalf of the Sovereign, has normally been replaced from 1967 (to save debating time) by the A. being given by Letters Patent, i.e. the Lord Chancellor in the Lords, and the Speaker in the Commons, make a formal announcement that A. has been given.

ASSISI (ahsē′sē). Town of Umbria, Italy, 12 m E.S.E. of Perugia. It is the birthplace of St. Francis and the Franciscan monastery, completed in 1253 contains his tomb. The churches of St. Francis are adorned with frescoes by Giotto, Cimabue, and others. Pop. *c*. 30,000.

ASSJUT. Alternative transliteration of ASYUT.

ASSIZES. In Britain, the courts held by the judges of the High Court in each co. to try civil and criminal cases. They were abolished under the Courts Act (1971). *See* LAW COURTS.

ASSOCIATION FOOTBALL. *See* FOOTBALL.

ASSOCIATED STATE of the United Kingdom. Status proposed in a British Colonial Office White Paper in 1965, as a solution for the problems of the Leeward and Windward Is. It involves full internal self-govt., leaving Britain responsible for external relations and defence, and was first adopted by Antigua in 1966.

ASSUAN. Alternative transliteration of ASWAN.

ASSUMPTION. Principal feast of the Blessed Virgin in the R.C. Church, held on 15 Aug., when her translation into heaven is commemorated.

ASSY. Village and sanatorium in Haute-Savoie, France, 3,280 ft. above sea level, where the church of Notre Dame de Toute Grace, begun in 1937, consecrated 1950, is adorned by Braque, Chagall, Matisse, Derain, Rouault, and other artists.

ASSYRIA. Empire of antiquity in the Near East. The land of A. originally consisted of a narrow strip of alluvial soil on each side of the Tigris, starting where the Lower Zab joins the river, and reaching to the foothills beyond Dur-Sharrukin, the old city of Sargon. The area was settled about 3500 B.C., and the empire collapsed in 612 B.C.

Sumerian civilization in Mesopotamia came to an end about 2500 B.C., with the rise to power of Sargon of Akkad; for nearly 200 years A. was subject first to the dynasty of Akkad and then to the Gutians, barbarians from the north. The first Assyrian kings are mentioned during the wars following the decline of the 3rd dynasty of Ur. For many centuries yet, however, A. was under Babylonian and subsequently Egyptian suzerainty. About 1450 B.C. a fresh resurgence of A. began. Under king Ashur-uballit (reigned *c*. 1380–1340 B.C.) the future greatness of A. as a military power was laid. His work was continued by Adad-nirari I, Shalmaneser I, and Tukulti-enurta I, who conquered Babylonia and assumed the title of king of Sumer and Akkad. During the reign of Nebuchadrezzar I (1150–1110 B.C.), A. was subject to Babylonia, but Tiglath-pileser I threw off the yoke. In the Aramaean invasions, most of the ground gained was lost. From the accession of Adad-nirari II in 911 B.C. A. pursued a triumphant course of expansion and conquest, culminating in the mastery of Elam, Mesopotamia, Syria, Palestine, the Arabian marches, and finally of Egypt. Of this period the O.T. records and many 'documents' such as the Black Obelisk celebrating the conquest of Shalmaneser III in the 9th cent. B.C. survive.

The reign of Ashur-nazir-pal II (885–860 B.C.) was spent in unceasing warfare, in which he is said to have introduced 'frightfulness' as evidenced by many bas-reliefs. Shalmaneser III warred against the Syrian states. At the battle of Qarqar (854 B.C.) the Assyrian advance received a setback, and there followed a period of decline. The final period of Assyrian ascendancy began with the accession of Tiglath-pileser III (746–728 B.C.). Sargon, Sennacherib, Esarhaddon, and Ashurbanipal raised A. to the highest peak of its glory, culminating in the conquest of Egypt by Esarhaddon in 671 B.C. From this time the empire seems to have fallen into decay, and a union of Nabopolassar of Babylonia and Cyaxares of Media led to its destruction. Nineveh was destroyed, and A. became a Median province and subsequently a principality of the Persian empire.

Much of Assyrian religion, law, social structure and artistic achievement was based on, or derived from, neighbouring sources. The Assyrians adopted the cuneiform script invented by the Sumerians, and took over the Sumerian pantheon, although their national god, Ashur (Assur), assumed the chief place in the cult. They adopted in the main the Sumerian structure of society. The famous library of Ashurbanipal excavated at Nineveh witnesses to the thoroughness with which Babylonian culture was being assimilated. See BABYLONIA.

ASTAIRE, Fred (1899–   ). American dancer. B. in Omaha, Nebraska, he danced in partnership with his sister Adele A. (1898–   ) from 1916 until his mar. with Lord Charles Cavendish, younger son of the Duke of Devonshire, in 1932. Entering films in 1933, he appeared in *Roberta, Top Hat, Follow the Fleet, Easter Parade, Funny Face*, and others which contained many sequences designed by himself. Most famous of his later partners was Ginger Rogers.

ASTARTE. Semitic goddess, the Ashtoreth of the Bible. She was the embodiment of the female principle, a great nature goddess watching over fertility, and her rites provided occasion for sexual licence.

ASTATINE. Symbol At, at. no. 85, at. wt. 210; halogen-like and highly radioactive. It is artificially made by bombarding bismuth in a cyclotron.

A'STER, or Starwort. Genus of plants of the Compositae, belonging to the same division as the daisy. The sea aster (*A. tripolium*) grows wild on sea cliffs in the S.W. of England, but many more species are familiar as cultivated garden flowers. These include the Michaelmas Daisy (*A. tradescanti*). The China aster (*Callistephus hortensis*) belongs to a closely allied genus; it was introduced to Europe from China and Japan in the early 18th cent.

ASTEROIDS. The As., more properly known as Minor Planets, are small bodies circling the Sun between the paths of Mars and Jupiter – though a few, such as Eros, depart from the main swarm and may approach the Earth fairly closely. The largest A., Ceres, is 430 miles in diameter, and was discovered by Piazzi in 1801. It has been suggested that the As. were formed as the result of the break-up of an old planet or planets, but proof of this theory is very difficult to obtain. Only one A. (Vesta) is ever visible to the naked eye. See ICARUS.

ASTHMA (asth'- or as'ma). Disease distinguished by recurring attacks of breathlessness, caused by a spasm of the diaphragm or breathing tubes, or congestion of the membrane lining the tubes. *Ordinary A.* is essentially a reaction to a foreign protein, e.g. dust, eggs, milk, and the hair or scurf of an animal. As such it belongs to the same group of diseases as hay-fever, nettlerash, and some forms of epilepsy – the so-called allergic diseases. *Cardiac A.* is a distinct

ASSYRIA. A temple statue (*left*) of Ashur-nazir-pal II and (*right*) a bas-relief of a priest, wearing divine winged apparel and a bird-headed mask, taken from the royal palace at Nimrud and now in the British Museum.

condition, in which the breathlessness is caused by a form of heart disease.

ASTI (ahs'tē). City of Piedmont, 30 m. S.E. of Turin, on the Tanaro. It is the seat of a bishopric and has a Gothic cathedral. The sparkling wine of Asti prov. is famed. Pop. (1961) 60,217.

ASTON, Francis William (1877–1945). British physicist. From 1910 he worked in the Cavendish Laboratory, Cambridge. He pub. his *Isotopes* and received the Nobel Prize for chemistry in 1922. His researches were of the utmost value in the development of atomic theory.

ASTOR, John Jacob (1763–1848). American millionaire. B. near Heidelberg, in Germany, he set up as a fur trader in America, operating from the Great Lakes to the Pacific. He increased his wealth enormously by astute investment, and d. worth $30 million. His eldest son, WILLIAM BACKHOUSE A. (1792–1875), became known as the 'landlord of New York', and made a further fortune by land deals.

ASTOR, William Waldorf, 1st visct. (1848–1919). Great-grandson of John Jacob A. (q.v.), he was an American diplomat and writer before becoming a naturalized Briton in 1899. In 1917 he was made a visct. His son, WALDORF ASTOR, 2nd visct. (1879–1952), was Cons. M.P. for Plymouth 1910–9, when he succeeded to the peerage. He was chief proprietor of the *Observer*, Lord Mayor of Plymouth, 1939–44, and was keenly interested in the Turf.

He m. in 1906 Nancy Witcher Langhorne (1879–1964), LADY ASTOR. B. in Virginia, U.S.A., she succeeded her husband as M.P. for Plymouth (1919–45), and was the 1st woman M.P. to take her seat in the House of Commons. An opponent of the Drink Trade, she was a famous political hostess, and govt. policy was said to be decided before the S.W.W. at her Cliveden (q.v.) house parties. Their eldest son WILLIAM ASTOR, 3rd visct. (1907–66), was a Cons. M.P. 1933–45 and 1951–2, and was succeeded by his only son WILLIAM ASTOR, 4th visct. (1951–   ); another son DAVID ASTOR (1912–   ) ed. the *Observer* from 1948.

JOHN ASTOR, 1st baron A. of Hever (1886–1971), younger son of the 1st visct., was Unionist M.P. for Dover 1922–45, and as principal proprietor of *The Times* 1922–66 played a great part in securing for that newspaper a position of unrivalled influence.

ASTRAKHAN (ahstrahkhahn'). City in the R.S.F.S.R., on the delta of the Volga, cap. of A. region. Anciently a Tartar cap., it became Russian in 1556. It is the chief port for the Caspian fisheries. Pop. (1967) 361,000.

ASTROLOGY (astrol'oji). So-called art or science of foretelling the future from the positions of the stars (Gk. *astron*, star; *legein*, speak). The superstitious belief that the fortunes of men and nations are affected for good or evil by the movements of the stars and planets flourished in ancient Babylon. It spread to the Mediterranean world, and was widely held among the Greeks and Romans. During the Middle Ages A. had a powerful vogue, and astrological beliefs are frequently encountered in Elizabethan and Jacobean literature. In spite of the rise of modern science, popular interest in A. has never completely died. The 1st edition of *Old Moore's Almanac* appeared in 1700, and there have been annual editions since. Astrological forecasts are a prominent feature in popular newspapers and journals.

The astrologer 'casts a horoscope' based on the date and hour of his subject's birth, i.e. draws a diagram showing the position at that moment of the sun and moon, the planets, and the 12 signs of the Zodiac. These heavenly bodies are supposed to represent different character traits and influences, and by observing their positions and inter-relations the astrologer professes to assess the person's character and to foretell the main outlines of his career.

ASTRONAUT. U.S. term for man making flights into space. *See* SPACE RESEARCH.

ASTRONOMER ROYAL. Title of the astronomer in charge of the Royal Observatory estab. at Greenwich, England, in 1675. Since 1958 the observatory has been located at Herstmonceux Castle, Sussex, to avoid the obscuring smoke and lights of London.

The A.R. besides his strictly astronomical work has various public duties relating to weather, time, Summer Time, and the broadcast time signal (rhythmic and pips). The A.R. for Scotland is Prof. H. A. Brück.

ASTRONOMERS ROYAL			
John Flamsteed	1675	Sir W. H. M. Christie	
Edmund Halley	1720		1881
James Bradley	1742	Sir Frank Dyson	1910
Nathaniel Bliss	1762	Sir H. Spencer Jones	
Nevil Maskelyne	1765		1933
John Pond	1811	Sir Richard Woolley	
Sir Geo. Biddell Airy	1835		1956
		Sir Martin Ryle	1972

ASTRONOMY. The science that deals with the celestial bodies – the Sun; the Moon; the planets and other members of the Solar System; the stars, and the galaxies. It is concerned with the positions and motions of these bodies; with the explanation of their motions; with their distances, sizes, masses, temperatures and physical conditions.

The oldest branch of A. – *observational A.* – is concerned with the appearances of the celestial bodies, and so provides the fundamental data. This leads on to *theoretical A.*, which deals with the interpretation of the observations according to mathematical and physical principles; the detailed mathematical explanation of the motions of the celestial bodies is known as *celestial mechanics*, and studies of the constitution of stars and galaxies come under the heading of *astrophysics*. Much more recently, *radio A.* has been developed, together with *radar A.*; the instruments used here are quite different from those of optical A., but have provided a great deal of information which could not have been obtained in any other way. The latest branch of astronomical science

is *rocket A.*, in which scientific instruments are flown beyond the dense lower layers of the Earth's atmosphere. Equipment has also been flown successfully by balloons up to altitudes of 80,000 ft.

There can be little doubt that A. is the oldest science in the world, since there are observational records from Babylonia, China and Ancient Egypt. The first true astronomers, however, were the Greeks, and the work of men such as Thales, Pythagoras, and Hipparchus will always be remembered. The Greeks knew that the Earth is a sphere, and not flat, as earlier peoples had believed; Eratosthenes of Cyrene even measured the size of the Earth with considerable accuracy. Star-catalogues were drawn up, the most celebrated being that of Hipparchus. Fortunately, the work of the Greek philosophers was summarized by Ptolemy of Alexandria in a great book which has survived in its Arab translation, the *Almagest*. The main defect of Greek A. was that the Earth was still regarded as the centre of the universe – though even this had been doubted by some philosophers, notably Aristarchus of Samos, who maintained that the Earth moves round the Sun.

Ptolemy, the last famous astronomer of the Greek school, died in or about the year A.D. 180, and little progress was made for some cents. When A. revived, it did so by way of the Arabs, who carried out theoretical researches from the 8th and 9th cents., and who also produced good star-catalogues. Unfortunately, true A. was handicapped by a general belief in the pseudo-science of astrology, and this continued to be the case until the end of the Middle Ages.

The dawn of a new era came in 1543, when a Polish canon, Copernicus, pub. a work entitled *De Revolutionibus Orbium Coelestium*, in which he demonstrated that the Sun, not the Earth, is the centre of the planetary system. Copernicus was wrong in many respects – for instance, he still believed that all celestial orbits must be perfectly circular – but he had taken the fundamental step. Tycho Brahe, of Denmark (q.v.), increased the accuracy of observations by means of improved instruments, allied to his own personal skill, and his observations were used by the German mathematician Johann Kepler (q.v.) to prove the validity of the Copernican system. However, there was considerable opposition to the idea of removing the Earth from its proud position in the centre of the universe; the Christian Church was openly hostile, and, ironically, Tycho Brahe never accepted the idea that the Earth could move round the Sun. Yet before the end of the 17th cent. the theoretical work of Sir Isaac Newton had placed celestial mechanics upon a really firm footing.

The telescope was invented in or about 1608, by Hans Lippershey in Holland, and was first applied to astronomy by the Italian scientist Galileo (q.v.) in the winter of 1609–1610. Immediately Galileo made a series of spectacular discoveries. He found the 4 satellites of Jupiter, which gave strong support to the Copernican theory; he saw the craters of the Moon, the phases of Venus, and the myriad faint stars of the Milky Way. His telescope was feeble by modern standards, and magnified only 30 times, but before long larger telescopes were built, and official observatories were established. Greenwich Observatory, for example, dates from 1675.

Galileo's telescope was a *refractor*; that is to say, it collected its light by means of a glass lens or object-glass. Certain difficulties led Newton, in 1671, to develop the *reflecting telescope*, in which the light is collected by means of a curved mirror. (Newton was not the first to suggest this principle, but he seems to have been the first to construct such an instrument.) Modern telescopes are of tremendous size. The largest refractor, at Yerkes Observatory, has a 40-inch lens, and the Hale reflector at Palomar, in the U.S.A., has a mirror 200 in. in diameter.

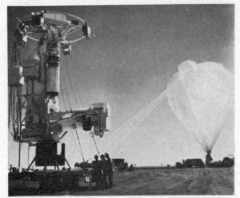

ASTRONOMY. Ready for launching at the Palestine Balloon Flight Station, Texas, the 36-inch telescope Stratoscope II which weighs 6,300 lb. is seen parked near the balloon inflation area prior to attachment to the flight train. Lifted to a height of 79,000 ft. it was then used to make an infra-red study of Mars and came down near Pulaski, Tennessee.
Photo: U.S. National Science Foundation.

Theoretical researches continued, and astronomy made rapid progress in all directions. New planets were discovered – Uranus in 1781, by Herschel, and Neptune in 1846, by Adams and Le Verrier; even more significant was the first measurement of the distance of a star, in 1838, when the German astronomer Bessel established that the star 61 Cygni lies at a distance of about 11 light-years. (A light-year is the distance travelled by light in one year; it is equal to about 5,880,000,000,000 miles.) Astronomical spectroscopy was developed, first by Fraunhofer in Germany and then by men such as Secchi and Huggins, while Kirchhoff successfully interpreted the spectra of the Sun and stars; and by the 1860s good photographs of the Moon had been obtained, so that by the end of the cent. photographic methods had started to play a leading role in research. Today, it is probably true to say that almost all serious work is carried out by photographic methods, and it is seldom that visual observations are made through the world's largest telescopes.

William Herschel (q.v.), probably the greatest observer in the history of A., investigated the shape of the star-system or galaxy during the latter part of the 18th cent., and concluded that the stars are arranged roughly in the form of a double-convex lens. Basically, Herschel was correct, though it is now known that he was wrong in placing the Sun near the centre of the system; in fact, the Sun is well out toward the edge, and lies some 25,000 to 30,000 light-years from the galactic nucleus. Herschel also studied the luminous 'clouds' or nebulae, and made the tentative suggestion that those nebulae capable of resolution into stars might be separate galaxies, far outside the Galaxy in which the Solar System is situated. It was not until 1923 that Hubble (q.v.), using the 100-in. reflector at the Mount Wilson Observatory, was able to prove the correctness of this view. It is now known that the 'starry nebulae' are galaxies in their own right, and that they lie at immense distances. The brightest galaxy visible from Europe, the Great Spiral in Andromeda (faintly visible to the naked eye), is more than 2,000,000 light-years away; the most remote galaxy so far measured lies at about 5,000 million light-years. It has also been found that the galaxies tend to form groups, and that each group is receding from each other group, so that the whole universe is in a state of expansion.

In the present cent. A. has made remarkable progress, and made use of new tools such as radio-astronomy and rockets which allow observation beyond Earth's shielding atmosphere. Yet we still know very little about the way the universe came into existence, and in the 1960s A. was to a certain extent in a state of flux. The modern concept of the structure of the universe rests largely on Hubble's Law, based on the observation of ordinary galaxies some few hundred thousand light years away, which relates the distance of an object to the amount spectra shift towards red—the red shift. However, objects such as quasars, discovered by optical and radio astronomers in the 1960s, have been shown to have wide variations in individual characteristics, e.g. one quasar may have differing red shifts for different aspects of its spectrum.

ASTROPHYSICS. The science that is (a) physical astronomy, the study of the physical conditions in the heavenly bodies; and (b) astronomical physics, a branch of physics in which the behaviour of matter and radiant energy is studied under conditions unattainable on the earth. From this point of view a star or a nebula is a special laboratory in which extremes of temperature and density unknown in terrestrial laboratories are reached, and the effect of these conditions on the familiar elements of chemistry is ascertained. An approach to these extreme conditions is attempted in thermonuclear machines.

ASTU'RIAS. An ancient Spanish prov., once a kingdom. The eldest son of a king of Spain was called prince of A. It corresponds to the modern prov. of Oviedo.

ASTU'RIAS, Miguel Angel (1899–   ). Guatemalan author and diplomat. He has pub. poetry, Guatemalan legends, and novels, such as *The President* (1946), in which he has attacked Latin-American dictatorships and 'Yankee imperialism'. He became ambassador to France in 1966 and in 1967 was awarded a Nobel prize.

ASUNCION (ahsōōntheōn'). Cap. of the S. American rep. of Paraguay, on the Paraguay river. Founded in 1537, it is a commercial centre with good docks. There are 2 univs. Pop. (1962) 288,882.

ASWAN (ahswahn'). Town of the United Arab Rep., in Upper Egypt, cap. of the sparsely populated administrative division of A. It stands near the 1st or

ASTRONOMY. The centre of the galaxy lies in the direction of Sagittarius (the Archer), which is therefore the richest part of the Milky Way. The galactic nucleus can never be seen because light from it is blocked by obscuring material, but it may be studied by means of radio telescopes, since radio waves are not similarly blocked. In this photograph of the Small Star Cloud in Sagittarius it is also possible to see dark patches, representing nebulae which have no suitable stars to excite them to luminosity.
Courtesy of Lick Observatory, Univ. of California

lowest cataract of the Nile, and has famous ruins. Pop. (1960) 48,000. The A. High Dam (1960–70) some 5 m. upstream has a storage capacity of 5,500 m. cu. metres and maintains the level of the Nile constant throughout the year without flooding.

ASYUT (ahsyoot'). City of the United Arab Rep., in Upper Egypt, cap. of A. prov. It is near the Nile, 200 m. S. of Cairo. An ancient Graeco-Egyptian city, it has many tombs of 11th and 12th dynasty nobles. Asyut Univ. was founded 1957. The A. barrage (1902: later much enlarged) supplies much of Middle Egypt with irrigation water. Pop. (1960) 122,000.

ATACAMA (ahtahkah'mah). Extensive desert in S. America, covering large areas of northern Chile. Inland are mountains, and the coastal area is rainless and barren. Silver and copper mines are worked, and in the N. Chile coastal province of A. are extensive nitrate deposits.

ATAHUALPA (ahtahwahl'pah) (*c.* 1502–33). Last of the Incas of Peru. He was taken prisoner in 1532 when the Spaniards arrived, and agreed to pay a huge ransom, but was accused of plotting against Pizarro and sentenced to be burnt. On his consenting to Christian baptism, the sentence was commuted to strangling.

ATALA'NTA. In Greek mythology, a huntress of Arcadia who declared that a suitor must first compete with her in a foot race; if he lost he must die. Milanion received from Aphrodite three golden apples which he dropped one by one during the race. A. stopped to pick them up and Milanion won.

ATATÜRK (1881–1938). Name assumed by Mustafa Kemal Pasha, Turkish statesman and soldier. B. at Salonika, the son of a customs official, he distinguished himself at a military academy, but was banished in 1904 to Damascus for having joined a revolutionary society, Later he was pardoned and promoted, and was largely responsible for the successful defence of the Dardanelles against the British in 1915. In 1918 he was sent into Anatolia to carry through the demobilization of the Turkish forces in accordance with the armistice terms, but instead estab. a provisional govt. opposed to that of Constantinople (under Allied control), and in 1921 led the Turkish armies against the Greeks who had occupied a large part of Asia Minor. He checked the invaders at the 21-day battle of the Sakaria, 23 Aug. to 13 Sept. 1921, for which he was granted the title of Ghazi (the Victorious) by the Assembly, and within a year had finally expelled the Greeks from Turkish soil. War with the British was averted by the statesmanship of K. and Gen. Harrington, and Turkey in Europe passed under K.'s control. On 29 Oct. 1923, Turkey was proclaimed a rep. with Kemal as 1st president. A one-party dictatorship was set up and a policy of consistent and radical westernization was embarked upon. In 1934 Kemal adopted the surname of Atatürk (Head of the Turks).

ATHANASIAN CREED. One of the three ancient creeds of the Christian Church consisting in the main of a definition of the doctrine of the Trinity. Although not written for many years after the death of Athanasius, it came to be attributed to him as he was the chief upholder of Trinitarian doctrine.

ATHANA'SIUS (*c.* 298–373). Christian bishop of Alexandria and reputed author of the Athanasian creed. Probably b. at Alexandria, he was a disciple of St. Anthony the hermit, and became early prominent in the great Arian controversy. Arianism was officially condemned at the council of Nicaea in 325, and in 328 A. was appointed bishop of Alexandria. Banished in 335 by the emperor Constantine because of his intransigence towards the defeated Arians, in 346 he was restored to his see, but suffered three more banishments before his final reinstatement about 366.

A'THEISM (Gk., without god). Disbelief in, or denial of, the existence of God or gods. A. takes many forms and expressions. *Dogmatic A.* asserts that there is no God. *Sceptical A.* maintains that the finite mind of man is so constituted as to be incapable of discovering that there is or is not a God. *Critical A.* holds that the evidence for Theism is inadequate. This is akin to *Philosophical A.* which fails to find evidence of a God manifest in the universe. *Speculative A.* comprises the belief of those who, like Kant, find it impossible to demonstrate the existence of God – although, again like Kant, they may believe in the existence of God on other grounds.

There were Atheists in ancient Greece, e.g. Democritus, Leucippus, and their followers of the materialistic schools. In Rome the outstanding A. was Lucretius. The early Christians were called Atheists by the pagans since they denied the familiar gods of the Roman world; and in the centuries of Christian domination the term A. was applied in a similarly opprobrious fashion by the members of one sect and church to those of other sects and churches. Buddhism has been called an atheistic religion since it does not postulate any Supreme Being. The Jains are similarly atheistic; and so are those who adopt the Sankhya system of philosophy in Hinduism. Following the revolution of 1917 Soviet Russia became definitely atheistic.

A'THELNEY, Isle of. 'Island' of firm ground, rising *c.* 40 ft. above the surrounding marshland, *c.* 7 m. from Taunton in Somerset, England: the name means 'isle of princes'. In 878 Alfred the Great built a fort here as his guerrilla H.Q. against the Danes, and the legend of his burning the cakes is set on A. *See illus.* p. 76.

ATHELSTAN (*c.* 895–939). King of the Mercians and West Saxons. Son of Edward the Elder and grandson of Alfred the Great, he was crowned king in 925 at Kingston-on-Thames. He subdued parts of Cornwall and Wales, and in 937 defeated the Welsh, Scots, and Danes at Brunanburh.

ATHE'NA. Greek goddess, identified with the Roman Minerva, and supposed to have been b. from the head of Zeus fully grown and fully armed. She was the maiden goddess of wisdom and of the arts and crafts, and also goddess of war and protectress of the city of Athens, where was her most famous temple – the Parthenon or Maiden's Temple.

ATHENS. Capital city of modern Greece and of ancient Attica. Situated 5 m. inland N.E. of its port of Piraeus on the Gulf of Aegina, it is built around the rocky hills of the Acropolis (412 ft.) and the Areopagus (370 ft.), and is overlooked from the N.E. by the hill of Lycabettus (909 ft.). It lies in the S. of the central plain of Attica watered by the mountain streams of Cephissus and Ilissus.

The Acropolis (q.v.) dominates the city. Here stand architectural remains of the great days of ancient Greece, e.g. the Parthenon, the Erechtheum, and the temple of Athena Nikē. Near the site of the ancient Agora or market-place stands the Theseum, and S. of the Acropolis is the theatre of Dionysus. To the S.E. stand the gate of Hadrian and the columns of the temple of Olympian Zeus. Near by is the marble stadium built about 330 B.C. and restored in 1896.

Site first inhabited *c.* 3000 B.C. A. became the capital of a united Attica before 700 B.C. Captured and sacked by the Persians in 480, subsequently under Pericles it was the first city of Greece in power and culture. After the death of Alexander the Great the city fell into comparative decline, but it flourished as an intellectual centre until A.D. 529, when the philosophical schools were shut down by Justinian. In 1458 it was captured by the Turks who held it until 1833; it was chosen as the cap. of modern Greece in 1834. Among the modern buildings are the Royal Palace, and several museums. Pop. Greater A. (including Piraeus) (1961) 1,837,041.

ATHLETICS. The practice of athletic games – i.e.

games of skill and endurance, such as hurdling, running, javelin throwing, etc. – and physical exercises. The Greeks were among the first to organize athletic games; the first Olympic games were held about 2,500 years ago. The Romans usually held their games at the festivals of the gods. The Olympic Games (q.v.) were revived in 1896 and the Commonwealth Games are run along similar lines. In Britain, where A. proper is limited to field and track events, the Amateur Atheletic Association (1880) is the leading body. In the U.S., where team games are included, leading associations incl. the Amateur Athletic Union (1888) and – typical of the American interest in intercollegiate competition – the National Collegiate Athletic Association.

ATHELNEY. In 1693 the superbly worked 'Alfred Jewel' was found some miles W. of the Isle of Athelney. About 2½ in. long, it may have been the head of a bookmark and is of green, red and blue cloisonné enamel work: round the gold rim are the words Ælfred mec heht gewyrcan—Alfred had me made.

MEN'S WORLD ATHLETIC RECORDS

High Jump:
　7 ft. 5¾ in. V. Brumel (U.S.S.R.), 1963.

Long Jump:
　29 ft. 2½ in. B. Beamon (U.S.A.), 1968.

Triple Jump:
　57 ft. 0¾ in. V. Saneyev (U.S.S.R.), 1968.

Hammer:
　245 ft. 0 in. A. Bondarchuk (U.S.S.R.), 1969.

Discus:
　224 ft. 5 in. L. Silvester (U.S.A.), 1968.

Javelin:
　304 ft. 1 in. J. Kinnunen (Finland), 1969.

Pole Vault:
　18 ft. 0¼ in. Chris Papanicolaou (Greece), 1970.

Hurdling:
　120 yds. 13·2 sec. M. Lauer (Germany), 1959; L. Calhoun (1960), E. McCulloch (1967), E. Hall (1969), all U.S.A.
　440 yds. 48·8 sec. B. Mann (U.S.A.), 1970.

Walking: ·
　20 miles. 2 hrs. 31 min. 33 sec. A. Vedyakov (U.S.S.R.), 1958

Running:
　100 yds. 9·1 sec. R. Hayes (1963), J. Hines (1967) C. Greene (1967), J. Carlos (1969), all U.S.A., and H. Jerome (Canada), 1966.
　220 yds. T. Smith (U.S.A.), 1966.
　440 yds. 44·7 sec. C. Mills (U.S.A.), 1969.
　880 yds. 1 min. 44·9 sec. J. Ryun (U.S.A.), 1966.
　1 mile. 3 min. 51·1 sec. J. Ryun (U.S.A.) 1967.
　3 miles. 12 min. 50·4 sec. R. Clarke (Australia), 1966.
　6 miles. 26 min. 47·0 sec. R. Clarke (Australia), 1965.

ATHLONE. Town (U.D.) in Westmeath, Rep. of Ireland, on the Shannon, well known for its tweeds. The broadcasting station of Radio Eireann is near by. Pop. (1961) 9,624.

ATHOS. A peninsular promontory on the Macedonian coast of Greece. Its peak is a white marble pyramid, 6,670 ft. high. The promontory is occupied by a community of 20 Basilian monasteries inhabited by some 3,000 monks and lay brothers. No female creature is allowed within the peninsula.

ATKINS, Robert (1886–1972). Brit. actor-producer, remarkable for his series of Shakespeare and other plays at the Open Air Theatre, Regent's Park from 1933.

ATKINS, Tommy. Popular name for the British soldier. The earliest discoverable use of the name is in a specimen form included in an official handbook circulated by the War Office at the end of the Napoleonic War. A story that T.A. was a British soldier mortally wounded under Wellington in the Netherlands in 1794, and that the Duke chose his name to be used in an army document some 50 years

later, seems to have originated in an article by Col. Newnham-Davis in Printer's Pie.

ATKINSON, Sir Harry Albert (1831–92). New Zealand statesman. B. at Chester, he emigrated to N.Z. in 1855, entered Parliament in 1863, and from 1874 was thrice Prime Minister, and 4 times Treasurer.

ATLANTA. Cap. and largest city of Georgia, U.S.A. Founded as Terminus in 1837, and re-named in 1845, it was nearly destroyed in 1864 during the American Civil War. It has 2 universities and a college founded in 1885 for Negro students. Nearby Stone Mountain Memorial (190 ft. × 305 ft.), the world's largest stone carving, shows Jefferson Davis, Robert E. Lee, and Stonewall Jackson on horseback. Artists were Gutzon Borglum 1923–5, Augustus Lukeman 1925–8, and Walter Hancock 1963–70: the original design incl. many more figures. Pop. met. area (1970) 1,373,629.

ATLANTIC, Battle of the. Name given to the continuous battle fought in the Atlantic Ocean throughout the S.W.W. (1939–45) by the Royal Navy, the Merchant Navy, and Coastal Command aircraft, under the operational control of the Admiralty, against the sea and air power of Germany.

The battle opened on the first night of the War, when on 4 Sept. 1939 the Donaldson liner, Athenia, sailing from Glasgow to New York, was torpedoed by a German submarine off the Irish coast. The Germans tried U-boats, surface-raiders, indiscriminate mine-laying, and aircraft, but every enemy method was successfully countered by, e.g., the convoy system and degaussing. Outstanding incidents were the engagements in which the armed merchantmen Rawalpindi (23 Nov. 1939) and Jervis Bay (5 Nov. 1940) were sunk by German warships, and the destruction of the great German battleship Bismarck on 27 May 1941. The total number of U-boats destroyed by the Allies during the whole war was nearly 800. No fewer than 2,200 convoys of 75,000 merchant ships crossed the Atlantic.

ATLANTIC CHARTER. Declaration issued by Winston Churchill and President Roosevelt following meetings on board H.M.S. Prince of Wales and the U.S. carrier Augusta, in Aug. 1941. It stated that Britain and the U.S.A. sought no territorial aggrandizement; desired no territorial changes not according with the wishes of the peoples concerned; respected the rights of all peoples to choose their own form of government; wished to see self-government restored to the occupied countries; would further access by all states to trade and raw materials; desired international collaboration for the raising of economic standards; hoped to see a peace affording security to all nations and enabling them to cross the seas without hindrance; and proposed the disarmament of the aggressor states as a preliminary to general disarmament.

ATLANTIC CITY. City of U.S.A. on the coast of New Jersey, celebrated seaside and pleasure resort. Pop. (1960) 59,544.

ATLANTIC COLLEGE. International educational experiment conceived by Kurt Hahn (q.v.) and Air Marshal Sir Lawrence Darvell. The first A.C. (for boys of 17–18 drawn from N. America and Europe) was opened in 1962 in St. Donat's Castle (once owned by W. R. Hearst, q.v.), 14 m. W. of Cardiff, Wales, which was bought for the college by Antonin Besse.

ATLANTIC OCEAN. The sea lying between Europe and Africa on the E., and America on the W., and probably named after the fabulous island or continent of Atlantis. It extends from the Arctic to the Antarctic Ocean, being divided by the Equator into the North A. and South A., with a total area of 31,500,000 sq. m. Its average depth is just over 2,000 fathoms (more than 2 miles). Running N.–S. along the middle of the ocean is the Mid-Atlantic Ridge which separates two large troughs in each of which the depth reaches more than 4,000 fathoms. The N. Atlantic is the saltest of the main oceans, and the tides are larger than those of other oceans.

ATLANTIS. An island continent, which according to Plato once existed in the Atlantic opposite the Straits of Gibraltar, but foundered about 9,600 B.C. as a result of submarine convulsions. The story (as originally told by Egyptian priests to Solon) may refer to the volcanic eruption *c.* 1500 B.C. of Santorin (of which the is. Thera and Therasis *c.* 70 m. N. of Crete are the remains), causing the collapse of the empire of Minoan Crete by fire and tidal wave.

A'TLAS. In Greek mythology, one of the Titans who revolted against the gods; as a punishment A. was compelled to support the heavens upon his head and shoulders. Growing weary, he asked Perseus to turn him into stone, and he was transformed into Mt. Atlas. The use of the word to denote a book of maps was introduced in the 16th cent. by Mercator; such books had a frontispiece showing Atlas supporting the globe.

ATLAS. Mountain system of N. W. Africa, stretching for about 1,500 m. from the Atlantic coast of Morocco to the Gulf of Gabes, Tunisia, and lying between the Mediterranean on the N. and the Sahara on the S. Geologically the A. mts. compare with the Alps in age, but their structure is much less complex. They are recognized as the continuation of the great Tertiary fold mountain systems of Europe.

ATMOSPHERE. The air which surrounds and forms a permanent covering of the earth's surface. It is a mixture of gases which show no measurable variation near the surface of the earth except for the water vapour. The constitution of dry air from which all water vapour has been removed is as follows (percentage by volume): nitrogen 78·09; oxygen 20·95; argon 0·93; carbon dioxide 0·03. Included in the above are minute quantities of other gases, e.g. neon, helium, krypton, hydrogen, xenon, ozone, and radon, each less than 0·0001.

Atmospheric pressure is normally equivalent to 14·73 lb. per sq. in. but varies slightly. It decreases steadily as higher altitudes are reached.

ATOLL. *See* CORAL REEFS.

ATOM (Gk. *atomos*, indivisible). Name given to the very small, discrete particles of which all matter is composed. There are 100 kinds of A. which differ in chemical behaviour, and correspond to the 100 elements which cannot be broken up by chemical means into anything simpler.

Belief in the existence of As. dates back to the days of the ancient Greek natural philosophers, but it rested on entirely circumstantial evidence, since As. are much too small to be seen even by the microscope; the largest is only about a hundred-millionth of an inch across. Furthermore, they are in constant motion. Of recent times, however, various methods for detecting the presence of single As. have been devised, all making use of effects which can be produced by the energy of a rapidly-moving A. Rutherford showed that As. of certain radio-active elements shoot out spontaneously the so-called alpha rays, single As. of helium issuing with a speed of about 10,000 m. a sec. At this speed an A. has sufficient energy to produce a tiny speck of light when it hits a thin layer of phosphorescent zinc sulphide. Each A. causes a splash of light, and this momentary scintillation can be observed with a microscope. It is then possible to determine its path.

Until near the end of the last century it was believed that every A. was a complete unbreakable entity. Since then the modern theory of atomic structure has been worked out, largely by Rutherford, who by experiments with alpha particles showed that every A. consists of a very minute particle, only one 10,000th as big across as the atom, called the *nucleus*, surrounded by a distribution of particles of negative electricity called *electrons*.

All electrons have identical mass and charge. The different properties of the various chemical elements are due to the different number of electrons in the atom of each element. The simplest element, hydrogen, contains 1 electron; each atom of carbon contains 6; the most complex A. known in nature, that of

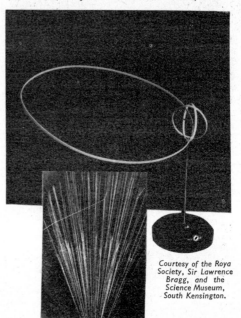

Courtesy of the Royal Society, Sir Lawrence Bragg, and the Science Museum, South Kensington.

ATOM. Lithium has the at. no. 3, and the path of the three electrons round the nucleus is shown by the white bands of the model: two move in compact circles, one in a wide ellipse. Below, a photograph of alpha-rays from thorium C[1]. One of the rays strikes the nucleus of a nitrogen atom, causing a transmutation. The ray is absorbed and a hydrogen proton ejected causing the transverse streak seen upper left.

ATOMIC ENERGY. The U.K. was a pioneer from 1955 in the conversion of nuclear fission energy into electricity with the Calder Hall type reactor. A major advance upon this type, however, was the gas-cooled reactor at Windscale, Cumberland, seen above.   *Photo: U.K.A.E.A.*

uranium, has 92. The mass of an A. of any kind is several thousand times as great as the mass of the electrons it contains. Moreover, As. in their normal state have no excess of electric charge. Save in hydrogen, each nucleus is composed of 2 kinds of particle, *protons* and *neutrons*. Each proton has a positive electric charge, equal in magnitude but opposite in sign to that of the electron; the neutrons have no charge. Proton and neutron have nearly equal mass, and this is about 1839 times as great as the mass of the electron. Since the proton and electron charges are equal and opposite and the A. as a whole has no charge, the number of protons within the nucleus of any A. must equal the number of electrons outside the nucleus. The number of units of positive charge (protons) in the nucleus is called the *atomic number*.

The problem of the basic structure of the neutrons and protons that make up atomic nuclei will be brought nearer solution when some fundamental (sub-atomic) particles discovered in recent high energy physics research are better understood. They incl. anti-particles (such as the anti-proton and anti-neutron) which are opposite in some properties but identical in others to known charged and neutral particles; hyperons, with masses greater than protons; and mesons, with masses intermediate between electrons and protons.

As. which have the same number of protons but differ in their number of neutrons are called *isotopes*; these have identical chemical properties since they have the same number of electrons. Most of the chemical elements consist of mixtures of two or more isotopes; e.g. about 1 atom in 4,000 of natural hydrogen contains 1 neutron in addition to the single proton that forms the nucleus of the ordinary hydrogen A. This kind of hydrogen is called heavy hydrogen or deuterium, and is denoted by the symbol H^2 as opposed to H^1 for the more plentiful isotope. At the other end of the list, natural uranium consists of 3 isotopes, U^{234}, U^{235}, and U^{238}, the last forming over 99 per cent of the mixture.

As. as a whole are held together by the electrical forces of attraction between each negative electron and the positive protons within the nucleus. The latter *repel* one another with relatively enormous forces; a nucleus holds together only because other forces, not of a simple electrical character, attract the protons and neutrons to one another. These additional forces act only so long as the protons and neutrons are virtually in contact with one another. If, therefore, a fragment of a complex nucleus, containing some protons becomes only slightly loosened from the main agglomeration of neutrons and protons, the strong natural repulsion between the protons will cause this fragment to fly apart from the rest of the nucleus with high speed, carrying with it energy that is very much greater than the energy released in chemical

reactions between As. – reactions which involve only the weak forces existing between the outer electrons of the As. It is by such fragmentation of atomic nuclei (*nuclear fission*) that 'atomic energy' (more strictly nuclear energy) is released.

Some of the most complex natural nuclei, e.g. those of uranium and radium, are radioactive, that is, they spontaneously disintegrate with the emission of a fragment containing 2 neutrons and 2 protons, a so-called alpha particle. If a large number of As. of say U^{238} are considered, about half of them will have disintegrated after about 4,000 million years; for radium the corresponding hard-life is c. 1,600 years.

ATOM BOMB. *See* BOMB.

ATOMIC ENERGY. Energy obtained from the inner core or nucleus of atoms, as contrasted with the energy released in chemical processes, which is derived from the electrons surrounding the nucleus.

If a high-speed alpha particle strikes another nucleus it can cause it to disintegrate, e.g. by the emission of a proton or a neutron. The released neutron, having no electric charge, can pass freely through matter unless it strikes a nucleus which it can easily enter since the protons do not repel it as they would a positively-charged particle. It may leave the nucleus again, or may stay in it, in which case it may or may not cause a practically immediate nuclear disintegration. What actually happens depends on the kind of nucleus it strikes and the velocity with which it strikes it. If a neutron enters a nucleus of U^{235} the latter may undergo fission into 2 roughly equal fragments which fly apart, while at the same time a small number of free neutrons (often 2 or 3) are released and travel out through the material. If the material is pure U^{235}, then they may enter other nuclei, causing further fissions, more released neutrons, and so on; an ever-branching 'chain' of nuclear fission spreads with great rapidity through the material with enormous evolution of energy. A certain minimum amount of U^{235} is required to support the nuclear explosion; this critical amount is a military secret. In practice 2 lumps of the materials, each smaller than the critical size, are brought close together, forming a lump above the critical size; as soon as a neutron enters the system, there will be a nuclear explosion. A slow controllable chain reaction may be produced in a *uranium pile*, made of alternate lumps or rods of pure uranium metal and of a material called a moderator. The first successful pile contained 6 tons of uranium metal, with carbon as the moderator. Since the persons operating the pile must be protected from the radiations arising from the fission process and from secondary causes, the pile must be enclosed by thick walls weighing many tons. This fact precludes the use of atomic energy in e.g. motor-cars, but it may be used in ships. The cost of construction is also so great that the use of uranium piles as generators of heat is unlikely at present to mean a large drop in electric-power costs. But it does deprive the steady reduction of coal and oil reserves of much of its menace; and it may be of the greatest significance to countries without these natural sources of power.

Beside producing power, the uranium pile may be used for the production of new radioactive substances that are made from ordinary chemical elements by the action of neutrons (which the pile provides in very great number). An example is radioactive phosphorus, of great value as a 'tracer element' in biological research. First commercial use of a nuclear explosion was in the release of natural gas deposits in New Mexico, 1967. *See* BOMB.

ATOMIC ENERGY ORGANIZATIONS. Atomic energy and its applications are normally controlled by national govt. organizations.

The nominated U.K. organization is the United Kingdom A.E. Authority (q.v.) with H.Q. in London. The major Commonwealth countries have their own organizations, in particular: A.E. of Canada Ltd., the Australian A.E. Commission, the Pakistan A.E. Commission, and the Indian Dept. of A.E. Most other leading countries have nuclear energy programmes and national organizations, the largest of these being the United States A.E. Commission, the U.S.S.R. State Committee of the Council of Ministers, the French Commissariat a l'Énergie Atomique, the Swedish organization AB Atomenergi, the Italian Atomic Energy Commission, the Spanish Junta de Energia Nuclear, and the Japanese Atomic Energy Authorities.

In addition the Common Market countries support a joint organization called Euratom, and there is a more broadly based and informal association under O.E.C.D. auspices known as the European A.E. Agency. The International A.E. Agency in Vienna, estab. in 1957, acts as a general clearing house on international matters, and provides a forum for technical discussion. It is guided by a Scientific Advisory Committee of the Sec. Gen. of the U.N.

International organizations exist for research in nuclear physics, the major ones being at Dubna (q.v. in Russia, and Geneva (C.E.R.N., q.v.). Other international organizations exist for co-operative research in the use of isotopes.

ATOMIC NUMBER. The number of electrons, or, what is its equivalent, the positive charge on the nucleus, of an atom. The 103 elements are numbered 1 (hydrogen) to 103 (lawrencium) in the Periodic Table. See CHEMISTRY and INORGANIC CHEMISTRY.

ATOMIC TIME. The measurement of the radia-

tions which atoms emit or absorb, made on the assumption that their properties are constant, as a standard of time. Such measurement can be rapidly and conveniently made in the case of atoms of caesium, and provides a degree of precision far beyond that of the rotation of the earth: it was adopted as world standard 1964.

ATOMIC WEIGHT. The least weight of a chemical element that is present in a molecular weight of any of its compounds. A.Ws. are relative numbers or ratios, not absolute weights. Formerly the A.W. of hydrogen, the smallest element, was taken as unity but it has been found more convenient to take the A.W. of oxygen as exactly 16, when that of hydrogen is $1 \cdot 008$. The absolute weight (or mass) of a hydrogen atom is $1 \cdot 6 \times 10^{-24}$ grams.

ATONALITY. In music, name given to a modern system of harmony, in which there is an absence of key. Towards the end of the 19th cent., the chromaticism of such composers as Wagner had the effect of leading the music farther and farther from the original key. Scriabin's later work showed a distinct tendency towards A., and he was the first to attempt to formulate it into a system by building up his harmonies on certain 'synthetic chords'. The system which is now generally called the atonal system, however, was that worked out by Arnold Schönberg about 1911, and finally perfected by him about 1923. This is more correctly called the 'twelve-tone system'; Schönberg and his followers repudiate the term A. as meaningless. Their system, though totally different from that which underlies diatonic harmony, is by no means arbitrary

ATOMIC ENERGY. Operating at considerably reduced cost, as against the Calder Hall type, the Windscale reactor began feeding the National Electricity Grid in 1963. Key: 1, Reactor vessel; 2, Graphite moderator; 3, Fuel element channels; 4, Neutron shield; 5, Hot box; 6, Concentric gas duct; 7, Heat exchanger; 8, Gas circulator; 9, Refuelling floor; 10, Refuelling machine; 11, Transit station for irradiated fuel; 12, Carousel for storage of irradiated fuel; 13, Containment building; 14, Personnel air lock; 15, Goods air lock; 16, Test loops; 17, Fuel element building; 18, Clean fuel preparation room; 19, Stringer breakdown cave; 20, Reactor control room; 21, Turbine hall; 22, Cooling towers; 23, Gas discharge treatment plant; 24, CO_2 and CO plant.
Photo: U.K.A.E.A.

but is bound by strict rules. The chief exponents of A. are Schönberg, Alban Berg, von Webern, and Křenek.

ATÖ'NEMENT. Literally, a bringing to be 'at one', i.e. reconciliation. In Christian theology, it is the doctrine that Jesus Christ suffered on the Cross as the means of effecting reconciliation and forgiveness between God and man.

ATONEMENT, Day of. Jewish religious fast held on the 10th day of Tishri (Sept.–Oct.), the 7th month of the Jewish year.

ATROPINE (a'tropin). An alkaloid, the active principle of deadly nightshade, or belladonna, named from the Greek *Atropos*, one of the three Fates who cut men's lives short. Usually given as atropine sulphate, it is a mild local anaesthetic.

ATTAR OF ROSES (Pers. *attar*, essence). Perfume derived from the essential oil of roses, obtained by crushing and distilling the petals of the flowers.

ATTENBOROUGH, Richard (1923–). British actor and film producer. Outstanding among his modern, naturalistic roles was Pinkie in *Brighton Rock* (1943); later films incl. *The Guinea Pig*, *Brothers in Law* and *The Angry Silence* (1959: co-producer). His brother **David A.** (1926–) led zoological expeditions to Indonesia, New Guinea, Madagascar, etc., was controller BBC 2 (television) 1965–8, and then became director of programmes, television.

ATTERBURY, Francis (1662–1732). C. of E. divine and politician. Taking holy orders in 1687, he was appointed a royal chaplain by William III. Under Queen Anne he received rapid promotion, becoming bishop of Rochester in 1713. His Jacobite sympathies prevented his attaining to the primacy, and in 1722 he was sent to the Tower and subsequently banished. He was a friend of Pope and Swift.

ATTICA. District of ancient Greece, washed on two sides by the Aegean Sea. It is a prefecture of modern Greece with Athens as its cap.

A'TTILA (c. 406–53). King of the Huns, called the 'Scourge of God'. Becoming king in 434 of hordes of Huns roaming the area from the Caspian to the Danube, he embarked on a career of vast conquests ranging from the Rhine to Persia. In 451 he invaded Gaul, but was defeated near Châlons-sur-Marne by the Roman and Visigothic armies under Aëtius and Theodoric. In 452 he led his Huns into Italy and only the personal intervention of Pope Leo I prevented the sacking of Rome. He returned to Pannonia and d. on the night of his marriage with Ildico.

A'TTIS. A Phrygian god, whose death and resurrection symbolized the end of winter and the arrival of spring. Beloved by the goddess Cybele, he was driven mad by her as a punishment for his infidelity, and castrated himself and bled to death. His worshippers sought identification with the god by castrating themselves.

ATTLEE, Clement Richard, 1st earl (1883–1967). British Labour statesman. B. in Putney, the son of a solicitor, he was ed. at Haileybury and Oxford, and practised at the Bar 1906–9. Social work in E. London and co-operation with the Webbs in Poor Law reform led him to become a Socialist: he joined the Fabian Society and the I.L.P. in 1908. He became sec. to Toynbee Hall in 1910 and lecturer in social science at the London School of Economics in 1913. After distinguished service in the F.W.W. he was mayor of Stepney 1919–20; Labour M.P. for Limehouse 1922–50 and for W. Walthamstow 1950–5.

In the 1st and 2nd Labour Govts. he was Under-Sec. for War (1924), and Chancellor of the Duchy of Lancaster and P.M.G. (1929–31). In 1935 he became Leader of the Opposition. In the wartime Coalition Govt. he was Lord Privy Seal (1940–2), Dominions Sec. (1942–3) and Lord Pres. of the Council (1943–5), combining the office of Deputy P.M. with both these latter posts. In July 1945 he became P.M. after a

Labour landslide in the general election, and introduced a sweeping programme of nationalization and a whole new system of social services. The govt. was returned to power with a much reduced majority in 1950 and was defeated in 1951. Following his resignation as P.M., he was awarded the O.M. and in 1955 accepted an earldom, on his retirement as Leader of the Opposition. His books incl. *The Labour Party in Perspective* (1937) and *As it Happened* (1954), an autobiography.

LORD ATTLEE
Photo: Daily Herald

ATTORNEY (ater'ni). Person appointed by another to do certain acts in his stead. In Britain the term is largely obsolete, but the head of the English Bar and principal law officer of the Crown is still known as the *A. General*: he is usually prominent in politics. In the U.S. an A. combines the functions of barrister and solicitor: the *A. General*, a member of the cabinet and appointed by the pres., is the chief law officer of the govt. and head of the dept. of justice.

ATTWELL, Mabel Lucie (1879–1964). British artist, illustrator of many books for children, incl. her own stories and verse. Her apple-faced children are inimitable and have been reproduced on numerous souvenirs. She m. in 1908 Harold Earnshaw who d. in 1937.

AUBE (ōb). River of N.E. France, a tributary of the Seine, giving its name to a dept. It is about 150 m. long.

AUBER (ōbār'), Daniel François Esprit (1782–1871). French operatic composer. B. at Caen, he studied under Cherubini. Of his about 50 operas, *The Dumb Girl of Portici* (1828) and the comic opera *Fra Diavolo* (1830) are best known.

AUBERT (ōbār'), Louis (1877–1968). French composer. B. near St. Malo, he composed in the Spanish idiom, particularly 'Habanera' (1919); also orchestral music and the opera *La Forêt bleue*.

AUBREY (aw'bri), John (1626–97). British antiquary. B. in Wilts, he studied law, but became dependent on patrons such as Ashmole and Hobbes. He pub. *Miscellanies* (1696) of folklore and ghost-stories, whilst the material he collected for surveys of Surrey and Wilts appeared posthumously in 1719 and 1862 respectively. His *Brief Lives* (pub. 1898) contain intimate notes on celebrities of his time. A. was the first to claim Stonehenge as a Druid temple.

AUBRIETIA (awbrē'sha). Genus of spring-flowering dwarf perennial plants of the Cruciferae order, trailing in habit and bearing purple flowers. It was named in 1763 by Adanson after Claude Aubriet (c. 1665–1742), painter for the French Royal Garden.

AUBUSSON (ōbüsoň'). Town in the dept. of Creuse, France, famous for its carpets and tapestry, the industry dating from the 15th cent. Pop. (1962) 6,279.

AUCH (ōsh). French town, cap. of the dept. of Gers. It was the capital of Armagnac and of Gascony, and has a fine Gothic cathedral. Pop. c. 16,500.

AUCHINLECK (awk'inlek), Sir Claude John Eyre (1884–). British soldier. Son of a colonel in the Royal Artillery, he was G.O.C.-in-C. Southern Command in England in 1940, C.-in-C. in India in 1941, and in the Middle East 1941–2. During the summer of 1942 his army was forced back to the Egyptian frontier by Rommel, but there made a magnificent stand. Handing over the command of the 8th Army to Montgomery, he was appointed in 1943 C.-in-C. in India for the second time. In 1946 he was promoted to field marshal, and retired in 1947.

AUCKLAND, George Eden, 1st earl of A. (1784–1849). British statesman. He became Tory M.P. in 1810, and 1835–41 was Governor-General of India. Auckland in N.Z. is named after him.

AUCKLAND. Largest city of New Zealand. It stands between Waitemata and Manukau Harbours on the A. peninsula, and is an important port and industrial and commercial centre. Founded 1840 (cap. of N.Z. till 1865), A. has a univ. (1882), Anglican and R.C. cathedrals, and internat. airport (1965) at Mangere. Pop. (1967) 565,500. *See* map below.

AUCTION. The sale of property in public, usually to the highest bidder. Auctioneers must take out an annual licence. There are usually conditions of sale by which all bidders are bound. A bid may be withdrawn at any time before the auctioneer brings down the hammer, and the seller is likewise entitled to withdraw any lot before the hammer falls. It is illegal for the seller or anyone on his behalf to make a bid for his own goods unless his right to do so has been reserved and notified before the sale. A reserve price is kept secret, but the amount of an upset price is made public before the sale. An A. where property is first offered at a high price and gradually reduced until a bid is received is known as a *Dutch A.*

AUCTION BRIDGE. Card Game played by two pairs of players. A development of bridge, it originated in India among members of the Indian Civil Service, reached England in 1903, and was first played at the Portland Club in 1908. Its chief characteristic is that trumps are decided by preliminary bid or auction. In 1929 it was largely supplanted by Contract Bridge (q.v.).

AUDE (ōd). River of S.E. France, 130 m. long, which gives its name to a dept. Carcassonne is the chief town on it.

AUDEN (aw'den), **Wystan Hugh** (1907–). Anglo-American poet. B. in York and ed. at Oxford, he was with C. Day Lewis and Spender (qq.v.), one of the 'committed' poets of the thirties, and pub. his 1st volume in 1930. By the time of *Look Stranger* (1926) much of the earlier obscurity of manner had been discarded, and noteworthy later books are *The Quest* (1941), with some fine sonnets: *Another Time* (1940),

excellent conversational verse; *The Age of Anxiety: A Baroque Ecologue* (1947), and *The Shield of Achilles* (1955). Representing a new departure in drama, both in idea and method, were *The Dog Beneath the Skin* (1935), *The Ascent of F6* (1937), and *On the Frontier* (1938), written with Christopher Isherwood (q.v.). In 1939 he became assoc. prof. of English Literature at Ann Arbor Univ., Michigan, and subsequently adopted American citizenship, but in 1956–61 returned to Oxford as prof. of poetry. A. is a poet of great satiric and lyric gifts, although not free from carelessness and cheap effects. By his daring technique, evolved under the influence of Hopkins and Eliot, he cleared the way for younger writers. His effect on modern drama is undeniable.

AUDENARDE. French form of OUDENAARDE.

AUDITOR. A person whose duty it is to examine accounts. In the U.K. the Companies Act 1948 requires that the accounts of companies to which it applies must be audited annually, that the As. must report to the members stating whether they have obtained all the information required and whether the company's balance sheet exhibits a true view of the company's affairs.

AUDUBON (aw'dūbon), **John James** (1785–1851). American naturalist. B. in Santo Domingo, the son of a French sailor and a Creole woman, he was ed. in Paris and became a trader in Kentucky. In 1827 he pub. the first parts of his *Birds of North America*, with a remarkable series of colour plates. Later he produced a similar work on American quadrupeds. The National A. Soc. (originating 1886) has branches throughout the U.S. and Canada for the study and protection of birds. (*see* illus. p. 82)

AUER (ow'er), **Leopold** (1845–1930). Hungarian violinist. A pupil of Joachim, he played in concerts with Brahms and Liszt, taught the violin at St. Petersburg from 1868, conducted the court concerts (1887–92), and emigrated to New York in 1918.

AUER VON WELSBACH (ow'er-fon-vels'bahkh) (1858–1929). Austrian chemist and inventor. B. at Vienna, he was a research worker in pure chemistry and invented the incandescent gas-mantle and many other lighting improvements.

AUGIER (ōzhē-ā), **Émile** (1820–9). French dramatist. B. at Valence, he studied law but turned to the stage after the success of his verse-play *La Ciguë* in 1844. His best-known play, *Le Gendre de M. Poirier* (1854), written in prose in collaboration with Jules Sandeau, a realistic delineation of bourgeois society, has become a classic.

AUGSBURG (owgs'boorg). German city in Bavaria at the confluence of the Wertach and Lech, 32 m. N.W. of Munich. It is named *c.* 800 after the Roman emperor Augustus who founded it in 15 B.C. During the Middle Ages its merchants, particularly the families of Fugger and Welser, were world-famous. During the S.W.W. the Messerschmitt and other engineering works were frequently bombed. Pop. (1966) 212,549.

The *Confession of A.* was a statement of the Protestant faith as held by the German Reformers, presented to Charles V at the Diet of A. in 1530. It is the accepted statement of the creed of the Lutheran Church.

AUGURS (aw'gerz). College of Roman priests who interpreted the will of heaven from traditional signs

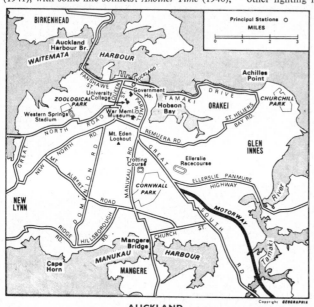

AUCKLAND

or 'auspices', chief of which were the flight of birds, the entrails of animals sacrificed, and the direction of thunder and lightning. Their advice was sought before the commencement of battle, and on other important occasions. Consuls and other high officials had the right to consult the auspices themselves, and a campaign was said to be conducted 'under the auspices' of the general who had thus consulted the will of the gods.

AUDUBON. 'The Wild Turkey Cock'. New York Historical Society, N.Y. City.

AUGUSTINE (awgus´tin) (A.D. 354–430). Christian saint, theologian, and a Father of the Church. B. at Tagaste, Numidia, of Roman descent, he studied rhetoric in Carthage where he became the father of a natural son, Adeodatus. He lectured at Tagaste and Carthage and for 10 years was attached to the Manichaean heresy. In 383 he went to Rome, and on moving to Milan came under the influence of Ambrose. After prolonged study of Neo-Platonism A. was converted to Christianity and was baptized by Ambrose together with his son. Resigning his chair in rhetoric, he returned to Africa, his mother St. Monica dying at Ostia on the journey, and settled at Tagaste. His son d. at 17. In 391, while visiting Hippo, A. was ordained priest. In 395 he was given the right of succession to the bishopric of Hippo, and in 396 succeeded to the office. He d. at Hippo during its siege by the Vandals.

Many of A.'s books resulted from his share in 3 great controversies: he refuted Manichaeism; attacked and did much to eliminate Donatism (conference of Carthage, 411); and devoted the last 20 years of his life to the Pelagian controversy, in which he maintained the doctrine of original sin and the necessity of divine grace. He estimated the number of his works at 230, and also wrote many sermons, as well as pastoral letters. A.'s most famous productions are his 'Confessions', his spiritual autobiography, and the influential *De Civitate Dei* (City of God) vindicating the Christian Church and Divine Providence in 22 books.

AUGUSTINE, St. (d. A.D. 604). First archbishop of Canterbury. Originally prior of the Benedictine monastery of St. Andrew, Rome, he was sent to convert England by Pope Gregory I. Landing at Ebbsfleet, Thanet (597), he soon baptized Ethelbert, King of Kent. He was consecrated bishop of the English at Arles (597) and appointed archbishop in 601. In 603 he attempted unsuccessfully to unite the Roman and native Celtic churches at a conference on the Severn. A. was the founder of Christ Church, Canterbury (603), and the abbey of SS. Peter and Paul, now the site of St. A.'s Missionary College. His festival is celebrated on 26 May.

AUGUSTINIANS. Name applied to all religious communities which follow the Rule of St. Augustine of Hippo. It includes the Canons of St. Augustine, Augustinian Friars and Hermits, Premonstratensians, Gilbertines, and Trinitarians.

AUGUSTUS (63 B.C.–A.D. 14). First of the Roman emperors. Caius Julius Caesar Octavianus was the son of a senator who married a niece of Julius Caesar, and he became his great-uncle's adopted son and principal heir. Following Caesar's murder, Octavian (as he was styled) formed with Mark Antony and Lepidus the triumvirate which divided the Roman world between them, and proceeded to eliminate the opposition. Antony's victory in 42 over Brutus

and Cassius brought the Republic to an end. Soon after Antony became enamoured of Cleopatra and spent most of his time at Alexandria, while Octavian consolidated his hold on the western part of the Roman dominion. War was declared against Cleopatra, and the naval victory at Actium in 31 left Octavian in unchallenged supremacy, since Lepidus had been forced to retire.

After his return to Rome in 29 B.C., Octavian was created *princeps senatus*, and in 27 he was given the title of Augustus (venerable). He then resigned his extraordinary powers, and received from the Senate in return the proconsular command, which gave him control of the army, and the tribunician power, whereby he could initiate or veto legislation. In his programme of reforms A. received the support of 3 loyal and capable helpers, Agrippa, Maecenas, and his wife, Livia, while Virgil and Horace acted as the poets laureate of the new regime. A firm frontier for the empire was established: on the N., the friendly Batavians held the Rhine delta, and then the line followed the course of the Rhine and Danube; on the E., the Parthians were friendly, and the Euphrates gave the next line; on the S., Africa was protected by the desert, on the W. were Spain and Gaul. The provinces were governed either by imperial legates responsible to the *princeps*, or by proconsuls appointed by the Senate. The army was made a profession, with fixed pay and length of service, and a permanent fleet was established. Finally, Rome itself received an adequate water supply, a fire brigade, a police force, and a large number of public buildings.

The years after 12 B.C. were marked by private and public calamities: the marriage of A.'s daughter Julia to his stepson Tiberius proved disastrous, while a serious revolt occurred in Pannonia in A.D. 6, and in Germany 3 legions under Varus were annihilated in the Teutoburg Forest in A.D. 9. A. d. a broken man, but his work remained secure. He was an enlightened and generous patron of literature and the arts, and the period of his rule lives in history as the Augustan Age. Our illus. shows Augustus wearing the diadem of a Hellenistic king, which he would not have dared to wear in Rome.

AUK (awk). Family of diving birds (Alcidae) allied to the gulls, and generally included with them in the plover order (Charadriiformes). They are marine birds feeding upon fish, and are confined to the northern hemisphere. The largest of the family, the Great Auk (*Plautus impennis*), became extinct after 1844. It could not fly, but other As. use their wings for flying short distances, and as oars in the sea. The smallest is the Little A. (*Alle alle*), which is a winter visitor to Britain. Other members of the family are razorbills, guillemots, and puffins.

AULD (awld) **LANG SYNE** (Scottish for 'old long since' or 'long ago'). Title of a song written by Robert Burns, c. 1789, and based on lines attributed to Sir Robert Aytoun; it is sung at the conclusion of social gatherings, and is set to an old Scottish air.

AULD REEKIE ('Old Smoky'). Scottish dialect name formerly applied to Edinburgh, on account of its smokiness and dirty streets.

AUGUSTUS, a gem cameo

AUNG SAN (1914–47). Burmese statesman. Imprisoned for his nationalist activities while a student in Rangoon, he escaped in 1940 to Japan, returned to lead the Burma Independence Army, which assisted the Japanese invasion of 1942, and

sexual maturity and lay eggs, without attaining to the salamander form.

AXUM. Alternative transliteration of AKSUM.

AYALA Y HERRERA (ärrä'rah), **Adelardo Lopez de** (1828–79). Spanish dramatist, poet and politician, b. at Guadalcanal. Of his plays, *Rioja* (1854) is his masterpiece. Among his lyrical works the *Epistola* ranks first.

AYE-AYE (ī-ī). A lemur (*Daubentonia* or *Chiromys madagascariensis*) from Madagascar, the sole representative of a special family, distinguished by having its front teeth adapted for gnawing like those of the Rodentia. It is about the size of a cat.

AYESHA (ah'yesha) (c. 611–c. 678). Favourite wife of Mohammed, whom she m. when she was 9. Her father, Abu-Bekr, through her influence became Caliph on the Prophet's death in 632.

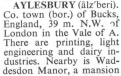

AYE-AYE.

AYLESBURY (ālz'beri). Co. town (bor.) of Bucks, England, 39 m. N.W. of London in the Vale of A. There are printing, light engineering and dairy industries. Nearby is Waddesdon Manor, a mansion in the French Renaissance style bequeathed to the nation in 1957 by James de Rothschild (q.v.). It contains art treasures collected by the family which rival those of the Wallace Collection in magnificence. Pop. (1961) 27,891.

AYLWARD, Gladys (1902–70). British missionary, naturalized Chinese and known as Ai-weh-deh 'the virtuous one'. Originally a parlour maid, she went to China in 1930 by a very dangerous route and during the Sino-Japanese war spied for the Nationalists until, with a price on her head, she led 100 children across the mtns. to Thailand in 1940. She continued her work in Formosa.

AYR (ār). Co. town (royal burgh) of Ayrshire, Scotland, at the mouth of the r. Ayr. The 'Auld Brig' was built in the 15th cent., the 'New Brig' in 1788 (rebuilt 1879). A. has associations with Robert Burns. Pop. (1961) 45,297.

AYRSHIRE. County of S.W. Scotland, with a 70 m. coastline on the Firth of Clyde. The principal hills are in the S. and S.E., the rivers are short and unnavigable. Loch Doon is 5 m. long. The climate is mild, and suited to dairying. The A. breed of cattle originated here. The A. coalfield is one of Scotland's largest, and deposits of ironstone have given rise to iron and steel industries. At Prestwick is an important airport.

Ayr is the co. town; other towns are Ardrossan, Kilmarnock, Saltcoats, and Troon. Area 1,134 sq. m.; pop. (1961) 342,855.

AYRTON (ār'ton), **Hertha** (1854–1923). British scientist and inventor. B. at Portsea, *née* Marks, she was ed. at Girton Coll., Cambridge, and in 1885 m. Prof. W E. Ayrton (1847–1908). She wrote *The Electric Arc* (1902), and invented the A. anti-gas fan, used in the trenches in France in 1916.

AYRTON, Michael (1921–). British artist. B. in London, he studied both there and in Paris, and has varied gifts as a sculptor, painter, theatre designer and book illustrator. Particularly notable are his designs for the revival of Purcell's *Fairy Queen* at Covent Garden (1946 and 1951) and his pictures and bronzes on the theme of Icarus (1962).

AYTOUN (ā'ten), **Sir Robert** (1570–1638). Scottish poet, one of the first of Scots to write in graceful English. His love poems are his best work. James I knighted him, and gave him employment.

AYTOUN (ā'toon), **William Edmonstoune** (1813–65). Scottish poet, b. in Edinburgh, chiefly remembered for his *Lays of the Scottish Cavaliers* (1848), and for the *Bon Gaultier Ballads* (1855), which he wrote in collaboration with Sir T. Martin.

AYURVEDA (ah'yurvēda). Ancient Hindu system of medicine, the main principles of which are derived from the Vedas. In India there are numerous Ayurvedic hospitals, dispensaries, etc.

AZAD (az'ahd), **Abdul Kalam** (1888–1958). Indian Congress politician. B. at Mecca and ed. at the El-Azhar Univ. in Cairo, he became prominent in Calcutta in the civil disobedience movement, founded and ed. nationalist papers, was interned and imprisoned several times, and was pres. of the Indian National Congress. He was Min. of Education 1947–58.

AZA'LEA. Group of plants of the order Ericaceae, closely related to Rhododendron, in which genus they are now generally incl. There are several species, natives of Asia and N. America, and from these many cultivated varieties have been derived which make fine ornamental shrubs —particularly the Japanese As. Several species are highly poisonous.

AZAÑA (athah'nyah), **Manuel** (1881–1940). Spanish statesman. Originally a civil servant, he made his reputation as a man of letters. He opposed Primo de Rivera and on the proclamation of the republic in April 1931 became War Minister. He succeeded Zamora as premier in Oct., and in 1936 he was elected Pres. of the republic. After Franco's triumph he withdrew to France.

AZARI'AH, Vedanayakam Samuel (1874–1945). Indian Christian divine. Son of an Indian clergyman of the C.M.S., he was ordained in 1909 and in 1912 was appointed bishop of Dornakal, the 1st Indian to become a bishop of the Anglican Church in India.

AZERBAIJAN (ahzerbījahn'). Constituent S.S.R. of U.S.S.R. in the S.E. of Europe on the S.W. shore of the Caspian Sea. Area 33,100 sq. m. It is heavily forested and has large mineral deposits, particularly petroleum. Baku, the cap., is one of the chief centres of Soviet oil production. Artificial irrigation is used, chiefly for cotton production. Pop. (1967) 4,800,000.

Also 2 admin. provs. of N.W. Persia: eastern A. (cap. Tabriz) and western A. (cap. Rezayeh).

AZHAR (azahr'), **El.** Moslem mosque and univ. at Cairo. Founded by Jawhar, C.-in-C. of the army of the Fatimid caliph, in 970, it is claimed to be the oldest univ. in the world. It became the centre of Islamic learning, with several subsidiary foundations, and is primarily a school of Koranic teaching.

AZI'LIAN. Name given to an archaeological period following the close of the Old Stone (Palaeolithic) Age, and regarded as one of the cultures of the Mesolithic Age. It was first recognized by Ed. Piette at Mas d'Azil, a village in Ariège, France.

AZINCOURT. Alternative spelling of AGINCOURT.

AZORES (azorz'). Group of 9 islands in the N. Atlantic, belonging to Portugal, divided into 3 admin. districts. Area 922 sq. m. Of the pop. (1967) of 318,558, more than half live on the is. of San Miguel, on which is the chief tn., Ponta Delgada (pop. 22,448). The islands are volcanic in origin, and have a genial climate. Known to the Carthaginians, they were rediscovered in the 14th cent. and annexed by the Portuguese c. 1430. Europe's most westerly land,

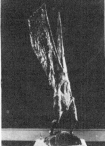

MICHAEL AYRTON. This striking interpretation in bronze of the Icarus legend stands 67 in. high.
Photo: David Farrell.

AZORES. The scenery ot St. Michael's at once betrays the volcanic origin of these islands, further from the mainland than any other Atlantic group. The traditional costumes are particularly attractive.   *Courtesy of the Portuguese State Office.*

they were used as an air base in the S.W.W. to protect Allied shipping, and a French missile-tracking station was estab. 1966 on Flores, the most westerly is.

AZORÍN (athorin'). Pseudonym of José Martínez Ruiz (1873–1967). Spanish author. B. in Alicante prov. he studied law, but soon devoted himself to literature. His work was as influential as it is rich and varied in form and incl. vols. of critical essays and short stories, plays and novels, such as the autobiographical *La voluntad* (1902) and *Antonio Azorín* (1903) – the author adopted the name of the eponymous hero of the latter as his pseudonym.

A'ZOV. Inland sea of the U.S.S.R., forming a gulf in the N.E. of the Black Sea.

A'ZTECS. An American Indian race, predominant in Mexico at the time of the Spanish conquest in 1519. They belonged to the racial stock of Nahuan; and coming from the north in A.D. 1325 they settled on the marshy island of Tenochtitlan in the lake of Tezcoco, and on piles driven into the lake bed reared the city of Mexico-Tenochtitlan (the site of Mexico City). They adopted an agricultural basis of life, and in other ways adopted the civilization of the people whom they had politically supplanted, the Toltecs, who in turn had derived their culture from the Maya people of Guatemala.

Under Montezuma I, who reigned from 1440, the A. power was extended over the greater part of what is now central and southern Mexico. Their rule was so oppressive, however, that Montezuma II, who reigned from 1502, was able to put up only very slight resistance to Cortez and his Spanish men-at-arms when they landed at Vera Cruz in 1519. Montezuma was slain and Tenochtitlan was stormed.

The civilization of A. Mexico is chiefly exemplified by its architecture, the massive and substantial character of which is to be observed in the remains of its pyramid temples or Teocallis, immense piles which only slave labour on a huge scale could have raised. The palaces were on a similar gigantic scale, the roads excellent. The govt. was an elective monarchy. Metals were not yet in use for practical purposes, although gold, silver, and copper were used for ornament; tools and weapons were of stone, flint, or obsidian. The jeweller's art had reached a high degree of excellence. The system of writing was a mixture of the hieroglyphic and pictographic. The religion was picturesque but terrible, and there was a system of wholesale human sacrifice. The chief gods were Uitzilopochtli, the national or tribal deity; his brother, Tezcatlipoca, representative of drought; Tlaloc, the rain god; and Quetzalcoatl, the Toltec deity who became chief patron of A. civilization.

AZUELA (ahthoo-ā'lah), **Mariano** (1873–1952). Mexican novelist and physician. His finest work, *Los de Abajo* (1915), was inspired by the 1910 revolution. In several novels A. portrayed Mexican low life in the cities. His later works reflected the contemporary political and social problems of his country, e.g. *El camarada Pantoja* and *La nueva burguesía*.

B Second letter of the alphabet. It corresponds to the Greek *beta* and the Semitic *beth*; and as written in the modern W. European alphabet is derived from the classical Latin.

BĀ'AL. Semitic word meaning 'lord' or 'owner', used as a divine title of their chief male gods by the Phoenicians, Canaanites, etc. Generally deities of fertility, their worship was often orgiastic and of a phallic character, and was strongly denounced by the Hebrew Prophets.

BAALBEK (bahl'bek). City of ancient Syria, in modern Lebanon, 36 m. E.N.E. of Beirut. There are magnificent ruins of Baal temples. The Greeks identified Baal with Helios, the sun, and renamed B. Heliopolis.

BA'BBITT, Irving (1865–1933). American literary philosopher. B. at Dayton, Ohio, he became prof. of French literature at Harvard (1912). In his *Rousseau and Romanticism* he regarded the Romantic exaltation of the Ego as having led to a confusion of values in art and politics. He opposed to it his own doctrine of 'Humanism', which represents a reaction against 19th cent. ideas.

BĀ'BEL. Hebrew name for Babylon, chiefly associated with the TOWER of B., which, in the Genesis story, was erected in the plain of Shinar by the descendants of Noah. The site has been identified with the temple of E-sagila in Babylon and the mound of Birs Nimrud (Borsippa) near the city.

BABEL, Isaak Emmanuilovich (1894–1939/40). Russian Jewish writer. B. in Odessa, he was an ardent supporter of the Revolution and fought with Budyenny's cavalry in the Polish campaign of 1921–2, an experience which inspired *Konarmiya* (1926: *Red Cavalry*). Best known of his other works is *Odesskie rasskazy* (1924: *Stories from Odessa*), which brilliantly conveys the life of the Odessa Jews.

BAB-EL-MANDEB (bahb-el-mahn'deb). Strait separating Arabia and Africa, and joining the Red Sea and the Gulf of Aden.

BABER (bah'ber) or **Babar** ('Tiger'). Title given to Zahir ud-din Mohammed (1483–1530), first Great Mogul of India. He was the great-grandson of Tamerlane, and at the age of 12 succeeded his father as ruler of Ferghana (Turkestan). In 1526 he defeated the emperor of Delhi at Panipat, captured Delhi and Agra, and estab. a dynasty which endured until 1858.

BABEUF (bahböf´), **François Noël** (1760–97). French revolutionary journalist. In 1794 he founded in Paris a paper, later known as the *Tribune of the People*, in which he demanded the equality of all men and the abolition of property. For conspiring against the Directory he was guillotined.

BÁBÍ FAITH, The. Religion founded by Mírzá 'Ali Muhammad (1819–50), known as the Báb ('The Gate'). A native of Shiraz, Persia, he was originally a Moslem, but taught that Islam was not the final revelation of God to men, and revealed a new scripture containing laws abrogating those of the Koran. He was shot by orders of the govt. at Tabriz, and his followers were savagely persecuted. The Bábí Faith developed later into the Bahá'í Faith (q.v.).

BABIRUSA (bahbiroo´sa). A wild pig (*B. alfurus*), found in Celebes, characterized by the great development in the male of the upper tusks which grow upwards through the skin of the snout, and curve back towards the forehead.

BABOO´N. A large monkey (*Papio*) found in Africa, S. of the Sahara and in S. Arabia, given the popular name 'dog-faced monkey', because of its elongated muzzle. Well-known species are: the chacma from S. Africa, the small ginger-coloured B. of Guinea, the yellow B. of E. Africa, the olive green Anubis B., ranging from E. Africa to Nigeria, and the Hamadryas or sacred B. from Abyssinia and S. Arabia.

BA´BYLON. Cap. of ancient Babylonia, on the left bank of the Euphrates. The site is in modern Iraq, 60 m. S. of Baghdad and 5 m. N. of Hillah (pop. 50,000), which is built chiefly from the ruins of Babylon. B. first rose to importance under Hammurabi, and under Nebuchadrezzar I it was a magnificent city. The site of the famous Hanging Gardens, probably built by Nebuchadrezzar II, has not been determined.

BABYLO´NIA. The great alluvial plain of Mesopotamia, watered by the rivers Euphrates and Tigris, now forming the principal portion of Iraq. In the O.T. it is frequently referred to as the plain of Shinar, Babel, and 'the land of the Chaldees'. In history it was the centre of the Babylonian (and later the Assyrian) empire.

The history of B. is bound up with that of the city of Babylon. B. lay at the meeting-point of 2 great avenues of commerce, the one connecting her with the Mediterranean and Egypt, the other with the Black Sea. Her rise to supremacy followed the penetration of the western Semites into Mesopotamia, and their eventual triumph over the Sumerians. They founded the 1st Amorite dynasty of Babylon in 1950 B.C. Under Hammurabi (1791–1750 B.C.) the 1st Babylonian empire reached on the S.W. to the borders of Syria. From 1650 B.C. the kings of the 1st Sea-land dynasty ruled for 368 years. There followed a period of Kassite domination, which lasted for 576 years. The Kassites are generally supposed to have been an Aryan people. The letters from Tell el-Amarna and from the Hittite archives at Boghaz-Keui throw a good light on the history of their later monarchs. The period was terminated in 1174 by an Elamite invasion.

During the next 300 years B. struggled against the advancing power of Assyria. From 732 until 612 B.C. Babylonia was a subject prov. of the Assyrian empire, and her continued resistance was one of the causes of the downfall of Assyria.

The Neo-Babylonian empire was estab. by Nabopolassar, whose son, Nebuchadrezzar II, raised it to a pitch of prosperity and greatness beyond any it had known. Babylonian rule was extended over the whole of Mesopotamia; Egypt became a tributary; Babylon was rebuilt, fortified, and adorned with magnificent buildings; Jerusalem was captured in 586 B.C., and a large part of the population of Judah carried into exile. After Nebuchadrezzar's death there was a swift decline. In 539 B.C. Babylonia became a prov. of the Persian empire.

The civilization of B. was largely derived from the Sumerians. Their cuneiform or wedge-shaped writing was taken over, and the Sumerian language continued to be used for religious purposes. The Sumerian pantheon was also adopted, together with the chief myths, such as those of the Creation and the Deluge, and the epic of Gilgamesh. Babylonian religious ideas and conceptions of the universe passed into Hebrew culture, and into Europe by way of Greece.

BABYLONIAN CAPTIVITY. The period spent by the Jews in Babylon following the capture of Jerusalem by Nebuchadrezzar the Babylonian emperor, in 605, 597 and 586 B.C. Traditionally it lasted 70 years, but Cyrus permitted the exiles to return to Jerusalem in 536 B.C. The term is applied to the period 1309–77, when the popes were exiled to Avignon.

BACAU (bahk´ow). Town of Rumania, cap. of a region, 155 m. N.N.E. of Bucharest, on the Bistrita. It has petroleum wells. Pop. (1966) 73,481.

BACCARAT (bakarah´). Card game popular with gamblers at Continental casinos, but illegal in England if played for stakes. The more usual variety is *chemin de fer*.

BACCHUS (bak´us). Greek and Roman god of wine, also known in Greece as Dionysus. In Gk. legend B. was the son of Zeus and Semele. He toured the cities of Greece, bringing the gift of the vine to those who welcomed him, and overwhelming those who opposed him with madness and intoxication. The worship of B. took the form of wild and licentious revels, called *Bacchanalia*.

J. S. BACH

BACH (bahkh), **Johann Sebastian** (1685–1750). German composer. B. at Eisenach, in Thuringia, he came of a distinguished musical family. At 15 he became a chorister at Lüneburg, and at 19 organist at Arnstadt. Subsequent appointments incl. positions at the ducal court of Weimar, and finally, in 1723, that of musical director at St. Thomas's choir school in Leipzig, where apart from his brief visit to the court of Frederick the Great of Prussia in 1747, he remained until his death. B. m. twice, and had numerous children, many of whom died in infancy. His 2nd wife, Anna Magdalena Wülkens, was a soprano singer; she also acted as his amanuensis, when in later years his sight failed.

B.'s music represents the culmination of the polyphonic style of the 17th and early 18th cents., but it was not until the time of Mendelssohn that it began to be generally known and appreciated. Since then both appreciation of his work and careful scholarship in regard to his texts have steadily and rapidly increased, and the extent of his influence on later musicians can hardly be overestimated.

His sacred music incl. the 190 church cantatas, the Easter and Christmas oratorios, the 2 great Passions, according to St. Matthew and St. John, and the Mass in B minor. *Phoebus and Pan* is a secular dramatic cantata. His orchestral music incl. the 6

D

Brandenburg concertos, and other concertos for clavier and for violin and 4 orchestral suites. B.'s keyboard music, for clavier and for organ, is of equal importance and incl. the collection of 48 preludes and fugues known as *The Well-tempered Clavier*, the Goldberg variations, the Italian concerto, and the French and English suites. Of his organ music the most important examples are the choral preludes. His music also incl. chamber-music and songs, and 2 important works written in his later years illustrate the principles and potentialities of his polyphonic art – the *Musical Offering* and *The Art of Fugue*.

His eldest son, **Wilhelm Friedemann B.** (1710–84), although famous as an organist, improviser, and master of counterpoint, had an unsuccessful career owing to his dissipated habits. J.S.B.'s 3rd and musically most important son, **Karl Philip Emanuel B.** (1714–88), b. at Weimar, studied music under his father, was appointed court musician to Frederick the Great, then Crown Prince, and became a member of the royal household on the latter's accession in 1740. He wrote over 200 pieces for the clavier, and pub. an important critical textbook on its technique. From 1768 he was Kapellmeister at Hamburg. His church music incl. the oratorio *The Israelites in the Wilderness*. He is important as a pioneer of the new 'harmonic' (as opposed to 'polyphonic') music, and Mozart, Haydn, and Beethoven all owed a considerable debt to him. J.S.B.'s 11th son **Johann Christian B.** (1735–82), b. at Leipzig, became well known in Italy as a composer of operas. In 1762 he was invited to London, where he remained till his death and enjoyed great popularity, both as a composer and performer.

BACILLUS (basil'us). Lat. diminutive of *baculus*, rod; the larger, rod-like forms of bacteria (q.v.).

BACKGAMMON. Game played by 2 persons with a board, pieces or draughtsmen, and a pair of dice. From time immemorial it has been popular in the Middle East, and the Romans had a game like it. It was widely played in England in the 18th cent., was fairly popular during the Victorian age, and very much so after the F.W.W. in both Europe and America. In France B. is known as *tric-trac*.

BACKHAUS (bak'hows), **Wilhelm** (1884–1969), German pianist, a virtuoso interpreter of Beethoven.

BACON, Delia (1811–59). American writer on Shakespearian subjects. In her *Philosophy of the Plays of Shakespeare Unfolded* (1857) she popularized the theory that the plays attributed to S. were written by Bacon and a group of associates.

BACON, Francis (1561–1626). English statesman and philosopher. Youngest son of Sir Nicholas B., the Elizabethan statesman, he was b. in London, ed. at Cambridge, called to the Bar in 1582, and in 1584 became an M.P. Although Lord Burleigh was his uncle, his political ambitions were frustrated and he attached himself to the Earl of Essex. Yet when Essex was disgraced and tried for his life in 1599, B. acted with the prosecuting counsel and in 1601 did much to secure his conviction as a traitor. On the accession of James I, his fortunes improved. He was knighted in 1603, in 1607 became Solicitor-General, and in 1613 Attorney-General. Lord Keeper in 1617, in the next year he was appointed Lord Chancellor and raised to the peerage as Lord Verulam. In 1621 he was

FRANCIS BACON
Photo: N.P.G.

created Viscount St. Albans; but in the same year he was accused in the House of Lords of taking presents from suitors in cases that he had tried. He offered no defence and was ordered to be fined £40,000, imprisoned indefinitely, and banished from Parliament and the Court. After a few days in the Tower he was allowed to retire to Gorhambury, but never again held office.

B.'s brilliant political career was overshadowed at the last by the misfortunes that his alleged malpractices brought upon him. In literature his fame is far more secure. His famous *Essays or Counsels, Civil and Moral*, a series of short discourses upon truth, death, revenge, friendship, etc., appeared in 1597. In 1605 he pub. *The Advancement of Learning* which gave a general view of his ideas upon scientific method, set out more fully in the *Novum Organum Scientiarum* of 1620. B. sought a means of building a natural science which should not be merely theoretical or philosophical, but the principal means of enlarging man's knowledge and power. Among his other writings are a history of Henry VII, a collection of apophthegms, and the *New Atlantis*, a description of a scientific Utopia.

For the theory that Bacon wrote the plays which are attributed to Shakespeare, *see* BACONIAN THEORY.

BACON, Francis (1910–). British artist. B. in Dublin, he was largely self-taught, beginning to paint *c.* 1930 and holding his 1st one-man show in London in 1949. His work is characterized by lurid colour, and terrifyingly blurred and featureless figures *Study after Velasquez* (1951) and *Mad Dog* (1952) are in the Tate Gallery, and *Studies of the Human Body* (1947 in the National Gallery of Victoria, Melbourne.

BACON, Sir Nicholas (1509–79). English statesman. B. at Chislehurst, he received grants of Church lands from Henry VIII, held leading legal posts under Mary, and on Elizabeth's accession became Lord Keeper of the Great Seal and a knight. One of his 8 children was Francis B., the philosopher-statesman.

BACON, Roger (*c.* 1214–92). English philosopher and pioneer scientist. B. in Somerset, and ed. at Oxford and Paris, he became a Franciscan friar and until *c.* 1251 was in Paris lecturing on Aristotle. Then he wrote a number of works in Latin, e.g. *On Mirrors, Metaphysical Questions, On the Multiplication of Species*, etc., and in 1266, at the invitation of his friend Pope Clement IV, he began his *Opus Majus*, a compendium of all branches of knowledge. In 1268 he sent this with his *Opus Minus* and other of his writings to the Pope. In 1277 he was condemned by the Church and imprisoned for 'certain novelties', but was released in 1292. One of the most original and bold thinkers of the Middle Ages, B. foresaw the magnifying property of convex lenses, the extensive use of gunpowder, and the possibility of mechanical boats and flying machines.

BACONIAN THEORY. The theory that the plays and poems generally attributed to Shakespeare are really the work of Francis Bacon. The theory is said to have been first suggested by the Rev. James Wilmot, a Warwickshire parson, in 1785, but the 1st full and definite claim for the Baconite authorship was made by William Henry Smith in 1856. Since then a considerable literature on the subject has sprung up, especially in U.S.A., and in England the Bacon Society, founded in 1886, exists for furthering these views. *See* BACON, Delia.

BACTERIA. Minute organisms, consisting of a single cell composed of protoplasm. Their place in nature lies between the simplest vegetable organisms, such as the fungi and algae, and the simplest of the microscopic animals, the protozoa, and they are usually classified as plants, although they have no chlorophyll and so are unable to synthesize food from simple organic materials. They are exceedingly numerous, and are present everywhere; and the

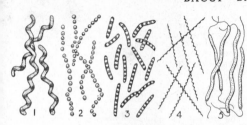

BACTERIA. I, Spirilla. 2, Cocci. 3, Bacilli. 4, Spirochaetae. 5, Vibrios.

names germs, microbes, bacilli, micrococci, and micro-organisms are popularly applied to the group.

CLASSIFICATION. According to their shape there are 5 main classes, viz. (1) *Cocci*, round or oval, e.g. streptococci, in which the cells are held together in chains, and staphylococci, which grow in clusters; (2) *Bacilli*, rod-like or, rather, cylindrical, straight or slightly curved; (3) *Vibrios*, rigid, curved rods, usually with a flagellum (whip) at one end; (4) *Spirilla*, curved and rod-like, with tufts of flagella at the ends; and (5) *Spirochaetae*, non-flagellate, spiral or undulatory.

STRUCTURE. As seen under the microscope, B. are minute, transparent cells, usually colourless, con-sisting of a mass of protoplasm often surrounded by a wall of sticky material. No nucleus as commonly recognized in other cells has been satisfactorily demonstrated. The unit of bacterial measurement is the micron ($\mu = 1/1000$ mm.). On an average, about 2,500 of the larger forms may measure $1/10$ in. if placed end to end. *Reproduction* is by fission. Cell division may occur every 20 minutes or so, so that an enormous bacterial population may be produced in a few hours. A single specimen may become 16 millions in a day. In the laboratory B. are grown on culture media, extracts of plant, animal, or fish. Heat and drying are destructive to B., and so is light, particularly short ultra-violet rays.

DISTRIBUTION. B. are universally present in nature and their action in breaking down complex sub-stances forms an essential part of the cycle of chemical events occurring in nature, in which plants take from the soil and air simple compounds and synthesize complex substances used by animals as food and built up by them into the complex compounds. Parasitic B. must have living hosts. Saprophytic B. flourish in non-living or inorganic matter. The soil is the great reservoir of the latter; surface soil con-tains up to 20 million or more B. per gramme. Water is full of B. and has to be purified to eliminate those forms harmful to man. B. are essential in the making of butter and cheese, curing tobacco, tanning leather, retting flax, and in a great many other industrial processes. Sewage disposal is greatly facilitated by the work of aerobic and anaerobic B.

Among harmful B. are those which cause the common cold, pneumonia, diphtheria, scarlet fever, measles, tuberculosis, enteric fever, venereal diseases, anthrax, cholera, etc. Infection is often spread by flies and human 'carriers'.

BA'CUP. Market town (bor.) in E. Lancs, England, 19 m. N.N.E. of Manchester. Cotton-spinning and weaving, calico-printing, shoemaking, and iron-founding are industries; there are coal mines and stone quarries in the vicinity. Pop. (1961) 17,295.

BADAJOZ (bahdah-hōs'). Spanish city, cap. of the prov. of the same name, on the Guadiana. It has the ruins of a Moorish castle; the cathedral dates from the 13th cent. An ancient Roman city, because of its strategic position near the Portuguese frontier it has often been besieged; Wellington stormed it in 1812 with the loss of 59,000 British troops. Pop. (1960) 96,152.

BADDELEY (bad'li), **Hermione** (1906–). British actress. Specializing in revue, she is as famous for her wit off-stage as on, and has appeared in the U.S. Her sister Angela B. (1904–) is also a well-known actress.

BADEN (bah'den). Former state of S.W. Germany, which had Karlsruhe as its cap. B. was captured from the Romans in 282 by the Alemanni, later it became a margravate, and in 1806 a grand duchy. A state of the German empire 1871–1918, then a rep. and under Hitler a *Gau*, it was divided between the *Länder* of Württemberg-Baden and Baden in 1945, and in 1952 made part of Baden-Württemberg (q.v.).

BADEN. Old Swiss town in Aargau canton, 14 m. N.W. of Zurich, with hot sulphur baths much visited since Roman times. It produces aluminium, chemicals, clothing and food products. Pop. *c.* 13,000.

BADEN-BADEN. Health resort in Baden-Württ-emberg, Germany, at the entrance to the Black Forest, 8 m. E. of the Rhine. The medicinal waters of the spa have been famed for centuries. Pop. (1960) 40,000.

BA'DEN-PÖ'WELL, Robert Stephenson Smyth, 1st baron (1857–1941). Soldier, and from 1920 'World-Chief Scout'. B. in London, he was ed. at Charter-house and commissioned in the Hussars in 1876. Worldwide fame came to him for his gallant defence of Mafeking during the S. African War. Invalided home, he was knighted in 1909, and retired in 1910 with the rank of lieut.-general. Earlier he had written *Scouting for Boys* (1908), and he now set about the establishment of the Boy Scouts movement which speedily spread throughout the Empire and beyond. In 1929 he was made Baron B.P. of Gilwell, and in 1937 received the O.M.

His sister, **Agnes B.-P.** (1854-1945) was a pioneer woman balloonist and aeronaut, and assisted him in the formation of the Girl Guides in 1910.

BADEN-WÜRTTEMBERG (bah'den vür'temberg). Land of S.W. Germany formed in 1952 (following a plebiscite) by the merger of the Länder Baden, Württemberg-Baden, and Württemberg-Hohenzol-lern. The Rhine forms its W. and S. boundaries, and the river valley is devoted to vine and fruit-growing, much of the state is rich agricultural country and forestry is carried on. Textiles, chemicals, iron and steel goods, clocks (espec. in the Black Forest), electrical equipment, etc. are produced. The cap. is Stuttgart. Area 13,400 sq. m.; pop. (1966) 8,534,100.

BADGER. Mammal of the weasel family, but with larger jaws and molar teeth of a crushing type adapted to a more vegetable diet, and short strong legs with long claws suitable for digging. It has long coarse hair grizzled with black on the upper side, the underside and legs are black. The face is white with a broad black stripe on each side. The common B. (*Meles meles*) is *c.* 3 ft. long. Harmless and of nocturnal habits, it spends the day in deep burrows, called a 'set'. It feeds on insects and roots, but also eggs, mice, and young rabbits.

The so-called sport of *badger-baiting* has been prohibited in Britain since 1850.

BAD HOMBURG. *See* HOMBURG.

BA'DMINTON. Game played by 2 or 4 players with rackets and shuttlecocks, usually indoors. The name is derived from B. House, the Gloucester-shire seat of the duke of Beaufort, where B. originated in the 1860s. The 1st rules were drawn up in 1876, and the B. Association was formed in 1895.

BADOGLIO (bahdō'lē-oh), **Pietro** (1871–1956). Italian soldier. A veteran of campaigns against the tribes of Tripoli and Cyrenaica, he in 1935 replaced de Bono as C.-in-C. in Ethiopia, adopting ruthless measures to break patriot resistance, and being created Viceroy of Ethiopia and Duke of Addis Ababa in 1936. Always unfavourable to Fascism, he succeeded Mussolini as P.M. from July 1943 to June 1944.

BAEDEKER (bād'-), **Karl** (1801–59). German publisher. B. at Essen, son of a publisher and printer, he estab. himself at Coblenz in 1827, and started the famous series of travel guides, recording nothing he had not seen himself. The firm (carried on by his descendants) removed to Leipzig in 1872, was completely destroyed in 1943, and was re-estab. nr. Hamburg after the S.W.W.

BAEKELAND (bāk'-), **Leo Hendrik** (1863–1944). American chemist. B. in Ghent, he went to U.S.A. in 1889, and undertook research on photographic materials, inventing Velox paper. His subsequent researches covered the fields of plastics, electrochemistry, organic chemistry, synthetic resins, and electrical insulation. He also invented bakelite.

BAER (bār), **Karl Ernst von** (1792–1876). German zoologist. B. in Estonia, he held scientific posts at Königsberg and St. Petersburg, and was the founder of comparative embryology.

BAFFIN, William (1584–1622). English navigator and explorer, a Londoner by birth. In 1612 he was chief pilot of an expedition in search of the N.W. passage, and in 1613–4 commanded a whaling fleet near Spitzbergen. In 1615 he became pilot for Robert Bylot on the *Discovery* examining Hudson Strait. In 1616 they discovered Baffin Bay and reached Lat. 77° 45', which for 236 years remained the 'furthest north'. After 1617 B. transferred his services to the E. India Co. and made surveys of the Red Sea and Persian Gulf. In 1622 he was killed in an Anglo-Persian attack on Ormuz.

BAGATE'LLE. A game resembling billiards, played on a board with numbered cups instead of pockets. The object is to drive the 9 balls into the cups. In *ordinary B.* each player sends all the balls up in turn. In *French B.* 2 or 4 players, playing alternately, take part.

BAGEHOT (baj'ot), **Walter** (1826–77). British economist. Manager of the London office of his family banking house, he pub. a masterly analysis of the London money market *Lombard Street* (1873). Other books incl. *The English Constitution* (1867), a classic explanation of the political system at the end of the Palmerstonian era, and *Physics and Politics* (1869), applying the laws of natural selection to the development of human communities. He ed. *The Economist* from 1860.

BA'GGARAS. A Beduin tribe whose home is in the Nile Basin, principally in Kordofan, W. of the White Nile. They are Mohammedans, chiefly occupied in cattle-breeding and big-game hunting. Physically they are of a very fine type. The British soldier nicknamed them 'Fuzzy-wuzzies' on account of their mop-like hair fashions.

BAGHDAD (bahgdahd'; Eng. bag'dad). Cap. of Iraq, on the Tigris. B. was founded in the very early days of history; it was a route centre of great importance, a commercial and intellectual centre during the 8th–9th cents. The present city was founded in 762 and enlarged by Harun-al-Rashid. It was overrun in 1258 by the Mongols, who destroyed the irrigation system. In 1639 it was taken by the Turks. During the F.W.W. B. was captured by Gen. Maude in 1917, and in 1921 was made cap. of the new country of Iraq. Pop. (1967) 1,007,605.

Of the old city of 'Arabian Nights' fame not much remains; the modern city is one of metalled roads, railway stations, public buildings, etc. The univ. was opened in 1958. B. is still a great centre of communications.

The **Baghdad Pact** was a treaty made in B. in 1955 between Turkey and Iraq to which Britain, Pakistan, and Persia later adhered. Iraq withdrew from it after the revolution of 1958 and the remaining allies renamed their group the Central Treaty Organization (CENTO) in 1959. The U.S.A. signed bilateral agreements of co-operation.

BAGHDAD RAILWAY. German project to link Berlin with the Mosul petroleum fields. The part of the line in Anatolia was completed in 1896; then the project was held up by opposition from other Powers. In 1911–4 the Germans completed the section from Baghdad to Samarra. During the F.W.W. the British extended the line to Kala Shargat (and also built a narrow gauge line S. from Baghdad to Basra). The last section of the B.R. was completed 1936–40.

BA'GNOLD, Enid (1896–). British author, who m. Sir Roderick Jones of Reuters. Her novel *National Velvet* (1935) achieved great success as a play, and *The Chalk Garden* (1954), staged both in London and N.Y., was a delicate essay in character study.

BAGPIPE. Musical instrument of ancient origin, being known to the Romans and ancient Egyptians and found in different forms in various parts of Europe, as well as in the British Isles. It is developed from the primitive reedpipe, but is distinguished by the presence of a bag for the supply of wind, a chanter or melody pipe and drones, which emit one invariable note and supply a ground-bass. The Scotch B.P. is regarded as the national instrument, and the chanter pipe has a compass of 9 notes. The compass of the Irish bagpipe is wider.

BAGPIPE. The massed pipe bands of the Queen's Own Cameron Highlanders and the Seaforth Highlanders are stirringly impressive as they march past Inverness Castle.
Photo: George Outram & Co. Ltd.

BAGRI'TSKY, Eduard (1895–1934). Pseudonym of the Soviet poet Eduard Dzyubin. One of the Constructivist group, he pub. a vol. of verse, *South-West*, the heroic poem *Lay About Opanas*, and collections of verse called *The Victors* and *The Last Night*.

BAGUIO (bagwi'o). Summer resort of the Philippine Rep., in Luzon, 125 m. N. of Manila, 4,500 ft. above sea-level. Pop. c. 40,000.

BAHADUR SHAH II (1775–1862). Last of the Mogul emperors of India. He reigned, though in name only, and under the British, as king of Delhi 1837–57, when he was hailed by the mutineers as an independent emperor at Delhi. After the Mutiny he was deported to Rangoon.

BAHÁ'Í FAITH, The. Religion founded in Persia by Bahá'u'lláh (1817–92) as a continuation of that of the Báb (*see* BÁBÍ FAITH). He taught that divine revelation continues from age to age, and that

Muhammad though a great Prophet was not the only or the final one. Bahá'u'lláh was succeeded in the leadership by his son 'Abdu'l-Bahá (d. 1921), who was knighted by the British in 1920 for his services during the F.W.W. The latter's grandson, Shoghi Effendi (1896–1957), then became 'Guardian of the Cause': on his death the succession was disputed. An international council now presides. Followers of the B. Faith claim it incorporates what is best in all religions. It stresses the oneness of mankind regardless of race, colour, class, or creed.

BAHAMAS (ba-hah'maz). Group of islands in the British W. Indies, off the S.E. coast of Florida. They comprise 700 is. and about 200 cays. Only 21 are inhabited. The total land area is 4,404 sq. m.; and of the pop. of 142, 846 (est.) in 1966 not more than 15 per cent were white. Tomatoes, salt, timber, crawfish are exported, but the tourist trade is of supreme importance.

The B. were visited by Columbus in 1492. During the 17th and 18th cents. the British and Spanish held them alternately until they became British in 1783. The chief islands are New Providence, on which stands Nassau, the cap.; Grand Bahama, Abaco, Eleuthera, Cat, Andros, Exuma, Mayaguana (on which a site was leased for 99 years to U.S.A. for a naval base in 1940), Crooked, Long, Great Inagua, and San Salvador. Internal self-govt. was introduced 1964 and there are a Senate and House of Assembly. In 1967 the first Negro P.M. (Lynden O. Pindling) took office.

BAHAWALPUR (bah-hahwahlpoor'). Town of the Punjab, Pakistan, once cap. of a former state of B. It is on the Sutlej, 50 m. S. of Multan, and has textile factories and rice mills. Pop. (1961) 326,671.

BAHIA (bah-ē'ah). Coastal state of N.E. Brazil, 1st part of the country sighted by Portuguese navigators in 1500. Apart from the fertile plain, it is for the most part a barren plateau. B. produces 90 per cent of Brazilian cocoa. Its cap. is Salvador (formerly also called B.). Area 217,670 sq. m.; pop. (1967) 6,885,000.

BAHIA BLANCA. Industrial town in S. Argentina, on the Naposta, 3 m. from its mouth. It has extensive dockyards and is a meat-packing centre. Pop. (1960) 150,000.

BAHR, Hermann (1863–1934). Austrian author and dramatist. He wrote social dramas in the manner of Ibsen and Strindberg, but was most successful with amusing and witty comedies such as *Der Krampus* (1902) and *Das Konzert* (1909).

BAHREIN (bahrān'). Group of islands in the Persian Gulf, 20 m. E. of the Arabian coast. On the largest island, also called B., is the cap. Manama. B. has been inhabited for 5,000 years. The Arabs seized it in the 7th cent., it was occupied by Portugal 1521–1602, after which it was disputed by various countries until in 1861 the ruling sheikh placed it under British protection. Long famous for its pearls, it became an important centre of production and refining of petroleum after the discovery here of this mineral in 1932. B. planned to join the Fed. of Arab Emirates (q.v.) Persia abandoned claims to the reversion of sovereign rights in B. in 1970. Area 231 sq. m. Pop. (1965) 182,203.

BAIKAL (bī'kahl). Largest freshwater lake in Asia, deepest in the world (up to 5,710 ft.), in the R.S.F.S.R. between Irkutsk region and Buriat-Mongol A.S.S.R. Fed by more than 300 rivers, it is drained only by the Lower Angara. Area 12,150 sq. m.; length 390 m.

BAIKONOUR (bīkohn'ōr). Small coalmining town in Kazakh S.S.R., 30 m. W. of Karakpai, in W. Karaganda region. It has been used as the launching point for Russian cosmonauts.

BAIL. The setting at liberty of a person in the custody of the law on an undertaking, usually backed

BAILEY BRIDGE. Components in use on a building site.
Courtesy of Acrow Engineers Ltd.

by some security, given either by him or by someone else, that he will attend at a court at a stated time and place. If he does not attend, the bail is 'estreated', i.e. forfeited.

BAILE ATHA CLIATH. Official Irish name of DUBLIN from 1922.

BAILEY, Sir Donald Coleman (1901–). British engineer, inventor during the S.W.W. of the Bailey Bridge. Made up of interlocking sections, speedily manhandled, the bridges can be easily transported and erected: the girders are built up from prefabricated panels and all parts are interchangeable. He was Dean of the Royal Military College of Science 1962–6.

BAILEY, Henry Christopher (1878–1961). British author. B. in London, he specialized in crime and mystery, his *Mr. Fortune* stories being particularly famous.

BAILLIE, Isobel (1895–). British soprano. B. in Hawick, Scotland, she became celebrated for her work in oratorio, her voice having a singularly pure quality. She was prof. of singing at Cornell Univ. 1960–1.

BAILLY (bahyē'), **Jean Sylvain** (1736–93.). French astronomer, who wrote on the satellites of Jupiter and the history of astronomy. Early in the French Revolution he was president of the National Assembly and mayor of Paris, but resigned in 1791 and was guillotined during the Terror.

BAILY (bā'li), **Edward Hodges** (1788–1867). British sculptor of bas-reliefs on Marble Arch and the figure of Nelson in Trafalgar Square, London.

BAILY, Francis (1774–1844). British astronomer, originally a stockbroker and actuary. In 1836 during an eclipse of the sun he noticed *Baily's beads*, due to the breaking-up of the solar crescent into separate portions of light by prominences on the moon.

BAIN, Alexander (1818–1903). Scottish philosopher. Originally a weaver, b. at Aberdeen, in 1845 he became prof. at Glasgow, and in 1860 prof. of logic and English at Aberdeen. He wrote *Logic* (1870). *Mind and Body* (1872), and founded the journal *Mind*.

BAINBRIDGE, Kenneth Tompkins (1904–). American physicist. B. in Cooperstown, N.Y., he worked at the Cavendish Laboratory, Cambridge, 1933–4. Returning to America, he taught at Harvard, and directed the Alamogordo atom bomb test in 1945. He has also carried out research in radar, and since 1961 has been George Vasmer Leverett prof. of physics at Harvard.

BAINES, Sir Frank (1877–1933). British architect, designer of the Imperial Chemicals building on Millbank, Westminster and restorer of Westminster Hall.

BAINTON, Edgar Leslie (1880–1956). British composer. B. in London, he was a pupil of Stanford, and is remembered for his choral symphony *Before Sunrise*, and a *Concerto-Fantasia* for the piano. As Director of the State Conservatorium of Music in Sydney, N.S.W. 1934–46, he did much for Australian music.

BAINVILLE (bañvēl'), **Jacques** (1879–1936). French historian, editor of the Royalist *Action Française* from 1899. He wrote *L'histoire de deux peuples* (1915), in which he analysed the antagonism of France and Germany, and *Histoire de France* (1923).

BAIRD, John Logie (1888–1946). British pioneer of

JOHN LOGIE BAIRD
Bronze by D. Gilbert.
Photo: N.P.G.

television. B. at Helensburgh, Scotland, he held a business post in London, but retired owing to ill-health in 1922, and began to work on television. In 1926 he demonstrated the transmission of detailed human faces before the Royal Institution, and in 1928 transatlantic television. Television was adopted for broadcasting by the German Post Office in 1929, and immediately afterwards by the B.B.C. Later the B.B.C. used B.'s system in conjunction with the Marconi-E.M.I. system, but shortly before the S.W.W. the latter system was exclusively adopted. In 1941 he demonstrated television in natural colour. From 1941 B. was consulting technical adviser to Cable and Wireless Ltd.

BAIREUTH. Alternative form of BAYREUTH.

BAIRNSFATHER, Bruce (1888–1959). British artist, celebrated for his 'Old Bill' cartoons of the F.W.W. In the S.W.W. he was official cartoonist to the U.S. Army in Europe, 1942–4.

BAJA CALIFORNIA. Mexican name of LOWER CALIFORNIA.

BAKER, Sir Benjamin (1840–1907). British civil engineer. B. in Somerset, he was chief assistant to Sir John Fowler in building the Metropolitan and District Railway, London, and with Fowler designed the Forth Bridge (1890) and the original Aswan Dam, Egypt.

BAKER, Sir Herbert (1862–1946). British architect. In 1892 he went to S. Africa, where he designed the Union Buildings and Govt. House, Pretoria, cathedrals in Pretoria, Rhodesia, and Cape Town, Rhodes's tomb in the Matopos and memorial on Table Mountain. Before the F.W.W. he went to India, where he helped Sir Edwin Lutyens in designing the New Delhi. In London he reconstructed the Bank of England, and designed India House, Africa House, and Church House, Westminster. He was knighted in 1926.

BAKER, Josephine (1905–). Coloured American singer and dancer. B. in Missouri, she joined a troupe of Negro actors at 13. In 1925 she rose to fame at the Folies Bergère in Paris and has toured the world.

BAKER, Richard St. Barbe (1889–). British forestry expert, founder of the Men of the Trees Society, which in 1932 became world-wide. In 1959 he settled in New Zealand.

BAKER, Sir Samuel White (1821–93). British explorer. B. in London, he founded an agricultural colony in Ceylon, built a railway across the Dobruja, and in 1861 set out to discover the source of the Nile. In 1863 he met Speke and Grant, who had anticipated him, but he pushed on into Central Africa to be the first to sight the Albert Nyanza and to find that the Nile flowed through it. His wife, Florence von Sass, accompanied him. In 1869–73 he was Gov.-Gen. of the Nile equatorial regions.

BAKEWELL, Robert (1725–95). British agricultural pioneer. B. at Dishley, Leics, he introduced the fine new Leicestershire breed of sheep, and a breed of cattle known as the Dishley or Leicestershire long-horn.

BAKEWELL. Market town (U.D.) in Derbyshire, England. Close by are Chatsworth House and Haddon Hall. It has textile industries founded by Arkwright (q.v.). Pop. (1961) 3,603.

BAKST, Léon (1866–1924). Russian artist whose real name was Rosenberg. B. at St. Petersburg, he displayed remarkable gifts as a theatrical designer, and from 1900 was scenic artist to the Imperial theatres. In 1909 he painted the scenery for Diaghilev's Russian ballets. The latter part of his life was spent in Paris, and he exercised worldwide influence on the decorative arts of the theatre.

BAKU (bahkoo′). Cap. city of the Azerbaijan S.S.R. (U.S.S.R.), on the Apsheron peninsula, in the Caspian Sea. It is the principal centre of the Russian oil industry, which began here in the 1870s. Pipelines lead to Batumi on the Black Sea. B. is also chief port on the Caspian. Pop. (1967) 1,196,000.

BAKUNIN (bahkoon′yĕn), **Mikhail** (1814–76). Russian anarchist. B. in the Tver prov. of a noble family, he served in the Imperial Guard, but, disgusted with Tsarist methods in Poland, resigned his commission, and travelled abroad. In 1848 he was expelled from France as a revolutionary agitator. For his share in a brief revolt at Dresden in 1849 he was sentenced to death. The sentence was commuted to imprisonment, and he was handed over to the Tsar's government and sent to Siberia (1855). In 1861 he managed to escape to Switzerland, where he became recognized as the leader of the anarchist movement. In 1869 he joined the 'First International', but after stormy conflicts with Marx, was expelled in 1872. He had a large following, particularly in the Latin countries. He wrote books and pamphlets, including *God and the State.*

BALA (bah′lah). Town (U.D.) in Merionethshire, N.-Wales, 18 m. N.E. of Dolgellau. During the 18th and 19th cents. it was renowned for its educational and religious associations. Pop. (1961) 1,603. **B. Lake** (Llyn Tegid) is the largest natural lake in Wales.

BALACLAVA (balaklah′va). Town in Ukraine S.S.R., in the Crimea, 6 m. S.E. of Sevastopol, which gives its name to a battle fought on 25 Oct. 1854, during the Crimean War, rendered famous by an ill-timed but gallant charge of the British Light Brigade of cavalry against the Russian entrenched artillery. About 700 all ranks were engaged; only 195 returned.

BALAKIREV (bahlah′kĕrev), **Mily Alexeievich** (1837–1910). Russian composer, b. at Nijni-Novgorod. At St. Petersburg he won fame as a pianist, attached himself to Glinka, estab. the Free School of Music (1862), which stressed the national element, and was director of the Imperial Chapel 1883–95. He wrote orchestral and pianoforte music and songs, all imbued with the Russian national character and spirit.

BALALAIKA (balalī′ka). Musical instrument, not unlike a guitar, much used by Russian peasants. It has a triangular sound box and 2, 3 or 4 strings played by plucking with the fingers.

BALANCE OF PAYMENTS. Summary of the financial results of economic relations between one country and the rest of the world over a certain period, usually a year. It consists in effect of 2 lists: on the one side, of the transactions which give rise to a demand for foreign currencies, i.e. to pay for which pounds have to be sold for dollars, francs, etc.; and on the other, of those transactions which are payable in sterling, i.e. foreign currencies have to be sold for pounds.

BALANCHINE (balantshin′), **Georges** (1904–). American choreographer. B. in St. Petersburg, he left Russia after the revolution, and was ballet master for Diaghilev 1925–9. In 1933 he went to U.S., became an American citizen, and since 1948 has been artistic director of the N.Y. City Ballet Co. He staged the ballet *Slaughter on Tenth Avenue* for *On Your Toes* (1936): others incl. *The Prodigal Son, Serenade,* and *Ballet Imperial.*

BALANOGLO′SSUS. Genus of marine wormlike animals which, with a few near allies, forms the class Hemichordata or Enteropneusta, the lowest division of the Chordata. They burrow in sand or mud at the sea bottom, live at moderate depths, and are found in the warm and temperate parts of the world.

BALBŌ′A, Vasco Nuñez de (c. 1475–1517). Spanish conquistador and discoverer of the Pacific Ocean. He went to the West Indies and in 1510 joined the expedition which conquered the isthmus of Darien. In 1513 he set out across the mountains, and reached the further shore on 29 Sept. He was made Admiral of the Pacific and Gov. of Panama, but was removed by intrigues at the Spanish court, imprisoned and executed.

BALCHIN, Nigel Marlin (1908–70), British author. During the S.W.W. he was engaged on scientific work for the army with the rank of brigadier, and estab. his reputation as a novelist with *The Small Back Room* (1943), dealing with the psychology of the 'back room boys' of wartime research.

BALCON, Sir Michael (1896–). British film producer. His films incl.: *The Lavender Hill Mob*, *The Cruel Sea*, and *The Long and the Short and the Tall*.

BALDER (bawl′der). In Norse mythology, the son of Odin and Frigga and husband of Nanna, and the best, wisest, and most loved of all the gods. He was killed, at Loki's instigation, by a twig of mistletoe shot by the blind god Hödur.

BALDNESS. Loss of hair from the scalp. It is common in elderly persons from the natural failure of nourishment in the hair follicles. Total or partial B. may be caused by excessive oily secretion of the skin; skin infections; tumours, and many other diseases. Hair may fall out as a result of fever, operation, shock, nervous disorder, failure of the thyroid gland (myxoedema), and other causes of poor health.

BALDWIN I (1058–1118). Son of the count of Bouillon in the Ardennes, he accompanied his brother Godfrey on the 1st Crusade in 1096 and became King of Jerusalem in 1100. The kingdom he founded endured for nearly a century.

BALDWIN, James (1924–). American author. A Negro, b. in Harlem, N.Y., he has been active in the civil rights movement. He has written plays, e.g. *The Amen Corner* (1955); vols. of essays, e.g. *Notes of a Native Son* (1955) and *The Fire Next Time* (1963); and novels, e.g *Going to Meet the Man* (1965).

BALDWIN, Stanley, 1st earl B. of Bewdley (1867–1947). Conservative statesman. B. at Bewdley, Worcs, he was the only son of A. Baldwin, M.P., of the iron and steel company known as Baldwin's Ltd. In 1908 he was elected Unionist M.P. for Bewdley, and in 1916 he became parliamentary private secretary to Bonar Law. He was Financial Secretary to the Treasury 1917–21, and then was appointed to the presidency of the Board of Trade. In 1919 he gave to the Treasury £150,000 of War Loan for cancellation, representing about 20 per cent of his fortune. He took a leading part in the disruption of the Lloyd George Coalition, and became Chancellor of the Exchequer in Bonar Law's Cons. admin. As such he negotiated, on the advice of Montagu Norman, the war debts settlement with the U.S.A. On Bonar Law's retirement in 1923, B. became P.M., and later in the year he 'went to the country' in search of a mandate to introduce a measure of Protection, which was necessary to counter the wave of unemployment. The result was adverse, and early in 1924 B. resigned. After the fall of the MacDonald admin., B. became Premier for the 2nd time, holding office until 1929. His premiership was marked by the General Strike of 1926, the Trade Disputes Act of 1927, the grant of widows' and orphans' pensions, and the securing of complete adult suffrage in 1928. In 1931 MacDonald formed in conjunction with B. a Nat. Govt. in which B. was Lord President of the Council. In 1935 B. became P.M. for the 3rd time; he retained the post until 1937, when he made place for Neville Chamberlain, he himself going to the House of Lords as an earl. His handling of the situation that arose from the abdication of Edward VIII was generally applauded, but his attitude towards the dictator powers of Germany and Italy was much criticized.

BÂLE. French form of BASLE.

BALEA′RICS. Group of islands off the E. coast of Spain; they were conquered by Aragon in the 14th cent. The largest are Majorca (on which is the cap., Palma), Minorca, Iviza, Cabrera, and Formentera. Area 1,935 sq. m.; pop. (1960) 443,327.

BALEWA. See TAFAWA-BALEWA.

BALFE (balf), **Michael William** (1808–70). British composer. B. at Dublin, he was a violinist at Drury Lane, London, when only 16. In 1825 he went to study in Italy, and in 1846 he was appointed conductor at Her Majesty's Theatre. He composed operas of which only *The Bohemian Girl* is now remembered.

BALFOUR, Arthur James, 1st earl of (1848–1930). British Cons. statesman. Son of a Scottish landowner, he was elected a Conservative M.P. in 1874. In Lord Salisbury's ministry he was Sec. for Ireland (1887) and for his ruthless vigour was called '3loody B.' by the nationalists. In 1891, and again in 1895, he became 1st Lord of the Treasury and leader of the Commons, and in 1902 he succeeded Salisbury in the premiership. His cabinet was divided over Chamberlain's Tariff Reform proposals, and at the 1905 elections suffered a crushing defeat. B. retired from the party leadership in 1911. In 1915 he joined the Asquith coalition as 1st Lord of the Admiralty, and he was Foreign Sec 1916–19; as such he issued the 'B. Declaration' of 1917 in favour of a national home in Palestine for the Jews and signed the Treaty of Versailles. He was Lord Pres. of the Council 1919–22 and 1925–9, and received the O.M. in 1916 and an earldom in 1922. He was also a distinguished philosopher, and wrote *A Defence of Philosophic Doubt* (1879), *Foundations of Belief* and *Theism and Humanism* (Gifford Lectures, 1914).

BALFOUR DECLARATION (1917). Letter written on 2 Nov. 1917 by A. J. Balfour, then British Foreign Sec., to Lord Rothschild, chairman of the British Zionist Federation, stating that 'His Majesty's Govt. view with favour the establishment in Palestine of a national home for the Jewish people': this eventually led to the foundation of the modern Jewish State of Israel in 1948.

BALI (bah′lē). Mountainous volcanic island of Indonesia, separated from Java by the mile-wide B. Strait. The climate is equable, the soil fertile, and the vegetation luxuriant. Tropical produce grows to perfection. The Balinese are noted for their fine physique, and the women are often remarkably beautiful. They are Hindus in religion, devoted to the drama and music, and their dances are world-famous. They are skilled craftsmen in gold and silver work, wood-carving, and weaving.

A Hindu culture, brought by settlers from India, was estab. in B. by the 7th cent. A.D. From time to time B. was subject to Javanese princes, but its warlike inhabitants were difficult to control, and in the 17th cent. the kings of B. ruled Lombok and a small part of E. Java. B. remained independent until 1856 when the Dutch occupied it.

B. Strait, between B. and Java, was the scene on 19–20 Feb. 1942 of a naval action between Japanese and U.S. and Dutch forces which served to delay slightly the Japanese invasion of Java.

The cap., Den Pasar, has an airfield. Area 2,240 sq. m.; pop. (est.) 1,100,000.

BALIKESIR (bahlikesēr′). Turkish town, cap. of an isl. of the same name, 80 m. S.W. of Bursa. It trades in silk and opium, and has silver mines near by. Pop. (1965) 69,300.

BALIKPAPAN. Port and petroleum centre of E. Borneo, in Kalimantan, Indonesia. It has an airfield. Pop. (est.) 30,000.

BALKANS (bawl′kanz) (Turkish for mountains). Peninsula in S.E. Europe stretching into the Mediterranean between the Adriatic and Aegean Seas. It is joined to the rest of Europe by a broad isthmus 750 m.

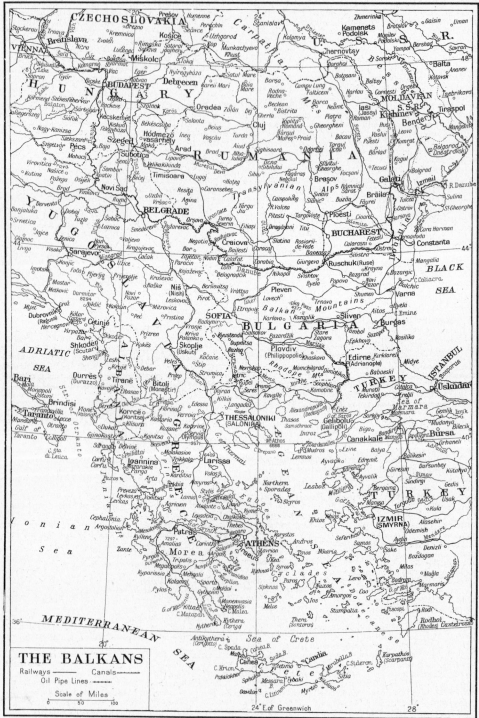

THE BALKANS

Railways ———   Canals ———
Oil Pipe Lines ········

Scale of Miles

0   50   100

Geographia Ltd.

wide between Rijeka on the W. and the mouth of the Danube on the Black Sea to the E. The plains of the Save–Danube basin in the N. are cut off from the influence of the sea by the complex of mountains (the Balkan Mountains) and valleys which forms the main bulk of the peninsula. The much dissected coastline of Greece allows the marine influence to penetrate far inland in the S. There are few navigable rivers.

The people are of great ethnic diversity, the remains of wave after wave of invasion, and speak a variety of languages. Most of them belong to the Greek Orthodox Church: a few are R.C., and in Turkey-in-Europe and in Bulgaria are a number professing Islam. Included in the B. are Greece, Albania, Bulgaria, Turkey-in-Europe, most of Yugoslavia, and part of Rumania (*see* these countries).

BALKAN WARS (1912–13). Two wars which resulted in the expulsion of Turkey from all but 9,068 sq. m. of Europe. The 1st, in 1912, of Bulgaria, Serbia, Greece, and Montenegro against Turkey, forced the Turks to ask for an armistice, but the peace negotiations, in London, broke down when the Turks, while agreeing to surrender all Turkey-in-Europe W. of Adrianople (Edirne), refused to give up that city. In Feb. 1913 hostilities were resumed, Adrianople fell on 26 March and on 30 May by the Treaty of London Turkey retained in Europe only a small piece of eastern Thrace and the Gallipoli peninsula.

In the 2nd Balkan War, June-July 1913 – among the victors – Bulgaria attacked Greece and Serbia which were joined by Rumania. Bulgaria was defeated, and Turkey secured from that country the cession of Adrianople.

BALKA′SH. Lake in the Kazakh S.S.R. (U.S.S.R.). It is 375 m. long, receives several rivers, but has no outlet. It is very shallow and is frozen throughout the winter. Area, about 6,680 sq. m. On its N. shore is the town of B., founded in 1928, pop. (est.) 75,000, engaged in refining copper mined near by.

BALL, John (d. 1381). English agitator, a priest and prominent leader of the Peasants' Revolt of 1381. At Blackheath he preached from the text 'When Adam delved and Eve span, Who was then the gentleman?' When the revolt collapsed he was taken prisoner and executed.

BALLAD (bal′ad). Type of popular poetry. Derived from Late Lat. *ballare*, 'to dance', the B. was primarily intended for singing at the communal ring-dance, the refrains representing the chorus.

Of simple metrical form and dealing with some strongly emotional event, the B. is half-way between the lyric and the epic. The majority of Bs. date from the 15th cent. but were not collected until modern times, the most famous collections being Bishop Percy's *Reliques of Ancient Poetry* (1765), Scott's *Minstrelsy of the Scottish Border* (1802–3), and Prof. F. J. Child's *English and Scottish Popular Ballads* (1857–9). Opinion is divided as to whether the authorship of the Bs. may be attributed to individual poets or to the community. Later Bs. tend to centre round a popular folk-hero, as in the case of the *Gest of Robyn Hode* and in the American cycles concerning Jesse James and Yankee Doodle. Other later forms are the 'broadsheets' with a satirical or political motive, and the testamentary 'hanging' Bs. of the condemned criminal. Poets of the Romantic movement both in England and in Germany were largely influenced by the B. revival, e.g., the *Lyrical Ballads* (1798) of Wordsworth and Coleridge. Other writers of modern Bs. include Keats, Southey, Rossetti, S. Dobell, Tennyson, Morris, and Kipling.

BALLADE (balahd′). Poetic form developed in France in the later Middle Ages from the popular ballad, and generally consisting of 1 or more groups of 3 stanzas of 7 or 8 lines each, followed by a shorter stanza or envoy. The last line of the 1st stanza is repeated as a refrain in each succeeding verse including the envoy. The B. was revived in the 19th cent. by Banville, A. Lang, E. Gosse, and Henley. Also a music form of story-like type, notably used by Chopin.

BALLANCE, John (1839–93). N.Z. statesman. B. in Ulster, he migrated to N.Z., founded and ed. the *Wanganui Herald*, held many cabinet posts, and was P.M. 1891–3.

BALLANTYNE (bal′antīn), **Robert Michael** (1825–94). British writer of stories for boys. B in. Edinburgh, a nephew of Scott's publishers, James and John B., he went to Canada as a boy and spent 6 years as a trapper in lonely outposts for the Hudson's Bay company. He produced over 100 spirited tales, incl. *The Young Fur Traders*, *Coral Island*, and *Martin Rattler*.

BALLARAT. Largest inland town in Australia, in Victoria, 66 m. W.N.W. of Melbourne, an industrial and railway centre. The discovery of gold here led to the founding of the town in 1851, and gold long remained its chief product. Pop. (1961) 54,913.

BALLET (bal′ā). A theatrical representation combining music and movement in a complex form of dancing. Some such form of entertainment existed in ancient Greece, but the germ of B. as it is known today was brought to France by Catherine de Medici, in the form of a spectacle combining singing, dancing, and declamation.

The first important dramatic B. was mounted in 1581 by Baltasar de Beaujoyeux, and was performed by male courtiers, ladies of the Court forming the *corps de ballet*. In 1661 Louis XIV founded *L'Académie Nationale de Musique et de la Danse*, from which all subsequent B. activities throughout the world can be traced. Long flowing court dress was worn by the dancers. In the 1720s Marie-Anne Camargo, the first ballerina, shortened her skirt to reveal her feet, thus allowing greater movement *à terre* and the development of dancing *en l'air*. In the early 19th cent. a Paris costumier, Maillot, invented tights, thus completing muscular freedom. The first of the great B. masters was J. G. Noverre (1727–1810). Great contemporary dancers were Vestris, Heinel, Dauberval, and Gardel. Carlo Blasis (1803–78) is regarded as the father of classical B.

ROMANTIC BALLET. The great Romantic era of Taglioni, Elssler, Grisi, Grahn, and Cerrito began about 1830, but survives today only in *Giselle* (1841) and *La Sylphide* (1832). The calf-length classical white dress was introduced together with dancing *en pointe*. The technique of the female dancer developed, but the men were reduced to partners.

Russian B. was introduced to the West by Diaghilev (q.v.) who set out for Paris in 1909 at about the same time that Isadora Duncan, a rigid opponent of classical B., was touring the Continent. Associated with

BALLET. Ulanova in Giselle, one of her greatest roles, supported by Fadeyechev and the Bolshoi company, as they appeared at Covent Garden, taking London by storm in 1956.
Photo: Houston Rogers.

BALLET. A remarkable partnership: Margot Fonteyn and Rudolf Nureyev create the leading roles in *Marguerite and Armand*, based by Frederick Ashton on the novel by Dumas, *La Dame aux Camélias.*   *Photo: Houston Rogers.*

him were Michel Fokine, Nijinsky, Pavlova, Massine, Balanchine, Lifar, and Bs. presented by his co. before its break-up on his death in 1929 incl. *Les Sylphides, Schéhérazade, Petrouchka* and *Blue Train.*

In the U.S. Balanchine estab. in 1933 the School of American B. and the de Basil Ballets Russes de Monte Carlo and Massine's Ballet Russe de Monte Carlo also carried on the Diaghilev tradition: since 1948 the N.Y. City Ballet with Maria Tallchief, Nora Kaye, and choreographer Jerome Robbins, under the guiding influence of Balanchine, has developed a genuine American classic style. *See* also GRAHAM, Martha.

In Britain Marie Rambert initiated in 1926 the Ballet Club which developed into the Ballet Rambert, and in 1930 Arnold Haskell and Ninette de Valois formed the Camargo Society, but the modern national co. the Royal Ballet (so named 1957) grew from foundations laid by Ninette de Valois in 1928. British dancers, incl. Margot Fonteyn, Beryl Grey, Alicia Markova, Anton Dolin, Michael Somes, Elaine Fifield and Antoinette Sibley.

In Russia B. continues to flourish, the 2 chief cos. being the Kirov and Bolshoi. Best known ballerinas are Ulanova and Plisetskaya (qq.v.), and among the men Rudolf Nureyev, now dancing in the West.

The best-known systems of dance notation are *Labanotation*, developed by Hungarian Rudolf Laban (d. 1958), and the much simpler Benesh System, using symbols on a horizontal stave, developed by husband and wife Joan and Rudolf Benesh.

BALLI′STICS. The study of the motion of projectiles. Internal B. deals with the motion of a projectile inside a gun; exterior B. with the trajectory of the projectile through the air; and terminal B. with the motion and effect at the target end. The Bs. of a gun are affected from day to day by the temperature of the charge, barometric pressure, and the wind. Range tables contain information enabling the gunner to allow for these variations.

BALLOON. A bag of impermeable fabric, which rises from the ground when filled with a gas lighter than air. The first successful balloon experiment was made by the Montgolfier brothers in 1783 at Annonay near Lyons. The first human ascents were made in Montgolfier Bs. by Pilâtre de Rozier at Paris later in the same year. These Bs. were filled with heated air,

but hydrogen was soon substituted. The French Revolution led to the first use of the B. in war for observation purposes.

Bs. were used in the Italian war of 1859 and the American Civil War, while during the siege of Paris in 1870 they proved of value for conveying passengers out of the city. A B. corps was added to the British Army in 1890, and served in the S. African War.

The scientific possibilities of the B. were early recognized. Ascents made by H. T. Coxwell and J. Glaisher in 1862–6 provided valuable observations on the constitution of the atmosphere, and attempts were made at aerial photography. In 1901 an altitude of 34,500 ft. was reached. In 1892 the use of unmanned Bs. carrying automatic recording instruments was introduced. In 1932 Prof. Piccard in a B. equipped with an airtight spherical gondola reached 53,000 ft.; in 1935 the American army balloonists Anderson and Stevens reached 72,395 ft. and carried out investigations into cosmic rays. An unsuccessful attempt was made in 1897 by S. A. Andrée to reach the North Pole by B. Before the S.W.W. B. races were held annually for the Gordon-Bennett Cup. In both World Wars, Bs. linked by cables – a B. barrage – were used to protect London from dive bombing. Bs. are still often used in research: see illus., p. 74.

BALMO′RAL CASTLE. Royal residence in Scotland on the Dee, 6½ m. N.E. of Braemar, Aberdeenshire. The castle, built of granite in the Scottish baronial style, is dominated by a square tower and circular turret rising 100 ft. It was rebuilt 1853–5 by Prince Albert, who bought the estate in 1852.

BALSAM. Name given in medicine to many resins and oils obtained from various plants, in particular the B. of Tolu obtained from the tree *Myroxylon toluifera*, and B. of Peru from the trunk of *M. pereirae*. Bs. have a pleasant fragrance and some have pain-relieving properties.

The name B. is also given to plants of the genus *Impatiens*, which are generally herbaceous annuals with white or red flowers.

BALTIC. Large shallow arm of the North Sea, extending N.E. from the narrow Skaggerak and Kattegat, between Sweden and Denmark, to the Gulf of Bothnia between Sweden and Finland. Its coastline is 5,000 m. long, and the sea, including the Gulfs of Riga, Finland, and Bothnia, has an area of 163,000 sq. m. Its shore-line is shared by Denmark, Germany, Poland, U.S.S.R., Finland, and Sweden. Many large rivers flow into it, including the Oder, Vistula, Niemen, W. Dvina, Narva, and Neva. Tides are hardly perceptible, and weather is often stormy and navigation dangerous. Most ports are closed by ice from Nov.

BALLOON. A contemporary print illustrates the ascent from Dover on Jan. 7, 1785 of J. P. Blanchard and J. Jeffries in their hydrogen-filled balloon. Landing near Calais, they achieved the first aerial crossing of the English Channel.
Courtesy of the Science Museum, South Kensington

till May. The Kiel canal links the B. and the North Sea, and the Göta canal connects the two seas by way of the S. Swedish lakes.

BALTIC, Battle of the (1801). Name given to the naval battle fought off Copenhagen on 2 April 1801, in which a British fleet under Sir Hyde Parker, with Nelson as second-in-command, annihilated the Danish navy.

BALTIC PORT. English name of PALDISKI, translation of its German name Baltisch Port.

BALTIC STATES. Collective name sometimes used for Estonia, Latvia, and Lithuania (qq.v.).

BALTIMORE. City and port of U.S.A. and largest city in Maryland State, on the W. shore of Chesapeake Bay, at the mouth of the Patapsco, 38 m. N.E. of Washington. Named after the founder of Maryland, Lord Baltimore (1606–75), the city of B. dates from 1729 and was incorporated in 1797. It is an important commercial, industrial, and educational centre. A road tunnel under B. harbour (opened 1957) relieved a bottle-neck between Washington and N.Y. Pop. met. area (1970) 2,043,667.

BALUCHISTAN (baloochistahn′). A large, mountainous area of Asia, from 1970 a province of W. Pakistan. It is contiguous on the W. with Persia and Afghanistan. Before 1947 it consisted of (i) British Baluchistan, ceded to Britain 1876, 1879, 1891 (9,084 sq. m.); (ii) British leased and tribal territories (45,372 sq. m.); (iii) the states of Kalat (cap. Quetta), Makran, Las Bela, and Kharan (79,546 sq. m.). British controlled B. was included in Pakistan in 1947, the states joined that country in 1948. B. was in 1955 formed into two divisions of W. Pakistan, Quetta (area 53,115 sq. m.; pop. 1961, 633,i18) and Kalat (area 72,944 sq. m.; pop. 1961, 530,893). The majority of the people are Moslems and many are nomads; the desert country and poor rainfall limit possibilities for agriculture. Coal and chromite are worked, and natural gas is being piped from Sui in the N.

BALZAC (bahlzahk′), **Honoré de** (1799–1850). French novelist. B. at Tours, the son of the director of the city hospital whose real name was Balssa, he studied law and worked as a notary's clerk in Paris, but turned to literature. His 1st attempts included tragedies such as Cromwell and novels pub. pseudonymously with no great success. A venture in printing and publishing (1825–8) involved him in a lifelong web of debt, but in 1829 he achieved his 1st success with Les Chouans and Physiologie du mariage. This was the beginning of the long series of novels the Comédie humaine, which according to the complete plan of 1842 was to consist of 143 vols. depicting 19th cent. French life in every conceivable aspect, but of which only some 80 were completed. They incl. studies of human folly and vice such as the miser in Eugénie Grandet (1833), the monomaniac of La recherche de l'absolu (1834), the weak loving father of Père Goriot (1834), the jealous Cousine Bette (1846), and the acquisitive Cousin Pons (1847); and analyses of professions or ranks such as the commercial traveller of L'illustre Gaudissart (1833), the doctor of Le médecin de la campagne (1833), the great business man of La maison de Nucingen (1838), and the cleric of Le curé de village (1839). Apart from the novels stand the collection of Rabelaisian Contes drôlatiques (1833).

In 1833, before the death of his patroness, Mme de Berny, who figures in Le Lys dans la vallée (1836), B. met the Polish countess Evelina Hanska; he m. her 4 months before his death in Paris. He was buried in Père Lachaise cemetery.

BALZAC, Jean-Louis Guez de (1594–1654). French writer. B. near Angoulême, he was one of the first members of the Académie Française; his Lettres (1624) had a great influence on French prose.

BALZAN, Eugenio (1874–1953). Italian philanthropist, managing editor of Corriere della Sera, Milan, for 30 years. His fortune was used by his dau., at his request, to estab. the Eugenio B. Foundation in 1962. Prizes are awarded annually either individually in (1) literature, art, philosophy; (2) peace, the humanities; (3) natural science; or one single prize. Single prizes went to the Nobel Foundation (1962) and to Pope John (1963).

BAMBERG. German city on the Regnitz. 33 m. N. of Nuremberg, Bavaria. The cathedral, built by Henry II in 1004, contains sculptures of the 13th cent., and the castle is renowned. Pop. (1960) 73,547.

BAMBOO′. Group of plants (Bambuseae), belonging to the family of the grasses (Gramineae), found in tropical and sub-tropical countries, and remarkable for the relatively gigantic size which they attain. The stems are hollow and jointed, and can be put to a number of uses. The young shoots are eaten in China; paper is made from the stem.

BANANA (banah′na). Tropical plant (Musa sapientum of the family Musaceae) producing a fruit which has been used for human food since before written history. It originated in the moist tropical

BANANA. Known from ancient times in Asia, the banana is now cultivated extensively in other parts of the world and Queensland's fertile soil is ideal. Plants die once they have fruited and are left to rot, after being cut down, so that they enrich the soil. *Courtesy of Agent-General for Queensland.*

regions of southern Asia, was carried to Africa by Arab traders, established in the Canary Is. by the Portuguese about 1482, and from there was introduced to the New World. It was scarcely known in Britain prior to 1890, and the first direct shipment of a full cargo of Bs. from Jamaica reached Bristol in 1901.

The B. plant reaches 15 to 30 ft. in height; it is not a tree, because there is no wood in it. Each plant bears a single bunch of Bs., made up of 6 to 9 'hands' or clusters, each containing from 12 to 18 Bs. or 'fingers'. For export, the fruit is cut green and transported in special refrigerated ships: some is sun-dried. The greatest B. farms in the world are in Jamaica.

BANARAS. Another transliteration of VARANESI.

BANBURY. Town (bor.) of Oxon, England, on the Cherwell, 20 m. N. of Oxford. It is famous for its cake and ale, and also for the B. cross of the nursery rhyme, which was removed in 1602, but replaced by a new one in 1858. Pop. (1961) 20,996.

BANCA. Alternative form of BANKA.

BANCROFT, George (1800–91). American diplomat and historian. A Democrat, he was sec. of the navy 1845, when he estab. Annapolis as the U.S. Naval Academy, and as acting sec. of war (May 1846) was instrumental in bringing about the occupation of California, and gave the order to Zachary Taylor to cross the Texas border which started war with Mexico. He wrote a History of the United States (1834–76).

BAND. Section of the full orchestra, e.g. the string band, the woodwind, the brass and the percussion. For outdoor performances Military Bs., comprising both woodwind and brass instruments, developed in the 18th cent., and from 1857 training has been given at Kneller Hall. *Brass Bs.* grew to great popularity in England during the 19th cent., especially in the factory and colliery districts of the north. The National Brass B. contests were instituted at the Crystal Palace in 1900, and are held annually in London: famous names are those of Foden's, the Black Dyke, and the Fairey Aviation Bs. Composers of Brass B. music include Bantock, Bliss, Holst, Elgar, and Vaughan Williams.

BANDA, Hastings Kamuzu (1905–). Malawi statesman. B. in Nyasaland, at 12 he worked as an interpreter in the Rand goldmines, S. Africa, going in 1923 to the U.S. to take a degree in philosophy at Chicago and medicine at Nashville. He went to Edinburgh in 1941, taking an L.R.C.P. there, and practised in the N. of England and London for several years. During this time in London he played a leading part in founding the Nyasaland African National Congress, which he led from Ghana in 1955, returning to Nyasaland in 1958. When the state of emergency was declared there in 1959 he was arrested and the Congress declared illegal. Released in 1960, he became leader of the recently formed Malawi African Congress, taking part in the London talks on Nyasaland's new constitution, and became P.M. in 1963 and pres. of the Rep. of Malawi 1966.

BANDAR ABBAS. Persian port on the Ormuz strait, Persian Gulf; formerly called Gombroon, it was renamed and made prosperous by Shah Abbas I (1587–1629). Its summer pop. is *c.* 10,000; winter, *c.* 15,000.

BANDARANAIKE (bondrahnī'ahkah), **Solomon West Ridgeway Dias** (1899–1959). Ceylonese statesman. Ed. at Oxford, he was called to the English Bar, and in 1925 returned to practise law in Ceylon. An ardent nationalist he founded in 1951 the Sri Lanka Freedom Party and in 1956 became P.M., pledged to a socialist programme and a neutral foreign policy. He failed to satisfy extremists and was assassinated by a Buddhist monk. In 1940 he had m. **Sirimavo Ratwatte** (1916–) and on his death she entered politics, campaigning for the continuation of her husband's policies. The first woman in the world to hold such office 1960–5 and from 1970.

BANDAR SHAH. Persian port on the Caspian Sea, 200 m. N.E. of Tehran, and northern terminus of the Trans-Iranian railway. It was a lease-lend supply port for the Russian armies 1941–5.

BA'NDICOOT. Small marsupial mammal of the Peramelidae family, inhabiting Australia, Tasmania, and New Guinea. There are several species, approximately the size of a rabbit and mainly insectivorous. They live in burrows.

BANDUNG. City of Indonesia, a commercial centre and cap. of W. Java prov. It has technical and medical institutions, an airfield, and a powerful radio station. Pop. (est.) 1,046,189.

BANFF. Royal burgh and holiday resort of Scotland, co. town of Banffshire, at the mouth of the Deveron. Pop. (1961) 3,329.

BANFF. Health and pleasure resort in Alberta, Canada, on the Bow. It is the railway and road centre for the Rocky Mountains national park. Lake Louise is near by. Pop. *c.* 2,500.

BANFFSHIRE. Maritime county of N.E. Scotland stretching from the Cairngorms to Moray Firth. Agriculture, cattle-rearing, fishing, and whisky distil-

ling are the chief occupations. Rivers incl. the Deveron, Spey, and Avon. The co. town is Banff, and other towns are Keith, Macduff, and Buckie. Pop. (1961) 46,400.

BANGALORE (bangaloor'). Cap. of the Indian state of Mysore, formerly the largest British cantonment in S. India. It is an important airport, railway junction, and industrial town. Pop. (1961) 907,627.

BANGKO'K. Cap. and chief port of Thailand (Siam) on the Menam, 25 m. from the Gulf of Siam. It has a royal palace, 5 univs., many industries, and an important airport. It was estab. as the cap. by Phra Chao Tak in 1769, after the Burmese had burned down the former cap. Avuthia *c.* 40 m. to the N. also on the r. Menam Chao Phya. The temple, Wat Phra Keo, within the palace walls, contains an image in jasper of Buddha: also famous is Wat Arun with a 243 ft. high tower. Pop. (1956) 1,328,228.

MRS. BANDARANAIKE
Courtesy of the Ceylon Govt.

BANGLADESH (bangladäsh'). Rep. of the Indian sub-continent: the name means 'Bengal Nation'. Until 1972 it was known as East Pakistan (*see* PAKISTAN), and had been formed on independence in 1947 from the eastern part of the Bengal prov. of British India and the Sylhet district of Assam. Part of the alluvial plain of the Ganges-Brahmaputra river system, with an annual rainfall of 100 in., B. is subject to devastating cyclones. The main crops are rice, tea in the hills and jute in the plains, although the market for jute has been affected by the development of artificial fibres. B. has little industry, and her smaller share of Pakistan's development funds, although her jute exports supplied a large part of Pakistan's foreign exchange and she had a larger pop. than West Pakistan, led to agitation for autonomy. Sheikh Mujibar Rahman proclaimed secession in 1971, and following a brief civil war, in which she received Indian aid, E. Pakistan became an independent state in 1972 as Bangladesh, and some 10 m. refugees returned home across the Indian border. The cap. is Dacca, and the chief port is Chittagong. There is a pres., but power rests with the parliament, and Sheikh Mujib became the first P.M. in 1972.

Area 54,501 sq. m.; pop. (1972) 75,000,000, of whom 65,000,000 are Moslem. Bangladesh became a member of the Commonwealth in 1972.

BANGOR. Cathedral city, seaport, and bor. of Caernarvonshire, N. Wales, seat of the Univ. College of N. Wales. There is an export trade in slate. The cathedral, begun in 1496, was restored 1866–80. Pop (1961) 13,977.

BANGOR. Seaside resort (bor.) on Belfast lough, co. Down, N. Ireland. 12 m. N.E. of Belfast. Pop. (1961) 23,860.

BANJERMASIN (bahnyermah'sin). Town and port of Indonesia, in Kilimantan, Borneo. It exports petroleum, rubber, etc. Pop. (1960) 180,000.

BANJO. Musical instrument usually with 4 or more strings. The notes are stopped by the left hand while the strings are plucked by the thumb or fingers of the right, or with a plectrum. It was taken to U.S.A. by Negro slaves and Negro minstrels introduced it into England about 1846.

BANKA. Island of the Rep. of Indonesia off the E. coast of Sumatra. It is one of the world's largest tin producers. Pangkal Pinang is the chief town, and Mintok the cap. and chief port. Area 4,610 sq. m. Pop. (est.) 205,000.

BANKING. A manual ledger-keeper formerly took several minutes to post entries which an electronic computer deals with in a few millionths of a second. Carefully designed characters (right) are used to print in special ink across the lower edge of a cheque the serial number of the item, the bank and branch number, the account number and – at a later stage – the amount. These can be detected and interpreted by electronic machines, known as M.I.C.R. (Magnetic Ink Character Recognition): the electronic cheque sorter/reader (left) sorts 700 items per minute into branch and account order and, under control of the central computer, records all the details on magnetic tape. The system originated in the U.S.A. and was first used in Europe by the Westminster Bank.
Courtesy of the Westminster Bank.

BANKHEAD, Tallulah (1903- 68). American actress. B. in Alabama, dau. of Senator Wm. B. Bankhead, she became a radio, stage, and screen star. Celebrated for her wit, she appeared with success in *Private Lives* and as Sabina in *The Skin of Our Teeth*.

BANKRUPTCY. The process by which the property of a person unable to pay his debts is taken from him and divided rateably among his creditors. Proceedings may be instituted either by the debtor himself (voluntary B.) or by any creditor for £50 (or $1,000 in the U.S.) or over (involuntary B.).

BANKS, Sir Joseph (1743–1820). British naturalist and explorer. B. in London, he accompanied Capt. Cook round the world, 1768–71, played a leading part in the development of New S. Wales, was a principal founder of the Botanical Gardens at Kew, introduced fresh food and plants into various parts of the world, and was President of the Royal Society from 1778.

BANKING. Banks are essentially intermediary financing institutions which do not own the larger part of the funds they employ, but owe them in turn to others. A country's monetary supplies are commonly controlled by entrusting the issue of notes to a central bank.

Modern B. originated with the Lombards who disappeared from England at the time of the Reformation, their place being taken by the goldsmiths, who received money for safe custody from their clients, and lent it out again to approved borrowers – the 1st cheques being their 'notes' or receipts. Firms so specializing developed into private banks. The *Bank of England* was founded with govt. backing in 1694, but private banks continued to flourish until the Napoleonic wars: joint-stock B. was legalized in 1826 but such banks were not permitted to operate in London, hitherto the Bank of England's preserve, until 1833. The Bank Charter Act of 1844 practically concentrated the note issue in the Bank of England, **but joint-stock banks expanded through the cheque** system, the present British 'Big Four' – the result of a long process of amalgamation – being Barclays, Lloyds, Midland, and National Westminster Bank Group. All have subsidiaries at home and abroad. Besides a number of other general bankers, there are also some 'merchant bankers' primarily concerned with commerce. In 1946 the Bank of England, till then a private corporation, was nationalized, but this marked no substantial change of function. In Europe there are similar central banks, but in the U.S. it was only in 1914 that a series of independent bank failures led to the estab. of the *Federal Reserve*

System. All national banks (those chartered by the Federal controller of the currency) are compulsory members: for state banks (those chartered by individual B. depts.) membership is optional. Co-operation between the Federal Reserve System and the U.S. treasury is close, especially since the 1933 crisis in B.: there is no one central bank, but the country is divided into 12 districts each with a Federal Reserve Bank.

Banks obtain payment of the cheques and bills of exchange, etc., drawn upon each other, through a *Bankers' Clearing House*. In the U.K. each bank has an account at the Bank of England, and the daily balances of amounts due and receivable are made by transfer through these accounts: the London clearing house was estab. 1770 and there are others in the chief provincial cities. The N.Y. clearing house dates from 1853, and each great city of the U.S. has its own.

The *International Bank for Reconstruction and Development* was estab. in 1945 as a result of the Bretton Woods Conference of 1944 and is popularly known as the 'World Bank': its H.Q. is in Washington. It aids international investment for production purposes, supplementing private investment from its own capital in order to improve the balance of world trade and living standards everywhere. The *Economic Development Institute* (estab. 1956) is an offshoot where economic planning can be studied by representatives of member countries, and there is an *International Centre for Settlement of Investment Disputes* (1966) with the pres. of the World Bank as chairman: both are in Washington. See UNITED NATIONS.

BANK RATE. The advertised minimum rate at which the Bank of England will discount Treasury Bills and approved bills of exchange. It provides an important means of economic control since the rates of other banks for loans, deposits, etc., are normally based on this rate.

BANNISTER, Roger (1929–). British doctor and athlete. On 6 May 1954, at Oxford, he became the 1st man in the history of athletics to run the mile in under 4 min., his time being 3 min. 59·4 sec. In 1963 he became physician to the Nat. Hospital for Nervous Diseases, London.

BANNOCKBURN. Town in Stirlingshire, Scotland, where on 24 June 1314 Robert Bruce completely defeated an army of English invaders under Edward II. It manufactures woollen goods. Pop. *c.* 5,000.

BA'NTENG. A species (*Bibos banteng*) of wild ox ranging from Indo-China through Burma to Java and Borneo. Its colour varies from pale brown to almost black; its height is about 5 ft.

BANTING, Sir Frederick Grant (1891–1941). Canadian scientist, discoverer with Prof. Macleod, Dr. Best, and others, of the insulin treatment for diabetes (1922), for which in 1923 he and Macleod received a Nobel Prize. B. was killed in an aeroplane crash in Newfoundland.

BANTOCK, Sir Granville (1868–1946). British composer. B. in London, he became known as a conductor of musical comedy and modern Eng. music, and was prof. of music at the Univ. of Birmingham 1908–34. He was knighted in 1930. His works incl. the choral symphony *Atlanta in Calydon, Hebridean Symphony*, and a setting of *Omar Khayyám*.

BANTU (ban'too). A group of related languages, spoken by predominantly Negroid peoples widely spread over the greater part of Africa S. of the Sahara. The word comes from the Zulu, and illustrates the inflexional use of the prefix which is the main structural peculiarity of B.: *ba-ntu*, people; *mu-ntu*, a man, etc. The origin of the B.-speaking peoples may have been in N. Central Africa. The B.-speaking natives of S. Africa are officially styled Native.

BANVILLE (boṅvēl'), **Théodore Faullain de** (1823–91). French poet, dramatist, and novelist. B. at Moulins, he made his name among the French Romantic poets with many vols. of verse such as *Les Cariatides* (1841). Of his plays *Gringoire* (1866) is the best-known.

BA'NYAN. A tree (*Ficus benghalensis*) of the tribe Moraceae. Its roots grow down from its spreading branches, forming supporting pillars which have the appearance of separate trunks.

BANYAN, held a sacred tree by Hindus.

BAOBAB (bah'obab). Tropical African tree (*Adansonia digitata*) of the family Bombaceae. Its trunk grows 30 ft. thick, and it is one of the largest trees known.

B.A.O.R. Short for British Army of the Rhine, the name adopted in 1945 for the occupation forces in Germany, which had previously been called the British Liberation Army.

BAPTISM (Gk. *baptizo*, I dip, submerge). Immersion in or sprinkling with water, particularly as a religious rite of initiation. In antiquity and among primitive peoples the practice has been widespread; in some of the mystery religions blood took the place of water. B. was universal in the Christian Church from the first days, being administered to adults and by immersion. The B. of infants was not practised until the 2nd cent., but became general in the 6th. B. by sprinkling (christening) when the child is named is now general in the West except for some sects, notably the Baptists (q.v.), where complete immersion of adults is the rule. The Eastern Orthodox Church also practises immersion.

BAPTISTS. A world-wide Christian community, practising baptism by immersion of believers only on profession of faith. They stand in the Protestant and evangelical tradition, seek their authority in the Bible, emphasize the right of the soul to an immediate relation to God, and conceive the Church as a fellowship of the spiritually regenerate.

BARBARY APE

Bs. originated among the English Separatists who took refuge in Holland in the early 17th cent., the first English B. being Rev. John Smyth, a Cambridge scholar and an ordained minister of the C. of E. The first Baptist Church in America was organized on Rhode Island in 1639 by Roger Williams. In the 19th cent. there was considerable B. development on the continent of Europe. There are virile B. communities in the Commonwealth. Of the world total of *c.* 23,000,000, some 21,000,000 members are in the U.S. and *c.* 314,000 in the U.K.

The Baptist Missionary Society, formed in 1792 under the inspiration of William Carey, pioneered in the modern missionary movement. In 1905 the Baptist World Alliance was formed.

BARBA'DOS. Most easterly is. of the W. Indies, British since 1627, which became independent within the Commonwealth in 1966. It lies in the Atlantic to the E. of the Windward Is. The volcanic soil is fertile, and produces sugar, cotton, tobacco, indigo, and arrowroot. Bridgetown is the chief port and city. There is a Senate and an elected House of Assembly dating from 1627. Area 166 sq. m.; pop. (1967) 250,000.

BARBARO'SSA. Name given to the German emperor Frederick I (q.v.), and also to two brothers who were Barbary pirates: Horuk was killed by the Spaniards in 1518, Khair-ed-Din took Tunis in 1534, and d. at Constantinople in 1546. The name means 'red beard'.

BARBARY. Traditional name for N. Africa W. of Egypt and N. of the Sahara, named after the Berbers, its principal inhabitants. *See* CORSAIRS.

BARBARY APE. Species (*Macaca sylvana*) of monkey, native to the mountains of Algeria and Morocco; introduced into Gibraltar, it is the only kind of monkey now found wild in Europe. Yellowish brown, the species has no visible trace of a tail. Legend has it that if the colony dies out, Britain will lose Gibraltar.

BARBASTE'LLE. Species (*Barbastellus barbastella*) of bat found in Britain and neighbouring parts of Europe. Although it is only the size of a mouse, its wings have a span of some 10 in.

BAR'BEL. Genus of freshwater fish (*Barbus*) of the carp family (Cyprinidae), so called because of the soft appendages near the mouth (Lat. *barba*, beard).

BARBE'LLION, W. N. P. Pseudonym of Bruce Frederick Cummings (1889–1919), British biologist and diarist. He held an appointment at the Natural History Museum, London, and was the author of the remarkable *Journal of a Disappointed Man*.

BARBER, Anthony (1920–). Brit. Cons. politician. Chairman of the party organisation 1960–70, he suceeded McLeod at the Exchequer in 1970.

BARBIRO'LLI, Sir John (1899–1970). Brit. conductor. B. in London, of French and Italian stock, he made a name as a cellist, and founded the B. Chamber Orchestra in 1925. He was permanent conductor to the N.Y. Philharmonic Symphony Orchestra 1937–42, and to the Hallé Orchestra, Manchester, 1943–58 becoming principal conductor (1958–68), then conductor laureate for life. He was knighted in 1949. His style had a temperamental brilliance.

BARBIZON (bahrbēzoṅ). French village on the outskirts of Paris near the forest of Fontainebleau

BARBIROLLI. Meticulous in preparation as in performance, Barbirolli working on the score of Vaughan Williams Fifth Symphony in the recording studio. *Photo: Godfrey MacDomnic.*

famous for its association with the artists of the 'Barbizon School' who included Millet, Rousseau, Corot, Daubigny, and Courbet.

BARBOUR (bar'ber), **John** (*c.* 1316–95). Scottish poet. He was archdeacon of Aberdeen after 1357, and held small posts at court. His chronicle-poem *The Brus* is almost the first Scottish poem.

BARBUSSE (bahrbüs'), **Henri** (1874–1935). French novelist and poet, b. at Asinères. He wrote novels of an extreme realistic type – *L'enfer* (1909), *Nous autres* (1914) – served in the F.W.W., and pub. in 1916 *Le feu* (Under Fire), a grim story of trench-warfare. In his later work he became more and more a radical political propagandist.

BARCELONA (bahrselō'nah). Largest port, chief commercial and industrial centre, and 2nd city of Spain, on the Mediterranean coast, 3 m. N. of the mouth of the Llobregat. It was founded in the 3rd cent. B.C., and its importance grew until in the 14th cent. it had become one of the leading trading cities of the Mediterranean. As the chief centre of anarchism and Catalonian nationalism it was prominent in the overthrow of the monarchy in 1931, and was the last city of the republic to surrender to Franco in 1939.

It has a Gothic cathedral. The city centre is the Plaza de Cataluña, the largest square in Spain, into which run the Rambla promenades. A remarkable modern building is the Templo Expiatorio de la Sagrada Familia, designed by Gaudi. The univ. was founded in 1450. The docks can accommodate the largest vessels. Industries include textiles, engineering, chemicals, etc. Pop. (1965) 7,655,603.

BARCLAY, Robert (1648–90). Scottish Quaker. B. in Moray, he joined the Society of Friends in 1667, engaged ably in numerous controversies, and suffered considerable persecution. He is esteemed the greatest apologist of the Quaker faith for his *Apology for the True Christian Divinity* (1678).

BARÉA, Arturo (1897–1957). Spanish writer, subsequently a British subject. He fought with the Republican forces during the civil war, and in 1937, his health having failed, he settled in Paris. Living in extreme want and misery, he wrote the autobiographical *The Forge* (1941): other works incl. *The Track, Lorca, The Clash,* and *The Broken Root.*

BAREBONE, Praise God (*c.* 1596–1679). English preacher of the Parliamentary party. A London leather-seller by trade, in 1653 he became a member of the new House of Commons, and in derision the Parliament was nicknamed 'Barebone's Parliament'.

BAREILLY (barālē'). City of India in the state of Uttar Pradesh near the Ramganga. It is an important

rly. junction and manufacturing centre. Pop. (1961 273,204.

BARENTS (bah'rents), **Willem** (d. 1597). Dutch explorer, who in 1594–7 made 3 expeditions from Holland in search of a N.E. passage. He d. in course of the last. Barents Sea is named after him.

BARÈRE DE VIEUZAC (bahrār' de vē-özahk'), **Bertrand** (1755–1841). French revolutionary. He presided over the National Convention when Louis XVI was sentenced to death. For his part in the Terror he was sentenced to deportation in 1795, but escaped. He was employed as a secret agent by Napoleon.

BARHAM, Richard Harris (1788–1845). British writer and antiquary. He took holy orders and became priest-in-ordinary to the Chapel Royal. He is best known for his verse tales pub. in *The Ingoldsby Legends* under his pseudonym Thomas Ingoldsby.

BARI (bah'rē). Italian port and airport on the Adriatic, 69 m. N.W. of Brindisi. It is the commercial centre of Apulia and has a cathedral, a castle, and a univ. founded 1924. Pop. (1961) 311,268.

BARING, Maurice (1874–1945). British writer. 4th son of the 1st Lord Revelstoke, he was in the diplomatic service 1898–1904, and made a reputation by his work as a press correspondent during the Russo-Japanese and 1st Balkan wars. He pub. poetry, novels, plays, studies of Russian and French literature, and the autobiography *The Puppet Show of Memory.*

BARING-GOULD, Sabine (1834–1924). British writer, rector of Lew Trenchard in N. Devon from 1881. He was prolific in novels, books of travel, mythology and folklore, and wrote the words of 'Onward, Christian Soldiers'.

BARIUM. A metallic chemical element, symbol Ba, at. no. 56, at. wt. 137·36. The name comes from the Greek word for 'heavy', since the presence of B. was first discovered in barytes or heavy spar. It is silver-white in colour, oxidizes very easily, and is a little harder than lead. Being heavy, B. sulphate is added to a meal to reveal abnormalities in the digestive tract during radiography. B. is very important since, with strontium, it forms the emissive surface in every small thermionic valve and cathode-ray tube.

BARK, or Cortex. The outer rind of the stems of plants, strictly speaking the outer covering of the stems of dicotyledonous plants, especially those of a woody and perennial growth (trees and shrubs). True bark consists of dried-up tissues, and its production is assisted by the formation of a layer of cork outside the growing part of the stem. B. has many economic uses. Some kinds have medicinal qualities, e.g. cinchona (quinine), cascara, and angostura.

BARKER, George (1913–). British poet. His verse has been compared to that of the surrealists, and, though uneven, has great vividness of imagery. His work incl. the long poem *Calamiterror* (1937), *The True Confession of George Barker* (1950), and *Collected Poems,* 1947–50.

BARKER, Sir Herbert Atkinson (1869–1950). British manipulative surgeon. He studied under his cousin, J. Atkinson, whose practice he took over in 1904, and achieved thousands of cures by his unorthodox methods. He was subject to bitter attack from the medical profession until late in his life: he was knighted in 1922, retiring in 1925. A series of films made at St. Thomas's Hospital, London, perpetuates his techniques.

BAR-LE-DUC (bahr-le-dük'). Capital of Meuse dept., France, on the Ornain, 124 m. E. of Paris; famous for its preserves, wines, etc. Pop. (1962) 20,168.

BARLETTA. Italian port on the Adriatic, 34 m. N.W. of Bari. It has a Romanesque cathedral and a good harbour, and exports wine, oil, and sulphur. Pop. (1960) 69,700.

BARLEY. Genus of cereals (*Hordeum*) belonging to the family Gramineae. The cultivated B. comprises 3 species – six-rowed barley (*H. hexastichon*), four-rowed barley or Scotch Bigg (*H. vulgare*), and two-rowed barley (*H. distichon*).

B. was one of the earliest cereals to be cultivated, and no other cereal can thrive in so wide a range of climate. Polar barley is sown and reaped well within the Arctic circle in Europe. B. is no longer much used in bread-making, but finds a wide use for pig, horse, and cattle foods. Its main importance, however, is in brewing and distilling.

BARLOW, Sir Thomas (1845–1945). Royal physician to Queen Victoria, Edward VII, and George V. It was for his work in the treatment of child diseases that he became most famous. He was the first to define 'rickets' as infantile scurvy, due to the lack of certain food-elements.

BARMEN. Former German city in the Rhineland, in 1929 joined with Elberfeld to form Wuppertal (q.v.).

BARNABAS. Christian saint and apostle, mentioned in Acts as a 'fellow-labourer' of Paul; he went with Mark on a missionary journey to Cyprus, his birthplace. His feast-day is 11 June.

BARNACLE. Marine crustacean of the order Cirripedia. The larval form is free-swimming, but after a time it settles down, and fixes itself by its head to a stone, floating wood, etc. The animal then becomes a sedentary creature, enclosed in a shell through the opening of which the cirri protrude. By means of these food is swept into the mouth. The true barnacles (*Lepadidae*) are fixed on long fleshy stalks, and include the common goose barnacle (*Lepas anatifera*) which grow on ships.

GOOSE BARNACLES

BARNARD, Christiaan. *See* HEART.

BARNARD CASTLE. Market town (U.D.) on the Tees, here crossed by an old bridge, 17 m. W. of Darlington. The castle is now a ruin. Here is Bowes Museum. Pop. (1961) 4,969.

BARNA'RDO, Thomas John (1845–1905). British philanthropist. B. in Dublin, he became a doctor in the east end of London. In 1867 he opened the first 'home' at Stepney Causeway, still the H.Q., and more than 100 others before he died.

BARNATO (bahrnah'tō), **Barnett Isaacs** (1852–97), known as Barney Barnato. Jewish diamond magnate and financier. B. in London, he went to S. Africa as an entertainer and conjuror, entered the diamond trade at Kimberley, changing his real name Isaacs to B., and in 1881 launched a company which was amalgamated with the De Beers Co. in 1888. He committed suicide by jumping overboard when returning from the Cape.

BARNAUL (bahrnah-ool'). Admin. centre of Altai Territory, R.S.F.S.R. (U.S.S.R.), situated where the r. Barnaulka enters the Ob. Originally a mining town founded 1730, it has cotton mills and food-packing factories. Pop. (1967) 395,000.

BARNES, Ernest William (1874–1953). British modernist churchman. A lecturer in mathematics at Cambridge 1902–15, he was an ardent advocate of the significance in modern religion of scientific thought. In 1924 he became bp. of Birmingham and outraged many by his controversial views, as in *The Rise of Christianity* (1947), expressing doubt as to miracles, the virgin birth, and so on.

BARNES, Thomas (1785–1841). British journalist, editor of *The Times* from 1817, developing it into a most powerful organ of informed opinion.

BARNES, William (1800–86). Dorsetshire poet. B. at Rushay, of farming stock, he became a solicitor's clerk, and then master (1823–62) of a private school at Mere, later at Dorchester. In 1838 he entered at

Cambridge to study theology, and was ordained as vicar of Whitcombe in 1847. From 1862 he was rector of Winterbourne Came, where he d. He issued three collections: *Poems of Rural Life in the Dorset Dialect* (1844 and 1862), *Hwomely Rhymes* (1859), and *Poems of Rural Life in Common English* (1868). An ardent philologist, he pub. grammars and glossaries of the Dorset dialect.

BARNET. Bor. in the N. of Greater London, England. Pop. (1964) 318,051.

In the Battle of B., on 14 April 1471 the Lancastrians under Warwick the Kingmaker were completely defeated by the Yorkists under Edward IV, Warwick himself being killed.

BARNSLEY. Town (co. bor.) in the W. Riding of Yorkshire, England, 15 m. N. of Sheffield. Situated on one of Britain's richest coalfields, it has iron and steel, glass and paper-making industries. Pop. (1961) 74,650.

BARNSTAPLE (bahrn'stapl; locally bar'um). Fishing port (bor.) on N. Devon coast, England, at the mouth of the Taw, which is crossed by an ancient 16-arch bridge. Pop. (1961) 15,907.

BA'RNUM, Phineas Taylor (1810–91). American showman, who after an adventurous career exhibited 'Tom Thumb', toured U.S.A. with Jenny Lind, and in 1871 established the 'Greatest Show on Earth', comprising circus, menagerie, and exhibition of 'freaks', conveyed in 100 railway cars.

BARO'DA. Town in Gujarat state, Rep. of India, 248 m. N. of Bombay, on the Vishnamitri. It has fine modern buildings and a univ. founded in 1949. It is a railway junction. Pop. (1961) 295,304.

B. was formerly the cap. of B. princely state, one of the most important and enlightened in India. A scattered state, it had an area of 8,236 sq. m. and a pop. of some 3,000,000. Its ruler was called a Gaekwar, from the family name, Gaekwad.

BAROJA (bahrokh'ah), **Pío** (1872–1956). Spanish novelist of Basque extraction and anarchist sentiments. His books incl. a trilogy dealing with the Madrid underworld, *La lucha por la vida* (1904–5), and *Memorias de un hombre de acción*, extending to a score of vols.

BARO'METER (Gk. *baros*, weight; *metron*, measure). An instrument for measuring the pressure of the atmosphere. The most common form is the *mercury*

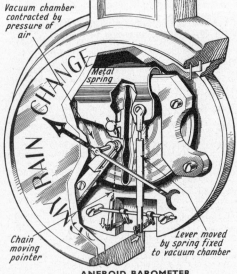

ANEROID BAROMETER

B., the principle of which was discovered by Torricelli in 1643. This is made by filling with mercury a clean dry glass tube about 36 in. long, closed at one end, and inverting it with the open end dipping into a vessel of mercury. The level of the mercury in the tube falls until it is about 30 in. or 76 cm. above the surface of the mercury in the open vessel, leaving a vacuum at the top of the tube. The pressure of the atmosphere on the mercury in the open vessel is thus balanced by the weight of the mercury column in the tube, the height of which is, therefore, a measure of the atmospheric pressure.

A more compact form is the *aneroid B.*, in which variations in the atmospheric pressure cause changes in the distance between the sides of a shallow cylindrical metal box which is partly exhausted of air. These small movements are magnified by a series of levers, so as to cause the rotation of a pointer pivoted at the centre of a circular calibrated scale.

A rise of 1,000 ft. in altitude measured from sea-level corresponds approximately to a change in pressure of 1 in. of mercury, but the relation between height and pressure depends very largely on atmospheric temperature.

BA'RON. Lowest rank in the peerage (q.v.) of the U.K., above a baronet and below a viscount. The 1st English barony was created in 1387, but Bs. by 'writ existed earlier.

BARONET. Hereditary title signifying a rank below that of a baron and above a knight. It was instituted by James I as a means of raising money.

BARONS' WAR. In English history, the civil war between the barons led by Simon de Montfort and Henry III. The former won the battle of Lewes in 1264, but at Evesham in 1265 the position was reversed, Montfort being slain.

BARO'QUE. Term used to denote a style of architecture, characterized by bizarre or fantastic ornamentation which prevailed on the Continent during the 17th and 18th cents. The term perhaps derives from the Span. *barrueco*, meaning an irregular-shaped pearl. The most famous exponents of B. were Giovanni Bernini and Francesco Borromini.

BARO'TSELAND. A north-west prov. of the Rep. of Zambia. Once a native kingdom, B. came under British protection at the request of Lewanika (c. 1860–1922), its ruler or litunga, in 1890 and on the establishment of Zambia in 1964 the reigning litunga (Sir Mwanawina Lewanika III) and his council were to remain the principal local authority in B. The admin. centre is Mongu; the litunga's cap. is Lealui. The Barotse are of fine physique; cattle are the chief form of wealth. Area 44,920 sq. m.; pop. (1965) 390,600.

BARRA. Most southerly of the larger Outer Hebrides is., in Inverness-shire, Scotland, separated from S. Uist by the Sound of B. The is., about 8 m. by 4 m., is barren; Castlebay harbour is a base for the herring fleet. Area 35 sq. m.; pop. (1961) 1,467.

BARRACUDA (barakoo'dah), **Barracouta.** Large carnivorous pike-like fish (*Sphyraena barracuda*) of the family Sphyraenidae, found in the warmer seas of the world. It is esteemed for food, and its skin is used for polishing wood.

BARRANQUILLA (bahrahnkēl'yah). Chief port, airport and city of Colombia, S. America, near the mouth of the Magdalena. Pop. (1964) 498,301.

BARRAS (bahrrahs'), **Paul François Jean Nicolas, Count** (1755–1829). French revolutionist. B. in Provence, he fought against the English in India, was elected to the National Convention in 1792, and helped to overthrow Robespierre (1794). In 1795 he became a member of the *Directoire*. In 1796 he brought about the marriage of his former mistress, Joséphine de Beauharnais with Napoleon, and assumed dictatorial powers. After Napoleon's *coup d'état* of 19 Nov. 1799, B. fell into disgrace.

BARRAULT (bahroh'), **Jean Louis** (1910–). French actor-director. He was producer-director to the Comedie-Française 1940–6, and was director of the Théâtre de France (formerly Odeon) from 1959 until dismissed 1968 because of statements made during the occupation of the theatre by student rebels. His films incl.: *La Symphonie fantastique, Les Enfants du Paradis* (1944) and *La Ronde* (1950).

BARREL ORGAN. Portable musical instrument consisting of a cylinder containing an arrangement of pins and staples which, on the handle being turned, raise keys which open pipe valves, thus admitting air from the wind chest.

BARRÈS (bahres'), **Maurice** (1862–1923). French novelist and political writer. From 1905 he was the spokesman of Alsace-Lorraine, then under the German yoke. His most enduring work is *Le Romain de l'energie nationale.*

BARRIE, Sir James Matthew (1860–1937). Scottish novelist and playwright. B. in Kirriemuir, Angus, he entered journalism in Nottingham in 1883, and settled in London in 1885. He became known by his studies of Scottish rural life in *Auld Licht Idylls* (1888), and *A Window in Thrums* (1889) which began the vogue of the Kailyard school. His 1st novel, *The Little Minister,* was dramatized in 1897 and, together with *The Professor's Love Story* (1894), estab. his reputation as a playwright. The most important of his later plays are: *Quality Street* (1901), *The Admirable Crichton* (1902), *What Every Woman Knows* (1908), *Dear Brutus* (1917), and *Mary Rose* (1920). The perennial children's play, *Peter Pan* (1904), was drawn from an idea in the *Little White Bird* (1902), and followed by *Peter Pan in Kensington Gardens* (1906) and *Peter and Wendy* (1911),

SIR JAMES BARRIE
Photo: George Outram & Co.

Other works incl. a biography of his mother, *Margaret Ogilvie* (1896), the novels *Sentimental Tommy* (1896) and *Tommy and Grizel* (1900), and his address on 'Courage' (1922), delivered on his installation as Lord Rector of St. Andrews. He was made a bart. in 1913 and received the O.M. in 1922. In our illus. he holds his godson, the Hon. Angus Ogilvy (q.v.).

BARRISTER. A person entitled to plead for others at the bar of a court of law. The bar is a division, indicated by a rail, separating the judges and officers of the court from the Bs. and public. Bs. remain outside the bar until they become Queen's Counsel, when they are called 'within the bar'.

In order to become a B. a man or woman must become a student at one of the Inns of Court, pass certain examinations, and 'keep terms', usually 12 in number, after which he or she may be called to the bar on the payment of certain fees. The Benchers of the Inn exercise disciplinary control over the members of the Inn, and can disbar any member, with an appeal to the judges.

In the higher courts only a B. can be heard on behalf of a litigant. With a few exceptions a B. cannot act for a client unless he is instructed by a solicitor.

BARROW, Isaac (1630–77). English mathematician and churchman. Appointed first Lucasian prof. of mathematics at Cambridge in 1664, he resigned in favour of his pupil, Isaac Newton, in 1669.

BARROW. A burial mound, usually composed of earth, but sometimes of stones, examples of which are found in many parts of the world. There are 2 main types, long and round.

The *long barrow* is held to be the earlier, dating from the New Stone Age. Sometimes it may be a mere mound, but usually it contained a chamber of wood or stone slabs in which were placed the bodies of the deceased. Such are especially common in the southern counties from Sussex to Dorset. They seem to have been communal burial-places of the long-headed Mediterranean race.

Round barrows were the work of the round-headed or 'beaker' folk of the early Bronze Age. The commonest type is the bell B., consisting of a circular mound, enclosed by a ditch and an outside bank of earth. Many dot the Wiltshire downs. In historic times certain of the Saxon and most of the Danish invaders were barrow-builders.

BARROW. Most northerly town of the U.S.A. on Point B. on the N. Coast of Alaska. The average winter temperature is 30° below zero, but it is heated by natural gas. It is the world's largest Eskimo settlement and oil strikes in Prudhoe Bay have brought added prosperity. Pop. (1970) 2,500.

BARROW-IN-FURNESS. Seaport (co. bor.) in Lancs, England, at the S. end of the Furness peninsula. High-quality iron ore, formerly mined locally, founded B.'s fortunes. B. has large docks, shipbuilding yards, iron and steel foundries, heavy engineering works, clothing and textile factories, paper works, paper factories, etc. Vickerstown on Walney Is. is a residential suburb. Pop. (1961) 62,824.

BARRY, Sir Charles (1795–1860). British architect, designer of the Houses of Parliament, Westminster (1840–60); he was knighted in 1852.

BARRY. Comtesse du. *See* DU BARRY.

BARRY. Port (bor.) in Glamorganshire, Wales, 8 m. S.W. of Cardiff. The 1st docks were built in 1889 for coal export. From fewer than 500 in 1881, the pop. grew to 42,039 in 1961. BARRY Is. is 1 m. offshore.

BARRYMORE. American family of actors, the children of British-born Maurice B. and Georgie Drew, both stage personalities. Lionel B. (1878–1954) 1st appeared on the stage with his grandmother, Mrs. John Drew, in 1893. After studying art in Paris, he returned to the stage, and from 1909 made numerous films. Ethel B. (1879–1959) played with Irving in London in 1898 and in 1928 opened the Ethel B. Theatre in N.Y.; she also appeared in many films from 1914. John B. (1882–1942), a vitally flamboyant personality, appeared on stage and screen, often with his brother and sister.

BART (bahr), **Jean** (1651–1702). Naval hero of France. B. at Dunkirk, the son of a fisherman, he served in the French navy, and harassed the British fleet in many daring exploits.

BARTH (bahrt), **Karl** (1886–1968). Swiss Protestant theologian. B. at Basle, he held chairs of theology in Germany from 1921, and 1935–62 was prof. at Basle. His *Epistle to the Romans* (1919) and *Church Dogmatics* (13 vols. 1932–67) gained him an international reputation.

BARTHOLDI (bahrtol'de), **Auguste** (1834–1904). French sculptor. He completed the statue of Liberty overlooking New York harbour in 1884.

BARTHOLIN (bahr'tōlēn), **Caspar Thomeson** (1655–1738). Danish anatomist who gave his name to the B. glands and the Duct of B. in the human body.

BARTHOLOMÉ (bahrtolomã'), **Paul Albert** (1848–1928). French artist and sculptor, whose *Aux Morts* in the Père Lachaise cemetery, Paris, became world-famous.

BARTHOLOMEW. Christian saint and one of the 12 apostles. Legends relate that after the Crucifixion he took Christianity to India, or that he was a missionary in Asia Minor and Armenia, where he suffered martyrdom by being flayed alive. The Catholic Church commemorates him on 24 Aug.

On St. Bartholomew's day in 1572 occurred the famous MASSACRE OF ST. B., when numbers of the French Huguenots were slaughtered by order of the queen-mother, Catherine de' Medici.

BARTHOU (bährtoo'), **Jean Louis** (1862–1934). French statesman. From 1894 he held many Cabinet posts including the premiership in 1913. In 1934, when Foreign Minister, he was assassinated, together with King Alexander of Yugoslavia, in Marseilles.

'BARTIMEUS'. Pen-name of the novelist L. A. Ritchie (q.v.).

BARTLETT, John (1820–1905). American publisher and author. B. in Massachusetts, he entered business as publisher and bookseller there, and in 1855 pub. his *Familiar Quotations* and in 1894 his Shakespeare concordance; both works have been reprinted many times.

BARTÓK (bor'tōk), **Béla** (1881–1945). Hungarian composer, b. in Transylvania. He was regarded as a child prodigy, studied music at Budapest, and collaborated with Kodály in research into Hungarian folk music, which coloured his later compositions. His large output includes string quartets, violin and piano concertos, orchestral suites, and operas. When Hungary joined Germany in the S.W.W., B. went to America. He d. in New York.

BARTOLOMMEO (bahrtōlommã'ō), **Fra** (1475–1517). Florentine painter, known also as BACCIO DELLA PORTA. He owed much to Leonardo da Vinci. Albertinelli assisted him in painting the fresco of the 'Last Judgment' in Santa Maria Nuova. Deeply moved by Savonarola's death, he entered a Dominican convent, but he soon turned again to painting. His figure of St. Mark is regarded as his greatest achievement.

BARTOLOZZI (bahrtōlot'se), **Francesco** (1727–1815). Italian engraver. After working in Rome, he was invited to London in 1764 by George III's librarian, and executed many works for the king.

BARTON, Sir Edmund (1849–1920). Australian statesman. B. at Sydney, N.S.W., he was leader of the Federation movement from 1896, and first P.M. of the Commonwealth of A. (1901–3). On his retirement, 1903, he became a High Court Judge.

BART'S. Short for St. Bartholomew's Hospital, in Smithfield, one of the great teaching hospitals of London, England. It was founded as part of a priory by Rahere in 1123, and re-founded by Henry VIII at the Reformation.

BARUCH (barook'), **Bernard Mannes** (1870–1965). American business man and economic adviser. Under Wilson and F. D. Roosevelt he held many economic appointments. In 1946–7 he was U.S.A. representative on the United Nations Atomic Energy Commission, and at its first meeting put forward the U.S. Government's proposals for control of atomic energy. His autobiography, *My Own Story* and *The Public Years*, was pub. 1957–60.

BASALT. The commonest basic lava. Composed chiefly of labradorite feldspar and ferrous and magnesium silicates, Bs. are usually dark grey, but may be green, brown, or black. The ground mass may be glassy or finely crystalline, sometimes with large crystals embedded. Bs. have been extruded at frequent intervals throughout geological time, and a substratum of B. may underlie the earth's crust. Generally B., when erupted, spreads out in a wide sheet of no great thickness; but successive eruptions in the same area may form sheets of substantial depth, as in the great plateaus of Colorado and the Indian Deccan. In the Tertiary epoch a great B. plateau, remnants of which are seen on the W. coast of Scotland and in N.E. Ireland, stretched from Britain to Iceland and Greenland. As the molten lava shrinks and solidifies it may form hexagonal columns, as in the Giant's Causeway in Antrim.

BASEBALL. The national summer game of the U.S.A., thought by some authorities to have evolved from the English game of rounders, while others claim that it originated in New York, U.S.A. in 1839.

It is played with a bat and ball between 2 teams,

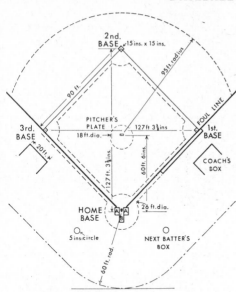

BASEBALL. The 'diamond'

each of 9 players. The field of play is marked with the form of a diamond 90 ft. square. One corner – marked with a five-sided whitened rubber slab – is called home base, the other three corners – 1st, 2nd, 3rd bases – are marked by white canvas bags 15 in. square which must be securely attached to the ground. Continuations of the lines of the diamond are marked from 1st and 3rd bases, and are known as 'foul lines'.

The side taking first innings bat in regular succession. The opposing side taking the field are: the pitcher, near the centre of the diamond; the catcher, behind the home base; 1st baseman, near the 1st base, which is to the right of the catcher; 2nd and 3rd basemen, near the 2nd and 3rd bases; short stop (infielder) about midway between 2nd and 3rd basemen; and outfielders at right, centre and left.

The pitcher may deliver the ball either under or over arm. The batsman tries to make a 'fair hit' which means that the ball must fall within the diamond or beyond, but within the 'foul lines'. If his strike is successful the batter tries to make a 'run' which is a complete circuit of the diamond from home base to 1st, 2nd, 3rd bases in regular order and back to home base. This may be in one dash called a 'home run' or by stopping in the circuit at any other base as a safety point.

He is declared out if, (1) he fails to hit the ball after 3 attempts, (2) he strikes the ball in the air and it is caught by a fielder, (3) he is touched by the ball in the hand of one of his opponents while he is between bases, and (4) a fielder standing on one of the bases catches the ball before he reaches the base. A batter may only run for 'fair hits', but he may be put out on a 'foul hit' if the ball is caught before it reaches the ground. The main duty of the infielders is to put out the batsman by touching him with the ball held in the hand, while he is running between the bases, or reaching a base with the ball before the batsman can get there; either method puts the batsman out. The out-fielders' duty is to catch or stop long hits and return them to 'basemen'.

The 1st batter is followed by the other members of his team in rotation until 3 members of the batting side are put out: the opposing team then take their turn. This continues until 9 equal innings have been

played and the team scoring the most runs wins the game. The game may be controlled by one umpire, but 2 are more usual for important matches.

The ball is formed by yarn wound on a core of cork or rubber and covered with two strips of white horsehide. The weight is between 5 and 5¼ oz. and the circumference 9 to 9¼ in. The bat is round, not more than 2¾ in. in diameter at its thickest part and not more than 42 in. long.

B. was first played in 1839 at Cooperstown, N.Y., the field being laid out by Abner Doubleday, who organized the game. The 100th anniversary of the game was celebrated at Cooperstown in 1939 with the dedication of the Hall of Fame and National Museum of B. The Select Five, the players whose performances were thought to have stamped them as the greatest players of all, were: Ty Cobb (1886–1961), Babe Ruth (q.v.), Christy Mathewson, Honus Wagner, and Walter Johnson, chosen in that order. The Knickerbocker Club, the 1st to be founded, was formed in New York by Alexander J. Cartwright in 1845. The National Association of Baseball Players was formed in 1858 and the 1st professional team was Cincinnati's Red Stockings (1869).

The 1st serious effort to introduce B. to Britain was made in 1917, when a demonstration match was played at Lord's cricket ground. In 1924, England played France at Stamford Bridge. B. Leagues were formed in London and the chief provincial cities, and by 1939 there were 360 teams. During the S.W.W, the presence of great numbers of American soldiers in U.K. led to a considerable increase in the game's popularity.

BASEL. German form of BASLE.

BA'SHKIR. A.S.S.R. of the R.S.F.S.R., on the W. slopes of the S. Ural Mts. Grains and sunflower seeds are grown; metals worked include iron, copper, gold; petroleum is raised; and the forests in the N.E. produce timber. Ufa is the cap. Area 55,400 sq. m.; pop. (1967) 3,757,000.

BASHKIRTSEFF (bahshkēr'tsev), **Maria Constantinova** (1860–84). Russian artist and diarist. After studying singing, she turned to painting while at Paris in 1877, and 3 years later began to exhibit at the Salon. She is chiefly known as a writer of letters and of a diary.

BASIC ENGLISH. Named from the initial letters of British-American-Scientific-International-Commercial, it is a simplified form of English, devised as an international auxiliary language. With a vocabulary of 850 words, including only 18 verbs, it expresses more advanced meanings by a combination of these with the 600 nouns or 20 prepositions and adverbs, e.g. 'buy' becomes 'give money for'.

The originator was C. K. Ogden, who began his researches in 1926, and was joined by I. A. Richards. In 1947 the British govt. purchased the copyright and the B.E. Foundation was estab. to promote its use.

BA'SIL (*c* A.D. 330–379). Christian saint, founder of the Basilian monks, and known as THE GREAT. B. at Caesarea, Asia Minor, he studied at Constantinople and Athens, visited the hermit saints of the Egyptian desert, entered a monastery in Asia Minor about 358, and developed a monastic rule I ased on community life, work, and prayer. These ideas form the basis of monasticism in the Greek Orthodox church, and influenced the foundation of similar monasteries by St. Benedict. Elected bishop of Caesarea in 370, B. opposed the heresy of Arianism. He wrote many theological works and composed the 'Liturgy of St. Basil', in use in the Orthodox church.

BASIL. A plant (*Ocimum basilicum*) of the family Labiatae. A native of India, it is cultivated in Europe as a potherb and for seasoning.

BASILDON. Town in Essex, England, developed from 1949 under the New Towns Act, 1946, as a residential and industrial centre round the ancient village of B. with its 15th-cent. church. Pop. (1961) 88,459.

BASILICA. Type of Roman public building; a large roofed hall flanked by columns generally having an aisle on each side, used for judicial or other public business. The earliest known B., at Pompeii, dates from the 2nd cent. B.C. The type was adopted by the early Christians for their churches.

BASINGSTOKE. Market town (bor.) of Hants, England, on the Loddon, 45 m. W.S.W. of London. Its first charter was granted in 1227, but there are pre-historic and Roman remains. Basing House, in the vicinity, was renowned for its long defence, 1643–5, against the Parliamentarians. Agricultural implements, motor vehicles, etc., are made. Pop. (1961) 25,940.

BASKERVILLE, John (1706–75). British printer. He began his career as a footman, became a writing-master in Birmingham, and from 1750 onwards experimented in casting types. In 1756 he pub. a 4to edition of Virgil, which was followed by 54 books remarkable for their craftsmanship.

BASKETBALL. Indoor game very popular in U.S.A. and Canada, invented by Dr. J. A. Naismith, of Springfield, Mass., a Y.M.C.A. instructor, in 1891. It is played by 2 teams of 5, substitutes being allowed during play. The object is to throw the ball, similar to a round football, into a basket suspended against a board, 10 ft. from the ground, at each end of the court. The ball is played by hand only. Most famous of all teams is the Harlem Globe-trotters.

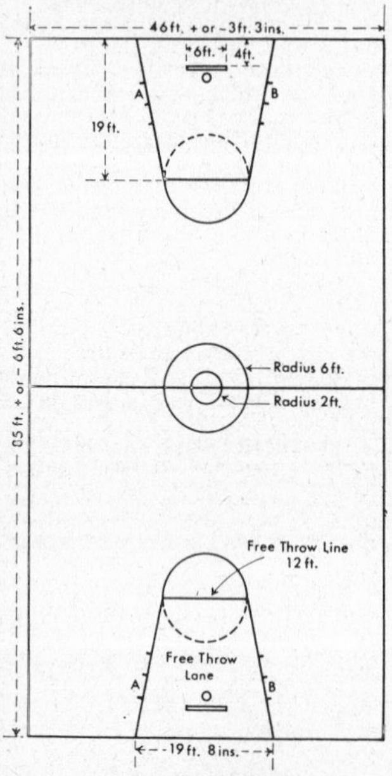

BASLE. Conventional English form of the name of the 2nd city of Switzerland (Basel in German, Bâle in French). Situated on the Rhine, on its right-angled bend at the S. end of the middle Rhine plain, it is one of the greatest route centres of Europe, and also a great banking and commercial centre. The Bank for International Settlements was estab. here in 1930. B. manufactures textiles, particularly silks and ribbons, machinery, chemicals, clocks and watches, foodstuffs, etc.

B. was a strong military station under the Romans. In 1501 it joined the Swiss confederation, and later developed as a centre of the Reformation. The 11th cent. cathedral was rebuilt after an earthquake in 1356. The town hall dates from the 16th cent., and the univ. from the 15th. Pop. (1966) 212,800.

BASQUES (baskz). A people inhabiting the Spanish prov. of Alava, Vizcaya, and Guipúzcoa, and part of the French dept. of Basses-Pyrénées, in the angle of the Bay of Biscay. They may be a remnant of the ancient Iberians, or they may belong to an even earlier stock. They first appeared in history in 778, when they annihilated the rearguard of Charlemagne's army at Roncesvalles, and slew Roland. The B.

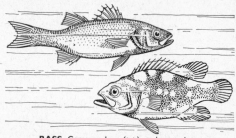

BASS. Common bass (*top*), and stone bass.

provinces gradually came under the crown of Castile. They retained their ancient privileges of self-govt. through their elected *juntas*, which confirmed or rejected the decrees of the Cortes. During the Carlist revolts of 1833–9 and 1873–6 they took the losing side, and their privileges were greatly curtailed. They were restored by the republic of 1931, and this led them to rally to the Republic when the Civil War began. They were crushed by Franco in 1937, their privileges suppressed, and the use of their language forbidden, but in 1968 activities by the terrorist organization ETA (for Euzkadi, the Basque homeland, and Freedom) led to a state of emergency in Guipuzcoa.

Iron ore, most of which is shipped to Britain, is mined in the Basque country; agriculture is technically backward, but its people are fine seamen and fishermen. They have their own customs, dances, ball game (pelota), and national dress. Their language (Eskuara, unrelated to French or Spanish) has to some extent been reinstated as a govt. conciliatory measure: its most typical expression is the long romantic verse dramas, *pastorales*, performed at open-air festivals. The Bs. are devout Catholics.

BA′SRA. City of Iraq, and its only port available for ocean steamers, situated near the Shatt-al-Arab, 60 m. from the Persian Gulf. It is an important railway and air centre; shipping trade is largely with India. Petroleum is worked in the vicinity. The irrigated areas round B. produce the world's finest dates. Pop. (1967) 423,000.

BASS (bas). Various species of fish of the order Percomorphi. The species *Morone labrax* belongs to the family of sea-perches (Serranidae), and is found In shoals off the Mediterranean and Atlantic coasts. *See* GROUPER.

BASSEIN (bahssān′). Port of Burma, on the B. river, 70 m. from the sea. A military and trade centre, it was founded in the 13th cent. and taken by the British in 1852. It has a teachers' training college. Pop. (1967) 90,000.

BASSES-ALPES. Dept. of FRANCE.

BA′SSET. A French hound for hunting the hare on foot, introduced into Britain in 1866. It is heavy and short-legged, and remarkable for its great powers of scent and for excelling in hound 'music'.

BA′SSET HORN. Wood-wind instrument, said to have been invented in 1770 by a clarinet-maker of Passau, Bavaria. It consists of a cylindrical tube of wood ending in a metal bell, and is the tenor of the clarinet family.

BASSOO′N. Wood-wind instrument of the oboe family, of which it is the bass. It is descended from the bass pommer, which was about 6 ft. in length and perfectly straight, whereas the B. is doubled back on itself. Its tone is rich and deep.

BASS ROCK. Islet in the Firth of Forth, Scotland, about 350 ft. high and 1 m. in circumference. It has a lighthouse, and is inhabited by hosts of sea birds.

BASSE-TERRE (bāhs tār′). Cap. and port of the French overseas dept. of Guadeloupe. Pop. (1967) 13,978.

Diagram labels (BASKETBALL court):
46 ft. + or –3 ft. 3 ins.
6 ft. 4 ft.
A   B
19 ft.
Radius 6 ft.
Radius 2 ft.
Free Throw Line 12 ft.
Free Throw Lane
A   B
19 ft. 8 ins.
05 ft. + or –6 ft. 6 ins.

BASKETBALL

BASSETERRE. Cap. and port of St. Kitts in the Leeward Is. Pop. (1960) 15,897.

BASTIA (bahstē'ah). Largest town, and commercial centre of Corsica, France. Pop. (1962) 50,881.

BASTILLE (bastēl'). Name given to the castle of St. Antoine, part of the fortifications of Paris, which was used for centuries as a State prison; it was singled out for the initial attack by the revolutionary mob, which set in train the French Revolution, on 14 July 1789. Only 7 prisoners were found in the B. when it was stormed; the governor and most of the garrison were killed; the B. was razed to the ground.

BASUTOLAND (bahsoō'tōland). *See* LESOTHO.

BAT (Chiroptera). An order of mammals distinguished by having the fore-limbs converted into wings capable of sustained and rapid flight. These wings consist of a thin hairless membrane stretched between the limbs and the body and between 4 of the fingers of the hand, which are greatly lengthened for that purpose, and cleft to the wrist. The thumb is free and is furnished with a sharp claw to help in climbing. The hind feet have 5 toes provided with sharp hooked claws, which suspend the animal head downwards when resting.

LONG-EARED BAT

Bats are nocturnal, and those native to temperate countries hibernate in winter. They form the most widely distributed order of mammals, their power of flight taking them all over the world where there are trees, and to oceanic islands which other mammals cannot reach. Bs., like whales and dolphins, use a type of echo-location system.

There are 2 main groups: the large fruit-eaters (*Megachiroptera*), also called Flying Foxes, of Africa, S. Asia and Australia, and the smaller insect-eaters (*Microchiroptera*), of which there are some 600 species, found in all temperate and tropical regions.

BATAAN. Peninsula on Luzon, Philippine Rep., W. of Manila Bay, which was gallantly but in vain defended against the Japanese by American and Filipino troops from 1 Jan. to 9 April 1942.

BATAVIA. Dutch name for DJAKARTA.

BATES, Mrs. Daisy (1861–1951). Friend of the aborigines of Australia. B. Daisy O'Dwyer-Hunt at Tipperary, Ireland, she visited Australia in 1884, and from 1899 spent her life amongstt he Aborigines. She wrote *Passing of the Aborigines* (1939), and compiled a native dictionary.

BATES, Herbert Ernest (1905–). British author. After brief experience in provincial journalism and, as a clerk, he pub. his 1st novel *The Two Sisters* in 1925: numerous successors incl. *The Purple Plain* (1947) and *The Darling Buds of May* (1958). He also excels in the short story and during the S.W.W. pub. under the pen-name 'Flying Officer X' several vols. dealing with the lives of R.A.F. personnel.

BATH. Largest town (city and co. bor.) in Somerset, England, on the right bank of the Avon, 10 m. S.E. of Bristol. A health resort, it claims the only natural hot springs (120° F.) in Britain, used both for bathing and drinking. The Romans built round the spa the city of Aquae Sulis; the ruins of the great temple and rectangular bathing pool are the finest Roman remains in Britain. During the Middle Ages it became an important walled city; the springs were Crown property, but were administered by the Church. Of medieval B. little remains but the Abbey, a fine Perpendicular structure with fan tracery. Early in the 18th cent. B. was transformed by the organizing ability of Beau Nash, the business acumen of Ralph Allen, and the architectural genius of the two John

BATH. Built to the design of John Wood, junior, the Assembly Rooms were restored in 1963 under the guidance of Oliver Messel (q.v.) to their original form, before the many minor alterations made to the interior in the 19th and 20th centuries. One of the three main rooms is the ballroom seen above, lit by the magnificent original chandeliers salvaged from the ruins.
Courtesy of the Bath City Council

Woods. Guests of high rank thronged the city. The Assembly Rooms (opened in 1771) were the finest suite of 18th cent. entertainment rooms in England until destroyed by German air attack in 1942; reconstructed, they were re-opened 1963. The Grand Pump Room was rebuilt in 1796. Pulteney Bridge is flanked by shops and houses. There is an annual music festival. Spa treatment is still carried on, but the establishment of Bath Univ. of Technology in 1966 is symptomatic of the growth of engineering industries. Bath stone, oolitic building stone is quarried nearby. There is a botanic garden in Victoria Park. Pop (1961) 80,856.

BATH, Knights of the. British order of knighthood, believed to have been founded in the reign of Henry IV (1399–1413). It was formally instituted in 1815, and since 1847 it has incl. civilians. There are 3 grades: Knights of the Grand Cross (G.C.B.), Knights Commanders (K.C.B.), and Knights Companions (C.B.).

BATHURST (bath'urst). Cap. (created a city in 1965) of Gambia, W. Africa, on the is. of St. Mary, at the mouth of the Gambia, it has an airport. Pop. (1963) 40,017.

Another B. is a town of N.S.W., Australia, on the Macquarie. It is the centre of a mining region, and manufactures railway equipment, boots and shoes, soap, etc. Pop. (1968) 17,330.

BATHYSCAPHE and BATHYSPHERE. Types of diving apparatus used to investigate animal life and conditions at great depths in the ocean. For the bathyscaphe *see* PICCARD, and for the spherical bathysphere BEEBE, CHARLES WILLIAM.

BATIK. Javanese technique of applying coloured designs to fabric. The portions which it is desired to protect from the action of a given dye are covered with wax. This is practised throughout Indonesia, and was introduced into Europe by the Dutch.

BATLEY. Old town (bor.) in W. Riding, Yorks, England, 6 m. S.S.W. of Leeds. It is the centre of the heavy woollen and shoddy industries. Pop. (1961) 39,390.

BATTEN, Jean (1909–). N.Z. aviator. B. in New Zealand, she joined the London Aeroplane Club, and obtained her pilot's licence in 1930. She flew solo from England to Australia in 1934 and back in 1935 – the 1st woman to make the return journey, and estab. several world records.

BATTENBERG, Prince Louis Alexander (1854–1921). Admiral of the Fleet. Son of Prince Alexander of Hesse (1823–88) and his morganatic wife, the Polish countess Julia Theresa von Hauke (1825–95),. who was created princess of Battenberg, in the Prussian province of Hesse-Nassau, in 1858, he became a naturalized British subject, entered the R.N. in 1868, m. in 1884, Princess Victoria of Hesse, daughter of Queen Victoria's daughter Alice, and was 1st Sea Lord, 1912–14. In 1917 he renounced his German titles, adopted the surname Mountbatten (q.v.) and was created 1st Marquess of Milford Haven (q.v.).

The 2nd son of Prince Alexander, ALEXANDER JOSEPH (1857–93), became Prince Alexander I of Bulgaria. The 3rd son, Prince HENRY MAURICE (1858–96), m. in 1885 Queen Victoria's youngest daughter, Beatrice (d. 1944), became governor of the Isle of Wight and of Carisbrooke, took part in the Ashanti war, and d. at sea; his daughter, Victoria Eugénie Julia Ena, m. Alfonso XIII of Spain.

BATTERSEA. Former bor. of London, merged in the new Inner London bor. of Wandsworth, on the S. bank of the Thames. Battersea Park has a popular funfair, and other features of the district incl. B. power station, the B. Dogs' Home (1860), Clapham Junction Station, and London Heliport, opened in 1959. Pop. (1964) 335,367.

BATTLE. Small town in Sussex, England, the name of which is derived from the battle of Hastings, 1066, which was fought in the neighbourhood. B. Abbey, a girls' school, incorporates part of the abbey built by William the Conqueror. Pop c. 5,000.

BATTLE CRUISER. A type of warship now obsolete with the displacement and armament of a battleship, and the speed and protection of a cruiser.

BATTLESHIP. Type of warship now obsolete, but formerly predominant over all others in armour and fire-power: it has been superseded by the aircraft carrier. *See* WARSHIP.

A lineal descendent of the wooden walls of the sailing-ship era, the 1st modern B. was H.M.S. *Dreadnought* (1906) with a displacement of 17,900 tons, an armament of ten 12-in. guns, armour belt of 11 in., and a speed of 21 knots. Last of Britain's Bs. was the *Vanguard* (commissioned 1946), 42,000 tons, with eight 15-in. guns in twin turrets and sixteen 5·25-in. guns: she cost £11,000,000.

BATUMI (bahtōōm'i). Chief town of Adzhar A.S.S.R. Georgia, S.S.R., an important port on the S.E. of the Black Sea. Linked with the oilfields of the Baku area by railway and pipelines, it has large oil-cracking plants. Pop. (1967) 100,000.

BAUDELAIRE (bōdlār'). **Charles Pierre** (1821–67). French poet. B. at Paris, he was sent to India (1841–

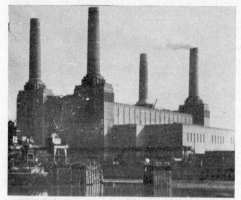

BATTERSEA. Completed in 1954, the power station is a striking example of the application of modern architecture to industry.   *Courtesy of General Electric Co.*

BAUXITE. As well as being used in making aluminium, bauxite is an important raw material for abrasive, refractory and chemical industries. This electrically-powered bucket wheel-excavator for extracting the ore is as high as a six-storey building and moves on double crawler tracks 6 ft. high.
Courtesy of Demerara Bauxite Company Ltd.

–3) by his guardians as a check to his dissipation, but remained so extravagant on his return that his inheritance was placed in the hands of a trustee. He joined the revolutionaries in 1848. His first book of verse, *Les Fleurs du Mal* (1857), caused considerable scandal, and was condemned by the censor as endangering public morals: author and printer were fined, and the most offensive pieces suppressed. In 1949 this sentence was quashed.

B. combined concentrated rhythmic and musical perfection with a morbid romanticism and eroticism which found beauty in decadence and evil. His later works incl. translations of E. A. Poe, whom he greatly admired; *Paradis artificiels, opium et haschisch* (1860), based on his own experience; an appreciation of *Richard Wagner et Tannhäuser à Paris* (1861); and *Petits poèmes en prose* (1868). His excesses impaired his health, and he spent the last 2 years of his life in hospitals at Brussels, where financial difficulties had driven him, and at Paris, where he d. B. prepared the way for Rimbaud, Verlaine, and the Symbolist school.

BAUDOUIN (bōhdoo-an') (1930–). King of Belgium. In 1950 his father, Leopold III (q.v.), relinquished to him his constitutional powers, and B. was known until his succession in July 1951 as *Le Prince Royal*. In 1960 he m. Fabiola de Mora y Aragòn (1928–), member of a Spanish noble family and author of fairy tales for children.

BAUHAUS (bow'hows), **Staatliches.** The 'State Building House' was founded in 1919 in an attempt to fuse all the arts and crafts in a unified whole, by the architect Walter Gropius (q.v.) at Weimar. Moved to Dessau in 1929, it closed under Nazi pressure in 1933. Klee and Kandinsky (qq.v.) were among its teachers. The Hochschule für Gestaltung at Ulm inherited the B. tradition, but closed in 1968 rather than accept the decision of the Baden-Württemberg State Legislature that it should combine with the local coll. of engineering.

BAUM (bowm), **Vicki** (1896–1960). American author. B. in Vienna, where she was an actress, she developed a distinctive technique, manipulating numerous characters in authentic settings. The success of *Grand Hotel* (1929) in America, both as book and play, led her to become a U.S. citizen.

BAUR (bowr), **Ferdinand Christian** (1792–1860). German theologian and Biblical critic, b. near Stuttgart. From 1826 he was professor of theology at Tübingen. Influenced by Schleiermacher and Hegel,

B. developed a system of theology from which the supernatural element had been completely expunged, and detected in the N.T. writings a long and bitter conflict between Petrinism (Jewish) and Paulinism (Gentile), in the early Christian Church. B. advanced his views in works which carried the fame of the 'Tübingen School' into every quarter.

BAUXITE (boks'ĭt). The most widely known ore of aluminium, providing the major part of the world's supplies of that metal; it is named from the district of Les Baux, near Arles, in the S. of France, where it was first discovered. Bauxite ($Al_2O_3 \cdot 2H_2O$) contains aluminium oxide, generally contaminated with compounds of iron, which give it a red colour.

BAVARIA (Ger. Bayern). The largest of the *Länder* of W. Germany with its cap. at Munich. Area 27,230 sq. m.; pop (est. 1966) 10,216,800. The greater part of B. is in the Danube basin; it is predominantly an agricultural country, although there are many towns with important industries. The main uranium deposits of W. Germany are in the Fichtelgebirge in the N.E. About 70 per cent of the people are Roman Catholics. The original Bavarians were Teutonic invaders from Bohemia who occupied the country at the end of the 5th cent. A.D. They were later ruled by dukes who recognized the supremacy of the Emperor. The House of Wittelsbach ruled parts or all of B. from 1181 to 1918; Napoleon made the ruler a king in 1806. In 1871 B. became a state of the German Empire. The last king, Ludwig III (1845–1921), abdicated in 1918, and B. declared itself a rep.

BAX, Sir Arnold Edward Trevor (1883–1953). British composer. B. in London, he studied at the R.A.M., was knighted in 1937 and became Master of the King's Musick in 1943. Composed in almost every branch except opera, his works show a strong Celtic, especially Irish, influence, and were often based on Celtic legends. They incl. *The Garden of Fand* (a symphonic poem), *Tintagel* (an orchestral tone poem), and 'Coronation March', his last, played in Westminster Abbey for the Coronation of Queen Elizabeth II. His brother Clifford B. (1886–1962) was a writer and dramatist.

BAXTER, George (1804–67). British inventor in 1834 of a special process for printing in oil colours, which he applied successfully in book illustrations.

BAXTER, Richard (1615–91). English churchman. B. in Salop, he took orders in the C. of E. in 1638, became minister at Kidderminster, and during the Civil War he was a chaplain in the parliamentary army.

BAVARIA. Standing in the Alpine foothills, almost 3,000 ft. above sea level, Neuschwanstein Castle was created for Ludwig II by Dollmann, Riedel, and Hofman to rival the 11th cent. Wartburg, whose design it closely follows. It reproduces faithfully the fairytale beauty of a typical German medieval castle. *Courtesy of the German Tourist Information Bureau.*

Ill-health caused his retirement to Rouse-Lench, Worcs, where he composed that Puritan classic *The Saints' Everlasting Rest* (1650). After the Restoration he lived in London and was a royal chaplain. In 1662 the Act of Uniformity drove him out of the Church. In 1685 he was tried before Judge Jeffreys for alleged sedition, and imprisoned for nearly 18 months.

BAY. Name applied to various species of laurel (*Laurus*) and some other plants. The victor's laurel of the ancients was the sweet bay (*L. nobilis*), a native of S. Europe. Its aromatic evergreen leaves are used in cookery, for flavouring.

BAYAR, Celâl (1884–). Turkish statesman. A follower of Atatürk, he was P.M. 1937–9, and in 1946 founded the Democratic Party. He succeeded Inönü as pres. in 1950 and was re-elected in 1958, but in 1960 was arrested following the military coup which overthrew the Menderes govt. and imprisoned on a charge of treason. In 1963 his release led to riots and he was re-imprisoned until 1964.

BAYARD (bā'ahrd), **Pierre du Terrail** (Chevalier) (1473–1524). French soldier. B. in Dauphiné, he served under Charles VIII, Louis XII, and Francis I, and was killed in action at the crossing of the Sesia in Italy. His heroic exploits in battle and in tournaments, his chivalry and magnanimity, won him the name of 'knight without fear and reproach'.

BAYERN. German form of BAVARIA.

BAYEUX (bahyö'). French town in Calvados dept., on the Aure, 18 m. N.W. of Caen. The fine cathedral is mainly 13th cent. Gothic. In the museum is the B. Tapestry (*see below*). B. was the first town in W. Europe to be liberated by the Allies, 7 June 1944. Pop. (1962) 10,641.

BAYEUX 'TAPESTRY'. A linen sampler, made about A.D. 1080, which gives a vivid pictorial record of the invasion of England by William the Conqueror in 1066. It is 231 ft. long and 20 in. wide, embroidered with woollen threads in blue, green, red, and yellow, and contains 72 separate scenes with descriptive wording in Latin. *See illus.* HAROLD II.

BAYLE (bāl), **Pierre** (1647–1706). French critic and controversial writer. Son of a Calvinist pastor, he held chairs of philosophy at Sedan and Rotterdam. Suspected of rationalist views, he was suspended in 1693. Three years later appeared his *Dictionnaire historique et critique*, which had a wide influence, particularly on the French Encyclopaedists.

BAYLEBRIDGE, William (1883–1942). Australian poet and author. His study of the F.W.W. from the Australian viewpoint, *Anzac Muster* (1922), is a notable prose work.

BAYLIS, Lilian Mary (1874–1937). British theatrical manager. A niece of Emma Cons, who in 1880 took over the Royal Victoria Hall (Old Vic), in Waterloo Road, London, she was well known as a child violinist and afterwards as a concert entertainer. Under her management (from 1898) the Old Vic theatre became a home of Shakespearian drama, and Sadler's Wells theatre, rebuilt in 1926, a home of opera and ballet. She was made a C.H. in 1929.

BAYONNE (bahyon'). Fortified French town in Basses-Pyrénées dept., 3 m. from the mouth of the Adour, near the Span. frontier. It is a centre of Basque life. Iron and steel works, linen, leather, and other factories lie just outside the town. The bayonet was invented here. Pop. (1968) 42,743.

BAYOU (bī'-oo). Corruption of Fr. *boyau* 'gut': in southern U.S.A. an oxbow lake or marshy offshoot of a river. Bs. may be formed, as in the lower Mississippi, by a river flowing in exaggeratedly wide curves in flat country, and then cutting a straight course across them in time of flood, so leaving 'loops' of dead water behind.

BAYREUTH (bī'roit). German town in Bavaria, 42 m. N.E. of Nuremberg, famous for its Wagnerian associations. The Wagner Theatre was opened in

BEACHY HEAD. The cliff top lighthouse of 1831 was easily obscured by low cloud and the Bell Tout lighthouse (1902) which replaced it is off the shore. In 1690 a French fleet, intended to support a Jacobite rising, defeated the English and Dutch in the Battle of Beachy Head but no rebellion followed.   *Courtesy of the Eastbourne Publicity Department.*

1876, and here the Wagner festivals are held, attracting music-lovers from all over the world. Pop. (1954) 60,774.

BAYROUT, BAYRUT. Other forms of BEIRUT.

BAZAINE (bahzăn′). **Achille François** (1811–88). Marshal of France. B. at Versailles, he enlisted as a private soldier in 1831 and had a rapid rise. He commanded the French troops in Mexico in 1862–7, and was made a marshal in 1864. In the Franco-Prussian War B. commanded the 3rd Corps of the Army of the Rhine, allowed himself to be cooped up in the fortress of Metz, and capitulated on 27 Oct. 1870, with nearly 180,000 men. For this in 1873 he was court-martialled and sentenced to death; the sentence was at once commuted to 20 years' imprisonment. In 1874 he escaped to Spain.

BEACHY HEAD. Between Seaford and Eastbourne in Sussex, the eastern termination of the S. Downs, and the loftiest headland (531 ft.) on the S. coast of England. The lighthouse off the shore is 125 ft. high.

BEACONSFIELD (bě′konzfēld), **Benjamin Disraeli,** earl of (1804–81). Conservative statesman and novelist. The son of Isaac D., a distinguished Jewish man of letters, he was baptized a Christian at the age of 13. He was ed. at a private school, and after a period in a solicitor's office wrote the novel *Vivian Grey* (1826) and others, and the brilliant pamphlet *Vindication of the English Constitution* (1835). D. entered parliament in 1837 after 4 unsuccessful attempts, and 2 years later he m. Mrs. Wyndham Lewis, widow of a parliamentary colleague.

Excluded from Peel's government of 1841–6, D. formed his 'Young England' group to keep a critical eye on Peel's conservatism. Its ideas were expressed in the novels *Coningsby* (1844), *Sybil* (1845), and *Tancred* (1847). When Peel decided in 1846 to repeal the Corn Laws, D. opposed the measure in a series of witty and effective speeches; Peel's govt. fell soon after, and D. gradually came to be recognized as the leader of the Conservative Party in the Commons. He gave his own account of these events in his *Life of Lord George Bentinck* (1852).

During the next 20 years the Conservatives formed short-lived minority govts. in 1852, in 1858–9, and in 1866–8, with Lord Derby as P.M. and D. as Chancellor of the Exchequer and leader of the Commons. In 1852 D. first proposed discrimination in income tax between earned and unearned income, but without success. The 1858–9 govt. legalized the admission of Jews to parliament, and transferred the govt. of India from the E. India Co. to the Crown. In 1866 the Conservatives took office after defeating a Liberal Reform

Bill, and then attempted to secure the credit of widening the franchise by the Reform Bill of 1867. On Lord Derby's retirement in 1868 D. became P.M., but a few months later he was defeated at a general election. During the 6 years of opposition which followed he pub. another novel, *Lothair* (1870), and estab. a Conservative Central Office, the prototype of modern party organizations.

In 1874 he took office with a majority of 100. Some useful reform measures were carried, such as the Artisans' Dwelling Act, which empowered local authorities to undertake slum-clearance, but the outstanding feature of the government's policy was its Imperialism. It was Disraeli's personal initiative which purchased from the Khedive of Egypt a controlling interest in the Suez Canal, conferred on the Queen the title of Empress of India, and sent the Prince of Wales on the first royal tour of that country. The Bulgarian revolt of 1876 and the subsequent Russo-Turkish War of 1877–8 provoked the most famous of the political duels between Disraeli and Gladstone. The crisis was concluded by the Congress of Berlin (1878), where B.—he had accepted an earldom 2 years before—was principal British delegate, and whence he brought home 'peace with honour'. The government was defeated in 1880, and a year later B. d. after writing *Endymion*. He was the founder and chief inspiration of the modern Conservative Party.

BEACONSFIELD (be′konzfēld). English town in Bucks 23 m. W.N.W. of London. Edmund Waller and Burke lived in B., and Benjamin Disraeli, whose seat was Hughenden Manor in the neighbourhood, took his title from it. In 1949 the Manor was opened as a Disraelian Museum. Pop. (1961) 10,019.

BEADLE (bēdl), **George Wells** (1903–   ). American biologist. B. at Wahoo, Nebraska, he was prof. of biology at the California Inst. of Technology 1946–61, and in 1958 was awarded a share of a Nobel prize for his work with Edward L. Tatum in biochemical genetics. In 1961 he was appointed President of the Univ. of Chicago.

BEAGLE. A miniature fox-hound used for hunting the hare on foot. Of terrier size, the B. can be of any recognized foxhound colour.

BEALE, Dorothea (1831–1906). British pioneer in feminine education. Dau. of a London doctor, she became a teacher at the Queen's Coll. for Ladies, and as headmistress of the Ladies' Coll. at Cheltenham from 1858 was influential in raising the standard of women's education.

BEAN. Name given to the seeds of various leguminous and other plants, which are rich in nitrogenous or proteid matter, and are grown both for human consumption and as food for cattle and horses. The broad bean (*Vicia faba*) has been cultivated in Europe since prehistoric times. The French bean, kidney bean, or haricot (*Phaseolus vulgaris*) is possibly of S. American origin; the runner bean (*P. multiflorus*) is closely allied to it, but differs in its climbing habit. Among Bs. of importance in warmer countries are the Lima bean (*P. lunatus*) of S. America and the soya of China and Japan (*Glycine soja*).

LORD BEACONSFIELD, the youthful dandy. *After Maclise   Photo: N.P.G.*

BEAR. Large or medium sized, heavily-built mammal, forming the family Ursidae of the order Carnivora, distinguished by their protrusible lips, very short tail, and broad plantigrade feet armed with long, non-retractile claws; the teeth too are characteristic. Bs. are chiefly vegetarian in diet, breed once a year, and usually have 2 cubs in the litter.

The brown and grizzly bears (*Ursus arctos*) extend from Europe through Central Asia into N. America, and are represented by many local races. The colour varies from blackish or reddish brown to grey. The best-known races of the Old World, the typical brown B. of Europe (*U.a. arctos*), the paler Syrian B. (*U.a. syriacus*), the Kashmir Red B. (*U.a. isabellinus*), and the Tibetan Blue B. (*U.a. pruinosus*) are about 3 ft. at the shoulder, but in Alaska the brown Bs. are bigger, 4 ft. or over at the shoulder.

BEAR. Left to right: black, grizzly and polar.

These Bs. are very alike in habits. They hibernate where it is very cold in winter, and eat vegetable food, insects, fish, and small mammals, but sometimes raid farm property, and carry off cattle, pigs, or other livestock. Consequently, and also because of the value of their skins, they have become greatly reduced in numbers. They rarely attack man, except when cornered.

The grizzly B. (*U.a. horribilis*) of N. America is closely related to the brown bear, which it resembles in size, appearance, and habits. There are several races, chiefly inhabiting the Rocky Mountains; but it has been exterminated in many districts. Stories of its ferocity have probably been exaggerated. The N. American black B. (*Euarctos americanus*) stands only about 2½ ft. high. Other species are the Himalayan Black B. (*Selenarctos tibetanus*), the Malayan B. (*Helarctos malayanus*), the sloth B. (*Melursus ursinus*) of Hindustan and Ceylon, and smallest of all, the spectacled B. (*Tremarctos ornatus*) of S. America.

Lastly there is the polar or white B. (*Thalarctos maritimus*) distinguished by its white coat, inability to climb, and hairy soles of the feet—characters that are adaptations to arctic life. Its prey comprises fish, seals, and stranded whales. It will also eat seaweed and, in the summer, lichen and grass. This is one of the largest Bs., a good sized male being 4 ft. high and up to 9 ft. in length.

A still larger B. was the extinct cave B. (*U. spelaeus*) of prehistoric Europe.

BEAR BAITING. Brutal sport once popular in Europe; the bear was chained to a stake and baited by dogs. It was abolished in Britain in 1835.

BEAR, Great and **Little.** Two constellations, in Lat. called *Ursa major* and *minor* (q.v.).

BEARD, Charles Austin (1874–1948). American historian, author of *The Economic Interpretation of the Constitution, The Rise of American Civilization*, etc. Staunchly isolationist, he opposed Roosevelt and the entry of the U.S. into the S.W.W.

BEARDSLEY, Aubrey Vincent (1872–98). British black-and-white artist. A musical phenomenon as a boy, he began to study art at the age of 19 and developed an unconventional style which evoked much criticism. In 1894 he became prominent as illustrator

to the *Yellow Book*. He became a R.C. in 1897, and d. at Mentone of consumption.

BEARS AND BULLS. *See* STOCK EXCHANGE.

BEAS (bē'as). One of the 5 rivers which give its name to Punjab, B. is an upper tributary of the Sutlej. The ancient Hyphasis, it marked the limit of the invasion of India by Alexander the Great.

BEASLEY (bēz'li), **John Albert** (1895–1949). Australian Labour leader. Strongly anti-Communist, he was Min. of Supply and Shipping 1941–5 and played a great part in Australia's war effort. He was High Commissioner in London from 1946.

BEATIFICATION. *See* CANONIZATION.

BEATING THE BOUNDS. Ancient custom in the English countryside. On Holy Thursday the parish clergyman, with village officials and a number of boys, perambulate the bounds of the parish, the boys beating the corners, etc. with peeled willow-wands. In olden days the boys themselves were beaten.

BEATITUDES (bē-at'itūdz; Latin *beatitudo*, blessedness, or happiness). The sayings of Jesus reported in Matt. v, 1–12; Lk. vi, 20–38, depicting the spiritual qualities which are to characterize members of the Kingdom of God.

BEATON (bē'ton), **Sir Cecil Walter H.** (1904–). British photographer and designer. B. in London, he was educ. at Harrow and Cambridge and has produced notable portrait studies; settings for plays and films, e.g. the London and N.Y. production of *My Fair Lady*; and scenery and costumes for ballets. Among his books is *Cecil Beaton's Diaries 1922–39* (1961).

BEATON (bē'ton or bā'ton), **David** (1494–1546). Scottish cardinal and statesman. A chief min. of James V, he was made prim. ate of Scotland in 1539. Under Mary Queen of Scot. he opposed the alliance with England, persecuted the Reformers, and was assassinated by a band of fanatics at St. Andrews.

BEATRIX (bē'atriks) (193.–). Crown Princess of the Netherlands. The eldest dau. of Queen Juliana (q.v.), she achieved great popularity, but when in 1966 she m. W. German diplomat Claus von Amsberg

BEATON. In the winter garden of his Wiltshire home, Cecil Beaton relaxes in a setting as delicately exotic as any of his stage designs. His pug dog Sambi is equally content.
Courtesy of Cecil Beaton.

(1926–), created Prince Claus of the Netherlands, there was initially some opposition: their eldest child is Prince Alexander (1967–).

BEATTY (bē'ti), **David**, 1st earl (1871–1936). British admiral. Entering the navy in 1888, he commanded the cruiser squadron 1912–16, and bore the brunt of the Battle of Jutland. In 1916 he succeeded Jellicoe in command of the Grand Fleet, and in 1918 received the surrender of the German Fleet, being subsequently made Admiral of the Fleet and receiving an earldom and the O.M.

BEAUFORT SCALE. System of recording wind velocity, devised in 1806 by Admiral Sir Francis Beaufort (1774–1857), who became hydrographer to the Royal Navy in 1829. It consists of the numbers 0–17, calm being indicated by 0 and a hurricane by 12: 13–17 indicate degrees of hurricane force. In 1874 it received international recognition.

BEAUHARNAIS (bō-ahrnā'), **Alexandre** (1760–94). French viscount, who served in the American War of Independence, joined the popular party in the early days of the Revolution, but was guillotined for lack of zeal. He m. Joséphine Tascher de la Pagerie, afterwards wife and empress of Napoleon I, and had two children: **Hortense** (1783–1837), who m. in 1802 Louis Bonaparte, a younger brother of Napoleon, and became the mother of Napoleon III, and **Eugène** (1781–1824), who was made a prince by Napoleon and viceroy of Italy in 1805. After 1814 he lived in retirement in Bavaria.

BEAULIEU (bew'li). English village and parish in Hants, 6 m. N.E. of Lymington. An abbey founded 1204 is the home of Lord Montagu of Beaulieu. Here is the Montagu Motor Museum. Pop. *c.* 1300.

BEAUMARCHAIS (bōmahrshā'), **Pierre Augustin Caron de** (1732–99). French dramatist. B. in Paris, the son of a watchmaker named Caron, he attracted the notice of Louis XV and was given a court appointment. He m. a wealthy widow, assumed the title of de Beaumarchais, won a fortune by speculation, and on his wife's death made another good match. His great comedies *Le barbier de Seville* (1775) and *Le Mariage de Figaro* (1778, but prohibited until 1784 because of revolutionary tendencies) are best known in England by the operatic versions of Rossini and Mozart. Louis XVI entrusted B. with secret missions, and he was responsible for the shipment of arms to the American colonies during the War of Independence, conducting a private traffic with great profit. Accused of treason in 1792, he fled to poverty in Holland and England. In 1876 he returned to Paris where he died.

BEAUMONT, Francis (1584–1616). English poet and dramatist. B. at Grace Dieu, Leics, the son of a judge and brother to the poet Sir John B. (1583–1627), he studied law and in 1602 pub. a love-poem *Salmacis and Hermaphroditus*. From *c.* 1608 he collaborated with John Fletcher, with whom he lived until the latter's marriage in 1613. The best of their joint works are: *Philaster* (*c.* 1610), *The Maid's Tragedy* (*c.* 1611), and *A King and No King* (*c.* 1611). The *Woman Hater* (*c.* 1606) and *The Knight of the Burning Pestle* (*c.* 1607) are ascribed to B. alone. B. had greater powers of thought and versification than Fletcher, as well as excelling in plot construction. He was buried in Westminster Abbey.

BEAUNE (bōn). French town in the dept. of Côte d'Or, 23 m. S. by W. of Dijon, a centre of the Burgundy wine trade. Pop. (1962) 15,882.

BEAUTY CULTURE. The art of improving the physical appearance.

The practice of painting the face, of dressing the hair, and of using lotions and perfumes to enhance natural beauty dates back to ancient times. Unguent jars, still fragrant with musk, were found in the 4,000-year old tomb of King Tutankhamen. Cosmetics, oils for the skin, perfumes, and aromatic

BEAUTY CULTURE. Living in the eastern part of Cape Province are the Xhosa, a group of Bantu-speaking tribes. The women paint their faces with ochre, achieving an effect that resembles the mud-pack of the European beauty salon.
Courtesy of SATOUR.

baths were known to the Egyptians. Henna, which is still used as a hair dye, was used in the time of Cleopatra to colour the finger and toe nails. The Greeks used perfumes, many of which were imported from Egypt, and also experimented with hair dyes and bleaches. They introduced cosmetics into the Roman Empire, and by the time of Nero it was common for Romans of both sexes to use perfumes, and to indulge in luxurious baths. Kohl was used for painting the eyes, pumice powder for whitening the teeth, and *fucus* as a rouge for the lips and cheeks.

Cosmetics were first used in Britain at the time of the Roman occupation, but they were uncommon until many cents. later. During the 11th and 12th cents. the Crusaders brought all kinds of perfumes and cosmetics from the east. In Elizabethan times powders, rouges, and eye cosmetics were popular; ladies-in-waiting took milk baths; Mary, Queen of Scots, bathed in wine. These practices were suppressed during the Commonwealth, but were revived under Charles II. Small-pox scars and the ravages of other diseases were concealed by means of heavy make-up.

Herbal lotions and packs were later sold to improve the complexion, but it was not until the 20th cent. that make-up became generally accepted by women of all classes. The manufacture of cosmetics has now developed into a major industry, and many women pay regular visits to beauty salons, not only for treatment for their hair (the 1st permanent 'wave', created in 1905 by Charles Nessler, was a painful 9-hr. operation), but for massage, skin conditioning, facial treatment and manicure. Since the S.W.W. toilet preparations for men have become increasingly popular, and modern fashions with their revealing lines and emphasis on active leisure clothes have dictated greater attention to the body as well as the face for both sexes. Salons specializing, not merely in getting rid of excess fat, but in developing perfect proportions and fitness by exercises and other means, have multiplied.

BEAUVAIS (bōvā'). French town, cap. of Oise dept., 42 m. N.N.W. of Paris. The cathedral (1247–1558) is one of the noblest in France, and the town is famous for its carpets, rugs, and hand-made tapestries. Pop. *c.* 30,000.

BEAUVOIR (bohvwahr'), **Simone de** (1908–). French writer, who taught philosophy at the Sorbonne 1931–43. Her books incl. a number of novels illustrating philosophical theories, e.g. *All Men are Mortal* (1947); *The Second Sex* (1949), a sensational attack on the man-made world of values women must inhabit;

Les Mandarins (1954), a novel of post-war Parisian intellectualism with characters resembling Camus, Koestler and Sartre. Essential to an understanding of her work are the 2 autobiographical vols. *Memoirs of a Dutiful Daughter* and *The Prime of Life*.

BEAVER (bē'ver). Sole representative of the family Castoridae of the order Rodentia; found in Europe, Central Asia, and North America, and distinguished mainly by its broad, flat, scaly tail and webbed hind feet—adaptations to aquatic life.

The European B. (*Castor fiber*) survives in Central Asia and, under strict protection, in small numbers in the Elbe and Rhine, and in Norway and elsewhere in Europe. The American B. (*Castor canadensis*) is widely distributed in N. America. Both species have a coat of thick brown fur impervious to water, grow to 3½ ft., including the tail, attain a weight of 50 lb., and live from 12 to 15 years. There are usually 4 young born in the spring in a 'lodge' of logs and mud.

The B. is a valuable fur-bearing animal, and also yields castoreum, secreted by glands at the base of the tail, which is used for perfumes.

BEAVERBROOK, William Maxwell Aitken, 1st baron B. (1879–1964). Canadian newspaper proprietor. B. at Maple, Ontario, he made his fortune by a merger of the principal Canadian cement firms in 1910, when he settled in England and became a Conservative M.P. A close association with Bonar Law and other Conservative leaders gave him a strong influence in the F.W.W., and he received a peerage in 1917 and became Min. of Information in 1918. From 1919 he was in full control of the policy of the *Daily Express*, soon after founding the *Sunday Express* and buying the *Evening Standard*. In 1929–31 he launched a campaign for Empire Free Trade and against Baldwin's leadership of the Conservative Party, while during the 1930s he advocated a policy of 'splendid isolation' in Europe. In the S.W.W. he was Min. of Aircraft Production 1940–1, Min. of Supply 1941–2 and Lord Privy Seal 1943–5. The B. press campaigned vigorously against British entry into the Common Market in 1962–3. Among his books are *Men and Power* (1956) and *The Decline and Fall of Lloyd George* (1963). He made munificent gifts to New Brunswick Univ., and in 1954 estab. in London an educational trust, the B. Foundation, to which he turned over his newspaper holdings. He was succeeded by his son **Sir Max Aitken** (1910–), who renounced the peerage.

BEBEL (beh'bel), **Ferdinand August** (1840–1913). German Social Democratic leader. B. at Cologne-Deutz, the son of a N.C.O., he collaborated with Liebknecht, and was elected to the Reichstag. He condemned Bismarck's *kulturkampf*, spoke for the Paris Communards in 1872, and was imprisoned. Under Bismarck Socialism was proscribed, but after his fall, B. made the party a powerful organization.

BEBINGTON. English town (bor.) on the left bank of the Mersey estuary, Cheshire, just S. of Birkenhead. It incl. Port Sunlight, and manufactures soap, candles, margarine, oils, etc. Pop. (1961) 52,202.

BECCARIA (bekahrē'ah), **Cesare**, marquis of (1738–94). Italian philanthropical writer. B. in Milan, he pub. in 1764 a treatise on *Crimes and Punishments*. His arguments against torture and capital punishment, and in favour of education as a means of preventing crime, had their effect upon penal codes, and his phrase 'the greatest happiness of the greatest number', shortly became the watchword of Bentham, Romilly, and the English Utilitarians.

BECHSTEIN (hekh-stin), **Karl** (1826–1900). German pianoforte-maker, founder of the Berlin firm which bears his name in 1856.

BECHUANALAND. See BOTSWANA.

BECKET, Thomas (1118–70). English churchman. The son of a rich Norman merchant, he passed from the service of Theobald, Archbishop of Canterbury, to that of Henry II, who created him Chancellor of England in 1155. When he became Archbishop of Canterbury in 1162 he devoted all his energy to resisting royal encroachments on the privileges of the clergy, and as a result Henry's friendship turned to bitter hatred. His opposition to Henry's attempt by the Constitutions of Clarendon (1164) to bring the clergy under the jurisdiction of the royal courts provoked open hostility between them, and B. fled to France. He returned in 1170 when a reconciliation was patched up; but the quarrel soon broke out again, and 4 knights, encouraged by a hasty outburst of the king's, murdered B. in Canterbury Cathedral. He was canonized in 1172, and his shrine remained a popular object of pilgrimage until the Reformation.

BECKETT, Samuel (1906–). Irish dramatist, who settled in Paris as a disciple of Joyce, and published a number of novels and some verse. He made a world reputation with his play *Waiting for Godot* (1952), in which two tramps wait endlessly for 'Godot' and debate equally endlessly. Later plays incl. *Fin de Partie* (End Game: 1957). Nobel prizewinner 1969.

BECKFORD, William (1760–1844). British writer and eccentric. B. at Fonthill, Wilts, he inherited an immense fortune, became a M.P. in 1784, but shortly afterwards was obliged to leave England owing to scandals in his private life. *Vathek*, a fantastic Arabian Nights' tale, was pub. in Paris in 1787. In 1796 B. returned to England, rebuilt Fonthill Abbey, and filled it with fantastic curiosities. This he sold in 1822, and retired to Bath.

BECKMANN, Max (1884–1950). German artist. B. in Leipzig, he was driven from Germany in 1933 by political persecution and d. in N.Y. His experiences during the F.W.W. induced a bitterly realistic spirit, which gave way in later work to a hauntingly dream-like quality. He is an outstanding artist of the later phase of Expressionism.

BECQUEREL (bekrel'), **Antoine Henri** (1852–1908). French physicist, renowned for his discovery in 1896 of the *Becquerel rays*, the first indications of radio-activity: these were later re-named gamma rays. He shared with the Curies the Nobel Prize for physics in 1903.

BEDDOES, Thomas Lovell (1803–49). British poet and dramatist. A romantic, working under the influence of the Elizabethan dramatists, he started his most famous play, the incoherent *Death's Jest Book*, in 1825, but it was not pub. until 1850, much revised. From Oxford he had gone on to medical studies in Germany, and practised as a physician in Zurich until driven out by political events in 1839. After several suicide attempts, he succeeded in poisoning himself with curare. His lyrics and various dramatic fragments are now highly regarded by connoisseurs.

BEDE (bēd) (*c.* 673–735). English theologian and historian, known as the Venerable Bede. B. at Monkwearmouth, Durham, he entered the local monastery at the age of 7, later transferring to Jarrow, where he became a priest *c.* 703. He devoted his life to writing and teaching, the most famous of his pupils being Egbert, archbishop of York. He wrote many scientific, theological and historical works, the most celebrated being his *Historia Ecclesiastica Gentis Anglorum*, finished in 731. He d. and was buried at Jarrow, but his remains were removed to Durham in the 11th cent.

BEDFORD, John Robert Russell, 13th duke of (1917–). British nobleman. He succeeded his father, a noted naturalist, in the title in 1940. Under his aegis the family seat at Woburn in Bedfordshire has been restored to its former glory and both the house and grounds are visited by thousands annually.

BEDFORD. English town (bor.), co. town of

BEDFORDSHIRE Woburn Abbey near the village of Woburn was built in the 18th century on the site of a Cistercian abbey granted in 1547 to John Russell, later 1st earl of Bedford, so that little of the original structure survives. The surrounding park, as developed by the 13th duke of Bedford, includes a zoo and attracts as many visitors as the house.
Courtesy of the Duke of Bedford.

Bedfordshire, on the Ouse, 23 m. W.S.W. of Cambridge. Primarily an agricultural market town, it also makes agricultural implements and bricks, and has engineering shops. Bunyan began to write *The Pilgrim's Progress* in B. jail; Bunyan Meeting House stands on the site of the barn in which he preached. Bedford School dates from the 12th cent.; endowed in the 16th by Sir William Harpur, it is one of several run by the Harpur Trust. Pop. (1961) 63,317.

BEDFORDSHIRE (Beds). A S. midland county of England, lying mainly in the Ouse basin, and for the most part lowland, devoted to agriculture. Chief towns are Bedford, the co. town; Luton (largest town), Dunstable, and Leighton-Linslade. Area 477 sq. m.; pop. (1967) 598,220.

BEDLAM. Popular name of Bethlehem hospital, the oldest public lunatic asylum in Europe with the exception of that of Granada in Spain. It was originally founded in Bishopsgate, London, as a priory in 1247, was incorporated by Henry VIII in 1547, and was removed to Moorfields in 1675, in 1815 to Lambeth, and in 1930 to West Wickham, near Croydon.

BEDLINGTON. Breed of terrier dog supposed to have been produced by the Northumberland pitmen of about 100 years ago. It has much in common with the Dandie Dinmont, though in conformation like the greyhound. The colours are blue or liver.

BEDSTRAW. Name of a genus of plants (*Galium*) of the madder family (Rubiaceae). The yellow-flowered *G. verum* (Our Lady's B.) is the typical species. *G. mollugo*, with white flowers is also common in England. *G. aparine* is the goose-grass, or cleavers.

BEE. Four-winged stinging insect forming the super-family Apoidea of the order Hymenoptera. More than 12,000 species are known, but fewer than 5 per cent are social in habit.

The eggs of bees are laid in chambers or cells, each nest containing several or, as in the Hive B., many thousands of cells. Nectar and pollen are the staple food. Nectar is regurgitated as honey before being supplied to the larvae.

The *solitary bees* comprise ordinary males and females and do not live in communities. Some of the commonest are the species of *Halictus, Andrena*, and *Osmia*, important agents in pollinating fruit blossoms in early spring. Many of these bees make tunnels in the ground; others use existing cavities in wood or bramble stems, crevices in masonry, etc. The Mason B. (*Chalicodoma*) of S. Europe makes dome-like nests of soil and pebbles. The Leaf-cutting Bs. (*Megachile*) nest in hollow stems, in posts, or in the ground. There are also Bs. that lay their eggs in nests of other species, and are in fact 'cuckoo' bees, or parasites, whose larvae destroy those of their hosts.

The *social bees* include the Bumble Bs. (q.v.) or

BEE. Far removed from the traditional straw 'skep' is this modern hive (left) in the Israeli Government's Experimentation and Breeding Apiary at Zerifin which is even handled mechanically. On the right are the worker (*top*), shown much enlarged, but actually the smallest of the three, drone (*lower left*) and queen (*lower right*) of the Hive Bee.
Courtesy of the Government of Israel and the British Bee Research Association.

Bombidae; the Hive B. and related kinds (*Apis*) and the so-called Stingless Bs. (*Melipona* and *Trigona*) of the tropics. Like other social insects they live in communities, and the life of the female parent is prolonged so that she is able to co-operate with her offspring to the benefit of the colony.

The *Hive B.* (*Apis mellifera*) has perennial colonies, and a flourishing hive will number 50,000 to 80,000 bees. The vast majority are workers (infertile females): the drones (males) are considerably larger and stouter with large eyes, while the queen can be recognized by her longer abdomen, which reaches beyond the closed wings. The comb is made of wax (secreted by glands between the segments of the abdomen in the worker) and composed of a large number of typically hexagonal cells, arranged in two series, and placed back to back. A large number of these are used for rearing the brood, others are for storing honey and pollen. The queen lays an egg in each brood cell and the incubation period is about 3 days; the complete development of the queen takes 16 days, a worker 3 weeks, and a drone 24 days. Fertilized eggs develop into workers, or queens, and the unfertilized eggs produce drones. The larvae are fed at first on 'royal jelly', a glandular product of the workers. Those destined to grow into queens receive this diet until full grown. New colonies are estab. by swarming, and this event follows the emergence of a daughter queen. The swarm consists of the original queen accompanied by a host of workers, the new queen remaining in the hive. She takes her marriage flight at any early opportunity and is followed by a retinue of eager drones. Mating occurs in mid air, after which the young and now fertilized queen returns to the hive.

BEEBE (bē'bē), **Charles William** (1877–1962). American naturalist and explorer, leader of many scientific expeditions in tropics, the first to descend in a bathysphere (q.v.) to observe life in ocean depths.

BEECH. Genus of trees (*Fagus*), of which the common B. (*F. sylvatica*) grows as a forest tree throughout Europe. Its wood rots easily, but is used for making small objects for household use. The nuts or mast are a food for pigs.

BEECHAM, Sir Thomas (1879–1961). English conductor. Grandson of Thomas B. (1820–1907), founder of the pharmaceutical firm, and son of Sir Joseph B., bt. (1848–1916), b. at St. Helens, Lancs. As conductor to the B. Orchestra (formed 1908) and the B. Opera Co. (formed 1915; later the British National Opera Co.), he introduced new life into the world of British music, and in 1911 brought the Russian ballet to England. At his death he was still conductor of the Royal Philharmonic Orchestra, which he had founded in 1947. Renowned as an interpreter of Mozart and Verdi, he estab. the musical reputation of Delius, of whom he pub. a biography in 1959, by his ceaseless advocacy. He was k. in 1916, succeeded his father as 2nd bt. in the same year, and in 1944 pub. the autobiographical *A Mingled Chime*.

BEECH. The tree with eaves and mast.

SIR
THOMAS BEECHAM

His mischievous wit, fiery temper, and personal magnetism rendered him an unforgettable figure.

BEECHER, Lyman (1775–1863). American Presbyterian divine, one of the most influential pulpit orators of his time. He was the father of Harriet Beecher Stowe (q.v.), and of Henry Ward B. (1813–87), Congregational minister, pastor of Plymouth church, Brooklyn, N.Y., from 1847, a leader in the movement for the abolition of slavery, and an eloquent preacher.

BEECHING, Richard, baron (1913–). British scientist and administrator. A director of I.C.I. 1957–61 and 1965–8, he was chairman of Brit. Railways Board 1963–5, when the *B. Report* (1963) planning concentration on inter-city passenger traffic and a freight system was controversial.

BEERBOHM, Sir Max (1872–1956). English writer, the half-brother of the actor-manager Sir Herbert Beerbohm Tree (1853–1917). B. in London, he contributed to *The Yellow Book*, publishing the essays later ironically as *The Works of Max Beerbohm* (1896), and succeeded Shaw as dramatic critic to the *Saturday Review*. A superb stylist, B. produced one novel *Zuleika Dobson* (1911), parodies—*A Christmas Garland* (1912), and vols. of exquisite caricatures, e.g. *The Poet's Corner* and *Rossetti and his Circle*. From 1910 he lived in Rapallo, Italy, and was knighted in 1939. *See* illus. WILDE, Oscar.

BEERSHE'BA. Market town and road centre in Israel, cap. of the Negev, 45 m. S.W. of Jerusalem. A settlement from the Stone Age, in the 1950s B. developed industrially. Pop. (1967) 67,500.

BEET. Genus of plants (*Beta*) of the order Chenopodiaceae. *B. vulgaris* grows wild on seashores in many parts of the Old World; several varieties are cultivated for their fleshy taproot, such as the red beet and the mangold-wurzel, or for their leaves, such as the white or spinach-beet. The sugar-beet (q.v.) is the variety with the greatest commercial importance.

BEETHOVEN (beht'hōven), **Ludwig van** (1770–1827). German composer. B. at Bonn, 16 Dec. 1770, he was the son of a singer at the court of the archbishop-elector of Cologne, in whose household his mother also had a place. He was taught by his father, later by the court organist, and before he was 12 B. was made deputy organist and was already a busy composer. In 1787 he visited Vienna and had lessons from Mozart, and in 1792 the elector sent him to Vienna again to study under Haydn. There he became well known as a pianist and teacher, and benefited from the patronage of aristocratic enthusiasts—this in spite of his uncouth manners, unattractive appearance, eccentric habits, and ungovernable temper. By 1802 he was already troubled by deafness which steadily increased until it became total. It induced in him a feeling of terrible isolation, of spiritual loneliness and despair. A 'testament' written to his brothers in 1802 bears witness to the depth of his affliction. Family troubles increased his difficulties, especially the shiftless conduct of a nephew whose guardian he was. But, in spite of everything, he continued to compose even though now quite incapable of hearing his own works played. His music won European fame, and it was highly appreciated in England; the Royal Philharmonic Society commissioned several works, including the 9th Symphony, and sent him £100 during his last illness. *See* illus. under MUSIC.

B.'s work may be divided into three periods. In the

first his debt to Mozart and Haydn is obvious, though the distinctive features of his own individual style are already apparent. Here belong his early symphonies, chamber music, and piano sonatas. In the 2nd period he developed to the full his dynamic technique and powers of symphonic construction, displayed in e.g. the great *Appassionata* sonata the incidental music of *Egmont*, the opera *Fidelio*, and such symphonies as the *Eroica*, originally intended to be dedicated to Napoleon. The works of this period merge into those of the last, which show a greater complexity and breadth of construction, and an increased use of polyphony. Throughout, the development of B.'s music was essentially classical, but in the realm of the symphony he completely revolutionized the whole treatment of form, until it became dynamic and dramatic. A parallel development is to be discerned in his sonatas. His fine piano concertos, notably the 4th in G major and the 5th (*Emperor*), his string quartets, and a number of songs, should also be mentioned.

BEETLE. The common name of insects forming the order Coleoptera (Gk. *koleos*, a sheath, *pteron*, a wing). The ordinal name is in allusion to the fore-wings, which are horny or leathery sheaths or *elytra*. When closed the elytra meet in a straight line down the middle of the back and protect the membranous hind-wings folded beneath them. Other characteristics are their biting mouth-parts, antennae with a number of segments, and a large mobile prothorax.

Bs. pass through complete metamophosis. The larvae are very varied in form, but generally bear legs or rudiments of them. The hind-wings are the functional organs of flight; the elytra take no part in propulsion, they merely act as planes.

Bs. include some of the largest and also some of the most minute of all insects. Thus the Hercules B. (*Dynastes hercules*) measures up to 6 in. long, while some members of the family Trichopterygidae are mere specks. About 250,000 different Bs. are known, forming the largest single order in the animal kingdom.

In habit Bs. are more especially ground insects, but several families are aquatic, and great numbers of species live in close association with plants. Other kinds live in timber and in dried stored products. The carnivorous habit of seeking and devouring living prey occurs in the ground Bs., tiger Bs., ladybirds, and in water Bs. of the family Dytiscidae. The leaf Bs. or Chrysomelidae and the weevils or Curculionidae are plant feeders. Others such as the bark Bs. or Scolytidae feed in their larval stages on the wood or bark of trees. Wireworms, or injurious larvae of click Bs., and chafer larvae are root-feeders, whose activities cause great losses to farmers and others. A great and diverse assembly of Bs., and especially their larvae, feed upon decaying organic matter. Thus the Silphidae include many carrion feeders, e.g. the burying Bs. Hosts of rove Bs. or Staphylinidae frequent refuse of all kinds; and many such as the Scarabaeidae, are dung Bs. The glow-worms and fire-flies are Bs. belonging to the families Cantharidae and Elateridae respectively.

BRENDAN BEHAN. A sketch by Paul Hogarth (q.v.).

Many Bs. are highly injurious, e.g. the asparagus B. and the Colorado potato B., the apple blossom weevil in England, the cotton boll weevil in U.S.A., and the palm-weevil of the tropics. The death-watch and powder-post Bs. bore into furniture and rafters. The grain weevils and meal worms attack stored meal and grain.

BEETON, Mrs. (Isabella Mary Mayson) (1836–65). British expert in housewifery, compiler of *Beeton's Household Management* (1859) known as Mrs. Beeton's cookery book. She was the wife of Samuel Orchart B. (1831–77), a prominent publisher.

BEGONIA. Genus of plants of the family Begoniaceae. There are numerous species, natives of the tropics, esp. S. America and India. They have flesny succulent leaves, and the flowers are often brightly coloured.

BEHAN (bē'an), **Brendan** (1923–64). Irish author and playwright. B. in Dublin, he joined the Irish Republican scout organization, *Fianna*, when only 7, becoming an I.R.A. member in 1937. Sentenced to 3 yrs. Borstal training almost immediately on his arrival in England in 1939 (for carrying explosives), he was deported on release to Dublin. Involved in an Easter Day parade incident there which resulted in the shooting of a policeman, he was sentenced in 1942 to 14 yrs. imprisonment, but released in 1946. A house-painter by trade, he started writing in 1951, achieving success with the play *The Quare Fellow* (1956), based on his prison experiences. Other works incl. the autobiographical *Borstal Boy* (1958), the play *The Hostage* (1958), and *Brendan Behan's Island* (1962). A

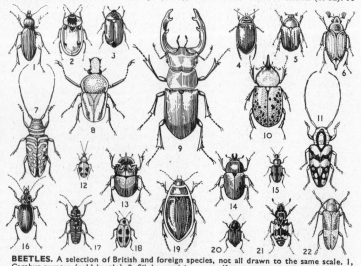

BEETLES. A selection of British and foreign species, not all drawn to the same scale. 1, Carabus auratus (gold beetle). 2, Silpha quadripunctata (four-spot carrion beetle). 3, Anomala frischii. 4, Acilius sulcatus. 5, Cetonia aurata (rose beetle) .6, Melolontha vulgaris (common cockchafer). 7, Sternotomis calliaudi. 8, Ranzania petersiana. 9, Lucanus cervus (stag beetle). 10, Dynastes tityus (tityus beetle). 11, Geloharpya insignis. 12, Callistus lunatus. 13, Copris lunaris (lunar-headed dung beetle). 14, Geotrupes stercorarius (dor beetle). 15, Panagaeus crux-major. 16, Carabus nemoralis. 17, Clytus arcuatus. 18, Endomychus coccineus. 19, Dytiscus marginalis. 20, Silpha sinuata. 21, Necrophorus mortuorum. 22, Saperda carcharius.

raconteur of genius, B. had the gift of language, and great warmth of personality.

BEHA'VIOURISM. A school of psychology originating in America early in the 20th cent. The Behaviourists set out to study human personality objectively by observation of the actual behaviour of men and women; and they make no use of terms such as 'mental', 'consciousness', 'emotion', and 'instinct', which they consider misleading. B. thus stands in strong contrast both to the older introspective psychology and also to the psychoanalysts who emphasize the concepts of mental conflict and unconscious desires. The leading exponent of the B. school was the American professor J. B. Watson, whose *Psychology as the Behaviourist Views It* (1913) gave the first general statement of its principles. Behaviourists maintain that all human activity can ultimately be explained in terms of conditioned reactions or 'reflexes' and habits formed in consequence.

BEHRING, Emil von (1854–1917). German bacteriologist, the founder of the science of immunology.

BEHRING (or Bering), Vitus Jonassen (1680–1741). Danish navigator. In 1728 he sailed from Kamchatka northward along the Siberian coast to 67°N., and proved that Asia and America are not connected, giving his name to B. Straits. In 1741 he sighted Alaska.

BEILBY, Sir George Thomas (1850–1924). Scottish chemist who originated the therm system of charging for gas.

BEIRA (bā'rah). Port at the mouth of the r. Pungwe, Mozambique, chief outlet for Malawi, Rhodesia, and Zambia, with which it is linked by rail. Pop. (1950) 41,876. Developed by a British co., it was taken over by the Portuguese in 1949.

BEIRUT (bāroot'). Cap. and chief sea and airport of Lebanon, 60 m. N.W. of Damascus. It is an important educational centre in the Levant, with 3 univs. (French, U.S., and Lebanese State). Pop. (est.) 500,000.

BEITH (bēth), **John Hay.** *See* HAY, IAN.

BEIT-LAHM. Transliteration of Arabic form of Bethlehem.

BELASCO, David (1859–1931). American playwright whose plays incl. *Madame Butterfly* (1900), and *The Girl of the Golden West* (1905), both of which served Puccini as libretti for operas.

BELÉM. Brazilian port, naval base, and air centre, cap. of Pará state. It was founded c. 1615 as Santa Maria de Belém do Grās Pará, often abbreviated to Pará. Pop. (1960) 402,170.

BELFAST (belfahst'). Cap. of N. Ireland. It stands where the Lagan enters B. Lough, 12 m. from the open sea. The principal buildings incl. the City Hall (1906); St. Anne's Protestant Cathedral (begun in 1899); Queen's University; B. museum and art gallery;

BEIRUT. One of the most cosmopolitan of cities, Beirut is beloved of the mystery novelist, and real-life incident sometimes follows the same pattern, as in the Philby case. In Maarad Street busy shops and offices rise side by side with the minarets of mosques.   *Courtesy of the Embassy of Lebanon*

BELFAST. Queen's University gives an impression of mellowed antiquity, but was actually founded as a college of the Royal University of Ireland in 1845, attaining university status in 1909.   *Courtesy of the Northern Ireland Tourist Board*

B. castle, a modern building on Cave Hill, presented by the Earl of Shaftesbury in 1934; the new Parliament House of N. Ireland at Stormont, 5 m. S. of B. (1928–32); the Grand Opera House; and Ulster Hall. B. is the most important industrial centre and port of all Ireland. Its chief industries are shipbuilding and the manufacture of aircraft, linen, and tobacco; there are distilleries. The earliest town grew up around a castle built in 1177 by John de Courcy. It was granted a charter in 1613, made a bor. in 1840, and a city in 1888; its chief magistrate became Lord Mayor in 1892. Pop. (1961) 415,039.

BELFORT (belfor'). French town, cap. of the territory of B., commanding the important route-way between the Vosges and the Jura mountains. Pop. (1962) 51,280.

BELGAUM (belgawm'). Chief town of B. dist., in Mysore state, India. Pop. (1961) 127,885. Part of B. district (Marathi-speaking) incl. the town of B. is claimed by Maharashtra: a commission appointed to settle the dispute ruled against Maharashtra 1967.

BELGIAN CONGO. *See* CONGO, Republic of.

BELGIUM. European state bordering the North Sea, lying between the Netherlands on the N. and France on the S., with Germany and the duchy of Luxemburg on the E. It is mainly low-lying, though in the S.E. the Ardennes rise in the Botrange to 2,283 ft. Parts of the plain are naturally fertile, others are dry and sandy, but by reclamation, fertilization, and irrigation have been made productive. The coast is backed by sand dunes, and sand also occurs on the Campine Heaths in the N. The plain is watered by the Scheldt and its many tributaries, and by the Sambre and Meuse. The Ardennes have a heavy rainfall and are forested.

POPULATION. In 1960 the pop. of B. was estimated at 9,178,154. Less than one-tenth of the total is employed in agriculture, more than one-quarter in mining and industry. The majority are Roman Catholics. There are univs. at Louvain, Brussels, Ghent, and Liège. French and Flemish are both official languages, but from 1963 the language of admin. and instruction has been decided according to a linguistic frontier: Flemish in Flanders and French in Wallonia, with the Brussels zone (prov. of Brabant) multi-lingual. Area 11,775 sq. m.

ECONOMICS. The fertile parts of the Belgian plain produce large crops of sugar beet, cereals, esp. wheat, root and forage crops, and flax, while excellent dairy cattle and pigs are reared. Orchards and market gardens abound, the countryside being divided into small hedgeless fields. Rye, oats, and root crops are

BELGIUM. The kitchen of the Maison du Roi, now the city museum, in the Grande Place, Brussels. It is built on the site of the house in which Egmont and Horn (qq.v.) spent heir last night before execution.
Courtesy of Belgian National Tourist Office.

raised in the dry sandy places. On the good pastureland of the Ardennes region cattle are reared. There are extensive deposits of coal, Mons, Charleroi, and Liège being the principal mining towns; Seraing, Verviers, and Namur are industrial centres making chemicals, glass, zinc, machinery, and metal goods. B. has a large textile industry, which developed from the old Flanders textile trade. Ghent, Tournai, Kortrijk, and Verviers are the main centres. Brussels is the cap., Antwerp by far the most important port. On the North Sea are several small ports, e.g. Ostend and Zeebrugge, and holiday resorts, e.g. Blankenberghe and Knokke.

ADMINISTRATION. B. is a kingdom with a Senate and Chamber of Representatives, elected on a basis of proportional representation by universal suffrage (women received the vote in 1948).

History. Julius Caesar conquered the lands occupied by the Celtic Belgae, and they were incorporated in the Roman Empire in 15 B.C. The Franks overran the area from the 3rd cent. onwards. The peace and order estab. by Charlemagne fostered the growth of such towns as Ghent, Bruges, and Brussels; following the division of his empire in 843 the area was incl. in Lotharingia. By the 11th cent. 7 feudal states had emerged: the counties of Flanders, Hainault, and Namur, the duchies of Brabant, Limburg, and Luxemburg, and the bishopric of Liège, all nominally subject to the French kings or the German emperor, but in practice independent. From the 12th cent. a flourishing economic life developed; Bruges, Ghent and Ypres became centres of the cloth industry, while the artisans of Dinant and Liège exploited the copper and tin of the Meuse valley. During the 15th cent. the states came one by one under the rule of the dukes of Burgundy, and in 1477, by the marriage

of Mary, heiress of Charles the Bold, duke of Burgundy, to Maximilian, Archduke of Austria, passed into the Habsburg dominions.

Other dynastic marriages brought all the Low Countries under Spain, and in the 16th cent. the religious and secular tyranny of Philip II led to general revolt in the Netherlands; the independence of the N. as the Dutch Republic was recognized in 1648; the S., reconquered by Spain, remained Spanish until the Treaty of Utrecht, 1713, transferred it to Austria. The Austrian Netherlands was in 1797 annexed by revolutionary France and incorporated in France. The Congress of Vienna reunited the N. and S. Netherlands as one kingdom under William, Prince of Orange-Nassau; but historical differences, and the fact that the language of the wealthy and influential in the S. was (as it remains) French, made the union uneasy. A rising in 1830 of the French-speaking part of the people in the S., and continuing disturbances, led in 1839 to the recognition by the Great Powers of the S. Netherlands as the independent and permanently neutral kingdom of Belgium, with Leopold of Saxe-Coburg (widower of Charlotte, dau. of George IV) as king, and a parliamentary constitution. Leopold II (reigned 1865–1909) acquired the Congo, annexed to B. as a colony in 1908, given independence in 1960.

Although Prussia had been a party to the treaty of 1839 recognizing Belgium's permanent neutrality (Bethmann Hollweg's 'scrap of paper'), Germany invaded Belgium in 1914 and occupied a large part of it until 1918. Again in 1940 B. was overrun by the Germans, to whom Leopold III surrendered. But his govt. escaped to London, and inside B. there was a strong resistance movement. After B.'s liberation by the Allies, 1944–5, the king's surrender gave rise to acute controversy, ended only by his abdication in 1951 in favour of his son Baudouin (q.v.). Subsequent important issues have been the independence of the Belgian Congo (*see* CONGO), and the flaring of Flemish and Walloon nationalism, the govt. falling on the linguistic issue as affecting Louvain Univ. (q.v.) in 1968.

THE ARTS. The declaration following the revolution of 1830–9, that French was the only official language (it remained so until 1898), actually stimulated interest in the Flemish language (in its written form, the same as Dutch). J. F. Willems (1793–1846) brought out a magazine which revived medieval Flemish works; H. Conscience (1812–83) and J. T. van Ryswyck (1811–49) pub. novels in Flemish; K. L. Ledeganck (1805–47), Prudens van Duyse (1804–59), Jan de Beers (1821–88) wrote poetry. Later writers were Albrecht Rodenbach (1856–80), Pol de Mont (1857–1931), Cyriel Buysse (1859–1932). Writers in French

BELGIUM. Contrasting with the ornate medieval beauty of the older Brussels is the simple modernity of Le Mont des Arts, with the Congress Hall in the centre of the picture.
Courtesy of Belgian National Tourist Office.

BELGRADE. Tree-lined Teraziji Street has a number of modern hotels, including the Moscow on the left and the Belgrade to the right.
Courtesy of Yugoslav National Tourist Office.

have included Georges Eekhoud (1854–1927), who wrote of Flemish peasant life; Émile Verhaeren and Maurice Maeterlinck (qq.v.).

The noted composer César Franck (1822–90) was of Belgian birth; Eugène Ysaÿe (1858–1931) was a famous violinist. Belgian painting has its roots in the Flemish Art (q.v.) of medieval and later times; best known modern painter is James Ensor (q.v.).

BELGRADE. Cap. of Yugoslavia and of Serbia, one of the federal reps. of Yugoslavia. At the junction of the Save with the Danube, the city is an important inland port and exchange centre. It was formerly defended by walls, and an old citadel still stands on a 200 ft. cliff. Except for brief intervals, it was in Turkish hands from 1501 to 1867; in 1878 it became the cap. of newly independent Serbia. Pop. (1961) 598,346.

BELISARIUS (c. 505–65). General under the emperor Justinian (q.v.).

BELITUNG. Island of Indonesia famous for its tin, discovered in 1759 and developed by the Dutch. The cap is Tanjongpandan. Area 1,850 sq. m.

BELIZE (belēz). Cap. and chief port of British Honduras, on the Caribbean Sea at the mouth of the B. river. In 1961 B. was wrecked by a hurricane and a new cap. 50 m. inland was begun in 1967. Pop. (1966) 38,482.

BELL, Alexander Graham (1847–1922). British inventor. B. in Edinburgh, he was ed. at the Univ. of Edinburgh and London, and in 1870 went 1st to Canada and then to the U.S. where he opened a school for teachers of the deaf in Boston in 1872, and in 1873 became prof. of vocal physiology at the univ. there. In 1876 he patented his invention of the telephone, and later experimented with a type of phonograph and in aeronautics.

BELL, Sir Charles (1774–1842). British surgeon. His greatest discovery, made in 1807, was of the sensory and motor nerves of the brain.

BELL, Gertrude Margaret Lowthian (1868–1926). British traveller, who from 1899 spent most of her time in the Near East. In 1913 she set out from Damascus to the interior of Arabia, and was the 1st European woman to arrive at Haïl since Lady Anne Blunt in 1879. She worked in the British intelligence service during the F.W.W. For some years she exercised dominating influence as Oriental Secretary of the High Commissioner of Iraq, and to her Feisal largely owed his throne. Her *Letters* are famous.

BELL, Henry (1767–1830). Scottish steamship pioneer, who designed the *Comet*, a 40-foot steamship launched on the Clyde in 1812; it had a 3 h.p. engine and a speed of 7 m. an hour.

BELL. Instrument of hollowed metal struck to pro-

duce a musical sound. The oldest inscribed B. is that cast in 698 by Hirokuni Tsukishinenomura for the Myoshinji Temple, Kyoto. The earliest-dated English B. (1296) is at Claughton, Lancs. The largest B. in the world is the Tsar Kolokol (King of bells) in the Kremlin, Moscow; cast in 1734 for Nicholas II, it weighs 220 tons and stands on the ground where it fell when being hung. Famous English Bs. are Great Paul in the clock tower of St. Paul's, the largest in England; Big Ben (q.v.); Great Peter at York and Great Tom at Oxford. The Peace B. at the U.N. headquarters in N.Y. was cast in Japan in 1952 from coins given by 64 countries, incl. a medal offered by the Pope.

BELLADO′NNA. Deadly nightshade (*Atropa belladonna*). The leaves, which contain the alkaloids hyoscyamine, atropine, hyoscine, and belladonnine, are dried and powdered. The plant and all its preparations are highly poisonous.

BELLARMINE (bel′armin), **Roberto Francesco Romolo** (1542–1621). Italian theologian, cardinal, and controversialist. He taught at the Jesuit College in Rome, and became archbishop of Capua in 1602. *Disputationes de controversiis fidei christianae* (1581–93) is his chief work. He was canonized in 1930. Drinking jugs known as Bs., because bearing a caricature likeness of the cardinal, were originally designed by the Protestant party in the Netherlands.

BELLAY (belā′), **Joachim du** (1522?–60). French poet and prose-writer, who pub. the great manifesto of the new school of French poetry, the Pléiade: *Défense et illustration de la langue française* (1549).

BELLFLOWER. A genus of plants (*Campanula*) incl. the harebell and the Canterbury Bell.

BELLINI (belē′nē). A family of Venetian artists. **Jacopo B.** (c. 1400–70) was founder of the Venetian School. Only 5 of his paintings – a 'Crucifixion' and 4 'Madonnas' – have survived. There are, however, 2 books containing his drawings – one in the British Museum, the other in the Louvre. His elder son, **Gentile B.** (c. 1429–1507), was a painter of great achievement and versatility. In 1474 he was commissioned to assist in the decoration of the Great Hall of Council in the Ducal Palace, and later he worked in the court of Mohammed II at Constantinople. A portrait of the Sultan is in the National Gallery, London. His other important works incl. paintings of processional groups in che Academy at Venice, the 'Adoration of the Magi' in the National Gallery, London, and 'St. Mark Preaching at Alexandria' (1505), in the Brera, Milan. His younger brother, **Giovanni B.** (c. 1430–1516), studied under his father. His early works show the influence of the Paduan School, particularly of his brother-in-law, Mantegna. He was one of the 1st painters to work in oil, and executed altarpieces. *See* ITALIAN ART.

BELL. A grand carillon of 53 bells for the National Episcopal Cathedral in Washington is seen here in the workshop of the founders at Loughborough, England, ready for testing. The largest has a diameter of 8 ft. 8 in. and weighs 11 tons and the smallest has a diameter of 7¼ in. and weighs 15 lb.; the total weight is c. 60 tons. Each bell not only has all its harmonics in tune, but is in accurate tune with all the others in the carillon.
Courtesy of John Taylor & Company.

BELLINI, Vincenzo (1801–35). Italian composer, of the operas *La Sonnambula*, *Norma*, etc.

BELLINZO′NA. Cap. of Ticino canton, Switzerland, on the Ticino, 10 m. from Lake Maggiore. It is the road and rail junction for the St. Gotthard pass. Pop. (1960) 13,435.

BELLOC, Joseph Hilaire Pierre (1870–1953). Author, the son of a French barrister and an English mother, he became a naturalized British citizen in 1902. In 1911 he founded the *Eye-Witness* in collaboration with C. Chesterton, with whom he also wrote a political work entitled *The Party System*. With G. K. Chesterton he advocated a return to the Distributist theories of the late Middle Ages, in place of modern capitalism or socialism. His literary versatility is shown by his nonsense verse, by his historical studies, incl. *Danton, Robespierre, James II*, and a *History of England*, by satires such as *Mr. Clutterbuck's Election*, and by *The Path to Rome*, a walker's classic.

CHESTERTON, BELLOC and BARING
H. J. Gunn.   Photo: N.P.G.

BELLOT (belō'), **Joseph René** (1826–53). French Arctic explorer, who discovered Bellot Strait, and lost his life while searching for Franklin.

BELLOW, Saul (1915–). American novelist. Building on the firm base of Jewish tradition, he is intensely concerned with moral issues, and esp. in later books, gives full rein to rhetoric: *The Victim* (1947), *The Adventures of Augie March* (1953), and *Herzog* (1964); and the play *The Last Analysis* (1965).

BELL-RINGING. Change-ringing is a truly British art and was introduced by Fabian Steadman, a Cambridge printer, in the 17th cent. The method he perfected was named after him and is rung at the present day. Change-ringers are organized into Diocesan and County Guilds, the oldest being the 'Ancient Soc. of College Youths' (estab. 1637), responsible for ringing at St. Paul's Cathedral, Westminster Abbey, and Southwark Cathedral. On the Continent and in America, the most common form of B.R. is by the Carillon, which comprises a set of 12–70 stationary Bs., operated by a clavier. The keys are wooden levers, operated by hands and feet, and are connected by wires to the clappers of the Bs.

BELL ROCK. Another name for INCHCAPE ROCK.

BELLS. Nautical term applied to half-hours of watch. A day is divided into 7 watches, 5 of 4 hours each and 2 of 2 hours. Each half-hour of each watch is indicated by the striking of a bell, 'eight bells' being the end of the watch.

BELSEN. See CONCENTRATION CAMPS.

BELTANE (bel'ten). Celtic name for the 1st day of May, formerly one of the Scottish quarter days. The ancient feasts held on this day were marked by the kindling of B. fires on the hillsides.

BELY, Andrey. Pseudonym of the Russian Symbolist writer Boris Nikolaevich Bugaev (1880–1934). He travelled widely, dabbled in anthroposophy (*see* Steiner, Rudolf), and sympathized with the ideals of the Revolution. His works incl. vols. of verse, original in content and form: *The Silver Dove* (1910) and *Petersburg* (1912), novels; and vols. of brilliant memoirs incl. *On the Border of Two Centuries* (1929) and *Between Two Revolutions* (1933).

BENARES. Another transliteration of VARANESI.

BENAVENTE Y MARTINEZ (mahrtē'neth), **Jacinto** (1866–1954). Spanish playwright, founder of a modernist drama of ideas. Of some 50 plays, the best-known is *Los intereses creados* (The Bonds of Interest: 1907). He was awarded a Nobel prize in 1922.

BEN BELLA, Mohamed (1916–). Algerian leader. B. at Marnia, Algeria, he served in the French Army, but was increasingly convinced of the necessity of Algerian independence, and helped to found the Organisation Spéciale. Imprisoned in 1950, he escaped in 1952 to Cairo to found the National Liberation Front (F.L.N.). He was re-arrested in 1956, but became P.M. of independent Algeria from 1962 until overthrown by Col. Boumedienne in 1965.

BENBOW (ben'bō), **John** (1653–1702). English admiral. He ran away to sea as a boy, and from 1689 served in the Royal Navy. He fought at Beachy Head (1690), La Hogue (1692), and d. of wounds received in a great fight with the French off Jamaica.

BENCHLEY, Robert (1889–1945). American humorist. B. at Worcester, Mass., he went to N.Y. in 1916 as a journalist and was drama editor to the *New Yorker* 1929–40. His books incl. *Of All Things* (1921) and *Benchley Beside Himself* (1943) and his film skit *How to Sleep* illustrates his superb ability to extract humour from daily living.

BENDA, Julien (1867–1956). French writer. B. in Paris, of Jewish stock, he ed. the *Cahiers de la Quinzaine* 1910–4, attacked Bergson's philosophy, and in 1927 pub. a manifesto on the necessity of devotion to the absolute truth which he felt his contemporaries had betrayed *La Trahison des clercs* (The Treason of the Intellectuals, 1927). His last book *La Grande Epreuve des démocraties* (1942) was smuggled to N.Y. from Nazi-occupied Paris.

BE'NDIGO. Name under which the British pugilist Wm. Thompson (1811–89) was known. He won his first prize fight in 1832 and fought his last in 1850. Subsequently he was a popular figure and preacher, and B. in Australia is said to be named after him.

BENDIGO. Gold-mining city and county in Victoria, Australia, on the flank of the Australian Great Divide, about 75 m. N.N.W. of Melbourne. In 1851 alluvial gold was discovered here, and a 'rush' followed. Pop. (1961) 40,309.

BENDS. Caisson disease. Paralytic affliction of divers, arising from too rapid release of nitrogen after solution in the blood under pressure. Immediate treatment is compression and slow decompression in a special chamber.

BENEDICT, Ruth (1887–1948). American anthropologist. B. in N.Y., she taught at Columbia Univ. from 1922, and was a pioneer in the integration of human personality and cultural forms (*Patterns of Culture*, 1934), and the application of anthropological methods to contemporary cultures.

BENEDICT, St. (c. A.D. 480–c. 544). Founder of Christian monasticism in the West, and of the order of the Benedictine monks. B. of wealthy parents at Nursia, he was sent to be ed. in Rome, but fled from that city and spent 3 years in ascetic solitude. He founded 12 monasteries near Subiaco, and later migrated to Cassino, and founded the monastery of Monte Cassino. Here he wrote out his rule for monastic life, and was visited shortly before his death by the Ostrogoth king Totila, whom he won to the Christian faith. In 1964 he was proclaimed patron saint of Europe.

BENEDICT XV (1854–1922). Pope from 1914. During the F.W.W. he endeavoured to remain neutral, and his papacy is noted for the renewal of British official relations with the Vatican, suspended since the 17th cent.

BENEDICTINES. Religious order of monks and nuns in the R.C. Church, founded by St. Benedict at Subiaco, in Italy, in the 6th cent. St. Augustine brought the order to England. At the beginning of the

14th cent. it was at the height of its prosperity, and medieval civilization was largely its creation. At the Reformation there were nearly 300 B. monasteries and nunneries in England, all of which were suppressed. The English novice house survived in France, and in the 19th cent. monks expelled from France removed to England and built abbeys at Downside, Ampleforth, and Woolhampton. The monks from Pierrequi-vive, who went over in 1882, rebuilt Buckfast Abbey in Devon on the ruins of a Cistercian monastery. Celebrated Benedictine monasteries in the U.S. are at Latrobe, Pennsylvania, and St. Meinrad, Indiana.

BENELUX. Name for the BElgium, NEtherlands, LUXemburg customs union, agreed to by the exiled governments of those countries in 1944, and ratified by them after the war. Owing to post-war economic difficulties, it did not come into full effect until 1960.

BENEŠ (ben'esh), **Eduard** (1884–1948). Czech statesman. A devoted pupil and friend of Thomas Masaryk, he followed him into exile in 1915, became sec. of the Czechoslovak national council in Paris, and in 1918 Min. of Foreign Affairs in the Czechoslovak govt. recognized by the Allies. He returned with Masaryk to Prague, and was For. Sec., playing a leading part in the Little Entente and League of Nations affairs until 1935, when he was elected Pres. of the rep. on Masaryk's retirement. After the Munich Conference he was compelled to resign through German pressure and left the country. He became leader of the Czechoslovak freedom movement in 1939 and set up a provisional Czechoslovak govt. in London. In 1945 he returned to Czechoslovakia, but ill-health and dislike of Communist measures led to his resignation on 7 June 1948.

BENÉT (benā'), **Stephen Vincent** (1898–1943). American writer, whose best-known work is *John Brown's Body* (1928), a poem dealing with the American Civil War.

BENEVE'NTŌ. Town in Campania, Italy, cap. of B. prov., 35 m. N.E. of Naples, with many ancient remains. Its 12th cent. cathedral was almost completely destroyed in the fighting in 1943. Pop. (1961) 54,744.

BENGAL (bengawl'). Former presidency and later prov. of British India at the head of the Bay of B., in the N.E. of the Indian peninsula. In 1947 the prov. was divided, W. Bengal going to India, E. Bengal to Pakistan.

In the north B. touched the Himalayas, but for the most part it consists of a vast alluvial plain which owes its existence to the silt brought down by the Ganges and Brahmaputra. The annual rainfall is 100 in. or more. The main crops are rice, jute in the plain, tea in the hills; jute manufacture is the most important industry. In W. Bengal there are iron smelting and steel rolling mills; but the great majority of the people all over B. is employed on the land.

EAST BENGAL. This, with the Sylhet division formerly in Assam, constitutes the prov. of E. Pakistan. *See* PAKISTAN.

WEST BENGAL. State of the Republic of India; area 33,829 sq. m.; pop. (1961) 34,926,279. Adjoining its cap., Calcutta, is Howrah, chief jute manufacturing centre of India.

BENGHAZI (bengah'zē). Mediterranean seaport in N. Africa, joint cap. with Tripoli of Libya. It changed hands between Axis and British forces a number of times during the S.W.W. Pop. (est.) 80,000.

BENGUELA (bengāl'a). Town on the coast of Angola, W. Africa, 20 m. S.W. of Lobito Bay. It has an airport and is the W. terminus of B. railway which links it with the central African lines. Pop. (1951) 14,690.

BEN GU'RION, David (1886–). Israeli statesman. B. in Plonsk, Poland, he settled in Palestine in 1906, but was exiled by the Turks as a Zionist in 1915. In America he became an organizer of the Jewish Legion in which he served under Allenby. He was chairman of the Jewish Agency for Palestine 1935–48, and in 1948 proclaimed the independence of Israel. Leader of the Mapai (Labour) party, he was P.M. and Min. of Defence 1949–53 and 1955–63. He led a breakaway Labour Party (Rafi) 1965–7.

BENIN (benēn'). Town and airport of Nigeria, cap. of the Mid-Western state. Once centre of the kingdom of the Beni, noted for its well-organized but cruel govt. (human sacrifice by crucifixion was common), it was a slave-trading port, and made handsome brassware and ivory carvings. Pop. (est.) 54,000.

BENJAMIN. O.T. character, youngest son of Jacob and Rachel, and founder of the tribe of Israel which bore his name.

BENJAMIN, Arthur (1893–1960). Australian pianist and composer. B. at Brisbane, he taught composition at the R.C.M. from 1926, where Britten was one of his pupils. His works incl. *Jamaica Rumba* inspired by a visit to the W. Indies in 1937; operas incl. *A Tale of Two Cities* (1953); and a harmonica concerto for Larry Adler.

BENJAMIN OF TUDELA (toodhā'lah) (d. 1173). Jewish rabbi and traveller. B. in Navarre, Spain, he was the author of a famous *Itinerary*, the first work to give an account of the Far East.

BENN, Anthony Wedgwood (1925–). British Labour politician. Elder surviving son of 1st visct. Stansgate, a Labour peer, he succeeded his father in 1960, but never used the title or took his seat in the Lords. He attempted renunciation in 1955 and 1960, and in 1963 was the first person to disclaim his title under the Peerage Act, when he re-entered the Commons. He succeeded Cousins as Min. of Technology (and Power 1969–70) in 1966.

BENN, Gottfried (1886–1956). German expressionist poet. A doctor, he pub. his first poems *Morgue* in 1912, served in the F.W.W. and subsequently was attracted to the Nazi Party by their kindred belief to his own in the primitive. After the S.W.W. he returned to the forefront of German literature with *Statische Gedichte* (1948), an autobiography *Doppelleben* (1950) and other works.

BENNETT, Donald (1910–). Australian air vice-marshal, known as Pathfinder Bennett. B. in Australia, he joined the R.A.A.F. in 1930 and in 1938 broke the world's long-distance seaplane record with a flight from Dundee to S. Africa. During the S.W.W. he helped develop Bomber Command's Pathfinder Force and the Atlantic Ferry organization.

BENNETT, (Enoch) Arnold (1867–1931). British novelist. B. at Hanley, Staffs, son of a solicitor in whose office he started work, he settled in London in 1893 as a journalist, becoming editor of *Woman* in 1896. His 1st successful novel was *The Grand Babylon Hotel* (1902), but his best books are those set among the 5 towns of the Potteries he knew so well, e.g. *Anna of the Five Towns* (1904), *Sacred and Profane Love* (1905), *The Old Wives' Tale* (1908) – his masterpiece, dealing with the lives of 2 sisters – and the trilogy *Clayhanger, Hilda Lessways* and *These Twain* (1910–15). Of his ventures into drama the more successful were *What the Public Wants* (1909) and *Milestones* (1912: with E. Knoblock): a notable late novel is *Riceyman Steps* (1923). Our illus. shows the plaque in Wedgwood black basalt erected in 1962 in the main square of Burslem, heart of the 'Five Towns'.

ARNOLD BENNETT
Courtesy of Wedgwood.

BENNETT, Floyd (1890–1928). American airman who accompanied Admiral Byrd on his flight to the N. Pole in 1926. He d. at Quebec from exposure suffered when flying to relieve Irish and German airmen stranded on Greenly island.

BENNETT, Henry Gordon (1887–1962). Australian general. He was G.O.C. of the Australian forces in Malaya, 1941–2. He escaped from Singapore (for which he was criticized at the time, but an official enquiry in 1945 exonerated him), commanded the 3rd Australian Corps, and pub. *Why Singapore Fell* (1945).

BENNETT, James Gordon (1841–1918). American journalist, who succeeded his father as manager of the *New York Herald* and was responsible for sending Stanley in search of Livingstone (1870).

BENNETT, Richard Bedford, 1st viscount (1870–1947). Canadian statesman. In 1905 he was leader of the Conservatives in the 1st legislative assembly of Alberta; and in 1911 entered the Canadian parl. as Cons. M.P. for Calgary. He was Min. of National Service in 1917 and Attorney-Gen. in 1921. In 1927 he became leader of the Cons. party, and was P.M. 1930–5. An ardent supporter of imperial preference, he was chairman of the Imperial Economic Conf. at Ottawa, 1932. Defeated at the general election of 1935, he retired from parl. in 1938, and lived in England. He was created a visct. in 1941.

BENNETT, Sir William Sterndale (1816–75). British composer. His original gifts were stifled as prof. of music at Cambridge from 1856 and principal of the R.A.M. from 1866. His works incl. *The Wood Nymphs* and *The Woman of Samaria*: he was knighted in 1871.

BEN NEVIS (nev′is). Highest mountain (4,406 ft.) in the British Isles, in the Grampians, Inverness.

BENOÎT (benwah′), **Pierre** (1886–1962). French novelist. His fondness for exotic travel is reflected in his prolific output which incl. *L'Atlantide* (1919) and *Les Plaisirs du voyage*; *Axelle* (1928) is a remarkable story of a French prisoner-of-war in Germany.

BENSON, Edward White (1829–96). British churchman, 1st headmaster of Wellington Coll. 1859–68, and, as Archbishop of Canterbury from 1883, responsible for the 'Lincoln Judgment' on questions of ritual in 1887. His eldest son Arthur Christopher B. (1862–1925) Master of Magdalen Coll. from 1915, collaborated with Lord Esher in editing Queen Victoria's correspondence.

BENSON, Sir Frank (1858–1939). British actor-manager whose repertory company, founded 1884, schooled many leading actors and actresses. He was responsible for the Stratford-on-Avon Shakespeare festivals for many years, and was knighted in 1916 by George V, following his performance in Julius Caesar.

BENTHAM, Jeremy (1748–1832). British philosopher and legal reformer. He rose to fame by the publication in 1776 of his *Fragments on Government*. He declared that the 'utility' of any law is to be measured by the extent to which it promotes the pleasure, good, and happiness of the people concerned, and the essence of his 'Utilitarian' philosophy is found in the pronouncement in his *Principles of Morals and Legislation* (1789), that the object of all legislation should be 'the greatest happiness of the greatest number'. He made suggestions for the reform of the poor law (1798), which formed the basis of the reforms enacted in 1834, and in his *Catechism of Parliamentary Reform* (1817) he proposed annual elections, the secret ballot, and universal manhood suffrage. He was also a pioneer of prison reform. In economics B. was an apostle of *laissez-faire*, and in his *Defence of Usury* (1787) and *Manual of Political Economy* (1798) he contended that his principle of 'utility' was best served by allowing every man to pursue his own interests unhindered by restrictive legislation. He was made a citizen of the French Republic in 1792.

BENTINCK, Lord George (1802–48). British Cons. politician. From 1846 he was the leader of the Protectionists after Peel, the Cons. leader, had repealed the corn laws. He was a great friend of Disraeli, and was well known on the Turf.

BENTINCK, Lord William Cavendish (1774–1839). Son of the 3rd duke of Portland, in 1827 he became Gov.-Gen. of Bengal and in 1833 the 1st Gov.-Gen. of India.

BENTLEY, Edmund Clerihew (1875–1956). British author of the classic detective story *Trent's Last Case* (1912) and inventor of the 4-line doggerel verse known as the 'clerihew', as used in *Baseless Biography* (1939).

BENTLEY, John Francis (1839–1902). British architect of the R.C. cathedral at Westminster.

BENTLEY, Phyllis (1894–　). British novelist. B. in Halifax, she has written novels with a Yorkshire industrial background incl. *Inheritance* (1932), and is an expert on the Brontës, e.g. *The Young Brontës* (1960).

BENTLEY, Richard (1662–1742). British classical scholar, famous for his pioneer work in textual criticism and for his controversy (1697–9) with Charles Boyle, in which he demonstrated the spuriousness of the *Letters of Phalaris*, a collection of 148 letters supposed to have been written by the Sicilian tyrant of that name in the 6th cent. B.C. From 1700 he was master of Trinity Coll., Cambridge.

BENZ (bents), **Karl** (1844–1929). German automobile engineer. B. in Karlsruhe, in 1878 he built his first model engine, and in 1885 produced his first motor-car, one of the first cars to be driven by an internal combustion engine.

BENZAL′DĒHYDE ($C_6H_5.CHO$), or oil of bitter almonds. A clear colourless liquid with the characteristic odour of almonds. It occurs free in certain leaves, such as the cherry, laurel and peach, and in a combined form in certain nuts and kernels. It can be extracted from such natural sources, but the product of commerce is nearly always synthetic, being made from toluene.

BEN′ZĒNE (C_6H_6). A clear liquid hydrocarbon of characteristic odour, occurring in coal tar. Although useful as a motor fuel, it is more important as a solvent and a starting substance for the synthesis of many important chemicals.

BENZINE. A distillate of petroleum, used in dry-cleaning and in plastics.

BENZŌ′IC ACID (C_6H_5COOH). A white crystalline solid, sparingly soluble in water, and used as a permitted food preservative for certain articles. It is obtained chemically by the direct oxidation of benzaldehyde and occurs in certain natural resins, some essential oils, and in the compound state as hippuric acid.

BEN′ZŌIN, or **Gum Benjamin**. A resin obtained by making incisions in the bark of *Styrax benzoin*, a

BEN NEVIS. Seen from across Loch Eil the heights of Ben Nevis have a sombre beauty. *Photo: George Outram & Co. Ltd.*

tree native to the E. Indies. It has a fragrant smell, and is used in the preparation of cosmetics, perfumes, and incense.

BEN ZVI (zvē), **Izhak** (1884–1963). Israeli statesman. B. at Poltava, he was active in the Zionist movement in the Ukraine. In 1907, he went to Palestine and was deported together with Ben Gurion in 1915 and, like him, served in the Jewish Legion under General Allenby. In 1952 he succeeded Ben Gurion as pres. of Israel and was re-elected in 1957 and 1962.

BEOGRAD. Another form of BELGRADE.

BEOWULF (bā'ōwulf). Old English poem (composed c. 700), the only complete surviving example of Germanic folk-epic. It is extant in a single MS. copied c. 1000 in the Cottonian collection of the British Museum. The hero B. delivers the Danish king Hrothgar from the water-demon Grendel, and his monstrous mother, and, returning home, succeeds his cousin Heardred as king of the Geats. After 50 years' prosperity, he is killed in slaying a dragon.

BÉRANGER (behroñzheh'), **Pierre Jean de** (1780–1857). French poet, famous for his light satirical *chansons*, treating of love, wine, popular philosophy, and politics. Fined and imprisoned for his republican and Bonapartist views in 1821 and 1825, he was elected to the Constituent Assembly in 1848, but resigned after a few days. *Derniers chansons* and *Ma biographie* appeared in 1857.

BERBERA (ber'bārah). Seaport of Somalia, N.E. Africa, with the only sheltered harbour on the S. side of the Gulf of Aden. British 1884–1960, it exports sheep, cattle products, ghee, frankincense, and myrrh. Pop. summer, 15,000; winter, 30,000.

BERBERS. A people of N. Africa, who since prehistoric times have inhabited Barbary, the Mediterranean coastlands from Egypt to the Atlantic. Their language is Berber, and about one-third of the Algerians and nearly two-thirds of the Moroccans speak it. B. customs are best preserved in the mountain communities, e.g. the Kabyles of Algeria, and the Rifs of the Atlas ranges in Morocco.

BERCHTESGADEN (berkh'tesgah'den). Village in S.E. Bavaria, N. of the Königssee. It has rock-salt mines. Hitler's country residence, the Berghof, stood near by at the base of Obersalzberg, his private retreat at its top. B. was several times bombed by the Allies during the S.W.W., and was captured by U.S. troops on 4 May 1945. Pop. (1960) 5,000.

BERDIANSK. Older name of OSIPENKO.

BERDICHEV. Town of the Ukrainian S.S.R., U.S.S.R., 30 m. S.W. of Zhitomir, scene of bitter German-Russian battles in 1943–4. The town is a railway junction and commercial centre. Pop. (est.) 75,000.

BERDYAEV (berdyah'yef), **Nikolai Alexandrovich** (1874–1948). Russian philosopher. B. in Kiev, he often challenged official viewpoints and although appointed prof. of philosophy in 1919 at the univ. of Moscow, his defence of religion caused his exile in 1922. He based his ideas on Russian Orthodox Christian thought, and a conception of the operation of the spirit of God in history was their focal point. His books incl. *The Meaning of History* (1923) and *The Destiny of Man* (1935).

BERESFORD, John Davys (1873–1947). British novelist. Having practised as an architect for some years, he turned to literature in 1906 and achieved a remarkable success with the trilogy *Jacob Stahl, A Candidate or Truth* and *Goslings* (1911–13), in which the hero was an architect. Among his other works are: *The Hampdenshire Wonder* (1911), the story of a precocious boy who absorbed the contents of an encyclopaedia at one reading, and a number of books dealing with abnormal psychology, e.g. *If This Were True* (1944).

BERESFORD, William Carr, 1st visct. (1768–1854). British general, one of the most famous British

commanders in the Peninsular War. He reorganized the Portuguese army in 1809, and was in command at the battle of Albuera (1811).

BERET (ber'i). Round, flat cap or bonnet, originally worn by the Basques. During the S.W.W. maroon coloured Bs. were worn by the airborne troops (hence their name 'Red Devils'), black by the tank corps, green by the commando units, and blue by the R.A.F. Regiment.

BEREZNIKI. Town in the R.S.F.S.R., on the left bank of the Kama r., 90 m. N.N.E. of Perm. Formed in 1932 by the amalgamation of several older towns, it has giant chemical works based mainly on local salt and potash deposits. Pop. (1967) 134,000.

BERG, Alban (1885–1935). Austrian composer. B. at Vienna, he studied under Schönberg, and was associated with him as one of the leaders of the atonal school of composition. His most successful work was the opera *Wozzeck*, a grim story of working-class life, first produced in 1925.

BERGAMA. See PERGAMUM.

BER'GAMO. City and episcopal see of Lombardy, cap. of B., prov. Italy, 27 m. N.E. of Milan. There is a textile industry, specializing in silks. Originating with paintings donated by Count Giacomo Carrára in 1796, the Accademia Carrara now contains one of the finest collections in N. Italy. Pop. (1961) 113,512.

BERGAMOT. Tree of the genus citrus (*C. bergamia*); from the rind of its fruit a fragrant orange-scented essence used as a perfume is obtained. The sole source of supply is southern Calabria, but the name comes from the town of Bergamo, in Lombardy.

BER'GEN. Second largest city in Norway, on a deep sound sheltered by islands, about 100 m. N. of Stavanger. It is the westernmost port of Norway, with an airport, and has a great tourist traffic. There are shipbuilding yards and engineering works; fishing is important. Pop. (1967) 117,465.

BERGEN-OP-ZOOM (bergh'en-op-zōm'). Town in N. Brabant province, Netherlands, at the junction of the E. Scheldt and the Zoom, 32 m. E. of Flushing. There are anchovy and oyster fisheries, and large pottery works. Pop. (1967) 38,155.

BERGIUS (ber'gē-oos), **Friedrich** (1884–1949). German research chemist, who received the Nobel Prize for chemistry in 1931. He invented processes for converting coal into oil, and wood into sugar.

BERGMAN (bär'yman), **Ingmar** (1918–). Swedish theatre and film producer. B. at Uppsala, he was educated at Stockholm univ., and subsequently directed at the theatres of Helsingborg, Gothenburg and Malmo. From 1963 to 1966 he was Head of the Royal Dramatic Theatre, Stockholm. His films have an international reputation and incl. *Summer Interlude* (1950), *The Seventh Seal* (1956), and *Through a Glass Darkly* (1962).

BERGMAN (bergman), **Ingrid** (1917–). Swedish actress. B. in Stockholm, where she was trained at the school of the Royal Dramatic Theatre, she is best known for her films, such as *Intermezzo* (1939), *Joan of Arc* (1948), *Anastasia* (1957), and *Goodbye Again* (1961). She m. in 1937 Dr. Peter Lindstrom, leaving him for the film producer Roberto Rossellini whom she m. in 1950, and in 1958 m. a Swedish impresario Lars Schmidt.

BERGSON (bergson'), **Henri** (1859–1941). French philosopher. B. in Paris of Anglo-Jewish parentage, he became a naturalized French citizen. He was prof. of philosophy at the Collège de France (1900–21), and in 1928 was awarded the Nobel Prize for literature. Under the Pétain govt. in the S.W.W., he refused exemption from certain anti-Jewish regulations, being unwilling to accept any privileged treatment.

For B. time, change, and development were the essence of reality and he considered that time was not a succession of distinct and separate instants, but a continuous process in which one period merged imperceptibly into the next. His books incl. *Time and Free Will* (1889), *Matter and Memory* (1896), and *Creative Evolution* (1907). In the last-named he expressed his dissatisfaction with the materialist account of evolution popularized by such thinkers as Herbert Spencer, and attempted to prove that all evolution and progress are due to the working of the *élan vital* or life-force.

BERIA, Lavrenti (1899–1953). Soviet politician. B. in Georgia, of peasant parentage, he became head of the Soviet police force and Minister of the Interior. On Stalin's death he, with Malenkov and Molotov, formed a virtual triumvirate, but later he was shot after a secret trial.

BERI-BERI. Endemic polyneuritis, an inflammation of the nerve endings, mostly occurring in the tropics and resulting from deficiency of Vitamin B.

BERIOZO'VA, Svetlana (1932–). British ballerina. B. in Lithuania, she was brought up partly in the U.S. and has danced with the Royal Ballet since 1952. Her style has a lyrical dignity and she excels in *The Lady and the Fool, Ondine,* and *Giselle.*

BERKELEY (bark'li), **George** (1685–1753). Irish bishop and idealist philosopher. He pub. several of his main philosophical works between 1707, when he became a fellow of Trinity Coll., Dublin, and 1712, when he left Dublin for England. In 1713 he was presented at Court by his friend, Swift, and from 1713 till 1720 he travelled on the Continent. In 1721 he returned to Ireland, became successively dean of Dromore and dean of Derry, and in 1723 inherited a considerable property from Miss Vanhomrigh (Swift's 'Vanessa'). His project to found a college in Bermuda did not materialize, and after spending some years at Rhode Is. he returned to England in 1731. In 1734 he became bishop of Cloyne, where he stayed until his retirement in 1752.

It was as a philosopher and as a critic of the empiricism of Locke that B. became famous. He was unable to accept Locke's theory that our ideas are representations of real objects, and he propounded as an alternative his famous theory of 'Subjective Idealism', according to which all objects exist simply in the mind of the beholder, and 'to be' means simply 'to be perceived'. This theory is contained in his *New Theory of Vision* (1709), *Principles of Human Knowledge* (1710), and *Hylas and Philonous* (1713).

BERKELEY (berk'li). On San Francisco Bay in California, U S.A. it is the seat of the Univ. of California, famous particularly for its atom research. *See*

BERLIN. Symbol of a divided Germany, the Berlin Wall dates from the sealing off of the border between East and West Berlin on 13th August, 1961. The pavement only of the Bethanien-Damm in the Kreuzburg district is still open to West Berliners: on the right is the wall of Bethany Hospital and in the background – also on the Western side – is St. Thomas's Church.　　*Courtesy of the German Embassy.*

BERKELIUM in table of transuranium elements. Pop. (1960) 111,268.

BERKELEY, Lennox (1903–). British composer. He studied with Nadia Boulanger in Paris 1927–33, and excels in composition for the human voice. His works incl. *Three Poems of St. Teresa* for contralto and strings, operas (*Nelson* and *Ruth*), and 2 symphonies.

BERKSHIRE (bark-). English co. lying S. of the Thames between Wilts and Surrey. Its northern boundary follows the Thames for about 100 m. B. is composed partly of lowland but from W. to E. run the B. downs, and in the extreme S. is Inkpen Beacon, 954 ft., one of the highest points of the chalk downs of England. In the N. the river Ock, a tributary of the Thames, flows through the Vale of the White Horse

BERLIN. The Congress Hall in West Berlin was a gift of the U.S. government in 1957. Originally built for the Interbau Exhibition in which architects of some 100 nations took part, it is the scene of many international conventions.
Courtesy of the German Tourist Information Bureau.

with its figure of a horse, 374 ft. long, cut from the chalk of the hillside. British and Roman remains are numerous. The co. is agricultural. The famous B. pigs are reared particularly near Faringdon. Windsor Forest in the E. and the pine woods of Bagshot Heath in the S.E. cover a considerable area. Reading, the co. town, is the only large industrial centre; smaller towns incl. Abingdon, Maidenhead, and Windsor on the Thames; and Newbury on the Kennet. Area 725 sq. m.; pop. (1967) 598,220.

BERLE (bur'l), **Adolf Augustus** (1895–). American lawyer and diplomat. In 1927 he became prof. of law at Columbia Univ., and under Roosevelt was Sec. of State (1938–44). He was chairman of Kennedy's Task Force in Latin America in 1961 and in the same year became consultant to the Sec. of State.

BE'RLIN, Irving (1888–). Pseudonym of Israel Baline, American composer. B. in Russia, he settled in the U.S. in 1893. His international song hits incl. *Alexander's Ragtime Band, Always, What'll I do?, Everybody's Doing It.* Among his stage musicals are *Annie Get Your Gun* and *Call Me Madam.*

BERLIN. City of Germany, on the Spree, cap. of united Germany from 1871 to 1945. First mentioned *c.* 1230, the city grew out of a fishing village, joined the Hanseatic League in the 15th cent., became the permanent seat of the Hohenzollerns, and was cap. of the Brandenburg electorate 1486–1701, of the kingdom of Prussia 1701–1871. From the middle of the 18th cent. it grew rapidly, developing into an important commercial and cultural centre.

After the S.W.W., B. was divided into 4 sectors – British, U.S., French, and Russian – and until 1948 was under quadripartite govt. by the Allies; in that year the Russians withdrew from the combined board

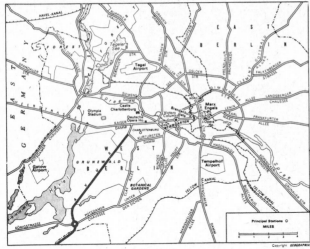

BERLIN

and created a separate municipal govt. in their sector. The other 3 sectors (W. B.) were made a Land of the Federal Rep. in May 1949, and in Oct. 1949 E. B. was proclaimed cap. of E. Germany.

In the S.W.W. air raids and conquest by the Russian army 23 April – 2 May 1945 destroyed much of B., but Unter den Linden, the tree-lined avenue once the whole city's focal point has been restored and new projects undertaken on both sides of the wall. In West B. the fashionable shopping area incl. the Kurfürstendamm and Europa-Centre; the Alexander-platz complex has a giant hotel and television tower; and the Hansa quarter is a striking residential district. Notable buildings incl. the Kaiser-Wilhelm Gedachtniskirche (rebuilt 1959–61, but with its ruined 19th cent. tower); Reichstag (former parliament building); Schloss Bellevue (Berlin res. of the pres.); Schloss Charlottenburg (housing several museums); Congress Hall; restored 18th cent. State Opera, new Komische Oper, and Philharmonic concert hall; 20th Century Art Gallery and Dahlem picture gallery. The Tiergarten (zoo) has the largest aquarium in Europe. The attractive environs of B. inc. the Grunewald forest and Wannsee lake. There is an airport at Tempelhof. Industries incl. machine tools, electrical goods, paper and printing. Pop. (1966) W. B., 2, 185,400; E. B. 1,080,726.

BERLIN, Congress of. Congress of the European Powers held at Berlin in 1878 under the presidency of Bismarck, to determine the boundaries of the Balkan states after the Russo-Turkish war. Beaconsfield attended as Britain's chief envoy, and declared on his return to England that he had brought back peace with honour.

BERLIOZ (berlē-ōz'), **Hector** (1803–69). French composer. He studied music at the Paris Conservatoire. His cantata, *La Mort de Sardanapale*, gained the *prix de Rome* in 1830, and he spent 2 years in Italy. In 1833 he m. Henrietta Smithson, an Irish actress playing Shakespearian parts in Paris, but there was a separation in 1840. After some years of poverty and public neglect, B. was invited by Schumann to Germany in 1842, and there conducted his own works with triumphant success. Subsequently he made successful visits to Austria, Russia, and England. In 1854 he m. Marie Rechio, a singer.

B. was the founder of modern orchestration. He wrote symphonic works such as *Symphonie fantastique* and *Roméo et Juliette*, built upon a literary or dramatic programme. His dramatic cantatas include *La damna-tion de Faust* and *L'enfance du Christ*, and his sacred music, a *Te Deum* and a *Requiem* in memory of the French soldiers killed in Algeria. He wrote 3 operas, *Béatrice et Bénédict*, *Benvenuto Cellini*, and *Les Troyens à Carthage*.

BERMU'DA. British colony consisting of more than 300 small islands and islets, of which only about 20 are inhabited, in the W. Atlantic, 580 m. E. of N. Carolina. The islands are composed of coral sand, and the entire chain, 22 m. long, is connected by bridges and causeways. Only a fraction of the area is cultivable, and B.'s largest industry is tourism. B.'s chief export is lily bulbs and blooms, the U.S. being the main importer. Hamilton is the chief town.

B. is named after Juan Bermudez, a Spaniard who visited the islands in 1515, and was settled by British colonists early in the 17th cent. During the S.W.W. sites were leased to the U.S.A. as naval and air bases. The colony is governed by a gov. with executive and legislative councils, and a house of assembly elected by universal suffrage. Area 21 sq. m. Civilian pop. (1966) 49,092.

BERNADETTE (bernahdet') (1844–79). French saint. B. at Lourdes in the French Pyrenees. In Feb. 1858 she had a vision of the Virgin Mary in the grotto of Massabielle, which was later opened to the public by command of Napoleon III. Many sick who were dipped in the water of a spring there were said to be cured. A church built on the rock above the grotto became a shrine of international celebrity. At the age of 20 B. became a nun at Nevers, and nursed the wounded in the Franco-Prussian War. She d. of tuberculosis.

BERNADOTTE, Count Folke (1895–1948). Nephew of the King of Sweden and president of the Swedish Red Cross. In 1945 he conveyed Himmler's offer of capitulation to the British and U.S. govts., and in 1948 was U.N. mediator in Palestine. He was assassinated by Stern Gang terrorists.

BERNADOTTE (bernahdot'), **Jean-Baptiste Jules** (1764–1844). Marshal in Napoleon's army who in 1818 became Charles XIV of Sweden. Hence, B. is the family name of the present royal house of Sweden.

BERNADETTE. The grotto where Bernadette oubirous saw her visions. Candles burn beneath a statue of the Virgin and high on the rock to the left are the crutches left as a votive offering by those who have been cured.

BERNAL, John Desmond (1901–71). British scientist. Having studied and taught at Cambridge, he became prof. of physics (1938) crystallography (1963) at Birkbeck Coll., London. He carried out research on the structure of both simple and complex substances and, starting with carbon, metals and water, went on to vitamins, hormones, proteins, viruses, and,

BERNE. Founded by Duke Berchtold in 1191 as a military stronghold, Berne is built on a narrow rocky peninsula 120 ft. above the river Aar. Not a single foot of ground is unused, and only a few narrow lanes break between the closely ranged houses. *Courtesy of the Swiss National Tourist Office.*

recently, studies of structure of liquids. His books incl. *The Social Function of Science* (1939), *The Freedom of Necessity* (1949), and *World Without War* (1958).

BERNANOS, Georges (1888–1948). French author. B. in Paris, he achieved fame in 1926 with *Sous Le Soleil de Satan* (The Star of Satan). His strongly Catholic viewpoint emerged equally in his *Journal d'un Curé de Campagne* (1936: The Diary of a Country Priest). After Munich he went into voluntary exile in Brazil, and in the S.W.W. strongly supported de Gaulle, writing his *Lettre aux Anglais* in support of the Allied cause in 1942.

BERNARD, Claude (1813–78). French physiologist. He made many valuable physiological discoveries particularly in connection with the liver, the blood, and the nervous system, and wrote a *Physiologie expérimentale* (1865), which is a standard work.

BERNARD, Tristan (1866–1948). French dramatist and novelist. His comedy, *Le fardeau de la liberté* (1897), was the 1st of a series of successful dramas, including light pieces such as *Le danseur inconnu* (1907), the larger satire of *Monsieur Codomat* (1907), and the brilliant *Triplepatte*.

His son, **Jean-Jacques B.** (1888–), showed in the cynical humour of his early plays the influence of his father. In 1921 he established his reputation with *Le feu reprend mal*, dealing with the return of a soldier from prison-camp; later plays include *L'âme en peine* (1926), and *Le jardinier d'Ispahan* (1939). He has also pub. novels, essays, and *Le camp de la mort lente*, 1941–2.

BERNARD OF CLAIRVAUX (1090–1153). French saint and theologian. He entered the monastery of Cîteaux in 1113, and 2 years later founded and became first abbot of the monastery of Clairvaux, in Champagne. He did much to reinvigorate the Cistercian Order, and many new houses sprang up in France and beyond. In 1146 he preached the 2nd crusade, and induced Louis VII of France and Conrad III of Germany to take the cross. B.'s numerous Latin writings have been often printed and translated, and include letters, sermons, theological treatises, and hymns. He was canonized in 1174.

BERNARD OF MENTHON (923–1008). Christian saint. B. in Savoy, he became archdeacon of Aosta and founded in 962 the St. B. hospices on the passes of the Pennine Alps, which bear his name. The St. Bernard dogs kept by Augustinian monks in the hospice of the Great St. B. have saved many travellers from death from exposure or starvation.

BERNE (bärn). Cap. of the Swiss Confederation, and of B. canton, lying 43 m. S.S.W. of Basle, on the Aar. Its principal features include a minster (begun in 1421), the Town Hall (1406), the Univ. (founded 1834). It makes textiles, chocolate and other foods, and light metal goods; it is the seat of the Universal Postal Union.

The city was founded in 1191, and made a free imperial city by Frederick II in 1218. It joined the Swiss Confederation in 1353, soon taking the lead, and in the 16th cent. championed the Reformed religion. The seal of B. shows a bear; the bear-pit in the city has been one of its sights since the 16th cent. Pop. (1966) 166,000.

BERNERS, Gerald Hugh Tyrwhitt-Wilson, 14th baron B. (1883–1950). British composer. In addition to music for the opera *Le Carrosse du Saint-Sacrement*, ballets such as *The Triumph of Neptune* and *Cupid and Psyche*, he wrote books, incl. *A Distant Prospect*, and was also an artist.

BERNHARD (1911–). Prince of the Netherlands. Formerly Prince B. of Lippe-Biesterfeld, he m. Princess Juliana (q.v.) in 1937. When the Germans attacked Holland in 1940, B. led the defence of the royal palace at The Hague. He escaped to England in 1940, and next year became liaison officer for the Netherlands and British forces, playing a part in the organization of the Dutch underground. Interested in the arts and sciences, he also promoted the expansion of his country's trade which followed the S.W.W.

BERNHARDT, Sarah. Stage name of the French actress Rosine Bernard (1845–1923). B. in Paris of Jewish parentage, she studied at the Paris Conservatoire, made her début with the Comédie Française in 1862 and came to be recognized as the greatest actress of her day. Her great roles incl. the heroine of Racine's *Phèdre*, Dona Sol in Hugo's *Hernani*, Hamlet (1899) and the duc de Reichstadt in Rostand's *L'Aiglon* (1900). In 1882 she m. a member of her own company, Jacques Damala (or Daria), but they separated the next year. Although she lost her right leg as the result of an accident in 1915, B. continued to act. Her autobiography *Ma Double Vie* appeared in 1907.

BERNINI (berně'ně), **Giovanni Lorenzo** (1598–1680). Italian architect, sculptor, and painter; one of the great masters of the baroque style. His most famous piece of sculpture is his 'Apollo and Daphne', while his architectural masterpiece is the colonnade surrounding the piazza outside St. Peter's in Rome.

BERNOULLI (bernoolyē'). Swiss family of mathematicians. **Jacques B.** (1654–1705) is remembered for his work relating to 'curves', and for his discovery of *Bernoullian numbers*, a complex series of fractions of considerable value in higher mathematics and the theory of numbers. **Jean B.** (1667–1748), his brother, discovered the exponential calculus. Jean's son, **Daniel B.** (1700–82), was professor of mathematics at St. Petersburg, and later held chairs at Basle. When only 24 he invented a clepsydra for recording time at sea, and he made discoveries relating to the inclination of the planets, the tides, etc.

BERNSTEIN, Henri (1876–1953). French dramatist. Earlier plays such as *The Secret* (1913) were marked by much violence, though the later, e.g. *The Promise* (1934), emphasize the psychological. On the fall of France he temporarily emigrated to the U.S.

BERNSTEIN, Leonard (1918–). American composer, conductor and pianist. B. at Lawrence, Mass., he was ed. at Harvard Univ. and the Curtis Inst. of Music. In 1958–69 he was Music Director of the

BERNSTEIN. Noted for his versatility and ability to appeal to the popular as well as the 'classical' audience, Bernstein is a brilliant executant. He is also well known for his children's concerts. *Photo: Godfrey MacDomnic.*

N.Y. Philharmonic Orchestra, and has conducted other major orchestras throughout the world. His works incl. symphonies – *Jeremiah* (1942), *The Age of Anxiety* (1949); song cycles – *I Hate Music* (1943), *La Bonne Cuisine* (1949); and scores for musicals – *Wonderful Town* (1953) and *West Side Story* (1957).

BERRY. Family name of Viscount Camrose and Viscount Kemsley. *See* KEMSLEY, Lord.

BERSAGLIERI (bersahlyā'rē), (Ital., sharp-shooters). A *corps d'élite* in the Italian army, first raised in Sardinia in 1836.

BE′RSEKER. In Scandinavian myth the Bs. were warriors subject to fits of insensate fury, during which they were immune to s word and flame—hence to 'go berserk'.

BERTHELOT (bertlō′), **Marcellin Pierre Eugène** (1827–1907). French chemist and politician. He became Min. of Public Instruction in 1886, and Foreign Min. in 1895. He investigated organic compounds and heat and wrote *Mécanique chimique*, etc.

BERTHIER (bertiã′), **Alexandre** (1753–1815). Marshal of France, he fought under Lafayette in America, and became one of Napoleon's most trusted generals. He came to terms with Louis XVIII after Napoleon's fall and retired to Bamberg, where he committed suicide or was assassinated.

BERTHOLD (bert′-hold), (*c.* 1220–72). German Franciscan, whose missionary work led him through all upper and central Germany. His sermons contain important information about medieval life.

BERTHOLLET (bertolã′), **Claude Louis** (1748–1822). French chemist. With Lavoisier and others he undertook the revision of chemical nomenclature, and was the first to suggest chlorine gas as a bleaching agent. His chief work was *Essai de statique chimique.*

BERTILLON (bertē′yoṅ′), **Alphonse** (1853–1914). French criminologist, who became head of the Identification Dept. of the Préfecture of Police in Paris. He invented a system of identification of criminals by careful measurement of certain parts of the body which do not change after full growth.

BERTRAND (bertroṅ′), **Henri Gratien, count** (1773–1844). French soldier, one of Napoleon's marshals. He went with Napoleon to Elba in 1814, served with him in the Waterloo campaign, and accompanied him to St. Helena. In 1840 he brought Napoleon's remains to Paris.

BERTRAND DE BORN (*c.* 1140–*c.* 1215). Provençal troubadour. He was viscount of Hautefort in Perigord, accompanied Richard Coeur de Lion to the Holy Land, and d. a monk.

BERWICK (ber′ik), **James Fitzjames, duke of** (1670–1734). French marshal. Natural son of the duke of York (afterwards James II of England) and Arabella Churchill, sister of the great duke of Marlborough, he was made duke of B. in 1687. After the revolution of 1688 he served under his father in Ireland, joined the French army, fought against William III and Marlborough, and in 1707 defeated the English at Almansa in Spain. He was killed at the siege of Philippsburg.

BERWICKSHIRE (ber′ik). Co. of S.E. Scotland, between the Lammermuir hills and the river Tweed, forming the boundary with England. It has a rocky and inhospitable coast, and includes the 3 districts of the Merse in the S., one of the richest plains in Scotland; Lammermuir, chiefly pastoral, to the N.W., with the hills of the same name, averaging 1,000 ft. in height; and Lauderdale, in the S.W. Its streams are tributaries of the Tweed. Two-thirds of the county is under cultivation, and fishing is an important industry. The county town is Duns. Area 457 sq. m.; pop. (1961) 22,441.

BERWICK-UPON-TWEED (be′rik). Seaport and fishing town (bor.) of England, at the mouth of the Tweed, Northumberland, 3 m. S.E. of the Scottish border. Held alternately by the English and Scots for centuries, B. was in 1551 made a neutral town; it was attached to Northumberland in 1885. The Old Bridge (1611–34) over the Tweed, with 15 arches, remains, but was superseded in 1928 by the Royal Tweed Bridge in reinforced ferro-concrete which carries the Great North Road. The Royal Border railway bridge, constructed by Robert Stephenson, was opened in 1850. The town has iron foundries and shipbuilding yards, salmon and other fisheries. Pop. (1961) 12,166.

BERYL (ber′il). Species of precious stone; silicate of beryllium and aluminium. B. usually occurs as green hexagonal crystals sometimes of large size, found chiefly in granites and pegmatites; the dark green crystals are termed emeralds and the light blue-green aquamarines.

BERYLLIUM (Glucinum). Light silvery hard metallic element, at. wt. 9·013, at. no. 4, symbol Be, sp. gr. 1·84. Its chief uses are as a source of neutrons when bombarded; windows of X-ray tubes, being highly transparent; toughening copper for high-grade gear-wheels and spark-free tools; and as a neutron reflector, moderator, and uranium sheathing in nuclear reactors.

BERZE′LIUS, Jöns Jakob (1779–1848). Swedish chemist. In 1818 he was appointed secretary of the Stockholm Academy of Sciences. His special study was the determination of atomic and molecular weights, and his tables, pub. in 1818 and 1826, comprised more than 2,000 chemical substances. He invented the system of chemical symbols now in use, and discovered several elements.

BES. Egyptian god of recreation, music, and dancing, sometimes also associated with childbirth. He was usually represented as a grotesque dwarf wearing a crown of feathers.

BESANÇON (bezoṅsoṅ′). Cap. of Doubs dept., France, 38 m. S.W. of Belfort, on the Doubs. The fortress, on a rock 387 ft. above the town, was fortified by Vauban. The Roman remains include an amphitheatre, aqueduct; and triumphal arch of Marcus Aurelius. B. has also an 11th and 12th cent. cathedral. Watchmaking is the principal industry. B. is a great route centre. Pop. (1968) 113,220.

BESANT (bez′ant), **Annie** (1847–1933). British theosophist. In London, *née* Wood, she m. in 1867 the Rev. Frank B., who obtained a separation in 1873. She became closely associated with Charles Bradlaugh (q.v.) and with the Fabian Society. About 1889 she came under the influence of Mme Blavatsky, and henceforth was an enthusiastic theosophist. She went to India, founded the central Hindu college at Benares, and in 1917 was president of the Hindu

BETHLEHEM. The grotto beneath the Church of the Nativity is one of the most sacred places in Christendom. The star under the altar is said to mark the actual spot of the Nativity.

National Congress. In 1926–7 she visited England and America with J. Krishnamurti, a young protégé in whom she recognized the new Messiah. She wrote many books on theosophical subjects and an autobiography (1893).

BESANT, Sir Walter (1836–1901). British author. He collaborated with James Rice in novels such as *The Golden Butterfly* (1876), and produced an attack on the social evils of the E. End, *All Sorts and Conditions of Men* (1882), and an unfinished *Survey of London* (1902–12). He was a founder of the Soc. of Authors.

BESIER, Rudolf (1878–1942). British playwright, author of the perennially popular *Barretts of Wimpole Street* (1930).

BESSARABIA. Territory of E. Europe. Annexed by Russia in 1812, after the 1917 revolution B. broke away and its union with Rumania was agreed to by the Allies in a treaty signed in Paris in 1920. Russia never recognized this cession, and in 1940 reoccupied B. Rumania ceded the area to the U.S.S.R. by the peace treaty of 1947, and it was incorporated partly in Moldavia, partly in Ukraine, S.S.R.s. Area and pop. in 1939, 17,100 sq. m. and 3,200,000. Kishinev is the chief town.

BESSEL, Friedrich Wilhelm (1784–1846). German astronomer. Director of the newly-estab. observatory at Königsberg from 1813, he pub. in 1818 a catalogue of more than 3,000 stars and by his systematic research founded modern precision astronomy.

BE′SSEMER, Sir Henry (1813–98). British civil engineer and inventor of the *Bessemer Process* (1856) for converting molten pig-iron into steel.

BEST, Charles Herbert (1899–   ). Canadian physiologist, who was one of the team of Canadian scientists under the leadership of Sir Frederick Banting, whose researches resulted in 1922 in the discovery of insulin as a cure for diabetes. A Banting-Best Dept. of Medical Research was founded in Toronto, and B was its director 1941–67.

BETA PARTICLES. Electrons emitted from nuclei of radioactive substances undergoing spontaneous disintegration. Streams of B.P. are called beta rays.

BE′TEL-NUT. Fruit of the areca palm (*Areca catechu*), used as a masticatory by peoples of the East: chewing it results in blackened teeth and the mouth is stained deep red.

BETHE (bāt′e), **Hans Albrecht** (1906–   ). German-American physicist. A refugee from Hitler in 1933, he taught first in Britain, then in the U.S.A. where he became prof. of theoretical physics at Cornell in 1937. He worked on the first atom bomb, and was in 1967 awarded a Nobel prize, especially for his discoveries concerning energy production in stars.

BE′THLEHEM. Small town of ancient Palestine 6 m. S. of Jerusalem, the reputed birthplace of Jesus Christ, and of King David. It contains the Church of the Nativity, used by Latins, Greeks, and Armenians, beneath the choir of which is the Grotto of the Nativity, much visited as a place of pilgrimage. In the N.W. stands a square-domed building said to mark the site of Rachel's tomb. In 1099 the Crusaders captured B., and Baldwin I was crowned king of Jerusalem there. On its site, in Jordan, is the modern town of Beit-Lahm. Pop. (est.) 10,000.

BETHLEHEM. City of Penn., U.S.A., on the Lehigh r., 50 m. N.W. of Philadelphia. It is the site of a chief plant of the B. Steel Corporation, one of the largest steel companies in the world. Pop. (1960) 75,408.

BETHMANN HOLLWEG (beht′mahn-holveg), **Theobald von** (1856–1921). German statesman who succeeded Prince Bülow as Imperial Chancellor in 1909. At the outbreak of the F.W.W. he defended Germany's invasion of Belgium and Luxemburg. He was dismissed in 1917.

BETHNAL GREEN. See LONDON.

BÉTHUNE (bātün′). Town in Pas-de-Calais dept. France, 20 m. N.N.W. of Arras, on the richest coalfield in France. Pop. (1962) 24,655.

BETJEMAN, Sir John (1906–   ). English poet and essayist, originator of a peculiarly English light verse, nostalgic and delighting in Victorian bric-à-brac, Neo-Gothic architecture, and so on. His *Collected Poems* appeared in 1968 and a verse autobiography *Summoned by Bells* in 1960. Knight bachelor 1969.

BE′TONY. Plant (*Stachys betonica*) of the family Labiatae, a hedgerow weed in Britain. It has a hairy stem and leaves and dull purple flowers, and was formerly supposed to have curative properties.

BETTERTON, Thomas (*c.* 1635–1710). British actor. A member of the Duke of York's company

BETJEMAN. A moment's pause in the shade on a walk down a typical English lane. Closing the vista is one of the village churches that are among the poet's 'loves'.
Photo: Cecil Beaton.

after the Restoration, he attracted the attention of Charles II, and was particularly famous in such parts as Hamlet and Othello.

BETTI, Ugo (1892–1953). Italian poet and dramatist. In daily life a magistrate, his clear-eyed view of things as they are is shot through with poetry. His best-known plays are *The Queen and the Rebels* (1949) and *The Burnt Flower-Bed* (1951).

BETTING. The staking of money, etc., on the result of some future event, generally of a sporting character, e.g. horse-racing, dog-racing, etc. In Britain only credit B. and B. on the course (whether by ready money or on the Tote, q.v., on approved courses on specified days) were formerly legal, but the B. and Gaming Act of 1960 legalized off-course cash B. and the establishment of B. Offices licensed by local authorities, and in 1966, a B. Duty (by 1970 6% of stake money) was imposed. Football 'pools' pay a 25% duty on the stake money, and by the Pool B. Act (1954) a company or person promoting such a business must register with the local authority to whom annual accounts are submitted. The amount of the money prizes is determined by the number of successful forecasts of the results of matches received by the promoter except in fixed odds B.

BETWS-Y-COED (betoos'-a-koid). Welsh village and tourist centre (U.D.) on the r. Conway, Caernarvonshire, in Snowdonia National Park. Pop. (1961) 778.

BETTY, William Henry West (1791–1874). British boy actor, called the 'Young Roscius', after the greatest comic actor of ancient Rome. First appearing in Belfast aged 11, he was enthusiastically received for 6 yrs, especially in Shakespeare. As an adult actor he was not remarkable.

BeV. Symbol for one billion electron volts or 10^9 electron volts.

BEVAN, Aneurin (1897–1960). British Labour politician. B. at Tredegar, Mon., the son of a miner, he entered the pit at 13, later becoming a miner's agent. In 1929 he became M.P. for Ebbw Vale, holding the seat for the rest of his life, and with the establishment of the weekly *Tribune* became prominent in Labour journalism. As Min. of Health 1945–51, he started post-war rehousing and inaugurated the Health Service, and was Min. of Labour Jan.-April 1951, resigning because his opinions increasingly diverged from official Labour policy. As leader of the 'Bevanites' he conducted lively skirmishes, but in Nov. 1956 became 'Shadow' Foreign Sec., having reached a working arrangement with Gaitskell. He was a superb orator. *See* LEE, JENNIE.

BEVATRON. Massive apparatus for accelerating protons and other atomic particles. It is situated at the Radiation Laboratory of the Univ. of California, Berkeley, and was designed to produce 6BeV protons.

BEVERIDGE, William Henry, 1st baron (1879–1963). British administrator and economist. His active interest in social reform began with his sub-wardenship of Toynbee Hall in 1903. In 1908 he joined the Civil Service and acted as Lloyd George's lieutenant in the social legislation of the Liberal govt. before the F.W.W. He was at the Board of Trade until 1916, for most of the time as Director of the newly-established Labour Exchanges. Leaving the Civil Service in 1919, he was director of the London School of Economics until 1937 when he was Master of University Coll., Oxford (until 1944). He was chairman of the Committee on Social Insurance and Allied Services (1941), and practically all his recommendations for a unified and greatly improved system of Social Security were at once accepted in principle by the Churchill Govt. and embodied in later legislation. In 1944 he was elected Liberal M.P. for Berwick-upon-Tweed, but lost his seat in the general election of 1945. He had been knighted in 1919, and was created baron in 1946. His most influential book was *Full Employment in a Free Society* (1944).

BEVERLEY. Co. town (bor.) of E. Riding of Yorkshire, England, 8 m. N.N.W. of Hull. The minster was built in the 13th-15th cents. B. is an agricultural centre, and makes wire rope, motor accessories, agricultural implements, etc. Pop. (1961) 16,024.

BEVERLY HILLS. Residential city adjoining Los Angeles, California, U.S.A., mainly inhabited by film actors. Pop. (1960) 30,817.

BEVIN, Ernest (1881–1951). Labour statesman and Trade Unionist. B. at Winsford, Som, the son of a farm labourer, he worked on a farm as a boy, and was ed. chiefly at evening classes in Bristol. At 29 he became a trade union official, and was largely responsible for the creation of the Transport and General Workers' Union. In 1920, at an official enquiry into dock labour, he won the title of 'Dockers' K.C.' From 1921 until 1940 he was gen. sec. of the T.G.W.U. In 1940 he was returned as Labour M.P. for Wandsworth, having been already appointed by Churchill Min. of Labour and National Service, and a member of the War Cabinet. He organized the system of choosing boys ('B. boys') of all classes by ballot to work in the mines. He was For. Sec. in the Labour Govt. of 1945, resigning owing to ill-health in 1951, when he became Lord Privy Seal.

BEWICK (bū'ik), **Thomas** (1753–1828). British artist. B. nr. Newcastle upon Tyne, where at 14 he was apprenticed to an engraver, his wood engravings of animal life are masterly, e.g. *British Birds* (1797–1804).

BEXHILL. English seaside resort (bor.) 5 m. W.S.W. of Hastings, Sussex. Here is the De la Warr Pavilion, built 1937. Pop. (1961) 28,926.

BEYROUT. Alternative form of BEIRUT.

BEZA (properly De Bèsze), **Théodore** (1519–1605). French reformer. He settled at Geneva, where he attached himself to Calvin, and succeeded him in 1564 as head of the reformed church at Geneva, which post he resigned in 1600. He wrote in defence of the burning of Servetus (1554), translated the N.T. into Latin, and presented in 1581 a 5th cent. Graeco-Latin MS. of the Gospels and the Acts, the *Codex Bezae*, to Cambridge univ.

BÉZIERS (behziä'). Town in Hérault dept., S. France, on the Canal du Midi. It was a Roman station. Pop. (1968) 80,492.

BÉZIQUE (behsēk'; Fr. *bésigue*). Card game, supposed to have originated in Spain, and introduced into England in 1861. About 1869 it became very popular in the London clubs. *Rubicon B.* has a code of laws promulgated by the Portland Club in 1887.

BHAGALPUR. Town in Bihar state, India, 120 m. E.S.E. of Patna. It has Jain temples, and makes silks. Pop. (1961) 143,994.

BHA'GAVAD-GITA (-gē'tah) (The Song of the Blessed). Religious and philosophical Sanskrit poem forming an episode in the 6th book of the Mahabharata, one of the 2 great Hindu epics. It is the supreme religious work of Hinduism.

BHAMO (bhahmō'). Town in Burma, 30 m. S.W. of the nearest point of the Chinese frontier, 300 m. N.E. of Mandalay. It stands at the head of navigation of the Irrawaddy r. Pop. c. 10,000.

BHARAT. Hindi name of INDIA.

BHATGA'ON. Town in Nepal, 7 m. S.E. of Katmandu. It dates from the 9th cent., is a religious centre, and possesses a palace with golden doors. Pop. *c.* 85,000.

BHAVE (bahvā), **Acharya Vinoba** (1895–). Indian leader. A disciple of Gandhi, he founded in 1951 the Bhoodan 'land gift' movement, in which wealthy people give land for the use of the poorer classes: 5 million acres have so far been given.

BHAVNAGAR. Seaport, railway terminus, and

airport of Gujarat, India, in the Kathiawar peninsula on the Gulf of Cambay. It makes and exports textiles, and was cap. of the former Rajput princely state of B. Pop. (1961) 177,488.

BHŌPA′L. Cap. of Madhya Pradesh, India. It stands on the N. slopes of the Vindhya Hills, has an airport, and is developing rapidly as an industrial centre-making textiles, chemicals, jewellery, etc. It was cap. of the former princely state of B. Pop. (1961) 225,460.

BHUBANESWAR (boobahnesh′wah). Cap. of Orissa, Rep. of India. A place of pilgrimage and centre of Sivá worship, it has temples of the 6th–12th cents., and was cap. of the Kesaris (Lion) Dynasty of Orissa 474–950. Utkal Univ. (1843) was removed from Cuttack to B. in 1962. Pop. (1961) 38,374.

BHUMIBOL ADULYADEJ (poo′mipol adoo-leah′desh) (1927–). King of Thailand. Ed. in Bangkok and Switzerland, he succeeded on the assassination of his brother in 1946, formally taking the throne in 1950.

BHUTAN (bhootahn′). Independent state in the S. slopes of the Himalayas, between Tibet and Assam. It is very mountainous. The climate is varied, depending on the altitude. The dominant people are of Tibetan origin, and speak a Tibetan dialect. In religion they are nominally Buddhists. Maize and rice are grown in the valleys of tributaries of the Brahmaputra. Tasichozong and Punakha are 2 of the chief fortresses of the country. Treaties of 1865 and 1910 with the British govt. were replaced in 1949 by one with India, under which B. receives a subsidy and is guided in external relations by the Indian govt. The cap. is Thimphu. Area c. 16,800 sq. m.; pop. c. 700,000.

BIAFRA (bē-af′rah), **Rep. of.** State proclaimed in 1967 when the predominantly Ibo Eastern Region of Nigeria seceded under Lt.-Col. Odumegwu Ojukwu, an Oxford-educated Ibo. On the proclamation of B. civil war ensued with the rest of the Federation, but in a bitterly fought campaign Federal forces had confined the Biafrans to a shrinking area of the interior by 1968. and by 1970 B. ceased to exist.

BIA′LIK, Hayyim Nachman (1873–1934). Hebrew poet, greatly responsible for the modern renaissance of the Hebrew language. B. in S. Russia, he wrote Zionist poems in Hebrew and, leaving Russia in 1921, estab. a publishing firm in Tel Aviv.

BIALYSTOK (byah′lüstok). City of Poland, cap. of B. region, 105 m. N.E. of Warsaw. Dating from 1310, it makes woollen textiles, chemicals, tools, etc. Pop. (1966) 142,000.

BIARRITZ (bē-ahrēts′). French seaside resort and spa on the Bay of Biscay, in Basses-Pyrénées dept., 5 m. S.W. of Bayonne. Pop. (1962) 25,514.

BIBE′SCO, Princess. See ASQUITH.

BIBLE (bībl; Gk. *ta biblia*, the books). Collection of books comprising the authoritative documents of the Jewish and Christian religions, and divided into the Old Testament or 'Covenant', the Apocrypha, and the New Testament.

The O.T. contains those books recognized by the Jews and classified by them as: the Law (the Pentateuch or books of Moses; recognized soon after the return from captivity); the Prophets (Joshua, Judges, Samuel, Kings, Isaiah, Jeremiah, Ezekiel and the 12 minor prophets, Hosea to Malachi, recognized by the 3rd cent. B.C.); and the Hagiographa or Sacred Writings (including the remaining books; finally recognized c. A.D. 90–100).

The Apocrypha consist for the most part of the books of the Gk. Septuagint which were not included in the final Hebrew canon. Included in the Vulgate, and so recognized by Catholics as authoritative, they were excluded by Luther, and segregated by the English translators from Coverdale onwards. Many editions of the A.V. omit them. Texts of other apocryphal works, e.g. *The War between the Children of Light and*

BIBLE. Although Henry VIII had already broken with the Pope, Coverdale's Bible of 1535, illustrated here, was published on the Continent – probably being printed in Zurich.
Photo: The British and Foreign Bible Society.

the Children of Darkness, were found among the Dead Sea Scrolls (q.v.).

The N.T., containing those books recognized by the Church in the 4th cent. as canonical, is also divided into three parts: history, Matthew to Acts; epistles, Romans to Jude; and prophecy, Revelation.

A copy of the 'lost' *Gospel of St. Thomas*, also known as the *logia* or sayings of Jesus, was discovered by peasants in an earthenware jar in 1945 at Nag Hammadi, nr. Luxor. A 3rd or 4th cent. translation in Coptic of a Gk. original dating from about A.D. 135, it is variously regarded as authentic, or as more probably a later elaboration.

Text. The Hebrew text of the O.T. is that of the Massoretes, Jewish scholars who finally estab. it between about A.D. 500 and 900. The oldest dated MS. is A.D. 916, but there is evidence that a practically identical Hebrew text existed many cents. earlier, e.g. the Dead Sea Scrolls (of disputed date, but certainly hundreds of years earlier than any other bible MSS.) found in the caves of the Wadi Qumran from 1947 onwards. Of other versions of the O.T. the Gk. Septuagint is the chief. The MS. material for the Gk.

BOOKS OF THE BIBLE

Old Testament

Genesis	Nehemiah	Hosea
Exodus	Esther	Joel
Leviticus	Job	Amos
Numbers	Psalms	Obadiah
Deuteronomy	Proverbs	Jonah
Joshua	Ecclesiastes	Micah
Judges	Song of Solomon	Nahum
Ruth	Isaiah	Habakkuk
I & II Samuel	Jeremiah	Zephaniah
I & II Kings	Lamentations	Haggai
I & II Chronicles	Ezekiel	Zechariah
Ezra	Daniel	Malachi

Apocrypha

I & II Esdras	Song of the Three
Tobit	Children
Judith	Story of Susanna
Rest of Esther	Bel and the Dragon
Wisdom	Prayer of Manasses
Ecclesiasticus (of Jeremiah)	I & II Maccabees
Baruch, with the Epistle	

New Testament

Matthew	Galatians	Philemon
Mark	Ephesians	Hebrew
Luke	Philippians	James
John	Colossians	I & II Peter
Acts of the	I & II Thessalonians	I, II & III John
Apostles		
Romans	I & II Timothy	Jude
I & II Corinthians	Titus	Revelation

text of the N.T. now consists of (1) papyri (2nd and 3rd cents.); (2) MSS. in capital or uncial writing, including the Codex Vaticanus and Codex Sinaiticus of the 4th cent.; (3) MSS. in minuscule writing (9th to 15th cent.). In addition there is the evidence of early translations, notably Jerome's Latin Vulgate (384–91).

English Translations. The 1st complete B. was produced by John Wycliffe (1380–2), from the Latin Vulgate. In 1525 Tyndale printed a version of the N.T., and in 1535 his disciple Coverdale pub. the first complete printed translation on the Continent (in England 1537). A revised version by Coverdale (the Great Bible), commissioned by Thomas Cromwell, was ordered to be placed in all churches in 1539. The Geneva Bible (complete 1560), prepared by the Protestant Marian exiles, was the first to adopt verse divisions and was not superseded until the A.V. of 1611 (subsequently revised: N.T. 1881, O.T. 1885, Apocrypha 1895).

For R.C. readers the Douai B. (N.T. 1582 and O.T. 1609–10) and the version by Mgr. Ronald A. Knox (N.T. 1945, O.T. 1949; also from the Vulgate) are approved, and the Jerusalem B. (from the original languages) which was published in 1966. Later Protestant versions are that of James Moffatt (1935), the American Rev. Standard Version (1946–57; modified for R.Cs. 1966), *Phillips' N.T. in Modern English* 1958), and the New English B. (complete 1970).

BIBLE SOCIETIES. Societies founded for the promotion of the translation and distribution of the Scriptures. The largest is the British and Foreign B.S., founded in 1804.

BIBLICAL CRITICISM. The subject is generally treated under 3 main headings: (1) *lower or textual C.*, which is directed to the recovery of the original text; (2) *higher or documentary C.*, which is concerned with questions of authorship, date, and literary sources; and (3) *historical C.*, which seeks to ascertain the actual historic content of the Bible, aided by archaeological discoveries and the ancient history of neighbouring peoples.

BICARBONATE OF SODA ($NaHCO_3$). A white crystalline compound more properly called sodium bicarbonate. It neutralizes acids and is used in medicine as an antacid. It is also used in baking powders and in effervescing drinks.

BICHAT (bēshah′), **Marie François Xavier** (1771–1802). French anatomist and physiologist. In 1800 he became physician at the Hospital at Lyons, and he is regarded as the chief founder of general anatomy.

BICYCLE. See CYCLING.

BIDAULT (bēdoh′), **Georges** (1899–). French statesman. Before the S.W.W. he made a reputation as a journalist, fought in the 1940 campaign and also in the resistance movement. As a leader of M.R.P., he held office as P.M. and For. Min. in a number of unstable administrations of 1944–54. As head of the *Organisation de l'Armée Secrète* from 1962, in succession to Salan, he left the country, but was allowed to return in 1968.

BIDEFORD (bid′iford). English port (bor.) on the N. Devon coast, 8 m. S.W. of Barnstaple, on the estuary of the Torridge. B. had a large ocean-going trade in the Middle Ages, and is still used by ships of 500 tons; it makes boots, furniture, clothing, etc. Pop. (1961) 10,265.

BIEL. German form of BIENNE.

BIELEFELD (bē′lefeld). Manufacturing town in N. Rhine-Westphalia, Germany, 34 m. E. of Münster, at the foot of the Teutoburger Wald. Pop. (1966) 170,624.

BIELORUSSIA. See WHITE RUSSIA.

BIELOSTOK. Russian form of BIALYSTOK.

BIENNE (byen′). Swiss town and lake in Berne canton, in the Jura mountains, 17 m. N.W. of Berne. The town stands at the N. end of Lake B., and is the centre of a watchmaking industry. Pop. (1966) 60,900.

BIERCE (bĭrs), **Ambrose (Gwinett)** (1842–1916?). American author. B. in Ohio, he served with the Union army in the Civil War, and spent most of his life as a journalist in San Francisco. He established his reputation as a master of supernatural and psychological horror by his *Tales of Soldiers and Civilians* (1891), and *Can Such Things Be?* (1893). In 1913 he disappeared on a secret mission to Mexico.

BI′GAMY. The offence of marrying another person when one's husband or wife is still alive, and the marriage has neither been dissolved nor annulled. It is a good defence to a charge of B. to prove that the husband or wife of the person charged with the crime has been continually absent for the previous 7 years and has not been known to be alive within that time by the accused, or to prove that the accused genuinely believed on reasonable grounds that his or her husband or wife was dead, even though 7 years have not elapsed. Although a person proving any of these defences is not guilty of B., the second marriage will still be invalid. The maximum penalty for B. is 7 years' imprisonment. The position in the U.S. is similar.

BIG BEN. Bell in the clock tower of the Houses of Parliament, cast at the Whitechapel Bell Foundry in 1858, and popularly known as 'B.B.' after Sir Benjamin Hall, First Commissioner of Works at the time. It weighs $13\frac{1}{2}$ tons.

BIGHORN. The Rocky Mountain sheep (*Ovis cervina*); a large sheep, with massive horns, which inhabits the Rockies from Mexico to Alaska.

BIHA′R. State of India, stretching across the Ganges valley from Nepal to Orissa. For the most part it is a flat and fertile plain, and densely populated. Rice, maize, wheat, jute, tobacco, etc., are grown, and some artificial irrigation has been developed. Coal is mined, and B. is India's richest iron-producing area, with iron and steel plants at Jamshedpur. Patna is the cap. Area 67,000 sq. m.; pop. (1961) 46,457,042.

BIJAPUR (bējahpoor′). Ancient Indian city in Mysore state. Once the cap. of the Muslim kingdom of B., it has imposing buildings. Pop. (1961) 78,854.

BIKANER (bikanēr′). City in Rajasthan, India, 170 m. N. of Jaipur. Once the cap. of the Rajput state of B., it has Jain monasteries and defensive walls. It makes leather goods, soap, electrical appliances, etc. Pop. (1961) 150,494.

BIKINI (bēkē′ni). Island and atoll in the Marshall Islands, Pacific. In the atoll in 1946 atomic bomb tests were carried out by the U.S.A. See BOMB.

BILBAO (bilbah′ō). Cap. of Biscay prov. and an important port of N. Spain, 44 m. W. of Santander, on the r. Nervión. There are rich iron deposits near, and much iron ore is exported to S. Wales. B. also exports wine, lead, olive oil; and has large iron and steel works, chemical, cement and food factories. Pop. (1965) 359,407.

BILBERRY (Whortleberry, or Blaeberry). Plant (*Vaccinium myrtillus*) of the family Ericaceae closely resembling the cranberry, but distinguished by its bluish berries.

BILDERDIJK (bil′derdīk), **Willem** (1756–1831). Dutch poet. B. at Amsterdam, he became an advocate at The Hague, but was exiled in 1795 after the French invasion. Recalled in 1806, he became King's Librarian and President of the Royal Institute. His works include religious and love lyrics of great beauty, the didactic *Disease of the Learned* (1807), and the unfinished epic *De Ondergang der Eerste Wereld* (1820).

BILE. A brownish fluid secreted by the liver, also called gall. B. is contained in a small pear-shaped bag on the under-surface of the liver called the gall-bladder, and plays an important part in the digestive processes of the intestines.

BILHARZIASIS. A group of diseases caused by small parasitic worms or flukes which may invade the body in tropical and sub-tropical countries. These flukes are of 3 principal kinds: *Bilharzia haematobia*, which causes leakage of blood into the urine; *B. mansoni*, which causes dysentery; and *B. japonica*, which causes cirrhosis of the liver and dropsical swelling of the abdomen (ascites).

BILLIARDS. Indoor game of skill played with cues and composition balls on a heavy rectangular table covered by green cloth.

There are pockets at each corner and in the middle of each long side of the table, and the surface is marked out with a baulk line, a semicircle known as the 'D', and 4 spots. Three balls are used, a red and two white, and one of the latter has a spot for easy identification. Points are scored by the cannon, i.e. by the cue (player's) ball hitting the other 2 balls successively, or by winning and losing hazards, the former being made by striking the cue ball against one of the object balls, and sending it into a pocket, and the latter by pocketing the cue ball after hitting one of the object balls. Points are awarded for cannons and for going in off, or pocketing, the white and red balls. The amateur game is usually played for 100 up. The player continues until the end of his break, i.e. until he fails to score, when his opponent takes over.

The origin of the game is obscure, but it has been played in England and France for many centuries. The earliest known rules were printed in 1650.

BILLINGHAM. District of Teesside C. B. in Yorks. N. Riding, 3½ m. N.W. of Middlesbrough. In 1920 it was a small town; development in the 1920s of large works producing fertilizers led to its growth. Pop. (1961) 32,130.

BILLINGS, Josh. Pseudonym of Henry Wheeler Shaw (1818–85). American humorous writer. His popular *Josh Billings, His Sayings* (1865) depended largely for its humour on mis-spelling, puns, and malapropisms.

BILLINGSGATE. Originally one of the gates of the city of London giving on to the Thames just below London Bridge. Near by there is a fish-market dating from the 9th cent. The language of the porters was frequently commented upon by 17th cent. writers, until the word has come to mean foul language.

BILLION. In British usage, a million million (1,000,000,000,000); but in U.S.A. and France, a thousand million (1,000,000,000), which in Britain is a milliard.

BILLITON. Another form of BELITUNG.

BILL OF EXCHANGE. A form of commercial credit instrument, defined in Britain by the Bills of Exchange Act, 1882, as an unconditional order in writing addressed by one person to another, signed by the person giving it, requiring the person to whom it is addressed to pay on demand or at a fixed or determinable future time a certain sum in money to or to the order of a specified person, or to bearer. A *cheque* is a B. of E. drawn on a bank payable on demand. U.S. practice is governed by the Uniform Negotiable Instruments Law, drafted on the same lines as the British, and accepted by all states by 1927.

BILL OF RIGHTS (1689). The Act embodying the Declaration of Rights drawn up by the House of Commons and presented to William of Orange and his wife before they ascended to the throne as William III and Queen Mary in place of James II. It declares the following illegal: the suspension of laws by royal authority without consent of Parliament; the power to dispense with laws; the establishment of special courts of law; levying money by royal prerogative without the consent of Parliament; the raising or keeping of a standing army in time of peace within the kingdom without such consent. The right to petition the King, the freedom of parliamentary elections, freedom of speech in parliamentary debates, and the necessity for frequent parliaments, are also asserted.

BILLROTH (bil'rōt), **Theodor** (1829–94). Viennese surgeon. B. in the island of Rügen, he became professor in Zürich (1859) and Vienna (1867) universities. He was an outstanding figure among the surgeons of his time, and an authority on military surgery.

BILSTON. Ancient English town in Staffs, 10 m. N.W. of Birmingham, making japanned and enamelled ware, glass, etc.; once a centre of heavy industry. Pop. (1961) 33,077.

BIMETALLIC STRIP. Strip made from 2 metals each having a different coefficient of thermal expansion which therefore deflects when subjected to a change in temperature. Used widely for temperature measurement and control.

BIMETALLISM. That monetary system in which gold and silver both circulate together at a ratio fixed by the State, are coined by the Mint on equal terms, and are legal tender to any amount. Advocates of B. have argued that the 'compensatory action of the double standard' makes for a currency more stable than one based only on gold, since the changes in the value of the two metals taken together may be expected to be less than the changes in one of them.

BI'NARIES. Name given to stars that can be seen close together, with optical aid, and gravitationally connected. B. move together through the heavens like other stars, having their own proper motion; but in addition, they move round their common centre of gravity, performing a revolution in a period that may vary from a few days to hundreds of years.

BINARY NUMBER SYSTEM. A system in which numbers are represented by combinations of successive power of 2, i.e. 1, 2, 4, 8, 16, etc. (cf. decimal system where successive powers of 10 are used). Some examples of binary numbers are:

Decimal notation	Binary notation
5	$101 = 1 \times 2^2 + 0 \times 2^1 + 1 \times 2^0$
14	$1110 = 1 \times 2^3 + 1 \times 2^2 + 1 \times 2^1 + 0 \times 2^0$
43	$101011 = 1 \times 2^5 + 0 \times 2^4 + 1 \times 2^3 + 0 \times 2^2 + 1 \times 2^1 + 1 \times 2^0$

This system is widely used in electronic digital computers.

BINARY STAR. A star made up of 2 separate components, moving round their common centre of gravity. In some Bs. (e.g. Gamma Virginis) the components are virtually equal, and widely separated; with others (e.g. Sirius) one component is very much brighter than the companion. The theory that a B. results from the fission of a formerly single star has now been generally rejected. Famous Bs. incl. Mizar, in the Great Bear; Castor, in the Twins; and the brilliant southern star Alpha Centauri. With some Bs. there are more than 2 components, and Castor, for instance, is a complex multiple system.

BINDING (bin'ding), **Rudolf Georg** (1867–1938). German poet and novelist. B. at Basle, he pub. several vols. of verse, and finely-constructed short novels. After 1933 he supported the Nazi regime.

BINET (bēnēh'), **Alfred** (1857–1911). French psychologist. He was director of the laboratory of psychology and physiology at the Sorbonne from 1892, and in 1904 became a member of a commission on education of backward children. Together with Simon he pub. in 1905 the Binet-Simon tests of intelligence, designed to distinguish between children who were backward through mental deficiency and those backward through laziness or ill-health.

BING, Sir Rudolf (1902–). Brit. impresario. B. in Vienna, he fled to England in 1933, and in 1946 founded the Edinburgh Music Festival. In 1950–72 he was manager of the Metropolitan Opera, N.Y.

BINGO. Game played with cards divided into numbered squares. Each player has 1 or more cards and when the 'caller' draws numbered discs from a bag, numbered balls from an automatic machine, etc., he marks off such numbers as appear on his cards. On achieving a full line (horizontal and sometimes also diagonal), the player shouts 'Full House' or 'House', and may win a prize. Long known as a children's game (lotto), and played in the forces as 'housey-housey', it became a gambling craze in the 1960s in Britain, especially among housewives.

BINOCULAR. An optical instrument for the viewing of an object with both eyes, e.g. field-glasses and opera-glasses. The first B. telescope was constructed by a Dutchman, J. Lippershey, in 1608, but interest then lasted until 1823, when the Dutch binocular telescope was re-invented by a Viennese optician, J. Voigtlaender. Later development was largely due to E. Abbé, of Jena, who at the end of the last cent. designed prism Bs. that foreshadowed the instruments of today, in which not only magnification but stereoscopic effect is obtained.

BINOMIAL. In algebra, an expression consisting of 2 terms, as $a + b$, $a - b$. The BINOMIAL THEOREM discovered by Newton and first pub. in 1676, is a formula whereby any power of a B. quantity may be found without performing the progressive multiplications.

BINTURONG. Small mammal (*Arctictis binturong*) with a shaggy coat, short muzzle, and tufted ears. The length of the head and body is about $2\frac{1}{2}$ ft. and the long prehensile tail measures some 2 ft. The B. is black to greyish black, and is a native of S.E. Asia, ranging from Assam to the Philippines. It sleeps in trees during the day and feeds at night on fruit, eggs, and small animals.

BINYON, Laurence (1869–1943). British poet. B. at Lancaster, son of a clergyman, he became keeper of Prints and Drawings at the British Museum (1932–3), and pub. studies of English and Eastern art. His verse vols. incl. *Lyric Poems* (1894) and *London Visions*, but he is best remembered for his fine ode *For the Fallen* (1914).

BIO-BIO (bē'o-bē'o) (Araucanian 'much water'). Longest river of Chile, *c.* 230 m. from its source in the Andes to its 2 m. wide mouth on the Pacific. Once forming the boundary of Araucanian territory, it is navigable by flat-bottomed craft for about 100 m. and is crossed at Concepción, 6 m. E. of its mouth, by a bridge built by British engineers in 1890.

BIOCHEMISTRY. Science concerned with the chemistry of living material and processes, subdivided into the study of fats, proteins, carbohydrates, enzymes, etc. Two principal aspects of this subject are the static, dealing with chemical composition and structure; and the dynamic, dealing with the processes by which food is built up into living matter and then broken down to waste products.

BIOGENESIS (-jen'esis). Biological term coined in 1870 by T. H. Huxley to express the hypothesis that living matter always arises by the agency of pre-existing living matter. The opposite idea, that of spontaneous generation or abiogenesis, i.e. that living things may arise out of non-living matter, was generally held until comparatively recently, but evidence is inconclusive.

BIOGRAPHY. The history of a person's life not written by himself. Among ancient biographers are Xenophon, Plutarch, Tacitus, Suetonius, and the authors of the Gospels. Medieval B. was devoted to religious edification and produced chronicles of saints and martyrs; among the Bs. of laymen are Einhard's *Charlemagne* and Asser's *Alfred*.

In England B. really begins with the early Tudor period and such works as Roper's *Sir Thomas More*. More frequent in the 17th cent., B. was established as an art by Johnson's *Lives of the Poets* and Boswell's *Johnson*. The 19th cent. is remarkable for such fine biographers as Southey, Lockhart, Moore, Mrs. Gaskell, J. Forster, G. H. Lewes, Morley, and Carlyle, but the general tendency was to irrelevant detail and the suppression of the more 'human' facts.

Lytton Strachey's *Eminent Victorians* opened the modern era of frankness, and the new development of the biographical novel was instituted by Maurois with his studies of Byron and Shelley. Orthodox 20th cent. writers include Churchill, John Buchan, David Cecil, Harold Nicolson, Aldous Huxley, Edith Sitwell, Una Pope-Hennessy, Carl Sandburg, Emil Ludwig, and Romain Rolland.

The earliest biographical dictionary in the modern sense was that of Pierre Bayle (1696), followed during the 19th cent. by the development of national Bs. on the Continent, and the foundation of the English Dictionary of National B. in 1882 and the Dictionary of American B. in 1928.

BIOLOGICAL SHIELD. Shield round a reactor to protect personnel from the effects of radiation.

BIOLOGY (bī-o'loji). The science of life. The word was first used by the German physician Treviranus in 1802, and was popularized by Lamarck. Strictly speaking, B. includes all the life sciences, e.g. anatomy and physiology, bacteriology, zoology and botany, ecology, genetics, biochemistry and biophysics, animal behaviour, embryology, and plant breeding.

Medical men, such as Hippocrates in the 5th cent. B.C., made the 1st accurate observations, describing medicinally useful plants and their properties, and Aristotle, in the 4th cent. laid the foundations of a philosophical approach. Attempts at a scientific physiology were bound to fail in the absence of scientific instruments, a tradition of experiment, and a body of organized knowledge with its own terminology. Galen, in the 1st cent. A.D., epitomized what was known of anatomy, but from A.D. 200 to 1200 no scientific advances were made, and only with the Renaissance did free enquiry again come into its own. The 16th cent. saw the production of encyclopaedias of natural history, such as that of Gesner (1516–65), and the beginnings of modern anatomy, notably at Padua under Vesalius (1514–64), who was succeeded by Fabricius. William Harvey, a student of the latter, laid the foundation of modern physiology by his work on the circulation of the blood. This was the first time that any basic function of the body had been scientifically explained, or that quantitative considerations were properly applied in B.

In the 17th cent. came the rise of scientific societies, such as Britain's Royal Society, and of scientific journals and museums. The use of alcohol for preserving specimens was a great step forward, but the outlook in B. was transformed by the introduction of the microscope (Malpighi, Grew, Swammerdam, and Leeuwenhoek were pioneers). Meanwhile, in addition to the complex world revealed by the microscope, explorers had been discovering myriads of new plants and animals and by the early 18th cent. it had become urgent to find a means of classification, and Linnaeus introduced a binomial system. Under this, the name was reduced to 2 Latin or Latinized words – the 1st for the genus, or group of similar species, the 2nd for the individual species: later a 3rd or sub-specific name was added to distinguish differing geographical sub-groups.

In modern B. evolution (q.v.) is the guiding principle and this cent. has seen an all-out attack on the central problem – the mechanism of cellular inheritance. The genetic apparatus in the nucleus of a cell determines the character of the other materials there, and so rules its entire activity. The relationship between the genetic material or DNA (deoxyribonucleicacid) and the vital protein materials was long thought to be governed by a 'genetic code' and in 1961 a team of scientists at the Cavendish Laboratory, Cambridge (incl. F. H. C. Crick and S. Brenner), succeeded in breaking it. These advances in cell study (cytology), have been greatly assisted by the development of the electron microscope, which uses a beam of electrons instead of a light beam. *See also* ANATOMY,

BIOCHEMISTRY, DARWIN, PASTEUR, MICROSCOPE, etc.

BĪONO′MICS. Branch of biology which deals with the laws of life, as they affect organisms in relation to their environment and to each other. The study of heredity and of variation and the part these play in evolution are among the lines of research included.

BĪ′OPSY. Removal of tissue from a living body for the purpose of diagnostic examination.

BĪ′OSPHERE. Region of earth, air and water occupied by living organisms. Man-made modifications have unpredictable consequences, e.g. imbalance of carbon dioxide and oxygen in the atmosphere. Transatlantic jets burn 30 tons of oxygen per flight and produce carbon dioxide, and natural plant sources of oxygen are being reduced by expanding cities, etc.

BIRCH, John M. (1918–45). American Baptist missionary. B. in Georgia, he served in China, and during the S.W.W. was commissioned in the U.S.A.A.F. to carry out intelligence work behind the lines there. He was killed by Chinese Communists 10 days after the war ended. The ultra-nationalist *J. B. Society* (1958) was founded and named after him by retired sweet manufacturer Robert Welch of Boston, Mass.

BIRCH. Tree of the genus *Betula*, including about 25 species, found in the cool temperate parts of the northern hemisphere, of which the white or silver, *Betula alba*, is the best-known. It is of great importance to man, as its timber is quickgrowing and very durable. The bark is used for tanning and dyeing leather, and an oil is obtained from it.

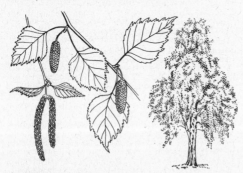

BIRCH. Silver birch, with male (below) and female catkins.

BIRD OF PARADISE. Family of birds (*Paradiseidae*) native of New Guinea and the neighbouring islands. The males are noted for the extreme beauty of their plumage; the females are inconspicuously coloured.

BIRDS. Warm-blooded, vertebrate animals clothed in feathers, and with their fore-limbs transformed into wings. They are oviparous, and feathers and scales originate as epidermal appendages. Except in brain development they are structurally as highly organized as mammals. Their behaviour is largely instinctive. Yet their body temperature is so much higher than that of mammals that they exhibit the emotional side of life in a far greater degree. Physically and mentally they have become highly specialized.

Primarily birds are divided into the *Archaeornithes* (also called Saururae): extinct forms with well-marked reptilian affinities, represented by a single genus, Archaeopteryx (q.v.) and the *Neornithes* or modern birds, which includes two distinct types. (a) The *Ratitae* are flightless and their breastbone resembles a flat bottomless raft (Lat. *ratis*); they comprise only 5 extant forms, viz. the ostrich, rhea, kiwi, emu, and cassowary. (b) The *Carinatae* comprise

CLASSIFICATION OF BIRDS
Passeriformes. Crows, jays, choughs, starlings, birds-of-paradise, orioles, finches, larks, pipits, wagtails, creepers, nuthatches, titmice, goldcrests, shrikes, waxwings, flycatchers, warblers, thrushes, wheatears, wrens, dippers, swallows, lyre-birds.
Apodiformes. Swifts, humming-birds.
Caprimulgiformes. Nightjars.
Trogoniformes. Trogons.
Coliiformes. Mouse-birds.
Coraciiformes. Hornbills, hoopoes, kingfishers, rollers, bee-eaters, etc.
Piciformes. Woodpeckers, barbets, toucans, etc.
Cuculiformes. Cuckoos, plantain-eaters.
Psittaciformes. Parrots and cockatoos.
Strigiformes. Owls.
Falconiformes. Vultures, eagles, hawks, falcons.
Ciconiiformes. Herons, storks, ibises, spoonbills, flamingoes.
Anseriformes. Swans, geese, ducks, mergansers, American screamers.
Pelecaniformes. Cormorants, darters, gannets, pelicans, frigate-birds, tropic-birds.
Procellariiformes. Petrels, shearwaters, albatrosses.
Sphenisciformes. Penguins.
Podicipediformes. Grebes.
Gaviiformes. Divers.
Columbiformes. Pigeons, dodo, sand-grouse.
Charadriiformes. Snipe, curlews, godwits, phalaropes, sandpipers, avocets, plovers, pratincoles, coursers, jaçanas, gulls, terns, auks, bustards, cranes, trumpeters, etc.
Gruiformes. Rails, crakes, moorhens, coots, etc.
Turniciformes. Hemipodes.
Galliformes. Grouse, pheasants, partridges, domestic fowl, turkeys, peacocks, curassows, etc.
Tinamiformes. Tinamous.

the vast majority of living and extinct birds, in which the breastbone is provided with a keel (Lat. *carina*) which amplifies the surface for attachments of the immensely developed muscles of flight. A widely accepted classification of Bs. is given in the Table.

In addition to their use in flight, feathers also give protection and regulate body temperature (ranging from 40° to 43°C.). The vocal apparatus is highly specialized, with no 'obstructions' to prevent free passage of the voiced current of air through the open mouth and, though the lungs are relatively small and inelastic, the air supply is reinforced through numerous air sacs, direct prolongations of the lungs. Besides song (used in courtship but continued while the female broods), there are call and alarm notes. Display of plumes and other ornamentations by the male before the female plays the major part in courtship.

Bs. benefit man by eating insect pests (it has been computed that the blue titmouse consumes *c*. 6½ million insects per annum), eliminating rodent pests in the case of birds of prey, and acting as scavengers. Their senses of smell and touch are little developed, but their hearing, despite no external ears, is excellent and even more so their sight – B. migrants are thought to be largely guided by landmarks. The average life-span is 2 to 6 years. *See* also ORNITHOLOGY.

BIRKBECK, George (1776–1841). British educationist. He helped to found the London Mechanics' Institution (1823)—a coll. of London Univ. from 1920 as *B. College.*

BIRKENHEAD, Frederick Edwin Smith, 1st earl of (1872–1930). British Cons. statesman. B. at Birkenhead and ed. at Oxford, he was called to the bar in 1899. He was

BIRD OF PARADISE

elected Cons. M.P. for a Liverpool seat in 1906, and fiercely resisted Lloyd George's budget of 1909 and the Parliament Act of 1910–11. When Home Rule for Ireland became a burning topic of debate, 'F.E.' joined with Sir Edward Carson in organizing armed resistance in Ulster, his activities earning him the sobriquet of 'Galloper Smith'. In 1915 he became Solicitor-General, and later in the same year Attorney-General. He was Lord Chancellor 1919–22, and Sec. for India 1924–8, and received an earldom in 1922.

BIRKENHEAD. English seaport and industrial town (co. bor.) in Cheshire, on the Mersey estuary opposite Liverpool, and 4 m. from the sea. The first settlement grew up round a Benedictine priory; as late as 1818 B. was a village. In 1824 William Laird estab. a small shipbuilding yard there, and in 1829 the first iron vessel in England was laid down at B. Wallasey dock, first of a series covering 800 acres, was opened in 1847, the docks are under the control of the Mersey Docks and Harbour Board. William Laird's yard was succeeded by the huge yards of Cammell Laird Ltd. B. was made a co. bor. in 1888.

Communications with Liverpool are by rail (via the Mersey Tunnel, 1886), by passenger ferries, and by Queensway, a four-road tunnel $2\frac{1}{4}$ m. long, opened in 1934. In 1860 B. had the first street tramways in Europe. Pop. (1961) 141,683.

BIRKETT, Norman, 1st baron (1883–1962). British barrister and judge. He appeared with Sir Edward Marshall Hall (q.v.) in many cases, became a judge of the High Court and was knighted in 1941, and in 1950–7 was a Lord Justice of Appeal. He was the last of the great pleaders who dominated the legal scene early this century.

BIRMINGHAM, George A. Pseudonym of Irish novelist James Owen Hannay (1865–1950). Son of a Belfast vicar, he was himself canon of St. Patrick's Cathedral, Dublin, 1912–21, and successively rector of Wells from 1924 and of Holy Trinity, Kensington, from 1934. His novels incl. *Spanish Gold* (1908) and *Laura's Bishop* (1949), and his play *General John Regan* (1913) was very successful: under his own name he wrote religious works.

BIRMINGHAM. Second largest city (co. bor.) in the U.K., 100 m. N.W. of London, and falling mainly in Warwickshire, though several of its suburbs are in Worcs and Staffs. It is among the largest manufacturing centres in the world, the principal industry being metal-working. Articles produced incl. pins, needles, wire, nails, screws, small arms, buttons, ironmongery and hardware, machinery, bicycles, cars, and railway engines and carriages. There are also chemical, rayon, rubber, plastic, glass, jewellery, and food industries. B. is a canal and railway centre and has an airport at Elmdon to the S.W.

B. has 2 univs., the Univ. of B (1900) and the Univ of Aston in B. (1966), a School of Music, and a repertory theatre founded by Sir Barry Jackson (q.v.). Few of the city's main buildings are of great age: the Anglican cathedral of St. Philip (1711–19); the R.C. cathedral of St. Chad (1839–41) and St. Martin's parish church (13th cent.). The re-developed site of the Bull Ring was opened as one of Europe's finest shopping centres 1964.

Settlement here dates from Roman times, and the name B. is of Saxon origin. It became a metal-working centre in the 16th cent. B. was made a co. bor. in 1888, a city in 1889. Area 80 sq. m.; pop (1961) 1,105,651.

BIRMINGHAM. Largest city in Alabama, U.S.A., a port and an airport. Founded in 1871, it is on important iron- and coalfields, and manufactures iron and steel goods, textiles, chemicals, building materials, etc. Pop. met area (1970) 729,984.

BI'ROBIJAN (-jahn). Town in Kharabovsk Terr., R.S.F.S.R., on the Bira r., 100 m. W. of Khabarovsk, cap. of the Jewish Autonomous Region 1928–51 (sometimes also called B.) of the R.S.F.S.R. It has sawmills and clothing factories. Pop. (1967) 46,000.

BIRTH CONTROL. See FAMILY PLANNING.

BISCAY, Bay of. Atlantic bay stretching between Point du Raz, France; Cape Ortegal, N. Spain; and Biarritz, S. France. It is roughly triangular in shape, the sides being about 400 m. long. At times the Bay is very rough, and ithas exceptionally high tides.

BISCUIT. A crisp, flat cake, consisting of flour, sugar, and fat. Other ingredients are used to give variety of flavour – e.g. eggs, milk, coconut, almonds, and spices. Bs. contain only a low percentage of moisture. They are, therefore, a concentrated food, and their food value, *c.* 2,000 calories per pound, is high.

BISHOP (Gk. *episkopos,* an overseer). A clergyman consecrated for the spiritual government or direction of a diocese or see; as such a B. ranks below an archbishop and above priests and deacons.

In N.T. times there was no clear distinction between Bs. and elders, but with the growth in influence and numbers of the Church, the B. became an increasingly important figure. Originally Bs. were chosen by the people, but in time the power of election passed to the other bishops of the province, and next to the cathedral chapter, subject to the veto of the metropolitan, and later of the Pope. Today in some R.C. countries the political authority has secured the right of appointment to bishoprics, but in other countries the Pope nominates the Bs.

Since 1534 the appointment of Bs. of the C. of E. has been vested in the Crown. Theoretically the cathedral chapter make the nomination, but in practice the selection is made by the Prime Minister, usually on the advice of the archbishops. There are 29 dioceses in the province of Canterbury and 14 in the province of York, and there are many suffragan Bs., i.e. Bs. in charge of parts of dioceses. There are 6 Bs. of the Church in Wales, and many Bs. in the Anglican Church in the Commonwealth.

In the Eastern Orthodox Church a B. is always chosen from the monastic orders, since he must be unmarried. There are also Bs. in certain of the Lutheran churches, the Moravians, and in the Methodist Episcopal Church in the U.S.A.

BISHOP, Sir Henry Rowley (1786–1855). British opera composer, now remembered mainly for his song *Home, Sweet Home.*

BISHOP, William Avery (1894–1956). Canadian air ace. B. at Owen Sound, Ontario, he won the V.C. in 1917, was promoted Air Marshal in 1939 and as Director of the R.C.A.F. in the S.W.W. played an important part in the Empire training scheme.

BISHOP AUCKLAND. English market and colliery town (U.D.) in Durham, 8 m. S.S.W. of Durham. The palace is the seat of the bishops of Durham. Pop. (1961) 35,276.

BISHOP'S STORTFORD (stor'ford). English market town (U.D.) in Herts., 30 m. N.N.E. of London, on the Stort. It is an educational centre. Cecil Rhodes was b. here. Pop. (1961) 18,308.

BISKRA (bēs'krah). Oasis, town, resort, and military station in a valley of the Aures mountains, Algeria bordering the Sahara. Pop. *c.* 40,000.

BISLEY. English village in Surrey, 3 m. W.N.W. of Woking. The National Rifle Association moved its ranges here from Wimbledon in 1890. Many military and civil shooting events are held here regularly; and rifle club members can receive instruction.

BI'SMARCK, Otto Eduard Leopold, Prince von (1815–98). German statesman. The son of a Brandenburg landowner, he studied law and was employed for a time in the civil service. He entered the Prussian Landtag in 1847, and during the revolution of 1848–9 upheld the principle of Divine Right. His experiences as Prussian envoy to the Federal Diet (1851–9) inspired his ambition to establish Prussia's hegemony inside Germany, and to eliminate the influence of Austria. After serving as ambassador to St. Petersburg and Paris, he was appointed For. Min. in 1862. He secured Austria's supporti n his war of 1863–4 with Denmark, but in 1866 he went to war with Austria and her allies. Prussia's victory brought about Austria's secession from the German Bund, and the unification of the N. German states in the N. German Confederation under B.'s chancellorship (1867). Napoleon III's alarm at this development enabled B. to manœuvre him in 1870 into the Franco-Prussian War. The proclamation of the German Empire in 1871 and the annexation of Alsace-Lorraine crowned his work. As Imperial Chancellor he sought to secure the peace settlement by forming the Triple Alliance with Austria and Italy (1882). At home he became involved in conflicts with the R.C. Church, and with the Socialist movement, in both of which he was defeated. William II dismissed him in 1890.

BISMUTH. A reddish white metal. It occurs in nature in the native condition (i.e. as the free metal), although ores (i.e. compounds of B.) are also known. It is used chiefly as a medicine and cosmetic. Being heavy, B. subnitrate is used as a shadowing agent in radiography of the digestive tract. B. is also strongly diamagnetic, the electrical resistance varying with magnetic field.

BI′SON. Genus of wild cattle, represented by 2 species, one European (*Bison bonasus*) and one N. American (*Bison bison*). They are mainly brown, and have short horns and a mane on the head and neck.

The *European B.*, or *Wisent*, is the larger, standing 6 ft. high and weighing nearly a ton. It is almost extinct, being now represented by a few protected herds. The *American B.*, or buffalo, has a more extensive mane and more sloping hind quarters than the European B., but its height seldom exceeds 5¾ ft. It formerly roamed the prairies in vast herds, but was nearly exterminated by the Indians and European settlers. The few remaining are now protected in Canada and the Yellowstone Park, U.S.A. It will cross with cattle, the resultant hybrid, known as 'cattalo', being fertile.

BITLIS. Town in Asiatic Turkey, cap. of B. il, 25 m. S.W. of Lake Van. It was the scene of a massacre of Armenians in 1895. Pop. (1965) il, 140,847.

BITOLJ (bitŏl). Town in S. Yugoslavia, 20 m. N. of the Greek frontier, noted for home-made mats and ropes. The Serbians captured it from the Turks in the Balkan War of 1912. Pop. (1961) 49,101.

BITTERN. Genus of birds (*Botaurus*) of the heron family (Ardeidae). The typical European species (*B. stellaris*) was formerly abundant in marshy country

in Britain and is now found, owing to protection, in the fens and elsewhere. It is a shy, solitary bird, smaller and more stoutly built than the heron, and its yellowish-brown plumage, streaked with black, renders it very inconspicuous. The male has a curious 'booming' cry. The smaller American species (*B. lentiginosus*) and the Little B. (*Ixobrychus minutus*) occasionally visit the British Isles.

BITTERSWEET. Name of a plant, the woody nightshade. *See* NIGHTSHADE.

BITU′MEN. An impure mixture of hydrocarbons, including such deposits as petroleum, asphalt, and natural gas, although sometimes the term is restricted to a soft kind of pitch resembling asphalt. Solid B. may have arisen as a residue left behind by the evaporation of petroleum. If evaporation took place from a pool or lake of petroleum the residue may form a pitch or asphalt lake like the famous asphalt lake of Trinidad. B. was used by the ancients as a mortar, and by the Egyptians for embalming.

BIZE′RTA. Mediterranean port in Tunisia, 37 m. N.W. of Tunis, most northerly town in Africa. It was founded by the Phoenicians. The French occupied it in 1881. Pop. (1966) 95,023.

BIZET (bēzeh′), **Georges** (1838–75), French composer. B. near Paris, he studied at the Paris Conservatoire and won the Grand Prix de Rome in 1857. On his return from Italy he became known as a pianist, and began to compose operas, among them *Les Pêcheurs de perles* (1863), *La jolie fille de Perth* (1867), and *Djamileh* (1872), which are still occasionally performed. He also wrote an overture to Sardou's play *Patrie*, and incidental music to Daudet's *L'Arlésienne*. The latter forms the material of two well-known orchestral suites. His operatic masterpiece *Carmen*, on a libretto founded on Prosper Mérimée's story, was produced a few months before his death in 1875.

BJÖRNEBORG. Swedish name of PORI.

BJÖRNSON (byern′son), **Björnst′erne** (1832–1910). Norwegian author. He became a journalist in Oslo, and made his name by the peasant-tale *Synnöve Solbakken* (1857) and the historical dramatic trilogy *Sigurd Slembe* (1862). B. directed the Bergen (1857–9) and Oslo (1865–7) playhouses, and advanced to realism in *The Newly Married Couple* (1865) and *A Bankruptcy* (1875). Later plays are *Leonarda* (1879) and *A Gauntlet* (1883), treating of sexual morality; the political *Paul Lange and Tora Parsberg* (1898), and *Beyond Human Power* (1883). He also wrote *Poems and Songs* (1870), and the novels *Flags are Flying in Town and Port* (1884), and *In God's Way* (1889). In 1903 he received a Nobel Prize.

BLACK, Davidson (1884–1934). Canadian anatomist. In 1927, when professor of anatomy at the Union Medical Coll., Peking, he unearthed the remains of Peking Man (q.v.), a very primitive type.

BLACK, JOSEPH (1728–99). Scottish physicist and chemist. B. at Bordeaux, of Scottish descent, he qualified as a doctor in Edinburgh. In chemistry he prepared the way for Cavendish, Priestley, and Lavoisier – and in physics, by his work on 'latent heat', he laid the foundation of the work of his pupil, James Watt.

BLACK-AND-TANS. Nickname of a specially raised force of military police employed by the British in 1920–1 to combat the Sinn Feiners in Ireland; the name was derived from the colours of the uniforms.

BLACKBERRY. Fruit of the bramble (*Rubus fruticosus*), a prickly shrub, closely allied to the raspberry. It is native to the northern parts of the Old World, is exceedingly abundant in Britain, and produces pink or white blossoms and edible black, compound fruit. Several varieties have been regarded as distinct species, e.g. the dewberry.

BLACKBIRD. British resident bird (*Turdus merula*) belonging to the thrush family (Turdidae). The male has coal-black plumage, set off by the yellow bill and eyelids; the hen is somewhat larger, her plumage is dark brown, and she has a dark beak. The eggs are pale sea-blue, freckled with reddish-brown, and there are 4 or 5 in a clutch. The B.'s song is rich and flute-like.

BLACKBUCK. An antelope (*Antilope cervicapra*) found in C. and N.W. India. It is related to the gazelles, from which it differs in having the horns spirally twisted. The males are black above and white beneath, whereas the females and young are fawn-coloured above. It is about 2½ ft. in height.

BLACKBURN. English town (co. bor.) in Lancs, 20 m. N.W. of Manchester. It became famous in the 17th cent. for its weaving of cotton checks, later superseded by a cotton-and-linen fabric called Blackburn greys. Pre-eminently a cotton-weaving town, B. also makes machinery, especially for its own industries, and mines coal. The diocese of B. dates from 1926. The town was made a bor. in 1851, a co. bor. in 1888. Pop. (1961) 106,114.

BLACKBUCK

BLACKCAP. *See* WARBLER.

BLACKCOCK. *See* GROUSE.

BLACK COUNTRY. Part of the English Midlands, lying about and to the N. of Birmingham, including S. Staffs and part of Worcs and Warwicks. It is a region of factories, ironworks, and coalmines, claypits, railways, and canals. It got its name from the smoke belching out of the vast number of chimneys.

BLACK DEATH. Modern name (first used in England in the early 19th cent.) for the great epidemic of bubonic plague, which spread from China to devastate Europe in the 14th cent. It completely demoralized society, and it is estimated that one-third to one-half of the population of England succumbed in 1348–9. The disease remained endemic in London for the next 3 cents., the last great outbreak being that of 1665, when *c.* 100,000 of the 400,000 inhabitants d. *See* PLAGUE.

BLACK EARTH. Name applied to the exceedingly fertile soil which covers a belt of land in Europe and Asia, extending from Bohemia through Hungary, Rumania, S. Russia, and Siberia, as far as Manchuria. It is a kind of loess (q.v.), and was laid down when the great Eurasian inland ice sheet melted at the close of the last ice age.

BLACKETT, Patrick Maynard Stuart, baron (1897–). British physicist. He worked with Rutherford at the Cavendish Laboratory 1923–33, and was prof. of physics at Manchester 1937–53 and the Imperial College of Science, London, 1953–65. He was awarded a Nobel Prize in 1948 for work in cosmic radiation and his perfection of the Wilson 'cloud-chamber'. He was Pres. R.S. 1965–70, was awarded the O.M in 1967 and became a life peer 1969.

BLACKFISH. Sea-fish (*Centrolophus niger*), of the family Stromateoidae, native to European seas. Wholly black, it is esteemed as food.

BLACK FOREST. Wooded mountainous region 100 m. long in S.W. Germany, bounded on the W. and S. by the Rhine, which separates it from the Vosges, and covering an area of about 1,800 sq. m., which falls in Land Baden-Württemberg.

BLACKHEATH. English common which gives its name to a residential suburb of London partly in Greenwich, partly in Lewisham. Wat Tyler encamped on B. in 1381.

BLACK HOLE OF CALCUTTA. Dungeon at Fort William, Calcutta, W. Bengal, 18 ft. by 14 ft. 10 ins., into which on the night of 20 June 1756 were thrust, by order of Suraj-ud-Dowlah, nawab of Bengal, 146 British prisoners taken when he sacked the factory there of the East India Co. Only 23 survived the night. Doubt has been cast on the story; but even Indian historians have come to accept that it has a foundation in fact.

BLACKMAIL (Fr. *máille*, 'rent' paid in labour or base coin). Legal term for the criminal offence of demanding anything of value with menaces of violence and other injury, or of exposure of some misconduct on the part of the victim (whether actually committed by him or not).

BLACK MARKET. Illegal trade in food or other rationed goods, such as petrol and clothing, during the S.W.W. and after.

BLACKMORE, Richard Doddridge (1825–1900). British novelist, author of *Lorna Doone* (1869), a romance of Exmoor in the late 17th cent., and of *Maid of Sker* (1872) and *Springhaven* (1887).

BLACK MOUNTAINS. Group of hills in Breconshire, Wales, overlooking the Wye valley in the N. Waun Fâch is 2,660 ft. high. In 1966 a network of beautiful passages and caves was discovered beneath them.

BLACKPOOL. Famous English seaside resort (co. bor.) in Lancs, 28 m. N. of Liverpool. It possesses many amusement facilities, incl. promenades 7 m. long, fun fairs, and a tower 500 ft. high. It was made a bor. in 1876, a co. bor. in 1904. Pop. (1961) 152,133.

BLACK POWER. During the 1960s existing civil rights organisations in the U.S.A. such as the National Association for the Advancement of Coloured People and the Southern Christian Leadership Conference were seen to be ineffective in producing major change in Negro status. It was then proposed by Stokely Carmichael that the concept of B.P. be adopted, i.e. the attainment of full citizenship by exploitation of political and economic power, abandonment of non-violence, and a move towards the type of separatism first developed by the Black Muslims. Negro leaders such as Martin Luther King rejected this approach, but nationwide influence was achieved by the Black Panther Party (so-named because the panther, though not generally aggressive, will fight to the death under attack) founded in 1966 by Huey Newton and Bobby Seale, which fully adopted it, and put forward as the ultimate aim establishment of a separate Negro state in the U.S.A. estab. by a Negro plebiscite under the aegis of the U.N. *See* MOSLEMS.

BLACK PRINCE. Name given to Edward (q.v.), Prince of Wales, eldest son of Edward III of England.

BLACK SEA. Inland sea in S.E. Europe, 164,000 sq. m. in area. It is linked to the N.E. with the Sea of Azov, and to the S.W. with the Sea of Marmara, and through the Dardanelles with the Mediterranean.

BLACKSNAKE. Non-poisonous snake (*Zamenis constrictor*), very common in the U.S.A. But in Australia the B. is *Pseudechis porphyriacus*, a highly poisonous species of the family Elapidae, allied to the cobra.

BLACK FOREST. In the south of the Black Forest, at Aeule, overlooking the Schluchsee, this farmhouse in traditional style and the delightful costume of its inhabitants are typical of this extremely beautiful part of Germany.
Courtesy of the German Tourist Information Bureau

BLACKSTONE, Sir William (1723–80). British jurist, remembered for his *Commentaries on the Laws of England* (1765–9). Called to the Bar in 1746, he became professor of law at Oxford (1758), and a Justice of the Court of Common Pleas (1770).

BLACKTHORN, or Sloe. Tree (*Prunus spinosa*) of the family Rosaceae, closely allied to the plum, and producing a cloud of white blossom on black, leafless boughs in early spring.

BLACKWATER FEVER. Form of subtertian malaria, characterized by the breakdown of the red blood corpuscles, which stain the urine a reddish brown. It is widespread on the E. and W. coasts of Africa, and in other malarial districts.

BLACKWELL, Elizabeth (1821–1910). First British woman doctor, and first woman to gain medical degree anywhere. Taken to the U.S.A. at 11, she became a teacher and qualified as a doctor there in 1849, being admitted to the English medical register in 1859.

BLACK WIDOW. Popular name of a poisonous species of N. American spider (*Lathrodectus mactans*). It is not so deadly as fiction suggests.

BLADDER. Hollow organ in which urine is accumulated. Situated in the pelvis, it is a round bag of muscle lined with mucous membrane. Urine enters the B. through 2 ureters, one leading from each kidney, and leaves it through the urethra; on emptying, the B. collapses in folds.

BLADDERWORT (-wert). Genus of carnivorous aquatic plants (*Utricularia*) of the family Lentibulariaceae, which feeds on small crustacea.

BLAGONRAVOV (blahgonrah′vof), **Anatoly Arkadievich** (1894–   ). Russian specialist in rocketry and instrumentation. B. at Ankov, he pub. in 1931 *Bases for Planning Automatic Weapons*, was awarded a Stalin prize in 1941 for his work on Soviet artillery and became head of the Soviet Academy of Artillery Science. He is believed to have directed the earth satellite programme leading to the launching of Sputnik I and II.

BLAKE, Robert (1599–1657). British admiral. He represented his native Bridgwater in the Short Parliament of 1640, and distinguished himself with the Parliamentary forces in defending Bristol (1643) and Taunton (1644–5). Appointed 'general-at-sea' (1649), he destroyed Prince Rupert's fleet off Cartagena in the next year. In 1652 he won several engagements against the Dutch before being defeated by Tromp off Dungeness, and revenged himself in 1653 by defeating the Dutchman off Portsmouth and the N. Foreland. In 1654 he bombarded Tunis, the stronghold of the Barbary corsairs, and in 1657 captured the Spanish treasure-fleet in Santa Cruz.

BLAKE, William (1757–1827). British poet and artist. B. in Soho, he was apprenticed to an engraver 1771–8, and studied at the Academy under Reynolds. The comparative simplicity of *Songs of Innocence* (1789) and *Songs of Experience* (1794) was lost in the 'prophetic' books portraying through mythological figures the conflict of restrictive morality and anarchical liberty, e.g. *Book of Thel* (1789), *Marriage of Heaven and Hell* (1793), and *Song of Los* (1795), for all of which he engraved illustrations. He kept a print-shop in London (1784–7), and received commissions from booksellers and others, but after the failure of his exhibition in 1809, retired (1810–17), until

WILLIAM BLAKE
Photo: N.P.G.

BLARNEY. When Dermot McCarthy refused to relinquish his castle to Elizabeth I, using one ingenious excuse after another, she angrily exclaimed 'More Blarney talk!' – and so the legend was born. The stone, itself unknown until the 18th century, is high in the battlements and to reach it the visitor must hang head downward. *Courtesy of the Irish Tourist Board.*

his final recognition in his last years. Later works include *Milton* (1803–8), the symbolic *Jerusalem* (1804–20), and the fragmentary *Everlasting Gospel*. His most celebrated illustrations are those to Young's *Night Thoughts*, Blair's *Grave*, the *Book of Job*, and Dante. Our illus. is a plaster cast of a life mask of 1823 made by J. S. Deville.

BLAMEY, Sir Thomas A. (1884–1951). Australian field-marshal. He was chief of the staff of the Australian Corps in 1918, and during the S.W.W. led the Australian Imperial Forces in the Middle East, becoming commander of the Allied Land Forces in the S.W. Pacific (1942–5).

BLANC (blon), **Louis** (1811–82). French socialist. In 1839 he founded the *Revue du progrès*, in which he pub. his *Organisation du travail*, advocating the establishment of co-operative workshops and other socialistic schemes. He was a member of the provisional government of 1848, and from its fall lived in England until 1871.

BLANCHARD (blonshahr′), **Jean Pierre** (1753–1809). French balloonist, who came to England to make the first balloon flight across the Channel with Dr. John Jeffries in 1785. He also made the first balloon flight in the U.S.A. in 1793. *See* BALLOON.

BLANE, Sir Gilbert (1749–1834). Scottish physician. He accompanied Admiral Rodney in the West Indies expedition of 1779, and by his advocacy of lime-juice as part of the men's diet was responsible for the elimination of scurvy.

BLANK VERSE. The unrhymed iambic pentameter or 10 syllable line of 5 stresses. Originated by the Italian Trissino, *c*. 1515, it was introduced to England by the Earl of Surrey, *c*. 1540, and developed by Marlowe. B. was used with increasing freedom by Shakespeare, Fletcher, Webster, and Middleton. It was remodelled by Milton, who was imitated in the 18th cent. by Thomson, Young, and Cowper, and revived in the early 19th cent. by Wordsworth, Shelley, and Keats, and later by Tennyson, Browning, and Swinburne. Modern exponents include Hardy, T. S. Eliot, and R. Frost.

BLANQUI (blonkē′), **Louis Auguste** (1805–81). French revolutionary politician who spent 37 years in prison. He invented the theory of the 'dictatorship of the proletariat', taken over by Marx.

BLANTYRE. Parish in Scotland on the Lanarkshire coalfield. Here David Livingstone was born. Pop. *c*. 18,000.

BLANTYRE. City in Central Africa, the principal commercial centre of Malawi, in the Shiré highlands. It has an airport and was named after Livingstone's birthplace. With Limbe it forms a municipality. Pop. (1966) 109,795.

BLARNEY. Small town with tweed mills in Co. Cork, Rep. of Ireland, 7 m. N.W. of Cork. High up in the wall of the 15th cent. castle is the *B. Stone*, reputed to give those kissing it wonderfully persuasive speech. Pop. c. 1000.

BLASIS (blahsē'), **Carlo** (1803–78). Italian *maître de ballet* of French extraction. He had a successful career as a dancer in Paris and in Milan, where he established a famous dancing school (1837).

BLASPHEMY (Gk. *blasphemia*, evil speaking). Written or spoken insult directed against God, Christianity, or the Church, religious beliefs or sacred things, with deliberate intent to outrage belief. B. is still an offence in English law.

BLAST FURNACE. Furnace in which the temperature is raised by the injection of an air blast. It is employed in the extraction of metals from their ores, particularly pig-iron from iron ore. The principle has been known for thousands of years, but the modern B.F. is a heavy engineering development combining a number of special techniques.

BLATCHFORD, Robert (1851–1943). British journalist. He founded and edited the popular Socialist weekly *Clarion* (1891–1910), and his articles in the *Daily Mail* prior to the F.W.W., in which he pointed out the German menace, caused him to be denounced as a warmonger.

BLAVA′TSKY, Helena Petrovna (1831–91). Russian theosophist. *Née* Hahn, she m. as a girl Nicephore B., a councillor of state, but separated from him after a few months and travelled widely. While in Tibet (1856), she was supposed to have been initiated into theosophy. In 1873 she experimented in spiritualist phenomena in N.Y., where she founded the Theosophical Society (1875), and in 1877 pub. her controversial *Isis Unveiled*. In 1879 she went to India, where in Adyar she reorganized the Theosophical Society.

BLAYDON. English coal mining and industrial town (U.D.) in Durham, on the Tyne 4 m. W. of Newcastle. Pop. (1961) 30,615.

BLEACHING. Decolorization of coloured materials. B. processes have been known from antiquity, especially those acting through sunlight. Both natural and modern chemical colouring matters usually possess highly complex molecules, the colour property often being due only to a part of the molecule. B. chemicals usually attack only that small part, giving another substance similar in chemical structure but colourless. The 2 main types of B. agent are the oxidizing (which add oxygen and remove hydrogen, and include the ultra-violet rays in sunshine, hydrogen peroxide, and chlorine), and the reducing which add hydrogen or remove oxygen, e.g. sulphur dioxide.

BLEAK. Species of freshwater fish (*Alburnus lucidus*), of the carp family (Cyprinidae), found in the rivers of northern and central Europe.

BLEEDING. Loss of blood (haemorrhage) due to injury or disease. Sudden and copious B. may cause death in a few minutes, and even slight B. may endanger life if unchecked for a considerable time. External B. is treated by closing the blood vessels leading to the wound by means of a tourniquet in the case of a limb, or by pads if on the body; internal B. demands hospital treatment. General symptoms of B. are as in shock.

BLENHEIM. German village in Bavaria on the left bank of the Danube, near which Marlborough defeated the French and Bavarians on 13 Aug. 1704. For *B. palace*, named after the battle, see MARLBOROUGH, duke of, and VANBRUGH, Sir John.

BLENNY. Family of fishes of world-wide distri-

BUTTERFLY BLENNY

bution (Bleniidae), distinguished by spiny fins and smooth body, belonging to the order Percomorphi. The Smooth B. or Shanny (*Blennius pholis*) is the most familiar in Britain.

BLÉRIOT, Louis (1872–1936). French aviator. He constructed a monoplane, and in it made the first flight across the English Channel, 25 July 1909.

BLESBOK (*Damaliscus albifrons*). Species of brownish antelope, c. 3 ft. high, related to the hartebeest (q.v.). Only a few protected herds survive N. of the Orange River in S. Africa.

BLESSINGTON, Marguerite, countess of (1789–1849). Irish writer. She m. as her 2nd husband the earl of B. in 1818, but in later years damaged her reputation by her association with Count D'Orsay. A queen of literary society, she pub. *Conversations with Lord Byron* (1834), travel sketches, and novels. Her husband d. 1829 and, bankrupt by 1849, she fled London for Paris in D'Orsay's wake, and there d.

BLIGH, William (1754–1817). British admiral. He accompanied Capt. Cook in his 2nd voyage (1772–4), and in 1787 commanded H.M.S. *Bounty* on an expedition to the Pacific. On the return voyage the crew mutinied (1789), and cast B. adrift with 18 men in a boat. The mutineers settled in Tahiti and on Pitcairn Is., whilst B. brought his boat 3,618 m. to Timor Is., near Java. Appointed Governor of N.S.W. in 1805, his discipline again provoked a mutiny (1808), but on returning to England he was made an admiral in 1811.

BLIGHT. A number of diseases of cultivated plants, mainly caused by parasitic plants (e.g. fungi of the family Erysiphaceae, which produce a whitish appearance on leaf and stem surfaces), or insects (e.g. Aphidae or green fly).

BLIGHTY (Hindustani, *bilāyati*, foreign). Popular name during the F.W.W. among British troops for 'home' or England.

BLIMP. In the F.W.W., British lighter-than-air aircraft were divided into A – rigid, and B – limp (i.e. without rigid internal framework). The barrage balloon is called a B. Low, the cartoonist, adopted the name for his famous character.

BLINDHEIM. Older form of BLENHEIM.

BLINDNESS. Absence of sight. Sudden B. is usually due to a general condition, such as hysteria (functional B.), sudden and severe internal bleeding,

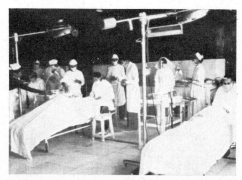

BLINDNESS. India, with more than 2,000,000 blind people, has to adopt special methods to deal with the problem. The excellent Sitapur Eye Hospital in Uttar Pradesh, under the direction of Dr. H. L. Patney, is set up for 'assembly line' operations for cataract, glaucoma, squint, corneal grafts and so on. *WHO photo by T. S. Satyan.*

brain wounds, etc. The main causes of gradual B. are trachoma, onchocerciasis, smallpox, glaucoma and cataract.

The first institution for the blind was estab. in the 4th cent. A.D., by St. Basil at Caesarea in Cappadocia. In 1260 the king St. Louis founded an asylum for the blind in Paris, which still exists. Education of the blind was begun by Valentin Haüy, who pub. a book with raised lettering (1784), and founded a school. There are now approx. 10,000,000 blind people in the world incl. 650,000 children, and measures to help them and avoid the incidence of preventible B. are co-ordinated by the World Council for the Welfare of the Blind. The most highly developed system of blind welfare exists in Britain which has in the Royal National Institute for the Blind (founded by Dr. T. R. Armitage in 1868) the largest organization of its kind in the world: other large organizations are St. Dunstan's (founded by Sir Arthur Pearson in 1915) for the blinded of both World Wars; the National Library (estab. 1882) and the Guide Dogs for the Blind Assocn.

BLINDWORM or **Slow Worm.** Harmless species of lizard (*Anguis fragilis*), common in Europe and Britain. Superficially resembling a snake, it is distinguished by its small mouth and movable eyelids.

BLISS, Sir Arthur (1891–). British composer. B. in London, and ed. at Rugby and Pembroke College, Cambridge, he became Master of the Queen's Musick in 1953. His music has a masculine individuality, and his works include *Colour Symphony* (1922), an experimental relation of tone and visual impressions; the ballets *Miracle in the Gorbals* (1944) and *Adam Zero* (1946); the opera *The Olympians* (1949); and dramatic film music, e.g. *Things to Come*.

BLISTER BEETLE. *See* CANTHARIDES.

BLITZKRIEG (Ger., lightning war). Name applied to a swift, shattering campaign, such as those of 1939–41, which resulted in the fall of Poland, France, Yugoslavia, and Greece, and the advance to Moscow.

BLITZSTEIN (blit'stīn), **Marc** (1905–64). American composer. B. in Philadelphia, he appeared as a child prodigy pianist at the age of six. He served with the U.S. Army 8th Air Force 1942–5, for whom he wrote *The Airborne*, a choral symphony. His operas incl. *The Cradle Will Rock* (1937) and *Reuben Reuben* (1953).

BLOCH (blok), **Ernest** (1880–1959). American composer. B. in Geneva, of Jewish parentage, he went to the U.S. in 1916 and became founder-director of the Cleveland Institute of Music (1920–5). He later taught at the San Francisco Conservatoire and the Univ. of Berkeley. His works incl. the lyrical drama *Macbeth* (1910), 5 string quartets, and *Rhapsodie Hebraique* (1951), and he often used themes based on Hebrew liturgical music and folk-song.

BLOCH, Felix (1905–). American physicist. B. in Zürich, he has been prof. of physics at Stanford Univ., U.S., from 1936, receiving a Nobel Prize jointly with E. M. Purcell in 1952, for his work on nuclear-magnetic precision measuring. In 1954–5 he was director-general of the Nuclear Research Centre at Geneva.

BLOCKADE. Obstruction of part of the coast of a belligerent by the ships of its opponent, so as to prevent any ships or aircraft having access to it. Before the F.W.W. such Bs. were maintained by vessels near the coast, but the development of mines and submarines made this impossible and a 'long distance' B. by cruiser 'cordon' was introduced to prevent access to Germany. In the S.W.W. the *Navicert System*

BLOEMFONTEIN. The Town Hall.
Courtesy of South Africa House.

made goods or ships which might ultimately reach the enemy, whether by neutral or enemy ports, liable to seizure unless possessing the necessary certificate.

BLOEMFONTEIN (bloom'fontän). Cap. of the Orange Free State, and judicial cap. of the Union of S. Africa. It lies on a plateau at 4,568 ft. above sea-level, 200 m. N.W. of Durban. Founded in 1846, B. was taken by Lord Roberts in 1900 during the Boer War of 1899–1902. Here is the appellate division of the supreme court of the Union of S. Africa; and the Univ. of the Orange Free State. General Hertzog airport, opened 1958, with a runway 8,400 ft. long, lies 6 m. E.N.E. Last home of the Republican Volksraad, the Town Hall on Pres. Brand Street is used for the Provincial Assembly. Pop. (1960) 145,273 (63,046 white).

BLOIS (blwah). Chief town of Loir-et-Cher dept., France, on the Loire, 35 m. S.W. of Orléans. It has a castle dating from the 13th cent. and makes shoes, porcelain, furniture, etc. Pop. (1962) 36,426.

BLOK, Alexander Alexandrovich (1880–1921). Russian poet. He was influenced by Soloviev, and having pub. the mystic *Verses about the Beautiful Lady* (1904), became the foremost Russian symbolist. Later works are the lyrical plays *Puppet Show* (1907) and *The Rose and the Cross* (1913), and the revolutionary poems *The Twelve* and *The Scythians* (1918).

BLONDIN (bloń-dań), **Charles.** Name assumed by the French tight-rope-walker, Jean François Gravelet (1824–97). He became world-famous when he crossed Niagara Falls on a rope at a height of 160 ft. in 1859, repeating the feat several times – blindfolded, wheeling a barrow, etc. He later performed in England.

BLOOD. Red liquid circulating in the arteries, veins, and capillaries of the higher animals, and the corresponding fluid in those lesser animals which possess a circulatory system. In man *c.* a 20th part of the body weight, the temperature of B. in health is *c.* 37°C (98·4°F). It consists of a colourless, transparent liquid called plasma, containing microscopic cells of 3 varieties: (1) Red cells, which form nearly one half of the volume of the B. A cu. mm. of B. contains *c.* 5,000,000. Their colour, actually a pale yellow, is caused by haemoglobin, which takes oxygen from the air in the lungs, and yields it to the body tissues. (2) White cells of different kinds. A cu. mm. of B. contains only *c.* 7,500, but some of them have the power to eat up invading bacteria and so protect the body from disease (phagocytes); others repair injured tissues. (3) Cells called blood platelets, which are manufactured in the bone marrow, and assist in the clotting of B.

Invading disease germs cause the B. to generate 'antibodies', which resist them and give the person immunity to the disease for a time. B. cells constantly wear out and die, and are replaced from the bone marrow.

BLOOD, Col. Thomas (*c.* 1618–80). Irish adventurer, whose most daring exploit was an attempt to steal the Crown Jewels from the Tower (1671).

BLOOD GROUPS. In 1900 Karl Landsteiner discovered that when the serum of one person's blood was mixed with the red cells of another, agglutination of the red cells would follow. He, therefore, divided human beings into 3 different B.Gs., and 2 years later a 4th was discovered. The serum of group A agglutinates the cells of group B, and vice versa; the cells of group O will not agglutinate in contact with any serum; those of group AB will be agglutinated by serum from an A or B person. B.Gs. are of great importance in B. transfusion and may be of use in cases of disputed paternity. Sometimes another agglutinogen is present in the B., the Rhesus factor. A woman who is Rh negative (lacking it), who becomes pregnant with a child who is Rh positive (possessing it), may in certain circumstances have developed antibodies which will pass into the blood stream of her child and kill it by destroying the red cells.

BLOODHOUND.

Ancient breed of dog. Black and tan in colour, it has long, pendulous ears, and distinctive wrinkles on the head. Its phenomenal powers of scent have been employed in tracking and criminal work from very early times.

BLOOD POISONING, or Toxaemia. Circulation of a dangerous quantity of poisonous substances in the blood. Such substances may be derived from outside, e.g. carbon monoxide and alcohol, but they are often due to toxins or poisons manufactured by invading microbes, e.g. the poisoning of a system from an abscess in the root of a tooth. When invading microbes penetrate the blood in large numbers and multiply the condition is known as septicaemia.

BLOOD PRESSURE, or tension, is due to the muscular action of the left side of the heart, which forces the blood out of the left ventricle into the arterial system, acting against the elastic muscular coats of the arteries, which tend to contract and to resist the passage of blood. B.P. is also modified by the degree of fluidity of the blood. It varies considerably, gives a valuable indication of the condition of a patient's health, and is measured in terms of the height in millimetres of the column of mercury which the blood will support. Persistent high B.P. shows disease of the arteries. A very high B.P., especially when the arteries are hard, brings with it a danger of apoplectic stroke, the bursting of an artery in the brain. A persistently low B.P. may be induced by certain diseases, general ill-health, etc.

BLOOD TESTS. Tests made to provide information of use to the doctor, and also to detect foreign substances such as poisons or alcohol in the blood. B.Ts. in commonest use are cell counts, determination of the time taken to coagulate, and the chemical measurement of the constituents of blood.

BLOOD TRANSFUSION. Injection of blood into the circulation in the treatment of conditions resulting from loss or impairment of blood, such as haemophilia, shock due to injury, poisoning by carbon monoxide, etc. The first human-to-human B.T. was made in 1818. Practically all B.Ts. are now made, not as formerly directly from donor to patient, but with stored blood (treated with sodium citrate to prevent clotting). Unless used within 3 or 4 weeks, the stored blood has its red cells removed, and the remaining liquid is reduced to powder. This dried plasma is kept for emergency use. During the S.W.W. Birmingham Univ. developed a blood plasma substitute, prepared by the large-scale fermentation of sugar.

BLOOM, Claire (1931–). British actress. B. in London, she made her reputation in Shakespearian roles such as Ophelia and Juliet. Her films incl. *Richard III* and *The Brothers Karamazov.* In 1959–69 she was married to the actor Rod Steiger.

BLOOM, Ursula. Maiden name of the authoress Mrs. Gower Robinson. Dau. of a country cleric, she took to writing in 1918 on the death of her 1st husband

2 years after their marriage. Besides more than 300 romances, she has produced several attractive vols. of reminiscences beginning with *Victorian Vinaigrette* (1956), and a life of her father *Parson Extraordinary*.

BLOOMER, Amelia Jenks (1818–94). American dress reformer and supporter of temperance and women's rights. She advocated, c. 1849, the wearing of a short skirt with loose trousers gathered at the ankles, hence the name 'bloomers'.

BLOOMSBURY. Parish in W.C. London, England, between Gower Street and High Holborn. It contains London Univ. H.Q., the British Museum, and the Royal Academy of Dramatic Art. Following the F.W.W. B. was the home of a number of writers, artists, etc., and is popularly connected with a type of intellectual.

BLOW, John (1648–1708). English composer. He was organist at Westminster Abbey, wrote anthems and other church music, and a masque, *Venus and Adonis*.

BLOY (blwah), **Léon-Marie** (1846–1917). French author. He became a clerk in Paris in 1863. Converted to mystic Catholicism c. 1870, he achieved a considerable reputation by his literary lampoons, etc., by 1890. Indifferent to politics and philosophy, and believing in the imminence of the Kingdom of Heaven, he taught the need for sharing in Christ's suffering. He wrote biographies, the novels *La Femme pauvre* and *Le Désespéré* and revealing Journals.

BLÜCHER (blükh'er), **Gebhard Leberecht von** (1742–1819). Prussian general field marshal, popular as 'Marshal Forward'. He took an active part in the patriotic movement, and in the War of Liberation defeated the French as C.-in-C. at Leipzig (1813), crossed the Rhine to Paris (1814), and was made prince of Wahlstadt (Silesia). In 1815 he was defeated by Napoleon at Ligny, but shared with Wellington the triumph of Waterloo.

BLUE. A sporting honour at Oxford and Cambridge, awarded to students representing their univ. in some game or form of athletics. It consists of a strip of light or dark B. ribbon, and is said to have originated with the 2nd Oxford and Cambridge boat-race in 1836.

BLUEBEARD. 'Hero' of a popular tale, best known from Charles Perrault's version (c. 1697). He murdered 6 wives in turn, who disobeyed his command not to enter a locked room, but was himself slain before he could kill the 7th. In Brittany B. has been identified with Gilles de Rais.

BLUEBELL. Name given in Scotland to the harebell (*Campanula rotundifolia*), and in England to the wild hyacinth (*Endymion nutans*), belonging to the family Liliaceae.

BLUEBIRD. An American bird (*Sialia sialis*) affectionately regarded as the herald of spring. Slightly larger than a robin, it has a similar reddish breast, the upper plumage being sky-blue. The song is sweet. *See* illus. p. 146.

BLUEBOTTLE. Species of fly (*Musca vanitaria*) of the order Diptera, allied to the house fly, but distinguished by its blue abdomen and loud hum.

It closely resembles other species, e.g. the larger blow-fly (*Sarcophaga carnaria*), which has a brownish-grey abdomen. All lay their eggs in animal flesh, either in carcases or wounds of the living beast.

BLUEBUCK (*Cephalophus monticola*). S. African antelope, only 13 in. high, and blue-grey in colour. It is related to the duikers, and is common in Natal.

Larva and pupa of the blue-bottle fly.

BLUEBIRD. A male alighting at its nest-hole, usually in a hollow tree, with food – often insects caught in the air, worms, larvae, fruit or seeds. *Photo: G. Ronald Austing.*

BLUECOAT BOYS. *See* CHRIST'S HOSPITAL.

BLUE GRASS. Dense, spreading grass which grows in clumps. The blue-tinged *Poa compressa* provides fine pasture for horses, and Kentucky, where it is abundant, is known as the B.G. state. Another species is totally green.

BLUE RIBAND. Term denoting the highest distinction in any particular sphere, derived from the B.R. of the Order of the Garter. The B.R. of the Turf is the Derby. The B.R. of the Atlantic is held by the vessel making the fastest crossing in both E. and W. directions: the *Queen Mary* 1938–52, and the *United States* from 1952. In 1935 an actual international trophy was presented by Harold K. Hales (1868–1942), but this was refused by the Cunard-White Star Co. and remained in abeyance until accepted by the United States Lines in 1952. It is awarded by an international committee.

BLUES. Type of popular jazz or rag-time music that consists of 3 lines of verse, the 2nd of which is a repetition, usually with variations, on the first, giving the singer time to improvise the last line. B. originated among the American Negroes, and the words are melancholy. Composers of B. include J. A. Carpenter, G. Gershwin, Milhaud, D. Ellington and W. C. Handy. Blues are primarily secular, e.g. the classic renderings of Bessie Smith (1894–1937), the religious equivalent being 'gospel' (Mahalia Jackson, q.v.), but a blending was achieved by blind, Georgia-born Ray Charles after the S.W.W., and from this in the 1960s developed 'soul', the raw, emotionalised joy and pain of daily living, as in the songs of Aretha Franklin (1942–).

BLUE STOCKING. Disparaging term for a learned woman. It originated *c.* 1750 in London with the literary gatherings of Mrs. Montagu, which were attended by Benjamin Stillingfleet, who wore unfashionable blue worsted stockings. Most famous of later B.Ss. is Hannah More.

BLUM, Léon (1872–1950). French Jewish statesman. He was converted to Socialism by the Dreyfus affair (1899), and in 1936 he became first Socialist Prime Minister of France. Again Premier for a few weeks in 1938, he was imprisoned in 1942 for his supposed responsibility for the fall of France, but released by the Allies in 1945. He was again Premier for a few weeks in 1946.

BLUNDEN, Edmund (1896–). English poet. B. in Kent, he served in France and Belgium in the F.W.W., and published the prose *Undertones of War* (1928). Ed. at Oxford, he returned there as fellow and tutor 1931–43, was professor of English at the Univ. of Hong Kong 1953–64, and prof. of poetry at Oxford 1966–68. His poetry is that of a countryman, shows

the influence of Clare, and besides 2 collected volumes incl. *A Hong Kong House* (1962).

BLUNT, Wilfred Scawen (1840–1922). British poet and traveller. In 1869 he m. Lady Anne Noel, Byron's granddaughter, with whom he travelled in Arabia, Syria, Persia, and Mesopotamia. Becoming a supporter of Arab aspirations, he sympathized with the Egyptian national movement in 1881–2, visited India twice, and tried to enter Parliament as an advocate of Irish Home Rule. He wrote many anti-imperialist books, and his poems (collected 1914) and prose diaries (1919–20) show vigorous individuality.

BLYTH. English seaport (bor.) in Northumberland, with coalmines and a shipping trade in coal. It is 12 m. N.E. of Newcastle upon Tyne. Pop. (1961) 35,933.

BOA. Name given to a family (Boidae) of non-poisonous snakes, natives of both hemispheres, and loosely to other large snakes which kill their prey by constriction, such as the python. Most common is the boa constrictor, which is found in tropical S. and C. America, reaches a length of 10 or 12 ft., and feeds on small animals and birds.

BOADICEA. *See* BOUDICCA.

BOAR, Wild. Name given to several members of the pig family. Best known are the Crested W.B. of India (*Sus cristatus*), and the European W.B. (*Sus scrofa*), from which the domesticated breeds derive. The darkish brown or grey coat is made up of coarse bristles overlying underwool. The W.B. is sturdily built, being *c.* 4½ ft. long and 3 ft. high, and possesses formidable tusks. Usually neither species is aggressive, roots and berries forming their chief diet.

BOATBILL. Bird (*Cancroma cochlearia*) of the heron family (Ardeidae), native to tropical America. It resembles the night heron, but is placed in a separate genus because of its broad, flattened bill.

BOAT RACE. Rowing race between Oxford and Cambridge Univ. crews. First held in 1829 at Henley, it has normally been held since 1845 during the Easter vacation on the Thames from Putney to Mortlake, on a course of just under 4¼ m. Up to 1970 there were 116 races: Cambridge won 64, Oxford 51, and 1 was a dead heat.

BOBRUISK'. Town in White Russia S.S.R., U.S.S.R.; on the Beresina, it is an important railway junction and a timber centre. Pop. (1967) 117,000.

BOA CONSTRICTOR

BOCCACCIO (bok-kah'chō), **Giovanni** (1313–75). Italian poet. The son of a Florentine merchant, he came to Naples in 1328, where he abandoned trade for literature, and fell in love with the unfaithful 'Fiametta', who inspired his early work. Before returning to Florence in 1341 he had written *Filostrato* and *Teseide* (used by Chaucer in his *Troilus and Criseyde* and *Knight's Tale*), etc. His great work is the *Decameron*, containing 100 stories told by 10 young people seeking refuge in the country from the plague: narrative skill and characterization compensate for their licentiousness, and Shakespeare, Chaucer, Dryden, and Keats were later indebted to them. B. was a friend of Petrarch, and sponsored Leon Pilatus' translation of Homer.

BOCCHERINI (bōkārē'nē), **Luigi** (1743–1805). Italian composer. Having studied in Rome, he was a great success in Paris in 1768, and held posts as court composer in Prussia and Spain. An outstanding 'cello player, he composed some 350 instrumental works, an opera, oratorios, etc.

BOCHUM (bokh'oom). German town in the Ruhr industrial district of N. Rhine-Westphalia, between Essen and Dortmund. Its metallurgical industries made it a frequent target for British bombers during the S.W.W. Pop. (1966) 353,796.

BODE (bō'de), **Johann Elert** (1747–1826). German astronomer. He was director of the Berlin observatory, and propounded *Bode's Law*, which states that the proportionate distances of the planets from the sun out to Uranus are found by adding 4 to each term of the series 0, 3, 6, 12, 24, etc., if the asteroids be included between Mars and Jupiter. The law breaks down for Neptune and Pluto, however.

BODENSEE. German name of LAKE CONSTANCE.

BODH GAYA. Another form of BUDDH GAYA.

BODIN (bodan'), **Jean** (1530–96). French political thinker. He became an attorney in Paris, and in 1574 pub. a tract explaining that prevalent high prices were due to the influx of precious metals from the New World. His *De la république* (1576) has been described as originating political economy.

BODLEY, Sir Thomas (1545–1613), English diplomat and scholar. He was employed by Queen Elizabeth on diplomatic missions, but retired in 1597, and began to restore the library at Oxford (originally founded by Humphrey, duke of Gloucester, in the 15th cent.), which was opened in 1602, and is named after him the Bodleian Library. He was knighted in 1604.

BODMIN. Co. tn. (bor.) of Cornwall, England, 30 m. W.N.W. of Plymouth. B. was a great agricultural market. Pop. (1961) 6,209. *B. Moor* to the N.E. is a granitic area, culminating in Brown Willy (1,375 ft.).

BODONI (bōdō'nē), **Giambattista** (1740–1813). Italian printer, who managed the printing-press of the duke of Parma and produced books, chiefly editions of the classics, that were magnificent specimens of the craft.

BOEHM (böm), **Sir Joseph Edgar** (1834–90). Sculptor. B. at Vienna of Hungarian parentage, he settled in England. Among his statues are those of Gordon in St. Paul's Cathedral and Wellington at Hyde Park Corner.

BOEHME (bö'me), **Jakob** (1575–1624). German mystic. He became a shoemaker in Görlitz, and although persecuted as a heretic after the appearance of his mystical *Aurora* (1612) continued to write theosophical treatises, which won followers in Germany, Holland, and England. He claimed divine revelation of the unity of everything and nothing, and found in God's 'eternal nature' a principle to reconcile evil and good.

BOEOTIA (bē-ō'shya). Ancient district of central Greece. The chief city was Thebes. The modern prefecture of B., pop. (1961) 114,474, has Levadeia as its cap.

BOER (bor; Dutch, farmer). Dutch settler in S. Africa. For BOER WARS *see* SOUTH AFRICA.

BOERHAAVE (boor'hahve), **Hermann** (1668–1738). Dutch physician. He was prof. of medicine, botany, and chemistry at the Univ. of Leyden, and made it the leading school of medicine.

BOETHIUS (bō-ēthius), **Anicius Manlius Severinus** (c. 480–524). Roman statesman and philosopher. He rose to high rank under the Gothic king Theodoric, but was eventually imprisoned on suspicion of treason, and executed at Pavia. While in prison he wrote his *De Consolatione Philosophiae*.

BOGART, Humphrey (1899–1957). American actor, celebrated in 'tough' parts. Entering films in 1930, he appeared in *The Petrified Forest, The Maltese Falcon, The Caine Mutiny*, and others.

BOGHAZKOI (bo'gahzkö'ē). Turkish village in Asia Minor, c. 90 m. E. of Ankara. It is on the site of Hattusas, the ancient Hittite capital about. c. 1640 B.C. Thousands of tablets discovered by excavations here over a number of years by the German Oriental Society revealed, when their cuneiform writing was deciphered by Bedrich Hrozný (1879–1952), a great deal about the customs, religion, and history of the Hittite people. Pop. (est.) 1,000.

BOGNOR REGIS (rē'jis). English seaside resort (U.D.) in Sussex, 66 m. S.W. of London, which owes the Regis in its name to the convalescent visit of George V in 1929. Pop. (1961) 28,144.

BOGORODSK. Name until c. 1930 of NOGINSK.

BOGOTÁ (bōgōtah'). Cap. of the S. American rep. of Colombia, on the edge of the plateau some 8,500 ft. above sea-level. Founded in 1538, it is an archiepiscopal see with a cathedral, 1563, and several univs. Industries include iron and steel, tobacco, textiles, clothing, leather, etc. Pop. (1964) 1,697,311.

BOHEMIA. Historic kingdom of Central Europe, consisting of a square block of highland bounded by the Bohemian Forest, the Erzgebirge, the Sudeten Mts., and the Moravian Heights, and drained by the Vltava River, on which Prague stands.

The name B. derives from the Celtic Boii, its earliest-known inhabitants. By the 5th cent. Czechs and other Slav peoples had conquered the country, which became Christian by the end of the 9th cent. The Bohemian princes were tributary to the emperor, but the native dynasty became extinct in 1306, and the crown passed to the House of Luxumburg, the 2nd of whom, Charles I (1346–78) was also emperor as Charles IV, and founded Prague Univ. in 1348. Under his son Wenzel (1378–1419) there was a strong reforming movement led by John Huss, whose burning at the stake caused a civil war. In 1457 George of Poděbrad became king, the first native ruler since 1306. He was followed by Vladislav of Poland, whose son Louis was killed at Mohács in 1526; the archduke Ferdinand of Austria was then elected king, and henceforth until 1918 B. was under Habsburg rule. The Hussites supported the Reformation, and a revolt in 1618 precipitated the Thirty Years War. The Battle of the White Mountain in 1620 ended Czech freedom. In 1918 B. became a province of the new rep. of Czechoslovakia; it was abolished as an administrative division in 1949.

BOHLEN (bō'len), **Charles Eustis** (1904–). American diplomat. Ed. at Harvard, he entered the Foreign Service in 1929, and in 1945 accompanied Roosevelt to the Yalta conference. Ambassador to the U.S.S.R. 1953–7, he was ambassador to France 1963–8, then Deputy Under-Sec. for Political Affairs 1968–9.

BOHR (bōr), **Niels** (1885–1962). Danish physicist; Nobel prizewinner 1922. After work with Rutherford at Manchester, he became prof. at Copenhagen in 1916 and founded the Institute of Theoretical Physics there, of which he became director, in 1920. He fled from the Nazis in the S.W.W. and took part in work on the atomic bomb in the U.S.A.

BOIARDO (bōyahrdō), **Matteo Maria,** count (1434–94). Ital. poet, famed for his *Orlando Innamorato* (1486).

BOIL. Inflamed nodule beneath the skin, formed by the infection of the root of a hair by a staphylococcus. Bs. are only likely to occur when general resistance is low, as in those who are fat, overfed, diabetic, or have mild blood-poisoning.

BOILEAU (bwalo'), **Nicolas** (1636–1711). French poet and critic. Called to the bar in 1656, he turned to literature on receiving a legacy. After a series of keen contemporary satires, his *Epîtres* (1669–77) led to his joint appointment with Racine as historiographer royal in 1677. Later works include *L'Art poétique* (1674), the mock-heroic *Le Lutrin* (1674–83), and a translation of Longinus *On the Sublime* (1674). The close friend of Racine, Molière, and La Fontaine, he was elected to the Academy in 1684.

BOILING POINT. For any given liquid, the temperature at which the application of heat raises the temperature of the liquid no further, but converts it to vapour. The B.P. of water under normal pressure is 100°C. or 212°F. The lower the pressure the lower the B.P. and vice versa.

BOIS-LE-DUC (bwah-le-dük). French form of 's Hertogenbosch.

BOITO (bō-ē-tō), **Arrigo** (1842–1918). Italian poet and composer. He wrote the operas *Mefistofele* (1868) and *Nerone*, and the libretti for his friend Verdi's *Otello* and *Falstaff*.

BOKHARA. Another form of BUKHARA.

BOLDREWOOD (bōl'der-), **Rolf** (1826–1915). Pseudonym of the Australian writer Thomas Alexander Browne. B. in London, he was taken to Australia in 1830, where he became a pioneer squatter, etc., and until 1895 was police magistrate in the goldfields. His novels of adventure include *Robbery under Arms* (1888), and *Miner's Right* (1890).

BOLĒ'TUS. Genus of European fungi, resembling mushrooms, and belonging to the Basidiomycetes. *B. edulis* is edible, but some species are poisonous.

BOLEYN (bool'in), **Anne** (*c.* 1507–36). Second queen of Henry VIII. The daughter of Sir Thomas B., she was m. to the king in 1533, and in the same year became the mother of the future Queen Elizabeth. Accused of adultery and incest, she was beheaded.

BOLINGBROKE, Henry St. John, visct. (1678–1751). British statesman and philosopher. He entered parliament as a Tory in 1701, became Sec. of War (1704–8), and For. Sec. in Harley's ministry in 1710.

ANNE BOLEYN
Artist unknown. *Photo:* N.P.G.

He was raised to the peerage in 1712, and in 1713 negotiated the Peace of Utrecht. He planned the restoration of the 'Old Pretender', and secured Harley's dismissal in 1714, but his plans were ruined by Anne's death only 5 days later and George I's peaceful succession, and he fled to France in 1715. Allowed to return in 1723, he worked for Walpole's downfall, but after 1739 lost all influence. His political writings, which influenced Disraeli, include *The Patriot King* and *Letters on the Study and Use of History*.

BOLIVAR (bōlē'vahr), **Simón** (1783–1830). S. American soldier-statesman, known as the Liberator. B. in Venezuela, he joined the patriots working for Venezuelan independence, and was sent to Britain in 1810 as the representative of their govt. Forced to flee to Colombia in 1812, he joined the revolutionists there, and invaded Venezuela in 1813. A bloody civil war followed and in 1814 B. had to withdraw to Colombia, and eventually to the W. Indies, whence he raided the Spanish-American coasts. In 1817 he returned to Venezuela to set up a provisional govt., crossed into Colombia (1819), where he defeated the Spaniards, and returning to Angostura proclaimed the rep. of Colombia, comprising Venezuela, New Granada, and Quito (Ecuador), with himself as president. The independence of Venezuela was finally secured in 1821, and in 1822 B. liberated Ecuador. B. was invited to lead the Peruvian struggle in 1823; and final victory having been won by Sucre at Ayacucho in 1824, he turned his attention to framing a constitution. In 1825 the independence of Upper Peru was proclaimed, which adopted the name Bolivia in B.'s honour.

BOLIVIA. Land-locked rep. of S. America. The main chains of the Andes run through the W. part, enclosing a great tableland at an elevation of 12,000 ft.

in which lie Lake Titicaca (only part of which is in Bolivia) and Lake Poopo. This region, on account of its height, is cold; it is inhabited chiefly by Sierra Indians engaged in agriculture and mining. The temperate region is formed by valleys between 4,500 and 7,500 ft., where wheat and maize are grown. Towards the E. are hot plains, densely wooded and sparsely populated, but being increasingly developed for rice, sugar, and cotton. The chief rivers are headstreams of the Amazon.

The basis of B.'s economy since colonial times has been the mining industry; silver was formerly the principal product, but today tin occupies first place. In the S., at Sanandita and Camiri, petroleum is worked. The chief railway connects La Paz with Antofagasta, on the Pacific coast of Chile. About 1,000 m. of the Pan-American Highway are in B. Air transport is costly but useful in reaching remote parts.

La Paz, the seat of govt., is situated more than 12,000 ft. above sea-level; the official cap. is Sucre; other towns are Cochabamba, Oruro, Potosi, and Santa Cruz. The pop. is principally R.C., but the Church was disestablished 1961. The official language is Spanish; the Indians speak Quichua or other Indian languages.

History. Before the Spanish Conquest in the 16th cent., B. formed part of the Inca empire. Independence was achieved in 1825, and the country was named in honour of Simón Bolivar, whose lieutenant, Sucre, was the first President. Originally possessing a narrow Pacific coast line, B. lost this in 1883 after its defeat by Chile. B.'s political history is troubled: from 1880 Simon Patino, the 'mining king', was for many years dominant in the state; and there was a disastrous war in the Chaco between B. and Paraguay (1932–5), the boundary line being fixed by arbitration only in 1938. Under President German Busch (1937–9) the oil industry was nationalized, and under Villaroel (1943 to 1946, when he was lynched) important social and economic reforms were initiated. A constitution adopted in 1947 provided for a directly elected President, National Congress and Chamber of Deputies, but in 1969 a 'leftist' military govt. overthrew the pres. Area 424,000 sq. m.; pop. (1964) 4,334,121.

BOLLANDISTS. Body of Belgian Jesuits who edit the *Acta Sanctorum*, the standard collection of saints'

BOLIVIA. Across Lake Titicaca the clear air enables mountains fifty miles away to be seen in detail. On the shore, alongside already completed craft, tortora reeds are piled ready for making into balsa rafts. Constructed in three days, they will last as many years, and are used by the Indians chiefly for punting in the shallow waters of the lake, though sometimes as sailboats.   *Photo:* Bell, Howarth Ltd.

lives. They are named after JOHN BOLLAND (1596–1665), who pub. the first 2 vols. in 1643.

BOLL-WEEVIL. Small American beetle (*Anthonomus grandis*) of the family Curculionidae: the female lays eggs in the unripe pods or 'bolls' of the cotton plant, and on these the larva feeds, causing great destruction.

BOLOGNA (bōlō′nyah). City of N. Italy, at the foot of the Apennines on the Reno and Savena, 50 m. N. of Florence. The city has 2 leaning towers, a cathedral, a univ. (founded in the 11th cent.), and many industries, principally concerned with foodstuffs. B. was the site of an Etruscan town, later of a Roman colony, became a rep. in the 12th cent., came under Papal rule in 1506, and in 1860 was united with Italy. Pop. (1966) 481,740.

BOLSHEVISM (Russ. *bolshinstvo*, a majority). Doctrines of the extreme Socialists or Communists who effected the Russian Revolution of 1917. The word came into use following a conference of Continental and British Socialists held in London in 1903, at which there was a split between the Russian Social Democratic party led by Lenin, and the moderate delegates. The former being in the majority were called *Bolsheviki*, and their opponents the *Mensheviki* (Russ. *menshinstvo*, a minority). Since 1952 Bolshevik is no longer the official alternative for Communist.

BOLSOVER (bōl′zover, or bow′zer). English coalmining centre in Derbyshire, 6 m. E. of Chesterfield. B. dates from the 11th cent. There are also limestone quarries nearby. Pop. (1961) 11,770.

BOLTON. Important textile-making town (co. bor.) in Lancs, England, 11 m. N.W. of Manchester. It became a co. bor. in 1888. Pop. (1961) 160,887.

BOLTON ABBEY. Ruins of a priory (begun *c.* 1150) on the r. Wharfe, 6 m. E. of Skipton, Yorks, England; name also of the neighbouring village.

BOLTZMANN, Ludwig (1844–1906). Austrian physicist and authority on the kinetic theory of gases. B.'s constant **k** (1·375 × 10⁻¹⁶ ergs per degree) is the ratio of the mean total energy of a molecule to its absolute temperature, and the principle of the equipartition of energy is known as B.'s law.

BOLZANO (boltsah′no). Town in Italy, in Trentino-Alto Adige region, on the Isarco at its confluence with the Talvera; formerly in Austria. Pop. (1966) 100,466.

BO′MA. Town in the Rep. of Congo (Kinshasa) on the estuary of the r. Congo, 55 m. from the Atlantic. It was the oldest European settlement in the Belgian Congo, of which it was the cap. until 1929. Pop. *c.* 11,000.

BOMB. An explosive projectile used in warfare. Aerial bombing started in the F.W.W. when the German Air Force carried out 103 raids on Britain, dropping 269 tons of bombs. In the S.W.W. nearly twice this tonnage was dropped on London in a single night, and at the peak of the Allied air offensive against Germany more than 10 times this tonnage was

BOMB. Extensive atom bomb tests were carried out by U.S. forces at Bikini atoll in the Pacific in 1946. On July 1 a bomb was exploded at a height of 1,000–1,500 feet above the assembled test fleet of 75 warships, and on July 25 a bomb was exploded under water. Beneath the vast atomic cloud the warships look like toys and the battleship *Arkansas* was sunk by the blast.
Photo: Keystone Press Agency Ltd.

regularly dropped in successive nights, on one target. Raids in which nearly 1,000 heavy bombers participated were frequent and the same town might be subjected to this terrible punishment by day and night.

They were delivered either in 'precision' or 'area' attacks and great advances were made in 'blind' bombing, in which the target is located solely by instruments and is not visible through a bomb-sight. In 1939 B.s were commonly 250 and 500 lb. but by the end of the conflict the 10-tonner was being produced, though even these paled beside the atom B. This derives its explosive force from nuclear fission as a result of a neutron chain reaction; 3 were exploded during the S.W.W.: 1st a test explosion on 16 July 1945, at Alamogordo, New Mexico, U.S.A.; then on 6 Aug. the 1st to be used in actual warfare was dropped over Hiroshima (q.v.) and 3 days later another over Nagasaki. These were 'nominal', i.e. nominally equal in destructive power to 20,000 tons of T.N.T. Russia 1st detonated an atom B. in 1949 and Britain in 1952 (in the Monte Bello Islands off Australia). Later developments have incl. the fusion or hydrogen bomb (q.v.), and by the 1960s intercontinental 100-megaton nuclear warheads could be produced (5,000 times more powerful than those of the S.W.W.) and the U.S.A. and U.S.S.R. between them possessed a stockpile sufficient to destroy all mankind. *See* FALLOUT.

Methods of delivery have also changed since Germany pioneered the V1 flying bomb and V2 rocket bomb, so that in the 1960s it was recognized that the era of bombers with free-falling bombs was over, and that future devel pment would lie with missiles launched from aircraft, land sites or submarines. The danger of such nuclear weapons naturally increases with the number of nations possessing the ability to produce them (France and China became nuclear powers in 1960 and 1964 respectively), and the possibility of 'policing' states to check on their testing of bombs has been complicated by the development of underground testing.

A non-proliferation treaty was signed in 1968 by U.K., U.S.A., U.S.S.R. and 56 other countries, not incl. France and China.

BOMBAY. Former presidency, later prov., of British India. It lay along the W. coast of the peninsula between Kutch and Mysore, and when incorporated in the Dominion of India in 1947 was interspersed by a number of semi-independent princely states which had been absorbed into the prov. by 1950. The Kathiawar peninsula was excluded from the state of Bombay constituted within the Rep. of India in 1950; as reconstituted in 1956, Bombay state re-absorbed Kathiawar and had added to it some lands in the E., but lost the area S. roughly of a line from Kolhapur to Sholapur cities to the state of Mysore. In 1960 this state of B. was divided, on a linguistic basis, into the 2 new states of Gujarat and Maharashtra (qq.v.). The city of B. was cap. of the presidency, the prov. and the states of B.

BOMBAY. Cap. and chief port of Maharashtra state, Rep. of India. B. occupies the former B. Island, joined by reclamation to Salsette Island to the N., with suburbs spreading northwards on Salsette. The great harbour lies on the E. of the city, facing the mainland, here some 7 m. away. Prominent features are the waterfront Gateway built to commemorate the landing of George V in 1911, the Univ. (founded 1857), Victoria railway terminus, and the General Post Office.

B. handles much of India's trade, and is the centre of the cotton and textile industries: other activities include dyeing, tanning, metal-working, banking, shipping, and engineering.

B. was founded in the 13th cent., came under Mogul rule, was occupied by Portugal in 1530, and passed to Britain in 1662 as part of Catherine of Braganza's wedding dowry. Pop. of Greater B. (1961) 4,146,491; area 91 sq. m.

BOMBOIS (bombwah'), **Camille** (1883–   ). French painter. Son of a barge-owner, he worked as a farm

BOMBAY. The Flora Fountain strikes a welcome note of coolness in this typical fine wide thoroughfare. Occasionally loads are still carried peasant-style on the head, but most of the hurrying white-clad figures are modern-style office workers.
Courtesy of High Commissioner for India.

labourer, and then joined a circus as a wrestler, later working as a navvy. He is self-taught and his circus scenes and landscapes have a naïvely attractive strength.

BONA. Another form of BÔNE.

BŌ'NA FĪ'DE (Lat. in good faith). Legal phrase signifying that a contract is undertaken without intentional misrepresentation.

BO'NAPARTE. Corsican family, originally of Italian origin, from whom Napoleon I (q.v.) was descended. Napoleon's father **Carlo B.** (1746–85), was a lawyer of Ajaccio, Corsica, and had a large family by his wife Letizia Ramolino (1750–1836), who joined Napoleon in Paris in 1799, and lived with him in Elba. Among their other children were **Joseph B.** (1768–1844), whom Napoleon made king of Naples in 1806, and of Spain (1808–13), and who fled to the U.S.A. on Napoleon's final surrender; **Lucien B.** (1775–1840), whose masterly handling of the Council of Five Hundred on 10 Nov. 1799 helped to secure Napoleon's success; **Louis B.** (1778–1846), whom Napoleon made governor of Paris in 1805 and king of Holland 1806–10; his son Charles Louis Napoleon became emperor of the French as Napoleon III (q.v.); **Caroline B.** (1782–1839), who m. Joachim Murat (q.v.) in 1800; and **Jerome B.** (1784–1860), who became king of Westphalia in 1807, and under Napoleon III was made marshal of France and president of the Senate. A grandson of Jerome by his first wife, Elizabeth Patterson of Baltimore, was Charles Joseph B. (1851–1921), Attorney-General of U.S.A. in the Roosevelt cabinet 1906–9. Jerome's son by his 2nd wife, Catherine of Württemburg, Napoleon Joseph Charles (1822–91), known as 'Plon-Plon', held office under Napoleon III, and his grandson Louis Jerome (b. 1914) is the present Bonaparte 'pretender'.

BO'NAR, Horatius (1808–89). Scottish divine (Free Church), and author of many hymns, including 'I heard the voice of Jesus say'.

BONAVENTURA (bōnahventōō'rah), **St.** (John of Fidanza) (1221–74). Italian R.C. theologian,

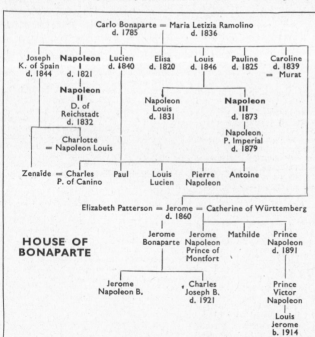

HOUSE OF BONAPARTE

Carlo Bonaparte = Maria Letizia Ramolino
d. 1785 — d. 1836

- Joseph, K. of Spain, d. 1844
- Napoleon I, d. 1821
  - Napoleon II, D. of Reichstadt, d. 1832
  - Charlotte = Napoleon Louis
- Lucien, d. 1840
  - Zenaïde = Charles, P. of Canino
  - Paul
  - Louis Lucien
  - Pierre Napoleon
  - Antoine
- Elisa, d. 1820
- Louis, d. 1846
  - Napoleon Louis, d. 1831
  - Napoleon III, d. 1873
    - Napoleon, P. Imperial, d. 1879
- Pauline, d. 1825
- Caroline, d. 1839 = Murat

Elizabeth Patterson = Jerome = Catherine of Württemberg
d. 1860

- Jerome Bonaparte
  - Jerome Napoleon B.
- Jerome Napoleon, Prince of Montfort
  - Charles Joseph B., d. 1921
- Mathilde
- Prince Napoleon, d. 1891
  - Prince Victor Napoleon
    - Louis Jerome, b. 1914

canonized in 1482. He entered the Franciscan order in 1243, became professor of theology at Paris, and in 1256 general of his order. In 1273 he was created cardinal and bishop of Albano, and d. at the 2nd Council of Lyons. His eloquent writings earned him the title of the 'Seraphic Doctor'.

BONDFIELD, Margaret Grace (1873–1953). British Socialist. From being a shop assistant she became a trade union organizer among women workers. She was a Labour M.P. (1923–4 and 1926–31), and was the 1st woman to enter the Cabinet – as Min. of Labour, 1929–31.

BONE, Sir Muirhead (1876–1953). British etcher. Famed for scaffolding subjects, such as his 'Great Gantry, Charing Cross', in the B.M., he was an official artist to the forces during the F. and S.W.W.s. His brother, Sir David William B. (1874–1959), a master mariner, wrote many books on life at sea.

BÔNE (bohn). Algerian seaport, in Constantine prov., 260 m. E. of Algiers. One of the best harbours on the African coast, it has industrial plants, flour mills, etc.; railway communication with Algiers and Touggart; and an airfield. It was occupied by the French in 1832, but since Algerian independence has been known by the Arabic form of its name Annaba— city of jujube trees. Pop. (1967) 165,000.

BONE. Hard animal tissue consisting of a network of fibres impregnated with salts of lime. A bone is a portion of B. tissue having a definite size and shape and forming part of the skeleton. Human beings have *c*. 200 distinct Bs. which form the hard core of the body, preserving its shape, and providing fixed points from which the muscles can work, and to which ligaments are anchored.

B. forms early in the unborn child. Plates of B., e.g. those forming the skull, develop from membrane; long Bs. from cartilage or gristle. B. is formed by the cells enlarging and depositing fine granules of phosphate and carbonate of lime in the spaces between them. The original membrane or cartilage disintegrates and is carried away. Experiments have been made in setting broken Bs. with plastic.

BONHAM-CARTER, Lady Violet. *See* ASQUITH OF YARNBURY, Lady.

BONHEUR (bonör'), **Rosa** (1822–99). French animal painter, who exhibited at the Paris Salon from 1841. Her best work is 'Horse Fair' (1853).

BONIFACE (bon'ifās). Name of 9 popes. The most notable was B. VIII (*c*. 1228–1303). Succeeding to the office in 1294, he exempted the clergy from taxation by the secular government by a bull of 1296. Philip the Fair of France and Henry III of England forced him to give way by excluding the clergy from certain lay privileges. His bull of 1302 asserting the complete temporal and spiritual power of the papacy was equally ineffective.

BONIFACE, St. (680–754). 'Apostle of Germany'. Originally named Wynfrith, he was b. in Devon and became a Benedictine monk. After a preliminary missionary journey to Frisia in 716, he was given the task of evangelizing Germany by Pope Gregory II in 718, and was appointed archbishop of Mainz in 746, but returned to Frisia 754 and suffered martyrdom near Dockum.

BONIN (bōnēn') and **Volcano Islands.** Island groups in the Pacific, *c*. 800 m. E. of the Ryukyu Is. The **B. Islands** number 27 (in 3 groups), largest being Chichijima: area 40 sq. m.; pop. (1968) *c*. 200. The **Volcano Islands** number 3, incl. Iwojima, scene of some of the fiercest fighting of the S.W.W.; total area 11 sq. m. The B. and V. Is. were under U.S. control, following the 1952 peace treaty, until returned to Japan in 1968.

BONINGTON, Richard Parkes (1801–28). British painter. His family settled in France in 1817 and he rapidly developed a talent for seascapes and landscapes in watercolour. In the last few years of his life

he also painted in oils, and excelled in depicting the transitory effects of light. The Wallace Collection has a fine selection of his work. He d. of tuberculosis.

BONITO (bonē'tō). Popular name of a smaller species of tunny not exceeding 3 ft. in length (*Thynnus pelamys*), belonging to the mackerel family (Scombridae), and common in tropical seas.

BONN. Cap. of the W. German Federal Rep. 15 m. S.S.E. of Cologne, on the left bank of the Rhine. An important Roman station, it was captured by the French in 1794, annexed by them in 1801, and was allotted to Prussia in 1815. Remarkable features are the cathedral (begun 11th cent.), the univ., the observatory, and Beethoven's birthplace. Industries have grown up in the suburbs, and in the S.W.W. B. was frequently bombed. B. was chosen W. German cap. in 1949. Pop. (1966) 138,515.

BONN. The cathedral. *Courtesy of the German Tourist Information Bureau.*

BONNARD (bonahr'), **Pierre** (1867–1947). French painter. One of the Nabi group led by Maurice Denis, he made an idea rather than an object his starting point, using colour with a decorative effect in street scenes of Paris, landscapes and interiors with figures.

BONSAI (bonsī). Dwarf tree cultivation. Formerly limited to Japan, which originated the practice, it has in recent years spread increasingly to the West. Collectors will pay as much as £1,000 for specimens which may be several hundred years old.

BOOK. Permanent portable written record. Early substances used in B.-making include leaves, bark, linen, silk, clay, leather, and papyrus. Early in the Christian era (*c*. 100–150), the codex or paged book, as against the roll, began to be adopted. Vellum was generally used for B. production by the beginning of the 4th cent. and its use lasted until the 15th, when it was superseded by paper.

BOOKBINDING. B. only emerged as a distinct art when printing made less expensive materials than precious metals and wood essential. The principal ornament of leather B., gold tooling, was probably introduced to Europe from the East by the Venetian Aldus Manutius, and adopted in England by Thomas Berthelet, binder to Henry VIII. Famous binders include Nicholas and Clovis Eve (16th cent.), Le Gascon, Samuel Mearne (17th cent.), A. M. Padeloup, N. D. Derôme, Roger Paynes (18th cent.), Francis Bedford (19th cent.), and T. J. Cobden-Sanderson, C. Ricketts (20th cent.). Modern cloth binding common to England and America was first introduced by Leighton in 1822, but since the S.W.W. synthetic bindings have been increasingly employed.

BOOKKEEPING. Keeping books of account, i.e., records of commercial transactions, in a systematic and accurate manner (*see* ACCOUNTANCY). The earliest-known work on double entry B. was by Luca Pacioli, pub. in Venice in 1494. The method which he advocated had, however, been practised by the Italian merchants for several hundred years before that date. The first English work on the subject, by the schoolmaster Hugh Oldcastle, appeared in 1543. Double entry is a system which recognizes the duality inherent in every business transaction, each item being entered in the books twice – as debit and as credit.

BOOK OF THE DEAD. Ancient book of the Egyptians, known to them as the *Book of Coming Forth by Day*, and forming a guide-book for the deceased through Hades to the kingdom of Osiris. It is extant in 3 main versions, known as the Heliopolitan,

Theban, and Saïte, and the oldest copies belong to the 3rd millennium B.C.

BOO'MERANG. Hand-thrown, curved, wooden missile used chiefly by Australian aborigines, usually 2–3 ft. long, and weighing about ¼ lb. One type returns after striking its objective, and a good thrower may achieve a 145 ft. return throw.

BOOLE, George (1815–64). British mathematician. Self-educated, he in 1847 pub. *The Mathematical Analysis of Logic* which estab. the basis of modern mathematical logic and was prof. at Queen's College, Cork, from 1849.

BOOT, Jesse. *See* TRENT.

BOOTH, Charles (1840–1916). British sociologist and shipowner. He conducted a remarkable investigation into the manner of living of the London poor, recorded in *Life and Labour of the People of London* (1891–1903). B. was also a pioneer in the old-age pensions movement.

BOOTH, John Wilkes (1839–65). American actor, who fired the shot which mortally wounded President Lincoln at Ford's Theatre, Washington, on April 14, 1865. He escaped with a broken leg, and was shot dead in a barn in Virginia on his refusal to surrender.

BOOTH, William (1829–1912). 'General' of the Salvation Army. B. at Nottingham, the son of a builder, he experienced religious conversion at the age of 15. For some time he did open-air preaching for the local Methodists, and for some years was a full-time minister of the Methodist New Connexion, but in 1861 he became an itinerant evangelist. In 1865 he founded in Whitechapel the Christian Mission which in 1878 became the Salvation Army. *In Darkest England, and the Way Out* (1890) contained proposals for the physical and spiritual redemption of the great mass of 'down-and-outs'. His wife Catherine (1829–90) *née* Mumford, whom he m. in 1855, became a public preacher in *c.* 1860, initiating the ministry of women.

Their eldest son, **William Bramwell B.** (1856–1929) became chief of staff of the S.A. in 1880 and was General from 1912 until his deposition (1929). **Evangeline B.** (1865–1950), 7th child of General William B., was a prominent S.A. officer, and 1934–9 was General. She became a U.S. citizen.

BOOTHBY, Robert John Graham, baron (1900–   ). Scottish politician. Ed. at Eton and Magdalen Coll., Oxon, he became a Unionist M.P. in 1924 and was P.P.S. to Churchill 1926–9. An ardent advocate of Britain's entry into Europe, he was British delegate to the Consultative Assembly of the Council of Europe 1949–57. In 1953 he was created K.B.E. and a life peer in 1958. A rebel of radical tendencies, a superb speaker and a powerful personality in British politics, he has embodied his views in the autobiographical *I Fight to Live* (1947) and *My Yesterday, Your Tomorrow* (1962).

BOOTHE, Clare (1903–   ). American writer. B. in N.Y., she entered journalism, was managing editor of *Vanity Fair* (1933–4), and made a sensational success with her plays, espec. the mordant *The Women* (1936) and *Margin for Error* (1939); and the book *Europe in the Spring/European Spring* (1940). A Republican, she was a member of Congress 1943–7, ambassador to Italy 1953–7, and ambassador designate to Brazil in 1959, when she resigned because of a political dispute over her appointment. She married 1935 Henry Robinson Luce (d. 1967), head of Time-Life Inc. until 1964.

LORD BOOTHBY

BOOTLE. English town (co. bor.) in Lancs, adjoining Liverpool, on the estuary of the Mersey. It has extensive docks, shipyards, foundries and factories, and was heavily bombed from the air by the Germans in 1941. It became a co. bor. in 1889. Pop. (1961) 82,829.

BOOTLEGGING. In the early days of U.S.A. the sale of intoxicating liquor to the Red Indians was prohibited but unscrupulous traders conveyed to them bottles of liquor hidden in the legs of their jack-boots. Thus originated the term B. which came into universal vogue during the period 1920–33 of nation-wide prohibition in the U.S.A.

BORAGE (bur'ij). A plant (*Borago officinalis*) cultivated in Britain and occasionally found wild. It has small blue flowers and rough hairy leaves.

BORAH, William Edgar (1865–1940). American Republican politician. B. in Illinois, he was a senator for Idaho from 1906. He is remembered as an arch-isolationist, one of those chiefly responsible for America's repudiation of the League of Nations.

BORAS (-os). Market town in Sweden, 45 m. E. of Gothenburg. Iron ore is mined, and artificial silk and textiles are manufactured. Pop. (1966) 69,443.

BORAX. Hydrated sodium borate, found as soft whitish crystals or incrustations on the shores of hot springs and lakes associated with recent volcanoes. Formerly much of the world's B. came from a salt lake in Tibet, but now it is largely derived from the mineral colemanite. B. is employed in glazing pottery and enamel ware, in calico printing, etc.

BORDEAUX. French city, seaport, and cap. of Gironde dept., on the Garonne, 60 m. from the sea. Situated in the fertile plain of Médoc, famous for its vineyards, B. is the port for S.W. France and the centre of the wine trade of the area. It has shipbuilding yards and food factories; a cathedral of the 12th–14th cents.; and a univ. founded in 1441. B. was under the English crown for 3 cents. until 1453. In 1914 and again in 1940 the French govt. was moved there in the face of German invasion. The Germans made it a submarine base, and it suffered heavy Allied air raids in 1944. Pop. (1968) 266,662.

BORDEN, Sir Robert Laird (1854–1937). Canadian Conservative statesman. B. at Grand Pré, he became one of Canada's leading barristers. From 1896 onwards he sat in the Canadian House of Commons; was leader of his party from 1901, and P.M. from 1911 until 1920.

BORE. A tidal wave which rushes up certain rivers with great violence, forming a wall of water stretching across the stream, sometimes with disastrous results to river craft. It occurs chiefly at spring tide in rivers with a funnel-shaped estuary quickly narrowing upstream so that the wave is steadily concentrated and attains a considerable height, e.g. the Severn B. and the very much larger Bs. on the Amazon and Yangtze-Kiang.

BORG OLIVIER (bawzh oliver'), George (1911–   ). Maltese statesman. In 1950 he succeeded Dr. Mizzi as leader of the Nationalist party, and was P.M. 1950–5 and from 1962. He sought closer links with the Common Market and asked in 1962 for Malta's independence within the Commonwealth.

BORGES (bor'khes), **Jorge Luis** (1899–   ). Argentinian poet and author. Grandson of an Englishwoman, and the son of a lawyer, he was encouraged by his father to write, and headed a youthful anti-traditionalist (Ultra-iste) movement. Under Peron he was deprived of his post as librarian, but in 1961 became Director of the National Library, Buenos Aires, where he is also prof. of English literature at the univ. His reputation rests chiefly on his short stories, *Ficciones* (1962) being the 1st vol. to appear in translation. He is almost blind.

BORGIA (bor'jah), **Cesare** (1476–1507). Italian cardinal and ruler. Illegitimate son of Rodrigo B., who became pope as Alexander VI in 1492, he was made a cardinal by his father at the age of 17, but resigned the honour in exchange for the post of captain-general of the papacy. He led a number of successful campaigns against the Italian city-republics and was suspected of aiming at the establishment of his own kingdom. In 1503 he nearly d. of the poison that killed his father. Faced by a powerful coalition, B. went to Spain and then to Navarre, and was killed at the siege of Viana. Execrated for his crimes and vices, he was yet a patron of the arts and a ruler of unusual ability.

BORGIA, Lucrezia (1480–1519). 5th child of Pope Alexander VI and sister of Cesare B., she was first married at the age of 12 and again at 13. Both marriages were annulled in turn by her father, and at 18 she was married to a Neapolitan noble, who 2 years later was murdered at the instigation of Cesare B. Finally in 1501 she was found a 4th husband in Alfonso of Este, who became duke of Ferrara in 1505. She encouraged authors and artists such as Ariosto and Titian.

BO′RGLUM, Gutzon (1871–1941). American sculptor. Of Danish stock, he was b. in Idaho. He developed a gift for monumental works reminiscent of the achievements of ancient Egypt, e.g. a 6-ton marble head of Lincoln at Washington and a series of giant heads of Washington, Jefferson, Lincoln and T. Roosevelt carved on Mount Rushmore. S. Dakota.

BORIC ACID (H_3BO_3). Also called boracic acid; an acid formed by the simple combination of hydrogen and oxygen with the non-metallic element boron. It is a weak antiseptic.

BORIS III (1894–1943). Tsar of Bulgaria from 1918, when he succeeded his father, Ferdinand I. From 1934 he was virtual dictator until his sudden and mysterious death following a visit to Hitler. His son Simeon II was Tsar until deposed in 1946.

BORIS GODUNOV′ (1552–1605). Tsar of Russia rom 1598, when he succeeded Fedor, son of Ivan the Terrible. He was a capable but tyrannical ruler, and he d. during a revolt led by one who professed to be Dmitri, a brother of Fedor and the rightful Tsar, whom B. is supposed to have murdered.

BORLAUG (bor′lowg), **Norman** (1914–). American scientist of Norwegian extraction, 'father of the green revolution'. Sent to Mexico 1944 by the Rockefeller foundation, he developed high-yielding strains of dwarf wheat invaluable for use with fertilisers and irrigation in countries such as India and Pakistan. He was awarded a Nobel peace prize 1970.

BORMANN, Martin (1900–). German Nazi politician, b. at Halberstadt. He took part in the abortive Munich Putsch of 1923, and rose to high positions in the National Socialist Party. After Hess's flight to England he became 'party chancellor' in May 1941. His fate after the fall of Berlin in May 1945 is uncertain; but he was tried in absence at Nuremburg (1945–6) and sentenced to death.

BORN, Max (1882–1970). Physicist. B. in Germany, he became British in 1939, and was Tait prof. of natural philosophy at Edinburgh 1936–53. In 1954 he was awarded a joint Nobel Prize for his fundamental work in quantum mechanics.

BO′RNEO. Large island in the E. Indies. Politically it comprises Kalimantan (Indonesian), Sarawak and Sabah (*see* MALAYSIA), and Brunei (British protected) (qq.v.). The name B. is a variant of Brunei, first reached by the Portuguese discoverers who gave the name to the whole island. Most of B. is forest-clad and mountainous (highest peak Kinabalu, 13,450 ft., in N. B.), but it has wide alluvial plains and low marshy shores with silted estuaries. The pop. consists of (1) Dayak tribes of the interior, an Indonesian people, animists and formerly head-hunters, who live by the sale of jungle produce, grow rice and maize, and fish; (2) Malays, a later coastal people, Moslems, who plant

fish, and trade; and (3) Chinese who started gold-mining and are now farmers and tradesmen. Area 290,000 sq. m.; pop. (1960 est.) 5,750,000.

BORNHOLM. Danish island in the Baltic Sea, 22 m. S.E. of the nearest point of the Swedish coast. Rønne is the cap. Area 227 sq. m.; pop. (1965) 48,744.

BORNU (bornoo′). A country of Africa lying W. and S. of Lake Chad, once a powerful Negro kingdom, absorbed in 1901 into (British) Nigeria, (French) Niger, and (German) Cameroons. It slopes from S.W. to N.E., and ranges from desert in the N. to scrubland in the S. Lion, gazelle, and other wild animals are found. Much of the land is fertile, and ground-nuts, millet, yams, cotton, etc., are grown. The inhabitants, converted to Islam in the 13th cent., have remained Moslem. Maiduguri is the chief town in Nigerian Bornu, area 45,900 sq. m.; pop. (est.) 1,050,000.

BOROBUDUR. Largest Buddhist monument in Java, 15 m. N.W. of Jokjakarta, built between A.D. 750 and 850, and one of the architectural wonders of the world.

BORODI′N, Alexander Porfirievich (1834–87). Russian composer. B. at St. Petersburg, the illegitimate son of a Russian prince, he became by profession an expert in medical chemistry, but in his spare time devoted himself to music. His principal work is the opera *Prince Igor*; left unfinished, this was completed by Rimsky-Korsakov and Glazunov. B.'s works include symphonies, songs and chamber music, and are characterized by the use of traditional Russian themes.

BORODINO (borōdĕ′nō). Russian village, 70 m. W. of Moscow, on the road to Smolensk, where on Sept. 7 1812 Napoleon defeated the Russian army under Kutusov.

BO′RON. A non-metallic element: symbol B.; at. wt. 10·82; atomic number 5. It is a maroon-coloured powder, made by heating a mixture of its oxide with magnesium at a high temperature. Very important in reactor engineering, it absorbs neutrons, transmuting to lithium isotope. Boral (alloy with aluminium) is an excellent shield for neutrons, and B. steel is used for reactor control rods. Arc-made B. carbide is used for steel-cutting tools.

BOROUGH (bur′u). In the U.K. an area of local govt., probably dating from the 8th cent., though estab. in the present form by the Municipal Reform Act (1835). Each has an annually elected mayor, aldermen (elected for 6 years, half retiring every 3 years) and councillors (elected for 3 years, one-third retiring annually); the mayor and aldermen are elected by the other aldermen and councillors, and the councillors directly by popular vote.

Municipal or non-county Bs., which incl. some of the most ancient, differ little in actual powers from district councils, but county Bs. are in effect county councils with similar powers. Under the reform of local govt. (q.v.) planned in 1971 'borough-style' authorities with powers for most purposes disappeared. *See* LONDON. A parliamentary B. is an urban constituency, a unit of political representation.

In the U.S. the name B. largely ceased to be used after the War of Independence: an interesting survival is the administrative subdivision of N.Y. City into the 5 Bs. of Manhattan, The Bronx, Brooklyn, Queens and Richmond.

BOROUGH, The. *See* SOUTHWARK.

BORROMEO (borōmā′ō), **Carlo** (1538–84). R.C. saint and cardinal. B. at Arona of noble Ital. stock, he was created a cardinal and archbishop of Milan by his uncle Pope Pius IV in 1560. B. wound up the affairs of the Council of Trent, and largely drew up the catechism that contained its findings. He lived the life of an ascetic, and in 1578 founded the community later called the Oblate Fathers of St. Charles. He was canonized in 1610. His feast day is 4 Nov.

BORROW, George Henry (1803–81). British author and traveller. B. at E. Dereham, Norfolk, he was articled to a Norwich solicitor, but having studied many languages, including Romany, came to London in 1824 as a translator before taking to the life of a wanderer in 1827. He travelled on foot through England, France, Germany, Russia, Spain, and the East, and acted as agent for the British and Foreign Bible Society for several years. On his marriage in 1840, he settled to writing at Oulton Broad, Norfolk, and produced *Zincali* (1840), an account of the Spanish gipsies, and *The Bible in Spain* (1843). In 1844 he toured the Balkans, and then pub. *Lavengro* (1851), and its sequel, *The Romany Rye* (1857), mingling autobiographical and fictitious material. A later work, *Wild Wales* (1862), was the result of a visit to that country. His knowledge of languages and gipsy lore was wide though unscientific, and he was unrivalled in the creation of the atmosphere of the open road.

BORROWDALE. Famous beauty-spot in the Lake District of England, 5 m. S. of Keswick, Cumberland, stretching from Derwentwater to Scafell Pike.

BORSTAL. A reformatory system estab. in Britain under the Prevention of Crimes Act, 1908, for the purpose of retrieving young persons of both sexes who have started on a career of crime, and first put into practice in 1902 at Borstal prison near Rochester in Kent. B. Institutions vary in type and are classified as 'open' (e.g. North Sea Camp, Lincs. and Hollesley Bay Colony, Suffolk) and 'closed' (e.g. Borstal, Kent, and Feltham, Middlesex). From 1963 the minimum age of entry has been 15.

BORZOI (Russ. for 'swift'). Russian species of greyhound, first seen in England in 1842, and widely known since 1890. Height for dogs 29 in. upwards at shoulder; long-haired; colour, white with black and tan markings.

BOSANQUET (bō′zanket), **Bernard** (1848–1923). Philosopher; prof. of moral philosophy at St. Andrews 1903–8. In 1911 and 1912 he delivered his Gifford lectures on *Individuality and Value* at Edinburgh. He wrote on logic and metaphysics, aesthetics, Plato's philosophy, and *Philosophical Theory of the State* (1899).

BOSCAWEN (boskō′en, -kaw′en), **Edward** (1711–61). English admiral who saw much service against the French in the mid-18th cent. wars. To his men he was known as 'Old Dreadnought'.

BOSCH (bos), **Jerom** (c. 1460–1516). Dutch painter named from his birthplace, 's Hertogenbosch. His works, of a bizarre and grotesque style, were greatly admired by Philip II of Spain. His Christian name Jerom is often given its Latinized form Hieronymus.

BOSE, Sir Jagadis Chunder (1858–1937). Indian physicist. B. nr. Dacca, he was prof. of physical science at Calcutta 1885–1915, and studied plant-life, especially the growth and minute movements of plants, and their reaction to electrical stimuli. He was knighted in 1917.

BOSE, Satyendranath (1894–). Indian physicist, formerly prof. of physics at the Univ. of Calcutta. With Einstein, he formulated the B.-Einstein law of quantum mechanics.

BOSMAN, Herman Charles (1905–51). S. African writer. Sentenced to death as a youth for shooting his stepbrother, he was reprieved and while serving 4 years' hard labour began to write. *Mafeking Road* (1947) is his best vol. of stories, and concerns an Afrikaner community of the backveld.

BOSNIA-HERÇEGOVINA (-hertsegō′vēna). Federal rep. of Yugoslavia, formed of the 2 provs. of B. and H. Sarajevo is the cap. Wild and mountainous with fertile valleys and forest lands in the E., it produces fruits, tobacco, wheat and other grains, pigs, cattle and sheep. Minerals incl. coal, iron, quicksilver; and there are steelworks and other industrial plants. A number of the inhabitants are Moslems. Area 19,745 sq. m.; pop. (1961) 3,274,886.

Both B. and H. formed part of Roman Illyria; in the 7th cent. they were conquered by the Slavs. B. was an independent kingdom for a short time in the 14th cent. Part of the Turkish empire from 1463, B. and H., still nominally Turkish, were placed under Austrian administration in 1878. Austria annexed the area in 1908, and in 1918 it was made part of the new kingdom of the Serbs, Croats, and Slovenes (renamed Yugoslavia 1931).

BOSPORUS. Strait *c.* 17 m. long joining the Black Sea with the Sea of Marmara, and forming part of the water division between Europe and Asia. Istanbul stands on its W. side. A suspension bridge (5,320 ft.) was under construction 1970–3.

BOSPORUS. Looking down on the strait over Istanbul's 5th cent. fortifications, from the Western (European) shore of the city to the Eastern (Asiatic) side. North of the city the Bosporus forms the 4 m. long, natural harbour of the Golden Horn.
Courtesy of the Turkish Embassy.

BOSSUET (bosü-eh′), **Jacques Bénigne** (1627–1704). French R.C. divine, pulpit orator, and theologian. B. at Dijon, he became a canon at Metz, moved to Paris in 1659, and was appointed to the Chapel Royal in 1662. Here he won fame by his *Oraisons funèbres*, delivered at the funerals of certain great personages. Then he became tutor to the young Dauphin. Appointed bishop of Meaux in 1681, B. became involved in the Gallican controversy between Louis XIV and the pope and did his best to effect a compromise. His *Exposition de la foi catholique* (1670) and *Histoire des variations des églises protestantes* (1688) are brilliant essays.

BOSTON. Cap. of Massachusetts, U.S.A., at the mouth of the r. Charles where it enters Mass. Bay. B. is a cultural centre, and has been the home of many literary and political figures. The inhabitants, for the main part descendants of the original New England settlers, were long regarded as the aristocrats of the U.S.A., but Irish, Italian, Polish and Czech immigrants have modified the former Puritan basis of the population. There are many fine buildings and historical landmarks, including B. univ., the public library, and the Statehouse on Beacon Hill, overlooking the city. The Boston Symphony Orchestra is world-famous. The Charles is spanned by many bridges, including Harvard, leading to the famous univ.

The industries incl. book publishing and printing, rubber manufacture, shoemaking, confectionery, and machinery.

The site was settled in 1630, and was named after B. in England. The attempt of the British govt. to levy a tax on tea led to the 'Boston Tea Party', 1773, when citizens disguised as Red Indians boarded ships carrying tea and threw it into the harbour. Bunker Hill, which gives its name to the 1st battle of the.

War of American Independence, is now within the city of B. Pop. met. area (1970) 2,730,228.

BOSTON. Seaport (bor. from 1544) in Lincs., on the Witham, 4 m. from its mouth. The church of St. Botolph is England's largest parish church, and one of its finest; its tower, known as 'Boston Stump', is a landmark for seamen. In 1882 a dock was built, and the river deepened for seagoing vessels. B. has water connections with all parts of the Fen country. Pop. (1961) 24,903.

BOSTON TERRIER. American breed of dog, but British in origin. It is on terrier lines, but with the short head of the bulldog. The coat is black with a white blaze on the head, white collar and 'socks'.

BOSWELL, James (1740–95). Scottish biographer and man-of-letters. B. at Edinburgh, the son of the judge Alexander B., Lord Auchinleck, he studied law but centred his ambitions on literature and politics. He first met Johnson in 1763 before setting out on the Continental tour during which he met Rousseau, Voltaire, and General Paoli, whom he commemorated in his popular *Account of Corsica* (1768). In 1766 he was admitted as an advocate, and in 1772 renewed his acquaintance with Johnson in London, as became his custom almost every year. Establishing a place in his intimate circle, he became a member of the Literary Club in 1773, and in the same year accompanied Johnson on the journey later recorded in the *Journal of the Tour to the Hebrides* (1785). On his succession to his father's estate in 1782, he made further attempts to enter Parliament, was called to the Eng. bar in 1786, and was Recorder of Carlisle 1788–90. In 1789 he settled in London, and in 1791 produced the greatest of Eng. biographies, the *Life of Johnson*. His long-lost personal papers were acquired for publication by Yale Univ. in 1949. *See* ISHAM, RALPH.

JAMES BOSWELL
By Reynolds, 1786.
Photo: N.P.G.

BOSWORTH. Last battle of the Wars of the Roses, fought on 22 Aug. 1485 near the village of Market B., 12 m. W. of Leicester. Richard III, the Yorkist king, was defeated and slain by Henry of Richmond, who became Henry VII.

BOTANY. The study of plants; this is subdivided into a number of smaller studies, e.g. the distinction of the differences and resemblances of plants is termed taxonomy, their external formation plant morphology, their internal arrangement plant anatomy, their microscopic examination histology, their life history plant physiology, and their distribution over the earth's surface in relation to their surroundings, plant ecology. Palaeobotany concerns the study of fossil plants, while economic B. deals with the utility of plants. Horticulture, agriculture, and forestry are specialized branches of B.

The most ancient botanical record is carved on the walls of the temple at Karnak, about 1500 B.C. The Greeks in the 5th and 4th cents. B.C. used many plants for medicinal purposes, the first Greek Herbal being drawn up about 350 B.C. by Diocles of Carystus. Botanical information was collected into the works of Theophrastus of Eresus (380–287 B.C.), a pupil of Aristotle, who founded the technical plant nomenclature. Cesalpino in the 16th cent. sketched out a system of classification based on flowers, fruits, and seeds, while Jung (1587–1658) used flowers only as his criterion. John Ray (1627–1705) arranged plants systematically, based on his findings on fruit, leaf, and

flower, and described about 18,600 plants. Swedish Carl Linné or Linnaeus (1707–78), who founded systematics, included in his classification all known plants and animals, working them into a rigid framework, and giving each a binomial descriptive label. Banks, Solander, Brown, Bauer, and others travelled throughout the world studying plants, and found that all could be fitted into a systematic classification based on Linnaeus' work. Linnaeus was also the first to recognize and accept the sexual nature of flowers, this work being followed up later by Sprengel, Amici, Robert Brown, and Charles Darwin. Later work revealed the detailed cellular structure of plant tissues, and the exact nature of photosynthesis and the manufacture of plant food. Sachs (1832–97) defined the function of chlorophyll, and the significance of plant stomata. Engelmann (1843–1909) worked on the effect of the spectrum on chlorophyll; the effect of nitrogen on plant life was revealed about the same time, and the study of plant functions has assumed a comprehensive form.

BOTANY BAY. Inlet on the E. coast of Australia, 5 m. S. of Sydney, N.S.W. Discovered by Capt. Cook in 1770, it was so named by him on account of the variety of plants found on its shores by Joseph Banks, the expedition's botanist. Chosen in 1787 as the site for a penal colony, it proved unsuitable, and the settlement was made where Sydney stands. But the name B.B. continued to be popularly used for any convict settlement in Australia.

BOT-FLIES. Group of dipterous insects, forming the family Oestridae. The larvae are parasitic, internally or externally, on horses, sheep, cattle and deer.

BOTHA (bō'ta), **Louis** (1862–1919). S. African soldier and statesman, b. at Greytown, Natal, of Boer parents. Elected a member of the Volksraad in 1897, he supported the more moderate Joubert

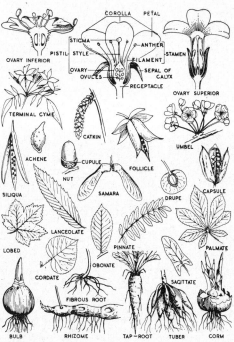

BOTANY. A selection from thousands of botanical terms.

against Kruger. On the outbreak of the Boer War he commanded the Boers besieging Ladysmith, and in 1900 succeeded Joubert in command of the Transvaal forces. For 18 months he engaged in guerrilla warfare, but eventually welcomed the conclusion of peace. In 1907 B. became Premier of the Transvaal and in 1910 of the first Union govt. On the outbreak of war in 1914 he rallied S. Africa to the Commonwealth, suppressed the Boer revolt under de Wet and conquered German S.W. Africa. At Versailles in 1919 he represented S. Africa.

BOTHWELL, James Hepburn, 4th earl of (*c.* 1536–78). Scottish nobleman, who is alleged to have arranged the explosion which killed Darnley, husband of Mary Queen of Scots, in 1567. Tried and acquitted a few weeks later, he abducted Mary, and (having divorced his wife) married her on 15 May. A revolt ensued, and B. was forced to flee to Norway and thence to Sweden. In 1570 Mary obtained a divorce on the ground that she had been ravished by B. before marriage. Later, B. was confined in a castle in Zeeland, where he d. insane.

BO- (abbr. of *Bodhi* 'wisdom' or 'enlightenment') **TREE.** Name given by Indian and Ceylonese Buddhists to the peepul or sacred wild fig (*Ficus religiosa*) under which Buddha (q.v.) was 'enlightened'. The B. planted *c.* 300 B.C. at Anuradhapura (q.v.) is still worshipped by pilgrims.

BOTSWA′NA. Country—formerly Bechuanaland —in S. Africa, lying between the Molopo on the S. and the Zambezi on the N., and S.W. Africa and the Transvaal on the W. and E. respectively. It came within the British sphere of influence in 1885, became a prot. in 1895, self-governing 1965, and in 1966 a rep. within the Commonwealth, as Botswana, with Sir Seretse Khama (q.v.) as pres. There is also a Nat. Assembly and advisory House of Chiefs. The cap. is Gaborone, pop. (1964) 18,000; the chief tribe is the Bamangwato, whose cap. is Serowe, pop. (1964) 34,182. Cattle are reared and livestock and products exported; field crops are undependable owing to irregular rainfall; industrial diamonds, copper and nickel were discovered 1968. Education is chiefly in missionary hands and most of the people profess Christianity. Area 275,000 sq.m.; pop. (1964) 543,105, incl. 3,921 Europeans.

BOTTICELLI (bottēchel′lē), **Sandro** (1444–1510). Florentine artist, real name Filipepi, but his elder brother's nickname B. 'little barrel' was passed on to him. He studied under Filippo Lippi, and was patronized by the Medici family. His *Primavera* (about 1477) treats a theme from classical mythology in a style which is both graceful and realistic. In 1481–2 he assisted with the decoration of the Sistine chapel in Rome. About 1494 he produced his illustrations of Dante. After the execution in 1498 of Savonarola, B. broke with the Medicis, and his 'Calumny of Apelles' (1498) is said to express his detestation of those who calumniated Savonarola. His pictures became more sombre and religious, though his 'Madonna of the Magnificat' shows all the grace and colour of which B. was capable.

BOTTLE-NOSE WHALE (*Hyperoödon rostratus*). Species of whale inhabiting the N. Atlantic. It has a swollen head with short jaws that project like a beak in a manner somewhat resembling the shoulder and neck of a bottle. It is from 20 to 30 ft. long, and feeds on cuttle-fish. It is hunted mainly for its oil.

BO′TULISM. A frequently fatal type of food poisoning due to *Clostridium botulinum*, which excretes one of the most powerful toxins known.

BOUCHER (boosheh′), **François** (1703–70). French painter. B. in Paris, he became director of the Gobelin tapestry works in 1755, and 10 years later court painter. He is famous for his paintings of maidens, shepherds, cupids, etc. *See* illus. p. 862.

BOUCHER DE CRÈVECOEUR DE PERTHES (boosheh′ de krăvker′ de părt), **Jacques** (1788–1868). French geologist, whose discovery of Palaeolithic hand-axes in 1837 led him to promote the recognition of man's history as ante-dating the popularly accepted limit of 4000 B.C.: he was attacked by traditionalists.

BOUDICCA (boodik′a) (d. A.D. 62). Queen of the Iceni, often referred to by the Lat. form Boadicea (bō-adisēah). Her husband, king Prasutagus, had been a tributary of the Romans, but on his death (A.D. 61), the territory of the Iceni was violently annexed, and B. was scourged and her daughters outraged. B. raised the whole of S.E. England in revolt, and before the main Roman armies could return from campaigning in Wales she burnt London and Colchester. Later the British were annihilated somewhere between London and Chester, and B. poisoned herself.

BOUDIN (boodin′), **Eugene** (1824–98). French painter, a fore-runner of Impressionism noted for his seascapes.

BOUGAINVILLE (boogaṅvēl′), **Louis Antoine de** (1729–1811). French navigator. After service with the French in Canada during the Seven Years War he sailed round the world, 1766–9. Several islands are named after him, and also the climbing plant *Bougainvillea*, a genus of the family Nyctaginaceae, native of

BOTTICELLI. Brilliant colour, rich moulding of the figure and exquisitely precise detail mark the work of Botticelli, whose art was ill-appreciated until the later 19th cent. by the art critics. Particularly attractive is the delicately pensive expression of Venus as she watches over the sleeping Mars.   *Photo: National Gallery.*

S. America, and cultivated for its conspicuous red, purple, or mauve bracts which cover the flowers.

BOUGHTON (baw′ton), **Rutland** (1878–1960). British composer. B. at Aylesbury, he is best known for his music drama *The Immortal Hour* (1914), with a text based on the work of Fiona Macleod.

BOUGIE (boozhē). Algerian seaport, 120 m. E. of Algiers, captured by the French 1833. The site has been occupied since Roman times. B. is linked by oil pipe-line with the Hassi Messaoud petroleum wells. Pop. (1967) 63,000.

BOULANGER (boolonzheh′), **George Ernest Jean Marie** (1837–91). French general. After service in Indo-China and N. Africa, he became Minister of War in 1886. He won immense popularity because of his anti-German speeches, and nearly provoked a war with Germany in 1887. In 1889 he was suspected of aspiring to dictatorial powers by a coup d'état, fled to London, and was tried in his absence for treason. He committed suicide in Brussels on the grave of his mistress.

BOULANGER ,**Nadia (Juliette)** (1887–). French music teacher. B. in Paris, she taught at the École Normale de Musique de Paris from 1920, and has had considerable influence on American composers such as Copland and Virgil Thomson through her work at the Conservatoire Américain de Fontainbleau. She is also a remarkable conductor.

BOULEZ (boo′lāz), **Pierre** (1926–). French composer. He studied with Messiaen, and is a devotee of the abstract in music. His works incl. *Le Visage Nuptial* (1946–50) for 2 solo voices, female choir and orchestra; *Le Marteau sans Maître* (1955) a cantata; and *Poésie pour Pouvoir* (1958) for orchestra and 8-track tape-recorder.

BOULOGNE-SUR-MER (boolōny′-sür-mār). French port and seaside resort on the English Channel, Pas-de-Calais dept., and French terminus of the cross-Channel steamboat service from Folkestone. It was a medieval countship, but became part of France in 1477. Napoleon gathered his forces there in 1804 intending to invade England. The chief local industries are fishing, fish curing, petroleum refining, food preserving. Pop. (1968) 49,276.

During the F.W.W. B. was a principal port of the B.E.F. In the S.W.W. it was evacuated by the British on 23 May 1940 and re-captured by Canadians on 22 Sept. 1944.

BOULT (bōlt), **Sir Adrian Cedric** (1889–). British conductor. B. at Chester, he studied at Leipzig, and was conductor of the B.B.C. Symphony Orchestra 1930–50 and the London Philharmonic 1950–7. He promoted the work of Holst and Vaughan Williams, and is a fine interpreter of Elgar. He was knighted in 1937.

SIR ADRIAN BOULT
Photo: Godfrey MacDomnic.

BOULTBEE, John (1747–1812). British sporting artist. He studied under Reynolds, and first exhibited at the R.A. in 1783, specializing in the hunting-field.

BOULTON (bōl′ton), **Matthew** (1728–1809). British engineer. B. at Birmingham, he continued his father's silver-inlaying business, financed James Watt's steam engine, and entered into partnership with him in 1775. They also produced the copper coinage issued in Britain in 1797. For a century B.'s coin-making machine was in use at the Royal Mint.

BOUNTY, Mutiny of the. *See* BLIGH.

BOURBON (boorbon′). A royal house of Europe whose members have occupied the thrones of France,

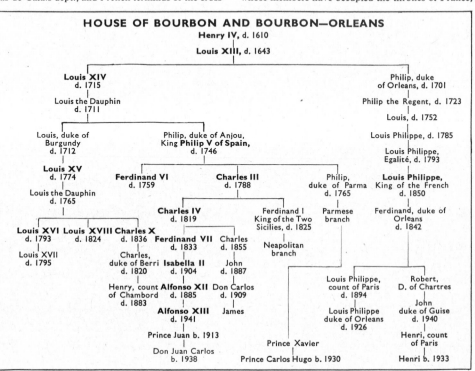

HOUSE OF BOURBON AND BOURBON—ORLEANS

Henry IV, d. 1610

Louis XIII, d. 1643

Louis XIV d. 1715 — Philip, duke of Orleans, d. 1701

Louis the Dauphin d. 1711 — Philip the Regent, d. 1723

Louis, d. 1752

Louis, duke of Burgundy d. 1712 — Philip, duke of Anjou, King **Philip V of Spain,** d. 1746 — Louis Philippe, d. 1785

Louis XV d. 1774 — Louis Philippe, Egalité, d. 1793

Louis the Dauphin d. 1765 — **Ferdinand VI** d. 1759 — **Charles III** d. 1788 — Philip, duke of Parma d. 1765 — **Louis Philippe,** King of the French d. 1850

Charles IV d. 1819 — Ferdinand I King of the Two Sicilies, d. 1825 — Parmese branch — Ferdinand, duke of Orleans d. 1842

Louis XVI d. 1793 — **Louis XVIII** d. 1824 — **Charles X** d. 1836 — **Ferdinand VII** d. 1833 — Charles d. 1855 — Neapolitan branch

Louis XVII d. 1795 — Charles, duke of Berri d. 1820 — **Isabella II** d. 1904 — John d. 1887

Henry, count of Chambord d. 1883 — **Alfonso XII** d. 1885 — Don Carlos d. 1909 — Louis Philippe, count of Paris d. 1894 — Robert, D. of Chartres

Alfonso XIII d. 1941 — James — Louis Philippe duke of Orleans d. 1926 — John duke of Guise d. 1940

Prince Juan b. 1913 — Henri, count of Paris

Don Juan Carlos b. 1938 — Prince Xavier

Prince Carlos Hugo b. 1930 — Henri b. 1933

Spain, Naples, and ruled several Italian duchies; the name comes from Bourbon l'Archambault, chief town of the feudal lordship of Bourbonnais in central France. Antoine de B. became king of Navarre by marriage in 1554, and his son became king of France in 1589 as Henry IV. The last of the French line was Louis-Philippe, who abdicated in 1848. The present B. Pretender to the French throne is Henry, Count of Paris.

The Spanish Bs. are descended from Philippe, duke of Anjou, younger son of Louis Dauphin of France (d. 1711); he became Philip V of Spain in 1700. The last Spanish king, Alfonso XIII, lost his throne in 1931, and the present B. Spanish Pretender is his son, Prince Juan.

BOURBON. Name 1649–1815 of RÉUNION.

BOURBON, Charles, duke of (1490–1527). He was made Constable of France for his courage at the battle of Marignano, 1515. Later he served the emperor Charles V, and helped to drive the French from Italy. In 1526 he was made duke of Milan, and in 1527 allowed his troops to sack Rome. He was killed by a shot Cellini claimed to have fired.

BOURDALOUE (boordahloo'), **Louis** (1632–1704). French Jesuit, divine and pulpit orator. B. at Bourges, he preached in Paris from 1669, and his sermons were extremely popular.

BOURGEOIS (boorzhwah'), **Léon Victor Auguste** (1851–1925). French statesman. Entering politics as a Radical, he defeated Gen. Boulanger in 1888, in 1895 was Prime Minister, and later served in many cabinets. He was one of the pioneer advocates of the League of Nations. In 1920 he received the Nobel peace prize.

BOURGEOISIE (boorzhwahzē'). The middle classes. The Fr. word originally meant the freemen of a borough. Hence it came to mean the whole class between the workers and peasants, and the nobility. B. has also acquired a contemptuous sense, as implying commonplace, philistine respectability. By socialists it is applied to the whole propertied class, as distinct from the proletariat.

BOURGES (boorzh). Historic French city, cap. of Cher dept., 125 m. S. of Paris. It has a Gothic cathedral and great art collections. B. is the seat of an archbishopric and an important literary and commercial centre. Pop. (1962) 63,479.

BOURGET (boorzheh'), **Paul** (1852–1935). French writer. B. at Amiens, he pub. some verse and then estab. his name as a critic with *Essais de psychologie contemporaine* (1883). His 1st novel, written in England, *L'Irréparable* (1884), dealt pessimistically with the psychological problems of the upper middle classes, as did its successors, incl. *Le Disciple* (1889) and the war novel *Le Démon du midi* (1914).

BOURGET (boor'zheh), **Le.** Civil and military aerodrome, 7 m. N.E. of Paris, estab. in 1914, the terminus of the London-Paris air service. Pop. (1962) 10,236.

BOURGUIBA (boor'gēbah), **Habib ben Ali** (1903–). Tunisian leader. Ed. at the Univ. of Paris, he became a journalist and was frequently imprisoned by the French for his nationalist aims as leader of the Néo-Destour party. He became P.M. in 1956, and Pres. and P.M. of the Tunisian Rep. in 1957.

BOURNEMOUTH. Popular English seaside resort (co. bor.) on Hampshire coast, in the valley of the r. Bourne. Chines interrupt the line of cliffs. The town is famous for the high standard of its music, and for a good Art Gallery, in which are paintings by Turner, Corot, etc. Pop. (1961) 153,965.

BOURNVILLE. A suburb of Birmingham, England, consisting of a housing estate (*c.* 1,000 acres in extent with some 3,000 houses) owned and managed by the Bournville Village Trust, founded by George Cadbury in 1900.

BOUTS, Dierick (*c.* 1400–75). Dutch painter. B. at

Haarlem, he settled before 1448 at Louvain, where he executed his finest works such as the 'Last Supper' and the 'Martyrdom of St. Erasmus'.

BOVET (bōveh'), **Daniel** (1907–). Swiss-born physiologist, who became an Italian citizen in 1947. He pioneered research in the antihistamine drugs used to combat allergies, and in 1957 was awarded the Nobel prize for medicine, following his development of a synthetic form of curare (q.v.). In 1947–64 he worked at the Istituto Superiore di Sanità, Rome, becoming prof. of pharmacology Univ. of Sassari 1964.

BOW BELLS. The bells of St. Mary-le-Bow church, Cheapside, London; a person born within their sound is considered to be a true Cockney. The church was nearly destroyed by bombs in 1941. The bells, recast from the old metal, were restored in 1961.

BOWDLER (bowd'ler), **Thomas** (1754–1825). British editor whose prudishly expurgated versions of Shakespeare and other authors gave rise to the verb 'bowdlerize'.

BOWEN (bō'en), **Elizabeth** (1899–). British novelist. B. in Dublin, she followed her 1st vol. of short stories *Encounters* (1923), with *Look at all those Roses* (1941), *Demon Lover* (1945) and others. Her novels incl. *Friends and Relations* (1931), *The Death of the Heart* (1938), *The Heat of the Day* (1949), and *The Little Girls* (1964). *Bowen's Court* (1942) is the story of her home in co. Cork.

BOWEN, Marjorie. *See* LONG, M. G.

BOWER-BIRD. Family of Australian birds (Ptilonorhynchidae), nearly allied to the birds of paradise; the males construct decorated bowers or playgrounds of sticks, grasses, etc., in which they pay court to the females.

BOWLES, Chester (1901–). American administrator. B. at Springfield, Mass., he was ed. at Yale, and entered advertising and market research. He held varied govt. posts 1943–6, was ambassador to India 1951–3 and from 1963, and was influential, as chairman of the Democratic Platform Committee, in drafting Kennedy's campaign programme. He was Under-Sec. of State Jan.-Nov. 1961, adviser to the Pres. on African, Asian and Latin American Affairs 1961–3 and ambassador to India 1963–9.

BOWLES, William Lisle (1762–1850). British poet. He pub. *Fourteen Sonnets* (1789), which influenced Wordsworth, Southey, and Coleridge.

BOWLS. Outdoor game played in England at least since the 13th cent. It is played on flat or crown greens with biased bowls of lignum vitae (4½–5¼ in. in diameter), and the object of the game is to draw each bowl as near as possible to the small white jack.

BOURNEMOUTH. Golden sands along the bay, and double tides, make Bournemouth an ideal resort for the swimmer. Zig-zag paths give easy access to the beach.
Courtesy of John Etches of Bournemouth.

The game can be played as singles, pairs, or rinks (4 men a side).

BOWRA, Sir Cecil Maurice (1898–1971). Brit. classical scholar. Warden of Wadham Coll., Oxford, from 1938, he pub. such outstanding studies as *Greek Lyric Poetry* (1936), *From Virgil to Milton* (1945), *The Romantic Imagination* (1950) and *Primitive Song* (1962). He was knighted in 1951.

BOX. Genus of shrub. and small trees (*Buxus*) of the family Euphorbiaceae. The common box (*B. sempervirens*) has compact evergreen foliage.

BOXER. Medium-sized dog of continental origin, with a short, smooth coat, and in a wide range of colour.

BOXER

BOXERS. Name given to bands of fanatical Chinese nationalists who in 1900 at the instigation of the Empress Dowager besieged the foreign legations in Pekin, and murdered European missionaries and thousands of Chinese converts. An international punitive force was dispatched, Pekin was captured on 14 Aug. 1900, and China agreed to pay a large indemnity.

BOXING. Fighting with the fists, originally using the bare knuckle and without 'rounds', though later each fall marked the end of a round and a fight of 276 such rounds is on record.

Jack Broughton (1705–89), English champion for many years, is said to have introduced gloves, though only for practice bouts. B. became popular with the nobility or 'Corinthians' (*See* JOHN JACKSON), but only lost its reputation for brutality with the introduction of the Queensberry Rules (drawn up by the 8th Marquess in 1866), which with certain modifications still obtain in Britain, but have been superseded in the U.S. by those of the Amateur Athletic Union of America. Official professional organizations are the B. Board of Control in Britain and the Nat. B. Assocn. and N.Y. State Athletic Commission in the U.S.: the British amateur body is the Amateur B. Assocn. B. champions are classified according to weight as heavyweight (no limit), light heavyweight (175 lb.), middle-weight (160 lb.), welter-weight (147 lb.), lightweight (135 lb.), featherweight (126 lb.), bantam-weight (118 lb.), and flyweight (112 lb.). Outstanding heavyweight champions have been John L. Sullivan (bare-knuckle champion) 1882–92, James J. Corbett (1st Marquess of Queensberry champion) 1892–7, Jack Dempsey 1919–26, Joe Louis 1937–49, Floyd Patterson 1956–9 and 1960–2, and Cassius Clay (q.v.) from 1964—all of U.S.A.

BOYCOTT, Charles Cunningham (1832–97). Land agent of Lord Erne in co. Mayo, Ireland, who strongly opposed the Irish Land League, with the result that the peasants refused to work for him; thus arose the word 'boycotting'.

BOYD ORR, John, 1st baron (1880–1970). Brit. nutritional expert, and advocate of world federalism. In 1936 he caused a sensation by proving in *Food Health and Income* that half the nation was under-nourished, and was director-general of the F.A.O. 1945–8. In 1949 he was awarded a Nobel peace prize.

BOYE, Karin (1900–41). Swedish poet and novelist. Her first poems appeared in 1922. Her novel *Kallocain* (1941) was concerned with totalitarian ideology.

BOYER (bwah-yeh'), **Charles** (1899–). French actor. Going to Hollywood in 1934, he made a reputation as 'the great lover' in such films as *Mayerling*.

BOYLE, Charles, 4th earl of Orrery (1676–1731). Irish soldier and diplomatist who was worsted in his dispute with Bentley over the authenticity of the *Letters of Phalaris*. The orrery, a contrivance for studying the solar system, is named after him.

BOYLE of Handsworth, Edward, baron (1923–). British Cons. politician. He entered parliament in 1950, and became Economics Sec. to the Treasury (1955–6) resigning at the Suez crisis; Parl. Sec. to the Treasury (1959–62), and Min. of Education (1962–4).

BOYLE, Kay. Pseudonym of the American author Baroness Joseph von Franckenstein (1903–). B. in St. Paul, Minnesota, she has written vols. of short stories such as *Wedding Day* (1930), and psychological novels incl. *Plagued by the Nightingale*.

BOYLE, Robert (1627–91). Irish natural philosopher, 7th son of the 1st earl of Cork. From 1654 he lived in Oxford. In 1659 he discovered the elasticity of air, and in 1662 enunciated *Boyle's Law*: that the volume of a gas varies inversely with its pressure. He was one of the founders of the Royal Society, and in 1661 pub. *The Sceptical Chemist*. He studied the Bible languages, and by his will founded the B. lectures for the defence of Christianity.

BOYNE. Irish river, 70 m. long, flowing past Drogheda into the Irish Sea. It gives its name to the battle fought on 11 July 1690, near Drogheda, in which James II was defeated by William III.

BOY SCOUTS. Non-military and non-political youth organization originating with an experimental camp held in 1907 for 24 boys from every class of society by Baden-Powell (q.v.) on Brownsea Is., Poole Harbour, Dorset. The island was in 1962 acquired by the National Trust. Baden-Powell's book *Scouting for Boys* (1908) led to the incorporation of the B.S. Assocn. by royal charter in 1912, and the movement has spread throughout the Commonwealth as well as to foreign countries. The corresponding organization for girls is the Girl Guides, inc. by royal charter in 1922. The scheme was introduced to the U.S. by William D. Boyce, a Chicago publisher who had visited England and met Baden-Powell and the Boy Scouts of America were inc. in 1910: a similar organization for girls, the Girl Scouts of the U.S.A., was founded in 1912. World membership: Scouts 10,000,000, Guides 6,000,000.

BOZEN. German form of BOLZANO.

BRABANÇONNE (brahboňson'), **La.** National anthem of Belgium, written and composed during the revolution of 1830.

BRABANT. District of W. Europe, comprising the Belgian provinces of Brabant and Antwerp and the Dutch province of N. Brabant. During the Middle Ages it was an independent duchy, and after passing to Burgundy, and thence to the Spanish crown, was divided during the Dutch War of Independence. The southern portion was Spanish until 1713, then Austrian until 1815, when the whole area was included in the Netherlands. In 1830 the influential French-speaking part of the pop. in the southern Netherlands rebelled, and when Belgium was recognized in 1839, S. Brabant was included in it. The Dutch prov. of N. Brabant has an area of 1,921 sq. m.; pop. (1966) 1,700,866; cap. 'sHertogenbosch. S. Brabant prov. Belgium, is 1,267 sq. m. in area; pop. (1966) 2,130,276; cap. Brussels.

BRABAZON OF TARA, John Theodore Cuthbert Moore-Brabazon, 1st baron (1884–1964). British pioneer motorist and the 1st English aviator. During the F.W.W. he was in the R.F.C. He was a Cons. M.P. 1918–29 and 1931–42, Min. of Transport 1940–1, of Aircraft Production 1941–2, and a peer from 1942.

BRACEGIRDLE, Anne (*c.* 1663–1748). English actress who made her first London appearance in 1680 and had a brilliant career on the stage until 1707, esp. in Congreve's plays, and she may have secretly married him.

BRACHIOPODA (braki-o'pōda), or Lamp-shells. Group of marine animals, usually treated as a separate, isolated phylum. They have 2 shells placed dorsally and ventrally, and are fixed to stones, corals, etc., by means of a stalk. The shell has something of the appearance of an ancient lamp. Some of the earliest fossils known belong to the B.

BRACKEN. Species of fern (*Pteris aquilina*), abundant in most parts of Europe. It has a perennial root-stock, which throws up large fronds.

BRACTON, Henry de (d. 1268). English judge, writer on English law, and chancellor of Exeter cathedral from 1264. He compiled an account of the laws and customs of the English, the first of its kind.

BRADBURY, Ray (1920–). American writer. B. at Waukegan, Illinois, he advanced from pulp magazine stories to science fiction on a serious level, with its basis in developments of existing inventions and mental attitudes: *The Martian Chronicles* (1950) and *Something Wicked This Way Comes* (1962).

BRADDON, Mary Elizabeth (1837–1915). English novelist, author of the sensationally successful murder story *Lady Audley's Secret* (1862). She m. publisher John Maxwell in 1874, and her son William Babington Maxwell (1876–1938) was also a popular novelist.

BRADFORD. English manufacturing and commercial city (co. bor.) of the W. Riding of Yorkshire, on the Brad 9 m. W. of Leeds. Since its first markets were granted in the 13th cent., B. has risen to be the world's leading wool-dealing centre and weaver of woollen fabrics. The first spinning factory was opened in 1798, and in 1825 came the power loom. There are many other industries. The cathedral is 15th cent.; the bishopric was created in 1919. The Exchange (1867) is the wool marketing centre. The Cartwright Memorial Hall (1904) contains the art gallery and museum. B. was made a co. borough in 1888, a city in 1897. The univ. (1965) originated in the technical coll. founded 1882. Pop. (1961) 295,768.

BRADFORD-ON-AVON. English town (U.D.) in Wilts, 6 m. S.E. of Bath. The Town Bridge has a chapel; the church of St. Lawrence is Saxon. Pop. (1961) 5,767.

BRADLAUGH (-law), **Charles** (1833–91). British freethinker and radical politician. He served in the army, was a lawyer's clerk, became well known on the platform and in journalism under the name of Iconoclast, and from 1860 ran the *National Reformer*. In 1880 he was elected Liberal M.P. for Northampton, but was not allowed to take his seat until 1886 as, being an atheist, he had expressed his unbelief in the efficacy of the oath and claimed to affirm instead.

BRADLEY, Francis Herbert (1846–1924). British philosopher. B. in Brecknock, he became a fellow of Merton Coll., Oxon, in 1870. In *Ethical Studies* (1876) and *Principles of Logic* (1883) he attacked the utilitarianism of J. S. Mill, and in *Appearance and Reality* (1893) and *Truth and Reality* (1914) he outlined his Neo-Hegelian doctrine of the universe as a single ultimate reality. His brother, **Andrew Cecil B.** (1851–1935), became professor of poetry at Oxford (1901–6). His *Shakespearean Tragedy* (1904) is a fine example of the philosophical and psychological approach to the dramatist.

BRADLEY, Henry (1845–1923). British philologist and lexicographer, b. at Manchester. He began work on the *Oxford English Dictionary* in 1883, became joint-editor in 1889, and in 1915 succeeded Sir James Murray as senior-editor. He wrote *The Making of English*.

BRADLEY, Omar Nelson (1893–). American general. In 1943 he commanded the 2nd U.S. Corps in Tunisia and Sicily, and in 1944 led the U.S. troops in the invasion of France. He was Chief of Staff U.S. Army 1948–9 and chairman of the Joint Chiefs of Staff 1949–53. He was appointed General of the Army in 1950.

BRADMAN, Sir Donald George (1908–). Australian cricketer, and formerly a stockbroker at Adelaide. B. in N.S.W. he played for Australia

1928–48 and was captain 1936–48. He has the highest aggregate score and greatest number of centuries in England v. Australia Test Matches.

BRAEMAR (brām-ahr'). District and village in Upper Deeside, Aberdeenshire, Scotland. Highland games are held here in August.

BRAGA (brah'gah). Portuguese city in Minho prov., 30 m. N.N.E. of Oporto. It is the seat of an archbishopric, the archbishop being primate of the Iberian peninsula. Pop. (1960) 40,977.

BRAGANÇA (brahgahn'sah). City in the N.E. corner of Portugal, the seat of a bishopric. It gave its name to the royal house of Portugal, whose members reigned 1640–1853; another branch were emperors of Brazil 1822–89. Pop. *c.* 7,500.

BRAGG, Sir William Henry (1862–1942). British physicist. B. in Cumberland, he was prof. of physics at Adelaide 1886–1908, Leeds 1909–15 and the Univ. of London from 1915. He was made K.B.E. in 1920, and received the O.M. in 1931. Apart from his numerous technical papers, he wrote many popular books incl. *The World of Sound* (1920) and *Concerning the Nature of Things* (1925). In 1915 he shared with his son **Sir (William)Lawrence B.** (1890–1971) a Nobel prize for physics for their research work on X-rays and crystal structure. B. in Adelaide, S. Australia, Sir Lawrence was Cavendish prof. of experimental physics at Cambridge 1938–53, and was Fullerian prof. of chemistry at the Royal Institution 1953–66 and scientific director 1954–66. He pub. many technical papers and books incl. *Atomic Structure of Minerals* (1937).

BRAHE (brah'e), **Tycho** (1546–1601). Danish astronomer. In 1576 Frederick II of Denmark gave him the island of Hven in the Sound, together with a pension. Here he erected the observatory of Uraniborg. In 1597 he quarrelled with the authorities, and eventually settled near Prague where Kepler became his assistant.

BRAHMA. In Hinduism, the Supreme Being, or Universal Soul, the Absolute, self-existing and eternal. When referred to in the masculine he is the creator who forms with Vishnu and Siva the 'Trimurti'.

BRAHMANISM. The earliest stage in the development of Hinduism (q.v.). Its sacred scriptures are the Vedas with their accompanying literature of comment and explanation known as Brahmanas, Aranyakas, and Upanishads.

BRAHMAPUTRA (-poot'ra). River in Asia which rises in the Himalayan glaciers as Tsang Po and runs for 900 m. through Tibet, to the mountain mass of Namcha Barwa. Turning S., as the Dihang, it enters India near Jido, and flows into the Assam valley near Sadiya. Now known as the B., it flows generally westward until shortly after reaching E. Pakistan it turns S. and divides into the B. proper, without much water, and the main stream, the Jamuna, which joins the Padma arm of the Ganges at Goalunda. The r. (1,800 m. long) is navigable for 800 m. from the sea.

BRAHMA SAMĀJ. Indian monotheistic religious movement, founded in 1830 in Calcutta by Ram Mohun Roy who attempted to recover the primitive simple worship of the Vedas and purify Hinduism. Under Debendra Nath Tagore and Keshub Chunder Sen the movement made considerable progress, and has continued to do so.

BRAHMS, Johannes (1833–97). German composer. B. at Hamburg, he attracted the attention of the great violinist Joachim in 1853 and was introduced by him to Liszt and Schumann. The latter in particular encouraged him. From 1872 B. made his home in Vienna. Though his music has many romantic qualities, it represents in essence a continuation of the classical tradition from the point to which Beethoven had brought it. As a composer of symphonic music and of songs, he is ranked with the greatest. Among his choral works the German

JOHANNES BRAHMS in his study.
Photo: Paul Popper.

Requiem is best known. He was famed as a pianist and as a performer and conductor of his own works.

BRAILA (brah-ē'lah). Rumanian commercial and naval port on the Danube, 106 m. from its mouth. It exports grain, is connected with the Rumanian oil fields and manufactures man-made fibres, iron and steel, construction machinery, etc. Pop. (1966) 138,587.

BRAILLE (brahy; Eng. brāl), **Louis** (1809–52). French inventor in 1829 of the system of lettering or embossed dots which is named after him. He himself was blinded at the age of 3.

BRAIN, Dennis (1921–57). British horn player. His father Aubrey Harold B. (1893–) was prof. of this instrument at the R.A.M., where B. studied under him. Hindemith and Britten wrote works specially for him as a soloist.

BRAIN, Walter Russell, 1st baron (1895–1966). British neurologist, consulting physician to the London Hospital and to Maida Vale Hospital for Nervous Diseases. His books incl. *Diseases of the Nervous System, Mind Perception and Science* (1951) and *Speech Disorders* (1961). Created a baron in 1962.

BRAIN. That part of the central nervous system contained within the skull. The B. weighs a little over 3 lb. and consists of a soft white substance which during life is almost fluid. The greatest part of this is contained in the 2 cerebral hemispheres, which are situated on either side of the middle line of the skull and together form the cerebrum or great B. The cerebellum or small B. lies below the great B. at the back of the head, within the occiput; it also consists of 2 hemispheres. The medulla (marrow), or hind B., is a short conical structure which connects the B. with the spinal cord. The pons (bridge) joins the lower parts of the cerebellar hemispheres. The mid-B. consists of 2 broad strands of nerve tissue which run from the centre of the cerebral hemisphere to the pons, and of the structures lying over these.

The surface of the cerebral hemispheres is wrinkled (convolutions) or furrowed (fissures). These hemispheres are divided into the frontal, temporal, parietal, and occipital lobes, and the frontal lobes are separated from the parietal lobes by the fissure of Rolando, which divides the B. into the effector area in front – the part which is concerned with action and the receptor area behind – the part which is concerned with receiving stimuli. The outer parts of all the convolutions are made of grey matter which consists of innumerable nerve cells. The remainder of the cerebrum is formed of white matter, made up of nerve fibres. These conduct impulses from the end organs all over the body to the cortex. They cross from one side to the other in the pyramid of the medulla, a fact which explains why each side of the brain governs the opposite side of the body.

The B. is enclosed by 3 membranes, which separate it from the skull. The cerebro-spinal fluid surrounds the whole of the B., spinal cord, and nerves, in a thin layer to form a kind of water-cushion in which the nerve tissues float.

There are 6 layers of B. cells, connected with certain functions. It is not possible to draw an exact map of the cerebral cortex, but many functions can be localized. Speech is governed by the left hemisphere in right-handed persons, and usually by the right hemisphere in left-handed persons.

BRAINE, John (1922–). British novelist. From Bradford grammar school he went on to selling furniture, working in a bookshop and as a laboratory assistant, before making a career as a librarian. His novel *Room at the Top* (1957), which estab. him as an author, created Joe Lampton, a typical modern go-getter.

BRAINS TRUST. Nickname applied to a group of experts who advised President F. D. Roosevelt on his New Deal Policy.

BRAITHWAITE, Dame Lilian (1873–1948). British actress, with a delightful technique in Noël Coward and Ivor Novello comedies: her latest success was as a lovable murderess in *Arsenic and Old Lace*. In 1943 she received the D.B.E.

BRAITHWAITE, Richard Bevan (1900–). British philosopher. Originally a physicist and mathematician, he was Knightbridge prof. of moral philosophy at Cambridge 1953–67 and has experimented in the provision of a rational basis for religion and moral choice.

BRAMAH, Ernest. Pseudonym of the British short-story writer Ernest Bramah Smith (1868–1948), creator of Kai Lung, a philosophically-minded Chinese, and of Max Carrados, a blind detective.

BRAMAH, Joseph (1748–1814). British inventor. B. near Doncaster, he became a cabinet-maker in London, and invented the B. lock (1784) and a hydraulic press (1796).

BRAMA'NTE (LAZZARI), Donato (c. 1444–1514). Italian architect and painter, whose real name was Donato d'Agnolo. B. at Urbino, he moved to Rome about 1500 and there under Pope Julius II commenced the rebuilding of St. Peter's.

BRAMBLING. A bird (*Fringilla montefringilla*) belonging to the finch family (Fringillidae) which visits Britain in winter, breeding in Asia and N. Europe.

BRAMWELL, George William Wilshere, 1st baron (1808–92). British judge. He was partly responsible for the Companies Act of 1862, and it was at his suggestion that limited liability companies were compelled to add the word 'Limited' to their title. He was made a peer in 1881.

BRANCUSI (brahn'koosh or brahnkoo'zi), **Constantin** (1876–1957). Rumanian sculptor. B. in S. Rumania, he studied at Bucharest before going to

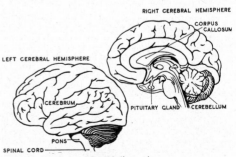

RIGHT CEREBRAL HEMISPHERE

CORPUS CALLOSUM

LEFT CEREBRAL HEMISPHERE

CEREBRUM

PITUITARY GLAND   CEREBELLUM

PONS

SPINAL CORD

BRAIN (human).

Paris in 1904. Important in his work are the abstractions of animal and bird form, such as his bronze 'Bird in Space' (1919). In 1927 this was assessed by the American Customs as a piece of metal not a work of art and therefore dutiable: the claim caused controversy and was over-ruled in 1928. Rodin had an important influence on his work.

BRANDENBURG. Former Prussian and German prov. The area, then inhabited by Slavonic tribes, was conquered in the 12th cent. by Albert the Bear. Frederick of Hohenzollern became margrave in 1415, and an elector of the Holy Roman Empire; the Elector Frederick III achieved the crown of Prussia in 1701. Potsdam was the cap. When Germany was united in 1871, Brandenburg became one of its provs. That part of it E. of the Oder came under Polish administration, in accordance with the Potsdam agreement, in 1945; the remainder became a Land of (E.) Germany, abolished in 1952 when its boundaries were obliterated in the newly created administrative districts of Neubrandenburg, Potsdam, Frankfurt-an-der-Oder, and Kottbus.

BRANDENBURG. Town in (E.) Germany, on the r. Havel, 36 m. W. of Berlin. Seat of a bishopric 949–1544, it makes textiles, motor cars, aircraft, etc. It gave its name to the former prov. of B. Pop. (est.) 65,000.

BRA'NDES, Georg Morris Cohen (1842–1927). Danish critic. He was belatedly appointed prof. of aesthetics in his native Copenhagen in 1902, but had previously played a major part in the Scandinavian literary awakening, and encouraged Lagerlöf, Björnsen, Ibsen and others.

BRA'NDO, Marlon (1924–). American actor. B. at Omaha, Nebraska, he studied at the Dramatic Workshop of the New School for Social Research, N.Y., and with Elia Kazan and Stella Adler. Best-known of the exponents of Method acting, his successes incl. *A Streetcar Named Desire* (both as film and play) and the films *The Wild One* and *The Fugitive Kind*.

BRANDT, Willy (1913–). German politician. He emigrated to Norway in 1933 as an anti-Nazi and anti-Communist, and was active in the resistance movement, resuming German citizenship 1947. Mayor of W. Berlin from 1957, he became chairman of the Social Democratic Party 1964, Vice Chancellor and Min. of Foreign Affairs under Kiesinger in 1966, and Fed. Chancellor 1969.

BRANDY. A potable spirit obtained by the distillation of the fermented juice of grapes or other fruits. The best and only genuine B. comes from true wine-producing countries. The finished product contains from 40 to 70 per cent ethyl alcohol by volume.

BRANGWYN, Sir Frank (1867–1956). British artist. Of Welsh extraction, he was b. at Bruges, where his father was working as an ecclesiastical architect. His talent coming to the notice of William Morris, he worked for him as a textile designer, then travelled widely, developing a sense of colour and power of large-scale decorative concepts unusual in British artists and greatly appreciated on the Continent. In 1925 he completed 5 of a series of panels for the Royal Gallery of the House of Lords, but these were rejected after much controversy and now hang in the B. Hall, Swansea. In 1932 he was commissioned to work on panels for Radio City, N.Y. His gifts were varied and he produced furniture, pottery, carpets, schemes for interior decoration and architectural designs, as well as the more expected book illustrations, lithographs and etchings. There is a B. Museum (1936) at Bruges, and at Orange, Vaucluse (1947). He was knighted in 1941.

BRANTING, Karl Hjalmar (1860–1925). Swedish Socialist statesman. In 1897 he was the 1st Social Democrat to be elected to the Swedish Second Chamber. In 1920 he formed Sweden's 1st Social Democratic Ministry, and was again Prime Minister in 1921 and 1924–5. In 1921 he was awarded the Nobel prize for peace.

BRANTÔME (broñtōm'), **Pierre de Bourdeille,** Seigneur de (*c.* 1540–1614). French historian, who accompanied Mary Stuart to Scotland, served in Malta, Italy, Africa, and Hungary, and in the Huguenot wars. His *Mémoires* give a vivid picture of his time.

BRAQUE (brahk), **Georges** (1882–1963). French artist. B. at Argenteuil, he was associated with Picasso in introducing the Cubist movement in 1908. Eliminating curved lines, he reduced the human figure, landscapes and everyday objects to geometrical shapes. About 1912 he was also the main initiator of *papiers collés* in which oddments of paper, wood, etc., are glued to a canvas and incorporated in the picture. His later works are less deliberately geometrical, and are sometimes realistic. He also produced engravings and sculpture, and in 1953 finished 3 ceiling paintings for the Louvre.

BRASI'LIA. Cap. of Brazil (construction begun 1957, inaugurated 1960), in the state of Goias, 600 m. N.W. of Rio de Janeiro and 3,000 ft. above sea-level. Juscelino Kubitschek de Oliveira, Brazilian President 1955–60, pushed through the idea, dating from 1823, of a completely new city bringing life to the interior. It was designed by Lucio Costa in the shape of a bent bow and arrow, and Oscar Niemeyer was chief architect. Pop. (1960) 141,172; it is planned to be *c.* 500,000.

BRASOV (brahshōv'). Rumanian town at the foot of the Transylvanian Alps, an important route centre, producing machine tools, industrial equipment, cement, and woollens, etc. It was called Urasul Stalin (Stalintown) 1948–56. Pop. (1966) 163,348.

BRASS. An alloy of copper and zinc, with not more than 5 or 6 per cent of other metals. The zinc content ranges from 20 to 45 per cent, and the colour of B. varies accordingly from coppery to whitish yellow. Bs. are characterized by the ease with which they may be worked into shape. They are strong and ductile, and resist many forms of corrosion. Usually they are classed into those that can be worked cold (up to 25 per cent zinc) and those which are better worked hot (about 40 per cent zinc).

BRA'SSICA. Genus of plants of the family Cruciferae. The best-known species is the common cabbage (*B. oleracea*) with its varieties broccoli, cauliflower, kale, brussels sprouts, etc.

BRATBY, John (1928–). British artist, popularly regarded as the leader of the 'kitchen-sink' school because of a preoccupation in early work with working-class domestic interiors. He has also pub.

BRASILIA. Among the many fine buildings of Brazil's new capital is the President's Palace, built 1960 to a design by Oscar Niemeyer. *Courtesy of the Brazilian Information Service.*

books illustrated by himself which have a similar bold energy of style, incl. *Breakdown* (1960). His wife **Jean E. Cooke** (1927–) is a sensitive artist in her own right.

BRATISLAVA (brahtislah'va). City and chief port of Czechoslovakia, on the Danube, 38 m. E. of Vienna. A trans-shipment centre, the town has engineering and chemical industries, oil refineries, shipbuilding yards, and the Slovak univ. founded in 1919. Pop. (1967) 277,000.

BRATTAIN (brat'un), **Walter Houser** (1902–). American physicist. B. in Amoy, China, son of a teacher, he joined 1929–67 the staff of Bell Telephone Laboratories. In 1956 he was awarded a Nobel prize jointly with William Shockley and John Bardeen for their work on the development of the transistor which replaced the comparatively costly and clumsy vacuum tube in electronics.

BRAUCHITSCH (browkh'itsh), **Walther von** (1881–1948). German field marshal. A staff officer in the F.W.W., he replaced in 1938 von Fritsch as C.-in-C. of the army and became a member of Hitler's 'secret cabinet council'. He was dismissed after the failure before Moscow in 1941. Captured in 1945, he d. before being tried.

BRAUN (brown), **Eva** (1910–45). German Nazi. B. at Munich, she became secretary to Hitler's photographer and personal friend, Hoffmann. Her name was associated with Hitler's for years, and she is supposed to have married him in the air-raid shelter of the Chancellory at Berlin on 29 April 1945. They then committed suicide together.

BRAUNAU (brow'now). Town and railway junction in Austria, on the Inn, which here forms the frontier with Bavaria, Germany. Adolf Hitler was b. here, 1889. It has an aluminium plant, tanneries, breweries, etc. Pop. *c.* 12,000.

BRAZIL. Largest of the S. American countries occupying the N.E. part of the great land mass. On the E. and N.E. it faces the Atlantic Ocean, being bordered on the landward side from N. to S. by French Guiana, Surinam (Dutch), British Guiana, Venezuela, Colombia, Peru, Bolivia, Paraguay, Argentina, and Uruguay; thus B. has a land frontier with all the S. American republics except Ecuador and Chile. It has a coastline 4,100 m. in length and an estimated area of 3,287,000 sq. m., making it the 4th largest country in the world, occupying nearly half the total area of S. America.

Geography. B. is a country of plains and plateaux. There are 3 main plains – those of the Amazon and Paraná-Paraguay rivers, and the coastal lowlands. The flat Amazon lowlands in the N. cover some 1,000,000 sq. m. Along the northern frontier are several chains of mountains averaging 3,000-5,000 ft. though Mt. Roraima (q.v.) rises to 8,625 ft. The whole E. and S.E. part of B. is occupied by a great system of scarps and plateaux with a tipped-up scarp edge along the S.E. coast, reaching over 9,000 ft. behind Rio de Janeiro (Pico da Bandeira, 9,462 ft.). B.'s largest river system is that of the Amazon. The São Francisco enters the Atlantic some 80 m. S.W. the Paraná, with its tributary the Paraguay, by the Plate estuary in Argentina. The Equator passes through N.B. and the Tropic of Capricorn through the S. The Amazon basin has a permanently hot, wet climate, and a dense tropical vegetation. Among the almost impenetrable Amazonian forests is found the Pará rubber tree, as well as the Brazil nut, rosewood, and other trees of commercial value. The S. uplands produce Araucaria pine and other timber suitable for furniture. Most of the plateau surface is covered with savanna grassland and scattered trees. In the N. the poor prairie country is dominated by cactus.

POPULATION. In 1967 the population of B. was 87,209,000. The Brazilians are mainly of Portuguese descent, though there is a considerable admixture

BRAZIL. Rising cloud-capped and uninhabited, the plateau of Mount Roraima (q.v.) is believed by the few Indians of the surrounding countryside to be the source of all diamonds in the area, but fear of the evil spirits said to haunt it prevents their venturing near it.
Photo: The Oxford & Cambridge Expedition to South America.

of Indian and Negro blood. In the interior are found native Brazilian Indians. During the past 60 years immigration from Europe and Japan has been considerable. The pop. is concentrated in the coastal areas. The official language is Portuguese. Elementary education is free and compulsory, but illiteracy remains wisedpread; there are 24 official and 10 Catholic universities.

Economic Development. B. is mainly an agricultural country, with the greatest world production of several crops, such as coffee and castor oil beans, and large crops of cocoa, sugar, and tobacco. Cotton is grown in the S., cacao in the S.E., manioc (tapioca) in the S. centre; non-cultivated products include maté in the S., rubber and B. nuts in the Amazon basin. The castor oil plant grows wild. Excellent cattle and sheep are reared and B. now surpasses Argentina as a livestock producer. Other products include oranges, bananas, rice, wheat, maize, and grapes. The country has large mineral resources, many of them undeveloped. The existing mines are mainly in the S. and S.E. Coal, iron, manganese, nickel, gold, bauxite, and others are worked. Diamonds are found at Diamantina in Minas Gerais, the principal mining state. Emeralds, sapphires, topaz, rock crystal, etc., are also found. Petroleum is worked in Bahia; and hydro-electric power has been developed on the São Francisco r. (Paulo Afonso Falls), the Sorocaba r., and elsewhere. Textiles, automobiles, trucks, and paper are produced. The rivers constitute a principal means of communication, extending with canals to close on 22,000 m. of navigable waterways. There is also a road system, rail network (concentrated in the S.E.) and air services.

TOWNS. The capital is Brasilia (q.v.). The former capital, Rio de Janeiro, has a fine harbour. São Paulo, with its port Santos, is the principal coffee town. Porto Alegre, Salvador, Maceió, Recife, Fortaleza, Belem and Manáus are ports. Bello Horizonte and Diamantina are mining towns.

ADMINISTRATION. Under the constitution of 1969 B. is a Federal Rep. (22 States, 4 Federal Territories and 1 Federal District) and the pres. is indirectly elected by an electoral college of all members of Congress (Senate and Chamber of Deputies) and State legislatures, themselves elected by universal suffrage (except for illiterates).

History. The first European to reach B. in 1500 is reputed to have been a Spaniard, Vicente Yanez Pinzon, and later in the year a Portuguese, Cabral, landed there. B. was claimed by Portugal, and in 1532 coastal settlements were established. From 1632 to 1654 the Dutch had a foothold in the N.E. Rio de Janeiro became the cap. in 1763. When Portugal was invaded by Napoleon, Queen Maria (d. 1816) and her court went to Rio in 1808. Her son, John VI, returned to Lisbon following a rising in Portugal in 1816, leaving behind as regent his son Pedro who in 1822 declared B. independent with himself as emperor. King John, by a treaty of 1825, was made emperor of B., but abdicated immediately in favour of Pedro. War with Buenos Aires from 1825 to 1828 deprived B. of the Banda Oriental prov. (Uruguay from 1828). From 1864 to 1870 B. and the Argentine were at war with Paraguay, which suffered a crushing defeat. The Republic of B. was proclaimed in Nov. 1889 as a result of the abolition of slavery by Pedro II, 1888. B. has a less turbulent later history than other S. American reps., but after the military revolution of 1964 a less democratic regime evolved.

BRAZZAVILLE (braht′sahvēl). Cap. · of the People's Rep. of Congo (in the French Community), a river port with an airport. Founded by the Italian Count Pierre Savorgnan de Brazza (1852–1905), employed in African expeditions by the French govt., it stands on the right bank of Stanley Pool, opposite Léopoldville, and is linked by railway with Pointe-Noire, at the mouth of the Congo, 240 m. to the W.S.W. It has foundries and railway repair shops, builds ships, and makes shoes, soap, furniture, bricks, etc. The Pasteur Institute here dates from 1908, the cathedral from 1892. B. was the African H.Q. of the Free (later Fighting) French during the S.W.W. Pop. (1965) 156,000.

BREAD. The product obtained by moistening flour, kneading the resulting dough, and baking. Unleavened B. contains no raising agent; leavened B. – the normal product – is usually raised with yeast.

B. consists essentially of flour, yeast, salt and water, with fat, milk powder, eggs and other ingredients added in some cases. Wheaten flour is usually used, but rye flour may be used instead, or in addition, in some countries. White B. is made from flour from which all the outer skins (or bran) have been extracted during milling, but brown and wholemeal incl. part or all of the bran respectively.

BREAD FRUIT. Fruit of a tree (*Artocarpus altilis*) of the fig and mulberry family (Moraceae). When toasted, it is said to taste like bread, and is an important article of food among the people of the South Sea Islands to which it is native.

BREAKING AND ENTERING. *See* BURGLARY.

BREAKSPEAR, Nicholas. The only Englishman to become Pope. *See* ADRIAN IV.

BREAM. Name given to 2 quite distinct groups of fishes – the freshwater B. belonging to the carp family (Cyprinidae) and the sea B. (Sparidae) – and various others, which have in common their more or less compressed form. The former Bs. are esteemed by anglers. The latter Bs. are carnivorous fishes, resembling the perch, and are good eating.

BREASTED (bres′ted), **James Henry** (1865–1935). American archaeologist. B. at Rockford, Illinois, he was diverted from entry into the Church to the study of egyptology, intent on linguistic sources, and pub. 5 vols. of *Ancient Records of Egypt* (1906–7). Backed by John D. Rockefeller, jr., he organized the Oriental Institute of Chicago, of which he was director 1919–35, acquired many antiquities for the univ. museum, and pub. the valuable *Development of Religion and Thought in Ancient Egypt* (1912), etc.

BREATHALY-SER. Instrument (invented by Bork-

BREAD FRUIT

enstein of Indiana) for checking the amount of alcohol drunk during a given period. Breath samples are taken, e.g. from a suspected drunken driver, in small self-sealing plastic bags, and are bubbled through a diluted solution of potassium dichromate in 50 % sulphuric acid. A built-in colorimeter then gives a reading of the degree of colour change in the yellow dichromate to blue, this change being brought about by the presence of alcohol in the air. Since it is known that one part of alcohol is present in air for every 2,100 parts in blood at a temperature of 34°C (the mean breath temperature), the amount of alcohol consumed can thereby be measured. In the U.K. their use was legalised in the Road Safety Act 1967.

BRECHT (brekht), **Bertolt** (1898–1955). German poet, playwright and theatre producer. B. of bourgeois family in Augsburg, he became known after the F.W.W. as a dissolute Bohemian out to shock and singing songs to a guitar accompaniment. *Drums in the Night* (1918) is a play with one of his typical returning soldier heroes; *The Threepenny Opera* an attempt to set Gay to a propagandist tune (*See* KURT WEILL); *Mother Courage* (1939) attacked war and inadvertently made a heroine of 'Mother Courage', actually intended as a symbol of the little people who make war possible; and *Galileo*. A Communist, he went into exile in Scandinavia and the U.S. under the Hitler regime. After the S.W.W. he became an Austrian citizen and eventually settled in E. Berlin to direct his own company, the Berliner Ensemble, founded 1949. His controversial influence has led to varying estimates of his permanent value.

BRECKNOCKSHIRE or **BRECONSHIRE**. Border county of Wales, bounded on the N.E. by the river Wye, and on the E. and S.E. by the Welsh border. Much of it is mountainous; in the E. the Black Mountains rise to 2,660 ft.; the Brecon Beacons reach 2,907 ft. Only one-quarter is tilled. The chief rivers are the Wye, the Yrfon, and the Usk. The co. town is Brecon; other towns are Builth Wells, Crickhowell, Hay. Area 733 sq. m.; pop. (1961) 55,544.

BRECON or **BRECKNOCK**. Welsh cathedral town (bor.) and co. town of Brecknockshire, situated on the Usk. It has ancient fairs, and the priory church of St. John became in 1923 the cathedral of the bishopric of Swansea and Brecon. Pop. (1961) 5,797.

BRECONSHIRE. *See* BRECKNOCKSHIRE.

BREDA (brādah′). Historic Dutch town in N. Brabant. Charles II made here the Declaration that paved the way for his Restoration in 1660. Pop. (1967) 119,289.

BREEDING. The rearing of animals or the cultivation of plants, using the crossing of different varities to change the characteristics of an existing breed or variety, or produce a new one. Cattle may be bred for increased meat or milk yield, sheep for thicker or finer wool, horses for speed or stamina, bees for better honey, etc. Plants, such as cereals, may be bred for disease resistance, heavier and more rapid cropping, and hardiness to adverse weather or climate. Radiation is among the plant breeder's new tools: *see* RICE. *See also* EUGENICS.

BREEDING. Process in a nuclear reactor in which more fissile material is produced than was used in the operation of the reactor. Thus thorium can be turned into uranium-233, or plutonium-239 from uranium-238, both by the fission of natural uranium-238. The need is to use rare natural fissionable material only to initiate breeding of new fissile material, which can continue the process indefinitely with abundant raw material.

BREMEN. City and seaport of Germany on the Weser, 43 m. from the open sea. It was one of the Hanseatic towns, and a free imperial city from 1646. In 1867 it became a member of the N. German Confederation, and in 1871 of the German Empire. During the S.W.W. it was repeatedly bombed, and was captured by the British 26 April 1945, when it was found to have suffered severe damage. The 15th cent. town hall, the 11th cent. cathedral, the Stadthaus, and the merchant hall were some notable old buildings. The industrial part of B. centres on the docks. Pop. (1966) 601,884. The Land of B. consists of the city of B. and Bremerhaven; area 156 sq. m.; pop. (1966) 749,600.

BREMERHAVEN. Port at the mouth of the Weser, Germany, serving as outport for Bremen, 34 m. S.S.E. Pop. (1966) 147,765.

BRENNAN, Christopher John (1870–1932). Australian poet. His poems, pub. in Sydney in 1913, clearly reveal the influence of the French symbolists.

BRENNER PASS (4,495 ft.). Lowest of the Alpine passes, it leads from Trentino-Alto Adige, Italy, to Austrian Tirol, and is about 12 m. long. It is traversed by the rly. from Verona to Innsbruck.

BRENTA'NO, Klemens (1778–1842). German poet, novelist, and dramatist. B. at Ehrenbreitstein, the son of an Italian merchant, he became a leader of the younger Romanticists. His poetry reflects the lyric note of the folk-songs which he and L. A. von Arnim (q.v.) collected (1805–8); his other works include the erotic novel *Godwi* (1802), the mystic religious poems *Romanzen vom Rosenkranz* (1852), and plays. He excelled in lyric narrative and in the popular fairy-story.

BRENTANO, Lujo (1844-1931). German economist, author of works on the medieval guilds, etc., and a prominent pacifist, and won a Nobel peace prize 1927.

BRENTWOOD. English town (U.D.), chiefly residential, in Essex, 18 m. N.E. of London. There is some light industry. Pop. (1961) 51,959.

BRESCIA (bre'shah). Italian city, the fort of the Brescian Alps, 52 m. E. of Milan. It is capital of B. prov., and an episcopal see. Pop. (1966) 197,501.

BRESLAU. German name of WROCLAW.

BREST. French naval base, commercial port, and town on Brest Roads, a great bay at the W. extremity of Brittany, 313 m. W. of Paris. The naval base is well equipped; and the commercial harbour handles a considerable trade. B. has iron and steel works, chemical factories, etc.

As the key to the Channel approaches, B. has changed hands many times. During the F.W.W. it was the port of disembarkation of American troops. In the S.W.W., it was in German occupation 1940–4 as a U-boat base. Pop. (1968) 154,023.

BREST. Town in White Russia S.S.R., U.S.S.R., on the r. Bug, 210 m. S.W. of Minsk. From 1921 to 1939 it was in Poland. The Treaty of Brest-Litovsk (an older name of the town) between Russia and the Central Powers was signed here in 1918 during the F.W.W. Pop. (1967) 91,000.

BRETON (breton'), **André** (1896–). French author. Among the leaders of Dada – *Les Champs magnétiques* (1921), an experiment in automatic writing, was one of the most notable products of the movement, he was also a founder of Surrealism, publishing *Le Manifeste du surréalisme* (1924). Of his other works, *Najda* (1928), the story of his love affair with a medium is the most striking.

BRETON. Celtic vernacular of Brittany, belonging to the Cymric group and closely related to the extinct Cornish tongue. It developed from the speech of British emigrants of the 5th and 6th cents. Although superseded by French in the upper prov., B. has never lost its foothold in Lower Brittany; and in the 19th cent. the Romantic revival led to the collection of popular folk-tales, legends, and ballads, followed by the rise of original national poets such as Jaffrennou and Berthou at the end of the century.

BRETTON WOODS. Township in New Hampshire, U.S.A., where an International Monetary Conference was held 1–22 July 1944, under presidency of Henry Morgenthau, U.S. Sec. to the Treasury. At the conclusion of the Conference a Draft of a United Nations' Monetary Agreement was published, providing for the creation of an international monetary fund. *See* MONEY.

BREUER (broi'-er), **Josef** (1842–1925). Viennese physician, a discoverer of the form of psychiatric treatment known as Psychoanalysis. He applied it successfully to cases of hysteria, and collaborated with Freud in *Studien über Hysterie* (1895).

BREUIL (broy), **Henri** (1877–1961). French prehistorian. B. at Mortain, the Abbé B. became prof. of historic ethnography and director of research at the Inst. of Human Palaeontology, Paris, in 1919. He is famed for his establishment of the genuine antiquity of Palaeolithic art and his stress on the anthropological approach to the early history of man.

BRE'VIARY (Lat., a summary or abridgement). The book of the canonical office in use in the R.C. church. It is usually in 4 vols., one for each season.

BREWER, F. Cobham (1810–97). C. of E. divine, historian, and popular writer. His best-known work is the *Dictionary of Phrase and Fable* (1870).

BREWING. The alcoholic fermentation of an aqueous extract of cereal grains with the addition of hops. The medieval distinction between beer containing hops and ale without hops has now fallen into disuse and in modern terminology beer is strictly a generic term including ale, stout and lager. However, it is usual in Britain to refer to ale as beer and to regard stout and lager as products different from beer. In this usage beer is light coloured and top fermented; stout is dark coloured and top fermented and also contains roasted malt or barley; and lager is light coloured and bottom fermented.

Before the middle of the 19th cent. brewing was localized and even many private houses and institutions made their own beer. With modern transport facilities, production tends to be concentrated in a few large breweries and the beers are nationally distributed. The character of different beers arose originally from the water from which they were brewed, e.g., Burton became the most famous centre for English ale brewing and Pilsen gave its name to the most widely drunk lager, but modern water treatment processes enable brewers to reproduce these beer types from almost any local water supply.

The B. process starts with malted barley which primarily consists of starch and diastatic enzymes. This malt is ground in a mill and mixed with hot water which allows the conversion of the starch to sugars by the enzymes. The aqueous extract of these malt sugars – the 'wort' – may be strengthened by the

BREMEN. Overseas Harbour is one of the most modern of the port's basins. Grain ranks high among Bremen's imports, as the giant elevator and silo in the background illustrate, and the famous A. G. Weser dockyards can be seen to the left of the silo. *Courtesy of the German Tourist Information Bureau.*

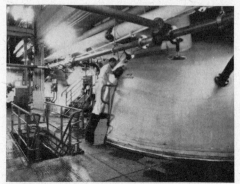

BREWING. The modern brewhouse looks more like a science laboratory, but the same traditional individual care is given to the product. Here inspection is made of the hops boiling in the coppers.   *Courtesy of Arthur Guinness Son & Co. Ltd.*

addition of other sugars such as glucose. It is boiled with hops, which act as a preservative, and give the resulting product a characteristic flavour. Apart from the use of other sources of starch, such as rice and maize and the use of different types and qualities of malt and sugars, the process for the production of beer, stout and lager need not vary greatly up to this point but thereafter the differences are more apparent.

The cooled, hopped wort is mixed either with top fermenting yeast (*Saccharomyces cerevisiae*) for English-type beer or stout, or with bottom fermenting yeast (*Saccharomyces carlsbergensis*) for lager. The fermentation by which the yeast converts the sugars to alcohol and carbon dioxide is, in the case of the English-type beer and stout a warm process (*c.* 60°F.) and in the case of the lager, a cold process (*c.* 45°F.). The finishing varies but, in general, consists of maturation followed by filtration. The length of maturation, and the degree of filtration all have a considerable effect on quality and flavour. Draught beer is filled into casks which are nowadays usually aluminium or stainless steel, together with enough carbon dioxide in solution to force the beer from the cask and give it a head in the glass. Bottled and canned beer also contains dissolved carbon dioxide but in these cases it gives additional sparkle and life.

BREWSTER, Sir David (1781–1868). Scottish physicist, famous for his discoveries regarding the diffraction and polarization of light.

BRE′ZHNEV, Leonid Ilyich (1906–). Russian politician. Son of a steelworker, he became an engineer and metallurgist. During the S.W.W. he was a political worker with the army and afterwards held party office in his native Ukraine. He succeeded Voroshilov as pres. of the U.S.S.R. (1960–4), and in Oct. 1964 succeeded Khrushchev as First Sec. (Gen. Sec. from 1966) of the Soviet Communist Party.

BRIAND (brē-oñ′), **Aristide** (1862–1932). French statesman. B. at Nantes, he became a journalist in Paris. An ardent socialist, he helped Jaurès to found *L'humanité*, and in 1902 was elected to the French Chamber. In 1906, as Minister of Public Instruction and Worship, he carried through the law separating Church and State. Henceforth he was one of the Radical Socialists. B. was several times Prime Minister: 1909–11, when he broke the railway strike of 1910 by mobilizing the strikers for army service; 1913, when he extended the period of military service from 2 to 3 years; 1915–17; 1921–2; 1925–6; and 1929. Subsequently he was often Foreign Minister. In 1925 he concluded the Locarno Pact, and in 1928 the Kellogg Pact; in 1930 he outlined his favourite scheme for the United States of Europe.

BRIANSK (brē-ansk′). Russian town and rly. junction in the R.S.F.S.R. on the Desna. It has foundries, sawmills, cement and brickworks, etc. Pop. (1967) 276,000.

BRIDGE. A construction which provides a continuous path or road over water, valleys, ravines, or above other roads. Bs. may be classified into 4 main groups: (1) the arch; (2) the girder; (3) the cantilever; and (4) the suspension B. Examples of these types are: (1) Waterloo B., London, and the Sydney Harbour B.; (2) the St. Louis Municipal B., crossing the Mississippi, which has 3 spans, each 668 ft., and carries a double deck with 2 railway lines and a road; (3) the Forth B. which is 5,440 ft. long, and has 2 main spans, each span consisting of 2 cantilevers, one from each tower; (4) the Golden Gate Suspension B., San Francisco, which has a gigantic span of more than ¾ m. Steel is pre-eminent in the construction of long-span Bs. because of its high strength-to-weight ratio, but in other circumstances reinforced concrete has the advantage of lower maintenance costs. Light alloy may be used in special cases. *See* TUNNEL for B.-TUNNELS.

BRIDGE (Straight Bridge). Card game, probably originating in Greece, which was introduced into Britain about 1880. From the Portland Club, where it was 1st played in 1894, it rapidly spread – to the detriment of whist – but about 1908 was superseded by its offspring, Auction B. *See* AUCTION B.; CONTRACT B.

BRIDGES, Robert Seymour (1844–1930). British Poet Laureate. B. at Walmer, he qualified as a doctor in London, but abandoned medicine for literature in 1882. His 1st vol. of poems in 1873 was followed by the sonnet-sequence *The Growth of Love* (1876), *Eros and Psyche* (1885), *Shorter Poems* (1896), and dramatic pieces such as *Prometheus the Firegiver* (1883), *Nero* (1885–94), and the masque *Demeter* (1904). In 1913 he was appointed Poet Laureate and became a founder of the Society for Pure English. He won popularity with his war anthology of prose and verse *Spirit of Man* (1916), followed by *New Verse* (1925), and *The Testament of Beauty* (1929), a long philosophical poem which won immediate currency. He was an eager experimenter in metre and was a friend of Hopkins (q.v.), whose poetry he pub. in 1918 when he felt that the time was ripe for such a daring new voice to be heard.

BRIDGET (453–523). A patron saint of Ireland, also known as St. Brigit or St. Bride. She founded a

BRIDGE. The Verrazano-Narrows Bridge, opened in 1964, is the world's longest with a centre span of 4,260 ft.—60 ft. longer than that of the Golden Gate Bridge. It spans the mouth of New York harbour, and was named after the Italian explorer who in 1524 was the first European to sail into the bay.
Courtesy of Amman & Whitney, Consulting Engineers.

church and monastery at Kildare, and is said to have been the daughter of a prince of Ulster.

BRIDGEWATER, Francis Egerton, 3rd duke of (1736–1803). Pioneer of British inland navigation. With James Brindley as his engineer, he constructed (1762–72) the B. canal from Worsley to Manchester, and thence to the Mersey, a distance of 42 m.

BRIDGMAN, Percy Williams (1882–1961). American physicist. B. at Cambridge, Mass., he was ed. at Harvard where he was Hollis prof. of mathematics and natural philosophy 1926–50 and Higgins univ. prof. 1950–4. His research in machinery producing high pressure led in 1955 to the creation of synthetic diamonds by General Electric.

BRIDGWATER. English seaport (bor.) in Somerset on the Parret, 33 m. S.W. of Bristol. The manufacture of bath-brick is the chief industry. Pop. (1961) 25,582.

BRIDIE, James. Pseudonym of Osborne Henry Mavor (1888–1951). Scottish dramatist. B. in Glasgow, where he became prof. of medicine at Anderson Coll., he achieved success in 1931 with *The Anatomist*, dealing with Burke and Hare. Later plays incl. biblical dramas in the modern idiom (*Tobias and the Angel*) and fantasies.

BRIDLINGTON. English market town and resort (bor.) in E. Riding, Yorks, 25 m. N.N.E. of Hull. B. Quay, a mile away, is a watering-place. Pop. (1961) 26,007.

BRIDPORT. English market town (bor.) in Dorset, 15 m. W. of Dorchester. Sailcloth, fishing nets and cordage are manufactured. Pop. (1961) 6,517.

BRIEUX (brē-ö′), **Eugène** (1858–1932). French dramatist, an exponent of the naturalistic problem play attacking social evils. His most powerful plays are *Les trois filles de M. Dupont* (1897); *Les Avariés* (1901; *Damaged Goods*), long banned for its outspoken treatment of syphilis; and *Maternité*.

BRIGGS, Henry (1561–1630). British mathematician. B. near Halifax, and ed. at Cambridge, he was Savilian prof. of geometry at Oxford from 1619. He is best known for his work in constructing the system of logarithms still in popular use.

BRIGHOUSE, Harold (1882–1958). British playwright. B. and bred in Lancs, in his most famous play *Hobson's Choice* (1916) he dealt with a Salford bootmaker's courtship, using the local idiom.

BRIGHOUSE. English market town (bor.) in the Yorkshire W. Riding, 5 m. N. of Huddersfield, with woollen and worsted factories. Pop. (1961) 30,783.

BRIGHT, Sir Charles Tilston (1832–88). British telegraphic engineer, who in 1858 succeeded in laying the first trans-Atlantic cable from Newfoundland to Ireland.

BRIGHT, John (1811–89). Liberal statesman. B. at Rochdale, the son of a Quaker millowner, he became a partner in his father's business. He was among the founders of the Anti-Corn Law League in 1839, and after entering parliament in 1843 led the struggle there for free trade, together with Cobden, which achieved success in 1846. His *laissez-faire* principles also made him a prominent opponent of factory reform. His influence was constantly exerted on behalf of peace, as when he opposed the Crimean War, Palmerston's aggressive policy in China, Disraeli's anti-Russian policy, and the bombardment of Alexandria. During the American Civil War he was outspoken in support of the North, and he was largely instrumental in securing the passage of the reform bill of 1867. He sat in Gladstone's cabinets as President of the Board of Trade 1868–70 and Chancellor of the Duchy of Lancaster 1873–4 and 1880–2, but broke with him over the Irish Home Rule Bill. B. owed much of his influence to his oratorical powers.

BRIGHT, Richard (1789–1858). British physician. He was for many years on the staff of Guy's hospital; 'Bright's Disease', an inflammation of the kidneys, is named after him.

BRIGHTON. Exotic as a fairy tale the Royal Pavilion was built 1784–1827 for the Prince of Wales. The original furnishings and decoration have now been restored, and the Banqueting Room is seen with the table magnificently set.
Photo: Brighton Corporation Royal Pavilion Committee.

BRIGHTON. English holiday resort (co. bor.) on the Sussex coast, 51 m. S. of London, seat of the Univ. of Sussex (1963). Originally a fishing village called Brighthelmstone, it became known as B. at the beginning of the 19th cent., when already it was a fashionable health resort. The Prince Regent, afterwards George IV, stayed there, and built the Pavilion which now belongs to the town and contains a concert hall, museum, assembly room, etc. B. has a sea frontage of 5½ m. Some of the buildings along and near the front are good examples of Regency architecture. There are 2 piers, parks, a racecourse, an aquarium, famous schools include B. Coll. and Roedean Girls' School. B. became a borough in 1854, and a co. bor. in 1888. Pop. (1961) 163,159.

BRILL. Flat-fish (*Rhombus laevis*) of the turbot genus, of a sandy brown colour, varied with white spots and darker brown on the upper side. It is abundant off the coast of Britain.

BRILLAT-SAVARIN (brē-yah′-sahvahrań′), **Anthelme** (1755–1826). French gastronomist, the author of *Physiologie de goût*, a witty guide to the pleasures of the table.

BRINELL HARDNESS TEST. The hardness of a substance is calculated from the area of indentation made by a 10 mm. hardened steel or sintered tungsten carbide ball under standard loading conditions in a test machine and is equal to the load (kg) divided by the surface area (mm²). Johann Auguste B. (1849–1925), inventor of the machine for testing metals and alloys in 1900, was a Swedish engineer.

BRINDISI (brin′dizi). Italian city and seaport on the Adriatic, in Apulia, 65 m. S.E. of Bari. One of the oldest Mediterranean ports, it was the terminus of the Appian Way from Rome. Its modern importance dates from the opening of the Suez Canal in 1869. It is the seat of an archbishopric, and has an 11th cent. cathedral and a 13th cent. castle. Pop. (1961) 70,084.

BRINDLEY, James (1716–72). British engineer. B. in Derbyshire, he was employed by the duke of Bridgewater for the construction of the Bridgewater canal, and played a great part in the rapid development of canal construction in Britain.

BRISBANE, Sir Thomas Makdougall (1773–1860). Scottish soldier and astronomer. After serving under Wellington, he was Gov. of N.S.W. 1821–5, and Brisbane in Queensland is named after him.

BRISBANE. Cap. and chief port of Queensland, Australia, on Moreton Bay, near the mouth of B. river, dredged to carry ocean-going ships. There are dry-docks, wharves, and warehouses, tobacco and shoe factories, breweries, and tanneries.

B. is a well-planned city, built on a plain backed by

BRISBANE. Rising above the fountain and palm trees of King George Square, the City Hall was completed in 1930. In pioneer days the site was a water-hole.
Courtesy of Agent-General for Queensland.

mountains. Among its notable buildings are the Parliament house and Govt. buildings, an Anglican and a R.C. cathedral, museums, etc. Ascot racecourse is to the E. Queensland univ. was estab. here in 1909. B. was named in 1824 after Sir Thomas B., (q.v.), who 1st had the site occupied as a penal colony, 1824–39, opened to free settlers 1842. Greater B. has an area of 385 sq. m.; pop. (1966) 777,935.

BRISSOT (brēsō′), **Jacques Pierre** (1754–93). French revolutionary leader. B. at Chartres, he became a member of the Legislative Assembly and the National Convention, but his party of moderate republicans – the Girondins, or Brissotins – fell foul of Robespierre and B. was guillotined.

BRISTOL. English city and seaport (co. bor.; also co. of itself) in Gloucestershire with some of its suburbs in Somerset, situated 8 m. from the mouth of the Avon on the Bristol Channel. It includes Avonmouth and Portishead Dock. Since Saxon times it has been a trading centre, and in the Middle Ages it handled important wool traffic. From B. John Cabot sailed to discover Newfoundland. In the 17th and 18th cents. B. developed a large commerce with the American colonies and the W. Indies, and it was to the fore in the slave trade.

The principal buildings incl. the cathedral and the 14th cent. church of St. Mary Redcliffe; the univ. (1909), technical colls., and many schools. At the junction of 2 modern motorways, B. plans further

BRISTOL. With a span of 702 ft., the Clifton Suspension Bridge, built by Brunel 1832–64, strides across the Avon gorge just below the city. Clifton itself, on the heights to the right, was a fashionable 18th cent. resort, and is now a 'prestige' residential suburb.   *Courtesy of Bristol Public Relations Office.*

dock development, and there has been rapid industrial expansion. Manufactures incl. aircraft engines, shoes, chocolate and cocoa, tobacco, chemicals, and there are nuclear and general engineering, printing and shipbuilding industries. Wines and spirits are imported. There is an airport at Lulsgate Bottom. Pop. (1961) 436,440.

BRISTOL CHANNEL. Seaward extension of the Severn estuary, 85 m. long, width 5 m. at first, opening to 43 m. between S. Wales, Lundy Island and N. Devon. It receives the rivers Usk, Wye, Severn, Avon, etc. and has very high tides.

BRITAIN, Ancient. The name B., indicating present-day England, Scotland and Wales, is derived from the Roman name Britannia which is in its turn derived from the ancient Celtic. Before the Celts arrived B. was inhabited for thousands of years by people who had already learnt to tame animals and to grow corn in a primitive fashion; built Stonehenge (perhaps about 1800 B.C.) and buried their chiefs in barrows. About 1000 B.C., Britain was conquered by the Celts, tall, fair-haired people who swept across from the Continent in 2 great waves of migration. First came the Goidelic Celts of whom traces may still be seen in the Gaels of Ireland and the Highlands; there followed the Brythonic Celts or Bretons who were closely allied in blood and culture to the Gauls of

BATTLE OF BRITAIN. In this series of air conflicts in 1940 the German attempt to destroy Britain's air bases and communications as a prelude to invasion was defeated, mainly by the gallantry of the pilots of R.A.F. Fighter Command. This vivid impression of the battle by Paul Nash is now in the Imperial War Museum.

France. The early British craftsmen were highly skilled in pottery and metal-work. Tin mines in Cornwall attracted merchant seamen from Carthage.

BRITAIN, Battle of. Air battle over Britain which lasted from 10 July to 31 Oct. 1940: one of the decisive battles of history. It has been divided into 5 phases: (1) 10 July-7 Aug., the preliminary phase; (2) 8–23 Aug., attack on coastal targets; (3) 24 Aug.–6 Sept., attack on Fighter Command airfields; (4) 7–30 Sept., daylight attack on London, chiefly by heavy bombers; and (5) 1–31 Oct., daylight attack on London chiefly by fighter-bombers.

At the outset the Germans were in a strong position. They controlled all the French and Dutch airfields, and the entire seaboard from North Cape to Hendaye. The front-line strength of the Luftwaffe was over 3,000 aircraft, and German industry was capable of producing over 1,000 operational types a month. As a preliminary to invasion the Germans launched a tremendous air attack on Britain, but failed to defeat the R.A.F.; and although they had assembled a great army, they had to abandon their plans.

The battle was won by the men of Fighter Command under Air Chief Marshal Sir Hugh (later Lord) Dowding. The number of German planes destroyed in the battle amounted to 1,733.

BRITISH ANTARCTIC TERRITORY. Colony created in 1962 from part of the Falkland Islands Dependencies. It consists of all British territories S. of lat. 60°S. and includes the S. Shetlands, area 1,800 sq. m., the S. Orkneys, 1,240 sq. m., and Graham Land. B.A.T. has no permanent pop. apart from the personnel of meteorological and other scientific stations.

BRITISH BROADCASTING CORPORATION (B.B.C.). *See* BROADCASTING.

BRITISH COLUMBIA. The Pacific coast province of Canada, lying between the Rocky Mts. and the sea; on the N.W. and on the S. it touches the U.S.A. It has 3 great parallel ranges – the Rockies, the Columbia mountain system, and the coast range – interspersed with valleys, lake basins, heavily timbered forests, rolling uplands, and plateaux. Mt. Fairweather on the Alaska border is 15,300 ft. The chief rivers are the Fraser and the Columbia, and there are more than 80 lakes. The coast is deeply indented.

The capital is Victoria, on Vancouver Island; the commercial metropolis is the port and city of Vancouver on the mainland. Other cities are New Westminster, formerly the capital, a freshwater port on the Fraser; Nanaimo, on Vancouver Island, centre of the coal-mining industry; Prince Rupert, centre of the halibut fishery; Nelson, on Kootenay Lake, centre of mining and lumbering; Vernon and Kelowna, both in the Okanagan, in the heart of the fruit-growing area; Trail, 50 m. S.W. of Nelson, headquarters of the Consolidated Mining and Smelting Co.; and Kamloops, at the confluence of the N. and S. Thompson rivers, a ranching and farming centre.

Vancouver Island was discovered by the Spanish in 1774. The territory was ceded to Britain in 1790, and entered the Canadian Confederation in 1871 as a province. B.C. has a Lieutenant-Governor and a legislative assembly, elected for 5 years, and is represented in the federal parliament by 6 senators

BRITISH COLUMBIA. The unspoiled coastline of the province is an increasing attraction to tourists. This is Breaker Beach, near Bamfield, on Vancouver Island.
Courtesy of the British Columbia Govt.

and 22 members of the House of Commons. There are 4 univs.: Univ. of B.C. at Vancouver (1908), Victoria (1963), Simon Fraser Univ. at Burnaby (1963), and Nelson (1963).

Area 366,255 sq. m.; pop. (1966) 1,873,674.

(BRITISH) COMMONWEALTH (OF NATIONS) On 15 May 1917 Jan Christian Smuts, then S. African Min. of Defence, and in London as representative of his country in the Imperial War Cabinet of the F.W.W., suggested that 'British commonwealth of nations' was the right title for the British Empire. The name was recognised in the Statute of Westminster (1931), but after the S.W.W. a growing sense of independent nationhood led to the simplification of the title to THE COMMONWEALTH.

The C. is now a free association of sovereign independent states, the full 'members of the C.', together with a number of dependent terrs., such as colonies and protectorates, which rank as 'C. countries'.

The members are: United Kingdom, Canada (1867), Australia (1901), New Zealand (1907), India (1947), Pakistan (1947), Ceylon (1948), Ghana (1957), Malaysia (1957–63), Nigeria (1960), Cyprus (1961), Sierra Leone (1961), Tanzania (1961–3), Western Samoa (1962), Jamaica (1962), Trinidad and Tobago (1962), Uganda (1962), Kenya (1963), Malawi (1964), Malta (1964), Zambia (1964) Gambia (1965), Singapore (1965), Guyana (1966), Botswana (1966), Lesotho (1966), Barbados (1966), Swaziland (1968), Nauru (1968), Tonga (1970), W. Samoa (1970), Fiji (1970).

In the case of C. countries which have reached self-governing maturity but are too small to bear the full responsibilities of 'members of the C.' there may be special status, for example, as an Associated State of the U.K. (q.v.) or 'special member', *see* NAURU.

There were 3 impulses behind the growth of the British Empire. The 1st, the impulse to seek freedom of religious practice, was the main element in the creation of the original colonies in N. America. The 2nd, the search for trade, had some part in N. America (notably through the Hudson's Bay Company) and was the overriding influence in the Far East and in many parts of Africa. The 3rd, which came into play in the 19th cent., was the urge felt by the Christian community in Britain to carry the gospel to the heathen; it resulted in the exploration and opening up of the interior of the 'dark continent' of Africa.

HISTORY. England, Wales, Ireland, and Scotland, the 4 countries of the British Isles, came under one sovereign with the accession of James VI of Scotland as James I of England in 1603; and it was in the reign of this monarch that, in 1607, the 1st successful English colony was founded overseas, in N. America at Jamestown, Virginia. British settlement spread up and down the E. coast of that continent until in 1664, when the British secured New Amsterdam (New York) from the Dutch, there was a continuous fringe of colonies from the present S. Carolina in the S. to what is now New Hampshire in the N. These colonies, and others formed later, had democratic institutions and a good deal of freedom, and it was the attempt of George III and his unwise minister Lord North to coerce their inhabitants into paying taxes to the home government that roused the colonists to resistance which came to a head in the War of American Independence, 1775–83, and led to the creation of a new independent state, the United States of America, from the 13 English colonies then lost.

But before this happened, the British had set up colonies and trading posts in other parts of the world, and conquered territories from other European empire builders. Settlements were made in Gambia and on the Gold Coast (1618) in Bermuda (1609) and others of the W. Indian islands; Jamaica was taken from Spain in 1655; Acadia (Nova Scotia) was secured from France by the Treaty of Utrecht, 1713, which recognised Newfoundland and Hudson Bay (as well as Gibraltar in Europe) as British. New France (Quebec), Cape Breton Island, and Prince Edward Island became British as a result of the Seven Years War, 1756–63.

In the Far East, the East India Company, chartered 1600, set up factories, as their trading posts were called, on the W. coast of India at Surat, 1612; on the E. coast at Madras, 1639; and on the Hooghli, one of the mouths of the Ganges, 1640. Bombay came to

THE COMMONWEALTH

	Area in 1,000 sq. m.	Pop est. in 1,000s	Capital
In Europe			
*United Kingdom			
England	50	45,374	London
Wales	7	2,701	Cardiff
Scotland	29	5,190	Edinburgh
N. Ireland	5	1,484	Belfast
Isle of Man	·227	50	Douglas
Channel Islands	·075	110	—
Gibraltar	·002	25	Gibraltar
*Malta and Gozo	·122	318	Valletta
In Asia			
Brunei	2	127	Brunei
*Ceylon	25	11,504	Colombo
*Cyprus	3	614	Nicosia
Hong Kong	·39	3,854	Victoria
*India	1,174	500,000	Delhi
Sikkim	2·7	162	Gangtok
**Jammu & Kashmir	86	3,584	Srinagar
*Malaysia, Fed. of			Kuala Lumpur
E. Malaysia	77	1,440	
W. Malaysia	51	8,415	
*Pakistan	365	93,720	Islamabad
*Singapore	·224	1,955	Singapore
In the Americas			
Bahamas	4	142	Nassau
*Barbados	·166	250	Bridgetown
Bermuda	·02	49	Hamilton
Brit. Honduras	9	114	Belize
*Canada	3,851	20,630	Ottawa
Falkland Islands	4·6	2	Stanley
*Guyana	83	674	Georgetown
*Jamaica	4	1,859	Kingston
*Trinidad & Tobago	2	973	Port of Spain
West Indies			
Leeward and			
Windward Is.	1	483	—
Cayman, Turks			
& Caicos Is.	·266	13	—

	Area in 1,000 sq. m.	Pop. est. in 1,000s	Capital
In the Antarctic			
Falkland Islands			
Dependencies	1·7	—	—
British Antarctic			
Territory	2	—	—
In Africa			
*Botswana	222	543	Gaberones
British Indian			
Ocean Territory	·072	1	Victoria
*Gambia	4	320	Bathurst
*Ghana	92	7,945	Accra
*Kenya	225	9,370	Nairobi
*Lesotho	12	967	Maseru
*Malawi	46	4,042	Zomba
*Mauritius	·72	773	Port Louis
*Nigeria, Fed. of	339	55,653	Lagos
Rhodesia	150	4,530	Salisbury
Seychelles	·089	47	Victoria
*Sierra Leone	28	2,183	Freetown
*Swaziland	6	389	Mbabane
*Tanzania	363	12,231	Dar-es Salaam
*Uganda	94	7,750	Kampala
*Zambia	290	3,700	Lusaka
In Australasia and the Pacific			
*Australia	2,974	12,000	Canberra
Dependencies	2,656	1,900	
*Fiji	7	483	Suva
***Nauru	·008	6	—
*New Zealand	104	2,676	Wellington
Dependencies	160	25	
Pitcairn	·001	·096	Adamstown
*Tonga	·27	77	Nuku'alofa
W. Pacific Islands	17	263	Honiara
*W. Samoa	1	131	Apia
	13,631·652	823,821·096	

*Independent members of the Commonwealth
**Disputed between India and Pakistan
***Special member

the British Crown in 1662, and was granted to the E. India Company for £10 a year. A struggle in the following century between the French and English E. India Companies ended in 1763 in the triumph of the English. The Company, subsequently involved in more than one war with Indian Princes, steadily increased its possessions and the territories over which it held treaty rights up to the eve of the Indian Mutiny, 1857. That rising was put down, but it resulted in the taking over of the govt. of British India by the Crown, 1858; Queen Victoria was proclaimed Empress of India on 1 Jan. 1877.

Constitutional development in Canada started with an act of 1791 which set up Lower Canada (Quebec), mainly French-speaking, and Upper Canada (Ontario), mainly English-speaking. In the American War of 1812, the U.S.A. assumed, erroneously as was soon apparent, that Canada would gladly join the Union; but there was nevertheless enough discontent there to lead in 1837 to rebellion in both Canadas. After the suppression of these risings, Lord Durham was sent out to advise on the affairs of British N. America; his report, published in 1839, became the basis for ihe future structure of the Empire. In accordance with tts recommendations, the 2 Canadas were united in 1840 and given a representative legislative council:

the beginning of colonial self-government. With the British N. America Act, 1867, the self-governing dominion of Canada came into existence; to the original union of Ontario, Quebec, New Brunswick, and Nova Scotia were later added further territories until the federal govt. of Canada controlled all the N. part of the continent except Alaska.

Far away in the Antipodes, colonization began with the need to find a place for penal settlement after the loss of the original American colonies. The 1st shipload of convicts was landed in Australia in 1788 on the site of the future city of Sydney; New South Wales was opened to free settlers in 1819; and in 1853 transportation of convicts was abolished. Before the end of the century 5 Australian colonies – N.S.W., W. Australia, S. Australia, Victoria, Queensland – and the island colony of Tasmania had each achieved responsible govt.; an act of the Imperial Parliament at Westminster created from them the federal commonwealth of Australia, an independent dominion, 1901. New Zealand, annexed in 1840, was at 1st a dependency of N.S.W.; made a separate colony in 1853, it was created a dominion 1907.

The Cape of Good Hope in S. Africa was occupied by 2 English captains in 1620; but neither the home govt. nor the E. India Company was interested. The

Dutch occupied it in 1650, and Cape Town remained a port of call for their E. India Company until 1795 when, French revolutionary armies having occupied the Dutch Republic, the British seized it to keep it from the French, and under the Treaty of Paris, 1814, bought it from the new kingdom of the Netherlands for £6,000,000. British settlement began in 1824 on the coast of Natal, proclaimed a British colony in 1843.

Resentment over the abolition of slavery (1833) in all British possessions led a body of Boers (Dutch for farmers) from the Cape to make the great trek north-eastwards, 1836, and found Transvaal and Orange Free State. Conflict between the British govt., which claimed sovereignty over those areas (since the settlers were legally British subjects), and the Boers culminated, after the discovery of gold in the Boer territories, in the S. African War of 1899–1902, which brought Transvaal and Orange Free State definitely under British sovereignty. Given self-govt. in 1907, they were in 1910, with Cape Colony (self-governing 1872) and Natal (self-governing 1893), formed into the Union of S. Africa, 4th dominion of the Empire.

The British S. Africa Company, chartered 1889, extended British influence over S. Rhodesia (a colony in 1923) and N. Rhodesia (a protectorate in 1924); with Nyasaland, taken under British protection in 1891, the Rhodesias were in 1953 formed into a federation (1953–63) with representative govt. Uganda was made a British protectorate in 1894, to put an end to inter-tribal wars. Kenya, formerly a protectorate, became a colony in 1920, certain districts on the coast forming part of the Sultan of Zanzibar's dominions remaining a protectorate.

In W. Africa, British control was extended from time to time in Gambia and the Gold Coast. Sierra Leone colony started in 1788 with the cession of a strip of land to provide a home for liberated slaves; a protectorate was established over the hinterland in 1896. British influence in Nigeria began through the activities of the National Africa Company (the Royal Niger Company from 1886) which bought Lagos from an African chief in 1861 and steadily extended its hold over the Niger Valley until it surrendered its charter in 1899; in 1900 the two protectorates of N. and S. Nigeria were proclaimed.

The F.W.W. ousted Germany from the African continent, and in 1921–2, under League of Nations mandate, Tanganyika was transferred to British administration, S.W. Africa to South Africa; Cameroons and Togoland, in W. Africa, were divided between Britain and France.

The establishment of the greater part of Ireland as the Irish Free State, with dominion status, came in 1922. A new constitution adopted by the Free State in 1937 dropped the name and declared Ireland (Eire) to be a 'sovereign independent state'; 12 years later S. Ireland became a republic outside the Commonwealth, though remaining in a special relationship with Britain.

British India was given independence in 1947 as the 2 dominions of India (predominantly Hindu in religion) and Pakistan (predominantly Moslem). A startling constitutional development came in 1950 with India's decision to become a republic but, with the full consent of the other members, to remain within the Commonwealth. This made it simple for Pakistan, a rep. from 1956, and Ghana (the former Gold Coast Colony), a dominion 1956, a rep. 1960, to remain members of the Commonwealth. Independence within the Commonwealth followed for Nigeria in 1960, for Sierra Leone in 1961, and the process continued. (For the position of other parts of the Commonwealth, see under separate headings.) This emergence of Commonwealth members inhabited by populations of non-British blood brought about changes of attitude within the group; and when the Union of S. Africa in 1961 adopted a republican form of govt., it decided, owing to the strong differences between its govt. and other members of the Commonwealth (incl. Britain) over 'apartheid' (total separation of different racial groups in the S.A. Republic), not to seek re-admission to the Commonwealth. Another crisis was provoked by Rhodesia's unilateral declaration of independence 1965. Mandatory sanctions were imposed by the U.N., and African and Asian states pressed for the solution of the problem by force. In Canada divisive nationalism, based on language and culture instead of 'colour', became vocal in the 1960s in Quebec.

Consultation at top level on major topics takes place at *Commonwealth Conferences* specially convened, but there was no permanent organisation until at the 1965 conference it was suggested, mainly by the Afro-Asian members, that one should be estab. on the lines of the United Nations. The unanimous choice as first Secretary-General of the *Commonwealth Secretariat* (H.Q. at Marlborough House, in London's Pall Mall) was Canadian diplomat Arnold Smith (1915–   ). The Commonwealth Office, formerly the only day-to-day link with the C. countries, was merged with the Foreign Office in 1968.

Bodies dealing with C. affairs incl. the *Royal Commonwealth Society* (1868), *Commonwealth Institute* (q.v.), *Commonwealth Development Corporation* (q.v.), and *Commonwealth Foundation* (1965) estab. to assist contacts between professional people and organisations in the C. countries. *See* COMMONWEALTH DAY.

BRITISH COUNCIL. Semi-official organization which was inaugurated in 1935 and granted a royal charter in 1940; has for its chief aims the promotion overseas of a wider knowledge of the U.K., excluding political and commercial matters, and the development of cultural relations with other countries.

BRITISH EMPIRE. A British order of chivalry, instituted by George V in 1917. There are military and civil divisions, and awards are made to men and women who have rendered distinguished servcie to the Empire at home or abroad. The ranks are: G.B.E., Knight Grand Cross or Dame Grand Cross; K.B.E., Knight Commander; D.B.E., Dame Commander; C.B.E., Commander; O.B.E., Officer; M.B.E., Member.

BRITISH EXPEDITIONARY FORCE (1939–40). British army that served in France and was evacuated, mainly from Dunkirk, in May–June 1940. It was commanded by Gen. Visct. Gort.

BRITISH COMMONWEALTH. The Commonwealth Institute, opened in Holland Park, Kensington, in 1962 has 3 tiers of exhibition galleries, an art gallery and a cinema.
Courtesy of John Laing & Son Ltd.

BRITISH GUIANA. *See* GUYANA.

BRITISH HONDURAS. British crown colony on the Caribbean Sea adjacent to Guatemala and Mexico. The coastal area is low and swampy, but inland it rises to mountains of considerable height. Numerous small rivers flow into Honduras Bay, on which stands Belize, the cap. and chief seaport. Most of the people are of mixed blood, descending from Negro slaves, native Indians, and British, Spanish, and German buccaneers and settlers. More than 90 per cent of the land is covered with forests, and much fine timber is exported. Tropical products are grown and cattle are reared. The climate is tropical.

Woodcutters from Jamaica were probably the first settlers about 1638. In the 18th cent. large numbers of Negro slaves were imported. The Spaniards continued to dispute possession of the country until 1798 when it came under British control; in 1862 it became a colony, subordinate to Jamaica, and in 1884 a separate colony. Under the constitution of 1964 it has a gov. and national assembly (House of Reps. and Senate). Guatemala lays claim to B.H. Area 8,867 sq. m.; pop. (1966) 111.255.

BRITISH INDIAN OCEAN TERRITORY. British colony in the I.O. estab. in 1965 to provide certain defence facilities for the govts. of the U.K. and U.S.A. It consists of the Chagos Archipelago *c.* 1200 m. N.E. of Mauritius, by which it was formerly admin., which has a pop. of 1,000; and the is. of Aldabra (pop. 100), Farquhar (172), and Desroches (112) some 300 m. northwards of Madagascar, which were formerly admin. by the Seychelles. The B.I.O.T. has its admin. centre at Victoria on Mahé in the Seychelles. Area 72 sq. m. incl. lagoons; pop. (1965) 1,400.

Diego Garcia, largest is. of the Chagos Archipelago, is on the direct staging route from the U.K. to Australia and the Far East, via the Red Sea, and has a good airfield site: the excellent harbour was used by the Navy in the S.W.W. Copra, salt fish, and tortoise shell are exported. Pop. *c.* 500.

BRITISH ISLES. Group of islands off the N.W. coast of Europe, consisting of Great Britain (England, Wales, and Scotland), Ireland, the Channel Islands, Orkney and Shetlands, Isle of Man, and many others which are included in various counties, e.g. Isle of Wight, Scilly Isles, Lundy Island, and the Inner and Outer Hebrides (qq.v.). The islands are divided from Europe by the North Sea, Strait of Dover, and English Channel, and face the Atlantic to the W.

BRITISH LEGION. Organization to promote the welfare of veterans of war service and their dependants. Estab. under the leadership of Haig in 1921 (royal charter 1925) it is open to both men and women; it is non-political. The sale on Remembrance Sunday of Flanders poppies made by disabled members raises much of its funds.

BRITISH MUSEUM. Largest and most important museum of the U.K. Founded in 1753 with the purchase of Sir Hans Sloane's library and art collection, and the subsequent acquisition of the Cottonian, Harleian, and other libraries, the B.M. was opened at Montagu House, Bloomsbury, in 1759. Rapid additions led to the construction of the present buildings (designed by Sir Robert Smirke) by 1852, with later extensions in the circular reading room (1857), and the N. wing or Edward VII galleries (1914). In 1881 the Natural History Museum was transferred to S. Kensington, and in 1906 and 1932 respectively provincial and London newspapers were stored at Colindale. The B.M. library receives a copy of every publication issued in the U.K., and as announced 1971, will eventually be re-housed on an adjoining site, when it will be known as the *British Library*: lending services will be concentrated in Boston Spa, Yorks.

BRITISH THERMAL UNIT (Btu). The amount of heat required to raise 1 lb. of water through 1°F.

BRITISH VOLUNTEER PROGRAMME. Name by which the various schemes under which volunteers from the U.K. are sent to work in overseas developing countries have been known since 1966. They number c.1000 graduates and c.500 school leavers or cadets annually, and serve up to 2 years. Voluntary Service Overseas (1958) is the best-known of these organisations, which inspired the American Peace Corps (q.v.).

BRITTAIN, Vera (1894–1970). British writer. B. in Staffs, she was a V.A.D. nurse 1915–19, and pub. a vol. of reminiscences *Testament of Youth* (1933) and a biography of her friend Winifred Holtby (q.v.) *Testament of Friendship* (1950).

BRITTANY. Ancient division and former independent duchy, later prov., of France, which covered its N.W. peninsula and in 1790 divided into depts. (Finistère, Côtes-du-Nord, Morbihan, Loire-Atlantique, Ille-et-Vilaine). The land is one of ridges and valleys; rivers are short and torrential. The sea is the dominating factor, and the Bretons are noted fishermen and mariners.

B. was the Roman Armorica, which was devastated by the Northmen after the Roman withdrawal. During the Angle and Saxon invasions of Britain, many Celts from that land joined their fellow Celts in B., which thus acquired its name. It became a duchy about 1000, lost much of its independence following the marriage in 1491 of Anne, Duchess of Brittany, to Charles VIII of France, and was formally annexed to the French crown in 1547. Rennes is the chief town; Brest is an important civil and naval port. The Breton language is close to Welsh and Cornish.

BRITTEN, Edward Benjamin (1913–). British composer. B. at Lowestoft, he was ed. at Gresham's School, Holt, and the R.C.M. In America when the S.W.W. broke out, he returned in 1942 and devoted himself to composing at his home in Aldeburgh, Suffolk, where he estab. an annual music festival. He is known for his songs – he has often accompanied the tenor, Peter Pears – and also for his operas, *Peter Grimes* (1945) based on a tale by Crabbe, the chamber opera *The Rape of Lucretia* (1946), *Billy Budd* (1951), and *A Midsummer Night's Dream* (1960). His oratorio *A War Requiem* (1962) was written for the dedication of Coventry Cathedral. He was awarded the O.M. 1965.

BRIXHAM. Seaside resort in the C.B. of Torbay Devon, England, 6 m. S.W. of Torquay. William of Orange (William III) landed here in 1688. Pop. (1961) 10,679.

BRNO. Industrial town and the 2nd city of Czechoslovakia, at the junction of the Svratka and

BRITTEN. Greatest in stature among modern English composers, Britten could also have made a pre-eminent name as pianist or conductor. He is here seen at rehearsal, for a B.B.C. concert with the London Symphony Orchestra.
Photo: Godfrey MacDomnic.

BRNO. Set in the beautiful Moravian countryside are the grounds of the International Trade Fair, first held in 1959 and now an annual event. On the left is the multi-storey administration building. *Courtesy of the Czechoslovak Travel Bureau.*

the Svitava. It has a fortress; the 15th cent. cathedral of St. Peter; a 16th cent. Rathaus; and a univ., founded in 1918. The Bren gun was first manufactured here. Pop. (1961 est.) 320,000.

BROAD, Charlie Dunbar (1887–). British philosopher. B. in London, he was ed. at Trinity Coll., Cambridge, and was Knightbridge prof. of moral philosophy at the univ. 1933–53. His books incl. *Perception, Physics and Reality* and *Lectures on Psychic Research* (1962), discussing modern scientific evidence for survival after death.

BROAD ARROW. The mark resembling an arrowhead placed on govt. stores. Of doubtful origin, the B.A. came into general use in the 17th cent. and is still used to mark govt. property, such as Post Office mail-bags, but it has long been abolished on prison dress.

BROADCASTING. The transmission of sound and vision programmes by radio. B. may be organized under complete state control, e.g. Soviet Union; or private enterprise, e.g. the U.S.A. where it is only limited by the issue of licences from the Federal Communications Commission to competing commercial companies; or operate under a compromise system, e.g. Australia (where official and commercial cos. compete), Canada (where a govt. corporation also sells time to advertisers) and Britain, where although sound broadcasting is entirely controlled by the B.B.C. (a centralized body appointed by the State and responsible to Parliament, but with policy and programme content not controlled by the State), there is also a commercial Independent Television Authority (1955). In Japan, which ranks next to the U.S. in the number of TV sets owned, there is a semi-governmental radio and television B. corporation (NHK) and numerous private TV cos. *See* RADIO and TELEVISION.

BROADMOOR. Place in S.E. Berks, England, the site of a special hospital opened 1863 for persons then described as criminally insane. It was transferred from Home Office to Min. of Health control in 1949, and in 1968 rebuilding was planned.

BROADS, The. A district of *c.* 5,000 acres in Norfolk and Suffolk, England, containing about 12 large freshwater lakes or 'broads' and many small ones. The largest B. is Hickling, 3 m. round. The total length of waterway available for light craft is some 200 m. The Bs. are famous as a holiday resort.

BROADSTAIRS. Seaside resort (U.D.) in N.E. Kent, England, 77 m. S.E. of London on the E. coast of Thanet. Pop. (1961) 16,979.

BROADWAY. Main street (18 m. long) of, and a great theatre and trade centre in, New York City.

BROCH (brokh), **Hermann** (1880–1951). Austrian novelist, best known for *Der Tod des Vergil* (1945: *The Death of Virgil*), a study of the last 18 hours in the poet's life, expressing his own sense of the inadequacy of poetry or any art as a full means of perception of truth. After a period under Nazi arrest he escaped to England and then to the U.S.A.

BROCK, Sir Thomas (1847–1922). British sculptor. B. at Worcester, he is known for his memorial to Queen Victoria in front of Buckingham Palace.

BROCKWAY, Fenner, baron (1888–). British Labour politician. During the F.W.W. he spent several

BROADCASTING. The radio 'chain' (1) a newsreader (2) the V.H.F. transmitting mast at Wrotham (3) the sound control room showing beyond the technical operations supervisor's desk, on the far right, the main contro desk with the simultaneous broadcast position (*right*) miscellaneous switching and monitoring position (*centre*, below the main source-to-destination indicator panel) and (*left*) a desk carrying some monitoring facilities as well as alarm lamps to indicate abnormal apparatus conditions: to the extreme left are 2 of the 3 two-channel control and monitor positions and (4) F.M. transmitters at Sutton Coldfield. *Courtesy of the British Broadcasting Corporation.*

years in prison as a conscientious objector, entered Parliament in 1929, and has campaigned vigorously for the freedom of colonial peoples. *Inside the Left* (1942) was a political autobiography. He became a life peer 1964.

BRO'DIE, Sir Israel (1895–). Chief Rabbi of the United Hebrew Congregations of the British Commonwealth 1948–65, and senior Jewish Chaplain to the Forces 1944–8. In 1964 he upheld the conservative position in the dispute over orthodoxy.

BRO'GAN, Sir Denis (1900–). British expert on French and U.S. affairs. B. in Glasgow, he became prof. of political science at Cambridge, and has pub. *The Era of Franklin D. Roosevelt* (1952), *The French Nation* (1957), *America in the Modern World* (1961), etc. He was knighted in 1963. His brother Colm B. (1902–) is well-known as a journalist.

BROKEN HILL. Mining town in N.S.W., Australia, in a district containing rich deposits of zinc, lead, tin, and silver. Pop (1966) 30,023.

Another BROKEN HILL (re-named **Kabwe** in 1967) is the H.Q. of Central Prov., Zambia. It is served by hydro-electric stations at Mulungushi and Lunsemfwa, and copper and cadmium are mined. Pop. 45,500.

BROMBERG. German name for BYDGOSZCZ.

BROMFIELD, Louis (1896–1956). American novelist. B. in Mansfield, Ohio, he studied agriculture at Cornell univ. and was subsequently to use the proceeds of his successful *The Rains Came* (1937) to estab. himself as a farmer. Some of his books have only the facility of the journalist, a profession he followed for some years, but exceptions are *The Strange Case of Miss Annie Spragg* (1928) and *Mrs. Parkington* (1943) dealing with the golden age of N.Y. society.

BRO'MINE. A chemical element, a dark brown-red liquid, very volatile, and with an unpleasant irritating smell – whence the name given to it in 1826 by its discoverer Balard (Gk. *bromos*, a stench). Its symbol is Br; atomic weight 79.92 and atomic number 35. It does not occur free in nature, but its compounds are found in sea water, mineral springs, etc.

Bromides, formed by combining metallic elements with B., are much used in photography, and potassium bromide and sodium bromide are used in medicine as sedatives.

BROMLEY. Bor. of Greater London from 1965, on the Ravensbourne. The palace of the bps. of Rochester (1777) is now a teachers' training college. H. G. Wells was born in B. Pop. (1967) 302,660.

BRONCHITIS. Inflammation of the bronchi. *Acute B.* is the most common acute disease of the lungs. It may be due to sudden exposure to cold, but is more usually caused by extension of a cold in the head. It may develop into *Chronic B.*

BRONOWSKI. Well known for his forthright appearances on television and radio in the U.K., Dr. Bronowski also has a reputation in the U.S. and in 1964 became deputy director Salk Institute for Biological Studies.

BRONOWSKI (bronof'ski**), Jacob** (1908–). British scientist. B. in Poland, he settled in England in 1920 and was ed. at Jesus Coll., Cambridge. In 1942 he became head of a number of mathematical units dealing with the statistical and economic effects of bombing. At the end of the war he was Scientific Deputy to the British Chiefs of Staff Mission to Japan. In 1959–64 he was Director-General of Process Development in the N.C.B. He is author of the classic radio ay *The Face of Violence* and of the philosophical

THE BRONTË SISTERS. Emily, Anne and Charlotte, painted by their brother Patrick Branwell c. 1835.
Photo: N.P.G.

treatise *The Western Intellectual Tradition* (1960).

BRONTË. Name of three sisters, famous as novelists: CHARLOTTE (1816–55), EMILY JANE (1818–48), and ANNE (1820–49). The daughters of an Irish clergyman, Patrick B. (1777–1861), they were b. at Thornton, near Bradford, whence in 1821 the family moved to Haworth. After their mother's death the sisters and their brother PATRICK BRANWELL (1817–48) were brought up by an aunt. In 1824 the older girls went to a school for clergymen's daughters, but were soon removed; Charlotte later described the school as 'Lowood' in *Jane Eyre*. For some years the sisters earned their living as governesses, and in 1842 Charlotte and Emily entered Mr. Héger's school at Brussels; Emily returned to Haworth on their aunt's death, but Charlotte, who had conceived a hopeless passion for Héger, did not finally leave Brussels until 1844. Meanwhile Branwell, who shared something of his sisters' genius, had become a drunkard and an opium addict. The sisters now discovered that each was secretly engaged in literary activity, and in 1846 they pub. a joint collection of poems under the pseudonyms of Currer, Ellis, and Acton Bell. Charlotte's first novel, *The Professor*, failed to find a publisher, though Emily's *Wuthering Heights* and Anne's *Agnes Grey* were accepted. *Jane Eyre*, issued in 1847, won a sensational success. During 1848–9 Branwell, Emily, and Anne all d. of consumption. *Shirley*, dealing partly with the Luddite riots, appeared in 1849, and *Villette* in 1853; it derives largely from Charlotte's Brussels experiences. Abandoning her anonymity, she visited London, and made the acquaintance of Thackeray, Harriet Martineau, and her biographer, Mrs. Gaskell. In 1854 she m. her father's curate, A. B. Nicholls, but their happy married life was cut short by her death a year later. Emily's only novel, *Wuthering Heights*, a share in which has been claimed for Branwell on insufficient evidence, is a work of strange, wild power unique in English literature. The same power is discernible in her poems, which are greatly superior to those of her sisters. Anne's two novels, *Agnes Grey* and *The Tenant of Wildfell Hall*, are mainly interesting through their author's association with her greater sisters.

BRONZE. Alloy of copper and tin, yellow or brown in colour; one of the first metallic alloys known to man. It is harder than pure copper and more suitable for casting. It contains 4–11 per cent of tin; for bell-metal, bronze containing 15 per cent or more of tin is used. Phosphor B. is hardened by the addition of a small percentage of phosphorus. Silicon B. (for telegraph wires) and aluminium B. are similar alloys of copper with silicon or aluminium, but usually contain no tin.

BRONZE AGE. Period of early history and pre-history when bronze was the chief material used for tools and weapons. It lies between the Stone Age and the Iron Age and may be dated 5000–1200 B.C. in the Near East, and about 2000–500 B.C. in Britain.

BRONZINO (bronzě'nō), Il (1503–72). Pseudonym of the Italian artist Agnolo di Cosimo, favourite painter of Cosimo I, duke of Tuscany. His portraits of the Medici circle have a simple elegance and incl. some attractive child studies. He was influenced by Michelangelo.

BROOK, Clive (1887–). British actor. B. in London, he is a polished stylist and appeared in films and plays on both sides of the Atlantic, e.g. *Second Threshold*.

BROOKE, Sir Basil. See BROOKEBOROUGH, VISCT.

BROOKE, Henry, baron B. of Cumnor (1903–). British Cons. politician. He entered Parliament in 1938, as Min. for Housing 1957–61 was responsible for the Rent Act (1957) providing for progressive relaxation of rent control, and 1962–4 was Home Sec. He was created a life peer in 1966.

BROOKE, Sir James (1803–68). British administrator, known as 'the white rajah'. B. nr. Benares, he served in the army of the East India Co. In 1838 he headed a private expedition to Borneo, where he helped to suppress a revolt, and in 1841 the Sultan gave him the title of Rajah of Sarawak. He was succeeded as Rajah by his nephew, SIR CHARLES JOHNSON B. (1829–1917), who in turn was succeeded by his son, SIR CHARLES VYNER B. (1874–1963), who in 1946 arranged for the transfer of Sarawak to the British Crown.

BROOKE, Rupert Chawner (1887–1915). English poet. B. at Rugby, where he was ed., he travelled abroad after a nervous breakdown in 1911, but in 1913 won a fellowship at King's Coll., Cambridge. Later that year he toured America (*Letters from America*, 1916), N.Z. and the S. Seas, and in 1914 became an officer in the Royal Naval Division. After fighting at Antwerp, he sailed for the Dardanelles, but died of blood-poisoning on the Greek island of Skyros, where he is buried. The 5 war sonnets pub. immediately after his death made him the symbol of the F.W.W. 'lost generation': 'Grantchester' and 'The Great Lover' are perpetual anthology pieces.

RUPERT BROOKE. Post-humous portrait by J. H. Thomas.   *Photo: N.P.G.*

BROOKEBOROUGH, Basil Brooke, visct. B. (1888–). Statesman of N. Ireland. Entering Parliament as a Unionist in 1929, he was Min. for Agriculture 1933–41, for Commerce 1941–5, and P.M. of N. Ireland 1943–63. He was a staunch advocate of strong links with Britain. He succeeded to his father's baronetcy in 1907, and was created a visct. in 1952.

BROOK FARM. Farm in W. Roxbury, near Boston, Mass., U.S.A., which in 1841–7 was the scene of a liberal communistic experiment led by George Ripley (1802–80), a former Unitarian minister. Financial difficulties and a disastrous fire led to the community's dissolution.

BROOKLANDS. Former motor racing track, 1 m. from Weybridge, Surrey, England, opened in 1907 as a testing-ground for motor-cars, and closed in 1946.

BROOKLYN. Most populous borough of New York City, U.S.A. Occupying the S.W. end of Long Island, on New York Bay and East r., it is connected with Manhattan Island by bridges, tunnels, and ferries. It is an important commercial and industrial centre; its waterfront, with many great docks, basins and wharves, extends to 33 m.; and at Wallabout Bay, East r., is the important Brooklyn U.S. Navy Yard.

B. is noted for the number and standard of its public buildings; cultural activities are the concern of the Brooklyn Institute, founded in 1823. Of the more than 60 parks, Prospect is the most important. Area 89 sq. m.; pop. (1960) 2,627,319.

BROOKS, Van Wyck (1886–1963). American critic. Though b. in New Jersey, B.'s spiritual home was New England, where he settled in Connecticut in 1920. He valued the 'rational intensity of the Puritan ideal' and his study *The Flowering of New England* (1936) was the first of a 5-vol. series covering American literature 1800–1915.

BROOKWOOD. Part of Woking, Surrey, England, the site of the first public crematorium in England, first used in 1885.

BROUGHAM, Henry Peter, 1st baron B. and Vaux (broom and vawks) (1778–1868). British statesman. B. in Edinburgh, he was a founder of the *Edinburgh Review* to which he contributed from 1802 onwards. From 1811 he was chief adviser of the Princess of Wales (afterwards Queen Caroline), and in 1820 he defeated the attempt of George IV to divorce her. He sat in Parliament 1810–12 and from 1816, and supported the causes of public education and law reform. When the Whigs returned to power in 1830, B. was made Lord Chancellor and created Baron B. and Vaux. His speeches in support of the Reform Bill were a notable effort, but his dictatorial and eccentric ways led to his exclusion from office when the Whigs next assumed power in 1835. After 1837 he took an active part in the business of the House of Lords.

BROUWER (brow'wer), Adriaen (c. 1605–38). Flemish artist. Influenced by Hals, with whom he may have studied, he developed an animated style of rendering peasant scenes. Avoiding bucolic romanticism, he captured in detail the squalid debauchery, and was himself said to have lived a Bohemian existence.

BROWN, Ernest William (1866–1938). British mathematical astronomer. Ed. at Cambridge, he devoted himself to the study of the lunar theory. His *Tables of the Motion of the Moon* was pub. by Yale univ., where B. was prof. of mathematics 1907–32. He also pub. *Planetary Theory* (1933).

BROWN, Ford Madox (1821–93). British painter. B. at Calais, he studied in Belgium, and later came to England where he was associated with the Pre-Raphaelites, though he did not actually join the movement. His best-known pictures incl. 'The Last of England' (Birmingham), and 'Christ Washing St. Peter's Feet' (Tate Gallery, London), and he had a gift for strong colour.

Lord GEORGE-BROWN

BROWN, George, baron George- (1914–). British Labour politician. Entering Parliament in 1945, he was briefly Min. of Works in 1951 and contested the leadership of the party on the death of Gaitskell. He was 1st Sec. of State and Min. for Economic Affairs 1964–6, and For. Sec. 1966–8. He was created a life peer in 1970.

BROWN, John (1800–59). American anti-slavery leader. B. in Connecticut, he settled as a farmer in Kansas in 1855. In 1856 he was responsible for the 'Pottawatomie massacre' when 5 pro-slavery farmers were killed. In 1858 he formed a plan for a refuge for runaway slaves in the mountains of Virginia. With 18 men, he seized, on the night of 16 Oct. 1859, the govt. arsenal at Harper's Ferry in W. Virginia, and resisted all attacks until on 18 Oct. U.S. marines under Col. Lee stormed the place. B. was seriously wounded. He was tried at Charleston and hanged on 2 Dec. In the northern states B. was quickly hailed as a martyr. The words of the song 'John Brown's Body' were written *c.* 1860, probably by Thomas B. Bishop: the tune is of uncertain origin.

BROWN, John (1810–82). Scottish essayist. B. in Lanarkshire, he became a physician at Edinburgh, and is remembered for his vols. of essays, *Horae Subsecivae* (Leisure Hours), pub. in 1858 and 1861.

BROWNE, E(lliott) Martin (1900–). British theatrical producer, famous for his presentation of T. S. Eliot's plays in London and N.Y. He was visiting prof. in religious drama at the Union Theological Seminary, N.Y., 1956–62.

BROWNE, Maurice (1881–1955). British actor-manager. With Harold Munro (q.v.) he gave encouragement to the Georgian poets, then went to the U.S. and founded with Ellen Van Volkenburg the influential Chicago Little Theatre in 1912. Among his London productions was the sensationally successful *Journey's End.*

BROWNE, Robert (1550–1633). English Puritan leader, founder of the Brownists. B. near Stamford, he took to preaching in Norwich, and was several times in prison in 1581–2 for attacking Episcopalianism. For a time he retired to Middelburg in Holland, but later made his peace with the Church and became master of Stamford Grammar School. From 1591 he was a rector in Northants.

The community which B. founded in Norwich and Holland continued on Nonconformist lines, developing into modern Congregationalism. In a work pub. in 1582 B. advocated congregationalist doctrine.

BROWNE, Sir Thomas (1605–82). English author and physician. B. in London, he travelled widely on the Continent as a student of medicine before settling at Norwich in 1637. He cultivated a personal mode of expression which still gives value to his main works: *Religio Medici* (1643), a justification of his profession; *Vulgar Errors* (1646), an examination of popular legend and superstition; *Urn Burial* and *The Garden of Cyrus* (1658); and *Christian Morals* (1717). He was knighted in 1671.

BROWNIAN MOVEMENT. When colloidal particles are suspended in a fluid medium they are subjected to impacts from the molecules of the medium and are in continuous random motion. This phenomenon was first observed by Robert Brown in 1827.

BROWNING, Elizabeth Barrett (1806–61). British poet. B. near Durham, *née* Barrett, she fell from her pony in girlhood and injured her spine, and was treated by her father as a confirmed invalid. In 1844 she pub. *Poems* (incl. 'The Cry of the Children'), which led to her friendship and secret marriage with Robert B. in 1846. The *Sonnets from the Portuguese* (1847) were written during their courtship and represent her work at its best. Freed from her father's oppressive influence, B.'s health improved, and during the years in Italy she wrote *Casa Guidi Windows* (1851), the poetic novel *Aurora Leigh* (1857), and other verse.

BROWNING, Sir Frederick Arthur Montague (1896–1965). British soldier, deputy commander of the 1st Airborne Army at Arnhem in 1944 and Chief-of-Staff S.E.A.C. 1944–6. He held posts in the Royal Household after retiring from the army in 1947, and from 1959 was Extra Equerry to the Queen and Duke of Edinburgh. *See* DAPHNE DU MAURIER.

BROWNING, Robert (1812–89). Poet. B. in Cam-

THE BROWNINGS. Bronze cast of the clasped hands of the poets by Harriet Hosmer, 1853.   *Photo: N.P.G.*

berwell, he wrote his first poem *Pauline* (1833) under the influence of Shelley; it was followed by *Paracelsus* (1835) and *Sordello* (1840), which marked the development of his use of psychological analysis and interest in obscure characters of literature and history. In 1837 he achieved moderate success with his play *Strafford*, and in the series of *Bells and Pomegranates* (1841–6), which contained *Pippa Passes* (1841), *Dramatic Lyrics* (1842) and *Dramatic Romances* (1845), he included the dramas *King Victor and King Charles*, *Return of the Druses* and *Colombe's Birthday*.

In 1846 he met Elizabeth Barrett, whom he m. the same year and took to Italy. Here he wrote *Christmas Eve and Easter Day* (1850); and *Men and Women* (1855), containing some of his finest love-poems and dramatic monologues, which were followed later by *Dramatis Personae* (1864), and *The Ring and the Book* (1868–9), based on an Italian murder story. After his wife's death in 1861 B. had settled in England and now enjoyed an established reputation, although his latest works such as *Red-cotton Night-Cap Country* (1873), *Dramatic Idylls* (1879–80), and *Asolando* (1889), still prompted opposition by their rugged obscurity of style. Although the charge of facile optimism is unfounded, B. is less valued today for his philosophy than for the range of his poetry. The *Pied Piper of Hamelin, Home Thoughts from Abroad, Rabbi ben Ezra*, etc., are constant anthology pieces.

BROWN SHIRTS. The S.A. (*Sturm-Abteilung*), or Storm Troops, the private army of the German Nazi Party; so called from their uniform.

BRUBECK (broo'bek), **Dave** (David Warren) (1920–). American jazz musician. B. at Concord, California, he studied the piano and worked under Darius Milhaud at Mills Coll., Oakland (1946–9), beginning to record in 1950. He is a jazz 'intellectual' and his quartet (formed 1951) combines improvisation with the disciplines of modern classical music.

BRUCE, David (1898–). American diplomat. B. in Baltimore, Maryland, where he practised law, he has been ambassador to France 1949–52, W. Germany 1957–60, and the U.K. 1961–9. One of the few Democrats to hold office in Eisenhower's administration, he was the President's special representative in Europe 1953–5, assisting the negotiations which led to the adoption of the Western-European Union Treaty.

BRUCE, James (1730–94). Scottish explorer. He was British consul at Algiers (1763–5), and then set out to explore the Roman remains in the Near East. Starting from Alexandria in 1768 he reached the source of the Blue Nile in 1770, and followed the river downstream to Cairo by 1773.

BRUCE, Robert (1274–1329). Scottish hero. He was the grandson of Robert de Bruce (1210–95), who unsuccessfully claimed the Scottish throne in 1290. B. shared in the national rising led by Wallace, and soon after the latter's execution in 1305 he rose again against Edward I, and was crowned king of Scotland in 1306. He defeated Edward II at Bannockburn in 1314, and in 1328 the treaty of Northampton recognized Scottish independence, and B. as king.

BRUCE, Stanley Melbourne, 1st visct. B. of Melbourne (1883–1967). Australian statesman. Called to the Bar in 1906, he practised in England until 1914. After serving in the F.W.W., he returned to Australia, where he was elected to the Commonwealth parliament in 1918 as a member of the National Party, becoming P.M. and Min. for External Affairs in a National-Country Party coalition (1923–9). He was Australian Minister in London (1932–3), and High Commissioner (1933–45), and 1951–61 was 1st Chancellor of the Australian National Univ., Canberra. In 1947 he received a viscountcy.

BRUCKNER (brook´ner), **Anton** (1824–96). Austrian composer. B. at Ansfelden, son of a country schoolmaster, he was a choirboy at the monastery of St. Florian where he later became apprentice organist. As cathedral organist at Linz 1856–68, he composed in his leisure time and was much influenced by Wagner, and from 1868 was at Vienna, where he became prof. at the Conservatoire in 1871. He wrote numerous choral works, and 9 symphonies, one unfinished.

BRUEGHEL (brö´khel), **Pieter** (c. 1525–69). Flemish painter, whose pictures of peasant life are distinguished by vividness of colouring and expression, and by a grotesque and often satirical humour. His son PIETER B. THE YOUNGER (1564–1637), called 'Hell' B., painted chiefly religious subjects; another son JAN B. (1568–1625), known as 'Velvet' B., was a painter of flowers, landscapes, and seascapes, and often collaborated with Rubens.

BRUGES (brüzh). City and episcopal see of Belgium, capital of W. Flanders province, 10 m. from the North Sea, with which it is connected by canal, and 58 m. N.W. of Brussels. It has its name from the many bridges that cross its many waterways. Among its notable buildings are the cathedral of St. Sauveur, dating from the 7th cent.; the church of Notre Dame, dating from the 8th cent.; the Hôtel de Ville, begun in 1376; and the famous belfry (13th cent.) above the Halles (markets). Medieval B. was the most important place in Flanders, with a thriving woollen industry, but was superseded by Antwerp and Amsterdam, though it is still important for textile and lace manufacturing. Pop. (1966) 52,249.

BRUGGE. Flemish form of BRUGES.

BRUMMELL, George Bryan (1778–1840). English man of fashion known as 'Beau' B. The friend of the Prince of Wales (later George IV), he was for several years the recognized leader of fashion. Eventually, however, his fortune was exhausted, he quarrelled with the Prince, and in 1816 fled to France.

BRUNEAU (brünō´), **Alfred** (1857–1934). French composer and critic. He is celebrated for his operas, the most famous being *Le Rêve* (1891), and *L'Attaque du Moulin*, with libretti supplied by his friend Zola.

BRUNEI (broonī´). State in N.W. Borneo, surrounded on all sides by Sarawak. It came under Brit. protection in 1885 and was occupied by the Japanese 1941–5. Under the constitution of 1959 (amended 1965), there is a Privy Council, Council of Ministers (elected) and Legislative Council (part nominated, part elected). The Mentri Besar, or chief minister, is appointed by the sultan, Hassanal Bolkiah (1922–   ), who succeeded on his father's abdication in 1967. Oil revenues provide excellent social services: other products are rubber and sago. The cap. is B. (Pop. 57,000) on B. river. Area 2,226 sq. m.; Pop. (1966) 127,195.

BRUNEL´, Sir Marc Isambard (1769–1849). Engineer and inventor. B. in Normandy, he served with the French navy until 1792, when he went to New York. Coming to England in 1799, he did engineering work for the Admiralty, improved the port of Liverpool, and planned a tunnel under the Thames from Wapping to Rotherhithe which was constructed 1825–43. He was knighted in 1841.

His son, **Isambard Kingdom B.** (1806–59), assisted his father in the Thames tunnel project, and in 1833 became engineer to the G.W. Railway, which adopted the 7 ft. gauge on his advice. In 1838 he designed the *Great Western* which was the first steamship to cross the Atlantic regularly, and sailed from Bristol to New York. His next ship,was the *Great Britain* (1845), the first large ship to be constructed of iron and to have a screw propeller; larger still was the *Great Eastern* (1858). Brunel Univ. (1966) at Uxbridge is named after them.

BRUNELLESCHI (broonel-les´kē) or **BRUNELLESCO** (-skō), **Filippo** (1377–1446). Italian architect. The first of the great Renaissance architects, he was a pioneer in the scientific use of perspective. His great work was the completion of the cathedral church of Santa Maria del Fiore in Florence.

BRUNETIÈRE (brüntyär´), **Ferdinand** (1849–1906). French critic. He became editor of the *Revue des deux mondes* (1893), and prof. at the École Normale (1886). He was a fearless critic.

BRÜNING, Heinrich (1885–1970). Ger. politician. Elected to the Reichstag in 1924, he led the Catholic Centre Party from 1929, and was Reich Chancellor 1930–2, when political and economic crisis forced his resignation. He then went to the U.S., but was prof. of political science at Cologne univ. 1951–5.

BRÜNN. German form of BRNO.

BRUNNER (broon´ner), **Emil** (1889–1966). Swiss theologian. Ordained a minister of the Reformed Church in 1912, he taught at Zürich 1924–53 and Tokyo 1953–5. B. was one of a group of Swiss pastors who combined after the F.W.W. to reject revelation through reason, and stress dependence on grace.

BRUNNER, Sir John Tomlinson (1842–1919). British industrialist. In 1873 he founded with Ludwig Mond the great chemical manufacturing firm of Brunner, Mond and Co., which was incorporated in Imperial Chemical Industries Ltd., in 1926.

BRUNO (broo´nō), **Giordano** (c. 1548–1600). Italian philosopher. He became a Dominican in 1563, but his sceptical attitude to Catholic doctrines compelled him to leave Italy c. 1577. After visiting Geneva and Paris, he lived in England (1583–5), where he wrote some of his finest works. He then returned to the Continent, and after much wandering was arrested in Venice by the officers of the Inquisition, who took him to Rome in 1593. He was imprisoned, but refused to renounce his heretical religious views and his

BRUNSWICK. Built in the 14th and 15th centuries, the Town Hall is a magnificent example of Gothic architecture.
Courtesy of the German Tourist Information Bureau.

belief in the Copernican system of astronomy, and was burnt at the stake.

BRUNO, St. (c. 1030–1101). Founder of the Carthusian order. B. in Cologne, he became a priest, and controlled the cathedral school of Rheims 1057–76. Withdrawing to the mountains near Grenoble, as a result of an ecclesiastical controversy, he founded the monastery at Chartreuse in 1084.

BRUNSWICK. District in the Land of Lower Saxony, (W.) Germany. Once an independent duchy, it became a rep. in 1918.

The city of B., on the Oker, 32 m. S.E. of Hanover, was one of the chief cities of N. Germany in the Middle Ages, and a member of the Hanseatic League. It was cap. of the duchy of B. from 1671. There is a technical univ. Pop. (1966) 231,785.

BRUSA. Alternative form of BURSA.

BRUSSELS. Capital city of Belgium on the Senne, 27 m. S. of Antwerp. Notable buildings incl. the 13th cent. church of Ste. Gudule; the 15th cent. Hôtel de Ville, and the Maison du Roi in the Grande Place; the Royal Palace and the Houses of Parliament dating from the 18th cent.; and the univ. founded 1834. B.'s manufactures incl. lace, textiles, silk goods, machinery,

BRUSSELS. The brilliant colour of its flower market and the ornate antiquity of the buildings which surround it make the Grande Place one of the most attractive squares in Europe.
Courtesy of Belgian National Tourist Office.

chemicals, pottery, clothing, furniture, and *objets d'art*. It has rail and air communications with all the capitals of Europe, and canals connect it with Antwerp and the sea. B. was a Roman settlement, and in the 16th cent. became one of the chief cities of the Low Countries. When these were divided between the Dutch Rep. and Spain, B. remained Spanish, and later became Austrian, then French. It was chosen as cap. of Belgium, recognized by the Powers as independent in 1839. In both World Wars it was occupied by the Germans. Pop. (1966) 1,074,586.

BRUSSELS, Treaty of. Pact signed in Brussels on 17 March 1948 by the Foreign Ministers of Britain, France, and the Benelux countries (Belgium, Netherlands, Luxemburg), which set up Western Union. The contracting parties pledged themselves to an economic, political, cultural, and military alliance for 50 years. The military side of the alliance was in 1950 merged in the North Atlantic Treaty (q.v.).

Following the London Conference of 1954 the German Federal Rep. and Italy entered Western Union (renamed Western European Union) in 1955. (W.) Germany agreed to limit its arms production; and Britain pledged itself to maintain 4 divisions and a tactical air force on the Continent of Europe.

BRUTUS (broo'tus), **Marcus Junius** (c. 78–42 B.C.). Roman leader. He sided with Pompey against Caesar

during the civil war, but on Pompey's defeat was pardoned by Caesar and raised to high office. He was, however, persuaded to become one of Caesar's assassins in the belief that the restoration of the rep. would follow. But the bulk of the army adhered to Caesar's lieutenant Antony, and Cassius and B. were defeated at Philippi in 42 B.C., whereupon B. committed suicide.

BRUXELLES. French form of BRUSSELS.

BRYAN, William Jennings (1860–1925). American Democrat politician. Elected to Congress in 1891, he made his name as an orator, and as champion of the 'free silver' movement. He was defeated as Democratic candidate for the presidency in 1896, 1900, and 1908, but was Wilson's Sec. of State 1913–15.

BRYANSK. *See* BRIANSK.

BRYANT, Sir Arthur (1899–). British historian, noted for his studies of Restoration figures such as Pepys and Charles II, and a series covering the Napoleonic Wars of which *The Age of Elegance* (1950) is the most effective. He was knighted in 1954.

BRYANT, William Cullen (1794–1878). American poet. After practising as an attorney, he became a journalist in New York in 1825, and from 1829 was editor-in-chief of the *New York Evening Post*. His verse combines appreciation of nature with Puritan idealism in ethics. His *Thanatopsis* is one of the earliest masterpieces of American poetry.

BRYCE, James, 1st visct. (1838–1922). British statesman. Prof. of civil law at Oxford 1870–93, he entered Parliament as a Liberal in 1880, holding office under Gladstone and Rosebery. An admirer of the U.S. and author of *The American Commonwealth* (1888), he was ambassador to Washington 1907–13, doing much to smooth U.S.-Canadian relations. He received the .M. in 1907 and viscountcy in 1913.

BRY'ONY. Two British climbing hedgerow plants. White B. (*Bryonia dioica*) belongs to the gourd family (Cucurbitaceae). Black B. (*Tamus communis*) is of the same family as the yam (Dioscoreaceae).

BRZESC NAD-BUGIEM. Polish name of BREST, White Russia.

BUBBLE CHAMBER. When an ionizing particle moves through a B.C., a vessel filled with a transparent highly super-heated liquid, it may start violent boiling along its path shown by a string of tiny bubbles. Photographic study of these tracks gives much information about the nature and movement of atomic particles and the interaction of particles and radiations. *See* GLASER, Donald.

BUBER (boo'ber), **Martin** (1878–1965). Israeli philosopher. B. in Vienna, he was driven from a professorship in comparative religion at Frankfurt by the Nazis, and taught social philosophy at the Hebrew Univ., Jerusalem, 1937–51. He attempted the re-appraisal of ancient Jewish thought in modern terms.

BUCCANEERS (Carib, *boucan*, wooden grid for smoking meat, the use of which was borrowed from  the natives of S. Domingo by early French hunters). Name given to the piratical rovers who infested the Spanish American coast in the 17th cent. Though mainly British, some were French, Dutch, and Portuguese; they were united in hatred of Spain and desire to plunder the Spanish Main. Among the most famous Bs. was Henry Morgan (q.v.). The ranks of the Bs. were divided by the outbreak of war between England and France in 1689, and the growth of

BRYONY. The white (*left*), and black forms.

naval power in the 18th cent. put an end to their activities.

BUCER (boots'er), **Martin** (1491–1551). German Protestant reformer. From 1549 he was regius prof. of divinity at Cambridge. He attempted to reconcile the viewpoints of Luther and Zwingli.

BUCHAN (buk'an), **Alexander** (1829–1907). Scottish meteorologist. He was sec. to the Scottish Meteorological Soc. from 1860, and evolved from tabulated records the series of 6 cold and 3 warm spells tending to occur between certain dates each year which are named after him.

BUCHAN, John, baron Tweedsmuir (1875–1940). Scottish statesman and author. Called to the Bar in 1901, he was Cons. M.P. for the Scottish Univs. (1927–35), and on his appointment as Gov. Gen. of Canada (1935–40) was raised to the peerage. In addition to biographies of Raleigh, Scott, Cromwell, Julius Caesar, and Augustus, he pub. thrilling adventure stories which won wide popularity and incl. *Prester John* (1910), *The Thirty-Nine Steps* (1915), *Greenmantle* (1916), *Huntingtower* (1922), *The Three Hostages* (1924), and *The House of the Four Winds* (1935); and the autobiographical *Memory Hold the Door* (1940).

BUCHAN (bukh'an) **NESS.** Most easterly cape of Scotland, in Aberdeenshire, 3 m. S. of Peterhead.

BUCHANAN (bukan'an), **George** (1506–82). Scottish humanist. Forced to flee to France in 1539 owing to some satirical verses on the Franciscans, he returned to Scotland c. 1562 as tutor to Queen Mary. He became principal of St. Leonard's Coll., St. Andrews, in 1566, and wrote *Rerum Scoticarum Historia* (1582).

BUCHANAN (bukan'an), **Jack** (1891–1957). British musical comedy actor. B. at Helensburgh, he played in London and N.Y. in *Charlot's Revue*, etc., and his songs such as 'Good-Night Vienna' epitomized the inter-war period.

BUCHAREST (bookarest'). Cap. of Rumania, on the Dombovita. Although open to the plains, except on the W. and S.W., it has a comparatively mild winter. Once a citadel built by Prince Vlad the Impaler to stop the advance of the Ottoman invasion in the 14th cent., it was the cap. of the Princes of Wallachia from 1698, and of Rumania from 1861. Little of the old

BUCHAREST. The characteristic houses of the Village Museum (1936) in Herastrau Park are furnished exactly as they were when inhabited, and form one of the most interesting open-air museums in the world.
Courtesy Rumanian Nat. Travel Office

town remains, but there are fine 17–18th cent. churches, the 18th cent. Mogosoaia Palace (now a museum), the univ. (1864), the Palace of the Grand Nat. Assembly, the Fine Arts Museum, Nat. Museum of Antiquities,

and the Cismigiu Gardens planned in the 19th cent. The international airport is at Baneasa. Pop. (1966) 1,650,000.

BUCHMAN (bōōk-), **Frank N. D.** (1878–1961). American evangelist. In charge of Christian work at Penn. State Coll. 1909–15, he visited Oxford in 1921 and gathered round him the 'Holy Club', nicknamed the 'Oxford Group' when a number of members visited S. Africa, noted for its group confessionals. In 1938 he launched in London the anti-Communist campaign for Moral Rearmament (M.R.A.).

BÜCHNER (bükh'ner), **Ludwig** (1824–99). German materialist philosopher. Forced to resign his lectureship in medicine at Tübingen university owing to the materialist views of his *Kraft und Stoff* (1855), he worked as a physician in Darmstadt and pub. several similar works. His brother **Georg B.** (1813–37), author of *Dantons Tod* and *Wozzeck*, was a dramatist.

BUCK (*née* Sydenstricker), **Pearl S.** (1892–). American novelist. Dau. of missionaries to China, she wrote novels of Chinese life, such as *East Wind – West Wind* (1930) and *The Good Earth* (1931), and received a Nobel prize in 1938.

BUCKINGHAM, George Villiers, 1st duke of (1592–1628). English courtier. Introduced to the court of James I in 1614, he soon became his favourite, being made earl of B. in 1617 and a duke in 1623. He failed to arrange the marriage of Prince Charles and the Infanta of Spain (1623), and on returning to England negotiated Charles's alliance with Henrietta Maria, sister to the French king. Following Charles's accession, B. attempted to form a Protestant coalition in Europe and Britain drifted into war with France, but he failed to relieve the Protestants besieged in La Rochelle (1627). His policy was attacked in Parliament, and when about to sail again for La Rochelle he was assassinated at Portsmouth.

BUCKINGHAM. Market town (bor.) of Bucks, England, on the Ouse. Primarily an agricultural centre, it has an Edward VI grammar school. Pop. (1961) 4,377.

BUCKINGHAM PALACE. The London home of the British Sovereign. Originally built in 1703 for the duke of B. it was bought by George III in 1762 and reconstructed by Nash 1825–36. It was permanently occupied by Queen Victoria, and in 1913 a new front was added. It was slightly damaged by bombs during the S.W.W.

BUCKINGHAMSHIRE (Bucks). S. midland county of England touching Northants in the N. and the Thames in the S. It is an agricultural county, the Vale of Aylesbury being particularly fertile. Woods are extensive in the N., and the S. is noted for its beech trees. The chief rivers are the Thames, Colne, Thame, Ouse and Ousel; the Grand Union Canal passes through the county. Manufactures include furniture, paper and agricultural machinery. The co. town is Aylesbury; other towns incl. Buckingham, High Wycombe, Slough, Beaconsfield, Eton, Marlow, Amersham. Area 749 sq. m.; pop (1967) 552,470.

BUCKLE, Henry Thomas (1821–62). British historian. The 1st 2 vols. of his unfinished *History of Civilization in England* (1857–61) were remarkable for pointing out the influence of food, soil, climate, etc. on the course of history.

BUCKTHORN. Genus of thorny shrubs (*Rhamnus*) of the family Rhamnaceae, of which 2 species, *R. catharticus* and *R. frangula* (alder B.), are British.

BUCKWHEAT. Plant (*Fagopyrum esculentum*) of the family Polygonaceae, producing a grain of high nutritive value for human and animal consumption, which can be grown on poor soil in a short summer.

BUDAEUS (boodē'-us). Latin form of the name of Guillaume Budé (1467–1540), French scholar. He persuaded Francis I to found the Collège de France, and also the library that formed the nucleus of the Bibliothèque Nationale.

BUDAPEST. City of central Europe, cap. of Hungary. It lies on the Danube, and consists of Buda on the right bank, which includes the former royal palace and coronation church, and Pest on the left, which includes the houses of parliament, palace of justice, govt. offices, etc. 8 bridges connect the 2 cities. Pest grew rapidly following the establishment of the Dual Monarchy in 1867 when it was made the cap. of Hungary and became the centre of agriculture and trade; it was united with Buda 1872. Between the wars many new industries incl. textiles and chemicals were estab. at B. There is a univ. (1635) and the technical univ. (1856) was reorganized 1967. In 1944–5 the city saw prolonged fighting between the German and Russian armies. Pop. Greater B. (1967) 1,969,000.

BUDDHA and **BUDDHISM** (boo-). Buddhism, one of the great world religions, originated in India, where it is now extinct, but has spread to other parts of Asia, where it exists in 2 forms. In Ceylon, Siam, Burma, and Indo-China that known as the School of the Elders (Theravada) prevails. Its followers are reckoned at 54 millions. A much later form known as Mahāyāna has spread throughout China, Korea, Japan, Tibet, and Mongolia, with some 470 million adherents.

Buddhism originated with Gautama (c. 563–c. 483 B.C.), the son of a king of the Sákyas, a tribe settled near modern Nepal, who was brought up in luxury, but at the age of 29 became aware of human ills and left his wife and home to seek a way of escape from the burdens of existence. After 6 years of extreme austerities he turned to meditation under a tree, the Bodhi tree (tree of Enlightenment) nr. Buddh Gaya, and became enlightened—hence his name Buddha (the Enlightened One). Enlightenment consisted of acquiring the four Truths: the fact of pain or ill; that pain has a cause; that pain can be ended; and the Noble Eightfold Way (right views, right intention, right speech, right action, right livelihood, right effort, right mindfulness, and right concentration) whereby pain may be ended. Adoption of the Way leads to a state of peace, Nirvana, the extinction of all craving for the things of sense, though not necessarily the annihilation of the individual. After his enlightenment, Buddha removed to Benares, where he began his teaching and founded the Sangha, or Order of monks. For the rest of his long life he moved here and there about N. India, but chiefly in the Magadha country (Bihar). He died at Kusinagara in Oudh at the age of 80. See LUMBINI.

The only complete canon of the Buddhist scriptures is that of the Singhalese (Ceylon) Buddhists, written in Pali, but other schools have essentially the same canon in Sanskrit. The scriptures are known as Pitakas or 'baskets', and there are 3 divisions: Vinaya or Discipline, listing offences and rules of life; Suitta (Discourse) or Dhamma (Doctrine), con-

BUDDHA. A bronze statuette from Kashmir just under 8 in. high, and of the 7–8th century.
Photo: British Museum.

taining an exposition of B. by Buddha and his disciples; and Abhidhamma or Further Doctrine, consisting of later discussions of the doctrine by various schools.

In common with other Indian religions, B. holds two fundamental doctrines, that of *karma* or action,

the belief that all deeds meet with reward or punishment in this life or in one and another of a long succession of lives; and that of transmigration or rebirth, according to which everyone is reborn in a happy or painful existence, wherein he experiences the fruit of past deeds. In Buddhism there is no belief in a permanent self. The object of the Noble Eightfold Way is to break the chain of *karma* binding the individual to rebirth, by attaining *Nirvana*, when there is final dissociation from the body.

About the beginning of the Christian era arose a new conception of Buddhism, known as *Mahayana*, 'the Great Career', in which the individual is exhorted not merely to attain Nirvana for himself, but to train to become a Buddha, and so save countless others. The elder school that prevails in Ceylon, Siam, and the East Indies is referred to as *Hinayana*, 'Base Career'. Those who set out on this 'Great Career' are called Bodhisattvas, and may be highly revered and even worshipped, much as are the gods of Hinduism. The original Buddhism, if not atheistic, at least found no place for God or gods. To this day the real strength of Buddhism lies in its lofty moral teaching, in particular its toleration and feeling of universal brotherhood, and in recent years there has been a growth of laymen's societies with temples of their own.

BUDDH GAYA (bood′gīa). Indian village 6 m. S. of Gaya, in Bihar, where Gautama became Buddha while sitting beneath a Bo (Bodhi) tree, of which a supposed descendant is still preserved there.

BUDENNY (boodyen′ni), **Simeon Mikhailovich** (1883–   ). Russian marshal. He entered the army in 1903, joined the Red Army in 1918, when he fought against the 'Whites' under Wrangel, and in 1920 in the Polish War. In 1935 he became a marshal, and in 1940 Commissar of Defence. In 1941 he commanded the Russian armies in the S.W. sector, and eventually joined in the victorious sweep westwards.

BUDGE, Sir Wallis (1857–1934). British orientalist. He was keeper of the Egyptian and Assyrian antiquities at the British Museum 1893–1924, conducted excavations in Egypt and Mesopotamia, and wrote largely on ancient Egypt and Assyria.

BUDGERIGAR (bujrigahr′). Small, hardy species of Australian parrakeet (*Melopsittacus undulatus*). Feeding mainly on grass seeds, it breeds freely in captivity, and while normally bright green, yellow, white, blue, and mauve varieties have been produced.

BUDOJOVICE. *See* CESKE BUDEJOVICE.

BUDWEIS. German form of Budejovice: *see* CESKE BUDEJOVICE.

BUENOS AIRES (bwā′nos īr′es). Cap. of the Argentine rep, largest city in the southern hemisphere, on the W. bank of the estuary of the Rio de la Plata, some 150 m. from the sea. Although founded in 1536, B.A. is almost entirely modern, its development dating from its establishment as the cap. of the Argentine rep. in 1853. It is laid out on the American 'gridiron' plan, and there are many fine thoroughfares: e.g. Avenida de Mayo and Avenida de Julio. In the Plaza de Mayo are the cathedral, govt. palace, treasury building, and municipal offices; the Palace of Congress is in the Plaza del Congreso. B.A. has a nat. univ. (estab. 1821) and a great many industrial and manufacturing establishments, incl. meat-packing plants. Hostile Indians caused the first settlers of 1536 to withdraw, but the site was re-occupied in 1586, and in 1776 was made cap. of the viceroyalty of Rio de la Plata. Pop. (1960) 3,200,000; of greater B. 7,200,000.

BUFFALO. City and port of U.S.A., in New York state, at the E. end of Lake Erie, close to the mouth of the r. Niagara. It is a leading commercial, industrial, and transport centre, with many large and small industries. Pop. met area (1970) 1,336, 601.

BUFFALO. Several species of wild cattle, mostly large, distinguished by their horns being flattened at

BUFFALO. The remarkable horns of these Cape buffalo meet in a helmet-like mass on the forehead and may measure 4 ft. across from the extremity of one outward curve to the other. Once there were herds several hundred strong, but shooting has reduced them to such small groups as this in Wankie National Park. *Courtesy of the High Commissioner for Rhodesia.*

the base and triangular in section. True Bs. are confined to the eastern hemisphere and fall into 2 distinct groups, African and Asiatic.

The typical African B. (*Synceros caffer*) inhabits open bush country, generally near rivers all over Africa S. of the Sahara. The Cape B. stands about 5 ft. in height, is black and has horns set close together to form a helmet-like mass on the forehead. Other races inhabit E. Africa. The dwarf B., sometimes called the bush-cow, is about 3½ ft. high. It is red, and lives in the Congo forest.

In Asiatic Bs., of which there are 3 distinct species, the head is relatively longer and the ears smaller. The common Indian B. or water-B. (*Bubalus bubalus*) is black and up to 5½ ft. high, with long, widely separated horns. They can be domesticated readily, and have been introduced into Australia, Italy, etc. The Tamarau or Philippine B. (*B. mindorensis*) is about 3½ ft. high, with short close-set horns growing backwards, and is intermediate between the Indian B. and the anoa (*B. depressicornis*), which inhabits Celebes and is about 3 ft. high. The so-called B. of America is the bison (q.v.).

BUFFET (büfeh´), **Bernard** (1928–). French artist. B. in Paris, he has exhibited annually since 1948, and besides oils and water colours, is known for his lithographs, book illustrations and murals. His rapidly produced canvases are pessimistic, reflecting a feeling of nausea at the unpleasantness of life.

BUFFON (büfoñ´), **Georges Louis Leclerc**, Comte de (1707–88). French naturalist. In 1739 he became keeper of the Jardin du Roi, and was elected to the Academy in 1753, when he delivered his *Discours sur le style*. He encouraged the popular study of natural history, and pub⁻ a 'Natural History' in 44 vols. (1749–1804).

BUG. Name loosely applied to various insects, and in the U.S.A. to various kinds of beetles (*Coleoptera*), but in England more particularly to the bed-bug and its allies, which form the sub-order Heteroptera of the order Hemiptera.

The bed-bug (*Cimex lectularius*) is a brownish, flattened, wingless insect, with an unpleasant smell, found in old houses, and issuing forth at night to suck the blood of sleepers. The Heteroptera include a number of families. Some are predatory, feeding on other insects; some suck the juice of plants, such as the squash B. (*Anasa tristis*) and the cotton stainer (*Dysdercus suturellus*); other Bs. such as the water-scorpions (Nepidae), water boatmen (Notonectidae), and pond skaters (Hydrometridae), are aquatic; and one genus (*Halobates*) is marine.

BUG (boog). Name of 2 rivers in eastern Europe. The West B. rises E. of Lvov, and flows past Brest to the Vistula some 20 m. below Warsaw. the South B. rises near Proskurov in the Ukrainian S.S.R. and flows S.E. to enter the Black Sea below Nikolaev.

BUGANDA (boog-). Region of Uganda, the largest of the 4 kingdoms recognized as in a federal relationship to the central govt. 1962–6, when its *Kabaka*, Sir Edward Mutesa II (1924–69) was also pres. Deposed under the 1966 constitution introduced by Milton Obote, he fled the country. The chief towns are Kampala, cap. of B. and of Uganda, and Entebbe (qq.v.). Area 26,000 sq. m.; pop. *c.* 1½ millions. The people are known as the Baganda.

BUGATTI (boogaht´ē), **Ettore** (1882–1947). Automobile designer and manufacturer of racing cars, b. in Milan. He designed his first car in 1899 and established a factory at Strasbourg (then German) in 1907. Refusing to work for Germany in the F.W.W. he went to Italy and then to France, where he was naturalized and produced many racing cars, etc.

BUGLE. Wind instrument, belonging to the brass family. It resembles the trumpet, but has a shorter tube and a less expanded bell, and is constructed of copper plated with brass. It has long been in wide use as a military instrument.

BUGLE. Perennial herb (*Ajuga reptans*) belonging to the family Labiatae, and common throughout Britain. B. has numerous running stems, leaves frequently tinged with red or purple, and a whorl of 6 or 10 blue flowers.

BU´GLOSS. Name of several plants of the family Boraginaceae, distinguished by their rough bristly leaves and small blue flowers.

BUHL (bool). Process of inlaying various metals, particularly brass and silver, into tortoise-shell or occasionally wood, which was invented by the Frenchman C. A. Boulle (1642–1732).

BUILDING SOCIETY. Institution which attracts investment, and from the proceeds makes advances on the security of first mortgage on property.

B.Ss. are mutual institutions and operate on public utility lines. They do not themselves engage in actual building operations today, but the first B.Ss. were directly concerned with the erection of houses. The first B.S. was estab. in Birmingham in 1781, and in 1836 the first Act of Parliament regulating their activities was passed. Among recent developments reflecting social change have been the increase of advances to mortgagors above the 80 per cent of the surveyor's valuation formerly usual, and the extension of the period of repayment beyond 20 years, consequences of higher house prices, longer expectation of working life, earlier marriage, etc. Most of the capital is provided by way of shares, attractive to small investors because income tax is borne by the B.S.: interest rates for borrowers are rendered less oppressive by income tax relief on mortgage repayments.

Originating in Britain, where there are c.500 with assets of some 6½ thousand million pounds, B.Ss. are now world wide, flourishing espec. in the U.S.A. and the Dominions.

BUISSON (büēsoñ´), **Ferdinand** (1841–1932). French pioneer of the idea of a league of nations. For 13 years he was president of the *Ligue des droits de*

BUG. I, Bed-bug; 2, Squash bug; 3, Froghopper; 4, Pond skater; 5, Leafhopper; 6, Boatman.

l'homme, which in 1916 placed on record B.'s view that permanent peace was possible only through a league of nations. He received a Nobel Prize in 1927.

BUJUMBURA (bōōjumbōō'rah). Cap. (formerly called Usumbura) of Burundi, on Lake Tanganyika. The univ. was founded 1960. There is a steamer service to Kigoma in Tanganyika, and an international airport. Pop. 70,000.

BUKHARA (bōōkhah'rah). Ancient city in Central Asia, formerly the capital of the independent emirate of B., annexed to Russia in 1868. It is the cap. of B. region, Uzbek S.S.R., in which it was included in 1924. On a branch of the r. Zarafshan, it is a great Islamic centre, has famous schools and colleges, and makes silk and cotton textiles, leather goods, etc. Pop. (est.) 60,000. Kagan, 9 m. to the S.E., called Novaya (new) Bukhara until *c.* 1935, grew up round the station on the Transcaspian railway.

BUKHAREST. *See* BUCHAREST.

BUKHOVINA (bōōkōvĕ'nah). Region covering *c.* 4,000 sq. m. in S.E. Europe. Part of Moldavia during the Turkish régime, it was ceded by Turkey to Austria in 1777, becoming a duchy of the Dual Monarchy, 1867–1918; then it was included in Rumania. North B. was ceded to Russia, 1940, and included in Ukraine S.S.R. as the region of Chernovtsy; the cession was confirmed by the peace treaty of 1947. The part of B. remaining in Rumania became the region of Suceava.

BULAWAYO (boolahwah'yō). City of Rhodesia and former cap. of Matabeleland, standing at an alt. of 4,450 ft. on the r. Matsheumlope, a trib. of the Zambesi. Founded on the site of the kraal, burned down 1893, of Lobenguela, the Matabele chief, B. has developed with the exploitation of goldmines in the neighbourhood. Notable buildings include Govern-

BULAWAYO. Laid out on a rectangular plan, Bulawayo has fine wide thoroughfares such as Abercorn Street. Arcades protect from the overhead sun, and market women still carry their traditional headloads.
Courtesy of the High Commissioner for Rhodesia.

ment House, once belonging to Rhodes, who is buried in the Matopo hills above B. It is the centre of the Rhodesian railway system and has an airport. Pop. (1967) 259,000 (incl. 52,000 Europeans and 7,000 non-African other races).

BULB. Instrument of vegetative reproduction characteristic of many monocotyledonous plants, e.g. daffodil, snowdrop, onion. It is composed of the fleshy leaf-bases of the previous year's plant, enlarged by the food material they contain for the nourishment of the new plant.

Bs. are grown on a commercial scale in temperate countries, e.g. in parts of E. Anglia (England), and particularly in Holland.

BULGA'NIN, Nikolai (1895–   ). Russian soldier. He helped to organize Moscow's defence in the S.W.W., became a Marshal of the Soviet Union in 1947, and was Min. of Defence 1947–9 and 1953–5. On the fall of Malenkov in 1955 he became 'P.M.' (Chmn. of Council of Ministers 1955–8) until ousted by Krushchev.

BULGARIA. Republic of S.E. Europe between the Danube on the N., Greece and Turkey-in-Europe on the S. The Balkan mountains form the backbone of the country, but in the S. between these and the Rhodope mountains is a stretch of low land drained into the Black Sea by the Maritsa and other rivers.

Divided from 1964 into 28 provs., B. is mainly agricultural, organised from 1970 into large 'agricultural–industrial complexes', with an ideal climate for cereals; crops include sugar beet, tobacco, rose oil. Exploitation of the forests (covering nearly a third of the country) and of minerals (iron, manganese, copper, lead, pyrites, etc.) is increasing. Textiles and chemicals, especially fertilizers, are the chief industrial products. Oil, discovered in the 1950s and 1960s, is refined at Pleven and Burgas, and a new industrial centre, Dimitrovgrad, was developed from 1947. The principal towns are Sofia, the cap.; Plovdiv, the agricultural centre; and the Black sea ports of Burgas and Varna. Area 42,796 sq. m. Pop. (1967) 8,334,000.

History. Under the Romans B. formed the prov. of Moesia Inferior. It was later occupied by Slavs who, conquered in the 7th cent. by the Bulgars from Asia, eventually absorbed the invaders though they gave their name to the country. In 865 Khan Boris adopted Eastern Orthodox Christianity (still the national religion), and under his son Simeon (893–927), who assumed the title of Tsar, B. became a leading power. In 1014 it was absorbed into the Byzantine empire, and although a 2nd Bulgarian empire was founded after the revolt of 1185, the last independent tsar died *c.* 1393, and B. passed under Ottoman rule until the national revival of the 19th cent. resulted in the creation of an autonomous principality under Turkish suzerainty in 1878, and the declaration of independence by Ferdinand I in 1908. In 1912–13 B. assisted in the defeat of the Turks, but was herself defeated in the 2nd Balkan war in 1913.

In 1915 B. entered the F.W.W. on the side of the Central Powers, and was again defeated; and in 1918 Ferdinand abdicated in favour of his son Boris III, who became virtual dictator from 1934. In 1941 B. became an ally of Germany, and German troops occupied the country, which declared war on Britain and the U.S.A., but never on Russia, though Russia, to compel B. to surrender, declared war against B. in 1943. King Boris d. in 1943 following a visit to Hitler; his son Simeon II lost his throne after a referendum, 1946, and a rep. was proclaimed. Following the 1947 peace treaties, which restored the frontiers of 1919 except that B. retained S. Dobruja ceded by Rumania in 1940, B. adopted a Communist constitution drawn up on the Russian model by Georgi Dimitrov (q.v.).

Language and Literature. Earliest of the Slavonic languages to be reduced to writing (9th cent.), Bulgarian is a member of the southern group, and is written in a modified Cyrillic character. Modern B. literature is not linked directly with the medieval, and was founded in the 19th cent. by Liuben Karavelov (1837–79), the epic poet Petko Slaveikov (1827–95), the lyric poet Christo Botev (1848–76), and the novelist and dramatist Ivan Vasov (1850–1921), who was also the first poet of liberated B. To the late 19th cent. belong Anton Strachimirov (1872–1937), Petko Y. Todorov (1879–1916), Pentcho Slaveikov (1866–1911), and Peyo K. Yavorov (1877–1914). Recent writers incl. Cyril Christoc, Dobre Nemirov, Nicolai Rainov, Georgi Karaslavov, Ludmil Stoianov, Dimiter Polianov, G. Meliv, Elin Pelin (pen-name of Dimitri Ivanov), and the women poets

Dora Gabe and Bagriana (pen-name of Elisabeth Belceva).

BULL, John. Typical Englishman, especially as represented in cartoons. The name came into popular use after the publication of Dr. John Arbuthnot's *History of John Bull* (1712) advocating the Tory policy of peace with France.

BULL, Olav (1883–1933). Norwegian poet. From his first vol., which appeared in 1909, he stood in the front rank of Norway's lyricists.

BULL, Papal. Document or edict issued by the pope; so called from the circular seals (medieval Lat. *bulla*) attached to them. Famous P.Bs. include Leo X's condemnation of Luther in 1520; and Pius IX's proclamation of papal infallibility in 1870.

BULL-BAITING. One-time popular Eng. sport in which a bull was set upon by a pack of vicious dogs. B. was made illegal in 1835.

BULLDOG. British dog of ancient but uncertain origin. Coming into prominence in the days of bull-baiting, it developed the characteristic underjaw which left the nostrils free for breathing whilst the dog retained its grip on the bull's throat. The head is broad and square, with a deeply wrinkled skull, small folded ears, and nose laid back between the eyes. The chest is broad, and the back, arched and tapering to the powerful hindquarters, marked by the distinctive short, thick, kinked tail.

BULLER, Charles (1806–48). British diplomat. He became private sec. to the Gov.-Gen. of Canada, Lord Durham, in 1838, and assisted him in preparing the report which resulted in the union of Upper and Lower Canada.

BULLER, Sir Redvers Henry (1839–1908). British soldier. Joining the army in 1858, he commanded the British armies in S. Africa against the Boers. Defeated at Colenso and Spion Kop, he eventually relieved Ladysmith but was superseded by Lord Roberts.

BULL-FIGHTING. Contests between men and bulls; the national sport of Spain and of Spanish S. America. It was common in Greece and Rome, and was introduced into Spain by the Moors in the 11th cent. B. takes place in an arena, or bull-ring, where a bull is let loose. The animal is at first tormented by men on horseback, called *picadores*, who wound it with lances, and then by the *banderilleros* who plunge darts into its neck. Finally the *matador* with his sword and muleta (a red cloth attached to a stick) enters. Lured by the red cloth, the enraged animal charges at the matador who steps aside, and deals the death blow by plunging his sword between the bull's left shoulder and the shoulder-blade.

BULLFINCH. Species of finch (*Pyrrhula pyrrhula*) of the family Fringillidae, distinguished by its thick-set form, silky plumage, and stout parrot-like bill. The male has a pinkish-crimson breast, grey back, and glossy black head, wings and tail. The B. is a common British resident.

BULLHEAD, or Miller's Thumb. Small freshwater fish (*Cottus gobio*), of no food value, with large, broad head, and sharp spines on the gill covers. The marine father lasher, or sting fish (*C. scorpius*), is of the same genus, and is so called because the male guards the eggs, and agitates the water with his tail to ensure them a supply of oxygen.

BULLITT, William Christian (1891–1967). American diplomatist, who was sent on a special mission to Russia by President Wilson in 1919, and was American ambassador to Russia 1933–6, and to France 1936–41. In *The Great Globe Itself* (1946), he argued that the Russian govt. aimed at world conquest.

BULLROARER. Australian aboriginal musical instrument; it consists of a piece of wood of varying size, which is fastened by one of its pointed ends to a cord, by which it is whirled round the head to create a whirring noice. Both among the aborigines and other primitive races the B. is of great magical significance.

BULL TERRIER. British dog, originating in the 1850s, of which there are 3 recognized varieties, the white, the coloured, and the miniature.

BÜLOW (bü'loh), **Hans von** (1830–94). German pianist and conductor. He studied under Wagner and Liszt, and in 1857 m. the latter's dau. Cosima. He was professor of pianoforte at the Stern conservatorium in Berlin (1855–64), and in 1864 obtained a post under Ludwig II of Bavaria, and was the first conductor of *Tristan* and the *Meistersinger*. His wife left him to live with Wagner whom she m. in 1870.

BULWER-LYTTON. *See* LYTTON.

BUMBLE-BEE. Family of social insects (Bombidae) belonging to the super-family Apoidea of the order Hymenoptera. They have broad hairy bodies, which are usually dark brown or black, banded with yellow or orange, and live in small colonies, usually underground. The queen lays her eggs in the hollow nest of moss or grass at the beginning of the season, and the larvae are fed on pollen and honey, and develop into workers. In the summer, males and perfect females are produced, and all die at the end of the season except the fecundated females, which hibernate, to form fresh colonies in the spring.

BUMBRY, Grace (1937–). American mezzo soprano. A Negress, b. in St. Louis, Missouri, she was ed. at Boston Univ. and Chicago's Northwestern Univ., and was a favourite pupil of Lotte Lehmann at the Music Academy of the West. In 1960–3 she joined the Basel Opera. Her roles incl. Amneris in *Aïda*, Carmen, and Eboli in *Don Carlos*.

BUNCHE (bunch), **Ralph** (1904–1971). American administrator, specializing in African and colonial affairs. A Negro and grandson of a slave, he was principal director of the U.N. Dept. of Trusteeship 1947–54, and then U.N. Under-Sec., acting as mediator in Palestine 1948–9 and as special representative in the Congo 1960. In 1950 he was awarded the Nobel peace prize.

BU'NIN, Ivan Alexeyevich (1870–1953). Russian writer. B. in Voronezh, he wrote realistic stories of peasant life: *Derevnya* (1910: *The Village*); and *Gospodin iz San Frantsisko* (1916: *The Gentleman from San Francisco*), dealing with the death of a millionaire on Capri, whic won him in 1933 a Nobel prize. Among later books *The Well of Days* (1930) has autobiographical elements and forms part of a longer work. He was also a poet and translated Byron and Longfellow.

BUNKER HILL. Small hill in Charlestown (now part of Boston), Mass., U.S.A., near which on 17 June 1775 the first considerable engagement was fought in the American War of Independence; the colonists were defeated.

BUNSEN (boon'sen), **Robert Wilhelm von** (1811–99). German chemist. He was prof. of chemistry at Heidelberg 1852–98, and is credited with the invention of the B. burner. His name is also given to the carbon-zinc electric cell which he invented in 1841 for use in arc-lamps. About 1859 he discovered 2 new elements, aesium and rubidium.

BUNTING. Group of birds usually treated as a

BUMBLE-BEE. Below: 1, pupa; 2, larva.

sub-family (Emberizinae) of the finches (Fringillidae), but of heavier build. The Bs. are best represented in the New World, though a number of species are native to the Old, 5 of which breed in Britain: the corn B. (*Emberiza miliaria*), the yellow B. or yellowhammer (*E. citrinella*), the cirl B. (*E. cirlus*), the reed B. (*E. schoeniclus*), and the snow B. (*Plectrophenax nivalis*).

BUÑUEL (boon'yōō-el), **Luis** (1900–). Spanish film director, famous for his controversial and often anti-clerical films, e.g., *L'Age d'Or* (1930), *Los Olvidados* (1950) and *Viridiana* (1961).

BUNYAN, John (1628–88). English author. B. near Bedford, the son of a tinker, he followed his father's trade, but at 16 was conscripted into the Parliamentary army. Released in 1646, he passed through a period of religious doubt before joining the fellowship of the Baptists in 1653. In 1660 he was committed to Bedford county gaol for preaching, where he remained for 12 years, refusing all offers of release on condition that he would not preach again. Chief of the books written during his confinement was *Grace Abounding* (1666) describing his early spiritual struggles. Set free in 1672, he was elected pastor of the Bedford congregation, but in 1675 was again arrested and imprisoned for 6 months in the gaol on Bedford bridge where he began *The Pilgrim's Progress* (1678). The book achieved instant success, and a second part followed in 1684. Among his many later publications only *The Life and Death of Mr. Badman* (1680) and *The Holy War* (1682) retain living interest.

JOHN BUNYAN
Photo: N.P.G.

BUOYANCY. The lifting effect of a fluid on a body wholly or partly immersed in it. This was studied by Archimedes in the 3rd cent. B.C. His principle states that the upward thrust or apparent loss of weight of a substance wholly or partly immersed in a fluid is equal to the weight of fluid displaced.

BURBAGE, Richard (*c.* 1567–1619). English actor. He is thought to have been the original Hamlet, Othello and Lear, and built the Globe Theatre *c.* 1599.

BURBANK, Luther (1849–1926). American plant breeder. B. in Mass., he evolved the B. potato in 1872, and 3 years later settled at Santa Rosa, Calif., where he originated many fruits, vegetables, and flowers.

BURBOT. See COD.

BURCHFIELD, Charles Ephraim (1893–). American artist. B. in Salem, Ohio, he is noted for landscapes and studies of small-town America, which made him a forerunner of the regionalist movement of the 1930s.

BURCKHARDT, Jakob (1818–97). Swiss historian and art-critic, b. at Basle, where in 1845 he became prof. of history. In 1860 he pub. *The Civilization of the Renaissance in Italy*, a standard work.

BURCKHARDT, John Lewis (1784–1817). Swiss traveller, whose intimate knowledge of Arabic enabled him to travel throughout the Middle East, visiting Mecca disguised as a Moslem pilgrim in 1814.

BURDETT, Sir Francis (1770–1844). English radical. He m. the wealthy Sophia Coutts, dau. of a banker, and having bought a parliamentary seat became a champion of liberal opinion. He was imprisoned in 1820 for censuring the Peterloo massacre, and agitated for parliamentary reform and R.C. emancipation. After 1837, however, he voted with the Conservatives. His dau. **Angela Georgina Burdett-Coutts** (1814–1906) was created a baroness in 1871 and was a financially able practical philan-

thropist. She was a close friend of Dickens. See COUTTS.

BURDOCK. A plant (*Arctium lappa*), of the family Compositae, a frequent roadside weed in Britain. It is a bushy herb, with hairy leaves, and ripe fruit enclosed in burs which are provided with strong hooks.

BURGAS (boor'gahs). Black Sea port of Bulgaria, handling a large export trade. There is an oil refinery (1963). Pop. (1965) 106,127.

BURGENLAND (boor'genlahnd). S.E. prov. of Austria, extending from the Danube southwards along the western border of the Hungarian plain. Extensive forests supply timber. Lignite, antimony, and limestone are worked. Eisenstadt (pop. *c.* 7,000) is the cap. Area 1,531 sq. m.; pop. (1961) 270,875.

BÜRGER, Gottfried August (1747–94). German poet, b. at Halberstadt. In 1773 he became famous with *Lenore*, and he also wrote many other ballads and lyrics.

BURGH (bur'o). A local govt. area in Scotland corresponding to the English borough. Each B. has a town council consisting of provost, magistrates, and councillors.

BURGH (boorg), **Hubert de** (d. 1243). Justiciar of England. He rose to high office under Richard I, and in 1215 was appointed chief justiciar. His defeat of the French fleet in the Straits of Dover in 1217 ended French intervention in England. Until his dismissal in 1232, he was Henry III's chief minister.

BURGHLEY (ber'li), **William Cecil**, baron B. (1520–98). English statesman. B. at Bourne, Lincs, and ed. at Cambridge, he became private sec. to the Protector Somerset, and in 1550 one of the king's secretaries. He was deprived of most of his offices under Mary, but on Elizabeth's accession he became one of her most trusted ministers. He was largely responsible for the religious settlement of 1559, and in 1560 persuaded Elizabeth to send an army to Scotland to support the reformers. He also took a prominent part in the events leading up to the execution of Mary Queen of Scots in 1587. In general he was an advocate of caution and moderation, and was at great pains to avoid any breach with Spain before the strength of England was fully prepared. In 1571 he was created Baron Burghley, and in 1572 Lord High Treasurer.

BURGLARY. Formerly the crime of breaking into any dwellinghouse by night, i.e. between 9 p.m. and 6 a.m., with intent to commit a felony: outside these hours the same act was called housebreaking. In 1969, under the Theft Act (1968), the distinction was abolished. B. (maximum sentence 14 years) and aggravated B. (involving the use of firearms, etc., and a maximum of life imprisonment) are limited neither by the type of premises or time of day. In the U.S.A. state law varies, but the crime of B. is not usually limited as it used to be in Britain.

BURGOS (boor'gōs). Spanish city, 135 m. N. of Madrid, cap. of B. prov. and former cap. of the old kingdom of Castile. The Gothic cathedral was built 1221–1567. Pop. (1964) 94,774.

BURGOYNE (bergoin'), **John** (1722–92). British soldier and dramatist. He served in the Seven Years War, and on the outbreak of the American War of Independence was given command of a force intended to invade the colonies from Canada, but was surrounded and surrendered at Saratoga in 1777. He wrote comedies, among them *The Maid of the Oaks* (1775) and *The Heiress* (1786).

BURGUNDY. Ancient kingdom and duchy of varying size in the valleys of the Saône and Rhône; later a prov. of France, divided in 1790 into the depts. of Ain, Côte-d'Or, Saône-et-Loire, and part of Yonne. The Burgundi were a Teutonic tribe and overran the country *c.* 400. From the 9th cent. to the death of the duke Charles the Bold in 1477, it was the nucleus of a powerful principality. On Charles's death the duchy was incorporated into France. The capital of B. was Dijon; the province is famous for its wines.

BURIAT (boo'rē-at). An A.S.S.R. within the R.S.F.S.R. In Central Asia with L. Baikal forming its western boundary, it adopted the Soviet system in 1920. Its name was shortened from Buriat-Mongol in 1958. It is largely steppe, and cattle-breeding is the chief occupation. Ulan-Ude is the cap. Area 135,700 sq. m.; pop. (1967) 780,000.

BURKE, Edmund (1729–97). British statesman and author. B. in Dublin and ed. at Trinity Coll., he settled in London in 1750, and achieved literary fame in 1756 by his *Vindication of Natural Society* and *Essay on the Sublime and Beautiful*. He entered Parliament as a Whig in 1765, and took a prominent part, as orator and pamphleteer, in the opposition to George III's attempts to dominate English politics and coerce the Americans, e.g. by his *Thoughts on the Present Discontents* (1770) and *Speech on Conciliation* (1775). He was paymaster of the forces in Rockingham's government of 1782, and in the Fox-North coalition of 1783, and after the collapse of the latter spent the rest of his career in opposition. He then threw himself into the attack on Hastings' misgovernment in India, and was among the managers chosen to conduct his unsuccessful impeachment. As a fanatical opponent of democracy, he denounced the French Revolution in *Reflections on the Revolution in France* (1790), which brought to an end his long friendship with Fox. He defended his conduct in his *Appeal from the New to the Old Whigs* (1791) and *Letter to a Noble Lord* (1796), and attacked the suggestion of peace with France in *Letters on a Regicide Peace* (1795–7). He retired in 1794 with a govt. pension to his estate at Beaconsfield, where he died. By modern Conservatives he is regarded as the greatest of their political theorists.

BURKE, Robert O'Hara (1820–61). Irish explorer. Going to Australia in 1853, he became inspector of police in Victoria, and in 1860 was chosen to lead an expedition into the interior. This ended tragically, Burke and his 2 companions perishing in the desert.

BURKE and HARE. Murderers. William B. and William H., two Irishmen living in Edinburgh, during 1827–8 murdered at least 15 people and sold their bodies to the anatomists. B. was hanged in 1829 on H.'s evidence. Hare is said to have died a beggar in London in the 1860s.

BURKE'S PEERAGE. Popular name of the annual *Genealogical and Heraldic History of the Peerage, Baronetage, and Knightage of the United Kingdom*, first issued by John Burke (1787–1848) in 1826.

BURMA. Rep. of S.E. Asia, lying between India and the Bay of Bengal in the W., China and Thailand in the E. Vast tracts of hill jungle lie on the Indian border, and great areas of mountains and gorges on the Chinese.

The geographical divisions are: (1) the coastal strip from Akyab to Cape Negrais, some 1,400 m. long and cut off from the rest of the country by (2) the Arakan mountains, except where the delta of the Irrawaddy gives entry into (3) the main plain of B., stretching N. from Rangoon 400 m. to Mandalay. To the E. of it lie (4) the Shan State, a tableland of hilly country. N. of Mandalay is (5) the Kachin State, 500 m. long and 200 m. broad, a country of jungle, mountains, and patches of cultivation in the river valleys. W. of the plain lie the Naga and Chin Hills, a similar waste of hill and jungle.

The largest river of B. is the Irrawaddy, its principal tributary the Chindwin. Flowing parallel to the Irrawaddy is the Sittang, whose mouth is only 50 m. E. of the Irrawaddy's; the Salween flows through the eastern part of the Shan State. Over half of B. is forested, the wetter parts with a dense tropical jungle, or a monsoonal forest, in which teak is found; the drier parts have a scrub vegetation merging into semi-desert.

The Burmese, most of whom are Buddhists, are the dominant people. The principal other peoples are the Karens, Shans, Kachins, Chins, and Arakanese.

B. is in the main an agricultural country, producing rubber, tobacco, ground-nuts, cotton, etc., and large quantities of rice (much of it exported). Rubies, sapphires, and jade, petroleum, wolfram, lead and tin are among its mineral products; teak is obtained from its forests. Area 261,789 sq. m.; pop. (1967) 25,800,000.

History. The Burmese date their era from A.D. 638, when they had arrived from the region where China meets Tibet, and were semi-savage. By 850 they had organized a little state in the centre of the plain at Pagan, and from 1044 until 1287 they maintained a hegemony over most of the area of B. as it now is, and developed a distinctive civilization, one of its chief characteristics being Buddhism, of the original Hinayana type, and the particular ecclesiastical architecture of the pagoda and monastery. In 1287 Kublai Khan's grandson Ye-su Timur occupied B. after destroying the Pagan dynasty. After he withdrew, anarchy supervened. From c. 1490 to 1750 the Toungoo dynasty maintained itself, with increasing difficulty; and in 1752 Alaungpaya once more unified the country and founded Rangoon as his cap. In a struggle with Britain, 1824–6, his descendants lost the coastal strip from Chittagong to Cape Negrais. The 2nd Burmese War, 1852, resulted in British annexation of Lower B. (the southern section of the plain, including Rangoon). Thibaw, the last Burmese king, precipitated the 3rd Burmese War, 1885, and the British seized Upper B., 1886. The country was united as a prov. of India until made a separate country with its own constitution in 1937. The Japanese invaded B. in 1941, and occupied the country 1942–5. Negotiations with Britain followed the liberation of B., and on 4 Jan. 1948 B. achieved complete independence outside the British Commonwealth.

Under the republican constitution of 1947 there was an elected pres. and parliament with a Chamber of Deputies and Chamber of Nationalities, but the constitution was suspended in 1962 and Gen. Ne Win headed a Revolutionary Council in establishing a socialist one-party state. There have been minority revolts, e.g. that of the Karens (q.v.) and border clashes with the Chinese.

BURNE-JONES, Sir Edward (1833–98). British painter and designer, b. at Birmingham of Welsh ancestry. Under Rossetti's influence he abandoned his intention of taking orders and devoted himself to art. He drew his inspiration from medieval ballads and legends, classical mythology, and the Bible. He received a baronetcy in 1894.

BURNET, Gilbert (1643–1715). British bishop and historian. B. in Edinburgh, he was ordained in the

BURMA. A market scene in Upper Burma.
Courtesy of the Burmah Oil Co. Ltd.

Episcopal Church of Scotland in 1661. He pub. his *History of the Reformation in England* in 1679. His Whig views having brought him into disfavour, he retired to The Hague on the accession of James II, and became the confidential adviser of Princess Mary and William of Orange. He returned to England with the latter in 1688, and was appointed bp. of Salisbury. His best-known work is his *History of His Own Time*.

BURNET, Sir Macfarlane (1899–). Australian virologist. He was awarded the O.M. in 1958 in recognition of his work on such diseases as influenza, polio and cholera, and 1944–65 was director of the Walter and Eliza Hall Inst. for Medical Research and prof. of experimental medicine at Melbourne. His books incl. *Viruses and Man* (1953) and *Integrity of the Body* (1962).

BURNETT, Frances Eliza Hodgson (1849–1924). Anglo-American writer. B. in Manchester, she lived in the U.S.A. from 1865. She wrote many novels and plays, and the famous children's story *Little Lord Fauntleroy* (1886).

BURNEY, Frances (Fanny) (1752–1840). British novelist and diarist. The dau. of Dr. Charles B. (1726–1814), historian of music, she belonged to the circle of Dr. Johnson, and achieved success with her first novel *Evelina*, pub. anonymously in 1778. She obtained a post at court 1786–91, and in 1793 m. the French émigré General D'Arblay. She pub. 2 further novels, *Cecilia* (1782), and *Camilla* (1796), and her diaries and letters appeared in 1842–6.

BURNHAM, James (1905–). American philosopher. B. at Chicago, he was a Rhodes scholar at Oxford. Prof. of philosophy at N.Y. univ. 1932–54, he argued in *The Managerial Revolution* (1941) that world control is passing from politicians and capitalists to the new class of business executives, the managers. Later books incl. *The Coming Defeat of Communism* (1950) and *Congress and the American Condition* (1959).

BURNLEY. Manufacturing town (co. bor.) in Lancs, England, 12 m. N.E. of Blackburn. It is an important cotton-weaving centre, and a large variety of cloths are manufactured. Pop. (1961) 80,588.

BURNOUF (bürnoof'), **Eugène** (1801–52). French orientalist. B. at Paris, he was prof. of Sanskrit at the Collège de France from 1832. He deciphered MSS., thus revealing to the western world the full Zoroastrian teaching for the first time.

BURNS, John (1858–1943). British labour leader. B. in Battersea and trained as an engineer, he was sentenced to 6 weeks' imprisonment for his part in the Trafalgar Square demonstration on 'Bloody Sunday' – 13 Nov. 1887 – and in 1889 was a leader of the strike securing the 'dockers' tanner' (wage of 6d. per hr.). In 1892 he entered Parliament as an Independent Labour M.P. and in 1906 was the 1st working man to be a member of the Cabinet (Pres. of the Local Govt. Board). In 1914 he was appointed pres. of the Board of Trade, but resigned on the outbreak of war.

BURNS, Robert (1759–96). Scottish poet. B. at Alloway, Ayrshire, the son of a farmer, he became joint tenant, after his father's death in 1784, with his brother in a farm at Mossgiel, where many of his best poems were written. In agriculture he proved less proficient and having in addition been crossed in his love for Jean Armour among others, he decided to emigrate to Jamaica. He was dissuaded by the success of his *Poems, chiefly in the Scottish dialect* (1786), which made him the lion of the Edinburgh season 1786–7. A 2nd enlarged edition in 1787 proved profitable, and in 1788 enabled him at length to marry Jean Armour and settle to farming at Ellisland, near Dumfries. In 1789 he obtained a part-time post as district excise-officer, and when his farm once more failed in 1791, he transferred to a full-time post.

B.'s fame rests equally on his poems and his songs,

of which he contributed some 300 to Johnson's *Scots Musical Museum* (1787–1803), and Thomson's *Scottish Airs with Poetry* (1793–1811); sometimes wholly original and at others combining inspiration from several popular versions, they attain lyric perfection. His English verse is negligible; the full vigour of his genius waited on his use of the Scots dialect as in 'Holy Willie's Prayer', 'Tam o' Shanter', and 'Jolly Beggars'.

BURNS. Injuries to the tissues caused by heat, light, or corrosive substances. A 'scald' is a burn caused by hot liquid or vapour; the nature of the injury is the same. Bs. include injuries made by invisible rays, whether these are of lower frequency than visible light (heat, infra-red), or of higher frequency (ultra-violet, X-rays, radium emanations).

Bs. are divided into two classes, superficial and deep, according to whether the skin is partially destroyed, or whether it is wholly destroyed and the muscle beneath it is damaged. All Bs. cause some degree of shock, and this is often more dangerous than the local effect. The treatment of a bad B. or scald is therefore first directed against shock and infection. The B. itself is treated with as little damage to sound tissue as possible. Oils, acids, dyes, and creams in great variety are applied, to exclude the air and prevent the absorption of noxious substances, ease pain, and encourage the natural repair of the skin and tissues.

BURR, Aaron (1756–1836). American politician. B. in New Jersey, he served on Washington's staff during the War of Independence, and in 1800 received the same no. of electoral votes as Jefferson in the presidential election. Through the influence of Alexander Hamilton the House of Representatives voted in favour of Jefferson (Feb. 17, 1801), but B. was vice-pres. 1800–4. B. never forgave Hamilton, whom he thought also prevented his becoming Gov. of N.Y. State in 1804, and killed him in a duel that year. As a result he became a social outcast, and had to leave the U.S.A. for some years following an attempt to raise an armed force for the invasion of Mexico.

BURRA, Edward (1905–). British artist. B. in Kensington, his work incl. genre watercolours with a humorous touch, as well as more dramatic works showing the influence of El Greco and Goya. Notable are 'Mexican Church' (1938) and 'Soldiers' (1942), both in the Tate Gallery.

BURROUGHS (bur'ōz), **Edgar Rice** (1875–1950). American novelist. B. at Chicago, he had a varied career, before writing a score of 'Tarzan' books, romantic stories of the adventures of an ape-man, which were widely popular, beginning with *Tarzan of the Apes* (1914).

BURROUGHS, William (1914–). American novelist. Member of a 'big-business' family, he was b. in St. Louis, Missouri, ed. at Harvard and has had a variety of jobs as reporter, advertising man, private detective, etc. Well known to devotees of the American 'beat' movement, he estab. his reputation with *The Naked Lunch* (1959) dealing with the world of the drug addict: *The Ticket that Exploded* (1962) is science fiction.

BURROUGHS, William Seward (1857–98). American inventor. A bank clerk, he patented an adding machine, which with many improvements and developments was successfully produced and marketed by the firm bearing his name.

BURSA. City in Turkey-in-Asia, 60 m. S. of Uskudar, cap. of B. il, and cap. of the Ottoman Empire 1326–1423. The commercial centre of a fertile district, it produces silk. Its port is Mudania, 16 m. N.W., on the Sea of Marmara. Pop. (1965) 212,500.

BURSLEM. Parish in Staffs, England, one of the most important towns of the Potteries. Formerly a separate borough, and included in the co. bor. of

Stoke-on-Trent in 1910, it began to make pottery in 1644.

BURT, Sir Cyril Lodowic (1883–). British psychologist, a pioneer in intelligence tests and psychological tests for special abilities in school-children. He worked with the L.C.C. Education Dept. 1913–32, and was prof. of education (1924–31) and psychology (1931–50) at London univ. He was knighted in 1946.

BURTON, Sir Richard Francis (1821–90). British traveller and orientalist. B. at Torquay, in 1842 he became a subaltern in the Indian army. He made himself master of 35 oriental languages. In 1853 he went on pilgrimage to Mecca; in 1854 he explored the interior of the Somali country, and in 1856 was commissioned by the Foreign Office to explore the sources of the Nile; with J. H. Speke he discovered Lake Tanganyika in 1858. From 1861 he was a British consul – from 1871 at Trieste, where he d. Every country of the many he visited was made the subject of a remarkable book, but he is chiefly remembered for his literal translation of the *Arabian Nights* (1885–8).

BURTON, Robert (1577–1640). English philosopher. B. in Leics, he was ed. at Oxford, and remained there for the rest of his life as a fellow of Christ Church. His fame rests on his *Anatomy of Melancholy* (1621), a remarkable compendium of information on the medical and religious opinions of the time.

BURTON UPON TRENT. Brewery centre (co. bor.) in Staffs, England, 123 m. N.W. of London. Other industries incl. copper, iron and boiler works. Pop. (1961) 50,766.

BURU'NDI. Country in central Africa, lying on the E. of Lake Tanganyika. Part of the former Belgian trust territory of Ruanda-Urundi (q.v.), it became independent 1962, and in 1966 the P.M., Captain Michel Micombero, deposed the King (Mwami Ntare V) and proclaimed himself pres. of the Rep. of B. Coffee, hides and livestock are exported. The chief towns are Bujumbura (cap., formerly called Usumbura) and Kitega (former royal cap.). Area 10,747 sq. m.; pop. (1965) 3,000,000.

BURY (ber'i). Cotton-spinning town (co. bor.) in Lancs, England, on the Irwell, 10 m. N. of Manchester. Other industries incl. calico-printing, dyeing and, engine-making. Pop. (1961) 59,984.

BURY ST. EDMUNDS. Market town (bor.) in Suffolk, England, capital of W. Suffolk. On the Lark, 28 m. E. of Cambridge, it is named after St. Edmund, the martyred king of E. Anglia, whose remains were re-interred here in 903. It makes agricultural implements, beet sugar, etc. There are remains of the once magnificent Benedictine Abbey founded in 1020. Pop. (1961) 21,144.

BUSBY (buz'bi), **Richard** (1606–95). English headmaster of Westminster school from 1640. Among his pupils were Dryden, Locke, Atterbury, and Prior, and he was renowned for his floggings.

BUSH, Alan Dudley (1900–). British composer. As a student under John Ireland, he experimented in 12-note composition, but has subsequently tried to keep his style simple in accordance with the ideas of Marxism, which he adopted when studying philosophy in Berlin. His works incl. the operas *Wat Tyler* (1953) and *Men of Blackmoor* (1956), both much more successful on the Continent than in Britain, and the *Byron*

Symphony (1962). Since 1925 he has been prof. of composition at the R.A.M., where he himself trained.

BUSHBUCK (*Tragelaphus*). African antelopes, with hairy tails and only a spiral twist in the horns. The largest species (*c.* 4 ft. high) is the mountain or Buxton's B. (*T. buxtoni*) of S. Abyssinia. The common B. (*T. scriptus*), the smallest species (less than 3ft. high), is found over most of Africa S. of the Sahara.

BUSHEL. A dry measure legally standardized in Britain in 1826 as the 'imperial bushel' of 8 gallons (or 4 pecks): some U.S. states have different standards according to the goods measured.

BUSHIDO (boo'shidō). Code of honour of the Japanese military caste of *Samurai*, analogous to the English conception of 'chivalry'.

BUSHIRE (boosher'). Port in Persia, on the Persian Gulf 140 m. S.E. of Abadan. Founded 1736, it was Persia's chief port until the rise of Abadan. It has an airfield. Pop. 30,500.

BUSHMEN. A nomadic race of hunters, living in the central parts of S. Africa, particularly the Kalahari Desert. They are thin and of small stature, with dark yellow skins, prominent cheekbones and a low skull. Only about 26,000 survive today. Their language, which is monosyllabic, has the same curious 'clicks' as that of the Hottentots. They have no tribal chiefs, live in holes in the ground or in reed huts, and wear rough skins. Ancient B. paintings found in mountain caves show remarkable artistic talent.

BUSHRANGERS. Australian armed robbers of the 19th cent. The first Bs. were escaped convicts. The last gang was led by the Kelly brothers in 1878–80. They form the subject of many Australian ballads.

BUSONI (booso'nē), **Ferruccio Benvenuto** (1866–1924). Italian pianist, composer, and musical critic. B. near Florence, he made his first public appearance at the age of 7. In 1891–3 he was at the Conservatoire of Boston, U.S.A., and later lived in Berlin, Bologna, and Zürich. Most of his music was for the piano, but he also composed several operas. As a critic he was influential in suggesting new standards of value.

BUSTAMA'NTE, Sir (William) Alexander (1884–). Jamaican statesman, *né* William Alexander Clarke. Of mixed blood, his father being Irish and his mother a mulatto, he adopted the name B. to show his opposition to racial discrimination. As leader of the Labour Party, he was chief min. 1953–5 and P.M. 1962–7, when Jamaica seceded from the proposed W.I. Federation following a referendum campaign headed by B. He was knighted in 1955.

BUSTARD. Family of large running birds (Otidae), with a superficial resemblance to turkeys, inhabiting dry plains in Europe, Asia, and Africa. The great B. (*Otis tarda*) and the little B. (*O. tetrax*) are occasional visitors to Britain.

BU'TANE. C_4H_{10} paraffin hydrocarbon b.p. 1°C, density at 0°C=0·60, obtained from petroleum distillation. It is liquefied under pressure in steel cylinders and used as fuel for industrial and domestic purposes, e.g. portable cooking stoves.

BUTE, John Stuart, 3rd earl of (1713–92). British Tory statesman. He succeeded his father in the title in 1723, and in 1737 was elected a representative peer for Scotland. Upon the accession of George III in 1760, he became the chief instrument in the king's policy for breaking the power of the Whigs and establishing the personal rule of the monarch through Parliament, and in 1762 was appointed Premier. His position as the king's favourite and the supplanter of the popular Pitt made him hated in the country. After the Seven Years War in 1763 he resigned.

BUTE. Scottish island in the Firth of Clyde, separated from Argyllshire by a narrow winding channel called the Kyles of B. It is 15½ m. long, has a fertile soil, and is a great holiday resort for Glasgow. Rothesay is the chief town. Area 47 sq. m.; pop. (1961) 9,779.

With Arran and other adjacent islands it forms the co. of B.; area 218 sq. m.; pop. (1961) 15,129.

BUTLER, Sir James Ramsay (1889–). British historian, Regius prof. of modern history at Cambridge 1947–54 and chief historian for the official military histories of the S.W.W. He was knighted in 1958.

REG BUTLER. At work in his studio on 'Fetish'.
Courtesy of Reg Butler.

BUTLER, Joseph (1692–1752). British theologian. In 1740 he became dean of St. Paul's, in 1747 refused the primacy, and in 1750 became bp. of Durham. He defined his philosophy in *Fifteen Sermons* (1726) and in his *Analogy of Religion* (1736) refuted Deism, attempting to prove that the element of revealed religion in Christianity is inherently probable even if not capable of logical proof.

BUTLER, Josephine Elizabeth (1828–1906). British social reformer. *Née* Grey, she was b. in Northumberland and m. Dr. Butler, later canon of Winchester. She agitated for the admission of women to higher education, helped to secure the Married Women's Property Act, worked for the improvement of the lot of 'fallen' women, and carried on a campaign against the Contagious Diseases Acts of 1864–9, which made women in garrison towns liable to compulsory examination for V.D. The Acts were repealed 1883–6.

BUTLER, Nicholas Murray (1862–1947). American educationist and political writer. B. in New Jersey, he became prof. of philosophy at Columbia univ. in 1890, and was pres. of the univ. 1901–45. He advocated women's suffrage and the repeal of prohibition, and worked for the improvement of international relations. In 1931 he was awarded half the Nobel peace prize.

BUTLER, Reg (1913–). British sculptor. B. in Herts, he held his 1st one-man show in 1949, and caused a sensation by winning the international Unknown Political Prisoner competition in 1953. He is primarily concerned with the human figure, using distortion to achieve striking effects.

BUTLER, Richard Austen, baron B. of Saffron Walden (1902–). British Cons. politician, known as 'Rab' from his initials. B. in India, he was ed. at Marlborough and Pembroke Coll., Cambridge and was M.P. for Saffron Walden 1929–65. As Min. of Education in the Coalition 1941–5, he was responsible for the 'Butler' Act of 1944 establishing the lines of post-war educational development, was Chancellor of the Exchequer 1951–5, and Lord Privy Seal 1955–9. A likely candidate for the premiership in 1957, he was given the additional post of Home Sec. under Macmillan, and in 1962 became Deputy P.M. with the new title of First Sec. of State. On the resignation of Macmillan in 1963, he again narrowly missed the premiership, but continued under Home as Sec. of State for Foreign Affairs until 1964. He became a life peer and master of Trinity Coll., Cambridge, in 1965.

BUTLER, Samuel (1612–80). English satirist. The son of a Worcs. farmer, he served in the household of the countess of Kent, and then of Sir Samuel Luke, a colonel in the Parliamentary army. After the Restoration he became secretary to the earl of Carberry. His poem *Hudibras*, pub. in 3 parts in 1663, 1664 and 1678, became immediately popular for its

biting satire against the Puritans. His prose *Characters* are also of high merit.

BUTLER, Samuel (1835–1902). British author. B. in Notts, the son of a clergyman, he refused to go into the Church, and became a sheep-farmer in New Zealand (1859–64). He made his name by the satirical *Erewhon* (1872) describing a visit to the imaginary country, Erewhon, i.e. Nowhere reversed. A sequel, *Erewhon Revisited*, was pub. in 1901. *The Fair Haven* (1873) was a satirical examination of the miraculous element in Christianity. *Life and Habit* (1877) and other works were devoted to a criticism of the theory of natural selection. In *The Authoress of the Odyssey* he maintained that the Odyssey was the work of a woman. B.'s fame was greatly increased by the posthumous publication of his *Note-books* and his largely autobiographical novel, *The Way of All Flesh*, written 1872–85; pub. 1903.

BUTLIN, Sir William Edmund (1899–). British pioneer of holiday camps. B. in S. Africa, he went in early life to Canada, but later entered the fair business in England. His chain of camps provide 'all-in' holidays with amusements, meals and sleeping chalets at an inclusive price. He was knighted in 1964.

BUTOR (bütor'), **Michel** (1926–). French writer. Ed. at the Univ. of Paris, he is a practitioner of the 'anti-novel' of which Robbe-Grillet (q.v.) is the theoretician. These incl. *Passage de Milan* (1954), *Degrés* (1960) and *L'Emploi du temps* (1963): *Mobile* (1962) is a vol. of essays.

BUTT, Dame Clara (1873–1936). British contralto. B. in Sussex, she had an unusually rich and powerful voice, and Elgar's *Sea Pictures* (1899) was specially written for her. She m. in 1900 the baritone Kennerley Rumford (1870–1957), and in 1917 became D.B.E.

BUTT, Isaac (1813–79). Irish politician. B. in Donegal, he taught political economy at Dublin univ., and founded in 1870 the Home Rule movement. He was ousted from the leadership of the parliamentary party by Parnell.

BUTTE (būt). City in Montana, U.S.A., 50 m. S.W. of the state capital Helena. Here are the copper smelting works of the Anaconda Mining Co., owners also of the copper, silver and other mines in the vicinity. B. was founded in 1864 during a rush for gold, soon exhausted; copper was found some 20 years later. Pop. (1960) 27,877.

BUTTER. A fatty dairy product made from milk by churning the cream. Besides the cow, the goat, sheep, ass, mare, camel, and buffalo have been used for milk production.

BUTTERCUP. Genus (*Ranunculus*) of the family Ranunculaceae, many species having divided leaves which have earned the alternative name of crowfoot, and shining yellow cuplike flowers. Common in Europe and Asia, and naturalized in N. America, are the bulbous B. (*R. bulbosus*), the creeping B. (*R. repens*), and the meadow crowfoot (*R. acris*); native to N. America are the marsh B. of the east (*R. septentrionalis*) and the California B. (*R. californicus*). The florists' B. is *R. asiaticus*.

LORD BUTLER
Photo: Daily Herald.

BUTTERFIELD, Sir Herbert (1900–). British historian, prof. of modern history at Cambridge from 1944 and Regius prof. 1963–7. His books incl. *The Origins of Modern Science* (1949), *George III and the Historians* (1957) and *International Conflict in the Twentieth Century* (1960).

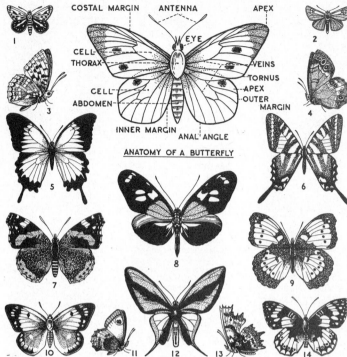

ANATOMY OF A BUTTERFLY

COSTAL MARGIN · ANTENNA · APEX · EYE · CELL · THORAX · VEINS · TORNUS · CELL · APEX · ABDOMEN · OUTER MARGIN · INNER MARGIN · ANAL ANGLE

BUTTERFLY. A small selection of the 68 British and many thousands of foreign species. Their names, habitat, and wing-span in inches are as follows. 1, *Cyclopides silvius*, Europe, 1⅛; 2, *Adopoea actaeon* (Lulworth skipper), England, 1; 3, *Argynnis adippe* (high brown fritillary), England, 2¼; 4, *Satyrus achine*, Europe, 2; 5, *Papilio ulysses*, New Guinea, 4½; 6, *Papilio marcellus* (zebra swallow-tail), N. America, 3; 7, *Pyrameis atalanta* (red admiral), Europe, Asia, N. and S. America, 2½; 8, *Heliconius burneyi*, Peru, 2¾; 9, *Precis octavia*, Africa, 2¼; 10, *Colias myrmidone* (dark clouded yellow), Europe, 2¼; 11, *Epinephele tithonus* (large heath or gatekeeper), England, 1⅞; 12, *Troides paradiseus*, New Guinea, 5¼; 13, *Polygonia c-album* (comma), England, 2; 14, *Melanargia larissa* (eastern marbled white), Europe, 2.

Grayling, together with the Heaths, Ringlets, and many others.

The family Pieridae includes the Whites, Clouded Yellows, Orange Tips, and their allies. The Garden or Cabbage Whites (*Pieris rapae* and *P. brassicae*) are among the few injurious species. The Lycaenidae are a large family that incl. the Blues, Coppers, and Hairstreaks. They are mostly rather small, often with metallic coloration. The Erycinidae are essentially S. American; the sole British representative is the Duke of Burgundy fritillary (*Nemeobius lucina*).

There occur different seasonal forms among certain Bs., e.g. the European Nymphalid B. *Araschnia levana*, whose spring form is known as *levana* whilst the summer form *prorsa* was considered to belong to a different species. Other Bs., such as the African *Papilio dardanus*, have several distinct forms of female and only one type of male.

Although the caterpillars of most Bs. feed upon flowering plants, those of a few kinds are carnivorous.

BUXTON. Market town (bor.) and spa in Derbyshire, England, 36 m. N.W. of Derby; the highest town of its size in England, 1,000–1,150 ft. above sea-level. Since Roman times its healing waters have been visited; there are private and public baths, and a hospital for the treatment of gout, rheumatism, etc. The town is also a popular winter resort. Pop. (1961) 19,236.

BUYSSE (boi'se), **Cyriel** (1859–1932). Flemish author, b. near Ghent. He wrote novels and short stories accurately delineating bourgeois Flemish life, e.g. *The Right of the Strongest* (1873).

BUZĂU. Rumanian town in Ploesti region, on the river B., a tributary of the Danube. It is an important railway junction and trade centre, and the seat of a bishopric. Petroleum is found nearby. Pop. (1967) 82,454.

BUZZARD. Name applied to the larger and heavier built hawks, particularly to the subfamily Buteoninae, allied to the eagles. The common B. (*Buteo buteo*) was formerly a common British bird, but is now found in only a few districts. The rough-legged B. (*Archibuteo lagopus*) is an irregular autumn visitor. The honey B. (*Pernis apivorus*) is very scarce as a breeding species. The bird called B. in America is the Turkey B. (*Cartharistes aura*), one of the New World vultures. *See* illus. p. 190.

BYBLOS (bib'los). Town (modern Jebeil), 20 m. N. of Beirut, Lebanon. Known to the Assyrians and Babylonians as Gubla it had a thriving export of cedar and pinewood to Egypt as early as 3000 B.C. In Roman times called B., it boasted an amphitheatre, baths and a temple dedicated to an unknown male god: excavation continues.

BUTTERFLY. Name given to those insects which form the series Papilionoidea (or Rhopalocera) of the order Lepidoptera, the remainder of the order consisting of the moths (q.v.). Like moths, Bs. are clothed with microscopic scales, and feed upon nectar and other fluid substances which they imbibe through a tubular proboscis formed by the greatly modified maxillae; but they are distinguished from moths by their clubbed antennae and in the absence of a frenulum from the hind-wings. They are essentially day-flying insects, whereas most moths are nocturnal. Metamorphosis is complete; the caterpillars are very diverse in form, and the pupae or chrysalids are usually without the protection of cocoons. The life of the adult insect is usually only a few weeks, but species which hibernate live until the spring or early summer when they lay their eggs.

The Skippers or Hesperiidae, the most primitive family of Bs., are characterized by all the veins in the fore-wings arising separately from the cell. In the remainder of the Bs. certain of the veins in the fore-wings are coincident and do not arise separately from the cell. The Swallow-tails or Papilionidae are a family of large or very large Bs., mainly tropical.

In the Nymphalidae, the largest family of Bs., with about 6,000 species, the fore-legs are so reduced as to be useless for walking. The subfamily Nymphalinae includes the Peacock, Purple Emperor, Tortoiseshells, Admirals and Fritillaries. The subfamily Satyrinae comprises the Meadow Brown,

BYDGOSZCZ (bid'goshch). Town in Poland, 65 m. N.E. of Poznan on the river Brda. It is an important railway and canal junction and was Prussian from 1772 to 1919, when it was restored to Poland. Pop. (1966) 258,000.

BYELORUSSIA. *See* WHITE RUSSIA.

BYELUY (byeh'lē), **Andrey.** Pen-name of the Russian poet and novelist Boris Bugaiev (1880–1934). A leader of the Symbolist poets, he also revolutionized Russian prose with the novels *Silver Dove* (1910) and *Petersburg* (1916), and the autobiographical *Kotik Letaev* (1922).

BYNG, John (1704–57). British admiral. When in 1756 the island of Minorca was invaded by the French, B. was ordered to sail to the relief of Fort St. Philip which was still resisting, but failed in the attempt. After the fort's fall he was court-martialled and condemned to death, and shot at Portsmouth.

BYNG OF VIMY, Julian Byng, 1st visct. (1862–1935). British general. A son of the 2nd earl of

BUZZARD

Strafford, he commanded the 3rd Cavalry Division in 1914, the Cavalry Corps in 1915, the IXth Army Corps at the Dardanelles, and the Canadian Army Corps in 1916–17 in France. After his victory at Vimy Ridge he took command of the 3rd Army, and in Nov. 1917 made the brilliant tank attack on Cambrai. He was Gov.-Gen. of Canada 1921–6, and was made a viscount in 1926, and a field marshal in 1932.

BYRD (bird), **Richard Evelyn** (1888–1957). American airman and explorer. B. in Virginia, he served in the navy from 1912. After an expedition to Greenland in 1925, on 9 May 1926, he flew to the N. Pole and back to Spitzbergen in 15½ hours. In 1928 he organized an expedition to the Antarctic, and in 1929 made a successful flight to the S. Pole. He made a 2nd expedition to the Antarctic in 1933–5, and discovered coal deposits 180 m. from the pole; in 1939 he was given command of an official expedition sent to the Antarctic by the U.S. govt., and in Dec. 1946 he led the largest expedition ever to visit the Antarctic.

BYRD, William (1543–1623). English composer, b. probably at Lincoln, where he became organist in 1563. He shared with Tallis the honorary post of

BYBLOS. In Roman times the city expanded rapidly, its new buildings including the magnificent amphitheatre excavated by Dunand shown here. Adjoining it were baths and a fine temple dedicated to an unidentified male god.
Courtesy of the Lebanese Embassy.

organist in Queen Elizabeth's Chapel Royal, and in 1575 he and Tallis were granted a monopoly in the printing and selling of music. B. was the founder of the English school of madrigal writers and also composed music for the virginals, but his church music represents his most important work.

BYRNES (burnz), **James Francis** (1879–). American statesman. B. at Charleston, S. Carolina, he sat in Congress as a Democrat 1911–25, and became Senator for S.

BYRON. In Albanian dress by Thomas Phillips, 1813. Photo: The National Portrait Gallery.

Carolina in 1931. In 1943 he was appointed Director of War Mobilization, and in 1944 the task of reconversion of industry to peace-time production was added to his office. From June 1945 to Jan. 1947 he was Secretary of State. His memoirs, *Speaking Frankly*, were pub. in 1947.

BYRON, George Gordon, 6th baron (1788–1824). British poet. Born in London, he succeeded his greatuncle in the title in 1798. He was ed. at Harrow and Cambridge, and pub. the juvenile poems *Hours of Idleness* in 1807. Their harsh criticism by the *Edinburgh Review* provoked his satire, *English Bards and Scotch Reviewers* (1809). He then undertook the tour of Portugal, Spain, and the Balkans, which he described in the first 2 cantos of *Childe Harold*. Their publication in 1812 made him famous overnight, while the series of Oriental verse romances which followed were even more successful. In 1815 he m. Anne Milbanke, but a year later a separation ensued which caused such a scandal that B. was hounded out of England. He first settled in Switzerland, where he met Shelley, and under his influence wrote *The Prisoner of Chillon* (1816), the 3rd canto of *Childe Harold* (1816), and *Manfred* (1817). The next 3 years he spent in Venice, where in spite of his debauched life he produced much of his finest work, incl. *Beppo* (1818), the 4th canto of *Childe Harold* (1818), and *Mazeppa* (1819), and began work on his masterpiece, *Don Juan* (1819–24). In 1819 he removed to Ravenna, as the lover of Countess Guiccioli, and there dabbled in Italian revolutionary politics, and wrote his rhetorical series of tragedies and the masterly *Vision of Judgment* (1822). He sailed for Greece in 1823, in order to aid the Greek struggle for independence, but d. of fever at Missolonghi in 1824. His writings, his life and his death contributed to make him the patron saint of romanticism and revolutionary liberalism in 19th cent. Europe.

BYZANTINE (bizan'tin) **ART.** A style of painting, architecture, etc., which originated in Byzantium (4th–5th cents.) and spread to Italy, throughout the Balkans, and to Russia, where it survived until modern times. It is a mixture of Greek and Oriental elements, and is characterized by the use of rich colours, particularly gold, geometrical designs on a flat surface, distorted figures, and (in architecture) the use of the dome supported on pendentives. Classical examples of B. architecture are St. Sophia, Constantinople, and St. Mark's, Venice. A modern example is Westminster Cathedral. The first great Italian painters to break away from the formalism of the B. style were Cimabùe and Giotto, who painted religious subjects in a naturalistic style.

BYZANTINE EMPIRE. The Eastern Roman Empire, with its capital at Constantinople (Byzantium). The Emperor Constantine removed his capital to Constantinople in A.D. 330, but it was not until 395 that the Empire was finally divided into E. and W.

halves. When the W. Empire was overrun by barbarian invaders, the B.E. stood firm, and Justinian I (527–565) temporarily recovered Italy, N. Africa, and parts of Spain. During the 7th cent. Syria, Egypt and N. Africa were lost to the Arabs, who twice besieged Constantinople (673–7, 718), but the Byzantines maintained their hold on Asia Minor. The Iconoclastic controversy of the 8th and 9th cents. brought the emperors into conflict with the papacy, and in 867 the Greek Church broke with the Roman. Under the Macedonian dynasty (867–1056) the B.E. reached the height of its prosperity; the Bulgars proved a formidable danger, but after a long struggle were finally crushed in 1018 by Basil II. After Basil's death the B.E. declined, and in 1071–3 the Seljuk Turks conquered most of Asia Minor. In 1204 the W. crusaders sacked Constantinople and set Baldwin of Flanders on the throne. The Latin Empire was overthrown in 1261, and the B.E. maintained a precarious existence, until in 1453 the Turks captured Constantinople. The B.E. rendered great services to civilization, as the guardian of Greek culture and Roman law during the Dark Ages, as the centre whence Christian civilization penetrated the Balkans and Russia, and as the bulwark of Christendom against Moslems and barbarians.

BYZANTINE LITERATURE. Written mainly in the Gk. *koinē,* a form of Greek accepted as the literary language of the 1st cent. A.D. and increasingly separate from the spoken tongue of the people, it is chiefly concerned with theology, history, and commentaries on the Greek classics. Its chief authors are the theologians St. Basil, Gregory of Nyssa, Gregory of Nazianzus, Chrysostom (4th cent. A.D.), and John of Damascus (8th cent.); the historians Zosimus (*c.* 500), Procopius (6th cent.), Bryennius and his wife Comnena (*c.* 1100), and Georgius Acropolita (1220–82); and the encyclopaedist Suidas (*c.* 975). Drama was non-existent and poetry, save for the hymns of the 6–8th cents., scanty and stilted, but there were many popular saints' lives.

BYZANTIUM. Ancient Greek city on the Bosphorus, founded by the Megarians *c.* 660 B.C. In A.D. 330 the capital of the Roman Empire was transferred there by Constantine the Great, who renamed it Constantinople (q.v.). Its Turkish name Istanbul (q.v.) is commonly used today.

C Third letter of the alphabet. It corresponds to Heb. *gimel* and Gk. *gamma,* both derived from the Semitic word for 'camel'. Originally representing a hard *g,* it was used by the Romans for *k* also.

In the Roman system the numeral C stands for a hundred; C. is also used for 'Celsius', formerly called 'Centigrade' in thermometer readings.

CABAʹL. A clique of scheming politicians; applied particularly to Charles II's ministry (1667–73) whose initials made up the word – C(lifford), A(shley), B(uckingham), A(rlington), and L(auderdale).

CABBAGE. A plant (*Brassica oleracea*) of the family Cruciferae, allied to the turnip and wild charlock. It is an important table vegetable, and the numerous cultivated varieties – all probably descended from the wild cabbage or seakale – include kail, Brussels sprouts, common cabbage, savoy, cauliflower, sprouting broccoli, and kohlrabi.

CABBALA. See KABBALA.

CABELL (kab'el), **James Branch** (1879–1958). American author. B. in Virginia, he wrote a series of ironically humorous novels set in the fictitious medieval country of Poictesme. Of these, *Jurgen* (1919) was prosecuted by the N.Y. Soc. for the Prevention of Vice, and naturally had assured success.

CAʹBER, Tossing the (Gaelic *cabar,* a pole). Scottish athletic sport. The C. is a tapering tree-trunk, some 20 ft. long. The tosser rests the C. on his shoulder, holding the thin end which he raises till it is about level with his elbow, runs forward as the C. begins to topple over, and hurls it into the air. A champion may achieve throws of over 40 ft.

CABET (kahbeh'), **Étienne** (1788–1856). French communist. B. at Dijon, he fled to England after the revolution of 1830, where he came under the influence of Robert Owen and his communistic ideals. Returning to France in 1839, he pub. a Utopian romance *Voyage en Icarie,* and in 1848 some 1,500 'Icarians' established a communistic colony in Texas. C. moved the colony to Illinois, but was expelled in 1856 and d. broken-hearted at St. Louis.

CABINET. In Britain the committee of ministers (selected by the P.M.) holding the most important executive offices, who decide the govt.'s policy. The C. system originated in the 'C. councils' (C. meaning a small room, and hence implying secrecy), or subcommittees of the Privy Council, which under the Stuarts undertook specialized tasks. Under William III it became customary for the king to select his ministers from the party with a parliamentary majority. When George I ceased to attend C. meetings, the office of P.M. came into being, to supply a chairman for C. meetings; Walpole is usually considered the first, although the office was not legally recognized until 1905. Cabinet policy is a collective one, and a vote of censure on one minister usually involves the whole C. Meetings are strictly secret, and almost invariably confined to members; minutes are taken by the Sec. of the Cabinet, a high civil servant. In the U.S.A. a C. system developed early, the term being used from 1793, though it is not responsible as in Britain for initiating legislation. Members are selected by the Pres. and, again contrary to British practice, may neither be members of either house of Congress nor speak there, being responsible to the Pres. alone.

CABIʹRI. Group of divinities worshipped in ancient times in Asia Minor and parts of Greece. They were demoniac powers of the underworld, and were believed to control fertility.

CABLE, George Washington (1844–1925). American novelist, b. in New Orleans. His *Old Creole Days* (1879) secured him recognition as an interpreter of a social system which ended with the Civil War, in which he fought as a Confederate cavalryman.

CAʹBOT, John (*c.* 1450–98). Genoese navigator and discoverer of the N. American mainland. He was naturalized a Venetian, and made many voyages to the Levant. In 1484 he moved to London; and in 1496 C. with his three sons was commissioned by Henry VII to discover lands hitherto unknown. On 2 May 1497, he sailed from Bristol, and after 52 days he landed on Cape Breton Island (which he thought was the N.E. coast of Asia). In 1498 he sailed again and touched Greenland.

His 2nd son, **Sebastian C.** (1474–1557) was cartographer to Henry VIII of England, and then similarly served Ferdinand of Spain. In 1526–30 he explored the Brazilian coast and the river Plate. Returning to England he planned a voyage to China by way of the N.E. passage, encouraged the formation of the Co. of Merchant Adventurers of London in 1551, and in 1553 and 1556 directed the Co.'s expeditions to Russia.

CABRINI (kahbrē′nē), **Frances** (1850–1917). The first R.C. saint in U.S.A. B. in Lombardy, she founded the Missionary Sisters of the Sacred Heart in America, and estab. many schools and hospitals in the care of her nuns. She was canonized in 1946.

CACCINI (catshē′nē), **Giulio** (c. 1545–1618). Italian singer and composer. From 1578 he was in the service of the duke of Tuscany at Florence, and his brief vocal compositions in recitative style paved the way for the growth of opera.

CACHALOT (kash′-) or **Sperm-whale** (*Physeter catodon*). The largest of the toothed whales. It has a large blunt snout, with the nostrils opening above at the tip, and an enormous head. The male may attain a length of 60 ft.; the female is only half that size. The C. favours the warmer oceans and is gregarious; it is much sought by whalers on account of its spermaceti.

CACTUS. 1, Cereus giganteus; 2, Opuntia dillenii (prickly pear).

CACTOBLASTIS. Genus of moths of the family Pyralidae. The most important species is *C. cactorum*, whose caterpillars feed on the prickly pear (*Opuntia*). For this reason they have been introduced into Australia in order to check the prickly pear menace.

CACTUS. Typical genus of plants of the family Cactaceae, and in common speech applied to the whole family. They are recognized by their woody axis being overlaid with an enlarged fleshy stem, which assumes various forms and is usually covered with spines. The leaves are usually very much reduced, and frequently are absent. The flowers are often large and brightly coloured. The fruit is fleshy and often edible, as in the case of the prickly pear.

The Cactaceae are a New World family, though some species are found in the warmer parts of the Old and others have been introduced from the New to the Old, e.g. in the Mediterranean area, and have become a pest. They grow in the driest and rockiest situations.

CADBURY, George (1839–1922). British manufacturer of cocoa and chocolate. The firm of C. was a pioneer in industrial welfare, and the garden village of Bournville (q.v.) was estab. for its workers.

CADDIS FLY. Common name for all the insects forming the order Trichoptera. They are moth-like in appearance, their wings covered with hairs, and their mouth-parts are of the biting type. They feed on the juices of plants. Their larvae are aquatic.

CADE, Jack (d. 1450). English rebel. A prosperous Kentish landowner, he took the lead when the men of Kent rose in 1450 against the misgovernment of Henry VI. He defeated the royal forces at Sevenoaks and occupied London, whereupon under promise of reforms and pardon the rebels dispersed. But C. was then hunted down and killed near Heathfield, Sussex.

CÁDIZ (Span. kah′dĕth). Spanish city and naval base, cap. and seaport of the prov. of C., standing on C. Bay, an inlet of the Atlantic, 64 m. S. of Seville. Probably founded by the Phoenicians about 1100 B.C., it was a centre for the tin trade with Cornwall. It was recaptured from the Moors by the king of Castile in 1262, and rose to great importance after

the discovery of America in 1492. The English burned it in 1596. Pop. (1965) 129,728.

CADMIUM. Symbol Cd., at. wt. 112·41, at. no. 48. C. is a soft silver-white metal. It is used in standard cells for the accurate determination of electromotive force (e.m.f.) in electroplating; as a constituent of one of the lowest-melting alloys; and in bearing alloys with low coefficients of friction. It is also used as control rods in nuclear reactors on account of its high absorption of neutrons. Its industrial importance has greatly increased in recent years.

CADWA'LADER (d. c. 634). Welsh hero. The son of Cadwallon, King of Gwynned, N. Wales, he defeated and slew Eadwine of Northumbria in 633. About a year later he was killed in battle.

CAECILIA (sēsi′lia). Typical genus of amphibians of the order Gymnophiona. Small worm-like animals, destitute of limbs, they have a wide distribution in tropical countries.

CAEDMON (kad′mon) (7th cent. A.D.). First English Christian poet. Bede says that he was a cowherd in the monastery of Whitby, when in a dream a stranger ordered him to sing, whereupon on waking he produced a poem on the Creation. Of this Bede appends a Latin translation, but the original Old English poem is preserved in some MSS. C. then became an inmate of the monastery and composed poems on sacred subjects.

CAEN (kaṅ). French town in Normandy, cap. of Calvados dept., on the Orne, 9 m. from the English Channel. St. Étienne church was founded by William the Conqueror, whose body was brought here after his death at Rouen. In the S.W.W. C. was severely damaged during the 5 weeks of heavy fighting that preceded its capture by the British 2nd Army on 9 July 1944. The univ., founded in 1432 by Henry VI of England, was among the casualties, but was rebuilt by 1957. C. is a business centre with ironworks and important industries. Its building stone is celebrated, and several English cathedrals are built of it. Pop. (1968) 110,262.

CAERLEON (kahrlē′on). Town (U.D.) in Monmouthshire, England, on the Usk, 3 m. N.E. of Newport. It was the site of a Roman legionary camp and there are remains of an amphitheatre. Pop. (1961) 4,184.

CAERNA'RVON (kahr-). Co. town (royal bor. since 1963) of Caernarvonshire, Wales, on the S.W. shore of the Menai Strait, 8 m. S.W. of Bangor. It was a Roman station and a market town and a port. The first Prince of Wales (later Edward II) was b. at C. Castle in 1284: the investiture of the Duke of Windsor as Prince was carried out in 1911, and that of Prince Charles planned for 1969. The Earl of Snowdon became Constable of the castle 1963. Pop. (1961) 8,998.

CAERNARVONSHIRE. Co. in N.W. Wales,

CAEN. The church of St. Étienne, or l'Abbaye-aux-Hommes where William the Conqueror is buried, is a fine example of Romanesque architecture, and dates from 1070.
Photo: Courtesy of the French National Tourist Office.

separated by the Menai Straits from the island of Anglesey, to which it is connected by the Menai bridge. The S.W. is extended in the Lleyn peninsula, 30 m. long, terminating in Bardsey Island. The N. of the co. is occupied by the Snowdon group of mountains. The tidal river Conway forms part of the E. boundary. In the Lleyn peninsula, barley and wheat are cultivated and cattle reared. In the N. are the great slate quarries of Penrhyn. The co. town is Caernarvon; other towns include Pwllheli, Nevin, Beddgelert, and the resorts of Bangor, Llandudno, Criccieth, Penmaenmawr, Betws-y-Coed, Capel Curig, and Llanfairfechan. Area 569 sq. m.; pop. (1961) 121,194.

CAERPHILLY (kahrfil'li). Market town (U.D.) in a colliery area, 7 m. N. of Cardiff, Glamorganshire, Wales noted for its mild C. cheese. The castle was built by Edward I. Pop. (1961) 36,008.

CAESALPINUS or CESALPINO (chesalpē'no), Andreas (1519–1603). Italian botanist and physician. Director of the botanical garden at Pisa, he prepared the way for the Linnean system of plant classification.

CAESAR. Name of one of the most powerful families of ancient Rome. The greatest of the line was Gaius Julius Caesar (q.v.), whose grand-nephew and adopted son Augustus assumed the name of C., and in turn passed it on to his adopted son Tiberius. Henceforth it was borne by the successive emperors, becoming a title of the Roman rulers. The titles Tsar in Russia and Kaiser in Germany are both derived from C.

CAESAR, Gaius Julius (c. 102–44 B.C.). Roman statesman, general, and founder of the Empire. Descended from a distinguished patrician family, his sympathies were from the first with the popular or democratic party. He m. Cornelia, daughter of Cinna, and refused to divorce her at Sulla's bidding – whereupon he had to flee to Bithynia.

In 65 B.C. he was elected Aedile and nearly ruined himself with his lavish amusements for the Roman population. In 63 he was elected chief pontiff, although he was a freethinker. Two years later he was appointed governor of Further Spain. Returning to Rome in 60, he formed with Pompey and Crassus the first triumvirate, and was given the two provinces of Cisalpine and Transalpine Gaul. For the next 13 years he was almost continuously engaged in campaigning in Gaul. He defeated the Germans under Ariovistus, and sold thousands of the Belgic tribes into slavery. In 55 C. crossed into Britain, and repeated his visit in the next year. Two years later the Gauls under Vercingetorix rose in revolt and in 51 C. crushed them completely. The series of

campaigns thus completed was described by C. himself in his Commentaries.

C.'s governorship expired in 49, and of his two partners Crassus was dead and Pompey was now a rival. He had many enemies in Rome, and Pompey was authorized to lead an army against him. Declaring 'the die is cast', C. crossed the Rubicon from Gaul into Italy, and the Civil War began. In 48 C. followed Pompey to Epirus, defeated him at Pharsalus, and chased him to Egypt, where he was murdered. For the next 9 months C. dallied with Cleopatra, by whom he had a son; then marching into Asia Minor, he defeated King Pharnaces in a lightning campaign which he described in the words Veni, vidi, vici (I came, I saw, I conquered). Returning to Italy, he moved from triumph to triumph over the Pompeian party, and in 46 he was firmly established in the seat of power at Rome. He planned to reform the calendar, take a census of the Empire, establish Roman colonies overseas, and improve the law of local govt., but the vigour with which he prosecuted his plans aroused a fear that he was aiming at a personal dictatorship. A band of disgruntled republicans with Brutus and Cassius as their leaders formed a conspiracy to kill him, and on 15 March 44 B.C. – the Ides of March – he was stabbed to death in the Senate House.

CAESAR, Irving (1895–). American lyricist, b. in New York of Rumanian parents. He has written songs, and the musical comedy, No, No, Nanette.

CAESAREA. See QISARAYA.

CAESAREAN SECTION. The removal of a child from the womb through an incision in the abdominal wall. Julius Caesar is said to have entered the world in this way: hence the name.

CAESIUM (sē'sium). Chemical element. Symbol Cs, at. wt. 132·91, at. no. 55. It is used in the manufacture of photo-electric cells. Highly radioactive C. (Cs-137, half-life 30 years), a waste product from nuclear power-stations, is used for mass radiation and sterilization of foodstuffs, and medically for irradiation of surface tumours. See CLOCKS.

CAETANO (kahetah'nō), Marcello (1906–). Portuguese statesman. Prof. of admin. law at Lisbon from 1940, he was asst. P.M. 1955–8, and succeeded Salazar as P.M. in 1968. His inaugural speech suggested a liberalisation of policy.

CAFETE'RIA (Span., a coffee-shop). A help-yourself restaurant; supposed to have originated in New York in the 1880's. The first English use of the word was about 1923.

CAFFEINE (kaf'fē-in) ($C_8H_{10}N_4O_2$). The most important member of a group of nitrogenous substances found in tea, coffee, etc., for whose stimulant effect it is partly responsible.

CAGLIARI (kahlyah'rē). City and archiepiscopal see of Sardinia, Italy, cap. of Sardinia and of C. prov., on the Gulf of C. The cathedral, completed 1312, was later modernized; the univ. was founded in 1626, Pop. (1961) 181,499.

CAGLIOSTRO (kahlyos'trō), Alessandro di, count (1743–95). Italian charlatan, whose real name was Giuseppe Balsamo. B. at Palermo, he travelled widely, married, and set up as a specialist in the occult. In Paris in 1785 he became involved in the affair of the Diamond Necklace (supposed to have been ordered by Queen Marie Antoinette, but in fact by a band of swindlers), and was imprisoned in the Bastille. Later he was arrested by the Inquisition in Rome. A sentence of death for freemasonry was commuted to one of life imprisonment. He d. in the fortress of San Leone. His Mémoires are not authentic.

CAGOULARDS (Fr., hooded men). Popular name for the Comité Secret d'Action Révolutionnaire, a French fascist organization formed in 1937. It was supplied with arms from Italy and Germany, and was responsible for the murder of Italian anti-Fascists and other outrages.

CAERNARVON. Begun in 1284 for Edward I, Caernarvon Castle is one of the glories of North Wales. The walls are still entire and are seven to nine feet thick, enclosing an area of some three acres.   Photo: Roy J. Westlake.

CAHORS (kah-ohr'). French city, cap. of Lot dept., on the r. Lot 60 m. N. of Toulouse. It is a market centre, and has an 11th cent. cathedral. Gambetta was b. here. Pop. (1962) 19,280.

CAILLAUX (kahyō'), **Joseph** (1863–1944). French statesman. Several times Min. of Finance and Min. for Foreign Affairs, he was P.M. 1911–12. In 1913, when he was Finance Min., his wife shot and killed G. Calmette, editor of *Le Figaro*, who had threatened to publish letters written by C. to her while she was still another man's wife. C. resigned and defended her on her trial, and she was acquitted. Suspected of defeatism during the F.W.W., he was arrested in 1918, tried and condemned to 3 years' imprisonment in 1920, but released the next day and fully amnestied in 1924. Subsequently he was again twice Min. of Finance.

CAIN. O.T. character, the first-born son of Adam and Eve. He murdered his brother Abel from motives of jealousy, as Abel's sacrifice was more acceptable to the Lord than his own, and so became the world's first murderer.

CAIN, James Mallahan (1892–). American novelist. B. at Annapolis, he entered journalism and is the author of *The Postman Always Rings Twice* (1934), *Double Indemnity*, and *Mildred Pierce* (1941).

CAINE, Sir Hall (1853–1931). British novelist. Though b. in Cheshire, he was of Manx parentage and the island figures largely in his rather melodramatic works which incl. *The Deemster* (1887), *The Bondman* (1890, also dramatized), *The Manxman* (1894), and *The Woman Thou Gavest Me* (1913). He lived with D. G. Rossetti in London for a time and pub. in 1882 *Recollections of Rossetti*. He was knighted in 1918.

ÇA IRA (sah ērah'). Song of the French Revolution, written by a street singer, Ladré, and set to an existing tune by Bécourt, a drummer of the opera.

CAIRN. British breed of terrier dog, the original terrier of the Scottish Highlands. It is shaggy, compact, and short-legged, weighing not more than 14 lb., and used in Scotland for going to ground to fox, badger, otter, etc.. among rocks and cairns.

CAIRNGORMS. Mountain group in Scotland, N. part of the Grampians, including Ben Macdhui (4,296 ft.), Braeriach (4,248 ft.), Cairntoul (4,240 ft.), and Cairngorm (4,084 ft.), which are the highest peaks in the Br. Isles with the exception of Ben Nevis.

CAIRNS. Seaport of Queensland, Australia, with a fine harbour, concerned largely with the export of sugar. Pop. (1961) 25,358.

CAIRO (kī'rō). Cap. of the United Arab Rep. and of Egypt, largest city in Africa, on the right bank of

CAIRO. Within the walls of the citadel built by Saladin in the 12th cent. are several mosques, the loveliest being that built of alabaster by Mohammed Ali. Its 2 slender minarets stand out, even among the 400 which pierce the sky over the city.
Courtesy of the Egyptian State Tourist Administration.

the Nile, 8 m. above the apex of the Delta, and 100 m. from the Mediterranean; the most important trading and distributing centre of the Near East and N. Africa.

El Fustat (Old Cairo) was founded by the Arabs *c.* A.D. 641, Cairo itself *c.* 1000 by the Fatimite ruler Gowhar. C. is 20 m. N. of the site of ancient Memphis, while outside C. at Gizeh are the Pyramids and the Sphinx. C. has many ancient buildings, incl. the citadel, the univ. (originally a mosque) of El Azhar, dating from *c.* 1000, and the mosques of El-Hakîm and Amru; modern buildings incl. the govt. offices, museums, hospitals, opera house. Parts of C. are still medieval; the modern quarters reflect the city's functions as a commercial, government, and tourist centre. At Helwan, 15 m. to the S., iron and steel works are planned (1968) to utilise power from the Aswan High Dam. Its people are predominantly of mixed Arab and pre-Arab blood. The majority are Moslems, but there is a considerable Coptic Christian community. Pop. (1960) 3,346,000.

CAISSON DISEASE. See BENDS.

CAITHNESS (kāth'nes). Co. in the extreme N.E. of Scotland. The low-lying N.E. part produces oats and vegetables. Towards the S.W. the land rises, and in the higher parts sheep are reared. The co. town is Wick; the only other town of importance is Thurso. Area 686 sq. m.; pop. (1961) 27,345.

CAIUS (kēs), **John** (1510–73). English doctor, physician to Edward VI, Mary, and Elizabeth. He extended in 1557 the building of Gonville (and Caius) College, Cambridge, founded by Edmund Gonville in 1348.

CALA′BRIA. Administrative region occupying the 'toe' of Italy; area 5,810 sq. m.; pop. (1961) 2,045,215. It contains the provs. of Catanzaro, Cosenza, and Reggio di C. In Roman times the name C. was given to the 'heel' of Italy.

CALAIS (kahlā'). Seaport and town in Pas-de-Calais dept., N. France, 148 m. N. by W. of Paris, and 25 m. E.S.E. of Dover across the English Channel. The old town is surrounded by the harbour and canals. It was taken by Edward III in 1347, and was held by the English until 1558. C. was in German hands from May 1940 till 1 Oct. 1944, when it surrendered to the Canadians. Pop. (1968) 74,624.

CALAS (kahlahs'), **Jean** (1698–1762). A French Protestant, who in 1761 was accused of murdering his son to prevent his joining the R.C. Church. In spite of his complete denials, he was found guilty and executed. His widow escaped to Switzerland, and enlisted the aid of Voltaire, who succeeded in getting the trial reviewed and Calas' innocence was proved. A grant was paid to the family by Louis XV.

CALCEOLARIA (kalsēolā′ria), also 'slipper flower' (Lat. *calceolus* 'slipper'). Genus of plants of the family Scrophulariaceae, native to S. America and including shrubby and herbaceous species. The brilliantly coloured flowers, much enlarged in highly cultivated greenhouse specimens, resemble pouches or 2-lipped slippers. Cs. were introduced to Europe *c.* 1830.

CALCITE (-s-). A form of calcium carbonate ($CaCO_3$) and the constituent of chalk, limestone, and marble. There are two distinct crystalline forms, viz. 'nailhead spar', where the crystals are flat and tabular in shape, and 'dog-toothed spar', with sharply pointed pyramidal crystals. Iceland spar, a variety of the first type, possesses the property of double refraction and is used in optical instruments. C. is one of the most abundant mineral constituents of the earth's crust.

CALCIUM. Chemical element, a silvery-white metal, one of the alkaline earth metals. Symbol, Ca; atomic weight 40·07; atomic number 20. It was discovered by Sir Humphry Davy in 1808 and is very widely distributed, mainly in the form of its carbonate $CaCO_3$ which occurs in a fairly pure condition as chalk and limestone. C. is an essential component of bones, teeth, shells and leaves. C. compounds are very important to the chemical industry and include lime (calcium hydroxide $Ca(OH)_2$); plaster of Paris (calcium sulphate $CaSO_4 2H_2O$); calcium hypochlorite $CaOCl_2$ a bleaching agent; calcium nitrate $(Ca(NO_3)_2 4H_2O)$ a nitrogenous fertilizer; calcium carbide CaC_2 which reacts with water to give acetylene (q.v.); calcium cyanamide ($CaCN_2$), the basis of pharmaceuticals, fertilizers and plastics incl. Melamine; calcium cyanide ($Ca(CN)_2$) used in the extraction of gold and silver and in electro-plating, and others used in baking powders, fillers for paints, etc.

CALCULATING MACHINES. *See* COMPUTER.

CALCULUS. Name given to the methods of calculation which are used to deal with such matters as changing speeds, problems of flight, varying stresses set up in the framework of a bridge, electrical circuits, and in general the study of quantities which are continuously varying.

The INTEGRAL C. deals with the method of summation or adding together of the effects of continuously varying quantities. The DIFFERENTIAL C.

CAITHNESS. The atomic power station on the lonely coastline at Dounreay. This fast fission breeder reactor was completed in 1959. *Photo: United Kingdom Atomic Energy Authority*

deals in a similar way with rates of change. Many of its applications arose from the study of speed. Each of these branches of the C. deals with small quantities which during the process are made smaller and smaller, hence both comprise the INFINITESIMAL C. Differential equations represent complex rates of change and integrals are the empirical solutions. If no known processes are available, the integrations are made graphically or by machine.

The C. originated with Archimedes in the 3rd cent. B.C. in the means he devised for finding the areas of curved figures and for drawing tangents to curves; but his ideas could not germinate until the 17th cent., when Descartes showed how geometrical curves could be described and analysed by means of algebraic formulae. Then Fermat and later Newton and Leibniz immensely advanced the study.

CALCUTTA. Great city of India, standing on the Hooghli, the most westerly mouth of the Ganges, some 80 m. N. of the Bay of Bengal. Across the river is Howrah (q.v.). C., which was the seat of govt. of British India from 1773 to 1912, is the cap. of the state of W. Bengal. Area 32 sq. m.; pop. (1961) 2,926,498.

C. is a city of palaces and slums. The quarter E. of the Maidan or Great Park was constructed during the British Raj and is western in style; it contains some splendid mansions. In the centre of the Maidan stands Fort William, begun by Clive in 1757 and completed in 1773. N. of it is Government House; oldest of several univs., C. Univ. has c. 100,000 students; Bose Research Institute; a famous Jain

temple, etc. Buildings in oriental style incl. some magnificent palaces of Indian princes. From its position as the natural outlet of the Ganges and Brahmaputra valley, C. has an enormous overseas trade, and is a great commercial and industrial centre.

C. was founded 1686–90 by Job Charnock, head of Hooghli factory of the East India Company, when Hooghli was attacked by Mogul troops. The original Fort William was completed in 1702. Suraj-ud-Dowlah captured C. in 1756, and a number of its citizens d. in the Black Hole of C. In 1757 it was recaptured by Clive, and the modern C. began with the erection of a new Fort William and the formation of the Maidan.

CALDECOTT, Randolph (1846–86). British book illustrator, best known for illustrations to Washington Irving and his work for children: *John Gilpin* and *The House that Jack Built.*

CALDER, Alexander (1898–   ). American artist. B. in Philadelphia, Pennsylvania, he studied as an engineer, but in 1923 turned to art and originated 'stabiles' in 1931, and in 1932 'mobiles', with which latter his name is usually associated. One of his most famous large-scale mobiles is 'Point 125' (1957) in the lobby of Idlewild Airport, N.Y.

CALDER, Alexander Stirling (1870–1945). American sculptor, b. at Philadelphia. His works incl. a statue of Washington in New York, and a head of Winston Churchill (1944).

CALDER, Ritchie, baron **Ritchie-** (1906–   ). British pioneer science reporter and author. He undertook a series of U.N. missions to help solve problems of underdeveloped countries by science and technology, and was prof. of international relations at Edinburgh 1961–7. His books incl. *The Life Savers* (1961) on modern drugs. He was created a life peer 1966.

CALDERON (kahldārōn'), **Ventura Garcia** (1886–   ). Peruvian novelist and short-story writer. His many stories dealing with the lives of the Peruvian natives are noteworthy for their colourful realism.

CALDERON DE LA BARCA, Pedro (1600–81). Spanish dramatist and poet. B. in Madrid, he studied law at Salamanca (1613–19). In 1620 and 1622 he was successful in the poetical contests at Madrid; and while still writing dramas served in the army in Milan and the Netherlands (1625–35). By 1636 his first vol. of plays was pub. and he had been made master of the revels at the court of Philip IV, receiving a knighthood in 1637. In 1640 he assisted in the suppression of the Catalan rebellion. After the death of his mistress he became a Franciscan in 1650, was ordained in 1651, and appointed to a prebend of Toledo in 1653. He

CALCUTTA. A view of the law courts.
Courtesy of the High Commissioner for India, London.

resumed playwriting when made honorary chaplain to the king in 1663. Many of these later dramas were *autos sacramentales*, outdoor plays for the festival of the Holy Eucharist. Most famous of his regular plays, of which some 118 survive, are the tragedies *El pintor de su deshonra*, *El Alcalde de Zalamea*, *El Médico de su honra* and *El Mayor monstruo los celos*; the historical *El Principe constante*; the dashing intrigue *La Dama duende*; the philosophical *La Vida es sueño*; and the religious *El Purgatorio de San Patricio*. He died in poverty.

CALDWELL, Erskine Preston (1903–   ). American novelist. B. in Georgia, he worked among the poor whites of the South as a journalist, cotton picker and stage assistant and achieved sensational success with *Tobacco Road* (1932), later dramatized and filmed, telling of a squalid share-cropping family in the back lands of the cotton country, which was banned in many places. Later books incl. *God's Little Acre* (1933) and *Trouble in July* (1940) analysing racial antagonism, and *The Weather Shelter* (1969).

CALDY ISLAND. Is. off the Pembrokeshire coast, Wales. The small Cistercian monastery is famous for its manufacture of perfume.

CALEDONIAN CANAL. A waterway across the N.W. of Scotland, linking the Atlantic and the North Sea. Of its length of 61 m. only a stretch of 23 m. is artificial, the rest being composed of lochs Lochy, Oich, and Ness. The C., now used chiefly by small pleasure steamers, etc., was built by Thomas Telford, 1803–23.

CALENDAR. A system devised for the distribution of time into periods convenient for the purposes of civil life. The word comes from the Lat. *kalendae* or *calendae*, the first day of each month on which solemn proclamation was made of the appearance of the new moon. All early Cs. except the ancient Egyptian were lunar. The C. in use over a great part of the world today rests on the Roman C. as revised by Julius Caesar and Augustus, but many modifications have been made in the course of time.

Quite early in their history the Romans had a civil year of 355 days; but the seasons depended on the solar year which was about 11 days longer than the lunar, and to bring the 2 years into harmony, additional days were intercalated. In 46 B.C. Caesar introduced the year of 365 days, and an extra day in every 4th year. He took the length of the solar year as 365 days, 6 hours. Actually, however, it is only 365 days, 5 hrs. 48 mins. 46 secs. and through the centuries the discrepancy mounted up until in the 16th cent. it amounted to 10 days. In 1582 Pope Gregory XIII proclaimed his Gregorian or New Style C., with the aim of putting the Julian error right and also to secure uniformity as to the date at which each year should be reckoned as beginning. At first only states in the Roman obedience accepted the new C., but in the 18th cent. Protestant states began to fall into line. Britain adopted it in 1751, by which date the accumulated error amounted to 11 days, so it was enacted that the day following 2 Sept 1752 should be renumbered 14 Sept. France, which had adopted the Gregorian C. in 1582, abandoned it from 1793 to 1805 in favour of the Revolutionary Calendar. Turkey and Russia did not adopt it until 1917, and the Eastern Orthodox Church in Russia and the Balkans not until 1923.

About 1930 the League of Nations decided that it would be advantageous to change to what is now called the World C., i.e. equal quarters perpetual, with an extra-calendrical day at the end of the year and a similar day in the summer every Leap Year. The proposal is still before the U.N. The 8-day week involved brought objections from orthodox Jewry.

CA'LGARY. Second city of Alberta, Canada, on the Bow, at the foot of the Rockies. It has grain elevators, flour mills, etc., and is a tourist centre. Fort Calgary was set up by the N.W. Mounted Police

CALIFORNIA. One of the loveliest and most important of the old Spanish Franciscan Missions is San Fernando, founded in 1797. The Convento or Long Building (1810–22), is famous for its façade of 19 arches and the adobe walls are 4 ft. thick.
Courtesy of the Mission San Fernando.

in 1875. The C.P.R. reached it in 1833, and C. rapidly developed. The Univ of C. became independent of Alberta Univ. 1966. Pop. (1969) 369,025.

CALHOUN (kalhōōn'), **John Caldwell** (1782–1850). American statesman. B. in S. Carolina, of Scots-Irish descent, he was elected Vice-President in 1824, and again in 1828. Throughout he was a defender of the 'States' Rights' as against the Federal Government and the institution of Negro slavery.

CALI (kahlē'). Industrial city of Colombia, S. America; capital of Valle Dept. It was founded in 1536. Sugar is manufactured. Pop. (1964) 637,929.

CALIBRA'TION. Comparison of scale marks with a standard, as in testing the accuracy of measuring instruments.

CA'LICO. A plain woven cotton material; the name derives from Calicut on the Malabar coast, an original source of Indian Cs.

CALIFORNIA. A Pacific state of the U.S.A., lying between Oregon and the Mexican province of Lower California. Its popular name is the 'Golden State' because of its gold mines, and as a result of a post-S.W.W. boom surpassed N.Y. as most populous state of the union 1964.

C. contains 2 great mountain ranges. The Sierra Nevada running along the eastern boundary with an average breadth of about 80 m., includes the Yosemite and other famous canyons, and its chief peak is Mt. Whitney (14,495), the highest mt. in the U.S.A. excluding Alaska. Along the coast is a series of disconnected ranges called the Coast Range, longer but lower than the Sierra Nevada. Between the 2 ranges lies the great valley of C., watered by the Sacramento, the San Joaquin, and tributaries which together drain most of the state.

Extending over nearly 800 m. from N. to S., C. has a varied climate, on the whole one of the best in the world. Vast quantities of fruit are produced and other temperate and sub-tropical produce. Petroleum refining, food canning, and meat packing are the main industries. At Hollywood is the film metropolis. Sacramento is the capital; but Oakland, San Diego, Longbeach, and the ports Los Angeles and San Francisco, are larger.

C. was first settled by the Spaniards in 1769. It formed part of Mexico from 1822 to 1848 when it was ceded to U.S.A. It became a state of the union 2 years later. The discovery of gold in 1848 led to the gold rush of the following year (the 'forty-niners') and mining has continued on a large scale, though petroleum has outstripped gold in importance. Area 158,693 sq. m.; pop. (1970) 19,953,134.

CALIFORNIA, Lower. *See* LOWER CALIFORNIA.

CALIFORNIUM. *See* TRANSURANIUM ELEMENTS.

CALI'GULA, Gaius Caesar (A.D. 12–41). Roman

emperor. The son of Germanicus, he ascended the throne in 37 on the death of Tiberius. He revealed a tyrannical character, and is reputed to have become mad. He was assassinated by an officer of his guard.

CALIPH (kā'lif; Arab. *khalifah*, successor). Title adopted by Mohammed's successors as civic and religious heads of the world of Islam. The first C. was Abu Bekr (d. 634). The caliphate was nominally elective, but became heredi-

JAMES CALLAGHAN
Photo: Daily Herald.

tary in practice, being held by the Umayyad dynasty 661–750, and then by the Abbasids. During the 10th cent. the political and military power passed to the leader of the C.'s Turkish bodyguard; about the same time an independent Fatimite caliphate sprang up in Egypt. After the death of the last Abbasid C. (1258) the title was claimed by a number of Mohammedan chieftains in Egypt, Turkey, and India. The most powerful of these were the Turkish sultans of the Ottoman Empire. In 1924 the last Turkish C. was deposed by Kemal Atatürk.

CALLAGHAN (kal'ahan), **(Leonard) James** (1912–). British Labour politician. The son of a chief petty officer in the R.N., in which he himself served during the S.W.W., he entered the Civil Service as a tax officer in 1929. In 1950–1 he was parliamentary and financial sec. to the Admiralty, and as Chancellor of the Exchequer 1964–7, he introduced a corporation and capital gains tax and in 1966, to promote the effective use of manpower, a selective employment tax. Resigning following devaluation in 1967, he became Home Secretary (1967–70).

CALLANDER. Scottish market town (burgh) and tourist centre in Perthshire. Pop. (1961) 1,654.

CALLAO (kahlyah'ō). Chief port of Peru, and cap. of the dept. (14 sq. m.) of the same name, 8 m. S.W. of Lima. C. was founded in 1537, and was rebuilt following its destruction by an earthquake and tidal wave in 1746. Pop. (1965) 266,700.

CALLAS, Maria. Stage-name of the lyric soprano Maria Calogeropoulos (1923–), b. in N.Y. of Greek stock. She studied at the National Conservatory, Athens, and made her début at 15, but fame eluded her until, under the management of G. B. Meneghini (whom she had m. in 1949), she was engaged by La Scala in 1951. With a voice of fine range and a gift for dramatic expression, she excels in opera, her roles incl. *Norma, Madame Butterfly, Aïda, Lucia* and *Medea.*

CALLES (kahl'yes), **Plutarco Elias** (1877–1945). Mexican general and statesman. He took part in the revolutionary movement of 1910, and was President of Mexico 1924–8. He fostered the infant labour-movement, and in an effort to reduce the economic power of the largely foreign-owned oil companies encountered strong opposition from the U.S.A. and Britain. In 1926 the Mexican Congress at his instigation approved acts to nationalize the property of the

MARIA CALLAS, in *La Traviata.*
Photo: Houston Rogers.

R.C. Church and restrict its activities, but subsequently a concordat was negotiated. He was exiled in 1936 and lived in the U.S. till 1941.

CALLIGRAPHY (kali'grafi). The art of beautiful writing, incl. both formal writing with an edged pen and informal writing. Modern letter forms have gradually evolved from originals which were shaped by the tools used to make them – the flat brush and chisel on stone, the stylus on wax and clay, and the reed and quill on papyrus and skin.

The principal formal hands used in early books were written in capital letters or majuscules. In the 4th and 5th cents. A.D. books were written in square capitals derived from classical Roman inscriptions of which the Trajan column is the outstanding example. The rustic capitals of the same period were written more freely, and the uncial capitals, more rounded, were used from the 4th to the 8th cents. During this period the cursive hand was also developing and the interplay of this with the formal hands, coupled with the need for speedier writing, led to the minuscule forms. During the 7th cent. the half-uncial was developed with ascending and descending strokes and was adopted by all countries under Roman rule. The cursive forms developed differently in different countries and in particular in Italy the beautiful italic script was evolved which became the model for italic type faces. The recent calligraphic revival in Britain was largely due to Edward Johnston (q.v.).

CALLI'MACHUS (c. 310–240 B.C.). Greek poet and critic. B. in Cyrene, he taught in Alexandria where he was head of the great library. He is best known for his epigrams.

CALLIOPE (kali'ōpē). In Greek mythology, the muse of epic poetry.

CALLOT (kahloh'), **Jacques** (1592–1635). French engraver and painter. He engraved about 1,600 pieces, of which the best known are his 'Miseries of War', his 'Sieges', 'Fairs', 'Temptation of St. Anthony', and 'Conversion of St. Paul'.

CALOMEL. Mercurous chloride, Hg_2Cl_2, a white, heavy powder, valuable as a purgative in infections of the bowel.

CALORIE (Lat. *calor,* heat). The unit of quantitative measurement of heat. The original small C. was the amount of heat necessary to raise 1 gramme of water through 1°C. But the word is nowadays nearly always used to signify the large C, or kilocalorie, the amount of heat required to raise 1 litre of water through 1°C. – chiefly by dietitians as a measure of the heat-giving properties of foodstuffs. 1 oz. of protein yields 120, carbohydrate 110, fat 270, and alcohol 200 large calories.

CALPE (kal'pē). Name of GIBRALTAR in antiquity.

CALTANISSE'TTA. Italian town in Sicily, cap. of C. prov., an episcopal see, 60 m. S.E. of Palermo. Sulphur is obtained, and there is a school of mining. Pop. (1961) 62,115.

CA'LVARY (Lat. *calvaria,* a skull). The place of Christ's execution at Jerusalem; also called Golgotha in Aramaic. Two chief sites are suggested. One is that where the Church of the Sepulchre now stands; the other, first suggested by General Gordon, is the skull-like hill beyond the Damascus gate. *See illus.* p. 198.

The name C. is further applied to a monument commemorating the Crucifixion.

CALVÉ (kahlveh'), **Emma** (1858–1942). French soprano, prima-donna, particularly famous for her interpretation of Carmen.

CALVIN, John (1509–64). Swiss reformer and theologian. B. at Noyon, Picardy, he studied theology and then law, and about 1533 adopted reformed opinions and soon came to the front as an evangelical preacher. In 1534 he was obliged to leave Paris and retired to Basle, where he studied Hebrew and wrote his *Institutes of the Christian Religion,* pub. in 1536. In the same year he accepted an invitation to go

CALVARY. The Church of the Holy Sepulchre, said to have been erected on the site of the Crucifixion. There are some topographical difficulties, but the tradition is continuous since the time of Constantine and may well be true.

to Geneva, and assist in the work of reformation. But in 1538 he was expelled because of public resentment at the many and too-drastic changes he introduced. At Strasbourg he m. a widow, and devoted himself to translating the N.T. In 1541 the Genevans invited him back. He accepted and established in the face of strong opposition a theocracy. The black mark on his rule is the burning of Servetus for heresy in 1553. He supported the Huguenots in their struggle in France, and afforded a refuge to English Protestants driven overseas by the Marian persecutions. His theological system is known as Calvinism (q.v.), and his Church government as Presbyterianism (q.v.).

CALVIN, Melvin (1911–). American chemist, prof. of chemistry (from 1947) and also director of the bio-organic chemistry group at the Lawrence Radiation Laboratory (from 1946), Univ. of California. An authority on photosynthesis, he received a Nobel prize in 1961 for research into the carbon dioxide assimilation of plants – a factor in plant growth.

CALVINISM. That interpretation of Christian doctrine that was formulated by John Calvin (q.v.) and became predominant in Scotland, parts of Switzerland and Holland, and has greatly influenced Protestant theology to the present time. Its central doctrine is that of predestination, by which is meant that certain souls (the elect) are predestined by God to salvation (although this does not obviate the need for faith and perseverance), whilst others are doomed to eternal damnation. C. stresses the total depravity of human nature, but insists that salvation is offered through the sacrifice of Christ, made only on behalf of the elect. Faith and repentance are also necessary, but the theory of irresistible grace implies that the operation of Divine grace which makes these possible is predetermined. C. is marked by logic and

lucidity, but even those churches originally C. in doctrine rarely accept it in its strict sense nowadays. Nevertheless during the present century there has been a marked revival of Neo-Calvinist thought, largely through the influence of Karl Barth (q.v.).

CALVINISTIC METHODIST CHURCH (Welsh Presbyterian Church). The only church of entirely Welsh origin, it arose from the work of Rev. Griffith Jones (1684–1761), and was first organized in 1743. From 1795 its members began to separate from the Church of England owing to persecution, and from 1811 it ordained its own ministers. Its members in 1960 numbered c. 150,000.

CAM. English river on which Cambridge stands; it rises near Ashwell, Herts, and flows through Cambridgeshire to join the Ouse 3½ m. S. of Ely. It is sometimes called the Granta.

CAMAGÜEY. City of Cuba, cap. of the prov. of C., in the centre of the island. It was founded c. 1514, and has a 17th cent. cathedral. Pop. (1960) 191,379.

CAMARGO (kahmahrgō′), **Marie-Anne de Cupis de** (1710–70). French dancer. B. in Brussels, she became a ballet star in Paris in 1726. She was the first ballerina to adopt a shortened skirt, and the first to attain the *entrechat à quatre.* She retired in 1751. The Camargo Society, founded in 1930, was named after her.

CAMBACÉRÈS (koṅbahsārās′), **Jean Jacques Regis de,** duke of Parma (1753–1824). French statesman. He came into prominence during the French Revolution and rose to an influential position under Napoleon. In 1815 C. went into exile, but regained his civil rights in 1818.

CAMBODIA. Republic of S.E. Asia, lying between Thailand on the W. and Vietnam on the E. and S., with a coast on the Gulf of Siam. It forms no geographical unit, but consists of (a) the low-lying middle valley of the Mekong; (b) the vast area, formerly a sea gulf, whose centre is the Great Lake or Tonle Sap; (c) the highlands adjoining the upper course of the Mekong; and (d) the mountains bordering the Gulf of Siam. The greater part of the surface is wild and uncultivated, but the central plain is immensely fertile, since in June the swollen Mekong causes the Great Lake to overflow and to inundate some 1,000 sq. m. of territory. When in October the flood waters retreat, a thick layer of fertilizing slime is left behind, and on this rice, maize, soya beans, tobacco, etc. are grown, rice being the chief product. Above the earth, perched high on stilts, are the houses of the Cambodians. Matches, cigarettes, bricks, textiles, etc., are manufactured on a small scale. The forests are valuable. Much dried fish is exported.

CAMARGO. Gay and wildly extravagant, she was almost the ruin of such admirers as Louis de Bourbon, comte de Clermont. Nicholas Lancret captures in this portrait the grace and fire, which owed something to her Spanish descent.
Reproduced by permission of the Trustees of the Wallace Collection.

Pnom-Penh is the cap.; other towns are Battambang, Kompong Chhnang, and Kompong-Cham. Kompong Son (formerly Sihanoukville), on the Gulf of Thailand, is a modern deepwater port.

The Cambodians are fundamentally an Indonesian people, but there has been much infiltration from India. The most ancient monuments date from the 7th cent. A.D., when the Khmers, the ancestors of the present Cambodians, had built up a remarkable civilization. After the 12th cent. the Khmer realm began to fade, and C. continued to decline. The king of C., formerly a vassal of Siam, in 1863 accepted the protection of France, which lasted until the Japanese overran the country in 1941 during the S.W.W. The independence of C. was recognised by France in 1955. Prince Norodom Sihanouk (1922– : elected king 1941) then abdicated to become P.M. as leader of the Popular Socialist Community. In 1960 he was created Head of State, but was deposed 1970 and set up a govt. in exile in China. U.S. and S. Vietnamese troops subsequently made large-scale attacks on N. Vietnamese bases in C., and a rep. was proclaimed Nov. 1970. The people are Buddhists of the Hinayana confession. Area 70,000 sq. m., pop. (1966) 6,260,000.

CAMBORNE. Market town in Cornwall, 10 m. W.S.W. of Truro. Tin is mined, and there is a noted mining school. With Redruth (q.v.) it forms a U.D., pop. (1961) 36,090.

CAMBRAI (coṅbrā´). French town in Nord dept., 37 m. S. by E. of Lille, on the Escaut (Scheldt). It is a centre for the manufacture of muslin, lace, and other delicate textiles (cambric is named after the town). Pop. (1962) 35,373.

During the F.W.W. C. was severely damaged while in German hands. It gives its name to 2 battles: (1) Nov.-Dec. 1917, when the 3rd Army under Byng

CAMBODIA. Side by side, the grace of a big ship and the beauty of 'The Floating Royal House', an effect typical of the country where land and water are almost interchangeable.
Courtesy of the Cambodian Dept. of Tourism.

nearly succeeded in recapturing C. in an engagement in which large numbers of tanks were used for the first time; (2) 26 Aug.-5 Oct. 1918, when C. was captured during the final British offensive.

CAMBRIDGE, Adolphus Frederick, 1st duke of (1774–1850). 7th son of George III, viceroy of Hanover 1816–37. His son George, 2nd duke of C. (1819–1904), as C.-in-C. of the British army 1856–95, was opposed to Cardwell's reforms; and his dau., Princess Mary, who m. the duke of Teck, was the mother of Queen Mary, consort of George V.

CAMBRIDGE. English city (bor.), co. town of Cambridgeshire on the Cam, 56 m. N.N.E. of London. The site was occupied as early as 100 B.C. and a Roman settlement grew up on a slight rise in the low-lying plain, commanding a ford over the river. There are many fine buildings, most of them connected with the univ.; the small Saxon church of St. Peter, and the round church of the Holy Sepulchre –

CAMBRIDGE UNIVERSITY. The Backs and King's College.
Photo: British Travel and Holidays Association.

the oldest of the 4 round churches in England; the Fitzwilliam museum, the Guildhall, the Leys and Perse schools, the Dunn Nutritional laboratory, the Folk museum, and the Arts theatre. It is a market town for local agriculture. Scientific instruments and machine tools are made, also jam, fertilizers and paper. Pop. (1961) 95,358.

CAMBRIDGE. City of Mass., U.S.A., facing Boston on the Charles r. It is a cultural centre, and sprang up round Harvard College (later univ.); there are many other educational institutions. Printing and publishing are industries. Pop. (1960) 107,716.

CAMBRIDGESHIRE and Isle of Ely. Low-lying fen co. of E. England. The only important hills are the Gog Magog, S.E. of Cambridge. The chief rivers are the Ouse and Nene. C. is one of the principal grain-producing districts and also produces fruit and dairy foods; sheep are reared. There is little manufacturing. The co. town is Cambridge; other towns incl. Wisbech, March, Soham, and the cathedral city of Ely. Area 831 sq. m.; pop. (1967) 296,930. *See* ELY, ISLE OF.

CAMBRIDGE UNIVERSITY. One of the oldest of European univs., founded probably in the 12th cent., though the earliest of the existing colls. was not founded until c. 1280–4: *see* Table, in which the women's colls. are marked by an asterisk. The Chancellor is the titular, and the Vice-Chancellor the active, head. The Regent House is the legislative and executive body, with the Senate as the court of appeal. Each coll. has its own corporation, and is largely independent. The head of each coll. (in the case of men's colls. usually called the master), assisted by a council of fellows, manages its affairs.

CAMBRIDGE COLLEGES

Peterhouse	1280–4	Sidney Sussex ...	1596
Clare	1326	Downing	1800
Pembroke ...	1347	Girton*	1869
Gonville and Caius	1348	Newnham* ...	1871
Trinity Hall ...	1350	Selwyn	1882
Corpus Christi ...	1352	Hughes Hall* ...	1885
King's	1441	St. Edmund's House	1896
Queens'	1448	New Hall* ...	1954
St. Catherine's ...	1473	Churchill ...	1960
Jesus	1496	Darwin	1964
Christ's	1505	Lucy Cavendish	
St. John's	1511	Collegiate Soc.*	1966
Magdalene ...	1542	Clare Hall... ...	1966
Trinity	1546	Fitzwilliam ...	1966
Emmanuel ...	1584	University ...	1966

CAMBY'SES (reigned 529–522 B.C.). Emperor of Persia. Succeeding his father Cyrus, he assassinated his brother Smerdis and conquered Egypt in 525. Here he outraged many of the native religious customs, and was said to have become mad. On his way back he d. in Syria by suicide or accident.

CAMDEN, William (1551–1623). English antiquary. B. in London, he pub. his *Britannia* in 1586, and became headmaster of Westminster School in 1593. The C. SOCIETY was founded in 1838.

CAMDEN. Industrial city of New Jersey, U.S.A., on the Delaware, connected with Philadelphia by a suspension bridge 8,536 ft. long (main span 1,750 ft.) opened in 1926. Pop. (1960) 117,159.

CAMEL. A large cud-chewing mammal (*Camelus*) of the order Artiodactyla with a humped back, and differing from typical ruminants by having a three-chambered stomach, tusk-like canines above and below and a similar isolated outer upper incisor, and by the two toes having broad soft soles for walking on the sand, and hoofs resembling nails. With the Llamas they constitute the sub-order Tylopoda.

There are 2 species, the Arabian one-humped C. or Dromedary (*C. dromedarius*) and the shorter-legged Central Asiatic or Bactrian two-humped C. (*C. bactrianus*). Both have long been domesticated. The dromedary is adapted to life in the sandy plains of Arabia and N. Africa, and is very hardy and capable of standing great privations. It feeds on desert vegetation and carries a reserve of fatty tissue in the hump, which it can draw on when needed.

BACTRIAN CAMEL

Cs. vary in colour from dark brown to light cream. From remote times they have been of great value to the tribes which domesticated them, and the wealth of chieftains was assessed by the herds of Cs. they owned. The walking pace of a C. is 3 m. an hour, and it can keep this up for 30 m. even when carrying 600 lb. A lightly built type of dromedary is capable of twice this speed when not heavily burdened.

CAME'LLIA. Genus of oriental evergreen shrubs of the family Theaceae, nearly allied to the tea plant. Numerous species, such as *C. japonica* and *C. reticulata* have been introduced into Europe.

CAMELOT (kam'elot). Legendary capital of King Arthur (q.v.). A possible site is the Iron-Age hill fort of South Cadbury Castle, nr. Yeovil in Somerset, where excavations from 1967 have revealed relics dating 3000 B.C. to A.D. 1100, incl. remains of a large 6th cent. settlement.

CAMEO. A precious stone on which a design is carved in relief. Cs. were used by the ancient Greeks and Romans as a means of decorating goblets, vases, etc., and were worn as personal ornaments.

CAMERA. *See* PHOTOGRAPHY.

CA'MERON, Basil (1884–). British conductor. B. at Reading, he conducted the symphony orchestras of San Francisco (1930–2) and Seattle (1932–8), and since 1940 has been an associate conductor of the London 'Proms'.

CAMERON, Charles (*c.* 1740–1812). Scottish architect. He studied architecture in Rome, and in 1779 was summoned to Russia by Catherine the Great. He designed part of the palace and built the cathedral of Tsarskoe Selo (Pushkin).

CAMERONIANS. Sect of Scottish Presbyterians named after Richard Cameron, a fanatical Covenanter who was slain in a skirmish in 1680. It came into being after the Revolution of 1688, when Presbyterianism was re-established in Scotland. But prelacy and dissent were also tolerated, and the Cs.

stood for the complete restoration of the Presbyterian system that was established by the National Covenant in 1638, reaffirmed by the Solemn League and Covenant of 1643, and had then existed up to 1649. In 1743 the Covenanters of the old and original school became the Reformed Presbyterians, and in 1876 most of them united with the Free Church of Scotland.

CAMEROON, Republic of. Country of W. Africa. The cap. is Yaoundé. It exports cocoa, coffee, palm-kernels and palm-oil, bananas, ground-nuts, cotton, and grows for home use cassava, millet, maize. Cattle, goats, and sheep are reared. Area 183,580 sq. m. Pop. (1968) 5,200,000

History. The Cameroons was a German possession, 1884–1916, when during the F.W.W. it was captured by Allied forces. After that war, it was in 1922 divided and admin. under League of Nations mandate by France and Britain which in 1946 placed their respective areas under U.N. trusteeship. French Cameroons was in 1960 proclaimed an independent rep. outside the French Community. British Cameroons consisted of 2 detached portions admin. from 1946 as part of Nigeria – the N. within the N. Region, the S. as a separate region. S. Cameroons received a ministerial form of govt. in 1958. Plebiscites were held in both parts in 1961; the N. chose to remain in Nigeria, the S. chose to join the Rep. of Cameroon.

CA'MISARDS. French Huguenots of the Cevennes, who following the revocation of the Edict of Nantes in 1685 rose in revolt and maintained a resistance until 1705, when they were crushed by a French army under Marshal Villars. They were named from the *camise*, a white peasant blouse which they wore.

CAMOENS (kam'ō-ens) or **CAMÕES** (Port. kah-moñ'ēsh), **Luis Vaz de** (1524–80). Portuguese poet. B. at Lisbon or Coimbra, of Galician descent, he studied at Coimbra, and *c.* 1545 went to Lisbon where he is said to have wooed a lady of the court to whom the *Rimas* are addressed. Banished from the cap. on some unknown cause, he served in Africa (1547–9) where he lost an eye fighting at Ceuta. Returning home, he wounded a king's equerry in 1552, and was released on condition of going to India. He arrived in Goa in 1553 and accompanied 2 military expeditions to the Red Sea and Persian Gulf, before being sent to Macao in an official capacity. In 1558 he was shipwrecked while returning to Goa, but the MS. of his epic poem *Os Lusiadas* was saved. In 1567 he left Goa for Mozambique, and by 1570 had reached Lisbon, where in 1572 he pub. the national epic of Portugal, the *Lusiads* (which tells of the voyage of da Gama and incorporates much of Portuguese history). He was granted a small pension in recognition of its success, but d. in poverty of plague. In 1880 his remains were taken to the national pantheon at Belem.

CA'MOMILE. Plant of the daisy (Compositae) family. The most important species *Anthemis nobilis* is a perennial herb common in Europe, the solitary flower-heads have yellow centres surrounded by white florets and when dried make a bitter tonic. It used to be thought that it grew faster the more it was trodden upon.

CAMO'RRA. Secret society in Naples and S. Italy. About 1820, prisoners in the Neapolitan dungeons banded themselves against their gaolers. On their release they maintained their unity, and dominated the life of Naples. They practised smuggling, robbery, and blackmail, and from 1848 went into politics. In 1911 the C. was suppressed.

CAMPAGNA ROMANA (kahmpahn'yah rōmah-nah). Lowland stretch of the Italian peninsula, incl. and surrounding the city of Rome. Lying between the Tyrrhenian Sea and the Sabine Hills to the N.E., the Alban Hills to the S.E., it is drained by the lower course of the Tiber and a number of small streams, most of which dry up in the summer. Prosperous in

Roman times, it became virtually derelict later owing to over-grazing, lack of water, and the arrival in the area of the malaria-carrying Anopheles mosquito. Extensive reclamation and drainage in the 19th and 20th cents. restored it to usefulness.

CAMPA'NA, Dino (1885–1932). Italian expressionist poet, whose life of world-wide wandering – its spirit expressed in *Canti Orfici* (1914) – ended in an asylum. He was 'discovered' only after the S.W.W.

CAMPANE'LLA, Tommaso (1568–1639). Italian philosopher. B. in Calabria, he became a Dominican in 1582 but developed heterodox views, and in 1598 was imprisoned on a charge of plotting to free Naples from Spanish rule. During his 28 years' imprisonment he wrote sonnets and philosophical works. After his release he went to Rome, and then to Paris, where he d. In philosophy he leaned towards neo-Platonism. His *Civitas Solis* is a description of an ideal state.

CAMPA'NIA. A prov. of ancient Italy, also a considerably more extensive region of modern Italy, embracing the provinces of Naples, Benevento, Caserta, Salerno, and Avellino. C. is extremely fertile, and is noted for its climate and scenery. The chief centre is Naples. Area 5,250 sq. m.; pop. (1961) 4,756,094.

CAMPANILE (kahmpahnē'le). Bell-tower erected near, or attached to, churches or town halls in Italy. The leaning tower of Pisa is a famous example; another is the great C. of Florence, 275 ft. high.

CAMPANULA'CEAE (Lat. *campanula*, 'a little bell'). Family of flowering plants, mainly found in the temperate regions of the N. hemisphere, e.g. the British harebell (*Campanula rotundifolia*), the garden Canterbury bell (*C. medium*) and the tall bellflower of the N. American woodland (*C. americana*).

CAMPBELL (kam'bel), **Alexander** (1788–1866). American religious leader. B. in Ireland, he emigrated to U.S.A. in 1809 and there founded with his father the Disciples of Christ (Campbellites): membership c. 2,000,000. He advocated what he believed was primitive Christianity and expounded his views in more than 60 vols. and innumerable sermons.

CAMPBELL, Sir Colin. See CLYDE, COLIN CAMPBELL, 1ST BARON.

CAMPBELL, Donald Malcolm (1921–66). British car and speedboat enthusiast. His father, Sir Malcolm C. (1885–1949) broke the world's land speed record in 1935 with his *Bluebird* at 301·1 m.p.h. and estab. a world water speed record in 1939 at 141·74 m.p.h. in a boat of the same name. Donald C. was invalided out of the R.A.F. in the S.W.W. and took up his

DONALD CAMPBELL. The engine of *Bluebird*: 1, Double bifurcated exhaust pipe; 2, Turbine casing; 3, Air intake; 4, Combustion chambers (8); 5, Igniter plug (2); 6, Blow-off valves; 7, Exhaust pipe thermocouple; 8, Oil drain pipe; 9, Fuel drain pipe; 10, Water spray ring; 11, Output shaft; 12, Mounting points (3). *Courtesy of Bristol Siddeley Engines Ltd.*

father's interests: in 1964 he set up the world water speed record of 276·3 m.p.h. on Lake Dumbleyung, Australia, with the turbo-jet hydroplane *Bluebird*. He was killed in an attempt to raise this record on Coniston Water, England.

The Proteus engine of his car *Bluebird* weighed 1¼ tons, was 8 ft. long and 39 in. in diameter, and produced 4,250 h.p. Driving all four wheels, it was placed in the centre of the car, immediately behind the driver, who could accelerate in 24 sec. from a standing start to 365 m.p.h. over a distance of 1½ m. It burned a distillate diesel fuel similar to paraffin, c. 1½ m. per gallon. He achieved the land speed record of 403·1 m.p.h. at Lake Eyre salt flats, Australia, 17 July, 1964. *See illus.* The car was accidentally wrecked in 1966.

CAMPBELL, Gordon (1886–1953). British vice-admiral. As commander of Q ships (warships masquerading as unarmed merchantmen, so luring German submarines to the surface) he destroyed numerous U-boats in the F.W.W. and won the V.C. He wrote *My Mystery Ships* (1928).

CAMPBELL, Mrs. Patrick (1865–1940). British actress, *née* Beatrice Stella Tanner. B. in London, she was selected by Pinero to play Paula in *The Second Mrs. Tanqueray* (1893); her other roles incl. Rosalind and Eliza Doolittle in *Pygmalion*, specially written for her by Shaw, with whom she conducted an amusing correspondence.

CAMPBELL, Roy (1901–57). S. African poet. B. at Durban, he became a professional jouster and bullfighter in Spain and Provence. He fought for Franco in the Spanish Civil War, and was with the Commonwealth forces in the S.W.W. He estab. his poetic reputation with the individualistic *The Flaming Terrapin* (1924): later vols. were the Byronic literary satire *The Georgiad* and the lyric *Talking Bronco*. He also pub. autobiographical books and translations from Baudelaire, St. John of the Cross, and Lorca.

CAMPBELL, Thomas (1777–1844). Scottish poet. Following the successful publication of his *Pleasures of Hope* in 1799, he travelled on the Continent, and there wrote some of his best poems, including 'Hohenlinden' and 'Ye Mariners of England'. In 1803 he settled (govt. pension from 1805) in London.

CAMPBELL-BANNERMAN, Sir Henry (1836–1908). British Liberal statesman, b. at Glasgow. He was Liberal M.P. for Stirling from 1868, Chief Sec. for Ireland in 1884–5, War Min. in 1886 and again in 1892–5, and leader of the Liberals in the House of Commons from 1899. In 1905 he became P.M., and led the Liberals to an overwhelming electoral victory in 1906. His period of office was marked by the grant of self-govt. to the S. African colonies, the Trades Disputes Act 1906, and the opening of the conflict between Commons and Lords that led to the Parliament Act of 1911. He resigned in 1908 and d. shortly afterwards.

CAMPBELTOWN. Scottish royal burgh, airport, and seaport on the E. coast of Argyllshire; it has a good harbour, distilleries, and fisheries. Pop. (1961) 6,525.

CAMPECHE (kahmpā'chā). Mexican port on the Gulf of C., capital of C. state, in the Yucatan peninsula. Seat of a univ., it was founded in 1540. Pop. (1960) 43,087.

CAMPENDONK, Heinrich (1889–). German painter. His work shows a close sympathy with the peasant life of Bavaria.

CAMPERDOWN. Dutch village in N. Holland prov., 8 m. N.W. of Alkmaar, off which on 11 Oct. 1797 the Dutch were defeated by a British fleet under Duncan.

CAMPHOR (kam'for). Volatile, aromatic ketone substance ($C_{10}H_{16}O$) obtained from the C. tree (*Cinnamomum camphora*), a member of the Lauraceae, native to S. China, Formosa, and Japan. The C. is distilled from chips of the wood of the root, trunk, and branches which are exposed to the action of steam, and afterwards refined.

CAMPI (kahm′pē). Family of Italian painters practising in Cremona in the 16th cent., the most famous being Giulio C. (c. 1502–72).

CAMPINAS (koṅpē′nahs). City of São Paulo state, Brazil, situated on the central plateau; a centre for the coffee-growing areas. Pop. (1960) 185,000.

CAMPION, Edmund (1540–81). English Jesuit and R.C. martyr. B. in London, he took deacon's orders in the English church, but fled to Douai, where in 1571 he recanted Protestantism. In 1573 he became a Jesuit at Rome, and in 1580 was sent to England as a missionary. He was betrayed by a spy in 1581, committed to the Tower, and hanged, drawn and quartered as a traitor. He was canonised in 1970.

CAMPION, Thomas (1567–1620). English poet and musician. He entered Gray's Inn in 1586 and later qualified as a doctor and practised in London. He pub. Latin *Poemata* (1595); *The Art of English Poesie* (1602); a textbook of music, and 4 *Bookes of Ayres* for which he composed both words and music.

CAMPION. Name given to several plants, belonging to the genera *Lychnis* and *Silene*, of the family Caryophyllaceae, e.g. the garden C. (*L. coronaria*), the wild white and red Cs. (*L. vespertina* and *L. diurna*) and bladder C. (*S. inflata*).

CAMPOBASSO (kahmpōbah′sō). Cap. of the Italian prov. of the same name, in Abruzzi e Molise, about 120 m. E.S.E. of Rome; it is noted for cutlery. Pop. (1961) 34,314.

CAMPS, Francis Edward (1905–). British pathologist. Trained at Guy's Hospital, where he was later house physician, he in 1963 became prof. of forensic medicine at London and pathologist to the Home Office. His books incl. a study of the Christie case and, in collaboration with Sir Bentley Purchase, *Practical Forensic Medicine* (1956).

CAMUS (kahmü′), **Albert** (1913–60). French writer. Of Breton and Spanish parents, he was b. in Algeria, became a journalist in Metropolitan France and was active in the S.W.W. Resistance, when he edited the clandestine *Combat*. *L'Étranger* (1942: *The Outsider*) tells of a meaningless killing in the harsh sun of N. Africa, and the same sense of the absurdity of the universe was expressed in the essays *Le Mythe de Sisyphe* (1942). Later books are the novel *La Peste* (1948: *The Plague*) and *L'Homme révolté* (1952: *The Rebel*), a study of the inevitable corruption of ideal revolutionary ideas by murder and oppression which marked the end of his association with Sartre. He was awarded a Nobel prize in 1957.

CANAAN (kā′nan). Area of the Palestinian coast inhabited as early as the 3rd millennium B.C. by the Canaanites, Semitic-speaking peoples of mixed race who were known to the Greeks of the 1st millennium B.C. as Phoenicians. *See* PHOENICIA.

CANADA. A federal union of 10 provs. and 2 territories, an independent community within the British Commonwealth of Nations, occupying (except for Alaska, U.S.A.), the entire northern half of N. America. N. and S. its territory extends from about the latitude of Rome to a few hundred miles short of the

CANADA. Forest covers a third of her land area and newsprint is her largest single export. In the pulp mill skilled hands guide the logs over the steam which enables the bark to be peeled off easily.
Photo by Malik, Ottawa.

DIVISIONS OF CANADA

	Area (sq. m.)	Population (1966)	Capital
Provinces:			
Alberta	255,285	1,463,203	Edmonton
British Columbia	366,255	1,873,674	Victoria
Manitoba	251,030	963,066	Winnipeg
New Brunswick	27,985	616,788	Fredericton
Newfoundland (incl. Labrador)	156,185	493,396	St. John's
Nova Scotia	21,068	756,039	Halifax
Ontario	412,582	6,960,870	Toronto
Prince Edward Island	2,184	108,535	Charlottetown
Quebec	594,860	5,780,845	Quebec
Saskatchewan	251,700	955,344	Regina
Territories:			
North-West Territories	1,304,903	28,738	Yellowknife
Yukon Territory	207,076	14,382	Whitehorse
	3,851,113	20,014,880	

N. Pole; E. and W. it stretches across 88° of longitude and embraces 5 Standard Time (hour) zones. It is divided from the U.S.A. by the 49th parallel of latitude in the W., the Great Lakes and St. Lawrence r. in the centre, and the 45th parallel to the northern hump of Maine in the E., the boundary on the Atlantic being the Saint Crois r. Of its area of 3,851,113 sq. m., c. 290,000 sq. m. are lakes and rivers.

Physical Features. In the N. and E. centre the old Precambrian continent, often called the *Canadian Shield*, has, broadly, the conformation of a great plain, and is profusely dotted with lakes and rock basins. While parts of it support productive forests, it is almost devoid of good agricultural soils; its riches lie in its minerals, furs, and hydro-electric water power. The *Appalachian Region* in Quebec, New Brunswick, and Nova Scotia consists for the most part of rounded hills and shallow valleys; it is productively forested, and contains considerable stretches and numerous pockets of fertile soil. The *St. Lawrence Lowlands*, an area which supports more than half the population, constitutes the southern interior of eastern central Canada. There are no elevated areas except a few intrusions of igneous rock near Montreal. The *Great Plains* or *Prairies* extend from the edge of the Canadian Shield to the Rocky Mts. There are 3 prairie steppes, roughly located in southern Manitoba, Saskatchewan, and Alberta respectively. Much of the soil is of great depth and very fertile. The *Cordilleran Region*, occupying British Columbia, the Yukon, and a narrow boundary zone of Alberta, consists of 'a sea of mountains' in 3 roughly parallel bands, the Rockies, the Selkirks, and the Coast Ranges. The highest peaks are in Yukon Territory, notably Mount Logan (19,539 ft.) and Mount St. Elias (18,024 ft.). British Columbia possesses fertile valleys devoted to fruit growing and dairying.

The chief coastal indentations are on the Atlantic side, where the Gulf of St. Lawrence and the St. Lawrence Waterway, opened 1959, give ready access by water to the heart of the Dominion. The inland lakes and waterways are remarkable for their number and size. The rivers incl. the St. Lawrence (1,900 m.), Saguenay, and Ottawa, flowing into the Atlantic; Nelson (360 m.), Churchill (1,000 m.), Saskatchewan (1,205 m.), Dubawnt, and Albany, flowing into Hudson Bay; the Columbia (1,214 m.), of which 459 m. is in C., and Fraser, flowing into the Pacific Ocean; Yukon (c. 1,900 m., some 700 m. in Canada), flowing into the Bering Sea; the Mackenzie (2,514 m.), Peace (1,054 m.), Back, Athabaska, Liard, and Coppermine, flowing into the Arctic Ocean.

CANADA. Specially prepared picnic and camping sites welcome tourists to Quebec province, such as this on Lac du Milieu in Chibougamau Reserve some 300 miles south-east of James Bay.   *Courtesy of Province of Quebec Film Bureau.*

While climatic conditions are very varied owing to C.'s vast area, the continental type predominates, and only the coastline of British Columbia enjoys a marine climate such as that of Britain and N.W. Europe. Over most of the central portion the ground is continuously snow-covered from the middle of November until late in March.

History. The first permanent settlements were established by Samuel de Champlain, a French explorer, in what are now Nova Scotia and Quebec province, on the sites of Quebec City and Montreal early in the 17th cent. From the outset the French colonies on the seaboard and along the St. Lawrence were bitter rivals of the English colonies to the S. The French régime was doomed to yield ultimately to the growing strength of the New England colonists and the sea-and-land power of Britain. In 1758 Wolfe captured Louisburg, the French stronghold, and a year later the citadel of Quebec. By the Peace of Paris (1763) C. was ceded to Britain. During and immediately after the War of American Independence (1775–83) large numbers of loyalists fled from the Union northward into what is now New Brunswick and Ontario, and, under the name of United Empire Loyalists, played an important part in the creation of these new provinces. In 1791 Canada was divided into (French-speaking) Lower Canada and (English-speaking) Upper Canada. The population was swelled by waves of migration from Great Britain and U.S.A., and by the time of Confederation (1867) there were a million people in Lower Canada and 1½ million in Upper Canada.

Meantime an effort to establish an agricultural colony on the Red River had been made by Lord Selkirk, 1811–12. Winnipeg was founded on the site of a fur-trading post, and a colony was estab. In 1866 two colonies on the Pacific side were united to form British Columbia.

Confederation of Upper and Lower Canada (now Ontario and Quebec), Nova Scotia, and New Brunswick was accomplished by the British North America Act, which came into force on 1 July 1867. Manitoba was created in 1870, and British Columbia joined the union in 1871. The Canadian Pacific Railway was completed in 1885. Prince Edward Island came into federation in 1873. The new provs. of Saskatchewan and Alberta were formed out of the N.W. Territory in 1905. A change of economic factors for the better about 1895 made it possible to throw open the vast region of fertile soil on the prairies for settlement; and the discovery of gold and other metals, the exploitation of forests for lumber and paper, the development of fisheries and tourist attractions, and heavy invest-

ment of capital from other countries in industrial plants, gradually transformed C. from a simple extractive economy to one of the important manufacturing and trading nations of the world. Quebec became strongly separatist in the 1960s, resenting English-speaking 'dominance' in Canada, and France fostered a closer association with Quebec in all fields.

People. The predominant racial stocks of C. are British (at the 1961 census, 7,996,669) and French (5,540,346). Nearly all French-speaking Canadians, who numbered 5,540,346 in 1961, are descendants of the few boatloads of emigrants from Normandy and other provinces of N.W. France who were settled in New France and Acadia by the French government in the 17th and 18th cents. The British stock is partly descended from the United Empire Loyalists who moved N. into C. from the U.S.A. during and after the War of American Independence, but in the main is the result of direct immigration. The 'Open Door' policy which began in the 1890s enriched the Canadian racial mosaic with a wide variety of European stocks.

The Eskimoes and Indians, aborigines of C., numbered 15,000 and 230,902 respectively in 1961.

There is no established or State Church.

Government. The Canadian constitution is partly written, partly unwritten. The British North America Act of 1867, and subsequent amendments, define and divide the fields of jurisdiction as between the central government and the 10 provinces. A Federal-Provincial Constitutional Conference (1968) agreed on establishing machinery competent to review the entire constitution, incl. 7 committees to study: language rights; a charter of human rights; federal-provincial powers; institutions such as the Senate and Supreme Court; regional and economic disparities; procedure for constitutional amendments; and federal-provincial relations.

The Federal Parliament at Ottawa consists of Queen, Senate, and House of Commons. Queen Elizabeth II of the U.K. is also Queen of Canada; she is represented in C. by her personal viceroy, the Governor-General, who acts as Chief of State in C. There is a Prime Minister of the Canadian Dominion, and there are Premiers in each prov. govt.

The Senate consists of 102 members nominated for life, the House of Commons of 264 members elected by universal suffrage for 5 years (unless previously dissolved). Broadly speaking, the Parliament possesses authority over all the large general matters of government.

Under the Canadian honours system (created 1967) no title is conferred, but recipients place the appropriate letters after their name: C.C. (Companion of the Order of C.), C.M. (Medal of Courage), S.M. (Medal of Service).

Provincial Governments. The Queen is represented in each prov. by a Lieutenant-Governor, appointed by the Gov.-Gen. in Council. The provincial govt. consists of the Lieutenant-Governor, the Executive Council and a Legislative Assembly (Quebec has, in addition, a Legislative Council). The provs. enjoy sovereign authority in all local matters.

Public education comes under the jurisdiction of the provincial govs. and there are 46 universities. In Quebec there are 2 distinct systems of education – Roman Catholic and Protestant.

Economic. Though during the S.W.W. employment in manufacturing for the first time exceeded that in agriculture, farming, including stock-raising and horticulture, continues to be of great importance. The chief cereal regions lie in the prairie provinces. Livestock are raised extensively. Milk production is the 3rd most valuable agricultural activity. Nova Scotia, Ontario, and British Columbia contain the chief fruit-growing areas. Alberta is the leading producer of wool. Fur-farming is an important industry in Prince Edward Island, Ontario, Quebec and Manitoba. C. supplies the British market with huge quantities of bacon and other pork products, beef, cheese, evaporated milk, dried eggs, dressed poultry and fruit and vegetable products.

Of the total area, 800,000 sq. m. is classified as bearing productive forests. The cutting of pulpwood for the manufacture of newsprint is a very important branch of Canadian forest operations.

Mining ranks second after agriculture. For a number of years C. has been among the world's leading producers of gold, but during the S.W.W. stress was shifted to base-metal production. C. produces 90 per cent of the world's supply of nickel. Uranium ore is mined near Great Bear Lake. The large iron and steel industries of Nova Scotia and Ontario depend on ore from Newfoundland, including Labrador, and elsewhere. Despite some of the largest coal deposits in the world, C. imports large quantities of coal and other fuels. Petroleum and natural gas are important products of Alberta and half the world's potash is in Saskatchewan. Water-power is the basis of a very large part of Canadian industry.

C.'s fishing grounds are among the most extensive and prolific in the world. Fur trade with the Indians led to the early exploration of C., but fur-trapping is now supplemented by fur-farmg.

In the 20th cent. C. has grown into one of the leading manufacturing countries of the world. Manufacturing is highly concentrated into Ontario and Quebec.

Communications. The 1st great period of railway construction was in the 1850s. Confederation was followed by rapid railway development, at first in the E., and then, after British Columbia agreed to enter the confederation if a railway link was provided, by the building of the Canadian Pacific Railway (q.v.) connecting Pacific with Atlantic coasts. During the F.W.W. 90 privately owned railway systems were taken over by the Canadian Govt. and, with the Intercolonial, welded into the greatest single transport enterprise in America (the Canadian National system).

The trans-Canada highway from Halifax, Nova Scotia, to Vancouver, British Columbia, is an all-weather, continuous motor road 4,195 m. long. The 1,257 m. of the Alaska Highway within Canada were absorbed in the Canadian road system in 1946. As in other countries with enormous distances, air transport has grown steadily in importance; scheduled air services cover some 31,544 m.

Art. Early painters of note included Cornelius Krieghoff (1812–72), who recorded *habitant* pioneer life; Antoine Plamondon (1804–95), a Quebec portrait painter; and Paul Kane (1810–71), painter of the Plains Indians. A native Canadian style developed with

CANADIAN ART. A pioneer of Canadian painting was the German-born Cornelius Krieghoff, who found his inspiration in the hard life of the early settlers. This characteristic 'Winter Landscape', in the National Gallery of Canada, is reminiscent of the Dutch art of the 17th cent.
Courtesy of National Film Board, Ottawa.

the landscapes of Tom Thomson (1877–1917) and the 'Group of Seven' – J. E. H. MacDonald (1873–1932), Franklin Carmichael (1890–1945), A. J. Casson, Lawren Harris, A. Y. Jackson, Arthur Lismer, and F. H. Varley – who worked as a group 1919–33.

Painters dependent on English or U.S. 19th cent. realism included Horatio Walker (1858–1938), William Brymner (1855–1925), and Homer Watson (1855–1936). Among Impressionist painters were A. Suzor-Côté (1869–1937), Clarence Gagnon (1881–1942) and, most important, J. W. Morrice (1865–1924). Followers of later movements were Emily Carr (1871–1945), Goodridge Roberts (1904–   ), David Milne (1882–1953), Stanley Cosgrove, P. E. Borduas (1905–60), Henri Masson, J. P. Riopelle, Alfred Pellan, Jacques de Tonnancour, and Harold Town.

Ecclesiastical wood-carving in the French Norman tradition has been continuous from the early 18th cent. Realist sculptors include Philippe Hébert (1850–1917), Walter Allward, Emmanuel Hahn (1881–1957), Elizabeth Wyn Wood, and Louis Archimbault.

20th cent. architecture has followed international style except in the prov. of Quebec which developed its own traditions.

Literature. ENGLISH. Canadian literature in English began early in the 19th cent. in the Maritime Provs. with the humorous tales of T. C. Haliburton (1796–1865); Charles Heavysege (1816–76), a poet of note, belonged to Kingston, Ontario. The later 19th cent. brought the lyrical output of Charles G. D. Roberts (1860–1943), Bliss Carman (1861–1929), Archibald Lampman (1861–99), and Duncan Campbell Scott (1862–1944).

Fiction begins with 'Ralph Connor' (the Rev. C. W. Gordon, 1860–1937), who wrote of pioneer life, and Gilbert Parker (1862–1932), whose field was the historical novel. Realism in fiction developed with Frederick P. Grove, Mazo de la Roche, and Morley Callaghan. They were followed by Robertson Davies, Hugh MacLennan (1907–   ), Mordecai Richler, E. A. McCourt, and W. O. Mitchell. The humorous works of Stephen Leacock (1869–1944) brought him world-wide fame.

Though their merits as poetry are not high, the verses of Robert W. Service (1874–1958), 'Bard of the Yukon', and W. H. Drummond (1854–1907), who affectionately satirized *habitant* life, maintained their popularity. Memories of the F.W.W. lived in the well-known poem 'In Flanders Fields' by John

CANADIAN PRIME MINISTERS		
Sir John A. Macdonald (Con.)	... ...	1867
Alexander Mackenzie (Lib.)	... ...	1873
Sir John A. Macdonald (Con.)	... ...	1878
Sir John J. Abbott (Con.)	... ...	1891
Sir John S. D. Thompson (Con.)	... ...	1892
Sir Mackenzie Bowell (Con.)	... ...	1894
Sir Charles Tupper (Con.)	... ...	1896
Sir Wilfrid Laurier (Lib.)	... ...	1896
Sir Robert L. Borden (Con.)	... ...	1911
Arthur Meighen (Con.)	... ...	1920
William Lyon Mackenzie King (Lib.)	... ...	1921
Arthur Meighen (Con.)	... ...	1926
William Lyon Mackenzie King (Lib.)	... ...	1926
Richard Bedford Bennett (Con.)	... ...	1930
William Lyon Mackenzie King (Lib.)	... ...	1935
Louis Stephen St. Laurent (Lib.)	... ...	1948
John G. Diefenbaker (Con.)	... ...	1957
Lester Bowles Pearson (Lib.)	... ...	1963
Pierre Elliot Trudeau (Lib.)	... ...	1968
Con. = Conservative.	Lib. = Liberal.	

McCrae (1872–1918). In the 'thirties poetry flourished in the work of E. J. Pratt (1883–) and the Montreal Group among whom were A. M. Klein, Frank Scott, A. J. M. Smith, P. K. Page and Patrick Anderson. Later prominent poets included Dorothy Livesay, Anne Marriott, Douglas LePan, Earle Birney (1904–), Roy Daniells, L. A. Mackay, and Jay MacPherson.

FRENCH. F.-X. Garneau's *Histoire du Canada* (1845–8) inspired a school of patriotic verse led by Octave Crémazie (1827–79) and continued by Louis Fréchette (1838–1908). A new movement began after 1900 with such poets as André Lozeau (1878–1924), Paul Morin, Robert Choquette (1862–1941), Alain Grandbois, St. Denys Garneau, Éloi de Grandmont, and Pierre Trottier. Fiction reached a high point with Louis Hémon (1880–1914) whose *Maria Chapdelaine* inspired many genre works. Outstanding later novelists are Germaine Guèvremont, Gabrielle Roy, 'Ringuet' (Philippe Panneton, 1895–), Robert Elie, Roger Lemelin, and Yves Thériault.

CANADIAN PACIFIC. Railway co. whose main line runs from Montreal to Vancouver, B.C.; other lines connect Montreal with St. John, N.B., and with most important towns in Canada and a number in north U.S.A. Miles operated in 1950 totalled 17,095 in C. and 4,762 in U.S.A. The plan to bridge C. by railway was brought into effect chiefly thanks to Donald A. Smith (later Lord Strathcona) and George Stephen (Lord Mount Stephen). The main line was completed in 1885; the first through train ran in 1886. The co. also owns hotels, ocean liners, and airways.

CANAL. A man-made waterway constructed for drainage, irrigation, or navigation.

Irrigation Canals carry water for irrigation from rivers, reservoirs, or wells, and are carefully designed to maintain an even flow of water over the whole length. These channels are found in all continents, but chiefly in tropical and sub-tropical lands where rainfall is scarce or non-existent. Irrigation canals fed from the Nile have maintained life in Egypt since the earliest times; the division of the waters of the Upper Indus and its tributaries for the extensive system of irrigation canals in W. Pakistan and Punjab, India, was for more than 10 years a major cause of dispute between India and Pakistan, settled at last by a treaty in 1960; the flourishing agriculture of the Murray basin, Victoria, Australia, and of the Great Valley of California, U.S.A., are examples of 19th and 20th cent. irrigation canal development.

Navigation Canals. The most remarkable ancient C. used for transport was the Grand Canal (q.v.) of China, of 850 m. total navigable length, and even today there is more traffic on the Cs. of China than on those in any other country.

Navigation Cs. must be at one level between locks. The channel of the C. has a flat bottom and sides which slope outwards from the bottom. The breadth of the bottom usually is at least twice the greatest breadth of any boat using the C.; the depth of water in feet at least 1½ times the draught of the vessel; the area of the waterway 6 times the greatest midship section of the vessel in the C.

Most C. barges are motor-driven, though the horse is still sometimes used for haulage on the smaller Cs. Tugs can be used only where there are no locks, or locks big enough to accommodate them. Electric traction, using rails on the tow path, has been used.

The first British C. (1761–76) was the Manchester-Worsley C. constructed by order of the 3rd duke of Bridgewater to carry coal from his collieries to Manchester. The engineer, Brindley, overcame great difficulties in the route. The major part of the 2,400 m. system now in use in Britain was nationalized in 1948. The largest C. is the Caledonian C., 61 m. long and remarkable for its locks.

Ship Canals are constructed to allow ocean-going

PRINCIPAL SHIP CANALS

Canal			Opened, year	Length, miles
North Sea (Netherlands)	...	...	1876	18
Corinth (Greece)	...	...	1893	4
Don-Volga (Lenin) (U.S.S.R.)		...	1952	63
Elbe and Trave (Germany)	...	...	1900	42
Göta (Sweden)	...	...	1832	240
Kiel (Germany)	...	...	1895	61
Manchester (England)	...	...	1894	35¼
Panama (Central America)	...	1914	50¼
Princess Juliana (Netherlands)		1935	20
St. Lawrence Seaway (Canada)	...	1959	180
Saulte Ste. Marie (U.S.A.)	...	1855	1¼
Saulte Ste. Marie (Canada)	...	1895	1
Suez (Egypt)	...	...	1869	103
Welland (Canada)	...	...	1929	25

ships either to reach inland centres (e.g. the Manchester Ship C.) or to reduce the distance by sea between 2 points by cutting across an isthmus (e.g. the Suez C.).

Belgium, France, Germany, and other countries in Europe have spent large sums of money on Cs. and ports. The Baltic Ship C. (1887–95) connects the Baltic with the N. Sea. The North Sea Ship C. unites the Ijsselmeer w th the N. Sea. The Russians have an extensive system of Cs. in Europe and Asia.

The St. Lawrence Seaway, started in 1954 and opened in 1959, extends from Montreal to Lake Ontario, 180 m.; with the deepening of the Welland C. and some of the river channels, it provides a waterway making it possible for ocean-going vessels to travel during the ice-free months between the Atlantic and Duluth, Minnesota, U.S.A., at the western end of Lake Superior, a distance of 2,342 m.

The N. Crimean C. (first section completed 1963) will link the Dnieper with the Black Sea and the Sea of Azov, and will be navigable for *c.* 125 m. of its 220 m. length.

CANALE'TTO, Antonio (1697–1768). Venetian painter. He painted many scenes of Venice, his works being remarkable for their handling of perspective and control of colour. He visited England in 1746 and 1753.

CANARIES. Group of volcanic islands belonging to Spain, 60 m. off the N.W. coast of Africa. There are 7 large and 6 small (uninhabited) islands, forming 2 provinces: Santa Cruz de Tenerife (Tenerife, Palma, Gomera, and Hierro), and Las Palmas (Gran Canaria, Lanzarote, Fuerteventura, and the uninhabited islets). Santa Cruz de Tenerife (1,238 sq. m.) has an est. pop. (1960) of 490,655, Las Palmas (1,569 sq. m.)

CANALETTO. Sharp and clear, with their meticulous detail and bright colour, the pictures of Canaletto bring 18th century Venice to life. This is 'A Fête on the Grand Canal'.
Reproduced by permission of the Trustees of the Wallace Collection.

CANBERRA. Twin buildings, housing the offices of the city administration, flank Civic Square at Civic Centre. The centre is the main commercial and retail shopping area of the town, which is Australia's largest inland city.
Courtesy of Australian News and Information Bureau.

of 453,793. Total area 2,807 sq. m.; pop. (1960) 908,718.

CANARY A bird (*Serinus canarius*) belonging to the finch family (Fringillidae). It is nearly allied to the European serin (*S.c. serinus*), which is now regarded as a sub-species only, but in a wild state is confined to Madeira and the Canary Islands. It was first bred in Europe as a cage-bird in Italy, in the 16th cent. As songsters, those known as rollers have the sweetest voice and the most sustained powers. They are bred in Germany, esp. in the Harz mts. British breeds include the Scotch fancies, Lizards, London fancies, and Yorkshires.

CANBERRA (kan'bra). Federal cap. of the Commonwealth of Australia, standing in the Australian Capital Territory enclosed within New South Wales, on a tributary of the Murrumbidgee; it was selected as capital in 1908. It contains the Parliament House, first used by the Commonwealth Parliament in 1927, the Australian Nat. Univ. (1946), and the C. School of Music (1965). Area (Australian Cap. Terr. incl. the port at Jervis Bay) 939 sq. m.; pop. (1967) 102,258.

CANCAN. A stage dance performed by a line of dancers or as a solo. It first appeared about 1830 in Paris and came to symbolize Parisian naughtiness. The music latterly associated with the C. is the *galop* from Offenbach's *Orpheus in the Underworld.* The high kick was a speciality of the C.

CANCER (kan'ser). A group of diseases due to the growth of malignant tumours; a malignant tumour. The chief varieties are *carcinoma*, which grows from skin or mucous membrane, and *sarcoma*, which grows from connective tissue. These 2 categories are subdivided according to the kind of tissue from which the growth takes place.

Although no known human form of C. has been directly proved to be caused by a virus, laboratory experiment has identified numerous C. viruses in animals. The viruses can alter inherited characteristics and are easily transferred, not only from cell to cell, but from one species to another, though their effect may be different. Cells affected by C. virus continue to live, but vary from the norm in a number of different ways, e.g. they may multiply lawlessly.

Taken in its early stages C. can be successfully treated by surgery, X-rays from electron tubes for deep therapy, or surface therapy with radioactive sources, the traditional radium being replaced by giant sources of radioactive cobalt or caesium, the latter coming from the 'waste' from nuclear power

stations. In suitable cases needles containing short-lived radioactive radon (from radium) can be implanted in tissue, or a cure may be effected by chemical means.

CANDELA OUTERIÑO, Felix (1910–   ). Mexican architect. Professor at the National School of Architecture, Univ. of Mexico, from 1953, he founded with his brother a firm specializing in the design and construction of reinforced concrete shell structures.

CA'NDIA. Italian name for the Greek island of CRETE, also formerly the name of the largest city, Heraklion, founded *c.* 824. It has many Venetian remains. Pop. (1961) 63,458.

CANDLE. A source of artificial light consisting of a rod or cylinder made of wax, tallow, or some other solid-fatty material, enclosing a wick of cotton or flax. There is a declining demand for household Cs., except for coloured and fancy Cs.

The traditional spermaceti C. flame used as a candle-power standard has been replaced by the *candela,* symbol cd, which is 1/60 of the intensity of one square centimeter of a blackbody radiator at the temperature of solidification of platinum (2046°K).

CANDLEMAS. In the Christian Church, the feast of the Purification of the Blessed Virgin Mary, or the Presentation of the Infant Christ in the Temple, celebrated on 2 Feb.

CANE. Name applied to the reed-like stem of various plants such as the sugar-cane and bamboo, but more particularly to the group of palms called rattans, consisting of the genus *Calamus* and its allies; their slender stems are dried and used for making walking sticks, baskets, and furniture.

CANEA (kahn'ya). Cap. and principal port of Crete, about midway along the N. coast. It was founded in 1252 by the Venetians, and is still surrounded by a wall. Vegetable oils, soap, and leather are exported. Heavy fighting took place round C. during the S.W.W., following the landing of German parachutists in May 1941. Pop. (1961) 38,268.

CANIDAE (kan'idē). Family of mammals belonging to the Carnivora, distinguished by their walking on the toes (digitigrade), having non-retractile claws and an elongated muzzle, and by other anatomical characters. The dogs, wolves, jackals, and foxes are typical members.

CANNAE (kan'ē). Ancient Italian town in Apulia, where in 216 B.C. Hannibal defeated the Romans.

CANNES (kahn). Town of the French Riviera in Alpes-Maritimes dept., one of the most fashionable and most popular holiday resorts of the Continent. Until 1834 it was only a little seaport, but then it attracted the patronage of Lord Brougham (who d. here) and other distinguished visitors, and soon a handsome new town (La Bocca) grew up facing the Mediterranean. Completion of the railway to C. in 1884 added to its popularity. It has a famous casino. Pop. (1968) 67,152.

CANNIBALISM. The practice of eating human flesh, also called anthropophagy. The name is derived from the Caribs, a man-eating tribe of S. American and W. Indian natives, who impressed themselves upon the conquering Spaniards by their savagery.

C. has been practised throughout the ages and in most parts of the world. It has religious and superstitious motives, but modern outbreaks, e.g. in Russia after the Revolution, in the Nazi concentration camps, and in China under Japanese rule, have been caused by overpowering hunger, and food C. is possibly the original form.

CANNING, George (1770–1827). British Tory statesman. The son of a barrister, he was ed. at Eton and Oxford, and in 1793 entered Parliament. His wit and eloquence, best shown in his verse satires and parodies contributed to the *Anti-Jacobin* (1797–8), made him extremely valuable to Pitt, who gave him

CANNING. The side seam of the can is soldered over a solder roll and one end is seamed on in a double seaming machine. The double seam combines with the sealing compound on the rim to give a completely hermetic seal, but the cans are additionally tested under air pressure, as seen here, and faulty cans are automatically rejected.
Courtesy of the Metal Box Company Limited.

several appointments. As For. Sec. 1807–10 C. was largely responsible for the seizure of the Danish fleet and British intervention in the Spanish peninsula, but his disapproval of the Walcheren expedition involved him in a duel with Castlereagh and led to his resignation. Except for the presidency of the Board of Control (1816–20) he held no further office until 1822, when on Castlereagh's death he again became For. Sec. He opposed the interventionist policy of the 'Holy Alliance' in Spain, and supported the national movements in Greece and the S. American republics. He succeeded Lord Liverpool as P.M. in 1827, and on the refusal of Wellington, Peel, and other Tories to serve under him formed a coalition with the Whigs. He d. in office a few months later.

His son **Charles John,** earl C. (1812–62), sat in the Lords from 1837 as visct. C. As Gov.-Gen. of India from 1856, he suppressed the Indian Mutiny with an unvindictive firmness which earned him the nickname 'Clemency C.' and became 1st Viceroy of India in 1858, receiving an earldom the next year.

CANNING. The art of preserving foods in hermetically sealed containers by the application of heat. In 1809 the Frenchman Nicolas Appert succeeded in preserving food in glass containers, and in 1810 the Englishman Peter Durand patented tin cans. In 1819 the 1st American C. factory was started in Boston by Underwood, an Englishman. The American Civil War stimulated the development of C. and there was phenomenal expansion following the introduction of scientific methods c. 1925.

Sterilization is achieved by heat, right up to the final sealing, but the very large radioactive sources becoming available from nuclear power stations open up the possibility of sterilization by blasts of electrons or gamma rays.

CANNING TOWN. Industrial area in the East End of London, England, part of the Greater London bor. of Newham, which rapidly developed during the latter half of the 19th cent. Here are chemical, iron, cable, etc., works and famous docks, viz. Victoria and the Royal Albert.

CANNOCK. Market town (U.D.) of Staffs, England, 8 m. N.W. of Walsall, on C. Chase, an

area of heath and woodland, and at one time a royal preserve, now a rich coalfield. Pop. (1961) 42,182.

CANO (kah′nō), **Juan Sebastian del** (d. 1526). Spanish voyager, for whom it is claimed that he was the first circumnavigator. He sailed with Magellan in 1519, and after the latter's death in the Philippines, brought the *Victoria* safe home to Spain.

CANOE (kanōō′). Lightweight boat of shallow draught, pointed at both ends and easily propelled by paddles or sails. Construction varies from the hollowed tree-trunk of African tribes to the framework covered with bark or skin used by the American Indians. Modern Cs. are often of lightweight wood construction, but various synthetic materials are increasingly used. Canoeing became a sport in the 19th cent. and the Royal C. Club in Britain was founded 1866.

CANON. In the Catholic Church, a clergyman holding a prebend in a cathedral or collegiate church. He lived within its precinct, and his life was ordered by ecclesiastical rules or canons. About the 11th cent. a distinction was drawn between *regular* or Augustinian canons who observed the rule, and *secular* canons who lived in the world, and were in effect the administrative officers of a cathedral, but in holy orders. Following the Reformation, all Cs. in England became secular Cs.; and the Cs., headed by the dean, are the resident ecclesiastical dignitaries attached to a cathedral and constitute the chapter.

CANON (of scripture). The collection or list of books of the Bible (q.v.) that are accepted by the Christian Church as divinely inspired and authoritative, i.e. the Old and New Testaments. The canon of the O.T. was drawn up at the assembly of Rabbis held at Jamnia in Palestine between A.D. 90 and 100; certain excluded books were included in the Apocrypha. The earliest list of N.T. books is known as the Muratorian Canon (c. A.D. 160–70). Athanasius promulgated c. 365 a list which corresponds with that in our Bibles.

CANONICAL HOURS. In the R.C. Church the daily set periods for the performance of devotion; matins and lauds, prime, terce (9 a.m.), sext (noon), nones (3 p.m.), evensong or vespers, and compline. In England C.Hs. are also those in which a marriage may legally be performed in a parish church, without a special licence (8 a.m.–6 p.m.).

CANONIZATION. Procedure in the Roman Catholic Church whereby one (or more) of her members is formally admitted into the Calendar of Saints. Formerly, under a system laid down mainly in the 17th cent., the long process of investigation was seldom completed in under 50 yrs., although in the case of a martyr the final stages were more speedy. In 1969 a simplified procedure was introduced whereby the investigation by the diocesan bishop where the candidate was born and that subsequently carried out by the Sacred Congregation of Rites, presided over by a cardinal at Rome, were merged. The gathering of proof is left to the bishop, the inquiry being based both on the writings, and on the life and virtues or martyrdom of the potential saint. The findings are then put before the Congregation for the Causes of Saints (created from the Sacred Congregation of Rites in 1969), and any objections are put forward by the *Promotor Fidei* (popularly 'devil's advocate'). On the papal ratification of the Congregation's verdict, as to the possession of heroic virtues and the reality of miracles, the stage of Beatification (allowing local veneration) is reached, and full C. follows after proof of further miracles. The ceremony takes place in the Vatican basilica. In the revised Calendar of Saints (1970) some, e.g. St. Christopher were removed as probably non-existent.

CANON LAW. The body of rules and regulations whereby the government of the Christian Church is carried on by ecclesiastics. Its origin is sought in the declarations of Christ and the Apostles, and through the succeeding centuries it has been in gradual but uninterrupted growth, under the guidance of the Papacy and the episcopate assembled in oecumenical councils. The earliest compilations were in the East, and the C.L. of the Eastern Orthodox Church is comparatively small and easy of access. In the course of centuries, a great mass of C.L. was accumulated in the Western Church, which in 1918 was condensed in the *Corpus juris canonici* under Benedict XV. Even so, however, this is supplemented by many papal decrees, etc.

The C.L. of the Church of England consists of canons pub. in 1604, a few of which have been revised, while 2 new canons were added in 1892 and 1921. In 1939 the archbishops appointed the Canon Law Commission, whose report appeared in 1947. Many of the canons of 1603 were found to be obsolete, and it was recommended that the majority of the remainder should be redrafted.

CANO'SSA. Ruined castle 12 m. S.W. of Reggio city in Reggio Emilia prov., Italy, where the emperor Henry IV did penance before pope Gregory VII in 1077, for having opposed him in the question of investitures.

CANOVA (kahnō'vah), **Antonio** (1757–1822). Italian sculptor. B. near Treviso, he traditionally modelled a lion in butter which brought his talent to notice, and his work has a sentimental delicacy which, though it led to the honour of executing the tombs of Clement XIII, Pius VII and Clement XIV, has not served his enduring reputation. 'Cupid and Psyche' in the Louvre and 'The Three Graces' at the Hermitage, Leningrad, are other famous pieces.

CANROBERT (koṅrobār'), **François Certain** (1809–95). Marshal of France. From 1835 he fought against the Arabs in Algeria, and in 1854–5 he held a command in the Crimean War. He distinguished himself on diplomatic missions, was made a marshal of France and senator, and fought again at Magenta and Solferino, and in the Franco-German war.

CANTAL (koṅtahl'). Range of mountains in central France which gives its name to Cantal dept. It is of volcanic origin. The highest point is the Plomb du Cantal, 6,096 ft.

CANTALOUP (kan'taloop). Name of several small varieties of the melon (*Cucumis melo*), distinguished by their small and round ribbed fruits.

CANTERBURY. City (county borough) in Kent, England, on the Stour, 62 m E.S.E. of London. C. is a cathedral city and the archdiocese of the primate of the Church of England, and also an old market town, the main trade being in hops, cattle, corn, and wool; brick-making and tanning are among its industries. From the time of the Norman conquest C. has been granted special privileges. Among its interesting features are the Dane John mound, remains of a Norman castle, fragments of the city wall and the great west gate, and the 18th cent. guildhall. Dominating all is the cathedral. Since A.D. 597 C. has been the centre of the English Church. The foundations of the present cathedral were laid by Lanfranc (1070–89), but the church has been rebuilt and added to, and its architectural styles range from Norman to Perpendicular. The King's School (1541) is built on the site of the monastery hall. The tombs incl. those of the Black Prince and Henry IV. Pilgrims were attracted to C. in the Middle Ages by the shrine of St. Thomas à Beckett, who was murdered in the N.W. transept of the cathedral, 1170. Such pilgrims are characterized in Chaucer's *Canterbury Tales*.

Excavation of areas bombed during Ger. air raids in the S.W.W. (espec. 1942) led to increased knowledge of the Roman city. The Univ. of Kent was estab. at C. in 1965. Pop. (1961) 30,374.

CANTERBURY, Archbishops of. The archbishop of C. is the Primate of All England, metropolitan of

CANTERBURY. St. Augustine's Chair in Canterbury Cathedral, used in the enthronement of all archbishops of Canterbury.   *Photo: British Travel and Holidays Association.*

the Church of England, and first peer of the realm, ranking next to royalty. He crowns the sovereign, has a seat in the House of Lords, and is a member of the Privy Council. His ecclesiastical province is all England with the exception of the 6 northern counties and Cheshire, and his diocese includes most of Kent and a small part of Sussex. He appoints to many livings, and is empowered to confer degrees (Lambeth degrees) in divinity, law and medicine. His seat is the Old Palace, Canterbury, with a 2nd residence at Lambeth Palace, London. He is appointed, in effect, by the Prime Minister.

The first A. of C. was Augustine, who was despatched from Rome by pope Gregory in A.D. 597 to convert the Anglo-Saxon kingdom of Kent. Archbishops appointed this cent. have been: Randal T. Davidson, 1903; C. G. Lang, 1928; Wm. Temple, 1942; G. F. Fisher, 1945, and A. M. Ramsey, 1961.

CANTERBURY PLAINS. District of South Island, New Zealand, nearly 4,000 sq. m. in extent, a rich area of grassland between the mountains and the sea. From here comes C. lamb.

CANTHA'RIDES (Blister Beetle, or Spanish Fly). Family of beetles (Coleoptera) belonging to the section Heteromera. *Cantharis vesicatoria*, the Spanish fly, is the best-known species; it is bright golden-green, and about ¾ in. long. The drug C., a dangerous aphrodisiac, is prepared from its dried body.

CA'NTILEVER. A horizontal beam fixed at one end to a rigid support and free to move at the other end. This type of structure is used widely in building and in C. bridges, where the projecting arms are built inwards from the piers to meet in the centre of the span, and in C. cranes where a straight steel truss rests on a central support.

CA'NTINFLAS. Stage-name of Mario Moreno Reyes (1911–). Of Mexican-Indian stock, he was b. in Mexico City, and ran away from school to join a travelling tent show. Greatest of the Latin-American stage and film comedians, he is also noted for his social work.

CANTON. Corrupt form of the name of Kwangchow, cap. of Kwangtung prov. China, and principal commercial city of S. China, on the Chukiang (Pearl river), about 75 m. N.W. of Hong Kong. It was the first Chinese port opened to foreign trade, the Portuguese visiting it in 1516, followed by British, French, and Dutch merchants. It was a treaty port from 1842 until occupied by the Japanese in 1938.

C. lies on both banks of a wide delta, the main section on the N. bank with industrial suburbs to the N., S., and S.W.; cotton, silk, and jute textiles, cement, paper, matches, lacquer work, and ivory engravings are among its products. C. is linked by railway with Hankow (completed 1936) and Peking, and has an airport; it is the focal point of river trade in the area. There are public parks, a leper hospital, a mint, pagodas, temples, and two universities. Pop. (1965) 3,000,000.

CANTON. Mfg. town of Ohio, U.S.A., in a rich mining and agricultural district. Pop. (1960) 113,631.

CANTON. In France, a subdivision of the arrondissement; in Switzerland, a C. is one of the 22 states forming the Confederation.

CANTON and ENDERBURY. Two atolls in the Phoenix group which forms part of the British colony of the Gilbert and Ellice Islands in the Pacific. In 1938 the U.S.A. claimed sovereignty over C. and E., and it was agreed that they should rank as a condominium for 50 years from 1939. C. airport is less used since the introduction of long-range jets.

CANUTE (c. 995–1035). King of England, Denmark, and Norway. Son of Sweyn, king of Denmark, he was baptized c. 1000, accompanied his father in his invasion of England in 1013, and on the latter's death in 1014 was hailed as king by the army. In 1016 he defeated Edmund Ironside at Assandun in Essex, and then ruled Mercia and Northumbria until on Edmund's death he succeeded to the whole kingdom, and proved himself a just and wise ruler. He invaded Scotland c. 1027, and forced King Malcolm to pay homage. In 1018 he succeeded his brother Harold as king of Denmark, and he conquered Norway in 1028. His empire fell to pieces, however, at his death. He was buried at Winchester.

CANYNGES, William (c. 1399–1474). English merchant. B. at Bristol, of which city he was 5 times mayor and twice the M.P. He was the greatest overseas merchant of his day, and rebuilt at his own expense St. Mary Redcliffe.

CA'NYON. Anglicized spelling of Span. *cañón*, a deep narrow hollow running through the mountains. There are many Cs. in the western States of the U.S.A. and in Mexico, e.g. the Grand C. of the Colorado, the C. in Yellowstone National Park, and the Black C. in Colorado.

CAPACITANCE, ELECTRICAL. The ratio of the electric charge on a body to the resultant change of potential. A capacitor (q.v.) has a C. of one farad when a charge of one coulomb changes its potential by one volt. The farad is an impractically large unit and capacitors normally used in electronic circuits are of the order of millionths of a farad (microfarads) or less.

CAPACITOR. Device for storing electric charge, consisting of conducting plates separated by layers of insulating material (dielectric). They may be flat or rolled up. Multiple air dielectric Cs. are commonly used as adjustable Cs. for tuning radio circuits. (Cs. were formerly called condensers.)

CAPE BRETON. Island forming part of the Canadian province of Nova Scotia, separated from the mainland by the narrow Gut of Canso, and bisected by a waterway. In the N. the surface is rugged, rising to 1,800 ft. at North Cape. The much indented coast has many fine harbours. The climate is mild, and very moist. Mineral wealth is considerable; timber is produced; the cod fisheries are highly important; agriculture is the basic industry. The chief towns are Sydney, Dominion, Inverness, Port Hood, and Glace Bay. The people are mainly of Scottish Highland descent. Some speak Gaelic.

The first English colony was estab. in 1629, but was driven out by the French. In 1763 C.B. was ceded to Britain; it was attached to Nova Scotia. Area 3,970 sq. m.; pop. (1961) 131,507.

CAPE COAST. Port of Ghana, West Africa, about 80 m. W. of Accra, superseded since 1962 by Tema. The town is built on a natural breakwater, adjoining which is the castle, 1st estab. by the Portuguese in the 16th cent. Pop. (1960) 41,143.

CAPE COLOURED. Descendants of mixed unions between Europeans and African peoples, living mainly in Cape Province, Rep. of S. Africa: in (1966) c. 1,800,000.

ČAPEK (chah'pek), **Karel Matěj** (1890–1938). Czech playwright. His great successes were *R.U.R.* (Rossum's Universal Robots) in 1921, in which the mechanical creations of the scientists develop souls and rebel against their masters, and, more bitterly satirical, *The Insect Play* also 1921 (written with his brother Joseph C., 1887–1945) prophetic of totalitarianism. He also wrote novels and an excellent biography of Masaryk.

CAPE OF GOOD HOPE. South African headland forming a peninsula between Table Bay and False Bay, Cape Town. Discovered by Bartholomew Diaz in 1488, it was named Cape of Storms, but afterwards given its present name by King John II of Portugal.

CAPE OF GOOD HOPE (Kaapland). A province – the parent state – of the Union of S. Africa, in the extreme S. of the African continent, named after the famous promontory. The Dutch occupied the Cape in 1650, and in 1652 laid out Capetown. The territory, first taken by the British in 1795 after the French Revolutionary armies had occupied the Netherlands, was sold to Britain for £6,000,000 in 1814. The Orange r. was proclaimed the N. boundary in 1825. Griqualand W. (1880) and the S. part of Bechuanaland (1895) were later incorporated; and Walvis Bay, although administered with S.W. Africa, is legally an integral part of Cape Province.

Physically the Cape consists of (a) a high plateau, the veld country, hilly and dotted with isolated kopjes, whose southern limit is the great escarpment which more or less parallels the coast and is called the Drakensberg, Stormberg, etc.; and (b) the area between the escarpment and the sea, comprising the Great Karoo, the S.E. region about Graaff Reinet, and the Coast Belt.

Rainfall is the dominating climatic factor; only the S.W. corner about Capetown has a copious and reliable (winter) rainfall, and here conditions favour the production of fruit and vegetables; the grapes are made into popular wines. The Karoo lends itself to extensive farming, in spite of droughts, since the scrub is nutritious animal food and the soil is fertile. The S.E. is an area of mixed farming, cattle and maize being the chief products. Kimberley, in Griqualand W., is the centre of great diamond workings; copper, asbestos, and manganese are also important.

The Cape was given self-government in 1872; it joined the Union in 1910. The chief towns are along the coast. Capetown, the cap., is also the legislative cap. of the Union of South Africa; Port Elizabeth and East London rank next in size. Other towns are Kimberley, the diamond metropolis; and the university towns of Grahamstown and Stellenbosch. Area 278,465 sq. m.; pop. (1960) 5,308,839 (977,377 white).

CAPER. A shrub (*Capparis spinosa*) of the family Capparidaceae, native to the Mediterranean region. Its buds and unripe fruit are preserved in vinegar and used as a condiment, known as capers.

CAPERCAILLZIE (kaperkāl'zi, -kāl'yi). Game bird (*Tetrao urogallus*), the largest member of the grouse family (Tetraonidae). The cock is as large as a hen-turkey, with dark iron-grey, brown and black plumage, glossed with green on the breast.

CAPET (kahpā'), **Hugh** (c. 938–96). King of France. He succeeded his father, Hugh the Great, as duke of France in 956, claimed the throne in

CAPETOWN. The oldest city of the republic, Capetown is built at the foot and on the lower slopes of Table Mountain (3,500 ft.), and is expanding seawards on the reclaimed land of Table Bay, seen in the foreground. Table Mountain offers difficulties, even for experienced climbers, and her streams supplement the city's water supplies.
Courtesy of South Africa Information Service.

987 on the death of Louis V, the last of the Carolingians, and maintained his claim against Charles of Lorraine, Louis's uncle. The dynasty he founded occupied the French throne until the Revolution.

CAPETANAKIS, Demetrios (1912–44). Greek writer. Born in Smyrna, he lived in Germany during the '30s and went to Britain in 1939, recording his experiences in *A Greek Poet in England,* ed. after his death by John Lehmann. He wrote in French, German and English, as well as Greek, and his English verse has a classic directness and simplicity of form.

CAPETOWN. City and oldest town of S. Africa, legislative cap. of the Union of S.A., and cap. of the province of Cape of Good Hope. It was founded in 1652 by Johan van Riebeek, of the Dutch East India Co., and later German and Huguenot refugees joined the small community. C. is a vitally important port and the modern harbour, continually improved, can accommodate vessels of large size. With the expansion of population, new suburbs are developed. The city is well planned, and contains many handsome buildings; they include City Hall, the Houses of Parliament, and the castle, begun in 1666. The university is situated in the grounds of Groote Schuur (great barn), Cecil Rhodes's home, designated by him to be the residence of the Premier. Most industries of C. centre round port activities, but the cultivation of fruit and flowers is also important. Pop. (1960) 731,484 (279,404 white).

CAPE VERDE ISLANDS. Archipelago belonging to Portugal in the Atlantic Ocean off the W. coast of Africa, about 350 m. W. of Cape Verde in Senegal, the most westerly cape of Africa. There are 10 inhabited islands, the largest and most populous being Santiago. The cap. is Praia. The population contains a large Negro element. A Portuguese dialect is spoken. Area 1,557 sq. m.; pop. (1960) 201,549.

CAPILLARY (Lat. *capillus,* a hair). One of the network of innumerable minute blood vessels situated between the small arteries and the small veins. Their size is about 8/1,000 of a millimetre. The term is also applied to any very fine-bore tube or cylindrical space of very small radius. C. pressure is pressure due to C. force, and capillarity deals with the effects of elevation or depression of fluids in fine Cs. the study of which throws much light on surface-tension phenomena, wetting of materials, soils, etc., and separation of gases through porous media.

CA'PITAL. In architecture, a stone placed on the top of a column, pier, or pilaster, and usually wider on the upper surface than the diameter of the supporting shaft. It consists of 3 parts: the top member called the *abacus,* a block which acts as the supporting surface to the superstructure; the middle portion known as the bell or *echinus;* and the lower part called the necking or *astragal. See* ORDER.

CAPITALISM. Name given to the economic system in which the principal means of production, distribution, and exchange are in private (individual or corporate) hands. Almost synonymous is 'private enterprise', since reliance is put on the enterprise of private individuals and business companies and firms for the satisfaction of the community's economic wants, and not on government and municipal activities. The 'profit motive' constitutes the prime stimulus to productive exertion, and the 'price mechanism' determines what things shall be made, in what quantities, and under what conditions. The rival system is Socialism or Communism, in which the State is the dominant factor.

CAPITAL PUNISHMENT. Punishment by death, a form of penalty common to all ages. In England at the end of the 18th cent. more than 200 offences, incl. petty theft, carried the death penalty, though in practice it was imposed only for some 25. From 1810 onwards Sir Samuel Romilly and others conducted a vigorous campaign for the mitigation of the penal laws; several acts were passed at intervals, each reducing the number of crimes liable to so drastic a penalty, until an act of 1861 left only murder, treason, piracy with violence, and the firing of government arsenals and dockyards punishable by death. Disuse abrogated its imposition for the last 2 offences and, except for a few executions for treason in time of war, all executions in Britain since 1838 have been for murder. Until 1866, they were carried out in public.

Under an act of 1931 no pregnant woman, and under one of 1933 no young person under 18, could be condemned to death. Agitation for the abolition of the death penalty led to the act of 1957, which introduced a distinction between 'capital' and 'non-capital' murders (committed in furtherance of theft; by shooting or some form of explosion; in resisting arrest or escaping from police custody; on a police or prison officer carrying out his duty) and others: execution was by hanging. In 1965 C.P. was abolished, initially for 5 years, and 'imprisonment for life' substituted.

In the U.S.A. there is no C.P. in 13 states: Alaska, Hawaii, Iowa, Maine, Michigan, Minnesota, New York (with exceptions), N. Dakota, Oregon, Rhode Island, Vermont, W. Virginia, and Wisconsin. In others it is imposed for first-degree murder, in some (e.g. Alabama, Georgia, Virginia) for rape, in some (e.g. Florida, Washington state) for kidnapping, in some (e.g. Kentucky, Texas) for armed robbery. Execution is by electrocution in 21; lethal gas in 9 hanging in 7; and in Utah by shooting or hanging.

Brazil, the Netherlands, and Norway are among countries which have abolished C.P.; New Zealand abolished it in 1941, reimposed it in 1950. In the U.S.S.R. crimes punishable by death (by shooting) incl. bribe-taking, theft and currency offences. France uses the guillotine (q.v.); Spain garrotting, a form of strangulation.

CAPONE (kapōn′), **Alphonse** (1898–1947). American gangster, called Al Capone, b. in Brooklyn, the son of an Italian barber. During the prohibition period C. built up a criminal organization in Chicago city. No charges could be sustained against him until 1931, when he received a 10-year sentence for evading the payment of income tax. He was released in 1939.

CAPORE'TTO. Village on the Isonzo, near to which in 1917 the Italians under Cadorna were defeated by the Austro-Germans under Below. Then in Hungary, it was in Italy from 1918 until

TRUMAN CAPOTE
Photo: J. R. Roustan.

trs. to Yugoslavia in 1947.

CAPOTE (kapō'tē), **Truman** (1924–). American novelist. B. in New Orleans, he uses a Southern setting in *The Grass Harp* (1951), etc., and set a trend in 'non-fiction' novels with *In Cold Blood* (1966), reconstructing a Kansas killing.

CAPP, Al. Pseudonym of the American cartoonist Alfred Caplin (1909–). B. in New Haven, Connecticut, he started his *Li'l Abner* strip in 1934 and the characters of the hillbilly community of Dogpatch, Kentucky, have passed into U.S. folklore.

CAPPADOCIA (kapadō'shia). In ancient geography, a mountainous district in the E. of Asia Minor bounded on the S. by the Taurus mts. and on the E. by the Euphrates.

CAPRA (kah'prah), **Frank** (1897–). American film director. Sicilian-born, but living in the U.S. from the age of 6, he won Oscars for such films as *Mr. Deeds Goes to Town* (1936) and *You Can't Take it With You* (1938), with sentimental, idealistic heroes.

CAPRI (kah'prē). Italian island at the S. entrance of the Bay of Naples, 20 m. S. of Naples. It has two towns, Capri and Anacapri, and is famous for its flowers, beautiful scenery, and ideal climate. Area 4 sq. m.; pop. about 8,000.

CAPRIVI (kahprē'vē), **Georg Leo**, Count von (1831–99). German Imperial Chancellor 1890–4.

CAPSICUM. Genus of plants of the nightshade family (Solanaceae), native of S. America. The fruit is exceedingly pungent, and is a source of cayenne pepper or red-pepper.

CAPSULE, SPACE. Vehicle launched by a rocket into space. It may be manned, in which case it contains all the instruments and accessories necessary for survival during launching, flight, re-entry into the atmosphere and recovery, or other projected programme.

CAPUA (kah'poo-ah). Italian town in Caserta province on the Volturno, in a fertile plain 27 m. N. of Naples. There was heavy fighting here in 1943 during the S.W.W., and the Romanesque cathedral was almost destroyed, Pop. (1960) 17,600.

CA'PUCHIN. A South American monkey (*Cebus*). Sometimes called the Sapajou. Some species have hairy 'cowls' on the forehead, thus giving rise to the popular name from a fancied resemblance to C. monks. They have prehensile tails used for climbing, and go about in troops, feeding on insects and fruit. The White-throated C. (*C. capucinus*) is a typical species; its head and body are about 18 in. long. The body is black with a white throat and cheeks.

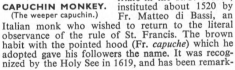

CAPUCHIN MONKEY.
(The weeper capuchin.)

CA'PUCHINS. Order of friars in the R.C. church, instituted about 1520 by Fr. Matteo di Bassi, an Italian monk who wished to return to the literal observance of the rule of St. Francis. The brown habit with the pointed hood (Fr. *capuche*) which he adopted gave his followers the name. It was recognized by the Holy See in 1619, and has been remarkable for its missionary activity. Despite stress on poverty and austerity, the order has attracted many members of the nobility. *See* FRANCISCANS.

CAPYBĀ'RA (*Hydrochaerus capybara*). The largest of the rodents and the only representative of the family Hydrochoeridae. It has scanty, coarse yellowish hair, and is about 4 ft. long with a large head and a very short tail, and may reach a weight of 100 lb. An expert swimmer, it herds in the forests of South America.

CA'RACAL (*Lynx caracal*). A species of wild cat, akin to the lynx. It lives in bush or desert country in Africa, Arabia, and India, where it was formerly tamed for the purpose of catching game. It is over 3 ft. long, has tufted blackish ears, and short fur, fawn above, and white with spots below.

CARACA'LLA, Marcus Aurelius Antoninus (A.D. 186–217). Roman emperor. He succeeded his father Septimius Severus in 211, ruled with great cruelty and ruinous extravagance, and was assassinated.

CARACAS (karah'kas). Chief city and cap. of Venezuela, on the Andean slopes, 11 m. by road S. of its port La Guaira on the Caribbean coast. It has many fine buildings. Founded 1560–67, it has several times suffered severely from earthquakes. Simon Bolivar was b. here. It makes cement, textiles, paper, tobacco, etc., and has an international airport. Pop. (1964) 1,000,000, metropolitan area 1,485,000.

CARAVAGGIO. Almost violent in its bold light and shadow and the dramatically posed figures, 'The Supper at Emmaus' is typical of the artist's powerful gifts.
Courtesy of the National Gallery.

CARA'CTACUS (d. *c.* A.D. 54). British chieftain, who resisted the Romans, A.D. 43–51, at the head of the tribes of S.E. Britain, but was defeated on the southern borders of Wales, and shown in Claudius's triumphal procession; in admiration for his courage Claudius released him, and he d. at Rome.

CA'RADON of St. Cleer, Hugh Foot, baron (1907–). British Labour politician, son of Isaac Foot (q.v.). As gov. of Cyprus 1957–60, he guided independence negotiations, was British representative on U.N. Trusteeship Council 1961–2 and in 1964 became Min. of State for Foreign Affairs and permanent British rep. at U.N., and was created a life peer.

CA'RAT. Unit of purity in gold. The carat implies a twenty-fourth part, and chemically pure gold is 24-carat. Jewellery is often composed of 22-carat or 18-carat gold, i.e. a mixture of 22 or 18 parts gold and 2 or 6 parts alloy. The metric C. of 0·200 grams is the unit of weight for diamonds and other precious stones.

CARAVAGGIO (kahrahvahd'jo), **Michelangelo Merisi da** (*c.* 1569–1609). Italian artist. B. at Caravaggio, near Milan, he developed a precocious talent and rapidly estab. a reputation for controversial realism. His life was equally adventurous—he killed a man in a brawl in 1606 and fled from Rome where the Cardinal del Monte had been his patron, working in Naples, Malta and Sicily. His works incl. 'The Supper at Emmaus' (National Gallery), 'The Entombment of Christ' (Vatican) and 'The Death of the Virgin' (Louvre).

CA'RAWAY. Genus of plants (*Carum*) of the family Umbelliferae. *C. carui*, of Europe and Asia, is cultivated for its fruit, known as C. seeds, which are aromatic and pungent, containing a volatile oil, and are used for flavouring and also in medicine.

CA'RBIDES. Compounds of carbon and one other chemical element, the 2nd element being a metal, silicon, or boron. They occupy an important place in chemical technology, particularly calcium C., which, as the generator of acetylene, acts as the starting-point of many basic organic syntheses. In recent years some metallic Cs. have come to hold a place of great importance in engineering technology on account of their extreme hardness and strength. The C. of tungsten and its ore, wolfram, is an essential ingredient of metallic C. tools as well as of ordinary high-speed tools.

CARBOHYDRATES. A group of compounds composed of carbon, hydrogen, and oxygen. On decomposition the Cs. yield water and a residue of carbon. Cs. include sugars – soluble crystalline compounds with a sweet taste; starches – more complex compounds, usually non-crystalline, and insoluble in cold water; and cellulose, which is fibrous and can be woven into textiles. Cs. form the chief foodstuffs of herbivorous animals.

CARBOLIC ACID. Phenol, C_6H_5OH. Extracted from coal tar, pure C.A. consists of colourless crystals, needle-shaped, which readily take up moisture from the atmosphere. The taste is pungent and slightly sweet and the smell strong and characteristic. It is a powerful and penetrating antiseptic, but because of its poisonous properties it is not now much used on human tissues. It is a strong disinfectant.

CARBON. Symbol C, at. wt. 12·011, at. no. 6. One of the most widely distributed non-metallic elements. It occurs free in nature as diamond and graphite (crystalline forms), in carbonaceous rocks such as chalk and limestone, as carbon dioxide in the atmosphere, as hydrocarbons in petroleum, coal and natural gas and as a constituent of all organic substances. *See* ORGANIC CHEMISTRY. In its amorphous form it is familiar as coke, charcoal, soot, etc.

Of the inorganic C. compounds, the most important is *carbon dioxide* (CO_2), a colourless gas with a very slightly acid taste, which is formed wherever C. is burned in an adequate supply of air. *Carbon monoxide* (CO) is formed whenever C. is oxidized in a limited supply of air. It is combustible, does not form an acid solution in water, and is tasteless. It is very poisonous owing to the stable compound it forms with the blood haemoglobin; it is the poisonous constituent of coal gas and motor-car exhaust fumes. *Carbon disulphide* (CS_2), a dense liquid with a sweetish odour, is the sulphur compound corresponding to the oxygen compound C. dioxide. An important group of compounds is known as the *carbon halides*, of which C. tetrachloride (CCl_4) is the best-known. Being non-inflammable it is used in certain fire appliances, but as it reacts with oxygen at high temperatures to produce phosgene ($COCl_2$), a poisonous war gas, the fumes are dangerous.

When added to steel C. forms a wide range of C. steels with useful properties. In pure form it is widely used as a moderator in nuclear reactors; as colloidal graphite (Dag, Aquadag) it is a good lubricant and, when deposited on a surface in a vacuum, obviates photoelectric and secondary emission of electrons. In the form of coal or coke (q.v.) C. is a widespread fuel. The isotope carbon-14 is greatly used as a tracer in biological research, since plants can be grown in an

CARDIFF. The pride of the city, in Cathays Park, the magnificent civic buildings, including the City Hall (1906) and the National Museum of Wales.
Photo: British Travel and Holidays Association.

atmosphere containing radioactive C. in carbon dioxide, which passes into chemicals derived from the plant and hence becomes a 'label'. Carbon-14 is also useful for dating, as in archaeology, e.g. on death wood ceases to take up carbon-14 from the air and that already taken up decays at a known rate, allowing the time which has elapsed to be measured.

Carbon fibres—fine, black, silky filaments produced by heat treatment from a special grade of Courtelle and bonded by resin—were developed at the Royal Aircraft Establishment, Farnborough, 1964–5. Light, wear-resistant, cheap to produce, and up to 8 times as strong as high-tensile steel, they are vital in the aerospace, car and electricity industries, manufacture of sports gear, etc.

CARBONARI (kahrbonah're). A political secret revolutionary society in southern Italy in the first half of the 19th cent. The first members were republican rebels against Murat, the Bonapartist king of Naples, who took refuge in the Abruzzi and called themselves C. ('charcoal burners'). Subsequently the C. rose more than once against the Bourbon king; and though driven underground, played a part in Mazzini's 'Young Italy' movement.

CA'RBONATES. Important group of minerals formed by the combination of carbon dioxide with a basic element. The carbon dioxide dissolved by rain falling through the air, and also liberated by decomposing animals and plants in the soil, forms with water carbonic acid, which unites with various alkaline basic substances to form Cs. Of these, calcium carbonate ($CaCO_3$) is the most important.

CARBORUNDUM. Silicon carbide (SiC). A hard black artificial compound of carbon and silicon, discovered in 1891 by E. G. Acheson. It is harder than corundum but not so hard as diamond.

CARBUNCLE. A mass formed by a cluster of boils, or a garnet cut to resemble it in the shape of a rounded knob.

CARBURATION. Regular combustion, usually in a closed space, of carbon compounds such as petrol, paraffin, or fuel oil; regulated combustion is distinct from much more rapid burning such as explosion or detonation, and the definition applies particularly to combustion in the cylinders of reciprocating petrol engines of the types used in aircraft, road vehicles, or marine vessels. The device by which the liquid fuel is prepared for combustion is termed the *carburetter*.

CARCASSONNE (kahrkahson'). City of S.W. France, cap. of Aude dept., on the r. Aude, which divides it into the ancient and modern town. Its medieval fortifications (much restored) are the finest in France. Pop. (1962) 43,709.

CARCHEMISH (kahr′k-). Ancient city on the right bank of the upper Euphrates, 50 m. N.E. of Aleppo, once the centre of a Neo-Hittite empire and in 605 B.C. the scene of a battle between Nebuchadnezzar and the Egyptians. On its site is the Turkish village of Karkamis; nearby on the Syrian side of the frontier is Jerablus.

CA′RDAN, Girolamo (1501–76). Italian physician, mathematician, philosopher, and astrologer, B. at Pavia, he became professor of medicine there in 1543, and wrote 2 important works on physics and natural science—*De subtilitate rerum* (1551) and *De varietate rerum* (1557).

CÁRDENAS, Lazaro (1895–). Mexican general and statesman. In early life a civil servant, he took part in the revolutionary campaigns 1915–29 that followed the fall of President Diaz, was President of the republic 1934–40, and introduced many Socialist measures. He was Min. of National Defence 1943–5.

CARDIFF. Capital of Wales and county town of Glamorganshire, on the Taff, with docks on the Bristol Channel. It is essentially a modern city, its importance dating from the opening of the docks in 1839. It also has an airport.

C.'s development was greatly helped by the 2nd marquess of Bute (1793–1848) and his trustees who extended the docks. The prosperity of this, one of the largest industrial and commercial centres of the British Isles, was built up on its coal export trade which in 1839 amounted to 165,880 tons, in 1913 to 10½ million tons. This trade began to decline in the 1920s and virtually ceased during the S.W.W., facing Cardiff's people with a serious struggle. Iron and steel exports continued to be extensive, and C.'s import trade grew, chief imports being timber, grain and flour, meat, tobacco. Industries include ship repairing, flour-milling, engineering, and the manufacture of paper, iron and steel goods, and enamel ware.

C. dates from Roman times, the later town being built round the Norman castle: this, the residence of earls and marquesses of Bute from the 18th cent., was given to the city in 1947 by the 5th marquess. In Cathays Park is a group of public buildings including the law courts and city hall, the Welsh national museum, registry of the university of Wales, Glamorgan county hall, Cardiff technical college and the university college of S. Wales, offices of the Welsh board of health, the Welsh national war memorial, and the Temple of Peace and Health. St. John's Church has a perpendicular tower. C. is the seat of an R.C. archbishopric. Llandaff, on the right bank of the Taff, seat of a bishopric from the 6th cent., was included in C. in 1922; its cathedral, virtually rebuilt in the 19th cent. and badly damaged in a German air raid, 1941, was restored 1948–57. It has a giant figure of 'Christ in Majesty' by Epstein. *See* illus. p. 396.

Constituted a county borough in 1888, made a city with a lord mayor by royal charter in 1905, C. was named capital of Wales in 1955. Area 28 sq. m.; pop. (1961) 256,270.

CARDIGAN. Cap. of Cardigan co., S. Wales, 3 m. from the mouth of the Teifi. The port is now little used. The Teifi has salmon fisheries. Pop. (1961) 3,780.

CARDIGANSHIRE. Welsh county, facing Cardigan Bay. It is mainly mountainous, rising to Plynlimmon (2,468 ft.) in the N.E., and is drained by the Rheidol, Ystwyth, Teifi, and Towy. The industries include salmon and longshore fishing, sheep rearing, woollens, and some agriculture. The co. has some fine scenery. Cardigan is the co. town; other towns are Lampeter and Aberystwyth. Area 692 sq. m.; pop (1961) 53,564.

CARDINAL. In the R.C. church, the highest dignitary next to the Pope. Originally a C. was any priest in charge of a major parish; but in 1567 the term was confined to the members of the Sacred College, and in 1586 their number was limited to 70 by Sixtus V, increased to over 125 under John XXIII and Paul VI. The Cs. assist the Pope in liturgical matters and in the temporal business of the Church, give their advice in all matters of doctrine, canonizations, and convocation of councils, and are responsible for electing the Pope from amongst their number. They are nominated and elected by the Pope and must come to Rome for the ceremony within a year, to receive the red hat which is the badge of office.

CARDUCCI (kahrdooch′ē), **Giosuè** (1835–1907). Italian poet. B. in Tuscany, he was appointed in 1860 professor of Italian literature at Bologna, and won a distinguished place by his lecturing and critical work, and also as a poet. His *Inno a Satana* (Hymn to Satan, 1865) was full of revolutionary feeling, and was followed by several other vols. of verse, in which his nationalist sympathies are apparent. He was awarded the Nobel prize for literature in 1906.

CA′RDUS, Sir Neville (1889–). British writer on music and cricket. B. in Manchester, he was a cricket professional at Shrewsbury school 1912–16, and was on the *Guardian* staff 1917–39 and from 1951. His books incl. an autobiography and a study of his friend of Sir Thomas Beecham (1961). Knighted 1967.

CARDWELL, Edward, visct. (1813–86). British Liberal statesman. He entered Parliament as a Peelite in 1842, and 1868–74 was Sec. for War under Gladstone, when he carried out many reforms, including the abolition of the purchase of military commissions and promotions.

CAREW (kār′i), **Thomas** (1595?–1638?). English poet. B. in Kent, he was in 1628 a gentleman of the privy chamber to Charles I, and was the most brilliant lyrist as well as the most deliberate and finished craftsman of the school of 'Cavalier Poets'.

CAREY, Henry (*c.* 1690–1743). British poet and musician, remembered for the song 'Sally in Our Alley'. 'God Save the King' (both words and music) has also been attributed to him.

CARICATURE. George IV – 'A Voluptuary under the Horrors of Digestion' by James Gillray.
Photo: Radio Times Hulton Picture Library.

CAREY, William (1761–1834). British missionary. An apprentice shoemaker, largely self-educated, he became a Baptist minister in 1786 and helped to found the Baptist Missionary Society in 1792. Going out to India in 1793, he founded a mission at Serampore in 1799, and was oriental prof. at Fort William College, Calcutta, 1801–30. He compiled dictionaries and grammars of many Indian languages and translated portions of the Bible into nearly 40 languages and dialects.

CARIBBE′AN. A sea forming that part of the Atlantic Ocean lying between the N. coasts of S. and Central America and the W. Indies, c. 1,700 m. long and 400 to 900 m. in width; here the Gulf Stream turns in the direction of Europe. Since the opening of the Panama Canal, the C. has become of great importance. It is named from the Caribs.

CARIBOU. See REINDEER.

CARIBS. Name given by Columbus to an aboriginal people of S. America and the islands of the W. Indies in the Caribbean Sea. They were cannibals, distinguished for their ferocity. In 1796 the English in the W. Indies deported most of them to Roatan Island off Honduras. They have since spread extensively in Honduras and Nicaragua. Reddish brown in colour, their features are mongoloid.

CARICATURE. The representation of persons or things by exaggerating characteristic features in such a way as to provoke ridicule or contempt. The word first came into use in England in its Italian form *caricatura* (from It. *caricare*, to exaggerate) c. 1680.

C. was not unknown to the Greeks and Romans. Grotesque drawings have been discovered in Pompeii and Herculaneum, and Pliny refers to a grotesque portrait of the poet Hipponax. Humorous drawings were executed by the Carracci and their followers (the Italian 'eclectic' school of the 16th cent.). Pictorial satire was common in England during the Civil War, but true C. begins with Hogarth: later exponents incl. Gillray, Rowlandson, Cruikshank, John and Richard Doyle, Leech, du Maurier, Tenniel, Phil May, Beerbohm, David Low, 'Vicky', 'Giles', Cummings, and Osbert Lancaster in England, and Jules Feiffer, Herb Block, Bill Mauldin and Saul Steinberg in the U.S.A. *See* illus. p. 213.

Charles Philipon (1800–62) founded in Paris in 1830 *La Caricature*, probably the 1st periodical to specialize in C.: notable later was *Punch* 1841.

CARINA′TAE. One of the two divisions into which the living members of the class Aves (Birds, q.v.) are divided. It includes all those which have a keel (Lat. *carina*) on the breastbone. These are the vast majority of the class, comprising all flying birds and the penguins.

CARINTHIA. An Alpine prov. of Austria, bordering on Italy and Yugoslavia in the S. Klagenfurt is the capital. Area 3,681 sq. m.; pop. (1961) 493,972.

CARISBROOKE. Village in the Isle of Wight, 1 m. S.W. of Newport, of which it is now a part. Its chief feature is the ruins of the castle in which Charles I was imprisoned (1647–8).

CARLILE (karlīl′), **Richard** (1790–1843). British Radical. His publication of the works of Paine (q.v.) and similar writers earned him successive prison sentences totalling more than 9 years, but though his

CARISBROOKE. Much of the castle has been restored, but the apartments where Charles I was imprisoned 1647–8 are still a ruin. Above can be seen the window, still largely in its original state, from which he made his second attempt at escape.
Photo: Central Office of Information.

THOMAS CARLYLE. By Sir J. E. Millais.
Photo: N.P.G.

stock was repeatedly seized he continued to publish, and issued his periodical *The Republican* from Dorchester gaol. He rendered great service to the cause of the freedom of the Press.

CARLILE, Wilson. *See* CHURCH ARMY.

CARLISLE (karlīl′). City (co. bor.) and county town of Cumberland, England, on the Eden, 8 m. S. of the Scottish border. It is an important railway centre; textiles, engineering, and biscuit making are the chief industries. The outstanding buildings are the cathedral and the castle, both dating from Norman times, but subsequently much added to. The bishopric dates from 1133. Pop. (1961) 71,112.

CARLISTS. Supporters of the Spanish pretender, Don Maria Isidro Carlos de Bourbon (1788–1855), who claimed the throne on the death of his brother Ferdinand VII in 1833, in opposition to his niece Maria Isabella who had been proclaimed queen. There ensued fighting between the Royalists, representing the more liberal elements, and the Carlists, particularly in the Basque provinces, and the revolt was not suppressed until 1839. Under successive descendants of Don Carlos the Cs. have continued to this day.

CARLOS I (1863–1908). King of Portugal, of the Braganza-Coburg line, from 1889 until he was assassinated in Lisbon with his elder son Luis. He was succeeded by his younger son Manoel.

CARLOS, Don (1545–68). Spanish prince. Son of Philip II, he was recognized as heir to the thrones of Castile and Aragon, but became a lunatic and had to be placed under restraint following a plot to assassinate his father. His story was made the subject of plays by Schiller, Alfieri, Otway, and others.

CARLOS, Don Juan (1938–). Heir to the pretender to the Spanish throne. In 1962 he m. Princess Sophia, eldest dau. of King Paul of the Hellenes. It is thought that he, rather than his father, Prince Juan, will eventually succeed to the throne, which Franco has said he will restore. *See* table under BOURBON.

CARLOW. Co. of Rep. of Ireland, in the prov. of Leinster. In the S. there is a long range of heights, rising to 2,610 ft. in Mt. Leinster, but the rest of the co. is a low-lying and undulating plain. The soil, watered by the Barrow and the Slaney, is fertile and dairy farming is important. The co. town is also C. Area 346 sq. m.; pop. (1966) 33,539.

CARLSBAD. German name of KARLOVY VARY.

CARLYLE, Thomas (1795–1881). Scottish author. B. at Ecclefechan in Dumfriesshire, he accepted a mathematical mastership at Annan in 1814, studying meanwhile for the Presbyterian ministry. In 1816 he transferred to Kirkcaldy where he met Edward Irving, and in 1818 to Edinburgh where, having given up thought of the Church, he combined study of the law with miscellaneous literary work. In 1821 he passed through the spiritual crisis described in *Sartor Resartus*, and after a period as a tutor secured the publication in London of his life of Schiller (1825), and a translation of Goethe's *Wilhelm Meister* (1824). He had first met Jane Baillie Welsh (1801–66) in 1821, and after their marriage in 1826 they moved to her farm at isolated Craigenputtock, where *Sartor Resartus* (1836) was written. In 1834 they removed to Cheyne Row, Chelsea, and in 1837 he established his reputation with the *French Revolution*, still unrivalled in vividness of narration. Of the series of lectures he gave (1837–40), the most successful were those *On Heroes, Hero-Worship, and the Heroic in History* (1841). At this period he also wrote *Chartism* (1839), attacking the doctrine of *laissez-faire*; *Past and Present* (1843), a comparison of labour in the 13th and the 19th cents.; and *Latter-Day Pamphlets* (1850), a criticism of popular government. The notable *Letters and Speeches of Cromwell* (1845) was followed by the miniature life of his friend *John Sterling* (1851). C. then began his monumental *History of Frederick the Great* (1858–65), and in the year of its completion was elected rector of Edinburgh university. After the death of his wife in 1866 he devoted most of his time to editing her letters and preparing the *Reminiscences*. The publication of these (in 1883 and 1881 respectively), and of the biography by Froude, caused a public outcry because of the rather unfavourable light thrown on C.'s character.

CARMAN, William Bliss (1861–1929). Canadian lyric poet. B. in New Brunswick, he became a journalist. His first vol. of verse, *Low Tide on Grand Pré*, attracted considerable attention in 1893. It was followed by *Songs from Vagabondia* (1894), *Ballads oj Lost Haven* (1897), and many more.

CARMA'RTHEN. Co. town (bor.) of Carmarthenshire, S. Wales, on the Towy, 8 m. from its mouth. It is a small port and a railway junction; parts of a Norman castle are incorporated in the co. gaol here. C. makes ropes and woollens. Pop. (1961) 13,249.

CARMARTHENSHIRE. County of S. Wales, bordering on the Bristol Channel; it is the largest co. in the principality. The N. and E. are hilly and wooded, with fertile valleys. Arable and pastoral farming are carried on. In the S.E. the Loughor valley has valuable anthracite seams, and Llanelly and Ammanford are engaged in coal- and iron-mining, tin-plate and other works. The Towy, Teifi, and Taf are the chief rivers. The co. town is Carmarthen; other towns are Kidwelly, Llandovery, Cwmamman. Area 919 sq. m.; pop (1961) 167,736.

CARMELITES or **White Friars.** Religious order of mendicants in the R.C. church. Traditionally they originated in the days of Elijah, who is supposed to have lived on Mt. Carmel in Palestine. Historically the first congregation was founded on Carmel by Berthold, a crusader from Calabria, about 1155. According to the rule which the patriarch of Jerusalem drew up for them about 1210, they lived as hermits in separate huts. About 1240 the Saracen conquests compelled them to move from Palestine, and they took root in the west, particularly in France and England, where the order became cenobitical and mendicant. There were many reform movements in the order's history, of which the most important was that initiated by St. Theresa. In 1562 she founded in Avila a convent where the rule was stricter than that hitherto observed, and with the co-operation of St. John of the Cross and others she established priories and further nunneries, whose members were called the Discalced or bare-footed Cs., to distinguish them from the senior branch of the Calced Cs. The Cs. have devoted themselves largely to missionary work and mystical theology. Their habit consists of a brown tunic with a white overmantle.

CARMO'NA, Antonio Oscar de Fragoso (1869–1951). Portuguese general and statesman. In 1926 he became P.M. and virtual dictator, and from 1928 he was Pres. of the Portuguese republic, being re-elected in 1935, 1942, and 1949.

CARNAC (kahrnahk'). Village in the dept. of Morbihan, France, 17 m. S.E. of Lorient. In the neighbourhood there is a fine collection of megalithic remains of the period 2000–1500 B.C., incl. various types of tomb and a series of stone alignments. In the largest of the 3 latter (Menec) well over 1,000 stones (2 to 13 ft. high) are arranged in 11 rows with a circle at the W. end. They were obviously used for processions, possibly linked with rituals for the dead. Pop. (1962) 3,641.

CA'RNAP, Rudolf (1891–). American philosopher, the world's foremost exponent of logical empiricism. B. at Wuppertal, Germany, he was a member of the Vienna Circle who adopted Mach (q.v.) as their guide, and in 1935 went to the U.S., where he was prof. of philosophy at the Univ. of California 1954–62. His books incl. *The Logical Syntax of Language* (1934), and *Meaning and Necessity* (1956).

CARNARVON, CARNARVONSHIRE. *See* CAERNARVON, CAERNARVONSHIRE.

CARNATION. Name given to the numerous double-flowered cultivated varieties of the clove-pink (*Dianthus caryophyllus*). They are divided into flake, bizarre, and picotees, according as the petals exhibit one or more colours on their white ground, or have it dispersed in strips, or as a border to the petals.

CARNÉ (kahrneh'), **Marcel** (1909–). French film director. A master of subtle depths of characterization, his films incl. *Quai des brumes* (1938), *Le Jour se lève*, and *Les Enfants du Paradis* (1944).

CARNEGIE (kahrneg'i), **Andrew** (1835–1919). Scottish-American millionaire. B. at Dunfermline, he was taken by his parents to U.S.A. in 1848, and at 14 became a telegraph boy in Pittsburg. Subsequently he became a railway employee, rose to be superintendent, and by the introduction of sleeping-cars and successful investments in oil, laid the foundations of a fortune. Next he concerned himself with the development of the Pittsburgh iron and steel industries, and built up a vast 'empire' which he disposed of to the U.S. Steel Trust in 1901. From that time he lived at Skibo castle in Sutherland, and devoted his wealth to philanthropic purposes, notably the provision and equipment of libraries, the endowment of universities, the Carnegie Hero Fund, etc. On his death the C. Trusts continued his benevolent activities. *Carnegie Hall* in New York, opened 1891 as The Music Hall, was renamed in 1898 in recognition of his large contribution to its construction.

CARNEGIE, Dale (1888–1955). American author and teacher. B. in Missouri, he planned a teaching career, but tried journalism and the stage before becoming Y.M.C.A. instructor on public speaking. An instant success, he achieved world fame with *How to Win Friends and Influence People* (1938).

CARNIOLA. A former crownland and duchy of Austria, most of which was included in Slovenia, part of the kingdom of the Serbs, Croats, and Slovenes (later Yugoslavia) in 1919. The westerly districts of Idrija and Postojna, then allocated to Italy, were transferred to Yugoslavia in 1947.

CARNI'VORA. An order of the mammalia, whose members are flesh eaters—though they are not the only animals which eat flesh and some of them are omnivorous or largely herbivorous. They are classified by variations in the skull and skeleton, the teeth, and various external features. There are 2 sub-orders, the Pinnipedia and the Fissipedia.

The *Fissipedia*, which are terrestrial, semi-arboreal, or amphibious, are sub-divided into 2 tribes, the Arctoidea and the Aeluroidea. The Arctoidea include the families of Ursidae or bears; the Canidae or dogs, wolves and foxes; the Procyonidae containing such dissimilar mammals as the racoon, coatimundi, kinkajou, and cacomistle; the Mustelidae including the otters, skunks and badgers, weasels and polecats; the Ailuropodidae containing the giant panda; the Ailuridae (common panda). The Aeluroidae incl. the Felidae or cats; the Hyaenidae comprising the hyaenas and aard-wolf; the Herpestidae containing the mongooses and suricates, the Cryptoproctidae containing only the fossa; the Viverridae containing the civets, genets, lingsangs, palm civets, binturong.

The 2nd sub-order, the *Pinnipedia*, with the limbs

paddle-like in adaptation to a marine habitat, is composed of modified descendants of the terrestrial Arctoid Fissipedia. They fall into 2 main groups. The first contains the Otariidae or sea-lions, and the Odobaenidae or walruses. The 2nd group is composed of the family Phocidae or true seals.

The geographical distribution of the C. is worldwide but for Australia and New Zealand, and our domestic pets include two typical representatives in the dog and the cat.

CARNOT (kahrnō'), **Lazare** (1753–1823). French general. He joined the army as an engineer, and at the Revolution earned the title of 'Organizer of victory', since he not only reformed French fighting methods, but also introduced efficient systems of supplying munitions, clothing, and especially food, to the troops. After the coup d'état of 1797 he went abroad, but returned in 1799 and was made War Minister 1800–1. In 1814 as gov. of Antwerp he put up a brilliantly successful defence. Minister of the Interior during the Hundred Days, he was proscribed at the Restoration and retired to Magdeburg, where he d. His great work on fortification (*De la défense de places fortes*, 1810) became a military textbook.

C.'s elder son, **Nicolas Leonard Sadi C.** (1796–1832), was the founder of thermodynamics. *See* C. CYCLE.

CARNOT, Marie Françoise Sadi (1837–94). French President. Grandson of Lazare Carnot, he entered the government service, was returned to the Assembly for Côte d'Or in 1871, and in 1887 was elected President. He successfully countered the Boulangist movement, and in 1892 the scandals arising out of French financial activities in Panama. He was assassinated by an Italian anarchist at Lyons.

CARNOT CYCLE. For a reversible heat engine a C.C. consists of the following changes, in the order stated, in the physical condition of a gas: (1) isothermal expansion (i.e. without change of temperature), (2) adiabatic expansion (i.e. without change of heat content), (3) isothermal compression and (4) adiabatic compression. The principles derived from a study of this cycle are important in the fundamentals of heat and thermodynamics. The absolute scale of temperature is based on this cycle.

CAROB TREE. Small tree of the Mediterranean region (*Ceratonia siliqua*), often called locust tree. The 8-in. pods are used as animal fodder and have been suggested as the 'husks' of the Prodigal Son and the 'locusts' eaten by John the Baptist in the wilderness.

CAROL I (1839–1914). King of Rumania. A prince of the house of Hohenzollern-Sigmaringen, he was invited to become Prince of Rumania, then under Turkish suzerainty, in 1866. In 1877, in alliance with Russia, he declared war on Turkey, and the treaty of Berlin recognized Rumanian independence; in 1881 C. was crowned king.

CAROL II (1893–1953). King of Rumania. Son of King Ferdinand, he m. Princess Helen of Greece, who bore him a son, Michael. In 1925 he renounced the succession, and settled in Paris with his mistress, Mme. Lupescu. Michael succeeded to the throne in 1927, but in 1930 C. returned to Rumania and was proclaimed king. In 1938 he introduced a new constitution under which he became practically absolute. He was forced to abdicate by the pro-German Iron Guard in Sept. 1940, and withdrew to Mexico with Mme. Lupescu, whom he m. in 1947.

CAROL. Originally a song associated with a round dance, the term came later to be applied to popular songs (as distinct from hymns) associated with the great annual festivals, such as May Day, the New Year, Easter, and Christmas.

Christmas Cs. were popular as early as the 15th cent. The custom of singing Cs. from house to house, collecting gifts, was associated with 'wassailing'. Many of the best-known Cs., such as 'God rest you

merry' and 'Noel', date back at least as far as the 16th cent. Others, such as 'Good King Wenceslas', have modern words but an ancient tune, and yet others are completely modern.

CAROLINA. *See* NORTH C. and SOUTH C.

CAROLINE OF ANSPACH (1683–1737). Queen of George II of Great Britain. The dau. of the Margrave of Brandenburg-Anspach, she m. George, Electoral Prince of Hanover, in 1705, and followed him to England in 1714 when his father became king as George I. As Princess of Wales she held a separate court at Leicester House and was the patron of many of the leading writers and politicians.

CAROLINE OF BRUNSWICK (1768–1821). Queen of George IV of Great Britain. Second dau. of Charles William, duke of Brunswick, and Augusta, sister of George III, she m. her first cousin the Prince of Wales in 1795, but following the birth of the Princess Charlotte a separation was arranged. When her husband ascended the throne in 1820 she was offered an annuity of £50,000 provided she agreed to renounce the title of queen and to continue to live abroad. She returned forthwith to London, where she assumed royal state. In July 1820 the Government brought in a bill to dissolve the royal marriage, but Lord Brougham's splendid defence led to the bill's abandonment. On July 19, 1821, she was prevented by royal order from entering Westminster Abbey for the coronation. She d. on Aug. 7, and her funeral was the occasion of popular riots.

CAROLINES. Scattered archipelago in Micronesia, Pacific Ocean, consisting of more than 500 coral islets, with a total area of 463 sq. m. The chief islands are Ponape, Kusai, and Truk in the eastern group and Yap and Palau in the western. They are well watered and productive. German from 1899, occupied by Japan 1914, and mandated by the League of Nations to that country in 1919, they were fortified, contrary to the terms of the mandate. Under Allied air attack in the S.W.W., they were not conquered. In 1947 they became part of the U.S. Trust Terr. of the Pacific Is. (q.v.). Pop. (1967) 61,500.

CAROLINGIANS. Frankish dynasty descending from Pepin the Short (d. 768) and named after his son Charles the Great (Charlemagne). The last of the Cs. was Louis V who reigned in France 966–87, and was followed by Hugh Capet.

CARO'SSA, Hans (1878–1956). German poet and novelist. B. at Bad Tölz in Bavaria, he became a physician like his father. His poetry, collected in 1938, and his novels *Eine Kindheit* (1922: *A Childhood*), *Der Arzt Gion* (1931: *Doctor Gion*) and *Rumanisches Tagebuch* (1924: *Rumanian Diary*) are stages in an autobiographical confession.

CARP. A genus of fresh-water fishes (*Cyprinus*) of the family Cyprinidae. *C. carpio*, the common species, found in most parts of Europe and Asia, has large scales, a long dorsal fin, and 4 barbels on its mouth. It prefers still waters, and is much esteemed as a food.

COMMON CARP

CARPACCIO (kahrpah'chō), **Vittorio** (*c.* 1465–1522). Venetian painter. His principal works were painted between 1490 and 1519, and are in Venice.

CARPATHIANS. A mountain chain of Central Europe, forming a great semicircle from the Bohemian massif, girdling the Hungarian Plain, to Orsova (90 m. E. of Belgrade) on the Danube. The total length is about 900 m.

CARPENTA'RIA. A great, shallow gulf opening out of the Arafura Sea on the N. of Australia, was discovered by Tasman in 1606 and named in 1623 in honour of Pieter Carpentier, Governor-General of

CARPET. The finest carpets in the world are the Persian, hand-tufted in the traditional manner (left). The closest machine-made type is the Axminster, seen (right) being manufactured on a wide gripper loom, which is also made of tufts inserted in the fabric, though these are bound down and not knotted.
Courtesy of the Wilton Royal Carpet Factory.

the Dutch East Indies. There is an Anglican bishop of C. with his seat on Thursday Is., Queensland.

CARPENTIER (kahrpaṅtyā'), **Georges** (1894–). French boxer. He worked in a coal mine as a boy, won the French boxing championship in every weight and division, knocked out Joe Beckett in 1919, held the world's light heavyweight championship 1920–2, and in 1921 was beaten by Jack Dempsey in New York.

CARPET. Thick textile fabric, generally made of wool, used for covering floors, stairs, etc. The earliest known Cs. are those excavated at Passypych in S.E. Siberia by Rudenko and date from *c.* 500 B.C., but it was not until the later Middle Ages that Cs. reached Western Europe from Turkey, Cardinal Wolsey being an eager buyer. Persian Cs., which reached a still unrivalled peak of artistry in the 15th and 16th cents., were rare in Britain until the mid-19th cent., reaching America a little later. The subsequent demand led to a revival of organized C.-making in Persia. Other countries with a long tradition of fine carpets are India, Pakistan, and China. Europe copied oriental technique, but developed western designs: France produced beautiful work at the Savonnerie and Beauvais establishments under Louis XIV and XV, and Exeter, Axminster, London and Wilton became famous British centres in the 18th cent., though Kidderminster is the biggest centre

CARPATHIANS. The highest group of the central Carpathians, the Tatra Mountains, lie partly on Czechoslovakia's northern frontier and partly in Poland. Štrbské Pleso Lake, 4,000 ft. above sea-level, is a popular Czech holiday resort.
Courtesy of the Czechoslovak Travel Bureau.

today. The 1st C. factory in the U.S.A. was estab. at Philadelphia, still a large producing centre, in 1791.

The 3 main types of machine-made Cs. today are the 'Wilton', remarkable for its fine, close texture and lending itself to design effects; the 'Axminster' which economizes in material, each tuft being on the surface with none hidden in the fabric as with 'Wilton'; and the 'tufted' Cs. The last-named are a postwar development, making wide use of the new synthetic fibres: the pile threads are looped through a hessian backing to which they are then anchored by a layer of rubber compound in the form of latex. Tufted Cs., originally inferior in quality and design now rival the traditionally woven Cs., and the latter have adopted the foam rubber and other backings first developed to give resilience, etc. to tufted types.

Cs. and rugs have also often been made in the home as a pastime, cross and tent stitch on canvas being widely used in the 18th and 19th cents.: famous among modern Cs. of this type were those produced by Queen Mary, consort of George V.

CARPET-BAGGER. Name given in U.S. history to the disreputable politicians and office seekers from the North who swarmed into the Southern States following the Civil War of 1861–5 and in co-operation with the local white riffraff (the 'scallawags'), and the Negroes, established governments which were a by-word for oppression and corruption. They were so called because they were supposed to own no property but what they carried in their carpet-bags.

CARPINI (kahrpē'nē), **Johannes de Plano** (*c.* 1182–1252). Franciscan friar and traveller. In 1245 Pope Innocent IV placed him in charge of a fact-finding mission to Mongolia, from which he returned in 1247. His history of the Mongols is a valuable piece of practical research.

CARRACCI (kahrah'chē). Three Italian painters who founded the eclectic school of painting, i.e. those who studied the works of the great masters and chose what they considered to be the chief merits of each and combined those in their own works. **Lodovico C.** (1555–1619), who lived at Bologna, was the initiator of the school. His nephews, **Agostino C.** (1557–1602) and **Annibale C.** (1560–1609), helped him in his work. The school is particularly well represented in Bologna.

CARRA'NZA, Venustiano (1859–1920). Mexican statesman. In 1917 he was elected President and during the F.W.W. kept his country neutral. He was killed in a revolution.

CARRARA (kahrah'rah). Italian town in the Apennines, 37 m. N.N.W. of Leghorn, with quarries of the finest white marble in the world. These were

worked by the Romans, abandoned in the 5th cent.
A.D., came into use again with the revival of sculpture
and architecture in the 12th cent. C. has a 13th cent.
Gothic church. Pop. (1951) 60,287.

CARREL (kahrel'), **Alexis** (1873–1944). French
surgeon and biologist, who emigrated to America
and in 1906 joined the New York staff of the Rockefeller Institute for Medical Research, winning the
Nobel prize in 1912 for his success in the surgery of
blood-vessels. Besides a number of medical books he
wrote *Man, the Unknown* (1935).

CARRHAE (kar'ē). Ancient town of N.W. Meso-
potamia in modern Turkey, called Haran in the O.T.
(Gen. 12), and scene of a battle in 53 B.C. in which a
Roman army under Crassus was wiped out by the
Parthians.

CARRICKFERGUS. Ancient market town and
seaport on Belfast Lough, Antrim, N. Ireland, 10 m.
N.E. of Belfast. Pop. (1961) 10,187.

CARRIER (kahryā'), **Jean Baptiste** (1756–94).
French revolutionary whose name is chiefly associated with the massacre of some 16,000 prisoners in a
few months, at Nantes. He was guillotined.

CARROLL, Lewis. Pseudonym of Charles Lut-
widge Dodgson (1832–98), mathematician and writer
of children's books. B. at Daresbury, Cheshire, he
became a lecturer on mathematics at Oxford and
published under his own name books on mathematics.
Alice's Adventures in Wonderland, under the pseudonym of L.C., appeared in 1865, and quickly became
popular. It grew out of a story told by Dodgson to
amuse 3 little girls, including the original 'Alice',
the dau. of Dean Liddell, Dean of Christ Church.
During his lifetime Dodgson refused to acknowledge
any connection with any books not pub. under his
own name, but a sequel, *Through the Looking Glass*,
followed in 1872. Among later works was the mock-
heroic nonsense poem 'The Hunting of the Snark'
(1876).

CARROLL, Paul Vincent (1900–68). Irish dramatist. B. nr. Dundalk, he became a schoolmaster
in Glasgow in 1921, where he helped to found the
Citizens' Theatre. His first play, *Watched Pot* (1931),
was followed by *Things That Are Caesar's* which won
a prize at the Abbey Theatre, *Shadow and Substance*
(1942), *The Wayward Saint* (1955) and others. He
did much to encourage good repertory.

CARRON, William, baron (1902–69). British trade
unionist. B. at Kingston-upon-Hull, he served his
apprenticeship with a general engineering firm, and

LORD CARRON

rose rapidly through the
ranks of the union move-
ment, becoming in 1956
pres. of the Amalgamated
Engineering Union. He was
created a life peer 1967,
and did much to increase
public understanding of
the constructive work of
trade unions.

CARROT. Genus of
plants (*Daucus*) belonging
to the family Umbelliferae.
The wild C. (*D. carota*) is
a common wayside and
meadow weed in Britain,
and ranges through Europe
and Asia as far as India.
Cultivated varieties have long, fleshy tap-roots.

CARSE OF GOWRIE (gow'ri). Fertile plain
bordering the Firth of Tay and divided between
Perthshire and Angus. It is 15 m. long, one of Scotland's most productive agricultural areas.

CARSON, Edward Henry, baron (1854–1935).
Irish politician and lawyer. As a member of both the
English and Irish Bars he made a great name in
criminal and civil cases; his part in the Oscar Wilde
trial was decisive. In the years before the F.W.W.
he was the leader of the Ulstermen in their resolve
to resist Irish Home Rule by force of arms if need be.
But on the outbreak of war he rallied Ulster to the
support of the Government, and took office under
both Asquith and Lloyd George (Attorney-General
1915, First Lord of the Admiralty 1916, member of
the War Cabinet 1917–18). He was an M.P. 1892–1921
and a Lord of Appeal in Ordinary, 1921–9.

CARSON, Rachel (1907–64). American naturalist. Aquatic biologist with the U.S. Fish and Wildlife
Service 1936–49, when she became its editor-in-chief
until 1952, she pub. in 1951 *The Sea Around Us*, and
in 1963 *The Silent Spring*, attacking indiscriminate use
of pesticides.

CARSON CITY. Cap. of Nevada, U.S.A. Smallest
of America's cap. cities, it was named after the famous
frontiersman Kit Carson (1809–68). Pop. (1960)
5,163. *See illus.* p. 780.

CARTAGE'NA. Spanish industrial city, seaport,
and naval base in the prov. of Murcia on the Mediterranean Sea. It was founded about 225 B.C. by the
Carthaginian Hasdrubal, and was then called New
Carthage; it continued to flourish under the Romans
and the Moors, and was conquered by the Spanish
in 1269. It has a 13th cent. cathedral and Roman
remains. Pop. (1965) 135,944.

CARTAGENA. City and seaport of Colombia,
cap. of the dept. of Bolivar. Founded in 1533, it was
taken by Drake in 1586. A pipe-line brings petroleum
here from the Baranco D'ermaja wells. Pop. (1964)
242,085.

CA'RTEL. An amalgamation of industrial businesses that falls short of a trust, in that the firms
comprising it retain their identity but pledge themselves to regulate output and to observe a common
price list so as to avoid undercutting.

CARTHAGE (kahr'thāj). In ancient geography, a
rich and powerful Phoenician city in N. Africa, on
the gulf of Tunis, *c.* 10 m. N. of modern Tunis.
C. is said to have been founded in 814 B.C. by
Phoenician emigrants from Tyre, led by the princess
Dido. It developed an extensive commerce throughout
the Mediterranean, and traded with the Tin Islands,
which have been located in Cornwall or in S.W.
Spain. After the capture of Tyre by the Babylonians
in the 6th cent. B.C. it became the natural leader of
the Phoenician colonies in N. Africa and Spain, and
there soon began a prolonged struggle with the Greeks
which centred mainly in Sicily, the E. of which was

*rushes and forget-me-nots, and the glass
table and the little door had vanished.*

*Soon the rabbit
noticed Alice, as
she stood looking
curiously about
her; and at once
said in a quick
angry tone, 'why,
Mary Ann! what
are you doing out
here? Go home this
moment; and look
on my dressing-table for my gloves and nosegay,
and fetch them here, as quick as you can*

LEWIS CARROLL. Part of a page from the autograph
manuscript of *Alice in Wonderland*, presented to the British
Museum in 1949 by a group of well-wishers in the U.S.A.
Photo: British Museum.

dominated by Greek colonies, while the W. was held by Carthaginian trading stations. About 540 B.C. the Carthaginians defeated a Greek attempt to land in Corsica, and in 480 a Carthaginian attempt to conquer the whole of Sicily was defeated by the Greeks at Himera. Eventually the Carthaginians came into conflict with Rome, and in the 1st Punic War (264–241 B.C.) they were defeated at sea and expelled from their strongholds in E. Sicily. Under Hamilcar Barca, they next proceeded to build up an empire and army in Spain, whence Hamilcar's son Hannibal launched the 2nd Punic War (218–201 B.C.); he crossed the Pyrenees and Alps and inflicted crushing defeats upon the Roman armies in Italy before being forced back to Africa and defeated at Zama (202 B.C.).

In the 3rd Punic War (149–146 B.C.), C. was finally defeated, and the city itself destroyed by the Romans in 146 B.C. About 45 B.C. Roman colonists were settled in C. by Caesar, and it rose to be the wealthy and important capital of the province of Africa. After its capture by the Vandals in A.D. 439 it was little more than a pirate stronghold. From 533 it formed part of the Byzantine empire until its final destruction by the Arabs in A.D. 698.

The population of C. before its destruction by the Romans is said to have numbered over 700,000. The constitution was an aristocratic republic with two chief magistrates elected annually, and a senate of 300 life-members. The religion was Phoenician, ncluding the worship of the goddess Tanit, the great god Baal-Hammon, and the Tyrian Meklarth: human sacrifices were not unknown. The real strength of C. lay in its commerce and its powerful navy; its armies were for the most part mercenaries.

When the French secured the protectorate of Tunisia in 1881, C. became the seat of an R.C. bishopric (1884) and the Cathedral of St. Louis was built upon the supposed site of the camp where Louis IX of France had d. in 1270. Modern C. is a pleasant villa suburb of Tunis.

CARTHUSIANS. Order of monks in the R.C. Church, founded by St. Bruno, who in 1084 estab. their first monastery on the bleak mountain plateau of Chartreuse, near Grenoble in Dauphiné. They lived in unbroken silence, abstained from all meat, took only one meal a day, and supported themselves by their own labours.

The first rule was drawn up by Guigo, the 5th Prior. Between then and 1681 a few important changes were made. The order was introduced into England about 1178, when the first Charterhouse was founded at Witham in Essex. They were suppressed at the Reformation, but there is a Charterhouse at Parkminster, Sussex, estab. in 1833.

The famous liqueur called Chartreuse was first made at La Grande Chartreuse after the Revolution to enable the monks to meet the rents which were newly imposed on them for their land. Most of the income is now given to charity.

CARTIER (kahrtyeh′), **Sir Georges Étienne** (1814–73). French-Canadian statesman. He fought against the British in the rebellion of 1837, was elected to the Canadian parliament in 1848, and was joint Premier with Sir John Macdonald 1858–62. He furthered railway development, and brought Quebec into the federation in 1867.

CARTIER, Jacques (1491–1557). French navigator. B. in St. Malo, he sailed in 1534 in search of a N.W. passage, and arrived at Newfoundland. On his 2nd voyage in 1536 he sailed up the St. Lawrence and named the Indian village of Hochelaga, Mount Royal (Montreal). In 1541 and 1543 he made further voyages to what was now French Canada.

CARTOON. A preliminary drawing on strong paper used as a design for oil painting, mosaic, and tapestry. When completed the drawing is transferred by tracing or pouncing to the surface on which the finished design, painting, etc., is to be executed. The term is commonly applied to carricatures (q.v.).

CARTWRIGHT, Edmund (1743‑1823). Inventor. B. in Notts, he went to Oxford and became a country rector, though he was also a farmer. In 1785 he patented a power-loom. He invented several other machines, but went bankrupt in 1793. In 1809 he received a government grant of £10,000.

CARUSO (kahroo′sō) (1873–1921). Italian operatic tenor. B. at Naples, he made his first appearance on the stage there at 21. In 1898 he achieved a great success at Milan, in Puccini's *La Bohème*. He subsequently won world-wide fame and appeared in many European and American cities.

CARVER, George Washington (c. 1864–1943). American Negro agricultural chemist. B. in Missouri of slave parents, he worked from 1896 at the Tuskegee Institute, Alabama. He advocated the diversification of crops in the South, especially the cultivation of the peanut from which he developed some 300 products, and was a pioneer in the field of plastics.

CARY (kā′ri), **Henry Francis** (1772–1844). British clergyman, asst. librarian at the B.M. 1826–37, and translator of *The Divine Comedy* (1805–12) in a spiritedly accurate version.

CARVER. Even at work in his laboratory in the Tuskegee Institute, this unassumingly brilliant scientist wore a few of the flowers he loved pinned to his cardigan.
Courtesy of the Tuskegee Institute.

CARY, Joyce (1888–1957). British novelist. B. at Londonderry, he was ed. at Clifton Coll. and studied art before going up to Trinity Coll., Oxford. In 1918 he entered the Colonial Service retiring 2 years later because of ill-health, but Nigeria, where he had served, gave a background to such novels as *Mister Johnson* (1939) concerning a half-educated African clerk. Other books are *Castle Corner* (1938) and *A House of Children* (1941), both with autobiographical elements; *The Horse's Mouth* (1944) telling the story of the outrageous Bohemian artist Gulley Jimson, and *The Captive and the Free* (1959) dealing with faith-healing and written when he was progressively paralysed by muscular atrophy.

CASABLA′NCA. Port on the Atlantic coast of Morocco, 200 m. S.W. of Tangier; it was occupied by the French in 1907 and developed by them until Morocco became independent in 1956. C. was the scene of the S.W.W. conference between Churchill and Roosevelt in Jan. 1943 which issued the Allied demand for unconditional surrender by Germany, Italy, and Japan. Pop. (1965) 1,177,000.

CASADESUS, Robert (1899–). French pianist and composer. B. in Paris, he was ed. at the Conservatoire and is a fine interpreter of Mozart. His own compositions incl. 4 symphonies and 3 concertos for piano and orchestra.

CASALS (kasals′), **Pablo** (1876–). Spanish violoncellist, composer and conductor. B. in Tarragona, he first appeared in Eng. in 1898 at the Crystal Palace and founded the Pau C. Symphony Orchestra of Barcelona in 1920. He was exiled by Franco in 1936 and now lives just over the Spanish border in France. He is regarded as the greatest living cellist and has written symphonic, chamber and choral works incl. the Christmas oratorio *The Crib*, which speaks much of his own exile.

CASANO′VA DE SEINGALT, Giovanni Jacopo (1725–98). Italian adventurer, author of memoirs largely concerned with his love affairs. B. at Venice, he

H

served in the household of Cardinal Acquaviva, and embarked upon a career of intrigue and adventure which took him into many parts of Europe, especially to Paris, Rome, Berlin, Warsaw, and Madrid. From 1774 he was a police spy in the Venetian service. In 1782 a libel got him into trouble, and after more wanderings he was appointed in 1785 Count Waldstein's librarian at his castle of Dux in Bohemia, where he wrote his *Memoirs* (pub. 1826–38): the unexpurgated text did not appear until 1960–1.

CASAUBON (kazoboń'), **Isaac** (1559–1614). French Protestant divine and classical scholar. He taught at the univs. of Geneva and Montpelier, went to London in 1610, became an English subject, and was made a prebendary of Canterbury.

CĀ'SĒIN. The coagulate protein of milk, familiar as cheese, where it is mixed with fat and water. It exists in milk, probably as a loose compound with calcium solids, and is obtained commercially by treating separated milk. It has a number of important commercial applications in the manufacture of glues, paints, distempers, artificial silk, and plastics.

CASE'LLA, Alfredo (1883–1947). Italian composer, pianist, conductor, and musical critic. He toured throughout Europe and America and composed numerous works, including operas, songs, etc.

CASEMENT, Roger David (1864–1916). Irish nationalist. While in the British consular service he exposed the ruthless exploitation of natives on the Belgian Congo and in Peru, and was knighted in 1911 (degraded 1916). During the F.W.W. he went to Germany in 1914 and attempted to induce Irish prisoners of war to form an Irish brigade to take part in a republican rising. He returned to Ireland in a submarine in 1916 (possibly to stop rather than lead the rising), was arrested, tried for treason, and hanged. The C. diaries, alleged to show that he was a homosexual and held by the British govt., have caused endless controversy. His remains were returned to Ireland by the British govt. in 1965 and rest in Glasnevin cemetery, Dublin.

CASE'RTA. Italian town, cap. of C. prov., in Campania region, 21 m. N.E. of Naples, with a palace completed for the Bourbons in 1774 which was made the seat of an air training academy in 1926, and during the S.W.W. was used as Allied h.q. in Italy 1943–5. At C. the Germans in Italy surrendered to Field-Marshal Alexander in 1945. Pop. (1961) 50,810.

CASEY, Richard Gardiner, baron (1890–). Australian Liberal Statesman. B. in Brisbane, he was 1st Australian Min. to the U.S.A. 1940–2, Min. of State in the Middle East, with a seat in the British War Cabinet, 1942–3, and Gov. of Bengal 1944–6. In 1949 he became Min. of Supply in the Menzies govt., Min. of Nat. Development in 1950, and Min. for External Affairs 1951; retiring 1960, he was created a life peer, and in 1965 became Gov.-Gen.

CASIMIR-PÉRIER (kahzēmēr'-pehryeh'), **Jean Pierre Paul** (1847–1907). 5th president of the French Republic. He was P.M. in 1893 and 1894, and in the same year was elected Pres. following Carnot's assassination, but resigned after 6 months.

CA'SLON, William (1692–1766). British type-founder. Showing Dutch influence, his graceful 'old-face' types were much used until the late 18th cent. and were revived in Britain and the U.S. in the mid-19th cent.

CASPIAN SEA. Inland sea lying between the S.E. and E. extremities of Europe (the Caucasus) and Asia. An underwater ridge separates it into two halves, of which the northern is very shallow. The Volga, Ural, and many other rivers empty into it, but it has no exit and is tideless. Its waters are salt and rich in fish. Except for its southern coast, which belongs to Persia, it lies within Soviet territory. Astrakhan and Baku are its chief ports. Its area is *c.* 155,000 sq. m., the

CASSATT. By her simple treatment of pleasant incident from everyday life the artist achieved an effortless grace and lingering charm, as in 'Summertime' painted *c.* 1895.
Courtesy of The Huntington Hartford Collection, Gallery of Modern Art.

largest inland sea in the world, but it is gradually shrinking, in the N. partly by artificial drainage.

CASSA'NDRA. In Greek legend, the dau. of Priam, king of Troy. She foresaw the doom of Troy, and became the booty of Agamemnon; she was murdered with him by Clytemnestra.

CASSATT (kasat'), **Mary** (1855–1926). American artist. In 1875 she went to Europe and finally settled near Paris. She is best known for her paintings of mothers and children in the Impressionist style.

CASSAVA (kahsah'vah), or **Manioc.** The starch-containing roots of plants of the S. American genus *Manihot*, which belongs to the family Euphorbiaceae. The bitter C. (*M. utilissima*) yields a meal called Brazilian arrowroot. Tapioca is prepared from it.

CASSEL. *See* KASSEL.

CASSIA. Bark of a plant (*Cinnamomum cassia*) of the family Lauraceae. It is aromatic, and closely resembles the true cinnamon, for which it is largely used as a substitute.

C. is also a genus of plants of the family Leguminosae, many of which have strong purgative properties and are the source of the laxative senna.

CASSIN (kahsań'), **René** (1887–). French lawyer. A Gaulliste from 1940 in the S.W.W., he was pres. of the European Court of Human Rights in 1965–8, and was awarded the Nobel peace prize 1968.

CASSINO. Italian town in the prov. of Frosinone, *c.* 50 m. N.W. of Naples, on the Rapido. Situated

CASSINO. Cassino and Monte Cassino, crowned with its ancient abbey, saw the fiercest fighting of the Italian campaign. After three major assaults, the positions were taken on 18. May, 1944. Here is the desolation after victory, painted by J. Stafford Baker.   *Courtesy of the Imperial War Museum*

at the foot of Monte C., it was the scene of heavy fighting during the S.W.W. in 1944, when most of the town was destroyed. It was rebuilt *c.* 1 m. to the N. The famous abbey on the summit of Monte C., founded by St. Benedict in 529, was destroyed by Allied bombardment in Feb. 1944 since it commanded the entrance to the Liri valley and was in German hands; rebuilding was completed in 1956. Pop. (1951) 18,734.

CASSIRER (kasē′rer), **Ernst** (1874–1945). German philosopher. B. at Breslau, he was interested in the philosophy of history and science, taught at Berlin and Hamburg, but was driven out by the Nazis, eventually settling in the U.S. His *Philosophy of Symbolic Forms* (1923) developed the ideas of Kant.

CA′SSIUS, Gaius (d. 42 B.C.). Roman soldier, one of the conspirators who slew Julius Caesar. He fought at Carrhae (53), and with the republicans against Caesar at Pharsalus (48), was pardoned and appointed praetor, but became a leader in the conspiracy of 44, and after Caesar's death joined Brutus. Defeated at Philippi (42), he killed himself.

CASSIVELAUNUS (kasēvelow′noos). Chieftain of the Catuvellauni, a tribe of Britons N. of the Thames, and leader of the resistance to Caesar in 54 B.C.

CA′SSON, Sir Hugh (1910–). British architect. Director of architecture for the Festival of Britain 1948–51, he was knighted in 1952, and in 1953 became prof. of interior design at the Royal Coll. of Art. His books incl. *Victorian Architecture* (1948).

CASSON, Sir Lewis (1875–1969). Brit. actor-producer. B. in Birkenhead, he made his first stage appearance in 1903, and from 1913 was a producer in London. His association with the Old Vic began in 1927, and he acted in many West End productions with his wife, Dame Sybil Thorndike (q.v.). He was knighted in 1945.

CASSOWARY (kas′o-weri). Genus of flightless ostrich-like birds (*Casuarius*), confined to Australia and the neighbouring islands, and allied to the emu. The C. can run and leap well. The wings are very small, and the plumage is a glossy black.

CASTALDI (kahstah′-dē), **Pamfilo** (1398–*c.*1474). Italian humanist, who is said to have been the real inventor of movable type printing.

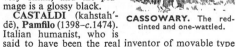

CASSOWARY. The red-tinted and one-wattled.

CASTANETS. Spanish musical instrument of percussion, consisting of a pair of hollow wooden shells, fastened together, bound round the thumb and 2nd finger of the hand. By striking them together a clicking sound is produced. They provide a rhythmical accompaniment to dancing, etc.

CASTE (kahst; Port., *casta*, race). A term generally used to denote the component groups of Indian or more particularly of Hindu society. In India the C. system is derived traditionally from the 4 classes of early Hindu society – Brahmans (priests), Kshatriyas (nobles and warriors), Vaisyas (traders and cultivators), and Sudras (servants), which were said to have originated from the head, arms, thighs, and feet respectively of Brahma, the Creator. A fifth class, the Untouchables, polluting on account of its origin, its occupations, or its mode of life, remained and still largely remains outside the pale of Hindu society, for although the Indian Constituent Assembly of 1947 abolished 'untouchability', and made discrimination against the Scheduled Castes or Depressed Classes illegal, and attempts have been made to enforce this, strong prejudice continues. The existing Cs. which number probably some 3,000, exclusive of sub-castes, are regarded as having come

into being by the interbreeding of these original groups, to form mixed groups of varying status.

The formation and development of the C. system owes a great deal to taboo, and it rests on a belief in pollution by touch, or even by sight, and in the necessity for purification from such contact. Internally each C. is generally broken up into sub-castes, often endogamous themselves, but often also with limited intermarriage. The 'Bhagavad Gita' lays down the principle that it is the first duty of every Hindu to follow the rules of his C., and a contentment with the C. into which each man is born is inculcated by the doctrine of *karma*. The belief in this doctrine alone makes tolerable the lot of those whose contact is deemed to be polluting to clean Hindus. While C. is opposed to western ideas, it may be claimed for the C. system that it has preserved a stable Indian society through the ages, given continuity to the exercise of industrial arts and crafts, and has provided a system of social providence and security.

CASTEL GANDOLFO (kahstel′ gahndohl′foh). Italian village 15 m. S.E. of Rome, with a castle, built by pope Urban VIII in the 17th cent., which is used by the Pope as a summer residence. The Vatican estab. an astronomical observatory at C.G. in 1936.

CASTELL′ANI, Aldo, marchese count (1877–). Italian physician. Prof. of tropical medicine at the Inst. for Tropical Diseases at Lisbon from 1947, he is noted for his work on sleeping sickness and yaws, and in dermatology and bacteriology.

CASTELNAU (kastelnoh′), **Édouard de Curières de** (1851–1944). French soldier, chief of staff to Joffre from Dec. 1915, whose name is linked with the defence of Verdun.

CASTELLÓN (kahstelyōn′) **DE LA PLANA.** Spanish city, cap. of Castellón prov., which faces the Mediterranean to the E. It is the centre of an orange-growing dist. Pop (1965) 76,780.

CASTELO BRANCO (kahstel′oo brahn′koo), **Camilo** (1825–90). Portuguese novelist. Illegitimate and soon an orphan, he had a dramatic life, and his works have a Balzac-type range, alternating in temper between mysticism and Bohemianism. They incl. *Onde está a felicidade?* (1856: *Where is Happiness?*); *Amor de perdição* (1862: *Love of Perdition*), written during his imprisonment for adultery and showing his obsession with love as a motive force; *Novelas do Minho* (1875), stories of the rural north; and *A brazileira de Prazins* (1882: *The Brazilian girl from Prazins*). Created a visct. in 1885. He committed suicide when overtaken by blindness.

CASTIGLIONE (kahstēlyoh′neh), **Baldassare, Count** (1478–1529). Italian author and diplomat. B. near Mantua, he served the duke of Milan, and in 1506 was engaged by the duke of Albino on a mission to Henry VII of England. While in Spain in 1524 he was created bishop of Avila. He pub. letters, poems in Lat. and It., and a picture of the perfect Renaissance gentleman *Il Cortegiano* (1528).

CASTIGLIONE, Giovanni Benedetto (1616–70). Italian painter and engraver, called Il Grechetto. B. at Genoa, he made a considerable reputation for his landscape paintings, and was also a very fine etcher. He d. at Mantua.

CASTILE (kastēl). Historic kingdom of central Spain, *c.* 50,000 sq. m. in area, consisting of 2 great basins, separated by the Sierra de Gredos and the Sierra de Guadarrama. The northern includes part of the Cantabrian mts., and reaches to the Bay of Biscay; it is drained by the upper Ebro, the upper Douro, and many tributaries. The southern is drained by the Tagus system and the Guadiana. The climate is continental and irrigation is essential to agriculture.

New C. occupied the S. basin, and Old C. the N. one. The kingdom grew from a small area in the N. In the 11th cent. Old C. was united with León; in 1085, the kingdom of Toledo was captured from the

Moors, becoming New C., with Toledo the cap. of the whole. Through the marriage in 1469 of Isabella, heiress of Castile, to Ferdinand, who became king of Aragon in 1479, C. and Aragon were united. *See* SPAIN.

The Castilian language is the standard form of Spanish. Principal town of C. is Madrid (in New C.); Valladolid, Burgos, and Santander are in Old C.

CASTILHO (kahstē′lyoh), **Antonio Feliciano de** (1800–75). Portuguese author, b. at Lisbon. Though blind from the age of 6, he became a prominent figure among the poets of the Romantic movement.

CASTLE, Barbara (1911–). Brit. Labour politician. Entering Parliament 1945, she was chairman of the Labour Party 1958–9, Min. of Overseas Development 1964–5 (only woman member of the Wilson cabinet), Min. of Transport 1965–8, and Min. for Employment and Productivity 1968–70.

CASTLE. A fortified building or stronghold of medieval times. The main parts of a Norman castle were: the keep, a square or oblong tower containing store rooms, dungeons, soldiers' quarters, etc.; the inner bailey or basecourt surrounding the keep;

CASTLE. Built *c.* 1131 by Fulc V (1090–1142), count of Anjou and from 1131 king of Jerusalem, Le Krak des Chevaliers some 48 m. S.E. of Jerusalem is an outstanding crusader castle. It illustrates the principle of mutual defence of all the parts of a stronghold which western engineers learnt from the Byzantines.
Photo: Aerofilms Ltd.

the outer bailey or 2nd courtyard separated from the inner bailey by a wall; the crenellated embattlements through which missiles were discharged against an attacking enemy; round towers known as bastions projecting from the walls; the postern gate used by messengers during a siege; the portcullis, a heavy grating which could be let down to close the main gate; and the drawbridge crossing the ditch or moat surrounding the castle. Sometimes a tower called a barbican was constructed over the gateway as an additional defensive measure.

Excavation of ancient Egyptian fortresses, e.g. that of Buhen in Nubia by Professor W. B. Emery (q.v.), has revealed complex structures which may have influenced the practice of medieval builders.

CASTLE CLINTON. Circular stone gun emplacement accommodating 28 pieces, built 1807–11 to the W. of Battery Park, Manhattan. As Castle Garden, from 1824 it was a place of entertainment, Jenny Lind being among performers here, and 1855–90 preceded Ellis Island as the New York immigration depot. From 1896 to 1941 it was an aquarium, and in the 1960s was being restored by the National Parks Commission as a national monument.

CASTLEFORD. Market town (bor.) on the Calder in the West Riding of Yorks, 10 m. S.E. of Leeds, England. It is a colliery centre and has brick, pottery, and glass works. Pop. (1961) 40,345.

CASTLEMAINE, Lady (1641–1709). Mistress of Charles II of England. B. Barbara Villiers, she m. in 1659 Roger Palmer (1634–1705) who in 1661 was created earl of C. For 10 years she held first place among the royal mistresses, and in 1670 she was made duchess of Cleveland; 3 of her sons were made dukes: Cleveland, Grafton, and Northumberland.

CASTLEREAGH (kahs′elrā), **Robert Stewart,** visct. (1769–1822). British Tory statesman. When his father, an Ulster landowner, was made an earl in 1796, he took the courtesy title of visct. C. In 1821 he succeeded his father as Marquess of Londonderry. He sat in the Irish House of Commons from 1790, and in 1797 became Chief Secretary in Ireland. He took a leading part in suppressing the rebellion of 1798, and by manipulation of the borough-mongers secured the passage in 1800 of the Act of Union. In the Parliament at Westminster he was War Secretary 1805–6 and again in 1807–9. In 1809 he fought a duel with Canning, the For. Sec., as a result of which they both resigned. C. returned to office in 1812 as For. Sec., devoted himself to the overthrow of Napoleon, represented Britain at the peace conferences, and used his influence to secure a just peace for France. Abroad his policy favoured the development of national liberalism, but at home he ruthlessly repressed the Reform movement. Popular opinion held C. responsible for the Peterloo massacre and the repressive legislation. Overwork and the realization of his unpopularity unsettled his mind, and on 12, Aug. 1822 he cut his throat with a penknife. His burial in Westminster Abbey was the scene of great popular rejoicing.

CASTLETON. Village in N. Derbyshire, England, centre for the Peak district. C. has the ruins of Peveril Castle, a small late-Norman keep standing on a limestone crag. Nearby are the notable Peak Cavern, Blue John, Speedwell, and Treak Cliff caves, and Mam Tor (1,700 ft.), 'the shivering mountain'.

CASTLETOWN. Town in the Isle of Man, formerly the island's cap., 10 m. S.W. of Douglas by railway. Nearby are King William's College (1668), the island's chief educational institution, and the I.O.M. airport. Pop. (1965) 2,378.

CASTOR and POLLUX. In classical mythology, the twin sons of Leda and brothers of Helen and Clytemnestra. They were called the *Dioscuri*, i.e. sons of Zeus, who had loved their mother in the guise of a swan. A temple was dedicated to them at Rome.

CASTŌ′REUM or **Castor.** Substance used in perfumery, consisting of the preputial follicles of the beaver.

CASTOR OIL. Oil obtained from the seeds of the C.O. plant or Palma Christi (*Ricinus communis*). This is a tall shrub of the family Euphorbiaceae, reaching a height of 6 or 8 ft., often cultivated as an ornamental garden-plant. The oil is used medicinally as a purgative.

CASTRATION. The removal of the testicles or ovaries. It prevents reproduction, and also much modifies the secondary sexual characteristics; e.g. in the male the voice may remain high as in childhood, and growth of hair on the face and body may become weak or cease, owing to the removal of the hormones normally secreted by the testes. In the woman it produces the change of life (menopause).

C. was formerly used to preserve the treble voice of boy singers or, by Moslems, to provide trustworthy harem guards: *see* EUNUCH. Today some Scandinavian countries use C. in the case of persistent male sexual offenders.

Male domestic animals, esp. stallions and bulls, are castrated to prevent undesirable sires from reproducing, to moderate their aggressive and savage disposition, and to make them produce more meat.

Cockerels are castrated (capons) to improve their flavour and increase their size.

CASTRES (kahstr). Town in Tarn dept., S. France, on the Agout, 43 m. E. of Toulouse. A thriving market centre, it makes textiles, furniture, tools, etc. C. adopted the Reformed religion in 1561. Pop. (1962) 40,005.

CASTRO RUZ, Fidel (1927–). Cuban Prime Minister. Of wealthy parentage C. was ed. at Jesuit schools and, after studying law at the Univ. of Havana, he gained a reputation through his work for poor clients. He strongly opposed the Batista dictatorship, and with his brother Raúl took part in an unsuccessful attack on the Army barracks at Santiago de Cuba in 1953. Although sentenced to 15 years' imprisonment, they were released after only 11 months. After spending some time in exile in the U.S. and Mexico, C. attempted a secret landing in Cuba in 1956 in which all but 11 of his supporters

FIDEL CASTRO
Courtesy of the Cuban embassy.

were killed. He eventually gathered an army of over 5,000 which overthrew Batista in 1959 and he became P.M. a few months later. His régime is socialist and he has declared himself a Marxist-Leninist. His younger brother Raúl was appointed Min. of Armed Forces in 1959.

CAT. A member of the mammalian family, Felidae, to which belong the lion, tiger, leopard, jaguar, puma, cheetah, etc. But the term is more usually confined to the smaller species, the domestic cat in particular.

Although Cs. have been domesticated since the time of the ancient Egyptians, their characters are so specialized and stable – in contrast with the dog – that only minor variants occur, e.g. the tail-less Manx C., which there is actually no reason to believe originated in the I.O.M. Cs. retaining the ancestral patterning of the coat, or modifications of it, are called 'tabbies', and may be 'striped' – when the pattern hardly varies from that of the European wild C. (*F. silvestris*) – or 'blotched'. Colours range through black, grey (divided into shades known as 'smokes', 'blues', 'chinchillas', and 'silvers'), white, cream, yellow and red (the last predominantly males); combinations of colours are frequent – red and black producing tortoiseshell (predominantly females). All are primarily classified as 'short-haired' or 'long-haired' (also known as Persian, though not known to have originated anywhere in the Middle East): the short-haired 'Abyssinian', 'Siamese', and Manx are separately judged. The National C. Club in Britain was founded in 1887.

CAT. Two domestic varieties, the exotic blue-eyed Siamese (left) and the blotched tabby.

CAT (Cat-o'-nine-tails). A whip with 9 knotted lashes used in the punishment of criminals. It is now very rarely used, for the Criminal Justice Act of 1948 abolished sentences of whipping except in cases of mutiny, incitement to mutiny, or gross violence to a prison officer. The sentence may be carried out then only after an order of a Visiting Committee or the Home Secretary.

CATACOMBS (kat'akōmz). Subterranean cemeteries. Most of the Christian Cs. belong to the 3rd and 4th cents. The name was first applied to the vaults beneath the basilica of St. Sebastian in Rome and afterwards to the network of tunnels there and to similar burial places in Naples, Syracuse, Egypt, etc., where the Christians buried their dead in niches hollowed in the walls. Mass was celebrated at the tombs of martyrs; they became places of pilgrimage; and in times of persecution the Christians would take refuge in the Cs. When Christianity became the State religion, the Christians began to bury their dead in cemeteries above ground.

CATALAN. A Romance language, belonging to the southern Gallo-Roman group, closely related to Provençal, of which it is usually considered a dialect. It is spoken in the N.E. and E. (Mediterranean) provinces of the Spanish mainland, the Balearic Isles, a corner of S.E. France, Andorra, etc.

CATALAUNIAN FIELDS. Plain near Troyes, France, scene of the defeat of Attila by the Romans and Goths under Aëtius in A.D. 451. The battle freed Europe from the danger of Asiatic domination.

CA'TALEPSY. In medicine, an abnormal state of complete suspension of the will in which the patient is apparently or actually unconscious and his limbs will remain in the position in which they are placed. He does not respond to stimuli, and the rate of his heart-beat and breathing is slow. A similar condition can be produced by hypnotism, but C. as ordinarily understood occurs spontaneously. It is seen in schizophrenia, hysteria, and sometimes in persons who have no other symptom of mental or nervous disorder. It is essentially an extreme form of resistive stupor, a defence against the environment or reality.

CATALONIA (Span. Cataluña). Old province and principality in N.E. Spain, bordering the Mediterranean on the E. and France on the N., divided into the provinces of Barcelona, Gerona, Lérida, and Tarragona, with a total area of 12,340 sq. m., and a pop. (1960) of 3,935,779. In the N. it is mountainous, but in the S. the Castellón mountains are broken through in by the lower Ebro, and the basin of its tributaries is arid. The soil is fertile, but the climate in the interior is arid. Coal, iron, wool, and cotton are imported, and C. leads Spain's industrial development, notably in textiles and shipbuilding. Barcelona is the chief town.

C. has a long tradition of semi-independence, and has often asserted itself against the purely Spanish influence in Madrid. This was much in evidence in the years that preceded the revolution of 1931, in which C. played a leading part on the republican side. C. was recognized in 1932 as an autonomous region of Spain, but following the civil war of 1936–9 its autonomy was abrogated.

CATA'LPA. Genus of trees found in N. America, China, and the West Indies, belonging to the Bignoniaceae. The common species, *C. bignonioides*, has been introduced into Europe. It has large, heart-shaped leaves, and white, yellow and purple streaked bell-shaped flowers.

CATA'LYSIS. Chemical process whereby the speed of a reaction is altered by means of the introduction of another substance into the system, this substance remaining chemically unchanged at the end of the reaction. Such a substance is called a *catalyst*, and in a broad analogy it may be compared with the oil which improves the working of a machine. The most important catalysts are those which increase the speed, i.e. *positive catalysts*, but in some reactions materials which slow down a reaction, i.e. *negative catalysts*, are important.

CATAMARA'N. Type of raft used in S. America and the E. and W. Indies, commonly consisting of a large centre log with 2 smaller ones lashed above it, the crew and cargo being carried between them. Double-hulled yachts designed on the same principle are the fastest craft in sailing and reach over 20 knots in the annual *Internat. C. Trophy* race (estab. 1961) at Thorpe Bay, Essex.

CATANIA (kahtah'nē-ah). Italian city, chief town of C. province in Sicily. It has Roman remains, including a great amphitheatre. The cathedral is part-Norman. It exports locally produced sulphur, asphalt, and fruits. Pop. (1961) 361,466.

CA'TARACT. Opacity of the lens of the eye. It sometimes occurs in children (lamellar C.), although the commonest form is senile C., occurring chiefly in persons over 50. Fluid accumulates between the fibres of the lens and gives place to deposits of albumen; these coalesce into rounded bodies; the lens fibres themselves break down, and areas of the lens become filled with opaque products of degeneration. The condition nearly always affects both eyes, but usually one more than the other. In most cases the treatment is to extract the lens. After the lens is removed the patient can see but cannot alter his focus, so he needs separate reading and distance glasses.

CATARRH. Discharge of fluid from mucous membrane; generally, an excessive secretion of mucous fluid, sometimes mixed with pus, from the nose (rhinitis).

CATCHMENT AREA. Area from which water is collected by a river valley.

CATECHISM. Instruction, usually in religion, by question and answer. Socrates used this method in his dialogues. A form of C. was used for the catechumens in the early Christian Church. Little books of C. became numerous at the Reformation. Luther pub. simple Cs. for children and unlearned people, and a larger C. for the use of teachers. The most popular R.C. catechism was that of Peter Canisius (1555); that with the widest circulation now is the 'Explanatory C. of Christian Doctrine'. Among the best-known Protestant Cs. are Calvin's Geneva C. (1537); that composed by Cranmer and Ridley with additions by Overall (1549–1661), incorporated in the Book of Common Prayer; the Presbyterian C. (1647–8); and the Evangelical Free Church C. (1898).

CATAMARAN. Japan's Sea Palace carries 300 passengers on Seto inland sea.
Courtesy of Japanese Embassy

CATECHU (kat'eshoo, -choo). An extract of the leaves and shoots of *Uncaria gambier*, an East Indian acacia It is rich in tannic acid, which is released slowly, a property which makes it a useful intestinal astringent in diarrhoea.

CATERPILLARS. The larvae of butterflies and moths. They are wormlike in form, and the body consists of 13 segments besides the head. The abdominal segments bear a varying number of pro-legs as well as the 6 true legs on the thoracic segments. The head has strong biting mandibles, silk glands and a spinneret. In many species the body is hairy, and the skin is often provided with scent and other glands. Many Cs. resemble the plant on which they feed, dry twigs, or rolled leaves. Others are brightly coloured and rely for their protection on their irritant hairs, disagreeable smell, or on their power to eject a corrosive fluid. Others again take up a peculiar 'terrifying attitude' when attacked.

Cs. emerge from the eggs which have been laid by the female insect on the food plant, and feed greedily, increasing greatly in size and casting their skins several times, until the pupal stage is reached.

CATFISH. Members of the order of Ostariophysi of the bony fishes; so-called because of the long feelers or barbels about the mouth, which give the effect of a cat's whiskers. The group includes several families of which most are wholly freshwater fishes.

In Britain the name C. is commonly given to the wolf-fish (*Anarrhichas lupus*), a sea-fish belonging to the blennies, and having nothing to do with the true C.

CATHARS or **Cathari** (medieval Lat., 'the pure'). A sect in medieval Europe usually numbered among the Christian heretics. They started about the 10th cent. in the Balkans where they were called Bogomils, spread to the southern countries of W. Europe where they were often identified with the Albigenses, and by the middle of the 14th cent. had been destroyed or driven underground by the Inquisition. It seems that they believed that this world is under the domination of Satan, and men and women are the terrestrial embodiment of spirits who were inspired by him to revolt and were driven out of heaven. At death the soul will become again imprisoned in flesh, whether of man or beast, unless it has been united in this life with Christ. If a man has become one of the C., death brings release, the Beatific Vision, and immortality in Christ's presence. Baptism with the spirit – the *consolamentum* – was the central rite, which was held to remedy the disaster of the Fall. The spirit received was the Paraclete, the Comforter, and it was imparted by imposition of hands. Those who received it were included among the Perfect, the ordained priesthood, were implicitly obeyed in everything, and lived lives of the strictest self-denial and chastity. The Believers or *Credentes* could approach God only through the Perfect.

CATHE'DRAL (Gk. *kathedra*, a seat or throne). Church containing the throne of a bishop or archbishop, which is usually situated on the S. side of the choir. There are Cs. in most of the important cities of Britain, and formerly they were distinguished as monastic and secular Cs., the clergy of the latter not being members of a regular monastic order. The term 'minster' applied to such Cs. as Lincoln and York does not imply that they were at one time monastic churches, but it originated in the name given to the bishop and C. clergy who were often referred to as a *monasterium*. After the dissolution of the monasteries by Henry VIII, most of the monastic churches were re-founded and are called Cs. of the New Foundation. Cathedrals of sees founded since 1836 incl. St. Albans, Southwark, Truro, Birmingham, and Liverpool. Among the most famous American cathedrals are: St. Patrick's and St. John the Divine, both in N.Y., and the Episcopal Cathedral of St. Peter and St. Paul, Washington, D.C. A cathedral is governed by a dean and chapter. *See* COVENTRY.

CATHER (kath'-), **Willa Sibert** (1876–1947). American novelist. Her books deal generally with

CATHERINE THE GREAT

immigrant life of the Midwest – *O Pioneers* (1913) and *Lucy Gayheart* (1935) – which she knew as a child in Nebraska, but *Sapphira and the Slave Girl* (1940) is set in her native Virginia.

CATHERINE I (1683–1727). Empress of Russia. A Lithuanian peasant girl, Martha Skavronsky m. a Swedish dragoon and eventually became the mistress of Peter the Great. In 1703 she was rechristened as Katarina Alexe·evna, and in 1711 the emperor divorced his wife and m. C. She accompanied him in his campaigns, and showed tact and shrewdness. In 1724 she was proclaimed empress, and after Peter's death in 1725 she ruled capably with the help of her ministers. She allied Russia with Austria and Spain in an anti-English bloc.

CATHERINE II, the Great (1729–96). Empress of Russia. Daughter of the prince of Anhalt-Zerbst, she married in 1745 the Russian grand duke Peter, who was an unbalanced weakling, and 6 months after his becoming Tsar in 1762 he was put out of the way. Henceforth C. ruled alone and proved capable and energetic. During her reign Russia extended her boundaries to include territory from Turkey (1774) and Sweden (1790), and profited by the Partitions of Poland.

C.'s private life was notorious throughout Europe, but she did not permit her amours to influence her policy. She admired and aided the Encyclopaedists, and corresponded with Voltaire and D'Alembert.

CATHERINE DE' MEDICI (de meh′dēchē) (1519–89). French queen, wife of Henry II and mother of Francis II, Charles IX, and Henry III. She was a daughter of Lorenzo de' Medici, and m. Henry in 1533. During the reigns of her sons she exercised a powerful political influence. At first she schemed with the Huguenots, but later bitterly opposed them, and the massacre of St. Bartholomew (1572) was largely her work. She was a patron of the arts.

CATHERINE OF ARAGON (1485–1536). First queen of Henry VIII of England. Daughter of Ferdinand and Isabella of Spain, she was betrothed at the age of 2 to Prince Arthur of England and m. him in 1501. He d. in 1502, and C. was then betrothed to his brother Henry, aged 11. When Henry became king in 1509, the marriage took place. C. bore 6 children, but only her daughter Mary lived. Henry desired a male heir, and in 1526 began to seek an annulment of his marriage on the grounds that the union with his brother's widow was invalid in spite of papal dispensation. When the Pope demanded that the case should be referred to him, Henry m. Anne Boleyn and afterwards received the desired decree of nullity from Archbishop Cranmer (1533). The Reformation in England followed. C. went into retirement, and was kept virtually a prisoner until her death.

CATHERINE OF BRAGANZA (1638–1705). Queen of Charles II of England. The daughter of John IV of Portugal, she m. Charles in 1662. Bombay and Tangier formed part of her dowry. Charles was occupied with his mistresses, and she lived in retirement. She had no children, but Charles opposed Shaftesbury's design for a divorce. Her liberty to practise her religion as a Catholic was resented. In 1692 she returned to Lisbon.

CATHERINE OF GENOA (1447–1510). Catholic saint. B. at Genoa of a noble family, she was m. at 16 and in later life devoted herself to the care of the sick, practised an inner life of deep meditation, and left two mystical treatises and a dialogue between the soul and the body. She was canonized in 1737.

CATHERINE OF SIENA (1347–80). Catholic saint and mystic, b. at Siena in Italy. She practised severe mortifications while still a child, and at the age of 16 became a Dominican tertiary. She attempted to reconcile the Florentines with the Pope, and persuaded Gregory XI to return to Rome from Avignon in 1376. In 1375 she is said to have received on her body the stigmata, the impression of Christ's wounds. Her *Dialogue* is a remarkable mystical work She was canonized in 1461.

CATHERINE OF VALOIS (1401–37). Queen of Henry V of England. The 3rd daughter of Charles VI of France, she was m. to Henry in 1420, and bore a son, Henry VI. Henry d. in 1422, and about 1425 she secretly m. Owen Tudor, by whom she had a son, Edmund, who became the father of Henry VII.

CATHERINE OF ARAGON
Photo: N.P.G.

CA′THODE. The electrode at which positive current leaves a device. It is the negatively charged electrode of an electrolytic cell, the electrode from which the primary stream of electrons is emitted in a vacuum tube, and the positive terminal of a battery.

CATHODE RAYS. Streams of negatively charged particles (electrons) emitted from the cathode of a discharge tube when sufficiently evacuated.

CATHERINE OF BRAGANZA
By J. Huysmans.
Photo: N.P.G.

CATHODE RAY TUBE. A special form of vacuum tube in which a beam of electrons is produced and focused on to a fluorescent screen. It is an essential component of television receivers and of oscilloscopes, instruments widely used in electronics for studying waveforms.

CATHOLIC CHURCH (Gk. *katholikos*, universal). Term applied to the whole body of the Christian Church (e.g. in the Apostles' Creed). By those Christians who accept the supremacy of the Pope, it is applied exclusively to themselves. Members of other churches, however, add the qualifying term Roman when speaking of them. *See* ROMAN-CATHOLICISM; OLD CATHOLICS.

CATHOLIC EMANCIPATION. Name given to a series of acts passed in Britain between 1780 and 1829 to relieve Catholics from the civil and legal restrictions accumulated from the time of Henry VIII.

CATILINE (kat'ilin). (**Lucius Sergius Catilina**) (*c.* 108–62 B.C.). Roman politician. An unscrupulous adventurer, of an impoverished patrician family, he followed a double failure to be elected to the consulship in 64/63 with a plot to seize control of the state. In 4 celebrated orations Cicero (q.v.) laid bare the conspiracy: several of C.'s followers were executed and C. d. in battle at the head of his revolutionary troops.

CATLIN, George (1796–1872). American authority on American Indian life. B. in Pennsylvania, he lived among the tribes 1832–40 and his paintings of them are in the U.S. National Museum, Washington.

CATLIN, Sir George Edward Gordon (1896–). British political scientist. He was prof. of politics at Cornell 1924–35 and Bronman prof. of political science at McGill univ. 1956–60: he is a strong advocate of Anglo-American co-operation and European unity. In 1925 he m. Vera Brittain (q.v.).

CA TŌ, Marcus Porcius (234–149 B.C.). Roman statesman. The son of a farmer, he served in the war against Hannibal, became consul in 195 B.C. and imposed a Roman peace upon the tribes of Spain. Appointed censor in 184 he used his powers to exclude from the senate all those members who fell short of the ancient Roman standards of dignity and moral uprightness. He was a keen farmer, and his treatise on agriculture is the earliest surviving work in Latin prose. Deeply impressed by the commercial prosperity of Carthage, which he visited in 157, he ended every speech in the senate by declaiming that 'Carthage must be destroyed'.

CATO STREET CONSPIRACY. An unsuccessful plot to murder Castlereagh and his ministers while they were dining with Lord Harrowby on 20 Feb. 1820, to capture the Bank and Mansion House, and to set London on fire, after which it was planned to set up a provisional govt. The conspirators were betrayed, and the 5 leaders were hanged and others sentenced to life transportation. The plot was hatched in Cato St., Edgware Rd., London. *See* THISTLEWOOD.

CATROUX (kahtrōō'), **Georges** (1879–1969). French general. After service in the F.W.W., he held commands in the colonies, and in 1940 joined De Gaulle, becoming his representative in the Near East. He was Gov.-Gen. of Algeria 1943–4, and was a member of the High Military Tribunal after the abortive military coup of 1962 in Algeria.

CATS (kahts), **Jakob** (1577–1660). Dutch poet. He became grand pensionary of Holland in 1636, and keeper of the great seal in 1648. In 1651 he retired to Zorgh-vliet, his home near The Hague, but was sent as ambassador to England in 1657. 'Father Cats' ranks in Holland foremost among the poets of the so-called Golden Age of literature.

CATS' CRADLES. Game played by one or more persons with a piece of looped string: world-wide in distribution it has magic connotations in some parts of the world, or may illustrate folktale events.

CATSKILLS. American mountain range, mainly in the state of New York; the highest point is Slide Mt. (4,204 ft.).

CATTARO. Italian form of KOTOR.

CATTERICK. Village and military camp in N. Riding of Yorks, on the Swale, 4½ m. from Richmond.

CATTLE. A group of large-sized ruminant Artiodactyla, including the buffaloes, bison, yak, gaur, gayal, and banteng, and the various familiar domesticated breeds. There are 2 main types of domesticated cattle, the European breeds and the zebus or sacred humped cattle of India, which are useful in the tropics for their ability to withstand the heat and diseases to which European breeds succumb. There is also in northern India a domesticated breed called the gayal descended from a wild species termed the gaur or tsain. A smaller related species, the banteng, has been domesticated in Java. The European breeds (*Bos taurus*) are descended from the extinct aurochs (*Bos primigenius*), which, although larger, resembled

CATTLE. Chillingham wild bull (left), and Indian humped bull.

the White Park Cattle formerly greatly prized in Britain, at Chillingham, Chartley, and elsewhere.

CATUL'LUS, Gaius Valerius (*c.* 84–54 B.C.). Roman lyric poet. B. at Verona, he moved in the best literary and political society of Rome and wrote lyrics describing his unhappy love affair with Clodia, wife of the consul Metellus. He journeyed to Asia Minor on the staff of the Roman governor Memmius, and near Troy visited the tomb of his brother for whom he wrote an epitaph full of sincere feeling. His longer poems include two wedding-songs. Many of his happiest poems are short verses to his friends.

CAUCASUS (kaw'-). Series of mountain ranges which traverse the area between the Black Sea and the Caspian Sea, in U.S.S.R. From its westerly extremity, S. of the estuary of the Kuban, it runs S.E. for 750 m., approaching the Caspian shore near the peninsula of Apsheron. The maximum width of the Great C. is about 140 m. The highest peaks include Elbruz (18,467 ft.), Jaikyl, Shkara, and several others, all higher than Mt. Blanc.

J. F. Blumenbach c. 1800 derived the white race of mankind from this area, hence the use of the word *Caucasian* to denote European types.

CAUCUS (kaw'-). Term originally used in Boston, U.S.A., in the 18th cent. for a meeting of the leaders of a political club or party designed to make arrangements for elections, etc. In England, it was first applied to the organization introduced by Joseph Chamberlain in 1878. Nowadays it means the powerful directive nucleus of a political party.

CAULAINCOURT (kohlaṅkoor'), **Armand Augustin Louis**, marquis de (1772–1827). French general and statesman. He was an aide-de-camp to Napoleon, accompanied him on the Russian campaign, and conducted his diplomatic negotiations during the concluding years of the Empire.

CAULIFLOWER. Variety of cabbage (*Brassica oleracea*), distinguished by its large flattened head of fleshy, aborted flowers, and by being less hardy than is the broccoli. It is said to have been introduced into England from Cyprus in the 16th cent.

CAVAFY, Constantinos (1863–1933). Greek poet.

An Alexandrian, he throws a startlingly up-to-date light on the Greek past, recreating the classical period with zest. In 1923 E. M. Forster translated *Pharos and Pharillon*.

CAVALIER. A term originally applied to horsemen of gentle birth, but referring in particular to the supporters of Charles I in the Civil War. Suckling, Lovelace, etc. are known as 'C. poets'.

CAVALLI (kahvahl'lē), **Francesco** (1620–76). Italian composer, organist at St. Mark's, Venice; 27 of his operas survive. C. was the first to make opera a popular entertainment.

CAVAN. Inland co. in that part of the prov. of Ulster that is included in Rep. of Ireland. The r. Erne divides it into a narrow peninsula, some 20 m. long, between Leitrim and Fermanagh – low-lying country for the most part – and an eastern section of wild and bare hill country. The soil is generally poor, and the climate moist and cold. Agriculture is the chief industry. The chief towns are Cavan, the capital, pop. c. 3,000. Kilmore, seat of R.C. and Protestant bishoprics, Virginia, etc. Area 730 sq. m.; pop. (1966) 54,022.

CAVE. A hollow in the earth's crust produced by the action of underground water or by waves on a sea coast. Cs. of the former type commonly occur in limestone, but not in chalk country where the rocks are soluble in water. A *pot-hole* is a vertical hole in rock caused by water descending a crack. C. fauna often show loss of pigmentation or sight, and under isolation specialized species may develop. *See* SPELEOLOGY.

Some of the most famous Cs. are the Mammoth C. in Kentucky, 4 m. in length and 125 ft. high; the Caverns of Adelsberg (Postumia) near Trieste which extend for many miles; Carlsbad C., the largest in America; the Cheddar Cs., Somerset; Fingal's C., Staffa, Scotland, famous for its range of basalt columns; and Peak Cavern, Derbyshire.

CAVE, Edward (1691–1754). British printer, founder under the pseudonym 'Sylvanus Urban' of *The Gentleman's Magazine* (1731–1914), the 1st periodical to be called a 'magazine'. Johnson was an influential contributor 1738–44.

CAVELL (kavl), **Edith Louisa** (1865–1915). British nurse. Dau. of a Norfolk clergyman, she was appointed matron at the new nurses' training institute in Brussels in 1907. In the F.W.W. this became a Red Cross hospital for both sides, and she with Philippe Baucq helped English and French soldiers to escape to the Dutch frontier. On 5 Aug. 1915 she was arrested; and after a court martial she and Baucq were condemned to death. She d. with heroic calmness. Since 1919 her body has rested beside Norwich Cathedral, and there is a statue of her in St. Martin's Place, London.

CAVENDISH. Pen-name of Henry Jones (1831–99), British authority on whist.

CAVENDISH, Lord Frederick Charles (1836–82). Second son of the 7th duke of Devonshire, he was appointed in 1882 chief secretary to the Lord-Lieutenant of Ireland, and on the evening of his arrival in Dublin was murdered in Phoenix Park with Burke, the Under-Secretary, by members of the society of 'Irish Invincibles'.

CAVENDISH, Henry (1731–1810). British physicist. A grandson of the 2nd duke of Devonshire, he devoted his life to scientific pursuits, living in rigorous seclusion at Clapham Common. He discovered the composition of nitric acid and the composition of water. The C. experiment was a device of his to discover the density of the earth.

CAVENDISH, Thomas (c. 1555–92). English navigator; commander of the 3rd circumnavigation of the world. He sailed in July 1586, touched Brazil, followed down the coast to Patagonia, passed through the Straits of Magellan, and sailed back via the Philippines, Cape of Good Hope, and St. Helena, reaching Plymouth after 2 years and 50 days.

CAVE TEMPLES. Examples of rock architecture, of which the finest are found in western India and the Deccan. *See* AJANTA and ELLORA.

CAVIARE (kavēahr'). Russian delicacy, obtained from the roe of the sturgeon. It is prepared by beating and straining the ovaries until the eggs are free from fats, etc., and then adding salt.

CAVITE (kahvē'teh). Town and port of the Philippine Republic, cap. of C. prov., Luzon, 8 m. S. of Manila. It was in Japanese hands Dec. 1941 to Feb. 1945 during the S.W.W. After the Philippines attained independence in 1946, the U.S.A. retained a military base here. Pop. (est.) 40,000.

CAVOUR (kahvoor'), **Camillo Benso**, count (1810–61). Italian statesman. B. at Turin, he served in the army in early life, and entered politics in 1847 as editor of *Il Risorgimento*. From 1848 he sat in the Piedmontese parliament, and held cabinet posts 1850–2. Becoming Prime Minister in 1852, he sought to secure French and British sympathy for the cause of Italian unity by sending Piedmontese troops to fight in the Crimean War. In 1858 he met Napoleon III secretly at Plombières, and planned with him the war of 1859 against Austria, which resulted in the union of Lombardy with Piedmont. The central Italian states also joined the kingdom of Italy, although Savoy and Nice had to be ceded to France as the price of acquiescence. With C.'s approval Garibaldi overthrew the Neapolitan monarchy, but to prevent him from marching on Rome C. occupied part of the Papal States, which with Naples and Sicily were annexed to Italy.

CĀ'VY (family Caviidae). Various kinds of short-tailed S. American rodents, of which the tame guinea pig (q.v.) is the most familiar kind.

CAWNPORE. Another form of KANPUR.

CAXTON, William (c. 1422–91). First English printer. B. in Kent, he was apprenticed to a London mercer (1438), and set up his own business in Bruges 1441–70. In 1471 he went to Cologne, where he learned the art of printing, and then set up his own press in Bruges in partnership with Colard Mansion. The first book from his press, and the first book printed in English, was C.'s own version of a French romance, *Recuyell of the Historyes of Troye* (1474). Returning to England in 1476 C. estab. himself in Westminster, where he produced the first book printed in England, *Dictes and Sayenges of the Phylosophers* (1477). Altogether he printed about 100 books, including editions of Chaucer, Gower and Lydgate, and translated many texts from the French or the Lat., in addition to revising others, e.g. Malory's *Morte d'Arthur*.

CAYENNE (kāyen'). Cap., chief port, and international airport of French Guiana, on C. island at the mouth of the r. C. Founded 1634 and destroyed by Indians, it dates actually from 1664; it was used as a penal settlement from 1854 to 1946. Pop. (1961) 18,635.

CAYENNE PEPPER, also known as chilly, Guinea pepper, or Spanish pepper. A condiment derived from the dried fruits of *Capsicum*, a genus of plants of the family Solanaceae. It is wholly distinct in its origin from true pepper. The capsicum is a herb or shrub, and bears pod-like fruits with a leathery envelope.

CAYLEY, Arthur (1821–95). British mathematician. Sadlerian prof. at Cambridge from 1863, he was the greatest pure mathematician of the cent. His books incl. *Elliptic Functions* (1876).

CAYLEY, Sir George (1773–1857). British pioneer in aeronautics. In 1804 he made the 1st model glider and his scientific writings were in advance of his age.

CAYMANS (kīmahnz'). Three low-lying islands in the W. Indies, 180 m. W.N.W. of Jamaica, discovered by Columbus in 1503. The inhabitants are chiefly concerned with catching and exporting turtles. Georgetown, the cap., is on Grand Cayman. Formerly a dependency of Jamaica, they were given their own administrative and legislative bodies by an act of the Imperial Parliament of 1958. Total area, 100 sq. m.; pop. (1960) 8,803.

CEBU (seboo'). Oldest city, founded 1565 as San Miguel, of the republic of the Philippines, on the island of C. (area 1,703 sq. m.), of which it is the chief port. Pop. (1960) 251,146.

CECIL (si'sil), **Lord David** (1902–). British critic. The younger son of the 4th marquess of Salisbury, he became Goldsmiths' prof. of English literature at Oxford in 1948. His books incl. *The Stricken Deer* (1929), dealing with Cowper, as well as studies of Jane Austen, Scott, and Hardy; and the subtly-penetrating *The Young Melbourne* (1939), with its sequel *Lord M.* (1954).

CECIL, Robert, 1st earl of Salisbury (?1563–1612). Son of Lord Burghley by his 2nd wife, he succeeded him as Sec. of State to Elizabeth, and was afterwards the chief minister of James I, who made him earl of Salisbury in 1605.

CECILIA (sesil'ia). Christian saint, martyred in Rome, in the 2nd or 3rd cent. Her later association with music may derive from the story that she sang hymns while undergoing torture.

CECIL OF CHELWOOD, Edgar Algernon Robert Cecil, 1st visct. (1864–1958). British statesman. Third son of the 3rd marquess of Salisbury, he was a Cons. M.P. 1906, sat as an Independent 1911–23, and was then created a visct. In the F.W.W. he was Min. of Blockade 1916–18, and in 1919 played a large part in drafting the Covenant of the League of Nations: he was awarded a Nobel peace prize in 1937.

CEDAR (sē'der). Genus of coniferous trees (*Cedrus*).

CEDAR. To the right, the leaves and cone.

The best-known is the C. of Lebanon (*C. libani*), which grows to a great height and age in the mountains of Syria and Asia Minor. Of the famous forests on Mt. Lebanon itself, only a few groups of trees remain. Together with the Himalayan C. (*C. deodara*) and the Algerian or Mt. Atlas order (*C. atlantica*), it has been introduced into England.

CELANDINE (sel'andīn). Name given to 2 plants belonging to different families, and resembling each other only in their bright yellow flowers. The greater C. (*Chelidonium majus*) belongs to the Papaveraceae, and is common in English hedgerows. The lesser C. (*Ranunculus ficaria*) is a member of the buttercup family, and is a familiar wayside and meadow plant.

CELEBES (selē'biz). Island of the Rep. of Indonesia, one of the Sunda group. It is mountainous and forested, but there are fertile valleys in which tropical produce grows abundantly. The majority of the people are Malayans of different tribes, among whom the Bugis and Macassars are Moslem, the Minahassa Christian. The semi-civilized Alfuoros remain in the wilder districts. Area 49,390 sq. m., with dependent islands 73,000 sq. m.; pop. (1961) 7,000,000.

CELERY (sel'eri). Genus of plants (*Apium*) of the family Umbelliferae. The common species (*A.*

graveolens) grows in ditches, salt-marshes, etc., and is coarse and acrid. In cultivation the acrid qualities are removed by blanching.

CÉLINE (sehlen'), **Louis Ferdinand.** Pseudonym of Louis Destouches (1897–1961). French novelist. B. in Paris, he studied medicine, and displays in his books a misanthropy contrasting sharply with his

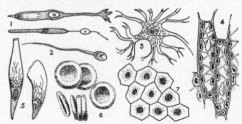

CELLS. I, Cone (above) and rod cells of retina; 2, Human spermatozoon cell; 3, Nerve cells; 4, Typical plant cells from a moss leaf; 5, Goblet cells of a frog; 6, Red cells from human blood; 7, Liver cells.

self-sacrificing career as a physician, notably *Voyage au bout de la nuit* (1932: *Journey to the End of Night*); *Mea Culpa* (1937) shows his disillusion with Soviet plans for human betterment.

CELL. A minute portion of living matter; the simplest living organism; the unit of physical life. Bacteria, amoebae, and certain other micro-organisms consist of single cells. Plants and animals are composed entirely of cells of various kinds. The body of a mammal (including that of the human species) originates from an organism consisting of a single cell – an ovum or egg-cell generated by the female and fertilized by fusion with a spermatozoon or seed-cell generated by the male. The fertilized ovum (embryo) is a microscopic body chiefly consisting of protoplasm, or clear jelly, the simplest form of living substance. The protoplasmic part of the cell is called the cytoplasm. It is enclosed in a membranous wall and contains a small spherical body called a nucleus – an essential part of most cells, without which they cannot reproduce. The only cells of the body which have no nucleus are the red blood cells. The nucleus of the embryo contains a denser spot called the nucleolus, but many other kinds of cells do not.

The composition of the protoplasm varies, but its breakdown products when the cell dies are mostly proteins. It contains also carbohydrates, fats, and the lipoids lecithin and cholesterin, besides inorganic salts such as the phosphates and chlorides of potash, soda, and lime. The cell wall in most animal cells is not a definite membrane, but the shape of the cell is maintained by surface tension or chemical action.

Cells reproduce by division, a complicated process which starts in the nucleus. The function of the cell is to convert energy from one form into another, e.g. food and oxygen into chemical energy.

Sexual reproduction is performed by the union of two special kinds of cells. When the human ovum is fertilized by fusion with a spermatozoon, the new cell contains the chromosomes from both – 48. The sex of the new individual is determined by the distribution of the special sex chromosomes. The ordinary cells of the female body have two X chromosomes; the cells of the male body have an X and a Y chromosome – two different types. The mature ovum contains one X chromosome and the mature spermatozoon contains either an X or a Y chromosome. If on fertilization two X chromosomes meet, the result is a female; if an X and a Y meet, the result is a male. All men thus inherit from their fathers one Y chromosome which gives their male characteristics: some (perhaps 1 in 300) inherit 2, which give added height, greater emotional instability, inability to bear frustration, and great aggressiveness. These men are often criminally violent, and possession of the Y-factor, immediately detectable under the microscope, has (as in France and Australia 1968) been successfully pleaded in mitigation in murder cases.

Ionization arising from gamma or X-radiation can damage Cs., and in the case of reproduction Cs. this may lead to disruption of the chromosomes and potential degradation of the offspring.

CELL (Electric). An apparatus in which chemical energy is converted into electrical energy; the popular name is 'battery', but this should be reserved for a collection of cells in one unit. E. Cs. can be divided into: (a) *primary*, which produce electric energy by chemical action and require replenishing after this action is complete; and (b) *secondary*, or accumulators, which are so constituted that the action is reversible, and the original condition can be restored by an electric current. The first battery was made by Volta in 1800. Types of primary cells are the Daniell, Lalande, Leclanché, etc., and the so-called dry cells; secondary cells include Planté, Faure, Edison, etc. Newer types incl. the Mallory (mercury depolarizer), which has a very stable discharge curve and can be made in very small units, e.g. for hearing-aids, and the Venner accumulator, which can be made substantially solid for some purposes.

CELLINI (chellē'nē), **Benvenuto** (1500–71). Italian artist, sculptor, and silversmith; also famous for his autobiography. B. in Florence, he was apprenticed to a goldsmith, and in 1519 went to Rome. C. claims to have killed the Constable de Bourbon during the siege of 1527. Later C. worked for the papal mint, and once was imprisoned on a charge of having embezzled pontifical jewels. In 1546 he began the bronze group of 'Perseus holding the head of Medusa', completed in 1554. He worked for a time in France at the court of Francis I, and finally settled in Florence in 1545, where he d.

CELLULOID (sel'ūloid). Transparent or translucent highly inflammable plastic material, now largely replaced by the non-inflammable cellulose acetate. C., chemically, is cellulose nitrate, and is formed by the action of nitric acid on cellulose in the presence of sulphuric acid mixed with camphor.

CELLULOSE. Complex carbohydrate material widely distributed in the plant kingdom, where it is the principal structural material. In various states of combination it is familiar as different kinds of wood; a purer form is cotton, and also paper and linen. It is present in nearly all plants, where it forms the harder parts, the cell walls, the fibres, etc.

CELSIUS. See CENTIGRADE.

CELTIC (keltik). A group of languages of the Indo-European family. They fall into two well-marked groups: the Goidelic consisting of the Gaelic language, under its 3 forms of Irish, Scottish, and Manx Gaelic, each with several sub-dialects; and the Brythonic, which includes Welsh, Cornish (extinct since *c.* 1800), Breton, and Gallic or Gaulish, the language of Gaul before the introduction of Latin, which seems to have died out in *c.* A.D. 600. The C. languages had formerly a much wider extension, as is seen by place-names in all parts of the British Isles, France, the N. of the Spanish peninsula, Switzerland, S. Germany, and N. Italy. Native C. speakers grow fewer, but measures to arrest a final decline were undertaken in the mid-20th century.

CELTIC ART. A style of art which originated in *c.* 500 B.C., probably on the Rhine, and spread westwards to Gaul and the British Isles, and southwards to Italy and Asia Minor until it was superseded by Roman influence (2nd–1st cent. B.C.). It is known conventionally as La Tène art, from a Swiss site where the best examples of the style were found. The chief characteristics are: linear designs – developing at a

CELTIC ART. A silver cauldron of the 1st century B.C. found at Gundestrup in north Jutland. At the rim it is 27 inches in diameter, and is richly ornamented.
National Museum, Copenhagen.

later state into intricate patterns – and the use of enamel and coral in the decoration of bronze objects.

A Late Celtic period existed only in the British Isles; it corresponds to a period of varying length according to regions in the Christian era, and is characterized by a rich decorative art, especially by enamelled horse-trappings and engraved mirrors.

CELTIC LITERATURE. The literature of the Celtic peoples is dealt with under the headings BRETON; CORNISH; IRISH; MANX; SCOTTISH GAELIC; WELSH.

CELTS (keltz). The name given, under various forms, by Greek and Roman writers to a people whose first-known territory was an area in the basin of the upper Danube and S. Germany. Here they were pioneers of the working of iron, and in the last 6 cents. B.C. elaborated the La Tène culture. They overran France, Spain, Portugal, N. Italy, sacked Rome in 390 B.C., the British Isles, and Greece. They appear never to have had a united empire, and their conquests were made by emigrant bands which effected permanent settlements in the lands named, as well as in the part of Asia Minor later known as Galatia from their name. The name C. was given by classical authors to a fair, tall people of N. Europe; and it was only gradually that they learned to distinguish the Cs. from the German tribes.

CEMENT (sement'). A bonding agent used to unite particles in one mass or to cause one surface to adhere to another. The term is applied to a variety of materials such as fluxes and pastes, and also bituminous products obtained from tar. In general, however, the name is more applicable to Portland C., a powder obtained from burning together a mixture of lime or chalk, and clay, which is the universal medium for building in brick or stone or for the production of concrete. In 1824 Joseph Aspdin, a Yorkshire bricklayer, discovered and patented the first Portland C., so named because of its resemblance in colour, in the hardened state, to the famous Portland stone. Today Portland C. is manufactured in huge quantities throughout the world. Chief centre of manufacture in the U.K. is the Thames valley.

CENOTAPH (sen'otaf; Gk. 'empty tomb'). Sepulchral monument to commemorate a person or persons whose remains are not actually buried at the site. The C. in Whitehall, London, for those who d. in both world wars, was designed by Sir Edwin Lutyens.

CENSOR (sen'-). High official at ancient Rome. Every 5 years 2 censors were elected to hold office for 18 months; besides completing a registration (*census*) of the citizen body, they revised the list of senators.

CENSOR. The psychic function by which, according to Freud and his followers, impulses arising in the sub-conscious mind are prevented from reaching consciousness if they are for some reason inacceptable, e.g. if they conflict with a moral sentiment, or would cause painful emotion. The rejection of psychic contents on these grounds is repression. *See also* Psychology (*psychoanalysis*).

CENSORSHIP. Supervision by some person or persons in authority of printed matter and other forms of publication with a view to suppressing anything considered immoral, subversive of the govt., or liable to undermine faith. The R.C. Church exercises a strict censorship, accepted by the faithful in every country, over all reading matter. In England, under the Tudors and Stuarts, the Crown claimed a monopoly of printing presses, and publication could be carried out only under licence until licensing was abolished in 1695. During both world wars, British defence regulations made it an offence to publish anything likely to be useful to the enemy, and censors were appointed to whom newspaper editors and others could submit material before publication, and much advantage was taken of their services; but such submission was not made compulsory. Laws relating to obscenity, libel, and defamation act in some respects as a censorship; they differ from one country to another, and much that would not be published in the U.K. because it would be libellous there can appear with impunity in e.g. the U.S.A. or France.

The C. of plays in the U.K. by the Lord Chamberlain (under the Theatres Act 1843) ended in 1968.

There is no official C. of films in either the U.K. or the U.S.A., but in both countries films are submitted before public presentation to bodies set up by the film industry: the British Board of Film Censors in the U.K., and a body popularly called the Hays Office (after its first president, 1922–45, Will H. Hays) in the U.S.A.

CENSUS. An official enumeration of the inhabitants of a country or state, together with certain other information regarding the age, sex, occupation, etc., of each individual. In most modern states a C. is taken at regular intervals, usually of 5 or 10 years. The first C. of England and Scotland was held in 1801, and since then the C. has been taken every 10 years except in 1941.

CENTAURS (sen'tawrz). In Greek legend, a race of creatures half-man and half-horse. They dwelt in the plains of Thessaly, and (apart from Chiron, the adviser of Hercules) they were noted for their lawless and turbulent character. The earliest representations of Cs. (c. 1800–1000 B.C.) were excavated near Famagusta in 1962, and are two-headed.

CENTAURY (sen'tawri). A plant (*Erythraea centaurium*) of the gentian family, Gentianaceae. It has numerous small red or pink funnel-shaped flowers, and is common in Britain in dry situations.

CENTIGRADE. The temperature scale in which one degree is taken as 1/100th part of the interval between two fixed points, melting ice (0°C), and steam over boiling water at standard atmospheric pressure (100°C). In 1948 the 9th General Conference on Weights and Measures decided that the term C. should be replaced by Celsius, the name of the Swede who invented the scale in 1742. The scale remains un-

CENTAUR. A two-headed centaur from Enkomi-Alasia. *Courtesy of Prof. C. Schaeffer.*

changed and one degree has the same magnitude as one degree of the Kelvin scale, which is based on the thermo-dynamic properties of an ideal gas and is independent of the physical properties of any medium. A temperature expressed on the Kelvin scale is numerically greater by 273·15 deg. than the same temperature on the Celsius scale.

CENTIPEDES (sen'tipēdz). Name of a class of animals (*Chilopoda*) of the phylum Arthropoda, having a distinct head and a single pair of antennae. They are distinguished from insects by their bodies being composed of numerous segments, all of similar form and bearing appendages, and from millipedes (*Diplopoda*) by the fact that there is only one pair of limbs to each segment. They are mostly nocturnal in their habits, predatory, and carnivorous, feeding on insects and worms, and are equipped with strong jaws provided with poison fangs. The bite of some of the larger species, found in warmer parts of the world, is painful and may be dangerous. Some of the tropical species, such as *Scolopendra gigas*, attain to as much as a foot in length. Several species are British, *Lithobius forficatus* being most common.

CENTRAL AFRICA, Union of. The Central African Rep., Chad, and Congo (Kinshasa) signed a protocol for the creation of a Union of C.A. in 1968: possible future members being Congo (Brazzaville), Rwanda and Burundi. It planned a common market and mutual assistance against aggression. H.Q. Bangui.

CENTRAL AFRICAN REPUBLIC. Name taken on achieving independence in 1960 by the former French territory of Ubangi-Shari. Its chief product is cotton. Area c. 240,000 sq. m.; pop. (1968) 2,000,000. The cap. is Bangui, pop. 238,000. C.A.R. is in the French Community and the Equatorial Union.

CENTRAL AMERICA. A geographical division comprising that portion of the American continent which connects Mexico with the Isthmus of Panamá. In itself it is also an isthmus, traversed by mountains that form part of the *cordillera*. It comprises British Honduras, the 5 republics of Guatemala, Honduras, Salvador, Nicaragua, and Costa Rica, and the republic of Panama, although this was never politically associated with the rest – before becoming an independent state in 1903 it was part of Colombia – which were included in the days of Spanish rule in the captain-generalcy of Guatemala.

CENTRAL CRIMINAL COURT. Court (usually known as the Old Bailey) which sits to try all treasons, felonies, and misdemeanours committed in the City of London, and the Greater London area. The C.C.C. was established in 1834, and is in effect London's Assize Court.

CENTRAL PROVINCES AND BERAR. *See* Madhya Pradesh.

CENTRAL TREATY ORGANISATION. *See* Baghdad.

CENTRIFUGE (se'ntrifūj). Apparatus for rotating containers at high speeds. One use is for separating

COUNTRIES OF CENTRAL AMERICA		
	Area Population in sq.m. (in 1,000s)	Capital
British Honduras	8,867　　114	Belize
Costa Rica	19,960　1,490	San Jose
El Salvador	8,260　3,036	San Salvador
Guatemala	42,042　4,575	Guatemala
Honduras	43,227　2,362	Tegucigalpa
Nicaragua	57,143　1,700	Managua
Panama	28,576　1,328	Panama
Panama Canal Zone	648　　 49	Balboa Heights
	208,453　14,654	

CERN. The 28 Gev proton synchrotron, forming part of the Cern laboratories at Meyrin, is the largest particle accelerator in Europe and is one of the two biggest in the world.
Courtesy of CERN.

substances of different densities. These substances (solid particles, colloids, liquids, gases or mixtures of these) are placed in the containers and the rotation sets up centrifugal forces in the whirling substances acting radially outwards, causing them to separate according to their densities. A common example is the separation of the lighter cream from the heavier milk in this way. The ultracentrifuge is a very high-speed C. and is used in colloid- and bio-chemistry. Large Cs. are used for physiological research, e.g. in astronaut training: testing bodily response to many times the normal acceleration due to gravity (g).

CEPHALONIA (sefalō'nia). Largest of the Ionian islands, off the W. coast of Greece. Area 260 sq. m.; pop. (1961) 46,302. Was devastated by an earthquake in 1953 which destroyed Argostolion, the cap., and Lixouri, and killed many of the inhabitants.

CEPHALO'PODA (sef-; Gk. 'head-footed'). Class of animals of the phylum Mollusca, including the octopus, cuttle-fish, squid, nautilus, etc. They are characterized by the inclusion of the mouth and head in the foot – hence the name – are exclusively marine, and have a very wide range.

CEPHALOSPORIN (sef'alo-). Antibiotic, also known as ceporin, extracted from cephalosporium mould. It was developed at Oxford by E. P. Abraham (q.v.) and others: Dorothy Hodgkin (q.v.) was associated in the early stages. C. is capable of destroying penicillin-resistant bacteria.

CERAMICS (seram'iks). In the widest sense any non-metallic mineral used in articles created from a powder and sintered at high temperatures. C. are divided into heavy clay products (bricks, roof tiles, drainpipes, sanitary ware), refractories or high-temperature materials (linings for furnaces used in steel-making, fuel elements in nuclear reactors), and pottery, which uses china clay, ball clay, china stone and flint. Pottery (q.v.) ranges from the opaque and porous earthenware well adapted to colour, through translucent white bone china (5% calcined bone) to finest porcelain (q.v.).

CERBERUS. In classical mythology, the many-headed watchdog at the gates of the underworld.

CEREALS (sē'rē-alz). Grain-bearing plants cultivated for food. The term relates primarily to barley and wheat, but may also be said to cover oats, maize, rye, millet, and rice. Cs. have been of the utmost importance in the history of human society, and different grain-bearing plants are characteristic of different civilizations in various parts of the world. *See* BREEDING.

CERES (sērēz). In Roman mythology, the goddess of agriculture, identified with the Greek Demeter.

CERIUM (sēr'-). The principal chemical element of the groups known as the rare earth metals, symbol Ce, at. wt. 140·13, at. no. 58. In the form of its oxide, C. helps to provide luminosity in gas mantles, and one of the most common uses of C. is as an alloy for 'flints' for cigarette lighters. Radioactive Ce-140 (half-life 9 months) is a fission product from nuclear power stations and may find a use in giant sources of limited life.

CERN (originally *Conseil Européen pour la Recherche Nucléaire*, but subsequently renamed *Organisation Européene pour la R.N.*, although still familiarly known as CERN). A European organization which came into being in 1954 as a co-operative enterprise among European govs. and is at present supported by contributions from 13 European member countries, to promote fundamental research in nuclear physics, and to provide the necessary high-energy machines too costly for an individual member country to support. The laboratories are situated at Meyrin near Geneva and the equipment includes a 600 million electronvolt synchro-cyclotron and a 28 thousand million electronvolt proton synchrotron, and large liquid bubble chambers, some of which have been specially brought to Geneva from other parts of Europe to use the beams from the high-energy machines.

CERNAUTI. Rumanian form of CHERNOVTSY.

CERVANTES (servan'tēz; Span. thervahn'thes), Miguel de Cervantes Saavedra (1547–1616). Spanish novelist, playwright, and poet. B. at Alcalá de Henares, he entered the army in Italy and in 1571 was wounded in the battle of Lepanto. In 1575, while on his way back to Spain, he was captured by Barbary pirates and was taken to Algiers, where he became a slave until ransomed in 1580. Returning to Spain he began to support himself by writing. He wrote several plays, and in 1585 his pastoral romance *Galatea* was printed. In 1587 he was employed at Seville in provisioning the Armada. He was more than once imprisoned for failures to make good deficiencies in the accounts of moneys he had received as a collector of taxes. He now sank once more into poverty, and little is known of the course of his life till *Don Quixote*, which had previously circulated in manuscript, appeared in 1605 and immediately achieved a great success. Within a few years it had been translated into English and French. In 1613 appeared his *Novelas Exemplares*, a collection of short tales; and in 1614 a burlesque poem, *Viage del Parnaso*, and a spurious 2nd part of *Don Quixote* which prompted C. to bring out his own authentic 2nd part, considered to be superior to the first in construction and in characterization. His last work was *Persiles y Sigismunda*.

CESKE BUDĚJOVICE. Town of Czechoslovakia, cap. of South Bohemian region. Dating from the 13th cent., it is a railway junction with some industry. Pop. (1967) 72,000.

CESTO'DA. Class of worms of the phylum Platyhelminthes. They include all those commonly called tape-worms (q.v.).

CETACEA (sitā'sha). A highly specialized order of purely aquatic fish-like mammals, including whales, dolphins, and porpoises. Fossil forms indicate their descent from an extinct group of the carnivora known as the creodonta. They can be readily distinguished from fish by their tail-fins, termed the 'flukes', being horizontal, not vertical. They are grouped in two sub-orders, the *Mystacoceti* or whalebone whales, including the rorqual and also the Greenland whale and the *Odontoceti* or toothed whales, including porpoises, dolphins, narwhal, etc. *See* WHALES.

CETEWAYO (setiwah'yō) (d. 1884). Ruler of Zululand, S. Africa, 1873–83, when he was expelled by his subjects. In 1879 he defeated the British at Isandhlwana, but was defeated himself at Ulundi.

CETINJE (tsetĕn'yĕh). Town of Montenegro, Yugoslavia, 12 m. E.S.E. of Kotor. Founded in 1484 by Ivan the Black, it was cap. of Montenegro until 1918. It has a palace built by Nicholas, the last king of Montenegro. Pop. (1953) 16,333.

CETTE. *See* SÈTE.

CEUTA (sū'ta). Spanish seaport and military base in Morocco, captured in 1580. It is 17 m. S. of Gibraltar and overlooks the Mediterranean approaches to the Straits of Gibraltar. Pop. (1960) 73,182.

CEVENNES (sehven'). Collective name given to a series of mountain ranges on the S., S.E., and E. borders of the Central Plateau of France.

CEYLON (sēlon'). Large island off the S.E. tip of India, formerly a British colony but created into a Dominion in 1948. In the 6th cent. B.C. the Sinhalese – an Aryan people from the N. of India – invaded and conquered it and today form 70% of the pop. (mainly Buddhist). Later migrations and invasions from India brought the Tamils, now just over 20% of the pop. (mainly Hindu). Only a handful of Veddas, the original inhabitants, survive in the jungle.

In a few hours the traveller can exchange the damp heat of Colombo (cap. and chief port) and the emerald paddy (rice) fields and rubber plantations of the low country for the cooler air of Kandy, the hill capital, set among wooded hills by a lake. From Kandy southwards the tea country opens out, with its hillsides covered with tea bushes. The hill station of Nuwara Eliya in the S.E. lies at over 6,000 ft. Mt. Pedrotallagalla (8,294 ft.) is the highest point in C.

The northern province of C., stronghold of the Tamils and Hinduism, is dry, sandy, and flat, and intensively cultivated. The tropical jungle in the S.E., and in the N. Central and Eastern provinces, contains the timber for which C. is famous – ebony, satinwood, rosewood, etc. These jungles are the home of big game. In the jungle country lie the ruins of the cities of Anuradhapura and Polonnaruwa.

The cultivation of rice and coconuts is the hereditary occupation of the villagers. British planters introduced coffee in the early 19th cent., but in 1870 a blight destroyed the entire crop. Cinchona was next introduced, followed by tea and rubber. In 1876, 70,000 seeds of *Hevea brasiliensis* were taken from the Amazon basin to Kew Gardens in England; 2,000 developed into plants which in 1877 were sent to C.: from that 2,000 sprang the trees of all the rubber plantations in C., the Dutch East Indies (Indonesia), and Malaya. The coconut industry has also greatly

CEYLON. Many of the people of Ceylon are Sinhalese, descended from colonists who left northern India to settle in the island in the 6th century B.C. Such wayside scenes are less frequent as mechanization proceeds.   *Courtesy, Tea Bureau.*

expanded. Minor products are graphite, cocoa, cinnamon, and precious stones. Pearl fishing is carried on in the Gulf of Manaar. C. is famous for its gold, silver, brass, ivory, and tortoise-shell work, basket and mat weaving. Modern industries incl. vehicle assembly and textiles, and tourism is developing.

History. The Sinhalese dynasty lasted 307 B.C.– A.D. 1815. The Portuguese in the 16th cent. were the first European invaders, but were ousted by the Dutch, who flourished until 1795 when, after the French Revolutionary armies occupied the Netherlands, C. was taken by the British. From 1815 C. was a crown colony with increasing powers of self-government until, under an act of the Imperial Parliament of 1947, C. became a dominion in 1948. In 1960 C. announced its intention of becoming a republic within the British Commonwealth; but internal disturbances in Tamil-speaking areas, following the decision in Nov. 1960 to replace English by Sinhalese as the official language of C., prevented the immediate realization of this intention. Area 25,332 sq. m.; pop. (1966) 11,504,100.

CÉZANNE (sehzahn'), **Paul** (1839–1906). French landscape, still-life, and portrait painter, the leader of the Post-Impressionist School. He was b. at Aix-en-Provence, where he studied and was on friendly terms with Émile Zola. In Paris he met Pissarro and other Impressionist painters, with whom at first he was in sympathy; but later he broke away from them and developed a style of painting which showed up their weaknesses. His aim was to give a sense of solidity which Impressionist paintings failed to give. His

CÉZANNE. Self-portrait in the Tate Gallery.

work has great influence on modern art.

c.g.s. SYSTEM. System based on the centimetre, gram and second as fundamental units of length, mass and time.

CHÂBLIS (shahblĕ'). Town in Yonne dept., France; the centre for the production of a white Burgundy wine of the same name. Pop. (1962) 1,687.

CHABRIER (shahbrē-eh'), **Emmanuel** (1841–94). French composer. Abandoning a post in the Ministry of the Interior to devote himself to music, he made his name with *España* (1883), an orchestral rhapsody, and the light opera *Le Roi malgré lui* (1887: 'King Against his Will'). He influenced French composers of the post-1918 era.

CHACMA. *See* BABOON.

CHACO (chah'koh). Prov. of Argentina, until 1951 a territory, part of Gran Chaco, a great zone, for the most part level, stretching into Paraguay and Bolivia. The prov., which includes many lakes and swamps, is partly unexplored. Much of it is forested, producing timber and quebracho; the chief crop is cotton. The cap. is Resistencia, in the S.E. Area 38,470 sq. m.; pop. (1965) 602,000,

The N. of Gran Chaco was the scene of the Bolivia-Paraguay war (over boundaries) of 1932–5, settled by arbitration in 1938.

CHAD (chahd), **Republic of.** Independent country of Africa, in the French Community, formerly a territory of France. It takes its name from Lake C. Much of it is desert, but in the Shari basin in the S. cotton and ground-nuts are grown; stock-rearing is important. Fort Lamy is the capital. Area 495,000 sq. m.; pop. (1965) 3,400,000.

LAKE CHAD, on the N.E. boundary of Nigeria, was

discovered in 1823; it varies in extent between rainy and dry seasons from 20,000 sq. m. to 7,000 sq. m.

CHADWICK, Sir Edwin (1800–90). British social and sanitary reformer. B. near Manchester, he became for a time a literary employee of Jeremy Bentham. In 1833 he was a member of, and from 1834 secretary of, the royal commission on poor law. His constant differences with his superiors were partly responsible for the break-up of the commission in 1846. C. also interested himself in drainage, water-supply, and sanitary problems, and was a commissioner to the Board of Health 1848–54.

CHADWICK, Sir James (1891–). British physicist. He studied at Cambridge under Rutherford, and in 1932 discovered the particle in an atomic nucleus which became known as the neutron, because it has no electric charge. In 1935 he was awarded a Nobel prize, and in 1940 was one of the British scientists reporting on the atom bomb. He was Lyon Jones prof. of physics at Liverpool 1935–48, and Master of Gonville and Caius Coll., Cambridge, 1948–59.

CHAETOGNATHA (kētog′natha) or **Arrow-worms**. Class of invertebrate animals of peculiar structure and uncertain position, consisting of *Sagitta* and 7 other genera, comprising 38 species. They usually measure from $\frac{1}{2}$ to $1\frac{1}{2}$ in. in length, occur in vast numbers on the surface of the sea, and form an important item in the food of fishes.

CHAETOPODA (kētop′oda). Division of annelid worms, distinguished from the Hirudinea by the presence of locomotive organs, in the form of paired bristles, borne on most of the numerous rings or segments into which the body is divided. They include two principal classes. The Polychaeta have many bristles, and include the marine bristle worms. The Oligochaeta, which have fewer bristles, include the earthworms and some freshwater species.

CHA′FER. Name given to several beetles of the section Lamellicornia, e.g. the cockchafer (*Melolontha vulgaris*); the summer C. (*Rhizotrogus solstitialis*), another common British species; and the rose C. (*Cetonia aurata*).

CHAFFINCH. A bird (*Fringilla coelebs*), well known as resident in Britain and Europe generally. The male is olive-brown above, with a bright chestnut breast, a bluish-grey cap, and two white bands on the upper part of the wing; the female is duller. The length is about 6 in. The C. is a good songster.

CHAGALL (shagal′), **Marc** (1889–). Russian artist. B. at Vitebsk, of Jewish parentage, he became a pupil of Bakst and from 1910 to 1914 studied in Paris. In 1922 he returned to France where he has since lived. A precursor of Surrealism, he breaks through the bounds of natural law to a dream world of floating animals and figures, and strange colours and juxtapositions of objects. He has also produced illustrated books—the Bible and La Fontaine's *Fables*.

CHAHAR. Former prov. of China, divided in 1947 between Inner Mongolia, Shansi, and Hopei.

CHAILLU (shahyü′), **Paul Belloni du** (1835–1903). American (French-born) traveller. B. in France, in 1855 he began a 4 years' journey of exploration in W. Africa. His *Explorations and Adventures in Equatorial Africa* (1861) relates amongst other things his discovery of the gorilla in Gabun.

CHAIN. Instrument of measurement used in land surveying, and hence a unit of land measurement. *Gunter's C.* is 66 ft. long and divided into 100 links. The *Engineer's C.* or *Ramsden C.* is 100 ft. long and divided into 100 links. In both cases the links are normally of steel wire. The former came to be adopted as the unit of land measurement; a C. is 22 yd., and 10 sq. C. make an acre (4,840 sq. yd.).

CHAIN, Ernst Boris (1906–). British scientist. B. in Berlin, son of a chemist and industrialist, he was driven to Britain by Nazi racial discrimination and

CHALK. Hill figures, formed by removing turf to show the underlying chalk, are a feature of English landscape. The White Horse on Bratton Hill near Westbury in Wiltshire is said to commemorate the victory of Alfred the Great over the Danes at Ethandun in 878. *Photo: Aerofilms Ltd.*

worked under F. Gowland Hopkins (q.v.) at Cambridge 1933–5. With Florey (q.v.) he initiated the work on penicillin which led to the discovery of its curative properties, and in 1945 shared the Nobel prize for physiology and medicine with Fleming and Florey. In 1961 he became prof. of biochemistry at Imperial College, London.

CHAITANYA (chītan′ya) (1486–c.1534). Indian mystic and philosopher, founder of a sect of Vaishnavas (devotees of Vishnu), numerous in Bengal. He was an eminent Sanskrit scholar, and advocated a religion of *bhakti* (personal devotion to the Deity), regardless of caste distinction.

CHAKA (chah′kah) (c. 1783–1828). Zulu chief who in the early years of the 19th cent. built up by conquest a powerful Zulu realm from the border of Cape Colony to the Zambesi. He was murdered.

CHALDAEA. See BABYLONIA.

CHALIAPIN (chahlē-ah′pēn), **Fyodor Ivanovich** (1873–1938). Russian singer. B. at Kazan of peasant parentage, he became a world-famous bass singer, and made his London début in 1913. His greatest role was that of Boris Godunov in Mussorgsky's opera. C. left Russia after the rise of the Soviet régime, and d. in Paris.

CHA′LICE (chal′is). Cup used in celebrating the Eucharist, sometimes of wood or pewter, but often of precious metal.

CHALK. A soft, fine-grained whitish rock composed of carbonate of lime, $CaCO_3$, formerly thought to derive from the remains of microscopic animal organisms or Foraminifera (foraminiferal ooze theory). In 1953, however, it was seen under the electron microscope to be composed chiefly of coccoliths, unicellular lime-secreting algae, and hence to be primarily a vegetable deposit. C. was laid down in the later Cretaceous period and covers a wide area in Europe. In England it stretches in a belt from Wilts continuously across Bucks and Cambs to Lincs and Yorks, and also forms the N. and S. Downs and the cliffs of S.E. England. C. is extensively quarried for use in cement, lime, mortar, etc.

CHALMERS (chah′merz), **James** (1841–1901). Scottish missionary-martyr. In 1866 the London Missionary Society sent him to the island of Rarotonga in the S. Pacific, and after 10 years there he was appointed to New Guinea. He was killed by cannibals on the is. of Goaribari.

CHALMERS, Thomas (1780–1847). Scottish divine. As minister of Tron Church, Glasgow, from 1815, he became noted for his eloquence and for schemes of social reform. In 1823 he became professor of moral philosophy at St. Andrews, and in 1828 of theology at Edinburgh. At the 'Disruption' of

NEVILLE CHAMBERLAIN. On his return from Germany in 1938, he waved aloft the Munich agreement which was to bring 'Peace With Honour'.   *Fox Photo, London.*

the Church of Scotland in 1843, C. withdrew from the church along with a large body of other divines, and became principal of the Free Church college.

CHÂLONS-SUR-MARNE (shaloń'-sür-mahrn'). Cap. of the dept. of Marne, France, about 90 m. E. of Paris, on the r. Marne. The seat of a bishopric, it has a fine 13th cent. cathedral. Pop. (1962) 45,348.

CHALON-SUR-SAÔNE (-sohn'). French town in the dept. Saône-et-Loire, on the Saône, about 80 m. N. of Lyons. It is an important manufacturing town and railway centre. Pop. (1962) 45,993.

CHAMBERLAIN, (Arthur) Neville (1869–1940). British Conservative statesman, younger son of Joseph C. and half-brother of Joseph Austen C. B. in Birmingham, of which he was Lord Mayor in 1915, he became Min. of Health in 1923, doing excellent work in slum clearance. After a brief space as Chancellor of the Exchequer he was Minister of Health again 1924–9. In 1931 he was Chancellor of the Exchequer in the National Govt., and in 1937 succeeded Baldwin as P.M. In an endeavour to close the old Anglo-Irish feud he agreed to the return to Eire of the ports occupied by the navy, and he made similarly friendly advances towards the dictators, Mussolini in particular. When in 1938 he went to Munich and negotiated with Hitler the settlement of the Czechoslovak question, he was ecstatically received on his return. Soon, however, he agreed that he had been tricked, and when Britain declared war on Sept. 3, 1939, he summoned the people to fight the 'evil things' that Hitlerism stood for. On May 10, 1940, he resigned, and became Lord President of the Council in the Churchill Cabinet, but d. on Nov. 9, 1940.

CHAMBERLAIN, Houston Stewart (1855–1927). German political theorist, one of the 'intellectuals' of Nazism. The son of an English rear-admiral, he lived in Germany and became a naturalized German citizen in 1916. His chief work, *Die Grundlagen des 19. Jahrhunderts* ('Foundations of the 19th Century'), was pub. in 1899. He m. Wagner's daughter Eva, as his 2nd wife, in 1908.

CHAMBERLAIN, Joseph (1836–1914). British statesman. B. in London, he entered in 1854 the screwmanufacturing business of his cousin Joseph Nettlefold at Birmingham. By 1874 he had made a sufficient fortune to devote himself entirely to politics; he early adopted radical views, and took an active part in local affairs. Thrice mayor of Birmingham, he carried through many schemes of municipal development. In 1876 he was elected M.P. for Birmingham as John Bright's colleague, and joined the republican group led by Sir Charles Dilke, the extreme left wing of the

Liberal Party. In 1880 he entered Gladstone's Cabinet as Pres. of the Board of Trade. The climax of his radical period was reached with the Unauthorized Programme of 1885, advocating free education, small holdings, graduated taxation, etc. In the next year he broke with Gladstone over Home Rule for Ireland, resigned from the Cabinet, and led the revolt of the Liberal-Unionists. In 1895 C. became Colonial Secretary in Salisbury's Cons. gov., and as such was responsible for relations with the Boer republics up to the outbreak of war in 1899. In 1903 he advanced proposals for Imperial Preference or 'Tariff Reform' as a general policy of imperial consolidation, and left the Cabinet in order to leave himself free to propagate his ideas. In 1906 a stroke was followed by the paralysis which kept him out of public life for his remaining years.

C. was one of the most colourful figures of British politics, and his monocle and orchid made him a favourite subject for political cartoonists.

CHAMBERLAIN, Sir (Joseph) Austen (1863–1937). British Conservative statesman. Elder son of Joseph C. he was elected in 1892 as a Liberal-Unionist M.P., and after holding several minor posts was Chancellor of the Exchequer 1903–6. During the F.W.W. he was Sec. of State for India 1915–17 and member of the War Cabinet 1918. He was Chancellor of the Exchequer 1919–21 and Lord Privy Seal 1921–2, but, as in 1911 (on Balfour's resignation), failed to secure the leadership of the party in 1922, as many Conservatives resented his share in the Irish settlement. He was For. Sec. in the Baldwin government 1924–9, and negotiated and signed the Locarno Treaty and the Kellogg Pact. After the formation of the Nat. Govt. in 1931 he was First Lord of the Admiralty for a few months.

CHAMBERLAIN, Owen (1920–). American physicist. At 22 he was working on the Manhattan Project, subsequently studied under Fermi (q.v.) and in 1958 became prof. at the Univ. of California. In 1959 he was awarded a Nobel prize with Emilio Segre for their work confirming the existence of the anti-proton.

CHAMBERLAIN, Lord. An administrative office in the royal household, responsible for engaging the staff, etc., and for appointing the tradesmen. New plays were submitted to the L.C.'s examiner for a licence before public performance until censorship ended 1968. The office is temporary, and its appointment is in the hands of the Government.

CHAMBERLAIN, Lord Great. The only Officer of State whose position survives from Norman times. His principal duties are to arrange Westminster Hall and the Houses of Parliament at the opening of the Houses by the monarch and to attend the sovereign at the coronation. He is also responsible for the ceremony at the creation of peers and bishops.

CHAMBER MUSIC. That class of music which is suitable for performance in a chamber, as opposed to that intended for the concert hall. As now used the term is applied to music written for a small combination of instruments, played with one instrument to a part. Many such combinations are possible, but of these the string quartet is the most important. A string quartet of G. Allegri (1582–1652) is believed to be the first example of its kind, while among English composers who wrote 'fantasy trios', or 'fancies', were Byrd and Orlando Gibbons. In the 17th and early 18th cents. C.M. generally had the harpsichord as a basis. The C.M. sonata with a figured bass accompaniment was established by the great Italian school of violinists – Vivaldi, Corelli, etc. From the 18th cent. onwards a new type of C.M. was first experimentally worked out by Haydn. In his string quartets each part plays, as it were, on equal terms, the keyboard instrument, as a basis, being eliminated. Haydn also developed the classical sonata form. His quartets influenced those of Mozart, who in turn influenced his master. The last quartets of Beethoven are the personal expression of his own individuality and show many striking departures from the original classical framework. In the 19th cent. C.M. found its way into the concert hall, and this effected a certain coarsening of the texture, and a quasi-orchestral quality, even in the work of Brahms. The early 20th cent. French school of Impressionists, represented by Debussy and Ravel, instituted changes in the classical framework, and during the period which followed various theories such as atonality, polytonality, etc., have found expression in C.M.

Modern composers of C.M. incl. Berg, Webern, Hindemith, Stravinsky, Prokoviev, Shostakovich, Kodály, Bartók, Ireland, Bliss, Tippett, Rubbra, Copland and Roy Harris.

CHAMBERS, Sir Edmund (1866–1954). British scholar, specializing in *The Elizabethan Stage* (1923); he also pub. studies of Coleridge and Arnold.

CHAMBERS, George (1803–40). British marine painter. B. at Whitby, Yorks, the son of a seaman, he excelled in battle scenes, e.g. 'The Bombardment of Algiers in 1816', Greenwich Hospital.

CHAMBERS, Sir (Stanley) Paul (1904–). British economist. Sec. and Commissioner of the Board of Inland Revenue 1942–7, he devised P.A.Y.E. (q.v.), and 1960–8 was chairman of Imperial Chemical Industries.

CHAMBERS, Sir William (1726–96). British architect. Sailing as supercargo to China at 16, he made drawings of Chinese subjects and his design for the Kew Gardens pagoda shows this influence, which he helped to popularize. His greatest work is Somerset House, London.

CHAMBÉRY (shonbārē'). Old capital of Savoy, now cap. of Savoie dept., France. The seat of an archbishopric, it is a railway junction and airport, with a number of industries; also a holiday and health resort. Pop. (1962) 47,447.

CHAMELEON (kamē'lēon). A family of lizards (*Chamaeleontidae*) of peculiar structure and remarkable for their faculty of colour-changing. The headquarters of the family is in Africa, but some species are found outside the limits of that region, including the common C. (*Chamaeleon chamaeleon*) of the Mediterranean countries, and there are also Indian representatives. The tail is long and highly prehensile, assisting the animal when climbing. The tongue is very long, protrusible, and covered with a viscous secretion; it can be shot out with great rapidity to a length of 7 or 8 in. and by means of it the C. captures insects. Cs. are entirely arboreal in their habits, and move very slowly. Their changes of colour are caused by changes in the intensity of light, of temperature, and of emotion, which affect the action of two layers of pigment-containing cells which lie underneath the skin.

CHAMINADE (shahmēnahd'), Cécile Louise Stéphanie (1857–1944). French composer. B. in Paris, she attracted the notice of Bizet, and made her appearance as a pianist when she was 18. Her best-known compositions are songs and piano pieces.

CHAMOIS (sham'wah) (*Rupicapra tragus*). A species of the so-called goat-antelopes, distinguished by vertical horns about 7 in. long and hooked backwards at the tip. It is brown, stands about 2½ ft. high, and inhabits the mountain ranges of S. Europe and Asia Minor. Its skin furnishes chamois leather.

CHAMONIX (shahmohnē'). Holiday resort at the foot of Mt. Blanc, in the French Alps. Pop. (1962) 7,966.

CHAMOIS

CHAMPAGNE (shampān'). Ancient province of France; parts of 10 depts. fall within the area, of which the chief are Ardennes, Marne (all), Haute-Marne, and Aube. The cap. was Troyes; Reims and Châlons are other important towns. C. consists of plains to the E. of the Paris basin, and is famous for its vineyards.

CHAMPAGNE. French wine, produced from specially fine grapes and blended wines, the former grown in a strictly defined area of the Marne region about Reims and Épernay in Champagne. Unlike other wines, fermentation takes place after the bottle has been sealed, this accounting for the effervescence.

CHAMPAIGNE, Philippe de (1602–74). French painter. Of Flemish origin, he settled in Paris at 19, and is famed for portraits, e.g. Richelieu. *See* p. 449.

CHAMPLAIN (shonplan'), Samuel de (1567–1635). French pioneer in Canada, soldier, and explorer. He served in the army of Henry IV and with an expedition to the W. Indies, and in 1603 began his exploration of Canada. In a 3rd expedition in 1608 he founded and named Quebec, and in 1612 was appointed Lieut.-Governor of French Canada.

CHAMPOLLION (shonpolyon'), Jean François, le Jeune (1790–1832). French Egyptologist, who in 1822 found the key to the decipherment of the Egyptian hieroglyphics on the Rosetta Stone (now in the British Museum).

CHANCELLOR, Lord High. A high state official who originally acted as royal secretary and keeper of the great seal. Until the 14th cent., the C. was always an ecclesiastic, who also acted as royal chaplain. Under Edward III the C. became head of a permanent court to consider petitions to the king, the Court of Chancery. Today he is a member of the cabinet, and goes out of office with it. In his legal capacity he may preside over the Court of Appeal, and appoints the judges and justices of the peace; he also acts as Speaker of the House of Lords. In order of precedence he comes after the Archbp. of Canterbury.

CHANCELLOR OF THE DUCHY OF LANCASTER. An honorary post held by a cabinet minister who has other non-departmental responsibilities. The C. was originally the king's representative controlling his lands and courts within the duchy.

CHANCELLOR OF THE EXCHEQUER. The cabinet minister responsible for the national economy. The office was originally established under Henry III, the C.'s task being that of keeper of the exchequer seal. Since the 19th cent. it has been a cabinet post, regarded as ranking next to that of Prime Minister.

CHANCERY. The court which, until the fusion of the courts in 1875 into the High Court of Justice and the Court of Appeal, administered the rules of equity as distinct from the rules of common law. It dealt with such matters as the administration of the estates of deceased persons, the execution of trusts, foreclosure of mortgages, partnerships, and the estates of infants. By the Judicature Act of 1873 it was established as a division.

CHANDERNAGO'RE. Indian city, 22 m. N. of Calcutta, in the state of W. Bengal. Formerly a French settlement it was ceded to India by treaty in 1952. Pop. (1961) 67,105.

CHANDIGARH. City of the Rep. of India, inaugurated 1953 to replace Lahore (cap. of British Punjab), which went to Pakistan under partition in

1947. Planned by Le Corbusier, in the foothills of the Himalayas 20 m. N. of Ambala, C. became the joint cap. of Hariana and Punjab in 1966, but from 1975 was to be cap. of Punjab only, being incorporated in that state. Pop. (1967) 89,000.

CHANDLER, Raymond (1888–1959). American thriller writer. B. in Chicago, he shared with Hammett (q.v.) the invention of tough crime writing and of the 'private eye' hero, such as his own Philip Marlowe. His books incl. *The Big Sleep* (1939), *Farewell, My Lovely* (1940) and *The Lady in the Lake* (1943).

CHANDOS (shan'dos, **Oliver Lyttelton**, 1st visct. C. (1893–1972). Brit. Cons. politician. Entering Parliament in 1940, he was Min. of Production 1942–5, and as Sec. of State for the Colonies 1951–4 coped with Mau Mau in Kenya and Communist terrorism in Malaya.

CHANDRAGUPTA MAURYA (called Sandrocottus by the Greeks). Ruled in N. India c. 321–c. 296 B.C. as king of Magadha.

CHANEY, James Eugene (1885–). American soldier. He commanded the U.S. Army Forces in Britain in 1941, and in 1945 was commanding general of the army forces which occupied Iwo Jima.

CHANGCHOW. Chinese city (now Lungki) in Fukien, 30 m. W. of Amoy, which has supplanted it as the commercial centre of the area; it produces satin, sugar, etc.; pop. (est.) 65,000. Another C. (now Wutsin) is in Kiangsu, 70 m. E.S.E. of Nanking, and on the Grand Canal; pop. (est.) 130,000.

CHANGCHUN. Chinese industrial city, in Kirin prov. A railway junction and the centre of an agricultural district, it makes machinery, motor vehicles, etc. As Hsingking (new capital) it was capital of Manchukuo 1932–45. Pop. (1965) 1,800,000.

CHANGSHA (chahngshah'). River port, on the Siangkiang, cap. of Hunan prov., China. It trades in rice, tea, timber, and non-ferrous metals; works antimony, lead, and silver; and makes porcelain and embroideries. Pop. (1957) 703,000.

CHANNEL ISLANDS. Group of islands lying in the English Channel, off the N.W. coast of France. Since the Norman conquest they have been a possession of the English Crown. They lie 50–100 m. S. of England and 10–30 m. N.W. of France. The largest is. are Jersey, Guernsey, Alderney, Sark, and Herm; there are besides a number of smaller islets and many rocks, the total area of the group being about 75 sq. m. French is the official language, though English is more widely used. English currency is used, in addition to local coinage. The is. have their own laws.

CHANNEL ISLANDS. An ancient cider press at Model Farm, St. Lawrence, on Jersey.
Photo: British Travel and Holidays Association.

Unless specially signified, the C.I. are not bound by Acts of Parliament. They are in the diocese of Winchester. They are the only part of the dukedom of Normandy still held by Britain. During the S.W.W. the Germans occupied the is. from June 30, 1940, until May 9, 1945. Pop. (1961) 110,503.

CHANNEL SWIMMING. The first to swim the English Channel was Capt. Webb on Aug. 25, 1875; he swam from Dover to Calais in 21 hr. 45 min. The fastest crossing (France to England) was by Yorkshireman Barry Watson, 1964, in 9 hr. 35 min. The first man to swim the channel in both directions was E. H. Temme, in 1927 and 1934, and the first to do so 'non-stop' was Argentinian Antonio Abertondo 1961.

CHANNEL TUNNEL. Proposed land link between England and France under the English Channel, first suggested by a Frenchman named Mathieu to Napoleon I in 1802. Another Frenchman, Thomé de Gamond (1807–75), put the idea to Napoleon III in 1856. Isambard Brunel and other British engineers became interested, and a convention between 2 countries was signed in 1875. Excavations were begun in 1882 near Dover and near Calais, but were abandoned a year later after a select committee of the House of Commons rejected the proposal on grounds of military hazard. In 1964 the British and French govts. decided on the construction of a rail T. to be completed by the early 1970s.

CHANNING, William Ellery (1780–1842). American Unitarian divine, a minister at Boston and a prominent advocate of the abolition of slavery.

CHANT. Word used in common speech to denote any vocal melody or song, especially of a slow and solemn character; but applied specifically to a type of melody used in the services of the Christian Church, which is specially adapted for singing the psalms, canticles and other non-metrical portions of the liturgy. The Ambrosian and Gregorian Cs. are forms of plainsong melody.

CHANTILLY (shonteye'). Town in Oise dept., France, 24 m. N.N.E. of Paris. Its racecourse is the centre of French horse-racing. Pop. (1962) 8,324.

CHANTREY, Sir Francis Legatt (1781–1841). British sculptor. Son of a carpenter, he was apprenticed to a Sheffield carver and gilder, but went to London in 1802 to study at the R.A. He made a reputation for his busts and statues of Wellington, Wordsworth, Scott (q.v.) and others, but is most celebrated for his child studies, notably the 'Sleeping Children' (1817) in Lichfield cathedral. The C. Bequest provides for the income from his private fortune to be used by the R.A. for the purchase of works of art for the benefit of the nation: these are housed in the Tate Gallery.

CHANUTE (shahnūt', **Octave** (1832–1910). French aviation pioneer. B. in Paris, he went to America and became the chief engineer of the Erie Railroad in 1872. He built several gliders in 1896, and had a marked success with a biplane, in which he completed over 700 glides.

CHAPEL ROYAL. The original C.R. of the English court, existing at least from 1135, was not a building but the royal retinue of priests, singers and musicians. In the 15th and 17th cents. the choirboys contributed to the development of the drama by their presentation of interludes, etc., and musicians attached to the C.R. have incl. Tallis, Byrd and Purcell. Today the name attaches to places of worship used by the royal household at Buckingham Palace, Hampton Court, Sandringham, Windsor Castle and the Tower of London (St. Peter ad Vincula).

CHAPLIN, Charles (1889–). British film actor-producer. B. in London, he 1st appeared on stage at 5, but made his world-wide reputation as the down-trodden trampish little character with smudge moustache, bowler hat and cane in silent films, e.g. *The Gold Rush* (1925), *The Circus* (1928), *City Lights*

CHARLES CHAPLIN. Wearing the costume familiar to millions, Chaplin in a bewildered moment in *Modern Times*. The waif round the corner is his third wife, Paulette Goddard.
Courtesy of the British Film Institute.

(1931) and *Modern Times* (1938), showing man's predicament in a machine age. In *The Great Dictator* (1940), guying Hitler, he spoke for the first time and in *Monsieur Verdoux* (1947) again abandoned his traditional costume. He has been 4 times married, his 3rd wife being Paulette Goddard and his 4th Oona, dau. of Eugene O'Neill (q.v.). In 1919 he was one of the founders of United Artists Corporation.

CHAPMAN, George (1559–1634). English poet, who was associated in London with Marlowe, and collaborated with Ben Jonson, but is best known for his fiery translation of Homer 1598–1624, which inspired Keats.

CHAR. Genus of fishes (*Salvelinus*) of the salmon and trout family (Salmonidae). *S. alpinus*, the typical species, is a marine form, but it enters rivers; and isolated colonies, each a distinct species or sub-species, have been formed in many European lakes. About 15 such have been distinguished in the British Isles.

CHARADRIIFORMES (karad′ri-ifor′mēz). Order of birds, including the plover family (Charadriidae) and their allies the snipe and sandpipers.

CHARCOT (shahrkoh′), **Jean-Martin** (1825–93). French neurologist. B. at Paris, he was prof. of pathological anatomy in the Univ. of Paris from 1860. He estab. the neurological clinic at the Salpêtrière, distinguished himself by his researches on the diseases of the nervous system, and initiated the scientific study of hypnotism.

CHARDIN (shahrdiṅ′), **Jean Baptiste Siméon** (1699–1779). French artist. B. in Paris, of a poor family, he is chiefly celebrated for his interiors and still-lifes of kitchen subjects – fruit and pots and pans.

CHARDONNE (shahrdon′), **Jacques**. Pseudonym of Jacques Boutelleau (1884–1968). French novelist, noted for his penetrating studies of married life, e.g. *Les Destinées sentimentales* (1934–5).

CHARENTE (shahroṅt′). French river, rising in Haute-Vienne dept. and flowing past Angoulême and Cognac into the Bay of Biscay below Rochefort. Its wide estuary is much silted up. Length *c.* 225 m. It gives its name to two depts., Charente and Charente-Maritime (formerly Charente-Inférieure).

CHARENTE-INFÉRIEURE. Former name of Charente-Maritime, a dept of FRANCE.

CHARING CROSS. District within the city of Westminster, London, lying around Charing Cross (main line) railway station. Its name is derived from one of the stone crosses built by Edward I at the resting-places of the coffin of his queen, Eleanor. The present cross is modern.

CHARLEMAGNE (char′lemän), or **Charles the Great** (742–814). King of the Franks and Roman emperor. The son of Pepin the Short, mayor of the palace in Merovingian Neustria, he was crowned by the Pope in 754 along with his father and his younger brother Carloman. When Pepin d. in 768, C. inherited the N. part of the Frankish kingdom, and when Carloman d. in 771, C. also took possession of his countries. In 770 he m. the dau. of the king of the Lombards, whom a year later he divorced.

He was engaged in his first Saxon campaign when the Pope's call for help against the Lombards reached him; he crossed the Alps, captured Pavia, and took the title of king of the Lombards. The pacification and Christianizing of the warlike pagan tribes of Saxons occupied the greater part of C.'s reign. The Westphalian leader Widukind did not submit until 785, when he received baptism. From 792 N. Saxony was subdued, and in 804 the country was finally pacified. In 777 the emir of Saragossa asked for C.'s help against the emir of Cordova. C. crossed the Pyrenees in 778, and reached the Ebro, but had to turn back from Saragossa. The rearguard action of Roncesvalles in which Roland, warden of the Breton March, and other Frankish nobles were ambushed and killed by Basque hordes, became immortal in the *Chanson de Roland*. In 801 the district between the Pyrenees and the Llobregat was organized as the Spanish March. The independent duchy of Bavaria was incorporated in the kingdom in 788, while the Avars, Turko-Finnish nomads inhabiting Hungary, were subdued in 791–6 and accepted Christianity. The supremacy of the Frankish king in the western world found outward expression in the bestowal of the imperial title: in Rome, during Mass on Christmas Day 800, pope Leo III crowned C. emperor.

C.'s activities were not confined to warfare. Jury-courts were introduced, the laws of the Franks revised, other tribal laws written down. A new coinage was introduced, weights and measures were reformed, and communications were improved. C. also took a lively interest in theology, organized the Church in his dominions, and furthered missionary enterprises and monastic reform. The 'Carolingian Renaissance' of learning began when he persuaded the Northumbrian Alcuin to enter his service in 781. C. gathered a kind of academy around him. He also collected the old heroic lays, began a German grammar, and promoted religious instruction in the vernacular. He died on Jan. 28, 814, at Aachen, where he was buried. Soon a cycle of heroic legends and romances developed round him, and these live on in epics of Ariosto, Boiardo, and Tasso.

CHARLEMAGNE PRIZE. Estab. by a no. of leading citizens in Aachen in 1949, it is awarded annually for services to European understanding and co-operation: winners incl. Churchill, Adenauer, Hallstein, Monnet, Schuman, Spaak and Heath.

CHARLEROI (shahrlrwah′). Belgian industrial and coal-mining town on the Sambre in Hainault prov. Pop. (1966) 24,895.

CHARLES I (1600–49). King of Great Britain and Ireland from 1625. B. at Dunfermline, the son of James VI of Scotland, he became heir to the throne on the death of his brother Henry in 1612. He went to Madrid in 1623 to urge his suit to the Infanta of Spain, but without success. In 1625 he became king, and m. Henrietta Maria, dau. of Henry IV of France. Friction with parliament began at once. The parliaments of 1625 and 1626

CHARLES I. After van Dyck. *Photo: N.P.G.*

were dissolved, and that of 1628 refused supplies until C. had accepted the Petition of Right. In 1629 it attacked C.'s illegal taxation and support of the Arminians in the Church, whereupon he dissolved parliament and imprisoned its leaders.

For 11 years he ruled without a parliament, raising money by expedients which alienated the entire nation, while the Star Chamber suppressed opposition by persecuting the Puritans. When C. attempted in 1637 to force a prayer book on the English model on Presbyterian Scotland he found himself confronted with a nation in arms. The Short Parliament, which met in April 1640, refused to grant money until grievances were redressed, and was speedily dissolved. The Scots then advanced into England, and forced their own terms on C. The Long Parliament met on Nov. 3, 1640, and declared extra-parliamentary taxation illegal, abolished the Star Chamber and other prerogative courts, and voted parliament could not be dissolved without its own consent. Laud and other ministers were imprisoned, and Strafford condemned to death. After the failure of his attempt to arrest the parliamentary leaders on Jan. 4, 1642, C. withdrew from London, and on Aug. 22 declared war on parliament by raising his standard at Nottingham. His defeat at Naseby in June 1645 ended all hopes of victory; in May 1646 he surrendered at Newark to the Scots, who in Jan. 1647 handed him over to parliament. In June the army seized him, and carried him off to Hampton Court. While the army leaders strove to find a settlement, C. secretly intrigued for a Scottish invasion. In Nov. he escaped to Carisbrooke; a Scottish invasion followed in 1648, and was shattered by Cromwell at Preston. In Jan. 1649 the House of Commons set up a high court of justice, which tried C. and condemned him to death. He was beheaded on Jan. 30 before the Banqueting Hall in Whitehall, and was buried in St. George's Chapel, Windsor.

CHARLES II (1630–85), King of Great Britain and Ireland from 1660. B. at St. James's Palace, the son of Charles I, he lived with his father at Oxford 1642–5, and after the victory of the parliament withdrew to the Continent. Accepting the Covenanters' offer to make him king, he landed in Scotland in 1650, and was crowned at Scone on Jan. 1, 1651. An attempt to invade England was ended on Sept. 3 by Cromwell's victory at Worcester. C. escaped, and after many adventures reached the Continent. For 9 years he wandered through France, Germany, Flanders, Spain, and Holland until the opening of negotiations by Monk in 1660 offered new hope. In April C. issued the Declaration of Breda, promising a general amnesty and freedom of conscience. Parliament accepted the Declaration; C. was proclaimed king on May 8, landed at Dover on the 26th, and entered London 3 days later.

Politically he had 3 aims: 'not to go on his travels again'; to make himself absolute; and to secure toleration, and if possible supremacy, for Catholicism. He hovered in religion between Catholicism and scepticism, but for his subjects he favoured the former as most consistent with absolute monarchy. For the present he entrusted the government to Clarendon, who arranged his marriage in 1662 with Catherine of Braganza, but his tutelage soon became irksome.

The disasters of the Dutch War furnished an excuse in 1667 for banishing him, and he was replaced by

CHARLES II. Artist unknown.   *Photo:* N.P.G.

the Cabal – Clifford and Arlington, both secret Catholics, and Buckingham, Ashley and Lauderdale, who had links with the Dissenters. In 1670 C. signed the Secret Treaty of Dover, the full details of which were known only to Clifford and Arlington, whereby he promised Louis XIV he would declare himself a Catholic, re-establish Catholicism in England, and support Louis's projected war against the Dutch; in return Louis was to finance C. and in the event of resistance to supply him with troops. War with Holland followed in 1672, and at the same time C. issued the Declaration of Indulgence, suspending all penal laws against Catholics and Dissenters. Parliament forced C. in 1673 to withdraw the Indulgence and accept a Test Act excluding all Catholics from office, and in 1674 to end the war with Holland. This broke up the Cabal, while Ashley (Lord Shaftesbury), who had learned the truth about the treaty, assumed the leadership of the opposition. Danby, the new chief minister, built up a Court Party in the Commons by wholesale bribery, while subsidies from Louis relieved C. from dependence on parliament. In 1678 Oates's announcement of a 'Popish Plot' released a wholesale panic, which Shaftesbury exploited to introduce his Exclusion Bill, excluding James, Duke of York, from the succession as a Papist; instead he hoped to substitute C.'s illegitimate son Monmouth. C. played for time, counting on a Royalist reaction and offering compromises which the opposition rejected. In 1681 his last parliament was summoned at Oxford; the Whigs attended armed, but when Shaftesbury rejected a last compromise, C. dissolved parliament and the Whigs fled in terror.

Henceforward C. ruled without a parliament. For money he relied on subsidies from Louis. When the Whigs plotted a revolt their leaders were executed, while Shaftesbury and Monmouth fled to Holland. Before C. d. in 1685 he had achieved his ambition to free himself from parliamentary control.

CHARLES (1948–). Prince of the United Kingdom, heir apparent to the British throne, and Prince of Wales. B. at Buckingham Palace on Nov. 14, 1948, he is the first-born child of Queen Elizabeth II and the Duke of Edinburgh. He entered Cheam School, Berks, in 1957 and in 1962 followed in the footsteps of his father to Gordonstoun. In 1958 he was created Prince of Wales (investiture 1969) and studied at Trinity Coll., Cambridge, 1967–70, subsequently serving in the R.A.F. and Royal Navy.

CHARLES. Name of 7 rulers of the Holy Roman Empire. CHARLES I was Charlemagne (q.v.). CHARLES II, THE BALD (823–77), the younger son of Louis I, the Pious, warred against his eldest brother the Emperor Lothair I, until the treaty of Verdun (843) assigned to C. the W. Frankish Kingdom, i.e. modern France and the Spanish March. He was crowned emperor at Rome in 875. CHARLES III, THE FAT (832–88), the youngest son of Louis the German, became king of the W. Franks in 885, thus uniting for the last time the whole of Charlemagne's empire. He was deposed in 887. CHARLES IV (1316–78), son of John of Luxemburg, king of Bohemia, was elected king of Germany in 1346, and in 1347 obtained power over all Germany. He founded the first German university, at Prague, in 1348. CHARLES V (1500–58): see below. CHARLES VI (1685–1740), the 2nd son of the emperor Leopold I, was put forward as the Austrian claimant to the Spanish dominions (see SPANISH SUCCESSION). In 1711 he abandoned Spain on becoming Holy Roman Emperor, and returned to Germany. CHARLES VII (1697–1745) was elector of Bavaria when Charles VI died, and contested the claim of the latter's dau., Maria Theresa, to the imperial crown. In 1742 he himself was crowned emperor.

CHARLES V (1500–58). Holy Roman Emperor. B. at Ghent, the son of Philip, son of the emperor

Maximilian, and Joanna of Castile, he was brought up in the Netherlands, which he inherited on his father's death (1506). In 1516 he inherited the possessions of his maternal grandfather Ferdinand V, consisting of Spain, Naples, Sicily, Sardinia, and the Spanish dominions in N. Africa and America. When Maximilian d. in 1519, C. came into possession of all the Habsburg dominions, and was elected emperor.

The rivalry of Francis I of France, originating in disputes over possessions in Burgundy and Italy, led to 4 wars, the outstanding events of which were the French king's defeat and capture in the battle of Pavia (1525), and the sacking of Rome – the Pope having become an ally of Francis – by Charles's troops in 1527. The series was concluded in 1544 by the treaty of Crépy-en-Valois in which C. renounced his claims on the duchy of Burgundy, but maintained his other Burgundian possessions and Milan. Francis never ceased to scheme against the emperor, and even allied himself with the Turks, who besieged Vienna in 1529 and again in 1532.

Meanwhile the religious movement started by Luther in 1517 was dividing the empire into two camps, and all Charles's efforts to reach a settlement, culminating in the diet of Augsburg in 1530, were unsuccessful. The Turkish threat obliged C. to conclude a truce with the Lutherans (1532), and not before the French wars had come to an end was he able to crush the Protestant League of Schmalkalden (1546–7). The Protestants then allied themselves with Henry II of France, and allowed him to take Metz, Toul, and Verdun. After years of struggle, the Protestants under Maurice of Saxony forced Charles by the treaty of Passau in 1552 to yield most of the Protestant demands. Disappointed and worn out, C. at last abdicated in favour of his son, Philip II, in the Netherlands (1555) and in Spain (1556), resigned the imperial crown into the hands of his brother Ferdinand, and passed the remainder of his days in the monastery of Yuste in Spain.

CHARLES (Karl) (1887–1922). Emperor of Austria and king of Hungary, the last of the Habsburg emperors. He succeeded his great-uncle, Francis Joseph, in 1916, at the height of the F.W.W., and in 1919 was forced to withdraw to Switzerland, although he refused to abdicate. In 1921 he attempted unsuccessfully to regain the crown of Hungary; and was deported to Madeira, where he d. He m. the Princess Zita of Bourbon-Parma, and their son, the Archduke Otto, maintains the Habsburg claims.

CHARLES. Name of 10 kings of France. Charles I was Charlemagne (q.v.) and for Charles II the Bald, see CHARLES, rulers of the Holy Roman Empire.

CHARLES III, THE SIMPLE (879–929), the son of Louis the Stammerer, was crowned at Reims in 893. In 911 he ceded what later became the duchy of Normandy to the Norman chief Rollo. CHARLES IV, THE FAIR (1294–1328), the last of the direct Capetian line, succeeded Philip V in 1322. CHARLES V, THE WISE (1337–80), acted as regent during the captivity of his father John II in England (1356–60), and became king in 1364. He renewed the war with England in 1369, and by 1380 had reconquered nearly all France. CHARLES VI (1368–1422) succeeded his father Charles V in 1380, but until 1388 France was governed by his uncles. In 1392 he went mad; his uncles regained power, and civil war broke out between the dukes of Orleans and Burgundy. Henry V of England invaded France in 1415, conquered Normandy, and in 1420 forced C. to sign the treaty of Troyes, which recognized Henry as his successor. Charles VII (1403–61), the son of Charles VI, was excluded from the succession by the treaty of Troyes, but on his father's death he was recognized as king by the S. of France. C. remained inactive until 1429 when Joan of Arc raised the siege of Orleans and had him crowned at Reims. C. organ-

ized France's first standing army, and by 1453 had expelled the English from all France except Calais. Charles VIII (1470–98) succeeded his father, Louis XI, in 1483. In 1494 he claimed the Neapolitan crown, invaded Italy, and entered Naples in 1495. Milan, Venice, Spain and the Emperor then formed a coalition against him; C. defeated the allies at Fornovo, but Naples was lost. He d. while preparing a 2nd expedition. Charles IX (1550–74), 2nd son of Henry II and Catherine de' Medici, succeeded his brother Francis II in 1560, but remained entirely under his mother's influence for 10 years, during which France was torn by religious wars. In 1570 he fell under the influence of the Huguenot leader Coligny, whereupon Catherine in alarm persuaded him to consent to the massacre of St. Bartholomew which led to a new religious war.

Charles X (1757–1836), grandson of Louis XV, and brother of Louis XVI and Louis XVIII, was known before his accession as Count of Artois. At the beginning of the Revolution he fled to England, where he remained until the fall of Napoleon. When he came to the throne in 1824 he attempted to undo the work of the Revolution. In 1830 there was a revolt, and C. again fled to England. He d. at Gorizia.

CHARLES. Name of 15 kings of Sweden. The first 6 were merely local chieftains. CHARLES VII reigned 1161–7. CHARLES VIII, elected king in 1448, was twice expelled by the Danes and twice restored before his death in 1470. CHARLES IX (1550–1611) was elected regent for his nephew Sigismund, king of Sweden and Poland, in 1595, and king in 1600. This involved him in war with Poland and Denmark. CHARLES X (1622–60) succeeded his cousin Christina in 1654. He waged war with Poland and Denmark, and in 1657 invaded Denmark from the S., leading his army over the frozen sea. CHARLES XI (1655–97), who succeeded in 1660, showed himself a remarkable general, and drastically reformed the administration. CHARLES XIII (1748–1818), who was elected king in 1809, became the 1st king of Sweden and Norway in 1814. CHARLES XV (1826–72) reigned over Sweden and Norway from 1859. For Charles XII and XIV see below.

CHARLES XII (1682–1718). King of Sweden. He succeeded his father Charles XI in 1697 and from 1700 was involved continuously in war with Denmark, Poland, and Russia. He won a brilliant succession of victories, until in 1709 while invading Russia he was defeated at Poltava, and forced to take refuge in Turkey until 1714. He was killed in 1718 while besieging Frederiksten.

CHARLES XIV (1763–1844). King of Sweden and Norway, originally Jean Baptiste Jules Bernadotte. B. at Pau, he entered the French army, won rapid promotion during the Revolutionary War, and was created a marshal of France by Napoleon. In 1810 he was elected crown prince of Sweden, under the name of Charles John. He brought Sweden into the alliance against Napoleon in 1813, as a reward for which Sweden received Norway. He succeeded to the throne in 1818, proved a capable ruler, and was the founder of the present dynasty.

CHARLES or Carlos. Name of 4 kings of Spain. CHARLES I was Charles V, Holy Roman Emperor (q.v.). CHARLES II (1661–1700) was the last of the Spanish Habsburg kings, 2nd son of Philip IV. He was an invalid and almost an imbecile from birth. On his deathbed he made a will leaving his dominions to Philip of Anjou, grandson of Louis XIV, which led to the War of the Spanish Succession. CHARLES III (1716–88), the son of Philip V, became duke of Parma in 1732, and in 1734 conquered Naples and Sicily. On the death in 1759 of his half-brother Ferdinand VI he became king of Spain, handing over Naples and Sicily to his son Ferdinand. During his reign Spain was twice involved in war with

CHARLESTON, S. CAROLINA. The neighbourhood is famed for its flowers, which are a tourist attraction. In spring the Magnolia Gardens have a splendid display of azaleas, magnolias and camellias.
Courtesy of the Magnolia Gardens, S. Carolina.

Britain, during the Seven Years War and the War of American Independence. At home C. carried out a programme of reforms and expelled the Jesuits. CHARLES IV (1748–1819) succeeded his father, C. III, in 1788, but left the government wholly in the hands of his wife and her lover Godoy. In 1808 C. abdicated in favour of his son Ferdinand. He became a pensioner of Napoleon, and d. at Rome.

CHARLES ALBERT (1798–1849). King of Sardinia. He showed Liberal sympathies in early life, and after his accession in 1831 introduced certain reforms. On the outbreak of the 1848 revolution he granted a constitution and declared war on Austria. His troops were defeated at Custozza and Novara, and in 1849 he abdicated in favour of his son Victor Emmanuel and retired to a monastery, where he died.

CHARLES AUGUSTUS (1757–1828). Grand Duke of Saxe-Weimar. He succeeded his father in infancy, fought against the French in 1792–4 and 1806, and is remembered as the patron and friend of Goethe.

CHARLES EDWARD STUART (1720–88), 'The Young Pretender'. He was b. at Rome, the son of James, the Old Pretender, and grandson of James II, and created Prince of Wales at birth. In July 1745 he sailed for Scotland, and landed in Invernessshire with 7 companions. On Aug. 19 he raised his father's standard, and within a week had rallied an army of 2,000 Highlanders. He entered Edinburgh almost without resistance, won an easy victory over General Cope at Prestonpans, invaded England, and by Dec. 4 had reached Derby, where his officers insisted on a retreat. The army returned to Scotland, and won a victory at Falkirk, but was forced to retire to the Highlands before Cumberland's advance. On April 16 at Culloden C.E.'s army was completely routed by Cumberland, and he himself fled. For five months he wandered through the Highlands with a price of £30,000 on his head before escaping to France. He visited England secretly in 1750, and may have made other visits. In later life he degenerated into a friendless drunkard.

CHARLES MARTELL ('the Hammer') (c. 688–741). Frankish ruler. An illegitimate son of Pepin of Heristal, he ruled the E. of the Frankish kingdom from 717 as mayor of the palace, and the whole kingdom from 731. His victory near Poitiers in 732 ended the Arab invasions of France.

CHARLES THE BOLD (1433–77). Duke of Burgundy. Son of Philip the Good, he inherited Burgundy and the Low Countries from him in 1465 and it was his ambition to create a kingdom stretching from the mouth of the Rhine to the mouth of the Rhône. He formed the League of the Public Weal against Louis

XI of France, invaded France in 1471, and laid the country waste as far as Rouen. His ambitions now united against him the Emperor, Lorraine, and the Swiss; he captured Nancy, but was defeated at Granson, and again at Morat (1476). Nancy was lost and while attempting to recapture it he was killed in battle. After his death his possessions in the Netherlands passed, by the marriage of his dau. Mary to Maximilian, to the Habsburgs.

CHARLES'S LAW. This law stated by Jacques Charles (1746–1823), French physicist, in 1787 and independently by Gay-Lussac in 1802 states that the volume of a given mass of gas at constant pressure increases by 1/273 of its volume at 0°C. for each degree Celsius rise of temperature, i.e. the coefficient of expansion of all gases is the same. The law is only approximately true and the coefficient of expansion is generally taken as 0·003663 per deg. C.

CHARLESTON. Main port and city of S. Carolina, U.S.A., dating from 1680. It has a fine sheltered harbour. In the vicinity are many historic houses and fine gardens. Pop. (1960) 65,925.

CHARLESTON. Chief city of W. Virginia, U.S.A., on the Kanawha. It is the centre of a district producing coal and natural gas. Pop. (1960) 85,796.

CHARLOCK or **Wild Mustard.** A plant (*Sinapis arvensis*) of the family Cruciferae. It is a common annual weed in Britain, reaching a height of 2 ft., and with yellow flowers.

CHARLOT (shahrloh'), **André** (1882–1956). Producer of plays and films. B. in Paris, he produced several witty revues in London and became a naturalized British subject in 1922. He went to America in 1937 and appeared in films.

CHARLOTTE (1896–   ). Grand Duchess of Luxemburg. Dau. of the Grand Duke William, she succeeded to the throne in 1919 on the abdication of her sister Marie Adélaide and m. Prince Felix of Bourbon-Parma. In 1961 she delegated her authority to her eldest son hereditary Grand Duke Prince Jean (1921–   ), abdicating in his favour 1964.

CHARLOTTE AUGUSTA, Princess (1796–1817). Only child of George IV and Caroline of Brunswick, and heir to the throne. She m. in 1816 Prince Leopold of Saxe-Coburg, but d. in childbed 18 months later.

CHARLOTTE SOPHIA (1744–1818). Queen consort. The dau. of the duke of Mecklenburg-Strelitz, she m. George III in 1761, and bore him 9 sons and 6 daughters.

CHARON (kā'ron). In Greek legend the ferryman of the souls of the dead over the river Styx.

CHARPENTIER (shahrpontyeh'), **Gustave** (1860–1956). French composer. His great success was *Louise* (1900), an opera dealing realistically with Parisian working-class life, to which he added a disappointing sequel *Julien* in 1913. In 1902 he founded an institution to give working-class girls free musical training.

CHARRON (shahron'), **Pierre** (1541–1603). French philosopher. He was a lawyer before he entered the Church. His first book, *Les trois Vérités* (1594), was a defence of belief in God, Christianity and Roman Catholicism. Yet in his *De la Sagesse* (1601) C. revealed himself as an advanced sceptic.

LESLIE CHARTERIS. On his right wrist the author wears a bracelet with the debonair, haloed pin-man familiar to readers all over the world as the emblem of the 'Saint'

CHARTERIS, Leslie (1907–   ). Anglo-American novelist. B. at Singapore, the son of a surgeon, he had a varied career in many exotic occupations which were

CHARTRES. A symphony of soaring columns, Chartres cathedral is sometimes considered the most beautiful in all France.
Photo: Mansell Collection.

to give authentic background to his some 40 novels of Simon Templar, the 'Saint' – gentleman-adventurer on the wrong side of the law – which have been translated into 16 languages and adapted for films, radio and television. These began with *The Saint Meets the Tiger* (1928). In 1946 he became a U.S. citizen.

CHARTIER (shahrtyeh'), **Alain** (c. 1392–c. 1430). French poet, b. at Bayeux. He was the author of *La Belle Dame sans Merci*, and many other works. In 1422 he wrote his *Quadrilogue invectif*, a conversation between France and the three estates (nobility, Church, and people), in which the ills of the time are trenchantly expounded.

CHARTISM. Radical British democratic movement, mainly of the working classes, which flourished c. 1838–50. It derived its name from the 'People's Charter', a programme comprising 6 points: universal manhood suffrage, equal electoral districts, vote by ballot, annual parliaments, abolition of the property qualification for M.Ps., and payment of M.Ps.

CHARTRES (shahrtr). Cap. of the dept. of Eure-et-Loir, N.W. France, 55 m. S.W. of Paris, on the Eure. Its cathedral of Notre Dame, completed about 1240, is a masterpiece of Gothic architecture. Pop. (1962) 33,992.

CHARTREUSE (shahrtröz'), **La Grande.** The original home of the Carthusian order of R.C. monks, estab. by St. Bruno c. 1084, in a remote valley some 14 m. N.N.E. of Grenoble (in modern dept. of Isère), France. The present buildings date from the 17th cent. The monks were expelled at the Revolution, returned 1816, were again expelled 1903, but, returning in 1940 as refugees from Italy, were allowed to remain. Since 1607 the monks have distilled a famous liqueur, here and at another house at Tarragona, Spain.

CHARYBDIS (karib'dis). In Greek mythology a whirlpool on one side of the narrow straits of Messina, Sicily, opposite the monster Scylla. Homer tells how the ship of Odysseus contrived to pass unscathed 'between Scylla and Charybdis'.

CHASE, James Hadley. Pen-name of René Raymond (1906–), who served in the R.A.F. during the S.W.W., and wrote *No Orchids for Miss Blandish* (1939), and other 'tough' novels with a great vogue.

CHASE, Stuart (1888–) American social scientist. From Harvard he entered his father's accounting firm, but made his name with *The Tragedy of Waste* (1925), a study of man in the machine age; *The Tyranny of Words* (1938) and *The Power of Words* (1954).

CHASING. Indentation of a design on metal by small chisels and hammers. This method of decoration was familiar in ancient Egypt, Assyria and Greece.

CHA'SUBLE. The outer garment worn by the priest in the celebration of the Mass. The colour of the C. depends on the feast which is being celebrated.

CHÂTEAU (shah'toh). Term originally applied to a French medieval castle, but now used to describe a country seat or important residence in France. The C. was first used as a domestic building in the late 15th cent.; by the reign of Louis XIII (1610–43) fortifications such as moats, keeps, etc., were no longer used for defensive purposes, but merely as decorative features.

CHATEAUBRIAND (shahtōbrē-oṅ'), **François René**, vicomte de (1768–1848). French author. He visited America in 1791, and returning to France, was exiled by the Revolution (1794–9). In exile he wrote *Atala* and the autobiographical *René*, which formed part of *Le Génie du Christianisme* (1802). He assisted the accession of Louis XVIII, under whom he held diplomatic appointments, and in 1849–50 his *Mémoires d'Outre Tombe* appeared. C. was an important precursor of Romanticism.

CHÂTEAUROUX (shahtohrōō'). Cap. of Indre dept., France, on the r. Indre. Dating from the 14th cent., it makes army cloth and has a national tobacco factory. Pop. (1962) 46,772.

CHÂTEAU-THIERRY (shahtoh'-tyärrē'). Town on the Marne, Aisne dept., France, the scene during the F.W.W. of a U.S. victory in 1918. Pop. (1962) 10,619.

CHATHAM, William Pitt, 1st earl of (1708–78). British statesman and orator. The grandson of Thomas Pitt, governor of Madras, he entered parliament in 1735 as M.P. for the family pocket borough of Old Sarum, and joined the 'patriots' in opposition to Walpole. After Walpole's fall in 1742 he attacked the policy of his successor, Carteret, during the War of the Austrian Succession, but in 1746 he was given a place in Pelham's Cabinet as Paymaster of the Forces; he refused to use this post, as was customary, to enrich himself, and contented himself with his legal salary. In 1755 he was dismissed from office for attacking the P.M., Newcastle, but the disastrous beginning of the Seven Years War led to a popular demand for his recall. He formed a govt. in 1756, but in 1757 was forced to form a coalition with Newcastle. His strategy and his choice of military and naval commanders were justified by brilliant success, culminating in the 'year of victories', 1759. By military and financial help to Frederick the Great he kept the French occupied in Europe, while Britain won the command of the sea and expelled the French from Canada and India, while at home he appealed to the patriotism of parliament and the nation by his eloquence and by such measures as the revival of the militia. In 1761 he was forced by George III to resign. He attacked the Peace of Paris in 1763, maintaining that Britain's gains were not proportionate to her efforts, and in 1766 formed an all-party government and accepted the title of earl of Chatham. Ill-health, however, kept him out of public life for 2 years, during which the govt. came more and more under the king's control, and in 1768 he resigned. During his last years he championed civil liberties, parliamentary reform and the rights of the American colonies against the king, although he rejected any suggestion of recognizing American independence. While making his last speech in the Lords, opposing the withdrawal of British troops from America, he collapsed (7 April 1778), and on 11 May he d. at Hayes. He was buried in Westminster Abbey.

CHATHAM. English seaport (bor.) and naval base on N. coast of Kent, on the Medway, adjacent to Rochester on the W. and Gillingham on the E. From 1958 C. naval base was reorganized as a sub-command under C.-in-C., Portsmouth. The Royal Dockyard (1588), employing 10,000 men, was converted to deal with the modern complex ships of the R.N., and H.M.S. *Pembroke* replaced the R.N. Barracks as accommodation for men from ships in refit. Pop. (1961) 48,989.

CHATTERJI (chat′erjē), **Bankim Chandra** (1838– 94). Indian novelist. B. in Bengal, where he estab. his reputation with his first book *Durges-Nandini* (1864), he became a favourite of the nationalists: *Ananda Math* (1882) contains the Indian national song 'Bande-Mataram'.

CHATTERTON, Thomas (1752–70). British poet. B. in Bristol, he became familiar with ancient documents he found in the church of St. Mary Redcliffe, and composed poems which he claimed as the work of Thomas Rowley, an imaginary monk of the 15th cent. Encouraged by his success in imposing on his Bristol acquaintance, he sent specimens to Horace Walpole, but was refused assistance when Walpole was advised by friends that these were forgeries. He then began contributing to periodicals in the style of Junius, and in 1770 went to London. Failing in success, he poisoned himself with arsenic. Although his modern productions show versatility and facility, his pseudo-medieval pieces are the proof of his genius, and greatly influenced the Romantic poets.

CHAUCER (chaw′ser), **Geoffrey** (c. 1340–1400). English poet. B. in London, he became a page in the household of Lionel, Duke of Clarence, by 1357, and in 1359 was taken prisoner in the French wars, although ransomed by Edward III in 1360. He m. Philippa Roet, whose sister later became the wife of John of Gaunt, and through her gained the patronage of the latter. C. held various court and official appointments, notably that of controller of customs in the port of London (1374), and was employed on missions abroad. In this way he visited Italy (1372–3), where he may have met Boccaccio and Petrarch, France and Flanders (1377), and Italy again in 1378. His early work is dominated by French influence, either in translation, as in his version of the *Romaunt of the Rose*, or in form, as with *The Boke of the Duchesse* (c. 1369). With his absorption of Italian influence came maturity, and such works as *Troilus and Criseyde* (adapted from Boccaccio), *The House of Fame, The Legend of Good Women*, and the *Knight's Tale* (also from Boccaccio). The last was to be merged in the great work

GEOFFREY CHAUCER
After T. Occleve.
Photo: N.P.G.

of C.'s final period, the *Canterbury Tales*, which was designed c. 1387, and envisaged a company of pilgrims beguiling their journey by telling stories. The descriptive prologue is a masterpiece of metre and characterization. He also wrote a prose translation of Boethius, and a treatise on the astrolabe for his small son. He is buried in Poets' Corner, Westminster Abbey.

CHAUVINISM (shōv′ —). A warlike fervour of patriotism: from Nicholas Chauvin, one of Napoleon I's veterans, and his fanatical admirer.

CHAVAN, Yeshwantrao Balwantrao (1914–). Indian statesman. A Mahratta from Satara, he was Chief Min. for Bombay 1956–60 and Maharashtra 1960–2; then in the Indian govt. Defence Min. 1962–6 and Min. of Home Affairs from 1966. Noted for his racial humanity, he is one of the most prominent of the new men emerging in the post-independence period.

CHÁVEZ (chah′vās), **Carlos** (1899–). Mexican composer. A student of the piano and of the complex rhythms of his country's folk music, he held his 1st public concert of his own work in Mexico City in 1921. He was founder-conductor of the Mexican Symphony Orchestra 1929–48, and founded the National Symphony Orchestra. His works incl. a number of ballets, 7 symphonies, and concertos for both violin and piano.

CHAYE′FSKY, Sidney (1923–). American playwright known as Paddy C. B. in the Bronx, he estab. his reputation with the television plays *Marty* and *Bachelor Party*, both successfully filmed (1955 and 1957 respectively). His characters have an inarticulate pathos and frustration well adapted to 'Method' acting, and are placed in a detailed urban setting.

CHEAPSIDE. A street running from St. Paul's Cathedral to Poultry, in the City of London, England. It was the scene of the 13th cent. 'Cheap', a permanent fair and general market.

CHECK. *See* CHEQUE.

CHEDDAR GORGE. It cuts through cliffs up to 800 ft. high.
Photo: A. W. Kerr.

CHEDDAR. Village of Somerset, famous for its gorge, caves, and fine cheeses. In 1962 excavation revealed the site of a Saxon palace.

CHEESE. A compact, concentrated food made usually from whole cows' milk, but also from the milk of goats, ewes, mares, buffaloes, reindeer, etc., and consisting of preserved milk solids. Its popularity is due to its palatability and its satisfactory nutritional quality; cheese such as Cheddar or Cheshire consists of approximately one-third protein, one-third fat, and one-third moisture. Furthermore, the highly nutritious non-bulky solid – 1 gallon of milk makes approximately 1 lb. of cheese – is easy to handle.

There are over 500 varieties of cheese, of which the greater number used to be made only in the districts after which they are named. The varieties are divided into 3 main groups: (1) hard pressed, e.g. Cheddar, Cheshire, Cantal, Parmesan, Gruyère, the most

THOMAS CHATTERTON. The poet's uncle was sexton at the church of St. Mary Redcliffe, Bristol (above), and old documents from the muniment room inspired his boyish imagination to the invention of Thomas Rowley, the beginning of a career of forgery.
Courtesy of Bristol City Public Relations Office.

important group, economically and nutritionally; (2) semi-hard, e.g. Stilton, Gorgonzola, Wensleydale, Roquefort, Pont l'Evêque, Gouda; (3) soft, e.g. Cambridge, York, Camembert, Coulommier, Brie.

CHEETAH (chē'tah). Member of the cat family (Felidae), also known as the hunting-leopard (*Cynaelurus jubatus*), used for  cents. in India and Persia for hunting game because of its phenomenal speed and comparative tractability. Standing about 1½ feet high, it is yellowish with black spots, and differs from other cats in having claws which are only partially retractile. It is found in open country in Africa and S.W. Asia, and S. Rhodesia has a specially handsome variety, the king C.

CHEFOO (chēfoō'). Ice-free port in Shantung prov., China, noted for the export of wild silk. It was formerly a treaty port. A railway linking it with Tsingtao was completed in 1955. Pop. *c.* 250,000.

CHEKA (chā'kah). Secret police operating in the Soviet Union 1918–23. The name is formed from the initials *che* and *ka* of the two Russian words meaning 'extraordinary commission', formed for 'the repression of counter-revolutionary activities and of speculation', and extended to cover such matters as espionage and smuggling. In 1923 the C. was replaced by the Ogpu and ultimately by the M.V.D. (q.v.).

CHEKHOV (chekhof'), **Anton Pavlovich** (1860–1904). Russian writer. B. at Taganrog, he qualified as a doctor in 1884, but devoted himself to writing short stories rather than medical practice. A collection *Particoloured Stories* (1886) consolidated his reputation, and gave him leisure to develop his style: *My Life* (1895), *The Lady with the Dog* (1898) and *In the Ravine* (1900). His 1st play *Ivanov* (1887) was a failure, as was *The Seagull* (1896) until revived by Stanislavsky in 1898 at the Moscow Arts Theatre, for which C. went to write *Uncle Vanya* (1899), *The Three Sisters* (1901) and *The Cherry Orchard* (1904). Not influential in Russian literature, he has been widely recognized abroad, espec. in Britain, where there is a tendency to over-solemnify. He relies on the creation of atmosphere and delineation of internal development, rather than external action.

CHEKIANG (chekyang'). The smallest, but densely populated, prov. of China, covering an area of 37,700 sq. m.; in 1968 it had a population of *c.* 31,000,000. The cap. is Hangchow. Among its products are rice, silk, cotton, jute, tea, fruits, lumber and fish; also some coal and salt.

CHELMSFORD. County town (bor.) of Essex, England, 30 m. N.E. of London. It is a market town of some importance, and manufactures radio parts, electrical apparatus, ball bearings, agricultural implements, etc. The name derives from the ford on the Chelmer. Pop. (1961) 49,810.

CHELONIA (kilō'nia). Order of reptiles, including the tortoises and turtles, and distinguished, among other characteristics, by their body protected by a bony carapace or shell, into which the head and limbs can be withdrawn.

CHELSEA. Formerly a met. bor., it was merged in 1965 in the new Royal Bor. of Kensington and C. (q.v.). The district of C. is immediately N. of the Thames, where it is crossed by the Albert and C. bridges. The Royal Hospital was founded by Charles II 1682 for old and disabled soldiers, 'Chelsea Pensioners'; the Physic Garden for botanical research was estab. in the 17th cent.; and the home of Thomas Carlyle in Cheyne Row is maintained by the Nat. Trust.

CHELTENHAM. English town on the Chelt, in Glos, at the foot of the Cotswolds. It is a spa and summer resort, and has many educational establishments, incl. C. Ladies' College, opened in 1854, and C. College, a public school for boys, founded in 1841. A Festival of Literature (estab. 1949) is held annually. Pop. (1961) 71,968.

CHELYABINSK. Industrial town of the R.S.F.S.R., cap. of C. region. It lies E. of the Ural Mountains, *c.* 150 m. S.S.E. of Sverdlovsk. It has ferrous and non-ferrous industries and engineering works, and makes chemicals, motor vehicles, and aircraft. Pop. (1967) 820,000.

C. region, area 33,900 sq. m., is an important iron-producing area, with manganese, chrome, nickel, limestone, and other mineral deposits also. An area devoted mainly to heavy industry, it includes Magnitogorsk. There is some agriculture in the E. Pop. (est.) 2,500,000.

CHEMISTRY. The science concerned with the composition of matter, and of the changes which take place in it under varying conditions.

The ancient civilizations were familiar with certain chemical processes, e.g. extracting metals from their ores, and making alloys. The alchemists were concerned with endeavouring to turn base metals into gold, and modern chemistry may be said to have evolved from alchemy towards the end of the 17th cent. Robert Boyle (1627–91) defined elements as the simplest substances into which matter could be resolved. The alchemical doctrine of the four elements (earth, air, fire, and water) gradually lost its hold, and the theory that all combustible bodies contained a substance called phlogiston was discredited by the experimental work of Black (1728–99), Lavoisier (1743–94), and Priestley (1733–1804), the last-mentioned discovering the presence of oxygen in the air. Cavendish (1731–1810) discovered the composition of water, and Dalton (1766–1844) put forward the atomic theory, which ascribed a precise relative weight to the 'simple atom' characteristic of each element. Much research then took place leading to the development in modern times of biochemistry, chemotherapy, plastics, etc.

All matter can exist in three states: gas, liquid or solid. It is composed of minute particles termed *molecules* which are constantly moving, and may be further divided into *atoms* (q.v.). Molecules which contain atoms of one kind only are known as *elements*, while those which contain atoms of different kinds are called *compounds*. The separation of compounds into simpler substances is analysis, and the building up of compounds from their components is synthesis. When substances are brought together without changing their molecular structure they are said to be *mixtures*. Chemical compounds are produced by a chemical action which alters the arrangement of the atoms in the molecule. Heat, light, vibration, catalyst, radiation or pressure, as well as moisture (for ionization), may be necessary to produce a chemical change.

To facilitate the expression of chemical composition, symbols are used to denote the elements. The symbol is usually the first letter or letters of the English or Latinized name of the element, e.g. C, Carbon; Ca, Calcium; Fe, Iron (Ferrum). These symbols represent one atom of the element; molecules containing more than one atom are denoted by a subscript figure, e.g. Water, H_2O. In some substances a group of atoms acts as a single atom, and these are enclosed in brackets in the symbol, e.g. $(NH_2)_2SO_4$, ammonium sulphate. The symbolical representation of a molecule is known as a formula. A figure placed before a formula represents the number of molecules of one substance present in another, e.g. $2 H_2O$, two molecules of water. Chemical reactions are expressed by means of equations, viz. $NaCl + H_2SO_4 = NaHSO_4 + HCl$. This equation states the fact that sodium chloride (NaCl) on being treated with sulphuric acid

TABLE OF CHEMICAL ELEMENTS

Name	Symbol	At. no.	Internat. at. wt.	Name	Symbol	At. no.	Internat. at. wt.	Name	Symbol	At. no.	Internat. at. wt.
actinium ...	Ac	89	227	gadolinium ...	Gd	64	157·26	potassium			
aluminium				gallium ...	Ga	31	69·72	(kalium) ...	K	19	39·100
(aluminum)	Al	13	26·98	germanium ...	Ge	32	72·60	praseodymium	Pr	59	140·92
americium ...	Am	95	(243)	gold (aurum)...	Au	79	197·0	promethium	Pm	61	(147)
antimony (sti-				hafnium ...	Hf	72	178·50	protactinium	Pa	91	231
bium) ...	Sb	51	121·76	helium* ...	He	2	4·003	radium ...	Ra	88	226
argon* ...	A	18	39·944	holmium ...	Ho	67	164·94	radon* ...	Rn	86	222
arsenic ...	As	33	74·91	hydrogen* ...	H	1	1·0080	rhenium ...	Re	75	186·22
astatine ...	At	85	(210)	indium ...	In	49	114·82	rhodium ...	Rh	45	102·91
barium ...	Ba	56	137·36	iodine ...	I	53	126·91	rubidium ...	Rb	37	85·48
berkelium ...	Bk	97	(249)	iridium ...	Ir	77	192·2	ruthenium ...	Ru	44	101·1
beryllium ...	Be	4	9·013	iron (ferrum)	Fe	26	55·85	samarium ...	Sm, Sa	62	150·35
bismuth ...	Bi	83	208·99	krypton* ...	Kr	36	83·80	scandium ...	Sc	21	44·96
boron ...	B	5	10·82	lanthanum ...	La	57	138·92	selenium ...	Se	34	78·96
bromine**	., Br	35	79·916	lawrencium ...	Lw	103	(257)	silicon ...	Si	14	28·09
cadmium ...	Cd	48	112·41	lead (plumbum)	Pb	82	207·21	silver (argen-			
caesium				lithium ...	Li	3	6·940	tum) ...	Ag	47	107·873
(cesium) ...	Cs	55	132·91	lutetium ...	Lu	71	174·99	sodium (natrium)	Na	11	22·991
calcium ...	Ca	20	40·08	magnesium	Mg	12	24·32	strontium ...	Sr	38	87·63
californium ...	Cf	98	(251)	manganese ...	Mn	25	54·94	sulphur ...	S	16	32·066
carbon ...	C	6	12·011	mendelevium	Mv	101	(256)	tantalum ...	Ta	73	180·95
cerium ...	Ce	58	140·13	mercury (hy-				technetium ...	Tc	43	(99)
chlorine* ...	Cl	17	35·457	drargyrum)**	Hg	80	200·61	tellurium ...	Te	52	127·61
chromium ...	Cr	24	52·01	molybdenum	Mo	42	95·95	terbium ...	Tb	65	158·93
cobalt ...	Co	27	58·94	neodymium ...	Nd	60	144·27	thallium ...	Tl	81	204·39
columbium, see				neon* ...	Ne	10	20·183	thorium ...	Th	90	232·05
niobium				neptunium ...	Np	93	(237)	thulium ...	Tm	69	168·94
copper				nickel ...	Ni	28	58·71	tin, (stannum)	Sn	50	118·70
(cuprum) ...	Cu	29	63·54	niobium, col-				titanium ...	Ti	22	47·90
curium ...	Cm	96	(247)	umbium ...	Nb	41	92·91	tungsten (wolf-			
dysprosium ...	Dy	66	162·51	nitrogen* ...	N	7	14·008	ram) ...	W	74	183·86
einsteinium ...	E	99	(254)	osmium ...	Os	76	190·2	uranium ...	U	92	238·07
Element 102	—	102	(254)	oxygen* ...	O	8	16·000	vanadium ...	V	23	50·95
erbium ...	Er	68	167·27	palladium ...	Pd	46	106·4	xenon* ...	Xe	54	131·30
europium ...	Eu	63	152·0	phosphorus ...	P	15	30·975	ytterbium ...	Yb	70	173·04
fermium ...	Fm	100	(253)	platinum ...	Pt	78	195·09	yttrium ...	Y	39	88·91
fluorine* ...	F	9	19·00	plutonium ...	Pu	94	(242)	zinc ...	Zn	30	65·38
francium ...	Fr	87	(223)	polonium ...	Po	84	210	zirconium ...	Zr	40	91·22

* = gas; ** = liquid; the remainder are solids. Atomic weights are for elements as found in nature, and those in parenthesis in the table are for the most stable isotope of the more recently discovered man-made elements which are represented only by unstable isotopes. They are International atomic weights 1959 based on oxygen 16·000. See also Transuranium Elements.

(H_2SO_4) is converted into sodium bisulphate ($NaHSO_4$) and hydrogen chloride (HCl).

Elements are divided into two classes: metals, having lustre, and being conductors of heat and electricity, and non-metals, which usually lack these properties. The Periodic System developed by Newlands (1863) and established by Mendeleyeef in 1869, classified elements according to their atomic weights, i.e. the least weight of the element present in a molecular weight of any of its compounds. Those elements which resemble each other in general properties were found to bear a relation to one another by weight, and these were placed in groups or families. Certain anomalies in this system were removed by classifying the elements according to their atomic number. The latter is the equivalent of the charge on the nucleus of the atom.

Organic Chemistry is that branch of C. which deals with carbon compounds. *Inorganic C.* deals with the description, properties, reactions, and preparation of the elements and their compounds, with the exception of carbon compounds. *Physical C.* treats of the particular changes which materials may undergo in special circumstances. Physical changes are changes of state only, the properties of the material remaining unaltered. This branch studies in particular the movement of molecules, and the effects of temperature and pressure, especially with regard to gases and liquids. *See* ORGANIC CHEMISTRY, INORGANIC CHEMISTRY, etc.

CHEMNITZ. Another name for KARL-MARX-STADT.

CHEMULPO. Chinese name for INCHON.

CHENGCHOW. Chinese town, made cap. of Honan prov. in 1954. It lies 40 m. W. of Kaifeng, the old cap., and is a railway junction and market town; it makes cotton textiles. Pop. (est.) 500,000.

CHENGHSIEN. Older name for CHENGCHOW.

CHENGTEH (chung'te). Chinese city, about 110 m. N.E. of Peking, formerly cap. of Jehol prov. (abolished 1955). Here the Manchu rulers of China had their summer residence. Pop. (est.) 60,000.

CHENGTU (chungdōō'). Walled city of China, cap. of Szechwan prov., seat of Szechwan univ. and a busy industrial centre with silk and other textile factories, engineering works, and railway workshops. Pop. (1957 est.) 1,107,000.

CHÉNIER (shehnyeh'), **André de** (1762–94). French poet, b. at Constantinople, son of a French father and a Greek mother. He began to write poetry in imitation of classical models, visited Italy and London, and in 1790 associated himself in Paris with the Feuillant Club, a group of constitutional royalists, and pub. political poems and prose. In 1793 he went into hiding, but continued to write, among other poems, his *Ode à Charlotte Corday*, and his *Ode à Versailles*. Finally he was arrested, and, on 25 July 1794, guillotined. While in prison he wrote some of his most famous poems, including the *Jeune Captive* and the political *Iambes*.

CHENNAULT (shen'awlt), **Claire Lee** (1890–1958). American airman. B. in Texas, he became aviation adviser to Chiang Kai-shek in 1937. In 1941 he founded the American Volunteer Group ('Flying Tigers') of airmen attached to the Chinese army fighting the Japanese, and was commander of the

14th U.S. Air Force in China 1943–5. *Way of a Fighter* (1949) is an autobiography.

CHENOPODIUM (keno-). Genus of plants, known as goose-foot. All-good, or Good King Harry (*C. bonus-Henricus*) is the most familiar species, a common wayside weed in Britain which was formerly cultivated, being used as a substitute for spinach.

CHEN YI (1905–72). Chinese soldier/statesman The son of a magistrate, he was awarded a scholarship for study in France. Returning to China, he became a member of the Communist Party in 1923 and then in 1927 of the political branch of the Chinese army. In the S.W.W. he was prominent in the campaigns against Japan, and in 1949 took Nanking and Shanghai from the Nationalists. In 1958–69 Chou En-Lai made him his own successor as For. Min., and he was thought a likely eventual successor to him as Premier, but in the Cultural Revolution he was under attack.

CHEPSTOW. Market town (U.D.) of Monmouthshire, England, 15 m. N.E. of Newport, on the Wye. The high tides (sometimes 50 ft. above low level) are the highest in Britain. C. has ruins of a castle, and those of Tintern Abbey are 4 m. N. of C. Pop. (1961) 6,041.

CHEQUE (chek). A form of bill of exchange, drawn on a bank by a depositor. It need not be on a special form, though this is usual. The essentials of a C. are that it should bear the date on which it is payable, name in words and figures a definite sum of money to be paid, to a named person or body or to bearer, to be signed by the drawer, and in the U.K. (not in U.S.A.) formerly bore a revenue stamp. It is then payable on presentation at the bank on which it is drawn. If the C. is 'crossed', it is not negotiable and can be paid only through a bank; in the U.S.A. a C. (spelled check) cannot be made non-negotiable. An Act of 1957 made endorsement of a C. paid into the payee's account unnecessary in the U.K.

CHEQUERS. Country seat of the Prime Minister for the time being of the U.K. It is an Elizabethan mansion in the Chiltern hills near Princes Risborough, Bucks, and was given to the nation by Lord Lee of Fareham under the Chequers Estate Act, 1917, which came into effect in Jan. 1921.

CHER (shār). French r. which rises in Creuse dept. and flows into the Loire below Tours. Length 220 m. It gives its name to a dept.

CHERBOURG (shārbŏŏr'). French port and naval station at the N. end of the Cotentin peninsula, in the dept. of Manche. It is one of the chief ports of call in France, particularly for liners making the Atlantic crossing, and has large shipbuilding yards. During the S.W.W., C. was captured in June 1944 by the Allies who thus gained their 1st large port of entry into France. C. was severely damaged; restoration of the harbour was completed in 1952. Pop. (1962) 40,018.

CHERENKOV, Pavel (1904–). Russian physicist. Ed. at Voronezh univ., he discovered in 1934 the *C. Effect*, important in atomic physics: when charged atomic particles pass through water or other media at a speed in excess of that of light itself, a bluish light is emitted. In 1958 C. and his colleagues Ilya Frank and Igor Tamm were awarded a Nobel prize. The C. Effect has also been claimed as the discovery of Fr. scientist Lucien Mallet.

CHERKASOV, Nikolai Konstantinovich (1903–66). Russian actor. Trained at the Leningrad Institute of Stage Art, he became in 1933 a member of the Leningrad State Pushkin Theatre of Drama. His roles incl. Peter I in Tolstoy's play and Krogstadt in Ibsen's *A Doll's House*, and he appeared in the title rôles of the films *Alexander Nevsky* (1938) and *Ivan the Terrible* (1945). He pub. interesting reminiscences *From an Actor's Notebook* (1951).

CHERKA′SSKY, Shura (1911–). Russian pianist.

Ed. at the Curtis Institute of Music, Philadelphia, he was a pupil of Hofmann, and has a remarkable technique.

CHERKA′SSY. Town on the Dnieper in the Ukrainian S.S.R., cap. of C. region; it has distilleries, flour mills, tanneries, and clothing factories. Pop. (est.) 52,000.

CHERNIAKO′VSKY, Ivan Danilovich (1908–45). Russian general. B. in the Ukraine, the son of a Jewish railwayman, he had a distinguished military career, and was promoted to major-general in 1942. He liberated Minsk, Vitebsk, and Vilna from the Germans, and led the invasion of East Prussia. He d. of wounds received in action.

CHERNIGOV (chernēgof'). Town on the Desna in the N. of the Ukrainian S.S.R., cap. of C. region. It has an 11th cent. cathedral. Lumbering, distilling, and food-canning are among its industries. Pop. (1967) 132,000.

CHERNOVTSY. City of the Ukrainian S.S.R., on the Prut r., cap. of C. region. It has a univ. founded 1875. It was in Rumania 1918–40. Pop. (1967) 175,000.

CHERRY. Sub-genus of trees (*Cerasus*) of the genus *Prunus* distinguished from the plums and apricots by their fruit, a drupe, being spherical and smooth, and not covered with a bloom. They are probably derived from the 2 species, the wild or dwarf C. (*Prunus cerasus*), and the gean (*P. avium*), which grow wild in Britain. The former is the ancestor of the 'sour Cs.' – morello, duke, and Kentish C., and the latter of the 'sweet Cs.' – hearts, mazzards, and bigarreaus. Besides those varieties which are grown for their fruit, others are well-known ornamental trees.

CHERUBINI (keroobē′nē), **Maria Luigi Carlo Zenobio Salvatore** (1760–1842). Italian composer. B. at Florence, his first opera *Quinto Fabio* was produced at Alessandria in 1780. In 1784 he went to London and became composer to the king, but from 1788 Paris became his permanent home. There he produced a number of dramatic works, e.g. *Médée* (1797), the ballet *Anacréon* (1803), and *Les deux Journées*. In 1809 with a Mass in F he began his career as a great church composer. In 1822 he became director of the Conservatoire at Paris; in 1835 appeared his treatise *Counterpoint and Fugue*; and in 1836 his Requiem in D minor was written.

CHERVIL. Genus of umbelliferous plants (*Chaerophyllum*). The garden C. (*C. cerefolium*) has leaves with a sweetish odour, somewhat resembling parsley. It is used as a garnish, and as a pot-herb.

CHERWELL (char′-), **Frederick Alexander Lindemann**, viscount C. (1886–1957). British physicist. Director of the Physical Laboratory of the R.A.F. at Farnborough in the F.W.W., he was personal adviser to Churchill on scientific and statistical matters during the S.W.W. He was prof. of experimental philosophy at Oxford 1953–6.

CHESHIRE, Geoffrey Leonard (1917–). British airman. Commissioned with the R.A.F. on the outbreak of the S.W.W., he  won the V.C., D.S.O. (with 2 bars) and D.F.C., and in 1945 was an official observer at the dropping of the atom bomb on Nagasaki: he retired in 1946. A devout Roman Catholic, he founded in 1948 the first C. Foundation Home for the Incurably Sick, an example followed in Britain, Europe and the Far East.

CHESHIRE. County in N.W. England, with a

CHESHIRE. Little Moreton Hall at Congleton, here seen from the south-east, is one of the finest examples of black and white timbering in England, and in its present form dates from the late sixteenth century. *Courtesy of the National Trust.*

coast on the Irish Sea. Most of it is a plain with fertile soil. The chief rivers are the Mersey, Dee, and Weaver. The inland waterways are important.

Textiles are made at Stockport, Stalybridge, Dukinfield, Hyde, Macclesfield, and Congleton. There are large tanneries at Birkenhead and Nantwich; shipbuilding yards about Birkenhead, which is an important port; locomotive works at Crewe. Soap, margarine, etc., are made in the Port Sunlight area. Coal is mined in E. Cheshire, and brine pumped up from a wide district near the Weaver is turned into salt, alkali, etc., at Northwich, Nantwich, and Winsford. Chief towns: Chester (co. town), Birkenhead, Stockport, Wallasey, Crewe, Hyde, Macclesfield. Area 1,015 sq. m.; pop. (1967) 1,486,470.

CHESIL BANK. A shingle bank extending *c.* 11 m. along the coast of Dorset, England, from Abbotsbury to the 'Isle' of Portland, breached by storms in 1954.

CHESS. A game of great antiquity, played by 2 players on a board of 64 squares alternating black and white. Each player has 16 pieces, the one side white and other red or black. These pieces are placed as shown in the accompanying diagram; and (reading from the white square on the player's right) they are: king's rook (or castle), king's knight, king's bishop, king, queen, queen's bishop, queen's knight, queen's rook. In front of these is a line of pawns. The object of the game is to force the king of the opposite side into such a situation that he can neither move nor remain without the danger of being taken by some other piece – this is called being in check. If the king cannot be removed out of check, the game is lost. Each of the pieces can move only in a particular way.

C. is a game that is capable of being recorded; the method usually used is by naming and numbering the squares. Strategy varies from the flexibly defensive, prevalent in the 1930s and again in the 1960s, to the strongly attacking style of the immediate post-S.W.W. period. The 1st international tournament was held in London in 1851.

CHESTER. English city and seaport (co. bor.), also co. town of Cheshire, situated on the Dee, 16 m. S. of Liverpool. Its name derives from the Roman *Castra Devana*, the 'camp on the Dee', and there are many Roman and later remains. The city walls are intact – a unique feature in England. The cathedral dates from the 11th cent. but was restored in 1876. The church of St. John the Baptist is one of the finest examples of early Norman architecture. The famous 'Rows' are covered arcades dating from the Middle Ages. From 1070 to the reign of Henry III, C. was the seat of a county palatine. In 1506 it was constituted a co. of itself, and in 1541 was erected into a bishopric by Henry VIII, who founded the King's School. The

town hall dates from 1869. Although the silting up of the Dee destroyed C.'s importance as a port, navigation has been greatly improved by dredging. Pop. (1961) 59,283.

CHESTERFIELD, Philip Dormer Stanhope, 4th earl of (1694–1773). English statesman and man of letters. B. in London, he sat in parliament from 1715, and in 1726 succeeded his father as 4th earl. As an opponent of Walpole, he was Lord-Lieutenant of Ireland in 1745 and a Sec. of State in 1746. He moved in the literary circle of Swift, Pope, and Bolingbroke, and is remembered chiefly for his *Letters to his Son* (1774) – his natural son, Philip Stanhope (1732–68).

CHESTERFIELD. Market town (bor.) of Derbyshire, England, 25 m. N. of Derby, on the Rother, a coal-mining and industrial centre. All Saints' church is renowned for its crooked spire. Pop. (1961) 67,833.

CHESTER-LE-STREET. Town in Durham, England, 6 m. N. of Durham on the Great North Road and in an important coal-mining area. Pop. (1961) 18,948.

CHESTERTON, Gilbert Keith (1874–1936). British author. B. in London, he studied art but quickly turned to journalism. His sympathies at this time were with the Socialist attempts to remedy the evils of capitalism, but he later found his own solution in Distributism. In poetry his best work is in satire, in the humorous *Wine, Water, and Song* (1915), and in *The Ballad of the White Horse* (1911). Among his best-known serious prose works are his studies of Browning (1903) and Dickens (1906); and the collections of essays *Twelve Types* (1902), *Heretics* (1905), and *A Short History of England* (1917). The most famous of his novels are the series dealing with the adventures of the naïve priest-detective, who first appeared in *The Innocence of Father Brown* (1911); but others incl. *The Napoleon of Notting Hill* (1904), *The Man who was Thursday* (1908), *The Flying Inn* (1914), and *The Man who knew too Much* (1922). In 1922 C. entered the R.C. Church, and in 1936 his autobiography appeared.

His brother **Cecil Edward C.** (1879–1918) fearlessly denounced corruption in professional politics. The latter's wife **Ada Elizabeth C.** (d. 1962) pub. *In Darkest London* (1926), the result of an investigation of down-and-out life which led to her foundation of the 'Cecil' houses for homeless women, and *The Chestertons* (1941).

CHESS. The position of the pieces at the opening of play.

CHESTNUT (ches'nut). Genus of trees (*Castanea*) belonging to the same family as the oak and beech (Fagaceae). The Spanish or Sweet C., *C. sativa*, produces a fruit that is a common article of diet in Europe and U.S.A., and its timber is also valuable. The Horse chestnut or *Aesculus hippocastanum* is quite distinct, belonging to a different family, Sapindaceae or Hippocastanaceae. Other Cs. are the American C., which is *C. dentata*; the Japanese C., *C. crenata*; and the Chinese C., *C. molissima*.

CHETWODE (chet'wood), **Philip Walhouse,** 1st baron (1869–1950). British soldier. Under Allenby he had an important part in the capture of Jerusalem, Damascus and Aleppo in the F.W.W., and was C.-in-C. India 1930–5. Promoted field-marshal in 1933, he was awarded the O.M. in 1936, and was created a baron in 1945.

CHEVALIER (shevahlyeh'), **Albert** (1861–1923). British music-hall artist. A Londoner, he performed from the age of 8, and was celebrated for coster songs, such as 'Knocked 'em in the Old Kent Road' and 'My Old Dutch', and sketches.

CHEVALIER, Maurice (1888–1972). French actor. B. in Paris, he became famous as dancing-partner to Mistinguett at the Folies Bergère, and made numerous films incl. *The Innocents of Paris*, which revived his song 'Louise', and *Gigi* (1958).

CHEVIOTS. Range of hills 35 m. long, forming for some 30 m. the border between England and Scotland. The highest point is the Cheviot (2,676 ft.). For centuries the area was a battleground of English and Scots.

CHEWING GUM. A confectionery mainly composed of chicle (q.v.), sweetened with various flavours. The first patent was taken out in the U.S.A. in 1871.

CHEYNEY, Peter. Pseudonym of British crime-novelist, Reginald Evelyn Peter Southhouse-Cheyney (1896–1951). B. in London, where he was ed. at the univ., he became an actor, then a journalist. *This Man is Dangerous* (1936) was his first success.

CHIANG KAI-SHEK (chyang kī-shek) (1887–). Chinese generalissimo and statesman. B. at Ningpo, he entered the Chinese military academy and in 1907 joined the revolutionary party of Sun Yat-sen. He took part in the Revolution of 1911, and served on Sun Yat-sen's staff at Canton, 1917–20. In 1925 he was made C.-in-C. of the Kuomintang armies in S. China and established a national government at Nanking, of which in 1928 he became President and Generalissimo. From 1931 he was continuously engaged in striving to unite the Chinese against the Japanese menace. In 1936 he was kidnapped by Chang Hsüeh-liang, the 'Young Marshal', but was released after 13 days. Following the 'incident' near Peking on 7 July 1937, C. conducted the war against the Japanese invaders and in the early years suffered many reverses. In 1937 he had to move the cap. to Chungking, and in the next year he resigned the presidency in order to devote himself entirely to military leadership. In 1943, however, he was re-appointed President of the Republic and of the Executive Yüan or cabinet, while retaining his post as Generalissimo. During the S.W.W. he met Roosevelt and Churchill in 1943, and in 1945 received the surrender of the Japanese in China. But almost at once the former struggle between the Kuomintang and the Chinese Communists was renewed. He temporarily resigned the presidency 1949–50, and the Communist victory limited his rule to Formosa.

Madame Chiang Kai-Shek (Soong Mayling, 1898–) was the 3rd dau. of Charles Soong, a Chinese merchant, was ed. in U.S.A., and is a distinguished

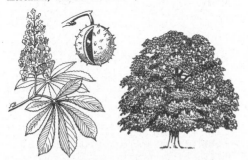

HORSE CHESTNUT, with foliage, flower and fruit.

sociologist. She assisted her husband in the foundation of the New Life Movement in 1934, designed to combat the opium habit and to encourage physical fitness, thrift, and public welfare, and accompanied her husband in most of his military and political journeys throughout China. During the S.W.W. she visited America and was prominent in the conferences at Delhi in 1942 and Cairo in 1943.

CHICAGO (shikah′gō). Second city in pop., third in area, of the U.S.A., in Illinois, on the S. shore of Lake Michigan. It covers just over 211 sq. m., and has a lake frontage of *c*. 25 m. The Chicago river cuts the city into three 'sides', joined by bridges and tunnels. The original lay-out of C. was rectangular, but many outer boulevards have been constructed on less rigid lines. As late as 1831 C. was still an insignificant village, but by 1871, when it suffered a disastrous fire, it was a city of more than 300,000 inhabitants. Rapid development began in the 1920s, and C. has become a series of towns rather than a centralized city. The old business and amusement centre was in the Loop; the newer business district lies to the north of it. C. was the original home of the skyscraper: the first was built here 1887–8, and during the years since many others have been erected, notably the Chicago Temple, the Tribune tower, the Wrigley building, the Civic Opera, and the Board of Trade offices. There are many fine parks, playgrounds and bathing beaches; cultural institutions incl. the Univ. of C., an art institute, a school of music, and a symphony orchestra.

C. is the greatest railway centre in the U.S.A.; the opening of the St. Lawrence Seaway in 1959 brought Atlantic shipping to its docks; it has two major airports and a number of smaller ones. It is the chief market in the U.S.A. for grain and livestock, and the biggest meat-packing centre. Its manufactures are on a colossal scale, steel (production capacity, more than 29,000,000 tons annually) being of outstanding importance. Government is by mayor and common council; the various social and racial groups in the city play an important part in local politics. Pop. (1970) 6,893,909.

The site of C. was visited by Jesuit missionaries in 1673, and Fort Dearborn, then a frontier fort, was built here in 1803. The World's Columbian Exhibition, commemorating the 400th anniversary of the discovery of America, was held in C. in 1893, and another great fair was held in 1933 and 1934. During the years of prohibition, 1919–33, the city became notorious for the activities of its gangsters.

CHICHEN ITZA (chechän′ etsa′). Maya city, Yucatan, Mexico, which flourished 11–13th cents. A.D. Excavated by Sylvanus Griswold Morley 1924–40, the remains incl. temples with magnificent sculptures and colour reliefs, an observatory, and a sacred well into which sacrifices, incl. human beings, were cast.

CHICHESTER, Sir Francis (1901–72). British yachtsman. B. in Devon, he became famous as a flier (1931 first E.-to-W. crossing of Tasman Sea in *Gipsy Moth*), and was knighted (K.B.E.) for his circumnavigation of the world in *Gipsy Moth IV* 1966–7.

CHICHESTER. English city and market town (bor.), cap. of W. Sussex, 69 m. S.W. of London nr. C. Harbour. It was an ancient Roman township and has a fine cathedral consecrated in 1108, later much rebuilt and restored; its spire is 277 ft. high. Other buildings are the guildhall, Vicars' Close, occupied by a theological college and the *Chichester Festival Theatre* (1962). Unique outside Italy are the remains (opened to the public 1968) of the Roman palace, built c. A.D. 80, at nearby Fishbourne. Pop. (1961) 20,118.

CHICKEN. *See* POULTRY.

CHICKEN POX. Varicella, an acute fever characterized by crops of small blisters and a rash. It is caused by an unknown virus, probably identical with that which causes shingles. One attack protects for life, probably against shingles as well. It chiefly attacks children under 10. The virus is probably air-borne, in the spray of coughing or speaking, but may also be transmitted on objects such as clothing or toys. The incubation period is 2–3 weeks.

CHICKWEED. A plant (*Stellaria media*) belonging to the pink family Caryophyllaceae. In Britain it is a common garden weed.

CHICLE (chik′l). Juice from the sapodilla tree of Central America. It is obtained by tapping, usually once in 5 years. Shortly after exposure, the juice hardens into gum. C. is the basis of chewing gum.

CHI′CORY. Plant (*Cichorium intybus*) belonging to the Compositae. It grows wild in Britain, mainly on chalky soils, and has large, usually blue, flowers. Its long tap-root is dried and roasted, to be mixed with coffee.

CHIFF-CHAFF. A bird (*Phylloscopus rufus*) of the warbler family (Sylviidae). It is olive-brown above and yellowish-white below, and is a summer migrant in England, being the first to arrive, about the middle of March.

CHIFLEY, Joseph Benedict (1885–1951). Australian Labour statesman. B. at Bathurst, N.S.W., of Irish descent, the son of a blacksmith, he became an engine-driver and was active with the Engine-Drivers' Union. Entering the Australian parliament in 1928, he was Min. of Defence in 1931–2, Treasurer in 1941–9, and Min. of Post-War Reconstruction in 1942–5. On the death of Curtin in 1945 he succeeded him as P.M. until Dec. 1949.

CHIHLI. Name of HOPEI prov., China, under Manchu; it means direct rule.

CHIHUAHUA (chēwah′wah). Mexican city, cap. of C. state, about 800 m. N.W. of Mexico City. It was founded 1707 and is the centre of a mining district. Pop. (1967) 221,500.

CHIHUAHUA. Breed of dog and one of the few varieties indigenous to the U.S.A., said also to be the smallest existing dog. Smooth and short-coated, prick-eared, skull large in comparison to body, in colour varied, it may weigh as little as 2 lb.

CHILBLAIN. A painful inflammation of the skin of the feet or hands, due to damp cold. The parts turn red, swell, itch violently, and are very tender. In a bad case the skin cracks, blisters, or ulcerates, or may even become gangrenous.

CHILDBIRTH. The expulsion of a child from its mother's body; labour. Normally a child grows within the womb (uterus) for 40 weeks from the date of conception; but birth may take place at any earlier time, and may be delayed by several weeks after the normal term. A child born before the end of the 7th month rarely survives. The birth of a dead child is called a stillbirth. Normal labour is spontaneous childbirth without assistance or complications.

CHILDE (chīld), **V. Gordon** (1892–1957). Australian archaeologist, director of the London Institute of Archaeology 1946–57. He discovered the prehistoric village of Skara Brae in the Orkneys, and in 1939 pub. *The Dawn of European Civilisation.*

CHILDERS (chil′derz), **Robert Erskine** (1870–1922). Irish Sinn Fein politician and writer. Before turning to Irish politics, he was a clerk in the House of Commons in London and author of the 'German spy' novel, *The Riddle of the Sands* (1903). In 1921 he was elected to the Irish parliament as a supporter of De Valera, and as a Republican took up arms against the Irish Free State in 1922. Shortly afterwards he was captured, court-martialled, and shot.

CHI′LE. S. American republic occupying the W. or Pacific slope of the Andes, S. of Peru. It is about 2,500 m. long, with an average width of 100 m. The country may be divided into 3 main areas: the chain of the Andes in the E., which extends through most of the length of C.; the central valley or tableland, and the coastal chain of mountains. The climate varies a great deal in different parts; the N. receives no rain and is desert, the S. is cold, wet, and heavily forested; the centre has a Mediterranean climate, and is the heart of C. This central area, which includes the largest cities – Santiago (the cap.), Valparaiso, and Concepción – is covered by farms and vineyards.

The principal rivers flow from E. to W.; they are short and of little importance for transport. The

CHILE. Lake Pehoe and the Paine mountains in the extreme south of Chile. Behind the Horns of the Paine, in the distance, are the famous Towers of Paine swept by 100-m.-an-hour winds: the central tower (8,760 ft.) was unclimbed until conquered by a British party in 1963.
Courtesy of Anglo-Chilean Society.

lakes are chiefly in the S. The chief ports from N. to S. are Arica, Iquique, Antofagasta, Coquimbo, Valparaiso, Talcahuano (port of Concepción), Puerto Montt, and Punta Arenas. There are 25 provs.

C. is the principal mining country in S. America. Sodium nitrate is found in Tarapacá and the Atacama desert; and in this region about 70 per cent of the world's iodine (an element which exists in nitrate deposits) is produced. Copper is mined in the mountainous region in the N. and is exported from Antofagasta and Tocopilla. Iron, coal, and many other minerals are worked.

The first European to see what is now Chile was Magellan who discovered and sailed through Magellan Strait in 1520. A Spanish expedition under Pedro de Valdivia founded Santiago in 1541. In 1810 there was a rising against Spain and a rep. was proclaimed; Spanish rule ended in 1818. The discovery of nitrates and guano in the borderlands to the N. led to disputes from 1866 onwards with Bolivia and Peru over frontiers which in 1879 came to war, ended in 1883 by a treaty under which C. gained Tacna (returned to Peru in 1929) and Arica provs. from Peru, Antofagasta prov. from Bolivia.

Salvadore Allende (1909–), elected pres. 1970, was the first Marxist .to be elected head of state by democratic vote in the Western world.

Govt. is by a president elected every 6 years by direct popular vote, and a national congress with senate and chamber of deputies, half the former and all the latter being re-elected every 4 years. The national language is Spanish; education is free and compulsory from 7–15. There are 8 univs., the oldest founded 1842. Area 286,400 sq. m.; pop. (1960) 7,339,546.

CHILLON (shē-yoń′). A fortress on an island rock at the E. end of Lake Geneva, Switzerland, made famous by a poem of Byron. It dates from the 8th cent.

CHILOPODA (kilo′poda). An important subdivision of the Arthropoda (q.v.) comprising the centipedes (q.v.).

CHILTERN HUNDREDS. The stewardship of the C.H. is a nominal office which may be accepted by a M.P. who wishes to resign his seat. Another is the stewardship of Northstead in Yorks

CHILTERNS. Range of chalk hills extending for some 45 m. in a curve from a point N. of Reading to the Suffolk border. The highest point is Haddington Hill near Wendover (857 ft.).

CHIMAERA (ki-mē′rah). Genus of fishes, typical

CHINA. A trio of lumbermen pause for a moment in their work, and provide an interesting study in facial expression.
Photo: Camera Press.

of the order Holocephali of the class Selachia. They resemble the sharks and rays in having a cartilaginous skeleton, and in laying large, single eggs, enclosed in a horny case. The Arctic C. or rabbit fish (*C. monstrosa*) is sometimes taken in British waters.

CHIMPANZEE (*Anthropopithecus troglodytes*). An anthropoid ape, which, apart from the gorilla, is the most man-like in structure. Like the gorilla it lives in the forests of West and Central Africa, but it is easily distinguished by its smaller size, larger ears, and unswollen nostrils. Its arms are somewhat shorter, reaching to the knees in the erect posture, and the hands and feet are narrower. An adult male is about 4½ ft. in the upright position and the female is some 6 in. shorter. Cs. feed mainly on fruit.

CHINA. Country of E. Asia, one of the largest in the world, and the most populous. The territory of the Chinese Rep. embraces the Chinese provs. (incl. former Manchuria) and bordering autonomous regions. Following the Communist conquest of the country in 1949, the provs. were several times re-organized.

Physical. China proper consists of 3 great river systems – the Hwang-Ho, or Yellow river, in the N.; the Yangtze-Kiang in central China; and the Si-Kiang in the S. Their basins are separated by mountain ranges. In the far N., beyond the Hwang-Ho, is the Mongolian plateau, merging into the loess-covered plateau of N.W. China. The S. part of the country is occupied by a rugged plateau, much dissected. In the W. is the Szechwan or Red basin, surrounded by mountains, except for the gorge where the Yangtze breaks through to the plain of central China. Beyond Szechwan, to the W., rises the lofty plateau of Tibet. Covering such a huge area, and with such varying surface conditions, C. has a very diverse climate, with Jan. temperatures below 0° F. in the N.E. and as high as 65° F. in Hainan. Rainfall is much heavier in the S. (85 in. at Pakhoi in Kwangtung, 14 in. at Tai-yuan in Shansi).

Originally much of C. was forested, but the Chinese have cut down the trees over large areas, and the torrential rains cause great erosion of the land, washing away crops and soil. Agriculture remains the main occupation of the people who farm the land

CHIMPANZEE

DIVISIONS OF CHINA			
Provinces	Area in sq. m.	Population (1968) in 1,000s	Capital
Anhwei ...	54,300	35,000	Hofei
Chekiang ...	37,700	31,000	Hangchow
Chinghai ...	278,400	2,000	Sining
Fukien ...	47,500	17,000	Foochow
Heilungkiang	179,000	21,000	Harbin
Honan ...	64,500	50,000	Chengchow
Hopei ...	83,700	43,000	Shihchiachuang
Peking*	3,386	7,000	
Tientsin* ...	1,200	4,000	
Hunan ...	81,100	38,000	Changsha
Hupei ...	72,600	32,000	Wuhan
Kansu ...	141,500	13,000	Lanchow
Kiangsi ...	63,600	22,000	Nanchang
Kiangsu ...	39,500	47,000	Nanking
Shanghai*	2,240	10,000	
Kirin ...	72,200	17,000	Changchun
Kwangtung	89,300	40,000	Kwangchow
Kweichow ...	67,100	17,000	Kweiyang
Liaoning ...	58,300	28,000	Shenyang
Shansi ...	60,700	18,000	Taiyuan
Shantung ...	59,200	56,000	Tsinan
Shensi ...	75,600	21,000	Sian
Szechwan ...	219,700	70,000	Chengtu
Yunnan ...	168,400	23,000	Kunming
Autonomous Regions			
Inner Mongolia	454,600	13,000	Huhehot
Kwangsi-Chuang	85,900	24,000	Nanning
Ningsia-Hui	25,640	2,000	Yinchuan
Sinkiang-Uighur	635,800	8,000	Urumchi
Tibet ...	471,700	1,000	Lhasa
	3,745,000	706,000	

Seat of Nationalist Government:

Formosa ...	13,890	13,000	Taipei

*Special municipalities

by hand, fertilizing it with human and animal manure, irrigating it with flood waters which deposit silt on the land, and conserving its productivity by careful rotation of crops. In the S. rice is the main crop and staple food material; to the N. this gives way to wheat, and N. again to millet. The soya bean is particularly important in the N., cotton in the Yangtze basin, tea in the centre and S., and groundnuts, maize, etc., in other parts. Silkworms are reared in the central parts. The chief animal is the pig, which provides valuable by-products such as bristles. Oxen and buffaloes are the draught animals in the S., and mules and horses in the N., but animal transport is nowhere as important as human labour. Sheep are kept in the N. and N.W., and chickens everywhere. Cattle are less important. Under the Communist régime irrigation and more intensive cultivation are being extended in the N.E. and N.W., and in the S. existing intensive cultivation is being increasingly aided by the use of farm machinery. Industrialization, stimulated in particular in Manchuria by the Japanese during their ascendancy in eastern China, was intensified by the Communists who from 1952 drew up five-year plans of industrial development affecting the areas N. of the Yangtze where C.'s most accessible raw materials – coal, iron, cotton, wool, petroleum – are concentrated. Most important of the coal deposits are those in Shansi and Szechwan; iron occurs in the N.E.; and tin, copper and other minerals are also found. The chief ports of C. are Shanghai, Canton, Tientsin, Foochow, and Amoy; inland centres incl. Peking, the capital, Nanking, Hankow, and Chungking. Fushun is a great oil-producing centre and Anshan produces iron and steel.

Government. After the Chinese Communists drove the remnant of the Nationalist Chinese forces from the mainland in 1949, they immediately introduced a Communist republican form of govt., ratified in 1954 by a national people's congress elected under Communist guidance from all over the country. Besides the people's congress, elected for 4 years and in theory the highest authority in the state, there is a state council and standing committees of the congress. The head of state is a chairman elected by the congress, but the Communist party wields the real power.

History. Chinese civilization is the oldest in existence. The social system which endured until this cent. was stabilized fully 3,500 years ago. The so-called Sage Kings (2800–2205 B.C.) were all associated with civilizing developments – agriculture, medicine, river conservancy, etc. There followed the Hsia dynasty (2205–1557 B.C.) of which little is known. Then came the Shang dynasty, whose artistic genius is illustrated in the still existing bronze vases; it was replaced about 1050 by the Chou dynasty, followed in 221 B.C. by the shortest and most remarkable of the dynasties, the Ch'in, comprising the reign of Shih Hwang Ti, who curbed the feudal nobility and introduced a widespread system of orderly government; he also built the Great Wall to keep out the northern barbarians. The next dynasty was the Han (206 B.C.–A.D. 220) under which the keeping of historical records was systematized and the idea of the unity of China was so firmly implanted that, though that unity has often been broken, it always re-asserted itself. After a period of division between N. and S. came the T'angs (618–906), the most brilliant centuries in China's history. After another period of disruption the Sungs ruled (960–1279) in an age of culture and refinement. The Mongols reigned from 1279–1368, when they were expelled by the 1st of the Mings (1368–1644); during their rule, in the 16th cent., Europeans began to arrive in China.

The last of the dynasties was the Manchu (1644–1912) which gave several great rulers to C., up to the empress dowager Tz'e Hsi who d. in 1908. Three years later revolution broke out, and in 1912 the infant emperor (*see* PU YI, HENRY) was deposed. The principal maker of the revolution was Sun Yat-sen, who became President of the Republic. He d. in 1925, and for years afterwards C. was distracted by civil war conducted by rival war lords. Then the country was divided between the nationalist Kuomintang under Chiang Kai-shek and the Communists, who received Russian support. In 1931 the Japanese began their penetration of Manchuria, and in 1937 the so-called 'China Incident' outside Peking marked the beginning of open war which continued until 1945 when C., as one of the Allied Powers, received the surrender of the Japanese. The Civil War was then resumed, and in 1949, following their elimination of Nationalist resistance on the mainland, the Communists inaugurated the People's Republic of China. The Nationalists retired to Formosa (q.v.).

Dissension developed in the Communist Party from 1957 when Mao Tse-tung (q.v.) attempted to achieve 'pure' Communist aims at home and abroad. He failed and moderate policies prevailed 1959–62 when Liu Shao Chi replaced him as chairman of the rep., but he struggled to regain power and launched 1964 the Great Proletarian Cultural Revolution, adopted as Party policy 1966 and put into force by the youthful Red Guards and adult Revolutionary Rebels. Widespread disturbances ensued 1967–8 and industry was disrupted. Relations with Britain and Russia de-

CHINESE ART. White horse, unglazed earthenware, T'ang dynasty.

teriorated sharply. Western influence in C. began with the arrival of the Portuguese at Canton in 1517. Spanish, Dutch, French, British, and Americans followed; and during the 19th cent. it seemed likely that C. would be partitioned amongst the Powers. Trade was conducted through Treaty Ports which were in the ownership or control of one or other of the Great Powers, and the Chinese customs were managed by British officials. The last Chinese effort under the Empire to throw off western influences was the Boxer rising of 1900, repressed by European troops. The Treaty Ports were abolished by new agreements made 1943–7.

Relations with Britain eased in 1970, though the ideological clash with the U.S.S.R. continued, and in 1972 rapprochement with America, with whom a cold war had been maintained since the establishment of the Communist regime, was symbolised by a visit of the U.S. pres. to Peking. Within C. disorder ceased, educational institutions were restored, and Lin Piao (q.v.) fell into disgrace.

Area and Population. The Chinese vary widely from province to province. The main barrier between the Chinese and other nations is the extreme difficulty of the language. Apart from Islam, which prevails in the remote N.W., 3 philosophical systems, Taoism, Confucianism, and Buddhism, flourished in pre-Communist China; a Chinese could profess all at once. Area 3,745,000 sq. m.; pop. (1968) 706,000,000.

CHINA CLAY. *See* KAOLIN.

CHINAWARE. *See* POTTERY.

CHINCHIL'LA (family, Chinchillidae). Name given to several species of South American rodents allied to porcupines. They have long hind legs, longish ears, and a bushy tail; vary in size from a large squirrel to a small rabbit, are very active, and live in groups in burrows and rock crevices in the Andes of Bolivia and Chile. The Common C. (*Chinchilla lanigera*) is famous for its beautiful, soft, silvery-grey fur.

CHINDITS. Name given to troops of the 3rd Indian Division (Long Range Penetration Group) under the command of Brigadier Wingate (q.v.) in the S.W.W. The name was derived from Chinthay, the mythical animal – half lion, half eagle – at the entrance of Burmese pagodas to scare evil spirits.

CHINESE ARCHITECTURE. Since early times Chinese buildings have been constructed chiefly of timber, and consequently they do not usually last long. There are few buildings which date back earlier than the Ming dynasty (1368–1644), but there are records, such as the Ying Tsao Fa Shih (Method of Architecture), pub. in A.D. 1103, which describe and illustrate early Chinese buildings. These records reveal that C.A. has remained very much the same in style throughout the ages. Chinese buildings usually face S., a convention which can be traced back to the 'Hall of Brightness', a famous building of the Chou dynasty (c. 1050–221 B.C.). One of the most characteristic features of C.A. is the curved roof, believed to have been imported with Buddhism from India.

The Chinese are also famous for their walls. The Great Wall of China was built, c. 228–210 B.C., by the Emperor Ch'in Shih Hwang Ti along the northern frontier as a defence against the hostile nomadic tribes of the north. The fine city wall of Peiping dates back to the Ming dynasty, as also do some of the buildings in or near Peiping, notably the Altar of Heaven, the ancestral temple of the Ming tombs, and the Five Pagoda Temple. The pagoda with its tiled roofs one above the other is typically Chinese.

CHINESE ART. During China's Stone Age painted pottery and jade objects were made, but there was not a Chinese culture until the acquisition of bronze. During the Shang period, which lasted till c. 1050 B.C., beautiful bronze vessels were produced, and motifs, such as the dragon, the elephant, and the ogre's mask, were already in use. Under the Chou dynasty a feudal system emerged, together with important developments in the field of art. Buildings were often decorated with mural paintings, and this art is said to have won the praise of Confucius. The brush had been used for painting on pottery, and lacquer workers used brushes as early as 2 or 3 cents. B.C. The use of finer brushes resulted in the invention by Mêng T'ien of the writing brush, c. 200 B.C., and the development of calligraphy, which the Chinese have long regarded as the greatest of the fine arts.

The Han period (206 B.C.–A.D. 220) was very important in art. Silk weavings appeared, glaze was used to brighten pottery, great architectural schemes were carried out, relief sculpture, portrait and other painting developed.

The first of the great painters whose name we know – Ku K'ai Chih – worked c. A.D. 350–400 in S. China. Some of his illustrations on the inscribed scroll entitled *The Admonitions of the Instructress to the Court Ladies* are in the British Museum.

During the T'ang period (618–906) the art of painting reached its zenith, and porcelain was perfected. This was a period of great expansion, and China began to take an interest in her neighbours, both oriental and occidental. The shapes of vessels show the influence of Persian designs. The Sung period (960–1279) is famous for its many beautiful landscape paintings, and its many animal, flower, and bird paintings which were executed with great delicacy and charm. An Imperial Academy of Painting was founded by the emperor Hui Tsung, who was himself a talented painter of birds. Then with the Mings (1368–1644) there was an outburst of patriotism which was reflected by artists and craftsmen in bold masses, free flowing line, and brilliant colour. Chinese architecture, pottery, and painting of the period display all these qualities. There was a flourishing trade in porcelain, and typical of the time are the large wine jars of sturdy design, tall and imposing vases with heavily outlined floral designs. Enamelling on metal was perfected.

The Ming dynasty was overthrown by invaders from Manchuria who proved to be excellent rulers. The Manchus fostered the arts and encouraged learning. Closer contact was made with western civilization. The two great liberal rulers of the period were K'ang Hsi, whose reign began in 1662, and Ch'ien Lung, who reigned from 1736 till almost the end of the 18th cent. Under K'ang Hsi porcelain became the most typical medium of expression. K'ang Hsi wares were chiefly the blue and white (called 'Nanking' in England), and the enamelled porcelains. During the 18th cent. there was a growing fad for intricacy of design. Although some fine pieces were produced during the reign of Ch'ien Lung, C.A. began to deteriorate, and it has never since recovered.

CHINESE LANGUAGE. Chinese is generally believed to belong to the Sinitic or Indo-Chinese family related to Tibetan, Burmese, Siamese, etc. Its chief characteristics are the possession of significant tones whereby the pitch or inflection of the voice entirely alters the meaning of a syllable, and monosyllabism. In course of time the spoken language has been affected by many innovations, but syllables which have become identical to the ear have remained distinguished to the eye. Thus the spoken language is distinguished from the written, and it was not until our own day that the spoken language has been given written form. The dialects of Chinese are many, and are so profoundly different as to constitute almost separate languages.

The classical written language has remained the same since about the 10th cent. A.D., while the spoken language moved further and further towards its modern form. Thus a good written style can be attained only after many years of study. After the establishment of the Republic, this was recognized as a hindrance to democratic development and Common Speech (Putonghua), based on the Peking dialect (Mandarin), was cultivated as a nat. spoken and written language. To speed reading and writing the characters, formerly vertical and read right to left, were from 1956 placed horizontally and read left to right, and c. 1,000 simplified characters were gradually introduced. A 25-letter Roman alphabet (excl. 'v'), introduced in primary schools 1957, is eventually to replace the old characters.

CHINESE LITERATURE. POETRY. Written in the ancient literary language understood throughout China, C. poems, often only 4 lines long, consist of rhymed lines of a fixed number of syllables, ornamented by parallel phrasing and tonal pattern. The oldest poems are contained in the *Book of Songs* (800–600 B.C.). Among the most famous C. poets are the nature poet T'ao Ch'ien (A.D. 372–427), the master of technique Li Po (701–62), the autobiographical Po Chü-i (772–846), and the wide-ranging Su Tung-p'o (1036–1101); and among the moderns using the colloquial language under European influence and experimenting in free verse are Hsu Chih-mo (1895–1931), and Pien Chih-lin (1910–).

PROSE. Typical C. history is less literary than an editing of assembled documents with moral comment, but the essay has long been cultivated under strict rules of form and style. Among the most famous essays is that of Han Yü (A.D. 768–824) *Upon the Original Way*, recalling the nation to Confucianism. Until the 16th cent. the short story was confined to the anecdote, startling by its strangeness, related in the literary language, e.g. those of the poetic Tuan Ch'eng-shih (d. A.D. 863), but after that time the more novelistic type in the colloquial tongue developed by its side. The C. novel has evolved entirely from the street storyteller's art, and has consequently always existed in the vulgar tongue. The early romances *Three Kingdoms*, *All Men are Brothers*, and *Golden Lotus* are anonymous, the earliest known author being Wu Che'ng-en (c. 1505–80); the most realistic of the great novelists is Ts'ao Chan (d. 1763).

20th cent. C. novels have largely adopted European form, and have been particularly influenced by Russia, as have the realistic stories of Lu Hsün (q.v.). In typical C. drama, the stage presentation far surpasses the text in importance (the dialogue was not even preserved in early plays), but the present cent. has seen experiments in the European mauuer.

CHINGHAI. Prov. of China, bordering Tibet; its chief products are grains and oil seeds. The cap. is Sining. Area 278,400 sq. m.; pop. (1968) 2,000,000.

CHINKIANG. Chinese city on the Yangtze-Kiang 40 m. N.E. of Nanking, at the point where the Grand Canal crosses the river. Once a British concession, it was opened to foreign trade in 1861, returned to China in 1927. Wheat, soya beans, rice are the principal items in its trade. Pop. (est.) 201,000.

CHINNERY, E. W. Pearson (1887–). Australian anthropologist. Official Adviser in Native Matters to the Commonwealth of Australia 1938–47, he was prominent in the discovery and pacification of cannibal and head-hunting tribes in the interior of New Guinea.

CHIOGGIA (kēoh'jah). City and port in N.E. Italy, 15 m. S. of Venice, built on C. island at the S. end of the Venice lagoon and connected by bridge with the mainland. Pop. (1960) 49,750.

CHIOS (kē'os). Greek island in the Aegean Sea,

CHIPMUNK

off the coast of Turkey. Cap. Chios, pop. (1961) 24,361. Area 321 sq. m.; pop. (1961) 62,090.

CHIPMUNK (*Tamias*). A kind of ground-squirrel found in N. America and E. Asia. Of small size and ornamented with white stripes, they are sometimes called striped gophers, and are distinguished from ordinary squirrels by having cheek-pouches. They inhabit woods, living in burrows or hollow logs. *See* illus p. 251.

CHIPPENDALE, Thomas (*c.* 1718–79). English cabinet-maker. The son of a joiner of Otley, Yorks, he went to London at the age of 20, and from 1753 had his workshop in St. Martin's Lane. His book *The Gentleman and Cabinet Maker's Director* (1754) was a landmark in furniture design, and illustrates his favourite styles – Louis XV, Chinese and Gothic. He worked mainly in dark mahogany.

THOMAS CHIPPENDALE. Mahogany bookcase in the Gothic style c. 1755 *Courtesy of the Lady Lever Collection.*

CHIPPENHAM (chip′nam). English market town (bor.) on the Avon in Wilts, 11 m. N.E. of Bath. Once a chief centre of the woollen trade, it produces condensed milk, bacon, etc., and has some light industry. Pop. (1961) 17 525.

CHIRGWIN, George H. (1854–1922). Music-hall artist; one of the most popular of all coon singers, and known as the 'White-Eyed Kaffir' from his trick of leaving one eye unblacked.

CHIRICO (kē′rēkō), **Giorgio de** (1888–). Italian artist. B. in Greece, of Italian parents, he was associated with the Dadaists and Surrealists, rearranging ordinary objects in unusual patterns. In more recent years he has revolted against 'modernism', producing a number of works in the style of Raphael. There are numerous striking self-portraits.

CHIRON (kī′ron). In Greek mythology, the wise centaur, son of Cronos and a sea nymph, and tutor of Jason, Achilles, and other heroes.

CHIROPODIST (kīrop′ōdist). One who is professionally concerned with the care and treatment of the hands and feet. The Society of Chiropodists functions in Britain under the Council for Professions Supplementary to Medicine. The first centre to provide treatment for the more common disorders of the foot was the Pedic Clinic in Bloomsbury, estab. in 1913 by E. G. V. Runting, which later became the London Foot Hospital.

CHIROPTERA (kīrop′terah). An order of mammals comprising the bats (q.v.), which are readily distinguished by the conversion of the fore-limbs into wings for the purpose of flight.

CHISINAU. Rumanian form of KISHINEV.

CHISLEHURST (chiz′lherst). District of the London bor. of Bromley. Camden Place (built by William Camden, q.v.) was the home of Napoleon III 1871–3. A nearby series of chambered caves, of unknown origin, were used as air-raid shelters in the S.W.W. and are open to the public.

CHISWICK (chiz′ik). An ancient English town, on the Thames, part of the Greater London borough of Hounslow from 1965. Hogarth, Barbara Palmer, duchess of Cleveland, and Whistler are buried at C., and it has other interesting associations.

CHITA. Russian town in eastern Siberia, cap. of C. region on the C. river. It is on the Trans-Siberian railway, and has engineering works, coal mines, etc. Pop. (1967) 201,000.

CHITAL (*Axis axis*), also known as the Axis or Spotted Deer. A medium-sized species of the deer family (Cervidae) inhabiting the jungles of India and Ceylon; it has white spots and resembles somewhat the fallow deer.

CHITRAL (chitrahl′). Former Indian princely state, merged in W. Pakistan in 1956. Area 5,700 sq. m.; pop. (1951) 105,724.

CHITTAGONG. Town and port in Bangladesh, the chief town of C. district. In 1967 a steel mill, and a power station fired by natural gas, were opened here. Pop. (1961) 364,205.

CHIVALRY (shiv′alri). Originally the knightly class of the feudal Middle Ages; subsequently the word came to mean the code of gallantry and honour that the knights were supposed to observe. The Court of C. endured from Edward III's reign to 1737.

CHIVE. A plant (*Allium schoenoprasum*) that sometimes grows wild in Britain, and is cultivated as a vegetable.

CHKALOV (chkah′lof). Name 1938–57 of ORENBURG.

CHLADNI (khlahd′nē), **Ernst Florens Friedrich** (1756–1827). German physicist, a pioneer in the field of acoustics.

CHLORAL (klor-) (CCl₃-CHO) or **Trichloracetaldehyde.** An oily colourless liquid with a characteristic pungent smell. It is very soluble in water, and its compound chloral hydrate is a powerful hypnotic.

CHLORATES. In chemistry, the salts of chloric acid, the common ones being those of sodium, potassium, and barium.

CHLORELLA (klore′la). A single-celled, freshwater green alga, 3–10 microns in diam., obtaining its growth energy from light. C. is capable of increasing its weight four-fold in a 12 hr. period, and already an essential tool for the study of photosynthesis in the laboratory, it may prove even more valuable as a staple foodstuff, particularly for space travellers. Although unpalatable, its nutritive content is high, consisting of 50% protein, 20% fat, 20% carbohydrate and 10% phosphate, calcium and other inorganic substances.

CHLORIDES (klor′ids). Salts of hydrochloric acid commonly formed by its action on various metals or by the direct combination of metal and chlorine.

CHLORINE (klor′ēn). A chemical element, a greenish-yellow gas with an irritating, suffocating smell. Symbol Cl; atomic weight, 35·457; atomic number 17. It rapidly attacks the membranes of the nose, throat, and lungs, producing bronchitis or pneumonia, and during the F.W.W. it was used as a weapon. It is never found uncombined in nature, but is widely distributed in combination with the alkali metals. Common or rock salt is sodium chloride. C. was discovered in 1774 by Scheele, but Sir H. Davy in 1810 first proved it to be an element. C. is an important bleaching agent and is used universally as a germicide for drinking water. It is also an oxidizing agent and finds many applications in organic chemistry.

CHLOROFORM. Trichloromethane, CHCl₃, with 1 or 2 per cent of alcohol to prevent it from decomposing on exposure to light. It is a clear, colourless liquid with a characteristic pungent, sweet, rather sickly smell and taste. It had been known to chemists long before David Waldie, chemist to the Apothecaries' Company of Liverpool, suggested to Professor James Young Simpson of Edinburgh in 1847 that it might be used as a general anaesthetic.

CHLOROMYCETIN (klō′rōmīsetin). Antibiotic which attacks viruses as well as bacteria, used in treatment of scrub-typhus, typhus and psittacosis.

CHLOROPHYLL (klo′rofil). The green colouring matter found in plants, being formed in the parts exposed to light. By its means, plants absorb and decompose carbon dioxide in order to produce oxygen and to form new organic substances.

CHOCOLATE. *See* COCOA.

CHODOWIECKI (kohdohvyets'kē), **Daniel Nicolas** (1726–1801). German painter and engraver. B. at Danzig of Polish descent, he is particularly famous for his engravings of scenes from the Seven Years War and the life of Christ, and for a picture of 'Jean Calas and his family'.

CHOIR (pron. and formerly spelt 'quire'). A trained body of singers, esp. as taking part in religious services, either leading the congregation or singing alone. The use of a C. in worship was taken over by the Christian Church from the Jews. In the Anglican Church, the C. consists, as a rule, of boys and men only, singing in 4 parts.

CHOISEUL (shwahzöl'), **Étienne François**, duke of (1719–85). French statesman. Originally a protégé of Mme de Pompadour, he became Minister for Foreign Affairs in 1758 and held this and other offices until 1770. He banished the Jesuits, and was a supporter of the *Philosophes*.

CHOLERA. Asiatic cholera, an acute epidemic disease, most common in India, due to a specific micro-organism (vibrio, spirillum) and characterized by violent diarrhoea, cramps, and a high death rate; this, however, has been reduced to about one per cent by Leonard Roger's treatment with copious injections of saline fluid.

CHOLESTEROL (koles'terol). Fatty alcohol occurring in bile and nervous tissue, and forming gall stones and causing arterio-sclerosis. Konrad Bloch (Harvard) and Feodor Lynen (Munich) received a Nobel prize 1964 for their research on C.

CHOPIN (shopań'), **Frédéric François** (1810–49). Polish composer. B. near Warsaw, the son of a French father and a Polish mother, he made his first public appearance as a pianist at the age of 9, and from 1831 made his home in Paris. Here he became well known in the fashionable salons, though he rarely performed in public. In 1836 Liszt introduced him to Mme Dudevant (George Sand, q.v.), with whom he had a liaison from 1839 which lasted for 7 years. At Majorca, George Sand nursed him – he was consumptive – and for a time he regained his health. He d. on 17 Oct. 1849 and was interred in Père Lachaise cemetery in Paris.

As a performer C. revolutionized the technique of pianoforte-playing. He excelled in the performance of his own works, and was at his best in the intimate atmosphere of a salon. As a composer, he made little attempt to handle the larger forms, but in his pieces for piano solo he is without a rival. These stand alone for their lyrical and poetic quality; in them Slavonic passion and melancholy are combined with French grace and refinement. Besides sonatas, his works incl. collections of waltzes, preludes, études, nocturnes, ballades, impromptus, fantasias, polonaises, and mazurkas.

CHORDATA (kordā'ta). The highest phylum of the animal kingdom, consisting of the Vertebrata, together with certain primitive forms lacking a true backbone, but agreeing in other characters, e.g. the sea squirts, lancelet, and Balanoglossus.

CHORLEY (chor'li). English town (bor.) in Lancs, 20 m. N.W. of Manchester. Cotton, chemicals, brassware, etc., are made. Pop. (1961) 31,262.

CHOSEN. Japanese name for KOREA.

CHOU EN-LAI (chō-enli) (1898–). Chinese statesman. B. in S. China, he was ed. at Nankai High School, and in Japan. After studying Communist organization in Europe, he became head of the political dept. of Whampoa Military Academy. Purged by Chiang Kai-shek in 1927 he went 'underground', and then during 1937–46 was Communist representative to the National Govt. at Nanking and Chungking. In 1949–58 he was Premier and For. Min. of the newly estab. People's Republic, becoming Premier of the State Council in 1958. He was a moderating influence in the Cultural Revolution 1966–8.

CHOUGH (chuf). Genus of birds (*Pyrrhocorax*) belonging to the crow family (Corvidae). The red-legged or Cornish C. (*P. graculus*) is now only rare and local in Britain. Its plumage is black, and the eggs are white, spotted with brown.

CHOW CHOW. Chinese breed of dog, popular in Britain as a pet. Its name is pidgin-English for 'food', and in China the C. is killed for human consumption. Its coat should be of one colour, and its chief peculiarity is its black tongue.

CHRÉTIEN DE TROYES (krehtē-ań' de trwah). Medieval French poet, b. in Champagne, about the middle of the 12th cent. His epics include *Le Chevalier de la Charrette*; *Perceval*, written for Philip, count of Flanders; *Erec*; *Yvain*, and other Arthurian romances.

CHRIST. *See* JESUS CHRIST.

CHRISTADELPHIANS (kristadel'fianz). A Christian religious denomination founded in Brooklyn, U.S.A., in 1848 by John Thomas (1805–71), an English medical student. They have no ministers or elders, hold to a strict literal interpretation of the Bible, and are millenarians. They are represented in Britain, the U.S.A., and other parts of the world.

CHRISTCHURCH (krIst'-). English town (bor.) in Hants, adjoining Bournemouth at the junction of the Stour and the Avon, with a fine Norman and Early English priory church. Pop. (1961) 26,498.

CHRISTCHURCH. City of South Island, New Zealand, on the Avon, 7 m. from its mouth. Principal city of the Canterbury plains, it has an Anglican cathedral, designed by Sir Gilbert Scott, and an R.C. cathedral; and is the seat of the Univ. of Canterbury. Pop. (1967) 163,800.

CHRISTENING (kris'ning). The Christian ceremony of baptism of infants, including giving a name.

CHRISTIAN. A professor of the religion founded by Jesus Christ. In Acts xi, 26, it is stated that the first to be called Christians were the disciples in Antioch.

CHRISTIAN. Name of 8 kings of Denmark and Norway. CHRISTIAN I (1426–81) was the first of the dynasty; in 1450 he established the union of Denmark and Norway which lasted until 1814. Under CHRISTIAN III, who reigned 1535–59, the Reformation was introduced. CHRISTIAN IV reigned 1588–1648, sided with the Protestants in the Thirty Years War, and founded Christiania (now Oslo, capital of Norway).

CHRISTIAN VIII was king of Denmark 1839–48. CHRISTIAN IX (1818–1906) was king of Denmark from 1863. His daughter Alexandra m. Edward VII of the U.K. and another m. Tsar Alexander III;

CHRISTCHURCH. A pleasant scene beside the Avon which could almost be in England in the spring.
Courtesy of the High Commissioner for New Zealand

his second son, George, became king of Greece. In 1864 he lost Schleswig-Holstein following a war with Austria and Prussia.

CHRISTIAN X (1870–1947) succeeded his father Frederick VIII as king of Denmark and Iceland in 1912. He m. Alexandrine, Duchess of Mecklenburg-Schwerin; and because of his democratic ways was highly popular. During the S.W.W. he was a semi-prisoner of the Germans in Copenhagen.

CHRISTIAN ACTION. Undenominational, non-party organization in Britain, founded in 1946 by Lewis J. Collins (q.v.), which aims at translating Christian teaching into action in local, national and international affairs. It opposes racial discrimination, aids refugees, relieves want and works for peace.

CHRISTIANIA. See OSLO.

CHRISTIANITY. One of the great world religions; regarded as having been founded by Jesus of Nazareth in the first third of the first Christian century. Like Buddhism and Islam it is a universal religion, claiming to be the true religion which ought to be believed by all men. It has, therefore, always been a missionary religion, and its expansion from its place of origin in Palestine is still in progress. Beginning as a religion of the Near East, it has become the religion of the West, and its central seat has been Europe. In fact C. has been the principal factor in Western culture. The last century has seen the greatest expansion of the Christian Church since its foundation.

C. includes a vast number of sects which represent different versions of the faith. The 3 main sections are: the Roman Catholic Church; the Eastern Orthodox Church; and the Evangelical communions which have since the Reformation repudiated the authority of the Pope. The schism between Eastern and Western churches was finally effected in 1054. The Reformation in the 16th cent. gave rise to 2 large groups of reformed churches – those which followed Luther and those which regarded Calvin as their teacher. The Protestant movement has since given birth to a very large number of smaller sects. Today there is a strong movement towards reunion, e.g. the presence of members of other churches as observers at the Vatican Council of 1962, and the reunion of the Anglican and Methodist churches discussed in 1963. The World Council of Churches (provisionally estab. 1938 and permanently 1948) has its H.Q. at Geneva, and incl. representatives of the Anglican, Eastern Orthodox, Protestant, and Old Catholic churches.

C. is grounded on the Bible, the N.T. in particular; in addition most Christians profess belief in the statements of the 3 creeds – the Apostles', the Nicene, and the Athanasian. Belief in God the Father, Who is all-good, all-wise and all-powerful, is the fundamental concept, combined with the doctrine of the Trinity, i.e. of the union of the three Persons of the Father, Son, and Holy Ghost in one Godhead. Only the comparatively few Unitarians reject the dogma of the divinity of Christ. Most Christians profess belief in the Incarnation and the Resurrection of Christ, although there are many Modernists of whom this can hardly be said. The universal belief of Christians is that Christ is the Redeemer, but there is no universal agreement as to the nature of the Atonement. Belief in a historical Fall in the Garden of Eden has declined since the propagation of the theory of Evolution in the last century.

Some churches are much more exclusive than others, and there is much dispute as to the number and meaning of the sacraments, but the Bible is accepted by all Christians as being, in some sense at least, authoritative and inspired. There are about 700 million Christians, of whom nearly half are returned as Roman Catholics. Rather more than 200 million are Protestants, and the rest are Eastern Orthodox, Copts, etc.

CHRISTIAN SCIENCE. The religion, or interpretation of the Christian religion, discovered and founded by Mary Baker Eddy (q.v.). It is regarded by Christian Scientists themselves as the restatement of primitive Christianity with its full gospel of salvation from all evil, including sickness and disease as well as sin. Christian Scientists believe that since God is good and is Spirit, matter and evil are not truly real; and the application of this belief constitutes C.S. practice. According to its adherents, C.S. healing is brought about by the operation of Truth in human conscience and not by mental suggestion, psycho-therapy, etc. In those who are properly attuned to the Divine Spirit there can be no place for evil, sin, and disease.

There is no ordained priesthood, but there are public practitioners of C.S. healing who are officially authorized and listed by the Church of Christ, Scientist, that was estab. by Mrs. Eddy in 1879. The Mother Church – the First Church of Christ, Scientist – is situated in Boston, Mass., U.S.A., and it has branches in most parts of the world. The textbook of C.S. is Mrs. Eddy's *Science and Health with Key to the Scriptures*, first pub. in 1875. Among the Christian Science publications is the *C.S. Monitor*, an international daily newspaper.

CHRISTIANS OF ST. THOMAS. Sect of Indian Christians on the Malabar coast; named after the apostle who is supposed to have carried his mission to India, although they were estab. in the 5th cent. by Nestorians from Persia. They now form part of the Syrian Church with their own patriarch.

CHRISTIE, Dame Agatha (1890–). British novelist, *née* Miller. B. at Torquay, she was later to use a

Photo: Angus McBean.

Devon setting in a number of books. Skilfully constructed and with strong characterization, her mystery novels began with *The Mysterious Affair at Styles* (1920), introducing Hercule Poirot, the Belgian detective. Outstanding among later books is *The Murder of Roger Ackroyd* (1926), much discussed because the narrator is the murderer, a device considered by purists to be illegitimate. Films have been made from her novels, and she has written a number of very successful plays, e.g. *The Mousetrap*. Her 2nd husband is the archaeologist, Sir Max Mallowan, whom she has accompanied on a number of Middle East 'digs'. Created D.B.E. 1971.

CHRISTIE, John (1882–1962). British patron of music. In 1934 he founded the Glyndebourne Festival, held in an opera house in the grounds of his country mansion, and in 1954 Glyndebourne Arts Trust Ltd. (a charitable trust) was estab. to continue his work.

CHRISTIE'S. Popular name for the firm of Christie, Manson, and Woods, Ltd., the principal art dealers in London. It was estab. by James Christie in 1766.

CHRISTINA (kris′tēna) (1626–89). Queen of Sweden. She succeeded her father Gustavus Adolphus in 1632, and until she was 18 the country was ruled by the great chancellor Oxenstjerna. In 1644 she assumed the royal power, and proved in many ways a wise and enlightened ruler. But she was extravagant and capricious, and refused to marry and thus secure the succession, as her ministers repeatedly advised her to do. At length she nominated her cousin Charles Gustavus as her successor, then she embarked upon a career of dissipation. In 1654 she abdicated and removed to Innsbruck, where she was received into the R.C. Church, and then maintained a court in Rome. Twice she returned to Sweden with a view to recovering the throne, but d. in Rome as a pensioner of the Pope.

CHRISTMAS. The mass of Christ; the day on which the birth of Christ is commemorated, constituting a feast of the Christian Church. The actual day of the Nativity has never been decided, and as late as the 5th cent. A.D. the feast was variously held on 25 Dec., 6 Jan., and 25 March; 25 Dec. the winter solstice was a highly significant date in pagan mythology – the Mithraists, for instance, kept it as the birthday of the 'Unconquered Sun' – and its increasing acceptance in the Western Church from the 4th cent. onwards owed much to the desire to facilitate the conversion of the pagans to Christianity. In Britain, 25 Dec. has been kept as a festival since long before the introduction of Christianity.

In the R.C. Church, the Church of England, and most of the Protestant denominations, Christmas Day is celebrated with religious services; and in most Christian countries it is kept as a public holiday. Many of the popular usages have a heathen origin. The yule log was taken from the pagan Norse festival. The holly, ivy, and mistletoe used to decorate churches and homes are symbols of fertility with their winter berries. Fir trees used to adorn the Roman Saturnalia, but the spread of their use as Christmas trees is said to date from their introduction to England from Germany by Prince Albert. Christmas puddings and cakes date from the Middle Ages. Carols were originally secular songs, until the Franciscans succeeded in giving them a religious application. Santa Claus is a corruption of St. Nicolaus, patron saint of children, whose feast is properly 6 Dec. The first Christmas card was designed in 1843, by J. C. Horsley, R.A.; the custom of sending them was estab. by 1870 in England, and spread to the U.S.A. a few years later.

CHRISTMAS. (i) Island in the Indian Ocean, c. 250 m. S. of Java. Uninhabited when discovered on Christmas Day 1643 by Capt. Wm. Mynors, it was annexed by Britain in 1888; Chinese labourers were brought in in 1897 to work the phosphate deposits. Japan occupied C. island 1942–5; it was transferred to Australia 1958. Area 64 sq. m.; pop. (1966) 3,381. (ii) One of the Line Islands, lying about 2° N.,157° W., area 220 sq. m.; pop. (1966) 356. Discovered on Christmas Eve 1777, by Capt. Cook, and annexed by Britain in 1888, it is the largest coral atoll in the Pacific. Copra is exported. Hydrogen bomb experiments were carried out here in 1957.

CHRISTOFF, Boris (1919–). Bulgarian bass singer. B. nr. Sofia, he gained a scholarship to study singing in Rome, and in 1946 made his début in opera. His roles incl. Boris Godunov, Ivan the Terrible and Mephistopheles.

CHRISTOPHE (krēstof'), **Henri** (1767–1820). Negro slave in the West Indies who was one of the leaders of the revolt against the French in 1790, and in 1812 was crowned king of Haiti. In spite of his capable rule he alienated support by his cruelty; when he was deserted by his troops he shot himself.

CHRISTOPHER. Patron saint of ferrymen and travellers. Traditionally he was a Christian martyr in Syria in the 3rd cent., and the best-known legend concerning him describes his carrying the Christ child over the stream; despite his great strength he found the burden increasingly heavy, whereupon he was told that this was no wonder as Christ was bearing the sins of all the world. See CANONIZATION.

CHRIST'S HOSPITAL. English public school for boys, generally known as the Blue Coat school from the blue gown which forms part of the boys' dress. Founded in 1552, it was removed from Newgate Street, London, to Horsham, Sussex, in 1902. At Hertford there is a girls' school on the same foundation. Coleridge and Lamb (qq.v.) were C.H. boys.

CHRŌMATO'GRAPHY. A method of analysing substances by spatial separation. It may be carried out either: (1) by passing solutions of different substances up a column of an absorbent when they will be separated according to their affinity for the absorbent; or (2) by putting drops of a mixture of components in solution on filter paper when the different components will be separated by differential diffusion through the paper (paper C.); or (3) by evaporating the liquid to be analysed into an inert gas which is allowed to flow into a partition column containing a substance, such as a high-boiling-point liquid, in which the materials of the sample have different partition coefficients, and are separated because they travel at different speeds (gas C.). These methods are extremely sensitive and enable very small quantities of substances to be detected and analysed.

CHROMIUM. Chemical element, symbol Cr, at. wt. 52·01, at. no. 24. A bluish-white metal capable of taking a high polish, and with a high melting-point, it is much used decoratively and (alloyed with nickel) for electrical heating wires. Resistant to abrasion and corrosion, it is used to harden steel, and is a constituent of stainless steel and many useful alloys. It is used extensively in C. plating and as a catalyst. Its most important compounds are sodium and potassium chromates and dichromates (for tanning leather) and potassium and ammonium chrome alums. It occurs chiefly as chrome iron ore: U.S.A., Rhodesia and India are the chief sources.

CHROMOSOMES. See GENETICS.

CHROMOSPHERE (krō'mosfēr). The upper portion of the sun's atmosphere, consisting mainly of hydrogen and ionized calcium. It may be observed through the spectroscope and visually when the sun is totally eclipsed.

CHRONOMETER. An instrument for measuring equal intervals of time with the greatest accuracy. Although its necessity is largely removed in these days of wireless telegraphy, ships at sea are still required by law to carry Cs. for navigation.

CHRYSANTHEMUM (krisan'thēmum). Genus of plants of the family Compositae, containing nearly 300 species, most of which have been developed by cultivation. The Chinese and Japanese varieties are derived by hybridization from C. indicum and C. morifolium. In the Far East the common C. has been cultivated for more than 2,000 years, and it is the national emblem of Japan. The first C. was introduced into England in 1789, but C. leucanthemum and C. segetum, the ox-eye daisy and the corn marigold respectively, are common weeds in Britain. Cs. may be grown from seed, but are more usually reproduced by cuttings or division.

CHRYSLER (krīs'ler), **Walter** (1875–1940). American industrialist, who produced the first C. car in 1924, and in 1925 founded the C. Corporation, which manufactures motor-cars, marine and industrial engines, etc.

CHRYSOLITE. See OLIVINE.

CHUANG CHOU, called Chuang Tzu ('philosopher Chuang') (c. 330–c. 275 B.C.). Chinese philosopher and essayist, he was a contemporary of Mencius, and the leading thinker of the Taoist school.

CHUB. A freshwater fish (Leuciscus cephalus) belonging to the carp family (Cyprinidae). It has a plump, thick body and heavy head, and is dark bluish or greenish on the back, with silvery sides.

CHUBB CRATER. Crater discovered in 1950 by a prospector, F. W. Chubb, in northern Quebec, c. 60 m. from Hudson Strait, Canada. Made by a meteor, in prehistoric times, it is 1,350 ft. deep with a rim 550 ft. above the local land level. In the centre is a lake 800 ft. deep.

CHUKO'VSKY, Kornei Ivanovitch (1882–1969). Russian critic and poet. The leading authority on Nekrasov, he was also an expert on the Russian language, e.g. Zhivoi kak zhizn (1963: Alife as Life), and beloved as 'Grandpa' K.C. for his nonsense poems

CHUNGKING. The rocky peninsula on which the city stands makes for great variation in level which it takes a modern highway to overcome. *Photo: Camera Press.*

which owe much to the English nursery rhymes and nonsense verse he admired.

CHUNGKING. City of W. China, in Szechwan prov. A former treaty port, opened to foreign trade in 1891, it stands at the confluence of the Yangtze-Kiang and the Kia-ling. For more than 4,000 years it has been an important commercial and route centre in one of the most remote and economically backward regions of China, and it remains a focal point of road, river and railway transport. Its manufactures incl. textiles, matches, iron and steel goods, chemicals; it exports tung oil, hog bristles, hides, etc., and is the seat of a univ. When both Peking and Nanking were in Japanese hands, it was cap. of China 1938–46; large sections of the town were destroyed by Japanese bombing, and more than 1,000 were killed in a fire in 1949. It was called Pahsien until 1936. Pop. (1960 est.) 2,165,000.

CHURCH, Richard (1893–1972). British man-of-letters. B. in London, and ed. at Dulwich Hamlet school, he entered the Civil Service at 16, retiring in 1933. Until then his chief published work had been as a subtly sensitive poet (*Collected Poems*, 1948) but in 1937 his novel *The Porch* was acclaimed. Among later works are 2 vols. of autobiography *Over the Bridge* (1955) and *The Golden Sovereign* (1957). He was also a noted essayist and literary critic.

CHURCH ARMY. Religious organization within the Church of England founded in 1882 by Wilson Carlile (1847–1942), a business man converted after the failure of his textile-firm, who took orders in 1880. Originally intended for evangelical and social work in the Westminster slums, it developed along Salvation Army lines, and has done much work among ex-prisoners and for the soldiers of both world wars.

CHURCH ASSEMBLY (or **National Assembly**). A body established by parliament in 1919, consisting of a House of bishops, a House of clergy, and a House of laity, which has power to frame legislation concerning the C. of E. Any measures it approves may become law when approved by both Houses of Parliament and given the Royal Assent.

RICHARD CHURCH

CHURCH COMMISSIONERS. *See* ANGLICAN COMMUNION.

CHURCH CONGRESS. Annual meeting, first held at Cambridge, in 1861, consisting of laymen and clergy of the C. of E. for the discussion of problems affecting the Church. It has no legislative authority.

CHURCH HISTORY. The Christian C. is traditionally said to have originated on the first Whitsun Day, but was only finally separated from the parent Jewish C. by the declaration of SS. Barnabas and Paul that the distinctive rites of Judaism were not necessary for entry into the Christian C.

For the 1st 2 cents. the C. was not much more than a spasmodically persecuted minority, but in the 3rd cent. more determined efforts to extirpate it were made under Severus, Decius, and Diocletian. Toleration was obtained by the victory of Constantine at Milvian Bridge (312), and Christianity became the estab. religion of the Roman Empire. Security and increasing wealth brought some deterioration, and the outbreak of heresies such as Montanism and Gnosticism, to which the C. opposed a developed creed, a canon of estab. scriptures, and her threefold ministry with its succession from the Apostles. Questions of discipline also threatened disruption within the C.; and to settle these Constantine called the Council of Arles (314), which was followed by the Councils of Nicaea (325), Constantinople (381), Ephesus (431), and Chalcedon (451). A settled doctrine of Christian belief evolved, but failed to prevent the schism of the churches of the East.

During the Dark Ages the Church, esp. as represented by the Celtic and Benedictine monks, preserved the best features of the Graeco-Roman civilization and taught the northern barbarians, e.g. SS. Colomba and Augustine in England. The C. fostered agriculture and education, and assisted the growth of the feudal system of which it formed the apex, as recognized by Charlemagne (800) in seeking coronation by the Pope.

The Middle Ages, despite an underlying unity symbolized by the theology of St. Thomas Aquinas, saw much controversy between secular and spiritual jurisdiction, e.g. Emperor Henry IV and Pope Gregory VII, Henry II of England and Becket. Moreover, increasing worldliness (against which the foundation of the Dominicans and Franciscans was a protest) and other ecclesiastical abuses, led to dissatisfaction in the 14th cent. and the appearance of the reformers Wycliffe and Huss.

In N. Europe the Renaissance brought a re-examination of Christian truth by More, Colet, and Erasmus; and with the advent of Luther, Calvin, and Zwingli came the Reformation, an attempt to return to primitive Christianity. In England Henry VIII and Elizabeth found a middle way between Romanism and Puritanism in the C. of England. During the 18th cent. Christianity was brought to the test of reason; the Scriptures were then examined on the same basis as secular literature, and the shock to orthodox belief was confirmed by the evolutionary theories of the 19th cent.

Meanwhile in England the Church of England suffered the loss of large numbers of Nonconformists, who estab. the denominations known today as the Free churches. In the 18th cent. arose the Methodist movement, and in the 19th cent. the Oxford movement led by Newman, Keble and Pusey, which eventually developed into present-day Anglo-Catholicism. Of the Presbyterian churches founded in the Reformation period the most important is the Church of Scotland. *See* CHRISTIANITY.

CHURCHILL, Charles (1731–64). British satiric poet. Once a clergyman in the C. of E., he wrote coarse and highly personal satires dealing to a large extent with political issues.

CHURCHILL, Lord Randolph Henry Spencer

(1849–95). British Cons. statesman. B. at Blenheim, son of the 7th duke of Marlborough, he entered parliament in 1874 as a Cons. M.P. After 1880 he formed the '4th party' with Drummond Wolff, Gorst, and Arthur Balfour, and in 1885 his policy of Tory democracy was widely accepted by the party. In 1886 he became Chancellor of the Exchequer, but resigned within 6 months because he did not agree with the demands made on the Treasury by the War Office and the Admiralty. He was a founder and the first member of the Primrose League, and was prominent on the Turf. He m. in 1874 Jenny Jerome, dau. of a wealthy New Yorker, and had 2 sons, the elder of whom was Winston C.

CHURCHILL, Winston (1871–1947). American novelist. B. at St. Louis, he wrote successful novels incl. *Richard Carvel* (1899), *Coniston* (1906), and *The Unchartered Way* (1941).

CHURCHILL, Sir Winston Leonard Spencer (1874–1965). British statesman. A descendant of the great duke of Marlborough, he was b. at Blenheim Palace on 30 Nov. 1874, being the elder son of Lord Randolph C. (q.v.) and his wife, Jenny Jerome. Ed. at Harrow, he was commissioned in the 4th Hussars in 1895 and saw active service in a series of minor campaigns. During the Boer War he was the *Morning Post*'s war correspondent and made a dramatic escape from imprisonment in Pretoria. In 1900 he was elected Cons. M.P. for Oldham, but he disagreed with Chamberlain's tariff reform policy, and joined the Liberals. In 1908 Asquith made him Pres. of the Board of Trade, in which capacity he introduced legislation for the establishment of Labour Exchanges. In 1910 he became Home Sec. and was present at the notorious incident in the East End of London known as the siege of Sydney Street, when he authorized the use of troops against some armed gangsters. Then in 1911 Asquith appointed him First Lord of the Admiralty with the instruction to put the fleet into a state of instant readiness for war. C. ordered naval mobilization on the eve of war without waiting for Cabinet authority, and early in the war sent the Naval Brigade to Antwerp. He was then involved in acute controversy over the Dardanelles operation which he sponsored, and when the first Coalition govt. was formed in 1915 he was excluded. Until the autumn of 1916 he served in the trenches in France as lieut.-col. of the 6th Royal Scots Fusiliers, but then resumed his parliamentary duties and was Min. of Munitions under Lloyd George in 1917, when he had much to do with the development of the tank. After the Armistice he was Sec. for War, 1918–21, and then as Colonial Sec. played a leading part in the establishment of the Irish Free State. During these post-war years he was active in support of the anti-Bolshevik (white) generals in Russia.

From 1922–4 C. was out of parliament, left the Liberals in 1923, and in 1924 was returned for Epping as a Constitutionalist. Baldwin made him Chancellor of the Exchequer, and he brought about Britain's return to the Gold Standard and was prominent in the defeat of the General Strike of 1926. In 1929–39 he was out of office as he disagreed with the Conservatives on India, re-armament, and Chamberlain's policy of appeasement.

On the 1st day of the S.W.W. C. went back to his old post at the Admiralty, and there he remained until 10 May 1940, when he was called to the Premiership as head of an all-party admin. On 13 May he presented himself to the House of Commons with the historic 'blood and tears, toil and sweat' speech. One of the decisive decisions of the war was his broadcast announcement on the evening of 22 June 1941, that Britain allied herself with the Soviet Union. He effected the closest personal contact with President Roosevelt, and in Aug. 1941 concluded with him the Atlantic Charter. On 20 Dec. 1941 he addressed a joint

SIR WINSTON CHURCHILL. Leader of Britain in her 'finest hour', he became in 1963 the first foreign national to receive honorary American citizenship by Congressional action.
Photo: Topix.

session of the American Congress. He travelled to Washington, Casablanca, Cairo, Moscow, and Teheran, meeting the other great leaders of the Allied war effort; and at Christmas 1944 he made a dramatic flight to Athens to avert civil war in Greece. In Feb. 1945 he met Stalin and Roosevelt in the Crimea, and agreed on the final plans for victory. On 8 May he announced the unconditional surrender of Germany.

Then on 23 May the Coalition was dissolved, and C. formed a 'caretaker' govt. drawn mainly from the Cons. Defeated in the gen. election in July, he resigned office to become Leader of the Opposition until the gen. election of Oct. 1951 brought his return to power as P.M. He received the O.M. in 1946, and was created K.G. in 1953. On 5 April 1955 he resigned.

Also a great writer, C. won the Nobel prize for literature in 1953. His 1st books were accounts of the campaigns in which he had participated. His life of his father was pub. in 1906, and his *World Crisis*, (4 vols., 1923–9) is a history of the F.W.W. In 1933–8 appeared his life of the Great Duke of Marlborough later followed by vols. of speeches, and Memoirs of the S.W.W. He was also a capable artist. He was buried at Bladon, nr. Blenheim Palace, and his home from 1922, Chartwell in Kent, was opened as a museum.

C. m. in 1908 Clementine Hozier (1885–), created G.B.E. in 1946 and in 1965 a life peeress as Lady Spencer-Churchill. Their children are: Diana (1909–63), who m. Duncan Sandys (q.v.) in 1935 (m. diss. 1960); Randolph (1911–68), Cons. M.P. 1940–5, well known as a journalist and author of studies of Eden (1959) and Derby (1960); Sarah (1914–), an actress, who m. Vic Oliver the musician and comedian in 1936 (m. diss. 1945), then Anthony Beauchamp, photographer, in 1949 (d. 1957) and in 1962 Lord Audley (d. 1963); and Mary (1922–) who m. in 1947 Christopher Soames (q.v.).

CHURCH OF ENGLAND. *See* ANGLICAN COMMUNION.

CHURCH OF SCOTLAND. *See* SCOTLAND, CH. OF.

CHU TEH (1886–). Chinese soldier-statesman. In 1922 he joined the Chinese Communists in Germany, was expelled from the country in 1925, and on his return to China was one of the organizers of the Nanchang Communist rising and formed the Chinese Red Army. C.-in-C. of the army from 1930, he became in 1954 vice-chairman of the Central People's Govt. Council and in 1959 (re-elected 1965) chairman of the Standing Committee of the People's Congress. In the Cultural Revolution he was denounced 1967.

CHUVASH (choovahsh'). An Autonomous Soviet Socialist Republic of the R.S.F.S.R. It lies W. of the Volga, some 350 m. E. of Moscow. The cap. is Cheboksary, the largest town Alatyr. Lumbering and grain-growing are important and there are phosphate and limestone deposits, and electrical and engineering industries. Area 7,100 sq. m.; pop. (1967) 1,192,000.

CIANO (chēah'noh), **Galeazzo** (1903–44). Italian Fascist politician. B. at Leghorn, the son of an industrialist, he entered the diplomatic service, and in 1930 m. Mussolini's dau. Edda. In 1936 he became Foreign Min., organized Italian intervention in Spain and the invasion of Albania, estab. the Rome-Berlin Axis in 1939, advocated the 'stab in the back' against France in 1940, and the invasion of Greece. But the war began to go badly, and in 1943 C. was removed from his post and given the office of ambassador to the Vatican. He voted against Mussolini at the meeting of the Fascist Grand Council on 25 July at which the Duce was overthrown, and went into hiding. Arrested by Fascists, he was tried for treason at Verona, found guilty, and shot. His diaries were pub. in Eng. in 1947.

CIBBER (sib'er), **Colley** (1671–1757). British actor and dramatist. B. in London, he joined Betterton's company in Drury Lane in 1690 and 3 years later produced his 1st play, *Love's Last Shift*. This was followed by *She Would and She Would Not*, *The Careless Husband* and *The Non-juror* (1717). His Whig sentiments secured him the post of Poet Laureate in 1730.

CICADA (sikā'da). A family of insects (Cicadidae) of the sub-order Homoptera of the order Hemiptera, nearly allied to the frog-hoppers. The adult insects live on trees, whose juices they suck, and are remarkable for the chirping noise made by the males.

CICERO (sis-), **Marcus Tullius** (106–43 B.C.). Roman orator, writer, and statesman. B. at Arpinum, he became an advocate in Rome, spent 3 years in Greece studying oratory, and after Sulla's death distinguished himself in Rome on the side of the popular party. In 63 B.C. he was appointed consul; later in the year he saved the Republic when it was threatened by Catiline's conspiracy. When the 1st Triumvirate of Caesar, Crassus, and Pompey was formed in 59, C. was exiled, and devoted himself to literature. On the outbreak of the Civil War in 49 he followed Pompey to Greece, but in 48 returned to Italy where he was well treated by Caesar. After the latter's assassination in 44 B.C. he took the lead in the Senate in an attempt to restore the republican form of govt., and in 14 great speeches he supported Octavian (the future Augustus) and denounced Mark Antony. These speeches are known as the Philippics after the denunciations of King Philip of Macedon by Demosthenes in the 4th cent. B.C. In the autumn of 43, however, Antony and Octavian came to terms and C. was killed while trying to escape to the East.

As a statesman, C. attempted unsuccessfully to carry out a moderate policy. His influence on the future of literature was immense. His speeches were soon recorded as models of Latin prose, and his philosophical essays are full of common sense and practical sympathies. His letters are of interest.

CID (Span., thēdh), **Rodrigo Diaz de Bivar** (c. 1040–99). Spanish national hero, was b. in Castile of a noble family, fought against the king at Navarre, and won his nickname *el Campeador* (the Champion) by killing the Navarrese champion in single combat. Eventually he became a soldier of fortune, and d. while defending Valencia against the Moors. 'The Cid' (the Lord) was a name given to him by the Moors, and he soon became a hero of romance.

CIDER (sīder). A fermented drink made from the juice of the apple. As a beverage it has been known for more than 2,000 years, and for many centuries it has been a popular drink in France and England, which are now its main centres of production. The French output is by far the greater, Normandy and Brittany being chiefly concerned. In a good year c. 30 million gallons are produced in Britain. The West of England from Hereford to Devon has long been famous for its C. Most of the apple crop is sold to factories estab. in the region and also in Kent and Norfolk. In the U.S.A. the term usually refers to unfermented apple juice.

CIGAR (sigahr'). Originally a sheath of palm leaves filled with tobacco, smoked by the Indians of Central and N. America. The modern C. is a compact roll of tobacco leaves. C.-smoking was introduced into Spain soon after the discovery of America, and then spread all over Europe. The 1st C. factory was opened in Hamburg in 1788, and about that time the taste for C.-smoking became well marked in England. The 1st Cs. were made by hand – as still are the more expensive Cs., incl. most of those made in Cuba – but in U.S.A. from about the 1850s various machine methods were employed. From about 1890 C.-smoking was gradually supplanted in popularity in England by cigarette-smoking. The 'little cigar' has been in some demand of recent years.

CIGARETTE. Literally, a little cigar. The 1st Cs. were the *papelitos* smoked in S. America about 1750. The habit spread to Spain, and then throughout the world, and is today the most general form of tobacco-smoking, the vast majority of Cs. being machine-made. In some countries, through the tax on tobacco, smokers contribute a large part of the national revenue, e.g. U.K. c. £885,000,000 and U.S. c. $2,000,000,000. The diagnosis that C.-smoking is a factor in the increase of lung cancer has led to much experimental work on methods for filtering potentially harmful substances.

CIGARETTE CARDS. Cards incl. in packets of cigarettes, and bearing printed views, drawings, portraits, etc. They are believed to have originated in the U.S.A. in the 1870s.

CILEA (chēlā'ah), **Francesco** (1866–1950). Italian composer. B. in Calabria, he was prof. at the Reale Istituto Musicale, Florence, 1896–1904. His great successes were the operas *L'Arlesiana* (1897) after Daudet and *Adriana Lecouvreur* (1902) after Scribe.

CIMABUE (chēmahboo'-eh), **Giovanni** (1240–c. 1302). Italian painter; the master of Giotto, and styled the 'father of Italian painting'. Among the best-known works attributed to him are a 'Madonna and Child' in the Uffizi, Florence, and other paintings of the same subject in the Louvre, Paris, and the National Gallery, London. C. was one of the 1st artists to paint from a living model.

CIMAROSA (chēmahroh'zah), **Domenico** (1749–1801). Italian composer of operas extremely popular in their day, of which the best is *Il Matrimonio Segreto* (1792: The Secret Marriage).

CINCHONA (sinkō'na). Genus of shrubs and trees belonging to the family Rubiaceae and growing wild in the Amazonian forests. From the bark of some species is produced quinine (q.v.), and C. culture has been introduced into India, Ceylon, the Philippines, and the E. Indies, with marked success.

CINCINNATI (sinsina'ti). American city in Ohio

on the Ohio. Founded in 1788, it became a city in 1819, and during the middle years of the 19th cent. grew rapidly as it attracted large numbers of European immigrants, particularly Germans. It has one of the finest railway stations in the U.S.A. and is well served by air. The symphony orchestra of the municipal univ. (oldest mun. univ. in the U.S.A.) is famous; there is also a R.C. univ. Among the chief industries are machine-tool, clothing, and furniture making, and meat-packing. Pop. met. area 1,373,629.

CINCINNATUS, Lucius Quinctius. Early Roman general, famous for his frugal simplicity. Appointed dictator in 458 B.C. he defeated the Aequi in a brief campaign, then resumed life as a yeoman farmer.

CINEMATO'GRAPHY. The technique of making and showing motion pictures. Images recorded on a continuous strip of film on a cellulose acetate (non-inflammable) base (instead of the highly inflammable celluloid base used in early days) are projected on to a screen sufficiently fast to give the impression of continuous motion owing to the facility of retention of normal vision. The standard speed is 90 ft. per minute. Film is usually handled in lengths from 400 to 2,000 ft. Sound, as a rule recorded separately on $\frac{1}{4}$ in. magnetic tape, but carried for reproduction on a narrow track alongside the picture film, is delivered from loudspeakers placed behind the screen and sometimes also about the auditorium.

CINEMATOGRAPHY. Circlorama – the completely circular cinema – as developed in Russia by E. Goldovsky.
Courtesy of Circlorama Theatre, London.

As a medium of popular entertainment, the cinema is a creation of the 20th cent., but the basis of virtually all cinematographic technique was contained in a patent filed in 1889 by William Friese-Greene of Bristol, England. By about 1926 film technique had been perfected as a vehicle for artistic experiment, and films of high quality were being made in France, Italy, Sweden, Germany, and elsewhere. Hollywood, Calif., U.S.A., once the undisputed film metropolis on account of its light and climate, has come to occupy a less commanding position with improvements in cameras and film sensitivity which have made it possible to take satisfactory pictures in any light and any location. Sound films were 1st publicly presented in 1928. Colour, 1st used before the F.W.W., was not fully developed until the 1930s. Much experiment has been carried out with a view to obtaining a stereoscopic effect; and wider screens, up to a series encircling the cinema, have been introduced in the effort to produce greater actuality. The standard cine-film is 35 mm. wide, but 70 mm. has been used, and 'sub-standard' film in 16 mm., 9·5 mm., and 8 mm. widths is manufactured for amateurs and for special, e.g. educational, films.

For film production, see FILM.

CINNABAR (sin'abar). Mercuric sulphide, HgS, the only important ore of mercury. The chief deposits are at Almaden in Spain. The mineral itself is used as a pigment, commonly known as vermilion.

CINNAMON (si'namon). Bark of a tree (*Cinnamomum zeylanicum*) which is a member of the family Lauraceae and is grown in Ceylon, Java, Brazil, W. Indies, etc. Oil of C. is obtained from the inner bark, and is used as a flavouring and in medicine.

CINQUEFOIL (singk'foil). Genus of plants (*Potentilla*) belonging to the rose family (Rosaceae). The typical species (*P. reptans*) seen on this page, is a creeping perennial, widely distributed throughout the British Isles, growing in pastures and meadows and on banks.

CINQUE (sink) **PORTS** (Fr. *cinq*, five). An association of ports in S. England, originally Sandwich, Dover, Hythe, Romney, and Hastings, to which were added later Rye and Winchelsea, and a number of other places. Founded probably in Roman times, they rose to importance after the Norman conquest, and until the end of the 15th cent. were bound to supply the ships and men necessary against invasion. The office of Lord Warden survives as an honorary distinction (Churchill 1941–65, Menzies from 1965); his official residence is Walmer Castle. The C.P. court has continued to deal with salvage cases.

CIRCUITS. Periodical travels by the judges of the Queen's Bench Division of the High Court through England and Wales to try civil and criminal cases at the assize towns. There are at present 7 Cs.: S.-Eastern, Western, Wales and Chester, Northern, N.-Eastern, Midland, and Oxford, each with its own set of barristers attached to it. There are 3 Cs., winter, summer and autumn, at each place.

CIRCUMCISION. Surgical operation, practised from early times and usually accompanied by ritual, consisting of the removal of a small part of the foreskin. Performed for sanitary reasons in infancy, it is sometimes necessitated on medical grounds. All Jewish and Mohammedan boys must be circumcised as a religious rite, and the custom prevails among Arabs, Australian aboriginals, Kaffirs, and Papuans.

CIRCUMCISION, Feast of. Anglican and R.C. religious festival, celebrated annually on 1 Jan. in commemoration of Christ's circumcision.

CIRCU'MFERENCE. In geometry, the curved line that encloses a plane figure, e.g. a circle, an ellipse. Its length varies according to the nature of the curve, and may be ascertained by the appropriate formula. Thus the C. of a circle is $2\pi r$, where r is the radius and $\pi = 3\cdot1415927\ldots$ or roughly $\frac{22}{7}$.

CIRCUMNAVIGATION. The 1st ship to sail round the world was the *Victoria*, one of the Spanish squadron of 5 vessels that sailed from Seville in Aug. 1519 under F. de Magellan (q.v.). Four vessels were lost on the way, but the *Victoria* arrived back in Spain in Sept. 1522. Magellan himself did not complete the voyage, as he d. in the Philippines in 1521. The 1st English circumnavigator was Drake in 1577–80.

CINQUEFOIL

CIRENCESTER (sis'iter). English market town (U.D.) in Gloucestershire on the Churn, 12 m. S.E. of Gloucester. It has Roman remains and was once a centre of the wool trade. The Royal Agricultural College nearby was incorporated in 1845. Pop. (1961) 11,836.

CIRL (serl) **BUNTING.** A bird (*Emberiza cirlus*), nearly allied to the yellowhammer, from which it is distinguished by the olive crown and black bib in the male. In Britain it is a local resident, found chiefly in Wales and the S.W.

CISTERCIANS (sister'sh-). A monastic order of the R.C. Church, estab. at Cîteaux in 1098 by Robert de Champagne, abbot of Molesme. Its purpose was to restore in its full rigour the rule of St. Benedict, and the Cs., living mainly by agricultural labour, were responsible for much of the advance in farming methods in the Middle Ages.

CITHARA (sith'ara), **Cithern**, or **Cittern.** Ancient musical instrument, resembling a lute but with a flat back. It was strung with wire and plucked with a plectrum or (after the 16th cent.) with the fingers. It is now obsolete, but the bandurria and laud, still popular in Spain, are instruments of the same type.

CITRUS. Picking the ripened crop in an ortanique orchard. A cross between an orange and a tangerine, the ortanique is produced only in Jamaica. *Courtesy of Alcan Jamaica Ltd.*

CITRIC ACID. An organic acid widely distributed in the plant kingdom, especially in citrus fruits. It is a white crystalline powder with an acid taste. At one time it was prepared from concentrated lemon juice, but now the main source is the fermentation of sugar with certain moulds. It is widely used in effervescent saline drinks, calico-printing, etc. Its chemical formula is $C_8H_8O_7$.

CITRUS. Genus of trees and shrubs, belonging to the family Rutaceae, and found in the warmer parts of the world, particularly Asia. They are evergreen and aromatic, and several species (orange, lemon, lime, citron, grapefruit, etc.) are cultivated for fruit.

CITY. Generally speaking, a large and important town. In the ancient world Cs. were states in themselves. In the early Middle Ages, Cs. were usually those towns which were episcopal sees, and to this day the English cathedral towns are called Cs. In present-day Britain the term is chiefly of historical and ceremonial importance. The official style of city has been conferred by royal authority on certain towns, e.g. Birmingham in 1889, Cambridge, 1951, which were not the seat of a bishop.

CITY, The. *See* LONDON.

CITY TEMPLE. Congregational church in London, sometimes called the 'cathedral of Nonconformity'. Founded in the City in 1640, it was transferred in 1874 to a new building at Holborn Viaduct. Destroyed in an air raid in 1941, it was rebuilt 1958.

CIUDAD BOLÍVAR (thē-oodadh′ bohlē′vahr). City of Venezuela on the Orinoco, *c.* 250 m. from its mouth, and linked with Soledad across the river by the Angostura bridge (1967) – first to span the Orinoco. Gold is mined in the vicinity. Pop. (1964) 87,928.

CIUDAD REAL (reh-ahl′). City of central Spain, capital of C.R. prov.. 107 m. S. of Madrid. Its chief feature is its huge Gothic cathedral. Pop. (1960) 37,081.

CIUDAD TRUJILLO. Trujillo City: name 1936–61 of Santo Domingo (q.v.).

CIVET (siv′et) or **Civet Cat** (*Viverra*). Mammals of the family Viverridae, related to the cats (Felidae), but distinguished principally by their longer head and jaws, numerous dog-like teeth, and by having a perfume gland in the inguinal region. There are many different kinds inhabiting tropical Asia and Africa. A few species are of commercial value on account of their perfume.

CIVIL AVIATION. Passenger and freight service organization, and aircraft development.

The International C.A. Organization (1947) has its H.Q. in Montreal, and is a U.N. agency. In the U.K. there are about 150 airports, those for London (Heathrow, Gatwick and a third to be designated) and Prestwick being managed by the British Airports Authority (1965), and 2 state airlines – British European Airways and British Overseas Airways – besides a number of independent companies.

Close co-operation is maintained with authorities in other countries, incl. the Federal Aviation Agency, which is responsible for development of aircraft, air navigation, traffic control and communications in the U.S.A.: the Civil Aeronautics Board is the American authority prescribing safety regulations and investigating accidents. There are no state airlines in the U.S.A., although many of the private airlines are large. The world's largest airline is the govt.-owned Aeroflot (U.S.S.R.).

INDIAN CIVET

With increasing traffic, control of air space is a major problem, and in 1963 Eurocontrol was estab. by Belgium, Britain, France, W. Germany, Luxembourg, and the Netherlands to supervise both military and civil movement in the air space over member countries. There is also a tendency to co-ordinate services and pool service and other facilities between national airlines, e.g. the estab. of Air Union by France (Air France), W. Germany (Lufthansa), Italy (Alitalia) and Belgium (Sabena) in 1963.

CIVIL DEFENCE. Organization of the civil population to mitigate the effects of enemy attack. In Britain the Min. of Home Security was constituted 1939 to direct Air Raid Precautions in the S.W.W., the country being divided into 12 regions, each under a commissioner to act on behalf of the central govt. in the event of cut communications. Associated with the 'air-raid wardens' were ambulance and rescue parties, gas officers, breakdown gangs, etc., and a Nat. Fire Service, based on existing local services, and *c.* 5,000,000 citizens were enrolled as firewatchers and firefighters. The C.D. services (the name being changed from A.R.P. in 1942) were stood down 1945, and the renewed requirement from 1949 that they be maintained by local authorities ceased in 1968 when the C.D. Corps and Auxiliary Fire Service were disbanded.

In the U.S.A. the Office of Civil Defense (1961) of the Dept. of Defense has a Staff College and 3 warning centres. Public shelter from fall-out is available for 160,000,000 and special attention is given to incorporating shelter in all new constructions.

CIVIL DISOBEDIENCE. Movement in India led by Gandhi (q.v.) and aimed at peaceful withdrawal of Brit. power.

CIVIL AVIATION. The complex of runways at London Airport, typical of the modern international airport.
Photo: Aerofilms Ltd.

CIVIL AVIATION. The Anglo-French Mach 2.2 supersonic airliner Concorde (*left*) leaves the main aircraft assembly hall at B.A.C. Filton Works, Bristol, in 1968. A cruising speed of 1,450 m.p.h. will cut transatlantic flying time from 7 to 3 hours. Built of aluminium alloy with titanium or stainless steel used in areas subject to high thermal stress, Concorde has an overall length of 170 ft. and a wingspan of 77 ft., and accommodation for *c.* 140 passengers. Powered by turbojets, its engines are mounted in pairs below the wings and a retractable visor, raised in supersonic cruise to reduce aerodynamic drag, can be lowered in subsonic flight to provide normal vision for the crew. The instrumentation and flight control lay-out (*right*) is incredibly complex.

Courtesy of British Aircraft Corporation

CIVIL ENGINEERING. That department of engineering that is concerned with such works as construction of roads, bridges, aqueducts, waterworks, tunnels, canals, irrigation works, harbours, etc. The professional organization in Britain is the Institution of Civil Engineers, which was founded in 1818 and is the oldest engineering institution in the world.

CIVIL LIST. The annual sum settled by Act of Parliament on the British sovereign at the beginning of each reign. It is charged on the consolidated fund and takes the place of certain hereditary revenues 1st surrendered by William IV to Parliament. Under the revised C.L. of 1971 the provision for Queen Elizabeth II was £980,000 free of tax. Annuities (taxed) which do not form part of the C.L., but are separately charged on the Consolidated Fund are paid to the Duke of Edinburgh £65,000; Prince Charles receives nothing, since he draws £105,000 from the Duchy of Cornwall (this represents only half the revenues, since the Prince voluntarily surrendered the other half on coming of age), but his widow would receive £60,000; Princess Anne £15,000 (after marriage £35,000); Queen Elizabeth the Queen Mother £95,000; Princess Margaret £35,000; and the Duke of Gloucester £45,000. Younger sons of the Queen receive at eighteen £20,000 (£50,000 after marriage).

There is no equivalent of the C.L. in the U.S.A. A President receives, by Act of Congress, a salary of $200,000 a year taxable plus $50,000 (also taxable) for defraying expenses connected with his official duties, and may spend up to $40,000 (not taxable) a year on travel and official entertaining expenses; ex-presidents receive a life pension of $25,000, plus free office space and post facilities, and up to $65,000 for office staff, and their widows a life pension of $10,000 a year. The Vice-Pres. has a salary of $62,500 and $10,000 expenses, all taxable.

CIVIL LIST PENSIONS. Pensions originally paid out of the sovereign's Civil List, but granted separately since the accession of Queen Victoria. They are paid to persons in need, who have just claims on the royal beneficence, who have rendered personal service to the Crown, or who have rendered service to the public by their discoveries in science and attainments in literature and art, etc. The sums paid amount to about £24,000 per annum. The recipients are nominated by the Prime Minister, and the List is approved by Parliament.

CIVIL SERVICE. The body of civilian staffs working in the different departments of state of a country. In England, civil servants were originally in the personal service of the sovereign. They were recruited by patronage, and many of them did little except nominal duties. The great increase in public expenditure during the Napoleonic Wars led to a move in Parliament for reform of the C.S., but it was not until 1854 that two civil servants, Charles Trevelyan and Stafford Northcote, issued a report as a result of which recruitment by competitive examination, carried out under the C.S. Commission (1855), came into force. Some appointments still went by patronage, but by *c.* 1900 competitive entry was the rule, even those recruited from time to time (e.g. during the world wars) on a temporary basis having to pass some form of examination.

The 2 main divisions of the British C.S. are the Home and Diplomatic services, the latter created 1965 by amalgamation of the Foreign, Commonwealth and Trade Commission Services. All are paid out of funds voted annually for the purpose by Parliament.

In 1968, following the recommendations of the Fulton Committee, responsibility for the C.S. was transferred to a new C.S. Dept. under the control of the P.M., which was to absorb both the C.S. Commission and the Treasury's responsibility for central management, its Permanent Secretary being designated Head of the Home C.S. The 1400 classes of civil servant were replaced by a unified grading structure, emphasis being placed on the professional rather than the 'all-rounder', and a C.S. College was estab. to develop training. Freer movement between jobs in the C.S. and in industry was to be maintained, and the long-standing devotion to secrecy and anonymity broken down.

Members of the British C.S. may not take an active part in politics.

In the U.S.A., until 1883 all C.S. posts were given as rewards for political services, and changed hands with a change of the party in power; the Pendleton Act 1883, estab. competitive examinations and permanency for certain posts, and that system has been steadily extended. The govt. agency concerned is the C.S. Commission.

CIVIL WAR. In English history, the name usually applied to the struggle in the middle years of the 17th cent. between the king and his Royalist supporters on the one hand, and the Parliamentarians (also called Roundheads) on the other. It falls into two parts. The first C.W. began on 22 Aug. 1642, when Charles I raised his standard at Nottingham, and was ended on 5 May 1646, when he surrendered to the Scottish army. The most important battles were Edgehill (23 Oct. 1642) which was indecisive, Marston Moor (2 July 1644) and Naseby (14 June 1645) both of which were great Parliamentary victories won largely by Cromwell. The second C.W. was the Royalist and Presbyterian rising of March to Aug. 1648, which was soon crushed by Cromwell and his New Model Army.

Extensions of the C.W. were Cromwell's invasion of Ireland, 1649–50, and the campaign in which he defeated the Royalists under Prince Charles (Charles II) at Dunbar, 1650, and Worcester, 1651.

CIVITAVECCHIA (chē'vētah-vek'kē-ah). Ancient port on the W. coast of Italy about 40 m. N.W. of Rome, the seat of a bishopric. Pop. (1960) 38,500.

CIZEK (tsizek), **Franz** (1865–1947). Czech educationist who revolutionized art training in children's schools. He opened the first juvenile art class in 1893, and encouraged children to draw what pleased them most. After the F.W.W. his pupils' work was exhibited in Britain and America.

CLACKMA'NNANSHIRE. Smallest of the Scottish counties, 54½ sq. m. in area, bordering on the Firth of Forth. In the Ochil hills sheep are pastured, and coal is mined in the Devon valley. The county town is Alloa. Pop. (1961) 41,391.

CLACTON-ON-SEA. Popular English seaside resort (U.D.) on the Essex coast, 12 m. S.E. of Colchester. Nearby is St. Osyth's priory (16th cent.). Pop. (1961) 27,543.

CLAIR (klär), **René.** Pseudonym of the French film producer René-Lucien Chomette (1898–). Originally a poet, novelist, and journalist, he produced the 1st sound film of artistic value *Sous les Toits de Paris* (1930): later were *The Ghost goes West* (1935) for Hollywood, and *Tout l'Or du Monde* (1963).

CLAIRVAUX (klärvoh'). Prison in Aube dept., France, 2 m. N. of Ville-sous-la-Ferté. It was formerly a Cistercian abbey, founded in 1115 by St. Bernard of Clairvaux, suppressed at the Revolution.

CLAM. Various bivalve molluscs. In England the name is usually given to the gaper (*Mya truncata*) and to other species of *Mya* and *Mactra*; in Scotland to the scallops (*Pecten*). They are used for bait and for human food.

CLAN. A patriarchal division of human society usually restricted to the clans of Scotland and Ireland, but similar institutions exist among many other peoples. In theory, all members of the C. are in common origin, tracing their descent from one ancestor from whom in general the name is derived, e.g. the clan MacGregor (son of Gregor) believed themselves to be descendants of Griogar, a son of King Alpin of Scotland, and the Irish O'Donnells were the grandsons of Donnell, i.e. Donald.

In Scottish history the Cs. played a prominent part until after the Jacobite rebellion of 1745, when their distinctive dress was prohibited and a determined attempt was made to break the allegiance of the clansmen to their chiefs. In modern times the chieftainship of some Cs. is still maintained as a title.

CLAPHAM. District of S.W. London, England, part of the Greater London bor. of Wandsworth. It incl. C. Common. C. JUNCTION has been called the busiest station in the world, since more than 2,500 trains pass through it in a day.

CLARE (*c.* 1194–1253). Christian saint. B. at Assisi, she became at 18 a follower of St. Francis, who founded for her the convent of San Damiano. Here were gathered the first members of the Order of *Poor Clares*. Canonized in 1255, she was in 1958 proclaimed by Pius XII the patron saint of television,

since in 1252 she saw from her convent sickbed the services celebrating Christmas in the Basilica of St. Francis at Assisi.

CLARE, John (1793–1864). Poet. B. near Peterborough, the son of a farm labourer, he passed most of his days in poverty. His *Poems of Rural Life* (1820), and *The Village Minstrel* (1821) were followed in 1827 by *The Shepherd's Calendar*. He was given an annuity from the duke of Exeter and other patrons, but had to turn to work on the land and spent his last years in Northampton asylum. His early life is described in his autobiography (1st pub. 1931).

CLARE. Co. in Rep. of Ireland, in the prov. of Munster, bounded on the W. by the Atlantic, with a wild and dangerous coastline. Inland C. is an undulating plain, with fringing mountains on the E., W., and N.W., the chief range being the Slieve Bernagh mts. in the S.E., rising to over 1,700 ft. The principal rivers are the Shannon and its tributary, the Fergus. There are more than 100 lakes in the co., Lough Derg is on its eastern border. The co. town is Ennis. At Ardnacrusha, 3 m. N. of Limerick, is the chief power station of the Shannon hydro-electric installations. The co. is said to be named after Thomas de Clare, an Anglo-Norman settler to whom this area was granted in 1276. Area 1,231 sq. m.; pop. (1966) 73,579.

CLARENCE. English ducal title, which has been conferred on a number of princes. The last was Albert Victor (q.v.), eldest son of Edward VII.

CLARENDON, Edward Hyde, 1st earl of (1609–74). Statesman and historian. He sat in the Short Parliament of 1640 and in the Long Parliament, where he attacked Charles I's unconstitutional actions, and supported the impeachment of Strafford. In 1641, however, he broke with the revolutionary party, and became one of the royal advisers. When war began he followed Charles to Oxford, and was knighted and made Chancellor of the Exchequer. On the king's defeat in 1646 he withdrew to Jersey, and in 1651 became chief adviser to the exiled Charles II. At the Restoration he was created earl of C., while his influence was further increased by the marriage of his daughter Anne to James, duke of York. The 'Clarendon Code' was designed to secure the supremacy of the C. of E., but his moderation earned the hatred of the extremists, and finally he lost the support of Charles by his openly expressed disapproval of his private life. The disasters of 1667, when the Dutch sailed up the Medway, brought about his downfall. His last years were passed in exile in France. He d. at Rouen, and was buried in Westminster Abbey. C.'s claim to literary fame rests on his *History of the Rebellion* (1702–4).

CLARENDON, George William Frederick Villiers, 4th earl of (1800–70). British Liberal diplomat. He was Lord Lieutenant of Ireland 1847–52, and in 1853 became For. Sec. His diplomatic skill was shown at the Congress of Paris, 1855. He was again For. Sec. in 1865–6 and 1868–70, and an outstanding achievement was the settlement of the *Alabama* dispute with the U.S.A.

CLARENDON, Constitutions of. A code of laws accepted by the royal council at C., near Salisbury, in 1164, and intended to regulate the relations between Church and State. Becket refused to accept the Constitutions, and his ensuing quarrel with Henry II led to his murder.

CLARET. Since the 17th cent. the English term for the light red wines of Bordeaux.

CLARINET. A single-reed woodwind instrument, invented in its present form by Joseph Christian Denner (1655–1707). It has a mouthpiece containing the reed, a cylindrical tube, and a bell-mouthpiece. The tube is pierced by 18 holes, of which 9 are closed by the fingers and 9 by keys. Its tone is full, mellow, and sweet.

CLARK, Kenneth, baron (1903–). Brit. art expert.

CLAUDE LORRAIN. 'A Seaport' shows the artist's inimitable handling of light and colour equally with the more familiar landscapes. *Courtesy of National Gallery.*

As director of the National Gallery (1934–45) he did much to humanize relations with the public and was Slade prof. of fine art at Oxford 1946–50 and 1961–2. Through television he has stimulated lay interest in art, and his books incl. *Leonardo da Vinci* (1939), *Landscape into Art* (1949), *The Nude* (1955) and *Looking* (1960). He was created a life peer 1969.

CLARK, Mark Wayne (1896–). American soldier. B. in New York, he fought in France in the F.W.W. and between the wars held various military appointments in U.S.A. In 1942, during the S.W.W., he became Chief of Staff for ground forces, led a successful secret mission by submarine to get information in N. Africa preparatory to the Allied invasion, and commanded the 5th Army in the invasion of Italy and the capture of Rome. He commanded the U.S. forces in Austria 1945–7, and succeeded Ridgway as C.-in-C. of the U.N. armies in Korea 1952–3. Among his many decorations is an honorary K.B.E. awarded in 1944.

CLARKE, Charles Cowden (1787–1877). Shakespearian scholar. Keats was a pupil at his father's school at Enfield, and C. encouraged his early love of letters and of poetry. C. m. in 1828 Mary Victoria Novello (1809–98), who produced in 1845 a *Concordance to Shakespeare's Plays*. Some of C's. lectures on Shakespeare and Molière were pub. and the Clarkes worked together on an annotated edition of Shakespeare, and in 1878 pub. *Recollections of Writers*. From 1861 they lived at Genoa.

CLARKE, Marcus Andrew Hislop (1846–81). Australian writer. B in London, he went to Australia when he was 18, and worked as a journalist in Victoria. He wrote *For the Term of his Natural Life* (1874), a powerful novel dealing with life in the early Australian prison settlements.

CLARKSON, Thomas (1760–1846). British philanthropist. From 1785 he devoted himself to a campaign against African slavery. He was one of the founders of the Anti-Slavery Society in 1823 and was largely responsible for the abolition of slavery in the British colonies in 1833.

CLASSICISM. In literature, music, and art, the opposite to Romanticism (q.v.). It may be said to denote that style which emphasizes the qualities considered as characteristic of Greek and Roman art, i.e. reason, objectivity, restraint, definiteness, strictness and simplicity of form – as opposed to those Romantic qualities supposed to be derived from Gothic art and literature.

CLAUDEL (klohdel'), **Paul** (1868–1955). French author. Entering the diplomatic service in 1892, he was ambassador to Tokyo, Washington and Brussels.

A fervent Catholic, he was influenced by the Symbolists and achieved an effect of mystic allegory in such plays as *L'Annonce faite à Marie* (1912) and *Le Soulier de satin* (1929), set in 16th cent. Spain. His verse incl. *Cinq Grandes Odes* (1910).

CLAUDE LORRAIN (klohd lorän') (1600–82). Properly Claude Gellée, a landscape painter of the French school, b. in Lorraine. In 1627 he estab. himself in Rome, where he executed several pictures for pope Urban VIII. He was the 1st great artist to devote himself entirely to landscapes, of which he painted about 400, and had an unequalled ability to render light and the atmosphere of a place at a particular time of day. His *Liber Veritatis* contains some 200 drawings after his finished works, useful for dating.

CLAUDIAN (klaw'dian), or CLAUDIUS CLAUDIANUS (d. 408?). Last of the great Latin poets. He was b. probably in Alexandria, and fl. at the end of the 4th cent. A.D. He wrote official panegyrics, and may have been a Christian.

CLAUDIUS (klaw'di-us) (10 B.C.–A.D. 54). Roman emperor. A nephew of Tiberius, he was made emperor by the soldiers in A.D. 41, though he was much more inclined to scholarly pursuits. For many years he was under the thumb of his 3rd wife Messalina, notorious for her debaucheries and intrigues, whom ultimately he had executed. He d. of poison. During his reign the Empire was considerably extended.

CLAUSEWITZ (klow'sewitz), **Karl von** (1780–1831). Prussian soldier and writer on war, b. near Magdeburg. Outstanding among his writings is *Vom Kriege* (Eng. ed. 'On War', 1873) which gave a new philosophical foundation to the science of war, and put forward a conception of strategy which was dominant at least to the time of the F.W.W.

CLAUSIUS (klow'zē-oos), **Rudolf Julius Emanuel** (1822–88). German physicist, one of the founders of the science of thermodynamics. In 1850 he enunciated its 2nd law: Heat cannot of itself pass from a colder to a hotter body.

CLAVERHOUSE (klä'ver-), **John Graham of,** visct. Dundee (*c.* 1649–89). Scottish soldier. Employed in the suppression of the Covenanters, he was routed at Drumclog in 1679, but 3 weeks later won the battle of Bothwell Bridge, in which the rebellion was crushed. Until 1688 he was engaged in the work of persecution, and as 'Bloody Clavers' he became an almost diabolical figure among the peasantry. In 1688 he took up arms in support of James II and defeated Mackay in the pass of Killiecrankie, but was mortally wounded.

CLAVICHORD. Stringed keyboard instrument, popular in the Middle Ages and in 18th cent. Germany. Notes are sounded by a metal blade striking the string. It was a forerunner of the pianoforte.

CLAY, Cassius. *See* ALI, MUHAMMAD.

CLAY, Frederic (1838–89). British composer. B. in Paris, he wrote light operas and the cantata *Lalla Rookh* (1877), after Moore, which incl. 'I'll Sing Thee Songs of Araby'.

CLAY, Henry (1777–1852). American statesman and orator. B. in Virginia, he was one of the founders of the Republican Party and thrice stood unsuccessfully for the presidency. He was chiefly responsible for the Missouri compromise of 1821 and for the compromise of 1850 that endeavoured to reconcile the interests of the slavery and anti-slavery parties in the U.S.A.

CLAUDIUS

CLAY, Lucius DuBignon (1897–). American general. B. in Georgia, he was Director of Material, in control of armaments, 1942–4; deputy military gov. of Germany 1945–7 under Eisenhower, and was then C.-in-C. of the U.S. occupation forces in Germany until retirement in 1949. He broke the Berlin blockade with the 'airlift', a term he brought into general use.

CLAY. A mud which has undergone a greater or lesser degree of consolidation. It may be white, grey, red, yellow, bluish, or black, and consists essentially of hydrated silicate of alumina, together with sand, lime, iron, oxides, magnesium, potassium, soda and organic substances. When mixed with water it is rendered plastic. The more important clays are adobe, alluvial, building, brick, cement, china, ferruginous, fusible, refractory, vitrifiable, fireclays, etc. Clays have an immense variety of uses, some of which, e.g. pottery and bricks, date back to prehistoric times. According to international classification, in mechanical analysis of soil C. has a grain size less than 0·002 mm.

CLAYTON, Philip Thomas Byard (1885–). C. of E. clergyman, founder-padre of Toc H. (q.v.). B. in Queensland, he became a curate at Portsea in 1910 and during the F.W.W. was an army chaplain in France and Flanders. He opened Talbot House in Poperinghe in Dec. 1915, and after the war refounded it in London as Toc H. He was vicar (1922–63) of All Hallows, Barking-by-the-Tower, London (bombed 1940 but restored 1965), which he made the Guild Church of Toc H. He was made a C.H. in 1933.

CLEANTHES (klē-an'thēz) (c. 300–220 B.C.). Greek Stoic philosopher. B. in the Troad, Asia Minor, he attended the lectures of Zeno for nearly 20 years, and on his master's death took his place as the recognized head of the Stoic school.

CLEETHORPES. English seaside resort (bor.) on the Humber estuary, 3 m. S.E. of Grimsby, Lincolnshire. Pop. (1961) 32,705.

CLELAND, John (1709–89). British author. Consul at Smyrna and one-time employee of the E. India Co. at Bombay, he wrote *Fanny Hill – Memoirs of a Woman of Pleasure* (1748–9) to extract himself from the grip of his London creditors. Called before the Privy Council, he escaped with a pension to prevent his falling into more mischief. The publishers of a reprint were in 1963 prosecuted in the U.S. (unsuccessfully) and in the U.K.

CLEMATIS. Genus of plants of the family Ranunculaceae. They are mostly climbing plants, and have a wide distribution. *C. vitalba* (traveller's joy or old man's beard) is the only British species. Many beautiful species are also grown in gardens, e.g. *C. flammula* (sweet virgin's bower), with small, white, very fragrant flowers, and *C. viticella*, whose bell-like, purple or pink, flowers hang downwards.

CLEMENCEAU (klemonsoh'), **Georges** (1841–1929). French statesman. B. in La Vendée, he was mayor of Montmartre, Paris, in the war of 1870, and in 1871 was elected a member of the National Assembly at Bordeaux. He was elected a deputy in 1876, and soon earned the nickname of 'The Tiger' on account of his ferocious attacks on politicians whom he disliked. At this time he was an extreme radical. In 1893 he lost his seat and spent the next 10 years in journalism. He was prominent in defence of Dreyfus. In 1902 he was elected senator for the Var, and henceforth was one of the most powerful politicians. He was P.M. 1906–9; and in 1917, in the darkest hour of the F.W.W., he was again called to the premiership. His appointment of Foch as generalissimo was a stroke of the 1st importance. Victory won, he presided over the Peace Conference in Paris, but failed to secure for France the Rhine as a frontier. In 1920 he resigned, and withdrew his candidature for the presidency of the Rep. for lack of support. C. founded and edited a succession of political papers, wrote novels and works of philosophy. *The Grandeur and Misery of Victory* (1930) was his final testament. In 1922 he toured U.S.A., pleading unavailingly for American co-operation in the new European order.

CLEMENS, Samuel Langhorne. *See* TWAIN, MARK.

CLEMENTI (klehmen'tē), **Muzio** (1752–1832). Italian pianist and composer. He conducted the Italian opera in London in 1777, and settled there in 1782 as a teacher and then as proprietor of a successful pianoforte and music business. He was the founder of the new technique of piano-playing, and his *Gradus ad Parnassum* (1817) is still in use.

CLEMENT OF ROME (fl. c. A.D. 96). Saint and Father of the Church. According to tradition he was the 3rd or 4th bp. of Rome, and a disciple of St. Peter. He wrote a letter addressed to the church at Corinth (First Epistle of Clement), and many other writings have been attributed to him.

CLEMENTS, Sir John (1910–). Brit. actor-producer. He founded the Intimate Theatre (1935) at Palmers Green, and excels in Shaw and Restoration Comedy. He m. in 1946 the actress, Kay Hammond.

CLEON (klē'on) (d. 422 B.C.). An Athenian demagogue and military leader in the Peloponnesian War. After the death of Pericles, to whom he was opposed, he won power as representative of the commercial classes and leader of the party advocating a vigorous war policy. He was killed fighting the Spartans at Amphipolis.

CLEOPATRA (c. 68–30 B.C.). Queen of Egypt, famous for her beauty. Upon the death of her father in 51 B.C. she ascended the throne in Alexandria together with her younger brother Ptolemy XII, whom she was expected to marry according to the tradition of the Pharaohs. In 49 B.C. Julius Caesar arrived in Egypt and she became his mistress, bore him a son, Caesarion, and returned with him to Rome. After Caesar's murder she returned to Alexandria and resumed her position as queen of Egypt. In 41 B.C. she met Mark Antony in Cilicia, who, after having m. Octavia, sister of Octavian, in 40, returned to the E. to live in sumptuous magnificence with C., who bore him 3 sons. In 32 B.C. open war broke out between Antony and Octavian (the future Augustus). In the crucial battle of Actium (31 B.C.), fought at sea off the W. coast of Greece, C. took to flight with her 60 Egyptian ships, whereupon Antony abandoned the struggle and followed her to Egypt. Next year they were besieged in Alexandria. Antony committed suicide, and C. killed herself by applying an asp to her bosom.

CLEOPATRA'S NEEDLE. Name given to each of 2 ancient Egyptian granite obelisks erected at Heliopolis 15th cent. B.C. by Thothmes III, and removed to Alexandria by Augustus c.14 B.C. — so, much older than Cleopatra's reign. One of the pair was taken to London in 1878 and erected on the Victoria Embankment; it weighs 186 tons and is 68½ ft. high. The other was given by the Khedive to U.S.A., and erected in Central Park, N.Y., in 1881.

CLERKENWELL. English parish, a watch-making centre, immediately N. of the City of London, in the bor. of Islington, Greater London. The gatehouse is all that remains of the 12th cent. priory of St. John of Jerusalem; in 1887 it became H.Q. of the St. John Ambulance Association.

CLERK MAXWELL (klark-), **James** (1831–79). British physicist. B. in Edinburgh, he was prof. of natural philosophy at Aberdeen 1856–60, and then of physics and astronomy at London. In 1871 he became prof. of experimental physics at Cambridge. C.M.'s short life was rich in contributions of the 1st order to every branch of physical science, particularly on gases, optics and colour sensation, electricity and magnetism. His theoretical work in the last sphere prepared the way for wireless telegraphy and telephony. His principal works incl. *Perception of Colour, Colour Blindness* (1860), *Theory of Heat* (1871),

Electricity and Magnetism (1873), *Matter and Motion* (1876).

CLERMONT-FERRAND (klermoń'-feroń'). French industrial city, capital of Puy-de-Dôme dept. Its rubber industry is the largest in France; motor-car tyres are manufactured. Other products incl. chemicals, preserves, foodstuffs, and clothing, and C.-F. is an important agricultural market. The Gothic cathedral is 13th cent. At a council at C. Urban II ordered the First Crusade in 1095. Pop. (1968) 148,896.

CLERMONT-GANNEAU (-gahnō'), **Charles-Simon** (1846–1923). French Orientalist. In 1868 he discovered the Moabite stone, then the oldest existing inscription in the Semitic language (9th cent. B.C.).

CLEVELAND, Stephen Grover (1837–1908). President of the U.S.A.; notable as the 1st Democratic pres. elected after the Civil War, and as the only pres. to hold office for 2 terms (1885–9 and 1893–7) which were not consecutive. He attempted to check corruption in public life, and in 1895 settled the Venezuela dispute with Britain.

CLEVELAND. District in the N. Riding of Yorkshire, England, incl. the C. hills, which contains one of the largest deposits of iron ore in the British Isles.

CLEVELAND. Largest city of Ohio, U.S.A., standing on Lake Erie at the mouth of the r. Cuyahoga, where the iron ore from the Lake Superior region is brought to meet the coal from the mines in Ohio and Pennsylvania. Its chief industries centre round the many great iron and steel works; petroleum refining is also important. C. is a railway centre and has an airport. Pop. met. area (1970) 2,043,797.

CLÈVES. French form of KLEVE.

CLIBURN, Van. Pseudonym of the American pianist Harvey Lavan C. (1934–). B. at Shreveport, Louisiana, he was trained at the Juilliard School of Music, New York, and in 1958 won the international Tchaikovsky piano competition in Moscow. He is a skilled interpreter of Rachmaninoff and Prokofiev.

CLICK-BEETLE or **SKIP-JACK.** Name given to the members of the family Elaterideae of beetles (Coleoptera), which can be recognized by their long, narrow, rather flattened bodies, short legs, and the lengthening of the hinder end of the thorax backwards into 2 sharp spines. They can get on to their feet again from lying on their backs, by jumping into the air and turning over, making loud clicks in the process. The larvae are known as wireworms.

CLIFDEN. Irish market town and port, in Galway, 43 m. N.W. of Galway town. The British airmen Alcock and Brown landed here on 15 June 1919, at the end of the 1st non-stop flight of the Atlantic.

CLIFFORD, William Kingdon (1845–79). British mathematician. B. at Exeter, in 1871 he became prof. of mathematics at Univ. Coll., London. As a mathematician he was considered to be in the front rank, and in philosophy his sceptical, even atheistic, *Essays and Lectures* (1879) had a wide sale and influence. Mrs. W. K. Clifford (d. 1929) was a well-known novelist and dramatist.

CLIMATE. The primary factors which determine the variations of C. over the surface of the earth are (a) the effect of latitude and the tilt of the earth's axis to the plane of the orbit about the sun ($66\frac{1}{2}°$); (b) the difference between land and sea; and (c) contours of the ground.

The amount of heat received from the sun varies in different latitudes and at different times of the year. In the equatorial region the mean daily temperature of the air near the ground has no large seasonal variation. In the polar regions the temperature in the long winter, when there is no incoming solar radiation, falls far below the summer value.

The temperature of the sea, and of the air above it, varies very little in the course of day or night, while the surface of the land is rapidly heated by sunshine and at night is rapidly cooled by radiation to a clear sky. In the same way, the annual change of temperature is relatively small over the sea, and great over the land. Thus the land is colder than the sea in winter, and warmer than the sea in summer. The winds which blow from the sea are warm in winter and cool in summer, while winds from the central parts of continents are hot in summer, and cold in winter.

On an average, air temperature falls off with height at a rate of approximately 1° F. per 300 ft. Thus places situated at an elevation above mean sea-level will usually have lower temperatures than places at a lower level. Even in equatorial regions, high mountains are snow-covered during the whole year. Rainfall is produced by the ascent of air. When an air current blows against a range of mountains, so that it is forced to ascend over the high ground, it gives rainfall, of amount depending on the height of the ground and the dampness of air.

The complexity of the distribution of land and sea, and the consequent complexity of the general circulation of the atmosphere, makes the distribution of the climate extremely complicated. Centred on the equator is a belt of tropical rain-forest which may be either constantly wet or monꓢoonal, i.e. seasonal with wet and dry seasons in each year. Bordering each side of this belt is a belt of savannah, with lighter rainfall, and less dense vegetation. After this usually comes a transition through steppe (semi-arid) to desert (arid), with a further transition through steppe to Mediterranean climate with dry summer, followed by the moist temperate climate of middle latitudes. Next comes a zone of cold climate with moist winter, but where the desert extends into middle latitudes the zones of Mediterranean and moist temperate climates are missing, and the transition is from desert to a cold climate with moist winter. In the extreme E. of Asia a cold climate with dry winters extends from about 70° N. to 35° N. The polar caps have tundra and ice-cap climates, with little or no precipitation.

CLIMATRON. The world's 1st completely air-conditioned and moisture-controlled display greenhouse, in the Missouri Botanical Garden, St. Louis, U.S.A., which shows tropical and semi-tropical vegetation of various kinds in environments exactly

CLICK BEETLE, with grub (wireworm) and pupa.

simulating natural conditions. The Geodesic dome, lined by a layer of Plexiglass suspended from the aluminium framework, is 70 ft. high and 175 ft. in diameter, and covers approx. ¾ of an acre. Two individual air-conditioning systems allow full variable climate control; tropical lowland jungle in the S.E.; oceanic (cool days, warm nights) in the S.W.; dry tropical (warm days, cool nights) in the N.E.; and tropical mountain forest in the N.W. Every 5 min. controlled lighting effects a transition through dawn, midday, afternoon, and moonlight. The C. was planned by Frits W. Went, Director of the Garden.

CLINO′METER. A hand surveying instrument for measuring angles of slope.

CLIVE, Robert, baron (1725–74). Soldier and statesman, founder of the British Empire in India. B. at Market Drayton, in 1743 he became a writer in the East India Company's service in Madras and was given an ensign's commission. In 1751, during a dispute over the succession to the Carnatic in which the French took the side of one claimant and the British of the other, C. marched from Madras with 500 men, seized Arcot, the cap. of the Carnatic, defended it for 7 weeks against 10,000 French and Indian troops, and then sallied out and relieved the British besieged in Trichinopoli. In 1753 C. returned to England a national hero.

In 1755 he went back to India as a lieutenant-colonel and governor of Fort St. David. In the next yr. the Nawab of Bengal, Suraj-ud-Dowlah, seized Calcutta, and shut up 146 British prisoners in the 'black hole' where all but 23 perished (20 June 1756). In Feb. 1757 C., with 1,900 men, defeated the Nawab's army of 34,000 men outside Calcutta, and forced him to make peace. In Europe the Seven Years War had begun; and C., discovering that Suraj-ud-Dowlah intended to assist the French, set out from Chandernagore with 3,200 men, and on 23 June completely defeated the Nawab's army at Plassey. By this victory Bengal practically fell to the East India Company.

In 1760 ill-health forced C. to return to England. In 1762 he was created Baron C. of Plassey. He returned to India in 1765 as Governor of Bengal and C.-in-C., and executed many great and necessary reforms. But he made many enemies, and on his return to England for the last time, in 1766, he was fiercely attacked and threatened with impeachment. In 1772–3 a parliamentary enquiry was held and he was virtually acquitted, but the charges preyed on his mind. In a fit of depression he committed suicide.

CLIVEDEN (cleev′den). National Trust estate in Bucks, England, on the Thames, 3 m. N.W. of Maidenhead. Bought in 1893 from the 1st duke of Westminster by the 1st viscount Astor, it was presented by the 2nd viscount to the National Trust in 1942. In the grounds is a hospital built by the Canadian govt. during the S.W.W. at a cost of £5,000,000 which was handed to the National Trust in 1946 as the Canadian War Memorial in Britain.

CLOCKS. Any device that can be used for measuring the passage of time, though by customary usage the word normally indicates that class of timepiece which consists of a train of wheels driven by a spring or weight. The purpose of a C. is to perform the subdivision of the day into smaller time intervals. In ancient Egypt the time during the day was measured by a shadow-clock, a primitive form of sundial, and at night the water-clock was used. Up to the late 16th cent. the only C. available for use at sea was the sandclock, of which the most familiar form is the hourglass. The Royal Navy kept time by half-hour sandglasses until 1839. During the Middle Ages various types of sundials were widely used, and portable sundials were in use from the 16th to the 18th cent. Watches were invented in the 16th cent. – the 1st were made in Nuremberg shortly after 1500 – but it was not until the 19th cent. that they became cheap

enough to be available to the ordinary man or woman. The 1st known public C. was set up at Milan in 1353; the 1st in England was the Salisbury cathedral C. of 1386. The time-keeping of both Cs. and watches was revolutionized in the 17th cent. by the application of pendulums to Cs. and of balance-springs to watches.

The marine chronometer is a precision timepiece of special design and of the finest workmanship, used at sea for giving Greenwich mean time. Electric timepieces were made possible by the discovery early in the last century of the magnetic effects of electric currents. One of the earliest and most satisfactory methods of electrical control of a C. was invented by Matthaeus Hipp in 1842. In the modern mains electric C., the place of the pendulum or spring-controlled balance-wheel is taken by a small multipolar synchronous motor which counts up the alternations of the mains electric supply, and then by a suitable train of wheels records the time by means of hands on a dial.

The quartz crystal C. (made possible by the piezo-electric property of certain crystals) has even greater precision, with a short-term accuracy of about one-thousandth of a second per day. More recently still it has been shown that resonances in some molecules, e.g. ammonia or caesium, come within the range of established radar techniques, and through positive rays and cavity resonance a link can be maintained with the molecular resonance and the frequency of an electric current. In this way time division accurate to one part in 10^{11} can be maintained for reference purposes.

CLOETE (klōōt), Stuart (1897–). S. African writer. B. in Paris, he served with the Coldstream Guards in the F.W.W., retiring in 1925 to farm for 10 years. His novels incl. *Turning Wheels* (1937), *The Mask* (1958), and *The Abductors* (1966).

CLOISTERS, The. Branch of the Metropolitan Museum of Art in Fort Tryon Park, upper Manhattan. Lovingly reassembled are parts of a number of medieval buildings transported to America from Europe, and priceless medieval tapestries, pictures, books, etc. are among the exhibits.

CLOSED SHOP. Name given to a company or firm, public corporation or other body which requires its employees to be members of the appropriate trade union. In the U.K., some organizations recognize only one union as a negotiating body for their employees, e.g. the London Transport Executive so recognizes the Transport and General Workers' Union. Trade unionism is strong enough in many factories (of e.g. the motor industry) for employees to insist that only trade union members shall be employed; but membership is not restricted to one union: such restriction results in what is properly a 'union' rather than a 'closed' shop. The C.S. was made illegal in the U.S.A. by the Taft-Hartley Act, 1947, passed by Congress over President Truman's veto.

CLOTH. *See* TEXTILES.

CLOTHES MOTHS. Moths of the family Tineidae. The larvae feed on clothes, upholstery, etc., and often do considerable damage. The lesser C.M. (*Tinea pellionella*) has yellow larvae.

CLOUDS. Water vapour condensed into minute water particles which float in masses in the atmosphere. Like fogs or mists, from which they are distinguished by the height at which they occur above the ground, they are formed by the cooling of air charged with water vapour which condenses generally on tiny dust particles.

Clouds are usually classified according to the height at which they occur. *Cirrus* and *cirro-stratus* clouds are met with at an average height of 30,000 ft. The former, sometimes called mare's-tails, consist of minute specks of ice and appear as feathery white wisps, while cirro-stratus clouds stretch across the sky as a thin white sheet. Three types of cloud are found at heights of 10,000–24,000 ft.: cirro-cumulus, alto-cumulus, and alto-stratus. *Cirro-cumulus* Cs. occur in small or large rounded tufts, sometimes arranged in the familiar pattern called 'mackerel sky'. *Alto-cumulus* clouds are similar but larger white clouds, also arranged in lines. *Alto-stratus* clouds are like heavy cirro-stratus clouds and may stretch across the sky as a grey sheet.

The lower clouds, occurring at heights of up to 7,000 ft., may be of 2 types, the strato-cumulus or the nimbus. The *strato-cumulus* Cs. are the dull grey clouds which give rise to a so-called 'leaden' sky which, however, may not yield rain. *Nimbus* Cs. are dark grey, usually shapeless, rain-clouds.

Two types of C., the *cumulus* and *cumulo-nimbus*, are placed in a special category because they are produced by diurnal ascending currents which take moisture into the cooler regions of the atmosphere. Cumulus Cs. have a flat base generally at a height of about 4,500 ft. where condensation begins, while the upper part is dome-shaped and extends to about 6,000 ft. Cumulo-nimbus Cs. have their base at much the same level, but extend much higher, often up to over 20,000 ft. Short heavy showers and sometimes thunder may accompany them. *Stratus* clouds, met with below 3,500 ft., have the appearance of sheets parallel to the horizon. They are, practically speaking, high fogs.

CLOUD CHAMBER. Apparatus devised by C.T.R. Wilson of Cambridge for tracking ionized particles. It consists of a vessel filled with air or gas, saturated with water vapour. When suddenly expanded this cools and a cloud of tiny droplets forms on the nuclei, dust or ions present. If single fast-moving ionizing particles are allowed to traverse a dust-free chamber just before expansion a trail of droplets will appear where the ionizing particles collide with the air or gas molecules, showing as visible tracks. Much information about interactions between particles and radiations has been obtained from photographs of these tracks. This system has been developed in recent years by the use of liquid hydrogen or helium instead of air or gas. See BUBBLE CHAMBER.

CLOUD CHAMBER. Following its sudden cooling, these tiny condensation trails were formed in the wake of a neutral hyperon particle.
Courtesy of Imperial College of Science and Technology.

CLOUET (klōō-eh´), **Jean** (*c.* 1486–1541). French artist, court painter to Francis I, known as Janet. He portrayed Francis and the members of his court with great skill. His son François (b. before 1522, d. 1572), also known as Janet, succeeded his father as court painter to Francis, holding the same office under Henry II and Charles IX. Both produced oils, chalk drawings and miniatures of exquisite life.

CLOUGH (kluf), **Arthur Hugh** (1819–61). British poet. B. at Liverpool, the son of a rich cotton merchant, he was at Rugby under Dr. Arnold, and at Oxford came under the influence of Newman. Eventually he became an unbeliever in religion, and many of his lyrics are marked by a melancholy scepticism. One of his best-known poems is the pastoral 'Tober-na-Vuolich'. (1848). *Amours de Voyage* (1849) is a novel in verse. His lyric 'Say not the struggle nought availeth' was made famous in the S.W.W. through a Churchillian quotation. He d. at Florence. His sister **Anne Jemima C.** (1820–92) was the first principal of Newnham Coll., Cambridge.

CLOVE'LLY. Village of N. Devon, England, famous for its steep cobbled main street which descends 400 ft. down the side of a beautifully wooded cliff. Pop. *c.* 550.

CLOVER. A genus of leguminous plants (*Trifolium*), of which there are a great number of species, found mostly in the temperate regions; 20 are British. Herbaceous plants, they have trifoliate leaves and roundish heads or a spike of small flowers. Many are cultivated as fodder plants. The most important is the Red C. (*T. pratense*). White or Dutch C. (*T. repens*) is common in pastures.

WHITE CLOVER

CLOVES. The unopened flower-buds of the clove tree *Eugenia aromatica*, a member of the order Myrtaceae. Their aromatic quality is shared to a large degree by the leaves, bark and fruit of the tree, which is a native of the Moluccas. Cs. are used for flavouring in cookery and confectionery. Oil of Cs., which has tonic and carminative qualities, is employed in medicine.

CLOVIS (465–511). King of the Franks. One of the Merovingians, he succeeded his father Childeric in 481 as king of the Salian Franks, defeated the Gallo-Romans near Soissons, and also the Alemanni near Cologne in 496, embraced Christianity and subsequently proved a powerful defender of orthodoxy against the Arian Visigoths, whom he defeated at Poitiers (507). He made Paris his capital.

CLUB. An association of persons for social intercourse, indulgence in sport or hobbies, discussion of matters of common interest, etc. There were Cs. of a sort in the ancient world, but the London Cs. of today developed from the taverns and coffee-houses of the 17th and 18th cents. The oldest is White's, evolved from a chocolate-house of the same name in 1693. Other famous London clubs incl. Boodles, 1762; Brooks's, 1764; the Portland (cards), 1816; the Athenaeum, 1824; the Garrick (dramatic and literary), 1831; the Carlton (Conservative), 1832; the Reform (Liberal), 1836; the Savage (literary and art), 1857; the Press Club, 1882; the Royal Automobile, 1897. Among women's clubs are the Forum (1919) and University Women's (1887).

The clubland of London is in the St. James and Pall Mall area, but there are clubs in all British cities and many towns. The Working Men's Club and Institute Union (1862) comprises more than 3,000 Cs. with approx. 2 million members.

Club life in the U.S.A. is common in pursuit of a particular interest, notably sports and country Cs., and such bodies as the Antique Automobile Club of America (1935). The Yale Club of New York and the Harvard Club of New York, drawing membership in the main from the universities from which they take their names, are more like a London C. than many so-called Cs. in America. The most prominent type of C. in the U.S.A., however, is the women's club, with regular lunches followed by lectures and debates;

this form of C. was well estab. all over the country when the Federation of Women's Clubs was formed in 1889.

CLUB MOSS. A class of flowerless plants (Lycopodiales) belonging to the Pteridophyta and allied to the ferns and horsetails. They have a wide distribution, but were far more numerous in Palaeozoic times, the Lepidodendroids of the coal measures being large trees. The living species are all of small size. The common C.M. or stag's horn moss (*Lycopodium clavatum*) is found on upland heaths.

CLUB-ROOT. Disease affecting cabbages, turnips, and allied plants. It is caused by one of the organisms known as Mycetozoa or slime-moulds – *Plasmodiophora brassicae*; this attacks the root of the plant, which sends out knotty outgrowths, and the whole plant decays.

CLUJ (kloōzh). City in Transylvania, Rumania, cap. of C. region, on the Somes, a communications centre for Rumania and the Hungarian plain. It is the seat of a bishopric, and of a univ. (1919) and polytechnic. Varied industry incl. machine tools, furniture, and knitwear. Pop. (1966) 222,652.

CLUNY (klünē'). Town in Saône-et-Loire dept., France, on the Grosne r. Here from 910 to 1790 was a celebrated abbey, foundation house of the Cluniac order, originally a reformed branch of the Benedictines; some remains of the abbey exist. C., once famous for lace, has an important cattle market. Pop. (1962) 4,412.

CLYDE, Colin Campbell, 1st baron C. (1792–1863). British soldier. B. at Glasgow, he entered the army in 1808, and served in the Peninsular War, in China 1842–6, the Sikh War of 1848–9, and during the Crimean War commanded the Highland Brigade at Balaclava. During the Indian Mutiny he was C.-in-C., raised the siege of Lucknow, and captured Cawnpore. He was created Baron C. in 1858 and promoted to field marshal in 1862.

CLYDE. Scottish river, one of the chief commercial waterways of the world. It rises in Lanarkshire in the Lowther hills, runs through Clydesdale, and after a course of 106 m. enters the Firth of Clyde, a broad tidal inlet nearly 40 m. wide at its southern end. Between Glasgow and Greenock some of the world's greatest shipbuilding firms are established. Among the chief towns on the C. are Lanark, Hamilton, Bothwell, Glasgow, Port Glasgow, and Greenock. Ayr is on the Firth in which are the islands of Bute and Arran and a number of smaller islands. The C. is connected to the Firth of Forth by the Forth and Clyde canal, 35 m., from Bowling to Grangemouth.

CLYDEBANK. Scottish burgh on the Clyde, Dunbartonshire. 6 m. W.N.W. of Glasgow. Shipbuilding

CLYDE. Celebrated for her busy shipbuilding yards, the Clyde still has scenery of lonely grandeur along her banks. In the foreground are the modern Lithgow yards at Port Glasgow, but beyond are the quiet hills.   *Courtesy of Lithgows Ltd.*

COACHING. Utility is forgotten in the fairy-tale splendour of the state coach of the Austrian emperors now preserved in the palace of Schönbrunn, Vienna.
Courtesy of Austrian State Tourist Department.

is the primary industry; at C. is the famous firm of John Brown & Co. Pop. (1961) 49,654.

CLYNES, John Robert (1869–1949). Pioneer of the British Labour movement. B. at Oldham, he began work as a piecer in a cotton mill, but entered Parliament in 1906, and was Home Sec. 1929–31. He was opposed to 'direct action' and to the extremism of the general strike of 1926.

CLYTEMNESTRA (klĭtemnest'ra). In Greek legend, daughter of Tyndareus and Leda, and wife of Agamemnon. Their children were Orestes, Electra, and Iphigenia. During her husband's absence at the Trojan war, C. was seduced by Aegisthus, and on his return murdered him with the connivance of her lover. C. and Aegisthus were eventually slain by Orestes.

CNOSSUS. Alternative form of KNOSSUS.

COACHING. Conveyance by a coach – a horse-drawn passenger carriage on 4 wheels, sprung and roofed in. Famous coaches still in use are those of the Lord Mayor of London (1757) and the state coach built in 1761 for George III. Stage coaches made their appearance in the middle of the 17th cent.; the first mail coach ran in 1784. Between about that time and 1840, when railways became the vogue, was the golden age of C. The main roads were kept in good repair by turnpike trusts, and large numbers of inns – many of which still exist – arose to cater for man and beast. The influence of coach design may be seen in the normal railway carriage.

COAL. Mineral substance of fossil origin, the result of the transformation of organic matter: the main types are anthracite (bright and with more than 90 per cent carbon), bituminous C. (bright and dull patches) and lignite (woody, grading into peat) and brown C. (no woody structure but only 70 per cent carbon). Fields are widely distributed in the temperate N. hemisphere, the greatest reserves being in Europe, W. Siberia and U.S.A.: the York, Derby and Notts. is Britain's chief reserve.

C. has probably been worked in England since Roman times and in the 2nd half of the 18th cent. became the basis of Britain's rise to industrial power. Since 1950 the use of natural gas as fuel and of oil for generating electricity, manufacturing gas, etc., has led to a steep decline in world demand for C. except in the less developed countries. World consumption is c. 2,000 million metric tons (Soviet Union and Communist Europe c. 850 million; W. Europe, incl. the U.K., c. 550 million; and N. America c. 350 million). Under the C. Industry Nationalization Act (1946) Britain's mines are admin. by the National C. Board.

Extraction may be by the single 'longwall' operation popular in the U.K. in which a section of the coal seam is opened out to form a straight face or wall, perhaps 100 yd. long, and is then steadily cut away day by day; by the 2-operation 'bord and pillar'

COAL. The Collins Miner, invented in 1955 by H. E. Collins, is specially designed for the economic extraction of coal from thin seams, along which the miner would once have had to crawl on his stomach. A remote-controlled cutting and loading machine, it extracts a stall (a long narrow excavation in the solid coal), and is here seen in trial operation above ground.
Courtesy of National Coal Board.

method almost universal in the U.S.A., by which the coal seam is divided into blocks by narrow roads driven at right angles to each other; or by 'opencast' stripping of the top soil over near-surface deposits, with the soil being replaced after mechanical removal of the coal layer.

COAL TAR. The black oily material resulting from the destructive distillation of coal in the gasworks. After distillation a number of fractions are obtained, viz. light oil, middle oil, heavy oil, and anthracene oil; the residue is called pitch. On further fractionation a large number of substances – some 200 have been isolated – used as dyes, in medicines, etc., are obtained.

COASTAL COMMAND. Combined British naval and R.A.F. system of defence organized during the S.W.W. (1939–45). It was divided into groups which worked in close co-operation with Naval Command, both services being directed from an Area Combined Headquarters. In addition to the groups which operated in England, N. Ireland, Scotland, and Wales, there was a separate group in Iceland and a station at Gibraltar.

COASTGUARD. Organization to prevent smuggling, assist distressed vessels, etc. In Britain the C. was originally formed to prevent smuggling after the Napoleonic Wars, but passed from the control of the Customs in 1856 to the Admiralty (to the Board of Trade 1923 – when it was re-organized as primarily a life-saving service – and in 1946 to the Min. of Transport). The U.S. Coast Guard (1915) has wider duties incl. enforcement of law and order on the high seas and navigable waters; prevention of smuggling; maintenance of lighthouses, buoys and bells; carrying out of an ice patrol for ships crossing the N. Atlantic, etc. It had its beginnings in the revenue cutter service estab. by Washington in 1790.

COATBRIDGE. Scottish royal burgh in Lanarkshire, 8 m. E. of Glasgow, on the Lanarkshire coalfield, with a large iron and steel industry. Pop. (1961) 53,946.

COATES, Eric (1886–1957). British composer. B. in Notts, he was viola player, but from 1918 devoted himself to composing, e.g. *The London Suite*, which incl. the 'Knightsbridge March'; 'The Teddy Bears' Picnic'; 'The Dam Busters March' and songs such as 'Sleepy Lagoon' and 'Souvenir'.

COATES, Joseph Gordon (1878–1943). New Zealand statesman. The son of a farmer, he was elected to parliament in 1911 as a member of the Reform Party. After serving in the F.W.W. he entered the Cabinet in 1919, and on W. F. Massey's death in 1925 succeeded him as P.M., holding office until 1928. In the coalition govt. of 1931 he was Min. of Public Works and was Min. of Finance and Transport 1933–5. In the War Cabinet formed in 1940 he was Min. for the Armed Forces, and d. while in office.

COATI (ko-ah'ti) (*Nasua*). A mammal of the order Carnivora, family Procyonidae, related to the racoon. It has a long tail and a long, flexible, pig-like snout, and its paws are furnished with long claws for climbing and digging. It is found in the forests of S. and Central America.

COBALT. Metallic element, closely resembling nickel in appearance, symbol Co, at. wt. 58·94, at. no. 27. It occurs in a number of ores, though not in great quantities, and is used as a pigment and in alloys: because it maintains its hardness at great heat, it is used to cement carbides in tools in the high-speed machining of metals. The chief sources of supply are the Rep. of the Congo and N. Rhodesia. Radioactive cobalt-60 (half-life 5·3 years) is produced by neutron radiation in heavy-water reactors, and is used in large sources for gamma-rays in cancer therapy, substituting for the much more costly radium. The C. 'bomb' contains C.-60 and is used in routine radiotherapy in hospitals.

COBB, John Rhodes (1899–1952). British racing motorist, who estab. the world record of 394·2 m.p.h. at Bonneville Salt Flats, Utah, U.S.A., on 16 Sept. 1947, broken by Campbell (q.v.) in 1964.

COBBETT, William (1763–1835). English politician and journalist. B. at Farnham in Surrey, the son of a farmer, he enlisted in the army in 1784 and saw service in Canada. Having obtained his discharge, he lived in U.S.A. as a teacher of English, and became known as a vigorous pamphleteer, at this time on the Tory side. In 1800 he returned to England, and in 1802 launched his *Political Register*, a weekly journal. Gradually C.'s views changed to out-and-out Radicalism, largely because of his increasing knowledge of the sufferings of the farm labourers whose champion he constituted himself. In 1809 he was imprisoned for having criticized the flogging of English troops by German mercenaries, and in the post-war years he became the protagonist of the working-class movement. From 1817 to 1819 he was in America, and on his return wrote the *Rural Rides* for his newspaper, which were collected in book form in 1830. Other notable books of his were an English grammar, a *History of the Protestant Reformation in England* (in which he attacked the Protestant version) and *Advice to Young Men*. He was a strong advocate of parliamentary reform, and sat in the Reformed parliament from 1832.

COBDEN, Richard (1804–65). British Liberal statesman. B. in Sussex, the son of a farmer, he became a calico manufacturer at Manchester. With other business men he founded in 1838 the Anti-Corn Law League and began his lifelong association with John Bright. In 1841 he was elected Liberal M.P. for Stockport, and until 1845 devoted himself to the repeal of the Corn Laws. A typical early Victorian radical, he believed in the abolition of class and religious privileges, a minimum of govt. interference, and the securing of international peace by disarmament and arbitration. He opposed trade unionism and most of the factory legislation of his time, because he regarded them as opposed to liberty of contract. His opposition to the Crimean War made him unpopular, but in 1859

Palmerston offered him a seat in the Cabinet, which he refused. C. was largely responsible for the commercial treaty with France in 1860.

COBDEN-SANDERSON, Thomas James (1840–1922). British bookbinder and painter. Influenced by William Morris and Burne-Jones, he opened his own workshop in Maiden Lane, Strand, in 1884, and soon established a reputation as a bookbinder with faultless technique and admirable taste. Later he founded the Doves Press (1900–16).

COBH (cōve). Irish seaport and market town on Great Island, in the estuary of the Lee, co. Cork, Rep. of Ireland. Pop. (1961) 5,266.

COBHAM, Sir Alan John (1894–). Pioneer of long-distance aviation. During the F.W.W. he served in the R.F.C., and then turned to civil aviation. By his tours with an aerial 'circus' he did much to make Britain air-minded. In 1926 he was made K.B.E.

COBLENZ. *See* KOBLENZ.

COBRA. Venomous snakes of the genera *Naja* and *Sepedon*, characterized by the fact that their necks are dilatable into a broad hood. They have cylindrical bodies with long tails and smooth scales. The Indian C., or Cobra da Capello (*Naja naja tripudians*), attains 7 ft., and is black to pale brown, with generally a spectacle-shaped marking on the upper surface of the neck. Its bite is deadly. The king C. or hamadryad (*N. hannah bungarus*) may be 14 ft. long, and is one of the fiercest and most aggressive of snakes. It is yellowish brown or olive, with black cross-bands, and feeds on other snakes. African Cs. include the Egyptian asp or hooded C. (*N. haje*) and the black-necked C. (*N. nigricollis*).

INDIAN COBRA

COBURG (koh'boorg). German town in Bavaria, on the Itz, 50 m. S.E. of Gotha. Formerly the capital of the duchy of C., it was part of Saxe-Coburg-Gotha 1826–1918, and a residence of its dukes. Pop. (1960) 44,000.

COBURN, Charles. Pseudonym of British music-hall artist Colin Whitton McCallum (1852–1945). Reared in the East End of London, he took his name from Coburn Rd., Bow. His favourite songs were 'Two lovely black eyes' (1886), written by himself, and 'The Man who broke the Bank at Monte Carlo'.

COCA. A S. American shrub (*Erythroxylon coca*) belonging to the Erythroxylaceae, whose dried leaves are the source of cocaine. It is cultivated in Bolivia.

COCAINE. The chief alkaloid found in the leaves of the coca tree. It is used in medicine to produce local anaesthesia, etc.

CŌCHABA'MBA. City in Bolivia, cap. of C. dept. At a height of 8,370 ft., it has a refinery linked by pipeline with the Camiri oilfields. Pop. (1965) 115,989.

COCHIN. Indian town and seaport, also fishing port and naval training base, in Kerala state, on the Malabar coast. It exports coir, copra, tea, spices; makes ropes, clothing, etc.; and has an airport and railway terminus. Vasco da Gama established a Portuguese factory at C. in 1502, and in 1530 St. Francis Xavier made it a missionary centre. The Dutch held C. 1663–1795 when it was taken by the English. Pop. (1961) 35,061: with the adjoining town of Mattancheri, 118,954.

COCHIN. Formerly princely state lying W. of the Anamalai hills in S. India; capital Ernakulam; area 1,480 sq. m. It was part of Travancore-Cochin from 1949 until merged in Kerala in 1956.

COCHIN-CHINA. Former French colony in Indo-China, from 1949 part of Vietnam (q.v.).

COCHINEAL (coch'inēl). Red dye obtained from the bodies of *Dactylopius coccus*, one of the scale-insects (Coccidae) belonging to the sub-order Homoptera of the order Hemiptera. It is a native of S. America, and feeds on various species of cactus.

COCHRAN, Sir Charles Blake ('C.B.') (1872–1951). British impresario, who promoted everything from wrestling and roller-skating to the introduction to London of the Diaghilev Ballet. C.'s 'young ladies' incl. many musical comedy stars of later years. He was knighted in 1948.

COCKATOO

COCKATOO'. A group of birds, forming the family (Cacatuidae) of the parrots (Psittaciformes), confined to Australia, New Guinea, and the Malay Archipelago, and chiefly distinguished by the long crests of erectile feathers. The sulphur-crested C. (*Cacatua galerita*) is white, with a yellow crest. A native of Australia, it is a familiar cage-bird. The black C. (*Calyptorhynchus funereus*) is also Australian, and the great palm C. (*Microglossus aterrimus*) is the largest member of the group.

COCKCHAFER. Species of beetle (*Melolontha vulgaris*) belonging to the Lamellicorn series of the order Coleoptera. It is about an inch long, and of a reddish-brown colour, with the breast covered with fine, greyish hairs. Cs. emerge in large numbers in May, hence the name May-bugs.

COCKCROFT, Sir John Douglas (1897–67). British physicist. B. at Todmorden, Yorks., he held an engineering appointment with Metropolitan-Vickers, and took up research work under Rutherford at the Cavendish Laboratory, Cambridge. He succeeded (with E. T. S. Walton) in splitting the nucleus of the atom for the first time in 1932, and in 1951 they were jointly awarded a Nobel prize. Succeeding Appleton as Jacksonian prof. of natural philosophy, Cambridge (1939–46), he was engaged in the S.W.W. on scientific work for the govt., latterly in connection with the atom bomb. He was director at Harwell 1946–58, and in 1960 became 1st Master of Churchill Coll., Cambridge. Knighted in 1948, he was awarded the O.M. in 1957.

COCKERELL, Sir Christopher (1910–). British engineer, inventor of the hovercraft (q.v.). From a first interest in radio, he switched to electronics, working with the Marconi Co. 1935–50. In 1953 he began work on the hovercraft, carrying out his early experiments on Oulton Broad, Norfolk, and 1958–66 was director of Hovercraft Ltd. Knighted 1969.

COCK-FIGHTING. The pitting of game-cocks against one another to make sport for onlookers and gamblers – a diversion now, in most countries, illegal because of its cruelty. It was extremely popular in feudal England. A royal cockpit was built in Whitehall by Henry VIII, and royal patronage continued in the next century. During the Cromwellian period it was banned, but at the Restoration it received a new lease of life until it was banned in 1849. The cockpits were stages of about 20 ft. in diameter. Fighting cocks were from one to two years of age when matched, and wore steel spurs, 1–2½ in. long, on their legs.

COCKLE. Genus of bivalve molluscs (*Cardium*) belonging to the Lamellibranchia and recognized by their prominently ribbed, heart-shaped shell. The common C. (*C. edule*) is found in large numbers on the British coasts, and is gathered for food (after boiling to destroy typhoid bacilli).

COCKNEY. A native of the city of London. According to tradition he must be born within sound of Bow bells (q.v.) in Cheapside. The term C. is also applied to the racy dialect of the Londoner, of which a striking feature is the C. rhyming slang.

COCKROACH. A sub-order of insects (Blattaria), commonly but wrongly called 'black beetles'; they belong to the order Dictyoptera and have nothing to do with the true beetles. In Britain only 2 small species, of the genus *Ectobia*, which do not enter human habitations, are truly native, but several species have been introduced with imported food, etc., and are great pests, e.g. common C. (*Blatta orientalis*) which is common in old houses, and nocturnal and omnivorous in its habits. It leaves a disgusting smell, caused by its saliva, on whatever it touches.

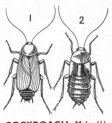

COCKROACH. Male (I), and female (2).

The so-called German C. (*Blattella germanica*) and the American C. (*Periplaneta americana*) are found in bakeries, warehouses, etc.

COCOA and **CHOCOLATE.** Food products both made from the cacao (or cocoa) bean, fruit of a tropical tree (*Theobroma cacao*) growing chiefly in W. Africa (Ghana, Nigeria), parts of S. America, the West Indies, Java, and Ceylon. Cacao is believed to be indigenous to the forests of the Amazon and Orinoco, and the use of the beans was introduced into Europe following the conquest of Mexico by Cortez in the 16th cent. A 'cocoa-house' was opened in London in 1657; others followed and became centres for the fashionable and the wits. In Mexico *chocolatl* (its native name) was mixed with hot spices, whisked to

COCOA. A Ghanaian farmer at work in a cocoa plantation. Some 20 ft. high when fully grown, the trees come into bearing about the 5th year. The 5–9 in. long pods contain 20–40 seeds, or beans, and there may be 2 or 3 harvests a year.
Courtesy of Cadbury Bros

a froth and drunk cold. Cocoa powder was a later discovery.

The cacao tree when fully grown is some 20 ft. high. It begins bearing fruit about the 5th year; this matures rapidly and takes the form of a pod, 5–9 in. long, containing 20 to 40 seeds (beans), embedded in juicy white pulp. The trees bear all the year round, and there are 2, sometimes 3, harvests. Preparation consists chiefly in roasting, winnowing, and grinding the nib (the edible portion of the bean). If drinking cocoa is required, a proportion of the cocoa butter is removed by hydraulic pressure and the cocoa which remains is reduced by further grinding and sieving to a fine powder. Chocolate, on the other hand, contains all the original butter.

COCONUT. Fruit of the palm (*Cocos nucifera*), native to India and S.E. Asia. The trees grow 60–80 ft., mature in 5–7 years, and bear up to 100 nuts a year until they are 70–80 years old. The kernel of the mature nut contains 70 per cent of oil and when dried this 'copra' is sold for use in making margarine and nut butter. The sap of the tree is fermented to produce a potent spirit, 'arrack', or may be boiled down to yield sugar, as in India. The leaves are woven into mats, baskets and sails, and the fibrous husk of the nut is used for mats, cordage and ropes. Indonesia,

COD The only freshwater member of the family, the burbot (*Lota lota*).

the Philippines, Malaysia, and Ceylon are among the chief exporters.

COCOS. Group of 27 small coral islands in the Indian Ocean lying some 1,720 m. N.N.W. of Perth, Australia. Discovered 1609, they had no inhabitants until 1826. Britain annexed them in 1857, and in 1955 transferred them to Australia. West Island is an important refuelling point for aircraft. Area 5 sq. m.; pop. (1966) 684 (210 Europeans).

COCTEAU (koktoh'), **Jean** (1891–1963). French writer of multifarious talents. Young in an era which worshipped youth, he produced Dadaist verse, a miscellany-novel *Le Potomak* (1919), ballets such as *Le Bœuf sur le toit*, or *The Nothing doing Bar* (1920), plays, e.g. *Orphée* (1926), and a mature novel of bourgeois French life, *Les Enfants terribles* (1929), which he made into a fine film in 1950. *Portraits-Souvenir 1900–1914* (1935) is autobiographical.

COD. The typical fish of the family Gadidae. The common species (*Gadus morrhua*) is found in the Atlantic and Baltic, and when freshly taken is brown to grey along the sides, with the belly shining white. The most important cod-fisheries are on the Newfoundland banks, Iceland, and the North Sea. The majority of the catch is salted and dried.

CODEX. An ancient book, with pages stitched together and bound, somewhat after the modern fashion; during the 2nd cent. A.D. codices began to replace the earlier rolls.

COD LIVER OIL. Oil obtained by subjecting fresh cod livers to pressure at a temperature of about 85°C. When prepared by modern methods, it is nearly tasteless and odourless and is highly nutritious. It is also a valuable source of the vitamins A and D.

CODY, Samuel Franklin (1862–1913). American aviation pioneer. B. in Texas, U.S.A., he spent his early days with a cowboy stage and circus act, and experimented with kites. At Farnborough, England, he helped design and build the *Nulli Secundus*, the 1st British dirigible. In 1908 he built an aeroplane, and in

W. F. CODY
Courtesy of Buffalo Bill Memorial Assoc.

1912 won a prize for the best British aeroplane. But whilst flying this machine he was killed.

CODY, William Frederick (1846–1917). American scout and showman known as Buffalo Bill from a contract he made with the Kansas Pacific Railway to supply buffalo meat to its labourers in 1867: he killed 4,280 buffalo in 18 months. He saw service against the Red Indians and from 1883 organized a 'Wild West' show with which he toured U.S.A. and Europe.

CO-EDUCATION. The teaching of boys and girls together, on equal terms and in the same classes. With the rise of modern national systems, economy dictated the adoption of C., as in 17th cent. Scotland and after the Education Act of 1870 in England. Yet it has never been universally approved, either in England or on the Continent, and segregation is still the general rule, particularly at the adolescent stage, and in the old-established schools. In 1954 the U.S.S.R. returned to her earlier co-educational system, partly abolished in 1944. In the U.S. 90 per cent of schools and colleges are co-educational, and an overwhelming majority of teachers are women.

COELACANTH (sē′lakanth). Archaic fish, formerly believed extinct. In 1938 a skin, in 1952 a complete fish, and subsequently other specimens, were obtained near Madagascar. It is directly related to the ancestors from whom human beings descend.

COELENTERATA (sēlenterā′ta). One of the phyla or primary divisions of the animal kingdom, distinguished from all the higher animals, or Coelomata, by having a single body cavity, which has only one opening, the mouth, through which food is taken into the body, and the waste products subsequently rejected. They thus correspond to the gastrula stage of the developing embryo of higher animals, and rank next in order above the Protozoa and sponges.

With one or two exceptions the C. are a marine group, and exhibit two main forms of organization: the free-swimming Medusa or jelly-fish form, and the fixed polyp. A special feature is the possession of special stinging cells, or nematocysts, by means of which they are able to paralyse their prey. Many C., e.g. the corals, build up skeletons for themselves from carbonate of lime.

The C. are divided into the 3 great classes of Hydrozoa, Scyphozoa, and Anthozoa (qq.v.). Sometimes a 4th class is added, the Ctenophora.

COFFEE. The seeds or berries of cultivated forms of *Coffea arabica, C. liberica* and allied species – natives of Africa and probably Arabia. Naturally growing 15–20 ft., the shrub is pruned to 6–10 ft. in cultivation, is in full bearing in 5–6 years and lasts for 30 years. C. is a tropical crop and does best on frost-free hillsides with moderate rainfall. The largest producer is Brazil; others are Colombia,

COFFEE. Plant, with berries.

Ivory Coast, Portuguese territories, Uganda, Mexico, El Salvador, Guatemala and Indonesia. Chicory (q.v.) is often mixed with C. to give it a distinctive bitter flavour and rich colour.

In Arabia C. drinking dates from about the 14th cent., but did not become common in Europe until 300 years later. In the 17th cent. C. houses were opened in London, but C. was largely superseded by tea until it began regaining ground in the 20th: in U.S.A. and on the Continent C. has always been more popular.

COGHILL, Nevill (1899–). British scholar, Merton prof. of English Literature 1957–66 and author of a modern English version of *The Canterbury Tales* (1951).

COGNAC (koṅyahk′). Town in Charente dept., France, 25 m. W. of Angoulême. Situated in a vinegrowing district, C. has given its name to a world-famous brandy. Pop. (1962) 21,081.

COHEN, Morris R. (1880–1947). American philosopher. B. in Russia, he emigrated to the U.S. as a boy and taught at the Coll. of the City of N.Y. 1912–38. A keen critic of anti-rational tendencies, he pub. in 1931 *Reason and Nature*.

COFFEE. The higher the altitude, within the limits of cultivability, the milder the coffee. This plantation is about 5 miles from Nairobi, and the Napier grass in the foreground is used for mulching.   *Courtesy of the Coffee Publicity Association Ltd.*

COIMBATORE (kō-imbator′). Indian city in Madras State on the Noyel r. It is a popular hill station and industrial centre. Pop. (1961) 285,263.

COIMBRA (koh-ēm′brah). Portuguese city on the Mondego r., 20 m. from the sea, cap. of C. district. It is an episcopal see, with 2 cathedrals; the university, founded at Lisbon 1290, was transferred to C. in 1537. C. was cap. of Portugal 1139–1385. Pop. (1960) 42,640.

COINS. *See* NUMISMATICS.

COKE, Edward (1552–1634). Lord Chief Justice of England. B. in Norfolk, he was called to the Bar in 1578, and in 1592 became Speaker of the House of Commons and Solicitor-Gen. In 1594 he was appointed Attorney-Gen., and as such conducted the prosecution at the trials of Essex, Raleigh, and the Gunpowder Plot conspirators. In 1606 he became Chief Justice of the Common Pleas, and began his struggle, as champion of the common law, against James I's attempts to exalt the royal prerogative. An attempt to silence him by promoting him to the dignity of Lord Chief Justice proved unsuccessful, and from 1620 he was a leader of the parliamentary opposition. Under Charles I he drew up the Petition of Right, and led the attack on Buckingham. His *Institutes* are a legal classic, and he ranks as the supreme common lawyer.

COKE, Thomas William, earl of Leicester of Holkham (1752–1842). British agriculturist, known as C. of Norfolk. He succeeded to his estates at Holkham

COLCHESTER. A medieval corner of the town – the Old Siege House. *Photo: British Travel and Holidays Association.*

in 1776, and devoted himself to agricultural improvements, and especially to improving the breed of sheep. He was M.P. for Norfolk for most of his life as a Whig, and was raised to the peerage in 1837.

COKE. A clean, light fuel produced by the carbonization of certain types or blends of coal. When this coal is strongly heated in airtight ovens, in order to release all volatile constituents, the brittle, silver-grey C. is left. It comprises 90 per cent carbon together with very small quantities of water, hydrogen, oxygen, etc., and makes a most useful industrial and domestic fuel. An inferior grade of C. is produced as a by-product in the manufacture of coal-gas.

COLBERT (kolbär'), **Jean-Baptiste** (1619–83). French statesman. B. at Reims, he entered the service of Mazarin, and after his death became Chief Minister to Louis XIV. In 1661 he set to work to reform the Treasury, and in 1665 was appointed Controller-General. The national debt was largely repaid, and the system of tax collection was drastically reformed. Industry was brought under state control, and a high standard of workmanship was insisted on. Shipbuilding was encouraged by bounties, companies were established to trade with India and America, and colonies were founded in Louisiana, Guiana, and Madagascar. Above all, C. tried to make France a naval power equal to England or Holland. He favoured a peaceful foreign policy, but in his later years was supplanted in Louis's favour by Louvois, who supported a policy of conquests.

COLCHESTER (kōl'chester). English town and river port (bor.) on the Colne, Essex, 50 m. E.N.E. of London. In an agricultural area, it is a market centre making clothing and with engineering and printing works. The Univ. of Essex (1962) is at Wivenhoe Park, 3 m. S.E. of Colchester.
C. goes back to the time of Cymbeline (c. A.D. 10–43). Made a colony of Roman ex-soldiers in A.D. 50, it became one of the most prosperous towns in Roman Britain despite its burning by Boudicca (Boadicea) in 61. Most of the Roman walls remain as well as ruins of the Norman castle, St. Botolph's priory, etc. Pop. (1961) 65,072.

COLD, Common. A minor disease caused by a variety of viruses, and which is a major cause of industrial absenteeism. Symptoms: headache, chill, nasal discharge, sore throat and occasionally cough. In 1962 the British C.C. Research Unit at Harvard Hospital, Salisbury, tested their 1st experimental vaccine against one virus strain.

COLE, George Douglas Howard (1889–1959). British economist. Active in the Guild Socialist movement, he was Chichele prof. of social and political theory at Oxford 1944–57, and pres. of the Fabian Soc. from 1952. His books incl. *The World of Labour* (1913), *The Simple Case for Socialism* (1935) and *Socialist Thought* (1953–8), 4 vols. He m. in 1918

Dame Margaret (1893–), dau. of R. W. Postgate (q.v.), and wrote with her detective stories and political works. D.B.E. 1970.

COLE'NSO, John William (1814–83). Anglican cleric. Bishop of Natal from 1853, he incurred furious attack from traditionalists by his *Pentateuch and Book of Joshua critically examined* (1862). Deposed in 1863 by the bishop of Capetown, he was reinstated on appeal to the Privy Council. He was later under attack for championing the Zulus against the white settlers.

COLEOPTERA. *See* BEETLE.

COLERAINE, Lord. *See* LAW, R. K.

COLERAINE (kōlrān'). Port (bor.) on the r. Bann, 4 m. from the sea, in co. Londonderry, N. Ireland. Steamers run to Glasgow and Liverpool; there is a linen industry and the New Univ. of Ulster (1968). Pop. (1961) 12,051.

COLERIDGE, John Duke Coleridge, 1st baron (1820–94). British judge. An eloquent pleader, he played a prominent part in the Tichborne case while at the Bar, and in 1880 became Lord Chief Justice. He was the great-nephew of the poet S.T.C.

COLERIDGE, Samuel Taylor (1772–1834). British poet, critic, and philosopher. B. 21 Oct. 1772 in Ottery St. Mary, Devon, he was a contemporary of Charles Lamb at Christ's Hospital, and while at Cambridge was driven by debt to enlist for a time in the Dragoons. In 1795, as part of a plan to found a communist colony in America with Robert Southey and others, he m. Sarah Fricker, from whom he afterwards separated. On the failure of this project, he turned to lecturing, and in 1796 pub. both the unsuccessful periodical *The Watchman* and his first vol. of *Poems.* In 1795 he had met Wordsworth, and now collaborated with him in the *Lyrical Ballads* (1798), in which the 'Ancient Mariner' appeared. 'Kubla Khan' and 'Christabel' were also written at this time. In 1798 he also visited Germany, becoming interested in German literature and philosophy, and 1800–4 he settled at Keswick, near Wordsworth, with whom he later quarrelled, and finally became enslaved by opium. He lectured in London during the next dozen years, and pub. another unsuccessful periodical, *The Friend*, in 1809. From 1816 he resided largely in the care of the physician James Gillman at Highgate, where his remarkable conversational powers attracted many young disciples.
His poetry is largely fragmentary, but unequalled in magic and music; and in criticism, the best of which is found in the *Biographia Literaria* (1817), lectures on Shakespeare, and *Table Talk*, he was the first to bring philosophical and psychological methods into the consideration of poetry. As a philosopher, he is less important as a creative thinker than as introducing idealistic German philosophy to England.
His eldest son, **Hartley C.** (1796–1849), was a poet of considerable power, especially in the sonnet, but ruined his life by intemperance; and his dau., **Sarah C.**

S. T. COLERIDGE
by Peter Vandyke, 1795.
Photo: N.P.G.

(1802–52), besides editing her father's works, was the author of the fairy-tale *Phantasmion* (1837).

COLERIDGE-TAYLOR, Samuel (1875–1912). Brit. composer. B. in London, he was the son of a West African Negro doctor and an English mother. While still a student at the Royal College of Music he had a symphony performed at St. James's Hall in 1896. His choral work *Hiawatha* (1898–1900), a setting in 3 parts of Longfellow's poem, won immediate popularity. He was a student and champion of trad. Negro music.

COLET, John (1467?–1519). English humanist. B. in London, he set out on a tour of the Continent in 1493 and in Italy fell under the influence of Savonarola. On his return in 1496 he was ordained, and began lecturing at Oxford on the Pauline epistles. His interpretation represented a reaction against the scholastic tradition, and Erasmus was strongly influenced by him. In 1505 C. became dean of St. Paul's and about 1508 refounded St. Paul's school. C. is the founder of modern biblical exegesis.

COLETTE (kolet'), **Sidonie-Gabrielle** (1873–1954). French writer. She was b. in the Burgundian countryside, whence she derived a great love of animals and natural scenery. At twenty she m. her 'Svengali', Henry Gauthier-Villars, a journalist known as 'Willy', who signed with his own name her 4 'Claudine' novels loosely based on her early life, which took Paris by storm. A period in music-hall as strip-tease artist and mime followed their divorce, but she continued to write, her later books incl. *Chéri* (1920) and *Le Fin de Chéri* (1926), dealing with a love affair between a young man and an older woman, and *Gigi* (1944). Her 2nd husband was the journalist Henri de Jouvenel (m. diss. 1925) and her 3rd Maurice Goudeket.

COLIGNY (kolēnyē'), **Gaspard de** (1519–72). French admiral and soldier, and prominent Huguenot. About 1557 he joined the Protestant party, and in 1569 achieved an advantageous peace. He became a favourite of the young king Charles IX, but on the eve of the massacre of St. Bartholomew's Day was killed by a servant of the duc de Guise.

COLI'TIS. Inflammation of the walls of the colon. Sulphonamides are among the drugs used in its treatment.

COLLAGE (kolahzh). Dada technique originated by Max Ernst, and named from the French for 'gluing' or 'pasting'. Disparate items such as fragments of newsprint or photographs are stuck alongside one another, and linked by brush or pencil to create a new artistic whole.

COLLECTIVE FARMS. System of farming developed in the Soviet Union. A C.F. is formed by a group of peasant farmers, who pool their land, horses, and agricultural implements, each household retaining as private property a plot of land and domestic animals for its own requirements. The profits of the farm are divided among its members in proportion to work done. This system has developed gradually since 1917, and became general after 1930. State farms also exist which are owned and run by the State, and employ their workers for wages. The State supplies the C.F.s with stock and equipment, and loans agricultural machinery as required. The system obtains in other Communist countries, and was adopted (1953) as an objective in China, but by 1954 had been considerably modified in Yugoslavia, Israel also has a large number of C.Fs.

COLLECTIVE SECURITY. The principle laid down in the covenant of the League of Nations, that all nations collectively should guarantee the security of each individual nation. When put to the test in Manchuria in 1931, in Abyssinia in 1935, in Spain in 1936, and in China in 1937, the principle was not enforced.

COLLEGE OF ARMS. *See* HERALDS' COLLEGE.

COLLIE. British sheepdog. There are 3 main varieties, rough, smooth, and bearded; and two lesser, the Welsh and Border Cs. Commonly known as the 'Scotch C.' the rough has been bred for centuries in the Highlands for herding. Of medium size, its long, narrow head and muzzle, and its strikingly handsome coat and colouring, are its chief features. The smooth variety differs in coat and colour. But the bearded C. resembles the Old English sheepdog.

COLLIER, Jeremy (1650–1726). Anglican divine. On the Revolution of 1688 he was one of the Nonjurors, refusing the oath of allegiance to William III, and was several times imprisoned. In 1696 he was outlawed for having granted absolution on the scaffold to 2 men who had tried to assassinate William. In 1698 appeared his *Short View of the Immorality and Profaneness of the English Stage*, aimed at Congreve and Vanbrugh, and temporarily effective. In 1713 he was consecrated a bishop of the Non-jurors.

COLL'IMATOR. An optical device for producing parallel light. A small point source or an illuminated slit is placed at the focus of a convex lens, from which the rays emerge parallel.

COLLINGWOOD, Cuthbert Collingwood, baron (1750–1810). British admiral. Entering the navy at the age of 11, he formed a close friendship with Nelson while serving in the W. Indies. He distinguished himself on the 'glorious 1st of June' and at St. Vincent, was promoted to Rear-Admiral in 1799, and was with the Channel fleet blockading Brest 1803–5, until Villeneuve's return from the W. Indies, when he blockaded him in Cadiz. Here he was joined by Nelson as his commander-in-chief, and after Nelson's death he took command at Trafalgar. He was buried beside Nelson in St. Paul's.

COLLINGWOOD, Robin George (1889–1943). British archaeologist and philosopher. Ed. at Oxford, where he was Waynflete prof. of metaphysical philosophy 1935–41, he was also an authority on Roman Britain. His works incl. *An Essay on Metaphysics* (1940) and an illuminating *Autobiography* (1939).

COLLINS, Lewis John (1905–). British churchman. While dean of Oriel Coll., Oxford (1938–48), he founded Christian Action (q.v.), and became in 1948 canon of St. Paul's. His support for the Aldermaston marches and other demonstrations has made him a controversial figure.

COLLINS, Michael (1890–1922). Irish Sinn Féin leader. B. in Co. Cork, he became an active member of the Irish Republican Brotherhood, and in 1916 fought in the Easter Rebellion. In 1918 he was elected a Sinn Féin member to the Dáil, and became a minister in the Republican Provisional Govt., and in 1921 he and Arthur Griffith were mainly responsible for the treaty which established the Irish Free State. In spite of the opposition of De Valera and the Republicans, he persuaded the Dáil to accept the treaty, and in 1922 became Min. for Finance in the Prov. Govt. During the ensuing civil war C. took command of the Free State forces, and crushed the opposition in Dublin and the large towns within a few weeks. When Griffith d. on 12 Aug., C. became head of the State and the army, but he was ambushed near Cork by fellow Irishmen 10 days later and killed.

COLLECTIVE FARM. In the Soviet Union it is planned that the economic prosperity engendered by such well-run collective farms as this should create conditions which will bring closer public ownership, with the eventual prospect of fusion into a single communist ownership.

COLLINS, William (1721–59). British poet. B. at Chichester, he was ed. at Winchester and Magdalen Coll., Oxford. His *Persian Eclogues* (1742) were followed in 1746 by the great series of endlessly imitated 'Odes', the best-known being 'To Evening'. After 1750 he became insane.

COLLINS, William Wilkie (1824–89). British novelist. Although called to the Bar, he turned instead to literature, and in 1860 contributed *The Woman in White* (a crime novel remarkable for its fat villain, Count Fosco) to Dickens' periodical *Household Words*. Best-known of his later books was *The Moonstone* (1868), with Sergeant Cuff, one of the first detectives in English literature. Still highly dramatic, his stories suffer for modern readers from repetition and very involved narrative technique.

COLLODI (kolō′di), **Carlo**. Pseudonym of Italian writer Carlo Lorenzini (1826–90), adopted from the birthplace of his mother. B. himself at Firenze, he was a journalist, and in 1881–3 wrote *The Adventure of Pinocchio* the children's story of a wooden puppet who became a human boy.

CO′LLOIDS. Non-crystalline substances of high molecular weight such as glue, egg-white, soaps, and starch which exhibit special properties in solution. A colloidal solution that retains the liquid form is known as a *sol*, but many Cs. can retain the colloidal state when in liquid form as a jelly or *gel*. The study of Cs. has thrown much light on the study of vital processes and has proved valuable in such industries as rubber and artificial silk.

COLMAN, George (1732–94). British dramatist, known as C. the Elder. His *The Jealous Wife* (1761) was based on *Tom Jones*, and he collaborated with Garrick in *The Clandestine Marriage* (1766). He managed Covent Garden Theatre 1767–74 and the Haymarket 1777–89. His son, **George C.** the Younger (1762–1836), took over the Haymarket from him and wrote the comedy *The Heir at Law* (1808).

COLMAN, Ronald (1891–1958). British actor. B. at Richmond, Surrey, he went to the U.S. in 1920 where his charm, good looks and speaking voice soon brought success in romantic Hollywood roles — *Beau Geste*, *The Prisoner of Zenda*, *Lost Horizon*, and *A Double Life* (1948), for which he received an Oscar.

COLMAR. French town, cap. of Haut-Rhin dept., between the Rhine and the Vosges mts. It is an industrial centre with an airport, and has a 13th–14th cent. minster. Pop. (1962) 54,264.

COLNE (kōn). English market town (bor.) in Lancs, 27 m. N. of Manchester. It is an important textile (cotton and artificial fibres) town. Pop. (1961) 19,410.

COLOGNE (kolōn′). German port, city, and archiepiscopal see in N. Rhine-Westphalia Land, on the left bank of the Rhine, 22 m. S. from Düsseldorf. It can be reached by ocean-going vessels and has developed into a great trans-shipment centre. It is the H.Q. of (W.) German civil aviation. Some 30 m. to the N. lies the Ruhr coalfield and C. has many industries based on Ruhr coal.

Founded by the Romans *c.* 38 B.C. and made a colony in A.D. 50 under the name Colonia Claudia Arae Agrippinensis (hence the name Cologne), it became an important Frankish city and during the Middle Ages was ruled by its archbishops. It was a free

COLOGNE. Beyond the express train, the spires of the cathedral.
Courtesy of the German Tourist Information Bureau.

imperial city from 1288 until the Napoleonic age. In 1815 it passed to Prussia. The great Gothic cathedral was begun in the 13th cent. but its towers were not built until the 19th cent. (completed 1880). C. univ. (1388–1797) was refounded 1919. C. suffered severely from aerial bombardment during the S.W.W.; some 85 per cent of the city was wrecked and its three Rhine bridges were destroyed. Pop. (1966) 859,830.

COLOMBES (kolônb′). Town in Seine dept., France, 5 m. N.W. of Paris; bicycles, chemicals, hosiery, perfumery, etc., are made. Pop. (1962) 77,090.

COLO′MBIA. S. American republic, in the N.W. corner of the continent, with coasts on the Pacific Ocean and Caribbean Sea. It is traversed by the Andes from N. to S. In the E. there are vast llanos and forested plains watered by tributaries of the Amazon and Orinoco. The Magdalena is an entirely Colombian river nearly 1,000 m. in length. Though C. is a tropical country its climate and temperature vary greatly according to the altitude.

The largest town is Bogotá, the capital; other important centres are Medellín, Barranquilla, the Caribbean port, and Cali. Some 60 per cent of the pop. are country-dwellers; and most of the people live at 4,000 to 9,000 ft. alt. Except for a few small isolated tribes, the indigenous peoples have been absorbed into the general population.

C. is the most important emerald-producing country in the world, and also ranks high as a producer of platinum; gold, silver, uranium are worked, and C. has many other minerals, including coal and iron. Petroleum is an important export, and some 25% is refined in C., chiefly at Barrancabermeja. Coffee and bananas are the chief crops grown for export; cotton, rice, tobacco, sugar are other important crops. Air transport has greatly simplified communications. An interoceanic seaway linking the Caribbean and Pacific via the Choco Valley, and formed by damming the Atrato and San Juan rivers, has been projected.

Primary education is free but not compulsory, and about 40% of the pop. are illiterate. The predominant religion is R.C., the language Spanish. There is a President and Congress composed of House of Representatives and Senate, all directly elected for 4 years. Women received the vote in 1954.

The land that is now C. was conquered by the Spaniards in the 16th cent. and from 1740 was the separate viceroyalty of New Granada. Simon Bolívar formed Greater C. in 1819, but after his death large parts split off. After several further changes of name, New Granada became in 1886 the republic of C.

Area 439,714 sq. m.; pop. (1967) 19,300,000.

COLOMBO. Capital and principal seaport of Ceylon, standing on the W. coast near the mouth of the Kelani. It is a port of call for liners on the Australian and Far East routes, and is one of the most important ports of the British Commonwealth. The harbour, started in 1875, was completed in 1912. The business quarter of the city contains the official residence of the governor, the chief government offices, etc. At C. also were Ceylon Univ. Coll. (1921) and Ceylon Medical Coll. (1870), united in 1942 to form the Univ. of Ceylon which was gradually moved to new buildings at Peradeniya near Kandy.

C. was mentioned as Kalambu in *c.* 1340, but the Portuguese renamed it in honour of Columbus. The Dutch seized it in 1656 and it was surrendered to Britain in 1796. Pop. (1963) 510,947.

COLOMBO PLAN. British Commonwealth plan for co-operative economic development in S. and S.E. Asia which came into operation in 1951. The plan covers large-scale irrigation and hydro-electric schemes, technical training, an Asian nuclear centre at Manila, etc., and is not limited to Commonwealth members.

COLO′N. City of Panama at the northern end of

COLOMBO. The House of Representatives.
Courtesy of the Ceylon Government.

the Panama Canal. Founded in 1850, and named Aspinwall in 1852, it was renamed C. in 1890 in honour of Columbus (Span. Colon). Once notorious for yellow fever, it has been transformed into a healthy and prosperous town. Adjoining is Cristobal, under U.S. control in the Canal Zone. Pop. (1968) 67,700.

COLONIAL OFFICE. The govt. dept. dealing with the colonial possessions of the Crown, originating in a committee of the Privy Council set up at the Restoration to deal with matters relating to the 'plantations'. In 1854 the Colonies became the entire charge of a principal Sec. of State. In the 20th cent. the growth of self-govt. led to diminishing responsibilities for the C.O., and in 1966 it was merged with the Commonwealth Office (q.v.), becoming the Dependent Territories Division.

COLONNE (kolon'), **Judas** (1838–1910). French violinist and conductor, known as Édouard C. He founded in 1873 the Concerts C., which he conducted till his death, and was an ardent advocate of Berlioz.

COLOPHON (kol'ofon). Originally an inscription on the last page of a book giving the writer or printer's name, place and year of publication, etc. In modern

COLORADO. The Dinosaur National Monument comprises almost 200,000 acres of country on the Green and Yampa rivers, with ancient river beds, and sandstone cliffs. Skeletons of prehistoric animals can be seen in situ, and the illustration shows the fossilized bones of a dinosaur being brought out in relief on the quarry face by skilled use of a hammer and chisel.
Courtesy of the U.S. National Park Service.

practice it is a decorative device on the title page or spine of a book, the 'trade-mark' of the individual publisher.

COLORADO (kolorah'dō). One of the mountain states of the U.S.A., west of the Mississippi basin in the Rocky Mountains. The eastern half is mainly rolling plains, but the west is mountainous with numerous peaks of more than 14,000 ft. The largest river is the Colorado, and this and other rivers travel in deep, narrow canyons. The state contains some of the finest mountain scenery in the world. A number of national parks have been set apart on the mountain slopes.

C. has great mining and smelting industries, coal, gold, silver, copper, uranium, etc., being produced. The world's largest molybdenum mine is at Climax. Agriculture is important. The cap. is Denver; other towns are Pueblo, Colorado Springs, Greeley, Trinidad, Boulder, and Fort Collins.

First settled by the Spanish, C. later attracted fur-traders. In 1858 gold was discovered and Denver was founded in the resulting gold rush. Later the immigrants turned to the mining of coal, silver, and lead, and to agriculture. C. became a state in 1876. Area 104,247 sq. m.; pop. (1970) 2,207,259.

COLORADO BEETLE. A beetle (*Leptinotarsa decemlineata*) of the family Chrysomelidae. A native of the U.S.A., it first appeared in England in 1933, and was at once dealt with as a menace to agriculture. It is a small, oval beetle, dark in colour with longitudinal yellowish stripes, and club-shaped antennae. The six-legged grub is orange-yellow. Both larvae and

perfect insects feed on the leaves of the potato, etc., and the damage done extends to the tubers.

COLORADO SPRINGS. Health resort in Colorado, U.S.A., 75 m. S.S.E. of Denver. At an alt. of nearly 6,000 ft., and surrounded by magnificent scenery, it is also a local trade centre.

COLORADO BEETLE with grub.

Pop. (1960) 70,194.

COLOSSEUM (kolosē'um). The largest amphitheatre in ancient Rome. Begun by the emperor Vespasian to replace the amphitheatre destroyed by fire in the reign of Nero, and completed by Titus in A.D. 80, it was 615 ft. long and 160 ft. high, and seated c. 50,000 people. Its ruins are amongst the most notable antiquities of Rome.

COLOSSUS OF RHODES. Bronze statue of Apollo erected at the entrance to the harbour at Rhodes 292–280 B.C. Said to have been about 100 ft. high, it was counted as one of the seven Wonders of the World, but in 224 B.C. fell as a result of an earthquake.

COLOUR. A quality of the visual sensation. It is not known what is going on in the mind of an observer when he sees a colour, but it is possible to analyse the quality of the light coming from a coloured object. Light consists of electro-magnetic radiations of various wavelengths or frequencies of vibration, and if a beam of light is refracted through a prism it can be spread out into a spectrum, each part of the spectrum corresponding to a particular wavelength. At the long-wave end of the spectrum there are the red radiations; at the short-wave end the violet colours; and in between are the orange, yellow, yellow-green, green, blue-green, and blue hues. Purples are a mixture of radiations from the two ends of the spectrum. When the surface of an object is illuminated by white light, some parts of the spectrum are absorbed, depending on the molecular structure of the material of the surface and of the dyes or pigments which may have been applied to it. Thus a red surface will absorb the light from the blue end of the spectrum, but have a high reflection for light at the long-wave end. Colours vary in brightness or luminosity, in hue, and in saturation – i.e. in the extent to which they are admixed with white.

COLOUR BLINDNESS. An incurable defect of vision which reduces the ability to discriminate one colour from another. In the most common types confusion among the red-yellow-green range of colours is very prevalent – e.g. many colour-blind observers are unable to distinguish red from yellow or yellow from green. The cause of congenital C.B. is not known, although it probably arises from some defect in the retinal receptors. Toxic conditions caused by excessive smoking, lead poisoning, etc., can lead to C.B. Statistics show that from 2 to 6 per cent of males suffer from the defect, but among women the number of cases is under 1 per cent.

COLOURS, Military. Flags or standards carried by regiments, so called because of the various combinations of colours employed to distinguish one regiment from another. Each battalion carries the Sovereign's colour – i.e. a Union Jack on a blue ground – and the regimental colour which bears the title, crest, and motto of the regiment with the names of battle honours. Rifle regiments do not carry colours.

COLT, Samuel (1814–62). American inventor of the revolver named after him (1835). At Hartford, Conn., his birthplace, he built up an immense arms-manufacturing business.

COLT'S FOOT. A plant (*Tussilago farfara*) of the family Compositae, common in Britain and growing on damp, heavy clay soils. Its bright yellow flowers somewhat resemble a dandelion.

COLUGO (*Galeopithecus*), sometimes called the flying lemur. An animal forming a special order of mammals, the Dermoptera; they are not related to the true lemurs. Cs. are about the size of a small cat, are chiefly vegetarian in diet, live in trees, and are active at night, sleeping during the day. They cling to the underside of branches with their sharp claws and cannot actually fly, but use an extensive flying-membrane to glide from branch to branch. The typical species is the flying lemur (*Galeopithecus volans*) from the forests of the Philippines.

COLUM, Padraic (1881–1972). Irish writer. He was associated with the foundation of the Abbey Theatre, Dublin, where his best-known plays *Land* (1905), *Fiddler's House*, and *Thomas Muskerry*, were performed. His *Collected Poems* (1932) show a homely lyric gift.

COLUMBA (521–97). Latin form of Colum or Colum-cille ('C. of the cell'). Irish saint and apostle of Scotland. B. in co. Donegal of royal descent, he founded monasteries and churches in Ireland. In 563 he sailed with 12 companions to Iona, and built there the monastery famous in the history of the conversion of Britain. He crowned king Aidan. In 1958 his cell, with the broad slab of rock on which he slept, was discovered.

COLUMBAN (543–615). Irish saint. B. in Leinster, he studied at Bangor, and *c.* 585 went to the Vosges with 12 other monks and founded the monastery of Luxeuil. Later he preached to the barbarians in Switzerland, then went to Italy, where he built the abbey of Bobbio in the Apennines.

COLUMBIA. River in western N. America, famous for salmon. It rises in B.C., Canada, and flows through Washington state, U.S.A., to the Pacific below Astoria. It is harnessed for irrigation and power by the Grand Coulee and other great dams.

COLUMBIA. U.S. city, cap. of S. Carolina, on the Congaree river. A distributing centre and seat of S. Carolina university, it makes textiles, fertilizers, hosiery, etc. Pop. (1960) 97,433.

COLUMBIA, District of. Seat of the federal govt. of the U.S.A. It is conterminous with the capital, Washington (q.v.).

COLUMBIFORMES. Order of birds including the various forms known as pigeons and doves (family Columbidae) together with the extinct dodo and solitaire (family Raphidae). The sand-grouse (Pteroclidae) are often added as a 3rd family.

COLUMBINE (kol′umbīn). A plant (*Aquilegia vulgaris*) belonging to the Ranunculaceae. It is a perennial herb, with deeply divided leaves, and purple flowers with spurred petals. It grows wild in woods and is a familiar garden plant.

COLU′MBIUM. See NIOBIUM.

COLU′MBUS, Christopher (1451–1506). Discoverer of America. B. at Genoa, he went to sea at an early age, and in 1478 settled in Portugal. Having come to the conclusion that Asia could be reached by sailing westward, he sought for many years for a patron to finance such a voyage. After many delays he won the support of the king of Spain, and on 3 Aug. 1492 sailed from Palos with 3 small ships. On 12 Oct. land was sighted (probably Watling Island), and within a few weeks Cuba and Haiti were also discovered. On his return to Spain in March 1493, C. was loaded with honours. During his 2nd voyage (1493–6) he discovered Guadalupe, Montserrat, Antigua, Porto Rico and Jamaica. In 1498 he discovered Trinidad, and sighted the mainland of S. America for the first time. He now became involved in quarrels among the colonists sent to Haiti, and in 1500 the governor sent him back to Spain in chains. Released and compensated by the king, he made his last voyage in 1502–4, during which he explored the coast of Honduras and Nicaragua in the hope of finding a strait leading to India. He d. in poverty in Valladolid, and lies buried in Seville cathedral. In many states of the U.S.A. *Columbus Day* (12 October) is a public holiday. In 1968 the site of the wreck of his flagship, *Santa Maria*, sunk off Hispaniola 25 Dec. 1492, was located.

COLUMBUS. Capital city of Ohio, U.S.A., on the rivers Scioto and Olentangy. It is the seat of the state univ., is near a coalfield and natural gas sources, and has diverse manufactures. Pop. met. area (1970) 904,715.

COLUMN. In architecture, a structure, round or polygonal in plan, erected vertically as a support for some part of a building. Cretan paintings reveal the existence of wooden Cs. in Aegean architecture, about 1500 B.C. The Hittites, Assyrians, and Egyptians also used wooden Cs., and in modern times they are a great feature in the monumental architecture of China and Japan. In classic architecture there are 3 principal types of Cs., viz. *Doric* which is a tapering shaft with a simple capital consisting of an echinus and abacus, and no base; the *Ionic* which is more slender than the Doric, its most distinctive feature being the capital which has 2 large volutes in the front and 2 at the back; and the *Corinthian* which is similar to the Ionic, but has a capital ornamented with conventional acanthus leaves. *See* ORDER.

COLWYN BAY. Seaside holiday resort (bor.) in Denbighshire, N. Wales. Pop. (1961) 23,090.

COMA (kō′ma). In medicine, a state of complete unconsciousness from which the subject cannot be roused even by powerful stimuli; and in optics one of the geometrical aberrations of a lens, whereby skew rays from a point object make a comet-shaped spot on the image plane instead of meeting at a point, hence the name.

COMBE (koom), **William** (1741–1823). Author of the *Tour of Dr. Syntax in Search of the Picturesque*, 1809–11. Written in doggerel verse, it owed its success largely to Rowlandson's illustrations.

COMBINATION ACTS. Laws passed in Britain in 1799 and 1800 making trade unionism illegal. Their introduction was the result of the anti Jacobin panic following the French Revolution, and the fear that the unions would become centres of political agitation. The unions continued to exist, but claimed to be friendly societies or went underground, until the acts were repealed in 1824, largely due to Francis Place.

COMBINED OPERATIONS. During the S.W.W. (1939–45), name given to the Command formed in Britain to plan and carry out raids on the enemy coasts, and to co-ordinate the activities of the land, sea and air forces engaged in these operations. The special troops trained to raid the enemy coast were known as Commandos (q.v.). Famous operations included the raid on Bruneval, St. Nazaire, and Dieppe. After the war a new School of C.O. was estab. at Fremington.

COMÉDIE FRANÇAISE (komehdē′ froṅsãz′). The French national theatre in Paris, formally estab. in 1680. Rules laid down by Napoleon in 1812 are still in force. It receives a govt. subsidy, and from Molière's time has been associated with the leading French dramatists and players.

COMENIUS (komē′nius), **Johann Amos** (1592–1670). Latinized name of the Czech educationist Komensky. B. in Moravia, he became the last bishop of the Moravian Brethren at Lissa in 1648. He revolutionized the teaching of languages, and his *Orbis sensualium pictus* was the first picture-book for children.

COMET. Mrkos' comet was one of the two naked-eye comets of 1957, and was quite conspicuous for a few days. Like all comets, it moves round the sun, but has a period of thousands of years, so that it will not re-appear in the foreseeable future.
Courtesy of Lick Observatory, Univ. of California.

COMET (Gk. *kome*, hair). A member of the Solar System, composed of relatively small particles surrounded by an envelope of tenuous gas. Some Cs. move round the sun in short periods, but the only periodical C. visible to the naked eye is Halley's, which has a period of 76 years and is due to return in the year 1986. Strictly speaking, all Cs. are periodical, but the 'great Cs.' have periods amounting to thousands or even millions of years, so that they cannot be predicted. Large Cs. have long tails, but the small, short-period Cs. are often tail-less. The last really brilliant C. appeared as long ago as 1910, but during recent years there have been several naked-eye Cs. Cs. used to be regarded with superstitious dread, but it is now known that they are completely harmless. Though they may be extremely large, they are of negligible mass.

COMFORT, Alexander (1920–). British poet and author. He qualified as a doctor at the London Hospital, where he lectured 1948–51, and was ranked among the 'new Romantic' poets during the S.W.W. He pub. *The Biology of Senescence* in 1956 and in 1966 became Director, Medical Research Council Group on Ageing, Univ. Coll., London.

COMINES (komēn′), **Philippe de** (c. 1445–1509). French statesman and historian. He was a minister of Charles the Bold, duke of Burgundy, but from 1472 was in the service of Louis XI of France. In 1489–91 he wrote his *Mémoires* (pub. 1524), one of the most valuable historical documents of the age.

COMINTERN. Abbreviation of Communist International. *See* INTERNATIONAL.

COMMAGER, Henry Steele (1902–). American historian. Born at Pittsburg, he became prof. of history at N.Y. univ. (1929–38) and at Columbia (1938–56). He estab. his reputation with *Growth of the American Republic* (1930–9, 2 vols.); later studies incl. *The American Mind* (1950).

COMMANDOS. British troops of Combined Operations Command who raided enemy-occupied territory in the S.W.W. The name was suggested by Lt.-Col. D. W. Clarke who, after Dunkirk, prepared a scheme for 'amphibious guerrilla warfare'. Among the most important C. raids were those on the Lofoten Islands (3–4 Mar. 1941), Vaagsö, Norway (27 Dec. 1941), St. Nazaire (28 Mar. 1942), and Dieppe (19 Aug. 1942). In 1940 Cs. were sent to the Middle East. One of their most daring exploits was the raid in Nov. 1941 on Rommel's H.Q. in the desert. Cs. were later active in other theatres of war, e.g. in French North Africa, Sicily, and Italy, and went into action on D-Day, taking part in some of the hardest fighting in Normandy. In Nov. 1944 Cs. took part in the capture of the island of Walcheren at the mouth of the Scheldt, and later distinguished themselves in the crossing of the Rhine. Cs. also fought in Burma. At the end of the war the army Cs. were disbanded, but the organization was carried on by the Royal Marines. The term C. originated in S. Africa, where it was used for Boer military reprisal raids against African tribesmen, and later, in the S. African War, against the British.

COMMISSIONERS FOR OATHS. In England persons appointed by the Lord Chancellor with power to administer the oath or take an affidavit. They are usually practising solicitors.

CO′MMŌDUS, Lucius Aelius Aurelius A.D. 161–92). Roman emperor from 180. Son of Marcus Aurelius, he proved an ignoble tyrant and was strangled by members of his household.

COMMON LAW. That part of the English law not embodied in legislation. In contrast with legislation, C.L. consists of rules of law embodied in judicial decisions. It is also described as 'unwritten law' as opposed to the 'written law' of legislation. English C.L. became the basis of law in the U.S.A.

With the growth of law reports grew the doctrine of 'judicial precedent', i.e., that, in deciding cases, the courts must have regard to the principles of law laid down in earlier reported decisions which relate to the same point, or to a similar point, in the particular case before them. This rule does not prevent the courts from making reasonable extensions of such principles to suit variant facts, or from laying down a new principle if the case before them is unconnected with any existing principle. Hence, the C.L. (sometimes also called 'case law' or 'judge-made law') is an important agency in keeping the law in harmony with the needs of the community, where no legislation is applicable, or where, if there is, its exact meaning has to be interpreted by the courts.

A narrower meaning of C.L. is that it comprises the law embodied in decisions of the C.L. Courts, as opposed to that contained in 'Equity', i.e. the decisions of the Court of Chancery.

COMMON MARKET. Another name for European Economic Community. *See under* EUROPE, Unification of.

COMMON PRAYER, Book of. The service book of the C. of E., based very largely on the Roman Breviary. The first Book of Common Prayer in English was that known as the First Prayer Book of Edward VI, pub.

in 1549. The Second Prayer Book of Edward VI appeared in 1552, but was withdrawn in 1553 on Mary's accession. In 1559 the Revised Prayer Book was issued, closely resembling that of 1549. This was suppressed by parliament in 1645, but its use was restored in 1660 and a number of revisions were made. This is the Book of Common Prayer still officially authorized, but a Revised Book was approved by the Church Assembly in 1927. This was twice rejected by the House of Commons, but in 1968 the Prayer Book (Alternative and other Services) Measure received the royal assent and opened the way for certain alternative services to be used.

COMMONS. Unenclosed wastes and pastures used in common by the inhabitants of a parish or district or the community at large. It is a popular misconception that a C. belongs to 'the public' and that therefore anyone may use it as he pleases. Cs. originated in the manorial system. In every manor there was a large area of unenclosed and uncultivated land over which the freeholders and copyholders had the right to take or use what the soil naturally produced.

COMMONS, House of. See PARLIAMENT.

COMMONWEALTH CONFERENCE. Popular name for a meeting between the Prime Ministers (or Defence, Finance, Foreign or other Mins.) of the sovereign independent members of the Commonwealth. Colonial Cs. had been instituted in 1887, also meeting in 1894, 1897 and 1902. The 1907 Conference resolved that Imperial Cs. be held every 4 years, and these met regularly till 1937 (the most notable being in 1926 which defined the relationship of the self-governing members of the Commonwealth). From 1937 the tendency was towards the present more informal discussions now known as C.Cs., but although these are purely consultative, the implementation of policies being decided by individual govts., results may be far-reaching. In 1971 the first C. C. to be held outside the U.K. was presided over by Lee Kuan Yew in Singapore.

COMMONWEALTH DAY. Celebrated on the official birthday of Elizabeth II, it was called Empire Day till 1958 and celebrated on 24 May (Qu. Victoria's birthday) till 1966. Its commemoration was advocated by Lord Meath to promote citizenship and knowledge of the Empire in schools, and the day was officially recognized by Canada in 1901, Australia and India in 1905, New Zealand in 1910 and the U.K. in 1916.

COMMONWEALTH DEVELOPMENT CORPORATION. An organization founded as the Colonial D.C. in 1948 to aid the development of dependent Commonwealth territories; the change of name and extension of its activities to include those now independent were announced in 1962. It works in close co-operation with the countries concerned.

COMMONWEALTH INSTITUTE. The major centre in the U.K. for information about the Commonwealth and its dependent territories, founded in 1887. It operates under the Min. of Education and Science, but is in effect independent and non-political, all the C. govts. contributing to its finances. The permanent galleries are in Kensington High St., see illus. p. 171.

COMMONWEALTH (RELATIONS) OFFICE. Govt. dept. formed in 1947 in succession to the Dominions Office to maintain relations between H.M. govt. in the U.K. and the govts. of the independent members of the Commonwealth. In 1966 the Colonial Office (q.v.) was merged with it, the word 'Relations' being dropped, and amalgamation with the Foreign Office as the Foreign and Commonwealth Office followed in 1968.

COMMUNE OF PARIS. The revolutionary govts. set up in Paris in 1789–94 and 1871. The former, a purely municipal govt. set up after the storming of the Bastille, played a prominent part in the French Revolution until the fall of Robespierre. The latter, a pro-

visional govt. of Socialist and left-wing Republicans, was elected in March 1871 after an attempt by the right-wing National Assembly at Versailles to disarm the Paris National Guard, and held power until May, when the Versailles troops captured Paris and massacred at least 20,000 people. It is famous as the 1st socialist govt. in history.

COMMUNICATIONS SATELLITE CORPORATION. Estab. by Pres. Kennedy in 1963 to provide satellites and ground facilities for international transmission of telephone, telegraph, television and other communications: 1st pres. Joseph V. Charyk.

COMMUNISM. The revolutionary socialist movement basing its theory and practice on the teachings of Marx (q.v.). The first organization of those sharing this outlook was the Communist League, for which Marx and Engels wrote the *Communist Manifesto* (1848), setting out the general theory of C. According to this, human society has passed through successive stages – primitive society, slavery, feudalism and capitalism; that each phase was at first progressive, but later became a drag upon human progress and had to be superseded by a higher phase, through the taking of power by a new class which represented the new social system. Capitalism, progressive in its early stages, appears as a barrier to progress in its monopoly stage, so that in order for mankind to advance the working class must take power, end the capitalist system of production for private profit, and build a socialist society based on common ownership of the means of production and a planned economy.

The Social Democratic parties formed in Europe in the 2nd half of last century professed to be Marxist, but their outlook gradually became 'reformist' – aiming at reforms of capitalist society rather than at the radical social change envisaged by Marx. The Russian Social Democratic Labour Party, however, led by Lenin, remained Marxist, and led the Russian workers in the November 1917 revolution, and in the subsequent building up in the Soviet Union of a socialist society on Marxist principles. It changed its name to 'Communist Party' to emphasize its difference from Social Democratic parties elsewhere. Revolutionary socialist parties and groups united to form Communist Parties in other countries (in Britain in 1920), and China, at first under Russian tutelage, swiftly emerged after the S.W.W. as a rival to the Soviet Union in world leadership. Both took strong measures to maintain or establish their own types of 'orthodox' C. in countries on their borders (U.S.S.R. in Hungary and Czechoslovakia, qq.v.) and China in Korea and Vietnam (qq.v.), and in more remote areas (U.S.S.R. in the Arab world and Cuba, and China in Albania); and both of them in the newly-emergent African countries.

By the late 1960s two issues were dominant. *Firstly*, whether the state requires to be maintained as 'the dictatorship of the proletariat' once revolution on the economic front has been achieved (so that classes may also be abolished beyond revival on the political, ideological, cultural and traditional fronts), or whether it may then become the state of the entire people: Engels, Lenin, Khrushchev, and Liu Shao-chi held the latter view, and Stalin and Mao Tse-tung the former. *See* CHINA, **History.** *Secondly*, the thesis maintained by Brezhnev in a Warsaw speech of 1968, that the Soviet Union was entitled to intervene militarily (as in Czechoslovakia) in any socialist country in which there was a threat of the restoration of capitalism: he was supported by Bulgaria, E. Germany, Hungary and Poland, condemned by Albania, China, West Germany, Rumania, Yugoslavia, and the British, French and Italian Communist Parties.

In the U.S.A. under the Internal Security Act of 1950 (known as the MacCarran Act: *see* MACCARRAN, PATRICK) all Communist organisations were required to register with the Attorney General and members might not hold a U.S. passport. However, in 1964 the Supreme Court reversed the conviction of the Communist Party for failure to register in 1962, and ruled the passport provision unconstitutional.

China has the largest Communist Party in the world (c. 17,000,000), next is the Soviet Union (c. 9,000,000); and outside the Communist world it is strongest in Indonesia (c. 2.000,000), Italy (c. 1,700,000), and France (c. 450,000).

CO′MMUTĀTOR. A device in an electric motor or generator whereby electric contact is made to the armature or rotor. It usually consists of a cylindrical insulator mounted on the armature shaft with metal contacts mounted on the insulator and connected to the armature coils through carbon or metal brushes. In a d.c. motor or generator the brushes and contacts are so arranged that the armature current is reversed at the appropriate time.

COMO (koh′moh). Italian city and episcopal see in Lombardy, cap. of C. prov., on Lake C. at the foot of the Alps. The r. Adda flows through the lake from N. to S., and the shores are famous for their beauty. C. has a marble cathedral (1396–1732), and is a tourist resort. Pop. (1961) 82,070.

CO′MORIN. The cape that is the most southerly point of India, in Madras state. Here meet the Indian Ocean, Bay of Bengal and Arabian Sea.

COMPANIES. Cs. may be either public (to which the general public is invited to subscribe) or private (the great majority), at least 7 members being required for the former and 2 for the latter. In the majority of

LAKE COMO, ringed by granite mountains 2,000–9,000 ft. high.
Courtesy of the Italian Cultural Institute.

Cs. in Britain the liability of the members is limited liability to the amount of their subscription, under the Limited Liability Act of 1855 (*see* BRAMWELL), by which British law came into line with Continental practice, which had already been largely adopted in the U.S. This limitation of liability is essential to commercial expansion when large capital sums must be raised by the contributions of many individuals. The affairs of Cs. are managed by directors, a public company having at least 2, and their accounts must be audited. *See* AUDITOR. The American equivalent of the company is the 'corporation', which has developed along similar lines although its activities are complicated on occasion by state law, i.e. a corporation of one state may not be allowed to operate in another.

In forming a company a Memorandum of Association is registered with the Registrar of Cs. which sets out its name and object, the country in which the registered office is situated, the share capital, and whether the liability of members is limited by shares, or guarantee, or is unlimited. Essential for private Cs. is the filing of Articles of Association containing the regulations governing their internal affairs. Every notice or advertisement offering shares or debentures for purchase or subscription is a 'prospectus' and must contain certain detailed information as provided in the C. Act, 1948, which also gives rulings for the annual presentation of balance sheets, etc.

COMPANIONS OF HONOUR. British Order of Chivalry, founded by George V in 1917. It is of one class only, and carries no title, but Companions append C.H. to their names. The number is limited to 65 and the award is made to both men and women.

COMPASS. An instrument for finding direction.

The most commonly used is a magnetic C. consisting of a thin piece of magnetic material with the north-seeking pole indicated, free to rotate on a pivot perpendicular to its length and mounted on a C. card on which the points of the C. are marked. When the C. is properly adjusted and used the north-seeking pole will point to the magnetic N. from which true N. can be found from tables of magnetic corrections.

Cs. not dependent on the magnet are gyrocompasses dependent on the gyroscope and radiocompasses, dependent on the use of radio.

COMPIÈGNE (koṅpē-äṅ′). Town with an airport in Oise dept., France, on the Oise near its confluence with the Aisne. It has an enormous château, built by Louis XV. Nearby is the forest of C. in a clearing of which the armistices of 1918 and 1940 were signed. Pop. (1962) 28,000.

COMPLEX. In psychology, a group of ideas and feelings which have become repressed because they are distasteful to the person in whose mind they arose; but which are still active in the depths of the person's unconscious mind, and which continue to affect his life and actions, even though he is no longer fully aware of their existence. Typical examples of a C. are the Oedipus C. and the Inferiority C.

COMPOSITAE. Family of Dicotyledonous flowering plants, characterized by having the flowers crowded into composite heads. It is the largest family of flowering plants, and the most highly advanced.

COMPTON, Fay (1894–). British actress, sister of Sir Compton Mackenzie (q.v.), and dau. of the celebrated actor Edward C. Equally at home in Shakespeare and modern roles, she has a fine voice.

COMPTON-BURNETT, Dame Ivy (1892–1969). English novelist. She relied on dialogue to show reactions of small groups of characters dominated by the tyranny of family relationships. Set at the turn of the century, they incl. *Pastors and Masters* (1925), *More Women than Men* (1933), *Mother and Son* (1955) and *The Mighty and Their Fall* (1961). D.B.E. 1967.

COMPUTER. Device for performing numerical calculations. There are 2 main types. In an *analog* C. numbers are represented by continuously variable physical quantities such as lengths, rotation of shafts or voltages. A common analog C. is the slide-rule, but modern ones are electronic. They contain various sub-units which perform the individual mathematical operations such as addition, multiplication and integration, and the machine is controlled, or programmed, by connecting together the appropriate wires on an external plugboard. The output is usually a curve tracer. They are not as accurate as digital C.s, but for some problems they are faster and are mainly used for solving differential equations, and simulating physical processes, so enabling models to be studied.

In a *digital* C. numbers are represented by discrete stable states, either mechanical or electrical, such as bead positions on a wire, toothed wheels, or, electronically, where devices can be in either the conducting or the non-conducting state. Examples are the abacus and conventional calculating machines. Charles Babbage, c. 1835, was the first to conceive the idea of building a large machine of this type to execute variable and extended sequences of operations; this machine used toothed wheels, but modern ones are electronic and can perform long and complicated sequences of numerical calculations on stored information under the guidance of a programme, or list of instructions to the computer, which is usually also stored internally, The first electronic machine was the Electronic Numerical Integrator and Calculator (ENIAC) built at the University of Pennsylvania in 1946. Normally, C.s work on the binary number system, and the essential parts are an arithmetic unit, a calculating unit and a store. Data is fed in by means of punched paper, punched cards or magnetic tape, and the output can be similar, or by electrical type-

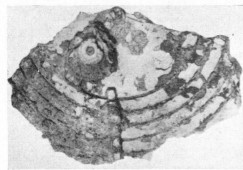 

COMPUTER. A bronze computer (left), the earliest known, made c. 30 B.C. and recovered from the wreck of an ancient Greek ship off the Mediterranean island of Antikythera in 1953; and (right) girl operators of the giant Ferranti Atlas computer at Manchester University, of which only a fraction can be seen.
Courtesy of Derek Price and Maurice Broomfield.

writer or line printer. Digital Cs. are in very wide use for scientific and business purposes, and modern machines can perform up to 1,000,000 operations per second.

COMSTOCK, Anthony (1844–1915). American agitator. B. in Conn., he served in the Civil War, founded in 1873 the New York Society for the Suppression of Vice, and crusaded against what he regarded as improper literature and indecent pictures.

COMTE (koṅt), **Auguste** (1798–1857). French philosopher, founder of Positivism or the Religion of Humanity. B. at Montpellier, he studied at the Paris École Polytechnique, being expelled for leading a student revolt in 1816, and began teaching mathematics in Paris. In 1818 he became secretary to Saint-Simon and was much influenced by him. He began lecturing on the 'Positive Philosophy' in 1826, but was almost immediately attacked by a nervous disorder and once tried to commit suicide in the Seine. On his recovery he resumed his lectures and mathematical teaching. His first great work, the *Cours de Philosophie Positive*, was pub. in 6 vols., 1830–42. In 1848 he founded the Positivist Society, out of which grew the Positivist Church, which secured members not only in France but in Brazil and England. His 2nd work of importance was the *Système de Politique Positive* (4 vols., 1851–4). For many years C. was in correspondence with J. S. Mill, who was the means of securing financial assistance from English sympathizers to enable him to carry on his work. C. d. of cancer and was buried in Père La Chaise cemetery in Paris. *See* POSITIVISM.

CONAKRY (kō′nakri). Cap. and chief port of Rep. of Guinea, linked by rail with Kankan. Bauxite and iron ore are mined nearby. Pop. (1964) 120,000.

CŌ′NANT, James Bryant (1893–). American educationist. Pres. of Harvard univ. 1933–53, he is celebrated for his studies of the American educational system.

CONCENTRATION CAMPS. Prison camps used by the Nazis for the detention, and later for the mass extermination, of the Jews and political opponents. In 1939 some 40,000 Germans were est. to be in C.Cs. and over 200,000 had previously passed through them. During the S.W.W. the numbers of inmates were swollen by many millions of Jews and political suspects from occupied Europe, and when Germany was over-run the Allies found 80,000 prisoners at Buchenwald, 30,000 at Belsen, 32,000 at Dachau, 16,000 at Mauthausen and 16,000 at Ebensee – all near to starvation and many diseased. At the Polish camps conditions were even worse: at Oswiecim the total number sent to the gas-chambers exceeded 4 million and medical experiments were carried out on living persons, and at Maidanek *c.* 1½ million people were exterminated, cremated, and their ashes used as fertilizers. Many camp officials and others responsible were executed by the Allies as war criminals. *See* EICHMANN.

CONCEPCIÓN (konthepthē-on′). City of Chile, capital of the province of C., near the mouth of the Bió-Bió in a rich agricultural district. Nearby are a coalfield and a large steel plant. Pop. (1966) 158,941.

CONCERTINA (konsertē′na). A wind musical instrument with free reeds consisting of 2 keyboards connected by expansible and folding bellows. It is played by compressing and expanding the bellows while at the same time pressing the knobs on the keyboard. By these means air is admitted to the reeds, which are set in vibration. The English C., or melodion, was invented by Wheatstone (q.v.) in 1829.

CONCERTO (konchär′tō). Composition, usually in 3 movements, for solo instrument or instruments and orchestra. Corelli and Torelli were early composers in the form, and Mozart wrote some 50 Cs. for various instruments. Modern C. composers incl. Schoenberg, Berg and Bartók, who have developed it along new lines.

CONCLAVE. Literally, a room locked with a key. Usually the word refers to the papal C. which is held in Rome immediately following the funeral of a pope. Wooden cells are erected inside the Vatican Palace near the Sistine Chapel, one for each cardinal, who is accompanied by his secretary and a servant, and all are sworn to secrecy on the deliberations. This section of the palace is then locked and no communication with the outside world is allowed until a new pope is elected, the result of each ballot being announced by a smoke signal – black for an undecisive vote and white when the choice is made.

CONCORD. Town in Mass., U.S.A., on the C. river, 20 m. N.W. of Boston. Site of the first battle of the War of American Independence, 19 April 1775, it also has associations with Emerson, Thoreau, Hawthorne, Louisa Alcott and her father. Pop. (1960) 12,517.

CONCORDANCE. Book containing an alphabetical list of the words in some important work with reference to the places in which they occur. The first C. was one prepared to the Vulgate by a Dominican in the 13th cent. The first to the English N.T. was pub. in 1535, and to the whole Bible in 1550. The most famous C. is A. Cruden's (1737), of which many editions have appeared. There are also C.s to Shakespeare, Milton, etc.

CONCO′RDAT. An agreement between the Pope

CONCORD. Preserved at Antiquarian House is a reproduction of Emerson's study. A typical New England room of
the period, it contains his books just as he left them.
Courtesy of Concord Antiquarian Society.

as head of the R.C. Church and the temporal ruler
of a state, concerning matters which are of mutual
concern, e.g. the appointment of the clergy, education, taxation, etc. The C. effected between Napoleon
and Pius VII in 1801 lasted in France until 1905.
Mussolini concluded a C. with the Holy See in 1929.

CONCRETE. A building material composed of
cement, sand, and crushed stone or gravel, mixed in
varying proportions so that when dry there results a
solid stone-like substance of very great durability.

C. was used by the Romans before 500 B.C., and
many examples of Roman work nearly 2,000 years
old still exist. In medieval times it was used for the
foundations, etc., of Westminster Abbey, Salisbury
and York Cathedrals, etc. C. of the type known today
was not used until the middle of the last century,
following the discovery of Portland cement by
Aspdin in 1824.

The life of C. is almost unlimited, and it is not
affected by extremes of weather conditions. Additional strength is imparted by the use of steel reinforcement in the form of rods from $\frac{3}{8}$ in. to 2 in. in diameter. Owing to its fireproofing qualities C. is frequently
used as a coating for steel structural bars.

Pre-cast C. units such as paving slabs, lamp posts,
drainpipes, walling blocks, etc., are now common, but
the more recent development of larger units not only
speeds the construction time of tunnels, blocks of
flats and offices, etc., but minimizes interruptions due
to bad weather. C. can be applied to other substances
by means of a cement coating, and coloured C. is
decoratively effective.

CONDÉ (kondeh'). A noble French family, related
to the house of Bourbon, The founder of the family,
Louis de Bourbon (1530–69), was an uncle of Henry IV
of France, and was prominent as a Huguenot leader in
the Wars of Religion. Louis II, called the Great C.
(1621–86), won brilliant victories during the Thirty
Years War at Rocroi (1643) and Lens (1648), rebelled
in 1651 and entered the Spanish service, was pardoned
in 1660, and commanded Louis XIV's armies against
the Spaniards and the Dutch.

CONDER, Charles (1868–1909). English artist who
painted in water-colour and oil, and executed a number of lithographs including the 'Balzac' (1899) and
the 'Carnival' sets (1905).

CONDILLAC (kondē-yahk'), **Étienne Bonnot de**
(1715–80). French philosopher, B. at Grenoble, of
noble parentage, he entered the Church and was
appointed tutor to Louis XV's grandson, the duke of
Parma. As a philosopher he mainly followed Locke,
but his *Traité de sensations* (1754) claims that all mental

activity stems from the transformation of sensations.
He was a collaborator in the *Encyclopédie*.

CONDITIONED REFLEX. A response to an
associated stimulus, e.g. a dog secretes saliva not only
at the sight of food but in answer to a bell rung at
mealtimes. It is considered to occur without conscious
learning as a result of nerve processes in the brain.
See BEHAVIOURISM and PAVLOV. Contrasted with the
C.R. is a *simple* or *unconditioned* reflex – an action
occurring automatically or intensively in immediate
response to a stimulus, without involving the higher
brain centres.

CONDOMINIUM. The joint rule of a territory by
two or more states. Examples include the Anglo-
Egyptian Sudan until 1953, the New Hebrides (administered by Britain and France), and Canton and
Enderbury Islands, in the Phoenix Group (under the
joint control of Britain and the U.S.A. for 50 years
from 1939).

CONDOR. Largest of all flying birds (*Sarcor-
hamphus gryphus*), one of the American vultures
(*Cathartidae*), 4 ft. long and with a 9–10 ft. wing span.
The plumage is black, except for a white frill at the
base of the neck which (like the head) is bare and
bright red. Ranging from Ecuador to Patagonia, the C.
hunts by sight and is carnivorous. Another species
(*Gymnogyps californianus*) frequents the mountains of
Lower California to Arizona.

CONDORCET (kondorsā'), **Marie Jean Antoine
Nicolas Caritat, marquis de** (1743–94). French philosopher and statesman. His essay on the theory of prob-
abilities (1785), contributed to the *Encyclopédie*, won
him a high reputation as a mathematician. He welcomed the Revolution in 1789, was elected to the
Legislative Assembly of 1791–2, and his plan for state
education (1792) formed the basis of the scheme
adopted. One of the Girondins, he opposed the execution of Louis XVI, and was outlawed. Whilst in hiding,
he wrote *Esquisse d'un tableau historique des progrès de
l'esprit humain*. Arrested at length, he was found
dead in his cell, probably having taken poison.

CONEY (kōn'i) **ISLAND.** Pleasure resort on a
peninsula in the S.W. of Long Island, New York
City, U.S.A., part of Brooklyn. It has a famous board-
walk 2 m. long.

CONFECTIONERY. A term of wide application
covering food preparations having sugar as the

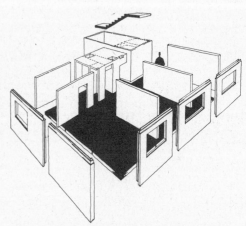

CONCRETE. The construction of flats from pre-cast concrete
units halves the time needed for erection and cuts costs. Under
the Bison wall-frame system – the first all-British method –
each flat comprises 21 units, and the first blocks were erected
in Kidderminster and Rugby in 1963. *Courtesy of Concrete Ltd.*

principal ingredient and comprising 2 main classes, (*a*) sweetmeats and (*b*) cakes and pastries.

Prior to the 19th cent., sweet manufacture was carried out by apothecaries, who produced sweetmeats to mask the taste of their drugs, and by the chefs attached to the courts of kings and nobles. The manufacture of sugar-coated nuts, etc., known as dragées, is said to have been introduced by a Roman, Julius Dragatus, about 177 B.C. Bon-bons were first made in France in the 13th

CONDOR

cent., pastilles in the 15th, and fondants in the 17th cent. The great present-day volume of manufacture is due to the introduction of automatic and semi-automatic machines about the middle of the 19th cent.

CONFEDERATION OF BRITISH INDUSTRY. Organization estab. in 1965, combining the former Federation of British industries (founded 1916), British Employers' Confederation, and National Association of British Manufacturers. The unified body voices general policy on economic, fiscal, commercial, labour, social and technical questions, and increased efficiency.

CONFESSION. The C. of sins originated with the Jews, and both John the Baptist's converts and the early Church practised public C. The Lateran Council of 1215 made auricular confession (the accusation by the penitent of himself of his sins to a priest who in Catholic doctrine is divinely invested with authority to give him absolution) obligatory once a year. Auricular C. is practised in Roman Catholic, Orthodox and most Oriental Churches and since the early 19th cent. has been revived in Anglican and Lutheran Churches.

CONFIRMATION. Rite by which a previously baptized person is admitted to full membership of the Christian Church. It consists in the laying on of hands by a bishop, in order that the confirmed person may receive the gift of the Holy Spirit. Among Anglicans, the rite is deferred until the child is able to learn a catechism containing the fundamentals of Christian doctrine, and an unconfirmed person is not usually allowed to receive Holy Communion.

CONFUCIANISM. The body of beliefs and practices that are based on the Chinese classics and are supported by the authority of Confucius, although he himself maintained that he was a transmitter rather than a creator. For some 2,500 years C. has been the religion of the great masses of Chinese.

The scriptures of C. are the 5 Chinese classics or canonical books, viz. the Shu King, or book of historical documents; the Shih King, or ancient poems; the Li Ki, or book of rites and ancient ceremonies and institutions; the Yi King, or book of changes; and the Annals of Lu, otherwise known as Spring and Autumn. Only the last may be attributed with any confidence to Confucius's authorship, but the material in the other books may owe something to his editing.

From these scriptures the Chinese in countless generations have derived their ideas of cosmology, political government, social organization, and individual conduct. The origin of things is seen in the union of Yin and Yang, the negative and positive principles. Human relationships follow the patriarchal pattern; until 1912 the emperor was regarded as the father of his people, appointed by heaven to rule. The Superior Man was the ideal human, filial piety was the virtue of virtues, and in general human relationships were to be regulated by the Golden Rule.

Accompanying this lofty morality is a kind of ancestor worship. Under the emperor, sacrifices were offered to heaven and earth, the heavenly bodies, the imperial ancestors, various nature gods, and Confucius himself. These were abolished at the Revolution in 1912, but ancestor worship (better expressed as reverence and remembrance) remained a regular practice in the home. Even under the modern régime C. has shown itself capable of continuing and even expanding in a nominally democratic world.

CONFUCIUS (*c.* 550–478 B.C.). Latinized form of K'ung Fu-tzu (K'ung the master), the Chinese sage whose name is given to Confucianism (q.v.). He was b. in Lu, a small state in what is now the province of Shangtung, and his early years were spent in poverty. At 15 his mind was 'set on learning'. At 19 he m., and about this time he was a minor official. Very early he began his career as a teacher, and gradually attracted a number of disciples on whose voluntary contributions he made a meagre living. In 517 there was an uprising in Lu, and C. spent the next year or two in the adjoining state of Ch'i, where the ruler treated him with marked respect. On his return he held aloof from public life until he was nearly 50, when he accepted the governorship of a small town and distinguished himself in the suppression of crime and in the promotion of morality. Then for 14 years he wandered from state to state accompanied by a handful of disciples. At last he returned to Lu and devoted himself to the revision of the ancient Chinese scriptures, some parts of which have been attributed, though on slight evidence, to his pen. At his death he was buried with great pomp, and his grave outside Kufow has remained ever since a centre of devout pilgrimage.

CONGER. *See* EELS.

CONGO. Second-longest river in Africa, and one of the longest in the world. It is more than 3,000 m. in length, draining an area of 1,425,000 sq. m.; at its mouth it is 7 m. wide. Its remotest headstream is the Chambezi, which rises between lakes Nyasa and Tanganyika. The Upper C. sweeps over the Stanley Falls, a few miles N. of the equator. Below the cataracts the Middle C. is navigable for 1,000 m. to Stanley Pool. This section forms a great arch towards the N., the main tributaries being the Lomami, Aruwimi, Chuapa, Ubangi, and Kasai. Below the Ubangi cliffs reduce the C. from 8 to 1 m. wide, and navigation is interrupted by a series of cataracts S. of Stanley Pool. Below the rapids, at Matadi, begins the 95 m.-long estuary which is navigable for ocean-going ships. The mouth of the river is continued 100 m. out to sea in a deep canyon on the continental shelf. Léopoldville and Brazzaville stand on the C. near Stanley Pool; Boma is a large port on the estuary.

The mouth of the C. was discovered by Diogo

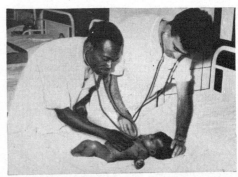

CONGO. Close collaboration between a doctor of the Swiss Red Cross and a Congolese auxiliary at Leopoldville.
Courtesy of WHO.

K

Cão in 1482; but not until the explorations of Livingstone and Stanley in the 19th cent. did the vast extent of the C. system become known.

CONGO, People's Republic of. Name assumed 1969 by the Rep. of C. (cap. Brazzaville), formerly French Middle Congo, which achieved independence in 1960. Lying N. and W. of the river Congo, it is in the French Community and the Equatorial Union. Its chief products are coffee and cotton. A railway, 320 m. long, connects Brazzaville with Pointe-Noire. Area c. 138,000 sq. m.; pop. (1966) 870,000.

CONGO, Republic of. Name taken by the former Belgian C. (cap. Kinshasa), on achieving independence in 1960. It occupies a large part of the C. basin. Its central area is a vast flat plain covered by dense forests and jungle swamps; but in the S. plateau country rises to 500–1,000 ft. In the extreme E. and S. the land rises to over 16,000 ft. in the Ruwenzori Mts., among which lies a chain of lakes including Albert, Edward, and Tanganyika. Climate on the plain is hot with heavy rainfall; on the plateau it is milder.

The people are for the most part Bantu of various tribes; numerous dialects are spoken, the chief being Kiswahili or Kingwana in the E., Tshiluba or Kiluba in the S., Lingala and Kikongo along the C. river. The republic is rich in vegetable and mineral resources; rubber, cotton, coffee, and oil palms are cultivated, and the timber of the forests is exploited. Minerals include copper, diamonds (chiefly of industrial quality), cobalt, uranium radium. Shaba (Katanga) in the S. has the principal mineral wealth, espec. copper.

The chief port, Matadi, and the second, Boma, lie on the Congo estuary. The C. river and its tributaries remain important means of transport. Area c. 900,000 sq. m.; pop. (1965) 15,627,000.

History. The C. basin was unknown territory until the explorations during the 1870s of Livingstone and Stanley (qq.v.). Leopold II, king of the Belgians, financed Stanley's journeys, and established personal rule over the so-called C. Free State, which was internationally recognized in 1885. Local wars occurred and were suppressed, and there was a good deal of oppressive exploitation of the inhabitants under Leopold's rule. In 1908 the Belgian government annexed the territory as a colony, and it was generally believed that from that time the Belgian C. was one of the best-administered colonies in Africa; but though peace was maintained, and the territory's resources were developed, the granting of complete independence to the colony in 1960 revealed that its people had been given no preparation for self-govt. Old tribal antagonisms revived, Belgian settlers were driven out, and rich Katanga sought to break away from the rep. A small U.N. force remained in C. till 1964, but civil unrest continued, and in 1965 Gen. Joseph-Désiré Mobutu (1930–   ) assumed the presidency by a coup. In 1966 he reduced the no. of provs. from 21 to 12—the cap. remaining an independent admin. unit—and renamed various towns Kinshasa (Léopoldville), Lubumbashi (Elizabethville), Kisangani (Stanleyville). A new constitution instituting a unitary state under a pres., with a unicameral legislature, and political parties limited to 2, was proclaimed after a referendum 1967. By 1968 order was largely restored, and power had been increasingly centralised by Mobutu; re-elected for 7 yrs. 1970. In 1971 C. became the *Rep. of Zaïre*, the C. river within C. also becoming known as the Zaïre river.

CONGREGATIONALISM. The form of church govt. adopted by those Protestant Christians known as Congregationalists, in which each congregation manages its own affairs. The first Congregationalists were the Brownists, named after Robert Browne, who in 1580 defined the congregational principle. In the next cent. they were known as Independents, e.g. Cromwell and many of his Ironsides, and in 1662 hundreds of their ministers were driven from their churches and estab. separate congregations. In Britain there are c. 3,000 Congregational churches, with many more in the Commonwealth. The Congregational Union of England and Wales (1832), like the Congregational Union of Scotland (1812; united 1896 with the Evangelical Union), has no control over individual churches but is simply consultative. In Canada the Congregationalists joined with the Methodists and Presbyterians in 1925 to form the United Church of Canada, and in the U.S. in 1957 they joined with the Evangelical and Reformed Church to form the United Church of Christ.

CONGRESS. National legislature of U.S.A., consisting of a House of Representatives (438 members, apportioned to the States of the Union on the basis of population, and elected for 2-year terms) and the Senate (100 senators, 2 for each State, elected for 6 years, one third elected every 2 years). Both representatives and senators are elected by direct popular vote. C. meets at Washington in the Capitol. Members of both houses receive a salary of $42,500, plus allowances.

CONGRESS OF INDUSTRIAL ORGANIZATIONS. *See* AMERICAN FEDERATION OF LABOR AND CONGRESS OF INDUSTRIAL ORGANIZATIONS.

CONGRESS PARTY. The Indian National Congress, founded by the Englishman A. O. Hume in 1885, was a moderate body until the F.W.W. when, under Gandhi's leadership, it began a campaign of non-violent non-co-operation. Declared illegal 1932–4, it polled 70 per cent of the votes at the 1937 elections and formed ministries in 9 out of 11 provs., and by 1939 had 6 million membership. Under Nehru's guidance, it was recognised as the paramount power in India at the granting of independence in 1947, and was returned to power at the elections of 1952, 1957, 1962 and 1967. In 1969 there was a split, and the section in opposition to the govt. became known as the 'Organization Congress'.

CONGREVE (kon′grēv), **William** (1670–1729). English dramatist and poet. B. nr. Leeds, he was a friend of Swift at Trinity Coll., Dublin, and in 1691 began studying law in London. He won immediate success with his first comedy *The Old Bachelor* (1693), which was followed by *The Double Dealer* (1694), *Love for Love* (1695) and the tragedy *The Mourning Bride* (1697). In 1698 he pub. a reply to Jeremy Collier's (q.v.) attack on the contemporary stage, and 2 years later his masterpiece, *The Way of the World*, appeared, but was at the time a failure.

Among the friends of his later years were the actress Mrs. Bracegirdle, and Henrietta, duchess of Marlborough, to whom he left his fortune. C. is the most brilliant of the Restoration comic dramatists, and achieves perfection of construction and style.

CONIC SECTIONS. The curves obtained when a cone is intersected by a plane; they were first discovered by the ancient Greeks and have been of great importance in mathematics. If the intersecting plane cuts both extensions of the cone it yields a hyperbola, if it is parallel to the side of the C. it produces a parabola; other intersecting planes produce circles and ellipses.

CONIFERAE (kōnif′erē) or **CONIFERALES.** Division of plants, forming the largest and most important order of the Gymnosperms, and contained in about 46 genera, and about 500 species. They are trees and shrubs, often of a characteristic pyramidal form, and the leaves are linear 'needles', or small and scale-like, usually evergreen. The reproductive elements are borne in male and female cones, and the pollen is distributed by the wind. They usually grow in forests, and are specially characteristic of the colder and temperate parts of the world, particularly the N. hemisphere.

The C. are divided into 5 families: the Araucariaceae, including the monkey-puzzle tree and the kauri pine; Podocarpaceae, including half-a-dozen genera of

CONNEMARA. Chequered by low drystone walls, sometimes enclosing no more than a few square yards of land, the countryside at Rossaveal – dotted with limewashed cottages – is a harmony of white and silver-grey.
Courtesy of the Irish Tourist Board.

trees, shrubs, or small undershrubs; the Pinaceae, including the spruce, pine, fir, larch, and cedar; the Cupressaceae, including the juniper, cypress, arbor vitae, umbrella-pine, and the gigantic *Sequoia*; and the Taxaceae, which includes the yew.

CONJUNCTIVÍTIS. Inflammation of the conjunctiva or membrane which covers the front of the eye.

CONKLIN, Edwin Grant (1863–1952). American biologist. B. and ed. in the state of Ohio, he was prof. of biology at Princeton (1908–33), and became known for his discoveries in embryology and in the mechanism of evolution and heredity.

CONNACHT. Province of Rep. of Ireland, consisting of the cos. of Mayo, Galway, Roscommon, Sligo, and Leitrim: area 6,611 sq. m., pop. (1966) 401,950. Mainly lowland, it is agricultural and stock-raising country with very poor land in the W. The chief rivers are the Shannon, Moy, and Suck, and there are a number of lakes. The chief towns are Galway, Roscommon, Castlebar, Sligo, and Carrick-on-Shannon. The Gaelic language has maintained itself better in C. than in the other provinces, and the C. dialect has been adopted as the standard of the national language.

CONNAUGHT AND STRATHEARN (kon'awt, strathern'), **Arthur William Patrick Albert**, duke of (1850–1942). 7th child and 3rd son of Queen Victoria, he was Gov.-Gen. of Canada 1911–16. He m. in 1879 Princess Louise of Prussia, and their only son, **Prince Arthur of C.** (1883–1938) was Gov.-Gen. of S. Africa 1920–3. The latter's wife, Alexandra (1891–1959), whom he m. in 1913, was a grand-dau. of Edward VII and Duchess of Fife in her own right.

CONNECTICUT (konet'ikut). One of the New England States of the U.S.A., bounded by the States of New York, Massachusetts, and Rhode Is., and Long Is. Sound. Most of it is plain, but there are highlands in the N.W. The chief rivers are the Connecticut, the Thames, the Naugatuck, and the Housatonic. The chief towns are Hartford (the cap.), New Haven, Bridgeport, Waterbury, and New Britain. C. is primarily an industrial state, and noted for its armament factories. Tobacco growing and dairying are important. Yale univ. at New Haven is world-famous. Settled in 1635 by Puritan colonists from Massachusetts, C. in 1639 adopted the famous Fundamental Orders, foreshadowing in many respects the United States constitution. It was one of the original 13 states of the American union.

Area, 5,009 sq. m.; pop. (1970) 3,032,217.

CONNELL, James (d. 1929). Irish socialist writer, remembered as the author of *The Red Flag*.

CO'NNELLY, Marc (1890–). American dramatist. B. in Penn., he became a reporter in Pittsburgh, and in 1930 won a Pulitzer Prize with *Green Pastures* –

banned in England because God was represented (as a venerable Negro), but a film version was shown.

CONNEMARA (konemah'rah). The western division of co. Galway, Rep. of Ireland, much visited by tourists for its wild scenery.

CO'NNOLLY, Cyril (1903–). English writer. As founder-editor of the literary magazine *Horizon* (1939–50), he exercised considerable critical influence. His books incl. *The Rock Pool* (1935), a novel of artists on the Riviera; *The Unquiet Grave* (1945), a vol. of essays under the pseudonym 'Palinurus'; *The Condemned Playground* (1946), parodies and satires; and *Ideas and Places* (1954), more essays.

CONNOLLY, James (1870–1916). Irish socialist and nationalist. B. in Ulster, he led, with James Larkin, the Dublin transport workers' strike of 1913, and helped to lead the Easter Rebellion of 1916, in which he was severely wounded. He was captured, court-martialled, and shot at Kilmainham gaol.

CONNOR, Ralph. Pseudonym of the Canadian writer, the Rev. Charles W. Gordon (1860–1937). A missionary to the miners and lumbermen of the Rockies (1890–3), and minister of a Presbyterian church in Winnipeg from 1894, he wrote novels drawing on this background, e.g. *The Sky Pilot* (1899).

CONQUISTADOR (konkistador'). Spanish word for 'conqueror', applied to such explorers and adventurers in the Americas as Cortes and Pizarro.

CONRAD. Name of several kings of the Germans. Conrad I (d. 918) succeeded Louis the Child, the last of the Ger. Carolingians, in 911, and during his reign the realm was harassed by Magyar invaders. **Conrad II** (d. 1039) reigned from 1024 and ceded the march Sleswick to Canute. **Conrad III** (1093–1152), the 1st king of the Hohenstaufen dynasty, was crowned at Aachen in 1138, and throughout his reign a fierce struggle between his followers, the Ghibellines, and the Guelphs, the followers of Henry the Proud, duke of Saxony and Bavaria, and his son Henry the Lion, continued. C. took part in the 2nd crusade. **Conrad IV** (1228–54), son of the emperor Frederick II, was elected king in 1237, and had to defend his right of succession against Henry Raspe of Thuringia and William of Holland. His son **Conradin** (1252–68), the last of the Hohenstaufen, was defeated and captured by Charles of Anjou at Tagliacozzo in 1268, and beheaded in Naples.

CONRAD, Joseph (1857–1924). British novelist. Of Polish parentage, he was b. Teodor Jozef Konrad Korzeniowski in the Ukraine, and was taken to Warsaw in 1861 by his father. He joined the French merchant marine in 1874, and transferred to the British service in 1878, when he first landed at Lowestoft with no knowledge of English. In 1886 he gained his master mariner's certificate and became a naturalized British subject, but retired from the sea in 1894 to write. His first novel, *Almayer's Folly*, appeared in 1895 and was followed by – among others – *An Outcast of the Islands* (1896), *The Nigger of the 'Narcissus'* (1897), *Lord Jim* (1900) and *Nostromo* (1904). Showing increasing power and mastery of technique, he not only brought home to English readers the mysteries of sea life and exotic foreign settings, but plumbed the psychological isolation of the 'outsider'. C.'s earlier period closes with the autobiographical *Mirror of the Sea* (1906). Among later books were *Under Western Eyes* (1911), with a Tsarist Russian background, *The Secret*

JOSEPH CONRAD
Etching by W. Tittle, 1924.
Photo: N.P G.

Agent (1907), and *Chance* (1914), his first popular success.

CONS, Emma (1838–1912). British philanthropist. B. in London, she devoted herself to social work, and in 1880 bought the Royal Victoria Hall and made it the home of Shakespeare and opera. *See* OLD VIC.

CONSANGUINITY. Relationship by blood, whether lineal, i.e. by direct descent, or collateral, i.e. by virtue of a common ancestor. The degree of C. is of importance in laws relating to the inheritance of property and also in relation to marriage, which is forbidden between parties closely related by blood.

CONSCIENCE (końsyońs′), **Hendrik** (1812–83). Flemish novelist. B. at Antwerp, he served in the Belgian army, and, fired by the desire to write in Flemish, he pub. in 1837 *In't Wonderjaar 1566*, a series of sketches of the War of Dutch Independence, and *Phantazy*. These were followed by many other works, notably *The Lion of Flanders* (1838) and *The Conscript* (1850). Long before his death C. was recognized as the creator of a national literature in a hitherto despised tongue.

CONSCIENTIOUS OBJECTORS. A term originally denoting parents who objected to compulsory vaccination, later applied to persons refusing compulsory service, usually in the army, on moral, religious or political grounds. When conscription was introduced in Britain in 1916, there were about 22,000 C.O.s. Nearly 7,000 were arrested and many were repeatedly sentenced by court-martial. When conscription was re-introduced in May 1939, tribunals were set up to decide the claims of C.O.s. In the S.W.W. about 3,500 C.O.s were sent to prison.

CONSCRIPTION. The system under which all able-bodied male citizens are legally liable to serve with the armed forces. It originated in France in 1792, during the Revolutionary War, and in the 19th cent. it became the established practice in almost all European states. C. was unknown in Britain before the F.W.W., although a campaign in its favour was carried on by Lord Roberts for some years. During F.W.W. it was introduced for single men between 18 and 41 in March 1916 and for married men 2 months later, but was abolished after the war. It was introduced for the first time in peace in April 1939, when all men aged 20 became liable to 6 months' military training. The National Service Act, passed in Sept. 1939, made all men between 18 and 41 liable to military service, and in 1941 women also became liable to be called up for the women's services as an alternative to industrial service. Men reaching the age of 18 continued to be called up until 1960.

In the U.S.A. C. was introduced during the Civil War. During the F.W.W. men of 18–45 were conscripted. Peacetime C. – the 'draft' – was first introduced in 1940, and since 1948 the balance of the armed forces has been maintained by the Selective Service System.

CONSERVATIVE PARTY. One of the 2 historic British parties, the name replacing 'Tory' in general use from 1830 onwards. Traditionally the party of landed interests, opposed to the *laissez-faire* of the Liberal manufacturers, it supported, to some extent, the struggle of the working-class against the harshness of conditions arising from the Industrial Revolution. The split of 1846 over Peel's corn-law policy led to 20 years out of office, or in office without power, until Disraeli 'educated' his party into accepting parliamentary and social change, extended the franchise to the artisan (winning considerable working-class support), launched imperial expansion, and estab. an alliance with industry and finance. The Home Rule issue of 1886 drove Radical Imperialists and old-fashioned Whigs into alliance with the Conservatives, so that the party had nearly 20 years of office, but Joseph Chamberlain's proposals for Imperial Preference and the general fear that Protection meant higher prices led to a Liberal landslide in 1906. The C.P. fought a rearguard action against the sweeping reforms which followed and only the outbreak of the F.W.W. averted a major crisis.

During 1915–45, except briefly in 1924 and 1929–31, the Conservatives were continually in office, whether alone or as part of a coalition, the main factor in maintaining this ascendancy being the break-up of the traditional 2-party system by the rise of Labour. At the elections following the end of the S.W.W. Labour swept to power, but the C.P. formulated a new policy in their Industrial Charter of 1947, visualizing an economic and social system in which employers and employed, private enterprise and the State, work to mutual advantage. Antagonism to further nationalization 1st reduced the Labour majority in the 1950 election, and in 1951 returned the Conservatives to power with a small majority. This was slightly increased in the general elections of 1955 and 1959 – despite such setbacks as Suez – because of maintained prosperity. Narrowly defeated in 1964 under Home (q.v.), the C.P. chose in 1965 its first elected leader, Edward Heath (q.v.) and was again defeated 1966, but in 1970 had an overall majority of 31. A dissident right wing developed from 1968: *see* POWELL, ENOCH.

JOHN CONSTABLE. Self-portrait in pencil and water colour.
Photo: N.P.G.

CONSTABLE, John (1776–1837). English landscape painter. B. at E. Bergholt, Suffolk, the son of a miller, he first worked in his father's mills, but in 1795 was sent to study art in London, where he copied Reynolds, painted religious pictures and studied Ruysdael. In 1799 he entered the R.A. schools and from 1802 exhibited every year in the R.A. His marriage to Mary Bicknell in 1816 followed a long period of waiting, due to her relatives' stubborn opposition. He was elected A.R.A. in 1819, and his picture 'The Haywain' created a sensation when exhibited in the Paris Salon in 1821. From 1830 to 1833 he was mainly occupied with the famous series of mezzotints engraved by David Lucas. His pictures are remarkable for the way in which they evoke a sense of warmth or coolness, according to the kind of weather he is depicting. Among the most famous are 'Flatford Mill' (1825), 'Stratford Mill' (1820), 'The Leaping Horse' (1825), 'The Cornfield' (1826), 'Dedham Vale', and 'Salisbury Cathedral' (1831).

CONSTANCE. Town in Baden-Württemberg, Germany, on the section of the Rhine joining Lake C. and the Untersee. Suburbs stretch across the frontier into Switzerland. C. has clothing, machinery, and chemical factories and printing works. The Council of C.,1414–17, ended the Great Schism, 1378–1417, with rival popes at Rome and Avignon. Pop. (1960) 52,000.

CONSTANCE, Lake (Ger. Bodensee). Lake lying between Germany, Austria, and Switzerland. It is 45 km by 8 m., and the Rhine flows through it.

CONSTANTA. Chief seaport of Rumania on the Black Sea, cap. of C. region. The exporting centre for the Rumanian oilfields, to which it is connected by pipeline, it has refineries, shipbuilding yards, and food factories. Pop. (1966) 150,436.

CONSTANTAN. A high-resistance alloy of approximately 40 per cent Ni and 60 per cent Cu with a very low temperature coefficient. It is used as a resistance wire in items of physical apparatus.

CONSTANT DE REBECQUE, Henri Benjamin (1767–1830). French writer and politician. B. at Lausanne, he travelled widely, began a liaison with

Mme de Staël in 1796, and in 1803 went into exile because of his liberal views. Returning to Paris on the fall of Napoleon in 1814, he advocated a constitutional monarchy, and after Waterloo he withdrew to London, where he pub. the autobiographical novel *Adolphe*. He went back to Paris in 1816, and for the rest of his life defended constitutional liberalism. His most ambitious work is *De la Religion* (1825–31).

CONSTANTINE XIII (1940–   ). King of the Hellenes. In 1964 he succeeded his father Paul I (q.v.) and later that year m. Princess Anne-Marie of Demark: his heir is Crown Prince Paul (1967–   ). In 1967 he went into voluntary exile.

CONSTANTINE, Sir Learie Nicholas (1902–   ). West Indian Test cricketer and barrister. One of the game's finest bowlers, he captained a Dominions team against England in 1945 and played as a professional in the Lancs League. He was Trinidad's 1st Commissioner in the U.K. (1962–4), and was created Life Peer 1969.

CONSTANTINE THE GREAT (*c.* A.D. 274–337). First Christian emperor of Rome, and founder of Constantinople. B. at Naissus (Nish, Yugoslavia), he was the son of Constantius. He was already well known as a soldier when his father d. at York in 306 and he was acclaimed by the troops there as joint-emperor in his father's place. His authority over Britain and Gaul was at first recognized by the other emperors, but a few years later Maxentius, the joint-emperor at Rome (whose sister C. had married), mobilized his armies to invade Gaul. C. won a crushing victory outside Rome at the Milvian Bridge (312). It was during this campaign that he was said to have seen a vision of the cross of Christ superimposed upon the sun, accompanied by the words, 'In this sign conquer'. By the Edict of Milan (313) he formally recognized Christianity as one of the religions legally permitted within the Roman Empire, and in 314 summoned the bishops of the western world to the Council of Arles. Since 312 C. had been sole emperor of the West, and by defeating Licinius, the emperor in the East, C. became sole ruler of the Roman world (324).

He now set to work to consolidate and reorganize his empire. He increased the autocratic power of the emperor, issued legislation which tied the farmers and workpeople to their crafts in a sort of caste system, and enlisted the support of the Christian Church. He summoned, and presided over, the first general council of the Church at Nicaea (q.v.) in 325.

C. moved his capital to Byzantium on the Bosphorus in 330 and renamed it Constantinople. In 337 he set out to defend the Euphrates frontier against the Persians, but d. at Nicomedia in Asia Minor.

CONSTANTINE. City of Algeria, cap. of C. dept. 200 m. E. of Algiers. An ancient town, it was captured by the French in 1837. Carpets and leather goods are made. Pop. (1967) 255,000.

CONSTANTINO'PLE. The former capital of the Eastern Roman and Turkish Empires, now generally called by its Turkish name, Istanbul (q.v.). It was founded by Constantine the Great by the enlargement of the Greek city of Byzantium in 328, and became the seat of the imperial government in 330. Its elaborate fortifications enabled it to resist a succession of sieges, but it was captured by crusaders in 1204, and was the seat of a Latin kingdom until in 1261 the Greeks recaptured it. An attack by the Turks in 1422 proved unsuccessful, but after a gallant defence lasting nearly a year another Turkish army took the city by storm on 29 May 1453.

CONSTELLATION. A group of stars. Many received their names in antiquity from some mythological figure with which they were associated. *See* ZODIAC. In 1930 the International Astronomical Union standardized the boundaries of 88 Cs., the chief being: NORTHERN: Andromeda, Aquila, Auriga,

Boötes, Cassiopeia, Cepheus, Corona Borealis, Cygnus, Draco, Hercules, Lyra, Ophiuchus, Pegasus, Perseus, Sagitta, Ursa Major, Ursa Minor. *Zodiacal:* Aquarius, Aries, Cancer, Capricornus, Gemini, Leo, Libra, Pisces, Sagittarius, Scorpius, Taurus, Virgo. SOUTHERN: Canis Major, Centaurus, Cetus, Corona Austrina, Corvus, Crater, Crux Australis, Eridanus, Hydra, Lepus, Lupus, Orion.

CONSTITUTION. The fundamental laws of a state, laying down the system of government, and defining the relations of the legislative, executive and judiciary to each other and to the citizens. The British C. is unique, in that it does not exist in the form of a single document; it consists rather of an accumulation of customs and precedents, which have arisen in the course of national development, together with a number of laws defining certain of its aspects. Among the most important of the latter are Magna Carta (1215), the Petition of Right (1628), and the Habeas Corpus Act (1679), limiting the royal powers of taxation and of imprisonment; the Bill of Rights (1689) and the Act of Settlement (1701), establishing parliamentary supremacy and the independence of the judiciary; and the Parliament Act (1911), limiting the powers of the House of Lords. The Triennial Act (1694), the Septennial Act (1716), and the Parliament Act (1911) limited the duration of parliament, while the Reform Acts of 1832, 1867, 1884, 1918, and 1928 extended the electorate. Relations between states of the Commonwealth are regulated by the Statute of Westminster (1931). By the Republic of Ireland Act (1948), S. Ireland ceased to be a member of the Commonwealth, but neither the Irish Rep. nor the U.K. regards the other as a foreign state. The adoption of Republican status by India (1950) and others does not affect their membership and they accept the Queen as Head of the Commonwealth.

The British C. is that of a parliamentary monarchy, sovereignty being vested in the Queen, Lords, and Commons. The legislature consists of the House of Lords and the elected House of Commons. The hereditary basis of the former has been modified by the creation of Life Peers and in 1968 measures were under consideration which would both further reduce its existing powers (amendment of bills and delay for one year) and reduce voting Peers. *See* PARLIAMENT. All legislation requires the royal assent (q.v.). The Queen, as the head of the executive, appoints her ministers, but since the revolution of 1688 it has become customary for her to choose them from the party commanding a majority in the Commons, on the advice of the leader of the party. The judges are appointed by the Crown for life, and can be removed only on a petition from both Houses.

The C. of the U.S.A., adopted in 1787, is the oldest written C. in existence. Subsequent modifications incl. the Bill of Rights, 1791 – this contained 12 amendments of which 10 were adopted, among them the '5th amendment' including the provision none should be compelled 'to be a witness against himself' which has frequently been quoted by those accused as Communists – the abolition of slavery 1865, equal rights for white and coloured 1870, and limitation of presidential terms to two, which came into effect in 1951 and was inspired by F. D. Roosevelt's unique achievement in being elected for a 4th term. *See* UNITED STATES.

Since the French Revolution almost all states have adopted written Cs. The present C. of the Soviet Union was adopted in 1936; it, too, is written.

CONSTRUCTIVISM. Art movement which arose in the 1930s out of cubism (q.v.), having as its aim the creation of works – sculpture, painting, etc. – which exist in their own right and are unrelated to natural forms. Among the chief exponents of the movement are N. Gabo, B. Nicholson, B. Hepworth, and Mondrian (qq.v.).

CONSUL. The chief magistrate of ancient Rome

Photos: L. Sharpes, F.A.D.O.

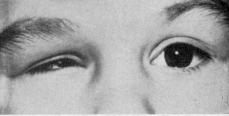

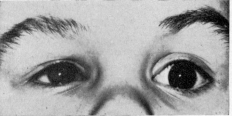

Courtesy of the Photographic Dept., Westminster Medical School.

CONTACT LENSES. *Far left* a Haptic lens and *to the right* a much-enlarged micro-corneal lens: the child illustrated is suffering from microphthalmos (the right eye is the size of a pea) combined with a squint, but in the lower picture has been fitted with a Haptic cosmetic contact lens giving full movement and the effect of correcting (by obscuring) the squint.

following the expulsion of the last king in 510 B.C. The Cs. were two annually elected magistrates, both of equal power; they jointly held full civil power at Rome, and the chief military command in the field. After the establishment of the Roman Empire the office became purely honorary. *See* FOREIGN OFFICE.

CONTACT LENSES. Lenses placed under the eyelids in contact with the eye, separated in most cases only by a film of tears. They may be used as a substitute for spectacles in the correction of refractive defects or, in special circumstances, as protective shells, or to correct cosmetic defects, or refractive errors which cannot be coped with by the normal spectacle lens. The earliest use of C.L. in the late 19th cent. was protective, or in the correction of corneal malformation, for it was not until the 1930s that simplification of fitting technique by taking eye impressions made their general use possible. Until the advent of the corneal lens after the S.W.W. the only lens used was the Haptic lens covering the whole eye. Since 1955 the modern micro-corneal lens has been developed, which is very much smaller than the cornea (average size 9·5 mm.).

CONTINENT. A major division of the land surface of the earth. There are 6 major Cs.: Europe, Africa, Australia, Asia, N. America and S. America. Antarctica and Greenland are referred to as Cs. on occasion. Each C. is continued under the sea in a *continental shelf*, which varies in width according to the nature of the coastline. The shelf reaches an approximate depth of 100 fathoms, then drops more sharply, by the *continental slope*, to the ocean deeps. That part of the earth's surface above sea-level is called the *continental area* and covers roughly five-sixteenths of the earth's surface. In 1915 Alfred Wegener (q.v.) put forward the hypothesis suggested by the way in which, for example, the shores of Europe/Africa and N./S. America fit together, that the continents had reached their present position by *continental drift*, following the split-up of 2 super-continents Laurasia in the N. and Gondwanaland in the S. Later research confirmed that Cs. 'float' on the rocks of the mantle of the Earth, proof of their movement coming from study of the magnetism of ancient rocks, etc., by Blackett, Runcorn and others. It is thought, for example, that the folding of the Himalayas was the result of the comparatively recent drifting together of India and Asia.

CONTRACEPTION. *See* FAMILY PLANNING.

CONTRACT. An agreement between two or more parties which will be enforced by law. Every agreement is not a C., which always consists of an offer and an acceptance of that offer. In English law a C. must either be made under seal (i.e. in a deed) or there must be consideration to support it, i.e. there must be some benefit to one party to the C. or some detriment to the other.

A C., even though it is made in the proper form and the parties to it have the necessary capacity, may be unenforceable because it is made under a mistake, misrepresentation, duress, or undue influence.

Cs. which are illegal are void. Among illegal Cs. are those to commit a crime or civil wrong, to trade with the enemy, immoral Cs., and Cs. in restraint of trade, i.e. Cs. by which a servant binds himself not to compete with his master after his service is over. Cs. by way of gaming and wagering are void.

CONTRACT BRIDGE. Probably the most popular card game, played all over the world since 1930. It originated in 1925 in a bridge game on a steamer *en route* from Los Angeles to Havannah, and was introduced to New York clubs by H. S. Vanderbilt, one of the players. Subsequently the most famous expert was Ely Culbertson (q.v.).

C.B. is a development of Auction B. and like it is based on whist. It is played by 2 pairs of players as partners, and its distinctive feature is that trumps are settled by a preliminary process of bidding. The partner of the caller is 'dummy', and his hand is laid face upwards on the table. Scoring is above the line for honours and below the line for tricks; only the tricks actually contracted for and won count towards the game. Each trick over six contracted for and won counts 30 if spades or hearts, and 20 if diamonds or clubs, are trumps; in no trumps, 40 is counted for the first trick and 30 thereafter. A game is won when a pair scores 100 points below the line, and the pair which first wins 2 games wins the rubber (500 points if 3 games have been played, 700 if only 2). Extra points are awarded for over tricks, small slam, grand slam, etc., and penalties are imposed for under tricks. Once the bidding has been completed, play is very much as in 'auction' or whist, although in the various highly complicated systems there are numerous 'conventions'.

CONVOCATION. In the Church of England, the synods of the clergy of the provinces of Canterbury and York. It is convened by the archbishops at the same time as Parliament begins a new session, and consists in each province of an Upper and Lower House, the one comprising the archbishop and bishops of the province, and the other the representatives of the lower clergy. From 1717 until 1852 it was indefinitely prorogued. The General Synod estab. 1970 took over the functions and authority of the Cs. of Canterbury and York which continued to exist only in a restricted form.

CONVO'LVULUS, or **Bindweed.** Genus of plants,

typical of the family Convolvulaceae. They are characterized by their twining stems, and by having their petals united into a tube. The common bindweed (*C. arvensis*), a trailing plant with handsome white or pink-and-white-streaked flowers, is a frequent weed in Britain.

CONVOY SYSTEM. The grouping of ships to sail together under naval escort in wartime. In the F.W.W. Royal Navy escort vessels were at first used only to accompany troopships, but the C.S. was adopted for merchant shipping when the unrestricted German submarine campaign opened in 1917. In the S.W.W. it was widely used by the Allies, and was generally successful, although there were heavy losses.

CONWAY. Welsh port (bor.) on the river C., in Caernarvonshire. The town is still surrounded by walls, and has ruins of a castle, rebuilt by Edward I in 1284. Pop. (1961) 11,392.

COOCH BEHAR. Town of W. Bengal, India, on the Torsa r., 88 m. S.E. of Darjeeling. A trade centre, it also makes leather goods. Pop. (1961) 41,922. It is the cap of C.B. dist., a former princely state merged in W. Bengal in 1950.

COOK, James (1728–79). British explorer. B. at Marton, Yorks., he joined the R.N. in 1755, and in 1768 was given command of an expedition to the S. Pacific to witness the transit of Venus. He sailed in the *Endeavour* with Joseph Banks and other scientists, reaching Tahiti in April 1769. The transit was observed in June, after which C. sailed round New Zealand and charted the coasts. He then went on to make a detailed survey of the E. coast of Australia, naming New South Wales, Botany Bay, etc., and arriving back in England on 12 June 1771.

Portrait by J. Webber.
Photo: N.P.G.

Now a commander, C. set out in 1772 with the *Resolution* and *Adventure* to search for the southern continent. The location of Easter Island was determined, and the Marquesas and Tonga Islands plotted. Among other discoveries were New Caledonia and Norfolk Island, and New Zealand was revisited. C. returned on 25 July 1775, having sailed 60,000 m. in 3 years.

The object of his 3rd and last voyage with the *Resolution* and *Discovery*, on which he set out 25 June 1776, was the discovery of the N.W. Passage from the Pacific end. On the way to New Zealand, he discovered several of the Cook or Hervey Islands and rediscovered the Hawaiian or Sandwich Islands. The ships sighted the American coast in lat. 45° N., and sailed N., making a continuous survey as far as the Bering Strait, when the way was blocked by ice. C. then surveyed the opposite coast of the strait (Siberia), and returned to Hawaii early in 1779. In Kealakekua Bay, one of the *Discovery*'s boats was stolen by the islanders, and C. was clubbed from behind on 14 Feb. in a scuffle on the beach when trying to recover it, and was buried at sea.

C. made enormous additions to geographical knowledge, was responsible for Britain's acquisition of the Australasian territories, and his accounts of his discoveries are classics.

COOK, Sir Joseph (1860–1947). Australian politician. B. in Staffs, he started work in a coal-mine at the age of 9, emigrated to Australia in 1885, and in 1891 was elected to N.S.W. legislative assembly. In 1901 he was elected to the first Commonwealth Parliament as a Liberal free trader, and 1913–14 was Prime Minister. In 1917 C. joined Hughes's coalition government, and was High Commissioner in London 1921–7.

COOK, Thomas (1808–92). Pioneer British travel agent, founder of Thos. C. & Son. B. in Derbyshire of poor parents, he started work at 10, and at 20 became a Baptist travelling missionary and temperance worker. He organized his 1st excursion in 1841 for a temperance meeting at Loughborough, and his 1st tour to Switzerland in 1863. Tours to America (1866), the Middle East (1868), and round the world (1872) followed. In 1884 C. was given charge of transport of Gordon's Sudan expedition.

His son, John Mason, and grandsons expanded the business. A Banking and Exchange Department was set up in 1879, and earlier C. had transported cattle to the Vienna Exhibition for Queen Victoria, thus laying the foundation for the Shipping and Freight Department. Travellers' cheques, known as 'circular notes', were introduced in the early 1870s.

COOKE, Alistair (1908–). American journalist. B. in England, he was ed. at Cambridge, Yale and Harvard, and estab. a reputation for humorously penetrating interpretation of American affairs for British readers and radio listeners. In 1948 he became chief U.S. correspondent of *The Guardian*.

COOKHAM-ON-THAMES. Village in Berkshire, England. The artist Stanley Spencer (q.v.) lived here for many years and a memorial gallery of his work was opened in 1962.

COOK ISLANDS. A group of 6 large and a number of small islands 1,638 m. N.E. of Auckland, N.Z.; total area *c.* 89 sq. m. Rarotonga is the chief, area 26 sq. m.; on it is Avarua, seat of govt. An air service is maintained between N.Z. and Aitutaki, another of the islands. The group was discovered by Capt. Cook in 1773, annexed to Britain in 1888, transferred to N.Z. in 1901, and given internal self-govt. in 1965. Pop. (1966) 19,251.

COOLIDGE, John Calvin (1872–1933). 30th President of the U.S.A. B. in Vermont, the son of a farmer and storekeeper, he became a lawyer and was Governor of Massachusetts in 1919, when he won fame by the vigour with which he crushed the Boston police strike. A Republican, he became Vice-President in 1921 and President, on the death of Harding, in 1923. He was re-elected in 1924, and his period of office was marked by great economic prosperity.

COOPER, Alfred Duff. See NORWICH, LORD.

COOPER, Gary (1901–62). American actor. B. in Montana, he epitomized the lean, true-hearted Yankee, slow of speech but capable of besting the 'badmen' in *A Bengal Lancer*, *Mr. Deeds Goes to Town*, *Sergeant York* (Academy award 1941), and *For Whom the Bell Tolls*.

COOPER, Dame Gladys (1889–1971). Brit. actress. B. at Lewisham, she was a polished stylist, and her parts ranged from Paula in *The Second Mrs. Tanqueray* (1922) to Mrs. St. Maugham in *The Chalk Garden* (1955). Created D.B.E. 1967. See MORLEY, ROBERT.

COOPER, Henry (1934–). Brit. heavyweight boxer. Noted for his left—Henry's hammer—he won the British and Empire titles in 1959, and the European 1964 and from 1968. In 1967 he became the first to win 3 Lonsdale belts outright.

COOPER, James Fenimore (1789–1851). American writer. B. in New Jersey of Quaker stock, he sailed before the mast to Europe and in 1808 became a midshipman. In 1811 he made a happy marriage, and spent most of the rest of his life on the family estate of Cooperstown. He wrote some 30 novels, 1st becoming popular with *The Spy* (1821). Most notable were the volumes of *Leather Stocking* stories (so called because they were linked by the figure of Hawk-eye or Leather Stocking) comprising *The Pioneers* (1823), *The Last of the Mohicans* (1826), *The Prairie* (1827), *The Pathfinder* and *The Deerslayer* (1841), all exciting

CO-OPERATIVE WHOLESALE SOCIETY. The C.W.S., which had its origins mainly in the N. of England, still has its headquarters in Manchester, and seen here is the new 14-storey office block, which also serves the C.I.S., and the New Century Hall (on the left), opened in 1963, which adjoin the old C.W.S. building.   *C.W.S. Ltd. (Manchester).*

stories of settlers and Redskins in the middle 18th century.

COOPER, Samuel (1609–72). English artist. He was probably b. in London, and his works – the finest of all miniatures – incl. portraits of Milton, Cromwell, and members of Charles II's court. Pepys commissioned him to paint his wife.

CO-OPERATION. The banding together of bodies of persons for mutual assistance in trade, manufacture, the supply of credit, or other services. In Britain the predominant type of C. is the Consumers' Co-operative Society, a retail trading concern whose shops sell at current market prices, but return the bulk of their profits (less any sums placed to reserve) to their members as 'dividends' on the sums spent there. Control is in the hands of a management committee elected by the members. Societies of this type in Britain have nearly 13,000,000 members, and in Scandinavia the rate is also high – in Denmark they cover approx. 45 per cent of the population. Usually the local societies are federated nationally in co-operative wholesale societies, which carry on wholesale trade and factory production. The original principles of consumers' C. were laid down in 1844 by the Rochdale Pioneers, under the influence of Robert Owen (q.v.). Producers' Co-operative Societies, formed on a basis of co-partnership among the employees, exist on a large scale in France, Italy, and the Soviet Union, but are of little importance in Britain. Agricultural Co-operative Societies have been formed in Britain for the collective purchase of seeds, fertilizers, etc., while societies for co-operative marketing of agricultural produce are prominent in the U.S., Ireland, Denmark, the British Commonwealth, and many other countries. Often both functions are discharged by a single society. Agricultural Credit Societies are strong in the peasant countries of Europe and Asia, including parts of India. The U.S. also has a Co-operative Farm Credit System.

CO-OPERATIVE COMMONWEALTH FEDERATION (C.C.F.). Canadian political party, in some measure the counterpart of the British Labour Party. It was formed after the depression of 1930, and was for a time a federation of Labour, Socialist, and Farmer parties. Its programme includes strict control or nationalization of monopolies, nationalization of the banking credit system, and the establishment of a system of social security with greatly improved social services. In 1944 C.C.F. secured a majority in Saskatchewan, and formed its first cabinet: still in power 1963.

CO-OPERATIVE PARTY. Founded by the C. movement in 1918 to maintain its interests and principles in Parliament and local governing bodies. Although it has rejected affiliation to the Labour Party, local branches are eligible for affiliation to local Labour parties, and seats in Parliament contested by agreement with the Labour Party.

CO-OPERATIVE WHOLESALE SOCIETY (C.W.S.). The largest co-operative organization in the world, this British concern is owned and controlled by 850 co-operative retail societies, who are also its customers. Founded in 1863, it acts as wholesaler, manufacturer, banker, etc., and has a share capital of over £31 million. It owns some 200 factories, farms and estates, in addition to offices and warehouses, etc., and has more than 54,000 employees.

COORG (koorg). Dist. of Mysore, India, formerly a princely state, merged in Mysore in 1956. It is agricultural; Mercara is the cap. Area 1,586 sq. m.; pop. (1961) 321,516.

COOT. Genus of birds (*Fulica*), belonging to the rail family (Rallidae) and closely resembling the moorhens in habits and appearance. The European species (*F. atra*) is common in Britain. Its plumage is sooty black, and there is a large, bare white patch on the forehead (hence 'bald as a coot').

COOTE, Sir Eyre (1726–83). Irish soldier. B. near Limerick, he took part in Clive's occupation of Calcutta and the battle of Plassey. In 1759 he was transferred to the Carnatic, where his victory in 1760 at Wandiwash, followed by the capture of Pondicherry, ended French hopes of supremacy. He returned to India as C.-in-C. in 1779, and several times defeated Hyder Ali, sultan of Mysore.

COPE. Ecclesiastical vestment. It is a semi-circular cape, without sleeves, worn by priests of the Western Church in processions and on certain other formal occasions, but not when officiating at Mass.

COPENHAGEN. Capital of Denmark, on the islands of Zealand and Amager. The harbour occupies the channel between the two islands and forms the headquarters of most of the Danish shipping lines.

COPENHAGEN. Seen across the Raadhuspladsen (Town Hall Square) is the Renaissance-style Raadhus (1901) with its easterly tower. At an annual gathering round the column surmounted by two Vikings with *lurs*, on the left; such long bronze trumpets, relics of prehistory, are still played. To the right of the Raadhus is Hans Christian Andersen's Boulevard and the Tivoli pleasure garden, with its open-air theatres, funfair, restaurants, ballrooms and concert hall.
Courtesy of the National Travel Association of Denmark

The centre of the city is the Kongens Nytorv, an irregular open space adjacent to the harbour, on which focus the main thoroughfares of the city. To the N.E. are the citadel and the royal palace at Amalienborg. Buildings round the square include the Charlottenburg palace (1672–83), occupied 1754 by the Academy of Arts, the Kunstudstilling (1883), Thotts Palais (c. 1685), the Royal Theatre, Foreign Office, etc. The cathedral church was rebuilt early in the 19th cent. The new town hall dates from 1901. The Christiansborg, in the Slottsholm, an island formed by an arm of the harbour, is used for meetings of parliament. The univ. was founded in 1479.

AARON COPLAND
Photo: Godfrey MacDomnic.

C. was a fishing village until 1167, when a castle was built on the site of the present Christiansborg palace by the bishop of Roskilde. A settlement grew up, and it became the Danish cap. in 1443. On 9 April 1940 C. was occupied by the Germans, remaining in their hands until 5 May 1945. Pop. (1965) 1,377,605.

COPENHAGEN, Battle of. Naval victory won on 2 April 1801 by a British fleet under Sir Hyde Parker and Nelson over the Danish fleet. Here it was that Nelson put his telescope to his blind eye and refused to see Parker's signal for withdrawal.

COPE'PODA. Sub-class of Crustacea, incl. a great variety of forms, nearly all microscopic, abundant in the sea and fresh water.

COPERNICUS, Nicolaus (1473–1543). Polish astronomer. B. at Thorn on the Vistula, then under the Polish king, he studied at Cracow and in Italy, and lectured on astronomy at Rome. On his return to Pomerania in 1505 he became physician to his uncle, the bishop of Ermland, and was made canon at Frauenburg, although he did not take holy orders. Living there until his death, he interspersed astronomical work with the duties of various civil offices. For 30 years he worked on the hypothesis that the motion of the earth was responsible for the apparent movements of the heavenly bodies, but his great work *De revolutionibus orbium coelestium* was not pub. until the year of his death. In this work he proved that the sun is the centre of our system, and he thus became a prime founder of modern astronomy.

CO'PLAND, Aaron (1900–). American composer. B. in N.Y., he studied in France with Nadia Boulanger, and in 1940 became instructor in composition at the Berkshire Music Center – from 1945 assistant director. C.'s early works, such as the piano concerto of 1926, were in the jazz idiom then popular in America, but he gradually developed a gentler style with a regional flavour drawn from American folk music. Later works incl. the ballets *Billy the Kid* (1939) – which contains a variant of the cowboy song 'Bury Me Not on the Lone Prairie' – *Rodeo* (1942) and *Appalachian Spring* (1944), based on a poem by Hart Crane; and *Piano Fantasy* (1957).

COPLEY, John Singleton (1737–1815). American artist. B. at Boston, Mass., of Anglo-Irish parents, he became the leading portraitist of the colonial period. From 1774 he lived mainly in England, where he also painted historical scenes incl. 'The Death of Chatham', which gained him his R.A.

COPPARD, Alfred Edgar (1878–1951). British writer. B. in Folkestone, he pub. his 1st collection of stories *Adam and Eve and Pinch Me* in 1921, and subsequently regularly pub. vols. of short stories, incl.

The Black Dog, which show a skilful unity of fantasy and realism. C. also wrote verse.

COPPÉE (kopeh'), **François** (1842–1908). French poet. He was a clerk in the War Office before his poems *Le Reliquaire* (1866) and *Les Intimités* (1867) established his reputation as one of the principal Parnassiens. He then maintained a steady output of moving verse, including *Olivier*, a long narrative poem; *Contes en vers*; *Le Passant*, his first dramatic poem; *L'Abandonnée*, *Les Jacobites*, etc.

COPPER. A chemical element, one of the earliest metals used by man. Chemical symbol Cu; at. no. 29; at. wt. 63·54. It is salmon pink, very malleable and ductile, and used principally on account of its toughness, softness, and pliability, high thermal and electrical conductivity, and resistance to corrosion. When alloyed with tin it forms bronze, a relatively hard metal, the discovery of which opened a new age in human pre-history.

Until about a century ago, Spain and Cornwall were the chief producers, but these are now of minor importance compared with the U.S.A. (which produces about a quarter of the world's output), Chile, Canada, Zambia, and the Katanga area of the Congo. C. is usually commercially extracted from C. pyrites. Large deposits containing C. sulphide occur in the Lake Superior district in N. America, and in Spain. Other ores from which C. is extracted include malachite, crysocolla, and atacamite.

COPPER HEAD. N. American snake (*Trigonocephalus contortrix*) belonging to the viperine section of the Ophidia, allied to the rattlesnake. It is about a yard long, and in colour coppery-brown, banded with reddish brown.

COPRA. Dried kernel of the coconut (q.v.).

COPTIC. The latest phase of the old Egyptian language, and still the ritual language of the Coptic Church. It is written in the Greek alphabet with the addition of 8 characters derived from the demotic. Of the several dialects, that of Upper Egypt, known as Sahidic, became the literary medium. The literature is wholly religious.

COPTS. The descendants of the ancient Egyptians who had accepted Christianity in the 1st cent. and refused to adopt Mohammedanism after the Arab conquest. Prior to the Arab conquest a majority of

COPPER. Part of the surface installations at Mufulira copper mine on the Copperbelt of Zambia. In the right foreground is a corner of the concentrator, where the ore-bearing rock from underground is crushed and ground, and the mineral fraction removed by a flotation process in which the mineral attaches itself to a froth which is dried and then sent to the smelter. Behind the concentrator is the power plant, now on emergency stand-by duties only, as the Copperbelt's main supplies come from the Kariba hydro-electric scheme on the Zambezi river. The smelter can be seen behind the power station. In the left foreground and middle distance are engineering workshops, and in the background the refinery, where anodes from the smelter are used to electro-plate pure copper cathodes. The pure cathodes are then melted and cast into suitable shapes for fabricators, the most common being the wirebar. *Courtesy of Rhodesian Selection Trust,*

Christian Egyptians had adopted Monophysite views, and when this doctrine was condemned by the Council of Chalcedon in 451 they became schismatic and were persecuted by the orthodox party, to which they were opposed on nationalistic as well as religious grounds. They therefore readily accepted Arab rule, but were later subjected to persecution by their new masters. They now form a small minority (*c.*1,300,000) of the population, mainly town-dwellers, and are distinguishable in dress and customs, but hardly in physical features, from their Mohammedan fellow-countrymen. They rarely marry outside their own sect. The head of the Coptic Church is the Patriarch of Alexandria.

COPYRIGHT. Generally speaking, the law of C. applies to literary, musical or artistic works, including plays, recordings, films, and radio and television broadcasts. It prevents the reproduction of the work, either whole or in part, without the consent of the author, but is essentially a safeguard, not for the basic idea or theme, but for the individual interpretation by the author, composer, or artist through which it takes on concrete form. For example, the basic plots of 2 novels might be identical without infringing the law of C., but should details in the descriptions and development of characters make it clear that one author had copied from the other, then C. would be infringed. Translations of literary works are also protected.

In 1952 agreement was reached by many nations to adopt the Universal C. Convention, its basic principle being that each contracting country should afford the authors of the other signatories the same protection that it gave its own. It came into force in the U.S.A. 1955, U.K. 1957: though not a signatory the U.S.S.R. made concessions. Revision of the Convention of Berne (1886, mainly European) at Stockholm 1967 introduced a controversial protocol allowing countries regarded by the U.N. as 'developing' to modify C. conditions extensively: Britain did not sign the protocol. Under English law, C. subsists for 50 years from end of year of author's death, or from date of publication, where posthumous. Duration of C. in the U.S.A. is for 28 years from date of publication, with a right to renewal for another 28, but the law is in process of being revised.

COQUELIN (koklaṅ'), **Benoît Constant** (1841–1909). French actor. B. at Boulogne, the son of a baker, he went on the stage in 1860 and for many years was associated with the Comédie Française, creating leading comic parts. In 1892 he formed his own company, and in 1897 created his greatest role, that of the hero in Rostand's *Cyrano de Bergerac*. His brother, ALEXANDRE C. (1848–1909), was also a versatile actor and a writer on stage subjects.

COQUES (kok), **Gonzales** (1614–84). Flemish artist. B. at Antwerp, he painted portraits and groups in the style of Van Dyck, whom he admired, and became known as the Little Van Dyck.

CORAL. Name given to the hard skeletons of various marine organisms, belonging to the phylum Coelenterata. Most of them are members of the class Anthozoa, but a few are placed in the Hydrozoa. The skeleton is composed of carbonate of lime extracted from the surrounding waters. In the simplest solitary Cs., such as the Devonshire cup coral (*Caryophyllia smithii*), the skeleton takes the form of a cup, into which the polyp can contract itself. The majority of Cs., however, form large colonies, and it is from the accumulated skeletons of these polyps that C.-reefs are built up. The red C. of the Mediterranean (*Corallium rubrum*) has been valued from very ancient times as an ornament.

CORALLI, Jean (1779–1854). French dancer and choreographer. B. in Paris of Italian descent, he made his début as a dancer in Paris in 1802. He composed *Giselle* (1841) and *La Péri* (1843), both for Grisi; *Le Diable Boiteux* for Fanny Elssler, and many other famous ballets.

CORAL REEFS are built up from the accumulated skeletons of marine organisms, including certain algae as well as Cs. These flourish in the warmer seas and at moderate depths. C. reefs take the 3 distinct forms of fringing reefs, barrier reefs, and atolls. *Fringing reefs* are so called because they are built up on the shores of continents or islands; the living Cs. mainly occupy the outer edges of the reef. *Barrier reefs* are separated from the shore by a salt-water lagoon, which may be as much as 20 or more miles wide; there are usually navigable passes through the barrier into the lagoon. The Great Barrier Reef, to the N.E. of Australia, is more than 1,000 miles long. *Atolls* resemble a ring surrounding a lagoon, and do not enclose an island; their origin is undecided.

CORAL SEA. Part of the Pacific Ocean lying between N.E. Australia, New Guinea, the Solomon Islands, New Hebrides, and New Caledonia. It contains numerous coral islands and reefs. The BATTLE

CORAL. Among the many types of coral found in the Great Barrier Reef are the more than seven beautiful varieties seen here. Some are capable of stinging and it is not uncommon to find a fish which has been stung to death.
Courtesy of the Agent-General for Queensland.

OF THE C.S. was fought 4–8 May 1942 and ended with the victory of American naval and air forces over a Japanese fleet. The first Allied success in the Pacific, it saved Australia from invasion.

CŌRAM, Thomas (1668–1751). British philanthropist. B. in Lyme Regis, he became a farmer and shipwright in Massachusetts, returned to England in 1703 and founded the Foundling Hospital in London in 1741. He nearly became bankrupt through his many philanthropic schemes and also promoted the settlement of Georgia and Nova Scotia.

COR ANGLAIS (kŏr-aṅglā') or **English Horn.** Musical instrument; it is not a horn, but a member of the oboe family, and its English origin is doubtful. A metal tube, bent backwards to the mouth of the player, contains the reed. The C.A. was introduced into the Orchestra in the time of Wagner, has an expressive tone, and is used in slow melodic passages.

CORBETT, Harvey Wiley (1873–1954). American architect. B. in San Francisco, he set a pattern in design by his economical exploitation of space for large structures, e.g. Bush House in London and his contribution to the Rockefeller Centre, N.Y.

CORBIÈRE (korbē-ār'), **Tristan** (1845–75). French poet. The merits of his *Les Amours jaunes* (1873) went unrecognized until Verlaine called attention to it in 1884. Many of his poems, such as *La Rhapsodie Foraine*, deal with life in his native Brittany.

CORBY. English industrial and iron-mining town

(U.D.) in N. Northants. The first blast furnace was built in what was then a village in 1910; from *c.* 1931 it began to grow, and with its development after the S.W.W. as a 'new town' its pop. rose from 16,743 in 1951 to 46,580 in 1967.

CORDAY (kordä´), **Charlotte** (1768–93). Frenchwoman who assassinated Marat. She belonged to the Girondist party and went to Paris in 1793 resolved to rid the country of one or other of the Jacobin leaders, Robespierre or Marat. Having secured admission to the latter's apartment, she stabbed him to the heart with a bread-knife as he was sitting in his bath. She was guillotined 4 days later.

CÓRDOBA. City of Argentina, cap. of C. prov., on the Rio Primero, here harnessed for power. Founded in 1573, it has a univ. founded 1613, a military aviation college, an observatory, and a cathedral. Pop. (1960) 589,000.

CÓRDOBA. Spanish city, cap. of C. prov., on the Guadalquivir. It has many Moorish remains. Its glory is the mosque, now a cathedral, founded by Abder-Rahman I in 785; it is 590 by 425 ft. and except for St. Peter's, Rome, is the largest Christian church in the world. C. was founded probably by the Carthaginians, and from 711 until 1236 was held by the Moors. Pop. (1965) 214,562.

CORE′LLI, Arcangelo (1653–1713). Italian composer and violinist. B. in Milan, he studied in Bologna and in *c.* 1685 settled in Rome, under the patronage of Cardinal Pietro Ottoboni, where he pub. his 1st violin sonatas. He was one of the first great violinists and his music, marked by graceful melody, incl. a set of concerti grossi and 5 sets of chamber sonatas.

CORE′LLI, Marie. Pseudonym of the British novelist Mary Mackay (1855–1924). Trained for a musical career, she turned instead to writing and from the appearance of *The Romance of Two Worlds* (1886) was highly popular, though literary critics were far from kind. Later books incl. *Barabbas* (1893), *The Sorrows of Satan* (1895), and *Temporal Power* (1902). After the F.W.W. her popularity declined, since her luscious style and undisguised moralizing did not suit the new age.

CORFE (korf) **CASTLE.** English village in the Isle of Purbeck, Dorset, built round the ruins of a Norman castle destroyed in the Civil War in 1646.

CORFU (korfōō´). Most northerly, second largest of the Ionian islands, also a nome of Greece, off the coast of Epirus in the Ionian Sea. The chief town, also C. (pop. 1961, 27,431), is a port and seat of an R.C. archbishopric. C. was colonized by Corinthians *c.* 700 B.C. Venice held it 1386–1797, Britain from 1815–64. Area 414 sq. m.; pop. (1961) 101,555.

CORINIUM. Roman name of CIRENCESTER.

CORINTH (kor′int), **Lovis** (1858–1925). German artist, a leader of German Impressionism. He painted fine portraits and religious pictures, e.g. 'Ecce Homo' (Basle Museum).

CO′RINTH. Ancient city of Greece, on the isthmus connecting the Peloponnesus with the mainland. The isthmus is rocky, and is now cut by the 4 m.-long C. canal, opened in 1893. C. was already a place of some importance in the 9th cent. B.C. At the end of the 6th cent. B.C. it joined the Peloponnesian League, and it took a prominent part in the Persian and the Peloponnesian wars. In 146 B.C. it was conquered by the Romans. St. Paul visited it, and addressed two epistles to the churches there. After many changes of ownership it became part of independent Greece in 1822. The most outstanding of C.'s ancient monuments is the ruined temple of Apollo (6th cent. B.C.). The city is cap. of the modern nome of C. Pop. (1961) 17,728.

CORK. The light cellular outer layers of the bark of the stems and roots of almost all trees and shrubs, which is impermeable by water. In particular, the word is used for the corky outer layers of the bark of

CORK. Overlooking the River Lee, on the site of the cathedral founded by St. Finbarr in the 7th century, the modern Protestant cathedral – rebuilt in the early French style in the 19th century – is still dedicated to the saint.
Courtesy of the Irish Tourist Board.

the cork-oak (*Quercus suber*), a native of S. Europe and N. Africa, which is cultivated in Spain and Portugal and provides the cork of commerce. Manufactured C. is C. ground up and then formed into sheets with a binder: it is much used for engine gaskets and isolation of vibration, as well as for heat insulation.

CORK. Co. of Rep. of Ireland, in Munster prov., with a coastline on the Atlantic Ocean. The co. is occupied by a series of ridges and vales, running from N.E. to S.W. Across its centre run the Nagles and Boggeragh mts., which separate the two main drainage systems, the Blackwater and the Lee. There are many smaller rivers, such as the Bandon, Ilen, etc. C. is an agricultural co., but there is some mining of copper, manganese, etc., marble-quarrying, and river and sea fishing. The co. town is Cork. Other towns are Cobh, Bantry, Youghal, Fermoy, and Mallow. Area 2,880 sq. m.; pop. (1966) 339,703.

CORK. City (co. bor.), episcopal see, and seaport of co. Cork, at the head of the long inlet of Cork harbour, on the Lee. It is the 2nd port of the Rep. of Ireland. The lower section of the harbour can berth liners, and the town has distilleries, shipyards, iron-foundries, etc. There is a Protestant cathedral dedicated to St. Finbarr, an R.C. cathedral of St. Mary and St. Finbarr. University College (1845) became in 1968 the University of Cork. The city hall was opened in 1937.

St. Finbarr's 7th cent. monastery was the original foundation of C. It was eventually settled by Danes, who were dispossessed by the English in 1172. Pop. (1966) 122,146.

CORMORANT. Genus of birds (*Phalacrocorax*) included with the gannets in the Pelicaniformes. They are divers, with long necks and strong, solid beaks. Of the 30 species, 2 are British. The common C., *P. carbo*, is a familiar sea-bird, and is black glossed with bronze. The shag or green C. (*P. graculus*) is rather smaller

CORMORANT

and has a greenish gloss on its plumage. Cs. feed on fish, and are proverbially voracious.

CORNCRAKE. *See* RAIL.

CORNEILLE (kornāy´), **Pierre** (1606–84). French dramatist. B. at Rouen, he had his first play *Mélite* performed in 1629. It was followed by others of skilful construction, which were approved by Richelieu, and gained him an appointment as one of the 5 poets engaged to mould the cardinal's ideas for the stage (1634). But C. proved intractable and was soon dismissed.

His first important play, the tragedy *Médée* (1635), was followed in 1636 by *Le Cid*, which achieved sensational success with the public, although it was fiercely attacked by Academicians under the influence of Richelieu. After 3 years' retirement, C. returned to the cardinal's favour and a pension with *Horace* (1639), which like all his later plays was based on Aristotle's unities. Continuing his success with *Cinna* (1640), *Polyeucte*, the comedy *Le Menteur*, and *Rodogune*, he was elected to the Academy in 1647. He then encountered a run of failures, and retiring from the stage in 1652 devoted himself to translation and criticism, notably his *Discours du poème dramatique*. He returned with *Oedipe* (1659), approved by Louis XIV, and *La Toison d'or* (1661). His last great play was *Sertorius* (1662), although he continued to write until 1674. His tragedies glorify the strength of will governed by reason, and although unequal in style and construction, established the French classical drama of the next two centuries.

His younger brother **Thomas Corneille** (1625–1709), wrote some 40 plays, of which the most famous are *Ariane* (1672), and *Comte d'Essex* (1678).

CORNELIUS (korneh'lē-oos), **Peter von** (1783–1867). German painter. B. at Düsseldorf, he went to Rome in 1811, and became one of the group of German painters who founded a new school of German art, being chiefly responsible for a revival of mural painting. Later he worked in Düsseldorf, Munich, and Berlin.

CORNELIUS NEPOS (1st cent. B.C.). Roman scholar, antiquarian, and biographer. He was a friend of Cicero; of his writings only 25 biographies have survived, and these have been much altered.

CORNELL, Katharine (1898–   ). American actress-manager. Of great dignity, she estab. her dual reputation with her production of *The Barretts of Wimpole Street* (1931); others incl. *Romeo and Juliet* and *Candida*.

CORNET. Musical instrument. Originally the name of a family of woodwind instruments; it now refers to the *Cornet à Pistons*, which is without fixed notes, notes of different pitch being obtained by overblowing and by means of 3 pistons. It is often used as a substitute for the trumpet in brass bands.

CORNFLOUR. The purified starch content of maize (Indian corn) used in milk puddings, etc.

CORNFLOWER. A plant (*Centaurea cyanus*) belonging to the Compositae. It is distinguished from the knapweeds by its deep azure blue flowers, and is a fairly common weed in cornfields in Britain.

CORNISH. An extinct branch of the Brythonic group of the Celtic languages, spoken in Cornwall till the beginning of the 19th cent. Written C. first appears in 10th cent. glosses and similar documents. C. verse is first represented by a (dramatic?) fragment of the 14th cent. and a slightly later poem on the Passion of Our Lord. There are a number of religious plays of the 15th and 16th cents. which draw on Lat. and Eng. sources. Later C. literature is scanty, and consists of an occasional folk-tale or poem and other scraps of verse and prose.

CORN LAWS. Laws to regulate the export or import of cereals, in order to maintain an adequate supply for the consumers and a fair price for the producers. For centuries they formed an integral part of the Mercantile System in England, and it was not until after the Napoleonic wars that they aroused any strong opposition. They were modified in 1828, again in 1842, and practically repealed by Peel in 1846, as being an unwarranted tax on food.

CORNWALL. County occupying the extreme S.W. of England and including the Scilly Is. It is surrounded by the Atlantic Ocean and the English Channel, except in the E. where it adjoins Devon. C. is renowned for its fine coastal scenery culminating in Land's End, and for its moorland stretches. Bodmin Moor rises to 1,375 ft. in Brown Willy; everywhere the co. is rugged and hilly. The main rivers are the Tamar, Fowey, Fal, and Camel. Creeks along the coast have given shelter to fishing fleets for centuries. The climate is mild and sunny, particularly in the south round Falmouth and Penzance (Cornish Riviera). Agriculture is general, and there are specialized 'pockets' for early vegetables. The Scilly Is. are famous for spring flowers. Among the rocks of C. there is considerable mineral wealth, the best-known deposits being those of tin. Exploited from the Bronze Age, they were for many years superseded by Malayan discoveries until renewed workings in the 1960s. Tungsten, lead, zinc, and silver are also mined. Kaolin occurs near St. Austell. The Cornish have been fishermen for many centuries. Tourism is important.

The co. town is Bodmin, though the administrative centre is Truro, which is also an episcopal see. Penzance and Falmouth are the principal ports; Bude, Padstow, Newquay, St. Ives, and Looe are fishing towns and holiday resorts. Launceston is a market town. Area 1,375 sq. m.; pop. (1967) 356,200.

CORNWALLIS, Charles, 1st marquess (1738–1805). British soldier, eldest son of the 1st earl C., he had a distinguished career in the army until 1781, when he and the force under his command were forced to surrender at Yorktown, thus virtually ending the War of American Independence. Subsequently he was twice Governor-General of India, and Viceroy of Ireland, and was made a marquess in 1793.

CORNWELL, John Travers (1900–16). British naval hero. Joining the Navy in 1915, he was rated as a 'boy' and won the V.C. for his gallant conduct on the *Chester* at the battle of Jutland. He was mortally wounded in the action.

COROMANDEL. The east coast of Madras, India.

CORONATION. The ceremony of investing a king with the emblems of royalty, as a symbol of his inauguration in office. The British C. ceremony combines the Hebrew rite of anointing, with customs of Germanic origin, e.g. the actual crowning and the presentation of the king to his subjects to receive homage. Its main features are the presentation to the people; the administration of the oath; the presenta-

Coronation chair and 'stone of destiny' in Westminster Abbey.

tion of the Bible; the anointing of the sovereign with holy oil on hands, breast, and head; the presentation of the spurs and the sword of state, the emblems of knighthood; the presentation of the armills, robe royal, the orb, the ring, the sceptre with the cross, and the rod with the dove; the coronation with St. Edward's Crown; the benediction; the enthroning; and the homage of the princes of the blood and the peerage. A queen consort is anointed on the head, presented with a ring, crowned, and finally presented with the sceptre and the ivory rod. Since the

C. of Harold in 1066 English sovereigns have been crowned in Westminster Abbey.

CORONEL. Port of Chile, off which on 1 Nov. 1914 a German squadron under Admiral von Spee defeated a technically inferior British squadron under Rear-Ad. Cradock, who went down with his ship.

CORONER. In England an officer appointed by a county council to inquire into the deaths of persons who have died suddenly by acts of violence, under suspicious circumstances, or in prison at the hands of the hangman. They may also inquire into instances of treasure trove. The office may date back to the days of King Alfred.

A C. is appointed for life, and must be a barrister, solicitor, or medical practitioner with at least 5 years' professional service. Some county councils insist on the double medical and legal qualification.

At an inquest, a C. is assisted by a jury of not less than 7 or more than 11 persons. Evidence is on oath, and medical and other witnesses may be summoned. If the jury return a verdict of murder or manslaughter, the C. can commit the accused for trial.

In Scotland similar duties are performed by the procurator-fiscal. In the U.S.A. coroners are usually elected by the qualified voters of the co.

CORONETS. 1, duke; 2, marquess; 3, earl; 4, viscount; 5, baron.

CORONET. A small crown worn by a peer at the Coronation and the state opening of parliament. A duke's C. consists of a golden circlet, above which are 8 strawberry leaves; a marquess's has 4 strawberry leaves with 4 points surmounted by pearls between them, an earl's 8 strawberry leaves with 8 tall points surmounted by pearls between them, a viscount's 16 small pearls, and a baron's 6 large pearls.

COROT (koroh'), **Jean Baptiste Camille** (1796–1875). French landscape painter. B. in Paris, he was at first employed in a linen-draper business there, but from the age of 26 devoted himself to painting, and became famous as one of the painters of the 'Barbizon school'. Though he exhibited regularly at the Paris Salon from 1827, his pictures did not begin to attract attention until he was about 60. He was one of the most poetical of landscape painters; much of his best work was executed in the early hours of the morning or at twilight.

CORPORATIVE STATE. A state in which the members are organized and represented not on a local basis as citizens, but as producers working in a particular trade, industry, or profession. The conception first appeared in modern politics in the theories of the Syndicalist movement of the early 20th cent., which proposed that all industries should be taken over and run by the trade unions, a federation of whom should replace the state. Similar views were put forward in Britain by the Guild Socialists. Certain features of Syndicalist theory were adopted and given a right-wing tendency by the Fascist régime in Italy, under which employers' and workers' organizations were represented in the National Council of Corporations, but this was completely dominated by the Fascist Party and had no real powers. Catholic social theory, as expounded in recent papal encyclicals, also favours the C.S. as a means of eliminating class conflict. Corporative institutions have been set up by the Franco and Salazar régimes in Spain and Portugal, under the influence of Fascist and Catholic theories. In Spain representatives of the national syndicates are included in the *Cortes*, and in Portugal a Corporative Chamber exists alongside the National Assembly.

CORPUS CHRISTI (Lat., Body of Christ). A feast celebrated in the R.C. and Greek churches, and to some extent in the Anglican Church, on the Thursday after Trinity Sunday. It was instituted in the 13th cent. through the devotion of St. Juliana, prioress of Mount Cornillon, near Liège, in honour of the Real Presence of Christ in the Eucharist.

CORREGGIO (kohr-rej'oh), **Antonio Allegri da** (c. 1494 – 1534). Italian painter, named after his birthplace near Modena. The son of a prosperous merchant, he came under the influence of Mantegna, Leonardo da Vinci, and Raphael, but developed a style of his own which is remarkable for its fine sense of colouring and its treatment of light and shade. His best-known works incl. 'Adoration of the Shepherds' or 'Night' in the Dresden Gallery, 'The Marriage of St. Catherine' in the Louvre, and 'Mercury instructing Cupid before Venus' and 'Ecce Homo' in the National Gallery, London.

CORREGGIO. 'Mercury instructing Cupid before Venus'.
Courtesy of the National Gallery.

CORREGIDO'R. Fortified island at the mouth of Manila Bay, Luzon, Philippine Rep. It became famous for its heroic defence in the S.W.W. by survivors of the Bataan campaign under Gen. Wainwright from 9 April until resistance ceased on 6 May 1942. U.S. parachute troops recaptured it 15 Feb. 1945.

CORRÈZE (korrāz'). River of central France flowing 55 m. from the Plateau des Millevaches, past Tulle, cap. of C. dept. (to which it gives its name), to join the Vézère. It is harnessed for power at Bar, 6 m. N.W. of Tulle.

CORRIENTES (korrē-en'tes). City of Argentina, cap. of C. prov., on the Paraná; an important river port in a stock-raising district. Pop. (1960) 57,000.

CORRO'BOREE. Dance of the Australian aborigines. Some Cs. record events in history; others have a religious significance, connected with fertility and rejuvenation, or are just theatrical entertainment.

CORSAIR. Sir F. Verney.

CORSAIRS (kor'sārz). Moorish pirates who from the 16th cent. onward plundered shipping in the Mediterranean and Atlantic. Although many punitive expeditions were sent against them, they were not suppressed until France occupied Algiers in 1830. Some Englishmen of good birth joined the Barbary pirates or C., e.g. the half-brother of Sir Edmund Verney (q.v.), Sir Francis Verney.

CORSE. French name of Corsica.

CORSICA. Island in the Mediterranean off the W. coast of Italy, and immediately N. of Sardinia. It forms a dept. of France, and is composed of a granitic plateau. The only part with a coastal plain is in the E. C. has a very favourable climate. Much of the land is covered by the characteristic maquis vegetation, herbs, evergreens, and bushes, but parts have fine chestnut forests and pine woods. Sheep are kept on the highland pastures, while on the coastlands wheat, vines, tobacco, olives, and fruits are grown. Fishing is important, marble is quarried; there is little industry.

The Corsican is renowned for his pride and dignity, his hospitality towards visitors, and formerly was famed for the relentless nature of the vendetta, or blood feud. The chief town and port is Ajaccio; other towns are Bastia, Bonifacio, Calvi, and Corte.

The first civilized inhabitants of C. were the Phocaeans of Ionia, who founded Alalia about 560 B.C. They were succeeded in turn by the Etruscans, the Carthaginians, the Romans, the Vandals, and the Arabs. In the 14th cent. C. fell to the Genoese, and in the second half of the 18th cent. Paoli led an independence movement. Genoa sold her rights to France in 1768 and French rule was eventually established. In the S.W.W. C. was occupied by the Italians 1942–3. Area 3,367 sq. m.; pop. (1962) 275,465.

CORT, Henry (1740–1800). British ironmaster. He invented the puddling process and developed the rolling mill in the manufacture of wrought iron, which were of vast importance early in the Industrial Revolution.

CORTES (kortehs'), **Hernando** (1485–1547). Spanish soldier. He went to the W. Indies as a young man, and in 1518 was given command of an expedition to Mexico. Landing with only 600 men, he was at first received as a god by the emperor, but was finally expelled from Mexico City by a revolt. With the aid of native allies he recaptured the city in 1521, and conquered the whole country. After ruling as governor for some years he returned to Spain, where he d., neglected by the court.

CORTISONE (**Compound E.**). Substance discovered by T. Reichstein of Basle, Switzerland, and put to practical clinical use for rheumatoid arthritis by P. S. Hench and E. C. Kendall in the U.S.A. (all 3 shared a Nobel prize in 1950). A product of the adrenal gland, it was first synthesized from a constituent of ox-bile, and is now produced commercially from a Mexican yam and from a by-product of the sisal plant.

CORTO'NA. Town in Arezzo prov., Italy, one of Europe's oldest cities. It is encircled by walls built by the Etruscans and has a medieval castle, and an 11th cent. cathedral. Pop. c. 5,000.

CORTOT (kortoh'), **Alfred** (1877–1962). French pianist and conductor. B. in Switzerland, he trained at the Paris Conservatoire, and became an unrivalled interpreter of Chopin, whose works he edited, and Schumann.

CORUMBÁ (koroombah'). Brazilian port on the Paraguay river, long disputed between Paraguay and Brazil, the commercial centre of Mato Grosso state. Pop. (1960) 20,000.

CORU'NDUM. Native aluminium oxide (Al_2O_3), occurring in cleavable masses or in pyramidal crystals. It includes the ruby and sapphire, and is next on the scale of hardness to diamond. It occurs as crystals distributed through granites, cyanites, and schists in many parts of the world.

CORUNNA (kohroon'yah). Town, cap. of C. prov., in the extreme N.W. of Spain. Its activities are for the most part based on the fisheries, but it has tobacco and match factories, sugar refineries, linen and cotton mills, etc. Nearby in 1809 was fought the battle in which Sir John Moore was killed. Pop. (1965) 185,142.

CORVETTE (korvet'). Term, now obsolete, for a class of vessels in the Royal Navy, which guarded convoys, etc., during the S.W.W. The term was a revival from the days of sail.

CORVIDAE. Family of birds including the crow, magpie, chough, and jay (qq.v.).

CORVO, Baron. See ROLFE, F. R.

CORYPHAENA (korefē'na). Genus of ocean fishes of the mackerel family, known to sailors as dorados or 'dolphins'. *C. hippurus*, the best-known species, is brilliant blue with golden reflections and deep blue spots. They grow to 6 ft.

COS. Fertile Greek island, one of the Dodecanese, in the Aegean Sea. It gives its name to the Cos lettuce. Area 111 sq. m.; pop. (1961) 20,000.

COSE'NZA. Italian town of Calabria at the junction of the Crati and the Busento, cap. of C. prov., an archiepiscopal see, and the burial place of Alaric. Pop. (1961) 77,590.

COSGRAVE, William Thomas (1880–1965). Irish statesman. B. in Dublin, he took part in the Easter Rebellion of 1916, and sat in the Sinn Féin cabinet of 1919–21. Head of the Free State govt. from 1922 until his defeat by De Valera in 1932, he led the Fine Gael opposition 1933–44, as did his son Liam C. (1920–   ) from 1965.

COSMETICS. See BEAUTY CULTURE.

COSMIC RADIATION. The so-called cosmic rays are not true rays, but high-speed particles (atomic nuclei) moving at tremendous velocities. The cosmic-ray primaries are relatively heavy, since the nuclei appear to have atomic weights as high as that of tin, and may well be dangerous to living matter; fortunately, the earth's atmosphere provides an effective screen, and the primaries are broken up, so that only their fragments reach the ground. The origin of C.R. is still rather uncertain. The sun is one source, but most of the cosmic rays come from beyond the Solar System. They were first studied by Millikan (q.v.) in 1925. Their energy far exceeds that of particles from a laboratory accelerator, and they present a marginal hazard to manned space flights.

COSMONAUT (kos'monawt) Russian term for man making flights into space. See SPACE RESEARCH.

COSSACKS. A section of the Russian population, of mixed descent, which originally held land in return for military service. Before 1917 C. households had a larger allotment of land than that of the ordinary peasant, and in return all the men were bound to serve in the army for 20 years. Their chief pursuits are agriculture and the breeding of sheep and cattle. Their fine horsemanship is proverbial.

COSTA, Lorenzo (1460–1535). Italian painter. A member of the Bolognese school, though b. in Ferrara, he painted notable frescoes at the Bentivoglio chapel in San Giacomo Maggiore.

COST ACCOUNTANCY. A specialized branch of accountancy concerned with ascertaining the cost of production of goods or services rendered at any and every stage of their production. Its aim is the securing of the maximum productive efficiency of the undertakings. The professional bodies in the U.K. are the Institute of Cost and Works Accountants (1919) and the Cost Accountants' Association (1937) and in the U.S. the National Association of Cost Accountants.

COSSACKS. Once a name to be feared, it now suggests to audiences throughout the world the thrill of watching their fiery dances. Here a star of the Ukrainian State Cossack Company demonstrates for his delighted fellow-troopers his skill in the *gopak*.   *Photo: Novosti Press Agency, Moscow.*

COTMAN. Water colour 'Greta Bridge', in the British Museum, which dates from c. 1806 and is powerfully effective in the simplicity of its design.

COSTA RICA (rē'kah). A Central American rep. lying between the Caribbean Sea and the Pacific. It was discovered by Columbus, and from 1563 until 1821 was under Spanish rule. Since then it has been independent. Its chief troubles have been boundary disputes with its neighbours.

Most of C.R. is an elevated tableland, and there are a number of high volcanic mountains. The chief river is the San Juan. The country is divided into 7 provs. The capital is San José, pop. (1967) 185,640; other towns are Cartago, Heredia, Alajuela, Liberia, Limón, and Puntarenas.

Agriculture is the principal industry, but much of the country remains to be cleared. The principal product is coffee, followed by bananas and cacao. There is gold, silver, etc., and mineral surveys are in progress: timber is produced.

C.R. is governed by a president and a single chamber, the Legislative Assembly, both elected for 4 years. Roman Catholicism is the state religion. The language is Spanish. There is a national system of education, and English is taught in all secondary schools. Area 19,690 sq. m.; pop. (1966) 1,490,000.

CO'STELLO, John Aloysius (1891–   ). Irish statesman, leader of the Fine Gael party. B. in Dublin, he was Attorney-General under Cosgrave 1926–32, and P.M. of the Rep. 1948–51 and 1954–7, and led the Opposition 1951–4 and 1957–9.

COSTER, Charles de (1827–79). Belgian writer. B. at Munich, he was one of a group of young writers who set out to produce a distinctively Flemish literature instead of using French. In *La Légende de Thyl Uylenspiegel* (1867) he achieved a true masterpiece.

COSTER, Laurens Janszoon (1370–1440). Dutch printer, b. at Haarlem. According to some authorities, he invented movable type, but after his death an apprentice ran off to Mainz with the blocks and, taking Gutenberg into his confidence, began a printing business with them.

COST OF LIVING. This phrase came into common use during the F.W.W., when it was desired to measure the rise in prices of goods in general consumption, partly as a guide to necessary increases in wages. In Britain the first C.O.L. index was introduced in 1914 and based on the expenditure of a working-class family of man, wife and 3 children; the standard is 100. This, officially known from 1947 as the *Index of Retail Prices*, has been revised from time to time, as a result of inflation and a general rise in prices. Supplementary to it in reaching estimates of C. of L. is the *Consumer Price Index*, calculated from 1938 on the expenditure of all consumers.

In the U.S. a Consumer Price Index, based on the expenditure of families in the iron, steel and related industries, was introduced in 1890. The modern index is based on the expenditure of the urban wage-earner and clerical-worker families in 46 large, medium and small cities, the standard being 100.

COSTUME. *See* DRESS.

COSWAY, Richard (1742–1821). British artist. Elected R.A. in 1771, he was the most accomplished of the 18th cent. miniaturists and painted the chief members of the Prince Regent's court.

COTMAN, John Sell (1782–1842). British landscape painter. B. at Norwich, he went to London to study c. 1798, returning to Norwich in 1807 as a drawing master. In 1834 Turner helped him to an appointment at King's Coll., London. He achieved a balanced harmony of forms in subdued tones, and was fond of depicting ships and bridges. His sons, Miles Edmund (1810–58) and Joseph John (1814–78) were also landscape painters.

COTONEASTER (kŏtōnē-as'ter). Genus of trees and shrubs belonging to the Rosaceae and closely allied to the hawthorn and medlar. Its leaves are simple and entire, and woolly beneath, and the conspicuous but small and unpalatable fruits persist through the winter.

COTONOU (kot'onoo). Chief port of Dahomey, on the Gulf of Benin. It is a road and rail centre, and has an airport. Palm products and timber are exported. Pop. (1965) 85,000.

COTOPA'XI. Formerly the world's highest active volcano (q.v.) situated to the S. of Quito in Ecuador. It is 19,347 ft. high, and was climbed first in 1872. Its name is Quechua and means shining peak.

COTSWOLDS (kots'wōldz). Range of hills in Gloucestershire, England, some 50 m. long, between Bristol and Chipping Camden. They rise to 1,070 ft. in Cleeve Cloud, near Cheltenham, but average 500–600 ft.

COTTA. German publishing house established at Tübingen in 1659. JOHANN FRIEDRICH C. (1764–1832) pub. the works of Schiller, Goethe, Jean Paul, etc., and founded the *Allgemeine Zeitung* (1798).

COTTBUS. *See* KOTTBUS.

COTTET (koteh'), **Charles** (1863–1925). French painter, best known for his paintings of life in the coastal region of Brittany.

COTTON, Sir Robert Bruce (1571–1631). English antiquary. At his home in Westminster he built up a fine collection of MSS. and coins, many of which had come from the despoiled monasteries. His son, Sir Thomas C., added to the library, and in 1700 it was bestowed on the nation by Sir John Cotton. Its contents are in the British Museum.

COTTON, Thomas Henry (1907–   ). British golfer. B. in Cheshire, he won the British Open Championship in 1934, 1937 and 1948.

COTTON. Commercial cotton mainly processed by industry consists of the fibres surrounding the seeds in the ripened fruit or boll. Most frequently cultivated is *Gossypium herbaceum*, believed to be of eastern origin, but introduced to America in the 18th cent. However, the longest fibres come from Sea Island Cotton (*Gossypium barbadense*), considered to be a native of the New World and now grown in the West Indies, which is so named from its early cultivation on the islands that fringe Georgia and South Carolina. Many cultivated cottons are hybrids.

The C. shrub grows 4–5 ft. and requires 200 days free from frost coupled with moderate rainfall or irrigation. Bright sunshine and rich soil are important for the ripening of the bolls. The C. seed is sown in March or April and the C. is picked in late summer or autumn. The principal C. lands of the world are in the sub-tropical regions. In the U.S.A. the principal States are in the South from the Carolinas and Georgia to Texas, Arizona and California, excluding the swampy Gulf Coast and Florida. The other main C.-growing areas in order of importance

COTTON. Each shrub produces some 20 flowers (left). The petals fall after only 3 days, leaving small green pods with 30–40 seeds in each, and every seed has soft downy hairs like those of dandelion clocks. After 2 months the swollen pods open (right), revealing the cotton. *Courtesy of The Cotton Board, Manchester.*

with regard to quantity, though not necessarily quality, are the U.S.S.R., China, India and Pakistan, Egypt and the Sudan, Brazil, Mexico, Peru, Tanganyika, Uganda and Kenya. *See* illus. under ALABAMA.

The staple length of C. varies quite considerably, ranging from short staple C. (about $1\frac{1}{8}$ in.) to long staple (up to $2\frac{1}{2}$ in.). Classification is by growth (country of origin), grade, and staple and 'character'. The grade depends on the colour, the amount of trash and foreign impurities present, and the quality of the ginning (the first process C. goes through to remove seeds, etc.). Character is judged by fibre strength, fibre fineness, the degree of uniformity in diameter and twist, and the ability of the fibres to hold or cling together.

C. may be classified in the country of origin and in the country of importation, and a certain amount is done in Liverpool. The C. industry in Britain grew up in Lancashire and remains there. Its varied products range from apparel fabrics and household and surgical textiles to industrial fabrics and Service equipment. In recent years increasing competition, both from cheap imports produced by the developing countries and from man-made fibres, has stimulated new developments in machinery, and in new processes and finishes, as well as combination of C. with synthetics. The Shirley Institute has a world-wide reputation for fundamental and applied research in C., silk, and man-made fibres.

COTTON SEED. A by-product of C. cultivation from which can be extracted a reddish oil containing glycerides of palmitic, oleic, stearic and linolic acids. Refined, it turns yellow and is used in the manufacture of edible products such as cooking fats, margarine and salad oils. Other derivatives are soaps, tars, paints, chemicals, etc. The C. cake is used as cattle food and as a fertilizer, since it contains nitrogen, phosphates and potash. Cotton seed flour blended with wheat flour is used by bakers and confectioners and the hard covering of the kernel is used for making insulating materials and fertilizers.

COTY (kohti'), **René** (1882–1962). French statesman. Of Norman stock, he studied law, entered Parliament in 1923 and in 1948 was elected to the Senate. He was last President of the 4th Republic (1953–9), being elected on the 13th ballot (the longest election in the history of the rep.), and was succeeded by de Gaulle.

COUCH GRASS. A plant (*Agropyron repens*), one of the commonest of the grasses (Gramineae). It is closely allied to wheat, but is generally regarded as an undesirable weed.

COUDENHOVE-KALERGI, Richard Nicolaus, count (1894–). Austrian writer. Founder-president in 1923 of the Pan-European Union, he has pub. many books advocating a federal Europe.

COUÉ (koo-eh'), **Emile** (1857–1926). French psychological healer, famous for his slogan, 'Every day, and in every way, I am becoming better and better'. 'Couéism' reached the height of its popularity in the 1920s.

COULOMB (koolon'), **Charles Auguste de** (1736–1806). French scientist, inventor of the torsion balance for measuring the force of electric and magnetic attraction. The name *coulomb* was given to the practical unit of quantity of electricity – the quantity conveyed by a current of one ampère in a second.

COUNCIL. In English local government, a popularly elected local assembly charged with the good government of the area within its boundaries, e.g. county C., city C., borough C., urban district C., rural district C., parish C. All members of the district and parish Cs. are styled councillors, but counties, cities, and boroughs have aldermen in addition. Councillors are directly elected, and sit usually for 3 years: aldermen are elected by the councillors from among their number. *See* COUNTY COUNCIL, etc.

COUNCIL FOR MUTUAL ECONOMIC ASSISTANCE (COMECON). Organization established in 1948 as the East European equivalent of the Marshall Plan. Members are Bulgaria, Czechoslovakia, German Democratic Republic, Hungary, Mongolia, Poland, Rumania, Soviet Union. In addition to fostering trade and industrial growth among themselves, they aim at expanding trade with 'capitalist' countries.

COUNCIL OF EUROPE. Body constituted in 1949 to secure 'a greater measure of unity between the European countries'. The first session of the Consultative Assembly opened at Strasbourg in August 1949, the members then being Great Britain, France, Italy, Belgium, the Netherlands, Sweden, Denmark, Norway, the Repub. of Ireland, Luxemburg, Greece, and Turkey; Iceland, W. Germany, Austria, Cyprus, Switzerland, and Malta joined subsequently. The Assembly operates through 12 general committees; a standing committee preserves its existence between sessions. Its seat is Strasbourg, France. Greece withdrew 1969 when govt. condemned as undemocratic.

COUNTER-ESPIONAGE. *See* SECRET SERVICE.

COUNTERFEITING. The production of fraudulent imitations, particularly of money. The problem is increased today by the rapidity with which large sums, produced by modern printing and photographic techniques, can be distributed over great distances. In the U.S.A. the Secret Service seizes some $10,000,000 of counterfeit notes annually.

COUNTERPOINT. In music, the combination of melodies to form an artistic and satisfying musical texture. Derived from the Lat. *punctus contra punctum*, 'note against note', it originated in Plainsong where 2 vocal lines, independent but sung simultaneously, produced a certain texture. The greatest period for C. was the 16th century.

COUNTESS OF HUNTINGDON'S CONNEXION. A Nonconformist denomination in England, founded by Selina, countess of Huntingdon, in the middle of the 18th cent. Calvinistic Methodist in theology, most of its 37 chapels are affiliated with the Congregational Union.

COUNTRY DANCING. *See* FOLK DANCING.

COUNTY. In Britain, an administrative unit, nowadays synonymous with 'shire', although historically the two had different origins. Many of the English cos. can be traced back to Saxon times, but a number have proved either too large or too small for modern administrative purposes, and others have cut across the lines of new development. In 1971 it was proposed to replace the existing 46 English admin. Cs. by 44 new county areas of local govt. (6 being 'metropolitan' on the plan of Greater London). Wales has 13, which it has been proposed to reduce by amalgamation to seven. Scotland has 33 civil counties (to become 8 regions and 49 districts), and N. Ireland 6, admin. and geographical Cs. The Irish Republic has 26 geographical and 27 admin. Cs.

COUNTY BOROUGHS. *See* BOROUGH.

COUNTY COUNCIL. The largest of British local govt. units. C.Cs. were established in 1888, and exist in every administrative county. *See* COUNTY.

The C.C. consists of a chairman, aldermen, and councillors. The chairman is elected annually by the whole council and may be paid. The aldermen are usually one-third the number of the councillors and hold office for 6 years, one-half retiring every 3 years, and are elected by the councillors from their own number, or from persons qualified to be elected councillors. Councillors are elected every 3 years by the local-government electors, who are now the same as parliamentary electors.

Powers of C.Cs. as envisaged 1971 incl. education, personal social services, police and fire services, overall planning and development, purchase and disposal of land, overspill housing, and building regulations; and (taken over from existing local authorities) weights and measures, clean air, refuse disposal, environmental health, and libraries. Revenue is derived from the county rate obtained by precept from the local authorities.

COUNTY COURT. An English court of law created by the County Courts Act, 1846. It exists to try civil cases, and actions on contract and most actions on tort may be brought before it if the claim does not exceed £400. C.Cs. are presided over by a paid judge sitting alone. An appeal on a point of law lies to the Court of Appeal.

COUPERIN (koopran'), **François** (1668–1733). French composer, called *le Grand*, as being the most famous of a distinguished musical family. B. in Paris, he held various court appointments and wrote exquisite pieces for the harpsichord.

COUPERUS (koo'-), **Louis** (1863–1923). Dutch poet and novelist. B. at The Hague, the setting of his 4-vol. *Books of the Small Souls* (1901–3), he also wrote historical novels of Xerxes, and Alexander.

COURBET (koorbeh'), **Gustave** (1819–77). French landscape and genre painter. From 1841 he was associated with the Barbizon school, and his paintings created a sensation at the Salon of 1850, because of their Impressionistic technique. Manet was influenced by him. In 1871 C. became a member of the Paris Commune and was sentenced to 6 months' imprisonment and a fine. His last years were spent at Vevey in Switzerland.

COURSING. The chasing of hares by greyhounds, not by scent but by sight, as a sport, and as a test of the greyhound's speed, etc. It is one of the most ancient of field sports. Since the 1880s it has been practised on enclosed or park courses. The governing body in Great Britain is the National Coursing Club, formed in 1858.

The C. season lasts September–March: the Altcar or Waterloo meeting, which decides the championship, is held in Feb. The Waterloo Cup race is known as the Courser's Derby.

COURTAULD, Samuel (1793–1881). British industrialist. He founded the firm of Courtaulds in 1816 at Bocking, Essex, which at first specialized in silk and crape manufacture, but from 1904 developed the production of viscose rayon. His great nephew, **Samuel C.** (1876–1947). was chairman of the firm from 1921, and in 1931 transferred his house and art collection to the Univ. of London as the C. Institute. The firm has more recently developed other man-made fibres.

COURT-MARTIAL. A court convened for the trial of persons subject to service discipline. British Cs.-M. are governed by the code of the service concerned – Naval Discipline, Army, or Air Force Acts – and in 1951 an appeal court was estab. for all 3 services by

the Cs.-M. (Appeals) Act. The procedure prescribed for the U.S. services is similar, being originally based on British practice.

COURTNEIDGE (kawrt'nēj), **Dame Cicely** (1893–). British actress. B. in Sydney, she estab. herself on stage and screen as a comedienne with a gift for rousingly tuneful songs. She is the wife of Jack Hulbert.

COURT OF SESSION. The supreme Civil Court in Scotland, estab. 1532. Cases come in the first place before one of the 8 Lords Ordinary, and from their decisions an appeal lies to the Inner House which sits in 2 divisions called the First and Second Division. From the decisions of the Inner House an appeal lies to the House of Lords.

COURT OF THE LORD LYON. Scottish heraldic body composed of 1 King of Arms, 3 Heralds, and 3 Pursuivants. It embodies the High Seanachie of Scotland's Celtic kings.

COURTOIS (koortwah'), **Jacques** (1621–76). French painter, known as Bourguignon or Il Borgognone, chiefly famous for his battle and siege scenes.

COURTRAI. Belgian industrial town on the Lys, in W. Flanders. It is connected by canal to the coast, and by river and canal to Antwerp and Brussels. It has a large textile industry, esp. damask, linens, and lace. Here in 1302 was fought a battle in which the Flemings of Ghent and Bruges defeated an army of French knights. Pop. (1966) 43,310.

COURTS, Law. *See* LAW COURTS.

COUSIN (koozan'), **Jean** (1501–89). French painter, engraver, and sculptor. He was a Paris goldsmith, and his stained-glass windows in the Sainte Chapelle at Vincennes are considered among the finest examples in France.

COUSIN (koozan'), **Victor** (1792–1867). French philosopher. B. at Paris, he became a lecturer at the Sorbonne when 23, and did much to introduce German philosophical ideas into France. In 1840 he was Minister of Public Instruction and reorganized the system of elementary education.

COUSINS, Frank (1904–). British trade union leader. B. in Notts., from the age of 14 he worked in the mines for 6 years. Moving into transport, he became organizer for the Road Transport Section of the Transport and General Workers' Union in 1938. Min. of Technology 1964–6, he resigned in protest over the 'prices and incomes' policy, and was Gen. Sec. of the T.G.W.U. 1956–64 and 1966–9. He became chairman Community Relations Commission 1968.

COUSTEAU (koostoh'), **Jacques-Yves** (1910–). French naval officer. Celebrated for his oceanographic researches in command of the *Calypso* from 1951, he shared in the invention of the Aqualung and was the first to use television under water. *The Silent World* (1953) and other books recount his adventures, and he pioneered in underwater archaeology.

COUTTS, Frederick (1899–). British Salvation Army officer. B. at Kirkcaldy, Scotland, he was principal of the Army's Training Coll. 1953–7, and then Territorial Commander of E. Australia from 1957 until his election as General of the Army (1963–9).

COUTTS (koots), **Thomas** (1735–1822). British banker. He estab. with his brother the firm of Coutts & Co. (one of London's oldest banking houses, first originating in 1692 in the Strand, which it has never left), becoming sole head on the latter's death in 1778. Since the reign of George III an account has been maintained there by every succeeding sovereign and other customers incl. Chatham, William Pitt, Fox, Wellington, Reynolds and Boswell. In 1920 the bank was affiliated to the National Provincial Bank Ltd., but retains a separate identity. One of his daus. m. Sir Francis Burdett (q.v.).

COUVE DE MURVILLE (koov de mürvēl'),

COVENTRY The new cathedral, consecrated in 1962, replaced the 14th cent. building destroyed in the air raids of 1940–1. Behind the High Altar is the world's largest tapestry, 'Christ in Majesty', designed by Graham Sutherland: measuring 75 ft. by 40 ft. it weighs nearly a ton and was woven at Felletin, in France. To the right and left may be seen some of the 8 stone mural panels, by Ralph Beyer.
Photo: P. W. & L. Thompson, Coventry.

Maurice (1907–). French diplomat. Holding a post in the Finance Ministry in 1940, he escaped in 1942 to the Free French in N. Africa, and was ambassador to the U.S. 1955–6, and W. Germany 1956–8. Always in close harmony with de Gaulle, he was appointed For. Min. on the latter's return to office in 1958 and was P.M. 1968–9.

COVENANTERS. The Presbyterian adherents of the National Covenant in 17th cent. Scotland. The National Covenant was occasioned by Charles I's attempt in 1637 to introduce a liturgy on the English model into Scotland. The Presbyterians revived the covenant drawn up by John Craig in 1581, swearing to uphold Presbyterianism, and added an appendix condemning recent innovations. This document was signed at Greyfriars' church, Edinburgh, on 28 Feb. 1638 and a general assembly abolished episcopacy. In 1643 the Cs. signed with the English parliament the *Solemn League and Covenant*, whereby they promised military aid in return for the establishment of Presbyterianism in England, and a Scottish army entered England and fought at Marston Moor.

At the Restoration Charles II revived episcopacy in Scotland, and ministers who resisted the change were evicted. Conventicles began to be held, and those who attended them were savagely persecuted. Rebellions followed in 1666, 1679, and 1685, and led to the intensification of persecution, but Presbyterianism was restored as the national religion of Scotland after the revolution of 1688.

COVENTRY (kuv'entri). City (co. bor.) in Warwickshire, England, on the r. Sherbourne, 18 m. E.S.E. of Birmingham. A priory was founded in 1043 by Leofric, earl of Mercia, whose wife was Lady Godiva (q.v.). C. was a centre of woollen and cloth manufacture to *c.* 1700; ribbons, silks, and cottons are still made. C.'s great engineering industry began with the manufacture of bicycles in 1870; it produces motor-cars, aeroplanes, bicycles, radio and electrical equipment, etc.

C., sometimes called the 'City of Three Steeples', was one of the most heavily bombed British cities in the S.W.W. The cathedral, built 1373–95 on the site of an earlier building, was destroyed in the air raid of 14 Nov. 1940, but its 303-ft.-high steeple survived and was incorporated in the plan of the new cathedral, prepared by (Sir) Basil Spence; permission to rebuild was given in 1952, and Elizabeth II laid the foundation stone in 1956. During the war, Christ Church also was demolished, though the 14th cent. spire remains.

Trinity Church (17th cent.), with the 3rd of the spires, was only slightly damaged. St. Mary's hall was built in 1394–1414 as a guild centre; of the old walls (1356) 2 gates remain. The Belgrade Theatre, a civic project, dates from 1958. Pop. (1961) 305,060.

COVERDALE, Miles (1488–1569). Translator of the Bible into English. B. in Yorks, he became a Catholic priest, but turned to Protestantism and in 1528 went abroad to avoid persecution. His translation of the Bible appeared in 1535 and was dedicated to Henry VIII – the first complete translation of the Bible to be printed in English. His translation of the psalms is that retained in the Book of Common Prayer. In 1539 he ed. the Great Bible which was ordered to be placed in churches. After some years in Germany, he returned to England in 1548, and in 1551 was made bishop of Exeter. Under Mary he again left the country, but in the early part of Elizabeth's reign he held the living of St. Magnus near London Bridge.

COWARD, Sir Noël (1899–). Brit. man-of-the-theatre. He first appeared on the stage in 1910, and estab. himself as a dramatist with *The Young Idea* (1921), going on to consolidate his reputation in the '20s and '30s with the sharp sophistication of *The Vortex* (1924); the brilliant comedy *Hay Fever* (1925); the revue *This Year of Grace* (1928); the operetta *Bitter Sweet* (1929); *Private Lives* (1930), which gave a great role to Gertrude Lawrence; and the sentimental *Cavalcade* (1931). Besides stage appearances in his own plays, etc., he acted in the film *In Which We Serve* (1942), which he also scripted, and wrote scripts for films of his later plays, *Blithe Spirit* (1941), a venture in spiritualism, and *This Happy Breed* (1942); and for the subtle *Brief Encounter* (1945).

COWES (kowz). Seaport and resort (U.D.) on the N. coast of the Isle of Wight, on the Medina estuary, opposite Southampton Water. It is the H.Q. of the Royal Yacht Squadron which holds the annual Cowes Regatta, and has maritime industries. In East C. is Osborne House (q.v.), used as a museum. Pop. (1961) 16,974.

COWLEY, Abraham (1618–67). British poet. Joining King Charles at Oxford in 1644, he fled to France after Marston Moor, and was employed in Royalist intrigues. He returned to England in 1655, and although arrested was released on bail, and in 1656 pub. his collected works, including the epic *Davideis*, 'The Mistress', 'Pindarique Odes', and 'Miscellanies'. Highly valued in his own day, his fondness for 'conceits' now makes him unreadable except in his lighter pieces and unstudied essays.

COWLEY FATHERS. Name given to senior members of the Society of St. John the Evangelist, a monastic order within the C. of E. founded by Richard Meux Benson (1824–1915); junior members are referred to as C. Brothers. Members take the vows of poverty, chastity, and obedience, and engage in evangelical and religious social work. The headquarters are at Cowley St. John, near Oxford.

COWPER, (koo'per), **William** (1731–1800). British poet. B. in Herts, he was called to the Bar in 1754, but suffered from intense melancholic depression, which in 1763 was aggravated to madness. While in a St. Albans asylum he underwent a great religious experience, and on his recovery in 1765 settled in Huntingdon with Mr. and Mrs. Unwin. On the death of the former, C. and Mrs. Unwin removed to Olney,

WILLIAM COWPER
By George Romney.
Photo: N.P.G.

where he was subjected to the evangelical influence of the converted slave-trader, the Rev. John Newton, with whom he collaborated in the *Olney Hymns* (1779). In 1773 C. suffered another attack of madness which prevented his marriage with Mrs. Unwin, but on the removal of the influence of Newton in 1779, C. turned to secular poetry, and in 1782 pub. *Table Talk*. This was followed in 1785 by *The Task* and *John Gilpin*, but in 1787 and 1794 he again suffered from insanity. Many of C.'s best minor poems belong to these later years, and in 1794 he received a state pension. The outstanding qualities of his poetry, delicate observation and kindly humour, are also present in his letters.

COWRY. A family of marine gasteropod molluscs (Cypraeidae), belonging to the Streptoneura. They are distinguished by the peculiar form of the shell, in which the last wall conceals the others, and the outer lip of the elongated border is bent in towards the inner. Cs. are shallow-water dwellers, and are found in many parts of the world, particularly in the Indian and Pacific Oceans. C. shells are often beautifully coloured and polished. They have been used as ornaments and charms, and were worn by women to produce fertility. They have also been used as money in the S. Seas.

COWSLIP. A plant (*Primula veris*) belonging to the Primulaceae, being placed in the same genus as the primrose. It is common in English meadows, and in some parts the flowers are made into C. wine. The oxlip (*P. elatior*) is closely allied to it.

COX, David (1783–1859). British artist. B. nr. Birmingham, the son of a blacksmith, he studied under John Varley and made a living as a drawing master. His water-colour landscapes have attractive cloud effects, and his renderings of scenes in N. Wales are excellent.

COXCIE (kok'sē), Michael (1499–1592). Flemish painter who came under the influence of Raphael, and was court painter to Philip II of Spain.

COXWELL, Henry Tracey (1819–1900). British balloonist. B. in Kent, he made his first balloon ascent in 1844, and in 1845 pub. *The Balloon*, the first British journal devoted to aeronautics. In 1852 he became a professional balloonist, and during the Franco-Prussian War he helped to found the first German balloon corps.

COYO'TE (*Canis latrans*). Name for several races of small wolf inhabiting N. America from southern Canada to Mexico, and representing the jackals of the New World. They live in burrows, and are a great nuisance to poultry farmers, but their food consists chiefly of hares, mice, and wild birds.

COYPU (koi'poo). S. American water rodent

COYPU. Although harmless in the Argentine, the C. developed in Britain – where it had no enemies to check its numbers – a dangerous liking for root crops and young corn. It also undermines marsh roadways and the banks of waterways.
Crown Copyright.

(*Myocaster coypus*) of the porcupine group, often 2 ft. long, excluding its scaly rat-like tail, and weighing more than 20 lb. It has webbed hind feet, a blunt-muzzled head on a short, thick neck, and its strong front teeth are orange-yellow. Most common in the Argentine, it feeds on water plants and lives either on flat nests of dry reeds above water-level or in burrows on river-banks. Introduced into East Anglia in the 1930s for its fur (nutria), the C. escaped, bred, and did such damage to growing crops and waterways that it was officially recognized as a pest in 1960.

COZENS (kuz'enz), Alexander (c. 1717–86). British artist. B. in Russia, he was rumoured to be a natural son of Peter the Great, but was probably the son of Richard C., employed by the Tsar as a shipbuilder. Coming to England in 1742, he taught at Eton and George III's sons were his pupils. He is famous for his water-colour landscapes done in brown, grey or black washes, and sometimes used blots as the inspiration of a study to be finished with brush or pen. His son, John Robert C. (c. 1752–97) was also a water-colourist, influencing Girtin and Turner, but became mentally unstable.

CRAB. Robber crab and the European edible crab.

CRAB. Name given to the crustacea of the sub-order Brachyura, and to many of the Anomura (hermit crabs, etc.) of the order Decapodoa. The true Cs. (Brachyura) are characterized by having the abdomen small, and tucked under the cephalothorax, which is covered with a broad carapace. They have 10 legs, of which the first pair are modified as claws, or nippers, and the remaining 4 pairs are used for swimming and walking. They are active, intelligent crustaceans, mainly carnivorous in their diet, and acting as scavengers. Most of them have a characteristic sidelong mode of progression. The young pass through a metamorphosis, the zoëa and megalopa stages, before the familiar adult form is reached; and growth, both in these larval free-swimming forms and the adult, is effected by periodic casting of the outer shell.

Cs. vary greatly in habit and type. Common between tide-marks in Britain and Europe is the shore or green C. (*Carcinus maenas*); species of commercial value incl. the British and European edible C. (*Cancer pagurus*) and the blue C. (*Callinectes sapidus*) of the American Atlantic coast; freshwater Cs. incl. the S. European river C. (*Thelphusa fluviatilis*); and the hermit Cs. have a soft, spirally twisted abdomen and rely on the empty shells of gasteropod molluscs such as the whelk and periwinkle to afford them protection. Some tropical hermit Cs. live most of their lives a considerable distance from the sea, and the robber C. (*Birgus latro*) – a member of the family that has developed armour on the upper surface of the abdomen – climbs palm trees for the nuts.

CRAB APPLE. The wild form (*Pyrus malus*) from which the cultivated apple has been derived; it differs chiefly in the smaller size and bitter flavour of the fruit, used in C.A. jelly. The tree is common in woods and hedgerows in Britain S. of Perthshire, and varies from a mere bush to 30 ft. in height.

CRABBE, George (1754–1832). British poet. B. in Suffolk, he was apprenticed to an apothecary and practised medicine until he went to London in 1780 and was assisted by Burke in furthering his literary career. In 1781 he took orders and pub. his first poem *The Library*, which was followed by *The Village* (1783), *The Parish Register* (1807), *The Borough* (1810), *Tales* (1812), and *Tales of the Hall* (1819). In 1782 C. became chaplain to the duke of Rutland, and in 1814 settled as vicar of Trowbridge. Reacting against the romantic idealized conception of country life, he dealt realistically with the agricultural poor.

CRACOW. Alternative form of KRAKOW.

CRAIG, Edward Gordon (1872–1966). British theatrical producer, actor, dramatist and writer. The son of Ellen Terry, he went on the stage at 6, and joined Irving's company in 1889. His first stage production, Purcell's *Dido and Aeneas* (1900), introduced new effects in staging and lighting. His sister, **Edith C.** (1869–1947), was also a stage designer and producer, and his son, **Edward Anthony C.** (1905–), working under the name Edward Carrick, is an artist and film and theatre designer.

CRAIGAVON (krägav'on), **James Craig**, 1st visct. C. (1871–1940). Irish Unionist statesman. B. in Co. Down, he was elected a Unionist M.P. in 1906, and when in 1914 Carson organized the Ulster Volunteers to resist by force the granting of Home Rule to Ireland, C. acted as his lieutenant. During the F.W.W. he raised the 36th (Ulster) Division. In 1921 he became the 1st Prime Minister of N. Ireland, and in 1927 was created visct.

CRAIK, Dinah Maria (1826–87). British novelist. B. at Stoke-on-Trent, the dau. of Thomas Mulock, an eccentric Irishman, she pub. *John Halifax, Gentleman* in 1857, still an English classic. In 1864 she m. G. L. Craik, partner in Macmillan's, the publishers.

CRAIOVA (krahyoh'-vah). Rumanian town near the r. Jiu, cap. of C. region. It is an important commercial and manufacturing centre. Pop. (1966) 148,821.

GORDON CRAIG
Courtesy of Helen Craig

CRAKE. See RAIL.

CRAMER (krah'mer), **Johann Baptist** (1771-1858). German musician. Brought to England as an infant, he founded the publishing firm of C. in 1824, and was a celebrated pianist and teacher.

CRANACH (krah'nakh), **Lucas** (1472-1553). German artist. B. at Kronach in Bavaria, he settled at Wittenberg in 1504 to work for the elector of Saxony. He was a close friend of Luther, whose portrait he painted several times, and his work is highly finished and gaily inventive in the use of classical themes. He produced numerous woodcuts and copperplates. His 2nd son **Lucas C. the Younger** (1516–86) had a similar style, and succeeded his father as director of the C. workshop.

CRANBERRY. A plant (*Vaccinium oxycoccus*) allied to the bilberry, and belonging to the heaths (Ericaceae). It is a small evergreen, growing in marshy places, and bearing small, acid, edible crimson berries.

CRANE, Hart (1899–1932). American poet. B. in Ohio, he had little education and at 15 was working in his father's sweet factory. His long heroic poem *The Bridge* (1930) lives only in parts. He drowned after jumping overboard from the steamer bringing him back to the U.S.A. after a visit to Mexico.

CRANE, Stephen (1871–1900). American writer. B. in N.J., he became a journalist, and won fame in 1895 with *Red Badge of Courage*, dealing vividly with the American Civil War.

CROWNED CRANE

CRANE, Walter (1845–1915). British artist. While apprenticed to W. J. Linton, the wood engraver, he came under pre-Raphaelite influence. He excelled as a book illustrator for children and adults, his finest work being for an edition of Spenser's *Faerie Queene* (1894–6).

CRANE. A family of birds (Megalornithidae), distinguished by long legs and neck, powerful wings. They are marsh- and plain-haunting birds, feeding on plants as well as insects, small animals, etc., fly well, and are usually migratory. They are found in all parts of the world except S. America. The common C. (*Megalornis grus*) is an occasional visitor to Britain, and is still common in many parts of Europe, and winters in Africa and India. It stands about 4 ft. high and the plumage of the adult bird is grey, varied with black and white, and a red patch of bare skin on the head and neck.

CRANE. Machine for raising, lowering, or placing in position, heavy bodies. The jib C. revolves, and an arm which juts from the base carries the load. The overhead travelling C., which is chiefly used in workshops, is mounted on rails laid on girders.

CRANE-FLY or **Daddy-Long-Legs.** Family of insects (Tipulidae), belonging to the Diptera. They have long, slender, and very fragile legs. The larvae of the typical genus (*Tipula*) are known as 'leatherjackets' and live underground, doing damage to the roots of plants, esp. grasses.

CRANE'S BILL. Plants of the genus *Geranium*, which contains about 300 species and is typical of the family Geraniaceae. They are so called because of the long, beak-like process which is attached to the seed-vessels. When ripe, this splits into spiral, coiling processes which jerk the seeds out, thus assisting in their distribution. The genus incl. 14 British species, including herb-robert (*G. robertianum*) and bloody C. (*G. sanguineum*).

CRANKO, John (1927–). British choreographer. Ed. in Capetown, where he worked with the univ. ballet, he joined Sadler's Wells in 1946 and was resident choreographer 1951-7. His authorship and production of the revue *Cranks* (1952) showed the

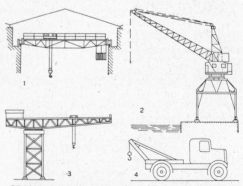

CRANE. *Top left* an overhead travelling model used in the factory to speed mass production; *top right* a portal crane for unloading cargo; *bottom left* cantilever crane essential for the new tall buildings of the modern city and *bottom right* the mobile crane indispensable on any building site.

same liveliness of invention and in 1961 he became ballet director to the Württemberg State Opera, Stuttgart.

CRANMER, Thomas (1489–1556). English churchman. B. in Notts, he went to Cambridge and was ordained a Catholic priest in 1523. In 1529 he suggested that the question of Henry VIII's marriage to Catherine of Aragon should be referred to the universities of Europe, and Henry received him into his favour. In 1530 and 1531 he was sent on foreign embassies, and in 1532 m. a German Lutheran. In 1533 he was appointed Archbishop of Canterbury, declared the King's marriage to Catherine of Aragon null and void, and crowned Anne Boleyn queen.

THOMAS CRANMER
By Gerlach Flicke
Photo: N.P.G.

Having by now adopted Protestant views, he encouraged the translation of the Bible, ordering a copy to be placed in every church, and issued an English litany, the basis of that now in use. Under Edward VI he was responsible for the issue of the Prayer Books of 1549 and 1552, and took a large part in their compilation On Edward's death he supported the movement to place Lady Jane Grey on the throne, and in 1553 was condemned to death for treason. Taken to Oxford, he was tried for heresy, found guilty, excommunicated, and degraded. He signed 6 recantations of his heresies, but when Mary refused to spare his life he repudiated them and was burnt at the stake.

CRASHAW, Richard (1613–49). English religious poet of the metaphysical school. B. in London, he pub. a book of Latin sacred epigrams in 1634. Developing Catholic leanings, he fled to France, and in Paris joined the R.C. Church, and his *Steps to the Temple* appeared in 1646. In 1649 he became sub-canon of the Holy House at Loretto, and d. there of fever or possibly of poison.

CRASSUS, Marcus Licinius (c. 108–53 B.C.). Roman general, statesman, and financier. He crushed the rising of gladiators and slaves under Spartacus in 71, and in 70 became consul with Pompey. In 60 he joined with Caesar and Pompey in the first Triumvirate and in 55 obtained a command in the East. Invading Mesopotamia, he was defeated by the Parthians, captured, and put to death.

CRATER LAKE. *See* CHUBB CRATER.

CRAWFORD, Francis Marion (1854–1909). American novelist. Son of the neo-classical sculptor Thomas C. (1814–57), he aimed solely at entertainment in his many stories which reflect his travels. Many have the background of Italy, where he was born and made his home from 1883, e.g. *A Roman Singer* (1884).

CRAWFORD, Joan (1908–). American actress. B. in Texas, she was originally a dancer, but made her name from 1925 in such strongly dramatic films as *Mildred Pierce* and *Whatever Happened to Baby Jane*.

CRAWFORD, Osbert Guy Stanhope (1886–1957). British archaeologist. He introduced aerial survey as means of finding and interpreting remains, an idea conceived in the F.W.W., and was founder-editor of *Antiquity* from 1927.

CRAWLEY. English town (U.D.) in W. Sussex, 7 m. N.E. of Horsham. A village until chosen in 1946 for development as a new town, it has a 16th cent. inn. Pop. (1961) 53,786.

CRAYFISH. Name given to freshwater crustaceans of the family Astacidae, which closely resemble the lobsters, and like them belong to the division Macrura of the order Decapoda. *Astacus pallipes* is common in rivers and streams in England and Ireland, living in burrows in the mud, and emerging chiefly at night. It is sometimes eaten in England.

The name C. or CRAWFISH is also given by fishermen to a marine Crustacean, the spiny or rock lobster (*Palinurus vulgaris*), which belongs to quite a different family of the Macrura. It is abundant on the S. and W. coasts of Britain; in France it is much valued for the table, and is known as *langouste*.

CREASY, Sir George (1895–). British admiral. In the S.W.W. he directed anti-submarine warfare 1940–2, and largely planned the naval operations of D-Day. He was C.-in-C. Portsmouth, and Allied C.-in-C. Channel Command under N.A.T.O. 1954–7, and in 1955 was promoted Admiral of the Fleet.

CRÉBILLON (krehbē'yoń), **Prosper Jolyot de** (1674–1762). French tragic dramatist. B. at Dijon, his *Idoménée* was produced in 1705, and *Rhadamiste et Zénobie*, his finest play, in 1711. Powerful friends at court advanced him in opposition to Voltaire, and his *Catalina* (1748) was a great success.

CRÉCY-EN-PONTHIEU (krehsē'-oń-pońtyō'). A village in Somme dept., France, about 11 m. N.N.E. of Abbeville, where in 1346 Philip VI of France was defeated by Edward III. Pop. (1962) 1,419.

CREDITON. English agricultural market town (U.D.) on the Creedy in Devon, traditionally the birthplace of St. Boniface. Pop. (1961) 4,422.

CREED, Frederick George (1871–1957). Canadian inventor. B. in Nova Scotia, he came to Britain in 1897 and perfected the teleprinter, or C. telegraphy system, first used in Fleet Street in 1912 and now used in newspaper offices all over the world.

CREEDS (Lat. *credo*, I believe). Name given to the verbal confessions of faith expressing the accepted doctrines of the Christian Church. The oldest is the APOSTLES' CREED, which, though not the work of the apostles, was probably first formulated in the 2nd cent. The full version of the Apostles' Creed, as now given, first appeared about 750. The use of Cs. as a mode of combating heresy was established by the appearance of the NICENE CREED, introduced by the Council of Nicaea in 325, when the Arian heresy was widespread. The Nicene C., as used today, is substantially the same as the version adopted at the Church Council at Constantinople in 381.

The so-called ATHANASIAN CREED is much later in origin than the time of Athanasius (d. 373) although it represents his views in a detailed exposition of the doctrines of the Trinity and the Incarnation. Some authorities suppose it to have been composed in the 8th or 9th cent. but others place it as early as the 4th or 5th cent. The only Creed recognized by the Eastern Orthodox Church is the Nicene.

CREEPER. A family of birds (Certhiidae) of the order Passeriformes, so named from their habit of creeping up the trunks of trees or other upright surfaces in search of insects which harbour in the crannies. Typical representatives are the tree C. (*Certhia familiaris*) and the wall C. (*Tichodroma muraria*).

CREEVEY, Thomas (1768–1838). British politician and diarist. B. at Liverpool, the son of a slave-trader, he entered parliament as a follower of Fox, m. a rich widow, and in 1830 became Treasurer of the Ordnance. His lively letters and journals give information on early 19th cent. society and politics.

CREIGHTON (krīt'on), **Mandell** (1843–1901). Anglican bishop and historian. B. at Carlisle, he became bishop of Peterborough and (1897) of London. His books include *The Age of Elizabeth* (1876), *History of the Papacy during the Reformation*, and a life of Wolsey.

CREMATION. The method of disposing of the dead by burning. The custom was universal among Indo-European peoples, e.g. Greeks, Romans, Teutons, etc., but was discontinued among Christians on account of the belief in the bodily resurrection of the dead. It is practised among primitive and advanced peoples of Asia and America.

C. was revived in Italy about 1870, and shortly afterwards introduced into England. The C. Society was formed in 1874, but it was not until 1885 that C. was legalized and the first crematorium in England was opened at Woking. In 1902 an Act of Parliament was passed, amended in 1952, to regularize C., and to permit burial authorities to establish crematoria, of which there are now 175 in Great Britain.

In the U.K. an application for C. must be accompanied by 2 medical certificates. C. is usually carried out by means of gas-fired furnaces, taking about 1½ hours to complete. Cremated ashes are scattered in Gardens of Remembrance or deposited in urns at the crematorium or in private graves.

The U.K. has the highest C. rate in the world (38·7 per cent), followed by Australia, N.Z., and Scandinavia. C. is also practised in most other European countries, the U.S.A., Rhodesia, South Africa, and Canada.

CRÉMAZIE (krehmahzē´), **Octave** (1827–79). French-Canadian poet. B. at Quebec, in 1862 he emigrated to France, where he d. in poverty. He wrote the patriotic *Chant du vieux soldat canadien* and *Promenade des trois morts.*

CREMO´NA. Italian city, capital of C. prov. in Lombardy, on the Po, 45 m. S.E. of Milan. It has a 12th cent. cathedral, and was a famous violin-making centre. Pop. (1961) 74,242.

CREOLE (krē´ōl). In the West Indies and Spanish America, people of European descent born in the New World; in Louisiana and other states on the Gulf of Mexico, either someone of French or Spanish descent, or (popularly) someone of mixed European and African descent. The French *patois* spoken in Louisiana is also known by this name.

CREOSOTE (krē´-osōt). A constituent of coal-tar and wood-tar used as a preservative and disinfectant.

CRESCENT. Term applied to the curved shape of the moon during its first quarter when its points or horns are seen at the left (in the N. hemisphere). Also applied to any object, symbol, etc., resembling the C. moon. Often associated with Islam, it was first used by the Turks on their standards after the capture of Constantinople in 1453, and appears on the flags of Pakistan and the United Arab Republic.

CRESS. Name given to several plants, mostly belonging to the Cruciferae, and characterized by a pungent taste, but especially to the common garden C. (*Lepidium sativum*). This is cultivated in Europe, N. Africa, and parts of Asia, the young plants being grown along with white mustard to be eaten while in the seed-leaf stage as mustard and cress'.

CRETE (krēt). Large island in the Mediterranean belonging to Greece, lying S.E. of the Greek mainland. Its backbone is a limestone ridge, rising into 4 main mountain groups; snow covers the highest peaks for most of the year. The valleys and lower slopes are very fertile, and produce the usual Mediterranean fruits, etc.

The chief towns are Canea, the capital, on the northern coast; Heraklion (formerly Candia), seat of the abp. of C. and formerly the capital; Rethymnon; and Hierapetra. Most of the people belong to the Eastern Orthodox Church.

Archaeologists have unearthed many traces of early civilization in C. beginning somewhere about 3000 B.C., before which time there are traces of a Neolithic population. Between about 1900 and 1400 B.C. was the flowering time of the Minoan culture, named after the legendary king Minos of Knossos (q.v.). About 1000 B.C. it was overthrown by Dorian invaders from Greece. Subsequent changes in ownership have been many. From 1669 to 1898 C. was under Turkish rule, and in 1913 it was allowed to join Greece.

During the S.W.W. an Allied force of Greek, British, and N.Z. troops under General Freyberg (q.v.) made a desperate stand against German airborne troops, 19 May–1 June 1941. The survivors withdrew to Egypt. Area 3,235 sq. m.; pop. (1961) 482,021.

CREUSE (kröz). River in central France flowing 140 m. generally N. from the Plateau des Millevaches to the Vienne r. It traverses Creuse dept., to which it gives its name. There is a hydro-electric station at Eguzon in Indre dept.

CREUSOT (krözö´), **Le.** Industrial and coal-mining centre in Saône-et-Loire dept., France. It has foundries, locomotive shops, armaments factories, etc. Pop. (1962) 33,779.

CREWE. English industrial town (bor.) in Cheshire, which owes its growth to its position as a railway junction. At C. are the chief construction workshops of British Rlys. Pop. (1961) 53,394.

CRICHTON (krīt´on), **James** (c. 1560–82). Scottish scholar. Commonly called 'the Admirable C.' because of his extraordinary gifts as a poet, scholar, and linguist, he was also an athlete and swordsman. According to one account he was killed at Mantua in a street brawl.

The killer is said to have been C.'s pupil, Vicenzo di Gonzaga, son of the Duke of Mantua, whose enmity had been aroused by his master's popularity.

CRICK, Francis (1916–   ). British molecular biologist. During the S.W.W. he worked on the development of radar, but from 1949 did research into DNA (deoxyribo-nucleic acid) at the Cavendish Laboratory, Cambridge. For his discoveries as to its molecular structure (the means whereby characteristics are transmitted from one generation to another), he was awarded a Nobel prize (with Maurice Wilkins of Harvard and John D. Watson of London) in 1962. He pub. *Of Molecules and Men* (1966).

CRICKET. Name applied to insects of the family Gryllidae, which are allied to the grasshoppers and like them belong to the order Orthoptera or Saltatoria. They have long, slender antennae, and the males make a chirping note by rubbing together their wing-cases, which are provided with special stridulating organs, the purpose being to attract the females. The latter have a long ovipositor, and the males, also, are provided with special organs for transferring the sperm to the female. They are typically subterranean insects, but the most familiar species, the house C. (*Gryllus domesticus*), about ½ in. long, is common in old houses and bakehouses in the Old and New Worlds. The field C. (*G. campestris*) is larger and darker, and lives in burrows in the ground;

CRICKET. Sir Donald Bradman (left) and W. G. Grace, two of the greatest batsmen of all time.

the American *G. assimilis* closely resembles it.

CRICKET. England's national summer game, played in the open air with bat and ball. Its origin is obscure, but some form of bat and ball game has been played since the 13th cent. In 1711 Kent played All England, and in 1735 a match was played between teams chosen by the Prince of Wales and the Earl of Middlesex. The Hambledon Club at Broad-Halfpenny Down in Hampshire was the first to be formed, in 1750. The Marylebone Cricket Club (M.C.C.) was established in Thomas Lord's ground in Dorset Square in 1787, and in 1814 it moved to St. John's Wood. Since then it has been the controlling authority, and its ground the acknowledged H.Q. of the game.

The rules of the game have been changed from time to time. At first the wicket consisted of only 2 stumps, first without, then with a single bail. The third stump was introduced in the middle of the 18th cent. The first rules of the game were drawn up in 1774. Only underhand bowling was allowed at first, but over-arm bowling was introduced in 1865. The game is played between 2 sides of 11 men each. Wickets are pitched at 22 yards apart. A batsman stands at each wicket and the object of the game is to score more runs than do the opponents. The bowler bowls to the batsman a stipulated number of balls (usually 6), after which another bowler bowls from the other wicket. A run is normally scored by the batsman after striking the ball, exchanging ends with his partner, or by hitting the ball to the boundary line for an automatic 4 runs. A batsman is usually got out by being (1) bowled; (2) caught; (3) run out; (4) stumped; (5) l.b.w. – when the ball hits his leg which is placed before the wicket. Games comprise either one or two innings per team.

Every year series of Test Matches are played among member countries of the Commonwealth, where the game has its greatest popularity: Australia, India, N.Z., Pakistan, U.K., and W. Indies; S. Africa, outside the Commonwealth from 1961, participated till 1968. *See* ASHES. In Britain there is a County Championship Table (1850), and a County Knock-Out Competition for the Gillette Cup. The Eton v Harrow (1805, in which Lord Byron played) and Oxford v Cambridge (1827) matches are social occasions.

Famous grounds, besides Lord's, incl. Kennington Oval, Old Trafford (Manchester), the Melbourne Ground and Sydney Oval (Australia); and the Wanderers' Ground (Johannesburg). Great cricketers have incl. W. G. Grace, Sir Jack Hobbs, W. R. Hammond, and Sir Len Hutton; the Australian Sir Don Bradman; the Indian K. S. Ranjitsinhji; the South African A. D. Nourse; and the West Indians Sir Leary Constantine, Sir Frank Worrell and Gary Sobers.

The game has suffered some diminution of popularity in recent years because of the growth of defensive tactics and the number of drawn games, and there have been moves to amend the rules.

CRIEFF (krēf). Small Scottish burgh and health resort on the r. Earn, Perthshire, with tanneries. Pop. (1961) 5,773.

CRIMEA. Peninsula on the N. shore of the Black Sea, forming a region of Ukraine S.S.R. Most of its surface is steppe, but the Kerch peninsula on the E. is rich in iron ore and petroleum is worked. The southern coastal strip has a Mediterranean climate and a fertile soil, making it a favourite health resort. The cap. is Simferopol. Sevastopol is a great port and naval base. Smaller places are Yevpatoria, Feodosia, Kerch, and Yalta, scene of an Allied conference in 1945.

At an early period the C. was colonized by the Greeks; overrun later by successive invaders, it was Turkish 1475–1774, then independent until seized by Russia in 1783. It was the republic of Taurida 1917–20, C. A.S.S.R. of the R.S.F.S.R. 1920–44. The Germans occupied it July 1942–May 1944; its Tatar inhabitants were afterwards deported for alleged collaboration (exonerated 1967) and it was reduced to the rank of a region, first of the R.S.F.S.R., from 1954 of Ukraine. Area 23,312 sq. m. Pop. (est.) 2,250,000.

CRIMEAN WAR (1854–6). The war arose nominally from a disagreement over the custody of the Holy Places at Jerusalem, actually from British and French mistrust of Russia's ambitions in the Balkans. Hostilities began in 1853 with a Russian invasion of the Balkans (whence they were compelled to withdraw by Austrian intervention) and the sinking of the Turkish fleet at Sinope. Britain and France declared war on Russia in 1854, and were joined in 1855 by Sardinia. The main military operations were the invasion of the Crimea, the siege of Sevastopol (Sept. 1854–Sept. 1855), and the battles of the Alma, Balaclava, and Inkerman, fought in 1854. The French lost 62,500 men, the British 19,600 – 15,700 of them by disease, a scandalous state of affairs that led to the organization of proper military nursing services by Florence Nightingale (q.v.)

CRIMINAL APPEAL, Court of. In England and Wales a court constituted under the Criminal Appeal Act of 1907 (amended 1908) and consisting of the Lord Chief Justice as president, and all the judges of the Queen's Bench Division. A similar court was estab. for Scotland in 1926.

CRIMINAL INJURIES COMPENSATION BOARD. In Britain the board estab. in 1964 to admin. the govt. scheme for compensation of victims of crimes of violence.

CRIMINAL INVESTIGATION DEPARTMENT (New Scotland Yard). Detective branch of the London Metropolitan Police, estab. in 1878, and comprising a force of 1,600 men, which is recruited entirely from the uniformed police and controlled by an Assistant Commissioner.

Some 600 men are stationed at New Scotland Yard, where are housed: the *Central Office*, which deals with international offences and serious crimes in London and the provinces, and controls the Flying Squad; the *Criminal Intelligence Department*, which studies criminals and their methods; the *Fingerprint Department*, which contains *c*. 1,750,000 prints of convicted persons; the *Criminal Record Office*, which has information on all known criminals, and pub. the 'Police Gazette' and a pawn list daily; the *Scientific Laboratory*, which also serves police forces in the Home Counties; the *Stolen Car Squad*; and the *Special Branch*, which deals with offences against the State. The remaining 1,000 detectives are stationed locally in the Metropolitan Police District. *See* SCOTLAND YARD.

CRIMINAL LAW. It is distinguished from Civil Law, which redresses the private wrong of the individual, by being the attempt of the State to preserve public order, at first by limitation of private vengeance, and later exclusively by state-inflicted punishment.

Prior to the Norman Conquest, machinery for the enforcement of C.L. was rudimentary, and rested on the organization of the local territorial unit, e.g. the hundred. The principal court was the shire court, at which the freemen of the county were represented, and in which the law was declared from oral tradition. The main tendency of Saxon times was to extend money penalties for all offences, except for those that were *botless*, for example, murder, arson, rape.

After the Conquest the Saxon conception of the king's peace, at first limited to the vicinity of the king's person, was extended to include the whole kingdom, and offences against this, together with the crimes that were *botless*, form the basis of modern C.L. Under Henry II more modern procedure was introduced into C.L. by the institution of a formal 'presentation' of persons suspected of felonies, i.e. homicide, treason, arson, before a grand jury, and their ultimate trial before one of the king's justices. Lesser offences or misdemeanours were for a time dealt with by the county courts, and later by the Justices of the Peace. The distinction between felonies and misdemeanours was afterwards lost, when, owing to the extreme penalties inflicted for the former, new crimes created by statute were commonly placed in the latter class.

Early law does not differentiate sharply between offences which are committed intentionally and those which cannot be attributed in law to the doer, but today the first test of criminal liability is guilty intention. This may be affected by the accused being an infant, e.g. it is presumed that no child under 14 may have guilty intention; by insanity; irresistible impulse (admitted as a defence in some states of America, although not in England); drunkenness (generally no excuse to a criminal charge, and sometimes an aggravation); necessity (apparently no defence in English C.L.); duress, i.e. coercion, or the threat of it.

During the last cent., however, a great many minor offences have been created by legislation which may be crimes of absolute liability, i.e. offences committed independent of any question of intention, e.g. selling adulterated food; or impose vicarious liability on certain persons, e.g. a publican is liable if his servant permits any unlawful game on licensed premises.

In the U.S.A. each of the States has its own individual body of C.L., but these have a common origin in English practice.

CRIMINOLOGY. The study of crime in its various forms; of its causation and prevention; of the types of individuals who commit crimes; and of the methods used in studying these problems. C. as an independent branch of scientific study dates from the first half of the 19th cent, but criminologic research remained a comparatively little-developed field in Britain until the continued increase of crime in the years following the S.W.W. prompted the endowment of an Institute of C. at Cambridge Univ. in 1959 by the Isaac Wolfson Foundation.

CRINOI′DĒA. Class of Echinoderms mainly known as feather-stars and sea-lilies. They are distinguished from the other living members of the phylum by being fixed by a stalk for at least part of their existence. The majority are known only as fossils.

CRIPPEN, Henry Hawley (1861–1910). British murderer. He killed his wife, variety artist Belle Elmore, and tried to burn the remains, but finally buried them in the cellar of his house in Hilldrop Crescent, Islington, London. Trying to escape to the U.S.A., with his mistress Ethel le Neve (dressed as a boy), he was arrested on board ship following a radio message to the captain. He was the first criminal captured 'by radio', and was executed at Pentonville.

CRIPPS, Sir (Richard) Stafford (1889–1952). British Labour statesman. The youngest son of the 1st baron Parmoor and Theresa Potter, sister of Beatrice Webb, he was called to the Bar in 1913, and during the F.W.W. served with the Red Cross in France, and later ran an explosives factory. Knighted in 1930, he was Solicitor-General in the MacDonald govt. and was elected a Labour M.P. in 1931. During the 1930s he became, as leader of the Socialist League, which he helped to found, an outstanding figure in the left wing of the Labour Party but was expelled from the latter in 1939 for supporting the proposal for a 'Popular Front' of all opposed to the Chamberlain appeasement policy, and was not re-admitted until 1945. In 1940 he was appointed British ambassador to Moscow and did much to improve Anglo-Soviet relations during a difficult period. On his return in 1942 he became Lord Privy Seal and Leader of the House of Commons, and shortly afterwards went to India to put forward proposals for a solution of the constitutional deadlock, but without success. From 1942 to 1945 he was Min. of Aircraft Production, and in the Attlee govt. made great efforts to curb inflation while Chancellor of the Exchequer from 1947 until his resignation for health reasons in 1950.

CRISPI, Francesco (1819–1901). Italian statesman. He took part in the Sicilian revolution of 1848 and in Mazzinian conspiracies, and organized Garibaldi's Sicilian expedition of 1860. In later life he abandoned his republican views, and as Prime Minister 1887–91 and 1893–6 relied on the right-wing parties for support.

CRITCHLEY, Alfred Cecil (1890–1963) Canadian soldier. B. in Calgary, and ed. in England, he served with the 1st Canadian Division and the R.F.C. in the F.W.W., and in 1939 became Air Commodore R.A.F.V.R., organizing the initial training of R.A.F. aircrews until 1943. He also opened Britain's 1st greyhound track at Manchester in 1926.

CRIVE′LLI, Carlo (c. 1430–c. 1493). Italian artist. B. in Venice, probably the son of a painter, he fled from his native city after a sentence for rape. His numerous paintings of sacred subjects are sharply defined and often incl. swags of realistic fruit.

CROATIA (krō-ā′shia). Federal republic of Yugoslavia. It has a long coastline on the Adriatic with the r. Drava forming its eastern boundary. Although the majority of the pop. is engaged in agriculture, coal, iron, and other minerals are mined, and there are various industries. The people are mainly Serbs and Croats (nearly 90 per cent), and about 75 per cent are R.C., most of the remainder being Greek Orthodox. Zagreb is the cap., other towns are Rijeka, Split, Dubrovnik, Zadar.

C. was in Roman times part of Pannonia, but in the 7th cent. was settled by Carpathian Croats. From 1102 it was for 800 years an autonomous kingdom under the Hungarian Crown. An Austrian crownland 1849, a Hungarian crownland 1868, it was included in the kingdom of the Serbs, Croats, and Slovenes (called Yugoslavia from 1931) in 1918. Area 21,720 sq. m. Pop. (1961) 4,148,122.

CRIVELLI. Detail, head of the Virgin, from the Demidoff altarpiece.
Courtesy of the National Gallery.

CROCE(krō′cheh),**Benedetto** (1866–1952). Italian philosopher. B. in the Abruzzi, he studied at Rome Univ. and continued as a private scholar in Naples. He was Min. of Public Instruction 1920–1, but the gradual hardening of his opposition to Fascism prevented his holding further office until he was briefly Min. without portfolio in Badoglio's cabinet in 1944. He was, however, allowed to pub. his journal *La Critica*, which he founded in 1903, and continued from 1945 as *Quaderni della Critica*.

C. like Hegel held that ideas do not *represent* reality but *are* reality; but unlike his master he rejected every kind of transcendence. For C. immediate experience generates whatever is, and ultimate reality is the active, changing, self-creative spirit. The bulk of his work consists of a detailed application of his theory of art as the expression of the creative mind. Nothing exists but present Mind, which is the product of the past and is greatly modified by its understanding of the past. In this sense all reality is history, and all knowledge is historical knowledge.

CROCKETT, Davy (1786–1836). American folk-hero. Tennessee-born, he was a Congressman (Democrat) 1827–31 and 1833–5. A series of books, of which he may have been part-author, made him into a mythical hero of the frontier, but their Whig associations cost him his office. He d. defending the Alamo during the war for Texan independence.

CROCKETT, Samuel Rutherford (1860–1914). Scottish novelist. Son of a Galloway farmer, he took orders in the Free Church, but later devoted himself

CROCODILE
Courtesy of the South African Information Service.

to novel writing, gaining success with *The Stickit Minister* (1893).

CROCKFORD, John. Managing clerk to Edward Cox, Sergeant-at-Law, who pub. in Britain in 1858 the 1st edition of *Crockford's Clerical Directory*, and who preferred to use his clerk's name because of his own official position, It has been pub. since 1921 by the Oxford University Press, and the anonymous prefaces have estab. an influential tradition.

CROCKFORD, William (1775–1844). British gambler. Son of a fishmonger, he founded in 1827 C.'s Club in St. James's Street, which became the fashionable place for London society to gamble.

CROCODILE. Name given to reptiles of the order Crocodilia, and esp. to that section which includes the genera *Crocodylus* and *Osteolaemus*, distinguished from the alligators and caimans by their short, triangular or rounded snout, and a notch in the upper jaw into which the 4th tooth in the lower jaw fits. There are about a dozen known species, found in the tropical regions of Africa, Asia, Australasia, and Central America. The largest is the salt-water or estuarine C. (*Crocodylus porosus*), which ranges from the eastern shores of India, through the Malay Region, to N. and E. Australia, New Guinea, and the Fiji Is. Lengths of 20 ft. or over are not uncommon. The Nile C. (*C. niloticus*) ranges from the Upper Nile to the Cape, incl. Madagascar.

The members of the order Crocodilia are distinguished by their more or less ponderous, lizard-like form, short legs and amphibious habits.

Cs. are generally sluggish when on land, but can move with considerable speed when alarmed. They are largely nocturnal, and wholly carnivorous, and will not hesitate to attack man. All the Crocodilia are oviparous; their eggs are relatively small and are covered with a hard, white shell.

CROCUS. Genus of plants of the family Iridaceae, natives of the N. parts of the Old World, esp. S. Europe and Asia Minor. During the dry season of the year they remain underground in the form of a 'corm', and produce fresh shoots and flowers in spring or autumn. At the end of the season of growth fresh corms are produced. Several species are cultivated as garden plants, the familiar mauve, white and orange forms being varieties of *C. vernus*, *C.*

versicolor, and *C. aureus*. To the same genus belongs the saffron (*C. sativus*). The so-called autumn C. or meadow saffron (*Colchicum*) is not a true C., but belongs to the Liliaceae.

CROESUS (krē'sus) (d. *c.* 546 B.C.). Last king of Lydia. He secured dominion over the Greek cities of Asia Minor, and welcomed at his court their wise men, among them Solon, the Athenian lawgiver, who warned him that no man could be called happy till his life had ended happily. Later C. was overthrown by Cyrus the Persian and condemned to be burnt to death. When on the pyre, he called three times the name of Solon; and Cyrus, having learnt the reason, was moved to spare his life. *See* NUMISMATICS.

CROFTS, Freeman Wills (1879–1957). Irish writer. B. in Dublin, he was a railway engineer until 1929, but pub. the first of many detective novels, *The Cask*, in 1919. He was precisely detailed in his settings and his detective, Inspector French, was a member of the British regular force.

CROKER, John Wilson (1780–1857). British Tory politician and writer. B. at Galway, he entered parliament in 1807, and was secretary to the Admiralty 1810–30. He regularly contributed to the *Quarterly Review* for many years; the best-known example of his criticism is his brutal attack on Keats's *Endymion*. He fiercely opposed the Reform Bill, and refused to sit in parliament after it was passed.

CROKER, Richard (1841–1922). American politician, known as 'Boss C.' B. in Co. Cork, he was taken to New York in infancy and there became 'Boss' of Tammany Hall, the notorious political organization of the Democratic Party (1886–1902).

Accused of every crime from corruption to murder, he was only once in prison, and lived from 1900 in retirement in England.

CROMAGNON (kroman'yoṅ). Name given to a race of prehistoric man, the first skeletons of whom were found in 1868 in the C. cave near Les Eyzies, in the Dordogne region of France. They are supposed to have been negroid and rather larger in build than modern man, and to have been possessed of considerable artistic gifts.

CRO'MARTY. *See* ROSS AND CROMARTY.

CROME, John (1768–1821). British artist, known as Old Crome. B. at Norwich, the son of a journeyman weaver, he was apprenticed to a housepainter. In his spare time he drew from nature, his work showing Dutch influence, and in 1803 founded the Norwich Society. Chiefly using oils, he also produced watercolours and etchings, and is important in the development of English landscape art. His most important

CROME. 'Back of the New Mills, Norwich', which is now in the Castle Museum of the city, probably dates from the period 1806–1814. In his work can be seen the transition from 18th century picturesque to 19th century romantic.

pictures incl. 'Mousehold Heath' (National Gallery), 'The Poringland Oak', and 'Carrow Abbey'.

CROMER, Evelyn Baring, 1st earl of (1841–1917). British statesman. A member of the banking family of Baring, he was appointed British commissioner of the Egyptian public debt office in 1877, and then financial member of the Viceroy of India's council in 1880. He returned to Egypt in 1883 as British agent and consul-general, and until his resignation in 1907 remained the real ruler of the country.

CROMER. Seaside resort (U.D.) and fishing port on the cliffs of Norfolk, 24 m. N. of Norwich. Pop. (1961) 4,895.

CROMLECH (krom′lek). A prehistoric burial-chamber, consisting of 2 or more upright stone slabs, on top of which a flat stone is placed as a roof. A well-known example is Kit's Coty House, near Aylesford, Kent.

CROMPTON, Richmal. Pseudonym of the British author R. C. Lamburn (1890–1969). B. in Lancs, and formerly a teacher, she is best known for her scape-grace schoolboy creation 'William'.

CROMPTON, Rookes Evelyn (1845–1940). British electrical engineer, founder of R. E. Crompton & Co., now Crompton Parkinson Ltd. He estab. the International Electrotechnical Commission (1906) to resolve problems of standardization, and was a pioneer in electric lighting and in public electricity supply.

CROMPTON, Samuel (1753–1827). British inventor. B. in Lancs, he invented in 1779 the 'spinning mule', an improved version of Hargreaves' spinning-jenny. His contribution to the supremacy of British manufactures was inadequately rewarded, and he d. in comparative poverty.

CROMWELL, Oliver (1599–1658). English soldier and statesman. B. at Huntingdon, the son of a small landowner, he was ed. at the local grammar school and at Cambridge. He represented Huntingdon in the parliament of 1628–9, and Cambridge in the Short Parliament of 1640, and the Long Parliament. Active in the events leading to the Civil War, he raised a troop of horse with which he did good work at Edgehill. After this experience he worked with the Eastern Association, raising more cavalry forces. These were chiefly responsible for the victory at Marston Moor in 1644, being called 'Ironsides' by Prince Rupert. By 1645, C. was the only member of either House allowed to retain his commission. The New Model Army was now raised, and under Fairfax and C. inflicted a decisive defeat on the royalists at Naseby.

Throughout 1646–8 C. worked to secure a constitutional settlement with the king acceptable to all parties. The 2nd Civil War of 1648, during which C. defeated a Scottish invasion at Preston, ended all hopes of a compromise; the army purged parliament of its Presbyterian right wing, a special commission, of which C. was a member, tried the king and condemned him to death, the monarchy and House of Lords were abolished, and a republic was set up. The democratic party or Levellers wished to go further, but in 1649 C. suppressed them and executed their leaders. During 1649–50 he crushed the resistance of the Irish clans and their royalist allies by terrorist methods. He then turned on the Scots, who had acknowledged Charles Ii, defeated them at Dunbar on 3 Sept. 1650, and a year later ended their attempt to invade England at Worcester.

In 1653 C. forcibly expelled the 'Rump' parliament,

OLIVER CROMWELL
After Samuel Cooper.
Photo: N.P.G.

whose corruption was discrediting the republic, and summoned a convention known as 'Barebone's Parliament', which was soon dissolved as too radical. Under a constitution drawn up by the army leaders, the Instrument of Government, C. assumed the title of Protector, with almost royal powers. A parliament which met in 1654–5 proved refractory; it was dissolved, and a period of military dictatorship followed. C.'s last parliament, that of 1657–8, offered him the crown, which only fear of the army's republicanism restrained him from accepting. His greatest achievement as a ruler was the broad, though not complete, system of religious toleration he established. His foreign policy restored English prestige, but its whole basis, of an alliance with France against Spain, was anachronistic. He d. at Whitehall on 3 Sept. 1658; his body was buried in Westminster Abbey, whence it was removed in 1661.

His eldest surviving son **Richard Cromwell** (1626–1712) succeeded him as Protector, but resigned in May 1659. After the Restoration he lived in exile until 1680, and subsequently in retirement in England. C.'s 4th son **Henry Cromwell** (1628–74) served in the Irish campaign and ruled Ireland 1655–9 with considerable success.

CROMWELL, Thomas, earl of Essex (c. 1485–1540). English statesman. B. at Putney, he entered Wolsey's service in 1514, and after his fall transferred to that of Henry VIII. He soon won his new master's favour, and from 1534 acted as royal secretary and the real director of government policy. Aiming at the establishment of an absolute monarchy unchecked by Church or parliament, he had Henry proclaimed head of the Church, suppressed the monasteries, ruthlessly crushed all opposition, and favoured Protestantism, which upheld the divine right of kings against the divine right of the Pope. The failure of Henry's marriage to Anne of Cleves, which C. arranged in 1539 to cement an alliance with the German Protestant princes against France and the Empire, brought about his downfall. In 1540, shortly after being created earl of Essex, he was accused of treason, attainted, and beheaded.

CRONIN, Archibald Joseph (1896–). British novelist. B. in Scotland, he practised as a doctor, and then in 1930 settled to creative writing. *Hatter's Castle* (1931), the story of a tradesman's lust for power, was immediately successful: later books incl. *The Citadel* (1937), exposing the methods of certain 'society doctors'. He is also the creator of 'Dr Finlay's Case-book', celebrated television series.

CRONJE (krõn′ye), **Piet Arnoldus** (c. 1840–1911). Boer general in the South African War of 1899–1902. In 1899 he besieged Mafeking and defeated Gatacre at Magersfontein, but early in 1900 he was surrounded by Kitchener's force near Paardeberg, and forced to surrender with 4,000 men.

CROOKES, Sir William (1832–1919). British scientist. B. in London, he was from 1856 engaged on scientific research. Among his many chemical and physical discoveries were the metal thallium (1861), the radiometer (1875), and C.'s high vacuum tube used in X-ray techniques. He was an authority on town sewage disposal, and interested in other problems, including dyeing and printing, artificial manures, and spiritualism (q.v.). Elected F.R.S. in 1863, he was awarded the O.M. in 1910.

CROQUET (krō′ke). Open-air game played with mallets and balls on a level grass lawn not less than 30 yd. long by 20 yd. wide. Two or more players try to drive the balls through a series of hoops set to a pattern on the ground, leading to the winning peg. During the game a player may have his ball advanced by his partner or retarded by his opponent. These conflicts are the chief interest of the game. C. was played in France (16th–17th cent.), and was popular in England during the 1850s, before being superseded by lawn tennis (c. 1875); but from the 1950s showed signs of revival.

CROSBY, Harry Lillis (1904–). American singer, known as 'Bing' C. B. at Tacoma, Washington, he started singing with dance bands in 1925 and achieved world success with such songs as *Pennies from Heaven, Blue Skies, White Christmas, The Bells of St. Mary's –* which were featured in films with the same titles. He also made a series of 'road' film comedies with Dorothy Lamour and Bob Hope, the last being *Road to Hong Kong*.

CROSS, Henri-Edmond. Pseudonym of the French Neo-Impressionist artist Henri Delacroix (1856–1910). His use of brilliant colour and solid form influenced Matisse and Fauvism (qq.v.).

CROSS (Lat. *crux*). Stake used in ancient times as an instrument of punishment; particularly, the C. on which Christ was crucified. It was commonly used by the Carthaginians, and the Romans employed it as a means of executing malefactors of the lowest class. The simplest form of cross (*crux simplex*) is an upright stake, without the transverse bar, on which criminals were bound or nailed. The form of C. best known in the West is the Latin cross, or *crux immissa*, which has a transverse bar fixed towards the top of the upright stake. The *crux commissa* or C. of St. Anthony has the transverse bar at the top of the stake. St. Andrew's C., or *crux decussata*, is formed of 2 diagonal beams, and the C. of St. George or Greek C. of equal upright and horizontal beams, intersecting at the centre.

The C. is the recognized symbol of the Christian faith, but long before the Christian era it was used as a religious emblem or for ornamental purposes. Traditionally, St. Helena, Constantine's mother, discovered the C. on which Christ was crucified when she made a pilgrimage to Jerusalem in 326.

CROSSBILL. Genus of birds (*Loxia*) of the finch family, distinguished by the crossed tips of the bill. This peculiar formation enables the C. to lever up the scales of pine cones and scoop out the seeds with its tongue. The common C. (*L. curvirostra*) of Europe also breeds in the Scottish Highlands and visits other parts of Britain; the adult male is orange crimson and the female and young are greenish. The smaller-billed *L.c. minor* is an American species, as is the rose-coloured *L. leucoptera*.

CROSSMAN, Richard (1907–). British Labour politician. Fellow and tutor of New Coll., Oxford, 1930–7, he entered Parliament in 1945. A 'Bevanite' (*see* ANEURIN BEVAN), he consistently opposed the Labour Party's official defence policy, and in 1960 left the shadow cabinet following a disagreement on this with Gaitskell, returning in 1963. He was Min. of Housing and Local Govt. 1964–6, Min. of Health and Social Security 1968–70, and editor of the *New Statesman* 1970–72.

CROSSWORD. Short for a crossword puzzle, consisting of a diagram divided with squares, some of which are cancelled, but the remainder are numbered and have to be filled in with the letters of words of which numbered clues ('down' and 'across') are given at the side. The modern vogue dates from 1923, when Cs. became very popular in U.S.A. and soon after in Britain.

CROUP. An obsolete name for diphtheria; but spasmodic croup is a distinct disease in which a child suffers frequent attacks of severe breathlessness. Treatment of the attack is by warm and cold bathing, but the cause is probably nervous.

CROW. Bird of the genus *Corvus* which also incl. the raven, rook and jackdaw, in the family Corvidae. The carrion C. (*C. corone*), resident in Britain, is wholly black, without the patch of bare white skin at the base of the bill which marks the rook – it is also less gregarious and more carnivorous. It is highly intelligent and sometimes destructive. The hooded or grey C. (*C. cornix*) takes its place in Ireland and parts of Scotland. The American C. (*C. brachyrhynchos*) is rather smaller.

CROWFOOT. Name applied to plants of the genus *Ranunculus*. Of this genus, some members are terrestrial, and have yellow flowers, while others are aquatic, and have white flowers, with only a touch of yellow at the base of the petals. In the former are included the buttercup, lesser celandine, and spearwort. The celery leaved C. (*R. sceleratus*) is a large annual, inhabiting ditches and pond-sides, the corn C. (*R. arvensis*) is found in cornfields. The water C. (*R. aquatilis*) has 3-lobed floating leaves with dentate margins, and thread-like submerged leaves.

CROWN. An official head-dress worn by a king or queen. The modern C. originated with the diadem, an embroidered fillet worn by eastern rulers, for which a golden band was later substituted. A laurel C. was granted by the Greeks to a victor in the games, and by the Romans to a triumphant general. Cs. came into use among the Byzantine emperors and the barbarian kings after the fall of the Western Empire. Perhaps the oldest in Europe is the Iron C. of Lombardy, made in 591. The C. of Charlemagne, preserved at Vienna, consists of 8 gold plates.

Before the Conquest kings of England certainly wore Cs., and from the Conquest to the Commonwealth each king had two Cs. The old regalia was broken up under the Commonwealth, and a new set had to be made after the Restoration. *See* REGALIA.

CROWN AGENTS FOR OVERSEAS GOVERNMENTS AND ADMINISTRATIONS. The officially appointed business and financial agents in the U.K. for many govts. (inside and outside the Commonwealth) and public authorities, incl. the U.N. The office originated in 1833 under the title C.A. for the colonies, and was assimilated to the Civil Service in 1909, though not forming part of it. Self-supporting, its funds are drawn from fees charged to clients.

CROWN COLONIES. British colonies which are under the direct legislative control of the Crown, and do not possess their own systems of fully responsible or representative government. They are administered either by a Crown-appointed governor or by elected or nominated legislative and executive councils with an official majority. Usually the Crown retains rights of veto and of direct legislation by orders in Council.

CROWN COURTS. Courts estab. under the Criminal Justice Administration Act in 1956 in Liverpool and Manchester, for Quarter Sessions and Assize Court work. *See also* LAW COURTS.

CROWN JEWELS. *See* REGALIA.

CROWN PROCEEDINGS ACT. An Act of Parliament passed in 1947 providing that, as from 1 Jan. 1948, the Crown (i.e. Government departments, etc.) may be sued like a private person.

CROWTHER, Geoffrey, baron (1907–72). British economist. Editor of *The Economist* (1938–56), he pub. *Ways and Means* (1936), *An Outline of Money* (1941), etc., and was created a Life Peer 1968.

CROYDON. Bor. of Greater London from 1965. Lanfranc's palace (11th cent.), residence of the Archbishops of Canterbury until c. 1750, survives in part. The Peggy Ashcroft (q.v.) Theatre was opened 1962. Opened 1920, C. airport was once one of the world's busiest: closed 1959. Office development to relieve congestion in central London has led to rapid growth. Pop. (1967) 328,290.

CRUCIFERAE (kroosi'ferē). Family of dicotyledonous flowering plants, so called because of the cross-like arrangement of their four petals. They are annuals or biennials, and comprise about 220 genera and 1,000–2,000 species.

CRUCIFIX (kroo'sifiks). A cross, or a representation of a cross, with the image of Christ on it.

CRUDEN (krōō'den), **Alexander** (1701–70). Scottish scholar who became a bookseller in London, and was the author of *The Complete Concordance of the Holy Scriptures*, first pub. in 1737. For much of his life he was mentally unbalanced.

CRUFT, Charles (1852–1938). British dog expert. He organized his first dog show in 1886, and henceforward annual shows were held in Islington – Cruft's being the premier event of the dog year in Britain.

CRUIKSHANK (krook'-), **George** (1792–1878). British caricaturist, painter and illustrator. B. in London, he illustrated children's books when still a youth, and at 19 began to contribute satirical drawings to periodicals. He owed much to Gillray for his mastery of technique, but his cartoons were not so coarse as those of his contemporary. His best-known illustrations include those for Dickens's *Oliver Twist*, and *Sketches by Boz*; *The Ingoldsby Legends*; Ainsworth's *Tower of London*, and works by Fielding, Smollett, and Sterne. He was an ardent teetotaller, and his oil-painting, 'The Worship of Bacchus', now in the National Gallery, illustrates the evils of drink.

CRUISER. *See* WARSHIP.

CRUSADES. The wars undertaken 1096–1291 to recover the Holy Land from the Moslems. The term was also applied to wars undertaken, with the blessing of the Church, against the Spanish Moors, the Baltic pagans, heretics, and excommunicated princes. The motives combining to produce them included religious zeal, the territorial ambitions of feudal princes, and the desire of the Italian cities to secure trading bases. The 1st CRUSADE 1095–9 was occasioned by the conquest of Asia Minor and the capture of Jerusalem by the Seljuk Turks; it resulted in the recovery of Jerusalem and the establishment of a chain of Latin kingdoms along the Syrian coast. The 2nd CRUSADE 1147–9, led by Louis VII of France and the Emperor Conrad III, was a complete failure. The 3rd CRUSADE 1189–92, led by Philip Augustus of France and Richard I of England, failed to recapture Jerusalem, which had fallen to Saladin in 1187. The 4th CRUSADE 1202–4, originally intended for Egypt, was diverted against Constantinople by the intrigues of Venice; the city was sacked, and its empire divided among the crusaders. The 5th CRUSADE 1218–21, again directed towards Egypt, captured Damietta only to lose it again. The 6th CRUSADE 1228–9 was led by the Emperor Frederick II, himself under excommunication at the time, who recovered Jerusalem from the Sultan of Egypt by negotiation. The city was finally lost in 1244. The 7th CRUSADE 1249–54 and the 8th CRUSADE 1270–2 were both led by Louis IX of France, with whom in the latter was associated Edward I of England. Acre, the last Christian fortress in Syria, was lost in 1291.

CRUSTACEA (krustā'shia). Class of animals in the phylum Arthropoda, comprising the crabs, lobsters, crayfish, prawns, and shrimps, besides a very large number of less familiar forms. The name is derived from the Lat., *crusta*, a shell or crust, as the stiff outer skin of chitin is further strengthened by lime salts, and forms a covering of shelly plates. C. are mostly aquatic and often develop by metamorphosis. The class is divided into 5 sub-classes: Branchiopoda, including certain shrimps and waterfleas; Ostracoda, minute forms with the body completely enclosed in a bivalved shell; Copepoda, minute forms with a simple unpaired eye and paddle-like two-branched feet; Cirripedia, the barnacles and acorn shells; and Malacostraca, comprising all the larger and better-known examples of the class, with the body divided into two regions, and the appendages sharply distinguished. Each of these sub-classes is further sub-divided into orders.

In point of size the C. have, probably, a greater range than any other of the major divisions of the animal kingdom, varying from less than one hundredth of an inch to as much as 11 ft.

Most of the C. live in sea water and are found all

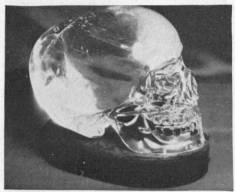

CRYSTAL. It may have taken 150 years to rub down with sand this 'skull of doom', reputed to be 3,600 years old. According to Maya legend, when a wise man grew too old he and an intelligent youth were laid together on the altar before the skull, and the High Priest performed a ceremony willing the elder man to die, his knowledge passing to the younger.
Courtesy of Miss A. Mitchell-Hedges.

over the world. There are a few terrestrial species, but most of these breed in water. The most familiar of the terrestrial C. are the woodlice, whose whole life is spent on the land.

Some varieties such as crabs, lobsters, etc., serve as human food, but the importance of the Cs. lies in the part they play in the 'food-chains' in the sea.

CRYOGENICS (krī-ōjen'iks). The science of very low temperatures (approaching the absolute zero) and its applications. C. includes the production of these low temperatures, the liquefaction of gases such as nitrogen, helium, hydrogen, etc. Most substances have peculiar properties at these low temperatures which in recent years have been exploited. These include the disappearance of electrical resistance (superconductivity) and the application of this phenomenon to the production of very intense magnetic fields, masers such as that used in connection with Telstar, and high-speed switching devices for computers.

CRYSTAL. Nearly all known substances, organic and inorganic, natural or artificial are crystalline; that is, they possess directional properties and their ultimate structure is a highly symmetrical arrangement of electrically-bonded atoms or molecules. A crystalline substance often grows with the characteristic shape of a geometrical solid called a crystal, which is bounded by plane surfaces termed 'faces'. Each geometrical figure or form, many of which may be combined in one crystal, consists of 2 or more faces, e.g., dome, prism, pyramid, etc. A mineral can often be identified by the shape of its crystals and the system of crystallization determined. A single crystal can vary in size from a sub-microscopic particle to a huge mass some hundred feet in length.

CRYSTALLO'GRAPHY. The scientific study of crystals, a type of solid body which shows a pattern of atoms extended in all directions. Scientific interest in crystals has greatly increased in recent years owing to the discovery of yet more remarkable properties possessed by them. Thus in 1912 it was found that the shape and size of the unit cell of a crystal can be discovered by X-rays and also the exact nature of the cell contents, thus opening up an entirely new way of 'seeing' atoms and how they cling together to form crystalline solids. This means of determining the atomic patterns in a crystal is known as X-ray diffraction. By this method it has been found that many substances have unit cells or boxes which are exact cubes, e.g. ordinary table salt (sodium chloride).

The unit boxes into which a crystal structure can be divided are not always cubic; many have boxes whose edges are all of different lengths and not all at right-angles to one another.

The interest of chemists now lies in a detailed study of the complex groupings which occur in living matter. It has recently been shown that even protein molecules of living matter can form crystals, and such compounds may now be studied by X-ray C. Another field of application of X-ray analysis lies in the study of metals and alloys. C. is also of use to the geologist, since X-ray analysis of crystals can tell how atoms are arranged in the rocks and soils. Many materials now examined by X-ray C. were until recently not even suspected of being crystals.

CRYSTAL PALACE. Building of glass and iron designed by Paxton, originally erected in Hyde Park, London, England, to house the Great Exhibition of 1851, transferred to Sydenham Hill 1854. Saturday concerts of symphonic music were held there 1855–1901, and a triennial Handel Festival took place 1859–1929. During the F.W.W. the C.P. was the depot of the Royal Naval Division, and after the war it housed the Imperial War Museum for a time, but was burnt down in 1936, except for one tower (demolished 1941). Sporting events, such as the Cup Final, had often been held in the grounds, and the site was acquired in 1952 by the London County Council for a National Youth and Sports Centre (opened in 1964 and covering c. 36 acres), a National Exhibition Centre being planned for 1970.

CTESIPHON (tes′ifon). Ruined city of the Sassanians 12 m. S.E. of Baghdad. A palace of the 4th cent. still has its throne-room standing, spanned by a single vault of unreinforced brickwork some 80 ft. across. *See* illus. under MESOPOTAMIA.

CU′BA. Largest of the islands of the West Indies; it lies across the entrance to the Gulf of Mexico; and is an independent republic. C. is long and narrow, and is mountainous at either end. For the rest there are large areas of well-watered, fertile plain, on which tropical agriculture flourishes. The staple products are tobacco and sugar: in 1960 C. was the largest producer of sugar in the world after the U.S.S.R. Tobacco is chiefly grown in the Vuelta-Abajo district in the W. Coffee, cocoa, pineapples, bananas, etc., are also exported. There is much valuable wood in the forests; the cedar is used locally for cigar-boxes. Working of iron, copper, nickel, etc., was developed chiefly by U.S. companies.

CRYSTAL. Using specially designed pressure vessels and control equipment, Standard Telephones and Cables Ltd. has perfected a process which permits the growth in less than a month of large pieces of radio quality quartz suitable for use in the manufacture of frequency control units. Against this the world's deposits of natural quartz crystals took over 3,000,000 years to form. *Courtesy of Standard Telephones and Cables Ltd.*

CUBA. One of the world's racial melting pots, the island ranges in its population from deepest black to white, with every shade in between. *Courtesy of the Cuban Embassy.*

C. is divided into 6 provs. The cap. is Havana. Roman Catholicism is the predominant religion and Spanish the official language. Commerce is chiefly with the U.S.A. About two-thirds of the people are descended from Spanish settlers, but there is a large Negro and mulatto pop. and an intermixture of races. A Socialist constitution has been promised at an unspecified date, and the general programme is Marxist-Leninist. There is a president, who appoints the Prime Minister (Castro) and a Cabinet.

C. was discovered by Columbus in 1492 and conquered by the Spanish some 20 years later. The import of African slaves began in 1523. After a long period of corrupt administration and civil war, the Cubans revolted in 1895. The blowing up of the U.S.S. *Maine* in Havana harbour in 1898 led to war, April–Dec., between Spain and the U.S.A. in which Spain was defeated and in the peace treaty acknowledged C.'s independence. A short period of U.S. military rule followed. A Cuban convention adopted a constitution in 1901, and in 1902 the U.S.A. withdrew and the first president was inaugurated. A corrupt regime forcibly established by Maj.-General Fulgencio Batista y Zaldivar in 1952 was forcibly overthrown in 1959 by Fidel Castro (q.v.) who introduced a violently anti-U.S.A. policy. C. is subject to hurricanes, and one in 1963 killed more than a 1,000 people, and destroyed roads and railways as well as 80 per cent of the coffee crop. *See* also PIGS, BAY OF.

Area 44,200 sq. m. including the Isle of Pines and adjacent islands; pop. (1967) 8,033,000.

CUBISM. Art movement arising out of Post-Impressionism. The term was first used in a derogatory sense by Henri Matisse in 1908 in his criticism of a picture by Georges Braque, who invented the Cubist technique; its chief exponent is Pablo Picasso.

C. is the artistic expression of reality by means of abstract forms. The cubist does not try to reproduce a photographic or impressionistic picture of an object – indeed, many of his pictures do not, at first sight, bear any resemblance to recognizable objects – but merely gives an impression of its solidity and abstract qualities. Thus Picasso cuts up human features into a number of geometrical forms.

Other exponents of C. incl. André Dérain, Fernand Leger, Albert Gleizes, and Francis Picabia.

CUCHULAIN (kuhōō′lin). Legendary hero, the chief figure in an important cycle of Irish legends. He is associated with his uncle Conchobar, king of Ulster, and his most famous exploits are described in the epic saga *Cow-reiving of Cuailgne*. He has been called the Irish Achilles.

CUCKOO. Large and important family of birds (Cuculidae), of which the common C. (*Cuculus canorus*) is the type. The latter breeds in Europe and N. Asia, and migrates S. in winter. Its name derives from its characteristic cry. The adult bird somewhat resembles a hawk in appearance, being bluish-grey above and barred beneath, and has a long rounded tail. The eggs are laid singly, at intervals of about 48 hours, and placed in the nests of small insectivorous birds. As soon as the young C. is hatched, it ejects all other young birds or eggs from the nest. It is useful to farmers, as it feeds entirely on insects, particularly hairy caterpillars.

The C. has played a great part in European folklore and literature, and has often been introduced into music and song.

CUCKOO. Young bird being fed by the much smaller reed-warbler.

CUCKOO FLOWER or **Lady's Smock.** A perennial plant (*Cardamine pratensis*) belonging to the Cruciferae, and in Britain common in moist meadows and marshy woods; it bears pale lilac flowers, which later turn white, from April to June.

CUCKOO-PINT, Wake-robin or **Lords-and-ladies.** A plant (*Arum maculatum*), belonging to the arum family, Araceae, of which it is the only British representative. The large arrow-shaped leaves appear in early spring, and the inflorescence is provided with a purplish appendix above and is enveloped by a leafy spathe. This latter forms a chamber which contains the flowers, protected by a ring of downward-pointing hairs. By means of these small insects are trapped, and effect the plant's fertilization. In autumn the bright red, berry-like fruit, which is poisonous, makes its appearance.

CUCUMBER. Name of a plant (*Cucumis sativus*) belonging to the same genus as the melon, in the gourd family (Cucurbitaceae). It is an annual climbing and trailing plant, with rough or bristly stem and five- or three-lobed leaves. The flowers are bell-shaped and borne on short stalks and are succeeded by the oblong fruit, which varies from 4 in. to 2 ft. in length.

CUDWORTH, Ralph (1617–88). English philosopher. B. in Somerset, he became master of Clare Hall and Regius professor of Hebrew at Cambridge in 1645. He was a leading Cambridge Platonist, and in 1654 became Master of Christ's. His most important work, *The True Intellectual System of the Universe*, a critique of atheism, appeared in 1678.

CUENCA (kwän'kah). City of Ecuador, cap. of Azuay prov. It was founded by the Spanish in 1557. Pop. (1966) 71,484.

CUENCA. Spanish city, cap. of C. prov., at the confluence of the Júcar and Huécar, 84 m. S.E. of Madrid. It has a 13th-cent. cathedral. The British captured it in 1706. Pop. (1960) 25,000.

CUI (kü-ē'), **Cesar Antonovich** (1835–1918). Russian composer. B. at Vilna, he became a military engineer. He wrote operas and orchestral suites, but is chiefly remembered for his piano pieces and songs.

CUIABÁ (kwē-yahbah'). Brazilian town, on the C. river, cap. of Mato Grosso state. Gold and diamonds are worked nearby. Pop. (1960) 62,726.

CULBERTSON, Ely (1891–1955). American contract bridge expert. In 1930 he became famous as the author of the C. approach-forcing system, and was largely responsible for the world-wide popularity of the game.

CULDEES (kul'dēz). Name given to an ancient order of Christian monks which existed in Ireland and Scotland from before the 9th cent. to about the 12th cent. A.D., when the Celtic Church, to which they belonged, was forced to conform to Roman usages. Some survived till the 14th cent., while at Armagh in N. Ireland they endured until the dissolution of the monasteries in 1541.

CULICIDAE (kūlis'idē). Family of insects of the order Diptera, incl. the various gnats, mosquitoes, and midges.

CULLINAN, Sir Thomas (1862–1936). S. African diamond miner. He discovered the Premier Diamond Mine, Pretoria, and the world's largest diamond was named after him. (*See* DIAMOND.) Uncut the C. Diamond measured 4½ by 2½ by 2 in. and was presented by the Transvaal govt. to Edward VII: one of the 2 main portions is in the Sovereign's sceptre and the other in the crown.

CULLODEN. Stretch of moorland in Inverness-shire, where the Young Pretender, Charles Stuart, was defeated in 1746 by the Duke of Cumberland.

CULLUM, Ridgwell (1867–1943). British novelist. B. in London, he travelled in various parts of the world, was a cattle-rancher in Montana, and played a part in risings of the Indians. From 1904 he lived in England, and devoted himself to writing, chiefly 'Western' adventure stories.

CULPEPER, Nicholas (1616–54). English medical writer and astrologer. B. in London, he set up there as a physician and astrologer in 1640, and in 1649 pub. a translation of the Pharmacopoeia of the College of Physicians.

CUMAE (kū'mē). Ancient city in Italy, on the coast 12 m. W. of Naples. A Greek colony founded c. 740 B.C., it was famous in the ancient world as the seat of the oracle of the Cumaean Sibyl.

CUMANS (kū'manz). A powerful Turki federation of the Middle Ages, which dominated the steppes in the 11th and 12th cents., and built an empire reaching from the Volga to the Danube. For a generation they held up the Mongol advance on the Volga, but in 1238 a Cuman and Russian army was crushingly defeated near Astrakhan, and 200,000 Cs. took refuge in Hungary, where they settled and where their language died out only about 1775. The Mameluke dynasty of Egypt was founded by Cuman ex-slaves. Most of the so-called Tartars of S. Russia were of Cuman stock.

CUMBERLAND, Ernest Augustus, duke of; king of Hanover (1771–1851). The 5th son of George III, he served in the Hanoverian army against the French 1793–5. In 1799 he was created duke of C. He was intensely unpopular, being a high Tory and an opponent of all reforms. On the death of William IV in 1837 he became king of Hanover, Victoria being excluded by the Salic Law, and had a stormy reign.

CUMBERLAND, Richard (1732–1811). British dramatist, author of some 50 sentimental plays, novels, and interesting memoirs.

CUMBERLAND, William Augustus, duke of (1721–65). British general. 3rd son of George II, he was created duke of C. in 1726. He fought at Dettingen in 1743, was defeated by Marshal Soaxe at Fonteyn in 1745, and in 1746 ended the Jacobite rising in Scotland by his victory at Culloden. His brutal repression of the Highlands earned him the nickname of 'Butcher'. In the Seven Years' War he surrendered with his army at Kloster-Zeven (1757).

CUMBERLAND. County of N.W. England, adjacent to the Scottish border on the N., and in the S. including part of the Lake District. In the E. the land rises to the Pennines, and in the N.E. are the Cheviot hills. In the N.W. is the fertile low-lying Solway plain, drained by the Eden and Liddel. The

CULLINAN DIAMOND
Found in 1905

mountainous mass is drained by many rivers, e.g. the Derwent, Esk, Eden, and nearly every valley is occupied by a lake, some of the best-known being Derwentwater, Bassenthwaite, Buttermere, Wastwater, etc. C. is rich in minerals; there are extensive coal and iron workings in the W. and S. Carlisle is the county town. After the Roman withdrawal, C. became part of Strathclyde, a British kingdom. In 945 it passed to Scotland, in 1157 to England; until the union of the English and Scottish crowns in 1603 C. was the scene of frequent battles between the two countries. Area 1,521 sq. m.; pop. (1967) 296,050.

CUNEIFORM. The king of Babylon worships at the shrine of the Sun-god (seated right) c. 870 B.C. A cuneiform inscription below records his restoration of the god's temple at Sippar.

CU'MBERNAULD. New town of Dunbartonshire, Scotland, 11 m. from Glasgow, and founded 1956 to take the city's overspill. In 1966 it won a prize as the world's best-designed community. Pop. (1968) 25,000; ultimately to be 100,000.

CUMMINGS, Bruce F. *See* W. N. P. BARBELLION.
CUMMINGS, Edward Estlin (1894–1962). American artist-poet. B. in Mass. and ed. at Harvard, he wrote much verse, characterized by a peculiar use of punctuation and typographical devices, and the French prison camp novel *The Enormous Room* (1922).
CUNARD (kūnahrd'), **Sir Samuel** (1787–1865). British shipowner. B. at Halifax, Nova Scotia, he prospered as a merchant and shipowner, went to England in 1838, and in 1839 founded with others the British and N. American Royal Mail Steam Packet Co., which eventually became the C. line.
CUNDALL, Charles (1890–). British artist. B. in Lancs, he studied at the Manchester School of Art and at the Slade School, and has produced landscapes and portraits. 'Bank Holiday' is in the Tate Gallery.
CUNEIFORM (kūnē'iform). An ancient system of writing formed of combinations of wedge-shaped strokes, usually impressed on clay. It was probably invented by the Sumerians, and was in use in Mesopotamia as early as the middle of the 4th millennium B.C. It was adopted and modified by the Assyrians, Babylonians, Elamites, Hittites, Persians, and many other peoples of different races and languages. In the 5th cent. B.C. it fell into disuse, but sporadically reappeared in later cents. B.C. The decipherment of the C. scripts was due to the efforts of G. F. Grotefend (1802) and H. C. Rawlinson (1846).
CUNNINGHAM, Allan (1784–1842). Scottish man of letters. B. in Dumfriesshire, he was apprenticed to a stonemason, and became clerk of works in Chantrey's studio in London. His best-known poem is 'A Wet Sheet and a Flowing Sea'.
CUNNINGHAM, Andrew Browne, 1st visct. C. of Hyndhope (1883–1963). British admiral. From the training ship *Britannia*, he entered the R.N. in 1898, served in the F.W.W. and as C.-in-C. in the Mediterranean 1939–42 maintained British control. He was Naval C.-in-C. of the Expeditionary Force to N. Africa in 1942 and Feb.–Oct. 1943 was C.-in-C. Allied Naval Forces in the Mediterranean and Admiral of the Fleet, receiving in Sept. the surrender of the Italian fleet. He succeeded Dudley-Pound as First Sea Lord and Chief of Naval Staff 1943–6, when he was created a visct. and awarded the O.M. His autobiography *A Sailor's Odyssey* (1951) records his story as the greatest fighting sailor since Nelson.

CUNNINGHAM, Sir John (1885–1962). British admiral. In 1940 he assisted in the evacuation of Norway, taking the Norwegian King to England in his flagship, and as 4th Sea Lord in charge of supplies and transport 1941–3 prepared the way for the N. African invasion in 1942. He was C.-in-C. Mediterranean 1943–6, 1st Sea Lord 1946–8, and became Admiral of the Fleet in 1948.
CUNNINGHAME GRAHAM, Robert Bontine (1852–1936). Scottish writer and politician. Of Scottish and Spanish descent, he travelled widely in C. and S. America, Spain and Morocco. He was a Liberal M.P. 1886–92, became president of the Scottish Labour Party in 1888, and in later life was associated with the Scottish Nationalist movement. His writings deal with Morocco, e.g. *Mogreb-el-Acksa* (1898), or Latin America, e.g. *A Vanished Arcadia* (1901). For using the word 'damn' in the House of Commons he was once suspended.
CUPAR (kōō'pahr). Scottish royal burgh and co. town of Fifeshire, on the Eden, 30 m. N.E. of Edinburgh. Pop. (1961) 5,495.
CU'PID. Roman name for the Greek god Eros (q.v.).
CU'PRITE. Red oxide of copper, Cu_2O, occurring crystalline in cubes or octahedra or massive. It resembles haematite in its reddish colour, but is much softer. In Arizona it is an important source of copper.
CUPRO-NICKEL. Copper alloy (75 per cent copper and 25 per cent nickel) substituted in the U.K. in 1946 for the 'silver' (50 per cent silver, 40 per cent copper, 5 per cent nickel and 5 per cent zinc) previously used in currency. The change was prompted by the rising cost of silver, obtained chiefly from the U.S. and paid for in dollars.
CURAÇAO. Island in the West Indies, one of the Netherlands Antilles (q.v.), to the legislature of which it sends 12 members. It lies in the Caribbean Sea, c. 40 m. N. of Venezuela. Area 210 sq. m. Pop. (1965) 136,289.
Willemstad, the cap., has a fine harbour. There is some agriculture, but the principal industry, dating from 1918, is the refining of petroleum from Venezuela. C., discovered in 1499, colonized by Spain 1527, annexed by the Dutch West India Company 1634, gave its name from 1924 to the group of islands renamed Netherlands Antilles in 1948.
CURAÇAO. Liqueur, originally the produce of the island of C. in the Netherlands W. Indies, but now made in other countries, notably Latvia. Both dry and sweet C. is produced and marketed, the alcohol content varying between 36 and 40 per cent.
CURARE (kūrah'ri). S. American native poison obtained from the bark of the tree *Strychnos toxifera* by macerating in water: used on arrow tips it paralyses the victim. An alkaloid derivative, curarine, is used as a muscle relaxant in surgical operations.
CURATE (kū'ret). Literally, a priest who has the cure of souls in a parish, and so used on the Continent. In England, however, it is generally applied to an unbeneficed clergyman who acts as assistant to a parish priest, more exactly an 'assistant C'.
CURÉ D'ARS (kūreh'-dahr'). Name by which the French R.C. saint Jean Baptiste Vianney (1786–1859) is generally known. He was ordained priest in 1815, and in 1817 was appointed to the obscure parish of Ars, in the dept. of Ain. There he remained for 40 years, and his good life and alleged miracles attracted crowds of pilgrims. He was canonized in 1925.
CURIA ROMANA. The judicial and administrative bodies through which the Pope carries on the government of the R.C. Church. It includes certain tribunals; the chancellery which issues papal bulls, and various offices including that of the Cardinal Secretary of State; and the Congregations, or councils of cardinals, each with a particular department of work.
CURIE (kūrē'), **Marie** (1867–1934). Polish scientist. B. in Warsaw (née Sklodovska), she went to study in

Paris in 1891, where she m. the scientist **Pierre
Curie** (1859–1906), in 1895. Impressed by the publication of Becquerel's experiments, Marie decided to investigate the nature of uranium rays; and in 1898 she reported the possible existence of some new powerful radioactive element in pitchblende ores. Her husband abandoned his own researches to assist her, and in the same year the existence of polonium and radium was announced, the pure elements being isolated in 1902. Both scientists refused to take out a patent on their discovery, and were jointly awarded the Davy Medal (1903) and the Nobel Prize for physics (1903; with Becquerel). In 1904 Pierre was appointed to a chair in physics at Sorbonne, and on his death in a street accident was succeeded by his wife. She wrote a *Treatise on Radioactivity* in 1910, and was awarded the Nobel Prize for chemistry in 1911. She d. a victim to the radiations among which she had worked in her laboratory, as seen below.

Her elder dau., **Irène C.** (1896–1956), m. in 1926 the physicist **Frédéric Joliot** (1900–59), who added the surname C. to his own. Together they made the discovery of the possibility of artificial radioactivity, i.e. that non-radioactive substances could be induced

to acquire the properties of radium after being submitted to bombardment by its rays. For this they received the Nobel chemistry award in 1935. Irène C. d. from leukaemia, caused by her work on radiation. Joliot-C. was prof. of physics at the Collège de France from 1937, but incurred official disapproval for his Communist sympathies from 1950.

Marie C.'s younger dau. **Eve-Denise** (1904–), pub. a biography of her mother in 1937, was a war correspondent in the S.W.W. and pub. *Journey Among Warriors* (1943).

CURIE. Unit of radioactivity equal to that emitted by one gramme of radium, named after Marie C.

CURITIBA (kōōrētē′ba). Brazilian city, cap. of Paraná state on the C. river. It has a univ. (1912) and makes paper, furniture, textiles, chemicals, etc. It dates from 1654. Maté is its chief export. Pop. (1960) 361,309.

CURIUM. Element at no. 96, at wt. 247, radioactive transuranic metal produced from americium and named after the Curies.

CURLEW (ker′lū). Genus of wading birds (*Nemenius*) of the snipe family Charadriidae, distinguished by their long curved bills. The typical European C. or whaup (*N. arquata*) breeds on upland moors, and is about 2 ft. long with brownish, mottled plumage. A more northern species is the smaller whimbrel (*N. phaeopus*), which also has a shorter bill. Closely allied is the American whimbrel (*N. hudsonicus*). The stone-C. or thick-knee (*Oedicnemus crepitans*) belongs to the Oedicnemidae, a family intermediate between plovers and bustards.

CURLING. Game played on ice with stones; sometimes described as 'bowls on ice'. One of the most distinctive national games of Scotland, where it probably originated, it has spread to many countries. It can also be played on artificial (cement or tarmacadam) ponds. Two tees are erected 38 yd. apart. There are 2 teams of 4 players. The object of the game is to deliver the stones near the tee, those nearest scoring. Each player has 2 stones, of equal size, fitted with a handle. The usual weight of the stone, which is shaped like a small flat cheese, is 36 to 42 lb. In Canada the weight is greater (about 60 lb.) and iron replaces stone. The stone is slid on one of its flat surfaces and it may be curled in one direction or another according to the twist given it as it leaves the hand. The match is played for an agreed number of heads or shots, or by time.

CURRAN, Charles (1921–). Brit. administrator. Director of External Broadcasting 1967, he became Director-General BBC in 1968.

CURRAN, John Philpot (1750–1817). Irish politician and lawyer. In 1783 he entered the Irish parliament, where he championed Catholic emancipation, although himself a Protestant, and parliamentary reform. Between 1794 and 1803 he delivered speeches in defence of the leaders of the United Irishmen.

CURRANT. Variety of grape first cultivated near Corinth (hence the name), with a small round seedless berry. Dried, these are used extensively in cakes and are grown on a large scale in Greece and California. Because of the similarity of the fruit, the same name is given to several species of shrubs in the genus *Ribes* (family Grossulariaceae). The red C. (*Ribes rubrum*) is a native of S. Europe, Asia and N. America, occasionally growing wild in Britain. The white C. is a cultivated, less acid variety, but the black C. (*R. nigrum*) is the most favoured for cooking. The flowering C. (*R. sanguineum*) is a native of N. America.

CURRENCY. See MONEY.

CURRENT. A body of water flowing in a particular direction. Oceanic Cs. are of two kinds, viz. drifts which are broad and move slowly, and streams which are narrow and move swiftly. Of stream currents the best-known is the Gulf Stream (q.v.).

CURTIN, John (1885–1945). Australian Labour statesman. B. in Victoria, he rose to prominence as a trade-union leader and journalist, entered the House of Representatives in 1928, and was elected leader of the Labour Party in 1935. Becoming Prime Minister in 1941, he organized the mobilization of Australia's resources to meet the danger of Japanese invasion, and was confirmed in office in 1943.

CURTIS, Lionel (1872–1955). British advocate of imperial federation and a world state. One of Milner's 'young men' in S. Africa after the Boer War, he pub. in 1916 *The Commonwealth of Nations* – the 1st time this term was used – arguing the federalist case.

CURTISS, Glenn Hammond (1878–1930). American aircraft-designer. B. in New York, he designed some of the earliest successful types of aeroplane, was the first man to pilot a seaplane with success (1911), and was concerned with the early development of flying boats; his N.C.4 model was the first plane of any kind to be flown across the Atlantic.

CURVE. In geometry, the locus of a point moving according to specified conditions. The best-known of all Cs. is the circle, which is the locus of all points equidistant from a given point (the centre). Other common geometrical Cs. are the ellipse, parabola, and hyperbola; these curves are produced when a cone is cut by a plane at different angles. Many Cs. have been invented for the solution of special problems in geometry and mechanics, e.g. the cissoid and the cycloid.

CURWEN (ker′wen), **John** (1816–80). British musician. A Nonconformist minister, he retired in 1864 to propagate the tonic sol-fa system of music notation which he adapted from that originated by Sarah Ann Glover (1785–1867).

CURZON, Clifford (1907–). British pianist. He studied in Berlin under Schnabel, and under Wanda Landowska and Nadia Boulanger in Paris, and became famous as an interpreter of Schubert and modern British composers.

CURZON LINE. The Polish-Russian frontier proposed by the territorial commission of the Versailles conference in 1919, based on the eastward limit of areas with a predominantly Polish population. It acquired its name after Lord Curzon (q.v.) suggested in 1920 that the Poles, who had invaded Russia, should retire to this line pending a Russo-Polish peace conference. The frontier established in 1945 in general follows the C.L.

CURZON OF KEDLESTON, George Nathaniel Curzon, 1st marquess (1859–1925). British Cons. statesman. Son of a clergyman, he entered Parliament in. 1886 and acquired an expert knowledge of Asian affairs by foreign travel 1887–94. Created baron C. in the Irish peerage on his appointment as Viceroy of India in 1899, he was the inaugurator of the North West Frontier prov. and of various reforms, but resigned in 1905 following a controversy with Kitchener. In 1911 he accepted an earldom and in 1921 a marquessate. He was For. Sec. 1919–22 and 1922–4, but on Bonar Law's resignation in 1923 he was bitterly disappointed when passed over for the premiership in favour of Baldwin.

CUSHIONCRAFT. *See* HOVERCRAFT.

CUSTARD APPLE. Name given to several tropical fruits, produced by trees and shrubs belonging to the genus *Anona*, of the family Anonaceæ. *A. reticulata,* the common C.A., or 'bullock's heart', bears a large, dark-brown fruit, containing a sweet reddish-yellow pulp. It is a native of the W. Indies.

CUSTOMS AND EXCISE. C. duties are taxes levied on certain imports, e.g. tobacco, wines and spirits, perfumery and jewellery; E. duties are levied on certain goods produced (e.g. beer) and incl. purchase tax; or on licences to carry on certain trades (sale of wines and spirits, etc.) or other activities (theatrical entertainments, betting, etc.) within a country. In the U.K. both come under the Board of C. and E.; in the U.S.A. E. duties are classed as Internal Revenue and C. are controlled by the C. Bureau.

CUTHBERT (d. 687). Christian saint. He was a shepherd of Northumbria till after a vision he entered the monastery of Melrose, travelled as a missionary far and wide, and because of his miracles was known as the 'wonderworker of Britain'. He became prior of Lindisfarne, but retired in 676 to Farne Island. In 684 he became bishop of Hexham and later of Lindisfarne. His body was removed to Durham in 995.

CUTTACK (kut-tak′). Indian city and minor port in Orissa state, of which it was the cap. until 1950. It is on the Mahanadi river delta. The old fort (Kataka) from which the town takes its name is in ruins. Pop. (1961) 146,590.

CUTTLE-FISH. Name applied to various ten-armed molluscs of the class Cephalopoda, chiefly those belonging to the family Sepiidae, which are distinguished by their internal calcareous shell (cuttlebone). The common European C.F. (*Sepia officinalis*) reaches a length of 6–10 in., and swims actively by means of the fins into which the sides of its oval, flattened body are expanded, and also jerks itself backwards by emitting a jet of water from its siphon.

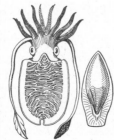

It varies from dark brown to grey, and is capable of rapid changes of hue. The large head is provided with conspicuous eyes, and 10 arms provided with suckers. Two of these are very much elongated, and with them the animal seizes its prey. The C.F. is provided with an 'ink-bag', from which a black fluid can be discharged into the water, whereby the animal can cover its retreat when alarmed; from this sepia, the well-known dark-brown pigment, is obtained.

CUVIER (küvyä′), **Georges,** baron (1769–1832). French comparative anatomist. In 1798 appeared his *Tableau élémentaire de l'histoire naturelle des animaux,* in which his scheme of classification is outlined. He was prof. of natural history in the Collège de France from 1799, and at the Jardin des Plantes from 1802; and at the Restoration in 1815 he was elected Chancellor of the University of Paris. C. was the first to relate the structure of fossil animals to that of their living allies. His great work, *Le Règne animal,* embodies a systematic survey of the animal kingdom.

CUXHAVEN (kooks′hahfen). German seaport on the S. side of the Elbe estuary, at its entrance into the North Sea. It acts as an outport for Hamburg. Pop. (1960) 50,000.

CUYP (koip), **Albert** (1620–91). Dutch artist. The son of Jacob Gerritsz C. (1594–1652), a landscape and portrait painter, he himself painted views of rivers remarkable for their purity of colour and simplicity of design, people on horseback, seascapes, etc. His 'Riders with the Boy and Herdsman' is in the National Gallery, and 'Piper with Cows' in the Louvre.

CUZCO (kooz′koh). City of S. Peru, cap. of C. dept., in the Andes, over 11,000 ft. above sea-level, some 350 m. S.E. of Lima. It was the ancient cap. of the Inca empire, and has many Inca remains as well as a fine Renaissance cathedral and other relics of the early Spanish conquerors. Founded in the 11th cent. by the first of the Incas, it was captured by Pizarro in 1533. The univ. was founded in 1598. Pop. (1965) 92,600.

CYANIDES (sī′anīdz). In chemistry, salts of prussic or hydrocyanic acid, produced when this is neutralized by alkalis. The principal are potassium, sodium, calcium, mercuric, gold, and cupric.

CYBELE (sib′elē). In the pantheon of W. Asia, the Great Mother Goddess, whose worship, originally of Phrygian origin, was introduced among the Greeks and Romans. The Greeks identified her with Rhea. The Corybantes celebrated her worship with wild orgiastic dances, and in Rome the Galli, the priests of her cult, castrated themselves in her honour. Attis (q.v.) was beloved by her.

CYBERNETICS (sīberne′tiks). Name, derived from the Gk. κυβερνήτης 'steersman', for the science concerned with how systems organize, regulate and reproduce themselves, and also how they evolve and learn. In the laboratory inanimate objects are created that behave like living systems, e.g. Ross Ashby's Homeostat, a behavioural model made up of 4 interacting regulators and an independent switching mechanism which changes the interconnections between these elements until a stable arrangement is reached. Its working is identical with a feature of the workings of a brain which is relevant to the control within a brain. The logical ultimate development of C. is the evolution of adaptive, decision-making machines operating at managerial level, e.g. able to assimilate data on the state of a factory and produce the correct solution to any aspect of inefficient working. Such control mechanisms would open the way to a new industrial revolution.

CYCADS (sī′kadz). An order of plants (Cycadales) belonging to the Gymnosperms. Some have a superficial resemblance to palms, others to ferns. There are 9 genera and about 80 species, natives of tropical and sub-tropical countries. The stems of many species yield an edible starchy substance resembling sago.

CYCLADES. One of the lesser Cyclades, Mykonos is famed for its tiny and varied Byzantine churches – about 365 – and its windmills, such as the one from beneath whose sails this photograph was taken.
Courtesy of National Tourist Organization of Greece.

CYCLADES (sik′ladēz). Group of about 200 Greek islands in the Aegean Sea, lying between Greece and Turkey. They include Andros, Melos, Paros, Naxos and Siros on which is the cap. Hermoupolis. Area 923 sq. m.; pop. (1961) 99,931.

CYCLAMATES (sīk′lamãts). Derivatives of cyclo-hexysulphamic acid used as cheap artificial sweeteners, because 30 times as sweet as sugar, without after-taste, and free of calories. In excess of 3 grams a day C. may be harmful, especially in the case of heart, circulatory or liver complaints. In the U.S.A., where they were discovered 1937, their use was banned 1970; the U.K. followed suit, also 1970.

CYCLAMEN (sik′lamen). Genus of perennial plants of the Primulaceae, with heart-shaped leaves and the lobes of the corolla twisted and bent back. The flowers are usually white or pink, and several species are cultivated.

CYCLING. Riding a bicycle for sport, pleasure or transport. The bicycle derived from the hobby-horse which consisted of 2 wheels connected by a wooden beam carrying a saddle. The rider propelled himself by thrusting his feet against the ground. By the 1860s it had assumed a practical form; being driven from the front wheel by pedals and cranks. Structural improvements, including wire wheels, metal frames, and solid rubber tyres followed in the 1870s and 1880s, and an increase in the diameter of the front wheel to gain extra speed, gave rise to the graceful 'penny-farthing'. Further developments led to the chain drive 'safety' bicycle, equipped with pneumatic tyres (J. B. Dunlop, 1888), which exists virtually unchanged to the present day. C. is now very popular for touring and racing both on road and track. A famous international race is the 'Tour de France' in 21 stages covering 2,500 m.

CYCLONE. See ANTICYCLONE.

CYCLOPES (sī′klōpēz). In Gk. mythology, a race of one-eyed giants, inhabiting Sicily. As described by Homer, they were savages, subsisting on their flocks of sheep and goats, but of cannibalistic propensities.

The name C. was also given to a legendary race of builders, supposed to have come from Thrace or Lycia, and to be responsible for the so-called Cyclo-pean walls, a feature of the prehistoric architecture of Mycenae and other places in Greece and Italy.

CYMBAL (sim′bel). Musical instrument of per-cussion, consisting of a pair of round metal plates, fastened to the hand with a leather strap, and struck together to produce a loud clashing sound.

CYNEWULF (kin′ewoolf) (fl. 750). Anglo-Saxon poet. He is thought to have been a Northumbrian monk, and is the undoubted author of 'Juliana' and part of the 'Christ' in the Exeter Book, and of the 'Fates of the Apostles' and 'Elene' in the Vercelli Book, in all of which he inserted his name in form of runic acrostics.

CYNIC (sin′ik). Originally the name of a school of ancient Greek philosophy, founded at Athens *c.* 400 B.C. by Antisthenes, a disciple of Socrates. He advocated a stern and simple morality, and a com-plete disregard of pleasure and comfort. His followers led by Diogenes (fl. 340 B.C.) not only showed a contemptuous disregard for pleasure, but despised all human affection as a source of weakness. Their 'snarling contempt' for ordinary men earned them the name of C., which in Gk. means 'dog-like'.

CYPRESS (sī′pres). Genus of coniferous trees (*Cupressus*) of the family Cupressaceae. There are 12 species, which are evergreen trees and shrubs, found mainly in the warm temperate regions of the N. hemisphere. They have minute scale-like leaves and small globular cones, made up of peltate woody scales, and exude an aromatic resin.

CYPRIAN (si′prian) (*c.* 210–258). Christian saint and martyr, one of the earliest Christian writers and bishop of Carthage about 249. His most famous work is a treatise on the unity of the Church.

CYPRUS (sī′prus). Large island in the E. Medi-terranean, some 40 m. S. of Turkey in Asia, 60 m. W. of Syria.

Much of the island is covered by 2 mountain ranges, between which lies the broad and fertile plain of Messaoria. Streams are small, and even the largest, the Pedias, may be dried up in summer. In ancient times C. was famed for its copper, and in modern times cuprous pyrites is the most important mineral worked. Other minerals are iron pyrites, asbestos chrome ore, and gypsum. The lack of water is being remedied by extensive irri-gation works; afforesta-tion is carried on.

The cap. is Nicosia; other towns are Limassol, Larnaca, Famagusta, and Kyrenia. Area 3,572 sq. m.; pop. (1967) 614,000, of whom *c.* 112,000 were Moslems, and all but a few of the remainder members of the Eastern Orthodox Church. Greek is the lan-guage of the mass of the people, Turkish that of the Turkish minority (*c.* 17½ per cent); English is spoken by the educated.

From the 15th cent. B.C. C. was colonized by a succession of peoples from the mainland. In the 8th cent. it was within the Assyrian empire, then the

CYCLING. The Moulton bicycle is a revolutionary design from first principles. With its small wheels and F-shaped frame, it has indepen-dent suspension to iron out road bumps. It is shown in racing form during a record breaking run from Cardiff to London in 1962.

Babylonian, Egyptian, and Persian. As part of Ptolemaic Egypt, it was seized by Rome in 58 B.C. The Lusignan family ruled it from 1191 until Venice captured it in 1489, and from 1571 it belonged to the Turks until in 1878 they surrendered its administration to Britain which annexed it in 1914, made it a colony in 1925 In 1954 Gk. Cypriots erupted into violence, demanding *enosis* (pron. en′ōsis, union with Greece), a movement which first developed *c.* 1930), the Turks

CYPRUS. The rough country of the Kyrenia range is ideal terrain for guerrilla warfare, and much Greek, Turkish and British blood has been spilt here.
Photo: Central Office of Information.

demanding partition. Negotiations between the British, Greek and Turkish govts. in 1960 led to the establishment of an independent rep. of C. (admitted to the Brit. Commonwealth 1961) with Archbishop Makarios, leader of the insurgents, as first pres. Britain retained 2 bases on the S. coast at Akrotiri and Dhekelia. From 1964 the U.N. maintained a peace-keeping force and by 1968 tension was less.

CYRANO DE BERGERAC (sērah'noh-de-berzher-ahk'), **Savinien** (1619–55). French writer. B. in Paris, he joined a corps of guards at 19, and performed heroic feats which made him famous. He wrote a comedy, *Le Pédant joué* (1654), classical tragedies, notably *Mort d'Agrippine* (1654), and scientific romances, *L'Histoire comique des Etats du Soleil* (1662) and *L'Histoire comique des Etats de la Lune* (1656). He is the hero of a well-known play by Rostand (q.v.).

CYRENAICA (sirēnā'ika). Area of E. Libya, N. Africa. The Greeks estab. colonies here in the 7th cent. which passed under the rule of the Ptolemys in 322 B.C., and in 174 B.C. became a Roman province. It was conquered by the Arabs in the 7th cent., by Turkey in the 16th and by Italy in 1912, when it was developed as a colony which became a prov. of the new kingdom of Libya from 1951 until it was split into a number of smaller divisions under the constitutional reorganization of 1963. Modern cities, rapidly growing following discoveries of oil, incl. Benghazi, Derna and Tobruk, and there are magnificent ruins at Cyrene, Apollonia, etc.

CYRENAICS (sīrenā'iks). A school of ancient Greek philosophy founded *c.* 400 B.C. by Aristippus of Cyrene. He regarded pleasure as the only absolutely worth-while thing in life, but taught that self-control and intelligence were necessary to choose the best pleasures.

CYRIL (sir'il) **OF ALEXANDRIA** (376–444). Christian prelate and saint. B. at Alexandria he was made archbp. in 412. He persecuted Jews and heathens, and his conjectured part in the death of Hypatia, the girl philosopher, aroused indignation. His violence arose out of hatred of heresy, but he himself was charged with unorthodoxy.

CYRIL and METHODIUS. Christian saints, apostles of the Slavs in the 9th cent. They were brothers, b. in Thessalonica, and were sent in 863 as missionaries to Moravia. They translated the scriptures and liturgy into Slavonic, and are said to have invented the Cyrillic alphabet, a variation of the Greek alphabet, with some additional signs, which is still in use among the Serbs, Bulgars, and Russians.

CYRUS (sī'rus) (d. 529 B.C.). The founder of the Persian empire. He became king of the Persians while they were still a small tribe of hardy warriors subordinate to the king of Media. In 550 B.C. he over-

threw his suzerain Astyages of Media, and in 546 captured Croesus, king of Lydia, and became master of the whole of Asia Minor, including the Greek cities on the coast. Finally in 539 he captured Babylon and added Babylonia and Syria to his empire. As part of his policy of toleration he allowed the exiled Jews to return to Jerusalem. He d. fighting in Afghanistan.

CZAR. *See* TSAR.

CZECH (chek). A member of the western branch of the Slavonic languages, spoken in the former provs. of Bohemia and Moravia, and in the Teschen dist., Czechoslovakia. Its closest allies are Polish and Sorb or Wendish. The Slav-speaking people seem to have established themselves in Bohemia in the 5th cent. A.D., displacing or incorporating earlier Celtic or Germanic inhabitants. Spoken by *c.* 10,000,000, it is closely related to Slovak, spoken by *c.* 4,000,000; and is the liturgical language of the Slovak Protestants.

CZECHOSLOVAKIA (chekōslōvah'kē-a). Federal republic of central Europe. Area 49,381 sq. m. Pop. (1967) 14,271,547.

C. may be divided into two main areas separated by the valley of the Morava. To the W. lies a densely populated area with good communications; to the E. a district that is sparsely populated and comparatively backward. The continental character of the climate increases towards the E.

Agriculture is highly developed. In the low-lying regions sugar-beet, wheat, maize, and barley are grown, in the higher parts potatoes, oats, and rye. Hops for the production of beer and for export are cultivated. Fruit is grown in many districts, and there are numerous vineyards.

Many of the important industries obtain their raw materials from agricultural products, e.g. the sugar and beer-brewing industries, the numerous factories for the production of preserved fruit, cheese, smoked meat. C. is rich in minerals, there are important coalfields at Most, Chomutoc, Kladno, Ostrava, and elsewhere; iron, silver, copper, lead, uranium, and rock-salt are mined. Parts of C. are among the most densely wooded regions of Europe, and the timber industry is important. Manufactures incl. machine tools, cars, glass, imitation jewellery, toys and woodware.

The capital is Prague; other large towns are Brno, Bratislava, Ostrava, and Plzen.

Government. Under the Federalization Law (1969) there is a pres. and a bicameral federal assembly: directly elected Chamber of the People (2 to 1 Czech majority) and Chamber of Nations (150 deputies:

CZECHOSLOVAKIA. Bohemian glass has been famous since the 14th cent. Today, traditional skills are passed on through special technical training centres, and here a student at the Železný Brod artcraft school puts the finishing touches to her graduation work.
Courtesy of the Czechoslovak Travel Bureau.

half chosen by each of the Czech and Slovak Nat. Councils), with safeguards to prevent domination by either nationality.

History. C. came into existence as an independent republic in 1918, after the break-up of the Austro-Hungarian empire at the end of the F.W.W. It consisted originally of the Bohemian crownlands (Bohemia, Moravia, and part of Silesia) and Slovakia, the area of Hungary inhabited by Slavonic peoples; to which was added as a trust part of Ruthenia when the Allies and Associated Powers recognized the new republic under the treaty of St. Germain-en-Laye. (For the earlier history of the regions concerned, see those headings.) Besides the related Czech and Slovak peoples, the country included substantial minorities of German origin long settled in the N., of Hungarian (or Magyar) origin in the S. But despite the problems of welding into a nation such a mixed group of peoples, until the troubled 1930s C., under the presidency of Thomas Masaryk (q.v.), made considerable political and economic progress.

The rise of Hitler to power in Germany produced a revival of opposition among the German-speaking part of the pop., and irredentism revived among the Magyar-speakers; in addition, the Slovakian national party demanded autonomy for Slovakia. These difficulties led on to crisis in 1938 and the Munich agreement (q.v.) between Britain, France, Germany, and Italy, made without consultation with or the consent of C., which detached from C. the Sudetenland and gave it to Germany. Six months later Hitler occupied all C. A government-in-exile under Beneš was estab. in London until the liberation in 1945 by Russian and U.S. troops. The same year saw some 2,000,000 Sudeten Germans expelled and Czech Ruthenia transferred to Ukraine S.S.R. Elections in 1946 gave the Left a slight majority and by 1948 the Communists were in full control (*see* MASARYK, JAN). The historic provs. were subsequently abolished, the country being divided into 10 regions plus Prague, and the 1960 constitution estab. a socialist rep., a unitary state of Czechs and Slovaks with equal rights, with a unicameral Nat. Assembly. A slight liberalization of the economy initiated 1965 became in 1968, under the leadership of Alexander Dubcek (1921–) the First Sec. of the Communist Party, a 'Socialist Democratic Revolution'. Its programme, incl. restoration of freedom of assembly, speech and movement, and restric-

tion of the secret police, was regarded with suspicion by the U.S.S.R., and in Aug. 1968 Soviet, Bulgarian, E. German, Hungarian and Polish troops invaded C. to restore the orthodox line. Nevertheless, C. went ahead with the adoption of a federal structure with equal status for Czechs and Slovaks, and attempted to retain some shadow of freedom of action.

Literature. Although Czech has the oldest of the Slavonic literatures, little remains before the 14th cent. when there was a rapid development of vernacular writing in prose and verse. But interest was soon absorbed in religious controversy, and after 1621 the native literature was suppressed by the Jesuits; Comenius (1592–1670), greatest of the early writers, was driven into exile. In the 18th cent. the national language was suppressed by the Austrian govt.; but in the early 19th cent. came a revival led by the scholar J. Dobrovský (1753–1829). Among the new writers were the poets Jan Kollár (1793–1852) and Karel H. Mácha (1810–36); the historian F. Palacký (1798–1876), and the novelist B. Němcová (1820–62). The leading figure of the mid-19th cent. was the critic and journalist Jan Neruda (1834–91). Towards the end of the 19th cent. Czech literature split into 2 groups. One, under the leadership of the poet and translator J. Vrchlický (1853–1912), turned westward; the other, represented by the poet S. Čech (1846–1908) and the patriotic historical novelist A. Jirásek (1851–1930), preferred to maintain the Slav tradition and looked rather to Russia. A more realistic approach was induced by T. Masaryk (1850–1937), who influenced the poet Jan S. Machar (1864–1942), and novelists such as K. M. Capek-Chod (1860–1927). Later writers included Karel Čapek (1890–1938), whose plays achieved international fame; and the novelists J. Hášek (1883–1923), V. Vančura (1891–1942), and I. Olbracht (1882–1952). Most popular of recent novelists is Ladislav Mnacko (1919–), who fled to Israel with his Jewish wife in 1967 in protest against govt. anti-Israeli policy.

CZERNY (cher′nē), **Karl** (1791–1857). Austrian composer and teacher of the pianoforte. B. at Vienna, he was a teacher when he was 14. He composed over 900 works, and is best known for his piano studies.

CZESTOCHOWA (chestokhoh′vah). Industrial town in Poland, 120 m. S.W. of Warsaw, making iron goods, chemicals, paper, cement, etc. It has a railway junction and an airport. Pop (1966) 176,000.

D Fourth letter of the alphabet, answering to the Semitic *daleth* and the Greek *delta*. In the Latin numeral system D stands for 500. In English money d. is the sign for a penny (Lat. *denarius*).

DAB. Species of flatfish (*Limanda limanda*) belonging to the plaice family (Pleuronectidae). Light brown or grey, with dull brown spots, it is commonly about 10 in. long.

DABCHICK or **Little Grebe.** Freshwater bird (*Podiceps fluviatilis*) belonging to the Podicipedidae. *See* GREBES.

DACCA (dak′ah). Capital of Bangladesh, 150 m. N.E. of Calcutta, on the Burhi Ganga. It makes jute goods, chemicals, muslin, etc. Chittagong and Chalna are its ports. The univ. was founded in 1921. Pop. (1961) 556, 712.

DACE. A freshwater fish (*Leuciscus leuciscus*) of the carp family (Cyprinidae). Common in England, it is silvery, and reaches a length of about 12 in.

DACHAU (dakh′ow). *See* CONCENTRATION CAMPS.

DACHSHUND (daks′) (Ger., badger-dog). Small hound of German origin, intended for use in badger digging, whence its name. Black-and-tan or self-coloured tan, it is long in body and short-legged.

DACOIT. Indian term for an armed robber, member of a gang numbering 5 and over: also used in Burma. Dacoity remained troublesome after India's independence, and a mission of reform by Vinoba Bhave (q.v.) in 1960 conspicuously failed.

D'ACOSTA, Uriel (*c.* 1590–1647). Jewish rationalist. B. in Oporto, he removed to Amsterdam, where he found himself in opposition to the Jewish authorities. Accused of atheism in a Christian court, he was excommunicated. Eventually he shot himself.

DADAISM. Irrational literary and artistic movement developed between 1915 and 1922, born of reaction and disillusion during the F.W.W. D. appeared almost simultaneously in New York, with Marcel Duchamp's exhibition of 'ready-made' sculptures; and in Zürich, the Rumanian poet Tzara with German writers Ball and Hillsenbeck founded the

'Cabaret Voltaire' in 1916, where works by Jean Arp, Max Ernst, Klee, Modigliani and Picasso were exhibited. D. was a preparatory phase in the development of Surrealism (q.v.).

DADDY LONG-LEGS. *See* CRANE FLY.

DAEDALUS (dē'dalus). In Greek mythology, an Athenian craftsman who constructed for King Minos the labyrinth in which the Minotaur was imprisoned, and fled from Crete with his son Icarus by means of wings made from feathers and fastened with wax. *See* AYRTON, MICHAEL.

DAFFODIL. Name given to several species of plants of the genus *Narcissus*, distinguished by their bell-shaped corollas. The common D. of N. Europe (*N. pseudo-narcissus*) has large yellow flowers, and grows from a large bulb. There are numerous cultivated forms.

DAGENHAM. Industrial locality on the N. bank of the Thames, divided between the Redbridge and Barking bors. of Greater London. It has a Ford factory and a famous band of girl pipers.

DAGHESTAN (dahgestahn'). An A.S.S.R. of the R.S.F.S.R., at the E. extremity of the Caucasus, bordering the Caspian Sea. It is mountainous, dissected by deep valleys and inhabited by numerous distinct peoples, each with its own language. Makhach-Kala, the cap., is a useful port on the Caspian, with petroleum refineries. D. was annexed from Persia in

DACCA. Opened in 1948, the Government Institute of Arts has been a constituent college of the University of Dacca since 1963, and offers its 200 students courses varying from ceramics to commercial art. In the approachway a scooter 'taxi' waits.
Courtesy of the Pakistan High Commission.

1723, made an autonomous republic in 1921. Area 14,700 sq. m.; pop. (1967) 1,361,000.

DAGLISH, Eric Fitch (1892–1966). British artist and author. B. in London, he wrote a number of natural-history books, and illustrated both these and such classics as Izaac Walton, Thoreau, Gilbert White, and W. H. Hudson with exquisite wood engravings.

DAGUERRE (dahgār'), **Louis Jacques Mandé** (1789–1851). French painter and pioneer of photography. He worked from 1829 with J. N. Niepce (d. 1833) who, like himself, had discovered the possibility of using sunlight to obtain permanent pictures. D. perfected the process, which was pub. in 1839 and is known as daguerreotype.

DAHLIA (dā'lia). Genus of plants of the family Compositae, named after Andrew Dahl, a Swedish botanist. There are 10 species of the genus, which is a native of Mexico, but was introduced to England in 1789. There are many cultivated forms.

DAHOMEY (dahō'mi). Republic in West Africa, between Nigeria and Ghana, with a short coast on the Gulf of Guinea. Much of D. is arid, but there are scattered forest areas producing palm kernels and palm oil, the chief export. The climate is tropical.

DAHOMEY On his rounds, one of the many African doctors trained at Dakar Medical School. *Courtesy of WHO.*

Porto Novo (pop. 65,000) is the cap.; other towns are Cotonu (largest port), Whydah, Abomey. Area 45,000 sq. m.; pop. (1965) 2,370,000.

The French signed a commercial treaty with the well-organized Negro kingdom of D. in 1851, made it a protectorate in 1863, a colony in 1894. On attaining independence in 1960 D. left the French Community. After a period of military rule 1965–8, and 1969, presidential govt. by rotation among members of a presidential council was introduced 1970.

DÁIL ÉIRANN (doil-ār'an). The lower house of the legislature of Eire. It consists of 144 members elected by adult suffrage on a basis of proportional representation.

DAIMLER (dīm'ler), **Gottlieb** (1834–1900). German motor-car pioneer. B. in Württemberg, he had engineering experience at the Whitworth works, Manchester, before joining in 1872 N. A. Otto of Cologne in the production of new-type gas engines. In 1886 he produced the first 'motor vehicle', and a motorbicycle. He is usually credited with the original invention of the internal combustion engine, though Benz and others were experimenting simultaneously. His patents, etc., were acquired in 1891 by the D. Co., later a subsidiary of Jaguar, and from 1966 part of British Motor Holding Ltd.

DAIREN (dīren'). Chinese port on Liaotung peninsula facing the Yellow Sea, in the prov. of Liaoning. It was leased to Russia in 1898, ceded to Japan in 1905 until in 1945 by a Russo-Chinese treaty it was made a free port, half the port installations being leased to Russia; under a second treaty, 1950, the status of D. was to be reconsidered after Russia and China had made peace with Japan. D. makes machinery, chemicals, textiles, etc., has petroleum refineries, soya-bean processing factories, and a naval

DAHLIA. Left to right: garden cactus, star, old-fashioned double dahlias.

dockyard. With Port Arthur (q.v.) it forms the municipal district of Lüta. Pop. (1960) 1,508,000.

DAIRYING. The business of producing and handling milk and milk products. Liquid whole milk is the nearest approach which is known to a perfect food. In England and Wales, over 70 per cent of the milk produced is consumed in its liquid form, consequently D. is dominated by the needs of the home liquid milk market, whereas countries such as New Zealand rely on easily transportable milk products such as butter, cheese, condensed and dried milk. It is now usual for dairy farms to concentrate on the production of milk and for factories to take over the handling, processing, and distribution of milk as well as the manufacture of dairy products. In Britain the Milk Marketing Board (1933), to which all producers must sell their milk, forms a connecting link between farms and factories. Research is carried out at the National Institute for Research in Dairying at Reading, the Hannah Dairy Research Institute in Scotland, etc. *See* MILK.

DAISY. Genus of plants (*Bellis*) of the family Compositae. The best-known species is the common D. (*B. perennis*), a British wild flower. A single white or pink flower-head rises from a rosette of spoon-shaped leaves. There are many cultivated varieties.

DA'KAR. Chief port and cap. of Senegal, W. Africa, on Cape Verde peninsula. Founded in 1862, it has an artificial harbour, extensive docks, and an airport. It is an industrial centre, and there is a univ. (1957). It was formerly the seat of govt. of French W. Africa. Pop. (1968) 450,000.

COMMON DAISY

DAKOTA. *See* NORTH DAKOTA; SOUTH DAKOTA.

DALADIER (dahlahdyeh'), **Edouard** (1884–1970). French statesman. Originally a teacher, he entered the Chamber as a Radical in 1919, and was P.M. Jan.–Oct. 1933 and Jan.–Feb. 1934. Once more Premier April 1938–March 1940, he was largely responsible both for the Munich Agreement and France's declaration of war on Germany, was arrested on the fall of France, and was a prisoner in Germany 1943–5. He was re-elected to the Chamber 1946–58.

DALAI LAMA (dahli' lah'mah), 14th Incarnation (1935–   ). Spiritual and temporal head of the Tibetan State until 1959. Enthroned in 1940, he temporarily fled 1950–1 when the Chinese overran Tibet, and in March 1959 made a dramatic escape from Lhasa to India, following a local uprising against Chinese rule. He then settled at Dharmsala, in the Punjab. In 1962 he pub. his autobiography *My Land and People*. *See* LAMAISM.

DALCROZE (dahlcrōz'), **Émile-Jaques**. *See* JAQUES-DALCROZE, ÉMILE.

DALE, Sir Henry Hallett (1875–1968). Brit. scientist. B. in London, he was director of the National Institute for Medical Research 1928–42 and in 1936 shared the Nobel prize for medicine with Otto Loewi of Graz for work on the chemical transmission of nervous effects. In 1942–6 he was prof. of chemistry at the Royal Institution, and was awarded the O.M. 1944.

D'ALEMBERT. *See* ALEMBERT.

DALGARNO, George (1626–87). Scottish schoolmaster and inventor of the first deaf-and-dumb alphabet (1680).

DALHOUSIE (dalhow'zi), **James Andrew Broun Ramsay**, 1st marquess and 10th earl of D. (1812–60). British administrator. He worked with Gladstone at the Board of Trade, succeeding him as pres. from 1845 until his appointment as Gov.-Gen. of India in 1847. For his successful handling of the 2nd Sikh War he received a marquessate, annexed the Punjab (1849) and, following the Burmese War, Lower Burma (1853). He also reformed the Army and Civil Service, and furthered social and economic progress before retiring in 1856.

DALI (dah'lē), **Salvador** (1904–   ). Spanish artist. B. near Barcelona, he came under the influence of the Italian Futurists, but in 1929 joined the Surrealists. A student of Freud, he claimed that his work could be appreciated only by the unconscious, and shocked the public into startled recognition of his gifts. His later work shows a reversion to classicism. He collaborated with L. Bunuel in surrealist films, and has designed ballet costumes and scenery. *Secret Life of S.D.* and *Diary of a Genius* (1966) are autobiographical.

DALIN (dah'lin), **Olof von** (1708–63). Swedish poet, essayist and dramatist. A civil servant at Stockholm, he became famous for the political satires *Story of the Horse* and *Aprilverk* (1738), and in 1751 was appointed tutor to the Crown Prince. He wrote tragedies and comedies in the French classical style.

DALKEITH (dalkēth'). Scottish burgh of Midlothian, 6 m. S.E. of Edinburgh, between the N. and S. Esk. Pop. (1961) 8,864.

DALLAN MAC FORGAILL (6th cent.). Irish poet, contemporary of Columba. His chief interest today is as the author of the *Eulogy of Colum Cille*, one of the earliest works in the Irish language extant.

DALLAS. Industrial city of Texas, U.S.A., an important railway centre with an airport in a large agricultural, mineral and petroleum area. It has a univ., and the annual Texas State Fair. Pop. met. area (1970) 1,539,372.

DALMATIA (dalmā'shia). Region of Croatia, Yugoslavia, area 4,956 sq. m.; pop. (est.) 800,000. The cap. is Split. It lies along the E. shore of the Adriatic and incl. a number of islands. The interior is mountainous. Important products are wine, olives, and fish. Notable towns in addition to the cap. are Zadar, Sibenik, and Dubrovnik. D. became Austrian in 1815, and by the treaty of Rapallo, 1920, went to the kingdom of the Serbs, Croats, and Slovenes (Yugoslavia from 1931), except for the town of Zadar (Zara), and the island of Lastovo (Lagosta) with neighbouring islets, given to Italy until transferred to Yugoslavia in 1947. D. was made a region of Croatia in 1949.

DALI. A surrealist treatment of a conventional subject, 'The Discovery of America by Christopher Columbus' dated 1959, results in a dreamlike atmosphere.
Courtesy of The Huntington Hartford Collection, Gallery of Modern Art.

DALMATIAN. Breed of dog, familiar as the 'spotted' or 'plum pudding' dog. Medium-sized and smooth-coated, white with characteristic liver or black spots, it is classified as a pointer.

DALMA'TIC. The outer liturgical vestment of the deacon in the R.C. Church; a mantle worn at Mass and in solemn processions.

DALNY. Russian form of DAIREN.

DALOU (dahloo′), **Jules** (1838–1902). French sculptor. Involved in the Commune rising of 1871 he fled to London, but returned in 1879 and after 20 years' work his 'Triumph of the Republic' was erected in the Place de la Nation.

DALTON, Hugh, baron (1887–1962). British economist. The son of a canon of St. George's, Windsor, he was called to the Bar in 1914, and in 1919 became a lecturer at the London School of Economics. He had been pres. of the University Fabians at Cambridge and in 1924 entered parliament as a Labour M.P., becoming an important figure in the '30s. Chancellor of the Exchequer in 1945, he resigned in 1947 following an indiscreet disclosure to a Lobby correspondent before a Budget speech. His name is associated with the $2\frac{1}{2}\%$ Irredeemable Treasury Stock known as 'Daltons', introduced in 1946 and bought by many savers, but rapidly depreciating in value. In 1960 he was created a life peer.

DALTON, John (1766–1844). British scientist. B. in Cumberland, he taught at New College, Manchester 1793–9, his 1st important work *Meteorological Observations and Essays* appearing in 1793. He is remembered for his tentative formulation of the atomic theory of chemical composition in 'Absorption of Gases' (1805), with a list of atomic weights, and elaborated in his *New System of Chemical Philosophy* (1808).

DALTON-IN-FURNESS. English town (U.D.) in Lancs, 4 m. N.E. of Barrow-in-Furness. Iron ore is mined. Pop. (1961) 10,317. Romney was b. and buried here.

DALY, Augustin (1838–99). American theatrical manager. Of Irish descent, he was at first a drama critic and playwright, then in 1879 built Daly's theatre in New York and another Daly's in London (1893–1939). His company was a great training ground for the American stage.

DALZIEL (dal′zĕl). British family of wood-engravers. George D. (1815–1902), Edward D. (1817–1905), John D. (1822–60), and Thomas Bolton D. (1823–1906), were all sons of Alexander D. of Wooler, Northumberland. George went to London in 1835 and was joined in due course by his brothers. They produced a large number of illustrations for the classics and magazines.

DAMAN. Another form of DAMAO.

DAMÃO (dah′mahñ). Former Portuguese settlement on the W. coast of India, at the entrance to the Gulf of Cambay, some 100 m. N. of Bombay. Area 149 sq. m.; pop. (1950) 63,521. It was annexed by India in 1961.

DAMARALAND. Central region of S.W. Africa, lying about Windhoek. It is inhabited by the Hereros (q.v.).

DAMASCUS. City of western Asia, the capital of Syria, said to be the oldest still inhabited city of the world. It stands on the Barada, 57 m. S.E. of Beirut, on the edge of a highly fertile area, and has rail connections with the chief cities of the Levant.

D. was an ancient city even in O.T. times. The Assyrians destroyed it in *c.* 733 B.C. In 332 B.C. it fell to one of the generals of Alexander the Great; in 63 B.C. it became Roman. In A.D. 635 it was taken by the Arabs, and has since been captured many times, by Egyptians, Mongolians, Turks, etc. During the F.W.W. it was taken by the British, 1918, and in 1920 became cap. of French-mandated Syria.

The 'street which is called straight' is associated with St. Paul who was converted while on the road to D. The most notable of the old buildings is the Great Mosque, completed as a Christian church in the 5th cent. A.D. The fortress dates from 1219. A Syrian univ. was founded in 1924. From ancient times, D. has been a trading centre and was once famous for its swords. Pop. (1965) 599,000.

DAMASK. In textiles: linen, cotton, silk, etc., fabrics that possess a figured pattern. The name derives from the city of Damascus.

DAMASKINOS (damaskē′nos) (1891–1949). Primate of the Greek Orthodox Church from 1938, and Regent of Greece 1945–6, following the withdrawal of the German forces and prior to the return of King George.

DAME. Legal title of the wife (or widow) of a knight or baronet, also of Dames of the Order of the British Empire. *See* CUSTOMARY FORMS OF ADDRESS.

DAMIEN (dahmyañ′), **Father** (1840–89). Belgian missionary; his original name was Joseph de Veuster. He entered the order of the Fathers of the Sacred Heart at Louvain, went to Hawaii, and from 1873 was resident priest in the leper settlement at Molokai; he became himself infected.

DAMIETTA. River-port of the United Arab Republic, in Lower Egypt on the E. branch of the Nile delta, 10 m. from its mouth. Pop. (1967) 97,000.

DAMOCLES (dam′ōklēz) (fl. 4th cent. B.C.). A courtier to the elder Dionysius, ruler of Syracuse. Having extolled the happiness of his sovereign, D. was invited by him to a great feast, and in the midst of his enjoyment beheld above his head a sword suspended by a single hair. He recognized this as a symbol of the insecurity of the great.

DAMODAR. Indian river flowing *c.* 350 m. from Chota Nagpur plateau in Bihar through Bihar and W. Bengal states to join the Hooghli 25 m. S.W. of Calcutta. Work on the major D. valley project for flood control, irrigation, and production of power began in 1948.

DAMPIER (dam′pēr), **William** (1652–1715). English explorer. B. in Somerset, he went to sea in 1668, led a life of buccaneering adventure, circumnavigated the globe, and pub. his *New Voyage Round the World* in 1697. In 1699 he was sent by the government on a voyage to Australia and New Guinea, and again circled the world. He accomplished a 3rd circumnavigation 1703–7, and on his final voyage 1708–11 rescued Alexander Selkirk, the original of Robinson Crusoe, from Juan Fernandez.

DAMROSCH (dam′rosh), **Leopold** (1832–85). German-American composer and conductor. B. at Posen, he held musical appointments at Weimar and Breslau, before emigrating to America in 1871 to become conductor at the Metropolitan Opera House, N.Y. His son WALTER D. (1862–1950), succeeded him at the Metropolitan Opera House and also conducted the New York Symphony Society 1885–1926, the N.Y. Oratorio Society, etc.

DAMS. Engineering structures built to hold up water so as to prevent floods, provide water for irrigation and storage, and produce hydro-electric power. The first of the modern scientifically designed Ds. was the Aswan Dam on the Nile, 600 m. above Cairo.

DAMSON. Variety of the plum distinguished by its small, oval fruit, which in colour ranges from yellow, through dark purple or blue to black.

DANA (dā′na), **Richard Henry** (1815–82). American author. Son of Richard Henry D., poet and essayist, he went to sea and worked his passage round Cape Horn to California and back, publishing in 1840 an account in *Two Years before the Mast.*

DANAE (dan′ā-ē). In Gk. mythology, dau. of Acrisius, king of Argos, who shut her up in a brazen tower because of a prophecy that her son would kill his grandfather. Zeus became enamoured of her and descended in a shower of gold, and by him she became the mother of Perseus.

DANBY, Thomas Osborne, earl of (1631–1712). British Tory statesman. Entering parliament in 1665, he acted 1673–8 as Charles II's chief minister, and in 1674 was created earl of D. He endeavoured to strengthen the Crown, although his foreign policy was hostile to France. In 1678 he was impeached, and sent to the Tower until 1684. In 1688 he signed the invitation to William of Orange which led to the Revolution, was again chief minister 1690–5, and in 1694 was created duke of Leeds.

DANCE, George (1700–68). British architect. He designed the Mansion House (1739). His son, GEORGE D. (1741–1825), succeeded him as architect to the City of London.

DANCE, Sir George (d. 1932). British playwright. B. at Nottingham, he became a successful dramatist and wrote *A Modern Don Quixote*, the first English musical comedy.

DANCING. Rhythmic movement of the body, usually performed in time to music by one, two or more people. Its primary purpose is not for exercise, but may be religious, magical, martial, social or artistic – the last 2 being characteristic of contemporary 'advanced' societies.

Dances have always tended to rise upward through the social scale, i.e. the medieval court dances derived from peasant country dances. One form of dance tends to typify a whole period, e.g. the galliard the 16th cent., the minuet the 18th, the waltz the 19th and the quickstep the 20th. In this cent. new dances have tended to reach Britain from the Americas, the pioneers in popularizing them being Vernon and Irene Castle and the Astaires. The 9 dances of the modern World Championships in ballroom D. are the standard 4 (waltz, foxtrot, tango and quickstep) the Latin-American styles (samba, rumba, cha-cha-cha, and paso doble), and the Viennese waltz: a British development since the '30s, which has spread to some extent abroad, is 'formation' D. in which each team (usually 8 couples) performs a series of ballroom steps in strict co-ordination. Popular dance crazes, also American imports, have been the jitterbug in the '40s, jive in the '50s and the twist in the '60s. There is also today a great interest in Old Time (lancers, polka, two-step) and sequence D. *See* BALLET.

DANCOURT (doṅkoor'), **Florent Carton** (1661–1725). French actor and dramatist, author of some 60 farcical comedies, the most notable being *Le Chevalier à la Mode* (1687).

DANDELION (dan'delī-on). Perennial British wild flower (*Taraxacum officinale*) belonging to the Compositae. The stout root-stalk rises from a rosette of leaves, deeply indented like a lion's tooth, hence the name (from Fr. *dent de lion*). The flower-heads are bright yellow. The fruit is surmounted by the hairs of the calyx which constitutes the familiar D. 'puff'. The milky juice of the D. has laxative properties, and the young leaves are sometimes eaten in salads.

DANCING. In Indonesia an honoured guest is still welcomed with the traditional dances. Here, in the Purwodiningratan Pavilion, Djakarta, the Sari Kembar dance is performed.
Courtesy of Indonesian Embassy.

DANDIE DINMONT

DANDIE DINMONT. Breed of terrier dog, which originated in the Scottish border country, and was made famous through the character Dandie Dinmont (and his terriers) in Scott's *Guy Mannering*.

DANDOLO. Celebrated Venetian family which produced 4 doges, of whom the most outstanding was Enrico D. (*c.* 1120–1205) who became doge in 1193. He greatly increased the dominions of the Venetian republic and accompanied the crusading army which took Constantinople (1203).

DANE, Clemence. Pseudonym of British author Winifred Ashton (1888–1965). Her many works include novels, such as *Regiment of Women* (1917) and *He Brings Great News* (1946), and plays, e.g. *A Bill of Divorcement* (1921), *Wild Decembers* (1932) – on a Brontë theme – and *Call Home the Heart* (1947).

DANIEL, Glyn (1914–). British archaeologist. University lecturer in archaeology at Cambridge from 1948, he has greatly assisted the development of the subject. His books incl. *A Hundred Years of Archaeology* (1950) and *The Idea of Prehistory* (1961).

DANIEL, Samuel (1562–1619). English poet and playwright. B. near Taunton, he was appointed in 1603 Master of Revels and entertained the court with his own masques and plays. The best-known of these is *Hymen's Triumph* (1615). The most popular of his works are his sonnets.

DANILŌ'VA, Alexandra (1906–). Russian dancer. B. in Pskoff, she was with Diaghileff's company 1925–9 and was prima ballerina of the Ballet Russe de Monte Carlo 1938–58.

DANINOS (dahnēnoh'), **Pierre** (1913–). French author. Originally a journalist, he was liaison agent with the British Army at Dunkirk in 1940, and created in *Les Carnets du Major Thompson* (1954) a humorous-type Englishman who caught the French imagination

DANISH LANGUAGE, LITERATURE, ART. *See under* DENMARK.

D'ANNUNZIO (dahnoon'tsyō), **Gabriele** (1863–1938). Italian writer. His 1st vol. of poetry, *Primo Vere* (1879), was followed by further collections of verse, short stories, novels, and plays, such as *La Gioconda* (1898) for Duse; *Francesca da Rimini* (1902), etc. After serving in the F.W.W., he led an expedition in 1919 to capture Fiume, which he held until 1921. He prepared the way for Fascism by his mystic nationalism, and was created Prince of Montenevoso in 1924.

DANTE ALIGHIERI (ahlēgi-ā'ri) (1265–1321). Italian poet. B. in Florence, he first met Beatrice in 1274 and conceived a love for her which survived her marriage to another and her death in 1290, as he described in *Vita Nuova* (*c.* 1295). In 1289 D. fought in the battle of Campaldino, won by Florence against Arezzo, and from 1295 took an active part in Florentine politics. In 1300 he was one of the 6 Priors of the Republic, and since he favoured the moderate White Guelphs rather than the Black, was convicted in his absence of misapplication of public moneys in 1302 when the latter became predominant. He spent the remainder of his life in exile, in central and N. Italy. His works include the prose philosophical treatise *Convivio* (1306–8); *Monarchia* (1310–13), expounding his political theories; *De vulgari eloquentia* (1304–6), an original Latin work on Italian, its dialects, and kindred languages; *Canzoniere*, containing his scattered lyrics; and the *Divina Commedia* (*c.* 1300–21) an imaginary journey through Hell, Purgatory, and Paradise, under the guidance of Reason and Faith, represented by Virgil and Beatrice respectively. It is the greatest poem of the Middle Ages.

DANTON (doǹtoǹ'), **Georges Jacques** (1759–94). French revolutionary. B. at Arcis-sur-Aube, he practised law, and during the early years of the Revolution he was one of the most influential men in Paris. He organized the rising of 10 Aug. 1792 which overthrew the monarchy, roused the country to expel the Prussian invaders, and procured the formation in April 1793 of the revolutionary tribunal and the Committee of Public Safety, of which until July he was the real leader. Thereafter he sank into the background. When he attempted to recover power, he was arrested and guillotined.

DANUBE. Second longest of European rivers. It rises on the E. slopes of the Black Forest, and flows for 1,750 m. across Europe to enter the Black Sea in Rumania by a swampy delta. The head of river navigation is Ulm, in Baden-Württemberg; Braila, Rumania, is the limit for ocean-going ships. Large towns on the D. include Linz, Vienna, Bratislava, Budapest, Belgrade, Ruse, Braila, and Galati. The D. is connected with the Main by canal, and thus with the Rhine system.

Navigation of the D. delta below Braila was in 1856 placed under an international commission and the Versailles Treaty, 1919, created another to maintain free navigation for all nations from Ulm to Braila; this was abolished by Germany in 1940. After the S.W.W. Russia was in a position to control the D. from Vienna to its mouth, and in 1948 called a conference of Danubian states which excluded non-Danubian countries from the commission and, in practice, from use of the river.

DANZIG. German form of GDANSK.

DAPHNE. Genus of shrubs, natives of the N. hemisphere of the Old World, and included in the Thymeleaceae. Best known of the 40 species is the British spurge laurel (*D. laureola*). The leaves are evergreen, the flowers green, and the berries black and poisonous.

D'ARBLAY, Madame. See BURNEY, FANNY.

DARDANELLES. Turkish strait that joins the Sea of Marmara with the Aegean Sea; its shores are formed by the Gallipoli (q.v.) peninsula on the N.W. and the mainland of Turkey-in-Asia on the S.E. It is about 47 m. long and 3–4 m. wide.

DAR ES SALAAM (dahr-es-salahm') (Arab., 'haven of peace'). Seaport and cap. of Tanganyika (also of Tanzania) on the E. coast of Africa. Univ. Coll. is a constituent coll. of the Univ. of E. Africa (1963) and there is a Technical College. Oil is refined and a pipeline (1968) runs to Ndola in the Zambian copperbelt, to which a road was completed 1966. There is also an airport and the TanZam railway to Zambia is under construction. Pop. (1967) 372,515.

DARFUR (dar'foor). Prov. in the W. of the Republic of Sudan, a vast rolling plain producing gum arabic; there is also stock raising. The cap. is El Fasher (pop. 30,000). D. was an independent sultanate until conquered by Egypt in 1874. Area 138,150 sq. m. Pop. (1967) 372,515.

DARIEN. Eastern prov. of Panama, cap. La Palma. Pop. (1968) 24,100. It produces timber, rice, and beans, and cattle are reared. The Gulf of D., part of the Caribbean, lies between Panama and Colombia.

The name D. was formerly used for the Panama isthmus, an attempt at colonization of which by Scottish emigrants in 1698–9 failed disastrously owing to Spanish hostility and the unhealthy climate.

DARIO (dahrē-oh'), **Rubén.** Pseudonym of the Nicaraguan poet, Felix Rubén Sarmiento (1867–1916). After holding various diplomatic appointments, he came to Madrid in 1892. He estab. the Modernist movement by his *Azure* (1888), a collection of prose and verse, and *Profane Prose* (1896). Greatest of the later works is *Songs of Life and Hope* (1905).

DARIUS I, the Great, king of Persia, 512–

DARIUS I
Courtesy of Imperial Iranian Embassy.

485 B.C. A member of a younger branch of the royal family of the Achaemenidae, he won the throne from the usurper Gaumata, reorganized the govt., and in 512 marched against the Scythians and subjugated Thrace and Macedonia. An expedition in 492 to crush a rebellion in Greece failed, and the army sent into Attica (490 B.C.) was defeated at Marathon. D. had an account of his reign inscribed on the mountain at Behistun, Persia. Our illus. shows a low-relief carving from Persepolis. Then, as now in the East, the parasol was a symbol of royal dignity.

DARJEELING (dahrjē'-ling). Town and hill-station in W. Bengal, India, c. 7,000 ft. above sea-level on the S. slopes of the Himalayas, and connected by rail with Calcutta, 369 m. to the S. It is the centre of a tea-producing district. Pop. (1961) 40,651.

DARLAN (dahrloǹ'), **Jean François** (1881–1942). French admiral and politician. He entered the navy in 1899, and in 1939 was appointed admiral and C.-in-C. He commanded the French navy 1939–40, took part in the evacuation of Dunkirk, and entered the Pétain Cabinet as Naval Minister. In 1941 he was appointed Vice-Premier, and became strongly anti-British and pro-German, but in 1942 he was dropped from the Cabinet by Laval. He was recognized as Chief of State by the Americans when they landed in French N. Africa, and was assassinated by a young Frenchman.

DARLEY, George (1795–1846). Irish poet. B. in Dublin, he became a journalist in London in 1822. His chief poem 'Nepenthe' (1839) was left unfinished; he also wrote lyrics and poetic dramas.

DARLING, Grace (1815–42). British heroine. She was the dau. of a lighthouse keeper on the Farne Islands. On 7 Sept. 1838 the *Forfarshire* was wrecked, and at considerable danger Grace and her father rowed to the wreck and 9 lives were saved. She was awarded a medal for her bravery.

DARLING. Australian river, a tributary of the Murray, which it joins at Wentworth; its length is 1,910 m. D. is also the name of a district of New S. Wales, a mountain range in W. Australia, and of Downs in S.E. Queensland. The name comes from Sir Ralph Darling (1775–1858), governor of N.S.W. 1825–31.

DARLINGTON, Cyril Dean (1903–). British geneticist. Director of the John Innes Horticultural Institution 1939–53, he was then appointed Sherardian prof. of botany at Oxford. His books incl. *The Evolution of Genetic Systems* (1939) and *Genus, Plants, and People* (1950). In 1941 he was elected F.R.S.

DARLINGTON, William Aubrey (1890–). British

DARJEELING. 'Darby and Joan'.
Photo: B. Deane.

author. Dramatic editor of the *Daily Telegraph* from 1925, he wrote the comic fantasy *Alf's Button* (1919), later staged and filmed.

DARLINGTON. English town (co. bor.) in Durham, on the Skerne, near its junction with the Tees. It has coal and ironstone mines, and makes iron and steel goods, woollens, etc. Pop. (1961) 84,162.

DARMESTETER (dahrmestetär'), **Arsène** (1846–88). French lexicographer and philologist. Of Jewish origin, he was professor at the Sorbonne, joint author with Hatzfeld of the *Dictionnaire général de la langue française* (1895–1900), and author of works on philological subjects. His brother, JAMES D. (1849–94), orientalist, pub. *Études iraniennes* (1883) and translated and commented on the *Zend Avesta*.

DARMSTADT. Town in the Land of Hessen, Germany, 18 m. S. of Frankfurt-am-Main. It has a ducal palace and a technical university. Its industries include iron founding and the manufacture of chemicals. Pop. (1966) 139,748.

DARNLEY, Henry Stewart or **Stuart**, lord (1545–67). 2nd husband of Mary, Queen of Scots. He was b. in England the son of the earl of Lennox and Lady Margaret Douglas, through whom he inherited a claim to the English throne. In 1565 he m. Mary, who was his 1st cousin. By the advice of her secretary, David Rizzio, Mary refused D. the crown matrimonial; in revenge D. led a band of nobles who murdered Rizzio in Mary's presence. Within a few days Mary and D. were reconciled, and a son, later James I and VI, was b. in June, but soon D. alienated all parties and a plot was formed against him by Bothwell. While he was lying ill at Kirk o'Field, a lonely house at Edinburgh, it was blown up on 10 Feb. 1567, D.'s body being found strangled in a neighbouring garden. Mary's share in the plot remains a subject of controversy.

DARROW, Clarence Seward (1857–1938). American lawyer. B. in Ohio, he appeared on behalf of labour organizations in many famous cases, notably the trial of Eugene Debs in 1895, and was counsel for the defence in the Loeb and Leopold murder trial of 1924, and the Dayton 'monkey' trial of 1925.

DARTFORD. English market town (bor.) in Kent, 17 m. E.S.E. of London, on the Darent, close to its union with the Thames. Manufactures cement, chemicals, and paper. The D. Tunnel (1963) runs under the Thames to Purfleet, Essex. Pop. (1961) 45,643.

DARTMOOR. Plateau of S.W. Devon, some 400 sq. m. in extent; 200 sq. m. lie 1,000 ft. or more above sea-level. D. is noted for its wild aspect. Rugged

DARTMOOR. One of a number of such broken granite masses, Haytor lies slumbering like a primeval beast. The moor, at once strangely beautiful and sinister, has captured the imagination of innumerable writers and artists.

Photo: Roy J. Westlake.

DARTMOUTH. The Pilgrim Fathers set sail in the *Mayflower* and *Speedwell* from Southampton on 5 August 1620, but had to put in at Dartmouth when the *Speedwell* was found to need repair. A second start was made from Monkey Quay, seen here, but bad weather drove them into Plymouth Sound where the *Speedwell* was abandoned. *Photo: A. W. Kerr.*

blocks of granite, or 'tors', crown its higher points, the highest being Yes Tor (2,029 ft.) and High Willhays (2,038 ft.). The chief rivers of Devon have their sources on D. There are numerous prehistoric relics. 365 sq. m. of D. is a National Park.

D. Prison, opened in 1809 originally to house prisoners-of-war, is at Princetown in the centre of the moor, 7 m. E. of Tavistock.

DARTMOUTH. English seaport (bor.) at the mouth of the Dart, 27 m. E. of Plymouth, on the Devon coast, a noted centre for yachting, with an excellent harbour. The Britannia Royal Naval Coll. dates from 1905. Pop. (1961) 5,757.

DARU (dahrü'), **Pierre Antoine**, count (1767–1829). French statesman. B. at Montpellier, he became one of Napoleon's ablest advisers and administrators, and at the Bourbon restoration was made a peer.

DARWEN. English town (bor.) on the D. river, Lancs, 23 m. N.N.W. of Manchester. Cotton and plastics are manufactured, coal mined, and stone quarried. Pop. (1961) 29,452.

DARWIN, Charles Robert (1809–82). British scientist; discoverer of the principle of natural selection. B. at Shrewsbury, the grandson of Erasmus D. (q.v.), he studied medicine at Edinburgh and theology at Cambridge. As naturalist on the surveying voyage in the southern hemisphere of H.M.S. *Beagle* 1831–6, he made the observations leading to his theory of modification of species. Having m. in 1839 his cousin Emma Wedgwood, he settled in Down, Kent, for the rest of his life. By 1844 he had enlarged his notes to a sketch of his conclusions, and in 1858 A. R. Wallace (q.v.) sent a memoir to D. embodying almost the same theory. In 1859 D. pub. *On the Origin of Species by Means of Natural Selection* which placed the whole world of living things in an intelligible pattern, a genealogical tree, but aroused bitter controversy because it did not agree with the literal sense of the Book of Genesis. D. himself played little part in the debates, but his *Descent of Man* (1871) added fuel to the theological

CHARLES DARWIN. By John Collier. *Photo: N.P.G.*

DARWIN. Named after Charles Darwin, who visited it in 1836 on his way to New South Wales, the city is the northern gateway to Australia. The way overland from the south was opened by John McDouall Stuart in 1861 and a 1,000-mile road (Stuart Highway) links it with Alice Springs.
Courtesy of Australian News and Information Bureau.

discussion in which T. H. Huxley and Haeckel (qq.v.) took leading parts. D. then devoted himself chiefly to botanical subjects till his death. He was buried in Westminster Abbey.

Of his 5 sons, several were eminent scientists, and his grandson SIR CHARLES D. (1887–1963), a theoretical physicist, was the chief organizer in S.W.W. of British atom-bomb research, and director of the N.P.L. 1938–49. Another grandson, BERNARD D. (1876–1963), was *The Times* golf correspondent 1907–53 and played for England 8 times.

DARWIN, Erasmus (1731–1802). British poet, physician and naturalist. B. in Notts, he practised as a doctor at Nottingham, at Lichfield, and at Derby. His most famous work was *The Loves of the Plants* which attempted to expound the Linnaean or sexual system of classification in verse.

DARWIN. Cap. and port of Northern Territory, Australia, in the N.W. of Arnhem Land, a centre for pearl shell, bêche-de-mer, and fish, founded in 1872 and named after Charles D. The N. terminus of a railway from Birdum, and an air station on the route from India, it was bombed by the Japanese in the S.W.W. Experiments in commercial fruit and vegetable growing are in progress in D. area. Pop. (1966) 20,412.

DASS (dahs), **Petter** (1647–1708). Norwegian poet of Scottish descent. He became a priest, and pub. *Den norska Dale-Vise* (Norwegian Song of the Valley) in 1696; other books, including his greatest poem, *Nordlands Trompet*, appeared posthumously.

DASYURUS (dasi-ū′-rus). Genus of marsupial cats. Nocturnal animals found in Australia and New Guinea, they are usually brown, spotted with white, and have a long fairly bushy tail, and feet adapted for climbing and running.

DATE. Genus of palms (*Phoenix*), of which *P. dactylifera*, a native of N. Africa, S.W. Asia, and parts of India, is the most important. It varies in height from 30 to 60 ft. The fruit are produced by the female tree in bunches,

DATE palm and fruit.

weighing 20–5 lb., and numbering 180–200 fruit. Ds. are an important source of food in the Near and Middle East, being exceedingly rich in sugar, and when dried are exported. Their juice is made into a kind of wine.

DAUBIGNY (dohbĕnyi′), **Charles François** (1817–78). French landscape painter. B. in Paris, he was associated with the Barbizon school, and is famed for his river scenes.

DAUDET (dohdeh′), **Alphonse** (1840–97). French novelist. He became a journalist in Paris. Among his works, which show a Dickensian realism, are the sketches *Lettres de mon moulin* (1866); *Tartarin de Tarascon* (1872) with its 2 sequels; *Fromont jeune et Risler aîné* (1874); the play *L'Arlésienne* (1872), for which Bizet composed the music; and *Souvenirs d'un homme de lettres* (1889). He m. in 1867 Julie Allard (1847–1940), who wrote verse and literary sketches under the name of Karl Steen. His brother **Ernest D.** (1837–1921), wrote historical works, novels such as *Thérèse*, and the autobiographical *Mon Frère et moi.* Alphonse D.'s son, **Léon D.** (1867–1942), also became a journalist, and founded in 1899, after the Dreyfus case, the militant royalist periodical *Action Française.* He wrote novels and philosophical treatises, and frank *Souvenirs* (1914). During the S.W.W. he was a collaborator.

DAUGAVPILS. Town in Latvia S.S.R., on the Daugava (W. Dvina). A fortress of the Livonian Knights, 1278, it became the cap. of Polish Livonia. There is a timber industry. Pop. (1967) 87,000.

DAUMIER (dohmyeh′), **Honoré** (1808–79). French artist. B. at Marseilles, he was taken to Paris as a child and entered a lithographer's studio. He became famous for his cartoons for *La Caricature*, *Charivari* and other periodicals, once being imprisoned for an attack on Louis Philippe. His output was enormous and incl. 4,000 lithographs, but his popular success hindered appreciation of his work as a painter, e.g. his realistic 'Les Bohémiens de Paris', 'Christ Mocked' and illustrations of incidents from Cervantes.

DAUPHIN (dohfań′). Title of the eldest sons of the kings of France from 1349 to 1830. It was originally attached to the rulers of the provinces of Vienne and Auvergne, known as the Dauphiné.

DAUPHINÉ (dohfĕneh′). Old prov. of France, comprising the depts. of Isère, Drôme, and Hautes-Alpes. After the collapse of Rome it belonged to Burgundy, then was under Frankish domination, afterwards part of Arles, it was sold by its ruler to France in 1349. The cap. was Grenoble.

DÁVAO. Town in the Philippine Republic, cap. of D. prov., at the mouth of D. river on the island of Mindanao. It is the centre of a fertile district and is a busy port. Pop. (1968) 298,300.

DA'VENANT, Sir William (1606–68). English poet and dramatist. B. at Oxford, he was rumoured to be a son of Shakespeare. In 1638 he became poet laureate, and during the Civil Wars was imprisoned by Parliament. His *Siege of Rhodes* (1656) is considered the first English opera.

DAVENTRY (dān′tri). English town (bor.) in Northants, 12 m. W. of Northampton, with boot and shoe manufactures. On Borough Hill to the S.E. a B.B.C. high-power, short-wave transmitter was built in 1925. Pop. (1961) 5,846.

DAVID (c. 1060–970 B.C.). Second king of Israel. Youngest son of Jesse of Bethlehem, while still a shepherd boy he was anointed by Samuel to succeed Saul. He played the harp before Saul to banish his melancholy, and later slew the Philistine giant, Goliath, with a sling and stone. Saul's son, Jonathan, became his friend, but Saul, jealous of his prowess, schemed to murder him. D. married Michal, Saul's dau., but following further attempts on his life went into exile until Saul and Jonathan fell in battle with the Philistines at Gilboa. D. was anointed king at

Hebron, took Jerusalem, made it his capital, and housed the Ark there. Absalom, his favourite son, led a rebellion but was defeated and slain. D. sent Uriah to his death in order that he might marry his widow. He probably wrote a few of the psalms, was a skilled harpist, and was celebrated as a secular poet.

DAVID (or **Dewi**) (fl. 5th–6th cent.). Patron saint of Wales, traditionally the son of a prince of Cardiganshire and uncle of King Arthur. He founded a monastery at Menevia, and presided over a synod at

DAVID with the head and sword of Goliath. After Domenico Feti at Hampton Court.
Victoria and Albert Museum.

Brefi and condemned the Pelagian heresy. It is said that D. was responsible for the adoption of the leek as the national emblem of Wales.

DAVID I (1084–1153). King of Scotland. The youngest son of Malcolm Ceanmhor and St. Margaret, he was brought up in the English court of Henry I, m. in 1113 Matilda, widow of the earl of Northampton, and in 1124 became king. He invaded England in 1138 in support of Queen Matilda, dau. of Henry I, but was defeated at Northallerton in the 'Battle of the Standard', and again in 1141.

DAVID II (1324–71). King of Scotland. Son of Robert the Bruce, he was m. at the age of 4 to Joanna, dau. of Edward II of England, and in 1329 succeeded to the throne. After the defeat of the Scots by Edward III at Halidon Hill, D. and Joanna were sent to France for safety. They returned in 1341 and in 1346 D. invaded England and was captured at the battle of Neville's Cross and imprisoned for 11 years. On Joanna's death in 1362 D. m. Margaret Logie, but divorced her in 1370.

DAVID (dahvēd'), **Félicien César** (1810–76). French composer. He travelled in Palestine, and became famous with the performance of his symphonic fantasy *Desert* (1844). He was one of the first Western composers to introduce oriental scales and melodies into his music.

DAVID, Gerard (c. 1450–1523). Flemish painter. The last great artist of the Bruges school, he is famous chiefly for his altar-pieces.

DAVID (dahvēd'), **Jacques Louis** (1748–1825). French painter. He studied under Boucher, won the Prix de Rome in 1774, and during the Revolution he was an ardent supporter of the republicans; he was elected to the Convention and a member of the Committee of Public Safety, and narrowly escaped the guillotine. His most famous paintings are 'The Sabine Women' and 'Mme. Récamier'. He became court painter to Napoleon, but was banished by the Bourbons and settled in Brussels.

DAVIDSON, John (1857–1909). Scottish poet. B. in Renfrewshire, he developed an interest in science as assistant to the public analyst at Greenock, spent some years as a schoolmaster, and in 1889 went to London. At first mildly successful with *Fleet Street Eclogues* (1893) he declined into poverty and drowned himself. The modern, realistic idiom of such a poem as 'Thirty bob a week' influenced Eliot.

DAVIDSON OF LAMBETH, Randell Thomas, 1st baron (1848–1930). British churchman. Of Scottish parentage, he was archbishop of Canterbury 1903–28, and took a leading part in the movement to reunite the Christian Churches and the passing of the Church Assembly (Powers) Act of 1919, presiding over the Assembly 1920–8. He was created a baron on his resignation.

DAVIES, Clement (1884–1962). British politician. B. in Montgomery, he was called to the Bar in 1909 and in 1929 entered politics as M.P. for his native co. He led the Liberal Party 1945–56, when he was succeeded by Grimond (q.v.).

DAVIES, Sir Henry Walford (1869–1941). English composer. B. in Salop of Welsh parentage, he was knighted in 1922, and was organist at St. George's Chapel, Windsor 1927–32. From 1934 he was Master of the King's Musick, and he was influential in the musical education of Britain through his attractive radio talks. His compositions incl. the cantata *Everyman* (1904), the 'Solemn Melody' for organ and strings, chamber music and part songs.

DAVIES, Joseph Edward (1876–1958). American diplomat. B. in Wisconsin, he was ambassador to the U.S.S.R. 1936–8 and Belgium 1938–9, and special asst. to Sec. of State Hull 1939–41. He was Roosevelt's special envoy to Stalin in 1943 and at the Potsdam Conference he was special adviser to the Pres.

DAVIES, Rhys (1903–). British author. B. in the Rhondda Valley, he wrote short stories and novels, such as *Marianne* (1951) and *Girl Waiting in the Shade* (1960), often in the Welsh dialect.

DAVIES, William Henry (1871–1940). British poet. B. in Mon. he went to America, where he lived the life of a 'hobo', and lost his right foot 'riding the rods'. Returning to England he raised the money to pub. his first vol. of poems, *Soul's Destroyer* (1906), as a wandering pedlar. G. B. Shaw recognized its merit and assured his success. D. pub. further vols. of simple direct verse and the prose *Autobiography of a Super-Tramp* (1908). Our portrait is by Dame Laura Knight.

DA VINCI. *See* LEONARDO DA VINCI.

DAVIS, Bette (1908–). American actress. B. in Mass., she entered films in 1930, estab. a reputation with *Of Human Bondage* as a forceful dramatic actress. Later films incl. *Dangerous* (1935) and *Jezebel* (1938), both winning her Academy Awards, *Private Lives of Elizabeth and Essex*, and *Whatever happened to Baby Jane* (1963).

DAVIS, Colin (1927–). British conductor. Musical director at Sadler's Wells 1961–5, and chief conductor BBC Symphony Orchestra from 1967, he was appointed in 1968 musical director of the Royal Opera from 1971.

DAVIS, Dwight Filley (1879–1945). American tennis player, donor in 1900 of the *Davis Cup* – more properly, the Dwight Davis International Bowl, competed for annually by the world's amateur lawn-tennis players. He was Gov.-Gen. of the Philippine Islands 1929–32, after being U.S. Sec. for War from 1925.

DAVIS, Elmer (1890–1958). American journalist. B. in Indiana, he was a Rhodes scholar at Oxford, and was associated with the *New York Times* 1914–24. He is remembered for his superb broadcast on Pearl Harbor and his campaign against McCarthy (q.v.).

DAVIS, Jefferson (1808–89). American statesman. B. in Kentucky, he served in the U.S. army before becoming a cotton planter in Mississippi. He sat in the Senate 1847–51, and was Secretary of War 1853–7. He returned to the Senate in 1857 as a leader of the Southern Democrats, and a defender of slavery; in 1860 he issued a declaration in favour of secession, and early in 1861 he was elected president of the Confederate States. During the Civil War he ably directed the home front, but his strategy was less

W. H. DAVIES

successful. He left Richmond on its fall in 1865, and shortly after was captured in Georgia, and spent 2 years in prison.

DAVIS, John (c. 1550–1605). English navigator and explorer. B. near Dartmouth, he sailed in search of a N.W. passage in 1585, and in 1587 sailed to Baffin Bay through the straits named after him. In 1588 he fought against the Armada. He was killed by Japanese pirates in the straits of Malacca.

DAVIS, John William (1873–1955). American diplomat. A popular ambassador to Britain 1918–21, he was one of Wilson's advisers at the Versailles Conference.

DAVISSON, Clinton (1881–1958). American scientist. B. in Illinois, he worked under O. W. Richardson at Princeton before joining the Bell Telephone organization in 1917, and proved de Broglie's theory that electrons – and therefore all matter – have wave structure: G. P. Thompson carried through the same research independently and in 1937 the 2 men shared a Nobel prize.

DAVITT, Michael (1846–1906). Irish revolutionary. B. in co. Mayo, he began work in a factory at the age of 10, joined the Fenians in 1865, and was sentenced in 1870 to 15 years' imprisonment for treason-felony. After his release in 1877 he and Parnell founded the Land League in 1879. Imprisoned several times for his share in the land agitation, he was a M.P. 1895–9.

DAVOS (dahvohs′). Town, 5,115 ft. high, in an Alpine valley in Grisons canton, Switzerland, famous as a resort for consumptives and as a winter-sports centre. Pop. (1960) 9,588.

DAVOUT (dahvōō′), **Louis Nicolas**, duke of Auerstädt and prince of Eckmühl (1770–1823). Marshal of France from 1804. He held high command in the *grande armée*, and distinguished himself at Austerlitz and in the campaign in Russia. His defence of Hamburg was renowned. D. rejoined Napoleon during the 100 Days, and in 1819 was made a peer.

DAVY, Sir Humphry (1778–1829). British chemist. Initially an apprentice surgeon, he also studied metaphysics, ethics and mathematics, before devoting himself to chemistry. While laboratory superintendent at the Bristol Pneumatic Institute he discovered the respiratory effects of 'laughing gas' (nitrous oxide) in 1799, and as a result was invited to the Royal Institution, London, where he became prof. of chemistry in 1802. He soon estab. a fine reputation for his lecturing and research, and at govt. request gave a course of lectures on agricultural chemistry (1803), later pub., which remained the standard work for nearly 50 years. During his classic 'Bakerian' lectures (1806–10) on electro-chemistry, he demonstrated his discovery of the metals sodium, potassium, calcium, magnesium, strontium and barium, by electrolysis. During a continental tour in 1813, with his assistant Faraday (q.v.), he investigated the electricity of torpedo-fish, burnt diamonds in oxygen to prove that they were made of carbon, and examined volcanic activity. On returning to England he investigated fire damp in coal mines and constructed the safety lamp, used from 1816. He was elected pres. of the Royal Society in 1820. Throughout his life he wrote poetry for relaxation.

DAVY JONES. Sailor's name, generally occurring in the phrase 'gone to D.J.'s locker' applied to those drowned at sea, and taken as the name of a sea-spirit or devil.

DAWES (dawz), **Charles Gates** (1865–1951). American statesman. In 1923 he was appointed by the Allied Reparations Commission president of the committee which produced the 'Dawes Plan' – aiming at securing that Germany should pay as much as possible as war debts. It was superseded by the Young Plan in 1929. D. was elected vice-president of the U.S.A. in 1924, received the Nobel peace prize in 1925, and was ambassador to Britain 1929–32.

DAWSON, Geoffrey (1874-1944). British journalist.

As editor of *The Times* 1912–19 and 1923–41 (the interval being caused by a difference of opinion with Lord Northcliffe), he exerted considerable influence, and used it against Edward VIII at the time of the Abdication Crisis.

DAWSON, Peter (1882–1961). Australian baritone, noted for marching songs, ballads, etc.

DAWSON. Canadian 'ghost town', cap. until 1953 of the Yukon Territory, at the junction of the Yukon and Klondike rivers, founded 1896 at the time of the Klondike gold rush when its pop. was 25,000; pop. (1966) 881.

DAY, Edith (1896–). American actress and singer. B. in Minneapolis, she appeared in the great musical successes *Rose Marie* (1925–6), *The Desert Song* (1927–8), and *Show Boat* (1928–9).

DAY, Thomas (1748–89). British author of the educational novel *Sandford and Merton* (1783–9), a children's classic for more than a century, he brought up 2 poor girls on his own educational principles, with a view to marrying whichever of the two should turn out the better. The scheme miscarried, however, and eventually he m. an heiress and lived in Essex and Surrey as a philanthropic farmer.

DAYAKS (dī′aks) or **Dyaks.** Semi-savage tribes of Borneo. They are taller and less dark-skinned than the Malays, and are skilled in many arts and crafts. For hunting purposes they use the blowpipe. The custom of head-hunting has tended to die out.

DAY-LEWIS, Cecil (1904–72). British poet. B. at Ballintubber, Ireland, he was ed. at Oxford and then became a schoolmaster, teaching at Cheltenham Coll. 1930–5. With Auden and Spender he was one of the influential Leftist poets of the 1930s, and first showed an individual quality in *From Feathers to Iron* (1931). In maturity he developed a gift for tangy, accomplished lyrics, and sustained narrative power, e.g. 'The Loss of the Nabara' in *Overtures to Death* (1938). Prof. of poetry at Oxford 1951–6, he pub. critical works, translations of the *Georgics* and *Aeneid*, and detective novels under the pseudonym Nicholas Blake. In 1968 he succeeded Masefield as Poet Laureate.

DAYTON. City of Ohio, U.S.A., producing precision machinery, household appliances, electrical equipment, etc. It has an aeronautical research centre and an R.C. university. It was the birthplace of Orville Wright (q.v.). Pop. met. area (1970) 842,147.

DAYTON. Small town in Tennessee, U.S.A., notorious as the scene of the trial (1925) of John T. Scopes, a science teacher at the high school, accused of teaching, contrary to a law of the State, that 'man is descended from the lower animals'. Scopes was fined $100, but this was waived on a technical point. Pop. (1960) 3,500.

DAYTONA BEACH. Popular U.S. seaside resort and motor-racing centre on the Atlantic coast of Florida. Pop. (1960) 37,395.

DAZAI, Osamu. Pseudonym of Shuji Tsushima (1909–48), Japanese author. His work reflects the drunkenness and drug addiction of his life, and his ultimately successful penchant for suicide. The title of his novel *The Setting Sun* (1947) has become in Japanese synonymous with the dead of the S.W.W.

D-DAY. Name given to the day – 6 June 1944 – when the Allied invasion of Europe took place during the S.W.W. It was originally fixed for 5 June, but owing to unfavourable weather the invasion was postponed for 24 hrs. See S.W.W. In military jargon D-Day was any day for which an operation was planned, but in ordinary usage it has acquired this specialized sense. See illus. p. 328.

D.D.T. (Dichloro-Diphenyl-Trichloroethane). Powerful insecticide, in the form of a white powder, discovered in 1940 by the Swiss firm J. R. Geigy. Effective against flies, mosquitoes, sand flies, lice, fleas, etc., it is valuable in the control of diseases such as malaria, typhus, yellow fever and plague

D-DAY. 6 June 1944 is one of the great dates of history that will never be forgotten. Between 6.30 and 7.30 a.m., after a tremendous sea and air bombardment, the spearhead of the liberating Allied forces secured a lodgement on the French coast between the Cotentin peninsula and the Seine estuary. Hitler's 'Fortress Europe' was breached, and victory was at last in sight. This painting by Barnett Freedman, now in the Imperial War Museum, shows the main beach-head at Arromanches 20 days later (D.20). The Mulberry harbours are in position and functioning, and the 'build-up' for the great push is in full swing.

which they spread. Unfortunately, there is evidence that these pests develop resistant strains in response.

DEACON. Third and last order of the Christian min. It dates from Apostolic times, and originally the Ds. were entrusted with the care of the material needs of the Christian community. Subsequently it became the preliminary stage to the priesthood, and in the C. of E. a candidate for holy orders is ordained D., proceeding to obtain priest's orders after a year. Ds. receive episcopal ordination and must be at least 23 years of age. In the Presbyterian and Free Churches a D. is a layman chosen to assist the min. In 1964 the Second Vatican Council approved in principle the estab. of a permanent·order of Ds., who might incl. married men of mature years.

DEACONESS. In the Christian Church, a woman specially trained and set apart for spiritual work, sick visiting, and charitable and welfare work in general. There were Ds. in the early Church, but as known today they are a modern institution. The order of Ds. was revived in the C. of E. in 1862; they are trained at special colleges and are licensed by the bishop in whose diocese they are chosen to serve. They are not allowed to administer the Sacraments, but may conduct public worship, preach, and hold special services. They achieved legal standing within the law of the Church 1968.

DEAD SEA. Large lake partly in Israel partly in Jordan; it is 46 m. long, about 8 m. wide, and lies 1,292 ft. below sea-level. The chief river entering it is the Jordan; it has no outlet to the sea, and the water is very salt.

DEAD SEA SCROLLS. Collection of ancient scrolls (some intact in their jars) and fragments of scrolls found in 1947 in a cave on the W. side of the Jordan 12 km. south of Jericho and 2 km. from the N. end of the Dead Sea. The jars are considered to date from *c.* 22 B.C. to A.D. 100. The fragments were painstakingly pieced together and deciphered. Five are in Syrian possession: five (incl. a complete Isaiah) are at the Hebrew Univ. of Jerusalem, which also acquired a 6th, the Temple Scroll, discovered 1967. *See* QUMRAN.

DEAFNESS. Absence or deficiency of the sense of hearing. It may be inborn and due to abnormality of development, but is usually caused by injury of disease of the inner ear. After the habit of speech has been fully formed, the ability to speak will be retained, and some relief may be given by electrical hearing aids (q.v.), but deafness in young children necessarily implies mutism as well unless special training is given.

DEAKIN, Alfred (1856–1919). Australian statesman. He was Attorney-General in the first Federal Cabinet of 1901, and P.M. 1903–4, 1905–8, and 1909–10. He favoured social reform and preference for Britain.

DEAKIN, Arthur (1890–1955). British trade unionist. Son of a cobbler, he made a name as a masterly negotiator and succeeded Bevin as sec. of the T.G.W.U. 1945–55.

DEAL. English port and resort (bor.) on the E. coast of Kent; one of the Cinque ports. Julius Caesar is said to have landed there in 55 B.C. The castle was built by Henry VIII and houses the town museum. Pop. (1961) 24,791.

DEAN. In the C. of E., the head of the chapter of a cathedral or collegiate church. A rural D. is a clergyman who is invested with jurisdiction or precedence over a division of an archdeaconry. There are also Ds. in the colleges of Oxford and Cambridge, being fellows charged with the maintenance of discipline; and in medical schools, univs., etc.

DEAN, Basil (1888–). British man-of-the-theatre. He made his début as an actor in 1906, and has since produced many West End successes, often under his own management. During the S.W.W. he was founder and director-general of ENSA, providing entertainment for the forces.

DEAN, Forest of. Wooded area in W. Gloucestershire, England, much of it Crown property. Iron and coal are mined.

DEARBORN. Motor manufacturing city in Michigan, U.S.A., 10 m. W.S.W. of Detroit. Settled in 1795, it was the birthplace and home of Henry Ford (q.v.) who built here the first Ford works. D. also makes aircraft parts, steel, bricks. Pop. (1960) 112,007.

DEAD SEA SCROLLS. Besides the leather scrolls found at Qumran, two originally of bronze were discovered embedded in the dust of the floor of Cave 3. As only metallic salts remained, the scrolls could not be unrolled, and Professor H. Wright Baker (right) of the Manchester College of Science and Technology solved the problem by bonding the salt crystals together and cutting the scrolls into strips with a tiny circular saw. The scrolls are apparently a record of the location of treasures of the Temple at Jerusalem, concealed in time of trouble, and never recovered, but the land-marks mentioned, and probably the treasure, have long since disappeared: a transcription from one segment is seen above.

Courtesy of Prof. H. Wright Baker.

DEATH. The permanent ending of all life processes in an animal or plant. The exact moment of its occurrence is sometimes uncertain, and modern resuscitation techniques render definition difficult, the one sure sign being putrefaction. The development of transplant surgery, however, led in 1968 to an agreed definition of D. by a conference at the World Health Organization H.Q. in Geneva: a potential donor is considered dead when his brain has totally and irreversibly ceased to work, i.e. there is no brain-body connection, muscular activity, blood pressure, or ability to breathe unaided by machine.

DEATH'S HEAD. A large species of moth (*Acherontia atropos*) of the hawk-moth family (Sphingidae). The fore-wings are mottled with yellow, brown, and black, and the hind-wings are dark yellow banded with black. The body is stout and hairy, of a dark yellow colour; black markings on the thorax often bear a striking resemblance to a skull, whence the name. It has a wing-span of nearly 6 in.

DEATH VALLEY. Narrow depression in S.E. California, U.S.A., 140 m. long, 4–16 m. wide, 280 ft. below sea-level, lowest point in N. America, bordered by mountains rising to 10,000 ft. above sea-level. It is desert most of the year (1·4 in. average annual rainfall) and is one of the world's hottest regions.

DEATH WATCH. Species of beetle (*Xestobium rufovillosum*) of the family Anobiidae. It bores in old furniture, etc., and the male, in order to attract the female, produces a ticking sound by striking its head upon a wooden surface; this is taken by the superstitious as a warning of approaching death.

DEAUVILLE (dohvēl'). Holiday resort of Normandy in Calvados dept., France, 25 m. N.E. of Caen, on the Eng. Channel and at the mouth of the Touques, opposite Trouville. Pop. (1962) 5,239.

DE BASIL, Wasily (*c.* 1886–1951). Russian impresario. Once colonel of a Cossack division, he became manager to the pianist Horowitz, and in 1932 (with René Blum) re-formed Les Ballets Russes de Monte Carlo, touring Europe and America, and initiating a great ballet revival.

DEBRÉ (debrā'), **Michel** (1912–). French statesman. B. in Paris, he escaped in 1940 to Morocco and from 1944 was a close associate of de Gaulle. On the latter's return to power in 1958 he became Min. of Justice and in 1959–62 was Premier Ministre, 1st to bear this title in modern times – the French 'Premier' formerly being called officially 'President of the Council of Ministers'. He was Min. of Economic Affairs 1966–8, Min. of Foreign Affairs 1968–9, and became Min. of Defence in 1969.

DEBRECEN (de'bretsen). Hungarian town, 120 m. E. of Budapest. It is a commercial centre, and has a univ. founded 1912. Pop. (1962) 136,719.

DEBRETT, John (1753–1822). London publisher who in 1802 pub. a *Peerage* followed by a *Baronetage* in 1808, still called by his name.

DE BROGLIE (de brōly'), **Maurice**, 6th duc (1875–1960). French scientist, noted for his work on atomic physics and X-rays. He was succeeded in the title by his brother **Louis Victor de B.**, 7th duc (1892–), well known for his research in nuclear physics and the relations between wave and corpuscular theories. The latter was awarded a Nobel prize in 1929, and became prof. of physics at Paris in 1932.

DEBS, Eugene Victor (1855–1926). American Socialist. B. in Indiana, he organized the American Railway Union in 1893, and was Socialist candidate for the presidency in every election from 1900 to 1920, except that of 1916. He opposed U.S. intervention in the F.W.W., and was imprisoned 1918-21.

DEBUSSY (debüsē'), **Claude Achille** (1862–1918). French composer. B. at St. Germain-en-Laye, he studied at Paris, and won the Grand Prix de Rome with his cantata *L'enfant prodigue* (1884). After studying in Rome and Russia, he returned to Paris and won fame with his *L'après-midi d'un faune* (1894). His opera *Pelléas et Mélisande* was 1st performed in 1902. He also wrote orchestral music and numerous piano pieces, chamber music, ballets, songs, etc. For his rejection of classical diatonic harmony he may be called the first of the modern composers.

DEBYE (debi'), **Peter** (1884–1966). Dutch-American physicist. Ed. at Munich, he subsequently held

DEATH'S HEAD MOTH, about half natural size.

professorships at Zürich, Utrecht, Göttingen, Leipzig and Berlin: in 1940 he went to the U.S. where he was prof. of chemistry at Cornell univ. 1940–52. A pioneer of X-ray powder photography, and famed for his work on polar molecules, dipole moments and molecular structure, he was awarded a Nobel prize in 1936.

DE'CALOGUE. The 10 commandments delivered by Jehovah to Moses, and stated in Ex. xx, 1–17, and Deut. v, 6–21. The D. is recognized as the basis of morality by both Jews and Christians.

DECA'PODA. An important order of crustaceans of the division Malacostraca. The name is derived from the limitation of the feet to 10. They are divided into Natantia (prawns and shrimps) and Reptantia (lobsters, crayfish, hermit-crabs, crabs).

DECATUR (dekä tur), **Stephen** (1779–1820). American naval hero. Of French ancestry, he was b. in Maryland and greatly distinguished himself in the war with Tripoli (1801–5), when he succeeded in burning the *Philadelphia*, which the enemy had captured. During the war with England he surrendered only after a desperate resistance in 1814, and in 1815 was active against the Algerian pirates. He was killed in a duel. He is famed for his toast which incl. the phrase 'our country, right or wrong'.

DE'CCAN. Triangular tableland in the peninsula of India, stretching between the Vindhya Hills in the N. and the Western and Eastern Ghats.

DECIBEL (des'ibel). A logarithmic unit, symbol dB, used to express ratios of power, voltage current or sound intensity. It is expressed as 10 times the logarithm to the base 10 of the power ratio, that is $10 \log_{10} p_1/p_2$ where p_1 and p_2 are the powers being compared. The unit is the tenth of a bel, and 3 dB is equivalent to roughly doubling the power.

Sound intensity which is proportional to the square of the sound pressure is often quoted in Ds. with reference to a standard intensity, which is usually taken to be a pressure of $0 \cdot 002$ dyn/cm². Hence a sound intensity corresponding to this pressure would, by definition, be 0 dB. *See* NOISE.

DECIMAL FRACTIONS (Lat. *decem*, ten). The system of fractions expressed by the use of the decimal point, which are in fact all those fractions where the denominator is 10, 100, 1,000 or any higher power of 10. Thus 3/10, 51/100, 23/1,000 are D.Fs. and are normally expressed as $0 \cdot 3$, $0 \cdot 51$, $0 \cdot 023$. The regular use of the decimal point appears to have been introduced about 1585, but the occasional use of D.Fs. can be traced as early as the 12th cent.

DECIMAL SYSTEM. A system of weights and measures, or coinage based on one standard unit (e.g. the metre, the dollar), which is divided into or multiplied by multiples of 10. Since the U.S.A. and France set the example in the late 18th cent., many leading countries of the world have adopted the D.S. for their coinage. Apart from Canada the Commonwealth has generally been slow to adopt decimal coinage, but India did so in 1957, Australia 1966, New Zealand (from 1967) and the U.K. announced in 1966 its adoption of the system in Feb. 1971 (£1 retained with 100 units: one new penny = 2.4d.). The D.S. of Weights and Measures, 1st suggested by James Watt, and 1st adopted by France during the Revolution, was being adopted in Britain 1970–5:90% of the world pop. either use or are committed to the system. In terms of relative efficiency, however, the Duodecimal System (q.v.) is superior.

DECIUS (dē'shius), **Gaius Messius Quintus Traianus** (A.D. 201–51). Roman emperor. He fought a number of campaigns against the Goths, but was finally beaten and killed by them near Abritum. He ruthlessly persecuted the Christians.

DECLARATION OF INDEPENDENCE. The statement issued by the American Continental Congress on 4 July 1776, renouncing all allegiance to the British Crown, and ending the political connection with Britain. Following a resolution moved on 7 June, 'that these United Colonies are, and of right ought to be, free and independent States', a committee incl. Jefferson and Franklin was set up to draft a declaration; most of the work was done by Jefferson.

The resolution was adopted by the representatives of 12 colonies, New York abstaining, on 2 July, and the Declaration on 4 July; the latter date has ever since been celebrated as the 'birthday' of the U.S.A. The representatives of New York announced their adhesion on 15 July, and the Declaration was afterwards signed by the members of Congress on 2 August.

DECLARATION OF RIGHTS. The statement issued by the Convention Parliament in Feb. 1689, laying down the conditions on which the crown was to be offered to William and Mary. Its clauses were later incorporated in the Bill of Rights (q.v.).

DECORATED. Name given in architecture to the 2nd period of English Gothic, covering the latter part of the 13th cent. and the 14th cent. Its chief characteristics are highly ornate window tracery, the window itself being divided into several lights by vertical bars called mullions; sharp spires ornamented with crockets and pinnacles; complex church vaulting; and slender arcade piers. Exeter cathedral is a notable example.

DEE, John (1527–1608). English alchemist and mathematician. B. in London, he lived for many years on the Continent, and claimed to have transmuted metals into gold. He long enjoyed the favour of Queen Elizabeth, but d. in poverty.

DEED. A legal document serving to pass an interest in property or to bind a person to perform or abstain from some action. Ds. are of two kinds: indentures and Ds. poll. Indentures are those which bind two parties in mutual obligations: Ds. poll concern one party only, as where a person changes his name.

DEEP FREEZING. Method of extremely rapid cooling of food to *c.* 300°F below freezing point, the temperature then being kept constant until the food is required. The real nutritive value and flavour of food is contained in the water or 'juice' which forms the greater part of it, and which is released in D.F. Thawing enables it to run away and escape, unless a temporary 'skin' is formed by cooking until the food can be served and eaten. Hence, thawing before cooking results in tasteless food without nourishment, whereas the reverse, allowing all the flavour to be released at once, may give a more palatable meal than with untreated food. First used in the U.S.A. in the 1930s, D.F. is not to be confused with the earlier practice of slowly chilling food to a few degrees below freezing, which is now recognized as harmful.

DEER. Family of ruminant hoofed mammals (Cervidae) akin to antelopes and cattle but distinguished by the presence of antlers in almost all species. In the typical D. the antlers are usually branched and with rough surfaces and are carried only by the male, but they occur in both sexes in the reindeer (*Rangifer tarandus*).

Most species of D. are forest-dwellers, and the family is distributed throughout Europe, Asia, and America; it is absent from Australia, and in Africa occurs only in Morocco, where the Red D. (*Cervus elaphus*) is found. This is the typical wild D. of Europe, including Great Britain.

DEERHOUND. Breed of dog traced as far back as the 14th cent., and formerly used for stag-hunting; similar to the greyhound, but of larger size, being 30 in. and upwards in height with a harsh, wiry coat.

DE FALLA, Manuel. *See* FALLA, MANUEL DE.

DEFAMATION. *See* LIBEL, SLANDER.

DEFENCE, Ministry of. British government dept.

DEER. Red deer (left) and fallow deer.

created in 1964, which absorbed the existing Ministry of D. (estab. after the S.W.W., in which the P.M. had been Min. of D. 1940–6, to assist co-ordination), and the 3 other depts. previously responsible: the Admiralty, Air Ministry, and War Office. It is headed by the Sec. of State for D., under whom are the Min. of D. for Administration and the Min. of D. for Equipment: individual Service Ministers were replaced 1967 by Under-Secs. for the Royal Navy, Army, and R.A.F. A new *Defence Council*—Sec. of State, Mins. of State, Chief of D. Staff and Chiefs of Staff, Permanent Under Sec. of State, Chief Scientific Adviser—controls major defence policy, replacing the Admiralty, and the Army and Air Councils. Management rests with the Admiralty, Army and Air Force Boards. This centralization was influenced by the example of the U.S.A., where the army, navy, and air force were unified by the National Security Act, 1947, under the **Dept. of Defense**, presided over by a Sec. of Defense with a seat in the President's Cabinet; each of the 3 services has a civilian sec. at its head, not of cabinet rank.

DEFENDER OF THE FAITH (Lat. *Fidei Defensor*). One of the titles of the English sovereign, conferred on Henry VIII in 1521 Pope Leo X in recognition of the king's treatise against Luther. It appears on British coins in the shortened form *Fid. Def.*

DEFFAND (deffon′), **Marie Anne de Vichy-Chamrond**, marquise du (1697–1780). French letter-writer. She held a salon in Paris, and is remembered for her letters, particularly those to Horace Walpole.

DEFLATION. *See* INFLATION.

DEFOE (defō′), **Daniel** *c.* (1660–1731). English novelist and journalist. B. in Cripplegate, the son of a butcher, James Foe. He was ed. for the Nonconformist min., but became a hosier. He took part in Monmouth's rebellion, and joined William of Orange in 1688. After his business had failed, he held a Civil Service post (1695–9). He wrote numerous pamphlets, and 1st achieved fame with the satire *The True-Born Englishman* (1701), followed in 1702 by the ironic *The Shortest Way with Dissenters*, for which he was fined, imprisoned, and pilloried. In Newgate he wrote his 'Hymn to the Pillory' and started a paper, *The Review* (1704–13). Released in 1704 he travelled in Scotland (1706–7), working to promote the Union, and pub. in 1709 *A History of the Union*. During the next 10 years he was almost constantly employed as a political controversialist etc. His version of the contemporary short story 'Apparition of Mrs. Veal' (1706) had revealed a gift for realistic narrative, and *Robinson Crusoe*, based on the story of Alexander Selkirk, appeared in 1719. It was followed among others by the pirate story *Captain Singleton* (1720); *A Journal of the Plague Year* and picaresque novels *Moll Flanders* and *Colonel Jack* in 1722, and *Roxana* (1724).

His last years were given to more 'solid' work, beginning in 1724 with *A Tour through the Whole Island of Great Britain*.

DE FOREST, Lee (1873–1961). American inventor. B. in Iowa, and ed. at Yale and Chicago univs. he perfected the audion tube and other radio inventions and also worked in television.

DE FRECE, Lady. *See* TILLEY, VESTA.

DEGAS (degah′), **Hilaire Germain Edgard** (1834–1917). French impressionist painter. B. in Paris, the son of a French father and a Creole mother from New Orleans, he abandoned law in order to study at the *École des Beaux-Arts*, where he came under the influence of Ingres. He worked in Italy for 5 years, and in 1870, during the Franco-Prussian War, he served in the National Guard. He avoided the Paris Salon, and became one of the chief exponents of the French impressionist technique, working almost exclusively in pastel, and devoting himself to studies of ballet, horses and jockeys, and representations of contemporary life. He was also a sculptor. He became blind, and d. in Paris.

DE GAULLE, Charles (1890–1970). French statesman. B. at Lille, he graduated from Saint-Cyr in 1911 and in 1916 was severely wounded and captured by the Germans. In his *The Army of the Future* (1934) he attacked French dependence on an 'impregnable' Maginot Line, and in 1940 refused to accept Pétain's truce with the Germans, becoming leader of the Free French in England. In 1944 he entered Paris in triumph and was briefly head of the provisional govt. before resigning in protest at the defects of the new constitution of the Fourth Republic in 1946. In 1947 he founded the Rassemblement du Peuple Français (R.P.F.) a non-party constitutional reform movement, and when bankruptcy and civil war loomed in 1958 D.G. was called by Coty to form a govt. As Premier he promulgated a constitution subordinating the legislature to the presidency and in 1959 took office as President. Economic recovery and eventual solution of colonial problems followed, but in pursuit of his Grand Design (q.v.) he opposed 'Anglo-Saxon' influence in Europe: *see* EUROPEAN UNION. Re-elected pres. in 1965, he quelled student-worker unrest which endangered the economy in 1968, and the Gaullist party, reorganized as *Union des democrates pour la Cinquième République*, won an overwhelming majority in the elections of the same year. In 1969 he resigned after the defeat of the govt. in a referendum on constitutional reform. A *Charles de Gaulle Institute* was established 1971 in Paris.

DEGAUSSING (dēgōs′ing). The neutralization of the magnetic field of a body by encircling it with a conductor through which a current is maintained. Ships were degaussed in the S.W.W. to avoid detonating magnetic mines.

DEGREE. The 360th part of the circumference of a circle; it is symbolized by the sign ° after a figure, e.g. 32°. It is subdivided into 60 minutes (1°=60′). A degree of latitude is the length along a meridian such that the difference between its N. and S. ends is 1°. A degree of longitude is the length between 2

DEGAS. A composition which catches the timeless pleasure of a child's summer day by the sea – 'Bains de mer; petite fille peignée par sa bonne'.   *Courtesy of the National Gallery.*

meridians making an angle of 1° at the centre of the earth. *Temperature* is also measured in Ds. but in this case the D. is divided decimally, not into minutes and seconds.

DE GRUNWALD, Anatole (1910–67). British film producer. Son of the historian Constantin de G., his successes incl. *Quiet Wedding*, *The Winslow Boy*, and *The Way to the Stars*.

DE HAVILLAND, Sir Geoffrey (1882–1965). British aircraft designer. Founder in 1920 of the De H. Aircraft Co., he had already designed planes for the F.W.W. Later were the *Moth*, the *Mosquito* fighterbomber of the S.W.W., and the post-war *Comet* – the world's first jet-driven air liner. He was knighted in 1944 and received the O.M. in 1962.

DEH'MEL, Richard (1863–1920). German poet. B. in Brandenburg, he wrote socialist poems, and was influenced by Nietzsche. He also wrote dramas, and the epic poem *Zwei Menschen* (1903).

DEHRA DUN (deh'rah doon). Town of India in Uttar Pradesh, capital of D.D. district. It has a military academy, a college, and a Sikh temple built in 1699. Pop. (1961) 158,599.

DEHYDRATION. Process whereby food is reduced to powder form by removing its water content. Research, begun in 1937, was carried on at the Cambridge Low Temperature Research Station and elsewhere and was stimulated by the need to save shipping space during the S.W.W. D. was applied to milk, butter, eggs, meat, fish, and vegetables, but there was loss of flavour until the process was perfected in the 1960s. In accelerated freeze drying (A.F.D.) food is quick-frozen to preserve the flavour, before being dehydrated in vacuo.

DEISM (dē'izm). Literally, belief in one Supreme Being; but especially a movement of religious thought in England in the 17th–18th cents., characterized by belief in the 'religion of nature' as opposed to the revealed religion of Christianity. The father of English D. was Lord Herbert of Cherbury (1583–1648), and the chief writers were John Toland (1670–1722), Anthony Collins (1676–1729), Matthew Tindal (1657–1733), Thomas Woolston (1670–1733), Thomas Chubb (1679–1747). Later, D. came to mean a belief in a personal deity who is distinct from the world and not very intimately interested in its concerns. *See* THEISM.

DEKKER, Edward Douwes (1820–87). Dutch writer, usually known as Multatuli. B. at Amsterdam, he was in the Dutch Civil Service in Java from 1838, and his novel *Max Havelaar* (1860) is an exposure of labour conditions in the Dutch Indies.

DEKKER, Thomas (*c.* 1572–*c.* 1632). English dramatist and pamphleteer. B. in London, he wrote realistic plays incl. *The Shoemaker's Holiday* (1600), *Old Fortunatus* (1600); *The Honest Whore* and *Roaring Girl* (both with Middleton); *Sir Thomas Wyat* (with Webster), *Virgin Martyr* (with Massinger), and *The Witch of Edmonton* (with Ford and Rowley).

DEKOBRA (dekohbrah'), **Maurice** (1885–). French novelist. B. in Paris, he became highly successful as a writer of cosmopolitan novels, such as *La Madone des Sleepings*, and *Hell is Sold Out*.

DE LA BECHE (de lah bāsh), **Sir Thomas Henry** (1796–1855). British geologist. A veteran of the Peninsular War, he produced the first series of geological maps covering England, and estab. in 1835 the Geological Survey on a permanent basis.

DELACROIX (delahkrwah'), **Ferdinand Victor Eugène** (1798–1863). French artist. Possibly the son of Talleyrand, whom he resembled, he was b. near Paris. Outstanding in his early romantically heroic style is 'Liberty Leading the People' (1831), and a visit to Morocco in 1832 (as a member of a French military mission) and to Spain introduced a colourfully exotic element to his work. He excelled in religious and historical subjects, animal studies, illustrations of

Shakespeare, Dante and Byron, and painted superb portraits of Paganini and Chopin. Leader of the romantic movement, he encountered great opposition to his daring use of colour and freedom of approach. His lithographs and murals are notable. As striking in his personality as in his work he kept a remarkable *Journal*.

DELAFIELD, E. M. Pseudonym of British writer Edmée Elizabeth Monica de la Pasture (1890–1943). Author of a number of psychologically competent novels, she is best remembered for her amusing *Diary of a Provincial Lady* (1931), skilfully exploiting the foibles of middle-class existence.

DE LA MARE, Walter (1873–1956). English poet. Of Huguenot descent, he was born in Kent, and wrote superlative verse for children, such as *Songs of Childhood* (1902), which appeared under the pseudonym Walter Ramal. Later vols. of poetry incl. *The Listeners* (1912) and *Collected Poems* (1942). He was also a gifted anthologist, as in *Come Hither* (1923) and *Behold this Dreamer* (1939), and wrote attractive prose, e.g. *The Memoirs of a Midget* (1921). He received the O.M. in 1953. He had a gift for the weirdly mysterious.

DELANE (delan'), **John Thaddeus** (1817–79). British journalist. As editor of *The Times* (1841–77), he 1st gave it international standing.

DE LA RAMEE, Louise. *See* OUIDA.

DELAROCHE (delarosh'), **Hippolyte**, called **Paul** (1797–1856). French artist. B. in Paris, he 1st exhibited in the Salon of 1822, and with his friends Géricault and Delacroix was in the forefront of the revolt against the classicism of David and his followers. D.'s historical paintings were very popular.

DE LA ROCHE (-rosh), **Mazo** (1885–1961). Canadian novelist, author of the 'Whiteoaks' series, a family chronicle of 3 generations on an estate in Ontario, ruled by an autocratic old lady.

DELAUNAY (delōneh'), **Robert** (1855–1941). French painter. B. in Paris, he made fruitful experiments in the constructive use of colour in nonrepresentational works and in subject pictures of runners, etc. His 'Windows' (1912) is believed to be the 1st Cubist painting in colour.

DE LAURENTIIS, Dino (1919–). Italian film director and producer. His depictions of Italian life *Bitter Rice* (1952) and *La Strada* (1956) have harsh realism, and he made the spectacular *Barabbas* and an attempt to film the scriptures in their entirety.

DELAVIGNE (delavēn'y), **Jean François Casimir** (1793–1843). French poet and dramatist. B. at Havre, he wrote *Vêpres siciliennes* (1819) and many other historical dramas.

DELHI. Among the many government buildings is the circular Parliament House at New Delhi, designed by Sir Herbert Baker, and surrounded by a continuous colonnade half a mile long, which was opened at the inauguration of the city as India's capital.   *Courtesy of Indian Press Information Bureau.*

DELAWARE. Atlantic maritime state of the U.S.A. It is divided into 2 physical areas, one hilly and wooded, and the other gently undulating. The state is generally agricultural. The chief towns are Wilmington, Dover (cap.), and Newark. D. is named after Lord de la Warr, Governor of Virginia 1610–18. The 1st settlers were Dutch and Swedes about 1638, but in 1664 the area was captured by the British. D. was made a separate colony in 1702, organized as a state in 1776; it was one of the original 13 states of the U.S.A.

FREDERICK DELIUS.
Drawing by James Gunn.
Courtesy of Mrs. Edward T. Clark.

Area 2,057 sq. m.; pop. (1970) 548,104.

DE LA WARR, Thomas West, baron (1577–1618). American colonial governor. Appointed Gov. of Virginia in 1609, he arrived in 1610 just in time to prevent the desertion of the Jamestown colonists and by 1611 had reorganized the settlement. Both the river and state of D. are named after him.

DELCASSÉ (delkahseh′), **Théophile** (1852–1923). French statesman. He became Foreign Min. in 1898, but had to resign in 1905 because of German hostility: and again 1914–15. To a large extent he was responsible for the *Entente Cordiale* with Britain.

DELE′DDA, Grazia (1875–1936). Italian novelist. B. in Sardinia, the setting of her most powerful, naturalistic novels, e.g. *Elias Portoliu* (1903) and *La Madre* (1920). She was awarded a Nobel prize in 1926.

DELFT. Town in the Netherlands in the prov. of S. Holland, 9 m. N.W. of Rotterdam, famous for its china. William the Silent (q.v.) was murdered at D., 1584. Pop. (1961) 74,454.

DELHI (de′li). Union territory of the Rep. of India from 1956. The chief town is Delhi, capital of the Republic. About 380 sq. m. are under arable agriculture, grains, sugar cane, fruits, and vegetables being the chief crops. Area 573 sq. m. Pop (1961) 2,658,612.

DELHI. Capital of the Republic of India. *Old D.* on the Jumna is an ancient city that was reconstructed by the emperor Shah Jehan in the 17th cent. and remained the capital of the Mogul Empire until the establishment of British rule in 1857. It is surrounded by a wall with 7 gates, and its chief features are the Red Fort, formerly the imperial palace (1638–48), and the Great Mosque (1644–58)

New D., on the Jumna 5 m. S.W. of Old D., was designed to house government departments when the capital of British India was moved in 1912 from Calcutta to D. George V laid the foundation stone in 1911. It was constructed to plans by Sir Edwin Lutyens and Sir Herbert Baker, and was inaugurated in 1931. It has an international airport 10 m. to the S.W.

Old D. is a centre of skilled craftsmanship (ivory carving, gold and silver embroidery, jewellery, etc.). New D. has a number of industrial concerns employing some 90,000 workers. The Univ. of Delhi was founded in 1922. Pop. of Old and New D. (1961) 2,061,758.

DELIBES (deleb′), **Léo** (1836–91). French composer of comic operas of a slight but charming character, incl. *Le Roi l'a dit* (1873) and *Lakmé* (1883), and ballets (*Coppélia*, 1870).

DELITZSCH (deh′lich), **Franz** (1813–90). German Lutheran theologian and Hebrew scholar, the virtual founder of the higher criticism of the Bible. His son **Friedrich D.** (1850–1922) was an eminent assyriologist.

DE′LIUS, Frederick (1863–1934). British composer.

B. at Bradford, son of a German-born wool merchant, he spent an abortive period in the trade and tried orange-growing in Florida, before going to study music in Leipzig in 1887. Encouraged by Grieg, he settled in Paris to work in 1888, and in 1903 m. the artist Jelka Rosen, the couple making their home at Grez-sur-Loing, where – after being blind and paralysed from 1925 – he d. His works incl. choral works (*Appalachia, Sea Drift, A Mass of Life, A Song of the High Hills*); the opera *A Village Romeo and Juliet* (1906) and music for the very popular play *Hassan* (1923); orchestral works such as *Brigg Fair* and *In a Summer Garden*; chamber music and songs. A shifting texture of harmonies, his music depends greatly on skilled interpretation, and his reputation owes much to the untiring advocacy of Sir Thomas Beecham (q.v.)

DELL, Ethel M. (1881–1939). British romance writer. B. in Streatham, she was sensationally successful with her emotional stories, in which the heroes were usually ugly: *Way of an Eagle* (1912), *The Keeper of the Door* (1915), and *Storm Drift* (1930).

DE′LOS. Greek island, smallest in the Cyclades group, in the Aegean. The great temple of Apollo (4th cent. B.C.) is still standing.

DELPHI (delfi). City of ancient Greece, situated in a rocky valley about 6 m. N. of the gulf of Corinth, on the S. slopes of Mt. Parnassus, site of a famous oracle. Here in the temple of Apollo was the *Omphalos* or conical stone supposed to stand at the centre of the earth; the oracle was interpreted by priests from the inspired utterances of the Pythian priestess. A European Cultural Centre was built nearby 1966–7.

DELPHI′NIUM or **Larkspur.** Genus of plants belonging to the Ranunculaceae. There are some 150 species, incl. rocket larkspur (*D. ajacis*), and great flowered larkspur (*D. grandiflorum*). *See illus. p. 334.*

DELTA. A triangular tract of land at a river's mouth, formed by deposited silt or sediment. Familiar examples of large Ds. are those of the Mississippi, Ganges and Brahmaputra, Rhône, Po, Danube, and Nile; the shape of the last-named is like the Greek letter △, and thus gave rise to the name.

DELVAUX (delvoh′), **Paul** (1897–). Belgian artist. A Surrealist, he uses bright colour, and against meticulously detailed backgrounds will place odd contrasts of nude and dressed figures.

DEMA′NT, Vigo Auguste (1893–). British churchman. Canon of St. Paul's 1942–9, he then became Regius prof. of moral and pastoral theology at Oxford. His books incl. *God, Man and Society* (1933), and *Religion and the Decline of Capitalism* (1952)

DEMERA′RA. River in Guyana, 180 m. long, which gives its name to one of the country's counties. Demerara county is the chief growing area for

DELPHI· Partly hewn from the hillside the stadium to the N.W. of the temple is well preserved. It is narrower than modern stadia, and the runners in foot-races turned a post at the far end.   *Courtesy of Professor Harold A. Harris.*

sugar-cane in the country, and D. sugar is named after it.

DEME′TER. Greek goddess of agriculture (equivalent to the Roman Ceres), dau. of Cronus and Rhea. By Zeus she became the mother of Persephone.

DE MILLE (demil′), **Cecil B. (Blount)** (1881–1959). American film director. B. in Mass., he entered films with Jesse L. Lasky in 1913 (with whom he later estab. Paramount), and was one of the founders of Hollywood's long supremacy. He specialized in biblical-type epics, e.g. *The Sign of the Cross* and *The Ten Commandments*.

DEMO′CRACY. As defined by Abraham Lincoln, 'Government of the people, by the people, for the people'. A distinction may be made between direct D., where the whole people meet for the making of laws or the direction of executive officers, and indirect D., where the people entrust such power to elected representatives. The most famous example of direct D. is that of Athens in the 5th cent. B.C. Direct D. today is represented mainly by the use of the referendum, as in Switzerland and certain states of the U.S.A. In the modern world D. has developed from the American and French Revolutions. Representative parliamentary government has existed in England since the 13th cent., but the working classes were excluded almost entirely from the franchise until 1867, and women were admitted and property qualifications abolished only in 1918.

Recent controversy has centred on the 'western' conception of D., as accepted in Britain, France and the U.S.A., and the 'eastern', as in the U.S.S.R. and Communist Asia and E. Europe. The former emphasizes the control of the govt. by the electorate and freedom of speech and the Press. The latter envisages economic control by the govt. for the benefit of the community, both political and economic power resting in the Communist Party under a single-party system.

DEMOCRATIC PARTY. One of the two great parties of the U.S.A. Founded by Jefferson in 1792 to defend the rights of the individual states against the centralizing policy of the Federalists, it tends to be the party of the 'small man', as opposed to the Republicans, the party of 'big business', but the divisions between the two are not clear-cut. Its stronghold is the Southern states, or 'solid south'. The D.P. held power almost continuously 1800–60, and later returned Cleveland, Wilson, F. D. Roosevelt, Truman, Kennedy, and Johnson. In the 20th cent. it has become associated with more liberal policies than the Republican.

DEMO′CRITUS (*c.* 460–361 B.C.). Greek philosopher and speculative scientist. B. in Thrace, he travelled widely in the E. in search of knowledge. His most important contribution to philosophy is the atomic theory of the universe.

DE MORGAN, William (1839–1917). British novelist and artist. Son of Augustus de M. (1806–71), a noted mathematician, he joined the pre-Raphaelite circle and, having rediscovered the secret of the bright blue and green glazes of medieval ceramists, produced tiles and pottery at his own factory. On his retirement in 1905 he attained a 2nd reputation with his novels *Joseph Vance* (1906) and *Alice-for-Short* (1907) – the latter having autobiographical interest.

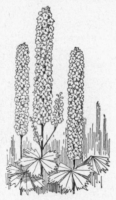

DELPHINIUM

DEMO′STHENES (*c.* 384–322 B.C.). Athenian orator and statesman. From 351 B.C. he led the party which advocated resistance to the growing power of Philip of Macedon and in his 'Philippics' incited the Athenians to war. This policy resulted in the defeat of Chaeronea in 338, and the establishment of Macedonian supremacy. After the death of Alexander he organized a revolt, and when it failed took poison to avoid capture by the Macedonians.

DEMO′TIC WRITING. A cursive script derived from Egyptian hieratic, itself a cursive form of hieroglyphic. D. documents are known from the 6th cent. B.C. to about A.D. 470. It was written horizontally, from right to left.

DEMPSEY, William Harrison (Jack) (1895–). American boxer. B. in Colorado of Irish-Scottish-American descent, he became world heavyweight champion in 1919, when he knocked out Willard. He defeated all challengers for the title until 1926, when he was beaten on points by Gene Tunney.

DENBIGH (den′bi). County town (bor.) of Denbighshire, Wales, in Clwyd valley. It is an agricultural centre, with a castle built in Edward I's reign. Pop. (1961) 8,044.

DENBIGHSHIRE. Co. of N. Wales, bordering the Irish Sea. The interior is hilly, rising to the Berwyn mts., over 2,000 ft., in the S. The chief rivers are the Clwyd, Conway, and Dee. The Vale of Clwyd is excellent agricultural land. Coal, lead, and limestone are obtained. The co. town is Denbigh; other towns are Wrexham, Ruthin, Llangollen, Abergele, and the coastal holiday resort of Colwyn Bay. Area 669 sq. m.; pop. (1961) 173,843.

DEN HAAG. Dutch form of THE HAGUE.

DENHAM, Sir John (1615–69) British poet. B. in Dublin, he was driven into exile as a Royalist in 1648, and at the Restoration was appointed surveyor-general of works. He achieved fame with *The Sophy*, a tragedy; his best-known poem, 'Cooper's Hill', is a graceful description of the Thames valley.

DE′NIER. System of measuring fine yarns, both natural and man-made, derived from the old French silk industry. The D. was an old French silver coin; it is the weight in grammes of 9,000 metres of yarn. Thus 9,000 metres of 15 D. nylon, commonly used in nylon stockings, weighs 15 g. and in this case the thickness of thread would be 0·00170 in.

DENIKIN (denē′kin), **Anton Ivanovich** (1872–1946). Russian general. He distinguished himself in the Russo-Japanese and the F.W.Ws. After the outbreak of the Revolution he organized a volunteer army of 60,000 'Whites', but in 1919 was routed and escaped abroad. He wrote a history of the Revolution and the Civil War.

DENIS (denē′), **Maurice** (1870–1943). French artist. His definition of a picture being primarily 'a flat surface covered with colours arranged in a certain order' is often quoted, but he lent importance to subject-matter by his later concentration on religious art.

DENIS, St. (Dionysius). 1st bishop of Paris and one of the patron saints of France. He was martyred by the Romans about A.D. 275.

DENMAN, Lady (1884–1954). British social worker. Dau. of 1st visct. Cowdray, she m. in 1903 Lord D., Gov.-Gen. of Australia 1911–14. She helped the spread of Women's Institutes (q.v.) in England and Wales, and was chairman of the Nat. Federation 1917–45. *Denman College*, named after her, provides training for members. She was also the organizer of the Women's Land Army in the S.W.W.

DENMARK. Kingdom of N.W. Europe, occupying the N. two-thirds of the Jutland peninsula and the islands lying between the peninsula and Sweden. It is a low-lying, flat country, the highest point being Mollehoj (561 ft.) in E. Jutland. The W. part is sandy, terminating in a sand-dune coast, behind which lies a succession of lagoons. The E. coast is broken by long inlets, on which are most of D.'s towns. The islands, largest of which are Fünen, Zealand, Lolland, Falster, are separated by narrow channels, e.g. Little Belt, Great Belt, and Bornholm some 100 m. to the E. The Sound separates Zealand from Sweden.

The country is poorly endowed with industrial raw materials, but has a very fertile soil and a mild climate. A highly advanced co-operative system of agriculture has been developed, and the land is intensively cultivated in this country of small holdings. Great quantities of bacon, eggs, butter, etc., as well as cereals and meat, are exported. The fishing industry is of importance. Food processing, manufacture of clothing, textiles, chemicals, and tobacco, and engineering, are among industries in the towns.

Copenhagen, the cap., on the island of Zealand facing Sweden, is connected with the mainland by rail and ferry. On Fünen is Odense. Esbjerg is an artificially constructed harbour on the W. coast. Aalborg is a port on the Limfjord, and Aarhus on the E. coast. There are ferry services with Norway and Sweden across the Skagerrak and Kattegat. D. is served by the Scandinavian Airlines System.

Government. D. is a constitutional monarchy. The House of Oldenburg ruled from the election of Christian I in 1448 as king of D. and Norway up to 1863 when the crown passed to the House of Schleswig-Holstein-Sonderburg-Gluckstein in the person of Christian IX. Margrethe II (1940–) succeeded 1972, D.'s 1st reigning queen for 500 years.

Three-quarters of the members of the single house, the Folketing, are elected by proportional representation on a basis of universal suffrage at 21 (until 1961, at 23); the other quarter of the seats is allotted to parties that receive insufficient votes to gain any elective seats. The Faeroes and Greenland (q.v.) each send two representatives to the Folketing. The Social Democrats, long the strongest party, though owing to P.R. they have not had a clear majority, gave way to a non-socialist coalition in 1968. Social security legislation is advanced and a good educ. system includes univs. at Copenhagen, Aarhus, and Odensee and people's high schools for adult educ.

Area 16,576 sq. m. Pop. (1967) 4,813,892.

History. The original home of the Danes was S. Sweden, whence they migrated in 5th and 6th cents. Ruled by local chieftains, they terrified Europe by their piratical raids in the 8th–10th cents. until Harald Bluetooth (c. 940–85) unified D. and estab. Christianity. Canute (1014–35) founded an empire embracing D., England, and Norway, which fell to pieces at his death. After a cent. of confusion D. again dominated the Baltic unde r Valdemar I, Canute VI, and Valdemar II (1157–1241). Domestic conflict then produced anarchy, until Valdemar IV (1340–75) restored order. D., Norway, and Sweden were united under one sovereign in 1397. Sweden broke away in 1449 and after a long struggle had its independence recognized in 1523. Christian I (1448–81) secured the duchies of Schleswig and Holstein, fiefs of the Holy Roman Empire, in 1460; they were held by his descendants until 1863. Christian II (1513–23) was deposed in favour of his uncle Frederick whose son Christian III (1534–59) in 1536 made Lutheranism the established religion. Attempts to regain Sweden led to disastrous wars with that country, 1563–70, 1643–5, 1657–60; equally disastrous was Christian V's intervention, 1625–9, on the Protestant side in the Thirty Years War.

Frederick III (1648–70) made himself absolute in 1665, and ruled through a burgher bureaucracy. Serfdom was abolished in 1788. D.'s adherence in 1780 to the Armed Neutrality against Britain resulted in the naval defeat of Copenhagen (1801), and in 1807 the British bombarded Copenhagen and seized the Danish fleet to save it from Napoleon. This

DENMARK. Modern methods and a rich soil make Denmark one of the world's biggest exporters of dairy and agricultural products. The gently undulating land of this small farm, with its windmill and trees, is typical of the Danish countryside.
Courtesy of the National Travel Association of Denmark.

'ncident drove D. into the arms of France, and the Allies at the Congress of Vienna took Norway from D. and gave it to Sweden, 1815. A liberal movement then arose, which in 1848–9 compelled Frederick VII (1848–63) to grant a democratic constitution. In 1848–50 the Germans in Schleswig-Holstein revolted with Prussian support, and in 1864 Prussia seized the provinces after a short war. N. Schleswig was recovered after a plebiscite in 1920. D. was occupied by Germany 1940–5, but a strong resistance movement was maintained.

Language. Danish, like the other languages of Scandinavia, belongs to the Germanic language group; it evolved from old Norse, becoming a separate language in the 11th and 12th cents. It was recorded on parchment in runic script towards the end of the 13th cent. and in the 14th began to be written in Latin script. By the beginning of the 16th cent. the characteristic accent with its glottal stop had become established. The literary language developed from the Jutland dialect during the 18th cent.

Literature and the Arts. Danish literature proper began to develop only in the 15th cent., a rhymed history, 1495, being the 1st book printed in the country; but much Danish folk-lore as well as history is preserved in the Latin chronicles of Saxo Grammaticus (12th cent.). In 1550 came a translation by Christian Pedersen of the Bible into the common tongue, literary interest in which was thus much stimulated. The 1st poet of note was A. K. Arrebo (1587–1637); T. Kingo (1634–1703) wrote hymns. Ludvig Holberg (1684–1754), writer of comedies and satires, held a dominating place in the early 18th cent.; later came J. Ewald (1743–81), a fine poet, and Johan Wessel (1742–85) a playwright. The 19th cent. produced several writers who achieved world fame: the story-teller H. C. Andersen (1805–75), the poet and philosopher S. Kierkegaard (1813–55), and the critic Georg Brandes (1842–1927). The playwrights J. Heiberg (1791–1860) and Kaj Munk (1898–1944); the poets H. Drachmann (1846–1908) and J. Jörgensen (1866–1956); the novelists K. Gjellerup (1857–1919), H. Oppidan (1857–1943), and J. Jensen (1873–1950) are other noted names in Danish literature.

D. Buxtehude (1637–1707) is a famous musician, Bartel Thorvaldsen (1770–1844) a famous sculptor. Painters of note were Jens Juel (1745–1802) and C. W. Eckersberg (1783–1853) who studied under David in Paris. The best-known piece of Danish sculpture is probably the Little Mermaid at Copenhagen, by E. Eriksen (1877–1959).

DENSITY. The D. of a substance is its mass per unit volume and in the metric system is usually measured in grammes per cubic centimetre. The specific gravity of a substance is the ratio of the D.

of the substance to that of water which is taken to be unity at 4°C. As the D. of water varies with temperature it is more convenient for precision work to deal with Ds. than with specific gravities.

DENT, Edward (1876–1957). British musicologist. Prof. of music at Cambridge 1926–41, he did much to foster opera in Britain, translated a number of librettos and pub. *Opera* (1941). He was founder-pres. of the International Society for Contemporary Music (1923).

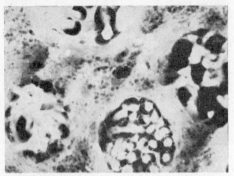

DENTISTRY. Section under a cavity of a tooth (x 7,500), showing bacteria in each of the dentinal tubules. These bacteria are surrounded by a 'matrix' they have formed for themselves, and which would, on the surface, be the basis for dental calculus.
Courtesy of Miss K. Little, Nuffield Orthopaedic Centre, Oxford.

DENT, Joseph Malaby (1849–1926). British publisher. He issued the 'Temple' Shakespeare (1893), launched the 'Temple' classics (1896), and with his son Hugh, and Ernest Rhys, planned the 'Everyman Library' of 1,000 classics of world literature.

DENTISTRY. The care and treatment of the teeth and their supporting tissues. The earliest dental school was opened at Baltimore in 1839; in Britain the 2 schools which were to become the modern Univ. College Hospital Dental School and the Royal Dental Hospital and School, both now under the Univ. of London, were estab. in 1859 and 1860 respectively. Since then schools have been opened at most of the univs. There is an International Dental Federation, founded in 1900.

DENVER. City of U.S.A., capital of Colorado on the South Platte river, and a commercial and industrial metropolis of the western U.S.A. It has a univ. Pop. met. area (1970) 1,240,316.

DE'ODAR. Species of cedar (*Cedrus deodara*), native to the Himalayas, Afghanistan, and N. Baluchistan. It forms forests at high elevations, and is a valuable timber-tree.

DEPI'LATORY. An instrument or substance used to eradicate growing hair. For ringworm of the scalp in children, X-rays or thallium acetate are generally employed, but the only sure method of removing facial hair for cosmetic reasons is the destruction of each hair root separately with an electrolytic needle or an electrocautery.

DEPTFORD (det'-). Locality in E. London, part of the Greater London bor. of Lewisham, bordering the S. bank of the Thames. Peter the Great worked in the dockyard at D., built 1513, closed 1869. The chief industries are marine engineering, chemicals, railway goods, etc.

DE QUINCEY (de kwin'si), **Thomas** (1785–1859). British author. B. in Manchester, he ran away from school there to wander and study in Wales. He then went to London where he lived in extreme poverty, but with the constant companionship of the young orphan Anne, of whom he writes in the *Confessions*. In 1803 he was reconciled to his guardians and was sent to Oxford, entering the Middle Temple in 1808. In 1809 he settled with the Wordsworths and Coleridge in the Lake District, and in 1816 m. Margaret Simpson. His addiction to opium had begun while he was at college, and in 1820 he removed to London where he pub. his *Confessions of an English Opium-eater* in 1821 in the *London Magazine*. He devoted the rest of his life to miscellaneous writing; most notable are his essays. In 1828 he moved to Edinburgh, where he died.

DERAIN (deraṅ'), **André** (1880–1954). French post-impressionist artist. He originally estab. himself as one of the leaders of the Fauve movement with a number of landscapes and studies of the Paris suburbs in 1905, and went on to produce work of astonishing diversity. His gift for fantasy emerged in his scenery and costumes for Diaghileff's ballet *La Boutique Fantasque*.

DERBY (dar'bi), **Edward Geoffrey Smith Stanley,** 14th earl of (1799–1869). British statesman. Son of the 13th earl, he entered parliament in 1820 as a Whig. In 1830 he became Sec. for Ireland, and in 1833 Sec. for the Colonies, introducing the bill for the abolition of slavery. He broke with the Whigs in 1834 and joined the Tories, the split in the Tory Party over Peel's free-trade policy giving him the leadership for 20 years, with Disraeli as his lieutenant in the Commons. He succeeded to the earldom in 1851. He was thrice P.M.: in 1852, in 1858–9, and 1866–8.

DERBY, Edward George Villiers Stanley, 17th earl of (1865–1948). British Cons. statesman. He became an M.P. in 1892 and succeeded to the earldom in 1908. In 1915 he was appointed director-general of recruiting, and was responsible for the system known as the Derby Scheme. In the Lloyd George coalition of 1916–18 he was Sec. for War, and held the same post

DERAIN. Painted c. 1904–6 'Barges on the Thames' is a superb early example of the Fauve manner, with its dynamic use of colour. *Photo: Temple Newsam House, Leeds.*

in 1922–4. In 1918–20 he was ambassador to France. He was well known on the Turf. He was succeeded by his grandson **Edward John Stanley, 18th earl of** D. (1918–).

DERBY. Co. town (co. bor.) of Derbyshire, England, on the Derwent, 14 m. W. of Nottingham. It is a great industrial centre, manufacturing locomotives and wagons, Rolls-Royce cars and aero-engines, Crown Derby china, electrical, mining and engineering equipment, chemicals, paper, etc. All

Saints church became the cathedral in 1927, when the diocese of D. was created. Pop. (1961) 132,325.

DERBY. The most important horse-race in England, run for the D. stakes (estab. by the 12th earl of D. in 1780) on the 2nd day of the Epsom summer meeting. The distance is 1½ m. (the record time being 2 min. 33·8 sec. by Mahmoud in 1936): the winning owner receives not less than £5,000, but the value of victory lies in prestige and use of the horse for breeding.

RECENT DERBY WINNERS

Year	Horse	Owner
1956	Lavandin	Pierre Wertheimer
1957	Crepello	Sir Victor Sassoon
1958	Hard Ridden	Sir Victor Sassoon
1959	Parthia	Sir Humphrey de Trafford
1960	St. Paddy	Sir Victor Sassoon
1961	Psidium	Mrs. A. Plesch
1962	Larkspur	R. R. Guest
1963	Relko	François Dupré
1964	Santa Claus	J. Ismay
1965	Sea Bird II	M. J. Ternynck
1966	Charlottetown	Lady Zia Wernher
1967	Royal Palace	H. J. Joel
1968	Sir Ivor	Raymond Guest
1969	Blakeney	Arthur Budgett
1970	Nijinsky	Charles Engelhard

DERBYSHIRE. Co. in the English midlands, lying to the S. of Yorks. The N.W. includes the S. end of the Pennines, with the Peak district (Kinder Scout, 2,088 ft.), a tract of desolate millstone-grit country. To the S. and E. the land is lower and flatter and yields heavy crops of cereals, etc. Dairy-farming is important. Sheep are grazed on the limestone hills. The principal rivers are the Derwent, Dove, Rother, and Trent. Coal occurs in the E. and S.W., iron is also mined, and there are large reserves of fluorspar. The chief towns are Derby (co. town), Buxton, Chesterfield, Glossop, and Ilkeston. Area 1,006 sq. m.; pop. (1967) 882,230.

DERMATÏTIS. Inflammation of the skin. It may occur in nearly any skin disease, but the best-known varieties, because of their legal implications, are those caused in persons engaged in occupations bringing them into contact with irritating substances such as dyes, paints, solvents or even flour, or in persons wearing clothing, such as woollen garments or fur coats, to which their skin is sensitive.

DERRY. See LONDONDERRY.

DERVISH. In Persia and Turkey, a religious mendicant, and throughout the rest of Islam a member of a Moslem religious brotherhood, not necessarily mendicant in character. The Arabic equivalent is *fakir*. There are various orders of Ds., each with its 'rule', and a special ritual. The 'howling Ds.' gash themselves with knives and claim miraculous healing powers.

DERWENTWATER. English lake in Cumberland in the Lake District, occupying part of the valley of the Derwent, which rises on Scafell Pike.

DESCARTES (dākahrt'), **René** (1596–1650). French philosopher. B. near Tours, he served in the army of Prince Maurice of Nassau, and in 1619, while travelling on the Continent, he experienced an illumination which determined him to apply the certain methods of mathematics to metaphysics and science. He settled in Holland in 1628, where he was likely to be free from interference by the ecclesiastical authorities. In 1649 he visited the court of Queen Christina of Sweden, and d. at Stockholm.

D.'s philosophical and scientific works were elaborated by application of the method of doubt, which eliminated everything except certain clear and distinct ideas, e.g. his own existence, which could not be denied because the very act of denial asserted his own existence (*Cogito ergo sum*, 'I think, therefore I am');

everything has a cause; nothing can result from nothing; and matter is extended substance. He aimed at showing that the entire material universe can be completely explained in terms of mathematical physics, on the basis of the fewest possible ultimates – his 'clear ideas' of extended substance and its ultimate properties, divisibility, and mobility. But although all matter is in motion, matter does not move of its own accord – the initial impulse comes from God; and he also postulated two quite distinct substances – spatial substance or matter, and thinking substance or mind. This dualism preserved him from serious controversy with the Church.

D. is regarded as the discoverer of analytical geometry and the founder of the science of optics. His works include *Discourse on Method* (1637), *Meditations on the First Philosophy* (1641), and *Principles of Philosophy* (1644), and numerous books on physiology, optics, geometry, etc.

DESCHAMPS (dāshoń'), **Eustache** (*c.* 1346–*c.* 1406). French poet. B. in Champagne, he was the author of more than 1,000 ballades, etc., and the *Miroir de Mariage*, an attack on women.

DESERT RATS. Popular name for the British 8th Army, originating from the shoulder-flash worn by the 7th Armoured Division showing a jerboa, or desert rat, a rodent noted for its prodigious leaps.

DE SICA (sē'ka), **Vittorio** (1901–). Italian director and actor. B. in Sora, Caserta, he achieved international fame in 1946 with *Bicycle Thieves*, a film of subtle realism. As an actor, he is skilled in comedy touched with pathos.

DESIGN CENTRE, THE. Estab. in the Haymarket, London, in 1956 by the Council of Industrial Design (an official body set up in 1944 to improve standards in British products), the centre displays goods such as building fittings, furniture, cutlery, etc., and includes in a Design Index selected examples of

DERBYSHIRE. On the Derwent, some 2½ miles from Bakewell, is Chatsworth House, begun in 1688 by William, 1st duke of Devonshire. It replaced an earlier mansion in which Mary Queen of Scots was five times a prisoner. Still the family seat, it is famed for its library, art gallery and gardens.
Courtesy of the Trustees of the Chatsworth Settlement.

good design. Since 1957 D. Awards have been given annually for 20 outstanding specimens. Scottish D.C. in Glasgow is run on similar lines. See illus. p. 338.

DES MOINES (de moin). Cap. and largest town of Iowa, U.S.A., on the D.M. river, a tributary of the Mississippi. It is an important road, railway, and air centre with many manufactures. Pop. (1960) 208,982.

DESMOULINS (dāmoolań'), **Camille** (1760–94). French revolutionary, who summoned the mob to arms on 12 July 1789, so precipitating the revolt that culminated in the storming of the Bastille. A prominent

Jacobin, he was elected to the National Convention in 1792, and his *Histoire des Brissotins* was largely responsible for the overthrow of the Girondins. But shortly after he went to the guillotine.

DESPIAU (dāpē-oh´), **Charles** (1874–1946). French sculptor, a pupil of Rodin; his portrait busts are among his finest works.

DESSALINES (desahlēn´), **Jean Jacques** (1758–1806). Negro emperor of Haiti. B. in Guinea, he was taken to Haiti as a slave, where he led the revolt against the French in 1791, and became emperor in 1804. He proclaimed himself emperor, as Jean-Jacques I, but was killed when trying to suppress a revolt.

DESSAU (des´ow). Town of Halle region, E. Germany, on the Mulde, 70 m. S.W. of Berlin, the former cap. of Anhalt duchy and state. It manufactures chemicals, machinery, chocolate, etc., and was the seat of the great Junkers aeroplane works. Pop. (1966) 94,000.

DESTOUCHES (dātoosh´). **Philippe Nicolas.** Pseudonym of the French dramatist, P. N. Néricault (1680–1754). B. at Tours, he wrote comedies of character in the manner of Molière, the most famous being *Le Glorieux* (1732).

DESTROYER. *See* WARSHIP.

DETAILLE (detahy´), **Jean Baptiste Édouard** (1848–1912). French painter who excelled in painting scenes of military life.

DETECTIVE FICTION. Novels of crime, in which a prominent part is played by an amateur or professional sleuth. The 1st great detective of fiction was E. A. Poe's Dupin in *The Murders in the Rue Morgue* (1841). The earliest English example was the Sergeant Cuff of Wilkie Collins (q.v.), but the real vogue of D.F. began with Sherlock Holmes (*see* Conan Doyle). More recent writers incl. Agatha Christie, Dorothy Sayers, F. W. Crofts, G. K. Chesterton (qq.v.), and Maurice Leblanc, whose Arsène Lupin was both criminal and detective. One striking departure was in books by Dennis Wheatley in which the reader was presented with data and clues to solve the problem himself. Successor to the more formal detective is the 'private eye' and adventurer-investigator of Charteris, Hammett, Chandler and others. *See* also SIMENON.

DETERGENT. In the broadest sense any cleansing agent including soap is a D., but the term is generally limited to a special class of surface-active agents. The common Ds. are made from fats or hydrocarbons and sulphuric acid, and their long-chain molecules have a type of structure similar to that of soap molecules - a salt group at one end attached to a long hydrocarbon tail'. The mechanism of removing dirt, which is generally attached to materials by oil or grease, is that the hydrocarbon 'tails' (soluble in oil or grease) penetrate the oil or grease drops, while the 'heads' (soluble in water but insoluble in grease) remain in the water, and being salts become ionized. Consequently the oil drops become negatively charged and tend to repel one another; thus they remain in suspension and are washed away with the dirt. They have the advantage over soap in that they do not produce scum by forming insoluble salts with the calcium and magnesium ions present in hard water.

Ds. were 1st developed from coal tar in Germany during the F.W.W., and synthetic organic Ds. came into ever-increasing use after the S.W.W. Domestic powder Ds. for use in hot water have alkyl benzene as their main base, but also incl. bleaches and fluorescers for the whiter-than-white look, perborates to free stain-removing oxygen, and phosphates and silicates to soften the water. Liquid Ds., an even more recent large-scale development, are based on ethylene oxide. Special low-temperature powders and liquids have been produced for use on delicate fabrics, washing woollens, etc. Use of Ds. rather than soap has been encouraged by the fact that the raw materials for the latter are actual or potential foodstuffs, but they also have their own special problems e.g. surface-active material escapes the normal processing of sewage and causes troublesome foam in rivers.

DETERMINISM. Psychological theory which maintains that all human actions are completely determined or caused by past conditions. It is the opposite of Free Will, and involves the denial of moral choice and responsibility; the causes which determine men's actions are not limited to their external circumstances, but incl. also their own past mental states and their motives. In antiquity the theory of D. was held by the Stoics. In Christian theology the Calvinist doctrine of Predestination is deterministic. Support for D. has been found in psychoanalysis.

DETROIT. City of Mich., U.S.A., situated on D. river. It was founded in 1701 and is the oldest city of any size W. of the original colonies of the coast. In 1805 it was completely destroyed by fire, but was soon rebuilt and is today a great industrial centre with major factories of Ford, Cadillac, Packard, and other famous cars. Pop. met. area (1970) 4,161,660.

DETSKOE SELO. *See* PUSHKIN.

DETTINGEN. Bavarian village where on 27 June 1743, in the War of the Austrian Succession, an army of British, Hanoverians, and Austrians under George II defeated the French under Noailles. It was the last battle in which a British sovereign took part.

DEUS, João de (1830–96). Portuguese poet, who with *Ramo de flores* (1875)—his greatest work—and *Folhas soltas* (1876) estab. himself as the most distinguished national lyrist of the period.

DEUTERIUM (dūtēr´ium). Heavy isotope of hydrogen, mass number 2, discovered in 1932 by Urey. Combined with oxygen it produces heavy water.

DEUTERON (dū´-). Nucleus of the deuterium atom, or the ion of deuterium. It is of mass 2 and carries a unit positive charge.

DE VALERA (de valá´ra), **Éamon** (1882–). Irish statesman. B. in New York, the son of a Spanish father and an Ir. mother, he was sent to Ireland as a child, and became a teacher of mathematics. He was sentenced to death for his part in the Easter Rebellion, but the sentence was commuted to penal servitude for life, and in 1917 he was released under an amnesty. In the same year he was elected M.P. for E. Clare, and president of Sinn Féin. In May 1918 he was re-arrested and imprisoned in Lincoln gaol, but in 1919 escaped to the U.S.A. Elected Pres. of the Irish Rep., he returned to Ireland in 1920, and directed the struggle against the British govt. from a hiding-place in Dublin. He authorized the negotiations of 1921, but refused to

accept the treaty which ensued. Civil war followed, and in 1923 De V. was arrested by the Free State govt., and spent a year in prison. In 1926 he formed a new party, *Fianna Fáil* ('soldiers of destiny'), which in 1932 secured a majority. De V. became P.M. and For. Min., and at once abolished the oath of allegiance and suspended payment of the annuities due under the Land Purchase Acts. In 1938 he negotiated an agreement with Britain, under which all outstanding points were settled. Throughout the S.W.W. he maintained a strict neutrality. He resigned after his defeat at the 1948 elections, but was again P.M. 1951–4 and 1957–9, when he retired. He was elected Pres. of the Rep. of Ireland in 1959: re-elected 1966.

DE VALOIS (de vahl′wah), **Dame Ninette** (1898–). Stage-name of the British dancer and choreographer Edris Stannus. B. in co. Wicklow, of Huguenot ancestry, she was a member of Diaghileff's Russian ballet, but from 1931 devoted herself (as director) to the development of the Vic-Wells Ballet, later the Royal Ballet, being created D.B.E. in 1951 and retiring in 1963. She was also founder of the Royal Ballet School, and created such ballets as *Job*, *Checkmate*, and *The Rake's Progress*. Both Frederick Ashton and Margot Fonteyn (qq.v.) were her protégés.

DE′VENTER. Town in Overijssel prov., the Netherlands, on the Ijssel, 28 m. S. of the Ijssel Meer. It is an agricultural and transport centre. Pop. (1967) 61,623.

DEVIL. In Christian theology, the supreme spirit of Evil, or an evil spirit generally. The D. or Satan is mentioned only in the later books of the O.T., written after the Exile, but the later Jewish doctrine is that found in the N.T. Jesus recognized as a reality the kingdom of evil, of which Satan or Beelzebub was the prince. The conception of the D. thus passed into the early Church; and theology till at least the time of St. Anselm represented the Atonement as primarily the deliverance, through Christ's death, of mankind from the bondage of the D. In the Middle Ages the D. in popular superstition assumed the attributes of the horned fertility gods of paganism, and was regarded as the god of the witches. The belief in a personal D. continued at the Reformation; Luther regarded himself as the object of a personal Satanic persecution. With the development of liberal Protestant theology in the 19th cent. came a strong tendency to deny the existence of a positive spirit of evil, and to explain the D. as merely a personification. But the traditional conception was never abandoned by the R.C. Church, and such present-day theologians as C. S. Lewis maintain the assumption of the existence of a power of positive evil.

DEVIL FISH. Name given to several marine animals, on account of their formidable and ugly appearance. These include the octopus, the angler-fish (*Lophius piscatorius*), and the largest rays.

DEVIL'S COACH-HORSE. A beetle (*Ocypus olens*) of the Staphylinidae. It is a common British species, black, very pugnacious, and feeding mainly on carrion. When alarmed it turns up the tip of its abdomen, and emits an evil-smelling fluid.

DEVIL'S ISLAND. Island of French Guiana, 27 m. N.W. of Cayenne. It was a convict settlement notorious for the terrible conditions of life there. Dreyfus was imprisoned 1895–9 on D.I. Transportation ceased in 1946; the remaining convicts were repatriated in 1950.

DE VINNE, Theodore Low (1828–1914). American printer, founder (1883) of the 'De V. Press', the most famous establishment of its kind in America, and a recognized authority on typography.

DEVIZES (dĕvī′zez). English agricultural town (bor.) in Wilts, seat of the co. assizes. Pop. (1961) 8,497.

DEVON. Co. in the S.W. of England, lying between Cornwall and Somerset, with a wild and rocky coast

DEVON. Seen from the emplacements of the citadel is Plymouth Hoe, where Sir Francis Drake played his famous game of bowls before his defeat of the Spanish Armada, and beyond is Drake's Island. From the re-erected Smeaton Lighthouse, which stood for 130 years warning ships on the Eddystone Reef, sightseers have a magnificent view of Plymouth and of the surrounding countryside. *Photo: R. J. Westlake.*

on N. and S. The N.E. is occupied by the mass of Exmoor, and towards the S. is the granite area of Dartmoor, culminating in High Willhays (2,039 ft.) and Yes Tor (2,028 ft.). Elsewhere, the co. is lower, and much of it is covered with rich red soil. There is a high percentage of pastureland, and in favoured areas of the S. coast specialized crops are grown. Devon cider is famous. Sheep are grazed on Exmoor and the drier parts of Dartmoor. The chief rivers are the Taw and Torridge, Axe, Otter, Exe, Teign, Dart, and the Tamar. Kaolin is worked in the S. Plymouth and Dartmouth have shipbuilding yards, and Honiton is known for its lace. The tourist industry is of great importance: leading resorts incl. Sidmouth, Exmouth, Teignmouth, Paignton, and Torquay in the S., and Lynton, Ilfracombe, Barnstaple, and Bideford in the N. Exeter is the co. town. Plymouth-Devonport forms the great naval centre. Area 2,591 sq. m.; pop. (1967) 869,840.

DEVONPORT. Port, a principal naval station with a royal dockyard and military centre at the head of Plymouth Sound, S. Devon. The 1st dockyard was built in 1689 by William III. In 1914 D. was incorporated with Plymouth (q.v.).

DEVONSHIRE, William Cavendish, 7th duke of (1808–91). British nobleman. He was largely responsible for the development of Eastbourne as an early example of town planning. His son **Spencer Compton Cavendish,** 8th duke of D. (1833–1908), was known from his father's accession to the title in 1858 as the marquess of Hartington. As a Liberal M.P., he held

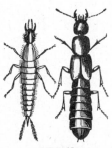

DEVIL'S COACH-HORSE
Larva and adult.

many cabinet posts until 1885, when he broke with Gladstone over the Irish Home Rule Bill, and became leader of the Liberal Unionists. He was Lord President of the Council 1895–1903, when, as a free trader, he resigned from Balfour's Cabinet.

Victor Christian Cavendish, 9th duke of D. (1868–1938), was the nephew of the 8th duke. He was Gov. Gen. of Canada 1916–21 and Colonial Sec. 1922–4. His son **Edward William Spencer Cavendish**, 10th duke of D. (1895–1950), became a Unionist M.P. in 1923, and was Under-Sec. for Dominion Affairs 1936–40, for India 1940–2 and for the Colonies 1943–5; he was succeeded by his son **Andrew Cavendish** (1920–   ) as 11th duke.

DEW (dū). Moisture which collects on the ground during clear, calm nights, particularly after a warm day. As temperature falls during the night the air and the water vapour it contains become chilled. Condensation takes place on the cooled surfaces of grass, leaves, etc. When the moisture begins to form, the surrounding air is said to have reached its dew-point. If the temperature falls below freezing point during the night, the dew will freeze, or if the temperature is low, and the dew-point is below freezing point, the water vapour condenses directly into ice; in both cases hoar frost is formed.

DEWAR (dū′ar), **Sir James** (1842–1923). Scottish chemist and physicist; Fullerian prof. of chemistry at the Royal Institution, London, from 1877. He invented cordite jointly with Abel (q.v.); and while working on the liquefaction of gases and low temperatures evolved the vacuum flask.

DE WET (de vet), **Christian** (1854–1922). Boer general and politician. B. in the Orange Free State, he served in the Boer Wars of 1880 and 1899; in 1907 became Min. of Agriculture in the Orange River Colony; and when the F.W.W. broke out in 1914 he headed a rising that was soon suppressed by Botha.

DEWEY (dū′i), **George** (1837–1917). American admiral. B. in Vermont, he was commander of the U.S. squadron which in 1898 during the Spanish-American War destroyed or captured the whole Spanish fleet in the battle of Manila Bay.

DEWEY, John (1859–1952). American philosopher. B. in Vermont, from 1904 he was prof. of philosophy at Columbia univ. D. early recognized that the exigencies of a modern democratic and industrial society demand new educ. technique. He expounded his ideas in numerous writings, esp. in *School and Society* (1899), and founded a progressive school in Chicago. A pragmatist thinker, influenced by William James, D. maintained that there is only the reality of experience, and made 'inquiry' the essence of logic. D.'s influence on American thought and educ. has been profound. His writings incl. *Experimental Logic* (1916), *Reconstruction in Philosophy* (1920), *Quest for Certainty* (1929), *Problems of Men* (1946), etc.

DEWEY, Thomas Edmund (1902–71). American Republican politician. B. in Michigan, he became a noted New York lawyer and was U.S. Attorney 1933–4. In 1935 he was appointed to conduct a special campaign against organized crime in New York, and was Gov. of the state 1942–54. He failed to defeat Roosevelt in the presidential elections of 1944, and Truman in 1948 – the closest contest since 1916.

DE WINT, Peter (1784–1849). English landscape artist. B. in Staffs, of Dutch descent, he was a notable water-colourist.

DHOLE. Wild dog of India, reddish-brown in colour, larger than the jackal, but, like it, hunting in packs.

DIABETES. A disease in which, owing to deficiency of the islets of the pancreas, the body cannot reduce sugars properly. It causes incapacity, weakens resistance to infection, and ends in death in coma unless treated by regulation of diet and regular dosage with insulin. The correct name is *diabetes mellitus*; *diabetes insipidus* is a distinct condition of unknown cause marked by the passage of abnormally large quantities of clear urine.

DIAGHILEFF (dĕah′gilef), **Sergei Pavlovich** (1872–1929). Russian impresario. B. in the prov. of Novgorod, he studied law at St. Petersburg, and in 1908 went to Paris and produced *Boris Godunov* with Chaliapin in the title role. In 1909 he founded the Ballet Russe, with its H.Q. in Monte Carlo, which he was to direct for 20 years. Its artists incl. Pavlova and Nijinsky, and Falla, Ravel and Stravinsky provided scores, so that 1st Paris, and then in 1911 London, were taken by storm.

DIALECTICAL MATERIALISM. The philosophy developed by Marx and Engels. From Hegel they derived the conception that all material and mental phenomena constitute a single system, developing through the tension between opposites, which resolves itself in a transition to a higher form of organization. But reversing Hegel's view, D.M. teaches that matter preceded mind, that in the course of evolution it gave rise to life, and subsequently to mind, and that the mental always remains a function of matter. D.M. assumes that things do not always remain the same, but possess latent potentialities which emerge as conditions change. What things are and how they behave depends on the relationships in which they are found, and only in relation to surrounding phenomena can they be understood. Institutions change their nature as social and political developments transform conditions. As one social order, by developing its internal contradictions, is compelled to change into a higher order, the new society will evoke new qualities in man, and transform law, politics, economics, morals, and art.

DIALYSIS. The separation of colloids and substances in solution by diffusion through a semipermeable membrane. The process is made use of in the artificial kidney machine for dialysing accumulated impurities, normally removed by healthy kidneys, out of the blood.

DIAMOND. A precious gem stone, the hardest natural substance known (10 on Mohs' scale). Composed of carbon, it crystallizes in the cubic system, other common crystals being octahedra and dodecahedra. The high refractive index of 2·42 and the high dispersion or 'fire' accounts for the display of colours seen in cut Ds. Rough Ds. are dull or greasy before

DIAMOND. The blue ground is first crushed and washed until completely disintegrated, and the resultant diamond-iferous concentrates are then passed over grease tables, like those seen here in the Premier Mine's recovery plant, Transvaal. The diamonds adhere to the grease and the residue is washed away.
Courtesy of the Anglo-American Corporation of South Africa.

being cut, and only some 20 per cent are suitable as gems. There are 4 chief varieties: well-crystallized transparent stones, colourless or only slightly tinted, valued as gems; *bort*, poorly crystallized or inferior Ds.; *balas*, an industrial variety, extremely hard and tough; and *carbonado*, or industrial D., also called black D. or carbon, which is opaque, black or grey, and very tough. *See* CARAT.

Ds. were known before 3000 B.C.; and until their discovery in Brazil in 1725 India was the principal source of supply. Today sources incl. S. Africa (1867), the Congo, Portuguese W. Africa, Tanganyika, Ghana, Brazil and Yakutia on the Siberian plateau (1954). They may be found as alluvial Ds., on or close to the earth's surface in river beds or dried water-courses, or on the sea bottom (off W. Africa); or else in 'pipes' composed of blue ground or kimberlite, where the original matrix has penetrated the earth's crust. In the latter case the blue ground is extracted, then washed until completely disintegrated, and the residue made to flow over vibrating, sloping tables where a layer of petroleum grease arrests the Ds. This involves wastage and x-ray sorting is being developed. Natural Ds. may be exhausted by 2000 unless new deposits are found: *See* GEM.

Famous rough Ds. incl. the Cullinan (3,025¾ carats, S. Africa 1905); Excelsior (995·2 carats, S. Africa 1893) and President Vargas (726·6 carats, Brazil 1938). Ds. are cut by the use of D. dust. The 2 most frequent forms of cutting gem Ds. were the 'brilliant' (for thicker stones) and the 'rose' for shallower ones, but in 1961 Arpad Nagy, a Hungarian merchant, evolved the 1st new method for 500 years, the 'princess'. To give full refraction of light the back of the D. is cut into angled and spaced grooves, and surface area becomes the criterion of value. *See* CULLINAN.

DIA'NA. Roman goddess identified with the Gk. Artemis. The dau. of Jove and twin-sister of Apollo, she was the goddess of hunting and of the moon.

DIARBEKIR. Town of Asiatic Turkey, cap. of D. il, on the Tigris. It exports copper, wool, mohair, etc. Pop. (1965) 102,600.

DIARRHOEA (dī-arē'-a). Excessive action of the bowels so that the motions are fluid or semi-fluid. It is usually due to irritation by a poisonous substance taken with the food or generated by microbes in the food itself (food poisoning), or by a disease organism, as in dysentery or cholera.

DIARY (dī'-ari). A daily record of personal events. The earliest D. extant in English is that of Edward VI, but full development of the form came in the 17th cent. with Pepys, Evelyn, and George Fox. The following cent. provides Swift's *Journal to Stella*, Boswell's *Journal of a Tour to the Hebrides* and the Ds. of John Wesley, Fanny Burney, and the country parson James Woodforde. Very detailed diaries were often kept in the 19th and early 20th cents., e.g. those of C. Greville, T. Creevey, Queen Victoria, Gladstone, Francis Kilvert, W. N. P. Barbellion, K. Mansfield, Sir Harold Nicolson, and Lady Cynthia Asquith. Foreign diarists include Emerson, Saint-Simon, Jules and Edmond Goncourt, Henri Amiel, Marie Bash-kirtseff, Gide, etc. A more modern development of the D. is the fictitious form, e.g. George and Weedon Grossmith's *D. of a Nobody*, E. M. Delafield's *Ds. of a Provincial Lady*, and A. Loos's *Gentlemen Prefer Blondes*.

DI'ATHERMY. The generation of heat in body tissues by the passage of high-frequency electric currents through the body between two electrodes placed on the body. In diathermic surgery one electrode is very much reduced for cutting purposes and the other correspondingly enlarged and placed at a distance on the body. The high-frequency current produces at the tip of the cutting electrode sufficient heat to cut tissues, or to coagulate and kill tissue cells, with less bleeding than in normal surgical methods.

DI'ATOMS. Class of microscopic algae, found in

all parts of the world. They consist of single cells, known as *frustrules*; the cell-wall is made up of 2 similar valves, which are usually impregnated with silica, and which fit together like the lid and body of a pill-box. Diatomaceous earths (diatomite) are made up of the valves of fossil Ds., and are used in the manufacture of dynamite and in the rubber and plastic industries.

DIAZ (dē'ahs), **Bartolomeu** (fl. 1481–1500). Portuguese explorer. He extended Port. explorations down the W. coast of Africa, discovered the Cape of Good Hope (1488) and a route round the S. extremity of Africa. He served under Vasco da Gama in 1497, and d. during an expedition led by Cabral, off the Cape of Good Hope.

DIAZ (dē'ahth), **José de la Cruz Porfirio** (1830–1915). Mexican President 1877–80 and 1884–1911. He gave Mexico its longest period of stable govt. but was at length driven from power and fled to Europe.

DIAZ DE LA PEÑA (dē'ahth de lah pān'yah), **Narcisse Virgile** (1807–76). French landscape and genre painter. B. at Bordeaux of Spanish parentage, he excelled as a colourist.

DIBDIN, Charles (1745–1814). British song-writer. B. at Southampton, his first operetta was produced at Covent Garden in 1762. He was later connected with Drury Lane and other theatres, and wrote the words and music of about 1,400 songs, including 'Bells of Aberdovey' and 'Tom Bowling'.

DIBELIUS (dēbeh'lē-oos), **Martin** (1883–1947). German Protestant theologian, who initiated the form criticism of the N.T. and wrote *From Tradition to Gospel, Gospel Criticism and Christology*, etc.

DICEY (dī'si), **Albert Venn** (1835–1922). British jurist, prof. of law at Oxford 1882–1909. His works incl. *Introduction to the Study of the Law of the Constitution* (1885).

DICK, Sir William Reid (1879–1961). British sculptor. B. in Glasgow, he became the most promi-nent representative of the classical school, was elected R.A. in 1928, and was pres. of the Royal Soc. of British Sculptors 1933–8. His dignified but rather colourless works incl. the George V memorial, Westminster; the Kitchener Memorial Chapel, St. Paul's; the Roosevelt statue, Grosvenor Square, and 'Godiva' at Coventry.

DICKENS, Charles (1812–70). British novelist. B. on 7 Feb. 1812, in Ports-ea, the son of a clerk, he received little systematic education, although a short period spent work-ing in a blacking factory in S. London, while his father was imprisoned for debt in the Marshalsea during 1824, was followed by 3 years in a private school. In 1827 he became a lawyer's clerk, and then after 4 years as a reporter in Doctors' Commons, became parliamentary re-porter for the *Morning Chronicle*, to which he contributed the *Sketches by Boz*. In 1836 he m. Katherine Hogarth, three

CHARLES DICKENS. By Ary Scheffer.
Photo: National Portrait Gallery.

days after the publication of the first number of the *Pickwick Papers*. Originally intended merely as an accompaniment to a series of sporting illustrations, the adventures of Pickwick outgrew their setting and established D.'s position as a writer. He followed up this success with *Oliver Twist* (1838), the first of his 'reforming' novels; *Nicholas Nickleby* (1839); *Barnaby Rudge* (1840), set in the period of the Gordon riots; and *The Old Curiosity Shop* (1841). In 1842 he visited the U.S.A., where his attacks on the pirating of English books by American publishers chilled his welcome; his experiences are reflected in *American Notes* and *Martin Chuzzlewit* (1843). In 1843 he pub. the first of his Christmas books, *A Christmas Carol*, followed in 1844 by *The Chimes*, written in Genoa during his first long sojourn abroad, and in 1845 by the even more successful *Cricket on the Hearth*. A venture as editor of the Liberal newspaper, *The Daily News*, in 1846 was short-lived, and *Dombey and Son* (1848) was largely written abroad. *David Copperfield*, his most popular novel, appeared in 1849, and contains many autobiographical incidents and characters.

Reverting to journalism, D. inaugurated the weekly magazine *Household Words* in 1850, reorganizing it in 1859 as *All the Year Round*; many of his later stories were pub. serially in these periodicals. His married life had long been unsatisfactory, and in 1856 he agreed with his wife on a separation: his sister-in-law remained with him to care for his children, while D. himself formed an association with the actress Ellen Ternan. In 1858 he began making public readings from his novels, which proved such a success that he was invited to make a 2nd tour of America in 1867. Among his later books are *Bleak House* (1853), which mirrors his legal experience; *Hard Times* (1854); *Little Dorrit* (1857), in which he evoked his memories of the Marshalsea prison; *A Tale of Two Cities* (1859), indebted to Carlyle's *French Revolution*; *Great Expectations* (1861); and *Our Mutual Friend* (1864). He d. at Gadshill, his home near Rochester, on 9 June 1870. *Edwin Drood*, left incomplete, was a mystery story influenced by the style of his friend, Wilkie Collins.

Dickens's life was written by John Forster (1872–4), who also edited his letters. He had 7 sons and 3 daughters. The 6th son was **Sir Henry Dickens** (1849–1933), an eminent barrister.

DICKENS, Monica Enid (1915–). British novelist. A great-granddau. of Charles D., she became a hospital nurse and wrote *One Pair of Hands, Happy Prisoner*, and *Flowers on the Grass*.

DICKINSON, Emily (1830–86). American poetess. B. in Mass., she had an unhappy love affair while visiting Philadelphia in 1854, and from 1862 lived in complete seclusion at Amherst. There she wrote a large number of short poems of an increasingly mystical character. During her lifetime very few of her poems were pub., but numerous vols. have since appeared, including *Bolts of Melody* (1947). D.'s poetry has been described as among the most remarkable ever written by a woman.

DICKINSON, Goldsworthy Lowes (1862–1932). British scholar. B. in London, he lectured at King's College, Cambridge (1896–1920), on modern political problems, and wrote on history, philosophy, religion, and the causes of war; one of his best-known books is *The Greek View of Life* (1896).

DICK-READ, Grantly (1890–1959). British gynaecologist. In private practice in London 1923–48, he developed the theory of natural childbirth, i.e. that by the elimination of fear and tension childbirth pain could be minimized and anaesthetics rendered unnecessary. He encountered much opposition, but his work was ultimately recognized. His theory is contained in *Natural Childbirth* (1933), *No Time for Fear* (1955), etc.

DICOTYLEDONS (dīkotilē'donz). In botany, class of Angiosperms, containing the great majority of flowering plants. They are characterized by the presence of 2 seed-leaves or cotyledons in the embryo, which is usually surrounded by an endosperm.

DICTATOR. Originally a Roman magistrate invested with extraordinary powers for 6 months in order to cope with a grave emergency, but in modern usage an absolute ruler possessing extra-constitutional powers. A king overriding the constitution and assuming extraordinary powers may constitute himself a D. Although dictatorships were common in Latin America during the 19th cent., the only European example during this period is the rule of Napoleon III. The crises following the F.W.W. produced many dictatorships in Europe; these included the régimes of Atatürk, Mussolini, Hitler, Pilsudski, Primo de Rivera, Franco, and Salazar.

DICTATORSHIP OF THE PROLETARIAT. Marxist term for a revolutionary dictatorship estab. after a socialist revolution, during the period of transition from capitalism to complete communism.

DICTIONARY. Book containing the words of a language, with their meanings – either definitions or equivalents in another language – usually arranged alphabetically. The term is also applied to books containing specialized information on some particular subject and to lexicons of the special terms of some particular art or science.

J. G. DIEFENBAKER
Courtesy of the High Commissioner for Canada.

The earliest Ds. in England were written for the purpose of explaining Latin words in English. Dr. Johnson's D. (1755) was the first standard English D.; it long held foremost place in English lexicography, as did that of Noah Webster (1828), in U.S.A. The Oxford *New English Dictionary* appeared in 10 vols., 1884–1928, and a revision began in 1958.

DIDEROT (dēderoh'), **Denis** (1713–84). French man of letters, b. in Langres. His first notable publication, *Les Pensées philosophiques* (1746), was burnt by order of the *parlement*. His *Lettre sur les Aveugles* (1749) was also condemned, and the author was imprisoned for several months. In 1749 he was commissioned to edit a vast Encyclopaedia, and obtained the collaboration of Voltaire, D'Alembert, Rousseau, Montesquieu, etc. They aimed not merely to impart information but to mould opinion, and although the *Encyclopédie* was often in danger of being suppressed, D.'s indomitable spirit had carried it through by 1772. D. also wrote novels, e.g. *Le Neveu de Rameau*; plays, e.g. *Le Fils naturel*; and criticism.

DĪDO. Phoenician goddess, legendary founder of Carthage. Virgil makes her fall in love with Aeneas.

DIDOT (dēdō'). Firm of French printers and publishers, founded in 1713 by François D. (1689–1757), and continued by successive generations up to Hyacinthe Firmin D. (1794–1880).

DIEFENBAKER (dēf'enbāker), **John George** (1895–). Canadian statesman. B. in Ontario, of Dutch-Scottish ancestry and son of a schoolteacher, he was ed. at the Univ. of Saskatchewan and made a brilliant reputation as a defence counsel after being invalided from the army in 1917. Cons. M.P. for Lake Centre 1940–53 and for Prince Albert from 1953, he succeeded George A. Drew as leader of the Progressive Cons. Opposition in 1956, and became P.M. in 1957. Since the govt. had not an absolute majority, D. went to the polls again in 1958, and the result was the greatest Cons. landslide in Canadian history. In 1963 he was defeated at the polls after strong Opposition criticism of his defence policy, and lost the party leadership in 1967 following his repudiation of a 'two nations' (*deux nations*) policy for the Canadian Confederation as a backward step. A 'radical' Tory, he has been emphatic in his belief in Commonwealth unity.

DIELE'CTRIC. A D., which is always an insulating material, is a substance capable of supporting electric stress. The D. constant of a substance may be measured by the ratio of the capacity of a capacitor with the medium as D. to that of a similar capacitor when the D. is replaced by a vacuum. Common examples of good insulators are ceramics, glass and paraffin wax.

DIELS (dēls), **Otto** (1876–1954). German chemist. He was prof. of chemistry at the Berlin univ. inst. 1906–15, and at Kiel univ. 1916–45. In 1950 he and his former assistant, Kurt Alder, were jointly awarded the Nobel prize for chemistry for their research into carbon synthesis.

DIEM, Ngo dinh. *See* NGO DINH DIEM.

DIEMEN (dē'men), **Anthony van** (1593–1645). Dutch admiral, b. at Kuilenberg. In 1636 he was appointed Governor-General of Dutch settlements in the E. Indies, and wrested Ceylon and Malacca from the Portuguese. In 1636 and 1642 he supervised expeditions to Australia, on the 2nd of which Abel Tasman discovered land which he named Van Diemen's Land, now Tasmania.

DIEN BIEN PHU (dyen byen foo'). Town of N. Vietnam, nr. the Laotian border, 200 m. from Hanoi. General de Castries and some 10,000 troops (metropolitan French, Vietnamese, Foreign Legionaries, and Africans from Morocco) were besieged in the Fr. Union fortress 13 March–7 May 1954 by the Communist Vietminh. Its fall led to the partition of Vietnam and indirectly to the end of the Fourth Republic in France.

DIEPPE (dē-ep'). Seaport at the mouth of the Arques, Seine-Maritime dept., N. France. From 1066–87 and 1135–1204 D. was in English hands. It has a good harbour, with sea services to Newhaven and elsewhere; fishing is carried on. There is an airport. Pop. (1962) 30,227.
During the S.W.W. the first Allied combined-operations raid was carried out on D. on 19 Aug. 1942; a force of 7,000, most of them Canadians, was put ashore and remained there for 9 hours. There were some 3,500 casualties.

DIESEL (dēzl) **ENGINE.** A type of internal combustion engine which burns heavy oil. Air, which is mixed with the oil, is compressed and thereby heated to the ignition temperature of the oil. The principle was invented in England by Herbert Akroyd Stuart 1864–1937) in 1890, and developed by Rudolf Diesel (1858–1913) in Germany. D., or compression ignition engines, are used for road, rail and marine transport.

DIET. A meeting or convention of the princes and other dignitaries of the Holy Roman (German) Empire.

DIETETICS. The science and practical application of the principles of diet or nutrition. Therapeutic D. is very important in the treatment of certain illnesses, e.g. diabetes, being used sometimes alone, and often in conjunction with drugs.

DIETRICH (dēt'rikh), **Marlene.** Stage-name of the German-American actress Magdalene von Losch (1902–). B. in Berlin, she won fame by her appearance with Emil Jannings in *The Blue Angel*, and went to Hollywood, becoming a U.S. citizen in 1937. Her husky, sultry singing voice added to her appeal.

DIEZ (dēts), **Friedrich Christian** (1794–1876). German scholar, founder of Romance philology. Prof. of modern literature at Bonn, he prepared a historical grammar (1836–44) and an etymological dictionary (1853) of the Romance languages.

DIFFERENTIAL CALCULUS. *See* CALCULUS.

DIFFERENTIAL GEOMETRY. An offspring of co-ordinate geometry and the differential calculus; it deals with the problems of curves and curvature, leads beyond the concepts of Euclidean geometry to those of Riemannian geometry, named after B. Riemann (1826–66), whose work in this subject is of inestimable value; joins hands with hyperspatial geometry; and ultimately touches upon Einstein's theory of relativity.

DIFFRA'CTION. The interference phenomena observed at the edges of opaque objects, or discontinuities between different media in the path of a wave train. The phenomena give rise to slight spreading of light into light and dark bands at the shadow of a straight edge. The D. grating is a device for separating a wave train such as a beam of incident light into its component frequencies (white light results in a spectrum). The regular spacing of atoms in crystals are used to diffract X-rays, and in this way the structure of many substances has been elucidated, including recently that of proteins. Sound waves can also be diffracted by a suitable array of solid objects.

DIFFUSION. Term used in physical chemistry to describe at least 3 similar processes: the spontaneous mixing of gases or liquids (classed together as *fluids* in scientific usage) when brought into contact without mechanical mixing or stirring; the spontaneous passage of fluids through membranes; and the spontaneous passage of dissolved materials both through the material in which they are dissolved and also through membranes.
One important application of the D. principle is for the separation of isotopes, particularly those of uranium. When uranium hexafluoride is forced through a porous plate the ratio of the 235 and 238 isotopes is changed slightly. With sufficient number of passages, the separation is nearly complete. There are large plants both in U.K. and U.S.A. for obtaining enriched fuel for fast reactors and the fissile uranium-235, originally required for the first atom bombs. Another application is the D. pump, used extensively in vacuum work, in which the gas to be evacuated diffuses into a chamber where it is carried away by the vapour of a suitable medium, usually oil or mercury.

DIFFUSIONISM. The theory that all civilization of a higher nature originated in one place, Egypt. The group of diffusionist anthropologists believe, and have produced considerable evidence to prove, that the culture of India, China, and Japan was spread by Phoenician commerce from Egypt, and on across the Pacific Ocean to Central America. Among the best-known supporters of D. are Elliot Smith, W. J. Perry, S. C. Gilfillan, and Griffith Taylor.

DIGGERS or **TRUE LEVELLERS.** A 17th cent. socialist sect who became prominent in April 1649, when, headed by Gerrard Winstanley, they set up communal colonies near Cobham, Surrey, and elsewhere. They were broken up by mobs and, being pacifists, made no resistance. Their ideas considerably influenced the early Quakers.

DIGITAL COMPUTER. *See* COMPUTER.

DIGITĂ'LIS. Genus of plants of the family Scrophulariaceae, incl. the foxgloves. The leaves are the source of the drug D.

DIGITALIS (Foxglove)

DIJON (dēzhon´). Capital of Côte d'Or dept., France, and once capital of Burgundy. It is 165 m. S.E. of Paris, has a large wine trade; the cathedral dates from the 13th cent., the univ. from 1722. Pop. (1968) 145,357.

DILHORNE, Reginald Edward Manningham-Buller, 1st visct. D. (1905–). British lawyer. Called to the Bar in 1927, he was elected Cons. M.P. for Daventry 1943–50 and South Northants 1950–62, and became Solicitor General 1951–4 and Attorney General 1954–62. In 1962–4 he was Lord Chancellor, and in 1964 created a visct.

DILKE (dilk), **Sir Charles Wentworth** (1843–1911). British Liberal politician. B. in London, he became an M.P. in 1868, and expressed republican, radical, and strong imperialist views. In 1885 his political career was ended by his involvement in a divorce case. In *Greater Britain* (1868) he advocated a union of the British Empire and the U.S.A.

DILL. A plant (*Anethum graveolens*) belonging to the family Umbelliferae and resembling fennel. It is a native of S. Europe and Africa. Oil of D. and D. water, prepared from the seeds, are used medicinally.

DILL, Sir John (1881–1944). British soldier-diplomat. An Ulsterman, he became C.I.G.S. in 1940 at the time of the evacuation from Dunkirk, and in 1941 was promoted field marshal and sent by Churchill on a special mission to Washington. Roosevelt had full confidence in him, and he attended the conferences at Casablanca, Quebec, Cairo and Teheran as senior British representative on the Combined Chiefs of Staff.

DINGO

DILLON, John (1851–1927). Irish nationalist. He was the son of John Blake D. (1816–66), one of the founders of the *Nation* and a leader of the 1848 rebellion. He entered parliament in 1880 as a follower of Parnell, took an activ epart in the Land League agitation, and was 4 times imprisoned. He remained a leader of the Irish group in parliament until 1918.

DILTHEY (dilt´hī), **Wilhelm** (1833–1911). German philosopher. Prof. at Berlin from 1882, he laid the philosophical foundations of what in opposition to the physical sciences he called *Geisteswissenschaften* (psychical sciences). He applied his analytical and descriptive psychology, centring round the concept of the *Erlebnis* (experience), to the lives and works of thinkers, poets, and musicians, and decisively influenced the course of literary studies in Germany.

DIMBLEBY, Richard (1913–65). British broadcaster and provincial-newspaper owner. He joined the B.B.C. in 1936 and estab. himself as the foremost commentator on royal and state events, and current affairs (*Panorama*), on radio and television.

DIMITROV, Georgi (1882–1949). Bulgarian Communist. He was elected a deputy in 1913, and from 1919 was a member of the executive of the Comintern. In 1933 he was arrested in Berlin and charged with others with having set fire to the Reichstag. So forceful was his defence that the court was obliged to acquit him, and he went to the U.S.S.R., where he was general secretary of the Comintern until its dissolution in 1943. He returned to Bulgaria in 1945 and in 1946 became P.M. He d. in Russia.

DINAN (dēnoń´). Town in Côtes-du-Nord dept., N. France, on the Rance, with an airport. Hosiery is made. Pop. (1962) 16,438.

DINANT (dēnoń´). Ancient town in Namur prov., Belgium, on the Meuse, a tourist centre for the Ardennes. It was almost destroyed by the Germans in August 1914. There are metal and woollen industries. Pop. *c.* 7,000.

DINGAAN (d. 1140). Zulu king. Obtaining the

Reconstruction of a giant dinosaur (*Diplodocus*) over 70 ft. long.

throne in 1828 by murdering his predecessor, he was noted for his cruelty. In warfare with the Boer immigrants into Natal he was defeated on 16 Dec. 1838 – 'Dingaan's Day'. Escaping to Swaziland, he was murdered there.

DINGLE, Herbert (1890–). British astronomer. Prof. of the history and philosophy of science at University Coll., London, 1946–55, he wrote *Modern Astrophysics* (1924), *Through Science to Philosophy* (1937), and *Practical Applications of Spectrum Analysis* (1950).

DINGLE. The most westerly town in Ireland, situated on an inlet of D. Bay, co. Kerry, Ireland. It was a Celtic fort, and is now a fishing and market town. Pop. (1960) 1,500.

DINGO, or **Australian Wild Dog** (*Canis dingo*). Descended from a domesticated breed introduced from Asia by the aborigines, it is about the size of a small wolf and pale yellow in colour.

DINOSAUR (dī´nosawr). Term used in a general way to denote a number of extinct reptiles belonging to the Mesozoic age, mostly of gigantic size – some were *c.* 70 ft. long and weighed about 35 tons – yet with very small brains.

DIOCLETIAN (dīoklē´shian), **Gaius Valerius** (A.D. 245–313). Roman emperor. B. in Dalmatia, he was proclaimed emperor in 284, and estab. a fourfold division of the Empire with two joint and two subordinate emperors. Under him there was a severe persecution of the Christians (303). In 305 he abdicated in favour of Galerius, and retired to his books and gardens at Salona, on the Dalmatian coast.

DI´ODE. An electronic device containing only 2 electrodes, an anode and a cathode, with marked unidirectional characteristics.

DIOGENES (dī-o´jenēz) (*c.* 412–323 B.C.). Ascetic Greek philosopher of the Cynic school, b. at Sinope. Legend has it that he lived in a tub in the temple of the Mother of the Gods. He was captured by

DINOSAUR. Footprints (measuring *c.* 10 in.) of three dinosaurs, probably carnivorous animals of the same general type as *Megalosaurus*, seen as if moving toward the camera. They were discovered in 1962 in the Middle Purbeck of Suttle's Quarry at Herston, nr. Swanage.
Photo: C. P. Nuttall by courtesy of the British Museum (Natural History).

pirates and sold as a slave to a Corinthian named Xeniades, of whose 2 sons he was appointed tutor. He spent the rest of his life in Corinth and won a great reputation for cynical wisdom.

DION (dē-oń'), **Albert de**, Comte (1856–1946). French pioneer of the motor industry. After producing a variety of steam vehicles, from bicycles to omnibuses (1880–95), he made (with M. Bouton) highly efficient light cars. He founded the Automobile Club of France.

DION CASSIUS (dī'on kash'ius) (**Cocceianus**) (c. A.D. 150–235). Roman historian. He wrote in Greek a Roman History, in 80 books (of which 26 survive), covering the period from the foundation of the city to A.D. 229, giving the only surviving account of Claudius's invasion of Britain.

DIONNE QUINTUPLETS. Five girls, b. at Callander, Ontario, in 1934, the daughters of Oliva and Elzire Dionne. They were greatly under weight at birth, and their survival was largely due to the doctor in attendance, Allan Dafoe. One sister d. in 1954.

DĪONY'SIA. Festivals of Dionysus (Bacchus) celebrated in ancient Greece, esp. in Athens. The most important were the lesser D. in December, chiefly a rural festival, and the greater D., at the end of March, when new plays were performed.

DĪONY'SIUS. Name of 2 tyrants of the ancient Greek city of Syracuse in Sicily. **D. the Elder** (c. 432–367 B.C.) seized power in 405. His first 2 wars with Carthage further extended the power of Syracuse, but in a 3rd (383–378) he was defeated. He was succeeded by his son, **D. the Younger.** Driven out of Syracuse by Dion in 356, he was tyrant again in 353, but in 343 returned to Corinth.

DIONYSIUS EXI'GUUS (c. A.D. 500). Greek monk and theologian, remembered as having for the first time dated the Christian calendar from the birth instead of the death of Christ.

DIONYSUS. *See* BACCHUS.

DIOPHANTUS (dī-ōfan'tus). Greek mathematician who lived at Alexandria c. A.D. 250 and wrote *Arithmetica*, a treatise on the theory of numbers, which is the first known work on problems in algebra.

DĪOPTRE. An optical unit in which the power of a lens is expressed as the reciprocal of its focal length in metres. The usual convention is that convergent lenses are positive and divergent lenses negative.

DIOR (dē-or'), **Christian** (1905–57). French fashion designer. He worked for Lelong 1942–6, estab. his own Paris salon in 1947, and made an immediate hit with the 'New Look' (very feminine after the stark wartime fashions) and a series of styles named after the letters of the alphabet Y, X, H, and A. A master of cut, he recorded his ideas in *Talking About Fashion* (1954).

DIPHTHERIA (difthē'ria). An infectious disease in which a false membrane forms on a mucous surface, usually in the throat, and death may result either from asphyxiation or from general collapse. The death rate has been much reduced by the discovery of an efficient antitoxin and a means of immunization and testing of susceptibility (Schick's method).

DIPLO'DOCUS. Genus of extinct reptiles, belonging to the division Sauropoda, whose fossil remains were found in the Upper Jurassic rocks of western U.S.A. They were of enormous size.

DIPLOMATIC SERVICE. *See* FOREIGN RELATIONS.

DIPLO'PODA. Class of Arthropods, commonly known as millipedes (q.v.).

DIPNOI (dip'nō-ī) (double breathers). An order of fishes, characterized, among other things, by having the swim bladder modified as a lung, so that when the rivers which they inhabit dry up in the hot season they are able to live buried in the mud. The living representatives of the group are hence called lung fishes or mud fishes.

DIPPER or **Water Ouzel.** Name of a bird (*Cinclus*

DIPPER

cinclus), the type of a small family (Cinclidae) of the order Passeriformes. They are allied to the wrens and thrushes, but are distinguished from all other members of the order by their aquatic habits.

DIPSOMANIA. A morbid craving for alcohol, usually appearing at intervals. It is considered to be a symptom of an underlying mental disturbance.

DI'PTERA. Order of insects, characterized by the presence of a single pair of wings, and having the mouth-parts modified for sucking. It comprises the two-winged flies.

DIRAC (dērak'), **Paul Adrien Maurice** (1902–). British physicist. Lucasian prof. of mathematics at Cambridge from 1932, he has done important work in the field of quantum mechanics, and was awarded the Nobel prize in physics in 1933.

'DISCOVERY'. The vessel in which Captain Scott, commanding the National Antarctic Expedition in 1900–4, sailed to the Antarctic and back. Moored nr. Waterloo Bridge, London, it is a recruiting H.Q. for the R.N. and Royal Marines.

DISCUS. Circular disc used in ancient times at gymnastic contests, esp. at the Olympic Games, and also in modern Olympic and other athletic games.

DISINFECTANT. An agent which kills or prevents the growth of germs. Since the introduction of carbolic acid (phenol) by Lister (q.v.) in the 1870s, many different types of D. have been developed for special purposes, e.g. treatment of cuts and burns; cleansing of clothes, bedding, food processing equipment, and medical and surgical instruments. *See* ANTISEPTICS.

DISNEY, Walt (Walter Elias) (1901–66). American film-maker. B. in Chicago, he estab. his own studio in Hollywood in 1923, and his first Mickey Mouse cartoon (*Plane Crazy*) appeared in 1928: among other notable creations was the surly Donald Duck. He developed the 'Silly Symphony', a new type of cartoon based on a musical element conceived in close association with the visual image, of which *Fantasia* (1940) was the culmination. His first feature-length cartoon was *Snow White and the Seven Dwarfs* (1938), followed by *Pinocchio* (1940), *Dumbo* (1940) and others. From 1953, when *The Living Desert* was shown, D.

WALT DISNEY. Here colour-stylist and background-artist Walt Peregoy works on one of the many background settings for the animated cartoon of King Arthur's boyhood, *The Sword in the Stone*, based on the book by T. H. White.

© *MCMLXII Walt Disney Productions.*

also made some remarkable nature-study films as well as features with human casts e.g. *The Swiss Family Robinson* (1960).

DISPLACED PERSONS. Citizens of occupied countries brought into Germany as slave labour during the S.W.W. The Allies found *c.* 7½ million, and when I.R.O. funds ran out in 1952 the remaining 100,000 became the responsibility of the country (chiefly W. Germany) in which they were living. The United Nations High Commissioner for Refugees, appointed principally to cope with Arab refugees (1951) after the establishment of Israel, helped with the remaining D.P. and later refugees, e.g. 200,000 Hungarians. The Germans who fled before the advancing Russians, and the Germans and German-speakers expelled from Poland, Czechoslovakia, and Polish-occupied E. Germany, are sometimes loosely referred to as D.P.: they numbered *c.* 9 million. By the late 1960s the problem was greatest in Africa (Congo, Nigeria, etc.) and Asia (Tibet, Chinese in Hong Kong, Vietnam, etc.).

DISRAELI. *See* BEACONSFIELD, EARL OF.

D'ISRAELI (dizrǎ'li), **Isaac** (1766–1848). British scholar. Son of a Spanish Jew, who had emigrated to England from Venice, he was the father of Lord Beaconsfield (q.v.) and author of *Curiosities of Literature* (1791–3 and 1823).

DISSENTERS. Those who dissent from the Established Church in England or in Scotland. Usually the term refers to those legally styled Protestant Ds., viz. Baptists, Presbyterians, and Independents (now known as Congregationalists).

DISTEMPER. A disease common in young dogs, characterized by catarrh, cough, and general weakness. It is caused by a virus, and is very contagious.

DISTRIBUTISM. The economic theory associated with G. K. Chesterton and Hilaire Belloc. They maintained that property is essential to liberty, criticized both capitalism and socialism on the grounds that both abolish liberty, and advocated guild relations in industry and peasant ownership of the land.

DISTRICT COUNCIL. In the local govt. of England and Wales, the governing body of a county district that is not a borough. It is a corporate body but not chartered, and has a chairman instead of a mayor. There are 2 types of D.C.: Urban Districts, established in populous areas and towns; and Rural Districts, which comprise a number of civil parishes (some with parish councils and others with parish meetings). Members of both types are elected in May for 3 years, and normally one-third of the members retire each year. The functions are varied, those of the U.D.C. being greater and more extensive than those of the R.D.C.; indeed, they are approximately the same as those of a non-county borough. The chief matters dealt with are public health and sanitation; provision of council houses; maintenance of unclassified, i.e. minor, roads, etc. Together with non-county boroughs, district councils constitute the lower of the 'two-tier' organization of which the upper tier is the county council.

DISTRICT OF COLUMBIA. *See* WASHINGTON.

DITZEN, Rudolf. *See* FALLADA, HANS.

DIU (dē'-oo). Island (7 m. long) and town, off the Kathiawar pen., N.W. India, formerly belonging to Portugal (*see* GOA). Salt is produced. Pop. 20,000.

DIVER, or **Loon.** A family of birds (Gaviidae) of the order Gaviiformes. They are confined to the N. hemisphere, and usually breed in fresh water, but at other seasons of the year are mainly marine in their habits. On land the birds are scarcely able to stand, but their flight is powerful and in the water they swim and dive readily.

DIVINATION. Art of ascertaining future events or eliciting other hidden knowledge by supernatural or irrational means. There are 2 main types of D. The first depends on the interpretation of the mechan-

ical operations of chance or natural law, and includes the casting of lots and ordeals by water, fire, single combat, etc.; consultation of texts obtained by a random opening of such books as the Bible, etc.; omens drawn from the behaviour of birds and animals; examination of the entrails of sacrificed animals; and the observation of the stars in astrology. On the borderline of the subjective forms of D. are fortune-telling by cards and palmistry; manipulation of a Bible and key or the reaction of a suspended ring; and the use of the divining rod in finding water, metals, etc. To the 2nd or almost entirely subjective class, which uses external aids only to a minor extent, belong clairvoyance by crystal gazing, etc.; oracular trance-speaking and automatic writing; necromancy, or the raising of the spirits of the dead; and dreams, often specially induced.

D. played a large part in the ancient civilizations of the Egyptians, Greeks, and Romans, and is still active throughout the world at every stage of culture.

DIVINE RIGHT OF KINGS. The political doctrine that monarchy is divinely ordained, hereditary right is indefeasible, kings are accountable to God alone for their actions, and rebellion against the lawful sovereign is thus a sin against God. The doctrine became prominent in 16th cent. Europe as a weapon against the claims of the Papacy, and in 17th cent. England was maintained by the supporters of the Stuarts in opposition to the democratic theories of the Puritans and Whigs.

DIVER

DIVORCE. The legal dissolution of a lawful marriage. In England, divorce could be secured only by the passing of a private Act of Parliament until the Matrimonial Causes Act, 1857, set up the Divorce Court and enacted that a wife could be divorced for adultery, a husband for adultery plus cruelty or desertion. An act of 1923 made adultery sufficient cause for divorce by either spouse; an act of 1937 (*See* A. P. HERBERT) extended the grounds of divorce to desertion for at least 3 years; cruelty; incurably unsound mind after detention for 5 years in a mental hospital; but laid it down that, except by leave of the court, no suit could be brought for the first 3 years of the marriage. Under the *Divorce Act* (1969) the sole ground for D. from 1971 is the irretrievable break-down of the marriage. The petitioner can estab. this by proof of the respondent's adultery, or other behaviour rendering it unreasonable to live with him or her; having lived apart for 2 years or (if the respondent objected to a decree), 5 years. Nicknamed the 'Casanovas' Charter', it aroused widespread opposition which proposals for more efficient financial safeguards for wives divorced against their will did not dispel. The act also laid greater stress than previously on facilities for reconciliation.

In the U.S.A. divorce laws differ from state to state. Everywhere adultery is a ground, in N.Y. until 1967 the only ground. Cruelty, desertion, alcoholism, drug addiction, insanity for varying terms (10 years in N. Carolina to 2 years in Nevada) are among additional grounds in other states. In W. Virginia there is no minimum residence required in adultery cases; minimum residence period in Nevada is 6 weeks, in other states from 3 months (Ark.) to 5 years (Maryland). Some states set a time period before re-marriage is permitted. The U.S. divorce rate in 1960 was 2·2 per 1,000 pop. (the marriage rate, 8·5 per 1,000) compared with ·5 per 1,000 divorce rate in 1890 (9·0 marriage rate).

In Canada D., except by special act of the federal parliament, is possible only in B.C., New Brunswick, Nova Scotia, and Prince Edward Is., which had D. laws before entering the Confederation in 1867.

A Muslim wife cannot divorce her husband, but the husband can divorce his wife by repeating the formula 'I divorce you' 3 times. The R.C. Church does not permit divorce, and none is allowed in Italy, Spain, or Portugal. Belgium allows divorce by mutual consent; in the Netherlands the court tries to bring the spouses together before pronouncing a decree. In France a divorce law which was part of the Napoleonic code was abolished 1816, reintroduced 1884. In Russia there is a tax on divorce, increased for second and later decrees.

DIXIE. Word of uncertain origin, denoting the southern states of the U.S.A.

DIYARBAKIR. Another form of DIARBEKIR.

DJAKARTA. Cap. of Indonesia, a city and seaport on the N.W. coast of Java. Govt. offices, the president's palace, a univ., and handsome residential buildings, all built by the Dutch, lie in the higher part of the town, the poorer quarters and business premises in the older low-lying part. D. was founded by the Dutch in 1610 and called Batavia from 1619 until 194?. A can il links it with its port at Tanjon Priok, 6 m. N.E. D. has shipbuilding yards and an airport. Pop. (1968) 3,500,000.

DJERBA (jer'ba). Island, linked to the mainland by a causeway in Roman times, off S. Tunisia. Rendered fertile by springs, it has been identified with the island of the lotus-eaters. Area 198 sq. m.; pop. (1966) 65,533.

DJIBOUTI (jibōō'ti). Port on the Gulf of Aden, founded 1888, and cap. of the Fr. Terr. of the Afars and the Issas (of Fr. Somaliland 1892–1967). It is linked by rail with Addis Ababa. Pop. (1966) 70,000.

DJILAS (jēl'as), **Milovan** (1911-). Yugoslav revolutionary. B. in Montenegro, he became a Communist while at Belgrade univ., and was closely assoc. with Tito in developing the policy which led to the break with Moscow in 1948. However, he became critical of the régime and was arrested and imprisoned in 1956: his books, *The New Class* (1957) and *Land Without Justice* (1958), and *Montenegro* (1964) a novel of the F.W.W., have been very successful in the West. He was released in 1966.

D.N.A. *See* NUCLEIC ACID.

DNEPRODZERZHINSK. Town in the Ukraine S.S.R., Russia, in the Dnieper, *c.* 30 m. N.W. of Dnepropetrovsk. There are chemical works, etc. Pop. (1967) 219,000.

DNEPROPETROVSK. Town in Ukraine S.S.R., Russia. On the right bank of the Dnieper, it is the centre of an important industrial region, linked with the Dnieper Dam, some 37 m. downstream. D., founded in 1786, was originally named Ekaterinoslav (Catherine's glory) after Catherine the Great. Pop. (1968) 837,000.

DNIEPER (dnē'per). Russian river, rising in the Smolensk region and flowing S. past Kiev, Dnepropetrovsk, and Zaporozhe, to enter the Black Sea E. of Odessa. Total length *c.* 1,400 m.

The **Dnieper Dam**, on the Dnieper opposite Zaporozhe, built 1928–32, to the design of the U.S. engineer Hugh Cooper, is one of the chief power structures of the U.S.S.R. It was breached by the retreating Russians in 1941, repaired by the Germans who damaged it more effectively in 1943. It was repaired 1944–7 with U.S. assistance.

DOBBS, Mattiwilda (1925-). American coloratura singer. B. in Atlanta, Georgia, she was the first Negro to sing at the Metropolitan Opera – in 1956 as Gilda in *Rigoletto*; other roles incl. the Queen of Night in *The Magic Flute*.

DOBELL, Sir William (1899–1970). Australian portraitist and genre painter. B. in New S., Wales, he

DJAKARTA. The oriental details of the building, reflected in the water, suggest that time stands still in Indonesia, but not far away are the office blocks, cars and trucks typical of any great modern city.   *Courtesy of Indonesian Embassy.*

worked as an architect until, in 1929, he won a travelling scholarship, and went to study art in England and in Holland. He returned to Australia in 1939, and during the S.W.W. became an official war artist. In 1943 (and twice subsequently) he won the Archibald Prize, and in 1948 the Wynne Prize. His best-known portraits incl. 'Joshua Smith', 'Margaret Olley', and 'Helena Rubinstein'. He was knighted in 1966.

DOBOUJINSKY, Mstislav (1875–1958). Russian-Lithuanian artist. B. in Leningrad, he was celebrated for his genre paintings, book illustrations (*Eugene Onegin*), and theatrical designs (*The Love of Three Oranges*, 1949).

DOBRÉE (dō'brā), **Bonamy** (1891-). British scholar. Prof. of English literature at Leeds 1936–55, he is best known for his complementary studies of Restoration comedy and tragedy (1924–9).

DOBRUJA (dōbroo'jah). District in the Balkans between the Danube, on the N. and W., and the Black Sea on the E. It is low-lying, partly marshland, partly fertile steppe land. Constanta is the chief town. D. was divided between Rumania and Bulgaria in 1878; in 1913 after the 2nd Balkan War Bulgaria ceded its part to Rumania, but received it back in 1940, a cession confirmed by the peace treaty of 1947.

DOBSON, Frank (1888–1963). British sculptor. Equally skilled in modelling and carving, he became pres. of the London Group in 1923, and attained European standing in 1924 when he exhibited with Epstein and others. He often used unusual stones, or metals such as oxidized silver.

DOCK. Name applied to a number of plants of the genus *Rumex*, belonging to the Polygonaceae. They are perennial herbs, natives of the temperate parts of the world, with lance-shaped leaves and small, greenish-coloured flowers. There are several British species and some 30 N. American.

DOCKS. Accommodation at ports for commercial and naval vessels. There are 2 types, viz. wet Ds. (or 'basins'), and dry Ds. (or 'graving Ds.'); the former type is used mainly for loading and unloading ships, the latter for the repair and examination of ships that need to be reconditioned.

The first enclosed wet D. in the world was completed in Liverpool in 1715. In 1686 the East India Co. considered a project to build the first dry D. in Bombay, but it was not commenced until 1748. Among the largest graving Ds. in the world is the King George V at Southampton. Completed in 1933, this D. is capable of accommodating vessels of 100,000 tons. It is 1,200 ft. long, 135 ft. wide and 45 ft. deep at spring tides.

M

DOCKS. The crowded panorama of London's dockland: 1, Royal Docks; 2, Tilbury Docks; 3, India and Millwall Docks; 4, Surrey Commercial Docks; 5, London and St. Katherine's Docks.

Photo by Aerofilms, reproduced by courtesy of the Port of London Authority.

Floating Ds. are built for the same use as the graving Ds. They are constructed of steel pontoons – hollow chambers – which are filled with water so that the floor of the D. sinks below the ship to be repaired. When the water is pumped out of the pontoons the D. rises, lifting the ship with it.

DODD, Charles Harold (1884–). British theologian. A Congregationalist, he was prof. of divinity at Cambridge 1935–49, and was general director 1950–65 of the New English Bible project, joint director from 1966 (N.T. translation pub. 1961).

DODDER. A genus of parasitic plants (*Cuscuta*), belonging to the bindweed family (Convolvulaceae). There are about 100 species, of wide distribution. The plant is without leaves or root, but has a slender stem which twines round that of some other plant, from which it draws its nourishment, penetrating its cells by means of suckers.

DODDS, Sir Charles (1899–). British biochemist. Courtauld prof. of biochemistry at London 1927–65, and pres. of the Royal Coll. of Physicians 1962, he was largely responsible for the discovery of stilboestrol, the powerful synthetic hormone used in treating prostate conditions and also for fattening cattle.

DODECANE'SE (Gk. '12 islands'). Group of islands of the Aegean Sea belonging to Greece. The inhabitants – mostly Greeks – are noted as spongefishers. Under Turkish domination from the 16th cent., the D. were occupied by Italy in 1912, and in 1947 were ceded to Greece. With Rhodes (q.v.) they were formed into a nome called D., area 1,036 sq. m.; pop. (1961) 122,346.

DODGSON, C. L. *See* CARROLL, LEWIS.

DO'DO. Bird (*Didus ineptus*) which formerly inhabited the island of Mauritius, but became extinct at the end of the 17th cent. It belonged to the pigeon order (Columbiformes), but is the type of a distinct family, Dididae. It was larger than a turkey, with a bulky body and very short wings and tail which rendered it incapable of flight.

DODSLEY, Robert (1703–64). British publisher. For a time he was a footman, and wrote *A Muse in Livery* (1732). Later he pub. Pope, Young, Grey and Goldsmith, and assisted in the production of Dr. Johnson's *Dictionary*. He wrote a number of plays and pub. a valuable collection of *Old Plays* (1744) and *Poems by Several Hands* (1748).

DOG. Member (*Canis familiaris*) of the family Canidae in the order Carnivora, which also incl. the jackals, wolves and foxes. Domestic Ds. have been in existence since prehistoric times, but it is hotly debated whether they derive by selective breeding

DODO

from the wolf. Wild Ds. are found in Africa, America, Asia and Australia.

There are some 400 different breeds of D. throughout the world, the Kennel Club (1873) grouping those eligible for registration (116 breeds) into sporting breeds (hound, gundog, and terrier) and non-sporting (utility, working, and toy); the American Kennel Club (1884) adopts the classification sporting Ds., hounds, working Ds., terriers, toys, and non-sporting Ds. The premier event of the D. year is Crufts Show, Olympia, London: *see* CRUFT, Charles.

DOGE (dōj). The chief magistrate in the ancient constitutions of Venice and Genoa. The first D. of Venice was appointed in A.D. 697 with absolute power (modified in 1297), and from his accession dates Venice's prominence in history. The last Venetian D., Lodovico Manin, retired in 1797.

DOGFISH. Name given to a number of fishes of the order Pleurotremata. They are essentially members of the various families of sharks, differing only in their smaller size. The piked D. or spur D. (*Squalus acanthias*) is viviparous, and is the most abundant species of the British coasts.

DOGGER BANK. Shoal in the North Sea, about 70 m. off the coast of Yorkshire. In places the water is only 6 fathoms deep, but the general depth is 10–20 fathoms; it is a well-known fishing ground. An indecisive naval action was fought near the D.B. in 1915 during the F.W.W.

DOGGETT, Thomas (d. 1721). British actor, b. in Dublin, whose memory has been preserved by the prize of 'D.'s Coat and Badge', given to the winner of a sculling race on 1 Aug., open to Thames watermen in the year following their apprenticeship.

DOGS, Isle of. District of E. London, England, part of the Greater London bor. of Tower Hamlets.

DOHNÁNYI (doh'nahnyi), **Ernst von** (1877–1960). Hungarian composer. B. at Pozsony, he made an international reputation as a pianist, and wrote music of a traditional style under the influence of Brahms,

DOGFISH

who encouraged his development. His best-remembered work is 'Variations on a Nursery Song'.

DOLCE (dol'che), **Carlo** (1616–86). Italian painter. His pictures are distinguished for tender beauty and modest colouring. 'St. Andrew' in the Pitti Palace, Florence, is considered his masterpiece.

DOLCI (dol'chē), **Danilo** (1924–). Italian social worker, best known for his activities in Sicily from 1952 in providing full employment in this perpetually depressed area. He has pub. *Waste* (1963) etc.

DÔLE (dohl). Town in Jura dept., E. France, on the Doubs and the Rhine-Rhône canal. It was the birthplace of Pasteur. Iron and steel goods, chemicals, etc., are manufactured, meat processed. Pop. (1962) 25,863.

DOLERITE (dol'erīt). A dark, heavy, coarsely crystalline rock, resembling basalt, but generally found as a dyke or sill intruded into other rocks and not as a volcanic lava.

DOLET (dohleh'), **Étienne** (1509–46). French scholar and printer, author of *Dialogus de imitatione Ciceroniana* (1535) and *Commentariolum linguae Latinae* (1536), etc. He was imprisoned for 'atheism' and burnt at the stake.

DOLGELLAU (dolgeth'lī). Market and co. town (U.D.) of Merionethshire, N. Wales, on the Wnion river, at the foot of Cader Idris. Pop. (1961) 2,267.

DOLIN, Anton. Stage-name of the British dancer and choreographer Patrick Healey-Kay (1904–). In 1915 he made his début as an actor and, after studying ballet with Nijinska, joined the Diaghileff Co. in 1923. Dancing leading roles in many classical and modern works, he later partnered Karsavina, and was *premier danseur* of the Vic-Wells Ballet 1931–5, when the Markova-D. Ballet was formed. With Markova he founded the Festival Ballet in 1950 and in 1962 was visiting Director of Ballet at the Rome Opera. His choreographic work incl. the ballet *Rhapsody in Blue*.

DOLMEN

DOLLAR. Name applied to many silver coins, and esp. to the standard unit of money in the U.S.A., adopted in 1785. The word is derived from the Germ. *Thaler*. The D. is also the money unit of Canada, Australia (from 1966), Hong Kong and Brit. Honduras, and there are dollars under various names of the Latin American republics.

DOLLFUSS, Engelbert (1892–1934). Austrian statesman. A Christian Socialist, he was appointed Chancellor in 1932, and in 1933 suppressed parliament and ruled by decree. Negotiations for an alliance with the Austrian Nazis broke down. On 12 Feb. 1934 he crushed the Social Democrats by force, and in May Austria was declared a corporative state. The Nazis attempted a coup d'état on 25 July; the Chancellery was seized and D. murdered. D., who was only 4 ft. 11 in. in height, was known as the 'pocket chancellor'.

DOLLOND, John (1706–61). British optician. The son of a Huguenot refugee silk-weaver, he made several important improvements in optical instruments, and in 1761 became an F.R.S., and optician to George III.

DOLMEN. Type of prehistoric monument, taking the form of a chamber built of large stone slabs, which are roofed over by a flat stone which they support. Ds. are grave chambers of the Neolithic period, found in Europe and Africa, and occasionally in Asia as far as Japan. In Wales they are known as cromlechs.

DOLMETSCH, Eugène Arnold (1858–1940). Swiss

musicologist, b. at Le Mans, who became anglicized. After studying music at Brussels and London, he started workshops at Haslemere, Surrey, for the making of harpsichords, clavichords, and other early instruments. With members of his family he instituted in 1925 an annual festival at Haslemere for the performance of early instrumental music, and in 1928 a D. Foundation was estab.

DOLPHIN (dol'fin). Genus of cetaceans, of which the typical member is the true, or common, D.

DOLPHIN

(*Delphinus delphis*), found in all temperate and tropical seas. Dark grey to black on the upper part the D. is whitish beneath, reaches some 7 ft. in length, and has about 100 teeth in its 6 in.-long 'beak'. Of high intelligence (they are popular performers in oceanariums), Ds. have been the subject of much research in recent years. They are thought once to have gone about on land (their flippers have the bone structure of a 5-toed limb and there are vestiges of hind limbs), and to have been covered with hair. They emit sounds (some audible to humans) which they use for echo-ranging or sonar, so that they can detect objects otherwise invisible in clouded water, and reach speeds in the water of 30 to 35 m.p.h. through specialized modifications of the skin, etc., which are not yet fully understood. In the U.S. the Ds. are often known as porpoises. The name D. is also given to the beautiful game fish *Coryphaena hippurus*, which may be up to 5 ft. long.

DOMENICHINO (-nēkē'noh), or **Domenico Zampieri** (1581–1641). Italian artist. B. at Bologna, he assisted Caracci in some of the frescoes at the Farnese, and in 1630 began work on the frescoes in the Capella del Tesoro in Naples. D.'s principal works incl. 'Adam and Eve' and the 'Martyrdom of St. Agnes'.

DOMESDAY BOOK. Record of the survey of England carried out in 1086 by officials of William the Conqueror. Its purpose was to provide the necessary information for the levying of the land-tax and other dues, and to ascertain the value of the crown lands. It also enabled the king to discover the wealth and power of his barons, and who were their vassals. Northumberland and Durham were omitted, and also London, Winchester, and certain other towns. The D.B. is preserved in 2 vols. at the Public Record Office, London. The name is derived from the belief that its judgment was as final as that of Doomsday.

DOMESTIC SERVICE. The oldest form of employment for women, it was generally ill-paid and little-esteemed, and the mobilization of women in the S.W.W. combined with later widened opportunities in other fields to shrink available labour. The National Institute of Houseworkers (1946) helped to raise

DOMENICHINO. Monsignor Agucchi, a patron for whom the artist executed many works in Rome and Naples.
Courtesy of the City Art Gallery, York.

prestige in Britain by issuing diplomas, etc., but a recent development both in the U.S. and Britain is the rise of the *au pair* girl. Generally from the Continent and studying the English language, she lives as family and receives pocket-money for her services, but increased labour-saving devices are the more usual answer to household problems.

DO'METT, Alfred (1811–87). British colonial politician and poet. B. in England, he emigrated to New Zealand in 1842, where he was P.M. 1862–3. He returned to England in 1871. His *Ranolf and Amohia* (1872) is an epic of Anglo-Maori life.

DOMINIC, St. (1170–1221). Founder of the R.C. order of preaching friars, called Dominicans. B. in Old Castile, he was sent by pope Innocent III on a mission to the Provençal Albigenses, and remained preaching among them 1205–15. In 1208 the pope substituted the Albigensian crusade to suppress the heretics by force, and this was supported by D. From D.'s mission grew the Dominican order, and in 1215 it was given premises at Toulouse. Pope Honorius III, in 1218, permitted D. to constitute his 'holy preaching' as an order, and by the time of his death it was estab. all over W. Europe. D. was canonized in 1234.

DOMINICA (dominē'ka). Island in the West Indies, most northerly of the Windward Is., about 29 m. long and containing the highest land in the group. It produces timber, limes, oranges, bananas, cocoa, and rum. The chief town is Roseau, on the W. coast; Portsmouth, the only other town, has a good harbour. D. was discovered and named by Columbus, 1493, and became British in the 19th cent. The last remaining Caribs (*c*. 500) have a reserve here. D. became an assoc. state of the U.K. 1967.

Area 305 sq. m. Pop. (1967) 69,780.

DOMINICAN REPUBLIC. Republic occupying the eastern two-thirds of the island of Hispaniola, W. Indies; formerly a Spanish colony, it is the oldest settlement of European founding in America. The land is mountainous, rising in the central range to 10,310 ft., and the most densely settled part is the long E.-W. valley between the central and N. ranges. The lower lands produce sugar, bananas, rice, tobacco, coffee, and cocoa; the soils of the S. parts are poorer and arid. The pop. is partly of Spanish descent, but mainly comprises people of mixed European, Indian, and African origin. The language is Spanish, and the state religion R.C. The cap. is Santo Domingo on the S. coast. Area 19,000 sq. m.; pop. (1960) 3,013,525.

Columbus discovered the island in 1492, and it was named Hispaniola ('little Spain'). After centuries of Spanish rule it became independent in 1821, and in 1844 the D.R. seceded from Haiti. It was occupied 1916–24 by the U.S.A. who landed troops when fighting broke out between rival factions in 1965: peace was restored 1966 and free elections held.

DOMINICANS. The order of friars founded by St. Dominic; they are also known as Friars Preachers, Black Friars, or Jacobins. The first house was estab. at Toulouse in 1215; in 1216 the order received papal recognition, and their rule was drawn up in 1220–1. They soon spread all over Europe, the first house in England being estab. at Oxford in 1221. The English Ds. were suppressed in 1559, but were restored to a corporate existence in 1622. Today the order is worldwide.

DOMINIONS. *See* BRITISH COMMONWEALTH.

DOMITIAN (dōmi'shian; A.D. 51–96). Roman emperor. B. at Rome, he became an emperor in 81. His reign was troubled by barbarian attacks on the Danube frontier, and in 88 the armies of the Rhine rose in revolt, but were quickly suppressed. From this time D. began a reign of terror, and was eventually assassinated.

DON. Russian river, rising in the Moscow region of the R.S.F.S.R., and entering the N.-E. extremity of

the Sea of Azov after a course of 1,200 m. In its lower reaches the D. is over 1 m. wide, and for about 4 months of the year it is closed by ice. The upper course is linked with the Volga by a canal.

DO'NAT, Robert (1905–58). British actor. B. in Manchester, he had a diffident charm in such roles as Gideon Sarn in *Precious Bane*, Cameron the medical student in *A Sleeping Clergyman* and the superannuated schoolmaster in *Mr. Chips* (also filmed).

DONATE'LLO, or Donato di Niccolo di Betto Bardi (1386–1466). Italian sculptor. With Brunelleschi he revived the classical style, and exercised a profound influence on the masters of the Italian Renaissance. After he had completed his studies in Rome he returned to his native Florence, where he executed many famous sculptures. Among his important works are: the 'David' at Florence; the equestrian statue of Gattamelata at Padua; the 'St. John' in Siena cathedral, etc.

DONATI (dohnah'tē), **Giovanni Battista** (1826–73). Italian astronomer. B. at Pisa, he was prof. of astronomy and director of the observatory of Florence from 1859, and carried out research on comets, stellar spectra, etc. He discovered 'D.'s Comet' on 2 June 1858.

DONBAS. One of the most important industrial regions in the Soviet Union. It incl. Donetsk and Voroshilovgrad regions in E. Ukraine and the W. part of Rostov region in the R.S.F.S.R. It is bounded by the Don and its trib. the Donets. About 40 per cent of the coal mined in the U.S.S.R. comes from the D., which has also extensive deposits of salt, mercury, lead, and other minerals.

DO'NCASTER. English town (co. bor.) in the W. Riding of Yorks, on the Don, and on the Great North Road, 156 m. N. of London. The principal manufactures are agricultural machinery, brass, wire, etc. Coal is extensively mined in the area. D. was a Roman station and received its first charter in 1194. D. owns a race-course, and it is here that the St. Leger Race is run every Sept., and the Lincoln (from 1965) in March. Pop. (1961) 86,402.

DONEGAL (don'ēgawl). Co. in Ulster, Rep. of Ireland, washed by the Atlantic on the N., W., and S.W. Most of it is mountainous, being geologically a continuation of the Highlands of Scotland. Agriculture is limited to the W. Sheep and cattle are kept. There is little industrial development, but tweed and linen are made. Deep-sea fishery is carried on. The r. Erne hydro-electric project (1952) involved the building of

DONEGAL. The hills are boldly picturesque and the strongly secured thatch of the whitewashed cottage is a reminder of the wild gales which sweep across from the Atlantic. The pleasing drystone walls are nowadays giving way to wire fencing.
Courtesy of the Irish Tourist Board.

large power stations at Ballyshannon. The co. town is Lifford. Area 1,865 sq. m.; pop. (1966) 108,549

DONEGAL. Market town and port of co. Donegal, Rep. of Ireland, at the head of D. Bay. Pop (1966) 1,100.

DONETS. River of the U.S.S.R. rising in Kursk region and flowing c. 670 m. to join the Don 60 m. E. of Rostov. In the bend formed by the Don and the D. lies one of the richest coalfields in Europe. See DONBAS.

DONETSK. City in the Ukrainian S.S.R., cap. of D. region, 380 m. S.E. of Kiev. In the Donbas, D. is a railway centre and has an airport. It has blast furnaces, rolling mills, and other works engaged in heavy industry. Founded in the 1870s by a Welshman named John Hughes, it was called Yuzovka after him; it was renamed Stalino c. 1935, Donetsk in 1961. Pop. (1967) 823,000.

JOHN DONNE
Portrait on loan to the N.P.G. from the collection of the Marquis of Lothian.

DO'NGOLA. Region of the Northern prov. of the Rep. of the Sudan, lying on both banks of the Nile. Its chief town is New D., some 45- m. above the 3rd cataract, which was founded c. 1812 to replace Old D., some 75 m. up river, destroyed by the Mamelukes. The latter was cap. of the Christian kingdom of D. 6th–15th cents. Area 27,520 sq. m.; pop. c. 150,000.

DÖNITZ (dön'its), **Karl** (1891–). German admiral who was C.-in-C. of the German navy, 1943–5, and succeeded Hitler as head of the state. At Nuremberg in 1946 he was sentenced to 10 years' imprisonment, and was released 1956.

DONIZETTI (donĕdzet'tē), **Gaetano** (1797–1848). Italian composer. B. in Lombardy, he composed 64 operas, of which the best known are *Lucrezia Borgia* (1833), *Lucia di Lammermoor* (1835), *La Fille du Régiment* and *La Favorita* (1840), and *Don Pasquale* (1843). They show the influence of Rossini and Bellini, and their chief feature is their unfailing flow of brilliant and expressive melodies.

DONKEY. Popular name for Ass (q.v.).

DONNE (dun), **John** (1571–1631). British poet. He was brought up in the R.C. faith, and matriculated early at Oxford to avoid taking the oath of supremacy. Before entering Lincoln's Inn as a law student in 1592 he travelled on the Continent. During his 4 years at the law courts he was notorious for his wit and reckless living. In 1596 he sailed as a volunteer with Essex and Raleigh, and on his return became private secretary to Egerton, Keeper of the Seal. This appointment was ended by his marriage to Ann More, niece of Egerton's wife, and they endured many years of poverty. The more passionate and tender of his love poems were probably written to her. In 1615 D. took orders in the C. of E. His wife d. 2 years later; and from 1621 to his death he was Dean of St. Paul's. His sermons place him among the greatest orators of his century, and his passionate poems of love and hate, violent, tender, or abusive, give him a unique position among English poets. His verse was not pub. in collected form until after his death.

DONNYBROOK. Locality, formerly a village, in co. Dublin, Rep. of Ireland, famous for riotous fairs, which were stopped in 1855. It is now part of Dublin city.

DONOGHUE (don'ohū), **Stephen** ('Steve') (1884–1945). British jockey. Between 1915 and 1925 he rode 6 Derby winners, thus beating Fred Archer's record of 5 Derby victories, and 1921–3 achieved the 'hat-trick' by winning 3 successive Derbys.

DOOLITTLE. Hilda (1886–). American poetess. She came to Europe in 1911, and was associated with Ezra Pound and the British writer, Richard Aldington (q.v., to whom she was m. 1913–37), in founding the Imagist school of poets, whose members advocated the presentation of a clear-cut visual image in poetry, and the writing of short, concentrated poems in free rhythms. Her books include *Sea Garden* and *Hymen*.

DOOLITTLE, James Harold (1896–). American aviator. In 1925 he won the Schneider Trophy Race, and in 1932 estab. world speed records for land planes. During the S.W.W. he led the U.S. bomber squadron which made a spectacular daylight raid on Tokyo in April 1942, and later held commands in N. Africa, the Mediterranean and Britain. He was created Hon. K.C.B. in 1945, and 1959–62 was chairman of the U.S. Space Technology Laboratories.

DOOMSDAY BOOK. See DOMESDAY BOOK.

DOON. River of Ayrshire, Scotland, which flows for 36 m. through loch D. to the Firth of Clyde.

DOONE. Family of freebooters who lived on Exmoor, according to legend, until they were exterminated in the 17th cent. They feature in Blackmore's novel *Lorna Doone* (1869). The D. Valley is near Lynton.

DOPPLER, Christian Johann (1803–53). Austrian physicist. He became prof. of experimental physics at Vienna, and formulated 'D.'s Principle', which states that in the same way as the pitch of a sound alters if the body from which it proceeds is moving relatively to a fixed observer, so the light from a moving star varies in colour.

The **D. Radar Navigational System** for aircraft is an airborne equipment requiring no ground installation. In a typical system 4 separate beams of microwave energy are radiated from an antenna in the aircraft to the surface of the earth and some of the energy is reflected back. Due to the D. phenomenon the frequency of the reflected signal from each of the 4 beams is shifted by an amount proportional to the velocity of the aircraft, and is modified by the angles of the various beams. This data is processed in a computer and enables the pilot to fix his position.

D.O.R.A. Short for the Defence of the Realm Act, passed in Nov. 1914, which conferred extraordinary powers on the Govt. with a view to the proper prosecution of the war.

DORCHESTER. Co. town (bor.) of Dorset, England, on the r. Frome, 7 m. N. of Weymouth. Roman remains include a theatre, encampments, and walls. Thomas Hardy was born nearby, and D. is the Casterbridge of the novels. Pop. (1961) 12,266.

DORDOGNE (-dōn'). River of France rising in Puy-de-Dôme dept. and flowing 300 m. to join the Garonne 14 m. N. of Bordeaux. It gives its name to a dept. and is harnessed for power.

DORDRECHT (-rekht). River port on an island in the Maas, S. Holland, Netherlands, 12 m. S.E. of Rotterdam. It is an inland port with shipbuilding yards and makes heavy machinery, plastics, etc. The first assembly of the United Provinces took place at D., 1572. Pop. (1967) 88,475.

DORÉ (dohreh'), **Gustave** (1832–83). French artist. B. at Strasbourg, he was a skilled lithographer at 11, and was also active as a painter, etcher, and sculptor. His lasting reputation rests on his illustrations for Rabelais (1854), Dante, Cervantes, the Bible, Milton and Poe, which range from the sardonically humorous to the dark and harrowing.

DŌ'RIANS. Race of ancient Greece. They entered Greece from the N. and conquered most of the Peloponnese from the Achaeans; this invasion appears to have been completed before 1000 B.C. Their chief cities were Sparta, Argos, and Corinth.

DORIC ORDER. *See* ORDER.

DORKING. English market town (U.D.) in the valley of the Mole, Surrey, near Box Hill, on the edge of the N. Downs. Pop. (1961) 22,594.

DORLING, Henry T. (1883–1968). British writer of nautical stories under the name 'Taffrail'. After some 30 years in the navy he retired in 1929, but served again in the S.W.W. Among his numerous books are *Dover-Ostend* (1933) and *The Navy in Action* (1940).

DORMAN, Sir Arthur (1848–1931). British ironmaster and colliery owner, co-founder with Albert de Lande Long of Dorman, Long and Co. The largest producers of structural steel in the country, the firm has built many great bridges, incl. Sydney Harbour Bridge.

DORMOUSE

DORMOUSE. Small group of rodents, akin to rats and mice, which comprise the family Muscardinidae. They can be distinguished by their hairy tails. They are arboreal and nocturnal and in cold latitudes hibernate in winter. The Common D. (*Muscardinus avellanarius*) is reddish fawn in colour.

DORNIER (-yeh), **Claude** (1884–1969). German aircraft designer. B. in Bavaria, he founded the D. Metallbau works at Friedrichshafen, Lake Constance, in 1922. He invented the seaplane and during the S.W.W. supplied the Luftwaffe with the 'flying pencil' bomber.

DORPAT. German name of TARTU.

D'ORSAY (dorsā′), **Alfred Guillaume Gabriel,** count (1801–52). French dandy. After serving in the French army, he accompanied the earl and countess of Blessington on a tour of Italy. For 20 years he resided with Lady Blessington in London at Gore House, where he became known for his taste and accomplishments. In 1849 he returned to Paris, and shortly before his death was appointed director of fine arts.

DORSET, Earl of. *See* SACKVILLE.

DORSET. Co. of S.W. England on the English Channel, between Hants and Devon. The centre is occupied by the chalky Dorset Heights, rising to over 900 ft. in the E. Elsewhere the co. is low-lying. Sheep and cattle are kept, and marble and building stones quarried. The co. town is Dorchester. Along the S. coast are many holiday resorts, incl. Lyme Regis and Weymouth. Other towns include Poole, Shaftesbury, and Sherborne. The co. contains the village and ruins of Corfe Castle and fine religious buildings, incl. Wimborne Minster. D. is the centre of Thomas Hardy's Wessex. Area 978 sq. m.; pop. (1967) 337,910.

DORT. Another name for DORDRECHT.

DORTMUND (dort′moond). Industrial centre in the Ruhr, Germany, 36 m. N.E. of Düsseldorf; it is the S. terminus of the D.-Ems canal with large docks and has an airport. D. owes its importance to the Westphalian coalfield, of which it is the largest mining town. D. was bombed repeatedly during the S.W.W. Pop. (1966) 654,541.

DŌRY or **John Dory.** A sea-fish (*Zeus faber*), the type of the family Zeidae and the order Zeomorphae; found in the Mediterranean and Atlantic. There are 9–10 spines on the dorsal fin, and bony plates on the abdomen and back. In colour D. is olive brown or dull grey, with a conspicuous blotch on each side of the body. It is an excellent food fish, and grows to about 20 in.

DOS PASSOS (dus-pas′sus), **John** (1896–1970). American author. B. in Chicago, he made a reputation with the war novels *One Man's Initiation* (1919), and *Three Soldiers* (1921). His acknowledged masterpiece is the *U.S.A.* trilogy (1930–6), which attains a panoramic view of American existence by placing fictitious characters against the real setting of newspaper headlines, and contemporary events.

DOSTOIEVSKY (dostōyef′skē), **Fyodor Mihailovich** (1821–81). Russian novelist. B. in Moscow, the son of a physician, he was for a short time an army officer. His first novel, *Poor Folk*, appeared in 1846. In 1849 D. was arrested as a Socialist revolutionary, and after being reprieved from death at the last moment was sent to the penal settlement at Omsk for 4 years, where the terrible conditions increased his epileptic tendency. Finally pardoned in 1859, he pub. the humorous *Village of Stepanchikovo*; *The House of the Dead* (1861), recalling his prison experiences; and *The Insulted and the Injured* (1862). Meanwhile he had launched 2 unsuccessful liberal periodicals in the 2nd of which his *Letters from the Underworld* appeared. Compelled to work by pressure of debt he quickly produced *Crime and Punishment* (1866), an analysis of a murderer's reactions, and *The Gambler* (1867), and then fled abroad from his creditors. He wrote *The Idiot* (1868–9), in which the hero is an epileptic like himself; *The Eternal Husband* (1870); and *The Possessed* (1871–2).

Returning to Russia in 1871 he again entered journalism and issued the personal miscellany *Journal of an Author* in which he discussed contemporary problems. In 1875 he pub. *A Raw Youth*, but the great work of his last years is *The Brothers Karamazov* (1880).

Remarkable for their profound psychological insight D.'s novels have greatly influenced Russian writers, and since the beginning of the 20th cent. have been increasingly admired and imitated abroad.

DOTTEREL. Bird (*Eudromias morinellus*) of the plover family (Charadriidae). About the shape and size of the golden plover, it is mostly plain brown in colour, with white eyebrows and breast-band. In Britain it is a summer migrant, frequenting moors.

DOUAI (doo-ā′). French industrial town on the r. Scarpe, Nord dept. It has coal-mines, iron foundries, breweries, etc. In the English R.C. college, founded there in 1568, removed to England 1903, the D. Bible was prepared. Pop. (1968) 49,187.

DORY

DOUBS (doo). French river rising in the Jura Mountains and flowing 260 m. to join the Saône at Verdun-sur-le-Doubs. It gives its name to a dept.

DOUGHBOY (dō′-). Nickname for U.S.A. soldiers in the two world wars. One derivation is from the large buttons on the uniforms of the soldiers of the American Civil War, which were so called. In the 17th cent. a D. was a dumpling.

DOUGHTY (dow′ti), **Charles Montagu** (1843–1926). British poet and prose-writer. B. in Suffolk, he travelled in Arabia, 1876–8, and recorded his experiences in antique prose in *Travels in Arabia Deserta* (1888). In 1906 appeared his epic *Dawn in Britain*, a chronicle of legendary British history.

DOUGLAS (dug′las), **Lord Alfred (Bruce)** (1870–1945). British poet. The 3rd son of the 8th marquess of Queensberry, he became closely associated in London with Oscar Wilde. This friendship led to Wilde's action for libel against D.'s father, and ultimately resulted in Wilde's own imprisonment. He discussed his relations with Wilde in his autobiography

(1929), and also in *Without Apology* (1938), and *Oscar Wilde: a Summing Up* (1940). In 1902 he m. the poetess Olive Custance, and in 1911 he became an R.C. A vol. of verse, *In Excelsis*, was pub. in 1924 and his complete *Sonnets and Lyrics* in 1935.

DOUGLAS, Clifford Hugh (1879–1952). British Social Credit theorist. Ed. at Cambridge, he was employed 1900–14 as a construction engineer on railways in India, Argentina, and Britain. In a series of works – *Economic Democracy, Credit Power, Social Credit* and *The Monopoly of Credit* – he put forward his economic theory of Social Credit, and in 1935–6 he acted as reconstruction adviser to the govt. elected in Alberta on a Social Credit (q.v.) programme.

DOUGLAS, Gavin (or **Gawain**) (1475–1522). Scottish poet. A son of the earl of Angus, he became bishop of Dunkeld in 1515, and was very active in Scottish politics. He wrote 2 allegories, *The Palace of Honour* and *King Hart*, but his best work is his translation of Virgil's *Aeneid*, the first Eng. version of one of the great classical poets.

DOUGLAS, George. Pseudonym of the Scottish novelist George Douglas Brown (1869–1902). B. in Ayrshire, he is chiefly famous for *The House with the Green Shutters* (1901), a grimly realistic study of Scottish provincial life.

DOUGLAS, Lloyd Cassell (1877–1951). American author. For many years a Lutheran and Congregationalist pastor, he achieved fame by his novels on religious themes, *The Robe* and *The Big Fisherman*.

DOUGLAS, Norman (1868–1952). English writer. His travel books, such as *Siren Land* (1911) and *Old Calabria* (1915), are witty and sensually appreciative, as is his most famous novel *South Wind* (1917). *Looking Back* and *Late Harvest* are autobiographical.

DOUGLAS OF KIRTLESIDE, William Sholto Douglas, 1st Baron (1893–1969). British air marshal. During the S.W.W. he was A.O C.-in-C. of Fighter Command 1940–2, Middle East Command 1943–4, and Coastal Command 1944–5. In 1946–7 he was Military Gov. of the British Zone of Germany, and in 1949–64 was chairman of B.E.A.

DOUGLAS. Cap. (bor.) of the Isle of Man, on the E. coast of the island. It is a holiday resort, and terminus of the shipping routes from and to Fleetwood and Liverpool. Pop. (1961) 18,837.

DOUKHOBORS (dōō′) or **Dukhobortzi.** Russian religious sect, also known as 'Christians of the Universal Brotherhood', some of their teachings resembling those of the Quakers. They were long persecuted, mainly for refusing military service – Tolstoy organized a relief fund for them – but in 1898 were permitted to emigrate and settled in Canada where they number *c.* 13,000, mainly in British Columbia and Saskatchewan. Refusing to send their children to school (where militarism might be taught) the extremist group, 'The Sons of Freedom', have staged demonstrations and terrorism in recent years leading to the imprisonment of *c.* 100 members of the sect by 1963.

DOULTON (dol′ton), **Sir Henry** (1820–97). British ceramist. He developed special wares for the chemical, electrical and building industries and in 1846 estab. the world's first stoneware drainpipe factory. From 1870 he created at Lambeth and Burslem a reputation for art pottery and domestic tablewares.

DOUMER (doomār′), **Paul** (1857–1932). French statesman. He was elected pres. of the Chamber in 1905, in 1927 became pres. of the Senate, and in 1931 Pres. of the Rep. He was assassinated by Gorgulov, a mad White Russian émigré.

DOUMERGUE (doomerg′), **Gaston** (1863–1937). French statesman. After holding many cabinet posts, he became in 1923 pres. of the Senate, and 1924–31 was Pres. of the Rep.

DOUW (dow) or **DOW, Gerard** (1613–75). Dutch painter. B. at Leyden, he studied under Rembrandt.

DOVER. The floodlit castle is a landmark for visitors arriving by sea. Built on a site fortified from very early times, it covers some 34 acres and is one of the finest examples of British medieval fortification, although considerable changes were made in the Napoleonic period under threat of invasion.
Photo: Ray Warner Ltd.

He was fond of painting half-length figures in window alcoves, and is famous for exactitude in detail.

DOVE. See PIGEON.

DOVER. One of the Cinque Ports (q.v.) market town, seaport, and municipal bor. on the S.E. coast of Kent, and the nearest point of Britain to the Continent, being only 21 m. from Calais. D.'s modern development has been chiefly due to the cross-Channel traffic, which includes train-ferry and other passenger and goods services. D., the terminus of Watling Street, was the Roman Portus Dubris. The beacon, or pharos, on the cliffs, built *c.* A.D. 50, is reputed to be one of the oldest buildings in Britain. The Lord Warden of the Cinque Ports is Constable of Dover Castle. D. is the main centre of the Channel coast defence system and during the S.W.W. suffered heavily from enemy shelling and aerial bombardment; 212 civilians were killed. Pop. (1961) 35,248.

DOVER, Strait of. Strip of water separating England from France, and connecting the English Channel with the North Sea. About 22 m. long, and 17 m. wide at the narrowest part (Dover to Cap Gris Nez).

DOWDEN, Edward (1843–1913). Irish critic and poet, who was prof. of English literature at Trinity Coll., Dublin, from 1867 till his death. He edited many of Shakespeare's plays, and wrote *Shakespeare: a Study of his Mind and Art* (1875).

DOWDING, Hugh Caswall Tremenheere, 1st baron (1882–1970). British air chief marshal. A member of the R.F.C. (later R.A.F.) in 1914, he was chief of Fighter Command at the outbreak of war in 1939, a post he held through the Battle of Britain. He retired in 1942 and was created a baron in 1943. He wrote works on spiritualism.

DOWLAND, John (1563–1626). English composer. He failed to estab. himself at Elizabeth's court – he was an R.C. convert – but later reverted to Protestantism and from 1612 was patronized by the Stuarts. He is remembered for his songs to lute accompaniment.

DOWN. Co. in the S.E. of N. Ireland, facing the Irish Sea on the E., and adjoining Armagh on the W., Antrim on the N. In the S. are the Mourne mts., in the E. Strangford sea lough. The co. town is Downpatrick. Area 952 sq. m.; pop. (1966) 286,930. See illus. p. 354.

DOWNING STREET. Street in Westminster, England, leading from Whitehall to St. James's Park, named after Sir George Downing (d. 1684), a diplomat under Cromwell and Charles II; No. 10 is the official residence of the Prime Minister. Poorly built, the D.S.

DOWN. With more than a dozen peaks rising to 2,000 ft. the Mountains of Mourne have inspired poets and songwriters and provide excellent climbing.
Courtesy of Northern Ireland Tourist Board.

and Old Treasury buildings were reconstructed in 1963 at a cost of £3 m.

DOWNPA'TRICK. Co. town of Down, N. Ireland, on the Quoile, 20 m. S.S.E. of Belfast. Pop. (1961) 4,196.

DOWNS, North and **South.** Two lines of chalk hills in S.E. England. They form two scarps which face each other across the Weald of Kent and Sussex, and are much used for sheep pasture. The N. Downs run from Salisbury Plain across Hampshire, Surrey, and Kent to the cliffs of S. Foreland. The S. Downs run across Sussex to Beachy Head.

DOWNS, The. Roadstead off E. Kent, England, between Deal and the Goodwin Sands; it is 8 m. long, 6 m. wide, greatest depth 72 ft. Several 17th cent. naval battles took place here, incl. a defeat of Spain by the Dutch in 1639.

DOWSON, Ernest (1867–1900). British poet. Perhaps the best of the 'decadent' poets of the 1890s, he suffered from tuberculosis, and in later life was very poor. His lyric 'Cynara' has a famous refrain: 'I have been faithful to thee, Cynara! in my fashion'.

DOXIADIS (doksēah'dis), **Constantinos** (1913–). Greek 'master-builder'. Trained as an architect-engineer, he was during the S.W.W. head of the Greek 'underground' Hephaestus, and 1948–51 was co-ordinator of the Greek Recovery Programme. He founded the Graduate School of Ekistics at Athens Technological Institute, where he is prof., and is also pres. of the Ekistic Centre of Athens, and consultant to many govts. He pub. *Architecture in Transition* (1963), and *Ekistics* (1968). *See* EKISTICS, ISLAMABAD.

DOYLE, Sir Arthur Conan (1859–1930). British writer. B. at Edinburgh, he qualified as a doctor, and practised at Southsea, 1882–90. Later he travelled in the Arctic and on the W. coast of Africa, and during the Boer War was senior physician of a field hospital in S. Africa. He wrote *The Great Boer War* (1900), and was knighted in 1902.

The first of D.'s books, *A Study in Scarlet*, appeared in 1887 and introduced to the public the famous private detective, Sherlock Holmes, and his ingenuous companion, Dr. Watson. Other books featuring the same characters followed, incl. *The Sign of Four* (1889), *The Hound of the Baskervilles* (1902), and *The Valley of Fear* (1915), as well as several vols. of short stories. D. also wrote historical novels (*Micah Clarke*, 1889, and *The White Company*, 1891) and scientific romances (*The Lost World*, 1912). In his later years he became a spiritualist.

DOYLE, Richard (1824–83). British caricaturist and illustrator. Son of John D. (1797–1868), a caricaturist known as H.B., he was b. in London and started work in his father's studio. He illustrated many books,

contributed to *Punch* (the original cover being his design), and painted fanciful pictures of witches and elf-like creatures.

D'OYLY CARTE, Richard (1844–1901). British theatrical manager, famous as the producer of the Gilbert and Sullivan operas at the Savoy theatre in London, which he built.

DRACHMANN (drakh'mahn), **Holger Henrik Herboldt** (1846–1908). Danish author. B. at Copenhagen, he pub. his first poems in 1872, and later became known as a novelist and playwright.

DRA'CO or **Flying Dragon.** Genus of small lizards, inhabiting the E. Indies, Malaya, etc., of which *D. volans* is the type. They are arboreal in their habits. The ribs are prolonged and support a parachute of skin, by means of which the animal is able to glide from bough to bough.

DRACO (7th cent. B.C.). Athenian statesman, the first to codify the laws of the Athenian city-state. These were notorious for their severity; hence Draconian, meaning particularly harsh.

DRAFT. *See* CONSCRIPTION.

DRAGON. In zoology, name given to two kinds of lizards, such as the flying D. (*see* DRACO), and the Komodo D. (*Varanus komodensis*). The latter is a species of monitor, and is the largest living lizard, reaching a length of 10 ft. It is an inhabitant of Komodo, Indonesia.

DRA'GONET. A family of sea-fishes (Callionymidae) allied to the blennies and gobies, and belonging to the order Percomorphi. Like their allies they are small fishes haunting rock-pools and coastal waters, and are distinguished by their large upturned eyes and mobile mouth.

DRAGON-FLIES. Insects found throughout the world which form the order Odonata. Mostly large and brilliantly coloured, Ds. have narrow, elongated bodies, prominent, protruding eyes and minute, bristlelike antennae. The mouthparts are modified for seizing and chewing, and have strong teeth. Their 2 pairs of approximately equal, membranous, glassy wings have a net-like venation.

The nearly 5,000 species of Ds. are classified in 2 main groups or sub-orders: the Anisoptera incl. the larger and stouter members, the Zygoptera the smaller and weaker kinds. They are often known as damsel-flies.

DRAGOON (dragoon'). Name derived from the 'dragon' or short musket used by the French in the 16th cent., and applied to a mounted soldier who carried this or some other infantry weapon. The name has been retained by certain regiments, though it no longer has its original meaning.

DRAKE, Sir Francis (*c.* 1545–96). English sea-captain. B. near Tavistock, he was apprenticed to the master of a coasting vessel, who left him the ship at his death. He accompanied Sir John Hawkins (q.v.) in 1567, and then after 2 voyages of reconnaissance he set out in 1572 to plunder the Spanish Main. He returned to England in 1573 with considerable booty. After serving in Ireland as a volunteer, he suggested to the Queen an expedition to the Pacific, and in Dec. 1577 he sailed in the *Pelican* with 4 other ships and 166 men. In Aug. 1578 the fleet passed through the Straits of Magellan in 16 days and was then blown S. to Cape Horn. The remaining ships became separated and returned to England, leaving the *Pelican*, now renamed the *Golden Hind*, alone in the Pacific. D. sailed N. along the coast of Chile and Peru, plundering

DRAGON as emblem. Top, Welsh; below, Chinese.

DRAGON-FLY. Resting after the tremendous effort of freeing itself from the pupa-case, the perfect insect waits for its wings to dry and harden. Below, the empty case still grips the stem, only the split thoracic cuticle showing the point of emergence.   *Photo: G. Ronald Austing.*

Spanish ships as far N. as California, and then, in July 1579, S.W. across the Pacific. He rounded the Cape in June 1580, and reached England in Sept. Thus the 2nd voyage round the world, the 1st made by an Englishman, was completed in a little under 3 years. When the Spanish ambassador demanded D.'s punishment, the Queen knighted him on the deck of the *Golden Hind* at Deptford.

In 1582 D. was chosen mayor of Plymouth, and in 1584–5 he represented Bossiney in parliament. In a raid on Cadiz in 1587 he burnt 10,000 tons of shipping, 'singed the King of Spain's beard', and delayed the Armada for a year. He was stationed off Ushant in 1588 to intercept the Armada, but was driven back to England by unfavourable winds. During the fight in the Channel he served as a vice-admiral in the *Revenge*. D. sailed on his last expedition to the W. Indies with Hawkins in 1595, and in Jan. 1596 d. on his ship off Nombre de Dios.

DRAKENSBERG (drah′kens-). Mountain range in S. Africa, on the boundary of Basutoland and Orange Free State with Natal; highest point is Mont aux Sources, 11,000 ft., near which is Natal National Park.

DRAMA. A story interpreted to an audience by actors, in which such elements as dancing, music, singing, etc., are only subsidiary.

ORIENTAL D. is characterized by fixed conventions and an avoidance of all semblance of reality. This is true in Japan of both the aristocratic *No* plays developed in the 14–16th cents. and of the popular *Kabuki* which originated in the 17th cent., and also applies to the less literate Chinese theatre and to Indian drama.

GREEK D. arose from the lyrical dithyramb chanted by a chorus in praise of Dionysus when, according to tradition, Thespis added a single actor. D. rapidly developed with the inauguration of the Athenian festivals: Aeschylus, Sophocles, and Euripides perfected tragedy, and comedy reached its greatest heights under Aristophanes and Menander.

All that survives of ROMAN D., e.g. the comedies of Terence, the farces of Plautus, and the tragedies of Seneca, is directly based on the Greek tradition.

MEDIEVAL. Something of the classical tradition was probably carried on into the Dark Ages by wandering entertainers. But in about the 10th cent. Church ritual began to assume dramatic form, and thence developed the mystery cycles and miracle plays. Essentially amateur productions, they were popular all over Europe in the 12th–16th cents.

RENAISSANCE. The rediscovery of classical D. brought a new beginning in the Italian courts at the end of the 15th cent., and at the same time the *commedia dell' arte*, depending on the actors' improvisation, was evolved among the people. This cleavage did not exist in Spain, where Lope de Vega and Calderón de la Barca were the outstanding dramatists.

In England, too, there was no rigid class demarcation. Early experiments in the morality, interlude, comedy, and tragedy, were followed by the work of the young univ. men. Lyly, Greene, Peele, Kyd, and Marlowe, which prepared the way for Shakespeare.

17TH CENT. In England tragedy declined, although erratic strength still appears in Webster, Massinger, Middleton, and Ford. New vitality in comedy came with the comedy of humours of Jonson, which, combining with the witty comedy of Beaumont and Fletcher, produced the early plays of Shirley, and the later Restoration works of Etherege, Wycherley, and Congreve. The playhouses became the resort of the courtier, so that although the comedy of manners flourished, there was no place for great tragedy, despite the efforts of Dryden, Otway, and Lee.

In France the intellectual interests of the age found expression after the middle of the cent. in the work of Corneille, Racine, and Molière.

18TH CENT. In this period less vital examples of the older types of tragedy and comedy were written by Sheridan, Goldsmith, Marivaux and Voltaire, but a new sentimental genre was exploited by Cumberland and Kelly in England; and by Diderot, Beaumarchais, Goldoni, and Lessing abroad. This sentimentalism was coloured by romantic aspirations in Schiller and Kotzebue.

19TH CENT. The most popular form was the melodrama, which left nothing behind of literary value. In France Victor Hugo gave full expression to romanticism, but otherwise it was the period of the sentimental problem drama represented by S. Knowles, B. Lytton, and Boucicault in England; and Hebbel, Augier, and Dumas fils on the Continent. The latent vitality of the latter was exploited by Ibsen and Strindberg, who secured the triumph of realism – a development paralleled less forcefully by Robertson, Pinero, and H. A. Jones in England; and by Sardou, Hervieu, Lavedan, Becque, Brieux, Sudermann, Hauptmann, and Wedekind in Europe.

20TH CENT. In Russia, the native realistic tradition combined with the inspiration of Ibsen to produce the Moscow Arts Theatre and Chekhov, and elsewhere the plays of Oscar Wilde, Shaw, Bridie and Pirandello

DRAMA. The Asolo theatre, originally built inside the great hall of Asolo Castle, near Venice, by Antonio Locatelli in 1798. It was torn down in the 1930s but in 1951 acquired for restoration, as seen above, in Florida.
Courtesy of the John Mable Ringling Museum of Art, Florida

also reflected a preoccupation with the individual in society. The cynical mood prevalent after the F.W.W. gave rise to the comedies of Coward and later Rattigan in England, and to the general trend elsewhere towards satire, experiment and fantasy shown in the work of Cocteau, Mayakovsky, and O'Neill, and in the early plays of Čapek, Brecht, Toller and Elmer Rice. With the advent of the Depression and the rise of Fascism, the latter writers became committed to action, and the 'thirties saw some of Brecht's best work, and the rise of the American playwrights, Odets, A. MacLeish and Irwin Shaw. The dramatists produced by the S.W.W. incl. Camus, Sartre, Anouilh and Salacrou. The nihilistic mood of the 'fifties was reflected by the 'Theatre of the Absurd' in work by Ionesco, Simpson and Beckett; this was accompanied by the more realistic drama of Osborne, Wesker, Pinter and John Arden in England, Brendan Behan in Ireland, Genet, Dürrenmatt and Ugo Betti on the Continent, and Miller, Jack Gelber and Tennessee Williams in America.

The re-association, begun by Claudel, of the poet and the playhouse in the 20th cent. led to the rise of the Irish Abbey Theatre, with plays by J. M. Synge and W. B. Yeats, and to the poetic drama of Lorca in Spain, and of T. S. Eliot, Spender, Auden and Isherwood, MacLeish and Fry, in England and America. The logical culmination of this trend was in the pure-sound plays of Dylan Thomas and Harold Pinter.

DRAPER, Ruth (1884–1956). American diseuse. Dau. of a N.Y. physician she developed technique of solo presentation of character studies, e.g. 'The German Governess' which won her a world-wide reputation.

DRAUGHTS, or **Checkers.** A game played by 2 players on a square checkered board of 64 squares. Each player has a set of 12 men which at the start of the game occupy alternate squares of the first 3 rows on 2 opposite sides of the board. A man may be moved forwards diagonally left or right to a contiguous and unoccupied square. When a man reaches the opponent's back line he becomes a king, and as a distinguishing sign another man of the same colour is placed on top of him. A king may move backwards as well as forwards. When there is a hostile piece on a contiguous square, and there is an empty square on the further side, the man or king may be moved to the empty square and the hostile piece removed from the board. If after making such a capturing move there is another hostile piece contiguous and with an empty square beyond it, such piece, being *en prise*, must be captured also. The object of the game is to leave the opponent without a move, either by capturing all his pieces or by blocking them so that they cannot move.

DRAVI'DIAN. Name applied to a group of non-Indo-Aryan peoples, inhabiting the Deccan and N. Ceylon. They generally are of darker skin and shorter stature than the Aryan types of the N., and developed their own style of temple architecture. The D. languages include Tamil, Telugu, Malayalam, and Canarese.

DRAYTON, Michael (1563–1631). English poet. B. in Warwickshire, he came to London in 1590, where he pub. a vol. of poems, *The Harmony of the Church* (1591), which was destroyed by order of the arch-bishop of Canterbury. After a collection of pastorals in 1593 came *Idea's Mirror* (1594); a series of English historical poems; *Poems Lyrical and Pastoral* (1606); and *Nymphidia* (1627), a fairy poem. His greatest poetical work was the topographical survey of England, *Polyolbion* (1613–22), in 30 books. D. was buried in Westminster Abbey.

DREAM. Fantasy experienced during sleep. Until the 18th cent. Ds. were closely studied, especially as indications of future events, a whole code arising for their interpretation, but then came to be regarded as an unimportant reaction to physical stimuli. In 1900 Freud revived the importance of Ds., concluding that they were an expression of unconscious wish-fulfilment, nightmares being failed Ds. induced by intense fear of 'repressed' impulses, since the function of Ds. is seen as simply an attempt to preserve the peace of mind essential for sleep. A thought of the previous day would become disturbing, by having forged a number of unconscious associations, and the D. mechanism would counter this by associating it with a basic emotional need (imagined as being gratified) and keeping it from consciousness by various disguises until the final product appeared as a dream. Most frequent on first falling asleep or just before waking, Ds. are not rapidly fleeting (as was once claimed), but occupy the same period of time as they appear to do to the dreamer. This is ascertainable by measurement of mental and physical activity during sleep, the sleeper reacting in the same way to D. stimuli as to real stimuli when awake.

DREISER, Theodore (1871–1945). American novelist, noted for his large-scale realism. B. in Indiana, he pub. in 1910 *Sister Carrie*, which was suppressed as immoral, and only became known with *Jennie Gerhardt* (1911). Later were the companion studies of big business *The Financier* (1912) and *The Titan* (1914), and his masterly study of an unscrupulous climber who ends as a murderer. *An American Tragedy* (1925), based on a real-life crime. In his later years he became a Communist. His brother, **Paul Dresser** (1857–1911), wrote popular songs such as 'On the Banks of the Wabash'.

DRESDEN. City of (E.) Germany, cap. of D. district, formerly cap. of Saxony. It is on the Elbe, 100 m. S. of Berlin, and is first mentioned in 1206 as a place fortified by the margraves of Meissen. D. became one of the most beautiful Ger. cities under the elector Augustus II the Strong (1694–1733), who made it a centre of art and culture, and erected the Zwinger and other rococo buildings. Count Brühl built a famous palace and the Brühl terrace. The museums contain well-known works of art. There is a conservatory of music and a technical coll. Manufactures incl. chemicals, machinery, glassware, musical instruments, and luxury goods. The manufacture of D. china, started at D. in 1709, was transferred to Meissen in 1710. Napoleon won a famous battle at D. 1813. D. was devastatingly bombed by the Allies on the night of 13–14 Feb. 1945, 6 sq. m. of the inner town being destroyed, more than 21,000 killed. The Russians took the city on 8 May. Pop. (1966) city, 505,188; dist. 1,889,779.

DRESS. The various garments which cover the human form. In ancient times D. usually remained

DRESS. A Victorian family at home in the parlour of c. 1855. On the right, mother and son are absorbed with one of the forerunners of the cinema and television – a stereoscope in which double-view photograph cards give an illusion of depth.
Courtesy of Bath Assembly Rooms, Museum of Costume.

DRESS. Ready for the afternoon visit c. 1900 superbly gowned by Worth.
Courtesy of Bath Assembly Rooms, Museum of Costume.

unmodified for cents. Greek D. was extremely simple; from the 7th to the 1st cent. B.C. the main D. for both men and women was the tunic, called the *chiton*, which consisted of a rectangular woollen cloth fastened on each shoulder by a pin. The male garment of the Romans was the *toga*, which was usually white.

MIDDLE AGES. During the Middle Ages costumes did not change much in style for cents., but differed widely from place to place. There was also a wide difference between the costumes of different classes. The typical head-gear was the hood. Women wore a veil or fold of mantle, but this was abandoned in the 15th cent. for various kinds of caps, some with horns, some with butterfly-wings of gauze. Fashion, in the modern sense, was evident in the 15th cent., the two main centres being Venice and Paris.

16TH CENT. In the 16th cent. all points became blunted. As an instance, in the previous cent. shoes were excessively pointed – men's shoes became so long that the points were curled up and attached to the knees – but in the 16th cent. they seemed for a time excessively wide. In the first part of the cent. women's clothes were bell-shaped and kept in position by petticoats. Later the ruff developed, and men wore the doublet, the legs being exposed and covered with tight-fitting hose.

17TH CENT. The main outlines of Elizabethan costume were retained during the reign of James I, but with the accession of Charles I costumes became more elegant. Women were not so tightly waisted. The short puffed breeches of the men extended downwards to the knee and were adorned with rosettes of ribbon, as were also the shoes. Puritans wore the same styles in general outline, but the materials were plainer. Cavaliers and Roundheads wore the same kind of wide-brimmed, high-crowned hat, but the Roundheads abandoned the plume. French modes were introduced at the restoration of Charles II, and the male costume became more elaborate than that under Charles I. Men began to wear flowing wigs in imitation of Louis XIV. During the rest of the cent. the costume of both sexes gradually stiffened, and the male D. began to consist of the 3 garments which, with various modifications, have remained the typical male attire ever since.

18TH CENT. Women's clothes ost some of their stiffness. Men's coats were richly embroidered, and the waistcoat assumed something of its present form. In the 1770s the head-dress of both men and women became very high – women's hair was sometimes dressed to the height of 2 or 3ft. and was crowned with ships, windmills, and various other ornaments.

DRESS. A lesson in the minuet c. 1760.
Courtesy of Bath Assembly Rooms, Museum of Costume.

Towards the end of the cent. men adopted the plain cloth of the English country gentleman, and wore a high-crowned hat.

19TH CENT. Trousers were worn by all classes, and men's clothes became more sombre in tone, until about 1850 black clothes were introduced for evening and formal wear. The top hat was by this time universal. Women's clothes were more varied than men's. The crinoline was introduced in the '40s, but was later replaced by the bustle. In the middle '90s the chief eccentricity was the leg-o'-mutton sleeve. Men's clothes developed a new informality with the introduction of the 'suit' and of the bowler hat and 'gent's boater'.

20TH CENT. During the Edwardian epoch men became more formal, and the frock coat was revived. Women had narrow waists, and wore much lace. The 'hobble' skirt, worn with a large hat, was introduced about 1910. By 1925 a new type of female D. appeared – the narrow straight garment extending down to the knees, and having the waist round the hips. Plus-fours were worn by men, and the Homburg or Trilby was introduced. In the '30s skirts grew longer, and after the S.W.W. austerity came the even longer skirts and femininity of the 1948 'New Look'. In the 1950s came the return to modified 'Edwardian' for men (so-called 'Teddy Boys'), and (for women) to the straight line and dropped waist of the '20s in the Dior H-look and A-line of 1954–5. Late in the 1950s the waist disappeared altogether with the advent of the 'Sack', and in the early 1960s of a modified and better-cut version of this – the 'Shift', and the hem-line rose to just below the knee. The development of man-made fabrics, and of the ready-to-wear industry catering largely for a young market, led in the mid-1960s to the 'swinging' era of London's Carnaby Street in Soho, and mini-skirts 8 in. and more above the knee.

DREW, George Alexander (1894–). Canadian Progressive Conservative politician. He entered the Ontario legislature in 1939, was provincial premier 1943–8, and 1949–56 was leader of the opposition in the Federal Parliament. In 1957–64 he was High Commissioner to the U.K.

DREYFUS, Alfred (1859–1935). French soldier. B. in Mulhouse of a Jewish family, he held a post in the War Ministry when in 1894 he was accused of betraying military secrets to Germany, court-martialled, and sent to Devil's Island. In 1896 it was discovered that the real criminal was a Maj. Esterhazy; the High Command nevertheless attempted to suppress the facts, and used forged documents to strengthen their case. After a violent controversy, during which Clemenceau and Zola were prominent among D.'s champions, a re-trial in 1899 found him guilty with extenuating circumstances and he received a pardon. In 1906 the Court of Appeal declared him innocent, and he was reinstated in his military rank.

DRIBERG, Thomas Edward Neil (1905–). British writer and Labour politician. A war correspondent during the S.W.W. and in Korea, he was elected M.P. for Maldon 1942–55 (as an Independent 1942–5) and Barking since 1959, becoming Chairman of the Lab. Party Nat. Exec. 1957–8. He is a contributor to many periodicals, has broadcast and appeared on television, and in 1956 pub. studies of Beaverbrook – he was on the staff of the *Daily Express* 1928–43 – and Guy Burgess.

DRILL. A large baboon (*Papio leucophaeus*) of W. Africa, characterized by a very short tail and a long prehensile great toe. Its face is black with no colouring as in the mandrill. It is mainly arboreal.

DRINKWATER, John (1882–1937). British poet. B. in Leytonstone, Essex, he was an insurance clerk for 12 years, before becoming associated as manager and producer with the Birmingham Repertory Co. His 1st vol. of verse appeared in 1906, and he contributed accomplished lyrics to *Georgian Poetry*. His outstanding revival of the chronicle play *Abraham Lincoln* (1918) won great success, and was followed by *Mary Stuart* (1921), *Oliver Cromwell* (1921), *Robert E. Lee* and *Robert Burns* (1925).

DROGHEDA (drokh′eda). Seaport (bor.) near the mouth of the Boyne, co. Louth, Rep. of Ireland. The town was stormed by Cromwell in 1649, and in 1690 it surrendered to William III after the battle of the Boyne. Pop. (1966) 17,908.

DROITWICH (droit′ich). English town (bor.) on the r. Salwarpe, Worcs, famous for its saline springs. There is a large B.B.C. station here. Pop. (1961) 7,975.

DRÔME. French river rising in Dauphiné Pre-Alps and flowing W.N.W. for 63 m. to join the Rhône below Livron. It gives its name to D. dept.

DRO′MEDARY (*Camelus dromedarius*). The Arabian one-humped camel. All Ds. are now domesticated and are suited to life in the sandy deserts of Arabia and N. Africa. The hump contains fatty tissue on which the D. subsists when food is scarce.

DRŎ′MŎRE. Town (U.D.) on the r. Lagan, co. Down, N. Ireland. An abbey was founded here *c.* 600, probably by St. Colman, and became a bishopric. The old cathedral was destroyed in 1641, and the existing one built in the 17th cent. by Bishop Jeremy Taylor (q.v.). The diocese was united with Down in 1842. Pop. (1961) 2,121.

DROPSY. An accumulation of lymph in body cavities or tissues. If in the abdomen, it is called ascites; if local, oedema. General D. is usually a sign of disease of the heart, kidneys, or lungs. Tapping or a drug which will dilate the blood-vessels sometimes gives relief.

DRO′SERA. *See* INSECTIVOROUS PLANTS.

DROSOPHILA (drōsof′ila). Genus of flies, belonging to the family Muscidae and the order Diptera. The best-known species is the fruit-fly, *D. melanogaster*. Because of the rapidity with which it can be bred, and its well-marked variations, it is most suitable for the study of the laws of heredity.

DROUET (droo-ā′), **Jean Baptiste**, Comte d'Erlon (1765–1844). French soldier. B. at Reims, he served in the Revolutionary and Napoleonic wars, and in 1834 became Governor of Algeria, and in 1843 was made a marshal.

DROWNING. *See* ARTIFICIAL RESPIRATION.

DRUGS, Misuse of. The taking of dangerous substances, some of which have medicinal value, for non-medicinal purposes: a problem since the earliest times, it is in the 20th cent. increasingly so. In the U.K. the Misuse of D. Act (1971) divided them into 3 categories according to their degree of harmfulness: (a) heroin, morphine, opium and other narcotics; hallucinogens (commercially developed after the S.W.W.) such as mescalin and LSD; injectable amphetamines, e.g. methedrine. (b) narcotics such as codeine and cannabis (*see* HEMP), and stimulants of the amphetamine type, e.g. Benzedrine, Dexedrine and Drinamyl (purple hearts). (c) less dangerous drugs of the amphetamine type. Hospitalisation is the most effective form of treatment, since psychological factors are almost always involved.

DROMEDARY

Most countries strictly control production and distribution by legislation. In the U.S.A. the Justice Dept. has its Bureau of Narcotics and Dangerous Drugs and, since 1972, a special Office of Drug Abuse Law Enforcement; and Scotland Yard has a Danger-ous Drugs Squad dealing with the problem. Internationally, a new Narcotics Control Board was estab. in 1965, and in 1971 a U.N. convention was approved on psychotropic substances (those affecting the central nervous system) to control hallucinogens, stimulants and tranquillizers. Burma is the chief source of smuggled narcotics.

DRU′IDISM. Ancient religion of the Celtic peoples of pre-Christian Britain and Gaul. The word is

DRUM. I, Drake's drum; 2, a specimen from Uganda; 3, this drum from Ashanti was sounded at human sacrifices.

generally connected with a root meaning 'oak', this tree being regarded as sacred. Druids taught the immortality of the soul and a reincarnation doctrine, and were also expert in astronomy; their chief religious rite consisted in the cutting off of a mistletoe bough from the sacred oak with a golden knife. They are supposed to have offered human sacrifices.

D. was stamped out in Gaul after the Roman conquest. In Britain their stronghold was Anglesey, where they were extirpated by Agricola. They also existed in Scotland and Ireland until the coming of the Christian missionaries. What are often termed Druidic monuments – cromlechs, stone circles, etc. – are of Neolithic origin, though they may later have been used for religious purposes by the Druids.

DRUM. Musical instrument of percussion. It consists of a piece of skin, parchment, plastic or nylon, which is struck with a stick or with the hands and thus set in vibration, and which is stretched over one or both ends of a wooden or metal frame acting as a resonator. Ds. were adopted into military bands from the Turks during the 18th cent.

DRUMMOND, William, called 'of Hawthornden' (1585–1649). Scottish poet. B. at Hawthornden, near Edinburgh, he became laird there in 1610. He was the first notable Scottish poet to adopt southern English as his mode of expression.

DRUMMOND, William Henry (1854–1907). Canadian poet. B. in Ireland, he practised medicine in Quebec prov., and his poems deal with the French-Canadian voyageurs and habitants he met: *The Habitant* (1897) and *The Voyageur* (1905).

DRURY LANE THEATRE (Theatre Royal, Drury Lane). London playhouse. The first theatre bearing this name opened in 1663 on the site of earlier playhouses; the present building dates from 1812.

DRUSES (droo′zēz). A religious sect of Syria and the Lebanon, founded in the 11th cent. A.D. They are monotheists, and their scriptures are drawn from the Christian gospels, the Pentateuch, the Koran, and the Sufi allegories.

DRYAD (drī′ad). In Greek mythology, a wood nymph; each tree was supposed to be personified in its own D. or nymph. They were sometimes called hamadryads.

DRY CLEANING. Method of cleaning textiles based on the use of volatile solvents, discovered by accident in 1849 when a French tailor, John Baptiste Jolly-Bellin, noted the cleansing effect on a portion of a tablecloth on which turpentine had spread from an overturned lamp; introduced into Britain in 1886. Under the 'charged system', a non-inflammable solvent (perchlorethylene) is used under strictly controlled conditions in closed machines. The older 'white spirit' method still accounts for 30 per cent of all D.C., but it is not fully automatic.

DRYDEN, John (1631–1700). British poet. B. at Aldwinkle, Northants, he came to London in 1657, and although in 1659 he pub. *Heroic Stanzas*, in memory of Oliver Cromwell, he hastened to celebrate the Restoration with *Astraea Redux* (1660). In 1663 he m. Lady Elizabeth Howard, and was already embarked on his career as a dramatist. He produced more than a score of plays, including the comedy *Marriage à la mode* (1672); *Tyrannic Love* (1669) and *The Conquest of Granada* (1669–70), which represent the culmination of 'Heroic Tragedy'; and *All for Love* (1678). Much excellent criticism is contained in the prefaces to D.'s plays and in his *Essay of Dramatic Poesy* (1668). D.'s work as a satirist and didactic poet begins with *Absalom and Achitophel* (1681), which was followed by *The Medal* (1682); *MacFlecknoe*; *Religio Laici*, a justification of Protestantism; and *The Hind and the Panther* (1687), a defence of Roman Catholicism, to which he was converted after the accession of James II. At the Revolution of 1688 D. as an R.C. was deprived of the laureateship to which he had been appointed in 1668, and having also lost his pension supported himself by writing for the stage, and by translations, notably that of Virgil (1697). Among his many other works are *Annus Mirabilis* (1667); his odes on 'St. Cecilia's Day' (1687), and to the 'Memory of Mrs. Anne Killigrew' (1686); and *Fables* (1699), verse paraphrases of stories from Chaucer, Boccaccio, and Ovid. D. was buried in Chaucer's grave in Westminster Abbey.

He was the greatest literary figure of his age; a master of all verse forms, he particularly excelled in the heroic couplet, and created modern English prose style.

DRY CLEANING. Some 700,000 garments are dry-cleaned daily in Britain, and more than 16 tons of solid dirt is removed from the cleaning fluid. The average recovered from a two-piece suit is 1½ oz.
Courtesy of the National Federation of Dyers and Cleaners.

DRY-POINT. A method of drawing on a metal plate with a sharp point; 'dry' indicates that no acid is used in its production. The incision made on the plate makes a furrow which turns up a rough edge or fringe of metal called the 'burr'. When the plate is inked for printing, the burr collects the ink and gives an effect of great richness and a soft velvety quality to the dark portions. Dürer made a few D.-Ps., and it was much used by Rembrandt in his later work, and in more recent times by J. M. Whistler, A. Legros, W. Strang, Muirhead Bone, F. Dodd, and H. Rushbury.

DRYSDALE, Sir George Russell (1912–69). Australian artist. B. in Sussex, England, he went to Australia as a child. He studied art in Melbourne, London and Paris, and became known particularly for his drawings and paintings of the Australian Outback. He was awarded the Wynne Prize in 1947 and in 1962 became a member of the Commonwealth Art Advisory Board. He was created knight bachelor 1969.

DU BARRY, Marie Jeanne Bécu, comtesse (1743–93), Mistress of Louis XV of France. The dau. of a dressmaker, she m. Comte Guillaume du B., and in 1769 was presented at court. She is said to have been strikingly handsome, not without wit, and frank to the point of vulgarity. She exercised great influence on Louis. On the latter's death in 1774 she was

DUBLIN. The Republic's High Court of Justice, known as Four Courts because it once housed the courts of Exchequer, Common Pleas, King's Bench and Chancery, was built 1786–1800 to the design of James Gandon and Thomas Cooley. Only the outer walls remained after heavy shelling by Michael Collins in 1922, but restoration was completed in 1931.
Courtesy of the Irish Tourist Board.

banished to a convent, but later went to live at Luciennes. At the Revolution she fled to London, but returned to Paris in 1793, when she was arrested and guillotined.

DUBCEK (dŏŏb'chek), **Alexander** (1921–). Czechoslovak statesman. A Slovak, he lived in the Soviet Union 1925–38, and during the S.W.W. was a resistance leader in the Tatra mtns. In 1968–9 he was First Sec. of the Czechoslovak Communist Party and launched a liberalisation campaign. He was arrested by invading Soviet troops but later released and appointed ambassador to Turkey in 1969.

DUBLIN. Cap. and co. bor. of Rep. of Ireland, at the mouth of the Liffey, on the coast of co. D., facing the Irish Sea. The greatest port of the republic, D. draws its exports from the whole state, and is the largest collecting and distributing centre. In D. is the world's largest brewery (Guinness); other industries include the manufacture of poplin and linen, biscuits, and machinery, and there are shipyards, flour-mills, railway yards, and engineering shops. The city is a great route focus, roads, railways, and canals converging there, and has a handsome airport. The river channel has been artificially deepened and miles of granite quays built.

The present city was founded in 840 by the Danes who were finally defeated in 1014 at Clontarf, a N. suburb of the city. From 1171, when Henry II landed in Ireland, D. was the centre of English rule until 1922; D. castle dates from 1200. The 18th cent. saw the architectural development of D. as it increased in importance. A good deal of damage was done to prominent buildings (e.g. the Custom House) in the rising of 1916 and in 1922. There are 2 cathedrals, both Protestant: St. Patrick's founded in 1190, Christ Church in 1038, rebuilt in 1172. Trinity Coll. (1591 Protestant) and Univ. Coll. (1851 R.C.) were merged 1968 as the Univ. of D. Other interesting buildings are the City Hall (1779), the Four Courts (1796), the Art Galleries and Museum, the General Post Office, the R.C. pro-Cathedral of St. Mary (1816), the Bank of Ireland (formerly the Parliament House), Leinster House, in which the Dáil Eireann sits. Area of the co. bor. 46 sq. m.; pop. (1966) 568,772.

DUBLIN. Co. of the Rep. of Ireland, facing the Irish Sea. It is level and low-lying, though in the S. it rises to 2,473 ft. in Kippure, part of the Wicklow mts. The only river of importance is the Liffey, which enters D. bay. Agriculture is chiefly directed towards supplying the needs of Dublin city. Dun Laoghaire is the only other large town. Area 356 sq. m.; pop. (1966) 795,047, incl. Dublin city.

DUBNA (doob'nah). Town in R.S.F.S.R., 25 m. W. of Tula. It is a metal-working centre, and nuclear research is also carried on. The Germans held it for a short time in 1941 during their attempt to capture Moscow. Pop. (est.) 10,000.

DUBOIS (dübwah'), **Jean Antoine** (1765–1848). French R.C. missionary in India, known as the Abbé D. On being ordained in 1792 he went to S. India and remained there until 1823. He adopted Indian dress and manners, and wrote *Hindu Manners, Customs, and Ceremonies* (1816).

DUBROVNIK. Yugoslav port on the Adriatic Sea. It was a Roman station, and after centuries as an independent rep. was under Austrian rule, 1814–1919. (1967) 19,000. *See* RAGUSA.

DUCASSE (dükas'), **Curt John** (1881–). French-American philosopher. B. at Angoulême, he became a U.S. citizen in 1910 and in 1929 prof. at Brown univ. His *Nature, Mind and Death* (1951) explores the possibility of survival through metempsychosis.

DUCCIO DI BUONINSEGNA (doo'choh dē bwonēnsen'yah) (*c.* 1255–1319). Italian painter, the earliest of the Sienese school. His greatest work is his altar-piece for Siena cathedral (1308–11). The Nat. Gallery acquired 'Virgin and Child with Four Angels', one wing of a diptych, 1968.

DUCE (doo'cheh). Ital. for 'Leader'. The title was bestowed on Mussolini by his followers, and was later adopted as his official title.

DUCK. Bird of the family Anatidae found mainly in the northern hemisphere. The family is a large one, and comprises several sub-families such as the geese (Anserinae), swans (Cygninae), mergansers (Merginae), surface-feeding Ds. (Anatinae), and diving Ds. (Nyrocinae).

The Anatinae are distinguished by the flattened bill, moderately long and covered with a soft skin except for the nail at the tip, and provided with lamellae through which the birds are able to strain their food from the water and mud. The front toes are

DUCKS. I, sheld-duck; 2, mandarin; 3, Pekin; 4, eider; 5, Indian runner.

webbed, and the small hind toe is free. They are mostly freshwater species, feeding on worms, insects. etc., as well as vegetable matter. The typical species is the wild D. or mallard (*Anas platyrhynchos*).

The diving Ds. (Nyrocinae), have the feet set farther back, and the hind toe lobed. The nail of the beak is usually prominent, and many of them are marine in their habits. The most familiar species is the tufted D. (*Nyroca fuligula*).

DUCKBILL. *See* PLATYPUS.

DUCTLESS GLANDS. Certain glands, including the pituitary, thyroid, parathyroid adrenal, and sex, in the human body which have no ducts or canals for carrying away their products. Known as internal secretions, the latter pass directly into the blood stream. Another name for D.Gs. is endocrine glands.

DUDINSKAYA, Natalya Mikhailovna (1912–). Russian dancer. Ed. at the Leningrad School of Choreography, she became prima ballerina of the Kirov Ballet, creating leading roles in Prokofiev's *Cinderella*, Glière's *The Bronze Horseman*, Soloviev-Sedoy's *Taras Bulba* (1956), etc.

VLADIMIR DUDINTSEV
Photo: Der Stern, Hamburg.

DUDI'NTSEV, Vladimir Dmitriyevitch (1918–). Russian writer. B. near Kharkov, he studied law in Moscow. In 1956 he pub. the controversial novel *Not by Bread Alone*, a product of the de-Stalinization era, which permits criticism of injustice and the bureaucratic attitude in the individual, although not of the Communist system in general.

DUDLEY. English industrial town (co. bor.), 8½ m. W.N.W. of Birmingham, in Staffs, with iron and steel, coal, brass, lime, and brick industries. Pop. (1961) 61,748.

DUFFERIN AND AVA (ah'va), **Frederick Temple Hamilton-Temple Blackwood**, 1st marquess of (1826–1902). British diplomat and administrator. Governor-General of Canada 1872–8, during his viceroyalty of India 1884–8 he annexed Upper Burma (1885), for which he was created marquess in 1888.

DUFFY, Sir Charles Gavan (1816–1903). Irish Nationalist. A journalist in Dublin, he founded the *Nation* as organ of the 'Young Ireland' movement, of which he was the leader. In 1852 he was elected M.P., but in 1856 emigrated to Australia, and in 1871 became premier of Victoria. He was knighted in 1873.

DUFY (düfē'), **Raoul** (1877–1953). French painter and designer. He was noted for his calligraphic style, varied use of colour, and for his pictures of sport and recreation.

DU'GONG. A mammal (*Halicore dugong*) of the order Sirenia, or sea-cows, found in the Indian seas. It sometimes attains a length of 7 to 8 ft., and has a tapering body with a notched tail and 2 fore-flippers. Leather, ivory, and oil are obtained from it, and its flesh is edible.

DUHAMEL (dü-ahmel'), **Georges** (1884–1966). French man-of-letters and doctor. He pub. vols. of verse, plays, etc., but is chiefly famous as a novelist. The cycle *Chronique des Pasquier* (1933–45), a bourgeois family saga, is among his best-known works.

DUIKERBOK (dīk'er-). Genus of African antelope, with a crested head, short conical horns in the males, and a large muzzle.

DUISBURG (doo'-is boorg). Industrial city of the Ruhr, Germany, at the confluence of the Rhine and the Ruhr. It is the largest inland port in Germany, with important coal-mines, iron and steel, chemical, shipbuilding and engineering industries. The N. suburb of Hamborn was incorporated in 1929, and until 1935 it was called D.-Hamborn. During the S.W.W., D. was heavily bombed from 1940 until its capture by U.S. troops after severe fighting 30 March 1945. Pop. (1966) 477,770.

DUKAS (dükahs'), **Paul** (1865–1935). French composer. B. in Paris, he was prof. of composition at the Paris Conservatoire, and composed the opera *Ariane et Barbe-bleue*, the ballet *Le Péri*, and the very popular orchestral scherzo *L'Apprenti Sorcier* (The Sorcerer's Apprentice).

DUKE (Lat. *dux*, a general). Highest title in the English peerage. It was unknown in England until 1337, when Edward III created his son Edward D. of Cornwall. The oldest Scottish duchy is Hamilton, 1643.

DUKES, Ashley. *See* RAMBERT.

DULCIMER (dul'simer). Musical instrument, consisting of a shallow box strung with wire strings which are struck with small wooden hammers.

DU'LLES, John Foster (1888–1959). American statesman. B. in Washington the s. of a Presbyterian minister, he was ed. at Princeton, the Sorbonne and George Washington univ., before being admitted to the Bar. At 19 he attended the Hague Peace Conference of 1907, and took part in the 1919 Paris Peace Conference. He was senior U.S. adviser at the U.N. founding conference in 1945 and was prominent in the drafting of the Japanese Peace Treaty in 1951. D. became Sec. of State in 1952 and criticized Britain's actions during the Suez crisis in 1956. Suffering from cancer, he resigned office and d. in 1959.

His brother, **Allen D.** (1893–1969), a lawyer, was director of the Central Intelligence Agency 1953–61.

DULUTH (dulooth'). U.S. port on Lake Superior, by the mouth of the St. Louis river, Minnesota. It manufactures steel. Pop. (1960) 106,884.

DULWICH. Suburb of London, England, part of the inner London bor. of Southwark. It contains D. College (founded 1619 by Edward Alleyn), the Horniman Museum (1901) with a fine ethnological collection, D. Picture Gallery (1814, rebuilt 1953

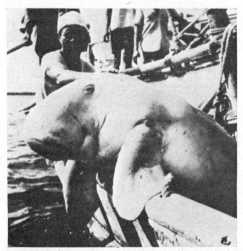

DUGONG. Slow-moving and harmless, the dugong is herbivorous and becoming rare. It is sometimes suggested as the original of the mermaid legend, but a close-up view is disillusioning. *Photo: Associated Press.*

after S.W.W. bombing), D. Park and D. Village, still pleasantly rural.

DUMAS (dümah'), **Alexandre** (1802–70). French novelist and dramatist, called D. the Elder. B. at Villers-Cotterets, he was the son of a French general, and through his paternal grandmother inherited a strain of Negro blood. When he was 20 he went to Paris, and in 1829 had a resounding success with his play *Henri III et sa Cour*. Another great success was *Antony* (1831), and altogether he wrote more than 20 plays. The famous historical novels began to appear in 1836, and in a vast output D. was assisted by collaborators, incl. Auguste Maquet. It was with Maquet's help that he wrote *Les Trois Mousquetaires* (The Three Musketeers, 1844) and its sequels; also in 1844 he pub. the *Comte de Monte-Cristo*. Another series centres round Henri IV, and a 3rd deals with the French Revolution, e.g. *Le Collier de la Reine* (The Queen's Necklace). Best known of the many other novels are *La Tulipe Noire* (The Black Tulip) and *Les frères Corses* (The Corsican Brothers). In 1832 appeared *Impressions de Voyage*, the first of a series of entertaining travel books. *Mes Mémoires* gives the story of his life to 1832. His natural son Alexandre D. the Younger (q.v.) was also a writer.

DUMAS, Alexandre (1824–95). French dramatist and novelist known as D. the Younger, to distinguish him from his father, Alexandre Dumas the Elder (q.v.). His novels and miscellaneous writings have been eclipsed by his plays, of which the first, *La Dame aux Camélias* (1852), had an outstanding success as the first important comedy of manners of the 19th cent. in France: the novel had appeared 1848.

DU MAURIER (dü mō'ryä'), **Dame Daphne** (1907–). British novelist; 2nd dau. of Sir Gerald du M. (q.v.). Her books incl. *Jamaica Inn* (1936), *Rebecca, Hungry Hill*, and *My Cousin Rachel*. Many have been successfully filmed. She has also pub. *Gerald, a Portrait* (1934) and the *Du Mauriers*. In 1932 she m. Lt.-Gen. Sir Frederick Browning. She was created D.B.E. 1969.

DU MAURIER, George Louis Palmella Busson (1834–96). British author and artist. B. in Paris, the son of a French refugee who became an English subject during the Revolution, he settled in London in 1860 and secured a place on the staff of *Punch*. Besides illustrating books and periodicals, he wrote novels: *Peter Ibbetson* (1891) and *Trilby* (1894) – story of a natural singer able to perform only under the hypnosis of Svengali, her tutor.

DU MAURIER, Sir Gerald (1873–1934). British actor-manager, son of George du M. He made his stage début in 1894, and in the following year appeared in the stage version of his father's *Trilby*. He subsequently appeared in many plays and films.

DUMBA'RTON. Co. town and royal burgh of Dunbartonshire, Scotland, sit. on the Clyde estuary, at the mouth of the Leven. It has shipyards, iron foundries, an aircraft factory, distillery, etc. Pop. (1961) 26,335.

DUMBARTON OAKS. An 18th cent. mansion near Washington, D.C., U.S.A., scene of a conference held 21 Aug–29 Sept. 1944, between Britain, the U.S.A., and the U.S.S.R. for preliminary discussions of the structure and aims of a new international league to enforce peace. After the Russians (who were not then at war with Japan) had left, a Chinese delegation arrived. The conference ended on 7 Oct., agreement having been reached for a draft programme for a conference held at San Francisco 25 April–25 June 1945, at which the United Nations was founded.

DUMFRIES (dumfrēs'). Co. town and royal burgh of Dumfriesshire, Scotland, on the r. Nith. It is a centre of tweed and hosiery manufacture, a market town, and a road and railway junction. Pop. (1961) 27,275. *See* illus. p. 362.

DUMFRIESSHIRE. Co. of S. Scotland, bordering

the Solway Firth and England on the S. It rises to 2,695 ft. in the N. (White Coomb). From the mts. dales run S. to the plain bordering the Solway Firth; e.g. Nithsdale, Annandale, and Eskdale. The chief towns are Dumfries, the co. town, Annan, Langholm, and Lockerbie. In the S.E. is Gretna Green. Area 1,072 sq. m.; pop. (1961) 88,423.

DUMOURIEZ (dümooryeh'), **Charles François du Périer** (1739–1823). French general. In 1792 he was appointed Foreign Minister, supported the declaration of war against Austria, and after the fall of the monarchy was given command of the army defending Paris; he won the battle of Jemappes, but was defeated at Neerwinden in 1793, and after intriguing with the Royalists he had to flee for his life. From 1804 he lived in England.

DUNANT (dünoñ'), **Jean Henri** (1828–1910). Swiss philanthropist; the originator of the Red Cross. B. at Geneva, he became a physician and witnessed the battle of Solferino (1859). He helped to tend the wounded, and described their distress in *Un Souvenir*

DUMFRIES. In the foreground Devorguilla's Bridge spans the Nith. One of the most ancient in Scotland, it was built of stone *c.* 1280 by Devorguilla the widowed mother of John de Balliol (king of Scotland 1292–6), she also founded Balliol College, Oxford.   *Photo: George Outram & Co. Ltd.*

de Solférino (1862) wherein he proposed the establishment of an international body for the aid of the wounded – an idea that was realized in the Geneva Convention of 1864.

DUNBAR, William (*c.* 1460–*c.* 1520). Scottish poet. Said to have become a Franciscan and to have travelled in France, he returned tô Scotland about 1500, and appears to have become prominent in the court of James IV. D. is generally accounted the greatest Scottish poet before Burns.

DUNBAR. Port, royal burgh, and resort in E. Lothian, Scotland, with 2 harbours. Pop. (1961) 4,003.

DUNBARTONSHIRE. Co. of W. Scotland bordering the N. bank of the Clyde estuary. The W. border runs through Loch Long, and the E. through Loch Lomond. The country is mountainous, rising to 3,092 ft. in Ben Vorlich, and provides fine highland scenery. A detached part is lower; coal is mined there at Kirkintilloch. Tourism is important. Along the Clyde are the industrial towns of Clydebank, Dumbarton (co. town), and Helensburgh. Area 246 sq. m.; pop. (1961) 184,546.

DU'NCAN, Adam, 1st visct. (1731–1804). British admiral. B. in Angus, he entered the navy in 1746, and served in the Seven Years War and the American War. D. successfully countered the mutiny of 1797 and defeated the Dutch fleet in the battle of Camperdown. He was created a visct. and retired in 1800.

DUNCAN, Isadora (1878–1927). American dancer. B. in San Francisco, she created a sensation by her lightly clad interpretations of Greek dances, reconstructed from vase paintings and other art relics. *My Life* (1928) is her autobiography.

DUNCAN, Sir Patrick (1870–1943). British statesman. B. in Banffshire, Scotland, he was one of Lord Milner's 'young men' in S. Africa, held high posts in the Transvaal, was a member of the first Union Parliament (1910), and Gov.-Gen. of the Union of S. Africa 1937–43.

DUNDALK (dundawk'). Co. town and seaport of Louth, Rep. of Ireland, at the mouth of the Castletown r. in D. Bay. It manufactures linen, cigarettes, etc., and has iron foundries. Pop. (1966) 20,002.

DUNDA'S, Henry, 1st visct. Melville (1742–1811). British Tory statesman. In 1791 he became Home Secretary, and carried through the prosecution of the English and Scottish reformers. After holding other high Cabinet posts, he was impeached in 1806 for corruption, and although acquitted on the main charge held no further office.

DUNDEE (dundē'). City of Scotland, royal burgh, and seaport on the N. side of the Firth of Tay, in Angus co. It is the chief centre of the British jute industry, and has engineering works and shipbuilding yards; linoleum, hemp, and linen factories; preserve, canning, and confectionery works; also fishing is carried on. D. is an important shipping and railway centre. The Firth, here 2 m. wide, is crossed by the Tay Bridge (railway) and the Tay Road Bridge (7,356 ft.) opened 1966. The principal buildings are the Episcopal cathedral, Caird Hall, the Albert Institute (1867), and the 15th cent. Old Steeple. The Univ. of Dundee (formerly Queen's Coll., founded 1881, and part of the Univ. of St. Andrew's from 1953) was estab. 1967. Pop. (1961) 182,959.

DUNDEE, Visct. *See* CLAVERHOUSE.

DUNDO'NALD, Thomas Cochrane, 10th earl of (1775–1860). British admiral. B. in Lanarkshire, he had a distinguished career in the navy, and in 1807 was elected Radical M.P. for Westminster, but in 1814 he was expelled from the navy and from Parliament for alleged connivance in a fraud. In 1817 he became commander of the Chilean fleet, and later commanded the Brazilian navy, 1823, and that of Greece 1827. He was reinstated in the British navy in 1832.

DUNE'DIN. City of South Island, New Zealand. Founded in 1848 by members of the Free Church of Scotland, it is a centre for railway, sea, and air services; makes woollens, boots, and steel; and is the seat of Otago univ. Pop. (1967) 109,400.

DUNFERMLINE (dunferm'lin). Royal burgh and manufacturing town in Fifeshire, Scotland, 12 m. N.W. of Edinburgh; it incl. the naval base of Rosyth. The chief industry is the manufacture of damask table linen. Pop. (1961) 47,159.

DUNGENESS (dunjenes'). Accumulation of shingle and sand which has been built up (and still forms) by deposition and sea currents on the S. coast of Kent, England. It has a lighthouse and a coastguard station and in 1959 was approved as the site of a nuclear power station. A bird sanctuary was established on D. in 1932.

DUNHAM, Katherine (1910–). American Negro dancer. B. in Chicago, she studied ethnology and dance at the univ. there and in 1938 went to the W. Indies to study negro dancing. In 1940 she began presenting her own dances, which portray ritualized emotion, and in 1945 she founded her own school and dance company.

DUNKIRK. Seaport of N. France in the Nord dept., on the Strait of Dover, 152 m. N. of Paris. Its harbour is one of the most important in France, and canals link the town with the industrial centres of Nord and Pas-de-Calais and other regions of France, and with Belgium. The chief industries incl. iron founding, shipbuilding, and fishing; and textiles, machinery, and soap are manufactured. The town grew up round the church of St. Éloi, founded in the 7th cent. During the F.W.W. the front was for most of the time close to D.; during the S.W.W. D. was the scene of one of the most momentous events in British history – the evacuation of the bulk of the B.E.F. and a large number of French troops, 337,131 in all. The port was reopened to shipping in 1946, and Dunkirk gives its name to the 50-year Anglo-French treaty of alliance signed there on 4 March 1947. Pop. (1962) 28,388.

DUN LAOGHAIRE (doon lã'reh). Port of Dublin, Rep. of Ireland, lying 6 m. S.E. of Dublin, known as Kingstown 1821–1922. It has regular sea services with Holyhead and Liverpool. Pop. (1966) 51,772.

DU'NLIN. A species of sandpiper (*Tringa alpina*) belonging to the snipe family (Scolopacidae). Very common as a shore bird on all coasts of the British Isles, it is about the size of a lark, and in summer is chestnut above, with a black patch on the breast.

DUNLOP, John Boyd (1840–1921). Scottish inventor. B. in Ayrshire, he practised as a veterinary surgeon in Belfast. To help his child win a tricycle race, he bound on rubber hose to the wheels and inflated it (1887). Later he took out a patent for pneumatic rubber tyres and was one of the founders of the D. Co. formed to market them.

DUNKIRK. Under a storm of shells and bombs the 'little ships' came across the Channel to the rescue. This historic photograph shows some of the troops waiting in orderly files for their embarkation.

DUNMOW (dun'mō). GREAT D. is an English market town on the Chelmer, Essex, on the site of a Roman station. LITTLE D., 2 m. away, is the scene of the annual D. Flitch trial. The ceremony, first held in 1244, consists of the presentation of a flitch of bacon to any married couple who 'will swear that they have not quarrelled nor repented of their marriage within a year and a day after its celebration'. Pop. Gt. D. *c.* 3,500.

DUNNE, Finley Peter (1867–1936). American humorist. B. at Chicago, he contributed (1891–1900) sketches to the *Times-Herald* of Chicago, supposed to be the work of Martin Dooley, an Irish-American saloon-keeper and philosopher with a gift for pungently humorous comment on the affairs of the day.

DUNNE, John William (1875–1949). British philosopher. In *An Experiment with Time* (1927) he developed *Serialism*, a theory framed to afford a rational explanation of phenomena ascribed to telepathy or clairvoyance. D.'s other important works incl. *The Serial Universe* (1934), *The New Immortality* (1938), and *Nothing Dies* (1940).

DUNSANY (dun-sā'ni), **Edward John Moreton Drax Plunkett,** 18th baron D. (1878–1957). Irish author. He succeeded his father in the barony in 1899, and became famous for his fantastic stories, notably the Jorkens series, and plays.

DUNS SCOTUS, John (*c.* 1265–*c.* 1308). Medieval scholastic philosopher, known as *doctor subtilis*. B. in Scotland, he became a Franciscan monk and was ordained in 1291. He studied and lectured at Oxford and Paris, and was later transferred to Cologne, where he d. D.S. wrote commentaries on the Bible and

Aristotle, and is generally regarded as the leader of the Franciscan school which criticized the Aristotelanism of the Dominican, St. Thomas Aquinas.

DUNSTABLE (dun'stabl). English town (bor.) in S.W. Beds, 30 m. N.W. of London. Whipsnade zoo is near. Printing, engineering, etc., are carried on. Pop. (1961) 25,618.

DUNSTAN, St. (*c.* 924–88). English prelate and statesman. B. near Glastonbury, the son of a West Saxon noble, he became a monk, and *c.* 945 was appointed abbot of Glastonbury. There he rebuilt the church and made the abbey a famous centre of education. Under Edred and Edgar he was chief minister, and in 959 he became bishop of London and in 961 archbishop of Canterbury.

DUNSTERVILLE, Lionel Charles (1865–1946). British soldier. He was a school friend of Rudyard Kipling, who had him in mind when creating the character of Stalky in *Stalky & Co.* In 1918 D. commanded an expedition to the Caucasus to save the Baku oilfields from the Turks and Bolsheviks, as described in *The Adventures of Dunsterforce* (1920).

DUNWICH (dun'ich). Village on the coast of E. Suffolk, England; all that remains of a once substantial town, gradually washed away and submerged.

DUODECIMAL SYSTEM. System of arithmetic notation using 12 as a base, superior to the decimal system in that 12 has a high divisibility (2, 3, 4, 6) and the gross (12 dozen) also has numerous divisors. D. societies exist for its promotion in the U.K. and U.S.

DUPARC (düpahrk') (**Marie Eugène**) **Henri** (**Fouques**) (1848–1933). French composer. B. in Paris, he studied under César Franck, and later helped to found the National Musical Society. His songs, hough only 15 in number, are of great importance for their high intrinsic quality and their place in the history of French song-writing.

DUPLEIX (düplăks'), **Joseph François** (1697–1763). French administrator. He first went to India in 1715 and became Governor-General of French India in 1742. He made it hĩs object to eject the British from India and to establish French supremacy in native politics. Clive's victory at Arcot in 1751 destroyed his plans, and in 1754 he was recalled.

DU PONT (düpoñ'), **Eleuthière Irenée** (1771–1834). American chemical manufacturer. B. in Paris where he studied gunpowder manufacture under Lavoisier (q.v.), he later managed his father's printing works, pub. counter-revolutionary pamphlets, but was forced by the Revolution to flee to America, there founding the chemical manufacturing firm of D.P. de Nemours at Wilmington, Delaware, in 1802. This firm has provided explosives for every war in which the U.S. has since been engaged and in 1950 was appointed by the U.S. Atomic Energy Commission to run its Savannah River plant. Nylon (1938), the first synthetic fibre, was a D.P. invention.

DUPRÉ (düpra'), **Marcel** (1886–1971). French composer. Director of the Paris Conservatoire 1954–6, where he was a prof. 1926–54, he was organist of St. Sulpice from 1934 and in 1961 was Pres. of the Académie de Beaux Arts. D.'s numerous organ works have enriched the instrument's repertory.

DURALUMIN. An aluminium base alloy containing copper, manganese, magnesium, silicon, and iron, Developed by a German engineer, Wilm, before the F.W.W., it possesses the remarkable property of 'age hardening', and is exclusively used in the rolled or forged condition.

DURAS (dürah'), **Marguerite** (1914–). French writer. Ed. at the Sorbonne, she graduated in law, and her works incl. short stories (*Des Journées entières dans les Arbres*), plays (*La Musica*), film scripts (*Hiroshima Mon Amour*), and novels such as *Le Vice-Consul* (1966), evoking an existentialist world from the actual setting of Calcutta.

DURAZZO. Italian form of DÜRRES.

DURBAN. A time exposure gives an air of magic to this picture of the popular winter holiday resort.
Courtesy of the South African Information Service.

DURBAN. Principal port of Natal, S. Africa, and second port of the rep. Founded in 1824 as Port Natal, it was renamed in 1835 after General Sir Benjamin d'Urban (1777–1849), lieut.-governor of the eastern district of Cape Colony 1834–7. D.'s exports consist of coal, maize, wool, etc., whilst heavy machinery and mining equipment for the Rand is imported. It is also an important holiday resort. Natal univ. (1949) is divided between Durban and Pietermaritzburg. Pop. (1960) 681,492, of whom 196,398 were white.

DÜRER, Albrecht (1471–1528). German engraver and painter. B. at Nuremberg, in 1486 he was apprenticed to Michael Wohlgemuth, a distinguished artist, and at the age of 13 he drew a portrait of himself from the mirror, the first self-portrait in the history of European art. After some years of travel, D. m. in 1494 Agnes Fey, whose portrait he drew many times. In 1494–5 he visited Venice. After his return to Nuremberg he executed a number of copperplates, and also his famous series of woodcuts of the 'Apocalypse'. His first important painting, The Adoration of the Magi', is dated 1504. In 1505 he went to Venice again, where he painted 'The Feast of the Rosary' and 'The Martyrdom of St. Bartholomew'. In 1512 he first became associated with the Emperor Maximilian I, for whom he did a great deal of work. In 1520 he travelled to the Netherlands, and became court painter to Charles V. He was a friend of Luther, and was greatly influenced by the Reformation. D.'s drawings and engravings are among the finest in the world.

DURGA (door'gah). Hindu goddess; one of the many names for Siva's wife.

DURHAM (dur'am), **John George Lambton**, 1st earl of (1792–1840). British statesman. He inherited a large estate while still a child, served in the army, became an M P. in 1813, and in 1816 m. Lord Grey's dau. In 1828 he was created baron D. and in 1830 became Lord Privy Seal and drew up the Reform Bill. Ambassador to Russia in 1832, he became an earl in 1833; and in 1837 went to Canada as Gov.-Gen., to deal with the situation created by the rebellions. His arbitrary methods were disowned by the govt. and he at once resigned. In 1839 he laid before parliament his *Report on the Affairs of British N. America*, which marks a turning-point in the history of the Empire; it advocated that the government of the colony should be entrusted to the colonists themselves, that Upper and Lower Canada should be united as a first step towards a federation of the N. American colonies, that emigration should be encouraged, and that the construction of railways should be undertaken.

DURHAM. Co. of N.E. England, lying between Northumberland and Yorks, and facing the North Sea. Towards the W. the land rises to the crest of the Pennines (2,452 ft.) and to the E. slopes down to a coastal plain. The N. part is drained by the Wear, and the S. by tributaries of the

LORD DURHAM
T. Phillips.
Photo: N.P.G.

Tees. Teesdale and Weardale contain some fine scenery. In the E. the soil is fertile; on the hills to the W. many sheep are pastured. D. contains one of England's richest coalfields, this being one of the main factors for the siting of some of the principal industrial areas in Great Britain. Industry is scattered over the coalfield, but is concentrated round the estuaries of the Tyne and Tees. Gateshead, S. Shields, Jarrow, and Hebburn are on the S. bank of the Tyne; Sunderland on the r. Wear, and in the S. are W. Hartlepool, Stockton on Tees, and Darlington. The co. town is Durham. Area 1,015 sq. m.; pop. (1967) 1,547,050.

DURHAM. City (bor.) and co. town of co. D., on the Wear. D. was founded in 995, when a church was built on an eminence almost surrounded by the river; the Norman cathedral was built on the same site, and with later additions is one of England's finest ecclesiastical edifices. The remains of Bede, who d. at Jarrow, were transferred to D. Cathedral in 1370. On the same hill stands the castle, built by William I in 1072; the univ. was founded 1832. The river is crossed by 3 bridges. Pop. (1961) 20,484.

DURKHEIM (dürkem'), **Émile** (1858–1917). French philosopher. Prof. of sociology at Paris from 1892, he maintained that human progress is mechanically determined, and stressed the importance of precision and scientific method in all social investigations.

DURRA doo'ra) or **Dourra.** Genus of grasses

The artist's father.　　　*Courtesy of the National Gallery.*

(*Sorghum*), also known as Indian millet, grown as cereals in parts of Asia, Africa, etc. *S. vulgare*, is the chief cereal of many parts of Africa.

DURRELL, Laurence George (1912–). English poet and novelist. B. in India, he was for a time in the Foreign Service, and has lived mostly in the E. Mediterranean countries about which he writes. His verse incl. *A Private Country* (1943), *Cities, Plains and People* (1946), and *On Seeming to Presume* (1948); and his tetralogy *Justine, Balthazar, Mountolive* and *Clea* (1957–60) made him one of England's leading novelists: on the Continent his reputation stands even higher. His brother, **Gerald Malcolm D.,** (1925–) is a zoologist and writer and runs the Jersey Zoological Park.

L. G. DURRELL

DÜRRENMATT, Friedrich (1921–). Swiss dramatist. The son of a Protestant pastor, he writes in German, and takes crime and violence as the mainstay of his grotesquely farcical tragedies. These incl. *The Visit* in which a millionairess corrupts a village by bribing the people to avenge her grudge against a girlhood lover, and *The Physicists* (1962), dealing with 3 normal nuclear physicists who take refuge from mad reality in a Swiss asylum.

DÜRRES (dōō′räs). Chief port of Albania, cap. of D. district, chief commercial and communications centre of the country with flour mills, soap and cigarette factories, distilleries and an electronics plant. It is 20 m. W. of Tirana. Pop. (1966) 45,935.

DUSE (dōō′se), **Eleanora** (1859–1924). Italian actress. B. in Lombardy, she began acting at the age of 4, and when 14 played Juliet in Verona. In 1879 her success in Zola's *Thérèse Raquin* led to her engagement as leading lady in Cesare Rossi's company. She estab. a reputation as one of the greatest actresses of all time. Her association with D'Annunzio began in 1897, and is recorded in his novel *Il Fuoco* (*The Flame of Life*). He wrote *La Gioconda* for her. She made her last London appearance in 1923, and d. during a visit to America.

DUSHANBE (dōōshan′bä). Cap. of Tadzhik S.S.R., U.S.S.R., and of D. region, *c.* 100 m. N. of the Afghan frontier and 200 m. S. of Tashkent. An important road, rail and air centre. D. has cotton mills, tanneries, meat-packing factories, printing works, etc., and is the seat of Tadzhik state univ. Developed as Stalinabad from 1929 on the site of the ancient village of D., it reverted to its old name in 1961. Pop. (1967) 332,000.

DÜSSELDORF. German industrial city on the right bank of the Rhine, 16 m. N.N.W. of Cologne, cap. of N. Rhine-Westphalia. It is a great river port, and a leading industrial centre of the Ruhr area. There are large iron foundries, engineering, textile, and chemical works, paper mills, breweries, etc. Art and cultural life make it an important city of W. Germany. Pop. (1966) 696,615.

DUSTBOWL. Name given to a large area in the U.S.A. covering western Kansas, and parts ('panhandles') of Oklahoma and Texas which lie just to the S. It is swept by winds from N. to S. The native grasses which formerly covered it and held down the soil were removed to make way for wheat-farming, and during the drought years of 1934–7 hundreds of tons of loose topsoil was blown away into the Gulf of Mexico. Many of the farmers abandoned their worthless farms and migrated westward (*see* Steinbeck) By planting trees as windbreaks and re-intro-

ducing suitable grasses, etc., much of the area has been rehabilitated.

DUTCH ART, LANGUAGE, LITERATURE. *See* under NETHERLANDS.

DUTCH EAST INDIES. *See* INDONESIA.

DUTCH GUIANA. *See* SURINAM.

DUTT, Toru or **Tarulata** (1856–77). Indian author and poetess. B. in Calcutta of a Christian family, she visited France as a young girl and later translated French poems and speeches into English. She also wrote a French novel, *Le Journal de Mlle. D'Arvers*, and, in English, *Ancient Ballads and Legends of Hindustan*.

DUUN, Olav (1876–1939). Norwegian novelist. B. near Trondheim, he made this neighbourhood the scene of all his novels. Best known are the series which tell the story of the Juvik family from about 1800 down to our own times.

DUVAL (düvahl′), **Claude** (1643–70). English highwayman. B. in Normandy, he came to England at the Restoration as a valet, but turned highwayman, and his gallantry was as famous as his robberies. He was hanged at Tyburn.

DUVEEN OF MILLBANK, Joseph D., baron (1869–1939). British art patron. Son of Sir Joseph D. (d. 1908), who estab. in 1866 an antique business in Hull and through whose generosity the Turner Wing at the Tate Gallery was completed, he was created a baron in 1933, taking his title from the site of the Tate, whose further extensions he financed. He also made lavish gifts to the National Gallery, National Portrait Gallery and British Museum, and endowed a chair of history of art at London univ.

DUVIVIER (düvivyeh′), **Julien** (1896–). French film director, of such French classics as *Poil de Carotte, Un Carnet de Bal, La Fin du Jour* (1938).

DVINSK. Russian name of DAUGAVPILS.

DVOŘÁK (dvor′zhahk), **Antonin** (1841–1904). Czech composer. B. near Prague, the son of a butcher, he early showed a talent for music, and in 1857 went to Prague. There he entered an organ school and supported himself by playing the viola in cafés, etc. In 1862 he joined the orchestra of the Prague National Theatre, later gained an appointment as a church organist, and also taught. A patriotic hymn for chorus and orchestra gained him popularity in 1872, and in 1875 an annual allowance from the Austrian govt. gave him financial independence. His series of Slavonic dances (1877) were a further success, and his *Stabat Mater* was performed by the London Musical Society in 1883. In 1892–5 he was director of the National Conservatory in New York. His interest in Negro music is evident in the *New World Symphony* (1893) and such works as the *Nigger Quartet*. In 1895 he returned to Prague, where he later became head of the Conservatoire. D. wrote 9 operas, incl. *The Water Nymph* (*Rusalka*); large-scale choral works, the *Carnival* and other overtures, violin and 'cello concertos, chamber music, piano pieces, songs, etc

DYE. Substance which, applied in solution to fabrics, imparts a colour resistant to washing. Direct Ds. combine with the material of the fabric, yielding a coloured compound; indirect Ds. require the presence of another substance (a mordan), with which the fabric must first be treated, and which will cause precipitation of the coloured compound in the fibres; vat Ds. are usually colourless soluble substances which on oxidation by exposure to air yield an insoluble coloured compound.

Naturally occurring Ds. incl. indigo, madder (alizarin), logwood and cochineal, but industrial Ds. are usually synthetic, and are classified according to the substances from which they are produced, or the characteristic chemical groupings in the molecules, e.g. the azo-dyestuffs, acridine, anthracene and aniline. Colour can now be diagnosed by photoelectric instruments which measure the red, blue and green contents: the recipe for producing it can then be calculated exactly by a computer.

DYER, Reginald Edward Harry (1864–1927). British soldier. During riots in Amritsar in 1919 he ordered troops to open fire on a dense crowd, 379 being killed and over 1,000 injured. Following an enquiry he was ordered to resign his commission, but there was widespread controversy as to the exact circumstances of the incident.

DYNAMICS. The branch of mechanics that deals with the mathematical and physical study of the behaviour of bodies under the action of forces which produce changes of motion in them.

DYNAMITE. A high explosive consisting of a mixture of nitroglycerine and kieselguhr; it was first devised by Alfred Nobel (q.v.).

DYNAMO (dī'namo), also called generator. A machine for transforming mechanical energy into electrical energy. Present-day Ds. work on the principles described by Faraday in 1830, that an electromotive force (e.m.f.) is developed in a conductor when it is passed through a magnetic field. A simple form of D. consists of a powerful field magnet, between the poles of which a suitable conductor, usually in the form of a coil(armature), is rotated. The mechanical energy of rotation is thus converted into an electric current in the armature.

DYNE (dīn). Symbol dyn. In physics, the absolute unit of force in the centimetre-gramme-second (c.g.s.) system; it is defined as the force which produces an acceleration of one centimetre per second per second in a mass of one gramme.

DYSENTERY (dis'enteri'). Infective ulceration of the large bowel, causing copious passage of blood and mucus (the 'bloody flux'). It may be due to *Entamoeba histolytica* (amoebic dysentery); a dysentery bacillus, especially *B. dysenteriae Shiga*; or a variety of intestinal worms.

DYSON, Sir George (1883–1964). Brit. composer. B. at Halifax, he was master of music at Winchester College 1924–37, then director, Royal College of Music, till 1952. He wrote choral and orchestral works.

DYSON, William Henry (1883–1938). Australian cartoonist. After working on papers in Melbourne and Sydney he went to London, where his best work was his political cartoons for the *Daily Herald*.

DYSPEPSIA (dispeps'ia). Disturbance of digestion. Of the numerous possible causes the chief are a faulty diet, excessive drinking or smoking, nervous disorder, general lack of tone with sagging of the stomach (visceroptosis), chronic inflammation of the stomach lining (gastritis), and cancer of the stomach.

DYSPROSIUM (disprō'zium). One of the yttrium group of rare earths (symbol Dy, at. no. 66, at. wt. 162·51) discovered in 1886 by Lecoq de Boisbaudran. The free element has not yet been isolated.

DZERZHI'NSKY, Ivan (1909–). Russian composer. Encouraged by Shostakovitch, D. has produced music for the mass audience, and is best known for his opera *Quiet Flows the Don* (1934).

DZUNGARIAN (dzōōngah'rēahn) **GATES.** Ancient route in central Asia on the border of Kazakh S.S.R. (U.S.S.R.) and Sinkiang-Uighur region (China), 290 m. W.N.W. of Urumchi. Long abandoned, since the Mongol hordes passed through on their way to Europe, it was surveyed by the Russians in 1953 as a possible railway route.

E The second vowel and fifth and most often used letter of our alphabet. In Lloyd's Register of Shipping it formerly represented a 2nd-class rating.

EAGLE. Name given to a number of genera of large birds of prey of the family Falconidae. The typical genus *Aquila* includes the golden E. (*A. chrysaëtus*). It has a wing-span of 6 ft. and is dark brown; in Britain it is now confined to the highlands of Scotland. The larger spotted E. (*A. clanga*), of Central Europe and Asia, is a very rare visitor to Britain.

The sea Es. (*Haliaëtus*) incl. the white-tailed sea E. (*H. albicilla*) which is now only an irregular visitor to Britain; mainly a carrion-feeder, it breeds on sea cliffs. The American white-headed sea E. or bald E. (*H. leucocephalus*) is the symbol of the U.S.A.; rendered infertile through the ingestion of agricultural chemicals, it is rapidly becoming extinct.

The E. was anciently regarded as sacred to Zeus, and the bearer of his thunderbolts. It was the standard of the Roman legions, and hence was adopted as an imperial symbol by the Russian, German, and Austrian empires, and also by Napoleon.

GOLDEN EAGLE

EAKER, Ira Clarence (1896–). American Air Force commander. B. in Texas, he entered the U.S. Army in 1917, served in the Philippines 1919–22, and achieved distinction as an air pilot. He commanded the 8th Air Force 1942–4, and also 1943–4 the U.S. Army Air Forces in U.K.

EAKINS, Thomas (1844–1916). American artist chiefly famous for his realistic portraits but who also painted accurate sporting pictures.

EALING. Residential district, bor. of Greater London, England. The first British sound-film studio was built here in 1931, taken over by the B.B.C. in 1956. Pop. (1967) 302,570.

EAMES, Charles (1909–). American designer. B. in the Middle West, in 1939 he won (with Eero Saarinen, q.v.) a furniture competition sponsored by the Museum of Modern Art, N.Y., with a design for a moulded plywood chair. Production difficulties having been solved by 1946, his new technique greatly enlarged the scope of furniture design. He is also noted for his sales and educational cartoon films, and designs for toys and exhibition stands.

EAR. The organ of hearing. The external ear (pinna) is a funnel to collect sound. From it a short tunnel leads to the middle ear (tympanum), a small cavity in the temporal bone from which the Eustachian tube runs to the back of the nose, connecting it with the outside air. The tough membrane of the eardrum completely separates the middle from the outer ear; it vibrates when struck by sound waves, and nerves convey the impressions to the brain.

EARHART, Amelia (1898–1937). American airwoman. B. in Kansas, she was the first woman to fly the Atlantic – in 1928, as a passenger from New-foundland to Burry Port, Wales; also the first woman to fly the Atlantic alone, in 1932 from Harbour Grace to Londonderry, in 15 hrs. 18 min. While making a Pacific flight in July 1937 she disappeared without trace. She was the wife of G. P. Putnam, American publisher.

EARL. In the British peerage, the 3rd title in order of rank, coming between marquess and viscount; it is the oldest of British titles, being of Scandinavian origin. The premier earl is Arundel, now united with the dukedom of Norfolk. An earl's wife is a countess.

EARL MARSHAL. In England, the 8th of the great Officers of State; the office has been hereditary since 1672 in the family of Howard, the dukes of Norfolk. The E.M. is head of the College of Arms, and arranges State processions and ceremonies.

EARLOM (er′lom), **Richard** (1742–1822). British mezzotint engraver, the first to use the point in mezzo-tint work. His engravings after Hogarth's *Marriage à la Mode* are best known.

EARLY ENGLISH. In architecture, name given by Thomas Rickman (1776–1841) to the first of the 3 periods of English Gothic. It covers the period from about 1189 to about 1280, and is characterized by lancet-windows without mullions often grouped in threes, fives, or sevens; the pointed arch; pillars of stone centres surrounded by shafts of black Purbeck marble; dog-tooth ornament, etc. Salisbury cathedral is almost entirely Early English.

EARTH. The planet on which we live: it is the 3rd planet outward from the sun, lying with its satel-lite, the moon, between Venus and Mars. Its path round the sun, i.e. that of its revolution, is an ellipse of which one focus is formed by the sun. The mean distance of the E. from the sun is about 93 million miles. The plane of its orbit is called the ecliptic, and it is inclined to the earth's equatorial plane at an angle of 23½°; it is this inclination that is responsible for the phenomena of the seasons. The E., moving at an average speed of 18½ m. a second, makes a complete circuit in the solar year, which measures 365 days 5 hr. 48 min. 46 sec. It has also a daily movement, rotating about its own axis in 23 hr. 56 min. 4·1 sec., which is responsible for day and night. By using atomic clocks it has been possible to prove that the E.'s rate of rotation is slowing down.

The E. is an oblate spheroid; its equatorial diameter is 7,926·7 m. and its polar diameter 7,900 m.; its equatorial circumference is 24,902 m. and its polar circumference 24,860 m. The area of the land surface of the globe is 57·5 million sq. m.; the sea floor covers 139·4 million sq. m. or over 70 per cent. The greatest known height on the E.'s surface is Mt. Everest, which reaches 29,002 ft. above sea-level; the greatest oceanic depth reached is 36,198 ft. in the Mariana trench, off Guam, in the S. Pacific, by the *Vityaz* (U.S.S.R.) in 1957.

The origin of the E. is disputed, one theory being that it may have been formed from a swarm of meteorites which arose when matter, drawn from the sun by the attraction of a passing star, condensed. It is thought to consist of an inner core extending *c.* 800 m. from the centre (possibly solid iron and nickel); an outer core *c.* 1,400 m. thick (possibly molten iron and nickel); and a mantle of solid rock *c.* 1,800 m. thick, separated from the outer crust (varying in thickness from 3 to 5 m. beneath certain points in the oceans to *c.* 30 m. beneath the continents) by the Mohorovičic Discontinuity (*see* MOHOLE). The age of the elements composing the crust and atmo-sphere is est. at 5,000 million years. Crustal move-ments have been intensively studied in recent years, and it is probable that in the last 150 million years Britain and N. America have moved from positions near the equator, with at the same time a widening of the gap between them of *c.* 1,000 m. An analysis of radioactive materials in the crust suggests that it was formed *c.* 2,800 million years ago.

EARTHQUAKE. A shaking or convulsion of the earth's surface, the scientific study of which is called seismology. Most Es. are due to sudden earth move-ments, generally along faults (fractures or breaks) in the strata – these tectonic Es. are the greatest and most widespread in their effects. Es. of one kind or another are constantly occurring, and severe Es. occur every fortnight or so. The great majority are in marine areas.

The chief zones of E. activity constitute two belts: (*a*) the circum-Pacific belt, running from the islands in the western Pacific to Japan, the Aleutians, and down the whole of the W. coast of the American continent to Antarctica; (*b*) the Mediterranean belt, which stretches from the Cape Verde Is. and Portugal along the mountain backbone of Europe into Asiatic Turkey, through the Himalayas to Indonesia, where it connects with the former belt. E. disaster areas incl. Tokyo and Yokohama and Agadir and Skopje (qq.v.).

EARTHWORMS. Name given to those members of the Oligochaeta which are mainly terrestrial in their habits. Es. are hermaphrodite, and deposit their eggs in cocoons. They live by burrowing in the soil, feeding on the organic matter it contains. They play a most im-portant role in the formation of humus, by irrigating

the soil, and levelling it by transferring earth from the deeper levels to the surface as castings. The common British Es. belong to the genera *Lumbricus* and *Allolobophora*. These are comparatively small, but some tropical forms reach 3 or 4 ft., and *Megascolides australis*, of Queensland, attains 11 ft. in length.

EARWIG. Insects, forming the family Forficulidae and order Dermaptera. The fore-wings are short and leathery, and serve to protect the hind-wings, which are large and are folded fan-wise when at rest. The family is represented in Britain by several species. It feeds at night on the tender parts of plants, flowers, etc., and also on other insects, dead or living. It rarely flies.

EASEMENT. In law, a class of rights which a per-son or persons may have over the land of another. The commonest example is a right of way; others are rights to bring water over another's land, and to prevent building up so as to exclude light from existing windows.

EAST. Point of the compass indicating that part of the horizon where the sun rises, i.e. when facing N., E. is to the right. The E. has held an important place in various religions; ancient pagan temples had their altars at the E. end, a practice bound up with sun-cult and sacrifices made facing the rising sun. In the 2nd cent. it became customary for Christians to wor-ship facing the E., and also to bury the dead with their feet towards the E., so that on the resurrection-morn they would be facing the quarter whence Christ was to come in glory.

EAST AFRICA. General term covering Kenya, Tanzania, and Uganda (qq.v.): in 1967 the EAST AFRICAN COMMUNITY superseded earlier organisa-tions for shared services in the three countries – com-munications, co-ordination of commerce and industry, finance, social and research services, and labour and industrial relations. The H.Q. is at Arusha in Tan-zania, and the Legislative Assembly has 9 members from each country. The *University of E.A.* (1963)

EASTBOURNE. The sun lounge on Grand Parade commands a fine view of the sea: at the rear still stands the Wish Tower, one of the martello defence chain against Napoleon.
Photo: H. C. Deal Ltd.

at Kampala, Uganda, has 3 constituent colleges—the Univ. Coll., Nairobi (1961), Univ. Coll., Dar es Salaam (1961), and Makerere Univ. Coll. (1949).

EAST ANGLIA. District of E. England, formerly a Saxon kingdom, roughly corresponding to Norfolk and Suffolk. Once almost isolated by fens and woods, E.A. remains a specialized region. The Univ. of E.A. was founded at Norwich in 1962.

EAST BENGAL. *See* BENGAL; PAKISTAN.

EASTBOURNE. English seaside resort in Sussex, 64 m. S.S.E. of London. The old town lies about a mile inland; the modern town extends along the coast for some 3 m., with a pier and fine marine parades; its development was largely due to the 7th duke of Devonshire. E. became a county borough in 1911. At E. the South Downs terminate in Beachy Head (q.v.). Pop. (1961) 60,897.

EASTER. Feast of the Christian Church, commemorating the Resurrection of Christ. Its English name is derived from Eostre, a goddess of Spring honoured by the pagan Anglo-Saxons during April. The festival grew out of the early Christians' observance of the Jewish Passover, and from very early times there has been considerable variation in the date of the annual celebration. By an Act of Parliament passed in 1752 Easter Day is the first Sunday after the full moon which happens upon or next after March 21, and if the full moon happens upon a Sunday then Easter Day is the Sunday following. Yet the full moon referred to is not the real moon, but a hypothetical one, and tables are given in the Book of Common Prayer for determining Easter in any given year. Easter may fall on one of 35 days from 22 March to 25 April, and several attempts have been made (e.g. in 1928) to avoid the inconvenience of a movable feast by establishing a fixed Easter. So far, however, ecclesiastical influence has told against it.

E. has been from ancient times the most important feast in the Christian year. Many popular customs, which probably go back to pagan times, are also associated with it throughout Europe, e.g. the giving of E. eggs. Eggs as a symbol of life and fertility, and the breaking of the chicken through the shell was taken as symbolical of Christ's resurrection.

EASTER. Island, about 64 sq. m. in area, in the S. Pacific Ocean, about 2,300 m. W. of Chile, to which country it belongs. It was discovered on Easter Sunday, 1722, and is famous for its huge carved statues and stone houses, the work of neolithic peoples who may have been of South American origin. Pop. (est.) 600, nearly all Polynesians.

EASTERN ORTHODOX CHURCH. The Christian Church of many nations inhabiting the eastern part of Europe and the N. and W. of Asia, including Greeks, Russians, Rumanians, Serbians, Bulgarians, Georgians, and Albanians; in the last 200 years it has spread into China, Korea, Japan, and Alaska, as well as among the tribes of Siberia and central Asia. Today it is a federation of self-governing Churches, some of which were founded by the Apostles and their disciples, which conduct services in their own language, and follow their own customs and traditions, but are in full communion with one another. The senior church of Eastern Christendom is that of Constantinople, whose chief bishop bears the title of oecumenical patriarch, and has primacy of honour.

The Church's teaching is based on the Bible; and the Nicene-Constantinopolitan Creed (325–81) is the only confession of faith used. The centre of Eastern worship is the Eucharist, celebrated with little change since the 6th cent. The ritual is elaborate, and accompanied by singing in which both men and women take part, but no instrumental music is used. Besides the seven sacraments the prayer book contains many other services for daily life. There is an impressive marriage service during which the bride and groom are crowned. There are many monasteries, the most famous being Mt. Athos in Greece, which has flourished since the 10th cent. During the last century contacts between Eastern and Anglican Christians have become more frequent, and several societies have been started for its promotion, e.g. the Fellowship of St. Alban and St. Sergius.

EAST INDIA COMPANY. An English commercial company that was chartered by Queen Elizabeth I in 1600 and given the monopoly of trade between England and the E. In the 18th cent. it became in effect the ruler of a large part of India, and a form of dual control by the Company and a committee responsible to Parliament in London was introduced by Pitt's India Act, 1784; following the Indian Mutiny in 1857, the Crown took complete control of the govt. of British India, and the India Act of 1858 abolished the Company.

EAST KILBRIDE. Town in Lanarkshire, Scotland, 7 m. S. of Glasgow, built under the New Towns Act, 1946. It enveloped Long Calderwood, birthplace of William and John Hunter. Construction started in 1949. It has a jet-engine factory (1953) and a laboratory of mechanical engineering. Pop. (1961) 31,972.

EASTLAKE, Sir Charles Lock (1793–1865). British artist. B. at Plymouth, he painted a famous study of Napoleon as a prisoner on board the *Bellerophon*. He became an R.A. in 1830, and P.R.A. in 1850.

EAST LONDON. Port and resort on the S.E. coast of Cape Province, S. Africa. It has a good harbour, is the terminus of a railway from the interior, and is a

EASTER. With only their heads above ground, a group of statues in their temporary positions, awaiting the completion of work on the backs before they were taken to temple platforms elsewhere on the island. *Courtesy of Thor Heyerdahl.*

leading wool-exporting port. Pop. (1960) 116,056 (49,295 white).

EAST LOTHIAN. A south-eastern county of Scotland lying between the Firth of Forth and the North Sea on the N. and Berwickshire on the S. The N. part is a broad plain, where agriculture is the leading industry; in the S. the land rises to the Lammermuir hills (1,749 ft.). The Tyne is the only important river. Coal, iron ore, and limestone are obtained. Haddington is the co. town. Area 267 sq. m.; pop. (1961) 52,653.

EASTMAN, George (1854–1932). American inventor and philanthropist. B. at Waterville, N.Y., he was interested in photography, and after manufacturing dry plates produced the first effective roll film in 1884 and in 1888 the 'Kodak' camera. He gave many millions of dollars to educational institutions.

EAU DE COLOGNE (ō de kolōn′). A refreshing perfume whose invention is ascribed to Giovanni Maria Farina (1685–1766) who moved from Italy to Cologne in 1709, and there manufactured the perfume.

EBBW (e′boo) **VALE.** Mining town (U.D.) in Monmouthshire, England; there are large iron, steel, and tinplate works. Aneurin Bevan (q.v.) was M.P. for E.V. 1929–60. Pop. (1961) 28,631.

EBERT (eh′bert), **Friedrich** (1870–1925). German statesman. B. at Heidelberg, he was a saddler, and was elected to the Reichstag as a Social Democrat in 1912. He opposed the F.W.W. and on the abdication of the Kaiser in Nov. 1918 became Chancellor and formed a provisional govt. In 1919 he was elected 1st Pres. of the rep. and was re-elected in 1922.

E'BONITE. A dark brown, horny substance produced by the prolonged heating of rubber with approx. half its weight of sulphur. It is mainly used as an electrical insulator.

E'BONY. Hardwood, obtained from trees of the genus *Diospyros* of the family Ebenaceae found in the tropics. It is very heavy, hard and black; takes a fine polish; and is used in cabinet-making, inlaying, and also for piano-keys, knife-handles, etc.

EBO'RACUM. Roman name for YORK. The archbp. of York subscribes himself 'Ebor'.

ÉBOUÉ (ehboo-eh′), **Félix** (1884–1944). French colonial governor, the first Negro to be appointed. He became Gov. of Guadeloupe in 1936, of Chad in 1938, and as a supporter of the Free French was made Gov.-Gen. of Equatorial Africa by De Gaulle.

ECCLES, Sir John Carew (1903–). Australian physiologist. A student of Sir Charles Sherrington (q.v.) he worked at Oxford until 1937, and was prof. of physiology at the Australian Nat. Univ., Canberra, from 1951–66, when he undertook research in Chicago for the American Medical Assocn. For his research on conduction in the central nervous system he was elected F.R.S. in 1941, and in 1963 shared the Nobel prize (with Hodgkin, q.v., and Huxley) for physiology and medicine.

ECCLES. English industrial town (bor.) in Lancs, 4 m. W. of Manchester, of which it forms a suburb. The town, noted for its cakes, makes cotton and other textiles. Pop. (1961) 43,184.

ECHEGARAY (āchägahrah′-i), **José** (1832–1916). Spanish dramatist. B. at Madrid, he became an engineer and professor of mathematics, and later was a cabinet minister, but is chiefly remembered as a playwright. He wrote some 60 dramas, the best of them being *O locura o santidad* (1877) and *El gran galeoto* (1881), and received the Nobel prize in 1904.

ECHIDNA (ekid′na) or **Spiny Ant-eater.** Name given to a family comprising 2 genera of mammals, in the order Monotremata, found in Australia and New Guinea. They slightly resemble the hedgehog,

are terrestrial in their habits, and subsist entirely upon ants, which they dig out by their powerful claws and lick up by their prehensile tongue. When attacked Es. roll themselves into a ball, or try to hide by burrowing in the sand.

ECHINODERMA or **Echinoderms** (eki′no-). One of the great phyla of the animal kingdom, divided into 5 main classes typified by the sea urchins (Echinoid), the starfish (Asteroid), the brittle star (Ophiuroid), the feather-star or sea-lily (Crinoid), and the sea-cucumber (Holothuroid). They are exclusively marine animals, and most of them have a body covered with knobs or spines (echinoderma – Gk. for 'prickle-skinned') and small stalked out-growths which normally keep them fixed to the sea bottom.

ECHO SOUNDING and ranging. Sonar equipment (SOund NAvigation and Ranging) is employed in underwater detection, ranging and depth measurement by means of a process similar to that used in radar. The time taken for an acoustic beam in the audible or supersonic range to travel to the underwater object, whose distance is required, and back to the source enables the distance to be found since the velocity of sound under water is known. *See* SONAR.

ECKHART (c. 1260–1327). German mystic, called Meister E. near Gotha, he became a Dominican, was provincial of the order for Saxony 1304–11, taught in Paris, Strasbourg, and Cologne, where in 1326 he was accused of heresy; in 1329 a number of his doctrines were condemned.

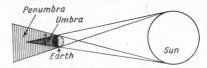

ECLIPSE OF THE MOON. The earth, moving between the sun and the moon, obscures its satellite at the apex of the *umbra*, or region in total darkness. The *penumbra* is the area in partial darkness surrounding the umbra.

ECLIPSE (ēklips′). Es. are of 2 kinds: solar and lunar. A solar E. occurs when the moon passes in front of the sun, and conceals it either totally or partially; during a total E. the sun's outer atmosphere (the corona) is visible to the naked eye. The next British total E. will take place in 1999. A lunar E. occurs when the moon passes into the shadow of the earth; direct sunlight is then cut off from the moon's surface, and the moon becomes dim until emerging from the shadow. Lunar Es. may be either total or partial.

ECO'LOGY. The study of living organisms as they exist in their natural habitats. The term was first introduced by the German biologist, Ernst Haeckel, in 1866, but it did not come into general use until the present cent. The field of E. embraces all living organisms, and therefore the human race; but in the latter case it merges with sociology, etc.

ECONOMICS. The scientific study (formerly known as 'political economy') of the production, distribution and exchange of 'wealth' – anything and everything conducive to material welfare. Notable economists incl. Adam Smith, Ricardo, Malthus, J. S. Mill, Marx, W. S. Jevons and J. M. Keynes (qq.v.). The chief point in dispute in modern times is the respective spheres of state and private enterprise.

ECUADOR (ek′wador). A republic of S. America, situated on the W. coast, across the equator (from which it derives its name), and bounded by Colombia and Peru. The capital is Quito, 8,400 ft. above sea-level.

E. falls into 4 zones: (1) The Andean region or Sierra, formed by the Eastern and the Western Cordillera (of which the highest mountain is Chimborazo, 20,700 ft.), with the inter-Andean valleys; this district supplies the principal agricultural produce for home consumption. (2) The tropical coastal region, which provides the main products for export. (3) The Oriente, stretching eastward from the Andes towards the Amazon basin, for the most part undeveloped tropical forest. (4) The Galapagos Islands, made up of 13 large and numerous smaller islands, and possessing rich fauna and vegetation and fishing grounds. Most important of E.'s rivers is the Guayas; Guayaquil, linked by road and rail with Quito, is the chief port.

E. is predominantly agricultural. The chief exports are cacao, bananas, and coffee. The minerals include petroleum, gold, sulphur, and copper. A rail connection between Quito and San Lorenzo was opened 1957 and a coastal highway is under construction.

Area (govt. est.) 116,270 sq. m.; pop. (1967 est.) 5,585,400, of whom 39 per cent are Indian, 41 per cent Mestizos, 10 per cent Mulattos and Negroes, and 10 per cent white. Spanish is the official language, but most of the Indians speak only Quichua. Roman Catholicism is the prevailing religion.

HISTORY. E. was conquered by the Incas shortly before the arrival of the Spaniards in the 16th cent. After an abortive revolt in 1809, E. became in 1822 part of Bolivar's republic of Colombia, seceding peacefully to become an independent republic in 1830. There have been many revolutions and the constitution of 1967 was devised to prevent rule by a military junta, as in 1963–6. There is a pres. elected for 4 yrs. and an elected chamber of deputies and senate. In 1942 E. ceded half her Amazonian terrs., occupied by Peru in 1941, but the agreement was denounced by E. in 1961 and 1967.

ECZEMA (ek'zēma). An allergic skin affection marked by itching, the formation of vesicles, and the exudation of fluid. It is often complicated by infection due to scratching. The treatment is that of the allergic condition.

E'DAM. Town in the Netherlands on the river Ij, N. Holland prov., famous for its round red cheeses. Pop. (est.) 4,000.

EDDA. Name given to 2 collections of early Icelandic literature, which together constitute our chief source for the old Scandinavian mythology. The term strictly applies to the *Younger* or *Prose E.*, compiled by Snorri Sturluson, a priest, about 1230. The *Elder* or *Poetic E.* is the name given to a collection of poems, discovered by Brynjólfr Sveinsson, about 1643, and written by unknown Norwegian poets of the 9th to 12th cents.

EDDINGTON, Sir Arthur Stanley (1882–1944). British astronomer. Prof. of astronomy at Cambridge from 1913, and director of the univ. observatory from 1914, he did work of the highest importance on the motions and equilibrium of stars, their luminosity and atomic structure, and became a leading exponent of Einstein's relativity theory. In his *Expanding Universe* (1933) he expressed the theory that in the spherical universe the outer galaxies or spiral nebulae are receding from one another. He was knighted in 1930 and received the O.M. in 1938.

EDDY, Mary Baker (1821–1910). American founder of the Christian Science movement. *Née* Baker, she was b. in New Hampshire, and was brought up as a Congregationalist. Her faith in Divine healing was confirmed by her recovery from injuries caused by a fall in 1866, and a pamphlet *Science of Man* (1869) was followed by *Science and Health* (1875), which she constantly revised until her death. In 1876 she founded the Christian Science Association, and among her disciples was A. G. Eddy, whom she m. as her 3rd husband in 1877. In 1879 the Church of Christ, Scientist, was estab., and although living in retirement after 1892 Mrs. E. continued to direct the activities of the movement until her death.

EDDYSTONE. Lighthouse in the English Channel, 9 m. off the coast of Cornwall and 14 m. S.S.W. of Plymouth, completed in 1882, the fourth on the E.

EDELWEISS

rocks, of whose presence its light warns mariners; it can be seen up to $17\frac{1}{2}$ m. away.

EDELWEISS (eh'del-vīs). Alpine plant (*Leontopodium alpinum*) belonging to the family Compositae. It has white flower-heads and grows at great heights.

EDEN, Sir Anthony. *See* LORD AVON.

EDEN. The 'garden' in which, according to the book of Genesis, Adam and Eve were placed after their creation, and from which they were expelled for disobedience. It is usually assumed that it was in Mesopotamia, and that two of its rivers were the Euphrates and the Tigris.

EDENTA'TA. An order of mammals, comprising the families of sloths, ant-eaters, armadillos, pangolins, and ant-bears. They are practically confined to South and Central America.

EDFU (ed'foo). Ancient town and trade centre on the left bank of the Nile, Upper Egypt, with an almost perfect Ptolemaic temple dedicated to Horus. Pop. (est.) 18,500.

EDGAR (944–75). King of all England from 959. Called the Peaceful, he was the younger son of King Edmund, and strove successfully to unite English and Danes as fellow subjects.

EDGEHILL. Ridge in S. Warwicks, England, where the 1st battle of the Civil War took place in 1642, between Royalists under Charles I and Parliamentarians under the Earl of Essex. The result was indecisive.

EDGEWORTH, Maria (1767–1849). Irish novelist. B. in Oxfordshire, she was the dau. of the writer, inventor and educationist, Richard Lovell E. (1744–1817). Her first novel, *Castle Rackrent* (1800), dealt with the Anglo-Irish country society, and was followed by the similar *The Absentee* (1812) and *Ormond* (1817), and the English *Belinda* (1801).

EDINBURGH, Philip, duke of. *See* PRINCE PHILIP. The dukedom of E. was first conferred in 1726 by George I on his eldest grandson, Frederick, who d. 11 months later and never became king. It was revived in 1866 for Victoria's 2nd son Alfred (1844–1900), and became extinct on his death.

EDINBURGH. City and capital of Scotland; co. tn.

EDINBURGH. The beauty and rich cultural life of this ancient city have earned her the title of 'Athens of the North'. Here, upon the high central embankment known as the Mound, are the National Gallery and Royal Academy of Scotland. To the right the Scott Memorial towers over Princes Street, one of the finest thoroughfares in Europe, and Edinburgh castle dominates the skyline to the left.
Courtesy of Edinburgh Corporation.

EDISON. In his physics laboratory at West Orange, New Jersey, the great inventor holds one of his 'Edison Effect' lamps. By his discovery of this 'effect' in 1880 he revealed one of the fundamental principles on which modern electronics rests.
Courtesy of U.S. Dept. of the Interior.

of Midlothian, near the S. shores of the Firth of Forth. The site during Roman times was occupied by British or Welsh tribes, and *c.* 617 was taken by Edwin of Northumbria, from whom the town took its name. The early settlement grew up round a castle on Castle Rock, whilst about a mile to the E. another burgh, called Canongate, grew up round the abbey of Holyrood, founded in 1128 by David I. It remained separate from E. until 1856. Robert Bruce made E. a burgh in 1329, and estab. its port at Leith. In 1544 the town was destroyed by the English. After the union with England in 1707, E. lost its political importance, but is still culturally pre-eminent. E. univ., with a famous medical school, dates from 1583 and Heriot-Watt Univ. (1885: univ. status 1966) is a technical institution.

E. castle contains St. Margaret's chapel, the oldest building in Edinburgh. The palace of Holyrood House was built in the 15th and 16th cents. The Parliament House, begun in 1632, is now the seat of the supreme courts. The episcopal cathedral of St. Mary, opened in 1879, and St. Giles parish church (mostly 15th cent.) are the principal churches. The two most renowned thoroughfares are Princes Street and the Royal Mile. The part known as New Town was started in 1767.

E. is not a great industrial city, but printing and book publishing are important. It attracts many tourists, especially to the annual E. festival, founded 1947. E. ranks as an independent co., and is administered by a town council of 70 members, presided over by the Lord Provost. The port of Leith was incorporated in 1920; the city covers *c.* 55 sq. m.; pop. (1961) 468,378.

EDIRNE (edĕr'ne). Turkish city, capital of E. il, on the Maritza, about 140 m. W.N.W. of Istanbul. Pop. (1965) 46,000.

EDISON, Thomas Alva (1847–1931). American inventor. B. in Ohio, of Dutch-Scottish parentage, he became first a newsboy and then a telegraph operator. His first invention was an automatic repeater for telegraphic messages, and was followed by over 1,000 others, including various telegraphic devices; the carbon transmitter (of assistance in the production of the Bell telephone); the phonograph; the incandescent lamp; a new type of storage battery; and the kinetiescopic camera, an early form of cinematography. He anticipated the Fleming diode thermionic valve.

EDMONDS, Walter Dumaux (1903–). American author of historical novels set in the 19th cent., such as *Drums along the Mohawk* and *Chad Hanna* (1940).

EDMONTON. Locality, once a town, part of the Greater London bor. of Enfield. Charles Lamb lived and d. here: the Bell inn is referred to in Cowper's *John Gilpin.*

EDMONTON. Capital of Alberta Province, Canada, on the N. Saskatchewan river. It is the centre for a mining and petroleum-bearing area to the N. and also for an agricultural and dairying region. Petroleum pipelines link E. with Superior, Wisconsin, U.S.A., and with Vancouver, B.C. Pop. (1966) 401,299

EDMUND (*c.* 840–70). King of East Anglia from 855. In 870 he was defeated and captured by the Danes at Hoxne, and martyred on refusing to renounce Christianity. He was canonized and his shrine at Bury St. Edmunds became a place of pilgrimage.

EDMUND IRONSIDE (*c.* 989–1016). King of England. The son of Ethelred the Unready, he led the resistance to Canute's invasion in 1015, and on Ethelred's death in 1016 was chosen as king by the citizens of London, while the Witan elected Canute. E. was defeated by Canute at Assandun (Ashington). Essex, and they divided the kingdom between them,

E'DOM. The southern district of Palestine, which stretched from the Dead Sea to the Gulf of Aqaba. The original settlers are supposed to have been descendants of Esau.

EDRISI (ĕdrē'sē) or **Idrisi** (*c.* 1099–1164). Arab geographer. B. at Ceuta, he became attached to the court of Roger II of Sicily, for whom he prepared a geographical account of the then known world, compiled in 1154.

EDUCATION. In its widest sense, E. begins at birth and continues so long as the mind is capable of receiving impressions The most primitive human groups have always prepared the young for the sort of life they have to live: had they not done so the group would soon have vanished; and some sort of instruction of the young is common among other mammals and birds. In the more restricted sense of imparting knowledge dependent on literacy, E. has become almost world wide.

Formal E. in the present-day sense is of European origin, though China can boast of an allied form of instruction dating from an imperial decree of 165 B.C. which set up open competitive examinations for the recruitment of members of the Civil Service. The earliest known European educational systems are those of ancient Greece – in Sparta, devoted particularly to development of military virtues, in Athens to the good of the rep. in a wider sense, but both, as in China, accorded only to the privileged few.

EDUCATION. Language learning the modern way. These American children use specially designed recorders, and the teacher (with headphones and microphone) stands in front of a console from where he controls the class.
Courtesy of Electronic Classrooms, Ltd.

Rome took over much of the Greek notion of E., as of so many other aspects of civilized life, and spread it over western Europe. With the barbarian invasions and the extinction of the Roman Empire, E. vanished from Europe, though monks preserved both learning and the Latin tongue. Charlemagne's monastic schools which taught the 'seven liberal arts' – grammar, logic, rhetoric, arithmetic, geometry, music, and astronomy – produced the 'Schoolmen' and the Scholastic Movement, which in the 11th to 13th cents. led to the foundation of the universities of Paris, Bologna, Padua, Oxford, Cambridge. The capture of Constantinople by the Turks in 1453 sent into exile across Europe the Christian scholars who had congregated there, and revived European interest in learning.

Until the 19th cent. in England no attempts were made to spread literacy downwards. The Factory Act of 1802 required owners of the newly rising factories to have children taught reading, writing, and arithmetic during the first four years of their apprenticeship: the clause was not everywhere observed, but it embodied a new principle. The British and Foreign Schools Society (1808) and the National Society for Promoting the E. of the Poor in the Principles of the Established Church (1811) set up schools in which the 'three Rs' as well as religious knowledge were taught. In 1862 govt. grants became available for the first time for schools attended by children up to 12. The Elementary E. Act of 1870 (Forster's Act) estab. district school boards all over the country whose duty was to provide accommodation for the elementary E. of all children not otherwise receiving E. Once the principle of elementary E. for all was accepted, the idea of higher E. for everyone capable of benefiting from it gradually asserted itself.

By the middle of the 20th cent., in most countries of the world E. was compulsory and supplied free from the age of about 6 up to 14 or 15, though the compulsion remained theoretic in, e.g., Mexico, Albania, Bolivia, where the country is difficult and there were not enough schools and teachers to provide for all the children who should have been at school. The decision of the Communist govt. of China in 1956 to introduce gradually a 25-letter alphabet based on the Latin alphabet, to replace the 30,000 symbols of Chinese script, was a first step towards universal literacy in China.

The increasing impact in the 20th cent. of science and technology on ways of life has led, especially in secondary and higher E., to increasing stress (some educationists think over-stress, to the impoverishment of the general intelligence of students) on scientific and technological knowledge, rather than the 'liberal arts', as the basis of instruction. This has been most noticeable in the U.S.S.R., though it has had a marked effect on E. in the U.S.A., and to a growing extent in the U.K.

In the U.K. the **Dept. of E. and Science** (1964, successor to the Board of E. 1899 and Min. of E. 1944), headed by a Cabinet Min., promotes 'the E. of the people of England and Wales and the progressive development of institutions devoted to that purpose'; the Scottish E. Dept., under the Secretary for Scotland, has a similar duty in Scotland; N. Ireland has its own Ministry of E.

In the U.S.A., E. is in the main the responsibility of the states, but the **Department of Health, Education, and Welfare** (1953), headed by a Secretary who is a member of the President's Cabinet, includes a Commissioner of E. responsible for federal aspects of the subject.

EDWARD I (1239–1307). King of England. The son of Henry III, he commanded the royal forces in the Barons' Wars of 1264–7, and was on a crusade when he succeeded to the throne in 1272. He estab. English rule over all Wales for the first time in 1282–4, and attempted to extend it to Scotland, at first by

EDWARD II. South-east of the market town of Berkeley is the castle of the same name, and it was in this room that Edward II was murdered after much earlier ill-treatment. In the Civil War the castle was under siege by the Parliamentarians for nine days before being taken.
English Life Publications Ltd.

securing a recognition of his overlordship from the Scottish king, and later by direct conquest. The Scots maintained a fierce resistance under the leadership of Wallace and Bruce, and the struggle was still undecided when he d. At home his reign is notable for the emergence of Parliament in roughly its modern form with the Model Parliament of 1295.

EDWARD II (1284–1327). King of England. B. at Caernarvon, he was created the 1st prince of Wales in 1301, and succeeded his father Edward I in 1307. He soon showed himself incompetent and frivolous, falling entirely under the influence of favourites, and his reign was occupied by struggles with the discontented barons. His invasion of Scotland in 1314, undertaken to suppress Bruce's revolt, resulted in the defeat of Bannockburn. E. was deposed in 1327 by his wife Isabella and her lover Mortimer, and murdered in Berkeley castle.

EDWARD III (1312–77). King of England. B. at Windsor, he succeeded his father, Edward II, in 1327, and assumed charge of the government in 1330. He began his reign by attempting to force his suzerainty on Scotland, winning a victory at Halidon Hill (1333). In 1337 he began the 100 Years War by claiming the French throne in right of his mother. During the 1st stage of the war E. defeated the French at Crécy (1346), won naval victories at Sluys (1340) and Winchelsea (1350), and captured Calais (1347), while his son, the Black Prince, defeated and captured the French king at Poitiers (1356). The war ended temporarily in 1360 with the treaty of Brétigny, by which E. surrendered his claim to the throne in return for Calais, Aquitaine, and Gascony. After its renewal in 1369 the French recaptured all the English dominions in France but Calais, Bordeaux, and Bayonne.

EDWARD IV (1442–83). King of England. He was the son of Richard, duke of York, and before his accession was known as earl of March. After his father's death E. occupied London in 1461, and was proclaimed king in place of Henry VI by a council of peers. His position was secured by the defeat of the Lancastrians at Towton (1461) and by the capture of Henry. He quarrelled, however, with Warwick, his strongest supporter, who in 1470–1 temporarily restored Henry, until E. recovered the throne by his victories at Barnet and Tewkesbury.

EDWARD V (1470–83). King of England. He succeeded his father, Edward IV, in 1483, but was deposed 3 months later in favour of his uncle Richard, duke of Gloucester. He is generally believed to have been murdered with his brother in the Tower of London by Richard's orders.

EDWARD VI (1537–53). King of England. The son of Henry VIII and Jane Seymour, he became king in 1547. The government was entrusted to his uncle the duke of Somerset,

EDWARD VI
Artist unknown.
Photo: N.P.G.

and after his fall in 1549 to the earl of Warwick, later created duke of Northumberland. While still a child, E. became a strong Protestant, and strongly supported the policy of advancing the Reformation adopted by both Somerset and Northumberland. He d. of consumption.

EDWARD VII (1841–1910). King of Great Britain and Ireland. B. at Buckingham Palace, the eldest son of Queen Victoria and Prince Albert, he received a careful education. In 1860 he made the first tour of Canada and the U.S.A. ever undertaken by a British prince. After his father's death in 1861 he undertook many public duties, although the Queen refused to allow him to take any part in political life. Nevertheless, he took a close interest in politics, and was on friendly terms with Gladstone, Chamberlain, and other party leaders. In 1863 he m. Princess Alexandra of Denmark, by whom he had 6 children. He toured India in 1875–6, played an active part in the life of society, and was a keen sportsman. He succeeded to the throne in 1901, and was crowned in 1902. His influence contributed to the *Entente Cordiale* of 1904 with France, and Anglo-Russian agreement of 1907.

EDWARD VIII (1894–1972). King of Great Britain and Ireland. Eldest son of George V, he was created Prince of Wales in 1910, received a naval training at Dartmouth and studied in Paris and at Magdalen College, Oxford. He saw active service in the F.W.W., and subsequently travelled widely both within and outside the Commonwealth. Succeeding to the throne on January 20, 1936, he showed great concern for the problems of the Glasgow slums and the distressed areas of S. Wales. In Nov. a constitutional crisis arose when he wished to marry Mrs.

EDWARD VIII. On a Christmas shopping expedition to London the duke and duchess of Windsor receive an affectionate welcome from the crowds. *Photo: Topix.*

Wallis Warfield (Simpson), an American, since it was felt that as she had been divorced she would be unacceptable as Queen. On Dec. 11, E. abdicated and left for France where the couple were m. June 3, 1937, at the Château de Candé, Tours. He received the title of duke of Windsor and was Gov. of the Bahamas 1940–5, subsequently settling in France. His autobiography *A King's Story* appeared in 1951.

EDWARD, called the **Black Prince** (1330–76). Prince of Wales. The eldest son of Edward III, he served at Crécy, and in 1356 defeated and captured the French king at Poitiers. He ruled Aquitaine as his father's representative 1362–71, and in 1367 invaded Castile and restored to the throne the deposed king, Pedro the Cruel. After attempting unsuccessfully to suppress a revolt in Aquitaine he was obliged by ill-health to return to England in 1371, and thereafter took little part in public life. The name 'The Black Prince', said to be derived from his black armour, was probably a later invention.

EDWARD the Confessor (d. 1066). King of England. The son of Ethelred II, he lived in Normandy until shortly before his accession in 1042. The government remained in the hands of Earl Godwin, and, after his death, of his son Harold, while E. devoted himself to religious exercises. E. was buried in Westminster Abbey, which he had rebuilt.

EDWARD the Elder (d. 924). King of England. The son of King Alfred, he succeeded him in 901. He crushed Danish risings and extended his kingdom to the Humber.

EELS

EDWARD the Martyr (c. 963–78). King of England. On the death of his father, King Edgar, in 975, his stepmother Aelfthryth attempted to secure the crown for her son Ethelred, but through Dunstan's influence E. was crowned king. In 978 E. was murdered, probably at Aelfthryth's instigation.

EDWARDS, Gus (1881–1945). American songwriter. His real name was Gustave Edward Simon. With Will Cobb, a writer of lyrics, he produced many popular songs, incl. 'Don't cry, little girl, don't cry'.

EDWARDS, Jonathan (1703–58). American divine. B. in Connecticut, he became in 1727 pastor at Northampton, Mass. Here he developed Calvinistic views of predestination and initiated the religious revival known as the 'Great Awakening'.

For 200 yrs. regarded as an anachronism, he has in the 20th cent. been recognized as a brilliantly original thinker. His important works are *The Freedom of the Will* (defending Determinism), *Nature of the True Virtue*, and *Religious Affections* (defending the emotive basis of religious experience).

EDWIN (c. 585–633). King of Northumbria from 617. He fortified Edinburgh, named after him, and was killed in battle with Penda of Mercia.

EECKHOUT (ek'howt), **Gerbrand van den** (1621–74). Dutch painter, b. at Amsterdam. Most of his paintings are of Biblical subjects.

EEKHOUD (ek'howd), **Georges** (1854–1927). Belgian poet and novelist. B. at Antwerp, he pub. his first poems *Myrtes et Cyprès* in 1877. His novels, e.g. *Kees Doorik*, describe rural Belgian life.

EEL. Fish of the order Apodes, characterized by a serpent-like body, small gill openings, and reduced fins. The common E. of European and African rivers (*Anguilla anguilla*) reaches a length of 5 ft. and weighs

12–15 lb. On becoming mature some 6 yrs. later, and assuming a silver breeding livery instead of their earlier yellowish colouring, these Es. were then thought to make their way back to the Sargasso Sea (from which they originally came as larvae) to spawn. It is now suggested, however, that these Es. cannot muster strength for the return journey and consequently never breed and that they are actually of the same species as the American common E. (*Anguilla rostrata*), although the latter may reach 4 times their weight because of more favourable conditions. The eggs of American Es. laid at the northern limits of the spawning grounds would be held in the Sargasso Sea for a year before being carried by the Gulf Stream to Europe, Africa and the Mediterranean; those laid at the southern limits would be carried much more rapidly to the richer feeding grounds of the American coasts by the Antilles and Florida ocean currents, with resultant differences in development.

The morays or painted Es. are represented by some 100 species in tropical and temperate seas; they are often brilliantly coloured and very fierce. The conger Es. are all marine and are distinguished from freshwater species by the total absence of scales, and are common on British coasts.

EEL-GRASS or Glass Wrack. A genus of plants (*Zostera*) belonging to the family Naiadaceae. *Z. marina* is the typical species. They are remarkable among flowering plants in being adapted for a marine life, being completely submerged at high tide.

EGAN, Pierce (1772–1849). Sporting writer. B. in London, he became a sporting journalist and wrote *Life in London* (1821), illustrated by Cruikshank.

EGBERT (d. 839). King of the W. Saxons. The son of Ealhmund, an under-king of Kent, he succeeded to the W. Saxon throne in 802, and by 829 he had united England for the first time under one king.

EGG. In animals, the ovum, or female reproductive cell. It corresponds to the sperm cell or spermatozoon of the male, and when fecundated by this develops by division into further cells, into the embryo.

EGGLESTON, Edward (1837–1902). American writer. B. in Indiana, he became a 'circuit rider', i.e. an itinerant pastor of small Methodist churches, and then a minister. His *Hoosier Schoolmaster* (1871) tells of life among backwoodsmen of Indiana.

EGMONT, Lamoral, count of (1522–68). Flemish patriot. B. in Hainault, he defeated the French at St. Quentin in 1557 and Gravelines in 1558, and became stadtholder of Flanders and Artois. From 1561 he helped to lead the movement against Spanish misrule, but in 1567 the duke of Alva was sent to crush the resistance, and E. was beheaded.

E′GRET. Genus of birds (*Egretta*) in which both sexes develop a long train of loose-webbed feathers during the breeding season. These snowy-white plumes were formerly so much in demand for hat ornaments that Es. were almost exterminated until the wearing of them was prohibited by law. The great white heron (*E. alba*) which grows to a length of 3 ft. and the little E. (*E. garzetta*), 2 ft. long, are found in Asia, Africa, S. Europe and Australia and rarely visit Britain.

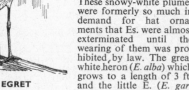

EGRET

EGYPT (ē′jipt). Country of N.E. Africa, lying between the Mediterranean in the N. and the Republic of Sudan in the S. Egypt consists in the main of a low plateau through which the Nile flows towards the N., depositing alluvium which forms a narrow strip of fertile land on both banks; here the great majority of the population is concentrated. This fertile strip is

EGYPT. The Great Sphinx, 189 ft. long, and with a shrine of the sun god Harmachis between its paws, was sculptured from an outcrop of rock used by the builders of the Great Pyramid of Khufu as a stone quarry. It is said to be a portrait of Khafra whose own pyramid (*right*) still has some of its original casing.
Courtesy of the Egyptian State Tourist Administration.

bounded on the E. by the Arabian and on the W. by the Libyan desert. Before reaching the Mediterranean the Nile forms a triangular delta with a width of 150 m. at the seaward end. Most of E. is almost rainless. The principal tree is the date palm. The ass, camel, sheep, and buffalo are the chief domesticated animals.

About 99 per cent of the population live in the cultivated area and in towns; 60 per cent of them are *fellahin* or peasants, living at a bare subsistence level. Most of them are Mohammedans, but about 1,500,000 are Coptic Christians.

AGRICULTURE. Rain being rare, cultivation depends, as from time immemorial, on the Nile, but control of its waters throughout the year, once largely wasted in a single annual flood, has been completed by the erection of the Aswan High Dam. Cotton accounts for ⅔ of exports, and wheat, barley, rice, vegetables and sugar cane are grown. Large landowners have been eliminated under Nasser by limitation of individual holdings to *c.* 100 acres.

INDUSTRY. Industrialisation has been accelerated under Nasser, and a programme of nationalisation of banks, manufacturing and trading concerns undertaken. Soap, sugar, flour, pottery, cement, and glass are produced. Ancient emerald mines are still worked, and other minerals incl. building stone, manganese, phosphate rock, talc and petroleum.

TOWNS. The capital is Cairo, at the head of the Nile delta. Alexandria and Port Said are Mediterranean ports, while Suez lies at the S. end of the Canal.

GOVERNMENT. The 1964 constitution, in force until a plebiscite ratifies a permanent one, provides for a Pres. nominated by the Nat. Assembly (elected by universal suffrage) and confirmed by plebiscite. The country is divided into 2 districts, Upper and Lower E., subdivided into governorates.

Area 386,198 sq. m.; pop. (1966) 30,083,000.

History. ANCIENT. The Egyptian state was founded *c.* 3200 B.C. by the semi-legendary Menes, who united Lower E., in the delta, to his own kingdom of Upper E. in the Nile valley. Following the Archaic Period of the 1st and 2nd Dynasties (32nd–29th cents.), the 'Old Kingdom' reached the height of its power under the 4th Dynasty kings, who built the great pyramids at Gizeh (*c.* 26th cent. B.C.), and then gradually sank into anarchy. Unity was recovered under the 11th and 12th Dynasties (the 'Middle Kingdom', c. 22nd–18th cents. B.C.); there followed another period of anarchy, resulting in the conquest of E. by the Semitic Hyksos. Their expulsion in 1580 B.C. marks the beginning of

EGYPT. A touchingly realistic example of Egyptian art – a limestone group found at Gizeh showing the dwarf Seneb and his family.   Photo: Cairo Museum.

the 'New Kingdom'. Under the 18th Dynasty (1580–1370) a succession of able kings, notably Thothmes III (reigned 1484–1451), founded an empire in Palestine and Syria extending to the Euphrates. The golden age of Amenhotep III probably continued under Ikhnaton (q.v.) – although it is thought by some historians that his neglect of imperial defence for religious reforms led to the loss of most of E.'s possessions in Asia – and also under the 19th Dynasty (Ramses II and Ramses III). However, during the 20th Dynasty there was undoubtedly a decline in Egyptian strength, and power within the country passed from the pharaohs to the priests of Ammon. Under the Late New Kingdom (1090–663 B.C.) E. was often divided between 2 or more dynasties; the nobles became virtually independent, and in the 7th cent. the Assyrians established their suzerainty over E. Psammetichus I (663–609) and his successors restored to E. its independence and unity, and attempted to restore the empire. This national revival ended when Cambyses in 525 brought E. under Persian rule, which survived, except for a period of independence c. 405–340, until Alexander conquered E. in 332. When his empire was divided E. went to Ptolemy, whose descendants ruled until Cleopatra's death in 30 B.C.

RELIGION. The prehistoric Egyptian religion turned on the worship of totemic animals believed to be the ancestors of the clan. Totems later developed into gods, represented with the heads of the animals sacred to them, e.g. the hawk was sacred to Ra and Horus, the ibis to Thoth, the jackal to Anubis. The cult of Osiris, who was murdered, was mourned by his sister and wife Isis, and rose again, as a fertility ritual similar to those of Tammuz and Dionysus; by a natural development Osiris became a god of the underworld. Under the 18th Dynasty a local deity of Thebes, Ammon, came to be regarded as supreme, a

reflection of recovered national unity. Ikhnaton attempted, without success, to establish the monotheistic cult of Aton, the solar disc, as the one national god. Immortality, conferred by the magical rite of mummification, was originally the sole prerogative of the king, but was extended under the New Kingdom to all who could afford it.

MEDIEVAL AND MODERN. After its conquest by Augustus in 30 B.C. Egypt passed under the rule of Roman, and later of Byzantine, governors, and after the Arab conquest of 641 under that of representatives of the Caliphs. Christianity succeeded paganism as the national religion, and was succeeded in turn by Islam. After the 9th cent. Egypt passed to a series of native dynasties, and in the 13th cent. to the Mamelukes, or military

EGYPT. Hippopotamus in faience, New Kingdom, decorated with water plants.
Photo: Cairo Museum.

aristocracy. The Turks conquered Egypt in 1517, but after 2 cents. of rule by Turkish pashas the Mamelukes regained control.

Contact with Europe began with Napoleon's invasion and the French occupation of 1798–1801. A period of anarchy followed, until in 1805 an Albanian officer, Mehemet Ali, was appointed pasha; the title was later made hereditary in his family. Under his successors large sums of British and French capital were invested in Egypt, while the opening of the Suez Canal in 1869 made the country of great strategic importance. Discontent with foreign domination led to a nationalist revolt in 1881–2, put down by British forces. Henceforward the govt. was mainly in the hands of British civilian agents who directed their efforts particularly to the improvement of E.'s finances. On the outbreak of the F.W.W. in 1914, nominal Turkish suzerainty was abolished and E. was declared a British protectorate. Post-war agitation by the nationalist Wafd party led the way to establishment of an independent kingdom in 1922 (see FUAD; FAROUK), Britain retaining responsibility for the military protection of E. In 1936 all British troops were withdrawn except from the Suez Canal zone. Following a military coup in 1952 the monarchy was abolished in 1953, and Gen. Neguib declared E. a republic with himself as president; Neguib was displaced in 1954 by his prime minister, Lt.-Col. Nasser. By an agreement reached that year the last British units left the canal zone on June 13, 1956; on July 26 Nasser nationalised the canal. Border clashes between

EGYPT. Alabaster lamp, tomb of Tutankhamen.
Photo: Cairo Museum.

Egyptian and Israeli patrols led in Oct. to an Israeli invasion of E., and joint Franco-British military intervention to protect the canal. Nasser immediately blocked it, but after the U.N. ended hostilities 3 weeks later, it was cleared under their auspices and traffic resumed: traffic was again interrupted 1967 as a result of renewed hostilities between E. and Israel (q.v.). Egypt was known as the United Arab Republic 1958–71, but the union with Syria which prompted the change broke down in 1961. However, in 1971 Egypt, Syria and Libya formed the Fed. of Arab Republics and E. was renamed the Arab Rep. of Egypt. By 1972 Anwar Sadat (1918–), who had succeeded Nasser as pres. in 1970, was planning complete union with Libya, whose oil resources would complement E.'s industrial capacity, and had expelled E.'s Soviet military advisers who had not enabled the conquest of Israel to be carried out. Within E. there was unrest, and the Arab Socialist Union remained the only permitted political party. *See also* SUDAN, Rep. of.

EGYPTO'LOGY. The study of ancient Egypt. Interest in the subject was first stimulated by Napoleon's expedition of 1798, during which the Rosetta Stone was discovered. As this contained the same inscription in Gk. as well as the hieroglyphic and demotic scripts, it afforded the clue to the decipher-ment of the Egyptian inscriptions. Excavation continued throughout the 19th cent., and gradually assumed a more scientific character, largely as a result of the work of Sir Flinders Petrie from 1880 onwards, and the formation of the Egyptian Exploration Fund in 1892. The most sensational discovery so far made was Tutankhamen's tomb in 1922, the only royal tomb with all its treasures intact. Special branches of E. developed in more recent years are the study of prehistoric Egypt, and the search for papyri, preserved by the dryness of the climate; besides ancient Egyptian writings, many lost Gk. and early Christian works have been recovered.

EHRENBURG, Ilya Grigorievich (1891–1967). Russian writer. B. in Kiev, he spent many years in France before returning permanently to Russia in 1940. Apart from his brilliance as a war correspondent during both world wars, he is noted for *The Adventures of Julio Jurenito* (1930), a satire on the post-war decay of European civilisation, *The Fall of Paris* (1942), and the controversial *The Thaw* (1954), which depicted artistic circles in the U.S.S.R., and contributed to the temporary slackening of literary restraint in the 1950s. He was awarded the Order of Lenin in 1944. He pub. 5 vols. of autobiography 1961–4.

EHRLICH (ehr'likh), **Paul** (1854–1915). German bacteriologist. B. in Silesia, he became director of the Royal Institute for Experimental Therapy at Frankfurt in 1906. He did some cancer research, but his most famous discovery was salvarsan, an arsenical compound of great value in the treatment of syphilis. With Mechnikov he shared the Nobel prize for physiology in 1908.

EICHENDORFF (ī'khendorf), **Joseph**, Freiherr von (1788–1857). German poet and novelist. B. in Upper Silesia, he held various judicial posts, wrote romantic stories, but is chiefly remembered as one of the greatest lyricists in the German tongue.

EICHMANN (īkh'man), **Karl Adolf** (1906–62). Austrian Nazi war criminal. As an S.S. official he was appointed in 1937 to study Zionist and Palestinian questions, promoted the Anschluss (q.v.) as a Gestapo agent, and in 1938 became head of the Bureau of Jewish Emigration in Vienna. Within 6 mths. in 1939 he organised the deportation of 35,000 Jews from Czechoslovakia, and later became chief of the Jewish Emigration Centre in Berlin and the Gestapo's office for the registration of Jews, combined and renamed the E. Department in 1941. Not only did his dept. organise special squads for exterminating Jews, but he personally supervised the despatch of 180,000–200,000 Hungarian Jews to the Auschwitz gas chambers, and on 2 occasions offered to 'sell' Jews to the Allies. In 1960 he was abducted from Argentina by Israeli agents, tried in Israel during 1961 for the extermination of 6 million Jews, and executed.

EIDER (ī'der), Large marine duck, *Somateria mollissima*, highly valued for its soft down, used in stuffing quilts and cushions. It breeds in northern latitudes, from the Farne Islands to Spitzbergen, and in Iceland and Norway it is bred for its down.

EIFFEL (ī'fel) **TOWER.** Iron tower in the Champ de Mars, Paris, built 1887–9 to the design of the French engineer Gustave Alexandre Eiffel (1832–1923) for the Exhibition of 1889. It is 984¼ ft. high.

EIGER. *See* ALPS.

EIGHTH ROUTE ARMY. The Chinese 'Red Army' formed in 1927 when the Communists broke away from Kuomintang and estab. a Soviet government in Kiangsi, in S.E. China. When the Japanese invaded China in 1937 it was recognised as a section of the national forces under the name 8th R.A.

EILAT (ālaht'). Port founded in 1948 at the head of the Gulf of Aqaba, Israel's only outlet to the Red Sea. Formerly a fishing village close to Aqaba, Jordan it, occupies the site of the biblical Elath (Deut. 2, v. 8) and is on a fine bay. There are copper mines and granite quarries nearby. Since 1957 E. has been linked to Beersheba and Ashdod, on the Mediterranean, by an oil pipeline, first begun following the Suez Canal crisis, and in 1958 the 148 m. Beersheba–E. highway was opened. Pop. (est.) 2,000.

EINAUDI (ānow'dē), **Luigi** (1874–1961). Italian statesman and economist. B. in Piedmont, he became a senator in 1919 and was professor of economics in several Italian universities until removed by the Fascists. In 1945 he was appointed governor of the Bank of Italy and in 1946 Vice-Premier. In 1948–55 he was President of the Italian Republic.

EINDHOVEN. Town in N. Brabant prov., the Netherlands, on the Dommel. It is a manufacturing centre, chiefly of electric light bulbs and equipment. Pop. (1967) 183,637.

EINSTEIN (īn'stīn), **Albert** (1879–1955). German-Swiss physicist, framer of the theories of Relativity (q.v.). B. at Ulm, in Württemberg, of Jewish stock, he lived with his parents in Munich and then in Italy. After teaching at the polytechnic school at Zürich he became a Swiss citizen and was appointed an inspector of patents at Berne. In his spare time he

took his degree of Ph.D. at Zürich, and some of his papers on physics were of so high a quality that in 1909 he was given a chair of theoretical physics at the university. After holding a similar post at Prague (1911), he returned to teach at Zürich (1912), and in 1913 took up a specially created post as director of the Kaiser Wilhelm Institute for Physics, Berlin. In 1905 he had pub. his first theory – the so-called special theory of Relativity – and in 1915 he issued his general theory. His latest conception of the basic laws governing the universe was outlined in his unified field theory made public in 1953; and of the 'Relativistic Theory of the Non-symmetric Field', completed 1955, E. wrote that this simplified the derivations as well as the form of the field equations and the whole theory becomes thereby more transparent, without changing its content. He received the Nobel prize for physics in 1921. He was deprived of his post at Berlin in 1933 and became professor of mathematics and a permanent member of the Institute for Advanced Study at Princeton, N.J., U.S.A., and during the S.W.W. worked for the U.S. Navy Ordnance Bureau. Besides his treatises on Relativity, he wrote *My Philosophy* (1933), *The World as I See It* (1935), and (with Leopold Infeld) *The Evolution of Physics* (1938).

EINSTEINIUM. *See* TRANSURANIUM ELEMENTS.

EIRE (ār'e). Irish name for Ireland (q.v.). It was used 1937–49 for the part of the island called the Irish Free State 1922–37.

EISENACH (ī'senakh). Town on the r. Hörsel, in Erfurt district, (E.) Germany, with pottery, worsted, and machinery industries. J. S. Bach was b. at E. Pop. (est.) 52,000.

PRESIDENT EISENHOWER. On a visit to London in 1959 the President (left) is welcomed by Prime Minister Macmillan. He received greater popular acclaim from the crowds than had ever before been accorded to a visiting head of state, and made a historic television appearance with Macmillan.
Photo: Topix.

EISENHOWER (ī'zenhower), **Dwight David** (1890–1969). 34th President of the U.S.A.; Supreme Commander of all the Allied armies in the west during the S.W.W. B. at Denison, Texas, he graduated at West Point Military Academy in 1915, but saw no active service during the F.W.W. In 1935 he served in the Philippines at Manila under MacArthur, and from 1940 held high staff appointments at Washington. In June 1942 he was sent to England as U.S. Commander in the European theatre. In Nov. 1942 he became C.-in-C. of the American and British forces on the occasion of the invasion of N. Africa, and in July 1943 he took command of the Allied invasion of Sicily. It was E. who announced the unconditional surrender of Italy on Sept. 8, 1943. In Dec. he was appointed Supreme Commander of the Allied invasion of Europe, and from Oct. 1944 he was in command of all the Allied armies in the west. After the war 'Ike', as he was familiarly styled by his men, was given an official reception in Washington; in Sept. 1945 he was appointed Military Governor of the U.S. zone of Germany, and in Nov. Chief of Staff of the American Army. In Dec. 1950 he became Supreme Allied Commander, Europe, resigning in 1952 when, as a Republican, he was elected President. Re-elected in 1956 (the first Republican since 1900 to hold the Presidency twice in succession), in 1957 he introd. his 'Eisenhower Doctrine', a policy of giving aid, in consultation with the U.N., to any Middle Eastern countries requesting it, especially against international Communist aggression. This was approved by the U.K. but denounced by certain M. Eastern countries, e.g. Egypt, as an excuse for extending American influence.

EISENSTEIN (ī'senstīn), **Sergei Mikhailovich** (1898–1948). Soviet film director. A pioneer in the use of editing techniques, notably montage (as a means of propaganda) in *The Battleship Potemkin* (1925), he was also noted for his costume dramas (with his own designs), and won the Order of Lenin in 1938 with *Alexander Nevsky*, the 1st part of a planned but uncompleted trilogy. The 2nd part, *Ivan the Terrible* (1944), was banned in Russia. He is also famous for his beautiful sense of composition.

EISTEDDFOD (īstedh'vod) (Welsh, 'sitting'). Traditional Welsh gathering for the encouragement of the bardic arts of music, poetry, literature, etc. The E. traditionally dates from pre-Christian times, but it was discontinued from the late 17th until the beginning of the 19th cent., since when it has been held annually. The meetings last 3–4 days. Musical and literary contests take place, prizes, medals, and bardic degrees being awarded. The culminating ceremony is that of the 'chairing' of the bard.

EKATERINBURG. Pre-revolutionary name of SVERDLOVSK.

EKATERINODAR. Pre-revolutionary name of KRASNODAR.

EKATERINOSLAV. Pre-revolutionary name of DNEPROPETROVSK.

EKISTICS (Gk. *oikos*, home). The science of human settlements, a term coined by C. A. Doxiadis (q.v.). It involves the full inter-relationship of man and his environment by the co-operation of architect, engineer, town-planner, sociologist, economist, etc.

E'LAND. S. African antelope (*Taurotragus oryx*). Pale fawn in colour, it is about 6 ft. high, and both sexes have spiral horns about 18 in. long.

ELASTICITY. The property possessed by a body of automatically recovering its original shape when deforming forces are removed. There are several types of E. According to Hooke's law for an elastic solid, the stress set up within the body is proportional to the strain to which it is subjected. Stress is measured as a force per unit area and strain as the change in length per unit length. The ratio of stress to strain is called the modulus of E., and the value of the stress at which the material ceases to obey Hooke's law is called the elastic limit.

ELATH. See EILAT.

ELBA. Rugged island in the Mediterranean Sea, 6 m. off the W. coast of Italy. Iron ore is exported from Portoferraio, the capital, to the Italian mainland, and there is fishing. E. was the place of exile of Napoleon 1814–15. Area 86 sq. m.; pop. (est.) 30,000. *See* illus. p. 378.

ELBE. One of the principal rivers of Germany, rising on the S. slopes of the Riesengebirge in Czechoslovakia, and flowing generally N.W. across the German plain to the North Sea. It is 725 m. long.

ELBERFELD. See WUPPERTAL.

ELBING. German form of ELBLAG.

ELBLAG. Polish river port 7 m. from the mouth of the r. E. which debouches into the Zalew Wislany (Frisches Haff). It has shipyards, engineering works, car and tractor factories, etc. Pop. 76,000.

EKISTICS. Designed by Doxiadis (q.v.), the Graduate School of Ekistics of the Athens Technological Institute was estab. at the foot of Mount Lycabettus in 1958, and has an international student body. In the background is the headquarters of Doxiadis Associates. *Courtesy of Doxiadis Associates.*

ELBA. Picturesque Porto Azurro, one of the unspoilt fishing villages on the island that was Napoleon's kingdom 5 May 1814 to 26 Feb. 1815.   *Courtesy of the Italian State Tourist Office.*

ELBRUZ. Highest mt. in Europe, 18,467 ft., in the Caucasus, Georgia S.S.R.

ELBURZ. Volcanic mt. range in N.W. Persia, close to the S. shore of the Caspian, rising in Mt. Demavend to 18,500 ft.

ELDER. In the Presbyterian Church the Es. or ruling Es. are laymen who assist the minister (or teaching E.) in the government of the church.

ELDER. Genus of small trees or shrubs (*Sambucus*) of the family Caprifoliaceae. The common *S. nigra*, found in Europe, N. Africa, and W. Asia, has a smooth bark, pinnate leaves, and in early summer bears heavy heads of small, sweet-scented, white flowers, which are succeeded by clusters of small, black berries. The most handsome species, the scarlet-berried *S. racemosa*, is found in parts of Europe, Asia and N. America.

ELDON, John Scott, 1st earl of E. (1751–1838), British Lord Chancellor. B. at Newcastle, he became an M.P. in 1782, and was Lord Chancellor in 1801–6 and 1807–27, during which period the rules governing the use of the injunction and precedent in Equity finally became fixed.

ELEANOR (el'anor) **OF AQUITAINE** (c. 1122–1204). Queen of Henry II of England. The dau. of the duke of Aquitaine, she m. Louis VII of France in 1137, but the marriage was annulled on grounds of consanguinity in 1151, and she shortly after m. Henry of Anjou, who in 1154 became king of England as Henry II.

ELEANOR OF CASTILE (d. 1290). Queen of Edward I of England. The dau. of Ferdinand III of Castile, she m. Prince Edward in 1254, and accompanied him on his crusade in 1270. She d. at Harby, Notts.

ELECTORS. The seven German princes who elected the emperor from the 13th cent. until the dissolution of the Holy Roman Empire in 1806. These were commonly the archbishops of Mainz, Cologne, and Trier, the king of Bohemia, the duke of Saxony, the margrave of Brandenburg, and the palatine of the Rhine.

ELECTRICAL ENGINEERING. Branch of engineering concerned with the electrical industry, embracing all aspects of electrical technology incl. radio and electronics.

ELECTRIC FISH. Name given to certain fish that have electricity-producing powers. The best-known example is the S. American *Electrophorus electricus*, in which the lateral tail muscles are modified to form electric organs; current passing from tail to head is strong enough to stun another animal.

ELECTRICITY. The fundamental constituent of matter. A general term used for all phenomena caused by electric charge whether static or in motion. The fact that amber has the power, after being rubbed, of attracting light objects, such as bits of straw and feather, is said to have been known to Thales of Miletus (600 B.C.) and to Pliny (A.D. 70). In his studies on these attractions, William Gilbert (1544–1603), Queen Elizabeth I's physician, found that many substances possess this power, and he called it electric after the Greek word meaning amber. The attracting power may be transferred by contact from one body to another by conductors, such as metals. On the other hand, paraffin wax, hard rubber and dry glass do not transmit the power, and are called insulators. It was not until the early 1700s that 2 types of E. were recognized, and that unlike kinds attract each other and like kinds repel. The charge on glass rubbed with silk came to be known as positive E., and the charge on amber rubbed with wool as negative E. These two charges were found to annul one another when brought together. In 1800, Volta found that a series of little cells containing brine, in which were dipped plates of zinc and copper, gave an

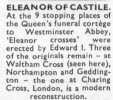

ELEANOR OF CASTILE. At the 9 stopping places of the Queen's funeral cortège to Westminster Abbey, 'Eleanor crosses' were erected by Edward I. Three of the originals remain – at Waltham Cross (seen here), Northampton and Geddington – the one at Charing Cross, London, is a modern reconstruction.

electric current, which later in the same year was shown to evolve hydrogen and oxygen when passed through water (known as electrolysis). Humphry Davy, in 1807, decomposed soda and potash, both thought to be elements, and separated the metals sodium and potassium; a discovery which led the way to electro-plating (q.v.). Other properties of electric currents discovered were the heating effect, now used in lighting and warming our homes, and the deflection of a magnetic needle, described by Oersted in 1820 and elaborated by Ampère in 1825. This work made possible the electric telegraph. For Michael Faraday the fact that an electric current passing through a wire caused a magnet to move suggested that moving a wire or coil of wire rapidly between the poles of a magnet would induce an

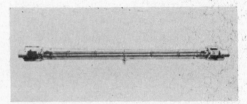

ELECTRICITY. The tungsten iodine lamp developed in the 1960s has double the life of conventional designs, since evaporated tungsten from the filament is redeposited by a reversible chemical reaction with iodine added to the gas filling. It also gives 15 per cent more light.
Courtesy of The British Lighting Council Ltd.

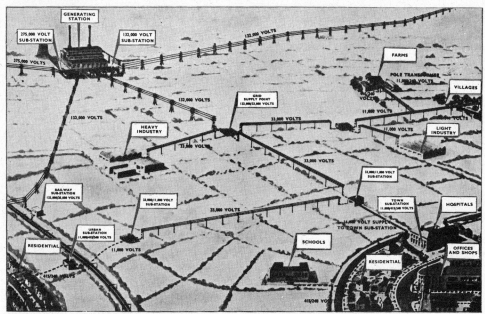

ELECTRICITY. Pressure must be varied to suit the needs of the area by transformers at the primary and secondary sub-stations, and ranges from the 33,000 volts required by heavy industry to the domestic 230/250 volts.

Courtesy of the Central Electricity Generating Board.

electric current. He did this in 1831, producing the first dynamo, afterwards the basis of electrical engineering. The characteristics of currents were crystallized by G. S. Ohm (*c.* 1827) who showed that the current passing along a wire was equal to the electromotive force (e.m.f., or driving press.) across the wire multiplied by a constant, which was the conductivity of the wire. The unit of resistance is named after Ohm, e.m.f. is named after Volta (volt), and current after Ampère (amp). The work of the late 1800s indicated the wide interconnections of E. (with magnetism, heat and light), and the discovery by J. Clerk Maxwell (*c.* 1855) of a single electromagnetic theory explaining both electric waves and light. The universal importance of E. was decisively proved, by the connection between atoms and E. The structure of the atom itself, hitherto thought to be the ultimate particle of matter, was found to be composed of a positively charged central core, the nucleus, about which negatively charged electrons rotate in various orbits. E. generated on a commercial scale was available from the early 1880s and used for electric motors driving all kinds of machinery; for lighting, by carbon arc, but later by incandescent filaments, first of carbon and then of tungsten, enclosed in glass bulbs partially filled with inert gas under vacuum. Light is also produced by passing E. through a gas or metal vapour, or a fluorescent lamp. Other practical applications include telephone, radio, television, X-ray machines, etc.

ELECTRICITY SUPPLY. The principal energy sources for E. generation are coal, water power, oil and natural gas, with contributions from wind power, geothermal power and. increasingly, nuclear energy. E. is generated as alternating current, usually in large turbo-alternators, because of the ease of changing the voltage (that is, 'pressure') for transmission and distribution. *See* RANCE.

Britain has one of the world's largest inter-connected E.S. systems, comprising large power stations feeding into a national grid: highest voltage 400,000. Coal, formerly the main fuel, was uneconomic by 1967 and being replaced by ever cheaper nuclear fuel. Elsewhere there are co-ordinated systems through transmission links, involving for example power pools of groups of undertakings in the U.S.A., and inter-country connections on the continent of Europe. Among specialized power units which convert energy directly to electrical energy without the intervention of any moving mechanisms, the most promising are thermionic converters. These may use conventional fuels such as propane gas, as in portable military power packs, or, when refuelling is to be avoided, expensive radioactive fuels, as in unmanned navigational aids, and spacecraft. *See* illus. p. 662.

ELECTROCA′RDIOGRAM. A recording on a chart of the electrical impulses from the heart, used to diagnose heart conditions, e.g. heart attacks.

ELECTROCUTION. Popular name for a method of execution in use in many of the states of the U.S.A. The criminal is strapped in a special electric

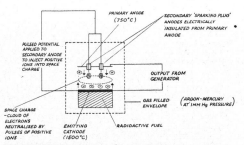

ELECTRICITY. Simplified general diagram illustrating the theory of a thermionic conversion triode using radioactive fuel.

Courtesy of the Fairey Co. Ltd

N

chair and an electric shock at 1,800–2,000 v. administered.

ELE'CTRŎDE. A conductor by means of which a current passes into or out of a substance, e.g. the electrodes of an electrolytic cell, an electric furnace, a discharge-tube, or a radio valve. The term is also applied to conducting elements separated by an insulating material as in a capacitor. *See also* ANODE and CATHODE.

ELECTRO-ENCEPHALO'GRAPHY. In E.-E. electrodes are fixed to the scalp and by means of electronic apparatus the electrical discharges of the brain can be studied. It is used in studying and diagnosing conditions in the brain, such as epilepsy and tumours.

ELECTRO'LYSIS. The production of chemical changes by ionic migration and discharge. Certain compounds, principally acids, bases, and salts, are decomposed by the passage of an electric current. Its most important application is in electro-plating.

ELE'CTROLYTE. A conducting medium or solution in which the electric current flows by virtue of chemical changes or decomposition and the consequent movement and discharge of ions in accordance with Faraday's laws of electrolysis (q.v.). The term E. is frequently used to denote a substance which, when dissolved in a specified solvent, produces a conducting medium. The term 'ionogen' has been suggested as an alternative to the term E. when used with this meaning.

ELECTROMAGNETIC INDUCTION. The production of an electromotive force in a circuit by a change of magnetic flux through the circuit. The e.m.f. so produced is known as an induced e.m.f., and any current that may result therefrom as an induced current. If the change of magnetic flux is due to a variation in the current flowing in the same circuit the phenomenon is known as self-induction; if due to a change of current flowing in another circuit, as mutual induction.

ELECTROMAGNETIC SYSTEM OF UNITS. A system of absolute electrical units (e.m.u.) based on the c.g.s. system (q.v.) and having, as its primary electrical unit, the unit magnetic pole. It involves the choice of the permeability of free space as a fourth fundamental unit.

ELECTROMAGNETIC WAVES. The 'waves' which occur in the natural process by which electric and magnetic effects are propagated. Electromagnetic waves are known as radio-waves, heat rays, infra-red rays, light, ultra-violet rays, X-rays, etc., depending on their frequencies.

ELECTROMOTIVE FORCE. That force (e.m.f.) which tends to cause a movement of electricity in a circuit. The electrical condition for generating electromagnetic energy by the transfer of electricity in a certain direction. It is measured by the amount of energy generated by the transfer of unit quantity of positive electricity in that direction. This direction is called the direction of e.m.f.

The e.m.f. in a circuit is the excess of the sum of the e.m.fs. of its constituent parts in one direction over the sum of those in the other direction. Symbol E or V. Practical unit: volt.

ELECTRON. An elementary particle containing the smallest known negative electric charge ($4\cdot803 \times 10^{-10}$ e.s.u.) and having a mass of $9\cdot11 \times 10^{-28}$ gram at rest.

ELECTRON GUN. A structure comprising a cathode and one or more electrodes for producing an electron beam. It is an essential part of many electronic devices such as cathode-ray tubes (television tubes), electron microscopes, etc.

ELECTRONICS. The branch of science which deals with the emission of electrons from conductors, with the subsequent motion of these electrons, and with the construction of electronic devices. From

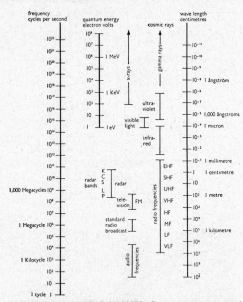

ELECTROMAGNETIC WAVES. Frequency spectrum of radiations from the sub-audible long waves (*bottom*), to the short wave cosmic rays (*top*).
Courtesy of Penguin Books from A Dictionary of Electronics *by S. Handel.*

1940 E. developed at an enormous rate due to the war-time need for radar (q.v.), and this impetus was maintained after the S.W.W. both for military and civil purposes. In the defence field E. forms an integral part of control and guidance systems for ballistic missiles, and methods for their detection, i.e. the Distant Early Warning system. Research into space requires the most advanced electronic techniques, for the control of artificial satellites from take-off to landing. In the civilian field E. played an integral part in the development of computers (q.v.). With the increasing complexity of electronic equipment there was an urgent need to save weight (in spacecraft) and bulk (in computers, etc.) which led to miniaturization. This has been possible due to the invention of the transistor (q.v.) and solid state circuitry (*see* SOLID CIRCUIT).

ELECTRON MICROSCOPE. An instrument similar to an optical microscope but using a beam of electrons instead of a beam of light, and electron instead of optical lenses. An electron lens is an electromagnetic or magnetic arrangement to control and focus the beam. Electrons are not visible to the naked eye, so instead of an eyepiece there is a fluorescent screen or a photographic plate on which the electrons are made to form an image. Since the wavelength associated with electrons is very much shorter than that of light much greater magnifications and resolutions are possible. Direct magnifications of 200,000 and total magnifications (after enlargement) of 3,000,000 have been achieved. The development of the E.M. has made possible the observation of very minute organisms, viruses, and even some molecules.

ELECTRON VOLT. A convenient unit for energy in atomic physics. It is the energy acquired by a particle carrying unit electronic charge when it falls through a potential difference of 1 volt, and is approximately equal to $1\cdot602 \times 10^{-12}$ erg.

ELECTRO-PLATING. The electro-deposition of metals upon metallic surfaces for decorative and/or

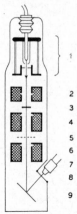

ELECTRON MICROSCOPE. A beam of electrons from the electron gun (q.v.) (1) pass through the electromagnetic lenses (2, 4, 6), and the whole microscope must be kept under high vacuum to allow free passage to these electrons. The condenser (2) concentrates the beam on the specimen (3), and the transmitted electrons are focussed by the objective (4) to form a magnified image on the intermediate screen (5) which is further enlarged by the projector (6). The electron image is projected on to the angled fluorescent viewing screen (9) converted to a visible image (as in a TV set) which the operator can view in the microscope (7) through the window (8).

protective purposes. A current is passed through a bath containing a solution of a salt of the plating metal, the object to be plated being the cathode; the anode is either an inert substance or the plating metal. Among the metals most commonly used for plating are zinc, nickel, chromium, cadmium, copper, silver, and gold. E. is used in the preparation of printers' blocks, gramophone records, and in many other processes.

In electro-polishing the object to be polished is made the anode in an electrolytic solution and by carefully controlling the conditions the high spots on the surface are dissolved away leaving a high-quality stain-free surface. This technique is useful in polishing irregular stainless steel articles, etc. In electro-refining the impure metal is made the anode with a thin sheet of pure metal as the cathode in an electrolytic bath. When a current is passed pure metal deposits on the cathode, leaving the impurities either as an insoluble sludge or in solution.

ELECTROSTATICS. That branch of electricity which deals with the behaviour of stationary electric charges.

ELECTROSTATIC SYSTEM OF UNITS. A system of electrical units (e.s.u.) based on the c.g.s. system (q.v.), and having, as its primary electrical unit, the unit of quantity of charge. It involves the choice of the permittivity of free space as a fourth fundamental unit.

ELEMENTS. *See* CHEMISTRY, INORGANIC CHEMISTRY and individual elements.

ELEPHANT. Name given to the 2 surviving species of the Proboscidea, the Asiatic (*Elephas maximus*)

ELEPHANT. Traffic problems in Africa sometimes differ from those of the rest of the world, and when a family of elephants chooses to cross the road in Kruger National Park they have absolute right of way.   *Courtesy of Satour.*

and African (*Elephas africanus*) Es. A full-grown E. is 8–10 ft. high, has a thick, grey, wrinkled skin, a large head, and a long trunk used to obtain food and water. The upper incisors or tusks, which grow to a considerable length, are a source of ivory. The African E. has very large ears and a convex forehead, and the Indian species has smaller ears and a flattened forehead. Es. are herbivorous, and live in herds. With a reputation for intelligence, the E. is quickly tamed, and in India, Burma and Siam is widely used for transport. The period of gestation is about 19–22 months (the longest amongst mammals) and the life span is probably about 60–70 yrs. Es. do not breed readily in captivity, and this, together with the (now illegal) slaughter of African Es. for ivory, is leading to their extinction.

ELEPHANTI'ASIS. In the human body, a gross local enlargement and deformity, especially of a leg, the scrotum, a labium of the vulva, or a breast. The commonest is the tropical variety due to infestation by the parasite filaria; the enlargement is due to chronic blocking of the lymph channels and consequent overgrowth of the skin and tissues.

ELEUSIS (elū'sis). Greek town in Attica nome, 11 m. N.W. of Athens, on E. Bay, with shipyards, olive-oil presses, cement and soap works, etc.; one of the oldest towns in Greece, with a famous temple of Demeter. Pop. 11,000.

EL FERROL DEL CAUDILLO. *See* FERROL.

ELGAR, Sir Edward (1857–1934). British composer. B. in Broadheath, Worcs., the son of an R.C. church organist and music-seller, E. had little formal musical education and he gained his first experience in conducting when appointed bandmaster of the staff of a lunatic asylum in 1879. He gained fame as a composer with his *Enigma* variations in 1899, and although his most celebrated work, the magnificent oratorio setting of Newman's *The Dream of Gerontius*, was a failure when performed in Birmingham the following year, it was a great success at Düsseldorf in 1902. Many of his earlier and hitherto unknown works were then performed and are now well known, incl. the popular *Pomp and Circumstance* marches. He was knighted in 1904, and became Master of the King's Musick in 1924. Among his later works are several oratorios, 2 symphonies, chamber music, songs and the tone-poem *Falstaff*.

SIR EDWARD ELGAR. Bust by P. Hedley, 1927. *Photo: N.P.G.*

ELGIN (el'gin). Scottish royal burgh and city, co. town of Moray, on the r. Lossie, with woollen mills, sawmills, whisky distilleries, etc. Pop. (1961) 11,971.

ELGIN MARBLES. Collection of ancient Greek sculptures mainly from the Parthenon at Athens, assembled by the 7th earl of Elgin. Sent to England in 1812, bought for the nation in 1816 for £35,000, they are now in the British Museum. *See* illus. p. 382.

ELGINSHIRE. Name until 1920 of MORAYSHIRE.

ELIJAH (elī'jah). Hebrew prophet during the reigns of Ahab and Ahaziah (*c.* mid-9th cent. B.C.). A native of Gilead and representative of Jehovah, he defeated the prophets of Baal, and was said to have been borne up to heaven in a fiery chariot in a whirlwind.

ELIOT, Charles William (1834–1926). American educator. B. in Boston, he was president of Harvard 1869–1909, and was mainly responsible for making it the leading establishment of higher learning in U.S.A.

ELIOT, George. Pseudonym of the British writer

ELGIN MARBLES. Housed in a gallery specially built, and opened in 1963, the marbles include this panel from the Parthenon frieze showing horsemen in the annual Panathenaic procession to the shrine of Athene in celebration of the union of Attica under Theseus.   *Photo: British Museum.*

Mary Ann Evans (1819–80). B. at Chilvers Coton, Warwicks, she received a strictly evangelical upbringing, but on moving to Coventry with her father in 1841 was converted to free thinking. In 1844 she undertook a translation of Strauss's *Leben Jesu*, and in 1850 began contributing to the *Westminster Review*, of which she became assistant editor under John Chapman 1851–3. At this period she made the acquaintance of Carlyle, Harriet Martineau, Herbert Spencer, and George Henry Lewes. Lewes was married but separated from his wife, and in 1854 E. entered upon a union with him which she regarded as a true marriage and which continued until his death. With Lewes' encouragement she pub. 'Amos Barton', the first of the *Scenes of Clerical Life*, in 1857 under the name of George Eliot. These were successful, and in the following years she won fame with *Adam Bede*, which like its successors, *Mill on the Floss* (1860) and *Silas Marner* (1861), was set in her native county. Less happy were *Romola* (1863), dealing with 15th cent. Italy, and *Felix Holt, the Radical* (1866), which entered the political field. Her next novel, *Middlemarch* (1872), returned to a Warwicks background and is now recognized as E.'s finest work and one of the greatest novels of the cent. Her final work, *Daniel Deronda* (1876), an impassioned plea against anti-semitism, tends to lose itself in obscurity. She also wrote some poetry. In 1880 she m. her old friend John Cross (1840–1924). *See* illus. p. 394.

ELIOT, Sir John (1592–1632). English statesman. B. in Cornwall, he became an M.P. in 1614, a vice-admiral, through Buckingham's patronage, in 1619, and in 1626 was sent to the Tower for demanding Buckingham's impeachment. In 1628 he was primarily responsible for the Petition of Right, and with other parliamentary leaders was imprisoned in the Tower in 1629, where, refusing to submit, he died.

ELIOT, Thomas Stearns (1888–1965). American-

born poet and critic; a British subject since 1927. B. at St. Louis, Missouri, he was ed. at Harvard, Paris, and Oxford. He settled in London in 1915 and was for a time a bank clerk, later lecturing and entering publishing. In 1917 E.'s first book of verse, *Prufrock and other Observations*, caused a sensation by its daringly experimental verse form and rhythms. His reputation was estab. by the desolate modernity of *The Waste Land* (1922). *The Hollow Men* (1925)

T. S. ELIOT
Photo: Angus McBean.

renewed the same note, but *Ash-Wednesday* (1930) revealed the change in religious attitude which led him to become an Anglo-Catholic. Among his other works are *Four Quartets* (1944), a religious sequence in which he seeks the eternal reality, and the poetic dramas *Murder in the Cathedral* (1935), *The Cocktail Party* (1949), *The Confidential Clerk* (1953), and *The Elder Statesman* (1958). In 1948 he received the O.M. and a Nobel prize: Medal of Freedom 1964.

ÉLISABETHVILLE. Town of the rep. of Congo (cap. Kinshasa), cap. of the prov. of S. Katanga, and centre of a great copper- and uranium-mining region. It was re-named Lubumbashi 1966. Pop. (est.) 130,000.

ELI'SHA. Hebrew prophet, the successor of Elijah in the mid-9th cent., B.C.

ELIZABETH I (1533–1603). Queen of England. The dau. of Henry VIII and Anne Boleyn, she was b. at Greenwich on Sept. 7, 1533. In Mary's reign her Protestant sympathies brought her under suspicion, and she lived in retirement at Hatfield until in Nov. 1558 she became queen. Her first task was to bring about a religious settlement sufficiently broad to exclude any extremists.

ELIZABETH I. Her court painter, Marcus Gheeraerts (1561–1635), shows the Queen, splendidly triumphant, before representations of the Armada, which is storm-tossed and defeated, to the right. Gheeraerts was later also court painter to James I. *Courtesy of the Duke of Bedford: Woburn Collection.*

Many unsuccessful attempts were made by Parliament to persuade E. to marry or settle the succession. Courtship she found a useful diplomatic weapon, and she sought emotional relief in flirtation with a succession of favourites, among them Leicester, Raleigh, and Essex.

The arrival in England in 1568 of Mary, Queen of Scots, and her imprisonment by E. caused a political crisis and a rebellion of the feudal nobility of the N. followed in 1569. Friction between English and Spanish seamen hastened the breach with Spain. When the Dutch rebelled against Spanish tyranny E. secretly encouraged them; Philip II retaliated by aiding Catholic conspiracies against her. This undeclared war continued for many years, until the landing of an English army in the Netherlands in 1585, and Mary's execution in 1587, brought it into the open. Philip's Armada, in 1588, met with total disaster.

The war with Spain continued with varying fortunes to the end of the reign, while events at home foreshadowed the conflicts of the 17th cent. Among the Puritans discontent was developing with E.'s religious settlement; and several were imprisoned and executed. Parliament showed a new independence, and in 1601 forced E. to retreat on the monopolies

Her Majesty Queen Elizabeth the Second.
Photo: Baron Studios.

question. Yet her prestige remained unabated, as was shown by the failure of Essex's rebellion in 1601.

ELIZABETH II (1926–   ). Queen of the U.K. The elder dau. of King George VI, Princess Elizabeth Alexandra Mary was b. at 17 Bruton Street, London, W.1., the home of her maternal grandparents, on April 21, 1926. She was ed. privately, and although she became heiress presumptive to the throne on King George's accession did not undertake any official duties until she was 16. During the S.W.W. she served in the A.T.S., and by an amendment to the Regency Act she became a State Counsellor on her 18th birthday, acting in this capacity during the King's visit to Italy in 1944. She m. her third cousin, the Duke of Edinburgh (*see* PHILIP), in Westminster Abbey on Nov. 20, 1947, and they have 4 children, Prince Charles Philip Arthur George, b. Nov. 14, 1948, Princess Anne Elizabeth Alice Louise, b. Aug. 15, 1950, Prince Andrew Albert Christian Edward, b. Feb. 19, 1960, and Prince Edward Antony Richard Louis, b. March 10, 1964. On the death of George VI in 1952 she succeeded to the throne while in Kenya with her husband at the beginning of a projected tour of Ceylon, Australia and N.Z. Since the Coronation in 1953 they have made a number of goodwill tours – in the Commonwealth, the U.S.A., etc. – with great success.

ELIZABETH (1900–   ). Consort of George VI. Born the Lady Elizabeth Angela Marguerite Bowes-Lyon, she is the 3rd dau. of the 14th Earl of Strathmore and Kinghorne (d. 1944), through whom she is descended from King Robert Bruce. Ed. privately, she spent most of her early life at her birthplace at her father's Scottish seat, Glamis Castle, Angus. On April 26, 1923, she m. Albert duke of York and their 2 children, Queen Elizabeth II and Princess Margaret [Rose], were b. in 1926 and 1930 respectively. When her husband ascended the throne as King George VI in 1936 she became Queen Consort, and was crowned with him in 1937. She adopted the style Queen Mother after his death.

ELIZABETH (1709–62). Empress of Russia. Dau. of Peter the Great, she carried through a palace revolution in 1741 and supplanted her cousin, the infant Ivan VI, on the throne. She possessed much of her father's energy and statesmanship, continued his policy of westernization, and allied herself with Austria against Prussia.

ELIZABETH (1843–1916). Queen of Rumania, consort of Carol I. Under the pen-name 'Carmen Sylva' she pub. many vols. of romances, verse, etc.

ELIZABETH. City in New Jersey, U.S.A., the first English settlement in N.J., 1664. It has motor-car and tool factories, oil refineries, chemical works, etc. Pop. (1960) 107,698.

ELIZAVETPOL. Former name of KIROVABAD.

ELK. Largest deer (*Alces alces*) inhabiting N. Europe, Asia, Scandinavia, and America, where it is known as the moose. It is brown in colour, stands about 6 ft. high at the shoulders, has very large palmate antlers, a fleshy muzzle, short neck, and long legs; and feeds on leaves and shoots.

ELKINGTON, George Richards (1801–65). Founder of the British electro-plating industry. B. in Birmingham, he inherited his uncles' silver-plating business there, and in partnership with his cousin, Henry E., developed commercially the application of electricity to metals.

ELLERMAN, Sir John Reeves (1862–1933). British ship-owner. B. at Hull, he formed the Ellerman line in 1901, which subsequently embraced shipping interests all over the world. He was created a bart. in 1905. His son, also **Sir John Reeves E.** (1909–   ), is a world authority on rodents.

ELLESMERE PORT. English town (bor.) on the Mersey and the Manchester Ship Canal, a petroleum importing and refining centre. Pop. (1961) 44,714.

ELLICE ISLANDS. *See* GILBERT AND ELLICE ISLANDS.

ELLINGTON, Edward Kennedy (1899–   ). American instrumentalist and composer, known as 'Duke' E. B. in Washington of part Negro origin, he became a pianist at night clubs and restaurants before forming his own band. Later he became one of the world's most famous composers of jazz. His works incl. *Creole Rhapsody* (1931) and *Black and Tan Fantasy* (1938).

ELLIPSE (eli′ps). In geometry, a closed curve which is the locus of a point which moves so that the sum of its distances from 2 fixed points, the foci, is constant. The diameter passing through the foci is

ELK

the major axis, and the diameter bisecting this at right angles is the minor axis.

ELLIS, Henry Havelock (1859–1939). British writer and sexologist. B. in Surrey, he studied medicine in London, spent 4 years as a schoolteacher in Australia, and later returned to England and qualified as a doctor. After only a short time in general practice he turned his attention to literary and scientific work. He is chiefly famous as the author of many works on the psychology of sex, incl. *Studies in the Psychology of Sex* (7 vols., 1898–1928), but he was also a literary critic and essayist of note.

ELLIS, Mary (1900–   ). American actress and vocalist. B. in New York, she first appeared on the stage in 1918, and made her reputation in a wide range of N.Y. productions, incl. *The Blue Bird* (1919) and *Rose Marie* (1924), in which she created the title role. She has frequently appeared in London – notably in *The Dancing Years* in 1939 and *Mourning Becomes Electra* (1955–6).

ELM, with flowers and fruit.

ELLIS, Vivian (1904–   ). British composer. He studied the piano under Myra Hess and composition at the R.A.M. and began his career as a concert pianist. Among his successes were the music for A. P. Herbert's *Bless the Bride* (1947) and *Water Gipsies* (1955), and the music and lyrics for *And So to Bed* (1951). He has also composed film music and songs.

ELLO'RA. Archaeological site in the N.-W. Deccan, Maharashtra State, India, with 35 cave temples – Buddhist, Hindu and Jain – varying in date from the late 6th cent. to the 9th cent. They incl. some of the greatest of India's architectural treasures: Visvakarma (an assembly hall *c.* 86 ft. long with a huge image of the Buddha), Tin Thal (a 3-storeyed Buddhist monastery cave), the Ramesvara cave (with beautiful sculptures) and Siva's Paradise, the great temple of Kailasa.

ELLSWORTH, Lincoln (1889–1951). American explorer. With Amundsen and Nobile he flew the dirigible *Norge* from Spitzbergen to Alaska in 1926, and in 1931 joined Wilkins in a trans-Arctic submarine expedition. He also made important flights into the Antarctic in 1935 and 1939.

ELM. A common genus (*Ulmus*) of trees of the Ulmaceae family, distributed throughout the temperate latitudes of the N. hemisphere, and in mountainous parts of the tropics. The common European E. (*U. campestris*) is distributed widely throughout Europe, N. Africa and Asia Minor and may grow to 150 ft.; its small, purplish-brown flowers are borne in tufts and appear before the leaves. Other species are the Scotch or wych E. (*U. montana*) found in N. Britain, where it is indigenous, and the N. American white E. (*U. americana*) and red or slippery E. (*U. fulva*). The fungus disease *Ceratocystis ulmi*, which first appeared in the Netherlands, has greatly reduced the numbers of E. trees in Europe and N. America.

ELMAN, Mischa (1891–1967). American violinist. Russian by birth, he received his musical education at Odessa and St. Petersburg and made his first professional appearance at Berlin in 1904 and in London the following year. A romantic player, he was noted chiefly for his rendering of Tschaikowsky. E. became American in 1923.

EL PASO (pah'soh). City of Texas, U.S.A., on the Rio Grande, at the foot of Mt. Franklin (7,100 ft.); it is the centre of a prosperous agricultural, mining, and cattle-raising area. Pop. (1960) 276,687.

ELPHINSTONE (el'finstōn), **William** (1431–1514). Scottish statesman and churchman. B. at Glasgow, he became bishop of Ross in 1481, held high ministerial posts, and estab. Aberdeen university in 1494.

EL SALVADOR *See* SALVADOR, EL.

ELSIE, Lily (1886–1962). English actress B. in London, she appeared in many pantomimes and light comedies on the English stage, notably in *A Chinese Honeymoon* in 1902, and as Sonia in *The Merry Widow* in 1907.

ELSINORE. Another form of HELSINGÖR.

ELSSLER, Fanny (1810–84). Austrian dancer, b. in Vienna. She and her sister, **Thérèse E.** (1808–78), were trained for the ballet at Naples. They usually danced together, and achieved an immense triumph in Berlin in 1830, and later appeared in other European capitals and in the U.S.A. Fanny m. a banker in 1851; Thérèse m. Prince Adalbert of Prussia.

ÉLUARD (ehlü-ard'), **Paul.** Pseudonym of the French poet Eugène Grindel (1895–1952). B. in Paris of working-class parents, he expressed the suffering poverty of the people in his verse, and was a leader of the Surrealists. He fought in the F.W.W. which inspired his *Poèmes pour la Paix* (1918), and was a member of the Resistance in the S.W.W. His other vols. incl. *Chanson complète, Au Rendezvous Allemand* and *Un Leçon de morale.*

ELVIN, Violetta (1925–   ). American ballerina. B. in Russia as Violetta Prokhorova, she was ed. at the Bolshoi Theatre School. She was prima ballerina with the Royal Ballet 1951–6, and has made such films as *The Queen of Spades.*

ELWES (el'wez), **Simon** (1902–   ). British portrait painter. He studied at the Slade and in Paris, and later became a successful portrait painter in England and the U.S.A. An official war artist in the S.W.W., he painted portraits of F.Ms. Sir William Slim, Smuts, and Lord Wavell.

ELY. City in Cambs on the Ouse, 15 m. N.N.E. of Cambridge. It was chief town of the former admin. co. of the Isle of E. The cathedral, which dates from the 11th cent., is one of the largest in England. E. is an agricultural town with beet-sugar works. Pop. (1961) 9,815.

ELY, Isle of. A former administrative co. of England, in the geographical co. of Cambs (q.v.), with which it was linked from 1964.

ELYOT, Sir Thomas (*c.* 1490–1546). English diplomat and scholar. In 1523 he was made clerk to the Privy Council by Wolsey, and in 1531 pub. *The Governour*, the first treatise on education in English.

ÉLYSÉE (ālēzā'), **Palace of the.** Building in Paris

ELY. The cruciform cathedral is seen from the bishop's garden to the south-east. Its 215 ft. octagonal tower, with partially detached side turrets, was designed by Alan of Walsingham, the sacrist 1322–8, to replace a Norman structure which collapsed in 1322.   *Photo: A. W. Kerr*

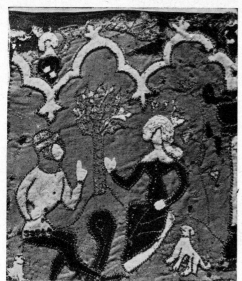

EMBROIDERY. A French 14th cent. embroidered wall-hanging, illustrating the story of Tristram and Iseult.
Courtesy of the Victoria and Albert Museum.

erected in 1718 for Louis d'Auvergne, count of Evreux. It was later the home of Mme de Pompadour, Napoleon I and Napoleon III, and in 1870 became the official residence of the presidents of France.

ELYSIUM (ili'zium), or the **Elysian Fields**. In classical mythology, a paradise (sometimes called the Islands of the Blessed) for those who found favour with the gods; it was situated near the r. Oceanus.

ELZEVIR (el'zevēr). Dutch printing house of the 17th cent., founded by **Louis E.** (1540–1617), b. at Louvain. Obliged to leave Belgium in 1580 on account of his Protestant and political views, he settled at Leyden as a bookseller and printer. Of his 7 sons, 5 went into the printing business. Among the firm's publications were editions of Latin, Greek, and Hebrew works, French and Italian classics, etc.

EMBA. River, 380 m. long, in the Kazakh S.S.R., Russia, draining into the N. part of the Caspian Sea. It flows through country rich in petroleum.

EMBROIDERY. The art of decoration by means of a needle and thread. Ancient Egypt, Greece, Phrygia, Babylon, and China were renowned for their E. There are many references to such work in the Bible. The earliest Anglo-Saxon work extant is the stole and maniple found in the tomb of St. Cuthbert at Durham (A.D. 905). E. has been used for the adornment of costumes, gloves, book covers, curtains, ecclesiastical vestments, etc. In Britain, early in the 20th cent., E. on canvas and linen for household purposes, together with appliqué, was popular.

EMBRYO'LOGY. The study of the changes undergone by living matter in the early life-history or ontogeny of a new individual, during the period in which it acquires the adult form of its species.

EMDEN. Port of Germany at the mouth of the r. Ems. Connected with the Ruhr by the Dortmund-Ems canal, E. became an importer of Scandinavian iron ore and timber, exporting Ruhr coal. Pop. (1966) 43,000.

E'MERALD. A precious stone, a bright, grass-green variety of beryl. It is transparent or translucent, and the finest come from Muzo, in Columbia. *See* RUBY.

EMERGENCE, or **Emergent Evolution.** Philosophical theory, propounded in the 20th cent. by C. Lloyd Morgan, S. Alexander, and C. D. Broad, who maintain that life 'emerges' or 'grows naturally' out of matter, and mind emerges out of life.

E'MERSON, Ralph Waldo (1803–82). American poet and essayist. B. at Boston, Mass., and ed. at Harvard, he became a Unitarian minister at Boston. In 1832 he resigned and went abroad, meeting Carlyle, who had a deep and lasting influence on his thought. On his return to America in 1833 he settled at Concord, where he led the Transcendentalists. He made a second visit to England in 1847, and incorporated his impressions in *English Traits* (1856). This had been preceded by two vols. of *Essays* (1841, 1844), and *Representative Men* (1850). Later works incl. *The Conduct of Life* (1860), *Society and Solitude* (1870), and *Letters and Social Aims* (1876). His verse (1847 and 1864) is remarkable for its quality of thought, and as a prose-writer E. possessed a brilliant and clear style.

EMERY, Walter Bryan (1903–71). British archaeologist. As director of the Egyptian Govt. survey of Nubia 1929–34, he made outstanding discoveries at Ballana and Qustol, and as field director of the Egypt Exploration Soc. from 1952 supervised the final survey of the country before it was flooded by the Nile waters following construction of the Aswan High Dam 1963–4. He was Edwards prof. of Egyptology, London, 1951–70, and d. while excavating the site of the tomb and temple of Imhotep (q.v.) at Sakkara. He pub. *Egypt in Nubia* (1965) etc.

E'MERY. A variety of corundum (q.v.), greyish-black and opaque, and containing a quantity of haematite and magnetite. Its hardness is second only to the diamond's, and it is much used as an abrasive.

ÉMINENCE GRISE (ehmēnoñs' grēz; Fr., 'grey eminence'). Name given to the Capuchin friar François Leclerc du Tremblay (1577–1638), who from 1612 was the intimate friend and adviser of Richelieu. Always he worked behind the scenes, and since his time the term *éminence grise* has been applied to other manipulators of power without immediate responsibility. He was also known as Père Joseph.

EMMET, Robert (1778–1803). Irish patriot. In 1803 he led an unsuccessful revolt in Dublin, was captured, tried, and hanged. His youth and courage have made him the best-loved of Ireland's heroes.

EMPE'DOCLES (c. 490–430 B.C.). Greek philosopher and scientist. He lived at Acragas (Agrigentum) in Sicily, and is famous for his analysis of the universe into the 4 elements – fire, air, earth, and water – which through the action of love and discord are eternally constructed, destroyed, and constructed anew. According to tradition, he committed suicide by throwing himself into the crater of Mt. Etna.

EMPI'RICISM (-isizm). Philosophical theory which maintains that all human knowledge is based ultimately on sense experience (Gk. *empeiria*, experience or experiment). It is the opposite of intuitionalism.

R. W. EMERSON
Photo: Concord Antiquarian Society, Mass.

EMPLOYERS' ASSOCIATIONS. Employers' organisations formed for purposes of collective action. In the U.K. there were formerly 3 main organizations, which in 1965 combined as the Confederation of British Industry (q.v.); one of the largest in the U.S.A. is the National Assoc. of Manufacturers.

EMPLOYMENT EXCHANGES. Agencies for

bringing together employers requiring labour and workers seeking employment. In the U.K. these may be organized by the State or a local authority, or as a business venture; a similar system operates in the U.S.A. Following the recommendations of the royal commission in England on the Poor Laws, a national system was estab. by the Labour Exchanges Act of 1909; this was originally controlled by the Board of Trade, but in 1917 control was transferred to the Ministry of Labour. When unemployment insurance was introduced in 1912 its administration was entrusted to the E.Es., which also became responsible during and after the S.W.W. for the registration of men and women for national service.

EMPSON, William (1906–). English poet. B. in Yorks, he has been prof. of English literature at Tokyo, Peking and from 1953 at Sheffield. His verse, *Collected Poems* (1955), is obscure and he has pub. unusual critical studies, e.g. *Seven Types of Ambiguity* (1930) and *The Structure of Complex Words* (1951).

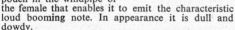

EMU (ē′mu). Bird of the *Dromaeidae* family of the *Ratitae* type. With the exception of the ostrich, the largest of living birds, it is found only in Australia and stands about 5 or 6 ft. high. The E. has small rudimentary wings, short feathers on the head and neck, and a curious bag or pouch in the windpipe of

EMU

the female that enables it to emit the characteristic loud booming note. In appearance it is dull and dowdy.

ENA′MEL. A vitrified substance used as a coating for pottery and porcelain; when transparent it is known as a 'glaze'. Also a vitreous substance of various colours used for decorative purposes on a metallic or porcelain surface. In *cloisonné* the various sections of the design are separated by thin metal wires or strips soldered to the metal base.

The art of enamelling dates back to ancient times, and is believed to be of Western Asiatic origin. The Egyptians, Greeks, and Romans enamelled their jewellery, and enamel-work dating from between the 6th and the 9th cents. has been found in the British Isles. Byzantium was famed for enamels from about the 9th to the 11th cents., the finest known work of this period being the famous altar-piece at St. Mark's, Venice, which was brought from Constantinople.

These were emulated in Europe, and some magnificent work was produced in Saxony, Brunswick, and in the Rhine valley. German enamellers were later employed in France, and during the 13th and 14th cents. the art was introduced into Italy. The chief centres of enamelling during the 15th and 16th cents. were the cities of Lorraine and Limoges. Enamelling was not introduced into China until about the 13th cent.

ENAMEL. The Castellain brooch in the British Museum, found in S. Italy and dated c. 600.

ENCAUSTIC PAINTING. A process of painting, commonly used in ancient times by the Egyptians, Greeks, and Romans, in which a medium consisting chiefly of wax was employed.

ENCKE (eng′keh), **Johann Franz** (1791–1865).

German astronomer. He was famed for his observations on comets, esp. the one of 1819 that bears his name, although it had been previously observed in 1786, 1795, and 1805.

ENCLOSURES. The conversion of common lands into private property, or the substitution of enclosed fields for the open-field system. This process, which has been almost entirely limited to England, began in the 14th cent. and became widespread in the 15th and 16th, the enclosed fields often being used for sheep-rearing. The distress thus caused led to serious rebellions in 1536, 1569, and 1607, while the numerous government measures against depopulation introduced during 1489–1640 were sabotaged by the land-owning J.Ps. A new wave of E. during 1760–1820 reduced the yeomanry to agricultural labourers, or drove them off the land. A reaction came after 1860, and in 1876 E. of commons was limited by statutes.

ENCYCLICAL (ensī′klikal). Ecclesiastical term, denoting a letter addressed by the Pope to all the bishops of the R.C. Church.

ENCYCLOPEDIA (ensiklope′dia). An alphabetical work of reference covering either the entire field of human knowledge or one specific subject. The earliest extant E. is the *Historia Naturalis* of Pliny the Elder (A.D. 23–79). The first alphabetical E. in English was the *Lexicon Technicum* (1704), compiled by John Harris. In 1728 Ephraim Chambers pub. his *Cyclopaedia*, which co-ordinated the scattered articles by a system of cross-references, and was translated into French (1743–5). This translation formed the basis of the *Encyclopédie* ed. by Diderot and d'Alembert, pub. 1751–72. By this time the system of engaging a body of expert compilers and editors was estab., and in 1768–71 the *Encyclopaedia Britannica* first made its appearance.

Famous foreign Es. incl. the Chinese E. (printed 1726); the German *Conversations-Lexikon* of Brockhaus; and the French *Grand Dictionnaire Universel du XIXᵉ Siècle* of Pierre Larousse (1865–76).

ENDIVE (en′div). Annual plant of the Compositae family, grown for use in salads and cooking.

ENDOCRINE GLANDS. *See* DUCTLESS GLANDS.

ENERGY. There are many forms of E. – the ability to do work – mechanical, electrical, chemical, thermal, nuclear, etc. According to the special relativity theory, E. and mass are equivalent, being related by Einstein's equation $E = mc^2$ where E is energy, m is the equivalent mass and c is the velocity of light.

ENFIELD. Bor. of Greater London, England. It has an old parish church and a grammar school founded in 1557, and incl. Edmonton (q.v.). At E. Lock is the Royal Small Arms factory. Pop. (1967) 266,640.

ENGELS, Friedrich (1820–95). German socialist. B. at Barmen, he was sent in 1842 to work in the family cotton-factory at Manchester by his father, and there he estab. contact with the Chartists, and collected material for his *Condition of the Working Class in England* (1845). In 1844 began his lifelong friendship with Marx, in collaboration with whom he worked out the materialist interpretation of history and in 1847–8 wrote the *Communist Manifesto*. Returning to Germany during the 1848–9 revolution, E. worked with Marx on the *Neue Rheinische Zeitung*, and fought on the barricades in Baden. After its defeat he returned to Manchester, and for the rest of his life largely supported Marx and his family. The lessons of 1848 he summed up in his *Peasants' War in Germany* (1850) and *Revolution and Counter-Revolution in Germany* (1851).

ENGINEERING. The design, construction and maintenance of works, machinery, and installations for civil or military purposes, e.g. roads, railways, bridges, harbour installations, engines, ships, aeroplanes generation, transmission and use of electrical power, and a very wide range of applications of science to civilization. To practise E. professionally a university or college training in addition to practical experience is required, but technician engineers usually receive their training through apprenticeships or similar training schemes. The main divisions of E. are aeronautical, chemical, civil, electrical, gas, marine, mechanical, mining, metallurgical, municipal, production, radio and structural E.

ENGLAND. A country of Europe, part of the United Kingdom of Great Britain and Northern Ireland. It occupies the largest part of the island of Great Britain, bounded on the N. by Scotland, on the W. by Wales; its E. coast is washed by the North Sea, its S. coast by the English Channel, and its W. coast by the Atlantic Ocean and the Irish Sea. Area 50,332 sq. m. incl. inland water; pop. (1967) 45,680,870.

Physical. The main physical features are, in the extreme N., the Cheviot Hills, and, southward, the Cumbrian Mountains and the Pennines which reach as far south as Derbyshire. The Welsh borderlands include Radnor Forest and the Black Mountains. In Devon and Cornwall, Dartmoor, Exmoor, and Bodmin Moor are other stretches of high land. The Cotswold Hills extend from Bristol into Lincolnshire; to the S.E., and separated by a broad vale, is a parallel line of hills, consisting of the Marlborough Downs, Chiltern Hills, and East Anglian Heights. Between London and the S. coast the N. and S. Downs enclose the Weald. At their W. end they are joined to Marlborough Downs by the extensive, low, chalk plateau of Salisbury Plain. Smaller groups of hills occur particularly in the W. Midlands, Dorset, and Somerset, and N.E. Yorkshire. The principal lowlands are the Vale of York, East Anglia, the Midlands, the London Basin, the Cheshire Plain, and Hampshire.

The whole of England is well watered, and the many good estuaries have encouraged the growth of great ports (London on the Thames, Bristol on the Avon, Liverpool on the Mersey, Hull on the Humber,

Newcastle on the Tyne). Of the rivers the most important is the Thames which flows from the Cotswolds to the N. Sea, passing through Oxford, Windsor, and London. The Severn rises in Wales and reaches the Bristol Channel below Gloucester. Other important rivers are the Trent and the Great Ouse, both flowing into the N. Sea, and the Mersey. A network of canals linking the ports with centres of industry, constructed in the 18th and 19th cents., lost importance with the growth of modern road and rail transport, but is being increasingly used for recreation and amenity. In the Cumbrian Mountains Windermere and other lakes are famed for their beauty. E. includes several smaller islands, among them the Isle of Wight and the Scilly Isles. (*See also* ISLE OF MAN.)

CLIMATE. The climate is temperate (mean coldest temperature about 5°C., warmest 15°C.), and for most of the year the country lies within the influence of the south-westerly variable winds which are cool and generally rain-bearing, though their impact changes unpredictably. Considerable seasonal and regional variations occur, and there are three climatic areas: (1) the west, with warm summers, mild winters, and abundant rainfall; (2) the south-east, with warm summers, cold winters, and less rain; (3) the north-east, with cool summers and cold winters. Throughout its length the W. coast is warmer than the E.

VEGETATION. E. was once a land of forests, with grasslands and bogs where the soil did not favour the growth of trees. Through the centuries the woodlands have been cleared until today they cover only a small percentage of their former area. The N. mountains lie within the sub-arctic belt of coniferous forests, while Sherwood, Dean, and the New Forests are deciduous. The oak and the beech are the most

ENGLAND. Rural serenity at Batemans, in the Sussex village of Burwash. Kipling made his home here when he retreated from Rottingdean, harassed by coachloads of sightseers from nearby Brighton.   *Photo: British Travel and Holidays Assn.*

common native species, but Forestry Commission plantations naturally tend to the more rapidly exploited conifers.

Economic Life. England is primarily industrial, relying on imports to fill many of her needs, and since the S.W.W. has encountered recurrent difficulties in achieving a 'balance of payments' by an expansion of exports. Her industrial power was first built on the reserves of coal in the N. and Midlands, the iron and steel industries which grew up nearby, and their dependent railway engineering works, shipbuilding yards, etc. These are all still of importance, as are the cottons of Lancs and the woollens of Yorks, but the emphasis has shifted to the newer and more diversified industries. These incl. the manufacture of cars and commercial vehicles; all types of aircraft; hovercraft; electronic, nuclear power and telecommunications equipment; mining, agricultural and textile machinery; scientific instruments; finished diamonds; fertilisers, and other chemical products, especially those from petroleum; all kinds of man-made fibres; paper, leather and plastic goods; pottery and glass – for industrial and personal use; film and television programmes; sound recordings; and fashion goods. Exports of these are supplemented by 'invisible earnings' from world-wide banking and insurance interests and overseas investments.

The recent tendency has been for new industry to concentrate in the S.E., but long-term govt. schemes to revitalise declining areas, such as the N.E. (*see* TEESSIDE), are proving successful. The govt. Industrial Reorganisation Corporation (1966) encourages efficiency and mergers to eliminate waste are frequent. New mineral surveys have revitalised old resources, e.g. Cornish tin and china clay resources; extended the scope of others, e.g. Yorkshire's potash and Derbyshire's fluorspar; and made entirely new discoveries, e.g. the oil and natural gas of the North Sea. The cap. is London, and other important towns are Birmingham, Bradford, Bristol, Canterbury, Coventry, Leeds, Leicester, Liverpool, Manchester, Newcastle, Norwich, Oxford, Plymouth, Portsmouth, Sheffield, Southampton, Stoke-on-Trent, Winchester and York.

The agricultural industry is increasingly mechanised, requiring fewer workers, and intensive. The chief crops are cereals (wheat, barley, oats and rye), vegetables (potatoes, beans, peas, cabbages, turnips), and sugar beet. Breeding cattle are exported and excellent meat, butter, cheese and milk produced on high quality grazing. Sheep are important both for meat and wool, and pigs for fresh meat and a bacon industry. Eggs and chicken, espec. on the controversial broiler-house system, are produced. Fruit – apples, pears, plums, cherries and strawberries – is grown in the southern half of the country; and tomatoes, salad crops, and flowers are grown under glass or in the open in favourable areas. Cod, haddock and herring are the chief catches in the great E. coast fishing ports, such as Hull, Grimsby, Yarmouth, and Lowestoft, and there are specialities such as oysters at Whitstable or lobsters in Cornwall.

Communications. The road and rail systems are being closely co-ordinated. British Rail (London, Midland, Western, Southern, Eastern and North-Eastern regions) provides fast passenger links between the principal towns, and freight-liner trains for goods, and the road system is being modernised with a series of fast motorways. Internal and external air services are good, and there has been general modernisation of seaports, besides such developments as the Milford Haven oil terminal and the bulk handling facilities at Immingham (q.v.).

Population. The English people are descended in the main from Anglo-Saxon and Danish stock, but with a British or Celtic strain surviving in the S.W. and on the Welsh border. Through the cents. there

has been an intermixture of Norman, French, Flemish, German and Jewish elements, and many have Scottish, Irish or Welsh blood in their veins. Before, during and after the S.W.W. there was a substantial influx of Continental refugees – Jewish, German, Polish, Lithuanian, Hungarian, Czech, etc. – and of people from the Irish Republic. Labour shortage in the 1950s and 1960s, and other special conditions, led to the arrival of the Italian and Spanish workers, and such increasing numbers from the West Indies, India, Pakistan and other Commonwealth countries that legislation was introduced to stem the flow. The table gives the administrative cos. as in 1971, when further reorganisation was projected (*see* COUNTY), with an est. pop. for 1967: census figs. were (1801) 8,892,536 and (1851) 17,927,609, both incl. Wales; (1901) 30,813,043, (1951) 41,572,585, and (1961) 43,874,061, all excl. Wales.

Religion. The Church of England (*see* ANGLICAN COMMUNION) is the estab. church, but there are substantial other Protestant and Roman Catholic denominations, as well as Jewish, Hindu, Moslem and other communities.

Language. English is universal, although Welsh, Yiddish, Hindi, Urdu, etc. may be spoken as a second language.

COUNTIES OF ENGLAND			
	Area in sq. m.	Population	Admin. H.Q.
Bedfordshire	477	432,940	Bedford
Berkshire	725	598,220	Reading
Buckinghamshire	749	552,470	Aylesbury
Cambridgeshire and Isle of Ely	831	296,930	Cambridge
Cheshire	1,015	1,486,470	Chester
Cornwall	1,375	356,200	Truro
Cumberland	1,521	296,050	Carlisle
Derbyshire	1,006	882,230	Matlock
Devonshire	2,591	869,840	Exeter
Dorset	978	337,910	Dorchester
Durham	1,015	1,547,050	Durham
Essex	1,419	1,268,610	Chelmsford
Gloucestershire	1,259	1,062,260	Gloucester
Hampshire	1,503	1,511,250	Winchester
Herefordshire	842	140,760	Hereford
Hertfordshire	632	881,870	Hertford
Huntingdonshire and Peterborough	486	189,560	Huntingdon
Kent	1,440	1,345,520	Maidstone
Lancashire	1,878	5,198,060	Preston
Leicestershire	834	723,730	Leicester
Lincolnshire:			
Holland	419	105,120	Boston
Kesteven	720	230,310	Sleaford
Lindsey	1,524	456,070	Lincoln
Greater London	616	7,880,760	London
Norfolk	2,054	593,990	Norwich
Northamptonshire	914	433,880	Northampton
Northumberland	2,019	828,290	Newcastle upon Tyne
Nottinghamshire	844	962,450	Nottingham
Oxfordshire	749	358,690	Oxford
Rutland	152	29,110	Oakham
Shropshire	1,348	326,010	Shrewsbury
Somerset	1,613	644,460	Taunton
Staffordshire	1,157	1,820,890	Stafford
East Suffolk	871	376,190	Ipswich
West Suffolk	611	155,240	Bury St. Edmunds
Surrey	650	985,930	Kingston upon Thames
East Sussex	824	717,800	Lewes
West Sussex	633	455,930	Chichester
Warwickshire	983	2,110,360	Warwick
Westmorland	789	68,030	Kendal
Isle of Wight	147	98,040	Newport
Wiltshire	1,344	479,080	Trowbridge
Worcestershire	703	669,400	Worcester
Yorkshire:			
East Riding	1,172	544,230	Beverley
North Riding	2,284	590,090	Northallerton
West Riding	2,798	3,782,590	Wakefield
	50,056	45,680,870	

ENGLEHEART, George (1752–1829). English miniature painter. B. at Kew, he studied under Joshua Reynolds and in 40 years painted nearly 5,000 miniatures incl. copies of many of Reynolds' portraits.

ENGLISH ART. Painting. Little can be said with authority about E. medieval painting – apart from some fine illuminated MSS. – since such few wall paintings, etc., as have survived have often suffered deliberate damage on religious grounds or been incompetently restored. In Tudor times painting became for the first time mainly secular, and the first well-known artist is Holbein, who came from Germany to paint the court of Henry VIII. Among his followers was the miniaturist Nicholas Hilliard, who estab. a tradition of English excellence in this field which was continued by Samuel Cooper, Richard Cosway and George Engleheart. The Flemish Van Dyck, employed as a court painter by Charles I from 1632, greatly influenced English portrait painters, as in turn did Sir Peter Lely and Godfrey Kneller.

ENGLISH ART. A pioneer of the truly English school of painting was William Hogarth. This is a detail from one of his famous series of 1734 Marriage à la Mode – the onset of dissolute boredom in the countess 'Shortly after the Marriage'.
Courtesy of the National Gallery.

William Hogarth was the first great English artist, Thomas Rowlandson following in the same tradition. More sedate are the famous painters of the 18th cent. conversation piece, the German-born Johann Zoffany and Arthur Devis. A truly indigenous form is the sporting picture, George Stubbs being the great 18th cent. master, although the Sartorius and Alken families also produced fine work, as did Sir Edwin Landseer in the next cent. and Sir Alfred Munnings in the 20th. George Morland's pictures of rural life have a similar vigorous realism.

Among the native portrait painters Sir Joshua Reynolds, Thomas Gainsborough – also a superb landscape artist – and Sir Thomas Lawrence hold high place in the late 18th and early 19th cents. Rather apart was the genius of the visionary William Blake and the water-colourist Samuel Palmer, who came under his influence. Among painters specializing in landscape in the same period were Richard Wilson,

Paul Sandby, Alexander Cozens, J. R. Cozens, John Crome, Thomas Girtin, J. S. Cotman, David Cox, Peter de Wint and – the giants in genius and influence – J. W. M. Turner and John Constable. *See* illus. p. 390.

In Victorian times the subject picture was popular and there was a pleasant domestic school which incl. J. C. Horsley. An outstanding group were the Pre-Raphaelites – Millais, Holman Hunt and Rossetti, but these and G. F. Watts, Ford Madox Brown, Lord Leighton and Sir Edward Burne-Jones have suffered in reputation in the 20th cent., although there are signs of a revival of interest.

J. M. Whistler, the American who introduced the doctrine of Art for Art's Sake and settled in Chelsea, had as his disciple W. R. Sickert, who also admired Degas and with Wilson Steer introduced Impressionism to England. Sickert headed the Camden Town group which incl. Spencer Gore and Harold Gilman. Among artists of the 20th cent. are Duncan Grant, Sir Frank Brangwyn, Sir William Nicholson, Augustus John, Paul Nash, Ben Nicholson, Christopher Wood, Graham Sutherland, Ivon Hitchens, Stanley Spencer, John Bratby, Francis Bacon and Victor Pasmore.

Sculpture. In addition to some early Celtic work, there are some fine medieval ecclesiastical sculptures, e.g. Wells Cathedral and the Henry VII chapel in Westminster Abbey. Foreign artists such as Roubillac were extremely popular in the 18th cent. but John Flaxman is the first outstanding English name. Well known in the 19th cent. were Sir Francis Chantrey, Alfred Stevens, and Lord Leighton, and Sir George Frampton at the turn of the cent. The 20th cent. has seen a remarkable flowering with the work of Epstein, Eric Gill, Frank Dobson, Henry Moore, Barbara Hepworth, Michael Ayrton, and Reg Butler.

Architecture. The main styles in English architecture are: Saxon, Norman, Early English (of which Westminster Abbey is an example), Decorated, Perpendicular (15th cent.), Tudor (a name chiefly applied to domestic buildings of the period, c. 1485–1558), Jacobean, Stuart (incl. the Renaissance and Queen Anne styles), Georgian, and the Gothic revival of the 19th cent. Notable architects incl. Wren, Inigo Jones, Vanbrugh, Hawksmoor. Sir Charles Barry, Sir Edwin Lutyens, Sir Hugh Casson, Sir Basil Spence, Sir Frederick Gibberd, and Denys Lasdun.

Universality of materials – steel, glass – has merged the English tradition with the international trend to austere skyscrapers, but recent years have seen such strikingly imaginative works as Coventry Cathedral by Sir Basil Spence, with the integrally designed tapestry by Graham Sutherland, and Liverpool Cathedral by Sir Frederick Gibberd, incorporating in the lantern 50-ft. high glass panels designed by John Piper.

ENGLISH CHANNEL. Stretch of water between England and France, leading in the W. to the Atlantic Ocean, and in the E. via the Strait of Dover to the North Sea. It is 280 m. long from W. to E.; 17 m. wide at its narrowest (Cap Gris Nez to Dover) and 110 m. at its widest (Ushant to Land's End). *See* CHANNEL SWIMMING and CHANNEL TUNNEL.

ENGLISH HISTORY. PREHISTORIC AND ROMAN BRITAIN. From c. 2500 Britain was inhabited by people who came from the E. and S.; they practised agriculture and left as their monument the long barrows in S. England. Another group, called 'beaker folk', introduced bronze-working c. 1800 B.C.; they constructed Stonehenge and other great religious structures. Several waves of Celtic invaders followed from c. 1000 B.C.; the use of iron was introduced c. 450 B.C. The Celts traded with Europe and their tribal organisation was developing into a system of kingdoms when Julius Caesar made his visits in 55 and 54 B.C. The Roman conquest began in A.D. 43.

ENGLISH ART. John Constable's pictures, mainly of East Anglia, seem to recapture completely the very essence of the English scene. Above is his 'Hay Wain', a treasure of the National Gallery.

and by A.D. 80 had reached the Scottish Lowlands. After a brief period of resistance Roman culture was accepted, the upper classes becoming completely Romanised. Christianity was introduced from Ireland in the 4th cent.

ANGLO-SAXON ENGLAND (407–1066). An obscure 200 years followed the withdrawal of the Romans in 407, during which the Germanic Angles and Saxons overran all England except Cornwall, Wales, and Cumberland; how far the Celts survived is uncertain. Roman partial military re-occupations possibly occurred 417–c. 427 and c. 450. In the 6th cent. Christianity was introduced among the pagan invaders by missionaries from Rome. England was divided into several kingdoms, the chief being Northumbria, Mercia, Kent, and Wessex, whose kings battled for supremacy until in 829 they all accepted Egbert of Wessex as overlord. His successors were confronted with the Danish raiders, and although Alfred expelled the Danes from Wessex in 878 he had to cede to them the N. and E. of England. During the 10th cent. this was reconquered and a real national unity achieved, but Danish raids began again in 991, and during 1016–42 England was ruled by Danish kings. Norman influence, predominant under Edward the Confessor led toward the Norman conquest of 1066.

EARLY MIDDLE AGES (1066–1307). As England advanced towards unity, the Anglo-Saxons had developed from a tribal society to a system somewhat akin to the feudalism introduced by the Norman kings. The contrast between the law and order they had established, and the disorder of Stephen's reign, made a return to a strong monarchy generally acceptable; nevertheless, when John attempted to claim more than was his due by feudal standards, barons, Church, and towns united against him to assert their privileges in Magna Carta (1215). This alliance was renewed against Henry III, in a struggle whence emerged the House of Commons, an assembly of knights and burgesses, side by side with the older baronial assembly, or House of Lords. The combination of king, lords, and commons began with Edward I's Model Parliament of 1295. Edward completed the conquest of Wales begun by the Normans, and attempted unsuccessfully to conquer Scotland. In Ireland Henry II had estab. a lasting colony in 1171.

LATER MIDDLE AGES (1307–1485). Dynastic, trade and other interests led to the 100 Years War with France (1338–1453). The financial problems created by this war enabled parliament to secure control of taxation, and of the king's choice of ministers by the weapon of impeachment. The later 14th cent. was filled with unrest. The Black Death (1348–9) created a serious labour shortage, and attempts to deal with it led to bitter class struggles, culminating in the Peasants' Revolt, 1381. In spite of the failure of the rising, serfdom steadily declined during the 15th

An Anglo-Saxon king consults with his witan, an early equivalent of a 'privy council', in this drawing in an 11th century manuscript in the British Museum. On the right, an execution in progress.

cent. Popular anticlericalism found expression in the
Lollard movement, which anticipated the Reformation. When Richard II moved towards absolutism,
parliament replaced him by Henry IV, who was
obliged to grant it unprecedented powers. Henry V's
attempt to conciliate the nobility by renewing the
French war ended in his son's reign in disaster, and
led directly to the Wars of the Roses (1455–85).
Order, restored by Edward IV, was maintained after
a change of dynasty by Henry VII, who broke the
political power of the feudal nobility.

TUDOR ENGLAND (1485–1603). Henry VIII followed
this up by bringing the Church under royal control,
repudiating the papal power, dissolving the monasteries, and confiscating their wealth. In this policy he
received the enthusiastic support of parliament and
the landowners, who benefited by the confiscated
lands. Under Edward VI the English Church adopted
Protestant doctrines; after a Catholic reaction under
Mary I, Elizabeth I adopted a compromise whereby
the Church's doctrines became Protestant and its
ritual semi-Catholic. These changes coincided with,
and encouraged, a movement whereby many of the
free peasantry who had arisen after the disappearance
of serfdom were evicted to make room for sheep-
farms. Modern capitalism began with the development of the woollen industry and of trade with
Russia, Turkey, and later with India. Trade rivalries
combined with political reasons to involve England
under Elizabeth I in war with Spain, whence the
country emerged as a major naval power.

Queen Elizabeth presides over parliament. An illustration
from Robert Glover's *Nobilitas Politica et Civilis* (1608).

Sir Robert Walpole – the first 'prime minister' – has a word
with the Speaker, Arthur Onslow. After Hogarth.

The accession in 1603 of James VI of Scotland as
James I of England united the crowns of the two
countries. *See* UNITED KINGDOM; also BRITISH
COMMONWEALTH; IRELAND; SCOTLAND; WALES.

THE ENGLISH REVOLUTION (1603–89). Under
James I the uneasy co-operation between king and
parliament, which had continued through the Tudor
period, ended. The gentry and merchants, enriched
by Church lands, enclosures, foreign trade, and
industry, took advantage of the Crown's financial
needs, produced by the inflation which followed the
import of American silver, to seize control of the
state machine. The issues were complicated by the
struggle between the State Church and the Puritans,
who became identified with the parliamentary
opposition. During the revolution of 1640–60 England
passed through civil war to republicanism, and thence
to military dictatorship. The Restoration of 1660
restored to the monarchy the show rather than the
substance of power. Charles II worked with considerable success to reverse the work of the revolution,
but James II's attempts to carry this process further
provoked a new revolution in 1688–9, which placed
political power in the hands of the Whig landowners
and merchants. Ireland, which had been finally conquered by the Tudors, rose for her independence in
1641 and 1689, only to be reduced to the status of a
colony. Meanwhile the foundations of the Empire
were laid in N. America and India, a process which
involved England in three wars with the Dutch. The
accession of James I had brought England and
Scotland under one king. Among the results of the
revolution of 1688 was the union of their parliaments
in 1707.

THE 18TH CENTURY (1689–1815). Another result of
1688 was the second 100 Years War with France,
the successor of Holland as England's commercial
and colonial rival. In this series of seven wars British
sea-power proved decisive, and the French were
ousted from N. America and India. At home the
supremacy of parliament found expression in the
establishment of cabinet government under Walpole
(1721–42). The power of the Whig landowning and
merchant oligarchy, supreme since 1714, was challenged by George III, and for 70 years (1760–1830)
the Tories were almost continuously in office. Those
years were troubled by the successful revolt of the
American colonies (1775–83) and the French Revolution (1789–99), which stimulated the growth of the
democratic movement in England. In Ireland a
powerful movement arose for complete independence,
which Pitt countered by carrying through a parliamentary union with Britain (1800). At home agriculture was revolutionised by a new wave of

enclosures, whereby the small farmer was driven off the land or reduced to being a landless labourer. At the same time mechanical progress and the rise of the factory system converted England from an agricultural to an industrial country without a serious rival. Two new classes emerged from the change, the industrialists and the exploited industrial workers, bitterly hostile to one another yet united in a demand for parliamentary reform.

THE 19TH CENTURY (1815–1900). The alliance of the industrialists with the Whigs produced a new

The Reform Bill of 1832 had abortive predecessors. Doyle's cartoon shows Lord Althorp, Chancellor of the Exchequer in Lord Grey's administration handing over the second Reform Bill to the Lord Chancellor, Lord Brougham, in the House of Lords. Like the first, it was rejected and it was the third Reform Bill which actually passed both houses.

party, the Liberals, who in 1832 carried a Reform Bill transferring political power from the aristocracy to the middle classes. For the next 40 years Liberalism, with its ideology of free trade and *laissez-faire*, was triumphant. The working classes, excluded from the franchise, created their own organizations in the trade unions and the Chartist movement, although the latter disappeared during the years of mid-Victorian peace and prosperity (1850–75). After 1875 Britain's industrial monopoly found rivals in Germany and the U.S.A., and she was obliged to seek new markets and sources of raw materials. The Conservatives made themselves the mouthpiece of the new imperialism, and launched Britain on a career of expansion in Egypt, S. Africa, and elsewhere. The outstanding feature of the history of the Empire in the 19th cent. was the development of Canada, New Zealand, Australia, and later of S. Africa, into self-governing dominions. The economic crisis of the later 19th cent., which encouraged imperial development, also induced the working classes, largely enfranchised in 1867 and 1885, to revive the militant trade unionism and political movement of Chartist days. From an alliance of trade unions and small socialist bodies emerged the Labour Party in 1900.

THE 20TH CENTURY. After 1900 Britain's commercial and colonial rivalry with Germany led to her abandonment of her traditional isolationist policy, and to her entry into the system of alliances dividing Europe and into a feverish armaments race. At home a Liberal government attempted to satisfy with social reforms a working class demanding a higher standard of living. In 1914 a general strike and a civil war in Ireland seemed imminent, and the F.W.W. created a host of new problems. During the post-war years Ireland won her independence, unrest swept India, and a wave of mass strikes culminated in the general strike of 1926. After a few years of comparative prosperity an unprecedented economic crisis devastated most of the world during 1929–31; among its results was the coming to power of the British National Government in 1931. The years that followed were dominated by the approach

of the S.W.W. of 1939–45. Like the F.W.W. this was followed by a general movement towards the Left throughout Europe, one feature of which was the return in 1945 for the first time of a Labour government with an overall majority, whose programme included nationalisation (q.v.) and a generally planned economy. The Conservatives returned to power 1951, Eden taking over from Churchill in 1955 until replaced, following Suez, by Macmillan in 1957. The latter's ill-health led to his replacement by Sir Alec Douglas-Home in 1963, and Labour, under Harold Wilson, narrowly returned to power in 1964. The Conservatives, under Edward Heath, were defeated by a larger margin in 1966, but won a small majority in 1970.

Neither party succeeded in solving the country's recurrent economic difficulties, though both attempted entry to the Common Market, and there was a similar confusion on defence commitments and other major issues. There was a blurring of party lines, and a tendency to political alienation in the country at large, but by 1970 there was a more vigorous clash of opinion.

SOVEREIGNS OF ENGLAND

West Saxon Kings

Egbert	829	Athelstan	925
Ethelwulf	839	Edmund	940
Ethelbald	858	Edred	946
Ethelbert	860	Edwy	955
Ethelred I	866	Edgar	959
Alfred the Great	871	Edward the Martyr	975
Edward the Elder	901	Ethelred II	978
Edmund Ironside	1016		

Danish Kings

Canute	1016	Harold I	1035	Hardicanute	1040

West Saxon Kings (restored)

Edward the Confessor	1042	Harold II	1066

Norman Kings

William I	1066	Henry I	1100
William II	1087	Stephen	1135

House of Plantagenet

Henry II	1154	Edward I	1272
Richard I	1189	Edward II	1307
John	1199	Edward III	1327
Henry III	1216	Richard II	1377

House of Lancaster

Henry IV	1399	Henry V	1413	Henry VI	1422

House of York

Edward IV	1461	Edward V	1483	Richard III	1483

House of Tudor

Henry VII	1485	Edward VI	1547
Henry VIII	1509	Mary I	1553
Elizabeth I	1558		

House of Stuart

James I	1603	Charles I	1625

The Commonwealth 1649–60

House of Stuart (restored)

Charles II	1660	William III and Mary II	1689
James II	1685	Anne	1702

House of Hanover

George I	1714	George IV	1820
George II	1727	William IV	1830
George III	1760	Victoria	1837

House of Saxe-Coburg

Edward VII	1901

House of Windsor

George V	1910	George VI	1936
Edward VIII	1936	Elizabeth II	1952

ENGLISH LANGUAGE. In its origin E. belongs to the western division of the Germanic languages. Towards the end of the 7th cent. 4 main dialects can be distinguished, the Jutish of Kent, the Saxon of the south, the S. Anglian or Mercian of the Midlands, and the N. Anglian or Northumbrian north of the Humber, which collectively form Anglo-Saxon or O.E. This tongue retained much of the complex Germanic grammar, and was inflectional.

King Alfred's active interest in literature made the W. Saxon dialect the prevailing literary language until the early part of the 10th cent.

The Norman Conquest did not at first greatly affect English, and it is possible that interaction with the related speech of the Danes settled in the country played the greater part in the dropping of many inflections and the creation of a much simpler language than O.E. by the end of the 12th cent.; but it had no standard form, and documents of the M.E. period (c. 1200–1400) are written in a variety of dialects. Thanks in particular to the influence of Chaucer, the dialect of London came to be accepted as a literary standard, an early indication of this being that Gower (c. 1330–1408), though of Kentish origin, wrote in the London, not the Kentish, dialect. This tendency was confirmed by the setting up in London in 1477 of the first printing press; Caxton, like Gower from Kent, used the London dialect in his publications in English. By c. 1650 printers had generally adopted a fixed orthography. But adoption of a standard form of written English did not abolish spoken dialects and local

The cabinet room at 10 Downing Street, the Prime Minister's residence, where modern English history is made. Covered in green baize, the table tapers at each end to allow the Prime Minister, who sits at the centre of one side (the armchair right), to see who is speaking.   *Photo: Crown Copyright.*

variations of pronunciation in different parts of E., many of which survive into the second half of the 20th cent. despite the widespread levelling influence of broadcasting. In the 1960s a regional 'accent' had become a social and career asset rather than a liability.

Almost purely Germanic at the time of the 5th cent. invasions, English borrowed certain Celtic and Latin words from the defeated inhabitants of Britain in the 6th to 10th cents. Many words used by the later Danish and Norse settlers passed into the general vocabulary, and from c. 1150 English absorbed a number of Norman-French words, particularly those concerning the Church, state, law, and feudal system.

From the middle of the 13th cent. the Romance element in E. is as important as the Germanic. These French borrowings closely resembled their Latin originals and prepared the way for continued and extensive Latinization of vocabulary. Greek words were also adopted, particularly with the growth of the various sciences from the 17th cent. During the 14th to 17th cents. words, many of them nautical, were adopted from the Low Countries and N. Germany, and from the 17th cent. onwards have been borrowed freely from every language, and also from other English-speaking communities, notably the

U.S.A. Surviving dialects often help to elucidate the history of pronunciation.

Spoken by perhaps 5,500,000 people in 1600, English is now the first language of more than 300,000,000, and the second of many others.

ENGLISH LAW. One of the 2 great European legal systems, Roman law being the other. E.L. has spread to the U.S.A., Canada, Australia, and New Zealand, and has greatly influenced Indian law. It has a continuous history dating from the local customs of the Anglo-Saxons, traces of which survived until 1925. After the Norman Conquest there grew up, side by side with the Saxon shire courts, the feudal courts of the barons and the ecclesiastical courts. From the king's council developed the royal courts, presided over by professional judges, which gradually absorbed the jurisdictions of the baronial and ecclesiastical courts. By 1250 the royal judges had amalgamated the various local customs into the system of Common Law, i.e. law common to the whole country. A second system known as Equity (q.v.) developed in the Court of Chancery, in which the Lord Chancellor considered petitions. In the 17th–18th cents. the Common Law absorbed the Law Merchant, the international code of mercantile customs.

During the 19th cent. virtually the whole of E.L. was reformed by legislation, e.g. the number of capital offences was greatly reduced. The Judicature Acts 1873–5 abolished a multiplicity of courts, and in their place established the Supreme Court of Judicature, organized in the Court of Appeal and the High Court of Justice; the latter has 3 divisions – the Queen's Bench, Chancery, and Probate, Divorce, and Admiralty Divisions. All Supreme Court judges may apply both Common Law and Equity in deciding cases. From the Court of Appeal there may be a further appeal to the House of Lords.

A unique feature of E.L. is the doctrine of Judicial Precedents, whereby the reported decisions of the courts form a binding source of law for future decisions. A judge is bound by decisions of courts of superior jurisdiction, but not necessarily by those of inferior courts.

ENGLISH LITERATURE. The earliest surviving O.E. poems – *Beowulf* and the epic fragments *Finnesburh, Waldhere, Deor* and *Widsith* – reflect the heroic age and Germanic legends of the 4th–6th cents., although probably not recorded until the 7th cent. Heroic elements also survive in several elegiac lyrics, e.g. *The Wanderer, The Seafarer,* and in many poems with a specifically Christian content, e.g. *The Dream of the Rood*; the Saints' Lives, e.g. *Elene,* by the 8th cent. poet Cynewulf; and the biblical paraphrases, e.g. *Genesis,* formerly attributed to Caedmon. These poems are all written in unrhymed alliterative metre. The great prose writers of the early period were the Latin scholars Bede, Aldhelm, and Alcuin, and it was left to Alfred to found the tradition of English prose with his translations and his establishment of the Anglo-Saxon Chronicle; other prose writers of the time are Aelfric and Wulfstan.

With the Conquest began the ascendancy of Norman-French in cultural life, and it was not until the 13th cent. that the native literature regained its strength. Prose was concerned chiefly with popular devotional use, but poetry emerged most typically in the metrical chronicles, e.g. Layamon's *Brut,* and the numerous romances based on the stories of Charlemagne, the Arthurian legends, the classical episodes of Troy, etc. First of the great English poets was Chaucer, whose early work was moulded by the predominant French influence, but who came to his maturity under that of Renaissance Italy. Of purely native inspiration was *The Vision of Piers Plowman* of Langland in the old alliterative verse, and the anonymous *Pearl, Patience,* and *Gawayne and the Grene Knight.*

Chaucer's mastery of versification was not shared by his much less effective successors, Lydgate, Occleve, and Hawes; most original of them was Skelton. More successful were the anonymous authors of songs and carols, and of the ballads, which (e.g. those concerned with Robin Hood) formed a complete cycle. Drama flowered in the form of miracle and morality plays, and prose, although still awkwardly handled by Wycliffe in his translation of the Bible, rose to a great height with Malory in the 15th cent.

SIR PHILIP SIDNEY.
By an unknown artist.
Photo: N.P.G.

The Renaissance, which had first touched E.L. through Chaucer, came to delayed fruition in the 16th cent. Wyatt and Surrey acclimatized the sonnet and blank verse in typically Elizabethan forms, and prepared the way for Spenser, Sidney, Daniel, Campion, etc. With Kyd and Marlowe drama emerged into theatrical form; it reached the highest level in Shakespeare and Jonson. Elizabethan prose is represented by Hooker, North, Ascham, Holinshed, Lyly, etc., but English prose reached full richness and variety in the 17th cent., which produced the Authorised Version of the Bible, Bacon, Milton, Bunyan, Taylor, Browne, Walton, and Pepys. Greatest of the 17th cent. poets were Milton and Donne; others include the religious writers Herbert, Crashaw, Vaughan, and Traherne, and the Cavalier lyrists Herrick, Carew, Suckling, and Lovelace. To the Restoration belong Butler (1612–80), poet, and Dryden, poet, dramatist, and critic, the founders of religious and political satire; the best of the court poets, Rochester; and the once popular Cowley, Waller, and Denham. Drama is represented by Dryden; Otway and Lee in tragedy; Etherege, Wycherley, Congreve, Vanbrugh, and Farquhar in comedy.

With the 18th cent. opened the Augustan Age in England. Pope perfected the poetic technique of Dryden; while in prose Steele and Addison evolved the form of the polite essay, Swift achieved supremacy in satire, and Defoe exploited his gifts as the genius of journalism. This cent. also saw the development of the novel through the long-drawn intricacies of Richardson to the robust narrative of Fielding and

ALEXANDER POPE.
Bust in terra cotta by Roubiliac.   *Photo: N.P.G.*

Smollett, the sentiment of Sterne, and the Gothic 'terror' of Horace Walpole. The standards established by the 'Augustans' were maintained by Johnson and the members of his circle – Goldsmith, Burke, Reynolds, Sheridan, etc., – but the 'romantic' element present in the work of the poets Thomson, Gray, Young, and Collins was soon to overturn them. The forgeries of Chatterton, Macpherson's *Ossian,* and the work of the Wartons are significant of the new attitude.

The poetry of Cowper, Blake, and Crabbe no longer fits into the old categories, and the *Lyrical Ballads* (1798) of Wordsworth and Coleridge forms the manifesto of the new age. Byron, Shelley, and

GEORGE ELIOT. Chalk drawing by Sir F. W. Burton.
Photo: N.P.G.

Keats form a second generation of Romantic poets. In fiction Scott took over the Gothic tradition from Mrs. Radcliffe, to create the historical novel, and the quiet genius of Jane Austen estab. the novel of the comedy of manners. Criticism attained new heights in Coleridge, Lamb, Hazlitt, and De Quincey.

During the 19th cent. the novel was further developed by Dickens, Thackeray, the Brontës, George Eliot, Trollope, and the lesser Disraeli, Reade, Kingsley, Bulwer Lytton, etc. The principal poets of the reign of Victoria are Tennyson, Browning, Arnold, the members of Rossetti's circle, Morris and Swinburne, and the solitary Fitzgerald. Among the other great prose writers of the era are Macaulay, Newman, Mill, Carlyle, Ruskin, and Pater. To the transition period at the end of the cent. belong the poetry and novels of Meredith and Hardy; the work of Butler and Gissing; and the plays of Pinero, Jones, and the Irishman Oscar Wilde.

The Victorian tradition in poetry was continued in the new cent. by Bridges; his contemporary Hopkins was a notable experimenter in verse forms. Kipling, Newbolt, Belloc, Davies, Hodgson, De la Mare, Housman, Chesterton, Masefield, Noyes, and Drinkwater were other poets of the opening cent. Best-remembered poets of the F.W.W. are Sassoon, Brooke, Owen, and Graves. Poets of the succeeding years incl. Dame Edith Sitwell, T. S. Eliot, Auden, Day Lewis, MacNeice and Spender. Unusual elements entered the novel with Henry James, Conrad, Kipling, and George Moore. New middle-class realism was in the novels of Wells, Bennett, E. M. Forster, and Galsworthy. Maugham, Hugh Walpole, James Joyce, D. H. Lawrence, Aldous Huxley, Priestley, Virginia Woolf, Christopher Isherwood, Evelyn Waugh, Graham Greene, and Ivy Compton Burnett are later writers of fiction. Writers for the English stage incl. another outstanding Irishman, Bernard Shaw, as well as Galsworthy, Maugham, Priestley, Barrie, Lonsdale, Coward, Graham Greene, Bridie, Rattigan, Emlyn Williams, and the writers of poetic drama, e.g. T. S. Eliot, Fry, Auden, and Isherwood. The '50s and '60s produced what has been called the 'kitchen sink' school of dramatists – e.g. Osborne and Wesker – and the English 'Theatre of the Absurd' in the plays of N. F. Simpson; other leading playwrights were Harold Pinter and John Arden. Post-S.W.W. poets included Thom Gunn, Roy Fuller, and Philip Larkin; and novelists of the same period were William Golding, Iris Murdoch, Angus Wilson, Muriel Spark, Lawrence Durrell, John Braine,

P. B. SHELLEY.
By George Clint, 1819.
Photo: N.P.G.

Kingsley Amis, C. P. Snow, Pamela Hansford Johnson, John Wain and Anthony Powell. Among prose writers of the cent. are W. H. Hudson, Lytton Strachey, T. E. Lawrence, Osbert Sitwell, Winston Churchill, G. M. Trevelyan, Arnold Toynbee, George Orwell, and Bertrand Russell. For other literatures in

English, *see under* AUSTRALIA, CANADA, IRELAND, NEW ZEALAND, SCOTLAND, SOUTH AFRICA, UNITED STATES OF AMERICA, WALES.)

ENGLISH - SPEAKING UNION. Society for promoting the fellowship of the English-speaking peoples of the world, founded in 1918 by Sir Evelyn Wrench.

ENGRAVING. The art of incising marks of any kind upon any hard substance, esp. on blocks of metal or wood for purposes of reproduction. There are three main types of printmaking: (1) relief prints made by means of woodcutting and wood engraving; (2) intaglio prints made by means of engraving and etching upon metal; and (3) surface prints made by means of lithography. *See* AQUATINT; DRY - POINT; ETCHING; MEZZOTINT.

ENNIS. Co. town (U.D.) of Clare co., Rep. of Ireland, on the r. Fergus, 20 m. N.W. of Limerick; it is a market centre, with flour mills; furniture is made. Pop. (1961) 5,678.

G. B. SHAW. Watercolour by Sir Bernard Partridge, 1925.
Photo: N.P.G.

ENNISKI'LLEN. Co. town (bor.) of Fermanagh co., N. Ireland, situated between the Upper and the Lower Lough Erne. It is a market town, with some light industry. Pop. (1961) 7,227.

ENNIUS (en'i-us), **Quintus** (239–169 B.C.). Early Roman poet. B. near Tarentum in S. Italy, he wrote tragedies based on Greek models. His epic poem, the *Annales*, deals with Roman history and earned him the name of 'father of Roman poetry'.

ENOSIS. See CYPRUS.

ENSCHEDE (ens'khedā). Textile manufacturing centre in Overijssel prov., the Netherlands. Pop. (1967) 136,503.

ENSOR, James, baron (1860–1949). Belgian artist. B. at Ostend, he became noted particularly for his dissonant use of colour and his 'decadent' and satiric pictures, whose skeletons and masked figures represented his view of humanity and its falsity. One of his best-known paintings is 'Entrance of Christ into Brussels' (1888).

ENTAIL. The settlement of land on a successive line of persons, usually the 'heirs of the body' of the settlor. 'Estates tail' are (1) general or (2) special. The former descend to the eldest child, regardless of sex, the latter to the eldest male child or the eldest female child or according to some other specific arrangement. Such settlements are increasingly rare in modern times, and the power to make them has often been destroyed by legislation, cf. restrictions in certain states of the U.S.

ENTE'BBE. Town in Uganda, on the N.W. shore of L. Victoria, 19 m. S.S.W. of Kampala. It lies 3,863 ft. a.s.l., and has technical schools, a botanical garden, and a first-class international airport. Founded 1893, it was the admin. centre of Uganda 1894–1962. Pop. (1967) 11,000.

ENTENTE CORDIALE (aṅtaṅt' kordē-ahl'). The 'friendly understanding' estab. between Britain and France in 1904, when France recognised Britain's 'special interests' in Egypt, while Britain professed herself disinterested in Morocco.

ENTE'RIC. A general name for infective fevers of the intestine, especially typhoid and paratyphoid.

ENTOMO'LOGY. *See* INSECT.

ENVER PASHA (1881–1922). Turkish statesman and soldier. He led the military revolt in 1908 which resulted in the Young Turk revolution, and was killed fighting the Bolsheviks in Turkestan.

ENWONWU (enwon'wu), **Ben** (1921–   ). Nigerian sculptor. B. in Eastern Nigeria, he became Federal Art Adviser to the Nigerian govt., and his works incl. a statue of Elizabeth II in the House of Representatives at Lagos, and a Risen Christ in wood in Ibadan univ. chapel.

ENZYMES. Organic catalysts secreted by living organisms, by means of which the various chemical changes necessary for life of the cell are controlled. Some are found in natural secretions, such as the digestive juices, pepsin and trypsin; more frequently they can be obtained only from the interior of cells. But there is a vast number of vegetable Es., e.g. diastase, which converts starch into sugar.

EOLITHS (ē'-oliths). The simplest and most primitive form of specially shaped stone implements, dating from the Tertiary period. Their recognition as artifacts was largely due to Benjamin Harrison in 1899 and Reid Moir more recently in E. Anglia.

E'OS. Greek goddess of the dawn, better known by the Roman name of **Aurora.**

EOTVOS (öt'vösh), **Roland von, Baron** (1848–1919). Hungarian scientist. B. at Budapest, he investigated problems of gravitation, and constructed the doublearmed torsion balance for determining variations of gravity.

EPAMINONDAS (ēpaminon'das) (*c.* 420–362 B.C.). Theban general and statesman, who won a decisive victory over the Spartans at Leuctra in 371, and fell in the moment of victory at Mantinea.

ÉPERNAY (ehpernā'). Town in Marne dept., France, centre of the champagne industry. Pop. (1962) 22,799.

EPHEDRINE (ef'edrin). A member of a group of drugs, called sympathomimetic amines, which incl. adrenalin and benzedrine. It occurs in the *Ephedra* genus of shrubs, found in warm temperate zones.

EPHESUS (ef'esus). Ancient city of Asia Minor, a centre of the Ionian Greeks, with a famous temple of Artemis (Diana). St. Paul visited the city and addressed one of his epistles to the Christians there. E. was destroyed by the Goths in A.D. 262.

EPIC. A narrative poem dealing at length with some great action such as the Babylonian *Gilgamesh,* Homer's *Iliad* and *Odyssey,* the Indian *Rāmāyana* and the *Mahābhārata,* and the Anglo-Saxon *Beowulf.* The primary or authentic epics were chanted at great feasts, and their main theme is always the deeds of heroes. The literary or secondary epic is written in imitation of the older epics, and is intended for reading. Virgil's *Aeneid* is the greatest Latin epic poem, and later examples are Milton's *Paradise Lost,* Tasso's *Jerusalem Delivered,* and Hardy's *Dynasts.*

EPICTE'TUS (fl. *c.* A.D. 90). Greek Stoic philosopher. B. at Hierapolis in Phrygia, he lived for many years in Rome as a slave, but eventually secured his freedom, attended the lectures of a Stoic, and became a Stoic philosopher himself. He taught that men are in the hands of an all-wise providence, and that they should endeavour to do their duty in the position to which they are called.

ENWONWU. The artist at work on a group.
Courtesy of the Nigerian Ministry of Information.

EPICURE'ANISM. System of philosophy named

after Epicurus (341–270 B.C.), a Greek philosopher who taught in Athens from 306 B.C. E. held human happiness to be the highest good, and his scheme of morality has been summed up in 4 canons: the pleasure which produces no pain is to be embraced; the pain which produces no pleasure is to be avoided; the pleasure is to be avoided which prevents a greater pleasure or produces a greater pain; and the pain is to be endured which averts a greater pain or secures a greater pleasure. His 'pleasure' was not sensual gratification, but the rational satisfaction of a healthy mind in a healthy body. The most distinguished Roman Epicurean was Lucretius.

EPIDAU′RUS. Ancient Greek city on the E. coast of Argolis. Originally famous for the temple of the god of healing, Asclepius, E. is now noted for its beautiful and well-preserved amphitheatre where the Nat. Theatre holds an annual festival.

EPIGRAM. A short poem, originally an inscription of a votive or funerary character, but later a short, witty, and pithy saying. The chief Latin epigrammatists were Catullus and Martial; in English literature the E. has been employed by Ben Jonson, Herrick, Pope, Swift, Prior, Landor, and Yeats.

EPI′GRAPHY (Gk. *epigráphein*, 'to write on'). The art of writing with a sharp instrument on hard, durable materials, and also the scientific study of that art. Epigraphical writings are called inscriptions.

E′PILEPSY. A chronic disorder marked by attacks of loss or alteration of consciousness, usually with convulsions, corresponding to a sudden release of psychic pressure. The cause may be hereditary defect, injury, or disease.

ÉPINAL (ehpĕnahl′). Capital of Vosges dept., France, on the Moselle. A cotton-weaving centre, it dates from the 10th cent. Pop. (1962) 34,806.

EPIPHANY (ēpi′fani). A feast of the Christian Church, held on Jan 6 in commemoration of the manifestation of Christ to the world.

EPI′RUS (Gk. 'mainland'). Country of ancient Greece; the N. part is in modern Albania; the remainder, in N.W. Greece, is divided into four nomes, Arta, Thesprotia, Yanina, Preveza. Area 3,572 sq. m.; pop. (1961) 351,161.

EPI′SCOPACY. That system of Church govt. in which administrative and spiritual power over a district (diocese) is held by a bishop. The Roman Catholic, Eastern Orthodox, Anglican and Protestant and Methodist Episcopal (U.S.) churches are episcopalian; E. also exists in some branches of the Lutheran Church, esp. in Scandinavia.

EPISTLE (epi′sl). In modern usage a word applied to letters of antiquity, or with a suggestion of pomposity and literary style. The best-known Es. are those contained in the N.T., and those of Horace, Boileau, Voltaire, Ben Jonson, Dryden, and Pope.

EPPING. English town (U.D.) in Essex, 16 m. N.E. of London. Pop. (1961) 9,998. EPPING FOREST, covering about 10 sq. m., was once a royal hunting ground; it became public property, controlled by the Corporation of the City of London, in 1882.

EPSOM. Old market town of Surrey, England, 15 m. S.S.W. of London. Epsom salts were obtained from its mineral springs from 1618, and it became a spa. Epsom Downs, 1½ m. to the S., is the site of a famous racecourse. With Ewell E. forms the bor. of E. and Ewell. Pop. (1961) 71,177.

EPSOM SALTS. Hydrated magnesium sulphate, $MgSO_4.7H_2O$, known as a saline purgative. The name is derived from a bitter saline spring at Epsom, Surrey, which contains the salt in solution, but the E.S. of commerce come from Germany and U.S.A.

EPSTEIN (ep′stīn), **Sir Jacob** (1880–1959). British sculptor. B. in New York of Russo-Polish parents, in 1904 he came to England, where most of his major work was done. In 1907–8 his series of figures for the British Medical Assoc.'s building in the Strand,

EPSTEIN. Above the nave of Llandaff Cathedral his sculpture 'Christ in Majesty', poised in mid-air, and appearing weightless.
Photo: British Travel and Holidays Association.

London, provoked a storm of criticism, as did the tomb of Oscar Wilde in Paris (1909). These were followed by, amongst others, the 'Rima' memorial to W. H. Hudson in Hyde Park, 1925; 'Genesis', 1931; 'Ecce Homo', 1933; 'Adam', 1939; 'Lucifer', 1945; the aluminium 'Christ in Majesty' for Llandaff Cathedral, 1957; and 'St. Michael and the Devil' for Coventry Cathedral, 1959. All his great sculptures were carved in stone or marble as expressions of human emotions, and their lack of the purely aesthetic conventions of form and elegance almost invariably aroused furious protest. E. became equally well known for his portrait busts, e.g. of Vaughan Williams, Einstein and Blake, whose vitality and insight earned him his reputation as a romantic sculptor. Knighted in 1954.

EQUATOR. The *terrestrial equator* is the great circle whose plane is perpendicular to the earth's axis, i.e. to the line joining the poles. Its length is 24,901·8 English miles, divided into 360° of longitude. The *celestial equator* or Equinoctial is the circle in which the plane of the terrestrial equator intersects the celestial sphere.

EQUATORIAL GUINEA. *See* GUINEA, Equatorial.

EQUATORIAL UNION. Group formed in 1960 by the Republics of Congo (cap. Brazzaville) and Chad and the Central African Republic (qq.v.).

EQUINOXES (ĕkwinoksĕz; Lat. 'equal nights'). The 2 points at which the sun during its apparent annual course among the stars crosses the celestial equator; when the sun is in either equinox the day and night are of equal length, 12 hours each, all over the earth.

EQUITIES. Stocks and shares (qq.v.) which differ from debentures and preference shares in not paying interest at fixed rates.

EQUITY (ek′witi). In law, a term denoting the mitigation of the ordinary rules of law where the application of these would operate harshly in a particular case; sometimes it is regarded as an attempt to achieve 'natural justice'. So understood,

E. appears as an element in practically all mature legal systems, and in a number of modern codes the judge is instructed to apply to the decision of particular cases both the rules of strict law and the principles of E.

In England E. originated in decisions of the Lord Chancellor's court, the Court of Chancery, on matters that were remitted to it because there was no remedy available in the Common Law courts, or the remedy there was inadequate. Gradually it assumed the appearance of a distinct system of legal rules, as precise and limited in their operation as the rules of Common Law, and developed by the same method as the Common Law, i.e. by the doctrine of judicial precedent. Thus, in the 19th cent., there existed 2 great systems of English law – Common Law and E. – side by side, and applied in separate law courts, until the Judicature Acts, 1873–5, established a single High Court of Justice, in which each judge was given full powers to apply both Common Law and E. to the decision of any case before him. Equitable principles exist side by side with principles of Common Law in many branches of the law, and particularly in the law of contracts, of real and personal property, and of torts (or civil wrongs). One of the greatest contributions made by E. to English law is the institution of the trust.

EQUIVALENT WEIGHT. A chemical term for the combining proportions of a substance by wt., relative to hydrogen as standard. The Gram E.W. of an element is the number of g. of that element which will combine with or replace 1 g. of hydrogen or 8 g. of oxygen.

ÉRARD (ārahr'), **Sébastien** (1752–1831). French musical-instrument maker. He set up as a manufacturer of pianofortes in Paris c. 1777, and invented (1823) the grand pianoforte with double escapement.

ERASMUS, Desiderius (?1466–1536). Dutch scholar and humanist. B. at Rotterdam, the illegitimate son of Rogerius Gerardus (whose story is told in Charles Reade's novel, *The Cloister and the Hearth*), he himself adopted the Latin-Greek name which means 'beloved'. As a youth he was a monk in an Augustinian monastery near Gouda, but in 1495, after becoming a priest, he went to study at Paris, and in 1499 paid the first of a number of visits to England. Here he met Linacre, More, and Colet, and for a time he was Lady Margaret professor of Divinity and of Greek at Cambridge. His pioneer edition of the Greek N.T. was pub. in 1516, and an edition of St. Jerome and the *Colloquia*, a series of dialogues on contemporary topics, in 1519. In 1521 he went to Basle, where he edited the Christian Fathers. More than 3,000 of his letters have survived.

The *Erasmus Prize* (1958) of 100,000 guilders (£11,500) is awarded annually to outstanding contributors to internat. understanding, usually in social or cultural fields, e.g. Martin Buber, Sir Herbert Read, Robert Schuman, Jan Tinbergen.

ERASTIANISM. The theory that the Church should be subordinated to the State. The name is derived from Thomas Erastus (1524–83), a German-Swiss theologian, who maintained in his writings that the Church should not have the power of excluding persons as a punishment for sin.

ERATO'STHENES (fl. 235 B.C.). Greek geographer and mathematician. His map of the ancient world was the first to contain lines of latitude and longitude; he calculated the earth's circumference with an error of less than 200 m.

ERBIUM. Metallic element; symbol Er, atomic number 68, at. wt. 167·27. It is one of the rare earths, and was discovered in 1843 by Mosander.

ERCKMANN-CHATRIAN (erk'mahn-shatrēoń'). Pen-name of 2 French writers in collaboration. Émile Erckmann (1822–99) and Alexandre Chatrian

(1826–90). Their work, dating from 1847, incl. many novels, e.g. the series dealing with the Napoleonic wars: *L'Ami Fritz* (1864), *Histoire d'un Conscrit de 1813*, and *Waterloo* (1865).

ERFURT (er'foort). City in (E.) Germany, on the Gera, cap. of E. district, in a rich agricultural area. Before the S.W.W., when it was virtually destroyed, it had a 13th cent. cathedral, a converted monastery where Luther resided for a time, and many other historic buildings. Pop. (1966) 191,887.

ERG. In physics, the unit of energy in the c.g.s. system. It is the energy expended when a force of 1 dyne is exerted through a distance of 1 cm. It represents a very small amount of work, ten million ergs being approximately equal to ¾ ft lb.

ERGONO'MICS. The study of the relationship between a man and his work. The main objective is to optimize the performance of a skill in the sense of mechanical efficiency, physiological compatibility (i.e. reducing muscular stress) and psychological effectiveness (i.e. reducing fatigue, coding displayed data to suit perceptual characteristics, taking account of peculiarities of memory). Some emphasis is laid upon dynamic systems, for example, in designing optimum instrument layout in vehicle control, but the science also deals with static optimization of work benches, furniture, and the whole environment.

ERGO'STEROL. The substance which, under the action of the ultra-violet rays in sunlight, gives rise to vitamin D – the vitamin which affects bone-formation and deficiency of which produces rickets. The sterol occurs in ergot (hence the name), in yeast, and in other fungi. The principal source of commercial E. is yeast.

E'RGOT. A parasitic fungus, *Claviceps purpurea*, which attacks the rye plant. It forms large grains usually black in colour from which E. alkaloids (used in childbirth) are extracted. Infected bread causes ergotism, with gangrene or convulsions.

ERHARD, Ludwig (1897–   ). German statesman. B. in Bavaria, he studied economics and sociology at Nuremberg and graduated in commercial science at Frankfurt. After holding posts in economic and industrial research work, he was elected to the Bundestag, as a member of the Christian Democratic Union, in 1949, becoming Min. for Economics the same year. He became Vice Chancellor in 1957, and succeeded Adenauer as Chancellor of the Federal Rep. (1963–6). The 'economic miracle' of W. Germany's recovery after the S.W.W. is largely attributed to E.'s policy of 'social free enterprise' (*Marktwirtschaft*).

LUDWIG ERHARD.
Courtesy of the Embassy of the Federal Republic of Germany.

ERICA (erī'ka). In botany, the heaths; the typical genus of the family Ericaceae. There are about 500 species, distributed through Africa and Europe.

ERICACEAE (erikā'sē-ē). Family of dicotyledonous flowering plants. They are herbs, small shrubs, or small trees, but mostly have woody, creeping stems and are often evergreen. Widely distributed in the cool and temperate parts of the world, they incl. the heaths and the rhododendron.

ERICSSON (er'ikson), **Leif**. Norse explorer who traditionally sailed W. from Greenland c. A.D. 1000 to find a country first sighted by one of his predecessors in 986. Landing with 35 companions in N. America, he called it 'Vinland', because he discovered grape vines growing, and spent a winter there. The story was confirmed in 1963 when a Norwegian expedition, led by Helge Ingstad, discovered remains of a Viking settlement (dated *c.* 1000) near the fishing village of L'Anse-aux-Meadows at the northern tip of Newfoundland.The Vinland Map (*c.* 1440, pub. 1965) gives further confirmation and names a co-explorer, Bjarni. *See* VINLAND.

ERIC THE RED (fl. 982–1000). The alleged discoverer of Greenland. According to a 13th cent. saga he was the son of a Norwegian chieftain, was banished

MAX ERNST. A pioneer of the Dadaist *collage* method, Ernst also used the Surrealist technique of *frottage*, by which lead rubbed over paper placed on an object, e.g. a piece of cloth, brings into relief the weave, etc., producing suggestive impressions of mysterious landscapes, forms, etc. The painting shown here is *La Ville Petrifiée*.
Courtesy Manchester City Art Gallery.

from Iceland *c.* 982 for homicide, sailed westward, and discovered a land which he called Greenland.

ERIDU (ā′ridoo). Ancient city of Mesopotamia, according to tradition the cradle of Sumerian civilization. On its site is the Iraqi village of Tell Abu Shahrain.

ERIE (ē′ri). City on the Pennsylvania bank of Lake E., U.S.A., with heavy industries and a trade in iron, grain, and freshwater fish. Pop. (1960) 138,440.

ERIE, Lake. Fourth largest of the 'Great Lakes' of N. America connected to L. Ontario by the Niagara river, on which are the famous falls, by-passed by the Welland Canal. It is 250 m. long.

ERIGENA (erē′jena), **Johannes Scotus** (*c.* 815–77). Medieval philosopher. He was probably an Irishman and according to tradition travelled in Greece and Italy before Charles the Bald invited him to France (before 847), where he became head of the court school. He is said to have visited Oxford, to have taught at Malmesbury, and to have been stabbed to death by his pupils. As a thinker he tried to combine Christianity with Neo-Platonism.

ERIN (ē′rin). Poetic name for Ireland derived from the dative case Érinn of the Gaelic name Ériu, possibly derived from Sanskrit 'western'.

ERITREA (ārētrā′-a). Prov. of Ethiopia with a coastline of 670 m. on the Red Sea. The interior is mountainous but the valleys and intermediate plains are cultivated with the aid of irrigation. The capital is Asmara, connected by rail to Massawa, the chief port. An Italian colony from 1889, E. was conquered by the British in 1941, and was under British military administration until 1952 when, following a decision of the U.N., it was federated with Ethiopia. E. enjoyed autonomous status 1952–62 and there was Moslem nationalist unrest 1966–7. Area 45,745 sq. m.; pop 1,104,000.

ERIVAN. Alternative transliteration of YEREVAN.

ERMINE (er′min). Name given to the stoat when in its white winter coat. In northern latitudes the coat becomes completely white, except for a black tip to the tail, but in warmer regions the back may remain brownish. The fur is used commercially.

ERNIE. Electronic Random Number Indicator Equipment. Machine designed and produced by the Post Office Research Station to select and print out a long series of random 9-figure numbers to indicate the prize-winners in the monthly premium-bond draws. Numbers are printed out every 2½ seconds.

ERNST, Max (1891–   ). French Surrealist painter. B. in Brühl, nr. Cologne, he studied philosophy at the Univ. of Bonn and first exhibited in Berlin in 1916. He was an active Dadaist and in 1922 went to Paris where he helped found the Surrealist movement in 1924. Exiled by the Nazis in 1933, E. went to New York, became a U.S. citizen in 1948 and French in 1958.

ERNST, Paul (1866–1933). German writer. He propagated heroic and classical ideals and a blending of 'Nordic' and Greek spirit. His most outstanding works incl. the drama *Demetrios* (1905), the critical essays *Der Weg zu Form* (1906), the partly autobiographical novel *Der Schmale Weg zum Gluck* (1903) and *Das Kaiserbuch* (3 vols., 1923–8), an epic.

E′ROS (Cupid, Amor). In the Hellenic and Roman pantheon, the god of love. Originally a god of fertility and son of Chaos, he is later described as the son of Aphrodite, and is represented as a youth blindfolded, armed with arrows and winged.

ERSE (ers). An early Scottish form of 'Irish', the word was applied in the 18th cent. English literary world to the Gaelic language of Scotland, and occasionally to the Irish Gaelic as well.

ERSKINE, Ralph (1914–   ). British architect. Trained at the Regent Street Polytechnic, he settled in Sweden in 1939, where his work has developed with particular emphasis on sub-arctic conditions. *See* illus. under SWEDEN.

ERSKINE, Thomas, 1st baron (1750–1823). British Lord Chancellor. B. in Edinburgh and called to the Bar in 1778, he appeared for the defence in a number of trials of parliamentary reformers for sedition, and when the Whigs returned to power in 1806 he became Lord Chancellor and a baron.

ERTZ, Susan. British writer. B. at Walton-on-Thames, she m. Major J. McCrindle in 1932. Her novels, incl. *Madame Claire* (1929) and *Frail Vessels* (1950), show a development of character against a detailed background.

ERVINE (er′vin), **St. John Greer** (1883–1971). British dramatist and novelist. B. in Belfast, he was primarily a dramatist and first gained success in 1911 with *Mixed Marriage* at the Abbey Theatre, Dublin. In 1915 he was manager of the Abbey Theatre, and his most important play, *John Ferguson,* was performed there the same year. E.'s other works incl. the plays *Anthony and Anna* (1926) and *Robert's Wife* (1937), novels, biographies and books on theatrecraft.

ERYSIPELAS (erisip′elas). An acute disease of the skin due to infection by a streptococcus. Starting at some point where the skin is broken or injured, the infection spreads, producing a swollen red patch with small blisters, and general fever.

ERZERUM (ār′zeroom). Turkish town, capital of E. il, a commercial centre at the meeting-place of routes from Europe and Asia, and seat of an Armenian bishopric. Pop. (1965) 106,300.

ERZGEBIRGE (ärz′gebērge). Mountain range – the 'ore mountains' – on the German-Czech frontier, where the rare metals uranium, cobalt, bismuth, arsenic and antimony are mined. Some 90 m. long, its highest summit is Mt. Klinovec (Keilberg) in Czechoslovakia, 4,080 ft.

ESAU (ē′saw; Heb. 'hairy'). O.T. character; the son of Isaac and Rebekah, and the elder twin brother of Jacob, who tricked Isaac into giving him the blessing intended for E. by donning goatskins.

Earlier E. had sold his birthright to Jacob for a 'mess of red pottage'. He was the ancestor of the Edomites. Typically he was a nomadic hunter, compared with Jacob the less barbaric pastoralist.

ESBJERG (ez'byerg). Port of Denmark on the W. coast of Jutland, and W. termination of the rail and ferry service across Denmark and Sweden to Stockholm. Pop. (1965) 55,882.

ESCALATOR. A mechanism consisting of a continuous series of steps (or trolleys), which travel in ascending or descending direction. Es. are driven by a motor generally housed in the upper landing. This motor drives the gears and the sprockets, which in turn operate the

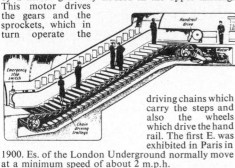

driving chains which carry the steps and also the wheels which drive the hand rail. The first E. was exhibited in Paris in 1900. Es. of the London Underground normally move at a minimum speed of about 2 m.p.h.

ESCAPE VELOCITY. The V. which would have to be imparted to a body in order for it to escape from the planet of origin, without the application of further power. In the case of the earth, E.V. is 7 miles per sec.; the value for the moon is $1\frac{1}{2}$ miles per sec., for Mars 3·1 miles per sec., and for Jupiter as much as 37 miles per sec.

ESCAUT. French form of SCHELDT.

ESENIN (yesay'nin), **Sergey** (1895–1925). Soviet poet. B. in Konstantinovo (renamed Esenino in his honour), of peasant stock, he went to Petrograd in 1915, attached himself to the Symbolists, greeted the Revolution, revived peasant traditions and folklore, and initiated the Imaginist group of poets (1919). Disillusioned by the political development, he went abroad, m. the American dancer, Isadora Duncan, and afterwards a granddau. of Leo Tolstoy, became the head of the Moscow bohemians and committed suicide.

E'SHER. English town (U.D.) in Surrey, on the Mole, 15 m. S.W. of London. There are some remains of Wolsey's palace. In the district is Sandown Park racecourse. Pop. (1961) 60,586.

E'SKILSTUNA (-toonah). Manufacturing town 52 m. W. of Stockholm, Sweden, with iron foundries, steel and armament works. Pop. (1966) 64,830.

ESKIMO. People inhabiting the Arctic coasts of N. America, the eastern islands of the Canadian Arctic, and the ice-free coasts of Greenland. Of uncertain origin, they are generally long-headed, of medium height, flat-faced, with prominent cheekbones, sallow complexion, dark eyes, and lank black hair. Traditionally, they construct their homes from stones, peat, bones, driftwood and skins – snow igloos being used only for temporary camps in winter travel

ESKIMO. Miniature stone carving: medicine man or shaman with drum.
Courtesy of the National Film Board of Canada.

– and rely on oil from blubber for light and heat and on their reindeer herds for all other wants. In practice this picture is increasingly modified as western civilization extends in the Arctic. The skill which the Es. show in the construction of their *kayaks* (skin-covered canoes) and in their remarkable small-scale carvings is easily adapted to the modern situation, and they are first-class mechanics.

The E. language possesses dialects, but has no striking divergencies. The conditions of their life make rather for individualism than distinctive tribal organization. The E. has belief in a soul, in survival after death, in taboos, charms and amulets and formerly in the medicine man or *angakok*, but Christianity has been adopted by many. They number *c.* 35,000.

ESKIMO DOG. Semi-domesticated dog kept by Eskimoes in Alaska for drawing sledges. They are strong and fierce, similar in appearance to sheepdogs.

ESKISEHIR. City in Turkey, 125 m. W. of Ankara, exports meerschaum, chromium, and magnesite; makes cotton goods, tiles; assembles aircraft. Pop. (1965) 174,500.

ESPA'RTO. A grass (*Stipa tenacissima*), native to S. Spain and N. Africa, now widely grown in dry, sandy situations throughout the world. The plant is 3 to 4 ft. high, producing greyish-green leaves up to 3 ft. long, which are used for paper-making, ropes, baskets, mats, cables, etc.

ESPEHAN. *See* ISFAHAN.

ESPERA'NTO. International language invented by Dr. L. L. Zamenhof of Warsaw (1859–1917), who pub. the first book on it in 1887. It consists of natural roots and develops on natural lines, and has a literature of original and translated works.

ESPINO'SA, Edouard (1872–1950). Maître de ballet. Son of Leon E. (1825–1903), who was a pupil of the early 19th cent. ballet masters, he became ballet master and principal dancer at various London theatres, wrote many books on ballet technique, and helped to found modern Br. ballet.

ESPARTO GRASS

ESPIONAGE. *See* SECRET SERVICE.

ESQUIMAULT (eskwi'mawlt). Canadian naval station, at S. of Vancouver Island, B.C. Pop. (est.) 6,500.

ESSAY. Literary form, dealing in a discursive meditative way with some particular subject; a personal note is more or less marked. The E. first became a recognized genre and name with the first edition of Montaigne's essays in 1580. Bacon's essays (1597) are among the most famous in English. Abraham Cowley, whose Es. appeared in 1668, was the first English essayist to bring ease and freedom to the genre, but it was with the development of periodical literature in the 18th cent. that the E. became a widely used form. The great names are Addison and Steele, with their *Tatler* and *Spectator* papers, and later Johnson and Goldsmith. A new era was inaugurated by Lamb's *Essays of Elia* (1820); to the same period belong Leigh Hunt, Hazlitt, Sainte Beuve and De Quincey and the Americans Emerson and Thoreau; Hazlitt may be regarded as the originator of the modern critical E., and his successors incl. Arnold and Gosse. Macaulay, whose Es. began to appear shortly after those of Lamb, presents a strong contrast in his vigorous but less personal tone. There was a considerable revival of the form during the closing years of the 19th and beginning of the 20th cent., in the work of R. L. Stevenson, Anatole France, Gautier, Sir Max Beerbohm, and later of Chesterton and Belloc. The literary journalistic tradition of the E. has been continued by E. V. Lucas, Robert Lynd, the American James Thurber, Sir Desmond MacCarthy, etc., and the critical essay by George Orwell, Cyril Connolly, F. R. Leavis, T. S. Eliot, etc. The E. was generally adopted in 19th cent. Europe as a vehicle for literary criticism, but the 'true' E. is usually regarded as being particularly English in spirit.

ESSEN. German city in North Rhine-Westphalia; centre of the great coal-mining and iron and steel industries of the Ruhr. The Krupps steel and armament plants here, largest in Germany, were repeatedly bombed during the S.W.W. Pop. (1966) 716,078.

ESSEN. The Altenessener Berkwerks.
Courtesy of German Information Bureau.

ESSENES (esēnz'). A body of pre-Christian Jewish ascetics in Palestine who regulated their life according to rules resembling those of later monasticism, and practised community of goods. It has been claimed that both St. John the Baptist and Christ himself may possibly have lived for a time among the E., perhaps at Qumran (q.v.), and sayings of Jesus seem to reflect both the influence of Essene teaching and antipathy to certain aspects.

ESSEQUIBO (esekē'bō). Principal river of Guyana. Navigable for 50 m., it rises in the Acari mts. on the Brazilian border and flows N. for *c.* 600 m.

ESSEX, Robert Devereux, 2nd earl of (1566–1601). English soldier and statesman. Eldest son of the 1st earl, he saw service in the Netherlands in 1585–6 and distinguished himself by his courage at the battle of Zutphen. From 1587 he became a favourite with Elizabeth, who created him Master of the Horse and a K.G. In 1599 he led an army against Tyrone in Ulster, but was outgeneralled, made an unauthorised truce with Tyrone, and returned without permission to England. He was forbidden to return to court, and Elizabeth's refusal to renew the monopoly of sweet wines he had enjoyed goaded him to madness. At the head of a body of supporters, he marched into the City, but was promptly arrested, tried for treason, and beheaded on Tower Green.

ESSEX, Robert Devereux, 3rd earl of (1591–1646). English soldier. Eldest son of the 2nd earl, he commanded the Parliamentary army at the drawn battle of Edgehill in 1642. Following a disastrous campaign in Cornwall, he resigned his command in 1645.

ESSEX. Co. of S.E. England, bounded on the S. by the Thames estuary, and on the E. by the North Sea. It is for the most part predominantly low-lying but undulating, the only high land is in the N.W. The N. two-thirds of E. belong geologically to E. Anglia: the soil is composed of the same highly fertile glacial clays which yield heavy crops of cereals, sugar beet, fruits, and vegetables. The southern part is composed of heavier clays, and was originally

ROBERT DEVEREUX, 2nd earl of Essex.
Photo: N.P.G.

ESSEX. The Cluniac Priory of St. Mary of Prittlewell, near Southend, was from the 12th century to its dissolution in the 16th the most wealthy community in the south-east of the county. Above the windows of the prior's chamber look down on the cloister garth.

densely forested. Parts of the forest remain, e.g. Epping Forest, but most has been cleared, and dairying is an important industry. In the S.W. the co. borders on Greater London. The co. town is Chelmsford; Colchester is the centre of an oyster industry; Southend, Brightlingsea, Clacton, Frinton, Dovercourt are seaside resorts; Harwich and Tilbury are ports. Area 1,419 sq. m.; pop. (1967) 1,268,610.

The Univ. of E. (1962) has its H.Q. at Wivenhoe Park, Wivenhoe, 3 m. S.E. of Colchester.

ESTATE. In law, the interest which a person has in any property. *Real E.* is an interest in any freehold land; *personal E.* the interest in any other kind of property.

ESTER. An organic compound formed by the reaction between an alcohol and an acid, with the elimination of water. Es. correspond to inorganic salts. They are important in explosives, plastics, photographic films, and rayon; vegetable and animal fats and oils; soaps, paints and varnishes; flavourings and perfume.

ESTHER. Chief character in the O.T. book of E., which relates that as consort of the Persian king Ahasuerus, she prevented the extermination of her people by the vizier Haman – a deliverance celebrated at the Jewish festival of Purim.

ESTIENNE (ātyen'; Latinized as **Stephanus**). French family of printers and scholars, who were estab. in Paris as printers in the 16th cent. ROBERT E. (1503–59) was the royal printer in Latin, Greek, and Hebrew, and on becoming a Protestant moved in 1551 to Geneva, where he produced the first Greek N.T. to be divided into verses.

ESTO'NIA (Estonian Soviet Socialist Republic). A constituent republic of the U.S.S.R., occupying the peninsula between the Gulf of Finland and the Baltic Sea, and bordering Latvia to the S. It is a low-lying extension of the Russian plain. The climate is suited to hardy agriculture, and the country is heavily forested. The capital is Tallinn, a port on the Gulf of Finland; Paldiski and Parnu are other ports; the largest town inland is Tartu, which has a university.

E. was Russian from 1721 until, following the Revolution of 1917, it won independence in 1920 after a struggle. In 1939 E. was occupied by Russia, and in 1940 became a S.S.R. of the U.S.S.R. The Germans overran E. in 1941, were ejected in 1944. The Estonian language is akin to Finnish. Area 18,300 sq. m.; pop. (1968) 1,304,000.

ESZTERGOM (es'ter-). Hungarian city on the Danube, 25 m. N.W. of Budapest, birthplace of St.

Stephen, and former ecclesiastical cap. of Hungary, with a fine cathedral. Pop. *c.* 25,000.

ÉTAPLES (ehtah'pl). Fishing port and seaside resort on the Canche estuary, Pas de Calais dept., France. During the F.W.W. it was an important British base and hospital centre. Pop. (1962) 8,647.

ETCHING. A print or impression on paper, taken from a metal (usually copper) plate, in which the picture has been 'etched' or bitten-in by means of some corrosive acid or chemical. The method was invented in Germany about 1500, the earliest dated print being of 1513. Whereas in the earlier method of engraving (q.v.) on metal the picture is cut into the metal surface by means of a sharp instrument called a burin or graver, used with a pushing action, in etching it is drawn on the plate by means of a sharp delicate metal point, which allows much greater

ETCHING. This example of the art – a portrait of Clement de Jonghe in the Victoria and Albert Museum – is the work of Rembrandt, its greatest master.

freedom of action. Among the earliest etchers were Dürer, van Dyck, Hollar, and Rembrandt. Since then great interest has been shown in it by many artists, e.g. Whistler, W. Strang, D. Y. Cameron, F. Brangwyn, W. Sickert, Muirhead Bone, etc.

E'THANE. A colourless, odourless gas, formula C_2H_6, b.p. 88°C., the second member of the series of paraffin hydrocarbons of the general formula C_nH_{2n+2}. Its chief importance is as a fuel in the form of natural gas.

ETHELBERT (*c.* 552–616). King of Kent, England. He succeeded his father, Eormenric, in 560, and gradually extended his authority over Middlesex, Essex, E. Anglia, and Mercia. He m. the Frankish princess, Bertha, who was a Christian, and favourably received St. Augustine in 597. In due course he was baptized.

ETHELRED I (d. 871). King of Wessex, England, elder brother of Alfred the Great. He succeeded his brother Ethelbert in 866, and his reign was spent in war with the Danish invaders. A defeat at Reading was followed by a victory at Ashdown.

ETHELRED II (968–1016). King of England; called the Unready, i.e. redeless, lacking in foresight. The son of King Edgar, he became king in 978 after the murder of his half-brother, Edward the Martyr. He tried to buy off the Danish raiders by paying Danegeld, and in 1002 ordered the massacre of the Danish settlers – so provoking an invasion by Sweyn of Denmark. War with Sweyn and Sweyn's son, Canute, occupied the rest of E.'s reign.

ETHER or **ETHYL ETHER.** $(C_2H_5)_2O$. Colourless, volatile, inflammable liquid, b.p. 35°C., slightly soluble in water, miscible with alcohol. It is prepared by treatment of ethyl alcohol with excess concentrated sulphuric acid at 140°C. It is used as an anaesthetic by vapour inhalation and as an external cleansing agent before surgical operations. It is also used as a solvent in the preparation of explosives and collodion and in the extraction of oils, fats, waxes, resins, and alkaloids.

The term E. is also applied to a series of organic compounds of the general formula R-O-R′, where R and R′ are different radicals.

ETHEREGE (eth'erej) or **ETHEREDGE, Sir George** (*c.* 1635–*c.* 1691). British dramatist. B. probably at Maidenhead, his first play, *Love in a Tub*, was produced in 1664, and was a great success. *She Would If She Could*, a lively but immoral piece, followed in 1667, and his best comedy, *The Man of Mode*, in 1676. E. is the founder of the comedy of intrigue.

ETHICAL MOVEMENT. Movement designed to establish, maintain, and further the moral or ethical factor as the real substance and fundamental part of religion. It had its rise in U.S.A. in 1876, when Felix Adler founded an Ethical Society in New York. In 1888 the first English E. Society was founded by Dr. Stanton Coit, the successor of M. D. Conway, at the Chapel in South Place, Finsbury, that became the South Place Ethical Society.

ETHICS. The branch of philosophy that is concerned with moral judgments of right and wrong, good and bad. So far as Europe is concerned, it may be said to have originated as a systematic intellectual study with Socrates in the 5th cent. B.C., but considerably earlier there was intense ethical speculation in India and China. Plato's *Republic* is an exposition of the nature of justice or righteousness, and ethical theory was advanced by Aristotle's *Nicomachean Ethics* and kindred writings. The Cyrenaics, Epicureans, and Stoics advanced theories that have been many times revived. The 'Christian ethic' is mainly a combination of N.T. moral teaching with ideas drawn from Plato and Aristotle. Hobbes, Shaftesbury, Hutcheson, Hume, and Bishop Butler are notable 17–18th cent. British ethical philosophers. One of the greatest individual contributors to ethical theory was Kant, with his 'categorical imperative'. The utilitarian ethic was ably expounded by Bentham, J. S. Mill, Sidgwick, and Herbert Spencer; they were opposed by such thinkers as F. H. Bradley and T. H. Green, who linked ethics with metaphysics, and emphasized the place of the individual in organized society. Leading modern ethicists are G. E. Moore, A. C. Ewing, C. D. Broad, and H. Rashdall.

ETHIO'PIA. In ancient geography, name given by the Greeks at first to the whole of N. Africa, later restricted to an area covered by present-day Nubia, Sennar, and Kordofan in the Republic of Sudan and the W. of the independent empire in N.E. Africa which is 20th cent. Ethiopia. E. consists of elevated plateaux and mountain ranges with a narrow coastal belt on the Red Sea, and is watered by the headstreams of tributaries of the Nile, e.g. the Takazze, the Abbai (which drains L. Tana, one of several large lakes), and the Blue Nile.

The northern part of the country is inhabited by Amharas, numbering about 2 million. Over half the population is made up of Gallas, an agricultural

ETHIOPIA. Addis Ababa is often the venue for conferences of African states. Emperor Haile Selassie (right) is here awarding an honorary degree to a visitor, President Tubman of Liberia.
Photo: Keystone

people of Hamitic origin. The E. part is settled by a number of Somali peoples. Other people represented include Negroes and Falashas, a Jewish group. The pop. generally adhere either to the Coptic Church or Islam, Christians predominating in some N. provs. and Moslems in some of the southern; there is also a pagan element. The economy is agricultural and pastoral, crops incl. coffee – the chief export – cereals, cane sugar, and oil seeds; and sheep, cattle and goats are raised, hides, etc., being exported. Some salt, gold and potash is worked, and there is thought to be other mineral wealth incl. oil. Addis Ababa (the cap.) is linked by rail with Djibouti, and by road with Asmara (which has a rail line to Massawa) and with Assab via Dessie. Dire Dawa is commercially important. Most populous of the 14 provs. are Hararge, Shoa, Tigre and Wollo; Eritrea (q.v.) gives E. a coastline. Pop. (1965) 22,590,400.

HISTORY. Long subject to Egypt, E. became independent about the 11th cent. B.C. Christianity was introduced from Egypt *c.* A.D. 330 and was adopted as the national religion, but the Arab conquests of the 7th cent. isolated E. from the rest of Christendom. Diplomatic relations were estab. *c.* 1500 by the Portuguese, and contact with Europe was renewed when the explorer Bruce arrived in 1769. Since 1850 Ethiopian history has turned on the attempt to establish the authority of the central government over the local chieftains. National unity was attained under Menelek (reigned 1889–1913). Italian penetration from Eritrea resulted in war in 1895–6, ending with the Ethiopian victory of Adowa. Menelek's successors were Lej Yasu, deposed in 1916, and the empress Zauditu; with her was associated Ras Tafari, who succeeded as Haile Selassie in 1930. E. was conquered by the Italians in 1935–6, but in 1941 Haile Selassie returned from exile and with the aid of British forces expelled the Italians. His policy, before and after his exile, aimed at strengthening the central government. Under the constitution of 1955, there is a Council of Ministers responsible to the Emperor, who also nominates the Senate, but the Chamber of Deputies, elected by universal suffrage for 4 years, has a gradually increasing power.

LANGUAGE AND LITERATURE. The various languages of Ethiopia constitute today the chief representatives of the S. branch of the Semitic family. The chief literary and the ecclesiastical language is Ge'ez; Amharic is the principal colloquial language of the highlands; other languages spoken include Tigrina, round Aksum, and Tigré in Eritrea, both dialects of Ge'ez. Ethiopian literature can be traced from the 5th cent. but apart from translations there are only a few chronicles, hymns, and diplomatic correspondence.

ETHNO'LOGY. That branch of anthropology that is concerned with the characteristics and distribution over the globe of the races of mankind; also of their cultural conditions and achievements.

ETHYL ALCOHOL. Colourless liquid C_2H_5OH with a pleasant odour, b.p. 78·5°C., density 0·789 g./ml. miscible with water or ether, and burning in air with a pale blue flame. The vapour forms an explosive mixture with air and may be used in high-compression internal combustion engines.

It is made by fermentation of many carbohydrates, by absorption of ethylene and subsequent reaction with water, or by the reduction of acetaldehyde in the presence of a catalyst. It is rapidly absorbed in the human body from the stomach and upper intestine and affects nearly every tissue, particularly the central nervous system. Tests have shown that the feeling of elation, etc., usually associated with drinking alcoholic liquors is due to the loss of inhibitions or removal of the restraining influences of the higher cerebral centres. It also results in dilatation of the blood vessels, particularly of the skin where a flushing is commonly observed. This loss of heat from the skin actually produces a physical cooling inside the body, despite the feeling of warmth experienced.

The digestive system is also affected and alcohol is absorbed unchanged from the gastro-intestinal tract into the circulation and intoxication depends on its degree of concentration. It can be detected and measured in the blood (legal limit for British motorists 80 mg in 100 millilitres) and in the breath.

E'TNA. Volcano on the E. coast of Sicily, 10,755 ft. in height (10,870 ft. in 1861) – the highest European volcano. There have been many violent eruptions.

ETON. English town (U.D.) in Bucks on the N. bank of the Thames, opposite Windsor. Pop. (1961) 3,901.

E. College, one of the largest and most famous of England's public schools, was founded in 1440 by Henry VI. The present constitution dates from 1871, and the governing body consists of a Provost appointed by the Crown and 10 fellows. The boys number over a thousand; seventy Collegers live in the College, the remainder, called King's Scholars and Oppidans, live in houses held by the masters. King George III's birthday is celebrated each year on June 4th. Famous old Etonians include Chatham, Wellington, Gladstone, Lord Avon, Macmillan, and Sir Alec Douglas-Home.

ETON. In the centre of the 'school yard' at Eton College stands a bronze statue of the founder, Henry VI, and behind is Lupton's Tower, commemorating Roger Lupton, provost of the college 1503–35, whose tomb is in the chapel.
Photo: A. W. Kerr.

ETRU'SCANS. Ancient people of northern Italy. Their chief settlements were the twelve cities of Etruria, including Volaterrae, Tarquinii, Clusium, Caere, and Vetulonia, each of which seems to have been independent. The height of their power was reached about 500 B.C. In 474 B.C. they were defeated by the Carthaginians in a naval battle off Cumae, and about 400 B.C. their northern conquests were lost by the irruption of the Celts into N. Italy. Thereafter the E. entered into a period of decline, and they gradually succumbed to the rising power of Rome.

Some knowledge of their art, religion, and language

has been obtained from excavated tombs. The principal medium is sculpture, but pottery, bronze-ware, and mural painting are also noteworthy. Etruscan religion seems to have been derived from Asia Minor, and shows many signs of Greek influence. The language, despite a large number of inscriptions, mainly funerary, and a certain number of words derived by the Romans from Etruscan, is still very imperfectly known.

ETTY, William (1787–1849). British artist. B. at York, he served 7 years' apprenticeship to a Hull printer, and in 1806 went to London at the invitation of his uncle, William E., himself a fine draughtsman. With Opie's aid he was admitted to the R.A. schools, becoming a student of Sir Thomas Lawrence in 1807, and first gained success at the Academy with 'Telemachus rescuing Antiope' in 1811. He visited Italy in 1816 and 1822, was elected R.A. in 1828, and lived in London until 1848 when he retired to York. In his work E. aimed to paint great moral truth and regarded his numerous nude paintings as a dedication to 'God's most glorious work'.

ETTY. A student of the Venetian masters, Etty captured a similar richness of flesh tints.
Photo: Victoria and Albert Museum.

ETYMO'LOGY. The branch of linguistic science which deals with the ultimate origin and history of individual words. It has 2 chief aspects: *phonetic*, dealing with the changes in sounds, and *semantic*, with the changes in meaning.

EUBOEA (ūbē'-a). Largest of the Greek islands. It lies off the E. coast of Greece, in the Aegean Sea, and is about 110 m. long. The chief town is Chalcis, connected by a bridge to the mainland. Area 1,450 sq. m. The nome of E., area 1,480 sq. m., includes several small islands and had a pop. (1961) of 165,758.

EUCALYPTUS (ūkalip'tus). Genus of trees of the Myrtaceae family, practically confined, in the natural state, to Australia and Tasmania, where they are commonly known as gum trees. About 90 per cent of Australian timber belongs to the E. group, which comprises about 400 species. EUCALYPTUS OIL, used in medicine, is obtained from the leaves of certain species by aqueous distillation.

EUCALYPTUS

EUCHARIST (ū'karist). The most solemn and universally observed of the Christian sacraments. The word comes from the Greek for 'thanksgiving', and refers to the statement in the Gospel narrative that Christ gave thanks over the bread and the cup. Other names for it are the Lord's Supper, Holy Communion, and (amongst Catholics) the Mass. Members of the C. of E. are required to participate in the E. at least 3 times a year, Easter to be one.

EUCKEN (oi'ken), **Rudolf Christoph** (1846–1926). German philosopher. B. in E. Friesland, he taught philosophy at Basle and Jena, and in 1908 was awarded the Nobel prize for literature. His systematic teaching is founded on the idealistic philosophy of Kant and Fichte, and centres round man's spiritual life which transcends nature, engages and brings into action all his faculties, and reaches perfection in religion. His memoirs were pub. in 1921.

EUCLID (u'klid) (fl. 300 B.C.). Greek mathematician, who lived at Alexandria and wrote the *Stoicheia* (Elements) in 13 books, of which 9 deal with plane and solid geometry, and 4 with arithmetic. His main work lay in the systematic arrangement of previous discoveries, and the geometrical books remained a standard textbook for over 2,000 years and were still in regular use in English schools in the present cent.

EUGÈNE (ūjèn') **of Savoy**, Prince (1663–1736). Austrian general. The son of Prince Eugène Maurice of Savoy-Carignano, he was b. in Paris. When Louis XIV refused him a commission he entered the Austrian army, and served against the Turks at the defence of Vienna in 1683, and against the French on the Rhine and in Italy 10 years later. In 1697 he expelled the Turks from Hungary by his triumph at Zenta. In the War of the Spanish Succession he shared with Marlborough in his great victories, and won many successes as an independent commander in Italy. He vainly protested against the dismissal of Marlborough, and suffered several defeats before the peace settlement at Rastatt in 1714. He again defeated the Turks in 1716–18, and fought a last campaign against the French in 1734–5.

EUGENICS (ūjen'iks). Term derived from the Greek for 'well born', coined by Sir Francis Galton (q.v.) for the science that he defined as the study of agencies under social control which may improve or impair the racial qualities of future generations either physically or mentally. The pioneer of the science was Galton.

EUGÉNIE (öjehnē') (1826–1920). Empress of the French. Dau. of a grandee of Spain, the count of Montijo, she m. in 1853 Louis Napoleon, soon after he became French emperor as Napoleon III. After Sedan she fled to England, and settled with him at Chislehurst. Later she lived at Farnborough, where she built a mausoleum in which she, her husband and her son, who was killed in the Zulu War, were buried.

EULER (oi'ler), **Leonhard** (1707–83). Swiss mathematician. B. at Basle, he became professor of physics at St. Petersburg in 1730. Summoned to Berlin in 1741 by Frederick the Great, he spent 25 years there and then returned to Russia. He laboured not only in pure mathematics, but also in astronomy, optics, etc.

EUMEN'IDES. In Greek mythology the Furies or spirits of vengeance, usually represented as winged women with snake-like hair. They were sometimes known as *Erīnyes* (Furies) and sometimes by the propitiatory name of E. (Kindly ones).

EUNUCH (ū'nuk; Gk. *eunoukhos*, one in charge of a bed). In Eastern countries originally a bedchamber attendant (generally a castrated male person) employed in a harem or zenana. Es. often filled high offices of state in China, India, Persia, etc. The *castrati* of Italy were famous throughout the cents. for the beauty of their voices, but on the accession of pope Leo XIII in 1878 the practice of castrating boys for this purpose ceased.

EURASIAN (ūrā'shan). In India and the E. Indies a term formerly used to denote a person born of a European and an Asiatic, and his or her progeny; it was almost exclusively derogatory and often insulting.

EURATOM (European Atomic Energy Community). *See under* EUROPE, UNIFICATION OF.

EURE (ör). French river rising in Orne dept. and flowing S.E., then N., to the Seine. Chartres is on its banks; length 70 m. It gives its name to two depts., E. and E.-et-Loire.

EURHYTHMICS (ūrith'miks). Practice of co-ordinated bodily movement as a help to musical development. It was founded by the Swiss musician

Jaques-Dalcroze (q.v.), prof. of harmony at Geneva. He devised a series of 'gesture' songs, designed to be sung simultaneously with certain bodily actions.

EURI'PIDES (*c.* 484–407 B.C.). Ancient Greek dramatist. The youngest of the 3 great tragedians of ancient Athens, he lived in retirement (apart from his normal terms of service with the Athenian conscript army) and wrote over 80 plays, of which 19 have survived. These show marked innovations in dramatic technique and in the treatment of dramatic themes, and E. was bitterly criticized for his 'impiety' and religious unorthodoxy, and for the sympathy he showed to slaves, beggars, and to women characters like Medea. All the plays are marked by realistic character drawing and, whereas earlier playwrights had presented ideal heroes, E. shows ordinary men and women as they really were. Towards the end of his life he went into voluntary exile at the court of Macedonia.

His surviving plays are: *Rhesus, Cyclops* (a satiric drama), *Alcestis* (438), *Medea* (431), *Hippolytus* (428), *Hecuba* (c. 426), *Children of Heracles* (c. 425), *Suppliant Women* (c. 424), *Madness of Heracles* (c. 423), *Andromache* (c. 420), *Ion* (c. 418), *Trojan Women* (415), *Electra* (c. 413), *Iphigenia in Tauris* (c. 413), *Helen* (412), *Phoenissae* (c. 410), *Orestes* (408), *Iphigenia in Aulis* (405), and *Bacchae* (405). There are verse translations of a number of these by Gilbert Murray.

EURŌ'PA. In Greek mythology, a maiden who was courted by Zeus in the guise of a white bull. She mounted on to his back, whereupon the god swam out to sea and transported her to Crete. As the name implies, E. personifies the European continent.

EUROPA NOSTRA (Our Europe). International federation estab. in 1963 by the representatives of 18 organizations (e.g. Italia Nostra, National Trust, Irish Georgian Soc., Vieilles Maisons Françaises) in 11 European countries to organize public opinion for the preservation of historic sites, buildings and monuments. The 1st pres. was Prince F. Caracciolo.

EUROPE. Continent forming the western extremity of the Euroasiatic land mass; the Ural Mountains are usually considered to mark its eastern limit, the frontier between the U.S.S.R. and Turkey and Persia its south-eastern. At one time the Caucasus Mountains were considered to mark the limit of Europe in this area, but the extension of European Russia into former Asiatic territories has pushed the line farther to the S. On all other sides E. meets the sea; it narrows towards the west. E., which forms about ⅕ of the world's land surface, has a length of about 2,400 m. from the North Cape to Cape Matapan, in S. Greece, and a breadth from Cape St. Vincent to the Urals of *c.* 3,150 m. The surface of the continent is divided into 3 main areas: (1) the North European Plain, which includes S. England and contains many great cities, such as London, Paris, Berlin, and Moscow, besides fertile agricultural lands; (2) the Central European Highlands, consisting of the Sierra Nevada, Pyrenees, Alps, Apennines, Carpathians and Balkans; and (3) the Scandinavian highland, including the N. of the British Isles.

The main rivers flow into northern or inland seas. The Volga, the Don, the Dnieper, the Northern Dvina, and the Western Dvina rise on the Valdaian plateau, to the N.W. of Moscow, and the Danube, the Rhine, the Rhône, the Po, and the Adige flow from the Alps.

E. has many lakes, notably Geneva, Constance, Lucerne, Neuchâtel, Maggiore, Garda, and Como in the Alps; Vänern, Vättern, Mälar, Mjosa, and Randsfjord in the peninsula formed by Norway and Sweden; Ladoga, Onega, Peipus, and Ilmen in N. Russia; Saïma and innumerable others in Finland. The largest islands are Spitsbergen, Iceland, Gt. Britain, Ireland, Sardinia, Corsica, Sicily, Novaya Zemlya, and Crete.

GEOLOGY. The oldest rocks found in Europe, those of the Archaean and Palaeozoic periods, cover most of the northern part of the continent including the N. and W. of Gt. Britain, and are also found in Brittany, Central France, and Spain. The more recent rocks of the Mesozoic and Cainozoic periods form a continuous belt in the central plain from the North Sea into Russia.

CLIMATE. Most of E. lies within the N. temperate zone, but parts of Norway, Sweden, and Russia are N. of the Arctic Circle. The British Isles and the western coastal areas of continental countries are washed by the Gulf Stream. There are four main climatic regions in E.: (1) southern in the Mediterranean region, characterized by an absence of rainfall in summer; (2) western, near the Atlantic and eastward to the Oder, with warm summers and cold winters, and rainfall evenly distributed throughout the year; (3) eastern or continental, with extremes of heat in summer and cold in winter; and (4) the sub-Arctic climate of the northern regions.

POPULATION. E. is remarkable for the high average density of its population. Several countries of the W. support an average of over 600 persons per sq. m. On the N. European Plain the highest densities are towards the W. There is a zone of high density along the S. edge of the plain, from the Ukraine to N.E. France, caused by the high quality of the soils and the occurrence of the major coalfields. Anthropologically 3 main racial types are found, though most Europeans show physically a blending of types. The 'Alpine' people, broad-headed and rather stocky, are found in Central E., especially the highlands. The 'Slavs' of Eastern E. are similar to the 'Alpine'. The 'Nordic' type of N.W. Europe have

EUROPE. Physical features of the continent.

COUNTRIES OF EUROPE

	Area in sq. m.	Population (in 1,000s)	Capital
Albania	10,629	1,914	Tirana
Andorra	191	5	Andorra la Vella
Austria	32,375	7,290	Vienna
Belgium	11,775	9,178	Brussels
Bulgaria	42,796	8,334	Sofia
Czechoslovakia	49,381	14,271	Prague
Denmark, inc. Faroes	17,116	4,813	Copenhagen
Finland	130,124	4,664	Helsinki
France	212,961	49,700	Paris
Germany, E.	41,636	17,080	East Berlin
Germany, W.	95,925	59,948	Bonn
Greece	51,182	8,614	Athens
Hungary	35,902	10,197	Budapest
Iceland	39,758	200	Reykjavik
Irish Republic	26,600	2,884	Dublin
Italy	116,365	53,649	Rome
Liechtenstein	61	20	Vaduz
Luxemburg	999	335	Luxemburg
Monaco	·575	22	Monaco-Ville
Netherlands	13,550	12,676	The Hague
Norway	125,068	3,769	Oslo
Spitzbergen (Svalbard)	24,000	3	Long Year City
Poland	120,360	32,065	Warsaw
Portugal	35,490	9,228	Lisbon
Rumania	91,700	19,287	Bucharest
San Marino	38	18	San Marino
Spain	194,424	32,275	Madrid
Sweden	173,629	7,894	Stockholm
Switzerland	15,941	6,071	Bern/Berne
Turkey-in-Europe	9,068	2,720	Ankara
United Kingdom	93,477	54,909	London
Gibraltar	2·25	25	Gibraltar
Malta	122	318	Valletta
U.S.S.R. in Europe:			
Armenia	11,500	2,306	Erivan
Azerbaijan	33,100	4,917	Baku
Estonia	18,300	1,304	Tallinn
Georgia	30,000	4,059	Tbilisi
Latvia	25,000	2,298	Riga
Lithuania	25,300	3,064	Vilna
Moldavia	13,100	3,484	Kishinev
R.S.F.S.R.	1,647,600	96,000	Moscow
Ukraine	232,000	46,381	Kiev
White Russia	80,500	8,820	Minsk
Vatican	·17	1	Vatican City
Yugoslavia	98,779	19,958	Belgrade
	5,027,324·995	627,463	

long heads, blond colouring, and blue eyes. The 'Mediterranean' type, found in the countries fringing that sea, are long-headed with dark hair and eyes.

LANGUAGES. Most European languages belong to the Aryan group. Celtic is still spoken to some extent in Wales, the Isle of Man, the Scottish Highlands, Ireland, and Brittany. The main divisions of the Teutonic group of languages are High and Low German; English; Dutch and Flemish; Scandinavian in Iceland, Denmark, Norway, and Sweden. Slav languages are spoken by Russians, Poles, Lithuanians, Letts, Wends, Czechs, etc., while French, Spanish, Portuguese, Italian, and Rumanian are Romanic languages. The few non-Aryan tongues include Magyar, Basque, and Turkish.

VEGETATION. S. of the Alps the trees are mainly evergreens. Rice, maize, millet, and wheat are among the cereals cultivated in this region, and olives, grapes, oranges, lemons, figs, and chestnuts thrive. Central E. is particularly rich in cereals and also produces large quantities of fruit. Most of its forests are deciduous, oak, beech, ash, etc. In the N. the chief trees are pines, larches, firs, birches, and willows.

MINERALS. Coal is abundant in Great Britain, Germany, France, Belgium, Czechoslovakia, Poland, and Russia; Great Britain, Germany, France, Belgium, Sweden, Austria, Czechoslovakia, Russia, and Spain have deposits of iron ore. Copper, lead, zinc, gold, platinum, silver, quicksilver, salt, sulphur, and graphite are all obtained in E. There are large oilfields in the Caucasus and W. Ukraine and both oil and natural gas offshore beneath the North Sea.

Industrialisation began in the W. where the aptitude of the people, presence of minerals that could be worked with comparative ease, and accessibility to overseas territories offering both raw materials and markets all helped the process; but after the F.W.W. industrial development spread eastwards, and was accelerated after the S.W.W. especially in Ukraine and other countries of the U.S.S.R. or under Russian influence.

RELIGION. The majority are Christian (45% Roman Catholic and 25% Protestant or Orthodox), the rest incl. Moslems in the Balkans and Caucasia, and in Britain; Jews; and – espec. in Communist countries – an increasing proportion of atheists.

ORGANISATION. As yet the European Community (see EUROPEAN UNION) is militarily inferior to both U.S.A. and U.S.S.R., and financially and industrially inferior to the U.S.A., but in trade it is the largest world importer of industrial and agricultural products, and of commodities from the developing countries. A customs union and common agricultural policy already exist, and there are plans for complete regulation of foreign trade and transport; full mobility of workers under uniform conditions of employment; united scientific and technical research; common tax laws, currency, social welfare, and civil and commercial law; and political institutions enabling E. to act as a single unit. The Action Committee for the United States of E. (1955) incl. 50 trade union and political leaders from the Six: Britain joined in 1968.

EUROPEAN HISTORY. Ancient. Throughout the many thousands of years of the Palaeolithic Age the inhabitants of E. lived by hunting or fishing; then came the Neolithic Age, during which agriculture and the domestication of animals began. The working of bronze, introduced into Crete from Egypt and Syria c. 3000 B.C., spread over the Mediterranean, and reached Britain and Germany after 1750 B.C.

Greece was overrun c. 1500 B.C. by Greek-speaking barbarians, who founded the Mycenaean civilisation, and c. 1100 B.C. subdued the Cretan Minoan civilisation. Iron-smelting, introduced into Greece from Armenia c. 1000 B.C., reached N. and W. Europe c. 750–500 B.C. New invaders overran Greece c. 1100 B.C. and destroyed the Mycenaean civilisation. In the city-states they established, monarchy gave place to the rule of a landed aristocracy, which with the growth of a merchant class yielded in turn to democracy. During the 6th–4th cents. B.C. the distinctively Greek culture arose, which the conquests of Alexander (334–323) spread over the Near East.

By the 3rd cent. B.C. the city-republic of Rome had become mistress of the Italian peninsula. The Carthaginian wars added Sicily and Spain to its empire, and in 146 B.C. Greece became a Roman province. Meanwhile the Celtic peoples of C. Europe had spread over what is now France, Britain, Ireland and N. Italy, and penetrated Spain. Rome subdued the Celts of Italy and Spain in the 2nd cent. B.C., France in the 1st, and Britain in the 1st cent. A.D. Under Augustus the Rhine and the Danube became the Empire's northern frontiers. Rome's conquests made possible not only the maintenance of order, the circulation of trade, and the diffusion of Graeco-Roman culture, but the dissemination of Christianity, the toleration of which Constantine ordered in 312. But the expansion of the Empire ended in the 2nd

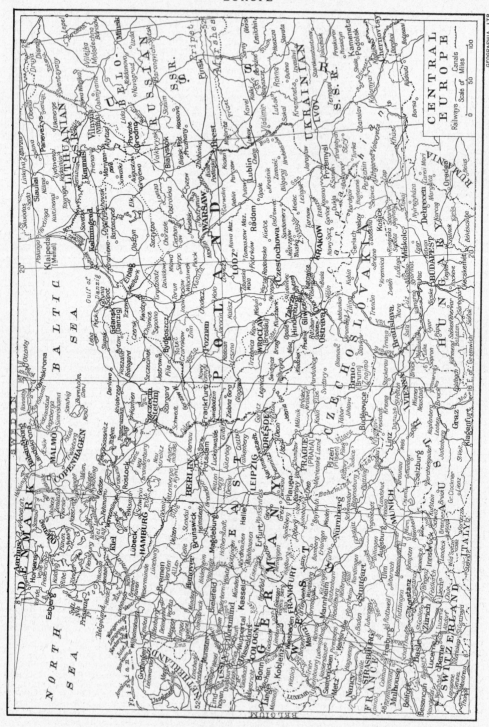

CENTRAL EUROPE

Railways — Canals
Scale of Miles
0   50   100

GEOGRAPHIA LT?

cent. A.D., and economic and administrative defects, added to the successive invasions by the barbarians on the northern frontiers, led to its disintegration.

Medieval. During the 4th–6th cents. W. Europe was overrun by Anglo-Saxons, Franks, Goths, and Lombards, although the traditions of Roman culture and administration were kept alive by the Church. In E. Europe the Empire survived, with its capital at Constantinople, whence Christianity reached the Balkans and Russia; the rival claims of the Pope and the Byzantine Patriarch led to a cleavage which became permanent in 1054. During the 7th–8th cents. Christendom was threatened by the Arabs, who conquered Spain.

Charlemagne united France, W. Germany and N. Italy, and in 800 received the title of emperor from the Pope. With the dissolution of his empire France and Germany came into existence as separate states. A period of confusion followed, accentuated by the Viking raids, during which the feudal system arose. As revived in 962 by Otto I the Empire was confined to Germany and N. Italy; he adopted for it the title Holy Roman Empire, used, long after the reality had become shadowy, until 1806. The claim to authority over secular princes put forward by Gregory VII (1073–85) and his successors provoked a conflict between empire and papacy which lasted for nearly 200 years and discredited both. Papal influence was strengthened by the Crusades (1096–1272), but the transfer of the papacy to Avignon (1309–71) and the Great Schism (1378–1417) weakened its prestige.

Town life and trade, which had declined under the barbarians, revived after Charlemagne's day. The revival began in the Italian cities, notably Venice, Genoa, Florence, and Milan, which traded with the Near East, and thence with C. Asia and China. From the 12th cent. these cities, like the German and Flemish cities, estab. themselves as self-governing republics, and in the 14th–15th cents. fostered the culture of the 'Renaissance'.

From the conflict of monarchy with feudal nobility centralised nation-states emerged in W. Europe in the 14th–15th cents.; a feature common to most of the new states was the existence of parliamentary assemblies, representing both landowners and cities. In E. Europe the political situation was unsettled by the Turkish conquest of the Balkans, culminating in the capture of Constantinople in 1453.

Modern. Throughout the 16th–17th cents. European politics turned on the rivalry of France and the Habsburgs, who held Spain and its empire, Austria, the Netherlands and the imperial crown, while after 1517 they were further complicated by the Protestant Reformation. Protestantism took 2 main forms: the more conservative Lutheranism, which was adopted by many German princes, and in Scandinavia; and the radical and democratic Calvinism, which gained many adherents in the Netherlands, Scotland, and France. The Catholic Church attempted to meet the challenge with the Counter-Reformation.

The struggle against Spain of the Netherlands and England in the later 16th cent. ended in the establishment of the United Provinces (or Dutch Rep.), 1648, and the emergence of the United Provinces and England as maritime powers. France was torn by religious wars (1562–98), until Henry IV introduced toleration and consolidated the absolute monarchy. Inside Germany the attempt of the Habsburgs to restore the power of Church and Empire led to the Thirty Years War (1618–48), as a result of which France succeeded Spain as the dominant power of Europe.

During the 17th cent. the supremacy of parliament was estab. in England; elsewhere, parliamentary institutions gave way to absolute monarchy, which found its supreme expression in Louis XIV of France (1643–1715). Until 1688 he successfully pursued an aggressive foreign policy but thereafter his ambitions

EUROPEAN HISTORY. The beginning of Germany's military domination of modern Europe. Bismarck, in light tunic, watches William I of Prussia proclaimed German emperor in the Hall of Mirrors at Versailles on 18 Jan., 1871, after the crushing defeat of France in the Franco-Prussian War. Painting by Anton von Werner.

united Europe against him. In N. Europe Sweden, after a cent. of glory, ceased to be a great power with the death of Charles XII (1697–1718), while 2 new powers arose: Russia, regenerated by Peter the Great (1682–1725), and Prussia. The rivalries of Prussia and Austria, and of Britain and France in India and Canada, produced the War of the Austrian Succession (1740–8), and the Seven Years War (1756–63); when they ended Prussia was estab. as a European power, and France had lost its colonial empire to Britain.

The spirit of revolt against absolute monarchy was voiced by the *philosophes*, whose humanitarian doctrines prepared the way for the French Revolution (1789–95). The opposition of the Austrian and Prussian monarchies provoked the wars of 1792–1815, during which the French armies spread revolutionary ideas throughout Europe. The dictatorship of the Jacobins (1792–4) saved France in 1792, but the Terror (1793–4) so terrified the bourgeoisie that they accepted the military despotism of Napoleon (1799–1814). His aggressions aroused throughout Europe a popular resistance which brought about his overthrow.

For 30 years the Holy Alliance attempted to hold back the popular movements which had arisen from the French and Industrial Revolutions, Liberalism, nationalism, and Socialism. In spite of the failure of the 1848 revolutions, by 1871 Germany and Italy were unified, and France was a republic.

With the Greek War of Independence (1821–9) the decadence of Turkey became evident. A struggle for the domination of the Balkans followed, in which Russia was matched at first against Britain and France, and later against Austria and Germany. The Balkan question, Franco-German hostility, and colonial rivalries divided Europe into 2 armed camps – the Triple Alliance (1882) of Germany, Austria and Italy, and the Franco-Russian Alliance (1891), with which Britain was linked by the Entente Cordiale, 1904, and an agreement with Russia, 1907. The last of a succession of international crises plunged Europe into the F.W.W. of 1914–18.

Russia became a Communist republic in 1917 and after the war Germany and Austria became democratic republics, Italy and Hungary Fascist dictatorships. The Austrian and Turkish empires disappeared, new states – e.g. Poland, Czechoslovakia, Yugoslavia – arising from the ruins. A new stage opened with Hitler's coming to power in 1933. Germany and Italy embarked on a policy of aggression in Spain, Austria, Czechoslovakia, and Albania, while Britain and France wavered between appeasement and resistance until the S.W.W. broke out in 1939. During 1939–41 Germany overran much of Europe, incl. most of European Russia. Germany's attack on Russia in June 1941, coupled with Japan's attack on the U.S.A. later that year, brought both Russia and the U.S.A. into the war and eventually turned the tide. Completely defeated, Germany and Austria were occupied by the Allied powers.

Russia emerged from the war as the greatest European power, with the small countries of E. Europe as satellites under Russian domination. Treaties of peace were concluded by the Allies in 1947 with Hungary, Italy, Finland, Rumania, and Bulgaria, in 1955 with Austria. The British, U.S., and French zones of (W.) Germany were recognized by those occupying powers in 1949 as the Federal German Republic; the Russian zone of (E.) Germany was proclaimed a separate democratic republic later the same year. Russian hostility to western Europe drew the countries of that part of the continent together and into close alliance with the U.S.A. (*see* NORTH ATLANTIC TREATY), but the closing of the gap between standards of life E. and W. of the Iron Curtain, reinforced by doctrinal

differences between the Soviet Union and China, led to a relaxation of the Cold War. Tension was renewed 1968 over Czechoslovakia.

EUROPEAN UNION. Since the break-up of the Roman Empire, which had united southern and western Europe, incl. Britain within the fence of Roman peace, the idea of a united Europe has been many times revived. Military reunions, such as those imposed by Charlemagne, Napoleon, and Hitler did not last, but peaceful achievement of the aim was advocated by Grotius (17th cent.), Kant (18th cent.), and Briand, Robert Schuman, Adenauer and de Gasperi (qq.v.) in the 20th cent. A start was made towards the end of the S.W.W. in the economic field through Benelux (q.v.). After the war came the European Recovery Programme (*see* MARSHALL, GEORGE C.) estab. as the Organization for European Economic Co-operation (OEEC) 1948, and renamed Organization for Economic Co-operation and Development (q.v.) in 1961. Also in 1948 the Brussels Treaty

The European School in Luxemburg for children of the staff of the European Communities represents the hope of a united continent.
Courtesy of the Information Service of the European Communities.

(q.v.) was signed, from which came Western European Union and the Council of Europe (q.v.).

The EUROPEAN COMMUNITY consists of the European Coal and Steel Community (1952), European Economic Community (EEC, popularly called the Common Market, 1957), and the European Atomic Energy Community (Euratom, 1957). These 3 share from 1967 the following institutions: a Commission (H.Q. Brussels, limited by 1970 to 9 members, which initiates Community action); Council of Ministers (H.Q. Brussels, consisting of a representative minister from each member govt. according to the subject discussed, which makes decisions on the Commission's proposals); European Parliament (H.Q. Luxembourg, with members nominated by the national parliaments, and provision for eventual direct election, which must be consulted on major issues and can dismiss the Commission by an adverse vote); and European Court of Justice (H.Q. Luxembourg, to safeguard interpretation of the Rome treaties, q.v.) The original members (the 'Six') were Belgium, France, W. Germany, Italy, Luxembourg, and the Netherlands; British applications for membership (by a Cons. govt. 1961 and Labour 1967) were blocked by France. However, a parallel trading group, the European Free Trade Assocn. (EFTA) had been estab. in 1959 by Austria, Britain, Denmark, Norway, Portugal, Sweden and Switzerland, who came to be known from their geographical relationship to the Common Market countries as the 'Outer Seven'. Linked with Britain in her final successful application for Common Market membership from 1973 were

Denmark, Norway (who withdrew after a referendum 1972) and the Irish Republic.

EURŌ'PIUM. An extremely rare chemical element. Symbol Eu; atomic number 63; atomic weight 152. It is of little importance at present.

EUSĒ'BIUS (*c.* 260–*c.* 340). Bishop of Caesarea from *c.* 313. Prominent in the Council of Nicaea, he wrote an Ecclesiastical History down to A.D. 324.

EUSTACHIO (ā-oostah'kē-ō), **Bartolommeo** (d. 1574). Italian anatomist, the discoverer of the Eustachian tube, leading from the middle ear to the pharynx, and of the Eustachian valve in the right auricle of the heart. He was physician to the popes.

EVANGELICALISM. The doctrines that distinguish those in the Christian churches who place supreme emphasis on the saving power of the blood of Jesus Christ shed for the redemption of mankind. Although in a sense all protestants are evangelical, the term often refers to Low Church Anglicans. (*See* ANGLICAN COMMUNION.) The World Evangelical Fellowship (founded 1951) unites churches and individuals who hold evangelical beliefs.

EVANGELIST (Gk. *euangelos* 'bringing good news'). Term used in the N.T. for one who is charged with a travelling mission to spread the gospel among the heathen. With reference to one of the authors of the four Gospels, it does not occur until the 3rd cent.

EVANS, Sir Arthur John (1851–1941). British archaeologist. B. in Herts, he was the son of Sir John E. (1823–1908), an authority on the Neolithic and Bronze Age periods in Europe. His excavation of Knossus (q.v.) on Crete resulted in the discovery of the pre-Phoenician Minoan script and in proving the existence of the Minoan civilisation of which all trace had disappeared except in legend. Notable among his pub. works are *Scripta Minoa* (1909) and 4 vols. on the *Palace of Minos*.

EVANS, Caradoc (1878–1945). Welsh novelist and playwright. B. in Carmarthenshire, he worked as a draper's assistant before entering journalism. His bitingly satirical novels, especially his first, *My People* (1915), and his play *Taffy* (1923) aroused much anger in Wales. His 2nd wife was the Countess Barcynska (Oliver Sandys q.v.).

EVANS, Dame Edith (1888–   ). British actress. B. in London, she is best known for her playing of Lady Bracknell in *The Importance of Being Earnest* (1939). A very versatile actress, she has appeared in Shakespeare, Restoration Comedy, Wilde and Shaw and in films.

EVANS, Sir E. R. G. R. *See* MOUNTEVANS.

EVANS, Maurice (1901–   ). American actor. B. in Dorset, he scored a success in *Journey's End* in 1929, and in 1935 went to the U.S., taking citizenship in 1941. His roles incl. Richard II and Macbeth as well as modern parts, e.g. *The Browning Version*.

EVA PERÓN. Name 1952–9 of LA PLATA.

EVATT, Herbert Vere (1894–1965). Australian Labour statesman. B. in N.S.W., he became a Labour member of the legislative assembly of N.S.W. in 1925 and was a justice of the High Court of Australia (1930–40). He was a member of the War Cabinet 1941–6, Min. for External Affairs 1941–9, and succeeded Chifley as leader of the Labour Party 1951–60. In 1960–2 he was Chief Justice of N.S.W.

EVE. *See* ADAM.

EVELYN, John (1620–1706). English diarist and author. B. in Surrey, he enlisted for 3 years in the Royalist army (1642), but withdrew on finding his estate exposed to the enemy and lived mostly abroad until 1652. He declined all office under the Commonwealth, but after the Restoration enjoyed great favour, received court appointments, and was one of the founders of the Royal Society. He was the friend of Pepys, and like him remained in London during the Plague and the Great Fire. Of his more than 30 books the most important is his diary, first pub. 1818, which covers the period 1640–1706.

EVEREST, Mount. The highest mountain in the world, in the Himalayan range on the Tibet-Nepal frontier (formerly 29,002 ft., but unofficially est. at 29,028 ft. – the range is said to be rising), it was named after Sir George Everest (1790–1866), Surveyor General of India. Among the most memorable expeditions to conquer E. are that of 1924 led by Col. E. F. Norton, when Mallory and Irvine were last seen at 28,239 ft., their fate being unknown; that led by Eric Shipton which discovered the southern route in 1951, opening the way to success, and the 1953 expedition led by John Hunt, when the summit was first reached by

EVEREST. Seen from the north, or Tibetan, side which is the one the Indian and Chinese expeditions claim to have attempted. Below are the tents of the unsuccessful British expedition of 1922, led by Brig.-Gen. Bruce, and incl. Mallory, Somervell, and Norton.

Photo: The Mount Everest Foundation.

the New Zealander Edmund Hillary and the Sherpa Tensing.

EVERSHED, John (1864–1956). British astronomer. B. in Surrey, he devoted himself to solar observations, surveying solar prominences in particular detail, and in 1909 discovered the radial movement of gases in sunspots ('E. effect'). He also gave his name to a spectroheliograph, the 'E. spectroscope'

EVESHAM (ēvz′-). English town (bor.) on the Avon, in S.E. Worcs, 14 m. S.E. of Worcester, in the fertile Vale of E. In the battle of E., 4 Aug. 1265, Edward, Prince of Wales, defeated Simon de Montfort, who was killed. Pop. (1961) 12,608.

EVEREST. The final ridge seen from the south shoulder, as Hillary and Tensing encountered it.
Photo: The Mount Everest Foundation.

EVOLUTION. Most usually, the organic E. of living creatures. Some conception of an evolutionary process may be traced in antiquity in writers such as Lucretius (1st cent. B.C.), but serious speculation was not renewed until the 18th cent. by Erasmus Darwin, grandfather of Charles Darwin, and Lord Monboddo. J. B. Lamarck in 1809 advanced a general theory of E., but the main contribution to the rise of evolutionary doctrine before Charles Darwin's *The Origin of Species* (1859) was the work of the geologist Lyell (q.v.). The evidence for continuous E. of living matter is provided by fossils, by vestigial organs or limbs in living species which are found to be fully functioning in other animals of similar construction, by geographical distribution and geology. Darwin assigned the major role in E. to natural selection, which resulted in the survival of the fittest, but the method by which E. takes place is still uncertain. Later followers of Lamarck maintain that an organism is moulded by its environment, to which it in turn endeavours to adapt itself, the consequent alterations in structure being transmitted to later generations – the concept of 'inheritance of acquired characters'. This theory is now largely discredited and it is thought that the vital factors in E. are the random changes in the hereditary constitution of an organism, upon which the environment may exert an encouraging or discouraging influence. A striking example of such changes in modern times is the rapid spread of the all-black form of *Biston* (*Amphi-*

EVOLUTION. On the left the peppered moth and its black form are seen at rest on a lichened tree-trunk, and on the right the two forms are side by side on a polluted oak trunk in Birmingham.   *Photo courtesy of H. B. Kettlewell.*

dasis) *betularia*, first observed in Manchester in 1848. Prior to this date, only the light-coloured form was known. This moth is invisible on lichened tree-trunks. The black form (*f. carbonaria*) has now replaced the light form through all industrial regions in Britain and elsewhere where trunks are black, up to a level of 98 per cent of the population. Kettlewell has shown that this represents a 30 per cent advantage; he has also suggested that there may be physiological differences between the two forms. This phenomenon is taking place in many different moth species. It is referred to as Industrial Melanism.

ÉVREUX (ehvrö′). Chief town of Eure dept., Normandy, France, on the Iton. It has an 11th cent. cathedral and a bishop's palace. Pop. (1962) 40,158.

EVZONES (ev′zōnz). Riflemen of the Greek army, characterized mainly by their picturesque dress with its spreading skirt.

EXCAVATOR. Machine designed for soil stripping, earth moving, ore extraction, etc., and usually of the track-mounted 'crawler' or more easily manœuvred and adaptable rubber-tyred type. Modern multi-storey concrete buildings which need very deep foundations have led to their increasing use on building sites.

EXCISE. *See* Customs and Excise.

EXCOMMUNICATION. The temporary or permanent exclusion of an offender from the rights and privileges of membership of a religious community. In the Middle Ages the popes claimed the right to excommunicate recalcitrant sovereigns, and the emperors Henry IV, Frederick I and Frederick II; and John, Henry VIII, and Queen Elizabeth I of England were among those excommunicated.

EXE′CUTOR. The person appointed by Will to carry out the testamentary instructions of the deceased. An E. can be appointed only by a Will or a Codicil to a Will, and he may refuse to act. The duties of an E. are to bury the deceased and to prove the Will and obtain a grant of probate thereof. He must then pay the deceased's debts from the estate, collect any monies due, and distribute the estate according to the testamentary directions.

EXETER, David G. B. Cecil, marquess of (1905–   ). Athlete and administrator. As Lord Burghley, he won 8 British championships and the 400 metre hurdles in the 1928 Olympic Games. He was a Cons. M.P. 1941–3, and succeeded his father as marquess in 1956.

EXETER. English city (co. bor.), co. town of Devon, on the Exe, 9 m. from its mouth. It is a rly. junction, and a market centre, and manufactures agricultural implements. The cathedral dates from 1280–1369 and was restored in the 1870s. There is an Elizabethan Guildhall; the grammar school was founded in 1332. E. is the seat of a university constituted in 1955, and of a bishopric. It was badly damaged by German air raids in 1942. Area 14 sq. m.; pop. (1961) 80,215.

EXHIBITION. Term used to denote a collection of works of art, industrial products, etc., displayed to the public at a museum, art gallery, etc. A national E. had been held in Paris as early as 1798, but the 1st great international E. was that held in London in 1851 under the patronage of the Prince Consort (*see* Crystal Palace). Notable later Es. were the one held in Paris in 1889, for which the Eiffel Tower was erected; the World's Columbian Exposition, held at Chicago in 1893; the British Empire E. at Wembley, 1924–5; the Festival of Britain, 1951 – for which the Royal Festival Hall on the South Bank of the Thames was built; and the 1964–5 World's Fair in New York.

EXISTENTIALISM. Philosophical system propounded about 1943 by the French philosopher J. P. Sartre. Its main tenet is that in all important matters 'Existence precedes Essence', or in simpler language 'Facts come before Ideas'. In the evolution of man the facts of human nature come first and it

EXHIBITION. The Canadian and Ontario pavilions at Expo 67, Montreal, dominated by the inverted steel pyramid (right) known as the Katimavik—Eskimo for meeting place.
Courtesy of the Centennial Commission, Ottawa.

is these facts which determine man's qualities, his purpose, and his 'essence'. Therefore E. is a philosophy which insists on facing the facts of man's nature. Historically speaking, E. is derived partly from the German philosopher Heidegger's cynical and subjective attitude to humanity, and partly from Kierkegaard's conception of man as an isolated and lonely individual dependent solely on God. Sartre himself ignores the religious element in Kierkegaard and is an example of atheist Existentialist, but it is possible to be a Christian Existentialist, e.g. Jaspers.

EXMOOR. English moorland in Devon and Somerset, near the Bristol Channel. The highest point is Dunkery Beacon (1,707 ft.), and much is over 1,000 ft. There are red deer and a native breed of pony. E. national park, 265 sq. m., covering all E. and the coastline from Minehead to Combe Martin, was designated in 1954.

EXMOUTH. English port (U.D.) and popular resort at the mouth of the Exe, S. Devon, 9 m. S.W. of Exeter. The docks were opened in 1869. Pop. (1961) 19,740.

EXPANDING UNIVERSE. In astronomy, a theory framed to account for phenomena exhibited by the extra-galactic nebulae (q.v.), viz. their even distribution through space, and the fact that the spectral lines in the light which they emit are displaced towards the long wave (red) end of the spectrum, of which the only known cause can be motion away from us. The theory of the E.U. interprets these observed properties – even distribution in space and 'red-shift' – as indicating an expansion of the universe, whereby every galaxy is receding from all the others.

EXPLOSIVES. Materials capable of a sudden release of energy and rapid formation of a large volume of gas, leading when compressed to the development of a high-pressure wave (blast). Combustion, explosion, and detonation differ essentially only in rate of reaction, and many explosives are capable under suitable conditions of undergoing relatively slow combustion. The explosive violence of atomic and hydrogen bombs arises from the tremendous amount of energy released by the conversion of mass into energy, according to Einstein's mass-energy equivalence, $E = mc^2$, where c is the velocity of light. It has been calculated that if it were possible to convert one pound of matter completely into energy it would be equivalent to eleven thousand million kilowatt hours of energy.

EXPRESSIONISM. Term applied to a style of painting, sculpture, or literary composition which is concerned with the inner world of feeling rather than the outer world of fact. An expressionist paint-

ing does not imitate nature but distorts natural appearance in order to convey what the artist feels about some subject; or it may consist purely of colours and forms which are entirely unrelated to nature, but express the mood of an artist. Some of Van Gogh's paintings may be described as 'expressionist'. Picasso in his picture of 'Guernica' expresses all the horror of war by means of distorted forms. Matisse's works are (in his own words) expressions of 'balance, of purity and serenity, devoid of any troubling subject matter'. The most important painters associated with the movement were Klee, Marc, Kandinsky, and Chagall.

EXTROVERT and **INTROVERT**. Two psychological types first defined by the Swiss psychologist C. G. Jung about 1916. The E. is the practical person whose energies are directed outwards towards the objective world; the soldier and the engineer are typical Es. The I., on the other hand, is the dreamer whose main energies are turned inwards in contemplation of his own imaginations and fancies; typical Is. include the poet and the musician.

EYCK (īk), **Van.** Family of early Flemish artists. **Hubert van E.** (c. 1370–1426) was probably b. at Maas Eyck or Alden Eyck on the Maas. Little of his work has survived. His 'Adoration of the Lamb', an altarpiece originally painted for Jodocus Vijdts who presented it to the cathedral of St. Bavon in Ghent, was finished after Hubert's death by his brother **Jan van E.** (c. 1390–1441), who like Hubert was court painter to Philip the Good, duke of Burgundy. He is chiefly famous for his portraits, painted with great care and exact likeness; his 'The Marriage of Giovanni Arnolfini' (1434) and 'Man in a Red Turban' are in the National Gallery.

EYE. The organ of sight. It is a roughly spherical

JAN VAN EYCK. 'The Marriage of Giovanni Arnolfini and Giovanna Cenami'. An inscription says 'Jan van Eyck was here', and it is thought he was a witness, being represented by one of the tiny figures in the circular wall mirror – reflected as if standing in the doorway.   *Courtesy of the National Gallery.*

o

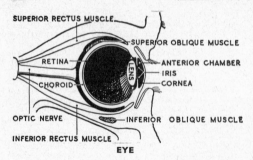

SUPERIOR RECTUS MUSCLE
SUPERIOR OBLIQUE MUSCLE
RETINA
ANTERIOR CHAMBER
LENS
IRIS
CHOROID
CORNEA
OPTIC NERVE
INFERIOR OBLIQUE MUSCLE
INFERIOR RECTUS MUSCLE
EYE

structure contained in a bony socket and having considerable freedom of rotatory movement. It is kept moist by the secretion of the lacrimal glands. Light enters it through the circular opening of the iris, passes through the lens, where it is focused, and strikes on the delicate inner membrane, the retina; thence the impulse is transmitted to the brain by the optic nerve.

EYEBRIGHT. Common wild flower of the genus *Euphrasia*, Scrophulariaceae family, found in fields throughout Britain. It is 2–6 in. high, bearing whitish flowers streaked with purple. The name indicates its former use as an eye-medicine.

EYRE (ār), **Edward John** (1815–1901). British colonial governor. B. in Yorks, he emigrated to Australia and made journeys into the interior, described in his *Expeditions into Central Australia*

(1845), and in 1864 became gov. of Jamaica. In 1865 he suppressed a Negro rising with harshness, was suspended and not reinstated.

EYRE. Lake in S. Australia, discovered by E. J. Eyre in 1840, area *c.* 3,000 sq. m. In dry seasons it is a salt marsh, in wet a lake; it was full in 1950 for the first time since its discovery.

EYSENCK (ī'senk), **Hans Jurgen** (1916–). British psychologist. Ed. at the Univ. of London, he became prof. of psychology there in 1955. He has attacked the usual methods of psychotherapy, notably Freudian psychoanalysis, pointing out that spontaneous remission would equally account for the cures claimed. Instead, he favours behaviour therapy which has links with J. B. Watson and Pavlov (q.v.), and advocates the treatment of symptoms rather than imaginary underlying causes.

EYSTON (ē'ston), **George Edward Thomas** (1897–). British racing motorist. He won many records in small cars at Brooklands and in 1937–8 took the world's land speed record 3 times, in U.S.A. *See also* SPEED RECORDS.

EZEKIEL (ezē'ki-el) (b. *c.* 622 B.C.). Prophet of the O.T. A priest of Jerusalem and member of the family of Zadok, he was carried into captivity with King Jehoiachin by Nebuchadnezzar in 597 B.C. While in Babylonia he preached the downfall of Jerusalem as retribution for the sins of Israel.

EZRA. Scribe of the clan of Zadok, who by permission of Artaxerxes led *c.* 1,500 Jews from Babylonia back to Jerusalem (458 B.C.) where he instituted reforms, including the eradication of intermarriage, and re-establishment of the Mosaic Law, as told in the O.T. book named after him.

F The sixth letter of the alphabet. Its capital form has changed little from what we see in the earlier Semitic alphabets.

FABER, Frederick William (1814–63). British hymn writer. A clergyman of the C. of E., he became an R.C. priest in 1845, and superior of the Oratory of St. Philip Neri (Brompton Oratory) in 1849. He wrote 'Hark, Hark, my Soul'.

FABERGÉ (fahbārjeh'), **Peter Carl** (1846–1920). Russian goldsmith. Of Huguenot descent, he was b. at St. Petersburg, and his workshops there and in Moscow were celebrated for the exquisite delicacy of their products, especially the use of gold in different shades. Among F.'s masterpieces was the series of imperial Easter eggs (illustrated), the first of which was commissioned by Alexander III for the Tsarina in 1884. He d. in exile.

FĀ'BIAN SOCIETY. Socialist propagandist and research organization, founded in 1884. Its name is derived from Fabius Cunctator (q.v.), and refers to the evolutionary methods by which it hopes to attain socialism by a succession of gradual reforms. In its early days it was dominated by Bernard Shaw and Sidney Webb: it still plays its part and in 1963 Harold Wilson first outlined in a F.S. meeting his plans for changing the machinery of British govt.

FAB'IUS. Name of an ancient Roman family, of whom the best known is **Quintus F. Maximus,** known as *Cunctator* (Delayer). As commander against Hannibal 217–214 B.C., he continually harassed his armies without ever risking a set battle.

FABLE. A story, either in verse or prose, in which the animal kingdom, and even inanimate objects, are

endowed with the mentality and speech of human beings in order to point a moral. The best-known Fs. include those of Aesop (5th cent. B.C.), Phaedrus and Avianus, La Fontaine, Gay, Lessing, etc.

FABRE (fahbr), **Jean Henri** (1823–1915). French entomologist, called the 'Insects' Homer' because of his remarkably vivid and intimate descriptions of wasps, bees, and other insects. B. in Aveyron, he became a schoolmaster but retired in 1871 to Sérignan. He pub. *Souvenirs entomologiques.*

FABRI'CIUS, Geronimo (1537–1619). Italian anatomist. He was prof. of surgery and anatomy at Padua from 1562, and did pioneer work that won him the title of the father of embryology.

FACTORY ACTS. Acts of parliament concerned with conditions of work, hours of labour, safety, and sanitary provisions in factories and workshops. The first was the Health and Morals of Apprentices Act 1802, and this was followed in 1819 by the Cotton Mills Act, which forbade the labour of children under 9 and reduced the hours of labour of those under 16 to 72 per week. Ashley's Act of 1845 forbade night work to women, and in 1847 Ashley (later the 7th earl of Shaftesbury) was responsible for passing the 10-hours bill. The first factory inspectors were appointed in 1833. Legislation was subsequently extended and consolidated, and by an act of 1963 offices, shops, and railway premises, in which conditions had often been unsatisfactory, were covered.

FADDEN, Sir Arthur William (1895–). Australian statesman. B. in Queensland, he became leader of the Country Party (1941–58), was briefly P.M. (Aug.–Oct. 1941), and Deputy P.M. 1949–58,

FABERGÉ. Easter gifts made for the Russian court, each a superb example of jeweller's and goldsmith's art. The coronation egg (right centre) is in red gold and lime-yellow enamel and just contains the yellow gold and strawberry enamelled coach to its left. *Courtesy of Wartski and Faber & Faber Ltd.*

when he was also Treasurer (a post he had previously held 1940–1).

FADEYEV, Alexander Alexandrovich (1901–56). Russian novelist. B. nr. Moscow, he enrolled at 17 among the partisans resisting Kolchak in E. Siberia and *Razgrom* (1927, The Rout) reflects his experiences. His novel of the S.W.W. *The Young Guard* (1945) was acclaimed, and he was gen. sec. of the Soviet Writers Union 1946–55, but then fell in disfavour. He took to drink and shot himself.

FAENZA (fah-en′tsah). City on the r. Lamone in Ravenna prov., Emilia-Romagna, Italy. It has many medieval remains, incl. the 15th cent. walls, and has been famous since the 13th cent. for 'faience pottery'. Pop. (1960) 51,000.

FAEROES (fār′ōs). Group of 21 islands (17 inhabited) belonging to Denmark, in the N. Atlantic, between the Shetlands and Iceland. The largest are Stromo, Ostero, Vaago, Sudero, and Sando, and the capital is Torshavn on Stromo. The principal industries are fishing, sheep-rearing, and the catching of sea-birds for their feathers. In 1948 the F. were granted home rule. Area 540 sq. m.; pop. (1968) 37,000.

FAGUET (fahgā′), **Émile** (1847–1916). French literary critic, author of *Histoire de la littérature française depuis le XVIIe siècle* (1885–94).

FAHRENHEIT (-hīt), **Gabriel Daniel** (1686–1736). German physicist, inventor of the Fahrenheit thermometric scale, in which freezing point of pot. chlor. was 0°, the freezing point of water was 32° and boiling point 212°. He was b. at Danzig, but lived mainly in England and Holland.

FAINTING. A sudden and temporary suspension of consciousness and movement, due to failure of the supply of blood, and consequently of oxygen, to the brain. The cause is generally a fall in blood pressure due to shock, heart disease, fatigue, privation, or – in air pilots – to the action of centrifugal force in drawing blood away from the head.

FAIRBANKS, Douglas (1883–1939). American actor. B. at Denver, Colorado, he starred from 1915 in films such as *The Three Musketeers, The Thief of Baghdad* and *Don Q*, and was the most famous of the silent screen's swashbuckling heroes. He and Mary Pickford, whom he m. in 1920, were idolized as 'the world's sweethearts'. His son by a previous marriage, **Douglas F.** (1909–), achieved similar screen renown in *Catherine the Great* and *The Prisoner of Zenda*. He was created an hon. K.B.E. in 1949 for his distinguished efforts in the Allied cause.

FAIRBANKS. Town in Alaska, U.S.A., on the Chena Slough, a trib. of the r. Tanana, terminus of the Alaska railway and of the Alaska Highway through Canada to Seattle. It is a centre for gold-mining and the fur trade and has sawmills. The University of Alaska is at College, 3 m. N.W. Pop. (1960) 13,311.

FAIRBRIDGE, Kingsley (1885–1924). S. African educationist. B. in S. Africa, he founded the Child Emigration Society in 1909 while studying at Oxford, after visiting slums in London and other cities, and originated a scheme for a group of schools, known as the Fairbridge Farm Schools, in Britain and the Dominions, intended to provide education and a career in the Doms. for deprived children.

FAIREY, Sir Charles Richard (1887–1956). British aircraft manufacturer. In 1915 he founded the F. Aviation Co. Ltd. at Hayes, Middlesex, which produced many famous models such as the Firefly, Albacore and Swordfish; he is also known as the inventor and developer of the wing flap.

FAIRFAX OF CAMERON, Thomas Fairfax, 3rd baron (1612–71). English soldier, C.-in-C. of the parliamentary army in the Civil War. With Cromwell he formed the New Model Army, defeated Charles I at Naseby, and suppressed the risings of 1648.

FAISAL, Ibn Abdul Aziz (1905–). King of Saudi Arabia. The younger brother of King Saud, on whose accession in 1953 he was declared Crown Prince, he has frequently represented his country at the U.N. He was P.M. 1953–60 and from 1962, when he also became C.-in-C. of the army: he has been continuously Foreign Min. since 1953. Remarkable for his balanced statesmanship, he has assisted the steady modernization of his country. In 1964 he emerged victorious from a lengthy conflict with his brother, the reactionary King Saud, and was proclaimed king.

FAIZABAD (fīzahbahd′). Town in Uttar Pradesh, India, at the head of navigation of the r. Gogra, cap. of F. district. Pop. (1961) 88,296.

FAKIR. In Oriental countries, a religious beggar, usually a member of a sect, order, or special caste. Originally a Mohammedan term for mendicants akin to dervishes, it is widely used in India for ascetics who practise varieties of self-torture.

FALAISE. French town 20 m. S.S.E. of Caen, in Calvados dept., Normandy. It is a market centre, and manufactures cotton and leather goods. The castle was that of the first dukes of Normandy, and William the Conqueror was b. at F. Pop. (1962) 6,711.

FALANGE ESPAÑOLA (fahlahn′khe espahnyō′-lah) (Spanish phalanx). Spanish Fascist Party, founded by José Antonio de Rivera, son of Primo de Rivera. It was closely modelled in programme and organization on the Italian Fascists, and on the Nazis. In 1937, when Franco assumed its leadership, it was declared the only legal party, and altered its name to Traditionalist Spanish Phalanx.

FALCON. Bird of the genus *Falco* in the family Falconidae. Of world-wide distribution, the Fs. are birds of prey with short, hooked beaks and sharp claws, remarkable for their keen sight and swiftness of flight. Notable are the wide-ranging peregrine (*F. peregrinus*), persecuted almost to extinction in Britain, of which there are American and Australian varieties, and which is blue-grey with dark markings

KING FAISAL
Courtesy of Aramco.

on the back and a white breast; the Scandinavian gyrfalcon (*F. gyrfalco*); the Greenland F. (*F. candicans*) almost white and lightest of the true Fs.; the 'saker' and the much smaller 'lanner', both Mediterranean species; the hobby (*F. subbuteo*); the merlin (q.v.); and the kestrel (q.v.) – all the last 3 breeding in Britain. *See* FALCONRY.

GREENLAND FALCON

FALCONRY. The use of specially trained falcons and hawks to capture birds or small mammals, practised from ancient times in the Near East, and introduced from the Continent to Britain in Saxon times. The Normans, the Tudors and Stuarts were all fond of F., but it fell into desuetude after the Civil War: in modern times revival has been attempted.

FALKIRK (fawl'-). Large burgh in Stirlingshire, Scotland, overlooking the fertile Carse of F. It is a centre of light-casting industry on the central coalfield; other industries include brewing and distilling, tanning, and the manufacture of chemicals and enamelled goods. Carron ironworks lie 2 m. N. Pop. (1961) 38,043.

FALKLAND (fawk'-), **Lucius Cary, 2nd viscount** (*c.* 1610–43). English royalist. Before the Civil War he earned a high reputation as a patron of literature and scholarship. Elected to the Long Parliament, he showed himself a zealous opponent of absolute monarchy, but the proposal to abolish episcopacy alienated him, and he went over to the king. Plunged into despair by his failure to secure a compromise peace, he flung away his life at the battle of Newbury.

FALKLAND ISLANDS. British Crown Colony in the S. Atlantic about 300 m. to the E. of the southern part of S. America. The islands are administered by a governor, with executive and legislative councils. There are 2 main islands, E. Falkland and W. Falkland, and a number of islets. Sheep are reared, and there are whale and seal industries, and surrounding seaweed beds are a potential source of alginates used in textile dyes and as a food additive. The cap. is Stanley (pop. 1,100), on the coast of E. Falkland. Area excl. dependencies 4,618 sq. m.; pop. (1966) 2,164; of S. Georgia, 22. Attached to the group are the dependencies of S. Georgia, and S. Sandwich islands. (*See also* BRITISH ANTARCTIC TERRITORY.)

The islands were sighted by Davis in 1592, claimed by Britain in the 18th cent., and colonized in 1833. Argentina has claimed them periodically (an armed group landed by air 1966), and there were govt. negotiations 1968. In 1948 both Argentina and Chile advanced claims on the Antarctic dependencies.

In the BATTLE OF THE FALKLAND ISLANDS, a British naval victory of the F.W.W. fought off E. Falkland on Dec. 8, 1914, a British force under Vice-Admiral Sturdee destroyed almost the entire German squadron commanded by Admiral von Spee that had just been successful in the battle of Coronel (q.v.).

FALLA (fahl'yah), **Manuel de** (1876–1946). Spanish composer. B. at Cadiz, he lived in France where he was influenced by the impressionists, esp. Debussy and Ravel. His first work of importance, the opera *La Vida Breve* (1905), was followed by the ballets *El Amor Brujo* and *The Three-Cornered Hat* (1919); *Nights in the Gardens of Spain*, songs, pieces for the piano and the guitar. The folk-idiom is an integral part of his compositions.

FA'LLADA, Hans. Pseudonym of the German novelist Friedrich Rudolf Ditzen (1893–1947), author of the novel *Kleiner Mann – was nun?* (*Little man, what now?*), treating the unemployment problem.

FALLO'PIUS, Gabriello (1523–62). Italian anatomist. He taught at Ferrara, Pisa, and Padua, and made a particular study of the generative organs; the Fallopian tubes are named after him.

FALL-OUT. Radiation scattered in the debris of a nuclear explosion. In war-time attack the first danger, provided that the blast and fire hazards have been survived, is gamma radiation. In tests, however, the deposit of F. on the ground is delayed, and the chief peril is from radioactive components, e.g. strontium, which either enter the body and cause cancer, or burn on contact with the skin.

Radiation is measured in Rads, and is cumulative in effect. Comparative safety lies below 100 R, though long-term genetic or carcinogenic changes are probable up to 300 R; deaths begin at 450 R and there is a 50 per cent chance of death occurring over a period of days or weeks.

FALLS, Cyril Bentham (1888–1971). British military expert. An official historian of the F.W.W., he was military correspondent of *The Times* 1939–53 and Chichele prof. of the history of war at Oxford 1946–53.

FALMOUTH. English seaport (bor.) on the S. coast of Cornwall, on the W. side of Carrick Roads, the estuary into which empty the Fal and other streams. Ship repairing and marine engineering are the main industries. Pop. (1961) 15,427.

FAMAGUSTA (fahmahgoos'tah). Seaport on the E. coast of Cyprus. The harbour is the only one on the island that can accommodate medium-sized vessels, and exports citrus fruits and other agricultural produce. To the N. the site of Enkomi-Alasia has yielded undeciphered inscriptions of *c.* 1200 B.C., etc. *See* illus. p. 230. Pop. (1966) 39,200.

FAMILY PLANNING. The spacing of the birth of children to safeguard the health of the mother and the balance of family life. The prevention of conception is opposed on religious grounds in that it is immoral to frustrate the natural purpose of the sexual relationship, but is often advocated by medical men to prevent the transmission of hereditary disease and by economists to mitigate poverty, especially in eastern countries such as India, which are undergoing a population 'explosion'. Birth control by contraception has only become a generally adopted practice, most commonly using some chemical or mechanical means, in the last few generations: in the 1960s an oral contraceptive taken by the woman to induce an extension

FALL-OUT. An American-designed fall-out shelter which provides for life to continue as usual. Beyond the far wall of the living space are (left to right) shower and sanitary facilities; kitchen with sink, water tanks and food storage; folding bed; and additional food stores. *Courtesy of Shelters for Living, Inc.*

of the 'safe period' was developed. *See also* ABORTION and STERILIZATION.

FANCY, The. Formerly the popular name for pugilists and for those who frequented the prize-ring.

FANGIO (fan'jō), **Juan Manuel** (1911–). Argentine racing motorist, 5 times world champion 1951–7, when he retired. His inspired, coldly brilliant, text-book precision is judged to have made him the finest racing driver of all time.

FANSHAWE, Sir Richard (1608–66). English poet. B. in Herts, he was an ardent Royalist, and after the Restoration was ambassador at Madrid. He translated Camoens' *Lusiad* (1655).

FANTIN-LATOUR (fontań'-lahtōōr'), **Henri** (1836–1904). French artist. B. at Grenoble, he excelled in lightly delicate still-lifes and flower paintings, genre pictures and portraiture. 'Homage to Delacroix' is a portrait group of Baudelaire, Champfleury, Legros, Whistler, and himself.

FARADAY, Michael (1791–1867). British chemist and natural philosopher. B. in London, the son of a blacksmith, he became a laboratory assistant to Sir Humphry Davy at the Royal Institution in 1813, and in 1827 succeeded him as professor of chemistry there. As early as 1812 he began researches into the problems of electricity, and in that year made his first electric battery. In 1821 he began experimenting on electro-magnetism, and ten years later discovered the induction of electric currents and made the first dynamo.

MICHAEL FARADAY. By Thomas Phillips, 1842. *Photo: N.P.G.*

Many more epoch-making discoveries in all fields of electricity followed; and in 1845 he began a second great period of research in which he discovered what he announced as the magnetization of light. He delivered highly popular lectures at the Royal Institution, and pub. many treatises on scientific subjects. In 1835 he was given a government pension, and in 1858 a house at Hampton Court, where he d. Deeply religious, he was a member of the Sandemanian sect. F.'s *laws of electrolysis* are (1) the chemical effect resulting from electrolysis is directly proportional to the quantity of electricity which has passed through the electrolyte; and (2) the quantity of each substance chemically changed, or liberated, at an electrode by the passage of a definite quantity of electricity is directly proportionate to the equivalent weight (q.v.) of the substance. F.'s *law of induced e.m.f.*, associated with him but not enunciated by him, is: the induced e.m.f. round any circuit is proportional to the rate of change of magnetic flux (q.v.) through the circuit. A *farad* is the practical unit of electrostatic capacitance and it is equivalent to 9×10^{11} E.S. units. It is the capacitance of a capacitor in which a charge of 1 coulomb produces a change of potential difference of 1 volt between its terminals.

FAR EAST. Geographical term for all that part of Asia lying E. of the Indian sub-continent. *See also* SOVIET FAR EAST and map p. 416.

FAREHAM. English market town (U.D.) in Hampshire, 6 m. N.W. of Portsmouth. It trades in bricks, wheat, coal, etc. Pop. (1961) 58,277.

FARGO, William George (1818–81). American pioneer expressman. In 1844 he estab. with Henry Wells (1805–78) and Daniel Dunning the first express company to carry freight west of Buffalo. Its success led to his appointment as sec. of the newly estab. American Express Co. in 1850, of which he was pres. 1868–81. He also estab. Wells Fargo & Co. (1851) carrying goods express between N.Y. and San Francisco via Panama.

Fargo, a town on the Red r., in North Dakota, is named after him. Pop. (1960) 46,662.

FARINA (fahrē'na), **Johann Maria** (1685–1766). Italian perfumer. A native of Novara in Piedmont, he settled in Cologne in 1709 and was the inventor of eau-de-Cologne.

FARINGTON, Joseph (1747–1821). English artist. Chiefly famous for his engraved views of the Lake District, he kept a diary (discovered in 1921) which illuminates the contemporary scene.

FARMAN (fahrmoń'), **Henry** (1874–1958). French air pioneer. In 1907 F. made his first flying experiments, and by 1909 F. had estab. a record by flying 100 m. He experimented with new models, and with his brother Maurice founded an aircraft works at Billancourt, important as the source of machines for the French army, and other countries, incl. England, which also made wide use of F.'s inventions, e.g. airscrew reduction gears, in the S.W.W.

FARNABY, Giles (*c.* 1550–1650). English composer. He is thought to have been b. in Cornwall and studied at Oxford. He composed pieces for the virginal, and for voices (madrigals).

FARNBOROUGH. English town (U.D.) in Hants, 3 m. N. of Aldershot. The mansion of Farnborough Hill was occupied by the Empress Eugénie, and she, her husband, and her son are buried in a mausoleum at the R.C. church she built. At F. is the Royal Aircraft Establishment. Pop. (1961) 31,437.

FARNE. Group of small rocky islands off the coast of Northumberland, England. An ancient chapel is said to be on the site of St. Cuthbert's hermitage. There are 2 lighthouses, that on Longstone being the scene of the rescue by Grace Darling (q.v.), 1838.

FARNESE (fahrneh'se). Name of a famous Italian family who held the duchy of Parma 1545–1731.

FARNHAM. English market town (U.D.) on the Wey, Surrey, 38 m. S.W. of London. The parish church was originally part of Waverley Abbey, which, founded in 1128, was the first Cistercian establishment in England. At Moor Park, Swift wrote some of his works. Pop. (1961) 26,927. Other English places called Farnham are in Dorset, Berks, Suffolk.

FAROE ISLANDS, FAROES. *See* FAEROES.

FAROUK (fahrōōk') (1920–65). King of Egypt. The son of Fuad (q.v.), he succeeded him in 1936. In 1952 he was compelled to abdicate, his own son Fuad being temporarily proclaimed in his stead. He adopted the title Prince of Egypt.

FARQUHAR (far'kar), **George** (1677–1707). Irish dramatist. B. in Londonderry, he became an actor in Dublin, but in 1698 went to London, where in 1699 his first play *Love and a Bottle* was produced. *The Constant Couple* (1700), was followed by a sequel *Sir Harry Wildair* (1701). The best of his later plays are *The Recruiting Officer* (1706), and *The Beaux' Stratagem* (1707).

FARRAGUT, David Glasgow (1801–70). American seaman. B. nr. Knoxville, Tennessee, son of a Spanish emigrant, he took New Orleans in 1862, after destroying the Confederate fleet, and in 1864 effectively put an end to blockade-running at Mobile, besides other dashingly heroic exploits. The ranks of vice-admiral (1864) and admiral (1866) were specially created for him by Congress.

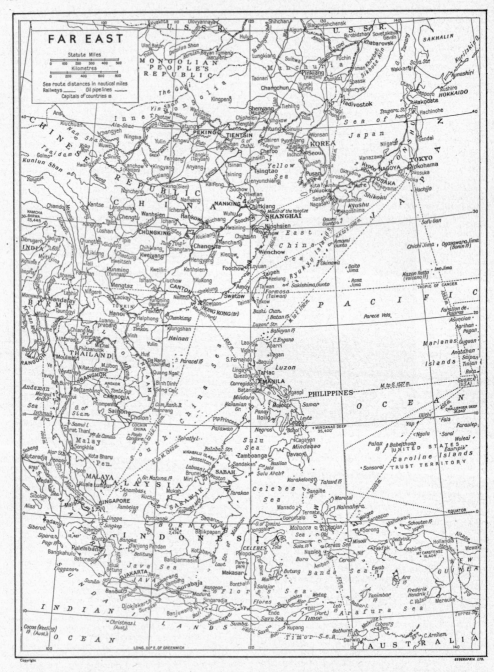

FARRAR, Frederick William (1831–1903). British churchman. Ordained in the C. of E. in 1854, he became headmaster of Marlborough Coll. (1871–6), and dean of Canterbury in 1895. He wrote a very popular *Life of Christ* (1874), and also school stories, notably the pious *Eric, or Little by Little* (1858) which later became a byword for moralizing sentiment.

FARRELL, James T(homas) (1904–). American novelist. B. in Chicago, he worked as a clerk, filling station assistant, and reporter. In his trilogy *Studs*

Lonigan (1932–5) he described a youth growing up in the district of the city in which he lived during the depression. Later books incl. *A World I Never Made* (1936), and other books protesting against social and economic handicaps.

FARS. Region, prov. No. 7, of Persia, on the N.E. shore of the Persian Gulf. The cap. is Shiraz; Bushire is the chief port. Wheat, barley, fruits, tobacco are grown. Persepolis (q.v.) is within the region. Pop. (1966) 1,600,000.

FARTHING. Formerly the smallest English coin, a quarter of a penny. It was introduced, originally as a silver coin, in Edward I's reign. The copper F. became general in Charles II's time, and the bronze in 1860. It became obsolete Jan. 1, 1961.

FASCES (fa'sēz). In ancient Rome, bundles of rods carried in procession by the lictors in front of the chief magistrates, as a symbol of their power over the lives and liberties of the people. An axe was included in the bundle. The F. were adopted by the Fascists as their badge.

FASCISM (fash'ism). The totalitarian nationalist movement founded in Italy by Mussolini; also similar movements elsewhere. Its units were originally called *fasci di combattimento, fascio* meaning a bundle or group; later it adopted as its emblem the *fasces* (q.v.). Between the 2 world wars F. movements arose in many other countries.

F. was essentially a product of the economic and political crisis of the inter-war years. It protected the existing social order by its forcible suppression of the working-class movement, and by providing scapegoats for popular anger in the Jew or the foreigner or the Negro: it also provided the machinery for the economic and psychological mobilization of the nation for war. In its propaganda it made great use of revolutionary phrases. Its ideology denied all rights to the individual in his relations with the State, personified in the infallible 'leader' (*Duce, Fuehrer*). Science, art, and education were brought under state control. Women were driven from economic and public life.

In Italy F. arose in 1919. In Oct. 1922 Mussolini was invited to take power by the king, and the Fascist régime ended with his fall in July 1943.

Outside Italy and Nazi Germany, Fascist or semi-Fascist régimes included the dictatorships of Horthy in Hungary, Pilsudski in Poland, Dollfuss in Austria, Franco in Spain, Salazar in Portugal, Pétain in France, and Perón in Argentina. The Fascist movements in Belgium, Holland, and Norway all assisted in the conquest of their countries by the Nazis. Sir Oswald Mosley's British Union of Fascists gained considerable notoriety 1932–9 and was revived as the Union Movement after the S.W.W., and in 1962 the National Socialist Movement was founded by Colin Jordan, having strong links with the U.S. Nazi Party (founded 1958) and led by George Lincoln Rockwell (assassinated 1967). Japanese F., which held power 1932–45, combined European ideas with emperor-worship, Shintoism, and feudal ideology.

FAST, Howard (1914–). American author. Long a member of the Communist Party, he broke away in 1957 on the suppression of the Hungarian revolt. His historical novels incl. *Citizen Tom Paine* (1943).

FAT. The principal component of the adipose tissue in animal bodies. In chemistry the name is applied to the glyceryl esters of certain fatty acids.

FATES. In Greek and Roman mythology, the spirits who determined the destiny of each newborn child, and in particular the length of its life. They are pictured as three old women spinning, their names being Clotho, Lachesis, and Atropos.

FATHER DIVINE. American Negro evangelist, George Baker (*c.* 1870–1965). As F.D., Dean of the Universe, he led the World Wide Kingdom of Peace (Christianity mixed with Judaism, etc.) from the 1920s: H.Q. Philadelphia, Penn, but with a famous 'Heaven' or religious community in Harlem, N.Y. His wife was known as Mother D.

FATHER-LASHER. Name given to 2 fish of the Cottidae family, *Cottus scorpius* and *C. bubalis*, which occur in British seas and are widely distributed.

FATHERS OF THE CHURCH. Name applied to certain teachers and writers of the early Christian Church, particularly eminent for their learning and orthodoxy, experience, and sanctity of life, who lived from the end of the 1st to the end of the 7th cent., a period of 600 years divided by the Council of Nicaea (325) into the Ante-Nicene and Post-Nicene Fathers. The most important of the Ante-Nicene Fs. are the Apostolic Fathers - Clement of Rome, Ignatius of Antioch, Polycarp of Smyrna, and 'Barnabas' - Justin Martyr, Tatian, Irenaeus, Clement, Origen, Tertullian, Cyprian, and Gregory Thaumaturgus. Of the Post-Nicene Fs. the most memorable are Cyril of Alexandria, Athanasius, John Chrysostom, Eusebius of Caesarea, Cyril of Jerusalem, Basil the Great, Ambrose of Milan, Hilary of Poitiers, Augustine, pope Leo I, Boethius, Jerome, Gregory of Tours, pope Gregory the Great, and Bede.

FATHOM. Unit of measurement, equal to 6 ft., used in taking marine soundings. The word originally meant the distance between the finger-tips with the arms outstretched. In mining and in handling timber F. signifies a measurement of 6 ft. square.

FATIMITES. Name given to a Moslem dynasty which was founded by Obaidallah, who claimed to be a descendant of Fatima, Mohammed's daughter, and her husband, Ali, in N. Africa in A.D. 909. In 969 Egypt was conquered and the dynasty continued until overthrown by Saladin in 1171.

FATTY ACIDS. Group of organic compounds, the higher members of which are found combined with glycerol in fats. They include formic acid, acetic acid, butyric acid, palmitic acid, and stearic acid.

FAULKNER, John Meade (1858–1932). English author. A remarkable stylist, he is best remembered for *The Lost Stradivarius* (1895), a ghost novel, *Moonfleet* (1898), a story for boys, and *The Nebuly Coat* (1903).

FAULKNER, William (1897–1962). American novelist. Son of a declined aristocratic family, he was b. in Mississippi, and aft r service in the R.C.A.F. and R.A.F. during the F.W.W. wrote prolifically but without publishing anything of importance, until his first novel of a war veteran, *Soldier's Pay* (1926). However, he did not strike his true vein until he returned to Oxford, the town in which he had spent his youth and on which he was to model Jefferson in the co. of Yoknapatawpha, the setting of his major novels. These began with *Sartoris* (1929); *The Sound and the Fury* (1929), dealing with a Southern family in decline and sometimes rated as his finest work; *As I Lay Dying* (1930); *Light in August* (1932), a study of segregation which concerned him deeply; *The Unvanquished* (1938), stories of the Civil War; and *The Hamlet* (1940), *The Town* (1957) and *The Mansion* (1959), a trilogy covering the rise of the materialist Snopes family. His experimental and turgid style - sentences sometimes running over a page - hindered popular recognition and a book such as *Sanctuary* (1931) was deliberately conceived as a horrific money-spinner. Also notable are *Intruder in the Dust* (1948), *Requiem for a Nun* (1953, dramatized 1955), and *The Reivers* (1962). In 1949 he was awarded a Nobel prize.

FAURÉ (fohreh′), **Gabriel Urbain** (1845–1924). French composer. A pupil of Saint-Saëns, he became prof. of composition at the Conservatoire in 1896, and was director 1905–20. He is remembered for his songs, chamber music, and a *Requiem* (1887).

FAUST (fowst). Legendary magician. The historical F. appears to have been a wandering mountebank, who appeared in Germany during the opening decade of the 16th cent. But earlier figures such as Simon Magus and Theophilus contributed to the F. legend. In 1587 appeared the first of a series of Faust books. Marlowe's tragedy of *Dr. Faustus* was acted in 1594. In the 18th cent. the story was a subject for pantomime in England, and puppet plays in Germany. In Germany the serious possibilities of the theme were first pointed out by Lessing; Goethe made F. a symbol of Man's striving after the infinite. Later Lunarcharski, Dorothy Sayers, and Paul Valéry took up the theme. F. has also inspired musical works by Schumann, Berlioz, Gounod, Boito, and Busoni.

FAUVISM. Art movement originating in Paris with the founding of the Salon d'automne in 1903, by Matisse and his friends. Their chief source of inspiration was the work of Van Gogh. Others who participated in the movement were Roualt, Derain, Bonnard, and Vlaminck. In 1905 the art critic L. Vauxcelles called the gallery in which they exhibited 'une cage aux fauves' (cage of wild beasts).

FAWCETT, Percy Harrison (1867–1925). British explorer. After several expeditions to delineate frontiers in S. America during the rubber boom, he set off in 1925, with his eldest son John and a friend, into the Mato Grosso to find the 'cradle of Brazilian civilization'. Their fate is unknown although F.'s younger son Brian F., who edited an account of his father's expeditions in *Exploration Fawcett* (1953), tried to follow up the trail.

FAWKES (fawks), **Guy** (1570–1606). English conspirator. B. at York, he was converted to Catholicism as a youth, served in the Spanish army in 1593, and in 1604 joined in the Gunpowder Plot to blow up the King and the members of both houses of Parliament. He was arrested in the cellar underneath the House on Nov. 4, 1605, tortured and executed.

FAYUM (fīyoom′). Prov. of Upper Egypt, S.W. of Cairo. Numerous very realistic mummy portraits of the 1st–4th cents. A.D. have been found here: they probably reflect Greek influence, since the area was largely settled by Greeks.

FAZ. See FEZ.

FÉCAMP (fehko′n). A seaport and resort of N. France, 22 m. N.N.E. of Havre in the dept. of Seine Maritime. The main industries are shipbuilding and fishing. Pop. (1962) 19,851.

FECHNER (fekh′ner), **Gustav Theodor** (1801–87). German psychologist. He became prof. of physics at Leipzig in 1834, but in 1839 through failing eyesight turned to the study of psychophysics, i.e. the relationship of physiology and psychology. He devised a method (Fechner's Law) for the exact measurement of sensation.

FEDDEN, Sir Roy (1885–). British aeroplane designer. As chief engineer of the Bristol Aeroplane Co., 1920–42, he was responsible for the design, etc., of the Bristol aero engines.

FEDERAL BUREAU OF INVESTIGATION (**F.B.I.**). Agency of the Dept. of Justice in the U.S.A. which investigates those violations of federal law not specifically assigned to other agencies, being particularly concerned with internal security, and which owes its unique position to the work of its director from 1924, J. Edgar Hoover (q.v.). Field divisions are maintained in over 50 major cities, and crime reports are turned over to it by more than 4,500 police agencies. There are *c.* 185,000,000 fingerprint cards on its files. Its Special Agents, known as G-men from the dept.'s code letter, are between 23 and 41 on entry, and

have special qualifications in law, accounting, or auditing. During the S.W.W. the F.B.I. shared espionage duties with the armed forces. In 1964 it was criticised by the Warren Commission for not having warned the Secret Service that Oswald was a potential threat to Pres. Kennedy.

FEDERALISM. A system of govt. under which two or more separate states unite under a common central gov., while retaining a considerable degree of local autonomy. A federation should be distinguished from a confederation, a looser union of states for mutual assistance. The oldest example of a federal state in Europe is Switzerland, which after 6 cents. as a confederation adopted a federal constitution in the 19th cent. The Soviet Union has been a federation since 1922, and the U.S.A. since 1789. Within the Commonwealth there are federal govts. in Canada (1867), Australia (1901), and Malaysia, linking Malaya, Singapore (till 1965), Sarawak and Sabah (1963). For latest developments in Europe, see EUROPEAN HISTORY.

FEDERAL UNION. See STREIT, CLARENCE.

FEDERATION OF BRITISH INDUSTRIES. See CONFEDERATION OF BRITISH INDUSTRY.

FEILING, Sir Keith (1884–). British historian. Chichele prof. of modern history at Oxford 1946–50, he pub. a 2-vol. history of the Tory Party 1640–1832 (1924–38), a study of *British Foreign Policy 1660–1672* (1930), and an interesting biography of *Neville Chamberlain* (1946). He was knighted 1958.

FEININGER (fī′-), **Lyonel** (1871–1956). American artist. B. in New York, the son of German immigrants, he worked for a time at the Bauhaus, and helped to found the Bauhaus in Chicago. Fond of the sea and ships, he portrayed them with romantic sensitivity in dreamlike translucence and purity of line.

FEISAL I (fī′sal) (1885–1933). King of Iraq. Descended from Mohammed, he was b. at Taif, represented Jiddah in the Turkish parliament of 1913, and became associated with the Arab national movement. Proclaimed king of Syria in 1920, he had to leave the country when it became a French mandate, but in 1921 was elected king of Iraq. His grandson **Feisal II** (1935–58) succeeded his father, King Ghazi, in 1939, and following the regency of his uncle Abdul Illah was king of Iraq 1953–8 and Head of State of the Arab Federation Feb.–July 1958. He was assassinated with his uncle when an army revolt estab. a rep.

FELDSPARS, FELSPARS. Important mineral group in rock formation, particularly of igneous rocks. They range through a great number of minerals, containing aluminium silicate and varying proportions of silicates of sodium, potassium, calcium, and barium; are white, grey, or pink in colour; and crystallize in the monoclinic or triclinic system.

FELIDAE (fēl′idē). Family of carnivores, which includes the lion, tiger, leopard, European wild cat, domesticated cat, etc.

FELIXSTOWE. Popular English holiday resort (U.D.) on the coast of Suffolk between the Orwell and Deben estuaries. The docks are increasingly important, and are being developed to rival Harwich. Pop. (1961) 17,254.

FELLINI, Federico (1920–). Italian film director. With strongly subjective poetic imagery, he has directed *I Vitelloni* (1953), *La Strada* (1954), *La Dolce Vita* (1960), and *8½* (1963) – i.e. he had by this time made 8½ films.

FELONY. A legal term for a wide variety of criminal offences. In Britain the original distinction, now mainly of historical interest, between felonies and misdemeanours, the 2 classes of criminal offences, was that Fs. were punishable by the forfeiture of the offender's whole property. Fs. were therefore the more serious offences. Under U.S. law, both State and

Federal, Fs. are defined as the most serious crimes, and the distinction is more logically sustained.

FÉNÉLON, François de Salignac de la Mothe (1651–1715). French writer and ecclesiastic. A son of the comte de Fénélon, he entered the priesthood in 1675 and in 1679 was made spiritual director to a sisterhood of ex-Huguenot proselytes, for whom he wrote his *Traité de l'Education des Filles* (1687). His *Démonstration de l'Existence de Dieu* was intended to bring the philosophy of Descartes into line with Catholic thought. In 1689 he was appointed tutor to the duke of Burgundy, grandson of Louis XIV, and wrote for him his *Fables, Dialogues des Morts, Télémaque*, and *Plans de Gouvernement. Télémaque* (1699) with its picture of an ideal commonwealth had the effect of a political manifesto, and Louis banished F. to Cambrai, where in 1695 he had been consecrated archbishop.

F's. mystical *Maximes des Saints* (1697) led to a quarrel with the Jansenists, rupture with Bossuet, and condemnation by pope Innocent XII.

FÉ′NIANS. Irish-American revolutionary secret society, founded in 1858 and named after the ancient legendary warrior band of the Fianna. It aimed at the establishment of an Irish republic. An attempt to invade Canada from the U.S.A. in 1866 and a rising in Ireland in 1867 failed completely, but the society continued down to the Irish civil war of 1922.

FENNEC. Species of fox (*Fennecus zerda*) found in the Sahara desert. Its coat is mainly pale fawn, and it has large ears.

FENNEL. Genus of plants (*Foeniculum*) of the Umbelliferae. The common F. is a perennial, reaching 2 or 3 ft. in height, and bearing large umbels of fragrant yellow flowers. It grows wild in S. Britain, and is used in cookery and sauces and as a garnish.

FENS. Level, low-lying tracts of land in E. England, W. and S. of the Wash, measuring some 70 m. from N. to S. with a maximum width of 35 m. They fall within the counties of Lincs, Hunts, Cambs, and Norfolk, consisting of a huge area once a bay of the North Sea, but now crossed by numerous drainage canals and forming some of the most productive agricultural land in Britain. The first drainage attempts were made by the Romans, but later attempts were unsuccessful until in 1634 the 4th earl of Bedford brought over the Dutch water-engineer Vermuyden who introduced Dutch methods. Burwell Fen and Wicken Fen, N.E. of Cambridge, have been preserved undrained as plant and animal reserves.

FERBER, Edna (1887–1968). American author. B. in Michigan, she was originally a reporter for the *Chicago Tribune*. Her novel *Show Boat* (1926) was adapted as an operetta by Jerome Kern and Oscar Hammerstein II, and her plays, in which she collaborated with G. S. Kaufmann, incl. *Dinner at Eight* (1932) and *Stage Door* (1936).

FERDINAND. Name of 3 Holy Roman emperors. **Ferdinand I** (1503–64) succeeded his brother Charles V as emperor in 1556. **Ferdinand II** (1578–1637), king of Bohemia and Hungary, succeeded his uncle Matthias as emperor in 1619, and by his fanatical Catholicism provoked the Bohemian revolt, which led to the 30 Years War. **Ferdinand III** (1608–57) succeeded his father Ferdinand II in 1637. The outstanding event of his reign was the conclusion of the 30 Years War in 1648.

FERDINAND (1861–1948). King of Bulgaria. Son of Prince Augustus of Saxe-Coburg-Gotha, he was elected prince of Bulgaria in 1887, and in 1908 proclaimed Bulgaria's independence of Turkey and assumed the title of Tsar. In 1915 he entered the F.W.W. as Germany's ally, and in 1918 abdicated and retired to Coburg.

FERDINAND I, called the Great (d. 1065). King of Castile. He united all N.W. Spain under his rule or that of his brothers, and began the reconquest of Spain from the Moors.

FERDINAND V of Castile, and **II** of Aragon (1452–1516). First king of all Spain. In 1469 he m. his cousin Isabella, who in 1474 succeeded to the throne of Castile. When in 1479 F. inherited the throne of Aragon the 2 great Spanish kingdoms were brought under a single government for the first time. The outstanding events of his reign included the introduction of the Inquisition in 1480, the expulsion of the Jews and the surrender of the Moors at Granada in 1492, Columbus' discovery of America, and the conquest of Naples in 1500–3.

FERDINAND (1865–1927). King of Rumania. He succeeded his uncle Charles I in 1914, and in 1916 declared war on Austria. The Allied victory was followed by the acquisition of Transylvania and Bukovina from Austria-Hungary and Bessarabia from Russia, and in 1922 F. was crowned king of All Rumanians.

FERGHANA (fergah′na). Town in Uzbek S.S.R., in the fertile F. valley, capital of the important cotton- and fruit-growing F. region; nearby are petroleum fields. Pop. (est.) 35,000.

FERGUSON, Harry (1884–1960). British engineer. B. in Co. Down, a farmer's son, he pioneered the development of the tractor, joining forces with Henry Ford in 1938 to manufacture in America. He also experimented in cars and aircraft machinery.

FERMANAGH (fermah′nah). Co. in the southern part of N. Ireland. The centre is occupied by a broad trough of lowland, in which lie Upper and Lower Loughs Erne. The highest points are Cuilcagh (2,188 ft.) and Belmore (1,312 ft.), and the main river is the Erne. The chief occupation is agriculture, and livestock are raised. The co. town is Enniskillen; smaller towns include Lisnaskea and Irvinestown. Area 657 sq. m.; pop. (1966) 49,876.

FERMAT (fermah′), **Pierre de** (1601–65). French mathematician. His method of calculating probability developed from his work with Pascal on the properties of numbers, and he is regarded as a founder of modern theory. His *Last Theorem*, though he himself may have discovered a complete proof, has never been demonstrated by anyone else.

FE′RMI, Enrico (1901–54). American physicist. B. in Rome, he was prof. of theoretical physics there 1926–38, when he settled in the U.S. The same year he was awarded a Nobel prize for having proved the existence of new radioactive elements produced by bombardment with neutrons and his discovery of nuclear reactions produced by slow neutrons. He was prof. at Columbia Univ., N.Y., 1939–42 and from 1946 at Chicago. The U.S. Atomic Energy Commission made a special award to him in 1954 for outstanding work in nuclear physics, and these annual awards have subsequently been known as F. Awards.

FERMOY′. Town (U.D.) on the r. Blackwater, co. Cork, Rep. of Ireland; once an important garrison town, it is a salmon-fishing centre. Pop. 3,200.

FERNANDEL (fernandel′). Stage-name of French comedian Fernand Contandin (1903–71), adopted because his mother-in-law used to refer to him as 'F. d'elle'. B. in Marseilles, he achieved an international reputation by his role as a country priest in *The Little World of Don Camillo* (1953) and as quins in *The Sheep has Five Legs* (1953). He had astonishing facial mobility.

FERNANDEZ (fernahn′deth), **Juan** (fl. 1570). Spanish navigator. As a pilot on the Pacific coast of S. America, he discovered in 1563 the islands off the coast of Chile that now bear his name; on one of these Alexander Selkirk, the original Robinson Crusoe, lived. In 1576 he may have sighted Easter Island, as well as Australia and New Zealand.

FERNANDO PO. Island in the Bight of Biafra, W.

Africa. It was discovered in the 15th cent., passed to Spain in 1778, and became one of the 2 overseas provs. of Spanish Guinea. In 1968 it became part of Equatorial Guinea (q.v.), of which its port of Santa Isabel is the capital.

FERNELEY, John (1782–1860). British artist. B. in Leics., he is famed for his hunting scenes.

FERNS. Name used loosely to cover all groups of the Pteridophyta, the best-known of which are the Equisetaceae (Horse Tail), Lycopodiaceae (Club Moss), and Selaginellaceae (Selaginella) families, and the Filicales, the true fern group.

The true Fs. are a group of non-flowering plants represented by about 150 living genera and a number of fossil forms; they are perennial herbs, with usually a low-growing rootstock, while the leaves, known as fronds, vary widely in size and shape.

Fs. are classified into 8 main families. By far the most common in Britain is the Polypodiaceae, in which are included the polypody (*Polypodium*), shield fern and male fern (*Aspidium*), hart's tongue (*Scolopendrium*), maiden hair (*Adiantum*), and bracken (*Pteris*).

FERNS. Left to right: common polypody, adder's tongue, hart's tongue, mountain buckler.

FERRAR, Nicolas (1592–1637). Founder of the Anglican monastic community at Little Gidding, Hunts, in 1625, which devoted itself to religious offices and the preparation of harmonies of the Scriptures, and was broken up by the Puritans in 1647.

FERRARA (ferrah′rah), **Andrea** (fl. 16th cent.). Italian armourer, who towards the end of the 16th cent. gained a European reputation as a swordmaker.

FERRARA. City and archbishopric in Emilia-Romagna dept., N. Italy, on a branch of the Po delta, 32 m. W. of the Adriatic Sea. It is the capital of F. prov., and has a Gothic palace and a cathedral, consecrated 1135. The free univ. was founded in 1391. F. is a trade and agricultural centre. Pop. (1966) 157,625.

FERRET. Small mammal of the Mustelidae family, related to the badger, weasel otter, and polecat. It belongs to the same genus, *Putorius*, as the last named, and may be described as a half-tamed albino polecat. It is about 14 in. long, with yellowish-white fur, and pink eyes. It is used to hunt rabbits, rats, etc.

FERRIER, Kathleen (1912–53). British contralto singer. B. in Lancs, and originally a student of the piano, she made a brilliant reputation in oratorio and opera. Notable appearances were in *The Rape of Lucretia* (1946) and *Das Lied von der Erde* (1947).

FERRIER, Susan Edmundstone (1782–1854). Scottish novelist. B. in Edinburgh, she became a close friend of Sir W. Scott. Her first novel, *Marriage*

FERTILIZER. Combine-drilling a cereal crop with fertilizer – Fisons 49.
Courtesy of Fisons Ltd.

(1818), was followed by *Inheritance* (1824), and *Destiny* (1831), all of which give a lively picture of Scottish manners and society.

FERRO-ALLOYS. Alloys of iron with a high proportion of manganese silicon, chromium, molybdenum, etc. They are used in the manufacture of alloy steels.

FERRŌ′L. City, port, and naval station on an inlet on the N.W. coast of Spain. It possesses a good sheltered harbour, whose narrow entrance is strongly guarded by forts, and there are shipbuilding and ship repairing industries, etc. Pop. (1965) 82,070.

FERTILITY DRUGS. Drugs developed in Sweden in the mid-1950s, the best-known being gonadotrophin. Made from hormone extracts (FSH and LH) taken from the human pituitary gland, it stimulates ovulation in women. In the 1960s it was still in the experimental stage and multiple births were a risk, e.g. the sextuplets born in Birmingham in 1968.

FERTILIZERS. Substances containing the twenty-odd chemical elements necessary for healthy plant growth, and which are used to compensate the deficiencies of poor soil or of soil depleted by repeated cropping. They may be (a) *Organic*, e.g. farmyard manure, composts, bonemeal, blood and fishmeal, which have been in immemorial use. (b) *Inorganic*, in the form of compounds, mainly of nitrogen, phosphate and potash, which have come into use on a tremendously increased scale since the S.W.W. The compounds are most frequently administered in solid form, but 'non-pressure' liquid Fs. are frequently used in market gardening and 'pressure' liquids, such as anhydrous ammonia (containing 82 per cent nitrogen), are being increasingly used on larger farms and by contractors.

FESCUE (fes′kū). Widely distributed genus (*Festuca*) of grasses. Two species are common in Britain: meadow F., which grows from 2 to 5 ft. high, and sheep's F., which is 6 in. to 2 ft. high.

FETI (fā′ti), **Domenico** (c. 1589–1624). Italian artist. B. in Rome, he became court painter in Mantua in 1613. He is chiefly remarkable for his small religious works with landscape settings which combine naturalism and sensitive colour.

FETISHISM. Belief in the supernormal power of some object, inanimate or otherwise, which is known as a fetish. Any object that can pass into the possession of an individual can become a fetish to him, but it may be communally owned. F. in some form is common to most civilizations. With the primitive races, e.g. the African Negro, F. is religio-magical.

FEUDALISM (fūd′-) (Lat. *feudum*, a fief). The system which arose during the 4th–10th cents., whereby land was held in return for service. Under it all land, in theory, belonged ultimately to the king, who might hold his kingdom from another king, and grant the use of the land and the right to exact services, and often to administer justice and levy taxes, to a tenant-in-chief, who in turn might grant portions of it to vassals, and so on. The most important of a vassal's obligations was that of military service. The economic basis of F. was the manor, cultivated by serfs bound to the soil, who held portions of the manor fields in return for labour services. The system declined from the 13th cent. onward, owing partly to the development of a money economy, partly to the many peasants' revolts of 1350–1550. In England serfdom became extinct in the 16th cent. and feudal dues paid by landowners to the Crown were abolished in 1660.

FEUERBACH (foi′erbahkh), **Ludwig Andreas** (1804–72). German philosopher, author of *Das Wesen des Christentums* (1841), trans. in 1853 by George Eliot under the title of *The Essence of Religion*. F. maintained that God is an outward projection of man's inner self; men have created an idea of ideal humanity which may replace God.

FEVER. Disorder due to raising of the body temperature above normal. It is generally the reaction of the organism to the presence in the blood stream of a foreign substance, usually a protein. This is most often produced by invading micro-organisms.

FEZ. Northern cap. of Morocco, a sacred Mohammedan city situated in a valley N. of the Great Atlas mts. It manufactures silk, woollen, and cotton goods, etc., and was originally the only place where the fez was made. The Kairwan Islamic Univ. dates from 859 and a second univ. was founded 1961. Pop. (1965) 249,000.

FEZZA′N. Desert area of *c.* 214,000 sq. m. in Libya with many oases. Formerly a prov., it was split into smaller divisions in the reorganisation of 1963.

FIANNA FAIL (fē-an′a foil) (Soldiers of Destiny). Irish republican party, founded by De Valera in 1926. It aims at the establishment of a united and completely independent all-Ireland republic.

FIBONACCI (fibonah′chē), **Leonardo** (fl. 13th cent.). Italian mathematician. He pub. his *Liber abaci* in Pisa in 1202, which led to the introduction of Arabic notation into Europe. From 1960 interest developed in his discovery of the *F. Numbers*, in their simplest form a series in which each number is the sum of its two predecessors (i.e., 1, 1, 2, 3, 5, 8, 13). They have unusual characteristics with possible applications in botany, psychology, astronomy, etc., for example, a more exact correspondence than Bode's Law to the distances between the planets and the Sun.

FIBRES, Man-made. The original stimulus to the development of extruded F. was the search for an alternative to carbon filaments in electric lighting, and Sir Joseph W. Swan patented an artificial silk in 1883, but the pioneer of commercial textiles was Count Hilaire de Chardonnet (1839–1924). Artificial silk, called rayon from 1926, began a social revolution in textiles, Courtaulds being the pioneers of the viscose process (patented by C. F. Cross and E. J. Bevan 1892). The revolution was completed by the introduction of the first fully synthetic fibre in 1938, nylon (q.v.) developed by DuPont. Today the 4 main fibre types are nylon; the acrylics used in knitwear (also developed by DuPont, e.g. Orlon 1944); the polyesters (e.g. Terylene, discovered by J. R. Whinfield and J. Dickson of the Calico Printers Association 1940 and developed by I.C.I.); and the spandex or elastomeric F. (e.g. Lycra, DuPont 1959) which replace traditional rubber yarns. The variants are as endless as their uses in clothes, carpets, industry, etc., but espec. notable are the foambacks or laminates, and texturised types (e.g. Crimplene 1959). A world-wide industry has resulted, since air-conditioning renders climate immaterial, and both raw materials and finished product are easily transported. *See* KNITTING.

FIBROSI′TIS. Inflammation and overgrowth of

fibrous tissue, especially of the sheaths of muscles; fibrositis is also known as muscular rheumatism.

FICHTE (fikh′te). **Johann Gottlieb** (1762–1814). German philosopher. B. in Silesia and ed. at Jena and Leipzig, he was an admirer of Kant and in 1792 pub. a *Critique of Religious Revelation*, a critical study on Kantian lines. While professor at Jena (1793–9), F. wrote a number of important works on the theory of knowledge. In 1799 he was accused of atheism, and was forced to resign his post. He moved to Berlin, where he lectured and devoted himself to public affairs. At the same time he delivered his *Addresses to the German People* on the foundations of true prosperity; his *Staatslehre* (Theory of Politics) describes a Utopian state founded on rational principles, but with a tendency towards dictatorship.

FIDEI DEFENSOR (fid′ē-ī dēfen′sōr). (Lat., 'defender of the faith'). The title conferred by pope Leo X upon Henry VIII of England in recognition of a treatise that the latter had written against Martin Luther. The title has ever since been included in the style of English sovereigns.

FIELDFARE. A bird (*Turdus pilaris*) of the thrush family (Turdidae), a winter migrant in Britain, breeding in Scandinavia, N. Russia, and Siberia. It has a slate-grey lower back, with black tail.

FIELDING, Gabriel. Pseudonym of British novelist Alan Gabriel Barnsley (1916–), descended from a brother of Henry F. (q.v.). He is best known for his trilogy about the Blaydon family *Brotherly Love* (1954), *In the Time of Greenbloom* (1956), *Through Streets Broad and Narrow* (1960).

FIELDING, Henry (1707–54). English novelist. B. in Somerset, he was a contemporary of the elder Pitt and H. Fox at Eton. In 1725 he attempted to abduct an heiress at Lyme Regis, and after some years of life as a man-about-town began writing for the stage, his chief successes in this medium being the burlesque *Author's Farce* (1730), and *Tom Thumb* (1730), and his adaptations from Molière. His first novel was *Joseph Andrews* (1742), a parody of Richardson's *Pamela*; it was followed by the ironic *Jonathan Wild the Great* (1743), and in 1749 by his masterpiece *Tom Jones*, 'a comic epic in prose'. F. had been called to the Bar in 1740, and in 1748 was appointed J.P. for Middlesex and Westminster. Here he was eminently successful, and his concern for social evils, especially prison conditions, emerges in his last novel *Amelia* (1751). In 1754 F. sailed to Portugal to improve his health, writing on the way *A Journal of a Voyage to Lisbon*, and d. and was buried at Lisbon two months after his arrival.

FIELD MARSHAL. Title given to the highest-ranking officer in the British Army, introduced from Germany by George II in 1736.

FIELD MOUSE. *See* MOUSE.

J. G. FICHTE. Drawing by Henschel.

FIELD OF THE CLOTH OF GOLD. Name given to the meeting between Henry VIII and Francis I of France in June 1520, between Guînes and Ardres, near Calais. The magnificence of the dresses was the origin of the name.

FIELDS, Gracie. Stage-name of British comedienne and singer Grace Stansfield (1898–). B. in Rochdale, she was originally a mill-girl, but her remarkable voice and personality soon brought her fame in the musical *Mr. Tower of London* (1918), and her film successes from 1931 incl. *Sally in our Alley. Sing as We Go, Keep Smiling*, etc. She lives on Capri.

FIELD STUDIES. The study of ecology, geography, geology, history, archaeology, and allied subjects, in their natural environment. The Council for the Promotion of F.S. was estab. in Britain in 1943, and Flatford Mill, Suffolk, was the first research centre estab.

FIESOLE (fē-ā′sōlā). Italian town 4 m. N.E. of Florence, with many Etruscan and Roman relics. The cathedral was completed 1028. Pop. (1960) 12,600.

FIFE, Alexander William George Duff, duke of (1849–1912). Son-in-law of Edward VII. He succeeded his father as 6th earl in 1879, and was created a duke in 1889 on his marriage to Princess Louise Victoria Alexandra Dagmar (1867–1931), later Princess Royal, eldest dau. of Edward VII. They had two daughters: Alexandra, duchess of F. in her own right (1891–1959), m. in 1913 Prince Arthur of Connaught (1883–1938); and Maud (1893–1945) m. Lord Carnegie, later 11th earl of Southesk.

FIFE. Co. in E. Scotland facing the North Sea and the Firth of Forth; the only high land is in the N.W. The chief rivers are the Eden and the Leven. Agriculture, linen-weaving, and coal-mining are important; the chief mining centres are Dysart, Leven, Dunfermline, Cowdenbeath, and Kirkcaldy. The co. town is Cupar. Area 504 sq. m.; pop. (1961) 320,541.

FIFE. A kind of small flute. Originally from Switzerland, it was known as the Swiss pipe and has long been used by British Army bands.

FIFTEEN, The. Name given to the Jacobite rebellion of 1715, which was led by the 'Old Pretender' (James Edward Stuart) and the earl of Mar, with the object of placing the former on the throne. Mar was checked at Sheriffmuir, and the revolt collapsed.

FIFTH COLUMN. A group within a country secretly aiding an enemy attacking from without. The term originated in 1936, during the Spanish Civil War, when General Mola boasted that the Franco supporters were attacking Madrid with 4 columns, and that they had a 'fifth column' inside the city. This technique was employed by the Nazis in the S.W.W.

FIFTH MONARCHY MEN. Revolutionary Puritan sect. Their name and theology were derived from the prophecies of the 4 monarchies in the O.T. book of Daniel, which they identified with Babylon, Persia, Greece, and Rome (including the papacy). The execution of Charles I they saw as the beginning of the downfall of Rome. At first they supported Cromwell's government, but later they plotted against him. A revolt in London in 1661 was soon suppressed.

FIG. Fruit of *Ficus carica*, the cultivated F. tree, and of a number of other species. The tree is grown particularly in Mediterranean lands, and in California, parts of Australia, S. Africa, etc. The fruit is exported fresh or dried; besides its use as a food, it is used in the preparation of laxatives.

FIGWORT. Genus (*Scrophularia*) of plants of the Scrophulariaceae family, including some common British weeds. The species F. grows 2 to 3 ft. high, with purplish flowers emitting a disagreeable smell.

FIG. 1, staminal (male) flower; 2, pistillate (female) flower; 3. section.

FIJI. Independent state which consists of about 322 mainly volcanic islands in the Melanesian archipelago, Pacific Ocean. About 106 is. are inhabited; the largest are Viti Levu (4,010 sq. m.), and Vanua Levu (2,137 sq. m.). The vegetation is tropical.

FIJI. The drinking of kava (q.v.) has great ceremonial importance. After the root and stem have been macerated in water, as seen here, the resultant liquor is a narcotic.
Photo: Aerofilms Ltd.

Jungle and forests, providing valuable timber, occupy generally the S.E. sides of the islands. The drier parts are under grass. Bananas, coconuts, sugar cane, rice, fruit, and vegetables are grown. Fishing is carried on. There is considerable industrial development, e.g. sugar and rice mills; copra, biscuit, and soap factories; and gold is mined. The cap. is the city of Suva, on Viti Levu.

The group was discovered by Tasman in 1643, visited by Cook in 1773, and ceded to Britain in 1874. The native peoples are of Negroid stock with a Polynesian admixture, but from *c*. 1880 Indians were introduced to work the sugar plantations and now outnumber them. There has been little intermarriage and there is racial tension: the Indians are industrially and commercially predominant and the Fijians own 80% of the land communally. F. attained Dominion status 1970, as an independent member of the Commonwealth, and there is a Gov.-Gen., Senate and House of Representatives elected on 3 communal rolls (Fijian, Indian, and other races). The Fijians are chiefly Methodist and the Indians Hindu. Area 7,036 sq. m.; pop. (1969) 525,000 (220,000 Fijians, 263,000 Indians).

FILEY (fīl′i). English seaside resort on the Yorkshire coast. Pop. (1961) 4,705.

FILLMORE, Millard (1800–74). 13th President of the U.S.A. B. in New York, he was elected Vice-President in 1848, and succeeded on the death of Zachary Taylor; he was President 1850–3. A Whig, he advocated reconciliation of North and South, and compromise on the slavery issue, and since he pleased neither side failed to gain renomination.

FILM. Roll of specially coated thin transparent material on which a series of photographs can be recorded (*see* CINEMATOGRAPHY), and, by the eye's persistence of vision, 'moving pictures' projected from it on to a screen. The first moving pictures were shown in the 1890s: Edison persuaded James J. Corbett (1866–1933), American world boxing champion (1892–7), to act a boxing match for a film. Lumière in France; R. W. Paul in England; Latham in the U.S.A. and others were making moving pictures of a few minutes' duration of actual events (e.g. the Derby, shown in London, on the evening of the race, 1896), and of simple scenes such as a train coming into a station.

In 1902 Georges Méliès of France made a fantastic story film, *A Trip to the Moon*, which ran in London for 9 months; and in 1903 Edwin S. Porter directed for Edison *The Great Train Robbery*, a story in a contemporary setting: it cost about £100, was shown all over the world, and earned more than £20,000.

For a number of years, films even of 'indoor'

happenings were 'shot' out of doors by daylight – and its admirable climate was the basis of Hollywood's outstanding success as a centre of film production, though the first film studio was Edison's at Fort Lee, N.J., U.S.A. In England, the pioneer company of Cricks and Martin set up a studio at Mitcham (where a romantic domestic drama, *For Baby's Sake*, was made in 1908).

D. W. Griffith. the great American director, revolutionized film technique and made it in essentials what it is today. He introduced, e.g., the close-up, the flash-back, the fade-out and the fade-in. His first 'epic' was *The Birth of a Nation* (1915), and his second, *Intolerance*, with magnificent and spectacular scenes in the Babylonian section that have never been surpassed, followed in 1916, at a cost (present values) second only to *Cleopatra* (1963).

At first, the players' names were considered of no importance, though one who appeared nameless in *The Great Train Robbery*, G. M. Anderson, afterwards became famous as 'Broncho Billy' in a series of cowboy films – the first 'Westerns'. The first 'movie' performer to become a name was Mary Pickford – cinemagoers found this young actress so attractive that they insisted on knowing who she was; and in the Hollywood of the 'twenties – helped to pre-eminence by the F.W.W. which virtually stopped film production in Europe – many stars were created: Rudolph Valentino, Douglas Fairbanks Sr., Lilian Gish, Gloria Swanson, Richard Barthelmess, and Greta Garbo outstanding among dramatic actors; Charles Chaplin, Harry Langdon, Buster Keaton, Harold Lloyd among comedians.

Concern for artistry began with Griffith; but developed in Europe, particularly Russia and Germany, whose directors exploited the film's artistic possibilities, during both the silent and the sound era. It is important to remember that silent films were never silent; there was always a musical background, integral to the film, whether played by the solo pianist in the suburban cinema, or the 100-piece orchestra in the big city theatre. The arrival of talking films (*The Jazz Singer*, 1928) proved a setback only to those artists with limited vision who exploited the mere novelty value of sound. Other directors, actors and actresses survived the transition and achieved a wider perspective by the marriage of sight and sound. Among the directors who succeeded were Jean Renoir in France, Lang and Murnau in Germany, Hitchcock in Britain and America, and Pudovkin and Eisenstein in Russia. After the S.W.W. Japanese films were first seen in the western world (although the industry dates back to the silent days),

and India produced some films of merit. Ingmar Bergmann (Sweden) and David Lean (England), were noteworthy post-war directors.

The introduction of sound banished from the screen a number of the silent stars and totally changed the style of acting from something close to mime to something more realistic even than that of the stage. It also brought to the screen many theatrical stars, e.g. in England Alec Guinness, Edith Evans, Laurence Olivier, Flora Robson, Ralph Richardson, Noël Coward. Stars made by the 'talkies' have included the Marx Brothers, Clark Gable, Katherine Hepburn, German-born Marlene Dietrich (U.S.A.); Raimu, Jean Gabin, Françoise Rosay, Fernandel (France); Peter O'Toole, Robert Donat, Tom Courtenay, Peter Sellers, Elizabeth Taylor, Richard Burton (Britain).

Apart from story films, the industry produces news films; 'documentaries', depicting factual life, of which the pioneers were the American Robert Flaherty (*Nanook of the North*, 1920, *Man of Aran*, 1932–4, etc.) and the Scottish John Grierson (e.g. *Drifters*, 1929, *Night Mail*, 1936); cartoon films, which achieved their first success with Patrick Sullivan's Felix the Cat (1917), later surpassed in popularity by Walt Disney's Mickey Mouse. To supply the needs of TV, some film studios switched over to producing short, often serial, pictures for that medium, making a story, or a section of a serial, in a few days (much as the earliest story films were made) instead of, as in feature films for the cinema screen, 'shooting' in a day no more material than will cover 90–120 seconds of showing time.

Interest in the history and development of film technique led to the formation in Britain of the British Film Institute (1933) with which is linked the National Film Theatre (1951) where borrowed films as well as the Institute's treasures are shown to members; the Film Library of the Museum of Art in N.Y.C. caters for a similar public.

In the 1950s the third phase of the cinema came with Cinemascope, which again gave greater artistic scope to the film-maker, just as sound had done in the 1920s. To meet increasing competition from TV for the viewing public, the cinema industry has countered, partly by the creation of smaller production companies centred round stars, directors and writers; and partly in the production of long-run, wide-screen spectaculars (block-busters) based on historical and biblical themes., e.g. *Cleopatra* (1963) costing £15,000,000 and the Russian version of *War and Peace* (1969) running over 6 hours. *See also* CENSORSHIP.

FINCH, Peter (1916–   ). British actor. B. in London, he was brought up in Australia, where he made his début in 1935. First appearing in London in *Daphne Laureola* in 1949, he has played in Shakespeare (Iago, Mercutio), and has achieved an international film reputation, notably in the title role of *The Trials of Oscar Wilde*.

FINCH. Name applied to birds of the family Fringillidae of the order Passeriformes. They have a short, stout, conical bill, and are mainly seed-eaters. The family is divided into 2 sub-families: the true Fs. (Fringillinae), e.g. chaffinch, goldfinch, canary, etc., and the buntings (Emberizinae).

BULLFINCH

FINE GAEL (fin′i gäl′) (United Ireland). Irish political party, formed in 1933 under the leadership of W. J. Cosgrave, who resigned in 1944, and led since 1965 by his son. Since the introduction of the republic by Costello, the basic conservatism of F.G. has weakened.

FILM. D. W. Griffith's *The Birth of a Nation* (1915) combined, in its story of the American Civil War, dramatic art and the potentialities of the cine-camera. The 'still' above shows the Ku Klux Klan. *Courtesy of the British Film Institute.*

FINGER PRINTS. A system of identification by means of the ridges on the skin of a person's finger tips. No two F.Ps. are exactly alike, and they remain constant in pattern throughout life. The classification was originated and practised in India and adopted by the police in England in 1901.

FINLAND. A republic of N. Europe lying N. of latitude 60°, one-third being N. of the Arctic Circle.

The Åland Islands, in the Gulf of Bothnia, are a Finnish dept. The many lakes form the principal means of communication, by water in summer; by ice in winter. Winters in F. are long and severe, and most of the harbours are icebound for at least 5 months. Over two-thirds of the land area is forested, the northern part having a tundra scrub vegetation.

FINLAND. Built on islands in the heart of the Saimaa lake area, Europe's largest inland waterway system, Savonlinna is the centre of many steamer routes. Established here in 1475 as an eastern frontier fortress, Olavinlinna Castle is one of Scandinavia's finest medieval monuments. The girl wears one of Finland's several national costumes.
Courtesy of the Finnish Tourist Information Centre.

The Saimaa Canal, linking the Saimaa lake area of Finland and the Gulf of Finland, but with half its length in the U.S.S.R., was modernized 1968.

Most of the population is Finnish-speaking, but about 8½ per cent speak Swedish, with a small number of Russian, German, and, in the N., Lapp speakers. The national religion is Evangelical Lutheran. There are 6 universities, one each at Helsinki, Jyvaskyla, Oulu and Tampere, and two at Turku.

Timber, pulp and paper industries are the mainstay of the economy, but there are metal and engineering industries, and copper and iron ore are mined. Many streams supply hydroelectric power. In modern design furniture, ceramics and glass, F. has a high reputation. Agriculture – cereals and dairy products – is confined to the better land of the south. The chief towns are Helsinki, the cap. and main port, Turku (former cap.) and Tampere, the largest industrial centre. The pres. is elected for 6 years, and appoints a Council of State, and there is a single legislative Chamber.

Area 130,124 (incl. 12,189 sq. m. inland water) sq. m.; pop. (1967) 4,664,000.

History. The Finns are of Asiatic origin and migrated to present-day F. in the 7th and 8th cents., finding there a people from whom the Lapps of today are probably descended. Sweden conquered and attempted to Christianize the Finns in the 12th cent., but it was some 150 years before they abandoned paganism. F. was part of the kingdom of Sweden for 600 years, but had a fair amount of self-govt. From early in the 18th cent. Russia and Sweden disputed possession of F. which in 1809 became a grand duchy of Russia with almost complete autonomy except in foreign affairs. A national movement secured the recognition of Finnish as the official language in 1863 (before that it had been Swedish). Later Russia attempted to reduce Finnish liberties, and after the Russian Revolution F. proclaimed itself an independent republic in 1917. In 1939 Russia attacked and defeated F. which in 1940 ceded territory N.W. of

Leningrad to Russia. In 1941 F. joined Germany in attacking Russia and advanced to its old frontier. The Russian offensive in 1944 regained the disputed land and led to an armistice by which, besides the cessions made in 1940, F. ceded the Petsamo area on the Arctic coast, giving the R.S.F.S.R. a frontier with Norway (cessions confirmed by the peace treaty between F. and the Allies, 1947).

LANGUAGE AND LITERATURE. Finnish, like Estonian, to which it is closely related, belongs to the Finno-Ugrian family of languages. Some fragments in Finnish have come down from the 12th cent.; the first book was an ABC published in 1544. A complete Bible in Finnish was issued at Stockholm in 1642. But the predominance of the Swedes and Swedish in F. inhibited the growth of a Finnish literature until the 19th cent. when it was launched with the publication in 1835 of Lönnrot's verse epic *Kalevala* (q.v.). The novelist Emil Sillanpää (1888–1964) was awarded a Nobel prize 1939.

MUSIC. F. gave to the arts a man of world fame in the person of the composer Sibelius (q.v.).

FINLAND, Gulf of. An eastern arm of the Baltic Sea, with U.S.S.R. on the S. and Finland on the N.

FINLAY, George (1799–1875). Historian chiefly remembered for his history of Greece from 146 B.C.

FINN MAC CUMHAILL (fin makool'). Hero of Gaelic folklore. He is believed to be identical with the general who organized a regular army for Ireland at the bidding of Cormac mac Airt (fl. *c.* A.D. 250), and his braves are sharply individualized.

FINSEN, Niels Ryberg (1860–1904). Danish physician. He was the first to develop light treatment scientifically, using artificial light, particularly the carbon arc. He received the Nobel prize in 1903.

FINUCANE, Brendan (1920–42). British air ace of the S.W.W. B. in Ireland, he shot down 32 enemy aircraft and damaged many others before being killed near Pointe du Touquet in France.

FIR. A term widely applied to trees of the order Coniferales, but correctly referring only to members of the genus *Abies* and a few other species. The F. is distinguished from the pine by bearing its needle-like leaves singly, trees of the genus *Pinus* bearing theirs in groups. The Fs. are pyramidal and ever-green, retaining their leaves for 6–9 years, but shedding a number every year, so that the tree is never without foliage. Common European Fs. include the silver F. (*A. pectinata*), spruce F. or Christmas tree (*Picea excelsa*), and Douglas F. (*Pseudotsuga Douglasii*). N. America has 10 native species.

FIRBANK, Ronald (1886–1926). English novelist. Set in the Edwardian decadent period, his work appeals to a small band of enthusiasts, but his malicious humour palls in large quantities. It incl. *Caprice* (1916), *Valmouth* (1918), set in an imaginary West Country, and the posthumous *Concerning the Eccentricities of Cardinal Pirelli* (1926).

FIRDOUSI (*c.* A.D. 940–1020). Persian poet, famous for the epic poem *Shahnama*, the Book of Kings, which relates the history of Persia in 60,000 verses.

FINLAND. Jean Sibelius.
Photo: Olav Gunuar.

FIREARMS. Weapons from which missiles are discharged by the combustion of an explosive. They are generally divided into 2 main sections: artillery (q.v.), (ordnance or cannon) which have a bore greater than 1 in., and small arms (q.v.), with a bore of less than 1 in. Although gunpowder was known 60 years previously, the invention of guns dates from 1300–25, and is attrib. to Berthold Schwartz, a German monk. *See also* PISTOL, MACHINE GUN.

FIRECLAY. A clay that is resistant to very high temperatures, and is therefore suitable for lining furnaces. Its refractory characteristics are due to its chemical composition, which contains a high percentage of silica and alumina and a low percentage of oxides of sodium, potassium, iron, calcium, etc. Fs. underlie the coal seams in the British Isles.

FIREDAMP. Gas which occurs in coal-mines and is explosive when mixed with air in certain proportions. It consists chiefly of methane (marsh gas) but always contains small quantities of other gases, e.g. nitrogen, carbon dioxide, hydrogen, and sometimes ethane and carbon monoxide.

FIREFLY. Popular name of certain beetles in the families Lampyridae and Elateridae. The genus *Pyrophorus*, in the latter family, contains many species which are usually found in western tropical countries. The main luminous organs are situated on the prothorax, and the light is thought to have some connection with the sexual activities of the insects. *See* GLOW-WORM.

FIRENZE. Italian form of FLORENCE.

FIRE PROTECTION. Fire constitutes a considerable cause of loss of life and one of the greatest causes of damage to property, and protection has always depended on a combination of public service and private enterprise. In Britain Acts of 1707 and 1774 required every parish to provide engines, hoses and ladders, but insurance cos. estab. their own more efficient brigades for the benefit of buildings bearing their own fire marks. The latter amalgamated in the 19th cent. to form the basis of the present-day service which is run by the local authorities who cooperate closely: experimentation in new methods, etc., is carried out at the Fire Research Station at Boreham Wood, in Herts. Similar services operate in other countries. Since early detection enhances the chance of success, a valuable method of protection for industrial and commercial buildings is by automatic sprinkler system: heat opens the sprinkler heads on a network of water pipes and immediately sprays the seat of the fire. In certain circumstances water is less effective and may be dangerous, e.g. for oil and petrol storage tanks foam systems are used, and, for

FIRE PROTECTION. A power-station fire being extinguished by a chemical foam. This consists of a 3 per cent solution of hydrolised proteins, e.g. horn or hoof meal, or animal blood, and hydrochloric acid, which is forced through a funnel and turned to foam by the power of the water jet.
Courtesy of the Yorkshire Evening Press.

FIREWORKS. A striking display on London's South Bank, mounted for the coronation of Queen Elizabeth II. To the left is the Royal Festival Hall, and beyond Hungerford Bridge the shadowy outline of County Hall.
Photo: Associated Newspapers Ltd.

plant containing inflammable vapours, carbon dioxide. Fire-resistant materials are also increasingly used in building construction. Forest Fs. and oil-well Fs. are among the most spectacular disasters, the latter often being tackled by international specialists

FIREWORKS. Pyrotechny, the art of firework-making. A firework consists of a container or 'case', usually cylindrical in shape and of rolled paper, enclosing a mixture capable of burning independently of the oxygen of the air, since it includes an ingredient holding a supply of oxygen which it readily gives up to the other burnable ingredients.

Fireworks may be divided into 2 main types: *Aerial*, e.g. the rocket, shell, etc., and *Ground F.* Rockets and other Fs. were used in warfare from earliest times, and during the S.W.W. they were employed for anti-aircraft defence, to propel bombs used by ground-strafing fighter aircraft, as signals and flares, etc.

FIRST AID. Action taken immediately after an accident in order to save the life of a victim, prevent further damage, or facilitate later treatment. A practicable technique is taught by the Red Cross Society and the Order of St. John of Jerusalem.

FIRST WORLD WAR. The war of 1914–18, fought between the Allied Powers (the British Empire, France, Russia, Italy, the U.S.A., Japan, Belgium, Serbia, Montenegro, Greece, Rumania, Portugal) and the Central European Powers (Germany, Austria-Hungary, Turkey, and Bulgaria).

Three main conflicts went to produce the war. The first arose from the French desire to recover Alsace-Lorraine, and the struggle of French and German industrialists to control the iron of Lorraine and the coal of the Ruhr. The second was caused by the desire of Russia to dominate the Balkans as an outlet to the Mediterranean, and of Germany to do the same as a step to economic control of the Near East. The third lay in the colonial ambitions of the Powers, who had partitioned Africa and divided China into spheres of influence, and especially in the ambitions of Germany, which had been left behind in the scramble. The Powers were divided into 2 rival alliances: the Triple Alliance of Germany, Austria, and Italy, formed in 1882, and the Triple Entente of Britain, France, and Russia, formed 1895–1907. The final crisis was caused by the murder of the heir to the Austrian throne at Sarajevo on June 28, 1914. Austria made this an excuse to declare war on Serbia on July 28. When Russia mobilized, Germany declared war on Russia and France, and

FIRST WORLD WAR. One of the maze of trenches on the western front in France and Flanders. In winter the men might be up to their armpits in water in low-lying sections.
Photo: Imperial War Museum.

invaded Belgium, whereupon on August 4 Britain declared war on Germany.

In spite of the resistance of the Belgian fortresses, the Germans advanced rapidly through Belgium, forcing back the French Army and the B.E.F., which had been positioned at Mons. On Sept. 6, when the Germans were a few miles from Paris, the Allied counter-attack opened on the Marne, and drove the Germans back to the Aisne. The Belgian Army, driven into Antwerp, evacuated it on Oct. 9 with British assistance, and retreated down the coast to join the Allies. By Oct. 19 the opposing lines had been extended to the sea at Nieuport, and the struggle had settled down into trench warfare. German attempts to break through at Arras and Ypres failed to change the situation.

An immediate offensive was launched by the Russians into E. Prussia, forcing the Germans to withdraw troops from the W., until stopped by Hindenburg's victory at Tannenberg (Aug. 26–30). The Russians also overran Galicia.

The German fleet early withdrew to its bases, and confined itself mainly to submarine raids and mine-laying. Australia, New Zealand, or Japanese forces soon occupied German Pacific possessions – Japan had declared war on Aug. 22. The German Pacific squadron escaped to the Atlantic and defeated a British squadron off Coronel on Nov. 1, but was itself destroyed on Dec. 8 off the Falkland Isles. By Sept. 1916 the German colonies in Africa were in Allied hands.

Throughout 1915 both sides made attempts to break through on the western front, with little result. These offensives incl. those made by the Allies at Neuve Chapelle (March), Vimy Ridge (May), and Loos (Sept.), and by the Germans at Ypres (April), during which poison gas was first used. In Dec. Sir Douglas Haig replaced Sir John French as British C.-in-C. On the eastern front German offensives by Mackensen in the S. and Hindenburg in the N. regained all that had been lost, and expelled the Russians from Poland.

Turkey, which entered the war on Nov. 1, 1914, launched an offensive in the Caucasus, and in 1915 unsuccessfully attacked the Suez Canal from Palestine. A British force invaded Mesopotamia, occupied Kut, and threatened Baghdad. A naval attack on the Dardanelles in Feb.–March, intended to open communication with Russia through the Black Sea, was followed by landings on the Gallipoli peninsula in April. Although further ground was gained in Aug., Gallipoli had to be evacuated in Jan. 1916.

Italy, hoping to secure control of the Adriatic, declared war on Austria in May 1915, while Greece, Bulgaria, and Rumania were still hesitating. The

German victories in the E. and the Gallipoli failure persuaded Bulgaria to join the German and Austrian attack on Serbia. The Serbian armies retreated to the Adriatic, and at Salonika finally joined the Allied forces, which had landed at the invitation of the pro-British Greek P.M. Venizelos.

The Germans opened 1916 on the western front with an attack in Feb. on the Verdun salient which continued till June, and 'bled France white', but failed to break through. The Allies replied with their offensive on the Somme, during which tanks were first used, and between July and Nov. carried their line forward 7 m. A further French offensive at Verdun in Oct.–Dec. recovered some lost ground. During June–Aug. the Russians' successful advance in S. Galicia encouraged the Rumanians to declare war and invade Transylvania. The Germans hit back from Transylvania and Bulgaria, and in Dec. occupied Bucharest.

In Mesopotamia a British force defended Kut against the Turks from Dec. 1915 to April 1916, when it had to surrender. The Arabs of the Hejaz rebelled against Turkish rule in 1916, and the revolt, aided by T. E. Lawrence, rapidly spread as far N. as Damascus; nevertheless, the Turks made another unsuccessful attack on the Suez Canal in August.

In Feb. 1915 the Germans announced they would use submarines to sink merchant-ships found in British waters, to which Britain replied by seizing all cargoes destined for Germany. The sinking of the *Lusitania* with many Americans on board aroused deep indignation in the U.S.A. and American protests forced Germany to abandon the submarine campaign in April 1916. On May 30 the High Sea Fleet put to sea, and the following day a general fleet action was fought off Jutland. Although the British losses were the heavier, the battered German fleet remained in port for the rest of the war. Renewed submarine warfare in Feb. 1917 resulted in the U.S.A. entering the war in April.

In March 1917 anti-war feeling led to the overthrow of the Russian monarchy. The attempts of the new Liberal government to continue the war destroyed its popularity, and on Nov. 7 the Bolsheviks took power with a programme of immediate peace. Fighting ceased on the eastern front in Dec., and in March 1918 peace was signed at Brest Litovsk. The example of the Russian Revolution did much to strengthen the anti-war movement in Germany.

Early in 1917 the Germans withdrew N. of the Somme to their new defences, the Hindenburg Line. The Allied offensive of April captured Vimy Ridge, but French losses were so heavy that widespread mutinies resulted. In June the British captured Messines Ridge and straightened out the Ypres salient, but an advance from Ypres towards the coast (Passchendaele offensive) in July–Nov. failed. The French during Aug.–Oct. recovered considerable

FIRST WORLD WAR. The war leaders at Downing Street in 1918: left to right, Marshal Foch, Georges Clemenceau, Lloyd George, Vittorio Orlando and Baron Sonino.
Photo: Central Press Photo.

ground before Verdun, and took the Chemin des Dames.

The war on the Italian front went on the whole in favour of the Italians, until in Oct. 1917 the Germans and Austrians attacked at Caporetto. The Italian line collapsed, and was pushed back beyond the Piave with very heavy losses. British and French troops were sent to the Italian front, and an Allied Council was set up to secure a unified strategy.

In Mesopotamia Gen. Maude captured Kut in Feb. 1917 and Baghdad in March. An advance from Egypt into Palestine, halted at Gaza in April, was resumed under Gen. Allenby in Oct., and captured Jerusalem in Dec.

The German submarine campaign reached its height in April 1917, when 196 British ships were lost, but the convoy system then put into operation caused losses to diminish steadily. The submarine was also combated by extensive mine-laying, while the naval raids on Zeebrugge and Ostend in April–May 1918 blocked 2 dangerous bases.

On the western front the Germans began what was intended to be the final offensive on March 21, 1918; by June the Allies had lost all they had gained since 1915, and the Germans had again reached the Marne. They had nowhere succeeded, however, in breaking the Allied line, and the Allies were now being reinforced by U.S. troops, who first saw fire in June. The danger forced the Allies to appoint a supreme commander, Gen. Foch, in April.

Greece had declared war in June 1917, when the Allies deposed the pro-German Constantine. In Sept. 1918 the Allies attacked Bulgaria, which quickly made peace, and in Oct. they expelled the Austrians from Serbia. An Austrian offensive on the Piave in June failed, and in Oct. the last Allied offensive on the Italian front began. On Nov. 3 Austria signed an armistice. In Palestine Allenby captured almost the entire Turkish army at Megiddo in Sept.; Syria was overrun, and Damascus and Aleppo surrendered. The Turkish army on the Tigris also surrendered, and Constantinople itself was threatened. Turkey signed an armistice on Oct. 30.

To a German offensive at Rheims on July 15 Foch replied on July 18 by an attack on the Marne, which by Aug. 3 had reached Soissons. On Aug. 8 a British attack at Amiens drove the Germans back 7 m. At the beginning of Sept. they were back behind the Hindenburg Line, which by the end of the month the British had broken. The Americans went into action as an independent army on the French right. During Oct. the Belgian coastline was occupied, the British reached the Scheldt, the French advanced over the Aisne, and the Americans down the Meuse.

Inside Germany revolutionary feeling was growing, and when on Oct. 29 the fleet at Kiel was ordered to prepare for sea, mutiny followed. Within a few days the revolution spread to all the main cities. Negotiations for an armistice began on Nov. 6; the Kaiser abdicated on Nov. 9, and on Nov. 11 the armistice was signed in the forest of Compiègne. Peace with Germany was signed at Versailles on June 28, 1919, and with Austria, Bulgaria, and Hungary respectively at St. Germain (Sept. 10), Neuilly (Nov. 27), and Trianon (June 4, 1920). A final settlement with Turkey was not reached until the Treaty of Lausanne was signed in 1923.

The Versailles Treaty was not signed by China, and on Wilson's submitting it to the U.S. senate it was rejected as insufficiently safeguarding American sovereignty in the League of Nations: instead a joint congressional resolution declaring peace with Germany and Austria was signed July 2, 1921 by Pres. Harding, and ratified by the senate Oct. 18. Strictly speaking, the U.S.A. was an 'associated' rather than an 'allied' power.

FIRTH, Raymond William (1901–). British anthropologist, prof. at London univ. since 1944, he has conducted social research surveys in Africa, Malaya, New Guinea, and Polynesia, and pub. many anthropological studies, incl. *Elements of Social Organization* (1951), and *Economics of the N.Z. Maori* (1959).

FISCHER (fi'sher), **Emil** (1852–1919). German chemist. Working with Julius Tufel, he produced synthetic sugars and from these the various enzymes. He was prof. of chemistry at Berlin from 1892, and a pioneer biochemist.

FISCHER, Hans (1881–1945). German chemist. Prof. at the Technische Hochschule at Munich, he received the Nobel prize in chemistry in 1930 for his discovery of the red colouring matter in blood.

FISCHER-DIESKAU (fisher-dē'skow), **Dietrich** (1925–). German singer. A baritone, he is a member of the Berlin and Vienna Operas, and has sung in concerts and festivals all over Europe. He is particularly famous for his interpretation of Schubertian songs.

FISH. Name applied to 3 classes of aquatic vertebrate animals. The body is adapted for freedom of movement in water. In most families the skeleton is composed of bone, but in the lamprey, shark and skate families it is of cartilage. The fins vary in

CLASSIFICATION OF FISHES

Class Marsipobranchii

Order, Hyperoartia; family: Petromysonidae; including lampreys.

Order, Hyperotreta; family: Myxinidae, including hag-fish, borer.

Class Selachii

SUB-CLASS, Euselachii

Order, Pleurotremata; 7 families, including the sharks, dog-fish, monk-fish or angel-fish.

Order, Hypotremata; 5 families including the rays, torpedo, skate, devil-fish.

SUB-CLASS, Holocephali; family Chimaeridae; Chimaera, rabbit-fish.

Class Pisces

SUB-CLASS, Palaeopterygii

Order, Chondrostei; family Acipenseridae; sturgeon.

SUB-CLASS, Neopterygii

Order, Isospondyli; 9 families, including the herring, sprat, shad, pilchard, sardine, anchovy, salmon, trout, char, grayling.

Order, Haplomi; family Esocidae; pike.

Order, Ostariophysi; 2 families including carp, goldfish, barbel, gudgeon, tench, minnow, chub, dace, roach, bream.

Order, Apodes; 6 families including eels, conger.

Order, Synentognathi; 3 families including skipper, gar-fish, flying-fish.

Order, Solenichthyes; 2 families including snipe-fish, pipe-fish, sea-horse.

Order, Anacanthini; 3 families including hake, cod, haddock, whiting, pollack, burbot.

Order, Zeomorphi; 2 families including John Dory, boar-fish.

Order, Percomorphi; 31 families including bass, perch, horse mackerel, bream, red mullet, wrasse, sand eels, weevers, mackerel, tunny, sword-fish, goby, dragonet, cat-fish, sticklebacks.

Order, Heterosomata; 3 families including turbot, brill, halibut, dabs, plaice, soles.

Order, Plectognathi; 3 families including trigger-fish, globe-fish or puffer, sun-fish.

Order, Pediculati; family: Lophiidae; angler, fishing-frog.

SUB-CLASS, Crossopterygii

Order, Actinistia; family: Coelacanthidae; coelacanth.

Order, Dipneusti; 2 families of lung-fishes.

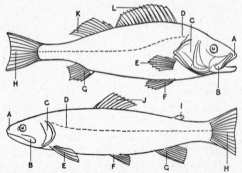

FISH. External features of perch (top) and trout. A, mouth; B, jawbone; C, gill-cover; D, lateral line; E, pectoral fin; F, pelvic fin; G, anal fin; H, caudal fin; I, adipose fin; J, dorsal fin; K, soft dorsal fin; L, spinal dorsal fin.

number. Those in front are termed the pectoral fins, and those beneath the abdomen the ventral fins; behind these appears the anal fin, and on the median line of the back the dorsal fin. The fins are composed of thin bones lightly covered with skin. Fishes are usually covered with scales of varying size and thickness, whose number remains constant throughout life. Along the side of most Fs. appears the 'lateral line' which is the chief sense organ; the number of scales appearing on this line is used as a means of identification of species.

Fs. breathe by means of gills, i.e. layers of tissue supported on bony arches, situated in the head. Water enters through the mouth and passes over the gills where the oxygen is absorbed by the blood vessels. The water then goes out through the gill slits at the sides of the head. Many Fs. have an air bladder; in the case of the lung-fishes this serves as a lung, but in other fishes it alters the specific gravity of the fish in accordance with the surrounding water.

The coloration of Fs. is usually such that it will conceal the animal in its surroundings, and in many varieties the colour changes with the background. At the spawning season, however, they display their colours, which often become much brighter. Reproduction is by means of eggs, which are frequently very small and numerous: some, e.g. guppies, are livebearers and the eggs hatch inside the body.

FISHER, Andrew (1862–1928). Australian Labour statesman. B. in Scotland, he went to Australia in 1885, and entered the Australian parliament in 1901. He was Prime Minister in 1908, 1910–13, and 1914–15, and then High Commissioner in London until 1921.

FISHER, Herbert Albert Laurens (1865–1940). British historian. B. in London, he was for most of his life a don at New Coll., Oxford. In 1916–22 he was President of the Board of Education in the Lloyd George Coalition ministry, and was mainly responsible for the 'Fisher' Education Act of 1918, intended to establish a really national system of education. Most important of his writings is a still useful *History of Europe* (1935). He received the O.M. in 1937.

FISHER, John (c. 1469–1535). British churchman. B. at Beverley, he was created bishop of Rochester in 1504, and was an enthusiastic supporter of the New Learning and a friend of More and Erasmus. But in 1535 he was tried on a charge of denying the royal supremacy and beheaded. Together with More he was canonized in 1935.

FISHER, John Arbuthnot, 1st baron (1841–1920). British admiral. Joining the navy in 1854, he served in the Crimean War, held various commands and was First Sea Lord 1904–10, when he carried out many

radical reforms and innovations, including the introduction of the Dreadnought battleship. He returned to the post in 1914, but resigned in the following year, disagreeing with Churchill over Dardanelles policy.

FISHER OF LAMBETH, Geoffrey Francis, baron (1887–). British churchman. Ordained in 1913, he was headmaster of Repton 1914–32, bp. of Chester 1932–9 and of London from 1939 until he succeeded Temple (q.v.) as abp. of Canterbury. He played a leading part in the World Council of Churches, was in 1960 the first holder of his office to visit the Pope for 600 years, and received a life peerage on retirement in 1961.

FISHGUARD. Seaport on the N. coast of Pembrokeshire, Wales, with ferry connections to and from Ireland. With Goodwick it forms U.D.; pop. (1961) 4,898.

FISHING AND FISHERIES. The increasing demand for fish as food has led to the development of improved marketing organizations for the catches, and of powerful ships with special refrigerating equipment, or fish-factory ships which enable filleting, processing, etc., to be done at sea, designed to exploit the deep-water resources out of reach of the smaller, older-type boats. Japan, with a population largely dependent on sea-food, has evolved new techniques for locating shoals (e.g. sonorific and radar methods) and catching them (e.g. electrical charges and chemical baits); and the North Sea countries have experimented with the artificial breeding of fish eggs and release of the small fry into the sea. The future lies with intensive breeding and farming in controlled areas, feeding and management of the 'herds' being effected by underwater workers. F. has a number of ancillary industries, e.g. net manufacture, and the processing of such by-products as oil, fish meal, glue and manure.

FISSION, Nuclear. See ATOMIC ENERGY.

FISTOULARI (fistoolah′rē), **Anatole** (1907–). Anglo-Russian conductor. B. at Kiev, he first conducted at 7, made an international reputation and in 1948 became a British subject. In 1946 he founded the London International Orchestra, and has since been its principal conductor.

FITZGERALD, Edward (1809–83). British poet and translator. B. in Suffolk, he lived a life of quiet study and retirement, and in 1859 pub. his poetic version of the *Rubaiyat of Omar Khayyam*, less a translation than an original creation.

FITZGERALD, Francis Scott Key (1896–1940). American novelist of the Jazz Age, b. in Minnesota. *This Side of Paradise* (1920) reflected his experiences at Princeton and made him known in the bright post-war society of the east. His most famous book is *The Great Gatsby* (1925), in which the narrator resembles his author, and Gatsby, the self-made millionaire, is lost in the soul-less 'Society' he enters.

FITZHERBERT, Maria Anne (1756–1837). Morganatic wife of the Prince of Wales, later George IV. She became Mrs. F. by her 2nd marriage in 1778, and after her husband's death in 1781 entered London society. She secretly m. the Prince of Wales in 1785, and finally parted from him in 1803. Henceforward she lived in retirement in Brighton.

FITZROY, Robert (1805–65). British vice-admiral and meteorologist. B. in Suffolk, he entered the navy in 1819, and in 1828 succeeded to the command of H.M.S. *Beagle*, then engaged on a survey of the Patagonian coast, and in 1831 was accompanied by Charles Darwin on a 5 years' survey. In 1843–5 he was Gov. of New Zealand.

FIVES. A game of handball played by 2 or 4 players in a court enclosed on 3 or 4 sides: the ball is struck by the hand. It dates from the 14th cent., and was probably derived from the French *jeu de paume.* The name F. may refer to the 5 fingers, or that there were originally 5 players, who had to make 5 points to win. In Britain the game is practically confined to public schools and colleges, and there are 3 main forms, viz. Eton F., Rugby F., and Winchester F.

FIVE-YEAR PLAN. An overall economic plan for an extended period with specific targets. From 1928 the basis of economic planning in the U.S.S.R., aimed particularly at developing heavy and light industry in a primarily agricultural country, the idea has since been adopted by other Communist countries, notably China, and is generally used as an incentive for increasing production, agricultural as well as industrial – not always successfully. The idea also became popular in western countries. The Russian 1966–70 plan aimed at 25% increase in agriculture and 50% in industry; this was shelved 1967 and even the one-year plans then adopted were reduced 1968.

FLAG. Plant of the *Iris* genus, which grows in damp places and in marshes in Britain and throughout Europe. It has a thick rootstock, from which rise stiff, blade-like monocotyledonous leaves, and stems about 2 ft. high. The flowers are large, and usually yellow. Cultivated varieties include the purple Garden F.

FLAGS in bloom.

FLAG. The British National F., the so-called 'Union Jack', unites the crosses of St. George, St. Andrew, and St. Patrick, representing England, Scotland, and Ireland; the Merchant F. places the National F. in the canton of a red F.; similarly placed on a large St. George's Cross it becomes the distinguishing F. of the Royal Navy. The Stars and Stripes, 'Old Glory', is the F. of the United States; the 50 stars represent the 50 States now in the Union, the 13 stripes the 13 original States. The F. of Russia places the crossed hammer and sickle, representing the workers of town and country, on the red F., the emblem of revolution. The Fs. of the Scandinavian countries bear crosses; the Danish 'Dannebrog' (strength of Denmark) is the oldest national F., used for 700 years. The Red Cross originated in Switzerland, and its emblem is the Swiss F. with its colours reversed.

A flag is flown upside-down as a signal of distress; is dipped as a salute; and when flown a little below the masthead is a sign of mourning. The 'Blue Peter', blue with a white centre, announces that a vessel is about to sail; a F. half red and half white that a pilot is on board. Many public bodies, as well as shipping lines and yacht clubs, have their own distinguishing Fs.

The British Royal Standard combines the emblems of England, Scotland, and Ireland; the United States Presidential Standard displays the American Eagle, surrounded by 50 stars.

FLAGELLANTS (flajel'-ants). Religious fanatics who either allow others to scourge them as a means of discipline and penance, or who scourge themselves. Such flagellation is known in many religions from ancient times, and there were notable outbreaks of this type of extremist devotion in Christian Europe

U.N. FLAG

in the 11th–16th cents.: it is still practised to a minor extent in some R.C. countries.

FLAGELLATA (flajelä'ta). Order of microscopic animals in the sub-kingdom Ptotozoa. The name is derived from the presence in each individual of one or more flagella – whip-like processes – usually at the front end of the body, which by actively lashing the water drive the protozoan forwards.

FLAGSTAD, Kirsten (1895–1962). Norwegian soprano singer. She was without rival in Wagnerian opera.

FLA'HERTY, Robert (1884–1951). American film director. B. in Michigan. he exerted great influence by his pioneer documentary of Eskimo life *Nanook of the North* (1920): later were *Man of Aran* and *Elephant Boy.*

FLAMBOYANT. In architecture, term applied to late Gothic style of French architecture, contemporary with the Perpendicular style in England. It is characterized by flame-like decorative work in windows, balustrades, and other projecting features.

FLAMEN (flä'men). The sacrificial priest in ancient Rome. The office was held for life, but was terminated by the death of the F.'s wife (who assisted him at ceremonies) or some breach of demeanour. At first there were 3 Fs., but another 12 were later added.

FLAMI'NGO (*Phoenicopterus*). A bird of the order Ciconiiformes. All members of the family (Phoenicopteridae) have very long legs and down-bent bills, specially adapted for sifting mud, from which they obtain their food of worms and molluscs, etc. They are able to swim and to fly, but usually confine themselves to wading. They live in large colonies, the nest being built of mud in shallow water, and are found in great numbers in the Carmargues, in S. America, etc.

The common F. (*P. roseus*) is white tinted with pink; the wings, as in all species, are bright red bordered with black.

FLAMMARION (flahmahrē-oñ'), Nicolas Camille (1842–1925). French astronomer. B. at Montigny-le-Roi, he joined the staff of the Paris observatory in 1858, and in 1882 estab. his own observatory at Juvisy. He wrote *L'Astronomie populaire* (1879) and many other popular expositions.

FLAMSTEED, John (1646–1719). First Astronomer Royal of England. B. near Derby, he was appointed astronomer to Charles II in 1675, and began systematic observations at Greenwich in the following year. From 1684 he was rector of Burstow in Surrey.

FLANAGAN, Bud. Stage-name of the British comedian Robert Winthrop (1896–1968). Leader of the 'Crazy Gang' (1931–62), he also played in variety all over the world, and with his partner Chesney Allen popularized such songs as 'Underneath the Arches'.

FLANDERS. A region of the Low Countries which in the 8th and 9th cents. extended from Calais to the Scheldt, and is now covered by the Belgian provinces of E. and W. Flanders, the French dept. of Nord, and part of the Dutch prov. of Zeeland.

W. Flanders lies along the coast of Belgium; cap., Bruges. Area 1,248 sq. m.; pop. (1966) 1,036,670. *E. Flanders* adjoins W.F. on the E.; cap., Ghent. Area 1,147 sq. m.; pop. (1966) 1,301,073.

FLANDRIN (floñdrañ'), Jean Hippolyte (1809–64). French artist. B. at Lyons, he painted battle-pieces and then, under the influence of Ingres, produced mural decorations with historical and religious subjects.

FLASH POINT. The temperature at which a liquid when heated under standard conditions gives off sufficient vapour to ignite on the application of a small flame. F.P. tests are carried out with the Pensky-Martens instrument. The Fire Point of the material itself is obtained by continuing the test and noting the temperature at which ignition occurs. For safe storage (fuel oil, etc.) the Flash and Fire Points must be high enough to reduce fire risks to a minimum, and such that no appreciable quantity of oils are driven off during exposure to the weather.

FLAUBERT (flohbãr′), **Gustave** (1821–80). French novelist. B. at Rouen, he entered Paris literary circles in 1840, but in 1846 retired to his native place, where he remained for the rest of his life. His masterpiece *Madame Bovary* appeared in 1857 and roused much controversy by its psychological portrayal of the wife of a country doctor, driven to suicide by a series of unhappy love affairs. *Salammbô* (1862) earned him the Legion of Honour in 1866, and was followed by *L'Éducation sentimentale* (1869), and *La Tentation de Saint Antoine* (1874). F. estab. himself as the master of the short story by his *Trois Contes: Un Cœur simple, Hérodias,* and *La Legende de Saint-Julien l'Hospitalier* (pub. 1877).

FLEMISH ART. 'Virgin and Child with Angels' by Quinten Matsys.   *Courtesy of the National Gallery.*

FLAX. A plant of the Linaceae family which yields valuable commercial products. The common F. or linseed plant (*Linum usitatissimum*) is of almost world-wide distribution. It has a stem 20–50 in. high, bearing small leaves and bright blue flowers. Apart from the fibres yielded by the stem, the seeds produce linseed oil and their residue forms cattle food. The long fibres are used in the manufacture of linen, the shorter fibres are made into twine, and the shortest of all used in paper manufacture. The chief producing areas are in Russia, Belgium, Holland, the Baltic countries, and Northern Ireland.

FLAXMAN, John (1755–1826). British sculptor. B. at York, he studied at the R.A. and for 12 years was employed by Wedgwood as a designer. He became an R.A. in 1800, and in 1810 he was appointed first prof. of sculpture at the academy. His best-known works incl. the monument to Reynolds in St. Paul's, and the statues of Burns and Kemble in Westminster Abbey.

FLEABANE. Plants of the genus *Erigeron*, Compositae family, resembling a dwarf michaelmas daisy.

FLEAS (*Siphonaptera* or *Aphaniptera*). Group of wingless insects, with mouth-parts adapted for sucking the blood of their host. The most important varieties are *Pulex irritans*, which lives on man, and the rat F. (*Xenopsylla cheopis*) which transmits plague.

FLECKER, James Elroy (1884–1915). British poet. B. at Lewisham, he entered the consular service, and

RAT FLEA AND LARVA

went to Constantinople in 1910 and in 1911 to Smyrna. In 1913 ill-health obliged him to visit Switzerland, where he d. of consumption. He pub. several vols. of verse, incl. *The Bridge of Fire* (1907), *The Golden Journey to Samarkand* (1913) and *The*

Old Ships (1915). He also wrote the dramas *Don Juan* and *Hassan*, the latter being performed in 1923 with incidental music by Delius.

FLEET STREET. Street in London, England, running from Temple Bar eastwards to Ludgate Circus, named after the River F. With adjoining streets it contains the offices and printing establishments of many of the leading British newspaper and press agencies.

FLEETWOOD. English fishing port (bor.) and holiday resort in Lancs at the mouth of the Wyre. Leather belting is manufactured and gravel deposits are exploited. Pop. (1961) 27,760.

FLEMING, Sir Alexander (1881–1955). British bacteriologist. B. in Ayrshire, he studied medicine in London, qualifying in 1906, and subsequently researching and lecturing in bacteriology and clinical pathology; he was prof. of bacteriology at London univ. 1928–48. His first notable discovery was lysozyme (1922), followed in 1928 by penicillin (q.v.), an antibiotic which saved many lives in the S.W.W. In 1945 he shared the Nobel prize with E. B. Chain and Sir Howard Florey, who had developed penicillin for practical use, and was knighted in 1944.

FLEMING, Ian (1908–64). British author. Son of an army officer, he was ed. at Eton, Sandhurst, and Munich and Geneva univs. After a number of years with Reuters, he worked successively with banking and stockbroking firms, and in the S.W.W. was personal asst. to the Director of Naval Intelligence. From 1953 he became famous as the author of suspense novels featuring the ruthless, laconic 'James Bond', Secret Service agent, No. 007.

FLEMING, Sir John Ambrose (1849–1945). British electrical physicist and engineer. B. at Lancaster, he was prof. of electrical engineering at Univ. College, London, 1885–1926, and was knighted in 1929. He was a pioneer in the development of the telephone, electric light, and radio.

FLEMISH. A branch of the West Germanic, or more especially the German division of the Germanic, languages (q.v.), spoken in the northern half of Belgium and in the Nord dept. of France. In opposition to the introduction of French as the official language in the F. provinces of Belgium after 1830 there arose a strong Flemish movement, led by scholars like J. F. Willems (1793–1846) and writers such as H. Conscience (1812–83), and although equality of French and F. was not achieved until

1898, it brought about a cultural and political revival of F. The F. movement was promoted for political reasons by the Germans in both world wars.

The great figures of F. literature are the poet Guido Gezelle, and the novelists Cyriel Buysse, Stijn Streuvels, and Felix Timmermanns.

FLEMISH ART. The style of painting developed in Flanders (Belgium) from the 14th cent. and distinguished by colourful realism, keen observation, and masterful technique. Hubert and Jan van Eyck made Bruges the first centre of F.A.; other schools arose in Tournai, Ghent, and Louvain. The great names of

FLIGHT. Orville Wright lies face downwards to pilot the Wright biplane making the first powered, sustained and controlled flight at Kittihawk, N. Carolina, on Dec. 17, 1903: he covered 120 ft. in 12 sec. To the right, on foot, is Wilbur Wright. *Photo: Crown Copyright.*

that period were Roger van der Weyden, Dierick Bouts, Hugo van der Goes, Hans Memlinc, and Gheerardt David. In the 16th cent. Italian influences made themselves felt, and the centre shifted to Antwerp, where Quinten Matsys worked. Whilst Jerome Bosch painted creatures of his own wild imagination, the pictures of P. Brueghel are faithful reflections of F. life. The Italian influence was strong

FLIGHT. The moment of release: U.S.A.F. rocket aircraft X-15, leaving the 'mother' plane, was piloted by Robert M. White at 4,105 m.p.h. on June 27, 1962. *Courtesy of U.S.I.S.*

in Mabuse, Jan Massys, and others. Peter Paul Rubens and his school created a new powerful style, which was continued by van Dyck, Jordaens, etc. Brouwer and Teniers kept up the earlier tradition.

FLENSBURG. Port on the E. coast of Schleswig-Holstein, N. Germany. Founded probably in the 12th

FLEUR-DE-LIS. Its development traced (left to right) the ir.s the fleur-de-lis on the seal of Louis VIII, and as it appears in modern heraldry.

cent., it has shipyards, breweries, etc., and is concerned with the Greenland whale fisheries. Pop. (1950) 102,045.

FLETCHER, Sir Banister Flight (1866–1953). British architect. The son of the architect Banister F. (1833–99), he was pres. of the R.I.B.A. 1929–31, and wrote a standard *History of Architecture on the Comparative Method.*

FLETCHER, Hanslip (1874–1955). British artist. He was noted for his architectural drawings, especially in *Changing London* (1943) and *Bombed London* (1948).

FLETCHER, John (1579–1625). English dramatist. B. at Rye, Sussex, he was left an orphan of restricted means when his father d. in disgrace with Queen Elizabeth. Of the 50 plays once attributed to his partnership with Beaumont (q.v.), only 7 are now generally recognized: the remainder are divided between F. and collaborators such as Massinger. Among those credited to F. alone are the pastoral drama *The Faithful Shepherdess* (1610), the tragedy *Bonduca* (c. 1614), and *Rule a Wife and Have a Wife* (c. 1624).

FLIGHT. The Hawker P-1127 strike aircraft was the first of the vertical take-off type to be designed for operational service and has been flying successfully since 1961. *Courtesy of Bristol Siddeley.*

FLEUR-DE-LIS (flör de lē; Fr. flower of the lily). A heraldic device which represents a lily, borne on coats of arms since the 12th cent., and adopted by the Bourbons of France.

FLIGHT, History of. The aeroplane is a development of the model glider, first flown by Sir George Cayley (1773–1857) in 1804, but not until the invention of the petrol engine did powered flight become feasible with the building of the Wright brothers' biplane in 1903. In Europe France led in aeroplane design (Voisin brothers) and Louis Blériot brought aviation to Britain by crossing the Channel in 1909. In that year A. V. Roe flew a motor-cycle-engined triplane and in 1911 Robert Blackburn produced two all-metal (steel) monoplanes and wireless telegraphy was demonstrated. In 1912 Sopwith and Bristol both built small biplanes and the first big twin-engined aeroplane was the Handley Page bomber in 1917.

The stimulus of the F.W.W. and rapid development of the petrol engine led to increased power (from 100 to 800 h.p. between 1917 and 1930) and speeds rose from 100 to 200 m.p.h. Streamlining then became imperative: non-essential excrescences were retracted into the body and wings and exposed parts were shaped to reduce drag, and eventually the biplane was replaced by the internally braced monoplane structure, e.g. the Hawker Hurricane and Supermarine Spitfire fighters and Avro Lancaster and Boeing Flying Fortress bombers of the S.W.W.

On May 15, 1941, the first British jet aircraft, the Gloster E. 28/39, flew from Cranwell, Lincs, powered by a turbo-jet i.c. engine invented by Sir Frank Whittle; the Heinkel He 280 twin-jet prototype also flew about this time. The rapid development of this new power-plant led to enormous increases in power and speed until air-compressibility effects were felt near the speed of sound. Twin-jet Meteor fighters were in use at the end of the war and the jet has now ousted the piston engine on nearly all military types and for civil use also, either as a turbo-prop or pure jet, since by flying high (50,000 ft.) these engines are more economical as well as more powerful.

To exceed sonic speed, mere retraction of excrescences was insufficient, and wings are now swept back, engines buried in wings, tail units and even bodies eliminated (all-wing, delta ∧ designs). Wings will certainly be made extremely thin, small, of new materials, and 'solid' construction for true supersonic aircraft. The research model X-15 has an immensely long pointed body with tiny, straight and extremely thin, solid steel aerofoils, and has flown at 4,000 m.p.h. (1962). The highest speed for a production plane (1959) was recorded by a Convair 106a at 2,455 m.p.h. In other fields, 1958 saw the inauguration of the first transatlantic jet service, a Comet IV of B.O.A.C.; in 1959 the first hovercraft (SR-NI) was demonstrated in the U.K. and vertical take-off aircraft were developed, e.g. Hawker P-1127 in 1961, which were also capable of supersonic level flight. Supersonic airliner projects are the Anglo-French Concorde (*see* CIVIL AVIATION); Russian Tu-144 (maiden flight 1968; 120 passengers, 1500 m.p.h., 4,000 m. range), and American Boeing-2707. Development of swing wing or variable geometry aircraft, capable of much higher speeds, encountered setbacks in both Europe and U.S.A. in the late 1960s. *See* AEROPLANE: BALLOON: GLIDING: JET PROPULSION.

FLINDERS, Matthew (1774–1814). British navigator. B. in Lincs, he joined the navy in 1789, and explored the Australian coasts, 1795–9 and 1801–3.

FLINT, Sir William Russell (1880–1970). Scottish artist. B. in Edinburgh, he was pres. of the Royal Soc. of Painters in Water Colours 1936–56: he was knighted in 1947.

FLINT. Town (borough) of Flintshire, N. Wales, on the left (S.W.) shore of the Dee estuary, 12 m. N.W. of Chester. A port until the silting up of the estuary, F. is the centre of a coal- and lead-mining area, with paper mills and chemical works. The castle was built by Edward I in 1276. Pop. (1961) 13,690.

FLINT. City of Michigan, U.S.A., on the F. river. Manufacture of motor-cars is the chief industry. Pop. (1960) 196,940.

Palaeolithic flint hand-axe and scraper.

FLINT. A compact, hard, brittle rock, brown, black, or grey in colour, found in nodules in chalk deposits. It consists of fine-grained silica, compressed into a homogeneous mass. When broken, the nodule has a shell-like fracture. Owing to their hardness, F. splinters are used for abrasive purposes, and when ground into powder for pottery manufacture. Flint implements made by chipping one F. against another were widely used by Palaeolithic and Neolithic Man. The earliest F. implements, belonging to the Palaeolithic Age, are simple, while those of the Neolithic Age are more expertly cut, and are often ground or polished. Such are found in many parts of Britain. In historic times they were used for making fire, by striking a F. against steel, which produces a spark, and for discharging guns. Cigarette-lighter Fs. are made from cerium alloy.

FLINTSHIRE. Smallest of the Welsh counties. Bordering the Dee estuary and the Irish Sea, with a detached part to the S., it is roughly rectangular. The

FLORENCE. The interior of the octagonal baptistery of St. John. Difficult to date, it may be 5th century, but was extensively restored in the 11th century. It has bronze doors by Andrea Pisano and Lorenzo Ghiberti.

central part is hilly, and the principal rivers are the Dee and Clwyd. The chief occupations are agriculture and coal-mining. The co. town is Mold; other towns are Flint, Holywell, Rhyl, and Prestatyn. Area 256 sq. m.; pop. (1961) 149,888.

FLODDEN. Site 3 m. S.E. of Coldstream, Northumberland, England, of the battle fought on Sept. 9, 1513, between the Scots under James IV and the English under the earl of Surrey, in which James and the flower of his nobility were slain.

FLOOD. The disaster which, according to Genesis, obliterated the human race except for a chosen few. *See* NOAH. Excavations at Ur by Woolley (q.v.) revealed an 8 ft. layer of water-laid clay, suggesting a local deluge prior to 4000 B.C. over an area *c.* 400 m. by 100 m. which may have been the origin of the story.

FLORA. Roman goddess of flowers, youth, and of spring. Festivals were held in her honour.

FLORENCE. City of central Italy on the Arno, 55 m. from its mouth; it is the capital of the province of F. and of Tuscany, a railway junction, and a manufacturing centre.

The Roman town of Florentia was built *c.* 187 B.C. on a former Etruscan site. It was besieged by the Goths, A.D. 405, visited by Charlemagne 786. In 1052, with the rest of Tuscany, F. passed to the countess Matilda of Tuscany. It was the scene of many later conflicts between the popes and the emperors, and was governed by nobles. 'Arti' or trade guilds began to grow up, until the feudal lords and the emperors were overcome, and in 1250 F. was proclaimed a republic. Ten years of Guelph supremacy made F. one of Italy's chief cities, but thereafter the struggle between papal supporters (Guelphs) and those of the emperors (Ghibellines) continued. From 1434 the city's history was bound up with the Medici family. In 1532 she lost her independence, and became capital of the duchy of Tuscany.

F. is famed for its art treasures; the Pitti Palace, the Uffizi Gallery, the cathedral of Santa Maria del Fiore, 1420–34, and many other fine buildings; and when the Allied forces approached the city in the summer of 1944 they received an order that 'the whole of F. must rank as a work of art of the first importance'. The Germans, on the other hand, planned and carried out the systematic destruction of five of F.'s historic bridges (they spared the Ponte Vecchio, with only a narrow footway between its old shops), and of medieval buildings along the Arno. Much was repaired, but in 1966 the worst floods for 700 years caused £57,000,000 damage to buildings and art treasures. Pop. (1961) 438,138.

FLOREY, Howard Walter, baron (1898–1968). British pathologist. B. in Australia, he was prof. of pathology at Oxford 1935–62. He began work on penicillin in 1938, and in 1945 won with Sir Alexander Fleming (q.v.) the Nobel prize for medicine. He was awarded a life peerage and O.M. 1965.

FLORIDA. The most southern state of U.S.A.; mainly a large peninsula jutting into the Atlantic which it separates from the Gulf of Mexico. For the most part rolling countryside, suitable for agriculture, it has many lakes in the central region; in the S. a great expanse of standing water, the Everglades, is being drained for agriculture; c. 2,000 sq. m. are preserved as a National Park. Rivers are of little importance, but swamps abound. Miami is the largest city; other towns are Tallahassee (the capital), Jacksonville and Tampa. Oranges, grapefruit, watermelon and vegetables are produced in great quantity; fish and shellfish are important; growing industries incl. food processing; chemicals and paper; and minerals incl. phosphate and rare earth metals. The U.S.A.F. Missile Test Centre is at Cape Kennedy. Area 58,560 sq. m. (incl. 4,298 sq. m. of water); pop. (1970) 6,789,443.

F. was named after the day of its discovery by Juan Ponce de Leon who landed there on Easter Day (Span. *Pascua florida*) in 1513. It became a state of the Union in 1845.

FLORIN. Coin, common to many European lands, first minted in Florence in 1252. The obverse bore the image of a lily, which led to the coin being called *fiorino* (from *fiore*, flower). This F. was a gold coin. The British silver F. of 2s. was first struck 1849.

FLORIO, Giovanni (c. 1553–1625). English translator. B. in London, the son of Italian refugees, he taught French and Italian at Oxford, but is best known for his translation of Montaigne (1603).

FLOTOW (floh'toh), **Friedrich, Freiherr von** (1812–83). German composer. Of his 18 operas only *Martha* (1847) is remembered.

FLOTSAM AND JETSAM. F.: goods found floating on the sea after a shipwreck. J.: goods deliberately sunk in the sea to lighten a vessel which is wrecked. Under British law F. and J. belong to the Crown, unless the true owner is known or a franchise has been granted to such goods.

FLOUNDER (*Pleuronectes flesus*). A species of salt- and freshwater flat-fish, whose skin varies in colour from black to grey, the underside being white. Both eyes are on the same side of the body. It is related to the dab and plaice and is used as a food.

FLOWER, Robin Ernest William (1881–1946). Celtic scholar and poet. B. in Yorks, he joined the staff of the British Museum in 1906 and was deputy keeper of MSS. 1929–44. His works include *Ireland and Medieval Europe* (1927), translations of Irish poetry and prose, and several vols. of original verse.

FLOWER. The blossom of a plant. The F. is a characteristic of the Phanerogams (flowering plants), its function being the production of reproductive organs and the formation of seed. The essential parts of the F. are the androecium, which includes the anthers (containing the pollen) or male nucleus, and the filaments on which they are borne; and the gynaecium, which consists of the ovary (containing ovules) or female nuclei and the style, culminating in the stigma.

FLUKE. Parasitic flat worm (*Fasciola hepatica*), belonging to the order Trematoda, that causes rot and dropsy of the liver, in sheep, cattle, horses, dogs, and man. Only the adult encysted stage of its life history is passed within the body, after ingestion by the host. The cyst dissolves in the stomach and the young fluke passes to the liver.

LIVER FLUKE

FLUORE'SCENCE. The process of emission of electromagnetic radiation resulting from the absorption of certain types of energy, in which case it is a luminescence lasting a minute fraction of a second after the exciting energy is removed. F. is also used to mean the radiation emitted as well as the emission process, and in X-ray F. it is the characteristic X-rays emitted when X-rays of a higher frequency are absorbed. This is used in analysis. F. is made use of in strip and other lighting, and was developed rapidly during the S.W.W. because of its greater efficiency of illumination, compared with the incandescent lamp. Other important applications are in fluorescent screens for television, cathode-ray tubes, etc.

FLU'ORIDES. Salts of hydrofluoric acid. F. occur naturally in all water to a differing extent. Pilot experiments in Great Britain, America and elsewhere have indicated that a concentration of fluoride of 1 part per million in water retards the decay of teeth in children by more than 50 per cent. If the natural concentration of F. is less than 1 part per million, the recommended policy of the Min. of Health in Britain is to add sufficient sodium fluoride to the water to bring it up to this amount, but implementation is entirely up to each local authority.

FLU'ORINE. Chemical element, symbol F., at no. 9, at. wt. 19, which was discovered by Scheele in 1771 and isolated by Moissan in 1886. It occurs naturally as the minerals fluorspar (CaF_2) and cryolite (Na_3AlF_6) and is a member of the halogen family. At ordinary temperatures it is a pale yellow, highly poisonous and reactive gas and it unites directly with nearly all the elements. Hydrogen fluoride is used in etching glass, and the Freons, which all contain fluorine, are widely used as refrigerants and propellants. Combined with uranium as UF_6 it is used in the separation of uranium isotopes.

FLUORSPAR or **Fluorite**. A cubic mineral (CaF_2), usually violet-tinted. The Blue-john from Derbyshire is a fibrous variety used as an ornamental stone. Colourless F. is used in the manufacture of microscope lenses, for the glaze on pottery, and in the Bessemer process of steel manufacture.

FLUSHING. Port on Walcheren Island, Zeeland, Netherlands, of great strategic importance, for it commands the entrance to the navigable Scheldt estuary, one of the principal sea entries to the continent of Europe. Before the S.W.W. the terminus of a regular sea service to and from Tilbury, England, it is a bathing resort with shipyards and railway workshops. De Ruyter was b. at F. The Dutch form of the name is Vlissingen. Pop. (1967) 38,564.

FLUTE. Genus of musical instruments, including the piccolo, the concert F., the bass or alto F., etc. They are cylindrical in shape, with a narrowed end, containing the aperture, across which the player blows. The air vibrations produce the note, which can be altered by placing fingers over lateral holes.

FLOWER. Some of the forms recognized by botanists. Regular: I, campanulate (bell-shaped); 2, rotate (wheel-shaped); 3, tubular; 4, urceolate (urn-shaped); 5, globular. Irregular: 6, papilionaceous (butterfly-shaped); 7, spurred; 8, personate (mask-like); 9, labiate (lipped).

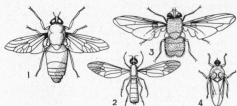

FLY. 1, horse fly; 2, soldier fly; 3, blow fly; 4, forest fly.

Certain keys can be depressed to extend the range of the F. to three octaves.

FLUX, MAGNETIC. *See* MAGNETIC FLUX.

FLY. Name given to the winged stage of many insects, such as dragon-fly, butterfly, caddis-fly, etc.: by zoologists it is used to mean a two-winged insect of the order Diptera. Flies form one of the largest orders of insects, and number about 90,000 described species, of which more than 5,200 inhabit the British Isles. They normally possess a single pair of membranous wings. Hind-wings are represented by a pair of knob-like organs borne on slender stalks. These are the halteres or balancers: they function in maintaining equilibrium during flight. The mouth-parts project from the head in the form of a proboscis. In most Fs. they are used for sucking in fluid substances, but in blood-sucking Fs. they are modified in order to pierce the skin of their victims.

Fs. undergo complete metamorphosis; their larvae are always without true legs, and the pupae are only rarely enclosed in cocoons. They are generally sombrely coloured, but some species are banded with yellow or white, others are metallic green or blue, while some are densely hairy. The sexes are usually very closely alike.

Fs. are usually classified into three sub-orders, viz. Nematocera, including the crane-flies, mosquitoes, midges, and gall-flies; Brachycera, including the horse-flies and robber-flies; and Cyclorhapha, including the house-fly, blow-fly, flesh-fly, etc.

FLYING LEMUR. Small insectivorous mammal, Colugo (q.v.), or Galeopithecus.

FLYNN, Errol (1909–59). Australian actor. B. in Tasmania, he tackled every kind of job before his good looks and gaily reckless personality attracted the film scouts. His films incl. *Captain Blood* (1935) and *The Master of Ballantrae* (1953). In his autobiographies he was characteristically frank.

FOCAL LENGTH (of a lens). The point to which a parallel beam of light is concentrated is termed the principal focus of a lens (q.v.) and the distance from the focus to the lens is the F.L. The F.L. depends on the refractive index of the material of which the lens is made and on the curvature of its faces.

FOCH (fosh), **Ferdinand** (1851–1929). Marshal of France. B. at Tarbes, he was commissioned in 1873, and was appointed to the general staff. At the beginning of the F.W.W. he defended Nancy; he was largely responsible for the victory of the Marne, and commanded on the N.W. front Oct. 1914–Sept. 1916. He was appointed chief of general staff in 1917, entrusted with the co-ordination of the Allied armies in March 1918, and created generalissimo in April. He launched the Allied advance in July which ended the war. After the war he received the O.M. and was made a field marshal.

FOG or MIST. Cloud which collects at the surface of the earth, composed of water vapour which has condensed on particles of dust in the atmosphere. Cloud and fog are both caused by the air temperature falling below dew point (*see* DEW). The thickness of F. is dependent on the number of water particles it contains. Usually, F. is formed by the meeting of 2 currents of air, one cooler than the other, or by warm air flowing over a cold surface. Sea Fs. commonly occur where warm and cold currents meet, and the air above them mixes. F. frequently forms on calm nights over the land, as the land surface cools more rapidly than the air immediately above it. Officially, F. refers to a condition when visibility is reduced to 1 kilometre (1,100 yards) or less, and mist or haze to that giving a visibility of 1–2 kilometres. A mist is produced by condensed water particles, and a haze by smoke or dust. Most industrial areas have a continual haze of smoke over them, and if the temperature falls suddenly, a dense yellow F. forms. To enable small bomber forces to take off in the S.W.W. from 1942 heat from petrol jets was used to clear F., the method being known as F.I.D.O. (Fog Intensive Dispersal Of), but it is too expensive for normal use. *See* SMOG.

FOGAZZARO (fogahtsah'roh), **Antonio** (1842–1911). Italian poet and novelist. B. at Vicenza, he pub. vols. of verse incl. *Valsolda* (1876), and in 1881 his first novel *Malombra*. His reputation was estab. by *Piccolo Mondo antico* (1896).

FOGGIA (fod'jah). City and episcopal see of Apulia region, cap. of F. prov., S. Italy. The cathedral, dating from *c.* 1170, was rebuilt after an earthquake in 1731. Pop. (1966) 134,581.

FOKINE (fokēn'), **Miche** (1880–1942). Russian choreographer. B. in St. Petersburg, he became chief choreographer to the Russian Ballet, and by his work with Diaghilev revitalized the art of ballet. His creations incl. the 'Dying Swan' for Pavlova; *Les Sylphides*, *Le Spectre de la Rose*, *Petrouchka*, *Carnaval*; and for the Ballet Theatre of N.Y. *Paganini* and *Barbe Bleu*. He d. in N.Y.

FOKKER, Anthony Herman Gerard (1890–1939). Dutch aeronautical engineer and aircraft designer; he founded aircraft factories in Germany and at Amsterdam. In 1924 he went to U.S.A. and became director of Atlantic Aircraft.

FOLEY, John Henry (1818–74). Irish sculptor. B. in Dublin, he first exhibited at the R.A. in 1839. His most important works include the statue of the Prince Consort for the Albert Memorial; statues of Burke and Goldsmith in Dublin, etc.

FOLIES-BERGÈRE (folē' berzhār'). Music-hall in Paris named after its original proprietor and famous for its lavish productions.

FOLK DANCE. A dance peculiar to a particular people, nation, or country. European F.Ds. are derived from the dances accompanying the native customs and ceremonies of pre-Christian times. Distinctive national characteristics are particularly noticeable in those countries which have had to struggle for national independence. F.D. has tended to die out in industrialized countries; its preservation

FOLK DANCE. The Morpeth Rant danced in the open air a festival organized by the English Folk Song and Dance Society. The old traditions take on new life as a relaxation from modern tensions.

in England was largely the work of Cecil J. Sharp.

FOLKESTONE (fōk'ston). English port and holiday resort (bor.) on the S.E. coast of Kent, 6 m. S.W. of Dover. There is a regular sea service between F. and Boulogne. Pop. (1961) 44,129.

FOLKLORE. The oral traditions and culture of the people. The term F. was coined in 1846 by W. J. Thoms (1803–85), but the founder of the scientific study of the subject was Jacob Grimm (1785–1863). The approach to F. has varied greatly: M. Müller (1823–1900) interpreted it as evidence of nature myths; J. G. Frazer (1854–1941) was the exponent of the comparative study of primitive and popular F. as mutually explanatory; Sir Laurence Gomme (1853–1916) adopted the historical method; and Malinowski and Radcliffe-Brown have examined the material as an integral element in a *living* culture.

FOLK SONG. Body of traditional song forming the spontaneous musical expression of a people. Many F.Ss. originated as a rhythmic accompaniment to manual work. Pure F.S. is melodic not harmonic, and the modes used are distinctive of the country from which it comes. The interest in ballad poetry in the later 18th cent. led to the discovery of a rich body of F.S. in Britain and on the Continent. In addition to Negro F.S., the cosmopolitan background of the U.S.A. has brought forth a wealth of material derived from European and S. American sources. A great revival of interest, starting in the 1950s, was led by Alan Lomax, John Jacob Niles, Theo Bikel, Pete Seeger, Woody Guthrie and Bob Dylan, and dealt with contemporary topics, e.g. atomic warfare and racial prejudice.

FONDA, Henry (1905–). American actor. He has appeared in both stage and screen versions of *Mister Roberts, Point of No Return*, and *Caine Mutiny Court Martial*, and was acclaimed for his production of the film *12 Angry Men*.

FONTAINEBLEAU (fontänblō). French town 37 m. S.S.E. of Paris, in Seine-et-Marne dept. It lies in one of the most beautiful forests of France, for long a favourite haunt of landscape painters. The town is renowned for its royal palace, founded in the 10th cent. Mme de Montespan lived there in the reign of Louis XIV and Mme du Barry in that of Louis XV. Napoleon signed his abdication there in 1814. Pop. (1962) 22,704.

FONTANA (fontah'nah), **Domenico** (1543–1607). Italian architect. He was employed by pope Sixtus V, and his principal works include the Vatican library, the completion of the dome and lantern of St. Peter's, and the royal palace at Naples.

FONTANE, Theodor (1819–98). German poet and novelist. B. in Brandenburg, he was one of the finest of modern ballad poets. In his later years he wrote realistic stories including *Irrungen, Wirrungen* (1888), and *Der Stechlin* (1899).

FONTANNE, Lynn. See ALFRED LUNT.

FONTENOY (fontnwah'). Village in Hainaut prov., Belgium, 5 m. S.E. of Tournai, where Marshal Saxe and the French defeated the British, Dutch, and Hanoverians under the duke of Cumberland in 1745.

FONTEYN, Dame Margot (1919–). British dancer. Née Margaret Hookham, she made her début with the Sadler's Wells Ballet in *The Haunted Ballroom* in 1934 and 1st appeared as Giselle in 1937, eventually becoming prima ballerina of the Royal Ballet. Technically impeccable and with unique beauty of line, she is supreme among the world's classical dancers. She was created D.B.E. in 1956, and since 1954 has been pres. of the Royal Academy of Dancing. In 1955 she m. Roberto E. Arias, Panamanian ambassador to the U.K. 1955–8 and 1960–2: a one-time political colleague shot and severely wounded him 1964. See illus. under BALLET.

FOOCHOW. Port and walled city, with extensive suburbs, on the r. Min cap. of Fukien prov., S.E. China. There is a naval dockyard at F., which exports tea, timber, leather, and lacquered goods. It was opened to foreign trade in 1842. Pop. (1965) 616,000.

FOOD. The general term for what is eaten by man and other creatures to sustain life. It is used in the formation and repair of body tissues, and for the production of heat and energy. Certain necessary chemical elements and complex groupings must be provided from which the body can make all it needs. These are the essential constituents: *proteins* for body building and repair, found in meat. fish, eggs, and some vegetables; *fats* to provide energy. e.g. butter, lard, and suet; *carbohydrates* also provide energy and are found in bread, potatoes, sugar, and cereals, which form the bulk of the diet; *vitamins* (q.v.) required only in small quantities to assist the body to make full use of its F.; *minerals*, also needed in small quantities, incl. salt; calcium (bone building) from milk; and iron (blood formation) from meats and green vegetables. The energy value of F. is expressed in calories.

FOOD POISONING. Acute illness caused by poisonous food, or by micro-organisms contained in food, or their products. Some fish and mushrooms are naturally poisonous. Lead or arsenic are sometimes introduced into food during manufacture. Preservatives have caused illness. Milk, oysters, etc., may carry typhoid fever. Uncooked meat may carry harmful organisms. Pork may carry the round-worm Trichinella. and rye the parasitic fungus ergot. The most dangerous food poison is the bacillus which causes botulism (q.v.).

FOOT, Isaac (1880–1960). British liberal politician. A staunch Nonconformist, an ardent collector of Cromwelliana, and an effective fighter against privilege, he held office (Min. of Mines 1931–2) only briefly. Of his sons **Sir Dingle F.** (1905–), once a Liberal, became in 1964 Solicitor-General in the Labour govt. and was knighted; and **Michael F.** (1913–) was a Labour M.P. 1945–55 and from 1960, and has been long assoc. with the Socialist weekly *Tribune. See also* CARADON, LORD.

FOOT AND MOUTH DISEASE. A highly contagious eruptive fever caused by a virus that attacks cattle and other animals, causing the milk yield of cows to deteriorate, and animals with young to abort. Control is by isolation and destruction of affected animals, or, on the Continent, inoculation.

FOOTBALL (American). Harvard university is said to have introduced the game to the U.S.A. in 1875. It is played on a field 330 ft. by 160 ft. marked in 5 yd. lines, with goal-lines at 10 yds. from each end. The goals and ball are as those used for English Rugby It is played between 2 teams, each of 11 men, made up of 7 linemen or forwards (a 'centre,' 2 'guards,' 2 'tackles,' 2 'ends'), a quarterback, 2 half-backs and a full-back. Each team's objective is to score most points.

AMERICAN FOOTBALL

A touch-down scores 6 points and allows the scoring team to try for an extra point. This they can do when the ball is put into play again on the 2 yds. line, by getting the ball over the line again by running or passing or by kicking a goal. A field goal (3 points) is scored by either a drop kick or place kick. A touch-down behind their own line by the defending team is called a 'safety' and scores 2 points to the other side. Padded clothing and helmets are worn and substitutes are allowed for injured players. Forward passing is allowed. Only the man with the ball may be tackled and his team-mates may run with him to block opponents from tackling. The side 'in possession' must make at least 10 yds. in every 4 attempts or the ball goes to the opponents. The game is divided into four 15-minute periods. Four officials are required to handle a college game. There are 3 sets of rules—collegiate, professional, and high school; they are very complicated and change from year to year.

FOOTBALL (Association). 'Soccer' has developed from robust, rural football of the past. In 1863 the Football Association was formed to co-ordinate existing rules. It is popular in every country in the world with the exception of the U.S.A.

The game is played between 2 teams each of 11 players, on a field 100–130 yds. by 50–100 yds. with a spherical, inflated leather ball, circumference 27 to 28 in. and weight 14 to 16 oz. The object of the game is to propel the ball with the feet or head through the opponents' goal, an area 8 yds. wide and 8 ft. high.

A team is broadly divided into defence, a goal-keeper, 2 full-backs, and 3 half-backs; and attack, 5 forwards. The 5 backs now generally each mark an opposing forward. The field has a half-way line, marked with a 10 yd.-radius centre circle, 2 penalty areas (each 44 yds. by 18 yds.), and 2 goal areas (each 20 yds. by 6 yds.). Corner kicks are taken from a 1 yd. segment, when the ball goes behind the goal-line off a defender; a ball kicked over the touch-lines is thrown in by one of the opposing side. The goal-keeper only is allowed to touch the ball with his hands, then only in his own penalty area and he must clear the ball after 4 paces. For major offences committed within defenders' penalty area, a penalty kick may be awarded by the referee to the attacking team. This is taken 12 yds. from the goal centre, with the goal-keeper only within the area. The game is started from the centre spot. It is played for 2 periods of 45 minutes each, the teams change ends at half-time. The game is controlled by a referee; 2 linesmen indicate when the ball is kicked into touch.

The Football Association Cup competition was inaugurated in 1872. The Football League was founded in 1888. The Fédération Internationale de Football Association (1904) organized in 1930 the first of the quadrennial competitions for the 'World Cup' or Jules Rimet trophy: winners 1930 Uruguay; 1934, 1938 Italy; 1950 Uruguay; 1954 Germany; 1958, 1962, 1970 Brazil; 1966 England: by their 3rd victory 1970 Brazil won the cup outright. The European Cup (1958) is contested annually.

FOOTBALL (Australian). Australia has its own code of football. It is played with 18 men a side, 2 reserves being allowed for each team. Each side is

FOOTBALL (Australian)

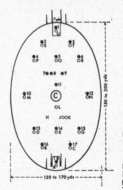

Black Team (attacking bottom goal): 1, Full-back; 2, Right full-back; 3, Left full-back; 4, Right half-back; 5, Centre half-back; 6, Left half-back; 7 and 8, Followers; 9, Rover (ruck); 10, Right centre (wing); 11, Centre; 12, Left centre (wing); 13, Right half-forward; 14, Centre half-forward; 15, Left half-forward; 16, Right full-forward; 17, Left full-forward; 18, Full-forward.

White team (attacking top goal): A, Full-back; B, Left full-back; C, Right full-back; D, Left half-back; E, Centre half-back; G, Right half-back; H, Rover (ruck); J to K, Followers; L, Centre; M, Left centre (wing); N, Right centre (wing); P, Left half-forward; Q, Centre half-forward; R, Right half-forward; S, Left full-forward; T, Right full-forward; U, Full-forward.

placed in 5 lines of 3 men each. Three men follow the ball all the time. The 2 goal-posts, at each end, are 20 ft. high and 7 yds. apart. On either side are 2 smaller posts. The football is oval, and weighs a little more than a Rugby ball. A goal (6 points) is scored when the ball is kicked between the goalposts, if it is not touched on the way. If the ball passes between a goal-post and one of the smaller posts, or hits a post, the score is a 'behind,' or one point. There are no scrums, line-outs, or off-side rules. A player must get rid of the ball as soon as he starts to run, by kicking, punching or bouncing it every 10 yds. No tackling is allowed as in Rugby. The Code originated on the Australian goldfields in the '50s of last century.

FOOTBALL (Rugby). 'Rugger' originated at Rugby school in 1823. The game takes place between 2 teams of 15 players a side, on a playing field not to exceed 110 yds. by 75 yds. with areas behind each goal terminated by a dead-ball line. The goal is 18 ft. 6 in. wide and the cross-bar 10 ft. from the ground, with goal-posts extending beyond this height. The object is to score goals or tries with an oval leather ball. A try is made by touching down the ball by hand over the opposing side's goal-line. A try is converted into a goal if a member of the scoring team kicks the ball through the goal-posts at any height above the cross-bar. The kick may be taken from any point on a line parallel to the touch-lines, passing through the point where the try was scored. Scoring is based on points, 3 for a try, 5 for a try converted into a goal, 3 for a drop goal, and 3 for a penalty or free kick.

The set scrummage, a feature of Rugger, is used to re-start the game after certain infringements of the laws. The 15 players on each side usually comprise 8 forwards, 2 half-backs, 4 three-quarter backs and 1 full-back. In all matches a referee and 2 touch-judges must be appointed or mutually agreed upon.

The Rugby Union, governing amateur Rugby, was formed in 1871. The Rugby League was founded in

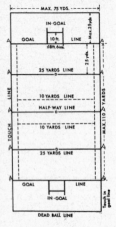

1895 and plays under Northern Union rules. In this game there are only 13 players a side.

FOOTE, Robert Bruce (1834–1912). British geologist. Going to India at 24 he spent 33 years with the geological survey and founded the study of the subcontinent's prehistory, discovering numerous sites and advancing theories that later excavation has confirmed.

FORAIN (foran'), **Jean Louis** (1852–1931). French artist. He excelled in Rembrandtesque lithographs and satirical etchings on subjects drawn from the law courts, politics, or the stage.

FORAMINI'FERA. Single-celled marine animals of the Protozoa enclosed by a thin shell.

FORBES, George William (1869–1947). Prime Minister of New Zealand at the head of a coalition government 1930–5, and subsequently leader of the opposition and of the National Party.

FORBES, (Joan) Rosita (1893–1967). British traveller. Her journeys were recorded in her many books, incl. *From the Red Sea to the Blue Nile* (1928) (Arabia), *The Forbidden Road – Kabul to Samarkand* (1937) (Afghanistan and Russia), and *Islands in the Sun* (1950) (W. Indies).

FORBES, Stanhope Alexander (1857–1947). Irish painter, b. in Dublin. He studied at the R.A. schools and in Paris; was a founder of the 'Newlyn school' and was elected R.A., 1910.

FORBES-ROBERTSON, Sir Johnston (1853–1937). British actor-manager. A pupil of Phelps, he acted under his own management from 1896, and was a striking Hamlet. He appeared with his wife Gertrude Elliot in a number of successes incl. Jerome K. Jerome's *The Passing of the Third Floor Back*, and Kipling's *The Light That Failed*. In 1931 he was knighted. His dau. **Jean F.-R.** (1905–62) also estab. a reputation as an actress, and her roles incl. *Hedda Gabler, The Constant Nymph*, and a highly successful *Peter Pan*.

FORCE. In mechanics F. is that which tends to change the state of rest or uniform motion of a body in a straight line and is measured by the product of its mass (m) and its acceleration (a). $F = ma$. See NEWTON, ISAAC.

FORD, Ford Madox (1873–1939). English writer, *né* Ford Madox Hueffer – he changed his name in 1919 – he was a grandson of Ford Madox Brown (q.v.). He was founder-editor of the *English Review* (1908), to which Hardy, D. H. Lawrence, and Conrad contributed. His verse is forgotten, but his novels incl. the historical trilogy *The Fifth Queen, Privy Seal* and the *Fifth Queen Crowned* (1906–8), dealing with Catherine Howard, and the war tetralogy *Parade's End* (*Some Do Not, No More Parades, A Man Could Stand Up* and *Last Post*, 1924–8), with its hero Christopher Tietjens.

FORD, Henry (1863–1947). American motor-car manufacturer. B. in Michigan, he built his first car in 1893 and 10 yrs. later founded the F. Motor Co. His model T (1908–27) was the first to be constructed by purely mass-production methods, and 15,000,000 of these historic cars were made. A pacifist, he visited Europe 1915–16 in an attempt to end the war, and in 1936 he founded with his son **Edsel B. Ford** (1893–1943) the philanthropic Ford Foundation. As pres. of the firm he was succeeded in 1919 by Edsel and in 1945 by his grandson **Henry F. II** (1917–): chairman 1960. In 1955 an annual Atoms for Peace prize was estab. as a memorial to Henry and Edsel, the 1st recipient being Niels Bohr (q.v.).

FORD, John (1586–1640). English poet and dramatist. B. in Devon, he was noted for an imaginative and dramatic study of incest between brother and sister in *'Tis Pity She's a Whore* (1633). The best of his other pieces are *The Broken Heart* (1633) and the chronicle play *Perkin Warbeck* (1634).

FORD, John (1895–). Irish-American film director. Active since the silent days, he was one of the original creators of the 'western'; *Stagecoach* being a masterpiece of the genre. His other films incl. *The Informer, Grapes of Wrath, Two Rode Together*, and he was co-director of the 1st cinerama story film *How the West was Won*.

FORDE, Daryll (1902–). British anthropologist. Prof. at London since 1945, he is known for his researches among N. American Indians and in Nigeria. His books include *Habitat, Economy and Society* (1934) and *African Worlds* (1953).

FOREIGN LEGION (*Légion Étrangère*). Popular name of the French *régiments étrangers*, formed in 1835. Men of any nationality may join the Legion, but the officers are French. Aubagne, nr. Marseilles is its H.Q.; till 1962 Sidi Bel Abbes, Algeria.

FOREIGN OFFICE. See FOREIGN RELATIONS.

FOREIGN RELATIONS. Formal relations between one sovereign state and another. In the U.K., F.R. are handled by the Foreign Office, a govt. dept. at the head of which is the Sec. of State for Foreign Affairs, with a seat in the cabinet, a dept. which dates from 1782. Before that there were 2 principal secs. of state, one of whom, the Sec. for the Southern Dept., dealt with home, Irish, and colonial affairs, and with relations with Mediterranean countries, while the other, the Sec. for the Northern Dept., dealt with relations with the rest of Europe. In 1782, the Southern Dept. became the Home Office and its foreign sections were transferred to the Northern Dept., which became the F. Office. The Sec. of State for Foreign Affairs (re-named in 1968 the Sec. of State for Foreign and Commonwealth Affairs) negotiates all treaties, and is responsible for all communications with foreign states and Commonwealth countries, and for the protection of British subjects abroad.

The Foreign Office worked 1943–65 through the Foreign Service, created by an amalgamation of the F.O. staff and the diplomatic, consular, and commercial diplomatic services, but from 1965 the overseas representational services of the Foreign Office and the Commonwealth Relations Office, together with the Trade Commission Service, were merged in the new H.M. Diplomatic Service. The Foreign and Commonwealth Relations Offices themselves, were amalgamated as the Foreign and Commonwealth Office in 1968. See CIVIL SERVICE.

In the U.S.A., F.R. are the concern of the State Dept. (1789). Thomas Jefferson, then Min. to France,

HENRY FORD with his first wife in his first car, built in 1893. From this model developed the Ford car and the great Ford Motor Co. Also in the photograph is Ford's grandson, Henry, who became chairman of the company in 1960.

was appointed Sec. of State by Washington in 1789 and took office in 1790. The Sec. of State is charged, under the direction of the President, 'with the duties appertaining to correspondence with the public ministers and the consuls of the United States, and with representatives of foreign powers accredited to the United States, and to negotiations of whatever character relating to the foreign affairs of the United States'.

Most other countries of the world have a Min. of Foreign Affairs who is a member of the cabinet (or equivalent body).

Up to the 18th cent. there was no specialized diplomatic body in any European country. After 1818 diplomatic agents were divided into: ambassadors, papal legates, and nuncios; envoys extraordinary and ministers plenipotentiary and other ministers accredited to the head of state; ministers resident; *chargés d'affaires* who may deputize for an ambassador or minister, or be themselves the representative accredited to a minor country. Heads of diplomatic missions are assisted by counsellors, secretaries, and attachés (military, labour, cultural, press, etc.). In 1925 eleven countries – Belgium, Brazil, France, Germany, Italy, Japan, Portugal, Russia, Spain, Turkey, and the U.S.A. – sent representatives of the rank of ambassador to one another; after the S.W.W. the representatives of a number of countries, incl. many formerly represented by a minister, envoy, or *chargé d'affaires* as well as newly created states, were elevated to the rank of ambassador. Consuls are state agents with commercial and political responsibilities in foreign towns, but are not 'travel agents'.

FORELAND, North and **South.** Headlands on the Kent coast, England. N.F., with one lighthouse, lies 2¼ m. E. of Margate; S.F., with two, lies 3 m. N.E. of Dover.

FORESTER, Cecil Scott (1899–1966). British author. His dual reputation rests on the varied excellence of such books as *Payment Deferred* (1926), a subtle crime novel; *Brown on Resolution* (1938), a study of patriotism; *The African Queen* (1938) and *The Earthly Paradise* (1940), dealing with Columbus: and on his series of the Napoleonic era covering the career – from midshipman to admiral – of the redoubtable Horatio Hornblower.

FORESTRY. The science of growing timber as a crop, made necessary by increasing demand for wood and the depletion of the world's timber reserves. Original forest areas have been drastically reduced during the last 3 cents., particularly in Europe, e.g. only 5% remains in U.K., 10–20% in France, Spain and Belgium and 50% in Sweden and Finland. The remaining productive forest area is about 18% of the earth's entire land surface. F. is complicated by the great life span of trees, and the vast areas involved, and its success depends upon sustaining the yield, by planting young trees to replace those cut down. Soft wood is the most commonly used timber and 80% of the world's trade is in conifers, used for paper pulp and construction, supplied by Sweden, Finland, and U.S.S.R. Temperate hardwoods from U.S.A. and Canada, used in furniture, railway sleepers, etc., account for another 18%, and tropical hardwoods of which there are great reserves in Africa, Asia, and S. America are the least used, only 2% being needed for special purposes. The value of trees extends beyond their worth as timber: they modify climate, prevent soil erosion etc., and reafforestation is of prime importance in countries such as Tunisia.

FORFAR. Co. town (burgh) of Angus, Scotland, 13 m. N.N.E. of Dundee. The chief industry is linen and jute manufacture. Pop. (1961) 10,252.

FORFARSHIRE. Name from 16th cent. until 1928 of ANGUS.

FORGERY. The falsification of any written instrument with intent to deceive. F. is not limited to spurious signatures.

FORGET-ME-NOT

FORGET-ME-NOT or **Scorpion Grass.** Common wild flower belonging to the Boraginaceae family (genus *Myosotis*) found in Europe, N. America, N. Asia, and Australia. The flowers are blue, pink, or white. The species *M. scorpioides* and *M. sylvatica* are much cultivated.

FORLI (forlē'). City and market centre in Emilia-Romagna region, Italy, cap. of F. prov. It has a cathedral, old churches, and a citadel. Felt, majolica, paper are made. Pop. (1966) 101,073.

FORMALDEHYDE. A gas, H_2CO at ordinary temperatures, condensing at −21°C. It has a powerful penetrating smell and burning taste. In aqueous solution it is used as a biological preservative.

FORMBY, George (1904–61). English comedian. Following the death in 1921 of his father George F. sen., one of music-hall's famed comedians, he appeared under a pseudonym for 18 months, until he had proved his worth. On stage and screen he estab. a reputation as the not-so-gormless Lancashire lad, and sang such songs as 'Mr. Wu' and 'Cleaning Windows', accompanying himself on the ukelele.

FORMENTOR PRIZES. So named from Cape F. on Majorca where the selectors first met, there are 2 awards of $10,000, both first given in 1961: the Prix F. is for an unpublished work of fiction, the MSS. being submitted by participating publishers and the winning book published simultaneously in the countries concerned; and the International Publishers' Prize is for any recently published work of fiction from any source.

FORMIC ACID (CH_2O_2). One of the fatty acids, a colourless, slightly fuming liquid that melts at 8°C and boils at 101°C. Specific gravity 1·22. It occurs

FORESTRY. Canada exceeds all other countries in her exports of both wood-pulp and paper, and is the source of more than half of all newspaper pages printed daily. Some lakes, such as this in the Gatineau pulpwood region of western Quebec, carry more than 150,000 cords of pulpwood on their frozen surfaces at the close of the cutting season.
Photo: Malak, Ottawa.

in stinging ants, nettles, sweat, and pine needles.

FORMO'SA. Island off the S.E. coast of China, separated from it by the F. Strait. F. was Chinese from 1683 until 1895 when it was ceded to Japan, becoming Chinese again after Japan's defeat in 1945. When the Communists conquered all the Chinese mainland in 1949 the Nationalist Govt. fled to F. where its status as the legal govt. of China continued to be recognized by the U.S.A. The cap. is Taipeh. It produces rice, tea, sugar, fruits, jute, camphor, etc.; there are flour mills, sugar refineries, cotton factories, glass and brick works, and some mining of copper, coal, aluminium, salt. With American assistance, F. has achieved independent economic prosperity and there is an efficient American-trained and equipped army, navy and air force. The Pescadores Is. some 35 m. W. of Formosa (area 50 sq. m.; pop. 110,000) are heavily garrisoned, as are Quemoy (60 sq. m.) and Matsu (11 sq. m.), from which loudspeaker propaganda and intermittent shelling are exchanged with the nearby mainland of China. Area 13,890 sq. m.; pop. (1966) 12,993,000.

FORRESTAL, James Vincent (1892–1949). American Democratic statesman. He served in the F.W.W. as a naval aviator, assisted Roosevelt from 1940 in work on national defence, and as Sec. of the Navy from 1944 visited the war zones, accompanying the assault troops at Iwo Jima. He was the first Sec. of the Dept. of National Defense (1947–9), a post created to unify the 3 services at the end of the S.W.W.

FORSSMANN, Werner (1904–). W. German heart specialist. In 1929 he originated by experiment on himself the technique of cardiac catheterization, passing a thin tube from an arm artery up into the heart itself and then having X-ray photographs taken. In 1956 he was awarded a joint Nobel prize with A. F. Cournand and D. W. Richards of America.

FORSTER, Edward Morgan (1879–1970). British author. B. in London and ed. at King's Coll. Cambridge, he pub. his first novel *Where Angels Fear to Tread* in 1905. He undermines the superficial situations of his plots with unexpected insights in *The Longest Journey* (1907), *A Room with a View* (1908), and *Howard's End* (1910). *A Passage to India* (1924), his most famous book, explores the relationship between English and Indians through the incident of a possibly non-existent assault on a stolid Englishwoman by the charming Dr. Aziz. Forster was concerned with the interplay of personality and the contrast between the contentional and the instinctive. His critical work incl. *Aspects of the Novel* (1927). Awarded O.M. 1969.

FORSTER, John (1812–76). British biographer and critic. Literary critic and later editor of *The Examiner*

(1847–56), he wrote (1872–4) a *Life of Charles Dickens* whose friend he was, which is a standard biography.

FORSTER, William Edward (1818–86). British reformer. He was a Bradford woollen manufacturer, who entered parliament in 1861 as a Liberal. In Gladstone's government of 1868–74 he was Vice-President of the Council, and secured the passing of the Education Act (1870) and the Ballot Act (1872). He was Chief Secretary for Ireland, 1880–2.

FORSYTHIA (forsi'thia). Flowering shrub, allied to the olive (Oleaceae family), frequently cultivated in British gardens; the bright yellow flowers appear in spring before the leaves.

FORTALEZA (fortahlä'zah). Cap. and port of Ceara state, Brazil. Pop. (1960) 514,818.

FO'RTAS, Abe (1910–). American lawyer. Partner in a Washington law firm, he became known in 1962 by the Gideon Case (in Florida a man named Earl Gideon had been convicted, after having been refused a lawyer, and appealed), in which he estab. that everyone had a right to legal counsel in a criminal trial. He became a member of the Supreme Court 1965, but resigned in 1969.

FORT DE FRANCE (for de froñs). Cap., chief commercial centre, and port of the French West Indian island of Martinique. Pop. (1960 est.) 60,648.

FORTH. River and firth in S.E. Scotland. Its headstreams rise on the N.E. slopes of Ben Lomond, near the Perth–Stirlingshire border, and it runs for about 45 m. to Kincardine, where it is crossed by a road bridge, and the Firth of F. begins; the Firth is *c*. 50 m. long and *c*. 16 m. wide where it joins the North Sea. At Queensferry near Edinburgh is the Forth Bridge (railway) opened 1890; a road bridge nearby was constructed 1958–64.

FORTH AND CLYDE CANAL. Canal, constructed 1768–90, across the lowlands of Scotland, connecting the Firth of Forth with the r. Clyde. It is 33 m. long, and runs from Grangemouth to Bowling.

FORT KNOX. U.S. army post and gold depository in Kentucky, established 1917 as a training camp. The depository was constructed 1936–7 and after the S.W.W. held gold valued at more than £3,000,000,000.

FORTU'NA. In Roman mythology, the goddess of chance and good fortune.

FORT WILLIAM. Scottish town and resort near the head of Loch Linnhe, Inverness-shire, below the south-west end of the Caledonian Canal. The fort was named after William III in 1690. Near are aluminium and chemical works, which use locally produced hydro-electricity. Pop. (1961) 2,715.

FORT WORTH. City of Texas, U.S.A.; it is one of the great grain and railway centres of the southern U.S.A. Pop. (1970) 757,105.

FORTY-FIVE, The. Name given to the Jacobite rebellion of 1745, led by Prince Charles Edward. With his army of Highlanders 'Prince Charlie' occupied Edinburgh and advanced into England as far as Derby, but then turned back. The rising was crushed by the duke of Cumberland at Culloden in 1746.

FOSSIL (Lat., *fossilis*, dug up). Organic remains which have been preserved in rocks; the majority are of marine origin or lived in swamps, lakes, etc. Fs. may be formed by refrigeration, e.g. the N. Siberian mammoths; the preservation merely of the skeleton; carbonization, e.g. wood and leaves converted into coal; the formation of a mould or cast round the organism; petrification, etc. Fs. provide evidence of the condition of the earth at successive epochs, and of the life-history of the world.

FOSTER, Myles Birket (1825–99). British artist. He produced mainly landscapes with figures, usually of children, at first as wood-engravings for illustrations, but after *c*. 1861 as paintings in water colours.

FOSTER, Stephen Collins (1826–64). American

FORTH. A marvel of bridge-building technique in the Victorian era, the railway bridge can be seen (right) beyond the new road bridge. *Courtesy of William Arrol Ltd.*

songwriter, author of 'The Old Folks at Home', 'My Old Kentucky Home', etc.

FOUCAULT (fookoh'), **Jean Bernard Léon** (1819–68). French physicist. He produced in 1851 the pendulum named after him, which demonstrates the rotation of the earth on its axis, and was the inventor of the gyroscope.

FOUCHÉ (foosheh'), **Joseph,** duke of Otranto (1759–1820). French statesman. B. near Nantes, he was elected to the National Convention, and organized the conspiracy which overthrew Robespierre. Napoleon employed him as Police Minister.

FOUGASSE (foogas'). Pseudonym of the British cartoonist C. Kenneth Bird (1887–1965). Art editor of *Punch* 1937–49, and editor 1949–53, he had a style distinguished by simple, bold outlines.

FOUNTAINS ABBEY. Cistercian abbey situated 8 m. N. of Harrogate, in the W. Riding of Yorks, England. It was founded *c.* 1132, and suppressed in 1540. A plan formed in 1946 to restore the ruins as a monastic establishment came to nothing.

FOUR FREEDOMS. President Roosevelt in his address to Congress on Jan. 6, 1941, defined the 'four essential human freedoms' as freedom of speech and expression, freedom of every person to worship God in his own way, freedom from want, and freedom from fear.

FOURIER (fooryeh'), **François Charles Marie** (1772–1837). French Socialist. B. at Besançon, he spent most of his life as a clerk, and d. at Paris. In his *Le nouveau monde industriel* (1829–30), he advocated that society should be organized in units of *c.* 1,800 people living and working in co-operation.

FOUR SQUARE GOSPEL ALLIANCE. Religious movement started in Ireland in 1915 and now organized in the Elim Four Square Gospel Alliance. It stresses the inspiration of the Bible, bodily healing through anointing with oil, adult baptism by immersion, the millennial return of Christ, etc.

FOURTEEN POINTS. The terms proposed by President Wilson of the U.S.A. in his address to Congress on Jan. 8, 1918, as a basis for the settlement of the F.W.W. that was shortly about to reach its climax. They included: open diplomacy; freedom of the seas; removal of economic barriers; international disarmament; adjustment of colonial claims; German evacuation of Russian, Belgian, French, and Balkan territories; the restoration of Alsace-Lorraine to France; autonomy for the Austro-Hungarian peoples and those under Turkish rule; an independent Poland; and a general association of nations. Many of the 'points' were embodied in the peace treaties following the war.

FOURTH (of July). Independence Day in U.S.A.; the anniversary of the day in 1776 when the Declaration of Independence was adopted by the Continental Congress.

FOURTH ESTATE. Name applied to the Press. The first to do so was Burke.

FOWEY (foi). English port and holiday resort (bor.) in Cornwall nr. the mouth of the Fowey estuary. It is being developed as an outlet for the Cornish clay mining industry. Pop. (1961) 2,237.

FOWLER, Henry Watson (1858–1933) and **Francis George** (1870–1918). British scholars, authors of a number of English dictionaries: *Modern English Usage* (1926), is the work of the elder brother.

FOWLIANG. *See* KING-TE-CHEN.

FOX. A dog-like carnivorous mammal; fem. vixen. *Vulpes vulpes*, the common European red fox, is reddish-brown, changing to white underneath, with a white-tipped tail. In Britain it is hunted as a sport. Silver or black F. is farmed for its pelt.

FOX, Charles James (1749–1806). English Whig statesman. The son of the 1st baron Holland, he entered parliament in 1769 as a supporter of the court, but in 1774 went over to the opposition. In 1782 he became Sec. of State in Rockingham's govt., but resigned when Shelburne succeeded Rockingham. He allied with North in 1783 to overthrow Shelburne, and formed a coalition ministry. When the Lords threw out F.'s bill to reform the govt. of India, George III dismissed the ministry, and in their place installed Pitt.

C. J. FOX. A contemporary caricature of Fox as Demosthenes satirizing his fondness for platform oratory. He was famous for his splendid debating powers and was a great rival of the younger Pitt.

F. now became leader of the opposition, although co-operating with Pitt in the impeachment of Hastings, etc. He welcomed the French Revolution, but the 'Old Whigs' deserted to the govt. in 1792, leaving F. and a small group of 'New Whigs' to oppose Pitt's war of intervention and his persecution of the reformers. On Pitt's death in 1806 a ministry was formed with F. as For. Sec., which at F.'s insistence abolished the slave trade. He opened peace negotiations with France, but d. before their completion, and was buried in Westminster Abbey.

FOX, George (1624–91). Founder of the Society of Friends. B. in Leics, he was apprenticed to a shoemaker, but in 1647 became a travelling preacher. In 1650 he was imprisoned for blasphemy at Derby, where the name of 'Quakers' was first applied to him and his followers, and altogether spent 6 years in prison. He later went on missionary journeys to the W. Indies, America, Germany, and Holland. His *Journal* appeared in 1694.

FOXE, John (1516–87). English Protestant propagandist. B. at Boston, he became a canon of Salisbury in 1563. His *Book of Martyrs* (1563), by its lurid descriptions of the Marian persecutions, helped to make hatred of popery a force in English life.

FOXGLOVE. Genus of flowering plants (*Digitalis*) of the family Scrophulariaceae found in Europe, W. Asia, and the Canaries; they bear showy spikes of bell-like flowers, varying from 1½ to 5 ft. in height. The wild species produce purple to reddish flowers.

FOXHOUND. Small hound specially trained for fox-hunting. It is a combination of the old southern hound, with its keen nose, and the speedy greyhound, and has been bred in England for over 300 years.

FOX-HUNTING. As a recognized sport, this dates from the last half of the 17th cent. In the 18th cent. it was practised by noblemen and country squires, but at the beginning of the 19th cent. it developed into a national pastime. Among the most famous 'hunts' are the Quorn, Pytchley, Belvoir, and Cottesmore. There is a recognized F.-H. season from the 1st Monday in November until the following April. F.-H. was introduced to the U.S. by early settlers from England, and continues in the south and middle-eastern regions.

FOX-TERRIER. A small, smooth- or rough-haired dog, originally used to run with the hounds but now kept mainly as a house dog.

FOX-TROT. Modern ballroom dance of transatlantic origin that made its appearance just prior to the F.W.W. Its name derives from the alternately rapid and slow movements of the fox.

FOYLE. Sea-lough on the N. coast of Ireland, traversed by the frontier of N. Ireland and the Irish Republic.

FRACTIONS. In mathematics a fraction is a number which indicates one or more equal parts of a whole. The usual way of denoting this is to place below a horizontal line the number of equal parts into which the unit is divided, and above the line the number of these parts actually comprising the fraction, thus ¾. Such fractions are called *vulgar Fs.* A *proper F.* is one in which the numerator is less than the denominator; an *improper F.* is one in which the numerator is greater than the denominator, e.g. ⅘. An improper F. can therefore be expressed as a mixed number, e.g. 1½.

A *decimal F.* is one in which the F. is expressed by figures written to the right of the units figure after a dot or point (the decimal point). The digits on the right of the decimal point indicate the numerators of vulgar Fs. whose denominators are 10, 100 . . .

FRA DIAVOLO (frah dyah'-). Name by which the Italian brigand Michele Pezza (1771–1806) was known. A renegade monk, he led a gang in the mountains of Calabria for many years, but was eventually executed at Naples. He has no link with Auber's opera.

FRAGONARD
'The Young Scholar.'
Courtesy of the Wallace Collection.

FRAGONARD (frahgonahr'), **Jean Honoré** (1732–1806). French artist. He studied under Boucher in Paris, and is famous chiefly for his light-hearted *rococo* paintings of love in romantic settings.

FRAMPTON, Sir George James (1860–1928). British sculptor. His most famous works are 'Peter Pan' in Kensington Gdns. and the Nurse Cavell memorial nr. St. Martin's, London.

FRANC. French coin, so named from *Francorum Rex* (king of the Franks) that was inscribed thereon about 1360, when it was a gold coin. The monetary unit as now known dates from the French Revolution. It is divided into 100 centimes, and there are also Belgian and Swiss francs.

FRANCE (froṅs), **Anatole.** Pseudonym of the French writer Jacques Anatole Thibault (1844–1924). B. in Paris, he pub. a critical study of Alfred de Vigny (1868), which was followed by several vols. of poetry and short stories. His earliest novel was *Le Crime de Sylvestre Bonnard* (1881): later books include *Thaïs* (1890), *Crainquebille* (1905), the satiric *L'île des Pingouins* (1908), and *La révolte des Anges* (1914), and the autobiographical series beginning with *Le Livre de mon Ami* (1885). He was elected to the French Academy in 1896, and in 1921 was awarded a Nobel prize for literature.

ANATOLE FRANCE, in middle life.

FRANCE. Republic of western Europe, bordering on Spain in the S.W., Italy, Switzerland, and Germany in the E., Belgium and Luxemburg in the N.E., and facing the Mediterranean, Atlantic Ocean, and English Channel on the S., W., and N. respectively. Area (incl. Corsica) 212,961 sq. m.; pop. (1967) 49,700,000. In 1881 the northern part of Algeria was made part of METROPOLITAN FRANCE, but achieved independence in 1962 as part of the new state of Algeria (q.v.).

PHYSICAL FEATURES. F. may be roughly divided into 2 parts: to the N. of a line from Bordeaux to Rheims, with a bay in the S.W. to include the basin of Aquitaine, are lowlands, while to the S. are highlands. The core of the mountainous area is the *massif central*. Westward, the mountains of Auvergne merge into the plateau of the Limousin and the hills of Quercy. To the E. the Auvergne merge into the Cevennes. The Pyrenees, forming a natural boundary between France and Spain, stretch from the Mediterranean to the Atlantic. The Alps, with their foothills and subsidiary ranges, cover most of F's. surface to the E. of the Rhône. The highlands of the S. are cut through by the valleys of the Rhône and the Aude. N. of the Rhône, the Jura mts. curve round to the Rhine at Basle. W. of the Rhine are the Vosges, merging into the Langres plateau in the N. The Ardennes farther N. abut on the low-lying country stretching to the North Sea.

With the exception of Sète, there is no natural harbour between the Spanish frontier on the Mediterranean and the Rhône estuary. Farther E. only Marseilles and Toulon are of importance. The principal port of S.W. France is Bordeaux on the Garonne, 60 m. from the sea. The shores of Brittany afford some of the best natural harbours, including Lorient and Brest. From Normandy, where Cherbourg is of great importance, to the Belgian frontier, most of the harbours are either in estuaries or are man-made. Of the 4 river systems, the Rhone rises in the Swiss Alps; and the Garonne, although the r. Garonne itself rises in the Pyrenees, draws much of its waters from the massif central, whence the Loire and Seine systems also rise.

Both in scenery and in climate F. is a land of contrasts. Normandy and Brittany may be compared for climate with Devon and Cornwall, while much of the N.E. endures sharp winters. S. of Lyon the climate merges into the Mediterranean zone. There is a noticeable difference in the flora of the N., which resembles that of southern England, and the S., in which the olive and the vine predominate.

AGRICULTURE. About one-third of the crops raised in F. are cereals, of which wheat is the most important, followed by oats, barley, and rye. Sugar beet is grown in the N.W. Among the other crops are flax, hemp, forage crops, hops, tobacco, colza, potatoes, fruits, of which the grape is most important: just over 3 million acres were under the vine in 1968, but the acreage is diminishing slowly (nearly 3¾ million acres in 1938). The principal wine-producing areas are the S. with Hérault dept. as a centre; the Bordeaux district; Touraine and Anjou; the Rhône valley; Burgundy; Champagne; Alsace; and the Charentes

FRANCE. Burgundy is one of the country's greatest wine-producing areas, and this is one stage in the pressing of the grapes. *Courtesy of the French Govt. Tourist Office.*

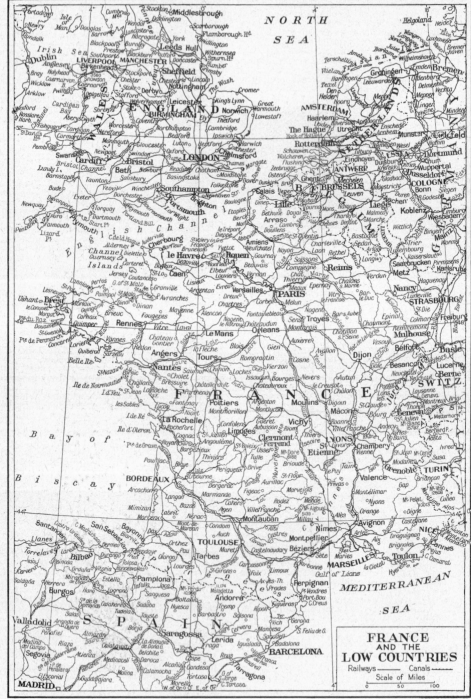

FRANCE
AND THE
LOW COUNTRIES
Railways ——— Canals ———
Scale of Miles
0   50   100

DEPARTMENTS OF FRANCE

	Area in sq. m.	Population (1968 census)	Capital		Area in sq. m.	Population (1968 census)	Capital
Ain	2,143	339,262	Bourg-en-Bresse	Lot-et-Garonne	2,078	290,592	Agen
Aisne	2,866	526,346	Laon	Lozère	1,996	77,258	Mende
Allier	2,848	386,533	Moulins	Maine-et-Loire	2,811	584,709	Angers
Alpes-de-Haute-				Manche	2,475	451,939	St. Lô
Provence	2,697	104,813	Digne	Marne	3,167	485,388	Châlone-sur-Marne
Alpes (Hautes-)	2,178	91,790	Gap	Marne (Haute-)	2,240	214,336	Chaumont
Alpes-Maritimes	1 660	722,070	Nice	Mayenne	1,986	252,762	Laval
Ardèche	2,144	256,927	Privas	Meurthe-et-Moselle	2,036	705,413	Nancy
Ardennes	2,027	309,380	Mezières	Meuse	2,408	209,513	Bar-le-Duc
Ariège	1,892	138,478	Foix	Morbihan	2,738	540,474	Vannes
Aube	2,327	270,325	Troyes	Moselle	2,403	971,314	Metz
Aude	2,448	278,323	Carcassonne	Nièvre	2,658	247,702	Nevers
Aveyron	3,385	281,586	Rodez	Nord	2,228	2,417,899	Lille
Belfort (territory)	235	118,450	Belfort	Oise	2,272	540,988	Beauvais
Bouches-du-Rhône	2,096	1,470,271	Marseilles	Orne	2,371	288,524	Alençon
Calvados	2,197	519,695	Caen	Paris, Ville de	40	2,590,771	—
Cantal	2,231	169,330	Aurillac	Pas-de-Calais	2,606	1,397,159	Arras
Charente	2,306	331,016	Augoulème	Puy-de-Dôme	3,090	547,743	Clermont-Ferrand
Charente-Maritime	2,792	483,622	La Rochelle	Pyrénées-			
Cher	2,819	304,601	Bourges	Atlantiques	2,978	508,734	Pau
Corrèze	2,272	237,858	Tulle	Pyrénées (Hautes-)	1,750	225,730	Tarbes
Corsica (Corse)	3,367	269,831	Ajaccio	Pyrénées-Orientales	1,600	281,976	Perpignan
Côte-d'Or	3,391	421,192	Dijon	Rhin (Bas-)	1,851	827,367	Strasbourg
Côtes-du-Nord	2,786	506,102	St. Brieux	Rhin (Haut-)	1,354	585,018	Colmar
Creuse	2,163	156,876	Guéret	Rhône	2,072	1,325,611	Lyons
Dordogne	3,550	374,073	Périgueux	Saône (Haute-)	2,074	214,176	Vesoul
Doubs	2,052	426,363	Besançon	Saône-et-Loire	3,330	550,362	Mâcon
Drôme	2,532	342,891	Valence	Sarthe	2,410	461,839	Le Mans
Essonne	699	674,157	Evry-Petit-Bourg	Savoie	2,388	288,921	Chambéry
Eure	2,330	383,385	Evreux	Savoie (Haute-)	1,775	378,550	Annecy
Eure-et-Loir	2,291	302 207	Chartres	Seine-Maritime	2,448	1,113,977	Rouen
Finistère	2,729	768,929	Quimper	Seine-et-Marne	2,275	604,340	Melun
Gard	2,270	478,544	Nimes	Seine-Saint-Denis	91	1,251,792	Bobigny
Garonne (Haute-)	2,457	690,712	Toulouse	Sèvres (Deux-)	2,337	326,462	Niort
Gers	2,428	181,577	Auch	Somme	2,443	512,113	Amiens
Gironde	4,141	1,009,390	Bordeaux	Tarn	2,231	332,011	Albi
Hauts-de-Seine	67	1,461,619	Nanterre	Tarn-et-Garonne	1,441	183,572	Montauban
Hérault	2,402	591,397	Montpellier	Val-de-Marne	94	1,121,340	Créteil
Ille-et-Vilaine	2,700	652,722	Rennes	Val-d'Oise	482	693,269	Cergy
Indre	2,664	247,178	Châteauroux	Var	2,333	555,926	Draguignan
Indre-et-Loire	2,377	437,870	Tours	Vaucluse	1,381	353,966	Avignon
Isère	3,316	768,450	Grenoble	Vendée	2,690	421,250	La Roche-sur-Yon
Jura	1,951	233,547	Lons-le-Saunier	Vienne	2,711	340,256	Poitiers
Landes	3,604	277,381	Mont-de-Marsan	Vienne (Haute-)	2,119	341,589	Limoges
Loir-et-Cher	2,478	267,896	Blois	Vosges	2,303	388,201	Epinal
Loire	1,852	722,383	St. Etienne	Yonne	2,892	283,376	Auxerre
Loire (Haute-)	1,930	208,337	Le Puy	Yvelines	876	853,386	Versailles
Loire-Atlantique	2,693	861,452	Nantes				
Loiret	2,629	430,629	Orléans		212,961	49,778,540	
Lot	2,017	151,198	Cahors				

(brandy). Silk is produced in 15 depts. Market-gardening and the growing of early vegetables are widespread. The richest pastoral areas are Normandy, Perche, and Flanders. Forestry and fishing are important. F. is self-sufficing in foodstuffs.

INDUSTRY. Minerals incl. coal in the N.E., the richest seams being in the Nancy and Longwy-Briey areas; iron and bauxite; and more recently oil from the Parentis field in the Landes; natural gas in the Lacq area in the Pyrenean foothills; and uranium near Autun, Clermont-Ferrand, Limoges and Nantes. Industry was formerly concentrated almost entirely in the N.E., Paris and Rhône valley areas, but under a series of post-war development plans new growth is being encouraged especially at the site of recent mineral discoveries, and hydroelectric stations now supply half the country's power. The chief manufactures are motor vehicles, radio and television sets, chemicals, textiles and processed foods.

GOVERNMENT Under the constitution of 1958, as amended 1962, the 5th Republic has a pres. directly elected by universal suffrage, a National Assembly and a Senate which incl. overseas representatives. In 1968 De Gaulle announced drastic reforms of the Senate (incl. its merger with the Economic and Social Council) and of regional govt. to be put to the nation in a referendum, in which he was defeated 1969.

POPULATION. With a basis of 'Alpine' and 'Mediter-ranean', the French show representatives of every European physical type. About half the pop. still lives near to the soil. The great majority of the pop. are Roman Catholics but there is no State Church. Protestants number c. 1 million.

The largest towns are Paris, Marseilles, Lyons, Toulouse, Bordeaux, Nice, Nantes, and Strasbourg. There are 95 depts., in each of which the central government is represented by a prefect and to facilitate economic planning is divided into 21 regions, each with a regional prefect who is also prefect of one of its depts.: Alsace, Aquitaine, Auvergne, Bourgogne, Bretagne, Centre, Champagne, Franche-Comté, Languedoc, Limousin, Loire (Pays de la), Lorraine, Midi-Pyrénées, Nord, Normandie (Haute), Normandie (Basse), Région Parisienne, Picardie, Poitou-Charentes, Provence-Côte d'Azur-Corse, Rhône-Alpes. See FRENCH HISTORY, LANGUAGE, LITERATURE, etc.

FRANCESCA (franhches'kah), Piero della (c. 1418–92). Italian artist. A member of the Umbrian school, he was one of the earliest painters in oils. His masterpiece is the series of frescoes of the Legend of the True Cross in the church of San Francesco, Arezzo. Described as the greatest geometrician of his day, he has since been called the first Cubist because of the geometrical construction of his work.

FRANCIS II (1768–1835). Holy Roman Emperor.

P

He succeeded his father, Leopold II, in 1792. During his reign Austria was 5 times involved in war with France, in 1792-7, 1798-1801, 1805, 1809, and 1813-14. He assumed the title of emperor of Austria in 1804, and abandoned that of Holy Roman Emperor in 1806.

FRANCIS I (1494-1547). King of France. He succeeded his cousin Louis XII, and from 1519 European politics turned on the rivalry between him and Charles V, which led to war in 1521-9, 1536-8, and 1542-4. In 1525 F. was defeated and captured at Pavia, and released only on signing a humiliating treaty. At home F. devel-)ped absolute monarchy.

FRANCIS I
Wallace Collection.

FRANCIS II (1544-60). King of France. He m. Mary, Queen of Scots, in 1558, and succeeded his father, Henry II, in 1559. He was completely under the influence of his mother, Catherine de' Medici.

FRANCISCANS, Friars Minor, or **Grey Friars.** R.C. order of friars founded in 1209 by Francis of Assisi (q.v.). Sub-divisions were the strict Observants, the Conventuals, who were allowed to own property corporately, and the Capuchins. The F. were noted for their preaching and ministrations amongst the poor, and included such scholars as Roger Bacon. There was also a Second Order of nuns known as Poor Clares after St. Clare (q.v.). The Third Order, or Tertiaries, consisted of lay men and women who adopted a modified form of the Franciscan régime, without abandoning business and family life.

FRANCIS FERDINAND (1863-1914). Archduke of Austria. He became heir to his uncle, the Emperor Francis Joseph, in 1889. While visiting Sarajevo on June 28, 1914, he and his wife were assassinated by Serb nationalists; Austria used the episode as an excuse for attacking Serbia, precipitating the F.W.W.

FRANCIS JOSEPH (1830-1916). Emperor of Austria-Hungary. He succeeded his uncle, Ferdinand I, on his abdication in 1848, and after the suppression of the 1848 revolution set out to estab. an absolute monarchy. But he was defeated in the Italian War of 1859 and the Prussian War of 1866, and had to grant Austria a parliamentary constitution in 1861 and Hungary equality with Austria in 1867. His only son committed suicide in 1889, and the empress was assassinated in 1897.

FRANCIS OF ASSISI (ase'sē) (1182-1226). Italian R. Catholic saint. The son of a wealthy merchant, his life was changed by two dreams during an illness following spells of military service when he was in his early twenties. He resolved to follow literally the behests of the N.T. and to live a life of poverty and service while preaching a simple form of the Christian gospel. F. attracted many followers, and in 1209 founded an Order of friars.

Many stories are told of his ability to charm wild animals and to influence men in all walks of life. In 1219 he went to Egypt to convert the Sultan, and

FRANCIS OF ASSISI

lived for a month in his camp. Returning to Italy, he resigned his leadership of the friars, and in 1224 he suffered a mystical experience during which he is said to have received the *stigmata* or 5 wounds of Christ. He d. at Assissi, and was canonized in 1228.

FRANCIS OF PAOLA (pow'lah), **St.** (c. 1416-1507). Founder of the R.C. Order of Minims (so called because they went further in austerity than the Franciscan 'Minors'), which received papal approval in 1474.

FRANCIS OF SALES (1567-1622). French R. Catholic saint. B. in Savoy, he became bishop of Geneva in 1602, and in 1610 he founded the Order of the Visitation, a congregation of nuns.

FRANCIUM. Element, at. no. 87, at. wt. 223. Discovered by Mlle Perey in 1939, it is a radioactive metal. *See* TABLE OF TRANSURANIUM ELEMENTS.

FRANCK (froṅk), **César Auguste** (1822-90). Belgian composer. B. at Liége, he became a teacher and in 1858 organist at the church of St. Clotilde, Paris. There he remained until his death. Much of his music is religious in character and subject. Best known are the Symphonic Variations for piano and orchestra, the violin sonata, and the oratorios *Redemption*, and *Les Béatitudes*, a choral masterpiece.

FRANCO BAHAMONDE, Francisco (1892-   ). Spanish dictator. B. in Galicia, he entered the army in 1910, served in Morocco, and was appointed Chief of Staff in 1935 and Gov. of the Canary Islands in 1936. Dismissed from this post by the Popular Front govt., he plotted an uprising with German and Italian assistance, and on the outbreak of civil war organized the invasion of Spain by Moorish troops and foreign legionaries. After the death of General Sanjurjo, he took command of the insurgents (Nationalists), proclaiming himself *Caudillo* (leader) of Spain, and the defeat of the Republic with the surrender of Madrid in 1939 brought all Spain under his govt. On the outbreak of the S.W.W., in spite of

Courtesy of the Spanish Embassy.

Spain's official attitude of 'Strictest neutrality', his pro-axis sympathies led him to send aid, later withdrawn, to the German side. At home, he curbed the growing power of the *Falange*, and in 1942 reinstated the *Cortes*, which in 1947 passed an act by which Spain became a realm, with F. as head of state for life and entitled to choose his successor. In spite of his attempts in the early 1960s to stabilize the economy and introduce some labour reforms, there was growing criticism of his régime even from its formerly firm supporters – the Church, Army and Civil Service.

FRANCO-PRUSSIAN WAR, 1870-1. *See* FRENCH HISTORY.

FRANK, Anne (1929-45). German diarist. B. at Frankfurt-am-Main, she fled to Holland with her family in 1933 to escape Nazi anti-Semitism. Under the occupation they remained in a sealed-off room in Amsterdam 1942-4, when betrayal resulted in Anne's death in Belsen concentration camp. Her diary during her period in hiding was pub. in 1947, and as a martyr to the Nazi régime she has been commemorated in the names of villages and schools for refugee children.

FRANK, Bruno (1886-1945). German author. B. at Stuttgart of Jewish parentage, he settled in Munich and emigrated to U.S.A. when the Nazis came to power. He made a name with historical novels such as *Tage des Königs* (1924), *Trenck* (1926), etc.

FRANK, Leonhard (1882-1961). German novelist.

Best known for his fervently anti-war *Der Mensch ist Gut* (1917; *Man is Good*), he also wrote *Die Ursache* (1920; *The Cause of the Crime*) and *Karl und Anna* (1927; dramatized 1929).

FRANKAU (fran′kō), **Gilbert** (1884–1952). British novelist, best remembered for *Peter Jackson, Cigar Merchant* (1919) which reflected in its setting his experience in his father's tobacco business. His dau. **Pamela F.** (1908–67) was also a novelist.

FRANKEL, Benjamin (1906–). British composer. Originally a watchmaker's assistant, he studied the piano in Germany, and continued his studies in London while playing jazz as a violinist in night-clubs. He has written numerous film scores, and chamber music of an individual, serious quality.

FRANKFURT-AM-MAIN. City of W. Germany, 45 m. N.N.E. of Mannheim. F. was a free city until in 1866 it was incorporated in Prussia. F.-am-M. is a very important commercial centre and inland port, with electrical and machinery industries, and the headquarters of the I.G. Farbenindustrie. Heavily damaged during the S.W.W., it became the H.Q. of the U.S. zone of occupation and of the Anglo-U.S. zone, 1947–9. Pop. (1966) 678,506.

FRANKFURT-AM-MAIN.
The original 16th cent. house where Goethe lived from his birth in 1749 until 1775 was destroyed by bombing in 1944. The new Goethehaus, opened in 1951, four years after its foundation stone was laid by André Gide, is a Goethe museum like its predecessor (opened in 1897), with archives and a library representative of German literature of the period.
Courtesy of the German Tourist Information Bureau.

FRANKFURT-AN-DER-ODER. City in E. Germany, 50 m. E.S.E. of Berlin, cap. of F. dist. Its industries include chemicals, iron and steel goods, particularly machinery, paper, and leather. Pop. (1966) 60,000.

FRANKFURTER, Felix (1882–1965). American lawyer. B. in Vienna, but ed. in U.S., he became an attorney in New York. He was prof. of administrative law at Harvard 1914–39, and was then appointed an associate justice of the Supreme Court (1939–62). As a teacher and author he made many important contributions to legal traditions and literature.

FRANKINCENSE. A resinous product obtained from trees of the *Boswellia* genus, Burseraceae family, natives of Africa, India, and Arabia, and used in incense.

FRANKLIN, Benjamin (1706–90). American states-man, scientist, and writer. B. in Boston of poor parents, he ran a printing business in Philadelphia so successfully that by 1749 he could retire and devote himself to science. His proof that lightning is a form of electricity, his discovery of the distinction between negative and positive electricity, and his invention of the lightning-conductor, made him internationally famous. He was elected to the Pennsylvania Assembly, and in 1754 put forward the first plan for a federation

BENJAMIN FRANKLIN.
Courtesy of the Pennsylvania Historical Society.

of the American colonies. As agent for Pennsylvania in London 1764–75, he used his influence to procure the repeal of the Stamp Act. Returning to America, he helped to draw up the Declaration of Independence, and as ambassador to France, 1776–85, negotiated an alliance with France and the peace settlement with Britain. He was president of Pennsylvania 1785–8, and took part in the drafting of the U.S. constitution. During his later years he wrote an autobiography.

FRANKLIN, Sir John (1786–1847). British explorer. B. in Lincs, he fought at Copenhagen and Trafalgar, took part in expeditions to Australia, the Arctic, and N. Canada, and in 1845 commanded an expedition in search of the N.W. Passage on which he perished. His fate remained a mystery until 1859, when records were discovered by a search party.

FRANKLIN. A district of Northwest Territories, Canada; area 549,253 sq. m.

FRANKS. A Germanic people from whom France derived its name. They overran Belgium and N. France in the 4th–5th cents.; their king, Clovis, accepted Christianity and founded the French monarchy. His successors extended their rule over all France and W. Germany. In France the Fs. and Gallo-Romans became fused in the 9th cent. into a single people speaking a modified form of Latin.

FRASER, Bruce Austin. 1st baron F. of North Cape (1888–). British admiral. Controller of the navy 1939–42, and responsible for its expansion in the S.W.W. and the development of special amphibious vessels, he next became successively C.-in-C. of the Home, British and Eastern Pacific fleets (1943–6), co-operating with the American fleet in the successful conclusion of the Japanese war. He was made a peer in 1946, Adm. of the Fleet in 1948, and was First Sea Lord 1948–51.

FRASER, Peter (1884–1950). New Zealand Labour statesman. B. in Scotland, he joined the I.L.P. in 1908. In 1910 he went to N.Z. and soon became prominent in the Labour movement there. He held various cabinet posts 1935–40, and was P.M. of the Dominion 1940–9.

FRASER. Canadian river, in British Columbia. It rises in the Yellowhead Pass of the Rockies and flows N!W., then S., then W. to the Strait of Georgia. It is 785 m. long and famous for salmon.

FRATERNITIES. Student societies peculiar to U.S. univs. and colls. Usually named with Gk. letters, they are nominally secret, with badge, passwords, motto and initiation rites, some of a degrading nature. They have a central governing body and a 'chapter' at each coll. Although mainly residential, some Fs. are purely honorary, membership being on the basis of scholastic distinction, e.g. Phi Beta Kappa, earliest of the Fs. founded at William and Mary Coll., Va., in 1776. Sororities are the feminine equivalent.

FRAUD. In law, to establish F., three things are essential: (1) The statement must be factually untrue and made with the intent that it should be acted upon; (2) the person making the statement knows it is untrue or remains deliberately careless whether it is true or not; (3) the party to whom the statement is made acts upon it to his detriment. A contract based on F. may be voided by the injured party in addition to his having an action for damages.

FRAUNHOFER (frown′hōfer), **Joseph von** (1787–1826). German physicist. B. in Bavaria, he was apprenticed to a glass cutter, and in 1807 founded an optical institute. The dark lines in the solar spectrum (F. lines), that revealed the chemical composition of the sun's atmosphere, were first accurately mapped by him.

FRAY BENTOS (frah′-ē bān′tos). River port in Uruguay, famous for its meat-packing industry, and particularly for corned beef. Pop. (est.) 10,000.

FRAZER, Sir James George (1854–1941). Scottish

anthropologist. B. at Glasgow, he was ed. at the univ.
and at Cambridge, and in 1890 won acclaim with *The
Golden Bough*. This study of primitive religion and
sociology on a comparative basis was a pioneer work,
still valuable although F.'s attitude was romantic
rather than scientific.

FRÉCHETTE (frehshet'), **Louis Honoré** (1839–
1908). French-Canadian poet. B. in Quebec, he
became a barrister, but owing to his advocacy of
Canadian union with U.S.A. was driven into exile there
until 1871. He sat in the Canadian parliament 1874–8.
His vols. of poetry *Les fleurs boréales* and *Les oiseaux
de neige* were crowned by the French academy in 1880.

FREDERICK I (*c.* 1123–90). Holy Roman Emperor,
known as **Barbarossa** (red-beard). Originally duke of
Swabia, he was elected emperor in 1152, and was
engaged in a struggle with the papacy 1159–77, which
ended in his submission; the Lombard cities, headed
by Milan, took advantage of this to establish their
independence of imperial control. F. joined the 3rd
Crusade, and was drowned in Asia Minor.

FREDERICK II (1194–1250). Holy Roman
Emperor, called 'the Wonder of the World'. Son of
Henry VI, he was elected emperor in 1212. He led a
crusade in 1228–9 which recovered Jerusalem by
treaty without fighting. At the same time he quarrelled with the Pope, and a feud began which lasted
at intervals till the end of his reign. F., who was a
complete sceptic in religion, was perhaps the most
cultured man of his age.

FREDERICK III (1831–88). King of Prussia and
German Emperor. The son of William I, he m.
Princess Victoria, eldest dau. of Queen Victoria, in
1858. In outlook he was a liberal, and frequently
opposed Bismarck's policy. He became emperor in
1888, but d. of cancer 3 months later.

FREDERICK VIII (1843–1912). King of Denmark.
He served in the war with Prussia in 1864, and shared
in the work of government until he succeeded his
father, Christian IX, in 1906. He was the brother of
Queen Alexandra, and the father of Christian X of
Denmark and Haakon VII of Norway.

FREDERICK IX (1899–1972). King of Denmark.
In 1935 he m. Princess Ingrid of Sweden, and suc-
ceeded his father, Christian X, in 1947. His eldest dau.
Queen Margrethe II, who succeeded him, m. 1967
Fr. diplomat Count Henri de Laborde de Montpezat
who took the title H.R.H. Prince Hendrik.

FREDERICK I (1657–1713). King of Prussia. He
became elector of Brandenburg in 1688, and assumed
the title of king of Prussia in 1701.

FREDERICK II, called **the Great** (1712–86). King

FREMANTLE. Most highly mechanized of Australia's ports,
Fremantle was further redeveloping her harbour facilities in
the 1960s, and rapidly expanding her population.
Courtesy of the Agent General for Western Australia.

of Prussia. He received a Spartan education from his
father, Frederick William I, and in 1730 was threatened with death for attempting to run away. Soon
after his accession in 1740 he attacked Austria, and
by the peace of 1745 secured Silesia. The struggle was
renewed in 1756–63, and in spite of assistance from
Britain F. had a hard task to hold his own against
the Austrians and their Russian allies; the skill with
which he did so proved him to be one of the great
soldiers of history. At home he encouraged industry
and agriculture, reformed the judicial system, fostered education, and established religious toleration.

FREDERICK WILLIAM. Name of 4 kings of
Prussia. **Frederick William I** (1688–1740), who succeeded in 1713, largely founded the Prussian army.
Frederick William II (1744–97), king from 1786,
waged war on the French Revolution. **Frederick
William III** (1770–1840), who succeeded him in 1797,
warred with France in 1806 and 1813–15. He permitted the abolition of serfdom and other reforms,
but in his later years persecuted the Liberals. **Frederick
William IV** (1795–1861), king from 1840, was a firm
believer in the divine right of kings; the Prussian
revolution of 1848 occurred during his reign.

FREDERICK WILLIAM (1620–88). Elector of
Brandenburg, called 'the Great Elector'. He succeeded to Brandenburg-Prussia in 1640, and by
successful wars with Sweden and Poland made it
the second state in Germany.

FREDERICK WILLIAM (1882–1951). Last Crown
Prince of Germany, eldest son of Wilhelm II. During
the F.W.W. he commanded a group of armies on
the western front. In 1918 'Little Willie', as he was
called in England, retired into private life.

FREDERICTON. Canadian city, cap. of New
Brunswick prov., on the r. St. John. The University
of New Brunswick, founded 1785, is at F., which is a
lumbering and mining centre. Pop. (1966) 22,460.

FREDRIKSSTAD. Norwegian port at the mouth
of the r. Glommen, dating from 1570, a centre of the
timber trade with shipyards. Pop. (1967) 30,006.

FREE CHURCHES. Those Protestant denomina-
tions in England and Wales, that, unlike the C. of E.,
are not established by the State. The chief are the
Baptist Union, the Congregational Union, the
Methodist Church, and the Presbyterian Church. In
1940 these joined for common action in the Free
Church Federal Council, representing some 7 million
Free Churchmen.

FREE CHURCH OF SCOTLAND. Name given to
the body of Scottish Presbyterians who seceded from
the Established Church of Scotland in 1843. In 1900
all but a small section that retains the old name
combined with the United Presbyterian Church to
form the United Free Church, which reunited with
the Church of Scotland in 1929.

FREEDMAN, **Barnett** (1901–58). British artist. He
produced posters, book illustrations and war studies
as an official Admiralty artist in the S.W.W., but is
chiefly remembered for his revival of lithography.

FREEDOM (**of a city**, etc.). In England the right
of participating in the privileges of a city or borough.
Persons possessing such are known as freemen. Birth,
apprenticeship, and marriage are qualifications and a
borough may admit distinguished persons as honorary
freemen. Before 1835 borough freedom was regulated
by the borough charter, and freemen enjoyed the
parliamentary vote, and a share in the income from
borough property.

FREEDOM, **Presidential Medal of.** Highest
civilian honour conferred in the U.S.A. in peacetime.
Instituted by Kennedy in 1963, it is awarded to those
'who contribute significantly to the quality of American life' and a list of recipients is pub. each Independence Day. It replaced the Medal of Freedom,
instituted 1945, which had been conferred on no
regular basis; only 24 awards had been made.

FREEFALLING. Sport also known as skydiving, which entails falling from an aircraft and then, by a correct positioning of the body, gliding down from anything up to 12,000 ft. until 2,000 ft. – the level at which a parachute must be opened. In 1960 J. W. Kittinger (U.S.A.) estab. a height record of 102,800 ft.

FREE FRENCH. Movement formed by Gen. de Gaulle in England in June 1940, consisting of French soldiers who continued to fight against the Axis after the Franco-German armistice. They took the name Fighting France in 1942 and served in many campaigns, among them Gen. Leclerc's advance from Chad to Tripolitania 1942, the Syrian campaigns 1941, the campaigns in the Western Desert, the Italian campaign, the liberation of France, and the invasion of Germany. Their emblem was the Cross of Lorraine (illus.), which was used by Joan of Arc.

FREEHOLD. An estate in land which is for an indefinite period and is therefore contrasted with a leasehold, which is always for a fixed term of years. In practical effect, a F. is absolute ownership.

FREEMAN, John (1915–). British diplomat. Editor of the *New Statesman* 1961–5, he also estab. a reputation in television interviews. He was High Commissioner in India 1965–8, and Ambassador to Washington 1969–71.

FREEMAN, Richard Austin (1862–1943). British novelist. Himself a doctor, he created a medical detective, Dr. Thorndyke, who appeared in numerous books: the model for his hero was the authority on poisons and medical jurist A. S. Taylor (1806–80).

FREEMASONRY. Linked national organizations open to men over 21, united by the possession of a common code of morals and beliefs, and of certain traditional 'secrets'. Apart from requiring a belief in the 'Great Architect of the Universe' and acceptance of its moral code, English F. maintains strict impartiality in politics and religion. F. is descended from an operative guild of masons which existed in the 14th cent., and by the 16th was admitting men unconnected with the building trade. The name 'freemason' may mean a full member of the guild, or one working in free-stone, i.e. a mason of the highest class. Modern F. originated with the formation of the 1st Grand Lodge, or governing body, in 1717, and during the 18th cent. spread from Britain to America, the colonies, and Europe. In France and other European countries, F. assumed a political and anticlerical character; it has been condemned by the papacy, and in certain countries was suppressed by the State. Both in Britain and the U.S.A. the freemasons maintain hospitals and institutions for their sick or aged members, and schools for their orphans.

FREESIA. Genus of plants of the Iridaceae family. It grows from a corm and produces funnel-shaped flowers in a wide range of colours.

FREETHOUGHT. The intellectual movement which arose in Europe following the Reformation, chiefly in critical opposition to the dogmatic statement of the Christian faith. In Britain it was represented by the Deists in the 17th and 18th cents., who were followed by Carlile, Holyoake, Bradlaugh, Lord Morley, J. B. Bury, Bertrand Russell, and many others. Its propagating organizations are the Rationalist Press Association and the Secular Society, and it found a historian in J. M. Robertson.

FREETOWN. Capital of Sierra Leone, W. Africa. It has an excellent harbour. Pop. (1963) 128,000.

FREE TRADE. International trade free from all tariffs except those levied for revenue purposes only. The case for F.T., first put forward in the 17th cent., received its classic statement in Adam Smith's *Wealth of Nations* (1776). The movement towards F.T. began with Pitt's commercial treaty with France in 1786, and triumphed with the repeal of the Corn Laws (1846). Britain's superiority to all rivals as a manufacturing country in the Victorian age made F.T. to her advantage, but when that superiority was lost the demand for Protection was raised, notably by Joseph Chamberlain. The Ottowa Agreements (q.v.) of 1932 marked the end of F.T. until in 1948 an international treaty, the *General Agreement on Tariffs and Trade* (GATT), came into operation. A drastic series of resultant international tariff reductions was agreed in the Kennedy Round Conference 1964–7, and an International Trade Centre was estab. in 1964 within the GATT organization to help developing countries. *See* also EUROPEAN UNION.

FREE WILL. The metaphysical doctrine that men are endowed with a Will as an independent faculty that enables them to choose between different courses of action. The theological dogma of F.W. states that man was so created by God that he may choose between good and evil. The opposite view is determinism (q.v.), necessitarianism, or predestination.

FREEZING. The change from a liquid to a solid state, as when water becomes ice. For a given substance, F. occurs at a definite temperature, known as the *freezing point*, that is invariable under similar conditions of pressure, and the temperature remains at this point until all the liquid is frozen. The amount of heat per unit mass that has to be removed to freeze a substance is a constant for each particular substance and is known as the latent heat of fusion. Water expands just before freezing point is reached. Ice is lighter than water, therefore: and if pressure is applied the freezing point will be lowered, as expansion is retarded. The presence of dissolved substances in the liquid also lowers the freezing point, the amount of lowering being proportional to the molecular concentration of the solution: 2 practical applications of this principle are seen in anti-freeze mixtures for car radiators and the use of salt to melt icy roads.

FREGE (frā'ge), **Gottlob** (1848–1925). German philosopher. The founder of modern mathematical logic, he pub. in 1884 *The Foundations of Arithmetic* which was to influence Wittgenstein. His work, neglected for a time, has attracted renewed attention in recent years in Britain and the U.S.

FREIBURG-IM-BREISGAU (frī'boorg-im-brīsgow). City in Baden-Württemberg, Germany. It is the seat of an archbishopric and a univ., and manufactures tobacco, paper, etc. Pop. (1966) 156,628.

FRÉJUS. French town in Var dept., the Roman Forum Julii, seat of a bishopric from the 4th cent. It was the scene of a disastrous flood in 1958, due to the bursting of a dam on the Reyran r., in which at least 300 were killed. Pop. (1962) 20,318.

FREMANTLE. Chief port of W. Australia, at the mouth of the Swan r., 12 m. S.W. of Perth. It has boat-building yards, sawmills, iron foundries, etc., and exports wheat and timber. Pop. (1967) 32,680.

FRENCH, Sir John. *See* YPRES, EARL OF.

FRENCH ANTARCTICA. Territory, in full French Southern and Antarctic Territories, created 1955 and consisting of Adélie Land, on the antarctic continent (136° to 142°E. long.), and the Kerguelen and Crozet archipelagos and Saint Paul and Nouvelle Amsterdam islands in the southern seas. It is admin. from Paris, but Port-aux-Français on Kerguelen is the chief centre, with several research stations. There are also research stations on Amsterdam and in Adélie Land, and a meteorological station on Possession Is. in the Crozet archipelago: Saint Paul is uninhabited. Total area 3,900 sq. m.; pop. *c.* 150 research workers.

FRENCH ART. Manet's last important work 'A Bar at the Folies-Bergère' dates from 1882. A performance is in progress and the mirror behind the barmaid reflects her back, her top-hatted customer and the audience.
Courtesy of Courtauld Institute Galleries, London.

FRENCH ART. Prior to the 15th cent. the artistic genius of the French was best expressed in architecture and sculpture. The miniatures of Jean Fouquet and the Limbourgs' *Très riches heures* stand out in the 15th cent. The 16th cent. artists were influenced by the Italians, but the miniature tradition was kept up by the Clouets and Corneille de Lyons. A great sculptor of the age was Jean Goujon. The most famous names of the 17th cent. include Poussin, Claude Lorrain, Philippe de Champaigne, Blanchard, and Bourdon.

In the 18th cent. F.A. became dominant throughout Europe. The great masters were Watteau, Chardin, Fragonard, Lancret, Boucher, and the sculptor Houdon. The neo-Classical school was founded by David. He was followed by Ingres. Delacroix was the leader of the Romantic movement. Géricault excelled as a history and animal painter.

The 19th cent. produced 2 famous schools of painting – the *Barbizon* and the *Impressionist*. The landscape painters of the Barbizon school incl. Millet, Corot, Daubigny, and Theodore Rousseau; the most famous Impressionists were Monet, Manet, Pissarro, Sisley, Degas, and Renoir. More subjective painters were Toulouse-Lautrec and Van Gogh, and it was the latter, with Cézanne and Gauguin, whose fresh approach to the technique of painting prepared the way for many 20th cent. developments. In the 1850s the graphic artists Daumier and Guys did their best work; and other outstanding artists were Courbet, the Douanier Rousseau, Bonnard, the *Pointillist* Seurat, and the sculptor Rodin.

The 20th cent. saw Paris as the home of 2 schools of painting in particular: Fauvism, showing the influence of Gauguin with his emphasis on pure colour, e.g. Matisse, Derain, Vlaminck, Dufy, and Friesz; and Cubism, deriving from Cézanne, and with exponents as diverse as Matisse and Derain, Picasso, Braque, and Juan Gris. Other notable artists are Chagall, the Dadaist Duchamp, the Surrealist Max Ernst, Rouault, Soutine, Utrillo, Modigliani, and Maillol the sculptor.

FRENCH COMMUNITY. Title taken by France and those overseas territories which adhered to it in the referendum held in 1958 on the proposed new constitution of the 5th Republic. *See* Table.

FRENCH GUIANA (gē-ah′nah). French overseas dept. in the N. of S. America, adjoining Surinam. Only *c.* 12 sq. m. is under cultivation, but the forests are rich in timber, gold is mined, and there is commercial shrimp fishing. The capital is Cayenne. Off the coast is Devil's Island (q.v.). Area 34,000 sq. m.; pop. (1961) 33,698 (incl. Inini).

THE FRENCH COMMUNITY

	Area in 1,000 sq. m.	Pop. in 1,000s	Capital
France	213	49,700	Paris
Overseas Depts.			
Guadeloupe	·69	316	Basse-Terre
Guiana	34	34	Cayenne
Martinique	·42	325	Fort-de-France
Réunion	·97	408	Saint-Denis
Overseas Terrs.			
Afars and Issas	8	108	Djibouti
Antarctica	4	—	Port-aux-Français
Comoro Is.	·82	244	Dzaoudzi
New Caledonia	8·55	89	Nouméa
Polynesia	1·52	100	Papeete
Saint-Pierre & Miquelon	·09	5	Saint-Pierre
Wallis & Fortuna Is.	·04	9	Matautu
Condominium			
New Hebrides	5·7	66	Vila
Members			
Equatorial Union			
Central African Rep.	238	2,000	Bangui
Rep. of Chad	496	3,400	Fort Lamy
Rep. of Congo	132	870	Brazzaville
Gabon	103	470	Libreville
Madagascar	228	6,336	Antananarivo
Rep. of Senegal	81	3,500	Dakar
	1,555·8	68,304	

Less formal links are retained in varying degrees with other former French possessions now independent: see *Cameroon, Dahomey, Guinea, Ivory Coast, Mali, Mauritania, Niger, Togo, Upper Volta.* See also *Sudan* and *O.A.U.*

FRENCH GUINEA. *See* Guinea.

FRENCH HISTORY. Before its conquest by Caesar (57–51 B.C.), France, then called Gaul, was occupied by independent tribes, mostly Celtic. During the 5 cents. of Roman rule they accepted Roman civilization and the Latin language. As the empire declined in the 5th cent. Germanic tribes overran the country, until a Frankish chief, Clovis (481–511), brought the other tribes under his rule and accepted Christianity. Under his successors, the Merovingians, the country sank into anarchy, until unity was restored by Pepin (741–68), founder of the Carolingian dynasty. Charlemagne (768–814) made France the centre of a great empire, but under his incompetent successors the great nobles became semi-independent, and the Norsemen invaded France and settled in Normandy. The first kings of the house

FRENCH HISTORY. The return of Louis XVI and his family to Paris in October 1789.

'Richelieu' by Philippe de Champaigne.
Courtesy of the National Gallery.

of Capet, which assumed the crown in 987, ruled only the district round Paris, and were surrounded by vassals stronger than themselves. During the 11th–13th cents. the royal power was gradually extended, with the support of the Church and the townspeople, but progress was later retarded by the 100 Years War (1337–1453). The restoration of the royal power was finally achieved by 1500, through the policies of Louis XI (1461–83) and the annexation of Burgundy and Brittany to the crown.

Charles VIII's Italian wars initiated a struggle with Spain for supremacy in W. Europe which lasted 2 cents. (1503–1697). Protestantism made considerable progress in France, and was adopted by a party of the nobles for political reasons; the result was a succession of civil wars, fought under religious slogans (1562–98). Henry IV (1589–1610) restored peace, established religious toleration, and made the monarchy absolute. His work was continued by the great ministers Richelieu and Mazarin, who by their intervention in the 30 Years War secured Alsace and made France the leading power in Europe. Louis XIV (1643–1715) embarked on an aggressive policy which united Europe against him; in his reign began the conflict with Britain which lost France her colonies in Canada and India. Misgovernment and unsuccessful wars aroused increasing discontent and resulted in the French Revolution (q.v.).

The revolution abolished feudalism and absolute monarchy, but failed to establish democracy. Foreign attempts at intervention led to wars (1792–1802, 1803–15), which gave Napoleon his opportunity to set up his military dictatorship. After Waterloo the Bourbon monarchy was restored. Charles X's attempt in 1830 to substitute absolute for limited monarchy provoked a revolution which placed his cousin, Louis Philippe, on the throne; he in turn was overthrown in 1848, and the 2nd Republic set up. Its president, Louis Napoleon, Napoleon I's nephew, restored the empire in 1852, with the title of Napoleon III. His ambitious foreign policy ended in defeat in the Franco-Prussian War (1870–1) and

the foundation of the 3rd Republic.

The new republic had an uneasy career, and on several occasions conflict between the clerical and militarist right and the Radical and Socialist left threatened civil war. Meanwhile a new colonial empire was being built up in Africa and Indo-China. After 1900 politics were largely dominated by the approach of the F.W.W. The war left France exhausted, and desperately seeking security in a system of E. European alliances. An unsuccessful Fascist coup in 1934 prepared the way for the victory in 1936 of a Radical-Socialist-Communist alliance, which introduced many social reforms; this broke down in 1938, and it was an alliance of the Radicals with the right which declared war on Germany in 1939. The German invasion of 1940 allowed the extreme right to set up a puppet dictatorship under Pétain, but resistance was maintained by the Free French under de Gaulle and the *maquis* until the liberation of 1944. The republic was re-established by a national govt., from which de Gaulle broke away to form a right-wing opposition in 1946–7, and the Communists were ejected in 1947. Open warfare with the Communists in Indo-China (q.v.) ended after 7½ years in the Geneva agreement of 1954, but a series of unstable govts. paved the way for the return to power of de Gaulle in 1958 and the inauguration of the 5th Republic. In 1962 independence was granted to Algeria (q.v.), and from 1963 France was economically strong. De Gaulle abroad offered friendship to W. Germany and E. Europe, condemned Israel and also the U.S. in Vietnam, opposed Britain's Common Market membership, and encouraged French-Canadian nationalism. Gaullists achieved only a bare majority in the 1967 elections, but in reaction to student unrest and mass strikes, achieved in 1968 the largest majority in Fr. republican history. In the new govt. then formed Couve de Murville (q.v.) replaced Pompidou (q.v.) as P.M. Continuing unrest led to a referendum 1969 on an increased degree of regional govt. and reform of the senate, and on the rejection of his proposals De Gaulle himself resigned and was succeeded by Georges Pompidou (q.v.).

FRENCH INDIA. Former French possessions in India consisted of Pondichéry, Chandernagore, Karikal, Mahé, and Yanaon (Yanam). By 1954 they had been transferred to India.

FRENCH LANGUAGE. One of the Romance languages, F. is a development of the Vulgar Latin used for ordinary intercourse in Roman Gaul. Dialects spoken N. of the Loire formed the *langue d'oïl* and to the S. the *langue d'oc*, and by 813, when an assembly of bishops at Tours decided to abandon Latin in their preaching, the tongue spoken in N. Gaul differed sufficiently from Latin for the existence of a F.L. to be affirmed. Modern F. was evolved from Francien, the dialect of the Île de France, which gained supremacy over other northern rivals in the 13th cent. Although the medium of a rich and varied literature, it remained a vulgar tongue until in 1539 the Decree of Villers-Cotterêts enforced F. as the vehicle of administration and justice.

From the beginning of the 17th cent. the F.L. became fixed: the F. Academy (founded in 1635) became its guardian, and Richelet's *Dictionnaire* (1680) stabilized its form and meaning. Developed by the *salons* and by the classical writers, F. became the polite language of Europe. The democratization of France at the Revolution assisted the gradual disappearance of the *patois*, and prepared the way for the rejuvenation of the romantic period.

Today F. is spoken not only in France but in the French Community and by several millions of Swiss, Belgians, and F. Canadians in the U.S.A. as well as in Canada.

FRENCH LITERATURE. The Middle Ages. The *Chanson de Roland* (c. 1080) is the greatest of the early *chansons de geste* which were superseded by the Arthurian romances (seen at their finest in the work of Chrétien de Troyes in the 12th cent.), and by the classical themes of Alexander, Troy, and Thebes. Other aspects of F. medieval L. are represented by the charming *Aucassin et Nicolette*, the allegorical *Roman de la Rose* of Guillaume de Lorris (*c.* 1230) and Jean de Meung (*c.* 1275), and the satiric *Roman de Renart*, the historians Villehardouin, Joinville, Froissart, and Comines, and the 1st great F. poet, François Villon.

Renaissance to the 18th cent. Greatest poet of the Renaissance is Ronsard, leader of the Pléiade, set between Marot who opens the 16th cent. and Régnier

MOLIÈRE

at its close. In prose the period produced the broad genius of Rabelais and the essayist Montaigne. In the 17th cent. came the triumph of form with the great classical dramatists Corneille, Racine, and Molière, and the graceful brilliance of La Fontaine, and the poet-critic Boileau. Masters of prose in the same period include the philosophers Pascal and Descartes; the preacher Bossuet; the critics La Bruyère, Fénelon and Malebranche; and La Rochefoucauld, Cardinal de Retz,

Mme de Sévigné, and Le Sage.

The 18th cent. was the era of prose, with Montesquieu, Voltaire, Rousseau; the scientist Buffon; the encyclopaedist Diderot; Vauvenargues; the novelists Prévost and Marivaux; and the memoir writer Saint-Simon, whose observations greatly illuminated the age.

The 19th and 20th cents. Poetry was reborn with the 'Romantics' Lamartine, Hugo, Vigny, Musset, Leconte de Lisle, and Gautier; novelists of the same school were George Sand, Stendhal and Dumas père, while criticism is represented by Sainte-Beuve, and history by Thierry, Michelet, and Taine. The realist novelist Balzac was followed by the school of Naturalism, whose representatives were Flaubert, Zola, the Goncourt brothers, Alphonse Daudet, Maupassant, and Huysmans. 19th cent. dramatists incl. Hugo, Musset, Dumas fils, and Mirbeau. Symbolism, a movement of experiment and revolt against classical verse and the materialist attitude, with the philosopher Bergson as one of its main exponents, found its first expression in the work of Gérard de Nerval, who was later followed by Baudelaire, Verlaine, Mallarmé, Rimbaud, Corbière, and

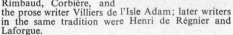

NATHALIE SARRAUTE

the prose writer Villiers de l'Isle Adam; later writers in the same tradition were Henri de Régnier and Laforgue.

In the late 19th and early 20th cents. drama and poetry revived with Valéry, Claudel, and Paul Fort, who advocated 'pure poetry'; other writers were the novelists Gide and Proust, and the critics Thibaudet (1874–1936) and later St. John Perse, also a well-known poet. The Surrealist movement, which developed from 'pure poetry' through the work of Éluard and Apollinaire, influenced writers as diverse as Giraudoux, Louis Aragon, and Cocteau. The in-

evitable literary reaction against the Symbolists incl. Charles Péguy, Rostand, Mme de Noailles, and Romain Rolland. 20th cent. novelists in the Naturalist tradition were Henri Barbusse, Jules Romains, Julian Green, François Mauriac, Francis Carco, and Georges Duhamel. Other prose writers are Maurois, Malraux, Montherlant, Anatole France, Saint-Exupéry, Alain-Fournier, Pierre Hamp, and J. R. Bloch, while the theatre flourished with plays by J. J. Bernard, Anouilh, Beckett, and Ionesco. The S.W.W. had a profound effect on French writing, and distinguished post-war writers incl. the Existentialist Sartre, and Camus, 'Vercors', Simone de Beauvoir, Alain Robbe-Grillet, Romain Gary, Nathalie Sarraute and Marguerite Duras.

FRENCH REVOLUTION. The revolution of 1789–99 which abolished feudalism and absolute monarchy in France. It began with the meeting in 1789 of the States General, later called the National Assembly. An attempt at counter-revolution was frustrated by the storming of the Bastille. The Assembly abolished feudal privileges and drew up a constitution which in 1791 was accepted by Louis XVI. Threats of foreign intervention led to war with Austria and Prussia in 1792. The monarchy was overthrown, the National Convention declared France a republic, and Louis was executed for treason. The democratic party, or Jacobins, estab. the dictatorship of the Committee of Public Safety, headed by Robespierre, and crushed opposition through the Revolutionary Tribunal. In 1794 the right overthrew Robespierre, and set up the Directory, which maintained a middle course between royalism and Jacobinism until Napoleon seized power in 1799.

FRENCH SOMALILAND. *See* SOMALILAND, FR.

FRENCH SUDAN. *See* MALI.

FRENCH WEST AFRICA. Former grouping of French colonies (Senegal, Guinea, Ivory Coast, Upper Volta, Dahomey, Sudan, Mauritania, Niger) administered by a governor-general from Dakar. It broke up following the birth of the Fifth Republic in 1958.

FRENEAU (frenō´), **Philip Morin** (1752–1832). American poet. Earliest outstanding poet of American birth, he was b. in N.Y. His *A Political Litany* (1775) was a mock prayer for deliverance from British tyranny, and he was twice captured by the British in voyages to and from the W. Indies, where some of his best poems were written.

FREQUENCY. The rate of repetition of a cycle; the reciprocal of the period. The unit of F. is the cycle per second (c/s), but in Continental literature it is known as the hertz (symbol Hz). Audio F. is F. within the range audible to the normal human ear; ultrasonic F. is above the audio F. range, and radio F. is any F. at which electromagnetic radiation is used for telecommunications. Radio Fs. are commonly given in thousands of cycles (kilocycles) per second, millions of cycles (megacycles) per second, or thousands of millions of cycles (kilomegacycles) per second. The standard F. for a.c. generation in the U.K. is 50 c/s.

See ELECTROMAGNETIC WAVES.

FRERE (frēr), **John** (1740–1807). British archaeologist. High Sheriff of Suffolk and M.P. for Norwich, he discovered at Hoxne, Suffolk, deposits of palaeolithic tools in 1790. His deduction that these must, from their situation, ante-date the conventional biblical time-scale was very much ahead of his era.

FRESCO (fres´kō). Term applied to a process of painting on plaster walls before the plaster is dry; also applied to the picture or design produced in this way. Some of the earliest frescoes are on the walls of the palace of Knossos in Crete.

FRESNAY, Pierre. Stage-name of French actor Pierre Laudenbach (1897–   ). His films incl. *La Dame aux Camélias, Monsieur Vincent, La Grande Illusion,* and *Les Aristocrates.*

FREUD (froid), **Sigmund** (1856–1939). Originator of psychoanalysis (q.v.). He was b. of Jewish parents in Freiberg, Moravia, and from 1860 lived at Vienna until, following the Nazi occupation in 1938, he migrated to London. He was influenced by Charcot and the researches into hysteria by the Viennese physician, Josef Breuer. With the latter he collaborated in the development of the cathartic method, which employed a hypnotic technique, but he soon abandoned hypnotism and developed the method of free association; this still remains the basic procedure in psychoanalysis. F.'s many books include *The Interpretation of Dreams* (1900), *The Psychopathology of Everyday Life* (1901), *Totem and Taboo* (1913), *The Ego and the Id* (1923), *The Future of an Illusion* (1927), and *Civilization and its Discontents* (1930). His dau. **Anna F.** (1895–   ), a naturalized British citizen, is a psychoanalyst and in 1938 became director of the Hampstead Child Therapy Clinic.

SIGMUND FREUD
Photo: Ernst Freud.

His grandson **Lucian F.** (1922–   ), son of Ernst F., is an artist noted for his portraits and still-lifes.

FREYBERG (frī'-), **Bernard Cyril**, baron (1889–1963). New Zealand soldier. B. in London, he was ed. at Wellington Coll., N.Z., and served in the F.W.W., becoming the youngest brigadier-general in the British Army; he won the V.C. and D.S.O. with 2 bars, and his courage became legendary. During the S.W.W. he commanded the N.Z. expeditionary force, and Allied forces in Crete in 1941, and later fought in the Western Desert and in Italy, receiving a third bar to his D.S.O. He was Gov.-Gen. of N.Z. 1946–52.

FREYTAG (frī'tahg), **Gustav** (1816–95). German writer. B. in Silesia, he was a journalist in Leipzig from 1848, wrote plays, a fine treatise on dramatic technique (1863), and the realistic novels *Soll und Haben* (1855), and *Die verlorene Handschrift* (1864). He also pub. a collection of historical documents, *Bilder aus der deutschen Vergangenheit* (1859–67); and a series of historical novels *Die Ahnen* (1872–80).

FRIAR (Lat. *frater*, Fr. *frère*). Name given to monks of all orders, but originally the title of members of

FRESCO. 'Isaiah' – one of Michelangelo's frescoes for the Sistine Chapel in the Vatican.

the mendicant orders, the chief of which were the Franciscans or Minors (Grey Friars), the Dominicans or Preachers (Black Fs.), the Carmelites (White Fs.), and Austin Friars (Augustinians).

FRIAR'S BALSAM. A compound tincture of benzoin. It is used (1) in boiling water as an inhalant, (2) internally, a few drops swallowed often on a lump of sugar against coughs and colds, and (3) externally to cover abrasions.

FRIBOURG (frēboor'). City in Switzerland, on the r. Sarine, cap. of F. Canton. Pop. (est.) 29,000. The leading products of the canton are cheese, esp. in the Gruyère district, timber, and tobacco. Area 645 sq. m.; pop. (1960) 159,800.

FRICK, Wilhelm (1877–1946). German Nazi leader. A Bavarian, he was among Hitler's earliest followers. As Reich Minister of the Interior (1933) he sponsored legislation against the Jews, the trade unions, and the Press. In 1943 he succeeded von Neurath as 'Protector' of Bohemia-Moravia. Arrested in 1945, he was tried at Nuremberg, found guilty, and hanged.

FRICTION. F. is the force which prevents one body sliding over another, and it occurs in solids, liquids, and gases. The coefficient of F. between 2 solid surfaces is equal to the force required to move one surface over the other, divided by the total force pressing the 2 surfaces together. F. is greatly reduced by the use of lubricants such as oil, grease, and graphite, and air bearings are now used to minimize the F. in high-speed rotational machinery. In other instances F. is deliberately increased by making the surfaces rough, e.g. brake linings, driving belts, soles of shoes, and tyres. F. is also important in problems of fluid flow.

FRIEDRICHSHAFEN (frē'drikshahfen). Town and tourist centre on the N.E. shore of Lake Constance, Baden-Württemberg, S. Germany. Zeppelins were made there. Pop. *c.* 28,000.

FRIENDLY SOCIETY. The F.S. movement arose mainly as an attempt to meet the needs caused by loss of income through sickness. In Great Britain the movement was the successor in this field of the great medieval guilds, but the period of its greatest expansion was in the late 18th and early 19th cents., following the passing in 1797 of the 1st legislation providing for the registration of F.Ss. There are now some 9,000 registered Ss. and their funds total *c.* £300,000,000: among the largest are the National Deposit, Odd Fellows, Foresters, and Hearts of Oak. In the U.S. similar 'fraternal insurance' bodies incl. the Modern Woodmen of America (1883) and the Fraternal Order of Eagles (1898).

FRIENDS, Society of. *See* QUAKERS.

FRIESE-GREENE (frēz-), **William** (1855–1921). British photographer and early experimenter in cinematography. Although his patent of 1890 was upheld in U.S. in 1910, the 1st functional moving-picture camera is generally credited to the French physiologist Marey, in 1888.

FRIESLAND (frēz'-). Province of the Netherlands, bordering the Ijssel Meer. Parts are below sea-level; reclamation of the former Zuyder Zee is adding to its agricultural area. The Frisian breed of cattle is famous. Leeuwarden is the cap. and largest town. Area 1,250 sq. m.; pop. (1966) 506,311

FRIESZ, Othon (1879–1949). French artist. One of the most robust of the Fauves, he was the son of a sea-captain and had an instinct for rich colour and volume in landscapes, still-life, or interpretations of figures, e.g. 'Bathers' and 'Portrait of the poet Fernand Fleuret'.

FRIGATE. Originally a small swift undecked sailing vessel, used in the Mediterranean. The name was first applied to a type of warship in the 18th cent. *See* WARSHIP.

FRINGILLIDAE (frinjil'idē). Family of birds in the order Passeriformes. They are small, hard-billed birds, living in the northern hemisphere, and include the finches, linnets, sparrows, buntings, etc.

FRISCH (frish), **Max** (1913–). Swiss writer. Ed. at Zürich univ. and technical high school, he was first a foreign correspondent and then an architect until 1955, when he had just estab. a reputation with his satirical novel *Stiller* (1954: *I'm not Stiller*). Among his works are the plays *Nun singen sie wieder* (1945), and *Andorra* (1961), and the novel *Homo Faber* (1957).

FRISIANS (fri′zians). Chain of low-lying islands lying 3 to 20 m. off the N.W. and N. coasts of the Netherlands and the N.W. coast of Germany, with a northerly extension off the W. coast of Denmark. They are divided between Germany, the Netherlands, and Denmark.

FRISIANS. A Germanic people who in Roman times occupied the coast of Holland, and may have taken part in the Anglo-Saxon invasions of Britain. Their language was closely akin to Anglo-Saxon, with which it formed the Anglo-Frisian branch of the West Germanic languages. It is almost extinct in the Ger. districts of E. Friesland, has attained some literary importance in the N. Frisian Is. and Schleswig, and developed a considerable literature in the W. Frisian dialect of the Dutch prov. of Friesland.

FRITH, William Powell (1818–1905). British artist. He was especially noted for his large-scale works with numerous accurately observed figures, such as 'Ramsgate Sands', bought by Queen Victoria; and 'Derby Day' in the Tate Gallery.

FRITILLARY. Name of several butterflies in the family Nymphalidae. All the Fs. are orange in colour with black markings, but vary in size, the silver-washed F. (*Argynnis paphia*) being the largest. The Fs. are common in British woodlands.

FRIULI-VENEZIA GIULIA (frē′oolē venet′sēah). Autonomous region of Italy, bordered on the E. by Yugoslavia. Formed in 1947 from the provs. of Udine and Gorizia, to which Trieste was added after its cession to Italy in 1954, it was granted autonomy in 1963. The name Friuli, derived from Forum Juli, a Roman settlement in the area, was long used for the greater part of the two provs. forming the region. Area 3,111 sq. m.; pop. (1961) 1,205,222.

FRO′BISHER, Sir Martin (*c.* 1535–94). English navigator. B. in Yorks, he made his first voyage to Guinea in 1554. In 1576 he set out in search of the N.W. Passage; and visited Labrador, and Frobisher Bay, in Baffin Land. A 2nd and 3rd expedition sailed in 1577 and 1578. F. served as vice-admiral in Drake's W. Indian expedition of 1585, and in 1588 was knighted for his share in the defeat of the Armada. He was mortally wounded in 1594 while attempting to relieve Brest.

FROEBEL (frö′bel), **Friedrich August Wilhelm** (1782–1852). German educationist. B. in Thuringia, he came into contact with Pestalozzi, and evolved a new system of education utilizing instructive play, described in *Education of Man* (1826), etc. In 1836 the first kindergarten was founded, in Blankenburg.

FROG. Amphibian of the family Ranidae with a world-wide distribution, especially abundant in tropical and sub-tropical areas and generally sharing with the toad (q.v.) a lengthy larval period, when the eggs hatch into fish-like 'tadpoles', which gradually lose their gill slits and tail and develop lungs and legs. The common English Grass F. (*Rana temporaria*) is typical of its genus; the body is yellowish-brown, short and stout; the eyes large and prominent; and the fore-limbs short, with only 4 fingers, whereas the hind-legs are long and powerful with 5 webbed toes enabling it to jump and swim rapidly It hibernates in winter, lives in damp places, migrating to water to spawn in the spring, and captures its prey (slugs, insects, etc.) by shooting out the tip of its tongue which carries a viscid secretion. Other species of

interest are the edible F. (*R. esculenta*), of England and Europe, of which only the legs are eaten; the bull-frog of eastern N. America (*R. catesbyana*), about 7 in. long (exclusive of the legs) and with a croak that carries for miles; and the flying Fs. of the Malayan area (*Rhacophorus*) which have completely webbed fore- and hind-feet which serve as 'parachutes'.

FROGBIT. Small water plant (*Hydrocharis*) with submerged roots, floating leaves, and small green and white flowers. It is common in England.

FROG-HOPPERS. Family of small brown insects (*Cercopidae*) in the division Exopterygota, which leap a considerable distance when touched, and live by sucking the juice from plants. The larvae, known as *froth-flies*, are pale green, and surround themselves with a mass of froth.

FROISSART (frwahsahr′), **Jean** (1338–1410). French chronicler. B. at Valenciennes, he became secretary to Queen Philippa, wife of Edward III of England. He travelled in Scotland and Brittany, accompanied the Black Prince to Aquitaine, and in 1368 was in Milan in the company of Chaucer and Petrarch. Later he entered the Church, and d. canon at Chimay. His *Chronique de France, d'Angleterre, d'Écosse, d'Espagne*, etc., records often at first hand the events of the years 1326–1400.

FROME (froom). English town (U.D.) on the river F., Somerset. It is a market centre, and has brewing, printing, and agricultural industries. Pop. (1961) 11,440.

FROMM, Erich (1900–). German-American psychoanalyst and philosopher. B. in Frankfurt, he has written a number of influential books on modern society and its standards incl. *Escape from Freedom* (1941), *The Sane Society* (1955), and *Sigmund Freud's Mission* (1959), in which he finds Freud 'a typical puritan'.

FRONDE. The French civil wars of 1648–53. They fall into 2 stages: the attempt of the Paris *parlement* in 1648–9 to limit the powers of the monarchy, and the revolt of the great nobles, headed by Condé, against the rule of Mazarin in 1650–3.

FRONTENAC ET PALLUAU (froṅtnahk′e pahlü-oh′), **Louis de Buade**, comte de (1620–98). Governor of French Canada. He began his military career in 1635, and was appointed Governor of Canada in 1672. Although efficient he quarrelled with the local

FROG. An American green frog, showing the powerful hind-limbs in action as it leaps. In swimming only these legs, with their webbed feet, are used and the forelegs are held tightly against the body.   *Photo: G. Ronald Austing.*

bishop and his followers and was recalled in 1682. A disastrous war with the Iroquois followed, and F. was reinstated in 1689.

FROST, David (1939–). British broadcaster. From Cambridge, he joined the B.B.C. and achieved celebrity with satiric late-night shows such as 'That Was the Week That Was' and controversial interview programmes, also telecast in U.S.A.

FROST, Robert Lee (1874–1963). American poet. B. in San Francisco, he had no formal ed. until 11, and 1900–12 farmed unsuccessfully in New Hampshire, combining this with teaching and writing poetry. In 1912 he sailed to England where he pub. *A Boy's Will* (1913), and with this and *North of Boston* (1914), estab. his reputation. Returning to the U.S. and to farming in 1915, he won Pulitzer poetry prizes with *New Hampshire* (1923), *Collected Poems* (1930), *A Further Range* (1936), and *A Witness Tree* (1942). He wrote with an American individuality and a simplicity that masked a penetrating vision.

ROBERT FROST

FROST. Condition of the weather when the temperature of the air is below freezing point (32°F.). Water in the atmosphere then freezes and crystallizes on exposed objects. As cold air is heavier than warm, *Ground Fs.* are the more common type. *Hoar F.* is formed by the condensation of water particles in the same way as dew collects.

FROSTBITE. Change produced in tissues by the action of cold, most common in the feet, hands, nose, and ears. The blood supply being cut off, the affected part starts to die (gangrene; necrosis). The treatment is massage with snow or cold water.

FROUDE (frood), **James Anthony** (1818–94). British historian. B. in Devon he was at first strongly influenced by the Oxford Movement, but subsequently became sceptical and was affected by the teaching of Carlyle. His *History of England from the Fall of Wolsey to the Defeat of the Spanish Armada* (1856–70) revealed his gift for dramatic realization of historic events. As Carlyle's literary executor he pub. his *Reminiscences* (1881) and the *Letters and Memorials of Jane Welsh Carlyle* (1883). He was prof. of modern history at Oxford 1892–4. His brother, **Richard Hurrell F.** (1803–36), collaborated with Newman in the Oxford Movement.

FRUCTOSE or **Fruit Sugar** ($C_6H_{12}O_6$). A sugar occurring with glucose in honey and cane sugar, and in grape juice, etc. It is somewhat sweeter than cane sugar, from which it is prepared on a large scale.

FRUIT FLY. A small yellow fly (*Drosophila melanogaster*) which breeds in fermenting fruit juices. Because of its rapid reproduction and simple structure – it has 8 chromosomes – it has been of great use to geneticists in the study of heredity.

FRUNZE (froon'ze). Capital (formerly Pishpek) of Kirgiz S.S.R., U.S.S.R., and F. region, situated in the fertile Chu valley. Its industries include the making of textiles, metal goods, and leather, and food preserving. A univ. was estab. in 1951. Pop. (1967) 396,000.

FRY, Christopher (1907–   ). British dramatist. Originally a teacher, he became by 1940 director of the Oxford Repertory Players, and after the S.W.W. was a leader of the revival of verse drama, notably *The Lady's Not for Burning* (1948), *Venus Observed* (1950), and *A Sleep of Prisoners* (1951). He has also translated plays by Anouilh and Giraudoux.

FRY, Elizabeth (1780–1845). British philanthropist. B. at Norwich, *née* Gurney, she joined the Society of Friends in 1798, and in 1800 m. **Joseph F.**, a London merchant. In 1810 she became a minister in the society. She first visited Newgate prison in 1813, and formed an association for the improvement of female prisoners in 1817. In 1818 she inspected the prisons of northern England and Scotland with her brother, **Joseph Gurney**, and their report pub. 1819

had great influence both at home and abroad. She subsequently travelled widely on the Continent. Her descendant, **Margery F.** (1874–1958), was a leading authority on penal reform and on social questions affecting women. She was principal of Somerville Coll., Oxford, 1926–31.

FRY, Roger Elliott (1866–1934). British painter and art critic. B. in London, he was chiefly responsible for introducing the French post-impressionist painters to England. His own paintings show a fine sense of design and mastery of technique. He was Slade prof. of Art at Cambridge from 1933.

FUAD I (foo'ahd) (1868–1936). King of Egypt. The son of the Khedive Ismail, he succeeded his elder brother, Hussein Kiamil, as sultan of Egypt in 1917, and when Egypt was declared independent in 1922 he assumed the title of king. **Fuad II** (1952–   ), grandson of Fuad I, was king of Egypt 1952–3 between the abdication of his father Farouk (q.v.) and the establishment of the republic.

FUCHS, Karl Emil Julius. *See under* SECRET SERVICE.

FUCHS (fookhs), **Sir Vivian** (1908–   ). British explorer. Before the S.W.W. he accompanied several Cambridge expeditions as geologist, exploring in Greenland and Africa as well as Antarctica, led the Falkland Islands Dependencies Survey from 1947–50, and was appointed director of the Scientific Bureau there in 1950. In 1957–8 he led the Commonwealth Trans-Antarctic Expedition and was knighted on his return. *See* ANTARCTICA.

FUCHSIA (fū'shia). Genus of exotic plants of the Onagraceae family, composed of a number of small shrubs native to S. America but frequently cultivated in Britain. The genus was named in 1703 after Leonhard Fuchs, German botanist (1501–66). The red, purple, or pink flowers hang downwards, and are bell-shaped.

FUEHRER (fü'rer), **Der.** German for 'the leader'; the name given to Adolf Hitler (q.v.) by his followers.

FUEL. Any source of heat or energy embracing the entire range of all combustibles and including anything which burns, i.e. nuclear Fs.

FUJIYAMA (fooji-yah'mah). Volcano on Honshu island, Japan, 60 m. W.S.W. of Tokyo; it rises in a snow-capped cone to 12,390 ft., and has a prominent place in Japanese art. A weather station was estab. on the summit in 1932.

FUKIEN (fookyen'). Province of S.E. China, bordering the Formosa strait, opposite the island of Formosa. Tea is the leading crop on the higher land, rice on the lowlands; timber, camphor, lacquer are also produced. The cap. is Foochow. Area 47,000 sq. m.; pop. (1968) 17,000,000.

FUJIYAMA. In Japan some 85 per cent of the country's total area is mountainous, and arable land is scarce. The average size of farms is less than 2½ acres and even steep slopes are cultivated so that Fujiyama itself, the country's highest mountain, overlooks terraces which resemble a giant staircase.
Courtesy of the Japanese Embassy.

FUKUOKA. Japanese industrial town and port on the N.W. coast of Kyushu island. Pop. (1965) 647,000.

FULBRIGHT, William (1905–). American politician. A Rhodes Scholar, he lectured in law at the Univ. of Arkansas 1936–9, and as a senator from 1945 was responsible for the *F. Act* (1946) which enabled thousands of Americans to study overseas and overseas students to enter the U.S. Chairman of the Foreign Relations Committee from 1959, he is a strong internationalist and supporter of the U.N.

FULHAM. *See* LONDON.

FULLER, Richard Buckminster (1895–). American architect. Charles Eliot Norton professor of poetry at Harvard 1961–2, he is the great exponent of the geodesic dome, e.g. the 277 ft. dome for the H.Q. of the American Soc. of Metals in Cleveland and the St. Louis climatron (q.v.).

FULLER, Roy (1912–). British poet and novelist. A London solicitor, he pub. his first *Poems* (1939), and in 1968 became prof. of poetry at Oxford. Later vols. incl. *Epitaphs and Occasions* (1951), *Brutus's Orchard* (1957) and *Collected Poems* (1962); and the novel *My Child, My Sister* (1965).

FULLER, Thomas (1608–61). English author. Rector at Broadwindsor, Dorset, from 1634, he served as a chaplain to the Royalist army, and at the Restoration became the king's chaplain. He is known for his *Worthies of England* (1662).

FULMAR (fool'-). Name given to several species of petrels of the family Procellariidae, which are similar in size and colour to the common gull. The F. (*Fulmarus glacialis*) is found in the N. Atlantic and visits land only to deposit its single egg. The giant Pacific F. (*Macronectes gigantea*) has a wingspan of 7 ft.

FULMAR

FU′LMINATES. The salts of fulminic acid (C:NOH), the chief being silver and mercury. They detonate, i.e. are exploded by a blow.

FULTON, Robert (1765–1815). American engineer and inventor. B. in Pennsylvania, he went to England in 1787 where he devoted himself to engineering in connection with inland navigation. In 1797 he moved to Paris where he produced a submarine, the *Nautilus*. After experimenting in steam navigation on the Seine in 1803, he returned to America and the first steam vessel of note, the *Clermont*, appeared on the Hudson in 1807, sailing between New York and Albany. The first steam warship was the *Fulton* of 38 tons, made in 1814–15.

FU′MITORY. Genus (*Fumaria*) of the plant family Fumariaceae, native to Europe and Asia. The common F. grows abundantly as a weed in Britain, and produces red or white flowers.

FUNCHAL (foońshahl′). Port, cap. of Madeira Is., overseas district of Portugal. It is on the S. side of Madeira, on a harbour capable of accommodating ocean-going ships. F. is popular as a holiday and health resort. Pop. (1967) 43,300.

FUNCHAL. Another name for MADEIRA.

FUNCTIONALISM. Term applied to a style of architecture and furniture characterized by a tendency to exclude everything that serves no practical purpose. It was a reaction against the 19th cent. practice of imitating earlier styles, and its finest achievements are in the realm of industrial building. Its leading exponents were the German Bauhaus school, and the Dutch group de Stijl; the most prominent architects in the field are Le Corbusier and Walter Gropius (qq.v.).

FUNDAMENTALISM. Name given to a religious movement which arose in U.S.A. just after the F.W.W.

and was characterized by insistence on complete belief in the literal inspiration of the Bible and such doctrines as the Virgin Birth, the physical resurrection of Christ, the Atonement, and the Bible miracles which were regarded as fundamental to the Christian faith. In 1925 F. was publicized by the 'Dayton Trial'. *See* DAYTON.

FÜNEN. German form of FYN.

FÜNFKIRCHEN (five churches). German name of PÉCS.

FUNGI. Wild ungi: left to right; common mushroom, shaggy cap, parasol mushroom, morel.

FUNGI (fun′ji). In botany, class of plants forming with the algae the Thallophyta. Unlike the algae they have no chlorophyll, and hence must get their food from organic substances. They are either parasites, living on living plants or animals, or saprophytes living on dead matter. F. include bacteria, the slime fungi, moulds, mildew, rusts and smuts, mushrooms, toadstools, puff-balls, etc. F. reproduce by means of spores. Some fungi are edible, but many are highly poisonous.

FUR. Animal skin bearing handsome hair worn for warmth: also, in the case of rarer species, regarded as a luxury, e.g. in ancient China, Greece and Rome,

FUNGI. The cultivation of mushrooms has reached the status of an industry, and grown in well-ventilated, steam-heated sheds, they give an all-year-round crop. There is no wasted space – other trays equally crowded are on the racks beneath these, where the fungi are ripe for gathering.
Courtesy of the Mushroom Information Bureau.

and as a status symbol in medieval Europe and, especially for women, in modern times. The modern F. trade originated with the exploitation of N. America from the late 17th cent. by the Hudson's Bay Co., etc.: the principal distributing centres are London, New York, and Leningrad. Mink (q.v.) is hard-wearing and long-lasting and has long been the most popular of the high-priced Fs., and lends itself to ranch breeding – more humane than trapping – but chinchilla and Russian sable are even more valuable. In the 1960s there was a trend in fashion towards longer-haired and colourful Fs. with deleterious effect on wild-life, e.g. the leopard. Artificial F. fabrics formerly offered little competition, but

FURNITURE. In the Middle Ages domestic furniture was frequently painted in bright colours, and the oak cupboard illustrated which is dated *c.* 1500 would have been decorated with sacred or heraldic subjects, long since worn away.

since the S.W.W. there has been increasingly successful use of synthetic fibres such as nylon.

FŪ'RIES. In Greek mythology, the Erinyes or Eumenides, the daughters of Earth or of Night, represented as winged maidens with serpents twined in their hair. They punished such crimes as filial disobedience, murder, and inhospitality.

FURLONG. A measure of length – 220 yds. or 40 rods, poles, or perches. 8 Fs. make one statute mile. Originally it was the length of the furrow in the common field characteristic of medieval husbandry.

FURNESS. Peninsula and district comprising the northerly detached portion of Lancashire, England, separated from the main part of the co. by Morecambe Bay. Barrow has iron and shipbuilding industries. F. abbey, now in ruins, was founded in 1127.

FURNITURE. Term that includes everything movable that is needed in buildings for human habitation and work. It includes those forms of F. which are used for (1) rest, e.g. chairs, couches, and beds; (2) work, e.g. desks and tables; (3) storage, e.g. chests and cupboards; and (4) decoration, e.g. picture frames. F. is made of a variety of materials incl. wood, metal, stone, glass, plastic, and textiles.

FURNITURE BEETLE. See WOODWORM.

FURSE, Roger (1903–). British stage designer. He designed the settings and costumes of many plays, incl. Old Vic productions of Shakespeare.

FURNITURE. Top of a marquetry table of the last years of Charles II: the flowers, of various woods, are inlaid on ebony.

FŪ'RTSEVA, Ekaterina (1910–). Russian politician. The only woman member of the presidium of the Communist Party of the Soviet Union, she became in 1960 Min. of Culture, and encouraged fuller international co-operation in this field.

FURTWÄNGLER (foort'vengler), **Wilhelm** (1886–1954). German conductor. He succeeded Nikisch at Leipzig, and with the Berlin Philharmonic Orchestra. His interpretations of Tchaikovsky and the German romantics, especially Wagner, were regarded as classically definitive. A denazification tribunal cleared him of the charge of having favoured the Hitler régime.

FUSAN. Transliteration of Japanese form of PUSAN.

FUSELI (fūz'eli) **Henry Johann Heinrich** (1741–1825). Swiss-born British artist whose work, influenced by Blake, had a fanciful macabre quality which later endeared him to the Surrealists.

FUSEL OIL ($C_5H_{12}O$), also called potato spirit. A liquid with a characteristic unpleasant smell, obtained as a by-product when distilling the product of any alcoholic fermentation, and used in paints, varnishes, essential oils, and plastics.

FUSHUN (foo-shoon). Great coal-mining centre in Liaoning prov., China, 25 m. E. of Shenyang. It has aluminium, steel, and chemical works. Pop. (1967) 1,000,000.

FUSIN (foo-sin). Industrial town in Liaoning prov., China, 95 m. N.W. of Shenyang. Pop. (1967) 500,000.

FUSION, Nuclear. See ATOMIC ENERGY.

FUST (foost), **Johann** (*c.* 1400–66). German printer and bookseller of Mainz. His partnership with Gutenberg (q.v.) ended in 1455. F. sued Gutenberg for debt, and with aid of his son-in-law, Peter Schöffer, carried on the business. He is supposed to have d. in Paris of the plague. He was often wrongly confused with the magician Johann Faust (q.v.).

FUTURISM. Literary and artistic movement which burst on Paris in 1909 with a general manifesto by F. P. Marinetti, Italian poet and mountebank, extolling 'a new beauty . . . a roaring motor-car, which

FURNITURE. Hepplewhite chair in painted satinwood with his favoured motif, the Prince of Wales feathers, forming the entire splat.

runs like a machine gun, is more beautiful than the Winged Victory of Samothrace . . . we wish to glorify war'. Together he and Carrà, Boccioni and

FURNITURE. Oak bed dated *c.* 1568 from Sizergh Hall Westmorland. With its inlays of various woods and the elaborate figures and panels of the back, it illustrates the importance attached to this article of furnishing by our ancestors.

FURNITURE. A walnut baby trotter of *c.* 1700: the upper ring opens to admit the child.

Russolo issued further manifestos praising the dynamism of modern life. These artists differed from Cubists in fragmenting their forms with penetrating shafts of light, which, together with their use of colour, infused a feeling of dynamic motion into their work. F. flourished until the advent of the F.W.W.

FYEN. Another form of FYN.

FYFE, David Maxwell. *See* LORD KILMUIR.

FYFFE, Will (1885–1947). Scots comedian. He began acting with his father's stock company but by 1921 had achieved great success on the halls, with his vividly portrayed character sketches. His greatest hit was the song 'I Belong to Glasgow'.

FYN (fin). Island forming part of Denmark; it lies between the mainland and Zealand. The cap. s Odense. Area 1,130 sq. m.; pop. (1967) 408,000.

FYZABAD. Another form of FAIZABAD.

G The 7th letter of our alphabet. It was formed by the Romans by adding a 'tail' to the letter C which represented the K sound.

GABÈS (gah'bes). Town and port on the Gulf of G., Tunisia, N. Africa, 70 m. S.W. of Sfax, standing on the site of the Roman town of Tacapae. G.'s chief product is dates. Pop. (1966) 76,356.

GABIN (gahbań'), **Jean.** Stage-name of French actor Jean Moncorgé (1904–   ), noted for the realism of his performances in such films as *Pépé le Moko* (1937), *Le Quai de Brumes* (1938), and *Le Jour se lève* (1939).

GABLE, Clark (1901–60). American actor. A star for more than 30 years in 90 films; he was celebrated for his romantic nonchalance and tough-with-women roles, e.g. as Rhett Butler in *Gone with the Wind*.

GABLONZ. German form of JABLONEC.

GABO, Nahum (1890–   ). Russian sculptor. One of the leading exponents of Constructivism, he left Russia in 1923 and settled first in London, in U.S.A. from 1946. In his sculpture he has made use of modern synthetic materials.

GABON (gahbōōn'). Republic on the Atlantic coast of Africa, S. of Cameroon. Formerly a French territory, it remained within the French Community on attaining independence in 1960. It has a broad coastal plain, rising to a hilly interior; the equator passes through it. Cocoa, coffee and timber are produced and minerals incl. manganese, uranium, oil and natural gas, and gold. The cap. and chief port is Libreville. Area 103,000 sq. m.; pop. (1965) 470,000.

GABOON, GABUN. Alternative forms of GABON.

GABOR (gah'bor), **Dennis** (1900–   ). Hungarian-British physicist. Ed. in Budapest and Berlin, he was engaged in industrial research in England 1934–48, when he became reader (1949) then prof. (1958–67) of applied electron physics at the Imperial College of Science and Technology. In 1958 he invented a type of colour TV tube, distinguished by its reduced depth, and simpler but more effective design. He was elected F.R.S. in 1956.

GABORIAU (gahbōrē-ō'), **Emile** (1835–73). French novelist. He found fame with *L'Affaire Lerouge* (1866), first of a detective series; he created the detective M. Lecoq.

GABRIEL. An archangel who is mentioned in the book of Daniel, and in the N.T. announces the birth of John the Baptist to Zacharias and of Christ to the Virgin Mary.

GADDI (gah'dē). Name of three Florentine religious painters, viz. **Gaddo G.** (*c.* 1260–1333), and his son **Taddeo G.** (1300–66) and grandson **Agnoli G.** (*c.* 1333–96).

GADE (gah'dheh), **Niels** (1817–90). Danish violinist and composer. He succeeded Mendelssohn as conductor at Leipzig and his most popular work is the overture *Echoes from Ossian*.

GADIDAE (gad'idē). Family of fish found in the northern hemisphere, incl. haddock, cod, and turbot.

GAELIC (gā'lik). One of the two main branches of the Celtic languages (q.v.), comprising Irish Gaelic, Scottish Gaelic, and Manx (qq.v.).

GAETA (gah-ā'tah). Italian seaport on the Gulf of G., 73 m. S.E. of Rome. The cathedral was consecrated in 1106. Pop. (1960) 20,000.

GAGA'RIN, Yuri (1934–68). Russian cosmonaut. B. in Smolensk Region, son of a collective farmer, he qualified as a foundryman. He became a pilot 1957, and joined the Communist Party in 1960. On 12 April 1961 he successfully completed the first manned space flight, orbiting the Earth at 18,000 m.p.h. He was killed on a routine training flight.

YURI GAGARIN

GAINSBOROUGH, Thomas (1727–88). British artist. B. at Sudbury, Suffolk, he began to paint while still at school, and in 1741 went to London where he learnt etching and studied at the Academy of Arts, but remained largely self-taught. In 1759 he settled at Bath, becoming famous as a painter of high society – his portraits of Sir Charles Holte, Garrick, and the 'Blue Boy' belong to this period. In 1768 he became one of the original members of the Royal Academy, and in 1774 went to London where his sitters incl. the royal family, Mrs. Siddons, Dr. Johnson, Burke, and Sheridan. His portraits are noted for their clear tones, graceful lines and a naturalistic approach, generally free from classical influence. In landscape, which he preferred to the portraiture which earned his living, he followed the Dutch as one of the first English artists to substitute real scenery for imaginary Italian.

GAINSBOROUGH. English town (U.D.) and canal trade centre on the r. Trent, Lindsey, Lincs. Agricultural implements are manufactured. Pop. (1961) 17,276.

THOMAS GAINSBOROUGH, after a self-portrait.
Photo: N.P.G.

GAITSKELL (gāt'skel), **Hugh Todd Naylor** (1906–63). British Labour statesman. Ed. at Oxford, he became head of the dept. of Political Economy at Univ. Coll., London, in 1938. In 1945 he was elected M.P. for S. Leeds, and was Min. of Fuel and Power 1947–50, when he succeeded Cripps, 1st as Min. of Economic Affairs and then as Chancellor of the Exchequer until Oct. 1951. When the 'Bevanite' controversy arose within the Labour Party, he took

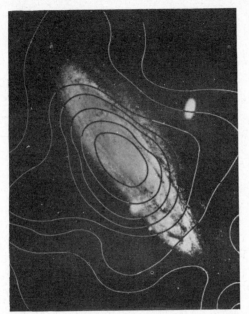

GALAXY. The radio corona of the Great Nebula in Andromeda (M 31), a galaxy similar to our own in its spiral structure and 2 million light-years distant, extends far beyond the visible nebula. The superimposed radio image shows some of the radio isophotes – contour lines along which radiation strength or radio brightness is everywhere equal – obtained by a survey using the Jodrell Bank 250 ft. reflector at a wavelength of 73 cm. The radiation is thought to be by cosmic ray electrons spiralling in magnetic fields.
Photograph by Mt. Wilson & Palomar Observatories.
Radio image by Jodrell Bank Observatory

the official line, and had a resounding victory over Bevan when elected party leader in 1955. His attempt in 1959 to modify party policy on nationalization and the split in 1960 between advocates of unilateral disarmament and the official multilateralist line threatened his position, but he was re-elected in 1960 and at his death had achieved undisputed authority. His wife, (Anna) Dora G., also keenly interested in politics, was created a life peer as baroness G. in 1964.

GALAPAGOS ISLANDS. Group of 13 large and many smaller islands in the Pacific Ocean, 695 m. W. of Ecuador, of which they form a prov. The cap. is San Cristobal, on San Cristobal Island. There are sulphur deposits. Area *c.* 3,000 sq. m.; pop. (1967) 3,100.

GALASHIELS (galashēlz'). Scottish town (burgh) in Selkirkshire, on Gala Water; famous for its tweeds. Pop. (1961) 12,374.

GALATEA (galatē'a). In Greek mythology, a sea nymph who loved Acis, and when he was killed by Polyphemus transformed his blood into the river Acis. Pygmalion made a statue (later named G.) which was brought to life by Aphrodite.

GALATI (galats'). Rumanian city on the Danube below its confluence with the Seret, cap. of G. region, an important river port with shipyards. Industries incl. iron and steel, notably the Gheorghe Gheorghiu-Dej works (1965), textiles, sweets and foodstuffs, perfumes and cosmetics. Pop. (1966) 151,349.

GALATIA. Ancient prov. of Asia Minor, occupying part of the inland plateau. It was occupied by the Gauls in the 3rd cent. B.C., and in 25 B.C. became a Roman province.

GALAXY. The star system in which the Solar System lies. It contains about 100,000 million stars, of which the sun is fairly typical, and also a vast quantity of interstellar matter, together with the concentrations of gas and dust known as *galactic nebulae.* The stars in our G. are arranged in the form of a double-convex lens, with a pronounced nucleus: the total distance from one side of the G. to the other is about 100,000 light-years.

Other Gs. are very remote from us, the Andromeda Spiral, one of the nearest, lies at a distance of over 2,000,000 light-years; only this and the 2 southern Nubeculae or Magellanic Clouds are visible to the naked eye, but the Palomar 200 in. telescope can photograph about 1,000 million separate Gs. They are of various types: spiral (radioastronomy investigations have estab. that our own has this structure), elliptical, and irregular. They tend to form groups and our own G. is a member of the so-called 'Local Group', of which other members are the Andromeda and Triangulum Spirals, the Nubeculae, and various dwarf Gs. such as the Sculptor System. Apart from the members of the Local Group, all the Gs. are receding from us at tremendous speeds: the most remote systems so far measured, 3C-295 in Boötes, is about 5,000 million light-years away, and is receding at almost 90,000 miles per second.

GALAZ. German form of GALATI.

GALEN (gā'len) (*c.* 130–*c.* 200). Greek physician. B. at Pergamum, Mysia, Asia Minor, he was accounted second only to Hippocrates among the physicians of antiquity. He was skilled in anatomy and physiology. Some 80 of his 500 treatises have survived.

GALICIA (galish'ia). Former kingdom and prov. of N.W. Spain, divided in 1833 into the provs. of Corunna, Lugo, Orense, and Pontevedra. Galicia was also the name of a prov. of central Europe, formerly a part of Austria, part of Poland after the F.W.W., divided 1945 between Poland and Russia. It occupied the northern slopes of the Carpathians, stretching southwards to the frontiers of Czechoslovakia and Rumania.

GALILEE (gal'ilē). A Roman prov. of Palestine, bounded by Samaria on the S., Phoenicia on the W., Coele Syria on the N., the r. Jordan on the E. The SEA OF GALILEE, a lake in the Jordan valley, lies 65 m. N. of the Dead Sea, and is frequently mentioned in the Gospels.

GALILEO (galēlā'ō) **Galilei** (1564–1642). Italian scientist. B. at Pisa, he studied at the univ. there, and was prof. of mathematics. An opponent's demonstration – by dropping 2 stones of unequal weight from the top of the Leaning Tower – confirmed his view that all falling bodies, great or small, descend with equal velocity, making him unpopular with the orthodox scientists, and he resigned his chair in 1591. From 1592 to 1610 he was prof. of mathematics at Padua. He improved the recently invented telescope, and with it was the first man to see satellites of Jupiter. His astronomical observations led him to accept the Copernican system, which he advocated in his *Dialogues on the two chief systems of the Universe,* pub. in 1632. The book was banned, and G. was summoned to Rome by the Inquisition, and eventually made to recant his views.

GALL (gahl), **Franz Joseph.** See PHRENOLOGY.

GALLAS. Race of Hamitic people inhabiting a large area of E. Africa in Abyssinia and Kenya.

GALLE (gahl'leh), **Johann Gottfried** (1812–1910). German astronomer, who in 1846 discovered the planet Neptune.

GALL FLY. Small hymenopterous insects of the family Cynipidae. They are similar in appearance to wasps and lay their eggs in leaves, twigs, or roots of plants causing galls, i.e. swellings of various kinds.

GALLICO, Paul William (1897–   ). American author. Of Italo-Austrian parentage, G. was b. in

PAUL GALLICO
Courtesy of Heinemann Publishers Ltd.

New York. Formerly a leading American sports columnist, he began writing fiction in 1936, and his books incl. *The Small Miracle* (1952), *The Snow Goose* (1941), and *Flowers for Mrs. Harris* (1958).

GALLI-CURCI (gahl′lē-koor′chē), **Amelita** (1889–1963). Italo-American coloratura soprano. Her superb technique allowed her voice to reach astonishing heights with a smooth, warm, and well-rounded tone, but her uncertain pitch made her records more effective than her concerts. She made her début in Rome (1909) as Gilda in *Rigoletto*, and from 1916 sang in U.S.A.

GALLIFO′RMES. The order of birds that includes the game birds.

GALLI′POLI. City and port in European Turkey, on the W. shore of the Dardanelles, giving its name to the peninsula on which it stands. In the F.W.W. an unsuccessful campaign was undertaken, from Feb. 1915 to Jan. 1916, first naval and then military with British Empire and French troops under Sir Ian Hamilton, to force these narrows and thus open up communication with Russia.

GALLIUM. Chemical element. Symbol Ga; at. wt. 69·72; at. no. 31. A grey metal liquid at near room temperatures, it is very scarce and was discovered in 1875 by Lecoq de Boisbaudtan.

GÄLLIVARE (galēvah′re). Iron-mining centre in a sparsely populated part of Swedish Lapland, 40 m. N. of the Arctic Circle. Pop. *c.* 3,300.

GALLON. A British liquid and dry measure. Its capacity is 4 quarts or 8 pints or 277·274 cu. in., and 2 gallons make a peck.

GALLOWAY (gal′ō-). An ancient district of S.W. Scotland comprising Wigtown and Kircudbright cos. noted for its horses and black, hornless cattle.

GALLS. On plants, vegetative growths caused by the presence of insects of the Cynipidae (gall fly, q.v.) family, which lay their eggs on the plant. An irritation is set up, and a swelling arises. The grubs live within the swelling. Among the commonest Gs. are bedeguar (on roses) and oak apples.

GALLSTONE. Biliary calculus; a hard, insoluble, pebble-like accretion formed in the human gall-bladder or bile duct by the precipitation of salts, chiefly cholesterol, from relatively stagnant bile. The size varies from a grain of sand to a walnut.

GALLUP, George Horace (1901–   ). American journalist and statistician, founder in 1935 of the American Institute of Public Opinion and deviser of the *G. Polls*, in which public opinion is gauged by questioning a number of representative individuals.

Bronze bust by David Evans, 1929. *Photo: N.P.G.*

GALSWORTHY (gawlz′-), **John** (1867–1933). British novelist and dramatist. B. at Kingston, Surrey, he pub. several novels and vols. of short stories before achieving success with *The Man of Property* (1906), the first instalment of *The Forsyte Saga* (1922), which included *In Chancery* and *To Let.* Soames Forsyte is the embodiment of the Victorian feeling for property, and the wife whom he also owns – Irene – was based on G.'s wife. Later additions to

GALWAY. Spanish arch, which has only its appearance to justify the name, used to be called 'the Arch Blind in One Eye' because one of its passageways was blocked. Built with the fort near the quay in 1590–1643, the *Canabhalla* once formed part of the town walls.
Courtesy of the Irish Tourist Board.

the series are *A Modern Comedy* (1929), which contained *The White Monkey*, *The Silver Spoon*, and *Swan Song*, and the short stories *On Forsyte Change* (1930). Among G.'s novels outside the Forsyte group are *The Country House* (1907), *Fraternity* (1909), *The Patrician* (1911), and *The Dark Flower* (1913). In 1906 G. also estab. himself as a dramatist with *The Silver Box*: later plays include *Strife* (1909), *Justice* (1910), *The Skin Game* (1920), *Loyalties* (1922), and *Old English* (1924). In all his work G. was deeply concerned with social conditions, and tackled problems such as the conflicts between employers and workmen, landed gentry and the manufacturers, and the prison system. He received the O.M. in 1929. His collected poems were pub. in 1934.

GALT, John (1779–1839). Scottish novelist. B. n Ayrshire, he moved to London in 1804 and 1826–9 was in Canada. He is best known for the *Annals of the Parish* (1821) in which he portrays the life of a Lowlands village, using local dialect.

GALTON, Sir Francis (1822–1911). British anthropologist. B. at Birmingham, he studied medicine, explored in Africa, made pioneer researches in meteorology, and then, under the influence of his cousin Charles Darwin, studied heredity. He wrote *Hereditary Genius* (1869), *Natural Inheritance* (1889), etc., and endowed a chair of Eugenics, a study he founded, at London. He was knighted in 1909.

GALVANI (gahlvah′nē), **Luigi** (1737–98). Italian scientist. B. at Bologna, where he taught anatomy, he discovered galvanic or voltaic electricity in 1762, when investigating the contractions produced in the muscles of dead frogs by contact with charged metal.

GALVANIZING. Process for rendering iron rust-proof, by plunging it into molten zinc (the dipping method), or by electro-deposition, in which zinc is electro-plated from aqueous solution.

GALVANOMETER. Instrument for indicating small electric current by means of its magnetic effect. There are many different types. The two main classes are (1) moving-magnet Gs. in which a small magnet is suspended at the centre of a coil of wire through which the current to be measured is passed and the resulting deflection of the magnet noted, and (2) moving-coil Gs. in which a small coil carrying a current to be measured is suspended between the poles of a permanent magnet and the deflection of the coil noted.

GALVESTON. City and port in Texas, U.S.A., at the entrance to G. Bay. It exports cotton, petroleum, wheat, timber; has dry docks, petroleum refineries, etc. It is subject to hurricanes, one in 1900 killing 8,000 people. Pop. (1960) 67,175.

GALWAY (gawl'wā). County of Rep. of Ireland on the W. coast, in Connacht. The E. part is low-lying. In the S. are the Slieve Aughty mts. W. of Lough Corrib is Connemara, a wild area of moors, hills, lakes, and bogs. In the S. is G. Bay with the Aran islands. The Shannon is the principal river. G. is the county town; other towns include Ballinasloe, Tuam, Clifden, and Loughrea, near which deposits of lead, zinc and copper were found 1959. Area 2,293 sq. m.; pop. (1966) 148,340.

GALWAY. Co. town and fishing port of G. co., Rep. of Ireland, on G. Bay, at the mouth of the Corrib. The Univ. Coll. became in 1968 the Univ. of Galway. Pop. (1966) 24,597.

GAMA (gah'mah), **Vasco da** (c. 1460–1524). Portuguese navigator. B. at Sines, he was chosen by Emanuel I to command an expedition sent in 1497 to discover the Cape route to India. The land he touched on Christmas Day, 1497, he named Natal. Crossing the Indian Ocean, he arrived at Calicut in May 1498, and arrived back in Portugal in Sept. 1499. In 1502 he founded a Portuguese colony at Mozambique and sacked Calicut in revenge for the murder of some Portuguese seamen. After 20 years of retirement, he was despatched to India again as Portuguese viceroy in 1524, but d. 2 months after his arrival in Goa.

GAMBETTA, Léon Michel (1838–82). French statesman. After Sedan he was one of the founders of the French Republic and organized a fierce resistance against the German invaders. In 1881–2 he was Prime Minister for a few weeks.

GAMBIA. State of W. Africa, comprising St. Mary's Island (area 29 sq.m.) on which is Bathurst, the cap., and a strip of up to 20 m. wide extending inland for about 200 m. on both sides of the river G. (area c. 4,000 sq. m.). The river is bordered by swamps from which the land rises to bush country. Ground nuts are the principal export.

British traders estab. a settlement in the area in 1618. G. was made a Crown Colony in 1888, and following the grant of self-govt. in 1963, became independent 1965 within the Commonwealth, and in 1970 adopted republican status. A treaty of Assocn. with Senegal was signed 1967. Pop. (1965) 320,000.

GAMBLING. The playing of games of pure chance into which skill does not enter, e.g. roulette and all games in which dice (or other mechanical means) are used to decide the chance; or wagering on some fortuitous event. In the U.K. the Betting and Gaming Act (1960) relaxed previous prohibitions and in 1966 licence duties on gaming were introduced; in the U.S.A. gambling is regulated by individual states.

GAME LAWS. In Britain the laws relating to game preservation and the punishment of poachers and trespassers 'in pursuit of game'. The Game Act, 1831, defines game as hares, pheasants, partridges, grouse, heath or moor game, black game, and bustards.

GAMELIN (gahmlaṅ'), **Maurice Gustave** (1872–1958). French general. French C.-in-C. and Generalissimo of the Allied armies in France in 1939, he was replaced by Weygand on the enemy breakthrough at Sedan in 1940, and tried as a scapegoat before the Riom 'War Guilt' court in 1942. He refused to defend himself, and was deported to Germany until released by the Allies in 1945.

GAMMA RADIATION. Very high-frequency electromagnetic radiation emitted by the nuclei of radioactive substances during decay, similar in nature to X-rays. *See* diagram under entry ELECTROMAGNETIC WAVES.

GANANA. Somali name of the r. JUBA.

GANDHI, Indira. *See* NEHRU.

GANDHI, Mohandas Karamchand (1869–1948). Indian social and political leader, called Mahatma (Great Soul) G. B. in the state of Porbandar, he studied law in London, and in 1893 went to S. Africa, where he stayed for some years successfully leading the Indian community in their passive resistance to discriminatory legislation. In the Boer and Zulu wars and in the F.W.W. he organized ambulance units before returning to India in 1915 to struggle for Indian home rule, by the method of 'non-violent non-co-operation' (*satyagraha*, defence of and by truth). In his choice of this method he was influenced by Christian and Tolstoyan ideals as well as by the traditions of his native Hinduism, and throughout his career he was consistent in his advocacy of peaceful resistance, even in the face of Japanese threats to India in the S.W.W. During a series of campaigns of non-co-operation 1920–44, in the course of which he was imprisoned several times, he estab. an influence over the British authorities, and over the Congress (nationalist) Party, which he was to retain all his life although never himself taking office; in the negotiations which eventually resulted in the attainment of independence in 1947 he played an active part behind the scenes. While developing (1932–9) his economic and educational plans for the benefit of the Indian masses, he undertook several 'fasts unto death' on behalf of the 'Untouchables', and during the last weeks of 1947 undertook fasts to end the rioting and anti-Moslem violence which followed Partition. These led to a great reaction in public feeling, but his advocacy of Moslem-Hindu friendship deeply offended the Hindu extremists, and he was assassinated by a Hindu nationalist on Jan. 30, 1948.

GANESA (ganā'sa). One of the principal Hindu gods, represented as elephant-headed, and worshipped as a remover of obstacles.

GANGES. Great river of India and Pakistan, the most sacred river of the Hindus. It rises in the Himalayas and pursues a course of 1,557 m. to reach the Bay of Bengal through a wide delta, the main stream flowing through E. Pakistan as the Padma and the

GANGES. The ghats or ritual bathing steps at Benares.
Photo: J. Allan Cash.

Meghna. At Allahabad it receives its chief tributary, the Jumna.

GA'NGRĒNE. Local death of tissues, due to destruction of tissue through injury, burning, freezing, etc.; poisoning; or failure of the blood supply, as where a bandage is too tight or the vessels are abnormally contracted, or where a vessel is blocked with a blood clot (thrombosis). The affected parts are painful and sensitive and feel cold, and their skin turns brownish or violet. The mass may become infected (wet G.). Amputation may be necessary.

GANJA. Former name of KIROVABAD.

GANNET or Solan Goose. Sea-bird (*Sula bassana*) in the family Sulidae. When full-grown it is white with black-tipped wings, but the young are speckled. It breeds on cliffs, the nest being roughly made of grass and seaweed. Only one white egg is laid.

GARAY (gor'oi), **János** 1812–53). A Hungarian writer, author of historical plays, stories, and lyrics.

GARBO, Greta. Assumed name of the Swedish actress Greta Lovisa Gustafsson (1905–   ). She was trained at the Royal Theatre dramatic school, Stockholm, made her first film *The Story of Gosta Berling* in 1924, and then went to the U.S.A., where she played in *The Torrent* (1926), becoming one of Hollywood's first 'stars'. Her later films incl. *Anna Christie* (1930), her first 'talkie', *Mata Hari* (1931), *Queen Christina* (1933), *Anna Karenina* (1935), *Camille* (1936), and *Ninotchka* (1939). A great personality rather than a great actress, she has become a legend.

GARBORG, Arne Evensen (1851–1924). Norwegian novelist, playwright, and poet, a pioneer in the literary use of 'new Norwegian', a language derived through the native *Landsmaal* dialect from old Norsk.

GARCIA LORCA (gahrthē'-ah lork'ah), **Federico** (1899–1936). Spanish poet. B. in Granada, he had a special affinity with the gipsies of the region, and his *Romancero gitano* (1928, *Gipsy Ballad-book*) has all the spirit of Andalusian songs. In 1929–30 L. visited New York, and his experiences are reflected in *Poeta en Nuevo York*. Returning to Spain, he founded a touring theatrical company and himself wrote plays such as *Bodas de sangre* (*Blood Wedding*) and *La Casa de Bernarda Alba* (*The House of Bernarda Alba*). His finest poem is his *Lament* for the bullfighter Sánchez Mejías. He was shot by the Falangists.

GARD (gahr). French river, 35 m. long, a tributary of the Rhône, which it joins 4 m. above Beaucaire. It gives its name to G. dept.

GARDEN, Mary (1877–1967). Scottish soprano singer. She went to the U.S. at six, and was star of the Chicago Opera 1910–31, finding her greatest role as Mélisande in Debussy's opera. She retired in 1931.

GARDEN CITY. Town built in a rural area and designed to combine town and country advantages, with its own industries, controlled developments, private and public gardens, cultural centre, etc. The idea was proposed by the Englishman Ebenezer Howard, who in 1899 formed the G.C. Association, and the first G.C. was Letchworth near Hitchin. A 2nd, Welwyn, 22 m. from central London, was started in 1919. The New Towns Act, 1946, provided machinery for developing new towns on some of the principles advocated by Howard (e.g. Stevenage, begun in 1947), and there have been various similar schemes in Europe and in the U.S., but on the whole these have not kept the economic structure, or the industrial self-sufficiency or the permanent rural belt which formed an integral part of Howard's original idea.

GARDINER, Samuel Rawson (1829–1902). British historian. Prof. of modern history at King's Coll., London, 1877–85, he was noted for his impartial objectivity, and especially for his well-documented series of books on the English Civil War period.

GARDINER, Stephen (*c.* 1493–1555). English churchman and statesman. After being secretary to Wolsey, he entered the king's service, became bishop of Winchester in 1531, and on Mary's accession was created Lord Chancellor. He played a prominent part in the attempted restoration of Catholicism.

GARDNER, Erle Stanley (1889–1970). American author. B. in Mass., he was in 1911 admitted to the California Bar, and in 1932 wrote his first crime story featuring the lawyer-detective Perry Mason, hero of film and television versions of later cases.

GARDNER, Dame Helen (1908–   ). British scholar. She specialises in the metaphysical poets, and has ed. the poetry and prose of Donne, and in 1966 became Merton Prof. of English Literature at Oxford. She was created D.B.E. 1967.

GARDNER, John (1917–   ). British composer. Prof. at the R.A.M. from 1956, he has produced a symphony (1947), the opera *The Moon and Sixpence* (1957), based on the Maugham novel; and other works incl. film music.

GARFIELD, James Abram (1831–81). 20th President of the U.S.A. B. in a log cabin in Ohio, he entered politics as a Republican and served with distinction in the Civil War on the side of the North. He was inaugurated President in 1881, but a few months later was shot in a Washington station by a madman.

GARGOYLE. Spout projecting from the roof-gutter of a building with the purpose of directing water away from the wall. The term is usually applied to the ornamental forms found in Gothic architecture; these were carved in stone and took the shape of fantastic animals, angels, or human heads.

GARHWA'L. Himalayan district of Uttar Pradesh, India. It contains several shrines sacred to Hindus, e.g. Badrinath and Kedarnath. Area 5,628 sq. m.; pop. (1961) *c.* 1,000,000.

GARIBALDI (gahrēbahl'dē), **Giuseppe** (1807–82). Italian patriot. B. in Nice, he became a sailor, and in 1834 joined Mazzini's Young Italy society. Condemned to death for treason, he escaped to S. America where he lived the life of a soldier of fortune. He returned to Italy during the 1848 revolution, served with the Sardinian army against the Austrians, and commanded the army of the Roman republic in its defence of the city against the French. He subsequently lived in exile until 1854, when he settled on Caprera. He again fought against the Austrians in

GAS. From the Sahara natural gas flows through a pipeline to Port Arzew on the Algerian coast, and is there liquefied at a temperature of −161°C and reduced to 1/600th of its original volume. Special tankers (*left*) then carry it to the Canvey Island methane terminal where frozen-ground storage units (*right*) 130 ft. in diameter and 130 ft. deep each have a capacity of 11 million therms of liquefied gas.

Courtesy of the Gas Council.

the war of 1859; and in 1860, at the head of his 1,000 Redshirts, conquered Sicily and Naples for the new kingdom of Italy. He led 2 unsuccessful expeditions to liberate Rome from papal rule in 1862 and 1867, served in the Austrian War of 1866, and fought for the French in the Franco-Prussian War.

GARLIC. Perennial plant of the Liliaceae family, the bulb of which has a strong odour and flavour. The edible G. is *Allium sativum*.

GARNET. A group of minerals used as gems and abrasives. They are usually pale pink to deep red, and are of common occurrence in gneiss and schist, crystallized limestones, etc.

GARO'NNE. River rising in the Spanish Pyrenees, then flowing N.W. through France to the Gironde estuary. Toulouse and Bordeaux are the chief towns on it. It gives its names to the depts. of Haute-Garonne, Tarn-et-Garonne, and Lot-et-Garonne.

GARRICK, David (1717–79). British actor. B. in Hereford, he was ed. at Lichfield grammar school and also briefly under Johnson, of whose circle in London he was to become a member, and both set out for the capital together in 1737. He made his début in 1741, and his Richard III and Lear brought him fame, so that he was engaged for Drury Lane. In 1747 he became joint-patentee of the theatre with his own co. The expressiveness and naturalness of his acting, and his gift of mimicry, broke startlingly with the traditional chanting delivery and he excelled in a variety of parts incl. Hamlet, Benedick, Archer in *The Beaux' Stratagem* and Abel Drugger in *The Alchemist*. He himself wrote plays, e.g. *The Clandestine Marriage* (1766, with Colman), and made numerous adaptations. He retired from the stage in 1766, but continued as a manager.

GARTER, Order of the. The senior British order of knighthood, founded by Edward III *c.* 1347. Its distinctive badge is a garter of dark blue velvet, with the motto of the order, *Honi soit qui mal y pense*, in gold letters, worn below the left knee. Membership is limited to 25 knights, and to members of the royal family and foreign royalties; appointments are made by the sovereign without ministerial recommendation. St. George's Chapel, Windsor, is the chapel of the order. *See* BLUE RIBAND.

GARY (gahrē´), **Romain** (1914–). French writer and diplomat. In the S.W.W. he served as a pilot with the Free French, then entered the diplomatic service and was consul-general in Los Angeles 1956–60. His novels incl. *Education Européenne* (1945) and *Les Racines du Ciel* (1956: *The Roots of Heaven*).

GARY. City of Indiana, U.S.A., at the southern end of Lake Michigan. It contains the largest steel and cement works in the world, those of the United States Steel Corporation. Pop. (1960) 178,320.

Insignia of the Garter

GAS. Word first used by J. B. van Helmont (1577–1644) for what may be defined as a form of matter that has neither volume nor shape, and such that when a given quantity of it is introduced into a vessel, it will fill the vessel completely. Gs. behave according to certain fundamental laws relating pressure, volume, and temperature. *See* BOYLE, R. and CHARLES'S LAW. Examples of gases are the elements hydrogen, helium, nitrogen, neon, etc., and among compounds, carbon monoxide, carbon dioxide, and nitrous oxide.

Natural gas is the gaseous form of the complex mixture of hydrocarbons called petroleum; crude oil is the liquid form, and bitumen the solid form, which is found at the surface when the lighter hydrocarbons have escaped to the atmosphere. Natural G. and oil are retained below the surface only if there is an adequate impervious capping layer laid down over the top of the accumulation, which is usually found in association with coal reserves. The capping is usually shale.

When oil deposits first began to be exploited the G. was regarded as a waste product, but since the S.W.W. has been increasingly utilized as fuel, and large deposits have been discovered, notably under the North Sea, in Siberia, in the Netherlands, North Africa, and Australia. Natural G. is usually 90% methane, but may also contain varying proportions of ethane, propane, and butane – used in the petrochemical industry – helium, hydrogen, sulphur, etc., all industrially utilizable.

For 150 years the traditional gas-making process was by coal carbonisation, but from *c.* 1960 the process has increasingly been based on oil, and then from 1965 increasingly on natural gas. *See* illus. p. 462.

GASCONY. Ancient province of S.W. France. Henry II of England gained possession of it through his marriage to Eleanor of Aquitaine in 1152, and it was often in English hands until 1451. It was united with the royal domain in 1607 under Henry IV.

GAS ENGINES. Type of internal combustion engine, in which gas (coal gas, producer gas, or gas from a blast furnace) is used as the fuel. The first practical G.E. was built in 1860 by Lenoir, and the type was subsequently developed by Otto.

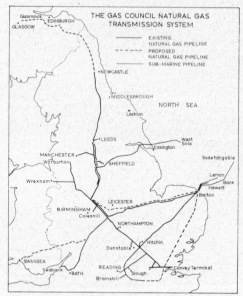

THE GAS COUNCIL NATURAL GAS TRANSMISSION SYSTEM

——— EXISTING NATURAL GAS PIPELINE
- - - - PROPOSED NATURAL GAS PIPELINE
——— SUB-MARINE PIPELINE

GAS. 'Orion' the jack-up type rig designed specifically for drilling in the North Sea, seen in operation.
Courtesy of the Gas Council.

GASKELL, Elizabeth Cleghorn (1810–65). British novelist. B. at Chelsea, *née* Stevenson, she was brought up by an aunt in Knutsford, Cheshire, the Cranford of her later writings. She m. William G., a Unitarian minister. Her first novel, *Mary Barton* (1848), depicts the problems of life among Manchester factory-hands. Her masterpiece was *Cranford* (1853), a delicate study of village life. Later books include *Ruth* (1853), *North and South* (1855), *Sylvia's Lovers* (1863–4), and the unfinished *Wives and Daughters* (1866). She was a friend of Charlotte Brontë, and her life of her is a standard work.

GASOLENE. A mixture of hydrocarbons derived from petroleum, whose main use is as a fuel for internal combustion engines. It is colourless and highly volatile. In U.S.A. petrol is called gasoline.

GASPERI (gahspä'rē), **Alcide de** (1881–1954). Italian statesman. Imprisoned by the Fascists 1926–8, he was released to work in the Vatican Library. A founder of the Christian Democrat party, he was P.M. 1945–53, and worked for European unification. *See* GAS WARFARE.

GAS POISONING. Intoxication by gas. House gas contains a high proportion of carbon monoxide, which combines with the haemoglobin of the blood and prevents it from taking up oxygen, so that death is caused by failure of oxygen supply to the brain. The skin of the victim is stained pink by the haemoglobin. *See* GAS WARFARE.

GASSENDI (gasendē'), **Pierre** (1592–1655). French philosopher, friend of Kepler and Galileo, prof. of mathematics from 1645 at the Collège Royal, Paris, and exponent of Epicurus.

GASTERO'PODA. Class of molluscs, including snails, whelks, etc. They have a well-developed head and a rough tongue, and move by means of muscular contractions of the ventral surface or 'foot'. Except in the very simplest forms, the body is asymmetrical.

GASTRITIS. Inflammation of the lining of the stomach. It may be caused by corrosive poisons (e.g. lysol, caustic soda, strong acids), too high a concentration of alcohol, or infection. Chronic gastritis, which is common and responsible for much indigestion, may be caused by habitual failure to masticate food properly, dietary indiscretions, and

excessive use of alcohol, medicines, tea, and coffee.

GAS WARFARE. The offensive use of G. to produce a toxic, irritant, or lethal effect on the human body. The idea of G.W. developed with industrial chemistry, so that by 1899 at The Hague Conference the use of toxic substances for war was foreseen by the Great Powers, who (with the exception of the U.S.) pledged abstinence from their employment. However, in 1915 during the F.W.W., the Germans launched a cylinder attack with chlorine against the Allies, who subsequently retaliated in kind. G. shells and mustard G. were also used, accounting for many casualties – immediate and long-term. Chlorine is an example of a lung irritant and mustard G. of a vesicant; other types incl. adamsite, a sneeze gas, and chloropicrin, a tear gas. Most insidious and difficult to detect are nerve Gs., found on German airfields after the S.W.W.; these attack the central nervous system through any moist surface of the body, esp. the eyes. In the S.W.W. there was no G.W. – largely because of more effective counter-measures, e.g. respirators to filter out the noxious substances.

GATESHEAD. English port and industrial town (co. bor.) in Durham, on the Tyne opposite Newcastle. It is an engineering centre, and has chemical, glass, railway workshops, shipyards, etc. Pop. (1961) 103,232.

GATUN (gahtōōn'). U.S. town in the Panama Canal zone, 7 m. S. of Colon on the Atlantic coast. Lake G. was created by the building of G. dam, part of the Panama canal works, on the r. Chagres. Pop. *c.* 3,000.

GA'TWICK. Location in Surrey, England, 27 m. S. of London, formerly noted for its racecourse, obliterated by the construction 1956–8 of Gatwick Airport, London.

GAUCHO (gow'chō). South American tribe, part Indian part Spanish, inhabiting the Argentine and Uraguayan pampas. They are nomadic, fine horsemen, and expert in the use of the lasso and bolas.

GAUDIER-BRZESKA (gōdyā'-bresh'ka), **Henri** (1891–1915). French sculptor. He studied art at Bristol, Nuremberg and Munich, and became a member of the English Vorticist movement. His sculptures incl. 'The Dancer' and 'The Embracers'.

GAUGE (gāj). A scientific measuring instrument, e.g. wire-G., pressure-G. The term is also applied to the width of a railway or tramway track, in England normally 4 ft. 8½ in. The original broad G. of the G.W.R. was 7 ft. On the Continent the 4 ft. 8½ in. G. is general, with the exception of Spain, Portugal, and U.S.S.R.: the standard G. is also used in N. America.

GAUGUIN (gōgań'), **Paul** (1848–1903). French artist. B. in Paris, he joined a banking firm, but threw up his career in 1881 in order to paint. After a visit to Martinique in 1887, he went to Pont Aven in Brittany, becoming the leading artist in the movement known as *Synthesism*. In 1891 he left Paris for Tahiti, where he remained from 1895 until his death, finding inspiration in the simple life and tropical colouring of the islands. A friend of Van Gogh, he disliked theories and rules of painting, and his pictures are Expressionist compositions characterized by his use

GAUGUIN. In a letter to a friend the artist wrote of this picture: 'I wanted to suggest by means of a simple nude a certain long-lost barbarian luxury. The whole is drowned in colours which are deliberately sombre and sad . . . As a title *Nevermore*: not the raven of Edgar Allan Poe, but the bird of the devil that is keeping watch.' Dated Tahiti, 1897, it was once in the collection of the composer Frederick Delius.
Courtesy of the Courtauld Institute Galleries, London.

of pure, unmixed colours. Among his most famous paintings is 'Le Christe Jaune'.

GAULS. The Celtic-speaking peoples who inhabited France and Belgium in Roman times. They were divided into several tribes, but united by a common religion controlled by the Druid priesthood. Certain tribes invaded Italy c. 400 B.C., sacked Rome, and settled between the Alps and the Apennines; this district, known as Cisalpine Gaul, was conquered by Rome c. 225 B.C. The Romans conquered S. Gaul between the Mediterranean and the Cevennes c. 125 B.C., and the remaining Gs. up to the Rhine were conquered by Caesar 58–51 B.C.

GAUR (gowr). Indian wild ox (*Bibos gaurus*). It is dark grey with white legs, measures nearly 6 ft. high, and has a ridge between the horns.

GAUSS (gows), **Karl Friedrich** (1777–1855). German mathematician and physicist. B. in Brunswick, he became professor of astronomy at Göttingen in 1807. His *Disquisitiones Arithmeticae* (1801) became a standard work on the theory of numbers. The unit of magnetic-field strength is known as a *gauss*, and the method devised to counter the German magnetic mine in 1939 was named *degaussing*.

GAUTIER (gōtyā'), **Théophile** (1811–72). French writer. Influenced by the Romantics, his poetry expresses his passion for beauty, and is distinguished by an instinct for descriptive language and imagery. He was a gifted prose writer also, his best-known novel being *Mlle de Maupin* (1835); soon after this he turned to journalism, writing short stories, dramatic and literary criticism and travel sketches.

GAY, John (1685–1732). British poet. B. at Barnstaple, he was the friend of Pope and Arbuthnot, and produced in his *Trivia* (1716) an excellent verse

picture of 18th cent. London. His *The Beggar's Opera* (1728), 'a Newgate pastoral' telling of the love of Polly for highwayman Capt. Macheath, has held the stage ever since and inspired Brecht (q.v.): it was the first opera in English (as opposed to Italian) and used English folk tunes. Its satiric political touches led to the banning of *Polly*, a sequel.

GAY, Noel (1898–1954). British composer, best remembered for his music for the Cockney musical *Me and My Girl* (1937) incl. 'The Lambeth Walk'.

GDANSK. A fountain in front of the beautiful Artus' Manor.
Courtesy of Orbis'

GAYA (gī'ah). Ancient Indian city, in Bihar state, cap. of G. div., 4,766 sq. m., which is famous for its association with Buddhism and includes Buddh Gaya (q.v.) with a temple dating back to 543 B.C. G. city contains a number of sacred shrines and is a place of pilgrimage. Pop. (1961) 150,884.

GAY-LUSSAC (gā-lüsahk'), **Joseph Louis** (1778–1850). French physicist and chemist. B. near Limoges, he became professor of physics at Paris in 1808. In 1804 he made balloon ascents to study the weather. He investigated the physical properties of gases and discovered new methods of producing sulphuric and oxalic acids.

GAZA (gah'zah). Town near the coast of S.W. Palestine, once chief of the 5 Philistine cities and scene of 3 battles in the F.W.W. Pop. 38,000. It was captured by Egypt on the proclamation of Israel 1948, and became cap. of the coastal *Gaza Strip* (area 100 sq. m.) where 200,000 Arab refugees remained. Israel invaded the strip 1956, and reoccupied it after withdrawal of U.N. troops 1967.

GAZIANTEP (gahzēahntep'). Turkish town, cap. of G. il, 115 m. E.N.E. of Adana. Industries incl. tanning and wine-making. Pop. (1965) 158,400.

GDANSK. Polish port, cap. of G. voivodship, on the r. Mottla, 8 m. S. of its mouth on the Gulf of G. The famous cathedral of St. Mary (protestant) dates from 1343, and G. retains some of its old city gates and many old buildings. It has a technical university, shipyards, machine and tobacco factories, breweries. A member of the Hanseatic League 1361, a free city under Polish protection from 1455 until occupied by Prussia 1793, created a free city under League of Nations protection 1919, G. was occupied by the Germans 1939, captured 1945 by the Russians who handed it over to Polish administration 1946. Pop. (1966) 324,000.

GDYNIA (gdin'ia). Polish port on the Gulf of Gdansk, founded in 1920 to provide newly consituated Poland with an outlet to the sea. Pop. (1966) 168,000.

GE (jē) or **GAIA**. Greek goddess of the earth. She arose from Chaos and produced Uranus and Pontus, respectively Sky and Sea. She was the mother of the Titans, the Cyclopes and of Cronus.

GECKO LIZARD. Small soft-skinned lizard in the family Geckonidae. They are common in warm climates, and have a large head, and short, stout body. Gecko is derived from the clicking sound which the animal makes.

GECKO LIZARD

GEELONG (gĕlong'). Port and city on an inlet of Port Phillip Bay, Victoria, Australia. It exports wool and wheat, and manufactures textiles, glass, fertilizers, etc. Prince Charles was a student at the C. of E. Grammar School, the 'Eton of Australia', in 1966. Pop. (1966) 104,974.

GEIGER (gī'ger) **COUNTER.** Geiger-Müller, Geiger-Klemperer, Rutherford-Geiger counters are devices often referred to under the generic name G.C. (derived from the name of **Hans G.** (1882–1945), one-time student of Rutherford and prof. of physics at Kiel who was active in their development). They are used for detecting and/or counting nuclear radiations and particles. The principle on which the G.C. operates is the detection of the momentary current which passes between electrodes in a suitable gas when a nuclear particle or a radiation pulse causes ionization in the gas. The electrodes are connected to electronic devices which enable the intensity of radiation or the number of particles passing to be measured.

GEISHA (gā'sha). Female entertainer (music, singing, dancing, etc.), in Japanese tea-houses and private parties. Gs. survive mainly as a tourist attraction.

GELBER, Jack (1932–). American playwright. Ed. at the univ. of Illinois, he was unknown until his very frank study of drug addiction *The Connection* was produced 'off-Broadway' in 1959.

GE'LDERLAND. Prov. of the Netherlands lying between the Ijssel Meer on the N.W. and the German frontier on the S.E. It is drained by the Ijssel, the Waal, and the Maas, and is a cattle-rearing area with flax, wheat, sugar beet, and tobacco as important crops. The scrubland in the N.W., called the Valuwe, is a favourite holiday district. The cap. is Arnhem; other towns are Nijmegen, Apeldoorn, and Zutphen. It includes part of the S.E. polder drained from the Zuyder Zee. Area 1,930 sq. m.; pop. (1966) 1,434,439.

GELIBOLU. Another form of GALLIPOLI.

GELLIVARE. Another form of GÄLLIVARE.

GELL-MANN, Murray (1929–). American Physicist. R. A. Millikan prof. of theoretical physics at the California Inst. of Technology from 1967, he was awarded a Nobel prize 1969 for his work on elementary particles and their interaction. He formulated in 1964 the theory of the 'quark' as the fundamental constituent of all matter and smallest particle in the universe.

GELSENKIRCHEN (gel'zenkèr'khen). City in the Ruhr, W. Germany, 6 m. N.E. of Essen, centre of the coal-mining area, with many iron and steel works. Pop. (1966) 362,508.

GEM. A mineral, precious by virtue of its composition, hardness, and rarity, cut and polished for ornamental use, or engraved. Of 120 minerals known to have been used as gemstones, only about 25 are in common use in jewellery; of these the diamond, emerald, ruby and sapphire are classified as precious, and the topaz, amethyst, opal, aquamarine, etc., as semi-precious. Among synthetic precious stones to have been produced successfully, on a commercial scale, are rubies and sapphires (first produced by the Frenchman Verneuil in 1904 and 1909 respectively), emeralds (first made by German scientists *c.* 1930), and diamonds (first made by G.E.C. in U.S.A. in 1955). Pearls are technically not Gs., though the term is sometimes extended to cover them.

GEMSBOK. See ORYX.

GENE (jēn). The unit of inherited material situated on the chromosome within the cell nucleus. It has a constant effect on the development of the individual bearing it, other conditions being constant. Gs. are indivisible, duplicate themselves, and are highly stable, though occasionally they mutate.

GĒNEA'LOGY. The study and tracing of family pedigrees. Formerly of limited aristocratic interest,

G. is increasingly popular both in Britain and the U.S.A. The Soc. of Genealogists in London (estab. 1911) with its library, thousands of family papers, marriage index (6,000,000 names of persons married before 1837), collection of parish register copies, etc., undertakes and assists research.

GENÉE (zhenā'), **Adeline.** Stage-name of the British dancer Dame Adeline Genée-Isitt (1878–1970). B. in Denmark, she went to London at 19 where she danced many years and was pres. of the Royal Adacemy of Dancing 1920–54, being created D.B.E. 1950. The *Adeline G. Theatre* (1967) at E. Grinstead, Sussex, commemorates her work.

GENERAL. An official of superior rank having wide authority. Usually in military sense – a G. officer commanding a body of troops larger than a regiment, or more than one arm of the service. In the British and U.S. armies the ranks are Maj.-G., Lt.-G. and G. Supreme commanders in Britain are field marshals, and in the U.S. Gs. of the army.

GENERAL ASSEMBLY. See SCOTLAND, CHURCH OF.

GENE'TICS. The scientific study of heredity, variation, development, and evolution. It accounts for the resemblances and differences to be found among organisms of related descent. Normal cells contain paired chromosomes, which separate during the formation of the germ cell, ultimately containing only one set. When male and female germ cells fuse, the chromosomes pair themselves off independently,

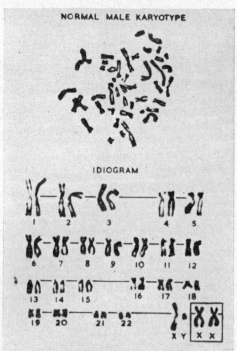

GENETICS. The number and shape of the chromosomes, formed by the linking together of the DNA molecules of a cell, are characteristic of a species. *Above* are the human chromosomes (male) in a very thinly spread-out skin cell grown in tissue culture. *Below* they have been provisionally arranged in order of size, though several of the same size have not yet been distinguished from one another. The last pair are the sex chromosomes, the male Y being very small, and the inset shows a slightly enlarged XX pair from a female cell.
Photo: Dr. D. T. Hughes, *Chester Beatty Research Institute*

and since they may be up to 100 in number the possible combinations are enormous (as enunciated by J. G. Mendel 1866), and account for the many differences in appearance among offspring in the same family; and between offspring and parents.

In 1962 the Nobel medicine and physiology prize was awarded to Francis Crick (molecular biologist at the Cavendish Laboratory, Cambridge), Maurice Wilkins (of the M.R.C. biophysics unit at King's Coll., London) and John D. Watson (prof. of biology at Harvard). Their researches on D.N.A. (deoxyribonucleic acid, a biological structure which makes transmission of characteristics possible) represents a breakthrough which may lead to an explanation of why species differ and why each individual is in some respect unique.

GENETIC EFFECT of radiation. Changes in the reproductive cells of living matter due to the absorption of ionizing radiations.

GENEVA (jenē´va). Swiss city, cap. of G. canton, on the shore of Lake G. It is a natural route focus, and is a cultural and commercial centre. Industries

GENEVA. The 'Palace of the Nations': the centre block is the headquarters of the W.H.O.
Courtesy of the World Health Organization.

incl. the manufacture of watches, scientific and optical instruments, foodstuffs, jewellery, musical boxes, etc. The site on which G. now stands was the chief settlement of the Allobroges; Caesar built an entrenched camp here. In the Middle Ages G. was controlled by the prince-bishops of G. and the rulers of Savoy. Under Calvin it became a centre of the Reformation 1536–64; the Academy, founded by him in 1559, became a univ. in 1892. G. was annexed by France in 1798; when freed in 1814 it entered the Swiss Confederation in 1815. In 1864 the International Red Cross Society was estab. at G. It was the H.Q. of the League of Nations whose properties at G. passed in 1946 into the possession of the U.N. Pop. (1960) 176,183.

GENEVA, Lake. Largest of the central European lakes. The northern shores are in Switzerland, and most of the southern are in France. It is 45 m. long and averages 5 m. wide. Area 225 sq. m.

GENEVA CONVENTION. An international agreement regulating the treatment of the wounded in war was reached at a conference held in 1864, and later extended to cover the treatment of the sick and prisoners and the protection of civilians in war-time. The rules were revised at conventions held in 1906, 1929, and 1949.

GENF. German form of GENEVA (Fr. Genève).

GENGHIS (jen´gis) **KHAN** (1162–1227). Mongol conqueror. Temujin, as he was originally called, was the son of a local chieftain. After a long struggle he estab. his supremacy over all the Mongol tribes by 1206, when he assumed the title of Chingis or 'perfect warrior'. He began the conquest of N. China in 1213, overran the empire of the shah of Khiva 1219–25, and invaded N. India, while his lieutenants advanced as far as the Crimea. At his death he ruled from the Yellow Sea to the Black Sea.

GENNESARET, Lake of. Another name for the SEA OF GALILEE.

GENOA (jen´ō-ah). City and seaport of N. Italy, capital of the prov. of G. and of the region of Liguria on the Gulf of G. It has become the chief commercial port of Italy with its fine harbour; its industries incl. shipbuilding, engineering, textiles, chemical works. Pop. (1966) 846,292.

GENOA. Built in 1155 for its defence against Frederick I, the city walls incorporate the Porto Soprano. In one of its twin 100 ft. high towers a guillotine – and later a gallows – were erected.
Courtesy of the Italian Cultural Institute.

GENOVA. Italian form of GENOA.

GENRE (zhaṅr). French word meaning 'kind', and originally used in conjunction with an adjective to describe certain 'kinds' of painting, e.g. *genre du paysage* (landscapes) or *genre historique* (historical paintings). But *genre* is now usually applied to a special kind of painting, one in which some scene of everyday life is depicted. The most famous G. pictures were painted by Flemish artists such as Pieter Brueghel and Adriaen Brouwer, and by Dutch artists such as Teniers and Frans Hals. Of the English G. painters the best-known incl. Hogarth, George Morland, William Mulready, and Sir David Wilkie.

GENTIAN (jen´shan). Alpine plant belonging to the Genus *Gentiana* of the Gentianaceae family. They grow abundantly in mountainous regions, esp. on the Swiss Alps; the flowers may be a brilliant blue, or white or yellow.

GENTILE, Giovanni (1875–1944). Italian philosopher and educationist. B. in Sicily, he became a prof. of philosophy in Rome in 1917, and developed Hegel's deification of the State in the direction of Fascism, which he supported from its earliest days. Under Mussolini he was Min. of Education. He was shot by anti-Fascists.

GENTILE DA FABRIANO (c. 1370–1427). Italian artist. B. at Fabriano, he has a lyric, poetical style in his great 'Adoration of the Magi' (1423), now in the Uffizi, and his altarpiece for the Quaratesi family (1425), of which the central panel is in the Buckingham Palace collection.

GENTILI (jentē´lē), **Alberico** (1552–1608). Italian jurist. He practised law in Italy, but having adopted protestantism was compelled to flee to England, where he lectured on Roman Law in Oxford. His *De Jure Belli libri tres* (1598) constitutes the real foundation of international law.

GENTLEMEN-AT-ARMS, Honourable Corps of. Estab. in 1509, the Corps is, next to the Yeomen of

GENTIAN

the Guard, the oldest in the British Army; it was reconstituted in 1862. It consists of army officers of distinction under a captain, a peer, whose appointment is political. Theoretically the first bodyguard of the Sovereign, its functions are ceremonial.

GENUS (jē′nus). A number of species in the animal or plant world, when recognized to be related, are grouped together into a genus; in the Linnean nomenclature each species is given 2 names, the former of which is that of the genus; e.g. the domestic dog is known biologically as *Canis familiaris.* Genera are grouped into families, and these into orders.

GEOGRAPHY. The study of the distribution and interrelation of phenomena connected with the earth's surface. The earliest geographers strove to determine the shape and size of the earth and the distribution of land and sea. The most notable were Herodotus (*c.* 484–*c.* 425 B.C.), Erastothenes (*c.* 284–204 B.C.), and Ptolemy (*c.* A.D. 150). During the 16th cent. the great cartographers Mercator, Hondius, and Blaeu made use of the information collected by explorers and travellers in the construction of their maps. Saxton and Speed contributed much to the map of England.

In 1488 Diaz discovered the Cape of Good Hope. The Atlantic crossing of Columbus in 1492 was followed by further exploration of the coasts of Africa, Asia, and America including Vasco da Gama's discovery of a sea-route to India (1497), and the circumnavigation of the globe by a ship of Magellan's fleet (1521): Magellan himself was killed in the Philippines, April 27, 1521. Hartogs discovered the W. coast of Australia (1616), Tasman reached New Zealand (1642). Cook sailed round New Zealand (1769), and explored part of the E. coast of Australia (1770). S. America was penetrated by Humboldt (1800), Africa by Livingstone and Stanley (mid 19th cent.). The N. Pole was reached by Peary (1909), and the S. by Amundsen (1911) and Scott (1912). Systematic survey of the bed of the ocean and life in the seas began with the *Challenger* expedition (1872–6).

G. in the 20th cent. has several branches: *Physical* geographers study landscapes and the natural processes by which they have been formed, including earth movements, and the effects of weather, running water, and moving ice. They are also concerned with weather and its causes, and with climate. *Economic G.* is concerned with the distribution and modes of occurrence of industrial raw materials; the means whereby they are assembled for manufacture, often over considerable distances; and the accessibility to markets for the finished products. It also includes natural factors governing agriculture, the crops produced and their markets; and the reasons for differences in types of farming in different areas. *Human G.* concerns man in relation to his environment, the distribution of settlement, urban and rural; and the special adaptations of different peoples and cultures to the conditions in which they live. *Historical G.* seeks to reconstruct the G. of past periods, e.g. the Norman

THE GEOLOGICAL TIME SCALE

Eras	Periods and Systems	Derivations of Names		Approximate dates in years	Distinctive Life
CAINOZOIC *Kainos or Cenos = recent Zoe = life (Recent life)*	QUATERNARY			*Present day*	
	Recent *or* Holocene	*Holos* = complete		25,000	Modern Man
	Glacial *or* Pleistocene	*Pleiston* = most		1,000,000	Stone-Age Man
			'cene' from *Kainos* = recent		
	TERTIARY				
	Pliocene	*Pleion* = more		15,000,000	
	Miocene	*Meion* = less		35,000,000	Pre-man
	Oligocene	*Oligos* = few		50,000,000	Mammals and
	Eocene	*Eos* = dawn		70,000,000	Flowering Plants

The above terms refer to the proportions of modern shells occurring as fossils in each sub-system

Eras	Periods and Systems	Derivations of Names	Approximate dates in years	Distinctive Life
MESOZOIC *Mesos = middle (Medieval life)*	CRETACEOUS	*Creta* = chalk	120,000,000	
	JURASSIC	*Jura* Mountains	150,000,000	Reptiles
	TRIASSIC	*Threefold* division in Germany	190,000,000	
	NEW RED SANDSTONE			
PALAEOZOIC *Palaios = ancient (Ancient life)*	PERMIAN	*Permia,* anc. kingdom E. of Volga	220,000,000	Amphibians and Primitive Plants
	CARBONIFEROUS	*Coal-bearing*	280,000,000	
	DEVONIAN *or*	*Devon* (marine sediments)	320,000,000	Fishes
	OLD RED SANDSTONE	(Land sediments of same period)		
	SILURIAN	*Silures,* anc. tribe of Welsh borders	350,000,000	Invertebrates
	ORDOVICIAN	*Ordovices,* anc. tribe, N. Wales	400,000,000	First appearance o
	CAMBRIAN	*Cambria* = Wales	500,000,000	abundant fossils

PRE-CAMBRIAN ERAS: sometimes described as:

PROTEROZOIC	*Proteros* =	Earlier		Scanty remains of
ARCHAEOZOIC	*Archaios* =	Primeval		Sponges and Seaweeds
EOZOIC	*Eos* =	Dawn	at least	No direct fossil
			1,750,000,000	evidence of Life

The term ARCHAEAN refers to the oldest Pre-Cambrian crystalline rocks of a given region

UNRECORDED INTERVAL (duration unknown)

ORIGIN OF THE EARTH   at least   2,000,000,000

Reproduced by courtesy of Prof. Arthur Holmes from Principles of Physical Geology. (T. Nelson)

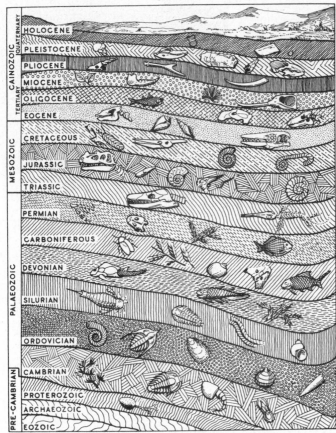

GEOLOGY. The long story of the earth written in its rocks and fossils.

The raw material of geological study is the rocks which are usually divided into three main groups: Igneous rocks are those resulting from the consolidation of molten rock substance or magma; Sedimentary rocks, those produced by the deposition of material derived in most cases by the wearing away of some existing rock; and Metamorphic rocks which are produced by the transformation of existing rocks as a result of changes in pressure, temperature, or composition. By the study of fossils, earthquakes, and volcanic activity, quarrying and mining operations, and the examination of rocks visible on the surface, the geologists have been able to classify the rocks into eras, periods, and systems, ranging from the Archaean (between 1,000 million and 2,000 million years ago) and our present position in the Quaternary. *See* TABLE.

GEOMETRY. That branch of mathematics which is concerned with the investigation of the properties of space. It probably originated in Egypt, in the land measurements made necessary by the periodic inundations of the Nile. Early geometers were Thales, Pythagoras, and Euclid (285 B.C.); the theorems of the last two still find a place in education. Analytical methods were introduced and developed by Descartes in the 17th cent. The subject is usually divided into pure G., which embraces roughly the plane and solid geometry covered by Euclid's 'elements'; and analytical or co-ordinate G. in which problems are solved by algebraical methods. Two-dimensional G. treats of figures on plane or spherical surfaces; and solid G. of three-dimensional figures. Of recent years, non-Euclidean geometries have been devised by the mathematician Riemann and others.

GEOPHYSICS. The study of the earth's surface and interior (incl. geodesy, seismology, vulcanology, glaciology, and oceanography) and of the phenomena of its atmosphere (incl. meteorology, geomagnetism, geo-electricity, and ionospheric physics). Internationally organized research is planned by the Comité Spécial de l'Année Géophysique Internationale (C.S.A.G.I.), e.g. in the International Geophysical Year of 1957–8.

GEORGE I (1660–1727). King of Great Britain. The son of the elector of Hanover, whom he succeeded in 1698, and a great-grandson of James I. He succeeded to the throne in 1714, but spent most of his reign in Hanover. He m. Sophia of Zell in 1682.

GEORGE II (1683–1760). King of Great Britain. He succeeded his father, George I, in 1727. Although he had little political ability, he distinguished himself as a soldier; his victory at Dettingen in 1743 was the last battle at which a British king commanded. He m. Caroline of Anspach in 1705.

GEORGE III (1738–1820). King of Great Britain. He succeeded his grandfather George II in 1760. From the beginning of his reign he set himself to dominate

period in England. *Regional G.* is the synthesis of all these for particular areas which have sufficient in common to be considered as units.

Cartography is the art and science of portraying as accurately as possible the surface of the earth, especially its physical features, and of expressing the findings of all branches of the subject in the form of maps.

GEOLOGICAL SURVEY. Great Britain was the 1st country to institute an official G.S. The 1st map, of part of Devon, was completed in 1834. The one inch to one mile survey of England was completed in 1883. A larger-scale survey of England, Wales and Scotland is in continuous progress.

GEOLOGY. The study of the earth, particularly the thin outer section, perhaps some 40 m. thick, known as the earth's crust. *Cosmical G.* is concerned with the earth's early history and the consequences of this. *Physical G.* deals with what goes on at the earth's surface – with the effect of earthquakes, volcanic eruptions, glacial action, denudation, and deposition, etc.; *Structural G.* with how rocks are put together to make the crust; and historical G. or *Stratigraphy* with the time relations of the rocks. *Economic G.* deals with the earth materials that are useful to man. Allied subjects are crystallography, mineralogy, and petrology, which study the components of the crust, and palaeontology, which deals with the development of life upon the earth.

GEORGE III
Photo: N.P.G.

parliament, and by wholesale bribery built up his own party, the 'king's friends'. His autocratic policy was largely responsible for the loss of the American colonies, and his influence was constantly exerted against Catholic emancipation and other reforms. He was subject throughout his life to attacks of lunacy, which in 1811 became permanent. He m. in 1761 Princess Charlotte of Mecklenburg-Strelitz.

GEORGE IV (1762–1830). King of Great Britain. He received a strict upbringing from his father, George III, and early reacted into a life of debauchery. He secretly m. an R.C. widow, Mrs. Fitzherbert, in 1785, but in 1795 he also m. Princess Caroline of Brunswick in return for a settlement of his debts. He acted as regent during his father's madness 1811–20, and succeeded him as king. On his accession in 1820 he attempted to divorce Caroline, but the project was dropped for fear of revolution.

GEORGE V (1865–1936). King of Great Britain. The 2nd son of Edward VII, he served in the navy until 1892, when on his elder brother's death he became heir to the throne. In 1893 he m. Princess May of Teck (Queen Mary) and had 5 sons and a dau. He succeeded his father in 1910 and was crowned in 1911. During the F.W.W. he paid several visits to the front, and concerned himself actively with war policy. During all the great crises of his reign, notably in 1910, 1914, and 1931, he played the part of a wise but unobtrusive counsellor.

GEORGE VI (1895–1952). King of Great Britain. The 2nd son of George V, he served in the navy in the F.W.W. (being present at the battle of Jutland) and then in the R.A.F.; subsequently studying at Cambridge. Created duke of York in 1920, he m. in 1923 the Lady Elizabeth Bowes-Lyon, and 2 dau. were born, Elizabeth (q.v.) in 1926 and Margaret [Rose] (q.v.) in 1930. On Edward VIII's abdication in 1936 he succeeded to the throne, and was crowned in 1937. With his consort he visited France (1938), Canada and U.S.A. (1939), and S. Africa (1947). During the S.W.W. he visited the Normandy and Italian battlefields. He was endeared to his people by an exemplary family life, a strong sense of duty, and the personal courage to overcome a speech impediment and endure ill-health.

GEORGE VI. He came to the throne at a time of national crisis and reigned through a troubled period in world history. He often referred to the sustaining happiness of his home life, and here we see him with his family in a detail from a painting (1950) by H. J. Gunn.
Photo: N.P.G.

GEORGIA. The climate is subtropical at Sukhumi and palm trees frame the entrance to the State Drama Theatre.
Photo: Novosti Press Agency.

GEORGE. Name of 2 kings of Greece. **George I** (1845–1913), 2nd son of Christian IX of Denmark, became king of Greece in 1863. He was assassinated at Salonika in 1913. **George II** (1890–1947) became king on the expulsion of his father king Constantine in 1922, but in 1923 was himself overthrown. He was restored by a military coup d'état in 1935, and soon abolished the constitution and set up a dictatorship under Metaxas (q.v.). He went into exile 1941–6.

GEORGE, Henry (1839–97). American land reformer. His solution of all economic problems by a 'single tax' on land values, expounded in *Progress and Poverty* (1879), attracted many people.

GEORGE, St. Patron saint of England. He is said to have been martyred at Lydda in Palestine, probably under Diocletian, but the other elements of his legend are of doubtful historicity. The story of St. G. and the Dragon, evidently derived from the Perseus legend, first appears in the 6th cent. The cultus of St. G. was introduced into western Europe by the Crusaders, and his feast day is April 23.

GEORGE (geh-ohr'ge), **Stefan** (1868–1933). German poet. His early poetry was influenced by the French Symbolists but his conception of himself as the seer and leader of a small band regenerating the German spirit first appears in *Der Teppich des Lebens* (1899). *Der Siebente Ring* (1907, *The Seventh Ring*) contains some of his finest verse and deifies the young man whom he sees as a substitute for Christ. *Das Neue Reich* (1928) shows his realization that the F.W.W. had failed to exert the purifying effect he had hoped for. He rejected Nazi overtures, and went to Switzerland, where he died.

GEORGE CROSS. The supreme civilian award in Britain for acts of the greatest courage in circumstances of extreme danger, instituted in 1940. It consists of a silver cross with a medallion in the centre bearing a design of St. George and the Dragon, and is worn on the left breast before all other medals except the V.C. The G.C. was conferred on the island of Malta in 1942. The **George Medal,** also instituted in 1940, is a civilian award for acts of great courage. The medal is silver and circular, bearing on one side a crowned effigy of the sovereign, and on the reverse St. George and the Dragon. It is worn on the left breast.

GEORGETOWN. Seaport and cap. of Guyana, near the mouth of the Demerara. Founded 1781, and named by the British, it was held 1784–1812 by the Dutch who re-named it Stabroek; it was ceded to Britain in 1814. Pop. (1966) 176,100.

GEORGE TOWN. Chief port of the Federation

of Malaysia, cap. also of Penang state, on the island of Penang. Its chief exports are rice, sugar, pepper, tin. Pop. (1967) 234,930.

GEORGIA. The most southern of the 13 original states of the U.S.A , it lies between S. Carolina and Florida on the Atlantic seaboard. The chief crops are cotton, maize. tobacco, sugar, and fruits. The chief cities are Atlanta, the capital, and Savannah. Named after George II, G. was founded by the English in 1733. Area 58,876 sq. m.; pop. (1970) 4,589, 575.

GEORGIA S.S.R. of the U.S.S.R., bordering Turkey and including Abkhaz A.S.S.R., Adzhar A.S.S.R. and S. Ossetian autonomous region. An area of mountain and plateau, it produces cereals, tea, mulberries (as food for silkworms), tobacco, fruit, etc. Manganese is the chief mineral resource; steel, cement, and fertilizers are among its manufactures. The cap. is Tbilisi. The Georgian language does not belong to the Indo-European language family; it has been preserved by the inhabitants of G., despite many invasions, for more than 2,000 years: there are several dialects. Area 29,400 sq. m.; pop. (1967) 4,610,000.

GERANIUM (jerā'nium) or **Crane's Bill.** Genus of plants of the Geraniaceae family. Many of the Gs. common in Britain are not members of the genus G., but of *Pelargonium*. *See* CRANE'S BILL.

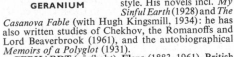

GERANIUM

GÉRARD (zhehrahr'), **François Pascal,** baron (1770–1837). French painter. He first exhibited at the Salon in 1791, became official portrait painter to Napoleon and to Louis XVIII, and produced a number of battle scenes.

GERHARDI, William Alexander (1895–   ). British novelist. B. in St. Petersburg, of English parents, he writes with a discursive, highly personal style. His novels incl. *My Sinful Earth* (1928) and *The Casanova Fable* (with Hugh Kingsmill, 1934): he has also written studies of Chekhov, the Romanoffs and Lord Beaverbrook (1961), and the autobiographical *Memoirs of a Polyglot* (1931).

GERHARDT (gār'haht), **Elena** (1883–1961). British soprano. B. at Leipzig, she was famous for her interpretations of *Lieder*.

GÉRICAULT (zhārikō'), **Jean Louis André Théodore** (1791–1824). French artist. An enthusiastic horseman – he d. as a result of a riding accident – he excelled in pictures introducing horses, e.g. 'The Riderless Horse Race' and 'The Derby at Epsom' – painted on a visit to England. His dramatic 'Raft of the Medusa', recording an incident in which shipwrecked seamen were deliberately set adrift, had political repercussions.

GERMAN, Sir Edward. Name used by British composer Edward German Jones (1862–1936). He studied at the R.A.M. and became a renowned theatrical conductor. His chief works are the operettas *Tom Jones* and *Merrie England*, and the incidental music to Shakespeare's *Henry VIII*. Besides these he wrote much instrumental, orchestral, and vocal music.

GERMAN. A branch of the Germanic group of the Indo-European languages, and more especially of its West Germanic division. The *High G.* of the S. and the centre differs from the *Low G.* of the N. chiefly in its having been affected by the 2nd or High German sound-shift which changed Germanic *b d g* to *p t k*; and, according to position, *p* to *pf* or *ff*, *t* to *z* (*ts*) or *zz* (ss), and *k* to *ch* or *hh*. *See* GERMANIC LANGUAGES.

GERMAN ART. Characterized always by intensity of feeling which finds expression in the mystic and in a realism pushed to the grotesque, G.A. also has a tradition of skilled craftsmanship. In the 13th cent. G.A. first emerged in the sculptures of Bamberg and Naumberg cathedrals, the wood carvings of Veit Stoss, sometimes claimed as Polish (Wit Swosz), and the bronzes of Peter Vischer. The earliest paintings resembled the miniatures of illuminated MSS, but with the series of panels of the life of Christ *c.* 1350 by the Master of Hohenfurth (Czech Vissy Brod), and the altar *c.* 1380

GERMAN ART. Superbly finished and glowing in colour, this 'Deposition' by the Master of St. Bartholomew (q.v.) shows the influence of the art of the N. Netherlands, where the artist worked as a young man.
Reproduced by courtesy of the Earl of Halifax.

for the monastery of Trebon by the Master of Wittingau (Czech Trebon), a high level was reached. To the 15th cent. belong the charming Stefan Lochner, the realists Hans Multscher (*c.* 1400–57) and Konrad Witz (*c.* 1400–*c.* 1446), and the painter-sculptor Michael Pacher (*c.* 1435–98). Incarnation of the Renaissance in Germany was Albrecht Dürer: other 16th cent. masters incl. Hans Baldung Grien (*c.* 1484–1545), Lucas Cranach, Albrecht Altdorfer,

GERMAN ART. Hans Holbein the Younger: a study of the artist's family 1528–9, now in the Musée de Beaux-Arts, Basle.

Grünewald, and Hans Holbein. The only notable name in the 17th cent. is that of Adam Elsheimer (1578–1610): in the 18th Chodowiecki's work is of historical value. Among the Romantics are the almost 'expressionist' portrait painter Philipp Otto Runge (1777–1810) and the landscapist Caspar David Friedrich (1774–1840). Max Liebermann (1847–1935) was the first to feel the influence of such foreign developments as Impressionism. At the turn of the cent. came Jugendstil (corresponding to French Art Nouveau), and then parallel with Fauvism the movement known as Die Brücke (The Bridge) which incl. Emil Nolde. Also important were the Blaue Reiter (Blue Rider) group – *see* KANDINSKY – and in architecture and the arts generally the Bauhaus (q.v.) was influential abroad.

GERMANY. Hitler and Mussolini stand side by side at the tomb of the Fascist 'martyrs' in 1938. The fanatic militarism which let loose on Europe the following year a tide of grotesque barbarity is symbolized in this picture.   *Photo: Keystone.*

GERMAN HISTORY. The W. Germanic tribes, originating in Scandinavia, early overran the region between the Rhine, Elbe, and Danube, where they were confined by the Roman power. In the 4th–5th cents. the Franks occupied Belgium and France, and there founded a kingdom which by Charlemagne's day had extended its authority over Germany. Under the Frankish kings the Germans accepted Christianity. After Charlemagne's death Germany was separated from France under its own kings while the local officials or dukes became virtually independent until the central power was restored by the Saxon dynasty (919–1002). Otto I, who in 962 revived the title of emperor, began the colonization of the Slav lands E. of the Elbe. This period of progress was ended by the feud between emperors and popes (1075–1250), which enabled the princes to recover their independence. A temporary revival of imperial power took place under Maximilian I (1493–1519), but he and his successor, Charles V (1519–56), were mainly concerned with dynastic interests outside Germany which brought them into conflict with France. The Reformation increased Germany's disunity, and led to the Thirty Years War (1618–48). The war not only reduced the Empire to a mere name, but destroyed Germany's economic and cultural life.

The rise of Brandenburg-Prussia as a military power began in the 17th cent., and reached its height under Frederick II (1740–86). Germany's regeneration was due, however, to Napoleon, who united W. Germany in the Confederation of the Rhine (1806) and introduced the ideas and reforms of the French Revolution: his reforms were subsequently imitated in Prussia. The Empire was abolished in 1806, and after 1815 Germany became a loose federation. In spite of persecution, the ideas of democracy and national unity spread, and inspired the unsuccessful revolutions of 1848. The growth of industry from 1850 also made national unity an economic necessity. Under Bismarck's leadership Prussia united Germany in 1871, after victorious wars with Austria and France. In the years following industry expanded greatly; the beginnings of a colonial empire and a fleet were made, and at home a powerful Socialist movement arose. Political, industrial, and colonial rivalries with Britain, France, and Russia all combined to produce the F.W.W.

In 1918 a revolution overthrew the monarchy, and the Socialists seized power, and estab. the democratic Weimar republic. The economic crisis of 1929–33 brought Germany near to revolution, until in 1933 the reaction manœuvred the Nazis into power. At home they solved the unemployment problem by a vast rearmament programme, abolished the democratic constitution, and ruthlessly destroyed all opposition; abroad the policy of aggression led to eventual defeat in the S.W.W. Germany was then divided, within her 1937 frontiers, into British, American, French, and Russian occupation zones until 1952.

Subsequent G.H. is overshadowed by the partition into the rival German Democratic Republic under a Communist régime and German Federal Republic under a Christian Democrat coalition, tension being periodically heightened by the anomalous position of Berlin (q.v.). *See* GERMANY. Economically the former encountered grave difficulties, until the revival of the mid-sixties. Under Adenauer and Erhard (qq.v.) the latter achieved an 'economic miracle' as a leading power of W. Europe (*see also* KIESINGER KURT). Rapprochement with France was followed up by Brandt (q.v.) with approaches to E. Europe.

GERMANI (gärmah′nē), **Fernando** (1906–   ). Italian organist. B. in Rome, he became prof. of organ music at the Conservatoire there in 1935.

FERNANDO GERMANI
Photo: Godfrey MacDomnic.

GERMANIC LANGUAGES. A branch of the Indo-European family. They are divided into: (1) *East Germanic*, consisting of Gothic, now extinct; (2) *North Germanic* or Scandinavian (Icelandic, Norwegian, Danish, Swedish); (3) *West Germanic*, divided into German, Dutch, Friesian, and English, the 2 last being somewhat more closely related between themselves. The chief feature which marks off the G.L. as a distinct group is the change in consonants collectively known as the Germanic sound-shift, and popularly referred to as *Grimm's Law*, whereby the Indo-European voiced aspirates became voiced spirants, later in certain cases voiced stops; p, t, and k changed to the corresponding unvoiced fricatives, and b, d, g to p, t, k respectively. There are certain exceptions to each of these rules, caused by the varying accent in Indo-European. Whereas in I.-E. the accent might fall on any syllable of the word, the G.L. stabilized it on the first syllable, the only exception being adverbial prefixes.

GERMANIUM. Chemical element, symbol Ge; at. no. 32; at. wt. 72·6, which was discovered in 1886. A grey-white, brittle, crystalline metal, it is in the silicon group, and its chemical and physical properties lie between those of silicon and tin. G. is widely used in the manufacture of transistors and rectifiers.

GERMAN LITERATURE. The fragmentary alliterative poem the *Hildebrandslied* (c. 800), the most substantial relic of the *Old High German* period, bears no comparison with the Old English literature of the same era, but in the *Middle High German* period there was a great flowering in the vernacular which had been forced into subservience to Latin since the early attempts at encouragement by Charlemagne. The court epics of Hartmann von Aue, Gottfried von Strassburg and Wolfram von Eschenbach in the early 13th cent. were modelled on the French in style and material, but the folk-epic *Nibelungenlied* revived the spirit of the old heroic Germanic sagas. Adopted – in the more limited meaning – from France and Provence, the *Minnesang* reached its height in the lyric poetry of Walther von der Vogelweide.

J. W. GOETHE. Sketched two months before his death by Schwerdgeburth.

Modern German literature begins in the 16th cent. with the standard of language set by Luther's Bible and then also came the climax of popular drama in the *Fastnachtsspiel* as handled by Hans Sachs. In the later 16th and early 17th cents. French influence was renewed and English influence, notably by troupes of players, was introduced: Martin Opitz's *Buch von der deutschen Poeterey* (1624), in which he advocates the imitation of foreign models, epitomizes the German Renaissance which was followed by the Thirty Years War vividly described in Grimmelshausen's *Simplicissimus*.

In the 18th cent. French Classicism predominated, extolled by Gottsched but opposed by Bodmer and Breitinger, whose writings prompted the Germanic *Messias* of Klopstock. Both Lessing and Herder were admirers of Shakespeare, and Herder's enthusiasm inaugurated the *Sturm und Drang* phase which emphasized individual inspiration, and his collection of folk songs was symptomatic of the feeling which inspired Bürger's modern ballad *Lenore*. Greatest representatives of the Classical period at the end of the cent. were Goethe and Schiller, but their ideals were combated by the new Romantic school which based its theories on the work of the brothers Schlegel, and Tieck, and which incl. Novalis, Arnim, Brentano, Eichendorff, Chamisso, Uhland, and Hoffmann.

With Kleist and Grillparzer in the early 19th cent. stress on the poetic in drama ends, and with Hebbel the psychological aspect becomes the more important. Notable c. 1830 was the 'Young German' movement led by Heine, Gutzkow, and Laube, which the authorities tried to suppress. Other excellent writers of the cent. incl. Jeremias Gotthelf, storyteller of peasant life; the psychological novelist Friedrich Spielhagen; the masters of the *Novelle*, Gottfried Keller and Theodor Storm, also both fine poets; and Wilhelm Raabe and Theodor Fontane, novelists of realism. Naturalistic drama found its chief exponents in Hauptmann and Sudermann. Influential in literature, as in politics and economics, were Marx and Nietzsche.

THOMAS MANN
Courtesy of Secker and Warburg.

Outstanding in the early years of the 20th cent. were the lyric poets Richard Dehmel, Stefan George, and Rainer Maria Rilke; von Hofmannsthal both poet and dramatist, and the novelists Thomas and Heinrich Mann, Ludwig Renn, E. M. Remarque, and Hermann Hesse. Just before the F.W.W. Expressionism emerged in the poetry of Georg Trakl, dominated the novels of Franz Kafka and the plays of Ernst Toller, Franz Werfel, Georg Kaiser and Karl Sternheim, and was later to influence Bertold Brecht. Under National Socialism many major writers left the country, others were silenced or ignored: to the period after the S.W.W. belong the Swiss dramatists Max Frisch and Friedrich Dürrenmatt, the novelists Heinrich Böll and Heimito von Doderer, and the poets Paul Celan and Günter Grass.

GERMAN MEASLES. Rubella; an acute infectious fever, usually of children, having an incubation period of 10–15 days. The first signs are slight fever, catarrh, and a general rash, paler than that of measles. The patient is usually well in 10 days, but in the case of a pregnant woman her unborn child may be affected.

GERMAN OCEAN. Ger. name for the North Sea.

GERMANY. Country of Europe, bounded to the N. by the N. Sea, Denmark, and the Baltic; to the E. by Poland, to the E. and S. by Czechoslovakia, to the S. by Austria and Switzerland; and to the W. by France, Luxemburg, Belgium, and the Netherlands. The surface is divided into (1) the lowlands in the N., forming part of the Great European Plain and traversed by the Northern and the Southern Ridge, two ranges of low hills, (2) the central mountains, and (3) the Alps with their foreland. The mountains of G. pivot on the Fichtelgebirge in N. Bavaria; to the N.W. of it are the Thuringian Forest and the Harz Mountains; to the N.E. the Erzgebirge; to the S. the Bohemian Forest; to the S.W. the Franconian and Swabian Juras, and the Black Forest; to the W. the Taunus Mts. In S.E. Bavaria the Alps culminate in the Zugspitze (9,700 ft.), G.'s highest mountain. The most important rivers are the Rhine, with its tributaries the Neckar, Main, Lahn, Moselle, Sieg, Ruhr, and Lippe; the Ems; the Weser; the Elbe; the Oder; and the Danube. S. Bavaria is noted for its lakes.

Economics. Wheat is grown in the fertile plains of N. Germany, but rye is much more extensively cultivated. Tobacco and hops are grown in Baden, Hessen, and Bavaria, while the Rhine, Main, and Moselle valleys are famed for their wines. Magdeburg is the centre of sugar-beet cultivation; potatoes are grown on the sandy tracts in the N. The Vierlande nr. Hamburg and the Spreewald nr. Berlin specialize in market gardening.

G. is well supplied with coal, mined in the Rhine-Ruhr district, which contains the largest field in Europe, in the Saar basin, and round Zwickau. Lignite is worked in central Germany, nr. Cologne, nr. Halle, and nr. Brunswick. Iron is found in the S. of the Ruhr district, nr. Hanover, and nr. Brunswick. G. also has supplies of rock salt (Halle), zinc (Aachen), copper (Harz), tungsten, lead, antimony, uranium, and other non-ferrous metals (Erzgebirge), petroleum (Emsland and Celle-Peine area), peat (Lüneburg Heath). The mineral springs of Baden-Baden, Wiesbaden, Ems, etc., are famous.

There is an excellent railway network, and c. 80,000 miles of roads, incl. *Autobahnen*, reserved for motor traffic. The main rivers are navigable; important canals incl. the Rhine-Herne, Dortmund-Ems, Mittelland, Kiel, and Ludwig – the last linking the Rhine and the Danube. Internal and external air services, centred on Cologne, are well developed in W. Germany.

The most extensive development of German industry is found in the Ruhr valley where the nearness of coal to iron deposits has encouraged the growth of a huge iron and steel industry. Here Essen, Solingen, and Remscheid are among the main manufacturing centres. Glass is manufactured at Dresden, fine china at Meissen, while Gotha is a centre for

DIVISIONS OF GERMANY

	Area in sq. m.	Pop. in 1,000s	Capital
Federal Republic of (Western) Germany Länder			Bonn
Baden-Württemberg ..	13,803	8,534	Stuttgart
Bavaria	27,240	10,217	Munich
Bremen	156	750	Bremen
Hamburg	288	1,847	Hamburg
Hessen	8,150	5,240	Wiesbaden
Lower Saxony ..	18,290	6,967	Hanover
North-Rhine-Westphalia	13,111	16,836	Düsseldorf
Rhineland-Palatinate ..	7,656	3,613	Mainz
Saarland	991	1,132	Saarbrücken
Schleswig-Holstein ..	6,054	2,473	Kiel
West Berlin ..	186	2,185	—
	95,925	59,794	
Democratic Republic of (Eastern) Germany* ..	41,636	17,080	East Berlin
	137,561	76,874	

*Divided 1945–52 into Länder (Brandenburg, Mecklenburg, Saxony, Saxony-Anhalt, Thuringia) based on the old duchies; re-divided 1952 into 14 districts (Bezirke) each named after its chief town: Dresden, Erfurt, Frankfort-on-Oder, Gera, Halle, Karl-Marx-Stadt (Chemnitz), Kottbus, Leipzig, Magdeburg, Neubrandenburg, Potsdam, Rostock, Schwerin, Suhl.
NOTE: More than 45,000 sq. m. (from which the German inhabitants fled during the S.W.W. or were subsequently expelled) were in Polish or Russian occupation.

pottery. There are huge chemical works at Leuna, nr. Leipzig; the textile industry is important at Wuppertal and Karl-Marx-Stadt, while Krefeld manufactures silk and velvet. Optical and scientific instruments are produced at Stuttgart and Dresden. Leverkusen, nr. Cologne, and Mannheim and Ludwigshafen specialize in artificial dyes. Tourism is important, especially in the Black Forest.

People and Government. The largest centres in G. are Berlin, Hamburg, Munich, Cologne, Essen, Düsseldorf, and Frankfurt-am-Main. Approximately two-thirds of the pop. are Protestants and one-third Catholics. A factor in the striking economic expansion of the W. German rep. in the post-war period was the influx of the foreign workers from Italy, Spain, etc. Important in European and also in world politics is the W. German pressure for a re-union of the two republics, which is linked to a varying extent with a revival of the German claim for restoration of the former frontier and the 'lost' territories sometimes incl. the Sudetenland.

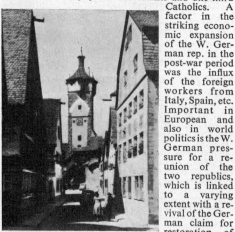

GERMANY. The Klingentor, one of the picturesque medieval gate towers of Rothenburg-ob-der-Tauber in Bavaria, once a free imperial city.
Courtesy of the German Tourist Information Bureau.

The *Federal Republic of Germany* was formed in 1949 by the union of the British, American, and French zones (excl. at that time Saarland, q.v.); it achieved full sovereignty and was recognized by the Western powers in 1955. The Russian zone, it was hoped, would eventually enter the Federal Republic. It has a parliament of 2 houses: the *Bundestag*, or federal diet, elected by universal suffrage for 4 years, and the *Bundesrat*, or federal council, consisting of the members of the govts. of the *Länder* or states. The pres. is elected for 5 years for a maximum of 2 terms by the federal assembly which consists of the *Bundestag* and an equal number of popularly elected representatives from the *Länder*. The govt. is headed by the federal chancellor, chosen by the *Bundestag*.

The *German Democratic Republic*, formerly the Russian zone, was also set up in 1949, but is recognized only by the Communist powers. Under the Constitution of 1968 there is a single-party, popularly elected people's chamber (*Volkskammer*) which nominates the members of the Council of State (supreme legislative and executive organ) and Council of Ministers. The Communist Party retains all real power. The pop. and economy were in decline, owing to emigration to the W., until 1964 but the mid-sixties saw a marked improvement in prosperity.

By the Potsdam Agreement, 1945, those parts of Germany lying E. of the Oder-W. Neisse rivers were placed (i) under Russian administration: the northern part of former East Prussia; (ii) under Polish administration: the southern part of former East Prussia and the territory lying between the pre-war and post-war frontiers of E. Germany. A treaty normalizing W. German–Polish relations in 1970 recognized the existing boundary on the Oder and western Neisse. *See also* BERLIN.

GERMISTON. S. African industrial town in the Witwatersrand gold-mining area, Transvaal. Pop. (1960) 204,605, of whom 84,419 were white.

GERM WARFARE. The use of biological agents to produce disease or death in man, animals, or crops. Of the 2 main types, the first comprises the use of hormones (normally used as weed-killers) to destroy crops; the second type consists of the living agents, e.g. disease-bearing insects, bacteria, viruses, and fungi. If the intention was to enfeeble the population and lower morale, agents causing sickness would be used, e.g. rabbit fever (tularemia) and undulant fever (brucellosis): but to kill, plague, typhus, cholera, and smallpox would need to be used. To be effective, such agents must be highly infective; able to withstand heat, light, and drying; rapidly disseminated; able to cause high initial mortality; and foreign to the part of the world against which they are directed, so that there is no natural immunity. The only protection is an informed populace and an alert and highly efficient public-health organization, adequately equipped.

GERONA (khārōn′ah). Rich prov. of Catalonia, Spain, producing copper, lead, cork, wine, etc.; bounded on the E. by the Mediterranean, on the N. by France. Its coast, the Costa Brava, is a tourist resort. Area 2,272 sq. m.; pop. (1960) 351,369. The cap. is G.; pop. (est.) 30,000.

GERRY (ger′i), **Elbridge** (1744–1814). American politician. Gov. of Massachusetts, in 1812 he had his men redraw the map of the state's senatorial districts to gain congressional election, the shape resembling a salamander: hence 'gerrymandering' to denote politic revision of electoral boundaries.

GERS (zhăr). Fr. river, 110 m. long, rising in the Lannemezan Plateau and flowing N. to join the Garonne 5 m. above Agen.

GERSHWIN, George (1898–1937). American jazz musician. B. in Brooklyn of Jewish parents, he composed popular jazz songs, notable for their instinctive rhythm and melody. He also wrote more serious music, in which he incorporated the essentials of jazz, e.g. the tone poem *An American in Paris*, *Rhapsody in Blue* (1924), and the opera *Porgy and Bess* (1935).

GESTAPO. An abbreviated form of *Geheime Staatspolizei*, the Nazi secret political police, formed in 1933. It was one of the organizations accused at the Nuremberg war-guilt trials (q.v.) in 1946, and was condemned.

GETHSEMANE (geth-sem′an-ee). Site on the Mount of Olives, just E. of Jerusalem, of the garden in which, according to tradition, Judas betrayed Jesus. When Jerusalem was divided in 1948 between Israel and Jordan, G. fell within Jordanian territory.

GETTY, John Paul (1892–). American millionaire, pres. of the G. Oil Co. from 1947, and founder of the J. Paul Getty Museum, California, noted for its 18th cent. French furniture and tapestries and an art collection ranging the 15–17th cents.

GETTYSBURG (get′iz-). Borough of south Pa., U.S.A., where in 1863 the battle of G. was fought. It was a Northern victory, and marked the turning-point of the American Civil War. The site is a national cemetery at the dedication of which Lincoln delivered his famous G. address Nov. 19, 1863. Pop. (1960) 7,960.

GEYSER (ga′ser). A natural spring which, at more or less regular intervals, explosively discharges into the air a column of steam and hot water. One of the best-known Gs. is Old Faithful, in Yellowstone National Park, Wyoming, U.S.A.; Gs. occur also in New Zealand and Iceland.

SIR FREDERICK GIBBERD. To the left is the Metropolitan Cathedral of Christ the King, Liverpool.
Photos: Lotte Meitner-Graf (portrait) and Henk Snoek·

GEYSER. Pohutu, the largest geyser in the Whakarewarewa group at Rotorua in New Zealand, dwarfs the spectators. The Maori guide wears the traditional cloak of Kiwi feathers, the *kakahu*, now rare and highly valued. *Courtesy of the High Commissioner of New Zealand.*

GHA′NA. Republic within the British Commonwealth, in W. Africa, formed by the former British colony of the Gold Coast and the part of Togoland formerly under British trusteeship. It achieved independence in 1957, entered into union with Guinea, 1958, and became a republic in 1960. The cap. is Accra. The name is derived from the ancient Sudanese empire of G. (fl. 4th–10th cent. A.D.), whose capital was Timbuktoo. The chief exports are cocoa, timber, diamonds, manganese, bauxite, and the gold which gave G. its European name; maize, rice, cassava, millet and tobacco are grown for home consumption.

The rule of Pres. Nkrumah (q.v.) was ended by a military coup in 1966, and under a new constitution for promulgation on return to civil rule in 1969, there was provision for a pres. without executive power and an elected nat. assembly.

Area 92,000 sq. m.; pop. (1966) 7,945,000, the great majority fetishists.

GHENT. Cap. of E. Flanders, Belgium, at the junction of the rivers Scheldt and Lys. G. is connected with the Scheldt estuary by ship canal. It has cotton and linen factories, sugar refineries, tanneries, iron foundries, etc. The university, founded in 1816, became Flemish in 1930. The earliest parts of the cathedral of St. Bavon date from *c.* 940: and the town hall from the 15th cent. Pop. (1966) 157,048.

GHETTO. The quarter of a town set aside by law for Jewish residence, and enclosed by gates and walls. The G., the origins of which go back to the Middle Ages, was first enforced by papal bull in Italy in 1555. It was largely swept away at the time of the French Revolution, save in eastern Europe, but was revived by the Germans 1940–5. Also used

generally for any minority slum quarter in a city.

GHIBERTI (gēber′tē), **Lorenzo** (1378–1455). Italian sculptor. A goldsmith by training, he created in the bronze doors for the baptistry of Florence – his native city – one of the most beautiful works of the Italian Renaissance. He also wrote *Commentarii* on art history.

GHIRLANDAIO (gērlahndah′yō), **Domenico.** Name by which the Florentine painter Domenico Bigordi (*c.* 1449–94) is known. He painted chiefly frescoes in his native city of Florence.

GIANT'S CAUSEWAY. Stretch of columnar basalt on the N. coast of Antrim, N. Ireland, forming a headland jutting out to sea. It was formed by an outflow of lava in Tertiary times which has solidified in polygonal columns.

GIBBERD, Sir Frederick (1908–). British architect and town planner. His works incl. the new town of Santa Teresa, Venezuela, and the R.C. Cathedral, Liverpool. Knighted 1967.

GIBBON, Edward (1737–94). British historian. B. at Putney, he was withdrawn from Oxford owing to his conversion to Roman Catholicism in 1753. Sent to Lausanne by his father, he was reconverted in 1754, met Voltaire in 1757, and fell in love with the future Mme Necker, from whom parental disapproval parted him. Setting out on a tour of Europe in 1763, he conceived the idea of *The History of the Decline and Fall of the Roman Empire*, while in Rome in 1764. The first vol. appeared in 1776, and was immediately successful, although he was compelled

GHENT. A fine specimen of the small medieval fort, the Rabot narrowly escaped destruction in 1540 when Charles V destroyed the defence system of Ghent. He had not forgotten the defeat of his ancestors, Frederick III and Maximilian of Austria, in 1488 by the men of the city under Philip van Cleef. *Courtesy of Belgian National Tourist Office.*

to reply to attacks on his account of the early development of Christianity by a *Vindication* (1779). The work was completed in 1788. From 1783 he had lived in Lausanne, but returned to England and d. in London.

GIBBON, Lewis Grassic. Pseudonym of Anglo-Scottish novelist James Leslie Mitchell (1901–35). His great work was the trilogy *A Scots Quair* (*Sunset Song, Cloud Howe* and *Grey Granite*, 1932–4), set against the background of the countryside and towns of eastern Scotland where he was born and bred. Written in a unique prose style, and reflecting the author's left-wing ideas, it won high praise. Under his real name he wrote *Spartacus* (1933), which deals with the great Roman slave rebellion of 73–71 B.C.

GIBBON. Genus of apes (*Hylobates*). The body is hairy except for the buttocks, which distinguishes them from other families of apes. They have long limbs, no tail, and are arboreal in habit, but when on the ground walk upright. They are found from Assam, through the Malay peninsula to Borneo.

GIBBONS, Grinling (1648–1721). Woodcarver and sculptor – his origin – English or Dutch – is disputed. On the recommendation of Evelyn, he worked for Charles II and from 1714 was master carver to George I. For Sir Christopher Wren he did work on St. Paul's cathedral choir, and country houses such as Petworth have fine examples of his carvings of flowers, birds, and foliage executed in great detail and with exquisite delicacy.

GIBBONS, Orlando (1583–1625). English composer. B. at Cambridge, he was the most distinguished of a family of musicians, and was appointed organist at Westminster Abbey in 1623. His finest works are his madrigals and motets.

GIBBONS, Stella Dorothea (1902–). British novelist. B. in London, she became a journalist, and is best known for her *Cold Comfort Farm* (1932), a satire on the regional novel.

GIBBS, Sir Philip (1877–1962). British writer known for his novels of contemporary life between the world wars, and for *The Street of Adventure*, a fictional account of his experiences in Fleet Street.

GIBEON. Biblical city, noted for its fine wine, the modern Arab village of Al Jib, 8 m. N. of Jerusalem, built on a rocky hill. Excavation has revealed tunnels through 389 ft. of solid rock justifying ancient traditions of the city's remarkable water system, and the water was found still sweet after 2,500 years of closure.

GIBRALTAR (jibrawl'tar). **City of.** Naval and air base, and fortress occupying a rocky promontory near the extreme S. of Spain. The town is on the N.W. side, and the harbour is enclosed by moles, and covers 440 acres.

Captured by Sir George Rooke in 1704, G. was ceded to Britain under the Treaty of Utrecht (1713); Spanish attempts to retake it incl. the siege of 1779–83. Following abortive Anglo-Spanish negotiations in 1966, a referendum in 1967 resulted in an overwhelming majority in G. for continued assocn. with Britain. In 1969 G. ceased to be a Crown Colony, becoming known as the *City of G.* Under the new constitution there is a Gov. and an elected House of Assembly of 15 members. Area 2½ sq. m.; pop. (1966) 25,184. *See* BARBARY APE.

GIBRALTAR, Strait of. The strait between N. Africa and Spain which forms the western entrance to the Mediterranean Sea from the Atlantic. It varies in width from 9 to 23 m. and is 35 m. long.

GIBSON, Charles Dana (1867–1944). American illustrator. B. in Mass., he became famous for his portrayal of an idealized type of American young woman, known as the 'Gibson Girl'.

GIBSON, Guy (1918–44). British airman. A wing commander of the R.A.F. in the S.W.W., with D.S.O., D.F.C., and bars, he took a leading part in the breaching of the Möhne Dam in 1943, for which he was

GIBRALTAR. With the rocky height near Ceuta on the African shore, Gibraltar formed the Pillars of Hercules regarded by ancient mariners of the Mediterranean as the limits of the known world.   *Photo: Anne Bolt.*

awarded the V.C. He was killed when his plane crashed over Holland returning from a raid.

GIBSON, Wilfred (1878–1962). British poet. His best poetry is concerned with human nature, and often with the landscape and people of his native Northumberland, as in *The Stonefolds* (1907), and *Krindlesyke* (1922).

GIDE (zhēd), **André** (1869–1951). French author. B. in Paris, of a Calvinist family, he pub. his first book *Les Cahiers d'André Walter*, a complex psychological confession, in 1891. In later books, *L'Immoraliste* (1902), *La Porte étroite* (1909), *La Symphonie pastorale* (1919), the autobiographical *Si le grain ne meurt* (1926), and his one real novel, *Les Faux-Monnayeurs* (1926, *The Coiners*), he develops the themes of self-fulfilment and renunciation, the 2 extremes between which he himself swung. His openly confessed homosexuality, dating from earliest youth, did not prevent the award to him in 1947 of a Nobel prize. The *Journal* (1939), with later supplements, is on the same level as his novels.

Courtesy of Secker and Warburg.

GIDEONS INTERNATIONAL, The. A Christian business and professional men's association with *c.* 20,000 members in more than 50 countries, which aims at winning the lost for Christ, founded in 1899, at Jamesville, Wisconsin. It is most celebrated for its scripture programme, which incl. the placing of Bibles in hotel and motel rooms: total distribution since 1908 *c.* 7,000,000 Bibles and 45,000,000 N.Ts. The International H.Q. is at Nashville, Tennessee and the name derives from the might of the minority illus. by the Biblical story of Gideon.

GIELGUD (gēl'good), **Sir John** (1904–). British actor-producer. A great-nephew of Ellen Terry (q.v.), he made his début at the Old Vic in 1921, attracted notice as Romeo in 1924, and created his most famous role as Hamlet in 1929. He has since produced and appeared in numerous plays incl. many by Chekhov and Shakespeare. His film roles incl. Clarence in *Richard III* (1955) and the Earl of Warwick in *St.*

Joan (1957). His elder brother **Val G.** (1900–) was Head of B.B.C. Sound Drama 1929–63, and has written plays and novels.

GIESSEN (gē'sen). Manufacturing town on the Lahn, Germany, 34 m. N. of Frankfurt-am-Main. It has a famous univ. founded 1605. Pop. (1960) 64,750.

GIFFARD (zhifahr'), **Henri** (1825–82). French inventor. In 1852 he constructed and successfully

SIR JOHN GIELGUD.
Photo: Angus McBean.

demonstrated at Paris the first airship, a balloon driven by a light-weight steam engine.

GIGLI (jēl'yi), **Benjamino** (1890–1957). Italian tenor. From his operatic début in 1914, he was specially successful in roles from Puccini, Gounod, and Massenet. His sensuous lyrical voice was unforced and perfect throughout its range.

GIJÓN. Ancient seaport in northern Spain, in Oviedo prov. Pop. (1965) 141,488.

GILBERT, Sir Alfred (1854–1934). British sculptor and goldsmith, b. in London, best known for his 'Eros' (memorial fountain to the 7th earl of Shaftesbury) in Piccadilly Circus, London. He was elected R.A. in 1892, and was knighted in 1932.

GILBERT, Cass (1859–1934). American architect. B. in Ohio, he was famous for his 'skyscrapers', incl. the Woolworth Building, New York.

GILBERT, Sir Humphrey (*c.* 1539–83). English navigator. B. at Dartmouth, the half-brother of Sir Walter Raleigh, he sailed from Plymouth for Newfoundland in 1583, and landed at the site of St. John's, taking possession in the queen's name – whence Newfoundland claims to be the oldest British colony. His ship foundered on the return voyage.

GILBERT, Sir William Schwenk (1836–1911). British humorist and dramatist. B. in London, he was called to the Bar in 1863, but in 1869 pub. a collection of his humorous verse and drawings, *Bab Ballads* – 'Bab' being his own early nickname – which was followed by a 2nd vol. in 1873. His collaboration with Arthur Sullivan (q.v.) in their great series of comic operas dates from 1871. The popularity of these was due as much to G.'s witty lyrics and plots as to Sullivan's music, but personal relations between the 2 men were often cool. He was knighted in 1907.

GILBERT AND ELLICE ISLANDS. British colony in the western Pacific consisting of the Ellice islands, the Line islands (Fanning, Washington, and Christmas), Ocean island, the Phoenix group, the Gilbert islands, etc. Total area, 395 sq. m.; pop. (1966) 51,900.

GILES (jīlz), **Carl Ronald** (1916–). British cartoonist for the *Daily* and *Sunday Express* from 1943, especially noted for his 'typical' British family complete from realistic infants-in-arms to a redoubtable grandma.

GILGAMESH. Hero of Sumerian, Hittite, Akkadian and Assyrian legend. The 12 verse 'books' of the *Epic of G.* were recorded in a standard version on a dozen cuneiform tablets by Assurbanipal's scholars in the 7th cent. B.C. and the epic itself is older than the *Iliad* by at least 1,500 years. One-third mortal and two-thirds divine, G. is Lord of Uruk, and his friend Enkidu (half beast, half man) dies for him: the incident of the Flood was later drawn upon by O.T. writers.

GILL, Eric (1882–1940). British sculptor and engraver. After 2 years at Chichester art school, and a few yrs. in an architect's office, he studied lettering at the Central School, under Edward Johnston, who decisively influenced him, before beginning his artistic

career carving inscriptions for tombstones; his interest in lettering and book production later led him to invent 4 new type-faces. Among his best-known sculptures are the 'Stations of the Cross' in Westminster Cathedral (begun 1913); 'Christ driving the moneylenders from the Temple' at Leeds univ. (1922–3); and the sculptures on Broadcasting House, London (1933). He also did numerous wood engravings, distinguished by their precise, clear-cut lines. His autobiography was published in 1940.

GILLEN, Francis James (1856–1912). Australian ethnologist. B. near Adelaide, he obtained a unique knowledge of the aboriginal peoples of the interior. In 1902 he and Baldwin Spencer conducted an ethnological expedition across Australia to the Gulf of Carpentaria, and collaborated in writing *Native Tribes of Central Australia*, etc.

GILLETTE (jilet'), **King Camp** (1855–1932). American inventor of the G. safety-razor.

GILLINGHAM (jil-). Town (bor.) in N. Kent, England, near the mouth of the Medway. It includes Chatham dockyard. Pop. (1961) 72,611.

GILLRAY, James (1757–1815). English caricaturist. His 1,500 cartoons, full of broad humour and keen satire (1779–1811), were aimed at the French, George III, politicians, and social follies of his day. He died after 4 years' insanity.

GILPIN, William (1724–1804). British artist. Vicar of Boldre from 1777 and a keen educationist, he is remembered as the inventor of the 'picturesque', establishing precise rules for the production of this effect in his essays. He pub. accounts of his summer tours with aquatint drawings. His brother **Sawrey G.** (1733–1807) was a sporting artist, producing hunting scenes and assisting other artists, such as Turner, by painting animals in their pictures.

GILROY, Norman Thomas (1896–). R.C. archbishop of Sydney from 1940, and first Australian cardinal, appointed 1946.

GILSON (jēlsoñ'), **Etienne** (1884–). French historian and philosopher, prof. of medieval philosophy at the Sorbonne 1921–32 and prof. at the Collège de France 1932–51. His greatest works are *The Spirit of Mediaeval Philosophy* (1932), *God and Philosophy* (1941), and *Elements of Christian Philosophy* (1959).

GIN (jin). A potable spirit, prepared by distilling a mash containing maize, malt, and rye, and flavouring it with juniper, etc. In Holland it is called geneva, a corruption of the French *genièvre*, juniper.

GINGER (jin'jer). Spice derived from the underground stem of *Zingiber officinale*, a reed-like perennial plant, native to S.E. Asia, which grows 3 ft. high, rarely producing flowers.

GINGER ALE and **BEER.** Sweetened, carbonated, and non-excisable beverages, aerated by fermentation or artificial means. They include ginger rhizome flavouring, sugar, syrup, harmless acid and colouring. The only difference between them is the employment of bitters in the preparation of G.B.

GI'NGKO. Tree (*Gingko biloba*), also known from the resemblance of its leaves to those of the maidenhair fern – though much enlarged – as the maidenhair tree. A 'living fossil', unchanged since prehistoric times, now only cultivated in Japan and China. First planted in England in the 18th cent., it does well in towns, e.g. Cardiff and New York. In 200 years it may reach *c.* 100 ft., and the fruits have edible kernels, although the pulp is poisonous.

GINGOLD, Hermione (1897–). English actress. She has acted in all media, but is noted for her biting satire as a comedienne, especially in intimate review, e.g. the *Sweet and Low* series 1942-6.

GINNER, Charles (1878–1952). British painter. B. at Cannes, he settled in London in 1910, and was one of the London Group from 1914. He was noted for the treatment of buildings in his landscapes.

Q

GIOLITTI (jōlit′i), **Giovanni** (1842–1928). Italian statesman. B. at Mondovi, he was P.M. in 1892–3, 1903–5, 1906–9, 1911–14, and 1920–1. He opposed Italian intervention in the F.W.W.

GIONO (jō′nō), **Jean** (1895–1970). French novelist, whose books are chiefly set in Provence. *Que ma joie demeure* (1935: *Joy of Man's Desiring*) is an attack on life in towns and a plea for a return to country life. In 1956 he pub. a defence of Gaston Dominici, who allegedly murdered an English family on holiday, maintaining that the old farmer exemplified the misunderstandings between town and country people.

GIORGIONE (jorjō′ne) (1478–1511). Name by which the Venetian artist, Giorgio of Castelfranco, is known. He was a leader of the High Renaissance, and influenced Titian and others. His masterpiece is the 'Madonna and Child Enthroned with Two Saints', an altar-piece for the church of Castelfranco.

GIOTTO (jot′tō) **DI BONDŌ′NE** (1266/76–1337). Italian painter, sculptor, and architect. B. at Vespignano, N. of Florence, he infused new life into Italian art, painting in a naturalistic style and depicting sacred personages as real people. He is chiefly famous for his frescoes in churches at Assisi, Padua, and Florence. In 1334 he was appointed master of the cathedral at Florence and official architect of the city. He collaborated with Andrea Pisano in decorating the cathedral façade with statues, and designed the Campanile, which was completed after his death. *See* ITALIAN ART.

GIRAFFE (jiraf′). Tallest mammal, in the family Giraffidae. It measures over 18 ft. in height, the neck accounting for nearly half this amount. The G. has 2 small skin-covered horns on the head and a long tufted tail. The skin has a mottled appearance and is reddish brown and cream. Gs. are now found only in Africa, S. of the Sahara Desert.

GIRAFFE. Specimens from northern Africa tend to have white 'socks', which show particularly on the forelegs of the animal illus. here. The young are born singly and in 3 days are able to trot almost at adult pace.

GIRA′LDUS CAMBRE′NSIS (Gerald the Welshman) (*c.* 1146–1220). Welsh bishop and historian. B. in Pembrokeshire, he was elected bishop of St. David's in 1198. One of the foremost Latinists of his age, he wrote a history of the conquest of Ireland by Henry II and *Itinerarium Cambrense.*

GIRAUDOUX (zhērohdōō′), **Jean** (1882–1944). French diplomat, author of light-weight novels, e.g. *Simon le pathétique* (1918), an autobiographical window on adolescence, and plays incl. the humorous renderings of Greek legends *Amphitryon 38* (1929) and *La guerre de Troie n'aura pas lieu* (1935).

GIRGENTI. Another form of AGRIGENTO.

GIRL GUIDES. A youth organization for girls estab. in 1910 by Lord Baden-Powell and his sister, Agnes Baden-Powell. As reorganized 1967 it has 3 branches: Brownie G. (7–11), Guides (10–16), and Ranger G. (14–20) with adult leaders known as Guiders. The World Assocn. of G.G. and Girl Scouts (the name by which they are known in U.S.A.) ensures international co-operation.

GIRO (ji′rō). System of receiving and making payments through a current account with the Post Office. Beginning in Austria in 1883, it spread through W. Europe, and was introduced in the U.K. in 1968 (H.Q. Bootle). The name derives from Gk. *guros* 'circle', since the money goes round and round.

GIRONDE (zhēroṅd′). Navigable French estuary off the Bay of Biscay, formed by the mouths of the Garonne and Dordogne rivers. It is 50 m. long and 2 to 6 m. wide. It gives its name to the largest dept. of France.

GIRON′DINS. The right-wing republican party in the French Revolution, so called because a number of their leaders came from the Gironde. They were driven from power by the Jacobins in 1793.

GIRTIN, Thomas (1775–1802). English painter. The poetic spirit and technical innovations of this friend and contemporary of Turner revolutionized landscape painting in water-colour, and were part of the romantic attitude of the early 19th cent.

GISSING, George Robert (1857–1903). British author. B. in Yorks, he taught for many years in London and the U.S.A., leading a life of near destitution. His first novel, *Workers in the Dawn*, appeared in 1880 but it was not until *Demos* (1886), which dealt with socialist ideas, that G. became at all widely read. Among his later books are *New Grub Street* (1891), the autobiographical *Private Papers of Henry Ryecroft* (1903), and a study of Dickens. His books depict, with a realism and sincerity born of experience, the degrading effects on men and women of the struggle against circumstances and poverty.

GIULINI (gūlē′ni), **Carlo Maria** (1914–). Italian conductor. Principal conductor at La Scala, Milan, 1953–5, he is the outstanding conductor today of Italian grand opera, e.g. Verdi's *Don Carlos* at Covent Garden in 1958. He is also a fine interpreter of modern composers, as well as of Brahms, Haydn and Mozart.

CARLO MARIA GIULINI
Photo: Godfrey MacDomnic.

GLACE (glas) **BAY.** Port on Cape Breton Island, Nova Scotia, Canada, centre of a coal-mining area. Pop. (1966) 23,516.

GLĀ′CIER. A compacted mass of ice which originates in mountains in the snowfields above the snowline, where the annual snowfall exceeds the annual melting and drainage. It moves slowly down a valley or depression, and is constantly replenished from its source. The scenery produced by the passing of Gs. is characteristic. When a G. moves over an uneven surface crevasses are formed in it; if it reaches the sea it breaks up to form icebergs.

GLADIĀ′TORS. Professional fighters, recruited mainly from slaves, criminals, and prisoners of war, who fought to the death for the entertainment of the ancient Romans. The custom, which originated in the practice of slaughtering slaves on a chieftain's grave, was introduced into Rome from Etruria in 264 B.C., and survived until the 5th cent. A.D.

GLADIŌ′LUS. Genus of plants of the Iridaceae (Iris) family. The tall leafy stems arise from corms and bear a spike of brightly coloured, irregular flowers. The perianth is funnel-shaped, and in the cultivated varieties may be any shade but blue.

GLADSTONE, William Ewart (1809–98). British Liberal statesman. B. in Liverpool, the son of a rich merchant, he was ed. at Eton and Oxford, and entered parliament as a Tory in 1833. In Peel's govt. he was Pres. of the Board of Trade 1843–5, and Colonial Sec. 1845–6. He left the Tory Party with the Peelite group in 1846, and after 1859 identified himself with the Liberals. He was Chancellor of the Exchequer in Aberdeen's govt. 1852–5, and in Palmerston and Russell's govts. 1859–66. Becoming P.M. in 1868–74, he carried through a series of important reforms, incl. the disestablishment of

W. E. GLADSTONE
By G. F. Watts
Photo: N.P.G.

the Church of Ireland, the Irish Land Act, the abolition of the purchase of army commissions and of religious tests in the universities, and the introduction of elementary education and of vote by ballot.

During Disraeli's govt. of 1874–80 G. strongly resisted his imperialist and pro-Turkish policy, and by his Midlothian campaign of 1879 helped to overthrow him. G.'s second govt. of 1880–5 was confronted with difficult problems in Ireland, Egypt and S. Africa, and lost prestige through its failure to relieve Gen. Gordon. Returning to office in 1886, G. introduced his Home Rule Bill, which was defeated by the secession of the Liberal Unionists, and he thereupon resigned. After 6 years' opposition he formed his last govt. in 1892; his 2nd Home Rule Bill was rejected by the Lords, and in 1894 he resigned. He is buried in Westminster Abbey.

GLADWYN, Hubert Miles Gladwyn Jebb, 1st baron G. (1900–). British diplomat. From Eton and Magdalen Coll., Oxford, he went on in 1924 to the diplomatic service, and as counsellor from 1943 attended the conferences of Quebec, Cairo, Tehran, Dunbarton Oaks, Yalta, San Francisco and Potsdam. He was permanent representative at the U.N. 1950–4, then British ambassador to France until his retirement in 1960.

GLAMIS (glahmz). Village in Angus, Scotland, near which is G. castle, seat of the earl of Strathmore and Kinghorne, and birthplace of Princess Margaret.

GLAMO'RGANSHIRE. County of S. Wales lying between Brecknock and the Bristol Channel. The southern part, the Vale of Glamorgan, is a low-lying, fertile area devoted to mixed farming. The northern part is occupied by part of the Welsh mountains, and in the valleys coal is mined. The principal coal-mining towns are Rhondda, Aberdare, and Merthyr Tydfil. Other industries include tin-plating at Swansea and Cardiff; copper at Swansea, Port Talbot, and Neath; shipbuilding and engineering at Cardiff; Margam has the largest steel rolling mills plant in Europe. Cardiff is the chief port and county town. Area 818 sq. m.; pop. (1961) 1,227,828.

GLASER, Donald A. (1926–). American physicist. B. in Cleveland, he was ed. at the Case Inst. of Technology and in 1960 became prof. at the Univ. of California. In 1960 he was awarded a Nobel prize for his invention of the 'bubble chamber' (q.v.) for observing high-energy nuclear phenomena. By using a pressurized liquid medium instead of a gas, it overcomes drawbacks inherent in the earlier 'cloud chamber'.

GLASGOW, Ellen (1874–1945). American novelist. B. in Virginia, in her novels she contrasts the traditional Southern life with the new industrialism; they incl. *Virginia* (1913), and *In this Our Life* (1941).

GLASGOW (glahs'gō). Third city of the United Kingdom; royal burgh (since 1454), city, and port on the Clyde, 22 m. from its mouth in Lanark, Scotland. G. is Scotland's leading commercial centre, and focus of one of the world's greatest industrial areas. The river channel has been blasted and dredged, and can accommodate ships drawing 25 ft. Shipbuilding is one of the most important industries; ships of all classes, incl. the *Queen Mary* and *Qu. Elizabeth* (I and II), come from the Clyde. Other industries incl. iron and steel, engineering, chemicals, leather, tobacco and textiles. G. is the seat of G. univ. (1450),

GLASGOW. Ships, cranes, smoke and cloud formations over the hills on the horizon blend in this view of the city from Meadowside into unexpected harmony.
Photo: George Outram & Co. Ltd.

housed in buildings designed by Sir Gilbert Scott, and of the Univ. of Strathclyde (1963), formerly the Royal Coll. of Science and Technology. The cathedral of St. Mungo (patron saint and founder of the city in the 6th cent.) was built in the 12th–13th cents. The Cross Steeple is all that remains of the old Tolbooth (c. 1628). Other buildings incl. the Royal Exchange, the Stock Exchange, the County Buildings, and many museums, galleries, theatres, etc. The Clyde is crossed by several wide bridges for road and rail; Glasgow has a local airport at Renfrew, 5 m. W.N.W.; Prestwick international airport is 28 m. S.S.W. The city is administered by a Lord Provost and corporation. Progress has been made in slum clearance, notably in the Gorbals district.

Little is known of the history of the early settlement until the 12th cent. About 1180 it was made a burgh of barony and granted a market. In 1300 Wallace defeated the English there. In 1893 G. was made a co. of a city with the Lord Provost acting as Lord Lieutenant. Area 62 sq. m.; pop. (1961) 1,054,913.

GLASS. An inorganic substance in a condition which is continuous with its liquid state, but which, as the result of having been cooled from a fused condition, has become for all practical purposes rigid. As such, it is transparent or translucent and may become to some extent opaque. It is a mixture of

GLASS. In a special clay furnace the ingredients of crystal glass – sand, potash, lead oxide and powdered glass – are first melted down. The 'gatherer' then takes just the right quantity of molten glass on the tip of his blowing iron and starts to blow the form.
Courtesy of Steuben Glass

silicates of lime, soda, and potash, to which are added metallic oxides, for colouring and opacity, and borates, phosphates, etc., for special purposes.

There are three main divisions of manufactured glass. Blown G. contains silica, potash, and lead oxide, which are mixed with broken G. (cullet) in crucibles, heated therein till viscous, when the G. is blown or drawn into tube. Plate G., which required grinding and polishing, has since 1959 been replaced by float G., produced by allowing the molten G. to flow out of the furnace into a chamber 150 ft. long containing molten tin, where it is 'fire-polished' by heating from above and cooled, solidifying at a much higher temperature than the tin. Optical G., homogeneous and transparent, is cooled slowly in crucibles, re-heated, and then subjected to prolonged cooling.

Modern advances have led to safety G., laminated G., ultra-violet ray G., heat-treated G., and G. fibres. These fibres were first manufactured as a heat-insulating material, later for vibration control. They have recently been developed as yarn for electric motor and domestic appliances, dress materials, etc.

The decorative use of G. is very ancient, blown G. reaching perfection in 18th dynasty Egypt, the Chinese excelling in imitation of rare stones, and the Graeco-Roman era being represented by the Portland vase (q.v.). High points in later glassware are the Byzantine G. mosaics, medieval European stained G., the delicate filigree of 15th cent. Venice, and English table glass of the 18th cent. Engraved G. by individual artists (e.g. Laurence Whistler, and the products of the Steuben works in the U.S.) is today often used for presentation pieces, the methods being diamond-point engraving (developed in 16th cent. Italy) and copperwheel engraving (originating in Bohemia): the commercial processes are sand-blasting and acid etching.

GLASTONBURY. Market town (bor.) in Somerset, England. Nearby are 2 excavated lake villages thought to have been occupied for c. 150 years before the Romans came to Britain.

The first church on the site was traditionally founded in the 1st cent. by Joseph of Arimathea: the ruins of the great Benedictine abbey built in the 10th–11th cents. by Dunstan (q.v.) and his followers were excavated in 1963 and the site of the grave of King Arthur and Queen Guinevere was thought to have been identified. Pop. (1961) 5,796.

GLAUBER'S SALT. Crystallized form of hydrated sodium sulphate, first described by J. R. Glauber (1604–68), German chemist. It is used as an aperient.

GLAZUNO'V, Alexander Constantinovich (1865–1936). Russian composer. B. at St. Petersburg, he studied under Rimsky-Korsakov, and became director of the St. Petersburg Conservatoire in 1905. In 1928 he settled in Paris. G. composed 8 symphonies, a violin concerto, symphonic poems, etc.

GLEIWITZ. German form of GLIWICE.

GLEIZES (glez), **Albert** (1881–1953). French artist. An exponent of Cubism, exhibiting at the Salon des Indépendants in 1911, he pub. in 1912 *Du Cubisme* – the first book of Cubist theory. Influenced by medieval art, he returned to the Catholic Church soon after settling in southern France in 1939, and his later work is mainly on religious themes.

GLENCOE (glenkō'). Glen in N. Argyll, Scotland, where members of the Macdonald clan were massacred in 1692, John Campbell, earl of Breadalbane. being the chief instigator. A chairlift to the plateau above it, for use in winter sports, was completed in 1960.

GLENDOWER, Owen (c. 1359–c. 1415). Welsh hero. He headed a revolt against the English in N. Wales, and defeated Henry IV in three campaigns, 1400–2. But from 1405 the struggle went against him and Wales was reconquered by 1413.

GLIDING. The art of using air currents to fly heavier-than-air craft without engines. Technically speaking G. involves the gradual loss of altitude: gliders designed for soaring flight (utilizing air rising up a cliff face or hill, warm air rising as a 'thermal' above sun-heated ground, etc.) are known as sailplanes. Pioneers incl. Cayley, Lilienthal, Chanute, Montgomery, and Orville Wright, who made the first soaring flight of any duration (9 min. 45 sec.) in the U.S.A. in 1911. The British G. Assoc. dates from 1929. Launching may be by rubber catapault from a hilltop; by a winch which raises the glider like a kite; or by aircraft tow. In the S.W.W. towed troop-carrying gliders were used by the Germans in Crete and the Allies at Arnhem. Distances of well over 500 m. and heights of over 46,000 ft. have been attained.

GLIÈRE (glē-âr'), **Reinhold** (1875–1956). Russian composer. B. at Kiev, of Belgian descent, he was director of the conservatoire in his native city 1914–20. He then returned to Moscow as head of the music section of the Dept. of People's Education, and made a close study of folk-music, as is shown by his opera *Shah Senem* (1925), based on an Azerbaijan folk-tale. Also notable for their fine grasp of orchestral effect are his symphonies and the symphonic poem *Les Sirènes* (1908).

GLINKA, Michael (1803–57). Russian composer. B. near Smolensk, he broke away from the prevailing Italian influence, and turned to Russian folk-music as the inspiration of *A Life for the Tsar* (1836). His later works incl. another opera *Russlan and Ludmilla* (1842), and the orchestral *Kamarinskaya*.

GLIWICE (glēvē'tse), Town in Polish-occupied Silesia, with coal-mining, iron, steel, and electrical industries. Pop. (1966) 164,000.

GLOBE THEATRE. Octagonal theatre open to the sky, built by Burbage, Shakespeare, and others in 1599 on the Bankside, Southwark, and burnt down in 1613.

GLOBIGERINA (glōbijerī'na). Genus of Foraminifera which are preserved in chalk. The conical spiral shells accumulate at the bottom of deep seas, forming 'G. ooze'.

GLOUCESTER (glos'ter), **Henry William Frederick Albert,** duke of (1900–). 3rd son of George V. Created duke of G. in 1928, he followed an army career until 1936, and was Gov. Gen. of Australia

GLENCOE. The unhappy memories of the glen find no reflection in the enjoyment of the hikers and campers who make it the focal point of their Easter week-end.
Photo: George Outram & Co. Ltd.

1945–7. He has represented George VI and Elizabeth II on many official occasions. In 1935 he m. Lady Alice Montagu-Douglas-Scott, dau. of the 7th duke of Buccleuch, by whom he has 2 sons, Prince William (1941–) and Prince Richard (1944–).

GLOUCESTER. City, port, co. borough and co. town of Glos, England, on the Severn. Industries incl. aircraft works, carriage and wagon works, making of agricultural machinery, etc. The cathedral, founded 1022 as the church of a Benedictine abbey, has many later additions. Other notable buildings include the 'New Inn' (1450). Robert Raikes founded the first Sunday school in G. in 1780. Pop. (1961) 69,687.

GLOUCESTER. The earlier parts of the cathedral are Norman, but there are later additions in a variety of Gothic styles. The monks of the abbey used to wash in this lavatorium in the cathedral cloisters, while above them rose the splendour of some of the earliest fan tracery known.
Photo: A. W. Kerr.

GLOUCESTERSHIRE. English county in the W. Midlands. The Cotswolds run across it from S.W. to N.E.; the highest point is Cleve Cloud (1,070 ft.). To the W. and N. of the Cotswolds is the broad, fertile Vale of Gloucester, drained by the Severn and its tributaries, and extending to the S.W. into the Vale of Berkeley. Coal is mined in the Forest of Dean, but G. is primarily an agricultural co. The chief industrial centre is Bristol, with its outport Avonmouth; other towns include Gloucester (the co. town), Stroud, Cheltenham, Tewkesbury, and Cirencester. Area 1,259 sq. m.; pop. (1967) 1,062,260.

GLOVE-BOX. A form of protection used when working with certain radioactive materials. Gloves fixed to ports in the walls of a box allow manipulation of work within the box. Contamination through inhalation of fine air-borne particles of poisonous alpha-active or other materials is prevented by maintaining a slight vacuum inside the box, so that any air flow is inwards.

GLOVE-BOX. Aseptic manipulation in the preparation at the Radiochemical Centre, Amersham, of iodinated human serum albumin, an isotopically labelled compound used in medical diagnosis.
Courtesy of U.K. Atomic Energy Authority.

GLOW-WORM. The wingless female of various luminous beetles in the family Lampyridae. The luminous organs are situated under the abdomen, and seem to have a sexual significance. The species are distributed throughout Europe and Siberia. Other species in the family are found in the western hemisphere, notably *Luciola italica*, both sexes of which are winged and give light. See FIREFLY.

GLUBB, Sir John Bagot (1897–). British soldier, known until the general abolition of the title

GLOW-WORM. Female (left) and male.

in 1952 as G. Pasha. As O.C. the Arab Legion 1939–56 he was its creator in its modern form. He was dismissed in 1956 as a result of anti-British sentiment in Jordan, and created K.C.B.

GLUCK (glook), **Christoph Willibald** (1714–87). German composer. B. at Weidenwang, nr. Neumarkt, Bavaria, he studied music at Prague, Vienna, and Milan, came to London in 1745 to compose operas for the Haymarket, but returned to Vienna in 1746. He was knighted by the Pope, and in 1756 settled at Vienna as Kapellmeister to Maria Theresa. In 1762 his *Orfeo ed Euridice* revolutionized the whole 18th cent. conception of opera. G. threw overboard the traditional operatic conventions and restrictions and gave free scope to dramatic effects of a serene and classic beauty. *Orfeo* was followed by *Alceste* (1767) and *Paris ed Elena* (1769). *Iphigénie en Aulide* (1774), produced in Paris, gave rise to furious controversies in which G. had the support of Marie Antoinette, whilst his Italian rival Piccini was patronized by Mme Du Barry. With *Armide* (1777) and *Iphigénie en Tauride* (1779) G. won a complete victory over Piccini. He d. at Vienna.

GLUCOSE ($C_6H_{12}O_6$). Form of sugar, also known as grape-sugar or dextrose. It is present in the blood, and in honey and fruit juices. In more complex formations it occurs as cellulose, starch, and glycogen,

GLOUCESTERSHIRE. Stone-built houses and a clear village stream make Upper Slaughter a place of quiet beauty in spring.
Photo: Roy J. Westlake.

and it is usually prepared by hydrolysis from cane sugar or starch. Generally a yellowish syrup, it may be purified to a white crystalline powder.

GLUE. Gelatine in its crude, commercial, and industrial form, employed as an adhesive, made from bones, fragments of hide, and fish offal. Modern developments in adhesives incl. the thermo-setting synthetic rubber and plastic compounds used to replace welding in bonding various car components, etc.

GLYCERINE (glis'erin), **GLYCEROL** ($CH_2OH.CHOH.CH_2OH$). Colourless, viscous, odourless, sweetish liquid b.p. 290°C., m.p. 18°C., miscible with water and alcohol, insoluble in ether. Obtained from vegetable and animal oils and fats (by treatment with acid, alkali, superheated steam or an enzyme, or by fermentation of glucose), it is used in the manufacture of high explosives, in antifreeze solutions, to maintain moist conditions in fruits and tobacco, in cosmetics, etc.

GLYCOL (gli'kol) ($CH_2OH.CH_2OH$). Colourless, odourless, viscous liquid with a sweetish taste; b.p. 197°C.; m.p. −17°C.; miscible with water and alcohol; density 1·115 g/ml. It is used in antifreeze solutions, in the preparation of ethers and esters, especially for explosives, and as a solvent; a substitute for glycerol.

GLYN (glin), **Elinor** (1865–1943). British writer. Her novel of an exotic love-affair, *Three Weeks* (1907)

scandalized Edwardian society, as did her passion for
tiger skins, and the beauty of her white skin and red
hair; her admirers incl. Lord Curzon. Her biography
was written by her grandson **Sir Anthony G.** (1922–   ),
also a novelist: *The Ram in the Thicket* (1957), *Kick
Turn* (1963), and *The Terminal* (1965).

GLYNDEBOURNE (glīnd-). An English estate nr.
Lewes, Sussex, where is an admirably equipped opera
house estab. by J. Christie (q.v.) for staging new and
old operatic works at an annual summer festival.

GNAT. Family of flies
(Culicidae) in the order
Diptera, also known as
mosquitoes. The eggs are
laid in water, where they
hatch into worm-like larvae,
which after passing through
a pupal stage emerge as
perfect insects. Well-known
species are the Common
G. (*Culex pipiens*), abundant in England; the carrier
of malaria (*Anopheles maculipennis*); and the banded
mosquito (*Aedes aegypti*) which transmits yellow
fever. Only the female is capable of drawing blood,
since the male possesses no piercing mandibles.

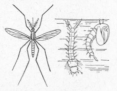

GNAT, with larva and pupa.

GNEISS (nis). Metamorphic rock, often found
in association with schists and granites. It has a
foliated structure, consisting of an alternation of
micaceous and granular bands. Garnets commonly
occur in G.

GNOSTICISM (nost'isizm). Name applied to a
religious movement contemporary with the rise of
Christianity, that is sometimes regarded as a series
of Christian heresies, but is better represented as an
attempt to form a synthesis of Christian theology,
Greek philosophy, and elements derived from the
ancient mystery cults of the Mediterranean world.
The Gnostics maintain that they possess an esoteric
knowledge of the inner meaning of religion, the
gnosis, by means of which they were able to attain
to illumination and immortality. They conceived the
world as a series of emanations or aeons proceeding
from the highest of several gods, and they recognized
a clear distinction between spirit and essentially evil
matter. The Albigenses and other heretics were
probably inheritors of Gnostic ideas, as were the
Sufis, or mystics of Islam.

GNU (noo). A large, white-tailed S. African antelope (*Connochaetes gnu*). Also a larger brindled gnu
(*Gorgon taurinus*) of central and E. Africa.

GOA (gō'ah). Former Portuguese prov. in India, it
included besides Goa proper, on the Malabar coast,
the settlements of Diu and Damao. Although it had
been Portuguese since 1505, from 1950 India demanded its transfer to her, and when Portugal refused,
first set up a land blockade (1954), then forcibly
seized G. (1961), incorporating it in the Rep. of India
(1962): G. rejected by referendum a merger with
Maharashtra (1967) and remains a Union Territory.
Area 1,426 sq. m.; pop. (1960) 625,831.

GOAT. Genus of ruminants (*Capra*), similar in
appearance to the sheep. It is probably Persian in
origin, but various species are now found in all parts
of the world. Gs. are frequently kept for milk, but
the Angora and Cashmere Gs. produce mohair.
There are many species of G.; the English type
(*Capra hircus*) is usually brown, sometimes with
white patches, has short hair and tapering horns.
Gs. are usually bearded and the males have an unpleasant smell. The Rocky Mountain G. of America
and the Ibex are wild varieties.

GOBELIN (goblań'). Name of a French tapestry
manufactory, originally founded as a dyeworks in
Paris by Gilles and Jean G. about 1450. The firm
began to produce tapestries in the 16th cent., and
in 1662 the establishment was purchased by Colbert

for Louis XVI. With the support of the State it still
continues to make tapestries.

GŌ′BI. Desert in Asia lying partly in the Mongolian People's Republic, partly in Inner Mongolia
region, China. It extends *c.* 500 m. from N. to S., and
1,000 m. from E. to W. The sandy, waterless part
occurs in the S.W., while the rest is a succession of
stony plains and ranges of hills. In some parts sheep
and cattle are reared, and where water is available for
irrigation crops are grown by the nomadic Mongol
and Kalmuck inhabitants. In the desert, relics of
prehistoric cultures have been discovered.

GOBINEAU (gŏbēnō′), **Joseph Arthur,** comte de
(1816–82). French diplomat and writer. His most
influential work was his *Essai sur l'inégalité des
races humaines* (1855), where he maintained the
doctrine of the innate superiority of the white or
'Aryan' race. This quasi-scientific thesis fitted well
with the rising nationalist spirit in Germany.

GOD. The Supreme Being: the Creator, Sustainer,
and Ruler of the universe. It used to be thought that
the idea of God was divinely revealed to man at an
early stage of his history, and that this original
monotheism degenerated into polytheism. The view
most generally held nowadays is that the God-idea
has arisen in the course of ages, and that it may be
traced perhaps to a kind of primitive fetishism. The
next stage was probably the deification of the forces
of nature, as in the Vedic hymns and in the mythology
of ancient Greece. A riotous polytheism followed,
out of which men here and there – the Hebrew
Prophets in particular – gradually evolved the concept of One God, who is all-good, all-powerful, all-
wise. The study of the God-idea is the subject of
theology and of the science of religion, although the
latter word may comprise world-faiths such as
Buddhism in which there is, at least in the earliest
form, no God or gods. Deism is the name given to
that system of monotheism in which God is regarded
as the Creator but as working only through the laws
of nature, whereas Theism holds that He is still
actively interested in His creation. Pantheism is the
identification of God and the universe. In the course
of cents. the conception of God as a Person has been
spiritualized, and in Christianity He is revealed as
a Trinity of Persons (not a triad of three gods as in
present-day Hinduism or in ancient Egypt). In the
Gospel of St. John, God is identified with Love.

GO′DALMING. English town (bor.) on the river
Wey in Surrey. It has tanning, hosiery, paper, and
agricultural industries. Charterhouse school was
moved there from London in 1872. Pop. (1961)
15,771.

GODDARD, Rayner, baron (1877–1971). British
judge. Son of a solicitor, he was Lord Chief Justice
1946–58, and estab. his reputation beyond the courts
for pithily lucid judgments.

GODDEN, Rumer (1907–   ). British author. B. in
Sussex, she spent much of her youth and later life in
India, as is reflected in the background of her novels
Black Narcissus (1939) and *The River* (1946).

GODFREY, William (1889–1963). British cardinal.
B. in Liverpool, he was domestic prelate to pope
Pius XI 1930–8, titular archbishop of Cius 1938–53
and Apostolic Delegate to Britain 1938–54. Abp. of
Liverpool from 1953 until he succeeded Cardinal
Griffin as abp. of Westminster in 1956, he was
created cardinal in 1958, and was a member of the
Preparatory Commission for the Second Vatican
Council.

GODFREY DE BOUILLON (*c.* 1060–1100).
Crusader. The 2nd son of Count Eustace II of
Boulogne, with his brothers Baldwin and Eustace he
led in 1096 a force of 40,000 Germans to take part in
the 1st Crusade. After Jerusalem was taken in 1099,
he was elected its ruler, but refused the title of king.

GŌDĪ′VA, Lady. Wife of Leofric, earl of Mercia,

who founded a Benedictine monastery at Coventry during the 11th cent., where she was buried. According to legend, the earl promised to remit a heavy tax imposed upon the people of the town if his wife rode naked through the streets at noonday. This she did, but by arrangement the people remained indoors; with the exception of 'Peeping Tom', who bored a hole in his shutters, and was struck blind.

GOD SAVE THE KING/QUEEN. The British national anthem. The origin of both tune and words is obscure; the former resembles a composition by John Bull (1563–1628) and a number of other 16th cent. works. The words can also be traced in various forms back to the 16th cent. The song assumed substantially its present form during the 1745 rebellion, when it was used as an anti-Jacobite Party song. The tune has been used for patriotic songs in the U.S.A. ('My country, 'tis of thee') and Germany.

GODWIN (d. 1053). Earl of Wessex from 1020. Secured succession to throne in 1042 of Edward the Confessor, to whom he m. his dau. Edith, and whose chief minister he became. King Harold was his son.

GODWIN, William (1756–1836). British philosopher and novelist. At first a Nonconformist minister, he later became an atheist and a philosopher, achieving fame in 1793 through his *Enquiry concerning Political Justice*, which advocated an anarchic society based on a faith in man's essential rationality. He subsequently pub. *Caleb Williams* (1794), a story written in illustration of his theories, and many other works. His first wife, the feminist Mary Wollstonecraft (1759–97), whose *Vindication of the Rights of Women* (1792) demanded equal educational opportunities for men and women, d. in giving birth to a dau., later Mary Shelley.

GOEBBELS, Paul Josef (1897–1945). German Nazi leader. B. in the Rhineland, he became a journalist, joined the Nazi Party in its early days, and was given control of its propaganda in 1929. On becoming Minister of Propaganda in 1933, he brought all cultural and educational activities completely under Nazi control, and built up sympathetic movements abroad to carry on the 'war of nerves' against Hitler's intended victims. On the capture of Berlin by the Allies he poisoned himself.

GOERING, Hermann Wilhelm (1893–1946). German Nazi leader. B. in Bavaria, he served in the F.W.W. as an ace flyer. He joined the Nazi Party in 1922, and organized and commanded the S.A. (Storm Troops). Appointed P.M. of Prussia and Min. of the Interior in 1933, he arranged the Reichstag fire, and directed the reign of terror which followed. As Commissioner for Aviation he built up the Luftwaffe, and in 1936 he became director of the four-year plan for war preparations. He later lost favour with Hitler, and was expelled from the Nazi Party in 1945. He was tried at Nuremberg as a war criminal in 1945–6 and condemned to death, but poisoned himself shortly before the execution was due.

GOES (gōōs), **Hugo van der** (c. 1440–82). Flemish artist. B. probably in Ter Goes, he spent his later years in a monastery subject to fits of insanity. His works, e.g. the Portinari altar-piece now in the Uffizi and the 'Death of the Virgin' at Bruges, have great emotional impact.

GOETHE (gö'te), **Johann Wolfgang von** (1749–1832). German poet and man-of-letters, statesman and natural philosopher. B. in Frankfurt-am-Main, he first discovered his poetic vocation while studying law at Leipzig; to this period belong the *Laune des Verliebten*, *Die Mitschuldigen* and the book of lyrics *Annette*. After meeting Herder at Strasbourg (1770–1) he shook off the influence of French rococo and became the leader of the 'Storm and Stress' movement, writing the dramas *Götz von Berlichingen*, *Faust* (not completed until 60 years later), *Clavigo*, *Stella*; and the novel *Die Leiden des*

Van GOGH
Self-portrait.
Courtauld Institute Galleries, London.

Jungen Werthers (1774). In 1775 G. moved to Weimar, entering the service of the Duke Karl August, and his administrative duties there helped him to discipline his genius. A visit to Italy (1786–8) inspired *Römische Elegien* (1795), which was followed by the classical dramas *Iphigenie* (1787) and *Tasso* (1790), and by the novel *Wilhelm Meister* (1794). The 1st part of *Faust* was pub. in 1808, but the 2nd did not appear until 1831. Among G.'s later works were the poetic *West-Östlicher Divan* (1819), the novel *Die Wahlverwandschaften* (1809), and the autobiographical *Dichtung und Wahrheit* (1811–33).

GO'GARTY, Oliver St. John (1878–1957). Irish writer. An ear, nose, and throat specialist with a large Dublin practice, G. was a member of the literary circle which incl. Yeats, George Moore, and Joyce, and figures in *Ulysses* as Buck Mulligan. A wit and a poet, he wrote several books incl. the autobiographical *As I was going down Sackville Street* (1937). He took an active interest in Irish politics, being a senator of the Irish Free State 1922–36.

GOGH (khokh), **Vincent Van** (1853–90). Dutch painter. B. at Zundert, he tried various vocations, working for a time as a schoolmaster in England, before he took up painting. He studied under Van Mauve at The Hague. In 1886 he went to Paris where he became a friend of Gauguin, and the two painters worked together for a short time in Arles, Provence. One of the leaders of the Post-Impressionist painters, he executed still-lifes, portraits, and landscapes, some of the best-known being 'Landscape with Cypress Trees', 'The Yellow Chair', and 'Sunflowers', all of which are in the Tate Gallery. He spent the last years of his life in asylums, and committed suicide. Our illus. shows him in 1889 bandaged and convalescent after a violent scene with Gauguin – with whom he had been living – in which he cut off a piece of his own ear.

GO'GOL, Nicolai Vasilyevich (1809–52). Russian writer. B. nr. Poltava, he tried several careers before entering the St. Petersburg Civil Service. His first collection of stories, *Evenings on a Farm near Dikanka* (1831–2), had an immediate success, and his second, *Mirgorod*, was warmly praised by Pushkin. Later were *Arabesques* (1835), one of the world's great short stories, 'The Cloak', and his great comedy *The Inspector General* (1836), an attack on bureaucracy. From 1835 he had been a restless traveller in Europe, and it was in Rome that he completed the earlier part of his masterpiece, the picaresque novel *Dead Souls* (1842), depicting Russian provincial society.

GOITRE. Name applied to a swelling on the front of the neck caused by an enlargement of the thyroid gland. Simple G., or Derbyshire Neck, occurs in certain hilly regions and has been attributed to a deficiency of iodine in the soil, a micro-organism infesting the drinking water, or lack of sunlight. In Exophthalmic G., also known as Graves's disease, the enlargement of the

GOGOL. By the Ukrainian poet-artist T. G. Shevchenko.
Photo: Novosti Press Agency.

thyroid gland is accompanied by protrusion of the eyeballs, palpitation, etc.

GOLD. A heavy, valuable, yellow metallic element, with symbol Au, atomic number 79, and atomic weight 197·0. G. has long been valued for its durability, malleability, and ductility, and because it may be easily recognized. It is unaffected by temperature changes and is highly resistant to acids. Its main uses are in coin and jewellery.

South Africa produces almost 75 per cent (30,500,000 fine oz. p.a.) of the world's G. and other major producers are the Soviet Union, Canada, U.S.A., and Australia. For manufacture, G. is alloyed with another strengthening metal, fineness being measured by the parts of pure G. in 24. *See* CARAT.

GOLD. Miners drilling in a gold-bearing layer on the Ventersdorp Contact Reef in the Transvaal.
Courtesy of the Anglo-American Corp. of S.A. Ltd.

GOLD COAST. Name given by Europeans, on account of the alluvial gold washed down by the rivers, to part of the W. coast of Africa, from Cape Three Points to the mouth of the Volta r. Portuguese and French navigators visited this coast in the 14th cent., and in 1618 the British set up a trading settlement which developed into the colony of the Gold Coast (24,000 sq. m.); with its Ashanti and Northern Territories dependencies plus British Togoland it became Ghana (q.v.) in 1957.

GOLDCREST. The smallest British bird (*Regulus cristatus*), it is sometimes called the golden-crested wren, but has no link with the wrens. Olive green, with a bright yellow streak across the crown, it builds usually in conifers.

GOLDEN CALF. Image made by Aaron in response to the request of the Israelites for a god, when they despaired of Moses' return from Mt. Sinai. The image was destroyed when Moses did return, but similar ones were made later. The platform of the one Jeroboam I set up at Dan was thought to have been excavated in 1970.

GOLDEN FLEECE. In Greek legend, the F. of the ram Chrysomallus, which hung on an oak tree at Colchis guarded by a dragon, and was taken by Jason and the Argonauts. It is also the name of an order of knighthood formerly awarded in Spain and in Austria, which was instituted by Philip the Good, duke of Burgundy, in 1429, and freshly inaugurated in Vienna in 1713 by Charles VI.

GOLDEN ROD. Popular name for the tall, leafy perennials of the *Solidago* genus of the Compositae. Each stem bears a head consisting of a great number of small yellow flowers.

GOLDEN GATE, California, U.S.A. Strait linking San Francisco Bay and the Pacific, spanned by a

bridge which was completed in 1937, which has a single span of 4,200 ft.

GOLDFINCH. Songbird (*Carduelis carduelis*) commonly found in Europe and N. Africa, and in many other parts of the world. It is brilliantly coloured – black, white, and red about the head, and gold and black wings. Most Gs. leave Britain in the autumn.

GOLDFISH. Fish of the carp family (*Carassius auratus*) found in eastern Asia. Greenish brown in its natural state, it has for cents. been bred by the Chinese, taking on highly coloured and freakishly shaped forms. In Japan G. breeding developed rapidly among low-class warriors dismissed by their feudal lords on the Emperor's restoration in 1868, and keeping them became an almost universal Japanese hobby: today enormous quantities are shipped abroad.

GOLDING, Louis (1895–1958). British novelist. A descendant of Russian refugees, he was at his best in portraying life in the Jewish community of his native Manchester disguised as 'Doomington', as in *Magnolia Street* (1932).

GOLDING, William (1911–). English poet and novelist, whose books have a deep moral significance, e.g. *Lord of the Flies* (1954) in which savagery takes over among a group of English schoolboys on a Pacific island and *Pincher Martin* (1956), flashbacks of a drowning man.

GOLDŌ'NI, Carlo (1707 –93). Italian dramatist. B. at Venice, he wrote popular comedies for the Sant'Angelo theatre, incl. *Don Giovanni Tenorio* (1736), *La bottega di caffè*, *La locandiera*, *La casa nova*, etc. In 1761 G. moved to Paris, where he directed the Italian theatre, gave It. lessons at the court, and d. in extreme poverty.

GOLDSMITH, Oliver (1728–74). British author. B. in Ireland, the son of a clergyman, he was ed. at Trinity Coll., Dublin and went to Edinburgh to study medicine in 1752. After 18 months he proceeded to Leyden, but left without a degree and wandered through France, Switzerland, and Italy. Returning to England in 1756 he became an usher, before settling to hackwork from which he never escaped, e.g. his *History of England*, and *Animated Nature*. His earliest work of literary importance was *The Citizen of the World* (1762), a series of letters by an imaginary Chinese traveller. In 1761 he met Johnson, and became a member of his 'club'. In 1764 he estab. his reputation with his poem *The Traveller*, and followed it with his collected essays in 1765, and his novel,

The Vicar of Wakefield (1766), sold according to Johnson's account to save him from imprisonment for debt. A further poem, *The Deserted Village* (1770), was followed by his dramatic masterpiece, *She Stoops to Conquer* (1773), which far exceeds the earlier comedy, *The Good-Natur'd Man* (1768).

GOLD STANDARD. The linking of money with

the value of gold. Before the F.W.W. a number of countries were on the G.S.; in Britain, e.g., gold sovereigns and half-sovereigns worth their face value were in circulation, and banknotes were freely convertible into gold coin. Gold coin was called in at the beginning of the F.W.W. and was not re-issued. Under the gold bullion standard (in operation in Britain 1925–31) notes were convertible at the central bank (in Britain, the Bank of England) into gold bullion, and gold bullion could be freely imported and exported. Neither of these forms exists any longer; but the par values of the currency units of the member countries of the International Monetary Fund (which incl. nearly all members of the U.N. not in the Communist bloc) are fixed in terms of gold and of the U.S. dollar, so that they are also related to the price at which the U.S.A. deals in gold with central banks and official monetary authorities ($35 per oz 1934–72, then $38). This fixed price is maintained to encourage stability, but the internat. gold crisis of 1968 led to a two-tiered price system, that of the official and free markets. During the crisis the statutory requirement that the U.S. govt. hold a 25% gold backing for the money supply was abolished. From 1965 Gen. de Gaulle made repeated demands for return to the G.S.

GOLDSTONE. Village in Calif., U.S.A., 100 m. N.E. of Los Angeles, site of a satellite tracking station.

GOLDWATER, Barry (1909–   ). American Republican politician. Senator for his native Arizona 1953–64 and from 1969. He opposes govt. intervention in economic life. As presidential candidate in 1964, he was badly defeated by Johnson.

GOLDWYN, Samuel (1882–   ). American film producer. B. in Warsaw, he emigrated to the U.S.A. in 1896 and became a pioneer film-maker. He is famed for his 'goldwynisms', e.g. 'Anyone who visits a psychiatrist should have his head examined.'

GOLF. A game consisting of hitting a ball from a starting tee into a standard-sized hole (4¼ in. diam. and at least 4 in. deep) by means of various clubs; 18 such holes played constitute a round. In 'medal-play' the competitive object is to take fewer strokes than an opponent, but in match-play the result depends on the winner of individual holes. The ball, which must weigh not more than 1·62 oz. and not be smaller than 1·62 in. diam., is now composed of elastic thread

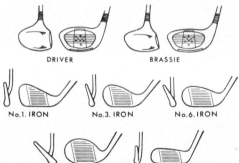

DRIVER   BRASSIE

No.1. IRON   No.3. IRON   No.6. IRON

No.9. IRON   PUTTER

wound round a soft core, with a vulcanized rubber outer covering. The clubs, 14 in a full set, are of 2 types. The woods, driver, brassie, spoon and No. 4 wood, now mostly with steel shafts, are the most powerful and are used for initial tee drives and long 'fairway' play; they are capable of 300 yd. shots. The irons, with steel heads and shafts, are numbered 1 to 9 according to the shape of the blade. No. 1 is set upright and is most powerful; No. 9 is set back the farthest. High-numbered irons are used for gaining

height rather than distance. The putter is reserved for shots when the ball is on the green – the small area surrounding each hole. After raising the ball for play from each tee it may not again be touched by hand but must be played as it lies.

Holes vary from 100–500 yds., the majority being nearer 300 yds. They consist of a platform tee, a main fairway, where grass is cut short and which is bounded by rough grass, and the green. Sand bunkers are laid at vulnerable points, often ringing the green. A course now measures about 6,000 yds. for which leading players return scores of under 70. For average players, handicaps are employed as a method of matching unequal opponents.

Originally an ancient game of Scotland, G. has spread during the last century to all parts of the world. The Royal and Ancient Club at St. Andrews was founded in 1754. Open and Amateur championships for men and a Women's Championship attract many foreign entrants, the U.S.A. now dominating the standard. Famous winners of the 'Open' have been W. Hagen, R. T. Jones (U.S.A.), and T. H. Cotton (Britain). G. is very popular in Japan.

GOLIATH. The giant champion of the Philistines, who, according to I Sam., xvii, was slain with a stone from a sling by David in single combat before the opposing armies of Israelites and Philistines.

GOLLANCZ, Sir Victor (1893–1967). British left-wing writer and publisher. Founder in 1936 of the influential Left Book Club.

GÓMEZ (gō'meth), **Juan Vicente** (1857–1935). Venezuelan statesman. Elected president in 1910, he remained virtual dictator until his death.

GOMULKA, Wladyslaw (1905–   ). Polish politician. Several times imprisoned for revolutionary activities in the inter-war years, he was a resistance leader during the S.W.W. A leading member of the United Workers Party from 1945, he was expelled in 1949 for anti-Stalinist deviationism and imprisoned without trial 1951–6. He was then elected 1st sec. of the U.W.P., an appointment heralding the change towards 'an independent road to socialism'. Although re-elected 1959, 1964 and 1969, he resigned following food price riots in 1970.

GONADOTRO'PHIN. See FERTILITY DRUGS.

GONCHAROV, Ivan Alexandrovitch (1812–91). Russian novelist. B. at Simbirsk, he became a civil servant. His first novel, *A Common Story* (1847), was followed in 1858 by his humorous masterpiece, *Oblomov*, which summarized the indolent and impotent determinism of Russian landed gentry.

GONCOURT (goṅkoor'), **de**, the brothers **Edmond** (1822–96) and **Jules** (1830–70). French writers. They collaborated in producing a compendium, *L'Art du XVIIIe Siècle* (1859–75), and various historical studies which like their *Journal* (1887–96), obtained their effect by cumulative detail. Their joint novels include *Renée Mauperin*, *Germinie Lacerteux*, and *Madame Gervaisais* (1869). Edmond continued to write after his brother's death, e.g. *Chérie* (1884). Edmond de G. founded the *Académie Goncourt*, opened in 1903, which awards an annual prize to the author of the best novel of the year.

GONDAR. City of Ethiopia situated *c.* 7,500 ft. above sea-level, 24 m. N. of Lake Tana. It is capital of the prov. of Begemdir. Pop. (1965) 29,600.

GONDWA'NALAND. See WEGENER.

GONORRHOEA (gonorē'a). Infection by the gonococcus, the commonest form of venereal disease. It is usually transmitted by sexual intercourse, but sometimes, especially in children, by contact with an infected person. A copious opaque discharge from the infected part appears in a few days and infection of the eyes must be guarded against. G. is increasingly resistant to penicillin and streptomycin, but in 1963 a new antibiotic actinospectacin effected cures by a single injection.

GOOD FRIDAY (probably a corruption of God's Friday). In the Christian Church, the Friday before Easter, which is kept in memory of the Crucifixion.

GOODHART, Arthur Lehman (1891–). American jurist. He was prof. of jurisprudence at Oxford 1931–51. His books incl. *English Law and the Moral Law* (1953) and *Law of the Land* (1966).

GOODMAN, Benny (1909–). American clarinetist, the 'king of swing'. B. in Chicago, he has had his own band since 1934, and has made celebrated recordings, e.g. 'Blue Skies' and 'King Porter Stomp'. Bartók's *Rhapsody* for clarinet and violin was written for him.

GOODMAN, Nelson (1906–). American philosopher. Prof. of philosophy at the Univ. of Pennsylvania from 1951, he is especially concerned with the theory of knowledge and problems of language, e.g. *Fact, Fiction and Forecast* (1955).

GOODWIN SANDS. Group of shoals about 6 m. off the E. coast of Kent, England, 8–10 m. from N.–S. The sands are exposed at low tide, but despite lightships and buoys, ships frequently go aground. According to legend, the sands represent the submerged island of Lomea, which in the 11th cent. belonged to earl Godwin.

GOODWOOD. The Sussex seat of the duke of Richmond and Gordon, 3½ m. N.E. of Chichester, England. On the downs adjoining is G. Park and racecourse, where horses have been raced since 1802. There was a motor-racing track 1948–66.

GOODYEAR, Charles (1800–60). American inventor, who developed vulcanized rubber in 1839.

GOOLE. English market town and port (bor.) at the junction of the Don and Ouse, 24 m. W. of Hull, in Yorks, W. Riding. It is connected with the North Sea by the 47 m.-long Humber estuary, and its industries include shipbuilding and -repairing, flour-milling, making of fertilizers and clothing. Pop. (1961) 18,875.

GOONHI'LLY. Post Office satellite tracking station in Cornwall, England. It is equipped with a communications satellite transmitter-receiver in permanent contact with most parts of the world, and able to handle 500 transatlantic telephone calls and a television channel simultaneously.

GOOSANDER. Fish-eating duck (*Mergus merganser*). The drake has a black and grey back, black and white wings, and a green head; the rest of the body is white with a rosy tinge. The duck, sometimes known as the Dun-diver, has a chestnut head, and a long crest, which is absent in the male.

GOOSE. Name given to birds forming the sub-family Anserinae. Both sexes are similar in appearance; they have short, webbed feet, placed nearer the front of the body than in other members of the order Anatidae, and the beak is slightly hooked. They feed entirely on grass and plants, 'grey' geese being very destructive to young crops. The commonest variety is the grey-lag G. (*Anser anser*) which is the ancestor of the tame goose. This is the only variety which nests in Gt. Britain. The genus also includes the bean G. (*A. fabalis*), the pink-footed G. (*A. brachyrhynchus*), and the white-fronted G. (*A. albifrons*), all of which breed in the Old World, and visit Britain in winter. The G. builds a nest of grass and twigs on the ground, and from 5 to 9 eggs are laid, white or cream-coloured, according to the species.

GOOSEBERRY. Edible fruit of *Glossularia reclinata*, a low-growing bush allied to the currant bushes. The bush is straggling in its growth, bearing straight sharp spines singly or in groups, and rounded, lobed leaves. The flowers are green, and hang on short stalks. The fruits are generally globular, green, and hairy, but there are reddish and whitish varieties.

GOOSSENS, Sir Eugene (1893–1962). British composer and conductor, member of a remarkable musical family of Belgian extraction that settled in Britain in 1873. He wrote chamber music, operas (*Judith* and *Don Juan*), and symphonies, and is remembered as one of Beecham's young men in the great days of Beecham opera and as conductor of the Sydney Symphony Orchestra 1947–56. His brother **Léon G.** (1897–) is a celebrated oboist.

GOPHER (gō'fer). N. American rodent. It is a burrowing animal, and does much damage to crops.

GORDIMER, Nadine (1923–). S. African writer. Her 1st novel appeared in 1953, *The Lying Days*, and has been followed by a number of others incl. *Occasion for Loving* (1963) and vols. of short stories (*Friday's Footprint*). She gives a delicately observant picture of S. African life.

GORDON, Adam Lindsay (1833–70). Australian poet. B. in the Azores, he was sent to Australia in 1853, and lived a varied life as mounted policeman, sheep farmer, politician, etc. *Sea Spray and Smoke Drift*, a collection of some of his best poems, was pub. in 1867, followed in 1870 by *Bush Ballads and Galloping Rhymes*. He committed suicide.

GORDON, Charles George (1833–85). British general. B. at Woolwich, he joined the Royal Engineers in 1852, and served in the Crimean War, and in the Chinese War of 1860. In the latter he suppressed the Taiping rebellion and became known as 'Chinese G.' In 1874 he went to Egypt, and 1877–9 was governor of the Sudan. He spent the next few years in India, China, Ireland, Mauritius, the Cape, and Palestine. He was sent back to the Sudan in 1884 to rescue English garrisons which were at the mercy of native rebels under the Mahdi, but was himself besieged by the Mahdi's army in Khartoum. A relief expedition under Wolseley arrived on Jan. 28, 1885, to find that Khartoum, after a siege of 10 months, had been captured, and G. killed, 2 days before.

GORDON, Douglas (1909–). British radiologist, holding appointments at Moorfields Eye Hospital, Willesden General Hospital, and the West End Hospital for Neurology and Neurosurgery. He began research in medical ultrasonics in 1953. In 1962 he invented the ultrasonic tomograph which achieved a major advance in medical diagnosis by showing details not demonstrable by X-rays.

GORDON, Lord George (1751–93). Protestant fanatic, who organized the Protestant protest against the Catholic Relief Act of 1778, which led to the disgraceful 'Gordon Riots'. G. was tried for treason, but acquitted. G. and the 'No Popery' riots figure in Dickens' *Barnaby Rudge*.

GORDON, John Rutherford (1890–). British journalist. He worked on the *Evening News* and the *Daily Express*, before becoming editor (1928) and editor-in-chief (1957) of the *Sunday Express* of which his column 'Current Events' is a well-known feature. He is a trustee of the Beaverbrook Foundation.

GORDON, Richard O. (1921–). British author. After qualifying and practising as a doctor, he pub. a series of light-hearted novels on the career of a young medical aspirant beginning with *Doctor in the House* (1952).

GORDONSTOUN. Public school nr. Elgin, Morayshire, Scotland, founded by Kurt Hahn (q.v.) in 1935, which emphasizes a spartan outdoor life and achievement of objectives, e.g. in mountain-climbing and sailing. Prince Philip and Prince Charles were both ed. there. The estate was formerly the seat of the Gordon Cumming family, Sir William Gordon Cumming, 4th bt., being the centre of the baccarat scandal of 1890 when he was accused of cheating in a game which included the Prince of Wales (Edward VII), who gave evidence in the subsequent court case.

GORE, Charles (1853–1932). Anglo-Catholic churchman. The first head of Pusey House, Oxford, he edited the volume of theological essays *Lux Mundi* (1890), founded in 1892 the Community of the

GORILLA. A study at the Crystal Palace grounds in Belgian fossil marble by sculptor David Wynne (q.v.). Weighing two and a half tons, it shows the knuckle-walking stance usually adopted. *Courtesy of David Wynne.*

Resurrection that was est. at Mirfield in 1898, and was successively bishop of Worcester (1902), the new diocese of Birmingham (1905), and Oxford (1911–19). His many books include the trilogy, *Belief in God, Belief in Christ,* and *The Holy Spirit and the Church.*

GORE, Frederick Spencer (1878–1914). British artist. He studied at the Slade, and his paintings show the influence of Sickert, and of the Post-impressionists Cézanne and Gauguin. In 1911 he became the 1st Pres. of the Camden Town Group.

GORGAS, William Crawford (1854–1920). American military doctor, who cleared the Panama Canal Zone of malaria and yellow fever, and discovered that the latter is transmitted by the mosquito.

GO′RGON. In Greek mythology, Stheno, Euryale, and Medusa, the 3 daus. of Phorcys and Ceto, who were possessed of wings, claws, enormous teeth, and snakes in place of hair. So terrible was the face of Medusa (the only one who was mortal) that the sight of it, even after her death at the hands of Perseus, turned the gazer to stone.

GORGONZO′LA. Town in Lombardy, Italy, 12 m. N.E. of Milan, famous for its cheeses. Pop. (1960) 8,750.

GORILLA. Largest of the anthropoid apes (*Gorilla gorilla*) found in the dense forests of W. Africa. The mountain species (*G. berengei*) is slightly larger and heavier.

GORILLA. The erect, breast-beating position, usually denoting excitement rather than rage.

The G. stands about 5½ ft. high, the female being smaller, and the body is covered with blackish hair, silvered on the back. The family unit is a male with several females and their young ones: the males are said to sleep on the ground and the females and young

in stoutly built nests in trees, used only for a nights. The G. is chiefly vegetarian and will not attack man except in self-defence, but is rapidly dwindling in numbers despite stringent protection.

GORIZIA (gŏrēt′sē-ah). Town in Friuli-Venezia-Giulia region, N. Italy, cap. of G. prov., 20 m. E.S.E. of Udine. During the F.W.W. a number of battles were fought round it. Pop. (1961) 41,854.

GORKY, Arshile (1904–48). American artist. B. in Armenia, he went to the U.S.A. in 1920 and was an initiator of Abstract Impressionism, his work having a broodingly introspective quality.

GORKY, Maxim. Pseudonym of the Russian writer Alexei Peshkov (1868–1936). B. at Nijni-Novgorod, now renamed G. in his honour, he is unique in playing an equally important part in his country before and after the Revolution, which he strongly supported, enduring exile 1906–13 for his revolutionary principles. Intimate contact with men and life during his restless wanderings in search of work in S.E. Russia gave G. a strong sense of reality, coupled with a romantic dream of a different world and a better life. This duality pervades such a play as *Na dne* (1902: *The Lower Depths*). Despite the terrible pressure of events, G. never lost his faith in the human

MAXIM GORKY
Photo: Novosti Press Agency.

race, e.g. *Chelovek* (1903: *Man*), a prose poem; *Mat* (1907: *Mother*), a novel celebrating the potential power of the industrial proletariat; the recollections *Detstvo* (1913: *My Childhood*), and *Yegor Bulychov* (1932), a play forming part of an unfinished trilogy. He suffered from tuberculosis and stayed in S. Italy in 1922–8, but then returned to a hero's welcome.

GORKY. Town in the R.S.F.S.R., cap. of G. region, situated at the junction of the Oka and Volga. An ancient city with a kremlin or castle, it was, as Nijni-Novgorod, long famous for its great annual fair. It remains a great trade centre, making also motor-cars, locomotives, aeroplanes, etc. It has a univ. Its name was changed in 1932 in honour of Maxim Gorky who was b. there. Pop. (1967) 1,100,000.

GÖRLITZ. Manufacturing town in E. Germany, 55 m. E. of Dresden. Pop. (1960) 90,800.

GORLOVKA. Industrial town and railway junction in the Ukrainian S.S.R. Pop. (1967) 348,000.

GORSE, Furze, or **Whin.** Genus of plants (*Ulex*) of the Leguminosae family, consisting of thorny shrubs with spine-shaped leaves densely clustered along the stems, and bright yellow flowers. The gorse bush (*U. europaeus*) is an evergreen, and grows on heaths and sandy areas throughout western Europe, and abundantly in Britain.

GORST, Sir John Eldon (1835–1916). British statesman. In New Zealand 1860–5, he was influential in negotiations with the Maoris, and returning to England reorganized the Conservative Party for Disraeli's victory in 1874. He was a member of Randolph Churchill's Fourth Party 1880–4, but later became a Liberal.

GORT, John Vereker, 1st visct. G. (1886–1946). British soldier. He succeeded his father as 6th visct. G. in the peerage of Ireland in 1902, won the V.C. in the F.W.W., and as C.I.G.S. from 1937 commanded the B.E.F. 1939–40, conducting a fighting retreat to the Channel and Dunkirk. He was Gov. of Gibraltar in 1941, of Malta 1942–4, and High Commissioner for Palestine 1944–5. He was created field marshal (1943) and a visct. in the British peerage in 1945.

GORTON, John Grey (1911–   ). Australian Liberal statesman. Son of a Victorian fruit-grower, he studied at Oxford, and served in the R.A.A.F. during the S.W.W. He was Min. for the Navy 1958–63; became Min. for Interior and also for Works 1963; and was Min. for Education and Science 1966–8, and then P.M. on the death of Holt (q.v.) until he resigned in 1971.

GOSCHEN (go'shen), **George Joachim,** 1st visct. (1831–1907). British Liberal politician. He held several cabinet posts under Gladstone 1868–74, but broke with him in 1886 over Irish Home Rule. In Salisbury's Unionist govt. of 1886–92 he was Chancellor of the Exchequer, and 1895–1900 was 1st Lord of the Admiralty.

GOSHAWK. Bird (*Accipiter gentilis*) used in falconry; similar in appearance to the peregrine falcon, but with short wings and short legs.

GOSPEL. Word used in the N.T. generally to signify the message of salvation; later it was applied to the 4 written Gs. of Matthew, Mark, Luke, and John. Although the first 3 give approximately the same account or synopsis (thus giving rise to the name Synoptic Gs.), their differences from John have raised many problems, discussed in a vast literature.

The so-called 5th G., or G. of St. Thomas, is a 2nd cent. collection of 114 sayings of Jesus found in a Coptic translation in one of 13 papyrus codices, discovered in Upper Egypt in 1946, which were apparently the library of a Gnostic community. Strongly influenced by Gnostic teaching, it is nevertheless interesting for comparison with the canonical Gs.: there is no reason to believe that it was written by St. Thomas, the name being used merely to give authority.

GOSPORT. English port (bor.) and naval depot to the W. of Portsmouth harbour, Hants. Pop. (1961) 62,436.

GOSSE (gos), **Sir Edmund William** (1849–1928). English author. Son of a marine biologist, who was a member of the Plymouth Brethren, G.'s childhood was shadowed by the narrow tenets of the sect in Victorian times, and in his one great original book *Father and Son* (published anonymously in 1907) he describes the conflict between the generations, even where affection exists. G. worked as a librarian, first at the British Museum, and from 1904–19 in the House of Lords, and was knighted in 1925. He was influential as a critic and an authority on French and Scandinavian literature.

GÖTEBORG. Swedish port at the mouth of the Göta and at the W. end of the Göta canal. Pop. (1966) 443,292.

GOTHA (gō'tah). Town in E. Germany, at the N. edge of the Thuringian forest, 15 m. W.S.W. of Erfurt. It was a former cap. of the duchy of Saxe-Coburg-Gotha, and has a castle and 2 observatories; it makes pottery, soap, aircraft, etc. The *Almanach de G.*, an annual survey of the royalty, aristocracy and diplomatic ranks of Europe, first appeared at G. in 1764. Pop. (1966) 60,000.

GOTHENBURG. German form of GÖTEBORG.

GOTHIC ARCHITECTURE. The various styles of architecture which are grouped under the heading of Gothic have certain features in common, viz. the vertical lines – tall pillars, spires, etc. – which take the place of the horizontal lines of previous styles, the pointed arch, rib vaulting, and the flying buttress. G.A. originated in Normandy and Burgundy in the 12th cent., and prevailed in W. Europe until the 16th cent. when classic architecture was revived. The term Gothic was at first used disparagingly of medieval art by Renaissance architects.

In France, G.A. may be divided into 4 periods, viz. (a) early Gothic, 1130–90, when ogival vaults were introduced; (b) lancet Gothic, 1190–1240, when pointed arches were tall and narrow; (c) radiating Gothic, 1240–1350, which takes its name from the

A superb example of Perpendicular Gothic architecture, Winchester cathedral (1475). The lines of the vertical tracery give an effect of lacework in stone.   *Photo: A. W. Kerr.*

series of chapels which radiate from the cathedral apse; and (d) late Gothic or the Flamboyant style, 1350–1520. Examples of the different periods are (a) Notre Dame, Paris (begun 1160); (b) Chartres (begun 1194); Bourges (begun 1209); Rheims (begun 1211); and Amiens (begun 1221); (c) Sainte Chapelle, Paris (1226–30); and (d) St. Gervais, Paris.

In Italy Gothic had a classical basis. A notable example of Italian Gothic is Milan cathedral.

The Gothic style in Germany appeared, until the end of the 13th cent., to have been imported from France, e.g. Cologne cathedral, the largest in N. Europe, was built after the model of Amiens (q.v.).

In England the Gothic style is divided into Early English (1200–75), Decorated (1300–75), and Perpendicular (1400–1575), qq.v.

GOTHS. An E. Germanic people who settled on the shores of the Black Sea, about the 2nd cent. A.D. One branch, the Ostrogoths, was conquered by the Huns *c.* 370, while another, the Visigoths, migrated to Thrace. The latter raided Greece and Italy under Alaric (395–410), sacked Rome, and set up a kingdom in S. France. Expelled thence by the Franks, they estab. a Spanish kingdom which lasted until the Moorish conquest of 711. The Ostrogoths regained their independence in 454, and under Theodoric conquered Italy in 488–93; they disappeared as a nation after Justinian reconquered Italy in 535–55.

GOTLAND. Swedish island in the Baltic Sea. Its cap. is Visby. Area 1,220 sq. m. Pop. (1966) 53,738.

GOTTFRIED VON STRASSBURG (fl. *c.* 1210). German poet, author of *Tristan und Isolde.* Hardly anything is known about his life, but he may have been a member of one of the patrician families of Strasbourg. His unfinished *Tristan* epic, which shows a formal refinement and splendour of diction unprecedented in Ger. epic poetry, is a free version of that of the Anglo-Norman Thomas (*c.* 1170).

GOTTHELF, Jeremias. Pseudonym of the Swiss novelist Albert Bitzius (1797–1854). B. at Murten, he became in 1832 pastor of Lützelflüh. His masterpiece is considered to be *Uli der Knecht* (1841).

GÖTTINGEN. W. German univ. town in Lower Saxony on the Leine, 26 m. N.E. of Kassel. The univ. was founded in 1734 by George II of England, elector of Hanover, and became a famous seat of learning. The main industry is printing and publishing; scientific instruments and chemicals are made. Pop. (1966) 112,172.

GOTTSCHED (got'shed), **Johann Christoph** (1700–66). German author and critic. B. in east Prussia, he taught philosophical subjects and poetry at Leipzig from 1725, and for nearly 20 years exercised almost dictatorial powers as a literary critic.

GOTTWALD (got'vahlt), **Klement** (1896–1953). Czechoslovak Communist. B. of a peasant family in Moravia, he joined the Czechoslovak Army on its formation in 1918, and became gen. sec. of the Communist Party in 1929. In the same year he was elected to parliament. In 1938 he went to Moscow, but returned to Czechoslovakia in 1945, and in 1946 became P.M. of a coalition govt., and in 1948 succeeded Beneš as President. He estab. a dictatorship.

GOUDA (gow'da). Dutch town in S. Holland prov., 12 m. N.E. of Rotterdam; it is famous for its round flat cheeses. Pop. (1967) 46,823.

GOUDY, Frederic William (1865–1947). American type-designer and printer. B. in Illinois, he designed over a hundred type faces which profoundly influenced magazine advertising in the U.S.

GOUGH (gof), **Sir Hubert** (1870–1963). British general. As commander of the 5th Army (1916–18), he was blamed for the German break-through on the Somme and superseded, but it was subsequently admitted that the number of his troops was far from sufficient to hold such a length of front: he was created G.C.B. in 1937.

GOUJON (goozhoñ'), **Jean** (1515–66). Considered to be the finest French sculptor of the 16th cent., he executed work in Rouen cathedral and the Louvre.

GOULBURN. Australian town, in N.S.W., 137 m. S.W. of Sydney. A railway junction, it is an agricultural centre with brick and tile factories, pottery works, boot factories, etc. Pop. (1966) 20,849.

GOULD (goold), **Sir Francis Carruthers** (1844–1925). British artist, known as F.C.G. B. at Barnstaple, he was the first English caricaturist to contribute a daily cartoon to a newspaper, *The Westminster Gazette*, and became famous for his cartoons of political subjects.

GOULD, Jay (1836–92). American financier. B. in New York, he set up as a stockbroker in 1859, and in 1868 was elected president of the Erie rly. In 1872 he was compelled to resign following the discovery that he had issued large amounts of fraudulent stock. Some years earlier his speculations in gold had caused a financial panic on 'Black Friday', Sept. 24, 1869. Subsequently he developed a large railway system in the S.W. states.

GOULD, Nathaniel (1857–1919). British novelist, famous as 'Nat' G. *The Double Event* (1891), pub. during a 10-year stay in Australia as a journalist, was an immediate success. He wrote some 130 popular novels of the Turf.

GOUNOD (goonoh'), **Charles François** (1818–93). French composer. B. in Paris, he studied at the Conservatoire and in Rome. His first opera, *Sapho*, was produced in Paris in 1851, and was followed by an operatic version of Molière's *Le Médecin malgré lui*, *Faust* (1859), *Philémon et Baucis* (1860), and *Roméo et Juliette* (1867). He also wrote sacred songs, masses, and an oratorio, *The Redemption*.

GOURD (gōrd). Name applied to various members of the plant family Cucurbitaceae, including the melon, pumpkin, etc. In a narrower sense, the name applies only to the genus *Lagenaria*, of which the bottle G. (*L. vulgaris*) is best known.

GOURMONT (goormoñ'), **Rémy de** (1858–1915). French writer. B. in Orne dept., he was one of the founders in 1890 of the *Mercure de France*, of which he eventually became editor. His literary criticism was reprinted in *Promenades Littéraires* (1904–28) and other vols., and he also wrote *La Culture des Idées* (1900) and novels.

GOUT. Disease due to excess of uric acid in the blood, and almost entirely confined to men. The tendency to it may be inherited. It usually appears between 30 and 50. Attacks are brought on especially by sweet wines, beer, and meat. A typical attack comes suddenly in the night with inflammation of a big toe joint and fever. The disease may become chronic and shorten life by affecting the kidneys. Commonly there is a generalized inflammation of the joints. Treatment aims at removing, more recently at preventing, the deposits of urate of soda in the system by diet and drugs.

GOW, Niel (1727–1807). Scottish violinist. B. near Dunkeld, he was famed as a player and composer of

GOYA. Detail of the Wellington portrait stolen in 1961 and recovered in 1965. *Courtesy of the National Gallery*

reels; nearly 100 tunes are attributed to him. His 4 sons were also musicians, and 1784–1822 the family pub. the Gow collection of Scottish airs.

GOWER, John (*c*. 1330–1408). British poet. B. in Kent, he was a friend of Chaucer and wrote in English a long poem, *Confessio Amantis*, and other poems in French and Latin. He was buried in Southwark cathedral.

GOYA Y LUCIENTES (gō'yah ē loothē-en'tes), **Francisco José de** (1746–1828). Spanish painter and etcher. B. in Aragon, of humble parentage, he lived a wild and dissolute life in Madrid, and for a time joined a troupe of bull-fighters, thus obtaining a knowledge of the bull-ring that he employed in some of his finest etchings. After studying art in Italy he returned to Spain, was employed on a number of paintings for the royal tapestry manufactory, and in 1786 became court painter to Charles IV. He is famous for his portraits of 4 successive kings of Spain and of many other great personages, and for his etchings, 'The Disasters of War', depicting the horrors of the French invasion of Spain, 1808–14.

GOZZI (got'sē), **Carlo**, Count (1720–1806). Italian dramatist. B. at Venice, he wrote plays based on fairy tales, among them *Re Turandote*, basis of operas by Busoni and Puccini.

GPU. *See* M.V.D.

GRAAF, Regnier de (1641–73). Dutch physician at Delft, who wrote a treatise in 1663 on the pancreatic secretions, and in 1672 discovered the follicles of the female ovary that are named after him.

GRACCHUS, Tiberius (163–133 B.C.) and **Gaius** (153–121 B.C.). Roman agrarian reformers. Tiberius, when elected tribune in 133, attempted to end the process whereby the small farmers were being ruined by the competition of large estates cultivated by slave labour. He introduced an agrarian law for the resumption by the state of public lands in private hands and their redistribution in small lots, but was murdered by a mob of landowners. His brother Gaius, elected tribune in 123 and 122, revived the agrarian law, and introduced a sweeping programme of social and political reforms. Outlawed by the Senate, he committed suicide.

GRACE, William Gilbert (1848–1915). British cricketer and physician. B. at Downend, Glos, he began playing in first-class matches at 15, and was captain of the Gloucester County team, 1870–99, when he became manager of the London County Club. He took several teams to Australia and U.S.A. In 1871 he scored 2,739 runs in the season, and by 1900, when his career as a first-class cricketer ended, he had scored over 54,000 runs. *See* CRICKET.

GRACES. Three goddesses of ancient Greece, who were the personifications of light, joy, and fertility, and the inspirers of the arts, the sciences, and all graceful activities. Their names were Aglaia, Euphrosyne, and Thalia.

GRAEME (grām), **Bruce.** Pseudonym of the novelist Graham Montague Jeffries, best known as the creator of the adventurous character 'Blackshirt' (1925).

GRAFTON, Augustus Henry, 3rd duke of (1735–1811). British statesman. Grandson of the first duke, who was the son of Charles II and Barbara Villiers, duchess of Cleveland, he became 1st Lord of the Treasury in 1766 and acting Prime Minister 1767–70.

GRAFTON. Town of N.S.W., Australia, on the r. Clarence, 45 m. from its mouth; it is an important dairying and sugar centre, with bacon factories, tanneries, etc. Pop. (1966) 15,944.

GRAHAM, Billy (1918–). American evangelist. Of Scottish-Irish parents, he was brought up in N. Carolina, and at 17 was converted at a revival. He has crusaded, holding emotional mass meetings, throughout the U.S. and in Britain.

GRAHAM, Martha (1894–). American choreographer and dancer. B. in Pittsburgh, she became a Broadway cult in the 'twenties because of her break with tradition and her repertoire incl. *Appalachian Spring* (score by Aaron Copland) and *Clytemnestra* (1958), one of a number of classical theme dances.

GRAHAME (grā'-am), **Kenneth** (1859–1932). British author. B. at Edinburgh, son of an advocate, he worked at the Bank of England 1878–1908. The early vols. of sketches of childhood, *The Golden Age* (1895) and *Dream Days* (1898), were followed by his masterpiece *The Wind in the Willows* (1908), an animal fantasy originally created for his little son. It has been successfully staged in A. A. Milne's dramatization: *Toad of Toad Hall.*

GRAHAME-WHITE, Claude (1879–1959). Pioneer British airman and engineer. Owner of one of the first petrol-driven cars in England, he was in 1909 the first Englishman to be granted an aviator's proficiency certificate.

GRAHAM LAND. Peninsula of the Antarctic continent, formerly a dependency of the Falkland Islands and from 1962 part of the British Antarctic Territory (q.v.). Discovered by John Biscoe in 1832, it was thought to be an archipelago until 1934; it is mountainous and covered with ice and snow.

GRAHAMSTOWN. Town in Cape Prov., S. Africa, 85 m. W.S.W. of East London. It has 2 bishops, Anglican and Roman Catholic, and is the seat of Rhodes University (1951; founded 1904 as Rhodes Univ. College). Pop. (1960) 32,195 (10,500 white).

GRAIL, Holy. The dish or cup used by Christ at the Last Supper, which, together with the spear with which He was wounded at the Crucifixion, appears as an object of quest by King Arthur's knights in certain stories incorporated in the Arthurian legend. According to one story, the Blood of Christ was collected in it by Joseph of Arimathea at the Crucifixion, and he brought it to Britain.

GRAINGER, Percy Aldridge (1882–1961). Australo-American composer. B. in Melbourne, he was a sensitive and technically brilliant concert pianist. His interest in folk music led to his making many popular settings, e.g. *Molly on the Shore* and *Shepherd's Hey.*

GRAM/GRAMME. In the metric system the unit of mass, i.e. the thousandth part of the standard kilogram mass.

GRAMPIANS. Mountain mass separating the Scottish Highlands from the Lowlands; it contains the highest peaks in Scotland, e.g. Ben Nevis.

GRAMPUS. A cetacean (*Grampus orca*) of the Delphinidae or dolphin family. It breeds in Arctic regions and preys on other members of the same family – dolphin, seal, porpoise, and whale – and is 20 to 30 ft. long. It is black above and white beneath.

GRANADA (granah'da). Ancient kingdom and modern prov. of S.E. Spain and their capital. G. was the last territory in Spain held by the Moors, and did not surrender until 1492. The prov. includes mts. in the Sierra Nevada rising to over 11,000 ft. The dry summers make artificial irrigation necessary; sheep and goats are reared, and sugar refining is the principal industry. Area 4,838 sq. m.; pop. (1960) 769,408.

The city is famous for its Moorish buildings, among them the Alhambra; it also has a cathedral, built 1523–1703, and a university. Pop. (1960) 157,178.

GRANADA. A city of Nicaragua, cap. of G. dept. Founded in 1524, it has shipyards, sugar refineries, clothing, soap, and furniture factories; and a cathedral. The univ. founded here in 1846 was moved to León in 1951. Pop. (1963) 40,092.

GRANADOS, Enrique (1867–1916). Spanish composer. A brilliant pianist, he was inspired by the work of Goya to write his important piano work *Goyescas* (1911), converted to an opera in 1916. He d. when the liner in which he travelled back from its performance in N.Y. was torpedoed by a German submarine.

GRANBY, John Manners, marquess of (1721–70). British soldier. His head appears on many inn-signs in England as a result of his popularity as a commander of the British forces fighting on the Continent in the Seven Years War.

GRAN CHACO. *See* CHACO.

GRAND CANAL. Waterway in China connecting the Hwai Ho and Hai Ho river systems. It runs from Hangchow to Tientsin. The middle section was already in use in 480 B.C.; the S. section was built in the 7th cent. A.D., the N. in the 13th. It is silted up between Lintsing and Tsining.

The chief canal in Venice is also called the GRAND CANAL.

GRAND CANYON. Great, many-coloured gorge through which flows the Colorado r., in Arizona, U.S.A. It is 4–18 m. in width, reaches depths of more than a mile, and is 217 m. long; made a national park 1919.

GRAND COULEE. Dam on the Columbia river, Washington state, U.S.A. Completed 1942, 550 ft. high and 4,173 ft. long; powerplants will eventually produce some 10,000,000 kilowatts.

GRAND DESIGN. Plan attributed by Sully to Henry IV of France, and rendered abortive by his assassination, for a great Protestant Union against the Holy Roman Empire; the term is also applied to Pres. de Gaulle's vision of France's place in a united Europe.

GRAND FALLS. Town of Newfoundland, Canada, site of large paper and pulp mills. Pop. (1966) 7,451.

GRAND NATIONAL. A steeplechase (1839) run at Aintree during the Liverpool Spring meeting in March or April; the course of about 4 m. 856 yd. has 30 formidable jumps and casualties are not infrequent.

GRAND PRIX DE PARIS (groṅ prē de pahrē'). The Continental horse-race which most nearly approximates to the English Derby. It is run on the Paris racecourse in June over a distance of 1 m. 7 furlongs, and is for 3-year-old colts and fillies.

GRAND RAPIDS. City in Michigan, U.S.A., on the Grand r., noted for furniture; makes also motor bodies, plumbing fixtures, paints, etc. Pop. (1960) 177,313.

GRAND TOUR. In the 17–18th cents. the tour of Europe which finished the education of wealthy young men. A *G.T. of Space* was planned 1968 by Wernher von Braun (q.v.) for 1977, when it should be possible to send a spacecraft to the outer edges of the solar system, and when the planets would be in a favourable relative position reached once every 175 years.

GRAND UNION CANAL. The longest artificial inland waterway system in Britain, running from London to Birmingham, Leicester, Loughborough, etc.; total length with branches 240 m.

GRANITE (gra'nit). An acidic igneous rock, of plutonic origin, occurring in intrusions in many parts of the British Isles. The rock is coarse-grained, the characteristic minerals being quartz, feldspars, particularly orthoclase, and mica. It often comprises the core of a range of mountains, the surrounding rocks having been metamorphosed by the heat of the intrusion. Granitic areas produce a very characteristic scenery type, e.g. in the Grampians and Scottish Highlands, the Lake District, Dartmoor, Bodmin Moor in Cornwall, the Mourne mountains, etc. *See* FELDSPAR.

GRANT, Cary. Stage-name of American actor Archibald Leach (1904–). B. in Bristol, England, he went to the U.S. in 1921, becoming a citizen in 1942. Since entering films in 1932 he has estab. himself as the most skilled of light-comedy actors, e.g. *Notorious* (1946 with Bergman) and *A Touch of Mink* (1962).

GRANT, Duncan (1885–). Scottish painter. A member of the 'Bloomsbury' group which incl. Roger Fry and Virginia Woolf, he shows in later work, e.g. 'Snow Scene' (1921), the influence of the Post-impressionists, esp. Cézanne. He also designed carpets, pottery, etc.

GRANT, Ulysses Simpson (1822–85). American general and 18th President of the U.S.A. The son of an Ohio farmer, he had an unsuccessful career in the army 1839–54 and in business, and on the outbreak of the Civil War received a commission on the Mississippi front. He took command there in 1862, and by his capture of Vicksburg in 1863 brought the whole Mississippi under Northern control. Appointed commander-in-chief in 1864, he slowly wore down Lee's resistance, and in 1865 received his surrender at Appomattox. He was elected Pres. in 1868 and 1872, and carried through a liberal reconstruction policy in the S., although he failed in his attempts to suppress political corruption.

GRANTHAM (grant'-am). Market town (bor.) on the river Witham, Kesteven, Lincs, England. It was founded in Saxon times, and has always been the market centre for the surrounding agricultural area. Pop. (1961) 25,030.

GRANVILLE, Granville George Leveson-Gower, 2nd earl G. (1815–91). British Liberal statesman. Son of the 1st earl, whom he succeeded in 1846, he was For. Sec. in 1851, 1870–4, and 1880–5.

GRANVILLE-BARKER, Harley (1877–1946). British theatre director and dramatist. During 1904–18 he produced, with J. E. Vedrenne, plays of Shaw, and introduced works of Galsworthy, Housman, and Masefield with simple provocative productions and new scenic and lighting principles. His own plays incl. *The Voysey Inheritance* (1905), *The Madras House* (1907) and *Waste* (1909). A scholarly work, *Prefaces to Shakespeare*, was pub. 1927–45.

GRAPE. *See* VINE.

GRAPEFRUIT. Common name for the large yellow fruit of *Citrus paradisi*, grown chiefly in Florida, California, S. Africa, and the W. Indies.

GRA'PHITE, Plumbago or **Black Lead.** Crystalline form of carbon. Iron-grey to black, with a metallic lustre, it splits up easily into flakes, each flake breaking into smaller flakes – the property which is responsible for its wide use as a lubricant. G. occurs in veins in gneiss, crystalline limestone, and metamorphic rocks. So far it has proved an essential element for the moderator in certain types of nuclear power reactors and will be so used in the new nuclear power stations coming into use in Britain. For this application it is essential that impurities are present to less than a few parts per million. The powdered carbon is compressed and heated several times in a coke furnace. It is then cleaned up and accurately machined.

GRASMERE (gras'mēr). English lake and village in the Lake District, Westmorland. Wordsworth lived near and is buried in the churchyard. With Ambleside and some smaller areas, G. village was in 1935 formed into the Lakes U.D.; pop. (1961) 6,061.

GÜNTER GRASS
Courtesy of Secker and Warburg Ltd.

GRASS (grahs), **Günter** (1927–). German sculptor and writer. B. in Danzig, he studied at the art academies of Düsseldorf and Berlin, worked as a writer and sculptor, first in Paris and later in Berlin, and in 1958 won the coveted 'Group 47' prize. The grotesque humour of his novel *Die Blechtrommel* (*The Tin Drum*: 1963) is again shown in many of his poems. G. has also written plays, incl. *Onkel, Onkel* (1958).

GRASSE (grahs). Town in Alpes-Maritimes dept., S. France, 8 m. N.N.W. of Cannes. Around the town, orange blossom and roses are grown for the production of perfumes. Pop. (1962) 27,226.

GRASSES. Plants belonging to the Gramineae family; the most important and one of the largest of the families of monocotyledonous plants. They are distributed throughout the world, and include all the cereals, the grasses of meadows and pastures, and other plants of economic importance, including sugar cane, the bamboo, the reed, etc. The leaves of G. are long and narrow, with parallel veins, the lower part enclosing the stem in a sheath. The stem is mainly hollow, and the flowers are borne in one or more spikelets, terminating the stem. The fruit is single seeded, and is known as a caryopsis. It contains a small embryo set at the base of a hard, albuminous endosperm. When the flower is ready for pollination, the large stamens break through to the outside of the spike and shed their pollen outside.

GRASSES. I, Cockfoot; 2, Yorkshire fog; 3, perennial rye; 4, rough-stalked meadow.

GRASSHOPPERS. Insects of the order Orthoptera,

usually with strongly developed hind legs which enable them to leap. The short-horned Gs. (Acridiidae) incl. the locust (q.v.), and all members of the family feed voraciously on vegetation. The femur of each hind leg in the male usually has a row of protruding joints which produce the characteristic chirping when rubbed against the hard wing veins. Eggs are laid in a small hole in the ground, and the unwinged larvae become adult after about 6 moults. There are several sober-coloured, small and harmless species in Britain. The long-horned Gs. (Tettigonidae) have a similar life-history, but differ from the Acridiidae in having long antennae, etc., and in producing their chirping by the friction of the wing covers over one another. The large green G. (*Phasgonura viridissima*), 1½ in. long, is a British species of this family, which also comprises the N. American katydids (Phanopterinae), notable stridulators.

LONG-HORNED GRASSHOPPER

GRASS SNAKE. Harmless reptile (*Tropidonotus natrix*), commonly found in wet districts of England and Scotland. Attaining 3–6 ft., it is olive-brown or grey with black spots above and mottled white below, with a yellow and black collar. It feeds on frogs or fish, one meal often sufficing 1–2 months, and the soft oval eggs – about an inch long and numbering 1–4 dozen – are laid in July/August.

GRATTAN, Henry (1746–1820). Irish statesman. B. in Dublin, he entered the Irish parliament in 1775. As leader of the opposition he secured the abolition of all claims by the British parliament to legislate for Ireland in 1782. Although he strongly opposed the Act of Union, he sat in the British parliament from 1805.

GRAUBÜNDEN. German name of GRISONS.

's GRAVENHAGE. Formal Dutch name of THE HAGUE.

GRAVES, Robert Ranke (1895–). English poet and author. B. in London, he was the son of the Irish writer Alfred Perceval G. (1846–1931) whose songs and poetry contributed largely to the Celtic revival. He was severely wounded on the Somme in the F.W.W. and his frank autobiography *Goodbye to All That* (1929) is one of the outstanding war books. In 1927 he joined Laura Riding (q.v.) in directing the Seizin Press and collaborated with her in several books. His first book of verse was *Over the Brazier* (1916) and other vols. followed incl. *Collected Poems* (1959). Particularly striking are his novels of Imperial Rome, *I Claudius* and *Claudius the God* (1934) and *They Hanged My Saintly Billy* (1957), a defence of William Palmer, a forger and supposed poisoner of 14 people, hanged in 1856. He is an avid student of myth and has published notable volumes of literary criticism: he was prof. of poetry at Oxford 1961–6.

GRASS SNAKE

GRAVESEND. English river port and market town (bor.) in Kent, on the Thames estuary. It is the Thames Pilot Station, and has a ferry service to Tilbury. Pop. (1961) 51,388.

GRAY, Thomas (1716–71). English poet. B. in London, he formed at Eton a close friendship with Horace Walpole, with whom in 1739 he started on a tour of France and Italy, vividly described in his letters. In 1741 he returned to London, where he lived for a year, making occasional visits to his mother and sister at Stoke Poges; to this period belong the 'Ode on a Distant Prospect of Eton College' and the 'Hymn to Adversity'. In 1748 his first poems appeared anonymously in Dodsley's *Miscellany*, and in 1750 he wrote the 'Elegy written in a Country Churchyard' at Stoke Poges. A vol. of *Poems* was pub. by Dodsley in 1752, and in 1757 Walpole issued G.'s Pindaric Odes, 'The Bard' and 'The Progress of Poesy' from his private press.

GRAYLING. Freshwater fish (*Thymallus thymallus*) of the family Salmonidae. It is found locally in England and has been introduced into Scotland. It exhibits a coloration shading from purple to pink, and may be distinguished by its long dorsal fin.

GRAZ (grahts). Capital of Styria prov., Austria, on the Mur at the foot of the Styrian Alps. It has a 15th cent. cathedral and a univ. founded 1573. Pop. (1961) 237,041.

GRAZIANI (grahtsē-ah'nē), **Rodolfo** (1882–1955). Italian general. With experience in colonial warfare

GREAT BARRIER REEF. One of Australia's playgrounds, the reef is a paradise for the yachtsman and naturalist. Here are Lindeman Island and, in the background, Royal Seaforth Island. *Courtesy of the Agent-General for Queensland.*

in Libya, Cyrenaica, and Abyssinia, G. became G.-in-C. of Italian forces in N. Africa in the S.W.W., but was soundly beaten by Wavell (1940), and subsequently superseded. Later, as Defence Min. in the new Mussolini govt. he failed to reorganize a Republican Fascist army, was captured by the Allies (1945), tried by an Italian military court, and finally released in 1950.

GREAT BARRIER REEF. A collection of coral reefs and islands stretching for about 1,200 m. at a distance of 10–30 m. from the E. coast of Queensland, Australia, and forming an immense natural breakwater.

GREAT BRITAIN. Name used for England, Scotland, and Wales, and the adjacent islands, that came into official use in 1603, when the English and Scottish crowns were united in the person of James VI of Scotland, I of England. With Northern Ireland it forms the United Kingdom.

GREAT CIRCLE. A plane cutting through a sphere, and passing through the centre point of the sphere, cuts the surface along a G.C. Thus, on the earth, all meridians of longitude are half G.Cs.; of the parallels of latitude, only the Equator is a G.C. The shortest route between 2 points on the earth's surface is along a G.C.

GREAT DANE. A large dog popular in Britain. It has a long head, deep-set eyes, and small ears, straight legs and short hair. The average height is 30 in.

GREAT GRIMSBY. *See* GRIMSBY.

GREATHEAD, James Henry (1844–96). British engineer. B. in Cape Colony, he came to England and developed the Greathead shield system of tunnelling, which he used in constructing the London 'tubes'.

GREAT LAKES. Series of 5 freshwater lakes along the U.S.-Canadian border, comprising Lakes Superior, Michigan, Huron, Erie, and Ontario. All are connected and inter-connected by rivers and canals. The

GREAT WALL OF CHINA. The square watch towers built at intervals served as signal-fire stations, and the whole was carefully sited to follow the contours of the landscape. It has been well restored under the Communist régime.
Photo: Camera Press.

lakes, lying in a plain, are invisible from a few miles' distance; they are drained by the St. Lawrence.

GREAT RIFT VALLEY. Geological feature whose eastern arm stretches from the Sea of Galilee on the Israel-Jordan frontier (historically Palestine), through the Red Sea to near Kilimanjaro in E. Africa, and the W. from L. Albert to the mouth of the Zambezi. Total length about 5,000 m.

GREAT WALL OF CHINA. System of frontier defences in N. China consolidated to a continuous wall c. 450 m. in length under the Ch'in dynasty in 214 B.C. It consists of a brick-faced wall of earth and stone c. 25 ft. high and interspersed with square watch towers, eventually extended to c. 1,400 m., and intended to prevent incursions by Turkish and Mongol tribesmen.

GREAT YARMOUTH. *See* YARMOUTH.

GREBES. Aquatic birds of the family Podicipedidae. The legs are placed far back on the body, causing the birds to stand upright like penguins. There are 5 European species, the best-known being the Little G. or Dabchick (*Podiceps fluviatilis*).

GREAT CRESTED GREBE

GRECO (gre'kō), **El.** Name given to the Spanish immigrant artist Doménico Theotocopuli (1541–1614) because of his birth in Crete. Some time before 1570 he travelled to Venice, where he studied under Titian, and while visiting Rome was influenced by the works of Michelangelo. In 1575 he first went to Spain, where he found the spiritual atmosphere suited his deeply religious temperament, and settled in Toledo. His works have a fanatic intensity, an almost lurid sense of colour, and exaggeratedly elongated forms, e.g.

GREECE. A steep grey-blue rock rising abruptly from the green Saronic Sea, the island of Hydra produced from such fishing villages as Vlychos the patriots and sea captains who bore the brunt of the Greek War of Independence.
Courtesy of the National Tourist Organization of Greece.

'The Burial of Count Orgaz' and 'The Agony in the Garden'.

GRECO, Emilio (1913–). Italian sculptor. B. in Sicily, he became prof. at the Naples Academy of Fine Arts, and from 1943 has worked in Rome. His works incl. the Pinocchio monument at Collodi and bronze doors for Orvieto cathedral.

GREECE. Independent kingdom of Europe in the southern Balkans. The country is mainly composed of the complicated series of mountain ridges and enclosed valleys forming the Pindus mountains. The coastline is very broken, and is lined with scores of islands. Although winters are cold in the N., southern G. has a typical Mediterranean climate. G. is mainly an agricultural country, growing, chiefly for export, tobacco, olives, and fruits, particularly currants. Meat, wheat, and flour have to be imported. Wine and olive oil are produced; and there are textile and chemical factories; smelting and shipbuilding are carried on.

The capital is Athens, of which Piraeus, its port (formerly distinct), forms part; other towns are Corinth, Thessaloniki, Kavalla, Kalamai, Trikkala, Larissa, and Patras. Area 51,182 sq. m.; pop. (1966) 8,614,000, some 95 per cent of whom belonged to the Eastern (Greek) Orthodox Church. Under the constitution overwhelmingly approved by referendum in 1968, G. is a crowned democracy with a unicameral legislature of 150 elected by universal suffrage, voting being obligatory. *See* GREEK ART, HISTORY, etc.

GREEK ARCHITECTURE. The architecture of Greece stands foremost among the arts of the world as the most perfect. It is divided into 3 styles, viz. Doric, Ionic, and Corinthian. Of these the Doric is the oldest; it is said to have evolved from a former timber prototype. The finest example of a Doric temple is the Parthenon at Athens (447–438 B.C.). The origin of the Ionic is uncertain. The earliest building in which the Ionic capital appears is the temple of

The Acropolis of Athens restored as a citizen would have seen it on emerging from the great entranceway, the Propylaea. Centre, the great statue of Athena Promachus (the Champion), behind it the Erechtheum, and to the right, the Parthenon.

Hellenistic bronze head in the British Museum of an African from Cyrene. It shows excellent balance of elaborate detail-treatment against simple and harmonius general effect.

Diana at Ephesus (530 B.C.). The famous gateway to the Acropolis at Athens (known as the Propylaea) has internal columns of the Ionic order. The most perfect example is the Erechtheum at Athens. The Corinthian order belongs to a later period of Greek art. The most important example of the order is the temple of Jupiter (Zeus) Olympus at Athens (174 B.C.), completed under Roman influence in A.D. 129. The Mausoleum at Halicarnassus (353 B.C.) was one of the Seven Wonders of the World. *See* ORDERS.

GREEK ART. The sculpture, painting, vases, gems, etc., produced in Greek cities during the first millennium B.C. Chronologically G. A. can be divided into Archaic (to 530 B.C.), Classical (530–320 B.C.), and Hellenistic (320 B.C.–A.D. 1).

By *Archaic* G.A. is meant the period beginning with the geometric style (900–700 B.C.) in which decoration consists of geometric elements – circles, triangles, etc. – followed by a transition to more naturalistic decoration showing the influence of Oriental, Egyptian, and Cyprian art, and ending with the red-figure style of vase painting (530 B.C.).

The *Classical* period may be subdivided into (a) Post-Persian, a name given to the art of the first half of the 5th cent. B.C. when archaic conventions were abandoned for three-dimensional composition; (b) Periclean art which is sunnier and freer than previous styles – e.g. heavy ornate drapery gives way to more decorative flowing folds; (c) the period of the Sophists when Periclean 'beauty with extravagance' is dissolved into the two extremes of emotional realism and luxuriant artificiality; and (d) the mid-4th cent., the period of the great sculptors Praxiteles, Skopas, and Lysippos, and the great painters Pausias, Nikias, and Apelles.

The *Hellenistic* period saw an increase in the variety of types of sculpture, painting, etc. Works produced during the period include the Tanagra terracottas, the Victory from Samothrace, the altar of Zeus (Pergamum), etc.

GREEK HISTORY: Ancient. The first Greek civilization, that known as Mycenaean (fl. *c.* 1600–1200 B.C.), owed much to the Minoan civilization of Crete, and may have been produced by the intermarriage of Greek-speaking invaders with the original inhabitants. From the 14th cent. B.C. a new wave of invasions began. The Achaeans overran Greece and Crete, destroying the Minoan and Mycenaean civilizations, and penetrated Asia Minor; to this period belongs the siege of Troy (*c.* 1180). The latest of the invaders were the Dorians (*c.* 1100), who settled in the Peloponnese and founded Sparta. An obscure period followed (1100–800) during which the great city-states arose. The mountainous geography of Greece pre-

Head of a statue of Hermes by Praxiteles, discovered at Olympia in 1877.

vented the cities from attaining any national unity, and compelled them to take to the sea. During the years 750–550 the Greeks not only became great traders, but founded colonies around the coasts of the Mediterranean and the Black Sea, in Asia Minor, Sicily, S. Italy, S. France, Spain, and N. Africa. The main centres of Greek culture in the 6th cent. were the wealthy Ionian ports of Asia Minor, where Greek philosophy, science, and lyric poetry originated.

Most of the Greek cities passed from monarchy to the rule of a landowning or merchant oligarchy, and thence to democracy; in many states a 'tyranny', or rule of a popular dictator, formed an intermediate stage between oligarchy and democracy. Thus Athens passed through the democratic reforms of Solon (594), the enlightened 'tyranny' of Peisistratus (560–527), and the establishment of democracy by Cleisthenes (*c.* 507). Sparta remained unique, a state in which a ruling race, organized on military lines, tyrannized over the original population.

After 545 the Ionian cities fell under the suzerainty of the Persian empire. Aid given them by Athens in an unsuccessful revolt in 499–494 provoked Darius of Persia to invade Greece in 490, only to be defeated by the Athenians at Marathon and forced to withdraw. Another invasion by Xerxes, after being delayed by the heroic defence of Thermopylae by 300 Spartans, was defeated on sea at Salamis in 480, and on land at Plataea in 479. The Ionian cities were liberated, and formed a naval alliance with Athens, the Confederacy of Delos. Pericles, the real ruler of Athens 461–429, attempted to convert this into an Athenian empire. and in addition to form a land empire in Greece,

PERICLES

Mistrust of his ambitions led to the Peloponnesian War (431–404), which destroyed Athens' political power. In 5th cent. Athens, Greek tragedy, comedy, sculpture, and architecture reached their height, and Socrates and Plato founded moral philosophy.

After the Peloponnesian War, Sparta became the leading Greek power, until she in turn was overthrown by Thebes (378–371). The constant wars between the cities gave Philip II of Macedon (358–336) his opportunity gradually to establish his supremacy over Greece. His son Alexander overthrew the decadent Persian empire, conquered Syria and Egypt, and invaded the Punjab. After his death in 323 his empire was divided among his generals, but his conquest had nevertheless spread Greek culture all over the Near East.

During the 3rd cent. B.C. the cities attempted to maintain their independence against Macedon, Egypt, and Rome by forming federations, e.g. the Achaean and Aetolian Leagues. Roman intervention began in 212, and ended in the annexation of Greece in 146 B.C. Under Roman rule Greece remained important mainly as a cultural centre, until Justinian closed the univ. of Athens in A.D. 529.

Medieval and Modern. Medieval Greek history begins with Constantine's grant of toleration to Christianity in 313, and the transference of the capital of the Roman Empire to Constantinople in 330. In 1453 the Turks captured Constantinople, and by 1460 they had conquered all Greece.

Except for the years 1686–1715, when the Morea was occupied by the Venetians, Greece remained

Turkish until the outbreak of the War of Independence in 1821. British, French, and Russian intervention in 1827, which brought about the destruction of the Turkish fleet at Navarino, led to the establishment of Greek independence in 1829. Prince Otto of Bavaria was placed on the throne in 1832; his despotic rule provoked a revolution in 1843, which set up parliamentary government, and another in 1862, when he was deposed and replaced by Prince George of Denmark. Relations with Turkey were embittered by the Greeks' desire to recover Macedonia, Crete, and other Turkish territories with Greek populations; a war in 1897 ended in disaster, but the Balkan Wars (q.v.) of 1912–13 won for Greece most of the disputed areas.

In a period of internal conflict from 1914, two monarchs were deposed, and there was a republic 1923–35, when a military coup restored George II (q.v.), who estab. in the following year a dictatorship under Metaxas.

An Italian invasion in 1940 was successfully resisted, but a German *blitzkrieg* in 1941 overwhelmed the Greeks, despite British assistance. On the German withdrawal in 1944, British troops occupied the country and assisted the royalists against the left-wing groups in the civil war which had broken out. A plebiscite in 1946 led to the return of George II, succeeded on his death in 1947 by his brother Paul. The Cyprus dispute (q.v.) and economic problems meant that Constantine XII succeeded to a troubled situation in 1964. In 1967 a bloodless army coup led to the formation of a National Govt., and the eventual flight of the King, after failing in a counter-coup. A regent (Gen. Zoitakis) was appointed, and a new constitution was approved by referendum under martial law in 1968, which curtailed civil liberties.

GREEK LANGUAGE. A member of the Indo-European family of languages. Of the ancient Gk. dialects, the Attic form of Ionic had won the supremacy over the other dialects (Aeolic, Arcadian, Doric) by the 4th cent. B.C. and a common tongue, based on Attic, spread to the colonies, to Mesopotamia, Syria, Egypt, etc. Modern Gk. uses the ancient Gk. alphabet, but the language has undergone decisive changes in phonetics and grammar. There is a 'purist' movement which aims at a return to the classical standard, but the vigorous and freely developed 'popular' language of everyday speech holds the field in poetry and fiction.

GREEK LITERATURE. Ancient. The three greatest names of early G.L. are those of Homer (fl. *c.* 950 B.C.), author of the epic *Iliad* and *Odyssey*; Hesiod (fl. 800 B.C.), whose *Works and Days* deals with agricultural life; and the lyric poet Pindar (b. 522 B.C.). Prose came to perfection with the historians Herodotus (b. 485 B.C.) and Thucydides (460–400 B.C.) The 5th cent. also saw the development of the Athenian drama through the works of the tragic dramatists Aeschylus (b. 524 B.C.), Sophocles (b. 495 B.C.), and Euripides (480–406 B.C.), and the comic genius of Aristophanes (*c.* 445–385 B.C.). After the fall of Athens came a period of prose with the historian Xenophon (434–353 B.C.), the idealist philosopher Plato (b. 427 B.C.), the orators Isocrates (436–338 B.C.) and Demosthenes (*c.* 383–322 B.C.), and the scientific teacher Aristotle (b. 384 B.C.).

After 323 B.C. Athens lost her political importance, but was still a university town with teachers such as Epicurus (341–270 B.C.), Zeno, and Theophrastus,

SOPHOCLES. An imaginary portrait of the Hellenistic period in the B.M.

STRATIS MYRIVILIS
Portrait by Paul Bret, 1938.

and the comic dramatist Menander (342–291 B.C.). Meanwhile Alexandria was becoming the centre of Greek culture: the court of Philadelphus was graced by scientists such as Euclid, and the poets Callimachus, Apollonius, and Theocritus. During the 2nd cent. B.C. Rome became the new centre for G.L., and Polybius, the historian, spent most of his life there; in the 1st cent. B.C. Rome also sheltered the poets Archias, Antipater of Sidon, Philodemus the Epicurean, and Meleager of Gadara, who compiled the first *Greek Anthology*. In the 1st cent. A.D. Latin writers overshadow the Greek, but there are still the geographer Strabo (63 B.C.–A.D. 21), the critic Dionysius of Halicarnassus (fl. 10 B.C.), the Jewish writers Philo Judaeus and Josephus, the N.T. writers, and the biographer Plutarch (A.D. 45–125). A revival came in the 2nd cent. with Lucian (A.D. 125–95). To the 3rd cent. belong the historians Cassius Dio and Herodian, the Christian fathers Clement and Origen, and the neo-Platonists. For Medieval G.L., *see* BYZANTINE LITERATURE.

Modern. After the fall of Constantinople, the Byzantine tradition was perpetuated in the classical Gk. writing of e.g. the 15th cent. chronicles of Cyprus, various historical works in the 16th and 17th cents., and educational and theological works in the 18th cent. The 17th and 18th cents. saw much controversy over the various merits of the Gk. vernacular ('demotic'), the classical language ('katharevousa'), and the language of the Church, as a literary medium. Adamantios Korais (1748–1833), the first great modern, produced a compromise language, and was followed by the prose and drama writer, and poet, Alexandros Rhangavis ('Rangabe') (1810–92), and many others. The 10th cent. epic of *Digenis Akritas* is usually considered to mark the beginnings of modern Gk. vernacular literature, and the demotic was kept alive in the flourishing Cretan lit. of the 16th and 17th cents., in numerous popular songs, and in the Klephtic ballads of the 18th cent. With independence in the 19th cent. the popular movement became prominent with the Ionian poet Dionysios Solomos (1798–1857), Andreas Kalvos (1796–1869), and others, and later with Iannis Psichari (1854–1929), short-story writer and dramatist, and the prose writer Alexandros Papadiamandis (1851–1911), who influenced many younger writers, e.g. Konstantinos Hatzopoulos (1868–1921), poet and essayist. After the 1920s, the novel began to emerge with Stratis Myrivilis (q.v.) and others. Truly national drama in the demotic, apart from that in 17th cent. Crete, only appeared in the late 19th and early 20th cents., with Iannis Kambissis (1872–1902), Spyros Melas (1880–   ), and Gregorios Xenopoulos (1867–1951). Vernacular poetry, esp. the lyric, flourished in the 20th cent., espec. in the group incl. the popular poet Georgios Drosinis (1859–1951), and Kostis Palamas (1859–1943), poet and prose writer, Angelos Sikelianos (1884–1951), and Georgios Seferis (q.v.); the modern generation of poets incl. Odysseus Elytis (1912–   ). Other notable 20th cent. writers are Nikos Kazantzakis (1885–1957), and Konstantinos Karafis (1868–1933).

GREELEY, Horace (1811–72). American journalist. B. in New Hampshire, he became founder and editor of the *New York Tribune* (1841), helped to found the Republican Party, supported Lincoln, and advocated a vigorous conduct of the Civil War.

GREEN, John Richard (1837–83). English historian.

Forced to abandon a clerical career by ill-health in 1869, he devoted himself to a *Short History of the English People* (1874), immediately popular as the earliest complete study from the social viewpoint.

GREEN, Julian (1900–). American author. B. in Paris of American parents, he has written almost all his works in French, but is a U.S. citizen. His novels, which incl. *Le Visionnaire* (1934), and *Le Malfaiteur* (1958), explore the possibilities and dangers of freedom for the human spirit. An R.C., he differs from the 'Catholic novelists' in imposing no artificial conclusions on his plots. He has also pub. his *Journal* (1938–58), and several plays, incl. *Sud* (1953).

GREEN, Thomas Hill (1836–82). British philosopher. B. in Yorks, he was prof. of Moral Philosophy at Oxford from 1878. He gave a new direction to 19th cent. philosophical thought by showing the limitations of Spencer and Mill, and advocated the study of Kant and Hegel. His chief works are *Prolegomena to Ethics* (1883) and *Principles of Political Obligation* (1895).

GREENAWAY, Kate (1846–1901). British artist and illustrator. B. in London, she became famous for her drawings of children, which are full of charm and humour. In 1877 she first exhibited at the R.A., and began her collaboration with the colour printer Edmund Evans, with whom she produced a number of books, incl. the popular *Mother Goose*.

GREENE, Graham (1904–). English author. B. at Berkhamsted, son of a headmaster, he was ed. at Oxon. He was then on the staff of *The Times* 1926–30, literary editor of the *Spectator* 1940–1, and during the S.W.W. served in the Foreign Office. Intensely concerned with religious issues – he is an R.C. convert – he creates characters dominated by the conflict of right and wrong. His novels incl. *Brighton Rock* (1938) depicting race-gang warfare, *The Power and the Glory* (1940), *The Heart of the Matter* (1948), *Our Man in Havana* (1958) and *A Burnt-Out Case* (1961), set in a leper colony in Africa. Rather less effective, but still thought-provoking, are his plays, e.g. *The Living Room* (1953) and *The Potting Shed* (1957). His brother **Sir Hugh Carleton G.** (1910–) was director-gen. of the B.B.C. 1960–8.

GREENFINCH. Bird (*Ligurinus chloris*), also known as the green linnet, common in Europe and N. Africa. The male is green with a yellow breast and the female a drab greenish-brown.

GREENLAND. Arctic island forming a Danish prov. It lies between the North Atlantic and Arctic Oceans. The whole of the interior is covered by a vast ice-sheet. Large deposits of lead are known to exist. The Greenlanders are of mixed Eskimo, Danish and other European stocks. Area *c.* 826,000 sq. m. Pop. (1965) 39,600.

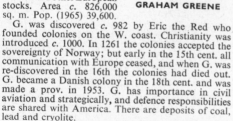

GRAHAM GREENE

G. was discovered *c.* 982 by Eric the Red who founded colonies on the W. coast. Christianity was introduced *c.* 1000. In 1261 the colonies accepted the sovereignty of Norway; but early in the 15th cent. all communication with Europe ceased, and when G. was re-discovered in the 16th cent. the colonies had died out. G. became a Danish colony in the 18th cent. and was made a prov. in 1953. G. has importance in civil aviation and strategically, and defence responsibilities are shared with America. There are deposits of coal, lead and cryolite.

GREENOCK. Scottish seaport (burgh) and industrial centre in Renfrew. Industries incl. shipbuilding, engineering, sugar refining. Pop. (1961) 74,578.

GREENSHANK. Greyish bird (*Tringa nebularia*) of the sandpiper group. The name is derived from its long olive-green legs, which distinguish it from the redshank. It breeds in Scotland and N. Europe.

GREENWICH (grin′ij). Inner bor. of Greater London, England. The Blackwall tunnel connects G. to the N. bank of the Thames.

Charles II built *G. Hospital* to designs by Inigo Jones on the site of an earlier palace, where Henry VIII, Mary, and Elizabeth I were born, and Edward VI died. A hospital for superannuated seamen 1705–1869, it became the Royal Naval College 1873. The *Cutty Sark*, most celebrated of the great tea clippers, is preserved as a museum of sail. The Royal Observatory (founded here in 1675), source of British Standard Time, has been moved to Hurstmonceux (q.v.), but the G. meridian (0°) remains unchanged. Part of the buildings have been taken over by the National Maritime Museum, and named Flamsteed House after the first Astronomer Royal. Pop. (1967) 231,150.

GREENLAND. The men work on their sturdy canoe and a local girl shows off the national costume.
Courtesy of the National Travel Association of Denmark.

GREENWOOD, Arthur (1880–1954). British Labour statesman. He was Min. of Health 1929–31, and while deputy leader of the Labour Party, 1935–9, was an outspoken critic of govt. appeasement policy. During the S.W.W. he was Min. without Portfolio 1940–2, and was chairman of the Labour Party 1952–3.

GREENWOOD, Walter (1903–). British novelist and playwright. B. at Salford, he had repeated experience of unemployment to give authenticity to his novel *Love on the Dole* (1933), later dramatized and filmed.

GREET, Sir Philip Ben (1857–1936). British actor-manager. He was noted for his interpretations of Shakespearian roles, and his 'Players' were a training ground for many British actors, e.g. Harley Granville-Barker (q.v.). He was knighted in 1929.

GREGG, Sir Norman (1892–1966). Australian ophthalmic surgeon. He discovered in 1941 that German measles in a pregnant woman could cause physical defects in her child. Knighted 1953.

GREGORY. Name of 16 popes. **Gregory I** or St. GREGORY THE GREAT (*c.* 540–604), a Roman patrician, was elected pope in 590. He asserted the supremacy of Rome over the other patriarchates of the Church, and within Italy assumed an almost imperial position, making peace and war and negotiating with kings as an equal. In 596 he sent St. Augustine's mission to England. **St. Gregory VII** or HILDEBRAND (*c.* 1023–85) acted as chief minister to several popes before his election in 1073. His claim to a power superior to that of kings, including the right to depose them, and his denial that laymen could make appointments to ecclesiastical offices, involved him in conflicts with many rulers, while his attempts to suppress simony and enforce clerical celibacy raised him enemies within the Church. In 1077 he forced the emperor Henry IV to wait in the snow at Canossa for 4 days, dress·d as a penitent, before receiving pardon. G., driven from Rome, d. in exile. **Gregory XIII** (1502–85), who was elected in 1572, introduced in 1582 the reformed calendar known as the Gregorian.

GREGORY, Isabella Augusta, Lady (1852–1932.)

Irish playwright, *née* Persse, associated with W. B. Yeats in the creation of the Abbey Theatre (1904). B. in Co. Galway, she m. in 1881 Sir William G. She wrote many plays, incl. the comedies *Spreading the News* and *Rising of the Moon*, and the tragic *Gaol Gate* and *Grania*. Her *Journals 1916–30* were pub. 1946.

GREGORY, John (1879–1958). American sculptor. He studied in London, Paris and Rome and his works incl. exterior panels for the Folger Shakespeare Library, Washington.

GREGORY OF TOURS, St. (538–94). French bishop and historian. B. at Clermont-Ferrand, he was elected bishop of Tours in 573. His *History of the Franks* is of historical value.

GRENĀ'DA. One of the Windward Is., an associated state of the U.K. from 1967, producing cocoa and spices. The chief towns are St. George's, the capital, and Gouyave. Area 133 sq. m. Pop. (1963) 91,967.

GRENFELL, Joyce (1910–). British comedienne, *née* Joyce Phipps, she m. Reginald Pascoe G. in 1929. Noted for her use of comic monologue and for her facial expressions, she appeared first in revue and since 1949 in films, incl. the St. Trinians series.

GRENFELL, Julian Henry Francis (1888–1915). British soldier-poet. Eldest son of Lord Desborough, he d. of wounds in the F.W.W., and is remembered for his poem 'Into Battle'.

GRENOBLE (grenōbl'). Capital of Isère dept., on the Isère, 60 m. S.E. of Lyons, S.E. France, with a 11th cent. cathedral and a univ. The chief industry is glovemaking. The Franco-German *Paul Langevin-Max von Laue* (qq.v.) *Institute* (1967) carries out fundamental research into nuclear and solid body physics. Pop. (1968) 161,616.

GRENVILLE, George (1712–70). British Whig statesman. He entered parliament in 1741, and was P.M. and Chancellor of the Exchequer 1763–5. His govt. is notable for the prosecution of Wilkes in 1763, and the Stamp Act of 1765, which precipitated the American War of Independence.

GRENVILLE, Sir Richard (*c.* 1541–91). English naval hero. B. of an old Cornish family, he commanded the fleet sent by his cousin, Sir Walter Raleigh to colonize Virginia in 1585, and organized the defence of W. England in 1586–8. In 1591 he sailed to the Azores as 2nd-in-command to Lord Thomas Howard to intercept a Spanish treasure-fleet. Cut off by the Spaniards from the main force, G. commanded the *Revenge* (500 tons) in a fight against 15 Spanish ships for 15 hours. When most of his crew were dead and he was fatally wounded, he ordered the master-gunner to blow up the ship. The crew surrendered, however, and G. was taken aboard the Spanish flagship, where he d.

GRENVILLE, William Wyndham, baron (1759–1834). British Whig statesman. The son of George Grenville (q.v.), he was raised to the peerage in 1790, and in 1806–7 headed the 'All the Talents' coalition.

GRESHAM, Sir Thomas (*c.* 1519–79). English economist. B. in London, the son of Sir Richard G., Lord Mayor in 1537, he was admitted to the Mercers' Co. in 1543, and in 1566–8 paid for the building of the first Royal Exchange He bequeathed money and his house to found G. College, and his name has been given to *Gresham's Law*, which asserts that bad money tends to drive out good money from circulation.

GRETCHANINOV (grechanēn'of), **Alexander Tikhonovich** (1864–1956). Russian composer of church music and songs, and of the opera *Dobrinia Nikitch* (1903) in which Chaliapin played the leading role.

GRETNA GREEN. Scottish village in Dumfries, just over the border from England, which became famous as a centre for runaway marriages after 1754, when an act of 1753 forbidding clandestine marriages in England became effective. In 1856 a law was passed requiring 3 weeks' previous residence in Scotland, and the wedding traffic almost ceased.

GREUZE (grӧz), **Jean Baptiste** (1725–1805). French

painter. B. at Tournus, he gained sudden success with 'A Father Explaining the Bible to his Children' in the Salon of 1755. Mainly a genre painter, he also produced a number of portraits and his best-known works incl. 'Innocence' and 'The Broken Pitcher'.

GREVILLE, Charles Cavendish Fulke (1794–1865). British diarist. He was Clerk of the Council in Ordinary 1821–59, an office which brought him into close contact with all the noted personalities of the court and of both political parties. This gives the *Greville Memoirs 1817–60* unrivalled interest.

BERYL GREY Superbly elegant in *The Sleeping Beauty*.
Photo: Houston Rogers.

GRÉVY (grehvē'), **François Paul Jules** (1807–91). French statesman. A lawyer, he was Pres. of the republic 1879–87.

GREY, Beryl (1927–). British ballerina. Making her début with the Sadler's Wells Co. in 1941, she was their prima ballerina 1942–57, then danced internationally, becoming artistic director, London Festival Ballet 1968. Tall for a ballet dancer, and with impeccable technique, she excels in dramatic character parts, e.g. the Black Queen in *Checkmate*, Queen Myrtha in *Giselle*, and the dual role in *Swan Lake*.

GREY, Charles, 2nd earl (1764–1845). British Whig statesman. He entered parliament in 1786, and in 1806 became 1st Lord of the Admiralty in the 'All the Talents' ministry, succeeding Fox as For. Sec. soon afterwards. He was P.M. 1830–4, and in 1832 carried the great Reform Bill.

His son **Henry,** 3rd earl G. (1802–94) served under him as Under-Sec. for the Colonies 1830–3, resigning because the Cabinet would not back the immediate emancipation of slaves, was Sec.-at-War 1835–9, and Colonial Sec. 1846–52. He was unique among statesmen of the period in maintaining that the colonies should be governed for their own benefit, not that of the mother country, and in his policy of granting self-govt. wherever possible. Yet he advocated convict transportation, and was in opposition to Gladstone's Home Rule policy.

GREY, Sir George (1812–98). British colonial governor. B. at Lisbon, he became Gov. of S. Australia in 1841, and of New Zealand in 1845. He succeeded in restoring prosperity to both colonies, and won the gratitude of the Maoris by his care for them. Sent to Cape Colony as Governor in 1853, he quelled a Kaffir rising. Returning to New Zealand as Gov. in 1861, he was P.M. there 1877–9.

GREY, Lady Jane (1537–54). Queen of England. B. in Leics, the dau. of Henry G., duke of Suffolk, and a great-grand-dau. of Henry VII, she was m. in 1553 to Lord Guildford Dudley, son of the duke of Northumberland, and shortly after Northumberland persuaded Edward VI to make a will bequeathing the crown to her, setting aside the claims of his sisters Mary and Elizabeth. When Edward d. on July 6 Jane reluctantly accepted the crown and was proclaimed queen 4 days later. Mary, however, received universal support and G. was executed on Tower Green.

GREY, Zane (1875–1939). American author of 'Westerns', e.g. *Riders of the Purple Sage* (1912). B. in Ohio, he was a dentist.

GREYHOUND. Ancient breed of dog, with a long narrow muzzle, slight build, and long legs, renowned for its swiftness. As its sense of smell is defective, it hunts by sight. The English G. has smooth sandy or slate-grey hair, and weighs 50–60 lb. Other varieties incl. the delicate Italian G., Borzoi, and Afghan hound. *See* WHIPPET.

GREYHOUND

GREYHOUND RACING. A sport held on circular enclosed tracks where Gs. pursue a mechanically propelled hare. It attained popularity in England and U.S.A. after the F.W.W.

GREY OF FALLODON, Edward Grey, 1st visct. (1862–1933). British Liberal statesman. For. Sec. in Campbell Bannerman's govt. in 1905, he followed up Lord Lansdowne's entente with France and concluded an entente with Russia in 1907. Despite worsening relations with Germany after Agadir in 1911 he tried to secure a settlement, and in 1914 commented: 'The lamps are going out all over Europe; we shall not see them lit again in our lifetime.' Eye trouble forced his retirement in 1916, when he accepted a peerage.

GRIEG (grēg), **Edvard Hagerup** (1843–1907). Norwegian composer. B. at Bergen, he studied at Leipzig Conservatoire and in Copenhagen, and settled as a teacher and conductor at Christiania in 1867. He won success with his incidental music for *Peer Gynt* (1876). His works, often inspired by the folk tunes of his country, include a piano concerto, the Holberg Suite for strings, songs, etc.

GRIERSON, Sir Herbert (1866–1960). British scholar. Prof. of English at Aberdeen 1894–1915 and Edinburgh 1915–35, he was noted as an expert on the 17th cent. and his edition of Donne (1912) helped to estab. the poet's modern reputation.

GRIERSON, John (1898–1972). Brit. film producer. B. in Perthshire, he was a sociologist who pioneered the documentary film in Britain. Used as a social force, it is 'the creative treatment of actuality'. He directed *Drifters* (1929) and produced (1930–5) *Industrial Britain, Song of Ceylon, Night Mail*, etc. During the S.W.W. he created the National Film Board of Canada.

GRIFFES, Charles Tomlinson (1884–1920). American composer, remembered for his symphonic poem *The Pleasure Dome of Kubla Khan*.

GRIFFIN, Bernard (1899–1956). British cardinal. He first made his mark as an administrator while auxiliary bp. of his native Birmingham (1938–44), then succeeded Hinsley as abp. of Westminster and was created cardinal in 1944. He encouraged Ronald Knox in his biblical translation.

GRIFFITH, Arthur (1872–1922). Irish statesman. B. in Dublin, he joined the Fenians, and in 1899 founded a nationalist paper, *The United Irishman*. He was a leader of Sinn Féin, and was imprisoned several times. Released in July 1921, he headed the delegation which signed the treaty setting up the Irish Free State in Dec. He was elected pres. of the Dail in 1922, but died soon after.

GRIFFITH, David Wark (1875–1948). American film director. Son of a Kentucky colonel, he was an actor then a director, making many hundreds of 'one reelers' (12 min.) 1908–13, in which he introduced the now current techniques of the flash-back, cross-cut, close-up and longshot, completely breaking with theatrical tradition. His masterpiece *Birth of a Nation* (1915) estab. the film as a work of art and entertain-

EDVARD GRIEG
Photo: Elliot & Fry.

ment, and was followed by the mammoth *Intolerance* (1916), and *Broken Blossoms* (1919). In decline, from the advent of 'talkies', he d. in poverty.

GRILLPARZER (gril'pahrtser), **Franz** (1791–1872). Austrian poet and dramatist. B. in Vienna, he followed his sensational tragedy *Die Ahnfrau* (1817) with the classical *Sappho* (1818) and the trilogy *Das goldene Vliess* (1821). His historical tragedies *König Ottokars Glück und Ende* and *Ein treuer Diener seines Herrn* (1826) both involved him with the censor. Two of his greatest dramas followed, *Des Meeres und der Liebe Wellen* (1831), returning to the Hellenic world, and *Der Traum, ein Leben* (1834). The bitter cycle of poems *Tristia ex Ponto* (1835) followed an unhappy love-affair. G. is Austria's finest dramatic poet.

GRIMA'LDI, Joseph (1779–1837). British clown. B. in London, the son of an Italian actor, he appeared on the stage when 2 years old, and since his day the clown has been called 'Joey'. His best part was in *Mother Goose* at Covent Garden in 1806.

GRIMM, Jacob Ludwig Carl (1785–1863) and **Wilhelm Carl** (1786–1859). German philologists and folklorists. Brothers, they collaborated in the world-famous *Fairy Tales*, ed. medieval texts, and collected the historical legends *Deutsche Sagen* (1816–18). Jacob's chief work was his *Deutsche Grammatik* which gave the first historical treatment of the Germanic languages (q.v.).

GRI'MMELSHAUSEN (-howzen), **Hans Jacob Christoffel von** (*c.* 1625–76). German author of the great realistic picaresque novel *Der Abenteuerliche Simplicissimus* (*The Adventurous Simplicissimus*: 1669), whose hero shares his own experiences as a soldier in the Thirty Years War.

GRI'MOND, Joseph (1913–). British Liberal politician. Ed. at Eton and Balliol Coll., Oxford, he was called to the Bar in 1937 and became M.P. for Orkney and Shetland in 1950. Succeeding C. Davies (q.v.) as leader of the party 1956–67, he aimed at making it 'a new Radical Party to take the place of the Socialist Party as an alternative to Conservatism', and in the 1959/64 general elections the no. of Lib. votes increased, falling a little 1966. In 1938 he m. Laura, dau. of Lady Asquith of Yarnbury (q.v.).

GRIMSBY. English port (co. bor.) in Lindsey, Lincs, at the mouth of the Humber, 15 m. S.E. of Hull. It is the most important fishing port in the British Isles, and its fleets sail as far afield as the Arctic Ocean and the Mediterranean. Pop. (1961) 96,665.

GRIQUALAND (grē'kwa-) **EAST** and **WEST.** Two districts of Cape Prov., South Africa. *G. East*, part of the Transkeian Territories (q.v.), lies S. of Natal and Lesotho, and Kokstad is the chief town. *G. West* is to the W. of the Transvaal and Orange Free State, the chief town being Kimberley. Both were named after their Griqua inhabitants, of mixed Hottentot and Dutch descent.

GRIS (grē), **Juan.** Pseudonym of the Spanish-born artist José González (1887–1927), who settled in Paris at 19 and became the exponent of analytical Cubism. His dissertation *Les Possibilités de la Peinture* (1924) was influential.

GRI'SEWOOD, Frederick (1888–). British broadcaster. Attached to the B.B.C. as announcer and commentator 1929–48 – being associated particularly with the 'Scrapbook' series, 'The World Goes By', and 'Our Bill' – he later became a freelance.

GRISI (grē'sē), **Giulia** (1811–69). Italian opera singer. B. in Milan, she gained world-wide recognition as a brilliant soprano, and m. the Italian tenor Mario (q.v.). Her cousin **Carlotta G.** (1819–99) was a celebrated dancer.

GRISONS (grēzoṅ'). Largest of the cantons of Switzerland. There are many tourist resorts, such as Davos, St. Moritz, and villages in the Engadine. The capital is Chur. Area 2,746 sq. m.; pop. (1960) 147,458.

GRIVAS (grē'vahs), **George** (1898–). Greek

underground fighter. B. in Cyprus, he took Greek nationality in 1919, led an underground resistance known as X in Athens during the S.W.W., and in 1954–9 was leader as 'Dighenis' of the Eoka movement in Cyprus, and C.-in-C. Gk. Cypriot Forces, Cyprus, from 1964.

GROCK. Stage-name of the Swiss clown Adrien Wettach (1880–1959). Once tutor to the children of Count Bethlen, later P.M. of Hungary, he was a masterly acrobat, tight-rope-walker and juggler.

GRO'DNO. Industrial and market town in White Russia, cap. of G. region, on the Niemen, 10 m. E. of the Polish frontier. Once part of Lithuania, it was a

GROSBEAK

meeting place of the diet after the union of Poland and Lithuania in 1569. The 1793 partition of Poland gave it to Russia; it was ceded to Poland 1923, ceded back to Russia 1945. Pop. (1967) 90,000.

GROMYKO (grome̅'ko), **Andrei** (1909–   ). Russian diplomat. B. in White Russia and originally an economist, he was ambassador to the U.S. 1943–6 and to the U.K. 1952–3. As U.N. representative 1946–58 he was celebrated for the frequency with which he said 'niet' (he exercised the Soviet veto 26 times), and his appointment as For. Min. in 1957 (after being 1st deputy from 1953) was regarded as a return to Stalinist traditions.

GRO'NINGEN. N.E. prov. of the Netherlands. Parts are below sea-level, and stretches of fen inland have been reclaimed. Natural gas deposits (discovered 1962) are the world's largest outside U.S.A. Area 867 sq. m.; pop. (1966) 508,173. The cap., also G., is a market centre; pop. (1967) 156,208.

GRO'PIUS, Walter Adolf (1883–1969). German-American architect. Founder-director of the *Bauhaus* Weimar (1919–28), he exerted great influence through his concepts of team architecture, and the application of artistic standards to industrial production. Later he left Germany, and 1937–52 was prof. of architecture at Harvard where he designed the Harvard Graduate Center (1949–50). He was founder (1946) of The Architects Collaborative (U.S.).

GROS (grō), **Antoine Jean,** baron (1771–1835). French historical painter. B. in Paris, he is best known for his pictures of scenes in the Napoleonic wars.

GROS'BEAK. Name given to several thick-billed birds. The pine G. (*Pinicola enucleator*), also known as the pinefinch, breeds in Arctic forests; its plumage is similar to the crossbill's. The scarlet G. (*Zamelodia ludoviciana*) is a native of N.E. Europe and N. Asia; it has a rose-red breast and brown wings and tail.

HUGO GROTIUS
By J. Van Mierevelt.

GROSSMITH, George (1847–1912). British actor. From journalism he turned to the stage, and in 1877 began his long association with the Gilbert and Sullivan operas, in which he created a number of parts. He collaborated with his brother **Weedon G.** (1853–1919) in the comic *Diary of a Nobody* (1894). The latter was also an artist, and actor-manager.

GROTE (grōt), **George** (1794–1871). British historian. One of the founders of London univ., he glori-

GROUPER. Hand-feeding ensures fair shares, otherwise this fine specimen might lose his lunch to the dolphins hovering in the background.
Courtesy of Marine Studios, Marineland, Florida.

fied Athenian democracy in his *History of Greece* (1846–56).

GROTEFEND (grōt'efent), **George Frederick** (1775–1853). German scholar. A student of the classical rather than the oriental languages, he nevertheless ingeniously solved the riddle of the cuneiform script as used in ancient Persia: decipherment of Babylonian cuneiform followed on the basis of his work.

GROTIUS (grō'shius), **Hugo** (1583–1645). Dutch jurist and statesman. B. at Delft, he became a lawyer, and later received political preferments. In 1618 he was arrested as a republican and sentenced to imprisonment for life: his wife contrived his escape in 1620, and he settled in France, where he composed the *De Jure Belli et Pacis* (1625), a classic of international law, and 1634–45 was Swedish ambassador in Paris.

GROUND-NUT. Name given to the fruit of a number of plants, but especially to that of the annual *Arachis hypogaea* in the family Leguminosae (which is also known as the pea-nut, earth-nut or monkey-nut), because the pods – borne on stalks after the death of the flower – bury themselves in the earth to ripen. A native of S. America, though now widely grown in all tropical countries, the plant is 1–2 ft. high, and the nuts are a valuable source of vegetable oil. A British govt. scheme for mass cultivation in Tanganyika, 1947–51, resulted in a loss of between £30 million and £40 million.

GROUPER. Name given to a number of species of sea bass (Serranidae) found in warm waters off the Atlantic coast of America. The spotted giant G (*Promicrops itaiara*) is 6–8 ft. long, may weigh over 700 lb., and is sluggish in movement. Formerly primarily game fish, they are now commercially exploited as food.

GROUSE. Game birds of the sub-family Tetraoninae, common in N. America and northern Europe. Among the most familiar are the red G. (*Lagopus scoticus*), a native of Britain; the ptarmigans (q.v.); the ruffed G. (*Bonasia umbellus*), common in N. American woods; and the

RED GROUSE

capercailzie (*Tetrao urogallus*) and the blackcock (*T. tetrix*), both known in Britain. G. are shot over dogs or by driving in Britain 12 Aug.–10 Dec.

GROZNY. Russian industrial town, cap. of Chechen-Ingush A.S.S.R., on the r. Assa, a trib. of the Terek. It is about 90 m. W. of the Caspian Sea, and is the centre of an important petroleum field; pipelines link it to Mahachkala on the Caspian Sea and Tuapse on the Black Sea. Pop. (1967) 331,000.

GRUNDY, Mrs. The personification of British respectability. She is first mentioned in Thomas Martin's play *Speed the Plough* (1798), when though she does not actually appear she is constantly appealed to as one who knows the proprieties.

GRÜNEWALD (grün'evalt). German artist identified in 1938 as Mathis Gothardt Neithardt (*c.* 1460–1528). Little is known of his life, but his work shows extremes of emotion with terrible religious intensity. Last and most important of the Gothic painters in

GRUNEWALD. The 'Mocking of Christ' (1503) in the Alte Pinakothek, Munich, showing the keen sensitivity of the artist.

Germany, he achieved his masterpiece in the expressive Isenheim altar-piece now in the Colmar Museum.

GRUYÈRE (grü-yār'). District in Fribourg canton, Switzerland, famous for its cheese.

GUADALAJARA (gwah'dalakhah'ra). Mexican city, capital of the state of Jalisco; 300 m. W.N.W. of Mexico City. Pop. (1967) 1,183,000.

GUADALCANAL (gwah'-). British protected island, largest in the Solomons, S.W. Pacific. Invaded by the Japanese in Jan. 1942, it was the scene of bitter fighting between them and U.S. forces, which landed in Aug., eventually annihilating the Japanese, Feb. 1943. Area *c.* 2,500 sq. m.; pop. (est.) 15,000.

GUADELOUPE (gwahd-loop'). French West Indian overseas dept. in the Lesser Antilles, consisting of the islands of Guadeloupe proper and Grande-

Terre, separated by the narrow Rivière Salée channel. With 5 other small islands the area is 688 sq. m. The cap. is Basse-Terre, on Guadeloupe proper, and the pop. (1965) 316,000.

GUAM (gwahm). American island in the W. Pacific, the largest of the Mariana group. Agaña is the cap., Piti the port of entry. A naval station and radio centre, G. was ceded to U.S.A. by Spain in 1898, and occupied by Japan 1941–4. Area 206 sq. m.; pop. (1966) 79,000.

GUARDI (gwahr'dē), **Francesco**(1712–93).Italian artist. He was once regarded merely as a follower of Canaletto, but his brilliant evocations of his native Venice, using an almost impressionist technique, are now highly valued.

GUARESCHI (gwahres' ki), **Giovanni** (1909–68). Italian author. B. at Parma, he studied law, but after the S.W.W. became editor of the magazine *Candido*. In this his short stories of the friendly feud between

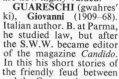

GIOVANNI
GUARESCHI

parish priest Don Camillo and the Communist mayor, originally written in haste as space-fillers, first appeared. Collected vols. incl. *The Little World of Don Camillo* (1951).

GUARNIERI (gwahrnyā're). Celebrated family of violin-makers at Cremona, of whom Giuseppe Antonio G. (1687–1745) produced the finest models.

GUATEMALA (gwahtāmah'la). A republic of Central America, adjoining Mexico, British Honduras, Honduras, and Salvador. It is divided into the great plain of Petén to the N., the Pacific and Caribbean lowlands, and the central region of volcanic mountains and high valleys. Coffee, cotton, bananas, and sugar are the chief products. Of the pop. (est. at 4,575,000 in 1966) over half are pure Indians, the rest, mixed Indian and Spanish (*ladinos*), providing the ruling classes. The cap. and commercial centre is G. city (pop. 580,000), which is 4,880 ft. above sea-level in a wide plateau traversed by the Rio de las Vacas.

The republic was founded in 1839, and its boundaries were not settled until 1936. Vague claims are maintained over British Honduras. Under the constitution of 1965, govt. is by a pres. (elected for 4 yrs.) council of state with the vice-pres. as chairman, and a congress. Voting is compulsory for all literate men

GUATEMALA. The villagers of San Antonio Palopo, 70 m. from Guatemala City, fill their water jars beside beautiful volcano-ringed Lake Atitlan.   *Pan American Photograph.*

and women over 18; optional for the illiterate (more than 70 per cent). There is extreme political instability, and from 1960 right and left-wing guerrillas were in competition. Political assassination, e.g. the U.S. ambassador 1968, is commonplace.

GUAYAQUIL. The Malecón 'Simón Bolívar', a broad boulevard extending along the Guayas River.
Courtesy of the Ecuador Govt.

GUAYAQUIL (gwī-ahkē′). City and chief port of Ecuador nr. the mouth of the Guayas. Pop. (1966) 680,000.

GUBEN (gōō′ben). Town in Polish-administered Germany, 28 m. S. of Frankfurt-an-der-Oder. Pop. (est.) 45,000.

GUDGEON (guj′en). Freshwater cyprinid fish (*Gobio gobio*) found in Europe and N. Asia on the gravel bottoms of streams. Olive-brown, spotted with black and attaining *c*. 8 in., it has a distinctive barbel at each side of the mouth.

GUELDER ROSE or **Gelder Rose.** Flowering shrub (*Viburnum opulus*) of the Caprifoliaceae (honeysuckle) family. The wild variety bears its flowers in a head, followed by a cluster of blackish-red berries. The flowers of the garden shrub are enlarged and grouped into a heavy globular head.

GUELDERS. *See* GELDERLAND.

GUELPH (gwelf). River port of Ontario, Canada, 43 m. W.S.W. of Toronto. It is an agricultural centre, exporting fruit, grain, and livestock, with textile, furniture, soap, etc., factories. Pop. (1966) 51,377.

GUELPHS AND GHIBELLINES (gib-). Names of rival parties, originally in 12th cent. Germany, and later in medieval Italy. They were the partisans of the rival German houses of Welf, dukes of Bavaria and later of Saxony, and of the lords of Hohenstaufen and Waiblingen, who struggled for the imperial crown after the death of Henry VI in 1197, until the Hohenstaufen died out in 1268. In Italy, the papalists were known as Guelphs and the imperialists as Ghibellines.

GUERNICA (gernē′ka). Spanish town, in Biscay prov. Under its famous oak the Castilian kings formerly swore to respect the rights of the Basques. G. was destroyed in 1937 by German bombers fighting for Franco, an event which inspired a famous painting by Picasso. Rebuilding was completed in 1946. Pop. (1965) 7,000.

GUERNSEY (gern′zi). One of the Channel Islands, second in area to Jersey. The island specializes in the cultivation of grapes and tomatoes under glass, and also produces flowers and vegetables, as well as its own breed of cattle. G., which has belonged to the English Crown since 1066, was occupied by German forces 1940-5. Pop. (1961) 45,028; area 25 sq. m. St. Peter Port is the cap. and chief harbour: there is an airport at La Villiaze.

GUEVARA (gevah′rah), **Ernesto 'Che'** (1928–67). Argentine revolutionary. B. in the Argentine, he was trained as a doctor, but in 1953 left the country because of his opposition to Peron. In effecting the Cuban revolution of 1959, he was second only to Castro and his brother, but in 1965 moved on to fight against white mercenaries in the Congo, and then to Bolivia, where he was killed in an unsuccessful attempt to lead a peasant rising. His revolutionary technique using minimum resources has been influential, but his orthodox Marxism has been obscured by romanticising disciples.

GUIANA (gē-ah′nah). *See* FRENCH G., GUYANA, *and* SURINAM.

GUIDO. *See* RENI.

GUIENNE (gē-en′). Old prov. of S.W. France that formed with Gascony the duchy of Aquitaine. Its cap. was Bordeaux. It became English in 1154 and passed to France in 1451.

GUILDFORD (gil′ford). Historic co. town (bor.) of Surrey, England, on the river Wey, where it cuts through the N. Downs, to the E. of the Hog's Back, 29 m. S.W. of London. It has 16th and 17th cent. buildings, and ruins of a Norman castle. The cathedral, started in 1936, was consecrated in 1961: grouped below are the buildings of the Univ. of Surrey (1966), specializing in technology. Yvonne Arnaud (1895–1958), the sophisticated comedy actress, was b. in G. and a theatre (1964) is named after her. There is a cattle market and industries include flour-milling. Pop. (1961) 53,977.

GUILDS, or **Gilds.** Medieval associations, particularly of craftsmen or merchants, formed for mutual aid and protection and the pursuit of a common purpose, religious or economic. Gs. fulfilling charitable or religious functions, such as the maintenance of schools, roads, or bridges, the assistance of members in misfortune, or the provision of masses for the souls of dead members, flourished in England from the 9th cent. down to 1547, when they were suppressed.

The earliest form of economic G., the *G. Merchant*, arose in the 11th–12th cents.; this was an organization of the traders of a town, who had been granted by charter a practical monopoly of its trade. As the merchants often strove to exclude craftsmen from the G., and to monopolize control of local government, the *Craft Gs.* came into existence in the 12th–13th cents. These, which included journeymen and apprentices as well as employers, regulated prices, wages, working conditions and apprenticeship, prevented unfair practices, and maintained high standards of craftsmanship; they also fulfilled many social, religious and charitable functions. By the 14th cent. they had taken control of local government, ousting the G. Merchant.

After the 16th cent. the position of the Gs. was undermined by the growth of the domestic system, which removed industry into the country. where G. regulations had no force, and of the factory system.

GUILLEMOT (gil′emot). Diving sea-fowl of the auk family, which breeds in large numbers on the rocky N. Atlantic coasts. The common G. (*Uria aalge*) has a sharp bill and short tail, and sooty-brown and white plumage. Gs. build no nest, but lay one large, almost conical, egg on the rock.

GUILLEN (gēyen′), **Jorge** (1893–). Spanish poet, who has lived in the U.S.A. since 1938 as a teacher of Spanish. His single vol. of verse was *Cántico* (1928) progressively enlarged to 1950.

GUILLOTINE (gilotēn′). A beheading instrument, introduced in France during the Revolution, and named after Joseph Ignace Guillotin (1738–1814), a physician, who in 1789 advocated the adoption of such a machine; it was first used 25 April 1792. It consists of an oblique-edged knife which falls between two grooved posts on to the victim's neck. It is still used in France and other countries.

GUINEA (gin'i). English gold coin, not minted since 1817, when it was superseded by the gold sovereign. The term continued in use – signifying 21s (£1.05) – for professional fees and for limited commercial purposes.

GUINEA. Rep. of W. Africa. Formerly a French colony, it left the French Community after a referendum in 1958, but the official language is still French and there is co-operation in other fields. There is a pres. (Sékou Touré 1961, re-elected 1968), and a single-party Nat. Assembly. In 1966 the deposed pres. Nkrumah of Ghana was declared joint head of state.

The chief products incl. rice, palm kernels, coffee and pineapples; and the chief minerals are bauxite, iron ore, and diamonds. The cap. is Conakry. Area 95,000 sq. m.; pop. (1965) 3,500,000.

GUINEA, Equatorial. The 2 overseas provs. of Spanish Guinea achieved independence in 1968 as Equatorial Guinea, which comprises the mainland terr. of Rio Muni (area 10,040 sq. m.; pop. 183,000, chief town Bata) and the is. of Fernando Po (area 779 sq. m.; pop. 61,000) together with the 4 smaller is. of Annabon, Corisco, Elobey Grande and Elobey Chico. The port and cap. is Santa Isabel on Fernando Po. Products are cocoa, coffee, bananas and high-grade timber. Under the constitution of 1968 E.G. is a unitary state. Total area 10,852 sq. m.; pop. (1968) 245,000.

GUINEA COAST. Geographical name for the coast of W. Africa from Gambia to Cape Lopez.

GUINEA-FOWL Gallinaceous bird (*Numida*), of the family Phasianidae. The plumage is slate-grey with white spots, and the head is crowned with a bony crest or tuft of feathers. The commonest variety is the African *N. meleagris*, introduced to poultry farms.

GUINEA PIG. Small vegetarian rodent in the family Caviidae. The domestic species is probably derived from the Peruvian cavy (*Cavia cutleri*), and may be black, white, or brown. They breed readily and are extensively used in laboratory experiments.

GUINNESS (gin'es), **Sir Alec** (1914–). British actor. A Londoner, he joined the Old Vic in 1936, played Hamlet in modern dress in 1938 and gave another unorthodox portrayal in 1951. He is celebrated for the humorous versatility of his characterizations, e.g. *Kind Hearts and Coronets* (a film in which he played a number of related characters); and his subtlety, as in the film *The Bridge on the River Kwai* (1957), and his interpretation on stage of Lawrence of Arabia in *Ross* (1960). He was knighted in 1959.

GUISE (gü-ēz'). French noble family, prominent in the period of religious wars in the 16th cent. **Francis** (1519–63), the second duke, commanded against the Huguenots, and was assassinated by a anatic. His son, **Henry** (1550–88), 3rd duke, was largely responsible for the massacre of St. Bartholomew. He, too, was assassinated.

GUITAR (gitahr'). A musical instrument, resembling the violin in appearance, but the playing is effected by plucking the six strings. Of great antiquity, it is traditionally the instrument of Italy and Spain, but since the S.W.W. has been revived as a concert instrument, e.g. by the British guitarist Julian Bream, who has done so much to encourage contemporary compositions for it. The comparative ease with which it can be used to provide a strumming accompaniment has also led in the 1960s to its great vogue with 'pop' groups who use 'electric' Gs. to obtain a harsh, amplified sound.

GUIZOT (gēzō'), **François Pierre Guillaume** (1787–1874). French statesman and historian. B. at Nîmes, he was a Protestant, and 1812–30 was prof. of modern history at the Sorbonne. He wrote on the history of civilization, and became P.M. in 1847. His resistance to all reforms led up to the Revolution of 1848.

GUJARAT (goojraht'). State of the rep. of India, formed in 1960 on a linguistic basis (the majority of the inhabitants speaking Gujarati) from the northern part of former Bombay state. It covers the Kathiawar peninsula, Kutch, Baroda, Surat, and neighbouring territory. The cap. is Ahmedabad, to be replaced by Gandhinagar, 13 m. to the N. Area 72,154 sq. m.; pop. (1961) 20,633,350.

GUJRANWA'LA. City of W. Pakistan, 40 m. N. of Lahore. Industries incl. textiles, metallurgy, brassware, etc. Pop. (1961) 196,154.

GULF STREAM. The most pronounced element in the circulation of the upper waters of the North Atlantic, and the most widely known of the permanent ocean currents. The name is often applied to the whole of the surface-current which issues from the Gulf of Mexico through the Strait of Florida, flows northwards off the E. coast of the U.S.A., and crosses the Atlantic in several branches, one of which skirts the British Isles to enter Norwegian waters and so on to the Arctic Ocean, but should properly be restricted to that part of the current between Cape Hatteras, U.S.A., and the Grand Banks of Newfoundland. The average width of the stream is about 130 miles, and the annual mean temperature of the surface-water in its central part is about 78° F. The continuation of the G.S. in the G.S. Drift is a prime cause of the mild winter climate of N.W. Europe.

GULL. Seabird of the Laridae family. A typical G. of the genus *Larus* is the black-headed G. (*L. ridibundus*), common in Britain, which is grey and white with (in summer) dark brown head and red beak; it breeds in large colonies on marshland, making a nest of dead rushes, averaging 3 eggs. Allied are the larger laughing G. of America, and the great black-headed G. (*L. ichthyaëtus*) of Asia. Other notable Gs. are the herring G. (*L. argentatus*), often known in the U.S. as the harbour G., which has white and pearl-grey adult plumage and yellow beak; and the oceanic great black-backed G. (*L. marinus*), found in the Atlantic and upwards of 2½ ft. long.

GUMS. The soft tissues surrounding the bases of the teeth. They are liable to inflammation due to prolonged use of medicines containing mercury, bismuth, etc., or to infection by microbes from food deposits and tartar, or by Vincent's angina. Pyorrhoea is a general infection of the margins extending down the walls of the teeth. Gumboil is a local infection of one gum.

GUMS. Complex hydrocarbons formed by many plants and trees, particularly by those from dry regions. Tasteless odourless substances, insoluble in alcohol and ether but generally soluble in water, Gs. are used for adhesives, sizing fabrics, in confectionery, medicine and calico printing.

There are 5 main groups: (1) plant and tree exudates such as acacia (G. arabic, one of the most common), ghatti (British Indian G.), tragacanth (Bassorin); (2) marine plant extracts such as agar-agar, Irish moss, algin; (3) seed extracts such as guar, locust kernel, locust bean, quince seed; (4) fruit and vegetable extracts such as the pectins and (5) processed gums such as dextrins and cellulose ethers.

GUN. See ARTILLERY, SMALL ARMS PISTOL, MACHINE G.

GUNMETAL. An alloy of copper and tin, usually in the proportions of about 90 and 10 per cent respectively, with small quantities of zinc or lead. A tough metal, it is used in castings, etc.

GUNN, Sir James (1893–1964). British artist. A skilled interpreter of likenesses, he produced many royal portraits (*see* illus. pp. 124, 333, 468). He was knighted in 1963.

GUNPOWDER. Oldest known explosive, a mixture of sulphur, saltpetre, and charcoal. Though no longer used as a propellant, it is in wide use for blasting and fireworks.

GUNPOWDER PLOT. The Catholic conspiracy to blow up James I and his parliament on 5 November 1605. It was discovered through an anonymous letter sent to Lord Monteagle, and Guy Fawkes was found in the cellar beneath the House, ready to fire a store of combustibles. Several of the conspirators were slain, and Guy Fawkes and 7 others were executed. The searching of the vaults of parliament before the opening of each new session, however, was not instituted until the 'Popish Plot' of 1678.

GU'NTHER, John (1901–70). American journalist. Overseas correspondent for leading journals, covering events such as the London Blitz, he became famous for his vols. of reportage, e.g. *Inside Europe* (1936).

GUREV (gōō'yef). Port in Kazakh S.S.R., cap. of G. region, on the Ural r. near its mouth on the Caspian Sea. Founded in 1640, it has become an important petroleum-refining centre linked by pipeline with oil-fields to the E.N.E. on the Emba r. and with Orsk. Fishing and fish-curing are other industries. Pop. (est.) 70,000.

GURKHAS (goor'kahz). The ruling Hindu caste in Nepal. In the military sense soldiers recruited since 1815 from Nepal for service in British India and also overseas (e.g. in France in the F.W.W.) and officered only by British or Nepalese. After Indian independence in 1947 a depot was still maintained in Nepal for recruiting to the *Brigade of G.* in the British Army. Their bravery is legendary.

GURNARD. Genus of coastal fish (*Trigla*) in the family Triglidae, which creep along the sea bottom by means of 3 finger-like appendages detached from the pectoral fins. They are both tropic and temperate zone fish, half a dozen species being found in British waters, where they are trawled for food.

GUSTAVUS V (1858–1950). King of Sweden. Son of Oscar II, he m. Princess Victoria (1862–1930), dau. of the Grand Duke of Baden, in 1881, thus uniting the reigning Bernadotte dynasty with the former royal house of Vasa. He succeeded his father in 1907, and thus had one of the longest reigns in modern history. His son **Gustavus VI** (1882–) is an eminent archaeologist and expert on Chinese art. His first wife was Princess Margaret of Connaught (1882–1920), and in 1923 he m. Lady Louise Mountbatten (1889–1965), sister of Earl Mountbatten of Burma. His heir is his grandson, Crown Prince Carl Gustaf (1946–).

GUSTAVUS ADOLPHUS (1594–1632). King of Sweden. Son of Charles IX, whom he succeeded in 1611, he waged successful wars with Denmark, Russia, and Poland, and in the Thirty Years War became a champion of the Protestant cause. Landing in Germany in 1630, he defeated Wallenstein at Lützen on 6 Nov. 1632. but was killed in the battle. He was known as the 'Lion of the North'.

GUSTAVUS VASA (1496–1560). Son of a nobleman, he led the Swedish movement of independence against the Danes, and in 1523 was elected king of Sweden. Under him Lutheranism was established as the State religion.

GUTENBERG (goot'en-), **Johann** (*c.* 1400–68). German printer, considered the inventor of printing from metal movable types. B. at Mainz, he lived at Strasbourg, and about 1448 was in Mainz where, with Johann Fust as a partner, he carried on a printing business The partnership was dissolved through monetary difficulties, but G. set up another printing press. He is believed to have printed the Mazarin and the Bamberg Bibles. *See* COSTER, LAURENS JANSZOON.

GUTHRIE, Sir Tyrone (1900–71). British man-of-the theatre. Administrator of the Old Vic and Sadler's Wells 1939–45, he was associated with the founding of the Shakespeare Festival at Stratford, Ontario, in 1953, and noted for such experiments as *Hamlet* in modern dress in 1936.

GUTTA-PERCHA. The coagulated juice of various tropical trees belonging to the Sapotaceae family. G.P. is similar to rubber, but is thermoplastic and when stretched will not spring back to its original shape. Its chief use is in insulating cables.

GUY, Thomas (1644–1724). British philanthropist. Son of a lighterman, he began business in 1668 as a bookseller in the City, dealing mostly in Bibles which he imported from Holland. He built and endowed G.'s Hospital, London, from his profits.

GUYANA (gē-ah'nah). Country of S. America between Surinam and Venezuela, formerly known as Brit. Guiana. Most of the crops (sugar, rice, coconuts, coffee and fruits) are grown in the low coastal region; gold, diamonds, and bauxite are worked in an intermediate area; and the hinterland is mountain and savannah. The chief rivers—Demerara, Essequibo, and Berbice—give their names to the 3 counties into which G. is divided; chief towns are Georgetown, the cap., New Amsterdam, Springlands, and Bartica. First settled about 1620 by the Dutch West Indian Co., G. was captured by the British 1796 (formally ceded 1814), attained independence as Guyana 1966, and in 1970 was proclaimed a 'co-operative republic' within the Commonwealth. Area *c.* 83,000 sq. m.; pop. (est. 1966) 674,680: 50% are East Indians brought in to run the sugar estates after abolition of slavery; some 30% Negroes concentrated in the towns; 5% Amerindians of the interior: and the rest Portuguese and of mixed blood. There is a unicameral Nat. Assembly, elected by proportional representation. Party divisions tend to be racial: the predominantly Negro *People's Nat, Congress* led by Forbes Burnham (P.M. from 1966; re-elected 1968) and Indian *People's Progressive Party* (*see* JAGAN, CHEDDI).

GUYS (gēs), **Constantin** (1805–92). French artist. He was with Byron at Missolonghi and during the Crimean War sent sketches to the *Illustrated London News*. His delicately realistic drawings of Parisian life, ranging from high society to the street corner, were not fully appreciated until the mid-20th cent.

GWALIOR (gwah'lior). Indian city in Madhya Pradesh, 215 m. N. by E. of Bhopal. It contains Jain and Hindu monuments and was formerly in the princely state of G. Pop. (1961) 300,513.

GWYN, Nell (Eleanor) (1651–87). English actress. As a girl she was an orange-seller at Drury Lane Theatre, but became an actress in 1665. Her dramatic gifts tended to low comedy, and Dryden was particularly appreciative of her talent, and wrote her suitable parts. She became the mistress of Charles II in 1669, and had 2 sons by him, the elder of whom was created duke of St. Albans in 1684. The relationship continued until Charles's death, and almost his last wish, made to the duke of York, was 'Let not poor Nellie starve'. She outlived Charles by 2 years only, and was buried at St. Martin-in-the-Fields, London. She was largely instrumental in the establishment of the Royal Hospital for old soldiers at Chelsea.

GYMNASTICS. Performance of physical exercises to promote health, so named from Gk. *gymnos*, 'naked', all ancient Greek athletics having been performed stripped and the *gymnasia* being schools for training competitors for public games. In the 19th cent. the cult was first revived since ancient times in Germany as an aid to military strength, and was also taken up by educationists incl. Froebel and Pestalozzi, becoming a recognized part of the school curriculum in the present century. International competition is governed by the rules of the *Fédération Internationale de Gymnastique* (1923) which organizes the Olympic G.

section and world championships every 4 yrs, 2 yrs after the Olympics. *See* PHYSIOTHERAPY.

GYMNOSPERMS. Plants whose seeds are not borne within a fruit. They form one of the major divisions of the flowering plants, the other being the Angiosperms, in which the ovules are enclosed in an ovary which ripens to form the fruit. Pollen is carried directly on to the gymnospermous ovule on the scale of the cone; after pollination the cone scales close until the seed is ripe. There are 3 orders: Coniferales (the pines), Cycadales, and Gnetales.

GYÖRGY (jör′j), **Paul** (1893–   ). American doctor. B. in Hungary, he was director of pediatrics at Philadelphia Genera Hospital 1957–63 and was discoverer and co-discoverer of Riboflavin, Pyridoxine and Vitamin H (Biotin).

GYPSIES. A wandering folk, scattered over most parts of the world, whose name is a corruption of 'Egyptian'. The name they apply to themselves is Rom, which may be derived from Romanoi, the name assumed by the inhabitants of the Byzantine Empire in which the Gs. are believed to have originated. In the 14th cent. they crossed the Bosphorus into Europe and settled in the Balkan peninsula. During the next cent. they spread over Germany, Italy, and France, and they arrived in England about 1500. A long period of persecution followed, including accusations of cannibalism and child-stealing, and they are still suspected of petty thefts in country districts. Their customs and faiths are a medley of beliefs and superstitions gathered from different countries. Gs. are small, dark, and are associated with many crafts; often they are hawkers of their own wares. G. women are renowned for fortune-telling. They live nomadically, nurture an inherent gift of music, and favour gay attire.

The G. language, known as Romany, has relations with the Indo-Aryan group, and some of its words correspond with words in Hindustani. All the countries through which the Gs. have passed have added to their word-stock, Greek and Slavonic being the chief.

GYPSUM (jip′sum). Mineral of common occurrence, composed of hydrated calcium sulphate, $CaSO_4.2H_2O$. It has a number of commercial uses. A fine-grained G., called alabaster, is used for ornamental work, and burnt G. is known as plaster of Paris, since it was obtained for a long time from the G. quarries of the Montmartre district.

GYROSCOPE (jīr′o-). In its simplest form, a

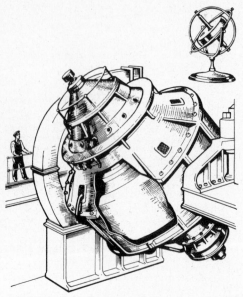

GYROSCOPE. The familiar model (top), and a huge gyroscopic ship's stabilizer.

mechanical instrument consisting of a heavy wheel mounted on an axis which is fixed in a ring, which ring in turn is capable of rotation about another axis, fixed in another ring capable of rotation about a third axis. The whole is arranged so that the 3 axes of rotation in any position pass through the wheel's centre of gravity. The wheel is thus capable of rotation about 3 mutually perpendicular axes, and its axis may take up any direction. The G. is used as a stabilizing device. If the axis of the spinning wheel is displaced a restoring movement is developed which returns it to its initial direction. Important practical applications of the G. are seen in the gyro-compass, the gyropilot for automatic steering, gyro-directed torpedoes.

GYULA FEHÉRVÁR. Magyar name of ALBA IULIA.

H Eighth letter of the Roman alphabet, representing an aspirate in all modern alphabets derived from the Latin except in those languages, especially the Romance languages, where the aspirate is lost. The 'dropping of initial h', often regarded as a corruption in modern dialects, is a phenomenon traceable at least as far back as Tudor times.

HAAKON (haw′kon) **VII** (1872–1957). King of Norway. B. Prince Charles, the 2nd son of Frederick VIII of Denmark, he m. in 1896 Princess Maud (1869–1938), youngest dau. of Edward VII of the U.K. He was elected king of Norway in 1905 on the separation of that country from Sweden, and at his coronation in 1906 he took the name of H. When the Germans invaded Norway in 1940 he refused to surrender; and, when armed resistance in Norway was no longer possible, carried on the struggle from Britain until his triumphant return in 1945.

HAARLEM (hahr′lem). Town in the Netherlands, in N. Holland prov., 12 m. W. of Amsterdam, with which it is connected by canal and railway. At Velsen to the N. a 2 m. road-rail tunnel runs under the North Sea Canal and is an important link between N. and S. Holland. H., a famous centre for bulbs, has also textile factories and printing works. The Frans Hals Museum is at H. Pop. (1967) 172,268.

HABEAS CORPUS (hā′bēas kŏr′pus) (Lat. 'have the body'). In England a writ directed to a person who has custody of a prisoner, ordering him to produce the prisoner before the court issuing the writ, and to explain why the prisoner is detained in custody. H.C. may be claimed by any prisoner except those charged with treason or felony, to whom certain reservations apply. The H.C. Act of 1679, mainly due to Lord Shaftesbury, clarified and helped to enforce traditional rights with regard to detention by public authorities, and the Act of 1816 dealt with the detention by private authorities. The H.C. Act of 1679 is valid in Wales and the Channel Is., and that of 1816 also in the I. of Man; the main principles of H.C. were adopted in the U.S.; and there are equivalents in Ireland, and in the Scottish Wrongous Imprisonment Act, 1701. A writ of H.C. cannot, since 1862, run from England to any English colony or dominion which has its own courts with authority to grant H.C. In a national emergency the H.C. Act can be suspended.

HABER (hah'ber), **Fritz** (1868–1934). German chemist. He was known for his work on gases, the preparation of synthetic ammonia, nitro-benzene, etc., and in the F.W.W. he devised gas masks.

HABSBURG or **Hapsburg.** European royal family, to which the former imperial house of Austria-Hungary belongs. The name comes from the family castle in Switzerland. The Hs. held the title of Holy Roman Emperor 1273–91, 1298–1308, 1438–1740, and 1745–1806. They ruled Austria from 1278, and in 1806 adopted the title of emperor of Austria, which they held until 1918. The archduke Otto, son of the last emperor, Charles, is the present H. pretender.

HACHETTE (ahshet'), **Louis Christophe François** (1800–64). French publisher and bookseller, who founded in Paris in 1826 the business known by his name. The London branch dates from 1859.

HACKNEY. Inner bor. of Greater London. In the E. lie the H. marshes bordering the river Lea, and to the W. are H. downs. Pop. (1967) 249,140.

HADDINGTON. County town of E. Lothian, Scotland, on the Tyne, 10 m. W.S.W. of Dunbar, birthplace of John Knox. It is an agricultural centre. Pop. (1961) 5,506.

HADDINGTONSHIRE. Name until 1921 of EAST LOTHIAN.

HADDOCK. Important food fish (*Gadus aeglefinus*), one of the Gadidae family of marine carnivorous fish, found off the N. Atlantic coasts. H. may be eaten fresh, but split and smoked H., especially from Finnan, near Aberdeen, is a delicacy.

HĀ′DĒS. In Greek mythology the underworld where the spirits of the departed went after death, usually depicted as a cavern or pit underneath the earth. It was presided over by Pluto, and its entrance was guarded by the three-headed dog Cerberus.

HADHRAMAUT (hahdrahmawt'). District in S. Arabia, forming part of the Protectorate of South Arabia, and ruled by Arab leaders maintaining protective treaty relations with Britain. Parts of the interior are still relatively unknown except to Arab traders; British explorers who have penetrated it incl. H. St. John Philby, Bertram Thomas and Freya Stark.

HĀ′DRIAN (A.D. 76–138). Roman emperor. B. in Spain, he was adopted by his kinsman, the emperor Trajan, whom he succeeded in 117. He abandoned Trajan's conquests in Mesopotamia, and adopted a defensive policy which included the building of H.'s Wall in Britain.

HADRIAN'S WALL. Roman fortification built in A.D. 122–6 to mark the northern boundary of Britain, and abandoned *c.* 383. The wall, of which major sections still exist, was formerly thought to be only

HADRIAN. Bronze recovered from the Thames at London, now in the British Museum.

HADRIAN'S WALL. Striding across the Northumbrian hills, the wall was built as a defensive measure against the warlike tribes to the north. This recently uncovered section, in the wall-mile 45–46, at Haltwhistle, is one of the most impressive and best preserved. *Photo: Crown Copyright.*

73½ m. long, running from Wallsend on the Tyne to Bowness on the Solway, but excavations 1954–62 confirmed that it extended another 40 m. to Maryport and possibly farther south.

HAECKEL (ha'kel), **Ernst Heinrich** (1834–1919). German scientist and philosopher. B. at Potsdam, he became in 1865 prof. of zoology at Jena, and for more than 50 years laboured to propagate his recapitulation theory of evolution.

HAEMATITE or **HEMATITE** (hem'atīt). Ferric oxide, Fe_2O_3, a valuable iron ore, containing 70 per cent of iron and a low proportion of phosphorus.

HAEMOGLOBIN (hēmoglō'bin). The colouring matter of the red blood cells, which makes the blood red. As it carries oxygen to all the cells of the body, it is necessary to life.

HAEMOPHILIA (hēmofil'ia). A tendency to uncontrollable bleeding through deficiency in the blood of the normal clotting substances. It is hereditary, occurs only in males, and is transmitted through the mother. In 1957 the Lister Inst. for Preventive Medicine developed an effective antidote – an injectable solution containing 10 times the anti-haemophilic factor of healthy blood.

HAEMORRHAGE (hem'orij). Loss of blood from the circulation. It is 'manifest' when the blood can be seen, as when it flows from a wound, the female genital tract, or piles, or is vomited, spat out or passed in the urine. Haemorrhage is 'occult' when the blood is lost internally, as from an ulcer or cancer of the stomach or an internal injury. The condition produced by severe haemorrhage is shock, by slow haemorrhage anaemia. The chief remedies are blood transfusion and the administration of iron.

HAEMORRHOIDS (hem'oroids). See PILES.

HAFFKINE (-kīn), **Waldemar Mordecai Wolff** (1860–1930). Russian bacteriologist. B. in Odessa, he assisted Pasteur in Paris 1889–93, and was director of the British govt. laboratory in Bombay 1893–1915, where he produced a vaccine (1893) offering temporary immunity against cholera.

HAFI′Z (*c.* 1300–88). Persian poet. B. in Shiraz, he became prof. in a Dervish college there. His fame rests on his *Diwan*, a collection of short odes, some extolling the pleasures of life, others satirizing his fellow Dervishes.

HAFNIUM. Metallic element; symbol Hf, atomic number 72, atomic weight 178·6. It was discovered by the Danish chemists D. Coster and G. von Hevesy. It occurs in zircon, and its properties and compounds resemble closely those of zirconium. It is highly absorbent of neutrons, and could be used, if available, for control rods in nuclear reactors.

HAGANA'H (Heb. 'defence'). Zionist military organization in Palestine. It originated under Turkish rule as a force of armed watchmen protecting Jewish settlements. The British authorities tolerated its existence, and many of its members served in the British forces during the S.W.W. In 1945–7 it condemned the terrorist activities of Irgun Zvai Leumi and the 'Stern Gang', and confined its opposition to the British authorities to passive resistance. It formed the basis of the army of the Rep. of Israel.

HAGEN (hah'gen). Industrial centre of the Ruhr, W. Germany, with iron and steel works, textile mills, etc. Pop. (1966) 202,083.

HAGENBECK (hah'gen-), Carl (1844–1913). German zoo proprietor. He enlarged the collection of animals he inherited from his father and founded in 1907 H.'s Zoo, nr. his native Hamburg. He was a pioneer in the display of animals in comparative freedom, against a natural setting.

HAG-FISH (*Myxine glutinosa*). One of the Cyclostomata, found in temperate seas and common off the E. coast of Scotland. It is eel-shaped and has toothed jaws, and bores into the body of a fish on which it feeds.

HAGGADAH (hagah'da). The part of the Talmudic literature not given to religious law (the *Halacha*), but devoted to stories of heroes, folklore, etc.

HAGGAI (hag'i). Minor O.T. prophet (520 B.C.) devoted to promoting the rebuilding of the Temple.

HA'GGARD, Sir Henry Rider (1856–1925). British novelist. B. in Norfolk, he held colonial service posts in Natal and the Transvaal 1875–9, then returned to England to read for the Bar. He turned his S. African experience to good use in his romantic adventure tales *King Solomon's Mines* (1885), *She* (1887) and many others; he also wrote on agricultural questions.

HAGGIS. Popular Scottish dish, of ancient origin, consisting of a sheep's or calf's heart, liver, and lungs, etc., minced up with onion, oatmeal, suet, spice, pepper and salt, and boiled in the animal's stomach.

HAGUE, La. Cape at the N.W. of Manche dept., France.

HAGUE (hāg), **The.** Seat of Govt. of the Netherlands, and cap. of S. Holland prov.; situated 2½ m.

THE HAGUE. Once surrounded by a moat and access still gained through medieval gateways, the government buildings of the Binnenhof (or 'inner court') are the heart of The Hague. Glimpsed to the right is the Ridderzaal (Knight's Hall) built in 1252 and scene of the opening of Parliament. Here the states of the Netherlands abjured their allegiance to Philip II of Spain.

from the North Sea, and linked by canal and railway with Rotterdam and Amsterdam. The H. is reputed to be the richest of Dutch cities, and has many fine buildings. The H. is the seat of the U.N. International Court of Justice. Pop. (1968) 576,200.

HAGUE CONFERENCES. Two international conferences held at The Hague in 1899 and 1907 to discuss means for the prevention of war or the mitigation of its horrors. The first resulted in the setting up of The Hague Tribunal for the settlement by arbitration of international disputes; this body was absorbed, 1946, by the International Court of Justice set up by the United Nations.

HAHN, Kurt (1886–). German educationist. Founder and headmaster (1920–33) of Salem School in Germany, after his expulsion from Germany by Hitler he founded Gordonstoun (q.v.) and was headmaster 1934–53. He returned to Salem 1953, and was co-founder of the Atlantic College project (q.v.) in 1960. He is also assoc. with the Outward Bound schools, whose mountain rescue teams, etc., incorporate his educational theories on training.

HAHN, Otto (1879–1968). W. German physical chemist. B. at Frankfurt-am-Main, he worked with Rutherford and Ramsay, becoming director of the Kaiser-Wilhelm Inst. for Chemistry in 1928. With Strassmann (1938) he discovered nuclear fission of uranium when bombarded with neutrons, which led to the A-bomb, first used in 1945, when he received the Nobel prize for chemistry. In 1957 he was among the W. German scientists who refused to co-operate in the development of nuclear weapons.

HAIFA (hi'fa). Principal port of Israel, on the S. shore of the Bay of Acre, at the foot of Mt. Carmel. It has a fine harbour and an institute of technology, and is the terminus of a 600 m.-long pipeline from Iraq, which fell into disuse in 1948 owing to Arab-Israeli hostility. Pop. (1967) 207,500.

HAIG, Douglas, 1st earl (1861–1928). British soldier. B. at Edinburgh, he served in the Omdurman and S. African campaigns, and in the F.W.W. commanded the 1st Army Corps 1914–15, and the 1st Army in 1915 until he succeeded French as C.-in-C. the same year. His Somme offensive in the summer of 1916 made considerable advances only at heavy cost, and his Passchendaele offensive (July–Nov. 1917) achieved little at huge loss. He then loyally supported Foch in his appointment as supreme commander and in his victorious 1918 offensive, and it was his foresight which persuaded Foch to extend his attack N., so breaking the Hindenburg Line. Created field marshal in 1917, and awarded the O.M., an earldom, and £100,000 in 1919, he retired in 1921 and devoted himself to ex-service interests as 1st pres. of the British Legion. He has been stringently criticized, however, for the appalling losses on the Somme and at Passchendaele by modern historians, even though allowance be made for the unprecedented circumstances.

HAILE SELASSIE (hi'lē sela'sē) (1891–). Emperor of Ethiopia. The son of Ras Makonnen, nephew of the emperor Menelek, he was appointed heir to the empress Zauditu in 1916 and undertook a programme of reforms, among them the abolition of the slave trade in 1923. His proclamation as king in 1928 placed all power in his hands, and on Zauditu's death in 1930 he became emperor. He made a noble but unavailing plea to the League of Nations against Italian aggression, and after the conquest of his country 1935–6 lived in England until his restoration in 1941. In 1952 he ratified the re-integration with Ethiopia of Eritrea.

HAILSHAM, Douglas McGarel Hogg, 1st visct H. (1872–1950). British lawyer and Cons. politician, son of Quintin Hogg and father of Quintin McGarel Hogg (qq.v.). Entering parliament in 1922, he was Attorney-General 1922–4 and 1924–8. Created a baron (1928) and visct. (1929), he was Lord Chancellor 1928–9 and 1935–8, and Sec. of State for War 1931–5.

HAILSHAM. Market town of Sussex, England, in the Cuckmere valley, 7 m. N. of Eastbourne. St-

Mary's church (Perpendicular) and Michelham Priory (13th cent.) 2 m. to the W. are notable. Pop. of R.D. (1961) 42,372.

HAINAN (hīnahn'). Large island off the Luichow peninsula, China, in the prov. of Kwangtung. The N. is low-lying, the centre and S. are mountainous. The rainfall is high and the valleys and coastal areas are productive, the principal crop being rice. The farmers are principally Chinese settlers, but aboriginal tribes survive in the mountains which have valuable timber resources. Kiungshan is the cap. and port. Area 13,000 sq. m.; pop. (1967) 3,000,000.

HAINAUT (hānō'). Province of S.W. Belgium, adjoining France. It is low-lying, drained by the Scheldt and Sambre, and crossed by several canals. There are important coalfields and much iron and steel is produced. Mons is the capital; Charleroi, Tournai, and Soignies are industrial centres. Area 1,436 sq. m.; pop. (1966) 1,331,953.

HAIPHONG (hīfong'). Chief port of N. Vietnam, on an arm of the Thaibinh r. delta, near the Gulf of Tonkin, 60 m. E.S.E. of Hanoi. It has shipyards and cement and textile factories. When Indo-China was French it was a naval station. Pop. (1960) 369,248.

HAIR. A fine structure proceeding from the skin and consisting of a root which is embedded in the follicle, a cavity in the second layer (true skin); and a shaft composed of horny material. A H. grows from the root, and consists of 3 layers: the cuticle (outer), cortex (middle), and core (inner). The colouring matter is in the 2 outer layers. The Hs. of different species of animals differ and are distinguishable under the microscope. Most diseases of H. are due to faulty nourishment or pests, e.g. ringworm.

HAIRDRESSING. The latest style in Carthage in the 2nd cent. A.D.

The care and arrangement of the H. has been of social importance from the most ancient times, cf. the elaborate hairstyles of ancient Egypt and Assyria, and among the most primitive tribes. The H. may indicate age-group (the Victorian girl was adult once her hair was 'up'), marital status (African tribes), political allegiance (Roundheads and Cavaliers), rank (the styles, sometimes 2 ft. high, developed among the 18th cent. aristocracy of France, and imported to England), mourning (the shaven heads of ancient Greeks and Hebrews), disgrace (women collaborators in the S.W.W. were often shaven by their compatriots), and religious vocation (the tonsure of the R.C. and E. Orthodox Churches). The modern western styles for women, increasingly adopted throughout the world, tend to daytime simplicity, with avoidance of any 'crimping' in the permanent waving (often replaced by special methods of cutting), and more elaborate evening creations made feasible by 'lacquers' or sprays, and often supplemented by nylon or real hair 'switches', etc. Besides semi-permanent and permanent 'rinses', there are hair dyes of every colour – blue, pink, and green not excepted – and, for complete transformation, full wigs. Similar tendencies, usually at a discreet level, are seen among men. *See* BEAUTY CULTURE.

HAIRE, Norman (1892–1952). Australian gynaecologist, obstetrician, and sexologist. He settled in England in 1919, and in 1921 helped to found the Walworth Welfare Centre, the first in Britain to give advice on contraception.

HAIRSTREAKS. Group of butterflies (q.v.), belonging to the Blues (Lycaenidea), and represented in both temperate and tropical regions. Most of them are brownish in their adult form, and they are nearly all tailed. They incl. the purple H. (*Thecla quercus*) in which the usual brownish-black colouring is shot with purple, and which is found throughout Europe.

RIDER HAGGARD relaxing in his garden.

HAITI (hā'ti). Republic in the western part of the West Indian island of Hispaniola. Ceded to France by Spain in 1697, it gained independence in 1804 under Dessalines (q.v.), who was followed by a colourful series of 'monarchs', until H. became a republic in 1859: H. embraced the whole island 1821–93 (*see* DOMINICAN REPUBLIC). H. was occupied by the U.S.A. 1915–34.

H. is mountainous, but well-wooded with fertile plains, and under French rule was prosperous, although subject to hurricanes. Subsequent mismanagement and the falling value of its chief products (coffee, sisal, sugar, and bauxite) make it a poor country, but indications suggesting varied mineral resources are being followed up. The cap. is Port au Prince. Under the revised constitution of 1964 there is a pres. and single-chamber legislative elected for 6 years, and candidates may be re-elected indefinitely. Pres. François Duvalier came to power in 1957 and was created Life Pres. in 1964. The official language is French, but the majority speak the Créole dialect. There is acute racial tension between this predominantly Negro majority and the mulatto bourgeoisie, and political plots are frequent. Area 10,710 sq. m.; pop. (1966) 4,500,000.

HAKE. Important food fish (*Merluccius vulgaris*) of the Gadidae family, found in N. European and N. American waters. Its silvery, elongated body attains 3–4 ft., and it consumes quantities of herring.

HAKLUYT (hak'loot), **Richard** (*c.* 1553–1616). English geographer. B. in London, he entered the Church and became archdeacon of Westminster in 1603. H. lectured on cartography at Oxford, became geographical adviser to the E. India Co., and was an original member of the Virginia Co. His chief work is his great compilation, *The Principal Navigations, Voyages and*

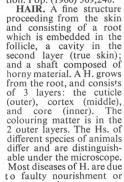

HAKE

Discoveries of the English Nation (1589–1600), in which he was assisted by Raleigh.

The *Hakluyt Society* (founded in 1846) pub. original accounts of journeys and geog. records.

HAKODATE (hahkōdah′teh). Japanese city on the S. coast of Hokkaido island. It has an excellent harbour. Pop. (1965) 252,000.

HALBERSTADT (hahl′berstaht). E. German town at the northern foot of the Harz mts., 30 m. S.W. of Magdeburg. There is a fine Gothic cathedral. Pop. (1966) 60,000.

HALDANE (hawl′dān), **John Burdon Sanderson** (1892–1964). British biologist. The son of J. S. Haldane, he was professor of genetics (1933–7) and biometry (1937–57) at London, when he acquired Indian citizenship and became research prof. at the Indian Statistical Inst. until his resignation in 1961. He pub. several collections of popular scientific essays incl. *Possible Worlds* (1927) and *Fact and Faith* (1934) and later works, such as *Science Advances* (1947), are written from the Marxist standpoint. He was chairman of the *Daily Worker* editorial board 1940–9.

HALDANE, Richard Burdon, visct. (1856–1928). British Liberal statesman. As War Minister 1905–12 he carried out an extensive scheme of army reforms, and was Lord Chancellor 1912–15. He later joined the Labour Party, and was again Lord Chancellor in the 1924 Labour govt. He pub. a number of philosophical works, written from a Hegelian standpoint. His brother **John Scott H.** (1860–1936) was an eminent biologist.

HALE, Sir Matthew (1609–76). British lawyer. Called to the Bar in 1637, he was counsel to many prominent public men, incl. Laud. He sided with Charles I for a time, and then was a member of both Cromwell's and Richard Cromwell's parliaments. At the Restoration he became Chief-baron of the Exchequer and in 1671 Lord Chief Justice.

HALE, Sarah Josepha Buell (1788–1879). American poetess, author of 'Mary had a Little Lamb' (1830).

HALES TROPHY. *See* BLUE RIBAND.

HALÉVY, Élie (ahlehvē′) (1870–1937). French historian. The son of Ludovic H., in 1898 he became a professor at the École Libre des Sciences Politiques at Paris. Of his many books the best-known is *Histoire du Peuple Anglais au XIXe Siècle* (1913–23).

HALÉVY, Jacques François (1799–1862). French composer. Of many operas, the most well-known was *La Juive* (1835).

HALEVY, Ludovic (1834–1908). French dramatist and author. B. in Paris, the son of the dramatist Léon H. (1802–83), he collaborated with Hector Crémieux in the libretto for Offenbach's *Orpheus in the Underworld*, and in partnership with Henri Meilhac (1831–97) produced comedies and operettas, including *La Belle Hélène*, *Le Petit Duc*, and *Frou-Frou* (1869). Alone, he wrote *Monsieur et Madame Cardinal* (1873), *L'Abbé Constantin* (1882), etc.

HALE-WHITE, William. *See* MARK RUTHERFORD.

HALFAYA (hahlfī′-ah). Narrow pass between 2 rocky promontories on the N. coast of Egypt near the Libyan frontier. A strongly fortified position, it was the scene of bitter fighting during the S.W.W., when it became known to the British 8th Army as Hell-fire Pass.

HALF-LIFE. The time in which the strength of a radioactive source decays to half its original value. It may vary from millionths of a second to thousands of millions of years.

HALF-TONE. A device used in printing by which the intensity of a printed colour can be varied from full strength to the lightest shades although only one colour of ink and one of paper is used. In this encyclopaedia, for example, the H.-T. illustrations contain not only black and white but every shade between, although all are printed in black ink on white paper. The picture to be reproduced is photographed through a screen ruled with a rectangular mesh of fine lines, which breaks up the tones of the original into dots which vary in size according to the intensity of the tone. In the darker shades the dots are large and run together, in the lighter shades they are small and separate. The frequency of lines on the screen governs the frequency of the dots to facilitate printing on a variety of paper surfaces. In this book the half-tone blocks are made with 100 dots to the inch, whatever size the dots may be. The process is particularly useful in colour printing. *See* PROCESS ENGRAVING.

HALIBUT. Valuable food fish (*Hippoglossus vulgaris*) of the family Pleuronectidae. Largest of the flat fish, it may reach 7 ft. and weigh 200–300 lb., and is very dark mottled brown or green above and pure white beneath. It prefers the colder seas from the English Channel to the Arctic.

HALICARNA′SSUS. Ancient city of Asia Minor. The tomb of Mausolus, built *c.* 350 B.C. by widowed Queen Artemisia, was one of the 7 wonders of the world. Herodotus was born here.

HALIFAX, Charles Montagu, earl of (1661–1715). English financier. Appointed Commissioner of the Treasury in 1692, he raised money for the French war by instituting the National Debt, and in 1694 carried out William Paterson's plan for a national bank (the Bank of England), and became Chancellor of the Exchequer. In 1695 he reformed the currency and issued the first 'Exchequer Bills', and in 1696 inaugurated the Consolidated Fund, used to pay interest on foreign loans. He was created a baron in 1700, and at the accession of George I became again 1st Lord of the Treasury and was made an earl.

HALIFAX, Edward Frederick Lindley Wood, 1st earl of H. (1881–1959). British Cons. statesman. Son of the 2nd visct. H., he was an M.P. from 1910 until 1925, when he was created baron Irwin and succeeded Reading as Viceroy of India (1926–31), doing much to further independence. As For. Sec. 1938–40 he was associated with 'appeasement', but was created an earl in 1944 in recognition of his services to the Allied cause while ambassador to the U.S. 1941–6, and received the O.M. in 1946.

HALIFAX, George Savile, 1st marquess of (1633–95). English statesman. He entered parliament in 1660, and was raised to the peerage by Charles II. He strove to steer a middle course between extremists, and became known as 'the trimmer'. He played a prominent part in the revolution of 1688.

HALIFAX. English manufacturing town (co. bor.) on the Hebble, W. Riding of Yorks. The town's leading industry is the woollen textile trade. The parish church is Perpendicular Gothic and Piece Hall, a market, was built in 1799. Pop. (1961) 96,073.

HALIFAX. Capital city of Nova Scotia, and Canada's chief winter port. Founded in 1749, it has a fine harbour and is a naval station with dock and shipyards. Industries include lumber, foundries, and sugar refineries. It is the terminus of the 2 great transcontinental railways. Pop. (1966) 198,193.

HALITO′SIS. Offensive breath. It may be due to dirty teeth, disease of the mouth, throat, nose, or lungs, or disturbance of the digestion.

HALL, Edward (*c.* 1498–1547). English chronicler. His history of England since Richard II, *The Union of the Noble Families of Lancaster and York* (1542), was used by Shakespeare.

HALL, Sir Edward Marshall (1858–1927). British criminal lawyer. Called to the Bar in 1883, he made a great reputation by his histrionic handling of evidence and skill in cross-examination: among his most famous briefs was the Seddon poisoning case. He was knighted in 1917.

HALL, Peter Reginald Frederick (1930–). British theatre director. One of the liveliest minds of the British stage, he was in 1960–8 director of the Royal Shakespeare Theatre at Stratford and developed the

Aldwych Theatre as a London 'annexe'; his striking productions incl. *Waiting for Godot* (1955), *Troilus and Cressida* (1960) *A Midsummer Night's Dream* (1962), and *The Collection* (1962). He became co-director of the Royal Shakespeare Co. in 1968.

HALL, Radclyffe (*c.* 1886–1943). British author: full name Margaret R.H. Ed. at King's Coll., London, and in Germany, she pub. some verse, estab. her reputation with the novel *Adam's Breed* (1926), and roused bitter controversy by the subject-matter of *The Well of Loneliness* (1928) – female homosexuality.

HALLAM, Henry (1777–1859). British historian. He was called to the Bar, but a private fortune enabled him to devote himself to historical study from 1812 and his *Constitutional History of England* (1827) estab. his reputation. His eldest son, the poet Arthur Henry H. (1811–33), was commemorated by Tennyson in the elegiac *In Memoriam*.

HALLE. E. German industrial and university town, cap. of H. dist., on the Saale, 20 m. N.W. of Leipzig. The production of salt from brine springs is important among many industries: lignite is mined. The univ. was founded in 1964. Pop. (1966) 276,009.

HALLÉ (hal'ā), **Sir Charles** (1819–95). Anglo-German musician. B. in Westphalia, he moved to London in 1848, estab. a reputation as a pianist, and in 1853 went to Manchester, where he founded the H. Orchestra in 1857.

HALLEY, Edmund (1656–1742). English astronomer. B. in London, he became friendly with Sir Isaac Newton, whose *Principia* he financed. He is remembered as having observed H.'s Comet in 1682 and for accurately predicting (in 1704) that it would reappear in 1759. He was Astronomer Royal from 1720.

HALL MARK. Instituted in the year 1300 for the prevention of fraud, H.Ms. are, in the U.K., the official marks stamped on gold and silver wares after the articles have been rigorously tested. Authorized Assay Offices exist at Goldsmiths' Hall, London, at Birmingham, Sheffield, Edinburgh, and formerly at other towns with distinguishing marks and the complete H.M. also contains a maker's mark, the date letter, a mark guaranteeing the standard and, from 1784 to 1890, a mark indicating that duty had been paid. In the U S. local equivalents of the H.M. developed in the 18th–19th cents., and in the 19th cent. the words coin (900 parts silver to 100 parts alloy) and sterling (925 silver to 75 copper) were added: since 1906 this marking has been federally supervised, as is the marking of gold articles with the degree of purity expressed in carats (q.v.).

HALLOWE'EN. The evening of 31 Oct., immediately preceding Hallowmas or All Saints' Day, the Christian festival kept in honour f all the saints. Many of the customs associated with the festival date back to pre-Christian days.

HALLSTATT (hahl'shtaht). Village in Upper Austria, 30 m. S.W. of Salzburg. The salt workings date from prehistoric times, and there have been distinctive archaeological finds, notably in a cemetery of more than 3,000 graves discovered in 1846, of a transitional Celtic civilization – between the Bronze and Iron Ages – known as the H. culture.

HALLSTEIN (hahl'shtīn), **Walter** (1901–). W. German expert in international law, he was prof. at Rostock 1930–41 and Frankfurt 1941–4. At the Schuman Plan conference in 1950 he led the German delegation and was Sec. of State, Foreign Office, 1951–8. In 1958–67 he was pres. of the commission of E.E.C., and in 1961 was awarded a Charlemagne prize.

HALS (hahls), **Frans** (1580/81–1666). Dutch portrait and genre painter. B. at Antwerp, he was carefree and irresponsible, and some of his best-known pictures are of tavern scenes. Though some would place him next to Rembrandt for his skill as a portrait painter, others have criticized him for his lack of insight in delineating character. In his ability to seize

and set down a passing mood he anticipated the French Impressionists. His principal works are at Haarlem, but his famous 'Laughing Cavalier' is in the Wallace Collection, London.

HALSBURY (hawlz'-), **Hardinge Stanley Giffard,** 1st earl of (1823–1921). British lawyer. Called to the Bar in 1850, he entered parliament in 1877, and was raised to the peerage in 1885. With 2 short interruptions he was Lord Chancellor 1885–1905.

HALS. 'Woman with a Fan'. *Courtesy of the National Gallery.*

HALSEY, William Frederick (1882–1959). American admiral. Entering the navy in 1905, he was appointed to command of the Third Fleet in the S. Pacific in 1942 and compelled the Japanese to withdraw 1943–4. On his flagship, the *Missouri*, the Japanese signed the surrender document ending the S.W.W.

HAMBLEDON. English village in S.E. Hants, famous in the history of cricket. In its prime the original H. cricket club was strong enough to beat any other team in England; its last important match was at Lord's in 1793, and it was disbanded in 1796. It played on Broadhalfpenny Down until *c.* 1782 then on Windmill Down. A H. cricket club continued to exist after the disbandment of the famous one.

HAMBOURG, Mark (1879–1960). Russian-born pianist who became a British citizen. He specialized in the Romantics – Grieg, Rachmaninov, and Tchaikovsky – and his own compositions incl. *Variations on a Theme of Paganini,*

HAMBURG. W. German city and port, cap. of H. Land, with which it is contiguous, on the right bank of the Elbe estuary at the head of tidal navigation, 75 m. from the N. Sea. It is the largest port of Continental Europe and incl. the industrial suburb of Altona. Pop. (1966) 1,847,267.

HAMBURG. With harbour basins, shipyards, docks, and wharves extending over ten miles along the banks of the river Elbe, Hamburg plays an important role in internation transit trade, and tugs and launches move busily between the large ocean-going ships. In the background is St. Michael's church. *Courtesy of the German Tourist Information Bureau.*

H. was an archbishopric from 834. From its alliance with Lübeck in 1241 the Hanseatic League arose. In 1510 the emperor Maximilian I created it a free imperial city, and in 1871 it became a state of the German Empire. During the S.W.W. it was the target of concentrated air attacks, and when, on 3 May 1945, it

R

surrendered to the British 2nd Army, nearly half the city's buildings were in ruins. There is a univ. (1919) and the H. Schauspielhaus is one of the rep.'s leading theatres. Shipyards demolished by the Allies in 1946 were re-equipped in 1953.

The *hamburger* (chopped beef and seasoning fried as a flattened round) is said to have been invented by the medieval Tartar invaders of the Baltic area. Sailors from H. took the idea home, but although naturalized in the 19th cent. in the U.S.A. by German immigrants, the H. dropped out of use in Germany until reintroduced in the 1960s via England.

The LAND OF HAMBURG consists of the city and surrounding districts. Area 288 sq. m.; pop. (1966) 1,847,300.

HAMELN (hah'meln). Town on the Weser, W. Germany, 25 m. S.W. of Hanover. Buildings of interest include the Rattenfängerhaus (rat-catcher's house) and the minster. The town is famous for the Pied Piper legend. Pop. (1960) 52,000.

HAMILCAR BARCA (*c*. 270–228 B.C.). Carthaginian general, father of Hannibal. From 247 to 241 he harassed the Romans in Italy, and then led an expedition to Spain where he d. in battle.

HAMILTON, Alexander (1757–1804). American statesman. B. in the W. Indies, he served during the War of Independence as captain and from 1777 to 1781 was Washington's secretary and aide-de-camp. After the war he practised as a lawyer. He was a member of the Constitutional Convention of 1787, and in the *Federalist* influenced public opinion in favour of the ratification of the constitution. H. was Sec. of the Treasury, 1789–95, and proved an able controller of the national finances. He led the Federal Party, and incurred the bitter hatred of Aaron Burr when he cast the deciding vote against Burr and in favour of Jefferson for the presidency in 1801. Eventually fought a duel with Burr, was wounded, and died the next day.

HAMILTON, Lady Emma (*c*. 1765–1815). British courtesan. *Née* Lyon or Hart, the dau. of a Cheshire blacksmith, she obtained employment in London, and in 1782 became the mistress of Charles Greville, and in 1786 of his uncle Sir William Hamilton (1730–1803), the British envoy at Naples. She at once became a leading figure in the society of Naples, and Hamilton married her in 1791. After Nelson's return from the Nile in 1798 she became well known as his mistress and her dau. by him, Horatia, was b. in 1801. After

LADY HAMILTON by George Romney

the death of Hamilton and Nelson, Lady H. was imprisoned for debt, but later escaped to Calais where she d. in poor circumstances.

HAMILTON, Iain Ellis (1922–). Scottish composer. Glasgow-born he worked as an aircraft engineer 1939–46, and studied at the R.A.M. 1947–51. Intensely emotional and harmonically rich, his works incl. the striking viola and 'cello sonatas, a ballet (*Clerk Saunders*), the *Pharsalia* cantata, and symphonies.

HAMILTON, Sir Ian (Standish Monteith) (1853–1947). Scottish soldier. He was chief-of-staff and deputy to Lord Kitchener, C.-in-C., in the S. African War. In 1914 he was C.-in-C. of the Home Defence Army and in 1915 he led the land operations in Gallipoli. He had become a full general in 1914.

HAMILTON, James Hamilton, 1st duke of (1606–49). Scottish royalist. He acted as Charles I's adviser on Scottish affairs and in 1639 commanded an army against the Covenanters. Subsequently he took part in the negotiations between Charles and the Scots. During the 2nd Civil War he led the Scottish invasion of England, but was captured at Preston and executed.

HAMILTON, Patrick (1904–62). British novelist and dramatist. He specialized in suspense, notably in the plays *Rope* (1929), based on the classic murder case of Loeb and Leopold (*see* DARROW, CLARENCE), and the Victorian *Gaslight* (1937); and the radio dramas *To the Public Danger* and *Money with Menaces* (1939).

HAMILTON, Sir William (1788–1856). British philosopher. Prof. of history (from 1821) and of logic and metaphysics (1836–56) at Edinburgh, he greatly influenced the 19th cent. Scottish school. His chief work was the *Philosophy of the Unconditioned* (1829).

HAMILTON, Sir William Rowan. *See* QUATERNIONS.

HAMILTON. Town (burgh) in Lanark, Scotland, nr. the Clyde, 10 m. S.E. of Glasgow. Among its industries are textiles, engineering, etc. Pop. (1961) 41,968.

HAMILTON. Chief city of Wentworth co., Ontario, Canada. It lies nr. Lake Ontario, 40 m. to the W. of the Niagara Falls, possesses a large hydro-electric plant. and manufactures agricultural implements. It is the seat of a univ. Pop. (1966) 449,116.

HAMILTON. Town on the Waikato river, North Island, New Zealand. Waikato Univ. was estab. here 1964. Pop. (1967) 65,800.

HAMILTON. Cap. of Bermuda, on Bermuda Island. Pop. (1966) 3,000.

HAMM (hahm). Town on the river Lippe, North Rhine-Westphalia, W. Germany, 19 m. N.E. of Dortmund. H. has wire and machine factories, railway repair shops, and the rly. marshalling yards are among the largest in Europe: during the S.W.W. they were frequently bombed. Pop. (1960) 68,000.

HAMMARSKJÖLD (ha'mershold), **Dag** (1905–61). 'World civil servant.' Son of a Swedish P.M., he taught economics at Stockholm univ. and, although an Independent became Assist. For. Sec. in 1949 and Min. of State in 1951. In 1953 H. was elected Sec.-Gen. of U.N. and unanimously re-elected in 1958. He dealt with the Suez Crisis (1956) in which he opposed Britain, and his attempts to solve the problem of the Congo, where he was killed in a plane crash, were strongly attacked by the Soviet Union.

HAMMERFEST. Town on Kvalö island off the N.W. coast of Norway; the northernmost town of Europe. Whaling is carried on. Pop. (1960) 5,600.

HAMMERHEAD. Several species of shark in the genus *Sphyrna*, characterized by a hammer-shaped head. and found in tropical seas.

HAMMERSMITH. Bor. of Greater London, England, lying between Kensington and the Thames on the S. The H. suspension bridge was completed

1887. St. Paul's School at H. from 1883 was moved to Barnes 1968, also in the bor. are the Lyric theatre, Olympia, and the White City Stadium. Pop. (1967) 211,720.

HAMMERSTEIN, Oscar. *See* RODGERS, RICHARD.

HAMMETT, Dashiell (1894–1961). American crime-novelist, a pioneer of the tough-guy school, who had himself been a 'private eye'. His best books were *The Maltese Falcon* (1930) and *The Thin Man* (1932).

HAMMOND, Joan (1912–). Australian soprano. As a violinist she played with the Sydney Philharmonic Orchestra for 3 yrs., made her concert début as a singer in London with the *Messiah* in 1938, and in 1939 made her début in opera in Vienna.

HAMMOND, John Lawrence (1872–1949). British historian of the Industrial Revolution, on which he wrote jointly with his wife Barbara H. (1873–1961), whom he m. in 1901. Their works incl. *The Village Labourer, 1760–1832* (1911), *The Rise of Modern Industry* (1925) and *The Bleak Age* (1934).

HAMMOND, Walter R. (1903–65). British cricketer. Capt. of Gloucestershire 1939–47, he became the English cricket capt. in 1938, leading the team in the 1946–7 test series in Australia. A great batsman, his most famous feat was the scoring of over 1,000 runs in 3 weeks in 1927.

HAMMURABI (hamōōrah'be). King of Babylon (reigned *c.* 1792–50 B.C.) of the 1st or Amorite dynasty. He expelled the Elamites and united the country, but is best remembered for his legal code, a consolidation of material already traditional, which survives in several copies: the punishments are bloodthirsty.

HAMPDEN, John (*c.* 1594–1643). English statesman. The son of a wealthy landowner, he was b. at Great Hampden, Bucks, sat in the parliaments of 1621, 1625, and 1626, and became conspicuous when in 1627 he was imprisoned for refusing to pay a forced loan. His refusal in 1636 to pay Ship Money made him a national figure. In the Short and Long parliaments he proved himself a skilful debater and parliamentary strategist. Charles's attempt to arrest him and four other leading M.Ps. made war inevitable. He raised his own regiment on the outbreak of hostilities, and on 18 June 1643 was mortally wounded at the skirmish of Chalgrove Field.

HAMPSHIRE. Co. of southern England lying west of Sussex and Surrey and with a coast on the English Channel. The geographical county includes the Isle of Wight (q.v.). H. is crossed by the downs, while in the S.W. is the New Forest. Sheep are reared on the downs. In the lower parts, wheat, hay, and fodder crops, fruit, etc., are grown and cattle are pastured. The chief rivers are the Test, Itchen, Avon and Stour. The co. town is Winchester; Southampton is a great maritime centre, Portsmouth and Gosport are naval ports, at Fawley is a large petroleum refinery and Bournemouth is a holiday centre. Area 1,503 sq. m.; pop. (1967) 1,511,250.

HAMPSTEAD. Locality in the bor. of Camden, Greater London. Famous for its picturesque village atmosphere, it is fashionable and expensive, and reaches 443 ft. a.s.l. in parts. **H. Heath** is an open space of *c.* 250 acres; **H. Garden Suburb** originated 1907.

HAMPTON. City of S.E. Virginia, U.S.A., estab. 1610, lying on H. Roads, the lower James river estuary. H. Institute (1868) is a famous Indian and Negro educational institute. Pop. (1960) 89,259.

HAMPTON COURT PALACE. Palace erected in H.C. Park, on the N. bank of the Thames, in the Greater London bor. of Richmond-upon-Thames, England, by Cardinal Wolsey in the early 16th cent. In 1526 he presented it to Henry VIII, who added the chapel and the Great Hall. The later additions made by Wren for William III included the Fountain Court, and the E. and S. fronts.

HAMSTER. The H. (*Cricetus frumentarius*) of Europe and N. Asia is the typical member of the

cricetine group of rodents. The thickset body is about 10 in. long, and the tail *c.* 2 in., and the fur usually golden-brown above and darker below. It excavates cleanly kept

HAMSTER

and complex chambered burrows 1–2 ft. deep in summer, and 3–6 ft. deep in winter, when it hibernates. It is prolific.

HAMSUN (hahm'soon), **Knut** (1859–1952). Norwegian novelist. The son of a farmer, he suffered from poverty, twice emigrating to the U.S., and his novel *Sult* (1890: *Hunger*) had a terrible truth which at once made him famous. Of his later books *Growth of the Soil* (1917), after which he received a Nobel prize, in 1920, was the best. His ideas were in sympathy with Nazism in some respects and in 1946 he was fined for collaboration.

HANCOCK, Tony (1924–68). British radio and television comedian. In 'Hancock's Half Hour', etc., he was the little man whose romantic ideas and schemes were always at odds with everyday life.

HA'NDEL, George Frederick (1685–1759). German-born composer, who became a British subject in 1726. B. at Halle, he abandoned the study of law at the univ. in 1703, to become a violinist at Keiser's Opera House in Hamburg, where his first opera *Almira* was performed in 1705. Visits to Italy (1706–10) inspired a number of operas and oratorios, and in 1711 his opera *Rinaldo* was performed in London. Appointed Kapellmeister to the elector of Hanover in 1709, he took French leave in 1712 to settle in England, and was for a time in disgrace when the elector succeeded as George I in 1714. However, he wrote for him in 1715 the 'Water Music' and from 1720 directed the opera at the King's Theatre, Haymarket. The rivalry of the fashionable Italian composer Bononcini, and Gay's ridicule in *The Beggar's Opera* (1728), led him to abandon Italianate opera for English oratorio.

HANDEL. Portrait by Thomas Hudson, 1756.
Photo: National Portrait Gallery.

Saul and *Israel in Egypt* (both 1739) were unsuccessful, but his masterpiece *Messiah* was acclaimed on its first performance in Dublin in 1742 and maintains unrivalled popularity. His great contribution is to choral music, later oratorios incl. *Samson* (1744), *Belshazzar* (1745), *Judas Maccabaeus* (1747) and *Jephtha* (1752). From 1751 he became totally blind, and throughout his career suffered financial difficulty.

HANDLEY, Tommy (1896–1949). British comedian. B. in Liverpool, he became famous for his immensely popular radio programme 'ITMA' (It's That Man Again) with its catch-phrases, e.g. 'After you, Claud', and such characters as 'Mrs. Mop' and 'Mona Lot': it ran from 1939 till his death.

HANGCHOW'. Chinese port at the mouth of the Tsientang, at the head of H. Bay. The capital of Chekiang prov., it lies 110 m. S.W. of Shanghai at the S. end of the Grand Canal. It is a tourist centre with silk, jute, and tea industries; trade is mainly inland. Pop. (1957) 784,000.

HANGING. Suspension by the neck usually with a noose. The base of the tongue is forced into the back of the throat and blocks the air passages; the large blood-vessels supplying the brain are shut off and the vagus nerve and carotid arteries are compressed, causing the heart to stop. Unconsciousness and death therefore follow very quickly. In judicial hanging the condemned person is allowed to drop about six feet so that the powerful jerk of the tightened rope breaks his neck.

HANKEY, Maurice Pascal Alers, 1st baron (1877–1963). British administrator, 'the man with a million state secrets'. Son of a British emigrant to Australia, he was in 1916 appointed Sec. of the Cabinet by Lloyd George, the 1st 'outsider' regularly to attend its meetings. For assistance in organizing Allied victory in the F.W.W. he was awarded £25,000, the only civilian officer to be so recognized. He was knighted in 1919, and raised to the peerage in 1938.

HANKO (hahnk'ō). Port at the end of H. peninsula on the S.W. coast of Finland. It is kept ice-free all the year. Finland leased H. to Russia 1940–4. Pop. (est.) 7,000.

HANKOW. *See* WUHAN.

HANLEY. *See* STOKE-ON-TRENT.

HANNAY, James Owen. *See* BIRMINGHAM, G. A.

HANNIBAL (247–182 B.C.). Carthaginian general, the son of Hamilcar Barca (q.v.). Chosen as general by the army in 221 he besieged Saguntum (in Spain) in 219, whereupon the Romans declared war on Carthage. H. then fought a brilliant campaign in Italy, culminating in his victory at Cannae (216). However, he failed to capture Rome, and after spending some years in S. Italy was recalled to Carthage in 203 to meet a Roman invasion which culminated in H.'s defeat at Zama (202). He then became head of the Carthaginian government, but was exiled in 196 at the wish of the Romans, fleeing to the court of Antiochus in Asia Minor. He poisoned himself in Bithynia to avoid extradition to Rome.

HANOI (hanō'i). Capital of N. Vietnam, on the Song-ka, *c.* 100 m. from its mouth. It is a trade and communications centre with an airport; is the seat of a univ.; and produces textiles and beer. It was the cap. of French Indo-China, 1902–45. Pop. (1967) 850,000.

HA'NŌVER. W. German city, at the junction of the Leine and Ihme, capital of the Land of Lower Saxony. It is an important river and canal port with a noted institute of technology and many industries, incl. the making of machinery, vehicles, electrical equipment, rubber, textiles, chocolate, biscuits, tobacco; and petroleum refining. The seat of a Lutheran bp., it is first mentioned in 1163, was chartered 1241, passed to Brunswick 1369, joined the Hanseatic League 1386. Pop. (1966) 540,723.

From 1692 H. was the cap. of the former electorate (after 1815, kingdom) of H. George Louis, elector of

H., great-grandson of James I, became king of the U.K. in 1714, and the ruler of the 2 countries was the same person until Victoria's accession in 1837 when H., where a woman could not hold the throne, passed to her uncle Ernest Augustus, duke of Cumberland. His son, George V of H., was forced by Bismarck to abdicate in 1866, H. becoming a prov. of Prussia. In 1946 H. was merged with Brunswick and Oldenburg to form the Land of Lower Saxony.

HANSARD. Name given to the official report of the proceedings of the British parliament. Luke H. commenced printing the *House of Commons Journal* in 1774, but the first 'official' reports were pub. from 1803 by Cobbett, who during his imprisonment of 1810–12 sold the business to his printer, Thomas Curson H., son of Luke H. The publication of the debates remained in the hands of the family until 1889, and is now the responsibility of the Stationery Office. The name H. was officially adopted 1943.

HANSEATIC (hansēat'ik) **LEAGUE.** A medieval confederation of N. German trading cities. The earliest association had its headquarters at Wisby; it included over 30 cities, but was gradually supplanted by that headed by Lübeck. Hamburg and Lübeck estab. their own trading-stations in London in 1266 and 1267 respectively, which coalesced in 1282 with that of Cologne to form the so-called Steelyard. There were 3 other such stations: Bruges, Bergen, and Novgorod. At its height in the later 14th cent. the H.L. included over 70 towns, among them Lübeck, Hamburg, Cologne, Breslau, and Cracow. The basis of its power was its monopoly of the Baltic trade and its relations with Flanders and England.

The decline of the H.L. from the 15th cent. onwards was due to the movement of trade routes, and to the development of national states. The last general assembly (1669) marks the end of the League.

HANSOM, Joseph Aloysius (1803–82). British architect. His works incl. the town hall of Birmingham (1831), but he is remembered as the introducer of the H. cab in 1834.

HANUMAN (ha'noomahn). The monkey god and king of Hindustan. He assisted Rama to recover his wife Sita, abducted by Ravana of Lanka (Ceylon).

HANSOM CAB

HANWAY, Jonas (1712–86). British traveller – he wrote of his experiences in Persia – and advocate of prison reform. He is believed to have been the first Englishman to carry an umbrella.

HANYANG. *See* WUHAN.

HAPSBURG. *See* HABSBURG.

HARA-KIRI (harahkir'i). Form of suicide by disembowelment prevalent in Japan, usually to avoid capture or other ignominy. It dates back to the Middle Ages and was widely practised by the Japanese forces during the S.W.W. It is more correctly called *seppuku*.

HARA'PPA. Archaeological site in W. Pakistan with remains of the Indus Valley Civilization (q.v.). Of the series of great mounds, the most important is the Citadel – the ramparts still rising 50 ft. above the level of the plain – which Sir Mortimer Wheeler identified in 1946.

HARAR (hahrahr'). Chief town of H. prov. in E. Ethiopia. The city stands 220 m. E. of Addis Ababa, and is a caravan centre; coffee is the chief product of the area. An ancient walled city, it is the Moslem centre of Ethiopia. Pop. (1960) 40,000.

HARBIN. Chinese city, cap. of Heilungkiang prov., on the Sungari. A railway and river centre, it makes

HARBIN. A skilled worker at the Sputnik Bearings Plant passes on her experience to others. *Photo: Camera Press.*

machinery, linen, etc. Its growth began with the opening of the Chinese Eastern Railway in 1897. Pop. (1965) 1,600,000.

HARCOURT, Sir William Vernon (1827–1904). British Lib. statesman. A barrister, he first made a name by his opposition to recognition of the Southern States as belligerents in the Civil War, entered parliament in 1868, and was appointed Solicitor-General and knighted in 1873. Under Gladstone he was Home Sec. 1880–5, and Chancellor of the Exchequer 1886 and 1892–5. He was disappointed in his hopes to succeed him as P.M. His son **Lewis Vernon H.,** 1st visc. (1863–1922), was Colonial Sec. 1910–15.

HARDICANUTE (hahr′dikanūt′) (c 1019–42). King of England. The son of Canute, he ascended the throne in 1040 and was a harsh ruler.

HARDIE, James Keir (1856–1915). British socialist. B. in Lanarks, he worked in the mines as a boy, and in 1886 became Sec. of the Scottish Miners' Federation. In 1888 he was the 1st Labour candidate to stand for Parliament and was a chief founder of the I.L.P. in 1893. A pacifist, he desperately opposed the Boer War, and the flame of his idealism in his work for socialism and the unemployed made his name a legend: he was M.P. for West Ham 1892–5 and for Merthyr Tydfil from 1900.

HARDING, William Gamaliel (1865–1923). 29th President of the U.S.A. B. in Ohio, he entered the U.S. Senate in 1914 as a Republican, and opposed the Peace Treaty of 1919. In 1920 he was elected President of the U.S.A. He concluded the peace treaties of 1921 with Germany, Austria, and Hungary, and in the same year called the Washington Conference. After the conference there were charges of corruption among members of his Cabinet.

HARDING OF PETHERTON, John, 1st baron (1896–). British field marshal. Chief-of-staff to Alexander in Italy in the S.W.W., he was C. in C. B.A.O.R. 1951–2, and C.I.G.S. 1952–5. As Gov. of Cyprus 1955–7, during part of the period of terrorism and political agitation prior to independence (1960) he was responsible for the controversial deportation of Makarios (q.v.) from Cyprus in 1955, and for the reorganization of the security forces to combat the Eoka terrorists.

HARDINGE (hahr′ding), **Henry,** 1st visct. (1785–1856). British soldier and administrator. He was Sec. for War 1828 and 1841–4; Chief Sec. for Ireland 1830 and 1834–5; introduced many reforms as Gov.-Gen. of India 1844–8; and was C. in C. of the British Army 1852–6. He was created a visct. in 1846 and a field marshal in 1855. His grandson, **Charles H.,** 1st baron H. of Penshurst (1858–1944), was ambassador to Petrograd 1904–6 and Paris 1920–3, and Viceroy of India 1910–16. The latter's son, **Alexander H.,** 2nd

baron (1894–1960) ,was private sec. to Edward VIII, his warning letter to the King during the Abdication Crisis causing much subsequent controversy, and to George VI 1936–43.

HARDWAR (hurdwahr′). Indian town in Uttar Pradesh, on the right bank of the Ganges, one of the holy places of the Hindu religion and a pilgrimage centre. The Kumbhmela festival, held every twelfth year in honour of Siva, is the most important and attracts some million pilgrims. The name means door of Hari (or Vishnu). Pop. (1961) 58,513.

HA′RDWICKE, Sir Cedric Webster (1893–1964). British actor. Possessed of caustic wit and impressively sardonic appearance, he excelled in such roles as the father in *The Barretts of Wimpole Street* (1930–1) and King Magnus in *The Apple Cart* (1931): his films incl. *Nell Gwynn* and *Richard III.* He was knighted in 1934.

HARDY, Thomas (1840–1928). British poet and novelist. B. nr. Dorchester in the heart of the 'Wessex' which was to form the background of his novels, he was trained as an architect. His first success was *Far From the Madding Crowd* (1874), followed among others by *The Return of the Native* (1878), *The Mayor of Casterbridge* (1886) and *The Woodlanders* (1887) – all remarkable for the background contrast of richly humorous rustic characters, for the brooding intensity of human loves and hates played out before the onrush of the harshly indifferent force that H. believed governs the world. *Tess of the D'Urbervilles* (1891) – subtitled 'A Pure Woman' – outraged public opinion by portraying as its heroine a woman who had been seduced, and the even greater outcry which followed *Jude the Obscure* (1895) helped reinforce H.'s decision to confine himself to verse. Beginning with *Wessex Poems* (1898), he pub. several vols. of lyrics and a gigantic blank-verse panorama of the Napoleonic wars, *The Dynasts* (1904–8). In 1910 he was awarded the O.M.

THOMAS HARDY

HARDY, Sir Thomas Masterman (1769–1839). British sailor. He entered the navy in 1781, and at Trafalgar was Nelson's flag-captain in the *Victory*, attending him during his dying moments. He was promoted rear-admiral in 1825, and became 1st Sea Lord in 1830.

HARE, Robertson (1891–). British actor, celebrated for his lugubriously comic roles in such Aldwych farces as *Rookery Nook* and *Cuckoo in the Nest* and typified by his catch-phrase 'Oh calamity!' He excels as the henpecked husband or the prim cleric.

HARE. Rodent of the family Leporidae, incl. the species not classified as rabbits. The common H. (*Lepus europaeus*) is found in England, and southern and central Europe and the smaller blue or mountain H. (*L. timidus*) in Scotland and Scandinavia. The H. is found in most parts of the world and those of the very north, the polar (*L. articus*) and Greenland (*L. groenlandicus*) Hs., turn white in winter.

HAREBELL. Wild flower (*Campanula rotundifolia*), sometimes called the bluebell of Scotland. It bears a group of blue bell-shaped flowers on a stem, with heart-shaped leaves at the base, and is found in the N. of the northern hemisphere, the Rockies, and Sierra Nevada.

HARE-LIP. A deformity of the face consisting of a cleft in the upper lip and jaw. The cause is failure of union between the right and left sections of the jaw. The cleft may extend back into the palate. Surgery and re-education can often provide a remedy.

HAREWOOD (har'wood), **George Henry Hubert Lascelles**, 7th earl of H. (1923–). The elder son of the 6th earl and H.R.H. Princess Mary, the Princess Royal, he served in the Grenadier Guards in the S.W.W. and was a P.O.W. 1944–5. A patron of music, he ed. the magazine *Opera* 1950–3 and was in 1961–5 artistic director of the Edinburgh Festival. His brother, **Gerald David Lascelles** (1924–), is an ardent supporter of jazz.

HARFLEUR (ahrflör'). Port on the N. side of the Seine estuary, Seine-Maritime dept., France. During the Middle Ages it was leading port of N.W. France. Pop. (1962) 10,514.

HARGEISA (hahrgās'a). Second-largest town of the Somali Rep., connected by air service to Aden and Asmara and by highway to Berbera and Addis Ababa. Pop. (est.) 50,000.

HARGRAVES, **Edmund Hammond** (1815–91). British discoverer of the Australian goldfields. B. in Hants, he found gold in the Blue Hills of N.S.W. in 1851, was made temporary Commissioner of Crown Lands and given a govt. award of £10,000.

HARGREAVES, **James** (d. 1778). British inventor. B. nr. Blackburn, he became a weaver, and in 1760 was co-inventor of a carding machine. About 1764 he invented his 'spinning-jenny', which enabled a number of threads to be spun simultaneously by one person.

HARIANA. *See* PUNJAB.

HARKNESS, **Edward** (1874–1940). American railway magnate and philanthropist, who in England founded the Pilgrim Trust (£2,000,000, of which both capital and income may be used to promote the well-being of the U.K.) in 1930.

HARLECH. Town in Merionethshire, Wales, 10 m. N.N.W. of Barmouth. On a rock are the ruins of the castle, built in Edward I's reign. Pop. 1,096.

HARLEM (hahr'lem). District of Manhattan, New York City, with a large Negro population.

HARLEY, **Robert**, 1st earl of Oxford (1661–1724). British Tory statesman. He was Speaker of the Commons from 1701 to 1705 and entered the govt. in 1704 as Sec. of State. In 1708 the Whigs procured his dismissal, but in 1710 he returned to power as Chancellor of the Exchequer, and became subsequently a peer, received the Garter, and occupied the office of Lord Treasurer. In 1714, however, he was dismissed. After the accession of George I he was accused of treason, and imprisoned until 1717.

HARLOW. English market town (U.D.) in Essex, 5 m. N. of Epping. It was chosen in 1946 for development as a new town. Pop. (1961) 53,475 (5,771 in 1951).

HARMONICA. Name given to a variety of musical instruments of varying periods, incl. sets of musical glasses (graded in size or containing varying quantities of water) played with wetted fingers or small hammers – both Mozart and Beethoven composed for these; and the mouth organ. The latter, said to have been invented by Wheatstone (q.v.) in 1829, consists of a narrow box containing a metal plate in which there are a number of slots, each having a small metal reed affixed – the size of the reed is varied according to the note to be produced. Easily mastered by the amateur, it can by a few be used at the level of a concert instrument, e.g. Larry Adler.

HARMONIUM. Musical instrument: a pipeless, reed-vibrated organ, worked by air compression with a 5-octave keyboard and an air chamber filled by the action of foot-worked pedals.

HARMONY. The art of combining musical sounds into chords, and the moving from one chord to another. It is distinguished from counterpoint (q.v.), the combination of harmonic textures. H. first took the form of added parts moving parallel to a plainsong. New chord forms appeared in the 16th cent., when the shortcomings of the ecclesiastical modes became more and more apparent, resulting in the evolution of modern major and minor scales. J. S. Bach advanced consonance and dissonance, while chromatic notes began to appear. The practical advancement of H., by Beethoven, Wagner, Stravinsky, etc., has frequently aroused the hostility of academic critics, as it still does in the case of the atonality, abandonment of a fixed key note, and double and treble tonality of Bartók and Holst. Our universal diatonic scale was nearly attained by Pythagoras and perfected by Zarlino.

HARMSWORTH, Alfred. *See* LORD NORTHCLIFFE.

HARNACK (hahr'nahk), **Adolf von** (1851–1930). German Protestant theologian. B. at Dorpat, he held chairs of ecclesiastical history at Leipzig, Marburg, and Berlin. His main work is a history of Dogma (1886–90), and his approach to Christian history and dogma was realistic and critical.

HARNESS RACING. Sport popular in the U.S. and Canada, originating in the 18th cent., in which standardbred horses (rather sturdier than thoroughbreds) pull two-wheeled sulkies on which the driver sits. They compete in trotting (in which the diagonally opposite legs move forward simultaneously) and pacing (in which the 2 right legs, then the 2 left legs, are alternately moved forward) races and the winner may be decided by the best 2 out of 3 heats. The most famous race (trotting) is the Hambletonian at Goshen, N.Y., named after the mid-19th cent. horse Hambletonian, from which 90 per cent of modern standardbreds are said to descend in the male line. Attempts to popularize H.R. in Britain have failed, but it flourishes in Australia, France, Italy and Sweden.

HARNETT, **William Michael** (1841–92), American artist, celebrated for his trompe-l'oeil still-lifes.

HARNEY, **William** (1895–1962). Australian authority on the aborigines. B. in Queensland, he spent many years among the tribes, accepted as one of themselves. In 1940 he became patrol officer and Protector of Aborigines in the Northern Territory.

HAROLD I (d. 1040). King of England, known as 'Harefoot'. The illegitimate son of Canute, he claimed the throne on his father's death in 1035, and in 1037 was elected king.

HAROLD II (*c.* 1022–66). King of England. The son of Earl Godwin, he was early appointed earl of E. Anglia. He succeeded his father in 1053 in the earldom of Wessex and became the most powerful man in England. Soon after 1063 William of Normandy tricked him into swearing to support his claim to the English throne. In Jan. 1066 H. was elected king by the Witan; William began to prepare an invasion

HAROLD II. Shipwrecked on the Norman coast, Harold had little option but to take an oath dictated by Duke William (left) which would assure his rival the English throne. Only later did he discover the sacredness of the relics in the caskets on which he had sworn.

With the assistance of Tostig, H.'s brother, the king of Norway, Harald Hardrada, invaded Northumbria; H. marched north, and routed the invaders at Stamford Bridge on 25 Sept. Three days later William landed at Pevensey; H. took up his position at Battle. The battle of Hastings (14 Oct. 1066) ended with the death of H.

HARP. Musical instrument, the largest to be plucked by hand. It consists of 46 strings, stretched between an upright triangular frame, and is provided with several pedals at the base. These are used to alter the pitch of the instrument.

HARPENDEN. English town (U.D.) in Herts, 25 m. N.N.W. of London. Nearby is the Rothamsted agricultural experimental station, founded 1843. Pop. (1961) 18,218.

HARPIES. In classical mythology originally feminine wind-spirits. In later legend they became rapacious monsters who retained their human heads but possessed the bodies of vultures.

HARPSICHORD. Keyboard musical instrument popular in the 16–18th cents., until its supersession by the piano. The strings were plucked by quills, not struck by hammers.

HARPUR, Charles (1817–68). Australian poet. B. in N.S.W., he was brought up in the bush, and became a sheep farmer. He pub. *Thoughts: a Series of Sonnets* (1845), but displayed a more native talent in the later collections. His most famous poem is the 'Creek of the Four Graves'.

HARRER, Heinrich (1912–   ). Austrian author and explorer. His books incl. *Seven Years in Tibet* (1953) and *The White Spider* (1958), a history of the north face of the Eiger, which he was the 1st to climb in 1938.

HARRIER. Genus (*Circus*) of birds of prey in the family Accipitridae. They are found throughout the world, and 3 species occur in Britain: the moorland hen H. (*C. cyaneus*), Montagu's H. (*C. cineraceus*), and the marsh H. (*C. aeruginosus*).

HARRIER. A dog hunting the hare by scent. It resembles a foxhound, though smaller and slower.

HARRIER

HARRIMAN, (William) Averell (1891–   ). American administrator. S. of Edward H., founder of the Union Pacific Railroad, of which H. became chairman in 1932, he was ed. at Yale. Originally a Republican he became a Democrat in 1927, and was apt. by Roosevelt State Director of the National Recovery Administration in 1933. During the S.W.W. he was active in the admin. of Lease-Lend (q.v.) and was present at the Atlantic Charter (q.v.) meetings in 1941. Ambassador to the U.S.S.R. 1943–6 and to Great Britain for a few months, in 1946, he headed the European division of E.C.A. 1948–50 (M.S.A. 1951–3), and was Gov. of New York 1955–8. He was Asst. Sec. of State for Far Eastern Affairs 1961–3, Under-Sec. for Political Affairs 1963–4, and ambassador-at-large 1961 and 1965–9.

HARRINGTON, James (1611–77). English political philosopher, author of *Oceana*, describing an ideal republican commonwealth.

HARRINGTON, Sir John (1561–1612). English courtier, who translated Ariosto's *Orlando Furioso* (1591) at the command of Queen Elizabeth.

HARRIS, Sir Arthur Travers (1892–   ). British air marshal. He served with the R.F.C. during the F.W.W. and in the S.W.W. was deputy chief of the air staff 1940–1 and C.-in.-C. of Bomber Command 1942–5, becoming known as 'Bomber H.'. Since 1945 he has been Marshal of the R.A.F. and in 1953 he received a baronetcy.

HARRIS, Frank (1856–1931). Irish journalist. B. in

HARRIS. Woven by the island crofters on traditional looms, Harris tweed is in modern times in demand throughout the world.   *Photo: George Outram & Co. Ltd.*

Galway, he was active both in New York and London and wrote ephemeral fiction. He is best remembered for his highly coloured biographies of Wilde and Shaw, and his sensational autobiography, *My Life* (1926), banned in the U.K. and U.S.

HARRIS, Joel Chandler (1848–1908). American writer. B. in Georgia, he first pub. his 'Uncle Remus' stories in the Atlanta *Constitution*, which he edited 1890–1905; these tales were written in Negro dialect and gained worldwide popularity. His autobiography, *On the Plantation*, appeared in 1892.

HARRIS, Paul P. (1868–1947). American lawyer, founder of Rotary. B. in Wisconsin, he became a lawyer in Chicago in 1896, where he founded the first Rotary Club in 1905, and the International Association in 1912.

HARRIS, Roy (1898–   ). American composer. B. in Oklahoma, son of a farmer and an English-born mother, he served in the F.W.W., was then a truck-driver until 1921, when he studied music at the Univ. of California. Notable among his symphonies are the Third, Fifth and Sixth ('Lincoln'), and among other works his cantata *Abraham Lincoln walks at Midnight* and the orchestral piece *When Johnny Comes Marching Home*.

HARRIS. Southern part of Lewis-with-Harris Island, in the Outer Hebrides, in Inverness co., Scotland. It is a barren stretch, cultivated by crofters; sheep are reared on the rough upland pastures. *Harris tweed* is made from the hand-woven wool of the blackface or Cheviot sheep. Tarbet is the chief town. Area 176 sq. m.; pop. (1961) 3,285.

HARRISMITH. Town in the Orange Free State, S. Africa, 45 m. N.W. of Ladysmith; it is a market centre and a health resort, and is named after Sir Harry Smith (1787–1860), Governor of the Cape 1847–52. Pop. (1960) 12,786 (3,200 white).

HARRISON, George Bagshawe (1894–   ). British scholar. Prof. of Michigan univ., U.S.A., 1949–64, he has pub. many studies on Shakespeare and other Elizabethan subjects, incl. *A Companion to Shakespeare* (with Harley Granville-Barker: 1934), and three Elizabethan Journals.

HARRISON, Rex Carey (1908–   ). British actor. Lancashire-born, he had his first big success in *French Without Tears* (1936), and subsequently often appeared in London and New York, notably as Prof. Higgins in the musical *My Fair Lady* (1956). His films incl. *Blithe Spirit* (1944), and the role of Caesar in *Cleopatra* (1962). He was previously m. to actress Lilli Palmer (1943–57) and Kay Kendall (1957 until her d. in 1959), and in 1962 m. Rachel Roberts.

HARRISON, William (1773–1841). 9th Pres. of the U.S.A. B. in Virginia, he entered the army, became gov. of the newly formed Indiana Territory, and was elected Pres. in 1840, but d. a month after taking office. His grandson, **Benjamin H.** (1833–1901), a Republican, served as 23rd Pres. of the U.S.A. from 1889 to 1893.

HARRISSON, Tom (1911–). British biologist and sociologist. He took part in various scientific expeditions, living for a year among the cannibal mountain tribes of Malekula, New Hebrides, and in 1937 he founded with Charles Madge (1912–) Mass Observation, a statistical study of the British.

HARROGATE. English town (bor.) and spa in the W. Riding of Yorks, 14 m. N. of Leeds. H. is a tourist resort and holiday centre. Pop. (1961) 56,332.

HARROW. Bor. of Greater London, England. The parish church was founded by Lanfranc in the 11th cent. H. school was founded by John Lyon in 1571, and opened in 1611; it became a leading public school during the 18th cent.; among its former scholars are Byron, Sheridan, Peel, Palmerston, and Sir Winston Churchill. Pop. (1967) 208,200.

HARSCH, Joseph Close (1905–). American journalist. He worked with the N.B.C. 1953–67, and then became commentator for the American Broadcasting Company. His incisive interpretation of events has also earned him a reputation in Britain, where he received part of his education at Cambridge.

HART, Basil Henry Liddell. *See* LIDDELL-HART.

HART, Judith (1924–). British Labour politician and sociologist. She became M.P. for Lanark 1959, was Min. of Social Security 1967–8, Paymaster-General with Cabinet rank 1968–9, her assignment incl. decentralization of govt., and Min. of Overseas Development 1969–70.

HARTE, Francis Bret (1839–1902). American author. B. in Albany, N.Y., he became a gold-miner in California at the age of 18. While secretary of the California Mint (1864–70) he founded the *Overland Monthly* (1868), in which he pub. short stories of the pioneer West, e.g. 'The Luck of Roaring Camp', and poems, e.g. the 'Heathen Chinee'. In 1878 he entered the consular service, and after his retirement in 1885 settled in England, where he d.

HARTEBEEST. Name given to various species of African antelope, particularly the Caama (*Bubalis caama*). It is a brownish-red, and about 4 ft. high.

HARTFORD. Capital of Connecticut, U.S.A., on Connecticut r. It is a centre of the insurance business and of various manufactures, e.g. aircraft engines, typewriters and tools. Pop. met. area (1970) 657,104.

HARTLEPOOL (hart'li-). English port (bor.) on the N. side of H. Bay, Durham. The old town, dating from 640, is built on a promontory. H.'s industries include shipbuilding and engineering, and fishing. Pop. (1961) 17,674.

WEST HARTLEPOOL is a seaport (co. bor.) which developed with the development of the Durham coalfield. It lies S.W. of Hartlepool and has shipbuilding yards, paper factories, breweries, etc. Pop. (1961) 77,073. Called the Hartlepools, H. and W. H. together form a bor. constituency.

HARTMANN, Karl Robert Eduard von (1842–1906). German philosopher. His *Philosophy of the Unconscious* (1869) derived its pessimistic idealism from Hegel and Schopenhauer; and in it he maintains that the unconscious, composed of will and reason, is the absolute of existence.

HARTMANN, Nicolai (1882–1950). German philosopher, noted for his *Ethics* (1925) and his exposition of essentially insoluble metaphysical problems, e.g. free will, regarded as implied in any system of morality.

HARTY, Sir Hamilton (1880–1941). Irish conductor and composer. He settled in London in 1900 as an accompanist and, later, as a conductor, becoming conductor to the Hallé Orchestra, Manchester, 1920–33. His works include the tone poem 'With the Wild Geese'; 'Irish Symphony'; and the choral work 'The Mystic Trumpeter' (Whitman).

HARUNAL-RASHID(ha-roon'ahl-rah'shēd)(763–809). Caliph of Baghdad. B. near Teheran, he succeeded his brother in 786, and was a lavish patron of music, poetry, and letters.

HARVARD. Senior univ. and oldest educational institution in the U.S.A., founded in 1636 at New Towne (later Cambridge), Mass., and named after John Harvard (1607–38), who bequeathed half his estate (valued at £799 17s. 2d.) and his library to it.

HARVEST-BUG or **Harvest-mite.** Scarlet or rusty brown mites belonging to the Trombidiidae family of the Acari order of the Arachnida. Common in summer and autumn, they are parasitic, and their bites are intensely irritating to humans.

HARVESTMEN. An order (Opiliones) of the Arachnida; found in late summer and early autumn, they may be distinguished from true spiders by the absence of a waist or constriction in the oval body. They are carnivorous, and are found from the Arctic to the tropics; the long-legged H. (*Phalangium*) is often found in Britain.

HARVEY, William (1578–1657). English physician who discovered the circulation of blood. In 1609 he became physician to St. Bartholomew's hospital in London, and in 1615 lecturer at the College of Physicians. His theory of circulation was pub. in 1628. He was physician to James I and Charles I, and was in attendance on the latter at the battle of Edgehill.

HARWELL. Main research establishment of the United Kingdom Atomic Energy Authority (q.v.), close to the village of H. in Berkshire, after which it is often called. It has many reactors, chemical and metallurgical laboratories, workshops and the reactor school. The main objectives are basic research, provision of technological information to produce isotopes, and investigation of the possibilities of nuclear energy as a source of power.

HARWICH (ha'rij). English seaport (bor.) on the Essex coast, occupying a peninsula at the E. end of the Stour and Orwell estuary. Ferry services run to ports in the Netherlands, Belgium, and Denmark. Pop. (1961) 13,569.

HASDRUBAL (d. 207 B.C.). Carthaginian general, the brother of Hannibal (q.v.). He remained in command in Spain in 218 when Hannibal invaded Italy, and, after fighting there against the Scipios until 208, marched to Hannibal's relief. He was defeated and killed on the Metaurus.

HAŠEK (ha'sek), **Jaroslav** (1883–1923). Czech writer. B. in Prague, he became a bank clerk, and in 1909 the facetious editor of the entirely serious journal *The Animal World*. In 1915 he was called up, deserted to the Russians at the battle of Chorupan, later fighting in the Czech legion and eventually joining the Bolsheviks. His comic masterpiece is the unfinished *The Good Soldier Schweik*, based on his earlier experiences, which was condemned by authority as detrimental to discipline.

HASHISH. *See* HEMP.

HASKELL, Arnold Lionel (1903–). British balletomane, joint founder in 1930 with Philip Richardson of the Camargo Society. His books incl. *Ballet*.

HASLEMERE. English town (U.D.) in Surrey, between Blackdown (918 ft.) and Hindhead (854 ft.), two barren heaths. The Dolmetsch family, musicians and instrument-makers, estab. their workshops at H. and have held an annual music festival from 1925. Pop. (1961) 12,528.

HASSALL, John (1868–1948). British artist. B. at Deal, he farmed in Manitoba, studied art at Antwerp and Paris, and in London became the 'king of poster artists', e.g. the 'So bracing' poster of Skegness. The author **Christopher V. H.** (1912–63) and **Joan H.** (1906–), the wood engraver, are his son and dau.

HASSAN II (1930–). King of Morocco, 17th

WARREN HASTINGS. By Tilly Kettle. *Photo: N.P.G.*

monarch of the Alouite dynasty. He personally suppressed the Rif revolt of 1958–9 and directed rescue operations in the Agadir earthquake 1960, and succeeded to the throne on the death of his father Mohammed V in 1961, also taking over the premiership. In 1962 he introduced his country's first constitution and in 1965 became P.M.

HASTINGS, Francis Rawdon-Hastings, 1st marquess of (1754–1826). British soldier and statesman. He was Gov.-Gen. of Bengal 1813–21, and received in 1816 his marquisate for his successful war against the Gurkhas of Nepal. By his victory in 1817–18 over the Mahrattas he estab. British supremacy in C. India, and secured Singapore in 1819.

HASTINGS, James (1852–1922). Scottish biblical scholar. A minister of the Scottish Free Church 1884–1911, he compiled a *Dictionary of the Bible* (1898–1904), *Encyclopaedia of Religion and Ethics* (1908–22), etc.

HASTINGS, Sir Patrick (1880–1952). British barrister. Becoming a K.C. in 1919, he appeared in the Vaquier (1924) and Rouse (1931) trials and was knighted in 1924. A Labour M.P. 1922–6, he was Attorney-General in the first Labour govt., and achieved success as a playwright with *The Blind Goddess* (1947).

HASTINGS, Warren (1732–1818). British administrator. B. in Oxon, he went to India in 1750 as a clerk in the E. India Co.'s service. His services during the war in Bengal attracted Clive's attention, and in 1761 he was promoted to the council at Calcutta. After leave in England 1764–9 he received an appointment at Madras, and in 1772 was appointed Gov. of Bengal; this title was exchanged in 1774 for that of Gov.-Gen. of India. His aggressive war against the Rohillas, and the hanging of a Brahman who had accused H. of forgery, aroused a strong opposition against him. When in 1780 the Indian empire was threatened by the French and their ally Hyder Ali of Mysore, H. saved the situation by prompt action. He resigned and returned to England in 1785. He was impeached in 1788 for corruption and cruelty, but acquitted in 1795. His remaining years were spent at his seat at Daylesford, Worcs.

HASTINGS. English holiday resort (co. bor.) and one of the Cinque Ports, in Sussex. The battle of H. on 14 October 1066 took place on the hill of Senlac, 6 m. inland. Ruins of the Norman castle stand on the West Cliff. St. Leonards, formerly a separate resort, is within the bor. of H. It is scheduled for major redevelopment. Pop. (1961) 66,346.

HATAY (hat'ī). Turkish il on the E. Mediterranean coast. Its cap. is Antioch, chief port Iskenderun (q.v.). It was included in French-mandated Syria in 1919,

made an autonomous sanjak in 1937, restored to Turkey 1939. Area 2,200 sq. m.; pop. (1965) 482,936.

HATFIELD. Town in Herts, England, 5 m. E. of St. Albans, formerly Bishop's H., after a palace for the bishops of Ely erected there in the 12th cent. This residence passed to the Crown in 1538, and was given to Robert Cecil, earl of Salisbury, in exchange for Theobalds in 1607. The present mansion, seat of the marquess of Salisbury, but partly a museum and art gallery, was completed in 1611, and is a fine specimen of Jacobean architecture. The Coll. of Technology became a polytechnic (q.v.) in 1969. Pop. (1961) 20,504.

HATHAWAY, Ann (1556–1623). Englishwoman, dau. of a yeoman farmer, who m. Shakespeare in 1582. Her cottage at Shottery was bought and restored by the trustees of Shakespeare's birthplace in 1892.

HATHOR. Sky goddess worshipped in ancient Egypt. On her head she usually wears a cow's horns with the solar disc.

HATTERAS. U.S. cape on the Atlantic coast, N. Carolina, site of many shipwrecks. H. Inlet is a noted fishing ground.

HAUPTMANN (howpt'mahn), **Gerhart** (1862–1946). German dramatist and novelist. B. in Silesia, he turned from sculpture to literature, and in 1889 pub. the first of his naturalistic dramas, *Vor Sonnenaufgang*; the greatest and most powerful of the works that followed is *Die Weber* (1892). His comedy, *Der Biberpelz* (1893), has retained its place on the German stage. Subsequently H. turned to historical, mystical and allegorical, and legendary subjects, and besides many more plays wrote the novels *Der Narr in Christo Emanuel Quint* (1910), *Atlantis* (1912), and *Der Ketzer von Soana* (1918), and an epic poem *Till Eulenspiegel* (1927). Later he treated autobiographical themes (*Die Finsternisse*, 1937), and themes of classical antiquity. He was awarded a Nobel Prize in 1912.

HAUSA (how'saz). Mohammedan Negro people of W. Africa, chiefly inhabiting N. Nigeria. The H. language is accepted as a *lingua franca* over much of W. Africa; it is assigned to the Hamitic family.

HAUSHOFER (hows'höfer), **Karl** (1869–1946). German originator of the science of geopolitics. B. in Munich, he became a major-gen. in the Bavarian Army, and from 1921 was prof. of geography at Munich, providing Nazi ideology with the theory of *Lebensraum* (living space). He committed suicide.

HAUSSMANN (ōsmahn'), **Georges Eugène**, baron (1809–91). French administrator, chiefly famous for his re-planning of Paris. He became a prefect of the Seine in 1853, and widened streets, laid out boulevards and parks, and improved the water supply.

HAUTES-ALPES. Dept. of FRANCE.

HAVANA. Capital, commercial centre, and chief port of Cuba, situated on the N. coast of the island,

HAVANA. In the 17th century the Spanish gold fleets made their rendezvous here, but in the lay-out of the magnificent modern city it is the influence of the U.S.A. which is predominant in its planning. *Courtesy of the Cuban Embassy.*

HAWAII. Waikiki beach with Diamond Head in the background. *Pan American photograph.*

occupying a peninsula W. of the excellent harbour. Ancient buildings incl. the palace of the Spanish governors, and the stronghold of La Fuerza (1583). H. was founded on the S. coast in 1515, transferred to present site 1519. The Univ. of H. was founded in 1728. In 1898 the blowing up of the U.S. battleship *Maine* in the harbour precipitated the Spanish-American war. Chief manufactures are cigars and tobacco. Pop. (1960) 787,765.

HA'VANT. English town of pre-Roman origin in Hants, 1 m. N. of Hayling Is. With Waterloo it forms an U.D. Pop. (1961) 74,564.

HA'VELOCK, Sir Henry (1795–1857). British soldier. He saw service in Burma 1824–6 and in the Afghan War of 1839. On the outbreak of the Indian Mutiny in 1857 he was engaged in Persia, but returning to India he retook Cawnpore and relieved Lucknow, but d. of dysentery soon after.

HAVERFORDWEST. Co. town (bor.) of Pembroke, 7 m. N.N.E. of Milford Haven, Wales, founded by Flemings in the 12th cent. Pop. (1961) 8,872.

HAVERGAL, Frances Ridley (1836–79). British hymn-writer. B. in Worcs, dau. of the composer the Rev. William Henry H. (1793–1870). She pub. *Ministry of Song* (1870) and many other vols.

HAVRE (ahvr), **Le.** French port on the N. bank of the Seine estuary in the dept. of Seine-Maritime. During the S.W.W. it was taken by the Germans 14 June 1940; retaken by the Allies 12 Sept. 1944. By 1957 it had been reconstructed. Noted for its docks and shipbuilding yards, H. has regular sea communications with British ports. Pop. (1968) 199,509.

HAWAII (hawī-i). 50th state of the U.S.A. It consists of a chain of islands in the N. Pacific of which the chief are H., Maui, Oahu, Kauai, Molokai, Lanai, Niihau, and Kahoolawa. They are volcanic, and H. itself contains Mauna Kea (13,784 ft.), one of the world's highest island mountains, and Mauna Loa (13,680 ft.), the world's largest active crater. Lake Waiau on Mauna Kea is the highest lake in the U.S.A. (13,020 ft.), and Ka Lae (South Cape) on H. is the southernmost point of the U.S.A. In Oahu are the cap., Honolulu, and the naval base Pearl Harbor, the Japanese attack on which, 7 Dec. 1941, brought the U.S.A. into the S.W.W. The climate is tropical and the flora rich and varied. The chief products are sugar and pineapples. The chief industry is tourism, but fishing, handicrafts, etc., are carried on.

Capt. Cook landed in the islands (which he named Sandwich Islands) in 1778, but navigators from Europe are thought to have visited them in the 16th cent. The original population, estimated at 300,000 in 1778, was Polynesian; the number of people with aboriginal blood was about 105,000 in 1960, including those (the majority) of only partly Hawaiian ancestry. After 1852 immigration was encouraged, and the population is now heterogeneous, Japanese blood predominating. H. was a kingdom until 1893, became a rep. 1894, which ceded itself to the U.S.A. in 1898 and was admitted to the Union in 1959. Area 6,439 sq. m.; pop. (1970) 769,913.

HAWARDEN (har'den). Town 6 m. W.S.W. o Chester, on a tributary of the Dee, Flintshire, N. Wales. For many years H. Castle (1752) was the home of W. E. Gladstone. St. Deiniol's theological library, founded by Gladstone, is at H. Pop. (est.) 8,000.

HAWFINCH (*Coccothraustes coccothraustes*). Bird of the family Fringillidae of the order Passeriformes. Its plumage is brown and grey with a steel-blue patch on the wing and a white-tipped tail. It is found throughout central and S. Europe and Asia Minor, and in Britain.

HAW-HAW, Lord. *See* JOYCE, WILLIAM.

HAWICK. Burgh in Roxburgh, Scotland, on the r. Teviot, 10 m. S.W. of Jedburgh. It makes woollens. Pop. (1961) 16,204.

HAWK. Name of various birds of prey in the family Falconidae, excluding eagles and vultures. They have an untoothed bill and short wings.

HAWKE, Edward, 1st baron (1705–81). British admiral. In 1759 he destroyed in Quiberon Bay the French fleet which had been intended to cover an invasion of Britain. He was 1st Lord of the Admiralty 1766–71, and in 1776 was created a baron.

HAWKER, Robert Stephen (1803–75). British poet. B. in Devon, he became vicar of Morwenstow, Cornwall, in 1834, and introduced the harvest festival now generally adopted. His *Cornish Ballads* (1869) contains the 'Song of the Western Men'.

HAWKES, Jacquetta (1910–). British author. Dau. of Sir F. G. Hopkins (q.v.), she m. in 1933 Prof. Christopher H., with whom she collaborated in *Prehistoric Britain* (1944), and is a keen anthropologist and archaeologist. Following the dissolution of this marriage, she became the wife of J. B. Priestley (q.v.) in 1953, with whom she has also collaborated.

HAWKINS, Sir Anthony Hope. *See* HOPE, A.

HAWKINS, Henry, baron Brampton (1817–1907).

HAWK. At rest, but still alert, a pair of N. American redtailed hawks (*Buteo borealis*), so known because of their rich-brown unbarred tails, visible even at a great distance as they wheel in flight. *Photo: G. Ronald Austing.*

British lawyer. He became a barrister in 1843, a judge of the Queen's Bench Division in 1876, and in the same year was knighted. He appeared for the defence against Arthur Orton (q.v.).

HAWKINS, Jack (1910-). British actor-producer. A student of Italia Conti, he estab. a reputation in courageous, masculine, 'British' roles e.g. the film *The Cruel Sea*: later films incl. *Ben Hur* and *Lawrence of Arabia* (1962).

HAWKINS, Sir John (1532–95). English navigator. B. in Plymouth, he made 2 successful voyages to the Guinea coast, but a 3rd in 1567, in which he was accompanied by his cousin Francis Drake, ended in the almost complete destruction of his fleet. In 1573 he became treasurer (later comptroller) of the navy, and in 1588 was knighted for his services against the Armada. He d. while on an expedition to the W. Indies.

HAWKINS, Sir Richard (c. 1562–1622). English navigator. The son of Sir John H., he sailed to the W. Indies with his uncle, William H., in 1582, and in 1588 was given a command against the Armada. In 1593 he set out on an expedition against Spanish possessions, was captured in 1594, and not released until 1602. In 1603 he was knighted, and in 1604 became M.P. for Plymouth and vice-admiral of Devon.

HAWK-MOTH. Family of moths (Sphingidae) incl. some 1,000 species distributed throughout the world, but mainly tropical. The death's head H. (q.v.) is the largest of British moths; and the eyed H. (*Smerinthus ocellatus*), with a purplish spot on the hind wings, is another British species. The European pine H. (*Sphinx pinastri*) has larvae which may devastate Continental forests. Some S. American Hs. closely resemble humming birds and the humming bird H. (*Macroglossa stellatarum*) is found in southern England.

HAWKSMOOR, Nicholas (1661–1736). English architect. He entered Wren's office at 18, and assisted him at the City churches, Greenwich Hospital and St. Paul's. Later he was joint architect with Vanbrugh of Castle Howard and Blenheim. Until recently the originality of his work has been undervalued, but in 1962 the **H. Society** was founded to promote its study. His dramatic style can be seen in our illus. of Christchurch, Spitalfields, London, built 1723–9.

Courtesy of the Warburg Institute.

HAWORTH (how'orth), **Sir Walter Norman** (1883–1950). British chemist. He was Director of Chemistry at Birmingham univ. (1925–48). His success in synthesizing Vitamin C. gained him a Nobel prize in 1937.

HAWORTH. Small English town in Yorkshire (W.R.), 4 m. S. of Keighley of which it forms part. The parsonage that was the home of the Brontës is a museum. Pop. (est.) 6,000.

HAWTHORN. Common name for shrubs and trees of the *Crataegus* genus, of the Rosaceae family. The common H., may or whitethorn (*C. oxyacantha*), a thorny shrub or small tree growing 10–12 ft. in height, bears clusters of white or pink flowers followed by groups of red berries. It is indigenous to Britain and much of Europe, N. Africa and W. Asia, and has been naturalized in N. America and Australia.

HAWTHORNE, Nathaniel (1804–64). American author. B. at Salem, Mass., he was strongly impressed in boyhood with the Puritan tradition of the area. His early attempts at writing stories and sketches were

HAWTHORN

financially unrewarding, but he won immediate success with *The Scarlet Letter* (1850), a story of the retribution overtaking the parents of an illegitimate child, written while working as a customs official (surveyor of the Port of Salem 1846–9). Later were *The House of the Seven Gables* (1851), *The Blithedale Romance* (1852) and such vols. of tales for children as the classic legends of *Tanglewood Tales* (1853).

HAWTREY, Sir Charles (1858–1923). British actor-manager, famous for his comedy role of Douglas Cattermole in *The Private Secretary* (1883).

HAY, Ian. Pseudonym of British novelist and playwright Maj.-Gen. John Hay Beith (1876–1952). He wrote the light comedies *Tilly of Bloomsbury* (1919), *Housemaster* (1936) and *The White Sheep of the Family* (1951: with L. Du Garde Peach); and the non-fiction war book *The First Hundred Thousand* (1915).

HAY, Will (1888–1949). British comedian, celebrated as the incompetent schoolmaster of St. Michael's on music-hall and screen: he was also a notable amateur astronomer.

HAYDN (hīdn), **Franz Joseph** (1732–1809). Austrian composer. B. in Lower Austria, he was Kapellmeister 1761–90 to Prince Esterházy at Eisenstadt and Esterház, where he had ample opportunity to develop his native originality. He visited London in 1791–2 and again 1794–5, and to these visits we owe the 'Surprise', 'Military', 'Clock', 'Drum-roll', 'London', and 'Oxford' symphonies. For the Eng. public also were written the still popular oratorios *The Creation* and *The Seasons*.

H. established the regular symphonic form and the composition of the orchestra which were to be used by Mozart and Beethoven. He was the first great master of the quartet. He wrote operas, church music, pieces for various instruments, and songs, and composed the 'Emperor's Hymn', subsequently adopted as the Ger. national anthem.

HAYDON, Benjamin Robert (1786–1846). British artist. B. at Plymouth, he settled in London and became celebrated for his gigantic canvases, attempts at 'high art', incl. 'Christ's Entry into Jerusalem' (1820, now in Philadelphia). He is now better appreciated in genre pictures, e.g. 'The Mock Election' and 'Chairing the Member'; and for his lively autobiography and journals. Perpetually harassed financially, he shot himself.

NATHANIEL HAWTHORNE by Charles Osgood. *Courtesy of the Essex Institute.*

HAYEK (hī-ek), **Friedrich August von** (1899-). Austrian economist. B. in Vienna, he taught at the L.S.E. 1931–50, becoming a British subject in 1938, and was prof. of social and moral science at the Univ. of Chicago 1950–62. His *The Road to Serfdom* (1944) was a critical study of socialistic trends in Britain.

HAYES, Evelyn. Pseudonym of the New Zealand poet Mary Ursula Bethell (1874–1945). Though b. in England, she went out to N.Z. while still a child and pub. 3 vols. of verse *From a Garden in the Antipodes* (1929) and *Day and Night* (1939).

HAYES, Helen (1900–). American actress. Her stage successes include *Mary of Scotland, Victoria Regina,* and Harriet Beecher Stowe in *Harriet* (1943–5); her films incl. *Farewell to Arms* and *Anastasia.*

HAYES, Rutherford Birchard (1822–93). 19th President of the U.S.A. B. in Ohio, he was a major-general in the Civil War and prominent Republican politician. During his presidency (1877–81), the army of occupation was withdrawn from the southern states and the Civil Service reformed.

HAY-FEVER. An acute watery catarrh produced by pollen, etc., in the specially sensitive. As in asthma, nettle-rash and other allergic diseases, large quantities of fluid are released from the blood at the place where the foreign protein (in this case the pollen) enters. Remedies are detection and avoidance of the offending pollen, antiseptic sprays, zinc ionization, ephedrine, and desensitization by vaccine.

HAZEL. Popular name for shrubs or trees of the *Corylus* genus, Betulaceae family, also called filbert (the official U.S. name) and cobnut. The nuts are enclosed by a husk.

HAZLITT, William (1778–1830). British writer. B. at Maidstone, son of a Unitarian minister, he himself thought of entering the ministry and dabbled in portrait painting, but ultimately settled to writing in which he had been encouraged by Coleridge. Going to London in 1812 he worked for the daily press and magazines, incl. the *Edinburgh Review,* writing from the liberal viewpoint. He was a superb controversialist, with a unique, clear, hard-hitting prose style which served him equally well in his critical essays: *Characters of Shakespeare's Plays* (1817–18), *Lectures on the English Poets* (1818–19), *English Comic Writers* (1819) and *Dramatic Literature of the Age of Elizabeth* (1820). Other notable works are his *Table Talk* (1821–2); *The Spirit of the Age* (1825), perceptive appreciations of his contemporaries; and the curious *Liber Amoris* (1823) record of his infatuation with the dau. of a tailor with whom he lodged. The latter affair was sandwiched between his 2 marriages: 1st to a friend of Mary Lamb in 1808 (divorce 1822) and 2nd to a widow in 1824, who left him on the return from their honeymoon trip to Italy. His invective, scathing irony and gift for epigram were symptomatic of a temperament which, though sincere, was ill-fitted to cope with ordinary people and ordinary life.

HEADACHE. Discomfort in the head. It is due to irritation of different nerves by a variety of possible agents. The cause may be quite trivial; otherwise anxiety causes a more constant headache, migraine, severe periodical one-sided attacks. Other causes are disease of the sinuses, rheumatism, irritation of the brain linings (meninges), injury, tumour of the brain, kidney disease, hardening of the arteries, malaria, gout, diabetes, poisoning by alcohol, lead, etc., eye trouble, heart disease, digestive disorder, etc.

HEALEY, Denis (1917–). British Labour politician. He was sec. of the International Dept. of the Labour Party from 1946 until he entered Parliament in 1952, and 1964–70 succeeded Thorneycroft as Min. for Defence. He was in charge of the reduction of British forces under the policy of concentration on Europe and withdrawal E. of Suez.

HEALTH INSURANCE. *See* INSURANCE.

HEALY, Timothy Michael (1855–1931). Irish nationalist. B. at Bantry, he entered parliament in 1880, and after 1890 became prominent as an opponent of Parnell. He was first Gov. Gen. of the Irish Free State, 1922–7.

HEARD, (Henry Fitz) Gerald (1889–1971). British author. He began his career as a journalist, frequently broadcast 1930–4, and later settled in California. His books incl. *The Social Substance of Religion, Emergence of Man,* and *Science in the Making*; in writings such as *Desert Dialogue* he preached a mystical creed of oriental origin.

HEARD, William Theodore (1884–). British cardinal. Ordained 1918 he worked in Bermondsey, London, 1921–7 when he became auditor of the Sacred Rota (dean 1958) in Rome. In 1959 H. became the first Scottish cardinal for nearly 150 years.

HEARD and McDONALD ISLANDS. Group of is. in the southern Indian Ocean, *c.* 2,500 m. S.W. of Fremantle, discovered 1833, annexed by Britain 1910 and transferred to Australia 1947. Heard Is. (*c.* 26 m. by 12 m.) is glacier-covered, although the volcanic mtn. Big Ben (9,000 ft.) is still active: there is a weather station (1947). Shag Is. is 5 m. to the N. and the craggy McDonalds are 26 m. to the W.

HEARING AIDS AND CORRECTORS (Electrical). Devices for increasing the sound pressure over that normally received by the ear. They consist of a complete reproducing system of microphone, amplifier and loudspeaker. With the development of transistors, miniature components, and batteries, these can now be made very small and cordless. They may be worn in the ear, under the hair or incorporated in spectacles, hairslides, earrings, etc. There are 2 main types, in which either the receiver fits directly into the outer cavity of the ear and actuates the ear-drum by air conduction, or it fits behind the ear and transmits sound vibrations through the mastoid bone.

HEARN, Lafcadio (1850–1904). British-Japanese writer. Son of an Irish regimental surgeon and a Greek, he was b. in the Ionian Is. After working in the U.S. as a newspaperman, he settled in Japan, lectured at the Imperial Univ., Tokyo, 1896–1903, m. a Japanese and became a Japanese subject. He pub. *Glimpses of Unfamiliar Japan* (1904).

HEARST, William Randolph (1863–1951). American newspaper proprietor, celebrated for his introduction of banner headlines, lavish illustration, and the sensational approach known as 'yellow journalism'. A campaigner in numerous controversies, and a strong isolationist, he is the reputed original of *Citizen Kane* (*see* WELLES, ORSON). He collected art treasures, antiques, and castles – one of which, San Simeon in California, is a state museum.

EDWARD HEATH
Photo: Vivienne

HEART. The muscular organ which supplies blood to all parts of the body. Hollow and pear-shaped, it contains two pairs of chambers divided by a vertical muscular wall. The upper pair, the auricles, are smaller and communicate through valves with the lower and larger pair, the ventricles. When the heart beats its muscle contracts strongly (systole) and the following actions occur. The auricles feed blood to the ventricles, which contract an instant later, and the left ventricle pumps blood into the aorta – the main artery through which the whole of the body except the lungs is supplied. The heart muscle itself is supplied with blood through the coronary arteries, leading from the aorta. Valves prevent the blood from returning after the impulse. At the same time the right ventricle pumps used blood to the lungs through the pulmonary artery to be aerated. After the heart's contraction it dilates (diastole) and refills, used blood from the veins entering the right auricle and aerated blood from the lungs entering the left auricle. The timing of the heart's beat is regulated by its own local nervous system. Heart disease is due chiefly to disease or overwork of its muscle, defects of its valves, or disorder of its nervous system.

The first transplant of a human H. was carried out 3rd Dec. 1967 at Groote Schuur Hospital, Cape Town, by Christiaan N. Barnard, when Louis Washkansky received the H. of a woman, but d. 18 days later of pneumonia.

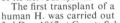

HEART. A, vena cava; B, aorta; C, pulmonary artery; D, pulmonary vein; E, right auricle; F, left auricle; G, right ventricle; H, left ventricle.

HEARTBURN. Irritation of the gullet by excessively acid stomach contents. The acid may be the hydrochloric acid which is a normal part of the digestive fluid, but present in excess. This is often associated with duodenal ulcer, and the pain is worst when the stomach is empty, and is relieved by eating. The acid may, on the other hand, be one of the organic acids produced by fermentation when the hydrochloric acid is deficient, e.g. lactic, acetic, and butyric acids. This is common in pregnancy.

HEAT. A form of energy which by its addition to or abstraction from a body causes a rise or fall in its temperature. It always tends to flow from a region of higher temperature to one of lower temperature. The effect of heat on a substance may be simply to raise its temperature, to cause it to expand, to melt it if it is a solid, to vaporize it if it is liquid, or to increase its pressure if it is a gas.

The quantity of heat is measured by the extent to which it will raise the temperature of a standard substance. See BRITISH THERMAL UNIT.

The name *specific heat* is given to the ratio between the heat required to raise the temperature of a given mass of a substance through a given range of temperature, to the heat required to raise the temperature of an equal mass of water through the same range. For example, the specific heat of copper is 0·095, i.e. it requires 0·095 Btu to heat 1 lb. of copper through 1 deg F. The *mechanical equivalent of heat* is the ratio of the amount of work done to the quantity of heat produced.

There are three ways by which heat may be transferred from one place to another, viz. (a) *convection* – transmission through a fluid or a gas by currents, as when the air in a room is warmed by a fire or radiator, or the water is heated in a domestic hot-water system; (b) *conduction* – when the heat passes from one part of a medium to neighbouring parts with no visible motion of the medium accompanying the transfer of heat, as when the whole length of a metal rod is heated when one end is held in a fire; (c) *radiation*. Radiant heat is of the same nature as light. It can pass through a vacuum, travels at the same speed as light, can be reflected and refracted, and does not affect the medium through which it passes.

HEATH, Edward Richard George (1916–). British Cons. politician. In the Administrative Civil Service 1946–7, he entered parliament in 1950, becoming Parl. Sec. to the Treasury and Govt. Chief Whip (1955–9), Min. of Labour (1959–60) and, as Lord Privy Seal (1960–3), was responsible for the negotiations concerning Britain's projected membership of the E.E.C., winning the Charlemagne prize in 1963. He was Sec. for Industry, Trade and Regional Development, and Pres. of the Board of Trade 1963–4, and succeeded Home as Cons. leader 1965, the first elected leader of his party. Defeated in 1966, he achieved a surprise victory in 1970, with an overall majority of 30.

HEATH and HEATHER. Popular names for plants of the *Erica* genus, Ericaceae family; also used for the common ling (*Calluna vulgaris*). In Britain the most common species is the bell heather, *E. cinerea*.

HEATHROW (hēth'rō). Location in the Greater London bor. of Hounslow, England, site of Heathrow Airport, London, opened 1946.

HEAT-STROKE. An acute seizure resulting from paralysis of the heat-regulating mechanism. The most usual cause is hard work in a hot, wet, still atmosphere. Drinkers and sufferers from malaria and other fevers are especially liable. The patient feels ill with headache, weakness and giddiness, and falls unconscious. The skin feels hot and very dry, and the temp. may rise to 112°F (44·4°C). Life may be saved by prompt spraying with cold water in a cool draught, blood-letting, saline injections, and heart stimulants.

HEAVEN. In the theology of Christianity and most of the other world religions, the place of the blessed in the next world. Many attempts have been made, particularly by Christian and Moslem writers, to describe its joys, but modern theologians usually prefer to describe it as a place or state in which the soul sees God as He really is – enjoys the Beatific vision.

HEAVISIDE, Oliver (1850–1925). British physicist. His theoretical studies of electricity pub. in *Electrical Papers* (1892) had considerable influence on long-distance telephony. In 1902 he predicted the existence of an ionized layer of air in the upper atmosphere which was verified by Kennelly (q.v.) and was later known as the Kennelly-H. or H. layer but is now called the E layer. Deflection from it makes possible the transmission of radio signals round the world, which would otherwise be lost in outer space, and its presence is connected with the phenomenon of radio fading. See IONOSPHERE.

HEAVY WATER. Deuterium oxide (D_2O), i.e. water containing deuterium (q.v.) instead of hydrogen (mol. wt. 20 against 18 for ordinary water). Its chemical properties are identical with those of ordinary water, its physical properties differ slightly, density at 25°C, 1·1056; m.p. 3·8°C; b.p. 101·42°C; temperature of maximum density 11·6°C. It occurs in ordinary water in the ratio of about one part by weight of deuterium to 5,000 parts by weight of ordinary hydrogen and can be concentrated by electrolysis, the ordinary water being more readily decomposed by this means than the H.W.

HE'BE. In Greek mythology, the goddess of youth, dau. of Zeus and Hera, and handmaiden of the gods.

HEBER, Reginald (1783–1826). British churchman and hymn writer. He took orders in the C. of E. in 1807, and in 1823 became bp. of Calcutta. Most famous of his hymns is 'From Greenland's Icy Mountains'.

HEBREW. The language of the O.T.; a branch of the Semitic languages, and closely related to Aramaic. By the 1st cent. A.D. it had become the language of the schools, being supplanted by Aramaic as the language of the people. The majority of the roots are triconsonantal, and the modifications of the sense are effected by changing the vowels, or adding prefixes or affixes. The script, written from right to left, originally represented only the consonants; in the 7th and 8th cents. systems of vocalization by means of adding points and strokes were devised.

HEBRIDES. The scattered houses of Digg Village in the north of the Isle of Skye. In the background is Quiraing, rising to 1,779 ft. *Photo: George Outram & Co. Ltd.*

During the 18th and 19th cents. an improved Hebrew, based on classical models, was evolved and adapted to a mod. literature of Jewry. The rise of Zionism gave it great impetus, and it is the nat. language of Israel.

HE′BRIDES. Group of over 500 islands off the W. coast of Scotland. They are divided into the *Inner H.*, including Skye, Mull, Jura, and Islay, and the *Outer H.* (separated from Inner H. by the Little Minch) incl. Lewis-with-Harris and N. and S. Uist. They are administratively divided between the cos. of Inverness, Argyll, and Ross and Cromarty. Fewer than 100 of the H. are inhabited. The principal industries are cattle and sheep raising, distilling, and the production of Harris Tweed. Measures to stem depopulation incl. a fisheries scheme for Lewis-with-Harris, and the estab. of the main site for testing British guided missiles at Geirnish on S. Uist. The H. were settled by Scandinavians in the 6th–9th cents., and passed under Norwegian rule from *c.* 890 till 1266. Area *c.* 2,800 sq. m. Pop. (1961) 48,113.

HE′BRON. City of Jordan, 20 m. S.S.W. of Jerusalem. The traditional sites of the tombs of Abraham, Isaac, Jacob, and their wives are shown within the mosque. Pop. (1966) 43,000.

HEB-SED. Festival celebrated by the kings of ancient Egypt, apparently commemorating Menes' union of Upper and Lower Egypt.

HE′CATE. Greek goddess of witchcraft and magic, sometimes identified with Artemis and the moon.

HE′CTARE. Unit of area in the metric system (Gk. *hekaton* 100) equalling 100 ares or 10,000 sq. metres or 2·471 acres. Trafalgar Square was laid out as one H., the only square in London conforming to metric.

HECTOR. Legendary Trojan prince, the son of Priam, who during the siege of Troy was the foremost warrior on the Trojan side until he was killed by Achilles.

HE′CUBA. Legendary Trojan queen, the wife of Priam and mother of Hector and Paris. After the fall of Troy she was carried off by the Greeks.

HEDGEHOG. Mammal (*Erinaceus europaeus*) common in Europe, western Asia, Africa, and India. The body is about 10 in. long and the tail 1½ in. It is speckled-brown in colour, has a pig-like snout, and is covered with sharp spines. When alarmed it can roll the body into a ball.

HEDGE SPARROW. European bird (*Prunella modularis*) similar in size and colouring to the sparrow, but with slate-grey head and breast, and more slender bill. It nests in bushes and hedges.

HEDIN (hedēn′), **Sven Anders** (1865–1952). Swedish explorer. B. in Stockholm, he travelled through Persia and Mesopotamia in 1885-6, and conducted three expeditions during 1893–1908 to Central Asia and Tibet, during which he explored the sources of the Brahmaputra and Sutlej and made many valuable geographical and geological discoveries. His books incl. *Through Asia* (1898); *Transhimalaya* (1909-12); and *Southern Tibet* (1917–22).

HE′DONISM (Gk. *hēdonē*, pleasure). The ethical theory that pleasure or happiness is, or should be, the chief end of life. Hedonist sects in Greece were the Cyrenaics, who held that the sentient pleasure of the moment is man's only good, and the Epicureans, who advocated the pursuit of pleasure under the direction of reason. Modern hedonistic philosophies, such as those of Bentham and Mill, regard the happiness of society as the aim, and not that of the single individual.

HEEM (hām), **Jan Davidsz van** (1600–83/4). Dutch painter. He worked in Utrecht, his birthplace, and at Leyden, where he was influenced by Rembrandt. He was a master of still-life, and formed its tradition. His son Cornelius (fl. 1658–71) was a flower painter.

HEE′NAN, John Carmel (1905–). R.C. abp. of Westminster. B. at Ilford, Essex, he was ordained in 1930 and spent 17 years in London's East End, becoming superior of the Catholic Missionary Soc. in 1947. He became bishop of Leeds in 1951 and succeeded Godfrey as abp. of Liverpool (1957) and Westminster (1963). Created cardinal 1965.

HEGEL (heh′gel), **Georg Wilhelm Friedrich** (1770–1831). German philosopher. B. at Stuttgart, he lectured at Jena and Nuremberg, and was prof. of philosophy at Heidelberg 1817–18, and at Berlin 1818–31. His writings incl. *The Phenomenology of Spirit*, *Logic*, *Encyclopaedia of the Philosophical Sciences* (1817), and *Philosophy of Right*. His German disciples split into 'Right Hegelians', who like H. himself championed religion, the Prussian State and the existing order, and 'Left Hegelians', among them Marx, who used **H.**'s dialectic to show the inevitability of radical change and criticized both religion and society.

H. conceived of consciousness and the external object as forming a unity, in which neither factor can exist independently. Mind and nature are two abstractions of one indivisible whole. Thus the world is the unfolding and expression of one all-embracing absolute idea, an organism constantly developing by its own internal necessity so as to become the gradual embodiment of reason. The laws of thinking are in principle the laws of reality, e.g. logic must reflect the contradictions within nature, whereby everything not only is something, but is striving to become something else. The whole of history is realization of the Absolute through phases of culture, each of which is embodied in a great nation. Each system by its own development brings about its opposite (antithesis), and finally a higher synthesis unifies and embodies both.

HE′GIRA or **HEJIRA** (Arabic, 'flight'). Name given to the Mohammedan era. The word denotes the escape of Mohammed from Mecca to Medina on 16 July, A.D. 622, the date when the era begins. The Mohammedan year is indicated by the letters A.H. *anno hegirae* (Latin, in the year of the H.).

HEIDEGGER (hī′deger), **Martin** (1889–). German philosopher. A student of Husserl, he pub. his influential *Sein und Zeit* (*Being and Time*) in 1927, but his arguments tend to be illogical. Often regarded as the chief exponent of existentialism, he denies ever having been an existentialist.

HEIDELBERG (hid′el-). W. German town on the

S. bank of the Neckar, 12 m. S.E. of Mannheim. H. univ., the oldest in Germany, was estab. in 1386. The town is overlooked by its ruined castle, built in the 13th–17th cents., 330 ft. above the river. Pop. (1960 est.) 127,595.

HEIFETZ (hī'fets), **Jascha** (1901–   ). Violinist. B. at Vilna, he first performed at the age of 5, and before he was 17 had played in most European capitals, and in America, where he settled.

HEILBRONN (hīl-). W. German town on the r. Neckar, in Baden-Württemberg. Pop. (est.) 66,000.

HEILUNGKIANG (hīloongkēang). Most northerly Chinese prov. which takes its name from the Amur r. (in Chinese Heilungkiang, black dragon r.) on its N. border. Wheat, oats, soya beans, sugar beet, flax are grown; gold and coal mined; there is also a lumber industry. Harbin is the cap. Area 179,000 sq. m.; pop. (1968) 21,000,000.

HEINE (hi'ne), **Heinrich** (1797–1856). German poet. N. at Düsseldorf, of Jewish parents, he pub. his

HEIDELBERG. Built round a central courtyard – seen here – the residence of the Prince-Electors, 13th–17th cents., is a mixture of Gothic, Renaissance (the Ottheinrich building on the left) and Baroque architecture. Partially destroyed by the French in 1689, it was finally reduced to a ruin by lightning in 1768, but has since been partly restored. A great wine-cask in the cellars holds 58,118 gallons.
Courtesy of the German Tourist Information Bureau.

first book of poems in 1821. His *Reisebilder*, which announced his revolutionary sympathies, appeared in 1826, and the *Buch der Lieder* in 1827. After 1831 he lived mainly in Paris, as a correspondent for German papers, but the publication of his writings was forbidden on political grounds in 1835. Later poems include the satire *Atta Troll* (1847), and *Romanzero* (1851). From 1848 he was confined to his bed by spinal paralysis. Much of his prose is topical journalism, but displays his characteristic gifts of fancy, irony, and satirical humour.·

HEINKEL (hīn'kel), **Ernst** (1888–1958). German aircraft designer. He founded his firm in 1922, and was credited with the first aircraft catapult and the first jet aircraft 1939 (developed independently of the Whittle jet of 1941). During the S.W.W. he was Germany's biggest producer of warplanes.

HEISENBERG (hī'sen-), **Werner Carl** (1901–   ). German physicist. B. at Würzburg, he was director of the Max-Planck Institute for Physics at Göttingen 1946–58 and at Munich from 1958. The originator of quantum mechanics and of the principle of indeterminacy in physics, he was awarded a Nobel prize in 1932. In 1958, in conjunction with W. Pauli of Zürich, he announced a theory which helps to resolve the contradictions hindering understanding of the atomic particles discovered since the S.W.W., and leads towards the discovery of a single natural law accounting for the existence of all known particles as well as those which may yet be discovered. The theory is expressed in the formula:

$$\gamma_r \frac{\partial}{\partial x_v} \psi + l^2 \gamma_\mu \gamma_5 \psi \left(\psi^+ \gamma_\mu \gamma_5 \psi\right) = 0$$

HEJAZ (hejahz'). Part of Saudi Arabia, lying along the shores of the Red Sea. It consists of a coastal plain rising sharply to a line of mountains parallel to the coast, and in the E. a desert plateau. Where water is available for irrigation wheat, barley, fruit, and date palms flourish. The chief towns are the holy cities of Mecca (the cap.) and Medina, and the port of Jedda. The desert areas are inhabited by wandering Bedouin. H. was under Turkish rule from 1517 until 1916, when Hussein revolted and made himself king of H. He was forced to abdicate in 1924 by Ibn Saud, sultan of Nejd, who in 1925 proclaimed himself king of H., and in 1932 changed the name of his united dominions to the kingdom of Saudi Arabia. Area *c.* 150,000 sq. m.; pop. *c.* 2,000,000.

HEL or **HELA**. Norse goddess of the underworld.

HELEN. In Greek mythology the dau. of Zeus and Leda, and the most beautiful of women. She m. Menelaus, king of Sparta, but during his absence eloped with Paris, prince of Troy, whereupon the Greek princes sent their expedition against Troy to recover her. After the Trojan war H. returned to Sparta with Menelaus.

HELENA, St. (*c.* 247–327). Mother of the emperor Constantine the Great, and according to legend the discoverer at Jerusalem of the True Cross of Christ.

HELENSBURGH (hel'enzburu). Scottish seaside resort (burgh) in Dunbartonshire on the N. shore of the Firth of Clyde, 7 m. N.W. of Dumbarton. Pop. (1961) 9,605.

HELICOPTER. An aircraft with one or more power-driven horizontal rotors that enable it to take off and land vertically, to move in any direction or to remain stationary in the air. If power fails during flight the rotor will continue to turn freely, if disengaged from the engine, providing lift as the H. descends, so permitting a safe emergency landing. Hs. are useful for lifesaving during floods, medical evacuation, communications, firefighting, etc.

HELIGOLAND. Small island in the North Sea off the mouth of the Elbe. It was taken from the Danes in 1807 by the British, who ceded it to Germany in 1890.

HELICOPTER. Its manœuvrability fits the helicopter for myriad tasks from sea rescue to crop spraying. Here one is being used to control potato blight in Shropshire, since the chemical solution can be applied more evenly and speedily in this way than by any other method.
Courtesy of Fisons Pest Control Ltd.

The Germans strongly fortified it, and used it as a naval base in both world wars. The fortifications were destroyed in 1947. Area 150 acres; pop. (est.) 3,000.

HELIOʹPŌLIS. Chief centre of the worship of the sun-god Ra in ancient Egypt, near the modern village of Matariah, *c*. 6 m. N.E. of Cairo: it appears in the Bible as On.

HĒʹLIOS. The Greek sun-god, who was thought to make his daily journey across the sky in a chariot.

HĒʹLIOTROPE. Genus of plants of the Boraginaceae family (*Heliotropium*), a few of which are found in Europe. The forked spikes of blue, lilac, or white flowers, and also the leaves, alter their position constantly so as to face the sun. The garden H. (*H arborescens*) was introduced into Europe from Peru.

HĒʹLIUM (Gk. *helios*, the sun). Symbol He, at. wt. 4·003, at. no. 2. Evidence of its existence in the sun was first obtained by Janssen in 1868 from a line in the solar spectrum and Ramsay isolated it in 1895. H. is a colourless, odourless, inert, non-inflammable and very light gas. It is present in natural gases issuing from the earth in Kansas and other parts of N. America, in radioactive minerals and in small quantities in the atmosphere, and is obtained by compression and fractionation of the natural gas. When ionized, by losing its two electrons in a high electric field, H. becomes identified with the alpha-particles ejected by many natural and man-made isotopes. Because of its short de-ionization time it is used in thyratrons. H.-oxygen atmospheres are used in high-pressure breathing work, as required by divers. H. being less soluble than nitrogen in blood it does not give rise to the 'bends'. Liquid H. is very important in cryogenics (q.v.). It is of value in nuclear work on account of its very low cross-section for absorbing neutrons, and because it is a good heat-transfer medium.

HELL. In the Bible, the word is used to translate Hebrew and Greek words all meaning the place of departed spirits, the abode of the dead. In popular speech, however, H. is the place in which unrepentant sinners suffer the eternal torments of the damned. Vivid descriptions of the physical and spiritual pains of H. have been frequently given by theologians, but during the last century the tendency, save among Roman Catholics, has been to regard H. as a legendary conception, or at least as a state rather than a place. The idea of H. is also contained in Islam and most of the other great religions.

HELL. Tourist resort in Michigan (q.v.).

HEʹLLEBORE. Plants of the genus *Helleborus*, Ranunculaceae family. The green H., or bear's-foot, flowers in early spring, and has pale yellowish-green flowers. Stinking H. produces a flower stem up to a foot tall, with drooping pale green flowers.

HEʹLLEBORINE. Name applied to several British wild flowers, principally of the *Epipactis* genus of the Orchidaceae. Broad H. bears greenish-purple flowers. Marsh H. grows in moist places, producing pink or white flowers. The white H., red H., and narrow H. (with white flowers) belong to the genus *Cephalanthera*, and are less common in Britain.

HELLENES (helʹēnz). The name by which the ancient Greeks knew themselves, and which is still used by the modern Greeks. Their country is called Hellas.

HELLESPONT. The ancient name for the Dardanelles (q.v.).

MARSH HELLEBORINE

HELSINKI. The cathedral (built 1838–52) forms part of the Great Square designed as an architectural whole by the Finnish architect Engel. Originally called the Great Church it became a cathedral in 1959 after a redistribution of bishoprics.
Courtesy of the Finnish Travel Information Centre.

HELLMAN, Lillian (1905–). American playwright. B. in New Orleans, she worked as a journalist in New York before achieving fame as a dramatist. Her plays, which are largely concerned with contemporary political and social issues, incl. *The Children's Hour* (1934), *The Little Foxes* (1939), *Watch on the Rhine* (1941), and *Toys in the Attic* (1960).

HELMHOLTZ, Hermann Ludwig Ferdinand von (1821–94). German scientist. B. at Potsdam, he became prof. of physics at Berlin. In 1847 he pub. an epoch-making treatise on the conservation of energy. He investigated the mechanics of vision, wrote a *Manual of Physiological Optics* (1856–66), invented the ophthalmoscope, and in his *Doctrine of the Sensations of Tone* (1862) gave a complete study of sound.

HEʹLMONT, Jean Baptiste van (1577–1644). Belgian scientist. B. in Brussels, he studied at Louvain, and practised medicine at Vilvorde, near Brussels. He was the first to realize that gases exist apart from the atmosphere, and claimed to have invented the word 'gas'. He was a pioneer experimental biologist, and his carefully controlled 5-year experiment on tree growth was a model of sound scientific method.

HEʹLOTS. The class of slaves in ancient Sparta, who probably represented the aboriginal inhabitants. Their cruel treatment by the Spartans became proverbial.

HELPMANN, Sir Robert (1909–). Australian dancer, choreographer and actor. B. in Adelaide, he was the leading male dancer with the Sadler's Wells Ballet 1933–50, successfully partnering Margot Fonteyn (q.v.) in the war years. He has made many stage and screen appearances as actor and dancer and since 1950 has also worked as a producer; he is noted for his gift for mime and for his dramatic sense, also apparent in his choreographic work, e.g. *Miracle in the Gorbals* (1944). Knighted 1968.

HEʹLSINGBORG. Port on the S.W. coast of Sweden, facing Helsingör across the Sound. Industries incl. copper-smelting, rubber and chemical manufacture, and sugar refining. Pop. (1966) 79,460.

HELSINGFORS. Swedish name of HELSINKI.

HEʹLSINGÖR. Port on the N.E. coast of Denmark, linked by a ferry with Helsingborg across the Sound, here only 3 m. wide. It has shipbuilding yards. Shakespeare made it the scene of *Hamlet*. Pop. 25,000.

HEʹLSINKI. Capital city and port on the S. coast of Finland. Its natural harbour has to be kept open by ice-breakers in winter. There are many fine modern buildings, among them the parliament house. Older buildings incl. the cathedral and the univ. Pop. (1967) 679 337.

HELVE'LLYN. Peak of the English Lake District (3,118 ft.) between Thirlmere and Ullswater.

HELVETIA (helvēsh'a). Region, corresponding to W. Switzerland, occupied by the Celtic Helvetii in the 1st cent. B.C.–5th cent. A.D. In 58 B.C. Caesar repulsed their invasion of southern Gaul at Bibracte (nr. Autun) and H. became subject to Rome.

HELVETIUS (elvehsē-us'), **Claude Adrien** (1715–71). French philosopher. B. in Paris, he became a farmer-general of taxes in 1738. In *De l'Esprit* (1758) he maintained that self-interest, however disguised, is the mainspring of all human action, and that since conceptions of good and evil vary according to period and locality there is no absolute good or evil.

HE'LY-HUTCHINSON, Victor (1901–47). British composer. He was prof. at Birmingham 1934–44, when he succeeded Bliss as B.B.C. director of music, and his light-heartedly witty compositions incl. settings of Lear's nonsense rhymes.

HEMANS (hem'anz), **Felicia Dorothea** (1793–1835). British poetess, *née* Browne. B. in Liverpool, she pub. many vols. of sentimental verse which attained great popularity. Her best-known poem is 'Casabianca'.

HEMEL HEMPSTEAD (hem'el hemp'sted). English town (bor.) in Herts, 25 m. N.W. of London, on the r. Gade. Dating back to Norman times, H.H., with a pop. of 20,000, was chosen for development under the New Towns Act, 1946. Paper, clothing, brushes, etc. are made, and there are breweries and tanneries. Pop. (1961) 55,164.

HEMINGWAY, Ernest (1898–1961). American novelist. B. in Illinois, the son of a doctor, he became a newspaper correspondent in Kansas City. Wounded while serving as a volunteer ambulance man in Italy during the F.W.W., he used these experiences for his war book *Farewell to Arms* (1929). He was much influenced by Gertrude Stein (q.v.) who introduced him to bull-fighting, the theme of his first novel *Fiesta* (1926: U.S. *The Sun Also Rises*) and of *Death in the Afternoon* (1932). *For Whom the Bell Tolls* (1940), has a Spanish Civil War setting, and he served as a correspondent both in this conflict and in the S.W.W. His passion for big-game hunting emerges in short stories, such as 'The Snows of Kilimanjaro' and 'The Short Happy Life of Francis Macomber', and *The Old Man and the Sea* (1952), telling of the duel between a Cuban fisherman and an enormous fish. In 1954 he was awarded a Nobel prize for his 'forceful mastery, which has created a new style in the contemporary art of narration'. His simple, curt sentences attracted imitation. He d. in a gun accident.

ERNEST HEMINGWAY
Photo: John Antill.

HEMI'PTERA (or **Rhynchota**). Order of insects with mouth-parts adapted for feeding by puncture and suction. There are 2 sub-orders, the Homoptera (q.v.) and the Heteroptera (including the bedbug, cotton stainer and chinch bug).

HEMLOCK. Genus of plants (*Conium*) of the Umbelliferae, the only important species being common H. (*C. maculatum*), found in Britain and Europe, and naturalized in the Americas. Reaching 3–5 ft., it bears umbels of small white flowers, and the whole plant, but especially the root and fruit, is poisonous, causing paralysis of the nervous system. The ancient Greeks used it as a mode of capital punishment (*see* SOCRATES).

HEMP. Annual plant (*Cannabis sativa*) of the Urticaceae family cultivated in most temperate countries for its fibres, produced in the outer layer of

HEMLOCK with seed pod and enlarged flower.

the stem (*c.* 3–15 ft. high), and used in ropes, twines and, occasionally, in a type of linen or even lace. Russia is the largest producer, Italy has the finest quality, and it is important in N. India and the U.S.A. Dried leaves or resin form a hallucinogen which may be smoked, made into a drink, or eaten. Use of the drug results in loss of inhibitions, uncontrolled giggling and talking, distortion of perception of space and time, and impairment of judgment and memory. Long-term effects have yet to be fully studied, but it soon creates great psychological dependence. H. is also known as bhang (India), dagga (S. Africa), hashish (Arabia), kif (N. Africa), and pot or marijuana (in W. hemisphere).

The name H. is extended to similar types of fibre, e.g. sisal H. or henequen (obtained from the leaves of *Agave rigida* and other species native to Yucatan and cultivated in many tropical countries) and manila H. (from a plant native to the Philippines and Moluccas).

HENBANE. Wild plant (*Hyoscyamus niger*) common on waste ground in Britain, central and S. Europe, and W. Asia. A branching plant, 1–4 ft. high, it has hairy leaves and a nauseous smell. The yellow flowers are bell-shaped. It is sometimes grown for medicinal purposes, but its use is dangerous.

HENDERSON, Arthur (1863–1935). British Lab. statesman. B. in Glasgow, he worked 20 yrs. as an iron-moulder in Newcastle, entered parliament in 1903 and did much for Lab.'s political organization. He was Home Sec. in the first Lab. govt. in 1924, and was For. Sec. 1929–31, when he accorded the Soviet govt. full recognition. For his constant endeavour to secure international limitation of arms he was awarded a Nobel peace prize in 1934.

HENDERSON, Sir Nevile Meyrick (1882–1942). British diplomat, ambassador to Germany from 1937, who delivered Chamberlain's ultimatum to Hitler in 1939: a supporter of 'appeasement', he was bitterly disillusioned, cf. his *Failure of a Mission* (1940).

HENDON. English residential district on the r. Brent, in the bor. of Barnet, Greater London. Its aerodrome, opened 1910, closed 1957, was the scene of the annual R.A.F. display 1920–37. The Metropolitan Police Coll. was opened in 1934.

HENDY, Sir Philip (1900–). British art historian. He was curator of paintings, Museum of Fine Arts, Boston, Mass., 1930–3; Slade professor of Fine Art at Oxford 1936–46; and in 1946–68 was director of the National Gallery.

HENIE (hen'i), **Sonja** (1913–69). Norwegian skater. Norwegian champion at 11, she won 10 world championships and 3 Olympic titles, turning professional in 1936 and making numerous films.

HENLEIN (-līn), **Konrad** (1898–1945). Sudeten-German Nazi leader. He led from 1923 the Sudeten-German athletic movement, which in 1933 emerged openly as the Nazis' agent inside Czechoslovakia. Condemned to death in 1938 for ordering an armed revolt, he fled to Germany, but after Munich returned as gauleiter of Sudetenland. He became commissioner for Bohemia 1939–45. Captured by the Allies in 1945, he committed suicide.

HENLEY, William Ernest (1849–1903). British poet and journalist. B. at Gloucester, he was early crippled by the amputation of one foot owing to tuberculosis. He was a voluminous writer of verse, besides criticism and miscellaneous journalism, but only his *vers libre* experiments in *Hospital Sketches* are of much interest. He was closely associated with Stevenson, with whom he wrote *Deacon Brodie* (1892) and other plays.

HENLEY-ON-THAMES. English town (bor.) in Oxon, 6 m. N.N.E. of Reading. It stands at the foot of the Chilterns on the left bank of the Thames, which is crossed by a fine stone bridge. It is famous for its annual regatta, held first in 1839, and taking place usually in July. Pop. (1961) 9,131.

HENNA. Small shrub (*Lawsonia inermis*) found in Persia, India, Egypt and N. Africa. The leaves and young twigs are ground to powder, mixed with hot water to a paste and applied to the fingernails and hair of women, and beards of men, giving an orange-red hue. The colour may then be changed to black by applying a preparation of indigo.

HENRIETTA MARIA (1609–69). Queen of England. The daughter of Henry IV of France, she m. Charles I in 1625. As she used her influence to encourage him to make himself absolute, she became highly unpopular, and had to go into exile 1644–60. She returned to England at the Restoration, but retired in 1665 to France.

HENRY I (1068–1135). King of England. The youngest son of William I, he succeeded his brother William II in 1100, and won the support of the Saxons by granting them a charter and marrying a Saxon princess. He was an able administrator, who built up a professional bureaucracy and estab. the system of sending out itinerant justices.

HENRY II (1133–89). King of England. The son of Matilda, daughter of Henry I, and of Geoffrey of Anjou, he inherited Normandy and Anjou, and acquired Poitou, Guienne, and Gascony by marriage. He succeeded Stephen as king in 1154, and successfully restored order and curbed the power of the barons. His attempt to bring the Church courts under royal control led to a long struggle with Becket, after whose murder it had to be abandoned. During his reign the English conquest of Ireland began.

HENRY III (1207–72). King of England. He succeeded his father John in 1216, and assumed royal power in 1227. His subservience to the papacy and generosity to foreign favourites provoked many protests from the barons, who in 1264 rebelled under de Montfort's leadership, defeated H. at Lewes, and held him a prisoner. After the royalist victory at Evesham in 1265 H. was restored to the throne.

HENRY IV (1367–1413). King of England. The son of John of Gaunt, he took an active part in politics under Richard II, and was banished in 1398. He returned in 1399, headed a revolt, and was accepted as king by parliament. His reign was troubled by baronial rebellions and Glendower's rising in Wales, and in order to win support he had to conciliate the Church by a law for the burning of heretics, and to make many concessions to parliament.

HENRY V (1387–1422). King of England. The son of Henry IV, he devoted his life after 1400 to war and statecraft, and succeeded to the throne in 1413. He invaded Normandy in 1415, captured Harfleur, and defeated the French at Agincourt. In 1417–19 he overran Normandy and captured Rouen, and in 1420 he was recognized as his heir by the French king.

HENRY VI (1421–71). King of England. He succeeded his father Henry V in infancy, and came of age in 1442. He identified himself completely with the party opposed to the continuation of the French war, and after his marriage in 1445 was dominated by his wife, Margaret of Anjou. The unpopularity of the government, especially after the loss of the English conquests in France, encouraged the duke of York to claim the crown, and although York was killed in 1460 his son Edward proclaimed himself king in 1461. H. was captured in 1465, and although temporarily restored to the throne in 1470 was again imprisoned in 1471 and soon murdered.

HENRY VII
Photo: N.P.G.

HENRY VII (1457–1509). King of England. The son of Edmund Tudor, earl of Richmond, he was descended through his mother Margaret Beaufort from John of Gaunt. He spent his early life in Brittany, until in 1485 he landed in England, raised a rebellion, and defeated and killed Richard III at Bosworth. He was recognized as king by parliament, although Yorkist rebellions continued until 1497, and by means of the Star Chamber restored order after the Wars of the Roses. By the confiscation of rebels' property, heavy fines, and forced loans he accumulated a large fortune, which rendered him practically independent of parliament.

HENRY VIII (1491–1547). King of England. He succeeded his father Henry VII in 1509, and m. Catherine of Aragon, the widow of his brother Arthur. During the period 1511–29 he pursued an active foreign policy, largely under the guidance of Wolsey. In 1529, as Wolsey had failed to persuade the Pope to grant H. a divorce, he was disgraced. With parliament's approval H. renounced the papal supremacy, proclaimed himself Head of the Church, and dissolved the monasteries; in this policy his chief assistant was Thomas Cromwell. H. nevertheless remained orthodox in theology, and while executing as traitors R.Cs. who denied the royal supremacy he also burned Protestants for heresy. Catherine was divorced in 1533, and H. m. Anne Boleyn, who in 1536 was beheaded for adultery. H.'s 3rd wife, Jane Seymour, d. in 1537. Anne of Cleves he m. in 1540 in pursuance of Cromwell's policy of allying with the German Protestants, but rapidly abandoned this policy, divorced Anne, and beheaded Cromwell. His 5th wife, Catherine Howard, was beheaded in 1542, and the following year he m. Catherine Parr, who survived him.

HENRY. Name of 4 kings of France. HENRY I (1008–60), who succeeded in 1031, spent much of his reign in a struggle with William the Conqueror, duke of Normandy. HENRY II (1519–59), who succeeded his father Francis I in 1547, captured Metz and Verdun from the emperor, and Calais from the English. He was killed in a tournament. HENRY III (1551–89), who succeeded his brother Charles IX in 1574, became involved in a struggle both with the Huguenots, headed by Henry of Navarre, and the Catholic League, headed by the duke of Guise. Expelled from Paris by the League in 1588, H. allied with the Huguenots, but was assassinated by a monk while besieging Paris. HENRY IV (1553–1610), the son of Antoine de Bourbon and Jeanne, queen of Navarre, was brought up as a Protestant, and from 1576 led the Huguenots in the wars of religion. Having succeeded Henry III in 1589, he settled the religious question by himself accepting Catholicism, while granting toleration to Protestants. He restored peace and strong government to France, and brought back prosperity by measures for the promotion of industry and agriculture and the improvement of communications. He was assassinated in 1610 by an R.C. fanatic.

HENRY VIII
Photo: N.P.G.

HENRY. Name of 7 Holy Roman Emperors. HENRY I, called THE FOWLER (*c.* 876–936), became duke of Saxony in 912, and German king in 919. HENRY III (1017–56), who succeeded in 1039, raised the Empire to the height of its power, and extended its authority over Poland, Bohemia and Hungary. HENRY IV (1050–1106), who succeeded in 1056, was involved from 1075 in a struggle with the papacy under Gregory VII. HENRY V (1081–1125), son of Henry IV, continued the struggle with the Church until a settlement on the investitures question was reached in 1122. HENRY VI (1165–97) inherited Sicily by marriage in 1189, and the Empire from his father Frederick I in 1190. As part of his plan for making the Empire universal he captured and imprisoned Richard I of England, and compelled him to do homage. HENRY VII (*c.* 1269–1313), originally count of Luxemburg, was elected emperor in 1308, and attempted unsuccessfully to revive the imperial supremacy in Italy.

HENRY, Joseph (1797–1878). American scientist. B. at Albany, N.Y., he became prof. of natural philosophy at Princeton 1832–46, and secretary of the Smithsonian Institution in 1846. He invented the first electromagnetic motor in 1829, and a telegraphic apparatus; he also discovered the principle of electromagnetic induction, simultaneously with Faraday, and the phenomenon of self-induction. He later estab. a nation-wide meteorological service, investigated the properties of sound-waves in fog, and perfected a system of fog signals. His name is given to the unit of electrical induction.

HENRY, O. Pseudonym of the American short-story writer William Sydney Porter (1862–1910). B. in N. Carolina, he worked in Texas as a bank clerk and a journalist, and was imprisoned for 3 years on a charge of embezzlement. After his release he lived in New York, devoting himself entirely to the short story, and pub. several collections, beginning with *Cabbages and Kings* (1904) and *The Four Million* (1906). His stories, which deal mainly with New York or southern and western life, are marked by a brilliant colloquial style, skilled construction with 'twist' endings, and a deep sense of pity.

HENRY, Patrick (1736–99). American statesman. He is remembered as an orator, espec. his speeches against the Stamp Act 1765 telling George III 'If this be treason, make the most of it!' and supporting the arming of the Virginia militia 1775 'Give me liberty or give me death!' He was governor of the state 1776–9 and 1784–6.

HENRY, William (1774–1836). British chemist. In 1803 he formulated *Henry's law*: when a gas is dissolved in a liquid at a given temperature, its weight is in direct proportion to the gas pressure.

HENRYSON, Robert (*c.* 1430–*c.* 1505). Scottish poet. His works incl. lively versions of Aesop and the *Testament of Cresseid*, a continuation of Chaucer.

HENRY THE NAVIGATOR (1394–1460). Portuguese prince. The son of John I, he devoted himself largely to the promotion of exploration and colonization. Under his patronage Portuguese seamen explored and colonized Madeira and the Azores, and sailed down the African coast almost to Sierra Leone.

HENSCHEL (hen'shel), **Sir George** (1850–1934). British conductor and baritone singer of Polish descent. He became the first conductor of the Boston Symphony Orchestra in 1881, founded the London Symphony Orchestra, and composed a Requiem Mass, songs, an opera, etc.

HENSON, Herbert Hensley (1863–1947). British churchman. An Anglican of the Broad Church school, he was bishop of Durham 1920–39. A masterly preacher, he published an unusual autobiography, *Retrospect of an Unimportant Life* (1942–3).

HENZE (hen'tse), **Hans Werner** (1926–). German composer. Well known for his operas *Boulevard Solitude* (1952: based on *Manon Lescaut*) and *King*

Stag (1956), and for his ballet *Ondine* (1958), he shows in his music the influence of Schoenberg, and he often uses a modified 12-note technique (dodecaphony). He became prof. of composition at Academy Mozarteum, Salzburg, 1961.

HEPBURN, Audrey (1929–). American actress B. in Brussels, she was originally a student of ballet, a training which emphasized her gamine grace in films such as *My Fair Lady* (1964).

HEPBURN, Katharine (1909–). American actress. B. in Connecticut, her gangly grace and husky voice brought stardom in such films as *Morning Glory* (1933), *Philadelphia Story* (1940), *African Queen* (1952).

HEPHAESTUS (hǐfěst'us). Greek god of fire and metal craftsmanship, identified with the Roman Vulcan. The son of Zeus and Hera, he was lame and was m. to Aphrodite.

HEPPLEWHITE, George (d. 1786). British craftsman. In his furniture workshop at St. Giles, Cripplegate, in London, he developed a simple elegant style, especially in his chairs, often with shield- or heart-

HEPWORTH. Seen here at her studio home at St. Ives, Cornwall, the artist looks at a favourite item of her collection, an oval sculpture in stone, which with its title 'Delos' recalls the island birthplace of Apollo. *Courtesy of Barbara Hepworth.*

shaped backs. He worked mainly in mahogany or satinwood, and his characteristic decorations of feathers, shells, or wheat-ears were inlaid or painted, rather than carved. *See illus.* p. 455.

HEPTARCHY (hept'arki). Term coined by 16th cent. historians to denote the 7 Saxon kingdoms supposed to exist prior to A.D. 800: Northumbria, Mercia, E. Anglia, Essex, Kent, Sussex, and Wessex.

HEPWORTH, Dame Barbara (1903–). British sculptor. B. at Wakefield, she studied at Leeds School of Art and the Royal College of Art, and since 1939 has lived in Cornwall. Although she has worked in such media as reinforced concrete, bronze, wood and aluminium, her favourite is stone. She was m. 1st to sculptor John Skeaping and 2nd to Ben Nicholson (q.v.): both marriages were dissolved.

HE'RA. Greek goddess. The sister and consort of Zeus, she was the mother of Hephaestus, Hebe, and Ares. The protectress of women and marriage, she was identified with the Roman Juno.

HERACLI'TUS (*c.* 540–475 B.C.). Greek philosopher. B. at Ephesus, he maintained in his chief work, *On Nature*, that the ultimate principle is fire, and that everything is in a state of eternal flux, producing a notably coherent system.

HERAKLION. Largest city of Crete, formerly known as Candia (q.v.) Pop. (1961) 63,458.

HERALDS' COLLEGE or **College of Arms.** English heraldic body formed in 1484 by Richard III incorporating the heralds attached to the Royal Household; reincorporated by Royal Charter of Philip and

Mary in 1555. There are 3 Kings of Arms, 6 Heralds, and 4 Pursuivants, who specialize in genealogical and heraldic work. The College establishes the right to bear Arms, and the Kings of Arms grant Arms by letters patent. In Ireland the office of Ulster King of Arms was transferred in 1943 to the College of Arms in London and placed with that of Norroy King of Arms, who now has jurisdiction in Northern Ireland as well as in the north of England.

HERAT (heraht'). Cap. of H. province, Afghanistan, on the N. banks of the Hari Rud. A principal road junction, it was a great city in ancient and medieval times. Pop. (1965) 62,000.

HÉRAULT (ārō'). River in S. France, 78 m. long, rising in the Cevennes and flowing into the Gulf of Lyons near Agde. It gives its name to a dept.

HERB. A plant which does not possess a permanent woody stem, the parts above ground dying every winter. Also a plant with a sweet, bitter, aromatic, or pungent taste, used in cookery, medicine, or perfumery.

HERBART, Johann Friedrich (1776–1841). German philosopher and educationist. B. at Oldenburg, he became professor at Königsberg in 1809 and at Göttingen in 1833, founded a school of philosophy specializing in psychology, and was interested in educational theory by contact with Pestalozzi.

HERBERT, Sir Alan Patrick (1890–1971). Brit. author. A contributor to *Punch* from 1924 as A.P.H., he was noted for his satiric wit and humorous verse, and the variety of his talents, e.g. the amusing novel *The Water Gypsies* (1930), the comic opera *Tantivy Towers* (1931), and the revue *Big Ben* (1946). On a more serious plane, he was a campaigner for marriage-law reform, and as an Independent M.P. (1935–50) introd. the Matrimonial Causes Bill. *See* DIVORCE. He was knighted in 1945.

HERBERT, George (1593–1633). English poet. He became in 1619 orator to Cambridge university, and in 1625 a prebendary in Hunts, where his friends incl. Donne, Walton, and Bacon. After ordination in 1630 he became vicar of Bemerton, Wilts, and d. of consumption. His vol. of religious poems, *The Temple*, appeared in 1633. His brother, **Lord Edward H. of Cherbury** (1583–1648), was also a poet and religious philosopher and in his *De veritate* (1624) propounded a theory of natural religion, which makes him the founder of English Deism.

HERBERT OF LEA, Sidney Herbert, 1st baron (1810–61). British statesman. He was Sec. for War in Aberdeen's Liberal-Peelite coalition of 1852–5, and during the Crimean War was responsible for sending Florence Nightingale to the front. After the war he supported army reforms and became a peer in 1861.

HERB ROBERT

HERB ROBERT. Common wild flower of the Geraniaceae family (genus *Geranium*), found through out Europe, central Asia, and N. America. About 12 in. high, it bears hairy leaves and small purplish flowers, and has a reddish hairy stem. When rubbed, the leaves have an unpleasant smell.

HERCEGOVINA, HERZEGOVINA. *See* BOSNIA-HERCEGOVINA.

HERCULANEUM. Ancient city of Italy between Naples and Pompeii. H. was overwhelmed during the eruption of Vesuvius (A.D. 79), which also destroyed Pompeii. It was excavated from the 18th cent. onward.

HERCULES (Gk. Heracles). Greek hero, the son of Zeus and Alcmene, famed for his strength. While serving Eurystheus, king of Argos, he performed the celebrated 12 Labours which included the cleansing of the Augean stables. The *Pillars of H.* are the great rocks guarding the entrance to the Mediterranean-Gibraltar and Ceuta.

HERDER, Johann Gottfried von (1744–1803). German poet, critic, and philosopher. B. in E. Prussia, he studied at Königsberg, where he was influenced by Kant, became pastor at Riga, met Goethe in Strasbourg (1770), and in 1776 was called to Weimar as court preacher. H.'s critical writings indicate his intuitive rather than reasoning trend of thought. He gave considerable impulse to the Storm and Stress movement in Ger. literature. He collected folk songs of all nations (1778) and in the *Ideen zur Philosophie*

der Geschichte der Menschheit (1784–91) he outlined the stages of cultural development of mankind.

HÉRÉDIA (ehrehdē-ah'), **José Maria de** (1842–1905). French poet. B. in the W. Indies, he came to France in 1850 and became one of the 'Parnassien' school of poets, led by Leconte de Lisle. His *Les Trophées* (1893) is mainly a series of sonnets.

HEREFORD (her'e-). English city (bor.), co. town of Herefordshire, on the Wye, 24 m. N.W. of Gloucester. The present cathedral was begun in 1079. The cathedral school was founded in the 14th cent. Pop. (1961) 40,431.

HEREFORDSHIRE. County of England adjacent to the Welsh border. It consists of broken hilly country, drained by the picturesque Wye and its tributaries. On the E. border the Malvern hills rise to Worcestershire Beacon, 1,395 ft. Pears, apples, and hops are grown, but most of the land is under pasture on which are reared the famous Hereford cattle. The co. town is Hereford; other towns incl. Leominster, Ross, and Ledbury. Area 842 sq. m.; pop. (1967) 140,760.

HEREROS (her'ārōz). A nomadic Bantu-speaking people living in S.W. Africa.

HERESY. A doctrine or system of thought opposed to orthodox belief, especially in religion, e.g. those held by the Gnostics, Arians, Pelagians, Montanists, Albigenses, Waldenses, Lollards, Anabaptists, Unitarians, Quakers, etc.

HEREWARD (her'e-), called the Wake (fl. 1070). English patriot. A small Lincs. landowner, he led a rebellion against Norman rule in 1070. William the Conqueror captured his stronghold in the Isle of Ely in 1071. H. escaped with a few companions, and his fate is obscure. *See* CHARLES KINGSLEY.

HERFORD. W. German town in North Rhine-Westphalia. Industries include textiles, machinery, foodstuffs and furniture. Pop. (1960) 55,500.

HERGESHEIMER, Joseph (1880–1954). American novelist. B. at Philadelphia, he is best remembered for his picturesque interpretation of the American past in *The Three Black Pennys* (1917) and *Head Java* (1919).

HERIOT, George (1563–1624). Scottish goldsmith. In 1597 he was appointed goldsmith to Anne of Denmark, consort of James VI, and in 1601 became jeweller to the king. His fortune founded the Heriot Trust which helped endow Heriot-Watt Univ., Edinburgh.

HERKOMER, Sir Hubert von (1849–1914). British artist. B. in S. Bavaria, he went to England in 1857, established his reputation with 'The Last Muster', exhibited at the R A. in 1875, and was elected R.A. in 1890. He was Slade prof. at Oxford 1885–94. His portraits are considered his best works.

HERMAPHRODĪ´TUS. In Gk. mythology, the son of Hermes and Aphrodite. He was beloved by a nymph whose prayer to the gods for perpetual union with him was answered in that she and H. became one body, but possessed of the characteristics of both sexes. Hence the modern 'hermaphrodite'.

HERMES. In Gk. mythology, the son of Zeus and Maia and messenger of the gods, usually appearing with winged sandals and bearing a staff around which serpents are coiled. He is identified with the Roman Mercury. He was also the god of thieves, travellers, and merchants.

HERMIT CRAB. Genus of crustaceans (Paguridea). The abdominal segments are not encased as in true crabs, but the H.C. lives in the shell of a gastropod. They are found on the coasts of Europe, America, and the West Indies, usually in close association with sea-anemones and sponges.

HE´RMON (Arab. Jebel esh-Sheikh). Snow-topped mtn. (9,232 ft.), the highest in Syria. It is the traditional scene of the transfiguration of Jesus.

HERNÁNDEZ (ārnahn´dãth), **José** (1834–86). Argentine poet. B. near Buenos Aires, he lived among the gauchos on the pampas in his youth, and his epic *Martín Fierro* (1872–8) is the greatest example of *gauchesca* literature.

HERNE (her´ne). Industrial town of the Ruhr, North Rhine-Westphalia, W. Germany. Pop. (1960 est.) 113,252.

HERNE BAY. English seaside resort (U.D.) in Kent, on the estuary of the Thames. Three m. to the E. is Reculver, site of a Roman station. Pop. (1961) 21,273.

HERNIA. Protrusion of a part of the bowel through a weak spot in the abdominal wall, usually in the groin or navel. The appearance is that of a rounded, soft tumour.

HERO and LEANDER. In ancient Gk. story, H. was the priestess of Aphrodite at Sestos on the Hellespont. She was loved by Leander, who visited her nightly by swimming across the strait from Abydos on the opposite shore. One stormy night he was drowned; and H. cast herself into the sea out of grief.

HERO of Alexandria. A Greek mathematician and writer, probably of the 2nd cent. A.D., who invented an automatic fountain, and perhaps a kind of stationary steam-engine.

HE´ROD (74–4 B.C.). King of the Jews; known as HEROD THE GREAT. The son of Antipater, he was declared king of Judea by the Romans in 40 B.C., and with Antony's assistance estab. his government in Jerusalem in 37 B.C. He rebuilt the Temple at Jerusalem, but his Hellenizing tendencies made him suspect to orthodox Jewry. His last years were akin to a reign of terror, and St. Matthew alleges that he ordered the slaughter of all the infants in Bethlehem to ensure the death of Christ, whom he visualized as a rival. His son **Herod Antipas** was tetrarch of Galilee and Peraea, 4 B.C.–A.D. 39. He m. Herodias, the divorced wife of his half-brother Herod Philip, and ordered the execution of John the Baptist. Christ was brought before him on Pontius Pilate's discovery that He was a Galilean and hence of Herod's jurisdiction. In A.D. 38 H.A. went to Rome to solicit the title of king, but Caligula was prejudiced against him, and he was banished. The rock citadel of Massada, built by Herod 37–31 B.C., was excavated 1963–4: there were important finds of ancient texts; mosaic floors and decorated walls of the royal palace; reservoirs, etc.

HEROD AGRIPPA I (d. A.D. 44). Jewish ruler of Palestine under the Romans. A grandson of Herod the Great, Caligula made him a tetrarch in Palestine, and Claudius gave him the title of king. He put St. James to death and imprisoned St. Peter. His son **Herod Agrippa II** (d. A.D. 100) as king of Chalcis assisted Titus in his siege of Jerusalem, and on the fall of the city in A.D. 70 went to Rome, where he d. St. Paul defended himself before him in A.D. 60.

HERO´DOTUS (*c.* 484–*c.* 424 B.C.). Greek historian and prose writer, who travelled widely, recording in his history observations of habits and creeds of many races. After 4 years in Athens, he settled in S. Italy in 443 at Thurii, apparently staying there the rest of his life. His history, written lucidly and with charm, deals with the Greek-Persian struggle which culminated in the defeat of the Persian invasion attempts in 490 and 480 B.C. The majority of the work is devoted to an early perspective history of the states involved. H. was the first historian to apply a critical sense.

HEROIN (her´ō-in). Diamorphine hydrochloride, an alkaloid obtained from morphine. A white crystalline powder, it depresses the nerve centres controlling breathing and is valuable as a sedative in conditions producing a cough, but the danger of addiction has led to its being banned for medical use in most countries, incl. the U.S., though not in the U.K. *See* DRUGS, MISUSE OF.

HÉROLD (ārold´), **Louis Joseph Ferdinand** (1791–1833). French operatic composer. His fame chiefly rests on the opera *Zampa* (1831).

HERON. Large bird in the group Ardeidae, which also includes bitterns, egrets, night-herons, and boat-bills. The Common H.

(*Ardea cinerea*) nests in Europe and Asia in large colonies at the tops of trees. The bird has a long neck and long legs. The plumage is chiefly grey, but there are black patches on the sides and a black crest. The legs are olive-green, and the beak yellow, except during the breeding season when it is pink. It is a wading bird, but is rarely seen to swim or walk. It feeds on fish, frogs, rats, and other small animals.

HERPES (her´pēz). Shingles; a disease in which red spots and small blisters appear on the skin over a set of nerve endings, accompanied by much neuralgic pain and irritation. The most usual positions are over the ribs like a girdle, the forehead and the limbs. Some authorities think that it is caused by the same virus as chickenpox.

HERRERA (errā´ra), **Francisco** (1576–1656). Spanish artist, surnamed **El Viejo** (the Old). B. in Seville, he is remarkable for his realism, and skilled use of light and shade. His son Francisco H. (1622–85), called **El Mozo** (the Young), also b. in Seville, was remarkable for his still-lifes.

HERRICK, Robert (1591–1674). English poet. B. in Cheapside, London, he was a friend of Ben Jonson.

In 1629 he became vicar of Dean Prior, near Totnes. He pub. *Hesperides* (1648), a collection of sacred and pastoral poetry unrivalled in lyric quality.

HERRING, John Frederick (1795–1865). British sporting artist. B. in Surrey, he is famous for his paintings of the winners of the St. Leger at Doncaster.

HERRING. One of the most important food fish (*Clupea harengus*), the leading member of the Clupeidae. A salt-water fish, it swims close to the surface and may be 10–18 in. long. A silvered greenish-blue, it has only one dorsal fin and one short ventral, and there are no spines on the fins.

Young Hs. *c.* 2 in. long largely compose the delicacy known as 'whitebait'.

The H. is found in large quantities off the shores of Britain, Scandinavia, the E. coast of N. America, the White Sea, and in the Sea of Japan, but not in the Mediterranean.

HERRIOT (ārē-ō′), **Édouard** (1872–1957). French Radical statesman. An opponent of Poincaré, especially his advocacy of French occupation of the Ruhr, he was briefly P.M. in 1924–5, 1926, and 1932. As Pres. of the Chamber in 1940 he opposed the policies of the Vichy govt., was arrested and later taken to Germany until released in 1945 by the Russians. He was Pres. of the Natl. Assembly 1947–53, and France's rejection of the E.D.C. treaty was attributed to a speech of his in 1954.

HERSCHEL, Sir William (1738–1822). British astronomer. B. at Hanover, he went to England in 1757, earning his living as a musician, whilst instructing himself in mathematics and astronomy. In 1781 he discovered Uranus, and later several of its satellites. During his appointment as astronomer to George III from 1782 he discovered the motion of the double stars round one another, and recorded it in his *Motion of the Solar System in Space* (1783). He constructed a 4 ft. telescope, of 40 ft. focal length, at Slough, in 1789, and discovered infra-red solar rays in 1800. His son **Sir John Frederick William H.** (1792–1871) was also an astronomer and estab. an observatory near Capetown in 1834, where he discovered thousands of close double stars, clusters and nebulae, reported in 1847. His inventions incl. astronomical instruments, sensitized photographic paper, and the use of sodium hyposulphite for fixing it.

SIR W. HERSCHEL

HERSEY, John (1914–). American writer. B. in China, he joined the staff of *Time*, and during the S.W.W. was on Bataan (*Men on Bataan*, 1942), with the American troops in Africa and Italy (*A Bell for Adano*, 1944), and investigated the effects of the Hiroshima atom bomb (*Hiroshima*, 1946).

HERTER, Christian Archibald (1895–1966). American statesman. Following a diplomatic career after the F.W.W., he became assistant to Sec. of Commerce H. Hoover 1921–4, and was elected to the Mass. House of Representatives (1931–43), when he became a Congressman (1943–53). He was Under Sec. (1957–9), then Sec. of State (1959–61), and became Chairman of the Atlantic Council of the U.S. in 1961, and Special Representative for Trade Negotiations in 1962.

HERTFORD (harf′). Co. town (bor.) of Herts, England, on the Lea; 2 m. S.E. of the town is Hailey-bury Coll. H. has brewing and brick industries. Pop. (1961) 15,734.

HERTFORDSHIRE. County of S.E. England, lying N. of Greater London. Across the co. from S.W. to N.E. run the Chiltern Hills. H. is drained by the Colne, Lea, and Stort, and is predominantly an agricultural county. On the chalk uplands sheep are grazed, while elsewhere the principal crops are wheat, oats, roots, beans, and potatoes. In the S.W. fruit is grown; other specialized products include flowers, early vegetables, and watercress. Dairy cattle are pastured by the Stort and Colne. The co. town is Hertford; other towns include St. Albans, Watford, Bishop's Stortford, Letchworth, and Hemel Hempstead. Area 632 sq. m.; pop. (1967) 881,870.

'sHERTOGENBOSCH (s-her′tögenbosh) (Fr., *Bois-le-Duc*). Capital of N. Brabant, Netherlands, 28 m. S.S.E. of Utrecht. There is a 14–15th cent. cathedral. Pop. (1967) 79,151.

HERTZ (her′ts), **Heinrich** (1857–94). German physicist. Continuing the work of Clerk Maxwell (q.v.) in electromagnetic (*Hertzian*) waves, he prepared the way for radio communication, and showed that their behaviour resembled that of light and heat waves.

HERTZOG (her′tsōg), **James Barry Munnik** (1866–1942). South African statesman. B. in Cape Colony, of Boer stock, he was a general in the S. African War, and in 1910 became Min. of Justice under Botha. In 1913 he formed the Nationalist Party, and in 1914 opposed S. African participation in the F.W.W. After the 1924 elections H. became P.M., and in 1933 his party and General Smuts's S. African Party were merged as the United S. African National Party. In Sept. 1939 his motion against participation in the S.W.W. was rejected, and he resigned.

HERZEN (her′tsen), **Alexander Ivanovich** (1812–70). Russian revolutionary writer. Persecuted for his opinions, he left Russia in 1847, and in 1852 settled in London. His *Memoirs* are valuable. He d. in Paris.

HERZL (hertsl), **Theodor** (1860–1904). Founder of the Zionist movement. B. at Budapest, he became a successful playwright and journalist, but the Dreyfus case convinced him that the only solution to the problem of the Jews was their resettlement in a state of their own in Palestine. His *Jewish State* (1896) launched political Zionism.

HE′SIOD (*c.* 700 B.C.). One of the earliest of the poets of ancient Greece. He is supposed to have lived a little later than Homer, and according to his own account he was b. in Boeotia. He is the author of *Works and Days*, a poem that tells of the country life, and the *Theogony*, an account of the origin of the world and of the gods.

HESPE′RIDES. In Gk. mythology, the maidens who, far away in the west, guard the tree that produces golden apples.

HESS, Dame Myra (1890–1965). British pianist. A pupil of Tobias Matthay, she organized the popular National Gallery concerts in London in the S.W.W., and was created D.B.E. in 1941. She was well known for her interpretations of Beethoven, and for her piano transcription of the Bach chorale 'Jesu, joy of man's desiring'.

HESS, Walter Richard Rudolf (1894–). German Nazi leader. He fought in the F.W.W. and joined the Nazi Party in 1920. Imprisoned with Hitler 1923–5, he became his private sec., taking down *Mein Kampf* from his dictation. In 1932 he was appointed deputy to the Fuehrer, and in 1939 was nominated as Hitler's successor after Goering. He was head of the *Ausland* organization responsible for fifth-column activities abroad. On 10 May 1941 he landed by air in Britain with compromise peace proposals, and was held a prisoner-of-war till 1945, when he was tried at Nuremberg and was sentenced to life imprisonment.

HESSE, Hermann (1877–1962). German-born

writer who became a Swiss citizen in 1923. A conscientious objector in the F.W.W. and a pacifist opponent of Hitler, he pub. short stories, poetry and novels, e.g. *Peter Camenzind* (1904) and *Unterm Rad* (1906). Later works, such as *Das Glasperlenspiel* (1943), tend towards the occult. He received a Nobel prize in 1946.

HE′SSEN. State (Land) of W. Germany, estab. in 1946. The cap. is Wiesbaden. About a quarter of the working pop. is engaged in agriculture, chief products being wheat, rye, oats, and potatoes, with dairying important; chemicals, motor-cars, and machines are made, and there are electrical engineering works. Area 8,145 sq. m.: pop. (1966) 5,239,700.

The Land of Hessen occupies generally the area of 2 former territories: (1) **Hesse**, a state divided into 2 separate parts by a strip of Prussian territory, the S. portion consisting chiefly of the valleys of the Rhine and Main, the N. being dominated by the volcanic Vogelsberg (2,532 ft.). Darmstadt, the cap., Giessen, Mainz, and Worms were among its towns. (2) **Hesse-Nassau**, a prov. of Prussia, a hilly region with rich timber, metal, and vine resources. Kassel, Fulda, Frankfurt, and Wiesbaden were the main towns.

HE′STIA. In Gk. mythology, the goddess of the hearth. She was a daughter of Cronos (Saturn) and Rhea, and the Romans identified her with Vesta.

HEUSS (hois), **Theodor** (1884–1963). W. German statesman. A member of the Reichstag from 1924 until in 1933 the Nazi régime forced him to withdraw from public life, he led the Free Democratic Party 1948–9 and was elected Federal President in 1949.

HEWLETT, Maurice Henry (1861–1923). British writer. He gained success as a novelist in the medieval romance *The Forest Lovers* in 1898. His later works incl. *Richard Yea-and-Nay* (1900), *The Queen's Quair* (1904), and a vol. of verse, *Song of the Plow*.

HEXHAM. English town (U.D.), on the S. bank of the Tyne, Northumberland, 20 m. W. of Newcastle. St. Wilfrid founded a church and monastery here in 674. The present church is an excellent example of Early English. Pop. (1961) 9,897.

HEYDRICH (hīd′rikh), **Reinhard** (1904–42). German Nazi terrorist. Whilst deputy 'protector' of Bohemia and Moravia from 1941, he was ambushed and killed by 3 members of the Czech forces in Britain, who had landed by parachute. Reprisals followed incl. several hundred executions and the massacre of Lidice.

HEYER (hī′er), **Georgette** (1902–). British novelist. Well known for her historical novels, e.g. *The Spanish Bride*, and for her light-hearted Regency romances, e.g. *Faro's Daughter*, she also writes contemporary detective stories.

HEYERDAHL (hī′-), **Thor** (1914–). Norwegian ethnologist. Ed. at the Univ. of Oslo, he was a paratrooper with the Free Norwegian forces in the S.W.W., and achieved world fame with the Kon-Tiki Expedition of 1947. With 5 companions he built a balsawood raft and sailed from Peru to the Pacific Is. along the Humboldt Current, proving it feasible that the light-skinned Polynesians, whose origin is disputed, could have been migrants from S. America. He wrote a celebrated account of the voyage and also *Aku-aku* (1957), a study of the mysterious history of Easter Is.

HEYSE (hī′se), **Paul Johann Ludwig** (1830–1914). German poet, novelist, and dramatist. B. at Berlin, he was called to Munich by Maximilian II in 1854. He translated Italian poets, but ranks foremost as a writer of short stories (*L'Arrabbiata*, 1855, etc.).

HEYSHAM. See MORECAMBE AND HEYSHAM.

HEYWOOD, Thomas (c. 1570–c. 1650). English dramatist. B. in Lincs, he became an actor in London, and wrote or adapted over 220 plays. Among them are the *Foure Prentises of London* (1615), the chronicle *Edward IV* (1599), *The English Traveller* (1633), and his masterly domestic tragedy, *A Woman kilde with kindnesse* (1607).

HEZEKIAH (hezēkī′ah). King of Judah 719–699 B.C.; son of Ahaz, and father of Manasseh. Against the advice of Isaiah he rebelled against Assyrian suzerainty in alliance with Egypt, but was defeated by Sennacherib. He carried out religious reforms.

HIAWATHA (hīawaw′tha). North American Indian teacher and Onondaga chieftain of the 15th or 16th cents. who welded the Six Nations of the Iroquois into the league of the Long House. Longfellow's epic *Hiawatha* (1855) was based on the data collected by Henry R. Schoolcraft (1793–1864).

HIBBERT, Robert (1770–1849). British merchant. B. in Jamaica, in 1847 he founded the Hibbert Trust, the funds of which were to be applied to the propagation of Christianity in its broadest and simplest form. The Hibbert Lectures and the *Hibbert Journal*, founded in 1902, are financed by the Trust.

HIBI′SCUS. Genus of the Malvaceae (mallow) family, ranging from large herbaceous plants to trees. Favourite ornamental plants because of their brilliantly coloured (red through to white) bell-shaped flowers, they incl. the rose of Sharon (*H. Syriacus*) and the rose of China (*H. rosa-sinensis*). Some tropical

HEYERDAHL. Named after the legendary Kon-Tiki (q.v. the raft was modelled on a design in use by the Indians when Europeans first reached Peru. She was built of nine 2 ft. thick balsa logs, each 30 to 45 ft. long, and lashed to balsa crossbeams supporting a plaited bamboo deck and an open bamboo hut.
Courtesy of Kon-Tiki Huset, Oslo.

species are also useful, e.g. *H. esculentus*, of which the edible fruit is known in the W. Indies as the gobbo; *H. tiliaceus*, which supplies timber and fibrous bark to S. Sea islanders; and *H. sabdariffa*, cultivated in the W. Indies and elsewhere for its fruit.

HICCUP, or Hiccough. Sharp noise caused by a sudden spasm of or irritation to the diaphragm with closing of the windpipe, commonly due to digestive disorder, etc. The remedy for ordinary H. is to cause a feeling of suffocation by breathing into a paper bag.

HICHENS, Robert Smythe (1864–1950). British novelist. He travelled widely in the Middle East, as reflected in the best-seller *The Garden of Allah* (1905): other books incl. *Bella Donna* (1909).

HICKEY, William (1749–1830?). British writer. Ed. at Westminster School, he was intended to follow his father as an attorney in England but dissipation led to his being packed off first to the East Indies and then to Jamaica, before he finally made good at the Indian Bar. His *Memoirs*, written in retirement, give one of the raciest accounts of the age. *See illus.* p. 530.

HICKOK, James Butler 'Wild Bill' (1837–76). American frontiersman. In the Civil War he was a sharpshooter and scout for the Union army, and then served as marshal in Kansas, killing many desperadoes. A legendary figure, he was shot from behind in Deadwood, S. Dakota.

HICKORY. Common genus (*Carya*) of trees native to N. America. It provides a valuable timber, and all species bear nuts, although some are inedible. The

WILLIAM HICKEY
Courtesy of the National Gallery of Ireland.

pecan (*C. illinoensis*) is widely cultivated in the S., and the shagbark (*C. ovata*) in the N.

HICKS, Edward (1780–1849). American self-taught artist, remembered for his numerous versions of a picture based on Isaiah 11, 6–9, 'The Peaceable Kingdom': from 1810 he was an itinerant Quaker preacher.

HIEROGLYPHIC (hī-eroglif′ik). One of the most important ancient systems of writing, originating in

'Cleopatra' in hieroglyphic characters.

Egypt. It was in existence about the middle of the 4th millennium B.C., and did not develop into a proper 'alphabet'. On the whole, picture-signs, triliteral, biliteral, and uniliteral signs and determinatives were combined into a complicated script, and this was maintained during 3,500 years. The latest H. inscriptions belong to the 3rd cent. A.D. The direction of writing is normally from right to left, the signs facing the beginning of the line. The 'Rosetta Stone' of 197 B.C., carved in H., Demotic, and Greek, furnished the key to decipherment, which was mainly due to J. F. Champollion in 1822.

HIGH COMMISSIONER. The representative of one independent Commonwealth country in the cap. of another. Equal in rank to ambassadors (q.v.), they have the same duties and powers.

HIGHGATE. District of N. London, England. It has associations with Dick Whittington, Andrew Marvell, Nell Gwynn, and others; George Eliot and Karl Marx are among the many famous buried in H. cemetery. The highest part, H. Village, is 426 ft. a.s.l. It is mainly in the bor. of Haringey.

HIGHLANDS. A broken plateau of ancient rocks occupying all Scotland N. of the boundary Helensburgh to Stonehaven, except Buchan, Caithness, and the Moray Firth plains. Ben Nevis (4,406 ft.) is the highest of many peaks. Glaciation has straightened and deepened the valleys, where lie many lochs. Their primitive scenery has made the H. famous for

holidays, fishing, and shooting. Habitation is limited mainly to crofters farming impoverished land. Throughout history, H. language and race have been distinguished from that of the Lowlands. *See* SCOTTISH GAELIC. The traditional *H. Games* incl. athletic events, e.g. tossing the caber (a tree trunk), dancing, and bagpipe playing.

The problem of depopulation and general decline has been tackled by the Highland Development Board (1965). The tourist and fishing industries are being promoted, and in the longer term the Moray Firth area is planned for development as a linear city by the controlled expansion of a dozen towns from Tain to Inverness, with an eventual pop. of 300,000. Cheap hydroelectric power would serve aluminium smelting, petrochemical works, etc.

HIGHLANDS. Celebrated by Sir Walter Scott in *The Lady of the Lake*: the Trossachs and Loch Ard.
Photo: George Outram & Co. Ltd.

HIGHWAY. In British law, any road over which an inalienable right of way has been estab., as by 21 years' uninterrupted use. In American usage, any one of the national trunk roads, controlled and partly sponsored by the Federal Govt. After the Roman exodus English roads were sadly neglected until the 16th cent. when parishes were made responsible in their localities, and in the 18th and 19th cents. when turnpike trusts maintained Hs. outside towns, and charged tolls. Development was delayed because of competition from water and rail transport, but from 1888, when County Councils took over, using the methods of Telford and McAdam, communications improved, particularly between towns. The Central

HIGHWAY. Britain's first national highway exclusively for motor traffic, the London-Birmingham M1, of which the main section was opened in 1959.
British Travel and Holidays Association

Govt. assumed entire responsibility for trunk roads in 1946. In America early European settlement was along the seaboard, and the sea provided the means of communication. With migration inland, development in 18th and 19th cents. was similar to that in England. The first real impetus to improved Hs. came with the bicycle and was strengthened by the increasing use of motor-cars. They were built by the State Govts. rather than the towns (1891–1913), but intracontinental Hs. were undertaken under the Federal Aid bills of 1916–21. Recognition of the need for rapid, efficient Hs. in Europe came between the wars – the *autostrada* in Italy and the *autobahn* in Germany; but belatedly in Britain, with the *motorway*, constructed after the S.W.W.

HIGHWAY CODE. A code of rules for the guidance of pedestrians, motorists and others using the roads, pub. by H.M.S.O. for the Min. of Transport.

HIGHWAYMEN. Term applied to thieves on horseback who robbed travellers on the highway, those who did so on foot being known as footpads. With the development of regular coach services in the 17th and 18th cents. their activities became notorious, and the Bow Street Runners were organized to suppress them. Favourite haunts were Hounslow and Bagshot heaths, and Epping Forest, and they continued to flourish well into the 19th cent. Among the best-known H. were Jonathan Wild, Claude Duval (1643–70), John Nevison (1639–84), the original hero of the 'ride to York', Dick Turpin (1706–39), and his partner Tom King, and Jerry Abershaw (*c*. 1773–95).

HIGH WYCOMBE (wi'kom). English market town (bor.) in a valley in the Chilterns, 9 m. N.E. of Henley, in S.W. Bucks. Famous for the manufacture of furniture, particularly chairs, H.W. is also an agricultural centre. Pop. (1961) 50,301. Near H.W. is West W.. a small village owned by the National Trust.

HIJACKING. *See* PIRACY.

HILDEBRAND. *See* GREGORY VII.

HILDESHEIM (hil'des-him). Town of Lower Saxony, W. Germany, at the foot of the Harz mts. A bishopric from the 9th cent., H. became a free city of the Holy Roman Empire in the 13th cent. It was under Prussia 1866–1945. Until devastated in the S.W.W., it contained many fine medieval buildings. Pop. (est.) 75,000.

HILL, Adrian Keith Graham (1895–). British painter and etcher. During the F.W.W. he was an official artist on the Western Front.

HILL, Archibald Vivian (1886–). British physiologist. He was prof. at Manchester 1920–3, London 1923–5, research prof. at Cambridge 1926–51, and has served on many governmental and scientific committees. For his work on the mechanism of muscle contraction he was awarded a Nobel prize in 1922.

HILL, Charles, baron H. of Luton (1904–). British doctor and Cons. politician. Wartime 'radio doctor', he was Postmaster Gen. 1955–7, Min. of Housing 1961–2, Chairman I.T.A. 1963–7, and Chairman of Govs. of B.B.C. from 1967: life peer1963.

HILL, Octavia (1838–1912). British housing reformer. Influenced by the Christian Socialist movement, and shocked by slum conditions, she bought houses in Marylebone, which she let in good condition and at moderate rents to working-class tenants; she was also joint founder of the National Trust (q.v.).

HILL, Sir Roderic Maxwell (1894–1954). British airman. He served with the R.F.C. in the F.W.W., and took charge of the Experimental Flying Dept. at Farnborough (1917–23). In the S.W.W. he was director-gen. of aircraft research and development 1940–1, commanded the Air Defence of Great Britain 1943–4 and was A.O.C. Fighter Command 1944–5. Knighted in 1944, he became air chief marshal in 1947.

HILL, Sir Rowland (1795–1879). British reformer. In a pamphlet 'Post Office Reform' he proposed the introduction of the penny pre-paid post (letters had

previously been paid for by the recipient on a rate varied according to distance) initiated in Jan. 1840. He was sec. to the Post Office 1854–64.

HILLARY, Sir Edmund (1919–). New Zealand mountaineer and apiarist. B. in Auckland, he served in the R.N.Z.A.F. during the S.W.W. Gaining his first mountaineering experience in New Zealand, he was one of the reconnaissance party to Everest in 1951, and in 1953, together with the Sherpa Tensing, conquered the summit. As leader of the N.Z. section at Scott Base of the Commonwealth Transantarctic Expedition 1957–8, he was the first man to reach the South Pole overland since Scott (q.v.) on 3 Jan. 1958: on the way he was laying depots for Fuchs's (q.v.) completion of the crossing of the continent.

HILLER, Wendy (1912–). British actress. An excellent character actress, she has played successfully parts as varied as Sally Hardcastle in *Love on the Dole* (1935), Catherine Sloper in *The Heiress* (1947), and Eliza in the film of *Pygmalion* (1938).

HILLIARD, Nicholas (*c*. 1547–1619). The earliest English miniaturist, and the first great painter of the English school. B. in Exeter, he became miniaturist and goldsmith to Queen Elizabeth.

HILLIER, Tristram (1905–). British painter. B. in Peking, he lived and worked in England; and France, at Dieppe. His landscapes and Surrealist pictures are remarkable for the careful rendering of detail.

HILLMAN, Sidney (1887–1946). American trade unionist. Emigrating to the U.S. from Lithuania at 20, he built up the powerful Amalgamated Clothing Workers of America and in 1935 helped found the C.I.O. He was closely associated with F.D.R. in drafting much New Deal labour legislation.

HILTON, Conrad Nicholson (1888–). American hotelier. From 1919 he estab. numerous luxury hotels in the U.S., and after the S.W.W. built up a world chain, the largest in existence. *See illus.* p. 544.

HILTON, James (1900–54). British novelist. Lancashire-born, he was to settle in Hollywood as one of its most successful script writers, e.g. *Mrs. Miniver*. His books incl. *Lost Horizon* (1933), envisaging Shangri-la, a remote district of Tibet where time stands still; *Mr. Chips* (1934), a portrait of an old schoolmaster; and *Random Harvest* (1941).

HILVERSUM. Town in N. Holland prov. of the Netherlands, 17 m. S.E. of Amsterdam. Besides being a summer resort, H. is the chief centre of Dutch broadcasting. Pop. (1961) 101,985.

HIMACHAL PRADESH (himah'chel predash'). State of the Rep. of India, between Punjab and Tibet. Created as a union territory in 1948, it was to attain full statehood in 1971. Certain hill areas were transferred from the Punjab to H.P. in 1966. The cap. is Simla. The state is agricultural (maize, wheat, fruit), with coniferous forests supplying timber. Industries are limited to handicrafts. Area 10,879 sq. m.; pop. (1961) 1,350,000.

HIMALA'YA (abode of snow). System of mountain ranges of central Asia, lying along the S. edge of the Tibetan plateau in an E.–W. arc convex to the S. In the most northerly range, average alt. 20,000 ft., a number of peaks exceed 25,000 ft. including Everest (29,028 ft.), the highest mountain in the world; K.2 or Godwin-Austen (28,278 ft.), the highest mountain within the British Commonwealth; and Kanchenjunga (28,146 ft.). The local pron. is himah'lia.

HIMMLER, Heinrich (1900–45). German Nazi leader. B. at Munich, he joined the Nazi Party in its early days, and became leader of the S.S. in 1929, and chief of the Bavarian police in 1933. His promotion in 1936 to the command of all German police forces, including the Gestapo, made him one of the most powerful men in Germany, and during the S.W.W. he replaced Goering as Hitler's second-in-command. In April 1945 he made a proposal to the Allies that Germany should surrender to Britain and the U.S.A. but not to Russia, which was rejected. He was captured in May, and committed suicide.

HINCHINGBROOKE, Victor Montagu, Visct. *See* SANDWICH, 10th earl of.

HINCKLEY. English market town (U.D.) in Leicestershire, 12 m. S.W. of Leicester. It manufactures boots, shoes, and hosiery. Pop. (1961) 41,573.

HINDEMITH (-mit), **Paul** (1895–1963). German composer. A fine viola player, he led the Frankfurt Opera Orchestra at 20, and taught composition at the Berlin Hochschule for music 1927–33, when the modernity of his work, e.g. the *Philharmonic Concerto*, led to a Nazi ban. In 1939 he went to the U.S., where he taught at Yale, and in 1952 became prof. of musical theory at Zürich. His works incl. many for chamber ensemble and orchestra, and the operas *Cardillac* (1926, revised 1952) and *Mathis der Maler* (1938).

HINDENBURG, Paul Ludwig Hans von Beneckendorf und von (1847–1934). German soldier and statesman. B. at Posen of a Prussian junker family, he was commissioned in 1866, served in the Austro-Prussian and Franco-German wars, and retired in 1911. Given the command in E. Prussia in Aug. 1914, he received the credit for the defeat of the Russians at Tannenberg, and was promoted to supreme commander and made a field marshal. Henceforward he and Ludendorff practically directed Germany's policy until the end of the war. He was elected Pres. of the German rep. in 1925, and re-elected in 1932. He invited Hitler to assume the Chancellorship in Jan. 1933, and his last public act was to congratulate him on the 'blood-bath' of June 1934. He d. on his Prussian estate, and was buried at Tannenberg.

HINDENBURG. Name given in 1915 to ZABRZE in honour of General H. H.: reverted to its old name in 1945.

HINDI. An Indian language, comprising an Eastern and a Western variety, ultimately derivable from Sanskrit, but descended from different Prakrit dialects. From Western H. Hindustani (q.v.) was derived; it is the official language of the Rep. of India.

HINDUISM. The religion of the Hindus; but the term includes the religious beliefs and also the system of caste and other social customs which have been inherited through the ages. Brahma, the Supreme Spirit, always existing and eternal, the original cause and the final home of everything that is, is envisaged as existing in and working through a triad of gods (the Trimurti), known as Brahma the creator, Vishnu the preserver, and Siva the destroyer and also the generator of new life. Vishnu and Siva are the principal objects of popular adoration, and the Vaishnavas and Saivas are the chief religious sects. Vishnu is considered to have been incarnated in a number of *avataras*, one of whom, Krishna, is perhaps the most popular deity. In addition to these principal gods, there is a vast host of minor divinities, demons, ghosts, and spirits, etc., who are popularly worshipped. But educated Hindus regard these and the Trimurti as expressions of the one great, all-comprehending Supreme Spirit.

The basic theological beliefs are the transmigration of souls, and *Karma* (deed), according to which a man's position in this life is affected by what he has done in an immensely long succession of past existences, and will affect his position in countless lives to come. The practice of H. is a complex of rites and ceremonies performed within the framework of the caste system under the supervision of the Brahman priests and teachers. Temple worship is almost universally performed, and there are many festivals. Benares is the principal of the holy cities, and the Ganges is the holiest river. In India and the rest of Asia there are over 400 million Hindus.

HINDU KUSH (hin'doo koosh). Range of mountains in central Asia running W.S.W. from the Pamir region to the Koh-i-Baba. a distance of about 500 m.

HINDU KUSH. Once one of the loneliest places in the world, it was a major obstacle to trade and communications between central and southern Asia until the completion in 1964 of the Salang Tunnel and a new highway system from Kabul to the Oxus valley via Doshi.
Courtesy of the Afghan Publicity Bureau.

The highest summit is Tirich Mir, 25,260 ft., in W. Pakistan.

HINDU MAHASABHA. Hindu communal organization. Founded in 1908, it supported the movement for national independence, but differed from the Congress Party in its more conservative political and social policy, and in its emphasis on purely Hindu communal claims, as opposed to the Congress policy of Hindu-Moslem co-operation. The H.M. opposed the partition of India in 1947, and one of its members assassinated Gandhi.

HINDUSTANI. An Indian language, called by Indians Urdu. Originally the language of the bazaars of Delhi, and a local variety of Western Hindi, it was adopted by the troops of the Mogul Empire, and rapidly became a *lingua franca* throughout India.

HINKLER, Herbert John Louis (1892–1933). Australian pilot who in 1928 made the first solo flight from England to Australia. He was killed while making another attempt to fly to Australia.

HINSHELWOOD, Sir Cyril (1897–1967). British chemist. Dr. Lee's prof. of chemistry at Oxford 1937–64, he was awarded a Nobel prize in 1956 (jointly with Nikolai Semenov of Russia) for discoveries in the field of chemical kinetics, and was pres. of the Royal Society 1955–60. His works incl. *The Chemical Kinetics of the Bacterial Cell* (1946).

HINTON, Christopher, baron H. of Bankside (1901–). British nuclear industrialist. An apprentice in a railway workshop, he won a scholarship to Cambridge, and was prominent in the British development of commercial power. From 1957–64 he was first chairman of the C.E.G.B. He was created a life peer 1965.

HIPPARCHUS (hipahr'kus) (*c*. 555–514 B.C.). Greek tyrant. Son of Pisistratus (q.v.), he was assoc. with his elder brother Hippias as ruler of Athens 527–14. His affection being spurned by Harmodius, he insulted the latter's sister, and was assassinated by Harmodius and Aristogiton.

HIPPA'RCHUS (fl. 160–145 B.C.). Gk. astronomer, a native of Nicaea in Bithynia. He invented trigonometry, calculated the lengths of the solar year and the lunar month, discovered the precession of the equinoxes, made a catalogue of 800 fixed stars, and advanced Eratosthenes's method of determining the situation of places on the earth's surface by lines of latitude and longitude.

HIPPO'CRATES (*c.* 460–*c.* 357 B.C.). Gk. physician commonly styled the Father of Medicine. B. in the island of Cos, he practised and taught medicine in his native place, travelled in the mainland of Greece, and d. in Thessaly. He was the author of a number of medical works, and set a high standard of professional ethics. For more than 2,000 years the Hippocratic Oath has epitomised the medical ethic.

HIPPO'LYTUS. In Gk. mythology, son of Theseus. He was accused by his step-mother Phaedra of dishonourable advances, and Theseus placed a curse on him. By the agency of the god Poseidon he was killed while riding in his chariot near the sea. Later he was proved innocent and restored to life.

HIPPOPO'TAMUS (Gk., river-horse). Large mammal of the family Hippopotamidae. The common H. (*H. amphibius*) is found in Central Africa. It is 14 ft. long, 4 ft. high, weighs between 3 and 4 tons, and has a slate-grey skin. The pygmy H. (*H. liberiensis*) inhabits W. Africa. Hs. are good swimmers, but leave the water at night to graze.

HIRE PURCHASE. The system of retail trading whereby the purchaser contracts to make partial payments at fixed intervals over a certain period, and the way in which most durable consumer goods are paid for. Increasing rapidly after the F.W.W., the H.P. debt outstanding in U.S.A. rose from $3,000 million in 1929 to $95,000 million in 1969, at annual interest rates of 15–18 per cent. The amount owing in Britain in 1969 was nearly £1,000 million, comparable with the cost of the entire National Health Service. H.P. is still expanding and covers an increasingly wide range of goods and services, from cradle to grave.

HIROHITO (hērōhē'tō) (1901–). Emperor of Japan. In 1921 he was the 1st Japanese crown prince to visit Europe, and in 1926 succeeded his father Yoshihito. After the defeat of Japan in 1945 he

HIPPOPOTAMUS. Keeping a moist skin is essential for the health of the hippopotamus, but this family party in the Kruger National Park make a pleasure of necessity, although keeping a wary eye for intruders. *Courtesy of Satour.*

formally rejected belief in the divinity of the emperor and Japanese racial superiority, and accepted the 1946 constitution greatly curtailing his powers. The Imperial Palace, destroyed by fire in air raids 1945, was rebuilt within the same spacious wooded compound at a cost of £13,000,000: completed 1969. Distinguished as a botanist and zoologist, H. has pub. several books.

HIROSHIMA (hēro'shima). City and port on the S. coast of Honshu, Japan; during the S.W.W. H. was utterly devastated on 6 Aug. 1945 by the first atomic bomb to be used in war-time. The bomb, dropped by parachute from an American Super-Fortress flying at 30,000 ft., exploded 1,000 ft. above the city. Over 4 sq. m. was obliterated, with very heavy damage outside that area. Casualties totalled 136,989 out of a pop. of 343,000; 78,150 were found dead and others died later.

By 1947 many temporary buildings on the site were inhabited; by 1955 substantial reconstruction had made H. once more a prosperous port and commercial centre with by 1965 a pop. of 504,000.

HISPANIŌ'LA. W. Indian is., the 1st landing place in the New World of Columbus, 6 Dec. 1492. It is divided into Haiti and the Dominican Rep. (qq.v.).

HISPANO-SUIZA. Motor-car designed by a Swiss engineer Marc Birkigt (1878–1947), who emigrated to Barcelona where he founded a factory which produced cars *c.* 1900–38, which were popular among the cognoscenti, incl. Alphonso XIII of Spain, after whom the 1911 sports model was named. During the F.W.W. a Paris factory produced the famous light-alloy aero-engine used by the 'stork' squadron of the French air force, whose emblem, a flying stork, became the mascot of later cars, which incorporated improvements based on war-time experience and incl. the '37·2' and 9 litre V12, still of legendary fame for their handling, elegance and speed.

HISS, Alger (1904–). American politician. B. in Baltimore, he was one of the bright young men recruited under Roosevelt's New Deal. While pres. of the Carnegie Endowment for International Peace 1946–9, he denied before a federal grand jury having in 1938 passed secret State Dept. papers to Whittaker Chambers (an editor of *Time* and a self-confessed Communist). An inconclusive trial for perjury in 1949 was followed by his conviction in 1950: he was released from prison in 1954. His actual guilt is still hotly disputed.

HISTORY. The written record of the development of human societies. The earliest surviving historical records are the inscriptions denoting the achievements of Egyptian and Babylonian kings. As a literary form H. begins with Herodotus (*c.* 484–425 B.C.), who first passed beyond the limits of a purely national outlook. Thucydides (*c.* 471–401 B.C.) brought to H. not only literary gifts but the interests of a scientific investigator and political philosopher. Later Greek H. degenerated into rhetoric, nor was Roman H. free from this vice; Sallust (86–35 B.C.) preserved the scientific spirit of Thucydides, but Livy (59–17 B.C.) and Tacitus (*c.* A.D. 54–118), in spite of their great powers, tended to subordinate truth to patriotic or party considerations. Medieval H. suffered from its domination by a ready-made religious philosophy imposed by the Church. English chroniclers of this period are Bede (673–735), William of Malmesbury (d. 1143), and Matthew Paris (d. 1259). France produced great chroniclers of contemporary events in Froissart (1337–1401) and Comines (1447–1511).

The Renaissance revivified H. both by restoring classical models and by creating the science of textual criticism. A product of the new secular spirit is Machiavelli's *History of Florence* (1520–3). The Reformation, especially in Germany, furthered the cause of scientific H. by sending controversialists back to the original documents, while in England the constitutional controversies of the 17th cent. performed a similar service. The 18th cent. 'enlightenment' finally disposed of the attempt to explain H. in theological terms, but it made little progress in the search for an alternative philosophy, although it produced one masterpiece in Gibbon's *Decline and Fall of the Roman Empire* (1776–88). The most remarkable attempt to formulate a philosophy of H., that of Vico (1668–1744), remained almost unknown until the 19th cent. Romanticism left its mark on H. in the tendency to exalt the contribution of the individual 'hero', and in the introduction of a more colourful and dramatic style and treatment, variously illustrated in the works of Michelet, Carlyle, and Macaulay.

During the last cent. H. has been revolutionized. The deciphering of the Egyptian and Babylonian inscriptions opened up a new world. The researches of archaeologists have enabled us to trace the development of prehistoric man, and have revealed forgotten civilizations such as that of Crete. The anthropological studies of primitive society and religion, headed by Frazer's *Golden Bough*, have laid bare the bases of later forms of social organization and belief. The changes brought about by the Industrial Revolution, and the accompanying rise of political economy to the status of a science, forced the historian to turn his attention to economic questions. Marx's attempt to find in economic development the most important, though by no means the only, determining factor in social change, an argument partly paralleled in Buckle's *History of Civilization* (1857), has influenced all serious historians since. A comparative study of civilizations is offered in A. J. Toynbee's *Study of History* (1934–54).

HITCHCOCK, Alfred (1899–). British film director. Experienced in many branches of the film industry, he is a master of suspense and film technique, and his films incl. *Thirty-nine Steps* (1935), *Rebecca* (1940), *Rope* (1948), *Strangers on a Train* (1951), *Rear Window* (1954), *Vertigo* (1958), *Psycho* (1960), *The Birds* (1963).

HITCHENS, Ivon (1893–). British artist. B. in London, the son of a painter, he held his 1st one-man exhibition in 1925. Remarkable for his sensuous use of paint, he is equally successful in the flower study or landscape as in murals for the English Folk Dance Society (1954) or the Univ. of Sussex (1963).

HITCHIN. English market town (U.D.) in Herts, 30 m. N.N.W. of London, with a Perpendicular style parish church. Eugene Aram (q.v.) at one time lived in Golden Square. The cultivation and distillation of lavender, introduced here from Naples in the 16th cent., still continues. Pop. (1961) 24,243.

HITLER, Adolf (1889–1945). German dictator. B. at Braunau-am-Inn, in Austria, the son of a customs official, he spent his early years in poverty in Vienna and Munich. After serving as a volunteer in the German army during the F.W.W., he was employed as a spy by the military authorities in Munich, and in 1919 joined in this capacity the German Workers' Party, founded by Anton Drexler. By 1921 he had assumed its leadership, renamed it the National Socialist German Workers' Party, provided it with a programme, and rallied a following. Having led an unsuccessful rising at Munich in 1923, he was sentenced to 9 months' imprisonment, during which he wrote his political testament, *Mein Kampf* (*My Struggle*). The party achieved national importance only in 1930, when the big industrialists began to support it; by 1932, although Hindenburg defeated H. in the presidential elections, it formed the largest group in the Reichstag. As the result of an intrigue directed by von Papen, H. became Chancellor in a Nazi-Nationalist coalition on 30 Jan. 1933.

The opposition were rapidly suppressed, the Nationalists removed from the govt., and the Nazis declared the only legal party. In 1934 H. succeeded Hindenburg as Head of the State, with the title of Fuehrer. Meanwhile, the drive to war began; Germany left the League of Nations, conscription was reintroduced, and in 1936 the Rhineland was occupied. H. and Mussolini, who were already co-operating in Spain, formed an alliance in 1937. The new year saw the annexation of Austria, and the cession of Sudetenland under the Munich agreement. The rest of Czechoslovakia was annexed in March 1939. The non-aggression pact with Russia in Aug. was followed in Sept. by the invasion of Poland and the declaration of war by Britain and France. (*See* SECOND WORLD WAR.) H. narrowly escaped death in 1944 from a bomb explosion prepared by high-ranking officers. On 29 April 1945, when Berlin was largely in Russian hands, he m. Eva Braun in the Reichschancellery, and on the following day committed suicide with her, both bodies afterwards being destroyed by burning.

HITTITES (hit'īts). A group of peoples who inhabited Asia Minor and N. Syria from the 3rd to the 1st millennium B.C. The original Hs., a people of Armenoid type, inhabited a number of city-states in E. Asia Minor, one of which, Hatti, gained supremacy over the others. An Indo-European people invaded the country *c.* 2000 B.C., made themselves the ruling class, and intermarried with the original inhabitants. Hatti, then known as Hattushash, became the capital of a strong kingdom, which overthrew the Babylonian empire. After a period of eclipse the H. New Empire became a great power (*c.* 1400–1200 B.C.) which successfully waged war with Egypt, until it was overthrown by the so-called Sea Peoples. Small H. states then arose in N. Syria, the most important of which was Carchemish; these were conquered by the Assyrians in the 8th cent. B.C., Carchemish in 717.

The Hs. used a cuneiform script, modelled on the Babylonian for ordinary purposes, and a 'hieroglyphic' script for monumental inscriptions. The H. royal archives were discovered at Hattushash in 1906–7, and deciphered in 1915 by Hrozný.

HOANG-HO. Another form of HWANG-HO.

HOARE, Sir Samuel. See TEMPLEWOOD.

HOATZIN (hō-at'sin). Tropical S. American bird (*Opisthocomus hoatzin*), the only representative of its family and resembling a small pheasant in size and appearance: adults are olive with white markings above and red-brown below. The young are hatched naked, and have well-developed claws on the 'thumb and index fingers' of the wing, so that they can crawl reptilian-fashion about the tree – a reminder of their ancestry. On account of its strong musky smell, the H. is known in British Guiana as the 'stink-bird'.

HOBART. Capital of Tasmania, Australia, situated on the estuary of the river Derwent, on the S. coast.

HOBART. From Mount Wellington the bright lights of the port area can be seen to the far right, and the circle to the left is the Tasmanian Cricket Association Ground. The Floating Bridge over the Derwent leads to the spreading residential suburbs, and in the distance beyond Mount Rumney are the lights of the airport. *Courtesy of the Mercury, Hobart.*

Founded in 1804, the city was called after Lord H., who was Secretary of State for the Colonies at the time. It has a fine harbour. Pop. (1959) 109,200.

HOB'BEMA, Meindert (1638–1709). Dutch landscape painter. B. at Amsterdam, he came under the influence of Ruysdael, and his pictures show the peace and charm of the Dutch countryside. Most of his best works, incl. his masterpiece, 'Avenue at Middelharnis' (National Gallery, *see* illus. p. 535) are in English galleries.

HOBBES, Thomas (1588–1679). English political philosopher. B. near Malmesbury, he was ed. at Oxford, and as a strong royalist withdrew to Paris in 1640, and was tutor to the exiled Prince Charles 1646–8. He pub. mathematical and scientific works and classical translations, but his most important work was his *Leviathan* (1651), an exposition of the totalitarian state.

HOBBS, Sir John ('Jack') (1882–1963). British cricketer. A most accomplished batsman, he achieved

197 centuries and 61,221 runs in first-class cricket. He played for England 1907–30, and for Surrey from 1905 until his retirement in 1935.

HO′BŌKEN. City and port of New Jersey, U.S.A., on the Hudson, adjoining Jersey City. H., incorporated 1849, is on the site of a Dutch farm destroyed by Indians in 1643. Pop. (1960) 48,441.

HOCHE (ōsh), **Lazare** (1768–97). French general. Commissioned in 1792 from the ranks, in 1793 he commanded the Fr. army in Lorraine, expelling the

HOBBEMA. Dated 1659 'Avenue at Middelharnis' shows a scene on Over Flakkee, then and subsequently an island off southern Holland, until in the 1960s by reclamation part of the mainland. *Courtesy of the National Gallery.*

Prussians, and in 1796 commanded an unsuccessful attempt to invade Ireland.

HOCHHUTH (hohkh′hoot), **Rolf** (1933–). Swiss dramatist. Municipal playwright at Basle from 1963, he is best-known for the controversial *Soldiers* (1968), with its implication that Churchill was involved in a plot to assassinate Sikorski (q.v.).

HO CHI-MINH (1892–1969). N. Vietnamese politician. B. in N. Vietnam, he was trained in Moscow, headed the Communist Vietminh from 1941, and, having campaigned against the French 1946–54, became Pres. and P.M. of the Democratic Rep. at the armistice. Aided by the Communist bloc, he did much to develop industrial potential, and although he relinquished the premiership in 1955, he was re-elected Pres. in 1960.

The *Ho Chi-Minh Trails*, the N. Vietnamese troop and supply routes to the interior of S. Vietnam through Laos, led to S. Vietnamese military intervention in Laos in 1971.

HOCKEY. A game using hooked sticks, not unlike the modern ones, was played by the ancient Greeks, and under the names of 'hurley' and 'shinty' a primitive form of the game was played in Ireland and Scotland. Modern H. dates from 1886 when the Men's H. Association rules were drafted.

It is played between 2 teams, each of not more than 11 players. The ground is 100 yds. long and 55–60 yds. wide. Goals, 7 ft. high by 4 yds. wide, are placed within a striking circle of 16 yds. radius, from which all shots at goal must be made. The white ball weighs

5½ to 5¾ oz., its circumference being 8 13/16 in. to 9¼ in., and the stick must not exceed 2 in. in diameter or 28 oz. in weight. Game is started by a 'bully-off' in which the centre-forwards strike the ground and the other's stick 3 times before playing the ball. The ball may be stopped with the hand, but not held, picked up, thrown or kicked, except by the goalkeeper in his own striking circle. If the ball is sent into touch, it is returned to play by a 'push in'. The game is divided into two 35 min. periods; it is controlled by two umpires, one for each half of the field. The women's game is governed by the All England Women's Hockey Association founded in 1895.

HOCKNEY, David (1937–). British artist. Trained at Bradford School of Art and the Royal College of Art, he made his first reputation in the Young Contemporaries Show of 1961. His work is colourful, inventive and innocently joyous, as in his representations of water.

HODGKIN, Sir Alan Lloyd (1971–). Brit. physiologist. Both H. and A. F. Huxley, former students of Lord Adrian (q.v.), were engaged in research on the mechanism of conduction in peripheral nerves 1946–60, during which they elected F.R.S., and in 1963 with Sir John Eccles (q.v.) shared the Nobel prize for physiology and medicine. He was elected pres. of the Royal Society 1970.

HODGKIN, Dorothy Crowfoot (1910–). British chemist. Wolfson research prof. of the Royal Society at Oxford Univ. from 1960, she was awarded a Nobel prize 1964 for work on the determination by X-ray studies of the structure of important biochemical compounds, e.g. vitamin B12, a liver extract used in combating pernicious anaemia, and penicillin. She m. in 1937 Thomas Lionel H. (1910–), lecturer in the govt. of new states, Univ. of Oxford, from 1965. In 1965 she was awarded the O.M.

HODGKINS, Frances (1870–1947). New Zealand landscape and still-life artist. She eventually settled in Paris and did some of her best work between the ages of 60 and 70. Her paintings have a poetic quality.

HODGSON, Ralph (1871–1962). British poet. B. in Yorks, he is best remembered for the anthology pieces 'The Bull' and 'The Song of Honour' in *Poems* (1917). He was an expert breeder of bull-terriers and lived in the U.S. in later life.

HOE (hō), **Richard March** (1812–86). American inventor. He was the head of a New York press-manufacturing business who invented the rotary press in 1846, and also a device to fold newspapers as they came from the press.

HOFFA, James Riddle (1913–). American trade unionist. Pres. of the 1½-million-strong International Brotherhood of Teamsters (expelled from the A.F.L.-C.I.O. in 1957 and banned from re-entry) from 1957, he was indicted by a Federal Grand Jury in 1962 for accepting more than $1,000,000 in illegal payments and charged by the Senate Permanent Subcommittee on Investigations with defiant indifference to the interests of his members and to misuse of union funds by corrupt officials. In 1964 he was sentenced to 8 yrs.' gaol for trying to bribe the Federal Court Jury in 1962 hearing a conspiracy charge against him.

HOFFMAN, Paul Gray (1891–). American administrator. B. in Chicago, he was chairman of the Studebaker Corporation from 1953 and of the combined Studebaker-Packard corporation 1954–6. In 1959 he was appointed managing director of the newly created U.N. Special Fund for economic assistance to under-developed countries, and became administrator United Nations Development Programme in 1966.

HOFFMANN, Ernst Theodor Amadeus (1776–1822). German composer and writer. A lawyer in Berlin, he enjoyed great success with his opera *Undine* (1816) and his *Fantastic Tales* inspired Offenbach's *Tales of H.*

HOFMANN, Josef Casimir (1876–1957). Polish pianist, a U.S. citizen from 1926. A student of Rubinstein, and a brilliant executant, he also wrote a symphony and 5 concertos.

HOFMANNSTHAL (hŏf'mahnstahl), **Hugo von** (1874–1929). Austrian poet. B. in Vienna, he reflects in his lyrics and lyrical plays (*Der Tor und der Tod*, 1893, etc.) the melancholy of a waning culture. His dramas deal with themes of classical antiquity or of the Middle Ages (*Jedermann*). He also wrote librettos for a number of operas by Richard Strauss.

HOGARTH, William (1697–1764). British artist and engraver. B. in London, he was apprenticed to an engraver, and from 1720 studied painting with Sir James Thornhill whose daughter he clandestinely married in 1729. His *A Harlot's Progress* (1731), a series of 6 pictures, engraved in 1732, estab. his fame and was followed by *A Rake's Progress* (1735); his masterpiece *Marriage à la Mode* (1745); *Industry and Idleness* (1749) and *The Four Stages of Cruelty* (1751). His penetrating satire of the follies and vices of his age, command of group composition and skill in genre painting are uniquely English in tone. In portraiture he has a sympathetic directness that did not appeal to the fashionable world of his time. **Paul H.** (1917–), British artist-reporter, is his descendant. He has pub. vols. of drawings of people and landscapes in 3 continents, and has made a name as a book illustrator for Dickens, O. Henry, Brendan Behan (q.v.), etc.

The artist at work in his studio, a self-portrait. *Photo: N.P.G.*

HOGBEN, Lancelot (1895–). British scientist. Prof. of social biology at London 1930–7, natural history at Aberdeen, and zoology (1941–7) and medical statistics (1947–61) at Birmingham, he is skilled in popularization, e.g. *Mathematics for the Million* (1936): other books incl. *Chance and Choice* (1950–5) and *Mathematics in the Making* (1960).

HOGG, James (1770–1835). Scottish poet, known as the 'Ettrick Shepherd'. B. in Ettrick Forest, Selkirkshire, he worked as a shepherd at Yarrow (1790–9), and until 30 was illiterate. His *Scottish Pastorals* (1801) are now forgotten, but his novel *Confessions of a Justified Sinner* (1824) is a masterly portrayal of personified evil.

HOGG, QuintinMcGarel (1907–). British Cons. politician, son of Lord Hailsham (q.v.) and grandson of Quintin H. (1845–1903), the merchant philanthropist who in 1882 estab. in Regent Street, London, a Youths' Christian Institute from which the Regent Street Polytechnic, and similar institutions for technical education, developed.

A fellow of All Souls Coll., Oxford, 1931–8, H. was then an M.P. until he succeeded his father as 2nd visct. Hailsham in 1950,

renouncing the title in 1963 to re-enter the Commons. He was First Lord of the Admiralty 1956–7 and Min. of Education from 1957 until his appointment to the newly created post of Min. of Science and Technology 1959–64. A member of the Tory Reform Committee, he in 1947 pub. *The Case for Conservatism* and is remembered for his rallying the party conference at Blackpool in 1958 by ringing a handbell. In 1970 he re-entered the Lords as Lord Chancellor and a life peer, Baron Hailsham of Marylebone.

HOGGAR. Another form of AHAGGAR.

HOGMANAY (hog'manā). Scottish name for the last day of the year and also for the oatmeal cakes given to the children as they go from house to house singing carols.

HOHENSTAUFEN (hŏ'enstowfen). Name of a German princely family, members of which held the title of Holy Roman Emperor 1138–1208 and 1214–54. The most notable of the H. emperors were Frederick I, Henry VI, and Frederick II (qq.v.).

HOHENZOLLERN (hŏ'entsollern). Name of a German family, originating in Württemberg, the main branch of which held the titles of elector of Brandenburg from 1415, king of Prussia from 1701, and German Emperor from 1871. The last emperor, William II, was dethroned in 1918. Another branch of the family were kings of Rumania 1881–1947.

HOKKAIDO (hoki'dō). Most northerly of the 4 main islands of Japan, separated from Honshu on the S. by Tsugaru Strait and from Sakhalin on the N. by Soya Strait. Snow-covered for 6 months of the year, H. was little developed until the Meiji Restoration of 1868 when disbanded Samurai were settled. Natural resources incl. coal, mercury, manganese, oil and natural gas, timber and rich fisheries. Intensive exploitation followed the S.W.W. incl. heavy and chemical industrial plants, development of electric power, and dairy farming. The cap. is Sapporo, founded 1871, which is the centre of the road system and site of H. Univ. (1918): pop. (1965) 821,000. An artificial harbour has been constructed at Tomakomai, and an undersea rail tunnel is planned to link Hakodate with Aomori (Honshu) by 1975. Area *c.* 30,300 sq. m.; pop. (1968) 5,000,000 incl. 16,000 Ainus (q.v.).

HOKUSAI (hŏ'kōōsahi) (1760–1849). Japanese artist. B. at Yedo, he was originally a student of engraving. Very prolific, he produced vital interpretations of everyday Japanese life in prints, water-colours and book illustrations, and was equally at home with a picture on a grain of rice or more than life-size figures.

HOLBACH (ōlbahk'), **Paul Heinrich Dietrich, baron d'** (1723–89). French materialist philosopher. B. in the Palatinate he settled in Paris and became a naturalized Frenchman. He contributed articles on scientific subjects to the *Encyclopédie*, and pub. the *Système de la Nature* (1770).

HOLBEIN (hol'bīn), **Hans, the Younger** (1497–1543). German painter. B. at Augsburg, he was the son and pupil of **Hans H., the Elder** (*c.* 1460–1524), who was also b. at Augsburg, and whose masterpiece is the altar-piece of St. Sebastian (1515) in the Munich

HOLBEIN THE YOUNGER
A study of Christina of Denmark (1523–90) who married in 1534 the duke of Milan. *Courtesy of the National Gallery.*

Pinakothek. In 1515 H. went to Basle, where he became friendly with Erasmus, and in 1517 to Lucerne, where he painted the façades of houses. He was working in Basle again 1519–26, and to this period belong the wood engravings for the *Dance of Death*. He also executed title pages for Luther's translation of the N.T. and More's *Utopia*, and did a number of woodcuts of O.T. subjects. One of his most famous works is the 'Meyer Madonna', a fine altar-piece at Darmstadt. In 1527 he came to England, and in 1536 became court painter to Henry VIII. He d. of the plague. *See* illus. p. 469.

HOLBERG, Ludwig von, baron (1684–1754). Danish historian and dramatist. B. in Bergen, he travelled widely 1704–16, and subsequently obtained professorships at Copenhagen univ. It was at this time that he determined to found a Danish literature written in the vernacular. He produced many dramatic and satirical works between 1719 and 1731, and 1721–7 directed the Copenhagen theatre.

HOLBROOKE, Josef (1878–1958). British composer. His romantic works, e.g. 'The Raven', a symphonic poem, the operatic trilogy *The Cauldron of Annwen* and quantities of chamber music were the height of fashion in the post-Victorian period. He was also well known as a critic.

HOLDEN, Charles (1874–1960). British architect, remembered for his Underground stations, incl. Piccadilly, and the buildings of the Univ. of London.

HOLFORD, William Graham, baron (1907–   ). British architect. B. in Johannesburg, he was Lever prof. of civic design at Liverpool from 1936, where he had studied and was to plan the nuclear laboratories, and in 1948 became prof. of town planning at London. His varied work has been influential: he was pres. R.I.B.A. 1960–2 and was created a life peer 1965.

HOLINSHED, Ralph (*c.* 1520–*c.* 1580). English chronicler. B. probably in Cheshire, he went to London as assistant to a printer, and pub. in 1578 2 vols. of the *Chronicles of England, Scotland and Ireland*, which were largely used by Shakespeare.

HOLLAND, Henry Richard Vassall Fox, 3rd baron H. (1773–1840). British Whig statesman. The son of the 2nd Lord Holland, he became Lord Privy Seal in 1806–7. His seat at Holland House was for many years the centre of Whig political and literary society.

HOLLAND, Sidney George (1893–1961). New Zealand statesman. In 1940 he succeeded to the leadership of the National Party, then in opposition, but was P.M. 1949–57.

HOLLAND, North and **South.** Two provs. of the Netherlands. N.H. occupies the peninsula jutting northwards between the North Sea and the Ijsselmeer. Most of it is below sea-level, protected from the sea by a series of sand dunes and artificial dykes. The cap. is Haarlem; other towns are Amsterdam, the largest and most important, Hilversum, Den Helder, and the cheese centres Alkmaar and Edam. Area 1,016 sq. m.; pop. (1966) 2,200,602.

S.H., to the S. of N.H., is also low-lying. The Hague is its cap.; other important towns are Rotterdam, Leyden, Gouda, and Delft. Dairy cattle are reared and dairy products are important; there are petroleum refineries at Rotterdam, distilleries at Schiedam. Area 1,085 sq. m.; pop. (1966) 2,902,572.

Because the provs. of N. and S. H. have always been the wealthiest part of the Netherlands (q.v.), the name HOLLAND is frequently used for the whole country – even by Dutchmen.

HOLLAND, Parts of. Separate administrative co. within Lincolnshire, England. The principal town is Boston. Area 419 sq. m.; pop. (1967) 105,120.

HOLLAR, Wenceslaus (1607–77). Bohemian engraver. B. at Prague, he went to England in 1637, and was appointed drawing master to the Prince of Wales. He made numerous plates of views of London and of various other cities which he visited.

HOLLY. Trees and bushes of the *Ilex* genus of the Aquifoliaceae family. The evergreen European H.

(*I. aquifolium*) may grow 60–80 ft. high and has a smooth grey bark and highly polished leaves, wavy and spined at the edges. The small whitish flowers, borne in May, are followed by scarlet berries. Branches of both the British and American species are used for Christmas decoration.

HOLLYHOCK. Garden perennial, *Althaea rosea*, of the Malvaceae family. Originally a native of Asia, the H. was introduced into Britain some 3 cents. ago. The flower spikes are up to 10 ft. high.

HOLLYWOOD. Suburb of Los Angeles, California, U.S.A., from 1911 the centre of the U.S. film industry. The film stars' homes are chiefly situated at Beverly Hills nearby.

HOLMES, Oliver Wendell (1809–94). American writer. B. at Cambridge, Mass., he became prof. of anatomy at Dartmouth (1838–40) and at Harvard (1847–82). In 1857 he founded with Lowell the *Atlantic Monthly*, in which were pub. the essays and verse collected in 1858 as *The Autocrat of the Breakfast-Table*, a record of the imaginary conversation of boarding-house guests. This was followed by *The Professor at the Breakfast-Table* and the novel *Elsie Venner* (1861).

HOLMIUM (Lat. *Holmia* for Stockholm). Symbol Ho, at. wt. 164·94, at. no. 67. Discovered by Cleve in 1897, H. is one of the rare earth metals and has not yet been isolated. It occurs in various minerals such as gadolinite.

HOLOGRAPHY. The technique of reconstructing a 3-dimensional image from the reflected waves of a source of single frequency: it operates equally well in sound and light. It is thought that bats owe their ability to weave through wire obstructions etc. to a system of bioholography.

HOLST, Gustav Theodore (1874–1934). British composer. B. at Cheltenham, of Swedish descent, he studied at the R.C.M. under Stanford, became a trombonist, and was a teacher in London and Reading. He composed operas (*Sāvitri, At the Boar's Head*, etc.), ballets, choral works ('Hymns from the Rig Veda', 'The Hymn of Jesus', etc.), orchestral suites (among which is 'The Planets'), songs, etc.

HOLT, Harold Edward (1908–67). Australian statesman. B. in Sydney, son of a teacher, he was Min. of Labour 1940–1 and 1949–58, and Federal Treasurer 1958–66, when he succeeded Menzies as P.M. He was drowned in a swimming accident.

HOLTBY, Winifred (1898–1935). British novelist. An ardent advocate of women's freedom and racial toleration, she is best known for her novel *South Riding* (1936), set in her native Yorkshire. *See also* VERA BRITTAIN.

HOLYHEAD (hol'ihed). Seaport (U.D.) on the N. coast of H. Island, off Anglesey, Wales. H. Island is linked by road and railway bridges with Anglesey, and there are regular sailings between H. and Dublin. Pop. (1961) 10,408.

HOLY ISLAND. English island 2 m. off the coast of Northumberland, to which it is connected by a causeway. St. Aidan founded a monastery there in 635. HOLYHEAD ISLAND is sometimes called Holy Island.

HOLY LAND. *See* PALESTINE

HOLYOAKE, George Jacob (1817–1906). British progressive. B. in Birmingham, he early became an Owenite and a Chartist, and in 1842 was imprisoned

HOLYROOD, and on the floodlit balcony the Queen.
Photo: George Outram & Co.

for blasphemy in a public lecture. He invented the term 'secularism' as a definition of his views, was largely responsible for the abolition of the newspaper tax in 1855, and supported the co-operative movement.

HOLYOAKE, Keith Jacka (1904–). New Zealand National Party statesman. Great-grandson of an English settler of 1842, he worked at 12 on his father's farm and became a successful sheep farmer. Entering parliament in 1932, he was deputy P.M. and Min. for Agriculture 1949–57, and succeeded Sir Sidney Holland (q.v.) as P.M. for 2 months in 1957. Favouring a property-owning democracy, he was returned to power in 1960, 1963, 1969, retiring 1972.

HOLY OFFICE. The Inquisition (q.v.).

HOLY ORDERS. The estate or condition of Christian priests, conferred by the laying on of hands of a bishop. In the C. of E. there are three orders – bishop, priest, and deacon; but in the R.C. Church H.O. include, in addition, sub-deacons, acolytes, exorcists, readers, and door-keepers.

HOLY ROMAN EMPIRE. Name applied to the empire of Charlemagne and his successors, and to the German Empire 962–1806, both being regarded as a revival of the Roman Empire. *See* GERMAN HISTORY; CHARLEMAGNE; HABSBURGS; etc.

HOLYROOD HOUSE. Royal residence in Edinburgh, Scotland. The palace was built (1498–1503) on the site of a 12th cent. abbey by James IV. It has associations with Mary Queen of Scots and Charles Edward, the Young Pretender.

HOLY SHROUD. *See* TURIN.

HOMBURG. Town and spa at the foot of the Taunus mts., W. Germany; has given its name to a soft felt hat, made fashionable at H. by Edward VII. Pop. (est.) 25,000.

HOME (hūm), **Sir Alec** (Alexander) **Frederick Douglas-** (1903–). British Cons. politician. Ed. at Eton and Christ Church, Oxford, he was M.P. for Lanark 1931–45 (being P.P.S. to Neville Chamberlain 1937–9), and from 1950 until he succeeded his father as 14th earl of H. in 1951: he had previously been known by the courtesy title Lord Dunglass. After being Min. of State for Scotland 1951–5, he was Sec. of State for Commonwealth Relations 1955–60, and Foreign Affairs 1960–3. He was chosen to succeed Macmillan as P.M. 1963, when he renounced his peerages, failed to win the 1964 general election, and resigned as Cons. leader 1965. In 1970 he became

SIR ALEC DOUGLAS-HOME
Photo: Photo Centre Ltd.

Sec. for Foreign and Cw. Affairs. His younger brother **William Douglas Home** (1912–) has stood several times unsuccessfully for Parliament, and has written a number of plays, e.g. *The Chiltern Hundreds, The Reluctant Debutante,* and *The Reluctant Peer.*

HOME. Daniel Dunglas (1833–86). British spiritualist medium: related to the earls of H. Evidence of his levitation was attested to in U.S.; and in England, by Lord Lindsay, Lord Adare and Sir William Crookes. He held *séances* before sovereigns of France, Prussia and Holland (1857–8), and while in Italy became a Roman Catholic, but in 1864 was expelled from Rome as a sorcerer.

HOME COUNTIES. Name given to the counties in close proximity to London, viz. Herts, Essex, Kent, Surrey, and formerly Middlesex.

HOME GUARD. Unpaid force formed in Britain in May 1940 to repel the expected German invasion, and known until July 1940 as the Local Defence Volunteers. It consisted of men of 17–65 who had not been called up, formed part of the armed forces of the Crown, and was subject to military law. Over 2,000,000 strong in 1944, it was disbanded 31 Dec. 1945, but revived in 1951, then placed on a reserve basis in 1955, and ceased activities in 1957.

HOME OFFICE. Govt. Dept. estab. in 1782; it deals with all the internal affairs of England and Wales except those specifically assigned to other Depts. The Home Secretary, the head of the Dept., holds cabinet rank, and is the channel of communication between the sovereign and his subjects. The chief matters with which the H.O. is concerned are advising on the exercise of certain prerogative powers of the Crown, the administration of justice (including supervision of the Borstal system), prisons, police administration, the Fire Service, Civil Defence, the care of children deprived of normal home life, the control and naturalization of aliens, duties in relation to Parliament and local govt. (elections and bye-laws) and the Race Relations Board. There is a separate Sec. of State for Scotland, and, since 1964, for Wales. The Home Sec. has certain duties in respect of N. Ireland, the Channel Islands, and the Isle of Man.

HṒMER. Legendary Greek epic poet, the traditional author of the *Iliad* and the *Odyssey.* According to tradition he was a blind wandering minstrel; seven cities claimed to be his birthplace, while he has been given dates ranging 11th to 7th cent. B.C.

The *Iliad* tells of an incident of the siege of Troy, the wrath of Achilles and the death of Hector; the *Odyssey* of the wanderings of Odysseus after the siege, and his return to Ithaca.

HOMER. A bust in the Louvre.

Both formed part of a cycle of epics on the siege of Troy, the remainder of which has been lost. The capture of Troy *c.* 1200 B.C. was an episode in the Achaean invasions of Asia Minor. Songs glorifying princely houses, combining historical elements with myth and folklore, arose at the courts of Achaean chieftains, and assumed artistic form at the hands of professional bards in the Ionian trading cities. In the course of transmission they were greatly modified, e.g. only slight traces of human sacrifice remain. Peisistratus, tyrant of Athens, is said to have first collected the complete texts from reciters at the Panathenaian festival *c.* 550 B.C. and committed them to writing. Early quotations show many variations from the received texts, which may have been produced by Alexandrian editors 3rd–2nd cents. B.C.

Modern Homeric criticism began in 1795 with

Wolf's *Prolegomena*, which attempted to prove that the *Iliad* was derived from earlier ballads. The origin of the poems remains a subject of controversy; in its later stages the controversy has been much affected by excavations at Troy, Mycenae, and in Crete.

HOMER, Winslow (1836–1910). American artist. B. in Boston, he estab. his reputation as a realist genre painter with 'Prisoners from the Front' (1866). He is celebrated for his farm and sea scenes, and for water-colours (influenced by English practice) of free brilliance, as in his West Indian studies.

HOME RULE. The slogan of the Irish nationalist movement 1870–1914; it stood for the repeal of the Act of Union, and the establishment of an Irish parliament within the framework of the British Empire. The slogan was popularized after 1870 by Isaac Butt and Parnell, his successor in the nationalist leadership. Gladstone's H.R. bills of 1886 and 1893 were both defeated; Asquith's H.R. bill became law in 1914, but was suspended during the F.W.W. After 1918 the demand for an independent Irish republic replaced that for H.R.

HOMOEOPATHY (homi-o'pathi). A system of medicine, introduced by the German physician Samuel Hahnemann (1755–1843), based on the treatment of morbid conditions by what would induce such diseases in healthy bodies, and on the administration of simple drugs in small quantities only. It is opposed to allopathy (q.v.).

HOMO'PTERA. Sub-order of insects in the order Hemiptera (q.v.), generally distinguished from the Heteroptera by the uniform consistency of the front wings. It includes the cicadas, aphides, and scale insects.

HOMOSEXUALITY. Sexual propensity for the same sex, often considered an inborn genetic variant, but more probably a circumventive adaptation for coping with fears of heterosexuality. The Sexual Offences Act (1967) legalized homosexual acts between consenting adults in private in England and Wales.

HOMS. City, cap. of H. dist., in Syria, near the Orontes, 55 m. N.E. of Tripoli. It is the trade centre of an area producing silk, cereals, fruit; and makes silk textiles and jewellery. Zenobia, queen of Palmyra, was defeated at H. by Aurelian in 272. Pop. (1960) 148,386

HONA'N. Prov. of N. China, crossed by the Hwang-ho. The cap. is Chengchow. It produces grain, cotton, soya beans, tobacco, ground-nuts, cotton textiles, processed foods. Area 64,500 sq. m.; pop. (1968) 50,000,000.

HONDECOETER (hon'dekooter), **Melchior** (1636–95). Dutch artist. B. at Utrecht, he became famous for his paintings of birds.

HONDO. Another name for HONSHU.

HONDU'RAS. Central American republic. The country is mountainous, the loftiest range being the Montañas de Selaque, rising to c. 7,000 ft. The extensive forests are exploited for mahogany and other valuable timber; rich mineral deposits incl. gold and silver. The country is well watered, and agriculture is important, the chief product being bananas; others are coffee, maize, sugar cane, and cattle. Road and rail links are limited, air transport being more usual, consequently the mineral potential is unexploited. The cap. is Tegucigalpa.

H. was discovered by Columbus in 1502, and first settled by Spaniards in 1524. Freedom from Spain was gained in 1821, and H. left the Fed. of Central America to become an independent state in 1838. A military coup in 1963 was followed 1965 by a return to constitutional rule. There is a single Congress of Deputies, elected by popular vote (men and women over 18) for 6 years, as is the president. Area 43,227 sq. m.; pop. (1966) 2,362,800.

HONDURAS, British. *See* BRITISH HONDURAS.

HONEGGER, Arthur (1892–1955). Swiss composer.

B. at Le Havre, he was ed. at Zürich and Paris, and in the 1920s joined the group of French composers known as *Les Six*. Later his work became more deeply expressive, and is very varied in form, e.g. opera (*Antigone*), ballet (*Skating Rink*), oratorio (*Le roi David*), programme music ('Pacific 231' inspired by a railway engine), and the *Symphonie liturgique*.

HONEY (hu'ni). A sweet sticky liquid manufactured in the hive by bees from nectar collected from flowers. It is stored in the honeycombs as a food for the bees' future use, but as more H. is produced than is needed, the surplus may be removed for human use. H. consists of various sugars, particularly levulose and dextrose, with enzymes and various other constituents such as colouring matter, acids, pollen grains, etc.

HONEYSUCKLE

HONEY-EATER, or **Honey-Sucker**. Name given to Australasian birds in the family Meliphagidae. They possess small tongues by means of which they can collect nectar from flowers.

HONEYSUCKLE. Popular name for plants of the *Lonicera* genus of the Caprifoliaceae family. The common British H., or Woodbine (*L. periclymenum*), is a climbing plant with sweet-scented flowers, purple and yellow-tinted outside and creamy-white inside. The N. American trumpet H. (*L. sempervirens*) is very handsome and incl. scarlet and yellow varieties.

HONFLEUR (oñflör'). Seaport on the N. coast of France, on the S. shore of the Seine estuary opposite Le Havre, in Calvados dept. Much of its trade is carried on with England. Pop. (1962) 9,132.

HONG KONG (Cantonese, 'fragrant harbour').

HONAN. The steep curved road leading to Sanmen gorge, where the first major water conservancy undertaking was constructed on the main course of the Hwang Ho (Yellow river), comprising a dam and a hydro-electric power station.
Photo: Camera Press.

s

HONG KONG. More than 140,000 of the colony's population lives aboard junks and sampans, a big junk carrying up to 40 people – plus cats, dogs, and chicken – a complete floating home and family.
Courtesy of Gov. Information Services, Hong Kong.

British Crown colony on the S.E. coast of Kwantung prov., China. The colony incl. Hong Kong Is., Stonecutters' Is., the ceded territory of Kowloon and the New Territories. H.K. is. was ceded to Britain in 1841 (confirmed by treaty 1842), Kowloon peninsula was added in 1860, and in 1898 Britain obtained a 99 years' lease of the New Territories, which incl. Mirs Bay, Deep Bay, the remainder of the Kowloon peninsula, and numerous islands. The harbour is one of the finest in the world. The cap. is Victoria on the N. coast of the island. Local industries incl. shipbuilding, but most important is textiles, followed by plastics. It is one of the greatest ports in the world, and a large proportion of the imports and exports of S. China are here transhipped. Govt. is by a Governor, with Executive and Legislative Councils. From 1941 until 1945 it was occupied by the Japanese. There were severe Communist-inspired riots 1967. Area 391 sq. m.; pop. (1966) 3,834,000.

HONITON. English market town (bor.) on the Otter, Devon, 16 m. E.N.E. of Exeter, famous for its pillow lace. Pop. (1961) 4,724.

HONOLULU (honōloo′loo). Capital city and port of Hawaii, U.S.A., on the S. coast of Oahu. Noted for its beauty and tropical vegetation, it is a holiday resort, with some industry. 7 m. S.W. is Pearl Harbor with naval and military installations. Pop. (1960) 294,179.

HONOURS LIST. In the U.K. the military and civil awards approved by the Sovereign at the New Year, on her official birthday (celebrated on some selected date in June), and also on other special occasions.

HO′NSHU (Mainland). Principal is. of Japan. It lies between Hokkaido on the N. and Kyushu on the S. A chain of volcanic mts. extends the length of the is., which is subject to frequent earthquakes. Tokyo and Yokohama stand on a triangular plain. On the Inland Sea in the S. are the ports of Osaka, Kobe, Kure, and Hiroshima. Honshu is linked with Kyushu by the 2 m. Shimonoseki Tunnel and in 1963 work began on the Seikan Tunnel, 23 m. long (14 m. under the sea), to create a similar link with Hokkaido. Area

88,919 sq. m., incl. 382 smaller islands. Pop. (est.) 65,000,000.

HO′NTHORST, Gerard van (1590–1656). Dutch artist, especially noted for his portraits.

HOOCH (hōkh), **Pieter de** (1629–after 1683). Dutch painter. B. in Rotterdam, he came under the influence of Jacob Le Duck, Kick, and Vermeer. He is famous for courtyard and garden scenes and interiors.

HOOD, Samuel, 1st visct. (1724–1816). British admiral. B. in Dorset, he distinguished himself at Dominica in 1782, being created a baron, and was created visct. after his brilliant handling of the Mediterranean command 1793–4. He was a masterly tactician.

HOOD, Thomas (1799–1845). British poet. B. in London, he entered journalism, and edited periodicals, e.g. *Hood's Magazine* (1843). Although best known by his comic verse, e.g. 'Miss Kilmansegg', he also wrote such universally known serious poems as 'Song of the Shirt' and 'Bridge of Sighs'.

HOOGHLI. Indian r. and town, in West Bengal. The r. is the western stream of the Ganges delta. The town is on the site of a factory set up by the E. India Co. in 1640 which was moved to Calcutta, 25 m. downstream, 1686–90. Pop. (1961), with Chinsurah, 83,103.

HOOKE, Robert (1635–1703). British experimental physicist, elected to the Royal Society in 1663, becoming also its curator for the rest of his life. His inventions incl. a double-barrelled air-pump, the spirit-level, marine barometer, and sea gauge.

HOOKER, Richard (1554–1600). English theologian. B. nr. Exeter, in 1585 he became Master of the Temple and in 1591 rector of Boscombe, near Salisbury, where he commenced *The Laws of Ecclesiastical Polity*, a defence of the episcopalian system of the C. of E. He became rector of Bishopsbourne, near Canterbury, in 1595, and d. there.

HOOKER, Sir William Jackson (1785–1865). British botanist. As 1st director of Kew Gardens from 1841, he estab. its reputation and stimulated botanical exploration overseas: Mount H. in the Rockies was named after him. He was succeeded in the directorship (until 1855) by his son **Sir Joseph Dalton H.** (1817–1911) who consolidated his work, and pub. such works as *Genera Plantarum* (1862–83 with George Bentham). Notable among his expeditions was that to the Himalayas (1846–9) from which he brought back many rhododendrons, etc. He was awarded the O.M. in 1907.

HOOK OF HOLLAND. Small peninsula and village in S. Holland, Netherlands, important as the terminus for a sea service with England (Harwich, Parkeston Quay); in Dutch, Hoek van Holland, meaning corner of Holland.

HOOPER, John (c. 1495–1555). English Protestant reformer and martyr. B. in Somerset, he adopted Zwinglian views, he was appointed in 1550 bishop of Gloucester, and in 1555 was burnt for heresy.

HOOPOE (hōō′pōō). Bird (*Upupa epops*) in the order Coraciiformes. About the size of a missel thrush, it has a long thin bill and a bright buff-coloured crest which expands into a fan shape as the bird alights. The wings are banded with black and white, and the rest of the plumage is black, white, and buff.

HOOPOE

HOOVER, Herbert Clark (1874–1964). 31st President of the U.S.A. As a mining engineer he travelled widely before the F.W.W., during which he organized relief work in occupied Europe; a talented administrator, he was subsequently associated with numerous international relief organizations, and became Food Administrator for the U.S. 1917–19. Sec. of Commerce 1921–8, he then defeated the Democratic candidate for the Presidency, 'Al' Smith, but lost public confidence after the stock-market crash of 1929, when he opposed direct govt. aid for the unemployed in the depression that followed, and in 1933 was succeeded by Roosevelt. In 1946 the U.S. govt. appointed him chairman of the committee co-ordinating world food supplies.

HOOVER, John Edgar (1895–1972). American lawyer. B. in Washington, he became in 1921 assistant to William J. Burns and in 1924 succeeded him as director of the F.B.I., which he reorganized to reach a new peak of efficiency and comprehensiveness, e.g. the finger-print file was enlarged to over 100 million. He estab. a reputation for utter impartiality.

HOOVER DAM. U.S. dam on the Colorado r., between Arizona and Nevada. It is 726 ft. high (highest in the U.S.A.), 1,244 ft. long at the top, and was completed in 1936. The water it impounds forms Lake Mead, 115 m. long; it is used for flood and river control, irrigation, power production, and navigation. H.D. was started in 1928 during Hoover's presidency, and was named after him; the Wall Street collapse in 1929 and subsequent depression made him so unpopular that the dam was renamed Boulder Dam when it was opened. Hoover's recovery of public respect as chairman of the U.S. famine emergency committee in 1945–6 led to the restoration of the dam's original name by Truman in 1947.

HOPE, Anthony. Pseudonym of British novelist Sir Anthony Hope Hawkins (1863–1933). B. in London, he is best known for his romance *The Prisoner of Zenda* (1894), set in the imaginary Balkan state of Ruritania, and its sequel *Rupert of Hentzau* (1898). His *Dolly Dialogues* (1894) are a social satire.

HOPE, Bob. Stage-name of comedian Leslie Townes H. (1904–), b. in Britain but taken to the U.S. in 1907. The most expert exponent of the dead-pan wisecrack, he has made numerous films, incl. the celebrated 'Road' series with Dorothy Lamour and Bing Crosby (q.v.), with whom he sustains a constant mock-feud.

HOPEI. Prov. of N.E. China, mountainous in the N. and W. The cap. is Tientsin; Peking is a special municipality within H. It produces wheat, cotton, fruit, oilseeds, coal, iron, gold, salt; and makes cement and textiles. Area 84,900 sq. m.: pop. (1968) 43,000,000.

HOPKINS, Sir Frederick Gowland (1861–1947). British biochemist. Prof. at Cambridge from 1914 and Sir William Dunn prof. 1921–43, he revolutionized the conception of the sources of muscular energy and oxidation of tissues, and did fundamental research on vitamins. In 1929 he was awarded the Nobel prize for medicine, and in 1935 the O.M. His dau. is Jacquetta Hawkes (q.v.).

HOPKINS, Gerald Manley (1844–89). British poet. B. at Stratford, Essex, he was converted in 1866 to the Church of Rome, and in 1868 began training as a Jesuit. He preached and ministered as a priest in Ireland and England and subsequently taught. He d. of typhoid. His poetry is profoundly religious and records his struggle to gain faith and peace, but also shows great freshness of feeling and delight in nature. A complete edition was issued by Robert Bridges in 1918. His employment of 'sprung rhythm', allied to the Old and Middle English alliterative verse, has greatly influenced later 20th cent. poetry. His *Journals and Papers* were published in 1959, and three volumes of letters 1955–6.

HOPKINS, Harry L. (1890–1946). American states-man. B. in Iowa, he became in 1935 head of W.P.A. (Works Progress Administration). After a period as Sec. of Commerce 1938–40 he was appointed super-visor of the Lend-Lease programme in 1941, and undertook wartime missions to Britain and Russia.

HOPPNER, John (1758–1810). British artist. B. in London, he was ed. at the R.A. by George III, and specialized in portraits, notably of the royal prince sses, William Pitt, Lord Grenville, Rodney and Nelson. He became portrait painter to the Prince of Wales in 1789 and R.A. in 1795. Lawrence was a rival.

HOP FRUITS

HOPS. Female cone-heads of the hop plant, *Humulus lupulus*, Moraceae family. The plant has a perennial rootstock, climbs by a twining stem, and produces green leaves and small flowers. H. grow in rich soil throughout Europe and N. America, and are picked and dried in oast houses. They are used as a tonic, and as a flavouring in beer.

HORACE (ho'ras) **(Quintus Horatius Flaccus)** (65–8 B.C.). Roman poet. B. at Venusia, S. Italy, the son of a freedman, he fought with the republicans at Philippi, lost his estate, and was reduced to poverty. Virgil introduced him *c.* 38 to Maecenas, who gave him a small estate and procured him the friendship and patronage of Augustus. His Satires, pub. 35–30 B.C., survey the follies of contemporary society. His lyrical poems, the Epodes and the 4 books of Odes (*c.* 24–15 B.C.), written in a variety of metres, deal with both personal and political themes. In later life H. wrote his Epistles, a series of verse letters, and the critical treatise in verse *De Arte Poetica*. His works are distinguished by their style, their wit, and their good sense.

HORDER, Thomas Jeeves, 1st baron (1871–1955). British physician. He attended Edward VII, Edward VIII, George VI, and Elizabeth II, and was a determined opponent of the Health Service as lowering professional standards.

HORE-BELISHA (hawr-belē'sha), **Leslie**, baron (1895–1957). British politician. A National Lib., he was Min. of Transport 1934–7, introducing 'B. beacons' to mark pedestrian crossings, and as War Min. from 1937, until removal by Chamberlain in 1940 on grounds of temperament, introduced peace-time conscription in 1939. He was created a peer in 1954.

HOREHOUND. Genus of plants (*Marrubium*) of the Labiatae family. The common H. (*M. vulgare*), found in Europe, N. Africa and W. Asia and naturalized in N. America, has a thick hairy stem and clusters of dirty-white flowers: it has medicinal uses.

HORI'ZON. The distance to which one can see across the surface of the sea or a level plain, i.e. *c.* 3 m. at *c.* 5 ft. above sea level, and just over 40 m. at 1,000 ft.

HO'RMONES. Products of the endocrine glands. The chief are those of the thyroid, parathyroid, pituitary, suprarenal, pancreas, ovaries, and testicles. They have been called 'blood messengers'. Their purpose is to bring about changes in the functions of various organs according to the body's requirements. Their combined action and interaction are delicately balanced and closely bound up with those of the nervous system. Generally speaking, the pituitary gland, in the skull, is the 'leader of the orchestra';

HOREHOUND

the thyroid secretion determines the rate at which the organism shall live; the suprarenal secretion prepares the organism for 'fight or flight'; and the sexual secretions govern the reproductive functions. Most hormones are complex chemical substances, and many diseases due to deficiency of one or other of them can be relieved with hormone preparations

HORMUZ. Another form of ORMUZ.

HORN, Philip de Montmorency, count of (1518–68). Flemish statesman. He held high offices under Charles V and Philip II, and from 1563 he was one of the leaders of the opposition to the rule of Cardinal Granvella and to the introduction of the Inquisition. In 1567 he was arrested together with Egmont, and both were beheaded in Brussels.

HORN. A family of musical instruments. They originated from animal horns, and are divided into the modern French H., hunting H., and natural H. They are circular in shape, and generally over 11 ft. long, with a narrow mouthpiece ($\frac{1}{4}$ in.) widening to a 12–14 in. bell. The natural H. is now replaced by the more varied valve or French H.

HORN, Cape. Most southerly point of the American continent, in the Chilean part of the archipelago of Tierra del Fuego. It was named in 1616 by its Dutch discoverer Willem Schouten (1580–1625) after his birthplace (Hoorn).

HORNBEAM. Genus of trees (*Carpinus*) of the Betulaceae division of the Amentaceae (catkin) family. The common H. (*C. betulus*) is found in woods and hedges throughout the temperate parts of Europe and Asia, and is planted in Britain. It is a small tree with a twisted stem and smooth grey bark. The leaves are oval and hairy on the undersurface. The flowers are borne in catkins, and the fruits are small nuts borne in groups.

HORNBILL. Birds of the family of Bucerotidae, found in Africa, India and Malaya, and so called from the powerful bill surmounted by a bony growth or casque. The H. nests in holes in trees where the female is voluntarily immured, herself assisting in the plastering over of most of the entrance, and fed by her mate throughout incubation.

HORNBLENDE. Mineral of the Amphibole group. It is greenish black, with a glassy, translucent appearance, and is found in the Scottish Highlands, the Alps, N. America, etc.

HORNER, Arthur (1894–1968). British trade union leader. B. in S. Wales, he became a miner, joined the I.L.P. in 1912, and was imprisoned during the F.W.W. as a conscientious objector. In 1923 he became a Communist. He was pres. of the S. Wales Miners' Federation 1936–46, and gen. sec. of the National Union of Mineworkers 1946–59.

HORNET. *See* WASP.

HORNIMAN, Annie Elizabeth Fredericka (1860–1937). British repertory-theatre pioneer. The dau. of Frederick John H. (1835–1906) founder in 1897 of the H. Museum at Forest Hill, London, she subsidized the Abbey Theatre, Dublin, and founded the Manchester repertory (1907–21). Her brother, **Roy H.** (1872–1909), was an actor and author of *Israel Rank* (1907), in which the hero gains a coronet by poisoning relatives standing between himself and a title (filmed as *Kind Hearts and Coronets*).

HORNET

HORNUNG, Ernest William (1866–1921). British novelist, creator of Raffles, the gentleman-burglar, and his assistant Bunny in *The Amateur Cracksman* (1899). The idea originated with Conan Doyle, H.'s brother-in-law, who suggested counterparts of Holmes and Watson on the wrong side of the law.

HO'ROSCOPE. The relative position of the stars

HORSE, and, drawn to the same scale, Eohippus (Dawn Horse).

and planets at the moment of birth, used by astrologists to forecast the future of the subject. *See* ASTROLOGY. To cope with increased demand in the 20th cent. the casting of Hs. has been computerized in the U.S.A.

HO'ROWITZ (-vits), **Vladimir** (1904–   ). American pianist. B. in Kiev, he made his début in the U.S. in 1928 with the N.Y. Philharmonic Orchestra. He is a masterful technician. In 1933 he m. Wanda, dau. of Toscanini.

HORROCKS, Sir Brian Gwynne (1895–   ). British soldier. He served in the F.W.W., and in the S.W.W. was a Corps Commander under Montgomery at Alemein and with the British Liberation Army in Europe, reaching the rank of lieut.gen. His TV programmes on military history, etc., have been popular.

HORROCKS, Jeremiah (1619–41). English astronomer who first made observations of the transit of Venus.

HORSE. Ungulate mammal (*Equus caballus*) of the family Equidae. The evolution of the H. has been traced from the Eocene age; it is thought to have originated in Asia or Africa, and it was early domesticated as a beast of burden. The teeth became adapted to cropping close grass, and the feet to swift running. The horse now stands on one toe (the hoof), the other toes having been reduced to small digits or splints. The Equidae also includes the zebra, ass, and quagga. The wild horse (*Equus przewalskii*) is now found only in Mongolia. Domesticated breeds are divided into 3 groups – riding, carriage, and carthorses. Riding Hs. incl. the thoroughbred and hunter, which are derived from the Arab H. Carriage Hs. incl. the Hackney, Cleveland Bay, and Coachhorses; the Shire H., Clydesdale, and Suffolk Punch are incl. in the category of carthorses. *See* PONY.

The young male H. is called a colt, and the female a filly; the adult male is called a stallion and the female a mare. There is a large vocabulary covering the coloration, peculiarities of shape, and measurement of Hs. The unit of height, termed a hand, is 4 in. London's 1st annual International H. Show was held in 1907, but the American National H. Show, held annually in N.Y., dates from 1883.

HORSE, Master of the. In England an official responsible for the royal stables, and head of one of the departments of the royal household.

HORSE CHESTNUT. Tree common throughout Britain and the temperate regions. The generic name is *Aesculus*. The common H.C. (*A. hippocastanum*) is a fast-growing tree reaching a height of 60 ft. or more. The scented, white or pink flowers are borne in May and June in spikes. The fruits, known to schoolboys as 'conkers', are hard, brown and shiny, and are borne in green spiky cases. *See* CHESTNUT.

HORSE-FLY or **Forest Fly.** Insect (*Hippobosca Equina*) of the family Tabanidae. Yellowish-brown, it feeds by sucking blood from the flanks of horses.

HORSE GUARDS. Name given to a building in Whitehall, London, England, erected in 1753 by Vardy from a design by Kent, on the site of the Tilt Yard of Whitehall palace. This spot has been occupied by the Household Cavalry or 'Horse Guards' since the Royal Horse Guards were formed in 1661.

HORSE RACING. Sometimes called the national sport of England, where it had its origin in organized form, it has been popular there since at least the 12th cent. and was greatly encouraged by the Stuarts, James I instituting H.R. on Newmarket Heath, where it developed further under Charles I and Charles II, and Queen Anne having Ascot racecourse laid out in 1711. All English thoroughbreds, and through them most of the world's best horses, descend in direct male line from 3 Arabian Hs. introduced in the 18th cent., the Byerly Turk, Darley Arabian, and Godolphin

HORSE RACING. Hyperion, famed thoroughbred who won the 1933 Derby in the record time of 2 min. 34 sec.

Arabian, and towards the end of that cent. the principal flat races were estab. (Derby, Oaks, St. Leger, 2,000 Guineas, 1,000 Guineas, and Ascot Gold Cup): the Jockey Club (1751) is the governing body and the season is March-Nov. Steeplechasing was not regularized as a sport until the 19th cent., the most important event being the Grand National (q.v.) at Aintree (1839): Liverpool then became the chief seat of steeple-chasing, for which the season is August Bank Holiday to Whitsun, and the governing body is the National Hunt Committee. Certain rules governing H.R. generally were laid down by Parliament in 1740, and incl. the basis of the present weight-for-age scale. Bookmaking is subject to legal provisions (*see* BETTING) and the law does not recognize betting debts unless incurred with the Totalizator (q.v.). The chief courses are Epsom, Newmarket, Ascot, Goodwood, Doncaster, Sandown Park, York, and Aintree.

H.R. has spread all over the world, to France, Australia, S. America, and the U.S.A., where it was introduced by Col. Richard Nicolls, commander of the English forces invading New Amsterdam (New York) in 1664, who laid out a 2-mile course very near the present one at Belmont Park. Now a year-round institution, race meetings may last 50–60 days and – also in contrast to English practice – are run over shorter distances, and from mechanical starting gates or stalls (this method, almost universal elsewhere, was first used for all British classic races in 1967): there is no centralized governing body. The scale of

American H.R. (c. 20,000 races) dwarfs that of other countries, betting on the Totalizator (the only legal method) is on an immense scale, and prize money may reach $75,000, especially in such classics as the Coaching Club Oaks, Belmont Stakes, and Withers Stakes at Belmont Park; the Preakness Stakes at Pimlico (Baltimore) and the Kentucky Derby at Louisville. *See also* HARNESS RACING.

HORSERADISH. Plant (*Cochlearia armoracia*) of the Cruciferae family, native to S.E. Europe and naturalized in Britain and America. The thick, cream-coloured and tapering root is used in pharmacy and cookery (a piquant condiment with beef).

HORSETAIL. Genus of plants (*Equisetum*) which, with certain fossil forms, constitutes the family Equisetaceae. The common H. (*E. arvense*) is a frequent weed in Britain and N. America. The giant H. (*E. telemateia*) has sterile stems up to 10 ft. high and occurs both in the Old World and on the N. American Pacific seaboard.

HORSHAM. English town and market centre (U.D.) on the r. Arun, in W. Sussex, 16 m. S.E. of Guildford. Christ's Hospital is c. 2 m. S.W. Pop. (1961) 21,155.

HORSLEY, Colin (1920–). New Zealand pianist. B. at Wanganui, he was ed. at the R.C.M., where he became prof. in 1953.

HORSLEY, John Calcott (1817–1903). English artist. B. in London, he was a skilled painter of attractive domestic scenes on the Dutch model and of portraits: his frescoes for the Houses of Parliament are less happy. He became R.A. in 1856, and pub. *Recollections* (1903). *See* CHRISTMAS CARD.

HORST-WESSEL-LIED. Song introduced by the Nazis as a 2nd German national anthem. The text was written by Horst Wessel (1907–30), a Nazi 'martyr', to a traditional tune.

HORTHY DE NAGYBANYA (hortē de nodybahn'yo), **Nicolas** (1868–1957). Hungarian statesman. Leader of the counter-revolutionary 'White' govt., he became regent in 1920, on the overthrow of the Communist Bela Kun régime by Rumanian intervention. He pursued a moderate policy, trying (although allied to Hitler) to retain independence of action: in 1944 his country was taken over by the Nazis and he was deported to Germany. Liberated by the Americans, he subsequently lived in exile.

HORTICULTURE. The art of growing flowers, fruit, and vegetables. Courses in H. usually include outdoor gardening, poultry farming, and hothouse care. In Britain the Royal Horticultural Soc. (1804) holds shows at Westminster, and has gardens at Wisley, in Surrey. In the U.S.A. there is no general organization like the R.H.S., but many local societies based upon geography and particular crops, e.g. American Rose Society and Mass. Fruit Growers Association, as there are also in Britain.

HŌ'RUS. Hawk-headed Egyptian god, the son of Isis and Osiris. The Greeks called him Harpocrates.

HOSPITAL. Institution for the care of the sick and injured. In ancient times temples of deities such as Aesculapius (q.v.) offered facilities for treatment, and the Church had by the 4th cent. founded Hs. for lepers, cripples, the blind, and sick poor. The oldest surviving H. in Europe is the Hôtel Dieu, Paris; in Britain the most ancient are St. Bartholomew's (1132) and St. Thomas's (1200); and in N. America the H. of Jesus of Nazareth, Mexico (1524). Medical knowledge advanced during the Renaissance, and Hs. increasingly became secularized following the Reformation. In the 19th cent. real progress was made in H. design, administration and staffing, cf. Florence Nightingale, and in the 20th there has been a dominant trend to specialization.

In Britain Hs. have formed part of the National Health Service since 1948 and give free treatment, although most also provide for some private patients and there are a number of private nursing homes and clinics. In the U.S.A. the Hs. may be public (federal or state) or private (voluntary, i.e. non-profitmaking, and proprietary, i.e. profitmaking. Patients usually pay for treatment, but from 1966 the over-65s have come under the state Medicare H. insurance scheme, to which workers and employers contribute. Most other Americans belong to voluntary H. insurance schemes, e.g. the non-profitmaking Blue Cross (1929) and the Blue Shield (1917).

HOTEL. A house providing for the lodging and refreshment of travellers. European Hs. tend to be smaller (up to 500 rooms), and have more personal service, whereas the American (up to 3,000 rooms) rely much more on mechanization. In the absence of an international rating system, guides are pub. on a national basis, and incl. R.A.C. and A.A. (Britain), Michelin (France), Warter (Germany), and A.A.A. tour book (U.S.A.). *See* MOTEL.

HOTEL. Overlooking London's Hyde Park, the Hilton has 30 storeys and is 328 ft. high. It has 512 bedrooms, 5 restaurants and one of Europe's largest ballrooms.
Courtesy of Hilton Hotels International.

HO'TTENTOTS. S. African people inhabiting the S.W. corner of the continent when Europeans first settled there. They were a pastoral race, composed of Bushmen and Bantu, who have now largely mixed with Dutch and other blood; the Namaqua tribe approximates nearest to the original H. The language bears a resemblance to Bushman, and has mainly monosyllabic roots with explosive consonants which produce peculiar clicking sounds.

HOTTER, Hans (1909–). German bass singer, noted for his Wagnerian roles.

HOUDIN (oodań'), **Robert.** Name assumed by the French conjuror Jean Eugène Robert (1805–71). B. at Blois, he opened a miniature Theatre of Magic in Paris in 1845, and obtained celebrity by his use of electromagnetism, and by many ingenious tricks.

HOUDINI (hoodě'nē), **Harry** (1874–1926). American escapologist and conjuror. B. in Wisconsin, he attained fame by his escapes from ropes and handcuffs. He also reproduced some of the phenomena of spiritualist séances by purely mechanical means.

HOUDON (oodoń'), **Jean Antoine** (1741–1828). French sculptor. His works include busts of Lafayette, Napoleon, and Rousseau.

HOUGHTON (how'ton), **William Stanley** (1881–1913). British playwright. He wrote a number of plays with a Lancashire setting, notably *Hindle Wakes* (1912), whose theme, novel at the time, concerns a girl who refuses to marry the man who has seduced her.

HOUGHTON-LE-SPRING (hō'ton-). English market town (U.D.) and coal-mining centre in Durham, 6 m. N.E. of city of Durham. Pop. (1961) 31,049.

HOULT (hōlt), **Norah.** Irish novelist. B. in Dublin, she was orphaned at 10 and became a journalist, working first for the *Sheffield Telegraph.* Her vol. of grimly realistic short stories, *Poor Women* (1928), and her several novels, incl. *Father and Daughter* (1957) and *Husband and Wife* (1959), strike the same note.

HOUNSLOW. English garrison town and borough of Greater London, England. Situated at the junction of the Bath and Exeter roads, it was an important coaching station, and H. Heath was a resort of highwaymen. Pop. (1967) 206,870.

HOUSE, Edward Mandell (1858–1938). American Democrat politician, friend and adviser of President Wilson. In 1917 he represented the U.S.A. in the Supreme War Council at Versailles, and subsequently played an important part in the Peace Conference. His *Intimate Papers of Col. House* – the 'Col.' was an honorary title – appeared 1926–8.

HOUSE FLY and larva.

HOUSE FLY. Insect (*Musca domestica*) belonging to the order Diptera. It breeds in stables, garbage dumps, etc., and is most abundant in summer. The female lays about 150 eggs at a time, and may produce 1,000 in a lifetime. It has a dark grey, hairy body, with compound eyes, and feeds through a proboscis. The H. is responsible for carrying a number of diseases, notably typhoid fever.

HOUSEHOLD, Royal. *See* ROYAL HOUSEHOLD.

HOUSEMAID'S KNEE. Inflammation and enlargement of the prepatellar bursa, a small fluid cushion beneath the skin in front of the kneecap.

HOUSING. It is only in the last 100 years that H. has become a matter of state concern, legislation in Britain beginning with measures passed from 1851 and first consolidated in the H. of the Working Classes Act (1890). Private enterprise still provides a proportion of British H., but flats and houses to rent – intended for lower-income groups – are built on a large scale by local authorities under the direction of the Min. of H. and Local Govt. Local authorities also have wide powers to ensure that all existing houses are well maintained, to clear and redevelop unhealthy or congested areas, to abate overcrowding, and to assist private owners and landlords to improve and convert their property.

Whether operating on a free-enterprise or Communist basis, all modern states have found some

HOUSING. Side by side on the Loughborough Estate at Lambeth, London, are traditional two-storey houses and tall blocks of flats designed by the council architect's department.
Courtesy of Greater London Council.

degree of state provision or subsidy essential, as in the U.S. through the Housing and Home Finance Agency, with special consideration for 'senior citizens', etc. Nevertheless, growth of population tends always to outstrip any provision made, especially at the income level where it is most needed, and increasing attention is being given to replacing traditional methods by mass-production factory techniques which can make features such as central heating, well-designed plumbing units, etc., available at a fraction of normal cost, and reduce work on site to a minimum.

HOUSMAN, Alfred Edward (1859–1936). B. in Worcestershire, he was ed. at Oxford, and wrote most of the poems of *A Shropshire Lad* (1896) while working as a clerk in H.M. Patents Office from 1882. Apparently simple, these poems bear the mark of his brilliant classical scholarship and he became prof. of Latin at Univ. Coll., London, in 1892 and held a similar post at Cambridge from 1911. He pub. no more verse until *Last Poems* (1922) and *More Poems* (1936), but greatly influenced the 'Georgian' school. His brother, **Laurence H.** (1865–1959), wrote the anonymous novel *An Englishwoman's Love Letters* (1900) and plays, e.g. *Victoria Regina*; his collected poems appeared in 1938.

HOUSTON (hoo'ston). City and port of S.E. Texas, U.S.A., connected to the Gulf of Mexico by a ship canal 58½ m. long. H. is a major petroleum centre, with large refineries, and natural gas and sulphur are also exploited. Chemicals, petrochemicals, plastics, synthetic rubber, electronic instruments, etc., are pro-

HOVERCRAFT. This Vickers VA-3 travels at a height of 8 in. and cruises at 60 knots. The lift fans and propulsion drives are powered by 4 gas-turbine engines, and direction is controlled by a pair of upright forefins and a pair of af rudders: length 54 ft. 9 in., width 26ft. 11 in. and cushion area 895 sq. ft.
Courtesy of Vickers-Armstrong.

duced, and H. is an important agricultural centre, espec. for rice. The Univ. of H. dates from 1934.

H. was founded 1836 and named after Gen. Sam Houston (1793–1863) who won Texan independence from Mexico. It is often known as Space City from the Manned Space Center nearby. Pop. met. area (1970) 1,958,491.

HOVE. English seaside resort (bor.) on the Sussex coast, adjoining Brighton. Pop. (1961) 72,843.

HOVERCRAFT. Amphibious vehicle riding on an air cushion, free of all contact with the surface beneath. Although H. need a smooth terrain when operating overland, it need not be metalled, and snow and ice present no difficulties, but they are at present best adapted to use on lakes, sheltered coastal waters, river estuaries and swamps. A first experimental passenger ferry service, between Rhyl and Wallasey, was operated in the summer of 1962. The H., owing to its lack of dependence on harbours is specially useful in under-developed countries. *See* COCKERELL.

HOWARD, Catherine (d. 1542). Queen of England, the daughter of Lord Edmund H., she was m. to Henry VIII in 1540. In 1541 Cranmer accused her to Henry of unchastity before marriage. In 1542 her adultery was also discovered, and she was beheaded.

HOWARD, Sir Ebenezer (1850–1928). British housing reformer, founder in 1899 of the Garden City Association. He was knighted in 1927.

HOWARD, John (1726–90). British philanthropist. On his appointment as high sheriff for Bedford county in 1773, he undertook a tour of English prisons which led to 2 acts of Parliament in 1774, making gaolers

salaried officers and setting standards of cleanliness. After touring Europe in 1775 he pub. his *State of the Prisons in England and Wales, with an account of some Foreign Prisons* (1777). He d. of typhus fever while visiting Russian military hospitals at Kherson in the Crimea. The *Howard League for Penal Reform* (1866) exists to continue his work.

HOWARD, Leslie. Stage-name of British actor Leslie Stainer (1893–1943). He starred in the films *The Petrified Forest, The Scarlet Pimpernel, Pygmalion,* and *Gone with the Wind,* and he was also a talented director and producer. His plane was shot down on his return from a lecture tour in Spain and Portugal, and it has been suggested that the Germans imagined that Churchill was on board.

HOWARD, Trevor Wallace (1916–). British actor. B. at Margate, he was ed. at Clifton Coll., and served with the 1st Airborne Division in the S.W.W. His style of acting ranges from the reckless bravura of *The Devil's General* (1953) to the quiet impact of the film *Brief Encounter* (1945).

HOWARD OF EFFINGHAM, Charles, 2nd baron and 1st earl of Nottingham (1536–1624). English admiral. The son of the 1st baron and a cousin of Queen Elizabeth, he served as ambassador to France 1559, and as Lord High Admiral 1585–1618 commanded the fleet which defeated the Armada. In 1596 he co-operated in the expedition against Cadiz.

HOWE, Elias. *See* SEWING MACHINE.

HOWE (how), **Julia Ward** (1819–1910). American poet and philanthropist. B. in New York City, she m. Samuel Gridley H. in 1843, and ed. with him an anti-slavery newspaper. In 1862 she pub. the 'Battle Hymn of the Republic', sung to the tune of 'John Brown's Body'. Later she advocated women's suffrage and prison reform.

HOWE, Richard, earl (1726–99). British admiral. The son of the 2nd viscount H., he saw service in the War of the Austrian Succession and the 7 Years War, and was promoted to vice-admiral in 1775. In 1776 he was given command of the N. American station, and in 1782 he relieved Gibraltar. He was 1st Lord of the Admiralty 1783–8, and in 1788 was created an earl. On the outbreak of the French Revolutionary War he took command in the Channel, and in 1794 won the victory of the 'Glorious 1st of June'.

HOWE, William, 5th visct. (1729–1814). British general. Younger brother of Earl Howe (q.v.), he fought at Bunker Hill. As C.-in-C. of the British forces in America, he captured New York, defeated Washington at Brandywine Creek and Germantown in 1777, and then settled in Philadelphia while the Americans regrouped at Valley Forge. He resigned 1778 because of lack of support from the home govt.

HOWELLS (how'elz), **William Dean** (1837–1920). American novelist. B. in Ohio, he became a journalist, and wrote novels remarkable for their analytic realism, e.g. *Their Wedding Journey* (1872), and the autobiographical *Years of My Youth* (1916).

HOWITZER. A piece of ordnance in use since the 16th cent. for steep angle descent in sieges, and much developed in the F.W.W. for demolishing the fortresses of the trench system. *See* FIREARMS.

HOWRAH. City of W. Bengal, India, on the right bank of the Hooghli, opposite Calcutta. The cap. of H. dist., it has jute and cotton factories, rice, flour and saw mills, chemical factories, engineering works, etc. H. suspension bridge, opened in 1943, spans the r. Pop. (1961) 514,090.

HOXHA (haw'ja), **Enver** (1908–). Albanian statesman. Once a schoolmaster, he founded the Albanian Communist Party in 1941, and headed the liberation movement of 1939–44. He was P.M. 1944–54, combining this with For. Affairs 1946–53, and from 1954 was First Sec. of the Albanian Party of Labour. In policy his closest links are with the Chinese Communists.

HOYLAKE. English resort (U.D.) at the N.W. end of the Wirral peninsula, Cheshire, famous for its golfing facilities. Pop. (1961) 32,268.

HOYLE, Edmund (1672–1769). British authority on card games, his *Short Treatise on Whist* (1742) being the first standard account.

HOYLE, Sir Fred (1915–). Brit. astronomer. Ed. at Cambridge, he became Plumian prof. of astronomy and experimental philosophy there in 1958. His radio talks and such science fiction as *The Black Cloud* (1957) and *Ossian's Ride* (1959) have estab. his popular reputation, and he is noted for his contribution to cosmological theory (continuous creation) and such books as *Nuclei and Quasars* (1966).

HROTSVITHA (hrots'vēta) (*c.* 935–*c.* 1002). German nun, Latin poet, chronicler, and the first dramatist of the Middle Ages. B. of a noble Saxon family, she belonged to the convent of Gandersheim.

HSINGKING. Japanese name of CHANGCHUN.

HSIUNG, Shih I (1902–). Chinese dramatist. B. at Nanchang, he worked in theatre management at Peking and Shanghai, and subsequently lectured at Peking univ. He achieved a great success in London, in 1934, with *Lady Precious Stream*, an English adaptation of an ancient Chinese comedy.

HSÜAN CHUANG (or **Yüan Chuang**) (*c.* 600–64). Chinese Buddhist monk, traveller, and scholar. B. near Honan, he walked to India in 629, and in 631–3 he was in Kashmir. In 645 he returned to China with numerous religious relics and works of art, and wrote an account of his travels.

HUAMBO. *See* NOVA LISBOA.

HUANG-HO. Another form of HWANG-HO.

HUASCARAN (ōō-ahskahrahn'). Extinct volcano in the Andes, highest mountain in Peru (22,000 ft.). An avalanche of ice, snow, and rocks in 1962 overwhelmed the village of Ranrahirca and killed some 2,500 there and in the surrounding countryside.

HUBBARD, Elbert (1856–1915). American writer and publisher. B. in Illinois, he is remembered for the essay 'A Message to Garcia' (1899) dealing with an heroic incident of the Spanish-American War.

HUBBARD, Hesketh (1892–1957). British artist, best known for his oil paintings of architectural subjects which recall Canaletto.

HUBBLE, Edwin Powell (1889–1953). American astronomer. His researches with the Mount Palomar telescope confirmed the theory, enunciated by de Sitter *c.* 1917, that the universe is expanding. He postulated that the outward velocity of a receding stellar system is proportional to its distance – H.'s law – accepted as valid until the mid-1960s. *See* ASTRONOMY. He was astronomer at the Mount Wilson Observatory, California, 1919–53.

HUCH (hookh), **Ricarda** (1864–1947). German poet and novelist. Her novels (*Erinnerungen von Ludolf Ursleu dem Jungeren*, *Aus der Triumphgasse*, *Vita somnium breve*, etc.) show great narrative power and mastery of diction. She developed a new form of historical novel in a Garibaldi cycle (1906–7), etc., pub. works on Luther and Bakunin, and studies of the romantic movement.

HUCHOW. Name until 1912 of WUHING.

HUDDERSFIELD. English industrial town (co. bor.) in the W. Riding of Yorkshire on the r. Colne. It has canal connections with Manchester and other N. of England centres. An Anglo-Saxon village, by the end of the 18th cent. H. was a thriving centre of the woollen manufacture and trade to which is now added engineering and numerous other industries. Pop. (1961) 130,302.

HUDDLESTON, Trevor (1913–). British churchman. As provincial of the Community of the Resurrection in S. Africa 1949–56, he strongly opposed apartheid and expressed his views in *Naught for Your Comfort* (1956). He was bp. of Masasi 1960–8, when he became bp. of Stepney.

HUDSON, Henry (d. 1611). English explorer. Under the auspices of the Muscovy Company in 1607 and 1608 he made unsuccessful attempts to reach China by way of the N.E. passage along the N. of Asia. In 1609 he was commissioned by the Dutch East India Co., and in Sept. reached New York Bay and sailed 150 m. up the river which now bears his name. In 1610 he sailed from London in the *Discovery* and entered what is now the Hudson Strait. The ship was icebound for the winter in the present Hudson Bay. Next spring some of the crew mutinied, and H. and 8 others were turned adrift.

HUDSON, William Henry (1841–1922). Anglo-American author. B. at Florencio near Buenos Aires, of American parents, he was inspired by recollections of early days in Argentina to write his romances *The Purple Land* (1885) and *Green Mansions* (1904), with

its bird-like heroine 'Rima', and his autobiographical *Far Away and Long Ago* (1918). His middle and later years were spent in England, and in 1900 he became British by naturalization. He wrote several books on birds, and was a sympathetic interpreter of the English countryside, e.g. *Nature in Down-Land* (1900) and *A Shepherd's Life* (1910). His birthplace has been preserved as a museum since 1956.

W. H. HUDSON

HUDSON. River of the U.S.A. at whose mouth New York City stands. It rises in the Adirondacks, and flows almost due S. for 300 m. to the Atlantic. Discovered in 1524, it was explored in 1609 by Henry Hudson (q.v.), in whose honour it was named.

HUDSON BAY. Extensive inland sea of N.E. Canada, connected to the Atlantic by Hudson Strait, and to the Arctic by Foxe Channel. Its area is *c.* 476,000 sq. m., its length from N. to S. 850 m., width 600 m.

HUDSON'S BAY COMPANY. A chartered company founded by Prince Rupert in 1670 to trade in furs with the Red Indians. In 1783 the rival North-West Fur Company was formed, but in 1851 this became amalgamated with the H.B.C. which lost its

HUDSON'S BAY COMPANY. At Spence Bay on Boothia Peninsula in the North-west Territories the treeless desolation of the Arctic is relieved by the traditional red and white of the Company buildings – the manager's house, the store and the warehouse.
Courtesy of George Hunter for Hudson's Bay Company.

monopoly in 1859. It is still Canada's biggest fur co., but today sales of general merchandise, in towns through large modern dept. stores, oil and natural-gas interests, etc., are more important.

HUÉ (hoo-ā'). Town in S. Vietnam, formerly cap. of Annam (Central Vietnam), 8 m. from the China Sea. The Citadel, within which is the Imperial City enclosing the palace of the former emperor, lies to the W. of the Old City on the N. bank of the Huong (Perfume) River; the New City, incl. the univ., is on the S. bank. H. was once an architecturally beautiful cultural and religious centre, but large areas were devastated, with many casualties, during the Battle of H. 31 Jan.–24 Feb. 1968 when U.S. and S. Vietnamese forces retook the city after Viet Cong occupation by infiltration. There is an airport. Pop. (1968) 145,000.

HUELVA (wel'vah). Prov. in the S.W. of Spain, bordering the Gulf of Cadiz on the S. and Portugal on the W. The Sierra de Aracena occupies the N., which is heavily wooded. Copper and manganese are mined. In the low-lying S., fruit is grown. Area 3,894 sq. m.; pop. (1960) 399,934. The cap. is Huelva, a seaport near the mouth of the Rio Odiel. Pop. (1965) 86,795.

HUESCA (wes'kah). Prov. of N. Spain, stretching northwards to the French frontier along the crest of the Pyrenees. Huesca (pop. (1950) 21,332), an episcopal see, is the cap. Area 6,052 sq. m.; pop. (1960) 233,543.

HUGGINS, Sir Godfrey. See LORD MALVERN.

HUGGINS, Sir William (1824–1910). British astronomer. He built a private observatory at Tulse Hill, London, in 1856, where he embarked on research in spectrum analysis that marked the beginning of astrophysics: he was also a pioneer in photographic astronomy. Knighted in 1897, he was awarded the O.M. in 1902.

HUGHES, Richard Arthur Warren (1900–). British author, chiefly known for his study of childhood, High Wind in Jamaica (1929), and Don't Blame Me (1940).

HUGHES, Thomas (1822–96). British author. Called to the Bar in 1848, he became a county court judge in 1882. He joined the Christian Socialists, and became principal of the Working Men's College in London. He is chiefly remembered for his boys' book, Tom Brown's School Days (1857), a story of Rugby under Arnold. It had a successor, Tom Brown at Oxford (1861).

HUGHES, William Morris (1864–1952). Australian statesman. B. in London, he emigrated to Australia in 1884 and was elected in 1894 to the N.S.W. parliament. In 1901 he joined the Commonwealth House of Representatives, and in 1904 became Min. for External Affairs. Attorney-General in 1908–9, 1910–13, and 1914–21, he acquired a national reputation, and in 1915 succeeded Fisher as P.M., proving a vigorous war leader. Originally Labour, he headed a National cabinet. He represented Australia at Versailles, and resigned in 1923, but held many other cabinet posts 1934–41.

HUGO (ügō'), Victor Marie (1802–85). French poet, novelist, and dramatist. B. at Besançon, the son of one of Napoleon's generals, he pub. Odes et Poésies diverses in 1822, and estab. himself as the leader of French Romanticism with the verse play Hernani (1830). Later plays include Lucrèce Borgia (1833), in which the courtesan Juliette Drouet, who was his mistress for 50 years, appeared, and Ruy Blas (1838). Of his 25 vols. of verse Odes et Ballades, Les Chants

VICTOR HUGO

du Crépuscule (1835), and Les Rayons et les Ombres (1840), may be mentioned. In 1841 he was elected to the academy, became a peer in 1845, but was banished in 1851 for opposing Louis Napoleon's coup d'état, and settled in Guernsey, where he wrote the vols. of verse Les Contemplations (1856) and La Légende des Siècles. His great series of novels began with Notre Dame de Paris (1831), and included Les Misérables

S. G. HULME-BEAMAN
Courtesy Mrs. S. G.
Hulme-Beaman.

(1862), Les Travailleurs de la Mer (1866), L'Homme qui rit and Quatre-Vingt-Treize (1874). On the fall of the empire in 1870 H. returned to France, later becoming a senator. He d. in Paris and was buried in the Panthéon.

HUGUENOTS (hū'genots). Name applied to the French Protestants in the 16th cent.; probably a corruption of Ger. eidgenossen, 'confederates'. Mainly Calvinists, they were severely persecuted under Francis I and Henry II, but the massacre of St. Bartholomew in 1572 and the 30 years of religious wars which followed failed to exterminate them. In 1598 the former Huguenot, Henry IV, granted a measure of toleration by the Edict of Nantes, and although they lost military power after the revolt at La Rochelle 1627–9, the Hs. were still tolerated by Richelieu and Mazarin. In 1685 Louis XIV revoked the Edict of Nantes and attempted their forcible conversion, with the result that 400,000 left France, and many settled in England.

HUHEHOT. City cap. of Inner Mongolia autonomous region, China, centre of a farming district. The name means blue city. Pop. (est.) 200,000.

HULBERT, Jack (1892–). British comedian, celebrated in musical comedy and revue. His wife is Cicely Courtneidge (q.v.), and his brother Claude H. (1900–64) was a well-known comedian.

HULL, Cordell (1871–1955). American statesman. B. in Tennessee, he was a member of Congress 1907–33, and, as Roosevelt's Sec. of State 1933–44, was identified with the 'good neighbour' policy, and opposed German and Japanese aggression. In his last months of office he paved the way for an international security system and was called 'father' of the U.N. He was awarded the Nobel peace prize in 1945.

HULL. English city (co. bor.) in the East Riding of Yorks. One of the main U.K. ports and the chief port of N.E. England, it stands on the N. bank of the Humber estuary, some 22 m. from the North Sea, and possesses up-to-date docks (236 acres). It is a very important fishing port, the world's largest centre of the seed-crushing and oil-extracting industry, and has paint, chemical, and many other industries. Notable buildings incl. Holy Trinity Church (13th cent.), the Guildhall City Hall and the Ferens Art Gallery. Hull univ. (1954) was founded 1928 as a univ. coll. A suspension bridge across the Humber is planned. Incorporated in 1576, H. was made a co. bor. in 1888 and a city in 1897. Since 1914 it has had a lord mayor. Pop. (1961) 303,268.

HULME (hüm), Henry Rainsford (1908–). British mathematical physicist and astronomer. He worked for the Admiralty in the S.W.W., and afterwards became chief of nuclear research at the Atomic Weapons Research Establishment.

HULME (hüm), Thomas Edward (1881–1917). British philosopher, critic and poet. He was killed on active service in the F.W.W., but his Speculations (1924) influenced T. S. Eliot, and his few poems originated the Imagist movement.

HULME-BEAMAN (hüm-bē'man), Sydney George

(1887–1932). British author. B. in Tottenham, London, where he was ed. at the grammar school, he was briefly a clerk before taking up a commercial career. He wrote a series of plays, performed in the puppet theatre he made and operated himself with beautiful hand-carved puppets, which were set in 'Toytown', and incl. such characters as Larry the Lamb, Ernest the Policeman and His Worship the Mayor.

HUMAN BODY. The physical vehicle of human consciousness. It develops for nine months in the womb from the single cell of the fertilized ovum, through all the stages of human evolution, and reaches maturity between 18 and 24 years of age.

Structure. The bony framework (*skeleton*) consists of 200 bones, over half of which are in the hands and feet. The skull is mounted on the spinal column,

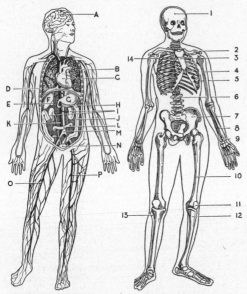

HUMAN BODY. The drawing on the left shows the principal physiological features. A, brain; B, lungs; C, heart; D, diaphragm; E, gall bladder; F, liver; G, stomach; H, pancreas; I, kidneys; J, large intestine (partly cut away); K, great vein; L, small intestine (partly cut away); M, large artery; N, bladder; O, femoral vein; P, femoral artery. The drawing on the right shows the skeleton. 1, skull; 2, collar-bone or clavicle; 3, breast-bone or sternum; 4, humerus; 5, ribs; 6, spine or vertebral column; 7, pelvis; 8, radius; 9, ulna; 10, femur; 11, kneecap; 12, tibia; 13, fibula; 14, shoulder blade.

a slightly undulant chain of 24 vertebrae. The ribs, 12 on each side, are articulated (jointed) to the spinal column behind, and the upper 7 meet the breast-bone (sternum) in front. The lower end of the spine rests on the triangular sacrum, to which are attached the two hip-bones (ilia), which are fused in front (symphysis pubis). Below the sacrum is the tail-bone (coccyx). These last 4 bones constitute the pelvis. The shoulder blades (scapulae) are held in place behind the upper ribs by muscles, and connected in front to the breast-bone by the two collar-bones (clavicles). Each carries a cup (glenoid cavity) into which fits the upper end of the arm-bone (humerus). This articulates below with the two forearm-bones, the radius and the ulna. The radius is articulated at the wrist to the bones of the hand. The upper end of each thigh-bone (femur) fits into a depression in the hip-bone; its lower end is articulated at the knee to both the leg-bones (tibia and fibula), which are articulated at the angle to the bones of the foot.

Bones are held together by joints (articulations) Some, but not all, of these allow movement of one bone on the other. At a moving joint the end of each bone is formed of tough, smooth cartilage, lubricated by synovial fluid. Points of special stress are reinforced by bands of fibrous tissue (ligaments).

Muscles (flesh) are bundles of fibres which have the power of contracting and relaxing. They perform all the movements of the body whether of bones or of organs. Muscles under voluntary control are attached to bones (skeletal or voluntary muscles). Those not under voluntary control (involuntary muscles) are found in internal organs and the walls of blood vessels. Muscle bundles are wrapped in thin, tough layers of connective tissue (fascia); these are usually prolonged at the ends into strong, white cords (tendons, sinews) or sheets (aponeuroses), which connect the muscles to bones and organs and through which the muscles do their work. Membranes of connective tissue also wrap the organs and line the interior cavities of the body, and secrete lubricating fluid (serum). Blood vessels, branching into multitudes of very fine tubes (capillaries), supply all parts of the muscles and organs with blood, which carries the oxygen and food necessary to their life. The food passes out of the blood to the cells in a clear fluid (lymph); this returns with waste matter through a system of lymphatic vessels to the large veins below the collar-bones (subclavian), and thence to the heart. A finely branching system of nerves regulates the function of the muscles and organs, and makes their needs known to the controlling centres.

The skull contains the brain, which with the spinal cord comprises the *central nervous system.* This governs the voluntary processes of the body. The spinal cord runs down within the vertebrae of the spinal column for about 17 inches, after which a fine terminal filament continues through the rest of the spine. The central nervous system is composed of nerve cells, the bodies of which form the grey matter and the fibres the white. The cell bodies are disposed over the surface of the brain and the interior of the spinal cord; the fibres run together into nerve trunks, which extend all over the body. The inner spaces of the brain and the cord contain cerebro-spinal fluid. On the sides of the spinal column are situated about 22 pairs of nerve junctions (sympathetic ganglia): these, with certain other nerves, make up the *autonomic nervous system,* which governs the involuntary processes of the body. These processes are further regulated by the hormones secreted by the endocrine glands.

The upper part of the trunk, enclosed by the ribs (thorax), contains the *lungs* and the *heart* lying between them. The thorax has a stout muscular floor, the diaphragm, which with the rib muscles expands and contracts the lungs in the act of breathing. The part of the trunk below the diaphragm, the abdomen, contains the *digestive organs* (stomach and intestines), the liver, spleen and pancreas, the urinary organs (kidneys, ureters and bladder), and, in the woman, the *reproductive organs* (ovaries, uterus, and vagina). In the man the prostate gland and seminal vesicles only of the reproductive system are situated in the abdomen, the testicles being housed in the scrotum, which, with the penis, is suspended in front of and below the abdomen. The bladder empties through a small channel (urethra); this in the female opens in the upper end of the vulval cleft, which also contains the opening of the vagina, or birth canal. In the male the urethra is continued into the penis. In both sexes the lower bowel terminates in the anus, a ring of strong muscle situated between the buttocks.

Cavities of the body opening on to the surface are coated with *mucous membrane,* which secretes a lubricating fluid (mucus). The exterior surface of the body is coated with *skin.* Within the skin grow the sebaceous glands, which secrete sebum, an oily fluid which makes the skin soft and pliable, and the sweat glands, which secrete water and various salts. From the skin grow hair, chiefly on the head, in the armpits, and around the sexual organs; and nails shielding the tips of the fingers and toes; both these structures are modifications of skin tissue. The skin also contains nerves of touch, pain, heat and cold.

Respiration and Circulation. Like an engine, the body derives energy from the combination of carbon, supplied in the food, with oxygen supplied in the air it breathes. The left side of the heart pumps blood through a system of arteries to all parts of the body, through which it circulates in a network of fine capillary vessels. These lead into veins, by which the blood returns to the right side of the heart, which pumps it to the lungs. Here it passes through minute vessels in which it comes into contact with air drawn through a network of tubes (bronchi) into a multitude of small air cells. The blood gives up carbon dioxide, receives oxygen, and returns to the left side of the heart to be sent again round the body. The beat of the heart is controlled by involuntary nerves; the expansion and contraction of the lungs are partly controlled by the will and partly involuntary.

Digestion. Food is mixed with saliva in the mouth by chewing and is swallowed. It enters the stomach, where it is gently churned for some time and mixed with acid gastric juice. It then passes into the small intestine. In the first part of this, the duodenum, it is more finely divided by the juice of the pancreas and of the duodenal glands and mixed with bile from the liver, which splits up the fat. The jejunum and ileum continue the work of digestion and absorb most of the nutritive substances from the food. The large bowel (colon) completes the process and ejects the useless residue.

The Urinary System. The body, to be healthy, must contain water and various salts in the right proportions. The blood is therefore filtered in the two kidneys, which remove such water and salts as are not needed. These, with a yellow pigment derived from bile, are the urine, which passes down through two fine tubes (ureters) into the bladder, a reservoir, from which the urine is emptied at intervals (micturition) through the urethra.

Heat Regulation. Heat is constantly generated by the combustion of food in the muscles and glands, and dissipated through the skin by conduction to the clothing and evaporation of sweat, through the lungs in the expired air, and in the other excreted substances. The body works best at a temperature of about 100° F. (98·4° F. in the mouth). This level is maintained by a nerve centre in the brain, which regulates the activity of the skin and lungs. *See* articles on various parts, etc., of the body. For Reproduction, *see* SEX AND REPRODUCTION.

HUMAN RIGHTS, Universal Declaration of. Proclamation by the U.N. General Assembly in 1948 which incl. assertion of the rights to life, liberty, education and equality before the law; to freedom of movement, religion, association, and information; and to a nationality.

HUMBER. An estuary formed by the Trent and Ouse, lying between Yorks and Lincs on the E. coast of England. On its banks are the ports of Hull and Grimsby. It is 37 m. long, 1 to 8 m. wide.

HUMBERT I (1844–1900). King of Italy. Son of Victor Emmanuel II, he saw service during the war of National Liberation and became king on his father's death in 1878. He was assassinated by an anarchist. For Humbert II *see* UMBERTO II.

HUMBOLDT (hoom'bolt), **Friedrich Heinrich Alexander,** baron von (1769–1859). German scientist. B. in Berlin, he explored the regions of the Orinoco and the Amazon, 1800–4, and on his return devoted 21 years to writing an account of his journeys. His greatest work, *Cosmos* (1845–62), is an account of the physical sciences. His elder brother, **Wilhelm** (1767–1835), held diplomatic and political posts. An eminent philologist, he was a pioneer in the study of Basque and the languages of the Orient and the S. Sea Is.

HUMBOLDT CURRENT. Cold ocean current flowing N. from the Antarctic along the W. coast of S. America to S. Ecuador, then westwards. It is named after Baron von H., the explorer who charted its course, and reduces the temperature of the coasts past which it flows, making the W. slopes of the Andes arid because winds are already chilled when they cross the coast.

HUME, David (1711–76). Scottish philosopher and historian. B. at Edinburgh, he studied in France and in 1739 pub. his treatise on *Human Nature,* followed in 1741 by *Essays Moral and Political.* In 1751 appeared his *Inquiry into the Principles of Morals,* an exposition of the Utilitarian philosophy. In 1752 he became librarian to the Faculty of Advocates in Edinburgh. His *History of England* reaches from the Roman period to 1761. His essays criticized belief in miracles and other Christian dogmas.

HUME, Fergus (1859–1932). British writer. Ed. in New Zealand, he returned to his native England in 1888: his *Mystery of a Hansom Cab* (1887) was one of the first popular detective stories.

HUME, Joseph (1777–1855). British Radical politician. B. at Montrose, he went out to India as an army surgeon in 1797, made a fortune, and on his return bought a seat in parliament. In 1818 he secured election as a Philosophic Radical and supported many progressive measures. His son **Allan Octavian H.** (1829–1912) was largely responsible for the establishment of the Indian National Congress in 1885.

HUMIDITY. Absolute H. is the quantity of water vapour in a given volume of the atmosphere, but the more useful quantity is the relative H. which is the ratio of the amount of water vapour in the atmosphere to the saturation value at the same temperature. At the dew-point the relative H. is 100 per cent. Measurements of relative H. are generally made with a wet and dry bulb thermometer (technical name psychrometer). *See* HYGROMETER.

HUMMING BIRD. Name given to many birds forming the family Trochilidae and found in America; they derive their name from the sound produced by the rapid vibration of their wings. They are brilliantly coloured, and have a long tongue with which they obtain nectar from flowers and capture insects.

HUMPERDINCK (hoom'perdink), **Engelbert** (1854–1921). German composer. B. at Siegburg, he studied music in Munich and in Italy and assisted Rich. Wagner at Bayreuth. Fame came to him with his musical fairy operas, *Hansel and Gretel* (1893), *Königskinder,* etc.

HUMPHREY (hum'fri), **Hubert** (1911–). American Democratic statesman. B. in Dakota, son of a chemist, he taught political science at the Univ. of Minnesota. Senator for Minnesota from 1948, he became 1965 vice-pres. to Johnson, and as the Democratic candidate, 1968, campaigned on 'law with justice and equality', but was defeated by Nixon.

HUMMING BIRD

HUNAN (hoonahn'). Prov. of central China lying S. of the Yangtze-kiang. Most of it is broken mountainous country, watered by the Siang-kiang and the Yuan-kiang, both of which flow into Tungting lake, a natural overflow reservoir of the Yangtze. Changsha is the capital; other cities are Siangtan and Hengyang. Rice, coffee, sweet potatoes, bamboo, etc., are grown; and there are non-ferrous metals, especially antimony and mercury. Area 81,100 sq. m.; pop. (1968) 38,000,000.

HUNDRED YEARS WAR. Name given to the struggle between England and France that was carried on from 1337 to 1453. It began with the claim of Edward III, through his mother, to the crown of France, and at the outset the English were victorious at the naval battle of Sluys in 1340 and on land at Crécy in 1346 and Poitiers in 1356. After 1369 the tide turned in favour of the French, and when Edward III d. in 1377 only Calais, Bordeaux, and Bayonne were in English hands. A state of half-war continued for many years until Henry V invaded France in 1415 and won a victory at Agincourt. After his death his brother Bedford was generally successful until Joan of Arc raised the siege of Orléans in 1429. Even after her capture and death the French continued their successful counter-offensive, and in 1453 only Calais was left in English hands.

HUNGARIAN or **Magyar.** One of the few languages spoken in Europe that are not of Indo-European stock; with Finnish and Estonian it belongs to the Finno-Ugrian family. Its vocabulary is basically Finno-Ugrian, although many words are importations from Iranian, Slavonic, Turkish, and modern European languages.

HUNGARY. Republic of central Europe, bordering on Czechoslovakia in the N., Rumania in the E., Yugoslavia in the S., and Austria in the W. Area 35,902 sq. m.; pop. (1967) 10,197,000, of whom more than 90 per cent were Magyar-speaking. H. consists mainly of the plains of the middle Danube; the river forms the N.W. boundary with Czechoslovakia, then turns S. and, through Budapest, the cap., flows right across the country in a southerly direction. The Great Hungarian Plain, watered by the r. Tisza and its tributaries, lies E. of the Danube. Once almost exclusively vast pastures, it is now for the most part under cultivation. For part of its course the Drava forms the southern boundary with Yugoslavia. N .of Lake Balaton, the largest of

HUNGARY. The Fisherman's Bastion gives a fine view over Budapest. Built in the Romanesque style at the end of the 19th century, it was so named because it was the duty of the fishermen's guild to man it in time of war.
Courtesy of the Hungarian News and Information Service.

the central European lakes, in the S.W. of the country, stretches the mountainous Bákony forest, between which and the Danube lies the Little Hungarian Plain. There is a large timber industry.

Agriculture is still important; main crops incl. wheat, maize, rye, barley, potatoes, and sugar beet.

Wine comes from N. of Lake Balaton and from the N.E. hills (Tokay). Horses, cattle, sheep, and pigs are reared. Fishing is important in the Danube and Tisza and Lake Balaton. Minerals incl. oil and natural gas, coal, iron, and bauxite; the chemical, machine and electric power industries are being rapidly expanded and textiles, cement, sugar, etc., are produced. The chief univs. are at Budapest, Debrecen, Szeged, and Pécs.

HUNGARY. Stove tile of the early 15th century, decorated with openwork tracery.
Courtesy of Corvina Press.

History. Originally inhabited by Celtic and Slavonic tribes, H. was partly occupied by the Romans and after their withdrawal was overrun by Germanic tribes, by the Huns, and by the Avars. The Hungarian state was founded in the 9th cent. by the Magyars, a federation of Finno-Ugrian tribes under a chieftain named Árpád. St. Stephen (997–1038) adopted the title of king, and estab. Latin Christianity. After the house of Árpád died out in 1301, H. came under the rule of foreign princes. The Turks were held at bay by John Hunyadi and his son, Matthias Corvinus (1458–90), but in 1526 the Turks annihilated the Hungarian army at Mohács, King Louis II being accidentally drowned as he fled, and secured the centre and S. of the country. The Habsburgs estab. themselves in the N. and W., while semi-independent princes under Turkish suzerainty ruled Transylvania, which had been part of Hungary since its conquest by St. Stephen in 1000 (it became part of Rumania in 1920). Habsburg attempts to suppress Protestantism and the privileges of the nobles led in the 17th cent. to several revolts, ruthlessly put down. By 1697 the Habsburgs had driven out the Turks and secured the whole of H., confirmed by the peace of Karlowitz, 1699. A peasant rising under Rakoczi led to the granting of a constitution in 1711 by Charles III of H. (VI of Austria).

After 1815 a national renaissance began, under the leadership of Kossuth. The revolution of 1848–9 proclaimed a republic and abolished serfdom, but with the help of Russia Austria suppressed the revolt. Francis Joseph in 1867 gave H. autonomy within the Dual Monarchy (*see* AUSTRIA; AUSTRIA–HUNGARY). In 1918, in the last days of the F.W.W., H. was proclaimed a republic, and for a few weeks in 1919 was ruled by a Bolshevik govt. under Bela Kun, who, following a coup d'état, escaped to Russia. A popularly elected assembly in 1920 chose Admiral Horthy (q.v.) as regent for an unnamed king; he remained in power until 1944. After 1933 H. fell more and more under German influence and, having joined Hitler in the invasion of Russia in 1941, was overrun by the Red Army 1944–5. Horthy fled, and a provisional govt. distributed land to the peasants, later reclaimed for collectivisation. An elected assembly inaugurated a rep. in 1946; it soon fell under Russian Communist domination, although only 70 Communists had been returned out of a total of 409. A popular rising in 1956 was harshly suppressed by Russian forces. Slightly more widely-based elections were held 1967 and far-reaching economic reforms were launched 1968.

Literature. After the H. state was estab. in 895, and Christianity adopted in *c.* 1000, Latin chronicles and devotional works dominated the lit. until *c.* 1500. The political upheavals which followed the battle of Mohács (1526) inspired the 16th, 17th, and early 18th cent. chronicle songs and folk poetry which helped preserve the national identity; notable writers in the vernacular were the poet Baron Bálint Balassa (1551–94) and the religious controversialist Cardinal Péter Pázmány (1570–1637). The reconstruction period after 1711 lacks imaginative inspiration, and the following era of foreign influence and stimulation initiated the 19th cent. renaissance. Dominating figures were Ferenc Kazinczy (1759–1831), the Romantic poet Mihály Vörösmarty (1800–55), such popular nationalist poets as Sándor Petőfi (1823–49) and János Arany (1817–82) and the novelist Mór Jókai (1825–1904); later realist novelists were Kálmán Mikszáth (1847–1910) and Ferenc Herczeg (1863–1950). The novelist Zsigmond Móricz (1879–1942), and the poets Endre Ady (1877–1918) and Mihály Babits (1883–1941) belong to the early 20th cent. revival; contemporary writers incl. the poets Gyula Illyés (1902–) and Lőrincz Szabó (1900–57), novelist János Kadolányi (1899–) and playwright Ferenc Molnár (1878–1952).

HUNGARY. An 18th century carved honeybread mould.
Courtesy of Corvina Press.

The Arts. Besides music (*see* BARTÓK and KODÁLY) H. excels in crafts such as glass, pottery and metalwork, in which there is a modern revival. *See* PERCZ, János.

HUNS. Name applied to a number of nomad Mongol peoples who first appeared in history in the 2nd cent. B.C. as raiding across the Great Wall into China. They entered Europe c. A.D. 372, settled in Hungary, and imposed their supremacy on the Ostrogoths and other Germanic peoples. Under the leadership of Attila they attacked the Eastern Empire, invaded Gaul, and threatened Rome, but after his death in 453 their power was broken by a revolt of their subject peoples. The White Hs. or Ephthalites, a kindred people, raided Persia and N. India in the 5th–6th cents.

HUNT, (Henry Cecil) John, baron (1910–). Brit. soldier/mountaineer. He served with the K.R.R.C. in India, before commanding the 11th batt. in 1944, and the 11th Indian infantry brigade 1944–6. An experienced mountaineer, he led the successful British conquest of Everest in 1953. He became chairman of the Parole Board 1967 and pres. Council for Volunteers Overseas 1968. He became a life peer 1966.

LORD HUNT

HUNT, James Henry Leigh (1784–1859). British poet and essayist. B. at Southgate, Middx, he began to edit *The Examiner* in 1808 and in 1813 was sentenced to 2 years' imprisonment for an attack on the Prince Regent, which made him widely acclaimed in radical circles. His narrative poem *The Story of Rimini,* written in prison, appeared in 1816. In 1822 he visited Byron and Shelley in Italy, and in 1828 H. pub. *Lord Byron and some of his Contemporaries.* Hampered by sickness and poverty, he was granted a civil-list pension in 1847. He did much to widen the public taste for early English and Italian poetry; but his own best work is largely in narrative verse.

HUNT, William Holman (1827–1910). British artist. B. in Cheapside, London, he first exhibited at the R.A. in 1846, and in 1848 helped to found the Pre-Raphaelite Brotherhood. In 1854 H. travelled to Syria and Palestine to paint realistic pictures of Biblical subjects. His most famous work, 'The Light of the World' (1854), is in Keble Coll., Oxford, a replica of it (1904) in St. Paul's.

W. H. HUNT. 'The Scapegoat', dated 1854, was the first of a series devoted to the presentation of Biblical history, the mountains of Edom being realistically portrayed. The frame bears the two quotations: 'Surely He hath borne our Griefs, and carried our Sorrows; yet we did esteem Him stricken, smitten of God, and afflicted', and 'And the Goat shall bear upon him all their Iniquities unto a Land not inhabited'.
Courtesy of the Lady Lever Collection.

HUNTER, John (1728–93). British surgeon and physiologist. B. in Lanarkshire, he became house-surgeon at St. George's hospital, London, in 1756, collaborated with his brother William in the anatomical school; and from 1768 was surgeon. He experimented extensively on animals, collected a large number of specimens and preparations (Hunterian Collections), now in the Royal College of Surgeons, and greatly furthered the art of surgery.

His brother **William H.** (1718–83), anatomist and obstetrician, became prof. of anatomy in the Royal Academy in 1768, and pres. of the Medical Society in 1781. His collections are now in the Hunterian museum of Glasgow univ.

HUNTINGDON, Selina Hastings, countess of (1707–91). British Methodist; founder of the Countess of Huntingdon's Connexion (q.v.). Dau. of Earl Ferrers, she m. in 1727 the 9th earl of Huntingdon (d. 1746). In 1739 she became a Methodist, and was one of the most important and influential disciples and supporters of Whitefield and the Wesleys.

HUNTINGDON. County town of Huntingdonshire, situated on the Ouse, 16 miles N.W. of Cambridge. It is a market town and has a number of light industries. A bridge (1332) connects H. with Godmanchester, the 2 towns having been united into a single bor. in 1961. The grammar school (founded 1565) attended by Pepys and Cromwell, dates from the 12th cent. and was formerly part of the medieval hospital: it was opened in 1962 as a Museum of Cromwelliana. Pop. (1961) 8,812.

HUNTINGDON. The Museum of Cromwelliana.
Courtesy of the County Records Dept.

HURSTMONCEUX. First built in 1446 by Sir Roger de Fiennes, a hero of Agincourt and Treasurer of the Household to Henry VI, the castle has been completely restored (left) and since 1958 has been the home of the Royal Greenwich Observatory (above).

Photos: A. W. Kerr and British Travel and Holidays Association.

HUNTINGDONSHIRE and Peterborough. English co. bounded by Beds, Northants, Lincs, and Cambs, and watered by the Ouse. A large part consists of rich fenland. Much of the co. is now arable, but the western areas still support herds of cattle. Though largely agricultural, the co. has important brickworks at Fletton and paper is manufactured at St. Neots. Huntingdon, the co. town, is becoming a centre for light industries. Other centres are Peterborough, the largest town, Ramsey, St. Ives and Godmanchester. H. is noted for its magnificent medieval church spires. Area 486 sq. m.; pop. (1967) 189,560.

HUNTINGTON, Ellsworth (1876–1947). American geographer. His research and explorations in Mesopotamia, Turkestan, Palestine, and Asia Minor were chiefly concerned with climate and its relation to human activities, and the distribution of civilizations.

HUNYADI (hoon'yodi), **János Corvinus** (1387–1456). Hungarian statesman and general. B. in Transylvania, reputedly the natural son of the emperor Sigismund, he campaigned successfully against the Turks. He had just driven them from before Belgrade when he d. of the plague.

HUPEI (hoo'peh). Prov. of central China, through which flow the Yangtze-kiang and its tributary the Han-shui. In the W. the land is high, the Yangtze breaking through from Szechwan in gorges, but elsewhere the prov. is low-lying fertile land. In summer rice and cotton are the principal crops, in winter cereals, beans, and vegetables. The greatest urban centre is Wuhan, the cap. Area 72,600 sq. m.; pop. (1968) 32,000,000.

HU'RONS. French nickname (*hure*, head of pig, etc.) for the Wyandot, nomadic Red Indian tribes related to the Iroquois, and living near Lakes Huron, Erie and Ontario in the 16–17th cents. They were decimated by the Iroquois, but some still survive in Quebec and Oklahoma. *Lake Huron*, second largest of the Great Lakes (q.v.), has an area of 23,010 sq. m., of which 13,900 sq. m. are in Canada.

HURRICANE. A violent revolving storm. The name is derived from a Carib word *huracan*, and applied originally only to the W. Indies, but is now used in many countries, though in the E. Indies and the China Seas similar storms are known as typhoons. Hs. are accompanied by a fall in pressure, and winds of up to 100 m.p.h. or more. They have a revolving speed of 10–15 m.p.h., and blow at over 75 m.p.h. On the Beaufort Scale it is force 12; the severer stages of H. are force 13 (83–92 m.p.h.), 14 (93–103), 15 (104–114), 16 (115–125) and 17 (126–136).

HURSTMONCEUX (hurstmonsoo'). English village, in Sussex, 7 m. N. of Eastbourne, with a 15th cent. but greatly restored castle. To this the Royal Greenwich Observatory moved from Greenwich, 1950–7.

HU SHIH (1891–1962). Chinese scholar and philosopher. An adviser of Chiang Kai Shek, though critical of the Kuomintang's curtailment of civil liberties, he was ambassador to the U.S. 1938–42. Largely through his influence as prof. at Peking Nat. Univ. 1917–26, the Mandarin dialect was abandoned for the colloquial *pai-hua* in modern Chinese writing.

HUSS, John (*c.* 1373–1415). Bohemian reformer. B. in S. Bohemia, he was ed. at Prague univ. of which he became rector in 1402. He attacked ecclesiastical abuses and was excommunicated. His preaching attracted popular support, and in 1411 Prague was laid under a papal interdict. In 1413 he was summoned to appear before the Council of Constance. There he defended Wycliffe and rejected the Pope's authority, and was burnt at the stake on 6 July 1415.

His followers were known as *Hussites*, and from a body of religious reformers they developed into a nationalist party opposed to German and papal influence in Bohemia. War began in 1419, and the Bohemians were for some years successful under the leadership of Žižka. Subsequently the movement split; and Roman Catholicism was re-established in 1620. The traditions of one section, the Taborites, are carried on by the Moravian Church.

HUSSEIN I
Courtesy of the Jordan Embassy.

HUSSEIN Ibn Ali (hoosān') (*c.* 1854–1931). King of the Hejaz. B. in Mecca, he was appointed Sherif of Mecca in 1908. After negotiations with the British he headed an Arab revolt in 1916, and with the aid of T. E. Lawrence raised an army against the Turks. He assumed the title of king of the Hejaz in 1916, but in 1924 was driven out by the Wahabis under Ibn Saud. He d. in Transjordan. His great-grandson **Hussein I** (1935–), grandson of Abdullah (q.v.), succeeded his father Talal as king of Jordan in 1952 on the latter's declared incapacity. Opposed to the Nasser-dominated U.A.R., he is nevertheless an Arab nationalist and remains unreconciled to the creation of the Jewish State of Israel. In 1958 he formed with Faisal II of Iraq the short-lived Arab Union. He m. as his 2nd wife 1961 Antoinette Gardiner, dau. of a former member of the British Army Advisory Mission, who became a Muslim and took the name Muna el-Hussein.

HUSSERL (hoos'-), Edmund Gustav Albrecht (1859–1938). Austrian philosopher. Prof. at Freiburg from 1916, he was the founder of phenomenology which gave birth to gestalt psychology and influenced Heidegger.

HUSTON, John (1906–). American film director. Son of the actor Walter H. (1884–1950), he has a powerful technique at its best in The Maltese Falcon (1941), The African Queen (1951), and Moby Dick (1956).

HUTCHESON, Francis (1694–1746). Founder of the Scottish school of philosophy. B. in co. Down, Ireland, he was prof. of moral philosophy at Glasgow 1729–46 and in various writings developed the doctrine that man has an inherent 'moral sense'. His System of Moral Philosophy appeared in 1755.

HUTCHINSON, Arthur Stuart Menteth (1879–1971). Brit. journalist, and author of the bitter novel of war and disillusionment If Winter Comes (1921).

HUTCHINSON, John (1615–64). British soldier. Colonel H. held Nottingham, as governor, for Parliament from 1643 until sent to sit in the Long Parliament in 1646. A signatory of Charles I's death warrant, though he disapproved of Cromwell's seizure of power, he was imprisoned and d. in Sandown castle. The Memoirs by his wife present a classic picture of the Puritan gentleman.

HUTTEN (hoot'en), Ulrich von (1488–1523). German humanist. B. nr. Fulda, he was crowned poet laureate by the emperor Maximilian in 1517, became enthusiastic follower of Luther, wrote violent satires against the monks; eventually found refuge in Zürich.

HUTTON, Barbara (1912–). American heiress, grand-dau. of F. W. Woolworth (q.v.), the original 'poor little rich girl', whose consecutive m. to Prince Alexis Mdivani, Count von Reventlow, Cary Grant, Prince Igor Troubetzkoy, Porfirio Rubirosa and Baron von Cramm ended in divorce: in 1964 she m. Prince Pierre Raymond Doan Vinh of Viet-Nam.

HUTTON, James (1726–97). Scottish geologist, the 'founder of geology'. In 1785 he developed the Huttonian theory of the igneous origin of many rocks.

HUTTON, Sir Leonard (1916–). British cricketer. B. in Yorks, he captained England in 23 Test matches and was the 1st professional to captain England (1952–6).

HUXLEY, Aldous (1894–1963). British author, grandson of Thomas H. and brother of Julian H. (qq.v.). From Eton and Balliol, where his education had been hampered by a disease of the eyes that permanently affected his sight, he went on to literary journalism, a Sitwellian book of verse The Burning Wheel (1916) and a witty first novel Crome Yellow (1921). Satiric disillusion continued throughout Antic Hay (1923), Those Barren Leaves (1925) and Point Counter Point (1928) with its impression of D. H. Lawrence, whose letters he edited. The fantasy Brave New World (1932) reproduced the unlikable human race by mass production in the laboratory, and H.'s sensitivity to the foul and disgusting in life led him to a retreat symbolized by his emigration to California in 1938 and a devotion to mysticism which ended in his experiments with mescalin recorded in The Doors of Perception (1954). His other works incl. Grey Eminence (1941), a study of Richelieu's adviser Père Joseph; stimulating travel books such as Jesting Pilate (1926) and Beyond the Mexique Bay (1934); essays,

The Olive Tree (1936) and piquant short stories, e.g. 'The Gioconda Smile' which was successfully staged and filmed.

HUXLEY, Elspeth Josceline (1907–). British authority on African affairs, author of such books as White Man's Country (1933), a study of the makings of Kenya, and also of novels.

HUXLEY, Sir Julian (1887–). British biologist and writer. Son of Leonard H. (1860–1933), editor of the Cornhill Magazine, half-brother of the eminent physiologist Andrew Fielding H. (1917–) (see A. L. HODGKIN); and a grandson of Thomas Henry H., he was prof. of zoology, King's Coll., London, 1925–7; Fullerian prof. of physiology in the Royal Institution, 1926–9; and secretary of the Zoological Society of London, 1935–42. In 1946–8 he was Director-Gen. of the United Nations Educational, Scientific and Cultural Organization (UNESCO). His books incl. Essays of a Biologist (1923), Religion without Revelation (1927), The Science of Life (with H. G. and G. P. Wells; 1929), Evolution, The Modern Synthesis (1942), Soviet Genetics versus World Science. He was one of the original members of the B.B.C. Brains Trust.

HUXLEY, Thomas Henry (1825–95). British scientist, humanist, and agnostic thinker. B. at Ealing, he graduated in medicine in 1845, and 1846–50 was surgeon to H.M.S. Rattlesnake on a surveying expedition in the South Seas. In 1851 H. was made F.R.S., and in 1854 became lecturer in Natural History in the Royal School of Mines, later prof. at the Royal Coll. of Science. Following the publication of The Origin of Species in 1859, he won fame as 'Darwin's bulldog', and for many years was the most prominent and popular champion of Evolution. He wrote Man's Place in Nature (1863), and textbooks on physiology, and innumerable papers. In 1869 he coined the word 'agnostic' to express his own religious attitude; and his later books, e.g. Lay Sermons (1870), Science and Culture (1881), and Evolution and Ethics were expositions of scientific humanism. He was president of the Royal Society 1883–5, and received many academic honours. In 1892 he became a Privy Councillor. His Life and Letters by his son Leonard H. was pub. in 1900.

HUYGENS (hē'genz), Christiaan (1629–95). Dutch physicist. B. at The Hague, he developed several of Galileo's ideas, propounded the undulatory theory of light, and discovered polarization. In 1660 he visited England and was made an F.R.S.

HUYSMANS (üismoňs'), Joris Karl (1848–1907). French novelist. B. in Paris of Dutch ancestry, he spent 30 years as a civil servant. Marthe (1876), the story of a courtesan, was followed by other realistic novels. His greatest work is La Cathédrale (1898), a symbolist novel dealing with Chartres.

HWA'NG-HŌ (Yellow River). One of the great rivers of China, some 2,740 m. long. The name comes from the quantity of yellow loess carried by the river in suspension. The river rises in the Kuen-lun ranges of western China, and flows across China with a very tortuous course to reach the Yellow Sea in the Gulf of Pottai. The principal tributary is the Wei-ho. Chief towns on the river are Kaifêng, and Tsinan. The river, called 'China's sorrow', frequently overflows and has several times changed its lower course and mouth.

HWANGSHIH. Industrial city in Hupei, China, c. 50 m. S.E. of Wuhan, formed in 1950 by the union of 2 riverside towns to exploit local iron ore, previously exported. It was completed in 1961–2.

HWLFFORDD. Welsh name of HAVERFORDWEST.

HYACINTH (hi'asinth). Popular spring flower belonging to the family Liliaceae, grown from a bulb, and producing large cylindrical heads of pink, blue, or white sweetly scented flowers. Cultivation has reached its highest development in Holland, particularly around Haarlem. The original plant, Hyacinthus orientalis, resembles the bluebell or wild H.

HYACINTHE, Père. Name borne by the French preacher Charles Loyson (1827–1912), when he was a Carmelite monk. One of the most famous pulpit orators of the day, he denounced ecclesiastical abuses with great boldness and was excommunicated in 1869. In 1872 he m. an American, and in his latter years was a Liberal Catholic curate in Paris and Geneva.

HYDASPES. Classical name of r. JHELUM.

HYDE, Douglas (1860–1949). Irish scholar and statesman, known in Gaelic as 'the lovely little branch'. Founder-pres. of the Gaelic League 1893–1915, he was Pres. of Eire 1938–45. His works incl. *Love Songs of Connacht* (1894).

HYDE PARK. One of the largest open spaces in London, England. It occupies *c.* 350 acres in Westminster (373 before the Park Lane traffic scheme was carried out). It adjoins Kensington Gardens (264 acres), and incl. the Serpentine (32 acres). Here was held in 1851 the Great Exhibition. Rotten Row is a famous riding track.

HYDERABAD. Capital city of the Indian state of Andhra Pradesh on the Musi, a tributary of the Kistna. Most famous of its buildings is the Jama Masjid mosque. Pop. (1961) 1,252,337.

H. was formerly cap. of the princely state of H. which occupied the greater part of the Deccan, and was by far the largest of the Indian princely states. The majority of its people were Hindu, but the ruler, called the Nizam, belonged to a Moslem dynasty. Relations between the Nizam and the British had been regulated by a series of agreements; and when the partition of British India was pending in 1947 the Nizam declared his wish to assume complete independence. This the new govt. of India would not allow; and after being subjected to a show of force the Nizam acceded to India in 1950, H. becoming a state of the Union. In 1956 the state disappeared from the map: it was divided between Bombay state (included in that part of it in 1960 created Maharashtra), Mysore, and Andhra.

HYDERABAD. City of W. Pakistan. H. was the capital of Sind until 1843, when Sind was conquered by the British. Still a military headquarters, it has many industries and a medical school. Pop. (1961) 434,537.

HYDER ALI (hī'der ah'lē) (*c.* 1722–82). Indian Moslem warrior. In command of the army in Mysore from 1749, he became the actual ruler of the state 1759 and rivalled British power in the area until his triple defeat by Sir Eyre Coote in 1781 during the Anglo–French wars. He was the father of Tippoo (q.v.).

HYDRA (hī'dra). Genus of freshwater animals, simplest of the order Hydrozoa. The body is a double-layered tube (with 6–10 hollow tentacles round the mouth) measuring $\frac{1}{2}$ in. extended but capable of contracting to a small knob. Multiplication is by the formation of buds, by division into 2 or more pieces, and by sexual reproduction (there are no organs except those of reproduction). Usually fixed to waterweed, the H. feeds on minute animals which are caught and paralysed by the stinging cells on the tentacles.

HYDRANGEA (hidrān'-jya). Flowering shrub (*Hydrangea macrophylla*) of the Saxifragaceae family and native to Japan, so named from the Gk. for water vessel, after its cup-like seed capsules. Also called hortensia, it normally produces round heads of pink flowers, but these may be blue if certain chemicals, e.g. alum or iron, are in the soil.

HYDRAULICS (hīdraw'-liks). The science that

HYDRA. Specimen with: A, vegetative buds; B, with sex cells (1, egg; 2, sperm) and C, contracted.

HYDRAULICS. A tidal model of the Tees estuary, built in one of the large wave basins at the Department of Scientific and Industrial Research, Hydraulics Research Station, Wallingford, Berkshire, England. The model has been used to determine the feasibility of maintaining, under the action of waves and tidal currents, a deepened channel across the bar at the entrance to the estuary.   *Courtesy of Hydraulics Research Station.*

deals with the dynamics of liquids (hydrodynamics) especially as applied to engineering. It generally refers to the study of water and falls into 2 main branches: *hydrostatics*, which deals with the equilibrium of liquids and the laws relating to liquid pressure, and incl. the study of pressure on submerged areas of any shape or inclination (water gates, dams, tanks, divers, diving bells, hydraulic presses, etc.), the measurement of pressure by means of manometers or pressure gauges, and buoyancy and flotation problems; and *hydrokinetics*, which deals with the problems of liquids in motion and incl. flow of all different types (from steady uniform to unsteady non-uniform) through pipes, conduits, orifices, nozzles, weirs, etc., discharge of water through siphons, valves, branching or looping lines, flow of water in rivers, problems connected with hydraulic turbines, pumps, and other machinery.

HYDROCEPHALUS (hīdrosef'alus). Excess of fluid within the skull; 'water on the brain'. In infants it may be congenital and was once commonly due to tubercular inflammation of the brain membranes (meninges), or to blocking by local inflammation of the channel between the ventricles of the brain and the spinal column. The head is much enlarged, and the condition may be fatal; but sometimes can resolve spontaneously or be treated by surgical inclusion of a valve.

HYDROCHLORIC (hīdrōklōrik) **ACID** (HCl aq.). A chemical reagent, known also as muriatic acid or spirits of salts, consisting of gaseous hydrogen chloride in water. H.A. is used extensively in industry in reactions with metals, e.g. the recovery of zinc from galvanized scrap iron and the production of chlorides and chlorine. Highly corrosive, it will attack most metals and dissolve metallic oxides. Oxidizing agents react with it to form chlorine, the salts of H.A. being known as chlorides.

HYDROCYANIC (hīdrosī-a'nik) **ACID.** Also known as prussic acid, H.A. is a solution of hydro-cyanic gas (HCN) in water and is a colourless, highly poisonous, volatile liquid with a characteristic smell of bitter almonds. Hydrogen cyanide is made by the reaction of sodium cyanide with dilute sulphuric acid and is used for fumigation. It forms a series of salts called cyanides, sodium cyanide being used in the cyanide process for extracting gold and silver from ores.

HYDRODYNAMICS. Science of fluids in motion. The theory of H. is concerned almost entirely with perfect fluids, such as water, alcohol, and ether, and indeed most liquids which are not classed as viscous fluids (i.e. fluids in which change of form takes place gradually, as is the case with pitch). The perfect, or inviscid, fluid, cannot sustain any tangential stress.

HYDRO-ELECTRIC POWER. Electricity generated by water power. The first large H.E. installation was completed at Niagara in 1892: outstanding modern schemes incl. Hoover Dam and the Tennessee Valley Authority (U.S.); Bratsk on the Angara and Kuibyshev on the Volga (U.S.S.R.); Kitimat (Canada); Kariba and Volta in Africa; Snowy Mountains (Australia); the Tata plants at Bombay; the Shannon scheme in the Irish Rep. and the Ben Nevis plant in Scotland.

HYDROGEN (hĭ′drojen) (Gk. *hydro*, water, and *genes*, forming). Symbol H; at. wt. 1·008; at. no. 1. Colourless, odourless and tasteless, it is the lightest known gas. It does not support combustion but burns in air to form water, and when mixed with air or oxygen forms an explosive mixture. H. was first recognized as a substance by Cavendish in 1766 who called it 'inflammable air'.

H. occurs chiefly in combination with oxygen as water, with carbon as hydrocarbons, and in most organic substances, particularly those used for foods and fuels, and in many minerals. It is manufactured by many processes among which are the action of steam on heated carbon, the electrolysis of water, the reaction of acids on certain metals. The isotope deuterium, at. wt. 2·0147, was announced by Urey in 1932, and tritium, at. wt. 3·0170, in 1934.

HYDROPONICS. Open-air gravel culture in Japan. At regular intervals pumps automatically discharge liquid fertilizer into concrete-lined beds of gravel, producing a larger, heavier crop of lettuce in a shorter time than obtained by conventional methods. The plants are clean, easily gathered and fertilizer costs are halved since none escapes into the ground.
Courtesy of the Embassy of Japan.

The many commercial uses of H. incl. the production of high-temperature flames for welding, cutting, and melting metals; the fixation of atmospheric nitrogen by the Haber ammonia process; the hydrogenation of fats and oils, e.g. in the preparation of margarine; the production of methyl alcohol by catalytic reaction with carbon monoxide; and the filling of balloons. Ordinary town gas contains about 50 per cent H.

When an atom of H. is ionized by losing an electron it becomes a proton. H. is the fuel of the stars, releasing energy turning to helium in their interiors.

HYDROGEN BOMB. Large-scale explosion resulting from the thermo-nuclear release of energy when hydrogen nuclei are condensed to helium nuclei. This is the continuing reaction in the sun and other stars, but on earth could result from the triggering of tritium (hydrogen isotope of atomic weight 3·0170) by an ordinary atom bomb. The first H.B. was exploded at Eniwetok Atoll by the U.S. in 1952.

HYDROGRAPHY. The study of the waters of the earth's surface – the sea, lakes, and rivers. It includes their physical properties and boundaries, the conformation of the sea floor, particularly the arrangement of deeps, shoals, sandbanks, etc., the measuring of currents, tides, and all movements within the water, effects of surface winds, and the mapping and charting of hydrographical features.

HYDROLYSIS (hĭdro′lisis). The term applied to a chemical reaction in which decomposition into simpler forms is effected by the action of water or its ions. H. occurs in the case of certain inorganic salts in solution; in nearly all non-metallic chlorides, in esters, and in other organic substances. It plays an important part in the utilization of food materials by the body.

HYDRO′METER. Instrument used to measure the density of liquids compared with that of water, usually expressed in grammes per cu. cm. The H., based on the theory that any body floating in a liquid equals in weight the volume of the displaced liquid, consists of a thin glass tube ending in a sphere which leads into a smaller sphere, the latter being loaded so that the H. floats upright, sinking deeper into lighter liquids than heavier. The density of the liquid is inversely proportional to the volume immersed, and is revealed by the graduated scale marked along the thin tube.

HYDROPHOBIA (hĭdrofō′bia). Rabies, a disease of animals transferable to man by biting. The saliva of the sick animal, usually a dog or wolf, carries the virus. If the wound is cauterized at once or proper serum treatment (Pasteur) is given, the disease may be prevented; otherwise the patient will die after a painful illness, marked by spasms of the throat brought on by drinking or the sight of water.

HY′DROPHONE. An underwater microphone and ancillary equipment which converts water-borne sound waves into electrical signals, originally developed to detect enemy submarines.

HY′DROPLANE. Specially constructed motor boats which skim over the surface of the water when driven at high speed.

HYDROPŌ′NICS. The cultivation of plants without soil, using specially prepared solutions of mineral salts. J. von Sachs in 1860 and W. Knop in 1865 developed a system of plant culture in water whereby the relation of mineral salts to plant growth could be determined, but it was not until about 1936 that large crops were grown by H. methods, at first in California, but since in many other parts of the world.

HYDROSTATICS. The science which deals with the mechanical problems of fluids in equilibrium. i.e. in a static condition. An important practical application concerns the problems connected with floating bodies, as in shipbuilding. Another is concerned with the design of dams.

HYDRO′XĬDE. The term applied to a compound containing one or more hydroxyl (OH) groups, generally combined with a metal. The most important Hs. are caustic soda, caustic potash, and slaked lime.

HYDROZŌ′A. Class of mainly marine animals in the phylum Coelenterata (q.v.).

HYENA (hĭ-ēna). Genus of quadrupeds, of which there are 3 living species, the striped H. (*Hyaena Striata*) found in India and northern Africa; the allied brown

HYENA. Both the brown and striped species have disproportionately short back legs, which affects their gait, but the spotted hyena, seen here in the Kruger National Park, is much better balanced. It is also much the largest and strongest of the three.
Courtesy of Satour.

H. (*H. brunnea*) found on the S. African coasts; and the spotted H. (*H. crocuta*) common S. of the Sahara. Remarkably strong, both in its bone-cracking jaws and muscular power, the H. has always had value as a scavenger, though it will also attack live cattle and sometimes human beings.

HYÈRES (ē-ār′). French town in the dept. of Var. It has a mild climate, and is a popular winter health resort, with some industry: e.g. olive-oil presses; export of violets, strawberries, vegetables. Pop. (1962) 33,693.

HYGIEIA (hēj-ē′ya). In Gk. mythology, the goddess of health, the dau. of Aesculapius.

HYGIENE (hījēn). The science of health, whose aim is the preservation of health, the prevention of disease, and the prolongation of life by proper attention to physical laws. It is chiefly concerned with such external conditions as the purity of air and water, sunlight, the cleanliness of body and dwelling-place, dietary rules, conditions of labour and recreation, etc.

HYGROMETER (hīgrom′-). Instrument for measuring the absolute or relative humidity (q.v.) of the atmosphere. The relative humidity is usually measured by means of a special type of H. consisting of 2 identical mercury thermometers, the bulb of one being dry and that of the other kept moist by a covering of muslin dipping into a reservoir of water. The evaporation from the wet bulb cools that thermometer relatively to the dry one, and tables are supplied giving values of the relative humidity at the temperature of the dry bulb for various values of the difference of temperature between the 2 thermometers.

HYKSOS (hik′sōz) ('Shepherd kings' or 'princes of the desert'). A Semitic people which overran Egypt in the 18th cent. B.C. and established their own dynasty, which lasted till 1580 B.C.

HYLTON, Jack (1892–1965). British impresario. Originally famous from 1922 as a band leader, he in later years concentrated on presenting such shows as *Salad Days* and the *Crazy Gang* series.

HYMANS (ēmoṅs′), Paul (1865–1941). Belgian statesman. He entered the Chamber in 1900 as a Lib., and acted as Belgian Minister in London during the F.W.W. He was For. Min. 1918–20, 1924–5, 1927–34, and 1934–5.

HYMEN (hī′men). In Greek mythology, the son of Apollo and one of the Muses, he was the god of marriage and in art is represented as a youth carrying a bridal torch.

HYMENO′PTERA. Order of insects, including ants, bees, etc., with a waist, and the saw-flies without a waist. They have 4 membraneous wings. The female possesses an ovipositor or a sting, and the mouth-parts of both sexes are suited to biting or sucking. They go through a complete metamorphosis.

HYMNS. Any compositions celebrating a deity which are intended to be sung or chanted. The use of Hs. has been common to most great ancient and modern religions. Christian hymnology originates with the O.T. psalms, those in the N.T. following closely in the same tradition. From the 4th cent. Latin was used as well as Greek in hymn-writing. St. Ambrose is thought to have introduced congregational singing and the full development of church music. In the 6th cent. pope Gregory the Great instituted the more severe mode of the Gregorian chant. Greatest of the medieval hymn-writers was the 12th cent. Adam of St. Victor.

The earliest English hymn is the 7th cent. fragment by Caedmon, but in general hymn-writing in the vernacular waited on the Reformation, and even in the 18th cent. Church of England services relied on the metrical psalms of Sternhold and Hopkins, and of Tate and Brady. Among 17th cent. writers are Herbert, Baxter, Ken, and Bunyan. In 1737 the first modern hymn book was pub. by John and Charles Wesley; other writers are Toplady, Newton, the poet Cowper, Watts, and the Taylor sisters. To counterbalance the Nonconformist predominance of the 18th cent. the 19th produced Heber, Newman, Keble, Lyte, and many others. Anglican worship is based on the *Hymns Ancient and Modern* (1861), ed. by Sir H. W. Baker, and notable for translations of ancient hymns, often by J. M. Neale. Most famous of the Scottish writers is Horatius Bonar. The popular H. was developed in America by Moody and Sankey, and in England by the Salvation Army. Richest of the Continental countries in Hs. is Germany, with writers such as Luther and Gerhardt.

HYRAX

HYNDMAN, Henry Mayers (1842–1921). British Socialist. He was a Tory democrat before he came across Marx's *Capital*, which converted him to scientific socialism. In 1881 he was a founder of the Democratic Federation which in 1884 became the Social Democratic Federation. He wrote *England for All* (1881), and devoted his life to Socialist propaganda.

HYOSCINE (hī-osīn) or Scopolamine ($C_{17}H_{21}O_4N$). An important alkaloid used for its hypnotic powers, in medicine in combination with morphine, to produce 'twilight sleep'.

HYPATIA (hīpā′shia) (A.D. 370–415). Greek woman philosopher, b. at Alexandria. She studied Neo-Platonism at Athens, and succeeded her father Theon as prof. of philosophy at Alexandria. St. Cyril, bishop of Alexandria, becoming jealous of her influence, denounced her as a pagan enchantress, and inspired a mob of monks to murder her.

HYPHASIS. Classical name of the r. BEAS.

HYPNO′TICS. Substances which produce a state like natural sleep. They depress the brain centres governing consciousness and mental activity. Taken in excess they suspend sensation and the power of movement, or even the action of the lungs and heart. The best-known are the alcohols, chlorals, and barbiturates.

HY′PNOTISM. The production of a state in which consciousness and will are suspended but other functions are not impaired. The patient is then extremely susceptible to suggestion and will carry out orders at once or long after he has been awakened, and may be made insensible to pain. The H. Act 1952 controlled exploitation of H. as entertainment.

HYPODERMIC (hīpo-) SYRINGE. An instrument used for injecting fluids beneath the skin. It consists of a small graduated tube of glass and sometimes also of metal, with a close-fitting piston and a nozzle on to which a hollow needle can be fitted. Various types incl. disposable plastic, and automatic spring-loaded H.Ss.

HYPO′TENUSE. The side of a right-angled triangle opposite the right angle. *See also* PYTHAGORAS.

HYPÔTHE′RMIA. Use of cooling anaesthesia – also known as hibernation – to lower the temperature of the body for heart surgery and to tide over a dangerous phase of illness. Notable cases incl. that of Mrs. Ellen Moore, unconscious for 169 days after head injury, who was kept in a virtual state of H. for a week at Newcastle General Hospital. Her child was afterwards born normally. The body's metabolism slows down at low temperatures, and less strain is imposed upon the vital organs, particularly the brain and the heart.

HYPSOMETER (hipsom′-). A double steam vessel for testing the accuracy of a thermometer at the boiling point of water. It was originally used for determining heights by changes in the b.p. with changes in pressure – hence the name from the Gk. *hypsos*, height.

HYRAX (hī′raks). Order of mammals (Hyracoidea) found in Africa and Syria. They are about the size of a rabbit, with a plump body, short legs, and brownish fur. There are 4 toes on the front limbs, and 3 on the hind, each of which has a hoof. They are good climbers, and live among rocks and in desert places.

HYSSOP (his′op). Herb (*Hyssopus officinalis*) of the Labiatae family, once grown for its medical properties. It produces small blue flowers and narrow, pointed, aromatic leaves. Hedge H. (*Gratiola officinalis*) belongs to the Scrophulariaceae.

HYSTERE′CTOMY. Surgical removal of the womb, usually for fibroid or malignant tumours.

HYSTĒ′RIA. A nervous disorder in which the patient simulates various kinds of disabilities in order to avoid responsibility or an unpleasant situation. In contrast with the deceptions of the malingerer, those of the hysteric are involuntary and for the most part unrealized. The commonest symptoms include paralysis of one or more limbs, deafness, blindness, dumbness, recurrent cough, vomiting, and general illness. The object of the hysterical reaction is to enable the hysteric to be dependent on others without loss of self-regard. The patient is commonly extremely selfish, self-centred and emotionally insincere and immature.

HYSSOP

HYTHE (hīdh). English seaside resort (bor.), one of the Cinque Ports on the S. coast of Kent, 5 m. W. of Folkestone. Pop. (1961) 10,028.

I Ninth letter of the Roman alphabet, deriving, as regards its form, from the sign for one of the several breaths of the Semitic languages. Its vocalic value was first given it by the Greeks.

IAŞI (yashe). Rumanian city, 10 m. W. of the Prut, cap. of I. region. There are machine, chemical and textile industries, and a univ. (1860). Pop. (1966) 160,880.

IBADAN (ebah′dahn). Largest city in Nigeria, in the S.W., 100 m. N.N.E. of Lagos. It is a trading centre – palm oil, cotton and tobacco, and has a univ. (1962). Pop. (1963) 600,000.

IBÁÑEZ (ēvahn′yeth), **Vincente Blasco** (1867–1928). Spanish novelist and politician. B. at Valencia, he played an active part in revolutionary politics. His novels incl. *Blood and Sand* (1913), and *The Four Horsemen of the Apocalypse* (1918).

IBĒ′RIA. Name given by ancient Greek navigators to the Spanish peninsula, derived from the r. Iberus (Ebro). Anthropologists have given the name Iberians to a pre-Celtish Neolithic race, traces of whom are found in the Span. peninsula, S. France, the Canary Is., Corsica, and part of N. Africa.

I′BEX. Wild goat (*Capra ibex*), native to the snowy regions of the Alps. The name has also been applied to the Asiatic ibex (*C. sibirica*).

IBI-GAMIN. Another name for KAMET.

I′BIS. Genus of wading birds related to the storks and herons, but having a long curved beak. Various species occur in the warmer regions of the world, including the scarlet I. of America and the glossy I. found in all 5 continents. The sacred I. of ancient Egypt (*I. aethiopica*) is still found in the Nile basin.

IBIZA. Spanish form of IVIZA.

IBN BATUTA (bahtoo′tah), properly Abu Abdallah Mohammed (1304–77). Arab traveller who wrote on the history of Islam in the post-Mongol period.

IBN SAUD (sowd) (1880–1953). King of Saudi Arabia. His father was the son of the sultan of Nejd, at whose capital, Riyadh. I.S. was born. In 1891 a rival tribe seized Riyadh, and I.S. went into exile with his father, who resigned his claim to the throne in his favour. In 1902 I.S. recaptured Riyadh and recovered the kingdom, and by 1921 he had brought all C. Arabia under his rule. In 1924 he invaded the Hejaz, of which he was proclaimed king in 1926. Nejd and the Hejaz were united in 1932 in the kingdom of Saudi Arabia.

IBSEN, Henrik Johan (1828–1906). Norwegian poet-dramatist. B. at Skien, he failed entry to Christiania univ. 1850, and was dramatic adviser to theatres at Bergen and Christiania, producing *The Vikings in Helgeland* (1858), *The Pretenders* (1864), and other plays. His satirical *Love's Comedy* (1862) aroused opposition, and the years 1864–91 he mainly spent abroad, in Italy or Germany. The first plays written abroad were the great verse dramas *Brand* (1866) and *Peer Gynt* (1867).

The political satire *The League of Youth* (1869) began the series of realistic dramas which revolutionized the European theatre. There followed *The Pillars of Society*; *A Doll's House*; *Ghosts*, which aroused furious opposition; I.'s rejoinder, *An Enemy of the People* (1882); the satiric tragi-comedy *The Wild Duck* (1884); *Rosmersholm* (1886); *The Lady from the Sea* (1888); and *Hedda Gabler* (1890). In 1891 I. returned to Norway, recognized at last as her greatest living writer. His last plays were *The Master Builder* (1892), which recaptures the poetic spirit of his earlier work; *Little Eyolf* (1894); *John Gabriel Borkman* (1896); and *When We Dead Awaken* (1899), a final statement of his philosophy.

I′CARUS. Asteroid *c.* 1 m. in diameter, discovered 1949 and named after the son of Daedalus (q.v.), whose orbital plane intersects with that of Earth. Its orbital period is 409 days and it passes through the plane twice a year. Unlike planets, asteroids are subject to severe orbital perturbations, and collision is theoretically possible.

ICE. The solid formed by water when it freezes. It is colourless, crystalline, and shapes hexagonally. The freezing point, adopted as a thermometric standard, is 0° for the Centigrade and Réaumur scales, and 32° for the Fahrenheit. I. expands in the act of freezing, becoming less dense than water (0·9175 at 0°C). The absorption of heat on melting, and its expulsion on freezing, are expressed as the latent heat of fusion of I.

ICEBERG. A constant hazard to shipping, icebergs drift with the sea currents, sometimes with more than two-thirds of their mass submerged, but they often assume shapes of great beauty, as here off the Greenland coast.
Courtesy of the National Travel Association of Denmark

ICE AGE. The earlier part of the Pleistocene period in geology, immediately preceding historic times. N. Europe and America underwent glacial conditions similar to the polar regions. The American mountains show signs of former glacial activity and the ice-sheet spread over N. Europe, reaching Ireland and the Atlantic, leaving its remains as far S. as Switzerland, Several ice ages are distinguished, and man was contemporary with at least the later glaciations.

ICEBERG. A floating mass or hill of ice, rising sometimes to 270 feet above the sea. Polar glaciers which reach the coast become extended into a broad foot; as this enters the sea, masses break off and drift towards temperate latitudes, becoming a menace to shipping. The sinking of the *Titanic* in 1912 was caused by collision with an iceberg.

ICE-CREAM. A dairy product composed mostly of milk, with sweetening added. The milk is pasteurized, homogenized, then whipped and frozen. To these basic ingredients flavouring may be added after the mixing process, when the I. emerges partially hard. Its final hardening is achieved in containers in which it is kept for several hours at about −10° F. Traditionally a trade in the hands of Italian immigrants, the making of I. became a mechanized industry first in the U.S.A. and then in the 1920s–30s in Britain, with rapid post-S.W.W. expansion. This involved the production of new-type 'hard' I. adapted for storage and transport, but from the mid-1950s a soft I. frozen on the premises where it is sold has regained popularity.

ICE HOCKEY. Game played on ice between 2 teams, each of 6 players. Derived from ordinary H., the game was 1st played on ice in Canada in 1867, and is the national sport.

The skating space or rink is 61 m. long and 30 m. wide, divided into 3 zones by 2 blue lines. The goals

(1·22 m. high by 1·83 m. wide) stand at either end of the rink on lines which are 4 m. from the ends of the rink. All players wear protective clothing. The 6 players are: Goal Keeper, Right Defence, Left Defence, Centre, Right Wing and Left Wing, and 8 reserves are allowed to each team. The puck (a rubber disc) must not be passed forward from one zone to the other between 2 players of the same side, and must precede the attacking players into the attacking zone. The puck must be kept continually in motion. Rough tackling is prohibited. The game is increasingly popular in Britain.

IÇEL. *See* MERSIN.

ICELAND. Island forming an independent repub. in the N. Atlantic just S. of the Arctic Circle and 230 m. S.E. of Greenland. In the main, it is a plateau of volcanic rocks of some 2,500 ft. in height rising to 6,952 ft. in the ice-sheet of Vatnajökull. Short, turbulent rivers and waterfalls are numerous. There are over 100 volcanoes, of which some 25 have been active in historical times. Fields of lava cover hundreds of square miles, and hot springs are numerous. More than three-quarters of I.'s area is unproductive, wild, and inhospitable.

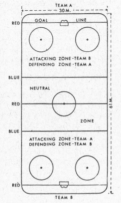

ICELAND. Active volcanoes show that the forces which formed our globe are still at work here. In the early Tertiary period the Brito-Arctic basalt region may have linked Iceland with Greenland and Britain.   *Courtesy of Icelandair.*

The climate is mild and wet. The pop. is almost all Icelandic. Reykjavik, the cap., is the only large town. There is an aluminium plant, and plans to use I.'s hydro-electric and geothermal power for heavy industry. Fishing is the chief occupation, cod and herring being the principal exports. There are no railways, but there are regular air services within I. and abroad.

Norse voyagers had probably visited I. before 874, when a few hundred settlers arrived. In 930 the first general assembly or Althing founded the republic of I. In 1000 the people adopted Christianity, and in c. 1263 submitted to the authority of the king of Norway. Norway, and with it I., came under Danish rule in 1381. I. remained attached to Denmark after Norway became independent in 1814; it received its own legislature (Althing) in 1871, home rule in 1903, and in 1918 was recognized by Denmark as independent (except for foreign affairs), but linked with Denmark by having the same king. After the German invasion of Denmark in 1940, a small British force was sent to help in the defence of I., which in 1941 proclaimed itself an independent rep., a status confirmed by an act of the Althing in 1944. U.S. troops, who took over the defence of I. in 1942, were withdrawn after the end of hostilities. I., a founder member of N.A.T.O., accorded the use of Keflavik to that body as a base, and forces from the U.S.A. were re-established there. Area 39,758 sq. m.; pop. (1968) 199,526.

ICELANDIC. The I. language is the most archaic of the Scandinavian group, and has retained many primitive forms. Early I. literature is mainly anonymous, and seems to have arisen in the Norse colonies in the British Isles. It consists largely in the 2 Eddas (q.v.), and in numerous narratives in prose and verse called *sagas*, among which the *Saga of Burnt Nial* is the best. Ari Thorgilsson (1067–1148) composed a history of the kings of Norway; the *Landnámabók*, narrating the early settlement of Iceland, was the work of a number of writers. Snorri Sturlason wrote the later, or prose, Edda, based partly on Ari. After a period of translation and adaptation of medieval romances, there followed, from 1300, a long eclipse of I. literature, which was ended by hymn-writers of the Reformation. A renaissance took place in the 19th cent., especially in the fields of lyric poetry and the novel, and in the 20th Laxness (q.v.) is outstanding.

ICELAND MOSS. Lichen (*Cetraria islandica*) – not a moss – which is common in I., and in other mountainous areas of the northern hemisphere. A lightish brown and 3–4 in. high, it can be processed as a foodstuff.

ICELAND SPAR. Form of calcite (q.v.) originally found in Iceland. The crystals cleave into perfect rhombohedra; in its purest form, which is not uncommon, I.S. is quite transparent, and is used in optical instruments.

ICHANG (ēchang'). Port at the head of navigation of the Yangtze Kiang, in Hupei prov., China. Coal and iron are found nearby; it handles rice, tea, cotton and other products of the locality, and has an airport. Pop. *c.* 80,000.

ICHNEUMON FLY. Name given to parasitic flies in the family Ichneumonidae. There are several thousand species in Europe, N. America and other regions. The eggs are laid in the eggs, larvae or pupae of insects, usually in the order Lepidoptera.

ICKES (ik'is), **Harold L.** (1874–1952). American Democratic statesman. He was Sec. of the Interior from 1933, and an outspoken supporter of the 'New Deal' reforms, but after Franklin Roosevelt's death he came into conflict with Pres. Truman, and in Feb. 1946 resigned.

ICON. Representations in the Greek or Orthodox Eastern Church of Christ, of an angel or a saint, in painting, low relief or mosaic. A *riza*, or gold and silver covering which leaves only the face and hands visible, and often adorned with jewels presented by the faithful in thanksgiving, is often added as a protection. One of the most famous Is. is the Virgin of Kazan (q.v.).

ICONIUM. Ancient city of Asia Minor. St. Paul visited it. In the 12th cent. under the Seljuk Turks it achieved great prosperity, but later decayed with the Seljuk state. Konya (q.v.) occupies the site.

ICONOCLASTS (Gk. image-breakers). Name applied in the 8th and 9th cents. to the Christian party in Byzantium, who refused to tolerate the use of images in churches. In 843 the Is. were finally defeated. The same name was applied to those opposing the use of images, etc., at the Reformation.

IDAHO. A N.W. state of the U.S.A. Much of I. is mountainous arid land, drained by waterways on which many rapids and waterfalls prevent navigation. The Snake is the chief river. The climate is generally mild. The chief towns are Boise (the capital), Pocatello, and Idaho Falls. The Mormon Church is the chief religious denomination. Lumbering, agriculture, and livestock raising are the leading industries, the chief crop being wheat. Minerals include lead, zinc, antimony, silver, gold, and copper. I. was admitted into the Union in 1890. Area 83,557 sq. m.; pop. (1970) 713,008.

IDDESLEIGH (id'zli), **Stafford Henry Northcote,** 1st earl of (1818–87). British Cons. politician. He collaborated on the report (1853–4) which led to the reform of the conditions of entry into and promotion in the Civil Service. As Chancellor of the Exchequer 1874–80, he introd. the New Sinking Fund (1876) to provide for the reduction of the national debt. He was For. Sec. 1886–7.

IDENTIKIT. The inventor (left) studies a set of cards, together with Peter Pitchess, Sheriff of Los Angeles County, who carried out the preliminary testing and worked out the operational procedures.

IDENTIKIT. System aiding the identification of 'wanted' criminals. Witnesses select from cards, each bearing a variant drawing of a single feature (hair, eyes, nose, mouth, etc.), their choices resulting in a composite likeness which is then photographed and circulated. Evolved by Hugh C. McDonald (1913–), it was adopted in Los Angeles in 1959, and first used with success in Britain in a murder hunt in 1961.

IDES (īdz). In the calendar of ancient Rome, the 15th day in March, May, July, and October, and the 13th day in all the other months. The word originally indicated the day of the full moon. Julius Caesar was assassinated on the I. or 15th March, 44 B.C.

IDRISS I (1890–). King of Libya. Mohammed Sayed Idriss el-Senussi succeeded his uncle in charge of affairs of the Senusiya Order in 1916, became amir of Cyrenaica and 1951–69 was king of Libya.

IF (ēf). Small French is. in the Mediterranean about 2 m. off Marseilles, with a castle, Château d'If, built *c.* 1529. This was used as a state prison, and is the scene of the imprisonment of Dantès in Dumas' *Count of Monte Cristo*.

IFNI. Territory in N.W. Africa held by Spain from 1860 (it became an overseas prov. 1958) until 1969, when it was transferred to 'Morocco. The pop. are nomadic Berbers, and camels, goats, and sheep are raised. The cap. is Sidi Ifni, pop. 16,000. Area 741 sq. m.; pop. (1968) 40,000.

IGARKA (ēgahr'ka). River port on the r. Yenisei, Krasnoyarsk Territory, R.S.F.S.R. The exporting centre for central Siberia, it was founded in 1929, and handles timber floated 1,000 m. down the river, coal from Tunguska, and wheat from S. Siberia. It has an airport. Pop. (est.) 25,000.

IGNATIUS (ignā'shius) (1st–2nd cent. A.D.). Early Christian Father. Traditionally he was a disciple of St. John the Apostle and the successor of St. Peter as bishop of Antioch. He was thrown to the wild beasts at Rome *c.* A.D. 115–17. Seven Epistles attributed to him are generally regarded as genuine.

IGNIS FATUUS. Name applied to the pale flame sometimes seen over marshy land and thought to be caused by the spontaneous combustion of methane. It is also known as will-o'-the-wisp.

IGUANA

IGUANA. Lizard of the family Iguanidae, which incl. *c.* 700 species and is chiefly confined to the Americas. The common I. (*Iguana iguana*) of Central and S. America may reach 6 ft. and is a favourite food of the Indians.

IGUA′NODON. Amphibious reptile belonging to the herbivorous dinosaurs (q.v.), whose remains are found in strata of the Lower Cretaceous age. The I. varied in length from 16 to 32 ft., and when standing upright reached a height of some 13 ft. It walked on its hind legs, balancing its body by its long tail.

IJSSELMEER (e′selmäer). Lake in the Netherlands, the remains after land reclamation of the former Zuider Zee, which was cut off from the North Sea in 1932 by the closing of a dyke more than 21 m. long from N. Holland via the former is. of Wieringen to Friesland. By 1944 the water of the lake had become fresh. Area 470 sq. m.

IKEBA′NA. The Japanese art of flower arrangement. It dates from the 7th cent. when arrangements of flowers were placed as offerings in Buddhist temples, a practice learned from China. In the 15th cent. I. became a favourite pastime of the nobility. Oldest of modern Japanese I. schools is Ikenobo at Kyoto (7th cent.), and there is an I. International.

IKHNA′TON. Pharaoh of Egypt of the 18th dynasty, son of Amenhotep III (q.v.), with whom he may have ruled jointly for a time. One of his wives was Nefertiti, by whom he had 6 daus., and who is frequently represented with him. Two of his daus. were m. to his successors Smenkhare and Tutankaton (later Tutankhamen, q.v.), but though he developed (rather than originated) the cult of Aten or Aton, changing his name from Amenhotep to I., it is unlikely that he neglected imperial affairs.

ILBERT, Courtenay Adrian (1888–1956). British horologist. His lifelong interest culminated in ownership of the finest private library and the best representative collection of clocks and watches in the world. Acquired by the B.M. in 1958, the latter incl. Mudge's lever clock and Mary Qn. of Scots' hour-glass.

ÎLE-DE-FRANCE (êl-de-froñs). District and former prov. of France, bounded by the Marne, Seine, and Oise, with Paris as its centre, from which the early kings spread their authority over the country.

ILFRACOMBE (-koom). English holiday resort (U.D.) on the N. coast of Devon, 9 m. N.N.W. of Barnstaple. Pop. (1961) 8,701.

ILKESTON. Market town (bor.) in Derbyshire, England. Hosiery and lace are manufactured, and there are coal-mines. Pop. (1961) 34,612.

ILKLEY. English spa (U.D.) in Yorks W. Riding, on the r. Wharfe. The famous Ilkley Moor stretches southwards. I. was a Roman military station, and there are Saxon crosses. Pop. (1961) 18,519.

ILLE (êl). French r.; 28 m. long, which rises in Lake Boulet and enters the Vilaine at Rennes. It gives its name to the dept. of Ille-et-Vilaine.

ILLINGWORTH, Leslie (1902–). British political cartoonist, long a contributor to *Punch* and on the staff of the *Daily Mail* from 1929.

ILLINOIS (illinoi′). North-central state of the U.S.A., forming part of the great central prairie. The chief rivers are the Mississippi, Illinois, Ohio, and Rock. The soil is fertile and much land has been reclaimed through drainage. I. is an important agricultural state. The chief industries are slaughtering and meat-packing, centred at Chicago. Minerals include coal, petroleum, and pig-iron. The chief towns include Chicago (2nd largest in the U.S.A.), Peoria, Rockford, East St. Louis, and Springfield, the capital.

The first Europeans to reach I. were French missionaries in the 17th cent. I. became part of the French province of Louisiana, 1712, but in 1763 was ceded to Britain. In 1783 it passed to the U.S.A., and was admitted to the Union in 1818. Area 56,400 sq. m.; pop. (1970) 11,113,976.

ILLY′RIA. Name anciently given to the region lying along the E. coast of the Adriatic from the Corinthian Gulf northwards. It was conquered by Philip of Macedon, and became a Roman province in A.D. 9. Several Roman emperors came from Illyria.

ILMENITE (ilmenīt). Ore of iron, composed of the oxides of iron and titanium, FeO. TiO$_2$, with some magnesia. The mineral is black, with a metallic lustre, and closely resembles haematite.

ILYU′SHIN, Sergei Vladimirovich (1894–). Soviet aircraft designer. Ed. at the Air Force Engineering Academy, he became prof. at the N. E. Zhukovsky Air Force Engineering Academy. He is known for such aircraft as the *Moscow* (IL-18) a turbo-prop. airliner (1957).

IMAGE RETAINING PANEL. Metal-ceramic type plate with a fluorescent phosphor layer, electrically operated and responsive not only to visible light but to X-rays, near infra-red, ultra-violet, and nuclear radiation. The image lasts for some 30 min., but the plate is rendered blank and re-usable by switching

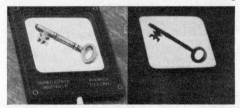

IMAGE RETAINING PANEL. An ordinary door-key is placed on the panel in ordinary light (left) and when the light is switched off and the key removed an image is printed on the plate (right), the remainder of which glows with a yellowish light.   *Courtesy of Thorn Electrical.*

off the current. It has great potentialities in the fields of cancer surgery (when used with the electron microscope), radiography (when immediately visible X-ray images might be produced with less than the usual dosage), nucleonics, laser research, etc.

IMAGISTS. Name given to a school of poets which flourished in England and America from 1909 to 1917. It originated with T. E. Hulme and incl. F. S. Flint, Richard Aldington and T. S. Eliot in England, and Ezra Pound, 'H.D.' (Hilda Doolittle) and Amy Lowell in America. It inculcated precision of language and the use of clear, hard images.

IMA′GO. The sexually mature stage of an insect.

IMAM (imahm′). Arabic word denoting: (1) one of the 4 successors of Mohammed or one of the 4 leaders of the orthodox sects; (2) one of the great leaders of Shi'ites; or (3) one who leads the prayers in a mosque.

IMBROS. Greek name of a Turkish is. in the Aegean. Occupied by Greek forces during the F.W.W., I. passed to Turkey in 1924 under the Treaty of Lausanne, 1923. Area 108 sq. m.; pop. (est.) 6,500.

IMHOTEP (fl. *c.* 2800 B.C.). Egyptian physician. Adviser to King Zoser (3rd dynasty), he is thought to have designed the step-pyramid at Sakkara, and was later worshipped as son of the god Ptah, being identified by the Greeks with Aesclepius (q.v.). In 1964 excavation at the N. Sakkara necropolis was begun by W. B. Emery (q.v.) to find the tomb of H., an ancient centre of healing: remarkable works of art and other remains were recovered.

IMMACULATE CONCEPTION. A dogma of the R.C. Church which states that the Virgin Mary was by a special act of grace preserved free from original sin from the very moment of her conception. This article of the Catholic faith was for cents. the subject of heated controversy, but became a dogma in 1854.

IMMIGRATION and **EMIGRATION.** The movement of people into a foreign country in which they intend to settle. Notable immigrants into Britain incl. the Flemish weavers, and wool-traders of the 16th cent.; the French Protestants persecuted after the Edict of Nantes in 1685; refugees from eastern Europe in the 2nd half of the 19th cent.; from Nazi Germany between 1933 and 1939, and from many European countries during and after the S.W.W. It is est. that the U.K. absorbed c. 1,000,000 Commonwealth immigrants 1953–68, many from the overpopulated W. Indies, India and Pakistan, and the govt. est. that by 1985 there would be c. 2,500,000 coloured immigrants and their descendants in the U.K. This raised problems of housing, education, etc., hence the I. acts of 1962/8 and the single system of control estab. by the I. Act of 1971: see ALIEN, KENYA. From 1815 until the S.W.W. some 20,000,000 people emigrated from the U.K. to countries outside Europe. In the 1960s the annual emigration figure rose to 300,000, about two-thirds going to Commonwealth countries, notably Australia and Canada, and there was concern because of the selective 'Brain Drain' to N. America, where c. 40,000 doctors, engineers, scientists, and technologists emigrated 1961–8. The U.S.A. has received emigrants on a larger scale than any other country, c. 44,500,000 from the end of the American War of Independence until 1969.

I′MMINGHAM. Seaport in Lindsey, Lincolnshire, England, on the Humber estuary 5 m. N.W. of Grimsby. Built 1906–12, it developed rapidly, and following construction (1968) of the largest bulk handling shipping terminal in Europe, was expected to be Britain's premier port, in terms of tonnage handled, by the 1970s.

IMMU′NITY. Resistance to poison or, more usually, to infection. Natural immunity is in the inborn power to resist microbes or their toxins; but I. can be acquired by an attack of the disease, e.g. a person rarely contracts smallpox or typhoid fever twice; by repeated exposure to small doses of infection, e.g. the resistance of the normal person to tuberculosis; or by treatment (artificial I.), e.g. vaccination against smallpox, inoculation against typhoid. Artificial I. is either active, when the resistance is developed in the body as a reaction to the organism or its toxins; or passive, as when a quantity of serum from an immune person or animal is injected into the body. The real nature of I. is still a matter of theory.

IMPEACHMENT. A judicial procedure whereby ministers and high officers of state are brought to trial before the House of Lords for serious offences, the Commons acting as prosecutors. Before the rise of the cabinet system, I. provided a means whereby parliament could control the king's ministers. The first example occurred in 1376. Later Is. were those of Bacon (1621), Strafford (1641), and Warren Hastings (1788). Under the U.S. constitution persons may be impeached by the House of Representatives and tried by the Senate; the best-known example is the trial of Pres. Andrew Johnson in 1868.

IMPERIAL COLLEGE OF SCIENCE AND TECHNOLOGY. Institution estab. at S. Kensington, London, in 1907, for advanced scientific training and research, applied especially to industry. It is part of the Univ. of London.

IMPERIAL CONFERENCE. See COMMONWEALTH CONFERENCE.

IMPERIALISM. In its original sense, the system of government by an emperor, or a policy of colonial expansion, I. is often used to denote any policy of political, military or economic expansion carried out at the expense of weaker peoples. The heyday of

British I. was between c. 1880 and 1900. but since the S.W.W. the increasing demand for self-determination has led to independence in most of the colonial countries, and as regards Britain a furtherance of the Commonwealth at the expense of the Empire. From the growing consciousness of her new-found strength in the 1890s, the U.S.A. began to look outward. After the Spanish American War, the Philippines, Puerto Rico and Guam were obtained, the Hawaiian is. annexed, and the Panama Canal zone acquired in 1903. The Philippines became a repub. in 1946, Puerto Rico a Commonwealth in 1952, and Hawaii the 50th state of the Union in 1959. Communist countries have developed their own variants of I.

IMPERIAL WAR MUSEUM. National museum founded in 1917, as a memorial to the men and women of the Empire in the F.W.W. Its scope has since been extended to incl. records of all operations fought by British forces since 1914, incl. the S.W.W. Its present building (formerly the Royal Bethlehem, or Bedlam, Hospital) in Lambeth Rd., London, was opened 1936.

IMPETI′GO. A minor skin disease of children. Pimples appear, usually on the face, and start to

IMPERIAL COLLEGE OF SCIENCE AND TECHNOLOGY. New construction in Prince Consort Road reflects the spirit of expansion: to the left is the Physics Building, and to the right the Hill Building, named after Sir Roderic Hill (q.v.), departments of aeronautics and chemical engineering and technology.
Courtesy of the Imperial College of Science and Technology

exude pus; they break, run together, and dry into yellow crusts, which eventually fall off and leave no scar unless scratched. The cause is infection by a streptococcus, sometimes introduced by louse bites, and later a staphylococcus. It is highly contagious.

I′MPHAL. Indian city, cap. of Manipur state (former hill state), 140 m. E.S.E. of Shillong. It is a road and trade centre. In 1944, when the Japanese invaded Assam, it was besieged from March to June, but held out with the help of supplies dropped by air. Pop. (1961) 132,000.

IMPRESSIONISM. Movement in painting which originated in France in the 1860s, its chief exponents being Manet, Monet, Degas, Renoir, and Pissarro (qq.v.). They sought to capture a fleeting aspect of some scene, guided not by their memory or knowledge of the object, but painting it as though seen for the first time. In nature, they argued, colour is an illusion created by the play of light upon an object, and there are no outlines. Colours are modified by atmosphere and the inclination of the sunlight at different times of day, and even shadows are not entirely colourless. The Impressionists did not mix their pigments but dabbed them side by side on the canvas in the pure state. Their technique was influenced by the work of Constable and Turner, and also by contemporary spectroscopic discoveries.

The starting-point of the movement was the *Salon*

des Refusés, an exhibition in 1863 of work rejected by the official Salon, followed by their own exhibitions 1874–86. Their work aroused fierce opposition; the term I. was first used abusively to describe Monet's painting 'Impression, Sunrise'. Among their followers

IMPRESSIONISM. Exhibited in Paris at the first Impressionist Exhibition in 1874 was *La Loge* ('The Box') by Renoir. The models were the artist's brother Edmond, and the Montmartre model Nini. *Courtauld Institute Galleries, London. Photo: © by S.P.A.D.E.M., Paris, 1964.*

were the American Whistler (q.v.), who introduced the term into England, and the Englishmen Sickert and Wilson Steer (qq.v.).

IMROZ. Turkish form of IMBROS.

INCANDE'SCENCE. The emission of light from a substance in consequence of its high temperature. The colour of the emitted light from liquids or solids depends on their temperature, and for solids generally the higher the temperature the whiter the light. Gases may become incandescent through ionization as in the glowing vacuum discharge tube. The oxides of cerium and thorium are highly incandescent and for this reason are used in gas mantles. The light from a filament lamp is due to the I. of the filament, rendered white-hot when a current is passing through it.

INCARNATION (Lat. *caro*, flesh). In Christian theology, the doctrine that the Second Person of the Trinity assumed human form and human nature as Jesus Christ. I. is also a feature of many other religions, e.g. Hinduism.

INCAS (ing'kahs). Name ordinarily given to the population of Peru before the coming of the Spaniards, but rightly restricted to the ruling caste; the ruler himself was known as the Inca. They probably entered Peru from the S.E. *c.* 1100. Children were bound to follow their ancestral occupation, and all products were the property of the State. The official religion was sun-worship. The Is. mummified their dead. They had no system of writing, but reached a high level in architecture, pottery, weaving, etc.

INCENDIARY BOMB. Usually dropped by aircraft, I.Bs. containing inflammable matter were used in the F.W.W., and in the S.W.W. were a major weapon in attacks on cities. To hinder firefighters,

delayed-action high-explosive Bs. were usually dropped with them.

INCEST. Sexual intercourse between persons so related that marriage between them is barred by law. I. is biologically undesirable because hereditary weaknesses are emphasized by inbreeding, and sociologically because it affects the emotional stability of the family unit.

INCH. In *place-names* in Scotland and Ireland, an islet or land by a river. As a measure of *length*, it is a twelfth of a foot. As a measure of *rainfall*, it is the amount which would cover the ground to a depth of one inch, if none of the water was evaporated, absorbed, or ran off.

INCHCAPE ROCK. Islet to the S.E. of Arbroath, Angus, Scotland, 12 m. out to sea, on which stands a lighthouse, built 1807–11. It is also called Bell Rock because of a warning bell placed there by the abbot of Aberbrothock (Arbroath).

INCHON. Port and summer resort on the W. coast of S. Korea, 20 m. W.S.W. of Seoul. Its ice-free harbour was opened to foreign trade in 1883. It has steel mills and textile and match factories, etc. Pop. (1966) 528,579.

INCOME TAX. Direct tax levied on annual income which, so far as the tax is concerned, may incl. the value of receipts other than in cash. In the U.K., the rate of tax and allowances vary from time to time; they are set out yearly in the annual Finance Act which implements the recommendations agreed to by the House of Commons in the Budget presented to it by the Chancellor of the Exchequer. William Pitt introduced an I.T. 1799–1801 to finance the wars with revolutionary France; it was re-imposed 1803–16 for the same purpose, and was so hated that all records were destroyed when it came to an end. Peel reintroduced the tax in 1842 and it has been levied ever since, becoming a more and more important part of govt. finance. At its lowest, 1874–6, it was 2d. in the £; at its highest, 1941–6, 10s. in the £. *See* P.A.Y.E.

In the U.S.A. every citizen or resident with a gross income of $600 or more must file a report for federal income-tax consideration unless he or she was 65 before the end of the tax year, when a return has to be made only if the gross income is $1,200 or more. Rate of tax, which is reckoned on a percentage basis, and allowances, are fixed by Congress from year to year. A state I.T. also is levied in all the states except Conn., Fla., Ill., Maine, Nev., Ohio, Pa., R.I., S.Dak., Tex., Wash., and Wyo.; the amount of tax and allowances vary from state to state. There is some adjustment between federal and state taxes in states which levy an I.T.

Most countries levy I.T., generally considered as bearing less heavily on the poor than indirect taxes: *see* TAXATION. However, in Communist states in which the salaries of most workers are fixed by the state, I.T. becomes illogical. From 1960 the U.S.S.R. gradually began abolition, factory and office workers becoming exempt, and higher grades – to reduce differentials – having their salaries reduced by the amount of tax they would otherwise have paid.

I'NCUBUS. A male spirit who in the popular belief of the Middle Ages cohabited with women in their sleep. Witches and demons were supposed to result from such intercourse.

INCUNA'BULA. Bibliographical term signifying the books printed during the 15th century.

INDEMNITY. An undertaking to compensate another for damage, loss, trouble, or expenses, or the money paid by way of such compensation. An *Act of I.* is one passed with the object of relieving persons from certain penalties to which they have become liable, or to legalize transactions which infringe the law.

INDEPENDENCE. Residential and industrial city in Missouri, U.S.A., lying E. of Kansas City. Pres.

Harry S. Truman spent his boyhood at I., and later made it his home; 3½ million documents relating to his presidency were in 1957 deposited (*see* MISSOURI) in the Harry S. Truman Federal Library. I. was made a city during the gold rush of 1849. Industries incl. making of steel and Portland cement, petroleum refining, flour milling. Mormons are the largest religious group in the pop., which in 1960 was 62,328.

INDEPENDENCE DAY. The day (4 July) on which the Declaration of Independence of 1776 is commemorated in the U.S.A. It is a public holiday.

INDEPENDENT LABOUR PARTY. Soc. party, founded at Bradford in 1893. In 1900 it joined with trade unions and Fabians in founding the Labour Representation Committee, the nucleus of the Lab. Party. Many members left the I.L.P. to join the Com. Party in 1921, and in 1932 all connections with the Lab. Party were severed. After the S.W.W. it consistently dwindled. *See* MAXTON.

INDEX. In finance, usually the selection of 30 leading industrial ordinary shares used by the *Financial Times* as an indicator of the general movement of the Stock Exchange market; the U.S. equivalent is the *Dow Jones Index. See* also COST OF LIVING.

INDEX LIBRORUM PROHIBITORUM. The list of books formerly officially forbidden to members of the R.C. Church. The process of condemning books and bringing the Index up to date was in the hands of a congregation of cardinals, consultors, and examiners from the 16th cent. until 1966.

INDIA. Geographical and historical name for the great S. Asian peninsula or sub-continent lying between the Himalayas and the Indian Ocean. It incl. the reps. of India and Pakistan, and the state of Kashmir, in dispute between them. Ceylon lies off its S.E. point; the princely states of Sikkim, Bhutan, and Nepal and Chinese-controlled Tibet lie to the N. Total area 1,620,000 sq. m.; pop. (1968) *c.* 720,000,000.

Physical. The country is in the form of a large triangle based on the Himalaya mountains, the Arabian Sea lying on the W. coast, and the Bay of

INDIA. Typical of rural India is the bo-tree (q.v.) which serves as the village meeting-place. Here in its shade, beside the mud-walled huts, teaching is given. *Photo: S.P.G.*

Bengal on the E. It has common land frontiers with Persia, Afghanistan, China (Tibet), and Burma. There are 3 main geographical divisions: (1) The Himalayas, a vast crescent-shaped range including the highest mountains in the world. (2) The river plains, extending across the widest part of the country and comprising the systems of the Indus, the Ganges, and the Brahmaputra. This region is the most populous. (3) The Deccan or southern tableland, which forms the greater part of the peninsula proper. The northern side of the tableland is formed by the Vindhya mts. The other

sides of the triangular plateau are formed by the E. and W. Ghats.

Climate. In the N. the peninsula has a continental climate, with considerable variations of temperature between winter and summer, when the thermometer at Jacobabad in W. Pakistan may reach 127°F in the shade. In the S. the climate is more equable, though the winter temperature at Bombay (well within

INDIA. In spite of government endeavour, water supplies are still short in the great cities, as here in Calcutta, so that even hydrants connected to untreated river-water are eagerly used, with a resultant spread of water-borne disease.
Courtesy of W.H.O.

the tropics) has been as low as 52° F. Rainfall varies greatly, but is constantly heavy in Bengal and in upper Assam (average at Cherpunji, 400 in. annually); while the monsoon brings heavy seasonal rain to the alluvial plains south of the mountains. Farther south there is an arid region, with waterless deserts. The weather system of the peninsula falls into 2 parts. N. of the Vindhyas there is copious rainfall during the S.W. monsoon; to the south the rains are more moderate, but the monsoon continues some weeks longer. The cold months in the peninsula are Jan. and Feb.; March, April, and May are hot. In June, July, Aug., Sept., and Oct. comes the S.E. monsoon, which is reversed during the remaining 2 months.

Peoples. Descendants of the earliest known inhabitants, a Negrito or Negroid people, are still found in scattered tribes in S. India; the Andamanese also belong to this group. Southern India is mainly inhabited by Dravidians, and the Aryo-Dravidian (Hindustani) type is found in the Ganges valley. People of Indo-Aryan stock occur in Kashmir and neighbouring regions, and Scytho-Dravidian and Mongolo-Dravidian peoples inhabit regions east of the Indus and Bengal respectively. In the N.W. Turco-Iranian types prevail, and Mongolians have penetrated into the N.E.

Vast areas of the sub-continent are fertile, and some areas less fertile naturally have been made so by artificial irrigation. Agriculture is the chief occupation in both republics. Minerals exist in considerable quantity: e.g. coal, iron ore, manganese, petroleum, and their exploitation is being developed. Both India and Pakistan have ambitious plans for developing hydro-electric power.

History. The earliest Indian civilization was that of the Indus valley (*c.* 2500–*c.* 1600 B.C.); this may have been built up by the Dravidians, the ancestors of the main people of the S. From *c.* 1500 B.C. waves of Aryans entered I. from the N.W., and gradually overran the N. and the Deccan, intermarrying with the Dravidians. From their religious beliefs developed the system of Brahmanism; this was periodically modified by reforming movements, the most important of which, Buddhism and Jainism, arose c. 500 B.C. The sub-continent, except the far S., was first unified under the Mauryan emperors (321–184 B.C.), one of whom, Asoka (264–c. 227), who was a Buddhist, ranks among the most enlightened rulers in history. The N. was not again united until the period of the Gupta dynasty (c. A.D. 300–500), 'the golden age of Hinduism'; its rule was ended by the raids of the White Huns, which plunged I. into anarchy.

During the 11th and 12th cents. raids on I. were made by Moslem adventurers, Turkish, Arab, and Afghan, and in 1206 the first Moslem dynasty was set up at Delhi. The next 3 cents. witnessed the establishment of Moslem rule throughout the N. and the Deccan, although the S. maintained its independence under the Hindu Vijayanagar dynasty (14th–16th cents.). The most brilliant period of Moslem India began with the founding of the Mogul empire by Babur in 1527, and its consolidation by his grandson Akbar (1556–1605). After 1707 the Mogul empire (which lasted nominally until 1858) fell into decline, and a period of anarchy ensued.

Portuguese, Dutch, French, and English traders had been establishing trading bases on the coast since the 16th cent. During the Seven Years War (1756–63) the E. India Co., eliminating their French rivals, made themselves masters of Bengal and the Carnatic, and within a cent. direct or indirect British rule was established all over I. After the mutiny of 1857–8 the rule of the E. India Co. was abolished, and I. passed under the British crown. National feeling found a rallying-point in the National Congress (founded 1885), and from 1906 onward periodic waves of nationalist agitation – after the F.W.W. under the leadership of Gandhi – swept the country. These were met by concessions in the direction of self-govt., culminating in 1947 in the division of British I. into the dominions of India (predominantly Hindu) and Pakistan (predominantly Moslem). See INDIA OF THE PRINCES.

INDIA, UNION OF. Rep. in Asia. Covering the greater part of the Indian sub-continent, it incl. the most fertile areas, in particular the Ganges valley. Agriculture, long handicapped by the social, religious and economic system and the small-size holdings, has achieved a rising standard of technology since independence, although failure of the monsoon (as in 1965/6 and 1966/7) is still a near disaster. Rice, wheat and cereals are grown, and industrial crops incl. cotton, jute, tea, oil seeds, and cane sugar. Industry has been modernized and expanded, and alongside the Tata iron and steel works at Jamshedpur on the Bihar coalfield, there are new industrial complexes such as Hindustan Steel, with plants at Rourkela, Bhilai and Durgapur, which is also I.'s largest supplier of nitrogenous fertilizers. Machinery and machine tools, petroleum products, textiles, etc., are produced, and hydro-electric installations have been built and extended, espec. in the Deccan.

On coming into existence in 1947, as the Dom. of India, the Union consisted of the former Brit. Provs.: the United Provs. (Uttar Pradesh), Bihar, Bombay, Central Provs., Orissa, Madras, most of Assam, W. Bengal and E. Punjab; by 1950 all the princely states within this area (see INDIA OF THE PRINCES, also KASHMIR) had been absorbed by the Union. In 1950 I. became a rep. within the Brit. Commonwealth. Internal developments have since incl. reorganization of some states on linguistic and other grounds, fluctuating violence in communal disturbances between Hindu and Moslem, and the emergence in the late 1960s of regional agitation, as in Assam and Maharashtra, against immigrants from other states. Relations with Pakistan have continued to be complicated by such issues as Kashmir and Kutch (q.v.), and there

has been border tension with Communist China. The Congress Party has maintained political supremacy, though by 1968 less undisputedly: see GANDHI, NEHRU, SHASTRI, INDIRA GANDHI. Hindi is the official language of the Union, but English has continued as an additional official language.

THE UNION OF INDIA			
States	Area in 1,000 sq. m.	Pop. in millions	Capital
Andhra Pradesh	106·2	35·98	Hyberabad
Assam	38·4	11·07	Shillong
N.-E. Frontier Agency	31·4	·53	
Bihar	67·2	46·46	Patna
Gujarat	72·2	20·63	Ahmedabad
Hariana	17·6	7·0	Chandigarh
Himachal Pradesh*	10·9	1·35	Simla
Kerala	15·0	16·90	Trivandrum
Madhya Pradesh	171·2	32·37	Bhopal
Maharashtra	118·7	39·55	Bombay
Manipur *	8·6	·78	Imphal
Meghalaya *	8·7	·79	Shillong
Mysore	74·2	23·58	Bangalore
Nagaland	6·3	·37	Kohima
Orissa	60·2	17·54	Bhubaneswar
Punjab	29·2	11·80	Chandigarh
Rajasthan	132·1	20·15	Jaipur
Tamil Nadu	50·3	33·68	Madras
Tripura *	4·0	1·14	Agartala
Uttar Pradesh	113·6	73·75	Lucknow
West Bengal	33·8	34·92	Calcutta
Union Territories			
Andaman and Nicobar Is.	3·2	·06	Port Blair
Chandigarh	·01	·09	—
Dadra and Nagar Haveli	·19	·06	Silvassa
Delhi	·6	2·65	—
Goa, Daman and Diu	1·4	·63	Panjim
Laccadive, Minicoy and Amindivi Is.	·01	·02	Kavaratti Is.
Pondicherry	·2	·37	—
	1,175·41	435·22	

N.B. This table, in which pop. figures are based on the 1961 census, does not include Jammu and Kashmir (q.v.) in dispute between India and Pakistan: India occupies 53,065 sq. m.; pop. 3,560,976. * Statehood pending 1971.

A pres., elected for 5 years by an electoral college, is head of state; there is a cabinet under a P.M. – a post first held by Nehru (q.v.); parliament consists of the House of the People, Lok Sabha, directly elected, on a basis of adult suffrage, for 5 years, and the indissoluble Council of States, Rajya Sabha, indirectly elected, one-third of whose members retire every 2 years. Delhi is the cap.; other large cities are Calcutta, Bombay and Madras. Area 1,173,639 sq. m.; pop. (1968) 520,000,000; rising by 3 m. in a year, so that a massive family planning programme is under way.

INDIA'NA. E. north-central state of the U.S.A. The surface is undulating prairie, except in the S. along the r. Ohio where there is a range of hills. The chief rivers are the Wabash and its tributaries. The soil is fertile, and agriculture is an important industry. The chief crops are maize, winter wheat, rye, and oats. Tobacco also is cultivated. Mineral products incl. coal, limestone, natural gas, and petroleum; steel, agricultural machinery, motor-cars, refrigerators and other domestic appliances are manufactured. The chief towns are Indianapolis, the cap., Fort Wayne, Gary, South Bend, Evansville, and Hammond. In the early 18th cent. French traders reached I., and the first settlements were established in 1731–5. It was admitted to the Union in 1816. Area, 36,291 sq. m.; pop. (1970) 5,193,669.

INDIANA'POLIS. Capital and largest city of Indiana, U.S.A. There is a large grain trade, and industries include meat packing and chemical and motor-vehicle manufacture. I. is a centre of communications. Pop. met. area (1970) 1,099,628.

INDIAN ART. The history of Indian art may be traced back to the ancient Indus valley civilization of *c*. 3000 B.C., which seems to have had a definite influence on the Brahmanical art of later periods. The

INDIA. The Hindu festival of Dasahra, with giant effigies of the demon Ravana and his two brothers ready for ceremonial burning. *Photo: Press Information Bureau, Govt. of India.*

Maurya period (3rd cent. B.C.) has its most notable example in the palace of Asoka, and was characterized by sculptured gateways and reliefs. The Kusana and Andhra periods (1st–4th cents. A.D.) led to the mature and voluptuous art of the Gupta period, which spread widely over S.E. Asia. Mathura, Sarnath, Ajanta, and Aurangabad were centres of Buddhist sculpture, and remarkable examples of Brahmanical art were also produced. The same tradition led in the 6th and 7th cents. to the painting of frescoes, usually depicting incidents in the legends of the Buddhist, Hindu, and Jain religions. The 7th cent. saw the highest peak of I.A.; the magnificent rock sculpture of the descent of the Ganges at Mamallapuram bears witness to the virility of this period. Medieval art gradually lost the simplicity and force of the classical period, and while continuing on the same general lines tended to become more and more elaborate. Sculpture was generally of a religious character, but the Gujarat school also excelled in decorating dwelling houses. A brilliant school of miniature paintings arose in 16th cent. Rajputana. The Moguls introduced a school of painting based on Persian forms; Indian artists absorbed and expanded this art with great technical virtuosity.

After a period of decline I.A. has enjoyed a renaissance in modern times, e.g. the work of Abanindranath Tagore and his brother Gaganendranath (qq.v.), Amrita Sher-Gil, Jamini Roy, and Sailoz Mookherjee.

INDIAN CORN. See MAIZE.

INDIAN LANGUAGES. Languages spoken in India total 220, falling into 5 main groups. Much the most important is the Indo-European or Aryan, languages belonging to which are spoken by over 230,000,000 people. This group includes Hindi (q.v.), Pushtu, Pali, Urdu, etc., and is ultimately derived from the ancient Sanskrit. Its range includes the whole of N. India. Dravidian languages come next, with about 64,000,000 speakers, mainly in the south, where they include the 4 literary languages. Dravidian tongues are also used in the hills of central India, and an isolated pocket exists in Baluchistan. The Tibeto-Chinese group includes no fewer than 145 languages, some of which are spoken in Assam and on the slopes of the Himalayas. Other groups are the Austro-

Asiatic (Mon-Khmer 550,000 and Munda 3,974,000) and Karen (1,114,000). For the use of English, *see under* INDIA *and* PAKISTAN.

INDIAN LITERATURE. For the literature of ancient India *see* SANSKRIT; VEDA; PALI; PRAKRIT. The great no. of Indian languages and the wealth of the literary output in India through medieval to modern times makes any brief survey impossible. Among recent developments the emergence in the last cent. of Bengali as an important literary tongue is remarkable, cf. the work of philologist Ram Mohan Roy, founder of Brahma Samaj (q.v.), who paved the way for such writers as novelist Bankim Chandra Chatterji (q.v.) and Romesh Chunder Dutt (1848–1909). A token of the reputation of Bengali among literatures of the modern world was the award to Rabindranath Tagore of a Nobel prize in 1913: notable among later writers are the poets Buddhadeva Bose and Amiya Chakravarty. Hindi has been developed rather as a political weapon than a literary medium during the struggle for independence and its aftermath, but especially important as literary languages are Urdu (the novelist Prem Chand and poet-philosopher Iqbal, q.v.) and Gujarati (the poet Nanalal Devi and the writings of Gandhi). The long association with Britain has estab. English as almost a native tongue for many Indians, and writers in English – though wholly Indian in the character of their work – incl. the novelist Dhan Gopal Mukerji, the poet Sarojini Naidu (1879–1949), Sri Aurobindo (1872–1950), and Dom Moraes, and Nehru. Tagore wrote little creatively in English, but translated many of his own works.

INDIAN MUTINY. The revolt against the British in India of the Bengal army in 1857–8. The movement was confined to the N., from Bengal to the Punjab, and C. India; it drew its main support from the army and the recently dethroned princes, but in certain areas it developed into a peasant rising or a general revolt. Outstanding episodes were the seizure of Delhi by the rebels and its siege and recapture by the British, and the defence of Lucknow by a British garrison. The I.M. led to the substitution in 1858 of direct administration by the Crown for the rule of the E. India Co.

INDIANS. Blackfeet Indian in ceremonial costume. *Courtesy of the Museum of the Plains Indian, Montana.*

INDIAN OCEAN. Ocean lying between Africa and Australia, with India to the N. In the S. it merges into the Antarctic seas, the arbitrary boundary being a line from Cape Agulhas to S. Tasmania. Area 28,350,000 sq. m.; average depth is 13,000 ft.; the deepest known part is Java Trench (24,440 ft.), off the S. coast of Java. *See* BRIT. I.O. TERR.

INDIANS, American. Name given to the pre-European inhabitants of America. Their ancestors, who entered America in successive immigrations via the Bering Straits, did not belong to one ethnic stock, although a Mongoloid strain predominated. Stature differs widely, and, if Eskimoes are included, the A.Is. include some of the shortest as well as (in Patagonia) some of the tallest races. There is also a great cultural diversity; the very low culture of the Is. of the N.

coast of S. America and the Eskimoes, among whom the means of subsistence was hunting or food-gathering, at the one extreme and at the other the civilizations of the Mayas (later adopted by the Aztecs), and of Peru, which produced works of very great artistic worth. Totemism (q.v.), is a notable feature in the social organization. In religion, while Mexico had advanced to an anthropomorphic pantheon, and the Incas worshipped the sun, the majority of the peoples remained at the stage of formless animism. The number of A.Is., also referred to as Amerindians, is estimated to be c. 10 million: those in U.S.A. number (1968) c. 600,000.

INDIA OF THE PRINCES (Indian states). Name formerly applied to the 562 native states ruled by Indian princes. Occupying an area of 715,964 sq. m. (45 per cent of the total area of pre-partition India) and with a population of over 93 million they were inextricably mixed up with the former British provs. Most of the states were Hindu, and their rulers mainly Rajputs (q.v.). When India was overwhelmed by the Moslems, the Rajput states in the deserts of the N.W., the outer Himalayas, and the central highlands, were saved by their isolation and by the fine fighting qualities of their inhabitants. As the Mogul empire disintegrated other states were set up by soldiers of fortune, e.g. Baroda, Hyderabad, Gwalior, Indore, Bhopal, Patiala, Bahawalpur, and Kolhapur: Mysore, Travancore, and Cochin were also non-Rajput states. At partition of British India in 1947 the princes were given independence by the British govt., but were advised to adhere to either India or Pakistan. Between 1947 and 1950 all except Kashmir (q.v.) were incorporated in the one or the other country.

INDIGESTION. *See* DYSPEPSIA.

I'NDIGO. Deep violet-blue dye originally obtained from plants of the *Indigofera* genus of the Leguminosae, but now replaced by the synthetic product.

INDIUM. Soft, silvery, malleable, rare metallic element; symbol In, at. wt. 114·82, at. no. 49. Discovered in 1863 by Reich and Richter, it was named I. after its indigo-blue spectrum. It occurs in minute traces in zinc ores, etc., and is obtained by electrolysis from solutions of complex salts. Due to its large neutron capture cross-section, I. is used to monitor the neutron emission from reactors. Other uses. incl. the manufacture of junctions in semi-conductor devices, and corrosion-resistant coatings for aircraft sleeve bearings.

INDO-ARYAN LANGUAGES. One of the 2 branches of the Aryan group of the Indo-European family, the other being the Iranian (q.v.). Aryan tribes entered India c. 2000–1500 B.C., and from the latter date comes the earliest specimen of I.-A., the *Rig-Veda*. Its language, called Vedic, is distinguished from Sanskrit, the later classical language which represents a codification of the language in use on the watershed between the Indus and the Ganges; Sanskrit has remained in use for sacred and literary purposes. Buddhism and Jainism were important in the development of local forms, or Prakrits, which are the direct ancestors of the modern Aryan vernaculars of N. India. They fall into 2 major groups – the languages of the centre: W. Hindi (whence Hindustani or Urdu), E. Hindi, Punjabi, Gujarati, and Rajasthani, while Sinhalese, spoken by the greater part of Ceylon, is a descendant of the now extinct Pali; and those of the outer band: Kashmiri, Lahnda, Sindhi, Marathi, Bihari, Bengali, and Assamese.

INDO-CHINA, French. Former collective name for a group of Asian countries that became independent after the S.W.W. *See* CAMBODIA, LAOS, VIET-NAM.

INDO-EUROPEAN (Indo-Germanic). Name of one of the world's largest families of languages, to which English and the majority of modern European languages belong. The common I.-E. language must have begun to split into branches as early as 2000 B.C.

What we know of its phonology, syntax, morphology, and vocabulary is a reconstruction, based on a comparison of the features of those languages now existing, or which have died out in historical times.

In classifying the I.-E. languages, use is made of the broad cleavage resulting from the different treatment of the palatal stops, which in one group, called the *centum* languages (from the Lat. for 100), have become simple velars, and in the other, the *satem* group (from the Zend form of the same word), have become fricatives. In the main, the former group is found W. of a line from the S.E. corner of the Baltic Sea to the head of the Adriatic, but including Greek; the latter E. of that line.

INDONESIA. The constant threat of disaster from the volcano of Mt. Merapi shadows the lives of the Javanese whose villages and rice terraces are hidden by the forests at its feet.
Courtesy of Indonesian Embassy.

INDONE'SIA, Republic of. Asian state composed of the E. Indian islands of Sumatra, Java, Madura, the Lesser Sundas (Nusa Tenggaru), the Moluccas (Maluku), Celebes (Sulawesi), and c. 3,000 smaller islands, together with Kalimantan (S. part of Borneo) and W. Irian (W. part of New Guinea).

Before the S.W.W. the rep. formed the Netherlands Indies, occupied 1942–5 by the Japanese who actively promoted the movement for independence from the Dutch. At the end of the fighting, the rep. of I., incl. all the Netherlands Indies except western New Guinea, was proclaimed, and was recognized by the Dutch in 1949; a union set up between the two countries at the same time was abrogated by I. in 1956. Under the leadership of Pres. Sukarno (q.v.), the rep. laid claim to Netherlands New Guinea which in 1962 was ceded to the U.N., in 1963 to Indonesia, but the 'confrontation' of Malaysia over Sabah and Sarawak 1963–6 ended in *détente*. This was a consequence of a revision of policy by Gen. Soeharto (q.v.) who took power 1966 and banned the Communist Party. He became pres. 1968, and elections were planned for 1971. Wild inflation was stemmed, aid was granted by the West for development, and commerce began to return to normal.

Agriculture is the chief industry, important products being sugar, rice, tea, coffee, cassava, sweet potatoes, and soya beans. Plantation-grown rubber, copra, tobacco, coconut oil, kapok, and pepper are valuable exports. Tin and petroleum are the principal minerals; textiles, paper, matches, and chemicals are made. The cap. is Djakarta: other towns incl. Surabaya, Semarang, and Bandung. Area 895,000 sq. m.; pop. (1967) 112,300,000.

INDO'RE. Indian city in Madhya Pradesh, on the Malwa plain, N. of the Vindhya hills. It is the seat of several colleges, and has a fine palace, residence of the maharaja when I. was cap. of the former princely state of I. Pop. (1961) 395,035.

INDRA. Hindu deity of the early Vedic era. He was the god of the firmament and thus the god of all-pervading power, and is depicted as a man on a white elephant. In one of his 4 arms he carries a thunderbolt.

INDRE (andr). French r. rising in the Auvergne mountains and flowing for 115 m. generally N.W. to join the Loire below Tours. It gives its name to the depts. of Indre and Indre-et-Loire.

INDU'CTANCE. Either that property of an element, or circuit, which when carrying a current is characterized by the formation of a magnetic field and the storage of magnetic energy; or the magnitude of the capability of an element or a circuit to store magnetic energy when carrying a current.

INDU'CTOR. An element possessing the characteristic of inductance.

INDULGENCES (Lat. *indulgere*, to grant). According to the R.C. Church the total or partial remission of temporal punishment for sins which remain to be expiated after penitence and confession has secured exemption from eternal punishment. The doctrine of I. began as the commutation of the Church penances for sin, such as fasting, for suitable works of charity or money gifts to the Church, and became a great source of church revenue. The system was grossly abused, and the height of degradation was reached when abp. Albert of Mainz and Magdeburg sold Is. through the agency of the Dominican Tetzel. This trade in Is. roused Luther in 1517 to draw up his 95 'Theses' and initiate the Reformation. The Council of Trent in 1563 recommended moderate retention of Is., but the Vatican Council debated continuance 1965.

I'NDUS. River of Asia which rises in Tibet in glaciers on the N. slopes of Kailas range in the Himalayas, flows N.W. across Kashmir, then turns S.W. to flow through W. Pakistan to the Arabian Sea which it enters through a delta, 125 m. wide, below Hyderabad. It is *c.* 1,800 m. long, and with its 5 tributaries forms a river system with twice the annual flow of the Nile. The lower I. has an extensive irrigation system dependent on the Lloyd barrage (1932), but the

INDUSTRIAL REVOLUTION. Child abour, an accompaniment of the earlier stages of Britain's industrial revolution, still exists in the East, but this little girl is not unhappy as she deftly spins.   *Courtesy of Malaya House.*

system for the upper I. area was cut in two by the partition of Punjab in 1947. A treaty of 1960 allotted India the use of the 3 eastern rivers (Ravi, Beas and Sutlej) and Pakistan the 3 western (Indus, Jhelum, and Chenab), and initiated a development plan.

From *c.* 2500–*c.* 1600 B.C. the lower Indus valley was the site of a prehistoric civilization of city-dwellers, destroyed and overrun by Aryan invaders from the N. *See* INDUS VALLEY CIVILIZATION.

INDUSTRIAL REVOLUTION. The sudden acceleration of technical development which occurred in Europe from the late 18th cent., and which transferred the balance of political power from the landowner to the industrial capitalist, and created an organized industrial working class. The great achievement of the first phase (to 1830) was the invention of the steam engine in Britain, originally developed for draining mines (*see* NEWCOMEN), but rapidly put to use in factories and in the railways (*see* WATT, ARKWRIGHT, CROMPTON, and TREVITHICK). In the second phase, from 1830 to the early 20th cent., the I.R. enlarged its scope from Europe to the world, with some initial exploitation of 'colonial' possessions by European powers as a preliminary to their independent development, and the internal combustion engine and electricity were developed. Then in 1911 Rutherford split the atom at Manchester and the prospect of nuclear power opened, and electronic devices were developed which made possible automation (q.v.), with the eventual prospect of even managerial decision-making being in the hands of 'machines'. *See* CYBERNETICS.

INDUS VALLEY CIVILIZATION. The culture of prehistoric N.W. India, which flourished in the 3rd millennium B.C. Complete, well-planned cities have been unearthed, notably Harappa in the Punjab and Mohenjo Daro in Sind. Sculptures in alabaster and marble, jewellery, etc., bear witness to a high civilization. There are evidences of a flourishing economy based on agriculture and cattle rearing; spinning and weaving and manufacture of cotton were practised. It seems that the founders of the I.V.C. were of the dolichocephalic Mediterranean type of S. Asia and Europe, who came in from the W. They used on seals an indigenous – hitherto undeciphered – script.

INDY (andē'), Vincent d' (1851–1931). French composer. B. in Paris, he studied under César Franck, and was one of the founders of the *Schola Cantorum,* in which the ideals of Franck were embodied. His works incl. operas (*Fervaal*), symphonies, tone poems (*Istar*), chamber music, etc.

INFANT. *See* MINOR.

INFANTE and **INFANTA** (Lat. *infans,* an infant). Title given in Spain and Portugal to the sons (other than the heir-apparent) and daughters respectively of the sovereign. The heir-apparent in Spain bore the title of Prince of the Asturias, and the title of I. was also given to other members of the royal family.

INFANTICIDE. In modern states the killing of children is a criminal offence, but it was a recognized practice until recent times as the simplest method of population control in India and China, and among ancient peoples incl. the Greeks. Girls were the most frequent victims, but in communities where bride-prices were high they might be regarded as the greater asset and boys were disposed of.

INFANTILE PARALYSIS. *See* POLIOMYELITIS.

INFANT MORTALITY. The number of infants

INFANT MORTALITY

Per 1,000 Births*

Africa			Europe	
Mali	250†	(1960)	Irish Rep.	30·5
N. America			Italy	40·5
Canada	27·2		Sweden	15·5
U.S.A.	25·3		United Kingdom	22·1
S. America			Eng. and Wales	21·4
Chile	116·2		Scotland	26·5
Asia			N. Ireland	26·6
India	145·9	(1958–9)	U.S.S.R.	32
Europe			Yugoslavia	82·2
Germany (E)	33·3		**Oceania**	
,, (W)	31·7		Australia	19·5
France	25·9		N.Z.	20·3

*Unless otherwise stated, figures are for 1961.
†Highest in the world.

dying under one year of age. Improved nutrition and medical care have considerably lowered figures throughout the world, e.g. in the 18th cent. in the U.K. 50 per cent. died, compared with under 2¼ per cent in 1961. The table incl. I.M. figures for selected countries to give a world range.

INFECTION. Invasion of the body by micro-organisms. These may be viruses (q.v.) or bacteria (q.v.) incl. cocci and bacilli. Among other diseases, viruses cause smallpox, chickenpox, shingles, measles, mumps, German measles, infantile paralysis, influenza, colds, and sleeping sickness; cocci cause diseases with short incubation periods and acute fever, e.g. scarlet fever, meningitis, and gonorrhoea; bacilli cause diseases with long incubation periods and course, e.g. diphtheria, whooping cough, and typhus. Both cocci and bacilli tend to be carried by immune persons. The effects of I. are due to the body's reaction to the poisons (toxins) produced by the organisms (*see* IMMUNITY). I. may be contracted from a sufferer from the disease; or from a carrier who may be immune or developing the disease himself or convalescent; or from contaminated objects, such as food, drink, bedclothes, or books; or from discharges, such as spray expelled in coughing or sneezing (common cold), or spittle (tuberculosis), or faeces (typhoid). Some infections are carried by insects (malaria by the mosquito, typhus by the louse), or on the feet of flies (food poisoning). Some may be introduced through a breach in the skin, e.g. gonorrhoea and lockjaw (tetanus). Contagion is infection by direct contact.

INFELD, Leopold (1898–1968). Polish physicist. He held a Rockefeller scholarship at Cambridge 1933–5, and was prof. of applied mathematics at Toronto 1939–50, and at Warsaw from 1950. A former sec. and the biographer of Albert Einstein, he pub. *The World in Modern Science* (1934) and *The Evolution of Physics* (1938), with Einstein.

INFERIORITY COMPLEX. Term used in psycho-analysis for a complex pattern of richly emotional ideas connected with what the patient rightly or wrongly believes to be his inferiority. In order to compensate for his inferiority he often tends to assume an opposite character.

INFLAMMATION. The reaction of tissues to injury. This may be caused by violence, a foreign body, poison, or invasion by harmful bacteria. The signs are heat, swelling, redness, pain, and loss of function. These result from the pouring of white blood cells and lymph into the affected region, with the object of combating the injurious agent and repairing the damage. Collections of dead white cells form the thick, yellowish fluid called pus. When the body's local defences win the fight the inflammation resolves. When they lose it, the I. spreads and may endanger life.

INFLATION and DEFLATION. Economic terms. I. is an abnormal increase in the quantity of money relative to the available supply of goods – 'too much money chasing too few goods', tending to decrease purchasing power; and D. is the reverse process, when the supply of money is contracted, thus increasing its purchasing power. Both these conditions can only exist when currency is not fixed to a gold or silver standard. Rising prices caused by moderate I. tend to stimulate producers and lower unemployment, but at the same time are detrimental to those living on fixed incomes. When carried to extremes, such as after the F.W.W., I. spirals uncontrollably upward until the fall in the value of the currency issued becomes more rapid than the quantitative increase in the currency issued. In present-day practice, govts. attempt to minimize I. by restricting credit and maintaining adequate reserves of gold. Since the S.W.W. the general trend has been one of I.

INFLUENZA. An acute infectious fever caused by Pfeiffer's bacillus or a filtrable virus. Incubation takes 2–5 days. The first signs are usually headache, catarrh, fever, shivering, and aching. The onset is sharp and the whole attack clear-cut, as distinct from the heavy cold often miscalled influenza. Bronchitis or pneumonia may follow, or the brain or stomach may be chiefly affected. A malignant type occasionally becomes epidemic, e.g. in 1918 and the milder 'Hong Kong' 'flu of 1968–9; a World I. Centre, financed by W.H.O. is at Mill Hill, N. London.

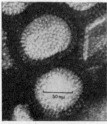

INFLUENZA. Made visible by the electron microscope, influenza virus particles are seen in this micrograph at a magnification of 600,000x, the bar being 50 millimicrons, i.e. 500 Angström units.
Photo: R. W. Horne, *Cavendish Laboratory, Cambridge.*

INFORMATION, Central Office of. The central British govt. agency set up in 1946 to produce and distribute publicity information on behalf of other govt. depts. and to provide them with technical advice for home and overseas purposes. It also aims to promote Britain overseas by pub. literature, providing radio, television and press material, arranging tours for official visitors to the U.K., etc.

INFRA-RED RADIATION. Invisible electromagnetic radiation of wavelength between about 0·75–1,000 microns (1 micron is a millionth of a meter), i.e. between the limit of the red end of the visible spectrum and the shortest microwaves. All bodies above the absolute zero of temperature absorb and radiate I-R.R. Absorption spectra are made use of in chemical analysis, particularly for organic compounds, and objects which radiate I-R.R. can be photographed or made visible in the dark, or through mist or fog, on specially sensitized emulsions. This is important for military purposes. I-R.R. is also used in medical photography and treatment, in industry, astronomy and criminology. The strong absorption of many substances for I-R.R. is a useful method of applying heat, as in baking and toasting.

INGE (ing), **William Ralph** (1860–1954). British churchman. Prof. of divinity at Cambridge 1907–11 and dean of St. Paul's 1911–34, he earned the title 'the gloomy dean' by his pessimistic criticism of modern life. His works incl. *Outspoken Essays* (1919 and 1922). He was created a K.C.V.O. in 1930.

INGERSOLL, Robert Hawley (1859–1928). American watch manufacturer. B. in Delta, Michigan, he pioneered mass-production methods, with his famous one-dollar watch (1892).

INGHELBRECHT, Désiré-Émile (1880–1965). Fr. composer and conductor. Appointed to the Opéra in 1945, he has written of his work there in *Le Chef d'orchestre parle au public* (1957), etc. His compositions incl. *Cantique des Créatures de S. François d'Assise* (1919); the ballet *El Greco* (1920); and *Les Heures claires* (1961), songs based on poems by Verhaeren.

INGLEBOROUGH. Hill, 2,373 ft. in height, in the W. Riding of Yorks, England, with remains of an Iron Age town on top. I. cave is 1,000 ft. in length.

INGOLSTADT. Town on the Danube, dating from 1250, 43 m. N.N.W. of Munich, W. Germany. The industries incl. foundry work and manufacture of machinery. Pop. (1960) 50,700.

INGRES (aṅgr), **Jean Auguste Dominique** 1780–1867). French painter. After studying under David (1797–8) he worked in Rome (1806–20) and Florence (1820–4), executing some of his finest portraits. In 1826 he became prof. of fine arts at the Academy in Paris, and in 1832 director of the French Academy in Rome, returning to Paris in 1841. His draughtsmanship, whether in his highly finished portraits or his female nudes, e.g. 'Odalisque' (1814) and 'La Source' (1856), is superb.

INITIATIVE and **REFERENDUM.** Devices whereby the voters may play a direct part in making laws. In the case of the *Initiative* a proposed law is drawn up and signed by petitioners, and submitted to the legislature. A *Referendum* may be taken on a law that has been passed by the legislature but which will not become operative until the people have expressed their will concerning it. If the R. gives an affirmative vote, then the law is confirmed and comes into force.

Switzerland was the pioneer in these devices, but both have been introduced into a number of the states and cities of U.S.A.

Another device is the *Recall*, whereby the voters are given the opportunity of demanding the dismissal from office of officials.

INK. The various kinds of ink include: (1) *writing inks*, the essential ingredients of which are hot-water extract of galls or some other vegetable material furnishing gallic acid, tannic acid, and other essentially phenolic compounds; (2) *copying and stamp-pad inks*, consisting of concentrated solutions of basic dyes in a hygroscopic medium; (3) *marking inks*, solutions of silver or copper compounds, with the possible addition of aniline; (4) *printing inks*, the chief ingredients of which are resin, soap, and a drying oil in which a colouring matter is mixed.

INKERMAN. A battle of the Crimean War, fought on 5 Nov. 1854, during which an attack by the Russians on I. ridge, occupied by the British army besieging Sebastopol, was repulsed.

INLAND REVENUE, Board of. British govt. dept. formed in 1849 and controlling the income tax, surtax, certain minor taxes, death duties, and stamp duties on documents. Its H.Q. are at Somerset House, London.

INNOCENT III (1161–1216). Pope. B. at Anagni, he was elected pope in 1198. He was successful in asserting the power of the papacy over secular princes, and played a decisive role in the struggles over the imperial succession. His greatest triumph was over King John, whom he compelled to accept Langton as archbishop of Canterbury, and to hold England as the Pope's vassal. I. promoted the 4th Crusade, and crusades against the pagan Livonians and Letts, and the Albigensian heretics.

INNOCENTS' DAY or **Childermas.** Festival of the Catholic Church, celebrated on 28 Dec. in memory of the children who were slaughtered by Herod following upon the birth of Jesus Christ.

INNS and **INNKEEPERS.** An I. may be defined as a house whose owner is according to law prepared to provide shelter and refreshment to all travellers able and willing to pay a reasonable price for the accommodation offered. An innkeeper is bound in law to receive and to provide this accommodation for every guest, so far as he is able, unless the guest be drunk, disorderly, or suffering from infectious disease. Is. differ from hotels in the U.S. only in being picturesque buildings set in attractive surroundings.

INNSBRUCK (-brook). Town on the r. Inn, cap. of Tirol, Austria. I. is a tourist centre, and important as a route junction, esp. as the junction for the Brenner Pass. I. is the seat of a univ. founded 1677. Ancient monuments incl. a 16th cent. Franciscan church. Pop. (1961) 100,699.

INNS OF COURT. Voluntary societies which have the power to call law students to the English Bar. There are now 4, viz. Lincoln's Inn, Gray's Inn, Inner Temple, and Middle Temple; each pursues its separate existence, though joint lectures are given, and a common examination board has been formed. Each is under the administration of a body of Benchers.

INOCULATION. The injection into the body of dead organisms, toxins, antitoxins, etc., with the object of producing immunity by provoking a mild attack of the disease.

INÖNÜ, Ismet (1884–). Turkish statesman. B. in Smyrna, he was a close associate of Atatürk, and as C.-in-C. against the Greeks won the battle of I., from which he took his surname. Appointed For. Min. in 1922, he signed the Treaty of Lausanne, was P.M. 1923–37, and succeeded Atatürk as pres. (1938–50). He then led the opposition (Republican People's Party) until the 1960 military revolution and 1961–5 was P.M. of a coalition govt.

INORGANIC CHEMISTRY. Science dealing with the preparation and properties of the elements and their compounds, except those carbon compounds considered in Organic Chemistry (q.v.). Many groups of analogous compounds exist, the oldest known being acids, bases, and salts. Acids usually have a sour taste, change blue vegetable colours (e.g. litmus) red, and react with alkalis to form salts. Alkalis restore the colours of indicators changed by acids, with which they react to form salts. All acids contain hydrogen. Acids containing oxygen are called oxyacids; those of the same element may contain different amounts of oxygen, the name then ending in -ous and -ic when less or more oxygen is present; the names of the corresponding salts end in -ite and -ate. Salts are formed by the replacement of the acidic hydrogen by a metal or radical. Oxides are classified into: (i) acidic oxides, forming acids with water; (ii) basic oxides, forming bases (containing the hydroxyl group OH) with water; (iii) neutral oxides; and (iv) peroxides (containing more oxygen than the normal oxide). Acidic and basic oxides combine to form salts, whilst in the reaction between acids and bases water is formed as well. An acid containing in the molecule one, two, or three atoms of replaceable hydrogen is called mono-, di-, or tribasic, respectively. If only part of the hydrogen is replaced, an acid salt is formed. A basic salt is usually a compound of a normal salt (in which all the acidic hydrogen is replaced) with excess of base. Other groups are the compounds of metals with halogens (fluorine, chlorine, bromine, and iodine), called halides (fluorides, chlorides, bromides, and iodides), and with sulphur (sulphides). It is usual in the chemistry of non-metallic elements to discuss their compounds with hydrogen, oxygen, and halogens; and in describing the metals to deal with their oxides, halides, and oxysalts (carbonates, nitrates, sulphates, etc.).

INNSBRUCK. Seen from the City Tower the 3,000 gilded copper shingles of the Goldenes Dachl gleam high above the arcaded streets of the old town. It was added to the Fürstenburg as a royal box for Maxmilian I when viewing entertainments in the street below.
Courtesy of Austrian State Tourist Department.

The basis of the modern description of the elements is the Periodic Table, given on p. 570. In this, the elements are arranged in the order of increasing atomic weight with one or two inversions (e.g. tellurium and iodine), or more correctly in the order of atomic number (nuclear charge). The continuous sequence of elements then breaks up into 7 periods and 8 groups, the members of a group and the subgroups (a) and (b) into which each is divided showing related chemical properties. The Roman numeral at the top of each group is equal to some valency (sometimes the minimum, as in group I, sometimes the maximum, as in groups VI and VII, of the elements it contains). *See also* table on page 244.

The sequence of atomic numbers shows that there

PERIODIC SYSTEM OF THE CHEMICAL ELEMENTS

IA	IIA	IIIA	IVA	VA	VIA	VIIA	VIII			IB	IIB	IIB	IVB	VB	VIB	VIIB	O
H 1																	He 2
Li 3	Be 4					*— metals —*						B 5	C 6	N 7	O 8	F 9	Ne 10
Na 11	Mg 12				*transition elements*							Al 13	Si 14	P 15	S 16	Cl 17	Ar 18
K 19	Ca 20	Sc 21	Ti 22	V 23	Cr 24	Mn 25	Fe 26	Co 27	Ni 28	Cu 29	Zn 30	Ga 31	Ge 32	As 33	Se 34	Br 35	Kr 36
Rb 37	Sr 38	Y 39	Zr 40	Nb 41	Mo 42	Tc 43	Ru 44	Rh 45	Pd 46	Ag 47	Cd 48	In 49	Sn 50	Sb 51	Te 52	I 53	Xe 54
Cs 55	Ba 56	La 57	Hf 72	Ta 73	W 74	Re 75	Os 76	Ir 77	Pt 78	Au 79	Hg 80	Tl 81	Pb 82	Bi 83	Po 84	At 85	Rn 86
Fr 87	Ra 88	Ac 89	Th 90	Pa 91	U 92												

increasingly electropositive (left), *non-metals* (right), *increasingly electronegative*

Rare Earths (Lanthanides)	La 57	Ce 58	Pr 59	Nd 60	Pm 61	Sm 62	Eu 63	Gd 64	Tb 65	Dy 66	Ho 67	Er 68	Tm 69	Yb 70	Lu 71
Transuranics (Actinides)	Ac 89	Th 90	Pa 91	U 92	Np 93	Pu 94	Am 95	Cm 96	Bk 97	Cf 98	Es 99	Fm 100	Md 101	No 102	Lw 103

are now no 'missing' elements, nos. 43, 61, 85, 87, etc., all highly radioactive, having been made. The last period contains similar elements, and since preceding periods contain 2, 8, 8, 18, 18, and 32 elements, it would be expected that the last should be a very long period and 11 elements beyond uranium have been prepared artificially (plutonium, neptunium, americium, curium, berkelium, californium, einsteinium, fermium, mendelevium, nobelium, and lawrencium. Research continues, as in the unsuccessful attempt at Berkeley in 1968 to find traces of no. 110 – thought to be relatively stable – in platinum ore.

The modern quantum theory of the atom (unlike the old Rutherford-Bohr theory) is able to give a satisfactory explanation of the numbers 2, 8, 18, and 32, of elements in the periods, and the structures of the shells of electrons in practically all atoms are known from the spectroscopic data; the explanation of the appearance of the 15 rare earth elements in period 6 is due to the filling up of an incomplete inner shell by successive additions of electrons as the atomic number increases in steps, whilst the outer valency shell, on which the chemical properties depend, remains unaltered. Elements, the atoms of which have incomplete inner shells, are called transitional elements in the wider sense: they include, besides the rare earths proper, and the group VIII metals, the elements from scandium to zinc, from yttrium to cadmium, and from hafnium to mercury, inclusive.

INQUEST. In English law, an inquiry held by a coroner (q.v.).

INQUISITION. An ecclesiastical tribunal in the R.C. Church, charged with the suppression of heresy. Its existence is usually dated from the Synod of Toulouse in 1229. The *Medieval I.* operated mainly in France and Italy, and to a lesser extent in the Empire and Spain; it never gained a footing in England. The Reformation led to a great revival in its activity in Italy and Spain. The I. or Holy Office (renamed Sacred Congregation for the Doctrine of the Faith 1965) still deals with ecclesiastical discipline, its jurisdiction confined to the Vatican City.

The *Spanish I.* was reorganized in 1480 under royal, not papal, control. Its jurisdiction was extended in the 16th cent. to the Spanish colonies in America. Executions continued until 1781. Napoleon suppressed it in 1808, but it was restored by Ferdinand VII in 1814, only to be abolished again in 1834.

Trials by the I. were conducted in secret, and torture was used to force the prisoner to admit his guilt. Those who confessed were condemned to flogging, fines, or penances; the obstinate to imprisonment or to death by burning. *See* INDEX.

INSANITY. Social inadequacy due to mental disorder. The word as used popularly has much the same meaning as the legal term mental disease, formerly lunacy. This means a condition which renders the patient so dangerous to himself or others or both, or so helpless, that he should be placed under care. Many mentally diseased or disordered persons are not socially inadequate. In medicine the corresponding term is psychosis.

INSECT. Small invertebrate animal whose body is divided into head, thorax, and abdomen. The head bears a pair of feelers or antennae, and attached to the thorax are 3 pairs of legs and usually 2 pairs of wings. Is. are placed in the class Insecta of the phylum Arthropoda, and their scientific study forms that branch of zoology termed Entomology. About 1,000,000 species are known, and several thousand new ones are discovered every year. Is. vary in size

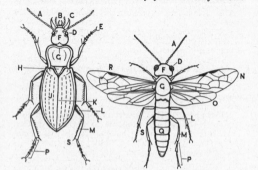

INSECT. Diagrams of Coleopterous and Hymenopterous insects. A, antenna; B, palpi; C, mandible; D, compound eye; E, claw; F, head; G, thorax; H, scutellum; J, elytra; K, suture; L, femur; M, tibia; N, fore-wing; O, hind-wing; P, tarsus; Q, abdomen; R, stigma; S, spur.

very considerably from 0·007 in. to 13 in. in length.

The skeleton is almost entirely external and is composed of chitin. It remains membranous at the

CLASSIFICATION OF INSECTS

Class – INSECTA

Sub-class Apterygota

Thysanura	Three-pronged bristle-tails
Diplura	Two-pronged bristle-tails
Protura	Proturans
Collembola	Springtails

Sub-class Pterygota

Division I. Exopterygota

Orthoptera	Grasshoppers, locusts, crickets, etc.
Dictyoptera	Cockroaches, praying mantids
Phasmida	Stick and leaf insects
Grylloblattodea	Few primitive, secondarily wingless forms
Plecoptera	Stone-flies
Isoptera	Termites or white ants
Embioptera	Web-spinners
Dermaptera	Earwigs
Ephemeroptera	May-flies
Odonata	Dragon-flies
Psocoptera	Psocids or book-lice
Anoplura	Sucking or true-lice and bird-lice
Thysanoptera	Thrips
Hemiptera	Plant-bugs, cicadas, leaf-hoppers, aphids, etc.

Division 2. Endopterygota

Neuroptera	Lace-wings, alder-flies, etc.
Mecoptera	Scorpion flies
Trichoptera	Caddis-flies
Lepidoptera	Butterflies and moths
Coleoptera	Beetles
Strepsiptera	Stylops
Hymenoptera	Saw-flies, ants, bees, wasps, ichneumon flies, etc.
Diptera	Two-winged or true flies
Aphaniptera	Fleas

joints, but elsewhere is hard and gives attachment to the muscles and other internal organs.

The head is its feeding and sensory centre. It bears the antennae, eyes, and mouth-parts. By means of the *antennae*, the I. detects odours and experiences the sense of touch. The *eyes* comprise *compound eyes* and simple eyes or *ocelli*. The compound eyes are formed of a large number of individual facets or lenses. There are about 4,000 lenses to each compound eye in the house-fly. The mouth-parts include a *labrum* or upper lip; a pair of principal jaws or *mandibles*, used for seizing and crushing the food; a pair of accessory jaws or *maxillae*; and a *labium*, or lower lip. The mouth-parts are modified in Is. which feed upon a fluid diet.

The *thorax* is the locomotory centre, and is made up of 3 segments – the *pro-*, *meso-*, and *metathorax*. Each bears a pair of legs and, in flying insects, the 2nd and 3rd of these segments also bears a pair of wings. Legs vary greatly in form according to use. *Wings* are outgrowths of the integument of the meso- and metathorax. A wing is composed of an upper and a lower membrane, and between these 2 layers it is strengthened by a framework of chitinous tubes known as *veins*. The venation or arrangement of this framework is of great importance in the classification of insects. The hind-body or abdomen is the metabolic and reproductive centre: it is here that digestion, excretion, and the sexual functions take place. Usually the abdomen consists of 10 segments. In the female there is very commonly an egg-laying instrument or *ovipositor*, and many insects have a pair of tail feelers or *cerci*. Most insects breathe by means of fine air-tubes called *tracheae* which open to the exterior by a pair of breathing pores or *spiracles*.

Growth and metamorphosis. When ready to issue from the egg the young I. forces its way through the *chorion*, or egg-shell, and growth takes place in cycles that are interrupted by successive moults. After moulting the new cuticle is soft and pliable and able to adapt itself to increase in size and change of form. Moulting is caused by a hormone discharged into the blood. The growth changes constitute metamorphosis.

Most of the lower orders of Is. pass through a direct or incomplete metamorphosis. The young closely resemble the parents and are known as nymphs. The transformation to adult stage is gradual and feeding goes on throughout life.

The higher groups of Is. undergo indirect or complete metamorphosis. They issue from the eggs at an earlier stage of growth than nymphs and are termed *larvae*. The life of the I. is interrupted by a resting *pupal* stage when no food is taken. During this stage the larval organs and tissues are transformed into those of the *imago* or adult. Before pupating the I. protects itself by selecting a suitable hiding place, or making a cocoon of some material which will merge in with its surroundings. When an I. is about to emerge from the pupa it undergoes its final moult, which consists in shedding the pupal cuticle. When in the adult stage the I. no longer grows or moults.

Reproduction is by diverse means. In most Is. mating occurs once only, and death soon follows. Many Is. are pests which may be controlled by chemical pesticides (which may also kill useful Is.), importation of natural predators (which may themselves become pests), or more recently use of artificially reared sterile Is., either the males only or in 'population flushing' both sexes, so sharply reducing succeeding generations.

The classification of Is. (*see* accompanying Table) is largely based upon characters of the mouth-parts, wings and metamorphosis.

INSECTIVOROUS PLANTS. Plants which attract and trap small insects, and digest them. Unique for their ability to use animal protein as a source of nitrogen, they are common to marshy ground where there is a shortage of nitrogen. The sundews (*Drosera*) are of world-wide occurrence, and the largest species, *D. gigantea*, found in Australia, can reach a height of

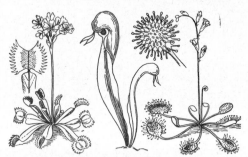

INSECTIVOROUS PLANTS. Left to right: Venus' fly-trap; side-saddle flower; sundew.

3 feet. The butterwort (*Pinguicula*) found in Britain, produces a rosette of pale green leaves, each with turned-up edges, and a greasy surface covered with tiny points to trap insects. Bladderworts (*Utricularia*) q.v. are floating plants growing in quiet waters or muddy soils, and trap insects by small green bladders among the leaves. The Venus' fly trap (*Dionaea*) is common in S. America, and pitcher plants (*Nepenthes*) are native to the wet tropics of the Old World.

INSEMINATION, Artificial. The artificial introduction of semen to the reproductive tract of the female to effect fertilization. Largely used as a means of improving cattle herds through outstanding sires, it has also been used in the case of human beings. Semen may sometimes be obtained from the husband – A.I.H(usband). - or from a stranger who usually remains unknown except to the doctor involved – A.I.D(onor). Further developments of A.I. are the possibilities of pre-determination of the sex of the child, the light 'y' chromosome sperms rising and the heavier 'x' chromosome sperms sinking (*see* GENETICS), and of external fertilisation of eggs which might then be either reimplanted in the womb or eventually grown to maturity in the laboratory.

INSTALMENT CREDIT. *See* HIRE PURCHASE.

I'NSŪLIN. The hormone secreted by the islets of Langerhans in the pancreas. It is necessary for the utilization of sugar, by the body and its deficiency causes diabetes. McLeod, Banting, and Best discovered its existence in 1921 and how to extract it and use it in the treatment of diabetes.

INSURANCE. By a contract of I. the insured party is guaranteed a specified indemnity in return for valuable consideration, otherwise known as the premium, which is scientifically calculated on the basis of experience in proportion to the risk involved. As practised by I. companies, mutual associations and societies, I. can be classified under the headings: fire, marine, accident and life – the last division being distinguished by the term 'assurance'. An assurance policy guarantees the payment of a definite sum upon the occurrence of a specific event which is accepted as being inevitable, e.g. death, whereas I. is strictly the provision effected by prudent men against a fortuitous and 'unexpected' contingency.

The practice of I. is strictly governed by various cor-related common-law principles, of which indemnity is the most important. This ensures that an insured person shall not be more than fully indemnified, thus preventing anyone profiting, as a result of his loss or misfortune, from the I. fund of which the I. co, is the trustee. It is also affected by various statutes, e.g. in Britain the Road Traffic Act (1960), which requires drivers of certain classes of vehicles to effect valid third-party cover. In Britain the Min. of Social Security (1966) admin. under the Nat. I. Acts of 1946–68 industrial injuries, maternity, sickness, unemploy-ment, widow's benefits, etc., and family allowances and retirement pensions, but in 1968 there were pro-posals for a new scheme of Nat. I. based on earnings-related benefits and contributions. *See* LLOYDS.

INTAGLIO (intal'yō). Term applied to an engraving which is cut into some material. It is applied more specifically to a gem which has a pattern cut into one surface. In printing, the term is applied to a process in which ink is laid in incisions and hollows on the plate, as in etching, photogravure, etc.

INTELLIGENCE, Military and Political. *See under* SECRET SERVICE.

INTELLIGENCE TESTS. *See* MENTAL TESTS.

INTEREST. Payment for the use of borrowed money or capital. It is calculated at so much per cent (U.K. £100; U.S. $100; etc.) per annum. The money lent is called the principal, and principal and interest equal the amount. *Simple Interest* is charged on the principal alone. *Compound I.* is charged on the amount of principal and interest as and when it falls due.

INTERIOR DECORATION. The decoration of the inside of a building. Among early names associated with I.D. in England are those of Inigo Jones and Grinling Gibbons, but the first architects to design a building as an integrated whole were the Adam brothers, e.g. Syon House, Middlesex. Craftsmen who have given their names to different styles of furniture design include Chippendale, Hepplewhite and Sheraton. In Victorian times William Morris became famous for his designs of carpets, wallpaper, furniture, etc. Associated with him were the Pre-Raphaelites: Burne Jones, D. G. Rossetti, and others.

In more recent times the trend has been to a less ornate and more functional style, fostered by the interaction of architects and designers working in teams, whether to remodel existing interiors, e.g. Misha Black and Hugh Casson, in British post offices, or in new buildings, e.g. Gio Ponti's Pirelli building (Milan) Oscar Niemeyer's capital city of Brasilia; and the many works of Le Corbusier (France), Eero Saarinen, and Skidmore Owings and Merrill (U.S.A.).

INTERLAKEN (in'terlahken). Town and tourist centre on the Aar between lakes Brienz and Thun, Switzerland. The site was first occupied in 1130 by a monastery, suppressed in 1528. Pop. (1960) 4,738.

INTERNAL COMBUSTION ENGINE. An engine in which energy supplied by a burning fuel is directly transformed into mechanical energy by the controlled burning of the fuel in an enclosed cylinder behind a piston. The term is usually applied to the petrol engine.

INTERNATIONAL, The. Name given to a number of international bodies set up by Socialist and labour organizations to co-ordinate their policies. The 1st International (International Working Men's Associa-tion) was formed in London in 1864, under the virtual leadership of Karl Marx (q.v.). The 2nd (Socialist) International, founded in 1889, was a loose federation of national Socialist parties, which lasted until 1939. The 3rd (Communist) International, generally known as the Comintern, was founded at Moscow in 1919. Like the 1st I. it had a common programme and a strongly centralized leadership, and after the triumph of Hitler in 1933 it advocated a 'popular front' of Communists, Socialists, and Liberals against Fascism. In 1943 it was dissolved. The 4th Inter-national, founded in 1936, consists of a number of groups supporting the policy of Trotsky (q.v.).

INTERNATIONAL ATOMIC ENERGY AGEN-CY. Estab. 1957, it has its H.Q. in Vienna, and is responsible for research centres in Austria and Monaco, and the Internat. Centre for Theoretical Physics (1964) in Trieste. It advises and assists member states in the development and application of nuclear power and guards against its misuse.

INTERNATIONAL BANK for Reconstruction and Development. Estab. in 1945 as a result of the Bretton Woods Conference of 1944, and related to the U.N., it facilitates productive investment among its mem-bers, and fosters the long-range growth of international trade. The H.Q. are at Washington. Membership is dependent on participation in the International Monetary Fund (1945) which encourages co-operation on monetary problems, e.g. convertibility and stability of currencies. Affiliated to the I.B. are the International Finance Corporation (1956), promoting economic development in less developed areas by making investments in private enterprise without government guarantee; and the International Develop-ment Association (1960), assisting on a more flexible basis such essential projects in undeveloped countries as water supply, sanitation and highways, which may not be directly productive or revenue-producing. *See* BANKING.

INTERNATIONAL BRIGADE. The international volunteer force which fought on the republican side in the Spanish Civil War of 1936–9.

INTERNATIONAL CIVIL AVIATION ORGAN-IZATION. Estab. in 1947 (provisionally 1945) and related to the U.N., it encourages safety measures, and uniform regulations in the operation of air services: simplified procedures for customs, immigra-tion and public health; and more safely efficient techniques and equipment.

INTERNATIONAL COURT OF JUSTICE. In-ternational court at The Hague, the main judicial organ of the U.N. Its statute follows closely that of the *Permanent C of J.*, set up in 1921, which was associated with the League of Nations.

INTERNATIONAL DATE LINE. A modification of the 180th meridian which marks the difference in

The international date line, at which a day is lost or gained.

time between E. and W. The date is put forward a day when crossing the Line going W., and back a day when going E.

INTERNATIONALE. International Communist anthem with words by Eugène Pottier (1871) and music by Pierre Degeyter (*c.* 1891): it was the nat. anthem of the U.S.S.R. 1917–19 Dec. 1943.

INTERNATIONAL GEOPHYSICAL YEAR (I.G.Y.). Over 250 observatories in 60 countries co-operated during the sunspot maximum period of 1 July 1957–31 Dec. 1958 in studying the region of the earth's atmosphere extending upwards from about 70 km. (45 miles). Valuable scientific data collected incl. information about the various layers of ionization (q.v.) in the atmosphere, irregular patches of the ionosphere (q.v.), and extra levels associated with disturbances on the sun.

INTERNATIONAL LABOUR ORGANIZATION. An organization, with H.Q. at Geneva, which formulates standards for labour and social conditions, to be ratified by member-states. An independent body, first estab. in 1919, it was assoc. with the League of Nations, and in 1945 became affiliated to the U.N.

INTERNATIONAL LAW. That body of law or collection of rules regarded by civilized states as binding in their relations with each other. The chief framers of modern I.L. were classical jurists, e.g. Hugo Grotius (q.v.), who believed in the uncodified and continually evolving 'law of nature' of reasonable man as a member of society. Its most fundamental rules, covering not only political matters and the conduct of war but broad questions of human welfare, are elucidated in treaties and pacts between countries. The weakness of I.L. is that no body has yet proved strong enough to impose its rulings, although the L. of N. (q.v.) made several attempts and the U.N. (q.v.) has succeeded to some extent.

Space research has further enlarged the scope of I.L. On the analogy of the high seas outside territorial limits being regarded as the common property of all states, it has been accepted practice since the F.W.W. that each state has absolute sovereignty over air space (the upward limit being undefined in view of the newness of the problem), but that air space over unclaimed territory and the open sea is free for all. Outer space is being customarily treated as free for all, subject only to its use by rockets and satellites of one state having no harmful effect on any other state over which they pass – or which pass under them. Other planets – should these prove available for appropriation – would preferably be internationally controlled. Britain, U.S.S.R., and U.S.A. signed a treaty 1967 banning nuclear weapons from outer space and in 1968 reached agreement on the rescue and return of astronauts, etc.

INTERNATIONAL SETTLEMENTS, Bank for.

Although originated in 1930 to handle the reparation transactions arising from the Young Plan, the bank lost this business with Germany's default, but continued to operate by providing a foreign exchange reserve for central banks and by supplying funds to aid weakened currencies. In addition since the S.W.W., it has been financial agent for the Marshall Plan, O.E.E.C., etc. Its H.Q. are in Basle.

INTERNATIONAL TRADE UNIONISM. The first internat. body was the *I. Fed. of Trade Unions* (1913), estab. with the beginning of companies with world-wide operations, able to switch their activities to countries where unionism is weak. The modern organisations are the *Internat. Confederation of Free Trade Unions* (I.C.F.T.U. 1949), which incl. the A.F. of L./C.I.O. and T.U.C.; *World Fed. of Trade Unions* (W.F.T.U. 1945), Communist-dominated; and *World Confederation of Labour* (W.C.L. 1920), mainly Roman Catholic

INTERPLANETARY MATTER. Material distributed in space, between the planets. It was formerly thought that space must be entirely empty, but this view is now known to be wrong; the material in the Solar System is very thinly spread, but it is still very appreciable. Studies of the interplanetary material have been carried out with the aid of lunar and planetary probes, but information is incomplete.

INTERPOL. Abbreviation of *International Criminal Police Commission*, founded following the Second International Judicial Police Conference (1923) with its H.Q. in Vienna, but reconstituted after the S.W.W. with its H.Q. in Paris: it has an international criminal register, fingerprint file and methods index.

INTERTYPE. A machine for composing printing type, similar to linotype (q.v.).

INTESTINES. The bowels; the digestive tract below the stomach. The small intestine (20 ft. in man), consists of the duodenum, jejunum, and ileum; the large intestine (5 ft.) of the caecum, colon, and rectum. Both Is. are muscular tubes comprising an inner lining which secretes alkaline digestive juice, a sub-mucous coat containing fine blood vessels and nerves,

a muscular coat with an inner layer of circular and an outer of longitudinal fibres, and a serous coat covering all. The muscle contracts in a series of waves (peristalsis) so as to pass the contents slowly along. The whole tract is supported by a strong band or sling of connective tissue (peritoneum) carrying the blood and lymph vessels and nerves (mesentery, omentum); this keeps the organs in place and isolates infection by pouring out lymph and sealing off the affected region.

INTESTINES. l, stomach; 2 and 8, small intestine; 3, gall-bladder; 4, transverse colon; 5, ascending colon; 6, coecum; 7, appendix; 9, descending colon; 10, rectum.

INTOXICATION. Affection by a poison (toxin); in popular language usually by alcohol, but scientifically also by poisonous substances, including those generated within the body, e.g. in an abscess under a tooth, or in an inflamed appendix.

INVALIDES, Hôtel des (ōtel' dăzaṅvahlēd'). Large building in Paris, S. of the Seine. It was founded in 1670 as a home for disabled soldiers. The church Dôme des Invalides contains the tomb of Napoleon I. The military gov. of Paris has his H.Q. at the I.

INVERCARGILL. City at the extreme S. of South Island, New Zealand. I. is situated on a deep inlet, and is the centre of a great grazing area. It has sawmills, meat-packing plants, and in 1968 a smelter was planned at nearby Bluff to process alumina from Queensland. Pop. (1967) 47,100.

INVERNESS. An inlet o fthe sea, Loch Nevis has an austerely breathtaking beauty. *Photo: George Outram & Co. Ltd.*

INVERNE'SS. Co. town (royal burgh) of Inverness-shire, Scotland. Situated in a sheltered position at the mouth of the Ness, I. is a railway junction and a tourist centre for the Highlands (q.v.). Sheep and wool are gathered in from all parts of the Highlands for the annual market. Industrial activity incl. tanning, engineering, railway workshops, distilling, and tweed manufacture. Pop. (1961) 29,773.

INVERNESS-SHIRE. Largest of the Scottish counties. It is a Highland co., including within its boundaries the highest peak in Britain, Ben Nevis (4,406 ft.), and some of the islands of the Hebrides. Striking across the co. from N.E. to S.W. is Glen More, occupied by the Moray Firth, Loch Ness, Loch Lochy, and Loch Linnhe, with their connecting rivers. The glen has been utilized by the Caledonian Canal. The main rivers are the Spey, Nairn, and Findhorn. Little of the co.'s surface is suitable for agriculture. On the moors sheep, Highland cattle, and Highland ponies are raised. There are fishing industries centred on Fort William and in the Hebrides, and other industrial development includes distilling, woollen manufacture, and aluminium processing, brewing, and spinning. The principal centres are Inverness, the co. town, and Fort William. Area 4,211 sq. m.; pop. (1961) 83,425.

INVESTMENT TRUST. *See* SAVING and TRUST.

INYŌKE'RN. Village in the Mojave desert, California, U.S.A., 45 m. N.N.W. of Mojave. It is the site of a U.S. Naval Ordnance test station at which research is carried out in rocket flight and propulsion. Founded in 1944, it is the centre of a military reservation covering some thousand sq. m.

I'O. In Gk. legend, the dau. of Inachus, king of Argos. She was beloved by Zeus, who (to evade the jealousy of Hera) transformed her into a heifer. She finally recovered her original human form on the banks of the Nile, and bore a son to Zeus.

IODINE (I'odin). A non-metallic element (Gk. *iodes* violet) discovered by Courtois in 1811: symbol I, at. wt. 126·91, at. no. 53. It is a violet-black lustrous solid volatilizing at ordinary temperatures to a bluish-violet gas with an irritating odour, and forming a characteristic blue colour with starch. Not found in the free state, it occurs in saltpetre and as iodides in sea-water from which it is taken up by seaweeds and sponges and may be extracted from their ashes. Most of the world's supplies were formerly extracted from Chile saltpetre deposits but the current process, using finely divided silver on brines from salt wells, has greatly increased production and lowered cost. It is used in photography, externally in medicine (tincture of I. is an alcoholic solution) as an antiseptic, and also internally; and in chemicals and dyes. It collects in the thyroid gland; lack of it producing goitre, and excess myxoedema. Iodine-131 (a radio-active isotope) is widely used in medical diagnosis, research and treatment.

IO'DOFORM (CHI_3). An antiseptic which crystallizes into yellow hexagonal plates. It is soluble in ether, alcohol, and chloroform, but not in water.

I'ON. An atom or group of atoms which carries a positive or negative electric charge. When neutral atoms or molecules lose valence electrons, positive Is. are formed, when they gain valence electrons, negative Is. are formed. In general salts such as chlorides, sulphates, nitrates, etc., dissolve in water to form both positive and negative Is. in equal quantities, the metal I. being the positive one. Gaseous Is. may be produced by the action of radiation or charged particles.

IO'NA. Island of the Inner Hebrides, Scotland, in Argyll co., separated from the Ross of Mull by the narrow Sound of Iona; a rocky stretch of land of some 2,200 acres, the highest point rising to 332 ft. Patches of grassland are used as grazing for cattle and sheep, agriculture and fishing are the principal occupations of the people. In 563 St. Columba founded a monastery which became a great centre of Celtic Christianity, it was destroyed in 807 by Norse pirates. A new Benedictine monastery (founded 1203) was the seat of the bishopric of Sodor 1499–1578, but later fell into ruin. Restoration began shortly after it was presented to the Church of Scotland by the duke of Argyll in 1899, and, from the establishment of the I. Community in 1938, was completed by them. Pop. (1961) 130.

IONESCO (ēones'kō), **Eugène** (1912–). French playwright. B. in Rumania, and for a time prof. of literature at Bucharest, he settled in Paris in 1938. Barely staged and allegorical in content, his plays incl. *Les Chaises* (*The Chairs:* 1952), in which a senile married couple converse, and *Rhinocéros* (*The Rhinoceros:* 1959), an attack on totalitarianism, in which every character except one turns into a rhinoceros.

IO'NIA. District on the W. coast of Asia Minor, inhabited in classical times by Greeks of the Ionian branch. It incl. a number of cities, e.g. Ephesus, Miletus, and later Smyrna, which were subject in turn to Lydia, Persia, Macedonia, and Rome (133 B.C.)

IO'NIAN ISLANDS. Group of islands off the W. and S. coasts of Greece consisting of Corfu, Cephalonia, Zante, Ithaca, Levkas, and Paxo. In 1815 they became a British protectorate, but were ceded to Greece in 1864. Area 860 sq. m.; pop. (1961) 212,277.

IONIAN SEA. That part of the Mediterranean that lies between Italy and Greece, to the S. of the Adriatic and containing the Ionian islands.

IONIDES, Basil (1884–1950). British architect. B. in London, he was chiefly famous for his interior

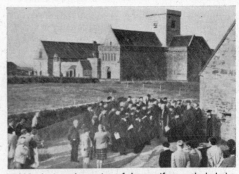

IONA. Against the setting of the cruciform cathedral they have helped to restore, members of the Iona Community – a religious brotherhood for training students – gather round their founder, George Macleod (q.v.), at their 21st anniversary celebration. *Photo: W. Pintail.*

decoration, e.g. the Savoy Theatre and Claridge's restaurant in London.

IONĪZÁ'TION CHAMBER. Device for measuring the amount of ionizing radiation. The radiation ionizes gas in the chamber and the ions are collected and measured as an electric charge.

Ī'ONĪZING RADIATION. Radiation which knocks electrons from atoms during its passage, thereby leaving ions in its path. Electrons and alpha-particles are much more ionizing than are neutrons or gamma-radiation (q.v.).

IO'NOSPHERE. The ionized layer of the earth's outer atmosphere, in which free electrons are normally present in sufficient quantities to modify the propagation of radio waves traversing it. There are 3 regions, approx. spherical and concentric, lying 30–100 m. from the earth's surface. Knowledge of the I. is important for radio communication and space travel. The lower regions (*see* KENNELLY-HEAVISIDE LAYER) are investigated by sending out radio waves and receiving them back at different places, after they have been reflected and refracted between the I. and earth. The upper boundaries of the I. are investigated with radio sounding from above, by satellites. A great deal of information is being collected in this way concerning daily and seasonal variations. The I. is assumed to be produced by absorption of the sun's ultra-violet radiation.

I O U. Short for 'I owe you'. A written acknowledgment of debt, signed by the debtor.

Ī'ŌWA. North central state of the U.S.A. A prairie tableland, it is drained by tributaries of the bordering Mississippi and Missouri, and has great climatic extremes. I. is chiefly devoted to agriculture, esp. maize, and stock raising, with its accompanying industries of meat packing and the manufacture of dairy products. The chief mineral product is coal. First visited by Frenchmen in 1673, I. was admitted to the Union in 1846. The chief cities are Des Moines, the capital, Sioux City, Davenport, Cedar Rapids, and Waterloo. Area 56,280 sq. m.; pop. (1970) 2,825,041.

IPECACUANHA

IPECACUANHA (ipikakū-a'na). A small shrubby plant (*Psychotria ipecacuanha*) found in Brazil and Colombia. The root, used in medicine, acts as an emetic and in lesser amounts as a digestive aid and expectorant.

IPHIGENIA (if ijēnī'a). In Gk. mythology, the dau. of Agamemnon and Clytemnestra.

IPPOLITOV-IVANOV Michael (1859–1935). Russian composer. B. in Gatchina, he studied under Rimsky-Korsakov, and became prof. at the Moscow Conservatoire. In 1894 appeared his most popular work, *Caucasian Sketches*.

IPSWICH. Co. town (co. bor.) of Suffolk, England, on the Gipping (Orwell), 16 m. N.E. of Colchester. I. is a market town with a civic coll. opened 1961, and has engineering works, and manufactures agricultural machinery, fertilizers, electrical apparatus, clothing, sacking, tobacco, etc. Pop. (1961) 117,325.

IQBAL, Sir Muhammad (1876–1938). Indian poet and thinker. B. in the Punjab, he became prof. of. philosophy at Lahore, and was knighted in 1923. He was influenced by Nietzsche, and expressed his philosophy in *Reconstruction of Religious Thought in Islam*, etc. An I. Society was formed in 1948.

IQUIQUE (ēkē'kā). City and seaport of Chile, cap.

of the prov. of Tarapaca. It exports nitrate of soda, from the desert region. Pop. (1966) 48,000.

IQUITOS (ēkē'tōs). Peruvian river port on the upper Amazon, cap. of Loreto dept. The town is a general clearing house for most of eastern Peru. Pop. (1965) 66,000.

IRAN. Persian name for PERSIA.

IRANIAN. The I. language, formerly known as Persian, is the literary language of modern Iran or Persia. Its earliest remains are the Old Persian inscriptions and the Zoroastrian scriptures. Old Persian was a highly inflected language, akin to Sanskrit, but modern I. is as lacking in grammatical forms as English. Written in the Arabic alphabet, it has incorporated a high percentage of Arabic words. *See also* PERSIAN.

IRAQ (ērahk'). Republic in the Middle East. Flowing across the country are the 2 great rivers Tigris and Euphrates. Rising on either side of the river-plain is plateau country. A great part of I. has a hot desert climate with a scanty rainfall. Natural vegetation of I. is greatly restricted, and cultivation is dependent in the main on artificial irrigation. The plain of I. is potentially highly fertile, much of its surface receiving a new covering of alluvium with each year's floods. In winter, wheat and barley are the main crops, while in summer rice, cotton, and maize are grown, and I. produces most of the world's dates. Sheep, goats, horses, donkeys, and camels are reared. There is a large construction industry and further industrial development is being encouraged by Soviet aid. There are rich oilfields; those at Kirkuk, found 1927, are connected by pipe-lines to the Mediterranean; other deposits have been found since. The cap. is Baghdad; Basra the chief port. Area 172,000 sq. m.; pop. (1965) 8,261,527.

History. Formerly a Turkish prov., I. became a British mandate after the F.W.W. In 1921 the Emir Faisal was elected king and in 1924 adopted a parliamentary constitution. The mandate ended in 1932, and Faisal was succeeded by his son Ghazi (reigned 1933–9) and grandson Faisal II, whose authority was exercised by his uncle Prince Abdul Illah during a regency which lasted till 1953. In 1958 both uncle and nephew were assassinated in a coup d'état, and I. was declared a rep. with General Kassem as P.M. A second coup organized by the military under Ahmed Bakr and the *Baath* Party (Socialist Party of the Arab Renaissance) led to the execution of Kassem 1963. Violent political disagreements ensued, and in 1968 Pres. Bakr also assumed the premiership, taking immediate steps to deal with the urgent problem of the Kurds. *See* KURDISTAN.

IRAWADI. Alternative form of IRRAWADDY.

IRELAND, John (1879–1962). British composer. B. at Bowden, Cheshire, he studied under Stanford at the R.C.M., returning as prof. of composition (1923–39), when his pupils incl. Britten, Searle and Arnell. Strongly self-critical, he destroyed much early work, but is revealed at his best in the mystic orchestral prelude *The Forgotten Rite* (1915) and piano solo *Sarnia* (1941), both inspired by his love for the Channel Islands where he lived for many years. Himself a brilliant pianist, he also wrote a fine Piano Concerto (1930) and other piano music (incl. London Pieces, 1919, and his Trio No. 3, 1938), as well as chamber music in which the piano takes the leading role. Notable, too, are his choral setting of John Addington Symonds 'These Things Shall Be' (1937), and song settings, e.g. Masefield's 'Sea Fever'. *See* MOERAN.

IRELAND, William Henry (1777–1835). British forger. The son of the engraver Samuel I., he forged deeds supposedly signed by Shakespeare, and the pseudo-Shakespearean drama *Vortigern*, unsuccessfully produced by Sheridan in 1796. He subsequently pub. a full account of his frauds.

IRELAND

Provinces and Counties*

	Area in sq. m.	Pop. (1966 census)	County Town
ULSTER			
Antrim	1,122	712,954	Belfast
Armagh	489	125,031	Armagh
Down	952	286,930	Downpatrick
Fermanagh	657	49,876	Enniskillen
Londonderry	804	174,345	Londonderry
Tyrone	1,218	135,634	Omagh
N. Ireland	5,242	1,484,770	Capital: Belfast
Cavan	730	54,022	Cavan
Donegal	1,865	108,549	Lifford
Monaghan	498	45,732	Monaghan
MUNSTER			
Clare	1,231	73,579	Ennis
Cork	2,880	339,703	Cork
Kerry	1,815	112,785	Tralee
Limerick	1,037	137,357	Limerick
Tipperary	1,643	122,812	Clonmel
Waterford	710	73,080	Waterford
LEINSTER			
Carlow	346	33,539	Carlow
Dublin	356	795,047	Dublin
Kildare	654	66,404	Kildare
Kilkenny	796	60,463	Kilkenny
Laoghis	664	44,595	Portlaoghise
Longford	403	28,989	Longford
Louth	317	69,519	Dundalk
Meath	903	67,323	Trim
Offaly	771	51,717	Tullamore
Westmeath	681	52,900	Mullingar
Wexford	908	83,437	Wexford
Wicklow	782	60,428	Wicklow
CONNACHT			
Galway	2,293	148,340	Galway
Leitrim	589	30,572	Carrick-on-Shannon
Mayo	2,084	115,547	Castlebar
Roscommon	951	56,228	Roscommon
Sligo	694	51,263	Sligo
Irish Republic	26,601	2,883,930	Capital: Dublin

*Including county boroughs

IRELAND. One of the British Isles, lying to the west of Great Britain, from which it is separated by the Irish Sea. It is divided into 4 provs.: Ulster, Leinster, Munster, and Connacht; 2 states, Northern Ireland and Rep. of Ireland (*see* table, and under those heads).

The centre of Ireland is a lowland, mainly 200–400 ft. high, but hills are present especially round the coasts, although there are few peaks above 3,000 ft. high, the highest being Carrantuohill (the inverted reaping hook), 3,414 ft., in Macgillicuddy's Reeks, co. Kerry. The entire western coastline is an intricate alternation of bays and estuaries. Several of the rivers flow in sluggish courses through the central lowland, and then cut through fiord-like valleys to the sea. The Shannon in particular falls 100 ft. in its last 16 m. above Limerick and is harnessed at Ardnacrusha (1929) for production of electricity.

The lowland bogs, which cover parts of central Ireland, are intermingled with fertile limestone country where dairy farming is the chief occupation. The bogs are an important source of fuel, in the form of peat, I. being poorly supplied with coal.

The climate is mild, moist, and changeable. The annual rainfall on the lowlands varies from 30 in. in the E. to 80 in. in some western districts, but much higher falls are recorded in the mountains, and as a result it gained the name 'the emerald isle'.

History. In prehistoric times I. underwent a number of invasions from Europe, the most important of which was that of the Gaels in the 3rd cent. B.C. Gaelic I. was divided into kingdoms, nominally subject to an *Ardri* or High King; the chiefs were elected under the tribal or Brehon law, and were usually at war with one another. Christianity was introduced by St. Patrick in c. A.D. 432, and during the 5th–6th cents. I. became the home of a high civilization, sending out missionaries to Britain and Europe. From c. 800 the Danes began to raid I., and later to colonize, founding Dublin and other coast towns, until they were decisively defeated by Brian Boru at Clontarf in 1014.

Anglo-Norman adventurers invaded I. in 1167, but by the end of the Middle Ages English rule was still confined to the Pale, the territory around Dublin. The Tudors adopted a policy of conquest, confiscation of Irish land, and plantation by English settlers, and further imposed the Reformation and English Law on I. The most important of the plantations was that of Ulster, carried out under James I in 1610. The Irish in 1641 took advantage of the opening struggle in England between king and parliament to begin a revolt which was crushed in 1649 by Cromwell, the estates of all 'rebels' being confiscated. Another revolt in 1689–91 was also defeated, and the R.C. majority held down by penal laws. The subordination of the Irish parliament to that of England, and of Irish economic interests to English, led to the rise of a Protestant patriot party, which in 1782 forced the British government to remove many commercial restrictions and grant the Irish parliament its independence. This did not satisfy the mass of the people, who in 1798, influenced by French revolutionary ideas, rose in rebellion, but were again defeated; and in 1800 Pitt induced the Irish parliament to vote itself out of existence by the Act of Union, effective 1 Jan. 1801, under which Ireland was given parliamentary representation at Westminster.

The national movement was revived by O'Connell (q.v.), who secured Catholic emancipation in 1829, and raised the demand for repeal of the union. The Young Ireland and Fenian movements, which organized revolts in 1848 and 1867 respectively, adopted a completely separatist policy. The agitation of the Fenians, and later of the Land League (founded 1879), combined with the parliamentary tactics of Parnell (q.v.), drove Gladstone in turn to disestablish the Irish Church, carry 2 Land Acts safeguarding tenants' rights, and introduce 2 unsuccessful Home Rule Bills. Conservative governments sought to conciliate the peasantry by enabling them to buy their holdings. A new Home Rule Bill in 1912 nearly led

IRELAND. The famed subtropical beauty of Killarney's lakes gives little hint of the intensive industrialization overtaking the surrounding area. No motor transport is allowed to penetrate here and the tourist makes use of a modified version of the traditional jaunting car. *Courtesy of the Irish Tourist Board.*

to civil war between armed nationalist and N. Irish Unionist volunteers. Its outbreak was postponed by the F.W.W., but a rebellion took place in Dublin at Easter 1916, and during 1919–21 the Irish Republican Army waged war on the British govt. This was ended by the treaty of 1921, which divided I. into the Irish Free State and N. Ireland.

IRELAND, Republic of. A sovereign independent state, occupying the larger part of Ireland.

The Republic consists of 26 geographical counties. The pres. (Eamon de Valera 1959, re-elected 1966) is elected by direct vote for 7 years, and there is a House of Representatives (Dáil Éireann) and Senate (Seanad Éireann) elected on a system of proportional representation. The prime minister (Taoiseach) is John Lynch (q.v.) and Fianna Fáil (q.v.) has been the ruling party 1932–48, 1951–4, and from 1957. See also FINE GAEL. The official language is Irish (q.v.), but English is recognized as a second official language. Approx. 93 per cent of the inhabitants are Roman Catholics. Area 26,601 sq. m.; pop. (1966) 2,883,930.

The country came into existence in 1922 as the Irish Free State, with dominion status in the British Commonwealth. A govt. formed by Cosgrave (q.v.) met with a good deal of violent opposition from Irish republicans. De Valera (q.v.) came to office in 1932, and in 1937 introduced a new constitution in which the description Free State was dropped and Eire (Ireland) was declared a sovereign independent state under a president. But the British govt., with the agreement of the other Commonwealth govts., continued to regard Eire as a member of the Commonwealth. Eire was neutral during the S.W.W. When an Irish govt. led by J. A. Costello (q.v.) passed legislation which took it, as the Republic of Ireland, outside the Commonwealth in 1949, the British govt. passed legislation maintaining for Irish citizens in the U.K. most of the advantages of British subjects, and a free trade area was estab. with the U.K. 1966. There is an increasing drift from the land, and growing industrial development by British, U.S. and Continental firms. The chief industries are food processing, brewing and distilling; engineering, vehicle assembly and tyres; mining and electronics, chemicals and tobacco. Tourism is important.

IRENAEUS (irēnē'us), **St.** (c. 130–202). Bishop of Lyons. Probably a native of Smyrna, Asia Minor, he laboured in missionary work among the Gauls, and went to Rome to try to secure better treatment of the Montanists. He became B. of L. on his return, and wrote against Gnostics and Valentinians.

IRE'NE. Greek goddess of peace (Roman 'Pax').

IRENE (c. 752–803). Consort of the eastern Roman emperor Leo IV. A poor orphan girl of Athens, her beauty and gifts won the love of the Emperor, who m. her in 769. On his death in 780 she became regent until 802, when her many cruelties led to her banishment. The Greek Orthodox Church canonized her.

IRETON, Henry (1611–51). English general. In 1642 he joined the Parliamentary forces and fought at Edgehill (1642), Gainsborough (1643), and Naseby (1645). He m. Oliver Cromwell's dau. in 1646. After Naseby I., who was opposed to the extreme Republicans and Levellers, strove to reach a compromise with Charles I, but he subsequently played a leading part in the trial and execution of the latter. I. went to Ireland with Cromwell and in 1650 became lord-deputy there. He d. after the capture of Limerick.

IRIAN. Indonesian name for NEW GUINEA.

IRI'DIUM. Chemical element. Symbol Ir, at. wt. 192·2, at. no. 77. Discovered by Tennant in 1803, I. is a metal of the platinum family; white, very hard and brittle, and usually alloyed with platinum or osmium. It is used for points of fountain-pen nibs, compass bearings, parts of scientific apparatus, and surgical tools. Under neutron bombardment I. becomes a most useful source of gamma rays for industrial radiography, especially for steel up to 2 in. thick, the half-life being 74 days.

IRIS. Plants bearing large flowers of various colours. The plants belong to the monocotyledonous family Iridaceae, Iris genus. The leaves are long and narrow, tapering to a point, the flowers have coloured sepals and petals, and stigmas enlarged into petalloid form which hide the stamens. See FLAG.

IRIS. The coloured part of the eye surrounding the pupil. It contains radiating muscle fibres which dilate and circular ones which contract the pupil in response to the stimulus of light or accommodation to longer or shorter distance.

IRISH. Irish Gaelic is the chief representative of the Gaelic branch of the Celtic languages. Its history falls roughly into 3 periods: Old Irish, from about the 7th to the middle of the 9th cent. A.D.; Middle Irish, from the 9th to the 12th cent.; and Modern Irish from the 13th cent. onwards. In the last period it is usual to distinguish Early Modern Irish, up to the 17th cent. The language of the Ogam inscriptions is earlier than Old Irish.

In spite of efforts to restore I. as the language of Eire there is as yet no standard modern I. which must be studied in its dialects. These are the Southern, the Western, and the Northern, and represent groupings of the cos. of Waterford, Cork, Kerry, Clare; Galway, Mayo; Donegal – the cos. to which I. has been driven back during the course of cents.

I. has been taught in all govt.-subsidised schools since 1922, and is the first official language of the rep., but the number of Irish speakers in genuine Irish-speaking districts (the Gaeltacht) is small and by 1965 only 10,000 children spoke it at home.

Literature. Early Irish literature consists of the sagas which are mainly in prose and a considerable body of verse. The chief cycles are that of Ulster, which deals with the mythological Conchobar and his followers, and the Ossianic, which has influenced European literature through MacPherson's version.

Early Irish poetry has a unique lyric quality and consists mainly of religious verse and nature poetry, e.g. St. Patrick's hymn, Ultán's hymn to St. Brigit, etc. A large amount of pseudo-historical verse is also extant, ascribed to such poets as Mael Mura (9th cent.), Mac Liac (10th cent.), Flann Mainistrech (11th cent.), etc. Religious literature in prose incl. sermons, saints' lives, e.g. those in the *Book of Lismore* and in the writings of Mícheál Ó Cléirigh (17th cent.), and visions. History is represented by annals and by isolated texts like the *Cogad Gaedel re Gallaib*, an

IRISH. Poet and prose writer Pádraic O'Conaire (1882–1928), who travelled the roads with his little donkey, is commemorated by this monument in Galway City.
Courtesy of the Irish Tourist Board.

account of the Viking invasions by an eye-witness.
The Early Modern Irish period is often referred to as the Classical age of Irish literature. The 'official' or 'court' verse of the 13th to 17th cents. was produced by a succession of professional poets, notably Tadhg Dall Ó Huiginn (d. *c.* 1617) and Donnchadh Mór Ó Dálaigh (d. 1244); and Geoffrey Keating (d. *c.* 1646) wrote in both verse and prose.

The bardic schools ceased to exist by the end of the 17th cent. Metre became accentual, and not as before syllabic. The greatest exponents of the new school were Egan O'Rahilly (early 18th cent.), and the religious poet Tadhg Gaelach Ó Súilleabháin. The present revivalist movement has produced writers such as Brian Ó Nualláin, Maurice Ó Sullivan and Thomas Ó Crohan.

IRISH REPUBLICAN ARMY. Extremist organisation, formed Jan. 1919, dedicated to the creation of a united Irish Republic. Its activities in England and Ireland led to stringent measures by the British govt., and it was declared illegal in Eire in 1939. Terrorism sporadically continued, and the I.R.A. was active in the Civil Rights disorders in N. Ireland from 1968, when a bitter division developed between the 'official' organisation, using slightly more regular means, and the 'provisionals' committed to indiscriminate assassination and bomb outrages.

IRISH SWEEPSTAKE. *See* under LOTTERY.

IRISH TERRIER. A brown or reddish-brown Irish breed of dog. The coat is rough, the head long and narrow, forelegs straight and strong, chest narrow, and back straight.

IRKUTSK (irkootsk´). City of the R.S.F.S.R., cap. of I. region, S. Siberia, situated on the Angara river, 45 m. N.W. of Lake Baikal. I., founded in 1652, began to grow after the Trans-Siberian railway reached it in 1898. Coal is found nearby; iron and steel, machine tools and gold-dredging machinery for the goldfields lying to the N., and timber are among its products. The city is a cultural centre with a univ. founded in 1918. Pop. (1967) 409,000.

IRON. The most widely spread of all metals except aluminium (Anglo-Saxon iron; Lat. *ferrum*), symbol Fe, at. wt. 55·85, at. no. 26, said to have been worked into implements by the Egyptians *c.* 3,000 B.C. It is always extracted from 4 main ores: (1) *magnetite*, a black oxide with as much as 68 per cent of iron, found in Swedish Lapland and the Urals; (2) *hematite* or kidney ore, another oxide, red in colour, with as much as 50 to 60 per cent of iron, found W. of Lake Superior, in the Ukraine, in Spain, in Brazil, and in Algeria and Tunis; (3) *limonite*, a brown oxide, with 35 per cent of iron, found in Luxemburg and Lorraine; and lastly (4) *siderite*, a carbonaceous ore, with about 26–42 per cent of iron worked in Yorks, Leics, and Northants. It was the manufacture of steel on a large scale that made the modern demands for I., which is the basis of all steel. Apart from constructional uses, when mixed with carbon and other elements, I. is most important chemically. In electrical equipment, it forms the basis of all permanent and electromagnets and the cores of transformers and magnetic amplifiers. I. is used for anodes in electronic rectifiers, because it is not corroded by mercury. Traces of I. salts in glass give a sharp cut-off for short U.V. rays, and the I.-arc contains a large collection of reference wavelengths useful in spectroscopy.

IRON AGE. Period in which mankind's weapons and tools were of iron, beginning *c.* 1000 B.C.

IRON CROSS. A Prussian decoration, instituted in 1813 and consisting of a Maltese cross of iron, edged with silver. *See* illus. under MEDALS.

IRON CURTAIN. In Europe after the S.W.W. the division between democratic West and Communist E.; first used by Churchill in speech at Fulton, Missouri, 1946.

IRON GATE. Narrow passage, interrupted by rapids, in the Danube below Orsova in Rumania. A

hydro-electric scheme undertaken 1964–70 by Rumania and Yugoslavia transformed the gorge to a 90 m. long lake and eliminated the rapids as a navigation hazard. An archaeological survey before flooding revealed 1965 Europe's oldest urban settlement, Lepenski Vir (6th millenium B.C.).

IRON GUARD. Rumanian Fascist organization, founded in 1927 by Corneliu Codreanu. Violently nationalist, anti-democratic and anti-Semitic, under German pressure I.G. members became in 1940 the nucleus of the govt. Fascist Party. However, on the forced cession of N. Transylvania, R.'s most valued possession, to Hungary, the I.G. overthrew King Carol II, and initiated a reign of terror against the former régime, culminating in an extremist revolt (1941) against the German-controlled govt., which suppressed the revolt and the organization.

IRON PYRITES. Common ore of iron, being the sulphide FeS_2, with about 46 per cent iron content. A brass-yellow, metallic mineral resembling gold (hence 'fool's gold'), it occurs in cubic crystals.

IRONSIDE, William Edmund, 1st baron (1880–1959). British field marshal, C.I.G.S. from 1938 until Dunkirk, and then for 2 months C.-in-C. Home Forces. He was created field marshal in 1940 and a baron in 1941. His diaries 1937–40 were pub. 1962.

IROQUOIS (irohkwoi´). Confederation of N. American Indians. Always friendly to the British and Dutch, they played a most important part in the Anglo-French American wars. They now live in reservations on the Canadian-U.S. border.

IRRADIATION. The process of exposing to radiation with a definite purpose in view. Ultra-violet I. is used in the food and pharmaceutical industries for making vitamin products. X-radiation and radiation from radium and radioactive isotopes are used in industry and medicine for diagnostic photography and in the treatment of certain malignant conditions. Radiation from particle accelerators and nuclear reactors is used in industry, agriculture and medicine; for making radioactive isotopes; and for preservation and sterilization of foods, drugs and prepacked surgical requirements. Gamma rays are used to control infestation in stored grain and other foodstuffs; I. with electrons, gamma-rays or neutrons is used to produce desired properties in plastics.

IRRAWADDY. Chief river of Burma. Its sources are the Mali and N'mai rivers. It crosses the centre of Burma, and flows roughly N. to S., for 1,300 m. into the Bay of Bengal. The chief tributaries are the Chindwin and Shweli.

IRRAWADDY. The fertile soil of the valley and plain of the great river formed the cradle of Burma's civilization, and its waters are still the country's main highway.
Courtesy of the Burmah Oil Co. Ltd.

IRRIGATION. The supplying of water, generally by artificial means, necessary to promote agriculture. The annual overflow of the Nile in Egypt and of the Tigris in Iraq are examples of natural I. Primitive methods of artificial I. have been used in China, India, Mesopotamia, and Egypt since very ancient times, but 19th and 20th cent. development of engineering techniques made possible construction of immense dams for the conservation of water for I. (many also serve other purposes, e.g. production of hydro-electric power, flood control, river regulation). The first constructed to promote I. was the Aswan dam in Egypt, opened 1902: another notable example was the Lloyd Barrage, opened with an accompanying system of canals in 1932 at Sukkur on the Indus (then in British India, after 1947 in Pakistan). A number of dams in the U.S.A. include irrigation among their uses, e.g. Hoover, Colorado r. (1936); Grand Coulee, Columbia r. (1942); Shasta, Sacramento r. (1945); Folsom, American r. (1955). The immense works started in Australia in 1955 for the diversion of the upper waters of the Snowy r. through the Snowy Mountains into the Murrumbidgee were undertaken to provide irrigation (and power) in Victoria and N.S.W. Rather more than a tenth of the land under cultivation in Israel is made usable by artificial I., and artificial I. schemes have been introduced in the Asiatic republics of the U.S.S.R., e.g. in the Syr Daria valley of Kazakh S.S.R.

IRVING, Edward (1792–1834). Scottish minister. Originally a schoolmaster at Haddington, where his pupils incl. Jane Welsh, the future wife of Carlyle, he moved to London in 1822 as a Presbyterian minister. Excommunicated in 1831 for heretical views regarding the humanity of Christ, he constituted in 1835 the Catholic Apostolic Church. Twelve 'apostles' were nominated, the last of whom d. in 1901, and the liturgy is characterized by elaborate ceremonial. The principal church of the body, also known as 'Irving-ites', is in Gordon Square, London.

IRVING, Sir Henry. Stage-name of the British actor John Brodribb (1838–1905). After acting in the provs., he went to London in 1866, and in 1871 began his long connection with the Lyceum Theatre, where he estab. his reputation in *The Bells*, and by his unconventional performance as Hamlet. In 1878 he became manager of the Lyceum, and engaged Ellen Terry as his leading lady, a partnership which lasted until I.'s death. The Lyceum became celebrated for superb and well-mounted productions, incl. *The Merchant of Venice*, with I.'s unusual and sympathetic portrayal of Shylock, *Henry VIII*, *Lear*, and Tennyson's *Becket*. I.'s acting, coloured by his strong personality, was noted for its versatility, spirit and originality; he was knighted in 1895, the first actor ever to be so honoured.

IRVING, Washington (1783–1859). American author. B. in New York City, of English parents, he pub. in 1809 a mock-heroic *History of New York*, supposedly written by the Dutchman 'Diedrich Knickerbocker'. In 1815 he went to England where his publications incl. the *Sketch Book of Geoffrey Crayon, Gent.* (1820), which contained such stories as 'Rip van Winkle' and 'Legend of Sleepy Hollow', and displayed the delicate humour and clear style which are characteristic of his work. He later visited Spain where he wrote amongst other books a *Life of Columbus* (1828), before returning to America in 1832. He was U.S. ambassador to Spain 1842–6. His last years were given mainly to his biographies of Goldsmith (1849) and George Washington (1855–9).

IRWIN (er'win), **Margaret** (d. 1967). Brit. historical novelist. She m. in 1929 the artist J. R. Monsell, and gives a skilled and well-documented interpretation of the Tudor and Stuart periods, e.g. *The Proud Servant* (1934), dealing with Montrose; *The Gay Galliard* (1941), the love story of Mary Queen of Scots; and a

trilogy *The Story of Elizabeth Tudor* (1944–53). *That Great Lucifer* (1960) is a biographical study of Raleigh.

ISAAC (ī'zak). Hebrew patriarch, only son of Abraham and Sarah, and father of Jacob and Esau.

ISAACS, Jorge (1837–95). Colombian poet and novelist. B. at Cali, of Jewish extraction, he pub. *Poesías* (1864), and *María* (1867), a novel of life in his native valley in the Cordilleras.

ISABE'LLA (1451–1504). Queen of Castile, known as Isabella the Catholic. She m. Ferdinand of Aragon in 1469, and in 1474 became queen of Castile in her own right on the death of her brother Henry IV. Thus the crowns of the 2 Christian states in the Spanish peninsula were united. She was largely responsible for the establishment of the Inquisition in Castile and the persecution of the Jews, and gave financial encouragement to Columbus.

ISABELLA II (1830–1904). Queen of Spain. She succeeded her father Ferdinand VII in 1833. The Salic Law banning a female sovereign had been abrogated by the Cortes, but her succession was disputed by her uncle Don Carlos. After 7 years of civil war the Carlists were worsted. She abdicated in favour of her son Alfonso XII in 1870.

ISABEY (ēzahbā'), **Jean Baptiste** (1767–1855). French portrait painter. B. at Nancy, he studied under David, and became court painter to Napoleon, and later to the Bourbon sovereigns. His son EUGÈNE I. (1804–86), was a historical painter.

ISAIAH (īzī'ya). O.T. prophet of the 8th cent. B.C. The son of Amoz, he was probably of high rank, and lived largely in Jerusalem. His call to prophecy is thought to have come *c.* 740, and he saw Assyria as the avenging weapon of Jahweh whom the Israelites had forsaken.

ISE (ēs'ā). Prov. of Honshu Is., Japan, centre of the Shinto cult. The shrines, of which the most sacred is that of the sun-goddess at Yamada, are rebuilt every 20 yrs. in the strict early tradition of a thatched hut in perfected form.

ISÈRE. River of S.E. France rising near the Italian frontier and flowing 180 m. generally W., to enter the Rhône 7 m. above Valence. A dam was completed in 1952 to harness its rapid flow for electricity. It gives its name to the dept. of I.

ISFAHAN (ēsfah-hahn'). City of Persia, chief town of the prov. of I. and Yazd on the Zaindeh r. The city reached its greatest prosperity and splendour when Shah Abbas I (1586–1628) made it the Persian capital. After the onslaught of the Afghans in 1722 its political significance diminished, and the cap. was

ISFAHAN. Iran's principal industrial city, developing apace under the guidance of the Shah, still preserves the best of the past in the Great Square with its trees and fountains and beautiful buildings. *Courtesy of Imperial Iranian Embassy.*

moved to Tehran. Notable features are the Great Square, the Grand Mosque, and the Hall of the Forty Pillars. Pop. (1964) 339,909.

I'SHAM, Ralph (1890–1955). American financier. A collector of books and MSS., he was responsible for the acquisition in 1927 and 1930 of the neglected private papers of James Boswell (q.v.), from his descendant Lord Talbot of Malahide, and for the discovery and publication of further papers, e.g. those found by Prof. Abbott at Fettercairn House in 1931.

I'SHERWOOD, Christopher William Bradshaw (1904–). English novelist. Ed. at Cambridge, as described in the autobiographical *Lions and Shadows* (1938), he later spent a fruitful period in Germany which inspired *Mr. Norris Changes Trains* (1935) and *Goodbye to Berlin* (1939). Returning to England, he collaborated with Auden (q.v.) in 3 verse plays. He then went to Hollywood as a scriptwriter, and joined the Huxley-Beard group, who were practising a form of Yoga in the Californian desert, and from 1944 collaborated with Swami Prabhavananda in a translation of the *Bhagavad-Gita*, etc.

ISHMAEL (ish'mā-el). O.T. character, the son of Abraham and Hagar, his wife's Egyptian handmaid, and regarded as the father of the Arab people. Driven out into the desert with his mother because of Sarah's jealousy, Ishmael grew up to be a famous archer in the wilderness of Paran. Mohammed claimed to be his descendant.

ISHTAR or **Istar**. The 'Lady of Heaven', the chief goddess in the Babylonian and Assyrian pantheon. She was identified with Astarte.

I'SINGLASS. Pure form of gelatin obtained from the cleaned and dried swimming-bladder of various fish, particularly the sturgeon. I. is used in the clarification of wines and beer, and in cookery.

I'SIS. The principal goddess of ancient Egypt. She was the dau. of Geb and Nut (earth and sky), and as the sister-wife of Osiris searched for his body after his death at the hands of his brother Set. Her son Horus then defeated and captured Set, but cut off his mother's head because she would not allow Set to be killed. She was later identified with Hathor (q.v.). The cult of Isis ultimately spread to Greece and Rome.

ISIS. Name sometimes given to the upper stretches of the Thames, England, above Oxford.

ISKENDERUN (iskenderoon'). Town and naval base in Hatay, Turkey. It is the main port for the area, with an oil pipeline to Batman, and was founded by Alexander the Great, 333 B.C. Pop. (1960) 24,000.

I'SLAM (Arabic for 'submission' i.e. to the will of Allah). One of the great world religions, also known as Mohammedanism, after its founder the prophet Mohammed (q.v.). The fundamental beliefs are contained in the creed: There is no God but Allah, and Mohammed is the Prophet or Apostle of Allah. The Oneness of God is emphasized [cf. the Christian Trinity], as are his omnipotence, beneficence, and inscrutability. He only is divine and idolatry or saint-worship is therefore regarded as blasphemous. Mohammedans (Muslims or Moslems) also believe in the Creation, the Fall of Adam, the Angels and the Jinn (q.v.), Heaven and Hell, a Day of Judgment, God's predestination of good and evil, and in a succession of scriptures revealed by Allah to a line of prophets, incl. the Pentateuch given to Moses, and the Gospel of Jesus; the ultimate and perfect revelation is in the Koran (q.v.) of Mohammed. The latter embodies the Islamic Law (the Shari'a or 'Highway'), which can be clarified by reference to the *sunna* (practice) of the Prophet, as transmitted by his Companions: the *Sunni* sect also employ *ijma'* (endorsement by universal consent of practices and beliefs not warranted by the Koran or the sunna).

Each individual Muslim is personally responsible for his religious life; there is no separate 'church'

organization or privileged priesthood, although the descendants of Mohammed, the *Hashim* family, are a class apart and wield great influence. Five practical obligations – 'The Pillars of the Faith' – are demanded of each Muslim: recitation of the Creed, at least once, and with understanding and faith; worship of Allah at the 5 appointed times each day, facing towards Mecca, the Holy City (q.v.); almsgiving; fasting from day-break till sunset throughout the month of *Ramadan* for all Muslims except the sick, travellers, soldiers on active service, etc.; and at least once in his lifetime the pilgrimage to Mecca.

The law also covers the institutions of the seclusion and veiling of women, marriage, divorce, inheritance, etc.; requires the circumcision of all male Muslims; authorizes up to 4 wives; forbids wine, the flesh of swine, usury, etc. The Koran recognizes slavery, but only of non-Muslim captives; the white slaves (*mamlucks*), usually Turks, in the Islamic slave-army were often manumitted and received administrative appointments, occasionally founding their own dynasties, e.g. the slave kings of Delhi and the Mame-lukes (q.v.) in Egypt. (*See also* JANISSARIES.) The duty of the Holy War or *jihad* against Unbelievers as the enemies of Allah was once preached and practised, and Arabic conquests spread I. to Asia, Russia, N. Africa, Spain (expelled 15th cent. A.D.), Pakistan and India, the Balkans, Indonesia and China. The last Holy War, however, proclaimed by the sultan of Turkey in 1914 against the Allies in the F.W.W., was of little importance, and I. has since lost influence in the Balkans; it has, however, been spread in the last 2 cents. by immigrant groups, and missionary work, e.g. by the Ahmadiyya (q.v.) movement, to the rest of Africa, and to N. and S. America. The number of Muslims is est. at c. 430 millions, of whom c. 12 m. are in Europe, c. 328 m. in Asia, and c. 88 m. in Africa.

The supreme political and religious ruler of the I. Community was the Caliph (q.v.), aided by the Vizier (wazir 'helper'). The 3 main sects into which I. became divided, the *Sunnis* (the majority party), the *Shiahs* or *Shi'ites* (qq.v.) and the *Kharijites*, originated in differing theories on the office of the Caliph, but have since developed differences in theology, etc.; later sects incl. the *Wahhabis* (q.v.) and the *Ahmadiyas*. I. was distinctive as a comprehensive political, legal and social system based on a religion, as opposed to a religious institution contained within a secular state. In the last 2 cents., nationalism, in e.g. Turkey, India and Pakistan, has often come before the ideal of a united Islam, and this, together with western influence on systems of govt., has led to basic changes in secular matters.

ISLA'MABAD. Cap. of Pakistan from 1967, in the Potwar district of W. Pakistan, at the foot of the Margala Hills and immediately N.W. of Rawalpindi. Designed by Doxiadis (q.v.) it is well landscaped and the Civic Centre on Capital Avenue is a notable feature. Pop. (1966) 30,000.

ISLAY (i'lā). Most southerly island of the Inner Hebrides, Scotland, forming part of the co. of Argyll, separated from Jura by the Sound of Islay. The principal towns are Bowmore and Port Ellen. Area 235 sq. m.; pop. (1961) 3,866.

ISLE OF ELY. *See* ELY, ISLE OF.

ISLE OF MAN. Island in the Irish Sea lying almost equidistant from Scotland to the N., Ireland to the W., Wales to the S., and England to the E. Nearly 50 per cent of the island is cultivated, oats being the principal crop. The cap. is Douglas; other towns incl. Ramsey, Peel, and Castletown. Shipping and air services link the I. of M. with England, Scotland and Ireland. The island is a popular holiday resort, and annual motor-cycle races are held.

Among the island's fauna is the tailless Manx cat. Pile dwellings, etc., show evidence of prehistoric settlement, and Christianity spread throughout the

ISLE OF MAN. The island's sailing centre is Port St. Mary, set among beautiful scenery on the south coast, overlooking the Calf of Man. To the south of the town, on Spanish Head, one of the Armada ships was wrecked.
Courtesy of Isle of Man Tourist Board.

island during the Celtic period. For *c.* 500 years Man and some of the Scottish islands were nominally under the Norwegian kings. Magnus, last king of Man and the Isles, d. in 1265 and *c.* 1266 M. passed to Scotland. From 1290 English and Scottish rule alternated; in 1406 the Stanley family were granted the territory by Henry IV, but were succeeded in 1736 by the dukes of Atholl, when the island became a great smuggling centre. In 1866 the I. of M. obtained home rule. The govt. is composed of a Crown-appointed Lieut.-Gov., the Legislative Council, and the representative House of Keys. Together these make up the Tynwald Court, which passes laws subject to the Royal Assent. Acts passed by parliament in London do not affect the I. of M. unless it is specifically named. Area 227 sq. m.; pop. (1965) 50,423.

ISLE OF WIGHT (wīt). Island off the S. coast of England, geographically part of Hants, it is separate administratively. It is divided from the mainland by the Solent on the N.W. and Spithead on the N.E. The chalk cliffs of the S. coast end on the W. in the Needles. The island is composed of agricultural and sheep-grazing land, but there are many holiday resorts, e.g. Sandown, Ventnor, Ryde, Shanklin. Inland is Carisbrooke. The cap. is Newport: near Cowes, the chief port, is Osborne House. The Romans called the island Vectis, meaning 'separate division': it was conquered by Vespasian in A.D. 43. Area 147 sq. m.; pop. (1967) 98,040

I'SLINGTON. Inner bor. of Greater London, England, incl. the residential district of Canonbury, Pentonville and Holloway prisons, and the 'Angel' tavern. The 'Caledonian Market' held in the Metropolitan Cattle Market (1885–1939) sold everything from food to antiques: the site was acquired by the

ISLE OF WIGHT. The chalk downs which run across the island culminate in the west in the Needles. A lighthouse warns shipping to keep clear.
Photo: Aerofilms Ltd.

G.L.C. for housing, etc. 1964. Pop. (1967) 254,580.

ISMAIL (isma-ēl') (1830–95). Khedive of Egypt. A grandson of Mehemet Ali, he became viceroy of Egypt in 1863 and in 1866 received the title of Khedive from the Sultan. In 1875 Britain, at Disraeli's suggestion, bought the Khedive's Suez Canal shares for £3,976,582, and Anglo-French control of Egypt's finances was estab. In 1879 Britain and France persuaded the Sultan to appoint Tewfik, his son, Khedive in his place.

ISMAILIA (isma-ēlē'ah). Town on the shore of Lake Timsah, Lower Egypt, near the entrance into the lake of the Suez Canal. I. came into existence in 1863 as H.Q. for the construction of the canal, and was named after Ismail (q.v.). Pop. (1960) 111,000.

I'SOBAR. A line drawn on maps and weather charts linking all places with the same atmospheric pressure. When used in weather forecasting, the distance apart of the Is. is an indication of the barometric gradient. Where they are close together cyclonic weather is indicated, and where far apart anticyclonic. The pressures indicated on the met. charts have generally been corrected to sea-level.

ISO'CRATES (436–338 B.C.). Athenian orator. One of the pupils of Socrates, he started his celebrated school about 392 B.C. Hampered in public life by nervousness, he was unrivalled as a composer of literary speeches. Shortly after Philip's victory at Chaeronea, I. committed suicide.

ISOLA'TION. Segregation of persons exposed to or suffering from an infectious disease, to prevent its spread. Isolation or fever hospitals are kept by many local authorities for patients suffering from the notifiable infectious diseases.

ISOLATIONISTS. The section of opinion in the U.S.A. which up to 1941 opposed all American intervention in European politics. They were more numerous among the Republicans than among the Democrats, and drew their greatest support from the Republican stronghold of the Middle West.

ISO'MERISM. The existence of more than one compound having the same molecular composition and weight, but with different properties, due to the changed arrangement of the atoms in the molecules. Some organic compounds and complex inorganic salts exhibit this phenomenon.

ISOME'TRICS. System of muscular exercises without apparatus, e.g. by opposing one set of muscles to another.

ISOMOR'PHISM. Crystalline similarity in chemically related substances. In mathematics it means correspondence between the operations of groups.

ISO'PODA. Order of marine, freshwater, and terrestrial crustaceans, having no exoskeleton.

I'SOPRENE (C_6H_8). A volatile fluid which forms substances similar to rubber by polymerization.

I'SOTHERM. On a map, a line linking all places having the same temperature either at a given time, or over a given period. Is. may show either actual temperature relations, or temperatures reduced to sea-level readings, 1·5°C or 2·7°F (moist air) to 3°C or 5·4°F (dry air), is subtracted for every 1,000 ft. of altitude.

I'SOTOPES. Substances having different atomic weights, although chemically identical, with the same atomic number and occupying the same place in the periodic table of the elements, are said to be Is., i.e., the atoms which are Is. of a particular element have a varying number of neutrons in their nuclei, but the same number of protons and orbiting electrons. Is. were shown to exist at the beginning of this century from investigations of natural radioactivity, and their importance has grown enormously, many hundreds now being known. They may be stable or unstable, naturally occurring or man-made. When naturally occurring all the Is. of an element occur in a fixed proportion. Most of the man-made Is. in the U.K.

are made and distributed by the U.K.A.E.A. (q.v.).

ISPAHAN. *See* ISFAHAN.

I'SRAEL. Independent republic of S.W. Asia, part of Palestine (q.v.). It was set up in 1948 immediately on the ending of the British League of Nations mandate for Palestine, and was accepted as a member of the U.N. in 1949. The Law of Return, 1950, provides that 'every Jew shall be entitled to come to Israel as an immigrant'. The head of state is a pres. elected directly for 5 years: the first holder of the office was Chaim Weizmann (q.v.). A single-chamber parliament (Knesset) is elected on a system of proportional representation for 4 years by universal suffrage. There is a cabinet headed by a P.M. (a post first held by David Ben-Gurion, q.v.). I., at once attacked by neighbouring Arab states, succeeded in holding them at bay, and armistices were concluded in 1949 with Jordan, Lebanon, Syria, and Egypt. Intermittent incidents continued, however, with large-scale fighting against Egypt (q.v.) in the Sinai campaign 1956, and the Israeli-Arab war of 5-10 June 1967, when Israeli forces again under Major-Gen. Moshe Dayan overran the Sinai peninsula, gained control of the Old City of Jerusalem, conquered the whole of Jordan W. of the r. Jordan, and invaded Syria to within 40 m. of Damascus. Guerrilla operations against I. by the rival Arab organizations, Popular Front for the Liberation of Palestine and Al Fatah, continued, accompanied by reprisals by Israel: technically the attack is on Zionism not the Jews.

The cap. is (the Israeli part of) Jerusalem; other large towns are Haifa and Tel Aviv-Jaffa. Hebrew is the national language, Judaism the official religion; other beliefs are tolerated. Intensive efforts, incl. development of artificial irrigation (e.g. in the Negev), are making for an improved agriculture in this formerly poor country. The salt deposits of the Dead Sea are the chief mineral resource; copper is found in the S. near Eilat. Manufactures incl. textiles, chemicals, plastics, tobacco, and precision instruments. Area 8,000 sq. m.; pop. (1967) 2,657,000 (incl. 312,000 non-Jews.

Historically, ISRAEL was the name of the northern kingdom of Palestine formed by those Jewish tribes which, after the death of Solomon, seceded from the rule of his son Rehoboam, and elected Jeroboam as their king.

ISTANBUL (-bool′). City and chief seaport of Turkey, formerly cap. of the Turkish Empire. Occupying the site of the ancient Byzantium and Constantinople (qq.v.), I. stands on the western shore of the Bosphorus at the point where it enters

the Sea of Marmara, thus controlling the route between the Mediterranean and the Black Sea. To the N. of the promontory on which I. stands is the 4 m. long harbour of the Golden Horn. Surrounding the nucleus of the city on the promontory are a number of suburbs: Galata (the shipping and banking centre) and Pera (the European quarter) are N.E. of the Golden Horn, but W. of the Bosphorus; Uskudar (the industrial and commercial centre) lies on the E. (Asiatic) side of the Bosphorus. Industries are numerous and varied.

Famous monuments are the Great Mosque, formerly the church of St. Sophia, which was built by Justinian in the 6th cent. on the site of the building erected by Constantine and rebuilt by Theodosius II in 415; and the alleged sarcophagus of Alexander (*c.* 300 B.C.) and that of the emperor Constantine.

In 1453 the city, which for 11 cents. had been the capital of the Roman Empire, was taken by the Turks and remained capital of the Ottoman Empire until 1923, when Ankara became the capital of the Turkish republic. Pop. (1965) 2,230,911.

ITALIAN. One of the main Romance languages derived from Latin, which it closely resembles. It originated in its present form in Tuscany in the Middle Ages, acquiring prestige through its use by Dante, though the renewed use and influence of Latin during the Renaissance period tended to make of written Italian a stilted and artificial language bearing little resemblance to the popular tongue. By the middle of the 19th cent. Florentine usage had come to be universally accepted as a basis for the written language. However, outside Tuscany, dialect is still the general conversational medium. D'Annunzio (q.v.) coined many new words.

Literature. It originated in the 13th cent. with the Sicilian school which imitated Provençal poetry. The contemporary works of St. Francis of Assisi and Jacopone da Todi reflect the religious faith of the time. Guido Guinicelli (1230–*c.* 1275) and Guido Cavalcanti (*c.* 1250–1300) developed the spiritual conception of love and influenced Dante Alighieri, whose *Divina Commedia* is the greatest work of I.L. Petrarch was a humanist and a poet, while Boccaccio is principally known for his short stories.

The 15th cent. marked the beginning of the Renaissance. Boiardo dealt with the Carolingian epics in his *Orlando Inammorato* which was completed and transformed by Lodovico Ariosto as *Orlando Furioso*. Their contemporaries Niccolo Machiavelli and Francesco Guicciardini (1483–1540) are outstanding historians. Torquato Tasso wrote his epic *Gerusalemme Liberata* in the spirit of the Counter-Reformation.

The 17th cent. was characterized by the exaggeration of the poets Giovanni Battista Marini (1569–1625) and Gabriello Chiabrera (1552–1638). In 1690 the 'Academy of Arcadia' was formed: its members incl. Innocenzo Frugoni (1692–1768) and Metastasio. Other writers incl. Salvator Rosa, the satirist. During the 18th cent. Giuseppe Parini (1729–99) ridiculed the abuses of his day, while Vittorio Alfieri attacked tyranny in his dramas. Carlo Goldoni wrote comedies and Ugo Foscolo (1778–1827) is chiefly remembered for his patriotic verse. Giacomo Leopardi is not only the greatest lyrical poet since Dante, but also a master of Italian prose; the Romantic, Alessandro Manzoni, is best known as a novelist, and influenced amongst others the novelist Antonio Fogazzaro. A later outstanding literary figure and poet, Giosuè Carducci, was followed by the verbose Gabriele d'Annunzio, writing of sensuality and violence, and Benedetto Croce, historian and philosopher, who between them dominated I. literature at the turn of the cent.; other writers were the realist novelist Giovanni Verga, the dramatist Luigi Pirandello, and the novelists Ignazio Silone and Italo Svevo. Poets of the period jncl.

ISTANBUL. The Galata bridge crosses the Golden Horn to the part of the city built on the site of ancient Byzantium. It also serves to divide this splendid natural anchorage into an outer harbour, and inner harbour and naval port.
Courtesy of the Turkish Embassy

ITALIAN ART. Doge of Venice 1501–21, Leonardo Loredan ruled the great city-state at the turning point of its history. This portrait by Giovanni Bellini is one of the greatest of the age. *Courtesy of the National Gallery.*

Dino Campana, Giuseppe Ungaretti and among the modern school are Eugenio Montale and Salvatore Quasimodo. Novelists of the post-Fascist period, preoccupied with political and moral problems, incl. Alberto Moravia, Carlo Levi, Cesare Pavese (1908–50), Vasco Pratolini (1913–), Elsa Morante (1916–), Giuseppe Tomasi, Prince of Lampedusa, and the younger writer Italo Calvino (1923–).

ITALIAN ART. Italy is rich in examples of the Byzantine style of architecture which is a mixture of oriental and classical elements; such are the monuments of Justinian in Ravenna and the later church of St. Mark's in Venice. The Romanesque style was developed in Italy from the 10th to the 13th cents. Examples of this style are the churches of Lombardy; the baptistery, cathedral, and Leaning Tower of Pisa; and the cathedrals of Sicily. The Gothic period in Italy developed from the 13th to the 15th cents. It is based on Romanesque and differs a great deal from the Gothic style of northern Europe. Façades were elaborately decorated; mosaics and coloured marble were used, and sculpture – delicately carved – was placed around windows and doors.

The history of It. painting begins in the latter half of the 13th cent., or in Italian parlance the *Duecento*. Giotto is usually regarded as the first great Italian painter. He broke away from the traditional formal style, and created a world of beauty that is related to the world of everyday life. An earlier painter, Cimabue, may have been Giotto's master. Other great artists of the *Duecento* were the sculptors Niccola Pisano and his son, Giovanni, and the painter Duccio.

The most famous names of the 14th cent. – the *Trecento* – include the Florentines Bernardo Daddi (c. 1290–1348); Taddeo Gaddi and his son Agnolo; the Sienese Ambrogio and Pietro Lorenzetti; and the Veronese painter, Vittore Pisano.

The next period in I.A. is called the *Renaissance* (15th and 16th cents.), i.e. 'rebirth' of the classical spirit. The architectural style was developed by Brunelleschi and his contemporaries. The most famous achievement is the basilica of St. Peter's, Rome, with which Michelangelo's name is associated.

The great artists of the Renaissance include Ghiberti, the sculptor of the 'Doors of Paradise' of the Florentine baptistery; Donatello, the greatest sculptor of the period; Luca della Robbia; Masaccio, famous for his paintings in the Carmelite church, Florence; Fra Angelico; Uccello who achieved fame as a pioneer in scientific perspective; Pollaiuolo, another famous experimenter; the Bellini family; Mantegna; Andrea del Verrocchio, sculptor of the Colleoni memorial, the greatest equestrian statue of the Renaissance; Sandro Botticelli; Leonardo da Vinci, the great mind of the Renaissance; Michelangelo, the greatest artistic genius of the period; Raphael, painter of the 'Sistine Madonna'; Titian, who was supreme as a colourist; Tintoretto, who was Titian's pupil; Correggio; and Veronese.

The most famous names of the following *Baroque* period are those of the sculptor and architect Bernini, and in painting Caravaggio and the Caracci. The 18th and earlier 19th cents. were dominated by the Neo-Classic movement, seeking inspiration from the works of the past rather than life itself, and it was not until the rise of the Futurist (q.v.) school, e.g. Gino Severini (1883–), and the succeeding Metaphysical school, e.g. Carlo Carra (1881–) that a revival came. Modigliani is an outstanding figure at the beginning of the 20th cent., but the Fascist régime was no breeding ground for great art. In more recent years there have been a no. of interesting sculptors incl. Giacomu Manzu (1908–), Marino Marini, and Emilio Greco: Annigoni is a popular portrait painter.

ITALICS. *In printing, the letters sloping towards the right as used in this article. Nowadays they are usually employed, side by side with the erect Roman type, for purposes of emphasis and citation. Aldus Manutius (q.v.) of Venice first introduced italics of the lower case in 1501, and only later also replaced the Roman capitals by capitals of the I. type. Is. were soon in vogue in Italy and imitated in other countries.*

ITALY. Republic of S. Europe bordering on France, Switzerland, Austria, and Yugoslavia on the W., N., and E., and stretching S.E. as a long peninsula into the Mediterranean. Area 116,365 sq. m.; pop. (1967) 53,649,000.

I. is bounded on the N. by the semi-circle of the Alps, from just E. of Monaco on the W. to the Adriatic on the E.; elsewhere by the sea. The coastline measures about 4,500 m. The Alps, among which lie the famous lakes Maggiore, Lugano, and Garda, slope down to the northern plain which is drained by the Po and its tributaries, the Adige and the Piave.

The peninsula of central and southern I. consists of the Apennines, which diverge from the maritime Alps round the Gulf of Genoa, and their valleys and foothills. These mountains rise into isolated limestone peaks, such as the Gran Sasso (9,580 ft.). Of the rivers, the Tiber and the Arno, on which stand Rome and Florence respectively, are important. The rep. of I. incl. the large islands of Sicily and Sardinia and a number of smaller ones, among them Elba, Capri, Ischia, the Lipari Islands. I. contains the only active volcanoes in Europe: Vesuvius, Stromboli, and Etna.

The climate is a good deal hotter in the S. than in the N. where some of the Alpine heights are covered with perpetual snow. The northern plain has a continental climate – hot in summer, cool in winter. In the peninsula the surrounding sea tempers summer heat; heavy snowfalls are common in winter in the mountainous backbone of the country. The chief rains, varying from 30 in. in the lowlands to upwards of 50 in. in the mountains, fall during Feb.–March.

The cap. is Rome; other large cities incl. Milan, Turin, Florence, Bologna, Verona, Padua, and Ferrara, and the ports of Genoa, La Spezia, Leghorn, Naples, Reggio di Calabria, and Palermo to the W.; Taranto on the S.E.; Brindisi, Bari, Ancona, Venice and Trieste on the E. coast.

The main rail lines are state-owned, and electrified and re-equipped since the S.W.W.; there is a motorway system, and Alitalia (chief airline) is state-run.

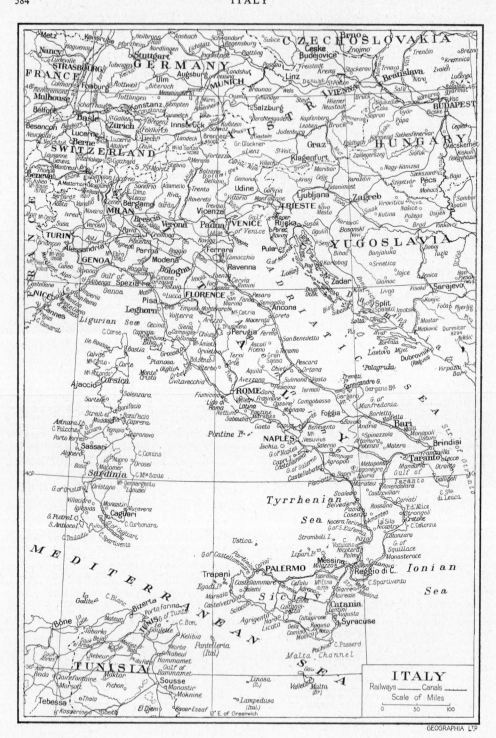

ITALY

Railways ——— Canals ———

Scale of Miles

0   50   100

GEOGRAPHIA LTD

Economics. A quarter of the working population is engaged in agriculture. The continental plain, the area round Naples and Tuscany, is very fertile. Wheat is the most important cereal and maize is cultivated as an alternative crop. Rice is grown in Lombardy, Piedmont and elsewhere. The vine is cultivated throughout I. Olive oil and chestnuts are universal foods; the orange, lemon, fig, and almond are important in the S. I. produces more silk than any other European country. Hemp, flax, and cotton are grown. Cattle, sheep, goats, and pigs are reared. Emilia and Lombardy produce famous cheeses.

I. has few minerals. Volcanic products include sulphur (Sicily), borax (Tuscany), pumice and lava stone. Tuscany has rich mercury deposits. Sardinia is rich in lead, copper and zinc, and Elba in iron. Carrara and Siena produce marble. Petroleum and natural gas are worked in Sicily; there are small deposits of coal in Sardinia and of lignite in Arezzo, Pisa, and Grosseto; this scarcity of coal has encouraged the development of water power which provides three-quarters of the electricity available. Formerly industry was concentrated in the N., but the state steelworks at Taranto form the focus for large-scale development in the poorer S. Other industries are textiles (cotton, silk, woollen, and man-made fibres), chemicals, motor vehicles, leather goods, food-processing, etc.

Government. I., which had been a monarchy since its unification in 1870, became a rep. in 1946 (*see*

REGIONS OF ITALY

	Area in sq. m.	Pop. (1961 census)	Capitals
Abruzzi e Molise	5,881	1,584,777	Aquila
Apulia	7,470	3,409,687	Bari
Basilicata	3,856	648,085	Potenza
Calabria	5,812	2,045,215	Reggio di Calabria
Campania	5,249	4,756,094	Naples
Emilia-Romagna	8,553	3,646,507	Bologna
Friuli-Venezia Giulia	3,111	1,205,222	Udine
Latium	6,630	3,922,783	Rome
Liguria	2,089	1,717,630	Genoa
Lombardy	9,191	7,390,492	Milan
Marches	3,742	1,347,234	Ancona
Piedmont	9,804	3,889,962	Turin
Sardinia	9,301	1,413,289	Cagliari
Sicily	9,923	4,711,783	Palermo
Trentino-Alto Adige	5,256	785,491	Trento
Tuscany	8,877	3,267,374	Florence
Umbria	3,265	788,546	Perugia
Valle d'Aosta	1,260	99,754	Aosta
Veneto	7,095	3,833,837	Venice
	116,365	50,463,762	

History below). It has a parliament of 2 houses – a Chamber of Deputies elected by universal direct suffrage for 5 years and a Senate elected for 6 years. The head of state is a Pres. elected for 7 years by a joint session of the houses of parl.; he must secure a two-thirds majority. He is assisted by a cabinet led by a P.M., and may dissolve parl. except during the last 6 months of his term of office.

Under the Italian constitution of 1947 there are 20 regions (incl. Molise, *see* Table, 5 being special regions with a higher degree of autonomy (Friuli-Venezia Giulia, Sardinia, Sicily, Trentino-Alto Adige, Valle d'Aosta) and 15 ordinary regions which elected their first regional councils in 1970. Under a treaty between the papacy and I. made in 1929, the Roman Catholic religion is the state religion; it is professed by more than 90 per cent of the people. Other faiths are allowed.

History. The varying peoples inhabiting I. – Etruscans in Tuscany, Latins and Sabines in middle

I., Greek colonies in the S. and Sicily, and Gauls in the N. – were united under Roman rule during the 4th–3rd cents. B.C. With the decline of the Roman Empire, and its final extinction in A.D. 476, I. became exposed to the attacks of the barbarians, and passed in turn under the rule of the Ostrogoths and the Lombards. The 8th cent. witnessed the rise of the papacy as a territorial power, the annexation of the Lombard kingdom by Charlemagne, and his coronation as emperor of the west in 800. Henceforward until 1250 Italian history turns in the main on the relations, at first friendly and later hostile, between the papacy and the Holy Roman Empire. During this

ITALY. The Italian architect of every period excels in the use of statuary and fountains to increase the effect of his work. Here is the Pretoria Fountain in Palermo, Sicily.
Courtesy of the Italian State Tourist Office.

struggle the Italian cities seized the opportunity to convert themselves into self-governing republics. By 1300 five major powers existed in I.: the city-republics of Milan, Florence and Venice; the papal states; and the kingdom of Naples. Their mutual rivalries and constant wars laid I. open during 1494–1559 to invasions from France and Spain; as a result Naples and Milan passed under Spanish rule. After 1700 Austria secured Milan and replaced Spain as the dominating power, while Naples passed to a Spanish Bourbon dynasty, and Sardinia to the dukes of Savoy. The period of French rule (1796–1814) temporarily unified I., and introduced the principles of the French Revolution, but after Napoleon's fall I. was again divided between Austria, the Pope, the kingdoms of Sardinia and Naples, and 4 smaller duchies. Nationalist and democratic ideals nevertheless remained alive, and inspired attempts at revolution in 1820, 1831 and 1848–9. After this last failure the Sardinian monarchy assumed the leadership of the national movement. With the help of Napoleon III the Austrians were expelled from Lombardy in 1859; the duchies joined the Italian kingdom; Garibaldi overthrew the Neapolitan monarchy; and Victor Emmanuel II of Sardinia was proclaimed king of Italy at Turin in 1861. Venice and part of Venetia were secured by another war with Austria in 1866; in 1870 Italian forces occupied Rome, thus completing the unification of I., and the Pope ceased to be a temporal ruler until 1929 (*see* VATICAN CITY). In 1878 Victor Emmanuel II died, and was succeeded by Humbert (Umberto) I, his son, who was assassinated in 1900. The formation of a colonial empire began in 1869 with the purchase of land on the Bay of Assab, on the Red Sea, from the local sultan. In the next 20 years the Italians occupied all Eritrea which was made a colony in

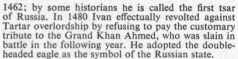

ITALY. Her place in the modern world is illustrated by the signature, on 25 March 1957, of the Rome treaty setting up the European Economic Community at the Palazzo dei Conservatori on the Capitoline Hill.
Courtesy of the Information Service of the European Communities.

1889. An attempt to seize Ethiopia was decisively defeated at Adowa in 1896. War with Turkey in 1911–12 gave Tripoli and Cyrenaica. I.'s intervention in the F.W.W. on the Allied side secured her Trieste, the Trentino, and S. Tirol. The post-war period was marked by intense political and industrial unrest, culminating in 1922 in the establishment of Mussolini's Fascist dictatorship. The régime embraced a policy of aggression with the conquest of Ethiopia in 1935–6 and of Albania in 1939, and I. entered the S.W.W. in 1940 as the ally of Germany. Defeat in Africa 1941–3 and the Allied conquest of Sicily in 1943 resulted in Mussolini's downfall; the new govt. declared war on Germany, and until 1945 I. was a battlefield between German occupying forces and the advancing Allies. In 1946 Victor Emmanuel III, who had been king since 1900, abdicated in favour of his son Humbert (Umberto) II, who abdicated later in the year, following a referendum in which 12,718,641 votes were cast for a rep., 10,718,502 for the monarchy; whereupon a rep. was proclaimed.

A peace treaty between I. and the Allies was signed and ratified in 1947. It deprived I. of its colonial empire and transferred to Yugoslavia Zara (Zadar) and part of Venezia Giulia; to France 4 small areas in the Alpes Maritimes; to Greece the Dodecanese. Trieste (q.v.), which the Allies proposed to make a free territory, was in 1954 returned to I. Post-war expansion and economic development has been rapid. The Christian Democrats (centre-left) have led numerous Coalitions since the S.W.W.; there is the largest Communist Party in W. Europe.

ITCH. Irritation of nerve endings in skin or mucous membrane not amounting to pain. 'The itch' is scabies, an eruption produced by the burrowing into the skin of the female of the minute parasite *Acarus scabiei.*

ITO (ē'tō), **Hirobumi,** Prince (1841–1909). Japanese statesman. He assisted in the modernization of the Japanese state, and between 1886 and 1901 he was 4 times P.M. He drafted the constitution of 1890, and the Anglo-Japanese Alliance of 1902 was largely his work. In 1906 he became resident-gen. in Korea, and was made a prince (1907). He was shot dead by a Korean at Harbin.

IVAN III (ēvahn') (1440–1505), called 'the Great'. Grand duke of Moscow, he succeeded his father in

ITCH MITE

1462; by some historians he is called the first tsar of Russia. In 1480 Ivan effectually revolted against Tartar overlordship by refusing to pay the customary tribute to the Grand Khan Ahmed, who was slain in battle in the following year. He adopted the double-headed eagle as the symbol of the Russian state.

IVAN IV (1530–84). Tsar of Russia, called 'the Terrible'. Son of the grand duke of Muscovy, he became grand duke on the death of his father in 1533 and was actual ruler from 1544. In 1547 he was crowned the first tsar of Russia, and embarked upon a period of internal consolidation and external conquest of Kazan, Astrakhan and W. Siberia. After 1560 he developed into a ferocious tyrant, and from 1564 he lived away from Moscow, his life being passed in alternate debauchery and religious austerities.

IVANOV (ēvahn'of), **Vsevolod Vyacheslavovich** (1895–1963). Russian novelist. B. in Siberia, he worked at a multitude of jobs before settling in Petrograd in 1921 to write. His most famous book is *Armoured Train 14–69* (1933), which was very successfully dramatized and represents the spirit of the insurgent proletariat.

IVANOVO. Cap. of I. region, R.S.F.S.R., 150 m. N.E. of Moscow; an industrial centre with textile, chemical, and engineering works. Pop. (1967) 398,000.

IVEAGH (ī'va), **Edward Cecil Guinness,** 1st earl of (1847–1927). British philanthropist. A son of Sir Benjamin G., he became chairman of the Dublin brewery, but retired in 1889. He estab. the Guinness' Trust for the building of working-class homes in Dublin and London, etc., and bequeathed Ken Wood, Hampstead, to the nation. He was created earl of Iveagh in 1919.

IVES (īvz), **Burl Icle Ivanhoe** (1909–). American singer. Making his début as an actor in 1938, he has appeared in musical and straight plays and in films, but is best known as a ballad singer to a banjo accompaniment, having made more than 300 records. He has pub. the autobiographical *The Wayfaring Stranger* (1948) and ed. collections of songs, e.g. *America's Musical Heritage.*

IVES, Charles Edward (1874–1954). American experimental composer, in daily life a business man, whose use of smaller intervals than the semi-tone rendered his songs and 5 symphonies hard to perform.

IVES, Frederic Eugene (1856–1937). American inventor. B. in Connecticut, he became manager of the photography laboratory at Cornell university, and there in 1878 invented a half-tone process. By 1886 he had evolved the half-tone process now generally in use. Among his many other inventions was the three-colour process of colour printing.

IVIZA (ēvē'thah). One of the Balearic is. in the Mediterranean Sea, lying 60 m. E. of Spain, to which it belongs. Area 221 sq. m.; pop. (est.) 37,000. The cap., also called I., has a 13th cent. cathedral. Pop. (est.) 14,000.

IVORY. The hard white substance of which the teeth of certain animals are composed. Most valuable are the tusks of the African and Indian elephants, in which the dentine is of unusual hardness and density. Articles manufactured from it include piano keys, billiard balls, and handles of cutlery, brushes, etc. I. has been used as a

IVORY. Pendant mask of the 16th century, representing an oba or king of Benin. *British Museum.*

medium for carving from prehistoric times in Europe, the Near East, and esp. in China and India.

Vegetable I. is used for buttons, toys, and cheap I. goods. It consists of the hard albumen of the seeds of a tropical palm (*Phytelephas macrocarpa*), which is imported from Colombia. Black Ivory was a euphemism for African slaves.

IVORY COAST (*Côte d'Ivoire*). Rep. in W. Africa lying between Liberia and Ghana. France secured trading rights on the coast in 1842, and occupied the interior in 1882, making it first a colony, later a territory. Given independence in 1960, it left the French Community and joined the W. African Entente. Behind the coastal plain, 40 m. wide and heavily forested, the country rises steeply to a plateau in the centre and to mountainous country in the N. The inhabitants are Negro in the coastal areas, primitive Senoufos and Baulé inland. Cocoa, coffee, millet, and maize are grown; mahogany is extracted from the forests, gold dredged from the rivers. The cap. is Abidjan. Area 224,000 sq. m.; pop. (1965) 3,840,000 (incl. 15,000 Europeans).

IVY. Genus of trees and shrubs (*Hedera*) of the Araliaceae family. The European I. (*Hedera helix*) has shiny, evergreen, triangular- or oval-shaped leaves and its clusters of small, yellowish-green flowers are followed by poisonous black berries. It climbs by means of root-like suckers put out from its stem, and is injurious to trees. Ground I. (*Nepeta hederacea*) is a small, creeping plant of the Labiatae family found both in Britain and N. America; and the N. American poison I. (*Rhus toxicodendron*), also known as poison oak, belongs to the Anacardiaceae.

IVY, with flower and fruits.

IXI'ON. In Greek mythology, son of a king in Thessaly and husband of Dia, who for his crimes was bound by Zeus to a fiery wheel which rolls endlessly through the underworld.

IXTAPAN DE LA SAL (ist'ahpan). Health resort, 45 m. from Toluca, Mexico. The radioactive waters are used in the treatment of rheumatism and skin ailments, and are sometimes identified with the legendary Aztec fountain of youth.

IZMIR. The grapes of the area are famous and the bunches are seen here carefully spread out by hand to dry in the hot sun to produce fine-quality raisins. *Courtesy of the Turkish Embassy.*

I'ZARD. A wild goat known as the Pyrenean ibex.

IZHEVSK (ēzhefsk'). Russian town, cap. of Urdmurt A.S.S.R., on the Izha, 150 m. S.W. of Perm. A metallurgical centre dating from 1760, it makes steel, agricultural and other machinery, and machine tools. Pop. (1967) 376,000.

IZMIR (ēzmēr'). Ancient port on the W. coast of Turkey-in-Asia, cap. of I. il. Originally a Greek colony founded *c.* 1000 B.C., it is mentioned as Smyrna in Revelation as the site of one of the Seven Churches of Christendom. After many vicissitudes (incl. destruction by Tamerlane in 1402), it was taken by the Turks in 1424. A rail terminus with modern harbour facilities, it exports wheat, dried fruit, textiles, etc., and has an oil refinery. Pop. (1965) 417,400.

J Tenth letter of the modern Roman alphabet. The modern Eng. value of *j* is that of a compound consonant, *d* followed by the sound *zh* (as in pleasure, pron. plezh'ur).

JABIRU (ja'biroo). Species of stork (*Mycteria americana*) found in America. It is 4–5 ft. in height with white plumage. The head is black and red.

JABLONEC (yah'blonets). Town in Czechoslovakia on the Neisse, 60 m. N.E. of Prague. From the 14th cent. jewellery and glass have been made. *See* illus p. 588.

JABORA'NDI. The dried leaves of several S. American plants which yield pilocarpine, an alkaloid which strongly stimulates sweat and saliva flow.

JA'CAMAR. Small Brazilian birds of the family Galbulidae. They have long sharp-pointed bills and paired toes. The plumage is brilliantly coloured.

JA'ÇANA. Wading birds in the family Parridae, found in S. America, Africa, India, and Australasia.

JACARA'NDA. Tree of the family Bignoniaceae found in Brazil, and also several other flowering trees with fragrant wood in the W. Indies and S. America.

JA'CINTH or **Hyacinth**. A red or yellowish-red gem which is a variety of zircon.

JACKAL (jak'awl). Member of the dog family (*Canis aureus*), found in S. Asia, Africa and Dalmatia. About 1½ ft. high and 2 ft. long, it is greyish-yellow. the fur darkening on the back. Nocturnal, it preys on smaller mammals and poultry, though packs will attack larger animals. It has a reputation as a scavenger and will follow lions and tigers to finish off the carcases of their kill.

JACKDAW. Species of crow in the genus *Corvus*, found in Europe and W. Asia. It is black, and nests in masonry.

JACKSON, Andrew (1767–1845). 7th Pres. of the U.S.A., b. in S. Carolina, he defeated the British at

New Orleans in 1815, and was elected Pres. in 1828. In 1832 he vetoed the renewal of the U.S. bank charter, and was re-elected, whereupon he continued his struggle against the power of finance.

JACKSON, Sir Barry Vincent (1879–1961). British theatre manager. B. in Birmingham, he founded the famous repertory theatre there in 1913 and became manager of the Court (1924) and Kingsway (1925) theatres in London. Knighted in 1925, he founded the Malvern Shaw Festival 1929–39, and reorganised the Stratford-on-Avon Memorial Theatre, laying the foundations for its present fame, while its director, 1946–8. He also translated many plays.

JABLONEC. Costume jewellery is one of Czechoslovakia's more important minor industries. The workers are mainly women who collect the components from Jablonex, the great firm controlling the industry, and make them up in their own homes. Here, the decoration of ear-rings is being skilfully carried out.
Courtesy of the Czechoslovak Travel Bureau.

JACKSON, John (1769–1845). British pugilist; known as 'Gentleman Jackson', he was champion 1795–1803. He taught Byron boxing.

JACKSON, Mahalia (1911–72). American contralto singer, noted as a gospel singer, some of her songs e.g. 'I Will Move on up a Little Higher', she wrote herself.

JACKSON, Thomas Jonathan, known as 'Stonewall' J. (1824–63). American Confederate general. After serving in the Mexican War of 1846–8, he became professor of military tactics at the Virginia military institute. In the Civil War he acquired his nickname and his reputation at Bull Run, from the firmness with which his brigade resisted the Northern attack. In 1862 he organized the Shenandoah valley campaign, and assisted Lee's invasion of Maryland. He helped to defeat Hooker's army at Chancellorsville, but was accidentally shot by his own men.

JACKSON. Cap. of Mississippi state, U.S.A., on the Pearl r. It dates from 1821 and was virtually destroyed by Sherman in 1863. The discovery of natural gasfields to the S. stimulated industry; products include lumber, furniture, cottonseed oil, iron and steel castings. Pop. (1960) 144,422.

JACKSONVILLE. City, port, and holiday resort of Florida, U.S.A., with some industry (cigars, furniture, boats, etc.). Founded in 1822, J. was named after Andrew Jackson (q.v.), then Gov. of Florida. To the N. the Cross-Florida Barge Canal links the Atlantic with the Gulf of Mexico, some 100 m. N. of Tampa. Pop. (1970) 513,439.

JACK THE RIPPER. Popular name for the unidentified murderer of 6 women prostitutes in the Whitechapel area of London in 1888: the mutilation of the bodies added to the sensation.

JACOB (jā′kob). Hebrew patriarch. The 2nd son of Isaac and Rebecca, he obtained the rights of seniority from Esau by trickery, and became a pastoral chief. He m. his 2 cousins Leah and Rachel, serving Laban 7 years for each. At the time of the famine in Canaan he joined his son Joseph in Egypt.

JACOBABAD (jāk′-). Town in W. Pakistan, 250 m. N.N.E. of Karachi, a railway junction and market centre. J. was laid out by (and named after) Gen. John Jacob as a frontier station when he was frontier commandant, 1847–58. It has a very small rainfall (c. 2 in. annually) and in May and June reaches the highest temperature in the Indian sub-continent – as much as 127°F. Pop. (1961) 90,049.

JACOBEAN. Term applied to a style of architecture

and furniture in favour during the reign of James I (1603–25). Following the general lines of Elizabethan design, it used classical features more widely. A fine example is Hatfield House, Herts.

JACOBINS (jak′obinz). A democratic republican club of the French Revolution, which originated at Versailles in 1789, but later moved to Paris where it rented a Jacobin (Dominican) friary. The name 'Jacobin' passed into general use for any supporter of revolutionary or democratic opinions.

JACOBITES. Those who continued to support the House of Stuart after the dethronement of James II in 1688 (Lat. *Jacobus*, James). Jacobitism was strongest among the Scottish Highlanders, who rose unsuccessfully under Claverhouse in 1689. James, the 'Old Pretender', headed a rebellion in Scotland and N. England in 1715, and in 1745–6 his son Charles Edward led a Scottish invasion of England which reached Derby. After the defeat at Culloden, Jacobitism disappeared as a political force.

JACOBS, William Wymark (1863–1943). British author. A professional civil servant, he was b. at Wapping and acquired an intimate knowledge of the docks and their 'characters', such as the rascally 'Bob Pretty', which he exploited in amusing short stories, e.g. *Many Cargoes* (1896) and *Light Freights* (1901). He excelled in the macabre, e.g. *The Monkey's Paw*.

JACOBSEN, Arne (1902–71). Danish architect. Noted for their simple elegance, his works incl. St. Catherine's Coll., Oxford, and the parliament building, Islamabad.

JACOPONE DA TODI (yahkopē′neh dah tō′dē) (c. 1230–1306). Italian religious poet. He was a Franciscan, and was imprisoned (1298–1303) for satirizing pope Boniface VIII. The authorship of the *Stabat Mater* has been ascribed to him.

JACQUARD (zhahkahr′), **Joseph Marie** (1752–1834). French inventor of the J. loom, enabling the most complex designs to be woven. He was bitterly attacked by his fellow weavers, but the basic principles of his invention are in universal use.

JACQUERIE (zhahkrē′). Name given to the French peasant rising of 1358. The word is derived from the nickname for the French peasant, *Jacques Bonhomme*.

JACQUES (jāks), **Reginald** (1894–). British musician. He founded and conducted the J. Orchestra and directed the Bach Choir 1932–60. He was the first Director Music to C.E.M.A. (now Arts Council) 1940–45, and has pub. vols. of carols and songs.

JADE (jād). Name given to various mineral substances, most commonly jadeite and nephrite,

JACQUARD. The culmination of a long series of inventions, the complicated Jacquard loom demands an alert and highly skilled operator. Each of the 2,000 or more threads is controlled individually through the 'harness'.
Courtesy of David Whitehead and Sons.

ranging from white to dark green according to the iron content. Long the hardest mineral known, its use by certain races is of ethnological interest and as a measure of their standard of civilization. The Chinese first discovered and used J., bringing it from E. Turkestan (so far as is known J. has never been found in China), and carried the art of J. carving to its peak: the Aztecs and Maoris have also used J. for ornaments, weapons and utensils since prehistoric times.

JAEN (hahen′). Capital of J. prov., S. Spain. The prov. is mountainous but fertile. Area 5,209 sq. m.; pop. (1960) 736,391. The city, an episcopal see, has remains of its Moorish walls and citadel, and makes textiles, leather, soap, alcohol. Pop. (1965) 70,300.

JA′FFA. Ancient port of Palestine dating at least from the 15th cent. B.C. It appears as Joppa in Egyptian records and in the Bible, and was captured by the Crusaders in the 12th cent. A.D., by Napoleon in 1799, and by Allenby in 1917. It was incl. in the rep. of Israel in 1948 and united with Tel Aviv in 1949 (*see* TEL AVIV-JAFFA).

JA′GAN, Cheddi (1918–). Guyanese politician Descended from Indian immigrants, J. was ed. at Queen's Coll., British Guiana, and in the U.S.A. In 1950 he became leader of the People's Progressive Party, with strong leftist tendencies, and in 1961–4 was the 1st P.M. of British Guiana and Min. of Development and Planning. His American-born wife, Janet J., is sec. of the party and in 1963–4 was Min. of Home Affairs.

JÄGER (yā′ger), **Gustav** (1832–1917). German naturalist and hygienist. He opposed the use of vegetable fibre for clothes, and the all-wool material 'Jaeger' was named after him.

JA′GUAR. Largest species of cat in America (*Felis onca*). It measures *c.* 4 ft. long excluding the tail. The ground colour of the fur varies from creamy white to brown or black, and is covered with black spots in rosettes.

JAHANGIR (-gēr′) ('Conqueror of the World'). Name adopted on his succession in 1605 by Salim (1569–1627), 3rd Mogul emperor of Delhi. Son of Akbar the Great, during his troubled and tyrannical reign he lost Kandahar to Persia in 1622; and as a result of his addiction to drink and opium he lost power also to his wife Nur Jahan ('Light of the World'). A literary and artistic connoisseur, he designed the beautiful Shalimar Gardens in Kashmir, and gardens and buildings in Lahore. *See* illus. p. 636.

JAHWEH. Another spelling of Jehovah (q.v.).

JAINISM (jā′nizm). A religion professed by about a million and a half Hindus, and sometimes regarded as an offshoot from Hinduism. Its sacred books record the teachings of Mahavira (599–527 B.C.), the latest of a long series of Tirthankaras, or omniscient saints and seers. B. in Vessali, now Bessarh, he became an ascetic at the age of 30, acquired omniscience at 42, and preached for 30 years.

Jains believe that non-injury to living beings is the highest religion and their code of ethics is based on sympathy and compassion. They also believe in 'karma' (q.v.). In J. there is no deity, and like Buddhism it is a monastic religion. There are 2 main sects: the Digambaras, who originally went about completely nude, and the Swetambaras.

JAIPUR (jīpoor′). Indian city, cap. of Rajasthan state, noted for the colour of its stone buildings – pink for Siva, with touches of yellow for Kali. It is a railway junction with some industry. Pop. (1961) 402,760. J. was formerly the cap. of the princely state of J., area 15,610 sq. m., merged in Rajasthan 1949.

JAKARTA. *See* DJAKARTA.

JAMAICA (jamā′ka). Largest is. in the British W. Indies, lying about 90 m. S. of Cuba, in the Caribbean

JAMAICA. The Blue Mountains to the N.E. of Kingston rise to the highest peak in the West Indies (7,388 ft.). Today the dramatic views attract the tourist, but in the 17th century they gave refuge to the escaped slaves (the Maroons) of the Spaniards, driven out by the British in 1658.
Courtesy of the Jamaica Tourist Board.

Sea. Of great natural beauty, J. consists of an elevated well-watered plain, bisected by the Blue Mts. running E. to W. which rise to 7,400 ft. The cap. is Kingston, founded 1693; the ruins of the nearby 'pirate city' of Port Royal, destroyed and partly submerged by an earthquake in 1692, with a loss of 2,000 lives, were excavated from 1965 by Robert Marx. The chief products are bananas, sugar, coffee, rum, citrus fruits, coconuts, and tobacco. Bauxite is a principal export.

Columbus discovered J. in 1494 and it remained Spanish until conquered by Britain in 1655. From 1666 to 1866 it was ruled by a gov. and council, part nominated, part elected. Representative govt. was estab. in 1884; self-govt. in 1957. J. entered the W. Indies Federation in 1958, but withdrew in 1961, and in 1962 was given independence; it remained within the British Commonwealth.

The name J. is from the aboriginal Xaymaca (land of wood and water). The aboriginal inhabitants of the island died out under the hard life imposed on them by the Spaniards, who began to import Negroes to work for them. Some 78 per cent of present-day Jamaicans are of Negro descent, with 17·5 per cent of mixed blood, 1 per cent white, the remainder E. Indian, Chinese, etc. English is the language. Area 4,411 sq. m.; pop. (1966) 1,859,072.

The Cayman Is. (q.v.) and the Turks and Caicos Is. (q.v.), formerly dependencies of J., were given separate administrations in 1958.

JAMES. Apostle and saint. A son of Zebedee, he was, like his brother John, a fisherman of Galilee. Called as a disciple by Jesus, he became a leader of the Church in Jerusalem after the Crucifixion, and was put to death by Herod Agrippa in A.D. 44. He is the patron saint of Spain. Another James, the son of Alphaeus, and also a disciple of Christ, is distinguished as 'J. the Little'. A third James was the Lord's brother, and is known as 'J. the Just'. Paul says that Christ appeared to him after the Resurrection, and that he was a leader of the Church in Jerusalem.

JAMES I and **VI** (1566–1625). King of England and Scotland. The son of Mary, queen of Scots, and Lord Darnley, he was proclaimed king of Scotland as J. VI upon his mother's abdication in 1567. After a troubled minority he assumed power in 1583; he estab. a strong central authority, and asserted the supremacy of the State over the Kirk. Succeeding Elizabeth as king of England in 1603, he alienated Puritan sentiment by his High Church views, and Parliament by his assertions of Divine Right. His unpopularity was increased by his fondness for favourites, and by his schemes for an alliance with Spain. He m. Anne of Denmark in 1589.

JAMES II and **VII** (1633–1701). King of England and of Scotland, the 2nd son of Charles I. In 1660 he m. Anne Hyde, by whom he had 2 daus., Mary and Anne. His 2nd wife was the Catholic Mary of Modena. Appointed Lord High Admiral at the Restoration, he was successful both as an administrator and as a commander in the Dutch Wars. His conversion to Roman Catholicism led to attempts to exclude him from the succession. After his accession in 1685 the failure of Monmouth's and Argyll's rebellions strengthened his position, but his attempts at arbitrary rule and his favour to Catholics produced a reaction against him, and in 1688 the Whig and Tory leaders united in an invitation to William of Orange to take the throne. J. fled to France. In 1689 he led a rising in Ireland, but was defeated at the battle of the Boyne (1690), and henceforward remained in exile in France.

JAMES. Name of 7 kings of Scotland. **James I** (1394–1437) was captured by the English on the way to France in 1406, and although he became king the same year was held a prisoner until 1424. Before returning to Scotland he m. Lady Jane Beaufort, and described his wooing in *The Kingis Quair*, a poem in the style of Chaucer. He was murdered by his nobles. **James II** (1430–60) succeeded his father James I, and took over the govt. in 1449. His reign was troubled and he was accidentally killed while besieging Roxburgh Castle. **James III** (1451–88) succeeded his father James II, assumed the royal power in 1469, and was murdered during a rebellion. **James IV** (1473–1513) succeeded his father James III. He m. Margaret, dau. of Henry VII, in 1503, but in 1513 he invaded England, and was defeated and killed at Flodden. **James V** (1512–42) succeeded his father James IV, and took power in 1528. The defeat of his army by the English at Solway Moss in 1542 hastened his end. For James VI and VII *see* JAMES I and II OF ENGLAND.

JAMES I (1208–76). King of Aragon, called 'the Conqueror'. Succeeding his father in 1213, he conquered the Balearic Is. and took Valencia from the Moors.

JAMES, Henry (1843–1916). Anglo-American novelist. B. in New York, the brother of the philosopher William J., he spent much of his youth in Europe. His first novel was *Roderick Hudson* (1876), which like *The American* (1877) and *The Portrait of a Lady* (1881) shows the impact of European culture on the American mind. Other novels of the middle years are the exclusively American *Washington Square* (1881) and *The Bostonians* (1886); and *The Tragic Muse* (1890), *The Spoils of Poynton* (1897), and *The Awkward Age* (1899), all with English backgrounds. Greatest of his later works were *The Wings of a Dove* (1902), *The Ambassadors* (1903), and *The Golden Bowl* (1904).

HENRY JAMES. By Sargent. Photo N.P.G.

Noteworthy are the short essay in the supernatural 'The Turn of the Screw' (1898), and his valuable literary *Notebooks*. After 1875 he resided permanently in Europe, becoming a naturalized British subject in 1915. His style became increasingly involved – the

HENRY JAMES. Lamb House at Rye, in Sussex, where the novelist made his home from 1896.
Photo: British Travel and Holidays Association.

stages wittily summarized as 'James I, James II and James the Old Pretender' – and he is popularly best known by the successful posthumous stage adaptations of his books, the medium being one in which he had always wanted to excel.

JAMES, Jesse (1847–82). American folk hero, who has inspired many books. B. on a Missouri farm, J. became, with his brother Frank (1843–1915), leader of the notorious Quantrill gang. Carrying out many daring bank and railroad robberies in the midwestern states, they caused numerous deaths and a large reward was offered for their capture. A hero even during his lifetime, he was killed by an accomplice. Frank was unconvicted and became a respectable farmer.

JAMES, Montague Rhodes (1862–1936). British theologian. Provost of King's Coll., Cambridge, 1905–18, and of Eton 1918–36, he pub. numerous Biblical studies, including the *Apocryphal New Testament* (1924). He was also a master of the uncanny, and the malevolent apparitions of *Ghost Stories of an Antiquary* (1904) and other volumes are unrivalled.

JAMES, William (1842–1910). American psychologist and philosopher, brother of Henry J. He turned from medicine to psychology and taught at Harvard 1872–1907. In 1890 appeared his *Principles of Psychology*, followed by *Will to Believe* (1897), and *Varieties of Religious Experience* (1902), one of the most important works on the psychology of religion. He expounded his pragmatic approach to metaphysics in *Pragmatism* (1907) and *Meaning of Truth* (1909).

JAMES EDWARD (1688–1766). The 'Old Pretender', called by Jacobites James III. The son of James II, he was b. at St. James's Palace, and after the revolution of 1688 was taken to France. He landed in Scotland in 1715 to head a Jacobite rebellion, but withdrew owing to lack of support. In his later years he settled in Rome.

JAMESON, Sir Leander Starr (1853–1917). British colonial statesman. B. in Edinburgh, he practised medicine in London and then Kimberley, where he became a friend of Cecil Rhodes. Early in 1896 he led the J. raid from Mafeking into Transvaal in support of the dissatisfied 'Uitlanders'. Surrendering, he was handed over to the British for punishment, but owing to ill-health he served only part of his sentence of 15 months' imprisonment. Returning to S. Africa, he succeeded Rhodes as leader of the Progressive Party in Cape Colony, where he was P.M. 1904–8. He was created a baronet in 1911.

JAMESON, Margaret Storm (1897–). British

writer. Her concern with the basic moral problems of contemporary life shows itself in such books as *In The Second Year* (1936). Well known also is her trilogy about the shipbuilding family of Herveys and Russells, which incl. *A Richer Dust* (1931).

JAMESTOWN. Site in Virginia, U.S.A., 37 m. N.W. of Norfolk, of the first permanent British settlement in N. America, estab. by Captain John Smith in 1607, and cap. of the British colony of Virginia 1624–99. In the nearby J. Festival Park there is a replica of the original Fort James, and models of the ships (*Discovery*, *Godspeed* and *Constant*), which carried the 105 pioneers.

JAMI (jaw'mē) (1414–92). Persian poet. B. at Jam in Khurasan, he embraced Sufism, and expressed its mystically romantic philosophy in his lyrics.

JAMMES (zhahm), **Francis** (1868–1938). French writer. B. at Tournay, he became a lawyer's clerk and estab. his reputation as a poet with the pastoral *De l'angelus de l'aube à l'angelus du soir* (1897). His increasingly Catholic outlook from 1905 is clearly shown in the poems of *Les Géorgiques chrétiennes* (1911–12) and the novel *Le curé d'Ozeron* (1918).

JAMMU (jumoo'). Winter cap. of the state of Kashmir (q.v.). It stands on the Tavi and is linked by road to Pathankot and India's rail system. An important drug research laboratory is situated at J. Pop. (1961) 108,562.

JAMNAGA'R. Indian city and port, in Gujarat state, on the Gulf of Kutch, 160 m. W.S.W. of Ahmedabad. It has textile mills, match factories, etc., and an airport. Pop. (1961) 147,420.

J., formerly cap. of the princely state of Nawanagar (of which the famous cricketer Ranjitsinhji, q.v., was maharajah), is sometimes called Nawanagar.

JAMSHEDPUR. City of Bihar, Republic of India. Begun in 1909, on land acquired in 1907, J. takes its name from the Parsee industrialist Jamsheedji Tata, founder of the great Bombay firm. The Tata iron and steel works at J. are based on the coal and iron of the neighbouring Chota Nagpur plateau. Pop. (1961) 332,134.

JANÁČEK (yah'nahchek), **Leoš** (1854–1928). Czech composer. He studied the organ at Prague before visiting Leipzig and Vienna in 1878; on his return he organized a series of popular concerts, presenting great masterpieces to his Moravian countrymen, and in 1881 founded and directed an organ school at Brno. He became director of the Conservatoire at Brno in 1919, and prof. at the Prague Conservatoire in 1920. His music, based on the rhythm and melody of the Moravian peasant speech and folk music, incl. arrangements of folk songs, many operas and choral works, e.g. *Jenufa* (1904); *Taras Bulba* for orchestra; and chamber music.

JANINA (yah'nēnah). Town in Epirus, Greece, near the Albanian frontier, cap. of J. Home and seat of an archbishopric; it makes silks. J. was famous as the stronghold of Ali Pasha, called the Lion of J., 1788–1818. Pop. (1961) 34,997.

JA'NISSARIES. Bodyguard of the sultan, the Turkish standing army 1330–1826. Until the 16th cent. it was recruited by taking Christian boys who received instruction in the Muslim faith. In 1826, when the sultan decided to raise a regular force, they revolted, whereupon they were suppressed.

JAN MAYEN (yahn mī-en). Norwegian island in the Arctic between Greenland and Norway, named after a Dutchman who visited it *c.* 1610. Area 144 sq. m.

JANNINGS (yahn'-), **Emil** (1886–1950). German actor. Best known for his playing of pathetic or tragic roles in the German films *The Last Laugh* (1924), *Variety* (1925), and *The Blue Angel* (1930).

JANSEN, Cornelius (1585–1638). Dutch theologian who became prof. at Louvain in 1630, and R.C. bishop of Ypres in 1636. J. gives his name to the

R.C. religious movement known as Jansenism, which originated with his *Augustinus* (1640), in which he argued that the teaching of St. Augustine on grace, free will, and predestination was opposed to the doctrines of modern theologians, especially the Jesuits. During the middle years of the 17th cent. the Church in France was distracted by the theological war of Jansenists and Jesuits. Pascal was an ardent Jansenist, together with the Arnaulds of the Port Royal circle. In 1713 a Jansenist work by Quesnel, the leader of the party, was condemned by pope Clement XI as heretical, and after Quesnel's death in 1719 Jansenism as an organized movement in France disappeared. But it survived in Holland where in 1723 a regular Jansenist church was estab. under the bishop of Utrecht.

JANUA'RIUS, St. (d. A.D. 305). Patron saint of Naples; also called San Gennaro. Traditionally, he was bishop of Benevento towards the end of the 3rd cenr. A.D. and suffered martyrdom under Diocletian.

JA'NUS. Roman god, the patron of the beginning of the day, month, and year. The first month of the year is named after him, and he is represented in art with 2 faces looking in opposite directions.

JAPA'N. An independent sovereign state of eastern Asia in the N. Pacific Ocean. J. consists of a chain of more than 1,000 islands running N. to S.W. and separated from the continent by the Sea of Japan. The chief islands are Hokkaido, Honshu (the mainland), Shikoku, and Kyushu (qq.v.). Total area, 142,680 sq. m.; pop. (1965) 98,281,955. The chief towns are Tokyo, Osaka, Nagoya, Kyoto, Yokohama, and Kobe.

The coastline is deeply indented, particularly on the Pacific shore where the Tuscarora Deep is one of the deepest sea-beds in the world. A mountain range traverses J. from N. to S.W., the highest peak being Fujiyama in Honshu, 12,390 ft. J. has a large number of active volcanoes and is subject to earthquakes. Extensive, well-watered plains divide the mountains. The main rivers are the Ishikari, *c.* 400 miles and the longest, in Hokkaido; the Shinano, Tone, and Yoshino in Honshu. Lakes are numerous.

By the 1960s the traditional products – rice, silk, and fish – accounted for less than 10% of her national output, and she was among the leading industrial nations, producing ships, motor vehicles, cameras, sewing machines, watches and clocks, electronic equipment, steel, textiles, plastics, paper, chemicals and cement. Minerals incl. some coal, of poor quality; oil and natural gas discovered on Honshu after the S.W.W. but insufficient to meet demand; copper, lead, manganese, iron, gold and silver. Hydro-electric and thermo-electric power is well-developed.

The Japanese are shorter than the Chinese and Koreans, but of similar build. There exists a physical difference between social classes, the majority being descended from the Malay or Indonesian race while the upper minority may have been of Manchu-Korean origin. Earlier than these types are the Ainu. The national religion is Shinto (q.v.), but its profession does not exclude acceptance also of Buddhism (introduced in 6th cent.); there are some half-million Christians (from 16th cent.).

Government. Under the constitution which came into effect in 1947, the Emperor divested himself of his former divine attributes and became a constitutional sovereign with no executive powers. Women received the vote, conscription was abolished (as was also the peerage), and human rights on Western lines were laid down. A cabinet led by a P.M. was given executive power; a house of representatives elected for 4 years and a house of councillors, one-half to be elected every 3 years, were given legislative power.

History. The Japanese nation probably arose from the fusion of 2 peoples, one coming from Malaya or

JAPAN. The Kofukuji Temple at Nara was originally a Buddhist monastery and guardian temple of the Fujiwaras who ruled the state from the 9th to 11th cents. It was so prosperous that it had 175 buildings under its management: one of the chief remaining structures is the five-storeyed pagoda seen here, built in 1426. *Courtesy of Japanese Embassy.*

Polynesia, the other from Asia, who conquered the original inhabitants, the Ainu. Japanese history remains legendary until the 5th cent. A.D., when the art of writing was introduced from Korea. After the introduction of Buddhism, also from Korea, in the 6th cent., Chinese culture became generally accepted, but although attempts were made in the 7th cent. to diminish the power of the nobles and set up a strong centralized monarchy on the Chinese model, real power remained in the hands of the great feudal families until modern times. In 1192 the ruling noble Yoritomo assumed the title of shogun (commander-in-chief), which until 1867 was usually borne by the real ruler of J. Intercourse with Europe began in 1542, when Portuguese traders arrived; they were followed by the Spaniards, and in 1609 by the Dutch. Christianity was introduced by Francis Xavier in 1549. During the 15th and 16th cents. J. sank into a state of feudal anarchy, until order was restored between 1570 and 1615 by 3 great rulers, Nobunaga, Hideyoshi, and Iyeyasu; the family of the last, the Tokugawa, held power until the abolition of the shogunate. The fear that R.C. propaganda was intended as a preparation for Spanish conquest led to the expulsion of the Spaniards in 1624, and the Portuguese in 1639, and to the almost total extermination of Christianity by persecution; only the Dutch were allowed to trade with J. under irksome restrictions, while Japanese subjects were forbidden to leave the country. This complete isolation continued until 1853, when the U.S.A. insisted on opening trade relations; during the next few years this example was followed by the European powers. Consequently the isolationist party compelled the last shogun to abdicate in 1867, and executive power was restored to the Emperor. During the next 30 years the privileges of the feudal nobility were abolished, a uniform code

of law was introduced, and a constitution was estab. in 1889. The army was modernized, and a powerful navy founded. Industry developed steadily and a considerable export trade was built up.

J.'s career of aggression began in 1894 when a war with China secured her Formosa and S. Manchuria, as well as control of Korea, which was formally annexed in 1910. A victorious war with Russia in 1904–5 gave J. the S. half of Sakhalin, and compelled the Russians to evacuate Manchuria. J. formed an alliance with Britain in 1902, and joined the Allies during the F.W.W.; at the peace settlement she received the German islands in the N. Pacific as mandates. The 1920s saw an advance towards democracy and party govt., but after 1932 the govt. assumed a semi-Fascist form. As a result of successful aggression against China in 1931–2 a Japanese puppet monarchy under Pu Yi, last Emperor of China, was estab. in Manchuria (*see* MANCHUKUO); war with China was renewed in 1937. J. entered the S.W.W. with the attack on Pearl Harbor on 7 Dec. 1941, and at first won a succession of victories in the Philippines, Malaya, Burma, and the Netherlands Indies. She was finally compelled to surrender in Aug. 1945; an Allied control commission took charge, and J. was under military occupation by Allied (chiefly U.S.) troops until April 1952 when the Japanese Peace Treaty came into force. After J.'s defeat, Korea was made independent; Manchuria and Formosa were returned to China; the islands mandated to J. after the F.W.W. were placed by the U.N. under U.S. trusteeship. Japan has successfully agitated for the return by the U.S.A. of the Ryuku Is., and the Bonin and Volcano Is (qq.v.), and has asked the Soviet Union to return the Northern Territories, i.e., the is. of Shikotan and the Habomai Group, and the southernmost Kuriles (q.v.), Kunashiri and Etorofu.

Following the S.W.W. Japan renounced nuclear weapons, but rapidly became Asia's leading economic power, extending aid to her neighbours. The Liberal Democrats (*see* SATO) are the leading party; the opposing Socialists are pro-Peking.

JAPAN, Sea of. The sea between Japan and the mainland of Asia.

JAPANESE. The language of Japan. Pure J. is usually considered a member of the Altaic group of languages, showing affinities with Korean. It is of simple, agglutinating structure. As the J. developed no script of their own, they adopted in the 3rd cent. the Chinese ideographs and adapted them, thus evolving an extremely complicated system. Later a simplified system (*Kana*) was introduced, but never ousted the old one. The language of today is a mixture of Japanese and Chinese, with borrowings from modern European languages.

JAPANESE ART. The main periods in the history of J.A. are: *Pre-Buddhist* (before 580): examples of Pre-Buddhist art and simplicity are the *haniwa*, clay grave figures, and *dôtaku*, bronze bells decorated with engravings. *Suiko* period (580–650): together with Buddhism, Korean temple builders, painters, etc., came to Japan. *Hakuohô* period (650–720): during this Japanese art was strongly influenced by Chinese. *Tempyô* period (720–810): in this 'blossom-time of Japanese civilization' there was still a strong Chinese influence, but native genius asserted itself, and a great amount of sculpture was produced. *Jogan* period (810–980): a transitional period in which the chief influences were the religious sects of Shingon and Tendai. *Fujiwara* period (980–1170): in this period of elegance and refinement elaborate temples and mansions were built. *Kamakura* period (1170–1350): a more vigorous style of art was adopted. Sculpture was characterized by great strength and solidity. *Ashikaga* period (1350–1570): Zen Buddhism influenced the art. The rapid ink sketch in line and wash introduced by Zen priests from China became popular. Pottery gained in importance from the introduction of the tea ceremony. *Momoyama* period (1570–1630): the brilliant Kano artists produced beautiful screens to decorate palaces and castles. *Tokugawa* period (1630–1867): colour prints were first produced. Famous artists were Matabei, Kôryusai, Kiyonaga, Utamaro, and Hokusai. *Meiji* period (1868–1912): the influence of Western art, especially Impressionism, is clearly discernible: well-known artists were Gaho (1835–1908) and Kogyo (1866–1919). *Showa* period (1926–): attempts were made by, e.g. Seiho (1864–1942), to adapt the Western methods of objective realism to the traditional J. variety, and by painters such as Taikan (1868–1958) to revive the traditional subjective style; younger painters, e.g. Kokei (1883–1957) tried to combine traditional and foreign styles. *See also* IKEBANA.

JAPANESE LITERATURE. Among its earliest survivals are the 8th cent. *Collection of a Myriad Leaves*, which incl. poems by Hitomaro and Akahito (the principal form being the *tanka*, a 5-line stanza of 5, 7, 5, 7, 7, syllables), and the prose *Record of Ancient Matters*. To the late 10th and early 11th cents. belong the women writers Sei Shōnagon and Murasaki Shikibu. During the 14th cent. the Nō drama developed from ceremonial religious dances, combined with monologues and dialogues. The 17th cent. brought such scholars of Chinese studies as Fujiwara Seikwa (1560–1619) and Arai Hakuseki (1657–1725). To this period belongs the origin of *kabuki*, the popular drama of Japan, of which Chikamatsu Monzaemon (1653–1724) is the chief exponent; of *haiku* (the stanza of 3 lines of 5, 7, 5 syllables), popularized by Matsuo Bashō (1644–94);

JUNICHIRO TANIZAKI
Courtesy of Higuchi Susumu

and of the modern novel, as represented by Ibara Saikaku (1642–93). Among those reacting against Chinese influence was the poet-historian Motoori Norinaga (1730–1801). The late 19th and early 20th cents. saw the replacement of the obsolete *Tokugawa* style as a literary medium by the modern colloquial language, and the influence of Western lit., esp. Russian, produced writers such as the 'Realist' Tsubouchi Shōyō (1859–1935), followed by the 'Naturalist' and 'Idealistic' novelists, whose romantic preoccupation with self-expression gave rise to the still popular 'I-novels' of e.g. Dazai Osumu (1909–48) and Ooka Shōhei (1909–). Reacting against the au obiographical school were Natsume Sōseki (1867–1916), Nagai Kafū (1879–1959), and Junichirō Tanizaki (1886–1965), who instead found inspiration in past traditions or in self-sublimation; later novelists incl. Kawabata Yasunari (1899–). Shimazaki Tōson (1872–1943) introd. Western-style poetry e.g. 'Symbolism', but the traditional forms of *haiku* and *tanka* are still widely used. Western-type, modern drama (Shingeki), inspired by Ibsen and Strindberg, has been growing since the turn of the century, and well-known dramatists incl. Junji Kinoshita (1914–).

JARNACH (yahr'nak), **Philipp** (1892–). Franco-Spanish composer. He studied in Paris and under Busoni, whose opera *Doktor Faust* he completed, in Berlin: his own compositions incl. a string quartet and orchestral works.

JARNEFELT, **Armas** (1869–1958). Finnish composer. B. at Vyborg, he became court conductor at Stockholm, and is chiefly known for his 'Praeludium' and the lyrical 'Berceu₋e'.

JA'RRAH. Wood of the tree *Eucalyptus marginata*

found in Australia; dark, close-grained, and durable.

JA'RROW. English industrial town (bor.) in co. Durham, on the S. bank of the Tyne, 6 m. E. of Newcastle and connected with the N. bank by the Tyne Tunnel (1967). It grew with the establishment in the 19th cent. of the Palmer shipbuilding yards, closed in 1933 during the great depression. J. was included in a 'special area', and steel rolling, ship repairing, tube manufacture, etc., were introduced. St. Paul's Church (686) was the home of Bede until his death. Pop. (1961) 28,752.

JARRY (zhahrē'), **Alfred** (1873–1907). French dramatist. His farce *Ubu Roi* (1896) foreshadows the Theatre of the Absurd, and satirises the bourgeoisie. Mère Ubu prods Père Ubu into making himself king by a coup, and his antics destroy the kingdom.

JASMINE or **Jessamine**. Genus of plants (*Jassminum*) of the Oleaceae family, found in many part-of the world, but mainly in the E. J. oil is used in perfumery. The common J. (*J. officinale*), a native of Persia and N. India, but naturalized in Europe, is a climber growing over 12 ft. high which bears clusters of white or yellow sweet-smelling flowers. The Chinese winter J. (*J. nudiflorum*) produces brilliant yellow flowers before its leaves appear.

JA'SON. In Greek mythology, the leader of the Argonauts who sailed to recover the Golden Fleece of the ram that had been carried away to Colchis. He escaped with the fleece and Medea, with whom he lived at Corinth; when he took a new bride she was slain by Medea's magic.

JA'SPER. Hard, compact variety of quartz, usually coloured red, brown or yellow. J. is opaque, and has been used as a gem.

JASPERS (yas'pers), **Karl** (1883–1969). German philosopher. B. at Oldenburg, he studied medicine and psychology, and in 1921 became prof. of philosophy at Heidelberg. Deprived by the Nazis in 1937, he was rescued in 1945 from the threat of death by the American occupation and 1948–61 taught at the univ. in Basle. His works incl. *General Psychopathology* (1913), *Man in the Modern Age* (1931), *The Great Philosophers* (1956) and *The Future of Mankind* (1958). As an interpreter of German existentialism, he was ranked next to Heidegger.

JASSY. Another form of IAŞI.

JA'TAKA. Name given to a collection of Buddhist legends giving an account of 547 previous incarnations of Buddha.

JAUNDICE. Yellowing of the skin and eyes. The usual cause is the presence of bile in the deeper layers, due to obstruction of the common bile duct, e.g. by gallstones, pressure of a growth on the duct, or swelling of the duct walls through catarrh; or to some disturbance of liver function which prevents the bile from ever reaching the ducts.

JAURÈS (zhohräs'), **Jean Léon** (1859–1914). French Socialist politician. B. in Tarn, he was a lecturer in philosophy at Toulouse until his election in 1885 as a deputy. In 1893 he joined the Socialist Party, and in 1904 founded *L'Humanité* and became its editor. An advocate of international peace, he was assassinated by a half-witted youth.

JAVA (jah'vah). The most important island of Indonesia, situated between Sumatra and Bali. With the is. of Madura, J. has an area of 51,032 sq. m. and a pop. (1967) of 72,600,000. Along the centre of J. extends a chain of mountains, sometimes rising to 9,000 ft., which incl. volcanoes. The highest mountain, Semeru, over 12,000 ft., is in the E. About half the island is under cultivation, the rest being thickly forested. Mountains and sea breezes prevent extreme heat, but humidity is high. as is rainfall in Dec. to March. Products incl. rice, coffee, cocoa, tea, sugar, rubber, quinine, teak, and petroleum.

The cap. of J. is Djakarta also the cap. of Indonesia; important ports are Surabaja and Semarang.

JAVA. The sun makes even the airy interior of this typical village-house in central Java unbearable, and a woman prepares batik in the open under the trees.
Courtesy of Indonesian Embassy.

The people, of Mongol affinities, comprise Javanese, Sundanese, and Madurese, with differing languages. The majority are Moslems. Fossilized remains of an animal (*Pithecanthropus erectus*) intermediate between the higher apes and man were discovered in 1891–2.

In central J. there are ruins of magnificent Buddhist monuments and of the Sivaite temple in Prambanan. J.'s last Hindu kingdom, Majapahit, was destroyed *c.* 1520 and followed by a number of short-lived Javanese kingdoms. The Dutch E. India company founded a factory in 1610, named Batavia. The British occupied J. in 1811, during the Napoleonic period, returning it to the Dutch in 1816. J. was occupied by the Japanese 1942–5, and after their defeat became part of the rep. of Indonesia (q.v.).

JAW. One of the bony structures, upper and lower, which hold the teeth and form the framework of the mouth. The upper jaw (maxilla) consists of 2 bones united in the middle at an early stage of development. They join the bones of the forehead and cheek and each contains a hollow space, the maxillary sinus. The lower jawbone, the mandible, is hinged at each side to the bone of the temple by ligaments.

JAWLE'NSKY, Alexei von (1864–1942). Russian artist. Associated with Kandinsky and Klee, he was later influenced by Matisse and developed a use of large areas of flat, bright colour reminiscent of peasant art. His later work has a mystic quality.

JAY. Genus of birds (*Garrulus*) of the crow family, confined to the Old World and common in Europe except in the far N. In the common J. (*G. glandarius*) the body is fawn with patches of white, blue and black on the wings and tail. Its own cry is a harsh screech, but it has considerable powers as a mimic. Allied is the common blue J. (*Perisoreus canadensis*), of N. America, rather drab-coloured and found in the pine forests.

JAZZ. A complete polyphonic, syncopated music originating in New Orleans between 1880–1900. The unusually favourable conditions were: the Spanish and later French domination of the city, with their musical traditions; the American brass band; and the still remembered 'Bamboula' chants from the Congo, whose mournful repetition and variations of short, insistent themes led easily to the blues. With no other entertainment available, music was an essential part of the bars, dance halls and bawdy houses of the red-light district, Storyville; as well as of picnic parties, weddings and funerals, where the marching bands led the procession to the cemetery playing hymns and slow blues, and then returned, swinging with the zest and fire of final salutation that could be heard miles away.

> 'What's that I hear, 12 o/c in the daytime – church bells ringin'?'
> 'Yes, indeed, somebody must be dead.'
> 'Ain' nobody dead. Somebody must be dead drunk.'
> 'No, I think there's a funeral.'
> 'Why looky here, I see there is a funeral.'
> 'I b'lieve I hear that trambone moan.'

The prodigious technique of early brass players was due to their natural talent, lack of awareness that their instruments had any limitations, and the competitive spirit that existed among bands. The exodus from New Orleans started in 1917, after the U.S. Navy caused Storyville to be closed. Joe Oliver, Fred Keppard, Louis Armstrong, et al., moved to Chicago and St. Louis, later spreading their influence to New York, where the more refined Fletcher Henderson orchestra was in vogue, succeeded by Paul Whiteman. Small dynamic groups survived the swing era of the 1940s, with the big bands of Goodman, Ellington and Herman, to emerge with increased vigour after the S.W.W., when J. had reached across Europe as far as Russia. Under the impetus of Charlie Parker, Dizzy Gillespie, Miles Davis, et al., J. has proliferated in an immense diversity of styles through which it is difficult to see the mainstream. From the revival of traditional J. in the 1950s – a romantic, unimaginative version of the original – to modern J. there is to be found an increasingly wide range of rhythmic and harmonic content, embracing such diverse elements as the Bach fugue, the Brazilian bossa nova and the atonalities of Bartók.

JEANS, Sir James Hopwood (1877–1946). British mathematician and astronomer. His original contributions incl. work in physics, on the kinetic theory of gases, forms of energy radiation; and in astronomy, on giant and dwarf stars, the nature of spiral nebulae, and the origin of the cosmos. His popular books on cosmogeny incl. *The Universe Around Us* (1929) and *The Mysterious Universe* (1930).

JEBEIL. *See* BYBLOS.

JEDBURGH (jed'buro). Scottish royal burgh and co. town of Roxburghshire, standing on Jed Water, 40 m. S.E. of Edinburgh. It has a ruined abbey founded by David I, and associations with Mary, Queen of Scots, Charles (the Young Pretender), and Burns. Pop. (1961) 3,647.

JEDDA. *See* JIDDA.

JEEP. The popular name for the General Purpose (G.P.) vehicle of the American Army. It is a small open vehicle which can be driven over rough ground.

JEFFERIES, John Richard (1848–87). British naturalist and writer. After an unsuccessful start, he gained a reputation as a writer in 1872, following a remarkable letter to *The Times* on the Wiltshire labourer. His intimate books on the countryside incl. *Gamekeeper at Home* (1878), *Wood Magic* (1881), *Life of the Fields* (1884); and the autobiographical *Bevis* (1882) and *Story of My Heart* (1883).

JEFFERS, John Robinson (1887–1962). American poet. B. in Pittsburgh, he had a complete mastery of free verse, and demonstrated a lone antagonism to human society which was echoed by the isolation of his home at Carmel in N. California. His vols. incl. *Tamar and Other Poems* (1924), *The Double Axe* (1948), and *Hungerfield and Other Poems* (1954).

JEFFERSON, Thomas (1743–1826). Third Pres. of the U.S.A. B. in Virginia, he pub. *A Summary View of the Rights of America* (1774) and as a member of the Continental Congresses of 1775–6 he was largely responsible for the drafting of the Declaration of

Independence. He was governor of Virginia 1779–81, ambassador to Paris 1785–9, and Secretary of State 1789–93. J. was the founder of the Democratic Party. He was elected Vice-President 1796–1801 and President 1801–9. *See* illus. under U.S. history.

JEFFREY, Francis, Lord (1773–1850). Scottish lawyer and literary critic. B. at Edinburgh, he was a founder and editor of the *Edinburgh Review* 1802–29. In 1830 he was made Lord Advocate, and in 1834 a Scottish law lord. He is chiefly remembered for his hostility to the romantic movement.

JEFFREYS, George, 1st baron (1648–89). British judge. B. in Denbighshire, he became Chief Justice of the King's Bench in 1683, and presided over many political trials, notably those of Sidney, Oates, and Baxter, becoming notorious for his brutality. In 1685 he was raised to the peerage, and conducted the 'bloody assizes' after Monmouth's rebellion, during which 320 rebels were executed and hundreds more flogged, imprisoned or transported. Created Lord Chancellor in 1685, he attempted to flee the country after the revolution of 1688, but was captured and d. in the Tower.

JEFFREYS, George (1889–1962). British evangelist and faith-healer. B. in S. Wales, he recovered from creeping paralysis by what he believed to be divine agency, and founded the Elim Foursquare Gospel Movement in 1914, resigning in 1939 to found the similar Bible Pattern Church Fellowship. Both movements are on revivalist lines, baptism is by total immersion, and many cures through prayer have been claimed.

JEHOL. Another name for CHENGTEH.

JEHOVAH. The principal name for God in the O.T., spelled JHVH or better YHWH in Hebrew; between these consonants were inserted the vowels of the word Adonai (Lord), but modern scholars incline to the pronunciation Jahveh or Yahweh.

JEHOVAH'S WITNESSES. Religious organization originated in the U.S.A. in 1872 by Charles Taze Russell (1852–1916). They attach great importance to Christ's second coming, said by Russell to have taken place invisibly in 1874, and by his successor 'Judge' Joseph Rutherford (d. 1942) in 1914. The ensuing Armageddon and Last Judgment, which entail the destruction of all except the faithful, is to give way to the Theocratic Kingdom. Their tenets, involving rejection of obligations such as military service, have often brought them into conflict with authority. The Watch Tower Bible and Tract Soc. and the Watch Tower Students' Assoc. form part of the movement. Membership *c.* 1,000,000.

JELGAVA (yel'gah-vah). City of the Latvian S.S.R., on the Aa, 25 m. S.W. of Riga. The centre of a fertile area, it has textile and timber mills and sugar refineries. J. was founded in 1265 by the Teutonic knights. Pop. (1967) 50,000.

JELLICOE, John Rushworth, 1st earl (1859–1935). British admiral. B. at Southampton, he entered the navy in 1872. As acting admiral, he commanded the Grand Fleet 1914–16, but the only action he fought was the battle of Jutland (q.v.). He was 1st Sea Lord 1916–17, organizing measures to combat the U-boat menace, and in 1918 was created visct. In 1919 he became admiral of the fleet and 1920–4 he was Gov.-Gen. of New Zealand, being made an earl in 1925.

JELLY-FISH. Class of marine animals in the group Coelenterata. The J. has an umbrella-shaped body composed of a semi-transparent gelatinous substance,

JELLY FISH

JERBOA

with a fringe of stinging tentacles. Most of them move freely, but some are attached by a stalk to rocks or seaweed. They feed on small animals which are paralysed by the stinging threads.

JENA (yeh'nah). Old town, first mentioned in the 9th cent., in E. Germany, 12 m. S.E. of Weimar. Here in 1806 Napoleon defeated the Prussians. Schiller and Hegel taught at the univ. which dates from 1558. The Zeiss firm of optical-instrument makers, founded 1846, is among its chief industries. Pop. (1966) 82,000.

JENKINS, Roy Harris (1920–). British Labour politician. Ed. at Balliol Coll., Oxford, he was a close friend of Gaitskell, and has pub. studies of Attlee, Asquith, etc. He was Min. of Aviation 1964–5, Home Secretary 1965–7, and succeeded Callaghan as Chancellor of the Exchequer (1967–70).

JENNER, Edward (1749–1823). British physician. He studied in London under John Hunter and practised all his life in Gloucestershire. From 1775 he made a special study of the cowpox, and in 1796 successfully inoculated a boy with matter taken from cowpox vesicles. He pub. his discovery that vaccination produced immunity from smallpox in 1798.

JENNER, Henry ('Gwas Myhal') (1849–1934). Cornish poet. He revived Cornish as a literary vehicle, and in 1904 pub. a handbook of the Cornish language.

JENSEN (yen'sen), **Johannes Vilhelm** (1873–1950). Danish poet and novelist. He pub. stories set in his native Jutland and *The Long Journey* (1908–22), an epic novel of man's evolution through the ages.

JERABLUS. *See* CARCHEMISH.

JERBO'A. Several genera of rodents, found chiefly in Africa and Asia, and mainly herbivorous and nocturnal. Most typical is the common Egyptian J. (*Jaculus aegyptius*) with a body *c.* 7 in. long and slightly longer tail. At speed it moves in a series of long jumps with its fore-feet held close to the body. *See* DESERT RATS.

JEREMI'AH. Hebrew prophet, b. near Jerusalem, whose ministry continued 626–586 B.C. During the siege of Jerusalem by Nebuchadnezzar, J. was imprisoned on suspicion of wishing to desert to the invader, but he was released on the city's fall, and retired to Egypt.

JEREZ DE LA FRONTERA (hereth' dä lah frontä'rah). Town in Cadiz prov., S.W. Spain, 14 m. N.E. of Cadiz, famed for sherry. Pop. (1965) 142,336.

JERICHO (jer'ikō). Ancient city in the Jordan valley, Jordan, 5 m. N. of the Dead Sea. It was the first of the Canaanite strongholds to be captured by the Israelites, the walls of the city falling down to the blast of trumpets. Excavations by successive archaeologists from 1907 at intervals onwards show that the walls of the city were destroyed many times; little is left of the Late Bronze Age city captured by Joshua. (*See* KENYON, K.) A short distance from the old site is a modern Arab village, in Arabic Eriha.

JERICHO. One of the Neolithic skulls with delicately moulded plaster features discovered during Kathleen Kenyon's excavations: apparently these were retained as mementoes of loved relatives.
Courtesy of Miss Kathleen Kenyon.

JEROME (jerōm') (*c.* 340–420). Christian saint and Father of the Church. B. at Strido, he was baptized at Rome in 360, and subsequently travelled in Gaul, Asia Minor, and Syria. Summoned to Rome as adviser to pope Damasus, he revised the Latin translation of the N.T. and the Latin psalter. On the death of Damasus in 384 he travelled to the east, and settling at Bethlehem translated the O.T. into Latin from the Hebrew. His Lat. versions form the basis of the Vulgate.

JEROME, Jerome K(lapka) (1859–1927). British author. After being successively clerk, teacher, and actor, he turned to journalism; his *Idle Thoughts of an Idle Fellow* (1889), a collection of essays on such subjects as 'Babies', 'The Weather', etc., and his *Three Men in a Boat* (1889), made his reputation as a humorist. His dramatized story *The Passing of the Third Floor Back* (1907) is more sentimental.

JERROLD, Douglas William (1803–57). British playwright and journalist. B. in London, he scored his greatest success as a dramatist with *Black-eyed Susan* (1829). He contributed to *Punch* from 1841.

JERSEY. Largest of the Channel Islands. Government is by a lieutenant-governor and an assembly. St. Helier is the capital. Farming is the chief occupation. J. was occupied by the Germans 1940–5. Area 45 sq. m.; pop. (1961) 63,345.

JERSEY CITY. City of New Jersey, U.S.A. It faces Manhattan Island, to which it is connected by tunnels. Its many industries incl. foundries, electrical apparatus, chemicals, cigarettes. The large dockyards form part of the port of New York. The site was first settled c. 1629. Pop. (1960) 276,101.

JERUSALEM (jerōō′salem). Ancient city of Palestine, divided in 1948 between the new rep. of

JERSEY. One of the sunniest places in the British Isles, Jersey has become a popular holiday resort. Here, overlooked by hotels, in St. Brelade's Bay, one of the series of large shallow sandy beaches in the south of the island, most water sports are enjoyed.   *Courtesy Jersey Tourism Committee.*

Israel and Jordan. In 1950 the Israelis proclaimed the New City, the western part which they then held, cap. of Israel, and following their capture of the Old City from the Jordanians in 1967, they amalgamated the 2 as a single municipality. It is not recognised as the cap. by the U.N. Pop. (1969) 275,000.

By 1400 B.C. J. was ruled by a king subject to Egypt. David made J. the cap. of a united Jewish kingdom c. 1000. Nebuchadnezzar captured J. in 586 B.C. and deported its population. Under Cyrus a new settlement was made, and c. 445 the walls were rebuilt. J. passed under Alexander the Great, and later was a pawn in the contest between the Syrian Seleucids and the Egyptian Ptolemies. In 63 B.C. Pompey captured J., and a Jewish revolt led to the city's utter destruction in A.D. 70 by Titus. On its site was founded in A.D. 130 the Roman city of Aelia Capitolina, which

was pillaged by the Persian Chosroës II in 615 while under Byzantine rule. J. was conquered by Islam in 637, and Turks and Egyptians held sway until the Crusaders took the city in 1099. Recaptured by Saladin in 1187, J. remained under almost unbroken Islamic rule, through the conquest by the Turks in 1517, until the British occupation in 1917.

There are 7 gates into the old city through the walls built by Selim I. From c. the 1920s, J. extended in modern suburbs, especially in the S. and W. Notable buildings incl. the Church of the Holy Sepulchre erected by Constantine in 335, and the Mosque of Omar, built in 691 and occupying the site of Solomon's temple. The Hebrew univ. of J. on Mount Scopus was opened in 1925. J. is a Holy City for 3 faiths: Christian, Hebrew and Moslem; it has R.C., Angli-

JERUSALEM. The old city seen from the Mount of Olives. Above its crenellated wall rises the Dome of the Rock, one of the most beautiful mosques in the world, built on the site of Abraham's intended sacrifice and of Solomon's temple.

can, and Greek bishops, and a Coptic Metropolitan. Freedom of access of all faiths to their Holy Places was guaranteed by Israel in 1967. *See* TEMPLE.

JERUSALEM ARTICHOKE. *See* ARTICHOKE.

JERVIS, John, earl of St. Vincent (1735–1823). British admiral. An efficient organizer and rigid disciplinarian with both officers and men, he secured the blockade of Toulon in 1795, and the famed defeat of the Spanish fleet off Cape St. Vincent (1797), in which Captain Nelson (q.v.) played a key part.

JERVIS BAY. Deep bay on the coast of New South Wales, Australia, 90 m. S.S.W. of Sydney. The Federal Govt. in 1915 acquired 28 sq. m. here to create a port for Canberra. J.B. forms part of Australian Capital Territory and is the site of the Royal Australian Naval College.

JESPERSEN (yes′-), **Jens Otto Harry** (1860–1943). Danish philologist. He wrote standard works on the English language and experimented with artificial languages, e.g. Novial.

JESUITS (jez′ū-its) or **Society of Jesus.** An R.C. religious order. Founded by Loyola (q.v.) in 1534, it received papal approval in 1540. Its main objects were defined as educational work, the suppression of heresy, and missionary work among the heathen. Its members are not confined to monasteries. Loyola infused into the order a spirit of military discipline; training is long and arduous. During the 16th and 17th cents. they achieved success as missionaries to Japan and China, in Paraguay, and among the Red Indians. From the beginning they aimed at political influence, and these activities resulted in their expulsion during 1759–68 from Portugal, France, and Spain, and in 1773 the Pope suppressed the order. It was revived in 1814, but has since been expelled from many of the countries of Europe and America.

The order has *c.* 36,000 members, incl. *c.* 20,000 priests, the remainder being students and lay members.

JESUS CHRIST (jĕz′us krīst) (4 B.C.–A.D. 29 or 30). Jesus – called in Hebrew the Messiah, and in Greek the Christ – was the founder of Christianity (q.v.). The main sources of information on His life and work are the 4 Gospels. B. in Bethlehem, the son of the Virgin Mary of the tribe of Judah and the family of David. He was brought up as a carpenter by Joseph (q.v.) at Nazareth. In A.D. 26 or 27 His cousin John the Baptist began his preparatory mission, and after baptism at his hands Jesus became fully conscious of His own purpose. The Galilean Ministry incl. 2 missionary journeys through the district and the calling of the 12 Apostles, and culminated in the feeding of the 5,000. His teaching is summarized in the Sermon on the Mount, and was illustrated by homely parables. His apparent disloyalty to the traditional religion roused the opposition of the dominant religious party, the Pharisees, who joined the secular party of the Herodians against Him. Consequently He retired to the non-Jewish territory of Tyre and Sidon, where He probably devoted Himself to training the disciples, and made Himself known to them as the expected Messiah.

He then returned to Jerusalem (probably in A.D. 29), entering the city a week before the Passover, acclaimed by the populace as the Messiah. Fearing popular anger, the Jewish authorities arrested Jesus privately, aided by the betrayal of Judas, and after a hurried trial He was condemned to death by the Sanhedrin. Ultimate confirmation of this sentence was wrung from the Roman procurator Pontius Pilate by stressing the threat to imperial authority of His teaching. Three days after the Crucifixion, the long series of reported miracles culminated in Christ's Resurrection and His later Ascension.

JET. Mineral substance similar in composition to lignite and anthracite; it occurs in quantity near Whitby and along the Yorkshire coast. Ornaments made of J. have been found in Bronze Age tombs.

JET PROPULSION. For aircraft propulsion, air is taken into a forward-facing intake, is heated and ex-

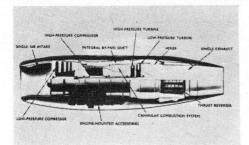

JET PROPULSION. Developed by Rolls-Royce, this Spey by-pass turbojet engine with a 10,000 lb. thrust was specially designed, by virtue of its low operating cost, for short- and medium-range aircraft. *Courtesy of Rolls-Royce Limited.*

panded by burning a fuel in it and the gases are ejected rearwards at very high speed through a converging duct. Propulsion is obtained not by pushing against the static air but by the reaction of accelerating the mass of gas rapidly rearwards. Thrust (*see* AEROPLANE) is proportional to the mass of gas ejected times the acceleration imparted to it. When the heating takes place simply in a divergent-convergent duct (i.e. an open-ended pipe having convex sides with ignition taking place at the widest section) the engine is known as a ram jet. This will not operate at low speeds due to insufficient dynamic head (ram) of air for compression, and although cheap, light, and

simple to make, possesses low combustion efficiency and is uneconomical in fuel. The usual turbo-jet uses a turbine-driven compressor to raise the comp. ratio and therefore the temperature (and expansion) of the gases. Some of the exhaust gas energy is extracted by the turbine, to drive the compressor by a shaft, the remaining gas velocity providing the jet thrust. Centrifugal compressors were first used because these had been well developed as superchargers on piston engines, but their compression ratio was limited to about 4:1; these engines were also large in diameter. Modern gas turbines use axial compressors having many stages and thus high compression ratios (e.g. 20:1), which thus exceed piston engines in expansion ratio and are thus much more economical in fuel. Axial jets are of small diameter (suitable for slim modern aircraft), but are longer and heavier. Several modern examples produce over 10,000 lb. thrust and consume less than 0·5 lb. fuel per lb. thrust per hour (≡ Diesel economy). Gas turbines driving propellers are incorrectly termed *prop-jets.* They do not propel by jet thrust, but most of the efflux energy is absorbed by the turbine to drive the propeller; these should be called *turbo-propeller* engines. J.P. is efficient only in fast, well-streamlined aeroplanes designed especially for these power plants.

Gas turbine engines are used in industry for generating electric power and as a stand-by source. They have been tried experimentally in motor-cars, the Rover B.R.M. gas turbine being the first to run at Le Mans (1963), when it covered 2,583 m. in 24 hours at an average of 107·84 m.p.h.

See FLIGHT, HISTORY OF.

JEVONS, William Stanley (1835–82). British economist. Prof. of logic and political economy at Manchester from 1866, and at London (1876–81). He introduced the concept of final or marginal utility into economic theory.

JEWEL, John (1522–71). English churchman. Going into exile under Mary, he was appointed bp. of Salisbury by Elizabeth in 1559, and by such works as his *Apologia Ecclesiae Anglicanae* (1562) estab. himself as a founder of English protestantism.

JEWETT, Sarah Orne (1849–1909). American writer. B. in Maine, she depicted the declining life of its small seaports, as in *Deephaven* (1877).

JEWISH AUTONOMOUS REGION. Part of Khabarovsk Territory, R.S.F.S.R., in the Far East, on the left bank of the r. Amur. The cap. is Birobidjan. Textiles, leather, and clothing are made; there is some non-ferrous metallurgy, light engineering, and agriculture, and timber is worked. The J.A.R. was estab. as a national district in 1928, made an autonomous region in 1934. Area 13,900 sq. m.; pop. (1967) 174, 000 incl. *c.* 15,000 Jews.

JEWS. Name given to the Semitic people, otherwise Israelites or Hebrews, who claim descent from the patriarch Abraham. Led by him they emigrated from Mesopotamia to Canaan *c.* 2000 B.C. During the Hyksos period some settled on the borders of Egypt and were put to forced labour, from which they were rescued by Moses, founder of their religion, who aimed at their establishment in Palestine. The main invasion *c.* 1274 B.C. was led by Joshua and during the period of Judges ascendancy was estab. over the Canaanites. Complete conquest of Palestine and the union of all Israel was achieved under David *c.* 1000 B.C., and Jerusalem became the capital. Solomon, David's son, succeeded and enjoyed a reputation for great wealth and wisdom, but his lack of a constructive policy led after his death to the secession of the north (Israel) under Jeroboam, only Judah remaining under the house of David. A new factor was introduced with the rise of Assyria: Israel purchased safety by tribute, and under Jeroboam II *c.* 785 reached her highest pitch of luxury, but the basis of her society was corrupt, and prophets such as Amos, Isaiah, and Micah predicted destruction. Retribution came at the hands of Tiglath-pileser and his successor Shalmaneser IV; the northern kingdom was organized as Assyrian provs. after the fall of Samaria in 721 B.C., although Judah was spared as an ally. When the Assyrian power waned, her place was taken by Babylonia, and in 586 B.C. Nebuchadnezzar took Jerusalem and carried off the major part of the population to Babylon.

Under Cyrus, the founder of the Persian Empire, they were allowed to return to Palestine; the Temple was restored in 520, and c. 444 Ezra promulgated the legal code which was to govern the future of the race. Alexander's conquest of the Persian Empire was followed by a struggle for Palestine between the Syrian Seleucids and Egyptian Ptolemies, and until the end of the 3rd cent. B.C. Palestine remained under the govt. of Egypt with a large measure of freedom. But with the advance of Syrian power Antiochus IV attempted intervention in Jewish internal quarrels, thus prompting the Maccabean revolt in 165 B.C. For a short time Judaea was practically an independent kingdom, but internal dissension led to Pompey's intervention in 63 B.C., and Roman suzerainty was estab. After the death of Herod in 4 B.C. one experiment in govt. followed another until the revolt of A.D. 66–70 led to the destruction of the Temple by Titus.

Further desperate revolts followed, but a new focus of Jewish national sentiment was found in the work of the Rabbi Johanan ben Zakkai (c. 20–90), and after his day the President of the Sanhedrin was recognized as the Patriarch of Palestinian Jewry. Greatest of these presidents was Rabbi Judah (c. 135–220), who codified the traditional law in the Mishnah. A decline followed the Christianization of the Roman Empire, and intellectual supremacy passed to the descendants of the 6th cent. exiles in Babylonia, who compiled the Babylonian Talmud.

European settlements also deteriorated under the Christianization of the Roman Empire, but Jewry enjoyed a golden era during the period of Islamic conquest, producing such men as the philosopher Saadiah, the poet Jehudah Ha-levi, the codifier Moses Maimonides, etc. In medieval Europe the Jews were increasingly separated from the general life and trade by measures which culminated in the 16th cent. institution of the Ghetto. This persecution has been periodically revived since the period of comparative enlightenment beginning with the extension of the rights of man to the Js. by the French Revolution in 1790. Under the Nazi régime, 1939–45, some 5,000,000 Js. were put to death in Europe, leaving 1,500,000 (with a similar number in Russia) out of a former 6,500,000. Zionism (q.v.) was an attempt to solve the Jewish problem. Outside Israel, the main centres of Jewry today are the U.S.A. (5,510,000) and the U.K. (450,000). See ANTI-SEMITISM.

JEW'S HARP. Musical instrument. It is a small iron frame, attached to which is a steel strip, to be twanged by the fingers, while the frame is gripped by the teeth. Only one fundamental note is available, but by changing the shape of the mouth a complete harmonic scale can be produced.

JEX-BLAKE, Sophia (1840–1912). British woman doctor. She studied medicine in Boston, U.S.A., and Edinburgh, and founded medical schools for women in London (1874) and in Edinburgh (1886), where she practised from 1878.

JHANSI (jahn'sē). Indian city in Uttar Pradesh, 178 m. S.W. of Lucknow, a railway and road junction, and a market centre. It was founded in 1613, and was the scene of a massacre of British civilians in 1857. Pop. (1961) 170,209.

JHELUM (jāl'um). One of the five rivers which give its name to Punjab. It is the ancient Hydaspes, on the banks of which Alexander the Great won a great victory in 326 B.C. The Mangla dam (1967), one of the world's largest earth-filled dams, stores flood waters for irrigation and hydro-electricity.

JIBUTI. See DJIBOUTI.

JIDDA (jed'a). Arabian seaport on the Red Sea, in Hejaz, a transit port for pilgrims to Mecca, 45 m. to the E.; it has an airport. It is linked by road with Mecca, Medina, Riyadh and Taif. Pop. (est.) 150,000, rising to 300,000 in the pilgrimage season.

JIHAD (jihahd'). Name given to the duty imposed by the Koran on all Mohammedans to wage war on those who reject Islam.

JIMÉNEZ (khēmān'eth), **Juan Ramón** (1881–1958). Spanish lyric poet. B. in Andalusia, he enriched his native inspiration by contact with the advanced circles of Paris and Madrid, and achieved in his diary of a newly married poet (Diario de un poeta recién casado, 1917) a break into new ground in Spanish literature. He left Spain during the civil war to live in exile in Puerto Rico: he has pub. more than 40 vols. mainly of verse. His poetry has great spirituality and artistic purity. Particularly famous are his odes to his donkey 'Platero'. He gained a Nobel prize in 1956.

JI'NGO. A noisy and bellicose patriot. The term originated in 1878, when Beaconsfield's pro-Turkish policy nearly involved Britain in war with Russia. His supporters adopted as their war-song a music-hall ditty containing the line, 'We don't want to fight, but by jingo if we do . . .' The word is possibly derived from Persian 'war' or Basque 'god'.

JI'NJA. Town in Eastern Province, Uganda, on the Victoria Nile. It has a large copper-smelting works, tobacco and textile factories, and a brewery; also an airfield. Nearby is the Owen Falls Dam, opened by Elizabeth II in 1954. Pop. (1965) 40,000 (8,000 Asians).

JINN (Djinn). In Mohammedan mythology, spirits which assume human or animal shapes.

JINNAH, Mohammed Ali (1876–1948). Indian statesman. He was ed. at Karachi and in England being called to the English Bar in 1896, and became

pres. of the Moslem League in 1916 From 1934 he was elected annually as pres., and popularized among Indian Moslems the idea of separate Moslem and Hindu states when British rule ended. His views on 'Pakistan' were recognized by the Cripps mission of 1942, and at the 1946 conferences in London he insisted that only partition could solve the Indian problem. J. became Gov.-Gen. of Pakistan on the transfer of power on 15 Aug. 1947.

JOACHIM (yō'akhim), **Joseph** (1831–1907). Hungarian violinist. He studied under Mendelssohn, first performed in England in 1844, and was the founder of the J. Quartet (1869–1907). His compositions incl. the 'Hungarian Concerto' and orchestral works.

JOAN. A mythical Englishwoman who was supposed to have become Pope in 855, as John VIII, and to have given birth to a child during a papal procession. The myth was exposed in the 17th cent.

JOANNINA. See JANINA.

JOAN OF ARC, St. (1412–31). French heroine. She was b. at Domrémy, on the Meuse, and was the daughter of a well-to-do farmer. In 1429 she went to Chinon, where she persuaded Charles VII she had received a divine mission to raise the siege of Orléans. At this time all France N. of the Loire was held by the English and their allies. Entrusted with a military command, J. raised the siege; defeated the English at Patay; and witnessed Charles's coronationat Reims.

The French henceforward took the offensive and by 1453 had expelled the English from France. J. failed to capture Paris, and in May 1430 was captured. She was found guilty of witchcraft and heresy. On 30 May 1431 she was burned by the English in Rouen market-place, her ashes being thrown into the Seine. An official inquiry in 1456 annulled her sentence, and in 1920 she was canonized.

JOB. An ancient chieftain in the land of Uz, usually dentified with Edom, whose name is given to a dramatic poem in the O.T. (probably 5th cent. B.C.). The book is one of the first attempts to explain the problem of human suffering in a world created and governed by God, who is all-powerful and all-good.

JOCKEY CLUB. See HORSE RACING.

JODHPUR (jŏdpoor′). Indian city in Rajasthan, formerly cap. of J. princely state, founded in 1459 by Rao Jodha. It is a market centre with notable buildings and is dominated by its red sandstone fort. The training college of the Indian Air Force is at J. Pop. (1961) 224,723.

JODL (yōdl), **Alfred** (1892–1946). German general. B. at Aachen, he drew up the Nazi government's plan for the attack on Yugoslavia, Greece, and the Soviet Union, and in Jan. 1945 became chief of staff. He headed the delegation which signed Germany's surrender at Reims on 7 May. He was tried at Nuremberg in 1945–6, and hanged.

JO'DRELL BANK. Site in Cheshire, England, of the giant radio-telescope belonging to Manchester univ. Completed in 1957 in time to track the orbit of the first sputnik, its 250 ft. diam. paraboloid reflecting bowl weighs 750 tons, and has a range 1,000 times greater than the best optical telescopes. See LOVELL, SIR BERNARD.

JOFFRE (zhofr), **Joseph Jacques Césaire** (1852–1931). French soldier. B. in the Pyrenees, he was made chief of general staff in 1911. The invasion of Belgium by the Germans in 1914 took him by surprise, but his successful stand on the Marne made him a national hero, and he received the supreme command of all the French armies. His failure to make adequate preparations at Verdun in 1916, and the disasters on the Somme, caused increasing discontent. In Dec. 1916 J. was replaced by Nivelle, although he received the honorary title of marshal of France.

JODRELL BANK. The world's largest radio-telescope, weighing 2,000 tons, is electrically powered, revolves on bogies (1) running in a circular track, and the bowl (2), with transmitting and receiving aerials (3) rotates on 2 massive trunnions (4). The control system – designed to counteract the earth's rotation – can follow a star or satellite continuously.

JOGJAKARTA. See JOKJAKARTA.

JOHANNESBURG (johan′-). Largest city of S. Africa, situated on the Witwatersrand in Transvaal and centre of the world's greatest gold-mining industry. Founded after the discovery of gold in 1886, the town was probably named after Jan (or Johannes) Meyer, first mining commissioner. Notable buildings incl. the law courts, Escom House (Electricity Supply Commission), the S. African Railways Administration Building, the City Hall, Chamber of Mines and stock exchange, the Witwatersrand (1921) and Rand Afrikaans (1966) univs., and the Union Observatory. J. is the Republic's biggest centre for local and overseas trade in primary and industrial products and is the most important rail centre. The Jan Smuts international airport, 18 m. N.W., came into use in 1954. The mines and railways have given rise to

JOHANNESBURG. White mounds of refuse from the gold-mine crushing machines.
Courtesy of the Anglo-American Corpn.

engineering works and there are meat-chilling plants, clothing factories, etc. Pop. (1961) 1,220,500 of whom 414,900 were white.

JOHN. Apostle and saint. The son of Zebedee and Salome, a sister of the Virgin Mary, he was b. in Judaea, and with his brother James became a Galilean fisherman and one of the first disciples called by Jesus. J. was present at the Last Supper and at the Trial, and to him Jesus entrusted His mother at the foot of the cross. According to tradition J. was the author of the 4th Gospel, the Johannine Epistles, and also of the Apocalypse.

JOHN. Name of 23 popes. JOHN XXII, pope 1316–34, who spent his papacy at Avignon, engaged in a long conflict with the emperor, Louis of Bavaria, and with the Spiritual Franciscans, who preached the absolute poverty of the clergy. 'JOHN XXIII', pope 1410–15, was a pirate before entering the Church. In an attempt to end the Great Schism he was elected pope by a council of cardinals at Bologna, but was deposed by the Council of Constance in 1415, together with the popes of Avignon and Rome. He is not recognized by the Church, and the title JOHN XXIII was assumed by Angelo Giuseppe Roncalli (1881–1963). B. near Bergamo, one of a peasant family of 13, he was ordained in 1904 and pub. studies of the work of Carlo Borromeo (q.v.). At 40 he was called to Rome and then as apostolic delegate to Bulgaria, Greece and Turkey gained an unusual knowledge of the Eastern Church. In 1944 he became Papal Nuncio

JOHN XXIII. In a special audience for the infirm the Pope gives his apostolic blessing to a crippled boy. His simple sincerity in such moments made him more especially the 'Pope of the People'. *Photo: Planet News.*

to France, in 1953 a cardinal and Patriarch of Venice, and in 1958 was elected Pope. Landmarks of his papacy were improved relations with the Soviet Union, establishment of R.C. hierarchies in newly emergent states, the encyclicals *Mater et Magistra* (*Mother and Teacher:* 1961) and *Pacem in Terris* (*Peace on Earth:* 1963) realistically outlining the role of the Church in modern conditions, and the summoning of the Second Vatican Council. Winner of the Balzan (q.v.) Peace Prize in 1963, J. used it to estab. the Pope John XXIII Peace Prize Foundation to make an award triennially.

JOHN (1167–1216). King of England. The youngest son of Henry II, he attempted to seize the kingdom during his brother Richard's absence at the Crusade. On Richard's death in 1199 J. was recognized as king by England and Normandy, while Anjou and Brittany supported the claim of his nephew Arthur. J. captured and murdered Arthur, but lost Normany to the king of France. J.'s refusal to recognize Langton as archbishop of Canterbury led to the imposition of an interdict on England, and to his excommunication so that in 1213 he surrendered his kingdom to the Pope and became his vassal. His tyranny led to the barons enforcing his signature of Magna Carta (q.v.) in 1215. His repudiation of the charter provoked a civil war which was still in progress when J. d. at Newark.

JOHN II (1319–64), king of France from 1350, was defeated and captured by the Black Prince at Poitiers in 1356. He was released in 1360, but having failed to raise the money for his ransom returned in 1364 to England, where he d.

JOHN III (1624–96), called Sobieski. King of Poland. A brilliant soldier, he was elected king in 1674. In 1683 he saved Vienna from the Turks, who were besieging it.

JOHN. Name of 6 kings of Portugal. John I (1357–1433), a natural son of Pedro I, was elected king by the Cortes in 1385. His claim was supported by an English army against his rival, the king of Castile, an event which marks the beginning of the Anglo-Portuguese alliance. John IV (1603–56), originally duke of Braganza, was elected king when the Portuguese rebelled against Spanish rule in 1640. John VI (1769–1826) acted as regent for his mother Maria I 1792–1816. He fled to Brazil when the French invaded Portugal in 1807, and did not return until 1822. On his return Brazil declared its independence, with J.'s elder son Pedro as emperor.

JOHN, Augustus Edwin (1878–1961). British painter. B. in Tenby, the son of a solicitor, he studied at the Slade, and in 1903 1st exhibited at the New English Art Club. Elected R.A. in 1928, he was awarded the O.M. in 1942. Typical of his portraits is 'The Smiling Woman' (his 2nd wife, Dorelia), and 'Galway', also in the Tate Gallery, exemplifies his gifted draughtsmanship as a mural artist. Himself an impressively picturesque figure, he was pres. of the Gypsy Lore Society, and in 1952 pub. a fragmentary autobiography *Chiaroscuro*.

His sister, Gwen J. (1876–1939), a Catholic convert, lived mainly in France, and was also a subtly talented artist. His son Sir Caspar J. (1903–) was First Sea Lord and Chief of Naval Staff 1960–3.

JOHN, Griffith (1831–1912). British Congregationalist missionary. He was ordained in 1855, and was the first missionary to visit central China.

JOHN, Sir William Goscombe (1860–1952). British sculptor His principal works incl. statues of Edward VII, George V and Queen Mary at Liverpool; and David Lloyd George at Caernarvon.

JOHN BULL. An imaginary figure used as a personification of England. The name was popularized by Dr. Arbuthnot's *History of J.B.* (1712). He is represented as a prosperous farmer of the 18th cent.

JOHN CHRYSOSTOM (345–407). Christian saint and Father of the Eastern Orthodox Church. B. at Antioch, he was a hermit of the desert before being appointed bishop of Constantinople in 398.

JOHN OF AUSTRIA, Don (1545–78). Spanish soldier, the natural son of Charles V. He won a great naval victory over the Turks at Lepanto in 1571.

JOHN OF DAMASCUS, St. (c. 676–c 754). Eastern Orthodox theologian. B. at Damascus, he ably defended image-worship against the Iconoclasts.

JOHN OF GAUNT (1340–99). English nobleman, duke of Lancaster from 1362. The 4th son of Edward III, he was b. at Ghent. During the last years of Edward and the minority of Richard II he acted as head of the government and provoked protests from parliament by the corruption of his rule.

JOHN OF THE CROSS, St. (1542–91). Spanish mystic. He became a Carmelite friar in 1564, and was several times imprisoned for attempting to impose the reforms laid down by St. Teresa. His *Obras espirituales* were pub. in 1618. His verse, full of spiritual ecstasy, is of great beauty.

JOHN O' GROAT'S HOUSE. Site in the N.E. of Caithness, Scotland, about 2 m. W. of Duncansby Head, proverbially regarded as the most northerly point of Britain.

JOHNSON, Amy (1904–41). British airwoman. B. at Hull, in 1930 she flew alone from Croydon to Australia in 19½ days, and in 1932 made a record-breaking flight to the Cape. She m. J. A. Mollison in 1932, with whom she flew the Atlantic in 1933. Her greatest achievement was her flight to the Cape and back in 1936. She was killed in an air crash while serving with the Air Transport Auxiliary.

JOHNSON, Andrew (1808–75). 17th President of the U.S.A. B. in N. Carolina, he was elected to Congress in 1843 as a Democrat, became Vice-President in 1864, and succeeded to the presidency on Lincoln's death, retiring in 1869. His conciliatory policy towards the seceded states involved him in a feud with the Radicals, culminating in his impeachment before the Senate in 1868, which failed by one vote.

JOHNSON, Celia (1908–). British actress. Making her début in 1928 as *Major Barbara*, she became known for the delicate subtlety of her performances, e.g. in *The Flowering Cherry* (1957) and the film *Brief Encounter* (1946). She m. in 1935 the author and traveller Peter Fleming (1907–71).

JOHNSON, Hewlett (1874–1966). British churchman. Dean of Manchester 1924–31 and of Canterbury 1931–63, he gained the title 'Red Dean' by his support of Anglo-Soviet friendship. His works incl. *The Socialist Sixth of the World* (1939).

JOHNSON, Lyndon Baines (1908–). 36th Pres. of the U.S.A. B. in Stonewall, Texas, he had to support himself from the age of 15, and worked his way through college, graduating in 1930. After teaching in 1931, he went into politics as sec. to a Texas Congressman, and was himself elected to Congress (1937–49), and to the Senate (1949–60). A gifted and persuasive orator, his appreciation that politics was 'one long accommodation of contesting forces' brought him to Democratic leadership of the Senate. He courageously assisted the passage of the first Civil Rights Bill in a hundred years, and cautiously restricted the right to filibuster. A Democratic nominee for Pres. in 1960, he agreed to stand as Vice-Pres., thus bringing crucial Southern votes for Kennedy and himself in the 1960 election. Following the assassination of Kennedy in 1963, he succeeded as president: re-elected 1964.

LYNDON JOHNSON
Courtesy of U.S.I.S.

In 1968 he declined the pres. nomination, and attempted to promote negotiations for peace in Vietnam by halting the bombing of N. Vietnam.

He m. in 1934 Claudia (1912–), *née* Taylor and intimately known as 'Lady Bird' J., also a Texan.

JOHNSON, Pamela Hansford. *See* SNOW, LORD.

JOHNSON, Samuel (1709–84). English lexicographer, author, and critic. B. in Lichfield, he became first an usher and then a literary hack. In 1736 he m. the widow Elizabeth Porter and opened a private school. When this proved unsuccessful he went to London with his pupil David Garrick, becoming a regular contributor to the *Gentleman's Magazine* and publishing the successful poem *London* in 1738. However, he still remained in miserable poverty with companions such as Richard Savage, whose Life he wrote in 1744. In 1755 he pub. his *Dictionary*, still interesting for the vigour of its definitions. While engaged on this he had also pub. the satire *Vanity of Human Wishes* (1749), seen the failure of his tragedy *Irene* (1749), and conducted the periodical The *Rambler* (1750–2), succeeded by *The Idler* (1758–60). In 1759 he wrote the philosophical romance *Rasselas*. He was awarded a pension in 1762, and his first meeting with Boswell in 1763 was followed by the formation of the 'Literary Club' in 1764, to which Reynolds, Burke, Goldsmith, and Garrick belonged. His edition of Shakespeare appeared in 1765. A visit with Boswell to Scotland and the Hebrides in 1773 was recorded in *Journey to the Western Isles of Scotland* (1775), and in 1779–81 were pub. *Lives of the Poets*, which contain his finest critical comments. J. was buried in Westminster Abbey and his house in Gough Square, London, is preserved as a museum.

JOHNSTON, Edward (1872–1944). British calligrapher. B. in Uruguay, he was an instructor at the R.C.A. from 1901, and is famous for his block letters designed in 1913 for London Electric Railways.

JOHNSTON, Sir Harry Hamilton (1858–1927). British explorer. In 1888 he founded the British protectorate over the Nyasa region in Central Africa, was commissioner of British Central Africa 1891–6, and saw service in Tunis and Uganda.

JOHN THE BAPTIST. Christian saint and prophet. The son of Zacharias and Elizabeth, who was a cousin of Christ's mother, he was a Nazarite from his birth. After preparation in the wilderness, he proclaimed the coming of Christ, baptizing Him in the Jordan. He was executed by Herod Antipas at the instigation of Salome.

JOHORE (johor'). State of the Federation of Malaysia. J. came under British protection in 1885. The southernmost point of the Asiatic mainland, J. is joined to Singapore by a causeway. Its products are rubber, tin, pineapples, copra, etc. The cap. is Johore Bahru. Area 7,321 sq. m.; pop. (1966) 1,278,289.

JOINT. An articulation; a structure in which 2 bones meet. Some joints allow no motion (e.g. the sutures of the skull); some allow a very small motion (e.g. the sacro-iliac joints in the lower back); but some other joints allow a relatively free motion. Of this 3rd class (diarthrodial) some allow a gliding motion (e.g. one vertebra of the

JOHN THE BAPTIST. By Rodin. Superbly interpreting the spirit of the apostle who sought to make men 'proselytes of righteousness', this bronze is in the Musée du Luxembourg.

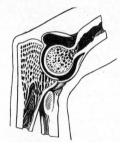

JOINT. A section through the left elbow joint.

spine on another); some have a hinge action (e.g. those of the elbow and knee); and others allow motion in all directions (e.g. the hip and shoulder joints), by means of a ball-and-socket arrangement. The ends of the bones at a moving J. are covered with cartilage for greater elasticity and smoothness, and enclosed in an envelope (capsule) of tough white fibrous tissue lined with a membrane which secretes lubricating (synovial) fluid. The J. is further strengthened by ligaments. Js. are easily injured, but heal readily unless infection is introduced.

JOINVILLE (zhwaṅvēl'), **Jean, Sire de** (1224–1317). French chronicler. B. in Champagne, he accompanied Louis IX on the crusade of 1248–54, which he described in his *History of St. Louis*.

JÓKAI (yoh'koi), **Mór** (1825–1904). Hungarian novelist. An active nationalist and partisan in the 1848 Revolution, he was later a Liberal member of parliament for 20 years and ed. several newspapers. His novels, e.g. *A Hungarian Nabob* (1854) and *Black Diamonds* (1870), reveal an exuberant imagination, and he often created in them an exotic, semi-scientific world of his own. He was also an essayist.

JOKJAKARTA (jokyōkahr'tah). Town in Java, Indonesia, 60 m. S. of Semarang. It has an airport and is the seat of a university. Pop. *c.* 300,000.

JOLSON, Al. Stage name of the American singer Asa Yoelson (1886–1950). B. in Russia, he became famous as a star of the early sound-films *The Jazz Singer* and *The Singing Fool*.

JŌ'NAH. Hebrew prophet, whose name is given to a book in the O.T. He was sent to prophesy destruction on Nineveh, was cast overboard, and is said to have spent 3 days and nights in the belly of a whale.

JONES, Daniel (1881–1967). British philologist. Prof. of phonetics at Univ. Coll., London, 1921–49, he produced many notable works incl. *Outline of English Phonetics*, *English Pronouncing Dictionary* and *Pronunciation of English* (1914). In 1950 he became Pres. of the International Phonetic Assoc.

JONES, Ernest (1879–1958). Welsh psychoanalyst. He wrote a monumental Life of Freud (1953–7), and from 1913 was engaged in introducing psychoanalysis into Britain and America.

JONES, Ernest Charles (1819–69). British Chartist. In 1848 he was sentenced to 2 years' solitary confinement for sedition. He was a friend of Marx, and the author of novels and poems.

JONES, (Frederick) Wood (1879–1954). British anatomist. Following anthropological studies in Nubia, he became prof. of anatomy at Manchester 1938–45, and at the Royal College of Surgeons, London, 1945–52. He wrote *Arboreal Man* (1916), *Man's Place among the Mammals* (1929), and the classic works on *The Hand* (1920), and *The Foot* (1944).

JONES, Henry (1831–99). British authority on card games, writing under the pen-name of 'Cavendish'. His 'Laws' of whist, piquet, and écarté appeared in 1862, 1873, and 1878 respectively.

JONES, Henry Arthur (1851–1929). British playwright. His first success was the melodrama *The Silver King* (1882); among his 60 other plays were *The Case of Rebellious Susan* (1894), *The Liars* (1897) and *Mrs. Dane's Defence* (1900), notable as an early realist-problem play.

JONES, Inigo (1573–*c.* 1652). English architect. B. in London, he studied in Italy, and was influenced by the works of Palladio. He was employed by James I in designing the scenery for Ben Jonson's masques, and in 1619 he designed his masterpiece, the banqueting-room at Whitehall; and the church of St. Paul, Covent Garden, London.

JONES, James (1921–　). American author. B. in Illinois, he was ed. at N.Y. univ., and was awarded the Purple Heart while serving with the U.S. Army 1939–44. *From Here to Eternity* (1951) attacked army-style conformity and *Some Came Running* (1958) the set attitudes of the Midwest.

JONES, John Paul (1747–92). American naval officer. B. in Kirkcudbright, he served at sea as a trader and slaver, but on his return to Scotland from the W. Indies, on a ship of which he had become master, he was accused of murdering one of the crew. Searching for evidence of his innocence, he returned to the W. Indies, but killed the leader of a mutiny and fled to his brother in Virginia, received a privateer's commission from Congress on the outbreak of the War of Independence in 1775. As head of a French naval expedition, he menaced British shipping 1779–81 and returned to America in 1781. He joined the Russian navy as a rear-admiral in 1788, fighting against Turkey, but lost Catherine's favour and d. in France.

JONGKIND (yong'kint), Johan (1819–91). Dutch artist. Settling in France in 1846, he was associated with the Barbizon group and developed in his landscapes in oil and water-colour delicate interpretation of light effects which influenced the Impressionists. His life was often wretched and he d. in an insane asylum.

JÖNKÖPING (yon'choping). Town at the S. end of Lake Vatter, Sweden, cap. of J. county. It is a great industrial centre. Pop. (1966) 53,765.

JON'QUIL. Name given to a species of the Amaryllidaceae family, *Narcissus jonquilla*, which has yellow flowers with an orange corona, and is found in S. Europe and Africa.

JONSON, Benjamin (1572–1637). English dramatist, poet, and critic. B. at Westminster, he entered the theatre as actor and dramatist in 1597. In 1598 he narrowly escaped the gallows for killing a fellow-player in a duel, and in the same year his *Everyman in His Humour* was produced, followed by *Everyman out of His Humour* (1599), *Cynthia's Revels* (1600) and *Poetaster* (1601). His first extant tragedy is *Sejanus* (1603), with Burbage and Shakespeare as members of the original cast. J. collaborated with Marston and Chapman in *Eastward Ho* (1605), and shared their imprisonment when official exception was taken to a derogatory reference to the Scots. There followed the great plays of his middle years *Volpone, or the Fox* (1606), *Epicoene, or The Silent Woman* (1609), *The Alchemist* (1610), *Catiline* (1611), *Bartholomew Fair* (1614). Meanwhile J. had made a great reputation in the presentation of masques, and produced some 30 such pieces before a quarrel with his associate Inigo Jones in 1630 lost him court favour. Failing health overshadowed his later plays, e.g. *The Staple of News* (1626). J. excelled in construction, and was the creator of the English comedy of humours. From 1630 he was virtually poet laureate; he is buried in Westminster Abbey.

JÓNSSON (yon'-), Einar (1874–1954). Icelandic sculptor. B. in Iceland, he developed a rugged austere style. His works incl. a statue of Thorfinnur Karlsefni (the 1st white settler in America, an Icelander) in Philadelphia.

JOOSS (yos), Kurt (1901–　). German choreographer, director of the Ballets Jooss, which he founded in 1932. In his ballet *The Green Table* (1932) he depicted the League of Nations, and in 1959 he revived Purcell's *The Fairy Queen*.

JOPPA. Ancient name of JAFFA.

JORDAENS (yor'dahns), Jakob (1593–1678).

Flemish painter. B. at Antwerp, he is noted for his realistic pictures of Flemish life.

JORDAN, Dorothea (1762–1816). British actress. She made her début in 1777, and retired in 1815. She was a mistress of the duke of Clarence (later William IV) by whom she had 10 children who were given the name FitzClarence.

JORDAN. River in the Levant. It rises on Mount Hermon in Syria at *c.* 1,800 ft. above sea-level and flows S. for some 200 m. through the Sea of Galilee into the Dead Sea, 1,290 ft. below sea-level. It occupies the northern part of the Great Rift Valley; its upper course forms the boundary of Israel with Syria and the kingdom of Jordan; its lower course runs through Jordan—W. bank occupied by Israel 1967.

JORDAN, The Hashimite Kingdom of. Independent country of S.W. Asia, bordered W. by Israel (with which J. shares the Dead Sea), N. by Syria, E. by Iraq and Saudi Arabia, S. by Saudi Arabia. It has a 15 m. coastline at the head of the Gulf of Aqaba, an inlet of the Red Sea, with one port, Aqaba. The cap. is Amman; other towns are Bethlehem, Jericho, Petra, and the eastern part of Jerusalem. The constitution of 1951 estab. a cabinet responsible to a parliament, consisting of ა senate nominated by the king and a lower house elected by manhood suffrage. Area 37,000 sq. m.; pop. (1966) 2,100,800, incl. 550,000 Arab refugees from Israel.

Much of J. is desert, though where there is water the soil is fertile; wheat, millet, sesame, olives and grapes are grown; cattle, sheep, camels, and goats are reared. About a quarter of the inhabitants continue to live nomadically. The potash of the Dead Sea and some phosphate deposits constitute the known mineral resources; prospecting for petroleum began in 1955. The general level of J. is 2,600 feet above sea-level, rising in the S. to over 5,000 ft. and sinking in the W. to the Dead Sea, 1,290 ft. below sea-level. The numerous *wadis* (river beds), most of which drain to the r. Jordan or the Dead Sea, are empty except for the brief period of the winter rains.

History. The area forming the kingdom of Jordan was occupied by the independent Nabataeans from the 4th cent. B.C., and perhaps earlier, until A.D. 106 when it became part of the Roman prov. of Arabia. It was included in the Crusaders' kingdom of Jerusalem, 1099–1187, and from the 16th cent. was ruled by the Ottoman Turks until the break-up of the Turkish Empire after the F.W.W. The League of Nations placed it in 1920 under British mandate as part of Palestine; but in 1923 Britain recognized the mandated territory E. of the Jordan r. as a separate country, Transjordan, under the Emir Abdullah. Transjordan was given full independence by a treaty of 1946, in which year Abdullah took the title king and changed the name of his country to the Hashimite Kingdom of Jordan (a name that came into general use only in 1949). Abdullah was a prime mover in the formation of the Arab League (q.v.), and in 1948 his forces invaded the newly proclaimed republic of Israel, occupying most of the area of Palestine (q.v.) which the United Nations had proposed to allocate to the Arabs. Abdullah made an armistice with Israel in 1949, but retained the part of Palestine (incl. eastern Jerusalem) which he had occupied, formally annexing it in 1950. Abdullah was assassinated in 1951; his grandson Hussein (q.v.) became king in 1952, his father Talal having been deposed owing to mental illness. J. fought in alliance with Egypt against Israel 5–10 June 1967, when all J. west of the r. Jordan as well as eastern Jerusalem (q.v.) was occupied by Israel. There was civil war between the govt. army and the Palestinian guerrillas in 1970.

JOSEPH. Hebrew patriarch, the elder of Jacob's sons by Rachel; he was sold by his envious brothers into slavery in Egypt. There he rose to high office under the Pharaoh, and succoured his father and brothers when they were driven by famine into Egypt.

JOSEPH. The husband of the Virgin Mary. He was a descendant of David, and a carpenter by trade. According to Catholic tradition, he had a family by a previous wife, and was an elderly man when he married Mary, who remained perpetually virgin.

JOSEPH, Sir Keith Sinjohn (1918–). British Cons. politician. A barrister and Fellow of All Souls, Oxon. (1946–60), he entered Parliament in 1956, becoming in 1962–4 Min. of Housing and Local Govt. and Min. for Welsh Affairs (1962), and Sec. of State for Social Services from 1970.

JOSEPH II (1741–90). Holy Roman Emperor. The son of the emperor Francis I and Maria Theresa, he succeeded his father as emperor in 1765, but only attained real power after his mother's death in 1780. He introduced a series of sweeping reforms, but his disregard of traditional privileges, etc., provoked revolts in Belgium, Hungary, and elsewhere.

JOSEPHINE (jō'zefĕn) (1763–1814). Empress of France. A native of Martinique, *née* Marie Josèphe Rose Tascher de la Pagerie, she m. in 1779 the vicomte Beauharnais, who was guillotined during the Revolution. In 1796 she m. Napoleon Bonaparte, with whom she was crowned empress in 1804. As she bore him no child, he divorced her in 1809, and she spent the rest of her life in retirement near Paris.

JOSEPH OF ARIMATHAEA. A wealthy Jew and member of the Sanhedrin, who was a secret supporter of Jesus, and on the evening of the Crucifixion begged his body of Pilate and buried it in his own tomb. According to tradition he brought the Holy Grail to England about A.D. 63 and erected at Glastonbury the first Christian church to be built in Britain.

JOSEPHUS (jōsē'fus), **Flavius** (A.D. 37–c. 100). Jewish historian. B. in Jerusalem, he became a Pharisee. On the outbreak of the Jewish revolt in 66 he was given the command in Galilee, but was defeated and captured. He won the favour of the emperor Vespasian and settled in Rome. He wrote *Antiquities of the Jews* to A.D. 66; *The Jewish War*; and an autobiography.

JO'SHUA. Hebrew general who led the Israelites after the death of Moses in the conquest and settlement of the land of the Canaanites (Palestine).

JŌS'IAH (b. 647 B.C.). King of Judah. Grandson of Manasseh and son of Amon, he succeeded to the throne when 8. The discovery of a Book of Instruction (probably Deuteronomy) during the repair of the Temple in 621 stimulated thorough reform, which included the removal of all sanctuaries except that of Jerusalem. J. was killed in a clash at Megiddo with Pharaoh-nechoh, king of Egypt.

JOSQUIN DES PRÉS (zhoskań' dā prā) (c. 1445–1521). Flemish composer of masses, a pupil of Okeghem; he also wrote secular songs.

JŌTUNHEIM (yö'toonhīm). Mountainous region in S. Norway, containing the highest mountains in Scandinavia, Glittertind (8,048 ft.) and Galdhopiggen (8,097 ft.).

JOUBERT (zhoobār'), **Joseph** (1754–1824). French thinker, famed for the posthumous *Pensées, essais maximes, et correspondance* (1842).

JOUBERT, Petrus Jacobus (1834–1900). Boer general, who led the Boer commandos against the British 1880–1, and on the outbreak of war in 1899 was nominal commander of the Boer forces.

JOUBERT (DE LA FERTÉ), Sir Philip (1887–1965). British air chief marshal. B. in Calcutta, he joined the R.F.C. in 1913 and was A.O.C.-in-C. Coastal Command 1936–7 and 1941–3, and A.O.C.R.A.F. in India 1937–9, being knighted in 1938. He was a well-known broadcaster and writer on R.A.F. subjects, and his books incl. *The Fated Sky* (1952) and *Birds and Fishes* (1960).

JOUFFROY d'ABBANS (zhoofrwah' dahboń'), **Claude** (1751–1832). French marquess and soldier,

U

who in 1783 built a small paddlewheel steamboat. By the French he is claimed as the founder of steam navigation.

JOUHAUD (zhoo-oh'), **Edmond** (1905–). French gen. B. near Oran, he escaped from German captivity in 1940 to become a resistance leader, and commanded the air force in Indo-China in 1954 and in Algeria 1956–8. Following the abortive 1961 coup in Algeria, he was second in command to Salan in the O.A.S. and in 1962 was condemned to death after his arrest in Oran. This unpopular sentence was commuted to life imprisonment and he was released 1967.

JOUHAUX (zhoo-oh'), **Léon** (1879–1954). French trade union leader, sec. of the Confédération Générale du Travail 1909–40. Arrested by the Vichy govt. in 1941, he was imprisoned in Germany until 1945. He was then joint sec. of the C.G.T. until his secession in 1947. He was awarded the Nobel peace prize in 1951.

JOULE, James Prescott (1818–89). British physicist. He was a brewery owner, but dedicated to precise scientific research, and his work on the relations between electrical, mechanical and chemical effects, led to the discovery of the first law of thermodynamics. He determined the mechanical equivalent of heat (J.'s equivalent); and the work done in one sec. by a current of 1 amp across a potential difference of 1 volt is known as the *joule*.

JOURDAN (zhoordoń'), **Jean Baptiste**, count (1762–1833). Marshal of France. B. at Limoges, he was made in 1793 C.-in-C. of the Army of the N., and defeated the Austrians at Wattignies and Fleurus. Napoleon created him a marshal of France.

JOURNALISM. The profession or occupation of writing for, and producing (as apart from printing), newspapers and other periodicals. The main divisions are editing, sub-editing, reporting and specialist writing.

In the U.K. student courses and courses for working journalists, e.g. at the Univ. of London, are arranged by the Nat. Council for Training of Journalists: the professional body is the Inst. of Journalists, and the Nat. Union of Journalists has *c*. 20,000 members. In the U.S.A. univ. training is the rule and prizes founded by Joseph Pulitzer (q.v.) and others maintain standards, so that journalists tend to stand in higher public repute. Television and radio newsmen were among the winners of awards given by the Newspaper Reporters of N.Y. City for the first time in 1967.

JOUVET (zhoo-veh'), **Louis** (1887–1951). French actor and director. Trained as a pharmacist, he turned to the stage, and was equally able to direct Molière or Giraudoux, whose genius he was early to recognize. Films he directed incl. *Carnet de bal* (1937) and *La Fin du jour* (1939).

JŌ'VIAN (331–64). Roman emperor. Captain of the imperial bodyguard, he was chosen emperor by the soldiers on Julian's death in battle with the Persians (363), and concluded a humiliating peace. He re-estab. Christianity as the state religion.

JOWETT (jō'et), **Benjamin** (1817–93). British scholar. Taking holy orders in 1842, he became in 1855 Regius prof. of Greek at Oxford, and in 1870 Master of Balliol. He was prominent in promoting univ. reform, incl. the abolition of the theological test for degrees, and trans. Plato, Aristotle and Thucydides.

JOWITT, William Allen, 1st earl (1885–1957). British Labour statesman. Called to the Bar in 1909, he was elected a Lib. M.P. in 1922 and a Lab. M.P. in 1929. He was Attorney General 1929–32, Solicitor General 1940–2, and then in turn Paymaster General, Min. without Portfolio, and Min. of National Insurance until 1945, when he was Lord Chancellor in the Labour Government until 1951.

JOYCE, Eileen. Australian pianist. B. in Tasmania, she incl. Schnabel among her tutors and made her début at the Proms under Sir Henry Wood. An attractively brilliant executant, she made the piano sound-track for *The Seventh Veil*.

JOYCE, James Augustin Aloysius (1882–1941). Irish writer. B. in Dublin, he studied medicine in Paris, but later became a teacher of languages. In 1907 he pub. a vol. of verse, *Chamber Music*, and in 1914 the realistic stories *Dubliners*. His *Portrait of an Artist as a Young Man* (1916) is semi-autobiographical and anticipates the advanced technique of *Ulysses* (1922), which records the events of a Dublin day, and mingles direct narrative with the unspoken and even unconscious reactions of the characters. The book was banned for obscenity in England and the U.S.A. *Finnegan's Wake* (1939), long known as *Work in Progress*, attempts a synthesis of all existence, using a polyglot language containing impressionistic compounds, e.g. 'polyfizzyboisterous'.

JOYCE, William (1906–46). Fascist. B. in New York, the son of a naturalized American of Irish birth, he was director of propaganda in the British Union of Fascists until 1937, when he formed the more openly pro-German National Socialist League. On the outbreak of the S.W.W. he went to Germany and regularly broadcast to Britain, being known as 'Lord Haw-haw'. Tried for treason at the Old Bailey in 1945, he was hanged.

JUAN FERNANDEZ ISLANDS (hoo-ahn' fern-ahndeth). A group of islands in the S. Pacific belonging to Chile. The most important are Santa Clara and Mas-a-Tierra (also sometimes called Juan Fernandez Island) where Alexander Selkirk (q.v.) was marooned 1704–9. The islands were named after the Spanish navigator who discovered them *c.* 1565.

JUAREZ (hoo-ah'reth), **Benito Pablo** (1806–72). Mexican politician, b. of Indian parents. He was governor of Oaxaca 1847–52, but was exiled by Santa Anna. He had a share in the successful revolt of 1855, and in 1858 was elected President of the republic. He declared war on France in 1862 when Napoleon III sent troops to Mexico and as constitutional President opposed the French-supported emperor Maximilian, who was executed in 1867. Juarez was re-elected President, and again in 1871.

JUBA (jōōb'a). River in E. Africa formed at Dolo, Ethiopia, by the junction of the Ganale Dorya and Dawa rivers. It flows S. *c.* 500 m. in a meandering course through the Somali Rep. (of which its valley is the most productive area) into the Indian Ocean 10 m. N.E. of Kismayu. When in flood it is 1,150 ft. wide, at other times *c.* 250 ft. A strip of country some 100 m. wide, on the right bank of the J., formerly called Jubaland, was in Kenya until transferred to (Italian) Somaliland in 1925.

JUBA. Town in Sudan Rep., cap. of Equatoria prov., on the left bank of the White Nile, at the head of navigation above Khartoum 750 m. N., J. is an admin. and trade centre, with an airfield. Pop. (1964) 15,000.

JUBBULPO'RE. City and district of Madhya Pradesh, Rep. of India. The city, with cotton and flour mills and a univ. coll., is a railway centre. Pop. (1951) 256,998.

JUDAH (joo'dah). District of S. Palestine, which after the death of Solomon adhered to his son Rehoboam and the Davidic line, whereas the rest of Israel elected Jeroboam as ruler of the northern kingdom. In N.T. times, J. was the Roman prov. of Judaea.

JUDAISM (joo'da-izm). Term signifying the distinctive religious beliefs and observances of the Jews. It is founded on the Torah, 'direction for living', which combines the Mosaic code and its oral interpretation. During the Babylonian exile of 586 B.C. the Jews preserved their individual mode of life, and with the return under Cyrus J. was estab. by the code of Ezra. The effect of the destruction of the Temple on J.

was countered by the rising importance of the synagogue, of home religious life, and of the lay rabbis.

The creed of J. is based on the fundamental concepts of one God, the revelation of His will in the Torah, and the special relationship of God and the Jewish people: its orthodox formulation is that of Moses Maimonides (1135–1204). Among the distinctive observances of J. are circumcision, the daily services in Hebrew, and the observance of the Sabbath (7th day of the week) and the 3 principal festivals, Passover, Pentecost, and Tabernacles. Dissenting movements in J. include the Pharisees, Sadducees, and Essenes of N.T. times; the 8th cent. Karaites; the Chasidism of the 18th cent.; the Reform movement begun in Germany in 1810 which reached England in 1842; and the more radical Liberal J. which developed in America and founded its first London synagogue in 1911.

JUDAS ISCARIOT (joo'das iskar'i-ot). The one of the 12 Apostles who betrayed Jesus. He was the treasurer of the little band, and at the last Passover arranged with the chief priests to betray Jesus for 30 pieces of silver. The betrayal effected, he was smitten with remorse and committed suicide.

JUDGE. A person invested with power to hear and determine legal disputes. In the U.K., Js. are chosen from the Bar, and those of the Supreme Court (except the Lord Chief Justice) and County Courts are nominated by the Lord Chancellor, who is a political appointee. In the U.S.A., apart from the Federal judiciary which are executive appointments, Js. in most states are elected by popular vote.

JUDICIAL SEPARATION. A decree of J.S. puts an end to the obligation of a married couple to cohabit, but does not dissolve the marriage or leave the parties free to marry again. A decree of J.S. may be granted on (1) any grounds which would support a petition for divorce; (2) failure to comply with a decree for the restitution of conjugal rights. As in divorce, J.S. may carry with it orders by the court as to alimony, the care and custody of children, etc. A decree of J.S. is also obtainable in the U.S.

JUDO (jū'dō). Synthesis of the most valuable methods from the many forms of jujitsu (jūjit'soo), the traditional Japanese skill of self-defence and offence without weapons, which was originally practised as a secret art by the feudal Samurai. In modern times J. has been adopted throughout the world as a compulsory subject in the armed forces, the police, and in many schools. When it is practised as a sport the 2 combatants wear special loose-fitting, belted-jackets and trousers to facilitate holds, and the falls are broken by a special square mat: when one

JUDO. Two experts – their black belts proclaiming their degree of efficiency – at the crucial moment in an inner thigh throw, called in Japanese *uchimata*.   *Photo: Philip G. Davis.*

estab. a painful hold that the other cannot break, the latter signifies his surrender by slapping the ground with a free hand. Degrees of proficiency are indicated by the colour of the belt: for novices white; after examination, brown (3 degrees); and finally, black (9 degrees). J. schools have been estab. in the U.S.A. and the U.K. since the beginning of this cent. and it is an increasingly popular sport. *Karate* (kahrah'te) is a purely offensive form of J. aimed at maiming or inflicting lethal blows. Resembling it, but even more deadly, is *Kung-fu*, developed in China *c.* 5,000 years ago.

JUGGERNAUT (jug'ernawt), or **Jagannath**. A name for Vishnu, the Hindu god, meaning 'Lord of the World'. His temple is at Puri, Orissa.

JUGOSLAVIA. *See* YUGOSLAVIA.

JUGULAR (jōō'gular). Belonging to the neck, especially of the external, anterior, and internal J. veins, through which the blood returns from the head and face towards the heart.

JUGU'RTHA (joo-) (d. 104 B.C.). King of Numidia in N. Africa, who, after a long resistance, was betrayed to the Romans in 107 B.C., and put to death by strangulation or starvation after being imprisoned in the underground prison beneath the Capitol.

JUIN (zhü-aṅ'), **Alphonse Pierre** (1888–1967). Marshal of France. Severely wounded in the F.W.W., he was a prisoner of the Germans (1940–1), but joined Giraud in N. Africa, and was C.-in-C. French forces in Italy in 1943 and chief of general staff 1944–7.

JU JITSU. *See* JUDO.

JUJUBE (jōō'joob). Tree of the *Zizyphus* genus in the family Rhamnaceae, and also its berry-like fruits. The Mediterranean species is *Z. vulgaris*; the Chinese (*Z. jujuba*) has fruit the size of small plums, known when preserved in syrup as 'Chinese dates', but the Indian (*Z. mauritiana*) has a more mediocre fruit. The name is also given to a type of mucilaginous sweet.

JULIAN (jōō'lyan) (*c.* 331–63). Roman emperor, called the 'Apostate'. B. in Constantinople, the nephew of Constantine the Great, he was brought up as a Christian, but in early life became a convert to paganism. Sent by Constantius to govern Gaul in 355, he was proclaimed emperor by his troops in 360, and was marching on Constantinople when in 361 Constantius's death allowed him to succeed peacefully. He revived pagan worship, and infuriated the Christians by refusing to persecute heretics. He was slain in battle against the Persians.

JULIANA (jōōlyah'na) (1909–). Queen of the Netherlands. The dau. of Queen Wilhelmina (1880–1962) and Prince Henry of Mecklenburg-Schwerin, she m. in 1937 Prince Bernhard of Lippe-Biesterfeld and has 4 daus.; the eldest and heiress to the throne is Crown Princess Beatrix (q.v.). During the German occupation of Holland 1940–5, when her mother withdrew her govt. to England, J. lived mainly in Canada. She was princess regent in 1947 and 1948 when her mother was in ill-health, and succeeded to the throne in September 1948 on Wilhelmina's abdication. In 1964 a constitutional crisis was precipated by the conversion to Roman Catholicism of her 2nd dau., Princess Irene (1940–), who m. Prince Carlos Hugo of Bourbon-Parma (1930–), son of the Carlist Pretender to the Spanish throne, Prince Xavier. The princess renounced her right of succession to the Dutch throne. *See* BOURBON table.

JULIUS (jōōl'yus) II. Pope 1503–13, was a politician who set himself to make the papal states the leading power in Italy, and formed international alliances first against Venice and then against France. He began the building of St. Peter's, Rome, in 1506, and was the patron of Michelangelo and Raphael.

JULY REVOLUTION. Name given to the Parisian revolution of 27–9 July 1830 which overthrew the restored Bourbon monarchy of Charles X, and substituted the constitutional monarchy of Louis Philippe, whose rule (1830–48) is sometimes referred to as the July Monarchy.

JUMPING HARE. S. African rodent (*Pedetes caffer*), similar in appearance and habits to the jerboa, but the head is like that of a hare.

JUMPING MOUSE. N. American rodent (*Zapus hudsonius*) in the jerboa family.

JUNAGADH (junah'gad). Indian city in the Kathiawar peninsula, Gujarat state. It has interesting caves and an old citadel, and one of King Asoka's rock edicts. Pop. (1961) 63,000.

J. was the cap. of the former princely state of J., area 3,337 sq. m., which after a show of force by India against its Muslim ruler, called the Nawab, and a plebiscite heavily in favour of accession to India, was merged in Saurashtra (q.v.) in 1948.

JUNCACEAE (jung-kā'-sē-ē). Botanical name for the rush family, represented by 2 British genera, *Juncus* (rush) and *Luzula* (woodrush). *See* RUSH.

JUNEAU (joonō'). Cap. and port of Alaska, U.S.A., on Gastineau Channel. Pop. (1960) 6,797.

JUNCACEAE
Hairy woodrush.

JUNG (yoong), **Carl G.** (1875–1961). Swiss psychologist. Like Freud he stressed the importance of unconscious memories and early childhood experiences, but he rejected Freud's excessive emphasis upon the sexual instinct. J. developed his own theory of analytical psychology, and wrote *Modern Man in Search of a Soul* (1933), etc.

JUNG (yoong), **Johann Heinrich** (1740–1817), called Stilling. German mystic writer. B. in Westphalia, he studied medicine at Strasbourg, where Goethe encouraged him to write his autobiography (1777–1817). He made a name with operations for cataract; turned to political economy, and propounded the belief in miracles and ghosts (*Theorie der Geisterkunde*, 1808).

JÜNGER (yüng'er), **Ernst** (1895–). German author. He used his experiences while serving during the F.W.W., in which he won the highest German military decoration, in such early books as *The Storm of Steel* (1920). Later he joined the ranks of Nazi thinkers, but *On the Marble Cliffs* (1939) renounces this creed: his diaries are impressive.

JUNIPER (jōōn'iper). Aromatic evergreen shrubs found throughout Britain, Europe, America, and temperate countries of the world. They are members of the Cupressaceae family, genus *Juniperus*.

JUNIUS (jōō'nyus), **Letters of.** A series of letters pub. in the *Public Advertiser* 1769–72, under the pseudonym J. Written in a pungent, epigrammatic style, they were intended to discredit the 'king's friends' in the interests of the opposition Whigs. The generally accepted theory attributes them to **Sir** Philip Francis.

JUNIPER

JUNKERS (yoong'kers), **Hugo** (1859–1935). German aeroplane designer. In 1919 he founded in Dessau the aircraft works named after him. J. planes, including dive bombers, night fighters, and troop carriers, were used by the Germans in the S.W.W.

JUNKERS. Name applied to a class of landed gentry in Prussia, given to reactionary views and policy. They constituted a large percentage of the officer corps of the Prussian army.

JUNO (jōō'nō). Roman goddess identified with the Greek Hera. The wife of Jupiter, the queen of heaven, she was especially the goddess of women.

JUNOT (zhünoh'), **Andoche**, duke of Abrantès (1771–1813). French gen. He served with Napoleon at Toulon and in Egypt, and in 1807 commanded the army invading Portugal. He was defeated by Wellesley at Vimeiro in 1808. Later he fell into disgrace, and committed suicide. His wife **Laure J.** (1783–1834) wrote memoirs.

JUPITER (jōō'piter), or **Jō've.** Chief god of the ancient Romans, identified with the Greek Zeus. Originally he was god of the sky and associated with the lightning and thunderbolt. Later he came to be known as the protector in battle and the bestower of victory. He was the son of Saturn, m. his sister Juno, and reigned on Olympus as lord of heaven.

JUPITER. The largest planet in the Solar System. Its diameter as measured through the equator is 88,700 miles, and it could contain over 1,300 globes the size of the Earth; its mass, however, is only 318 times that of the Earth, since the planet is composed largely or entirely of gas. Its internal constitution is still a matter for debate, but there can be no doubt that J. contains a great deal of hydrogen, together with hydrogen compounds such as ammonia and methane.

Despite its great distance from the Sun (483,300,000 m. on the average), J. is a brilliant object in the night sky, and is well seen for several months in each year. Telescopically it is of extreme interest, and even a small instrument will show the famous streaks known as 'cloud belts'. Particularly noteworthy, too, is the Great Red Spot, which seems to be semi-perma-nent. Its precise nature is unknown, but it is thought to be a solid or semi-solid body floating in J.'s outer gas. Sometimes, as in 1962, it is extremely conspicuous when seen with a moderate telescope.

JUPITER. Taken with a 36 inch refractor, this photo-graph shows the planet's famous cloud belts.
Courtesy of Lick Observatory, University of California.

J. takes 11·9 years to complete one journey round the Sun, but its axial rotation period is very short – less than 10 hours. The surface temperature never exceeds −200°F (−128·9°C), and J. is clearly unsuited for any form of life. Of the 12 satellites, 4 (Io, Europa, Ganymede and Callisto) are large, and are visible with any small telescope; they were discovered by Galileo in 1609–10. Radio signals emitted by J. are thought to depend on the position of Io and Europa.

JURA (joo'rah). Series of parallel mountain ranges running S.W.–N.E. along the French-Swiss frontier between the Rhône and the Rhine, a distance of 156 m. The highest peak is Crête de la Neige (5,654 ft.); several others exceed 5,000 ft. The J. mountains give their name to a dept. of France.

JURA (joo'ra) (Gaelic, meaning red deer). One of the Inner Hebrides, in Argyll co., Scotland, 143 sq. m. in area and mountainous, one of the twin peaks called the Paps of J. reaching 2,571 ft. J. is separated from the mainland by the Sound of J. Pop. (est.) 230.

JURINAC (yur'ēnats), **Sena** (1921–). Yugoslav soprano, well known for her interpretation of the composer in Strauss's *Ariadne*, and a member of the Viennese State Opera from 1944.

JURISPRUDENCE (jōōrisprōō'dens). The science of law in the abstract; that is, not the study of any particular laws or legal system, but of the principles upon which all mature legal systems are founded.

JURY. Body of laymen sworn to render a verdict in a court of justice. Of generally Germanic origin, the British J. probably derives most directly from the custom of the Franks, introduced into England by the Normans. Under the Plantagenets it developed from a body of neighbours, familiar with the people and background of the case – almost appearing in the character of witnesses – to an impartial panel render-ing a verdict based solely on evidence heard in court. In the U.K. the most important type (others are coroners' Js. and the now largely obsolete special Js. for important civil cases) are the common Js. which take part in the more important criminal and certain civil cases. Jurors are selected at random from men and women between 21 and 60, if they are parliamen-tary or local govt. electors (the basis of 'householder' qualification ended 1972), with exemption for certain classes, e.g. peers, doctors, M.P.s, ministers of religion, etc. Either prosecution or defence may challenge any juror as unsuitable. The verdict reached is conclusive, i.e. there can be no retrial on the same charge, and in England had always been unanimous (though Scotland had allowed simple majority verdicts in a J. of 15), but evidence of corruption and intimida-tion led to the Criminal Justice Act 1967, by which a majority of 10 to 2 convicts, and people with criminal convictions are disqualified from serving. Members of Js. are allowed certain expenses, etc.

The basic principles of the British system have been adopted in the U.S., most Commonwealth countries, and in some European countries, e.g. France. In the U.S.A. the use of a grand J. (abolished in England in 1933) has been retained, both at federal and state level: consisting of 23 persons it hears only evidence for the prosecution to decide whether there is a case to be referred for trial.

JUS PRIMAE NOCTIS (yoos prē'mī nok'tis) (Lat., right of the first night). The custom of allowing the lord to enjoy the wife of any of his tenants on the wedding night. It existed in Scotland until Malcolm III, in the 11th cent., enacted that the bridegroom might pay a sum of money in lieu; and a similar right has been discovered among many savage races.

JUSTICE OF THE PEACE. In England an unpaid magistrate appointed by the Lord Chancellor. Two or more Js. of the P. sit to dispose of minor charges (formerly their jurisdiction was much wider), to commit for trial by a higher court more serious ones, to grant licences for the sale of intoxicating liquor, etc. In the U.S.A., where they are in receipt of fees and are usually elected, their courts are the lowest in the States, and Js. of the P. deal only with minor offences, such as traffic violations: they may also conduct marriages.

JUSTINIAN I (483–562). Byzantine emperor. B. in Illyricum, he was associated with his uncle Justin I in the govt. from 518. He m. the actress Theodora, and succeeded Justin in 527. He recovered N. Africa from the Vandals, S.E. Spain from the Visigoths, and Italy from the Ostrogoths, largely owing to his great gen. Belisarius. The greater part of his reign was also taken up by an indecisive struggle with the Persians. J.'s religious zeal led him to build St. Sophia at Constanti-nople, and to close the univ. at Athens in 529. He ordered the codification of Roman law which has exercised a great influence on European jurisprudence.

JUSTIN MARTYR (c. 100–c. 163). Christian apologist, and a Father of the Church. B. in Palestine, he was converted to Christianity at Ephesus, and spent the rest of his life as an itinerant Christian missionary-philosopher. He was martyred in Rome.

JUTE (joot). Fibre obtained from 2 plants of the genus *Corchorus* – *C. capsularis* and *C. olitorius*. E.

J. is used for sacks and sacking, upholstery, webbing, twine, stage canvas, etc., but in uses such as bulk packaging, and tufted carpet backing, tends to be replaced by synthetic polypropylene. The world's largest produce of J. is E. Pakistan.

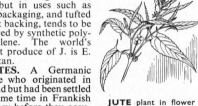

JUTE plant in flower

JUTES. A Germanic people who originated in Jutland but had been settled for some time in Frankish territory before they occupied Kent c. 450, according to tradition under Hengist and Horsa, and conquered the Isle of Wight and the coasts of Hants opposite in the early 6th cent.

JUTLAND. A peninsula of N. Europe between the N. Sea and the Kattegat. The S. belongs to Germany, whilst the N. part constitutes continental Denmark.

JUTLAND. The greatest naval battle of the F.W.W. fought between the British under Admiral Jellicoe and the Germans under Admiral Scheer, on 31 May 1916, off the W. coast of Jutland. After a battle-cruiser action between Beatty and Hipper, the former retired northward and drew the whole enemy fleet on to Jellicoe's battleships. Scheer, however, escaped a perilous situation by retreating S. During the night, with several encounters with British destroyers, he passed astern of Jellicoe's fleet and escaped, aided by the latter's lack of information. Yet J. was a decided British victory since the Germans never again ventured out to battle.

JUVENAL (jōō′venal) (c. A.D. 60–140). Roman satirist and poet. B. probably at Aquinum, he received a good education. Late in life his genius for satire brought him to the unfavourable notice of the emperor Domitian. 16 of his satires are extant, and they give a brutal and sometimes disgusting picture of the Roman society of his day.

JUVENILE DELINQUENCY. Offences against the law committed by young people. The Children and Young Persons Act (1969) introduced in Britain the gradual abolition of the prosecution of children up to the age of 14, and provided 3 options for Juvenile Courts in respect of all care and criminal proceedings involving children up to the age of 17: binding over of parents, supervision orders, and care orders. Community homes will replace the former approved schools, remand homes and probation hostels, and will be organized by regional committees set up by local authorities. The Act was strongly supported by police and child care officers, and there were plans to extend the police juvenile liaison scheme operating in Birmingham, Liverpool, and certain London areas, under which officers visit parents and children to warn of possible offences or give an informal caution when an offence has been committed. It was hoped that the system would reduce the number of children appearing in court.

Contrary to earlier belief, D. is not solely the product of poverty. It is more probable that the largest factor is family disorganization which creates emotional and psychological difficulties for the growing child. There is a higher D. rate in affluent countries, overcrowded urban populations have a higher rate, and the last year at school is at risk.

JUXON (juk′son), **William** (1582–1663). Archbp. of Canterbury. He became bishop of London in 1633, and acted as Lord High Treasurer 1636–41. He attended Charles I during his trial and on the scaffold, and was created archbp. of Canterbury in 1660.

JYLLAND (ju′lahn). The mainland of Denmark, the northern section of the Jutland peninsula (q.v.). The chief towns are Aalborg, Aarhus, Esbjerg, Fredericia, Horsens, Kolding, Randers and Vejle. *See also* JUTES.

K Eleventh letter of the Roman alphabet, in Eng. representing the unvoiced velar stop. It is silent before another consonant at the beginning of a word (e.g. in *knee*), a change accomplished, probably, in the 17th cent.

K2. Mountain (formerly Mt. Godwin-Austen) in the Karakoram range, N. Kashmir, 2nd highest in the world at 28,250 ft. It was first climbed 1954 by an Italian expedition.

KAABA (kah′bah). The oblong building in the quadrangle of the Great Mosque at Mecca (q.v.) into the N.E. corner of which is built the black stone declared by Mohammed to have been given to Abraham by Gabriel, and devoutly revered by Mohammedan pilgrims. The name means chamber.

KABALE′VSKY, Dimitri Borisovich (1904–). Russian composer. A pupil of Myaskovsky, he became prof. of composition at the Moscow Conservatoire in 1939, and has produced a Ukrainian folk-tune ballet *The Golden Spikes*; operas such as *The Master of Clamecy* (based on *Colas Breugnon* by Romain Rolland) and *Before Moscow*; and the patriotic suite *The People's Avengers* inspired by the struggle against the Germans, as well as concertos and symphonies.

KABBALA (kab′ala) (Heb., 'tradition'). Body of esoteric Jewish doctrine containing strong elements of pantheism, and akin to Neoplatonism. Among its earliest documents are the *Sefir Jezirah* (The Book of Creation), attributed to Rabbi Akiba (d. A.D. 120). The *Zohar* or Book of Light was first written in Aramaic about the 13th cent., and Kabbalistic writing reached its peak period between the 13th and 16th cents. The most notable writer was Moses ben Nachman (1195–1270).

KABUL (kah′bool). Cap. of Afghanistan and K. prov., on the K. r. 6,900 ft. a.s.l. Originally a walled city of importance throughout central Asia, it is a great marketing town, with match, woollen, furniture, and other factories, a military academy, and a univ. (1932). K. is the focal point for the Khyber Pass route to Peshawar, W. Pakistan. Pop. (1965) 450,000.

KABWE. *See* BROKEN HILL.

KABYLES (kabilz′). Group of Berber tribes in N. Africa, chiefly Algeria. Moslems, they formerly served as soldiers in the French forces. *See* ZOUAVES.

KÁDÁR (kah′dahr), **János** (1912–). Hungarian politician. A member of the underground in the S.W.W., he afterwards was a leader of the Communist régime (though himself imprisoned for deviation from 'Stalinism' 1951–3), but on the outbreak of the Hungarian revolt of 1956 declared the party dissolved. He then headed a govt. under Russian supervision 1956–8 and 1961–5, remaining in 1965 as 1st sec. of the Communist Party.

KAFFIR or **KAFIR** (kah′fer). Name given to the

Bantu-speaking peoples, incl. the Xhosa and Pondo tribes of Cape Province, living in much of S.E. Africa. They are primarily agriculturalists, raising cattle and grain. They should not be confused with the Kafirs (Arabic: 'infidels'), a mountain people living on the border between N.E. Afghanistan and Pakistan, so named because they refused to accept Islam until the 20th cent. They are now known as Nuri: 'people of light'. *See* illus. under BEAUTY CULTURE.

KAFKA, Franz (1883–1924). Czech novelist. B. at Prague, he worked for a time in an insurance office, but developed tuberculosis, and d. in a sanatorium nr. Vienna. He wrote in German and although short stories appeared during his lifetime he is chiefly remembered for his 3 long, but unfinished, allegorical novels *The Trial* (1925), *The Castle* (1926) and *America* (1927), which were pub. posthumously despite his instructions that they should be destroyed.

KAGAN. *See under* BUKHARA.

KAGANÔVICH, Lazar Moiseyevich (1893–). Soviet politician. He launched an industrialization drive in the cap. in the 1930s, and directed the construction of the Moscow 'underground' (subway). In 1942 he was prominent in the defence of the Caucasus. He was a member of the presidium and central committee 1953–7, when he was expelled (with Molotov and Malenkov) for 'persistent opposition' to party policy.

KAGAWA (kagah'wa), Toyohiko (1888–1960). Japanese Christian leader. After his conversion he studied in the U.S.A., founding in 1918 the organized Labour Federation and in 1928 the National Anti-War League, but during the S.W.W. he identified himself with the ruling party. He agreed with the Emperor's surrender in 1945, and, winning the support of Gen. MacArthur, continued his work.

KAGÔSHIMA. Port on K. Bay, Kyushu, Japan. The Satsumayaki porcelain is made there. Pop. (1965) 328,000.

KAIETEUR (kah-etoor') FALL. Waterfall on the r. Potaro, a tributary of the Essequibo, British Guiana. It is 822 ft. high – i.e. five times as high as Niagara.

KAIFÊNG (kïfung'). Ancient Chinese city, close to the Hwang-ho, formerly cap. of Honan prov. It lost its importance owing to the silting up of the waterway. K. was cap. of China 907–1127. Pop. (1953) 130,000.

KAIRWAN (kirwahn'). Moslem holy city in Tunisia, N. Africa, 80 m. S. of Tunis. Said to have been founded A.D. 671, K. ranks after Mecca and Medina as a place of pilgrimage. Pop. (1966) 82,300.

KAISER (kï'zer), Georg (1878–1945). German dramatist. B. at Magdeburg, after 3 years in Argentina as an engineer he became the leader of the Expressionist school in drama. He wrote *Von Morgen bis Mitternacht* (1918) and *Die Bürger von Calais*.

KAISER, Henry J. (1882–1967). American industrialist. He built up steel and motor industries, and his shipbuilding firms became famous for the mass production of vessels, incl. the 'liberty ships' – cheap, quickly produced, transport ships – built for the U.K. in the S.W.W.

KAISER. A title formerly borne by the Holy Roman Emperors, Austrian Emperors 1806–1918, and German Emperors 1871–1918. The word, like Tsar, is derived from the Lat. *Caesar*.

KAISERSLAUTERN (kï'zerslowtern). W. German town in the Rhineland Palatinate, 30 m. W. of Mannheim. It dates from 882; the castle from which it got its name was built by Frederick Barbarossa in 1152, destroyed by the French in 1703. K. makes textiles and sewing machines. Pop. (1960) 90,000.

KALAHARI (kahlahhah'rē). Desert region in Bechuanaland, S. Africa. The S.W. is a National Park.

KALE. A variety of cabbage (*Brassica oleracea*, variety *acephala*) grown as a winter vegetable. The commonest forms are the Scotch K. or borecole and curly K.

KALEVALA (kahlehvah'lah). Finnish national epic first formed from scattered legends and ballads by Elias Lönnrot in 1835. The hero of the poem is Väinamöinen, god of music and poetry.

KA'LGAN. Historic town and trade centre in Hopei prov., China, 100 m. S.E. of Peking, with which it is linked by railway. K. is on the border of Inner Mongolia and is the S. terminus of a motor road to Ulan Bator. It grew under the Manchu dynasty, and was the centre for the long-estab. overland tea trade from China to Russia. Pop. (1957) 230,000.

KALGOO'RLIE. Town of W. Australia, 340 m. E.N.E. of Perth. Gold has been mined there since 1893. Pop. (1966) 19,892.

KALI (kah'lē). In Hindu mythology, the wife of Siva. She is the goddess of destruction and death.

KÂLIDÂSA (kahlēdah'sah). The most famed of the writers is the 2nd epoch of Sanskrit literature, believed to have flourished about A.D. 375 at the court of King Vikramaditya at Ujjain. *Sakuntalâ* was his greatest play.

KALIMA'NTAN. Indonesian name of the S.E. part of Borneo, formerly Netherlands Borneo. It forms a prov. of the rep. of Indonesia and is for the most part low-lying, with mountains in the N.W. rising in Mt. Raya to 7,462 ft. The chief towns, both ports, are Banjermasin at the mouth of the Negara r., and Balikpapan, which is an important petroleum-producing centre. Area *c.* 210,000 sq. m.; pop. (1961) 4,500,000.

KALININ (kahlē'nin), Mikhail Ivanovich (1875–1946). Soviet statesman. B. in Tver prov. (later renamed K. in his honour), he was the son of a peasant, and as an active revolutionary suffered imprisonment, and was twice exiled to Siberia. Founder of *Pravda*, he was prominent in the October Revolution, and in 1919 became pres. of the Central Executive Committee of the Soviety Govt., then in 1937 pres. of the Presidium of the Supreme Soviet until his retirement owing to ill-health in 1946 – both posts were equivalent to Pres. of the U.S.S.R.

KALININ. City of the R.S.F.S.R., cap. of K. region. On the Volga, 100 m. N.W. of Moscow, and called Tver until 1933, it was renamed in honour of President K. It is an important transport centre. Pop. (1967) 311,000.

KALI'NINGRAD. City in the R.S.F.S.R., cap. of K. region, better known by its German name Königsberg. K. grew up round a castle dating from 1255, a seat of the Teutonic Knights. It was cap. of East Prussia until that area ceased to exist with its division between Russia and Poland in 1945, under the Potsdam agreement. It was renamed in honour of President Kalinin of the U.S.S.R. Pop. (1967) 261,000.

KALMAR (kahl'mahr). Port on the S.E. coast of Sweden. It has a match industry. Pop. (1966) 37,600.

KA'LMUCK. An A.S.S.R. of the R.S.F.S.R. Estab. on the Caspian Sea in 1935, it was abolished in 1943, and its inhabitants deported to Siberia for their alleged collaboration with the Germans during the battle of Stalingrad. It was restored in 1957. Pop. (1967) 248,000.

KA'LTENBRUNNER (-brooner), Ernst (1901–46). Austrian Nazi leader. After the annexation of Austria he joined Himmler's staff, and as head of the Security Police (S.D.) from 1943 was responsible for the murder of Allied soldiers, and of millions of Jews. He was tried at Nuremberg, and hanged.

KALUGA (kahloo'ga). Town in the R.S.F.S.R., on the Oka, 100 m. S.S.W. of Moscow, cap. of K. region. It has hydro-electric installations and engineering works, and makes telephone equipment, measuring devices, etc. Pop. (1967) 176,000.

KAMCHA'TKA. Mountainous peninsula of E. Asia; name also of a region of the R.S.F.S.R. covering the peninsula and the Chukchi and Koryak national districts. Agriculture is possible only in the S., and the inhabitants are fishermen and hunters. Petropavlovsk, cap. of region, is the only town.

KAMENEV, Leo Borisovich (1883–1936). Russian Bolshevik leader. He was elected pres. of the Moscow Soviet in 1918, and visited England in 1920, but was deported on a charge of attempting to subsidize the *Daily Herald*. After Lenin's death he sided with Trotsky. In 1936 he pleaded guilty to conspiring with the Germans and was shot, but his guilt remains controversial.

KAMET. Himalayan mountain (25,447 ft.), the first of over 25,000 ft. to be scaled by man. F. S. Smythe and Eric Shipton were in the group which made the ascent in 1931.

KAMPALA (kahmpähl′a). African town, commercial centre and, from 1962, cap. of Uganda, cap. of Buganda region and former residence of the Kabaka; *see* BUGANDA. It is linked by rail with Mombasa, and is a market for cotton, coffee, livestock, etc. Cigarettes are made. The Parliament buildings were opened in 1960. At Makerere, just N.W. of K., is the Univ. Coll. of E. Africa, founded in 1938. Pop. *c.* 200,000.

KAMPERDUIN. Dutch name of a village anglicized as CAMPERDOWN.

KANA′KA. Hawaiian word for man; applied to the natives of the South Sea islands.

KANAZA′WA. City of Honshu island, Japan, 100 m. N.N.W. of Nagoya. It has large textile and porcelain industries. Pop. (1965) 336,000.

KANCHENJU′NGA. Himalayan mountain (28,146 ft.), 75 m. E.S.E. of Everest. The summit was reached for the first time by a British expedition in 1955. Its name means '5 treasure houses of the great snows'.

KANDAHA′R. City of Afghanistan, *c.* 280 m. S.W. of Kabul, cap. of K. prov. and an important trading centre, with wool and cotton factories. It is surrounded by a 27 ft. high mud wall. On 1 Sept. 1880 the British under General (afterwards Lord) Roberts defeated the Afghans there. Pop. (1965) 115,000.

KANDI′NSKY, Vasily (1866–1944). Russian Ex-

KAMCHATKA. Volcanic springs have made Paratunka a favourite winter health resort, for swimming is possible all the year round despite ice and snow.

KANDY. Dancers.　　　*Courtesy of Ceylon Tea Centre.*

pressionist artist. B. in Moscow, he travelled widely abroad and by 1910 was producing completely non-representational work. In 1912 he pub. the influential *Concerning the Spiritual in Art* and was joint-originator with Franz Marc of the *Blaue Reiter* movement 1911–12. For some years he taught at the Bauhaus and, after its closure by the Nazis, settled in Paris. His use of colour, and ordered arrangement of spheres and rectangles, affected the work of many other artists.

KANDY (kahn′dē). Town of Ceylon, formerly cap. of the ancient kingdom of K. One of its temples contains an alleged tooth of Buddha and is one of the most sacred Buddhist shrines. At Peradenia, 3 m. away, are the Univ. of Ceylon and a botanical garden. Pop. (1963) 67,800.

KANGAROO′. Family of marsupials (Macropodidae) found in Australia and Tasmania. All are herbivorous and range from the musk K., similar in size to a large rat, through the medium-size wallabies – which extend their range to New Guinea – to the familiar great grey K. (*Macropus giganteus*) which stands 8 ft. high: some extinct forms must have reached 10 ft. or larger. The single young of the great grey K., born usually in Jan. after a very brief gestation period, is *c.* 1 in. long at birth and remains in the mother's pouch, with excursions as it matures, until Oct. The developed hind legs and strong tail enable them to travel at speed in long leaps. Adaptable to rain forest, rocky zones, or open grassland, the varied species of K. have tended to dwindle in number since they are hunted for furs, for damage to crops, or as a 'sport'.

KANI′SHKA (fl. *c.* A.D. 200). Indian king whose kingdom extended over Kabul, Kashmir, Gandhara, and E. to Benares. He was converted to Buddhism and held a council which codified Buddhist writings.

KANO′. State and town 705 m. N.E. of Lagos, N.

KANGAROO

Nigeria, W. Africa. (1) The state consists of a vast undulating plain, much of which is under cultivation. Area 16,625 sq. m.; pop. (1963) 5,775,000. (2) The town, cap. of K. state, is linked by railway with Lagos, and is an important centre for the Sudan; it makes cotton, silk and leather goods. Pop. (1963) 130,000.

KANPUR (kahn'poor). Indian city, on the Ganges, 45 m. S.W. of Lucknow, in Uttar Pradesh, cap. of K. district. It is an important commercial and industrial centre with cotton, woollen, and jute mills, chemical and plastics factories, iron and steel works. During the Indian Mutiny in 1857 it was the scene of a massacre of British civilians who had surrendered to Nana Sahib. Pop. (1961) 947,793.

KANSAS. Central state of the U.S.A. It is the principal winter wheat-producing area in the U.S.A. The chief rivers are the Missouri, Kansas, and Arkansas; the chief towns Kansas City, Wichita, Topeka (the cap.), and Hutchinson; and cattle, coal, petroleum, and natural gas are important; Wichita is a leading producer of aircraft. Area 82,276 sq. m.; pop. (1970) 2,249,071.

KANSAS CITY. Largest city of Kansas State, and next to Chicago the chief livestock centre of the U.S.A., situated at the confluence of the Kansas and the Missouri. Pop. met. area (1970) 1,240,575.

KANSAS CITY. City and port of Missouri, U.S.A., on the Missouri, adjoining K.C., Kansas. Its chief importance is in the distribution of agricultural implements, seeds and grain; in K.C., Mo., are most of the offices of the stockyards and packing factories in K.C., Kansas. Pop. (1960) 475,539.

KANSU (kahnsoo'). Prov. of N.W. China, mountainous in part and with an extreme climate. It is subject also to earthquakes – one in 1920 was said to have killed 120,000. K. incl. the chief Chinese petroleum field, production from which began in 1939; it also produces food crops and livestock, coal, salt, and soda. The ancient caravan route from China to central Asia through K. has been made into a motor road. The cap. is Lanchow. Area 141,500 sq. m.; pop. (1968) 13,000,000.

KANT, Immanuel (1724–1804). German philosopher. B. at Königsberg, he went to the univ. there, and in 1770 was appointed professor in logic and metaphysics. His first book, *Thoughts on the true estimates of living forces*, appeared in 1747, and the *Theory of the Heavens* in 1755. In the latter he combined physics and theology in an argument for the existence of God. Best-known of his works is the *Critique of Pure Reason* (1781), which was followed

KARAJAN. With sensitive hands the conductor emphasizes a point to Walter Legge in the discussion that arises on the playback of a recording.   *Photo: Godfrey MacDomnic.*

by the *Prolegomena* (1783), *Metaphysic of Ethics* (1785), *Metaphysic of Nature* (1786), *Of Practical Reason* (1788) and *Of Judgment* (1790). In 1797 ill-health led to his retirement. K. was a transcendental idealist, making a prime distinction between noumenon (object of purely intellectual intuition) and phenomenon (object of perception or experience); phenomena do not exist in themselves but only in relation to the mind. He identified practical reason with morality and the supreme cause is a moral cause. He gave the name of Categorical Imperative to the absolute unconditional command of the moral law, a law binding universally on every rational will.

KAOHSING. City and port on the W. coast of Formosa. Industrial products include aluminium ware, fertilizers, cement; there are also a petroleum refinery, iron foundry, shipyards, and food-processing factories. K. began to develop as a commercial port after 1858; its industrial development came about while it belonged to Japan, 1895–1945. Pop. (1966) 275,600.

KAOLAN. Name sometimes given to LANCHOW before 1946.

KA'OLIANG. Variety of millet grown in S. Manchuria and N. China as a foodcrop. The plants grow 10–12 ft. high. The stalks are used for thatch, matting, and fencing.

KA'OLIN or **China Clay.** A mineral named after the Kuling (Kaoling) range in China, where it was originally mined. It is hydrated aluminium silicate, and is also worked in England, the U.S.A., France, and other countries. K. is used for porcelain, in 'facing' paper, in making paint, and in cosmetics.

KA'PITZA, Peter (1894–). Russian scientist. B. in Kronstadt, he was asst. director of magnetic research at the Cavendish Laboratory, Cambridge, 1924–32, and was Messel research prof. of the Royal Society and director of their Mond Laboratory 1930–5. He then returned to Russia as director of the Inst. for Physical Problems, Academy of Sciences, 1935–46 and from 1955; edits their *Journal of Experimental and Theoretical Physics*; won state prizes in 1941 and 1943; and has written on magnetism and low temperature.

KAPOK (kah'pok). Silky hairs produced round the seeds of certain trees, particularly the K. tree (*Eriodendron anfractuosum*) of India, Java, and Malaya, and the silk-cotton tree (*Ceiba pentandra*), a native of tropical America. K. is used for stuffing cushions, mattresses, and life belts. Oil obtained

KANSAS. This unpretentious white-painted wooden house at Abilene is a typical Kansas home, and here President Eisenhower grew up. The town also has an Eisenhower Museum (1954) of trophies and a library (1962) of his records and memorabilia.   *Courtesy of The Eisenhower Foundation.*

from the seeds is used in food and soap preparation.

KAPP, Edmond Xavier (1890–   ). British artist. He first exhibited in 1919, and has produced portrait drawings, lithographs, still-life and flower pieces.

KAPP, Wolfgang (1868–1922). German politician who organized an armed rising in 1920. The 'Kapp Putsch' was foiled by a general strike of the workers of Berlin. K. fled to Sweden, was arrested on his return, and d. before his trial.

KARIBA. Officially opened in 1960, the dam has 2 generating stations with a joint capacity of 1,500 megawatts, and its wall provides an important road link between Southern Rhodesia and Zambia. The project will promote industrial expansion, and tourist resorts are planned on the lake. As many wild animals as possible were rescued from the inundated area in 'Operation Noah'.
Courtesy of the High Commissioner for Southern Rhodesia.

KARACHI (karah'chi). Chief seaport and former cap. of Pakistan, N. of the Indus delta. It has a fine harbour, and an international airport. Natural gas is brought to K. by pipeline from Sui, 350 m. to the N., and there is an oil refinery at nearby Korangi. Pop. (1961) 1,923,598.

KARAFUTO (kahrahfootō). Japanese name for the southern part of the island of Sakhalin (q.v.), annexed by Japan in 1905, restored to Russia in 1945.

KARAGA'NDA. Industrial town in Kazakh S.S.R., U.S.S.R., cap. of K. region, which produces coal, copper, tungsten, manganese, etc. Pop. (1967) 489,000.

KARAJAN (karayahn'), **Herbert von** (1908–   ). Austrian conductor. Originally a student of the piano, he was artistic director of the Vienna State Opera 1956–64, and of the Salzburg Festival from 1964. Exercising supreme dominance over his instrumental forces, he excels in conducting opera.

KARA-KALPAK (kah'ra kahlpahk'). A.S.S.R. of Uzbek S.S.R., U.S.S.R., called after the Kara-Kalpak people whose name means black bonnet. They live S. of the Sea of Aral and were subdued by Russia in 1867. An autonomous K.-K. region formed in 1926 within Kazakh A.S.S.R., transferred to the R.S.F.S.R. in 1930, made an A.S.S.R. in 1932, was attached to Uzbekistan in 1936. The cap. is Nukus. With the aid of artificial irrigation cotton, rice, wheat and other crops are grown : fish from the Aral Sea is canned at Muynak. Area 61,000 sq. m.; pop. (1967) 638,000 (c. 40 per cent Kara-Kalpaks).

KARAKŌ'RAM. Range of mountains in central Asia. The highest peak is K2 or Godwin-Austen (28,250 ft.). K. was also the name of Genghis Khan's capital, now in ruins.

The *Karakoram Highway* was constructed 1969–71 by Pakistan, branching from the Gilgit-Sinkiang road at Mor Khun in northern Kashmir to form a second link with Sinkiang.

KARA-KUM (kah'rah-koom'; Black Sands). Sandy desert occupying most of Turkmen S.S.R., U.S.S.R. Area c. 110,000 sq. m.

KARAMZIN (-zēn'), **Nikolai Mikhailovich** (1765–1826). Russian writer, author of *Letters of a Russian Traveller* (1797–1801), and an incomplete *History of the Russian State*.

KARA'TE. See JUDO.

KARBALA. See KERBELA.

KAREL (kah'rel), **Rudolf** (1880–1945). Czech composer. B. at Pilsen, he became a pupil of Dvořák at Prague, and prof. at the conservatoire. He d. in a concentration camp. His works include operas, a 'Renaissance' symphony, chamber music, etc.

KARELIA. A.S.S.R. of the R.S.F.S.R., formed in 1956 from the Karelo-Finnish S.S.R. set up in 1940 and adjoining the Finnish frontier. K. is rich in sources of water power and forest reserves and fisheries. The cap. is Petrozavodsk. Area 66,500 sq. m.; pop. (1967) 707,000.

KARENS (kahrenz'). People of the Far East, numbering perhaps 1½ million in all. Most of them live in E. Burma near the Thailand border, across which some of them are found, as also are some in the Irrawaddy delta. Their language belongs to the Sino-Thai family, and it is believed that they are descended from the Chinese driven S. by the Shan people. The K. strongly resisted integration in Burma after that country became independent in 1948, and Kantarawaddy, Bawlake, and Kyebogyi, three divisions of Burma formerly called the Karenni states, were in 1954 formed into the Kayah state (area c. 4,600 sq. m.; pop. c. 85,000), while parts of the districts of Toungoo, Thaton, and Amherst became the Kawthoolei state (area c. 11,600 sq. m.; pop. c. 400,000), both states having a measure of autonomy.

KARG-ELERT (ā'lert), **Siegfried** (1877–1933). German composer. Originally a pianist, he turned to composition under the advice of Grieg and produced much organ music.

KARIBA (karēb'a) **DAM.** Concrete dam in Northern Rhodesia on the Zambezi c. 220 m. W.N.W. of Livingstone, constructed 1955–60 for hydro-electric power. It is 420 ft. high and 1,900 ft. wide and created Lake K., 175 m. long and up to 40 m. broad with a volume of 130 million acre-feet, largest man-made lake at the time of its creation. Displaced African agriculturalists now fish the lake which has been specially stocked. K.D. was designed by the French engineer André Coyne (1891–1960).

KARIKA'L. Small port in India, 155 m. S. of Madras, at the mouth of the right distributory of the Cauvery delta. On a tract of land acquired by the French in 1739, it was transferred to India *de facto* in 1954, by treaty in 1956. See PONDICHERRY.

KARLFELDT, Erik Axel (1864–1931). Swedish poet. He estab. his reputation with *Fridolins visor*, and was awarded a Nobel prize in 1931.

KARL-MARX-STADT. Town in E. Germany, cap. of K. district, on the Chemnitz r., 40 m. S.S.E. of Leipzig. It is an industrial centre with engineering works, textile and chemical factories. Formerly called Chemnitz, it came within the Russian zone of occupation after the S.W.W. and was renamed in 1953. Pop. (1966) 294,900.

KARLOVY VARY. Spa in the Bohemian Forest, Czechoslovakia, famous from the 14th cent. for its alkaline thermal springs. Pop. (1967) 46,000. See p. 612.

KARLSBAD. German name of KARLOVY VARY.

KARLSBURG. German name of ALBA JULIA.

KA'RLSKRÖNA. Seaport and naval base on the S. coast of Sweden, the H.Q. of the Swedish navy since 1680. Pop. (1966) 37,800.

KARLSRUHE (-rōō-e). Town of Baden-Württemberg, W. Germany, 35 m. S. of Mannheim. K., founded 1715, is an important communication centre,

KARLOVY VARY. Czechoslovakia is famous for its mineral springs, and those at Karlovy Vary have been famous for more than 600 years. The largest, the Sprudel, produces some 400 gallons a day, the temperature reaching more than 70°C, and the water is effective against liver complaints.
Courtesy of the Czechoslovak Travel Bureau.

and has large railway shops, breweries, etc. Pop. (1966) 253,500.

KARLSTAD. Town in Sweden, cap. of Värmland county or Lan. It makes matches, machinery, etc. The conference which ended the union between Norway and Sweden was held there in 1905. Pop. (1966) 52,000.

KARMA (Sanskrit, action or fate). In Indian religion and philosophy, the sum of a man's actions that is carried forward from one existence to the next, and in so doing determines its character for good or for ill. In Hinduism and Jainism there is belief in an individual soul which inherits and passes on the load of K., improved or worsened as the case may be; in Buddhism, however, there is no conception of a permanent personality, but the K. is attached in some way to the *khandas* or elements, both physical and mental, which are carried on from birth to birth until the power that holds them together is dispersed in the attainment of Nirvana.

KA'RNAK. Village of modern Egypt, on the E. bank of the Nile, which gives its name to the temple of Ammon (constructed by Seti I and Rameses II) round which the major part of ancient city of Thebes was built. An avenue of recumbent rams leads to Luxor (q.v.).

KAROLYI (kah'rōli), **Mihály,** count (1875–1955). Hungarian statesman. He was P.M. of Hungary 1918–19, and was first pres. of the republic Jan.-March 1919. Exiled under the Horthy régime, he joined the Free Hungarian Movement during the S.W.W., and was ambassador in Paris 1947–9, but was later denounced by the Communists and lived in retirement.

KARRI (ka'ri). Giant eucalyptus tree (*E. diversicolor*) which grows in the extreme S.W. of W. Australia. Its height varies between 200 and 400 ft. Exceptionally strong, the timber is used for girders.

KARROO (karōō'). Two areas of semi-desert in Cape Province, S. Africa, divided into the Great K. and Little K. by the Swartberg. The two Ks. together have an area of over 100,000 sq. m.

KARS. Town in N.E. Turkey, cap. of K. il, bordering on Armenia S.S.R. It changed hands a number of times between Persia, Russia, and Turkey before being confirmed as Turkish in 1921. Pop. (est.) 32,000.

KARSAVINA (kahrsah'vēnah), **Tamara** (1885–   ). Russian dancer. She made her début at St. Petersburg in 1902, succeeding Pavlova as *première danseuse* in 1910; first appeared in London in 1909, and subsequently joined the Imperial Russian Ballet

Company. She was a great success in *Spectre de la Rose, Les Sylphides,* and *Scheherazade.*

KARSH, Yousuf (1908–   ). Canadian photographer. B. in Armenia, he makes use of strong highlights and shadows, and in 1933 opened his own studio in Ottawa. His 'bulldog' portrait of Churchill in the S.W.W. brought him world fame.

KARST. Name originally given to the barren limestone region along the N.E. shores of the Adriatic, and now applied to similar arid scenery throughout the world, e.g. the French Causses and Jura. Caves are a characteristic of K. lands.

KARTING. Miniature motor racing, originating in the U.S.A. *c.* 1955. More than 100,000 of these elemental racing cars, about 6 ft. long and 2½ ft. wide, were in use by 1959, when the sport was introduced into Britain. Powered by lawn-mower and motor-cycle engines, karts reach speeds of 80 m.p.h.

KASHAN (kahshahn'). Town in Persia, where some of the finest carpets are made. Pop. (1964) 60,500.

KASHGAR (kahshgahr'). Oasis town in Sinkiang-Uighur autonomous region, China, on the Kizil Daria, cap. of K. district which touches Kirghiz and Tadzhik S.S.Rs. and Kashmir. It is a trade centre for cotton, silks, and sheepskins. Pop. *c.* 80,000, most of them Uighur.

KASHMIR (kashmēr'). State in the Himalayas, in the N. of the Indian sub-continent, bordering Afghanistan and China; sometimes called Jammu and K. It is drained by the upper waters of the Indus and its tributaries Jhelum and Chenab. There are extensive forests, and rice, barley, raw silk, fruit, and vegetables are produced. Textiles are manufactured Srinagar, the summer cap., has an airfield; at Jammu, the winter one, there are hydro-electric installations. There are no railways in K., but there is a road, via an 8,100 ft. tunnel opened in 1956, from Jammu to Pathankot on the Indian frontier, and Gilgit in Azad K. was linked with Skardu in Chinese Sinkiang 1968. Most of the people are Moslem, but until 1952, when hereditary rule was abolished, were ruled by a Hindu maharajah. In 1947 their ruler acceded to India, but fighting developed between pro-Indian and pro-Pakistan factions, helped by Pakistani troops in the W., by Indian troops in the E. India brought the dispute before the U.N. in 1948, but, failing a settlement, open war broke out in 1965. In Jan. 1966 Ayub Khan and Shastri signed the *Declaration of Tashkent* pledging restoration of peaceful relations, but difficulties continued. Area 84,470 sq. m., more than a third occupied by Pakistan (Azad K.), the rest by India. Pop. (1961) 3,583,585.

KARROO. The name Karroo is also generally applied to the northern plains of Cape Province, and this scene in Griqualand West, near Kimberley, is typical. Low-growing grey-green shrubs, thorn trees and wild asparagus bushes flourish in the stony soil, and pointed kopjes break the skyline.
Courtesy of the South African Information Service.

KARTING. A sport for Everyman – and a sport of King Hussein of Jordan – shown racing at Biggin Hill, England.
Courtesy of Lambretta Concessionaires Ltd.

KA'SSEL. City in Hessen, W. Germany, dating from the 10th cent. It has engineering and locomotive works, etc. Pop. (1966) 213,000.

KASSE'M, Abdul Karim (1914–63). Iraqi politician. He became P.M. of the rep. in 1958, adopting a pro-Soviet policy. He pardoned the leaders of the pro-Egyptian party who tried to assassinate him in 1959, but was executed after the 1963 coup.

KASTAMONU (kahstahmōnoo'). Town by the Gok r., Turkey, cap. of K. il, with textile manufactures. Pop. (1960 est.) 15,000.

KÄSTNER (kest'ner), **Erich** (1899–). German writer. He has pub. satirical verse; *Fabian* (1931) a novel of post-war Germany; the widely trans. children's book *Emil and the Detectives* (1928); and *When I was a Little Boy* (1957) telling of his childhood in his native Dresden.

KATAEV (kahtah'yev), **Valentin Petrovich** (1897–). Soviet novelist and dramatist whose works incl. the novels, *The Island of Ehrendorf* (1924), *The Embezzlers* (1927) and *Lonely White Sail* (1937); and the play *Squaring the Circle*.

KATA'NGA. Prov. in the Rep. of Zaïre (re-named 1972 Shaba, from the Swahili 'copper') containing Lubumbashi, with some of the world's richest copper workings, and uranium and other minerals. K. unsuccessfully attempted secession 1960–3 under Moïse Tshombe (1919–69), P.M. of the Congo (q.v.) 1964–5. Pop. (1967) 1,853,000.

KATHIAWAR (kahtiawahr'). Peninsula on the W. coast of India. Within it were a number of princely states which formed the Western K. agency of British India, 1927–47, and, except for Ahmedabad and Aureli, the Saurashtra Union, 1948–56. The whole of K. (23,445 sq. m.) was added to Bombay state in 1956, and became part of Gujarat in 1960.

KATMANDU (kahtmahndōō). Cap. of the Himalayan state of Nepal, founded in the 8th cent. It has an airfield. Pop. (1961) 224,900.

KATOWICE (katovit'sa). City and chief town of K. voivodship (county), Poland. Anthracite and iron are mined and there are iron foundries, smelting works, and machine shops. Pop. (1966) 287,000.

KATRINE (kat'rin). Freshwater loch in the S.W. of Perth, Scotland, from which Glasgow draws most of its water supply. Area 5 sq. m.; length 8 m.

KATSURA (kahtsoo'rah), **Taro, Prince** (1847–1913). Japanese statesman. He received a military education in Prussia, reformed the Japanese army on modern lines, and was War Minister 1898–1901 and P.M. 1901–5 and 1908–11. The Anglo-Japanese alliance of 1902 was largely his work.

KA'TTEGAT. Sea passage between Jutland and Sweden. It is about 150 m. long, 85 m. at its broadest.

KATTOWITZ. German form of KATOWICE.

KATZ, Sir Bernard (1911–). British biophysicist. He studied at Univ. Coll., London and in 1952 became head of the biophysics dept. there. In 1970 he shared a Nobel prize with Ulf von Euler of Stockholm and Julius Axelrod of Maryland for work on the elucidation of the biochemistry of the transmission and control of signals in the nervous system, which is of vital importance in the search for remedies for nervous and mental disorders.

KAUFFER, Edward McKnight (1890–1954). American artist. He lived in England 1914–41, and was particularly famous for his posters.

KAUFFMANN (kowf'mahn), **Angelica** (1741–1807). Swiss artist. B. in Grisons, she lived in Italy until 1765 and in England 1765–81, where her neo-classical paintings became popular. She became one of the first R.As. in 1769 and returned to Rome in 1781.

KAUNAS. Town of the Lithuanian S.S.R., on the r. Nieman. It has a univ., opened 1922. Pop. (1967) 276,000.

KAUNDA (kah-oon'dah), **Kenneth David** (1924–). Zambian politician. Son of an African missionary, he was ed. at Lubwa Training School where he became a teacher (headmaster 1944–7), and was in 1950 founder-sec. of the Lubwa branch of the African Nat. Congress. In 1958 he founded the breakaway Zambia African Nat. Congress, but this organization was banned as subversive and K. imprisoned. On his release he founded in 1960 the United National Independence Party, became in 1963 Min. of Local Govt., and in 1964 first P.M. of N. Rhodesia, then first pres. of Zambia, re-elected 1968.

KAURI PINE (kow'ri). A New Zealand conifer (*Agathis australis*), it often reaches a height of 150 ft., and yields valuable softwood timber. *Kauri Gum*, the resinous deposit dug up in areas where K. forest existed previously, is used in varnishes.

KAVA (kah'vah). Non-alcoholic, intoxicating beverage prepared from the roots or leaves of a variety of pepper plant, *Piper methysticum*, in the S. Pacific islands.

KAVALA (kahvah lah). Seaport of Macedonia, Greece, cap. of K. nome, the centre of rich tobacco-growing country. Pop. (1961) 44,406.

KAVA'NAGH, Patrick (1905–67). Irish poet. Son of a farmer in co. Monaghan, he lived in Dublin from 1939. His poetry incl. *The Great Hunger* (1942) and *A Soul for Sale* (1947); *The Green Fool* (1938) is an autobiography, and *Tarry Flynn* (1948) an autobiographical novel.

KAWABATA, Yasunari (1899–1972). Japanese novelist. Influenced by the *Tale of Genji*, which he rendered into modern Japanese, his novels are delicate in technique, e.g. *Snow Country* (1947) and *A Thousand Cranes* (1952). He was awarded a Nobel prize 1968.

KATMANDU. On the tower of Bodnath pagoda, the eyes of Buddha symbolize supreme knowledge and divine benevolence.
Courtesy of W.H.O.

KAWASAKI (kahwahs-ahkē). Japanese city between Tokyo and Yokohama with a Buddhist temple to which pilgrimages are made on the 21st of Jan., March, May, and Sept. Pop. (1966) 855,000.

KAY, John (1704–after 1764). British inventor. In 1733 he patented his flying-shuttle, intended to speed up the work of the hand-loom-weaver, but was ruined by the litigation necessary to defend his patent, and in 1753 his house at Bury was wrecked by a mob, who feared the use of machinery would cause unemployment. He is said to have d. in poverty in France.

KAYAH STATE. *See* KARENS.

KAYAK (kī′ak). Long, and light, sealskin-covered boat used by Eskimo fishermen and sealers.

KAYE, Danny. Stage-name of American film and stage comedian Daniel Kominski (1913–). B. in Brooklyn, N.Y., of Russian extraction, he has made such films as *Wonder Man* (1944), *The Secret Life of Walter Mitty* (1946) and *Hans Christian Andersen* (1952). He excels in lunatic, apparently multi-lingual, monologue, etc.

KAYE-SMITH, Sheila (1888–1956). British novelist. B. in Sussex, she m. in 1924 T. Penrose Fry, an Anglican clergyman, and was converted with him to Roman Catholicism in 1929. Set against the background of her native co., her books deal with down-to-earth realities, notably *Joanna Godden* (1921), story of a successful sheep grazier: later are *The End of the House of Alard* (1923) and *The Treasures of the Snow* (1949). *Three Ways Home* is a spiritual autobiography.

KAZAKH S.S.R. (kahzahk′). Asiatic rep. of the U.S.S.R., bounded on the W. by the Caspian Sea. Predominantly low-lying, it rises in the E. and S.E. to the mountains of central Asia. Among its products are cotton, grain, and sugar beet; minerals incl. coal, petroleum, iron, copper, and lead. The cap. is Alma-Ata. Area 1,061,600 sq. m.; pop. (1968) 12,678,000 (of whom 30 per cent were Kazakhs and 51 per cent Russians and Ukrainians).

KAZA′N, Elia (1909–). American stage and film director. B. in Constantinople of Greek extraction, he became an actor, and made his name by his stage direction of *Skin of Our Teeth* (1942), *A Streetcar Named Desire* (1947), *Death of a Salesman* (1949), and *Cat on a Hot Tin Roof* (1955). His films incl. *A Tree Grows in Brooklyn* (1945), *Gentleman's Agreement* (1948), *Streetcar* (1951), *On the Waterfront* (1954), *East of Eden* (1954), and *Splendour in the Grass* (1962).

KAZAN (kahzahn′). Cap. of the Tatar A.S.S.R., R.S.F.S.R. Formerly a centre of Mohammedan culture, it is a busy marketing and transport centre with a univ.; its industries incl. tanning, motors, chemicals, and railway rolling stock. The 'Black Virgin of K.', housed in a specially built convent in the 16th cent., was removed to Moscow (1612–1917), where the great Kazan Cathedral was constructed to enshrine it in 1631. Pop. (1967)821,000.

KAZVIN (kahzvēn′). Town at the S. foot of the Elburz range, Persia, with an airfield. It is said to date from the 4th cent. Industries incl. rug weaving, distilling, cotton textile manufacture. K. is subject to earthquakes. Pop. (1964) 77,575.

KEAN, Edmund (1787–1833). British actor. B. in London, son of

KAZAN. Dating from the 14th cent. or earlier, the Virgin of Kazan, called 'black' because darkened with age, found a new home in 1963 in San Francisco. Besides numerous cures of the blind, the icon (q.v.) is credited with defeating by its presence both the Poles (1612) and Napoleon (1812) at Moscow. *Courtesy of Miss A. Mitchell-Hedges.*

a strolling actress, he made a sensationally successful London début as Shylock in 1814, and also excelled as Richard III and Othello. His son, **Charles John K.** (1811–68), made his stage début in 1827, and achieved fame as Hamlet in 1838. In 1842 he m. Ellen Tree (1805–80), who assisted his series of Shakespearian revivals as lessee of the Princess's Theatre, London, 1850–9.

KEARTON, Cherry (1871–1940). British naturalist, photographer, and author. B. in Yorks, he became well known for his films and photographs of wild life in Africa, Australia, etc.

KEATON, Buster. Stage-name of American comedian Joseph Frank K. (1896–1966). A sophisticated, deadpan actor, he began his screen career after the F.W.W. as stooge to 'Fattie' Arbuckle in the Keystone Kops comedies, and became one of the great silent-film comedians; his films incl. *Steamboat Bill Jr.* and *The General*, and later *Limelight* (1953) and *Round the World in 80 Days* (1957).

JOHN KEATS. A life mask. *Photo: N.P.G.*

KEATS, John (1795–1821). British poet. B. in London on 29 or 31 Oct. 1795, the son of a livery-stable keeper, he attended an Enfield private school before being apprenticed to a surgeon and becoming a student at Guy's Hospital (1815–17). He then abandoned medicine for poetry, publishing his first vol. in 1817, and *Endymion* in 1818: the latter was harshly reviewed by the Tory *Blackwood's Magazine* and the *Quarterly*, largely owing to K.'s friendship with the Radical, Leigh Hunt. In 1818 he wrote *Isabella*, and the first version of *Hyperion*; took a walking tour in Scotland which increased his tubercular tendency; and nursed his brother Tom, who d. of the same disease. To 1819 belong 'The Eve of St. Agnes', 'The Eve of St. Mark', his 'Odes', 'Lamia', and the new version of *Hyperion*. In this year also he fell hopelessly in love with Fanny Brawne. In 1820 he pub. a 3rd vol. of poems, and in Sept. sailed for Italy in an effort to recover his health. He d. in Rome. Valuable insight into K.'s poetic development is provided by his *Letters*, pub. in 1848.

KEBLE (kēbl), **John** (1792–1866). Anglican divine and religious poet. B. in Glos, he was ordained in 1815, and in 1827 pub. the vol. of poems *The Christian Year*. K. was prof. of poetry at Oxford, 1831–41; and his sermon on national apostasy preached in 1833 is taken as the beginning of the Tractarian movement. K. wrote 4 of the *Tracts for the Times*, and from 1835 was vicar of Hursley, in Hants. K. College, Oxford, was founded in 1870.

KEDAH (ked′a). State ruled by a sultan in the Federation of Malaysia. It was transferred by Siam to Britain in 1909, and was one of the Unfederated Malay States till 1948. The chief products incl. rice, rubber, tapioca, tin, and tungsten. Alor Star is the cap. Area 3,660 sq. m.; pop. (1966) 913,995.

KEELE. Town in N. Staffs, England, nr. Newcastle-under-Lyme, seat of Keele univ. (1962), founded in 1949 and opened in 1951 as the Univ. Coll. of N. Staffs: noted for originality and enterprise.

KEELING. Another name for the Cocos Islands.

KEENE, Charles Samuel (1823–91). British black-and-white artist. A talented wood-engraver and etcher, he was also well known for his spare line drawings in *Punch* (from 1851), distinguished by their acute and realistic observation of such familiar characters as cabmen, Thames anglers, and street boys.

KEEPER OF THE GREAT SEAL. An officer who

had charge of the Great Seal of England. During the Middle Ages the great seal was entrusted to the Chancellor. Later a special Lord Keeper was appointed to take charge of it, but since 1761 the posts of Chancellor and Keeper have been combined.

KEEWATIN (kēwah'tin). Eastern dist. of Northwest Territories, Canada, incl. the islands in Hudson and James Bays. The N. is an upland plateau, the S. low and level, covering the greater part of the Barren Grounds (Arctic prairies) of Canada. There are a number of lakes; trapping for furs is the main occupation. Trading posts incl. Chesterfield Inlet, Eskimo Point, and Coral Harbour, the last with an air base set up during the S.W.W. K. District was formed in 1876, under the administration of Manitoba; it was transferred to Northwest Territories in 1905, and in 1912 lost land S. of 60 deg. N. to Manitoba and Ontario. Area 228,160 sq. m.; pop. (1961) 2,345.

KEFALINIA. Italian form of CEPHALONIA.

KEFAUVER (kē'fawva), **Estes** (1903–63). American Democratic politician, known as the 'homespun Tennessean'. Son of a Tennessee dairy-farmer, he became a successful corporation lawyer and campaigned in a coonskin cap to enter Congress in 1939. Senator for his native state from 1949, he failed to gain acceptance as presidential candidate in 1952 and 1956, but made his mark in campaigning against organized crime, price-fixing and monopolies.

KEFLAVIK. Fishing port in Iceland, 22 m. W.S.W. of Reykjavik. It has a large international airport, built during the S.W.W. by U.S. forces (who called it Meeks Field). K. became a N.A.T.O. base in 1951, and a U.S. (N.A.T.O.) force was again estab. there. Pop. (1966) 5,422.

KEIGHLEY (kēth'li). English industrial town (bor.) in the W. Riding of Yorks. Manufactures incl. woollen and worsted goods, and machinery. Haworth, home of the Brontës, is part of K. bor. Pop (1961) 55,852.

KEITEL (kīt'el), **Wilhelm** (1882–1946). German field marshal. He was chief of the supreme command from 1938, and signed the unconditional surrender of the German forces at Berlin on 8 May 1945. He was tried at Nuremberg as a war criminal and hanged.

KEKULE (kek'oole), **Friedrich August** (1829–96). German chemist. B. at Darmstadt, he became prof. at Ghent in 1858, and at Bonn in 1865. His theory of molecular structure revolutionized organic chemistry (1858). In 1865 he conceived the novel idea of the ring structure of benzene from, it is said, a dream he had of a serpent catching its tail.

KELA'NTAN. State, ruled by a sultan, in the Federation of Malaysia. It was transferred by Siam to Britain in 1909, and until 1948 was one of the Unfederated Malay States. The cap. is Kota Bharu. The chief products incl. rice, rubber, copra, tin, manganese and gold. Area, 5,746 sq. m.; pop. (1966) 665,711.

KELLER, Gottfried (1819–1900). Swiss poet and novelist. B. at Zürich, he pub. his first vol. of *Gedichte* in 1846, another vol. of lyrics in 1851, and the outstanding educational and autobiographical novel, *Der grüne Heinrich*, in 1854–5. The first series of short stories, *Die Leute von Seldwyla* (1856), appeared at Zürich, where in 1861 he was made first sec. to the cantonal govt. After his retirement in 1876 there followed *Züricher Novellen* (1877), a story cycle, *Das Sinngedicht* (1881), the novel *Martin Salander*, etc.

KELLER, Helen Adams (1880–1968). American author. B. in Alabama, she lost the senses of sight and hearing through an illness when 19 months old, and of necessity remained dumb. Under the tuition of Anne Sullivan Macy, she became able to speak and graduated with honours at Radcliffe College in 1904. Her meeting with her teacher is described in William Gibson's play *The Miracle Worker* (1959), filmed in 1962. She pub. several books.

KELLERMANN, François Christophe de, duke of Valmy (1735–1820). French soldier, who in 1792 saved Paris by his victory at Valmy, and became one of Napoleon's marshals.

KELLOGG, Frank Billings (1856–1937). American Republican statesman. Ambassador to Great Britain in 1924, he was Sec. of State 1925–9, and was the author of the *Kellogg Pact* for the outlawry of war by the Great Powers, signed in Paris in 1928.

KELLS. Market town (U.D.) on the r. Blackwater, Meath, Rep. of Ireland. It was an ancient residence of the Irish kings. In the library of Trinity College, Dublin, is preserved the *Book of Kells*, an 8th cent. illuminated copy of the Gospels in Latin, written at a monastery of K. founded by St. Columba. Pop. (1961) 2,162.

KELLY, Edward (1854–80). Australian bushranger. The son of an Irish convict, he wounded a constable in 1878 while resisting the arrest of his brother Daniel for horse-stealing. The 2 brothers escaped and with two confederates carried out bank-robberies on the Victoria–New South Wales border. In 1880 K. was captured and hanged.

KELLY, Sir Gerald (1879–1972). British portrait painter. He was elected R.A. in 1930, and in 1945 completed State portraits of George VI and Queen Elizabeth, the Queen Mother. He succeeded Sir Alfred Munnings as President of the Royal Academy (1949–54).

KELLY, Grace Patricia (1928–). American film actress. B. in Philadelphia, she made her film début in 1951 in *Fourteen Hours*, and later starred in *High Noon* (1952), *The Country Girl* (1954) for which she received an Academy Award, and *High Society* (1955). In 1956 she m. Prince Rainier of Monaco (q.v.).

KELP. The powdery ash of burned seaweeds, a lesser source of iodine, also collectively the large seaweeds, particularly the *Fucaceae* and *Laminariaceae*.

KE'LSO. Market town on the Tweed, Roxburgh, Scotland. David I founded an abbey at K., 1120. Pop. (1961) 3,964.

KELVIN, William Thomson, 1st baron K. (1824–1907). British physicist. As prof. at Glasgow 1846–99, he was an inspiring teacher, and prodigious researcher in all aspects of physical sciences. Pioneer of the absolute scale of temperature, his work on the conservation of energy (1851) led to the 2nd law of thermodynamics. Popularly known for his contributions to telegraphy, he developed stranded cables and sensitive receivers, greatly improving transatlantic communications. Maritime endeavours led to a tide gauge and predictor, an improved compass, and simpler methods for fixing a ship's position at sea. He was pres. of the Royal Soc. 1890–5.

KEMA'L, Yasher (1922–). Turkish author. Once a field-labourer, then public letter-writer and shoemaker, he has pub. poetry and folklore collected during his wanderings in his native Anatolia. His first novel, trans. as *Memed, my Hawk* (1963), dealt with peasant life.

KEMBLE. British family of actors. **Roger K.** (1721–1802), a strolling player and travelling manager, had 12 children, one of whom was Mrs. Siddons (q.v.). **John Philip K.** (1757–1823), the 2nd child, made his début in 1776. In 1788 he became manager of Drury Lane, London, and in 1803 of Covent Garden. He retired in 1817 and lived at Lausanne. Strikingly handsome and intelligent, he was among the greatest English tragedians. **Charles K.** (1775–1854), a younger brother of the above, appeared with success in supporting roles 1792–1840. **Frances Anne (Fanny) K.** (1809–93), the elder dau. of Charles K., first appeared as Juliet at Covent Garden in 1829. After 1848 she made a great reputation by her Shakespeare readings.

KE'MEROVO. Coal-mining town in the R.S.F.S.R., cap. of K. region in W. Siberia and centre of Kuznetz coal basin; it has chemical and metallurgical factories. Pop. (1967) 358,000.

KEMPE. The tense moment in rehearsal when a difficult effect is exactly achieved.   *Photo: Godfrey MacDomnic.*

KEMPE (kemp), **Margery** (fl. 15th cent.). English religious writer, who lived at Lynn. Her account of her religious experiences forms the first English autobiography.

KE'MPE, Rudolf (1910–). German conductor. Specially noted for his appearances at the Salzburg and Edinburgh festivals and at Bayreuth, he is artistic director of the Royal Philharmonic, Tonhalle (Zürich), and Munich Philharmonic orchestras.

KE'MPENER, Peter de (c. 1503–80). Flemish painter. B. in Brussels, he worked in Seville 1537–62 and became known as Pedro Campaña. His masterpiece the 'Deposition from the Cross' (1548) is in Seville Cathedral.

KEMPIS. *See* THOMAS À KEMPIS.

KEMP-WELCH (-welsh), **Lucy Elizabeth** (1869–1958). British animal painter. B. at Bournemouth, she gained an international reputation with her pictures of horses, e.g. 'Colt Hunting in the New Forest' and 'Horses Bathing in the Sea', and became the first pres. of the Soc. of Animal Painters in 1914.

KEMSLEY, James Gomer Berry, 1st visct. K. (1883–1968). British newspaper proprietor. B. in Merthyr Tydfil, he built up with his brother Visct. Camrose (1879–1954), a large newspaper chain, and was from 1937 chairman of Kemsley Newspapers Ltd. and editor of the *Sunday Times*, until they were acquired by Roy Thomson (q.v.).

KEN, Thomas (1637–1711). English churchman and hymn-writer. He was bishop of Bath and Wells 1684–91, when he refused to take the oath of allegiance to William of Orange. His hymns incl. 'Awake my soul, and with the sun', and 'Glory to Thee, my God, this night'.

KENDAL. Town (bor.) on the r. Kent, Westmorland, England. Woollens (an industry introduced by Flemings in the 14th cent.), agricultural machinery, boots and shoes, etc., are made. Catherine Parr was born at K. castle. Pop. (1961) 18,595.

KENDAL, William Hunter (1843–1917). British actor. B. in London, the son of a painter named Grimston, he first appeared on the stage in 1862 and from 1866 appeared regularly in London. MADGE K., *née* Margaret Shafto Robertson (1849–1935), whom he m. in 1869, was a sister of T. W. Robertson, the dramatist, and made her first London appearance as Ophelia in 1865. Mr. and Mrs. Kendal played together in many famous parts, particularly in Shakespearian and the old English comedies. Mrs. K. retired in 1908 and received the D.B.E. in 1926.

KENDALL, Henry Clarence (1841–82). Australian poet. B. in New South Wales, he had a gift for lyrical expression of feeling inspired by the Australian countryside and domestic life, e.g. *Poems and Songs*, and *Songs from the Mountains* (1880).

KENILWORTH. Town (U.D.) in Warwickshire, England, famous for its Norman castle, which became a royal residence and was enlarged by John of Gaunt and later by the earl of Leicester. It was dismantled after the Civil War; the ruins were given to the nation by the 1st Lord Kenilworth in 1937. Pop. (1961) 14,427.

KE'NNAN, George Frost (1904–). American diplomat. For many years in the U.S. Foreign Service, he was ambassador to the U.S.S.R. 1952–3 and Yugoslavia 1961–3. He has taught at Princeton and Oxford, became prof. at Princeton in 1963, and is a world authority on the complexities of East-West politics. e.g. *Soviet American Relations 1917–20* (1956–8), *Russia and the West Under Lenin and Stalin* (1961) and *Memoirs 1925–50* (1967).

KENNEDY, David (1905–). American banker. A Republican, he was Sec. of the Treasury 1969–70, then becoming ambassador-at-large, working in the State Dept. on matters of internat. finance. He is not related to the family of Pres. Kennedy.

KENNEDY, John Fitzgerald (1917–63). 35th Pres. of the U.S.A. The 2nd son of Joseph Patrick K. (1888–1969), millionaire and ambassador to the U.K. 1938–40; he was b. at Brookline, Mass., and ed. at Harvard and the London School of Economics. A back injury received while playing football was worsened by service with the navy in the Pacific, when he was decorated for gallantry after a Japanese destroyer sank the torpedo-boat he commanded. Elected to the House of Representatives as a Democrat in 1947, he became a Senator in 1952, and in 1960 was elected to the presidency, defeating Nixon in one of the closest contests of U.S. history, the 1st R.C. and youngest man ever to be elected. Supported by the academics and intellectuals of the 'New Frontier', he pursued liberal domestic policies in civil rights, medical care for the aged, etc., and in foreign affairs adopted a firm but negotiable attitude, notably in the Cuban crisis of 1962 and in the signature of the nuclear test-ban treaty of 1963. Riding in an open car through Dallas 22 Nov. 1963 he was assassinated in full view of a television audience, shot (allegedly) by Lee Harvey Oswald, an ex-Marine and Marxist sympathizer, who was in turn shot dead at Dallas police H.Q. by a night-club proprietor, Jack Ruby. He was the author of *Why England Slept* (1940) and *Profiles in Courage* (1956). His wife, Jacqueline Lee Bouvier (1929–), whom he had m. in 1953, was noted for her restoration of the White House to the decor of 1880. Their children, Caroline (1957–) and John Fitzgerald, Jun. (1960–), became trend-setters for juvenile America. His

KENNEDY. The Kennedy family are noted for their close links, whether at work or play. Here in 1959 are the three brothers Robert (left), Edward (centre) and John during a recess in a hearing of the U.S. Senate Investigations Subcommittee.   *Courtesy of the U.S. Information Service.*

younger brother Robert Francis K. (1925–68) was ed. at Harvard and Virginia univs., and was admitted to the Mass. State Bar in 1951 and the U.S. Supreme Court in 1955. He was campaign manager for his brother in 1961, and as Attorney-General 1961–4 pursued a 'racket-busting' policy and promoted the Civil Rights Act of 1964. When Johnson preferred Hubert K. Humphrey for the 1964 Vice-Pres. nomination, K. resigned and became Senator for N.Y. In 1968 he campaigned for the Presidential nomination, but was assassinated by Sirhan Bissara Sirhan, a Jordanian Arab resident in the U.S.A. from 1957. In 1968 John F. Kennedy's widow m. Aristotle Onassis (q.v.).

His youngest brother Edward Moore K. (1932–) went into legal practice in Boston, joined with 'Bobby' K. in the management of J.F.K.'s pres. campaign, and in 1963 became the youngest U.S. Senator. His career suffered some setback from 1969, following his delay in reporting a car accident: see MARTHA'S VINEYARD. He was asst. majority leader in the U.S. Senate 1969–71.

The eldest of the 4 brothers, Joseph Patrick K., Jun. (1915–44), a naval airman, was killed in action in the S.W.W.

KENNEDY, Margaret (1896–1967). British writer, who made her name in 1924 with the novel *The Constant Nymph*. Her later works incl. the play *Escape Me Never* (1933) and the novel *Lucy Carmichael* (1951).

KENNEDY, Cape. U.S. promontory on the Atlantic coast of Florida, 228 m. N. of Miami. It is separated from the mainland by Banana r., Merritt is., and Indian r., and is marked by a lighthouse. Here also is the Atlantic Missile Range (1956), a proving ground for guided missiles, and a site of space-flight experiments from 1962 onwards. Formerly known as Cape Canaveral, it was re-named in 1963 by Pres. Johnson in honour of Pres. Kennedy.

KENNELLY, A. E. (1861–1939). American engineer. An assistant of Edison and later prof. at Harvard, he verified the existence of an ionized layer in the upper atmosphere in 1902, shortly before it had been predicted by Heaviside (q.v.) *See* IONOSPHERE.

KENNELLY-HEAVISIDE LAYER. The lower regions of the inosphere (q.v.) which absorb short radio waves, and reflect long radio waves, allowing their reception round the surface of the earth. The K.-H.L. approaches the earth by day, and recedes from it at night.

KENNET, Lady. *See* SCOTT, ROBERT FALCON.

KENNINGTON, Eric Henri (1888–1960). British painter, pastel artist and sculptor. An official war artist 1916–19 and 1940–3, he executed the British memorial at Soissons, the memorial to Thomas Hardy in Dorchester and various T. E. Lawrence memorials, incl. a bronze head in St. Paul's Cathedral and a recumbent effigy (1954) in the Tate Gallery.

KENNINGTON. Dist. in the bor. of Lambeth, Greater London, in which are K. Oval, headquarters of the Surrey Cricket Club, and K. Park, opened 1852, part of the former common on which the 1848 Chartist gathering took place.

KENSINGTON and CHELSEA, Royal Bor. of. Bor. of Greater London which contains K. palace, and the dists. of Notting Hill, Earl's Court, Brompton, and South K. (the chief museum centre of London, also having several learned institutions). West K. is in Hammersmith. K. gardens, 264 acres, are, except for the western strip containing K. palace, which is in K., in Westminster. *See* CHELSEA.

K. palace became a royal residence in the time of William III. Queen Victoria was b. there. Holland House, last of the great country mansions which once surrounded London, was destroyed during a German air raid in 1940: a youth hostel was opened on the site 1959 and the grounds are a public park.

KENT, Edward George Alexander Edmund 2nd, duke of (1935–). British prince, son of George

(1902–42), 4th son of George V, who was cr. duke of K. just before his m. in 1934 to Princess Marina of Denmark and Greece (1906–68). The second duke, who succeeded when his father was killed in an air crash on active service with the R.A.F., was ed. at Eton and Sandhurst, and then commissioned in the Royal Scots Greys. He represented the Queen at the Sierra Leone independence celebrations. In 1961 he m. Katharine Worsley (1933–) and his heir is George (1962–), earl of St. Andrews.

His brother, Prince Michael (1942–) became an officer with the Hussars in 1962. His sister, Princess Alexandra (1936–), who represented the Queen at the Nigerian independence celebrations, m. in 1963 Angus Ogilvy.

KENT, Rockwell (1882–1971). American artist, noted for his boldly grand landscapes and fine wood engravings.

KENT, William (1685–1748). British landscape gardener, influential in freeing the art from formalism. B. in Herts, he followed the landscapes of Claude and Poussin, with a fondness for classic temples. As an architect and sculptor (Shakespeare in Westminster Abbey) he was indifferent.

KENT and STRATHEARN, Edward Augustus, duke of (1767–1820). British general. The 4th son of George III, he m. Victoria Mary Louisa (1786–1861), widow of the Prince of Leiningen, in 1818, by whom he had one child, the future Queen Victoria.

KENT. Co. of S.E. England. Running N.W. to S.E. across the county are the N. Downs. S. of them is the Weald, agricultural land with orchards, hop fields, market gardens, etc. N.E. Kent produces fruit and wheat. K. is often called the 'Garden of England'. Romney Marsh in the S. is celebrated for its sheep. Industrial K. in the N.W. has large cement and paper-making industries. The principal rivers are the Darent, Medway, and Stour. Inland from Deal is an extensive coalfield.

The co. town is Maidstone; other important towns are Canterbury, Rochester, Chatham, Gravesend, Sheerness, and four of the Cinque Ports (Dover, Sandwich, New Romney, and Hythe). Coastal holiday resorts are numerous. In popular speech, a 'man of K.' hails from E. of the Medway, and a 'Kentish man' from the western part of the co. The Univ. of Kent at Canterbury was founded in 1965. Area 1,440 sq. m.; pop. (1967) 1,345,520.

KENT. Penshurst Place, of which the south front is here seen from the garden, is one of the county's loveliest houses. The birthplace of Sir Philip Sidney, it is now the seat of his descendant Visct. De L'Isle who in 1944 won the V.C. on the Anzio beachhead.   *Courtesy of Lord De L'Isle.*

KENTIGERN, St. (*c.* A.D. 518–603), also called 'Mungo', a nickname meaning 'dear friend'. First bishop of Glasgow, he was b. at Culross. The pagans forced him to flee to Wales, where he founded the monastery of St. Asaph. In 573 he returned to Glasgow, whose cathedral he founded.

KENTU'CKY. South-central state of the U.S.A., called the 'Blue Grass State' because of the richness of the grass in the 'blue grass' area. There are *c.* 800 m.

of river boundary, including the Ohio in the N.K. is famous for its caves. The chief products are tobacco, maize, livestock, coal, and petroleum. The chief towns incl. Frankfort (the cap.), Louisville, Covington, and Lexington. Area 40,395 sq. m.; pop. (1970) 3,219,311.

K. dam, 206 ft. high, 8,422 ft. wide, largest of those built by the Tennessee Valley Authority, is on the Tennessee r., 20 m. above its junction with the Ohio.

KEN WOOD. Estate and mansion in Camden, London, England, adjoining Hampstead Heath. The wood itself was bought for the public and opened in 1923; the mansion, built by Robert Adam, was bought by the Earl of Iveagh, who in 1927 left the house and 70 acres of land as public property. Total area 195 acres.

KE'NYA. Country in E. Africa with a coastline on the Indian Ocean; it rises from a coastal plain to a broad high plateau 3,000–10,000 ft. high, crossed by the Rift Valley. The chief r., the Tana, is navigable for about 150 m. from its mouth, The climate is tropical in the coastal plain, warm temperate in the highlands. Agricultural products incl. wheat, coffee, maize, sisal, cotton, coconuts, sugar cane; forests, some 3,000 sq. m. in extent, yield valuable timber. The cap. is Nairobi; Mombasa is the chief port. Area 224,960 sq. m.; pop. (1967) 9,370,000.

K. was made a British protectorate in 1895, a Crown colony in 1920. Following nationalist claims for independence from 1946 (*see* MAU-MAU), K. became independent 1963, and a rep. within the Brit. Commonwealth 1964. There is a pres. (*see* KENYATTA, JOMO), and from 1966 the House of Reps. and Senate were amalgamated in a single Nat. Assembly. Many Asians of Indian and Pakistani stock left K. 1967–8 as a result of the policy of Kenyanization in commerce and the professions, and went to Britain.

K. is a one-party state (from 1964), the *K. African Nat. Union* (KANU) being in control. There is considerable tribal tension, e.g. the assassination in 1969 of Tom Mboya (q.v.) a Luo, by a member of the dominant Kikuyu in 1969.

KENYA, Mt. Extinct volcano in E. Africa, from which K. is named. It is 17,040 ft. high, and was first climbed by Sir Halford Mackinder in 1899.

KENYA'TTA, Jomo. Name assumed by Kenya politician Kamau Ngengi (*c.* 1889–), *kenyatta* meaning 'beaded belt'. A member of the Kikuyu tribe, he was b. nr. Fort Hall, son of a poor farmer and grandson of a magician. Brought up at a Church of Scotland mission, he joined the Kikuyu Central Assocn., devoted to recovery of Kikuyu lands from white settlers, of which he became pres. He spent some years in Britain, and while a farm labourer during the S.W.W. m. an Englishwoman: he has had 3 African wives. Returning to Kenya in 1946 as pres. of the Kenya African Union (successor to the banned K.C.A.), he was in 1953 sentenced to 7 yrs. for his management of Mau-Mau (q.v.), though some doubt has been cast on his complicity. Released to exile in N. Kenya in 1958, he was allowed to return to Kikuyuland in 1961 and in 1963 became P.M. (also pres. from 1964) of independent Kenya. His policy is summarized by his slogans 'Uhuru na Moja' (Freedom and Unity) and 'Haram-

JOMO KENYATTA, a statue in Nairobi by Macdonald Reid in simulated bronze on a fibre-glass framework.
Photo: Central Press Photos Ltd.

bee' (Let's get going), and entails collaboration with the whites to ensure unbroken economic progress.

KENYON, Kathleen Mary (1906–). British archaeologist. Dau. of classical and biblical scholar Sir Frederic George K. (1863–1952), director and principal librarian at the British Museum 1909–30, she was ed. at Oxford, where she became principal of St. Hugh's Coll. in 1962, and lectured in Palestinian archaeology at the Inst. of Archaeology, Univ. of London, 1948–62. As director of the Brit. School of Archaeology in Jerusalem 1951–62, she showed that the double walls of Jericho, previously associated with Joshua, were of differing dates and belonged to an earlier period, and that a Neolithic settlement (the earliest known) had existed there *c.* 6800 B.C. Her books incl. *Digging Up Jericho* (1957).

KEPLER, Johann (1571–1630). German astronomer. B. in Württemberg, he became Tycho Brahe's assistant in 1600 and succeeded him as imperial mathematician in 1601. In his last years he was astrologer to Wallenstein. He d. at Ratisbon.

As the discoverer of the 3 laws of planetary motion that bear his name, K. ranks as one of the founders of modern astronomy. The laws are: (1) The

KENYA. While staying at Treetops, a game look-out first established by Sherbrooke Walker in 1932, Queen Elizabeth II succeeded to the British throne in 1952. Built on the site of a 'salt lick' which attracts numbers of elephant, rhinoceros, baboons and deer from surrounding Aberdare Forest, it was destroyed by Mau-Mau in 1954 but rebuilt in 1957.
Courtesy of Treetops, Nyeri.

orbit of each planet is an ellipse with the sun at one of the foci. (2) The radius vector of each planet describes equal areas in equal times. (3) The squares of the periods of the planets are proportional to the cubes of their mean distances from the sun.

KER (ker), **William Paton** (1855–1923). British scholar. B. at Glasgow, he was prof. of Eng. literature at Cardiff (1883–9), and London (1889–1922), and prof. of poetry at Oxford. His works incl. *Epic and Romance* (1897), *The Dark Ages* (1904), etc.

KE'RALA. State of the Rep. of India formed in 1956 from the former princely states of Travancore and Cochin (except for a small area in the E., transferred to Madras), plus a small area formerly in S. Madras. K. is noteworthy as the most literate state in India – more than 50 per cent of men, about a third of women. The name was that of an ancient kingdom in this area which came to an end in 1310 when it was conquered by Mohammedan invaders. Tea, spices, coconuts, oilseeds, and rice are grown; there are extensive mineral deposits (white clay, mica, graphite, lignite, etc.), and industry is developing under govt. encouragement. Political instability arises from strong religious and caste divisions. Area 15,000 sq. m.; pop. (1961) 16,903,715.

KE'RBELA. Holy city of the Shīite Moslems, 60 m. S.S.W. of Baghdad, Iraq. K. occupies the site of the battlefield where Husain, son of Ali and Fatima, was killed in A.D. 680 while defending his succession to the Kh.lifate. His tomb in the city is visited every year by many pilgrims. Pop. (est.) 120,000.

KERCH (kärch). Port in the Crimea, Ukraine S.S.R., at the E. end of K. peninsula, an important iron-producing area. Built on the site of an ancient Greek settlement, K. became Russian in 1783. Pop. (1967) 115,000.

KEREN. Small town and trade centre in Eritrea, Ethiopia, key point of the Italian defence line during the Italian occupation of E. Africa in the S.W.W. It fell to the British in March 1941. Pop. (est.) 10,000.

KERE'NSKY, Alexander Feodorovich (1881–1970). Russian politician. After holding several ministerial posts, he was premier of the 2nd provisional govt., before its collapse in Nov. 1917, during the Bolshevik revolution. He lived in the U.S.A. from 1918 where he wrote. lectured and did research on the provisional govt. era.

KERKYRA. Greek form of CORFU.

KERMAN (kärmahn'). Town in S.E. Persia, cap. of K. (no. 8) prov. It is a road centre and manufactures shawls, carpets, etc. Pop. (1964) 75,230.

KERMANSHA'H. Town of Persia, cap. of prov. no. 5 (covering Hamadan, K., and S. Kurdistan), which is on the borders of Iraq. The prov. is very fertile and inhabited mainly by Kurds. K. is noted for its carpets and weaving, there is also a large petroleum refinery. Pop. (1964) 130,000.

KERN, Jerome (1885–1945). American song-writer. He composed the popular operetta, *Show Boat* (1927), from which comes the song 'Ol' Man River'.

KE'ROSENE. Mineral oil, a mixture of liquid hydrocarbons of sp. gr. about 0·78 to 0·83 and flash point below 67° C., prepared by distillation from petroleum. It is used for illumination and heating, and in the U.K. is known as 'paraffin oil'.

KE'ROUAC, Jack (1923–69). American novelist. Of French-Canadian extraction, he was b. in Lowell, Mass., and by his football prowess was set for a univ. career. Instead he became a merchant seaman, then wandered the U.S. and Mexico making a living by a miscellany of jobs. His books are the continuing Odyssey of Jack Duluoz, king of the Beatniks, and incl. *On the Road* (1958), *The Dharma Bums* (1959), and *Big Sur* (1963), which shows the crack-up of his hero against a background of modern America, with its neonlit countryside and superhighways.

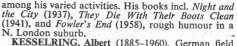

KEROUAC. The prophet of the beat generation, he rejected form in his life as in his work, and had mystic naïveté of approach.
Courtesy of André Deutsch Limited.

KERR (ker), **Deborah** (1921–). British actress. B. in Helensburgh, she made her stage début in London in 1938 and entered films in 1940. Her successes incl. *Black Narcissus, From Here to Eternity* (1953) and *The King and I* (1956). She is noted for the depth and restraint of her characterization.

KERRY. Co. in the prov. of Munster, Rep. of Ireland. Its W. coastline is deeply indented. The N. part is low-lying, but in the S. occur the highest mts. in Ireland; Macgillycuddy's Reeks rise to 3,414 ft. There are many rivers and lakes, incl. the famous lakes of Killarney. Tralee is the co. town. Area 1,815 sq. m.; pop. (1966) 112,785.

KERSH, Gerald (1911–68). British author. Of Russo-Polish origin, he was b. in England and had travelled widely, incl. service as a war correspondent among his varied activities. His books incl. *Night and the City* (1937), *They Die With Their Boots Clean* (1941), and *Fowler's End* (1958), rough humour in a N. London suburb.

KESSELRING, Albert (1885–1960). German field marshal. He commanded the Luftwaffe during the invasions of Poland and the Low Countries, 1939–40, and in the early stages of the Battle of Britain. Later he served under Rommel in N. Africa, took command in Italy in 1943, and was appointed C.-in-C. on the western front in March 1945. His death sentence for war crimes (1947) was commuted to imprisonment; he was released 1952.

KE'STEVEN, Parts of. S.W. area of Lincs, England, formed in 1888 into an administrative unit with county offices at Sleaford. Area 720 sq. m.; pop. (1967) 230,310.

KESTREL. Bird (*Falco tinnunculus*) in the family Falconidae, which breeds in the British Is. Its head and tail are bluish-grey, and its back is a light chestnut-brown with black spots.

KESWICK (kez'ik). Market town (U.D.) and tourist resort of Cumberland, England, in the Lake District near the N.E. shore of Derwentwater. Pop. (1961) 4,752. *Keswick Convention* is a meeting, held annually since 1875, of Evangelical Christians of all denominations.

KESTREL

KETCH, Jack (d. 1686). English executioner. He took over the post *c.* 1663, and carried out the executions of Lord Russell in 1683 and Monmouth in 1685. His name became a common nickname for an executioner.

KETELBEY (ketel'bi), **Albert William** (1885–1959). British composer, remembered for the orchestral pieces 'In a Monastery Garden' and 'In a Persian Market'.

KETONES. Organic compounds containing the carbonyl group CO, differentiated from aldehydes by uniting to 2 atoms of carbon instead of one of carbon and one of hydrogen. They are liquids or low-melting-point solids, slightly soluble in water, and form derivatives in acid solutions.

KETTERING. English industrial town (bor.) near the Ise, Northants, 13 m. N.E. of Northampton, with boot and shoe manufactures. Pop. (1961) 38,631.

KEW. Part of the bor. of Richmond-upon-Thames, in Greater London, containing Kew Palace, once a royal residence, and the Royal Botanic Gardens, which were opened to the public in 1841. In 1964 additional grounds were acquired at Wakehurst Place, Ardingly, Sussex. Kew Observatory is in the Old Deer Park.

KEY, Francis Scott (1779–1843). American author of 'The Star-Spangled Banner'. A lawyer by profession, he wrote the song while Fort McHenry was being defended against the British in 1814. It is (since 1931) the national anthem of the U.S.A.

KEYES (kīz), **Frances Parkinson** (1885–1970). American writer. B. in Virginia, she was the author of many romances, often set in the deep South, and including *River Road* (1946), and *Joy Street* (1951).

KEYNES (känz), **John Maynard**, 1st baron (1883–1946). British economist. B. at Cambridge, he was ed. at King's Coll., Cambridge, of which he became a Fellow. He held a Treasury appointment during the F.W.W., and took part in the peace conference as chief Treasury representative, but resigned in protest against the financial terms of the treaty. He justified his action in *The Economic Consequences of the Peace* (1919). His later economic works, e.g. *The General Theory of Employment, Interest, and Money* (1936), aroused much controversy by their proposals to prevent crises by control of credit and currency. During the S.W.W. he became a director of the Bank of England, and a member of the Chancellor of the Exchequer's consultative committee, and led the British delegation at the Bretton Woods (q.v.) Conference. In 1945 he negotiated the American loan agreement. He received a barony 1942. He m. dancer Lydia Lopokova in 1925.

KEY WEST. Town at the tip of the Florida peninsula, U.S.A. In 1967 it became the first in America to take all its fresh water from the sea. Pop. (1960) 33,956.

K.G.B. (*Komitet Gosudarstvennoye Bezhopaznosti*). The Russian secret police, known before 1953 as the M.V.D. (q.v.). Under the control of the State Security Committee, they are in charge of frontier and general security and the forced labour system. Earlier names for the secret police were the Okhrana under the Tsars; Cheka (q.v.) 1918–23; G.P.U. or Ogpu (*Obedinyonnoye Gosudarstvennoye Polititcheskoye Upravleniye*) 1923–34; N.K.V.D. (*Narodny Komisariat Vnutrennykh Del*) 1932–6; and M.V.D. (q.v.).

KHABARO'VSK. Town on the r. Amur, cap. of K. Territory in the far E. of the R.S.F.S.R. It has refineries for petroleum from Sakhalin, saw mills and flour mills, meat packing, and other industries. Pop. (1967) 420,000.

KHACHATURIAN (kachatiyūrē'an), **Aram Ilyich** (1903–). Russian composer. B. in Tiflis, he studied under Myaskovsky in Moscow, and has used folk themes to striking effect in concertos for violin and for piano, and the exotic ballet *Gayaneh* (1942), which incl. the 'Sabre Dance'.

KHAKI (kah'ki). Originally the sand- or dust-coloured uniforms worn by British and native troops in India *c.* 1850; recognized particularly in the S. African War as useful neutral camouflage, and adopted as standard throughout the world.

KHA'LIFA, The, or **Abdullah el Taaisha** (1846–99). Sudanese dervish leader. Succeeding the Mahdi as ruler of the Sudan in 1885, he was defeated by Kitchener at Omdurman in 1898; the K. escaped, but was killed at Kordofan.

KHAMA (kah'mah), **Sir Seretse** (1921–). Botswana politician. Son of the Bamangwato chief Sekoma II (d. 1925), he studied law in Britain and m. an Englishwoman, Ruth Williams. This m. was strongly condemned by his uncle Tshekedi K., regent during his minority, as contrary to tribal custom, and Seretse K. was banished in 1950, returning in 1956 on his renunciation of any claim to the chieftaincy, but in 1965 be became P.M. of Bechuanaland, and in 1966 pres. of the new rep. of Botswana and K.B.E.

KHA'MSIN (Arabic 'fifty'). Hot, dry, southerly winds which originate in the Sahara and blow across N Egypt during the spring and summer. The name is derived from the supposed average duration of the winds, i.e. 50 days.

KHAN, Ayub (1907–). Pakistani statesman. Ed. at Sandhurst, he became C.-in-C. of Pakistan's army in 1951, was Defence Min. 1954–5, and on the abrogation of the constitution by Pres. Mirza in 1958 became chief martial law administrator and himself Pres. on Mirza's resignation. Re-elected 1965, he met increasing opposition, announced 1969 that he would not be a candidate 1970 and resigned.

KHAN, Liaquat Ali (1895–1951). Indian statesman. Ed. at Allahabad and Oxford, he studied law, and in 1923 joined the Muslim League. He was deputy leader of the Muslim League Party 1941–7, and in 1947 became 1st P.M. of Pakistan. He was assassinated by a Muslim fanatic.

KHA'RGA. Oasis in the Western Desert of Egypt. Known to the Romans, it became in 1960 H.Q. of the

New Valley irrigation scheme. An area twice the size of Italy will be reclaimed for agriculture by use of newly located natural underground reservoirs.

KHA'RKOV. Industrial city of the Ukrainian S.S.R., cap. of K. Region, 250 m. E. of Kiev. It is an important railway junction, a great engineering centre, and has a large tractor-making plant. K., founded in 1654, has a univ. and an airport. Pop. (1967) 1,092,000.

KHARTOUM (-toom'). Cap. and trading centre of the Rep. of Sudan, at the junction of the Blue and White Nile, cap. of K. prov. K. was founded in 1830 by Mehemet Ali (q.v.). General Gordon (q.v.) was killed at K. by the Mahdist rebels in 1885. A new city was built after the site was recaptured by the British in 1898. Pop. (1961 est.) 117,685.

KHEDIVE (kedēv'). Title granted by the sultan of Turkey in 1867 to his viceroy in Egypt, and held by the latter's successors until 1914.

KHERSO'N. Town on the Dnieper r., Ukraine S.S.R., built by Potemkin as a naval harbour, cap. of K. region. Its industries incl. soap and tobacco manufacture and brewing. Pop. (1967) 222,000.

KHE SANH (kā san). U.S. Marine outpost 6 m. from the Laotian border and 14 m. S. of the demilitarized zone in N. Vietnam. Garrisoned by 4,000 Marines, it was under attack by 20,000 N. Vietnamese 21 Jan.–7 April 1968.

KHIVA (khē'vah). Town in Uzbek S.S.R., U.S.S.R., once the cap. of K. khanate, which submitted to Russian suzerainty in 1873. Carpets and textiles are made. Pop. (est.) 25,000.

KHORASAN (koorahsahn'). Prov. No. 9 of Persia, adjoining Afghanistan. It is mountainous, with salt wastes and desert, but has fertile valleys. Meshed is the cap. Area *c.* 125,000 sq. m.; pop. (est.) 1,800,000.

KHRUSHCHEV (krooshchov'), **Nikita Sergeyevich** (1894–1971). Soviet statesman. B. nr. Kursk, the son of a miner, he worked on the Donbas coalfield, and

NIKITA KHRUSHCHEV
Photo: Novosti Press Agency.

having taken a minor part in the Revolution joined the Communist Party in 1918 and fought in the Civil War. Rising in the party to full membership of the Politburo by 1939, he was assigned to organize the guerrilla defence of his native Ukraine in the S.W.W., and was chairman of the Ukraine Council of Ministers 1947–9. He became a member of the Presidium of the Supreme Soviet in 1952 and Sec. Gen. of the C.C.C.P. in 1953, following the formation of the Malenkov cabinet, and in 1958 succeeded Bulganin as Chairman of the Council of Ministers (P.M.). An original supporter of Stalin against Trotsky and Bukharin, he denounced the personality cult of Stalin and the latter's repressive measures in a secret session of the Soviet Communist Party in 1956 – many victims of the purges of the 1930s being subsequently released and others posthumously rehabilitated – and publicly repeated the charges in 1961, launching a de-Stalinization campaign. He believed that Communism would conquer in peaceful competition with Capitalism. He was compelled to resign 1964 because of mishandled foreign policy (e.g. his personal feud with Mao Tsetung, under-estimate of Chinese atomic progress, and hasty despatch of missiles to Cuba, later withdrawn), domestic failures (e.g. the agricultural crisis and his neglect of heavy industry), and personal failings (e.g. new personality cult and nepotism): by 1965 his reputation was to some extent officially restored.

KHUFU (koo'foo) (fl. *c.* 3000 B.C.). Egyptian king of Memphis, who built the largest of the Pyramids (*see* EGYPT illus.). The Gk. form of K. is CHEOPS

KHYBER (kīber) **PASS.** A defile 33 m. long through the mountain range which separates Pakistan from Afghanistan. The K.P. was used by Mahmud of Ghazni, Baber, Nadir Shah, and other invaders of India. The present road was constructed by the British during the Afghan Wars.

KIANGSI (kyangsē'). Prov. of S.E. China to the S. of the Yangtze-Kiang. Rice is the chief crop, coal and tungsten the chief minerals. The cap. is Nanchang. Area 63,600 sq. m.; pop. (1968) 22,000.000.

KIANGSU (kyangsoo'). One of the coastal provs. of China, on either side of the mouth of the Yangtze-Kiang. Much of the area is swampy, but in the S. is some very fertile land. Products incl. winter wheat, millet, soya beans; coal, iron, limestone; cement, ceramics, textiles. The cap. is Nanking; Shanghai is a special municipality within K. Area 39,500 sq. m.; pop. (1968) 47,000,000.

KIANGSU. Industrial China – a high-pressure compressor, key equipment of a 25,000 ton chemical fertilizer installation, being assembled by workers of the Chingyeh Machinery Works at Shangkai. Such large-scale production is being increasingly undertaken as the industrialization programme advances.
Photo: Camera Press.

KIBBU'TZ. Israeli communal collective settlement, with collective ownership of *all* property and earnings and collective organization of work; a modified version, the *Moshav Shitufi*, is similar to the Collective Farms (q.v.) of Soviet Russia. Other Israeli co-operative rural settlements incl. the *Moshav Ovdim* which has equal opportunity, and the similar but less strict *Moshav* settlement.

KIDD, William (*c.* 1645–1701). British pirate. B. in Greenock, he settled in New York. In 1696 he was commissioned by the Governor of New York to suppress pirates, but he became a pirate himself. Arrested in 1699, he was taken to England and hanged.

KIDDERMINSTER. Market town (bor.) on the Stour, Worcs, England, famous for carpets since *c.* 1735. Pop. (1961) 40,822

KIDNEYS. A pair of reddish-brown organs about 4½ in. by 1½ in., situated on the rear wall of the abdomen, which are responsible for water regulation, excretion of waste products and maintaining the homeostasis of the blood. Each K. consists of a number of long tubules; the outer parts filter the aqueous components of blood, and the inner parts selectively reabsorb vital elements, leaving waste products in the remaining fluid (urine) which is collected at the ends of the ducts and passed through the ureter to the bladder.

KIEL (kēl). Port of W. Germany on the Baltic 55 m. N. of Hamburg; cap. of Schleswig-Holstein prov. K. was heavily bombed during the S.W.W.,

and the *K. Canal*, *c.* 60 m. long, connecting the North Sea to the Baltic, opened 1895, was repeatedly mined. Pop. (1966) 270,000.

KIELCE (kē-'elt'se). Cap. of K. voivodship (co.), Poland, 70 m. N.E. of Krakow, an important railway junction. Pop. (1966) 109,000.

KIELLAND (chel'and), **Alexander** (1849–1906). Norwegian novelist. B. at Stavanger, where he became burgomaster, he shows in his novels, incl. *Garman og Worse* (1880), a fine psychological insight.

KIERKEGAARD (kye'-rkegawr), **Søren Aabye** (1813–55). Danish philosopher. B. in Copenhagen, where he spent most of his life, he was the son of a Jewish merchant, but was converted to Christianity in 1838, although he became hostile to the estab. Church, and his beliefs caused much controversy. His concept of man as an isolated individual before God is largely the basis of Existentialism (q.v.). He regarded sin as self-alienation, the cause of which is 'dread', and discarded the Bible and Reason as proof of God's existence, which he saw only in man's personal relationship with

KIERKEGAARD. Sketched by his cousin Christian Kierkegaard.
Courtesy of the Royal Danish Ministry of Foreign Affairs.

God. Very prolific, he pub. his first important work *Either-Or* in 1843, and notable later are *Concept of Dread* (1844) and *Post-script* (1846), which summed up much of his earlier writings. His many pseudonyms were sometimes used to argue with himself.

KIESINGER (kēs'-), **Kurt Georg** (1904–   ). West German statesman. A lawyer – member of the Nazi Party 1933–4, but later opposing Nat. Socialism –he joined the Christian Democratic Union after the S.W.W., became premier of Baden-Württemberg 1958 and succeeded Erhard as Federal Chancellor (1966–69).

KIEV (kē-et'). Cap. of the Ukrainian S.S.R., the 3rd largest city of the U.S.S.R. Situated at the junction of the Dnieper with the Desna, K. is a great route focus and marketing centre. It has a univ., an airfield, and a wide range of industries. The Slav domination of Russia began with the rise of K., the 'mother of Russian cities', founded in the 5th cent. and many times conquered and re-conquered. It was also the original seat of Christianity in Russia (988). Pop. (1967) 1,371,000.

KILDARE (kildār'). Co. of Leinster prov., Rep. of Ireland, S. of Meath. The north is wet and boggy, but in the E. and W. oats, barley, and potatoes, etc., are grown and cattle are reared. Area 654 sq. m.; pop. (1966) 66,404. The co. town, also K., has a 13th cent. cathedral. Pop. 3,800.

KILIMA-NJARO (kilimanjah'rō). Mountain mass in N. Tanganyika, Africa, with two extinct volcanic craters,. Kibo, the higher, rising to 19,300 ft., loftiest point in Africa. K. was first sighted by two German missionaries, Rebmann and Krapf, in 1847. Though less than 250 m. from the equator, it is crowned by glaciers and perpetual snow.

KILKE'NNY. Co. in Leinster prov., Rep. of Ireland, E. of Tipperary. K. is mainly devoted to agriculture, but in the N. coal is worked. Area 796 sq. m.; pop. (1966) 60,463. The co. town is K., situated on the r. Nore, with a cathedral. Pop. (1966) 10,000.

KILLA'RNEY. Market town of co. Kerry, Rep. of Ireland, the most famous beauty spot in Ireland. To the S.W. lie Macgillycuddy's Reeks, which incl. Carrantuohill, 3,414 ft., highest point in Ireland, and the K. lakes. Pop. (1966) 7,000. *See* illus. p. 576.

KILMA'RNOCK. Town (burgh) in Ayrshire, Scotland, 20 m. S.W. of Glasgow. Industries incl. coal mining and the making of locomotives, cranes, carpets, and hosiery. Pop. (1961) 47,509.

KILMUI'R, David Patrick Maxwell Fyfe, 1st earl K. (1900–67). British lawyer and Cons. politician. Called to the Bar in 1922, he became an M.P. in 1935 and was Solicitor-Gen. 1942–5 and Attorney-Gen. in 1945 during the Churchill govts. At the Nuremberg trials he was deputy to Sir Hartley Shawcross and for most of the time conducted the British prosecution. He was Home Sec. 1951–4 and Lord Chancellor 1954–62. In 1954 he was created visct. and in 1962 earl.

KILO. Prefix denoting in the metric system 1,000 units. *Kilogram* is a unit of weight equal to 1,000 grams or 2·205 lb. *Kilometre* is a unit of length equal to 3,280·89 ft. (approx. ⅝ m.). *Kiloton* is a unit of explosive force equivalent to 1,000 tons of T.N.T. used in describing atom bombs. *Kilowatt* is a unit of power equal to about 1⅓ horsepower.

KILVERT, Francis (1840–79). British clergyman and diarist. Unpub. until 1938–9, his *Diary: 1870–79* is a useful record of social life.

KIMBERLEY. In the chambering method of diamond mining used here, a grid of tunnels (each half pillar and half chamber) is developed at various levels in the pipe area. The chambered area is mined out beneath the pillars of the level above, so that the latter are undercut and collapse into the chamber below. The blueground is then loaded into trucks and hauled to the shaft. *Courtesy of the Anglo-American Corporation of South Africa.*

KI'MBERLEY. Diamond-mining town in Cape Prov., S. Africa, 95 m. N.W. of Bloemfontein. Apart from industries associated with diamonds, there are asbestos and manganese mines. The town was founded in 1871 and named after the 1st earl of K. who, as Sec. of State for the Colonies, placed the mines at that time under British protection; De Beers Consolidated Mines secured control of the mines in 1887. Pop. (1960) 77,180, of whom 23,987 were white.

KIMO'NO. Traditional costume of Japanese women, still retained for formal wear – the *homongi* or 'visiting dress'. For the finest Ks., which may cost several hundred pounds, a rectangular piece of pure silk (c. 36 ft. × 1·3 ft.) is cut into 7 pieces for tailoring, the brilliant colouring of the design (which must match perfectly over the seams and for which flowers are the favourite motif) then being painted by hand and enhanced by embroidery or gilding. The accompanying *obi* or sash is also embroidered.

KINCA'RDINESHIRE. Co. of E. Scotland. It is chiefly an agricultural region, but a large fishing industry is centred on Stonehaven, the co. town. Area 382 sq. m.; pop. (1961) 48,800.

KINE'TICS. Branch of dynamics dealing with the action of forces producing or changing the motion of a real body, as distinguished from kinematics, which deals with motion without reference to force or mass.

KING, Martin Luther (1929–68). American Negro leader. B. in Atlanta, Georgia, son of a Baptist minister, he also became a pastor. Preaching non-violence – he won the 1964 Nobel peace prize – he campaigned to end segregation. Riots across U.S.A. followed his being shot, and a white escaped convict, James Earl Ray, was arrested in England, extradited, and sentenced to 99 years' gaol in 1969.

KING, William Lyon Mackenzie (1874–1950). Canadian Lib. statesman. B. in Ontario, he was P.M. 1921–30 (excl. June-Sept. 1926) and 1935–48. He took part in the 1926 Imperial Conference which recognized the Dominion's equal status with Britain, and his proposals, that self-governing countries maintain close co-operation but be linked only by allegiance to the Crown, were incl. in the Statute of Westminster. He received the O.M. in 1947.

KING CRAB. Marine animal (*Limulus*) in the class Arachnida. The upper side of its body is entirely covered by a shell and it has a long spine-like tail. It is unable to swim and burrows in the sand, feeding on worms. K.Cs. measure up to 2 ft. long.

KINGCUP. Name given to several flowers of the Ranunculaceae family, particularly the buttercup and the marsh marigold.

KINGFISHER. European bird (*Alcedo ispida*), also found in parts of N. Africa and Asia. The plumage is brilliant blue-green on the back and chestnut beneath. Ks. feed upon fish and aquatic insects, etc. The nest is made of fishbones in a hole in a river bank.

KING-HALL, Stephen, baron (1893–1966). British publicist. He founded the K.-H. (later National) Newsletter (1936), and the Hansard Soc. (1944), and wrote on international politics: life peer 1966.

KINGLAKE, Alexander William (1809–91). British author. B. at Taunton, he wrote a delightful travel book of his Near East journeys, *Eothen* (1844), and an 8-vol. history of *The Invasion of the Crimea* (1863–87).

KING'S/QUEEN'S COUNSEL. In England, barristers appointed to senior rank by the Lord Chancellor and being 'called within the Bar'. They wear silk, as opposed to stuff gowns, and take precedence over the junior Bar.

KING'S COUNTY. Older name of OFFALY.

KING'S EVIL. The popular name in England for scrofula, which disease was supposed to be curable by the touch of the sovereign.

KIMONO.

KINGSFORD SMITH, Sir Charles Edward (1897–1935). Australian airman. He made many record flights: across the Pacific in 1928, Australia to England 1929, and a transatlantic flight in 1930. He was the first airman to circumnavigate the world, and was knighted in 1932. His plane was lost between Baghdad and Singapore in 1935.

KINGSLEY, Charles (1819–75). British Anglican churchman and author. B. at Holne, Devon. he became curate and then rector of Eversley, Hants (1842–75). His press articles and his campaigning novels *Yeast* (1848), and *Alton Locke* (1850), earned him the title of the 'Chartist clergyman'. His later books incl. *Hypatia* (1851), *Westward Ho!* (1855), a tale of Elizabethan seamen, and *Hereward the Wake* (1866): and for children *The Heroes* (1856) and *The Water-Babies* (1863). He was prof. of modern history at Cambridge 1860–9, and subsequently canon of Chester, and from 1873 of Westminster. In 1864 his controversy with J. H. Newman prompted the latter's *Apologia* (1864). His brother **Henry K.** (1830–76), novelist, b. in Northants, was involved in an escapade which led to his emigrating to the Australian goldfields (1853–8). His novels incl. *Geoffrey Hamlyn* (1859), based on his Australian experiences, and *Ravenshoe* (1862), dealing with the Crimea.

His younger dau. **Mary St. Leger K.** (1852–1931) m. a clergyman William Harrison and pub. under the pseudonym Lucas Malet novels such as *The Wages of Sin* (1891).

KINGSLEY, Mary Henrietta (1862–1900). British author and traveller. B. in Islington, the niece of Charles K., she recorded her experiences in *Travels in W. Africa* (1897), *West African Studies* (1899), etc. She d. of enteric fever while tending Boer prisoners in the Simon's Town hospital.

KINGFISHER

KING'S LYNN. English seaport (bor.) at the mouth of the Great Ouse, Norfolk. Its industries incl. fishing, shipbuilding, rope and boot and shoe making. Fanny Burney was b. at K.L. Plans gradually to move 3,500 families from London to K.L. were agreed between K.L. and the L.C.C. in 1962. Pop. (1961) 27,554.

KING'S MEDAL. Two awards initiated in 1945: K.M. for courage in the cause of freedom, and K.M. for service in the cause of freedom, designed for Allied or other foreign civilians who assisted Britain in the S.W.W.

KING'S/QUEEN'S PROCTOR. In England the official representing the Crown in matrimonial cases. His chief function is to intervene in divorce proceedings to stop a decree *nisi* being made absolute if he discovers that material facts have been concealed from the court or that there has been collusion, or adultery by the petitioner since the decree, or any other cause against the dissolution of the marriage.

KINGSTON. (1) Cap. of Jamaica, W. Indies. It has an excellent harbour on the S. coast and is the cultural and commercial centre of the is. K. was rebuilt after an earthquake in 1907. It was founded 1693–1703, and made cap. of Jamaica in 1872. Pop. (1967) 525,290. (2) City of Ontario, Canada, on Lake Ontario, seat of Queen's Univ., with shipbuilding yards, engineering works, and grain elevators. It grew from 1782 round the French Fort Frontenac, captured by the English in 1758, and was named in honour of George III. Pop. (1966) 59,004.

KINGSTON-UPON-HULL. Official name of HULL.

KINGSTON UPON THAMES, Royal Bor. of.

English market town, bor. of Greater London, on the S. bank of the Thames, 10 m. S.W. of London; here the Saxon kings were crowned. The industries of K. incl. metalworking, and the making of plastics and paint. Pop. (1967) 145,240.

KINGSTOWN. *See* DUN LAOGHAIRE.

KING-TE-CHEN. Chinese town (now Fowliang) in Kiangsi, 80 m. N.E. of Nanchang, near Kao Ling (high hill), a world-famous centre for porcelain. The imperial porcelain factories were set up at K. in 1004. The local kaolin has been worked out, but supplies are obtained from Kimen, S. Anhwei. Pop. (1957) 92,000.

KINRO'SS. Smallest but one of the counties of Scotland, situated between Perth and Fife, and containing Loch Leven. K. is chiefly an agricultural region; the cap., also K., makes linens and woollens. Area 82 sq. m.; pop (1961) co., 6,704; town, 2,365.

KINSALE. Seaport of Co. Cork, Rep. of Ireland, 14 m. S. of Cork. The *Lusitania* was sunk off K., 7 May 1915. Pop. (1961) 1,587.

KINSHASA. *See* LÉOPOLDVILLE.

KIPLING, Joseph Rudyard (1865–1936). British poet and author. B. in Bombay, the son of John Lockwood K. (1837–1911), curator of the Central Museum at Lahore (1875–93), he was ed. at the United Services College at Westward Ho, which provided the

By his cousin, Sir Philip Burne-Jones.   Photo: N.P.G.

background for *Stalky and Co.* (1899). His *Schoolboy Lyrics* were privately pub. in 1881, and he was engaged as a journalist in India 1882–9; during these years he wrote *Departmental Ditties*, *Plain Tales from the Hills*, *Soldiers Three*, *Under the Deodars*, *Wee Willie Winkie*, etc. Returning to London he pub. *The Light that Failed* (1890) and *Barrack Room Ballads* (1892), and m. in 1892 Caroline, the sister of the American Wolcott Balestier who collaborated with him in *Naulahka* (1891). He lived largely in the U.S.A. 1892–6, where he produced the short stories *Many Inventions* (1893), the 2 *Jungle Books* (1894–5), and *Captains Courageous* (1897). Prior to the F.W.W. he pub. *Kim* (1901), the *Just So Stories* (1902), *Puck of Pook's Hill* (1906), and *Rewards and Fairies* (1910); and in 1907 was awarded a Nobel prize. Later works incl. war books, *Letters of Travel 1892–1913* (1920), *Thy Servant a Dog* (1930) and the autobiographical *Something of Myself* (1937). His ashes rest in Westminster Abbey. Enjoying in his heyday an enormous popularity, and subsequently almost equal denigration for 'jingoist imperialism', he was yet a superb craftsman, and the variety and range of his achievement can still astonish. His is the ultimate distinction of being quoted daily by people who never realize whom they quote, or even that they do quote at all, e.g. 'The Ballad of East and West', 'Boots', 'If', 'Gunga Din', and 'Mandalay'.

KIRCHNER (kĕrkh'ner), **Ernst Ludwig** (1880–1938). German artist. With a number of other painters he formed the movement Die Brücke (The Bridge) in 1905, which was estab. in Berlin from 1911. Harsh, angular and distorted, his work changed from portraiture and city scenes to mountain landscapes when he settled in Switzerland on being invalided from the army in 1917. His work was attacked as degenerate under Hitler and he committed suicide.

KIRGHIZ S.S.R. A constituent rep. of the U.S.S.R., adjoining the frontier of Sinkiang-Uighur, China. Some two-thirds of the people are Kirghiz, belonging to the Mongolian Tartar family. The introduction of artificial irrigation and hydro-electric power, and of a number of Russian settlers, has modified their traditional nomadic way of living, but livestock breeding remains a principal industry. Wheat and other grains, fodder crops, tobacco, etc., are grown; there are sugar refineries, food, timber, and textile factories; and coal and petroleum are worked. The cap. is Frunze. Area 76,100 sq. m.; pop. (1968) 2,836,000.

KIRKCALDY (kirkaw'di). Royal burgh and seaport on the Firth of Forth, Fifeshire, Scotland. Manufactures incl. linoleum and paper. Pop. (1961) 52,371.

KIRKCUDBRIGHT (kirkoo'bri). (1) Co. in S. Scotland. Most of the county consists of rough pasture, or wasteland, but on certain reclaimed areas oats, root crops, and potatoes are grown. Area 900 sq. m.; pop. (1961) 28,877. (2) Co. town of K., on the Dee, at the head of K. bay. The name K. means 'chapel of Cuthbert'. Pop. (1961) 2,448.

KIRKUK (kirkook'). Town in N.E. Iraq, cap. of K. liwa. centre of a petroleum field connected with Tripoli (Lebanon) and Banias (Syria) by pipelines. Pop. (1967) 462,067.

KIRKWALL. Cap. and port of the Orkneys, Scotland, on the N. coast of Mainland. The cathedral of St. Magnus dates in part from 1137. Pop. (1961) 4,315.

KIRO'V, Sergei Mironovich (1886–1934). Russian Bolshevik leader. He joined the Bolsheviks in 1904, and took a prominent part in the 1918–20 civil wars. His assassination in 1934 led to the political trials held during the next 4 years.

KIROV. Chief town (formerly Vyatka) of K. region, R.S.F.S.R., annexed by Moscow 1489. A rail centre, it manufactures machine tools, etc. Pop. (1967) 302,000.

KIROVABAD (kĕrovahbat'). Important industrial town in Azerbaijan S.S.R., producing cottons and woollens and processed foods. Pop. (1967) 170,000.

KIRO'VOGRAD. Town on the r. Ingul in the Ukrainian S.S.R., U.S.S.R., cap. of K. region. On a lignite field, it processes food and makes agricultural machinery. Pop. (1967) 161,000.

KIRRIEMUIR (kirimū'er). Market town of Angus, Scotland, noted as 'Thrums' in Sir James Barrie's novels, and his birthplace. Pop. (1961) 3,485.

KIRTON. Another form of CREDITON.

KISFALUDY (kish'foloodi), **Károly** (1788–1830). Hungarian writer, the father of Hungarian drama, and founder of the periodical *Aurora* (1822). *Kisfaludy Társaság*, the leading literary society of the country, was founded in his memory.

KISHINE'V. Cap. of the Moldavian S.S.R., U.S.S.R. Founded in 1436, it became Russian in 1812. It was taken by Rumania in 1918; by the Russians in 1940, by the Germans in 1941, when it was totally destroyed; the Russians recaptured the site in 1944, and rebuilding soon began. It has cement and food factories. Pop. (1967) 302,000.

KITAKYU'SHU. Japanese city and port, on the Hibiki Sea, N. Kyushu, formed 1963 by the amalgamation of Moji, Kokura, Tobata, Yawata, and Wakamatsu. It is a great coal port for nearby mines and an industrial centre with steel mills and factories making cotton thread, plate glass, alcohol, etc. A tunnel (1942) links it with Honshu. Moji was opened to foreign trade in 1887. All the ports making up K. were heavily bombed from the air in 1945. Pop. (1965) 1,042,000.

KITCHENER. Canadian city and port in Ontario, 60 m. W.S.W. of Toronto. It has foundries, furniture factories, and other works based on power from Niagara Falls. Founded in 1806 as Sand Hills, it was renamed Berlin c. 1830, Kitchener in 1916. Mackenzie King was born at K. Pop. (1966) 93,255.

KITCHENER, Horatio Herbert, earl K. of Khartoum (1850–1916). British soldier. B. in Co. Kerry, he was commissioned in 1871, and transferred to the Egyptian Army in 1882. Promoted C.-in-C. in 1892, he crushed the Sudanese dervishes at Omdurman in 1898, re-occupied Khartoum, and also forced a French expedition to withdraw from Fashoda. During the S. African War he acted as Lord Roberts' chief of staff, and as C.-in-C. 1900–2 brought the war to a successful conclusion. He subsequently commanded the forces in India and acted as British agent in Egypt, and in 1914 received an earldom. Appointed War Minister on the outbreak of the F.W.W., he was drowned while on his way to Russia. He had been created field marshal in 1909.

KITE. Name of several birds of prey in the family Falconidae. The European species (*Milvus ictinus*) is a typical example, and may be distinguished by its forked tail. It is about 2 ft. long. Kites are rare in Britain, but are found in Europe, America, and India.

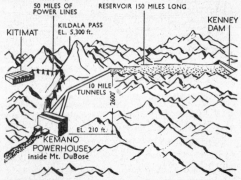

KITIMAT. The economic production of aluminium requires enormous quantities of hydro-electric power, and British Columbia has both the necessary tremendous water storage and towering mountains. The Kenney Dam on the Nechako river impounds the waters of a chain of lakes, and the flow has been reversed from E. to W. and tapped by a 10 m. tunnel through the mountains. Eventual capacity of the generators at Kemano is 2,240,000 h.p. and the fall of water through the penstocks is 16 times the height of Niagara. *Courtesy of Alcan.*

KI'TIMAT. Canadian town and port (founded 1955) at the head of Douglas Channel, 70 m. E.S.E. of Prince Rupert, British Columbia, through which alumina ships from Jamaica supply the Alcan aluminium smelter (ultimate annual production 550,000 tons per annum). The garden city of K. is 5 m. from the smelter. Planned pop. 50,000; (1961) 8,217.

KITTIWAKE. A sea-gull, *Rissa tridactyla*, found in North Atlantic regions. Other species are found in the North Pacific and Bering Sea.

KIUKIANG (kūky-ang′). River port in Kiangsi prov., China, on the Yangtze, c. 440 m. from its mouth. It deals in tea, tobacco, rice, etc., and was a treaty port from 1862 until the 1940s. Pop. (est.) 60,000.

KIUNGSHAN (ky-oong-shan′). Port of Hainan, Kwantung prov., China, near the mouth of the Nantur., a treaty port from 1876 until the 1940s. It is a trade centre with cotton, sugar, and vegetable-oil mills. Pop. (est.) 50,000.

KIUSHIU. See KYUSHYU.

KIUSTENDIL. See KYUSTENDIL.

KIWI (kē′wi). Native name for a genus of nocturnal flightless birds (*Apteryx*) confined to New Zealand. It has long and hair-like plumage, a very long beak, and the egg is larger, in relation to the size of the body, than that of any other bird.

KLAIPEDA (klī′peda). Seaport in the Lithuanian S.S.R., on the Baltic coast at the mouth of the Dange r., with iron foundries, shipbuilding yards, and other industrial works. It was founded in 1252 as the castle of Memelburg by the Teutonic Knights, joined the Hanseatic League soon after, and has changed hands between Sweden, Russia, and Germany. Lithuania annexed K. in 1923, and after German occupation 1939–45, it was restored to Lithuania. Pop. (1967) 125,000.

KLAPROTH (klahp′rōt), **Martin Heinrich** (1743–1817). German chemist. 1st prof. of chemistry in Berlin from 1810, he is famous for his discovery of the elements uranium, zirconium, cerium, and titanium.

KLAUSENBURG. German name of CLUJ.

KLÉBER (klehbär′), **Jean Baptiste** (1753–1800). French general. B. at Strasbourg, he served in the Austrian Army, returned to France in 1783, and dis tinguished himself in the Revolutionary Wars. He succeeded Napoleon as commander in Egypt in 1799, and was assassinated by a Turkish fanatic.

KLEBS, Edwin (1834–1913). German physician. B. at Königsberg, he was prof. of pathological anatomy at Zürich (1882), and discovered the diphtheria bacillus.

KLEE, Paul (1879–1940). Swiss artist. B. near Berne, he studied at Munich, Paris, and Rome. In 1920 he went to the Bauhaus in Weimar, and in 1922 he became a prof. at the Düsseldorf academy. When Hitler rose to power in 1933 he returned to Berne. K. dwelt in a dream world, and has been attacked for plagiarizing infant formulas, but many find his work full of profound sensibility.

KLEIST (klīst), (**Bernd**) **Heinrich Wilhelm von** (1777–1811). German dramatist. B. at Frankfurt-an-der-Oder, he wrote tragedies and a comedy *Der zerbrochene Krug* (1811) as well as stories and poems, but achieved only a posthumous reputation. In a suicide pact, he killed first a girl-friend, and then himself.

KLEIST, Ewald von (1881–1954). German field marshal. He planned the

KITTIWAKE

KIWI

attack on Poland in 1939, and took part in the invasions of Belgium, France, Yugoslavia, and Russia. In 1945 he was captured by the Allies, and d. in Russia.

KLE′MPERER, Otto (1885–). American conductor. B. in Germany, where he became noted for his interpretation of contemporary and classical (especially Beethoven) music, he was director of the Los Angeles Symphony Orchestra 1933–46.

KLEPTOMA′NIA. A symptom of insanity revealed by an overpowering desire to steal, and associated with many forms of mental aberration.

KLERKSDORP. Town of S. Africa, 100 m. S.W. of Johannesburg. Founded in 1837, it was the first Boer settlement in Transvaal; it is a cattle market and the centre of a gold-mining district. Pop. (1960) 43,067, including 19,017 white.

KLEVE (kleh′ve). Town in North Rhine-Westphalia, W. Germany, 35 m. N.W. of Duisburg, formerly cap. of the ancient duchy of Cleves (or K.), from which came Henry VIII′s 4th wife, Anne of Cleves. It was completely destroyed during the S.W.W. but subsequently rebuilt. Pop. (est.) 25,000.

KLONDIKE. District of Yukon, Canada, E. and S. of K. river. It was the scene of a gold rush in 1896, which brought some 30,000 people to the area, but by 1910 most of the gold had been removed and the pop. dwindled. Latterly, silver-ore has been found.

OTTO KLEMPERER
Photo: Godfrey MacDomnic.

KLO′PSTOCK, Friedrich Gottlieb (1724–1803). German poet. His religious epic *Der Messias* (1745–73) and his lyric odes, with their flexible, subtle metres, and impressionistic, subjective vocabulary, prepared the way for the great age of 18th cent. German literature.

KLUCK (klook), **Alexander von** (1846–1934). German general. He commanded the 1st army which in 1914 invaded Belgium, expelled the British from Mons, and advanced to within 30 m. of Paris. He was driven back by the Allies on the Marne.

KNAPWEED. Wild flower common in Britain, Europe, and W. Asia, known also as hardheads. A member of the Compositae family (*Centaurea nigra*), it produces hard, bract-covered buds which break into composite heads of purple flowers.

KNARESBOROUGH. English market town (U.D.) in the W. Riding of Yorks, 4 m. N.E. of Harrogate. Linen and textiles are made. The castle dates from c. 1070. Eugene Aram (q.v.) hid the body of his victim in St. Robert′s cave at K. Pop. (1961) 9,311.

KNEE. The hinge joint between the thigh bone and the shin bone. It consists, roughly, of two smooth, shallow cups (condyles of the tibia) within which fit two smooth rounded protrusions (condyles of the femur); in front, protecting it, is the kneecap.

KNELLER, Sir Godfrey (1646–1723). British portrait painter of German descent. Court painter to Charles II, William III and George I, he showed in his best works a strong grasp of character, e.g. the members of the Whig 'Kit-Cat Club'.

KNIGHT, Dame Laura (1877–1970). Brit. artist. She excelled in detailed, narrative painting of gypsies, of fairground and circus life, and of the ballet. *See* illus. p. 326. She m. in 1903 Harold K. (d. 1961), a portrait painter, and was created D.B.E. in 1929.

KNIGHTHOOD, Orders of. Fraternities carrying with them the rank of knight, admission to which is granted as a mark of royal favour or as a reward for public services. During the Middle Ages such fraternities fell into 2 classes, religious and secular. The first class, e.g. the Templars (q.v.), and Knights of St. John, consisted of knights who had taken religious vows and devoted themselves to military service against the Saracens or other non-Christians. The secular Os. probably arose from bands of knights engaged in the service of a prince or great noble, who wore his badge or the emblem of his patron saint. The Order of the Garter, founded *c.* 1347, is the oldest now in existence: there are 8 other British Os., those of the Thistle (founded 1687), St. Patrick (1788), the Bath (1725), the Star of India (1861), St. Michael and St. George (1818), the Indian Empire (1878), the Royal Victorian O. (1896), and the O. of the British Empire (1917). Most of the ancient European Os., such as the O. of the Golden Fleece, have disappeared as a result of political changes. A knight bachelor belongs to the lowest stage of K., i.e. is not a member of any specially named order.

KNIPPER, Lev Constantinovich (1898–   ). Russian composer. His early work shows the influence of Stravinsky, but after 1932 he became a 'popular' composer, as in the symphony *Poem of Komsomol Fighters* (1933–4) with its mass battle songs, etc. Best known in the W. is his song 'Cavalry of the Steppes'.

KNITTING. Hand-knitting (using one flexible or several straight needles) and crochet (in which the needle is hooked) are age-old crafts still widely practised as a hobby. K. was mechanized to produce stockings in the late 16th cent., and later developed to produce other types of garment, but the standard was generally uninspired until the introduction of synthetic yarns after the S.W.W. Brilliant dyes, and methods of texturizing, elasticizing, and stabilizing, revolutionized the industry, which rises towards a 50% share in the women's clothing industry and an increasing share in that of men.

KNOSSUS. Site in Crete occupied from *c.* 2500 B.C., where Europe's earliest civilization flourished (*see* MINOAN). Excavation of the palace of the legendary king Minos by Sir Arthur Evans 1900–25 revealed that the story of Theseus and the Minotaur kept in a labyrinth had a basis of fact in ancient ritual dances of youths and girls which involved somersaulting over a live bull's horns, and the maze-like palace lay-out.

KNOT. Bird (*Tringa canutus*) of the plover family. A wader, about the size of a thrush, it is brick-red in summer, drab in winter, and feeds on insects and molluscs. Breeding in the Arctic, Ks. travel widely in winter, to be found as far afield as Java, S. Africa, New Zealand, and Britain.

KNOT. The unit by which a ship's speed is measured, corresponding to 1 nautical mile per hour. The nautical mile is one minute of latitude, and although varying over the earth's surface, is in practice taken to be 6,080 ft. (1 kn.=approx. $1^1/_7$ m.).

KNOT. An intertwinement of parts of one or more ropes, cords, strings, etc., used to bind them together or to other objects. It is constructed so that the strain borne serves to draw it tighter. 'Bends' or 'hitches' are Ks. used to fasten ropes together or round spars, and splices are used to join 2 ropes together, end to end.

KNOWLES (nōlz), **James Sheridan** (1784–1862). Irish dramatist. Related to R. B. Sheridan (q.v.), he wrote plays, which were acted by, amongst others, Kean and Macready, and included *William Tell* (1825) and *The Hunchback* (1832).

KNOX, John (*c.* 1505–72). Scottish Protestant reformer. B. probably at Haddington, he was ordained priest, but afterwards was converted to Protestantism, probably by the reformer, George Wishart. After Wishart's execution in 1546 he went into hiding, but later joined a group of reformers who had seized the castle of St. Andrews, and at their request began to preach the reformed doctrines. When the castle was taken by the French in 1547, K. was sent to the galleys, and only released in 1549 at the intercession of the English govt. In England he exercised his influence to strengthen the Protestant element in the Prayer Book, in the compilation of which he assisted. He was made a royal chaplain in 1551. On Mary's accession he escaped and settled first at Frankfurt, where he was a pastor to English refugees, and later at Geneva, where he was associated with Calvin. In 1559 he returned to Scotland, and was chiefly responsible for the establishment of the Church of Scotland. His *History of the Reformation in Scotland* (1586) is one of the masterpieces of Scottish prose.

KOALA

KNOX, Ronald Arbuthnott (1888–1957). British R.C. scholar. Son of an Anglican bp. of Manchester, he became chaplain to the Univ. of Oxford following his ordination in 1912, but resigned in 1917 on his conversion to Rome and was Catholic chaplain 1926–39. His modern translation of the Bible (1945–9) had a masterly turn of phrase and was officially approved by the R.C. Church. He combined scholarship with a rare sense of humour, e.g. his dialogues *Let Dons Delight* (1939), and a reputation in detective fiction disapproved by his superiors.

KNOXVILLE. City of Tennessee, U.S.A., the centre of a mining and agricultural region of great beauty, seat of a univ. founded in 1794. Pop. (1960) 111,827.

KNUTSFORD. English town (U.D.) in Cheshire, 15 m. S.W. of Manchester, of which it is a residential district. Mrs. Gaskell, who lived at K. for 22 years and is buried there, wrote of it under the name Cranford. Pop. (1961) 9,389.

KOALA (kō-ahl'a). Marsupial (*Phascolarctos cinereus*) of the family Phalangeridae, found only in E. Australia and not easily kept in zoos because it feeds almost entirely on eucalyptus shoots. Resembling a small bear (2 ft. long), it has greyish fur which led to its almost complete extermination by hunters. Under protection from 1936 it has rapidly increased.

KOBE (kō'bi). Port on the S. coast of Honshu is., Japan, founded 1868. Industries include shipbuilding, iron and steel manufacture, sugar refining. Pop. (1965) 1,217,000.

KOBLENZ (kōb'lents). City of the Rhineland-Palatinate, W. Germany, at the junction of the Rhine and Mosel. It dates back to Roman times. It has shoe and cigar factories, paper mills, and other works, and is noted as a centre of the wine trade. K. was badly damaged in S.W.W. air raids. Pop. (1966) 102,792.

KOCH (kokh), **Ludwig** (1881–   ). German musician and naturalist, who settled in Britain in 1936. Originally a violinist and singer, he pioneered the recording and interpretation of bird-song.

KOCH, Robert (1843–1910). German bacteriologist. B. in Hanover, he isolated the tubercle bacillus in 1882, and invented the tuberculin test for cattle. In 1905 he received the Nobel prize for medicine.

KODÁLY, Zoltán (1882–1967). Hungarian com-

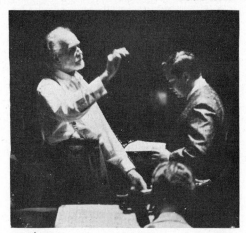

KODÁLY. Conducting a rehearsal of his own works at the Royal Festival Hall, the composer shows that eighty years put no limit to his finesse. To his right, the singer Dietrich Fischer-Dieskau studies a score. *Photo: Godfrey MacDomnic.*

poser. B. at Kecskemet, he studied at the Budapest Academy, where 1907–42 he was prof. of composition. With Bartok he collected Magyar folk music, and has written much chamber and instrumental music, the comic opera, *Háry János* (1926), 'Dances of Galanta', etc.

KŎ′DIAK. Island off the S. coast of Alaska, U.S.A., of which it forms part, site of the first white settlement in Alaska, 1784, and of a U.S. naval base. Area 5,363 sq. m. K. is the home of the world's largest bear.

KOESTLER (kerst′ler) **Arthur** (1905–). Anglo-Hungarian author. B. in Budapest and ed. as a scientist in Vienna, he became a foreign correspondent

KOBLENZ. In the 13th century the citizens built themselves new city walls and their overlords – Archbishop Hillin of Trier and his successors – strengthened their own defences at Ehrenbreitstein in retaliation. The castle, seen here on the farther (right) bank of the Rhine, is built on a cliff 400 ft. high, once the site of a Roman fort, and has since been much modified and reconstructed.
Courtesy of the German Tourist Information Bureau.

in the Middle East, and elsewhere, and later science editor for a German newspaper chain. He joined the Communist Party in 1931 and travelled in Russia and other Soviet countries, but was disillusioned a few years later and left, as described in *The God That Failed* (1950). His experiences while under sentence of death in Spain during the Civil War are told in *Spanish Testament* (1938: revised as *Dialogue with Death*) and inspired *Darkness at Noon* (1940). In 1940 he was imprisoned by the Nazis in France, the subject of *Scum of the Earth* (1941), but escaped to England and after the S.W.W. became a British subject. His later works incl. *Arrival and Departure* (1943), *The Yogi and the Commissar* (1945), both attacks on Communism; *The Sleepwalkers* (1959), a history of cosmology; *The Lotus and the Robot* (1960), exploring eastern philosophy; *The Act of Creation* (1964) analysing creativity; and *The Ghost in the Machine* (1967).

KOH-I-NOOR ('Mountain of Light'). A famous diamond, now one of the British Crown jewels. In 1849 it was presented to Queen Victoria by the East India Company.

KOHL-RABI (kōlrah′bi). A variety of kale (*Brassica oleracea*). The leaves shoot from a swelling on the main stem. The globular portion is used for food, and resembles a turnip.

KOKAND. Town of the Uzbek S.S.R., 330 m. E.N.E. of Bukhara, the centre of a fertile oasis. Industrial developments incl. a fertilizer factory, cotton and silk mills, and machine shops. K. was the cap. of K. khanate, annexed by Russia in 1876. Pop. (1967) 128,000.

KOKO′SCHKA, Oskar (1886–). Austrian painter. He studied in Vienna, and shocked public opinion by his first exhibition in 1907 and also by expressionist plays. Badly wounded as a cavalry officer in 1915, he taught at the Dresden Academy 1919–24, and subse-

KOESTLER

quently wandered the world, living in London during the S.W.W. His impressions of cities are brilliant with colour, and give the same impression of psychological penetration as his human portraits: he also makes skilled use of myth and allegory.

KOKSTAD. Chief town of Griqualand East, 110 m. S.W. of Durban, South Africa, a centre for wool, cattle, cheese, and grain. It was named after the last Griqua chief, Adam Kok III. Pop. (1961) 8,803, incl. 3,000 white.

KOKURA. *See under* KITAKYUSHO.

KŎ′LA. Peninsula in N. Russia, bounded by the White Sea on the S. and E., and by the Barents Sea on the N. It is coterminous with Murmansk region of the R.S.F.S.R. *See* MURMANSK.

KOLA NUT. The fruit of a W. African tree (*Cola acuminata*) cultivated in the S. and Central American tropics. The nut contains caffeine and is exported for use in refreshing beverages.

KO′LBENHEYER (-hī-er), **Erwin Guido** (1878–1962). German writer. B. at Budapest, in historical novels he interpreted life and thought of philosophers and mystics, e.g. Spinoza and Paracelsus. He also wrote the historical dramas *Giordano Bruno* (1893) and *Gregor und Heinrich* (1934).

KOLCHAK, Alexander Vasilievich (1875–1920). Russian admiral. He commanded the White forces in Siberia, and in 1918 proclaimed himself Supreme Ruler of Russia, setting up a provisional govt. at Omsk, and later at Irkutsk. He resigned in Denikin's favour, and was shot by the Bolsheviks.

KOLDEWEY (kōl′devä), **Robert** (1855–1925).

German architect and archaeologist, whose excavation at Babylon 1899–1917 illustrated a technique of stratification, etc., which inspired later workers.

KOLCHUGINO. See LENINSK-KUZNETSKY.

KOLHAPUR (kōlapoor'). Indian town in Maharashtra state, a trade, educational, and film-production centre, cap. of K. district. K. was formerly cap. of K. princely state, incorporated in Bombay state in 1949. Pop. (1961) 187,306.

KOLKHOZ. Russian term for collective farm (q.v.).

KOLLWITZ, Kaethe (1867–1945). German artist, chiefly famous for her drawings, etchings, etc., of social subjects. Her principal works are 'The Weavers', 'Peasant War', 'War', and 'Death'.

KÖLN. German form of COLOGNE.

KOLOZSVÁR. Hungarian name of CLUJ.

KOMSOMOL. The Russian name for the All-Union Leninist Communist Youth League. Membership is open to all young people between the ages of 14 and 26, and numbers several millions. Founded in 1918, it acts as the youth section of the Communist Party, and its activities include all forms of national service, e.g. the rebuilding of Stalingrad in 1942.

KONIEH. See KONYA.

KO'NIEV, Ivan Stepanovich (1898–). Soviet marshal. In the S.W.W. he was celebrated for his brilliant victory in 1943 in the Dnieper bend, liberating the Ukraine, and advanced to link with Anglo-U.S. forces approaching from the W.

KÖNIGSBERG. See KALININGRAD.

KONSTANZ. German form of CONSTANCE.

KON-TIKI. Legendary Sun King who ruled the country later occupied by the Incas (q.v.), and was supposed to have migrated, with certain white-skinned and bearded followers, out into the Pacific. See HEYERDAHL.

KONYA (kon'yah). City in Turkey-in-Asia, on the site of ancient Iconium (q.v.), cap. of K. il, c. 300 m. E. of Izmir. A market for a fertile area, it makes carpets and silks. At K. is the monastery of the Dancing Dervishes. Pop. (1965) 1,099,460.

KORAN. More properly, Quran, though both are transliterations; the sacred book of Islam (q.v.). Written in the purest Arabic, it contains 114 suras or chapters, and is stated to have been divinely revealed to the prophet Mohammed; the original is supposed to be preserved beside the throne of Allah in heaven.

KORDA, Sir Alexander (1893–1956). British film producer and director. B. in Hungary, he came to England in 1931 (naturalized 1936); his films incl. *The Private Life of Henry VIII* (1933), *The Third Man* (1950), and *Richard III* (1955).

KORDOFA'N. Prov. of the Rep. of Sudan, for the most part undulating plain with some higher ground. In the main pastoral, with cattle an important product, it incl. also extensive forests producing gum. Area 146,930 sq. m.; pop. (1964) 2,052,000.

KORE'A. Country in Asia occupying the peninsula projecting southwards from Manchuria, having the Yellow Sea on the W. and the Sea of Japan on the E. The N. border is mountainous, and a secondary range runs southward along the E. coast. There are large forest reserves in the N., while the streams provide hydro-electric power.

North K. has the country's chief deposits of iron and coal, and also has oil and barytes. First developed by the Japanese, its economy is increasingly industrial, iron and steel, textiles, cement, chemicals, etc., being produced. South K. is still chiefly agricultural (rice being the chief crop), but light industries, incl. consumer goods, fertilizers, electrical goods, etc., are developing: it also has the world's largest tungsten deposits. Cattle are reared on the W. lowlands, and fishing and whaling are important.

The principal religions are Confucianism and Buddhism. The chief towns of N. Korea are Pyongyang, the cap., and Wonsan; S. Korea has its cap. at Seoul, where there is a nat. univ., other centres being Pusan, Taegu, and Inchon. Area: S.K., 38,452 sq. m.; N.K., 46,814 sq. m. Pop.: S.K. (1966) 29,207,856; N.K. (1966) 12,500,000.

History. The foundation of the Korean state traditionally dates back about 2000 years B.C., to the dynasty of Tangun, followed by that of the Chinese Kija, which ruled from c. 1122 until the 4th cent. B.C. K. was subsequently distracted by internal war and invasion until the 10th cent. A.D. when it was united within the boundaries it subsequently retained. In the 16th cent. Japan invaded K. for the first time, later withdrawing from a country it had devastated. In 1905 Japan began to treat K. as a protectorate, and in 1910 annexed it. Many Japanese colonists settled in K., introducing both industrial and agricultural development. The Japanese in K. surrendered in 1945, but although Russia withdrew from K. north of the 38th parallel in 1948, and the U.S.A. from the south in 1949, the country remained divided. In 1950 the N. Koreans invaded South K., but the U.N. sent troops (mainly American) to drive them back and fighting was almost over when China intervened on the side of North K. The 1953 armistice restored the status quo.

North K. (Democratic People's Rep. of K.) has a Soviet-type constitution; South K. (Rep. of K.) a Pres. and Nat. Assembly. After Syngman Rhee (q.v.) South K. became more democratic under Gen. Pak Chung Hi (1962: re-elected 1963, 1967).

In 1968 the capture of the U.S. intelligence ship *Pueblo* by N. Korean patrols caused an international incident. The crew were held prisoner 11 months before release, and the ship was still detained: no disciplinary action was taken following a U.S. naval court of inquiry.

KOREAN. The language of Korea, written in Chinese characters from the 5th cent. to 1443, when King Sejong developed a remarkably advanced phonetic alphabet, and a native literature sprang up. It was later discouraged as 'vulgar letters' – Onmun – and banned by the Japanese, but revived after the S.W.W. as 'top letters' – Hangul – so that modern Korea has 85% literacy.

KORINTHOS. Greek form of CORINTH.

KORO'LEV, Sergei (1906–66). Russian designer of space-rockets. B. at Zhitomir, son of a teacher, he designed the first sputnik, the moon-rockets, and the manned space ships.

KORTRIJK. Flemish form of COURTRAI.

KOS. See COS.

KOSCIUSKO. Highest mt. in Australia, 7,328 ft., in New South Wales. (Sir) Paul Strzelecki, who was born in Prussian Poland, discovered K. in 1839 and named it after the Polish hero K. (q.v.).

KOSCIUSZKO (kosi-us'kō), **Tadeusz** (1746–1817). Polish leader of the revolutionary forces which fought against Russia in 1794. He was defeated by combined Russian and Prussian forces, and captured at Maciejowice, but was released in 1796.

KOSHER. Heb. for 'fit', as applied by Jews to meat slaughtered according to Mosaic law.

KOŠICE (kosh'itse). Town on the Hernad, Czechoslovakia, cap. of K. region. K., which makes textiles, is of strategic importance as a road centre; it has an airport. A large part of the pop. (1967) 112,000 is Magyar-speaking, and K. was in Hungary 1938–45.

KOSSUTH (kosh'oot), **Lajos** (1802–94). Hungarian patriot. He founded the paper *Pesti Hirlap*, in which he pleaded for social and national reforms, and in 1848 became pres. of the committee of national defence and virtual ruler of the country. In 1849 he proclaimed his country's independence of the Habsburgs. The Hungarians were later defeated by Austrian and Russian troops, and K. fled to Turkey. Later, he went to England.

KOSYGIN (koség'in), **Alexei Nikolaievich** (1904–). Russian politician. B. at Leningrad, he joined the

Red Army at 15, later becoming a textile engineering specialist and Min. for Light Industry 1948–53. Also an economic expert, he became a first deputy premier in 1960 and in 1964 succeeded Khrushchev as P.M. (chairman of the Council of Ministers).

KOTOR. Yugoslav port at the head of the Gulf of K., with one of the most sheltered harbours on the Adriatic, on the site of the Roman Ascrivium. It is the seat of Greek Orthodox and R.C. bishoprics. Pop. (est.) 8,000.

KOTTBUS (kot′boos). Town on the Spree, cap. of K. dist., E. Germany. A centre of rail and road communication, with an airport, K. makes cloth, carpets, hats, etc. Pop. (est.) 75,000.

KOTZEBUE, August Friedrich Ferdinand von (1761–1819). German dramatist. B. at Weimar, he served the tsar of Russia and was murdered at Mannheim while on a secret mission. He is chiefly remembered for his comedies *Der Wildfang* (1800), and *Die deutschen Kleinstädter* (1803).

KOVNO. Russian form of KAUNAS.

KOWEIT. See KUWAIT.

KOWLOON. Peninsula on the Chinese coast forming part of the British Crown Colony of Hong Kong (q.v.). The town of K. is a residential area.

KRAGUJEVAC (krahgooyāv′ats). Garrison town of Serbia, Yugoslavia. Pop. (1961) 52,491.

KRAKATOA. Is. volcano in Sunda Strait, Indonesia, between Java and Sumatra, whose eruption in 1883 caused widespread destruction and atmospheric phenomena. A tidal wave hit Java and Sumatra, where some 36,000 people were drowned.

KRAKOW (krak′ō). City of Poland, the cap. from *c.* 1300 to 1595, on the Vistula. K. is commercially important; railway wagons, paper, chemicals, etc., are made and there are tobacco and food factories. It has the second-oldest univ. in central Europe (1364), at which Copernicus was a student, and a fine 14th cent. Gothic cathedral. It forms the voivodship (co.) of K. City, pop. (1966) 525,000, and is cap. of K. voivodship, area 5,925 sq. m., pop. (1966) 2,143,000.

KRAKOW. In 1241 a bugler sounded the alarm from the tower of St. Mary's Church as the Tartars attacked the city and was killed before he finished the call. Today the same call is sounded every hour and is always suddenly broken off and left unfinished.
Courtesy of the Polish Travel Office 'Orbis'.

KRAMATORSK (krahmahtorsk′). Town in the Ukrainian S.S.R., in the Donbas, 52 m. N. of Donetsk. It produces coal-mining machinery, steel, and ceramics, and has railway repair shops. Pop. (1967) 136,000.

KRASNODAR. Cap. of K. territory of the R.S.F.S.R., U.S.S.R. Situated to the N. of the Caucasus, at the head of navigation of the r. Kuban, it is an important industrial town, connected by petroleum pipeline with the Caspian oilfields. Pop. (1967) 395,000. The territory produces hemp, maize, etc.

KRASNOYA′RSK. Cap. of K. territory of the R.S.F.S.R., U.S.S.R., on the r. Yenisei. The territory is an agricultural area of modern development. Gold was discovered near the town, founded in 1628, and besides locomotive works, paper and saw mills, cement factories, etc., K. has a gold refinery and hydro-electric installations. Pop. (1967) 557,000.

KREBS, Sir Hans (1900–). British biochemist. B. in Germany, he was prof. at Sheffield 1945–54, and Whitley prof. at Oxford 1954–67. In 1953 he shared a Nobel prize in medicine for discovering the citric acid or 'K' cycle – the route by which food is converted into energy by living tissues.

KREFELD (kreh′felt). Town near the Rhine, 32 m. N.W. of Cologne, W. Germany. An important industrial and textile centre and rail junction, it is on the Westphalian coalfield. K. was nearly destroyed during the S.W.W. Pop. (1966) 223,479.

KRIPS. Noted for the uninhibited vigour of his interpretations, Krips is caught in an expressive moment in the recording studio. *Photo: Godfrey MacDomnic.*

KREISLER (krīz′-), **Fritz** (1875-1962). Austrian violinist. The son of a Jewish doctor, and the youngest student ever admitted to the Vienna Conservatoire, he also studied in Paris under Massart and Delibes. He was specially noted for his interpretation of the concertos of Brahms and Beethoven, and Elgar's violin concerto is dedicated to him. His own compositions incl. the music for the operetta *Apple Blossoms* and the 'Caprice Viennois'.

KREMENCHUG (krämenchoog′). Town on the Dnieper, Ukrainian S.S.R., U.S.S.R. Industries incl. production of road-building machines, railway wagons, and processed food; lumber and grain are items in its trade; and it has hydro-electric installations. Pop. (1967) 129,000.

KŘENEK (shren′ek), **Ernst** (1900–). Austrian composer of Czech descent. B. in Vienna, he became internationally known through his jazz opera *Johnny Strikes Up* (1927), which was followed by *The Leap Over the Shadow, The Life of Orestes, Charles V*, etc. In 1938 he settled in U.S.A.

KREUTZER (krötsär′), **Rodolphe** (1766–1831). French violinist and composer of German descent, to whom Beethoven dedicated his violin sonata Op. 47, known as the K. Sonata.

KREUZNACH (kroits′nakh). W. German town in Rhineland Palatinate on the Nahe, 9 m. S. of Bingen, a spa and health resort. Pop. (1960) 35,000.

KRILIUM. Synthetic chemical, a powder developed by the Monsanto Chemical Co., U.S.A., and demonstrated in 1951, said to be a substitute for natural humus components. It is hoped to use it to increase the water-holding capacity of the soil, and its aeration, so reconditioning eroded desert areas.

KRIPS, Josef (1902–). Austrian conductor. B. in Vienna, he was conductor of the State Opera there 1933–8, returning to reorganize it in 1945, and conducted the London Symphony Orchestra 1950–4.

KRISHNA. A Hindu deity, the 8th incarnation of Vishnu, and hero of the Indian epic, *Mahabharata*.

KRI′SHNA ME′NON, Vengalil Krishnan (1897–). Indian politician. B. in Calicut, he went to London in 1924, where he studied political science at the univ. and was later called to the Bar. He was sec. 1929–47 of the India League, the cultural organization of the Indian Nat. Congress Party, which he developed into its chief mouthpiece in Europe. First High Commissioner for India in London, 1947–52, he was then deputy head, and later head, of the Indian delegation to the U.N., where he was active in arbitration during the Korean War and Suez Canal crises. In 1957 he became Defence Min., but resigned from the Cabinet in 1962 through pressure of public opinion over the Chinese advances on the Sino-Indian border. He is the leader of the extreme left wing of the Congress Party.

KRIVOI ROG. Town in the Ukrainian S.S.R., U.S.S.R., 80 m. S.W. of Dnepropetrovsk. The surrounding district is rich in iron ore, and there is a metallurgical industry. The name means 'crooked horn'. Pop. (1967) 498,000.

KRO̅NSTADT. Russian naval base on the is. of Kotlin in the Gulf of Finland, opposite Leningrad, founded by Peter the Great in 1703.

KROPO̅TKIN, Peter Alexeivich, Prince (1842–1921). Russian anarchist. B. in Moscow, he served in the army, did important survey work in Asia, joined the revolutionary party in St. Petersburg, and in 1874 was imprisoned. He escaped to England in 1876, and later moved to Switzerland. Expelled from Switzerland, he went to France, where he was imprisoned 1883–6. He then lived in England until 1917, when he returned to Moscow. Among his principal works are *Modern Science and Anarchism* and *Mutual Aid.*

KRUG (kro̅o̅g), **Julius Albert** (1907–). American engineer and administrator. He was chief power engineer of the Tennessee Valley Authority 1939–40 and Sec. of the Interior 1946–9.

KRUGER, Stephanus Johannes Paulus (1825–1904). President of the Transvaal Rep. B. at Colesberg, Cape Colony, he accompanied his family on the 'great trek' across the Vaal r., and soon became prominent in Transvaal politics. In 1863 he was appointed Cdr.-Gen. of the forces, in 1883 he was elected Pres., and re-elected in 1888, 1893, and 1898. His refusal to remedy the grievances of the Uitlanders (English and other non-Boer white inhabitants of the rep.) led to war with Britain in 1899. When Pretoria was occupied by British troops K. fled to Europe, where he pleaded vainly for European intervention. He d. in Switzerland.

KRUGER NATIONAL PARK. Game reserve in N.E. Transvaal, S. Africa, between the Limpopo and Crocodile rivers. It has an area of 8,000 sq. m.

KRUGERSDORP. Mining town in the Witwatersrand dist., Transvaal, S. Africa. Manganese and uranium are worked as well as gold. Pop. (1960) 89,493 (30,241 white).

KRUPP (kroop). German family of industrialists and armaments manufacturers. The Essen foundries were estab. by **Friedrich K.** (1787–1826), developed by **Alfred K.** (1812–57), the 'Cannon King', and the business further expanded by **Friedrich Alfred K.** (1854–1902), who took over the Germania shipbuilding yard at Kiel. His only child **Bertha** (1886–1957) m. in 1906 **Gustav von Bohlen und Halbach** (1870–1950), who became head of the firm. During the F.W.W. it advanced the construction of long-distance artillery, e.g. 'Big Bertha', and in the post-war years continued secretly to manufacture armaments – von Bohlen was a Hitler supporter. The K. works came under allied control in 1945, the Borbeck steel plant being given as reparation to the U.S.S.R. Gustav's son, **Alfried K.** (1907–67) who had controlled the firm from 1943, was imprisoned 1948–51, but attempted deconcentration of the K. assets failed. Just before Alfried's death in 1967, financial difficulties compelled his agreement to conversion of the firm to a public co. as the Friedrich K. Foundation.

KRYLOV (krēlof'), **Ivan Andrei** (1768–1844). Russian fabulist. He translated many of La Fontaine's fables, besides publishing his own original work, written in a colloquial style with familiar images, and satirizing bureaucracy and such everyday vices as greed, etc.

KRYPTON (Gk., hidden). A colourless, odourless, inert gas, at. wt. 83·8, at. no. 36, symbol Kr. It was discovered in 1898 by Ramsay and Travers in the residue from liquid air. Occurring in the atmosphere (*c.* 1 to 1,000,000), K. is used to enhance brilliance in miners' electric lamps, and in some gas-filled electronic valves.

KUALA LUMPUR (kwah'lah loom'poor). Cap. of Selangor, of the Fed. of Malaya and of Malaysia. It

KUALA LUMPUR. A ceremonial parade of Malay Regiment troops passes the Federal Secretariat, one of the city's distinctive landmarks, completed in 1897. The Regiment, which took an important part in jungle warfare against Communist terrorists, was started as an experiment and initially commanded by British officers. *Courtesy of Malaya House.*

does a large trade in tin and has an airport and is the seat of the Univ. of Malaya (1962). Pop. (1968) 500,000.

KUANYIN. The 'goddess of mercy' of the Chinese Buddhists; the Japanese worship her as Kwannon.

KUBAN (koobahn'). A river of the U.S.S.R., rising in Georgia and flowing about 500 m. N. and W. through the R.S.F.S.R. to the Black Sea. The name is also applied to the low-lying agricultural dist. of Krasnodar Terr. immediately N. of the Caucasus.

KUBELIK (koob'elēk), **Jan** (1880–1940). Czech violinist. He performed in Prague at the age of 8, and was one of the world's greatest virtuosos; he also wrote 6 violin concertos, etc. His son, **Rafael K.** (1914–), was musical dir. at Covent Garden 1955–8, and became in 1961 chief conductor Bayerischer Rundfunk, Munich.

KUBLAI (kooblī) **KHAN** (1216–94). Mongol emperor of China, grandson of Ghengis Khan. He succeeded his brother Mangu in 1259, estab. himself as emperor of the whole of China, and with little success attempted to extend his rule still further.

KUCHUK (kooch'ook), **Fazil** (1906–). Cypriot politician. B. in Nicosia, where he became a doctor, he was ed. at Istanbul and Lausanne univs., and in 1941–60 was ed. of the daily paper *Halkín Sesi* (Voice of the People), supporting the Turkish minority position. In 1960, as leader of the Nat. Turkish Party, he became vice-pres. of Cyprus.

KUFRA (koo'frah). Group of oases in the Libyan Desert, Libya, N. Africa, *c.* 740 m. S.E. of Tripoli. It was visited in 1921 by Rosita Forbes, and captured from the Italians by General Leclerc in 1941.

KUIBYSHEV (ko̅o̅'bishef, but anglicized kwē'-bishef). Cap. of K. Reg., R.S.F.S.R., U.S.S.R., an excellent river port, at the junction of the Samara with the Volga. K. is the centre of the fertile middle Volga plain; industries incl. making of aircraft, locomotives, cables, synthetic rubber, textiles; petroleum refining, quarrying; K. hydro-electric installation reached its projected capacity of 2·3 million kilowatts in 1957. Founded as Samara in 1586, it was renamed K. in 1935. K. was the provisional cap. of the U.S.S.R. 1941–3. Pop. (1967) 969,000. K. region produces oil shale, limestone, gypsum, etc., wheat sunflower seed, fruit, and livestock.

KUIBYSHEV SEA is an artificial lake in K. reg. created in the 1950s by damming the Volga r.; it is 300 m. long by 20–5 m. wide.

KU KLUX KLAN. American secret society. Two have existed; the first, estab. as a social club in Tennessee in 1865, later adopting hooded white robes, etc., developed into an organization for maintaining white supremacy in the S. and opposing the U.S. Congress reconstruction programme. It declined after the withdrawal of occupation forces from the S. in 1877. The 2nd K.K.K., formed in 1915 on an anti-Jewish-Catholic-Negro basis, also declined from 1928, till racial violence flared in the 1950s and 1960s.

KULAK (kōō'lak; literally 'fist'). Russian term for a rich peasant who could afford to hire labour, and often acted as village usurer. They resisted the Soviet govt.'s policy of collectivization, and in 1930 they were 'liquidated as a class', about a million families being banished to eastern Russia.

KUANYIN. This massive statue completed in 1961 towers 170 ft. above the top of Otsubo-Yama hill S.E. of Tokyo; and is meant to console the souls of those who died in the Second World War. Sightseers can climb to the head of the statue and look over Tokyo Bay. *Photo: Planet News*

KUMASI (koomah'sē). Town in Ghana, W. Africa, cap. of Ashanti reg. It trades in cattle, cocoa, and rubber, and has an aerodrome. In the 4th Ashanti War, 1900, Sir Frederic Hodgson, the Gov. of the Gold Coast Colony, his wife, his staff, and a small garrison were besieged in K. from March to July. K. is the seat of Kwame Nkrumah Univ. of Science and Technology (1961), founded as the K. College of Technology (1951). Pop. (1960) 190,323.

KUNG-FU. *See* JUDO.

KUNIYOSHI (kōōniyōsh'i), **Yasuo** (1893–1953). Japanese-born American artist. Going to the U.S.A. in 1906, he had a gift for fantasy and an exactly humorous precision, later approaching Surrealism.

KUN-LUN (kun-loon'). Name applied to mountain ranges on the N. edge of the great Tibetan plateau, stretching for 2,500 m. E. to W. Some of the summits exceed 20,000 ft.

KUNMING (koonming'). Cap. of Yunnan prov., China, seat of Yunnan Univ., an ancient city and an

important road, water, and railway centre, Chinese terminus of the Burma Road. K. stands on Lake Tien Chih. Chief industry is copper smelting with power from hydro-electric works built nearby in 1912. Pop. (1957) 880,000.

KU KLUX KLAN. The fiery cross associated with the society is raised during a Klan meeting at Maryville, Tennessee.
Photo: United Press International.

KUOMINTANG (National People's Party). Chinese nationalist party, founded by Sun Yat-sen (q.v.) in 1894, and responsible for the overthrow of the Manchu Empire 1912. In alliance with the Communists, the power of the warlords was broken and China unified during 1924–7, when Chiang Kai-Shek's right wing launched a reign of terror against the Communists, only interrupted to resist the Japanese invasion of 1937–45, and breaking out again 1945–9, when the K. were driven from the mainland to Formosa, q.v.

KUPRIN (koopryēn'), **Alexander Ivanovich** (1870–1938). Russian novelist. His most important book is the realist story of army life *The Duel* (1905). After 1917 he settled in Paris.

KURDISTAN (koordistahn'). Hilly region in S.W. Asia, S. of the mountains of Ararat, divided between Persia, Iraq, and Turkey. The area inhabited by Kurds in Persia was formerly the prov. of Ardelan, incl. in 1938 in the 5th prov., sometimes called Kermanshah; its chief town is Sanandaj or Sinneh. The Kurds of Iraq, in revolt 1961–70, obtained recognition of the existence of 2 nationalities in Iraq – Arab and Kurdish; representation in the govt.; and creation of an autonomous Kurdish area. The Kurds, a nomadic people, number 3,000,000.

KURE (koo're). Naval base and port 20 m. S.E. of Hiroshima, on the S. coast of Honshu, Japan. K. has shipyards and engineering works. The Japanese fleet surrendered in K. Bay to the Allies 14 Aug. 1945. Pop. (1965) 225,000.

KURILES (koor'ilz). Chain of c. 50 small islands stretching from the N.E. of Hokkaido, Japan, to the S. of Kamchatka. Some of them are of volcanic origin. They were discovered in 1634 by a Russian navigator and were settled by Russians. Japan seized them in 1875 and held them until 1945, when under the Yalta agreement they were returned to Russia. Japan claims return of the southernmost (Kunashiri and Etorofu), as having always been in the Japanese sphere and not properly part of the K. Area 5,700 sq. m.; pop. (est.) 15,000.

KUROPATKIN (koorōpaht'kin), **Alexei Nikolaievich** (1848–1921). Russian general. He won a high reputation during the Russo-Turkish War of 1877–8, was C.-in-C. in Manchuria in 1903, and resigned after his defeat at Mukden. During the F.W.W. he commanded the armies on the N. front until 1916, when he was appointed gov. of Turkestan.

KURSK (koorsk). Town dating from the 9th cent., cap. of K. reg. of the R.S.F.S.R., U.S.S.R. Industries incl. chemicals, machinery, alcohol, and tobacco. Pop. (1967) 249,000.

KÜRTEN, Peter (1883–1931). German criminal sadist, known as the 'Düsseldorf murderer'. From Feb. 1929 to May 1930 he terrorized Düsseldorf as a mass-murderer; arrested at last, he was found guilty of 9 murders and condemned to death.

KUSSEVI'TZKY, Sergei (1874–1951). Russian conductor. Originally a virtuoso of the double bass, he was noted for his interpretations of Russian works.

KUT-AL-IMARA (koot′-al-imah′ra). Town on the Tigris, Iraq, a grain market and carpet-manufacturing centre, cap. of Kut liwa. It was besieged Dec. 1915–April 1916, when Gen. Townshend with his force was compelled to surrender. Pop. (1967) 60,000. *Kut Barrage*, a dam across the Tigris, was opened 1939.

KUTCH (kooch), **Rann of.** Salt, marshy area in Gujarat state, India, which forms 2 shallow lakes, the Great Rann and the Little Rann, in the wet season, and is a salt-covered desert in the dry. It takes its name from the former prince'y state of K., area 16,724 sq. m., centrally admin. from 1950, which was ab̶sorbed in Bombay state in 1956 and became part of Gujarat state in 1960. An internat. tribunal awarded 90% of the R. of K. to India and 10% (*c.* 300 sq. m.) to Pakistan, the latter comprising almost all the elevated area above water the year round, in 1968.

KUTUSOV (kootoo′zof), **Mikhail Larionovich,** Prince of Smolensk (1745–1813). Russian field marshal. He commanded an army corps at Austerlitz, and the retreating army in 1812. After the burning of Moscow he harried the French throughout their retreat, and later took command of the united Prussian and Russian armies.

KUWAIT (koo′wăt). Sheikdom on the N.W. shores of the Persian Gulf. It is mainly low-lying desert

KUWAIT. The University of Kuwait (1966) at Shuwaikh on Kuwait Bay, a suburb of the capital: there is also a Kuwaiti Institute of Economic and Social Planning in the Middle East
Courtesy of Kuwait Oil Co., Ltd.

country inhabited by nomadic Bedouin. The sheik of K., to prevent possible pressure by the Turks (of whose empire K. was nominally a part), asked Britain for protection in 1897, and in 1899 a treaty was made giving Britain exclusive rights in K. K.'s independence under British protection was recognized in 1914, and in 1961 the treaty of 1899 was formally abrogated, K. becoming a member of the Arab League and of the U.N. General Kassem of Iraq refused to recognize K.'s independence, claiming it as part of Iraq. The

Iraqi threat was countered by the despatch of a British force for a few months, and by the non-recognition of the claim in the Arab world.

Formerly dependent on dhow building, pearling and maritime trading, this small, barren state assumed international importance following the discovery of a

KYOTO. The original Rokuonji Temple (popularly called the Gold Pavilion), surrounded by a beautiful garden, was built in 1394 at the foot of Kinugasayama Hill in thick forest, to the north of Kyoto. The present building, completed in 1955 on the same site, is an exact replica of the original, destroyed by fire in 1950.   *Courtesy of Japanese Embassy.*

rich petroleum field at Burgan in 1938 (production started in 1946) and subsequently also in the Kuwait-Saudi Arabian Neutral Zone. Since most of the royalties paid to the sheik (amounting to many millions a year) are used for social developments, K. is one of the best-equipped of the world's states in public works, medical and educational services. The giant tankers are accommodated at a man-made floating island terminal 555 yds. long 10 m. offshore, opened 1969. Area *c.* 5,800 sq. m.; pop. (1969) 733,000.

The cap., also called K., is a flourishing port and is being developed as an outstanding example of town planning. Its seawater distillation plant is the biggest in the world, and there are power stations supplying light industries. An impressive survival of the past is the 'Sif' palace on the seafront. Pop. (1969) 300,000.

KUZBAS. Industrial area in Kemerovo region, R.S.F.S.R., U.S.S.R., lying on the Tom r. to the N. of the Altai mountains. Development began in the 1930s. It takes its name from the old town of Kuznetsk: *see* LENINSK-KUZNETSKY; NOVO KUZNETSKY.

KUZNETSOV (koosnyetsof′), **Anatoli** (1930–). Russian writer. His novels *Babi Yar* (1966), describing the wartime execution of Jews at Babi Yar, nr. Kiev, and *The Fire* (1969), about workers in a large metallurgical factory, were seen as anti-Soviet. Visiting Britain in 1969, he was given permission to settle there.

KWANGCHOW. Chinese name for CANTON.

KWANGSI-CHUANG (kwahngsē′ chōō-ang′). Autonomous region of S. China bordering Vietnam. K.-C. covers the upper part of the basin of the Sikiang; it produces sugar cane, fruits, sandalwood, tung oil, tin, antimony, etc. The cap. is Nanning. Area 85,900 sq. m.; pop. (1968) 24,000,000.

KWANGTUNG (kwahntoong′). Prov. of S. China. In the S. it incl. the Luichow peninsula, and the island of Hainan. The prov. is drained by the Han and also by the Sikiang and its affluents converging on the Canton delta and estuary, where are Hong Kong and

Macao (qq.v.). Long ranges of hills run parallel with the coast. Rice, fruit, vegetables, silk, and manganese are produced. The coastal fishing industry is centred on Canton, cap. of the prov. Area 89,300 sq. m.; pop. (1968) 40,000,000.

KWANGTUNG was also the name of a Moslem enclave in Kansu prov., 45 m. S.S.W. of Lanchow, set up in 1953; and of a coal-mining district in Yunnan, 50 m. W. of Kunming. See also LAOTUNG PENINSULA.

KWEICHOW. Province of S. China, lying N.W. of Kwangtung. Drained by the Wu Kiang in the N., the Peipan Kiang in the S., it is noted for mercury; other products incl. rice, wheat, maize, tung oil, and silk. The cap. is Kweiyang. Area 67,100 sq. m.; pop. (1968) 17,000,000.

KWEISUI. Chinese name of HUHEHOT.

KYD, Thomas (c. 1557–95). English dramatist. He followed his father's profession as a scrivener, and c. 1588 wrote The Spanish Tragedy, which anticipated elements present in Hamlet.

KYŌ TO. Japanese city of Honshu situated near Biwa Lake, with which it is linked by canal. Among its industries are silk weaving and manufacture, embroidery, porcelain, and bronze and lacquer ware. K. was founded, as Uda, in the 8th cent. and was the Japanese cap. 794–1868. Pop. (1965) 1,365,000.

KYUSHU (kū'shoo). Most southerly of the main islands of Japan, separated from Shikoku and Honshu by Bungo Channel and Suo Bay, but connected to Honshu by a railway tunnel. The coast is very broken. The island is very mountainous, though the peaks are not very high. The active volcano Naka-dake (4,340 ft.) has the world's largest crater. There are coalfields, and gold, silver, iron and tin are mined. Agricultural products incl. rice, tea, and tobacco. The principal towns are Nagasaki, the cap. (q.v.), Kagoshima, Kumamoto, and Fukuoka. Area, incl. about 370 small islands, 16,247 sq. m.; pop. (est.) 12,937,000.

KYUSTENDIL. Town in S.W. Bulgaria, 43 m. S.W. of Sofia, notable for its hot springs. Pop. (est.) 20,000

L Twelfth letter of the Roman alphabet. The sound represented is one of the most stable in all languages; in some languages it tends to be lost between a back vowel and a consonant, as in Eng. 'half', 'should', etc.

LABELLED COMPOUND. A compound in which an isotope (usually radioactive) is substituted for a normal atom. Thus labelled, the path taken by the compound can be readily followed, and its quantity measured, by geiger counters, etc. This powerful and sensitive technique is used in science and industry.

LABIATAE. Family of dicotyledonous plants comprising some 200 genera with 3,000 species. Among their outstanding characteristics are the square stem, the hairy leaves, the arrangement of the flowers in small groups on the stem, and the hooded form of the petals. The family includes lavender, rosemary, thyme, sage and mint.

LABOUCHERE (la'booshār), **Henry Du Pré** (1831–1912). British journalist. A Liberal M.P. 1880–1905, he in 1877 estab. the weekly Truth, in which he exposed political, social and business scandals.

LABOUR DAY. The annual festival of the Labour movement, celebrated since 1890 on 1 May, or the first Sunday in May. In the U.S.A. and Canada L.D. is observed on the first Monday in Sept., and is a legal holiday.

LABOUR PARTY. British working-class and Socialist party. Although Keir Hardie and John Burns entered Parliament independently as Labour M.Ps. in 1892, it was not till 1900 that a conference representing the trade unions, the Independent Labour Party and the Fabian Society (qq.v.) founded the L.P., known until 1906, when 29 seats were gained, as the Labour Representation Committee. All but a pacifist minority of the L.P. supported the F.W.W., and in 1918 a Socialist programme was first adopted, with local branches of the party being set up to which individual members were now admitted. By 1922 the L.P. was recognized as the official Opposition, and in 1924 formed a minority govt. (with Liberal support) for a few months under J. R. MacDonald (q.v.). A second minority govt. in 1929 followed a conservative policy, completely failing to deal with unemployment, and in 1931 MacDonald and other leaders, faced with a financial crisis, left the party to support the National government. The I.L.P. (q.v.) seceded in 1932. In 1936–9 there was internal dissension on foreign policy, the leadership's support of non-intervention in Spain being strongly criticized, and Sir Stafford Cripps, Aneurin Bevan and others being expelled for advocating an alliance of all left-wing parties against the Chamberlain govt.

The L.P. supported the Churchill war-time coalition from 1940, in which most of its leaders held office, but in 1945 withdrew to win 393 seats and take office for the first time as a majority govt. with Attlee as P.M. It pursued a policy of developing the Welfare State by nationalization (q.v.) of essential services and industries, and establishment of a fully comprehensive system of national insurance (1946) and of the National Health Service (1948). Returned with a reduced majority in 1950, the L.P. was further weakened by the emergence of a dissident group under Aneurin Bevan, which incl. Harold Wilson, and was defeated in 1951. Disagreement over further nationalization, and multilateral or unilateral disarmament continued, but Gaitskell created a more united front and under Wilson, leader from 1963, Labour was in power 1964–70, pledged to national economic planning; greatly increased majority 1966.

Policy is decided by the annual conference of delegates from constituency organizations and the trade unions, who form a large part of the L.P.'s membership and by paying their union's political levy contribute a considerable proportion of its funds. In 1968 following clashes between policy decisions at the annual conference and those of the Labour govt., govt. mins. were to be asked by the L.P. nat. executive to explain such decisions as did not comply with those of the conference. The chairman and leader of the party is elected by the Parliamentary L.P. by ballot, and during periods in opposition there is an annual ballot to elect members of the Parliamentary Committee – popularly known as the Shadow Cabinet – who each take responsibility in opposition for one particular aspect of govt. The L.P., the T.U.C. and the Co-operative movement together form the National Council of Labour, in order to co-ordinate political activities and take joint action on specific issues. The Fabian Society is the most important affiliated political body.

LABRADO'R. Peninsula in N.E. Canada, lying between Ungava Bay on the N.W., the Atlantic on

LACE. Weighing 2 tons and with many thousands o moving parts, precision-made of metal, this modern Leavers machine can make all types of lace from narrowest edging to the widest flouncing of a bridal gown. It copes with all types of thread, natural or synthetic, produces a cobweb texture or rich, heavy styles, and colour is varied at will.
Courtesy of British Leavers Lace Publicity.

the E., and the Strait of Belle Isle on the S.E. Part of it is in the prov. of Quebec, part forms a division of the prov. of Newfoundland, from which it is separated by the Strait of Belle Isle. L. consists for the most part of a plateau sloping gently from the mountains which fringe the irregular coastline. Fishing, especially of cod, is the chief industry. Iron ore from deposits near the headwaters of Hamilton r., proved in 1950, is taken for shipment to the port of Seven Islands on the St. Lawrence by a railway completed in 1954. A considerable stand of virgin timber lies in S. L. and Churchill River (560 m.) is being developed for electric power. L. division of Newfoundland is *c.* 110,000 sq. m. in area; pop. (1966) 21,157.

LA BRUYÈRE (brüyär'), **Jean de** (1645–96). French essayist. B. in Paris, he studied law, took a post in the revenue office, and in 1684 entered the service of the house of Condé. His *Caractères* (1688), satirical portraits of contemporaries, made him many enemies.

LABUAN (lahboo-ahn'). A flat, wooded island off N.W. Borneo, ceded to Gt. Britain in 1846; made a Crown Colony in 1848; included in British North Borneo 1890–1906; a dependency of Singapore 1907–12; a separate colony again 1912 until occupied by the Japanese 1942–5; again part of British N. Borneo from 1946, and of Sabah, Fed. of Malaysia, from 1963. The chief town is Victoria, with a good harbour (pop. 1960 *c.* 3,200). Sago is produced; cattle and goats are raised. Area 35 sq. m.; pop. *c.* 10,000.

LABURNUM. Flowering tree (*Cytisus l.* or *L. vulgaris*) a member of the Leguminosae family, native to the mountainous parts of central Europe. The flowers, in long drooping clusters, are bright yellow and appear in early spring; some varieties have purple or reddish flowers. The seeds are poisonous.

LAC. Resinous incrustation exuded by the female lac-insects (*Coccus lacca*), which eventually covers the twigs of trees in India and the Far East. The gathered twigs are known as stick-lac, which yields a useful crimson dye and the commercial shellac formed by melting the separated resin, and spreading it into thin layers or flakes.

LACCADIVE (lak'adĭv), **MINICOY and AMIN-DIVI ISLANDS.** Group of 14 coral islands, 10 inhabited, in the Indian Ocean, 200 m. off the Malabar coast. Acquired by the British in 1877, they were attached administratively to Madras prov., later state, until 1956, when they were made a Union Terr. (admin. H.Q. Kavaratti Is.) of India. Coir and copra

from coconut plantations and fish are the chief products. Vasco da Gama discovered the islands in 1499. Laccadive is from Sanskrit Laksha 'divi' and means a hundred thousand islands. Area 11 sq. m.; pop. (1961) 24,108, most of them Moslems.

LACE. A plain or decorative textile fabric of an openwork or network type. Needle-point or point laces (which are a development of embroidery) were first evolved in Italy in the late 15th or early 16th cents., whence the craft spread to France and Germany, probably being brought to England by the Flemings. The other chief variety of L. is bobbin or pillow L., which is made by twisting threads together in pairs or groups, according to a pattern marked out by pins set in a cushion, and is said to have been invented by Barbara Uttmann (b. 1514) of Saxony: elaborate patterns may require 1,000 bobbins. From 1589 various attempts were made at producing machine-made L., and in 1809 John Heathcoat achieved success with a bobbin net machine: the principles of this system are kept in modern machines making plain net. The earliest machine for making true L., reproducing the movements of the fingers of the pillow-lace workers in twisting the threads together, was the invention of another Englishman, John Leavers, in 1813. It had a wooden frame and many of the moving parts were of wood (*see* illus.), but the principle involved is the same as in the modern machines at Nottingham, the great centre of machine-made L. Early Ls. were principally made from linen thread, enriched with gold, silver, or silk: later materials incl. cotton, wool, rayon, nylon, etc. Among the great centres of L.-making have been Venice, Alençon, and Argentan for point L., and Mechlin, Valenciennes, and Honiton for bobbin L.: both types are made at Brussels.

An early Leavers machine.
Courtesy of British Leavers Lace Publicity.

LACEWING FLY. Insect of the families Hemerobiidae (incl. the brown lacewings) and Chrysopidae (incl. the green lacewings or golden-eye flies), found throughout the world. So named because of the veining of their 2 pairs of semi-transparent wings, they have narrow bodies and long thin antennae. The eggs of the green lacewing are stalked.

LACHISH (lā'kish). Biblical city identified by Albright in 1929 as having occupied the mound of Tell ed-Duweir *c.* 25 m. S.W. of Jerusalem. Most notable find during excavations by J. K. Starkey 1932–8 was a no. of ostraca inscribed in Hebrew which antedate the final destruction of the city in 589 B.C. and are valuable for comparison with Hebrew MSS.

LACEWING. I, eggs; 2, larva; 3, cocoon; 4, fly.

LACHMANN (lahkh'-mahn), **Karl** (1793–1851). German philologist. From 1818 he lectured on philology at Königsberg and Berlin univs. He edited many Gk., Lat., and early German texts, among them the *Nibelungenlied*, the New Testament, and Lucretius, applying strict principles of textual criticism that set a standard for critical editions.

LACORDAIRE (lahkordär'), **Jean Baptiste Henri** (1802–61). French ecclesiastic. Formerly a lawyer, he was ordained priest in 1828, and became famous as a preacher. With Lamennais and Montalembert, he founded the journal *L'Avenir*, which in 1832 was condemned by the Pope on account of its radicalism.

LACQ. Small French town in Basses-Pyrénées dept., 15 m. N.W. of Pau. A small oilfield was struck at L., a village of 400 pop., in 1949; the discovery in 1951 of a natural gas deposit 11,500 ft. below the surface proved of much greater importance. The gas was extremely toxic, and it was 1957 before this could be overcome and the gas put into use. Pipelines laid or projected carry it to Nantes, Paris, Dôle, Grenoble, and intervening towns. Pop. (1962) 700.

LACQUER (la'ker). A varnish made from the sap of the lacquer-tree (*Rhus vernicifera*), and used for producing a highly polished surface on furniture and other articles. L. is often coloured red, blue, brown, etc., and successive coatings of the varnish are applied to the objects treated. The earliest specimens are Korean, whence the art spread to China and Japan. Many months are needed to produce the finest work.

LACROSSE. Canadian ball game. The name comes from the Fr. *la croix*, a bishop's crozier, which a L. stick somewhat resembles. The game was played by the Red Indians, both men and women, from whom the Canadians adopted it. Introduced into England in 1867, it became particularly popular as a women's game after 1900.

The stick or 'crosse' is a light staff of hickory wood, with the top bent in the form of a hook, from the tip of which a thong is drawn down and fastened to the shaft. Across the frame a loose network of hide is drawn. The ball, made of indiarubber sponge, weighs 5–5¼ oz., and is 7⅞–8 in. in circumference. The goals, 6 ft. by 6 ft., are placed 80 yds. apart, in a field 110 yds. long.

The team consists of 10 or 12 players, incl. the goalkeeper. To open play, the 2 centres 'face' the ball, and each tries to get it. The ball may be kicked, but not handled, except by the goalkeeper. A player may not be held, tripped, pushed, charged, or shouldered; a 'free position' may be awarded for a foul, or a player may be suspended. The game is controlled by a referee, and there is also an umpire at each goal. The playing time is 4 periods of 15 min. each.

LACTATION. The secretion of milk. In late pregnancy the cells lining the lobules inside the breasts undergo a change which makes them convert the blood into milk. The supply of milk starts shortly after birth with the production of colostrum, a clear fluid consisting largely of serum, which has a certain purgative effect needed by the infant. The milk becomes established in a few days, and will then continue practically as long as the child continues to suck.

LACTIC ACID. Three acids of the same composition. The ordinary acid is a colourless, almost odourless syrup, soluble in water, alcohol, and ether. It occurs in sour milk, wine, and certain plant extracts, and is always present in the stomach.

LACTOSE, or **Milk Sugar.** A disaccharide found in the milk of all animals. Cow's milk contains 4·5–5 per cent of the sugar. It is usually prepared from the whey obtained in cheese making.

LADAHK (ladahk'). Subsidiary range of the Karakoram and district of N.E. Kashmir on the border of Tibet. After the Chinese occupation of Tibet in 1951, China made claims on the area.

LADI'NOS. *See* GUATEMALA.

LADI'NS. Ethnic community in the Dolomites, descended from Etruscans and proto-Italic tribes of the Po valley, and speaking a language directly derived from Latin. Numbering *c.* 16,000, they have links with the Romansch-speakers of Switzerland.

LADOGA (lah'-), Lake. Largest lake in Europe, in the R.S.F.S.R., just N.E. of Leningrad. It receives the waters of the Svir, which drains L. Onega, and other rivers, and drains to the Gulf of Finland by the r. Neva. Lake L. forms a link in the White Sea–Baltic Canal. Area 7,100 sq. m.

LADRONES. Spanish name (meaning thieves) of the MARIANAS.

LADY. Feminine title of honour, correlative to that of Lord, and Sir. It is the correct title of the dau. of an earl, marquis or duke, and of any woman whose husband is above the rank of baronet or knight, and is also accorded by courtesy to the wives of these two latter ranks.

LADYBIRD. I, larva; 2, pupa; 3, beetle; 4, eggs.

LADYBIRD. A migratory beetle of the family Coccinellidae, red or yellow in colour, with black spots. There are several species which, with their larvae, feed upon aphides and scale-insect pests.

LADY DAY. 25 March, the festival of the Annunciation of the Virgin Mary. Until 1752 (when 1 Jan. was substituted) it was the beginning of the legal year in England, and it is still a quarter day.

LADYSMITH. Town in Natal, S. Africa, 115 m. N.W. of Durban, nr. the Klip. It was besieged by the Boers, 2 Nov. 1899–28 Feb. 1900, during the S. African War. L. was named in honour of the wife of Sir Harry Smith (q.v.). Pop. (1960) 22,997 (7,260 white).

LADY'S SLIPPER. Wild flower (*Cypripedium calceolus*) of the orchid family, found in Europe and N. Asia. It has purplish upper petals, with the lower part of the flower modified into a slipper-like sac, coloured yellow and flecked with purple.

LA FARGE (fahrzh'), **Oliver** (1901–63). American ethnologist and writer. He dealt in his best-known novel, *Laughing Boy* (1929), with the Navajo Indians.

LA FAYETTE (fayet'), **Marie Joseph Gilbert du Motier,** marquis de (1757–1834). French soldier and statesman. He fought against Britain in the American War of Independence. During the French Revolution he sat in the National Assembly as a constitutional royalist, and in 1789 was given command of the National Guard. In 1792 he fled the country after attempting to restore the monarchy, and was imprisoned by the Austrians until 1797. He supported Napoleon during the Hundred Days, sat in the Chamber of Deputies as a Liberal from 1818, and assisted the revolution of 1830.

LA FOLLETTE (fol'et), **Robert Marion** (1855–1925). American politician. Governor (1901–5) and republican senator (1905–25) for Wisconsin, he was a pacifist during the F.W.W. An advocate of public ownership of water power and railways, and public control of all national resources, he was rejected as presidential candidate by the Republican Party in 1924, and stood as a Progressive, receiving 5 million of the 29 million votes cast.

LA FONTAINE (fontän'), **Jean de** (1621–95). French poet. B. at Château-Thierry, from 1656 he lived largely in Paris, enjoying the friendship of Molière, Racine, and Boileau. His outstanding works are his *Fables* (1668–94), and his *Contes* (1665–74), a series of witty and improper tales in verse.

LAFORGUE (lahforg'), **Jules** (1860–87). French poet, whose technical innovations greatly influenced T. S. Eliot and also later French writers.

LA'GASH. Sumerian city 10 m. N. of Shatra, Iraq. Discovered (1877) and excavated by Ernest de Sarzec, then French consul in Basra, it was of great importance under independent and semi-independent rulers *c.* 3000–2700 B.C. Besides objects of high artistic value, it has provided *c.* 30,000 clay tablets giving detailed information on temple administration.

LAGER (lah′ger; Ger. *lager*, store). A light beer. After fermentation L. is stored at a low temperature for periods ranging from a few weeks to several months, and acquires its characteristic flavour. L. is particularly popular in Germany and the U.S.A.

LAGERKVIST, Pär (1891–). Swedish author. Recognition of his lyric poetry, dramas (*The Hangman*, 1935), and novels (*Barabbas*, 1950) has been hindered by their obscurity of expression, but in 1951 he was awarded a Nobel prize.

LAGERLÖF (lah′gerlöf), **Selma** (1858–1940). Swedish novelist. Originally a schoolteacher, she won fame in 1891 with a collection of stories of peasant life, *Gösta Berling's Saga*. Her later novels incl. *The Miracles of Antichrist* (1897) and *Jerusalem* (1901–2); she received a Nobel prize in 1909.

LÁ′GOS. Port and cap. of Nigeria, W. Africa, situated on an island in a lagoon. There is an excellent harbour, an aerodrome, and railway connection with the interior. There is a univ. (1962) with a large medical school. Pop. (1968) 700,000.

LAGRANGE (lahgroṅzh′), **Joseph Louis** (1736–1813). French mathematician. B. and ed. at Turin, where he received a professorship in 1754, he was appointed director of the Academy of Berlin in 1766. He settled in Paris as Louis XVI's guest in 1787, and received further honours from the revolutionaries and Napoleon. He presided over the commission which reformed the weights and measures in 1793. His chief writings are *Mécanique analytique* (1788) and *Théorie des fonctions analytiques* (1797).

LA GUARDIA (gwahr′di-a), **Fiorello Henrico** (1882–1947). American politician. B. in New York of Italian parents, he practised law, served in the Air Force during the F.W.W., and sat in Congress as a Republican. Elected mayor of New York in 1933 against the opposition of the powerful Tammany Hall machine, he cleaned up the administration, suppressed racketeering, and organized unemployment relief, slum-clearance schemes, and social services. Although

LAGOS. Receiving a guest in style in the capital involves a strenuous dance display, enjoyed by the performers as much as by the audience. *Courtesy of the Federation of Nigeria.*

nominally a Republican, he strongly supported the New Deal. In 1945 he refused to run for another term.

LA GUARDIA FIELD, a municipal airport of New York City in Queens Borough, opened 1939, was named in his honour.

LA HARPE (ahrp), **Jean-François de** (1739–1803). French dramatist and critic. B. at Paris; best remembered for his course of lectures at the Paris Lycée in 1786, pub. as *Cours de littérature ancienne et moderne*.

LA HOGUE (hòg). A naval battle fought off the Normandy coast in 1692 in which the combined English and Dutch fleets defeated the French.

LAHO′RE. City and cap. of W. Pakistan, seat of a univ. (1882). L. is divided into an old town enclosed by walls, and a modern quarter built on European lines. Industries incl. silk, cotton spinning and weaving, and metal-working. L. has many associations with the Mogul rulers Akbar, Jahangir, and Aurangzeb. Under British rule 1849–1947, L. was cap. of Punjab prov. Pop. (1961) 1,296,477.

LAHORE. One of the loveliest of oriental formal gardens, the Shalimar Gardens laid out in the late 17th century by Shah Jehan. *Courtesy of the Office of the High Commission for Pakistan.*

LAIBACH. German name of LJUBLJANA.

LAIRD, John (1805–74). British shipbuilder. B. at Greenock, he became a partner in his father's shipbuilding firm at Birkenhead, and was a pioneer in the building of iron ships. He was a Conservative M.P. 1861–74. His brother **Macgregor L.** (1808–61), a merchant of Greenock, became a pioneer of British trade with the Niger region of W. Africa.

LAISSEZ-FAIRE (lā′sehfair′). The theory that the State should refrain from all intervention in economic affairs. The phrase originated with the 18th cent. French economists, the Physiocrats, whose maxim was *laissez-faire et laissez-passer* (literally 'let go and let pass', i.e. 'leave the individual alone, and let commodities circulate freely'). Before the 17th cent. control by the guild, local authorities, or the State, of wages, prices, employment, the training of workmen, etc., was taken for granted. As capitalist enterprises developed in the 16th and 17th cents., entrepreneurs shook off the control of the guilds and local authorities, and the revolution of 1640–60 weakened the hold of the State on economic life. By the 18th cent. this process was complete.

The reaction against L.-F. began in the mid-19th cent., and found expression in the factory acts, etc. This reaction was inspired partly by humanitarian protests against the social conditions created by the Industrial Revolution, partly by the wish to counter the popular unrest of the 1830s and '40s by removing some of its causes. The last cent. has shown an ever-increasing degree of State intervention to promote social amelioration, which since 1945 has been extended into the field of nationalization of leading industries and services.

LAKE, Gerard, visct. (1744–1808). British general. After serving in America and the Low Countries, he defeated the Irish rebels at Vinegar Hill in 1798, and then had a distinguished career in India, defeating the Mahrattas in 1803 and capturing Delhi.

LAKE. Sheet of still water lying in depressed ground without direct communication with the sea. Lakes are common in glaciated mountain regions, along the course of gently declining rivers, and in low land near the sea. The main classifications are by origin as follows: glacial Ls., such as in the Alps; barrier Ls., formed by landslides, valley glaciers, etc.; crater Ls.; tectonic Ls., occurring in natural features. Most Ls. are fresh, e.g. the group incl. Superior, Michigan and Huron, but in hot regions where evaporation is excessive they may be salt, e.g. the Dead Sea. The 20th cent. has seen the creation of large artificial Ls. in connection with hydro-electric and other works, and also the eutrophication (a state of over-nourishment) of Ls. Agricultural fertilisers leach into them, causing an explosion of life, and the Ls. choke and die.

LAKE DISTRICT. The 700 sq. m. area in Cumberland, Westmorland, and N. Lancashire, embracing the principal English lakes separated by wild uplands rising to many peaks, incl. Scafell Pike (3,210 ft.).

Windermere, in the S.E., is connected with Rydal Water and Grasmere. The westerly Scafell range extends S. to the Old Man of Coniston overlooking Coniston Water, and N. to Wastwater. Ullswater lies in the N.E. of the district, with Hawes Water and Thirlmere nearby. The river Derwent flows N. through Borrowdale forming Derwentwater and Bassenthwaite. W. of Borrowdale lie Buttermere, Crummock Water, and, beyond, Ennerdale Water.

The contrasting scenery of lakes, rivers, and waterfalls in the dales, towered over by the proximate mountains, has many literary associations and in 1951 the L.D. was made a National Park.

LAKE DWELLINGS. Habitations built on piles driven into the bottom of a lake. Such villages are found in W. Africa, S. America, Borneo and New Guinea. Remains of Stone Age lake villages have been found in Switzerland, N. Italy, S. Germany, Austria and Hungary. A lake village of the 1st cents. B.C. and A.D. has been excavated near Glastonbury.

LAKE SUCCESS. Village in Long Island, New York, U.S.A., site 1946–51 of the secretariat of the United Nations. It makes aerial and naval instruments. Pop. (1960) 2,954.

LAKH, Lac, or **Lak.** Indian term for 100,000.

LAKSHMI (laksh'mē). Hindu goddess of good fortune, love and beauty, and the wife of Vishnu.

LALANDE (lahloñd'), **Joseph Jérôme de** (1732–1807). French astronomer. From 1762 he was professor of astronomy in the Collège de France, Paris. His popular writings, such as his *Traité d'astronomie* (1764), achieved a wide circulation. His planetary tables were long in use, and in his *Histoire céleste française* he catalogued over 47,000 stars.

LALLY (lahlē'), **Thomas Arthur,** comte de (1702–66). French general. The son of an Irish Jacobite, he accompanied Prince Charles Edward during the 1745 rebellion. Appointed commander of an expedition to India in 1756, he was compelled to surrender to the English in 1761. Hearing he was accused of treachery he returned to France to stand his trial, and was beheaded.

LALO (lahlō'), **Édouard** (1823–92). French composer. Of Spanish descent, he was originally a viola player. Best known of his works are: *Le Roi d'Ys* (1888), an opera, and his *Symphonie Espagnole*.

LAMAISM (Tibetan, *lama*, a superior priest). The religion of Tibet and Mongolia; a form of Buddhism belonging to the Mahayana school. Buddhism was introduced into Tibet in A.D. 640, but the real founder of L. was the Indian missionary Padma Sambhava who began his activity about A.D. 750. In the 15th cent. was founded the sect of Geluk-Pa (virtuous) by Tsongkhapa, which has remained the most powerful organization in the country. The Dalai Lama (q.v.), residing at the palace of the Potala at Lhasa, exercised both spiritual and temporal authority as head of the Tibetan State until 1959, and is considered an incarnation of Bodhisattva Avalokitesvara. *See also* PANCHEN LAMA. On the death of the Dalai Lama

great care is taken in finding the infant in whom he has been reincarnated.

L. formerly numbered 1 in 4 of the male population as a monk, but Chinese Communist rule is swiftly modifying this situation. Formerly frequent in the Tibetan countryside were the prayer-wheels (*see* illus.) and prayer-flags on which were inscribed prayers; when these were turned by hand or moved by the wind, great spiritual benefit was supposed to accrue.

LAMARCK (lamahrk'), **Jean Baptiste** (1744–1829). French naturalist. B. at Bazentin, he was forced by ill-health to abandon a military career, and studied medicine and meteorology before turning to botany. His *Flore française* (1773) won him admission to the Academy of Sciences. In 1781–2 he toured Europe, writing the *Dictionnaire de Botanique* and the *Illustrations de Genres* on his return. In 1792 he was appointed to a zoological chair at the Jardin des Plantes. His greatest works were his *Philosophie Zoologique* (1809) and the *Histoire naturelle des animaux sans vertèbres* (1815–22).

LAMARTINE (lahmahrtēn'), **Alphonse de** (1790–1869). French poet. B. at Mâçon, he achieved immediate success with his first vol. of musically romantic poems, *Méditations* (1820), which was followed by *Nouvelles Méditations* (1823), *Harmonies* (1830), *Recueillements* (1839), etc. He entered the Chamber of Deputies in 1833, and by his *Histoire des Girondins* (1847) influenced the revolution of 1848.

LAMAS, Carlos (1879–1959). Argentine lawyer. Prof. of international law and sociology at Buenos Aires univ., he was awarded the Nobel peace prize in 1936 for his arbitration in the Gran Chaco war between Bolivia and Paraguay.

LAMB, Charles (1775–1834). British essayist and critic. B. in London, he was ed. at Christ's Hospital, where he was a contemporary of Coleridge, and in 1792 became a clerk at India House. In 1796 he pub. some poems together with Coleridge, but in the same year his sister Mary (1764–1847) stabbed their mother to death in a fit of madness, and L. devoted his life to caring for her, since periodic recurrence of the attacks meant that she must at times be placed in an asylum. In 1807 he collaborated with Mary in the *Tales from Shakespeare*, and in 1808 pub. *Specimens of English Dramatic Poets* which assisted the revival of interest in Elizabethan playwrights. In 1820 he began contributing to the *London Magazine* the series of appealingly individual essays under the pseudonym of 'Elia', borrowed from an early office acquaintance, which were collected in 1823 and 1833. In 1825 L. retired from India House, and moved first to Enfield then to Edmonton, where both he and his sister are buried.

LAMB, Henry (1885–1960). Australian-born British artist. A student of medicine – he eventually qualified on service during the F.W.W. – he was an original member of the Camden Town Group in 1912. He was a sensitive portraitist, e.g. 'Lytton Strachey' and 'Lord David Cecil', and local genre artist, and his studies of soldiers in the S.W.W. (as official artist) are notable.

LAMBERT, Constant (1905–51). British composer and conductor. B. in London, he studied at the R.C.M. Often conductor for the Vic-Wells co., he wrote much ballet music – *Romeo and Juliet* (1926), commissioned by Diaghileff; *Pomona* (1927); *Horoscope* (1937); and *Tiresias* (1950). Other works incl. a setting of Sacheverell Sitwell's poem *The Rio Grande* (1929); the cantata *Summer's Last Will and Testament* (1936), songs and chamber music. *Music Ho!* (1936), is a book on contemporary music. His brother Maurice L. (1901–64) was a well-known sculptor.

LAMBERT, John (1619–83). English gen. B. in Yorks, he joined the parliamentary army in 1642, and distinguished himself as a cavalry commander at Marston Moor, Preston, Dunbar, and Worcester. He co-operated closely with Cromwell until 1657, when his opposition to Cromwell's proposed assumption of the title of king led to a breach. After the Restoration he was imprisoned for life.

LAMBETH. Borough of Greater London, England, opposite Westminster on the S. bank of the Thames. Notable buildings incl. L. Palace, with its 15th cent. Lollard's Tower, on a site which has been occupied by the chief residence of the archbishops of Canterbury from 1197; and County Hall, H.Q. of the G.L.C., opened in 1922. Pop. (1967) 338,130.

LAMBETH CONFERENCE. See ANGLICAN COMMUNION.

LAMBETH CROSS. Award instituted in 1942 by Lord Lang, the then archbishop of Canterbury, for bestowal upon distinguished prelates and laymen who have furthered the cause of Christian unity.

LAMBETH WALK. Name of a street in Lambeth, London, England, running between Black Prince Rd. and China Walk, Lambeth Rd., with an animated street market. It gave its name to a popular song and dance in the musical comedy *Me and My Girl* (1937).

LAMBURN, Richmal Crompton. See CROMPTON.

LAMELLIBRANCHIA (lamelibrang'kia). Class of molluscs, also known as bivalves, from the shell which consists of 2 valves joined by a hinge. There are many varieties, the best-known being cockles, mussels and oysters, usually found in shallow seawater.

LAMENNAIS (lahmenä'), **Hugues Félicité Robert de** (1782–1854). French philosopher. B. at St. Malo, he

LAMBETH. Seen from the Thames, Lambeth Palace; the hall to the left of the Tudor gatehouse houses a valuable library.
Photo: E. P. Olney.

took orders in 1815–16, and in 1817 pub. *Essai sur l'indifférence*, advocating extreme theocratic views. Later, however, he adopted strongly democratic opinions, and on their condemnation by the Pope in 1832 left the Church. His Christian Socialist views are expressed in *Paroles d'un croyant* (1834).

LAMMAS ('loaf-mass'). Medievai festival of harvest, celebrated on 1 Aug. At one time it was an English quarter day, and is still a quarter day in Scotland.

LAMMERMUIR HILLS (lammermür'). A range of hills dividing East Lothian and Berwickshire, Scotland, from Gala Water to St. Abb's Head.

LAMOUREUX (lahmoorö'), **Charles** (1834–99). French violinist and conductor. B. at Bordeaux, he founded the *Société de l'Harmonie Sacrée*, and the

Concerts Lamoureux (founded 1881) bear his name.

LAMPETER. Welsh market town (bor.) on the Teifi r., Cardiganshire. It has woollen mills and tanneries. St. David's Coll., for students of the Welsh Church, was founded there in 1822. Pop. (1961) 1,853.

LAMPREY (lam'pri). An eel-like fish belonging to the family Petromyzontidea. They feed on other fish by a type of parasitism, fixing themselves by the round mouth to their host and boring the flesh by their toothed tongue. The sea-L. is a food fish.

LAMPREY

LA'NARK. Royal burgh, the co. town of Lanarkshire, Scotland, 22 m. S.E. of Glasgow. The church of St. Kentigern is 12th cent. New L., nearby to the S., founded 1785, is known in connection with the Socialist experiments of Robert Owen. Pop. (1961) 8,436.

LA'NARKSHIRE. A southern inland county of Scotland drained by the Clyde. Mainly low-lying, it is the most densely populated of Scottish counties. Market gardening, fruit growing, stock raising, and dairy farming are carried on and the extensive industries incl. coal, iron and lead mining, shipbuilding, textile manufacture. The chief towns are Glasgow, Lanark, the co. town, Rutherglen, Motherwell, Hamilton, Coatbridge, and Airdrie. Area 879 sq. m.; pop. (1961) 1,626,317.

LANCASHIRE. A heavily populated county of England, situated between Yorks on the E. and the Irish Sea on the W. The coast is flat, with many estuaries and inlets. The chief rivers are the Mersey and Ribble. The many seaside resorts incl. Blackpool, Southport, and Morecambe. In the N. is Furness, which is separated from the rest of the county by Morecambe Bay; it is hilly and incl. the southern part of the Lake District. The great shipping centre is Liverpool; other ports incl. Manchester (via the Manchester Ship Canal), Barrow, Fleetwood, and Heysham. Formerly L. was the world centre of cotton manufacture, with heavy dependence also on iron and steel, shipbuilding, heavy engineering, and railway works. All have declined very sharply, but other existing industries, incl. chemicals, glass, and paper, have been expanded, and new ones introduced, i.e. Merseyside is now a leading car-manufacturing area. As a focus for further economic revival a new town, 'Ribbleton', is planned in the Preston, Chorley, Leyland area. The traditional co. town is Lancaster, but the admin. H.Q. is Preston. Area of county 1,878 sq. m.; pop. (1967) 5,198,060.

LA'NCASTER, House and Duchy of. A family descended from Henry III's son, Edmund, earl of L., which ruled England 1399–1461. The family estates passed by marriage to John of Gaunt (q.v.), who was created duke of L. in 1362. His son Henry IV obtained the throne in 1399. The 3rd Lancastrian king, Henry VI, was deposed in 1461 and murdered in 1471, and the Lancastrian claim passed to Henry of Richmond, a descendant of John of Gaunt, who became king as Henry VII in 1485.

The DUCHY OF L. became a county palatine, with its own courts outside the royal jurisdiction, in 1351; these rights have been attached to the Crown since 1399. The office of Chancellor of the Duchy of L. is generally held by a member of the cabinet.

LANCASTER, Joseph (1778–1838). British educationist. B. in Southwark, he founded a school there in 1801. His method. of teaching a group of monitors who then taught the rest, was used by the Royal Lancastrian Institution (re-named the British and Foreign Schools Society in 1812), founded in 1808.

LANCASTER, Osbert (1908–). British artist. Ed. at Charterhouse and Lincoln Coll., Oxford, he went on to study at the Slade, and has produced imaginative stage settings for Old Vic and Covent Garden productions. He is popularly best known for his 'pocket' cartoons in the *Daily Express* from 1939, which introduce a series of satirically amusing characters from the Establishment, e.g. Maudie Littlehampton and Canon Fontwater.

LANCASTER. Co. town (bor.) and city of Lancs, England, on the Lune. The castle and St. Mary's church are of interest, and there is also an R.C. cathedral, completed 1859, and L. univ. (opened 1964). Cotton and rayon spinning and the manufacture of linoleum, furniture, and plastics are carried on. Pop. (1961) 48,887.

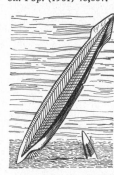

LANCELET. Animal (*Amphioxus*), sole representative of the class Cephalochordata or Leptocardia, one of the most primitive groups of the Chordata. Skull, vertebral column, centralized brain, and paired limbs are absent, but there is a notochord which runs from end to end of the body, a tail, and a number of gill-slits. L. is found in all seas; it burrows in the sand, but when disturbed swims freely. In its feeding habits it resembles the sea-squirts (Tunicata).

LANCELOT OF THE LAKE. The most celebrated of Arthur's knights, and the lover of Queen Guinevere. He was originally a folk-hero, and was introduced into the Arthurian cycle in the 12th cent.

LANCHESTER, Frederick (1868–1946). British aircraft and automobile engineer. In 1895–6 he built the first British petrol car and pub. works contributing to the development of aviation.

LANCHOW. Chinese city, cap. of Kansu prov., on the Hwang-ho, *c.* 120 m. S. of the Great Wall. An ancient walled town, it makes woollens, leather goods, cement, and chemicals, and has a large petroleum refinery started in 1956 to process oil brought by railway from the Yumen fields 500 m. N. L. is an important river, railway, and road junction, with a bridge across the river built in 1910; it has a univ. Pop. (1957 est.) 800,000.

LANCING, South. Resort in Sussex, England, on the English Channel, 3 m. E.N.E. of Worthing. To the N. is a well-known public school, St. Nicholas Coll. (often referred to as L. Coll.), founded 1848. Pop. (est.) 5,000.

LANCRET (loṅkreh'), **Nicolas** (1690–1743). French artist. B. in Paris, he was a follower of Watteau, painting graceful *fêtes galantes* and illustrating the amorous *Contes de la Fontaine*.

LANDAU (lan'dow), **Lev Davidovich** (1908–68). Russian theoretical physicist. B. in Baku, he was ed. at Leningrad univ., and in 1943 became prof. at Moscow. For his researches in the quantum theory, etc., he was awarded the Order of Lenin, and received a Nobel prize in 1962 for his theories on condensed matter, especially liquid helium.

LANDAU, Rom (1899–). British author. Originally a sculptor and art critic, he later wrote on religious subjects, subsequently becoming an expert on Islam and N. African studies and prof. at the Univ. of the Pacific 1956–67.

LANDES (loṅd), **The.** Sandy low-lying area in S.W.

France, along the Bay of Biscay, *c.* 5,000 sq. m. in extent. Formerly a furze- and heath-covered waste, it has in many parts been reclaimed by planting with pine and oak forests. It gives its name to a dept., and extends into the depts. of Gironde and Lot-et-Garonne. Arcachon is a well-known bathing resort. There is a testing range for rockets and missiles at Biscarosse, 45 m. S.W. of Bordeaux. For the oilfield in L. dept., *see* PARENTIS-EN-BORN.

LAND LEAGUE. Irish peasant organization, formed by Michael Davitt in 1879 to fight against evictions. It forced Gladstone's govt., by its skilful use of the boycott against any man who took a farm from which another had been evicted, to introduce a law in 1881 restricting rents and granting tenants security of tenure.

LANDLORD AND TENANT. The relationship which exists when an owner of land or buildings (the landlord) gives to another (the tenant) the exclusive right of occupation for a definite limited period, e.g. a year, a term of years, a week or a month. When the terms of the contract are embodied in a deed they are said to be covenants, and the whole agreement is termed a *lease*.

There was formerly freedom of contract between L. and T. in Britain, but wartime shortage of rented accommodation for lower income groups led to abuse by unscrupulous Ls. and from 1914 acts were passed affording protection for Ts. against eviction and rent increases. The shortage was aggravated by the S.W.W. and from 1939 Rent Acts were passed greatly increasing the range of dwellings so protected, but often bearing unfairly on good Ls. who were faced with increased maintenance costs, etc., and, because of inflation, a decreasing 'real' return on their investment. Extensive decontrol under the 1957 Rent Act led to hardship, and in 1965 a further act provided for security of tenure and rent control of furnished and unfurnished premises of a rateable value up to £400 per annum in London (£200 elsewhere). Later legislation tried to remedy defects and loopholes.

LANDOR, Walter Savage (1775–1864). British poet and author. B. in Warwick, he was expelled from Rugby and rusticated from Oxford owing to his uncertain temper. In 1795 he pub. his first *Poems*, followed by the epic *Gebir* (1798), and the verse drama *Count Julian* (1812). In 1808 he raised a force of volunteers to free Spain from Napoleon, and settled at Llanthony, S. Wales, in 1809–14. In 1811 he m. unhappily, and lived mainly in Italy 1814–35, when he settled in Bath until 1859. To this period belong the *Imaginary Conversations* (1824–46), *Pericles and Aspasia* (1836), *The Pentameron*, *The Hellenics* (1846–7), etc. Drawn into a libel action in 1858, he took refuge in Florence, where he d.

LANDOWSKA (landof'ska), **Wanda** (1877–1959). Polish-born harpsichordist, who settled first in France and from the S.W.W. in the U.S.A. Falla and Ravel wrote specially for her, and she estab. the reputation of the harpsichord as a contemporary instrument.

LANDRAIL. *See* RAIL.

LAND REGISTRY, H.M. State register of landowners voluntarily submitting titles to their land for examination and approval by the registrar on behalf of the State estab. in 1862. By the L.R. Act of 1897 the principle of compulsory registration was introduced, and any co. council or council of a co. bor. may apply for registration of title to be made compulsory on sale. Such registration makes the future buying or selling of land much easier and cheaper, since absolute titles granted by the L.R. (administered under the Lord Chancellor by the Chief Land Registrar) are guaranteed and lengthy examinations of title are unnecessary.

LANDSEER, Sir Edwin Henry (1802–73). British painter and sculptor. B. in London, he exhibited at the R.A. in 1815, and achieved **great** popularity with

LAND'S END. Granite cliffs thrust into the Atlantic and dangerous reefs lie close in, as well as the outer group marked by the lighthouse.   *British Travel and Holidays Association*

sentimental studies of animals, e.g. 'Dignity and Impudence'. A masterly draughtsman, he was elected R.A. in 1831 and knighted in 1850. Best known of his sculptures are the Trafalgar Square lions.

LAND'S END. A promontory of W. Cornwall, 9 m. W.S.W. of Penzance, the most westerly point of England. Its extension is a group of dangerous rocks, the Longships, a mile out, marked by a lighthouse with a light visible for 16 m.

LANDS'KRONA. Seaport of Sweden, on the Sound, 20 m. N. of Malmo. L. makes machinery, chemicals, etc., and has shipbuilding yards and sugar refineries. Charles XI defeated the Danes off L. in 1677. Pop. (1966) 31,960.

LANE, Edward William (1801–76). British orientalist. He visited Egypt 1825–8, 1833–5, and 1842–9, and pub. *Manners and Customs of the Modern Egyptian* (1836), a translation of the *Arabian Nights* (1838–40), and a monumental *Arabic-English Lexicon* (1863–92).

LANE-POOLE, Stanley (1854–1931). British numismatist, great-nephew of E. W. Lane (q.v.). B. in London, he held a post in the British Museum 1874–92, carried on archaeological research in Egypt and was prof. of Arabic at Dublin, 1897–1904. His works incl. *Egypt in the Middle Ages* (1901) and *Medieval India* (1902).

LANFRANC (lan'frangk) (c. 1005–89). Archbishop of Canterbury. B. at Pavia, he entered the monastery of Bec, Normandy, in 1042, and there opened a school which achieved international fame. His skill in theological controversy did much to secure the Church's adoption of the doctrine of transubstantiation. Appointed archbp. of Canterbury in 1070, he rebuilt the cathedral, replaced English clergy by Normans, enforced clerical celibacy, and separated the ecclesiastical from the secular courts.

LANG, Andrew (1844–1912). British author. B. at Selkirk, he went to London as a journalist in 1875. His writings include historical works, e.g. *History of Scotland* (1900–7) and *The Maid of France* (1908), a reply to Anatole France's life of Joan of Arc; anthropological essays, e.g. *Myth, Ritual and Religion* (1887) and *The Making of Religion* (1898), which involved him in controversy with Frazer; translations of Homer; verse and novels; and a series of children's books, beginning with the *Blue Fairy Tale Book* (1889).

LANG, Cosmo Gordon, 1st baron (1864–1945). British churchman. B. at Aberdeen, he was ordained in 1890. He was appointed suffragan bp. of Stepney in 1901, archbp. of York in 1908, and of Canterbury in 1928. He resigned in 1942, and was created a baron.

LANG, Fritz (1890–   ). American film producer and director, b. in Vienna. His early expressionist films, e.g. *The Niebelung Saga* (1923–4) and *Metropolis*

(1925) were made in Germany, whence he fled after his anti-dictatorial *Dr. Mabuse* (1933). In Hollywood he made *Fury* (1936), *You Only Live Once* (1937), and others with a strong sense of social realism, and after the S.W.W. worked again in Europe.

LANGE (lahn'ge), **Friedrich Albert** (1828–75). German writer on philosophy and sociology. B. at Wald, he was a schoolmaster and journalist, and in 1870 became a professor at Zürich. His best-known work is his *History of Materialism* (1866).

LANGEVIN (lonzhvan'), **Paul** (1872–1946). French physicist. A pioneer in the field of magnetic theory and the molecular structure of gases, he was prof. of general physics at the Collège de France. Arrested by the Germans as a anti-Fascist in 1940, on his release he escaped to Switzerland, returning after the liberation. *See* GRENOBLE.

LANGLAND, William (c. 1332–c. 1400) British poet. B. in the W. Midlands, possibly near Malvern, he took minor orders, and in later life settled in London. His alliterative *Vision concerning Piers Plowman* appeared in 3 versions c. 1362–c. 1398, but certain critics believe he was responsible only for the first of these. The poem forms a series of allegorical visions, in which Piers develops from the typical poor peasant to a symbol of Christ, and condemns the social and moral evils of 14th cent. England.

LANGLEY, Samuel Pierpont (1834–1906). American inventor. B. in Mass. he became professor of physics and astronomy at the Western Univ. of Pennsylvania in 1867, and sec. of the Smithsonian Institution in 1887. He carried on valuable research on the infra-red portions of the solar spectrum. In 1896 he launched a steam-driven aeroplane which flew for 90 seconds – the first flight made by an engine-equipped aircraft.

LANGMUIR, Irving (1881–1957). American scientist. Working for the General Electric Co. 1909–50, he invented the mercury vapour pump for producing high vacua and the atomic hydrogen welding process and was a pioneer of the thermionic valve. In 1932 he was awarded a Nobel prize for his work on surface chemistry.

LANGTON, Stephen (d. 1228). English churchman. B. in Lincs, he studied at Paris where he became chancellor of the univ., and in 1206 was created a cardinal. When in 1207 Innocent III secured his election as archbp. of Canterbury King John refused to recognize him, and L. was not allowed to enter England until 1213. He supported the barons in their struggle against John, and was mainly responsible for Magna Carta.

LANGTRY, Lillie (1853–1929). British actress. Greatly admired by Edward VII, she was known as 'the Jersey lily', having been born in the island.

LANGUAGES OF THE WORLD. They have been arranged, in a large number of cases, into language families on the basis of their genetic relationship, but many groupings are only tentative. Further information on the chief Ls. and L. families is to be found under their names.

Most practically important and thoroughly investigated is the Indo-European family, which comprises in the *centum* division Greek; the Italo-Celtic group (Latin, whence the Romance languages; Celtic, Gaelic, Manx, etc.); Germanic (Gothic, the North-Germanic or Scandinavian languages, and the West Germanic, including English, German, Flemish, Dutch, Afrikaans, etc.); and also Tocharian; and in the *satem* division Balto-Slavonic (Lithuanian, Russian, Polish, Slovene, Serbo-Croat, Bulgarian, etc.); Armenian Albanian; and the Indo-Iranian languages – Zend, Persian, Sanskrit, Pali, and the modern Indian languages. The Caucasian family includes Georgian and perhaps Basque. The Hamito-Semitic contains the Ethiopian tongues, Aramaic, Hebrew, Arabic with Maltese, and also Berber, Egyptian, Somali, etc.

The Finno-Ugrian family includes Finnish, Lapp, Estonian, Magyar or Hungarian. The Altaic family contains Turkish, Mongol, Manchu, etc. Eskimo and Aleut form one family, and Korean and Japanese another. In the Sinitic or Indo-Chinese family are placed Tibetan, Burmese, Chinese, Siamese, Annamese, etc. The Malayo-Polynesian family includes the languages of Malaya and the South Seas excluding New Guinea. Tamil is one of the languages in the Dravidian family. The languages of New Guinea and Papua, the Australian aborigines, the Bushmen and Hottentots, are placed in separate families. Yet other families comprise Bantu (Swahili, Zulu, etc.), Sudanian (Nuba, Ewe, Hausa, etc.), and the American (the 'Red Indian' tribes, the Maya, the Inca, etc.).

The most important languages numerically – in tens of millions of speakers – are: Chinese 70 (inclusive of Mandarin, Cantonese, etc.); English 30; Russian 18 (Great Russian only); Hindi 18; Spanish 18; German 12; Japanese 10; Bengali 10; Arabic 10; Portuguese 9; French 8; Malay 8; Italian 6.

LANIER (lanēr'), **Sidney** (1842–81). American poet. B. in Georgia, he served in the Civil War, and subsequently studied law, which he abandoned for music. His *Poems* (1877) contain some interesting metrical experiments, in accordance with his theories expounded in his *Science of English Verse* (1880), on the relation of verse to music.

LANSBURY, George (1859–1940). British Labour leader. B. in Suffolk, he worked for a time as a labourer, was a Labour M.P. 1910–12, and edited the *Daily Herald* 1912–22. He sat on Poplar borough council from 1903, and went to prison with most of the councillors in 1921 rather than modify the council's policy of more generous unemployed relief. Re-elected to parliament in 1922, he became Commissioner for Works 1929–31, and led the Labour Party in the House 1931–5. A pacifist, he resigned from the party leadership in opposition to the party's policy during the Ethiopian War.

LANSDOWNE, Henry Charles Keith Petty Fitzmaurice, 5th marquis of (1845–1927). British Cons. statesman. He was Gov.-Gen. of Canada 1883–8, Viceroy of India 1888–93, War Minister 1895–1900, and For. Sec. 1900–6; while at the Foreign Office he abandoned Britain's isolationist policy, by forming alliances with Japan and France. His publication in 1917 of proposals for a compromise peace led to a violent controversy.

LANSING. Capital of Michigan, U.S.A., at the confluence of the Grand and Red Cedar rivers. L. makes motor-vehicles, diesel engines, pumps, furniture, textiles, etc. Pop. (1960) 107,807.

LA′NTHANUM (Gk. *lanthano* to lie hidden). One of the cerium sub-group of the rare earths, it is a white metal: symbol La., at. wt. 138·92 and at. no. 57. Separated from ceria by Mosander in 1839, it occurs in nature in the cerite earths and resembles iron in its physical properties.

LAOIGHIS (lā-ish). Co. in Leinster prov., Rep. of Ireland. It is flat except for the Slieve Bloom mountains n the N.W. Sugar beet is grown and dairy farming practised. Woollens and agricultural implements are manufactured. Portlaoighise is the co. town. Area 664 sq. m.; pop. (1966) 44,595.

LAON (loń). Capital of Aisne dept., N. France, 75 m. N.E. of Paris. There is a fine 12th cent. cathedral. Pop. (1962) 27,268.

LAOS (lah′ōs). A mountainous kingdom in N.W. Indo-China, a protectorate of France 1893–1946, an associated state of the French Union from 1950 to 1954 when L. was accorded full independence. King Savang Vatthana (1908–) succeeded his father in 1959. The cap. is Vientiane.

Following the Geneva Conference agreement of 1954 establishing independence, civil war went on sporadically. The neutralist govt., headed by Prince Souvanna Phouma, negotiated the Vientiane Agreement 1957 with the Pathet Lao or Communist forces, re-named 1965 the Laotian People's Army, headed by Prince Souphanouvong, but a right-wing force, then headed by Prince Boun Oum, emerged. Further negotiations among the 'Three Princes' led to another agreement in 1962 (also not implemented). The 1967 elections confirmed Prince Souvanna Phouma in power. Intermittent warfare continued, the division of the country between Pathet Lao and govt. forces running N.W. to S.E. through its length, following approx. the cease fire line of 1962. The first of the Ho Chi-Minh Trails (q.v.) ran through the Pathet Lao section, and although branches of this were cut in 1971 by a successful S. Vietnamese thrust into L., a second trail, 60 m. W. and out of their reach, was then under construction.

LAO TZE (lah′ō-tsā′). Chinese philosopher, commonly regarded as the founder of Taoism (q.v.). Many legends gathered round him, but nothing certain is known of his life, and he is variously said to have lived in the 6th and the 4th cent. B.C. The *Tao Tê Ching*, the Taoist scripture, is attributed to him, but apparently dates from the 3rd cent. B.C.

LA PAMPA. *See under* PAMPAS.

LA PAZ (pahs′). City of Bolivia, the seat of government since c. 1900, although Sucre remains the official cap. Founded in 1548, La P. is 12,400 ft. above sea-level. It has a univ. and an airfield. Pop. (1965) 460,950.

LAPIS LAZULI (laz′ūlī) or **Lazurite.** Deep blue mineral used in inlaying and ornamental work, and in the manufacture of pigment. Chemically it consists of a sodium aluminium silicate with sodium sulphide. L.L. occurs in metamorphic limestones, and is found in Afghanistan, Siberia, Chile, and Persia.

LAPLACE (lahplahs′), **Pierre Simon,** marquis de (1749–1827). French mathematician and astronomer. B. in Normandy, he was appointed prof. of mathematics at the Paris École Militaire in 1767. He observed the motion of the moon, Jupiter, Saturn, etc., and won universal fame with his *Traité de Mécanique Céleste* (1799–1825).

LAPLAND. Region of N. Europe in Norway, Sweden, Finland and Russia without political definition. Within the Arctic Circle, L. has low temperatures, with 3 months' continuous daylight in summer

LAPLAND. For Lapps reindeer are the basis of a way of life, supplying skins for the traditional costume, still always worn on festive occasions, milk, meat, and bones and antlers to be turned into tools or tourist souvenirs. In winter they draw the *pulkka*, a boat-shaped snow sled on one runner. The man's hat, with its 4 points, is known as the Cap of the Four Winds.
Courtesy of the Finnish Travel Information Centre.

and 3 months' continuous darkness in winter. There is summer agriculture, incl. wheat, but the chief resources of L. are minerals (chromium, copper, iron, etc.), timber, hydroelectric power, and tourism. Of Mongolian stock, the true Lapps declined under successive invasions, and although now settled in special villages, form only a small proportion of the population, numbering c. 20,000. They live by hunting, fishing, reindeer herding, and handicrafts.

LA PLATA (plah'tah). Capital of Buenos Aires prov., Argentina, founded in 1882, 5½ m. from its port Ensenada. Industries incl. meat packing and petroleum refining. It has a univ. (1897). Pop. (1968) 400,000.

LA PLATA, Rio de. See PLATE, R.

LAPWING. Bird (*Vanellus vanellus*) of the plover family, so named from its slow flight. It is also known as the green plover and – from its call – as the peewit. Bottle-green above and white below, it inhabits moorland in Europe (incl. Britain) and Asia, making a nest scratched out of the ground.

LARCENY. Under the Theft Act (1968: effective 1969) the offence of L. was replaced by a wider definition of theft as the dishonest appropriation of another's property with the intention of depriving him of it permanently: maximum penalty 10 yrs. imprisonment. Until 1827 L. was divided into 'Grand L. punishable by death or transportation for life, and 'Petty L., when the articles stolen were valued under a shilling, and in the U.S.A. the distinction survives.

LARCH. Genus of trees (*Larix*) of the Coniferae family. The common L. (*L. europaea*) was introduced to Britain in the 17th cent. and grows 80–140 ft. The small needle-like leaves are replaced every year by new bright green foliage which later darkens. Closely resembling it is the tamarack (*L. americana*), and both are timber trees. The golden L. (*Pseudolarix amabilis*), a native of China, turns golden in autumn.

LARD. An edible fat prepared from the abdomen of pigs, but nowadays the term covers the whole body-fat of the pig. It is used in the manufacture of margarine, soap and ointment. Lard-oil, a clear, colourless liquid, is used for lubrication.

LARDNER, Ring (1885–1933). American short-story writer. A sporting correspondent, he based his characters on the people he met professionally and his collected vols. of short stories incl. his first *You Know Me, Al* (1916), *Round Up* (1929) and *Ring Lardner's Best Short Stories* (1938), all in a lively argot.

LA'RES. Roman household gods peculiar to each amily, and whose shrine was the centre of family worship.

LARISA (lahrēs'ah). Greek town, cap. of L. dept., Thessaly. In ancient Greece it was the seat of the Council of Thessaly. Pop. (1961) 55,733.

LARK. Songbird (*Alauda arvensis*) found in the northern hemisphere, and migrating south in winter. It is about 7 in. long, with light brown plumage, and nests on the ground. It mounts in the air almost vertically and sings as it rises.

LARKIN, Philip (1922–). British poet. Ed. at St. John's Coll., Oxford, he gained success in 1955 with his vol. of poems, *The Less Deceived*, remarkable for their clarity and sensitivity. His other works incl. his first book of verse *The North Ship* (1945), and the novels, *Jill* (1946) and *A Girl in Winter* (1947).

LARKSPUR. See DELPHINIUM.

LARNE. Seaport (bor.) of co. Antrim, N. Ireland, on Lough L., terminus of sea routes to Stranraer, Liverpool Dublin, etc. Pop. (1961) 16,313.

LA ROCHEFOUCAULD (rōshfookō), **François,** duc de (1613–80). French writer. B. in Paris, he became a soldier, and took part in the *Fronde*. His later years were divided between the court and literary society. His best-known work is his *Réflexions, ou Sentences et Maximes Morales* (1665), a collection of brief, epigrammatic and cynical observations on life and society.

LA ROCHELLE. See ROCHELLE, LA.

LAROUSSE (lahroos'), **Pierre** (1817–75). French grammarian and lexicographer. His *Grand Diction-naire universel du XIXᵉ siècle* (1865–76) was an epoch-making achievement and continues in subsequent revisions.

LARVA. The first form of an insect as it emerges from the egg, as a grub, maggot, or caterpillar. It differs considerably from the adult insect which appears after metamorphosis.

LARYNGITIS (larinji'tis). Inflammation of the lining membrane of the larynx (q.v.). The acute form is due to a cold, excessive use of the voice, inhalation of irritating smoke, etc. The voice may be completely lost. With rest the inflammation usually subsides in a few days.

LARYNX. A cavity at the upper end of the windpipe containing the vocal cords, by which sounds are produced. It is stiffened with cartilage and lined with mucous membrane.

LA SALLE (sahl'), **René Robert Cavelier,** Sieur de (1643–87). French explorer. B. at Rouen, he undertook 1670–83 a number of journeys which led to the discovery of Lakes Ontario and Erie and of the Ohio and the Mississippi. He annexed Louisiana and Illinois to the Crown of France, but during a final expedition was killed by his own men in Texas.

LASCAR. An E. Indian seaman. The word derives from the Persian *lashkar*, 'army', 'camp', and Ls. were originally an inferior class of sepoy.

LAS CASAS (lahs-kah'sahs), **Bartolomé de** (1474–1566). Spanish priest, the 'apostle of the Indians'. B. in Seville, he took R.C. orders in 1510, and sailed for the Spanish colonies in America, where he opposed the ill-treatment and enslavement of the native Indians, and in 1530 persuaded the government to forbid slavery in Peru. He also laboured as a missionary, his *Historia de las Indias* (1875–6) was never completed.

LAS CASES (lahs-kahz'), **Emmanuel Augustin Dieudonné Marin Joseph,** count of (1766–1842). French historian. B. in Languedoc, he was driven from France by the Revolution, but later held office under Napoleon, and accompanied him to St. Helena: expelled by the English governor in 1816, he pub. the controversial *Mémorial de Ste. Hélène* (1821–3).

LASCAUX (lahskō) **CAVES.** Series of caverns near Montignac, in S.W. France, discovered by chance by 4 boys in 1940. They contain many paintings of the Aurignacian period, especially of animals and hunting scenes; the oldest, which are the oldest paintings known, date probably 20,000 years back.

LA'SDUN, Denys (1914–). British architect. Ed. at Rugby, he has a versatile distinction in his work which incl. the Peter Robinson store in the Strand, the Royal Coll. of Physicians in Regent's Park, science buildings for Cambridge, part of the Univ. of Leicester and the complete development of the new Univ. of E. Anglia. In 1963 he was appointed architect for the National Theatre and Opera House on the South Bank.

LA'SER. Acronym for Light Amplification by Stimulated Emission of Radiation. Device for producing a narrow highly parallel beam of light, capable of travelling over vast distances without dispersion, and of being focused to give enormous power densities (10^8 watts per cm² for high-energy Ls.) and operating on a principle similar to that of the maser, q.v.

Many solid liquid and gaseous substances have been

used for L. materials incl. synthetic ruby crystal (used
for the first extraction of L. light in 1960 and giving a
high-power pulsed output) and a helium-neon gas
mixture, capable of continuous operation, but at a
lower power. In 1962 a L. was used to throw light at
the moon's surface, a reflection being detected 2½ sec.
later (Massachusetts Inst. of Tech.).

Some potential uses of Ls. are as flash bulbs in
high-speed photography, for communications (a L.
beam can carry much more information than present
radio waves), for cutting, drilling, welding, more
accurate radar, satellite tracking, and in medical and
biological research. In espionage, sound wave vibrations from the window glass of a room can be picked
up by reflected laser beam, extracted by a receiver
within horizon distance, and amplified. Believed to
be in the experimental stage, are X-ray Ls. which
would be incredibly destructive and render all types
of conventional weapon and defence obsolete.

LASHIO. Town in the Shan State, Burma, c. 125 m.
N.E. of Mandalay, with which it is linked by rail. L.
is linked by the Burma Road, constructed in 1938,
with Kunming in China.

LA'SKI, Harold (1893–1950). British political
theorist. Prof. of political science at the London
School of Economics from 1926, he taught a modified
Marxism, and pub. *A Grammar of Politics* (1925),
Liberty in the Modern State (1930) and *The American
Presidency* (1940). He was chairman of the Labour
Party 1945–6.

LASKI, Marghanita (1915–   ). British writer. She
was ed. in Manchester and at Oxford (reading
English); her first book was *Love on the Supertax*
(1944); later work incl. *Little Boy Lost* (1949), *The
Victorian Chaise Longue* (1953) and the play *The
Offshore Island* (1957). She is the niece of Harold L.
(q.v.).

LA SPEZIA. *See* SPEZIA, LA.

LASSALLE (lahsahl'), **Ferdinand** (1825–64). German Socialist. He took part in the 1848 revolution,
during which he met Marx, and in 1863 founded
the General Association of German Workers (later
the Social-Democratic Party). Besides carrying on a
tireless propaganda of speeches and pamphlets, he
secretly intrigued with Bismarck. He was killed in
a duel arising from a love-affair.

LASSUS, Orlande de (c. 1530–94). Flemish composer. B. at Mons, he pub. his first book of motets in
1556. Soon after he settled permanently in Munich.
His compositions include many songs and madrigals,
among them settings of poems by his friend Ronsard.

DENYS LASDUN. In a television interview Denys Lasdun
explains his approach. In the background is the plan for the
Royal College of Physicians, Regent's Park.
Courtesy of Granada Television.

LAS VEGAS. Night falls on the city of gamblers where pin
tables and fruit machines invade even the shops and railway
station. In the luxurious clubs roulette, baccarat, poker and
dice are the main forms of gambling. The name of the city,
ironically, means 'The Meadows'.   *Photo: Paul Popper Ltd.*

LAS VEGAS (lahs vāg'ahs). City of Nevada,
U.S.A., which has mushroomed since the S.W.W.
from a pop. (1941) 16,000 to (1960) 64,405, with est.
2,000,000 tourist visitors annually. It is the centre of
a vast recreation area, but is better known for its
nightclubs where performers are paid fabulous sums,
and for its gambling casinos in Fremont Street and
the 'Strip' outside the city.

LÁSZLÓ (lahs'lō) **(de Lombos), Sir Philip** (1869–
1937). British artist. B. in Budapest, he settled in
England in 1907, and was naturalized in 1914. He
was noted for his portraits, e.g. Edward VII and
Theodore Roosevelt.

LATAKIA. *See* LATTAKIA.

LATENT HEAT. Term first used by Joseph Black
(c. 1760) for the heat which changes the state of a
substance (e.g. in melting or vaporization) without
changing the temperature.

LATERAN CHURCH OF ST. JOHN The Pope's
cathedral as bishop of Rome. Little remains of the
ancient basilica built by Constantine, c. 324.

LATERAN TREATY. The treaty between the
Italian govt. under Mussolini and the Pope signed in
the L. Palace in 1929. Under it the Pope resigned all
claims to the former papal territories; the Vatican
City was recognized as an independent sovereign
state; and a concordat between Church and State
recognized Catholicism as the state religion of Italy
and made R.C. teaching compulsory in Italian schools.
This treaty was incorporated in the constitution of the
Italian rep. in 1947.

LATERITE (Lat. *later*, brick). A residual weathering product of basalts, granites and shales, forming
a clay-like rock impregnated with ferric hydroxide.
It is usually soft and friable, occurring in the
tropics.

LATEX. A lactiferous fluid of angiospermous
plants, an emulsion of various substances. It circulates longitudinally in branched tubes conducting
plastic substances and acting as reservoir. L. is exuded
from the Para rubber tree and worked into rubber.
Coagulation is prevented by ammonia or formaldehyde.

LATIMER, Hugh (c. 1490–1555). English Protestant reformer. After his conversion to Protestantism in 1524 he was several times imprisoned, but
was protected by Wolsey and Henry VIII. He was
appointed bp. of Worcester in 1535, but resigned in
1539. Under Edward VI his sermons denouncing
social injustice won him great influence. He was
arrested for heresy in 1553, and burned at Oxford.

LATIN. The language spoken by the Romans, and
the parent of the Romance languages, e.g. Italian,

French, Spanish, and Portuguese. As Lat. literature had an influence on all subsequent European civilization, L., even beyond the Middle Ages, remained for long as the vehicle for learned works; it is still the official language of the R.C. Church. The striking merits of L. are its clarity and conciseness. Like Greek it is a highly inflected language, i.e. the grammatical functions of nouns, verbs, pronouns, and adjectives in a sentence is indicated by terminations which vary according to the meaning.

L. was not native to Italy. It was brought there about 1000 B.C. by wandering tribes from the N. who settled in Latium near the mouth of the Tiber. With the growing power of Rome it spread throughout Italy, and other competing languages gradually disappeared (e.g. Oscan, Umbrian, Etruscan). The conquest of Spain and Gaul extended the use and influence of L. outside Italy, but the Roman hold on Britain (A.D. 43–A.D. 410) was not firm enough to submerge completely the Celtic speech of the islanders.

From the 3rd cent A.D. there has to be distinction between the literary or standard Latin used in speaking and writing by educated people, and the forms, generally known as Low or Vulgar L., spoken by ordinary people in the different parts of the western half of the Empire. A number of *patois* grew from the latter, and slowly became stabilized as the Romance languages.

LATIN AMERICA. The countries of S. and Central America (incl. Mexico) in which Spanish, Portuguese, and French are spoken. The L.A. Free Trade Association (1961: H.Q. Montevideo) links Argentina, Brazil, Chile, Colombia, Ecuador, Mexico, Paraguay, Peru, Uruguay, and Venezuela.

LATIN LITERATURE. Only a few hymns and inscriptions survive from the primitive period of L.L., before the 3rd cent. B.C. Greek influence began with the work of Livius Andronicus (c. 284–204 B.C.) who translated the *Odyssey* and Greek plays into Latin. Naevius and Ennius both attempted epics on patriotic themes; the former used the native 'Saturnian' metre, but the latter introduced the Greek hexameter. Plautus and Terence successfully adapted Greek comedy to the Latin stage. Lucilius (180–103 B.C.) founded Latin verse satire, while the writings of Cato were the first important works in Latin prose.

In the *De Rerum Natura* of Lucretius, the world's greatest philosophical poem, and the passionate lyrics of Catullus, Latin verse reached maturity. Cicero set a standard for Latin prose, in his orations, his philosophical essays, and his letters. To the same period belong the histories of Caesar.

The Augustan Age (43 B.C.–A.D. 17) is usually regarded as the golden age of L.L. There is a strong patriotic feeling in the work of the poets Virgil and Horace, and the historian Livy, who belonged to Augustus's immediate circle. Virgil produced the one great Latin epic in the *Aeneid*, while Horace brought a distinctive charm and polish to both the lyric and satire. Younger poets of the period were Ovid and the elegiac poets Tibullus and Propertius.

The 'Silver Age' of the Empire begins with the writers of Nero's reign: the Stoic philosopher Seneca, Lucan, author of the epic *Pharsalia*, the satirist Persius (A.D. 34–62), and, by far the greatest, the realistic novelist Petronius. At the end of the 1st and beginning of the 2nd cent. came 2 major writers, the historian Tacitus and the satirist Juvenal; other writers of the period were the epigrammatist Martial, the scientist Pliny the Elder, the letter-writer Pliny the Younger, the critic Quintilian, the historian Suetonius, and the epic poet Statius (c. 61–96).

The 2nd and 3rd cents. produced only one pagan writer of importance, the romancer Apuleius, but there were several able Christian writers, such as Tertullian, Cyprian, Arnobius (d. 327), and Lactantius (d. 325). In the 4th cent. there was something of a poetic revival, with Ausonius (c. 310–90) and Claudian, and the Christian poets Prudentius (c. 348–410) and St. Ambrose. The classical period ends, and the Middle Ages begin, with St. Jerome's translation of the Bible, and St. Augustine's *City of God*.

Throughout the Middle Ages Latin remained the language of the Church, and was normally employed for theology, philosophy, histories, and other learned works. Latin verse, adapted to rhyme and non-classical metres, was used both for hymns and the secular songs of the wandering scholars. Even after the Reformation Latin retained its prestige as the international language of scholars, and was used as such, e.g. by More, Bacon, and Milton.

LATITUDE and LONGITUDE. Latitude is the angular distance of any point from the equator, measured N. or S. along the earth's curved surface, equalling the angle between the respective horizontal planes. It is measured in degrees, minutes, and seconds, each minute equalling one sea-mile in length. For map-making latitude is based on the supposition that the earth is an oblate spheroid. The difference between this (the geographical) and astronomical latitude is the correction necessary for local deviation of plumb-line.

Longitude is the angle between the terrestrial meridian drawn from the pole, through a place, and a standard meridian now taken at Greenwich. All determinations of longitude are based on the earth turning through 360° in 24 hours, or the sun reaching 15° W. each hour.

LATITUDINARIANS. Name applied to those Anglican divines, e.g. Tillotson and Stillingfleet, who after 1660 regarded episcopal govt. and forms of worship as things indifferent, and favoured modifications to reconcile Dissenters to the Church.

LATIUM. Ancient division of central Italy, originally the territory of the Latinii. The modern Italian region of L. covers the provs. of Viterbo, Rieti, Rome, Frosinone, and Latina. Area 6,630 sq. m.; pop. (1961) 3,922,783; cap. Rome.

LATOUR (lahtoor'), **Georges de** (1593–1652). French artist. His name was unknown until discovered by an art historian in 1863 and in the 20th cent. nos. of pictures attributed to others were identified as his. He served as court painter to the king and to the duke of Lorraine, and is especially noted for his 'night' style using the light of shielded candles, etc.

LATTAKIA. Port in Syria, c. 70 m. E. of Cape Andreas, Cyprus, cap. of L. district. It trades in olive oil, sponges, and locally grown tobacco. A Phoenician city, it was the Roman Laodicea ad Mare. The Crusaders took it from the Byzantine Empire in 1103, and Saladin captured it in 1188. Pop. (1960) 67,600.

LATTER-DAY SAINTS. See MORMONS.

LATVIA. An S.S.R. of the U.S.S.R. It lies on the Baltic between Lithuania to the S., and Estonia to the N. L. is low-lying and watered by many rivers, e.g. the Daugava, and there are numerous lakes. Formerly dependent on agriculture and forestry, L. has become predominantly industrial since the S.W.W. and produces electric railway rolling stock, telephone equipment and radios, steel and rolled metal, fertilizers, paper, textiles, and cement. Riga is the cap.

Before the F.W.W. L. formed part of the Russian Empire, but in Nov. 1918 it was proclaimed an independent rep., recognized by Russia in 1920. In 1939 Russia demanded military bases, granted in a pact of mutual assistance; 1940 brought demands for free passage of Russian troops and the formation of a govt. friendly to the Soviet Union, in which 2 months later L. was incorporated as a constituent rep. It was in German occupation 1941–4, the last Germans in the country not surrendering until May 1945. Area 25,000 sq. m.; pop. (1968) 2,298,000.

LATVIAN or **Lettic.** One of the 2 surviving members of the Baltic branch of the Indo-European family, the other being Lithuanian. L. is known from 1585.

LAUD (lawd), **William** (1573–1645). English churchman. As archbp. of Canterbury from 1633, his High Church policy, his support for Charles I's unparliamentary rule, his censorship of the press, and his persecution of the Puritans all aroused bitter opposition, while his strict enforcement of the statutes against enclosures and of laws regulating wages and prices alienated the propertied classes. His attempt to impose the use of the Prayer Book on the Scots provoked a revolt which precipitated the English Revolution. Impeached by parliament in 1640 he was imprisoned in the Tower, condemned to death by a bill of attainder, and beheaded.

LAUDANUM (lawd'num). A solution of opium in alcohol (tincture).

LAUDER (law'der), **Sir Henry (Harry)** (1870–1950). Scots comedian. At first a mill worker and miner, he made his reputation with comic songs of his own composition such as 'Stop Yer Ticklin' Jock', and 'I Love a Lassie'.

LAUDER. Royal burgh in Berwickshire, Scotland, 23 m. S.E. of Edinburgh. It was at L. that Archibald Douglas, 5th earl of Angus, in 1482 seized and hanged the earl of Mar and other favourites of James III, thus earning his nickname of Archibald Bell-the-Cat. Pop. (1961) 597.

LAUDERDALE, John Maitland, duke of (1616–82). Scottish statesman. Formerly a zealous Covenanter, he joined the Royalists in 1647, and as High Commissioner for Scotland 1667–79 persecuted the Covenanters. He was created duke of L. in 1672.

LAUE (low-e), **Max Theodor Felix von** (1879–1960). German physicist. He was a pioneer in measuring the wavelength of X-rays by their diffraction through the closely spaced atoms in a crystal, leading to the powerful technique now used to elucidate the structure of complex biological materials, e.g. DNA (q.v.). Awarded Nobel prize 1914. *See* GRENOBLE.

LAUGHING JACKASS. Australian bird (*Dacelo gigas*), similar to a kingfisher, but feeding on insects and reptiles. The name is derived from its cry, but in Australia it is generally known as the Kookaburra.

LAUGHTON (law'ton), **Charles** (1899–1962). Anglo-American character actor. B. in Scarborough, he made his début in 1926, but devoted himself largely to film work from 1932. His most famous films were *The Sign of the Cross, The Private Life of Henry VIII, Mutiny on the Bounty* and *Rembrandt*. He m. the actress Elsa Lanchester (1902–   ) and both became U.S. citizens in 1950.

LAUNCESTON (lahn'ston). (1) English town (bor.) in Cornwall, 21 m. N.W. of Plymouth. There

LATVIA. The Komsomolskaya Embankment in Riga
Photo: Novosti Press Agency.

LAVA. Striking lava ormations at Höfdi in the south-east corner of Lake Myvatn, Iceland, nearly 1,000 ft. above sea-level. Elsewhere in the lake there are red and yellow sulphur springs.
Courtesy of Iceland Tourist Information Bureau.

are ruins of a Norman castle, besieged in the Civil War. Pop. (1961) 4,518. (2) Port in N.E. Tasmania, Australia, on the Tamar, founded 1805. Its industries incl. saw milling, engineering, furniture and pottery making; Tasmania's railway workshops are at L. Pop. (1966) 60,450.

LAURACEAE. A family of dicotyledonous plants containing over 1,000 species. They are evergreen and mostly aromatic. Two of the chief genera are *Cinnamomum* and *Laurus*.

LAURASIA. *See* WEGENER.

LAUREL. Name given to the bay (q.v.) and to evergreen species of the genus *Prunus* in the family Rosaceae, notably the common cherry L. (*P. laurocerasus*), introduced to Europe from Asiatic Turkey in the 16th cent., and a popular ornamental shrub in N. America and Britain. The leaves are either dark green or variegated with yellow, and the small flowers are followed by red berries: the whole plant is poisonous, containing hydrocyanic acid.

LAURENCIN (lorensin'), **Marie** (1885–1956). French artist. Working in her native Paris, she produced sensitively delicate portraits and theatrical decors, e.g. for Diaghilev's Russian Ballet in 1924.

LAURIER (lō'riā), **Sir Wilfrid** (1841–1919). Canadian statesman. B. near Montreal, he entered the Quebec legislature in 1871, and the Ottawa parliament in 1874, and became leader of the Liberal Party in 1887. As P.M. 1896–1911 – the first French-Canadian to hold the office – he supported imperial preference and the building of Canadian warships to co-operate with the British Navy, and sent Canadian troops to serve in the S. African War. He received the G.C.B. in 1897.

LAUSANNE (lōzahn'). Cap. of Vaud canton, Switzerland, above the N. shore of Lake Geneva. The opening of the Simplon railway tunnel in 1906 made L. an important point on the Paris-to-Milan main line. The cathedral church was consecrated in 1275, and L. univ. originated with an academy estab. 1537. At L. was signed in 1923 the peace treaty between Turkey and the Allies. Pop. (1960) 126,328.

LAVA. The molten substance emitted from a volcanic crater. Basic L. containing less silica than acid L., it flows greater distances, taking longer to solidify.

LAVAL, Pierre (1883–1945). French politician. B. near Vichy, he entered the Chamber of Deputies in 1914 as a Socialist, but after the F.W.W. moved towards the right. He was P.M. and For. Sec. in 1931–2, and again in 1935–6, his second period of office being marked by the Hoare-L. agreement for concessions to Italy in Abyssinia. He joined Pétain's govt. as Vice-Premier in June 1940; dismissed in Dec., he was reinstated by Hitler's orders as head of the govt. and For. Min. in 1942. His share in the deportation of French labour to Germany made him universally hated. On the Allied invasion he fled the country, but was arrested in Austria, tried for treason, and shot after trying to poison himself.

LA VALLIÈRE (lah vahlyār'), **Louise de La Baume Le Blanc**, duchesse de (1644–1710). Mistress of Louis XIV from 1661, to whom she bore 4 children. Created a duchess in 1664, she retired to a convent in 1674 when superseded by Mme de Montespan: she was slightly lame and had a sweetly winning personality.

LAVATER (lah'vahter), **Johann Kaspar** (1741–1801). Swiss writer. B. in Zürich, where he became a pastor, he is remembered mainly for his work on physiognomy, *Physiognomische Fragmente* (1775–8).

LA VENDÉE. See VENDÉE, LA.

LAVENDER. Sweet-smelling herb of the Labiatae family, genus *Lavandula*, a native of the western Mediterranean countries. The bush (*L. vera*) is low-growing with long, narrow, erect leaves of a silver-green colour. The flowers (borne on a terminal spike) vary in colour from lilac to deep purple, and are covered with small fragrant oil glands. The oil is extensively used in pharmacy and perfumes.

LĀ'VER, **James** (1899–). British art expert, noted for his studies of fashion and costume, and keeper of the depts. of engraving, illustration, design and paintings at the Victoria and Albert Museum 1938–59.

LAVOISIER (lahvwahzyā'), **Antoine Laurent** (1743–94). French chemist. B. in Paris, he was appointed a farmer-general of taxes in 1769, and director of the govt. gunpowder factory in 1775, and received other important appointments. During the Revolution he was arrested with the other farmers-general, who were hated for their extortions, and guillotined. Although he carried on useful research on meteorology and agriculture, his greatest contribution was the overthrow of the phlogiston theory (a weightless 'fire element' liberated during combustion), which had stifled the development of chemistry for over a century. He showed in 1772 that burned sulphur and phosphorus increased in wt. because they absorbed 'air', and later, in burning metals, that only a part of 'common air' was consumed, which he called oxygen (Priestley's dephlogisticated air); the non-vital air, or nitrogen, being left behind. With Laplace he showed that water was a compound of oxygen and hydrogen, and founded on his oxygen theory the basic rules of chemical combination which survive to this day.

LAW, **Andrew Bonar** (1858–1923). British Cons. statesman. B. in New Brunswick, he made a fortune in Scotland as a banker and iron-merchant, and entered parliament in 1900. Elected leader of the Opposition in 1911, he became Colonial Secretary in Asquith's coalition govt. 1915–16, and was Chancellor of the Exchequer 1916–19, and Lord Privy Seal 1919–21, in the Lloyd George coalition. He formed a Conservative cabinet in 1922, but resigned on health grounds in 1923.

LAW, **William** (1686–1761). English churchman. His Jacobite opinions caused him to lose his fellowship at Emmanuel Coll., Cambridge, in 1714, and later he became tutor in the household of Edward Gibbon, the grandfather of the historian, at Putney. After 1740 he lived in retirement at his birthplace, King's Cliff, Northants. His most famous work is *A Serious Call to a Devout and Holy Life* (1728), which influenced the Wesleys.

LAW. The body of rules and principles by which justice is administered in a state. The 2 main systems of European L. are Roman L. and English L. (qq.v.). English L. is (1) Common L., (2) Statute L. Common L. is unwritten and might be described as the basic code of justice necessary to any community. Statute L.

consists of the specific Acts of Parliament enacted from time to time to regulate particular matters. *See* INTERNATIONAL LAW.

LAW COURTS. At the head of the English legal system stands the House of Lords, which hears appeals in both civil and criminal cases. Below it, under the Courts Act (1971) are the Supreme Court of Judicature as the Court of Appeal (civil and criminal) and the High Court of Justice (civil), comprising the Chancery, Queen's Bench and Family Divisions. Equal in status with the High Court, under the Industrial Relations Act (1971) is the Nat. Industrial Relations Court. All criminal work not covered by the magistrates' courts was, under the new act, to be handled by the Crown Courts, organised in 6 circuits. The former assizes and quarter sessions, were to be abolished, and the criminal jurisdiction of the Central Criminal Court (Old Bailey) and the Liverpool and Manchester Crown Courts would also be absorbed. Cases would be allocated according to gravity among High Court and Circuit judges and Recorders (part-time judges with the same jurisdiction as Circuit judges). Solicitors were to be allowed to appear in and conduct cases in the Crown Courts, and solicitors as well as barristers of 10 yrs. standing became eligible for appointment as Recorders, who after 5 yrs. become eligible as Circuit judges.

County Courts (minor civil cases) would not be merged with the High Court, but would be served by Circuit judges. Minor criminal cases are heard by lay justices of the peace, exercising summary jurisdiction in petty sessions, or in London and certain larger provincial towns by stipendiary and metropolitan stipendiary magistrates.

At the head of the federal judiciary in the U.S.A. is the Supreme Court which also hears appeals from the inferior federal courts and from the decisions of the highest courts of the states. The U.S. Courts of Appeals – organized in circuits – deal with appeals from the U.S. District Courts in which civil and criminal cases are heard. State Courts deal with civil and criminal cases involving state laws, the lowest being those of the justices of the peace, etc.

LAWES, **Henry** (1596–1662). English composer. B. in Wilts, he became a gentleman of the Chapel Royal, pub. 3 collections of *Ayres and Dialogues* (1653–8), and wrote the music for Milton's *Comus* (1634).

LAWES, **Sir John Bennet** (1814–1900). British agriculturist. B. at Rothamsted, he produced 'superphosphate', the earliest patent manure in 1842, and in 1899 estab. the Lawes Agricultural Trust to supervise the work of the Rothamsted experimental station. He worked in collaboration with Sir Joseph Gilbert.

LAWLER, **Ray** (1911–). Australian playwright. B. in Melbourne, he became a factory hand at 13, then an actor. His play *The Summer of the 17th Doll* (1957) dealt with sugar cane-cutters on leave after the season's work and the passing of one man's physical supremacy: it was successful also abroad.

LAWLESS, **Emily** (1845–1913). Irish writer. B. in Ireland, the dau. of Lord Cloncurry, she wrote the novels *Hurrish* (1886) and *Grania* (1892), historical stories, and poems, *With the Wild Geese*.

LAW LORDS. The 9 Lords of Appeal in Ordinary, who, in England, together with the Lord Chancellor and other peers, make up the House of Lords in its judicial capacity. The L. L., who must have held judicial office or practised at the Bar for 15 years, hold the rank of baron. but their titles are not hereditary. They may now be 10 in number, and are never fewer than 7.

LAWN TENNIS. A racket-and-ball game invented in 1874 in England, and played on a level court. *See* diagram. The lively inflated rubber ball is about 2½ in. diam. and 2 oz. weight, and the racket about 27 in. long, with an oval head tightly strung with gut or nylon. The object of the game, which is called

L.T. on whatever surface it is played, is to hit the ball into the opponent's area in such a way that he cannot return it to the player's area. The court is divided along its length, and each point is started by one player (standing behind the base line, alternately on the left and right of his own area) serving the ball with a powerful overhead shot into a restricted part of the opponent's court diagonally opposite. The server is allowed 1 failure. The opponent must return the ball, after the first bounce, to any part of the server's area of the court, when play continues on both entire areas until the point is decided, the ball being played after

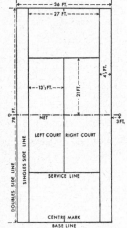

LAWN TENNIS COURT

the first bounce or volleyed in the air. The game is won by the first player to win 4 points (called 15, 30, 40, game) unless both players reach 40 (*deuce*) when a player needs 2 consecutive points to win. A *set* goes to the player who wins 6 games, but with a deuce provision at 5 all; and a match is 2 out of 3, or 3 out of 5 sets. A highly specialized sport, fostered by national and international bodies, in which Australian and American players predominate, its competition events incl. the Davis Cup (donated 1900) for international competition among men and the Wightman Cup (1923) for U.S. and U.K. women's teams. Formerly amateur, but professional from 1968, are The All England Championships at Wimbledon whose winners have incl., in the men's singles, F. J. Perry (1934–6). L. A. Hoad (1956–7), R. A. Laver (1961–2, 1968–9) and Roy Emerson (1964–5); and in the women's singles, Mrs. Wills Moody (1927–30, 1932–3, 1935, 1938), Miss Louise Brough (1948–50, 1955), Miss Maureen Connolly (1952–5), Miss M. E. Bueno (1959–60, 1964), Miss M. Smith (1963, 1965), Mrs. Billie-Jean King (1966–7, 1968), and Ann Jones (1969). *See* LENGLEN, SUZANNE.

LAWRENCE, St. (d. 258). Christian martyr. B. probably in Spain he became a deacon of Rome under Sixtus II, and when summoned to deliver the treasures of the Church displayed the beggars in his charge, for which he was broiled on a grid-iron.

LAWRENCE, David Herbert (1885–1930). British novelist and poet. B. in Notts, the son of a miner, he studied at Nottingham univ., and became a teacher. His earliest novel, *The White Peacock*, appeared in 1911, but he first attracted attention with the semi-autobiographical *Sons and Lovers* (1913). In 1914 he m. Frieda von Richthofen, who is the model for Ursula Brangwen in *The Rainbow* (1915), which was suppressed for obscenity, and in its sequel *Women in Love* (1921). His later years were largely spent in travel in Italy, Australia and Mexico, partly in search of health, partly in the hope of finding peace in a less

D. H. LAWRENCE

complex and materialistic society. His travels inspired the novels *Aaron's Rod* (1922), *Kangaroo* (1923), and *The Plumed Serpent* (1926), as well as *Etruscan Places* (1927–8), and other travel books. *Lady Chatterley's Lover* (1928) gave rise to a long controversy, and the unexpurgated edition was banned as obscene in the U.K. until 1960. It expresses rather crudely L.'s dominating conviction that emotion and the sexual impulse are creative and true to human nature, and therefore of paramount importance in our increasingly sterile and cerebral society. His philosophy and writing, often irrational and of uneven quality, are shown at their best in his poems, and short stories, e.g. 'The Woman Who Rode Away' (1926). L. d. of consumption near Nice.

LAWRENCE, Ernest O(rlando) (1901–58). American physicist. During his long period in California, he was prof. of physics from 1930 and director of the Radiation Laboratory from 1936, which he built up into a large, brilliant school for research in nuclear physics. His invention of the cyclotron pioneered the production of artificial radio-isotopes, and led to many new fields of investigation. He was awarded the Nobel prize in 1939.

LAWRENCE, Gertrude (1898–1952). English actress. B. in London, of Danish extraction, she estab. her reputation in the 1920s as a sophisticated stylist in revue and musical comedy. In later years she played mainly in New York. Her greatest success was *Private Lives* (1930–1) written specially for her by Noël Coward.

LAWRENCE, Sir Henry Montgomery (1806–57). British soldier. B. in Ceylon, the brother of John L., he entered the Bengal Artillery in 1823, and served in the Burmese War 1824–6 and the Afghan War, 1842. On the outbreak of the Mutiny he took charge at Lucknow and organized the defence of the residency, but was killed early in the siege.

LAWRENCE, John Laird Mair, 1st baron (1811–79). Viceroy of India. B. in Yorks, he began his Indian career in 1830, and in 1853 became chief commissioner for the Punjab. During the Mutiny he disarmed the mutinous troops in his area, and was largely responsible for the recapture of Delhi, and was viceroy of India 1864–9.

LAWRENCE, Sir Thomas (1769–1830). British painter. B. at Bristol, the son of an innkeeper, he entered the R.A. schools in 1787, and was elected R.A. in 1794, and P.R.A. in 1820. He succeeded Reynolds as principal painter to the king in 1792, and was knighted in 1815. He painted portraits of many of his famous contemporaries, incl. the series of pictures of Allied sovereigns and statesmen in Windsor Castle.

LAWRENCE, Thomas Edward (1888–1935). British soldier, known as 'Lawrence of Arabia'. B. in Wales, he studied at Oxford, and during 1910–14 took part in archaeological expeditions to Syria and Mesopotamia. Appointed to the military intelligence department in Cairo, he took part in negotiations for an Arab revolt against the Turks, and in 1916 attached himself to the Emir Faisal. He showed himself a guerrilla leader of genius, combining raids on Turkish communications with the stirring up of revolt among the Arabs. He joined the R.A.F. in 1922 as an aircraftman under the name Ross, transferring to the tank corps under the name T. E. Shaw in 1923 when his identity became known, then returning to the R.A.F. in 1925. He adopted the name Shaw by deed poll in

T E. LAWRENCE
Courtesy of Tate Gallery.

1927. In 1935 he was killed in a motor-cycling accident. His account of the Arab revolt, *Seven Pillars of Wisdom*, was pub. privately in 1926, was abridged as *Revolt in the Desert* (1927), and appeared in a public edition after his death in 1935. Richard Aldington's *Lawrence of Arabia: A Fictional Inquiry* (1955) only temporarily endangered L.'s reputation, but Lawrence's *The Mint* (pub. in a limited edition in 1936 and publicly in 1955) was a crude account of life in the ranks which caused much disappointment.

LAWRENCE. City of Kansas, U.S.A., seat of Kansas univ., opened 1866, and of Haskell Institute, largest Indian school in the U.S.A., opened 1884. L. has flour and paper mills, foundries, etc., and an army ordnance works. It was founded in 1854 by the New England Emigrant Aid Society, identified with the anti-slavery party. Pop. (1960) 32,858.

LAWRENCE. Town in Mass., U.S.A., established in 1845 to utilize power from the Merrimack Rapids on a site first settled in 1655. It makes woollens and other textiles, clothing, paper, radio equipment, etc. Pop. (1960) 70,933.

LA'XNESS, Halldor Kiljan (1902–). Icelandic author. B. in Reykjavik, the son of a roadmender, he deals in such books as *The Great Weaver of Cashmere* (1927) and *Happy Warriors* (1956) with Icelandic life in the epic narrative manner of the early sagas, and in 1955 was awarded a Nobel prize.

LAYAMON (fl. 1200). English poet. A priest of Arley Regis, Worcs. he wrote the *Brut*, a chronicle of *c.* 30,000 alliterative lines on the history of Britain from the legendary Brutus onwards, which gives the earliest version of the Arthurian story in English.

LA'YARD, Sir Austen Henry (1817–94). British diplomatist and archaeologist. B. in Paris, he travelled to the Middle East in 1839, conducted 2 expeditions to Nineveh and Babylon, 1845–51, and sent to England the specimens forming the greater part of the collection of Assyrian antiquities in the British Museum.

LAYE, Evelyn (1900–). British musical-comedy star. B. in London, she played in *Bitter Sweet* (London and N.Y., 1929–30), and has also appeared in such plays as *The Amorous Prawn* (1959). She m. the actor Frank Lawton in 1934.

LAY-READER. In the Church of England a layman permitted to read the lessons, or under licence from the bishop of the diocese to conduct morning or evening prayer.

LAZARISTS. Popular name for the Congregation of Priests of the Mission, an R.C. order founded by St. Vincent de Paul in 1626 in order to carry on religious teaching among the poor, and missionary work. The name is derived from the priory of St. Lazarus, their first house in Paris.

LAZIO. Italian form of LATIUM.

LEA. English river rising in Bedfordshire, flowing past Luton, Hertford and Ware, and bounding Herts and Essex, before it flows through Greater London to join the Thames at Blackwall. It is navigable for 28 m. The L. Valley Authority was estab. 1967 to make it a 'playground' for London.

LEACH, Bernard (1887–). British potter. His beautifully simple designs, influenced by a period of study in Japan, pioneered the modern revival of the art. He estab. the L. Pottery at St. Ives in 1920.

LEACOCK, Stephen Butler (1869–1944). British humorous writer. B. in Hants, he lived in Canada from 1876, and was head of the dept. of economics at McGill univ., Montreal, 1908–36. He pub. works on politics and economics, studies of Mark Twain and Dickens, but is best known for his humorous writings, such as *Literary Lapses* (1910), *Nonsense Novels* (1911), and *Frenzied Fiction* (1918).

LEAD. One of the 4 most used and produced metals, the end product of the uranium-radium and thorium series, symbol Pb (Lat. *plumbum*), at. wt. 207·21 and at. no. 82. Known since prehistoric times (mentioned in Exodus), it is a bluish-grey, and the heaviest, softest and weakest of common metals; it lacks elasticity and is a poor conductor of electricity. It is one of the cheapest shields for radio-active sources, and is widely used in plumbing (some Roman pipe drains are still in use), for containing corrosive liquids, for biological shielding, for cable coverings, storage batteries, ammunition and low-melting alloys. It is also used in the manufacture of lead tetraethyl, an anti-knock additive to petrol, and in paints, especially white L. (basic lead carbonate $PbCO_3$), sublimed white L. (lead sulphate $PbSO_4$), red L. (lead oxide Pb_3O_4), and chrome yellow (lead chromate $PbCrO_4$). Galena (PbS) is the principal mineral ore from which L. is obtained by a roasting process. Some L. salts are used in medicine as antiseptics and astringents. L. is a cumulative poison.

LEAF. Term applied to any lateral outgrowth on the stems of plants, but chiefly referring to those which constitute the foliage. Foliage leaves are composed of 3 parts: the *sheath* or leaf-base, the *petiole* or stalk, and the *lamina* or blade, the last-named being traversed by a network of veins. The chief leaf structures are: cotyledon (seed leaves); scale-leaf (on underground stems); foliage leaf (having the distinctive functions of assimilating carbon and other nutrient substances, the absorption of light, and constituting the respiring and transpiring organ of the plant); and bract (in the axil of which a flower is produced). A *simple* leaf is undivided, e.g. as in the aspen tree; a *compound* leaf is composed of several leaflets, e.g. the blackberry. Leaves that fall in the autumn are termed *deciduous*, and evergreens are *persistent*.

LEAF INSECTS. Family of insects (Phyllidae) of the order Phasmida, with a depressed and leaf-like body, remarkable for closely resembling the foliage on which they live. They are most common on islands from the Indian Ocean to the Pacific.

LEAGUE OF NATIONS. International organization for the prevention of war estab. in 1920 with H.Q. at Geneva, but superseded by the U.N. in 1945. Its Covenant, drawn up by a special commission of the Paris Peace Conference, presided over by Pres. Wilson, was incorporated in the Versailles and other peace treaties Members undertook to preserve the territorial integrity of all, and to submit disputes to the L. of N. or to arbitration.

Although successful in the humanitarian field (aid to refugees; international action against epidemics, drug traffic and slave trading; and improvement of working conditions through I.L.O., q.v.), it was hampered by internal rivalries and the necessity of unanimity on major political issues. No action was taken against Japan's aggression in Manchuria (1932); attempts to apply sanctions against Italy for her attack on Ethiopia collapsed (1935–6); no move was made against Germany for aggression in Austria, Czechoslovakia and Poland; and expulsion of Russia in 1939 had no effect on the Russo-Finnish War – Japan (1932) and Germany (1933) simply withdrew.

LEAKEY, Louis Seymour Bazett (1903–). British archaeologist. B. at Kabete, Kenya, he was ed. at St. John's Coll., Cambridge, and in 1958 made discoveries of gigantic fossils in the Olduvai Gorge (q.v.). He was curator of Coryndon Museum, Nairobi, 1945–61, and worked as a handwriting expert for Nairobi, C.I.D. 1943–51. Among his books are *Stone Age Africa* (1936) and *The Pleistocene Fossil Suidae of East Africa* (1958). His wife **Mary L.**, also an archaeologist, found the skull of an ape of the Miocene period on Rusinga Island, Lake Victoria: known as Proconsul, it is some 25,000,000 years old.

The discoveries in Kenya by L. and his wife in the field of human ancestry from 1959 incl. the oldest member of the stock which gave rise to true man *Kenyapithecus Africanus*, a pre-man 20,000,000 yrs.

old (Lower Miocene), pygmy-sized, omnivorous and without weapons or tools; and the earliest true man *Homo habilis*, 1,820,000 yrs. old, small-brained and upright, 3–4 ft. high, who used tools and talked.

LEAMINGTON (lem'-): officially **Royal L. Spa.** English spa and health resort (bor.) in Warwickshire on the Leam, adjoining Warwick. It caters extensively for visitors and also manufactures iron and bricks. Pop. (1961) 43,236.

LEAN, David (1908–). British film director. Beginning as a camera assistant in 1928, he was asst. director of *Pygmalion* (1938), and director of *Blithe Spirit* (1945), *Brief Encounter* (1946), *The Bridge on the River Kwai* (1957) and *Lawrence of Arabia* (1962). He was m. (1949–57) to the actress Ann Todd.

LEAR, Edward (1812–88). British artist and humorist. B. in Holloway, he first attracted attention by his paintings of birds, and later turned to landscapes. He travelled in Italy, Greece, Egypt and India, pub. books on his travels with his own illustrations, and spent most of his later life in Italy. A vein of fantastic humour appears in his *Book of Nonsense* (1846) which popularized the limerick.

LEASEHOLD. Called in law a 'chattel real', a L. is a tenancy of land from year to year, or for a term of years.

LEASE-LEND. Programme of mutual aid between Britain, the U.S.A., and the other Allies, carried out during the S.W.W. and begun under the Lease-and-Lend Act (1941–5), empowering the President to sell, exchange, transfer, lease, or lend war materials to any country whose defence he considered essential to the defence of the U.S.A. War supplies could thus be sent to Britain on a credit basis instead of the cash-and-carry system introduced by the Neutrality Act of 1939. In Feb. 1942, after the U.S.'s entry into the war, an agreement between Britain and the U.S. provided for mutual L.-L. assistance, and for collaboration to deal with post-war economic problems.

LEATHER. A material prepared from the skins of animals, birds, and fish. L. articles at least 7,000 years old still exist. Methods of preparation vary according to the type of hide or skin and the kind of L. required. 'Hides' are the coverings of larger animals, such as cattle, horse and buffalo; 'skins' those of the smaller, such as calf, pig, goat, and sheep.

Tanning, the 'oldest manufacturing process in the world', prevents a skin from putrefying and turns it into L. Skins from the slaughterhouse are salted for temporary preservation and on arrival at the tannery the surplus flesh, hairs and salt are removed, and the skins dipped in tanning solutions of gradually increasing strength – a process which may take many weeks. Vegetable tanning solutions are generally blends of bark, leaf or nut infusions from various trees, and chrome tanning (basic chromium sulphate) is used for shoe uppers. After drying L. may be dyed or sprayed to any colour; and mechanical treatments provide various physical properties and types of surface texture. In the U.K. 80 per cent of the L. industry's production is used for footwear, the remaining 20 per cent covers an ever-widening range of products incl. harness and saddlery, travel goods, handbags, clothing, upholstery for furniture and cars and industrial goods such as oil seals and drive belting.

LEATHERHEAD. English town (U.D.) in Surrey, 18 m. S.W. of London, on the Mole, at the foot of the N. Downs. Several industrial research stations are estab. there, and the Thorndike Theatre was opened 1968. *See* THORNDIKE, SYBIL. Pop. (1961) 35,554.

LEAVEN (lev'n). Element inducing fermentation; especially applied to the yeast added to dough in bread making. Hence it is used figuratively of any pervasive influence, usually in a good sense, although to the Hebrews it symbolized corruption, and unleavened bread was used in sacrifice.

LEAVIS, Frank Raymond (1895–). British scholar. A Fellow 1936–64, and Univ. Reader in English (1959–62) at Cambridge, he is well known for his editorship (1932–53) of the review *Scrutiny*, which he heiped found, and for his books of literary criticism, e.g. *New Bearings in English Poetry* (1932), *The Great Tradition* (1948), and *The Common Pursuit* (1952).

LE'BANON. A rep. in S.W. Asia, situated between the Mediterranean on the W., Israel on the S., and Syria on the E. and N. L. is a narrow strip of land, *c.* 130 m. long and 30 m. wide, lying between the ranges of the Anti-Lebanon and Mt. Hermon and the Mediterranean. The L. is also the name of a range running parallel to the sea and to the Anti-Lebanon down the centre of the country, and rising to 10,000 ft.; it was formerly famed for its cedars. Most of the rep. is hilly, except for the central valley of Bekáa. The main rivers are the Orontes and the Litani. Fruit, tobacco, silk, and cotton are the main products and the chief minerals are iron and lignite. Principal towns incl. Beirut, the capital and seat of 4 univs., Zahle, Tripoli, and Sidon (the last 2 towns being the terminals of oil pipelines). There are remarkable archaeological remains at Baalbek, Byblos and Tyre (qq.v.). Arabic is the official language, but French and English are widely used. Area *c.* 3,400 sq. m.; pop. (1963) 1,750,000, incl. 800,000 Christians of various denominations and 550,000 Moslems. About 88,000 Druses remained.

Before the F.W.W., Lebanon was part of the Ottoman Empire; it was placed under French mandate by the League of Nations in 1922 and was given a constitution in 1926. In 1941 Allied troops under General Catroux ousted the Vichy French administration and in 1944 the independence of L. was recognized. Under the constitution of 1947 there is a pres. who appoints the P.M. and Cabinet; the single chamber parliament is elected by universal adult suffrage. Divergent views on the Palestinian situation dominate the unstable political scene, but a Nat. Coalition was estab. 1969.

LEBDA. Older name of HOMS.

LEBEDEV (lebād'yef), **Peter Nikolaievich** (1866–1912). Russian physicist. While prof. at Moscow univ. 1892–1911 he succeeded in proving experimentally, and then measuring, the minute pressure which light exerts upon a physical body; confirming Clerk Maxwell's theoretical determination.

LEBENSRAUM (lehbensrowm') (Ger., living space). A slogan used by the Nazis to justify their annexation of neighbouring states and their demand for the return of the former German colonies, on the ground that Germany was over-populated.

LEBLANC (leblōn'), **Nicolas** (1742–1806). French chemist. B. at Issoudun, he became surgeon to the duke of Orleans. Having discovered a process (now superseded) whereby soda could be manufactured from common salt, he opened a factory near Paris, but his business was ruined by the Revolution, and he committed suicide.

LEBRUN (lebrun'), **Albert** (1871–1950). French statesman. He became Pres. of the Senate in 1931 and in 1932 was chosen as Pres. of the rep. In 1940 he handed his powers over to Marshal Pétain.

LE BRUN, Charles (1619–90). French painter. B. in Paris, he helped to found the Academy of Painting and Sculpture in 1648, and also the Gobelins tapestry works, of which he became a director. He excelled in elaborate historical paintings.

LE CARRÉ (le ka'rā), **John.** Pseudonym of British author David John Cornwell (1931–). After teaching at Eton, he was a member of the Foreign Service 1960–4. His books incl. *The Spy Who Came in from the Cold* (1963) and *A Small Town in Germany* (1968).

LECOCQ, Charles (1832–1918). Fr. composer, b. in Paris. He wrote some 40 comic operas, among them the popular *La Fille de Madame Angot* (1873).

LECONTE DE LISLE (lekoṅt-de-lēl), **Charles Marie René** (1818–94). French poet. B. on Réunion, he settled in Paris in 1846 and headed Les Parnassiens (q.v.) 1866–76. Distinguished by perfection of versification and form, his work drew inspiration from the ancient world, e.g. *Poèmes antiques* (1852), *Poèmes barbares* (1862) and *Poèmes tragiques* (1884).

LE CORBUSIER (korbüsyä'). Pseudonym of the French architect Charles Edouard Jeanneret (1887–1965). B. in Switzerland, he was originally a painter and engraver, but turned his attention to the problems of modern industrial society. For L.C. the house is a habitable machine which should be designed according to functional criteria. He won the contest for the Palace of the Nations at Geneva, devised town-planning schemes for Algiers, Barcelona, Buenos Aires, and Nemours (Algeria), and planned Cité Radieuse, Marseilles and Chandigarh, India. *Le Modulor* (1948) explains his mathematical system for proportioning and relating the parts of buildings.

LECOUVREUR (lekoovrör'), **Adrienne** (1692–1730). French actress. She gained fame at the Comédie Française, where she made her début in 1717, and had many admirers, incl. Voltaire. The duchesse de Bouillon, a rival mistress of Maurice de Saxe, is thought to have poisoned her.

LEDA. In Greek mythology the wife of Tyndareus and mother of Clytemnestra. She was loved by Zeus in the form of a swan, and by him became the mother of Helen of Troy, Castor and Pollux.

LEDBURY. Market town (U.D.) in Herefordshire, England, 13 m. E. of Hereford, and famous for its old timbered buildings, especially the market house. L. trades in cider. Pop (1961) 3,632.

LEDERBERG (lād'er-), **Joshua** (1925–). American geneticist. Prof. at Wisconsin 1954–8, and at Stanford from 1959, he shared a Nobel prize in 1958 with G. W. Beadle (q.v.) and E. L. Tatum, for his work on bacterial genetics.

LEDWIDGE, Francis (1891–1917). Irish poet. B. in co. Meath, the son of a peasant, he began writing poetry while working as a roadmender. He was killed in the F.W.W. His vols. of verse, incl. *Songs of the Fields* (1916), and *Last Songs* (1918), show an intimate lyrical quality.

LEE of Fareham (fahr'am), **Arthur Hamilton Lee, 1st visct.** (1868–1947). British statesman. B. at Bridport, Dorset, he became a Conservative M.P. in 1900, was civil lord of the Admiralty 1903–5, Min. of Agriculture and Fisheries 1919–21, and 1st Lord of the Admiralty 1921–2. He was well known as an art connoisseur and philanthropist. *See* CHEQUERS.

LEE of Asheridge, Jennie, baroness (1904–). British Labour politician. The dau. of a Fifeshire miner, she m. Aneurin Bevan (q.v.) in 1934. She was an M.P. 1929–31 and 1945–70, and 1964–70 was responsible for the Arts (from 1967 as Min. of State, Dept. of Education and Science). Life peeress 1970.

LEE, Nathaniel (c. 1653–92). English dramatist. B. at Hatfield, he was ed. at Westminster and Cambridge. After an unsuccessful attempt to become an actor, he wrote from 1675 a number of bombastic tragedies, the best of which was *The Rival Queens* (1677). His dissipated life led to temporary insanity, and he d. in a fit of intoxication.

LEE, Robert Edward (1807–70). American gen. B. in Virginia, he was commissioned in 1829, served in the Mexican War, and in 1859 suppressed John Brown's raid on Harper's Ferry. On the outbreak of

ROBERT E. LEE

the Civil War he joined the Confederates, and became military adviser to Pres. Davis. In 1862 he received the command of the army of N. Virginia and won the Seven Days' Battle against McClellan. During 1862–3 he made several raids into Northern territory, winning victories at Fredericksburg and Chancellorsville, but after his defeat at Gettysburg was compelled to take the defensive. He surrendered in 1865 at Appomattox Court House. He is recognized as one of the world's greatest strategists.

LEE, Sir Sidney (1859–1926). British man of letters. He joined the staff of the *Dictionary of National Biography* in 1883, and was joint editor with Sir Leslie Stephen in 1890, and editor from 1891. He pub. lives of Shakespeare (1898) and Queen Victoria (1902).

LEECH, John (1817–64). British caricaturist. B. in London, he studied medicine before turning to art. He illustrated many books, incl. Dickens' *Christmas Carol*, and during 1841–64 contributed *c.* 3,000 humorous drawings and political cartoons to *Punch*.

LEECHES. Worms in the class Hirudinea. They inhabit fresh water, and in tropical countries infest damp forests. As blood-sucking animals they are injurious to man and beast, to whom they attach themselves by means of a strong suctorial mouth. Formerly the medicinal leech (*Hirudo medicinalis*) was used for blood-letting. Some Ls. live in the sea, e.g. the rock L. which infests sharks, etc.

LEEDS. English city (co. bor.) in the W. Riding of Yorks on the Aire, principal seat of woollen manufacture, and market and rail centre with canal communication to Liverpool and Goole. L. has been connected with the woollen manufacture since the 14th cent. Engineering assumed primary importance

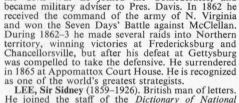

with the Industrial Revolution, but cloth and clothing manufacture remain the leading industries. Others incl. printing and the making of locomotives, machinery, aeroplane parts, chemicals, pottery, and glass. L. univ. was estab. in 1904. Pop. (1961) 510,597.

LEEK. Plant of the Liliaceae family. The cultivated L. (*Allium porrum*) is a variety of the wild *A. ampeloprasum* of Europe and Asia, and the lower leaf-parts are eaten as a vegetable. When fighting the Anglo-Saxons the Welsh, under St. David's instructions, wore Ls. in their hats and it remains their national emblem.

LEE KUAN YEW (1923–). Singapore statesman. A third generation Straits Chinese, he studied law at Cambridge, became a founder-member of the left-wing People's Action Party (P.A.P.), and P.M. of Singapore 1959.

LEEUWARDEN (lā'wahrden). City of the Netherlands, cap. of Friesland prov. Noteworthy buildings incl. the palace of the stadholders of Friesland, and the church of St. Jacob. L. is a marketing centre, and makes gold and silver ware. Pop. (1961) 83,161.

LEEUWENHOEK (lā'wenhook'), **Anthony van** (1632–1723). Dutch anatomist and pioneer microscopist. B. at Delft, he turned from business to microscopic research, investigated the structure of the red blood corpuscles, spermatozoa in animals, yeast, etc.

LEEWARD (loo'ahrd) **ISLANDS.** A general term for the N. half of the Lesser Antilles in the West Indies. The British L.I. comprise (i) Montserrat, area 32½ sq. m., pop. (1966) 14,464; (ii) Anguilla, area 50 sq. m., pop. 5,800; Nevis, area 50 sq. m., pop. 13,000; St. Kitts, area 68 sq. m., pop. 39,000; (iii) Antigua, area 108 sq. m., pop. 61,660; Barbuda, area 62 sq. m., pop. 1,000; Redonda, 1 sq. m., uninhabited. Products of the islands incl. sugar, molasses, cotton, citrus fruits, tomatoes, coconuts, and salt. The L.I., together with the British VIRGIN ISLANDS (q.v.), were until 1960 a single colony under a Governor appointed by the crown. Attempts at a general West Indies federation (1958–62) having failed, in 1967 the status of Associated State (q.v.) was granted to Antigua, and also to St. Kitts-Nevis-Anguilla. Anguilla then alleged domination by the St. Kitts federal admin. and in 1969 declared itself a rep., breaking all ties with Britain. A small British force was despatched to restore order and negotiations were opened.

LE FANU (lef'anoo), **Joseph Sheridan** (1814–73). Irish writer. B. in Dublin, he wrote novels and short stories, such as *The House by the Churchyard* (1863), *Uncle Silas* (1864), and *In a Glass Darkly* (1872), which rank high among stories of the mysterious.

LEFT WING. Term in politics used for the more radical parties. It originated in the French National Assembly in 1789, where the nobles sat in the place of honour on the president's right, and the third estate on his left; this arrangement has become customary in European parliaments, where the radicals sit on the left and the conservatives on the right. It is also usual to speak of the right, left, and centre, when referring to the different elements composing a single party.

LEGACY. A bequest of personal property made

LEEDS. The impressive Civic Hall opened by George V in 1933. *Courtesy of the City of Leeds.*

by a testator in his will and passing on his death to the legatee. Specific Ls. are definite named objects, e.g. a piece of jewellery. General Ls. are sums of money or items not specially identified, e.g. 'one of my clocks'. A residuary L. is all the remainder of the deceased's personal estate after the other Ls. have been distributed.

LEGEND (Lat. *legenda*, things to be read). Term originally applied to the books of readings designed for use in Divine Service, and afterwards extended to the stories of saints read at matins and at mealtimes in monasteries. The best-known collection of such stories was the 13th cent. *Legenda Aurea* by Jacobus de Voragine. The term has since extended its meaning to traditional stories about famous people.

LEGER (lehzheh'), **Fernand** (1881–1955). French artist. By 1911 he was exhibiting Cubist works, favouring espec. cylindrical and machine forms, and reducing his human beings to puppets. He designed settings for a no. of ballets, and was a decorative mural painter.

LEGHORN. Seaport of Tuscany, W. Italy, and the cap. of L. prov., 12 m. S.S.W. of Pisa. The modern town contrasts with the picturesque old fortress, dating back to before the 12th cent., and the new

fortress (16th cent.). L.'s prosperity developed under the Medici who built the first harbour. It has a naval academy, shipyards, iron and steel works, distilleries. and makes motor-cars, macaroni, glass, and copper goods. L. is also a popular resort. Pop. (1961) 159,973.

LEGION OF HONOUR (Légion d'Honneur). French military and civil order, founded by Napoleon in 1802. The pres. of the rep. is grand master, and administration is in the charge of the grand chancellor. Women are eligible and the 5 ascending grades are: chevalier, officer, commander, grand officer and grand cross. In 1963, owing to overcrowding of the lower grades, it was decided to limit award of the L. of H. to 'eminent' services, 'distinguished' and 'honourable' services to be rewarded by the newly created Order of Merit (Ordre de Mérite), which also replaced a number of other decorations awarded by the various ministries. Still retained was the *Palmes Académiques* awarded by the Min. of Education.

LEGITIMACY. Any child born anywhere in lawful wedlock is legitimate, unless the husband successfully repudiates paternity, a proceeding, in the interests of the child, which is not encouraged by the law. In England and Wales an illegitimate child was legitimated on the subsequent marriage of its parents, provided there was no impediment to such marriage at the time of the birth of the child, by an act of 1926 effective 1927; an act of 1959 legitimated an illegitimate child on the marriage of its parents even though at the time of the birth the father or mother was married to a third person. A legitimated person has all the rights and duties of one born in wedlock except that such a person cannot succeed to, or transmit, any dignity or title. The law relating to legitimation is not uniform in the U.S.A., but in general follows the line of the law in England.

LEGITIMISTS. The party in France which continued to support the claims of the house of Bourbon after the revolution of 1830. When the direct line became extinct in 1883 the majority of the party transferred their allegiance to the house of Orléans.

LEGOUVÉ (legooveh'), **Gabriel Jean Baptiste Ernest Wilfrid** (1807–1903). French dramatist. B. at Paris, author of *Adrienne Lecouvreur* (1849) and *Médée* (1855).

LEGROS (legrō'), **Alphonse** (1837–1911). Anglo-French artist. B. in Dijon, he began exhibiting in Paris in 1857, settled in England in 1863, was naturalized, and was Slade prof. at Univ. Coll., London, 1875–92. He painted portraits, landscapes, and figures, and was a distinguished etcher and sculptor.

LEGUMINOSAE. Family of dicotyledonous plants, containing 600 genera and 12,000 species. It includes trees, e.g. laburnum and acacia; bushes, e.g. gorse; garden flowers, e.g. lupin, sweet pea; vegetables, e.g. peas and beans; and wild plants, e.g. clover. In some species of L. leaves may be modified into tendrils which twine round other stems, affording support to the plant. Many species have characteristic flowers in which a large petal is flanked by 2 smaller ones, while in front 2 small petals form a boat-shaped shelter in which the 10 stamens are hidden. The seeds are carried in a pod. The roots of L. plants, e.g. clover, frequently bear small nitrogenous nodules, which restore nitrates to the soil.

LEHÁR (la'hahr), **Franz** (1870–1948). Hungarian composer. B. at Komárom, he studied at Prague conservatoire, intending to become a violinist, but abandoned this for conducting. He wrote many popular operettas, among them *The Merry Widow* (1905), *The Count of Luxembourg* (1909), *Gypsy Love* (1910) and *The Land of Smiles* (1923) and has also composed songs, marches, and a violin concerto.

LE HAVRE. *See* HAVRE, LE.

LEHMANN, **Lotte** (1888–). German-born American soprano. She excelled in Wagner and was the original Marschallin in *Rosenkavalier*.

LEHMANN (lā′man), **Rosamond Nina** (c. 1904–). British novelist, author of *Dusty Answer* (1927), *Invitation to the Waltz* (1932), *The Ballad and the Source* (1944), and *The Echoing Grove* (1953). Her sister, **Beatrix L.** (1903–), is a distinguished actress in such roles as Lavinia in *Mourning becomes Electra* and Miss Bordereau in *The Aspern Papers*. Her brother, **John Frederick L.** (1907–), a publisher, was founder-editor of *New Writing* in 1963 and ed. *London Magazine* 1954–61.

LEIBNIZ (līb′nits), **Gottfried Wilhelm** (1646–1716). German philosopher and mathematician. B. at Leipzig, he soon showed a versatile genius, and at the age of 20 was offered a professorship at the univ. of Altdorf. He dedicated his *Nova methodus docendi discendique Juris* (1667) to the elector of Mainz, who employed him on political missions. The French king invited L. to Paris, where he met Christian Huygens, who revived his interest in mathematical problems. About this time L. invented a calculating machine, and in 1673, while engaged on a political mission to London, was elected a fellow of the Royal Society. After his return to Paris, he resumed his mathematical investigations, and devised a new form of differential and integral calculus. He also left the service of the elector for that of the dukes of Brunswick-Luneburg. In his *Systema Theologicum* (1686), he sought to promote a reunion of the Protestant and Catholic Churches. *Essais de Théodicée sur la bonté de Dieu, la liberté de l'homme, et l'origine du mal* (1710), *La Monadologie* (1714), and *Principes de la nature et de la grâce* (1714), are his main philosophical works. In his view the universe consists of a number of monads in harmony with each other and with God; therefore this is the best of all possible worlds, and faith and reason are not in conflict.

LEICESTER (les′ter), **Robert Dudley**, earl of (c. 1532–88). English courtier. Son of the duke of Northumberland, he was created E. of L. in 1564. His good looks won him the favour of Queen Elizabeth, who might have married him if he had not been previously married to Amy Robsart. When his wife d. in 1560, Dudley was suspected of murdering her. Elizabeth gave him command of the army sent to the Netherlands in 1585–7, and of that prepared to resist the threatened Spanish invasion of 1588.

LEICESTER. English city (co. bor.) and co. town of Leics, on the Soar, 97 m. N.W. of London. As the Roman *Ratae Coritanorum*, estab. A.D. 50, it is one of the oldest towns in England. Its twice-weekly market dates from the 13th cent., and the guildhall (used as a town hall 1563–1876) from the 14th. Industries incl. the making of hosiery, boots and shoes, and elastic fabrics, and light engineering. The univ. (1957) was founded in 1918 as a univ. coll. The first excursion arranged by Thomas Cook was by rail from Leicester to Loughborough in 1841, fare 1s. Pop. (1961) 273,298.

LEICESTER OF HOLKHAM, earl of. *See* COKE.

LEICESTERSHIRE. A midland county of England. It is mainly low-lying. The Soar valley runs S. to N., dividing Charnwood forest from the E. uplands; other rivers are the Avon and Welland. The Angles reached L. in the 6th cent., and it was later subjugated by the Danes. Hosiery making, centred on Leicester and Loughborough, is the principal manufacture. The loamy soil affords rich pasture for cattle, and in the W. wheat and other cereals flourish. Hunting and horse breeding are popular, while the mineral resources incl. coal, limestone, and granite. The principal towns are Leicester, the co. town Loughborough, Hinckley, and Coalville. Area 834 sq. m.; pop. (1967) 723,730.

LEIDEN, LEIJDEN. Variant spellings of LEYDEN.

LEIF ERICSSON (līf er′ikson) (fl. 1000). Viking explorer, the son of Eric the Red, who colonized Greenland. He is said to have discovered 'Vinland', generally identified with Nova Scotia.

LEIGH (lē), **Vivien** (1913–67). British actress, *née* Hartley. A student at R.A.D.A., she rapidly achieved success in roles which demanded a combination of fragile beauty and vivacious fire, such as Sabina in *The Skin of Our Teeth*; *A Streetcar Named Desire* and *Caesar and Cleopatra* (both filmed), and the films *Lady Hamilton*, *Anna Karenina* and *The Roman Spring of Mrs. Stone*. She m. in 1932 Leigh Holman (div. 1940), and was the wife of Sir Laurence Olivier, with whom she played in *Antony and Cleopatra* etc., from 1940 to 1960.

LEIGH. English industrial town (bor.) in Lancs, 13 m. W. of Manchester. Its industries incl. textiles and coal mining. Pop. (1961) 46,153.

LEIGH-MALLORY, Sir Trafford (1892–1944). British air chief marshal. He served in the F.W.W., and subsequently held staff appointments. As A.O.C. Fighter Command 1937–41, he organized the defence during the Battle of Britain. He was C.-in-C. of Allied air forces during the invasion of France, and was killed in an air crash.

LEIGHTON (lā′ton), **Clare** (1899–). British artist, noted for the wood engravings with which she illustrates her own books, e.g. *Country Matters* (1937) and classics such as Hardy, and Emily Brontë.

LEIGHTON, Frederick, baron (1830–96). British artist and sculptor. B. at Scarborough, he spent most of his early life on the Continent, and achieved fame in 1855 with his 'Cimabue's Madonna Carried in Procession'. Most of his works represented historical, especially classical, subjects, e.g. 'Captive Andromache' (1888), 'The Bath of Psyche' (1890), and 'The Return of Persephone' (1891). He was elected R.A. in 1868, P.R.A. in 1878, and was raised to the peerage in 1896.

LEIGHTON (lā′ton), **Margaret** (1922–). British actress. Beginning in Birmingham's repertory co., she was soon a member of the Old Vic. Her controlled intensity of style suited such plays as Eliot's *The Cocktail Party*, Rattigan's *Separate Tables* and Tennessee Williams' *The Night of the Iguana*. Both her marriages, to Max Reinhardt and Laurence Harvey, were dissolved: she m. 1964 Michael Wilding.

LEINSDORF (līnz′-), **Erich** (1912–). Viennese-born American conductor. Greatly influenced by Toscanini, and noted for the superb precision of his renderings, he was with the Boston Symphony Orchestra from 1962.

LEINSTER (lin′ster). S.E. prov. of Rep. of Ireland, incl. the cos. of Longford, Westmeath, Meath, Louth, Offaly, Laoighis, Kildare, Dublin, Carlow Wicklow, Kilkenny, and Wexford (qq.v.). Area 7,581 sq. m.; pop. (1966) 1,414,361.

LEIPZIG (līp′tsig). Cap. of L. dist., E. Germany, 90 m. S.W. of Berlin, lying in a fertile plain. The old town has narrow streets with 16th and 17th cent. houses. Near the Gothic Rathaus (1558) is Auerbach's Hof, built about 1530. L. has musical associations with J. S. Bach and Mendelssohn. The 'Gewandhaus' concert hall was completed 1884, and the univ. founded in 1409. Before the S.W.W. L. was the centre of the German book trade. The famous L. fairs have been responsible for the growth of its varied manufactures, which incl. furs, leather goods, cloth, glass, motor-cars, and musical instruments. L. was the scene of Napoleon's defeat in the Battle of the Nations, 1813. Pop. (1966) 595,000.

LEITH (lēth). Scottish port, incorporated in Edinburgh in 1920, having been granted to Edinburgh as its port by Robert Bruce in 1329. L. stands on the S. of the Firth of Forth in Midlothian. Harbour accommodation is excellent, allowing much trade in the distilling industry centred here. Shipbuilding and engineering are other occupations.

LEITRIM (lē'trim). Co. in Connacht prov., Rep. of Ireland, bounded on the N.W. by Donegal Bay. The N. is tableland. The main rivers are the Shannon, Bonet, Drowes and Duff; Lough Allen divides it into two. The main products are potatoes, linen, woollens, and pottery, while coal, iron, and lead are mined and fish caught. The co. town is Carrick-on-Shannon. Area 589 sq. m.; pop. (1966) 30,572.

LEIX. Spelling from 1922–35 of LAOIGHIS.

LĒ'LAND, John (c. 1506–52). English antiquary. B. in London, he became chaplain and librarian to

LEITH. The port has large flour mills and a few of the granary workers take a moment of their lunch hour to look over the harbour. To right of centre a ship is supported in dry dock.
Photo: George Outram & Co. Ltd.

Henry VIII, and during 1534–43 toured England collecting materials for a history of English antiquities. His MSS. have formed a valuable source for scholars.

LĒ'LY, Sir Peter (1618–80). Anglo-German portraitist. B. in Westphalia, he came to England in 1641, and was employed both by Charles I and Cromwell. Charles II made him his court painter, and knighted him in 1679. His most famous paintings are those of the beauties of Charles II's court at Hampton Court.

LE MANS. See MANS, LE.

LEMBERG. German name of Lvov.

LEMMING. Small rodent found in America, N. Europe and Asia. The European lemming (*Lemmus lemmus*), common in Norway, is c. 5 in. long and yellowish brown. Periodically Ls. migrate towards the sea and are drowned in large numbers.

LĒ'MNOS. Greek island of volcanic origin, rising to 1,411 ft., in the N. of the Aegean Sea. Mulberries and other fruits and tobacco are grown, and sheep are reared. The main towns are Kastro and Mudros. Area 180 sq. m.; pop. (est.) 24,000.

LEMON, Mark (1809–70). British journalist, founder-editor of *Punch*, 1841–70.

LEMON. Fruit of the L. tree (*Citrus limone*). It may have originated in N.W. India, and was introduced into Europe by the Spanish Moors in the 12th or 13th cent. It is now grown largely in Italy, Spain, California, Florida, S. Africa, and Australia. The L. plant is low and straggling, growing to 10–12 ft. high. One tree may produce up to 3,000 fruit in a year. Imperfect fruit are used for the manufacture of citric acid and oil of lemon.

LEMPRIÈRE (lemprēr'), **John** (c. 1765–1824). British scholar. B. in Jersey, he became headmaster of Abingdon and Exeter grammar schools, and afterwards held livings in Devonshire. His *Classical Dictionary* (1788) was long a standard work.

LĒ'MUR. Sub-orders of Primates, Lemuroidea and Tarsioidea. The true Ls. inhabit Madagascar and the Comoro Islands, and certain allied species, e.g. the

LEMON

galagos and loris, are found in E. Africa and E. Asia. They are arboreal animals, valued for their long soft fur, and many species are nocturnal. They feed upon fruit, insects, birds, etc. The Ring-tailed lemur (*L. catta*) is often kept as a pet.

LĒNA. Longest river in Asiatic Russia, flowing generally N.E., then N.W. from the W. slopes of the Baikal mts. for nearly 3,000 m., during which it is ¹oined by innumerable tributaries to enter the Arctic Ocean by several mouths. It is ice-covered for 6 months of the year.

LE NAIN (nań), **Antoine** (1588–1648), **Louis** (1593–1648), and **Mathieu** (1607–77). French painters. The 3 brothers were b. at Laon, settled in Paris, and were among the original members of the French Academy. They painted portraits, but mainly devoted themselves to pictures of peasant life.

LENCLOS (loṅklō'), **Ninon de** (1615–1705). French lady of fashion. As the recognized leader of Parisian society, she was the mistress in turn of many highly placed men, including Condé and La Rochefoucauld.

LENGLEN (loṅgloṅ'), **Suzanne** (1899–1938). French woman lawn-tennis player, largely responsible for the rapid advance of the quality of women's tennis after the F.W.W. She won the Wimbledon championships 1919–23, and in 1925.

LENIN (lā'nin), **Vladimir Ilyich**. Pseudonym of Russian statesman V. I. Ulyanov (1870–1924). B. at Simbirsk (re-named Ulyanovsk in his honour), he was the son of a school-inspector. He practised law for a time, but after 1893 devoted himself entirely to revolutionary propaganda, and was banished to Siberia 1895–1900. After his release he ed. the Social-Democratic Party's paper *Iskra* (*The Spark*) from abroad, visiting London several times after 1902. In *What is to be done?* (1902) he maintained the revolution must be led by a disciplined party of professional revolutionaries; at the 1903 party congress in London this theory was accepted by the majority of delegates, who hence became known as Bolsheviks ('majority'). L. took an active part in the 1905 revolution, but after its defeat again had to leave Russia. In 1914 he settled in Switzerland, whence he attacked those

V. I. LENIN
Photo: Novosti Press Agency

Socialists who supported the F.W.W on the grounds that it was a purely 'imperialist' struggle; this view he expounded in his most important book, *Imperialism* (1917). On the outbreak of the revolution in March 1917 he returned to Russia, and put forward a programme of immediate peace and transfer of power to the Soviets. As a result, he had to go into hiding until 7 Nov., when the prov. govt. was overthrown and a Soviet govt. set up under L.'s presidency. Peace was concluded with Germany, but during 1918–21 the new régime was threatened by foreign intervention and 'White' uprisings. Even during the civil war many important reforms were achieved, including the division of large estates among the peasantry and the recognition of the equal rights of all the peoples of Russia, while L. was already planning large-scale electrification schemes. He also took the lead in founding the 3rd (Communist) International in 1919. His health was undermined by overwork and the effects of an attempt to assassinate him in 1918, and after 1922 he became an invalid. He d. on 21 Jan. 1924; his embalmed body was laid in a mausoleum in Red Square, Moscow.

His wife **Nadezhda Konstantinova Krupskaya** (1869–1939) worked with L. at St. Petersburg in the illegal Union for the Liberation of the Working Class, m. him in 1898, and shared actively in his work. Her *Memories of Lenin* throws much light on him, both as a political leader and as an individual.

LENINAKAN (lyenyinakahn'). Industrial town in Armenia S.S.R., U.S.S.R., 25 m. N.W. of Yerevan, a railway junction with textile factories and an electric power station. Founded in 1837 as a fortress called Alexandropol, it was virtually destroyed by an earthquake in 1926. Pop. (1967) 130,000.

LENINGRAD. Side by side along the Neva are Rastrelli's baroque Winter Palace (1754–62) with 700 rooms, and the Hermitage. The occupation of the Palace by the Bolsheviks on 25 October 1917 marked the victory of the Revolutionaries.
Photo: Novosti Press Agency.

LENINGRAD. Cap. of L. region of the R.S.F.S.R., 2nd city of the U.S.S.R. Cap. of the Russian Empire 1709–1918. It was founded as an outlet to the Baltic in 1703 by Peter the Great, who took up residence there in 1712. Originally called St. Petersburg, it was renamed Petrograd in 1914, and L. in 1924. It stands at the head of the Gulf of Finland, and is split up by the mouths of the Neva, which connects it with Lake Lagoda. The site is low and swampy, and the climate very severe.

L. was the centre of all the main revolutionary movements from the Decembrist revolt of 1825 up to the 1917 revolution. During the German invasion in the S.W.W. the city heroically withstood siege and bombardment from Sept. 1941 to Jan. 1944.

L. is famous for its wide boulevards; most of its fine baroque and classical buildings of the 18th and early 19th cents. survived the S.W.W. siege. L. has a univ. (1819) and is the seat of a Metropolitan of the Orthodox Church. Museums incl. the Winter Palace, occupied by the Tsars until 1917, the Hermitage, the Russian Museum (formerly Michael Palace), and St. Isaac's Cathedral. The oldest building in L. is the fortress of St. Peter and St. Paul, on an island in

the Neva, a dreaded political prison. L. became a seaport when it was linked with the Baltic by a ship canal built 1875–93, but for part of the year it is ice-blocked. It also has an airport. Its industries incl. shipbuilding and the manufacture of machinery and machine tools, chemicals, textiles, and textile machinery, diesel motors, tyres, and rubber boots. Pop. (1967) 3,665,000.

LENINSK-KUZNETSKY (lyen'yinskē kōōznyet'-skē). Town in Kemerovo region, R.S.F.S.R., on the Inya r., 200 m. S.S.E. of Tomsk. It is a mining centre in the Kuzbas, with a large iron and steel works; coal, iron, manganese, and other metals, and precious stones occur in the neighbourhood. Formerly Kolchugino, the town was renamed L.-K. in 1925. Pop. (1967) 140,000.

LĒNŌ, Dan (1861–1904). British comedian. Beginning as an acrobat, he became the idol of the music-halls, and the greatest of pantomime 'dames'.

LENS (loṅs). Coal-mining town in Pas-de-Calais dept., France. It was in German occupation and close to the front line from Oct. 1914 to Oct. 1918 in the F.W.W. when the town and its mines were severely damaged. In the S.W.W. it was occupied by the Germans May 1940 to Sept. 1944, but suffered less physical damage. Pop. (1968) 41,874.

LENS. A piece of a transparent medium such as glass with 2 polished surfaces – one of which may be concave or convex, and the other may be either plane, concave or convex – to modify the rays of light, which become more convergent or more divergent according to the type of L. they traverse. Convex Ls. converge the light and concave Ls. diverge it. They are essential parts of spectacles, microscopes, telescopes, cameras and almost all optical instruments. Compound Ls. for special purposes are built up from 2 or more Ls. made of glass (or other suitable medium) of different refractive index.

The image formed by a single L. suffers from several defects or aberrations, notably spherical aberration in which a straight line becomes a curved image, and chromatic aberration in which an image in white light tends to have coloured edges. Aberrations are corrected by the use of compound Ls. *See* FOCAL LENGTH of a lens, and (for electron L.) ELECTRON MICROSCOPE. In zoology a L. is the part of the eye which focuses the rays of light on to the cornea. *See* EYE.

LENT. In the Christian Church, the 40 days' period of fasting which precedes Easter, beginning on Ash Wednesday, but omitting Sundays.

LENTHALL (len'tawl), **William** (1591–1662). British lawyer. Speaker of the House of Commons in the Long Parliament of 1640–60, he took an active part in the Restoration.

LENTIL. Annual plant of the Leguminosae family (*Lens esculenta*) of which the small seeds are widely used for food. The plant, which resembles the vetch, is probably native to the shores of the Mediterranean. It grows 6–18 in. in height, and has white, blue, or purplish flowers. The pods are about 1½ in. long, containing 2 seeds. The commonest varieties are the greyish French L. and the red Egyptian L.

LENYA (lān'ya), **Lotte**. Stage-name of Austrian actress and singer Karoline Blamauer (1905–). M. to Kurt Weill (q.v.) in 1925, she was a soprano singer, and successfully appeared in several of the Brecht-Weill operas, notably *The Threepenny Opera* (1928) and *The Rise and Fall of the City of Mahagonny* (1930). In 1962 she appeared in the dramatic anthology *Brecht on Brecht* in N.Y. and London.

LĒŌ III, the Isaurian (c. 680–740). Byzantine emperor. A soldier who seized the throne in 717, he successfully defended Constantinople against the Saracens in 717–18, and attempted to suppress the use of images in church worship.

LEOMINSTER (lem'ster). English market town

(bor.) in Herefordshire 12 m. N. of Hereford on the Lugg. It has a fine church representing many styles, and trades in agricultural produce. Pop. (1961) 6,403.

LEÓN (lā-on'). (1) Cap. of L. prov., Spain, 2,700 ft. above sea-level. It is the see of a bishopric and has a Gothic cathedral (1199) and other fine ecclesiastical buildings. Pop. (1965) 83,770. (2) Prov. of N.W. Spain. Agriculture is the main occupation. Area 5,432 sq. m.; pop. (1960) 584,594.

The ancient kingdom of LEÓN, dating from the 10th century, incl. not only modern L. prov., but also modern Palencia, Valladolid, Zamora and Salamanca; in 1230 it was united with Castille.

LEÓN. City of Guanajuato state, Mexico, 230 m. N.W. of Mexico City. It dates from 1576 and has a fine cathedral. Pop. (1967) 306,700.

LEÓN. Cultural centre and univ. city of Nicaragua, founded in 1523. Pop. (1963) 61,650.

LEONARDO DA VINCI (vin'chē) (1452–1519). Italian painter, sculptor, architect, musician, engineer, and scientist. B. in Vinci, in the Val d'Arno, the natural son of a lawyer, he studied under Verrochio, and began to work as an independent artist *c.* 1477 under the patronage of Lorenzo the Magnificent. In 1482 he was employed at Milan by Lodovico Sforza as state engineer, court painter, and director of court festivities. He painted the 'Last Supper' on the wall of the refectory of Santa Maria delle Grazie, and devised an irrigation system for the plains of Lombardy. In 1500 L. returned to Florence, and in 1502 was employed by Cesare Borgia as architect and chief engineer. Commissioned to decorate one of the walls of the council hall in the Signoria, Florence, he chose the 'Battle of Anghiari' as his subject, but abandoned this work after spending 2 years on the cartoon. About 1504 L. completed his portrait of the wife of Zanoki del Giocondo, known as 'Mona Lisa', now in the

LEONARDO DA VINCI. A full-scale study (1499–1500) in charcoal on brown paper of 'The Virgin and Child with St. John the Baptist and St. Anne', a cartoon for a painting of the same subject in the Louvre, was acquired by the National Gallery in 1962.   *Courtesy of the National Gallery.*

Louvre. In 1513–15 he was in Rome. At the invitation of Francis I he went to France, and lived at the Château Cloux near Amboise, where he d. There is no other man in history who distinguished himself in so many different fields. *See* RENAISSANCE.

LEONCAVALLO (lāonkahvah'lō), **Ruggiero** (1858–1919). Italian operatic composer. B. at Naples, he played at restaurants, composing in his spare time, until in 1892 *I Pagliacci* was performed and immediately became popular. Of his other operas, only *La Bohème* and *Zaza* enjoyed some success.

LEONIDAS (d. 480 B.C.). King of Sparta. He was killed while defending the pass of Thermopylae with 300 Spartans, 700 Thespians, and 400 Thebans against a huge Persian army.

LEONOV (lā-ōnov'), **Leonid Maximovich** (1899–   ). Soviet writer. Although Communist in outlook, his works show the influence of Dostoievsky and have deep psychological insight, e.g. the novels *The Badgers* (1924), *The Thief* (1925), and *Skutarevsky* (1933), and the play *The Invasion*.

LEOPARD. Third largest of the cat family (*Felis pardus*), also known as the panther, found over almost all Africa and Asia. The ground colour of the coat is golden and the spots form rosettes which differ according to the variety: black Ls. are simply mutants and retain the patterning as a 'watered-silk' effect, and white specimens have been known. The L. varies in size from 5 to 8 ft., incl. the tail, which may measure 3 ft.

LEOPARD. Seldom a man-eater, he takes a heavy toll of cattle and dogs: black specimens are reputedly the more ferocious.
Courtesy of Satour.

Closely allied is the snow L. or ounce (*Felis uncia*) which has irregular rosettes of much larger black spots, and is a native of central Asia. The clouded L. or clouded tiger (*Felis nebulosa*) is rather smaller than the ordinary L., with large blotchy markings rather than rosettes, found in S.E. Asia.

LEOPARDI (lā-ōpahr'dē), **Giacomo**, count (1798–1837). Italian poet. B. at Recanati, of a noble family, he wrote many of his finest poems, incl. his great patriotic odes, before he was 21. His first collection, *Versi*, appeared in 1824, and was followed by his philosophical *Operette Morali* (1827), in prose, and *Canti* (1831). After 1830 his life was divided between Florence, Rome, and Naples, where he d. Throughout life he was tormented by ill-health, by the consciousness of his deformity (he was hunch-backed), by loneliness and a succession of unhappy love-affairs, and by his failure to find consolation in any philosophy. He has nevertheless been called the greatest lyric poet since Dante.

LEOPOLD. Name of 2 Holy Roman Emperors. Leopold I (1640–1705) succeeded his father Ferdinand III in 1657. The greater part of his reign was occupied by wars with Louis XIV of France and with the Turks. Leopold II (1747–92), son of Maria Theresa, succeeded his brother Joseph II in 1790. He adopted a hostile attitude towards the French Revolution which led to the outbreak of war a few weeks after his death.

LEOPOLD I (1790–1865). King of the Belgians. The son of the duke of Saxe-Coburg, he served against the French with the Russian Army 1813–14. He m. Charlotte, the dau. of George IV of the U.K., in 1816, but she d. in the following year. Elected to the throne when Belgium became independent in 1831, he proved a wise and liberal ruler. He exercised a great influence over his niece Queen Victoria.

LEOPOLD II (1835–1909). King of the Belgians. He succeeded his father Leopold I in 1865. He financed Stanley's explorations in Africa, which resulted in the foundation of the Congo Free State. This was ruled autocratically by L., who derived a huge fortune from it. The scandal caused by his maladministration resulted in its annexation as a Belgian colony in 1908.

LEOPOLD III (1901–). King of the Belgians. The son of Albert I, he succeeded his father in 1934. In 1926 he m. Princess Astrid of Sweden, who was killed in a motoring accident in 1935. When the Germans invaded Belgium in 1940, L. took command of the army, until the enemy compelled him to surrender. He was held a prisoner until 1945. In 1941 he made a morganatic marriage with Mlle. Baels, subsequently created the Princesse de Réthy. After his liberation a constitutional crisis arose, as the left-wing parties demanded his abdication in view of charges brought against his conduct in 1940; as a result, his brother Prince Charles was appointed regent. In 1950 L. was recalled, but national unrest led him to resign his powers to his son Baudouin.

LÉOPOLDVILLE. Cap. of the Rep. of Congo (q.v.), W. Africa, on the Congo; an inland port, linked by 2 petroleum pipelines with Matadi near the coast. It also has an international airport. Textiles, furniture, chemicals, palm oil are produced, and tugs and barges built. It was the base of a large U.S. force during the S.W.W. In 1966 it was renamed Kinshasa. Pop. (1967) 1,225,720.

LEPA'NTO. Italian name of the Greek port of Naupaktos, on the N. of the Gulf of Corinth. A famous sea battle was fought in the Gulf of Corinth off L., then in Turkish possession, on 7 Oct. 1571, between the Turks and Christian League forces from Spain, Venice, Genoa, and the Papal States which were commanded by Don John of Austria (q.v.). Instigated by pope Pius V, the League delivered a crushing blow to Moslem sea power. Cervantes was wounded in the battle, which is the subject of a stirring poem by G. K. Chesterton.

LEPIDOPTERA. *See* INSECT.

LE PLAY ('plī'), **Pierre Guillaume Frédéric** (1806–82). French engineer and sociologist. He became prof. of metallurgy at the Paris School of Mines in 1840, and in 1855 pub. *Les Ouvriers Européens.* Le P. and his followers stress the importance of a strong family organization, of religion, and of private property.

LEPROSY. A disease due to infection by the lepra bacillus. It is most common in hot, damp countries, especially Africa, but is found all over the world. In the nodular type the skin thickens, lumps appear all over it and break down into ulcers: the patient eventually dies of exhaustion, tuberculosis, or kidney disease. In the smooth type the microbe chiefly attacks the nerves of the skin, producing discoloured patches, loss of feeling, paralysis, and the death and shedding of fingers and toes. The bacillus may be transmitted by contact, or enter through stomach and lungs.

LE'PTIS MAGNA. Ruined city in Libya, near Homs and 75 m. E. of Tripoli. It was founded by the Phoenicians, then came under Carthage, and in 47 B.C. under Rome. Excavation in the 20th cent. brought to light remains of fine Roman buildings.

LE PUY. *See* PUY, LE.

LÉRIDA (ler'ēthah). Capital of L. prov. in N. Spain, on the Segre, 82 m. W. of Barcelona. The chief manufactures are leather, paper, glass, and cloth, L. was captured by Caesar in 49 B.C. It has a palace of the kings of Aragon. Pop. (1960) 63,850.

LE'RMONTOV, Mikhail Yurevich (1814–41). Russian poet and novelist. B. in Moscow, he received a commission in the Guards, but in 1837 was exiled to the Caucasus for a revolutionary poem on the death of Pushkin. The romantic scenery of the Caucasus deeply influenced his poetry. After returning to St. Petersburg in 1838 he pub. his psychological novel *A Hero of Our Times* and a vol. of poems. He was killed in a duel.

LERNER, Alan Jay. *See* LOEWE, Frederick.

LE SAGE (sahzh), **Alain René** (1668–1747). French novelist and dramatist. B. in Brittany, he early abandoned law for literature. His novels incl. *Le Diable boiteux* (1707) and his masterpiece *Gil Blas* (1715–35), much indebted to Spanish originals.

LESBOS. Greek island in the Aegean Sea, near the coast of Turkey, conquered by the Turks from Genoa in 1462, annexed to Greece in 1913. L. was an ancient Aeolian settlement, the home of Alcaeus, Sappho, and other literary celebrities. Mytilene is the cap. L. produces olives, wine, and grain. Area 675 sq. m. Pop. (1961) 140,144.

LESLIE, Sir John Randolph Shane (1885–). Irish author. B. in London, he became an R.C. convert in 1908, and strongly supported the nationalist and Celtic revivalist movements. He has pub. *Cantab* (1926), a satirical novel of Cambridge life; biographies, notably *The Skull of Swift* (1928); and vols. of verse. His dau. Anita Leslie is also an author: *Mrs Fitzherbert, Mr Frewen of England.*

LESOTHO (lesō'tō). Country, formerly known as Basutoland, bounded by the Orange Free State, Natal and Cape Prov., but not part of the Rep. of S. Africa. A Brit. prot. from 1868, it achieved self-govt. in 1965 under the Paramount Chief Moeshoeshoe II (1939–), and independence within the Commonwealth as the Kingdom of L. in 1966. In 1970 the first general elections resulted in the defeat of the govt., but P.M. Chief Leabua Jonathan suspended the constitution, the King going into exile for some months.

The land is mountainous, but maize and wheat are grown and erosion is being combated; sheep and goats supply wool and mohair for export; and diamonds are mined. Many of the men work in the Kimberley mines. The cap. is Maseru.

Area 11,716 sq. m.; pop. (1966) 967,760.

LESPINASSE (lāpinahs'), **Julie de** (1732–76). French authoress. B. at Lyons, an illegitimate dau. of the comtesse d'Albon, she was a friend of d'Alembert and other celebrities of the time, and is remembered for her correspondence, pub. in 1809.

LE'SSEPS, Ferdinand, viscomte de (1805–94). French diplomat and engineer. After serving as ambassador to Madrid 1848–9, he entered the service of the viceroy of Egypt, Said Pasha, and in 1854 obtained a concession for the construction of a canal across the isthmus of Suez. Work began in April 1859, completed Nov. 1869. *See* also PANAMA CANAL.

LE'SSING, Gotthold Ephraim (1729–81). German dramatist and critic. B. at Kamenz in Saxony, he studied at Leipzig, and subsequently lived in Berlin, Leipzig, and Hamburg. His dramatic masterpieces incl. *Miss Sara Sampson* 1755), the first German

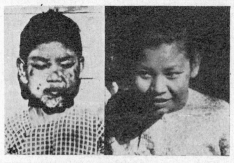

LEPROSY. Eight-year-old Ma Boke Sone on arrival (*left*) at the Roman Catholic Leprosy Institute in Rangoon, and three years later after sulphone drug treatment. *Courtesy of W.H.O.*

tragedy of common life; *Philotas* (1759) a one-act prose tragedy; the comedy *Minna von Barnhelm* (1767) with a Seven Years War background; the domestic tragedy *Emilia Galotti* (1772); and the verse play *Nathan der Weise* (1779) which treats the theme of religious tolerance. As a critic he decisively influenced the course of German literature with *Briefe, die neueste Literatur betreffend* (1759), in which Shakespeare is ranked above the French dramatists; with his masterpiece *Laokoon* (1766) in which he analyses the functions of poetry and the plastic arts; and with the *Hamburgische Dramaturgie* (1767–8) in which he re-interpreted Aristotle and again championed Shakespeare. His many theological and philosophical writings include *Ernst und Falk* (1777–80) in which he pleaded for tolerance and understanding in human affairs.

L'ESTRANGE (lestranj′), **Sir Roger** (1616–1704). English journalist. B. in Norfolk, he was active as a royalist during the Civil War, and was imprisoned 1644–8. He was appointed licenser of the press by Charles II, edited high Tory newspapers, and in 1685 was knighted. He lost his post as licenser in 1688, and was several times imprisoned for Jacobitism.

LESVOS. See LESBOS.

LETCHWORTH. English town (U.D.) in Herts, 35 m. N.N.W. of London, founded in 1903 as the first British garden city. The principal industrial products are clothing, furniture, scientific instruments, and light metal goods, and it is a printing centre. Pop. (1961) 25,515.

LĒ′THĒ. In Greek mythology a river of the underworld whose waters, when drunk, brought forgetfulness of the past.

LE TOUQUET. *See* TOUQUET-PARIS-PLAGE, LE.

LETTERS. The art of L.-writing was perfected by the Romans with Cicero, Pliny the Younger, and Seneca. Christianity introduced the pastoral L., of which the exponents include Basil, Chrysostom, and Gregory Nazienzen in the Eastern Church, and Ambrose, Augustine, Jerome, and Gregory in the West. Outside the Church the Middle Ages tended to produce mainly letters of state, apart from exceptions such as the correspondence of Héloïse and Abelard (12th cent.), and the Paston Ls. (15th cent.). To the Reformation period belong the notable correspondences of Erasmus, Luther, and Melanchthon. There was a steady development of English Ls. during the 16th and 17th cents. with Donne, Spenser, Sidney, Milton, Cromwell, Wotton, etc., while in France there were Pascal and Mme de Sévigné. Ls. reached its highest polish in the 18th cent. in the Ls. of Pope, Walpole, Swift, Mary W. Montagu, Chesterfield, Cowper, Gray, and the 'Ls. of Junius': Richardson adapted the form to the use of the novel. French L.-writers of the period incl. Bossuet, Voltaire, and Rousseau. Familiar names of the 19th cent. are those of Lamb, Byron, Keats, Fitzgerald, Stevenson; the American Emerson, and J. R. Lowell; the French George Sand, Saint-Beuve, and the Goncourt brothers; the German Schiller and Goethe; and the Swiss Gottfried Keller. In the 20th cent. we have T. E. Lawrence, G. B. Shaw and E. Terry, K. Mansfield, Rilke, etc. There are several collections of famous letters, e.g. E. V. Lucas's 'The Gentlest Art.'

LETTRES DE CACHET (let′r-de-kasheh′). French term for orders signed by the king and closed with his seal (*cachet*); especially orders under which persons might be imprisoned or banished without trial. They were used as a means of disposing of politically dangerous persons or criminals of high birth without the embarrassment of a trial. The system was abolished during the French Revolution.

LETTUCE (le′tis). Annual plant (*Lactuca sativa*) belonging to the Compositae family, and believed to have been derived from a wild variety, *L. serriola*. There are 4 common forms, the cabbage L., with round or loose heads, the Cos L., with long, upright heads, the asparagus L., with narrow leaves, and the cut-leaved L., with deeply serrated leaves.

LEUCITE (lū′sīt). Mineral occurring frequently in volcanic rocks of recent origin, and others low in silica content and rich in potash. It is dull white to grey, and usually opaque.

LEUCOCYTE (lū′kosīt). A white blood cell. The blood contains about 11,000 leucocytes to the cubic millimetre – about one to every 500 red cells. Generally speaking, the function of the white cells is to eat up invading bacteria and to repair the results of injury. The resistance of the body to injury and disease, therefore, depends on them. Their number may be reduced (leucopenia) by starvation, pernicious anaemia, and certain infections – e.g. typhoid and malaria. An increase in the numbers (leucocytosis) is a reaction to normal events such as digestion, exertion and pregnancy, and to abnormal ones such as loss of blood, cancer and most infections.

LEUKEMIA (lūkē′mia). A cancer-like disease of the blood, marked by an increase in the white blood cells. Though incurable it may be relieved and possibly controlled by X-rays and drugs. There may be an inherited proneness to L. which can be augmented by external factors such as high fever, and nuclear radiation.

LEVA′NT. Name applied to the E. Mediterranean region, or more specifically, to the coastal regions of Turkey-in-Asia, Syria, Lebanon, and Israel.

LEVELLERS. The democratic party in the English Revolution. They found wide support among the New Model Army, and the yeoman farmers, artisans, and small traders, and during 1647–9 proved a powerful political force. Their programme included the establishment of a republic, govt. by a parl. of one house elected by manhood suffrage, religious toleration, and sweeping social reforms. Mutinies by the Ls. in the army were suppressed by Cromwell in 1649, and the movement lost its importance, although it continued to exist until 1688.

LĒ′VEN, Alexander Leslie, 1st earl of (*c.* 1580–1661). Scottish general. After a distinguished career in the Swedish service, he led the Covenanters' army which invaded England in 1640. He also commanded the Scottish army sent to aid the English Puritans in 1643–6, and shared in the victory of Marston Moor. In 1641 he was created earl of L.

LEVEN. Burgh in Fifeshire, Scotland, at the mouth of the r. Leven. L. is a holiday resort, and manufactures ropes and linen. Pop. (1961) 8,872.

LEVEN, Loch. Lake in Kinross-shire, Scotland, area 6 sq. m. and 11 m. in circuit, with 7 islands, drained by the r. L. It is famous for trout. Mary Queen of Scots was imprisoned 1567–8 on Castle Island.

LĒVER, Charles James (1806–72). Irish novelist. B. in Dublin, he was ed. at Trinity Coll., and became a doctor. His rollicking novels of Irish and army life, such as *Harry Lorrequer* (1837), *Charles O'Malley* (1840), and *Tom Burke of Ours* (1844), achieved a remarkable popularity. His extravagance made it necessary for him to live on the Continent and support himself by incessant writing. In 1867 he became consul at Trieste.

LEVERHULME (lē′verhūm), **William Hesketh Lever, 1st visct. L.** (1851–1925). British manufacturer. B. in Bolton, he founded Lever Bros. Ltd. 1886 which became the leading soap business in the U.K. He founded the garden village of Port Sunlight, Cheshire, to house his factory workers. L. sat in Parl. as a Lib. 1906–9, and received a viscountcy in 1922.

LEVI, Carlo (1902–   ). Italian novelist. Originally a doctor, his books incl. *Christ Stopped at Eboli* (1946), *The Watch* (1951), and *Words are Stones* (1958).

LE′VITES. One of the 12 tribes of Israel, traditionally descended from Levi, one of the sons of Jacob. They were charged with the lesser services of the Temple, and the priesthood was confined to one Levite family, the descendants of Aaron.

LEVSINA. Another form of ELEUSIS.

LEWES (lū′es), **George Henry** (1817–78). British philosopher and critic. From acting he turned to literature and philosophy, his works incl. a *Biographical History of Philosophy* (1845–6), *Comte's Philosophy of the Sciences* (1853), *Aristotle* (1864), *Problems of Life and Mind* (1874–9), and *Life and Works of Goethe* (1855). He m. unhappily in 1840, and after meeting Mary Ann Evans (George Eliot) in 1851, left his wife in 1854 to form a life-long union with her.

LEWES. Ancient co. town (bor.) of Sussex and admin. H.Q. of E. Sussex, England, on the Ouse, 45 m. S. of London. Barbican House, near the castle, has a large collection of Sussex antiquities. Here Henry III was defeated by Simon de Montfort in 1264. Pop. (1961) 13,637.

LEWIS, Cecil Day-. *See* DAY-LEWIS, CECIL.

LEWIS, Meriwether (1774–1809). American explorer. Private sec. to Pres. Jefferson, he was commissioned with William Clark (1770–1838) to find a land route to the Pacific. He followed the Missouri River to its source, crossed the Rocky Mountains, and followed the Columbia River to the Pacific, then returned overland to St. Louis: 1804–6. He was rewarded with the governorship of the Louisiana Territory. His death, nr. Nashville, Tennessee, has been ascribed to suicide, but was more probably murder.

LEWIS, Clive Staples (1898–1963). British scholar. In 1954–63 he was prof. of Medieval and Renaissance English at Cambridge, and his books incl. the remarkable medieval study *The Allegory of Love* (1936); space fiction *Out of the Silent Planet* (1938); such individual essays in popular theology as *The Screwtape Letters* (1942) and *Mere Christianity* (1952); the autobiographical *Surprised by Joy* (1955) and books for children.

LEWIS, D(ominic) B(evan) Wyndham (1891–1969). Brit. writer. He made his name as the humorous columnist Timothy Shy of the *News Chronicle*, and as the biographer of Villon, Boswell and Molière.

LEWIS, John L(lewellyn) (1880–1969). American labour leader. B. in Iowa, son of a Welsh miner, he worked in the pits, and 1920–60 was pres. of the United Mineworkers of America. He was founder-pres. of the C.I.O. (*see* A.F.L./C.I.O.) in 1935, and was expelled from the A.F.L. Later he re-affiliated the U.M.W.A. to the A.F.L. until 1947, when it became independent.

LEWIS, Matthew Gregory (1775–1818). British author, known as 'Monk' L. from his terror romance *The Monk* (1795), which enjoyed a vogue.

LEWIS, Percy Wyndham (1884–1957). British author and artist. B. off Maine, in his father's yacht, he was ed. at the Slade and in Paris and pioneered on returning to England the new spirit of art which his friend Ezra Pound called Vorticism: he also ed. *Blast*, a literary and artistic magazine proclaiming its principles. His paintings were as boldly hard and aggressive as his literary style, his portraits being especially memorable, e.g. of Edith Sitwell and T. S. Eliot. Among his novels the best are *Tarr* (1918) and *The Childermass* (1928), but he also wrote a number of theoretical books, e.g. *Time and Western Man* (1927), and the autobiography *Blasting and Bombardiering* (1937) and *Rude Assignment* (1950). He has a controversial reputation, being assessed by some as a leading spirit

WYNDHAM LEWIS
Courtesy of Sir Edward Beddington Behrens.

of the early 20th cent.: the argument is generally sharpened by his support in the 1930s of Fascist principles. Our self-portrait, painted in 1920, is called 'Mr. Wyndham Lewis as a Tyro' – tyros being defined by the artist as 'immense novices [who] brandish their appetites in their faces, lay bare teeth in valedictory, inviting, or merely substantial laugh'.

LEWIS, Sinclair (1885–1951). American novelist. B. in Minnesota, he stayed for a time at Upton Sinclair's socialist colony in New Jersey, then became a freelance journalist. He made a reputation with *Main Street* (1920), depicting American small-town life; *Babbitt* (1922), story of a typical business executive, a real-estate man of the midwest caught in the conventions of his milieu which gave a new word to the American language; and *Arrowsmith* (1925), study of a scientist. His later books incl. *It Can't Happen Here* (1935), *Cass Timberlane* (1945), and *The God-Seeker* (1949). He received a Nobel prize 1930.

LEWIS. N. part of Lewis-with-Harris, the largest is. of the Outer Hebrides, off the W. coast of Scotland and to the N. of Uist. Lewis, incl. in Ross and Cromarty, is separated from Harris (q.v.) by a line joining Lochs Resort and Seaforth. Fishing is a main economic activity. Stornoway is the only centre of importance. Area 683 sq. m.; pop. (1961) 16,700.

LE′XINGTON. (1) Town, centre of the Bluegrass Country, Kentucky, U.S.A. Bloodstock is bred in the area, and races and shows are held. There is a tobacco market and the Univ. of Kentucky and Transylvania (1780). Pop. (1960) 62,810. (2) Town of Mass., U.S.A. Paul Revere (1735–1818), a Boston silversmith and member of the Sons of Liberty, was one of the official couriers who carried the news of the approach of British troops to Lexington and Concord on the night of 18 April 1775. Longfellow commemorated the event in 'Paul Revere's Ride'. The first shots of the American War of Independence were fired at L. next day. Pop. (1960) 27,691.

LEYDEN (lā′den). City of the Netherlands, in S. Holland prov., famed for its univ. founded by William the Silent in 1575. L. lies on the Old Rhine, 6 m. from its mouth, and is joined by canal to Haarlem, Amsterdam, and Rotterdam. L. manufactures linen and woollen goods, has many fine buildings, and has been a printing centre since the Elzevir works were set up in 1580. Rembrandt and Jan Steen were b. at L. Pop. (1967) 102,425.

LHASA (lah′sa). Cap. of Tibet, on a lofty plateau 11,830 ft. above sea-level and surrounded by mountains. Weaving, and the manufacture of pottery and gold and silver ware are carried on. It became in the 17th cent. the seat of the Dalai Lama, head of Lamaism; his palace, the 17th cent. Potala, standing 400 ft. above the town, is the most striking of a number of remarkable buildings; the

SINCLAIR LEWIS

Jokang temple of Buddha, which attracts many pilgrims, dates from A.D. 652. When the Chinese invaded Tibet in 1722 they destroyed the walls of L. which were not rebuilt. In 1950–1 the Chinese carried out a more determined conquest of Tibet; following an unsuccessful rebellion in 1959 the Dalai Lama fled to India. The monks who had formed the bulk of the pop. (est. at 50,000) were compelled to take up secular occupations.

LHOTE (lōt), **André** (1885–). French artist. B. at Bordeaux, he has been very influential through his treatises on art in which he explored questions of technique and ultimate artistic aims. His 'Rugby' in the Musée d'Art Moderne, Paris, is an excellent example of his use of colour and geometric style.

LHOTE, Henri. See SAHARA.

LIAO (lyow). River of N.E. China, The main headstream rises in the mts. of Inner Mongolia and flows E., then S. to the Gulf of Liaotung. It is c. 900 m. long and is frozen from Dec. to March.

LIAONING. Chinese prov. in the N.E. lying about the Gulf of Liaotung; it incl. Liaotung peninsula. The cap. is Shenyang; other large towns are Antung, Anshan, Port Arthur, Dairen. Agriculture is important, chief crops being millet, wheat, soya beans; heavy industry based on local coal and iron deposits, is found at Anshan. The name means peace of the Liao. Area 58,300 sq. m. Pop. (1968) 28,000,000.

LIAOTUNG PENINSULA. Promontory in N.E. China, lying between the Gulf of Liaotung on the N.W., Po Hai Strait on the S.W., and the Korea Sea on the S.E. A range of mts., rising to 4,490 ft., occupies the interior. The S.W. extension, which incl. Dairen and Port Arthur, leased by China to Russia in 1898, was taken over by Japan 1905–45; the Japanese called this area the Kwantung Peninsula. Liaotung means E. of the Liao.

LIAO-YANG (lyow-yahng′). City in Liaoning prov. (formerly Manchuria), China, on the Taitzu. Here in 1904 the Russians were defeated by the Japanese. Pop. c. 100,000.

LIBAU. German form of LIEPAJA.

LIBEL. One of the two types of defamation. In L. the defamatory statement is reproduced in a permanent form, the most common being by writing, in a newspaper, or by broadcasting. Libel is both a crime and a civil wrong, or tort (unlike slander (q.v.), which is a tort only). The more usual remedy is by civil proceedings, a criminal prosecution being resorted to only where the publication of the libel is likely to bring about a breach of the peace, as where it is so gross that there is a danger that the defamed person will assault the person responsible for publishing it. In civil proceedings, if the person publishing the libel proves its substantial truth, he escapes liability; but in criminal proceedings it is necessary to prove not only that the words used were true, but also that it was in the public interest that they should be known by the public.

The civil remedy for libel is extremely comprehensive, for proceedings may be brought not only against the person who was first responsible for the statement, but also against everyone who has subsequently repeated or published it. Moreover, a person may defame another of whose existence he is unaware, for the test is whether the words used could be regarded as applying to the plaintiff by reasonable men who knew him, but a defendant who can show he pub. the words innocently and without negligence may avoid liability if willing to pub. a reasonable correction and apology, and pay the plaintiff's costs.

Certain transactions and statements are 'privileged', either absolute or qualified. If a proceeding or statement is absolutely privileged, e.g. all proceedings in Courts of Justice, in Parliament, or in reports of parliamentary proceedings, no action can be brought for libel in respect of it, no matter how inaccurate or malicious the words were. Where a statement enjoys 'qualified privilege', a person who has been defamed by it must prove not only that the words used were untrue, but that the person uttering them had a malicious (i.e. an improper) motive. Another common defence to an action is 'fair comment on a matter of public interest'. Considerable latitude is allowed by the law to criticism of matters of general interest (including new books, plays and films, and all public sports and pastimes), but if facts are quoted they must be quoted with substantial accuracy, and the criticism must be reasonably temperate. In 1960s the stringency of English L. Law was widely attacked as limiting freedom of the press: in the U.S.A. the position is much more elastic.

LIBERALISM. The political and social theory associated with the Liberal Party in Britain, and similar parties elsewhere. L. developed during the 17th–19th cents. as the distinctive theory of the industrial and commercial classes in their struggle against the power of the monarchy, the Church, and the feudal landowners. In politics it stood for parliamentary govt., freedom of the press, speech and worship, and the abolition of class privileges; economically it was associated with laissez-faire, a minimum of state interference in economic life, and international free trade. In the late 19th and early 20th cents. these ideas were modified by the acceptance on the one hand of universal suffrage, hitherto opposed by most Liberals, and on the other of a certain amount of state intervention, in order to ensure a minimum standard of living and to remove extremes of poverty and wealth. The classical statement of Liberal principles is found in *On Liberty* and other works of J. S. Mill.

LIBERAL PARTY. One of Britain's 2 historic parties, the successor to the Whig Party (q.v.). The term 'L.', used officially from c. 1840 and unofficially from c. 1815, marked the transfer of control from the aristocrats to the more radical industrialists, backed by the Benthamites, Nonconformists and the middle classes. During the Ls.' first period of power (1830–41), they promoted parl. and municipal govt. reform and the abolition of slavery, but their utilitarian and laissez-faire theories led to the harsh Poor Law of 1834. Lib. pressure forced Peel to repeal the Corn Laws in 1846, thereby splitting the Tory Party, and except for 2 short periods the Ls. were in power 1846–66, but the only outstanding figure of the period, Palmerston, was very conservative and the only major change was the general adoption of free trade.

Extended franchise in 1867 and Gladstone's emergence as leader began a new phase, dominated by the 'Manchester school' with a programme of 'peace, retrenchment, and reform'. Gladstone's 1868–74 govt. introduced many important reforms, incl. elementary education and vote by ballot. The party's left, mainly composed of working-class Radicals led by Bradlaugh and Chamberlain, repudiated the laissez-faire ideology and inclined towards republicanism, but the Ls. were split over Home Rule in 1886 and many joined the Conservatives. Except for 1892–5, the Ls. remained out of power until 1906, when reinforced by Labour and Irish support they returned with a huge majority: Old-Age Pensions, National Insurance, limitation of the powers of the Lords, and the Irish Home Rule Bill followed.

From 1914 the L. Party declined, Lloyd George's alliance with the Conservatives 1916–22 dividing them between himself and Asquith, and although reunited in 1923 they continued to lose votes. In 1931 they joined the Nat. Govt., but broke away in 1932 in protest against a protectionist policy. The handful of L. members returned in 1950 and 1951 were only influential because of the narrow majority of the parties in power, but a L. 'revival' led by

Grimond resulted in an increased L. vote. In 1967 Grimond was succeeded in the leadership by Jeremy Thorpe (1929–).

LIBE′RIA. Rep. on the W. coast of Africa, between Sierra Leone and the Ivory Coast. The interior consists of a densely wooded plateau. The only navigable rivers are the St. Paul and the Cavalla. The main settlements are along the coast; here coffee, cacao, palm nuts indigo, yams, maize, sugar cane, sorghum, and rice are cultivated. Rubber produced from plantations worked under a concession granted in 1926, expiring 2025, by the Firestone Plantation Co. of Ohio, provides *c.* 10 per cent of U.S. rubber imports. Apart from Monrovia, the cap., the main ports are Robertsport, Marshall, Greenville, and Harper. There are some 1,200 m. of surfaced roads, and a freight railway, built in 1951, links the Bomi Hills iron-ore mines with Monrovia 40 miles distant. The political organization is modelled on that of the U.S.A., and English is the official language. Area *c.* 43,000 sq. m.; pop. (1966) 1,090,000 of whom *c.* 20,000 are Liberians proper, the remainder being indigenous peoples belonging to various tribes, some Moslem, some pagan; there are *c.* 6,000 white inhabitants.

L. began with a settlement made in 1822 near the present Monrovia by the American Colonization Society as a home for Negro freed slaves. The next years were occupied by a bitter struggle against the hostile natives. L. declared its independence in 1847. Large loans have been made by the U.S.A. There is a Pres. (*see* TUBMAN) and Cabinet on the U.S. model, Senate and House of Representatives.

LIBERTY, EQUALITY, FRATERNITY. The official motto of the French Republic, adopted in 1793 as a summary of the ideals of the revolution. The Vichy régime of 1940–4 substituted the phrase 'Work, family, fatherland'.

LIBREVILLE (lēbrvēl′). Cap. of Gabon, on the estuary of the r. Gabon. Founded in 1848 as a refuge for freed slaves, L. developed into a port. It has an airfield. Pop. (1965) 31,000.

LI′BYA. A sovereign independent state in N. Africa, bounded on the N. by the Mediterranean, on the W. by Tunisia and Algeria, on the S. by the reps. of Niger and Chad, and on the E. by the rep. of Sudan and Egypt. Until 1963 it comprised the federal provs. of Cyrenaica, Fezzan, and Tripolitania (qq.v.), but in the interest of overall unity was then divided into 10 admin. divisions. L. includes, from N. to S., a fertile undulating Mediterranean zone where fruits, particularly dates, and cereals thrive and many Italians settled; a sub-desert area where alfalfa is cultivated; the greater part of the Libyan desert, which is broken by fertile oases and the Fezzan mountains. L. is devoid of rivers. Oil, first discovered 1959, has provided unprecedented income growth; traditional industries incl. sponge and tunny fishing. The chief towns are Beida, the newly-built cap. near the coast of Cyrenaica, pop. 50,000; Tripoli and Benghazi, the former dual cap.; Misurata, Homs, Derna, Tobruk and Barce. There are magnificent archaeological sites, e.g. Leptis Magna (q.v.). Area 680,000 sq. m.; pop. (1967) 1,738,000.

L. has been held by the Romans, Vandals, Arabs, and in the 16th cent. by the Turks, who were ousted in 1911–12 by the Italians. L. was occupied in 1943 by British troops and in 1949 Cyrenaica (q.v.) achieved a measure of independence under British supervision. An independent kingdom under Idris from 1951, L. became a rep. after a military coup

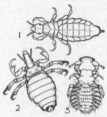

LICE. I, head louse; 2, pig louse; 3, peacock louse.

in 1969. British bases at Tobruk and El Adem were closed 1970.

LICE. Parasitic insects (Anoplura or Pediculidae). They have flat, segmented bodies without wings, and a sucking tube attached to the head, with which they suck the blood of mammals on whom they live. Several species occur on man including the hair-louse (*Pediculus capitis*), and the body-louse (*P. vestimenti*) which may be a typhus carrier. Most mammals have their own varieties of L. Bird-lice, or biting-lice, are a different insect (Mallophaga).

LICENCE. Document issued by some govt. or other recognized authority conveying permission to the holder to do something otherwise prohibited, and designed to facilitate accurate records, the maintenance of order, and collection of revenue. In Britain examples are those required for marriage, for keeping a dog or gun, and sale of intoxicating liquor.

LICHENS (lī′kenz). Group of plants, which consist of a fungus and an alga existing in a mutually beneficial relationship. They are found on trees, rocks, etc., and flourish under very adverse conditions. Some Ls. have food value (e.g. Reindeer moss and Iceland moss), others give dyes such as litmus, or are used in medicine, especially for lung diseases.

LICHFIELD. English city (bor.) in the Trent valley, Staffs, 15 m. S.E. of Stafford. The cathedral was started in the 13th cent., and the grammar school dates from the 15th. Dr. Johnson was b. at L., which

LICHEN. Top, Cetraria pyxidata; below, Evernia prunastri.

was founded in the 7th cent. by St. Chad. Pop. (1961) 14,077.

LICHINE (lichēn′), **David** (1910–). Russian dancer and choreographer. B. at Rostov, he studied under Nijinska and danced with the cos. of Ida Rubinstein, Pavlova, de Basil, for whom he created such early ballets as *Nocturne* (1933), and *de Cuevas*. Later works incl. *Graduation Ball* (1940) and *Harlequinade* (1950).

LIDDELL HART, Sir Basil Henry (1895–1970). Brit. military scientist. He retired as an army captain in 1927, and continued as military correspondent of the *Daily Telegraph* 1925–35, and *The Times* 1935–9. He was an early advocate of air power and a famed exponent of mechanized warfare. His books incl. biographies of *Scipio, Foch, T. E. Lawrence*; and *A History of the Second World War* (1961).

LIDICE (lē′dětseh). Czech mining village, completely destroyed by the Nazis on 10 June 1942 as a reprisal for the assassination of Heydrich. The 192 men of the village were all shot, the 196 women sent to concentration camps where 50 died, and the 105 children to Germany. After the liberation a model mining village was built near the site, which is marked by a monument. Karl Frank, a Sudeten German, was later tried, found responsible for the crime, and hanged at Prague in 1946. The name of L. was taken by many places abroad.

LIE (lē), **Jonas** (1833–1908). Norwegian author. B. at Eker, he gave up his legal practice in 1868, and achieved his most typical successes with his seafaring and folklore stories such as *Trolls* (1891–2), *Maïsa Jons* and *When the Iron Curtain Falls* (1901).

LIE (lē), **Trygve Halvdan** (1896–68). Norwegian statesman. He became sec. of the Lab. Party in 1926, was For. Min. in the exiled govt. 1941–6, when he helped keep the Norwegian fleet for the Allies, and 1st Sec.-Gen. of U.N. 1946–53.

LIEBERMANN (lēb′ermahn), **Max** (1847–1935). German impressionist painter. B. in Berlin, he is famed for his pictures of peasants at work in the fields, scenes in beer gardens, in factories, etc.

LIEBIG (lē'-), **Justus,** Baron von (1803–73). German chemist. After his discovery of the chemical composition of fulminates in 1824 he was appointed prof. at Giessen, and in 1852 at Munich. L. became a baron in 1845.

LIEBKNECHT (lēb'knekht), **Wilhelm** (1826–1900). German Socialist. He took part in the 1848 revolution, and subsequently lived in London until 1861, forming a close friendship with Marx. He was imprisoned for opposing the Franco-Prussian War. From 1874 he led the Social-Democrats in the Reichstag. His son, **Karl L.** (1871–1919), b. in Leipzig, entered the Reichstag as a Social-Democrat in 1912 and during the F.W.W. was imprisoned for organizing an anti-war demonstration. A founder of the German Communist Party, originally known as the Spartacus League, he led an unsuccessful Communist revolt in Berlin in 1919, and was murdered by army officers.

LIECHTENSTEIN (lēkh'tenstīn). Small European principality, situated between Austria and Switzerland. Vaduz is the cap. L. was formed in 1719 from the two counties of Schellenberg and Vaduz. L., which was in a customs union with Austria-Hungary 1876–1918, in 1924 joined the Swiss Customs Union. It is mountainous; the chief occupations are agriculture and cattle rearing. **Francis Joseph II** (1906–) succeeded to the princedom in 1938. Area 62 sq. m.; pop. (1967) 20,443.

LIE DETECTOR. Registering device for blood pressure, rate of breathing, etc., which tend to alter under stress of telling an untruth.

LIÈGE (lyāzh'). Cap. of L. prov., Belgium, 54 m. S.E. of Brussels, on the Meuse, a centre of iron and

LIÈGE. Today lawyers pace the cloistered courtyard of the magnificent Palace of the Prince-Bishops (built 1508–40), for the building now houses the law courts.
Courtesy of Belgian National Tourist Office.

armament manufacture, and of a coal-mining district; textiles, paper, and chemicals are other products. There is a univ. (1817) and a number of ancient churches, the oldest, St. Martin's, dating from 692. L., occupied by the Germans in both world wars, suffered severely economically, but was not badly damaged physically. Pop. (1966) 153,000.

LIEPAJA (lyä'pahyah). Port of the Latvian S.S.R., situated on a narrow peninsula between Lake L. and the Baltic. Shipbuilding, engineering, and the manufacture of steel, textiles, and chemicals are among its industries. The Knights of Livonia founded L. in the 13th cent. Pop. (1961) 76,000.

LIFAR (lē-), **Serge** (1905–). Russian dancer and choreographer. B. at Kiev, he studied under Nijinska, joined the Diaghilev co. in 1923 and was *premier maître de ballet* at the Paris Opéra 1947–58 and

LIFEBOAT. Modern lifeboats are unsinkable, but most are useless once capsized. Since the mid-19th century there have been self-righting boats, but their specialized shape lessened their seaworthiness. In the Oakley type (named after their designer, surveyor to the R.N.L.I.) reliance is placed instead on a water ballast tank over the keel which tips its contents into a side tank when the boat tilts beyond a certain angle. The 48 ft. 6 in. *Yarmouth* (I.O.W.), prototype of her class, rights herself in a few seconds and is the 1st lifeboat to carry radar – hitherto ineffective at sea-level in bad weather.
Courtesy of the Royal National Lifeboat Institution.

1962–63. A noted experimenter, he developed the importance of the male dancer in *Prometheus* (1929), produced his 1st ballet without music, *Icare*, in 1935, and pub. the same year the controversial *Le Manifeste du choréographie*.

LIFEBOAT. The first boat designed expressly for life-saving was built in 1789 and stationed at the mouth of the Tyne. In 1824 the Royal National L. Institution was estab. at the instance of Sir William Hillary: this service, manned by volunteers, is still, as it has always been, financed wholly by voluntary contributions. There are several types of L., ranging from 25 ft. to 52 ft., nearly all self-bailing. The U.S. Coast Guard, operating mainly inshore, tend to use self-righting boats, while U.K. vessels, having to travel farther out to sea, sacrifice self-righting ability for broader beam and greater stability. All boats now built have diesel engines. Equipment includes pistols or guns for firing life-lines, radio, searchlights, and oil sprays for smoothing the water; most Ls. carry a crew of 8 and can take on board 30–100 people.

LIFE INSURANCE. *See* INSURANCE and SAVING.

LIGAMENTS. Short bands of tough fibrous tissue connecting two bones at a joint, or holding an organ, such as the liver or uterus, in position.

LIGATURE. Suture (nylon, wire, etc.) binding a blood vessel, a limb, the base of a tumour, etc., chiefly so as to stop the movement through it of blood or other fluid.

LIGHT. Electromagnetic radiation in the visible range, i.e. from about 4,000 Å in the extreme violet to about 7,700 Å in the extreme red. See diagram of frequency spectrum of electromagnetic waves p. 380. L. is considered to exhibit both particle and wave properties and the fundamental particle or quantum of light is called the *photon*. The speed of L. in vacuo is approximately 186,000 miles/sec. or 3×10^{10} cm./sec. and is a universal constant denoted by c.

The L. year is the normal method of expressing astronomical distances and is the distance travelled by L. in one year, a distance of nearly 6 million million miles.

Newton was the first to discover, in 1666, that sunlight is composed of a mixture of L. of all different colours in certain proportions and that it could be separated into its components by refraction. Before his time it was supposed that refraction of L. actually produced colour instead of separating colours already existing. *See also* LENS.

LIGHTHILL, Michael James (1924–). British mathematician. After a brilliant academic career – he was in 1950 appointed prof. of applied mathematics in Manchester at 26 – he was elected F.R.S. in 1953, was director at Farnborough 1959–64, and Royal Soc. research prof. at Imperial Coll. from 1964.

LIGHTHOUSE. Structure carrying a powerful light to aid marine or aerial navigation. Among early Ls. were the Pharos of Alexandria (*c.* 280 B.C.) and those built by the Romans at Ostia, Ravenna, Boulogne and Dover. In England beacons burning in church towers served as Ls. until the 17th cent., and in the earliest Ls. such as the Eddystone, first built 1698, open fires or candles were used. Today dissolved acetylene or electricity is used, and the light of the burner or lamp is magnified and directed out to the horizon (or up to the zenith for aircraft) by a series of mirrors or prisms. For identification lights are individually varied, usually either flashing (the dark period exceeding the light) or occulting (the dark being equal or less): fixed lights are liable to confusion. Manned **lightships** replace Ls. where reefs, sandbanks, etc., make erection of a L. impossible; and, where it is impossible to maintain keepers, unattended light-buoys equipped for up to a year's service. In fog sound signals are made (horns, sirens, explosives), and in the case of lightbuoys, fogbells and whistles operated by the movement of the waves. In the U.K. there are 3 general authorities – Trinity House, Commissioners of Northern Ls., and Commissioners of Irish Lights: in the U.S.A. the supervisory authority is the Coast Guard.

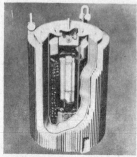

LIGHTHOUSE. Ten years' electricity without refuelling is supplied by this two-ton 'SNAP Seven-B' 60-watt nuclear generator (2 ft. 10 in. high) installed in a 50 ft. concrete-tower Coast Guard lighthouse at Baltimore in 1964. The 14 tubes in the centre contain strontium titanate fuel, and the 120 pairs of thermocouples surrounding them convert heat to electricity.
Courtesy of U.S.I.S.

LIGHTNING. A discharge of electricity, accompanied by a visible flash, between 2 clouds or a cloud and the earth, caused by a difference in potential. In dry weather the atmosphere has a positive potential with respect to the earth, increasing with distance. When the usual balance cannot be maintained, water particles coalesce to form drops, concentrating their charge, which under stress results in a flash of L. Forked L. gives the impression of sharp angles but is usually sinuous; sheet L. is usually a distant indefinite illumination. Thunder is the accompanying noise, augmented by echoing. Conduction of the discharge is most likely through isolated buildings or elevated conductors, lesser conducting suffering most damage.

LIGNITE. *See* COAL.

LILAC. A flowering shrub (*Syringa vulgaris*) of the family Oleaceae. The panicles of small white or purplish flowers are sweetly scented. The smaller Persian L. is also popular in gardens.

LILBURNE, John (*c.* 1614–57). English politician. He was imprisoned 1638–40 for circulating Puritan pamphlets, fought in the parliamentary army, and by his advocacy of a democratic republic won the leadership of the Levellers (q.v.). Under the Common-

LIMA. Dominating the main square, the Plaza de Armas, is the cathedral, consecrated in 1625. It contains the remains of Francisco Pizarro who laid its cornerstone on the same day that he founded the city. *Photo: Bell, Howarth Ltd.*

wealth he was twice tried for sedition and acquitted, and after his acquittal he was imprisoned 1653–5.

LILIACEAE (lili-ā'sē-ē). Family of bulbous plants, including a few shrubs. The genus *Lilium* is typical of the family, and incl. more than 50 varieties. They are monocotyledons, and the leaves may be alternate or in whorls. The stems are erect, the flowers usually appearing at the top. The flowers are regular and frequently bell-shaped. Many varieties are cultivated in gardens, including hyacinth, tulip, Madonna lily autumn crocus, etc.

Certain fibre-producing plants and the medicinal *Aloe* and *Colchicum* belong to this family, as do the food plants onion, garlic, leek and asparagus.

LILIENCRON (lēl'yenkrōn), **Detlev**, Freiherr von (1844–1909). German lyric poet. B. at Kiel, he served in the Prussian Army, and then sought his fortune in America. Returning to Holstein, he pub. his first vol. of verse. *Adjutantenritte* in 1883. It was followed by many others. He also wrote short stories, a humorous epic, a novel, and dramas.

LILIENTHAL (lēl'yentahl), **Otto** (1848–96). German aeronaut. He studied the flight of birds, and invented one of the earliest gliders, in which he made over 2,000 flights. He was killed when it crashed.

LILITH (Heb. *lilātū*, night). An Assyrian female demon; according to the Talmud she was the wife of Adam before Eve's creation. She was said to entice children to destruction.

LILLE (lēl). Cap. of Nord dept., N. France, on the Deûle, 154 m. N.N.E. of Paris. Lying in a rich agricultural and industrial plain, L. was long a fortress city, and became the seat of a bishopric in 1913. Its citadel, built by Vauban, and Palais des Beaux Arts, with its collection of pictures, are the most noted historical buildings, while public buildings incl. univs. and a Pasteur institute. There are many important industries and manufactures incl. locomotives, heavy machinery, coal mining, textiles, and sugar. Pop. (1968) 190,546.

LILLIE, Beatrice (1898–). British comedienne. B. in Toronto, she became celebrated in cabaret and for her one-woman theatre shows, in which she sings and displays a satiric talent of high order.

LILONGWE (lilong'wa). Town in Malawi, 150 m. N.W. of Blantyre and 50 m. W. of Lake Malawi, named 1964 as site of the new cap. (replacing Zomba) to be built 10 m. from the existing township. Pop. (1967) 20,000.

LILY OF THE VALLEY. Plant (*Convallaria majalis*) in the family Liliaceae, growing in woods in Europe, N. Asia, and N. America, and a common garden plant. The white flowers are scented.

LIMA (lē'mah). The cap. of the rep. of Peru, and

of L. dept., on the r. Rimac, 6 m. E. of the Pacific coast. Founded by Francisco Pizarro in 1535, it was rebuilt after destruccion by earthquake in 1746, and has a univ. dating from 1551. Manufactures incl. chemicals, textiles, glass, cement, etc. Of interest are the cathedral, the govt. palace (the rebuilt Palace of the Viceroys) and the ancient Inquisition building, now the senate house. Pop. (1960) 1,262,107. Limatambe airport lies to the S.E.

LIMASSŌ′L. Seaport of S. Cyprus, 38 m. S.S.W. of Nicosia, with a wine trade. Richard I m. Berengaria of Navarre at L., 1191. Pop. (1966) 48,100.

LIMBO (Lat. 'border' or 'edge'). In medieval theology, a region for the souls of those who were not admitted to the divine vision; the word was first used in this sense by Thomas Aquinas. *Limbus infantum* was a place where unbaptized infants enjoyed inferior blessedness; and *limbus patrum* was the place where the prophets and fathers of the O.T. dwelt. Also a West Indian dance in which the performer passes under a pole, the body being bent over backwards, and skilled exponents managing the feat when the pole is only a few inches from the ground.

LIMBURG. An ancient feudal duchy of Lower Lorraine, divided between the Netherlands and Belgium in 1839. The modern provs. are (1) Limbourg, a

LIME (Linden). Tree, flowers and fruit.

N.E. prov. of Belgium in part bounded by the Meuse, cap. Hasselt. Area 930 sq. m.; pop. (1966) 631,300. (2) Limburg, a S.E. prov. of the Netherlands, drained by the Maas and Roer, cap. Maastricht; it incl. the only Dutch coalfield. Area 857 sq. m.; pop. (1966) 980,300.

LIME. Citrus fruit (*Citrus aurantifolia*) regarded by some as a variety of the citron, *C. medica*, and a sub-variety of the sweet lime, *C. limetta*. It is a native of India and grows on small thorny bushes. The white flowers are succeeded by light green or yellow fruits resembling lemons but more globular in shape.

LIME. Calcium oxide (CaO), an alkaline earth, derived from the metal calcium. It is a white, powdery substance, sometimes known as quicklime. Slaked lime or hydrate of lime is calcium oxide combined with water (Ca_2OH). Carbonate of lime ($CaCO_3$) in the form of limestone or chalk is generally heated in kilns for the production of calcium oxide.

LIME or **Linden.** Genus of deciduous trees (*Tilia*) found in Europe, N. Asia, and N. America. They are distinguished by the light green leaves and yellowish sweet-smelling flowers, which hang in cymes from the leaf axil, accompanied

LILY OF THE VALLEY

by an oblong leaf or wing joined to the flower stalk at the base.

LIMEHOUSE. District of the Greater London bor. of Tower Hamlets. It borders on the Thames and the West India dock, and the population incl. many Chinese.

LIMERICK. Five-line nonsense verse, which first appeared in England *c.* 1820, and was popularized by Edward Lear. An example is:

There was a young lady of Riga
Who rode with a smile on a tiger;
    They returned from the ride
    With the lady inside
And the smile on the face of the tiger.

LIMERICK. Chief tn. and co. bor. in co. L., Rep. of Ireland, on the Shannon, 110 m. S.W. of Dublin. An ancient town, it was occupied by the Danes from *c.* 820 to *c.* 1100. The cathedral of St. Mary was built in the 12th cent., restored 1860. L. is the most important port on the W. coast. Pop. (1966) 58,082. The co. of Limerick, in Munster prov., is mainly level but rises in the S.E. to the Galty mts. The chief river is the Shannon. The Golden Vale is a fertile district, and the main occupation is farming. Area 1,037 sq. m.; pop. (1966) 137,357.

LIMERICK. The Treaty Stone, a rough block of limestone on which the Treaty of Limerick was signed in 1691, was mounted on a pedestal at the west end of Thomond Bridge in 1865. The liberties the treaty granted to Roman Catholics were never actually given. *Courtesy of the Irish Tourist Board.*

LIMESTONE. Name for sedimentary rocks composed chiefly of carbonate of lime ($CaCO_3$). They may be deposited under sea or fresh water, being the calcareous remains of many aquatic animals, such as crustacea, mollusca, foraminifera, etc. Corals build up into solid masses of limestone rock.

LIMITATION, Statutes of. Under English law Acts of Parliament limiting the time within which certain classes of action may be inaugurated, e.g. in simple contracts and most civil wrongs an action must be started by the aggrieved party within 6 yrs. In principle U.S. law is similar, but varies from state to state.

LIMITS, Territorial and **Fishing.** Traditionally T.L., over which a country has absolute jurisdiction, were set at 3 m. from the shore – the distance a gun could then reach – and under the Geneva Convention of 1882 T. and F.L. coincided at 3 m. However, modern warfare, new fishing methods, pollution dangers, and the value of minerals beneath the sea have led to internat. dispute and conferences in 1958 and 1960 failed to agree on the Geneva formula (T.L. 6 m. and F.L. 12 m.). Some Latin American countries have claimed T.L. of 200 m., and Canada claims an Arctic anti-pollution control belt of 100 m.

LIMNOS. See LEMNOS.

LIMOGES (lēmōzh′). Cap. of Haute-Vienne dept., France, 112 m. N.W. of Bordeaux on the Vienne. Its cathedral was begun in 1273. The Black Prince sacked L. in 1370. L. is the seat of a bishopric, and is famous for porcelain. Pop. (1968) 132,935.

LI′MONITE. Hydrated iron oxide. The mineral, also known as brown iron ore, is found in bog deposits.

LIMOUSIN (lēmoozań′), **Leonard** (*c.* 1505–*c.* 1577). French artist, the most famous enamel painter of Limoges. He was court painter to Francis I and Henry II, and produced portraits in enamel, vases, etc.

LIMPET. Species of gasteropod mollusc. It has a conical shell, and adheres firmly to rocks by the disc-like foot. They are marine animals, and the Common

L. (*Patella vulga.a*) remains in the inter-tidal area. They leave their fixed position only to obtain vegetable food, always returning to the same spot.

LINACRE (lin'aker), **Thomas** (*c.* 1460–1524). English humanist scholar and physician. In 1509 he became physician to Henry VIII, and in 1518 obtained from the king a charter constituting the Royal College of Physicians, of which he was the first president. He was one of the leading figures of the New Learning.

LIMPETS

LI'NAR ('line'+'star'). In astronomy, point sources discovered 1970 which emit with great energy at wavelengths characteristic of the spectral line of certain chemical compounds. Detectible in any weather, they have potential value in navigation.

LINCOLN (ling'kon), **Abraham** (1809–65). 16th Pres. of the U S A. B. in a Kentucky log cabin, he was almost entirely self-educated, but having qualified as a lawyer practised from 1837 at Springfield, Illinois. He sat, as a Whig, in the state legislature 1834–41 and in Congress 1847–9, and joined the new Republican Party in 1856. As a candidate for the Senate in 1858, he held a series of public debates with his opponent, Stephen Douglas, which won him the Republican candidature for the presidency in 1860. He was elected on a minority vote.

Between his election and his inauguration in March 1861, 7 slave states seceded from the Union, and were followed by 4 more. L.'s refusal to evacuate Fort Sumter gave the signal for civil war, which until 1863 went badly, and L. became extremely unpopular. His cabinet and generals were often insubordinate, and even disloyal, yet L. finally imposed his will on them so firmly that he was accused of aiming at dictatorship. The British govt. was hostile, and it took all L.'s tact to avert war. The abolitionists considered him lukewarm on the slavery question, for though he hated slavery he considered the fundamental issue to be the preservation of the Union.

Although his proclamation of 1863 freed slaves only in Confederate territory, he nevertheless advocated the constitutional amendment totally abolishing slavery. His view of the war is summarized in his speech at the dedication of the war cemetery at Gettysburg in 1863, in which he said it was being fought to preserve a 'nation, conceived in liberty, and dedicated to the proposition that all men are created equal', and to ensure that 'government of the people, by the people, for the people, shall not perish from the earth'. In 1864 he was re-elected by a 400,000 majority,

ABRAHAM LINCOLN. The president assassinated by John Wilkes Booth at Ford's Theatre in Washington D.C. on 14 April 1865, from a contemporary drawing. *Courtesy of U.S.I.S.*

and as victory approached he advocated a conciliatory reconstruction policy, 'with malice towards none, with charity for all'. Five days after Lee's surrender, L. was assassinated in a theatre at Washington by a Confederate fanatic, John Wilkes Booth. The L. Memorial (1922) consists of a large marble hall containing a 19 ft. seated statue of the pres. For the L. Center, *see* NEW YORK.

LINCOLN. City (co. bor.) co. tn. of Lincs, England, on the Witham, 130 m. N.N.W. of London. Remains exist of the Roman Lindum, and the cathedral, high above the town, built in the 11th–15th cents., contains the earliest Gothic work in Britain. Its bell, Great Tom of L., weighs 5½ tons. Agricultural machinery and implements are produced. Pop. (1961) 77,065.

LINCOLN. Cap. of Nebraska, U.S.A., seat of the state univ. The chief industry is flour milling. Lindbergh learned to fly at L. Pop. (1960) 128,521.

LINCOLNSHIRE. The 2nd-largest co. in England, stretching along 110 m. of its E. coast. The main rivers are the Humber, Trent, Witham, and Welland; the co. town is Lincoln. The fens cover a considerable area of L., which is divided into 3 administrative divisions: the Parts of Lindsey, Kesteven, and Holland (qq.v.). Area 2,663 sq. m.; pop. (1967) 791,500.

LIND, Jenny (1820–87). Swedish soprano singer. B. in Stockholm, she gained the name 'Swedish Nightingale' on account of her remarkable range.

LINDBERGH, Charles Augustus (1902–). American aviator. In 1927 he made the first solo non-stop flight across the Atlantic, and was created a colonel in the U.S. Army. Before America's entry into the S.W.W. he was prominent as an Isolationist. L.'s first-born son was kidnapped and killed in 1932; a case which led to the passing of the 'Lindbergh Law', making kidnapping a federal instead of a state offence, in the same year. The kidnapper, B. R. Hauptmann, was executed in 1936.

LINDEN TREE. *See* LIME.

LINDISFARNE. Another name of HOLY ISLAND. Northumberland.

LINDSAY, Nicholas Vachel (1879–1931). American poet. B. at Springfield, he adopted a wandering life, supporting himself by lectures and recitations of his own poetry. He gained recognition with *Congo and other Poems* (1914); later books incl. *Chinese Nightingale* (1917), *Johnny Appleseed* (1928), and the autobiographical *Handy Guide for Beggars*.

LINDSEY, Parts of. One of the 3 administrative cos. forming Lincs. Its administrative centre is Lincoln. Area 1,524 sq. m.; pop. (1967) 456,070.

LINEAR ACCELERATOR. A machine in which charged particles are accelerated to high speed in passing down a straight evacuated tube or waveguide. Acceleration of the particles is produced by electromagnetic waves in the tube or by electric fields.

LINE ISLAND. *See* GILBERT AND ELLICE ISLANDS.

LINEN. The yarn spun and the textile – one of the oldest known – woven from flax (q.v.). To get the longest possible fibres, F. is pulled (not cut) by hand or machine, just as the seed bolls are beginning to set. After preliminary drying, it is steeped in water so that the fibre can be more easily separated from the wood of the stem, then 'hackled' (combed), classified, drawn into continuous fibres, and spun. Bleaching, weaving, and finishing processes vary according to the final product, which ranges from sailcloth, canvas and sacking to cambric and lawn. Because of its length of fibre, L. yarn has twice the strength of cotton, and is superior in delicacy, so that it is especially suitable for lace making. It mixes well with synthetics.

LINGAM. A phallus, worshipped by the Hindus as the symbol of Siva, the god of destruction yet of generative power. Often it is combined with the Yoni, the female emblem.

LINGUA FRANCA. A simplified language or jargon used in intercourse between peoples of different language who are unable to acquire each other's languages correctly. The term, literally 'Frank language' (Frank being the general Arabic term for Europeans), was originally applied to the hybrid Italian which came to be used in trade in the eastern Mediterranean from Renaissance times onwards.

LINGUISTICS. The science of the phenomena of language in general. Language may be defined as the transmission of ideas by means of articulate sounds, but L. also includes written language, inasmuch as it begins by being dependent on the spoken words.

L. in its widest sense embraces a number of special studies, such as phonetics, etymology, semantics, and comparative grammar.

LINKLATER, Eric (1899–). Scottish writer. B. in Orkney, he set many of his stories in Scotland. A student of medicine at Aberdeen, he worked in Bombay as asst. ed. on the *Times of India*, and then returned to his old univ. to teach English for a year before going to the U.S. (1928–30), where he wrote the first of a series of light, sardonic novels which incl. *Juan in America* (1931), *Ripeness is All* (1935), and *Private Angelo* (1946). Among other works are the autobiographical *The Man on my Back* (1941) and the short stories *Sealskin Trousers* (1947).

LINKÖPING (lin'chöping). Town in Sweden, 107 m. S.W. of Stockholm. It is the seat of a Lutheran bishopric, and has a 12th cent. cathedral. Tobacco, hosiery, aircraft and engines are manufactured. Pop. (1966) 77,365.

LINLITHGOW, John Adrian Louis Hope, 1st marquess of (1860–1908). British administrator. The eldest son of the 6th earl of Hopetoun, he was first Gov.-Gen. of the Australian Commonwealth 1900–2. His son, **Victor A. J. Hope,** 2nd marquess (1887–1952), was viceroy and Gov.-Gen. of India 1936–43.

LINLITHGOW. Cap. of W. Lothian, Scotland, and royal burgh, 17 m. W. of Edinburgh. L. is a tourist centre and has distilleries. The ruined L. palace was at one time a residence of kings of Scotland; Mary Queen of Scots was born there. Pop. (1961) 4,327.

LINLITHGOWSHIRE. Former name of WEST LOTHIAN.

LINNAEUS (linē'us), **Carolus** (1707–78). Swedish botanist, ennobled in 1762 as Carl von Linné, Swedish form of his Lat. name. Son of a Lutheran pastor, he

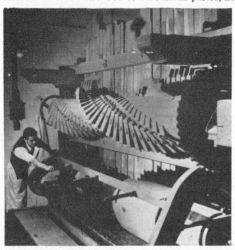

LINEN. The characteristic permanent natural sheen is achieved by 'beetling'. The cloth is wound on rollers and slowly rotated while being beaten with wooden blocks, a process which continues for up to 72 hours.
Courtesy of the Irish Linen Guild.

studied at Lund and at Uppsala, where he became asst. prof. of botany in 1730. An adventurous journey to Lapland in 1732 was followed by his *Flora Lapponica* (1737), and after spells in Holland and England he became in 1741 prof. of medicine (later botany) at Uppsala. In his *Species Plantarum* (1753) he achieved the concise method of naming plants and animals by genus, species, etc., which forms the basis of modern classification. His books, MSS. and specimens were bought by Sir J. E. Smith, founder of the Linnean Society (1788), and preserved in the Linnean Rooms, Burlington House, London. *See* CENTIGRADE.

LINNET. Bird of the finch family (*Linota cannabina*) common in Europe. Its colour changes with the seasons to brown, grey, or pink. It nests in bushes and feeds on fruits and insects.

LI'NOTYPE. A machine for composing printing types in solid lines or 'slugs'. The first composing machine to achieve enduring success, it is widely used for newspaper work and to a lesser extent for books. *See also* INTERTYPE.

LIN PIAO (lin pyow), **Marshal** (1908–71). Chinese soldier and politician. Vice-chairman of the Communist Party, and Vice-Premier and Min. of Defence from 1959, he was named as successor to Mao Tse-tung in 1969 but d. disgraced, in an aircraft crash.

LINSEED. Seeds of the flax plant (*Linum usitatissimum*), from which linseed oil is expressed, the residue being used as feeding cake for cattle. The oil is used in paint and varnishes, and in the manufacture of linoleum.

LINTON, William James (1812–97). British wood-engraver, one of the finest of his day, he illus. numerous books, and some of his best work was printed in the *Illustrated London News*; he pub. *Wood engraving: a manual of instruction* in 1884. In 1867 he went to the U.S.A. and founded a printing press in Connecticut.

LION. An adept tree-climber in the Kruger National Park.
Courtesy of Satour.

LINZ (lints). Cap. of Upper Austria, on the Danube. A river port, it grew up around the Roman fort Lentia. It is a tourist centre. Iron and steel, textiles, chemicals, etc., are manufactured. Pop. (1961) 196,206.

LION. Largest of the cat family (*Felis leo*), found in Africa and N.W. India and formerly more widely distributed. The coat is tawny, the young having darker stripe and spot markings which usually disappear in the adult, and the male has a heavy mane and a tuft at the end of the tail. Head and body measure *c.* 6 ft. with an additional 3 ft. of tail, the lioness being slightly smaller. Ls. commonly mate for life and produce litters of 2–6 cubs, and in the African interior often live in parties of several adult males and females with half a dozen young ones. Capable of short bursts of speed, they skilfully collaborate in stalking their prey which consists of the large herbivorous animals. Man-eating is usually the resort of old lions whose teeth and strength are failing.

LIPARI ISLANDS (lē'pahrē). Group of volcanic islands off the N.E. of Sicily, named Lipari, Vulcano, Stromboli, Salina, Panaria, Filicudi, and Alicudi. They were known to the ancients as the home of Aeolus, god of the winds. L., the largest island, contains the chief town of the same name (pop. 11,854). Area 44 sq. m.; pop. *c.* 18,000.

LIPCHITZ, Jacques (1891–). Lithuanian sculptor. He worked in Paris from 1909, becoming a member of the Ésprit Nouveau Group, and from 1941 in the U.S.A., where he became a citizen in 1957. His works range from the Cubist 'Femme Assise' (1916) to later more baroque studies of the human figure, his bronzes being especially fine.

LI'PPE. German r., rising in the Teutoburg Forest and flowing generally W. for 150 m. to join the Rhine at Wesel. It gave its name to a small state, area 470 sq. m., which was a sovereign principality from the 12th cent. until 1918, then a free state of the German rep.; united with Schaumburg under the Nazis to form a Gauleiter's district, it came under British occupation in 1945 and in 1946 was absorbed in the Land of North Rhine-Westphalia. Its cap. was Detmold. Prince Bernhard of the Netherlands belonged to the former ruling family of L.

LIPPERSHEY (lip'ershī), **Hans.** Dutch spectacle-maker who is said to have invented the telescope by chance, c. 1608.

LIPPI, Fra Filippo (1406–69). Italian painter, b. at Florence. His most important works are the frescoes in the choir of the cathedral at Prato, representing the lives of John the Baptist and of St. Stephen. L.'s 'Vision of St. Bernard', formerly attributed to Masaccio, is in the National Gallery, London. His son, **Filippino L.** (1457–1504), was also a painter, studied under Botticelli, and executed frescoes in the Carmine, Florence, and the 'Virgin and Saints' (Uffizi, Florence).

LIP READING. Interpretation of speech by observation of the lips, tongue, and facial expression, enabling a deaf person, when proficient in the art and when the other person fully co-operates, to carry on to some extent a normal conversation without the use of electrical or other hearing aids.

LIQUORICE (lik'ōris). Plant (*Glycyrrhiza glabra*) in the family Leguminosae, and the black, hard, sticks of paste prepared from boiled extracts of the crushed root, which are made into confectionery or, in pharmacy, for masking the bad taste of medicine.

LIRA (lēr'ah) (Lat. *libra*, pound). The standard unit of Italian currency, divided into 100 centesimi.

LISBOA. Portuguese form of LISBON.

LISBON (liz'bon). Cap. of Portugal from 1260, and of Estremadura prov. It lies in a beautiful position on the Tagus, which here forms a tidal lake and an estuary. Most of L. is built on low hills. Alfama dist. is the old town, with narrow streets, picturesque but poor. The centre of city life is the Cidade Baixa (lower city): an earthquake in 1755 destroyed this part of the city, with great loss of life; it was rebuilt rapidly at the expense of the marquis of Pombal. Points of interest incl. the Castelo de São Jorge, the cathedral, a Moorish citadel founded 1150, the monastery of São Vicente de Fóra and the church of Nossa Senhora do Monte, the palace of the National Assembly (formerly a Benedic-

LISBON. Built on the right bank of the river Tagus, Lisbon is an important fishing port. The catches are both valuable and varied and the fishmarket flourishes.
Courtesy of the Portuguese State Office.

tine monastery), the Palacio das Necessidades (formerly the royal palace, from which Manuel II, last king of Portugal, went into exile in 1910), the museums of ancient and of contemporary art, the botanical garden and Edward VII park, and the English cemetery, where Henry Fielding is buried. The city is the seat of an archbishopric and of a univ. (1911). It has a fine harbour and is the centre of an important fishing industry. Among industries are shipbuilding, sugar refining, and the manufacture of textiles, chemicals, paper, and pottery. Exports incl. wine, olive oil, and cork. The first section of an underground railway was opened in 1959; an electric railway links L. with the seaside resort of Estoril. The international airport of Portela lies 4 m. N.N.E. of L.

L., an important centre in Roman times, achieved its greatest prosperity in the 16th cent. In 1967 floods drowned c. 500 people in the worst disaster since the earthquake. Pop. (1960) 818,382.

LISBURN. Cathedral city and market town (U.D.) of co. Antrim, N. Ireland, seat of the bishopric of Down, Connor, and Dromore. L. is noted for its linens. Jeremy Taylor died there. Pop. (1961) 17,688.

LISIEUX (lēsyŏ'). Town in Calvados dept., France, 28 m. E.S.E. of Caen. Thérèse Martin (1873–97), popularly called the 'little flower', spent all but the first 5 years of her short life in the Carmelite convent of L., and was in 1925 canonized as St. Teresa of L.; her tomb attracts pilgrims. Pop. (1962) 22,472.

LIST, Friedrich (1789–1846). German economist. B. in Württemberg, he became a prof. at Tübingen univ. and a deputy in the Württemberg chamber, but was imprisoned in 1822 for his liberal views, and in 1825 emigrated to the U.S.A. He returned to Germany in 1832 as U.S. consul at Leipzig. He committed suicide. His *National System of Political Economy* (1841) greatly influenced German economic thought and practice.

LISTER, Joseph, 1st baron (1827–1912). British surgeon. He was prof. of surgery at Glasgow 1860–9, at Edinburgh 1869–77, and at King's Coll., London, 1877–92. The first to use antiseptic treatment for wounds, he introduced antiseptic surgery and the prevention of infection by the utmost cleanliness in the operating-room. He was pres. of the Royal Society 1895–1900, and was created baron L. of Lyme Regis in 1897. In 1902 he received the O.M.

LISZT (list), **Franz** (1811–86). Hungarian pianist and composer. B. at Raiding, he was originally taught by his father, but after his first public performance when only 9 he went to Vienna to study under Czerny and Salieri and at 11 claimed even Beethoven among his many admirers. Becoming possibly the greatest virtuoso pianist of all time, he travelled widely in Europe, producing an opera *Don Sancho* in Paris at 14. In 1833 began his 10-year affair with the comtesse d'Agoult, by whom he had 3 children and with whom he lived mainly in Switzerland (*see* WAGNER). As musical director and conductor at Weimar (1849–59), where he lived with the Princess Caroline Sayn-Wittgenstein, he was a propagandist of the music of Berlioz and Wagner. Retiring to Rome, he turned again to his early love of religion and in 1865 became a secular priest (hence his adoption of the title Abbé), but continued to teach, give concert tours and indulge in several love-affairs. He d. at Bayreuth.

L. greatly influenced many younger musicians, incl. Brahms, Bülow, and Grieg, and originated the symphonic poem. His most notable compositions are his lyrical, but often technically very difficult, piano works, incl. the popular *Liebesträume* and the *Hungarian Rhapsodies*, based on gipsy music. He also wrote a *Faust* and a *Dante* symphony; masses and oratorios; songs and piano arrangements of works by Beethoven, Schubert, Wagner, etc.

LI T'AI-PO (lē-tī-pō), or **LI PO** (705–62). Chinese poet. B. in Szechwan, he deals mostly with wine and other material joys of life, interspersing beautiful natural descriptions. His poems rarely exceed 12 lines. Li is said to have been drowned by falling from a pleasure-boat while drunk.

LITANY. In the Christian Church, a set form of responsive prayer or supplication.

LITERARY CRITICISM. The determination of the principles governing literary composition and their application. The earliest systematic L.C. was the work of Aristotle; among subsequent Greek writers is the anonymous author of the treatise *On the Sublime*, usually attributed to Longinus. The most important of the Latin critics were Horace and Quintilian. Medieval L.C. shows few original writers apart from Dante, but the Italian Renaissance produced a new type of Humanist C., beginning with Boccaccio, and the revival of classical scholarship exalted the authority of Aristotle and Horace. The spread of Renaissance ideas stimulated critics such as du Bellay in France and Sidney in England, and the increasing influence of classical writers illustrated in Jonson's work reached its apex in the neo-classicism of Boileau and Rapin, which affected Dryden. The neo-classic tradition was continued in the 18th cent. by Pope, Addison, and Johnson, and in France by la Harpe, Marmontel, and Voltaire. The Romantic reaction at the end of the 18th cent. was represented by Diderot in France, Lessing in Germany, and Wordsworth and Coleridge in England; other Romantic critics include Shelley, Hazlitt, Lamb, and de Quincey. A more scientific spirit was introduced by Sainte-Beuve, who was followed in France by Brunetière and Taine. To the later Victorian Age belong Carlyle, Arnold, and Pater, with Poe and Lowell in the U.S.A., and Tolstoy in Russia. Also influential in European thought were Georg Brandes and Benedetto Croce. English L.C. in the 20th cent. is represented by A. C. Bradley, Saintsbury, C. S. Lewis, T. S. Eliot, I. A. Richards, W. Empson, F. R. Leavis; and in the U.S.A. Edmund Wilson, Cleanth Brooks, and Lionel Trilling. Of other European literatures representative names are Emil Staiger (German), Emilio Cecchi and Umberto Ecco (Italian), Raymond Picard and Roland Barthes (French), Roman Jakobson (Russian), and Jan Kott (Polish).

LITHGOW, Sir James (1883–1952). Scottish ship-builder. Succeeding his father in the family firm at 25, he was director of merchant shipbuilding in the F.W.W., was bitterly attacked by Ellen Wilkinson and others for his share in rationalizing the industry between the wars, and in the S.W.W. was a most successful controller of merchant shipbuilding. He was succeeded by his son **Sir William L.** (1934–).

LI′THIUM (Gk. *lithos*, stone). The lightest metal known, symbol Li, at. wt. 6·940 and at. no. 3, it was discovered by Arfvedson in 1817. It has a silvery lustre, tarnishing rapidly in air so that it is kept under naphtha, is soft and ductile, and burns in air at 200° C. Never occurring free in nature, it is nevertheless widely distributed, traces being found in nearly all igneous rocks and many mineral springs. It is used to a limited extent in industry and in the production of tritium.

LITHO′GRAPHY. In printing, a process of graphic reproduction discovered by Aloys Senefelder in Munich towards the end of the 18th cent. It is a method of surface printing based on the principle that grease and water repel one another. The drawing is made with greasy ink on an absorbent stone; this is washed with water, and then inked, the watered parts repelling the ink, and the drawing (or greasy parts) attracting it. The drawing is then printed. It has enjoyed a revival in modern times, since it enables the collector to possess an artist's 'original' at a modest price. *See* FREEDMAN, BARNETT.

LITHUA′NIA. A Soviet Socialist Republic of the U.S.S.R. It is situated between Latvia on the N., White Russia on the E., Poland on the S., Kaliningrad region of the R.S.F.S.R. on the S.W., and the Baltic on the W. L. is flat and low-lying, with a few hills and numerous small lakes. It is watered by the Niemen and its tributaries. Forestry and agriculture are both of importance. Rye and oats are the chief grain crops; potatoes, vegetables and fodder crops are produced; poultry and eggs are exported. Industrial products incl. ships, textiles, sugar, bicycles, boots and shoes, and bricks. The cap. is Vilnius. Other towns incl. Kaunas, the seat of a univ.; and Klaipeda Area 25,300 sq. m.; pop. (1967) 3,064,000.

A grand duchy from the 13th cent., Christianized in the 14th, L. was united with Poland 1569–1776, when it passed to Russia. L. proclaimed its independence in 1918, recognized by Russia in 1920. L., like Estonia and Latvia, received demands in 1939 for military bases, in 1940 for the passage of Russian troops, and in 1940 was incorporated in the U.S.S.R. as a S.S.R.

LITHUANIAN. The language of the Lithuanians, an Indo-European tongue, retaining many very ancient features: the free accent, the full complement of cases in the noun, etc. It does not seem to have been reduced to writing before the 16th cent., and it is spoken by about 3 millions.

LITMUS. A colouring matter obtained from various lichens. The aqueous extract of L. is used as an indicator to test the acidic or alkaline nature of aqueous solutions; with acid it turns red, with alkali (hydroxyl) it turns blue.

LISZT. In Danhauser's portrait group the master, his piano ornamented by a bust of Beethoven, plays to his friends, the comtesse d'Agoult watching adoringly at his feet. Behind him sit Dumas and George Sand, and in the background (left to right) are Victor Hugo, Paganini and Rossini.
Photo: Bildarchivs der Österreichischen Nationalbibliothek

w

LITTLEHAMPTON. English seaside resort and port (U.D.) in Sussex, at the mouth of the Arun, 10 m. E.S.E. of Chichester. Pop. (1961) 15,647.

LITTLE ROCK. Cap. of Arkansas, U.S.A., and co. seat of Pulaski co. on the r. Arkansas, a centre for bauxite lumber, and cotton; there are foundries, machine shops, furniture and cotton factories, etc. Natural gas is used in home and industry, which gives the town clear air. Douglas MacArthur was b. at L.R. In 1958 considerable disorder arose when state and federal authority conflicted on school racial integration. Pop. (1960) 107,813.

LITTLEWOOD, Joan. British theatrical director. After early experience with the Manchester Repertory Theatre, she founded Theatre Workshop in 1945. With her professionally 'earthy' and vigorous productions at the Theatre Royal, Stratford (London), 1953–61 and from 1963, she broke through to fame, e.g. *A Taste of Honey* (1959), *The Hostage* (1959–60), *Fings ain't Wot They Used T'Be* (1960–1), and *Oh What a Lovely War* (1963).

LITTRE (lētreh'), **Maximilian Paul Émile** (1801–81). French philologist and philosopher. His *magnum opus* is the comprehensive *Dictionnaire de la langue française* (1863–72). A friend and admirer of Comte, he did much to disseminate the positivist philosophy.

LITURGY. In the Christian Church, a term originally limited to the celebration of the Eucharist, but now used of any or all services for public worship.

LIU SHAO-CHI (lē-ōō show-chē) (1898–). Chinese statesman. B. in Hunan, of peasant stock, he was ed. at the same school as Mao Tse-tung. In 1921 he joined the Communist Party, and later spent some years in Russia. In 1959 (re-elected 1965) he became Chairman (i.e. President) of the Republic in succession to Mao Tse-tung. Formerly a major party theoretician, he came under attack in the Cultural Revolution, and was removed 1968 from all govt. and party posts.

LIVER. The largest gland in man, wt. 3–4 lb. occupying the upper right-hand portion of the abdomen, below the diaphragm. A prodigious factory and storehouse, it makes the blood proteins (albumen, etc.) and antibodies; stores vitamins and food as glycogen, which is broken down to sugar and passed into the blood, to supply energy on demand to any part of the body. In addition to filtering and purifying the blood, the L. disposes of some waste products (e.g. urea) directly into the gut, to which it also supplies bile, an emulsifying agent which breaks fat down into minute droplets to aid its digestion.

LIVERPOOL, Robert Banks Jenkinson, 2nd earl of (1770–1828). British Tory statesman. He entered parliament in 1790, and was For. Sec. 1801–3, Home Sec. 1804–6 and 1807–9, War Min. 1809–12, and P.M. 1812–27. His govt. conducted the Napoleonic Wars to a successful conclusion, but its ruthless repression of freedom of speech and of the press aroused such opposition that during 1815–20 revolution frequently seemed imminent.

LIVERPOOL. City (1880) and seaport (co. bor.) in Lancs, England, on the right bank of the Mersey, 3 m. from the Irish Sea. Probably founded by the Norsemen, it became a bor. in 1207 and replaced Chester as a port for Ireland, but attained importance only under Charles II with the growth of trade with the American colonies and W. Indies. The first dock was opened in 1715 and during the 18th cent. L. became the main centre of the slave trade, and in the 19th and first half of the 20th cent. was notable as the exporting centre for the textiles of Lancs. and Yorks. Today, shortened lines of communication by motorway and freightliner train mean that more British exports of all kinds flow out through L. than by any other route and modernisation by the Mersey Docks and Harbour Board (1858) makes it Europe's major Atlantic port. There are some 38 m. of quayage with specialized berths for 'packaged softwood timber,

LIVERPOOL. A fine example of the half-timbered English house of the 17th century is Speke Hall, with lavish interior decoration in plaster and wood panelling and – a comment on the troubled times in which it was built – a roomy, well-concealed priest's hole.   *Courtesy of Liverpool Corporation.*

petroleum, bananas and other fruit, and the expanding 'container' trade with N. America, notably in the Seaforth dock 1967–71 which gives a 48-hr. turn-round. There are also modernized facilities for bulk cargoes and commodities which cannot be containerized, and for the conventional carrier to less developed areas as yet unable to handle container traffic, as in Africa, the Far East, and S. America, e.g. in the Birkenhead dock across the Mersey. Other imports incl. vegetable oils, grain, iron ore and other metals, sugar and cotton. Industries incl. flour milling, sugar refining, engineering, ship repairing, chemicals, tobacco, and extraction of vegetable oil, with modern factories on the industrial estates at Aintree, Kirkby and Speke. The 3 m. Mersey Tunnel (1925–34) links L. and Birkenhead, and a tunnel to Wallasey is under construction: there is an airport at Speke.

Outstanding buildings incl. Speke Hall, the 18th cent. Town Hall, St. George's Hall (1854) in the Greek style, the Walker Art Gallery (1877) with a fine collection, and the Dock Offices, Liver Buildings and Cunard Building on Pier Head. The Anglican Cathedral, designed by Sir Giles Gilbert Scott in the Gothic style and begun 1904, will be the largest church in England when complete; the R.C. Metropolitan Cathedral of Christ the King (*see illus.* p. 473) 1967, is circular and has a lantern-tower carrying 50-ft. glass panels designed by John Piper. The univ. (1881) received its charter 1903. Municipal area 43 sq. m.; pop. (1961) 747,490.

LIVERWORTS. Class of plants (Hepaticae) resembling mosses. They are of world-wide distribution in moist situations, and many are found in Britain.

LIVERY COMPANIES. The guilds of the City of London, whose members formerly wore a distinctive dress on special occasions. The companies have lost almost all their original industrial functions, but they still maintain their social activities. Most of them administer valuable charities often educational.

LIVINGSTONE, David (1813–73). Scottish missionary and explorer. B. at Blantyre, Lanarkshire, he

DAVID LIVINGSTONE
Photo: N.P.G.

worked in a cotton mill before studying medicine, Greek, and theology at Anderson's College, Glasgow. In 1838 he was accepted by the London Missionary Society, and in 1840 took his medical degree at Glasgow. L. was first sent to Bechuanaland. In 1844 he m. Mary Moffat, the daughter of the missionary Robert Moffat, and in 1849 discovered Lake Ngami. After a journey with him to the Upper Zambezi his wife and children fell ill and had to return to England. L.'s next journey took him to Loanda, where he arrived in 1854. In 1856 he followed the Zambezi to its mouth, and discovered the Victoria Falls before reaching Tete and Quilimane. During a visit to London he left the service of the London Missionary Society, and was appointed consul at Quilimane, being also chosen to lead an expedition to E. and Central Africa, which resulted in the discovery of lakes Shirwa and Nyasa and in the exposure of the slave trade. This journey was saddened by the death of his wife in 1862. In an attempt to find the sources of the Nile he ranged between lakes Nyasa and Tanganyika from 1866, reaching Ujiji in 1871. Here Stanley joined him, and together they explored N. Tanganyika. L. d. in May 1873 at Old Chitambo, Zambia. He was buried in Westminster Abbey in 1874.

LIVINGSTONE. Town, cap. until 1935, in Zambia, on the Zambezi, near Victoria Falls, founded 1905. L. (named after the explorer) is a tourist centre with an internat. airport (1950), game park, museum of arts and crafts, and a David Livingstone collection. Pop. (1963) 32,000.

LIVORNO. Italian form of LEGHORN.

LIVY (Titus Livius) (59 B.C.–A.D. 17). Roman historian, famous for his *History of Rome*, from the foundation to 9 B.C. It was composed of 142 books, of which 35 survive, viz., 1–10 and 21–45, covering the periods from the arrival of Aeneas in Italy to 293 B.C., and 218–167 B.C.

LIZARD. Order of reptiles, Lacertilia. The order contains 21 families and over 1,500 species. They are distributed throughout the temperate and tropical regions of the world, being most numerous in warmer climates. Most Ls. have scaly bodies, movable eyelids, and well-developed limbs. Some varieties, e.g. the British blindworm, are legless. The tail is often fragile, but a new tail grows if the old one is shed.

Ls. are generally terrestrial, and usually arboreal, but some are semi-aquatic and one is marine. Their diet varies, some being vegetarian, others feeding on insects, worms, or eggs, etc. They are usually oviparous, but in some varieties the young are completely developed before birth.

LIZARD

LIZARD POINT. The most southerly point of Cornwall and England. Lizard Town is the nearest village. The coast is broken into small bays, overlooked by 2 cliff lighthouses.

LJUBLJANA (lublyah'nah). Industrial city and cap. of Slovenia, Yugoslavia, with an 18th cent. cathedral and a medieval fortress. Cotton spinning and bell founding are among its industries; leather goods, beer, tobacco, machinery, chemicals are made. L. has a univ., founded 1919, and an airfield. Pop. (1961) 133,386.

LLAMA (lah'ma). S. American animal (*Lama huanacus glama*), used in Peru as a beast of burden. Ls. are white, with brown or black spots, very hardy, and require little food or water. They spit profusely when annoyed. The alpaca (q.v.), is an allied species.

LLANBERIS (lanber'is). Village in Caernarvon shire, Wales, point of departure for ascents of Snowdon. Pop. *c.* 2,300.

LLANDAFF (lan'daf). Part of the city of Cardiff, Glamorganshire, Wales, until 1922 a separate town, the seat of a bishopric from the 6th cent. The cathedral, restored 1844–69, badly damaged by a German land mine delivered in an air assault in 1941, was again restored 1948–60. A large figure, 'Christ in Majesty', by Epstein (q.v.), was placed within it.

LLANDUDNO (landid'no). Seaside resort (U.D.) in Caernarvonshire, Wales, near the mouth of the Conway. It incl. Great Orme's Head. The church of St. Tudno occupies the site of an oratory built by St. Tudno in the 7th cent. 'Lewis Carroll' frequently stayed at L. A garden city for the elderly was opened in 1960. Pop. (1961) 17,852.

LLANELLI (lane'lhi). Welsh seaport (bor.) in Carmarthenshire, by the Burry estuary, formerly Llanelly. Industries incl. tinplate and copper smelting, and L. is a colliery centre. Pop (1961) 29,994.

LLANES (lyah'nes). Seaport in Oviedo prov., N. Spain, on the Bay of Biscay. Pop. (1960) 25,000.

LLANFAIR P.G. (lan' vir-). Village in the S.E. of the Welsh island of Anglesey, 1 m. W. of Britannia railway bridge, and famous for its very small church. The first Women's Institute in Britain was founded at L. in 1915 by Mrs. Alfred Watt (1868–1948)

LLAMA

of Canada, where women's institutes had been started in 1897. The full name is Llanfairpwllgwyngyllgogerychwyrndrobwllllandysilliogogogoch (St. Mary's church in the hollow of the white hazel near to the rapid whirlpool of St. Tysillio's church, by the red cave).

LLANTWIT MAJOR (lan'twit). Welsh market town in Glamorganshire, 5 m. S.S.W. of Cowbridge. It was the site of a missionary centre and school established in the 5th cent. by St. Illtyd which became famous. On the coast, 2¼ m. W.S.W., is the 12th cent. St. Donat's Castle, bought by William Randolph Hearst in 1925, sold by his heirs in 1960 to the Atlantic College Foundation for use as an international school.

LLEWELYN (loo-el'in) I (d. 1240). Prince who became king of N. Wales in 1194, and extended his rule over all Wales not in Norman hands. His grandson, **Llewelyn II** (d. 1282), succeeded in 1246, and was compelled by Edward I in 1277 to acknowledge him as overlord and to surrender S. Wales. His death while leading a national uprising marked the end of Welsh independence.

LLEWELLYN, Richard. Pseudonym of the Welsh author and dramatist Richard Vivian Llewellyn Lloyd (1907–). He sprang to fame in 1939 with *How Green Was My Valley*, a novel about a S. Wales mining family: later came the plays *Poison Pen* (1937) and *Noose* (1947) and his novels *A Few Flowers for Shiner* (1950) and *Up, Into the Singing Mountain* (1960).

LLEWELYN-DAVIES, Richard, baron (1912–). British architect. Prof. at Univ. Coll., London, from 1960, he was consultant for the new offices of *The Times* in Printing House Square and the rebuilding of the London Stock Exchange. He was created a life peer in 1964.

LLOYD, Harold (1893–1971). American film comedian, noted for his 'trademark' of spectacles with thick horn rims, who appeared from 1913 in silent and talking films.

LLOYD, Marie. Stage-name of British music-hall artist Matilda Alice Victoria Wood (1870–1922). First singing at the Grecian music-hall in London's East End in 1885, she embodied the Cockney comedy of the 1890s.

LLOYD, (John) Selwyn Brooke (1904–). British Cons. politician. Ed. at Magdalene Coll., Cambridge, he became a barrister and in 1945 entered parliament. He was Min. of Supply 1954–5, of Defence 1955, and For. Sec. 1955–60, when he dealt with the Suez crisis. Appointed Chancellor of the Exchequer in 1960, he was responsible for the creation of the National Economic Development Council and combated inflation by an unpopular policy of wage restraint, and in 1962 was asked by Macmillan to resign. He returned under Home in 1963–4 as Lord Privy Seal and Leader of the Commons, becoming Speaker 1971.

LLOYD GEORGE, David, 1st earl L.-G. (1863–1945). Welsh Liberal statesman. B. in Manchester, son of a teacher, he became a solicitor, and in 1890 was elected M.P. for Caernarvon Boroughs, which he represented for 54 years. In parliament he made his reputation as a fiery Radical and Welsh Nationalist, and during the S. African War was prominent as a pro-Boer. In the Liberal cabinet of 1905 he became Pres. of the Board of Trade, and in 1908 Chancellor of the Exchequer; the most notable measures associated with his term of office were the introduction of old age pensions in 1908, and of health and employment insurance in 1911. His budget of 1909 provoked the Lords to reject it, and thereby led to the Parliament Act of 1911.

The F.W.W. brought him to the fore as the dominating figure in the cabinet. As Min. of Munitions 1915–16 he thoroughly reorganized the supply of arms and ammunition, shortage of which had created a national scandal. Succeeding Kitchener as War Min. in June 1916, he advocated a policy of diverting manpower to the eastern front which resulted in the Salonika expedition. By this time he had lost all faith in Asquith as a war leader; in Dec. the breach became an open one, and a new coalition was formed, with L. G. as P.M. His aim now became to secure a unified Allied command; this was achieved in May 1918, and enabled the Allies to withstand the last German offensive and conduct the war to a victorious conclusion. As one of the 'Big Three', L. G. was among those primarily responsible for the Versailles peace settlement. *See* illus. under FIRST WORLD WAR.

The 1918 elections gave the coalition a huge majority over the Labour Party and Asquith's Liberal followers, but it soon lost its prestige. The growth of unemployment, its interventionist policy in Russia, the use of the 'black and tans' in Ireland, and the failure of L. G.'s pro-Greek policy in the Near East, all lost it support, and in 1922 the Conservatives withdrew. The reunion of Asquith's and L. G.'s supporters failed to stimulate a Liberal revival, and within the party L. G. was widely distrusted. During 1931–5 he withdrew to lead a tiny opposition Liberal group within the Commons. He ceased to be an important figure thereafter, although he occasionally came to the fore, as when in 1940 he helped to overthrow the Chamberlain govt. He was raised to the peerage shortly before his death in 1945. His highly controversial war memoirs appeared in 1933–6. **Dame Margaret L. G.** (1864–1941), *née* Owen, whom he m. 1888, was created D.B.E. in 1919 for her social work for women and children.

His younger son **Gwilym L. G.**, visct. Tenby (1894–1967), entered parliament as a Liberal (Liberal-Cons. from 1951) in 1922, and was Parliamentary Secretary Min. of Food 1941–2, of Fuel 1942–5, and as Min. of Food 1951–4 was responsible for the abolition of food rationing. Home Sec. and Min. for Welsh Affairs 1954–7, he was created visct. in 1957.

L. G.'s younger dau. **Lady Megan L. G.** (1902–66) became a Liberal M.P. in 1929 and was deputy leader of the party from 1949 until her defeat in 1951.

Joining the Labour Party in 1955, she re-entered the House in 1957.

LLOYD'S. Insurance market and centre of the world's shipping intelligence in London, England. A corporation, the members of which, known as underwriters, issue insurance policies for their own account and risk. Business is only transacted through brokers who have been authorized by the committee to carry on business with Lloyd's underwriters. Underwriters must satisfy the committee annually that they are in every way fitted to undertake the financial responsibility which membership involves. Although originally predominantly marine, today there are few risks, life

LLOYD'S. The Underwriting Room: marine, motor and aviation business being transacted on the ground floor and fire, compensation, public liability and other non-marine business in the gallery. Underwriters sit at 'boxes' – so named from the days when customers sat at similarly shaped tables and benches in Edward Lloyd's 17th century coffee house. To the right is the rostrum at which the 'caller' sits to announce the names of brokers wanted by colleagues and above him is the Lutine Bell, rung when important announcements are to be made. *Courtesy of Lloyd's.*

assurance and financial guarantee apart, that cannot be effected. For two and a half cents. Lloyd's has been the centre for the diffusion of shipping information now collected by 1,500 agencies throughout the world.

In 1688 Edward Lloyd kept a coffee house in Tower Street, moving in 1691 to Lombard Street. Frequented by business men willing to insure against sea-risks, this became the acknowledged centre where insurers might be found. *Lloyd's News* incl. marine information in its single sheet which was 1st pub. in 1696, and *Lloyd's List and Shipping Gazette* started 1734 is still pub. The association, reorganized in 1811, became incorporated by Act of Parliament in 1871, and Lloyd's Act 1911 extended its powers, formerly confined to marine insurance. In 1928 L. moved to Leadenhall Street and still larger premises were opened in Lime Street in 1957.

LLOYD'S REGISTER OF SHIPPING. Founded in 1760, this international society for the survey and classification of merchant shipping provides rules for the construction and maintenance of ships and their machinery. It is governed by a large committee representing ship-owners, shipbuilders, marine engineers, and underwriters, and employs 850 surveyors. The register book, published annually, contains particulars of all known sea-going ships of 100 tons gross and over.

LOANDA. *See* LUANDA.

LOBACHE′VSKI, Nikolai Ivanovich (1793–1856). Russian mathematician. B. at Makariev, he was prof. of mathematics at Kazan univ. 1823–46, and is usually regarded as the founder of non-Euclidean geometry

LOBĔ'LIA. Genus of plants in the family Lobeliaceae, named after the botanist Matthias de Lobel. About 250 species are known, native of temperate and tropical regions. Some forms, especially those found in Africa, grow to the size of small trees.

LOBENGULA (lō-bengoo'la) (c. 1833–94). Matabele king. Succeeding his father in 1870, he accepted British protection in 1888, but in 1893 rebelled. He was defeated near Bulawayo.

LOBI'TO. Seaport of Angola, terminus of the Benguela railway, completed by the Belgians in 1931, which is linked through the copper-mining districts of Congo (Katanga prov.) and Zambia with Beira, Mozambique. The first harbour works at L. were completed in 1905. Pop. (1960) 32,000.

LOB-NOR. See LOP-NOR.

LOBSTER. A family of crustacea, Homaridae, found on the coasts of the N. Atlantic and Mediterranean, and used for food. They are distinguished by the pincers on the end of the first 3 pairs of legs, the front pair being very large. When living the outer cuticle is bluish black in colour, but turns red on boiling. They live in shallow water in rocky places, and are caught in wicker lobster-pots. *Homarus gammarus* is the common European lobster, which is usually sent to the market fresh.

LOCAL GOVERNMENT. That part of government dealing mainly with matters concerning the inhabitants of a particular district or place, together with those the administration of which parliament has delegated to local authorities.

HISTORY. The system of L.G. in England developed haphazard; in the 18th cent. it varied in the towns between democratic survivals of the guild system, and the narrow rule of small oligarchies. The Municipal Reform Act (1835) estab. the rule of elected councils, although their actual powers remained small. In the country L.G. remained in the hands of the J.P.s assembled in Quarter Sessions, until the L.G. Act (1888) set up county councils. These were given a measure of control over the internal local authorities, except the major bodies, which were constituted county boroughs. The L.G. Act (1894) set up urban and rural district councils, and, in the rural districts only, parish councils. Following the S.W.W. local govt. elections were increasingly fought on party lines, and there was a tendency for committees to proliferate.

In 1971 it was planned to re-organise English L.G. on a 2-level system with 44 county councils (incl. 6 metropolitan councils), based on existing areas, and c. 300 district councils (with provision for retention of 'borough' and 'city' traditions). For the first time urban and rural areas within the county boundaries would be linked together.

On the Continent, L.G. tends to be much more centrally directed and controlled, rather than the 'partnership' prevailing in England, e.g. France, Germany and the Soviet Union, although German cities have a tradition of independent action, as exemplified in Berlin, and France in 1969 was adopting a policy of regional decentralisation. In the U.S.A. a good deal of the English spirit of freedom survives, and the system shows evidence of the early type of settlement, e.g. in New England the town is the unit of L.G., in the South the co., and in the N. Central states the combined co. and township. A complication is the tendency to delegate power to special authorities in such fields as education.

LOCAL OPTION. The right granted by a government to the electors of each particular area to decide whether the sale of intoxicants shall be permitted.

Such a system has been tried in certain states of the U.S.A., in certain Canadian provs., and in Norway and Sweden.

LOCA'RNO. Health resort in the Ticino canton of Switzerland on the N. of Lago Maggiore, 12 m. W. of Bellinzona. Formerly in the duchy of Milan, it was captured by the Swiss in 1803. Pop. (1960) 10,155.

LOCARNO, Pact of. A series of diplomatic documents initialled at Locarno on 16 Oct. 1925, and formally signed in London on 1 Dec. 1925. The Pact settled the question of the Rhineland, and the powers – Britain, France, Belgium, Italy, and Germany – guaranteed the existing frontiers between Germany and France, and Germany and Belgium. The prime mover in the Pact was Austen Chamberlain. Following the signing of the Pact Germany was admitted to the League of Nations, but in 1936 the Nazis formally denounced the pact.

LOCHABER (lokhah'ber). Wild mountainous dist. of S. Inverness-shire, Scotland, including Ben Nevis. It is the site of hydro-electric installations, constructed 1926–41 at a cost of about £6,000,000.

LOCHNER (lokh'ner), **Stephan** (fl. 1400–51). German painter. He was b. on the Upper Rhine, and all his principal works are in the cathedral and museums of Cologne, incl. the 'Madonna in the Rose Garden', 'Adoration of the Kings', and 'Presentation in the Temple'. L.'s death marked the end of idealism in Rhenish painting, and the realism coming from the Netherlands took its place.

LOCKE, John (1632–1704). English philosopher. B. in Somerset, he studied at Oxford, practised medicine, and in 1667 became sec. to the earl of Shaftesbury. He consequently fell under suspicion as a Whig

LOCHABER. Beyond Corran Ferry the sun breaks through the rain clouds sweeping over the Ardgour Hills and touches Loch Linnhe to quicksilver.   *Photo: George Outram & Co. Ltd.*

and in 1683 fled to Holland, where he lived until the 1688 revolution. In later life he pub. many works on philosophy, politics, theology, and economics; these incl. *Letters on Toleration* (1689–92), *Two Treatises on Government* (1690), *Essay concerning Human Understanding* (1690), and *Some Thoughts concerning Education* (1693).

His *Treatises on Government* supply the classical statement of Whig theory, and enjoyed great influence in America and France. He maintains that governments derive their authority from the people's consent, and that they may overthrow any government threatening their fundamental rights. Among these rights he incl. religious freedom, although he would deny toleration to Catholicism and atheism as dangerous to society. His *Essay concerning Human Understanding*, which deals with the nature, origin, and limits of human knowledge, raised problems which dominated 18th cent. philosophy down to Kant.

LOCKHART, John Gibson (1794–1854). Scottish biographer and editor. He joined the staff of *Blackwood's Magazine*, to which he contributed his translations of 'Ancient Spanish Ballads'. In 1820 he m. Sophia, eldest dau. of Sir Walter Scott, whom he first met in 1818, and whose biography he pub. 1837–8. He edited the *Quarterly Review* (1825–53).

LOCKHART, Sir Robert Hamilton Bruce (1887–1970). Brit. diplomat. Entering the consular service in 1911, he was consul-general in Moscow 1915–17. He headed a mission to the Soviet govt. in 1918, and was arrested for a time until exchanged for Litvinov. He engaged in banking and journalism after the war, but returned to the Foreign Office in 1939, and was Deputy Under-Sec. of State 1941–5. His writings incl. *Memoirs of a British Agent* (1932).

LOCKJAW. *See* TETANUS.

LOCKSPEISER, Sir Ben (1891–   ). British engineer and administrator. After heading the air defence dept. at the Royal Aeronautical Establishment, Farnborough, 1937–9, he held successive research posts in the Air Ministry, and Min. of Aircraft Production, during the S.W.W., and was chief scientist to the Min. of Supply 1946–9, and sec. to Privy Council Commission for scientific and industrial research 1949–56. He possesses the rare capacity for combining administrative ability with scientific insight.

LOCKYER, Sir Norman (1836–1920). British astronomer. He was director of the observatory attached to the Royal Coll. of Science and prof. of astronomical physics 1885–1913, and director of the observatory at Salcombe Regis, Devon (now the N.L. observatory), from 1913. A pioneer of solar spectroscopy, he discovered helium in the sun's atmosphere (with Frankland) during the 1868 eclipse; was founder of the journal *Nature* (1869), and was knighted 1897.

LOCUST. Swarming grasshopper, with short antennae and auditory organs on the abdomen, in  the family Acrididae. When the larvae ('hoppers') emerge from the eggs, which are laid in the ground, they form into bands. As winged adults, flying in swarms, they may be carried by the wind hundreds of miles from their breeding grounds, and on alighting devour all vegetation. Ls. occur in nearly every continent, the migratory L. (*Locusta migratoria*) ranging from Europe across Russia to China, and even small swarms may cover several sq. m. and weigh thousands of tons. Control by spreading poisoned food amongst the bands is very effective, but it is cheapest to spray concentrated insecticide solutions from aircraft over the insects or the vegetation on which they feed. In dealing with the swarms shown in the illustration 7,000 galls. of insecticide (y-BHC and dieldrin) was sprayed during 6 days, killing *c.* 13,000 million Ls. weighing 52,000 tons, and the swarms decreased in size to 30 sq. m.

LODGE, Henry Cabot (1850–1924). American statesman. B. in Boston, he was a Republican senator from 1893 until his death. It was largely due to him that the U.S.A. refused to join the League of Nations. His grandson **Henry Cabot L.** (1902–   ) entered journalism, then became Republican senator for Mass. in 1936. Campaign manager for Eisenhower's nomination, he was a member of his cabinet and U.S. representative to the U.N. 1953–60. He was American ambassador to S. Vietnam 1963–4 and 1965–7, and in Bonn from 1968. In 1969 he took over from Harriman as Nixon's negotiator in the Vietnam peace talks, and became special envoy to the Vatican 1970.

LODGE, Sir Oliver Joseph (1851–1940). British physicist. B. in Staffs, he was prof. of physics at Liverpool 1881–1900, and principal of Birmingham univ. 1900–19. His place in physics rests chiefly on his

LOCUST. One of the Beaver aircraft used for spraying gets ready for take-off from Hargeisa airport in the Somali Republic. Darkening to a black cloud over the control tower, this swarm of desert locust (*Schistocerca gregaria*) is part of a group of swarms covering 150 sq. m.   *Photo: Desert Locust Survey.*

researches on radiation, and the relation between matter and ether. His investigations on the Hertzian waves led him to invent a coherer, which he used to accomplish wireless telegraphy. He pub. *Pioneers of Science* (1893); *Atoms and Rays* (1924); *Relativity* (1925), and many other scientific works. L. was a prominent psychical research worker, and wrote *Raymond* (1916); *The Reality of a Spiritual World* (1930), etc. His brother, **Sir Richard L.** (1855–1936), was prof. of history at Glasgow 1894–9 and Edinburgh 1899–1925.

LODGE, Thomas (*c.* 1558–1625). English author and dramatist. His romance *Rosalynde* (1590) was the basis of Shakespeare's *As You Like it*.

LODI (lō'dē). Town and episcopal see of Italy, 18 m. S.E. of Milan, a market for agricultural produce; fertilizers, agricultural machinery and textiles are made. Pop. (1960) 37,800. Napoleon's defeat of the Austrians at the battle of L. in 1796 gave him control of Lombardy. Napoleon was first called Le Petit Caporal at L.

LODZ. Town in Poland, cap. of L. voivodship, 75 m. S.W. of Warsaw. The centre of a group of industrial towns, it produces textiles and textile machinery, dyes, etc., and is the seat of a univ. (1945). A monument to Kosciuszko (q.v.), erected 1931, destroyed by the Germans 1939, was rebuilt 1958–60 under the direction of the same artist, Mieczyslaw Lubelski. Pop. (1966) 745,000.

LOEB (löb), **James** (1867–1933). American philanthropist. B. in New York, he became a member of a New York banking firm. A patron of art and science, he financed the L. Classical Library of texts and translations of Greek and Latin writers.

LOESS (lō'es). A yellow loam, accumulated by wind in periglacial regions during the ice ages. It usually attains considerable depths, and is very fertile. There are large deposits in central Europe, especially Hungary; in China and N. America.

LOEWE (lō), **Frederick** (1904–   ). American composer. B. in Austria, son of an operatic tenor, he studied music incl. the piano under Busoni, and in 1924 went with his father to the U.S.A. In 1942 he joined forces with Alan Jay Lerner (1918–   ), and their joint successes incl. *Brigadoon* (1947), *Paint Your Wagon* (1951), *My Fair Lady* (1956), and music for the film *Gigi* (1958).

LOFOTENS. Group of islands belonging to Norway with which are often included the Vesteralen group, off the N.W. coast of Norway. Hinnoy, in the Vesteralens, is the largest island of Norway. The seas surrounding the islands are an important fishing ground for cod and herring. Area 1,750 sq. m.

LOG. An apparatus for measuring the speed of a ship through water. For the original 'common L.', a piece of weighted wood (log-chip) attached to a line, knotted at intervals, was thrown off the rear of the ship, and its progress measured by timing the passage of the knots with a sand-glass. Modern Ls. use a propeller rotating a line attached to an indicator carried on board.

LOGANBERRY. Fruit first raised from seed by the American Judge J. H. Logan in 1881, a hybrid between a wild blackberry and a raspberry.

LO'GARITHMS. The exponents of powers to which an invariable number called the base has to be raised to produce the number of which it is the L. To multiply common numbers, their Ls. are added; to divide, they are subtracted; involution is done by multiplication, and evolution by division.

LOGIC (Gk. *logos*, reason). The science of accurate thought. The founder of L. as a separate branch of philosophy was Aristotle, whose treatises, known collectively as the Organon, provided the basis for a complete system. The medieval Church, concentrating on Aristotle's method of deduction from certain given premises, produced the modified system known as Scholasticism. This prevailed until the scientific spirit of the Renaissance produced the inductive method of Bacon, which works backward from the accumulated facts to the principle which accounts for them. Hobbes, Locke, and especially J. S. Mill, developed this form. To the school of rationalist philosophers inspired by Descartes belong Spinoza and Leibniz. Exponents of formal L. include Kant, Hamilton, Mansel, Lotze, and Herbart. Among later logicians are Bosanquet, Bradley, Johnson, Russell, and Whitehead.

LO'GOS (Gk. 'word' or 'reason'). A term in Greek, Hebrew and Christian philosophy and theology. It was used by Greek philosophers for the divine reason pervading the universe. Under Greek influence the Jews came to conceive of Wisdom as an aspect of God's activity. The Jewish philosopher Philo (1st cent. A.D.) attempted to reconcile Platonic, Stoic, and Hebrew philosophy by identifying the L. with the Jewish idea of 'Wisdom'. Several of the New Testament writers took over Philo's conception of the L, which they identified with Christ.

LOHENGRIN (lō'engrin). Name of Parsival's son, legendary Knight of the Swan and hero of a German epic of the late 13th cent., on which Wagner based his opera (1848).

LOIR (lwahr). French river, rising N. of Illiers in the dept. of Eure-et-Loir and flowing for 190 m. S.E., then S.W. to join the Sarthe near Angers. It gives its name to the depts. of Loir-et-Cher and Eure-et-Loir.

LOIRE (lwahr). The longest river in France, rising in the Cévennes at 4,430 ft., and flowing for 625 m. first N. then W. till it reaches the Bay of Biscay at St. Nazaire, passing Nevers, Orléans, Tours, and Nantes. It gives its name to the depts. of Loire, Haute-Loire, Loire-Atlantique, Indre-et-Loire, Maine-et-Loire, and Saône-et-Loire.

LOIRET (lwahreh'). River of France, 7 m. long. It rises near Olivet and joins the Loire 5 m. below Orléans. It gives its name to L. dept.

LOISY (lwahsē'), **Alfred Firmin** (1857–1940). French theologian. B. in French Lorraine, he entered the R.C. priesthood in 1879, and became a prof. at the Institut Catholique in Paris. His modernist views led to his dismissal in 1893, and eventually to his excommunication. He was prof. of Church history at the Collège de France 1909–32.

LŌ'KI. In Scandinavian mythology, one of the Aesir, but the cause of dissension among the gods, and the slayer of Balder. His children are the Midgard serpent Jörmungander which girdles the earth, the wolf Fenris, and Hela.

LOLLARDS. Name, probably meaning 'mutterers' given to the followers of Wycliffe (q.v.). They condemned transubstantiation, advocated the diversion of ecclesiastical property to charitable uses, and denounced war and capital punishment. Propaganda began *c.* 1377; after the passing of the statute *De Heretico Comburendo* (1401) many Ls. were burned, and in 1414 they raised an unsuccessful revolt in London. Lollardy lingered on in London and E. Anglia, and in the 16th cent. became absorbed into the Protestant movement.

LOMBARDS or **Langobards.** A Germanic people, originating on the Elbe, who invaded Italy in 568, and occupied Lombardy, which is named after them, and central Italy. Their kingdom was conquered by Charlemagne in 774.

LOMBARDY. Region of N. Italy, divided into the provs. of Bergamo, Brescia, Como, Cremona, Mantua, Milan, Pavia, Sondrio, and Varese. It incl. Lakes Como and Iseo, part of Maggiore on the W., part of Garda on the E., and is drained by the Po and several of its left-bank tributaries, incl. the Ticino. It has extremes of climate; vines, cereals, and the mulberry tree are cultivated, and silk is produced. Milan, the cap., is the centre of a highly industrialized area. In the N. the region is a much favoured holiday resort. The area was taken from the Roman Empire in 568 by the Langobardi or Lombards, from whom it took its name. In the Middle Ages it belonged to the dukes of Milan; later, in succession, to Spain, Austria, and Sardinia. Area 9,191 sq. m.; pop. (1961) 7,390,492.

LOMBO'K. Island of Indonesia. Mataram is the chief town, and Ampanam the chief port. It rises in Mt. L., a volcano, to 12,379 ft. Area 1,825 sq. m.; pop. 650,000.

Through L. Strait, between L. and Bali, runs Wallace's Line, discovered by the naturalist A. R. Wallace (1823–1913), to the W. of which the fauna and flora are predominantly Asian, to the E. predominantly Australasian.

LOMBRO'SO, Cesare (1836–1909). Italian criminologist. He became a prof. of mental diseases at Pavia in 1862. Subsequently he held chairs in forensic medicine, psychiatry, and criminal anthropology at Turin. His principal work is *L'uomo delinquente* (1889). He held that there was a physically distinguishable criminal 'type'.

LŌ'MOND. The largest freshwater Scottish loch, partly in Stirlingshire, partly in Dunbartonshire, 23 m. long and 5 m. at its widest point; area 27 sq. m. It

LOIRE. Most famous of the châteaux of the Loire, Chambord is a Renaissance miracle owing much of its design to the ideas of Francis I himself. For fifteen years 1,800 workmen toiled on its construction. *Courtesy of the French National Tourist Office.*

LOCH LOMOND. In the 13th century Vikings rowed across this 'queen of Scottish lakes' after dragging their ships across the narrow isthmus of Tarbet. Snow-capped in the background is 3,192 ft.-high Ben Lomond. *Photo: George Outram & Co. Ltd.*

contains 30 islands and is overlooked by Ben Lomond.

LONDON, Jack (1876–1916). American author. B. in San Francisco, he used his own adventurous life as the background of his most popular books, e.g. *The Call of the Wild* (1903), *White Fang* (1906) – the story of a dog – and *Martin Eden* (1909). Less familiar are the socialist ideas, influenced by Marx and Nietzsche, of *The People of the Abyss* (1903) and *The Iron Heel* (1907).

LONDON. The cap. of England, on the r. Thames, *c.* 50 m. W. of the sea at the Nore.

The City of London occupies the site of a nucleus dating from pre-Roman times. Area 677 acres; resident pop. (1967) 4,530 (daytime working pop. est. at 500,000). The City is the commercial and business centre of the U.K. Within its 'square mile' lie the Bank of England; the Royal Exchange, the Stock Exchange, the Baltic Exchange, etc.; Lloyd's; the head offices of the principal banks and insurance companies; the Bankers' Clearing House; the Central Criminal Court (popularly called the Old Bailey, from the street in which it stands) and the Inner and Middle

Temples; 3 food markets – Leadenhall (poultry), Billingsgate (fish), Smithfield (meat); and the H.Q. of the Port of London Authority. The Mermaid, first theatre within the City for 3 cents., was opened in 1959.

The City is governed by a corporation dating from the 12th cent. and unique in local govt.; it consists of 3 courts: (i) the Court of Aldermen, one for each of the 25 wards, elected for life; (ii) the Court of Common Hall, composed of freemen of the City Livery Companies, which chooses annually 2 Sheriffs and other officers, and nominates 2 Aldermen from among former Sheriffs for choice by the Court of Aldermen to fill the office of Lord Mayor; (iii) the Court of Common Council, composed of the twenty-five Aldermen, and 159 Common Councilmen elected annually on St. Thomas's Day (21 Dec.) by citizens who qualify as electors by paying rates on property in the City. This last is the local govt. authority for the City and sits at the Guildhall. The Lord Mayor (so called since the 16th cent. without specific grant of the title, which was formerly Mayor) presides over all 3 Courts, and he is also the chief magistrate. He takes office on 8 Nov. and his presentation to the Lord Chief Justice and swearing in at the Royal Courts of Justice (just beyond the City boundary, in Westminster) are the occasion of the annual Lord Mayor's procession, held on the next Saturday. The annual Lord Mayor's banquet at the Guildhall follows. The Lord Mayor's official residence is the Mansion House.

Greater London was redefined in 1965, following the recommendation of a Royal Commission, and enlarged to comprise the former co. of London, the major part of Middlesex, which also disappeared administratively, and parts of Essex, Herts, Kent, and Surrey. The overall authority is the G.L. Council, with 100 councillors (elected every third year) and 16 aldermen (chosen by the councillors for 6 years, half retiring every third year). Many of its responsibilities are shared with the 32 London Borough Councils, created by mergers which often aroused much opposition, e.g. the merging of Fulham, with admin. traditions going back to the 7th cent., in Hammersmith; and of Bethnal Green, Poplar, and Stepney as Tower Hamlets. The bors. each have 60 councillors, elected for three years, and up to 10 aldermen. *See* map. p. 675.

History. L. first appears in history as 'Londinium' in A.D. 61, when it was sacked by Boadicea. The

LONDON. The Household Cavalry ride out into the Mall, their helmets glinting softly in the light of a November fog. Alongside in no less strict uniform of pin-stripe suit, bowler hat and neatly furled umbrella, a City business man steps briskly out. This is London. *Photo: Godfrey MacDomnic.*

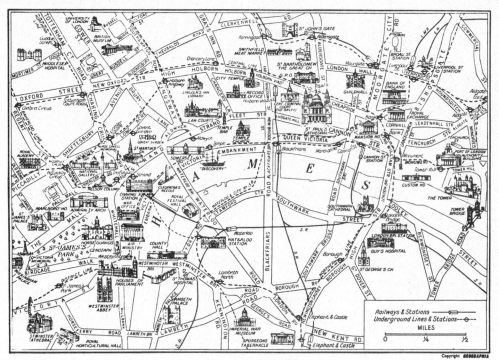

LONDON. The City and West End.

origin of the name remains uncertain. Roman L. was a walled city, and an important trading centre from which all roads radiated. It was the seat of a bishopric before 314. After an obscure period in the 5th–6th cents., L. reappears as the cap. of Essex. During the 9th–11th cents. it suffered greatly from Viking raids. The City secured rights of self-government in the 12th cent. and elected its first mayor in 1191, or perhaps earlier. Meanwhile Westminster, which grew up round the 7th cent. abbey, became the seat of govt. in the 12th cent., and of parliament in the 13th. The outstanding event of the 16th cent. was the dissolution of L.'s many monasteries. In the struggle against the Stuarts L. played a decisive part, and its trained bands distinguished themselves in the Civil War. The Great Plague of 1665 was followed by the Fire in 1666; rebuilding was entrusted to Wren and Robert Hooke, though the revolutionary plan made by Wren was not followed. The nobility in the 17th cent. abandoned the City as a residential district for Lincoln's Inn and Covent Garden, while in Hanoverian times they moved still farther W. In the 19th cent. the City lost its residential character altogether, and rail transport encouraged spreading suburbs. In the 20th cent. Mayfair and other central areas ceased to be mainly residential and were overtaken by offices, and commuter problems and road congestion correspondingly increased. Remedial measures after the S.W.W. incl. decentralisation of industry, offices and population to more than 30 other towns by special agreement; new residential projects within the area, e.g. the Barbican Scheme (*illus.* p. 1042), bringing residential population back to the City, and the creation of Thamesmead on reclaimed marshland near Woolwich for an eventual pop. of 80,000; improved bus and train services, and extension of tube facilities, e.g. the new Victoria Line opened 1969; and the G.L. Develop-

ment Plan (1969) envisaging three concentric rings of motorways. There are 2 airports (*see* GATWICK, HEATHROW) and a third (after rejection of the Stansted site 1969, as decided 1971) is to be sited at Foulness, Essex.

L. suffered slightly from air raids during the F.W.W. Raids during the S.W.W., which killed 29,890 people, injured 50,497, and destroyed or damaged many

The Boroughs of Greater London: figures indicate the number of councillors elected to the Greater London Council by each borough. Within the dotted line are the twelve Inner London Boroughs, and the City, an area which constituted the administrative County of London 1889–1965.

Reproduced, by permission, from The Times

famous buildings, fell into 3 main stages: day raids Aug.–Sept. 1940; night raids Aug. 1940–May 1941, incl. the fire raid on the City on 29–30 Dec.; and flying and rocket bombs June 1944–March 1945.

Architecture. L. contains specimens of all styles of English architecture since the 11th cent. Examples incl.: Norman: The White Tower, Tower of London; St. Bartholomew's, Smithfield; the Temple Church. Gothic: Westminster Abbey; Westminster Hall; Lambeth Palace; Southwark Cathedral. Tudor: St. James's Palace; Staple Inn, Holborn. 17th cent.: Banqueting Hall, Whitehall (Inigo Jones); St. Paul's, Kensington Palace, and many City churches (Wren). 18th cent.: Somerset House (Chambers); St. Martin-in-the-Fields; Buckingham Palace. 19th cent.: British Museum (classical); Houses of Parliament; Law Courts (Gothic); Westminster Cathedral (Byzantine). 20th cent.: County Hall; Bush House; Waterloo Bridge; Royal Festival Hall; Commonwealth Inst.

Commerce and Industry. Important from Saxon times, the Port of L. now extends 25 m. along the Thames from Tower Bridge to Tilbury, the docks having a water area of 688 acres. Notable modernisation incl. the extension of Tilbury in 1969 to cope with container traffic, and a plan to combine a new deep-water dock on the reclaimed Maplin Sands off Foulness Island with a 3rd London airport. The prime economic importance of L. is as an internat. banking, commercial, and financial centre, with high rents and decentralization thrusting larger-scale industry to the outskirts and beyond, e.g. printing, clothing, food processing, paper, chemicals, furniture, electrical and mechanical engineering, plastics, etc. Small-scale specialized products incl. finished diamonds (industrial and gem), jewellery, gold and silver work, furs, and haute couture and tailoring. There are also recording, broadcasting, television, and film studios; publishing offices, and the works and offices of the national press.

L. has long occupied a unique position in the nation's life as a centre of politics, administration, the law, fashion, pleasure, learning, and the arts. Its great public occasions range from Coronations to Cup finals, the Lord Mayor's show to the Royal Academy exhibition. It contains the headquarters of many learned and artistic societies; among its educational organizations are the British, Victoria and Albert, Natural History, and Science Museums, the National and Tate Galleries, and the Zoological Gardens. L. Univ. is the largest in Britain, while the Inns of Court have been the training-school for lawyers since the 13th cent. L. has been the main centre of English drama ever since its first theatre was built by Burbage in 1576.

LONDON. Canadian city in S. Ontario, on the r. Thames, 100 m. S.W. of Toronto. The centre of a good farming district, it has tanneries, breweries, and factories making hosiery, radio and electrical equipment, leather, shoes, etc. It dates from 1826 and is the seat of the Univ. of Western Ontario and of Anglican and R.C. bishoprics. It has an airport. Pop. (1966) 207,400.

LONDONDERRY. City, co. tn. (co. bor.) of co. L., N. Ireland, 63 m. N.W. of Belfast, on the Foyle. Developing from the monastery founded by Columba in the 6th cent., L. was defended by the Irish Protestants, who resisted the besieging army of James II from April to July 1689. During the S.W.W. L. was a base for U.S. ships on merchant convoy duty. Industries incl. textiles, food processing, light engineering, and chemicals. Civil rights disturbances 1968–9 led to a special Development Commission to 'transform economic and social conditions'.

The county of L. borders the Atlantic; its main river is the Roe. Cultivation is limited by the excessive rainfall. The capital is L. Area 804 sq. m.; pop. (1966) 118,664.

The town of L. was originally called Derry (Irish Dhoire, place of oaks); both town and county took the name L. when land belonging to the O'Neills was given to the City of London Corporation in 1609.

'LONDON GAZETTE.' Twice-weekly publication (which 1st appeared in 1666) of official announcements, service appointments, decorations, etc.

LONDON, Museum of. Formed by the amalgamation of the former Guildhall (Roman and medieval) and London (Tudor and later) Museums, announced in 1962: the exhibits of both, which complement each other, are being housed in a new building at the junction of London Wall and Aldersgate, nr. the Barbican.

LONDON UNIVERSITY. L.U. originated with the foundation in 1826 of University Coll., to provide university education free from religious tests. In 1836 a charter set up an examining body with power to grant degrees. L.U. threw open all degrees to women in 1878, being the first British univ. to do so. It ceased to be a purely examining body in 1900, when it took over the existing colleges. It also includes 20 medical schools. Among the chief colleges are University, King's, the Imperial College of Science and Technology, the London School of Economics, the School of Oriental and African Studies, Queen Mary, Birkbeck, and the 3 colleges founded for women: Royal Holloway, Bedford, and Westfield. There are *c.* 34,500 internal and *c.* 32,000 external students. The univ. headquarters are in Bloomsbury.

LONG, Huey Pierce (1893–1935). American 'Share the Wealth' demagogue, gov. of Louisiana 1928–31, when his rule was marked by reforms side by side with corruption and semi-Fascist tendencies. Elected to the senate in 1931 he was celebrated for his filibusters. He was assassinated. His son **Russell B. Long** (1918–), senator for Louisiana from 1948, was ousted as Democratic 'whip' by Edward Kennedy 1969.

LONG, Margaret Gabrielle (1888–1952). British author, *née* Campbell, who m. in 1917 as her 2nd husband Arthur L. Her first great success was the romantic historical novel *The Viper of Milan* (1917), pub. with many successors under the pseudonym Marjorie Bowen.

LONG BEACH. Coastal city of California, S. of Los Angeles, U.S.A. It is important both as an industrial centre and pleasure resort; Signal Hill oilfield, discovered in 1921, is within the city boundary. L.B. is subject to earthquakes, one in 1933 killing 130 and doing damage estimated at £10,000,000 Pop. met. area Los Angeles–L.B. (1970) 6,970, 733.

LONGCHAMP (lońshoń'). Pleasure resort and racecourse of Paris, France, in the Bois de Boulogne. It is on the site of a former nunnery founded in 1260, suppressed 1790.

LONGFELLOW, Henry Wadsworth (1807–82). American poet. B. in Portland, Maine, he was ed. at Bowdoin Coll., where he became prof. of modern languages (1829–35), and subsequently held a similar position at Harvard (1836–54). His first vol. of poems, *Voices in the Night*, appeared in 1839, and was followed by *Ballads and Other Poems* (1842), containing 'Excelsior' and 'The Wreck of the Hesperus'; *Evangeline* (1847); *The Golden Legend* (1851), based on the 12th cent. German work; *Hiawatha* (1855), a Red Indian epic; *The Courtship of Miles Standish* (1858); and *Tales of a Wayside Inn* (1863–74). His popularity in England is witnessed by the erection of a monument to him in Westminster Abbey.

LONGFORD, Frank (Francis) Aungier Pakenham, 7th earl of L. (1905–). Anglo-Irish Labour politician. Ed. at Eton and Oxford, he was brought up in High Tory Protestant circles but is a leading Catholic layman, worked in the Cons. Party Economic Research Dept. 1930–2, yet became a prominent member of the Labour Party (being personal assistant to Sir William Beveridge during the S.W.W.), was Min. of Civil Aviation 1948–51, Lord Privy Seal 1964–5, 1966–8; Colonial Sec. 1965–6 and Leader of the House of Lords 1964–8. His books incl. *Born to Believe* (1953) and *Five Lives* (1964), both autobiographical, and he is a keen advocate of penal reform. He m. 1931 Elizabeth Harman (1906–) who, as 'Elizabeth Longford' pub. such historical studies as *Victoria R.I.* (1964), and their eldest dau. Lady Antonia Fraser (1932–) pub. *Mary Queen of Scots* (1969).

LONGFORD. Co. of Leinster prov., Rep. of Ireland, whose rivers are the Camlin and Inny; the Shannon marks its W. boundary. There are several lakes. Area 403 sq. m.; pop. (1966) 28,989. The co. tn. is Longford, on the Camlin, seat of the bishopric of Ardagh. Pop. (1966) 3,500.

LONGINUS (lonjī'nus), **Cassius** (c. A.D. 213–73). Greek philosopher and critic. B. probably in Syria, he taught in Athens for many years. While journeying in the East, he became the teacher and adviser of Zenobia of Palmyra. On his instigation she rebelled against Roman rule, and when she was captured L. was put to death. The critical treatise *On the Sublime* is usually attributed to him.

LONG ISLAND. Is. forming part of the State of New York, U.S.A., separated from the mainland by Long Island Sound. There are many pleasure resorts, e.g. Jones Beach and Coney Island. In the W. are Brooklyn and Queen's, bors. of Greater New York City. Area 1,723 sq. m. Long Is. City, in Queen's, founded 1640 and a city in its own right 1870–98, is an industrial dist.

LONGITUDE. *See* LATITUDE AND LONGITUDE.

LONG PARLIAMENT. Name commonly applied to the parl. of 1640–60, which carried through the English Revolution. Its Royalist members withdrew in 1642, and the 'Presbyterian' right wing was excluded in 1648. The remaining members, known as the Rump, ruled England until they were expelled by Cromwell in 1653. The L.P. reassembled in 1659–60, and began the negotiations which led to the Restoration.

LONGWY (lonwē'). Fortified town in Meurthe-et-Moselle dept., N.E. France, on the Belgian frontier, and commanding the valley of the Chiers. It is among iron mines and has metallurgical works. Pop. (1962) 22,214.

LÖNNROT, Elias (1802–84). Finnish scholar. B. at Nyland, he travelled widely in Finland and Russia in search of Finnish folk-lore, and for the first time collected and pub. the national epic *Kalevala* (q.v.) in 1835. In 1854 L. became prof. at Helsingfors.

LONSDALE, Hugh Cecil Lowther, 5th earl of (1857–1944). British sportsman. He was an expert huntsman, steeplechaser, boxer, and yachtsman, and as president of the National Sporting Club laid down the rules of boxing and presented the 'L. belts'.

LOOFAH. Fruit of the herbaceous plant *Luffa cylindrica* in the gourd (q.v.) family. Its 'skeleton' is familiar in the bathroom.

LOOS, Anita (1893–). American author. B. in California, she scored her greatest success with the fictitious diary of a girl on the make, *Gentlemen Prefer Blondes* (1925).

LOOSESTRIFE. Plants of the Primulaceae family, e.g. the common L. (*Lysimachia vulgaris*) c. 3 ft. high on river banks in Britain with spikes of yellow flowers; wood L. or yellow pimpernel and creeping jenny: also the striking purple L. (*Lythrum salicaria*) in the family Lythraceae.

LOPE DE VEGA. *See* VEGA.

LÓPEZ (lō'pes), **Carlos Antonio** (1790–1862). Paraguayan statesman. He succeeded his uncle J. G. R. Francia as virtual dictator in 1840, and held supreme power until his death. He was succeeded by his son **Francisco Solano L.** (1827–70), who involved the country in a war with Brazil, Uruguay and Argentina

during which five-sixths of the pop. perished. He was himself killed in battle.

LOP-NOR. Series of shallow lakes with shifting boundaries in the Takla-Makan (desert) in Sinkiang-Uighur region, China. Marco Polo visited L.-N., then a single lake of considerable extent, c. 1273.

LOQUAT (lō'kwat). Evergreen tree of the Rosaceae family (*Eriobotrya japonica*) native to China and Japan, and known also as the Japanese 'plum'. The golden fruit is of delicate sweet-sour taste.

LORCA, Federico Garcia (1899–1936). Spanish poet. B. at Fuentevaqueros, he followed his first *Libro de Poemas* (1921) by *Canciones* (1926) and *Romancero Gitano* (1927). He visited New York in 1930, but returned to Spain in 1931 to found *La Barraca*, a touring theatrical company. Among his plays are *El Maleficio de la Mariposa* (1920), *Bodas de Sangre* (1933), *Yerma, Doña Rosita la Soltera*, and *La Casa de Bernada*. His finest poem is his 'Lament' for the bullfighter Sánchez Mejías. He was shot by the Falangists.

LORD. The prefix L. is used informally as an alternative to the full title of a marquess, earl, or viscount, and is normally so used in speaking of a baron, and as a courtesy title before the Christian and surname of the younger sons of dukes and marquesses. A bishop is formally addressed as the L. Bishop of A.

LORD-LIEUTENANT. The head of the magistracy of a county. This office, first instituted by Henry VIII, is usually held by a large landowner. Its duties included until 1871 responsibility for the co. militia. The L.-L. appoints the co. magistrates.

LORD MAYOR. *See* MAYOR.

LORD'S. Headquarters of the Marylebone Cricket Club, regulating body of English cricket since 1788, and also the county ground of Middx. Thomas Lord (1757–1832) first opened the ground in Dorset Square in 1787 and in 1814 it was removed to its present site in St. John's Wood.

LORDS, House of. *See* PARLIAMENT.

LORD'S SUPPER. *See* EUCHARIST.

LORELEI (-lī). A rock in the Rhine near St. Goar, W. Germany, which possesses a remarkable echo.

LORELEI. The dangerous cliff which rises 430 ft. above the river has found a permanent place in German song and story Heine's lyric 'Die Lorelei' being most famous of all.
Courtesy of the German Tourist Information Bureau.

According to a poem written by Brentano (q.v.) in 1802, a maiden who drowned herself because of an inconstant lover became a siren luring fishermen to destruction by her song, a story which developed into a legend used by several subsequent writers.

LORENZ, Konrad (1903–). Austrian ethnologist. Director of the Max Planck Institute for the Physiology of Behaviour in Bavaria from 1961, he is known for his attractive studies of animal behaviour *King Solomon's Ring* (1952) and *On Aggression* (1966).

LORENZETTI (lōrentset'ē), **Pietro** (c. 1280–1348). Italian painter. He was one of the earliest of Sienese painters, and his works incl. the 'Nativity of the Virgin' at Siena, and the altar-piece 'Madonna with Angels' in Florence. His younger brother, **Ambrogio L.** (c. 1300–48), is known for his allegorical pictures representing 'Good and Bad Government' at Siena.

LORE'TO. Place of pilgrimage in Ancona prov., Italy, containing the *Santa Casa*, or Holy House, of the Virgin, said to have been carried from Nazareth by angels in 1294, first to Dalmatia, and from there to L. Hence, Our Lady of L. is patron saint of aviators. Pop. (1960) 9,000.

LORIENT (lōryoṅ'). Seaport of W. France, 30 m. W.N.W. of Vannes. It is a naval station with state dockyards and a varied trade is conducted via its separate commercial port. Pop. (1968) 66,444.

LORRAIN, Claude. *See* CLAUDE LORRAIN.

LORRAINE. *See* ALSACE-LORRAINE.

LORRAINE, Cross of. A red cross with 2 horizontal crosspieces, on a blue ground. It was the emblem carried by Joan of Arc, and was adopted by the Free French forces in 1940. *See* illus. p. 447.

LORY. Group of Australasian, honey-eating parrots (family Loriidae) which are brilliantly coloured.

LOS ALAMOS. Military township in New Mexico, U.S.A., 25 m. N.W. of Santa Fé, where research and designing of the atom bomb were carried out (working on data provided by other research stations) 1943–5. It continued to be a centre of atomic and later of space research. Pop. (1960) 12,584.

LOS ANGELES (loss an-ja-les). City on the coast of S. California, in 1960 with the 3rd-largest pop. in the U.S.A. It has a pleasant climate, and with its suburb Hollywood (q.v.), 8 m. to the N.W., attracts many visitors. It is an important commercial port and a naval base; its industries incl. film making, petroleum refining and meat packing. Pop. (1970) 2,782,400; met. area L.A.–Long Beach 6,970,733.

L.A., founded in 1781, was then in Mexico; it was taken by a U.S. naval force in 1846 and annexed 1850. Its full name is El Pueblo de Nuestra Señora La Reina de los Angeles de Porciuncula (the village of Our Lady Queen of the Angels of Porciuncula).

LOS ANGELES, Victoria de (1923–). Spanish soprano. In opera her roles incl. Manon and Madame Butterfly, and she is celebrated for her concert renderings of Spanish songs.

LÖ'SEY, Joseph (1909–). American stage and film director. After studying medicine, literature and theatre, he produced several short films and plays, incl. *Payment Deferred* (1931) and *Galileo* (1947) – both with C. Laughton, on Broadway. In 1951 he settled in England, where some of his notable films inc. *The Servant* and *Secret Ceremony*.

LOSSIEMOUTH. Town in Morayshire, Scotland, on the Moray Firth, 5 m. N. of Elgin. Ramsay MacDonald was b. and buried at L. With Branderburgh, L. forms a burgh. Pop. (1961) 5,855.

LOSTWI'THIEL. English market town (bor.) and fishing port with a 13th cent. church, in Cornwall, on the Fowey, 5 m. S.E. of Bodmin. Pop. (1961) 1,954.

LOT (loh). French river, rising in the Cévennes in Lozère dept., and flowing for c. 300 m. in a westerly direction to join the Garonne at Aiguillon. It gives its name to the depts. of Lot and Lot-et-Garonne.

LOTHAIR I (795–855). Holy Roman Emperor. He was the son of Louis I, who in 817 associated him with himself in the govt. of the Empire. After Louis's death in 840 the Empire was divided between L. and his brothers, L. taking N. Italy and the Rhône and Rhine valleys.

LOTHAIR (825–69). King of Lotharingia. He inherited from his father, the emperor Lothair I, in 855 a district W. of the Rhine, between the Jura Mts. and the N. Sea. This became known after him as Lotharingia, later corrupted into Lorraine.

LOTHIAN (lōdh'ian), **Philip Henry Kerr, 11th** marquis of (1882–1940). British Lib. politician. He served in the S. African Civil Service 1905–10, and as Lloyd George's sec. 1916–21. He was ambassador to Washington 1939–40.

LOTHIAN, The. A name formerly applied to the S. Scotland cos. of Haddington, Edinburgh, and Linlithgow (E.L., Mid-L., and W.L.), also incl. Roxburghshire and Berwickshire. This area, part of the kingdom of Northumbria from 547, was annexed by the Scots in 1018.

LOTI (lohtē'), **Pierre.** Pseudonym of the French author Louis Marie Julien Viaud (1850–1923). B. at Rochefort, he was in the navy 1867–1910, becoming a captain in 1906. His novels reflect his knowledge of the sea, his masterpiece being *Le Pêcheur d'Islande*.

LOTTERY. Arrangement in which persons buying tickets are eligible to win prizes in a draw. In England, both govt. and private Ls. were held from the 17th cent. onwards, but cheating became so much of a scandal that an act of 1802 made illegal any L. not authorized by parliament; the last state L. was held in 1826. An act of 1934 permitted small Ls. or raffles at e.g. bazaars, and Ls. promoted for a society not connected with gaming, or among people working or living in the same premises; both types were subject to certain conditions, incl. the exclusion of money prizes. The Small Ls. and Gaming Act, 1956, gave a little more freedom, allowing money prizes up to £100, but again with stringent conditions. Premium Savings Bonds, introduced in 1956 (*see under* SAVING), were in the nature of a L.

Ls. are illegal in the U.S.A. and any lottery ticket found in the post is destroyed. But many countries still conduct state Ls., e.g. Italy and Malta. One of the most famous was the Calcutta' Sweepstake on the Derby, run by the Royal Calcutta Turf Club; its last pub. figures relate to 1929 when prize money totalled £135,000. The most successful of Ls. is undoubtedly the Irish Sweepstake, run under govt. auspices in aid of the nursing services in the Rep. of Ireland on 3 races in the course of the year; 25 per cent of the receipts, after deduction of expenses, go to the Hospitals Trust Board, the remaining 75 per cent being distributed in prizes which amount in total to £1,000,000 or more on each race. Sale of tickets in the U.K. is illegal.

LOTTO, Lorenzo (c. 1480–1556). Italian artist. B. in Venice, he was influenced by Raphael and Correggio; he produced many fine altar-pieces, and also remarkable portraits, e.g. 'Lucrezia' and 'The Protonotary' in the National Gallery. He ended his life among the monks of Loreto.

LOTUS. Genus of plants in the family Leguminosae, e.g. bird's foot trefoil (*L. corniculatus*); also the shrub

Nymphaea Lotus

Zizyphus lotus known to the ancient Greeks who used its fruit to make a type of bread and also a wine supposed to induce happy oblivion – hence L.-eaters; and the water-lilies *Nymphaea lotus*, frequent in Egyptian art, and *Nelumbium speciosum*, the sacred L. of the Hindus which (unlike the Egyptian) does not float but stands erect above the water.

LOUGHBORCUGH (luf'boro). English market town (bor.) in Leics, 10 m. N.W. of Leicester. Industries incl. engineering, bell founding, and the making of electrical apparatus and hosiery. L. Coll. of Technology (residential) was founded in 1918, expanded in 1959, became in 1966 L. Univ. of Technology. Pop. (1961) 38,621.

LOUIS I (778–840). Holy Roman Emperor, called **the Pious.** He succeeded his father Charlemagne in 814, and counts as Louis I of France.

LOUIS XIV. The King and his heirs by Nicolas Largillière (1656–1746), a portrait group that reflects no credit on 18th century health standards. The son, grandson and great-grandson depicted all died before Louis, and yet another great-grandson succeeded as Louis XV. *Reproduced by permission of the Trustees of the Wallace Collection.*

LOUIS. The name of 18 kings of France. The emperor Louis I (q.v.) counts as Louis I of France. **Louis V** (967–87), who reigned 986–7, was the last of the Carolingian dynasty. **Louis VII** (c. 1111–80), who reigned 1137–80, led the 2nd Crusade in 1147–9. **Louis VIII** (1187–1226) was invited to become king in place of John by the English barons, and unsuccessfully invaded England 1215–17. He succeeded to the French throne in 1223. **St. Louis IX** (1214–70), who succeeded him, was the ideal medieval king. He led a crusade to Egypt in 1248–50, but was defeated and captured by the Saracens, spending 4 years in captivity. He d. at Tunis while leading another crusade. **Louis XI** (1423–83), who succeeded to the throne in 1461, broke the power of the great nobles headed by Charles the Bold, duke of Burgundy, by a combination of force and unscrupulous intrigue. **Louis XII** (1462–1515) was known as duke of Orléans until he succeeded his cousin Charles VIII in 1499. Throughout his reign he was engaged in Italian wars. **Louis XIII** (1601–43) succeeded his father Henry IV in 1610, and assumed the royal power in 1617. During 1624–42 the control of his policy was entirely in the hands of Richelieu (q.v.).

LOUIS XIV (1638–1715). King of France. He succeeded his father Louis XIII in 1643, but until 1661 France was ruled by Mazarin (q.v.). After his death L. never appointed another prime minister, but planned and supervised the execution of his own policy, which was summed up in his saying *L'État c'est moi* (I am the State). His ministers were drawn from the middle classes, the greatest of them being Colbert, whose work was undone by L.'s policy of military aggrandizement. Louis attempted in 1667–8 to annex the Spanish Netherlands, but was frustrated by an alliance of Holland, England, and Sweden. Having detached England from the alliance, in 1672 he invaded Holland. Led by William of Orange, the Dutch stood firm, and a European alliance was formed against L.; the Peace of Nijmegen (1678) nevertheless brought considerable territorial gains.

War was renewed 1688–97 between L. and the Grand Alliance, including England, formed by William of Orange. On land the French were everywhere victorious, but in 1692 L.'s fleet was almost destroyed at La Hogue. L.'s acceptance in 1700 of the Spanish throne for his grandson led to the War of the Spanish Succession (1701–13). The Peace of Utrecht ended French supremacy in Europe. In 1660 L. m. the Infanta Maria Theresa of Spain, but he was greatly influenced by his mistresses, including Louise de la Vallière, Mme de Montespan, and Mme de Maintenon, whom he m. after his wife's death in 1683.

LOUIS XV (1710–74). King of France. A great-grandson of Louis XIV, he was only 5 when he came to the throne, and until 1723 the duke of Orléans was regent. L. was indolent and frivolous, and left the government in the hands of his ministers, the duke of Bourbon and Cardinal Fleury. On Fleury's death in 1743 he attempted to rule alone, but he fell entirely under the domination of his mistresses, Mme de Pompadour and Mme du Barry. His foreign policy proved humiliating for France, Canada and India being lost.

LOUIS XVI (1754–93). King of France. He succeeded his grandfather Louis XV in 1774. He was dominated by his queen, Marie Antoinette, and the finances fell into such confusion that in 1789 the States General were summoned, and revolution began. L. remained personally popular until in 1791 he attempted to flee the country; thereafter republicanism grew, and in Aug. 1792 the Parisians stormed the Tuileries and made the royal family prisoners. Deposed in Sept., L. was tried for treason and guillotined.

LOUIS XVII (1785–95). Nominal king of France. The son of Louis XVI, he was imprisoned with his parents in 1792, and probably d. in prison.

LOUIS XVIII (1755–1824). King of France. The younger brother of Louis XVI, he was known before 1795 as the count of Provence. He fled from France in 1791, and assumed the title of king in 1795. He lived in exile until he obtained the throne in 1814. Driven out again during the 100 Days, he returned after Waterloo. He pursued a liberal and conciliatory policy, attempting to restrain the violence of the ultra-royalists, until the assassination of the heir to the throne in 1820 led to a royalist reaction.

LOUIS (loo'is), **Joe.** Professional name of American boxer Joseph Louis Barrow (1914–   ). B. n r. Lexington, Alabama, he was world heavyweight champion 1937–49: the power of his blows earned him the nickname 'the brown bomber'.

LOUISIANA. South-central state of the U.S.A. bordering the Gulf of Mexico. Much of L. is occupied by the delta of the Mississippi. Mineral products incl. petroleum, sulphur, natural gas, salt; industries incl. petroleum refining, food processing, lumbering, paper making; agricultural products incl. rice, cotton, sugar, and maize. The cap. is Baton Rouge, and the largest city, New Orleans. Area 48,523 sq. m.; pop. (1970) 3,643,180.

L. takes its name from the old French prov. of LOUISIANA, explored by La Salle and claimed for Louis XIV, in whose honour he named it, in 1682. The prov. extended from the British colonies in the E. to the Spanish colonies on the W. and from what is now Manitoba to the Gulf of Mexico. France lost to Britain the part of L. east of the Mississippi in 1763, and it became part of the U.S.A. in 1783; the part west of the Mississippi, 828,000 sq. m. in extent, passed to Spain in 1762, but by a secret treaty of 1800 was restored to France. In 1803 Napoleon sold this area to the U.S.A. for £3,000,000; it was divided into the Territory of New Orleans, which became the state of L. in 1812, and the Territory of L., later to become the states of Arkansas, Missouri, Nebraska, Iowa, and S. Dakota, and part of N. Dakota, Minnesota, Kansas, Oklahoma, Colorado, and Wyoming.

LOUIS PHILIPPE (1773–1850). King of the French. The son of the duke of Orléans, he was known after 1785 as the duke of Chartres. He supported the French Revolution during its earlier stages, but fled the country in 1793, and until 1814 lived in exile. He identified himself with the Liberal opposition, and after the 1830 revolution became king. He relied for support on the rich bourgeoisie, and corruption discredited the régime. Overthrown in 1848, he escaped to England, where he d.

LOUISVILLE, City of Kentucky, U.S.A., on the Ohio, 95 m. S.W. of Cincinnati. It is an important industrial centre. The Kentucky Derby is held at L. in May each year. Pop. met. area (1970) 819,057.

LOURDES (loord). Place of pilgrimage in Hautes-Pyrénées dept., S.W. France. In 1858 a peasant girl, Bernadette Soubirous (1844–79), claimed to have experienced visions of the Virgin Mary beside the spring, which became credited with miraculous healing powers. An underground church, to hold 20,000 and dedicated to St. Pius X, was consecrated at L. in 1958. Pop. (1962) 16,376. *See* illus. under BERNADETTE.

LOURENÇO MARQUES (lōrań'so mahr'kes). Cap. of Mozambique, E. Africa, lying on Delagoa Bay. A well-planned city, it has many fine buildings. The starting point of a railway to Johannesburg, it handles a vast entrepôt trade; L.M. also has an international airfield. Pop. (1960) 441,360.

LOUTH (lowth). English market town (bor.) in the Parts of Lindsey, Lincs, 15 m. S. of Grimsby. The Cistercian abbey was founded *c.* 1140; Tennyson and his brothers attended the 16th cent. grammar school (rebuilt). Pop. (1961) 11,556.

LOUTH. Maritime co. of Leinster prov., Rep. of Ireland. For the most part undulating lowland, the co. is fertile. The chief industries are agriculture, linen manufacture and fishing. The co. town is Dundalk: 5½ m. to the S.W. is the village of L. Area 317 sq. m.; pop. (1966) 69,519.

LOUVAIN (loovań'). Town in Brabant prov. of Belgium, 15 m. E.N.E. of Brussels. The 15th cent. town hall is an excellent example of the late Pointed Flemish style. The chief industry is brewing. L. (Flemish Leuven) dates from 891, and had a pop. of more than 100,000 in medieval times when it was a cloth-making centre. The univ. (1426) is

THE LOUVRE
Courtesy of the French National Tourist Office.

just within the Flemish linguistic zone, and although formerly half the students were French-speaking, it was agreed in 1968, following bitter dispute, that the French-speaking faculties be removed to Walloon areas near Brussels. Pop. (1966) 32,125.

LOUVRE (loovr). Art gallery in Paris, containing one of the finest collections of paintings, sculptures, and art objects in the world; formerly a palace of French kings. Built on the site of a 13th cent. château, the L. is first mentioned in records of 1204. Napoleon converted the L. into a national art gallery. Two world-famous exhibits are the Venus de Milo and Leonardo da Vinci's 'Mona Lisa'.

LOVAT, Simon Fraser, 12th baron L. (*c.* 1667–1747). Scottish Jacobite. Throughout a political career lasting 50 years he constantly intrigued with both Jacobites and Whigs, and was beheaded for supporting the 1745 rebellion.

LOVELACE (luv'lās), **Richard** (1618–58). English poet. Owing to his responsibility for the Kentish Petition pleading for the re-establishment of the King's rule in 1642, he was committed to the Westminster gatehouse, where he wrote 'To Althea from Prison' etc. During a second imprisonment in 1648 he revised his *Lucasta: Epodes, Odes, Sonnets, Songs, etc.* (1649). He d. in poverty.

LOVELL, Sir Bernard (1913–). British astronomer. During the S.W.W. he worked at the Telecommunications Research establishment (1939–45), and in 1951 became prof. of radio astronomy at the Univ. of Manchester and director of Jodrell Bank Experimental Station. His books incl. *Radio Astronomy* (1951) and *The Exploration of Outer Space* (1961). He was knighted in 1961.

SIR BERNARD LOVELL, behind him the Jodrell Bank telescope.
Photo: Crown Copyright

LOVER, Samuel (1797–1868). Irish author. B. in Dublin, he became a miniature painter, and in 1835 settled in London where he conquered society by his singing of his own compositions, which he pub. in *Songs and Ballads* (1839), etc. He is also remembered for his humorous novels, *Rory O'More* (1837) and *Handy Andy* (1842).

LOVETT, William (1800–77). English Chartist. A cabinet-maker by trade, he drew up the People's Charter in 1838, led the 'moral force' Chartists, and was imprisoned 1839–40. His autobiography was pub. in 1876.

LOW, Sir David (1891–1963). New Zealand cartoonist. B. in Dunedin, he joined the *Sydney Bulletin* in 1911, and London *Star* (1919), the *Evening Standard* (1927–50), the *Daily Herald* (1950–3), and was with the *Guardian* from 1953 until his death. He was noted for his independence and radical views, and the bold, simple lines of his drawings and the gallery of characters he evolved, e.g. Colonel Blimp, Hit and Muss, and the T.U.C. horse, became world-famous. He was knighted in 1962.

LOW COUNTRIES. European region comprising the Netherlands and Belgium, sometimes extended to incl. Luxembourg.

LOWE (lō), **Sir Hudson** (1769–1844). British gov. of St. Helena, 1815–21. Charged with Napoleon's safe keeping, he was accused of unnecessary harshness. He served as gov. of Antigua in 1823 and commander of the forces in Ceylon 1825–30.

LOWELL (lō'-el), **Amy** (1874–1925). American poet. B. in Massachusetts, in 1913 she became attached to the Imagist group, succeeding Ezra Pound in its leadership. A distinguished experimenter in free verse, she pub. *Sword Blades and Poppy Seeds* (1914), and *What's o'Clock?* (1925); and *Tendencies in Modern American Poetry* (1917).

LOWELL, James Russell (1819–91). American author. B. in Massachusetts he was admitted to the

Bar 1840, and ed. *The National Anti-Slavery Standard* (1848–52). In 1848 he estab. his reputation with the satirical *Fable for Critics, The Vision of Sir Launfal*, and the first series of *Biglow Papers*. He succeeded Longfellow as prof. of modern languages at Harvard (1855–76), and was ambassador to Spain (1877–80), and to England (1880–5). Among his later works are the essays *My Study Windows* (1871).

LOWELL, Percival (1855–1916). American astronomer. In 1894 he founded the L. observatory at Flagstaff, Arizona.

LOWELL, Robert (1917–). American poet. A Bostonian, he broke the usual New England links to become a Roman Catholic in 1940 and a conscientious objector in the S.W.W. His vols. incl. *Land of Unlikeness* (1944), *Lord Weary's Castle* (1946), and *Notebook* (1970): tension in his verse derives from his quarrel with his Puritan cultural inheritance. *Life Studies* (1958) incl. an autobiographical prose study.

LOWELL. City of Massachusetts, U.S.A., at the junction of the Merrimac and Concord rivers. It manufactures cotton fabrics. Pop. (1960) 92,107.

LOWER CALIFORNIA. Long narrow peninsula, part of the rep. of Mexico. A mountain range, rising in places to 8,000 ft., runs down it. The climate is arid, but the soil is fertile where artificial irrigation is available, and citrus fruits, maize, grapes are grown. There are pearl fisheries and fishing grounds; and rich mineral deposits, little worked. The peninsula is divided into the state of Baja California (Lower California), cap. Mexicali; area 27,650 sq. m.; pop. (1967) 896,000; and the territory of Baja California Sur (S. Lower California), cap. La Paz; area 27,970 sq. m.; pop. (1967) 100,000.

LOWER SAXONY. Land of N.W. Germany, formed in 1946. Hanover is the cap. Area 18,290 sq. m.; pop. (1966) 6,967,200.

LOWESTOFT. Seaport and resort (bor.) in Suffolk, England, 118 m. N.E. of London, on Oulton Broad and the N. Sea. It is an important fishing and boat-building centre. Pop. (1961) 45,687.

L. Ness is the point farthest E. in England. In a naval battle fought off L. in 1665 the English under James, duke of York (afterwards James II), drove off the Dutch.

LOWRY, Laurence Stephen (1887–). British artist. B. in Manchester, he is most typical in his multi-figure industrial city scenes, simple and moving. He became R.A. 1962.

LOYALISTS or **Tories.** The colonists who opposed the break with Britain during the American War of Independence. Altogether they numbered about a third of the pop. After the war many of them removed to Canada, where they became known as 'United Empire Ls.'.

LOY'OLA, Ignatius de (Inigo Lopez de Ricalde) (1491–1556). Founder of the Society of Jesus, b. at the castle of Loyola in Guipuzcoa prov., Spain. He became a soldier and was wounded at Pampeluna. While he was recovering he read the Bible. The effect on him was so profound that he abandoned the army and retired to a mountain cave in order to meditate. He went on a pilgrimage to Jerusalem (1523), and later studied at Salamanca and Paris. He founded the Society of Jesus in 1534, and in 1541 became its first general. His *Spiritual Exercises* was pub. in 1548.

LOYSON, Charles. *See* HYACINTHE, PÈRE.

LOZÈRE (lōzār'). Section of the Cévennes Mts., S. France. It rises in Finiels to 5,584 ft., and gives its name to a dept.

LP (liquid petroleum) GAS, a by-product of oil refining, provides gas to 250 times its liquid volume. Butane, for domestic purposes, is increasingly used in remote areas, and propane has many specialized industrial uses, e.g. as an alternative to acetylene in metal cutting.

LSD (lysergic acid diethylamide). Hallucinatory drug, producing illusions of supernatural power, and other symptoms of insanity. Colourless, odourless, and non-addictive, it is easily synthesized and very dangerous in amateur experiment.

LUANDA, São Paulo de. Port and cap. of Angola, W. Africa. Founded in 1575, it exports coffee, sugar, palm oil, and diamonds, and petroleum is refined. Pop. (1967) 345,000.

LUA'NG PRABA'NG. Royal cap. of Laos (*see* VIENTIANE), on the upper Mekong. Pop. 30,000.

LUBBOCK, Percy (1879–1965). Brit. author. His books incl. the reminiscent *Earlham* (1922) and the influential *Craft of Fiction* (1921).

LÜBECK. Seaport of Schleswig-Holstein, W. Germany, on the Baltic Sea, on the Trave, 37 m. N.E. of Hamburg, founded in 1143. Its 5 main churches are fine Gothic examples, and its cathedral dates from 1173 Once head of the powerful Hanseatic League, it later lost much of its trade

LUBECK. One of the two surviving gates which once formed part of the fortifications surrounding the city, the beautiful 15th cent. Holsten Gate is built of brickwork in Gothic style.
Courtesy of the German Tourist Information Bureau.

to Hamburg and Bremen, but improved canal and port facilities helped it to retain its position as a centre of Baltic trade. The name L. is of Wendish origin, and means lovely one. L. was a free state of both the Empire and the Weimar Rep. Pop. (1966) 242,600.

LUBIS (lōō'-), **Mochtar** (1922–). Indonesian author. B. in Padang, Sumatra, he became editor-in-chief of the daily *Indonesia Raya*, and was imprisoned almost continuously without trial 1956–66 for criticism of the govt. and army. His novels incl. *Twilight in Djakarta* (1962) and *Road with No End* (1968).

LUBITSCH, Ernst (1892–1947). American actor and film director. He made his début as an actor in Berlin (1911), and in 1922 went to the U.S.A., where he directed films incl. *Ninotchka* and *Design for Living*.

LUBLIN (loob'lin). Polish town, cap. of L. voivodship, 95 m. S.E. of Warsaw. It existed in the 10th cent., and has an old castle and a 16th cent. cathedral. It is an agricultural trading centre, and bricks, aircraft, electrical goods, glass, etc., are manufactured. A council of workers and peasants proclaimed Poland's independence at L. in 1918; and a Russian-sponsored committee of national liberation, which proclaimed itself the prov. govt. of Poland at L. on 31 Dec. 1944, was recognized by Russia 5 days later. L. univ. was founded in 1918. Pop. (1966) 206,000.

L. voivodship is drained by the Vistula and the W. Bug; it incl. extensive forests. Area 9,602 sq. m.; pop. (1966) 1,911,000.

LUBRICANTS. Substances insinuated between moving surfaces to reduce friction. A solid L. is graphite (plumbago), either flaked or emulsified (colloidal) in water (aquadag) or oil (oildag). Semi-solid and liquid L. are more important, consisting of animal, vegetable, and mineral oils. The L. most used are recovered from petroleum distillation.

Extensive research has been carried out on chemical additives to reduce corrosive wear, prevent the accumulation of 'cold sludge' (often the result of stop-start driving in city traffic jams), keep pace with the higher working temperatures of aviation gas turbines, and provide radiation-resistant greases for nuclear power plants.

LUBUMBASHI. *See* ELISABETHVILLE.

LŬ'CAN or **Marcus Annaeus Lucanus** (A.D. 39–65). Latin poet. B. at Cordova, he was a nephew of the philosopher Seneca, and became a favourite of Nero's, until that emperor's jealousy of his poetic powers ended their friendship. He then joined in a republican conspiracy, and on its failure committed suicide. His unfinished epic *Pharsalia* deals with the civil wars between Caesar and Pompey.

LUCAS, Edward Verrall (1868–1938). British author. B. at Eltham, he joined the staff of *Punch* in 1902, later becoming assistant editor, and contributed to the *Sunday Times*. He produced over 100 books, incl. studies of Charles Lamb; vols. of essays such as *Old Lamps for New* (1911), and *Mixed Vintages* (1919); the novels *Over Bemerton's* (1908), and *Landmarks* (1914); and anthologies such as *The Open Road* (1899).

LUCAS VAN LEYDEN (līd'en) (*c.* 1494–1533). Dutch artist. B. at Leiden, he executed his first engravings when a boy, and was later influenced by Dürer, whom he met at Antwerp. His principal paintings incl. 'The Chess Players' (Berlin) and 'Virgin and Child' (Munich).

LUCCA (look'kah). City, of pre-Roman origin, in Tuscany, Italy, cap. of L. prov., a rep. 1369–1797. The city has many fine churches, with richly decorated exteriors, and its cathedral was begun in the 12th cent. Pop. (1961) 85,940.

LUCE, Henry Robinson (1898–1967). American journalist. The son of a missionary, he was b. at Tengchow, China. He went to the U.S.A. in 1912, and founded the magazines *Time* (1923), *Fortune* (1930), and *Life* (1936), retiring from their management in 1964. He m. Clare Boothe (q.v.).

LUCERNE. *See* ALFALFA.

LUCERNE (lūsern'). (1) Cap. and tourist centre of L. canton, Switzerland, standing on the Reuss, where it flows out of Lake L. Growing up round the Benedictine monastery, estab. *c.* 750, it owes its prosperity to its position on the St. Gotthard road and railway. There is a 17th cent. cathedral. Pop. (1960) 67,433.

LUCERNE. In spring the city has a particular charm. Mount Pilatus, at 6,995 ft. the 2nd-highest peak of the canton, looks down on the river Reuss, one of whose ancient wooden bridges can just be seen to the right.
Courtesy of Swiss National Tourist Office.

(2) Lake in central Switzerland, of great scenic beauty. Most famous of the surrounding mts. are the Pilatus and Rigi. It is 24 m. long with an area of 44 sq. m.

LUCIAN (loo'shian) (*c.* 125–*c.* 190). Greek writer. B. at Samosata in Syria, for a time he was an advocate at Antioch, but later travelled before settling in Athens *c.* 165. He d. in Egypt, where he occupied an official post. L. is chiefly remembered for his satirical dialogues, in which he pours scorn on all religions.

LUCK. Polish form of LUTSK.

LUCKNOW. Cap. city of Uttar Pradesh, Rep. of India, once cap. of the nawabs of Oudh. It lies on the Gumti, 43 m. N.E. of Kanpur. When the Indian Mutiny of 1857 broke out, the residency at L., already fortified and provided with stores by Sir Henry Lawrence, was besieged from 2 July (on which day Lawrence was wounded by a shell, dying 2 days later) until its relief by Sir Colin Campbell on 16 Nov. Notable buildings incl. the great mausoleum of Nawab Asaf-ud-Dowlah (1784), and a univ. founded in 1921, which incl. a medical college. Besides being an important rly. junction, L. has engineering, chemical, cotton, and leather industries, and vegetable oil works and railway workshops, and is noted for handcrafts in leather, embroidery, gold, silks, shawls, etc. Pop. (1961) 662,196.

LUCRETIA (lūkrē'shia). A Roman matron, the wife of Collatinus, said to have committed suicide after being ravished by Sextus, son of Tarquinius Superbus. According to tradition, this incident led to the dethronement of Tarquinius and the establishment of the Roman rep. in 509 B.C.

LUCRETIUS or **Titus Lucretius Carus** (99–55 B.C.). Roman poet and Epicurean philosopher. He is remembered for his splendidly sombre didactic poem *De Rerum Natura*, expounding his materialistic philosophy based on the notion that the whole universe is the result of combinations of atoms.

LŬCU'LLUS, Lucius Licinius (*c.* 110–56 B.C.). Roman general. As commander against Mithridates of Pontus 74–66 he showed himself one of Rome's ablest generals and administrators, until superseded by Pompey. He then retired from politics.

LUDDITES (lud'īts). Name given to those taking part in the machine-wrecking riots of 1811–16. Their main organizer, possibly an imaginary person, was referred to as General Ludd. The movement, which began in Notts and spread to Lancs, Cheshire, and Yorks, was primarily a revolt against the unemployment caused by the introduction of the new machines. Many Ls. were hanged or transported.

LUDENDORFF (lōōd'en-), **Erich** (1865–1937). German general. B. in Prussian Poland, he entered the army in 1883, and joined the general staff in 1894. As Chief of Staff to Hindenburg on the eastern front during the F.W.W. he was largely responsible for the German victory at Tannenberg in 1914. After Hindenburg's appointment as Chief of General Staff in 1916, and L.'s as Quartermaster-General, the two together largely decided German policy. After the war L. organized the Kapp putsch of 1920, took part in the Nazi rising at Munich in 1923, and sat in the Reichstag as a Nazi.

LÜDERITZ. Town and port on L. Bay, S.W. Africa, named after Adolf Lüderitz of Bremen, who settled here in 1883 and was drowned off the coast 3 years later. L. developed through the discovery of diamonds nearby; a fish-canning industry was started later. On the coast, 12 m. S. of L., Diaz placed a cross in 1488 on his return from rounding the Cape of Good Hope. Pop. (1960) 3,604 (1,117 white).

LUDLOW. English market town (bor.) in Shropshire, on the Teme, 26 m. S. of Shrewsbury. L. castle was founded *c.* 1085 by Roger de Lacy. Pop. (1961) 6,774.

LUDWIG (lood'vig). Name of 3 kings of Bavaria. **Ludwig I** (1786–1868) succeeded his father Maximilian Joseph I in 1825. His patronage of learning and the arts made Munich an international centre of culture. Although a liberal ruler, his association with the dancer Lola Montez destroyed his popularity and in 1848 he was compelled to abdicate. **Ludwig II** (1845–86) succeeded his father Maximilian II in 1864. He supported Austria during the Austro-Prussian War of 1866, but brought Bavaria into the Franco-Prussian War as Prussia's ally, and in 1871 offered the German crown to the king of Prussia. He became the patron of Wagner and built the Bayreuth theatre for him. Declared insane in 1886, he drowned himself soon after. **Ludwig III** (1845–1921) was proclaimed king in 1913, and abdicated in 1918.

LUDWIG, Emil (1881–1948). German biographer. B. in Breslau, of Jewish parents whose original name was Cohn, he became famous for his psycho-analytical studies of Goethe, Bismarck, Wilhelm II, Hindenburg, and Roosevelt. In 1932 he took Swiss nationality.

LUDWIGSHAFEN. Town in Rhineland Palatinate, Germany, on the Rhine opposite Mannheim. Through its harbour passes a large trade in iron, timber, coal, etc. Dyes, soda, chemicals, etc., are manufactured. Pop. (1966) 175,770.

LUFTWAFFE. The German air force reorganized in 1933 under Goering. The anti-aircraft defences and forces concerned with launching the V1 and V2 robots were also later included. Its first-line strength in 1938 was estimated at 3,000 planes, doubled by 1940. The total figures, however, were considerably higher. The 3 factors in the decline of the L. were the switch from airfield to city bombing of 1940, the fighter resistance and bomber retaliation of the R.A.F., and the increased British production figures.

LUGANO (loogah'nō). Lake, partly in Switzerland, partly in Italy, lying between Lakes Maggiore and Como, with an area of 19 sq. m. The town of L. stands on the lake in the Ticino canton, Switzerland, 39 m. N.W. of Milan. Both the town and lake are renowned for their beauty. Pop. (1960) 19,758.

LUGANSK. City in the Ukrainian S.S.R., cap. of L. region, on the r. Lugan, a centre of heavy industry making locomotives, mining machinery, etc. Its industrial importance started with the foundation of ironworks here in 1795 by an Englishman on behalf of the Czarist govt. L. was called Voroshilovgrad 1935–58. Pop. (1967) 339,000.

LUGARD, Frederick John Dealtry, 1st baron (1858–1945). British colonial administrator. He served in the army 1878–89, and then entered the service of the British E. Africa Co., for whom he took possession of Uganda in 1890. He later became High Commissioner for N. Nigeria (1900–7); Gov. of Hong Kong (1907–12); and Gov.-Gen. of Nigeria (1914–19). He received a barony in 1928. His *Dual Mandate* (1922) was an influential plea for development through the existing African system of chieftainship, rather than western democracy.

LUGWORM. Genus (*Arenicola*) of marine worms (also known as lobworms) common between tide-marks where their whereabouts are known by their castings. They are used by anglers as bait, but are useful – as are earthworms on land – for their cleansing and powdering of the sand, of which they may annually bring to the surface *c.* 1,900 tons per acre.

LU HSÜN. Pseudonym of the Chinese short-story writer Chon Shu-jêu (1881–1936). Grandson of a blameless official at the Manchu court who was executed by the empress dowager, he knew poverty in his youth. In 1926 he fled the long arm of the Peking govt. to become dean of the Coll. of Arts at Sun Yat Sen Univ. His 3 vols. of stories, *Call to Arms*, *Wandering*, and *Old Tales Retold*, reveal the influence of Gogol. His supreme mastery of the form is recognized by the Communist régime and he is widely read.

LUIK. Flemish name of LIÈGE.

LUINI (loo-ē'nē), **Bernardino** (*c.* 1475–*c.* 1532). Italian painter. B. at Luino on Lake Maggiore. His principal works incl. 'Presentation in the Temple', and

'Christ Teaching' (National Gallery).

LUKE, St. Traditionally the compiler of the third Gospel and of the Acts of the Apostles. He appears to have been a physician and to have accompanied Paul after the ascension of Christ. Of his life little is known, although it is surmised that he was a non-Jewish native of Antioch and that he d. in Bithynia at the age of 74.

LULEÅ (lool'ā-aw). Seaport of Sweden, on the Gulf of Bothnia at the mouth of the r. L. It ships iron ore and timber during the summer when it is free of ice. Pop. (1966) 35,450.

LULL, Raimon or **Raymond Lully** (Raimundus Lullus) (*c.* 1235–1315). Catalan mystic. B. in Majorca, he was a debauchee during his youth, but later turned to religion and travelled on missions among the Moslems. His Utopian novel *Blanquerna* (1283) and several poems ensure him a high place among Catalan writers.

LULLY (lülē), **Jean Baptiste** (1639–87). Italian-born French composer, *né* Giovanni Battista Lulli, who became a French citizen in 1661. B. in Florence, he went to France, and in 1653 became court composer to Louis XIV. He supplied music for Molière's plays, and also composed the first notable French opera *Les Fêtes de l'Amour et de Bacchus*.

LUMBÃ'GO. Aching and pain in the lower back. It may be due to spasm of the muscles protecting inflamed spinal joints, or the muscles may be made painful by rheumatism, chill, or the poison of a diseased appendix or other abdominal organ. One of the soft discs which form cushions between the vertebrae may be nipped by the bones.

LUMBINI (loombēn'ē). Birthplace of Buddha in the foothills of the Himalayas near the Nepalese-Indian frontier. A Sacred Garden and shrine was estab. 1970 by the Nepalese govt.

LUMIÈRE (lümyār'), **Auguste** (1862–1954) and **Louis** (1864–1948). French cinema pioneers and brothers. With their father they developed auto-chrome plates, the stereoscope, colour photography, and in 1894–5 improved the cinematograph sufficiently to herald their invention of the cinema; the production and exhibition of films for public entertainment.

LUMINAL. A proprietary name for phenobarbitone, a white colourless synthetic drug of the barbiturate group, used as a sleeping draught in some nervous disorders and given regularly to control epilepsy, or in the withdrawal treatment of drug addiction.

LUMINOUS PAINT. A preparation containing a mixture of pigment, oil, and a phosphorescent sulphide, usually of calcium or barium. After exposure to light it appears luminous in the dark. The L.P. used on watch faces is radioactive and does not require exposure to light.

LUMPA (loom'pah) **CHURCH.** Pseudo-Christian nationalist sect founded in Zambia in 1955 by Alice Lenshina (1919–), an African woman, *née* Lubishi, who m. a political organiser, Peter Mulenga: her assumed name Lenshina, is a corruption of Lat. *regina* queen. A 'holy war' in 1964 by the Lumpas resulted in *c.* 500 members being killed.

LUMUMBA (loōmoōm'bah), **Patrice** (1926–61). Congolese nationalist 'martyr'. B. in Kasai prov., a member of the Mutetela tribe, L. became a post-office clerk. He was imprisoned by the Belgians, but released in time to attend the conference which gave the Congo independence. In the subsequent general election in 1960 he led the National Congolese Movement to victory, but was murdered by the troops of Gen. Mobutu. Mobutu declared him a 'national hero' 1966.

LUNACHARSKY, Anatoly Vasilevich (1875–1933). Russian revolutionary and writer. Imprisoned during the 1905 revolt, he lived in exile until the 1917 revolution. As Commissar for Education 1917–29, he did much for the arts. He wrote 14 plays.

LUNARDI (loonarhr'dē), **Vincenzo** (1759–1806).

Italian balloonist. He came to London as sec. to the Neapolitan ambassador, and made the first balloon flight in England from Chelsea in 1784.

LUNAR PROBE. Vehicle intended to pass close to, orbit, or land on the Moon (q.v.). *Lunik I* (U.S.S.R.) passed by the Moon at less than 4,000 m. in Jan. 1959, sending back information about conditions in that region of space; *Lunik II* crash-landed on the surface Sept. 1959; *Lunik III* sent back in Oct. 1959 photos of that part of the Moon which is always turned away from Earth; *Ranger VII* (U.S.A.) crash-landed in the Sea of Clouds area July 1964 radioing back useful photographs; *Luna IX* (U.S.S.R.) made the first soft landing Feb. 1966, with an unmanned probe weighing 1¼ tons, and *Surveyor* (U.S.A.) followed in June 1966; *Zond V* (U.S.S.R.) was the first unmanned craft to go round the moon and back; and *Apollo VIII* (U.S.A.), carrying Frank Borman, James Lovell and William Anders, made the first manned lunar orbits 21–7 Dec. 1968. A manned landing followed in 1969.

LUND (loond). City in Sweden, 10 m. N.E. of Malmö. It has an 11th cent. Romanesque cathedral, and a univ. founded in 1666. The treaty of L. was signed in 1676 after Charles XI had defeated the Danes. Pop. (1966) 49,580.

LUNDY. Rocky island at the entrance to the Bristol Channel, 12 m. N.W. of Hartland Point, Devon, England, with an area of 1,047 acres. Formerly noted as a stronghold of privateers and pirates, L. also has prehistoric remains and the ruins of Marisco castle (11th–14th cent.). Pop. *c.* 40.

LÜNEBURG. Town of Lower Saxony, W. Germany, 30 m. S.E. of Hamburg. Formerly prominent in the Hanseatic League, it is an industrial centre making ironware, chemicals, etc., and gypsum and lime are mined. On L. Heath, S. of the town, all German forces in the Netherlands, N.W. Germany, Schleswig-Holstein, and Denmark (more than a million men) surrendered to Field Marshal Montgomery on 4 May 1945. Pop. (1960) 59,000.

LUNGS. The organs of respiration. They are 2, and occupy the thorax, the upper part of the trunk. They fit exactly into this conical space, but do not meet in the middle. The heart is placed between them. Their function is to remove the carbon dioxide from the blood and replace it with oxygen. At every beat the heart pumps blood into their veins, which divide into very small branches, where the blood is brought into contact with the air in the air cells at the ends of the smallest divisions of the air tubes (bronchi). The lung tissue, consisting of multitudes of air cells and blood vessels, is very light and spongy. Air is

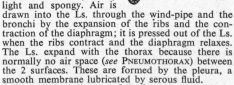

drawn into the Ls. through the wind-pipe and the bronchi by the expansion of the ribs and the contraction of the diaphragm; it is pressed out of the Ls. when the ribs contract and the diaphragm relaxes. The Ls. expand with the thorax because there is normally no air space (*see* PNEUMOTHORAX) between the 2 surfaces. These are formed by the pleura, a smooth membrane lubricated by serous fluid.

The principal diseases of the Ls. are tuberculosis, pneumonia, bronchitis, and cancer (qq.v.).

LUNN, Sir Arnold (1888–). British author. Son of Sir Henry L. (1859–1939), founder of the L. travel agency in 1892, he has written on mountaineering and skiing, and works of Catholic apologetics.

LUNT, Alfred (1893–). American actor. B. in Wisconsin, he went straight from school into the theatre, and in 1922 m. Lynn Fontanne with whom he subsequently co-starred in more than 30 brilliant

successes incl. *Design for Living* (1933), *There Shall Be No Night* (1940–1) and *The Visit* (1960).

LUPERCA'LIA. A Roman festival celebrated on 15 Feb. Goats and a dog were sacrificed, and the priests ran round the city carrying goatskin thongs, a blow from which was believed to cure sterility in women. The ritual probably combined fertility magic with charms conveying protection against wolves.

LUPESCU (loopes'koo), **Magda** (1900–). Wife of King Carol II (q.v.) of Rumania. Her long association with him was among the causes of his exile in 1926–30 and his abdication in 1940. They were m. in 1947.

LUPIN. Plants of the genus *Lupinus*, comprising about 200 species. They are native to Mediterranean regions and parts of N. and S. America, and have been naturalized in Britain. The spikes of pea-like flowers may be white, yellow, blue or pink. *L. albus* is cultivated in some places for cattle fodder, and for green manuring.

LU'PUS (L. vulgaris). Tuberculosis of the skin. The organism produces ulcers which spread and eat away the underlying tissues. Treatment by ultra-violet light is often effective. Lupus erythematosus is a chronic inflammation of the skin of the face, with red patches, usually on the cheeks and across the nose, with or without scales. The cause is unknown.

LURISTAN (looristahn'). Mountainous district in S.W. Persia, formerly a prov., inhabited by Lur tribes (est. at 500,000) who live by their sheep and cattle. Area 15,000 sq. m. In 1938 it became part of Province No. 6.

LUSA'KA. City (1960) and cap. of Zambia from 1964 (of N. Rhodesia 1935–64), 230 m. N.E. of Livingstone. A thriving commercial and agricultural centre, it has flour mills, tobacco factories, vehicle assembly, plastics and printing works. There are links by rail with Livingstone and the Congo, and in addition to the new road connection with Dar-es-Salaam, a railway is planned: L. has an internat. airport (1967). The Univ. of Zambia was estab. here 1966. At Kafue, 50 m. S., there is a vast hydroelectric and irrigation project, and textile, fertiliser, and steel industries. Pop. (1966) 151,400.

LÜSHUN. Chinese name of PORT ARTHUR, China.

LUSITA'NIA. Cunard liner, built in 1906, and sunk by a German submarine on 7 May 1915. About 1,200 lives were lost. This crime strengthened anti-German feeling in the U.S.A.

LÜ-TA. Name for the combined cities of PORT ARTHUR and DAIREN (qq.v.).

LUTE. Name given to a family of stringed musical instruments which was very popular in the 16–17th cents., and includes the mandore, theorbo, and chitta-rone. Ls. are pear-shaped and the strings are plucked with the fingers.

LUTHER (loōth'er), **Martin** (1483–1546). German reformer, usually regarded as the founder of Protestantism. B. at Eisleben, the son of a miner, he studied at the univ. of Erfurt, spent 3 years as a monk in the Augustinian convent there, and in 1507 was ordained priest. Shortly afterwards he attracted attention as a teacher and preacher in the univ. of Wittenberg; and in 1517, after returning from a visit to Rome, he attained nationwide celebrity for his denunciation of the Dominican monk Tetzel, who was one of those sent out by the Pope to sell 'indulgences' as a means of raising funds for the rebuilding of St. Peter's at Rome. On 31 Oct. 1517, he nailed on the church door at Wittenberg a statement of 95 theses on indulgences, and in the next year he was summoned to Rome to defend his action. His reply was to attack the papal system even more strongly, and in 1520 he publicly burnt in Wittenberg the papal bull that had been launched against him. Charles V summoned him to the Imperial Diet at Worms in 1521, where he refused to retract anything. On his way home he was taken into 'protective custody' by the elector of

Saxony in the castle of the Wartburg. Later he became estranged from Erasmus, and engaged in violent controversies with political and religious opponents. In 1525 he m. Catherina von Bora (1499–1552), an ex-nun. After the drawing up of the Augsburg Confession in 1530, he gradually retired from the Protestant leadership. His literary output was very great. His *Table Talk*, letters, sermons, and commentaries are still read, and his hymns sung, and his translation of the Scriptures into German may be said to mark the emergence of German as a modern tongue.

LUTHERANISM. That form of Protestantism that is derived from the life and teaching of Martin Luther (q.v.); it is sometimes called Evangelical to distinguish it from the other main branch of continental Protestantism, the Reformed. It is the principal form of Protestantism in Germany, and is the national faith of Denmark, Norway, Sweden, Finland, and Iceland. The organisation may be episcopal (Germany, Sweden) or synodal (Holland and U.S.A.): the Lutheran World Federation has its H.Q. in Geneva. The most generally accepted statement of Lutheranism is that of the Augsburg Confession (1530) but Luther's Shorter Catechism also carries great weight. L. is also very strong in the Middle West of U.S.A. where several churches were originally founded by German and Scandinavian immigrants. It is the largest Protestant body, incl. some 80 million persons, of whom 40 million are in Germany, 19 million in Scandinavia, 8½ million in U.S.A. and Canada and most of the remainder in central Europe.

LUTHULI (lōōtōō'li). **Albert** (1899–1967). S. African Negro leader. Ed. in an American missionary school, where he later taught, he was chosen as chief by his Zulu tribe, the Amkholwos, in 1936. In 1952 he was deposed by the Govt. when the African National Congress of which he was a member launched its defiance campaign. Elected pres. of the Congress a month later, he preached non-violence and multiracialism, and this led to the formation of the rival and militant Pan-Africanist Congress in 1958. He had been arrested in 1956, although never actually tried for treason, and from 1959 suffered certain restrictions. He was under suspended sentence for burning his pass when awarded the Nobel peace prize for 1960.

LUTINE. British bullion vessel lost off Holland 1799. Its bell, salvaged 1859, is at Lloyd's (q.v.).

LUTON. English industrial town (C.B.) in Beds, 33 m. S.W. of Cambridge. Hats, motor-cars, ballbearings, chemicals are made, and there is an airport. L. Hoo, a mansion built by Robert Adam 1762, was opened to the public by its owner, Sir Harold Wernher, in 1950. Pop. (1961) 131,505.

LUTYENS, Sir Edwin Landseer (1869–1944). British architect, whose works incl. country houses, the Whitehall Cenotaph, the govt. buildings of New Delhi, Liverpool R.C. cathedral and the British Embassy, Washington. Knighted 1918, he was P.R.A. 1938–44. His dau. **Elisabeth L.** (1906–), who m. Edward Clark (d. 1962) in 1942, is a composer.

LÜTZEN. Town in E. Germany, 12 m. S.W. of Leipzig, famous for the victory of 1632 of Gustavus Adolphus (q.v.), king of Sweden, over Wallenstein; Gustavus was killed in the battle. Here also Napoleon overcame the Russians and Prussians in 1813.

LUXEMBOURG. A prov. in the S.E. of Belgium. Its chief products are iron, slate, and manganese. The cap. is Arlon. Area 1,705 sq. m.; pop. (1966) 220,315.

LUXEMBOURG. Independent grand-duchy of Europe, situated between France, Germany, and Belgium. About a quarter of the pop. are engaged in agriculture, the chief crops being oats and potatoes. In the Esch-Alzette area mining of iron and steel production are important. The cap. is the city of L. on the Alzette; pop. (1967) 77,000. Most of the rivers flow into the Moselle which forms part of the eastern border of L. The people are of Low German

stock, with a language based on old Teutonic roots. The country is governed by a constitutional monarchy. Grand Duke Jean (1921–) succeeded to the throne in 1964 on the abdication of his mother Grand Duchess Charlotte (q.v.), dau. of Grand Duke William (d. 1912). Legislative power is vested in a Chamber of Deputies consisting of 56 members who are elected for 5 years. At the head of the govt. is the Min. of State. For the Customs Union between Belgium, the Netherlands and Luxembourg, *see* BENELUX. Area 999 sq. m.; pop. (1967) 335,000.

LUXEMBOURG, Palais du. Palace in Paris, France, in which the Senate sits. Built 1615 for Marie de' Medici by Salomon de Brosse, it was later enlarged: Watteau used the gardens in his backgrounds.

LUXEMBURG (looks'emboorg), **Rosa** (1870–1919). German Communist. B. in Poland, she settled in Germany *c.* 1895, and acquired German nationality by marriage. During the F.W.W. she co-operated with Liebknecht in anti-war propaganda and in founding the Spartacus League. She was imprisoned and wrote a series of prison letters. Released in Nov. 1918, she was murdered together with Liebknecht.

LU'XOR. Town of Upper Egypt, more correctly El-Aksur (The Castles), on the E. bank of the Nile, *c.* 450 m. S. of Cairo. Its ancient temple, to the S.W.,

LUXOR. Built by Amenhotep III and its decoration completed by Tutankhamen and Horemhab, the Temple of Luxor was dedicated to Amen, Mut and Khansu. An avenue of recumbent rams leads from its façade to the temples at Karnak.
Courtesy of the Egyptian State Tourist Administration.

is *c.* 300 yds. long and one of the greatest monuments of Thebes. The modern town has up-to-date hotels, bazaars, fine parks and an internat. airport.

LUZERN. German form of LUCERNE.

LUZON (loozon'). The largest and most northerly island of the Philippine Republic. It is mountainous, with a volcanic peak, Mayon (7,900 ft.). There are many rivers and lakes. Spanish settlers arrived in L. in the 16th cent. and the island belonged to Spain until it was ceded to the U.S.A. in 1898. Manila, with its suburb Quezon City, cap. of the republic, is on L., which was the scene of fierce fighting in 1942 and 1945 during the S.W.W.: *see* BATAAN and CORREGIDOR. Gold is produced and there is uranium at Larap in southern L. Area 40,420 sq. m.; pop. (est.) 8,000,000.

LVOV (lvof). City in the Ukrainian S.S.R., cap. of L. region. Founded in the 13th cent. by a Galician prince (the name means city of Leo or Lev), its German name is Lemberg. It was Polish until taken by Austria 1772; Polish again 1919–39, and then became part of the U.S.S.R. after the S.W.W. There are 3 cathedrals (Armenian, Greek and R.C.), and the univ. dates from 1661. It is a rail junction with an airport, and has textile, engineering and metallurgical industries. Pop. (1967) 502,000.

LWOW. Polish form of Lvov.

LYCANTHROPY (līkan'–). Human transformation to a werewolf; form of insanity involving this belief.

LYCEUM (līsē′um). An ancient Athenian gymnasium and garden, with covered walks, where Aristotle taught. It was S.E. of the city, and named after the nearby temple of Apollo Lyceus.

LYCEUM. London theatre, situated in Wellington Street, near the Strand. It was opened in 1809 (rebuilt 1834) and under the management of Henry Irving, (1878–1902), saw many of Ellen Terry's triumphs. After the S.W.W. it became a dance hall.

LYCURGUS (līker′gus). Spartan lawgiver. He is said to have been a member of the royal house, who, while acting as regent, gave the Spartans their constitution and system of education (9th cent. B.C.). Many scholars believe him to be purely mythical.

LYDGATE, John (c. 1373–c. 1450). English poet. B. probably at Lydgate, Suffolk, he entered the Benedictine abbey of Bury St. Edmunds, was ordained in 1397, and was prior of Hatfield Broadoak (1423–34). The friend of Chaucer, he produced numerous pedestrian works, often translations or adaptations, e.g. his *Troy Book*, and *Falls of Princes*.

LYELL, Sir Charles (1797–1875). Scottish geologist, whose *The Principles of Geology* (1830–3) estab. the conception of the earth's crust having been gradually brought to its present condition through millennia of change without sudden 'catastrophes'.

LYLY (lil′i), **John** (c. 1553–1606). English dramatist and author. B. probably in Canterbury, in his romance *Euphues, or the Anatomy of Wit* (1578), he popularized elaborate stylistic devices, and originated the word 'euphuism'.

LYME REGIS (līm rē′jis). English seaport and holiday resort (bor.) of Dorset. The duke of Monmouth landed at L.R. in 1685. Pop. (1961) 3,533.

LYMINGTON (lim-). Seaport (bor.) of Hants, England, 12 m. S.W. of Southampton. It is a yachting centre. Pop. (1961) 28.642.

LYMPH. A clear saline fluid which carries nutriment to the tissues and waste matter away from them. It exudes from the finest blood vessels into the tissue spaces between the cells all over the body, and bathes the cells, which take up from it the nourishment they require and excrete the waste. This is carried through lymph capillaries into larger lymph vessels (lymphatics). These lead to lymph glands, small round bodies chiefly situated in the neck, armpit, groin, thorax and abdomen. Their function is to generate lymphocytes – white blood corpuscles with a protective or repairing capacity – and to filter out harmful substances and bacteria. From the lymph glands, vessels carry the lymph to the thoracic duct and the right lymphatic duct, which lead into the large veins.

LYNCH, John ('Jack') (1917–). Irish republican statesman. Formerly Min. for Education 1957–9, Commerce 1959–65, and Finance, he succeeded Sean Lemass as P.M. and leader of Fianna Fail 1966.

LYNCHING. The execution of an alleged offender by a summary court having no legal authority. The origin of the term remains controversial. In the U.S.A. the custom originated on the frontiers, where no regular courts existed and outlaws and cattle thieves abounded. Recent examples have mostly occurred in the southern states, where it has been used ever since the Civil War as a means of keeping the Negroes in subjection. During 1882–1900 the annual figure for the U.S.A. varied between 96 and 231: the total 1900–61 was 1,992 (1,796 Negro and 196 white), and the recent average is 1 per annum.

LYND, Robert (1879–1949). British essayist, who often signed his work with the initials 'Y.Y.'. B. in Belfast, he became a London journalist, and is seen at his urbane best in the critical *The Art of Letters* (1921) and *Dr. Johnson and Company* (1928), and essay collections, e.g. *The Pleasure of Ignorance* (1921) and *Things One Hears* (1945).

LYNN. Industrial city of Massachusetts, U.S.A., situated on Massachusetts Bay. Mary Baker Eddy,

LYONS. A glimpse of the old quarter of the city where the inhabitants have a steep climb to reach their homes.
Courtesy of the French Government Tourist Office

founder of Christian Science, lived at L. Founded in 1629, it was called Saugus until 1673 when it was renamed after King's Lynn, England. Pop. (1960) 94,478.

LYNSKEY (lin′-), **Sir George Justin** (1888–1957). British judge. A judge of the High Court from 1944, he was chairman of the *L. tribunal* of 1948, appointed to inquire into irregularities in govt. depts. A chief witness was Sidney Stanley and a no. of resignations followed.

LYNTON and LYNMOUTH. Twin villages on the N. Devon coast, England, 14 m. E. of Ilfracombe. Lynton, at the top of a 400 ft. cliff, overlooks Lynmouth, at the base. Both are beauty spots. Severe floods in 1952 caused much damage in Lynmouth; 31 were killed, 42 houses and 2 bridges were destroyed, besides other damage. Lynton is a U.D., pop. (1961) 1,918.

LYNX. Genus of carnivorous mammals in the cat family. They do not occur in large numbers, but are widespread in N. temperate regions, where they are found in forests and rocky districts. The L. is larger than a wild cat, has a short tail and tufted ears. The fur is long and silky, usually reddish-brown or grey, with dark spots. The European L. (*Lynx borealis*), the Canadian L. (*L. canadensis*) and the Bobcat (*L. rufus*) of the U.S. are the usual sources of commercial furs.

LYON. French form of LYONS.

LYONS, Sir Joseph (1848–1917). British business man, the founder of the catering firm of J. Lyons and Co., Ltd., in 1894. B. in London, of Jewish extraction, he was at first an artist. L. was knighted in 1911.

LYONS, Joseph Aloysius (1879–1939). Australian statesman. After serving in the parliament of his native Tasmania as a Labour member from 1909, he was elected to the Federal Parliament in 1929, and became Postmaster-General and Minister for Works. In 1931 he resigned from the cabinet and formed the United Australia Party. After the general election in the following Dec., L. formed a coalition govt. with the Country Party, which was confirmed in office by the 1934 and 1937 general elections. He d. in office in April 1939. His wife **Dame Enid L.** (1897–) was first woman member of the House of Representatives and of the federal cabinet, and was created G.B.E. in 1937.

LYONS. Cap. of Rhône dept., and third city of France, at the confluence of the Rhône and Saône, 170 m. N.N.W. of Marseilles. The most notable buildings are the 19th cent. Notre Dame de Fourvière, the Gothic cathedral of St. Jean, and the church of St. Martin d'Ainay originating in the 6th cent. L. is the seat of an archbishopric, and a law and univ. centre. Formerly a chief fortress of France, L. is a road and rail centre, and is second only to Paris in commercial importance. L. is famous for silk and other fine textiles; it also makes chemicals, dyestuffs, machinery, etc., and has printing works. It was the ancient Lugdunum, taken by the Romans 43 B.C. Pop. (1968) 527,800.

LYRE. Stringed instrument of great antiquity. It originated in Asia, and was used in Greece and Egypt. It consisted of a soundbox with 2 curved arms joined by a crosspiece. There were 4 to 10 strings which were stretched from the crosspiece to a bridge near the bottom of the soundbox. It was played with a plectrum held with the right hand.

LYRE-BIRD. Genus of Australian birds (*Menura*), similar to a pheasant. The male has a large lyre-shaped tail, brilliantly coloured. They nest on the ground, and feed on insects, worms, and snails.

LYSANDER (līsan'der) (d. 395 B.C.). Spartan general. He brought the Peloponnesian War to a successful conclusion by capturing the Athenian fleet at Aegospotami in 405, and by starving Athens into surrender in the following year. He now aspired to make Sparta supreme in Greece, and himself in

LYRE-BIRD

Sparta; he set up puppet governments in Athens and her former allies, and intrigued to secure himself the Spartan kingship, but was killed in battle with the Thebans.

LYSE'NKO, Trofim (1898–). Soviet biologist. As director of the Institute of Genetics 1940–65, he enjoyed the support of Stalin for his neo-Lamarckian theory that plants and animals transmit to later generations characteristics acquired as a result of environmental changes – strongly opposed by orthodox scientists. In the new atmosphere under Khrushchev he lost ground, and was denounced under Kosygin in 1965.

LYTE, Henry Francis (1793–1847). British hymn writer. B. at Kelso, he was ordained in 1815, and in 1823 moved to the parish of Brixham. He d. in Nice. His best-known hymns are 'Abide With Me' and 'Praise, my soul, the King of Heaven'.

LYTHAM ST. ANNES (lidh'am). English resort (bor.) in Lancashire, on the Ribble, 6 m. S.E. of Blackpool. The Premium Savings Bond head office is at L.St.A. Pop. (1961) 36,222.

LYTTON, Edward George Earle Lytton Bulwer-Lytton, 1st baron (1803–73). British author. B. in London, he pub. his first poems in 1820, and in 1827 m. Rosina Wheeler, from whom he separated in 1836. His novels successfully followed every turn of the public taste and incl. *Falkland* (1827), the Byronic *Pelham* (1828), *Paul Clifford* (1830), *Eugene Aram* (1832), *The Last Days of Pompeii* (1834), *Rienzi* (1835), *The Last of the Barons* (1843), *Harold* (1848), and *The Caxtons* (1850). He also achieved success as a playwright with *The Lady of Lyons* (1838), *Richelieu* (1838), etc. He sat in Parl. as a Lib. 1831–41, and as a Cons. 1852–66, and was Colonial Sec. 1858–9. He was created a baron in 1866.

His only son **Edward Robert Bulwer-L.,** 1st earl of Lytton (1831–91), entered the diplomatic service and was Viceroy of India (1876–80), where he was noted for his controversial 'Forward' policy. He pub. verse under the pseudonym Owen Meredith, notably the lyric *Wanderer* (1857), and the epic *King Poppy* (1892). The 1st earl's son **Victor L.,** 2nd earl of L. (1876–1947), was Under-Sec. of State for India (1920–2) and Gov. of Bengal (1922–7). In 1932 he was responsible for the L. Report condemning Japanese aggression in Manchuria.

M The 13th letter of the Roman alphabet. It corresponds to the Gk. *mu* and the Semitic *mem*, and is almost always sounded as a voiced labial nasal. Finally, or before consonants, it disappears in French, Portuguese, and other languages, leaving a trace in nasalization of the preceding vowel. In Roman numerals M equals 1,000.

MAARTENS, Maarten. Pseudonym of the Dutch author Joost Marius van der Poorten Schwartz (1858–1915). He was b. in Amsterdam, and his works incl. *Sin of Joost Avelingh* (1890), a novel describing Dutch middle-class life, *God's Fool* (1892), and *Greater Glory* (1894), all written in English.

MAAS (mahs). River of the Netherlands, the lower course of the Meuse (q.v.).

MAASTRICHT (mahs'trikht). Capital of the prov. of Limburg, the Netherlands, on the Maas, near the Dutch-Belgian frontier. It dates from Roman times.

The manufactures incl. beer, paper, and earthenware. Pop. (1961) 91,157.

MAAZEL (mah'zel), **Lorin** (1930–). American conductor. B. in France, the son of an American singer, he studied the violin and was conducting symphony orchestras at 8. While studying at Pittsburgh univ., he also acted as associate conductor of the Pittsburgh Symphony Orchestra, and now tours the world: he is fond of Mozart opera. *See* illus. p. 688.

MABILLON (mahbēyoń'), **Jean** (1632–1707). French scholar, the greatest of the Maurists. B. nr. Reims, the son of a peasant, he became a Benedictine monk, and from 1664 worked at the literary centre of the Congregation of St. Maur, St. Germain-des-Près in Paris. He was the founder of the science of Latin palaeography, his *De re diplomatica* (1681) establishing the rules governing the authentication of medieval charters and MSS.

MABUSE (mahbüs'), **Jan.** Name adopted by

MAAZEL. When dealing with foreign orchestras and artists a highly developed linguistic gift helps to put his interpretation across.
Photo: Godfrey MacDomnic.

Flemish artist Jan Gossaert (*c.* 1472–*c.* 1534), derived from his birthplace, Maubeuge. His journey to Italy in 1508 with Philip of Burgundy started a vogue for Italian journeys and the Italian style. His works incl. 'The Adoration of the Magi' (National Gallery) and a no. of portraits, in which the hands are used to convey character. His colours are brilliant.

McADAM, John Loudon (1756–1836). Scottish engineer. B. at Ayr, he was appointed general surveyor of roads in 1827. The word 'macadamizing' was coined for his system of constructing roads of broken granite.

MACAO (mahkah'-ō). Portuguese overseas prov. on S. coast of China, *c.* 40 m. W. of Hong Kong, from which it is separated by the estuary of the Canton r. It consists of the town of M., occupying an island peninsula, and 2 small islands. M. was leased by the Portuguese in 1557, annexed by them in 1849, and recognized as Portuguese by treaty in 1887. Communist China occasionally exerts pressure (as in 1967), espec. as M. has many Chinese Nat. refugees, but encourages the transit trade carried on by Chinese merchants. Area 6 sq. m.; pop. (1965) 200,000.

MacARTHUR, Douglas (1880–1964). American gen. B. in Arkansas, the son of an army officer, he became Chief of Staff 1930–5. As commander of U.S. forces in the Far East he defended the Philippines against the Japanese 1941–2, escaped to Australia, and in March 1942 assumed command of the Allied forces in the S.W. Pacific. He was responsible for the reconquest of New Guinea in 1942–5 and of the Philippines in 1944–5, being appointed Gen. of the Army in 1944. After the surrender of Japan he commanded the Allied occupation forces there. During 1950 he also commanded the U.N. forces in Korea, but in April 1951, following his expression of views contrary to U.S. and U.N. policy, he was relieved of all his commands by Pres. Truman.

MACARTHUR, John (1767–1834). Founder of the Australian wool and wine trade. B. in England, he went to Sydney in 1790. In 1803 he introduced the breeding of fine wool sheep, and in 1817 planted the first vineyard of the colony.

MACA'SSAR. Town and seaport, cap. of the prov. of Celebes, on the is. of that name, Indonesia. It trades in coffee, copra, rice, pearls, rubber, spices, etc. The univ. was estab. 1956. Pop. (1967) 450,000.

MACAULAY, Dame Rose (1881–1958). British novelist. B. in Cambridge, she changed from the serious vein of her early novels to lightly touched satire of a muddled world, as in *Potterism* (1920) and *Keeping up Appearances* (1928). Her later books, very few being novels, incl. *The Writings of E. M. Forster* (1938), and *The Towers of Trebizond* (1956). Brought up in the Church of England, she returned to her lapsed faith through the influence of Father Hamilton Johnson: her letters to him were pub. in 2 vols. (1961–2). She was created D.B.E. in 1958.

MACAULAY, Thomas Babington, baron (1800–59). British historian, essayist, poet, and politician. B. in Leics, he was ed. at Cambridge, and in 1826 was called to the Bar. In 1825 he pub. in the *Edinburgh Review* his essay on Milton, which was followed during the next 20 years by numerous historical and critical essays. He entered parl. as a Whig or Lib. in 1830, and advocated parl. reform and the abolition of slavery. He spent 1834–8 in India as a member of the Supreme Council, and was mainly responsible for the Indian penal code He again sat in parl. 1839–47 and 1852–6, and in 1857 accepted a peerage. His only vol. of verse, *Lays of Ancient Rome*, appeared in 1842. The 4 vols. of his *History of England* (1848–61) were only completed to 1702. Although charged with showing dogmatism and Whig prejudices, it ranks as a literary masterpiece.

MACBETH (d. 1058). King of Scotland. The son of Findlaech, hereditary ruler of Moray, he was commander of the forces of Duncan, king of Scotia, whom he murdered in 1040. His reign was prosperous until Duncan's son Malcolm led an invasion and killed M. at Lumphanan. Shakespeare's tragedy (*c.* 1606) was based on Holinshed's *Chronicle*.

MacBRIDE, Seán (1904–   ). Irish politician. He was the son of Maud Gonne (1866–1953), a famous beauty who inspired poems and plays by Yeats, and Major John M., who was executed in 1916 for his part in the Easter Rebellion. M. served in the I.R.A., was called to the Irish Bar in 1937, and became a senior counsel in 1943. He founded the republican party *Clann na Poblachta* in 1946 (dissolved 1965), was elected to the Dáil the following year, and was For. Min. 1948–51 in the coalition govt.

MACCABEES (mak'abēz). Jewish family, sometimes known as the Hasmonaeans, founded by the priest Mattathias (d. 166 B.C.). He and his sons led the struggle for Jewish independence against the Syrians in the 2nd cent. B.C. Judas (d. 161) reconquered Jerusalem in 165 B.C., and Simon (d. 135) estab. Jewish independence in 142 B.C.

McCARRAN, Patrick (1876–1954). American Democrat politician, A lawyer, he became senator for Nevada in 1932, and as an isolationist strongly opposed Lend-Lease and sponsored in 1950 the McCarran-Walter Immigration Act, forbidding foreign seamen to land in the U.S. unless willing to submit to interrogation by immigration officers. *See* COMMUNISM.

McCARTHY, Eugene Joseph (1916–   ). American politician. A Democrat and R.C., he became senator, Minnesota 1959, and in 1968 was a candidate for the presidential nomination, advocating peace in Vietnam and a tackling of the 'deepening moral crisis in America'. He is not related to Joseph M. (q.v.).

McCARTHY, Joseph (1909–57). American Republican politician. A lawyer, he became senator for his native Wisconsin in 1946, and in 1950 caused a sensation by claiming to hold a list of *c.* 200 Communists working in the State Dept. He continued a not-uninfluential witch-hunting campaign – 'McCarthyism' – until censured by the senate in 1954.

MACCLESFIELD. English market town (bor.) in Cheshire, on the Bollin, about 18 m. N.E. of Crewe. It is an important manufacturing centre, the principal industry being the production of silk and other fibres. Pop. (1961) 37,578.

McCORMICK, Cyrus Hall (1809–84). American inventor. The son of a Virginian farmer, he invented a mechanical reaper in 1831.

McCORMICK, Robert Rutherford (1880–1955). American journalist. B. in Chicago, son of a former U.S. ambassador to Russia, he was admitted to the Bar in 1907. During the F.W.W. he served with distinction, rising to the rank of colonel, but his *Chicago Tribune* (of which he became pres. in 1911) was a vehicle for isolationist and anti-British sentiments, and '100 per cent Americanism'.

McCRACKEN, Esther Helen (1902–71). British dramatist, *née* Armstrong, who won fame with her 2 middle-class domestic comedies *Quiet Wedding* (1938) and *Quiet Week-end* (1941).

McCULLERS, Carson (1917–67). American novelist. B. at Columbus, Georgia, she wrote often through the eye of the abnormally simple or the child, as in *The Member of the Wedding* (1946) – a little girl wants to join her brother on his honeymoon – and *The Ballad of the Sad Café* (1951).

HUGH McDIARMID
Photo: George
Outram & Co. Ltd.

McDIARMID (makdur'-mid), **Hugh.** Pseudonym of the Scottish nationalist poet Christopher Murray Grieve (1892–). B. in Dumfriesshire, he worked for a time as a labourer: his nationalism emerges in 'A Drunk Man Looks at the Thistle' and his strongly Marxist views in his two 'Hymns to Lenin'. He is a forcefully gifted poet and his prose has the same idiosyncratic power: *At the Sign of the Thistle* (1934) and the autobiographical *Lucky Poet* (1943).

MACDONALD (mahk-donahl'), **Alexandre** (1765–1840). French soldier. He served in the Revolutionary Wars, and in 1809 was created a Marshal of France and duke of Taranto for his share in the victory of Wagram. He later fought in the Peninsular and Russian campaigns, and after the Restoration became a peer.

MACDONALD, Flora (1722–90). Scottish heroine who rescued Prince Charles Edward after the Battle of Culloden (1746), and, disguising him as her maid, escorted him from her home in the Hebrides to the mainland. She was arrested, but released in 1747.

MACDONALD, George (1824–1905). Scottish poet and novelist. B. in Aberdeenshire, he was the author of the poetic works, *Within and Without* (1855), *Phantastes* (1858), and the novels *David Elginbrod*, *Robert Falconer*, and *Donal Grant* (1883). He also wrote fairy tales, such as *At the Back of the North Wind* (1871).

MacDONALD, James Ramsay (1866–1937). British Lab. statesman. B. at Lossiemouth, the son of a labourer, he joined the I.L.P. in 1894 and became first sec. of the Lab. Party in 1900. He was elected to parl. in 1906, and led the party until 1914, when his opposition to the F.W.W. lost him his leadership. He recovered it in 1922, and in Jan. 1924 formed a govt. dependent on Lib. support, the withdrawal of which in Oct. forced him to resign. He returned to office in 1929, again as leader of a minority govt.; this collapsed as a result of the economic crisis in 1931, and M. left the Lab. Party to form a National govt. with Cons. and Lib. backing. He resigned the Premiership in 1935, remaining Lord President of the Council. His son, **Malcolm M.** (1901–), was a Labour M.P. (Nat. Lab. after 1931) 1929–35 and 1936–45. As Dominions Sec. 1935–9, he negotiated the Anglo-Irish agreement with de Valera; was the first senior min. to go out into the Commonwealth, as High Com. in Canada 1941–6; was Com.-Gen. for S.E. Asia 1948–55, High Com. in India 1955–60, Gov.-Gen. of Kenya 1963–4, returning as High Com. 1964–5, and Spec. Rep. in E. and Central Africa 1965–9. Awarded O.M. 1969.

MACDONALD, Sir John Alexander (1815–91). Canadian Cons. statesman. B. in Glasgow, he was taken to Ontario as a child. In 1857 he became P.M. of Upper Canada. He took the leading part in the movement for federation, and in 1867 became first P.M. of Canada. Defeated in 1873, he returned to office in 1878, and retained it until his death.

MacDOWELL, Edward Alexander (1861–1908). American composer. Encouraged by Liszt while in Germany, he showed much romantic feeling in his works which incl. the *Indian Suite* (1896), and piano concertos and sonatas. Prof. of music at Columbia univ., N.Y., 1896–1904, he had a mental breakdown in 1905.

MACEDONIA (masedōn'ēa). Name of an ancient country of S.E. Europe which lay between Illyria, Thrace, and the Aegean Sea. It is used for much the same area in modern geography: one of the fed. reps. of Yugoslavia and a prov. of Greece are both called Macedonia. The area is wild and mountainous; chief rivers are the Struma and the Vardar. Yugoslav M., area 9,925 sq. m.; pop. (1961) 1,406,000; cap. Skopje, is an under-developed region; chrome is the chief mineral worked, and tobacco is grown. Greek M., area 13,260 sq. m.; pop. (1961) 1,887,630; cap. Thessaloniki, is chiefly agricultural and grows rice.

MACEIO (mahsāyō'). Port of Brazil, cap. of the state of Alagoas. Cotton goods and machinery are exported, also cotton, sugar, and rum. Pop. (1960) 170,134.

McEVOY (mak'evoi), **Ambrose** (1878–1927). British artist, especially noted as a water-colourist and as a painter of delicately refined portraits of women.

MACGILLYCUDDY'S REEKS (makgilikud'iz-). A group of mts. lying W. of Killarney, in Co. Kerry, Ireland, which incl. Carrantuohill (3,414 ft.), the highest peak in Ireland.

McGINLEY, Phyllis (1905–). American writer of light verse. Canadian-born, she became a contributor to the *New Yorker* and has pub. many equally masterly collections of social satire: *One More Manhattan* (1937) and *The Love Letters of Phyllis McGinley* (1954).

McGO'NAGALL, William (1830–1902). Scottish poet, celebrated for the badness of his verse as the 'Great M.' Among his best-known works, a vogue of the 1960s, was an account of the Tay Bridge disaster of 1879. Quite humourless, he was often hoaxed, e.g. his journey to Balmoral in 1878 to see Qu. Victoria.

McGOVERN, George (1922–). American Democratic politician. Senator for S. Dakota from 1963, he became Democratic candidate in the presidential election of 1972 with the slogan 'Trust the People', promising to end the Vietnam War and heavily reduce American commitment in Europe.

MACH (mahkh), **Ernst** (1838–1916). Austrian philosopher. Originally a prof. of mathematics at Graz, he was prof. of philosophy at Prague 1867–95 and Vienna 1895–1901. An empiricist, he laid down that science was a record of facts perceived by the senses, and that acceptance of a scientific law depended solely on its standing the practical test of use: he opposed concepts such as Newton's 'absolute motion'.

MACH (mahk) **NUMBER.** System of speed measurement devised by Ernst Mach (*see* above), Austrian physicist and mathematician. The ratio of the speed of a body to that of sound in the undisturbed medium through which the body travels is its M.N. In an aircraft, when the M.N. passes through 1, i.e. when its velocity is greater than that of sound, it is said to have passed through the sound barrier.

MACHA'DO, Antonio (1875–1939). Spanish poet and dramatist. B. in Seville, he was inspired in his finest lyric verse, contained in *Campos de Castilla* (1912), by the Castilian countryside. His brother, **Manuel M.** (1874–1947), also b. in Seville, wrote verse on historic Spanish themes. The brothers collaborated in several plays, incl. *Desdichas de la Fortuna* (1926) and *La Lola se va a los Puertos* (1930).

MACHAR (makh'ar), **Jan Svatopluk** (1864–1942). Czech poet. B. in Bohemia, he achieved his masterpiece in the epic series 'Conscience of the Ages' incl. *Golgotha* (1901) and *In the Glow of the Hellenic Sun* (1906).

MACHAULT (mahshō'), **Guillaume de** (*c.* 1300–77). French poet and musician. B. in Champagne, he was in the service of John of Bohemia for 30 years, and later of King John the Good of France. He gave the forms of the *ballade* and *rondeau* a new individuality, and ensured their lasting vogue.

MACHEN, Arthur (1863–1947). Welsh author. Characterized by mystic symbolism and the supernatural, his writings incl. *House of Souls* (1906), *Angels of Mons* (1915; source of the famous legend), and *Green Round* (1933).

MACHIAVELLI (makē'ahvel'li), **Niccolo** (1469–1527). Italian statesman and author. B. in Florence, he became second chancellor to the Republic (1498–1512). With the accession to power of the Medici in 1512, he was arrested and imprisoned on a charge of conspiracy, but in 1513 released to exile in the country. He completed his *Il Principe* in 1513; this advocated a unified Italian state under a powerful ruler without reference to moral standards; in *L'Arte della guerra* (1520) he outlined the provision of an army for such a prince; and in *Historie fiorentine* analysed the historical development of Florence till 1492. Among his later works are the comedies *La Mandragola* (1524), and *Clizia*. The theories expressed in *Il Principe* and in his *Discorsi* (1531) influenced political science.

MACHINE GUN. Type of small arm (q.v.) perfected in the U.S. by Gatling in 1860. A number of barrels were arranged about a central axis, and the breech containing the reloading, ejection and firing mechanism was rotated by hand; shots being fired through each barrel in turn. The Maxim of 1883 was recoil operated, but some later types have been gas-operated (Bren) or recoil assisted by gas (some versions of the Browning). The sub-M.G., first exploited by Chicago gunmen in the 1920s, was widely used in the S.W.W., e.g. the recoil-operated Sten. *See* ROCKET.

MACHU PICCHU (mah'chōō pēk'chōō). Inca city, N.W. of Cuzco, Peru. It was discovered in 1911 by Hiram Bingham at the top of 1,000 ft. high cliffs, and contains well-preserved remains of houses, temples, etc.

McINDOE, Sir Archibald (1900–60). New Zealand plastic surgeon. B. at Dunedin, N.Z., he worked at the Mayo Foundation before joining St. Bartholomew's in 1930, and was subsequently surgeon-in-charge of the Queen Victoria Plastic and Jaw Injury Centre in Sussex. During the S.W.W. he became famous for his remodelling of the faces of badly burned pilots, forming for them the Guinea Pig Club. He was knighted in 1947.

MA'CINTOSH, Charles (1766–1843). Scottish manufacturing chemist, inventor of a waterproof fabric lined with a rubber solution, who gave his name (but spelt 'mackintosh') to raincoats made of it: other processes have largely superseded this method.

MACKAIL, John William (1859–1945). Scottish classical scholar, prof. of poetry at Oxford from 1906 and awarded the O.M. in 1935. His books incl. *Latin Literature* (1895) and studies of Virgil and William Morris. He m. in 1888 the only dau. of Burne-Jones, and novelist Denis M. (1892–1971) and Angela Thirkell (1890–1961), reviver of Trollope's Barsetshire as the setting of her novels, were their children.

McKAY, Claude (1890–1948). American Negro writer. B. in Jamaica, he pub. his first book of verse, *Songs of Jamaica*, in 1912, the year of his emigration to the U.S.A. Later books are the novels *Home to Harlem* (1928) and *Banana Bottom* (1933); the auto-biographical *A Long Way from Home* (1937), and the social study *Harlem* (1940).

MACKAY, Jessie (1864–1938). New Zealand poet. A journalist, she was at her best in 'Maori War Song' and 'Carol of Kossovo' (1915). An annual poetry prize is awarded in her memory by P.E.N. in N.Z.

MACKE (mahk'e), **August** (1887–1914). German artist, a member of the Blue Rider group. His poeticized canvases represent women, girls and children with French fluidity. He was killed in the F.W.W.

MACKENSEN (mahk'ensen), **August von** (1849–1945). German field marshal. B. in Saxony, in the F.W.W. he accomplished the break-through at Gorlice and the conquest of Serbia (1915), and in 1916 had a big share in the overthrow of Rumania. After the war M. retained his popularity to become a symbolical figure of the German Army.

MACKENZIE, Alexander (1822–92). British Lib. statesman. B. in Perthshire, he emigrated to Canada in 1842, entered parl. in 1861, and became Lib. leader in the Dominion parl. after 1867. He was P.M. 1873–8.

MACKENZIE, Sir Compton (1883–). Scottish author. From Magdalen Coll., Oxford, where he read history, he entered the army and, although invalided in 1915, returned to serve in Intelligence. By turns urbane and romantic, he pub. his first novel, *The Passionate Elopement*, in 1911; later successes incl. *Carnival* (1912), *Sinister Street* (1913–14), *Sylvia Scarlett* (1918), *The Four Winds of Love* (1937–45), and the richly comic *Whisky Galore* (1947). His memory is phenomenal, and his autobiography, planned as 10 'octaves' of *My Life and Times*, began in 1963. His sister is the actress Fay Compton (q.v.).

MACKENZIE, Henry (1745–1831). Scottish novelist. B. in Edinburgh, in 1771 he pub. *The Man of Feeling*, a novel with a sensitive, virtuous hero which popularized the cult of sensibility.

MACKENZIE, William Lyon (1795–1861). Canadian politician; grandfather of W. L. Mackenzie King. B. near Dundee, he emigrated to Canada in 1820, and in 1837 led a rising at Toronto. After its failure he lived in the U.S.A. until 1849, and 1851–8 sat in the Canadian legislature as a Radical.

MACKENZIE. River of the N.W. Territories, Canada, discovered by the British explorer, Sir Alexander Mackenzie (*c.* 1755–1820), in 1789; it flows from the Great Slave Lake to the Arctic Ocean, and is about 1,000 m. long. It gives its name to one of the 3 districts of N.W. Territories; area 527,490 sq. m.; pop. (1961) 14,895.

MACKEREL. Food fish (*Scomber scombrus*), found in N. temperate and tropical seas. It is blue with irregular black bands down its sides, the latter and the undersurface showing a pink metallic sheen. The chief M. fisheries of Britain are off the S.W. coast.

McKINLEY, William (1843–1901). Twenty-fifth pres. of the U.S.A. B. in Ohio, he was elected to Congress in 1876 as a Republican, and was Pres. in 1896 and again in 1900. His period of office was marked by America's adoption of an imperialist policy, as exemplified in the Spanish War of 1898, the annexation of the Philippines, etc. M. was assassinated by an anarchist at Buffalo in 1901.

McKINLEY, Mt. Highest peak (20,300 ft.) in N. America, situated in Alaska, U.S.A., named after Pres. William McKinley.

McLAREN, Jack (1887–1954). Australian writer of adventure tales, e.g. *Devil of the Depths* and the autobiographical *My Crowded Solitude*, describing his 8 yrs. living among the aboriginals of the Gulf of Carpentaria.

MacLEISH, Archibald (1892–). American poet. B. in Illinois, he was Asst. Sec. of State in 1944–5 and helped to draft the constitution of UNESCO. He made his name with a poem 'Conquistador' (1932), descriptive of Cortes' march to the Aztec capital, but his later plays in verse, *Panic* (1935) and *Air Raid* (1938), deal with contemporary problems. In 1949–62 he was Boylston Prof. of Rhetoric at Harvard, and his essays *Poetry and Opinion* (1950) reflect his feeling that a poet should be 'committed', expressing his outlook in his verse.

LORD MACLEOD
Photo: W. Pintail.

MacLEOD (maklowd′), **George Fielden, baron M. of Fuinary** (1895–   ). Scottish clergyman. Min. of Govan, Glasgow 1930–8, when he became leader of the Iona (q.v.) community, he was moderator of the General Assembly 1957. He succeeded to a baronetcy 1944 (title not used), and was created life peer 1967.

MACLEOD (maklowd′), **Iain Norman** (1913–70). British Cons. politician. Entering parl. in 1951, he was Min. of Health 1952–5, of Labour 1955–9, Colonial Sec. 1959–61, and Chancellor of the Exchequer 1970.

MACLISE (-lēs′), **Daniel** (1806–70). Irish artist. B. at Cork, he moved to London in 1827 and painted portraits of famous people, and historical pictures, incl. 'The Meeting of Wellington and Blücher after Waterloo', and 'Death of Nelson' for the Westminster Palace. He was elected R.A. in 1840.

MacMAHON (-oń), **Marie Edmé Patrice Maurice de** (1808–93). French soldier and statesman. His share in the victory of Magenta in the Franco-Austrian War of 1859 won him the titles of duke of Magenta and marshal of France. In the war of 1870 he was captured at Sedan, and after his release suppressed the Paris Commune. Elected Pres. of the Rep. in 1873, he worked for a royalist restoration, but was forced to resign in 1879.

McMAHON (makmahn′), **William** (1908–   ). Australian Liberal statesman. A lawyer and economist, he was Treasurer 1966–9, Min. for External Affairs 1969–71, and succeeded Gorton as P.M. on the latter's resignation 1971.

McMILLAN, Edwin Mattison (1907–   ). American physicist. Prof. at the Univ. of California from 1946, he shared a Nobel prize in chemistry with Seaborg (q.v.) in 1951, and in 1963 shared with I. Veksler, director of the Russian Joint Institute for Nuclear Research, ·an Atoms for Peace award for their independent arrival 20 years before at a method of overcoming the limitations of the cyclotron.

MACMILLAN, (Maurice) Harold (1894–   ). British Cons. statesman. Member of a family of publishers, he was ed. at Eton and Oxford and served with the Grenadier Guards in the F.W.W. Entering parliament as a Unionist (Stockton-on-Tees 1924–9 and 1931–45, and Bromley 1945–64), he held his first important post as Min. of Housing 1951–4, and was then Min. of Defence until he succeeded Eden as For. Sec. in 1955, and as Chancellor of the Exchequer 1955–7 introduced Premium Bonds. Taking over as P.M. in 1957, following Eden's resignation after Suez, he led his party to victory in the 1959 elections on the slogan 'You have never had it so good'. The Cyprus dispute had already been temporarily settled in 1959, but his realization of 'the wind of change' in Africa led to rapid recognition of the independence of new states, and though Britain's entry to the Common Market failed, the securing of the nuclear test-ban treaty just before his resignation through ill-health in 1963 counteracted to some extent the effect at home of the Vassall spy case and the Profumo scandal.

His only son, **Maurice Victor M.** (1921–   ), entered parl. in 1955 and in 1963–4 was Economic Sec. to the Treasury (Chief Secretary from 1970 in the Heath govt.).
See illus. under EISENHOWER.

MACMILLAN, Kirkpatrick (d. 1878). Scottish blacksmith who invented the bicycle in 1839. His invention consisted of a hobby-horse fitted with treadles, and propelled by pedalling.

McNAMA′RA, Robert Strange (1916–   ). American politician. Asst. prof. in business administration at Harvard 1940–3, he served with the Army Air Force 1943–6, and was with the Ford Motor Co. 1946–61 (pres. 1960–1). A Democrat, he was Sec. of Defense 1961–8, then Pres. of the World Bank.

MacNEICE, Louis (1907–63). Anglo-Irish poet. B. in Belfast, he was ed. at Oxford and lectured in classics at Birmingham 1930–6 and London 1936–40.

Free of the rigid political alignments of his contemporaries, he made his début with *Blind Fireworks* (1929) and developed a polished ease of expression, reflecting his classical training, in dealing with man in society, as in *Autumn Journal* (1939). Later vols. are the highly original *The Dark Tower* (1946), written for the B.B.C., for whom he wrote features 1941–9 'like a poet, but with a journalist's instinct for essence'; a verse translation of Goethe's *Faust*, and the radio play *The Administrator* (1961).

MÂCON (mahkoń′). Cap. of the French dept. of Saône-et-Loire, on the Saône, 45 m. N. of Lyons. A town dating from ancient Gaul, it is famous for wine. Pop. (1962) 27,669.

McPHERSON, Mrs. Aimée Semple (1882–1944). American evangelist and 'hot-gospeller'. She built the Angelus Temple in Los Angeles as the centre of the 'Four-Square Gospel', and visited London, New York, and Paris for 'revivalist' gatherings.

MACPHERSON, James (1736–96). Scottish author. B. at Ruthven, in 1760 he pub. *Fragments of Ancient Poetry collected in the Highlands of Scotland*, which was followed by the epics *Fingal* (1761) and *Temora* (1763), which he claimed as the work of the 3rd cent. bard Ossian. Challenged by Dr. Johnson, M. failed to produce his originals and a committee decided in 1797 that M. had combined fragmentary materials with ·oral tradition. Nevertheless, the works of 'Ossian' exercised a considerable influence on the development of the Romantic movement in Britain and abroad.

McQUAID, Charles (1895–   ). Irish R.C. churchman. A classical scholar, he was appointed abp. of Dublin and primate of Ireland in 1940, and exerts strong guiding influence on his flock.

MACQUARIE (makwor′ē), **Lachlan** (1761–1824). Scottish administrator who succeeded Bligh as governor of N.S.W. in 1808, and raised the demoralized settlement to prosperity. In 1821 he returned to Britain in poor health, exhausted by struggles with his opponents. Lachlan r. and M. r. and is. are named after him. **M. Island** is a Tasmanian dependency. Some 20 m. long by 2 wide, it is *c*. 850 m. S.E. of Hobart, and uninhabited save for an Australian govt. research station.

MACREADY, William Charles (1793–1873). British actor. In 1816 he made his début at Covent Garden, and rose to become England's leading actor. He was very successful as Macbeth, Lear, John, and Henry IV.

MacSWINEY, Terence (1883–1920). Irish patriot. Mayor of Cork, he was imprisoned by the English and starved to death after hunger-striking for 74 days, the longest fast in medical history.

M′TAGGART, John M′Taggart Ellis (1866–1925). British philosopher. Lecturer at Trinity Coll., Cambridge 1897–1923, he was influential as leader of the Hegelian school in England, e.g. *The Nature of Existence* (1921–7). Although an atheist, he believed in the immortality of the soul.

MADAGA′SCAR. Island off the S.E. coast of Africa, separated from the mainland by the Mozambique Channel. It was discovered by the Portuguese, Diego Diaz, in 1500. The interior is mountainous, the highest peak being Ankàratra (nearly 9,000 ft.). The lower regions are fertile, and there are dense forests round the coast. The only r. of any size is the Mangoka. The climate is tropical. Area 228,500 sq. m. For M.'s history, industry, etc., *see* MALAGASY REPUBLIC.

MADARIAGA (mahdahrē-ah′gah), **Don Salvador da** (1886–   ). Spanish author. Formerly active as a diplomat, he has been in exile since the Civil War as a

MADEIRA. Funchal rests at the foot of an amphitheatre of mountains, which rise to 4,000 ft. The cathedral is pleasantly unpretentious.   *Courtesy of the Portuguese State Office.*

liberal opponent of Franco. His books incl. *Anarchy or Hierarchy* (1937), *The Rise and Fall of the Spanish American Empire* (2 vols., 1947), and *Latin America between the Eagle and the Bear* (1962).

MADEIRA (madē′ra). Group of 5 Portuguese is., off the N.W. coast of Africa, 260 m. N. of Santa Cruz, Canary Is. Madeira, the largest, and Porto Santo are the only inhabited is. Their mild climate makes them popular winter resorts. Madeira wine is famous. The cap. is Funchal. Total area 308 sq. m.; pop. (1967) 269,770.

MAD′HYA BHA′RAT. State of the Rep. of India 1950–6. It was a union of 19 states of which Gwalior and Indore (qq.v.) were the most important; 5 other small states subsequently joined. M.B. had an area of 46,710 sq. m. and in 1956 was absorbed in Madhya Pradesh.

MADHYA PRADESH′. State of the Rep. of India, so named in 1950 when it consisted of the former British prov. of Central Provs. and Berar and the princely states of Makrai and Chattisgarh. In 1956 it lost some S.W. districts, including Nagpur (q.v.), and absorbed Bhopal, Madhya Bharat, and Vindhya Pradesh. The cap. is Bhopal; other large towns are Indore, Jabalpur, Ujjain and Gwalior. Area 171,210 sq. m.; pop. (1961) 32,372,408.

MADINET AL-SHAAB. *See* AL ITTIHAD.

MADISON, James (1751–1836). Fourth pres. of the U.S.A. In 1787 he became a member of the Philadelphia Convention and took a leading part in drawing up the U.S. constitution and the Bill of Rights. He became Sec. of State in Jefferson's govt. 1801–9, the main achievement of his ministry being the Louisiana Purchase; became Pres. in 1809; and was re-elected in 1812. During his period of office the U.S. became involved in the war with Britain of 1812–15.

MADISON. The cap. of Wisconsin, U.S.A., *c.* 120 m. N.W. of Chicago, situated between lakes Mendota and Monona, seat of the state univ. Pop. (1960) 126,706.

MADONNA (Italian, my lady). Italian name for the Virgin Mary.

MADRAS (mahdrahs′). City and port in the Rep. of India, the cap. of M. state. It lies on the Bay of Bengal, and is the 3rd city of the Rep. Cotton, cement, chemicals, and iron and steel goods are manufactured, and there is a brisk export trade. Fort St. George, nucleus of the city, and Government House, the governor's residence until 1947, then the seat of the legislature, are among the chief buildings. The univ. was constituted in 1857. Fort St. George was founded by the E. India Co. in 1639. Occupied by the French 1746–8, M. was shelled by the German ship *Emden* in 1914, the only place in India attacked in the F.W.W. Pop. (1961) 1,725,216.

MADRAS. State of the Rep. of India. It is bounded on the N. by Mysore and Andhra Pradesh, W. by Kerala, E. by the Bay of Bengal, S.E. by the Gulf of Manaar. The cap., also M., lies in the N.E., on the Coromandel Coast; Madurai, Tiruchirappalli, and Salem are other large towns. Area 50,331 sq. m.; pop. (1961) 33,686,953.

Agriculture is the chief occupation, rice, other grains, ground-nuts, sugar, and cotton the principal products. Cotton textiles and quinine are made. Some 10,000 sq. m. are forested. M. state is part of the former British presidency, later prov., formed from areas conquered in the 18th cent. from the French and from Tippoo Sahib (q.v.), area 126,000 sq. m. M. prov. became a state of the Rep. of India in 1950. The N.E. was detached to form Andhra Pradesh (1953); Kerala and Mysore were enlarged 1956 at the expense of M. and the Laccadives (q.v.) became a Union Terr.; and in 1968 M. was renamed Tamil Nadu.

MADRI′D. Cap. of Spain and of M. prov., on the Manzanares. It is built on an elevated plateau in the centre of the country, and has excesses of heat and cold. It first became important in the times of Charles V and Philip II; the original town was almost square, with rounded corners. The Puerta del Sol is the chief of many plazas, and in the Calle de Alcalá stands the Real Academia de Bellas Artes, founded in 1752. The famous Prado Museum (1785) is near the botanical garden. Some churches are historically interesting, and the royal palace, finished in 1764, contains a celebrated library and tapestry collection. M. has several schools of industry and art, and a univ. transferred from Alcalá de Henares 1836–7. Its suburbs have grown extensively, as have its industries, which incl. leather, chemicals, furniture, tobacco, and paper. During the civil war M. was besieged by the Nationalists 7 Nov. 1936 to 28 March 1939. Pop. (1965) 2,793,000.

The prov. of M. lies on slopes of the Guadarrama mts., with the Tagus as part of its S. boundary. Area 3,089 sq. m.; pop. (1960) 2,259,931.

MA′DRIGAL. In music, a form of composition for three or more voices without musical accompaniment. It originated in the Netherlands before the middle of the 15th cent., later becoming popular in Italy and in Elizabethan England. The chief English composers incl. Byrd, Weelkes, Kirbye, and Orlando Gibbons. The M. Society was founded in 1741.

MA′DURA. Island of the Rep. of Indonesia, off Surabaya, rising in the central hills to 1,545 ft. It produces rice, tobacco, salt, etc.; cattle breeding and fishing are carried on. Area 1,762 sq. m.; with off-

MADRAS. First constituted in 1857 as an examining body, Madras University now has some 60,000 students and includes a college of technology. Its buildings incl. the library and senate hall shown here.
Courtesy of Indian Information Bureau.

shore islands, more than 2,000 sq. m.; pop. (est). 2,000,000.

MADURAI (mudoorī'). Town on the r. Vaigai in Madras state, India, cap. of M. dist., site of the great Hindu temple of Sundareswara, and of M. Univ. (1966). Cotton textiles and brassware are made; rice, tobacco, spices exported. Pop. (1961) 424,975.

MAEANDER (mē-an'der). Anglicized form of the ancient Greek name of a river in Turkey-in-Asia (Turkish, Buyuk Menderes, great Menderes). It rises near Afhonkarahisar (in anc. Phrygia) and flows for *c.* 250 m. by a very winding course into the Aegean: hence the word 'meander'.

MAESTRICHT. See MAASTRICHT.

MAETERLINCK (maht'erlingk), **Maurice,** count (1862–1949). Belgian dramatist and philosopher. B. at Ghent, he went to Paris in 1887, and in 1889 produced

MADRID. Of the 16 original gates 3 survive. Here is the Alcala Gate in the fashionable Plaza de la Indepencia.
Courtesy of the Spanish Tourist Office.

the vol. of symbolist verse *Hothouses,* and the play *The Princess Maleine.* He achieved an international reputation with *Pelléas and Mélisande,* which inspired music by Debussy and Sibelius. Later plays incl. *Monna Vanna* (1902), *The Blue Bird, Mary Magdalene, The Betrothal,* and *The Burgomaster of Stilemonde* (1918), celebrating Belgian resistance in the F.W.W. – a theme which caused his exile to America in 1940. Among his philosophical works are *The Treasure of the Humble* (1896), *The Life of the Bee, The Buried Temple,* and *Death* (1912).

MAFEKING (maf'e-). A town in the N.E. of Cape Province, S. Africa, formerly the H.Q. of the administration of Bechuanaland Protectorate. It is chiefly famous for the siege during the South African War, when it was successfully defended against the Boers by a small garrison, under Baden-Powell, which held out from 12 Oct. 1899 until 17 May 1900. Pop. (1960) 8,280.

MAFIA (It. mafē'a; anglicized: maf'ēa). Originally a secret society of 15th cent. Sicily, hostile to the law and avenging their own wrongs by means of the vendetta. In the 19th cent. the M. was employed by absentee landlords to manage their *latifundia* (landed estates), and through terrorization, etc., soon became the unofficial ruler of Sicily. In spite of loss of power on the *latifundia,* which were expropriated and divided among the peasants after the S.W.W., the M. is still powerful in Sicily, especially in the towns, where they have turned their attention to industry. The govt. has

waged periodic campaigns of suppression, notably in 1927 and 1963–4. The M. has spread abroad, its biggest offshoot being in the U.S.A., where it is known as *Cosa Nostra* (It. 'our thing'), and is estimated to comprise 1 million citizens, with an annual income of over $40 billion. None but those of Italian descent is eligible for membership, organization is in 'families', each with its own boss or *capo,* and a committee of 12 bosses from N.Y., Chicago and other leading cities rules nationally. Activities range from 'protection' and illicit gambling to drug peddling and murder. In 1962–3 sensational revelations were made by Joe Valachi, who, while in Atlanta's Federal goal killed a fellow-prisoner, whom he thought had been detailed by the M. to kill him. Intimidation of witnesses prevents elimination of the M. and *Cosa Nostra.:* Nixon initiated a new campaign 1969.

MA'GADHA. A kingdom of ancient India, roughly corresponding to the middle and southern parts of modern Bihar; it witnessed many incidents in the life of the Buddha, and was the seat of the Maurya dynasty, founded by Chandragupta (q.v.).

MAGALLANES. Another name for PUNTA ARENAS.

MAGDEBURG (mahg'deboorg). Cap. of M. district, E. Germany, on the Elbe, 81 m. S.W. of Berlin. It has a Gothic cathedral, one of the few buildings to survive the Thirty Years War. Motor-cars, paper, textiles, machinery, etc., are produced, and there are sugar refineries. It dates from the 9th cent. and suffered heavy damage in the S.W.W. from Allied air attack and when captured by the U.S. 9th Army, 18 April 1945. Pop. (1966) 267,817.

MAGELLAN (majel'an), **Ferdinand** (*c.* 1480–1521). Portuguese navigator. He was brought up at court and entered the royal service, but later transferred his services to Spain. His proposal to sail to the E. Indies by the W. was accepted, and in 1519 he started from Seville. He discovered and sailed through *M. Strait,* crossed the Pacific, to which he gave its name, and in 1521 reached the Philippines. Here he was killed in battle: 18 of his companions reached Seville in 1522, completing the first voyage round the world. In 1964 the wreck of his flagship *Concepcion* was thought to have been located off Leyte in the Philippines where she was abandoned.

MAGENTA (mahjen'tah). Town in Milan prov., Lombardy, Italy, 15 m. W. of Milan, the scene of a victory by the French and Sardinians over the Austrians in 1859. Pop. (1960) 17,450.

MAGGIORE (mahjō're), **Lago.** Lake in Piedmont and Lombardy, Italy, and the Swiss canton of Ticino. Locarno is on its N. shore. It is 39 m. long, and $\frac{1}{2}$ m. to $5\frac{1}{2}$ m. wide, and is famous for the beauty of its scenery.

MAGGOT. Name of the footless larvae of insects, especially those of flies, a typical example being the larva of the blow-fly which is deposited on flesh.

MAGHREB (mah'greb). Name for N.W. Africa (Arabic 'west', 'sunset'): the M. powers – Algeria, Libya, Morocco, and Tunisia – agreed on economic co-ordination 1964–5.

MAGI (mā'jī). The name of the priesthood of the Persian (Zoroastrian) region, used in the Vulgate – where the authorized version gives 'wise men'. The three M. who came to visit the infant Christ with gifts of gold, frankincense, and myrrh were in later tradition described as 'kings'. The 'Adoration of the Magi' has inspired many artists.

MAGIC. The art of controlling the forces of nature by means of charms and ritual. It originated in the idea that like produces like, e.g. the ceremonial sprinkling of water will produce rain, a dance imitating a successful hunt will ensure success in hunting, to destroy the image of an enemy will cause his death. It is now generally accepted that most primitive religious practices are of magical origin. Under Christianity those still practising the ancient rites were persecuted as witches. Traces of M. still survive in folk-custom and in superstitions.

MAGINOT LINE (mahzhēnō′). French system of fortifications along the German frontier from Switzerland to Luxembourg. Built 1929–36 under the direction of the War Minister, André Maginot, it consisted of semi-underground forts armed with heavy guns, joined by underground passages, and protected by anti-tank defences. Lighter fortifications continued the line to the sea. In 1940 the Germans pierced the Belgian frontier line and outflanked the M.L.

MAGNA CARTA. The charter granted by King John in 1215. As a reply to his demands for excessive feudal dues and attacks on the privileges of the Church, Archbp. Langton in 1213 proposed to the barons the drawing up of a charter, and this John was forced to accept at Runnymede on 15 June 1215.

M.C. begins by reaffirming the rights of the Church. Certain clauses guard against infringements of feudal custom, e.g. the king shall not demand any grant beyond those customary, without the consent of his tenants-in-chief. Others are designed to check extortions by officials or maladministration of justice, e.g. no freeman to be arrested, imprisoned or punished except by the judgment of his peers or the law of the land, while others guaranteed the privileges of London and the cities.

As feudalism declined M.C. lost its significance, and under the Tudors was almost forgotten. During the 17th cent. it was re-discovered and re-interpreted by the parliamentary party. Four original copies exist, one each in Salisbury and Lincoln Cathedrals, and 2 in the British Museum.

MAGNANI (manyah′nē), **Anna** (1908–   ). Italian actress. B. in Alexandria of Italian immigrant parentage, she became famous for strongly emotional roles in e.g. *The Rose Tattoo* (filmed 1955), said to have been specially written for her by Tennessee Williams, and the film *The Fugitive Kind* (1960).

MAGNE′SIA. Magnesium oxide (MgO), obtained from the mineral periclase. It is formed when magnesium is burnt in air or oxygen, appears as a white powder or colourless crystals, and is used medicinally.

MAGNE′SIUM. A light, white, fairly tough metal, which tarnishes in air: symbol Mg, at. wt. 24·32 and at. no. 12. First found in Magnesia, a district in Thessaly, and widely distributed as the silicate, carbonate and chloride. It was recognized as an element by Black in 1755, isolated by Davy in 1808, and prepared in coherent form by Bussy in 1831. It is used in alloy, to strengthen aluminium for aircraft construction, and with uranium as a canning material in nuclear reactors. Its incendiary properties are used in flashlight photography, flares and fireworks.

MAGNETIC FLUX. A phenomenon produced in the neighbourhood of electric currents and magnets. The amount of M.F. through an area (measured in Maxwells) equals the product of the area and of the magnetic field strength at a point within that area.

MAGNETISM. Branch of science dealing with the properties of magnets and the magnetic fields. The lodestone acting as a compass, in that one pole seeks N., is thought to have been known to the Chinese, before (but not accepted in Europe until) the 12th cent. P. Peregrinus (fl. 13th cent.), an early experimentalist, inspired the work of William Gilbert (1546–1603) who described in *De Magnete* many fundamental properties of magnets and conceived of the earth itself as a magnet. Significant experiments were made in the 19th cent. by Coulomb, Gauss and Oersted (*see* ELECTRICITY). The general properties of magnets are that they align themselves on a N.–S. axis, the N. seeking pole facing N., but varying from the true geographic meridian (magnetic variation), like poles repel, and unlike poles attract. The force of attraction or repulsion between 2 poles varies inversely as the square of the distance between them.

Substances differ in degree and kind in their ability to be magnetized (permeability). Those substances, like iron, which have very high permeabilities, are said to be ferromagnetic. Apart from its universal application to dynamos, electric motors, switch-gear, and so forth, M. has become of considerable importance in modern science, incl. particle accelerators for nuclear research, memory stores for computers, tape recorders, cryogenics (q.v.) and investigations of matter and space.

MA′GNETITE. An important iron ore, magnetic iron oxide (Fe_3O_4). It is a black metallic mineral, strongly magnetic and sometimes possessing polarity (lodestone). It is widely distributed in igneous rocks.

MAGNI′TOGORSK. Town in Chelyabinsk region, R.S.F.S.R., 200 m. S. of Chelyabinsk town, on the r. Ural and the eastern slopes of the Ural Mountains. It was founded in 1931 to work the iron, manganese, bauxite, etc., in the district, and has blast furnaces and other metallurgical works producing steel, motorcars, tractors, railway waggons, etc. Pop. (1967) 352,000.

MAGNŌ′LIA. Genus of trees in the family Magnoliaceae, native to China, Japan, N. America, and the Himalayas. They vary in height from 2 ft. to 150 ft. The large single flowers are white, rose, or purple in colour.

MAGPIE. Genus of birds (*Pica*) in the Crow family. The Common M. (*Pica pica*) has black and white plumage, the long tail having a metallic gloss. It feeds on insects, snails, mice, etc., and is found in Europe, Asia, and N. Africa.

MAGRITTE (mahgrēt′), **René** (1898–1967). Belgian artist. A Surrealist, he used a visionary representationalism in such paintings as 'The Eye' (Museum of Modern Art, N.Y.) or the late 'Scheherazade'.

MAGYARS (mod′yars). The largest racial group of Hungary. *See* HUNGARY; HUNGARIAN.

MAHABHA′RATA (Great poem of the Bharatas). Sanskrit epic of 18 books probably composed in its present form *c.* 300 B.C. Forming with the *Ramayana* the 2 great epics of the Hindus, it deals with the fortunes of the rival families of the Kauravas and the Pandavas, and contains the Bhagavad-Gita (q.v.).

MAHABODHI. Another name for BUDDH GAYA.

MAHAN (mahan′), **Alfred Thayer** (1840–1914). American naval historian. His writings on naval strategy, notably *The Influence of Sea Power upon History, 1660–1783* (1890), and a *Life of Nelson* (1897), exercised great influence on the naval policies of several powers.

MAHAR′ASHTRA. State of the Republic of India formed in 1960 from the southern (predominantly Marathi-speaking) part of the former Bombay state. Bombay city is the cap.; other large towns are Poona, Nagpur, and Sholapur. It also includes the famous caves of Ajanta. Agriculture supports the majority of the people, cotton, rice, and ground-nuts being important crops. Cotton textiles are made extensively in Bombay and its environs. Area 118,717 sq. m.; pop. (1961) 39,553,718. *See* BELGAUM.

MAHĀYĀNA. *See* BUDDHISM.

MAHDI (Arab., he who is guided aright). The title of a coming messiah who will establish the reign of justice on earth. It has been assumed by many Moslem leaders, notably by the Sudanese sheik Mohammed Ahmed (1848–85), who headed a revolt in 1881 against Egypt and in 1885 captured Khartoum.

MAHLER, Gustav (1860–1911). Austrian composer. B. in Bohemia, of Jewish extraction, he studied at Vienna conservatoire, conducted in Prague, Leipzig,

Budapest, Hamburg (1891-7), and at the Imperial Opera, Vienna (1897-1907), and later went to the U.S.A., becoming chief conductor at the Metropolitan Opera House (1907), and director of the Philharmonic Orchestra, New York. Outstanding among his symphonies is the 4th; *Das Lied von der Erde* is a symphony for solo voices and orchestra; his songs and song-cycles incl. the moving *Kindertotenlieder*.

MAHO'GANY. Timber obtained from several genera of trees found in America espec. British Honduras. It is a warm red colour, very durable, and takes a high polish. True M. comes from the *Swietenia* but other types come from the Spanish and Australian cedars, the Indian redwood, and other trees of the family Meliaceae, native to Africa and the E. Indies.

MAHÓN (mahōn'). Cap. and port of the Spanish island of Minorca, probably founded by the Carthaginians. It was in British occupation 1708-56 and 1762-82. Pop. (1967) 16,550.

MAHRA'TTAS or **Marathas.** A mixed race living in W. and central India, and speaking the Marathi language. In the 17th and 18th cents. they formed a powerful military confederacy, which proved a dangerous rival to the Mogul emperors, until their power was broken by the Afghans in 1761. M. generals founded great states in the Deccan and central India, e.g. Indore, Gwalior, and Nagpur. A series of wars with the British, 1779-1817, ended in the annexation of most of their territory. *See* MAHARASHTRA.

MAIDEN CASTLE. Name of a prehistoric fort and successive later earthworks on Fordington Hill, near Dorchester, Dorset, England. A rampart, about 60 ft. high, encloses an area of 45 acres. The site was inhabited from Neolithic times (*c.* 2000 B.C.), and was stormed by the Romans A.D. 43.

MAIDENHAIR. A fern (*Adiantum capillusveneris*) with hair-like fronds terminating in small kidney-shaped pinnules containing the spores. It is widely distributed in America, and is sometimes found in the W. of the British Isles.

MAIDENHEAD. English town (bor.) and boating centre in Berkshire, 24 m. W. of London on the Thames. Two bridges, one of which was built in 1772, cross the river. Pop. (1961) 35,374.

MAIDS OF HONOUR. In Britain the immediate attendants on the person of a queen. They are chosen generally from the daus. and grand-daus. of peers, but in the absence of another title bear that of Honourable. Queen Elizabeth II was attended by 6 at her coronation.

MAIDSTONE. County town of Kent, England, on the Medway, 34 m. S.E. of London. There are the ruins of All Saints' Coll., founded in 1260, suppressed 1547, a 14th cent. church, and Chillington Manor House, an Elizabethan mansion, used as a museum and art gallery. Pop. (1961) 59,761.

MAIKOP (mī'kop). Cap. of Adyge autonomous region of the R.S.F.S.R. on the Bielaia r. It has timber mills, distilleries, tanneries, and tobacco and furniture are manufactured. M. petroleum fields, discovered in 1900, are linked by pipe-line with Tuapse on the Black Sea. Pop. (1967) 106,000.

MAILER, Norman (1923-). American novelist. Born in New Jersey, the son of a South African immigrant, he is best known for his novel of the S.W.W. *The Naked and the Dead,* (1949). He ran unsuccessfully for mayor of N.Y. 1969, campaigning for N.Y. as 51st state.

MAILLART (mahyahr'), **Ella 'Kini'** (1903-). Swiss traveller. She has travelled in Asiatic countries, and her books incl. *Forbidden Journey* (1937) and *The Land of the Sherpas* (1955).

MAILLOL (mahyol'), **Aristide Joseph Bonaventure** (1861-1944). French sculptor. B. at Banyuls, he was a painter and designer before turning his attention to sculpture and held his first exhibition in 1902,

Maillol's 'Striding Torso'.

becoming the leading sculptor in France. His principal works incl. the figure of 'Fame' for the Cézanne monument at Aix-en-Provence, and 'Flora' and 'Pomona' at Winterthur.

MAIL ORDER. Method of retail selling through specialized M.O. houses, by which the customer orders goods through the mail, usually with the aid of a glossy, illustrated catalogue. Originating as an organized business in the U.S., where the great distances made it a boon to isolated agricultural communities, it has expanded rapidly. Reduced prices to the consumer can follow from bulk buying and elimination of the middleman. Almost all the transactions are on credit, and sales are concentrated in clothing, footwear, household textiles and soft furnishings, though almost every known item is available by this method. In Britain M.O. has been comparatively slow to develop (3 per cent of retail sales in 1961) but is rapidly growing.

MAIMONIDES (mīmon'idēz), **Moses** (Moses Ben Maimon) (1135-1204). Jewish codifier and philosopher. B. at Cordova, he evolved a philosophy of religion of great significance. His Code of Jewish Law is known as the *Mishneh Torah*, and his philosophical classic is *The Guide to the Perplexed*.

MAINE. The north-easternmost state of the U.S.A., and the largest New England state. It has a rugged coast, and there are some 1,300 islands off the shore. The surface is undulating with a number of mountain peaks, culminating in Mt. Katahdin (5,273 ft.). There are many lakes. Rivers incl. the Penobscot and Kennebec. In the valleys dairy farming and market gardening are carried on. 25,000 sq. m. of M. are forested, and pulp and paper are the chief products; blueberries, apples and shell-fish are produced, and catering for holiday-makers is an important industry. The cap. is Augusta; the largest city, Portland. Area 33,215 sq. m.; pop. (1970) 993,466.

MAINE. Old French prov. bounded on the N. by Normandy, on the W. by Brittany, and on the S. by Anjou. The modern depts. of Sarthe and Mayenne approximately correspond with it.

MAINE. French river, 7 m. long, formed by the junction of the Mayenne and Sarthe; it enters the Loire below Angers, and gives its name to M.-et-Loire dept.

MAINTENON (mantnoń'), **Françoise d'Aubigné, marquise de** (1635-1719). Wife of Louis XIV. The dau. of a Protestant, she was m. in 1657 to the poet Scarron (1610-60). Louis XIV employed her as governess, gave her a title in 1678, and soon afterwards made her his mistress. After the death of his queen she was secretly m. to him *c.* 1685.

MAINZ (mīnts). Cap. of Rhineland-Palatinate, W. Germany, on the Rhine, 23 m. W.S.W. of Frankfurt-am-Main. In Roman times it was a fortified camp and became the cap. of Germania Superior. Printing was invented *c.* 1448 in M. by Gutenberg. The Romanesque cathedral was severely damaged in the S.W.W. Pop. (1967) 146,200.

MAISKY (mīs'kē), **Ivan Mikhailovich** (1884-). Soviet diplomat. A member of the revolutionary movement from 1899, he was twice exiled to Siberia and first visited Britain as a political refugee in 1912 as described in his *Journey into the Past* (1962), returning to Russia in 1917. After the revolution, he entered the diplomatic service, was Min. to Finland 1929-32 and ambassador to Britain 1932-43. He was assistant commissar for Foreign Affairs 1943–6 and has been a member of the Academy of Sciences since 1946. Among later vols. of reminiscences is *Who helped Hitler?*

MAIZE. Plant (*Zea mays*) of the grass family, cultivated by Amerindians – hence its alternative name of Indian corn or in U.S. usage 'corn' – and introduced to Europe by Columbus. It is now grown extensively in all subtropical and warm temperate regions, and is widely used as animal feed. Sweet corn, a variety in which sugar is not converted to starch, is a familiar vegetable (fresh, tinned or frozen): other varieties are made into hominy, polenta, popcorn, and corn bread. In the 1960s new hardy strains were being grown in S. England. Industrial uses incl. industrial alcohol, corn oil, and (from the stalks) paper and hardboard.

IVAN MAISKY

MAJO'LICA. A kind of enamelled pottery (q.v.), so-named from the Italian form of Majorca. The term is especially applied to the richly decorated enamel pottery produced in Italy 15th to 18th cents.

MAJO'RCA. Largest island of the Balearics, off the E. coast of Spain, of which they form a prov. M. rises in Puig Mayor to *c.* 5,000 ft. The soil is productive; olives, grapes, figs, oranges, etc., are grown; wine is made. Minerals incl. coal, iron, slate. Palma is the cap. Area 1,405 sq. m.; pop. (1960) 270,000.

MAKA'RIOS III (1913–). Cypriot Orthodox churchman. B. in Panayia, Paphos, he was ed. at Athens univ. and in 1950 became abp. and ethnarch in Cyprus. Active in support of the armed struggle for union with Greece, he was exiled to the Seychelles by the British govt. (1956–7). In 1960 he became pres. of the Rep. of Cyprus: re-elected 1968.

MAKHACH'KALA. City, cap. of Daghestan A.S.S.R., R.S.F.S.R., on the Caspian Sea, 90 m. E.S.E. of Grozny, from which pipelines bring petroleum to M.'s refineries; shipbuilding, meat packing, and the making of chemicals, matches, cotton textiles are other industries. M. was founded in 1844 on the site of a former camp called Petrovsk. Pop. (1967) 165,000.

MALABAR COAST. Name of the coastal area of

MAIZE. Among the world's major cereal crops, maize is continually extending its range of cultivation. Here it has been experimentally planted at Kpong in Ghana, and an agricultural assistant examines the cobs of the new crop.
Courtesy of Ghana Information Services.

Mysore and Kerala states, India, lying between the Arabian Sea and the Western Ghats. About 40 m. W. to E., 450 m. N. to S., it has fertile soil and heavy rains (80–120 in. a year) and produces food grains, coconuts, rubber, spices. Teak, ebony, and other woods are extracted from the mountain-side forests. Lagoons fringe the shore. A district of Madras transferred in 1956 to Kerala was called M.C.

MALACCA. State of W. Malaysia, Fed. of Malaysia. Portuguese from 1511, then Dutch from 1641, it was ceded to Britain in 1824, becoming part of the Straits Settlements. It produces rubber. Area 640 sq. m.; pop. (1966) 404,275 (about 70 per cent Chinese). The cap., also M., originated in the 13th cent. as a fishing village frequented by pirates, and developed into a trading port before Europeans reached the area. Pop. (1960) 72,000.

MA'LAGA. Spanish seaport, cap. of M. prov., on the Mediterranean, 65 m. N.E. of Gibraltar; its mild and sunny climate makes it a popular health resort; other industries incl. sugar refining, distilling, brewing, olive oil pressing, shipbuilding. It has an airport. Founded by the Phoenicians and taken by the Moors in 711, M. was cap. of the Moorish kingdom of M. from the 13th cent. until captured in 1487 by Ferdinand and Isabella who founded the parish church in 1490. Pop. (1960) 301,048.

MALAGA'SY REPUBLIC. Country occupying the island of Madagascar (q.v.). The cap. is Antananarivo; other towns are Majunga, Tamatave (chief port), Diégo-Suarez, Tuléas. Agriculture and cattle raising are the chief occupations, products incl. manioc, rice, coffee, ground-nuts, sugar cane. There is some mining (graphite, mica, phosphates, etc.); the forests have valuable timber, and industries such as textiles, cement, food-processing (espec. meat), machinery, etc., are being developed. Area 228,500 sq. m.; pop. (1966) 6,335,810.

The largest of a number of ethnic groups are the Hova (*c.* 1½ million), the lightest-skinned and probably most recent immigrants, who supplied the dynasty which ruled Madagascar from the late 18th cent. until it became a French colony in 1896, having been under French protection from 1890. During the S.W.W., the British, fearing a Japanese invasion, occupied the is. in 1942, the Free French taking over in 1943. It became an overseas terr. 1946, and in 1960 independent within the French Community as the M.R. There is a pres., nat. assembly and senate; and the official languages are French and Malagasy (Malayo-Polynesian).

MA'LAMUD, Bernard (1914–). American novelist. A teacher of English, he first attracted attention with *The Natural* (1952), taking a professional baseball player as his hero, but is more typically represented by *The Assistant* (1957), with its Yiddish-speaking immigrant characters, and *A New Life* (1962).

MALAN, Daniel François (1874–1959). S. African statesman. Originally a pastor of the Dutch Reformed Church, he was Min. of the Interior 1924–33. In 1933 he became leader of the Nationalist Party, which in 1940 combined with Hertzog's followers as the Reunited (*Herenigde*) National Party, and opposed participation in the S.W.W. M. was P.M. from 1948, until his retirement in 1954, and in 1951 his party united with the Afrikaner party as the new National Party, pledged to republicanism and *apartheid* (the territorial and political segregation of the non-white population).

MALĀ'RIA. Marsh ague; a recurring fever due to invasion of the blood stream by the minute parasite plasmodium. This develops in the stomach of the anopheles mosquito and passes into the blood when the insect pierces the skin to feed, enters the red corpuscles of the blood, completes its growth, and is then liberated into the blood stream, where its toxins cause the fever. In 1955 the W.H.O. began an urgent eradication campaign. The aim was to reduce mosquito numbers sufficiently to break the parasite's transmission cycle, and thus eliminate it, and was stimulated by the development of mosquito resistance to the new residual insecticides D.D.T., dieldrin, etc., and of parasite resistance to the drugs plasmoquin, atebrin, chloroquine – synthetics which avoid the disadvantages of quinine. Annual world deaths are still c. 1,000,000.

Anopheles mosquito

MALA′WI. Country in central Africa, known until 1964 as Nyasaland. The land area lies W. and S. of Lake M., which belongs to M., and incl. most of the Shiré basin and the Shiré Highlands. The cap. is Zomba (to be replaced by Lilongwe); other towns are Blantyre-Limbe, in the Shire Highlands, Fort Johnston on Lake M., Karonga, and Kota-Kota. The chief products are tobacco, cotton, tea, coffee, sugar cáne, and rice. Area 47,949 sq. m. (11,000 sq. m. water); pop. (1966) 4,042,412. M. was a Brit. protectorate from 1891, part of the Fedn. of Rhodesia and Nyasaland 1953–63, and became self-governing 1963, independent 1964, and a rep. (within the Commonwealth) 1966.

MALAWI, Lake. Formerly Lake Nyasa (q.v.).

MALA′Y PENINSULA. Southern projection of the continent of Asia lying between the Strait of Malacca, which divides it from Sumatra, and the China Sea. The northern portion is partly in Burma, partly in Thailand; the southern forms part of the Fed. of Malaysia (q.v.). The island of Singapore lies off its southern extremity.

The main physical feature is a central limestone range of wooded mountains, rising to above 7,000 ft. and flanked by undulating hills and alluvial plains. Mostly jungle-covered, they are watered by innumerable streams incl. the Perak, Bernam, and Muar on the W. and the Kelantan, Pahang, and Trengganu to the E. The extremely humid tropical climate has little difference between summer and winter, and there is a profusion of flora and fauna.

In ancient times the M.P. seems to have been dominated by various waves of immigrants from India, and was the centre (9th to 14th cents.) of Sri Vijaya, the great Malay Buddhist empire, which was ultimately overthrown by Majapahit, Java's last Hindu kingdom, which in its turn was destroyed by Islam.

MALAWI. Most of the country's tea is grown in the south in the Mlanje district, and this plantation lies at the very foot of 9,843 ft. high Mlanje Mountain, which rises rugged and cloud-capped.

Malacca became a centre of Islamic culture and an entrepôt for the spice trade, and a mighty Malay or Johore empire arose. Its growth was checked, however, by the conquest of Malacca by the Portuguese in 1511. In 1641 the Dutch ousted the Portuguese, and in 1773 the surrounding territory broke away from the Malay empire. Penang was founded by British interests in 1786, and Singapore in 1819. From 1874 Britain extended her control over the Malayan states, and before the S.W.W. the political organization of M. comprised the Straits Settlements (Singapore, Penang, incl. Prov. Wellesley, Malacca), the Federated Malay States (Perak, Selangor, Negri Sembilan, Pahang), and the Unfederated States (Johore, Kedah, Perlis, Kelantan, Trengganu). Occupied by the Japanese 1942–5, these various territories became in 1946 a crown colony, reorganized in 1948 as the *Federation of Malaya* which attained full independence 1957, and in 1963 (on the accession of Singapore, Sabah, and Sarawak) became known as Malaysia (q.v.).

MALAYSIA. Recent years have seen a spectacular revival of the ancient craft of the silversmith. Traditional methods are still used, and the individual pieces are the work of a single man, so that standards are high. *Courtesy of Malaysian Govt.*

MALAY′SIA. Federation in S.E. Asia, within the Brit. Commonwealth, formed in 1963 by the linking of the Fed. of Malaya, Sarawak, N. Borneo (then renamed Sabah), and Singapore (seceded 1965): its establishment was opposed by Indonesia, but militant 'confrontation' ceased 1966. Since 1966 the states of the former Fed. of Malaya have been known as West M., and Sabah and Sarawak as East M. The Supreme Head of the Federation is elected for 5 years by the rulers of the member states from among their number; the fed. parliament consists of a senate (partly elected, partly nominated) and a house of representatives elected by universal adult suffrage. The nat. language is Malay, usually written in Arabic characters, which belongs to the W. or Indonesian branch of the Malayo-Polynesian family of languages and originated in Malacca. English is also permitted officially in West M., and in East M. until the state legislatures decide. Islam is the official religion of West M.; East M. has no state religion.

Equatorial rain forest covers three-quarters of both East and West M., and besides the all-important rubber, copra, palm and coconut oil, timber, pineapples, kapok and rice (universally grown, but also imported) are produced. The chief mineral is tin, but gold, iron ore, bauxite, ilmenite, and coal are also mined, and there is petroleum in Sarawak. Industries are being developed to lessen M.'s dependence on raw material exports to more highly developed countries. Fishing is important. The cap. is Kuala Lumpur, also cap. of Selangor. Area 128,000 sq. m.; pop (1967) 10,000,000 (*c.* 1½ million in East M.), incl. 50%, Malays, 35% Chinese, 10% Indians and Pakistanis, and some 5% indigenous peoples of East M. A first 5-year plan (1966–70) gave priority to the development of E. Malaysia. Racial tension exists between Malays and Chinese, and Communist guerrilla activity on the Thai-M. border began in 1969.

MALCOLM (mal′kom) **III,** called **Canmore** (d. 1093). King of Scotland. The son of Duncan I, he became king in 1054. He was killed at Alnwick while invading Northumberland.

MA′LDĪVE ISLANDS. Group of coral atolls in the Indian Ocean, 450 m. S.W. of Ceylon, a republic since 1968. The Moslem inhabitants are famous as navigators and fishermen. The Is., which were a dependency of Ceylon 1645–1948, were under Brit. protection 1887–1965. An R.A.F. staging post estab. on Gan Island, in the S. of the group, in the S.W.W., was re-estab. in 1956 and its use guaranteed till 1986. There is a pres. and an elected legislature. Malé, on King's Island, is the cap. (pop. 8,000). Area 115 sq. m.; pop. (1972) 114,000.

MALDON. English market town (bor.) in Essex, at the mouth of the Chelmer, the scene of a battle with the Norsemen in 991. The town has a grammar school founded in the 16th cent. Laurence Washington, great-great-grandfather of George Washington, was rector of Purleigh nearby 1632–43; he is buried at M. Pop. (1961) 10,507.

MALEBRANCHE (mahlbroñsh′), **Nicolas** (1638–1715). French philosopher. B. in Paris, he joined the Congregation of the Oratory in 1660. His *De la Recherche de la Vérité* (1674–8), was inspired by Descartes: he maintained that exact ideas of external objects are obtainable only through God.

MALENKOV (mahl′yenkof), **Georgi Maximilianovich** (1901–). Soviet statesman. B. at Orenburg, he became chairman of the Council of Ministers (P.M.) in 1953, but resigned in 1955 following agricultural difficulties for which he confessed guilt. Since 1957 he has been manager of the Ust-Kameno-Gorsk power station. His second marriage was to Elena Khrushcheva, sister of Nikita Khrushchev.

MALET, Lucas. *See* KINGSLEY, CHARLES.

MALHERBE (mahlärb), **François de** (1555–1628). French poet and grammarian. B. in Caen, he became court poet in *c.* 1605 under Henry IV and Louis XIII. He advocated reform of language and versification and estab. the 12-syllable Alexandrine as the standard form of French verse.

MALI, Republic of. Inland country of W. Africa, the former French Sudan (*see* SUDAN), which became independent in 1960, outside the French Community. The name derives from the cap. of a medieval Negro kingdom on the Niger which fell before the attacks of other Negro tribes in 1500. M. covers the upper basins of the Senegal and Niger rivers, but is for the most part desert. Bamako, on the Niger, is the cap.; other towns are Mopti and Timbuktu. Cattle, sheep and camels are reared, but since independence rice and sugar-cane cultivation, and also some light industry, have been developed. A rail link Bamako-Conakry is planned to give M. access to the sea. In 1968 there was a military coup. Area 450,000 sq. m.; pop. (1967) 4,700,000.

MALIC ACID. A laevorotatory compound $C_4H_6O_5$, widely distributed in apples, plums, cherries, grapes, and other fruits. It is usually prepared from the unripe berries of the mountain ash, and has the appearance of colourless needle-like crystals.

MA′LIK, Yakob Alexandrovich (1906–). Soviet diplomat. B. in the Ukraine, he was permanent rep. U.N. 1948–53, and from 1968, and succeeded Gromyko as ambassador to London 1953–60. He was Deputy Foreign Min. 1946–53 and 1960–8.

MALINES (-lēn′), City in the prov. of Antwerp, Belgium, on the Dyle, 12 m. N.N.E. of Brussels. Once famous for its lace, called Mechlin (from Mechelen, the Flemish form of Malines), it makes furniture, carpets, textiles, etc., and is the seat of the archbishop-primate of Belgium. There is a famous carillon school and the cathedral contains Van Dyck's 'Crucifixion'. Pop. (1960 est.) 64,720.

MALINO′VSKY, Rodion Yakolevich (1898–1967). B. in Odessa, he became a farm labourer at 12 and after fighting in France during the F.W.W. served with the Foreign Legion until he joined the Red Army during the Civil War. Rising from the ranks to become major-gen. by 1940, he fought at Stalingrad, and, promoted marshal in 1944, commanded the advance through the Balkans to Budapest, and the Far Eastern army occupying Manchuria 1944–5. From 1957–67 he was Min. of Defence.

MALIPIERO mahlēpē-ā′rō), **Gian Francesco** (1882–). Italian composer. Prof. of the history of music at Padua from 1936, he has ed. Monteverdi and Vivaldi, and experimented with operatic treatment of Shakespeare's *Julius Caesar* and *Antony and Cleopatra*, etc.

MALLARMÉ (mahlahrmā′), **Stéphane** (1842–98). French poet. B. in Paris, he taught English there until 1892, and with Verlaine founded the Symbolist school. His belief that poetry should be evocative and suggestive was reflected in *L'Après-Midi d'un faune* (1876), which inspired Debussy. Later publications are *Poésies complètes* (1887), *Vers et prose* (1893), and the prose *Divagations* (1897).

MALLIA. Archaeological site 25 m. E. of Knossos on the N. coast of Crete. Excavated by the French since 1920, it has a palace, but the most striking feature is the *agora* or assembly place discovered in 1962. It provided the 1st evidence of civic institutions in Minoan Crete.

MALLORCA. Spanish form of MAJORCA.

MALLOW. Family of plants (Malvaceae) found in the N. hemisphere. The common M. (*Malva sylvestris*), native to Europe and naturalized in N. America, has 5-petalled, purple flowers and ivy-shaped leaves.

MALLOW

MALMÉDY (mahlmeh-dē′). Town in Belgium, situated in the deep valley of the Warche, 25 m. S.E. of Liège and 25 m. S. of Aachen. Given to Prussia in 1814, it became Belgian in 1920 after a plebiscite. It was a centre of fierce fighting during the German offensive in the Ardennes in Dec. 1944. Pop. (est.) 6,000.

MA′LORY, Sir Thomas (d. 1471). English author, most usually thought to have been the Warwickshire landowner of that name who was M.P. for Warwick in 1445, and in 1451 and 1452 was charged with theft, rape and attempted murder. He would have compiled his prose romance *Morte d'Arthur* during his 20 years in Newgate. It is a translation from the French modified by material from other sources, and deals with the exploits of Arthur's knights of the Round Table, the quest for the Grail, etc.

MALPIGHI (mahlpē′gē), **Marcello** (1628–94). Italian physiologist. B. near Bologna, he held professorships at Bologna, Pisa, and Messina, and made many discoveries in his study of animal and vegetable tissues by means of the microscope.

MALPLAQUET (mahlplahkā′). Village in Nord dept., France, about 6 m. N.W. of Maubeuge, where on

11 Sept. 1709 the Allies, under Marlborough and Prince Eugene of Savoy, defeated the French under Villars.

MALRAUX (mahlroh´), **André** (1901–). French novelist. B. in Paris, he studied art and oriental languages, then went with an archaeological expedition to Indo-China. Later he became involved in the Kuomintang revolution, and *La Condition humaine* (1933: *Storm over Shanghai*) drew on these experiences. *L'Espoir* (1937: *Days of Hope*) is set in Civil War Spain, where he was himself a bomber-pilot in the International Brigade. In the S.W.W. he was an ardent supporter of the Gaullist Resistance. During 1947–50 he pub. a 3 vol. study of the psychology of art, and 1960–9 was Min. of Cultural Affairs.

MALT. Grain, usually barley, which has been allowed to germinate and then dried. It is used for brewing and fermentation.

The barley must be perfectly matured, and the grain of uniform size and variety. After steeping in hard water for 2 or 3 days at a temperature of 50–5° F, the grain swells and becomes soft. It is then spread out on the growing floors and kept at a temperature of 50°F, where germination commences. After 10 or 12 days it is transferred to the drying kilns and roasted. When dried, it is removed, passed through a beating machine, which removes the rootlets, and stored in airtight containers. For use in brewing, the malt is crushed to a fine powder. M. is used for colouring and flavouring, and by fermentation with yeast to produce alcohol.

MALTA, G.C. Largest of a group of islands in the Mediterranean, situated 58 m. S. of Sicily and 180 m. N. of the N. African coast. It is 17 m. by 9 m. and fairly low-lying. M. was colonized in turn by Phoenicians, Greeks, Carthaginians, and Romans – St. Paul was shipwrecked here – and fell to the Arabs in 870. It was the headquarters of the Knights of St. John from 1530, became French in 1798, and British in 1814. M. was a vital naval link in the S.W.W., and was besieged and attacked by air with heavy loss of life, so that the island was awarded the George Cross in 1942. In 1947 limited self-govt. was granted, and in 1964 M. became independent within the British Commonwealth: there is a House of Representatives (50 members).

British defence cuts and the closure of the Suez Canal by Egypt led to economic crisis in 1967–8, but long-term recovery is based on increased tourism, industrial development, conversion of the naval dockyard to commercial use, and establishment of a new freeport zone (Medport) in Marsaxlokk Bay. Agriculture and fishing are important, and lace-making a traditional craft. Valletta is the cap. and Luqa airport was completed 1958. The official languages are English and Maltese, related to Arabic and having ancient Phoenician survivals, but much influenced by Italian. Area 95 sq. m. With the islands of Gozo (26 sq. m.) and Comino (1 sq. m.) the total area of M. is 122 sq. m.; pop. (1966) 318,109.

MALTA, Knights of. *See* ST. JOHN OF JERUSALEM.

MALTHUS (mal´thus), **Thomas Robert** (1766–1834). British economist and churchman. B. near Guildford, Surrey, he is famous for his *Essay on the Principle of Population* (1798; 2nd ed. 1803), in which he maintains that population increases in geometrical ratio, whereas the food supply increases in arithmetical ratio. Hence the necessity for checks, of which moral restraint is one the chief.

MALVERN, Godfrey Martin Huggins, 1st visct. M. (1883–1971). Rhodesian statesman. B. in Kent, and a doctor by training, he went out to S. Rhodesia in 1911, and continued in practice, after entering into politics in 1923. He was P.M. 1933–53 and strongly supported the creation of the Federation of Rhodesia and Nyasaland, of which he was P.M. 1953–6, and in 1955 was created visct.

MALVERN (mawl´vern). English spa and inland resort (U.D.) in Worcs, situated on the E. side of the Malvern Hills, 8 m. S.W. of Worcester. The Royal Radar Establishment is here. The M. Hills, which extend for 9 to 10 m., command a fine view. The highest point is Worcester Beacon, 1,395 ft. above sea-level. Pop. (1961) 24,373.

MALVINAS. Argentine name for FALKLAND Is.

MA´MELŪKES. Freed Turkish slaves who long dominated Egypt. They formed the royal bodyguard in the 13th cent., and in 1250 placed one of their own number on the throne. M. sultans ruled Egypt until the Turkish conquest of 1517, and they remained the ruling class until 1811, when they were massacred by Mehemet Ali.

MAMMALS or **Mammalia.** A classification, invented by Linnaeus in 1758. incl. all vertebrates which suckle their young. Most forms are viviparous, but there are still egg-laying species, e.g. marsupials.

MAMMOTH. Extinct elephant (*Elephas primigenius*) about the size of an Indian elephant, with a pointed skull, small ears, and spiral tusks about 10 ft. long. The body was covered with long fur. The M. was abundant in N. Europe in Pleistocene times.

MAMMOTH CAVE. Huge limestone cavern, in M.C. National Park (estab. 1936), Edmonson co., Kentucky, U.S.A. The main cave is 4 m. long, and rises to a height of 125 ft.; it is famous for its stalactites and stalagmites. Indian councils were once held here.

MAN, Origins of. Remains of the oldest member of the stock which gave rise to true man were discovered by L. S. B. Leakey (q.v.) in 1967. Fragments of the skull of Europe's earliest man were found 1965 at Vertsszöllös, 30 m. W. of Budapest: he belonged to the same species as Java and Peking Man (qq.v.) *See also* PILTDOWN.

MAN, Isle of. *See* ISLE OF MAN.

MANAGUA (mahnah´gwah). Cap. of Nicaragua, situated on the lake of the same name, about 25 m. N.W. of Granada. It was destroyed by earthquake in 1931, but was rebuilt. Pop. (1965) 275,000.

MANÁOS. Older spelling of MANÁUS.

MANÁUS (mahnah´os). Capital of Amazonas, Brazil, on the Rio Negro, near its confluence with the Amazon; though it is 1,000 m. from the Atlantic, it can be reached by sea-going vessels. Pop. (1960) 175,343.

MA´NCHA, La. Old prov. of Spain; the name, still used for the same district which covers the modern prov. of Ciudad Real and parts of Toledo, Cuenca, and Albacete, is derived from Arabic *al mansha*, the dry land.

MANCHE (monsh), **La.** French name for the English Channel (q.v.). It gives its name to a Fr. dept.

MANCHESTER. City (1853) and co. bor. (1889) of Lancashire, on the Irwell, 158 m. N.W. of London and 31 m. E. of Liverpool. Originally a Roman camp, M. is mentioned in Domesday Book, and by the 13th cent. was a centre for woollens. Its damp climate made it ideal for cotton, introduced in the late 16th cent., and in the 19th cent. (with a period of stagnation during the American Civil War which cut off supplies from the South) the M. area was the world centre of manufacture: in the 20th, espec. after the S.W.W., there was a sharp decline, and the disused mills were used to provide cheap premises for new industries. The varied products of the vast industrial area of which M. is the commercial centre, incl. road vehicles and tractors, aircraft, textile machinery, woollen and cotton goods, chemicals, iron and steel tubing, rubber, paper, flour and processed foods. There is a fine port with an extensive transit trade,

x

MANCHESTER. A great cultural as well as industrial centre, Manchester has a central library, opened in 1934, with more than half a million books (the circular building to the right). To the left is the high clock tower of the town hall, the new corporation administration block showing white at the rear, and the fine city art gallery is just a little farther beyond. Top centre is the modern skyscraper of the new G.P.O. building.   *Crown Copyright.*

which has encouraged M.'s growth as a financial, banking, and insurance centre. It is linked with the Mersey and the sea by the 35¼ m. M. Ship Canal (1894), and also served by the Bridgewater and other canals. Road and rail connections are highly developed, and M. Airport is of internat. standard.

M. has long been distinguished as a centre of radical thought (*see* PETERLOO), and in the *Guardian* (1821) has the one 'provincial' English newspaper of national standing. Culturally flourishing, it has the internat. Hallé Orchestra (1857); the City (1829) and Whitworth (1889) art galleries; the Central (1934) and John Rylands (1899) libraries; and Manchester Univ. (Owens Coll. 1851: univ. 1903) and Univ. Inst. of Science and Technology (1824: univ. 1966). Other buildings incl. the 15th cent. cathedral, Royal Exchange (1869), Town Hall (designed by Alfred Waterhouse), and the Free Trade Hall. Pop. (1961) 661,041.

MANCHUKUO (manchookwō′). Name of a puppet state set up in Manchuria by the Japanese in 1932 with Changchun (Hsinking) as its cap. and the last Chinese emperor, Henry Pu Yi, as ruler. It disappeared with Japan's defeat in 1945.

MANCHURIA (manchōōr′ēa). Region some 400,000 sq. m. in extent (formerly an administrative unit) in N.E. China, bounded by the R.S.F.S.R. to the N. and E., by Inner Mongolia autonomous region to the W., by Korea to the S. For the most part undulating plain, M. incl. 2 mountain ranges, the Khingan and the Changkwangsai Mountains, running N. and S. and rising to 8,000 ft. The climate is severe in winter, mild in summer: rainfall is scant, snowfall heavy. The chief rivers are the Amur and its tributaries the Sungari and Ussuri: the Amur and Ussuri (qq.v.) mark the N. and E. boundaries with the R.S.F.S.R. The mountains are forested, and lumbering is important; agriculture is well developed in the plains; crops incl. soya beans, sugar beet, millet, maize, wheat, barley, kaoliang, rice, and oats. Extensive deposits of coal and iron ores have given rise to a thriving iron and steel industry, concentrated in or near the Liao-tung peninsula (*liao* means iron). The main centres of pop. incl. Shenyang, the cap.; Dairen

and Port Arthur, both ice free ports; Changchun; Yungki; and Harbin, an important railway junction and centre for inland navigation on the Sungari.

Manchuria was originally inhabited by the nomadic Tungus, but in the 17th cent. the Manchus obtained control, and from 1644–1912 a Manchu dynasty occupied the imperial throne of China. Chinese colonization of M. began in the 18th cent. and gradually spread northwards, until by 1900 they formed 80 per cent of the pop. The few remaining Manchus are restricted to the Aigun area in the Amur valley; their language belongs to the Tungusic branch of the Altaic family.

Japan secured a part of S. Manchuria in 1895, and in 1898 Russia obtained the lease of the Kwantung peninsula for 25 years, which concession passed to Japan after her victory over Russia in the war of 1904–5. Both powers sponsored extensive railway construction in M. In 1931 the Japanese occupied M. and set up the puppet state of Manchukuo (q.v.), 1932. After the collapse of Japan in 1945, M. was returned to China, and the many Japanese who had settled there were expelled.

MANDAEANS (mandē′anz). The only surviving Gnostic sect; they live near the Euphrates, S. Iraq, and their sacred book is the *Ginza*.

MA′NDALAY. Chief town of Upper Burma, cap. of M. division, on the Irrawaddy, *c.* 370 m. N. of Rangoon. Founded by King Mindon Min in 1857, it was cap. of Burma 1857–85. It was severely damaged by fire in 1892, and devastated during the S.W.W. M. has many pagodas, temples, and monasteries. Pop. (1966) 316,796.

MA′NDARIN. Chinese official. The word was adopted in the 16th cent. from the Portuguese, its ultimate origin being Sanskrit *mantrin*, 'counsellor'. In China the Ms. were chosen from the 7th cent. by examination. The term M. was also applied to the group of dialects, of which the standard form is that of Peking; they have been since the Ming dynasty the standard language of Chinese officialdom.

MANDATE. Under the Treaty of Versailles the system whereby the administration of former German and Turkish possessions was entrusted to Allied States by the League of Nations, the latter being replaced as the responsible authority in 1945 by the U.N., when Ms. which had not achieved independence or self-govt. became known as Trust Territories (q.v.). S.W. Africa (q.v.) is an exception in that the Rep. of S. Africa does not recognize U.N. authority in this.

M. & B. The initials of May and Baker, a British firm of fine chemical manufacturers; the designation of a series of sulphonamide compounds invented by the firm. M. & B. 137 is soluseptacine, M. & B. 693 is sulphapyridine, and M. & B. 760 sulphathiazole.

MANDEL (mondel′), **Georges** (1885–1944). French politician, closely associated with Clemenceau, whose *directeur de cabinet* he was during the F.W.W. He became Colonial Min. in 1937 and Min. of the Interior in May 1940. Having opposed surrender to Germany, he was arrested by the Vichy govt. and shot by his German guards in Paris.

MANDELSHTAM, Osip Emilevich (1891–?). Russian poet. The son of a Jewish merchant, he was sent to a concentration camp by the Communist authorities in the 'thirties and the date and the manner of his death are unknown. His collected poems were pub. in 1928 and have a classic brevity that evades translation.

MANDEVILLE (man′devil), **Sir John.** Supposed author of a 14th cent. travel manual for pilgrims to the Holy Land, originally written in French and probably the work of Jean d'Outremeuse of Liège. As well as references to real marvels such as the pyramids, there are tales of headless men with eyes in their shoulders, etc.

MA′NDOLINE. A musical instrument descended

from the lute, so called because its body is shaped like an almond (It. *mandorla*). It has 8 or 10 strings.

MANDRILL. W. African baboon (*Papio maimon*). The nose is bright red and the cheeks striped with blue. There are red callosities on the buttocks; the fur is brown, with a yellow beard.

MĀ̄NĒS. The gods of the underworld in ancient Rome, later identified with the ghosts of the dead.

MANET (mahneh'), **Édouard** (1832–83). French painter. B. in Paris, he came under the influence of Velazquez and Hals, and exhibited with Monet, Renoir and Whistler at the *Salon des Refusés* in 1863.

MANDRILL

This exhibition marked the beginning of the Impressionist movement, of which M. was the leading spirit. He summed up his aims in the famous dictum, 'The principal person in a picture is the light.' His best-known works incl. 'Déjeuner sur l'herbe', 'Absinthe Drinker', 'Olympia', 'Fife Player', and 'Bar at the Folies-Bergère'. *See* illus. p. 448.

MANGAN, James Clarence (1803–49). Irish poet. B. in Dublin, after 10 years as a copying-clerk he became librarian at Trinity Coll., and entered the Irish Ordnance Survey Office in 1833. In addition to beautiful lyrics, e.g. 'Dark Rosaleen', he pub. vols of 'translations', e.g. *Anthologia Germanica* (1849).

MA'NGANĒSE (Lat. *magnes* magnet). A brilliant white metal, present in small quantities in most rocks: symbol Mn, at.wt. 54·94 and at.no. 25. Discovered by Gahn in 1774 by reducing the dioxide with carbon, M. has a high melting point and is normally very hard and brittle. Chemically it is very reactive, and combines readily with oxygen on heating. Chiefly used in alloys, espec. for M. steel which is very tough, it also serves as a depolarizer in dry batteries, and potassium permanganate (an oxidizing agent) is used as an antiseptic and in quantitative analysis.

MANGEL-WURZEL or **Mangold**. A variety of the common beet (*Beta vulgaris*) derived from the sea beet (*B. maritima*). It is used chiefly as feed for cattle and sheep.

MANGO. Tree (*Mangifera indica*) native to India but now widely cultivated for its oval fruits in other tropical and subtropical areas, e.g. West Indies. They do not travel well and in temperate countries are better known preserved unripe in pickles or chutney.

MA'NGROVE. Tree of the family Rhizophoraceae native to tropical coasts and estuaries where, by sending down roots from its branches, it rapidly forms close-growing M. swamps. Its timber is impervious to water and resists marine worms.

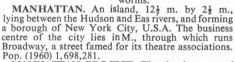

.MANGO|

MANHATTAN. An island, 12½ m. by 2½ m., lying between the Hudson and Eas rivers, and forming a borough of New York City, U.S.A. The business centre of the city lies in M., through which runs Broadway, a street famed for its theatre associations. Pop. (1960) 1,698,281.

MANHATTAN PROJECT. The development of

the atom bomb in the S.W.W. *See* FERMI, OPPENHEIMER.

MANICHAEISM (man'ikē-izm). Religion founded by Mani (Latinized as Manichaeus), who was b. in Mesopotamia *c.* A.D. 216, and proclaimed his creed in 241 at the Persian court. Returning from missions to China and India, he was put to death at the instigation of the Zoroastrian priesthood *c.* 276. Despite persecution M. spread and flourished until the 10th cent. Its fundamental tenet was that the material world is an invasion of the realm of light by the powers of darkness: particles of goodness imprisoned in matter were to be rescued by messengers such as Jesus, and finally by Mani himself.

MANILA (mahnē'lah). Former cap. and principal port of the Philippines, situated on Luzon. The new cap., Quezon City, is in a N.E. suburb of M. M. is cut in 2 by the r. Pasig; to the N. are the modern suburbs. The old city, which lay to the S., was reduced to rubble during the fighting between U.S. troops and Japanese in 1945. M. was founded in 1571 by Spain, and captured by the U.S.A. in 1898. It is subject to earthquakes. M. has distilleries, textile and tobacco factories, foundries, shipbuilding yards, etc. The natural harbour of M. bay, perhaps the finest in the

MANITOBA. The discovery of valuable mineral deposits has transformed the old conception of the northern areas as an unproductive wilderness. At Thompson, 400 miles north of Winnipeg, International Nickel operates the first fully integrated nickel-producing complex in the western world. The town which houses its workers is seen above.
Courtesy of the International Nickel Company (Mond) Ltd.

Far East, has contributed to the city's commercial importance. Pop. Greater M. (1968) 3,100,000.

MANING, Frederick Edward (1812–83). New Zealand author. B. in Dublin, he was taken to Tasmania in 1824, and in 1833 went to New Zealand, where he m. a tribal chief's dau. He was a judge in a native court 1865–81, and in 1863 pub. an account of Maori customs and traditions, *Old New Zealand*.

MANIOC. *See* CASSAVA.

MANIPUR (manipoor'). State (to be created in 1971) of the Rep. of India, lying to the E. of Assam, and bounded on the E. by Burma. Most of M. is mountainous and covered with dense forests, but there is a broad fertile valley which incl. Loktak Lake and Imphal, the cap., and produces large quantities of rice. M. first entered into treaty relations with Britain in 1762. It was the scene of very heavy fighting against the Japanese in March-April 1944. M. is the original home of polo. Area 8,620 sq. m.; pop. (1961) 778,318.

MANITŌ'BA. Prov. of Canada, situated midway between the Atlantic and Pacific. The territory was within the charter of the Hudson's Bay Company 1670–1869, the prov. being created 1870. It developed rapidly with mechanized grain-farming.

M. is mainly flat, with scattered hills. The prairie area lies to the W and S.W., while in the N.E. the surface is broken by marshes. The prov. has a

Hudson Bay coastline, and incl. 3 large lakes, Winnipeg, Winnipegosis, and Manitoba. The main rivers are the Assiniboine, Red, Nelson, and Churchill. The climate is continental. The provincial govt. at Winnipeg, the cap., is under a lieutenant-governor and a legislative assembly, while 6 senators and 14 M.P.s represent M. in the Dom. parliament. Wheat, flaxseed, etc. are grown; poultry reared; and almost half the land area being under timber, lumbering is important. Furs (wild and ranch-bred) and fisheries are also valuable. Minerals incl. nickel, copper, zinc, gold and silver. Industries incl. food processing, iron and steel, clothing, chemicals, electronic equipment, and space probes. After the cap. the chief towns are St. Boniface, St. James, Brandon, and St. Vital. Area 251,000 sq. m.; pop. (1966) 963,066.

MANKOWITZ (man'kŏvĭts), **Wolf** (1924–). British author. His novels incl. *Make Me An Offer* (1952) and *A Kid for Two Farthings* (1953)– both filmed; the musical plays *Expresso Bongo* and *Belle* (1961), based on the Crippen case; and studies of pottery and porcelain, espec. Wedgwood.

MANLEY, Gordon (1902–). British geographer. Appointed to the chair of environmental studies at the Univ. of Lancaster 1964, he is noted for his meteorological studies in N.W. England.

MANN, Thomas (1875–1955). German novelist and critic. Son of a Lübeck grain merchant, he worked in an insurance office in Munich and on the staff of the periodical *Simplicissimus*, then returned in imagination to his native Lübeck to portray in his first novel *Buddenbrooks* (1900) the decline of one of the great Hanseatic families. *Der Zauberberg* (1924: *The Magic Mountain*), set in a Swiss sanatorium and concerned with problems of life and death, prepared the way for the award to him in 1929 of a Nobel prize, but his opposition to the Nazi régime forced him to live abroad and in 1940 he became a U.S. citizen. Among his other most impressive works are the biblical tetralogy on the theme of Joseph and his brethren (1933–44), the political novel on the fate of modern Germany *Dr. Faustus* (1947), the comic masterpiece *Confessions of Felix Krull* (1954) and a number of short stories incl. 'Tonio Kröger' (1903) and 'Death in Venice' (1913).

His brother, **Henrich M.** (1871–1950) was also a novelist, his books incl. *Im Schlaraffenland* (1901), *Professor Unrat* (1904: *The Blue Angel*), depicting the sensual downfall of a schoolmaster; the happier *Die kleine Stadt* (1909); a scathing trilogy dealing with the Kaiser's Germany *Das Kaiserreich* (1918–25); and 2 vols. on the career of Henry IV of France (1935–8). He left Germany with his brother and d. in the U.S.A.

MANN, Tom (1856–1941). British Labour leader. In 1889 he achieved fame during the London dock strike. He was secretary of the I.L.P. 1894–6, and active in the Australian Labour movement 1902–10. He led the Syndicalist movement 1910–12, and in 1920 became a Communist.

MANNA. A sweetish exudation obtained from many trees such as the ash and larch, and used in medicine. The M. of the Bible is thought to have been from the tamarisk tree.

MANNERHEIM (mahn'erhīm), **Carl Gustav Emil von** (1867–1951). Finnish soldier-statesman. He served in the Russian Army during the F.W.W. After the establishment of a Finnish Socialist rep. in 1917 he formed a 'white' army, crushed the Socialists with German assistance, and during 1918–19 acted as regent. He commanded the Finnish armies during the Russian wars of 1939–40 and in 1941–4, and as president of Finland 1944–6 negotiated the peace settlement with Russia.

MANNHEIM. Town of Baden-Württemberg, W. Germany, at the confluence of the Neckar and Rhine. Heavy machinery, glass, earthenware, chemicals, etc.,

are manufactured. A fishing village from the 8th cent., M. was made a town in 1606. Pop. (1966) 329,301.

MANNIN, Ethel (1900–). British author. A Londoner of Irish stock, she became a journalist and pub. her first novel at 22. Her later prolific output, marked by the sincerity and independence which make her a self-styled anarchist, incl. travel books (Burma, India, Russia, Japan, the Middle East), vols. of autobiography, and many novels, e.g. *The Road to Beersheba* (1963), telling of the exodus before the Israeli advance.

MANNING, Frederic (1887–1935). Australian author, best known for his realistic novel of the F.W.W. *Her Privates We* (1930).

MANNING, Henry Edward (1808–92). British cardinal. Ed. at Harrow and Balliol, he left the Colonial Office for the Anglican Church, becoming in 1840 archdeacon of Chichester. In 1851 he was converted to Rome, founded in 1857 the congregation of the Oblates of St. Charles Borromeo, and in 1865 succeeded Wiseman as abp. of Westminster. An ardent defender of papal infallibility, he was created a cardinal in 1875, and crossed a polemical sword with Gladstone in *The Vatican Decrees* (1875).

MANOEL I (1469–1521). King of Portugal. He succeeded his uncle John II in 1495, and was known as 'the Fortunate', because his reign was distinguished by the discoveries by Portuguese navigators and the expansion of the Portuguese Empire.

MANOEL II (1889–1932). King of Portugal. He ascended the throne on the assassination of his father, Carlos I, in 1908; was driven out by a revolution in 1910, and lived in England.

MANOR. A type of estate which formed the basic economic unit under the feudal system in England. The M. lands consisted of the lord's demesne, the lands held by the free tenants and villeins, and the meadow and waste lands. Tenure of a M. carried with it the right to hold a manorial court, which dealt with petty offences and disputes.

MANRIQUE (mahnrē'ke), **Sebastião** (*c.* 1595–1669). Portuguese monk, who travelled throughout the East, pub. his *Travels* in 1649, and was murdered on a mission to London.

MANS (mon), **Le.** Car-racing circuit on which is held an annual 24 hr. endurance race (estab. 1923) for G.T. (grand touring) and sports cars, and their prototypes. Pop. (1968) 143,246.

MANSARD or **Mansart** (monsahr'), **François** (1598–1666). French architect. B. at Paris, he gave his name to the 'Mansard Roof', designed to give additional space to the upper storey of a building.

MANSBRIDGE, Albert (1876–1952). British educationalist. B. at Gloucester, he founded the Workers' Educational Assen. in 1903.

MANSFIELD, Katherine. Pseudonym of New Zealand writer Kathleen Beauchamp (1890–1923). B. nr. Wellington, New Zealand, she was ed. in London, to which she returned after a 2 year visit home, where she pub. her earliest stories. Her first marriage to George Bowden in 1909 was immediately disastrous, but a second to John Middleton Murry in 1913 endured. Her delicate artistry emerges not only in her vols. of short stories, e.g. *In a German Pension* (1911), *Bliss* (1920) and *The Garden Party* (1923), but in her *Letters* and *Journal*. She d. of tuberculosis.

MANSFIELD. English market town (bor.) in Notts, on the Maun, nr. a coalfield. The chief industries are the manufacture of textiles, boots, machinery, etc. Pop. (1961) 53,222.

MANSLAUGHTER. In both English and U.S. law the killing of a human being either (1) in a sudden affray, or (2) as an outcome of culpable negligence. Charges under the first head are closely allied to murder, and will only be M. if there is no evidence of premeditation.

MANSURA (mahnsŏŏ'rah). Town in Lower Egypt,

the cap. of Dakahlia prov. It lies on the Damietta branch of the Nile, and has a flourishing cotton industry. M. was founded c. 1220; St. Louis IX, king of France, was imprisoned in the fortress, 1250. Pop. (1960) 152,000.

MANTEGNA (mahntän'yah), **Andrea** (1431–1506). Italian painter of the Paduan school. B. at Vicenza, he came under the influence of Donatello, Uccello, Filippo Lippi, etc., and was the most important painter of the early Renaissance. His masterpiece is the 'Triumph of Caesar' (Hampton Court). The 'Madonna with John the Baptist and the Magdalen' (National Gallery), is one of the best preserved of all his works.

MANTES-LA-JOLIE. Town in the Seine-et-Oise dept. of N. France, on the Seine. William the Conqueror d. as a result of a fall from his horse at M. Pop. (1962) 19,227.

MANTIS. Insect of the family Mantidae. The praying mantis (*M. religiosa*) of S. Europe adopts an attitude characteristic of devotion while waiting for its prey – flies, grasshoppers, and caterpillars. The eggs are laid in September and hatch early in the following summer. Ms. have the power of changing their coloration in accordance with their surroundings. There are over 800 species.

MA'NTŪA. Cap. town of M. prov., Lombardy, Italy, standing on an island of a lagoon of the Mincio, 25 m. S.W. of Verona. Among the chief buildings are the cathedral, founded in the 12th cent., the church of St. Andrea, and Gothic palaces. Virgil was b. near M., which dates from Roman times. The industries incl. tanning and brewing. Pop. (1961) 32,687.

MANU (ma'noo). In Hindu mythology, the founder of the human race. His preservation by Brahma from a deluge has caused him to be compared with Noah.

MANUTIUS (manū'shius), **Aldus** (1450–1515). The most famous Italian Renaissance printer. He estab. his printing press in Venice in 1490, and was the first to print Greek books. He made Venice the chief publishing centre of Europe.

MANX. The Gaelic language of the Isle of Man. Known only from the 17th cent., it is nearer akin to Scottish Gaelic than to Irish, and has been considerably influenced by English. Manx-speakers have declined: nearly 5,000 in 1900 and c.150 in 1961. Original literature in M. consists mainly of ballads and carols (known as *carvels*). Bishop Phillips' Manx translation of the Prayer Book appeared in 1610, and the Bible was completed in 1775.

MANZŌ'NI, Alessandro, count (1785–1873). Italian writer, author of tragedies but best remembered for his historical love story *I Promessi Sposi* (1825–7).

MAORI (mowri). The aboriginal population of New Zealand. They came from E. Polynesia, according to tradition, c. 1350, and are tall and muscular, flat-nosed, with brown skin and black hair. At the time of the coming of Europeans they numbered c. 150,000. Their civilization was still neolithic, but they had acquired great skill in wood and stone carving and in weaving patterned cloth; women did most of the agricultural work, whilst the chief occupation of the men was warfare. The M. religion incl. some sort of belief in a supreme god, but was concerned mainly with placation of spirits who punished breach of taboo. The chief of a clan was held sacred. Not long ago in decline, their numbers are once more increasing, 200,000 (1967), and although they are full citizens of New Zealand there is some slight 'colour' difficulty.

MAO TSE-TUNG (mow tze-toong') (1893–). Chinese Communist statesman. B. in Hunan, he was a founder member of the Chinese Communist Party and became Chief of Publicity and Propaganda under Sun Yat-sen, but, sacked by Chiang Kai-shek, he became leader of the Communists in 1927. He led the 'long march' to Shensi in 1935 and secured an alliance

with the Kuomintang in 1936, but civil war resumed in 1945 and in 1949 M. became Chairman of the People's Govt. In 1954 he was re-elected after the adoption of China's new constitution, but resigned in 1958, though remaining chairman of the Party, and during the Cultural Revolution he inspired from 1966 the 'little red book' of thoughts from his writings was

its handbook. His 3rd wife, former actress Chiang Ching, played a leading role in the movement.

MAPLE. A deciduous tree of the genus *Acer* with opposite, stalked, palmately lobed leaves and green flowers, followed by two-winged samaras. There are about 115 species, chiefly in north temperate regions. The only British species is *A. campestre*; but *A. pseudoplatanus*, the sycamore or great maple, is naturalized. The sugar maple, *A. saccharatum*, is the N. American species, and the chief source of maple sugar.

MAQUIS (makē). Name of the scrub in Corsica, among which bandits sought cover. The term Maquis was popularly applied to members of the French Underground Movement (*Forces Françaises de l'Intérieur*) during the German occupation of 1940–5.

MARACAIBO (mahrahki'bō). Seaport dating from the 16th cent., chief town of Zulia, Venezuela, on the channel connecting Lake M. with the Gulf of Venezuela, seat of the Univ. of Zulia. M. makes cement, soap, chocolate, bricks, and has saw mills and tanneries; but its chief importance, from 1918, has been as a port for the export of petroleum; other exports are coffee, cacao, sugar, and hardwoods. Pop. (1967) 500,000.

MARACAIBO. Rising from the sea like 'trees' in some Martian landscape, the oil derricks of Lake Maracaibo are a symbol of Venezuela's mineral wealth.
Courtesy of the Venezuelan Embassy

MARA'S. Turkish town in the Taurus Mountains, cap. of M. il, about 55 m. N. of the Syrian frontier. An agricultural centre, it is on the site of an ancient Hittite settlement. Pop. (1965) 63,300.

MARAT (mahrah'), **Jean Paul** (1743–93). French revolutionary. B. in Switzerland, he practised medicine in Paris. After the outbreak of the Revolution he edited *L'Ami du peuple*, later renamed *Journal de la République Française*. He was the idol of the Paris working-classes, and in 1792 was elected to the National Convention and carried on a long struggle against the Girondins. He helped to bring about their overthrow in May 1793, but in July he was assassinated by the Girondin enthusiast, Charlotte Corday.

MA'RATHON. A plain in Greece on the E. coast of Attica, 25 m. N.E. of Athens, where in 490 B.C. the Greeks defeated the Persian invaders in one of the decisive battles of the world. The news of the victory was conveyed to Athens by a runner, sometimes called Pheidippides, who fell dead as he entered the city. His performance is commemorated by a *Marathon Race* of 26 m. 385 yds., first included in the Olympic Games at Athens in 1896.

MARBLE. A limestone of pleasant colour and pattern, which takes and retains a good polish. Most marbles were originally limestones of ordinary character which have undergone recrystallization under the action of metamorphism, e.g. the Carrara marbles. An exception is Purbeck M., which is clayey limestone containing abundant remains of the freshwater gastropoda Paludina.

MARBURG. W. German town in Hessen, on the Lahn, 50 m. N. of Frankfurt-am-Main, seat of a univ. founded in 1527 as a centre of Protestant teaching; Luther and Zwingli disputed on religion at M. in 1529. Manufactures incl. chemicals, machinery, pottery. Pop. (1960) 45,000.

MARC, Franz (1880–1916). German artist. Closely associated with Kandinsky in preparing the Blue Rider Album in 1911, he repeatedly used the symbolism of animals, e.g. 'The Tower of the Blue Horses'. He was killed at Verdun.

MARBURG. Originally the seat of a landgrave, the Gothic castle dominates the hill on which the old town is built and now houses the archives of Hesse. In its Knights Hall (1277–1312) the famous conference between Luther and Zwingli on Transubstantiation took place in 1529. On the left is the Church of St. Mary.

Courtesy of the German Tourist Information Bureau

MARCANTŌ'NIO (Marcantonio Raimondi) (c. 1480–c. 1530). Italian engraver. B. at Bologna, he was celebrated for his engravings of the works of Raphael, Michelangelo, Dürer, etc.

MARCEAU (mahrsoh'), Marcel (1923–). French mime. B. at Strasbourg, he is the creator of the clown-harlequin 'Bip', and of mime sequences such as 'Youth, Maturity, Old Age and Death'. See PANTOMIME.

MARCH. English market town (U.D.) in the fen country of the Isle of Ely, 24 m. N. of Cambridge. Pop. (1961) 13,119.

MARCHAND (mahrshoń'), Jean Baptiste (1863–1934). French general and explorer. In 1898 he headed an expedition from the French Congo which occupied Fashoda on the White Nile. The subsequent arrival of British troops under Kitchener resulted in a crisis which nearly led to war between Britain and France.

MARCHES. The boundary areas of England with Wales, and England with Scotland. In the Middle Ages these troubled frontier regions were held by lords of the marches, sometimes called *marchiones* and later earls of March. The first earl of March of the Welsh M. was Roger de Mortimer (c. 1286–1330); of the Scottish M., Patrick Dunbar (d. 1285).

M. is also the name in English of a region of N.E. Italy covering the provinces of Ancona, Ascoli Piceno, Macerata, and Pesaro e Urbino (in Italian, Marche pron. mahr'kā). Area 9,691 sq. m.; pop. (1961) 1,347,234.

MARCŌ'NI, Guglielmo (1874–1937). Italian pioneer in the invention and development of wireless telegraphy. B. at Bologna, in 1895 he estab. wireless communication over more than a mile near Bologna. In 1896 he came to England, and conducted successful experiments on the roof of the Post Office building in London, on Salisbury Plain, and across Bristol Channel, and in 1897 the company that is now Marconi's Wireless Telegraph Co. Ltd. was formed. In 1898 M. successfully transmitted signals across the English Channel, and in 1901 estab. communication with St. John's, Newfoundland, from Poldhu in Cornwall, and in 1918 with Australia. M. was an Italian delegate to the Peace Conference in 1919, received the Nobel prize for physics in 1909, and was made a senator and in 1929 a marchese.

MARCUS AURE'LIUS ANTONI'NUS (A.D. 121–180). Roman emperor and Stoic philosopher. B. in Rome, he was adopted, at the same time as Lucius Aurelius Verus, by his uncle, the emperor Antoninus Pius, whom he succeeded in 161. He conceded an equal share in the rule to Lucius Verus (d. 169). M. A. spent much of his reign warring against the Germanic tribes, and d. in Pannonia, where he had gone to drive back the invading Marcomanni. Although one of the best of the Roman emperors, he persecuted the Christians for political reasons. M. A. is famous for his philosophic 'Meditations'.

MARDIN (mahrdēn'). Turkish town, cap. of M. il, 50 m. S.E. of Dijarbakir. Overlooked by the ruins of a fortified castle, it is a market for the produce of the il. – onions, cereals, tobacco, mohair, etc. Pop. (1965) 392,875.

MARDUK. Chief god of Babylonia. Originally an inferior spirit connected with water magic, he became associated with Babylon, and on the rise of that city to greatness the priesthood gave him the qualities of a sun-god, recognizing him as creator of the earth and man.

MARE'NGO. Italian village in Piedmont, where on 14 June 1800 Napoleon inflicted a crushing defeat on the Austrians.

MARGAI (mahr'gī), Sir Albert Michael (1911–). Sierra Leone statesman. Son of a merchant and descendant of a Mende warrior chief, he qualified as a chemist, and also as his country's first barrister. In 1964 he succeeded his brother Sir Milton M. (1896–1964) who had founded the People's Party in 1951 and been first P.M. of independent Sierra Leone from 1961. In 1967 Sir Albert's govt. was not decisively returned at the elections, following an attempt to introduce a one-party state, and in 1968 he went to the U.S.A.

MARGARET, St. (c. 1045–93). Queen of Scotland. The grand-dau. of Edmund Ironside, she went to Scotland after the Norman Conquest, and soon after m. Malcolm III. Through her influence the Lowlands, hitherto purely Celtic, became largely Anglicized. The marriage of her dau. Matilda to Henry I united the Norman and English royal houses. She was canonized in 1251 in recognition of her benefactions to the Church.

MARGARET (1283–90). Known as the 'Maid of Norway', she was the dau. of Eric II, king of Norway, and Princess Margaret of Scotland. On the death of her grandfather, Alexander III, she became queen of Scotland, but d. in the Orkneys on the voyage to her kingdom.

MARGARET OF ANJOU (oṅzhōō') (1430–82). Queen of England. The dau. of René of Anjou, she was m. to Henry VI in 1445. After the outbreak of the Wars of the Roses in 1455, she acted as the leader of the Lancastrians, her one object being to secure the succession of her son, Edward (b. 1453). She withdrew to France in 1463, but returned during the Lancastrian reaction of 1471, only to be defeated and captured at Tewkesbury, where her son was killed. After 5 years' imprisonment she was allowed in 1476 to return to France, where she d. in poverty.

MARGARET (ROSE) (1930–). Princess of the

U.K. B. at Glamis Castle on 21 Aug. 1930, she is the younger dau. of George VI (q.v.). Religious and constitutional problems arose when it seemed possible that she might marry Group Captain Peter Townsend, former court equerry, who had been divorced, and in 1955 she announced her decision not to marry him. In 1960 she m. Anthony Armstrong-Jones, later created Lord Snowdon (q.v.), and is officially styled H.R.H. The Princess Margaret, Countess of Snowdon. They have a son, David, visct. Linley (1961–), and a dau., Lady Sarah Armstrong-Jones (1964–).

MARGATE. Famous English seaside resort (bor.) in Kent, a member of the Cinque Port of Dover. It has long promenades and fine sands. Pop. (1961) 45,708.

MARGRAVE. German title (equivalent of marquess) for the 'counts of the March', who guarded the frontier regions of the empire from Charlemagne's time. Later it was -borne by other territorial princes. The most important were the margraves of Austria and of Brandenburg.

MARGUERITE. Popular name for the *Chrysanthemum frutescens*, of the botanical family Compositae. It is a shrubby perennial bearing white ray-florets surrounding a yellow centre.

MARGUERITE D'ANGOULÊME (dongoolām') (1492–1549). Queen of Navarre, French poet, and author of the *Heptaméron*, an imitation of Boccaccio. The sister of Francis I, she was b. in Angoulême, and m. as her 2nd husband Henri d'Albret, king of Navarre, in 1527.

MARI (marē'). An A.S.S.R. of the R.S.F.S.R., in the E. of European Russia. The Volga flows through the S.W. of M., some 60 per cent of which is forested. The chief industries are lumbering, woodworking, paper making, and others associated with timber; grain, flax, potatoes, and fruit are grown. Yoshkar-Ola is the cap. About half the inhabitants are of Mari stock, a people conquered by Russia in 1552. M. was made an autonomous region in 1920, an autonomous rep. in 1936. Area 8,900 sq. m.; pop. (1967) 653,000.

MARIANAS (mahrē-ah'nahz). Scattered group of islands and atolls in the N.W. Pacific. The largest, Guam (q.v.), was ceded by Spain to the U.S.A. in 1898. Spain sold the remainder to Germany in 1899 for £840,000, and these in 1919 were mandated to Japan which, against the terms of the mandate, fortified them; in 1947 they were placed under U.S. trusteeship. They produce rice, maize, sugar, tobacco, etc. Magellan discovered them in 1521. During the S.W.W., U.S. Marines in severe fighting re-captured Guam and secured control of the rest of the archipelago, 1944–5. Pop. (1967) 10, 980 (excl. Guam). *See* PACIFIC IS. TRUST TERR.

MARIANNE Islands. Another form of MARIANAS.

MARIANSKE LAZNE (mahr'ēanskā lahz'nye). Spa in Czechoslovakia, internationally famous before the S.W.W. under its German name Marienbad. The water of its springs, which contains Glauber salts, has been used medicinally since the 16th cent. Pop. (1967) 8,500.

MARIA THERESA (1717–80). Austrian empress. The dau. of the Emperor Charles VI, she m. her cousin Francis of Lorraine in 1736, and succeeded her father as archduchess of Austria and queen of Hungary and Bohemia in 1740. Her claim was challenged by Charles of Bavaria, who was elected emperor in 1742, while Frederick of Prussia occupied Silesia. The War of the Austrian Succession followed, in which Austria was allied with Britain, and Prussia with France; when it ended in 1748, M. T. retained her heritage, except that Frederick kept Silesia, while her husband had succeeded Charles as emperor in 1745. Intent on recovering Silesia, she formed an alliance with France and Russia against Prussia; the

Seven Years War of 1756–63, which resulted, exhausted Europe and left the territorial position as before. After 1763 she pursued a consistently peaceful policy, concentrating on internal reforms; although her methods were despotic, she fostered education, codified the laws, and abolished torture. She also expelled the Jesuits. In these measures she was assisted by her son, Joseph II, who became emperor in 1765, and succeeded her in the Habsburg domains.

MARIBOR (mah'rēbor). Yugoslav town and resort in Slovenia, on the Drave, seat of a bishopric with a 16th cent. cathedral and some industry (boots and shoes, railway rolling stock are among products). M. dates from Roman times. Pop. (1961) 82,387.

MARIE (1875–1938). Queen of Rumania. The dau. of the duke of Edinburgh, 2nd son of Queen Victoria of the U.K., she m. Prince Ferdinand of Rumania in 1893, who was king 1922–7. She wrote a number of literary works, notably *Story of My Life* (1934–5). Her son Carol became king of Rumania, and her daus., Elisabeth and Marie, queens of Greece and Yugoslavia respectively.

MARIE ANTOINETTE (1755–93). Queen of France. The dau. of the Emperor Francis I and Maria Theresa, she m. in 1770 the dauphin, who 4 years later became king as Louis XVI. She forfeited her popularity by her frivolity, her extravagance, and her meddling in politics, often in Austrian interests. After the outbreak of the revolution in 1789 she exercised all her influence over her weak-willed husband to prevent concessions: she opposed Mirabeau's plans for a constitutional settlement, and brought about the unsuccessful flight to Varennes, which discredited the monarchy. She now relied on foreign intervention and when war with Austria began in 1792 betrayed the French plans to the enemy. In Oct. 1793 she was tried for treason and guillotined.

MARIE DE FRANCE (mahrē' de frons) (fl. c. 1150–1215). French poet. B. probably in Normandy, she is thought to have been the natural dau. of Geoffrey Plantagenet and half-sister to Henry II, and to have been abbess of Shaftesbury (1181–1215). She was the author of *Lais*, or verse tales, and *Ysopet* a collection of fables.

MARIE DE' MEDICI (mā'dēchē) (1573–1642). Queen of France. The dau. of the grand duke of Tuscany, she m. Henry IV of France in 1600, and after his murder in 1610 acted as regent for her son, Louis XIII. She left the government to her favourites, the Concinis, until in 1617 Louis seized power and put them to death. Reconciled to him in 1619, she lost all influence after the coming to power in 1624 of Richelieu.

MARIE LOUISE (1791–1847). Second wife of Napoleon I. The dau. of Francis I of Austria, she was m. to Napoleon in 1810 after his divorce from Josephine, and bore him a son, the king of Rome, in 1811. On his fall she returned to Austria. Granted the duchy of Parma in 1815, she proved a comparatively liberal ruler.

MARIENBAD. Ger. name of MARIANSKE LAZNE.

MARIETTE (mahryet'), **Auguste Ferdinand François** (1821–81). French Egyptologist. Beginning excavations in Egypt in 1850, he made many important discoveries, incl. the 'temple' between the feet of the Sphinx. He was the founder of the Egyptian Museum, Cairo, and Director of the Service des Antiquités from 1858.

MARIGOLD. Several plants of the Compositae family, espec. the pot M. (*Calendula officinalis*) in cultivation both in single and double forms for some 300 years, and the African M. (*Tagetes erecta*) and French M. (*T. patula*), both actually natives of Mexico.

MARIJUANA. *See* DRUGS and HEMP.

MARIN, John (1870–1953). American artist. B. in N.J., he was an architect's draughtsman until in 1899 he began to study art, living in Paris 1905–11. His finest works are his water-colour landscapes incl. studies of the Maine coast.

MARINES. Fighting men equally at home on land or sea, and because of their dual role of top calibre and esprit de corps. The Corps of Royal Marines (instituted 1664) is primarily a military force trained also for fighting at sea, providing commando units, landing craft, crews, frogmen, etc. The United States Marine Corps (estab. 1775) is primarily a naval force trained for fighting on land.

MARINE'TTI, Filippo Tommaso (1876–1944). Italian author. B. at Alexandria, in 1909 he pub. the first manifesto of 'Futurism'; he illustrated his theories in *Mafarka le futuriste* (1910), plays, and a vol. on theatrical practice (1916). He recorded his F.W.W. experiences in *Otto anime in una bomba* (1919), and welcomed Mussolini with *Futurismo e fascismo* (1924).

MARI'NI, Marino (1901–). Italian sculptor. He studied in Florence and Paris, and became prof. of sculpture at Monza (1929–40) and at the Brera Academy, Milan, from 1940. Influenced by primitive sculpture, he works in an elongated, elegant style, and is particularly well known for his bronze horses and riders and dancers.

MARIO (mah'rĕ-ō), **Giuseppe** (1810–83). Italian tenor. He made his début in Paris in 1838, appearing in London in 1839. He toured widely, and in 1844 m. the soprano, Giulia Grisi (c. 1811–69).

MARIONETTE. Type of puppet (q.v.), a jointed figure controlled from above by wires or strings. They early reached a high artistic level in Burma and Ceylon and at the courts of Italian princes in the 16th–18th cents., and Haydn wrote an operetta such as *Dido* for the Esterhazy M. theatre. In the 20th cent. there has been a revival, especially in television, and Ms. have reverted to being a popular rather than aristocratic entertainment.

MARIS. A family of Dutch painters of the 19th cent. JACOB M. (1837–99), was a genre and figure painter, b. at The Hague. His brother, MATTHEW M. (1839–1917), was a genre and landscape painter who worked in London, and another brother, WILLIAM M. (1844–1910), was a landscape painter.

MARISTS. Members of the R.C. congregation of Mary founded in France in 1816. The priests and lay members of the congregation conduct educational work, nurse the sick, and engage in missionary activities, particularly in N.Z. and the Pacific Is.

MARITAIN (mahretaṅ'), **Jacques** (1882–). French philosopher. Originally an exponent of Bergson, e.g. *La Philosophie bergsonienne* (1914), he later became the best-known of the Neo-Thomists applying to contemporary problems the creative techniques of medieval times, e.g. *Introduction à la Philosophie* (1920). Best of his later works is *Distinguer pour unir ou Les degrés du Savoir* (1932). He was prof. of philosophy at Princeton univ. 1948–52.

MARITIME TRUST. Equivalent of the National Trust (q.v.) in the world of ships, estab. 1970 to discover, repair and preserve vessels of historic scientific or technical interest: pres. the Duke of Edinburgh.

MARIUPOL. *See* ZHDANOV.

MĀ'RIUS, Gaius (155–86 B.C.). Roman military commander and statesman. B. near Arpinum, he served in Spain in 134, and in the Jugurthine War 109–106. He was elected consul 7 times, the first time in 107. He defeated the Cimbri and the Teutones 102–101. M. tried to deprive Sulla of the command in the East against Mithraidates, and as a result civil war broke out in 88. Sulla marched on Rome, and M. fled to Africa, but later Cinna held Rome for M. Cinna and M. created a reign of terror in Rome until the death of the latter.

MARIVAUX (mahrĕvō'), **Pierre Carlet de Chamblain de** (1688–1763). French novelist and dramatist.

He was b. in Paris, and his polished, sophisticated comedies, such as *Le Jeu de l'amour et du hasard*, *Les fausses confidences*, and *L'Épreuve*, gave the word *marivaudage* to the French language.

MARJORAM. Aromatic herbs of the Labiatae family. Wild M. (*Origanum vulgare*) is found both in Europe and Asia and has become naturalized n America: the culinary sweet M. is *Majorana hortensis*.

MARK. Christian apostle and evangelist, whose name is given to the 2nd Gospel. His first name was John, and his mother, Mary, was one of the first Christians in Jerusalem. He was a cousin of Barnabas, and accompanied Barnabas and Paul on their first missionary journey. Later, he was a fellow worker with Paul in Rome, and he seems to have attached himself to Peter as his interpreter after Paul's death. According to tradition he was the founder of the Christian Church in Alexandria, and Jerome says that he d. and was buried there.

The Gospel according to St. Mark is held to have been written A.D. 65–70, and used by the authors of the 1st and 3rd Gospels.

MARK ANTONY (Marcus Antonius) (83–30 B.C.). Roman statesman and soldier. He served under Julius Caesar in the later campaign in Gaul. As tribune he defended Caesar's interests at Rome during the civil war, and when consul (44 B.C.), tried to secure for Caesar the title of king. After Caesar's assassination, A. with Octavius and Lepidus formed a triumvirate, and in 42 B.C. A. assisted in the defeat of Brutus and Cassius at Philippi. During 41 B.C. A. toured the eastern provinces, where he met Cleopatra, with whom he fell in love. When the 3 triumvirs divided the empire between them, A. secured Egypt for his share. In 32 B.C. the Senate declared war on Cleopatra. Defeated by Octavius at the naval battle of Actium (31), A. committed suicide.

MARKHAM, Edwin Charles (1852–1940). American poet. B. in Oregon City, he became a schoolteacher. His vol. of poems, the democratic *Man with a Hoe* (1899), was followed by *Lincoln* (1901), etc.

MARKHOR (mahr'kor). Large wild goat (*Capra alconeri*), with spirally twisted horns and long shaggy coat. It is found in the Himalayas.

MARKIEVICZ, Constance Georgina, countess (d. 1927). Irish nationalist, *née* Gore Booth, who m. the Polish count M. in 1900. A prominent figure in the Irish national movement, she was a member both of the Irish Volunteers and Connolly's Citizen Army. She fought in the Easter Rebellion of 1916, and was sentenced to death; the sentence was commuted, and she was released in 1917. She was elected to parliament at Westminster as a Sinn Féin candidate in 1918, so becoming the first British woman M.P., but did not take her seat. From 1923 she was a member of the Dáil.

MARKOVA (markō'fa), **Dame Alicia.** Name assumed by British dancer, Lilian Alicia Marks (1910–). At 14 she was chosen by Diaghilev (q.v.) as ballerina in the D. Ballet Co., with which she danced until D.'s death in 1929, just before she was to dance her first major role. On returning to England, she devoted herself to the development of English ballet, joining in 1930 Marie Rambert's Ballet Club, and becoming in 1932 the first resident ballerina of the Vic-Wells Ballet. In 1935 she and Anton Dolin (q.v.), with whom she had a long partnership, formed their own company, and 1938–41 she danced with the new Ballet Russe de Monte Carlo, and until 1944 with Ballet Theatre U.S.A. On her return to Britain in 1949, she helped launch the Festival Ballet, to which she gave its name, and was its prima ballerina until 1952. She subsequently danced as guest artist with companies all over the world. The first English Prima Ballerina Assoluta in history, she was created D.B.E. in 1963, and in the same year became Director of the Metropolitan Opera Ballet of N.Y. Possessing an ethereal grace and lightness of movement, she is always associated with the great classical ballets in which she made her name, e.g. *Swan Lake, Casse-Noisette,* and, in particular, *Giselle.*

MARKS, Simon, 1st baron M. of Broughton (1888–1964). British chain-store magnate. The son of Polish immigrant Michael M., who started with Yorkshire-man Tom Spencer a number of 'penny bazaars' in 1887, he entered the business in 1907 and built up a chain of more than 200 stores. Selling specially manufactured goods of high quality, he achieved a democratic revolution in dress for men and women.

MARL. A sedimentary rock sometimes called a clayey limestone, and incl. various types of calcareous clays and argillaceous limestones. Ms. are commonly laid down in freshwater lakes, and are usually soft, earthy, and of a white, grey, or brownish colour. They are used in cement making and as a top dressing for farmland.

MARLBOROUGH, John Churchill, 1st duke of (1650–1722). English soldier. The son of an impoverished Cavalier, he rose rapidly in the army through the favour of James, duke of York, and received a barony in 1685. At the revolution of 1688 he deserted James for William of Orange, who rewarded him with the earldom of M., yet in 1692 he fell into disfavour for intriguing with the Jacobites. He had m. Sarah Jennings (1660–1744), the friend of the Princess Anne, and after Anne's accession was created a duke. In the War of the Spanish Succession, he commanded the English and Dutch forces. His victory at Blenheim in 1704 saved Vienna from the French, and was followed by further victories at Ramillies (1706), Oudenarde (1708), and Malplaquet (1709). The return of the Tories to power in 1710, and a quarrel between Anne and the duchess, resulted in the dismissal of M. in 1711, and his flight to Holland to escape prosecution for corruption. He returned in 1714. The magnificent mansion and estate of Blenheim, in Oxon, were granted in recognition of his services. His London home, *M. House* (1709), was designed by Sir Christopher Wren: it was afterwards leased by Queen Anne, and later provided a home for Queen Adelaide, Edward VII (as prince of Wales), and Queen Mary. In 1959 it was lent to the govt. by Elizabeth II to provide a Commonwealth meeting place in London (opened 1962). *See also* CHURCHILL, SIR WINSTON.

MARLBOROUGH. English market town (bor.) in Wilts, 76 m. W. of London. It has a 16th cent. grammar school, and M. Coll., opened in 1843, is a great public school. Pop. (1961) 4,843.

MARLOWE, Christopher (1564–93). English poet and dramatist. B. in Canterbury, the son of a shoemaker, he left Cambridge for London *c.* 1587, where he joined the earl of Nottingham's theatrical company. His 4 great plays, written 1587–93, are *Tamburlaine,* which gave blank verse the freedom of the English stage; *Dr. Faustus; The Jew of Malta;* and *Edward II.* His poems incl. versions of Ovid's *Amores,* and of Musaeus' 'Hero and Leander'. In 1593 he was involved, owing to statements made by Thomas Kyd under torture, in charges of atheism. A warrant had been issued for his arrest, when he was killed by Ingram Frisar in a Deptford tavern, apparently in a brawl over a reckoning, but possibly owing to political intrigue.

MA'RMARA. Small inland sea separating Turkey in Europe from Turkey in Asia, and connected through the Bosporus with the Black Sea, and through the Dardanelles with the Aegean. Length 170 m., breadth up to 50 m.

MARMONTEL (mahrmoñte'l), **Jean François** (1723–99). French novelist and dramatist. He wrote tragedies and libretti, and contributed to the *Encyclopédie;* in 1758 he obtained control of the journal *Le Mercure,* in which his *Contes Moraux* (1761) appeared. Other works incl. *Bélisaire* (1767), and *Les Incas*

(1777). He was appointed historiographer of France (1771), secretary to the Académie (1783), and Professor of History at the Lycée (1786), but retired in 1792 to write his *Mémoires d'un père* (1804).

MA'RMOSET. Small monkey in the family Hapalidae found in S. and Central America. Most species have characteristic tufted ears and handsome tail, and some are full-grown when the body is only 7 in. long. Best-known is the common M. or ouistiti (*Hapale jacchus*) of Brazil, often kept there as a pet.

MARMOT. A burrowing rodent of the genus *Marmotta,* living in snowy regions, extending from the Alps to the Himalayas, and also in N. America. *M. marmotta* is the typical M. of the Central European Alps. Ms. live in colonies, make burrows, one to each family, and hibernate.

American Marmot

MARNE (mahrn). French river which rises in the plateau of Langres and joins the Seine at Charenton near Paris. It gives its name to the depts. of Marne, Haute Marne, Seine-et-Marne and Val de Marne; and to 2 battles of the F.W.W. (q.v.).

MARONITES. Christian sect probably deriving mainly from refugee Monothelites of the 7th cent. They were subsequently united with the R.C. Church, and number *c.* 400,000 in the Lebanon and Syria with an equal no. scattered overseas in S. Europe, and the Americas.

MAROT (mahrō'), **Clément** (*c.* 1496–1544). French poet. B. at Cahors, in 1524 he accompanied Francis I to Italy, and was taken prisoner at Pavia, but was soon released, and by 1528 was a salaried member of the royal household. Suspected of heresy, he fled to Turin, where he d. His graceful, witty style has been a model for all later writers of light verse.

MARPLES, Ernest (1907–). British Cons. politician. Entering parliament in 1945, he was Postmaster General 1957–9, displaying a flair for organization and publicity, and as Min. of Transport (1959–64) introduced various measures to cope with London traffic, planned many new motorways, and was responsible for the Transport Act (1962) and for carrying out the drastic reorganization of the railways recommended by the Beeching Report, 1963.

MARPRELATE CONTROVERSY. Name given to a pamphleteering attack on the clergy of the C. of E. made in 1588 and 1589 by a Puritan writer or writers, who took the pseudonym of Martin Marprelate. The pamphlets were printed by John Penry, a Welsh Puritan. His press was seized, and he was charged with inciting rebellion and hanged in 1593.

MARQUAND, John Phillips (1893–1960). American writer. Originally famous for a series of stories featuring the Japanese detective 'Mr. Moto', he made a serious reputation with his gently satirical novels of Bostonian society – *The Late George Apley* (1937) and *H. M. Pulham, Esq.* (1941).

MARQUESAS (mahrkā'sahs). A mountainous archipelago in the central Pacific Ocean, extending over some 250 m., with a total area of 490 sq. m. and pop. (1962) 4,837. The 2 largest islands are Nuku-hiva and Hiva Oa. Mendaña discovered the southern M. in 1595 and named them in honour of his patron, the marquess of Cañete, Span. viceroy of Peru. Ingraham, an American, discovered the northern group in June 1791 and named these the Washington Islands; a month later this group was discovered by Marchand, a Frenchman, who named it Islands of the Revolution. Their native inhabitants are Polynesians. France annexed the islands in 1842 and used them as a penal colony until 1865.

MARQUESS or Marquis. Title and rank of a nobleman which in the British peerage ranks below a duke and above an earl. The first English M. was created in 1385, but the lords of the Scottish and Welsh 'marches' were known as *marchiones* before this date. *See* MARCHES. The premier English marquessate is that of Winchester, and the wife of a M. is a marchioness.

MARQUET (mahrkā'), **Albert** (1875–1947). French landscape painter. A friend of Matisse, he was associated with *Les Fauves*, but has his own individualistic style. His best-known paintings are of the quaysides and the river banks of the Seine.

MARQUETTE (mahrket'), **Jacques** (1637–75). French Jesuit missionary and explorer. Going to Canada in 1666, he explored the upper lakes of the St. Lawrence, and in 1673 made a remarkable voyage down the Mississippi.

MARQUIS, Donald Robert Perry (1878–1937). American author. B. in Illinois, he is chiefly known for his humorous creations, *Old Soak* (1921), portraying a hard-drinking comic, and *Archy and Mehitabel* (1927), the typewritten verse adventures of the cockroach, Archie.

MARQUISES. French form of MARQUESAS.

MARRA′KESH. City in Morocco, *c.* 130 m. S. of Casablanca, with which it is connected by railway. An important trade centre, it is the southern capital. It dates from 1062, but has a large modern quarter built since the French occupied M. in 1912. Pop. (1960) 242,000.

MARRAM-GRASS. A coarse perennial grass (*Ammophila arundinacea*) which flourishes on sandy patches and, because of its tough and creeping rootstocks, is largely employed to hold coast dunes in place, particularly in Holland.

MARRA′NOS. The descendants of the Span. Jews converted by force to Christianity in the 14th and 15th cents., who secretly preserved their adherence to Judaism and carried out Jewish rites. Under the Spanish Inquisition thousands were burned at the stake. M. refugees in the 17th cent. founded the Jewish communities in Amsterdam, London, etc.

MARRIAGE. For the community primarily the means of ensuring its own continuation under stable conditions for the care of the young, and because of its importance hedged round by conventions, customs, and religious and civil laws both in 'civilized' and 'primitive' communities. The modern tendency is to freedom of choice in a partner, but modified by age-limits, below which no M. is valid, e.g. in the U.K. for both sexes 16 and in the U.S.A. varying according to state, for example Georgia and Iowa allow girls to marry at 14; by degrees of consanguinity or other special relationships within which M. is either forbidden or enjoined; by economic factors such as ability to pay a father-in-law the required bride price, as in Africa; by rank, caste or religious differences; by medical requirements such as the blood tests of some states of the U.S.A.; by the necessity of obtaining parental, family or tribal consent; by the negotiations of a marriage broker in property-conscious and conventional societies, e.g. in Japan or formerly among Jewish communities; or colour, e.g. M. is illegal between European and non-European in S. Africa, and until 1967 between white and coloured in some Southern, and white and Mongolian in some Western, states of the U.S.A.

M. may be polyandrous or polygynous (qq.v.), but in modern times the emancipation of women in the W. has led to greater emphasis on M. as a personal relationship with monogamy increasingly the rule, e.g. even in Moslem countries such as Pakistan where the right of a man to have 4 wives has been much restricted. Women also approach equality in M. in other ways, e.g. married women were enabled to hold property in their own name in England by 1882; in California community property laws entail the equal division of all assets between the partners on divorce; and in England a woman may be required to support a husband unable to support himself, and may be awarded custody of children. Stress on the personal aspect, however, leads to easier divorce (q.v.) notably in the U.S.A. and increasingly in the U.K. so that re-marriage is more and more frequent for both sexes within the lifetime of the original partner. At the same time the community reacts towards maintaining the stability of the family unit, e.g. the Soviet Union has gradually modified (1926, 1936, and 1944) the original extreme freedom of divorce granted in 1917 at the Revolution, and the reluctance to legalize divorce by consent in England until the Divorce Act (1969).

In England Ms. can be effected according to the rites of the C. of E. or those of other faiths, or in a superintendent registrar's office, but in most European countries civil registration of M., as well as (or instead of) a religious ceremony is obligatory, but common-law Ms. (i.e. an agreement to marry followed by co-habitation as man and wife) are still recognized in e.g. Scotland, some states of the U.S.A. and the U.S.S.R. As a step to international agreement on M. law the U.N. in 1962 adopted a convention on consent to M., minimum age for M., and registration.

MARROW. In zoology, the soft vascular tissue in the central cavities of bones, composed largely of fat and white corpuscles. Another name for it is medulla.

In botany, Ms. are twining plants of the family Cucurbitaceae, producing large pulpy fruits used as a vegetable, and for making jams and preserves. There are bush Ms. and creeping or climbing Ms.

MARRYAT, Frederick (1792–1848). British naval officer and novelist. B. in London, he entered the R.N. in 1806 and rose to the rank of captain, but resigned in 1830 after the success of his 1st novel, *Frank Mildmay*. He wrote a number of popular adventure stories, incl. *Peter Simple* (1834), *Mr. Midshipman Easy*, and a series of boys' books, such as *Masterman Ready, Settlers in Canada*, and *Children of the New Forest* (1847).

MARS. The Roman god of war. The month of March is named after him.

MARS. The fourth planet in order of distance from the Sun. It has an average distance from the Sun of

141,500,000 m., and may approach the Earth to within 34,000,000 m., so that it is then closer than any planet apart from Venus; at such times it is extremely brilliant, and is always easy to recognize because of its strong red colour. It is, however, much smaller than Venus or the Earth; its diameter is 4,200 m., and its mass only 0·11 of that of the Earth.

MARS. Taken with a 36 inch refractor, this photograph shows the dark areas clearly, together with the southern polar cap.
Courtesy of Lick Observatory, Univ. of California.

In one way M. resembles the Earth. It has a rotation period of 24 hours 37 minutes, though its revolution period or 'year' amounts to 687 days.

Mariner VI and *Mariner VII* (U.S.A. 1969) photographed the surface from a height of 2,100 m., and it was found to be in large part heavily cratered, like the Moon, one crater being 24 m. wide. There are also plains, mountain ranges up to 6,000 ft., and a strange area of 470,000 sq. m. in the lower right quadrant is broken up in a way resembling nothing on Earth. The poles are covered by carbon dioxide ice, incl. perhaps some water ice. Neither probe recorded any of the so-called 'canals', straight streaks crossing the desert and dark regions, but photos taken by *Mariner IV* (1965) at 6,100 m. had shown what appeared to be ridges of natural formation. The atmosphere is almost wholly carbon dioxide with no nitrogen or oxygen, and is incapable of supporting life as we know it, although the dark patches, visible with a small telescope when M. is well placed, had been thought due to primitive vegetation. The temperature is low, ranging from a daytime maximum of 16°C to a night minimum of —67°C. An unmanned soft landing is planned 1973, and a manned landing before the end of the century.

The planet has 2 satellites. Phobos and Deimos, discovered by A. Hall in 1877; both are extremely small, with diameters of about 10 and 5 m. respectively.

MARSALA (mahrsah'lah). Italian seaport in the W. of Sicily, exporting the sweet, white M. wine. M. was a Carthaginian settlement. Its cathedral is dedicated to St. Thomas of Canterbury. Pop. (1960) 78,500.

MARSEILLAISE (mahrseyāz'), **La.** The French national anthem. The words and music were composed in April 1792 by Rouget de Lisle, an army officer stationed at Strasbourg, and were brought to Paris in Aug. by the volunteers from Marseilles, who led the storming of the Tuileries.

MARSEILLE (mahrsāy'). The chief seaport of France, and cap. of the dept. of Bouches-du-Rhône, on the Golfe du Lion, Mediterranean Sea, connected with the Rhône by a canal. Much of M.'s old quarter was destroyed by the Germans in 1943. M. is surrounded by hills, and offshore are several islands, incl. Île d'If with its famous castle. Principal buildings incl. the 19th cent. cathedral, the pilgrimage church of Notre Dame de la Garde, also 19th cent., the 13th cent. church of St. Victor, the 17th cent. town hall and the 18th cent. Grand Théâtre.

M. was founded by mariners of Phocaea in Asia Minor about 600 B.C. Under the Romans it was a free city. After suffering from several invasions, M. was repopulated, and for several cents. was a free city. In 1481 it was included in France. Its modern prosperity was enhanced by the French conquest of Algeria and the opening of the Suez Canal. There are many industries, incl. soap making, engineering, and shipbuilding. Pop. (1968) 889,029.

MARSH, Dame Ngaio (1899–). N.Z. novelist. Originally on the stage, and still with a lively interest in the theatre as a repertory producer, she went to England in 1928 and worked as an interior decorator. Her first detective novel *A Man Lay Dead* (1934) has had many successors. Created D.B.E. 1966.

MARSHAL. A title given in certain countries to a high officer of state, though originally it meant one who tends horses, in particular a farrier. The Earl Marshal (q.v.), is a high officer of state in England. The corresponding officer in Scotland was the Earl Marischal. The rank of a Marshal of the R.A.F. corresponds to that of Admiral of the Fleet in the navy and Field Marshal (q.v.) in the army. In the French Army the highest officers bear the designation of Marshal of France.

MARSHALL, Benjamin (1767–1835). British sporting artist. B. in Leics, he excelled in painting horses, and was a pioneer in sporting journalism. His best-known pictures incl. 'The Death of a Fox', 'Mameluke' and 'The Malcolm Arabian'.

MARSHALL, George Catlett (1880–1959). American soldier and statesman. B. in Pennsylvania, he was commissioned in 1901, served in the F.W.W., and in 1939 became chief of staff with the rank of general. On resigning in Nov. 1945 he became ambassador to China, attempting to secure a coalition between the Nationalist and Communist forces against Japan. He succeeded Byrnes as Sec. of State (1947–9), and as Sec. of Defence Sept. 1950–Sept. 1951 (a post never normally held by a soldier), backed Truman's recall of MacArthur from Korea. The Marshall Plan, initiated by him in a speech at Harvard in June 1947

and officially known as the European Recovery Programme, was in fact the work of a State Dept. group led by Dean Acheson. It set the pattern for the large-scale foreign aid by the U.S. which was subsequently widened in scope to cover the entire non-Communist world.

MARSHALL, John (1755–1835). American jurist. B. in Virginia, as chief justice of the Supreme Court 1801–35, he laid down interpretations of the U.S. constitution in a series of important decisions, which have since become universally accepted.

MARSHALL, John Ross (1912–). N.Z. Nat. Party statesman. Noted for his negotiations of a free trade agreement with Australia, he was deputy to Holyoake (q.v.) in both premierships and succeeded him 1972.

MARSHALLS. Two chains of islands in the W. Pacific Ocean, comprising Radak and the Ralik groups, with 13 and 11 islands respectively. Occupied by German traders in 1888, they were made a German colony in 1906; in 1919 they were placed under Japanese mandate, in 1947 under U.S. trusteeship. They export phosphates and copra. Two of the M. are Bikini (q.v.) and Eniwetok, a permanent testing ground for atomic weapons from 1947 (its 137 inhabitants were moved to Ujelong, another of the group). Pop. (1967) 18,925. *See* PACIFIC IS. TRUST TERR.

MARSH GAS. *See* METHANE.

MARSH MARIGOLD. Plant (*Caltha palustris*) of the buttercup family Ranunculaceae, known as the kingcup in England and as the cowslip in the U.S.A. The 5-sepalled yellow flowers are brilliant in moist sheltered spots in March.

MARSH MARIGOLD

MARSI'LIUS OF PADUA (1270–1342). Italian scholar. B. at Padua, he studied and taught at Paris, and in 1324 collaborated with John of Jandun in writing the *Defensor pacis*, a plea for the subordination of the ecclesiastical to the secular power. He played a part in the establishment of the Roman republic in 1328, and was made archbishop of Milan.

MARSTON MOOR. Battle fought in the Civil War on 2 July 1644 on M.M., 7 m. W. of York. The Royalists, under Prince Rupert and the duke of Newcastle, were completely defeated by the Parliamentarians and Scots, under Cromwell and Lord Leven. Lord Fairfax, on the right of the Parliamentarians, was routed; but Cromwell's cavalry charges were decisive.

MARSUPIA'LIA (Gk. *mar supion*, little purse or bag). An order of Mammalia, in which the female has a pouch in which she carries her young for some considerable time after birth. The chief members are the kangaroo, wombat, opossum, Tasmanian wolf, bandicoot, and wallaby.

MARTELLO TOWERS. Towers built along the coast, especially in Sussex and Kent, in 1804, as a defence against the threatened French invasion. The name is derived from a tower on Cape Mortella, Corsica, which was captured by the British with great difficulty in 1794, and was taken as a model. They are round towers of solid masonry sometimes moated, with a flat roof for mounted guns.

MARTEN. Small carnivorous mammals belonging to the Mustelidae family, genus *Mustela*. They live in wild and rocky regions in the warmer parts of the northern hemisphere, and are hunted for their fur. The pine-marten (*M. martes*), has long, brown fur,

MARTEN

and is about 2–2½ ft. long. It is found in Britain. The stone or beech M. (*M. foina*) is lighter in colour. The sable (*M. zibellina*) lives in E. Siberia, and provides the most valued fur. The largest is the pekan (*M. pennanti*), with black fur and reaching a length of 4 ft., of N. America.

MARTHA'S VINE-YARD. Island (20 m. long by 10 m. wide) off the coast of Cape Cod, Mass., where once lived the whaling captains whose houses are now owned by the wealthy as summer homes. Edward Kennedy and a girl companion, Mary Jo Kopechne, were involved in a car crash off nearby Chappaquiddick Is. in July 1969; the girl was drowned.

MARTIAL (mahr′shial) **(Marcus Valerius Martialis)** (c. A.D. 41–c. 104). Latin epigrammatist. B. in Bilbilis, Spain, he came to Rome in 64, where he lived by his literary and social gifts, retiring to his native place in 98. His poetry reflects contemporary Roman life, and although licentious, is unrivalled in correctness of diction, versification, and form.

MARTIAL LAW. As distinguished from military law, i.e. the law governing the conduct of the armed forces, whether within the realm or elsewhere, in peace or in war, the legal position as regards M.L. is difficult of definition in England. In effect, when war, rebellion, etc., are in progress in an area the military authorities are recognized as having powers to maintain order by summary means. In the United States M.L. is usually proclaimed by the pres. or the gov. of a state in areas of the country where the civil authorities have been rendered unable to act, or to act with safety. M.L., though neither in the constitution nor laid down in statutes, has frequently been used in the U.S., e.g. in Hawaii 1941–4 after the bombing of Pearl Harbor.

MARTIN DU GARD (mahrtiń′ dü gahr), **Roger** (1881–1958). French novelist. B. at Neuilly, of bourgeois stock, he realistically recorded the way of life of his class in the 8 vol. *Les Thibault* (1922–40). He was awarded a Nobel prize in 1937.

MARTIN, St. (c. 316–400). Bishop of Tours. B. in Pannonia, a soldier by profession, he was converted to Christianity, left the army, and lived for 10 years as a recluse. After being elected bishop of Tours c. 371, he worked for the extinction of idolatry and the extension of monasticism in France. He is usually represented as dividing his cloak with a beggar.

MARTIN V. Pope, 1417–31. A member of the Roman family of Colonna, he was elected during the Council of Constance, and ended the Great Schism.

MARTIN, Archer John Porter (1910–). British biochemist. He was staff member 1948–52, and head of the physical chem. div. at the Nat. Inst. of Med. Research, London, 1952–9, when he became director of Abbotsbury Laboratories Ltd. A specialist in a refined method of chemical analysis – chromatography (q.v.) – he shared a Nobel prize in 1952 with his colleague R. Synge.

MARTIN, (Basil) Kingsley (1897–1969). British author. Son of a Unitarian minister, he was ed. at Magdalene Coll., Cambridge, lectured in political science at the

KINGSLEY MARTIN
Caricature by David Low.

L.S.E. 1923–7 and after 4 years with the *Guardian*, ed. the *New Statesman* 1931–60, making it the voice of the Left. A hard-hitting controversialist, respected as much by opponents as supporters, he published such lively books as *The Triumph of Lord Palmerston* (1924, rev. 1963), a study of public opinion in England before the Crimean War, *The Press the Public Wants* (1947), *The Crown and the Establishment* (1962), and *Father Figures* (1966), and *Editor* (1968), vols. of autobiography.

MARTIN, John (1789–1854). British painter of landscapes and religious subjects. B. in Northumberland, he settled in London in 1806, and first exhibited at the R.A. in 1812. His pictures, such as 'Belshazzar's Feast' and 'The Deluge', show an exaggerated sense of drama. His brother, **Jonathan M.** (1782–1838), became a convert to Methodism, and followed up his warnings to the established clergy of judgment to come by setting fire to York Minster in 1829. He was condemned to an asylum.

MARTIN, Paul (1903–). Canadian Liberal statesman and lawyer. Entering parl. in 1938, he was Sec. of State 1945–6, Min. of Health 1946–7, Sec. of State for External Affairs 1963–8, and Min. without Portfolio from 1968.

MARTIN, Richard (1754–1834). Irish landowner, lawyer and humanitarian, known as 'Humanity Martin'. He founded the Royal Society for Prevention of Cruelty to Animals in 1824.

MARTIN, Sir Theodore (1816–1909). British man-of-letters. Under the pseudonym of 'Bon Gaultier', he collaborated with W. E. Aytoun in a collection of contemporary parodies, *Bon Gaultier Ballads*, in 1845.

MARTIN, Violet Florence (1862–1915). Irish novelist known under the pseudonym 'Martin Ross'. B. in Galway, she collaborated with her cousin, Edith Œ. Somerville, in novels of Anglo-Irish provincial life, e.g. *Some Experiences of an Irish R.M.* (1899), and *In Mr. Knox's Country*.

MARTIN. Several genera of birds, allied to the swallow, in the family Hirundinidae. The European house M. (*Delichon urbica*), a summer migrant from Africa, is blue-black above and white below, distinguished from the swallow by its shorter, less forked tail. The cup-like mud nest is usually constructed under the eaves of buildings. Best-known of other species are the brownish European sand M. (*Riparia riparia*), which tunnels 2–3 ft. to make a nest in sandy banks, also a migrant from Africa, and the common purple M. of N. America (*Progne subis*), a handsome steely-blue bird which often nests in hollow trees.

MARTINEAU (mahr′tinō), **Harriet** (1802–76). British author. B. at Norwich, she is mainly remembered for her children's stories, e.g. 'The Settlers at Home' and 'Feats on the Fiord', which appeared under the title of *The Playfellow* (1841).

MARTINET (mahrtineh′), **Jean** (d. 1762). French inspector-gen. of infantry under Louis XIV, whose constant drilling brought the army to a high degree of efficiency – hence the use of his name to mean a strict disciplinarian.

MARTÍNEZ RUIZ, José. *See* AZORÍN.

MARTÍNEZ SIERRA (marté′neth sĕ-er′rah), **Gregorio** (1881–1947). Spanish novelist and dramatist. B. in Madrid, he wrote more than 40 plays, in many of which he collaborated with his wife, Maria M. S.; they include *Canción de Cuña* (1911), and the ecclesiastical *El Reino de Dios* (1915).

MARTI′NI, Simone (c. 1284–1344). Italian painter

MARTINI. Dated 1342, 'Christ Found by his Parents In the Temple' is a late work which shows superbly the artist's gift for delicate portrayal of dramatic effect.
Courtesy of Walker Art Gallery, Liverpool

greatest of the Sienese school, whose influence was widespread. B. in Siena, he was a pupil of Duccio, but excelling his master in his development of line and colour. He painted a portrait of Laura for Petrarch and is commemorated by the poet in 2 sonnets. He d. at Avignon.

MARTINIQUE (mahr-tēnēk'). French island in the W. Indies (Lesser Antilles), an overseas dept. of France from 1 Jan. 1947, after being a colony from 1635. The cap. and chief commercial centre is Fort-de-France (pop. 90,000). Sugar, cocoa, rum, etc., are produced. M. was discovered by Spanish navigators in 1493. It is of volcanic origin and has several active volcanoes. *See* PELÉE, MONT. Area 420 sq. m.; pop. (1965) 325,000.

MARTINMAS. In the Christian calendar, the feast of St. Martin (11 Nov.). Fairs were frequently held on it, at which farm-workers were hired. In the Middle Ages it was also the day on which cattle were slaughtered and salted for winter consumption.

MARTI'NO, St. (1579–1639). Peruvian monk. The illegitimate son of a Spanish grandee and a freed Negro slave, he joined the Dominicans as a lay brother at 15, and estab. homes for Lima's abandoned children, caring also for stray animals. He became the first R.C. 'half-caste' saint in 1962.

MARTI'NSON, Harry (1904–). Swedish writer. B. in S. Sweden and orphaned at 7, he ran away to sea when only 14, travelling widely for 8 years as a sailor, and, at intervals, as a tramp. Forced by ill-health to leave the sea, he achieved success with his novel of tramp life, *The Road*, and, with *Aniara* (1956) a space-fiction epic poem which was adapted as an opera.

MARTYR (from the Gk. for 'witness'). In the Christian Church, one who voluntarily suffers death for refusing to renounce the Christian faith or a part thereof. The first recorded Christian M. was St. Stephen, who was killed in Jerusalem shortly after Christ's ascension.

MARVELL, Andrew (1621–78). English metaphysical poet and satirist. B. in Yorks, while tutor to the dau. of Lord Fairfax 1650–3 he wrote many of his finest nature poems, and was assistant to Milton as Latin Sec. to the Council of State 1657–60. He was M.P. for Hull from 1659, and devoted his last years mainly to verse satire and controversial prose works.

MARX (mahrks), **Karl Heinrich** (1818–83). German philosopher and Socialist. B. at Trèves, the son of a Jewish lawyer, he studied at Bonn and Berlin, and during 1842–3 edited the *Rheinische Zeitung* until its suppression. In 1844 began his life-long collaboration with Engels (q.v.), with whom he developed the Marxist philosophy, first formulated in their joint works, *The Holy Family* (1844), and *German Ideology* (1846), and M.'s *Poverty of Philosophy* (1847). Both joined the Communist League, a German refugee organization, and in 1847–8 they prepared its programme, 'The Communist Manifesto'. During the 1848 revolution M. ed. the *Neue Rheinische Zeitung*, until in 1849 he was expelled from Prussia.

He then settled in London where he wrote *Class Struggles in France* (1849), *The 18th Brumaire of Louis Bonaparte* (1852), *Critique of Political Economy* (1859), and his monumental work *Das Kapital* (1867: *Capital*). In 1864 the International Working Men's Association

was formed, whose policy M., as a member of the general council, largely controlled, and on behalf of which he wrote his defence of the Paris Commune, *The Civil War in France* (1871). Although he showed extraordinary tact in holding together its diverse elements, it was disrupted by the intrigues of the anarchists, and in 1872 collapsed. The 2nd and 3rd vols. of *Capital* were ed. from his notes by Engels, and pub. posthumously. M. was buried at Highgate.

MARX BROTHERS. Team of American film comedians, composed of 'Groucho' (Julius) (1895–), 'Harpo' (Arthur) (1893–1964), 'Chico' (Leonard) M. (1891–1961), and 'Zeppo' (Herbert) M. (1901–), who founded the Zeppo-M. agency in 1935 and appeared only in earlier films. Their best-known films incl. *A Night at the Opera*.

MARXISM. The philosophical system, also known as dialectical materialism or scientific Socialism, founded by Marx and Engels, and developed by Plekhanov, Lenin and Stalin. The main sources of Marx's thought were classical German philosophy, especially that of Hegel; English political economy, notably the works of Adam Smith and Ricardo; and the 'Utopian Socialism' of Saint-Simon, Fourier and Owen. M. is a complete and consistent philosophy, which has profoundly influenced current views on science, history, and literary criticism, even among non-Marxists. Modern British Marxist writers include C. Caudwell in philosophy, R. P. Dutt in politics, M. Dobb in economics, J. B. S. Haldane, J. D. Bernal, and H. Levy in science, V. G. Childe and C. Hill in history, and R. Fox, G. Thomson, B. Farrington and J. Lindsay in literary studies. *See* DIALECTICAL MATERIALISM; also COMMUNISM.

MARY (Blessed Virgin Mary). Mother of Jesus Christ. She was traditionally the miraculous child of Joachim and Anna in their old age; she m. Joseph, the carpenter of Nazareth, and accompanied him to Bethlehem. The question of her perpetual virginity (the 'brethren of Jesus' being presumed as the sons of Joseph by a former marriage) has occasioned much controversy, but is recognized as a dogma of the R.C. Church, as is her Immaculate Conception and bodily Assumption. Veneration of M. as a mediator has played an increasing part in worship since the Council of Ephesus, A.D. 431: Pope Paul proclaimed her 'Mother of the Church' 1964. *See* illus. p. 712.

MARY (1867–1953). Queen consort of George V (q.v.). The dau. of the duke and duchess of Teck, the latter a grand-dau. of George II, she became engaged in 1891 to the duke of Clarence, eldest son of the Prince of Wales (later Edward VII).

MARY I

After his death in 1892, she in 1893 m. his br. George, duke of York, who succeeded to the throne in 1910, and was crowned with him in 1911. She was noted for her gracious dignity, and was a renowned art connoisseur and needlewoman.

MARY I (1516–58). Queen of England. The dau. of Henry VIII by Catherine of Aragon, she was b. at Greenwich. When Edward VI d. in 1553, she secured the crown without difficulty in spite of the conspiracy to substitute Lady Jane Grey. In 1554 she m. Philip II of Spain, and as a devout Catholic obtained the restoration of papal supremacy. Although naturally humane, she sanctioned the persecution of Protestants which won her the nickname of 'Bloody M.'

MARY II (1662–94). Queen of England. The elder dau. of James II, she was m. in 1677 to her cousin, William of Orange. After the 1688 revolution she

MARY. 'The Immaculate Conception', a fervently devout interpretation by Velasquez.

accepted the crown jointly with William. During his absences abroad she took charge of the government, and showed courage and resource when invasion seemed possible in 1690 and 1692.

MARY, Queen of Scots (1542–87). She succeeded her father, James V, in infancy, and as a child was sent to France, where she m. the dauphin, later Francis II. After his death she returned in 1561 to Scotland, which, during her absence, had accepted Protestantism. She m. her cousin, the earl of Darnley, in 1565, but they soon quarrelled, and Darnley took part in the murder of M.'s secretary, Rizzio. In 1567 he was assassinated as the result of a conspiracy formed by the earl of Bothwell, possibly with M.'s connivance, and shortly after Bothwell carried M. off and m. her. A rebellion followed; defeated at Carberry Hill, M. abdicated and was imprisoned. She escaped in 1568, raised an army, and after its defeat at Langside fled to England. Elizabeth held her a prisoner, while the R.Cs., who regarded M. as rightful queen of England, formed many conspiracies to place her on the throne. The discovery that she was involved in Babington's plot led to her trial and execution at Fotheringay Castle in 1587.

MARY (1457–82). Duchess of Burgundy. The dau. of Charles the Bold, she m. Maximilian of Austria in 1477, thus bringing the Low Countries into the possession of the Habsburgs. and ultimately of Spain.

MARY (mah'rë). Town in Turkmen S.S.R., on the Murgab. It dates from the 19th cent. and lies 18 m. W. of the ancient city of Merv (q.v.). It makes textiles, carpets, and metal goods and has food factories. Pop. (1967) 58,000.

MARYBOROUGH. Australian coastal town in S.E. Queensland, near coal- and gold-mining fields. It has iron and steel foundries. Pop. (1966) 19,647.

MARYBOROUGH. PORT LAOIGHIS.

MARYLAND. An Atlantic state of U.S.A., between Pennsylvania and Virginia. It has a much-indented coastline, and is penetrated by Chesapeake Bay, a wide arm of the Atlantic. In the W. are wooded mountains and coal is mined; the centre is undulating wheatland, and on the coastal plains there are tobacco plantations, fruit orchards, etc. Fish is abundant, and oysters are very plentiful. The cap. is Annapolis; the largest city is Baltimore. The first settlers in M., 1634, were Roman Catholics, following the grant to Lord Baltimore in 1632 of a royal charter to establish a colony N. of the Potomac. They called their first township St. Mary's; it remained the cap. until displaced by Annapolis, 1694. M. was one of the 13 original states forming the Union. Area 10,577 sq. m.; pop. (1970) 3,922,399.

MARY MAGDALENE. Probably from Magdala, she is said in the Gospels to have had 7 demons cast out from her. She was present at the Crucifixion, and met the risen Jesus.

MARY OF MODENA (1658–1718). Queen consort of England and Scotland. The dau. of the duke of Modena, she m. James, duke of York, later James II, in 1673. The birth of her son, James, in 1688, which was widely believed to be fraudulent, gave the signal for the Revolution, and M. fled to France.

MASACCIO (mahsah'chō). Name given to the Florentine painter Tomaso di Giovanni di Simone Guidi (1401–28). B. nr. Florence, where, with his teacher Masolino di Panicale (c. 1384–1447), he executed his most famous work, the decoration of Santa Maria del Carmine. He was one of the first to apply the laws of perspective. had a good knowledge of anatomy and made effective use of light and shade.

MASA'DA. Rock fortress 1,300 ft. above the W. shore of the Dead Sea, Israel. Beseiged by the Romans A.D.72, its population of 953 committed mass suicide: the site was excavated 1963–5, incl. the palace of Herod.

MASAI (mahsī'). African people remarkable for their fine physique. Originally warriors and nomadic breeders of humped zebu cattle, on which they relied for their diet of milk, meat and blood, they disdained agriculture but are gradually adopting a more settled life. Their territory is divided between Tanganyika and Kenya, and at the time of independence in 1963 they unsuccessfully demanded its total inclusion in either one country or the other. Neither Negro nor Bantu, they speak a Hamitic language.

MASARYK (maz'erik), **Thomas Garrigue** (1850–1937). Czech statesman. B. of a humble Moravian family, he was apprenticed to a locksmith, but later studied at Leipzig and Vienna, and was a prof. at Prague univ. 1882–1911. On the outbreak of the F.W.W., he took the Allied side, and became a lecturer on Slavonic history and sociology at King's Coll., London. Always a champion of national minorities, he directed the Czech revolutionary movement, founding with Beneš and Stefanik the Czechoslovak National Council, and in 1918 was elected 1st pres. of the newly formed Czechoslovak Republic. He was thrice re-elected, but resigned in 1935 in favour of Beneš. His son **Jan Garrigue M.** (1886–1948) entered the Czech diplomatic service in 1918, and was Min. to Britain 1925–38. In 1940 he became For. Min. to the exiled govt. in London and continued to hold the post on its return to Prague in 1945, but when reorganization came following Communist pressure in Feb. 1948, he allegedly committed suicide. For 20 years no reference was allowed to be made to the Masaryks, but in the liberalisation of 1968 tribute was paid, and an official investigation into Jan M.'s death began.

MASCAGNI (mahskahn'yë), **Pietro** (1863–1945). Italian composer. B. at Leghorn, he became famous as the composer of the one-act opera *Cavalleria Rusticana*, first produced in Rome in 1890.

MASCARA'. Algerian wine trade centre, after which the cosmetic M. is named, 60 m. S.E. of Oran. It was the H.Q. of Abd-el-Kader (c. 1807–83) who fought the French invasion of Algeria 1830-47, M. being captured 1841. Pop. (1960) 45,000.

MASEFIELD, John (1878–1967). Brit. poet. B. at Ledbury, Herefordshire, he went to sea, and while in the U.S.A. worked as a barman in a New York saloon. Returning to England, he joined the *Manchester Guardian* before settling in London. He attracted notice by such vols. of poetry as *Salt Water Ballads* (1902), but fame came with the verse narrative of a drunkard's conversion *The Everlasting Mercy* (1911), with its forcefully colloquial language. Later were the Chaucerian *Reynard the Fox* (1919), and novels such as *Sard Harker* (1924) and *Badon Parchments* (1947); and he essayed drama in *Tragedy of Nan* and *Pompey the Great*. He was appointed Poet Laureate in 1930, and in 1935 was awarded the O.M.

MĀ'SER (Acronym for Microwave Amplification by Stimulated Emission of Radiation). A high-frequency amplifier or oscillator dependent on the quantum properties of electrons. By inverting the populations of a pair of electron spin energy levels (i.e. by making the upper level more densely populated than the lower one) the resonance absorption at a frequency corresponding to the energy difference can be changed to emission; an M. results from suitable coupling of this radiation to a microwave cavity or travelling wave structure. The population inversion can be achieved by beam focusing, as in a two-level ammonia gas M., or pumping at a different frequency between another pair of levels, as in a solid-state three-level M. This latter can be tuned magnetically and operates at liquid helium temperatures ($-269°C$); it is the most sensitive amplifier known.

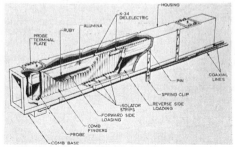

MASER. An L-band travelling wave maser operating at a frequency of about 1,420 Mc/s, which may be used for receiving weak signals from interstellar hydrogen in space. The signal enters through a small coaxial line, and travels about 250 times slower than the velocity of light along the copper comb-type structure from l.to r., where it is amplified 3,000 times by the ruby material and subsequently led out of the other coaxial line. *Courtesy of Bell Telephone Laboratories*

The two-level M. was first suggested in 1954 by C. H. Townes at Columbia univ. and independently the same year by Basov and Prokhorov in the U.S.S.R. The principle of the three-level M. was envisaged by Bloembergen in 1956 at Harvard and Bell Telephone Laboratories embodied it in a cavity M. in the same year and in a travelling wave M. in 1958. The principle has since been extended to other parts of the electromagnetic spectrum. (*See* LASER.) The ammonia M. is used as a frequency standard oscillator (*see* CLOCKS) and the three-level M. as a receiver for satellite communications and radio astronomy.

MASERU (maz'erōō). Cap. of Lesotho, S. Africa, on the Caledon r.; it is a trading centre and there is a univ. (1964) at Roma, 30 m. N. Pop. (1967) 10,000.

MASHŌ'NALAND. The E. part of Rhodesia, occupied by the Mashona tribes. It was granted to the British South Africa Company in 1889, and occupied 1890. The company ruled it until 1923 when it came within the self-governing colony of Southern Rhodesia. Here are the ruins of Zimbabwe (q.v.).

MASKELYNE (mas'kelin), **Nevil** (1732–1811). British Astronomer Royal from 1765, who devised such instruments as the prismatic micrometer, and was founder-editor of the *Nautical Almanac* from 1766. His scheme to measure the earth's density was put into practice in 1774.

MASON, Alfred Edward Woodley (1865–1948). British novelist and playwright. Originally an actor, he pub. his first novel, *A Romance of Wastdale*, in 1895, and won a great reputation with *The Four Feathers* (1902), a tale of the Sudan. One of the first authors to write detective stories with convincing characters, motivation, atmosphere, etc., he also created the detective Hanaud, who appears in *At the Villa Rose* (1910), *House of the Arrow* (1924), and *Prisoner in the Opal* (1929). Later novels incl. *Fire over England* (1936).

MASON AND DIXON LINE. In U.S.A., the boundary line between Maryland and Pennsylvania (lat. 39° 43′ 26·3″ N.), named after M. and D., English astronomers who surveyed it 1763-7. It became popularly regarded as dividing the slave states from the free before the Civil War, and generally the N. from the South.

MASQUE (mahsk). Form of amateur dramatic entertainment introduced into England from Italy during the reign of Henry VIII. It reached perfection in the Stuart period with the partnership of Inigo Jones and Ben Jonson. Based on a fairy or mythological theme, the plot was overshadowed by the elements of music, dancing, costume, and scenic design. The masked performers were drawn from the court nobility.

MASS. In physics, the quantity of matter in a body. The British unit of M. is the pound, i.e. the quantity of matter in a standard platinum cylinder preserved at the standards office at the Board of Trade; in the c.g.s. system it is the gramme, now defined as one-thousandth of the International Prototype Kilogram, which is a cylinder of platinum-iridium. M. determines the acceleration produced in a body by a given force working upon it, the acceleration being inversely proportional to the M. of the body. The M. also determines the force exerted on a body by the gravitational attraction of the earth, although this attraction varies slightly from place to place. At a given place, however, equal M. experiences equal gravitational forces, which are known as the weights of the bodies. M. may, therefore, be compared by comparing their weights at the same place, as in a balance.

MASS. In the Christian Church, the Eucharist, also known as the Lord's Supper, or Holy Communion; since the Reformation, the use of the word has been practically confined to the R.C. Church, but it is in use amongst Anglo-Catholics. R.Cs. believe that the M. is a real offering in which the bread and wine are transubstantiated, i.e. are converted into the body and blood of Christ. Changes were made to 'popularize' its celebration following the Second Vatican Council, e.g. the priest was to face the congregation, and English and other vernaculars could be used instead of Latin. Anglo-Catholics believe that Christ is really present under the forms of bread and wine. Protestants maintain that Christ's sacrifice was made on Calvary, and that Holy Communion is a commemorative rite.

Low M. is said by the priest without music; at high M. the priest is assisted by deacon and subdeacon, and there is incense and music.

MASSACHUSETTS (masachoo'sets). One of the New England states of U.S.A., facing the Atlantic

MASSACHUSETTS. Incorporated in 1861, the Massachusetts Institute of Technology has made a significant contribution to America's leading role in this field in the twentieth century. It was here in 1962 that light bursts were transmitted to the moon, the reflections being received through a telescope system at M.I.T.'s Lincoln Laboratory at Lexington.
Courtesy of Massachusetts Institute of Technology.

Ocean and incl. the 2 large islands of Nantucket and Martha's Vineyard. The N. coast is very rocky. Inland the country rises gradually to the Berkshire hills. There are many lakes, and the chief rivers are the Merrimac and the Connecticut. Agriculture is still important, but M. is largely industrial, e.g. electronics and communications equipment, shoes, textiles, and machine tools. Building stone is quarried. The cod fisheries have been famed for centuries. The famous M.I.T. (M. Institute of Technology, 1861) is at Cambridge, Mass., seat also of the Univ. of Harvard (1636).

The Pilgrim Fathers were the first settlers, at Plymouth in 1620, and the narrow Puritan outlook was long predominant. It was one of the original 13 states of the Union. The cap. is Boston. Area 8,257 sq. m.; pop. (1970) 5,689,170.

MASSA'WA. Chief port of Ethiopia, in Eritrea, on the Red Sea, with a good harbour. Salt is produced and pearl fishing carried on. One of the hottest inhabited spots in the world, the temperature reaching 100°F (37·8°C) in May, it was held by the Italians 1885–1941. Pop. (est.) 30,000.

MASSÉNA (mahsänah'), **André** (1756–1817). Marshal of France. He served in the revolutionary wars, and under Napoleon was created a marshal of France in 1804, duke of Rivoli in 1808, and prince of Essling in 1809. He was in command in Spain 1810–11.

MASSENET (mahsnä'), **Jules Émile Frédéric** (1842–1912). French composer. B. near St. Étienne, he composed many operas, incl. *Hérodiade* (known in England as *Salomé*), *Manon* (1884), *Le Cid* (1885), and *Thaïs*; and also ballets, oratorios and orchestral suites, incl. *Scènes pittoresques.*

MASSEY, Sir Harrie Stewart Wilson (1908–). Australian physicist. Prof. of mathematics at Univ. Coll., London, 1938–50, he was on a special mission to Berkeley, California, 1943–5, and in 1950 became Quain prof. of physics at London. He has written largely on atomic physics and was knighted in 1960.

MASSEY, Vincent (1887–1967). Canadian Liberal statesman. B. at Toronto of a wealthy family of agricultural-machinery manufacturers, he was ed. at the univs. of Toronto and Oxford. With the estate of his grandfather, Hart M. (1823–96), he helped estab. in 1918 the M. Foundation which has erected many educational buildings, incl. M. Coll., Univ. of Toronto; his father Chester D. M. becoming the Foundation's chairman, until he succeeded him in 1926. He entered politics in 1925 at the invitation of Mackenzie King, although they later often disagreed, and was Min. to the U.S.A. 1926–30, High Commissioner to the U.K. 1935–46, and was 1st Canadian-born Gov.-Gen. 1952–9. His brother, **Raymond M.** (1896–), an actor, became a U.S. citizen in 1944. He made his stage début in 1922, appeared in such films as *Things to Come* and *Mourning Becomes Electra*; and in the television 'Dr. Kildare' series played the revered Dr. Gillespie.

MASSEY, William Ferguson (1856–1925). N.Z. Conservative statesman. B. in Ireland, he entered the N.Z. parliament in 1894, was leader of the opposition in 1903, and was P.M. 1912–23.

MASSILLON (mahsēyoǹ'), **Jean Baptiste** (1663–1742). French Catholic cleric. Joining the Congregation of the Oratory at 18, he became bp. of Clermont in 1717, and was celebrated for his gently persuasive preaching.

MASSINE (mahsēn'), **Léonide** (1896–). Russian dancer and choreographer. He appeared with the Diaghilev Ballet Russe in Paris (1914–20), and subsequently danced leading roles with many major European and American companies, in particular the Ballet de Monte Carlo (1932–41), to which he was also Artistic Director and Choreographer; he was famous for his interpretations of character roles. His choreographic work incl. the first Cubist ballet *Parade* (1917); *The Three Cornered Hat* and *La Boutique Fantasque* (1919); *Le Sacré du Printemps* (1920); a ballet based on Berlioz' *Symphonie Fantastique* (1936); *Daphnis and Chloe'* (1944); and *Donald of the Burthens* (1951). He has appeared in films, e.g. *Red Shoes* (1948) and *Tales of Hoffmann* (1951).'

MA'SSINGER, Philip (1583–1640). English dramatist. B. at Salisbury, he settled in London *c.* 1606. His masterpiece is *A New Way to Pay Old Debts* (*c.* 1625), in which the usurer, Sir Giles Overreach, appears. He collaborated with Fletcher and Dekker, and some critics credit him with a share in Shakespeare's *Two Noble Kinsmen* and *Henry VIII.*

MASS OBSERVATION. Method of ascertaining general facts bearing on contemporary life, and also the name of a society founded in London in 1937 for this purpose, and employing a panel of observers and a number of trained investigators. *See* GALLUP and HARRISSON.

MASSON (mahsoǹ'), **André** (1896–). French artist. Joining the Surrealists in 1924, he often uses greenish-brown tints in his work, which strikes a philosophical note, and has been influential in the U.S.A.

MASSŌ'RAH. A collection of philological notes on the Hebrew text of the O.T. At first merely oral tradition, the M. was committed to writing in the Aramaic language at Tiberias in Palestine between the 6th and the 9th cents A.D.

MASS SPECTROMETER. An instrument in which positive ions (q.v.) of a material are separated by an electricmagnetic system which permits accurate measurement of the relative concentrations of the various ionic masses present, and detects non-radioactive isotopes.

MASSEY COLLEGE. Completed 1963 for the University of Toronto to the design of Ronald Thom.
Photo: Jack Marshall & Co. Ltd.

MASTER AND SERVANT. Although in Britain common law governs relations between employer and employee in circumstances not covered by special enactments, the latter cover an increasingly large field, e.g. the Wages Councils Act of 1945 which created councils empowered to fix wages and holidays in respect of certain trades and industries, the National Insurance (Industrial Injuries) Act of 1946, and the Contracts of Employment Act (1963) which requires a minimum period of notice to terminate employment for those employed for a qualifying period. In the U.S. wider scope is left for direct negotiation between employers and unions.

MASTER OF ST. BARTHOLOMEW (c. 1450–c. 1510). German artist of the Cologne school, named from his altar-piece of St. Bartholomew c. 1507, formerly in the Church of St. Columba, Cologne, but now in Munich. See GERMAN ART.

MASTER OF THE ROLLS. Title of an English judge ranking immediately below the Lord Chief Justice; he presides over the Court of Appeal, besides being Keeper of the Records and head of the Public Record Office.

MASTERS, Edgar Lee (1869–1950). American poet. B. in Kansas, he achieved fame with the free verse *Spoon River Anthology* (1915), in which the inhabitants of a small town tell of their frustrated lives. M. later pub. other collections of verse, novels and biographies.

MASTIFF. British dog, usually fawn, which was originally bred for sporting purposes. It has a large head, wide-set eyes, and broad muzzle.

MA'STODON. The primitive elephant, whose fossil remains have been discovered in all the continents except Australia, particularly in deposits of Pleistocene Age in the U.S.A. and Canada. It resembled the modern elephant, but was lower and longer; its teeth suggest that it lived on leaves in the primeval swamps and forests.

MASULIPATNA'M. Indian seaport in Andhra, at the mouth of the N. distributory of the r. Kistna. Its name means fish town, and it has a textile industry. Pop. (1961) 101,396.

MASU'RIAN LAKES. Lakes in Poland (former E. Prussia) which in 1914–15 were the scene of battles in which the Germans defeated the Russian invaders.

MATABELELAND (mahtahbā'le-). The western portion of Rhodesia, inhabited by Zulu tribes called Matabele. It consists of rich plains watered by tributaries of the Zambezi and Limpopo, with mineral wealth. The chief town is Bulawayo. M. was granted to the British S. Africa Company in 1889 and occupied in 1893 following attacks on white settlements in Mashonaland; in 1923 it was included in Southern Rhodesia.

MATA'DI. Chief port of Congo Republic (formerly Belgian Congo), on the Congo r. 70 m. from its mouth. It is linked by petroleum pipelines with Kinshasa and exports coffee, cacao, palm oil, cotton, copal, copper, etc. It has an airport. Pop. (1967) 47,000.

MATA'NZAS. Free port and cap. city of the prov. of M. on the N. coast of Cuba, chiefly engaged in the export of sugar. Pop. (1960) 82,700.

MATAPA'N. Southernmost cape of the mainland of Greece, off which, on 28 March 1941, during the S.W.W., a British fleet under Admiral Cunningham sank an Italian squadron.

MATCHES. A match is a small strip of wood (usually aspen) or taper tipped with combustible material for producing fire. Friction matches containing phosphorus were first made by Dr. Charles Sauria in France in 1831. A 'safety' match is one in which the oxidizing agent and the combustible body

are kept apart, the former being incorporated into the striking part, and the latter on to the side of the box.

MATÉ (mat'eh) (Paraguay tea). The dried leaves of the Brazilian holly (*Ilex paraguayensis*), an evergreen shrub akin to the common holly, that grows in Paraguay and Brazil. The Jesuits were the pioneers in its cultivation, and it is still sometimes called Jesuits' tea. After roasting, the leaves are powdered and the prepared infusion is drunk through a tube.

MATE'RA. Italian town, cap. of M. prov., in Basilicata region, seat of an archbishopric. Today some 18,000 people are still living in rock caves that have been inhabited from prehistoric times. M., an agricultural centre with flour mills, woollen factories, and potteries, has a 13th cent. cathedral. Pop. (1961) 38,233.

MATE'RIALISM. The philosophical theory that everything that exists can be explained in terms of matter and motion. Thus it excludes any form of supernaturalism, regarding 'matter' as the one ultimate fact and 'mind' as a product of matter. Like most other philosophical ideas, M. probably arose among the early Greek thinkers. The Stoics and the Epicureans were materialists, and so were the ancient Buddhists. Among modern materialists have been Hobbes, d'Holbach, Büchner, and Haeckel; while Hume, J. S. Mill, Huxley, and Herbert Spencer showed materialist tendencies.

MATHEMATICS. The science of spatial and numerical relations. Pure M. includes, as its main divisions, geometry, arithmetic, and algebra, the calculus, trigonometry, etc.; while mechanics, the mathematical theories of astronomy, electricity, optics, and thermodynamics, etc., are included in the heading of applied M.

Probably prehistoric man had learned to count at least up to the 10 represented by his fingers, and Chinese, Hindus, Babylonians, and Egyptians all evolved methods of counting and measuring which were of practical importance in their everyday life. The first theoretical mathematician is held to be Thales of Miletus (640–546 B.C.), to whom we owe the first theorems in plane geometry. His disciple, Pythagoras, established geometry as a recognized science among the Greeks, and the way that was prepared for the school of Alexandrian geometers that produced Euclid Archimedes, and others in the 4th and 3rd cents. B.C. Our present numerals are a Hindu-Arabic system which reached Europe about A.D. 1000. The Arab mathematicians of the Near East were the masters from whom European scholars learnt their science, and in the 15th cent. there began an uninterrupted development. Geometry was revivified by the invention of algebraical geometry by Descartes in 1637. Napier invented logarithms, and Newton and Leibniz the calculus. Lobachevski (1793–1856) rejected parallelism and developed non-Euclidean geometry, followed by Einstein in 20th cent.

MATILDA (1102–67). Queen of England. The dau. of Henry I, she m. the Emperor Henry V, and after his death Geoffrey Plantagenet, count of Anjou. Although the barons had recognized her as Henry's successor, on his death in 1135 they elected her cousin Stephen king. M. invaded England in 1139, and in 1141 was crowned queen. Civil war followed, until in 1153 Stephen was recognized as king, and M.'s son, Henry II, as his successor

MATISSE (mahtēs'), **Henri** (1869–1954). French artist. B. at Le Cateau Nord, after becoming an associate of the Salon, he was a member of the group known as *les Fauves*. One of the leading painters of the modern French school, he was essentially a designer or decorator, employing pure colour, distorting natural forms, and subordinating subject matter to pattern. In 1947–51 he designed and decorated a chapel for the Dominicans of Vence.

MATLOCK. English spa and market town (U.D.) in Derbyshire, 15 m. N. of Derby on the Derwent. It has famous warm springs. Pop. (1961) 18,486.

MATO GROSSO. State of Brazil, between Bolivia on the W. and the r. Araguaia on the E. There are extensive forests (the name means dense forest), from which maté, quebracho, rubber, timber, etc., are extracted; diamonds, silver, gold, lead and other minerals are found, sugar and tobacco are grown, cattle reared. The cap. is Cuiaba. Area 484,360 sq. m.; pop. (1967) 1,322,000.

MATRIARCHY (māt′riahrki). That form of social organization in which the mother and not the father is head of the family, and descent and relationship are reckoned through the female line. M., often associated with polyandry, has been found in certain parts of India, in the South Sea Islands, Central Africa, and among Indian tribes in N. America.

MATSYS (mahtsīs′) (also Massys or Metsys), **Quentin** (1466–1530). Flemish painter. B. at Louvain, he was influenced by the masters of the Italian Renaissance, and is famous for his sacred pictures, such as the triptych of the 'Pietà', in the Antwerp museum. He also painted portraits, incl. one of Erasmus, which he presented to Sir Thomas More.

MATTER. In physics, the 'stuff' out of which all objects outside the mind are considered to be composed. The history of science is largely taken up with accounts of theories of matter, ranging from the hard atoms of Democritus to the 'waves' of modern electrophysical theory. *See* ATOM, etc.

MATTERHORN. Famous mountain peak in the Alps on the Swiss-Italian border S.W. of Zermatt, first climbed by Edward Whymper in 1865. It is 14,782 ft. high. *See* illus. under ALPS.

MATTHEW. Christian apostle and evangelist, the traditional author of the 1st Gospel. He is usually identified with Levi, who was a tax-collector in the service of Herod Antipas, and was called by Christ to be a disciple as he sat at the receipt of custom by the Lake of Galilee.

MATTHEWS, Sir Stanley (1915–). British footballer. B. in Stoke-on-Trent, the son of a boxer, he played for his native city 1931–47, was then with Blackpool till 1961, returning to Stoke till 1965, and gen. manager of Port Vale 1965–8. The length of his career at international level, his deft ball control and the grace of his style, make him unique.

MATTHIAS CORVINUS (1440–90). Greatest of the kings of Hungary. The son of the great warrior, John Hunyadi, he was elected king in 1458. His aim of uniting Hungary, Austria. and Bohemia involved him in long wars with the emperor and the kings of Bohemia and Poland, during which, in 1485, he captured Vienna and made it his capital.

MATTINGLY, Garrett (1900–62). American historian. Prof. of European history at Columbia from 1948, he pub. *Catherine of Aragon* (1942) *Renaissance Diplomacy* (1955), and a fascinating study of *The Defeat of the Spanish Armada* (1959).

MATTO GROSSO. Older spelling of MATO GROSSO.

MAUBEUGE (mohbözh′). Fortified French town in the Nord dept., on the Sambre, and close to the Belgian frontier. In the F.W.W., it was captured and held by the Germans 1914–18; in the S.W.W., 1940–4. Pop. (1968) 32,028.

MAUDLING (mawd′-), **Reginald** (1917–). British Cons. politician. Called to the Bar in 1940, he entered Parl. in 1950, becoming Min. of Supply (1955–7), Paymaster-Gen. (1957–9), Pres. of the Board of Trade (1959–61), and Colonial Sec. (1961–2). In 1962–4 he was Chancellor of the Exchequer, and in 1965 was a close contender with Heath for the succession to Home as leader of the Cons. Party. In 1970–2 he was Home Sec. in the Heath govt.

MAUFE, Sir Edward (1883–). British architect. His works incl. the Anglican cathedral at Guildford,

REGINALD
MAUDLING
Photo: Walter Bird.

the Runnymede (q.v.) Memorial, and reconstruction of the war-shattered Gray's Inn and Middle Temple. He was knighted in 1954.

MAUGHAM (mawm), **(William) Somerset** (1874–1965). Brit. author. B. in Paris, he was ed. at King's School, Canterbury, and Heidelberg univ. before studying medicine at St. Thomas's Hospital. He practised for a year in the London slums, but after the success of his first novel *Liza of Lambeth* (1897) devoted himself to writing. *Of Human Bondage* (1915) has strong autobiographical elements, although whereas the hero was lame M.'s handicap had been a stammer; *The Moon and Sixpence* (1919), based on the life of Gauguin, was made into an opera by Gardner (q.v.), and *Cakes and Ale* (1930) satirizes Hardy and Walpole. Meanwhile M. had also been establishing a reputation as a fashionable dramatist, often having several plays running at the same time in the West End: *Lady Frederick* (1907), *The Circle* (1921) and *Our Betters* (1923). His cynical disillusion and urbanely ironic style is perhaps seen at its best in his short stories, e.g. *The Trembling of a Leaf* (1921) which incl. 'Rain', the story of an encounter between a missionary and a prostitute which has been dramatized and filmed. In the F.W.W. he was in Switzerland and Russia, where he was attempting to prevent the outbreak of revolution, as a secret agent – a role he again briefly played in the S.W.W. – and his adventures inspired the 'Ashenden' stories. His brother **Frederic Herbert**, 1st visct. M. (1866–1958), was a Judge of the High Court from 1928 and was raised to the peerage in 1939: and the latter's son **Robert**, 2nd visct. M. (1916–), is well known as an author under the name 'Robin M.', e.g. his novel *The Servant* (1948, filmed 1963).

MAU-MAU (mow mow). Terrorist secret society with Nationalist aims active in Kenya 1952–60. An offshoot of the Kikuyu Central Assocn., it was banned by the govt. at the outbreak of the S.W.W. Its members, chiefly of the Kikuyu tribe, were bound by oaths and ritual as repulsive as their methods of attack on white settlers, their cattle, and black Kenyans who opposed or refused to join them. In 1963 the independent Kenyan govt. offered free pardon to all M.-M. terrorists still outlawed.

MAUNDY THURSDAY. The Thursday before Easter. The name has been derived from the Lat. *mandatum*, the first word of the service chanted at the ceremony of washing the feet of pilgrims on that day, which was instituted in commemoration of Christ's washing the apostles' feet. The ceremony was observed in the Church from about the 4th cent., and performed by the English sovereigns until the time of William III. The rite of foot-washing was abandoned in 1754, but the Maundy money (M. pennies) is still presented in Westminster Abbey.

MAUPASSANT (mohpahson′), **Guy de** (1850–93). French author. B. in Normandy, he entered the Civil Service, and was encouraged in his literary ambitions by Flaubert. In 1880 he estab. his reputation with the short story *Boule de Suif*. His later works include many short stories and novels, such as *Une Vie* (1883), *Bel-ami* (1885), and *Fort comme la mort* (1889). Becoming insane in 1892, he d. in a Paris asylum.

MAURIAC (mohrē-ahk′). **François** (1885–1970). French novelist. B. in Bordeaux, he pub. his first important work *Le Baiser au lépreux* in 1922, which shows the conflict of an unhappy marriage. Similarly preoccupied with the irreconcilability of Christian practice and human nature are *Fleuve de feu* (1923), *Désert de l'amour* (1925), and *Thérèse Desqueyroux*. He was awarded a Nobel literary prize in 1952.

MAURICE, (John) Frederick Denison (1805–72). Anglican churchman. Son of a Unitarian minister, he was ordained in the C. of E. in 1834, but in 1853 was deprived of his professorships in English history and literature and divinity at King's Coll., London, following the publication of his *Theological Essays* attacking the doctrine of eternal punishment. He founded with Kingsley the Christian Socialist movement and promoted popular education. In 1866 he became prof. of moral philosophy at Cambridge.

MAURISTS. A congregation of French R.C. monks, belonging to the Benedictine order, estab. in 1621 at the Benedictine monastery of St. Maur-sur-Loire. Subsequently its chief house was in Paris, and there the M. fathers carried on literary and historical work, while still maintaining the strict monastic discipline. In 1792 the congregation was suppressed.

MAURITÃ'NIA. Republic of N.W. Africa, in full the Islamic Republic of M., lying N. of Senegal. Made a French protectorate in 1903, a colony in 1920, and an overseas territory in 1946, it was given independence in 1960, remaining within the French Community. Much of its 419,000 sq. m. lie in the Sahara Desert; very large deposits of iron ore and copper exist; most of its inhabitants (1965) 1,100,000 are nomadic and live by their flocks and herds. The cap. is Nouakchott. The name M. was that of the Roman prov. of N.W. Africa, so called from the Mauri, a Berber people who inhabited it.

MAURITIUS (mawrish'us). Island in the Indian Ocean, 550 m. E. of Madagascar, which was discovered, then uninhabited, by the Portuguese *c.* 1510; occupied by the Dutch 1598–1710; by the French 1715 until conquered by the British in 1810 and ceded to them 1814. In 1968 M. became an independent monarchy (with Elizabeth II as queen) within the Commonwealth. Sugar is the chief product. The cap. is Port Louis (pop. 135,000). There is a Gov.-Gen., Council of Ministers and Legislative Assembly. Area 720 sq. m.; pop. (1968) 773,000. Most numerous (c.350,000) are the Hindus, originally imported from India as indentured labour in the early 19th cent. after the abolition of slavery. Most important of several small is. dependencies is Rodriguez *c.* 350 m. to the E.: area 40 sq. m.; pop. (1968) 20,000: the Chagos Archipelago was transferred in 1965 to the British Indian Ocean Territory (q.v.). Official languages are English and French, Creole French being widely spoken. M. is subject to occasional devastating cyclones.

MAUROIS (mohrwah'), **André**. Pseud. of French author Émile Herzog (1885–1967). In the F.W.W. he was attached to the British Army, and the essays *Les Silences du Colonel Bramble* (1918) give humorously sympathetic observations on the British character. His novels incl. the semi-autobiographical *Bernard Quesnay* (1926), but he was best known for his fictionalized biographies, e.g. *Ariel* (1923), a life of Shelley, and for his essays on contemporary problems.

MAURRAS (mohrah'), **Charles** (1868–1952). French author and politician. B. in Provence, he became a journalist and an ardent royalist, as appears in such books as *Trois Idées politiques* (1898), and *L'Avenir de l'intelligence* (1905). In 1908 he joined with L. Daudet in the direction of the daily paper, *Action française*. He was jailed as a collaborator 1945–52.

MAVOR, O. H. *See* BRIDIE, JAMES.

MAWSON, Sir Douglas (1882–1958). Australian Antarctic explorer. B. nr. Bradford, he was taken to Sydney as a child, and qualified as a mining engineer. As a member of Shackleton's expedition of 1907–9, he discovered the South Magnetic Pole, and in an expedition of his own (1911–14) extended Australia's claim to sovereignty in the Antarctic to *c.* 2,720,000 sq. m. Prof. of geology and mineralogy at the Univ. of Adelaide 1920–53, he was knighted in 1914 and in 1954 his name was given to Australia's first permanent Antarctic base.

MAXIM, Sir Hiram Stevens (1840–1916). Anglo-American inventor. A naturalized Briton, he improved lighting methods, experimented with flight and invented the M. machine-gun.

MAXIMILIAN I (1459–1519). Holy Roman Emperor. The son of the Emperor Frederick III, he m. Mary of Burgundy in 1477, thus bringing the Low Countries under Habsburg rule, and became emperor in 1493. His dream of reviving the medieval empire involved him in long wars in Italy and Hungary with little result, but he made the Habsburgs the most powerful house in Europe, especially by marrying his son, Philip, to the heiress to the Spanish throne.

MAXIMILIAN (1832–67). Emperor of Mexico. The brother of the Emperor Francis Joseph of Austria, he was given command of the navy in 1854, and was gov. of Lombardy and Venetia 1857–9. He m. Princess Charlotte of Belgium in 1857. After the occupation of Mexico by French troops he accepted the title of emperor in 1864, but soon found himself a mere puppet in French hands. He met with resistance from the republicans under Juárez, and in 1866 French troops withdrew, at the demand of the U.S.A.; M., deserted, was captured by the republicans 1867 and shot.

MAXTON, James (1885–1946). British politician. He was a conscientious objector in the F.W.W. and was imprisoned for making a seditious speech in his native Glasgow, but entered Parl. in 1922 and was chairman of the I.L.P. 1926–46. His great sincerity attracted even those who could not share his views.

MAXWELL, James Clerk. *See* CLERK MAXWELL.

MAY, Phil (1864–1903). British artist. On the staff of the *Sydney Bulletin* 1885–8, he returned from Australia to Europe and in 1895 joined *Punch*. Well known for his vigorously vivid sketches of Bohemian and street life, he pub. *Phil May's Annual* 1892–1903.

MAY, Sir Thomas Erskine (1815–86). English constitutional jurist. Clerk of the House of Commons 1871–86, when he was created baron Farnborough, he wrote the standard *Treatise on the Law, Privileges, Proceedings, and Usage of Parliament* (1844).

MAYA (mah'yah). American Indian civilization of which remains are found in S. Mexico, Guatemala and British Honduras. Little survives of the earliest period from *c.* 500 B.C., but of the classic period *c.* A.D. 325-925 there are magnificent remains of buildings in stone (though metal tools were unknown to them), carved stelae, etc. They had a form of hieroglyphic writing, and were skilled in agriculture, mathematics and astronomy: their religion involved human sacrifice, but on a lesser scale than that practised by the Aztecs. Towards the end of this period there was an unexplained population movement away from the central area, and up till A.D. 1200 there was strong Mexican influence, subsequently thrown off. However, a general decline of the culture continued accompanied by civil wars, and the Spanish conquest in the 16th cent. completed its downfall, destroying much also of historical value incl. all except 3 of the ancient bark codices. *See* CHICHEN ITZA.

MAYA (mah'ya). Sanskrit word meaning 'illusion', applied frequently in Hindu philosophy, particularly in the Vedanta, to the cosmos which Isvara, the personal expression of Brahma or the Atman, has called into being. This is real, yet it also is illusion, since its reality is not everlasting.

MAYAKOVSKY, Vladimir (1893–1930). Russian poet. He combined revolutionary propaganda with efforts to revolutionize poetic technique, e.g. *150,000* (1920) and the dramatic poem *Mystery-Bouffe* (1918) on the October Revolution. He also wrote the satiric play *Klop* (1928: *The Bedbug*), taken in the West as an attack on philistinism in the U.S.S.R. He committed suicide.

MAY DAY. May 1, formerly the occasion for popular festivities, ultimately derived from pre-Christian magical rites. They included the maypole dance and the morris dance. May 1 is now the festival of the international Labour movement.

MAYENCE. French form of MAINZ.

MAYENNE (mahyen'). French town in M. dept., on the r. M., 40 m. N.W. of Le Mans. It is a market for the agricultural products of the vicinity, and has some textile industry. Its church dates from the 12th cent., its castle from the 13th. Pop. (1962) 11,163.

The r. MAYENNE rises in the W. of Orne dept., flows in a generally S. direction through the depts. of M. (to which it gives its name) and Maine-et-Loire for 125 m. to join the Sarthe just above Angers and form the Maine.

MAYER, Maria Goeppert- (1906–). American physicist. B. in Kattowitz, Poland, and ed. at Göttingen univ., she became a U.S. citizen in 1933, and was senior physicist at the Argonne Nat. Lab. 1946–60, and prof. in the Univ. of California (La Jolla) from 1960. For her discoveries in the theory of atomic nuclear shell structure, she was awarded a Nobel prize in 1963.

MAYFAIR. The fashionable quarter in the W. of London, England, vaguely defined as lying between Piccadilly and Oxford Street, and including Park Lane, but increasingly devoted to offices.

'MAYFLOWER'. Name of the vessel on which the 'Pilgrim Fathers' sailed from Plymouth, England, to Plymouth, Mass., founding the first colony in New England. The M. sailed with 102 passengers on 16 Sept. 1620 and landed at Plymouth Rock on 21 Dec. *Mayflower II*, a replica, re-enacted the original voyage in 1957, and was given as a token of goodwill by Britain to the U.S. to form part of a national shrine at Plymouth, Mass. *See* DARTMOUTH.

MAYFLY. Insects in the order Ephemeroptera (Gk. *ephemeros* lasting for a day, an allusion to the very brief life of the adult), found in many parts of the world. The larval stage, which can last as long as a year, is passed in water, the adult form developing gradually from the nymph through successive moults. The adult has transparent, net-veined wings, the hind pair being noticeably smaller, and 3 caudal filaments. Both nymphs and adults are important as food for fish, esp. trout.

MAYHEW, Henry (1812–87). British author of the classic social survey *London Labour and the London Poor* (1851–62).

MAYNOO'TH. Village in Co. Kildare, Rep. of Ireland, 13 m. W. of Dublin. St. Patrick's Coll. (1795) for the training of R.C. priests became an assoc. coll. of the Univ. of Dublin 1968.

MAYO, Katherine (1867–1940). American author and social reformer. B. in Philadelphia, in 1925 she attacked American maladministration in the Philippines in *Isles of Fear*, and in 1927 denounced child marriage in *Mother India*.

MAYO, Robert Hobart (1890–1957). British aircraft designer. He developed in the 1930s the Short-Mayo composite aircraft (a float seaplane carried on the back of a 'mother' flying-boat, the former being released at an agreed height and the latter returning to base). This device enabled a bigger fuel supply and payload to be carried by the seaplane.

MAYO, William James (1861–1939). American surgeon, founder with his brother, **Charles Horace M.**, of the M. Clinic (1889) in Rochester, Minnesota, and of the M. Association (1919) of which the income is devoted to the M. Foundation for Medical Education and Research. The latter's son, **Charles William M.** (1898–1968), became prof. of surgery, M. Foundation, in 1947.

MAYO. A western county of Rep. of Ireland in Connacht prov., facing the Atlantic Ocean and including Achill is. Much of it is wild and barren, and the coast is rocky. Castlebar is the co. town. Area 2,084 sq. m.; pop. (1966) 115,547.

MAYOR. The title of the principal officer of a municipal corporation of a city or bor. The title of Lord M. is borne by the chief magistrate of London, Belfast, Birmingham, Bradford, Bristol, Cardiff, Cork, Coventry, Dublin, Hull, Leeds, Leicester, Liverpool, Manchester, Newcastle-upon-Tyne, Norwich, Nottingham, Oxford, Plymouth, Portsmouth, Sheffield, Stoke-on-Trent, Westminster and York. There are also Lord Ms. in the 6 state caps. of Australia, and in Newcastle, N.S.W. In Scotland the title 'provost' is used instead of M. There are Lord Provosts for Aberdeen, Dundee, Edinburgh, Elgin, Glasgow, and Perth.

MAZARIN (mahzahrań'), **Jules** (1602–61). French statesman. B. at Piscina, he entered the papal diplomatic service, whence in 1639 he passed to that of France. He was created a cardinal in 1641, and succeeded Richelieu as chief minister in 1642. His policy of repressing the power of the nobility provoked the *Fronde* (q.v.), during which he was temporarily exiled. A great diplomatist, he conducted the Thirty Years War to a successful conclusion, and in alliance with Cromwell waged a victorious war against Spain.

MAZZINI (mahtsē'nē), **Giuseppe** (1805–72). Italian nationalist. B. at Genoa, he studied law and later joined the revolutionary society, the Carbonari. He was imprisoned in 1830, then went to France, where he founded 'Young Italy'. This was followed in 1834 by an international revolutionary organization, 'Young Europe'. For many years he lived in exile in France, Switzerland, and England, plotting uprisings in Italy, which all failed. In 1833 he was condemned to death in his absence by the Sardinian govt. On the outbreak of the 1848 revolution he returned to Italy, and for a few months in 1849 was at the head of the repub. govt. set up in Rome. After its overthrow he went into exile again. He achieved a widespread moral influence which was among the most potent factors making for Italian unity.

MBOMA. Another spelling of BOMA.

MBOYA (mboi-ya), **Tom** (1930–69). Kenya politician. Son of a Luo farmworker – he was the eldest of a family of 8 – he won a scholarship at Ruskin Coll., Oxford, and then returned to Kenya as an active labour leader. In 1960 he was among the founders of the Kenya African National Union (K.A.N.U.) a working alliance of the Kikuyu and Luo tribes. He was Min. of Lab. 1962–4, Justice 1963–4, and Economic Planning from 1964 until killed by a Kikuyu.

MEAD, Margaret (1901–). American anthropologist. Influential in questioning by comparative anthropology the conventions and customs of the West, she pub. *Coming of Age in Samoa* (1928), *Growing up in New Guinea* (1930), etc. She became Curator of Ethnology, American Museum of Natural History, N.Y. in 1964, and Chairman of Social Sciences at Fordham Univ. liberal arts college, Lincoln Center, 1969.

MEAD (mēd). Beverage made from honey and water fermented with yeast, drunk by the ancient Greeks and Britons, and still occasionally brewed in England.

MEAN. In mathematics, a specific related term intermediate between the first and last terms of a progression. The *arithmetic M.* is the average value of the quantities, i.e., the sum of the quantities divided by their number. The *geometric M.* is the corresponding root of the product of the quantities.

MEAN FREE PATH. The average distance travelled by a particle, atom or molecule between successive collisions.

MEANY, George (1894–). American labour leader. A plumber of Irish stock, he was pres. 1934–9 and sec.-treasurer 1949–52 of the N.Y. State Federation

MEDALS. Left to right: Legion of Honour (France); Iron Cross (Germany); Waterloo Medal, Victoria Cross, George Cross (U.K.); Medal of Honor (army and air force) and Medal for Merit (U.S.A.). *Courtesy of A. H. Baldwin Ltd., and Spink & Son Ltd.*

of Labour. He then succeeded J. L. Lewis as pres. of the A.F.L. (of the A.F.L./C.I.O., q.v., from 1955). In 1963 he was one of the 1st recipients of the Presidential Medal of Freedom.

MEARNS, The. Another name for KINCARDINE-SHIRE.

MEASLES. An acute infective fever caused by a virus, and transmitted usually by coughing, sneezing, etc. Symptoms are severe catarrh, small spots inside the mouth, and a raised, blotchy red rash appearing about the 4th day: patients are isolated for a fortnight. In white children it is comparatively a minor ailment, although serious complications may develop, but among some African peoples it is the most acute infectious disease.

By 1963 virus vaccines had estab. their usefulness in a number of countries.

See also GERMAN M.

MEAT. The flesh of animals taken as food. Modern means of preparation and transport have made its use widespread in all prosperous manufacturing areas, but many eastern peoples rarely or never eat M. Grasslands support mainly cattle and sheep, and grainlands support swine. Heavily peopled countries tend to specialize in high-grade beef or dairy cattle, confining sheep to the non-arable areas. Exporting countries incl. Argentina, Australia, New Zealand, Canada, U.S.A., and Denmark (chiefly bacon).

MEATH, Reginald Brabazon. See COMMONWEALTH DAY.

MEATH. Co. of Rep. of Ireland, in Leinster prov., facing the Irish Sea. It is mainly agricultural. The co. tn. is Trim. Area 903 sq. m.; pop. (1966) 67,323.

MEAT PACKING. Name given to the industry in the U.S.A. of preparing meat for consumption at a distance, particularly overseas. The industry depends on refrigeration, which was invented in 1861. Frozen beef was first sent to Smithfield from America in 1874. The first frozen meat was dispatched from Argentina in 1878 and from Australia in 1879. Chicago has the world's greatest M.P. plants.

MEAUX (moh). French town in Seine-et-Marne dept., 28 m. N.E. of Paris, centre of the Brie region, famous for its cheese; seat of a bishopric from the 4th cent. Thousands of peasants were killed at M. during the Jacquerie, 1358. Pop. (1962) 23,305.

MECCA. City of Arabia, the cap. of Hejaz and one of the caps. of Saudi Arabia, the holiest city of the Mohammedan world, where the Prophet was born. It stands in the desert, about 45 m. E. of Jidda, its port on the Red Sea, with which it is linked by an asphalted road, and long before the time of Mohammed was a commercial centre, caravan junction, and place of pilgrimage. In the centre of M. is the Great Mosque, in whose courtyard is the Kaaba (q.v.); it also contains the well Zam-Zam, associated by tradition with Hagar and Ishmael, and the Maqām Ibrāhīm, a holy stone supposed to bear the imprint of Abraham's foot. Pop. about 250,000.

MECHANICAL ENGINEERING. The design and production of machinery and mechanical contrivances used in connection with power generation, transport manufacturing processes, mining, drilling, etc.

MECHANICS. That branch of applied mathematics that deals with the motions of bodies and the forces causing them, and also with the forces acting on bodies in equilibrium. It is usually divided into dynamics and statics.

MECHELEN. Flemish form of MALINES. Mechlin is an older form of Mechelen.

MECKLENBURG. Historic name of an area lying along the Baltic coast of Germany. It was divided into 2 grand duchies, M.-Schwerin (5,068 sq. m.) and M.-Strelitz (1,131 sq. m.) which became free states of the Weimar Rep., 1918–34, when they were joined to form the state of M. After the S.W.W., M., incl. that part of Pomerania W. of the Oder, was in 1946 made a Land (area *c.* 8,800 sq. m.) of E. Germany. In 1952 the historic boundaries were swept away, and parts of M. were incl. in the regions of Rostock, Schwerin, and Neubrandenburg.

MEDAL OF HONOR. Award instituted by the U.S. Congress for the navy (1861) and army (1862) for gallantry in action. Although differing in design, both army and navy medals are bronze stars bearing Minerva encircled in their centres. *See* Medal illus.

MEDALS and DECORATIONS. Coins struck or cast in commemoration of victories, coronations, or other historic events, or issued in recognition of acts of gallantry, war service, or other public services, as distinct from those circulated as money. The commemorative M. originated in Italy in the 15th cent., reaching its highest artistic level in the work of Pisanello, etc. Other schools of medallists flourished in Germany in the 16th cent., and in France, England and Holland in the 17th.

Important Ms. for distinguished service incl. the British Victoria Cross (q.v., military, 1856) and George Cross and M. (q.v., mainly civilian, 1940); the American M. of Honor (q.v., military, 1861–2), Medal for Merit (civilian, 1942), Presidential Medal of Freedom (civilian, 1963), and Order of the Purple Heart (q.v., military, originally 1782, revived 1932); the French Legion of Honour (civilian and military, 1802) – previously weapons 'of honour' had been awarded – and Order of Merit (civilian and military, 1963); the German *Pour la Mérite* (civilian – since 1842 awarded for science and art – and military, 1740) and Iron Cross (q.v., military, 1813); the Italian Ms. for Military Valour (1833); U.S.S.R. Gold Star M. (civilian and military); and Belgian Order of Leopold (civilian and military, 1832). In addition there are a large number of campaign Ms. commemorating specific victories. The earliest one in England celebrated the defeat of the Armada, but until the 19th cent. Ms. were awarded only to officers. The first issued to all ranks was the Waterloo M. in 1816.

MEDAWAR (med'awahr), **Sir Peter** (1915–).

British scientist. As Jodrell prof. of zoology and comparative anatomy 1951–62, he was in 1960 awarded a Nobel prize for medicine (with Sir Macfarlane Burnet, q.v.) for his work in immunology, having discovered that the body's resistance to grafted tissue etc. is undeveloped in the new-born child. In 1962–71 he was director Nat. Inst. for Medical Research at Mill Hill, and was knighted 1965.

MEDĒ′A. In Greek legend, a sorceress, dau. of Æetes, king of Colchis. When Jason reached Colchis seeking the golden fleece, M. fell in love with him and by her magic helped him in his aim, and then fled with him on board the *Argo*. But when Jason married Creusa in her place, M. sent the bride a poisoned garment which caused her death, and killed the 2 children she had borne to Jason.

MEDELLIN (mādelyēn′). Capital of Antioquia dept., Colombia, lying at a height of 5,046 ft. The city has a univ. and is a large industrial centre. The seat of an archbishopric, it has a 17th cent. cathedral. Pop. (1965) 733,000.

MEDES (mēdz). An ancient Aryan people of W. Persia, on the borders of Mesopotamia. First heard of in the 9th cent. B.C. as tributaries to Assyria, their cap. was Ecbatana. In alliance with Babylon they destroyed Nineveh, the Assyrian cap., in 612, and extended their dominions as far as central Asia Minor. The Persians, who had been subject to the Ms., revolted in 550 B.C., and their king Cyrus became king of the Ms. and Persians, who rapidly merged.

MEDICI (mā′dēchē). A famous Florentine family. Its founder, **Giovanni** (1360–1429), acquired a fortune in commerce and banking, and exercised great political influence as a supporter of the popular party. His eldest son, **Cosimo** (1389–1464), dominated the govt. from 1434 onwards, and was succeeded by his son, **Piero** (1416–69), and his grandson, **Lorenzo the Magnificent** (1449–92). Both Cosimo and Lorenzo were munificent patrons of the arts, literature, and scholarship, while the latter was a poet of considerable ability; under their rule Florence was adorned with works of art, and became the centre of European culture. Lorenzo's son, **Giovanni** (1475–1521), became pope in 1513 as Leo X.

MEDICINE. The science and art of healing bodily and mental diseases; also any substance used in the treatment of disease. Taking the word in its former sense, M. covers every form of curative treatment, and also includes the study of the causes of disease and relative subjects. The basis of M. is anatomy or the structure and form of the body, and physiology, or the study of the body's functions. There are, however, many other sub-divisions, e.g. pathology, pharmacology, obstetrics, surgery, dentistry, etc.

M. as a scientific study had its rise in ancient Greece between 700 and 600 B.C., but the first Greek physician was Hippocrates (c. 460 B.C.). He it was who recognized that disease is the result of natural causes; and although his knowledge of the body was slight, he and his followers initiated the careful observation of symptoms out of which clinical M. has developed. In the Alexandrian age the city of Alexandria was the seat of a great medical school, and the knowledge acquired by the Alexandrian doctors was consolidated and extended by Galen, who lived in Rome in the 2nd cent. A.D. For more than 1,000 years Galen was chief medical authority, and it was not until the 16th cent. that any considerable additions were made to medical science. The discovery by Harvey in 1628 of the circulation of the blood was of epoch-making importance. John Hunter founded experimental and surgical pathology. Anatomists, botanists and chemists made valuable additions to the growing science, but it was in the 19th cent. that M. was revolutionized by the work of such men as Pasteur, Koch, Lister, and Manson.

In the 20th cent. spectacular advances have been made in the treatment and control of disease. Salvarsan (q.v.), 1909, was the first specific antibacterial agent, and the sulphonamides synthesized by G. Domagk in the 1930s were active against groups of pathogenic bacteria, as were the later antibiotics (q.v.) of natural origin (penicillin, streptomycin, tetracycline, etc.). As a result, pneumonia is no longer fatal, and tuberculosis can usually be cured. Diabetes, which prior to 1921 took its toll of the sufferer in under 5 years, can now be controlled indefinitely with insulin (q.v.). All branches of M. and surgery have benefited by the growth of effective nationwide blood-transfusion (q.v.) services. Prevention and control of viral diseases, such as influenza and polio (qq.v.), have been possible by large-scale inoculation with vaccines; and a dramatic increase in the understanding of the human mind has followed the work of Freud (q.v.) and his successors, in the many branches of psychiatry (q.v.), incl. the effective use of drugs. Transplant surgery (*see* HEART) rapidly developed in the 1960s.

MEDICINE HAT. Town in Alberta, Canada, 180 m. S.E. of Calgary, on the S. Saskatchewan r., a flour-milling centre; natural gas, coal, and oil shale occur in the vicinity. Pop. (1966) 25,574.

MEDINA (medē′nah). City of Arabia, about 220 m. N. of Mecca. To Mohammedans it is a holy city second only to Mecca, since it was here that the Prophet lived many years after he fled from Mecca, and here he died. The Mosque of the Prophet contains his reputed tomb, and those of Abu Bekr, Omar, and Fatima, Mohammed's daughter. M. is linked with Jidda by an asphalted road. Pop. c. 60,000.

MEDITERRANEAN. The inland sea that separates Europe from N. Africa, with Asia on the E. The Strait of Gibraltar connects it with the Atlantic; the Suez Canal links it with the Red Sea and the Indian Ocean. In the N.E., through the Dardanelles and the Sea of Marmara, it is connected with the Black Sea. Its name means surrounded by land, and on its shores western civilization was built up. Its chief divisions are the Tyrrhenian, Ionian, Adriatic, and Aegean seas, and its extreme length is 2,300 m. Shallows stretching from Sicily to Cape Bon in Africa divide it into an eastern and a western basin. It is saltier and warmer than the Atlantic, and nearly tideless. Area about 1,145,000 sq. m.

MEDLAR. A small European fruit tree (*Mespilus germanica*) of the family Rosaceae, with fruits resembling a small brown-green apple. These are eaten when decay has set in and the taste is agreeably acid.

MÉDOC (mehdok′). French dist. bordering the Gironde, N. of Bordeaux, famed for its wines; Margaux and St. Julien are 2 of the best-known varieties.

MEDUSA. *See* GORGON *and* JELLYFISH.

MEDWAY. River of S.E. England, rising in Sussex and flowing through Kent to Sheerness, where it enters the Thames. It is about 60 m. long, and divides the 'Men of Kent',

MEDLAR

who live to the east, from the 'Kentish men', who live to the west.

MEEGEREN (mā′-), Hans van (1889–1947). Dutch artist who faked Vermeers, incl. 'Christ at Emmaus', which was sold to Rotterdam's Boymann's Museum. Altogether his pictures brought him c. £500,000. He admitted the forgeries when he was arrested in 1945 for collaboration with the Nazis. After a year's imprisonment he d. penniless.

MEENEN. Flemish form of MENIN.

MEERSCHAUM (mērshawm; Ger. sea froth). A soft white mineral which, when dry, floats on the water; it is hydrated magnesium silicate, and is obtained chiefly from Asia Minor. It is used for pipe bowls and cigarette holders.

MEERUT (mē'rut). City of Uttar Pradesh, Rep. of India, where the Indian Mutiny began in 1857. It contains many mosques and temples, the Jama Masjid dating from 1019. Pop. (1961) 283,878.

MEGALITHIC MONUMENTS (Gk. *megas* great, and *lithos* stone). A term for all prehistoric remains consisting of large stones either standing upright and singly (menhirs), or in rows (alignments), stone circles, generally with a central 'altar stone', or built into the form of a hut. *See* DOLMEN.

MEGATHĒ′RIUM. Extinct quadruped of the order Edentata. Its skeleton has been found in Argentina.

MEGHALAYA. *See* ASSAM.

MEGI′DDŌ. Ancient Palestinian fortress, situated in the valley of Esdraelon. Here Thothmes III defeated the Canaanites, c. 1450 B.C.; Josiah was killed in battle, 609 B.C.; and Allenby broke the Turkish front in 1918.

MEHEMET ALI (mä′hemet ah′lē) (1769–1849). Pasha of Egypt. An Albanian, he commanded a Turkish regiment sent to Egypt in 1799 to fight the French, secured his election as pasha in 1805, built up an army and navy on European models, went to war with his overlord the sultan of Turkey in 1831 and 1839, and conquered the Sudan. He was the founder of the royal house (till 1953) of Egypt.

MEIGHEN (mē′-en), **Arthur** (1874–1960). Canadian Cons. statesman. Becoming M.P. in 1908, he was Solicitor-Gen. 1913–17 and was attacked for his promotion of conscription in 1917. P.M. 1920–1 and 1926, he led the Cons. Party in the senate 1932–41.

MEIJI TENNO. *See* MUTSUHITO.

MEILHAC (māyahk′), **Henry** (1831–97). French dramatist. He made his reputation with a long series of light comedies, of which *La Belle Hélène* and *Frou-Frou* (1869) are typical.

MEININGEN (mīn′-). Town in E. Germany, 29 m. S. of Eisenach. It was ounded in 982, and was cap. of the duchy of Saxe-M. 1680–1918. Pop. (est.) 24,000.

MEIR (mä-ēr), **Golda** (1898–   ). Israeli politician. B. in Kiev, she emigrated as a child to U.S.A., and settled in Palestine in 1921. A founder member of the Labour Party (Mapai), she was Min. of Labour 1949–56, Foreign Min. 1956–66, and became P.M. 1969.

MEISSEN (mī′sen). City in Dresden district, E. Germany, on the Elbe, 15 m. N.W. of Dresden. It was founded in 929 by Henry the Fowler, has a fine Gothic cathedral and is famed for its china, called Dresden from its original place of manufacture. Pop. (est.) 50,000.

MEISSONIER (māsonyä′), **Jean Louis Ernest** (1815–91). French painter. B. at Lyons, he is known for his small pictures, chiefly of scenes in the Napoleonic Wars, which he painted with great attention to detail. He was also a wood-engraver, and illustrated a number of books, e.g. *Paul and Virginia*.

MEISTERSINGERS (Ger. master singers). German lyric poets of the 14th to 16th cents. who formed guilds for the revival of minstrelsy at Nuremberg and elsewhere.

MEKNÈS (mek′nez). City in Morocco, 36 m. W.S.W. of Fez, in a fertile valley, one of the traditional caps. Pop. (1965) 205,000.

MEKO′NG. River of S.E. Asia, rising in Tibet and flowing for 2,800 m. generally S. into the South China Sea. The 4 riparian powers (Cambodia, Laos, Thailand, and S. Vietnam) are developing the lower M. for irrigation and power projects.

MELANCHTHON (melangk′thon), **Philip** (1497–1560). German Protestant reformer and theologian, whose real name was Schwarzerd. He was appointed prof. of Greek at Wittenberg in 1518, and helped Luther in preparing his German translation of the New Testament. From 1519 M. was a chief of the Reformers, and in 1521 he issued the first systematic formulation of Protestant theology. He composed the Augsberg Confession in 1530, and engaged in controversies with both Catholics and Protestants.

MELANE′SIA. A division of the islands in the central and western Pacific between Micronesia to the N. and Polynesia to the E. It embraces all the islands from the New Britain archipelago to the Fiji Islands, inhabited mainly by Papuans.

MELBA, Dame Nellie. Professional name of Australian soprano Helen Mitchell (1861–1931), prompted by her birthplace having been Melbourne. She made her operatic début in Brussels in 1887, and became the most renowned soprano of her day, notably as Donizetti's *Lucia*. In 1918 she was created D.B.E. (G.B.E. 1927). Her name has been given to fruit M., and M. sauce and toast.

MELBOURNE, William Lamb, 2nd visct. M. (1779–1848). British Whig statesman. In 1805 he m. Lady Caroline Ponsonby, who wrote novels under the title Lady Caroline Lamb and became infatuated with Byron from 1812, and from whom in 1825 he won a long fight for separation, following her becoming mad in the previous year. He had entered the Commons in 1806, became Irish Sec. in 1827, and succeeded his father in the title in 1828. He became Home Sec. in 1830 and was briefly P.M. in 1834, returning to office again as P.M. 1835–41. Falsely accused in 1836 of seducing C. E. S. Norton (q.v.), he lost William IV's favour, but was the confidential adviser of Victoria on her succession, teaching her statecraft.

MELBOURNE. Cap. of Victoria, Australia, on the Yarra, near its mouth. The settlement began in 1835, and was named M. in 1837, after Lord M.; its growth was accelerated by gold rushes, and M. is the second city of Australia. It was the seat of the Commonwealth government 1901–27, and its buildings incl. the Law Courts, Govt. Offices, Houses of Parliament, 2 cathedrals, and 3 univs. (Melbourne 1853, Monash 1958, and La Trobe 1964). Industries incl. engineering, food processing, clothing and textiles, and besides good road, rail, and air links, there are excellent dock facilities at Port M. Pop. (1966) 2,108, 499. *See* map p. 722.

MELILLA (melil′ya). Spanish town in Morocco, on the N.E. coast. An important military base, it was captured by Spain in 1496. Pop. (1960) 79,056.

MELLON, Andrew William (1855–1937). American banker, administrator, and philanthropist. B. at Pittsburgh, he entered the Thomas Mellon banking house which later became the Mellon National Bank, with M. as its president. He resigned in 1921 on his appointment as Secretary of the Treasury, and in 1932 was ambassador to Great Britain. In 1937 he gave his art treasures to the American people. The Nat. Gallery of Art, Washington, D.C. (1937), was built with funds given by M., who also donated his superb art collection, incl. 21 paintings from the Hermitage.

MELON. Twining plant of the family Cucurbitaceae. The Musk M. (*Cucumis melo*) and the Water M. (*Citrullus vulgaris*) are common edible varieties.

MĒ′LOS. Greek island in the Aegean Sea, one of the Cyclades. It was important in antiquity, and many fine works of art have been unearthed, notably the Venus de Milo, now in the Louvre. The cap. is Plaka. Area 60 sq. m.; pop. (est.) 6,000.

ME′LROSE. Scottish burgh in Roxburghshire, 30 m. S.E. of Edinburgh. The ruins of M. Abbey, founded in 1136, were immortalized by Sir Walter Scott. Pop. (1961) 2,133.

MELTON MOWBRAY. English market town (U.D.) in Leics, on the Eye, famous as a hunting and horse-breeding centre and for its pork pies. Pop. (1961) 15,913.

MELVILLE, Alan (1910–   ). British author, known

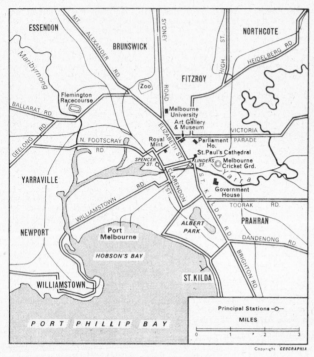

MELBOURNE

was town painter 1475–87, and some of his finest works are preserved in the Hospital of St. John, e.g. the 'Deposition' triptych (1480), the 'Adoration of the Magi' altar (1479), and the shrine of St. Ursula (1489). He has a serene delicacy of touch and invests his madonnas with a rich sensitivity of feeling.

MEMPHIS (mem'fis). Ruined city beside the Nile, 12 m. S. of Cairo, Egypt. Centre of the worship of Ptah, it was made the cap. of the united kingdoms of Upper and Lower Egypt by Menes, but was superseded by Thebes under the new empire in 1570 B.C. It declined and was subsequently used as a stone quarry, although the necropolis of Sakkara escaped damage under sand.

MEMPHIS. Largest city of Tennessee, U.S.A., on the Mississippi, an important cotton port. Pop. met. area (1970) 767,050.

MENAI (men'ī) **STRAIT.** Channel of the Irish Sea, dividing Anglesey from the Welsh mainland. It is about 14 m. long, and its greatest width is 2 m.; it is crossed by Telford's suspension bridge (1826), and R. Stephenson's tubular railway bridge (1850).

MENA'NDER (*c.* 342–291 B.C.). Greek dramatist. B. in Athens, he was the most popular exponent of the new comedy of manners, and his highly improbable plots later became fashionable. Only a few fragments of his 105 plays were known until the discovery in 1957 of the *Dyscholos* (Bad-tempered man). Many fragments have been recovered from papyri used as papier mâché for Egyptian mummy cases.

MENCIUS (men'shē-us; Latinized form of Mengtzu) (*c.* 372–289 B.C.). Chinese moralist. B. in Shan-Tung province, he founded a school in the tradition of Confucius. At the age of 40 he set out with his disciples to find a ruler who would put into practice his enlightened political programme. After 20 years he gave up the search and retired. His teachings (*Book of Mengtzu*) were collected after his death.

MENCKEN, Henry Louis (1880–1956). American critic, known from his birthplace as 'the sage of Baltimore'. His unconventionally phrased, satiric contributions to *Smart Set* and *American Mercury* (both of which periodicals he edited) roused great controversy. His best book was *The American Language* (1918 and often revised).

ME'NDEL, Johann Gregor (1822–84). Austrian monk, abbot of the Augustinian abbey at Brünn from

for revues, e.g. the *Sweet and Low* series; plays, e.g. *Simon and Laura* (1954, also filmed), and light-hearted novels.

MELVILLE, Henry Dundas, visct. M. (1742–1811). British Tory politician. B. at Edinburgh, he entered parl. in 1774, and as Home Sec. 1791–4 persecuted the parliamentary reformers. He was Sec. of War 1794–1801, and 1st Lord of the Admiralty 1804–5, and received a peerage in 1802. His impeachment for malversation in 1806 was the last in English history.

MELVILLE, Herman (1819–91). American author. B. in New York, in 1837 he sailed to Liverpool as a cabin-boy, as described in *Redburn* (1849), and in 1841 joined the crew of a South Seas whaler, an experience which inspired his masterpiece, *Moby Dick* (1851), story of the contest between Captain Ahab and a great white whale which has symbolic overtones. M. held a post in the New York customs 1866–85. His other books incl. *Typee* (1846), *Omoo*, *Billy Budd*, and several vols. of verse.

MELVILLE. Hanging above the desk at which he wrote *Billy Budd*, in the Herman Melville Memorial Room, this portrait of the author at about the age of 30 is the work of Asa W. Twitchell.
Courtesy of the Berkshire Athenaeum, Pitsfield, Mass.

MEMEL. German name of KLAIPEDA.

ME'MLING or MEMLINC, Hans (*c.* 1430–94). Flemish artist, b. probably at M. nr. Alkmaar. His masters are said to have incl. Lochner and van der Weyden. and in 1466 he settled in Bruges, where he

MEMLING. Outstanding, even among the many treasures of the ancient city of Bruges, is the Memling Museum, housed in a 13th cent. ward of the 12th cent. St. John's Hospital. It contains some of the artist's finest masterpieces, including the shrine of St. Ursula seen here.
Courtesy of Belgian National Tourist Office

1868. By experiments with generations of peas in the monastery garden he developed a theory of organic inheritance – Mendelism – governed by dominant and recessive characters. He pub. his results 1865–9, but his work remained unrecognized until the early 20th cent.

MENDELE'YEV, Dmitri Ivanovich (1834–1907). Russian chemist. The framer of the Periodic Law of the atomic weights of chemical elements, he was prof. at St. Petersburg univ. (1866–90), and wrote *Principles of Chemistry* (1868), etc.

MENDELSSOHN-BARTHOLDY, Jakob Ludwig Felix (1809–47). German composer. B. in Hamburg, the grandson of Moses M., he settled in Berlin. When 11, M. already had numerous compositions to his credit, and a few years later his output included symphonies, operas, etc. M. revered the great classical composers, esp. Bach. At the age of 17, M. wrote the overture to *A Midsummer Night's Dream*. M. visited England for the first time in 1829, and was enthusiastically received. During later visits to England, he conducted his two oratorios, *St. Paul* and *Elijah*, and was fêted. During a tour of Scotland he was inspired to write the overture *Fingal's Cave*, and a tour of Italy resulted in the *Italian Symphony*. He accepted important musical appointments at Düsseldorf, Leipzig, Berlin, and in 1843 founded the Leipzig conservatoire. Among M.'s most popular compositions are the piano pieces *Songs without Words*, numerous songs, an early *Octet*, and the *Serious Variations* and *Rondo Capriccioso*, both for piano.

ME'NDERES, Adnan (1899–1961). Turkish statesman. A law graduate and agricultural expert, he became P.M. of a democratic govt. in 1950 (re-electeα 1954 and 1957). In 1960, following an unrealistic economic policy, and a series of repressive measures against the opposition party and the freedom of the press, he was executed after an army coup.

MENDÈS (mondäs'), **Catulle** (1841–1909). French poet and author. B. at Bordeaux, of Jewish parentage, he wrote verse, novels, and plays of a voluptuous character. He m. the dau. of Théophile Gautier.

MENDÈS-FRANCE (-frahñs), **Pierre** (1907–   ). French statesman. A lawyer, he was P.M. and For. Min. 1954–5, when he concluded the war in Indochina, and granted Tunisian independence.

MENDICANCY. The solicitation of alms. A perennial problem, even in the Welfare State, M. is particularly widespread in eastern countries and has been fostered in Moslem lands by almsgiving being a religious obligation. Stringent measures are taken against M. in the U.S.S.R., and in Britain, where legislation began in the 14th cent., it is an offence to solicit alms on the public highway, to expose any sore or malformation to attract alms, or cause a child to beg, and begging letters containing false statements are also illegal.

MENDICANT ORDERS. In the R.C. Church, the 4 orders of Mendicant Friars – Franciscans, Dominicans, Carmelites, and Augustinian Hermits (Austin Friars) – all of which arose in the early and middle 13th cent., and were inspired by a resolve to return to the simplicity of primitive Christianity. The friars estab. themselves in the slums of the cities and towns, made poverty a virtue, and at first depended on alms, although in course of time they accumulated property. Hinduism also has many M.Os.

MENDOZA (mendō'thah), **Antonio de** (1490–1552). 1st Spanish viceroy of New Spain (Mexico) 1535–51. His rule was enlightened and the system he estab. lasted until the 19th cent. Appointed viceroy of Peru in 1551, he d. there.

MENDOZA (mendō'thah). Cap. of the Argentine prov. of the same name. It was founded in 1561 and has greatly developed owing to its position on the Trans-Andean railway. Pop. (1967) 109,150. The prov. is well irrigated, and produces wine, alfalfa,

olives, and cereals. Area 57,445 sq. m.; pop. (1965) 936,000.

ME'NELIK II (1844–1913). Negus (emperor) of Abyssinia from 1889. He defeated the Italians in 1896, and the independence of his country was fully recognized.

ME'NES. Traditionally, the 1st king of the 1st dynasty of ancient Egypt. He is said to have been the founder of Memphis and the organizer of the worship of the gods.

ME'NGER, Karl (1840–1921). Austrian economist. Prof. of economics at Vienna 1873–6 and 1878–1903, he developed the theory of marginal utility.

MENGS, Antony Raphael (1728–79). German painter. B. at Aussig in Bohemia, the son of a Danish painter, in 1741 he went to Rome, where he copied the works of Raphael, and in 1754 he became director of the Vatican school of painting. At the invitation of Charles III of Spain he travelled to Madrid in 1761, where some of his best works were painted, incl. the 'Triumph of Trajan' and the 'Temple of Glory'.

MENGTSZ (mung'tse). City of S. China, in Yunnan, 130 m. S.S.W. of Kunming, cap. of M. county. Lying at a height of 4,655 ft., it is a centre of tin and antimony mines; rice, tea, sugar cane, and fruit are grown in the vicinity, and lumbering is carried on. M. was opened to foreign trade in 1889. Pop. (est.) 200,000.

MENIN. Belgian textile-making town in W. Flanders, 7 m. S.W. of Kortrijk, on the Lys. The **Menin Gate** at Ypres (q.v.), on the road to Menin, commemorates 54,896 British soldiers missing in the battles of Ypres in 1914–18.

MENIN'DEE. Village and sheep centre of New S. Wales. Australia, on the Darling r. 65 m. E.S.E. of Broken Hill, centre of a water-conservation scheme conserving the waters of the Darling in M. Lake (60 sq. m.) and neighbouring lakes for irrigation.

MENINGI'TIS. Inflammation of the meninges, the lining membranes of the base of the brain and spinal cord. An acute attack can be caused by spread of infection from disease of the nose or ear, by other infections, such as influenza or typhoid fever, or by the organism of spotted fever (cerebro-spinal fever), so called because it also often produces a rash. The patient is very sensitive to light and cold, and resents being handled; he becomes delirious and his spine, with the neck and head, is curved backwards. Most acute cases are fatal, and recovery in the others takes a long time. More chronic forms are due to tuberculosis or syphilis.

MENKEN, Adah Isaacs (1835–68). American Jewish actress, whose name may originally have been Dolores Adios Fuertes, but who m. in 1856 A. I. Menken. B. in New Orleans, she made her most celebrated appearance (in Britain and the U.S.) in *Mazeppa*, strapped to a galloping horse while flimsily clad, and was also a dancer.

MENNOFER. Another name for MEMPHIS, Egypt.

MENNONITES. A Christian sect that originated in Zürich in 1523. They were baptists, and refused to hold civil offices and undertake military service. Similar sectarians in Holland found a leader in Menno Simons (1496–1559), and were named after him. After his death the Ms. spread rapidly, but their views led to persecution, and in 1683 a number of them settled at Germantown, Pennsylvania. Today there are more than a dozen separate Mennonite 'churches' in N. America. They are fundamentalists in theology, very simple in their ways of life, maintain their pacifism, and speak the languages of their ancestors.

ME'NOPAUSE. The change of life; the cessation of function of the female reproductive organs. The time of onset is usually about 45, but varies very much. Menstruation becomes irregular and ceases The 'change' is natural and usually uneventful, but some women suffer from troubles such as flushing, excessive bleeding, and nervous disorder.

MENORCA. Spanish form of MINORCA.

MENO'TTI, Gian Carlo (1911–). American composer. B. in Italy, he has lived in the U.S.A. since 1928. His operas are well known for their dramatic sense, excellent libretti (which he writes himself), and for the interdependence of words and music. Best-known are *The Medium* (1946); *The Telephone* (1947); *Amahl and the Night Visitors*, a Christmas story (1951); *The Consul* (1950); and *The Saint of Bleeker Street* (1954).

MENSHEVIKS. The right wing of the Russian Social-Democratic Party. They were so called because they formed the minority (Russ. *menshinstvo*) at the 1903 party congress, the left-wing majority being known as Bolsheviks. During the Russian revolution they succeeded in setting up a govt. in Georgia, and after its overthrow disappeared.

MENSTRUATION. The female period; the monthly discharge from the womb of blood and breakdown products of the lining which has been prepared for the development of an egg-cell if fertilized. It starts at puberty, about 14, and ends with the change of life (*see* MENOPAUSE). If conception has taken place, the discharge does not occur. Otherwise M. may fail (amenorrhoea) in association with anaemia, depression, certain glandular disorders, etc. It may be painful (dysmenorrhoea), usually because of spasm of the womb; or the loss may be excessive (menorrhagia) because of inflammation, etc., within the womb.

MENTAL DISORDER. Generic term for all forms of mental ill health, of which there are in law 4 main types: **mental illness** in which patients of normal intelligence become disordered; **severe abnormality** in which mental development is arrested to such an extent that the patient is incapable of leading an independent life, those formerly called idiots or imbeciles; **subnormality** in which special care and training can to some extent overcome the incomplete development of the mind, many of those formerly called feeble-minded; and **psychopathic disorder** in which the patient may or may not be of normal intelligence, but is characterized by extreme irresponsibility or abnormal aggressiveness which makes it unsafe for others as well as himself if he is not under treatment. Among disorders coming in the last category are: schizophrenia; paranoia, in which the patient builds up an elaborate delusional system; manic depressive insanity, an alternation between elation (mania) and depression (melancholia). *See* SEDATIVES.

MENTAL TEST. Scientifically standardized procedure for measuring a defined characteristic of the mind. Pioneer work was done by Sir Francis Galton and Binet; and later by Burt, Thorndike and others. M.Ts. may measure either intellectual ability or temperamental and moral qualities, and may be subdivided into those testing inborn or acquired characteristics; and cross-classified into those testing general qualities such as 'general intelligence' or more specialized aptitudes and propensities. The first large-scale use of intelligence Ts. for adults was for 2,000,000 drafted men in the U.S.A. in 1917. In industry aptitude tests, e.g. for manual dexterity, are practically useful, but conventional intelligence Ts., at one time favoured in deciding suitable education for eleven-year-olds, have drawbacks. Improved results may be contrived by practice; people with unconventional backgrounds are at a disadvantage, and original potentiality or 'creativity' cannot be measured: research is being directed to improved methods.

MENTHOL ($C_{10}H_{19}OH$). Peppermint camphor; an alcohol derivative of menthone. It occurs in peppermint and is responsible for the plant's odour.

MENTON (moňtoń'). Resort on the French Riviera, close to the Italian frontier, in Alpes-Maritimes dept., favoured with an agreeable climate. It belonged to the princes of Monaco until sold to France in 1861. Queen Victoria frequently visited it. Pop. (1962) 20,069.

MENTONE. Italian form of MENTON.

ME'NUHIN, Yehudi (1916–). American violinist. Of Russian-Jewish parentage, he gave his first concert at 8 and 2 years later toured Europe, dazzling the critics by his maturity and freshness of approach. He retired for a period of intensive study 1935–7, and achieved a depth of interpretation, as in the Elgar and Beethoven concertos, which made him among the world's greatest players. His sister **Hephzibah M.** (1921–) is a pianist and has often accompanied him,

MENUHIN. Recording Berlioz' 'Harold in Italy', Menuhin forsakes his usual instrument to play the viola obbligato.
Photo: Godfrey MacDomnic.

and his dau. Zamira m. in 1960 the Chinese pianist Fou Ts'ong (1934–).

In 1963 he founded the *Y.M. School* at Stoke D'Abernon, Surrey, a boarding school for talented young musicians, the only one of its kind outside Russia. In 1965 he was created hon. K.B.E.

MENZIES, Sir Robert Gordon (1894–). Australian statesman. A successful Melbourne lawyer, he entered politics in 1928, as Attorney-Gen in the federal parl. 1934–9, and in 1939 succeeded Lyons as P.M. and leader of the United Australia Party (1939–41). Leading the Opposition from 1943, he in 1944 initiated the formation of a new party—the Australian Lib. Party—to unite all anti-Lab. groups except the Country Party, and in 1949 became P.M. of a Lib.-Country Party coalition govt., being re-elected 1951, 1954, 1955, 1958, 1961, and 1963. Knighted 1963, he succeeded Churchill as Lord Warden of the Cinque Ports in 1965, and retired as P.M. 1966.

MEQUINES. See MEKNÈS.

MERCA'TOR, Gerardus (1512–94). Latinized form of Gerhard Kremer, name of the Flemish map-maker who devised 'M.'s projection' – the first map using it being pub. in 1568. *See* ATLAS.

MERCHANT NAVY. Ships owned by shipping companies and used as trading vessels to provide sea transport for passenger traffic and for export and import cargoes. The chief types of merchant ships are: (1) tramps, which may coast between home ports or carry bulk cargoes for voyages of up to 2 years from one port to another throughout the world; (2) tankers and other ships carrying a single specialized cargo; (3) cargo liners, combining cargo and passenger traffic on short or world voyages – liners carrying passengers only are decreasing in modern conditions. Among the most famous passenger ships are the 3 Cunard 'queens', *Queen Mary* (1936: 1019 ft. long and 81,237 tons gross) which in 1967 went to Long Beach, California, as a floating hotel; *Queen Elizabeth* (1940: 1031 ft., 82,998 tons), was in 1970 purchased by C. Y. Tung for a floating univ. and renamed *Seawise University*, a play on his own initials; and *Queen Elizabeth II* (1968: 963 ft., 58,000 tons); *France* (Fr. 1961: 1035 ft., 66,348 tons) and *United States* (U.S.A. 1952: 990 ft., 50,924 tons): see SHIP. The world's first atomic-powered merchant ship is the *Savannah* (U.S.A. 1959).

MERCIA (mer'shia). One of the Anglo-Saxon kingdoms, which at its greatest extent included all England between the Humber and the Thames, except E. Anglia. It first emerged *c*. 600, and in the 8th cent. dominated all England S. of the Humber. From *c*. 825 it came under the overlordship of Wessex. In 886 the E. of M. was included in the Danelaw.

MER'CURY. Roman god, identified with the Greek Hermes, and like him represented with the winged sandals and caduceus. He was the messenger of the gods.

MERCURY. The planet nearest to the Sun. Its distance from the Sun is 36,000,000 miles on the average, and its revolution period is 88 days; this was also thought to be the length of its axial rotation, so that it would always present the same face to the sun, the other being in perpetual darkness, but radar measurements have shown that it rotates once for every 2 orbits it makes round the sun, so that its day is double the length of its year. M. is a small planet, about 3,000 m. in diameter, and is practically devoid of atmosphere. The surface is thought to be rocky, resembling the Moon and Mars, and its temperature ranges from —160°C at midnight to 350°C at noon. M. is easily visible to the naked eye when well placed for observation, but is never conspicuous.

MERCURY. The only common metal liquid at ordinary temperatures, it was known to the ancient Chinese and Hindus, and is found in Egyptian tombs of *c*. 1500 B.C.: symbol Hg, at. wt. 200·61, at. no. 80. A dense, mobile, silvery liquid, it is found free in nature, but the chief source is the mineral cinnabar, HgS. Its alloys with other metals are *amalgams*. It is used in drugs and chemicals, for mercury vapour lamps, arc rectifiers, power-control switches, vacuum and other scientific apparatus, barometers, thermometers, etc.

MERCURY FULMINATE. Highly explosive compound used in detonators and percussion caps. It is a grey, sandy powder, and highly poisonous.

MEREDITH (mer'edith), **George** (1828–1909). British novelist and poet. B. in Portsmouth, he was ed. in Germany, articled to a London solicitor, but soon entered journalism, and in 1849 m. Mary Nicolls (d. 1861), the widowed dau. of Thomas Love Peacock, who left him in 1858. In 1851 he pub. *Poems* and in 1855 the prose romance, *The Shaving of Shagpat*. His first realistic psychological novel, *The Ordeal of Richard Feverel* (1859), was followed by *Evan Harrington* (1860), *Rhoda Fleming* (1865), *Harry Richmond* (1871), *The Egoist* (1879), *Diana of the Crossways* (1885), and *The Amazing Marriage* (1895). His later vols. of verse incl. *Modern Love* (1862) and *Poems and Lyrics* (1883). He was reader to Chapman and Hall 1862–94, and in 1867, 2 years after his marriage to Mary Vulliamy (d. 1885), made his home at Flint Cottage, Box Hill. In 1905 he received the O.M.

MEREZHKO'VSKY, Dmitri Sergeievich (1865–1941). Russian novelist. An early exponent of the 'modernist movement' of the 1890s, he wrote the trilogy *Christ and Anti-Christ* (1895–1905), and other historical romances. After the Russian revolution he lived in Paris.

MERGA'NSER. Genus of ducks, mainly marine. The goosander (*Mergus merganser*) is widely distributed in the N. hemisphere, though rare in Britain. *See* GOOSANDER.

MERGENTHALER (merg'entahler), **Ottmar** (1854–99). German-American inventor. B. in Hachtel, Württemberg, where he served his apprenticeship as a watchmaker, he went to U.S.A. in 1872 and there developed 1876–86 the first linotype (q.v.) machine: the principle of a circulating matrix is today universally used.

MERIDA (mer'ēdhah). Mexican city, cap. of the state of Yucatan and seat of a univ., it has a cathedral founded 1598. M., dating from 1542, is a centre of sisal industry. Pop. (1960) 170,513.

MERIDIAN. A great circle drawn on the earth's surface so as to pass through both poles, and thus through all places with the same longitude. Terrestrial longitudes are usually measured from Greenwich M. An astronomical M. is a great circle passing through the pole and the zenith. (*See* LATITUDE AND LONGITUDE.)

MERIMÉE (mehrēmeh'), **Prosper** (1803–70). French author. B. in Paris, he entered the public service, and under Napoleon III was employed on unofficial diplomatic missions. Among his best works are the stories *Colomba* (1841), dealing with a Corsican feud, and the Spanish *Carmen* (1846); and the witty and sceptical *Lettres à une inconnue* (1873).

MERINO (merē'no). Originally a term for sheep-pasture inspectors in Spain, M. now refers to a breed of sheep native to Africa. Its close-set, silky wool is of extremely good quality, and the M., now found all over the world, is the breed on which the Australian industry is built.

MERIO'NETHSHIRE. Co. in N. Wales, facing Cardigan Bay on the W. It has fine mountain and valley scenery, and includes Cader Idris and Bala lake. The Dee is the chief river. The co. is pastoral but slate and limestone are quarried. Dolgelley is the co. tn. Area 660 sq. m.; pop. (1961) 39,007.

MERIT, Order of. British order of chivalry, founded in 1902 by Edward VII and limited in number to 24. Though not a knighthood, it is very highly regarded. *See* LEGION OF HONOUR.

MERLIN. Small falcon (*Falco desalon*), which breeds in England and Scotland. Males are steel-blue

above and rufous below; females are brown. It nests in the heather. The N. American pigeon-hawk (*F. columbanus*) is similar.

MERMAIDS. In folklore, semi-human creatures who live in the sea; their form is that of a beautiful woman with the tail of a fish. The dugong and seal (qq.v.) have been suggested as possible origins for the legends.

MERLIN, an adult male.
Photo: G. Ronald Austing.

MEROE (mer'ō-ē.) Ancient city of the Rep. of the Sudan, on the Nile near Khartoum, cap. of Nubia *c*. 600 B.C. to A.D. 350. Tombs and inscriptions have been excavated, and because of its iron smelting slag-heaps, it has been called the 'Birmingham of ancient Africa'.

MEROVI'NGIANS. The name of a Frankish dynasty, derived from its founder, Merovech (5th cent.). His descendants ruled France from the time of Clovis (481–511) to 751.

MERSEY. English river formed by the union of the rivers Goyt and Tame at Stockport, flowing between Cheshire and Lancashire to form an estuary at Liverpool. The M. railway tunnel under the r. was completed in 1886; Queensway, a road tunnel linking Birkenhead and Liverpool, was opened in 1934.

MERSIN (mersēn'). Turkish port and market town, cap. of Içel il, and sometimes itself called Içel, on the Mediterranean, 40 m. W.S.W. of Adana. It exports chrome, copper, and agricultural produce, and has a large oil refinery, opened 1962, when built second in capacity in the Mediterranean area only to that of Naples. Pop. (1965) 87,300.

MERTHYR TYDFIL (mur'ther tid'vil). Welsh town (co. bor.) in Glamorganshire, on the Taff, 24 m. N.N.W. of Cardiff, in an iron and coal district. Between the 2 world wars it suffered heavily from unemployment. Pop. (1961) 59,008.

MERV. Oasis in Russian Turkmenistan, a centre of civilisation at least 1200 B.C., and site of a town founded by Alexander the Great. Old M. was destroyed by the Emir of Bokhara 1787, and the modern town of Mary (q.v.), founded by the Russians 1885, lies 18 m. W.

MÉRYON (mehryoń'), **Charles** (1821–68). French etcher. B. in Paris, son of an English father and French mother, he entered the navy, but left it in 1846, studied engraving, and began his famous series of etchings of Paris. He lived in poverty, and became mentally deranged.

MESCALIN. Drug derived from a turnip-shaped cactus (*Lophophora Williamsii*) of Texas and N. Mexico, known locally as peyote (pāyō'tā), etc. The tops, which scarcely appear above ground, are dried and chewed, or added to alcoholic drinks. Allegedly non-habit-forming and without after-effects, M. heightens the perceptions and is used by the Navajos of California and Indians of other states in the ceremonial of the Native American Church. It was used experimentally by Aldous Huxley (q.v.) and others.

ME'SHED. Capital of Prov. No. 9 (Khurasan) in Persia. It is the holy city of the Mohammedan sect of Shiahs, and is visited by about 100,000 pilgrims annually. It has a univ. of medicine and is linked by railway with Ashkhabad, cap. of Turkmen S.S.R. Pop. (1964) 312,186.

MESMERISM. Theory that a subject may be reduced to a state of trance by the consciously exerted 'animal magnetism' of the operator, in which the will-power of the former is entirely subordinated. It is named from the Austrian physician, Friedrich Anton Mesmer (1733–1815). B. at Weil, near Constance, he took a medical degree at Vienna, and conducted experiments there, at first with actual magnets. Driven from Vienna by the police, he settled at Paris in 1778, and created a fashionable sensation. An investigating committee denounced him as a charlatan in 1785, and he d. in Switzerland. M. is now popularly identified with hypnotism.

ME'SONS. Unstable particles with masses intermediate between those of the electron and the proton, found in cosmic radiation and emitted by nuclei under bombardment by very high-energy particles.

MESOPOTĀ'MIA. Classical name derived from

MESON. The discovery of the meson is illustrated here by the track (with mirror image) passing through the glass walls and copper cylinder of a Geiger-Müller counter in a magnetic field. Measurements of curvature and density of the track give particulars of the charge and mass of the particle.

MESOPOTAMIA. The ruined palace at Ctesiphon (.qv.).

the Greek for 'middle' and 'river' given to the land between the Euphrates and the Tigris. Here the civilizations of Sumer and Babylon flourished, and some consider it the original home of civilized man. It is part of modern Iraq.

MESOZŌ'A. Group of minute parasitic animals of the Metazoa. It is divided into 2 classes, the Rhombozoa and the Orthonectida.

MESSAGER (mesahzhā'), **André Charles Prosper** (1853–1929). French composer. He studied under Saint-Saëns. M. was successful with his light operas, such as *La Béarnaise* and *Véronique*.

MESSALINA, Valeria (*c.* A.D. 22–48). Roman empress. She was the 3rd wife of Claudius, and for some years dominated him. Her name has become a byword for immorality. In 48 she forced a noble to marry her, although she was still married to Claudius, and the latter had her executed.

MESSI'AH. Word derived from the Hebrew for 'the anointed', the Greek equivalent of which is Christ. The Jews from the time of the exile have looked forward to the coming of the M., who shall be a deliverer. Christians believe that the M. came in the person of Jesus Christ.

MESSIAEN (mesi-an'), **Olivier** (1908–). French composer. At the Paris Conservatoire he studied the organ, and for composition was a pupil of Dukas. In 1931 he became organist at the Trinité and prof. at the École Normale de Musique, etc. His works incl. the choral *Trois petites liturgies de la Présence Divine*; *La Nativité de Seigneur* for organ; and *Les Visions de l'Amen* for 2 pianos.

MESSINA (mesē'nah). Sicilian city in the N.E. corner of the is. It was an ancient Greek foundation before it was taken by the Carthaginians and then the Romans. In 1908 it was destroyed by an earthquake in which 77,000 were killed. The Straits of M. separate Sicily and Italy. Pop. (1961) 251,423.

MEŠTROVIĆ (mesh'trovitch), **Ivan** (1883–1962). Yugoslav sculptor. B. at Vrpolje in Dalmatia, he studied in Vienna and early in the cent. was leader of a nationalist art movement. In 1947 he went to the U.S. and was naturalized in 1954. His notable works incl. portrait busts of Rodin, Sir Thomas Beecham, Pres. Masaryk, etc.

META'BOLISM. The processes of building up and breaking down constantly taking place in living organisms to sustain life and growth. The 3 principal types relate to: green plants (based on photosynthesis in which complex organic substances are built up from water, carbon dioxide and mineral salts in the presence of chlorophyll and sunlight); plants not containing chlorophyll, e.g. moulds, yeasts, fungi, and bacteria, which secure energy by many different chemical transformations, e.g. oxidation of ammonia to nitrates; and animals dependent for food on complex compounds which they break down partially by digestion, and subsequently resynthesize. Thus animals are dependent on green plants either directly or indirectly.

METALIOUS, Grace (1924–64). American novelist, *née* de Repentigny. B. in Manchester, New Hampshire, she m. at 17 Christopher M. and, after writing many short stories uneventfully, struck the headlines with *Peyton Place* (1956), an exposé of life in a small New England town that roused a storm of protest.

METALLURGY. The art of working metals. Process M. is concerned chiefly with their extraction from the ores, and refining and adapting them for man's use, while physical M. is interested in their properties and application. The foundations of metallurgical art were probably laid about 3500 B.C. in Egypt, Mesopotamia, and India, where the art of smelting metals from ores was discovered, and gold, silver, copper, lead, and tin were worked. The smelting of iron appears to have been discovered about 1500 B.C., and the Romans hardened and tempered steel. From the fall of the Roman Empire until the latter part of the Middle Ages, the only advances in M. were due to the Arabian chemists.

Cast iron began to be made in the 14th cent., and in the 18th cent. we find the beginning of the modern blast furnace. The application of steam power resulted in an enormous increase in iron and steel production.

Metals can be extracted from their ores in 3 main ways: (1) dry processes such as smelting, volatilization or amalgamation, (2) wet processes involving chemical reactions, and (3) electrolytic processes.

METALS. Elements which are classified as Ms. have certain characteristics and physical properties which can be increasingly accounted for by modern theories based on studies of their atomic and sub-atomic structures. Ms. are good conductors of heat and electricity; opaque, but reflect light well; malleable, which enables them to be cold-worked and rolled into sheets; and ductile, which permits them to be drawn into thin wires. Generally hard, they are crystalline in their normal pure state, many of them mixing with one another to form alloys with properties depending on the proportions of their constituents. Their hardness, tensile strength, toughness, brittleness, etc., may be varied by physical means such as heat-treatment, work hardening, etc., but their physical properties, such as melting point, coefficient of thermal expansion, density, etc., are constant.

60 to 70 Ms. are known, but only the following are used in commerce: (i) *Precious Ms.:* gold, silver, mercury, platinum, and the platinum Ms., used principally in jewellery. (ii) *Heavy Ms.:* iron, copper, zinc, tin, lead, the common Ms. of engineering. (iii) *Raver heavy Ms.:* nickel, cadmium, chromium, tungsten, molybdenum, manganese, cobalt, vanadium, antimony, and bismuth; used principally for alloying with the heavy Ms. (iv) *Light Ms.:* aluminium and magnesium. (v) *Alkali Ms.:* sodium, potassium, lithium; and alkaline earth Ms.: calcium, barium, strontium, used principally for chemical purposes.

Other metals have come to the fore because of special nuclear requirements, e.g., technetium, produced in nuclear reactors, is corrosion-inhibiting; zirconium may replace aluminium and magnesium alloy in canning uranium in reactors; titanium is really tough and hard, titanium oxide finds wide application in artistic finishes, because of its inertness and whiteness. Of great importance are the carbides of titanium, zirconium, niobium, and hafnium, alone or in combination, because of their high melting points round 3,000°C.

METAMORPHISM. Geological term referring to the changes which have occurred in the rocks of the earth's crust, caused by increases of pressure or of temperature, or of both, since the rocks were formed.

METAPHYSICS. A branch of philosophy, concerned with the ultimate nature of reality. It has been maintained that no certain knowledge of metaphysical questions is to be had. Epistemology, or the study of how we know, lies at the threshold of the subject. M. is concerned with the nature and origin of matter and of mind, the interaction between them – i.e. the 'mind-body problem'; the meaning of time

and space, causation, determinism and free will, personality and the Self, arguments for belief in God, and human immortality.

The foundations of M. were laid by Plato and Aristotle. St. Thomas Aquinas, basing himself on the latter, produced a metaphysical structure that is accepted by the Catholic Church. The subject has been advanced by Descartes, Spinoza, Leibniz, Berkeley, Hume, Locke, Kant, Hegel, Schopenhauer, and Marx; and in modern times by Bergson, Bradley, Croce, M'Taggart, and Whitehead.

METASTASIO (metahstah'zē-ō). Pseudonym of the Italian poet, Pietro Trapassi (1698–1782). B. in Rome, from 1730 he was court poet at Vienna, and wrote numerous lyric dramas.

METAXAS, Joannis (1871–1941). Greek soldier and statesman. B. in Ithaca, he opposed co-operation with the Allies during the F.W.W. and was prominent in the restoration of the monarchy in 1935. To combat internal difficulties he estab. a dictatorship when he became P.M. in 1936, and introduced several important reforms. Refusing to abandon Greece's neutral position, he victoriously led the resistance to the Italian invasion in the S.W.W.

METAZŌ'A. One of the 2 main sections into which the animal kingdom is divided, the other being the protozoa. M. are multi-cellular, and include all the higher forms of animal life.

ME'TEOR. A small particle moving round the Sun. If a M. approaches the Earth to within 150 miles or so, it enters the upper atmosphere, and since it is moving very rapidly (at anything up to 45 m. per sec.) frictional heat is set up; the M. destroys itself in the streak of radiation known as a *shooting-star*. Most Ms. are smaller than grains of sand. They tend to travel in swarms, and when the Earth passes through a swarm the result is a shower of shooting-stars: the most famous annual shower is that of the Perseids, in early August There are sporadic or non-shower Ms., which may appear from any direction at any moment.

ME'TEORITE. A solid body which comes from space and lands on the Earth. Small Ms. are not uncommon, but large ones are extremely rare; during the present cent. there have been only 2 major falls, both in Siberia – one in 1908 and the other in 1947. The heaviest M. known is at Hoba West, in Africa, which fell in prehistoric times, and has a weight of over 60 tons. Ms. are fundamentally different from meteors or shooting-stars, and seem to be more nearly related to the minor planets or asteroids.

METEORO'LOGY. The scientific observation and study of the phenomena of weather. At meteorological stations readings are taken of the more important factors determining weather conditions. Atmospheric pressure is measured by a mercury barometer, temperature by a screened thermometer, humidity by a hygrometer, which expresses relative humidity as a percentage of the maximum. Winds are categorized by the Beaufort Scale, and the Beaufort weather code signifies every weather condition by suitable initials, with capitals denoting intensity. Cloud observations gauge how many tenths of sky are covered by each type, and rainfall is measured each 12 hours in a funnel. Specially equipped weather ships maintained by several nations incl. Britain, at a number of ocean stations (9 in N. Atlantic and 4 in N. Pacific), report on weather conditions and advise air traffic. They carry radar (q.v.) and twice daily make balloon soundings of wind, temperature and humidity at heights up to about 60,000 ft. All these data are reported to, and collated by, central agencies, e.g. Meteorological Office, London; U.S. Weather Bureau, Washington, and then pooled on an international basis, when all nations can be informed on weather conditions as they affect crops, storms, hurricanes, etc., enabling regular weather forecasts to be made. As a public service, these were established in the late 19th cent., when wireless telegraphy first permitted the rapid collection of weather reports from large areas. When the reports for successive standard observation times are displayed on a sequence of charts the situation, movement and development of various weather systems, such as cyclonic storms, becomes apparent. Forecasts are made by continuing their observed trend into the future, with a skill acquired as an art by long experience as much as by scientific understanding. The electronic computer has enabled a promising start to be made in the stupendous task of using physical laws to *calculate* the future trend and to give long-range weather forecasts. Much understanding of the earth's atmosphere, and its effect on weather, is gained from satellites, which signal back a wide range of information. The *World Meteorological Organization* (1950) has estab. weather centres at Suitland, Maryland, U.S.A.; Moscow; and Melbourne.

ME′TER. A general term for any instrument used for measurement, often compounded with a prefix to denote a specific type of M., e.g. ammeter, voltmeter, flowmeter, pedometer, etc. Ms. may not only indicate but also integrate and/or record measurements.

ME′THĀNE or **Marsh Gas** (CH_4). The simplest hydrocarbon of the paraffin series; a constituent of the gas which arises in marshy districts from the decomposition of vegetable matter in stagnant water, and also of the explosive 'fire damp' in coal mines. M. is also a product of the distillation of coal, lignite, peat, wood, etc. It is colourless, odourless, and lighter than air, burns with a faintly luminous flame, and explodes when mixed with air or oxygen.

METHODISM. The evangelical movement founded by John and Charles Wesley in 1739; the name was originally applied to the Wesleys and their circle at Oxford as a nickname. M. originated within the C. of E., and only in 1795 became a distinct body.

The doctrines of M. are contained in John Wesley's *Notes on the New Testament* and sermons. The form of church government is presbyterian in Britain, and episcopal in the U.S.A. The supreme authority is the annual conference, composed of equal numbers of ministers and laymen. Members are grouped under 'class leaders' and churches into 'circuits'. Disagreements have led to secessions, but the modern tendency is to reunion between the sects (as in 1932 in Britain and in 1939 and 1968 in the U.S.A.), and eventual merger with other Protestant denominations as a single Church (as in the union of Methodists, Presbyterians, and Congregationalists in Canada in 1925 as the United Church of Canada; the union of 7 major Protestant Churches, incl. the United Methodist Church, planned by 1980 in the U.S.A.; and the negotiations between the Methodist Church and the Anglican Communion in Britain).

METHODIUS. *See* CYRIL.

METHU′SELAH. One of the antediluvian patriarchs of Hebrew story. From the immense age with which he is credited, 969 years, M. has become the type of longevity.

METHYL ALCOHOL or **Methanol** (CH_3OH). The simplest of the monohydric alcohols, also known as wood alcohol, since it may be prepared by the dry distillation of hard woods. When pure, it is a colourless inflammable liquid with a pleasant odour and is highly poisonous. It is used in organic preparations, as a solvent (especially in the preparation of varnishes and lacquers), and for denaturing ethyl alcohol.

METHYLATED SPIRITS. Adulterated or 'denatured' alcohol, which has been rendered undrinkable, and is free of duty for industrial purposes. It is nevertheless drunk by advanced alcoholics, and eventually results in death.

METRIC SYSTEM. A system of weights and measures based on the *metre*, the unit of length based on the recommendations of a committee of the French Academy (1791) in a report to the National Assembly which fixed the standard of length as one ten-millionth part of the earth's meridian quadrant at sea-level determined from extensive geodetic surveys between Barcelona and Dunkirk. A subsequent redefinition still in use for some purposes is the distance at 0°C between the centres of 2 lines engraved on a bar of platinum-iridium in Paris, but in 1960 an internat. conference on weights and measures officially redefined it as the length measured in vacuo of 1,650,763·73 wavelengths of the orange-red radiation emitted by krypton (isotope 86) corresponding to the unperturbed transition between the $2p_{10}$ and $5d_5$ levels. The M.S. became legal in France in 1801 and obligatory in 1840.

The M.S. – SI or International System – is universally used for scientific work, is in general use on the Continent, and is in process of adoption throughout the world, 1975 being the guideline date for its adoption by British industry.

The main M. descriptions are: metre (symbol m) for length, litre (l) for capacity, gramme (g) for weight, newton (N) for force, joule (J) for energy, and watt (W) for power. They are preceded by the following expressions to multiply or divide them: mega (M) million times; kilo (k) thousand times, hecto (h) hundred times, deca (da) ten times, deci (d) tenth part, centi (c) hundredth part, milli (m) thousandth part, micro (μ) millionth part. All multiples and submultiples are decimal. *See* p. 1118.

METROPOLITAN OPERA COMPANY. Foremost opera co. of U.S.A., founded N.Y. 1883. The M.O. House (opened 1883) was demolished 1966, and the co. transferred to the New Met. in the Lincoln Center.

METSU (met′sü), **Gabriel** (1630–67). Dutch painter. B. at Leyden, he worked in Amsterdam from 1657. His pictures are usually of the anecdotal type and incl. 'The Duet' and 'Music Lesson', both in the National Gallery, London.

METTERNICH - WIN-NEBURG, Clemens Wenzel Lothar, prince (1773–1859). Austrian statesman. He was ambassador to France 1806–9, and Foreign Minister from 1809 until the 1848 revolution forced him to flee to England. At the Congress of Vienna in 1815 he advocated co-operation by the great powers to suppress democratic movements.

METZ. Cap. of Moselle dept., France, on the Moselle. It has a Gothic cathedral, is the centre of a rich agricultural region, and manufactures shoes, metal goods, and tobacco. It was long one of the great frontier fortresses of France. M. was a free city of the Holy Roman Empire until 1552, and was German 1871–1918. Pop. (1968) 107,537.

MEUNIER (mönyeh′), **Constantin Émile** (1831–1905). Belgian painter and sculptor. B. at Brussels, he is known for his paintings and sculptures of industrial life of Belgium.

MEUNIER. Typical of the sculptor's interest in 'the worker' is this fine impression of a stevedore, 'Le Débardeur'.
Courtesy of Belgian National Tourist Office.

MEURTHE (mört). French river, 102 m. long,

MEXICO. Mosaic inspired by pre-Colombian art is strikingly used in modern Mexican buildings such as the library of the Univ. of Mexico (1951–3) designed by Juan O'Gorman, Gustavo Saavedra and Juan Martinez de Velasco.
Courtesy of the Mexican Embassy.

which rises in the Vosges Mts. and flows in a generally N.W. direction to join the Moselle at Frouard, 5 m. N.N.W. of Nancy. It gives its name to the dept. of Meurthe-et-Moselle. M. was also the name of a French dept., part of which was lost to Germany in 1871; the remainder was incl. in M.-et-Moselle; when the part ceded in 1871 was recovered in 1919 it was added to Moselle dept.

MEUSE (mös). River which rises in the dept. of Haute-Marne, France, passes Verdun, and flows in a N. direction into Belgium, past Namur and Liège, then enters the Netherlands S. of Maastricht, flowing N., then W. to join the Waal near Gorkum. The Dutch form of its name is Maas. Of its total length of *c.* 560 m., 300 are in France, 120 in Belgium, 160 in the Netherlands. The M., which gives its name to a French dept., was a line of battle in the F.W.W. in 1914, and the S.W.W. in 1940.

MEW, Charlotte Mary (1870–1928). British poet. B. in London, after a lifelong struggle against poverty she received a Civil List Pension in 1923, but committed suicide after the death of her mother and sister. She pub. 2 vols. of sensitive verse, *Farmer's Bride* (1915) and *Rambling Sailor* (1929).

MEWAR. Another name for UDAIPUR.

MEXICO. Federal rep. of Central America, lying S. of the U.S.A.

Physical. The Gulf of California divides the mainland to the E. from the elongated, mountainous peninsula of Lower California to the W. The 2 ranges of the Sierra Madre enclose an extensive central plateau and meet near the isthmus of Tehuantepec, on which both coasts converge. None of the rivers is of any commercial importance. Climatically, the country is divided into: (1) *Tierra Caliente*, a low-lying, tropical region adjacent to the coasts and including the peninsula of Yucatan; (2) *Tierra Templada*, a temperate region including most of the plateau; and (3) *Tierra Fría*, a cold region rising above 6,000 ft., in which Mexico City is situated. Over much of M. the rainfall is very scanty.

Economic. M. is predominantly agricultural, but requires food imports. The main crops are maize (the staple food), beans, wheat, coffee, sugar, rice, bananas, tobacco, sisal, and cotton. Cattle are bred. Contour-ploughing, re-afforestation, and irrigation are being developed to conserve and extend cultivable land. Silver, gold, lead, zinc, arsenic, copper, iron ore and uranium are worked. The oil industry (nationalised 1938) is important and natural gas is supplied to U.S.A. Iron and steel, textiles, electrical goods, chemicals, etc., are increasingly produced, and traditional handicrafts in silver, pottery, weaving, leather, etc., supply valuable revenue. The chief

ports are Tampico and Vera Cruz, and communications by road, rail and air are excellent.

Political. M. comprises 29 states, 1 federal dist., and 2 territories. As amended in 1953, the federal constitution provided for a pres. popularly elected for 6 years and ineligible for re-election, and a congress consisting of a number of deputies elected for 3 years and a senate elected for 6 years. Men and women are eligible to vote at 18 if married, at 21 if unmarried.

Area and Population. The total area is 763,944 sq. m., and the pop. (mestizos, Indians, and whites), in 1967 *c.* 45,671,000. The official tongue is Spanish, but some 2,500,000 of the pop. (of whom perhaps half can speak Spanish) use Indian languages, among which Nahuatl is spoken by about 30 per cent; Mixtec (10 per cent); Maya (9 per cent); Zapotec (8 per cent); and Otomi (7 per cent). Most of the people are Roman Catholics, but Church and State have been separated since 1857, and Church activities are severely curtailed. Primary education up to 15 is free and in theory compulsory, but approx. half the pop. is under 15 and illiteracy is *c.* 20%.

Apart from Mexico City, the cap., the principal towns are Monterrey, Guadalajara, Puebla, San Luis, Potosi, Merida, and Veracruz. Tourism is increasingly important, the majority of visitors being from U.S.A., and resorts such as Acapulco are world-famous.

History. M. was the scene of the brilliant Indian civilizations of the Mayas, at its height *c.* A.D. 300–900, the Toltecs (*c.* 900–1100), and the Aztecs who settled on the central plateau, and whose last emperor, Montezuma II, was killed in 1520 during the Spanish invasion. M. became the viceroyalty of New Spain; Spanish culture and the Catholic religion were firmly established, and the natural wealth of the country was developed, but foreign rule became increasingly oppressive, and Spanish rule was ended in 1821. In 1824 a rep. was set up. Texas separated from M. in 1836, and New Mexico and California were ceded to the U.S.A. after the war of 1846–8. After 3 years of civil war, Benito Juarez established himself as ruler over the whole country in 1861. His repudiation of foreign debts led to foreign intervention, and in 1863 Maximilian of Austria was proclaimed emperor; but when the French troops supporting him were withdrawn, 1866, he was captured and executed, 1867. Juarez remained pres. until 1872. His successor, Lardo, was opposed by Porfirio Diaz who, entering Mexico City in force in 1876, was elected pres. 1877–80 and again in 1884 and at each succeeding election until forced to resign in 1911. The stability resulting from Diaz's dictatorship ended with his fall. But in 1920 a period of reconstruction began, based

MEXICO CITY. The Cathedral Square or Plaza de Armas is the heart of the city. The baroque cathedral itself is the greatest achievement of the colonial period. Its foundations having been laid *c.* 1562 and the building completed in 1813.
Courtesy of the Mexican Government Tourist Department.

on a new constitution of 1917 which expropriated owners of large estates and let the land to the peasants. Mexico declared war on the Axis powers June 1942, and was an original member of the United Nations.

MEXICO CITY. Cap. and largest city of Mexico, situated on the S. edge of the central plateau, at 7,400 ft. above sea-level near Lake Texcoco. It is spacious and regular, and the many fine buildings incl. the 16th cent. cathedral, the national palace, the national library, the Palace of Justice, and national univ. M.C. is an important cultural centre, a vital railway, road, and air service centre, and business and industrial development is growing. *See* illus. pp. 729 and 1104. The city dates from *c.* 1325, when the Aztec cap. Tenochtitlán was begun on an island in Lake Texcoco. This city was levelled in 1521 by the Spaniards, who in 1522 founded a new city on the site. The lake has gradually shrunk, and is some 2½ m. from the present-day M.C. Pop. (1968) 3,118,059.

MEYER (mī′er), **Conrad Ferdinand** (1825–98). Swiss poet and novelist. B. at Zürich, he abandoned law for literature after the success of his *Balladen* (1867). He continued to write verse, but also developed the short story and the novel. Among his fictitious reconstructions of history are *Jürg Jenatsch* (1876), *Der Heilige* (1880), and *Angela Borgia* (1891).

MEYERBEER (mī′-erbār), **Giacomo.** Adopted name of German composer Jakob Liebmann Beer (1791–1864). B. in Berlin, from 1826 he lived mainly in Paris, apart from his work after 1842 as general musical director in Berlin. A talented pianist, he became best known for his spectacular operas, e.g. *Robert le Diable* (1831) and *Les Huguenots* (1836).

MEYNELL (men′el), **Alice** (1847–1922). British poet, *neé* Thompson. She pub. *Preludes* (1875), and her collected poems appeared in 1923. Her essays incl. *Rhythm of Life* (1893), and *Second Person Singular* (1921). In 1877 she m. the Catholic author and journalist, Wilfrid M. (1852–1948) and with him befriended Francis Thompson. Her youngest son, **Sir Francis M.** (1891–), is a book designer, and in 1923 he founded the Nonesuch Press. He was knighted in 1946. Her 3rd dau., **Viola M.** (d. 1956), was a sensitive novelist, and also pub. a memoir of her mother (1929).

MEZZANINE (mez′anēn). Architectural term derived from the diminutive of the Italian word for middle; it is a low storey in a building between 2 higher ones.

MEZZOTINT (med′zo-). A method of etching in tone, widely practised during the 18th cent. A copper or steel plate is roughened by means of a rocking tool, which makes indentations and raises a 'burr'. The burr is then scraped away where lighter tones are wanted in the design. The process was used to reproduce the works of Turner, Reynolds, Constable, Romney, Lawrence and others.

MIAMI (mī-am′i). City and port in S.E. Florida, U.S.A., where the M. river enters Biscayne Bay. In 1895 'Fort Dallas' was a tiny hamlet, but with the coming of the railway and its incorporation as the City of M. (Seminole 'sweet water') in 1896, it grew rapidly as a centre for citrus fruit, tourism, and oceanographic research, and as a commercial and manufacturing 'Gateway to Latin America'. Many Cuban refugees (*c.* 125,000) settled here after 1959. Pop. met. area (1970) 1,259,176.

MIASKOVSKY, Nicolai (1881–1950). Russian composer. He studied music at St. Petersburg under Rimsky-Korsakov and others, and was a prolific composer of symphonies. Other works incl. the symphonic poem 'Nevermore' (after Poe). After the S.W.W. he became well known as a prof. of composition at the Moscow conservatoire, and was denounced by the Soviet authorities in 1948, together with Prokofiev, Shostakovich, et al., for 'formalism', i.e. for being supposedly too intellectual, too modern.

MICA. A group of minerals distinguished by their perfect basal cleavage causing them to split into thin flakes, and by their vitreous pearly lustre. They are found in schists, gneisses, and granites, and their good thermal and electrical insulation quality makes them valuable in industry. M. can be dated to a few thousand years by its geological context, and muon-neutrino tracks within it confirm evolutionary theories of the solar planetary system.

MICAH (fl. *c.* 700 B.C.). Hebrew prophet, whose writings in the O.T. denounce the oppression of the ruling class of Judah, and plead for justice.

MICHAEL. An archangel, referred to in the Book of Daniel as the guardian angel of Israel. In Revelation he leads the hosts of heaven to battle against Satan. In ecclesiastical art he bears a flaming sword.

MICHAEL (1596–1645). Tsar of Russia. He was elected tsar by a national assembly in 1613, at a time of anarchy and foreign invasion, and founded the house of Romanov, which ruled until 1917.

MICHAEL (1921–). King of Rumania. Son of Carol II, he succeeded his grandfather as king in 1927, but was displaced when his father returned from exile in 1930. In 1940 he proclaimed king again on his father's abdication, and in 1944 he overthrew the dictatorship of Antonescu and enabled Rumania to share in the final victory of the Allies at the end of the S.W.W. He abdicated and left Rumania in 1947.

MICHAELMAS DAISY. Popular name for *Aster tradescanti* and also for the sea aster or starwort.

MICHAELMAS DAY. Festival of St. Michael and all Angels, observed on 29 Sept., and one of the English quarter days.

MICHELANGELO (mīkelan′jelō) (1475–1564). Italian artist and poet, whose full name was Michelagniolo di Lodovico Buonarroti Simoni. B. near Florence, he studied painting under Domenico and David Ghirlandaio, and for a number of years lived in the palace of Lorenzo de' Medici. He worked in Rome 1496–1501, and again was chiefly in Rome 1508–64. His works of sculpture include the *Pietà*, David, and, for the tomb of pope Julius II, Moses, and the Slaves. In Florence he designed the Medici sepulchral chapel. His most important paintings are those on the ceiling and above the altar ('The Last Judgment') of the Sistine Chapel, Rome. In 1547 he was appointed chief architect of St. Peter's, and designed the dome. M. was the most gifted artist of the Italian Renaissance. He also wrote sonnets and madrigals, many of which were inspired by his friendship with Vittoria Colonna in his later years.

MICHELET (mēshlā′), **Jules** (1798–1874). French historian, prof. at the Collège de France from 1838. His *Introduction à l'histoire universelle* (1831), was followed by his masterpiece, the *Histoire de France* (1867); *Histoire de la révolution* (1853), etc.

MICHELSON, Albert Abraham (1852–1931). American physicist. Prof. at Chicago from 1892, he was the first American scientist to win the Nobel prize. He invented the M. interferometer, and in conjunction with E. W. Morley performed in 1887 the *Michelson-Morley Experiment* to detect the motion of the earth through the postulated ether. The failure of the experiment led to Einstein's theory of relativity.

MICHIGAN (mish′-). A north-central state of the U.S.A., consisting of 2 peninsulas separated by Lake M. and bordered by lakes Superior, Huron, and Erie, and Canada. The chief highlands are the Porcupine mts., and the rivers incl. the Muskegon, Grand, St. Joseph, Kalamazoo. The state, formerly agricultural, is now chiefly industrial, the motor-car industry being prominent. As the producer of iron ore, copper, cement, sand and gravel, gypsum, and salt, M. is one of the leading states in the Union. Detroit is the largest city; other cities are Grand Rapids, Flint, Saginaw, and Lansing (the cap.).

The area was explored by the French from 1618 onwards, their first permanent settlement being made

MICHIGAN. The whisky stills which flourished along this attractive creek in the mid.-19th cent. earned the little community growing up there the name of Hell. Not far from Detroit, Hell has a chain of beautiful lakes which make it today an up-and-coming tourist resort.
Courtesy of Hell Chamber of Commerce.

in 1668; it became British in 1763, was organized as a territory 1805 (M. territory, 1787, having incl. parts of other later states), and was admitted to the Union as a state 1837. Area 58,216 sq. m. incl. 1,194 sq. m. of inland water. Pop. (1970) 8,875,083.

LAKE M. is the 3rd largest of the great lakes of N. America, and the only one completely in the U.S.A. It is over 300 m. long, and has a water surface of 22,400 sq. m.

MICHIGAN CITY. City and port in the state of Indiana, U.S.A., lying on Lake Michigan, 40 m. E.S.E. of Chicago. It was founded *c.* 1830, and is a summer resort with metal and clothing industries. Pop. (1960) 36,653.

MICKIEWICZ (mitskē-ā′vich), **Adam** (1798–1855). Polish poet. B. in Lithuania, he was imprisoned and compelled to live for 5 years in Russia, owing to his revolutionary activities. There he pub. the narrative poem, *Konrad Wallenrod* (1828). He d. at Constantinople, while raising a Polish corps to fight against Russia in the Crimean War. The greatest of his later works is *Pan Tadeusz*, the Polish epic.

MI′CRŌBE. In biology, a microscopic organism, a germ, bacillus, micro-organism, or bacterium, instinct with life and power of multiplication. *See* BACTERIA.

MICROFILM RECORDING. Space-saving system for storing information by photographing books, documents, etc., on rolls of 16 or 35 mm. film.

MI′CRO′METER. An instrument for making very small measurements with the greatest accuracy. For astronomical use, it consists of 2 very fine wires, one fixed and the other movable, placed in the focal plane of a telescope; the movable wire is fixed on a sliding plate and can be moved parallel to the other until the object appears between the wires. The movement is then indicated by a scale on the adjusting screw. *M. gauges* are measuring gauges having their adjustment effected by an extremely accurate fine-pitch screw; they are of great value in engineering.

MICROMINIATURIZATION. The reduction in size and weight of electronic components and circuits to meet space, airborne and military needs, and for such devices as electronic computers in which the number of circuits is very large. By the use of transistors, ferrites and printed circuits the no. of components contained in a given vol. has multiplied 4 times; by M. techniques 40 times; and it may well be multiplied by 400 or more by the use of solid state circuits (q.v.).

MICRONE′SIA. That part of Oceania lying N. of Melanesia and incl. the Caroline, Marshall and Mariana groups of islands and the Gilberts. Guam, in the Marianas, belongs to the U.S.A.; the Gilberts are British; the remainder, mandated to Japan in 1919, were placed under U.S. trusteeship in 1947 and formed into the U.S. Pacific Islands Trust Territory.

MI′CROPHŌNE. The first component in a sound-reproducing system, whereby the mechanical energy of sound waves is converted into electrical energy for the purpose of transmission. One of the simplest is the telephone transmitter, invented by Bell in 1876, and other well-known examples are those used with broadcasting and sound-film apparatus.

MI′CROSCOPE. An optical instrument for magnifying small objects for detailed examination. A simple M. or magnifying glass has a single convex lens. A compound M. has 2 sets of lenses, an objective (4) and an eyepiece (5). Light from the source (1) is concentrated by the condenser (2) on to the object, mounted on a slide, resting on the stage (3). The objective (4) forms a real, inverted and magnified image of the object, just within the focal length of the eyepiece (5) which acting as a simple M. allows the operator to view the image. The focusing control (6) moves the lens barrel up or down, to focus on to the object. Compound lenses are always used, to reduce distortion of colour and shape to a minimum.

The electron M. (q.v.) is a modern development using an electron beam instead of light; and electromagnetic instead of optical lenses. It is up to 200 times (linear) more powerful than the optical M., and a recent development by E. W. Müller of Pa. State univ., the field ion M., uses ions as the travelling particles to determine atomic structure, and metal itself as their source. Magnifications up to $2\frac{3}{4}$ million are said to be possible.

MI′CRŌWAVE HEATING. Form of radio-frequency or dielectric H., using frequencies at least 20 times higher than usually employed. Instead of penetrating from the surface by conduction, heat is generated throughout an object simultaneously. It is used in instantaneous cooking of prepared foods, destruction of insects in grain, destruction of enzymes in processed food, liquid sterilization, pasteurization, and drying of timber and paper.

MI′DAS. King of Phrygia, who was granted the gift of converting all he touched to gold, and who, for preferring the music of Pan to that of Apollo, was given ass's ears by the latter. Also instrument (black box) recording flight data in planes.

MIDDELBURG. Town in Walcheren Island, Netherlands, cap. of Zeeland prov. It has engineering works and tobacco and furniture factories, and a 15–16th cent. Town Hall. Pop. (1967) 28,000.

MIDDLE AGES. A term which came into use in the 17th cent. for the period of European history between the fall of the Roman Empire and the Renaissance. It is usually regarded as beginning in the 5th cent. and ending in the 15th. Its distinctive features were the unity of W. Europe within the R.C. Church, and the feudal organization of political, social and economic relations.

MIDDLESBROUGH. Formerly a co. bor., it amalgamated in 1968 with Stockton on Tees, Redcar, Billingham, Thornaby and Eston to form the co. bor. of Teesside (q.v.), of which it is the commercial, social and cultural centre. Dating from *c.* 1830, it depended on the iron industry, shipbuilding and – from the 1920s – chemicals, and entered a depressed phase from the 1930s until diversification in the 1960s.

MIDDLESEX. English county, which disappeared as an administrative div. in the re-organization attendant on the creation of the new Greater London 1964–5. Contained within the Thames basin, and where not built over good agricultural land, it was

Y

settled in the 6th cent. by Saxon tribes, and its name comes from its position between the kingdoms of the E. and W. Saxons.

MIDDLETON, Sir Hugh (c. 1560–1631). London goldsmith, who between 1609 and 1613 built the New River Canal, whereby fresh drinking water was brought from wells in Herts to London.

MIDDLETON, Thomas (c. 1570–1627). English dramatist. B. in London, he produced numerous romantic plays and realistic comedies, both alone and in collaboration. Best-known are *A Fair Quarrel* and *The Changeling*, with Rowley; *The Roaring Girl* with Dekker; and *Women Beware Women*.

MIDDLETON. English market town (bor.) in Lancs, on the r. Irk, 6 m. N. of Manchester, with silk and cotton factories, printing works, etc. Pop. (1961) 56,674.

MIDDLETOWN. Name of a number of towns and villages in the U.S.A. The largest are M., an industrial city in Conn., on the Connecticut r., 14 m. S. of Hartford; it makes textiles, rubber products, clothing, chemicals, cigars, etc. A suspension bridge 3,420 ft. long, completed 1938, links it with Portland across the river. It dates from 1650. Pop. (1960) 33,250. Another M., in New York state, incorporated in 1888, is an agricultural centre with textile, machinery, paper, chemical, and other works. Pop. (1960) 23,475. M., a city in Ohio laid out in 1802, has steel-rolling and paper mills, tobacco and metal factories. Pop. (1960) 42,115.

For the 'M.' described by R. S. and H. M. Lynd, *see* MUNCIE.

MIDDLE WEST. Name given to a large area in the north-centre of U.S.A., usually taken as comprising the states of Ohio, Indiana, Illinois, Michigan, Iowa, Wisconsin, and Minnesota, and containing about a quarter of the total population. Lord Bryce, who first distinguished the area in 1888, said that the M.W. is the most distinctively American part of the U.S.A. It tends to be Republican and isolationist.

MIDGE. Name applied in popular speech to many gnat-like insects; in particular to the Chironomidae.

MIDLANDS. A section of England corresponding roughly to the Anglo-Saxon kingdom of Mercia. It is bounded on the N. by Yorks and Lancs, on the W. by Wales, on the S. by the Thames, and the E. by Norfolk, Suffolk, Essex, Herts, and Greater London.

MIDLŌ'THIAN. Scottish county lying S. of the Firth of Forth. In the S. are the Moorfoot and the Pentland hills. Rivers incl. the Gala, the N. and S. Esk, and the Water of Leith. The co. is largely agricultural, but coal is mined extensively on the N. Esk. In addition to Edinburgh, the co. town, the towns incl. Dalkeith, Musselburgh, and Penicuik. Area 366 sq. m.; pop. (1961) 580,332.

MIDNIGHT SUN. Phenomenon seen N. of the Arctic Circle and S. of the Antarctic Circle when the sun is above the horizon at midnight during summer.

MIDRASH (Heb., inquiry, searching out). Name given to the ancient Jewish homiletical commentaries on the Bible, in which allegory and legendary illustration are freely used. They were compiled principally in Palestine from the 4th cent. onwards.

MIDSHIPMAN. Officer in training in the R.N., ranking below the lowest commissioned officer. Ms. are often called 'snotties', traditionally because they wiped their noses with their sleeves rather than handkerchiefs. In the U.S. students training at the naval academy are called Midshipmen.

MIDSUMMER. The summer solstice, about 21 June, but M. Day is 24 June – a quarter day and the festival of St. John the Baptist.

MIDWAY. Circular atoll and island group in the N. Pacific, c. 1,200 m. N.W. of Hawaii. Discovered by the U.S.A. in 1859 and acquired by that country in 1867, M. became a point of call for trans-Pacific aircraft in 1935. M. was attacked without success by the Japanese in 1941. Area 2·2 sq. m.; pop. (1960) 416.

MIDWIFERY. Obstetrics; the assistance of women in childbirth. As one of the principal divisions of the qualifying course for medical practitioners, it incl. all sorts of treatment, medical and surgical, connected with birth, but the functions of a midwife are in most countries limited by law to the making of preparations and examinations, the giving of ordinary assistance and after-care, and the summoning of the doctor in an emergency. In England the local authorities conduct municipal M. services and license midwives for practice.

MIERIS (mē'ris). Name of a family of Dutch painters, of whom the most important was Franz van M. (1635–81). He painted small genre pictures distinguished by their polish and rendering of detail.

MIES VAN DER ROHE, Ludwig (1886–). American architect. Son of a stonemason, he was b. in Aachen, and was director of the Bauhaus 1929–33. He became prof. at the Illinois Institute of Technology (1938–58), for which he designed new logically functional buildings from 1941, and the bronze-and-glass Seagram building, N.Y.

MIGNARD (mēnyahr'), **Pierre** (1610–95). French painter. Known as 'Le Romain', he worked in Italy for 22 years, and subsequently in Paris, becoming an opponent of Le Brun. He painted many pleasant, graceful portraits of people of the day, e.g. Descartes, Molière, and Bossuet. The term 'Mignardise' (meaning sugar-sweet) is derived from his Italian-type Madonnas.

MIGNET (mēnyā'), **François Auguste Marie** (1796–1884). French historian. Notable for his sound judgment, he wrote a *Histoire de la révolution française* (1824), and *Histoire de Marie Stuart* (1851).

MIGNONETTE (minyonet'). Sweet-scented garden plant (*Reseda odorata*), bearing usually yellowish-green flowers in racemes, with abundant foliage. A native of N. Africa, it was brought to England about 1752.

MIGRAINE. Incapacitating disease, characterized by headaches, usually severe, and preceded in 75 per cent of cases by warning symptoms (disturbances of vision, especially flashing lights, and less frequently of sensation affecting the legs, arms or face). In 60 per cent of cases the headache is followed by nausea or vomiting. Preparations of ergotamine, taken early in the attack, are the best treatment, and in preventing attacks travel sickness compounds or, in 75 per cent of patients willing to take the drug all the time, l-methyl-D-lysergic acid butanolamide tartrate has proved beneficial.

MIGRATION. The seasonal movements of certain animals, particularly birds and fishes. Some fishes, notably eels and salmon, migrate at the breeding season. Many birds inhabiting temperate climates migrate in winter to warmer zones, usually travelling in large numbers. Observation of migrating birds is carried on chiefly from lighthouses, and the destinations, distance covered, and length of time taken have been ascertained by 'ringing' the legs of certain birds for identification.

MIHAILO'VICH, Draga (1893–1946). Yugoslav soldier. He served in the army of his native Serbia in the Balkan and F.W.Ws. After the German occupation of Yugoslavia in the S.W.W., he withdrew to the hills with his guerrilla troops ('Chetniks'), but his antipathy to the Croatian Tito's Communist resistance fighters, and the withdrawal in 1943 of the support of the Allies and the exiled Y. govt., forced him to accept aid from the Italians and Germans, and he was eventually captured and shot for treason.

MIKADO (mikah'dō). Title applied by foreigners to the Japanese emperor; the Japanese style is *tenno*.

MIKOYA'N, Anastasiy Ivanovich (1895–). Soviet statesman. B. at Tiflis, he was a prominent Bolshevik leader in Baku during the Revolution and was Min.

MILAN. Built in 1450 for Francesco Sforza on his succession to the duchy, the Castello Sforzesco was later decorated by Bramante and Leonardo da Vinci under the patronage of Lodovico. The 230 ft. Filarete tower, seen here, which ornaments one side of the open square it forms, was destroyed by an explosion in 1521 and rebuilt in 1904.
Courtesy of Italian Cultural Institute.

for Foreign Trade 1938–49 and for Home and Foreign Trade 1953–5. A member of the Presidium 1952–66 (of the Politbureau from 1934), he became a first Vice-Chairman (Deputy P.M.) in 1955 and was Pres. (Chairman of the Presidium) 1964–5.

MILAN (milan'). City of N. Italy, cap. of M. prov., on the r. Olona in the Plain of Lombardy. In the heart of the city is the Piazza del Duomo, at one end of which is the splendid Gothic cathedral – one of the largest Christian churches, with an area of 14,000 sq. yds., and capable of holding 40,000 worhippers. Begun in 1386, it was not finished until 1813, though St. Charles Borromeo consecrated it in 1577. The exterior is a mass of pinnacles, statues, etc. Nearby is the famous Scala opera house (1778). Other noteworthy buildings are the Palazzo Reale, the palace of the archbishop, the church of St. Ambrose (Ital. Ambrogio) with St. Ambrose's tomb, the Casa dei Borromei, the Brera picture-gallery, and the castle. Several 'skyscrapers' (one 400 ft. high with 31 stories) and an underground railway were constructed in the 1950s.

M., which is the seat of 2 univs., is also a great industrial centre, making aircraft, locomotives, motor-cars, bicycles, etc., and is the chief seat of the Italian textile industry. It was the ancient Mediolanum, and for cents. in the Middle Ages was an independent city-state under the Visconti and Sforza families. In 1859 it became part of the kingdom of Italy. Pop. (1961) 1,580,978.

MILDENHALL (mil'-). English market town in Suffolk, on the edge of M. Fen, 76 m. N.N.E. of London. In 1942 Roman silverware was dug up nearby, ascribed to the 3rd cent., and transferred to the British Museum in 1946. Pop. *c.* 7,000.

MILDEW. Name given to minute fungi, like a thin whitish coat, which appear as a destructive growth on plants, paper, leather, wood, etc., when exposed to damp. They incl. both parasites and saprophytes. *See* FUNGI.

MILE. Measure of length in English-speaking countries; 1,760 yds. (5,280 ft.). It is derived from the Roman M. of 1,000 paces. Considerably longer Ms. have been used in Ireland and Scotland. A nautical M. is 6,080 ft. A geographical M. is the length of 1 minute of latitude, and its mean length is 6,076·8 ft.

MILE END. A part of the Greater London bor. of Tower Hamlets in the district of Stepney in the East End. M.E. Green (later renamed Stepney Green) was the scene of Richard II's meeting with the rebel peasants in 1381, and the exercise ground of the train-bands.

MILES, Sir Bernard (1907–). British actor-producer. After repertory experience, he appeared in such parts as Briggs in *Thunder Rock* (1940) and Iago in *Othello* (1942), and his films incl. *Great Expectations* (1947). He founded a Trust which built the City of London's first theatre for 300 years, The Mermaid, opened in 1959 with the musical play *Lock Up Your Daughters*, and where he has since produced Mayakovsky's *The Bedbug* (1962), etc. He was knighted 1969.

MILETUS. Ancient Greek city in S.W. Asia Minor, which carried on an important trade with Egypt and the Black Sea. The scientists Thales, Anaximander, and Anaximenes were born at M.

MI'LFOIL. *See* YARROW.

MILFORD, Robin (1903–). British composer. He studied under Holst and Vaughan Williams at the R.C.M., and is best known for his songs and choral music, e.g. the oratorio *A Prophet in the Land* (1931).

MILFORD HAVEN, Louis Alexander, 1st marquess of (1854–1921). British sailor. B. Prince Louis of Battenberg (q.v.), he became a naturalized Briton in 1868, and entered the navy. In 1912 he was 1st Sea Lord, but he had to resign in 1914 owing to 'anti-German' agitation in the press. He gave up his German titles in 1917, assumed the surname of Mountbatten, and was made marquess of M.H. In 1921 he was appointed Admiral of the Fleet. He was the father of Earl Mountbatten, and the grandfather of the duke of Edinburgh. *See* also GUSTAV VI.

MILFORD HAVEN. Welsh seaport (U.D.) in Pembrokeshire, with a fine harbour comprising the estuary of the E. and W. Cleddau rivers. Here is a

MILDENHALL. In this silver dish from the treasure hoard, the central mask of Neptune with dolphins in his hair is surrounded by a frieze showing the triumph of Bacchus over Hercules. Dating from the 4th century A.D., it is almost two feet in diameter. *Photo: British Museum*

MILFORD HAVEN. This deep-water marine terminal (54 ft. minimum depth in the approaches) is able to accommodate the great super-tankers, and is one of Europe's largest oil ports. *Photo: Aerofilms.*

large petroleum refinery, and a specially built jetty for tankers, connected by a 62-mile pipeline with refineries at Llandarcy, near Swansea, where there are also petrochemical works. Pop. (1961) 12,802.

MILHAUD (mēloh'), **Darius** (1892–). French composer. In Brazil (19 7–19) he wrote the piano pieces *Saudades do Brasil*, before returning to France, where he became a member of the satirical group of composers 'Les Six', writing e.g. *Machines Agricoles* (1919), a setting of an agricultural catalogue, and the jazz ballet *La Création du Monde* (1923). He was associated with Paul Claudel (q.v.), with whom he collaborated in various ballets. In 1940 he went to the U.S. as prof. of music at Mills College, Calif., and became prof. of composition at the National Conservatoire in Paris in 1947. Much of his later work, which incl. chamber, orchestral, and choral music, is polytonal.

MILITARY LAW. *See* MARTIAL LAW.

MILITIA. A home-defence force, as distinguished from the Regular Army, consisting of ordinary citizens, with usually some military training, who are on call in emergencies.

King Alfred estab. the 1st M. or *fyrd*, in which every freeman was liable to serve. After the Conquest a feudal levy was estab. in which landowners were responsible for raising the men required. This in turn led to the increasing use of the general levy by English kings to combat the growing power of the barons. In the 16th cent., under such threats as the Spanish Armada, plans for internal defence relied increasingly on the M., or what came to be called 'trained bands', of the general levy. After the Restoration, the M. fell into neglect, but it was re-organized in 1757, and relied upon for home defence during the French wars; and in the 19th cent. it extended its activities abroad, serving in the Peninsular, Crimean and Boer wars. In 1852 it adopted a volunteer status, and in 1908 the M. was merged with the Territorial Army and the Special Reserve forces, to supplement the Regular Army, and ceased to exist as a separate force. In 1939 the name 'Militiamen' was given to the 6 month conscripts known as the 'Hore-Belisha Boys'.

The principle of a M. was introd. into the U.S. with the 1st settlers, who had to be able to defend as well as build their settlements. After an Act of 1792, it more or less replaced for a time the Regular Army, but was itself supplanted in the late 19th cent. by the volunteer National Guard units of individual states, which are under federal orders in emergencies, and are now an integral part of the U.S. Army. In Switzerland, the M. is the national defence force, and every ablebodied man is liable for service in it.

MILK. The secretion of the mammary glands of female vertebrate animals which suckle their young, for whom it is a complete food. The M. of cows, goats and sheep is consumed by man. In the U.K. the Food and Drugs Act of 1899 (amended 1939) empowered a standard to be fixed below which the fats and solids content of cows' M. should not fall; the same standard applies in the U.S.A. Preservatives were forbidden after 1912, and in 1913 the notification of cattle with tuberculosis became compulsory. M. from Tuberculin Tested herds is the highest type of raw M.; 'pasteurized' M. is partially sterilized; these and lower grades of M. are rated according to the number of bacilli per cu.cm.; 'homogenized M.' has the fat content broken down so that the cream can be evenly distributed. In the U.S., as in the U.K., there are stringent regulations for the hygienic preparation of M., grading, detection of adulteration, etc. Markets for M. were widened in the 1960s by 'long life' M. which, by special heat treatment, remains fresh in the hottest climate for 6 months without refrigeration. *See* DAIRYING.

MILKY WAY. The luminous band of light stretching around the heavens, and passing through constellations such as Cygnus (the Swan), Gemini (the Twins), Sagittarius (the Archer) and Crux Australis (the Southern Cross). It is composed of stars, together with bright and dark nebulae. These stars are not, however, packed closely together. When we look along the main plane of the Galaxy, we see many stars in more or less the same direction, and it is this which causes the M.W. appearance. In 1962 the magnetic field hitherto only conjectured as the cause of the M.W.'s spiral structure was measured by a research team at Jodrell Bank. It is thought that the 'translation' of the radio frequency of signals received from the M.W. into chemical formulae may reveal the presence of amino acids, the 'building blocks' of proteins and the origin of life. *See* illus. p. 74.

MILL, John Stuart (1806–73). British philosopher and economist. B. in Pentonville, the son of James M. (1773–1836), eminent Utilitarian philosopher, he proved a remarkably precocious student. In 1822 he entered the India House, where he became head of his department before retiring in 1858. In 1826, as described in his *Autobiography* (1873), he passed through a mental crisis; he found his father's bleakly intellectual Utilitarianism emotionally unsatisfying, and abandoned it for a more human philosophy influenced by that of Coleridge. So, too, in his social philosophy he gradually abandoned the Utilitarians' extreme individualism for an outlook akin to liberal socialism, while still laying great emphasis on the liberty of the individual; this change can be traced in the later editions of *Principles of Political Economy* (1848). He sat in Parliament as a Radical 1865–8, and introduced a motion for women's suffrage. His feminist views inspired his *On the Subjection of Women* (1869). His philosophical and political writings incl. *A System of Logic* (1843), *On Liberty* (1859; generally considered his masterpiece), and *Considerations on Representative Government* (1861).

MILLAIS (millā'), **Sir John Everett** (1829–96). British artist. B. at Southampton, he joined Holman Hunt and Rosetti in 1848, founding the Pre-Raphaelite Brotherhood, and all his best works were painted in the Pre-Raphaelite manner, e.g. 'Christ in the House of His Parents' (1850), 'Ophelia' (1852), and 'Autumn Leaves' (1856). In 1855 he m. Effie Gray, Ruskin's divorced wife. Although his early work had provoked fierce criticism, he later achieved great popularity with his story-pictures, such as the 'Boyhood of Raleigh' (1870), and 'The North-west Passage' (1874), sentimental child-studies, e.g. 'Bubbles' (1886), and

MILLAIS. His first essay in the Pre-Raphaelite style was 'Lorenzo and Isabella', an illustration of the story borrowed by Keats from the *Decameron*. It has all the mature characteristics of the school – dramatic portrayal of character and incident, and exquisitely finished detail.
Courtesy of the Walker Art Gallery.

portraits. He was created a bart. in 1885 and elected P.R.A. in 1896.

MILLAY (millā'), **Edna St. Vincent** (1892–1950). American poet. B. in Maine, she pub. her first collection of poems, *Renascence*, in 1917. This was followed by other vols. of direct emotional poetry, such as *The Harp-Weaver* (1922).

MILLBANK. Area bordering the Thames between the Houses of Parliament and Vauxhall Bridge, London, England. The Tate Gallery stands on the site of Millbank prison, built 1812–22, closed 1890, pulled down 1893.

MILLENNIUM. A period of 1,000 years, during which (so certain Christian sects believe), Christ will return to govern this earth in person. This belief, also called Chiliasm (from the Greek for 1,000), was widespread in the early days of Christianity. As hopes were disappointed, belief in the Second Coming tended to fade, but Millennarian views have been expressed at periods of great religious excitement, such as the Reformation. The Fifth Monarchy Men were millennarians, as are Jehovah's Witnesses.

MILLER, Arthur (1915–). American playwright. His concern with family relationships and contemporary American values is reflected in *All my Sons* (1947), and *Death of a Salesman* (1949), and *The Crucible* (1953) is an equation of the Salem witch hunt (q.v.) with political persecution of any age, with particular relevance to 'McCarthyism'. M. himself was convicted of Contempt of Congress in 1957 for refusing to reveal the names of those present at a meeting of Communist writers in 1947. He was m. (1956–61) to Marilyn Monroe (q.v.), for whom he wrote the film *The Misfits* (1960), in which she starred, and with whom Maggie in his play *After the Fall* (1964) has been popularly identified. Other notable plays incl. *A View from the Bridge* (1955).

ARTHUR MILLER

MILLER, Henry (1891–). American writer. B. in New York, he spent some years in the Paris underworld which provided material for the fictionalized *Tropic of Cancer* (1931), *Tropic of Capricorn* (1938) and *Black Spring* (1939). These were so out-spoken that the first could not appear in England until 1963,

and the 2nd was only pub. in the U.S. in 1961. *The Air-Conditioned Nightmare* (1945–7) records a trip across the U.S.A.

MILLES (miles'), **Carl** (1875–1955). Swedish sculptor. Intending to emigrate to Chile, he was sidetracked in Paris to the study of art, and came under the influence of Rodin and Meunier. His imaginatively stylized treatment of real and mythical animals, and of the characters of history and legend, make his work unique. Notable are his great basin fountains (e.g. the Poseidon at Gothenburg and the Folke Filbyter memorial at Linkoping), and the statue of Gustavus Vasa in the Northern Museum.

MILLET (millā'), **Aimé** (1819–91). French sculptor. B. in Paris, he first became famous with his statue of 'Ariadne' (1857). His other works incl. the 'Mercury' in the Louvre, and the colossal statue of Vercingetorix at Alise-Ste-Reine.

MILLET, Jean François (1814–75). French painter. B. in Normandy of a peasant family, he went to Paris to study in 1837. He settled at Barbizon, in the forest of Fontainebleau, in 1848, and there became the leader of a group of artists who concentrated on naturalistic paintings of peasant life and rustic scenery. He is best known for his studies of peasants, such as 'The Reapers' (1854), 'The Gleaners' (1857), 'The Angelus' (1859), and 'The Man with a Hoe' (1863).

MILLET. In botany, members of the family Gramineae (grasses), cultivated in various countries, the grains as a cereal food and the stems as fodder. The most important are *Panicum miliaceum*, extensively cultivated in the warmer parts of Europe, and *Sorghum vulgare*, also known as Durra (q.v.)

MILLIKAN, Robert Andrews (1868–1953). American physicist. B. in Illinois, he held chairs in physics at Chicago and Pasadena, California, and was best known for his atomic research, in which he made the most accurate measurement of the electronic charge of negative electricity (1917). He was awarded a Nobel prize in 1923.

MILLIN, Sarah Gertrude (1889–1968). S. African novelist, *née* Liebson, noted for her treatment of the problems raised by colour. Her first novel, *Dark River* (1919), was followed by *God's Step-Children*, *Three Men Die*, and *King of the Bastards*. She also pub. biographies of Rhodes and Smuts; a series of War Diaries; and the autobiography, *Night is Long*.

MILLIPEDE. Animal of worldwide distribution, in the class Diplopoda. It has a segmented body, each segment usually bearing 2 pairs of legs, and the head bears a pair of antennae. The class is divided into a number of orders; some species roll into a ball. Certain orders are provided with silk glands. Ms. feed on decaying vegetable matter, but some species injure crops by feeding on tender roots.

MILLS, John (1908–). British actor. Making his stage début in 1929, he entered films in 1933, and has appeared in *Great Expectations* (1947), *Scott of the Antarctic* (1949), *Town on Trial* (1958) and *Tunes of Glory* (1960); in 1961 he played in *Ross* on the N.Y. stage. His dau., **Hayley** (1946–), has appeared in many films since her first success in *Pollyanna* (1960).

MILMAN, Henry Hart (1791–1868). British Anglican churchman. Ordained in 1816, he became dean of St. Paul's in 1849. He is remembered for his controversial *The History of the Jews* (1829) – the first by an English churchman to treat the contents of the O.T. rationally – and for his standard *History of Latin Christianity* (1854–6).

MILNE, Alan Alexander (1882–1956). British author. Of Scots parentage, he became a journalist and joined *Punch* (1906–16). His plays, which mingle sentiment and whimsical absurdity, incl. *Mr. Pim Passes By* (1919) and *The Dover Road* (1922), but he is best remembered for the children's classics *When We Were Very Young* (1924), *Winnie-the-Pooh* (1926),

Now We Are Six (1927), and *The House at Pooh Corner* (1928).

MILNE BAY. Most easterly bay of New Guinea, *c.* 225 m. S.E. of Port Moresby. The Japanese made a landing here on 25 Aug. 1942, but were beaten off by the Australians.

MILNER, Alfred, visct. (1854–1925). British statesman. As Gov. of Cape Colony 1897–1901, he negotiated with Kruger on behalf of the Uitlanders, before the outbreak of the S. African War, and undertook, as Governor 1901–5, the remodelling of the civil admin. of the Transvaal and Orange River colonies after their annexation. His concept (later modified) of the Empire as a 'permanent and organic union', not an alliance of self-governing colonies, and his advocacy of colonial trade preferences, etc., influenced his disciples (Geoffrey Dawson, Lionel Curtis, etc.), known as M.'s Young Men. In 1916 he became a member of Lloyd George's War Cabinet, and as Sec. for War 1918–19, was largely responsible for creating a unified Allied command under Foch. He was created a visct. in 1901.

MILNES, Richard Monckton, 1st baron Houghton (1809–85). British writer and politician, best remembered as the first editor of the *Life, Letters and Literary Remains of Keats* (1848).

MILO. Italian form of MELOS.

MILTON, John (1608–74). English poet. B. in London, the son of a scrivener, he was ed. at Christ's Coll., Cantab. The best-known of his univ. poems are the ode 'On the Morning of Christ's Nativity' (1629), and his lines on Shakespeare. In 1632 M. retired to his father's house at Horton for 5 years of studious preparation for his poetic vocation, and there wrote the companion pieces *L'Allegro* and *Il Penseroso* (1632); the masque *Comus* (1634); and 'Lycidas' (1637), an elegy on the death of his friend, Edward King. In 1638–9 he visited France and Italy, where he met the imprisoned Galileo. Settling in London in 1640, he limited his creative writing during the next 20 years mainly to pamphlets. Among the chief of these are *Of Reformation Touching Church Discipline* (1641), one of several attacks on episcopacy; *Doctrine and Discipline of Divorce* (1643), and *Tetrachordon* (1644), both occasioned by the desertion of his Royalist wife, Mary Powell, whom he had m. in 1642; *On Education* (1644), a subject of which he had practical experience as tutor to his nephews and others; and *Areopagitica* (1644), a forthright defence of the freedom of the press. His only poetic productions during these years were his sonnets. He was reconciled to his wife in 1645, and 4 years after her death in 1652 m. Catherine Woodcock (d. 1658), and then in 1662 Elizabeth Minshull, who survived him. In 1649 he became Latin Secretary to the Commonwealth, and although blind by 1652, carried on his duties with the aid of assistants such as the poet A. Marvell. Although arrested at the Restoration, he was released on payment of a fine, and while living in obscurity began serious work on his long-projected epic. *Paradise Lost*, the story of the fall of mankind and the hope of ultimate redemption, appeared in 1667, and was followed by *Paradise Regained* and *Samson Agonistes*, a tragedy in the Greek tradition, in 1671. Among his other works are poems in Italian and Latin, the finest of the latter being the *Epitaphium Damonis*, lamenting the death of his friend, Charles Diodati; and a *History of*

JOHN MILTON
Photo: N.P.G.

Britain (1670). He d. from an attack of gout, and was buried in St. Giles, Cripplegate, London.

Our illus., showing M. at *c.* 21, may be the original 'Onslow' portrait, which passed from the poet's widow to Arthur Onslow the Speaker and was 'lost' after 1827: its history is unknown before 1939.

MILTON KEYNES (kēnz). New town, Bucks, England, planned 1969 on a grid lay-out as 'Los Angeles' in England. It is the H.Q. of the Open Univ. Eventual pop. 250,000.

MILWAUKEE (milwaw'kē). Largest city in Wisconsin state, U.S.A., on Lake Michigan, 85 m. N. of Chicago. With a fine harbour, it is a great grain- and coal-distributing port. Heavy machinery of many kinds is manufactured, and brewing and meat packing are important. Pop. met. area (1970) 1,393,260

MIMŌ'SA. Genus of the family Leguminosae, found in tropical and subtropical regions and ranging from shrubby plants to large trees. The flowers are small, fluffy, golden balls (tufts of stamens) and the leaves are pinnate, divided into a multiplicity of small leaflets. Certain species, e.g. the sensitive plant of Brazil (*M. sensitiva*), shrink as if withered on being touched, though rapidly recovering.

MI'NARET (Arab. *manāra*). A slender turret attached to a Mohammedan mosque. It has one or more balconies, from which the *muezzin* calls the people to prayer 5 times a day.

MINAS GERAIS (mē'nahs zherīs'). Inland state of Brazil, intersected by mountain ranges and deep valleys. Coffee, sugar, tobacco, etc., are grown in the lowlands and cattle are reared elsewhere; minerals incl. manganese and iron ores, gold, and diamonds. The cap. is Belo Horizonte. Area 224,700 sq. m.; pop. (1967) 11,440,000.

MIND. The presumed mental or psychical being or faculty that enables one to think, will, and feel; the seat of the intelligence and of memory; sometimes only the cognitive or intellectual powers as distinguished from the will and the emotions. The relation of M. to matter may be variously regarded. Materialists identify the two: mental phenomena equally with physical are to be explained in terms of matter and motion. Dualists hold that M. and matter exist independently side by side. Idealists maintain that M. is the ultimate reality, and that matter is the creation of intelligence, and does not exist apart from it. *See* PSYCHOLOGY.

MINDANAO (mindahnah'ō). The second-largest island of the Philippine Republic. It is very mountainous, rising in the active volcano Apo to over 10,000 ft., and is subject to severe earthquakes. Gold is worked. Chief towns are Davao and Zamboanga. Area 36,537 sq. m.; pop. *c.* 2,000,000.

MINDEN (min'-). Town of North Rhine-Westphalia, W. Germany, 35 m. W.S.W. of Hanover, on the Weser. The duke of Brunswick's Anglo-Allied army here defeated the French in 1759.

MINDORO (mindō'rō). Island of the Philippine Republic, S. of Luzon. Mount Halcon rises to 8,500 ft.; the cap. is Calapan. Area 3,759 sq. m.

MINDSZENTY, József (1892–). Hungarian archbishop, primate from 1945. Sentenced to life imprisonment in 1949 on a charge of treason by the Communist govt., he was released in 1956 when he was given asylum in the U.S. legation in Budapest. He has been the subject of much controversy.

MINEHEAD. English market town and seaside resort in Somerset, 21 m. N.W. of Taunton. Pop. (1961) 7,674.

MINERALOGY. The study of minerals. A mineral is a natural substance having a characteristic chemical composition. Most of them are crystalline, and in this they differ from rocks. The classification of minerals is based chiefly on their chemical constitution, viz. metallic, ionic, and molecular. In addition, their crystallographic and physical characters, their mode of formation and occurrence, form part of the study. In the case of minerals of economic importance a knowledge of mining and metallurgy is also needed.

MINERAL OIL. Term applied to oils obtained from mineral sources, e.g. coal, petroleum, as distinct from those obtained from vegetable or animal sources.

MINERAL WATERS. Waters with mineral constituents gathered from the rocks over which they flow, and classified by these minerals into earthy, brine, and oil M.Ws. Curative powers are believed to be attached to many M.Ws., the types of these medicinal waters being: alkaline (Vichy), bitter (Seidlitz), salt (Droitwich), earthy (Bath), sulphurous (Aachen), and special varieties, such as barium (Harrogate). The name M.Ws. is also applied to prepared drinks, artificially simulating the natural waters, and charged with carbon dioxide.

MINERVA. The Roman goddess of intelligence, and of the handicrafts and arts, identified with the Greek Athene. From the earliest times she had a temple on the Capitol in Rome.

MINHOW. Name 1934–43 of FOOCHOW.

MINIATURE PAINTING. The term 'miniature' is derived from the Lat. *miniare*, to paint with minium, i.e. a vermilion colour, and is usually applied to portraits of small dimensions; it was formerly used to describe little pictures in the initial letters and borders of medieval manuscripts.

Although practised with exquisite delicacy in Persia and India in the medieval period, M.P. did not reach its height in Europe until the 16th cent. with Hans Holbein the Younger. The first English miniaturist was Nicholas Hilliard (q.v.), later practitioners incl. Samuel Cooper, Richard Cosway and George Engleheart (qq.v.). Notable in France were Jean (1486–1541) and François (c. 1522–72) Clouet, Nicolas Lancret and Pierre Prud'-hon; in Spain Goya and in America C. W. Peale.

MINIATURE
Sir Walter Raleigh by Nicholas Hilliard.

Photography led to a decline in demand, but the art is still practised.

MINING. The extraction of minerals from the earth, carried on from the earliest times, e.g. Neolithic man's galleries through chalk with reindeer-antler picks and flint hammers and wedges, and Egyptian mining of turquoise in the Sinai Peninsula with copper implements during the First Dynasty. Modern M., in view of the growing scarcity of rich, shallow deposits, encounters increasing difficulties of exploitation, e.g. low-grade ores require new methods of mass working, such as the possibility of underground nuclear explosions to break up the rock; deposits at great depth necessitate new drilling methods and involve the overcoming of high temperatures (e.g. at 12,000 ft. the temperature will be c. 130°F); or deposits under the sea-bed will lead to the evolution of new techniques. Petroleum and natural gas are already extracted from the ocean floor, e.g. North Sea and off Venezuela. See IRON and COAL MINING.

MINK. Genus (*Mustela*) of the weasel family incl. the European M. *lutreola* and N. American M. *vison*. Up to 1½ ft. long, exclusive of their bushy tails which add another 9 in., they produce an annual litter of half a dozen in their riverbank burrows. The demand for their rich brown fur led to the estab. from the 1930s of M. ranches, and production of varying shades. 'Escapes' become a destructive pest.

MINNEAPOLIS. Largest city in Minnesota, U.S.A., on the Mississippi, seat of Minnesota univ. and of an important institute of arts. The main industry is flour milling; cream, electrical machinery, and motor-cars are also manufactured. It forms the large 'twin cities' area with St. Paul. Pop. met. area (1970) 1,805,081.

MINNESINGERS. German lyric poets of the 12th and 13th cents., who in their songs dealt mainly with the theme of courtly love without revealing the identity of the object of their affections. Among the best-known M. were Dietmar von Aist, Friedrich von Hausen, Heinrich von Morungen, Reinmar, and, greatest of all, Walther von der Vogelweide (q.v.).

MINNESŌTA. A N.-central state of the U.S.A. with innumerable lakes, and the sources of the Red, St. Lawrence, and Mississippi rivers. In the N. are pine-forests and the land is high; the remaining two-thirds are prairie. M. produces barley, flax seed, hay, rye, oats, potatoes, and wheat, and even more valuable livestock products – butter, milk, bacon, turkeys – but industry now leads farming. The chief industries are iron mining (60% of U.S. ore), food processing, farm and other machinery, pulpwood and paper. Minneapolis is the largest city, but St. Paul is the cap. Area 84,068 sq. m.; pop. (1970) 3,805,069.

MINNOW. Small fish (*Phoxinus phoxinus*) found in streams and ponds in Europe and Asia.

MINOAN. Name applied to the brilliant prehistoric civilization of Crete; it is derived from Minos, reputed son of Zeus, and the most famous of the legendary kings of Crete. No remains of palaeolithic man have as yet been found in Crete, but in the Neolithic Age some cents. before 3000 B.C. the island was peopled by men of non-Indo-European stock, coming probably from S.W. Asia Minor, and akin to the early Bronze Age inhabitants of the Gk. mainland. With the opening of the Bronze Age about 3000 B.C. the M. culture proper begins. This is divided into 3 main periods: Early M., c. 3000–2200 B.C.; Middle M. c. 2200–1580 B.C.; and Late M., c. 1580–1100 B.C. Each period is marked by cultural advances in copper and bronze weapons, pottery of increasing delicacy and intricacy of design, fresco-painting, and the construction of palaces (notably at Knossos, Phaistos, and Mallia), and of fine houses.

About 1400 B.C., in the late M. Period, the civilization was suddenly destroyed by earthquake or war. A partial revival continued till c. 1100 B.C.

In religion the Ms. seem to have worshipped principally a great mother goddess with whom was associated a young male god. The tales of Greek mythology about Rhea, the mother of Zeus, and the

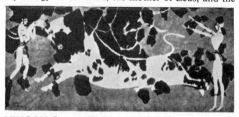

MINOAN. Fresco of bull-leaping by youths and girls from the palace at Knossus, suggesting that there was a foundation of fact for the legend of the Minotaur.

birth of Zeus himself in a Cretan cave seem to be based on M. religion. The Ms. left many documents, in the form of tablets written in a highly developed script, which were long undeciphered. See VENTRIS, MICHAEL, KNOSSOS and ATLANTIS.

MINOR. Under the Family Law Reform Act (1969) for England and Wales the age of majority in civil law was reduced to 18, and those under age are described as Ms. instead of infants. The act legalized marriage without parental consent, and the making of a valid will after the age of 18 (both already possible in Scotland), and enabled anyone over 16 to give valid consent to personal medical treatment. In the U.S.A. the age of majority is 21, except that in some states women attain it at 18, but reduction to 18 for all is proposed.

MINORCA. The second-largest of the Balearic islands in the Mediterranean, belonging to Spain. Area 271 sq. m.; pop. (1960) 60,000.

MINOTAUR. In Greek legend, a monster, half-bull and half-man, the offspring of Pasiphaë, wife of King Minos of Crete, and a bull. The M. was housed in a labyrinth, and provided with victims from 7 youths and 7 maidens sent as annual tribute from Athens. It was slain by Theseus, with the aid of Minos' dau., Ariadne. *See* Knossos, and illus. p .737.

MINSK. Cap. of White Russian S.S.R. Manufactures machinery, textiles, leather, etc. Dating back to the 11th cent. and in turn held by Lithuania, Poland, Sweden, and Russia, M. was destroyed by Napoleon in 1812. It is the seat of the White Russian state univ. Pop. (1967) 772,000.

MINSTER. Originally, a monastery, and in this sense often preserved in place names, e.g. Westminster; later the word was also applied to the church attached to a monastery, e.g. York Minster.

MINT. Genus of aromatic plants (*Mentha*) in the family Labiatae, widely distributed in temperate regions. The plants have square stems and creeping rootstocks, and the flowers grow in a terminal spike, usually pink or purplish. Garden mint (*M. viridis*) and peppermint (*M. piperita*), are the best-known.

MINT, Royal. Department which manufactures all British coins and also distinctive coinages, official medals and seals for the Commonwealth, foreign countries, etc. For cents. in the Tower of London, the R.M. was housed in a building on Tower Hill from 1810 until the new R.M. was opened at Llantrisant, Glamorgan, 10 m. N.W. of Cardiff in 1968. The nominal head is the Master and Worker, who is the Chancellor of the Exchequer, but the actual chief is the Deputy Master and Comptroller, a permanent civil servant. There are branches of the Mint at Melbourne and Perth, Australia. The equivalent in the U.S.A. is the Bureau of the M.

MINTO, Gilbert John Murray Kynynmond Elliot, 4th earl of (1845–1914). British statesman. He was Gov. Gen. of Canada 1898–1904, and Viceroy of India 1905–10. In India during a period of intense nationalist agitation, he collaborated with Lord Morley (q.v.) in the Morley-M. legislative reforms of 1909.

MINTON, John (1917–57). British artist. B. at Cambridge, he was well known as a stage designer, and illustrator. and for romantic landscapes.

MINTON, Thomas (1765–1836). British potter. B. at Shrewsbury, he at first worked under Spode, but in 1789 estab. himself at Stoke-on-Trent as engraver of designs (he was the first to devise the 'willow pattern') and in 1793 founded a pottery there producing exquisite bone china incl. much tableware.

MINUTEMEN. Originally the armed citizens who agreed to act 'in a minute' before the American War of Independence. The name was adopted 1959 by the right-wing organisation estab. by Robert DePugh, a Missouri manufacturer, to combat a Communist invasion or uprising. The New York police seized quantities of arms 1966, and DePugh was sentenced to 3 yrs. imprisonment.

MIQUELON ISLANDS (mēkloń'). Small group off the S. coast of Newfoundland which with St. Pierre (q.v.) form a French overseas territory. Cod fishing is the chief occupation; silver fox and mink are bred for their fur. Area 83 sq. m.; pop. (1967) 625.

MIRABEAU (mērahbō'), **Honoré Gabriel Riqueti,** comte de (1749–91). French statesman. The son of a Provençal nobleman, he had a stormy career before the Revolution, during which he was 3 times imprisoned, and passed several years in exile. In 1789 he was elected to the States General as a representative of the third estate. His eloquence won him the leadership of the National Assembly; nevertheless, he was out of sympathy with the majority of the deputies, whom he regarded as mere theoreticians, his own aim being to establish a parliamentary monarchy on the English model. From May 1790 he secretly acted as political adviser to the king.

MIRACLE (Lat. *miraculum*, a marvel). An event which seems to transcend the laws of nature, and is regarded as a manifestation of Divine power. Hume attacked the credibility of the miraculous, and there has been a marked decline in its evidential value. In our own day, however, C. S. Lewis and others have argued in favour of the reasonableness of miracles, given belief in a God who is still concerned for His creation.

MIRACLE PLAYS. Medieval religious dramas based on sacred writ or saints' lives, which were performed chiefly on festivals, such as Corpus Christi day or Easter, and reached their highest development in the 15th and 16th cents. Separate episodes were performed by the various guilds of the towns on mobile stages, and in some instances, e.g. the Wakefield, York, and Chester plays, almost complete cycles survive.

MIRANDOLA. See Pico della Mirandola.

MIRÓ (mērō'), **Gabriel** (1879–1930). Spanish author, celebrated for richly characterized novels of provincial life e.g. *Our Father Daniel* (1921).

MIRÓ, Joan (1893–). Spanish artist. B. at Barcelona, he was with Dali one of the main originators of the Surrealist movement. His pictures tend to spindly lines and blobs, and primitive colour, e.g. 'Still-life with an Old Shoe' and 'Dog Barking at the Moon '. He designed sets for the Diaghileff co.

MIRZAPUR (mērzahpōōr'). City of Uttar Pradesh, Republic of India, on the Ganges, *c.* 50 m. E.S.E. of Allahabad. It is a grain and cotton market, with bathing sites and temples on the river. Pop. (1961) 100,000.

MISCARRIAGE. *See* Abortion.

MISDEMEANOUR. *See* Felony.

MISERICORD or *Miserere.* In architecture, a bracket on the under-side of a hinged seat of the choir stalls in a church, used as a rest for a priest when standing during long services. Ms. are often decorated with carvings.

MISHIMA, Yukio (1925–70). Japanese author. He often chose homosexual themes, e.g. *Confessions of a Mask* (1949). Obsessed by the tradition of the Samurai, he founded a private army, the Association of Shields. With his followers he broke into a barracks, addressed the soldiers on the corruption of the nation, and committed hara-kiri.

MISHNA. A commentary on written Hebrew law, consisting of discussions between rabbis and handed down orally from their inception in A.D. 70 until *c.* 200, when with the Gemara, the discussions in schools of Palestine and Babylon on law, it was committed to writing to form the Talmud.

MISKOLC (mish'kolts). Town in Hungary, 90 m. N.E. of Budapest. Seat of a tech. univ. It trades in local wines and tobacco and makes textiles, furniture, paper, etc. Pop. (1963) 156,000.

MISR. Egyptian name for Egypt and the Egyptian name for Cairo.

MISSAL. In the R.C. Church, a service-book containing the complete office of Mass for the entire year. An easier, simplified M. introduced 1969 (obligatory from 1971) was the first major reform since 1570.

MISSIONS (Lat. *mittere,* to send). Organized attempts to spread religion among the unconverted. During the first 3 cents. Christianity was spread throughout the Roman Empire by missionaries, of whom the greatest was Paul. In the Dark Ages the new faith was spread beyond the Empire by men such as Gregory the Illuminator, Ulfilas, Chrysostom, Patrick, and Martin of Tours. And in addition to the great figures of medieval times, such as Columba, Aidan, Boniface, Cyril, etc., there were combined efforts of the Benedictine, Dominican and Franciscan orders. The explorations of the Renaissance opened new fields, and the foundation of the Jesuit order supplied such missionaries as Francis Xavier (1506–52). Gradually the Protestant churches also showed an interest in missions, the pioneer being the S.P.C.K., founded in 1698, and after 1731 the continental Moravians. In the late 18th and early 19th cents. many Protestant missionary societies were founded, incl. the Baptist (1792), the London (1795), and the Church (1799). Efforts were maintained throughout the cent., notably in the foundation of the China Inland Mission by J. H. Taylor (1865), but renewed impetus came from the career of David Livingstone, and since the World Missionary Conference at Edinburgh in 1910 there has been growing international co-operation. The 19th cent. also saw a growth of activity on the part of the R.C. and Eastern Orthodox churches.

MISSOURI. Truman went to the White House from Independence, and in 1957 the Harry S. Truman Library was dedicated there to house his papers and documents. Other presidential libraries, which form part of the U.S. National Archives, are the F. D. Roosevelt at Hyde Park, N.Y., Eisenhower at Abilene, Kansas, and Hoover at West Branch, Iowa.
Courtesy of Harry S. Truman Library.

Christianity's chief rival in the mission-field is Islam; particularly in Africa are there many Mohammedan converts.

MISSISSIPPI. With the Missouri, considered by some the longest river in the world. It is the main arm of the great river system draining the U.S.A. between the Appalachians and the Rockies, and was discovered in 1541 by the Spanish explorer Hernando do Soto at a point near present-day Memphis. The M. rises in the lake region of N. Minnesota, flowing through marsh and lakeland to St. Anthony Falls at Minneapolis. Below the tributaries Minnesota, Wisconsin, Des Moines, and Illinois, the confluence of the Missouri and M. occurs at St. Louis. The river turns at the Ohio junction, passing Memphis, and taking in the St. Francis, Arkansas, Yazoo, and Red tributaries, en route to its delta on the Gulf of Mexico beyond New Orleans. Length of M. proper, 2,348 m.; length of the Missouri and the Lower M., 3,643 m.

MISSISSIPPI. Built in 1858 by slave labour, the Old Court House at Vicksburg is now a museum containing Confederate and other memorabilia from the Indian and pioneer periods. Here the Confederate flag was lowered and the United States flag raised on 4 July 1863.
Courtesy of the Old Court House Museum.

MISSISSIPPI. A S. central state of the U.S.A., bounded on the W. by the M. river and on the S. by the Gulf of Mexico. It is mainly lowland, rising to 650 ft. in the N.E. Second only to Texas in cotton, M. also produces sweet potatoes, sugar, rice, pecan nuts, and soya beans. Oil and natural gas are exploited, and other industries incl. food processing, pulpwood and timber, chemicals, and canned seafood, based on Biloxi, also a holiday resort. A 'static test' rocket centre was estab. in Hancock co. 1967.

M. was traversed by De Soto in 1540, settled by the French in 1699, was English 1763–79, Spanish 1779–98, then part of the U.S. territory of M. (which incl. Alabama) until admitted to the Union in 1817. It was the second state to join the Confederacy, 1861; was re-admitted to the Union 1870. Jackson is the cap., Gulfport the chief harbour. Area 47,716 sq. m.; pop. (1970) 2,216,912.

MISSOURI (mizōō'ri). The longest tributary of the Mississippi in the U.S.A., rising in S.W. Montana among the Rockies, and flowing through N. and S.

Dakota, and Missouri; it forms the boundary between Nebraska and Iowa. The main towns in its course are Sioux City, Omaha, Kansas City, Kans., and Kansas City, Mo., its largest tributaries the Yellowstone, Platte and Milk. The M. is navigable to Fort Benton. Length from its formation at the Three Forks confluence to the Mississippi, 2,466 m. Total length from source of Red Rock r. 2,683 m. Dams provide flood control, irrigation, and electric power.

MISSOURI. A central state of the U.S.A., in the agricultural valley of the Mississippi, which forms the E. border. The M. river flows across the state from W. to E. In the S. rises the forested Ozark Plateau, while N. are praries. Maize, soya beans, and wheat are grown, and pigs, cattle and sheep are bred. Minerals incl. lead (largest U.S. producer), barytes, lime, coal and iron ore. Besides a large aerospace industry (space capsules, rocket engines, aircraft etc.), it has motor assembly plants, food processing, chemical, and cement works, and tourism, e.g. the Mark Twain State Park, is very important. The cap. is Jefferson City; other towns are St. Louis and Kansas City. Area 69,674 sq. m.; pop. (1970) 4,677, 399.

MISTINGUETT (mistaṅget'). Stage-name of the French actress and dancer Jeanne Bourgeois (1873–1956). A leading music-hall artist in Paris from 1899, she also appeared in revue at the Folies-Bergère, Casino de Paris, and Moulin Rouge, singing songs such as 'Mon Homme'. Maurice Chevalier often partnered her.

MISTLETOE. Parasitic plant (*Viscum album*) found in Europe. It occurs on deciduous and evergreen trees, most commonly on the apple, where it produces an evergreen bush. *See* DRUIDISM.

MISTRAL (mēstrahl'), **Frédéric Joseph Étienne** (1830–1914). Provençal poet. In 1854 he founded the literary society of the Félibrige, whose aim was the revival of Provençal. His works incl. the narrative poem *Mirèio*, the verse collection *Lis Isclo d'or*, and the blank-verse epic *Lou Pouèmo dóu Rouse*.

MISTRAL (mēstrahl'), **Gabriela.** Pseud. of the Chilean poet Lucila Godoy Alcayaga (1889–1957). B. at Vicuña, she became a teacher, estab. herself as her country's leading educationist, and represented Chile as consul in Lisbon, Los Angeles, Mexico, etc.

MISTLETOE

Her poetry, for which she was in 1945 awarded a Nobel prize, incl. *Sonetos de la Muerte* (1915: *Sonnets of Death*) and *Desolación* (1922).

MISTRAL. A cold, dry, northerly wind which occasionally blows during the winter on the Mediterranean coast of France. It has reached a velocity of 90 m.p.h. in the Rhône valley. ·

MITAU. German name of JELGAVO.

MITCHELL, Margaret (*c.* 1900–49). American novelist. B. in Atlanta, Georgia, she joined the *Atlanta Journal* as a reporter (1922–6) and in 1925 m. John R. Marsh. *Gone with the Wind* (1936), is a colourful novel of her home state in the Civil War period.

MITCHELL, Reginald Joseph (1895–1937). British aircraft designer. B. at Stoke-on-Trent, he joined Vickers in 1916, and became its chief designer in 1920. For his designs of the Schneider Trophy seaplanes he gained recognition by the Royal Aeronautical Society in 1927. Later designs incl. R.A.F. flying-boats and the Spitfire I fighter.

MITCHISON, Naomi Margaret (1897–). British novelist. B. at Edinburgh, she is a dau. of J. S. Haldane and sister of J. B. S. Haldane (qq.v.), and m. G. R. Mitchison (created life peer 1964) in 1916. Her novels, of which *The Corn King and Spring Queen* (1931), and *The Blood of the Martyrs* (1939) are best known, mainly deal with the ancient world.

MITE. In zoology, an order of minute Arachnida. There are many varieties, mostly parasites, which infest birds, animals, and plants, causing diseases and sometimes death.

MITFORD, Mary Russell (1787–1855). British author. B. in Hants, she is chiefly remembered for her sketches, *Our Village* (1824–32), describing Three Mile Cross, near Reading where she lived for years.

MITFORD SISTERS. Of the 6 daus. of the 2nd Baron Redesdale, the best-known are **Nancy** (1904–), author of the semi-autobiographical *Pursuit of Love* (1945) and ed. of, and one of the contributors to, *Noblesse Oblige* (1956), with its serio-comic definitions of 'U' (upper class) and 'Non-U' speech and behaviour; **Jessica** (1917–), author of the autobiography *Hons and Rebels* (1960) and *The American Way of Death* (1963), and m. 1st to her cousin Esmond Romilly, nephew of Winston Churchill, with whom in 1937 she ran off in a blaze of publicity to join the Republicans and report on the Spanish Civil War; and **Unity** (1914–48). who joined the British Union of Fascists in the 1930s, becoming associated with ·Hitler and other leading German Nazis. **Diana** m. Sir Oswald Mosley (q.v.).

MITFORD, William (1744–1827). British historian, author of a *History of Greece* (1784–1810), in which the anti-democratic attitude is marked.

MITHRADĀTĒS VI, called **the Great** (132–63 B.C.). King of Pontus from 120 B.C. His attempt to conquer all Asia Minor led to war with Rome in 88. He overran Asia Minor, massacred 80,000 Romans, and invaded Greece, but was defeated by Sulla and ultimately by Pompey. He was killed by a soldier at his own order.

MI'THRAS. Persian god of light, whose creed seems to have been an extension of the Zoroastrian dualism. M. represented the power of goodness, and promised his followers compensation for present evil

MITHRAS. Wearing a Phrygian cap, this marble head was found in the excavation of London's temple of Mithras.
Courtesy of the Guildhall Museum.

after death. His cult was introduced into the Roman Empire in 68 B.C., rapidly developed, particularly among soldiers, and by *c.* A.D. 250 rivalled Christianity in strength. M. was said to have captured and killed the sacred bull, from whose blood all life sprang, and a bath in the blood of a sacrificed bull formed part of the initiation ceremony. In 1954 remains of a Roman temple dedicated to M. were discovered on a site in the City of London, now occupied by Bucklersbury House, in front of which they were reassembled for permanent exhibition.

MITRE (mīt′er). The head-dress worn by bishops, cardinals, and mitred abbots at solemn services. There are Ms. of many different shapes, but in the western Church it usually takes the form of a tall cleft-cap. The M. worn by the Pope is called a tiara.

MITYLENE (mitilē′nē). Greek city and port, cap. of the island of Lesbos (to which the name M. is sometimes applied) and a centre of sponge fishing. It has an airport. Pop. (1961) 25,518.

MOA

MŌ′A. Group of extinct birds (*Dinornithes*), once found in N.Z. They varied from 2 to 12 ft. high, with strong limbs, a long neck, and no wings. They occurred as far back as the Pliocene age.

MŌ′AB. An ancient country situated E. of the southern part of the Jordan and of the Dead Sea, in the area of modern Jordan. The region is hilly and in parts is very fertile; cereals and vines were formerly cultivated. The inhabitants were closely akin to the Hebrews in culture, language, and religion, but were often at war with them. M. eventually fell to Arabian tribes. The MOABITE STONE, discovered in 1868 at Dhiban, dates from the 9th cent. B.C., and records the rising of Mesha, king of M., against Israel.

MOBILE (-bē′l). City and only seaport in Alabama, U.S.A., 135 m. E.N.E. of New Orleans. Founded 1702 by the French a little to the N. of the present city, M. was cap. of the French colony of Louisiana until 1763, then British until 1780, Spanish to 1813. It has a substantial import and export trade, and possesses dry docks; meat packing and manufacture of paper, cement, clothing, industrial chemicals, etc., are industries. Pop. (1960) 202,779.

MOÇAMBIQUE. Alternative spelling of MOZAMBIQUE.

MOCHA (mō′ka). Seaport of Yemen, near the mouth of the Red Sea, which gives its name to M. coffee. Once the chief port of Yemen, it declined as Aden and Hodeida increased in importance. Pop. (est.) 600.

MOCKING-BIRD. Genus of American birds (*Mimus*), related to the thrushes. Most familiar in the U.S.A. is *M. polyglottus*, brownish grey on the upper part, with white markings on the almost black wings and tail. It often nests in trees close to human homes and courageously defends its young.

MODDER. Tributary of the Riet, Orange Free State and Cape Colony, S. Africa. Near the village of M. River, a holiday resort at the junction of the M. and the Riet in Cape Colony, Lord Methuen defeated the Boers in 1899, to meet disastrous defeat 6 m. farther N. at Magersfontein 4 days later.

MŌ′DENA. City of Emilia, Italy, the cap. of the prov. of M. 23 m. N.W. of Bologna. There are many fine buildings, incl. the 12th cent. cathedral, the 17th cent. ducal palace, and the univ., founded 1683,

MODULE. 'Spider', the *Apollo IX* lunar module viewed from the command service module. Carrying 2 astronauts, it is flying upside down in relation to the earth below, with landing gear deployed and lunar surface probes or sensors extending out from the landing gear foot pads. *Courtesy of NASA.*

which is famed for its medical and legal faculties. Pop. (1961) 139,496.

MODERATOR. The material in a reactor used to reduce the energy, and hence the speed, of fast neutrons, so far as possible without capturing them. Slow neutrons are much more likely to cause fission in a U-235 nucleus than to be captured in a U-238 nucleus, so by using a M. a reactor can be made to work with fuel containing only a small proportion of U-235.

MODERATOR. One who presides over a meeting, especially in the Presbyterian and Congregational churches (e.g. the General Assembly of the Church of Scotland). Also applied to the chairman of town meetings in the U.S.A. and to the officials who superintend examinations at Oxford and Cambridge.

MODERNISM. In the C. of E. a development of the liberal church movement, known as M. since c. 1910, which attempts to reconsider Christian beliefs in the light of modern scientific theories and historical methods without abandoning the essential doctrines. Prominent Modernists incl. E. W. Barnes, J. A. Robinson, A. M. Stockwood, J. L. Wilson, and W. R. Inge. Similar movements exist in many nonconformist churches and in the R.C. Church. M. was condemned by pope Pius X in 1907.

MODIGLIANI (modēlyah'nē), **Amedeo** (1884–

MOCKING-BIRD. It earns its name by its mimicry of the songs of 20 to 30 other birds, and also of mechanical noises such creaking doors or hooters, but not human speech. *Photo: G. Ronald Austing.*

1920). Italian artist. B. in Leghorn, of Jewish family, he settled in Paris in 1906, became interested in primitive art, and in 1909 began to produce sculptures showing the influence of Negro masks. His originally conceived, strangely elongated portraits have a mournful attraction. Always penniless, and a prey to drink and drugs, he d. of tuberculosis and his pregnant mistress, Jeanne Hébuterne, threw herself to death from a window the next morning.

MO'DULE. Unit of measurement; used in architecture of the size of a structural part which governs the proportion of the remainder, and in space research, e.g. the 3 components in a spacecraft making a moon landing: command M. (working, eating, and sleeping compartment), service M. (containing electricity generators, oxygen supplies and manoeuvring rocket), and lunar M. (for landing astronauts on the surface and returning them to the command ship in lunar orbit).

MOERA'N, Ernest John (1894–1950). British composer. He received little formal education, but was influenced by Ireland, under whom he studied composition 1920–3, and by folk music in much of his early work. Valuable among his essentially lyrical,

MODIGLIANI. Nude, dated c. 1917.
Courtauld Institute Galleries, London, rights reserved A.D.A.G.P.

and often experimental, productions are a symphony (1937), violin and cello concertos, piano and orchestral music and songs.

MOFFAT, James (1870–1944). Scottish minister of the united Free Church. He pub. a colloquial translation of the Bible (N.T. 1899 and O.T. 1924).

MOGADISHU (mogudi-'shōō). Cap. and chief port of Somali Republic. It has a cathedral built 1925–8 and mosques dating back to the 13th cent. It also has an airport. Pop. (1967) 100,000.

MOGADO'R. Port in Morocco (Essouira), on the Atlantic, founded c. 1760. Pop. (est.) 32,000.

MO'GILEV. Town in White Russian S.S.R., 120 m. E. of Minsk, annexed by Russia from the Swedes in 1772. It makes tractors, clothing, furniture, etc. Pop. (1967) 164,000.

MO'GOK. Village of Burma, 71 m. N.N.E. of Mandalay, famous for its ruby and sapphire mines.

MOGULS (mōgulz'). A dynasty which ruled in N. India from the establishment of their empire by Baber in 1526 till the dethronement and imprisonment of the last M. emperor by the British in 1857. The emperors were called Ms. (Mongols) as being descendants of Tamerlane: among the greatest were Akbar (1542–1605), Shah Jehan (fl. 1614–66), and Aurungzebe (1618–1707).

MOHÁCS (mō'hahch). City on the Danube, Hungary, 110 m. S. of Budapest, famous for 2 battles, in 1526 the Turks beating the Hungarians, and in 1687 being beaten by the Austrians.

MO'HAIR. The hair of the Angora goat. Fine, white, and lustrous, the fibre is manufactured into fabric. Commercial M. is now obtained from crossbred animals, pure-bred supplies being insufficient. .

MOHA'MMED, Muhammad or **Mahomet** (Arab., 'praised') (c. 570–632). Founder of Mohammedanism or Islam (q.v.). B. in Mecca, he became a shepherd and caravan conductor, before obtaining leisure for meditation by his marriage with a wealthy widow in 595. He received his first revelation in 610, and after some years of secret teaching openly proclaimed himself the prophet of God, c. 616. The basis of his teaching was the Koran, a sacred work dictated by him to amanuenses while he remained in a state of trance. His increasing success in gaining converts led to persecution, and M. was forced to flee to Medina in 622. This flight – the Hegira – marks the beginning of the Mohammedan era. After the battle of Badr, 623, M. was constantly victorious, and in 630 he entered Mecca as the recognized prophet of Arabia. He d. at Medina, and was there buried.

MOHAMMED. Name of 6 sultans of Turkey. MOHAMMED II (1430–81), captured Constantinople in 1453 and conquered Greece. MOHAMMED VI (1861–1926), the last sultan, was deposed in 1922, and d. in exile.

MOHAMMEDANISM. *See* ISLAM.

MOHAWKS. Tribe of the Iroquois (q.v.).

MOHENJO DARO. One of the most striking features of the excavated city is the advanced drainage system. A covered drain runs the full length of this street and the houses had bathrooms. In the case of the Great Bath asphalt was used to make it watertight.   *Photo: J. Allan Cash.*

MOHENJO DARO. Site of a city of *c.* 2500–1600 B.C., on the lower Indus, Pakistan, where excavations from the 1920s have revealed the Indus Valley civilization (q.v.) Artistically remarkable are the soapstone seals – elephants, snakes, etc. M. has its own airport (1967).

MOHI′CANS and **Mohē′gans.** Two closely related N. American Indian tribes, akin to the Algonquins, who formerly occupied Connecticut and the Hudson valley. J. F. Cooper (q.v.) confused the 2 tribes.

MOHOLE. American project for drilling a hole through the earth's crust, so named from the discovery by the Yugoslav, Andrija Mohorovičić, of the Mohorovicic (abbr. Moho) Discontinuity, which marks the transition from the crust to the earth's first inner layer or 'mantle'. Initial tests were made in 1961 off Guadelupe Island in the Pacific, since the thickness of the earth's crust is least beneath the oceans, lessening to *c.* 3 m. in places. Expense and technical difficulties have indefinitely postponed achievement of the ultimate aim, but the cores already brought up have illuminated the geological history of the earth and aided the development of geophysics. Anti-Cosmos (launched 1967) is the Soviet equivalent.

MOHOLY-NAGY (mahoi′ noij), **Ladislaus** (1896–1946). Hungarian artist. Appointed by Gropius in 1923 prof. at the Bauhaus, he was noted for his work in photography – photo-montages, etc. – and in 1937 went to the U.S. where he founded the Institute of Design in Chicago.

MOHS (mōōs), **Friedrich** (1773–1839). German mineralogist. He devised in 1820 a scale classification of minerals in order of hardness, viz. diamond, corundum and sapphire, topaz, quartz, orthoclase, apatite, fluorite, calcite, gypsum, talc.

MOISEIWITSCH (moisā′vich), **Benno** (1890–1963).

Russian pianist. He went to England in 1908, and became a British subject in 1937. He was known for his rendering of the works of the Romantics.

MOISSON (mwahsoń′), **Ferdinand Frédéric** (1852–1907). French chemist. In 1886 he isolated fluorine, in 1892 invented the electric arc furnace, and in 1906 was awarded a Nobel prize. He also made tiny artificial diamonds.

MOJI. *See* under KITAKYUSHU.

MOLA′SSES. Strictly the drainings from raw cane sugar, but also used as a synonym for treacle (q.v.). M. from sugar cane produces rum on fermentation; that from beet sugar gives alcohol.

MOLDĀ′VIAN S.S.R. A constituent republic of the U.S.S.R. It is a fertile, well-watered plateau. Vineyards and orchards are its chief wealth; sheep and cattle are reared on the S. steppes. M. was created in 1940 from the former Moldavian A.S.S.R., and Bessarabia, ceded by Rumania in the same year, except the area bordering the Black Sea (added to Ukraine S.S.R.). Kishinev is the cap. Area, 13,100 sq. m.; pop. (1968) 3,484,000.

MOLE. Genus of mammals in the family Talpidae. The common M. of Europe (*Talpa europaea*) has a thick-set body *c.* 7 in. long, covered with soft dark fur. Purblind, it lives underground in circular grass-lined nests and excavates extensive tunnels in its search for worms and grubs, throwing up the earth at intervals in 'mole hills'. The short muscular forelimbs and shovel-like hind feet are adapted for burrowing. Some members of the family are aquatic, e.g. the American shrew M. (*Scalops aquaticus*).

MOLECULE. The smallest particle of any substance that can exist free yet still exhibit all the chemical properties of the substance. Molecules are composed of a number of atoms (q.v.) ranging from one atom in a helium molecule to many thousands of atoms in the molecules of complex organic substances. The composition of the molecule is determined by the nature of the bonds, probably electric forces, which hold the atoms together.

According to the molecular or kinetic theory of matter, molecules are in a state of constant motion, the extent of which depends on their temperature, and they exert forces on one another.

MOLIÈRE (mōlyär′). Pseudonym of the French dramatist Jean Baptiste Poquelin (1622–73). B. in Paris, he studied law before assisting his father in his trade as an upholsterer. In 1643 he became one of the founders of the *Illustre Théâtre*, of which he was later the leading actor, and in 1655 wrote his first play, *L'Étourdi*. He estab. his reputation with *Les Précieuses ridicules* (1659), which was followed by some 40 comedies, incl. *L'École des femmes* (1662), *Tartuffe* (1664), *Le Festin de Pierre* (1665), *Le Misanthrope* (1666), *Le Médecin malgré lui* (1666), *Georges Dandin*, *L'Avare* (1668), *Le Bourgeois gentilhomme* (1670), *Les Fourberies de Scapin* (1671), *Les Femmes savantes* (1672), and *Le Malade imaginaire* (1673). His fearless social satire exposed him to many attacks from his enemies, against whom he was consistently protected by Louis XIV.

M. introduced to the stage a new comedy, which relied not on the formal neatness of the Greek plots, but on the exposure of hypocrisy and cant in the eternally recurrent types of human character. *See* illus. p. 450.

MOLINOS (mōlē′nos), **Miguel de** (1640–97). Spanish mystic. B. near Saragossa, he settled in Rome after being ordained a R.C. priest, and wrote in Italian several devotional works, incl. the *Guida spirituale*, which aroused the hostility of the Jesuits, who caused him to be arrested in 1685. In 1687 he was sentenced to life imprisonment. His doctrine, known as Quietism, puts particular emphasis on disinterested love and on the attainment of a state of spiritual repose in which we can approach most closely to God.

MOLLUSCS. A large sub-division of the animal kingdom. The majority are marine animals, but some inhabit fresh water, and a few are terrestrial. They incl. shell-fish, snails, slugs, and cuttles. The body is soft, limbless, and cold-blooded. There is no internal skeleton, but most species have a hard shell covering the body. The shell takes a variety of forms, univalve (e.g. snail), bivalve (e.g. mussel), chambered (e.g. nautilus), and many other variations. In some cases, e.g. cuttle and squid, the shell is internal. There is a fold of skin, the mantle, which covers the whole body or the back only, and which secretes the calcareous

MOLLUSCS. Bivalve (above), and univalve.

substance forming the shell. The lower ventral surface forms the locomotory organ, or foot. Vary in diet, the carnivorous species feeding chiefly upon other members of the class. Some are vegetarian. Reproduction is by means of eggs, and is sexual.

Shellfish (oysters, mussels, clams, etc.) are commercially valuable, espec. when artificially bred and 'farmed'. The Romans, and in the 17th cent. the Japanese, experimented with advanced methods, and raft culture of oysters is now widely practised. The cultivation of pearls, pioneered by Kokichi Mikimoto, began in the 1890s and became an important export industry after the F.W.W.

CLASSIFICATION OF MOLLUSCA

Class Amphineura
Order, Polyplacophora; coat-of-mail shells.
Order, Aplacophora.

Class Gastropoda
SUB-CLASS, Streptoneura.
Order, Aspidobranchia; limpets, top shells, ear-shells.
Order, Pectinibranchia; rock snails, whelks, harp shells, cones, periwinkles.
SUB-CLASS, Euthyneura.
Order, Opisthobranchia; bubble shells, sea hairs, umbrella shells.
Order, Pulmonata; true snails and slugs, false limpets.

Class Scaphopoda
Family: Dentaliidae.

Class Lamellibranchia
Order, Protobranchia; Nucula.
Order, Filibranchia; common mussel, pearl oyster, scallops.
Order, Eulamellibranchia; freshwater mussel, cockle, razor shell, oyster, shipworms.
Order, Septibranchia; Poromya.

Class Cephalopoda
SUB-CLASS, Tetrabranchia; pearly nautilus.
SUB-CLASS, Dibranchia.
Order, Octopoda; octopus; argonaut.
Order, Decapoda; squids, cuttlefish.

MÓLNÁR, Ferenc (1878–1952). Hungarian novelist and playwright. His best novel is *Paul Street Boys* (1907), but he is most widely known for his plays, *Liliom* (1909), a study of a circus barker, adapted as the play *Carousel*.

MOLOCH (mō′lok), or **Molech**. A Phoenician deity worshipped at Jerusalem in the 7th cent. B.C., to which children were sacrificed.

MOLOKAI (mōlōkī′). A mountainous island of Hawaii state, U.S.A., lying S.E. of Oahu; Kamakou (4,960 ft.), is the highest peak. In 1873–89 Father Damien took charge of, and organized, the leper settlement, which is on the N. coast. at Kalaupapa. Area 259 sq. m.; pop. (1960) 5,000.

MO'LOTOV, Vyacheslav Mikhailovich. Name assumed by Soviet statesman V. M. Skryabin (1890–). Joining the Bolshevik Party in 1906 while a student at Kazan, he was 3 times exiled for revolutionary activities, and in 1921 was elected a member of the C.C.C.P., becoming a member of the Politbureau in 1929 (Presidium from 1952). He was Chairman of the Council of People's Commissars (P.M.) 1930–41, succeeded Litvinov as Foreign Commissar in 1939, Foreign Min. 1946–9 and 1953–6 and was first deputy premier 1953–7. After a few months as Min. of State Control 1956–7, he was one of the 'anti-party' group expelled from the govt. for Stalinist activities. He was Soviet Ambassador to Mongolia 1957–60, and was appointed Chief Permanent Representative to the International Atomic Energy Agency in Vienna (1960–2), shortly after Khrushchev's public denunciation of Stalinism and the beginning of his de-Stalinization campaign.

MOLOTOV. Name 1940–57 of PERM.

MOLTKE, Helmuth Carl Bernhard, count von (1800–91). Prussian general. B. in Mecklenburg, he entered the Prussian Army in 1821, became chief of the general staff in 1857, and was responsible for the Prussian strategy in the wars with Denmark (1863–4), Austria (1866), and France (1870–1). He was created a count in 1870 and a field marshal in 1871. His nephew, **Helmuth Johannes Ludwig von M.** (1848–1916), became chief of staff in 1906, and drew up the plans for the invasion of France carried out at the beginning of the F.W.W.

MÖLU'CCAS. Groups of islands, most of them volcanic, forming part of the Republic of Indonesia. The N. group comprises Morotai, Halmahera (the largest), Ternate, Tidore, Makian, Bachan, Obi Islands, Sula Islands; the S. group, Buru, Ceram, Amboina, Banda Islands, Kai Islands, Aru Islands, Tanimbar Islands, Babar Islands, Kisar, and Wetar. Pepper, cloves, nutmeg (especially from the Bandas) and other spices, for which the M. are still noted, attracted the Portuguese in the 16th cent. The Dutch acquired the M. in 1612 and held them until they were seized by the Japanese in 1942. Area *c.* 33,000 sq. m.; pop. (est.) 893,000.

MOLY'BDENITE. Molybdenum disulphide, MoS_2, the chief ore mineral of molybdenum. It possesses a hexagonal crystal structure, and has a metallic lustre resembling graphite.

MOLYBDENUM (Gk. *molybdos* lead). Very brittle and malleable white metal, an electric furnace product of molybdenite (MoS_2) and wulfenite, and one of many fission products from a nuclear reactor: symbol Mo, at. wt. 95·95 and at. no. 42. Discovered by Scheele in 1778, it has a melting point of 2,620°C, and is not found in the free state. Producing countries incl. the U.S.A., Canada and Norway. Important in producing specialized steels, it is also used for electrodes (since it is easily welded to soda and Pyrex glass and to other metals), and for filaments (alloyed with tungsten) in thermionic valves. In use as an aid to lubrication, M. disulphide (MoS_2) makes an outstanding reduction in surface friction between ferrous metals.

MOMBASA (mombah′sah). Port of Kenya, E. Africa, situated on M. island, and together with the adjacent port of Kilindini handling nearly all the foreign trade of Kenya and Uganda. It is the terminus of the Kenya and Uganda Railway, and has an airport. M. was cap. of the British E. Africa Protectorate 1888–1907. Pop. (1960 est.) 189,000 (4,900 white).

MOMENT. In physics and engineering the M. is

the product of a quantity and a distance. In particular the moment of a force about a point is the product of the force and the perpendicular distance from the point to the line of action of the force, and measures its turning effect or torque. The *M. of inertia* of a body measures its resistance to angular acceleration and depends on the particular axis of rotation being considered.

MOME′NTUM. The M. of a body is the product of its mass and its linear velocity; angular M. is the product of its moment of inertia (*see under* MOMENT) and its angular velocity. The M. of a body does no change unless it is acted on by an external force. The law of conservation of M. is one of the fundamental concepts of classical physics. It states that the total M. of all bodies in a closed system is constant and unaffected by processes occurring within the system.

MOMMSEN, Theodor (1817–1903). German classical scholar. He went to Italy in 1843, where he carried out researches on Roman inscriptions, and from 1858 was prof. of ancient history at Berlin. His monumental *Roman History* appeared 1854–6.

MONA. Another name for the ISLE OF MAN.

MO′NACO. Small principality, under French protection, on the Mediterranean, bounded by the French

MONACO. n the distance are Cap-Martin and Italy. Local law made the principality a haven of escape from heavy taxes elsewhere until friction with France led to a tightening of the regulations.　　*Courtesy of Consulat Général de Monaco.*

dept. of Alpes-Maritimes. M. comprises 3 communes, Monaco-Ville, Monte Carlo, and La Condamine. At the old town of M. is the palace, and a remarkable aquarium. M. is governed by a Ministry, Council of State, and elected National Council, under the authority of the reigning prince, Rainier III (1923–　), who succeeded his grandfather Prince Louis II in 1949. In 1956 he m. the American film star Grace Kelly (q.v.) and they have 3 children, Prince Albert Alexandre Louis Pierre (1958–　), the heir-apparent, and Princess Caroline (1957–　) and Princess Stephanie (1965–　). If the reigning House of Grimaldi were to die out, with no male or female heir, the principality would pass under French sovereignty. Area 368 acres; pop. (1962) 21,783.

MONAGHAN (mon′ahan). County of Ulster prov., Rep. of Ireland, watered by the Finn and Blackwater. Cereals are grown, and linen made. Area 498 sq. m.; pop. (1966) 45,732. The co. tn. is M.; pop. (1961) 4,010.

MŌ′NASH, Sir John (1865–1931). Australian general. B. in Melbourne, of Jewish descent, he entered the Australian army in 1887, and during the F.W.W. showed exceptional powers of generalship at Gallipoli and as commander of the Australian forces in France in 1918. M. Univ. nr. Melbourne (1960) was named after him.

MONASTICISM (Gk. *monachos*, monk). Method of religious life, by which the individual, under vows of poverty, chastity, and obedience, devotes himself

to the service of God in retirement. M. was known in pre-Christian times among the Jews, eg. the Essenes, and forms part of non-Christian religions, e.g. Buddhism. The institution of Christian M. is ascribed to St. Anthony in 3rd cent. Egypt, but the inauguration of communal life is attributed to his disciple, St. Pachomius. The full adaptation of M. to the conditions of western life was carried out by St. Benedict in the 6th cent., and the Benedictine Rule became general. In 910 the foundation of Cluny began the system of orders whereby each monastery was subordinated to the mother institution. During the Middle Ages other forms of M. were estab., incl. the eremitical Carthusians (1084), the Augustinian canons, who were clerics organized under a monastic system (11th cent.); the military Knights Templar and Knights Hospitaller (12th cent.); and in the early 13th cent. the 4 great mendicant orders, Franciscans, Dominicans, Carmelites, and Augustinians, who went out to work in the world.

M. reached the height of its influence during the 13th cent., declined during the 14th, and was severely affected by the Reformation. Renewed life came with the foundation of orders dedicated to particular missions, such as the great weapon of the Counter-Reformation, the Society of Jesus (1540). But the French Revolution exercised a repressive influence. Yet another revival came in the late 19th cent. and continues in the 20th, particularly in the active orders, although by the mid-20th cent. emphasis was moving to a combination of the active and contemplative life. Throughout the history of M. organizations for women have existed on parallel lines with those for men.

MONASTIR. Turkish name of BITOLJ.

MONCKTON of Brenchley, Walter Turner, 1st visct. (1891–1965). British lawyer and Cons. politician. Director-Gen. of the Min. of Information in the S.W.W., he was Min. of Labour 1951–55 and Defence 1955–6. He was created visct. in 1957.

MOND, Ludwig (1839–1909). British chemist. B. at Cassel, Germany, he moved to England in 1862, and, while partner in a chemical works at Widnes, perfected a process for recovering sulphur during the manufacture of alkali. In 1867 he became a British subject, and in 1873 helped to found the firm of Brunner, Mond and Co., which pioneered in the British chemical industry. M. was also instrumental in developing the Canadian nickel industry.

MONDRIAN (mon′drē-ahn), **Piet** (1872–1944). Dutch abstract painter. B. at Amersfoort, in 1917 he founded with Theo van Doesburg the review and movement known as *De Stijl* (The Style), which sought to apply the principles of geometrical abstract design to painting, sculpture, and architecture. Neo-Plasticism, which he founded in 1920, was a phase of *De Stijl*.

MONET (mōnā′), **Claude** (1840–1926). French Impressionist painter. B. at Paris, he studied under Boudin, and after spending 2 years in Africa with a French regiment, entered Gleyre's studio. He became a prominent member of the French Impressionist group, which incl. Manet, Degas, Renoir, and Sisley. He excelled in painting atmospheric effects, and was fond of depicting the same subject at different times of the day, e.g. his series of haystacks.

MONEY. Any commodity which by custom, convention, or law, serves as the common medium of exchange in a community. It may be in the form of gold, silver, copper, printed paper, or anything else; as long as it performs this primary function it ranks as money. Other functions are as a measure of value, i.e. a means of estimating the value of all other articles; a standard of value of deferred payments; and a store of value. Where M. is removed from country to country it performs yet another function; that of a transfer of value.

Until comparatively recently, most M. consisted of coins, and monetary theorists have described the properties that M. should possess as: general acceptability, durability, portability, homogeneity, divisibility, stability of value, indestructibility, and cognizability, etc. Gold and silver in practice have been found to answer best these requirements. In the early stages the precious metals passed current by weight and not by count, but the advantages of coined M. were made manifest much more than 2 thousand years ago. The Lydians in 7th cent. B.C. are supposed to have been the first to use coins. Very soon the right of coinage became, as it still is, the monopoly of the State.

Important in the study of M. is the QUANTITY THEORY according to which if the quantity of M. be increased above the real needs of the people, its value will be diminished; in other words, the price of commodities will rise, since the monetary unit will purchase less than it did before the amount of the circulating medium was increased. The principal factors that determine the value of M. at any given time are: the quantity of M. in circulation, and the quantity of goods and commodities on sale. There is, however, another element; account must also be taken of the velocity or rapidity of circulation, or number of times each unit of M. is used. M. hoarded or kept out of circulation, even if issued by the State mint or bank, can have no effect on the value of money in circulation, or on the prices of commodities.

At the present time coins are used as a rule only for small transactions. Far more important are the 2 forms of 'representative M.', viz. Government M. or bank notes, and bank M. transferred by cheques, Checks on the process of 'credit creation' or the creation of 'bank money' are the necessity on the banker's part to keep a balance sufficient to meet all demands for repayment, and in the U.K. the control exercised by the Treasury through the Bank of England.

INTERNATIONAL MONEY. The problems that faced nations after the S.W.W. of 1939–45 were not dissimilar to those that existed after the F.W.W. Disordered exchanges, depreciated monetary units, with the resulting interference with overseas trade, were the common experience. Various cures for these ills were tried, the suspension of the gold standard among them. Then in July 1944 a United Nations Monetary and Financial conference was held at Bretton Woods, New Hampshire, U.S.A., which led to the establishment of an International Bank for Reconstruction and Development, and the opening of the International Monetary Fund, in Washington, U.S.A., which is designed to assist in the smooth working of trade and in the prevention of crises, in addition to the preservation of exchange stability. The Fund system has many of the advantages of the gold standard, without its rigidity, but distorted balance of payments positions were a marked feature of the late 1960s, e.g. Britain struggling against an adverse balance and Germany in the reverse position. *See* BANKING, GOLD STANDARD, etc.

MONGŌ′LIA. A vast plateau region of E. central Asia, lying between L. Baikal and the Nan Shan mountains. The 3 physical divisions are: (1) the Gobi region, a long central depression within the plateau; (2) the N.W. mountains; (3) the S.E. mountains. The plateau climate is dry and subject to extremes of cold and heat, particularly in the Gobi region, where N.W. winds prevail; the N.W. and S.E. mountains receive the rainy winds. The inhabitants are Mongols, mainly nomadic and living in tents, who keep herds of horses, camels, cattle, goats, and sheep and are expert horsemen. The former organization of the Mongols under hereditary princes as a military society has broken down under Communist rule, as has the power of Islam and Lamaism (qq.v.), but in 1967 there was violent opposition to the Maoist Cultural Revolution in both Outer and Inner M. Discoveries made by expeditions in the 1920s confirmed that M. is a main area of world evolution, many remains being found of prehistoric animals and early human culture. The language of M. belongs to the Altaic family, and its literature is mostly colloquial fairy tales.

The name Mongols first appears in Chinese annals in the 6th cent., and their power reached its zenith under Genghis Khan, who became emperor in 1206, and his grandson, Kublai Khan (1216–94), the first Mongol emperor of China. Separation of the N. Mongols from the S. Mongols dates from the 14th cent., following the overthrow in 1368 of the Mongol dynasty of China by the Mings.

Inner Mongolia, the S. part of M., was made an autonomous region of China in 1947. To it in 1950 were added Hsingan and Liaopei, formerly provs. of Manchuria, and deducted Ningsia and Suiyuan. The last was restored to I.M. in 1954, and part of the former Jehol prov. was added in 1955. Only about 3 per cent. of the total area is cultivated, millet, soya beans, sugar beet, and oilseeds being grown. Timber is produced, and there are reserves of coal and iron ore little worked. The cap. is Huhehot (Chinese Kweisui). Area 450,000 sq. m.; pop. (1968) 13,000,000.

Outer Mongolia, the N. part of M., is bounded on the N. by the R.S.F.S.R., elsewhere by China. It was part of China from 1686 until given autonomy at the Chinese revolution of 1911–12. In 1924 it adopted the soviet system of government and proclaimed itself the Mongolian People's Republic. China recognized its independence in 1946, and M. has a mutual assistance pact with U.S.S.R. (1966). Agriculture is on the collective system, and new areas are being brought into cultivation. Minerals incl. gold, tungsten, uranium, coal and oil. Ulan Bator is the cap. and chief manufacturing centre, but industry is being developed at Darkhan (nr. Soviet border N. of the cap.) and Choybalsan (in the E.) mainly by Soviet aid. Area *c.* 6,000 sq. m.; pop. (1966) 1,120,000.

MO′NGOOSE. Mammal in the family Viverridae. The Indian M. (*Herpestes mungo*) is greyish in colour, about 18 in. long, with a long tail. It may be tamed, and is often kept for its ability to kill snakes. The Egyptian M. or Ichneumon is larger.

MONISM. In philosophy, the belief that the universe may be reduced to a single principle, whether mental, material, or other. It is thus opposed to dualism and pluralism.

MO′NITOR. Armoured vessel of light draught and slow speed, specializing in long-range coastal bombardment, which takes its name from the first of its class, the Federal turret-ship *Monitor*, used in the American Civil War. Ms. were largely used in the F.W.W., especially off the Belgian coast. None was built between the wars, but a few of the larger type were used in the S.W.W. The word M. also denotes a family of lizards (*see* DRAGON) and a professional listener to and reporter of broadcasts.

MONK, or **MONCK, George,** 1st duke of Albemarle (1608–69). English soldier. During the Civil War he fought for the king, but after being captured changed sides and took command of the parliamentary forces in Ireland. He served in Cromwell's Scottish campaign 1650, and at sea against the Dutch 1652–3, and under the Commonwealth became C.-in-C. in Scotland. Leading his army into England in 1660 he brought about the restoration of Charles II, and was created duke of Albemarle.

MONK, Maria (*c.* 1817–50). Claiming to have escaped from a Montreal nunnery, she pub. palpably alse *Awful Disclosures* (1836) of life therein.

MONKEY. Term usually applied to all the Primates, except man and the anthropoid apes. Ms. are numerous in tropical parts of Africa, S. America, and Asia, and are seldom found elsewhere.

MONKEY-PUZZLE TREE or **Chilean Pine.** Evergreen tree (*Araucaria imbricata*) native of Chile, first cultivated in Britain in 1796.

MONMOUTH, James Scott, duke of (1649–85). Leader of 'Monmouth's rebellion'. B. at Rotterdam, the natural son of Charles II by Lucy Walter, he was created duke of M. in 1663. He m. Anne Scott, countess of Buccleuch, and adopted her surname. The Whig opposition attempted unsuccessfully to secure him the succession to the crown by the Exclusion Bill, and in 1684, having become implicated in a Whig conspiracy, he fled to Holland. After James II's accession in 1685, he landed at Lyme Regis, claimed the crown, and raised a rebellion which was crushed at Sedgemoor, in Somerset. M. was captured and beheaded on Tower Hill.

MONMOUTH. Co. tn. (bor.) of Monmouthshire, Wales, 18 m. S. of Hereford, at the junction of the Monnow and the Wye, Henry V was born at M. Pop. (1961) 5,505.

MONMOUTHSHIRE. Co. of Wales, before 1970 for some purposes included in England. The chief rivers include the Wye and the Usk which flow into the Severn estuary on the S. border. Most of the co. is hilly (Chwasel y Fan in the Black Mts. is 2,228 ft.) and sheep farming is carried on. There are numerous orchards, and wheat, oats, and barley are grown. There are coal mines and iron works in the W. upland valleys. The co. tn. is Monmouth; other towns are Newport, Pontypool, and Abergavenny. Area 542 sq. m.; pop. (1961) 443,689.

MONOCOTYLEDON (monokotilē′don). Plants having one seed-leaf (cotyledon). The stems of such plants are usually hollow or soft, e.g. palms, bamboos, grasses, and cereal plants. The foliage leaves are parellel-veined.

MONOPHYSITES (mono′fisits). Christian heretics of the 5th–7th cents., who taught that Christ had one nature, in opposition to the orthodox doctrine laid down at the Council of Chalcedon in 451, that He had 2 natures, the human and the divine.

MONO′POLY. Originally a grant from the Crown conferring the sole right to manufacture or sell a certain article. The abuse of such grants, which were frequently made to royal favourites, provoked many protests from parliament under Elizabeth, James I, and Charles I. The term is applied today to business organizations or groupings of organizations, formed into trusts or cartels, strong enough to dominate particular industries and so restrict competition and control prices. In the U.K. the Ms. Commission (1948, reconstituted under the Restrictive Trade Practices Act 1956, which also created a special court to deal with restric-

tive agreements) inquires into such problems and makes recommendations to the govt. A familiar example is the enforcement by manufacturers of minimum resale prices, which was abolished, unless shown to be in the public interest, under the Resale Prices Act (1964), following the example of U.S.A. and Canada.

MONORAIL. Originally a device with wheels running on a single overhead rail, designed to carry light loads up to 1 ton, and when driven by electricity, called a telpher (the first of these having been invented in 1882). Since the S.W.W., however, the M. has been increasingly advanced as the solution to traffic problems in congested areas: Germany (Cologne) and Japan are pioneers in the field and Britain and U.S.A. also favour the idea. In undeveloped areas, e.g. E. Africa, the M. may be a practical means of linking mines, etc., to ports and railheads without the heavy cost of road and rail construction and maintenance in difficult country.

MONOTHEISM (mon′othē-izm). Belief in one God, as opposed to polytheism, the belief in many.

MONO′THELITES. Christian heretics of the 7th cent., who sought to reconcile the orthodox and Monophysite theologies by maintaining that while Christ possessed 2 natures He had only one will.

MONOTYPE (mon′otīp). Type-setting machine of American origin, commonly used for bookwork. It produces separate letters, and thus differs from the linotype machine, which produces type in solid lines called 'slugs'. The M. consists of a composing machine and a casting machine. The former has a keyboard, and by touching the keys the operator perforates a paper roll in the machine. The paper roll is then fed to the casting machine, which produces the separate types. The paper roll can be easily stored, and may be used several times. This encyclopaedia is an example of M. production.

MONRO (munrō′), **Harold** (1879–1932). British poet. He pub. vols. of verse, e.g. *Strange Meetings* (1917), and *Earth for Sale* (1928), but is best remembered for his foundation of the 'Poetry Bookshop' (1912), which issued the influential *Poetry Review* (1912), and the *Chapbook*.

MONROE, Harriet (1860–1936). American poet. B. in Chicago, she founded the magazine *Poetry* (1912), which published the work of A. Lowell, T. S. Eliot, R. Frost, E. Pound, and H. Crane.

MONROE, James (1758–1831). 5th pres. of the U.S.A. B. in Virginia, he served in the War of Independence, was Minister to France 1794–6, and during 1803 negotiated the Lousiana Purchase. He was Sec.

MONORAIL. Of French origin, the Safege monorail system has been adopted by Taylor Woodrow for development in the United Kingdom and Commonwealth. On the left a car runs on the test track at Châteauneuf-sur-Loire, near Orléans, and the cut-away (right) shows a section of the beamway rail and one of the two traction bogies. Each of these is fitted with two electric motors, mounted longitudinally, driving through a geared axle and differential. Enclosure of the bogies, together with the use of rubber tyres, ensures maximum use of the system in all weather conditions.

Courtesy of the Taylor Woodrow Group.

of State 1811–17, and was elected Pres. in 1816, and again in 1820. His name is associated with the *Monroe doctrine*, expressed in his message to Congress in 1823, when European intervention against the revolting Spanish colonies in S. America was proposed, in which he declared that the American continents 'are henceforth not to be considered as subjects for future colonization by any European powers', and that any attempt to extend European colonies in the Americas would be regarded as dangerous to U.S.A. peace and safety.

MONROE, Marilyn. Professional name of Norma Jean Baker (1928–62), American film actress and sex symbol. An illegitimate child, suffering wretchedly in early life, she first made her name in *The Asphalt Jungle*: later films incl. *The Seven Year Itch* and *Some Like it Hot*. Her second husband was Joe Di Maggio, the baseball star, and her third Arthur Miller (q.v.). She d. of an overdose of sleeping tablets.

MONROVIA (munrō′via). Port and cap. of the Liberian rep., Africa. M., founded in 1821, was named in honour of President Monroe (q.v.). Along the coast, 60 m. S.W., Buchanan handles iron exports from the Nimba mountains. Pop. (1967) 80,000.

MONS (monz). Cap. of the prov. of Hainault Belgium, situated in the centre of an extensive coalfield, and with textile and sugar industries. The retreat from Mons in Aug. 1914 followed the 1st important battle (23 Aug.) fought by the B.E.F. in the F.W.W. Pop.(1968) 27,710.

MONSARRAT, Nicholas (1910–). British author. B. in Liverpool, he served in the R.N. during the S.W.W., and made his name with the war novel *The Cruel Sea* (1951): later books incl. *The Story of Esther Costello* (1953), *The Ship That Died of Shame* (1959) and *Richer Than all His Tribe* (1968). He lives in Ottawa.

MONSOON (Arabic *mausim*, season). Term originally applied by the Arabs to a wind which occurs at fixed seasons in the Arabian Sea; now applied to any seasonal wind, particularly those which occur in India and the N. Indian Ocean.

MONSTERA. Plant of the Arum family (Araceae), a native of tropical America. The small flowers crowd

MONSTERA. Growing easily anywhere in the tropics, the Mexican *Monstera deliciosa* is familiar in Australian gardens and yields a pleasant fruit. Besides the fully ripe specimens, several unripe fruits (foreground) are still enclosed in their spathes.
Courtesy of the Agent-General for Queensland.

on thick, fleshy spikes, each enclosed by a large leaf. A striking feature is the drying up of areas between the veins of the leaves, which ultimately form holes and deep marginal notches.

MONSTRANCE. In the R.C. Church, a vessel used from the 13th cent. to hold the Sacred Host when exposed at Benediction or in processions.

MONTAGNA (montahn′yah), **Bartolomeo** (1450–1523). Italian painter. B. in Brescia, he was influenced by Carpaccio and Bellini, his most important work being the altar-piece executed for San Michele at Vicenza, now in Milan.

MONTAGU (mon′tagū), **Edwin Samuel** (1879–1924). British Lib. politician, the 2nd son of the 1st Lord Swaythling. Entering parl. in 1906, he was Sec. of State for India 1917–22.

MONTAGU, Lady Mary Wortley (1689–1762). British letter-writer and society poet. *Née* Pierrepont, she m. Edward Wortley M., ambassador to Constantinople. Returning to England in 1718, she introduced inoculation against smallpox, and quarrelled with Pope, her former friend and correspondent.

MONTAGU, Victor. *See* SANDWICH, Lord.

MONTAIGNE (montăn′), **Michel Eyquem de** (1533–92). French essayist. B. at the Château de Montaigne, near Bordeaux, he studied law, and in 1554 became a counsellor of the Bordeaux parlement. Little is known of his earlier life, except that he frequented the court of Francis II and tasted the pleasures of Paris. In 1571 he retired to his estates, relinquishing his magistracy, and in 1580 pub. the 1st 2 vols. of his *Essays*. He toured Germany, Switzerland, and Italy 1580–1, returning on his election as mayor of Bordeaux, a post he held till 1585. The 3rd vol. of *Essays* appeared in 1588. He d. of quinsy, and was buried in Bordeaux. The originator of the modern essay form, M. deals with all aspects of life in a mood of urbane scepticism, and as translated by John Florio in 1603, largely influenced English writers and thinkers.

MONTALE, Eugenio (1896–). Italian poet. His vols. of highly individual poetry – e.g. *Ossi di seppis* (1925: *Cuttlebones*), *Le Occasioni* (1939: *The Occasions*), *La bufera* (1956: *The Storm*) – reflect his concern with language and meaning, and explore with stoicism such experiences as isolation, uncertainty and exile, in the context of contemporary life.

MONTANA (montah′nah). State of the U.S.A., on the Canadian border. It is bisected by the Rocky Mts. and their subsidiary ranges: to the E. lies the Great Plains region. The chief rivers are the Missouri and Yellowstone. There is extensive irrigation, and wheat is the principal crop, but stock raising is also very important. Forestry supports timber, pulp, and plywood industries. M. is rich in minerals, espec. copper, first worked 1880: others incl. fluorspar, manganese, vermiculite, oil, and natural gas. The cap. is Helena. Area 147,138 sq. m.; pop. (1970) 694,409.

MONTANISM. A movement within the early Church which strove to return to the purity of primitive Christianity. Originating in Phrygia *c.* 156 with the teaching of a prophet named Montanus, it spread to Asia Minor, Rome, Carthage, and Gaul.

MONTAUBAN (montōbon′). Town of S. France, dating from 1144, cap. of the dept. of Tarn-et-Garonne, 31 m. N. of Toulouse, long a Protestant stronghold. Pop. (1962) 43,401.

MONT BLANC (mon blon). The highest mountain in the Alps (15,781 ft.). First ascended by Jacques Balmat and Dr. Michel Paccard in 1786. A 7½ m. road tunnel (1965) links France and Italy.

MONTBRETIA (-brĕsh′ia). Genus of plants (*Tritonia*) in the family Iridaceae. The yellow or reddish flowers are borne on long stems.

MONTCALM (montkahm′), **Louis-Joseph de Montcalm-Gozon,** marquis de (1712–59). French general. B. near Nîmes, he was appointed commander of the troops in Canada in 1756. He won a succession of victories over the British, but was defeated by Wolfe at Quebec, where he and Wolfe were slain.

MONTE CARLO. One of the 3 communes of Monaco (q.v.), famous for its gaming tables.

MONTE CRISTO. A small uninhabited island off the W. coast of Italy, 25 m. S. of Elba. It is chiefly famous because of Dumas' novel, *The Count of M. C*

MONTENE'GRO. Fed. rep. of Yugoslavia, between Bosnia-Hercegovina and Albania. Once part of Serbia, it became independent in the 14th cent. It never submitted to the Turks and the treaty of Berlin, 1878, recognized M. as a sovereign principality; Prince Nicholas took the title of king in 1910. M. sided with Serbia in the Balkan wars and in the F.W.W., when it was overrun by the Austrians. After the defeat of Austria in 1918, King Nicholas was deposed and M. voted in favour of joining the new Kingdom of the Serbs, Croats, and Slovenes (renamed Yugoslavia, 1931). The cap. is Titograd. Area 5,330 sq. m.; pop. (1961) 471,894

MONTERREY (mŏntārā'). Capital of Nuevo León state, Mexico. There are iron and steel works, food processing plants, etc., and a univ. (1933). It was founded as Léon in 1560, renamed M. in 1599. Pop. (1967) 900,600.

MONTESPAN (mŏntespoń'), **Françoise-Athénais de Pardaillan,** marquise de (1641–1707). Mistress of Louis XIV. The dau. of the duc de Montmartre, she m. the marquis de M. in 1663, became Louis's mistress in 1667, and in 1691 retired to a convent. Her 7 children by Louis were legitimized, but her influence over him waned following her engagement of the future Mme de Maintenon (q.v.) as their governess.

MONTESQUIEU (mŏnteskyŏ'), **Charles Louis de Secondat,** baron de la Brède et de (1689–1755). French philosophical historian. B. near Bordeaux, he became adviser to the Bordeaux parlement in 1714. After the success of his *Lettres persanes* (1721), he adopted a literary career. Later works are *Considérations sur les Causes de la grandeur des Romains et de leur décadence* (1734), and *De l'Esprit des Lois* (1748), a study of the principles of government.

MONTESSORI (montesaw'ri), **Maria** (1870–1952). Italian educationalist. B. near Ancona, she was the first woman to take a medical degree at Rome univ. (1894), and from experience with mentally deficient children evolved a system of spontaneous education adapted to normal infants, as described in her *Montessori Method* (1912).

MONTEUX (montö'), **Pierre** (1875–1964). French conductor. He estab. a reputation as conductor of Diaghilev's Russian Ballet 1911–14 and 1917, and Ravel's *Daphnis and Chloe* and Stravinsky's *Rite of Spring* were first performed under his direction. He then for many years conducted in America, notably with the San Francisco Symphony Orchestra 1935–52; and in 1961 became musical director and principal conductor to the London Symphony Orchestra Since 1942 he had been an American citizen.

MONTEVERDI, Claudio (1567–1643). Italian composer. B. at Cremona, while in the service of the duke of Mantua, he achieved fame with the operas *Orfeo* (1607) and *Arianna* (1608), and became musical director at St. Mark's, Venice, in 1613.

MONTEUX. One of the world's finest conductors, he was noted for the superb fire and clarity of his interpretations.
Photo: Godfrey MacDomnic.

MONTEVIDEO. The coastline of this region is unusual. The natural harbour at the heart of the city is almost circular in shape, and a chain of fine curved beaches converts the suburbs to fashionable bathing and pleasure resorts.
Courtesy of National Tourist Office of Uruguay.

MONTEVIDEO (montividä'-ō). Cap. and chief port of Uruguay, cap. also of M. dept., on the River Plate. Founded in 1726, M. is the seat of an archbishopric; it has a cathedral, a univ. (1849), and an international airport. The chief exports are beef and other animal products. Pop. (1967) 1,175,000.

MONTEZ, Lola. Stage-name of the adventuress Maria Gilbert (1818–61). B. in Ireland, she appeared on the stage as a Spanish dancer, and in 1847 became the mistress of King Ludwig I of Bavaria, whose policy she dictated for a year. Her liberal sympathies led to her banishment through Jesuit influence in 1848. She later acted in the U.S.A. and Australia, and d. in New York.

MONTEZUMA II (montēzoo'mah) (1466–1520). Aztec emperor of Mexico. He became emperor in 1502. When Cortes invaded Mexico in 1519 he made M. a prisoner, and shortly after the emperor was murdered by his subjects while attempting to dissuade them from attacking the Spaniards.

MONTFORT, Simon de, earl of Leicester (c. 1200–65). English statesman. The son of Simon de Montfort, leader of the crusade against the Albigenses, he came to England in 1230, and was granted the earldom of Leicester. From 1258 onwards he led the baronial opposition to Henry III's misrule, and in 1264 defeated and captured the king at Lewes. As head of the govt. in 1265 he summoned the first parl. in which the towns were represented. He was defeated and killed soon after at Evesham.

MONTGOLFIER (moṅgolfyä'), **Joseph Michel** (1740–1810), and **Étienne Jacques** (1745–99). French balloonists. The 2 brothers were papermakers of Annonay, near Lyons, where on 5 June 1783 they sent up a balloon filled with hot air. The first successful human flight was made in a M. balloon on 21 Nov. 1783. The M. experiments greatly stimulated scientific interest in aviation.

MONTGOMERY OF ALAMEIN, Bernard Law Montgomery, 1st visct. (1887–). British field marshal. The son of an Ulster clergyman, he was commissioned in the Warwickshire Regt. in 1908, and served in France during the F.W.W. At the beginning of the S.W.W. he was commanding the 3rd division, which formed part of the B.E.F. in France 1939–40, and he took part in the evacuation from Dunkirk. In Aug. 1942 he took command of the 8th Army, then barring the German advance on Cairo; the victory of El Alamein in Oct. turned the tide in N. Africa, and was followed by the expulsion of Rommel from Egypt and rapid advance into Tunisia. In Feb. 1943 M.'s forces came under Eisenhower's command, and during the following months were prominent in the conquest of Tunisia and Sicily and the invasion of Italy. He commanded the Allied armies during the opening phase of the invasion of France in June 1944, and from Aug. the British and Imperial troops which liberated the Netherlands, overran N. Germany, and entered

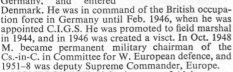

Denmark. He was in command of the British occupation force in Germany until Feb. 1946, when he was appointed C.I.G.S. He was promoted to field marshal in 1944, and in 1946 was created a visct. In Oct. 1948 M. became permanent military chairman of the Cs.-in-C. in Committee for W. European defence, and 1951–8 was deputy Supreme Commander, Europe.

MONTGOMERY. U.S. city, cap. of Alabama, on the Alabama r., 150 m. N.E. of Mobile. Settled in 1814, M. became the state cap. in 1847; it was the cap. of the Confederate govt. Feb.–May 1861. M. exports cotton and makes fertilizers, cigars, machinery, and cotton textiles. Pop. (1960) 134,393.

MONTGOMERYSHIRE. County of N. Wales. It is partly mountainous, but on the E. side there are fertile valleys. The principal rivers are the Severn, the Dovey, and the Vyrnwy. Most of the county consists of pastureland. The co. tn. is Montgomery; other towns are Welshpool and Newtown. Area 797 sq. m.; pop. (1961) 44,228.

MONTH. Originally the time between a new moon and the next, averaging 29½ days, now called a lunar M. The calendar M. is for convenience composed of a complete number of days, 30 or 31 (February 28), the extra 6 hours' time per year being added to February as a day each 4th or leap year.

MONTHERLANT (moṅterloṅ'), **Henri de Millon** (1896–). French author. B. in Paris, he was a Nazi sympathizer, and his novels, which are marked by an obsession with physical relationships, include *Aux fontaines du désir* (1927), and *Pitié pour les femmes* (1936). His tempered masterpiece is *Le Chaos et la nuit* (1963), drawn from one man's awareness of death.

MONTMARTRE (moṅmar'tr). Bohemian quarter of Paris, France, dominated by the basilica of Sacré Cœur, 1875. It is situated in the N. of the city on a 400 ft. high hill.

MONTPELLIER (moṅpelyā'). Cap. of the dept. of Hérault, France, 31 m. S.W. of Nimes. There is a 14th cent. cathedral and a univ. (1289) with a famous medical school. Industries incl. engineering, food processing, textiles. Pop. (1968) 161,910.

MONTREAL (montrē-awl'). Largest city, great inland port, and commercial centre of Canada, in Quebec prov., on the island of Montreal, at the junction of the Ottawa and St. Lawrence rivers. A number of bridges, incl. the Victoria Jubilee Bridge, spanning the St. Lawrence, link the city with the mainland. M. is linked with the inland canal system, and the Canadian National and Canadian Pacific Rlys. M. was founded as Ville Marie de Montréal in 1642 by Paul de Choméd. Sieur de Maisonneuve; suffered much from Iroquois hostility; and was the last place surrendered by the French to the British, 1760. Nevertheless, when troops of the rebel Continental Congress occupied M. 1775–6, the citizens refused to rise against the British. French remains the language of the majority of the pop. Mount Royal (or Mont Réal), 753 f., overlooks the city. M. is the seat of both R.C. and Anglican dioceses, and of the R.C. M. univ. (formerly

a branch of Laval) and the Protestant McGill and Sir George Williams univs. M. has excellent rail, waterway, dock and airline facilities (H.Q. of I.C.A.O.); and industries incl. aircraft, chemicals, oil refining and petrochemicals, flour milling, sugar refining, brewing and meat packing. Carefully preserving its old quarter, M. is also the modernest of cities, e.g. the Place Ville Marie project, consisting of a 45-storey skyscraper above a 7-acre plaza, with a weather-proof 4-level underground 'city' beneath: *c.* 40 acres of shopping arcades with 1½ m. of promenades; then 2 levels of parking space and service roads; and a bottom level for railway tracks and station platforms. The M. Internat. Exhibition (Expo 67) on 2 man-made is. in the St. Lawrence has been succeeded by the world's largest permanent exhibition. Pop. (1966) of met. area 2,436,817.

MONTREUX (moṅtrö'). Winter resort in Vaud canton, Switzerland, on the E. shore of Lake Geneva. Close by is the castle of Chillon. At the annual television festival (1961) the premier award is the *Golden Rose of M.* The *Convention of M.* in 1936 allowed Turkey to re-militarize the Dardanelles. Pop. (1960) 20,000.

MONTROSE (montrōz'), **James Graham,** marquess of (1612–50). Scottish soldier. The son of the 4th earl of M., he supported the Covenanters in their struggle against Charles I, but after 1640 went over to the king's side. In 1644 Charles created him a marquess and lieutenant-general in Scotland, whereupon he rallied the Highlanders and won a succession of brilliant victories. Defeated in 1645 at Philiphaugh, he escaped to the Continent. He returned in 1650, and after attempting to raise a rebellion was hanged at Edinburgh.

MONT ST. MICHEL (moṅ-saṅ-mēshel'). Small rocky island (165 ft. high), situated near the coast of Manche dept., France. It is famous for its Benedictine monastery, estab. in 708. *See* illus. p. 931.

MONTSERRAT. Mountain of Spain, 24 m. N.W. of Barcelona; so called because its uneven outline resembles the serrated edges of a saw (Sp. *monte serrado*). It rises to a height of 4,070 ft. The Benedictine monastery of M., built 2,910 ft. high on the mountain, contains a famous image of the Virgin.

MONTREAL. Seen from the Plaza, La Grande Salle, dominant structure of the Place des Arts, a multi-unit centre for the performing arts. It seats 3,000 and the stage for opera, ballet and drama converts easily for symphony concerts.
Courtesy of Panda Photography and Affleck, Desbarats, Dimakopoulos, Lebensold and Sise, Architects.

MONTSERRAT. Volcanic island in the British W. Indies, one of the Leeward group. It was discovered by Columbus (1493), who named it after the mountain in Spain. It was first colonized by the Irish, 1632. M.'s principal products are cotton and cottonseed, citrus and other fruits, and vegetables. The chief town is Plymouth (pop. 3,500). Area 32½ sq. m.; pop. (1966) 14,464.

MOON. A photograph (left) taken with a 36-inch refractor shows the various dark plains, together with mountain ranges and craters. The crater Tycho (lower part of the picture) is very prominent. In the right-hand photograph Earth, as seen by *Apollo* astronauts, rises above features near the eastern limb (as seen from Earth) of the Moon: the sunset terminator bisects Africa.
Courtesy of Lick Observatory and N.A.S.A.

MONUMENT, The. In London, England, overlooking Billingsgate, a column 202 ft. high, designed by Wren, and completed in 1677 to commemorate the Great Fire of London (1666), near the site of the house in Pudding Lane where the conflagration began.

MO'NZA. City in Italy, 9 m. N.E. of Milan. It was the capital of the Lombard rulers. The cathedral of San Giovanni, founded in 595, contains the iron crown of Lombardy. Pop. (1960) 80,000.

MOON. The only natural satellite of the Earth. Its average distance is 238,857 m., and its revolution period 27¼ days. Since it has no light of its own, and merely reflects the light of the Sun, it shows the familiar phases from 'new' to 'full'. Its diameter is 2,160 m., and its mass is $1/81$ of that of the Earth.

The surface of the M. contains large darkish areas, formerly regarded as liquid sheets and still known as 'seas', though for centuries now it has been known that there is no water anywhere on the M., and that the dark areas are simply plains, less mountainous than the rest of the surface. The brighter regions are very rough, and some of the lunar mountains are comparable with the highest peaks found on Earth. Hills and valleys are common, but the most interesting features are, without doubt, the craters, which range from vast plains more than 150 m. in diameter down to tiny pits. A typical crater has a raised, circular wall, and a floor deeply depressed below the level of the outer country. Once hot, turbulent and volcanic, the M. still has traces of a hot, central core, as well as traces of water vapour trapped in rocks at the time of its formation. Ages of the rocks brought back vary from 4½ to 2½ billion years, and analysis suggests that the M. was formed independently of Earth and later captured. The M. is almost or quite devoid of atmosphere, and this means that it is unsuitable for life in any form.

Because the M.'s axial rotation coincides with its revolution period, part of the surface is permanently turned toward the Earth, while another part – owing to various effects termed *librations* only 41% of the whole – is permanently averted: the latter is basically similar, though with fewer waterless seas. 'Soft landings' by lunar probes (q.v.) have shown that the surface consists of volcanic or lava-like rock, deeply pitted and strewn with small stones, and samples were brought back by *Apollo XI* (U.S.A. 16–24 July 1969) which achieved a M. landing near the lunar equator,

while Michael Collins remained on board the command module (q.v.) *Columbia*, Neil Armstrong and Edwin Aldrin descended in lunar module *Eagle* and walked on the surface at 9.17 p.m. 20 July.

The M. is the chief force in controlling the tides, but correlation of the weather with its changing phases is not proven, although rainfall records indicate that rain is more likely a few days after a new or full M.

MOONSTONE. Opalescent variety of potassium sodium feldspar, found in Ceylon or Burma, and distinguished by a blue, silvery, or red tint.

MOORE, George (1852–1933). Irish novelist. B. in Co. Mayo, he went to study art in Paris (1870), and pub. 2 vols of poetry there. His first novel, *A Modern Lover* (1883), was startlingly frank regarding sexual relationships and was followed by others, incl. *A Mummer's Wife* (1885); *Esther Waters* (1894); *Evelyn Innes* (1898); the religious *Brook Kerith* (1916); and *Aphrodite in Aulis* (1930). He also pub. the autobiographical *Confessions of a Young Man* (1888); *Memoirs of My Dead Life* (1906); and the trilogy of the Irish revival, *Hail and Farewell* (1911–14).

MOORE, George Edward (1873–1958). British philosopher. Educ. at Trinity Coll., Cambridge, he was prof. of philosophy at the univ. 1925–39, and ed. the journal *Mind*, to which he contributed important articles, 1921–47. His books incl. *Principia Ethica* (1903) and *Some Main Problems of Philosophy* (1953), but his chief influence was as a teacher with immense analytic power.

MOORE, Henry (1898–). British sculptor. B. at Castleford, Yorks, he studied at Leeds and the Royal College of Art, but learned more from the works of primitive artists in the British Museum and the simple forms of life in the Natural History Museum. He seeks to express his own emotional apprehension in term

'Three Standing Figures' by Henry Moore.

of the material in which he is working, and by his originality has encountered much hostility. His drawings are also of remarkable quality, especially his London air-raid-shelter scenes of the S.W.W. In 1963 he was awarded the O.M.

MOORE, Sir John (1761–1809). British general. B. at Glasgow, he entered the army in 1776, and served in the American and French Revolutionary Wars and against the Irish rebellion of 1798. In 1808 he commanded the army sent to Portugal; after advancing into Spain he had to retreat to Corunna, and was killed in the battle fought to cover the embarkation.

MOORE, Marianne (1887–1972). American poet. B. in Missouri, she edited the literary *Dial* (1925–9), and pub. vols. of intellectual verse of difficult form. e.g. *Observations* (1924), *What are Years* (1941), and *A Marianne Reader* (1961).

MOORE, Thomas (1779–1852). Irish poet. B. in Dublin, he went to England to study law in 1799, and in 1803 was appointed admiralty registrar in Bermuda, but left the post in charge of a deputy, whose subsequent embezzlement (for which he was held liable) sent him into exile on the Continent (1819–22). Among his works are the verse romance, *Lalla Rookh* (1817), the satirical *Fudge Family in Paris* (1818), *Loves of the Angels* (1823), the *Irish Melodies* (1807–35), upon which his reputation now mainly rests, and lives of Sheridan and Byron. His *Memoirs* appeared 1853–6.

MOOREHEAD, Alan McCrae (1910–). British journalist, brilliantly successful as foreign and war correspondent to the *Daily Express* 1936–45, whose books incl. *Mediterranean Front* (1941), *Montgomery* (1946), *Gallipoli* (1956), *The White Nile* (1960), and *Cooper's Creek* (1963), dealing with the Burke and Wills expedition of 1860.

MOORHEN. Common water fowl (*Gallinula*), about the size of a bantam, and found throughout the Old World. The M. is black with a red patch on the head and a white patch under the tail.

MOORS. Name (English form of Lat. *Mauri*) originally applied to the inhabitants of the Roman prov. of Mauritania, in N.W. Africa. Now applied to the people who live N. of the Sahara and W. of Tripoli, especially the people of Algeria and Morocco, who are principally of Arab and Berber origin. In the 7th cent. the Moors were conquered by the Arabs, and embraced the Mohammedan faith. The Arabs who occupied Spain from 711 to 1492 were called Moors (Sp. *moros*).

MOOSE. See ELK.

MOOSE JAW. Town in Saskatchewan, Canada, 40 m. W. of Regina. Settled in 1882, it is a railway centre and has an airport; also extensive stockyards, grain elevators, petroleum refineries, etc. Pop. (1966) 35,000.

MOOSONEE (moo'sonē). Village (pop. 300), in N.W. Ontario, near the mouth of the Moose r. on James Bay. It is a railway terminus and a trading post of the Hudson's Bay Company. On an island in the river opposite M. is Moose Factory (300) another Hudson's Bay Company trading post founded in 1671, later abandoned, and rebuilt 1730. Creation of a port at M. was begun in 1959.

MORAES (morãs'), **Dom** (1938–). Indian poet. B. in Bombay, son of Frank M. the writer and journalist, he travelled widely with his father, before going to the Univ. of Oxford in 1956. He writes in English, and his first book of poems *A Beginning*

(1956) won a Hawthornden prize. Later are *Poems* (1960), and *Gone Away* (1960), a description of his experiences on revisiting India in 1959.

MORAES (moorīs'), **Francisco de** (c. 1500–72). Portuguese writer. He wrote *Palmerin of England* (1567), one of the best chivalric romances.

MORALES (mōrah'les), **Luis de** (c. 1509–86). Spanish painter called *El Divino* (The Divine), because of his deeply religious nature. Most of his pictures are of sacred subjects.

MORALITY. Didactic medieval verse drama, in part a development of the Miracle Play (q.v.), in which human characters are replaced by personified virtues and vices. The M. flourished in the 15th cent., the most famous example being the *Everyman*.

MORĀ'VIA, Alberto. Pseudonym of Italian novelist Alberto Pincherle (1907–). The son of an architect, he was b. in Rome, publishing his first novel *The Indifferent Ones* (1932) to a burst of acclaim. However, his criticism of Mussolini's régime led to a stifling of his work by the govt. until after the S.W.W. Later books incl. *Woman of Rome* (1949), *Two Women* (1958) and *The Empty Canvas* (1961), a study of an artist's obsession with his model. He is noted for his bare and compelling narrative.

MORĀ'VIA. District of central Europe, part of Czechoslovakia, of which it formed a prov. 1918–49. After division into several regions named after their principal towns, M. was in 1960 re-divided into two: South M. (cap. Brno), area 5,800 sq. m.; pop. (1967 est.) 1,940,000; and North M. (cap. Ostrava), area 4,270 sq. m.; pop. 1,760,000. The principal river is the Morava. Forests cover about a quarter of M., which elsewhere is fertile, producing maize and the vine in the S., wheat, barley, rye, flax, sugar beet, etc., farther N. Coal and iron are mined.

By the end of the 6th cent. the Slavs had settled in M., they were converted to Christianity in the 9th cent., which became part of the German Empire under Charlemagne. In 874 the kingdom of 'Great Moravia' was founded by Sviatopluk. The country was conquered by the Magyars in 906, but became part of the Holy Roman Empire in 958; in 1029 it was incorporated in Bohemia, in 1526 was brought under the rule of the Habsburgs, and in 1849 became an Austrian crownland. It was incorporated in the new republic of Czechoslovakia in 1918.

MORĀ'VIANS. Protestant episcopal Church founded in Bohemia in 1457, as an offshoot of the Hussite movement. They suffered much persecution after 1620, and were held together mainly by the leadership of their bishop, Comenius (q.v.). Driven out in 1722 by further persecution, they spread over Germany and into England and N. America, while in 1732 missionary work among the heathen was begun. There are c. 60,000 Ms. in the U.S.A., and small congregations in England and on the Continent. Active missionary work is carried on.

MORAY FIRTH (mur'ā). Bay to the N. of Morayshire, Scotland. Its width at the entrance, between Burghead and Tarbat Ness, is 15 m.

MORAYSHIRE. County in the N. of Scotland. The principal rivers are the Spey and Findhorn. The county town is Elgin. Oats and barley are grown, and livestock are reared; the chief industry is whisky distilling. Area 476 sq. m.; pop. (1961) 49,156.

MORAZÁN (mōrahthahn'), **Francisco** (1792–1842). Central American statesman. B. in Honduras, he led the successful liberal-federalist revolt of 1827 against the cons. in Honduras and in Salvador and Guatemala in 1828 and 1829. Elected pres. of the Central American Confederation in 1830, he was re-elected in 1834, but Honduras, Nicaragua and Costa Rica seceded in 1838 and Guatemala in 1839. Attempting to hold the union together by force he was driven out by the Guatemalan dictator, Carrera, and a further attempt to revive union in 1842 ended in his capture and execution in Honduras. He is now the symbol of Central American unity.

MORBIHAN (morbē-oń'), **Gulf of.** Seawater lake, area 40 sq. m., in Brittany, W. France, linked by a channel with the Bay of Biscay. M. is a Breton word 'little sea'; the gulf gives its name to a dext.

MORDVI'NIAN A.S.S.R. Autonomous rep. of the R.S.F.S.R., lying W. of the Sura r. Forested in the W., it is fertile elsewhere and produces sugar beet, grains, potatoes, etc. Sheep are reared and dairy farming is important. Timber, furniture, and textiles are produced. Mordvinia was conquered by the Russians during the 13th cent. It was made an autonomous region 1930, an A.S.S.R. 1934. A state univ. was set up 1957. The cap. is Saransk. Area 10,100 sq. m.; pop. (1967) 1,010,000.

MORE (mōr), **Hannah** (1745–1833). British author. B. near Bristol, she went to London in 1774, and was one of the most brilliant 'blue-stockings'. After 1782 she again retired to the country to work among the poor and write such edifying books as *Coelebs in search of a Wife* (1809).

MORE, Henry (1614–87). Greatest of the Cambridge Platonists, he became a fellow of Christ's Coll. in 1639. His chief work is the *Divine Dialogues* (1688).

MORE, Sir Thomas (1478–1535). British statesman and author. B. in London, he studied under Linacre and Grocyn at Oxford, and was influenced in his religious beliefs by Colet. In 1497 he first met Erasmus, while studying law at Lincoln's Inn, and in 1504 entered parliament. From 1509 he was favoured by Henry VIII, and employed on foreign embassies, becoming a member of the privy council in 1518 and Speaker of the House of Commons in 1523. He was knighted in 1521, and on the fall of Wolsey became Lord Chancellor in 1529, but resigned in 1532 owing to his failure to agree with the king on his ecclesiastical policy and the marriage with Anne Boleyn. In 1534 he refused as a devout Catholic to take the oath of supremacy to Henry VIII as head of the Church, and after imprisonment in the Tower was executed. Among his writings are the Latin *Utopia* (1516), sketching an ideal commonwealth; the English *Dialogue* (1528), directed against Tyndale; and a *History of Richard III*. M. was canonized in 1935.

MŌR'ĒA. Name used under Turkish rule for the Greek peninsula of PELOPONNESE.

MORÉAS (mōrā-ah'), **Jean** (1856–1910). French poet. B. in Athens, he was a leader of the Symbolist movement, and formulated its principles in 1885 in *XIXe Siècle*. When Symbolism departed from these original tenets, M. founded the *école romane*, which returned to more traditional versification. His vols. of verse incl. *Les Syrtes, Le Pèlerin Passionné* and *Stances*.

MOREAU (mōrō), **Gustave** (1826–98). French painter. B. in Paris, he was influenced by Chassériau, and became a prof. at the *École des Beaux Arts*. His works incl. 'Jason and Medea' and 'The Young Man and Death'.

MOREAU, Jean Victor Marie (1763–1813). French general. B. at Morlaix, he served in the Revolutionary War, and won a brilliant victory over the Austrians in 1800 at Hohenlinden. His republicanism involved him in intrigues against Napoleon, for which he was banished. In 1813 he offered his services to the Allies, and was killed at the battle of Dresden.

MORECAMBE AND HEYSHAM. English port and seaside resort (bor.) of Lancs, situated on Morecambe Bay. Heysham was incorporated in the borough in 1928. Pop. (1961) 40,950.

MORE'L. Edible fungi. The common M., *Morchella esculenta*, grows abundantly in Europe and N. America. A yellowish-brown, its edible cap is much wrinkled and about an inch long. M. is used for seasoning gravies, soups, sauces, etc.

MORESBY, John (1830–1922). British naval 'explorer and author, remembered for his discovery in 1873 of the finest harbour in New Guinea, on which Port Moresby now stands.

MORGAN, Charles (1894–1958). British novelist. As a boy he spent 2 years as a midshipman, also serving in the navy in the F.W.W., and these experiences underlay his novel *The Gunroom* (1919), withdrawn owing to its frank revelations of naval life. He was captured at Antwerp, and interned in Holland, which provided the background of *The Fountain* (1932). Principal dramatic critic to *The Times* 1926–39, he joined the intelligence section of the Admiralty in the S.W.W. and these years inspired *The River Line* (1949: dramatized 1952). Other works incl. *Portrait in a Mirror* (1929); *The Flashing Stream* (1938), a play; and *The Voyage* (1940). His lucid style endeared him to France where he was highly honoured. He m. in 1923 Hilda Vaughan, novelist and playwright, a descendant of the 17th cent. Welsh poet Henry Vaughan.

MORGAN, Conwy Lloyd (1852–1936). Psychologist and biologist. B. in London, he became prof. at Univ. Coll., Bristol, in 1884, and was principal 1887–1909. In his *Introduction to Comparative Psychology* (1894) and *Animal Behaviour* (1900), he anticipated the work of Thorndike, Watson, and others. Best-known of his later books is *Emergent Evolution* (1923).

MORGAN, Sir Henry (c. 1635–88). Welsh buccaneer. Joining the W. Indies buccaneers, he warred against the Spaniards, capturing and sacking Panama in 1671. In 1674 he was knighted and appointed lieutenant-governor of Jamaica.

MORGAN, John Pierpont (1837–1913). American financier and philanthropist. B. in Conn., he built up one of the greatest international banking-houses, financing gigantic steel, shipping and railway enterprises. He was succeeded in this by his son, **John Pierpont M.** (1867–1943), who raised loans for the Allies during the F.W.W. He assisted the preparation of the Dawes Plan (1922), and was unofficial U.S. delegate to the Reparations Conference (1929). He presented his father's art collection and library to the American nation.

MORGAN, Lewis Henry (1818–81). American anthropologist. B. in New York state, he made a study of Indian society, and pub. *League of the Iroquois* (1851), followed by *Systems of Consanguinity and Affinity of the Human Family* (1869), and *Ancient Society* (1877).

MORGAN, Thomas Hunt (1866–1945). American biologist. B. at Lexington, he was prof. of biology at Bryn Mawr Coll. 1894–1904, when he transferred to Columbia univ. In 1933 he was awarded the Noble prize for medicine. He originated the theory of paired elements within the chromosomes which govern heredity, using a fruit fly (*Drosophila melanogaster*) in his experiments.

MORGAN, William de. *See* DE MORGAN, WILLIAM.

MORGANATIC MARRIAGE. Marriage between a man of royal birth with a woman of lower rank, who does not share his rank. The marriage is recognized by the Church, and the issue are legitimate, but they cannot succeed to the rank or possessions of their father.

MORGANTOWN. City in W. Virginia, U.S.A., founded 1767, seat of the Univ. of W. Virginia (1867) with its school of mines. Glass and clothing factories derive power from natural gas. Pop. (1960) 22,487.

MORGENSTERN, Christian (1871–1914). German poet, best remembered for his vols. of original nonsense verse, e.g. *Galganlieder* (1905) and *Böhmischer Jahrmarkt* (1938), but he also wrote love poetry, etc.

MORGENTHAU (-thaw), **Henry M.** (1891–1967). American statesman. Son of Henry M., prominent lawyer and financier, he was closely associated with the F. D. Roosevelt govt.'s measures for agricultural revival. As Sec. of the Treasury from 1934 to shortly after Roosevelt's death in 1945, he was mainly responsible for the administration's financial policy.

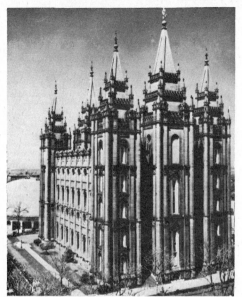

MORMONS. The Mormon temple at Salt Lake City, dedicated 1893, took forty years to build. Just beyond is the domed roof of the tabernacle (1870), which can seat 8,000.
Courtesy of Church of Jesus Christ of Latter-Day Saints

MORI'SCOS. Name given to Spanish Moslems who accepted Christian baptism, and their descendants. They were all expelled from the country in 1609.

MORISON, Stanley (1889–1967). Brit. typographer. Adviser to the Cambridge Univ. Press and Monotype Corporation, he designed Times New Roman (1932).

MORLAND, George (1763–1804). British painter. B. in London, the son of the artist Henry M., he first exhibited at the R.A. at the age of 10. After leaving home in 1784 he lived a dissolute life, but was a hard worker, sometimes painting 2 pictures a day. He excelled in country subjects showing gypsies, stable interiors, etc.

MORLEY, Christopher Darlington (1890–1957). American author. B. in Pennsylvania, he was best known for such novels as the fantasies *Where the Blue Begins* (1922), and *Thunder on the Left* (1925); the realistic *Kitty Foyle* (1939), and *Thorofare* (1942).

MORLEY, John, 1st visct. M. of Blackburn (1838–1923). British Liberal statesman and writer. He entered parliament in 1883, and was Sec. for Ireland in 1886 and 1892–5. As Sec. for India 1905–10, he prepared the way for more representative government. He was Lord President of the Council 1910–14, but resigned in protest against the declaration of war in 1914. He pub. lives of Voltaire, Rousseau, Burke, and Gladstone. He received a peerage in 1908.

MORLEY, Robert (1908–   ). British actor. With a presence and delivery which would have made him an ornament of the diplomatic corps for which he was originally intended, he excels in such roles as Oscar Wilde (both stage and screen), Sheridan Whiteside in *The Man Who Came to Dinner*, and the Prince Regent in *The First Gentleman*. He m. in 1940 Joan Buckmaster, dau. of Gladys Cooper.

MORLEY, Thomas (1557–*c.* 1603). English composer. He studied with Byrd, and became organist at St. Paul's, obtaining a monopoly of music printing. He wrote madrigals, and songs for Shakespeare's plays. His *Plaine and Easie Introduction to Practicall Music* (1597) is a useful historical source.

MORLEY. English industrial town (bor.) in the W. Riding of Yorks, 4 m. S.W. of Leeds. Woollen textiles are the chief manufacture; glass and leather are also made. Pop. (1961) 40,322.

MORMONS, or **Latter-Day Saints.** Religious organization founded by Joseph Smith (1805–44). B. in Vermont, he received his first call in 1820, and in 1827 claimed to have been granted the revelation of the *Book of Mormon,* which relates the supposed early history of America, and predicts the Millennium and the establishment of the New Zion there. The 'Church of Jesus Christ of Latter-Day Saints' (1830) was founded at Fayette, N.Y., and accepted the book as supplementing the Christian scriptures. Further settlements were rapidly estab. despite persecution, and Brigham Young and the Twelve Apostles undertook the first foreign M. mission in England, the earliest European converts reaching the U.S.A. in 1840. Their doctrines met with persecution, and Smith was killed in Illinois. To escape further persecution, Brigham Young led an emigration to the Valley of the Great Salt Lake in 1847 and in 1850 Utah was created a territory with Young as governor (1851–8). Most of the M. who remained in the Middle West (H.Q. Independence, Missouri) accepted the founder's son Joseph Smith (1832–1914) as leader, adopted the name *Reorganized Church of Jesus Christ of Latter Day Saints,* and claim to be the true successor of the original church. They do not accept the non-Christian doctrines later proclaimed by Young in 1852, notably that of polygamy, which Young attributed to the original founder in 1843 on no verifiable evidence: Smith is on record as condemning plural wives. The doctrine was formally repudiated by the Utah Mormons in 1890, and Utah was recognised as a State of the Union in 1896. The M. number *c.* 2,000,000; the Re-organized Church *c.* 170,000: both have branches in Britain.

MORNING GLORY. Plant (*Ipomoea purpurea*) of the family Convolvulaceae (*see* CONVOLVULUS), native to tropical America. It has dazzling blue flowers and small quantities of substances similar to LSD (q.v.) are found in the seeds of one variety.

MOROCCO (mŏrok'ō). Country in N.W. Africa; its Arabic name Al-Maghreb means farthest west. It has a long coastline to the N.W. on the Atlantic, continued in the N. on the Mediterranean. The High and Middle Atlas, rising to 15,000 ft., cross M. from S.W.

MOROCCO. European visitors mingle with the people of Tangier in the open-air market.
Courtesy of British European Airways.

to N.E.; farther S. is the Anti-Atlas range, and in the N. the Rif Mountains. Chief rivers are the Moulouya, flowing to the Mediterranean, the Sebou and er Abia, flowing to the Atlantic. Much of the land is fertile, the vine, the olive, figs, almonds, dates, citrus fruits, wheat, barley, linseed, and rice being grown; sheep, cattle, goats, mules, horses, and camels are reared. Mineral products incl. phosphates, anthracite coal, iron ore, manganese, antimony, lead, zinc, silver, and petroleum. Fishing (tunny and sardines) is important. Area (est.) 174,000 sq. m.; pop. (1965) 13,320,000, of whom the great majority are Berbers or Arabs with c. 220,000 Europeans and 18,000 Jews.

History. The sultan of M., last of the Barbary states to maintain independence, accepted French protection in 1912, and the country was divided into three zones: the special zone of Tangier, 240 sq. m. (internationalized 1925 under a treaty of 1923); a Spanish protectorate in the N., 11,000 sq. m.; the rest a French protectorate. The Spanish and later the French had to contend with serious armed opposition from the tribesmen, but after the surrender of Abd El-Krim (q.v.) in 1926 the country was pacified, and a number of French and Spanish colonists settled in M. The sultan continued to be recognized as ruler. After the S.W.W. there was widespread unrest in M. and in 1956 the country's independence was recognized by France, Spain, and the powers controlling Tangier. In 1957 the sultan Mohammed V (1909–61) changed his title to that of king; he was succeeded by his son Hassan II (1929–). The king usually lives at Rabat, but sometimes visits the other traditional caps., Fez (founded 808), Marrakesh (1062), and Meknes. Under the constitution of 1970 there is a single Chamber of Representatives, partly directly elected and partly by representatives of municipal councils, professional bodies and trade unions.

MO͞'RON. Adult with the mind of a 10-yr.-old.

MŌRŌ'NI (morō'nē), Giovanni Battista (c. 1525–78). Italian artist. His works incl. fine altar-pieces, and as a portrait painter, e.g. 'The Tailor' (Nat. Gallery) and 'A Gentleman in Adoration before the Madonna' (Nat. Gallery of Art, Washington), he influenced Van Dyck.

MO'RPETH. English market town (bor.) with iron and engineering works in Northumberland, situated on the Wansbeck, 15 m. N. of Newcastle. It grew up round the castle. Pop. (1961) 12,430.

MORPHEUS (mor'fūs). In Roman mythology the god of dreams or sleep.

MORPHIA (mor'fē-a). Name generally applied to the alkaloid morphine ($C_{17}H_{19}O_3N$), used to alleviate pain. It can be taken by mouth or injected.

MORRIS, William (1834–96). British poet, Social-ist and craftsman. B. at Walthamstow, he was ed. at Oxford, where he formed a lasting friendship with Burne-Jones, and was influenced by Ruskin and Rossetti. He abandoned architecture to study paint-ing, and in 1858 pub. his first book of verse, The Defence of Guenevere. He founded his own firm for the manufacture of furniture, wallpapers, church decorations, etc., in 1862, and did much to raise English standards of craftsmanship. He also pub. several more vols. of verse-romances, notably The Life and Death of Jason (1867), and The Earthly Paradise (1868–70). A visit to Iceland in 1871 inspired his greatest poem, Sigurd the Volsung (1876), and his translations of the Sagas. He joined the Social Demo-cratic Federation in 1883, left it as too moderate in 1884, and founded the Socialist League. To this period belong the romances, A Dream of John Ball (1888) and News from Nowhere (1891); the critical and socio-logical studies, Signs of Change (1888) and Hopes and Fears for Art (1892); and the narrative poem, The Pilgrims of Hope. Besides active journalistic and propaganda work, he founded the Kelmscott Press.

MORRIS, W. R. See NUFFIELD.

THE MORSE CODE

A ·—	J ·———	S ···	2 ··———
B —···	K —·—	T —	3 ···——
C —·—·	L ·—··	U ··—	4 ····—
D —··	M ——	V ···—	5 ·····
E ·	N —·	W ·——	6 —····
F ··—·	O ———	X —··—	7 ——···
G ——·	P ·——·	Y —·——	8 ———··
H ····	Q ——·—	Z ——··	9 ————·
I ··	R ·—·	1 ·———	0 —————

MORRIS DANCE. An English folk-dance which is still popular. It was usually danced by 6 men, one of whom wore girl's clothing. It probably originated in pre-Christian ritual dances.

MORRISON, Arthur (1863–1945). British novelist. B. in Kent, he became successively a civil servant and journalist, and wrote realistic studies of London slum life, Tales of Mean Streets (1894), A Child of the Jago (1896), and The Hole in the Wall (1902)

MORRISON, Robert (1782–1834). British mission-ary. B. in Northumberland, he was sent to Canton by the London Missionary Society in 1807, and pub. a Chinese translation of the N.T. and a Chinese Gram-mar in 1814, and a Chinese Dictionary in 1821.

MORRISON OF LAMBETH, Herbert Stanley Morrison, baron (1888–1965). British Lab. statesman. On leaving elementary school he became a shop assistant, was appointed sec. of the London Lab. Party (1915–45), and was a member of the L.C.C. 1922–45. Entering parl. in 1923, he was Min. of Transport 1929–31, Home Sec. 1940–5, and Lord Pres. of the Council and Leader of the House of Commons 1945–51, briefly succeeding Bevin as For. Sec. (Mar.–Oct. 1951). In 1955 he was defeated by Gaitskell in the contest for leadership of the party.

MORSE (mors), Samuel Finley Breese (1791–1872). American inventor of the magnetic telegraph. B. in Mass., in 1836 he produced the first adequate electric telegraph, and in 1843 was granted $30,000 by Congress for an experimental line between Washing-ton and Baltimore. His system was soon in general use, and in 1842 he experimented with telegraphy by submarine cable.

MORSE CODE. System of dots and dashes inven-ted by S. F. B. Morse, used for conveying messages by wireless, cable, etc. The dot is a signal of short dura-tion, the dash is three times this length. In the table above is the international M. alphabet.

MORTGAGE (mor'gej). A transfer of property – usually land – as a security for repayment of a loan. A M. of land is made by a deed which conveys the full ownership of the land to the mortgagee subject to the mortgagor's right to get his land back on payment of both principal and interest.

MORTLAKE. Locality of the Greater London bor. of Richmond-upon-Thames, ½ m. W. of Barnes Bridge, the finishing-point of the Oxford and Cam-bridge boatrace. It was once noted for tapestry.

MORTON, H(enry) V(ollam) (1892–). British author. Originally a journalist, he has written many books which vividly recall the past, incl. 'In Search of' England (1927), Scotland (1929), Ireland (1930), and Wales (1932); 'In the Steps of' St. Paul (1936) and Jesus (1953); and A Traveller in Rome (1957).

MORTON, John Bingham (1893–). British jour-nalist. Ed. at Oxford, he has contributed a humorous column to the Daily Express since 1924 under the pseudonym of 'Beachcomber', and has pub. many humorous novels, e.g. The Barber of Putney (1919); also several works on the French Revolution.

MORTON, John Maddison (1811–91). British dramatist, whose adaptation of the French farce, Box and Cox (1847), featured the proverbial pair of lodgers.

MOSCOW. The Kremlin from the Moskva river. The present walls date from 1492 in the reign of Ivan III, but the city gained its first wooden-walled 'little Kremlin' in 1156, built by George Dolgoruki, prince of Rostov who founded the city in 1147.
Photo: Novosti Press Agency

MOSAIC (mozāk'). A design or picture produced by inlaying variously coloured pieces of marble, stone, glass, or other substances, used chiefly for the decoration of floors and walls, especially in churches. M. was commonly used by the Romans for the decoration of their villas (e.g. Hadrian's villa at Tivoli), and by the Byzantines. The art was revived by the Italians during the 13th cent., when it was used chiefly for the decoration of churches. Examples of modern M. work may be seen in the hall of the Houses of Parliament, and in Westminster Cathedral.

MOSCICKI (mosytsi'tski), **Ignacy** (1867–1946). Polish statesman. Owing to his activities in the Polish nationalist movement, he was exiled 1892–1912. Elected President of Poland in 1926, after Pilsudski's death in 1935 he was virtual dictator. Following the German invasion of 1939 he resigned, and became a Swiss citizen.

MOSCOW (mos'kō). Russian city, cap. of the R.S.F.S.R. from 1918, of the U.S.S.R. from 1922; cap. also of the M. region, and of Russia from the 14th cent. until 1709, when Peter I transferred the cap. to St. Petersburg (renamed Leningrad in 1924). It stands on the Moscow r., 400 m. S.E. of Leningrad. The Kremlin (Citadel), which is situated on the northern bank of the r., is at the centre. First built in the 12th cent., it consists of a walled enclosure containing some of the most important buildings in M., including the cathedral of the Assumption of the Virgin; the cathedral of the Archangel Michael, which was the burial place of the tsars down to Ivan Alexeivich, brother of Peter the Great; the cathedral of the Annunciation; the Ivan Veliki tower (300 ft. high), a famine relief work commissioned by Boris Godunov in 1600; various palaces, incl. the former Imperial Palace, museums, and other buildings. The Tsar Kolokol (king of the bells), 200 tons (1735), is also in the Kremlin. The walls of the Kremlin are crowned by 18 towers and have 5 gates. Near the Kremlin stands the Kitai Gorod, containing various govt. offices. Lenin's mausoleum is in Red Square (near

the Kremlin), a famous open space in M. used for political demonstrations and processions. M. also has 2 univs., one of which was founded in 1755 and is the oldest in Russia, the other (32 storeys high) opened 1953; the Academy of Sciences, founded at St. Petersburg (Leningrad) 1726, moved to M. 1934; the M. Arts Theatre, founded 1898; and the state opera house. M. is the seat of the Patriarch of the Russian Orthodox Church; is linked with Stavropol by petroleum pipeline (300 m.), completed 1957; is the centre of the railway system, and has an international airport. An underground railway, opened 1935, later extended, is a tourist showpiece. M. is also the largest industrial centre of the U.S.S.R., producing machinery, electrical equipment, textiles, chemicals, and many food products. From its foundation in the 12th cent. the city has had a stormy history. It was burnt in 1571 by the Khan of the Crimea, and ravaged by fire in 1739, 1748, and 1753; in 1812 it was burnt by its own citizens to save it from Napoleon's troops, or perhaps by accident. In the S.W.W. Hitler's troops were within 20 m. of M. on the N.W. by Nov. 1941, but the stubborn Russian defence and severe winter weather forced them to withdraw in Dec.; the Germans were never able to make a fresh attempt to take M. Pop. (1968) 6,567,000.

MOSELEY (mōz'li), **Henry Gwyn-Jeffreys** (1887–1915). British physicist. He did valuable work on atomic structure, and in 1913 devised the series of atomic numbers. He was killed in action at Gallipoli.

MOSELLE (mōzel'). River, 320 m. long, which rises in the Vosges, France, and is canalized from Thionville to its confluence with the Rhine at Koblenz. It gives its name to the depts. of M. and Meurthe-et-Moselle.

MOSES (14th cent. B.C.?). Jewish lawgiver and judge who led the Israelites out of Egypt to the promised land of Canaan. According to the O.T., M. was hidden among the bulrushes on the banks of the Nile when the Pharaoh commanded that all new-born male Hebrew children should be destroyed. He was found by a dau. of Pharaoh, who reared him. Eventually he became the leader of the Israelites in the Exodus, and the 40 years' wandering in the wilderness. On Mt. Sinai he received from Jehovah the Ten Commandments engraved on tablets of stone, and died at the age of 120, after having been allowed a glimpse of the Promised Land from Mount Pisgah.

MOSES, Anna Mary (1860–1961). American artist, *née* Robertson, known as 'Grandma' M. Of Scots-

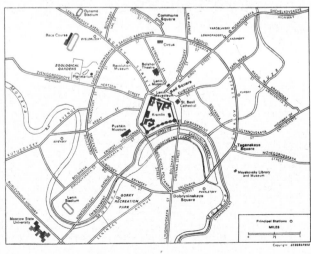

Irish ancestry, she began working as a serious artist only *c.* 1927, and rapidly achieved popularity by her colourful and simple scenes from American life.

MOSKVA. Russian form of Moscow.

MOSLEM LEAGUE. Formed 1906, it demanded an independent M. state in India in 1941, its pres. Jinnah becoming 1st pres. of Pakistan 1947. It continues to represent Ms. remaining in the Rep. of India.

MOSLEMS. Adherents of Islam (q.v.). An unorthodox variant of the creed is held by Negro extremists of the U.S.A., the *Black Muslims* or *Nation of Islam*, whose aims are segregation from white America in one or two separate and sovereign Negro states. Christianity is rejected as merely a means of continuing Negro subjection. The movement was founded by Wallace D. Fard, a pedlar who claimed to come from Mecca, and led from 1934 by the Hon. Elijah Muhammad (1898–), having its H.Q. in Chicago. Its growth from 1946 was due to Malcolm X (1926–65), *né* Little, son of a Baptist minister, who was converted while serving 7 yrs. imprisonment for larceny and reformed: *Autobiography* ed. Alex Haley 1965. In 1964 he broke away and founded his own Organization of Afro-American Unity, preaching 'active self-defence', but was shot: 3 Negroes, 2 being B.M., were convicted 1966.

MOSLEY (mōz'li), **Sir Oswald Ernald** (1896–). British Fascist. In parl. as a Unionist 1918–22, Independent 1922–4, and Lab. member 1924 and 1926–31, he then founded the British Union of Fascists. Interned during the S.W.W., he was released on health grounds in 1943, and resumed Fascist propaganda with his Union Movement. He m. in 1920 Lady Cynthia, dau. of Lord Curzon (d. 1933), and in 1936 Diana Freeman-Mitford. *See* Fascism and Mitford Sisters.

MOSQUE (mosk; Arabic *mesjid*, temple). Mohammedan place of worship. The earliest Ms. were based on the Christian basilican plan, but many different influences contributed towards their architectural development. Ms. vary a great deal in style in different parts of the world. Chief features are: the dome, the minaret, from which the faithful are called to prayer, the mihrab, or prayer niche, in one of the interior walls, showing the direction of Mecca, and an open court surrounded by porticos.

MOSQUITIA (mōsqētē'ah). An undeveloped, low-lying coastal region in Central America, partly in Honduras, partly in Nicaragua, on the Caribbean Sea. Most of its inhabitants are Mosquito (or Miskitto) Indians, and M. is sometimes called the Mosquito Coast. Mahogany and cedar are extracted from its forests, and there is some agriculture, coconuts, bananas, and tapioca being produced. M. was a British protectorate from 1655 until ceded to Honduras and Nicaragua in 1860.

MOSQUITO. Word of Spanish derivation often used in referring to species of gnat (q.v.).

MOSS, Stirling (1929–). British racing driver. Taking up racing in 1946, he was British National Champion 1950–2 and 1954–9, and winner of the European Grand Prix in 1961. Following serious injury in a crash at Goodwood in 1962, he concentrated on car design and race management.

MOSSA'DEQ, Mohammed (1880–1967). Persian P.M. 1951–3. He prosecuted the oil dispute with the Anglo-Iranian Oil Co., and when he failed in his attempt to overthrow the Shah was imprisoned: from 1956 he was under house arrest. *See* Abadan.

MOSSAMEDES (mōsam'idēz). Fishing and whaling port of Angola at the mouth of the Little Fish r. Pop. *c.* 5,000.

MOSSEL BAY. Port and bathing resort of S. Africa, in Cape Province. Pop. (est.) 12,000.

MOSSES. Class of small non-flowering plants (Musci) forming with the liverworts (q.v.) the lower order Bryophyta. M. are found throughout the world, especially where other vegetation is thin, and each plant comprises a rhizoid and a stem, with leaves on its lower portion and producing sexual organs at its tip. The peat or bog moss (*Sphagnum*) was formerly used for surgical dressings. Moss gardens are popular in Japan, the most famous being at the Moss Temple, nr. Kyoto.

MOSTAGANEM (mōstahgahnem'). Algerian town, cap. of M. dept. Founded 11th cent. it has distilling and metal-founding works, tobacco, cement, and other factories. It is linked by pipeline with the natural gas fields of Hassi Messaoud. Pop. (1966) 64,000.

MOSTA'R. Town of Bosnia-Hercegovina, Yugoslavia, 50 m. S.W. of Sarajevo, famous for its grapes and wines. On the site of a Roman fortress, M. is on a brown coalfield and produces aluminium and tobacco. Pop. (1961) 72,452.

MOSUL (mōs'ool). City in Iraq, cap. of M. liwa, situated on the right bank of the Tigris, opposite the site of ancient Nineveh and 220 m. N.N.W. of Baghdad. Once famous for muslin (q.v.), it is the centre of rich petroleum fields developed by a British company. M. remained Turkish until 1925–6. Pop. (1968) 388,000.

MOTEL. Type of hotel first developed (1928) in the U.S.A. by A. Heinemann which provides especially for the touring motorist. Accommodation consists of individual self-contained sleeping quarters with bath, toilet facilities and garage. Meals are generally obtainable at a central restaurant.

MOTHER OF PEARL. *See* Pearl.

MOTHERWELL & WISHAW. Burgh of Lanark, Scotland, 12 m. S.E. of Glasgow, possessing iron and steel works and coal mines. The two burghs were amalgamated in 1920. Pop. (1961) 72,799.

MOTHS. Insects forming the greater part of the order Lepidoptera. Normally distinguished

MOTHS. 1, Broad-bordered bee hawk-moth; 2, oleander hawk-moth; 3, six-spot burnet; 4, Austrian emperor; 5, tiger-moth; 6, swallow-tail; 7, great oak beauty; 8, magpie; 9, black arches; 10, green humming-bird hawk-moth; 11, small magpie; 12, thistle-ermine; 13, Kentish glory; 14, Aclius leto; 15, currant clearwing; 16, yellow underwing.

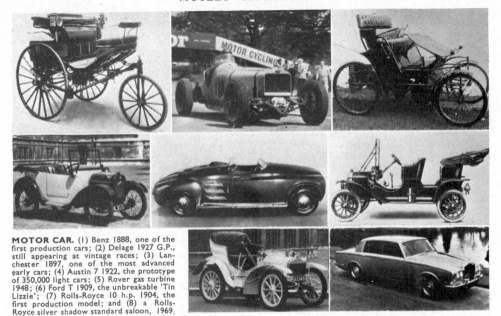

MOTOR CAR. (1) Benz 1888, one of the first production cars; (2) Delage 1927 G.P., still appearing at vintage races; (3) Lanchester 1897, one of the most advanced early cars; (4) Austin 7 1922, the prototype of 350,000 light cars; (5) Rover gas turbine 1948; (6) Ford T 1909, the unbreakable 'Tin Lizzie'; (7) Rolls-Royce 10 h.p. 1904, the first production model; and (8) a Rolls-Royce silver shadow standard saloon, 1969.
Courtesy of the Science Museum, London.
Rolls-Royce Ltd., Austins, Ford Motor Co. and Rover Car Co. Ltd.

from butterflies (q.v.) by the absence of a knob on the end of the antennae. When at rest, Ms. commonly hold their wings flat or sloping over the body; butterflies close them vertically. The wings are covered with flat, microscopic scales, but in the bee hawk-Ms. and the clearwings the scales are confined to certain areas. The mouth-parts are formed into a sucking proboscis, and certain Ms. have no functional mouth-parts, and, being unable to feed, rely upon stores of fat and other reserves built up during the caterpillar stage. In many cases the males are smaller and more brightly coloured than the females, and have the antennae branched or comb-like. In other cases, including the vapourer and winter Ms., the females have wings either absent or aborted to minute flaps.

Ms. vary greatly in size: thus the minute Nepticulidae sometimes have a wing-spread less than 3 mm., while the giant Noctuid or owlet M., *Erebus agrippina*, measures about 280 mm. (11 in.) across its extended wings. The largest British Ms. are the death's head and convolvulus hawk-Ms., which have a wing-spread ranging from $4\frac{1}{2}$ to $5\frac{1}{4}$ in.

Ms. feed chiefly on the nectar of flowers, on honey-dew, and other fluid matter: some, like the hawk-Ms., the Silver Y, and its relatives, frequent flowers and feed while poised with rapidly vibrating wings.

The larvae or caterpillars have a well-developed head, 3 thoracic and 10 abdominal segments. Each thoracic segment bears a pair of short legs, ending in single claws; a pair of sucker-like abdominal feet is present on segments 3 to 6 and 10 of the hind-body. In the family Geometridae the caterpillars bear the abdominal feet only on segments 6 and 10 of the hind-body. They move by a characteristic looping gait and are known as 'loopers' or geometers. Projecting from the middle of the lower lip of a caterpillar is a minute tube or spinneret, through which silk is emitted to make a cocoon within which the change to the pupa or chrysalis occurs. Silk glands are especially large in the silkworm M. Many caterpillars, including the geometers, which are eaten by birds, etc., are protected by their resemblance in both form and coloration

to their immediate surroundings. Others, which are distasteful to such enemies, are brightly coloured or are densely hairy.

Ms. are economically important, owing to the damage caused by the feeding caterpillars, e.g. the winter M. and the codling M., which attack fruit trees; the Mediterranean flour moth, which infects flour mills; and the several species of clothes Ms. At least 100,000 different species of Ms. are known.

MOTLEY, John Lothrop (1814–77). American historian and diplomat. B. in Boston, he was U.S. Min. to Austria 1861–7, and to Britain 1869–70. His masterpiece, *The Rise of the Dutch Republic* (1856), is no longer thought to give a true picture of the period.

MOTOR, Electric. A machine by which electrical energy is converted into mechanical power, which it supplies directly through motor-shaft, gearing, belt-drive, or other form of coupling. The 2 main types are direct-current and alternating-current Ms.

MOTOR BOAT. Small, water-borne craft powered by an internal combustion engine, either of the piston-petrol, compression-ignition oil, or gas-turbine type. Any boat not specially equipped as a M.B. may be converted by a detachable outboard motor. For increased speed, espec. in racing, M.B. hulls are designed to skim the water and reduce frictional resistance. Plastics, steel, and light alloys are now used in construction as well as the traditional wood. In recent designs, drag is further reduced with hydro-fins and hydrofoils, which enable the hull to rise clear of the water, at normal speeds. Notable events in M. or 'power-boat' racing incl. the American Gold Cup (1947) over a 90 m. course, and the Round-Britain race (1969).

MOTOR CAR. A self-propelled vehicle able to be run and be steered on normal roads. Although it is recorded that in 1479 one Gilles de Dom was paid 25 livres by the treasurer of Antwerp, for supplying such a vehicle, the 'father of the automobile' is generally agreed to be N. Cugnot's cumbrous steam carriage (1769), still preserved in Paris.

Steam was an attractive form of power to the

English pioneers, and in the 19th cent. practical steam coaches by Hancock and Goldsworthy Gurney were used for public transport, until stifled out of existence by punitive road tolls and legislation.

If another Parisian, Etienne Lenoir, made the first 'real' car in 1861, using electrically ignited petroleum vapour, Benz and Daimler can be said to be the first producers of cars for sale – from 1885; and Panhard 1890 (front radiator, engine under bonnet, sliding-pinion gearbox, wooden ladder-chassis) and Mercédès 1901 (honeycomb radiator, in-line 4-cylinder engine, gate-change gearbox, pressed-steel chassis) set the pattern for the modern car. Emerging with Haynes and Duryea in the early 1890s, U.S. demand was so fervent that 300 makers existed by 1895: many so ephemeral that there were 109 left in 1900.

Meanwhile in England cars were still considered to be light locomotives in the eyes of the law, and theoretically required a man to walk in front with a red flag. Despite this and other iniquities, which put U.K. development another 10 years behind all others, F. W. Lanchester in 1896 produced an advanced and reliable vehicle, later much copied. The period 1905–6 inaugurated a world boom continuing to the present. Among the legendary M.Cs. of this cent. are: De Dion Bouton, with the first practical high-speed engines; Mors, notable first for racing and later as a silent tourer (silentium mortis); Napier, the doughty 24 hr.-record holder at Brooklands in 1907, unbeaten for 17 years; the incomparable 'Silver Ghost' Rolls-Royce; the enduring Model T Ford (known to rivals as the car which popularized walking); and the many types of Bugatti and Delage, from record-breakers to luxury tourers.

After the F.W.W. popular motoring was inaugurated with the era of cheap light (baby) cars made by Citroën, Peugeot and Renault (France); Austin 7, Morris, Clyno, and Swift (England); Fiat (Italy), and the cheap though bigger Ford, Chevrolet and Dodge in U.S.A. The inter-war years saw a great deal of racing, and experience thus gained was of benefit to the everyday motorist in improved efficiency, relia-bility and safety; and also saw the divergence between the lighter, economical European car, with good handling; and the heavier American car, cheap and rugged, well adapted to long distances at speed.

One typical modern European design would have a semi-monocoque construction in which the body panels, suitably reinforced, support the road loads through independent front and rear springing systems, with seats located within the wheelbase for comfort. A vertical 4-cylinder engine is supplied with a suitable petrol-air mixture by the carburettor and cooled by water circulating through the engine block to a front-mounted radiator. From the rear of the engine power is transmitted through a clutch (which disconnects the engine from the rear wheels) to a 4-speed gearbox (which enables optimum engine speed to be maintained for varying road speeds) through a drive shaft to the differential gear, and thence to drive the rear wheels.

After the S.W.W. small European cars tended to be of 3 varieties – front engine and rear drive, front engine and drive, rear engine and drive – in about equal numbers. From the 1950s a creative resurgence has produced in practical form automatic transmis-sion for small cars, rubber suspension, and transverse engine mounting, self-levelling ride, disc brakes, safer wet-weather tyres; and the possibility of banishing reciprocating engine parts for ever, as shown by the Rover and Chrysler jet turbines, and the Wankel rotary engine. The prospect of world-wide anti-air-pollution laws led in the 1960s to renewed research on the steam car, and the electric 'city' car, limited in speed and range by the capacity of its batteries. See INTERNAL COMBUSTION ENGINE and HOVERCRAFT.

MOTOR CYCLE. A bicycle propelled by an internal combustion engine, usually single cylinder and air-cooled, which is noisy but lightweight and capable of high power and speed. M.Cs. are tradition-ally chain-driven, but there is now a tendency to employ shaft drive with a sprung rear wheel, and to improve comfort by employing two or more cylinders, and screens for the driver and saloon-type passenger sidecars. More recent developments are the powered cycle (less powerful and fast), and the motor scooter.

Most famous of the M.C. races is the Isle of Man Tourist Trophy (T.T.) race estab. 1907, but other popular types of event are reliability trials and scrambling or roughriding, and scooter rallies.

MOTORING. Between the 2 wars M. developed into a universal pursuit, whether for business or pleasure. The Min. of Transport was estab., roads were improved, and various laws and safety precau-tions imposed to govern the use of cars. A driver must possess a licence, and his vehicle be registered with the local licensing authority, displaying the number assigned to it. In 1953 a flat-rate duty was imposed, which affected engine and car design, and inadequately powered cars persist in Britain for economic reasons. The law also insists on insurance for third-party risks. Motorists are organized in the Automobile Association (A.A.), and the Royal Automobile Club (R.A.C.).

MOTOR RACING. Competitive events, beginning with a timed trial from Paris to Rouen in 1894, enjoy great popularity for spectator excitement and for manufacturer's and driver's prestige. Great road races have jncl. the mountainous Targa Florio (Sicjly), and Mille Miglia (Italy). The 24-hr. of Le Mans (1923) is the foremost proving ground for production cars. Famous circuits incl. Brands Hatch, Brook-lands (to 1939) and Silverstone, U.K.; Montlhéry, France; Nurburgring, Germany; and Indianapolis, U.S.A. In Grand Prix M.R. (1906) individual events in 10 different countries, notably the Monaco Grand Prix, count towards the world championship; multi-winners incl. J. Fangio (Argentine) 1951, 1954–7; J. Brabham (Australia) 1959–60, 1966; G. Hill (Brit.) 1962, 1968; and J. Clark (Brit.) 1963, 1965. For the driver of the production car M. rallies, often time-checked across a continent, are increasingly popular.

MOTOR SPEED RECORD. See SPEED RECORDS.

MOTTRAM, Ralph Hale (1883–1971). British author. B. at Norwich, he entered banking, but made his name as a novelist by his *Spanish Farm* trilogy 1924–6 promoted by his F.W.W. experiences.

MOULINS (mōōlah'). Cap. of the dept. of Allier, France; 90 m. N.W. of Lyons. It makes cutlery, textiles, glass, etc. M. was cap. of the old prov. of Bourbonnais 1368–1527. Pop. (1962) 25,671.

MOULMEIN (mowlmĭn'). Port in Lower Burma, on the Salween estuary, which exports teak and rice. Pop. (1967) 160,000.

MOUNTAIN ASH. Welsh coal-mining town (U.D.) in Glamorganshire, on the Cynon r., 18 m. N.N.W. of Cardiff. The Three Valleys Musical Festi-val is held annually at M.A. Pop. (1961) 29,590.

MOUNTAIN ASH or **Rowan.** Flowering tree (*Sorbus aucuparia*) of the family Rosaceae. Growing to a height of about 30 ft., it has pinnate leaves and large cymes of whitish flowers, followed by scarlet berries.

MOUNTAIN ASH

MOUNTBATTEN of Burma, Louis Mountbatten, 1st earl (1900–   ). British administrator. Son of Prin-cess Victoria, a granddau. of Queen Victoria, and Prince Louis of Batten-berg, marquess of Milford Haven (q.v.), Lord Louis entered the navy in 1913 and served in the F.W.W. After holding destroyer commands 1939–41 he was appointed Chief of Combined Operations in 1942 and C.-in-C. in S.E. Asia in 1943. He was responsible for the reconquest of Burma in 1944–5, and received the surrender of the Japanese S. armies at Singapore in Sept. 1945. He succeeded Lord Wavell as last Viceroy of India in March 1947, and on the transfer of power in Aug. became the 1st Gov.-Gen. of the Dominion of India until June 1948. Promoted Admiral of the Fleet in 1956, he was First Sea Lord 1955–9, and Chief of U.K. Defence Staff 1959–65, and Gov. of the Isle of Wight from 1965. He received a viscounty 1946, earldom 1947, and O.M. 1965. In 1922 he m. Edwina Ashley (1901–60), the elder dau. of the 1st baron Mount Temple.

MOUNTEVANS, Edward Ratcliffe Garth Russell Evans, 1st baron M. (1881–1957). British admiral. Joining the Antarctic Expedition of 1909, he took command after the death of Scott and wrote *South with Scott* (1921). In 1917 as commander of H.M.S. *Broke* he joined with H.M.S. *Swift* in the destruction of 6 German destroyers and was popularly known as 'Evans of the *Broke*'. He was created baron in 1945.

MOUNT VERNON. Village in Virginia, U.S.A., on the Potomac, 16 m. S. of Washington, D.C. The estate and house here which belonged to the Washington family, and was owned by George Washington from 1752 until he died there, 1799, is preserved as a national monument.

MOUSE. Small rodent of the Muridae family. The house M. (*Mus musculus*) is universally distributed; 3 in. long, with naked tail of equal length, with greybrown body, it nests in paper and straw. Commonly found in Britain are the long-tailed field M. (*Apodemus sylvaticus*), richer in colour, and the harvest M. (*Micromys minutus*), 2½–3 in. long. In the U.S.A. are found the short-tailed meadow M. (*M. riparius*), and the common white-footed M. (*Peromyscus americanus*) with rich fawn upper parts and snowy-white underparts and feet.

MOUTH. The cavity enclosed by the jaws, cheeks and palate. It is the outer end of the digestive and the respiratory tracts, and in addition to its part in masticating food, and in breathing, has a highly specialized mechanism for producing significant sounds. It is also largely responsible for facial expression, and plays a part in sexual activity. At the back of the M. is a passage (isthmus of the fauces) bounded on each side by 2 folds called the pillars of the fauces; between each pair of folds is one of the tonsils.

MOUTH ORGAN. See HARMONICA.

MOW'RER, Edgar Ansel (1892–). American newspaper columnist, author of *Germany Puts the Clock Back* (1932) and *An End to Make-Believe* (1961).

MOYNE (moin), **Walter Edward Guinness,** 1st baron M. (1880–1944). British Cons. politician. A son of the 1st Lord Iveagh, he was Min. of Agriculture 1925–9, and Col. Sec. 1941–2. Appointed resident Minister in the Middle East in 1944, he was assassinated in Cairo by members of the 'Stern Gang' of Jewish Zionists.

MOZAMBIQUE (mōzambēk'). Country of E. Africa, formerly a Portuguese colony, made an overseas prov. in 1951. M. was discovered by Vasco da Gama in 1498, and first colonized by the Portuguese in 1505. Since 1954 it has been divided into 9 districts: in 1970 Portugal announced the replacement of the govt. and executive councils by a local legislature, giving a measure of autonomy. A nationalist organization Frente de Libertação de Moçambique (Frelimo), operating from Tanzania, began guerrilla warfare in 1964. The cap. is Lourenço Marques. The principal rivers are the Zambezi and Limpopo. The chief products are sugar, cotton, maize, copra, sisal, and beeswax; coal, gold, silver, uranium, and asbestos deposits exist. Area 297,729 sq. m.; pop. (1965) 6,956,000.

MOZART (mō'tsahrt), **Wolfgang Amadeus** (1756–91). Austrian composer. B. at Salzburg, he showed astonishing precocity, and was trained by his father, Leopold M., who was also a professional musician and composer. With his sister, Maria Anna, he was taken on a number of tours (1762–79) in the course of which they visited Vienna, the Rhineland, Holland, Paris, London, and Italy. Young M. not only gave public recitals, but had already begun to compose a considerable amount of music. In 1770 he was appointed master of the archbishop of Salzburg's court band. He found the post uncongenial, as he was treated as a mere servant, and in 1781 he was suddenly dismissed. From then on he lived mostly in Vienna, and m. Constanze Weber in 1782. He supported himself as a pianist, composer, and teacher, but his lack of business acumen often rendered his existence a hard struggle. He composed prolifically, his works including 25 piano concertos, 25 string quartets, 40 violin sonatas; 49 symphonies, of which the most important are the E flat, G minor, and C major ('Jupiter') symphonies, all composed in 1787; a number of operas, including *Idomeneo* (1781), *Il Seraglio* (1782), *The Marriage of Figaro* (1786), *Don Giovanni* (1787), *Così fan tutte* (1790), and *The Magic Flute* (1791), and much other music. His Requiem was left unfinished at his death, and subsequently completed by a pupil. The composer had been in failing health, and regarded its commission (made by an eccentric nobleman in mysterious circumstances) as an evil omen. *See* illus. p. 763,

MTWARA. Seaport of Tanganyika, E. Africa, cap. of Southern prov., on Mtwara Bay. Opened in 1954, M. was the only deep-water port between Mombasa and Durban. It has an airport. Pop. (1968) 20,500.

MUCOUS (mū'kus) **MEMBRANE.** A thin skin containing cells which secrete mucus, a moistening and lubricating fluid. It is found on all internal surfaces of the body, such as the eyelids, breathing and digestive passages, and genital tract.

MUDFISH. N. American fish (*Amia calva*) having a highly developed air-sac, enabling it to live out of water for some time, The name is also applied to the lung-fish of the order Dipnoi.

MUDIE (mū'di), **Charles Edward** (1818–90). British publisher, who founded in 1842 M.'s lending library, which in Victorian days achieved outstanding success, but was closed in 1937.

MUEZZIN (mōō-ez'in). Mohammedan official who calls the faithful to prayer from the minaret or from the side of a mosque.

MU'FTI (Arabic, a magistrate). Mohammedan official who expounds the Islamic law. In Turkey the Grand Mufti had supreme spiritual authority in the state, but this office was abolished in 1924 after Turkey had been proclaimed a republic.

MUFTI OF JERUSALEM. Arab religious and political leader. Haj Amin el-Husseini (1899–), who was elected M. in 1921, assisted the Nazis in their subversive agitation in the Middle E. during the S.W.W., and subsequently directed anti-Zionist activities. Sought as a war criminal, and found but not arrested in Baghdad and Cairo, he now lives in Beirut.

MUGGERIDGE, Malcolm (1903–). British journalist, editor of *Punch* 1953–7, and known for his controversial views on the monarchy.

MU'GWUMP. In U.S. political history Republicans who voted for Cleveland, the Democratic candidate, rather than their own, hence 'non-party or neutral'. From Algonquian Indian 'chief'.

MUIR (mūr), **Edwin** (1887–1959). British writer. B. in Orkney, he became a clerk, then a journalist, and lived in Prague 1921–31. He translated the novels of Kafka (with his wife, Willa Anderson, whom he m. in 1919); wrote novels such as *The Three Brothers* (1931), criticism such as *The Structure of the Novel* (1928), and was a distinguished poet, e.g. *First Poems* (1925),

Variations on a Time Theme (1934) and *Journeys and Places* (1943).

MUIR, John (1810–82). Scottish Sanskrit scholar. He was attached to the East India Co. (1829–53), and founded a chair of Sanskrit at Edinburgh univ. in 1862. His greatest work was *Original Sanskrit Texts* (1858–70). His brother, **Sir William M.** (1819-1905), was a celebrated Arabic scholar. He was in the Indian govt. service 1837–76, and was principal of Edinburgh univ. 1885–1903.

MUI-TSAI (mōō-i-tsī). System formerly prevailing in Hong Kong whereby girls could be 'adopted' or, in effect, sold into a kind of domestic slavery. Legislation introduced in 1923 proved ineffective, and in 1938 the govt. ordered the compulsory registration of adopted girls as a preventive measure. At this time there were some 8,000–9,000 M. girls.

MUKDEN. Former and historical name of SHENYANG.

MULATTO (mūlat'ō). The offspring of parents, one of whom is a European and the other a Negro. *Mestizos* are of mixed European and South American Indian parentage.

MULBERRY. Genus of trees (*Morus*) of the family Moraceae, with a dozen species of which the best-known is black M. (*M. nigra*). Native to Persia, it was introduced into Britain in the 16th cent. It has heart-shaped toothed leaves, and spikes of whitish flowers. The fruit resembles a raspberry in appearance, but is a cluster of small berries. The leaves of the white M. (*M. alba*) are those chiefly used in feeding silkworms.

M. was also the code name for the 2 artificial harbours (one at the British and one at the American landing-place) which were floated across the Channel for the invasion of France in 1944.

MULE. Hybrid animal of the horse family, usually the offspring of a male ass and a mare.

MULFORD, Clarence (1883–1956). American author, whose 'Westerns' featuring ranch 'Bar 20' and 'Hopalong Cassidy' were filmed and televised.

MÜLHAUSEN. German form of MULHOUSE.

MÜLHEIM (mül'hīm). Town on the Ruhr, W. Germany, 16 m. N. of Düsseldorf. It is the centre of a coal-mining dist. and has ironworks. Pop. (1966) 190,230. Also the name of a former town on the Rhine (Mülheim-am-Rhein) merged with Cologne in 1914.

MULHOUSE (mül'ooz). Town in Haut-Rhin dept. France, 62 m. S.S.W. of Strasbourg. Cotton textiles, paper etc., are manufactured. Pop. (1962) 110,735.

MULL. Second-largest is. of the Inner Hebrides, Argyllshire, Scotland. It is separated by the Sound of Mull from the mainland. There is only one town, Tobermory. Area 367 sq. m.; pop. (1961) 2,342.

MU'LLAH. Name given to a judge of the Mohammedan sacred law; also a title of respect given to various other dignitaries who perform duties connected with the sacred law.

MULLEIN (mul'len). Plant (*Verbascum thapsus*) of the family Scrophulariaceae. It produces lance-shaped leaves a foot or more in length, and in the second year of growth a large spike of yellow flowers. Common in Britain, and found through Europe and Asia, it is naturalized in N. America.

MU'LLET. Two genera of food fishes found in river estuaries. The red M. (*Mullus*) contains about 40 species, is red with yellow stripes, and measures about 15 in. The grey M. (*Mugil*) includes about 70 species, which are found in temperate and tropical

MULLEIN

coastal regions. It is greenish above and grey below.

MULLIKEN, Robert Sanderson (1896–   ). American chemist and physicist. Professor at Chicago from 1931, he received a Nobel chemistry prize 1966 for his development of the molecular orbital theory.

MULLINGA'R. Co. tn. of Westmeath, Rep. of Ireland. It is an agricultural and trout-fishing centre and makes woollens; there is tanning and brewing. Pop. (est.) 5,500.

MULOCK. *See* CRAIK, Dinah.

MULREADY (mul'redi), **William** (1786–1863). Irish artist. B. in co. Clare, he painted genre pictures, e.g. 'Fair Time' and 'Roadside Inn', and illustrated books. In 1840 he designed the first penny-postage envelope, known as the 'Mulready envelope'. He was elected R.A. in 1816.

MULTAN (mooltahn'). City in W. Pakistan, on a site inhabited since the time of Alexander the Great, 190 m. S.W. of Lahore. Cap. of M. dist., it is a busy trade centre with shawl and carpet manufactures. Pop. (1961) 358,201.

MUMBLES. Welsh seaside resort 5 m. S.W. of Swansea, Glamorganshire, on Swansea Bay. The M. lifeboat is renowned for its work in the Bristol Channel area.

MUMFORD, Lewis (1895–   ). American sociologist. B. on Long Is., he ed. the *Dial* 1919, and studied architecture both in England and the U.S.A., having an especial concern with skylines. His books incl. *Technics and Civilisation* (1934), *The Culture of Cities* (1938), *The Condition of Man* (1944), and *The Conduct of Life* (1951).

MUMPS. An acute, highly infectious fever marked by painful inflammation and swelling of one or both of the glands situated in front of the ear (parotid). The cause is probably a virus. It is commonest in young children. Incubation is about 18 days, and isolation should last at least 3 weeks.

MUNCH (moonk), **Edvard** (1863–1944). Norwegian artist. The son of a physician, he studied in Paris, and achieved in his portraits and landscapes the expression of the spirit of the northern peoples.

MÜNCHEN. German form of MUNICH.

MUNCHHAUSEN (munkh'howzen), **Baron** (1720-97). German soldier. B. in Hanover, he had served with the Russian Army against the Turks, and after his retirement in 1760 told exaggerated stories of his campaigning adventures. This idiosyncrasy was utilized by the German writer, Rudolph Erich Raspe (1737–94), in his extravagantly fictitious account of the *Adventures of Baron M.* (1785), compiled while he was taking refuge in London from a charge of theft in his own country. The book was very popular, and was frequently enlarged by other hands.

MUNCIE (mun'sē). City in Indiana, U.S.A., on the White r., 55 m. N.E. of Indianapolis. Coal and natural gas provide power for glass, iron and steel, clothing, and other works. M. is the 'Middletown' of three social studies of a typical Middle W. town by R. S. and H. M. Lynd, published 1929, 1937, 1947 Pop. (1960) 68,603.

MUNICH (mü'nik). Cap. of Bavaria, W. Germany, on the Isar. It is famous for its magnificent buildings and art treasures, many of which it owes to the kings Ludwig I and Maximilian II of Bavaria. The cathedral is late 15th cent. The Old Pinakothek contains paintings by old masters, the New Pinakothek, modern paintings; there is a Bavarian National Museum, the Bavarian State Library, and the *Deutsches Museum* of science and technology. M. is the see of the R.C. archbishopric of Munich-Freising. It has a univ. (transferred to M. in 1826), and several other learned institutions. The principal industries incl. brewing and printing and the manufacture of stained glass, machinery, locomotives, and textiles. M. is also an important railway centre and has an international airport. Developed in 1158, M. became the residence of the dukes of Wittelsbach in the 13th cent. M. was the scene of the Nov. revolution of 1918, the 'Soviet' rep. of 1919, and the Hitler putsch of 1923. It became the centre of the Nazi movement, and the Munich Agreement of 1938 was signed here. During the S.W.W. parts of the town were completely destroyed by bombing. Pop. (1966) 1,235,600.

MUNICH. Snow lends enchantment to the neo-Gothic town hall on the Marienplatz. Designed by George Bauberrisser and built 1867–1908, it has a slender tower 280 ft. high, and the façade is decorated with statues of the dukes and electors of Bavaria. *Courtesy of the German Tourist Information Bureau.*

MUNICH AGREEMENT. The agreement between Britain, France, Germany, and Italy, signed by Chamberlain, Daladier, Hitler, and Mussolini, at Munich on 29 Sept. 1938, whereby the Sudeten-German dists. of Czechoslovakia were ceded under duress by that country to Germany without a plebiscite. Although the signatories all guaranteed the new Czechoslovak frontiers, Hitler seized the rest of the country in March 1939.

MUNKÁCSY (mōōn′kahchē), **Mihály.** Assumed name of the Hungarian painter Michael Lieb (1844–1900). B. at Munkács, he settled in Paris, and became famous for his genre and historical pieces, and such works as 'Last Day of a Condemned Prisoner' and 'Milton Dictating *Paradise Lost* to his Daughters'.

MUNNINGS, Sir Alfred (1878–1959). British sporting artist. B. at Mendham, Suffolk, he studied at Norwich and Paris, and in the F.W.W. was official artist to the Canadian Cavalry Brigade. Among his best-known pictures of racing and hunting incidents are 'Epsom Downs, City and Suburban Day' (Chantrey Bequest) and 'The Edge of the Wood' (Manchester Art Gallery). P.R.A. 1944–9, and knighted in 1944, he was famed for his outspoken dislike of 'modern art'.

MUNRO′, Hugh Hector. *See* SAKI.

MUNSTER. A prov. of Rep. of Ireland, containing the cos. of Clare, Cork, Kerry, Limerick, Tipperary, and Waterford. M. was a kingdom until the 12th cent. Area 9,316 sq. m.; pop. (1966) 859,316.

MÜNSTER. Town of N. Rhine-Westphalia, Germany, on the Dortmund-Ems Canal; formerly the cap. of Westphalia. The Treaty of Westphalia was signed simultaneously here and at Osnabrück in 1648. Seat of a univ. (1773) M. makes wire, cement, and iron goods and has breweries and distilleries. Damaged in the S.W.W., its ancient buildings, incl. the 15th cent. cathedral and town hall, have been restored. Pop. (1966) 200,300.

MUNTERNIA. Rumanian name of WALLACHIA.

MUNTHE (moon′te), **Axel** (1857–1949). Swedish writer. He became physician to the king of Sweden in 1903, and to the queen in 1908, but retired to live in the house called San Michele, on Capri. His celebrated *Story of San Michele* (1929) traces the history of his home.

MUNTJAC (-jak). Small deer (*Cervulus muntjac*) found in S.E. Asia. The buck has short spiked antlers, and two sharp canine teeth forming tusks.

MU′RAL PAINTING. (Lat. *murus*, wall). The decoration of walls, and, by extension, of vaults and ceilings, by means of fresco, oil, or encaustic methods. *See* ENCAUSTIC; FRESCO; and TEMPERA.

MURASAKI SHIKIBU (moorahsah′kē shik′iboo) (978–*c*. 1015). Japanese author, whose real name is unknown. Her greatest work is the *Tale of Genji*, the earliest realistic Japanese novel.

MURAT (mürah′), **Joachim** (1767–1815). King of Naples. The son of an innkeeper, he rose rapidly in the French Army through the friendship of Napoleon, and won the reputation of a dashing cavalry commander. He was made king of Naples by Napoleon in 1808, but deserted him in 1813 in the hope that the Allies would recognize him. In 1815 he attempted unsuccessfully to make himself king of all Italy, and when he landed in Calabria in an attempt to recover the throne he was captured and shot.

MURATORI (moorahtō′rē), **Ludovico Antonio** (1672–1750). Italian scholar. B. at Vignola, he entered the Church, and in 1700 became keeper of the archives at Modena. He pub. works on Italian history, and discovered the Muratorian Canon, a 2nd cent. document giving the oldest known list of books of the N.T. in order.

MURCIA (moor′thē-ah). Cap. of the Spanish prov. of M. on the Segura, 28 m. N.N.W. of Cartagena. The seat of a univ., M. was founded in 825 on the site of a Roman colony by Abd-ur-Rahman II, caliph of Cordoba; it has a 14th cent. cathedral; silks, metals, and glass are manufactured. Pop. (1965) 259,267.

MURDER. The unlawful killing of one person by another, who is of sound mind, has reached years of discretion, and acts with malice aforethought, express or implied.

MURDOCH (mer′dok), **Iris** (1919–). British novelist. B. in Dublin, she specializes in the chessboard intricacies of the adventures of a number of unconventional-type lovers, conveyed in witty prose with a degree of fantasy. Her books incl. *Under the Net* (1954), *The Sandcastle* (1957), *A Severed Head* (1961; dramatized by Priestley in collaboration with M. in 1963), and *An Unofficial Rose* (1962). A student of philosophy, she became in 1948 fellow of St. Anne's Coll., Oxford, and pub. in 1953 *Sartre, Romantic Rationalist*. She m. in 1956 J. O. Bayley.

MURDOCK, William (1754–1839). Scottish inventor. B. at Auchinleck, Ayrshire, in 1792 he first used coal-gas to illuminate his house and offices in Redruth, and in 1797 and 1798 he held public demonstrations of his invention.

MURGER (mürzhār′), **Henri** (1822–61). French writer. B. in Paris, he studied painting, and in 1848 pub. *Scènes de la Vie de Bohème*, which formed the basis of Puccini's opera, *La Bohème*. He d. of overwork and dissipation.

MURILLO, Bartolomé Estéban (1617–82). Spanish painter. B. at Seville, in 1642 he went to Madrid, where he was befriended by Velasquez, then at the height of his fame. After his return to Seville in 1645 he received many important commissions, and founded the academy there (1660). One of the leading painters of the Spanish school, he is famed for his religious and genre pictures.

MURMANSK. Seaport of the Russian S.F.S.R., on the Barents Sea. It is the only port on the Arctic coast of Russia which is ice-free at all times of the year. M. is cap. of M. region, which is coterminous with the Kola peninsula. It is linked with Leningrad by railway, and after the entry of Russia into the S.W.W. in 1941, supplies from Britain and later from the U.S.A. were unloaded at M. Pop. (1967) 279,000.

MURNAU (moor′now), **F. W.** Pseudonym of the German film director Friedrich Wilhelm Plumpe (1889–1931). His 'subjective' use of a moving camera to tell the story, through expressive images and without subtitles, in *The Last Laugh* (1924) made him famous. After making *Faust* (1926), M. went to the U.S.A., where his films incl. *Sunrise* (1927) and *Tabu*, filmed in Tahiti in 1931.

MURRAIN. *See* FOOT AND MOUTH DISEASE.

MURRAY, Gilbert (1866–1957). British scholar. B. in Sydney, N.S.W., he was taken to England in 1877, and was prof. of Greek at Glasgow univ. 1889–99 and at Oxford 1908–36. Author of *History of Ancient Greek Literature* (1897), he became best known for his fine verse translations of the Greek dramatists, espec. Euripides. He was awarded the O.M. in 1941.

MURRAY, Sir James Augustus Henry (1837–1915). Scottish philologist. B. near Hawick, he was pres. of the Philological Society 1878–80 and 1882–4, and compiled and edited the *New English Dictionary*, the 1st vol. of which was pub. in 1884 at Oxford.

MURRAY, or Moray, James Stuart, earl of (*c.* 1531–70). Scottish statesman. An illegitimate son of James V, he was among the leaders of the Scottish Reformation, and after the deposition of his half-sister, Mary, in 1567, became regent. He was assassinated by a supporter of Mary.

MURRAY. Principal river of Australia. It rises in the Australian Alps near Mt. Kosciusko, and flows W., forming the boundary between N.S.W. and Victoria. It reaches the sea at Encounter Bay, and is 1,600 m. long. Its chief tributaries are the Darling and the Murrumbidgee (qq.v.).

MURROW, Edward R. (1908–65). American radio commentator. S. of a N. Carolina farmer, he joined C.B.S. in 1935, becoming Foreign News Director. He broadcast memorably to America from London during the S.W.W., and helped to discredit Senator McCarthy on TV in 1954. Politically independent, he was Director of the U.S.I.A. 1961–4.

MURRUMBI'DGEE. River of N.S.W., rising in the Australian Alps, flowing N. to the Burrinjuck reservoir, and then W. to meet the Murray after covering 1,050 m.

MURRY, John Middleton (1889–1957). British writer. B. in Peckham of humble family, he won a scholarship to Oxford, and in 1913 m. Katherine Mansfield (q.v.), whose biography he wrote. He produced studies of Dostoievsky, Keats, Blake, and Shakespeare, poetry and an autobiographical novel *Still Life* (1916). For many years he was an ardent pacifist.

MUSCA'T AND OMAN (ōmahn′). Re-named in 1970 the *Sultanate of Oman*, it occupies the eastern corner of Arabia. A mountain range rising to more than 9,000 ft. runs from the N.W. to the S.E., but the coastal plain N.W. of Muscat is fertile and famous for its dates. The cap. is Muscat. Oil resources developed from 1967, have rendered the country wealthy, but modernisation was blocked by the reactionary sultan, who was deposed in 1970 by his son, who succeeded as Sultan Qaboos bin Said (1941–   ). A treaty of friendship between Britain and the sultanate was signed 195Γ. Area 82,000 sq. m.; pop. (1968) 750,000.

MUSCLE. Tissue with the special function of contraction. Every M. is made up of collections of large numbers of long spindle-shaped elastic cells, enclosed in coverings of connective tissue (fascia), and contracts and relaxes in response to the impulses reaching the nerves which supply it. All motion in the body is brought about by Ms., which are very numerous and varied in their shape, size and function. The Ms. which move the limbs and trunk in obedience to the will are called voluntary, and also striped, Ms. from the faint cross-shading visible under the microscope. Walls of blood vessels and intestines, hair follicles, the interior of the eye, etc., contain muscle not under the control of the will – involuntary or unstriped M. Muscular dystrophy (dis′trŏfē) is a progressive muscular weakness leading to premature death, more frequent in boys than girls.

MU'SES. In Greek mythology, the 9 minor divinities who inspired artistic creation. The offspring of Zeus and Mnemosyne, their names and spheres were: Clio (history), Euterpe (lyric poetry), Thalia (comedy), Melpomene (tragedy), Terpsichore (dancing), Erato (love poetry), Polyhymnia (sacred hymns), Urania (astronomy), and Calliope (epic poetry).

MUSIC. Consisting solely of percussion instruments, the Javanese gamelan orchestra sounds unusual to western ears. Instruments are often richly carved and painted: the saron, here being played so intently, is a type of xylophone made from pieces of bamboo.   *Courtesy of Indonesian Embassy.*

MUSHROOM. *See* FUNGI.

MUSIC. The art of combining sounds in melodic or harmonic combination, so as to express thought and feeling in an aesthetic form. The Gr. word *mousikē* covered all the arts presided over by the Muses, and not only music in the modern sense. Of ancient Greek music only a few fragments have survived, and scholars are not agreed as to how these are to be deciphered. The various civilizations of the ancient and modern world – such as the Chinese, Hindu and Arabic cultures – developed their own musical systems, which are based on scale-divisions often differing entirely from those we know in the west. It is in modern western civilization, however, that music has reached its most complex development. The history of this begins with the liturgical music of the medieval Church, which was derived partly from Greek, partly from Hebrew antecedents. The 4 scales, or modes, to which the words of the liturgy were chanted, were 1st set in order by St. Ambrose in A.D. 384. St. Gregory the Great (*c.* 540–604) added 4 more to the original Ambrosian modes, and this system forms the basis of the Gregorian plainsong still in use in the R.C. Church. Originally all chants were sung in unison, but *c.* 11th cent. counterpoint was introduced, notably at the monastery of St. Martial, Limoges, and in the late 12th cent. at Notre Dame in Paris by Léonin and Perotin the Great. Meanwhile the Provençal and French troubadours had developed a purely secular music, derived from church and folk music.

The 15th and 16th cents. have been called the Golden Age of contrapuntal or polyphonic music. One of the earliest names is that of John Dunstable (d. *c.* 1453), an Englishman, whose works influenced the Frenchman Guillaume Dufay (*c.* 1400–74) and in turn helped to produce the great achievements of the Flemish school whose members incl. Dufay's pupil Joannes Okeghem (*c.* 1420– *c.* 1495) and Josquin des Pré. Other notable composers were the Italian Palestrina and the Fleming Orlande de Lassus, who settled in Italy, the Spaniard Victoria and the Englishmen Tallis and Byrd. The

MUSIC. Beethoven, portrait possibly painted from life by Franz Lieder (1780–1859), in the collection of Mrs. Barcsai.

Elizabethan age in England was spec. notable for the flowering of the secular madrigal, and produced such great names as Thomas Morley, Orlando Gibbons, etc.

The beginning of the 17th cent. saw a remarkable development, arising from the ideas of the Florentine Academy, a group of artists and literary men who wished to revive the principles of Greek tragedy. This led to the invention of dramatic recitative, and the beginning of opera. The 1st great operatic composer was Monteverdi (1567–1643), but before the end of the cent. the form had evolved further in the hands of Alessandro Scarlatti in Italy, and Lully in France. In England a promising start was made by Purcell, but was ended by his premature death which marked a decline in English music. The 17th cent. was also important for the emancipation of instrumental music from purely vocal forms.

MOZART
Mozart Museum, Salzburg.

The early 18th cent. is dominated by the great figures of J. S. Bach and Handel. The former, perhaps the greatest of all composers, though comparatively neglected in his own day, possessed a complete mastery of harmony and counterpoint, and has exercised a far-reaching influence on the subsequent development of music. Handel is most noteworthy for his magnificently dramatic oratorios, but had at 1st written operas based on Italian models, which had then hardened into lifeless conventionality. However, against this, Gluck later exhibited an important reaction.

Bach's great achievements had been in the handling of contrapuntal forms, but the next generation, incl. his own sons, C. P. E. Bach and J. C. Bach, reacted against this way of writing, and began the development of sonata-form, which is the basis of the 'Classical' sonata, quartette, and symphony. In these fields perfection of style was reached by the Viennese school of Haydn and Mozart, who were followed by the commanding figure of Beethoven. With the latter, music assumed dynamic and expressive functions hitherto undreamed of, and the way was opened for the Romanticism of the 19th cent.

'Romantic' music, represented in its earlier stages by Schubert, Schumann, Mendelssohn, Chopin, and Weber, tended to be subjectively emotional. The resources of orchestral colour were increasingly exploited – particularly by Berlioz – and harmony became more and more chromatic in character. National characteristics also became prominent. Thus we have the intense Polish nationalism of Chopin, and the exploitation of Hungarian-gypsy music by Liszt. National schools of composers, such as the Russian, represented by Rimsky-Korsakov, Borodin, Mussorgsky, and, less typically, by Tchaikovsky; the Czech, represented by Dvořák and Smetana, and the Norwegian, represented by Grieg, also emerged. The most revolutionary changes were brought by Wagner into the field of opera, though the traditional Italian lyricism was still perpetuated in the line of Rossini, Verdi and Puccini. Wagner's contemporary, Brahms, stood for Classical discipline of form, though in other respects he, too, is deeply Romantic in feeling. The Belgian, César Franck, though he went far in the development of chromaticism, also renewed the tradition of polyphonic writing.

At the turn of the cent. there was a certain reaction against Romanticism and a tendency to experiment, which 1st became apparent in the French 'Impression-

ist' school, which incl. Debussy and Ravel. In Austria and Germany, Bruckner, Mahler and Richard Strauss, the last great representatives of Romanticism, were succeeded by the highly intellectual 'Atonal' school of Schönberg, Webern and Berg. Other experiments have incl. the 'Neo-Classicism' of Stravinsky, Bartók and Hindemith, and the work of the French group known as *Les Six*, which incl. Francis Poulenc and Darius Milhaud. The works of the Jewish composer, Bloch, are often influenced by Hebrew tradition. Sibelius's music blends Romanticism with a certain northern austerity.

The revival in British music begun by Sullivan, Stanford and Parry was continued in the early 20th cent. by Elgar, Delius and Holst. Among the many notable more recent composers in Britain are Vaughan Williams, William Walton, Benjamin Britten, Michael Tippett, Lennox Berkeley, Arthur Bliss, Eugene Goossens and Alan Rawsthorne; in America Aaron Copland, George Gershwin, Charles Ives, Gian Carlo Menotti and Stravinsky; in the U.S.S.R. Shostakovitch, Prokofiev and Khachaturian; in Germany Paul Hindemith, Werner Egk (1901–), Carl Orff (1895–), Hans-Werner Henze (1926–), and Karl Hartmann (1905–); in Italy, Francesco Malipiero; in Hungary Kodály.

MUSIC, Electronic. Musical sounds produced by audio frequency oscillations of signal generators, electro-magnetic instruments, etc. Henk Badings (1907–), a Dutch composer, has produced some of the most attractive romantic use of this, e.g., 'Capriccio for Violin and Sound Tracks'.

MUSICAL. A play interspersed with songs and dance sequences, which grew out of the similar, but more farcical, M. comedy, originally developed in the late 19th cent. from the French *opéra bouffe* at the Gaiety Theatre in London by George Edwardes, and spread to the U.S. It is still largely limited to English-speaking countries; notable writers incl. R. Friml, S. Romberg, J. Kern, I. Berlin, N. Coward, I. Novello, Cole Porter, Sandy Wilson and Lionel Bart. Whereas M. comedy was romantically escapist, Ms. tend since the S.W.W. to deal with contemporary problems, e.g., colour in *South Pacific* (1949) by Rodgers and Hammerstein and gang warfare in *West Side Story* (1957) by Leonard Bernstein.

MUSIC HALL. A theatre offering light entertainment consisting of 'turns', in which singers, dancers, comedians, acrobats, etc., perform in turn. The history of the M.H. begins in the 17th cent., when tavern-keepers acquired the organs which the Puritans had banished from churches. On certain nights organ music was played, and this practice resulted in the weekly entertainment known as the 'free and easy'. Certain theatres in London and the provs. then began to specialize in variety entertainment. The heyday of the M.H. was at the beginning of the present cent., when such artists as Albert Chevalier, Marie Lloyd, and Vesta Tilley performed to full houses. Later stars of M.H. have incl. Sir George Robey, Gracie Fields, the Crazy Gang, Ted Ray, and the American Danny Kaye. The cinema 'killed' M.H., but in the 1960s there were signs of a revival in the working men's clubs, espec. of the N. of England, and in public houses.

MUSICK, Master of the King's/Queen's. Appointment to the British Royal Household, the holder being responsible for composing appropriate music for state occasions. 1st M. of the K.M. was Nicholas Lanier (appointed by Charles I in 1625): Sir Arthur Bliss held the post from 1953.

MUSIL, Robert (1880–1942). Austrian novelist. B. at Klagenfurt, he devoted long years to *Der Mann ohne Eigenschaften* (3 vols., 1930–43: *The Man Without Qualities*), even then unfinished. Its hero combines the author's background of philosophical study and scientific and military training, and is preoccupied

2

with the problems of the self viewed from a mystic but agnostic viewpoint. M.'s reputation is largely posthumous.

MUSK. Perennial plant (*Mimulus moschatus*) of the family Scrophulariaceae. The small oblong leaves formerly exuded the musky scent which gave it its name, but within the last 20 or 30 yrs. the scent has disappeared. It has yellow flowers.

MUSK DEER. Small deer (*Moschus moschiferus*) native to Asia. It has no antlers, does not travel in herds, and is hunted for the musk secreted by an abdominal gland, and used as a medicine or a perfume.

MUSKE′G. Canadian word (of Cree Indian derivation) for swampland. There are some 500,000 sq. m. of M. in northern Canada.

MUSK OX. Animal (*Ovibos moschatus*) native to the Arctic regions of N. America. It displays characteristics of both the sheep and the ox, is about the size of domestic cattle, and has long brown hair. At certain seasons it exhales a musky odour.

MUSLIMS. *See* MOSLEMS.

MUSLIN (muz′lin). A light cotton fabric named after Mosul, in Iraq, where it was 1st made. Its manufacture was introduced into England from India during the 17th cent.

MUSQUASH (mus′-kwosh). Rodent (*Fiber zib-ethicus*), also named Musk Rat. About a foot long, its body is adapted to aquatic life, having webbed feet and a flattened tail. It builds up a store of food, plastering it over with mud, for winter consumption. The light brown fur is highly valued.

MUSSEL. Popular name for a number of bi-valve molluscs. Most notable of the sea Ms. is the edible *Mytilus edulis*, which is found in clusters attached to rocks around the Atlantic coasts in the N. hemisphere and the Mediterranean, and has a blue-black shell. The freshwater pearl Ms. (*Unio*) incl. the *U. margaritiferus* found in some N. American and European rivers.

MUSSELBURGH (mus′lburō). Town (burgh) in Midlothian, Scotland, 5 m. E. of Edinburgh. Here is Loretto public school. Pop. (1961) 17,273.

MUSSET (müsā′), **Alfred de** (1810–57). French poet, playwright and novelist. B. in Paris, he abandoned the study of law and medicine to join the circle of writers about Victor Hugo, and achieved success with the vol. of poems, *Contes d'Espagne et d'Italie* (1829). In 1833 he accompanied George Sand to Italy, and his *Confession d'un enfant du siècle* (1835) recounts the story of their broken relations. Most typical of his genius are the verse *Les Nuits* (1835–7) and the short plays *Comédies et proverbes* (1840).

MUSSOLINI, Benito (1883–1945). Italian dictator. B. in the Romagna, the son of a blacksmith, he worked in early life as a teacher and journalist, and became active in the Socialist movement, from which he was expelled in 1914 for advocating Italian intervention in the F.W.W. In 1919 he founded the *Fasci di Combattimento*, whose programme combined violent nationalism with demagogic republican and anti-capitalist slogans, and launched a campaign of terrorism against the Socialists. This movement was backed by many landowners and industrialists, and by the heads of the army and police, and in Oct. 1922 the king and the army leaders installed M. in power as P.M. In 1925 he assumed dictatorial powers, and in 1926 all opposition parties were suppressed. During the years that followed the entire political, legal and educ. system was remodelled on Fascist lines. In 1935–6 M. embarked on a career of conquest, with his successful invasion of Ethiopia;

this was followed by Italian intervention in the Spanish Civil War of 1936–9, and the conquest of Albania in 1939. This policy drew M. into close co-operation with Nazi Germany, and in June 1940 Italy entered the S.W.W. Italian defeats in N. Africa, the Allied invasion of Sicily, and rising discontent at home destroyed M.'s prestige, and in July 1943 he was compelled to resign by the Fascist Grand Council. He was released from his imprisonment by German parachutists in Sept., and set up a 'Republican Fascist' govt. in N. Italy. In April 1945 he and his mistress were captured at Lake Como by partisans while trying to flee the country, and shot. Their bodies were exposed to the execration of the mob in Milan. *See* FASCISM. His son, BRUNO M. (1915–41), served as a bomber pilot in Ethiopia, Spain, and Greece, and was killed in an air accident. His dau. EDDA, m. Count Ciano (q.v.). *See* illus. under GERMAN HISTORY.

MUSSORGSKY (moosorg′skē), **Modest Petrovich** (1839–81). Russian composer. B. at Karevo, he entered the army in 1856, but resigned his commission in 1858 to concentrate on music while working as a govt. clerk. His opera *Boris Godunov* was completed in 1869, although not produced in St. Petersburg until 1874. His other works incl. the incomplete operas *Khovanshtchina* and *Sorochintsy Fair*; the orchestral *Night on the Bare Mountain*: the suite *Pictures at an Exhibition*; and many songs. Some of his works were 'revised' by Rimsky-Korsakov, and only recently has their harsh and primitive beauty been recovered. M. d. in poverty, having taken to drugs.

MUSTAFA KEMAL. *See* ATATÜRK.

MUSTAGH. Another name for KARAKORAM.

MU′STARD. Annual plants of the family Cruciferae. The seeds of Black M. (*Brassica nigra*), and White M. (*B. alba*), are used in the production of table mustard, and are cultivated in Europe, N. America and England, where wild M. or charlock (*B. arvensis*) is also found. The seedlings of white M. are used as a salad food. M. is frequently grown by farmers and ploughed in to enrich the soil.

MUTATION. In heredity, a new characteristic which suddenly appears in the offspring of a plant or animal and which breeds true is said to be a M. This type of change is one of the bases of evolutionary theory. Mutational changes may be spontaneous, or induced, e.g. by radiation. *See* EVOLUTION.

MUTSUHITO (mootsoohē′tō) (1852–1912). Emperor of Japan. He took the title Meiji Tenno (enlightened peace), when he became emperor in 1867. During his reign Japan became a world power.

M.V.D. (Ministerstvo Vnutrennykh Del, Ministry for Internal Affairs). New title from 1968 for the already existing Ministry of Public Order, given in an attempt to strengthen the fight of the ordinary police/militia against increasing crime and hooliganism; also the title 1946–53 of the secret police, now the K.G.B. (q.v.).

MYCENAEAN (mīsinē′an) **CIVILIZATION.** The civilization, also known as the Aegean Civilization, which flourished in Crete, Cyprus, Greece, the Aegean islands, and W. Anatolia, c. 4000–1000 B.C. Its nature was 1st laid bare by the excavations of Schliemann at Troy, Mycenae (an ancient Greek city in Argolis), and Tiryns after 1870, and of Sir Arthur Evans in Crete after 1899. Originating in Crete, it spread into Greece c. 1600 B.C., where it continued to flourish, with its centre at Mycenae, after the decline of Crete c. 1400. It was finally overthrown by the Dorian invasions, c. 1100. The system of govt. was by kings, who also monopolized priestly functions; their palaces were large and luxurious, and contained highly efficient sanitary arrangements. Commercial relations were maintained with Egypt throughout. Pottery, fresco-painting, and metal-work reached a high artistic level.

MYERS, Frederic William Henry (1843–1901). British psychic investigator. B. at Keswick, he was one of the founders and the 1st pres. of the Society for Psychical Research. His book, *The Human Personality and its Survival of Bodily Death* (1903), is a classic of psychical research.

MYITKYINA (mitchĕ′na). Town, cap. of Kachin state and of M. district, in N. Burma. It stands at the limit of navigation of the Irrawaddy and is the terminus of a railway from Rangoon, 723 m. to the S. It was recaptured by the Allies from the Japanese in Aug. 1944 after 2½ months' siege. Pop. (est.) 10,000.

MYOPIA (mī-ō′pia). Short sight. It is due to the eye being slightly too large, so that the incoming light is focused before it reaches the retina. The error can be corrected by concave lenses.

MYRON (mī′ron) (fl. 500–440 B.C.). Greek sculptor. B. at Eleutherae in Boeotia, he is remembered for the Discobolus, or discus-thrower.

MYRRH (mer). Gum resin produced by a small tree (*Commiphora myrrha*), of the family Burseraceae, found in Abyssinia and Arabia. In ancient times it was used for incense and perfume, and in embalming.

MYRTLE (mer′tl). Genus (*Myrtus*) of evergreen shrubs in the family Myrtaceae. The common Mediterranean M. (*M. communis*) has oval opposite leaves and white flowers followed by purple berries, all of which are fragrant.

MYSORE (mīsor′). Indian city in M. state (of which it was formerly the cap.), 80 m. S.W. of Bangalore. Buildings incl. the fort and the univ. (estab. 1916). Pop. (1961) 253,865.

MYSORE. State in the Republic of India, bordered N. by Maharashtra, E. by Andhra Pradesh, S. by Kerala and Madras, W. by the Arabian Sea. Bangalore is the cap. It was formed in 1956 from the former princely states of M. (29,500 sq. m.) and Coorg (1,586 sq. m.) and districts transferred from Bombay and Madras states. Chief rivers are the Vistna, Tungabadhra, and Cauvery. Agriculture is the main occupation, rice and other grains, ground-nuts, and cotton being grown. Textiles, paper, metal goods, and sugar are produced. Gold, iron, asbestos, and manganese are among minerals worked. Area 74,210 sq. m.; pop. (1961) 23,586,772.

MYSTERY RELIGIONS. Cults of the ancient world open only to the initiated. The most important of such cults among the Greeks were the Eleusinian mysteries, celebrated annually in honour of Demeter at Eleusis, near Athens, and the Orphic mysteries, in honour of Dionysus. A number of Asiatic mystery cults, such as those of Attis, Cybele, Isis, and Mithras, attained great popularity under the Roman Empire. All these cults derived from primitive fertility rituals; their principal feature was a ritual drama, normally portraying the death and resurrection of the god, while a sacramental meal took place through which the initiate obtained communion with the god by feeding on his flesh and blood, hoping thereby to attain to life beyond the grave. These ideas strongly influenced early Christianity.

MYSTICISM. A mode of religious belief depending on personal spiritual experience of God as the ultimate reality, distinct from all references to thought or reason. The element of M. is common to all the higher religions – Hinduism, Buddhism, Judaism, Islam, and Christianity. M. was 1st introduced to W. Europe through Neoplatonism (q.v.) which was largely affected by Oriental schools of thought, and in its turn influenced the rise of Christian M. through the work of the pseudo-Dionysius the Areopagite. M. flourishes espec. in periods when a civilization is passing through a major crisis, as in Germany in the 14th–16th cents., when feudalism was breaking down, e.g. Thomas à Kempis and Jacob Boehme. Often M. assumed heretical forms, as with the Anabaptists and early Quakers, but the Counter-Reformation also produced mystics such as St. Teresa and St. John of the Cross. Mystical movements of the 17th cent. incl. those of the Quietists in France, and Henry More and the Cambridge Platonists in England, while the 18th cent. produced two great English mystics in William Law and William Blake. In the 20th cent. there has been a revival of M. in England and the U.S.A., largely due to Hinduism, which is expressed in the works of W. B. Yeats, Gerald Heard, and Aldous Huxley. The scientific study of M. was estab. by the work of Dean Inge, William James, and Evelyn Underhill, and valuable light has been thrown by the use of psychological methods.

MYTHOLOGY (Gk. *muthos*, fable). Science which attempts the interpretation of the stories invented by primitive peoples to express their imaginative conception of the origin of the universe, useful arts, etc., and assess their relationship to similar stories told by other races. The myth is distinguished from the legend (q.v.), which may have an ultimate basis in fact, by being purely fictitious. Great Ms. are those of Egypt, India, Greece, Rome, and Scandinavia.

MYTILENE, *See* MITYLENE.

MYXOEDEMA (miksidĕ′ma). A disease due to deficiency of the secretion of the thyroid gland chiefly seen in middle-aged women. The mind becomes dull, the temper irritable, and the memory is lost, there is a coarsening of the features, the skin becomes yellow and dry, and the speech thick. The condition can be improved by giving thyroid preparation.

MYXOMATŌSIS (mik′so-). A contagious filterable-virus infection of rabbits, causing much suffering, sometimes deliberately introduced to reduce rabbit population.

N 14th letter of the Roman alphabet, representing a dental nasal sound. In several Romance languages *n* in many circumstances disappears, with nasalization of the preceding vowel.

NAAFI. In full: Navy, Army, and Air Force Institutes. Non-profit-making association, providing canteens for H.M. Forces at home and overseas; its H.Q. is at Claygate, Surrey.

NABOKOV (nab′okof), **Vladimir.** Pseudonym of Russian author Vladimir Sirin (1899–). B. in St. Petersburg, he settled in the U.S.A. in 1940, and was prof. of Russian literature at Cornell univ. 1948–59, producing a fine translation and commentary on *Eugene Onegin* in 1963. He is also a noted lepidopterist, a pursuit which has something in common with his treatment of his fictional characters. His best-known books incl. *The Real Life of Sebastian Knight*

(1945), *Pnin* (1957) and *Lolita* (1955), story of the infatuation of the middle-aged Humbert Humbert for a precociously experienced child of 12 which added the word 'nymphet' to the language.

NĀ'DIR. Astronomical term denoting a point in the heavens diametrically opposite to the zenith.

NAEMEN. Flemish form of NAMUR.

NAEVIUS (nē'vius), **Gnaeus** (*c.* 265–*c.* 194 B.C.). One of the earliest Roman poets. He produced tragedies, comedies, and an epic on the Punic War.

NAEVUS (nē'vus). 'Port wine mark'; a bright red tumour of the skin, consisting of a mass of small blood vessels. A N. of moderate size is harmless. It can sometimes be treated by cutting out, burning with an electric needle, or freezing with carbon dioxide snow.

NAGALAND (nah'gah-). 16th state of the Rep. of India. It lies N. of Manipur and borders Burma on the E. The cap. is Kohima; area 6,366 sq. m.; pop. (1961) 369,200. Formerly part of Assam, N. is inhabited by Naga tribes once notorious as head-hunters. The British sent 18 expeditions against them 1832–87; and after India attained independence in 1947 they rose against their new ruler, who undertook military action against them 1955–6. Unable to repress them, the Indian govt. entered into negotiations with their leaders in 1960 and in 1962 passed an act giving them autonomy; the new state was inaugurated 1963, but resistance continued.

NAGASAKI (nahgahsah'kē). Seaport on Kyushu Is., Japan, destroyed by an atom bomb during the S.W.W. on 9 Aug. 1945. Of its pop. of 212,000, 73,884 were killed, 76,796 injured. N. was the only Japanese port open to European trade from the 16th cent. until other ports were opened in 1859. Coal is mined and there are iron works and shipbuilding yards. Pop. (1965) 405,000.

NAGOYA. Seaport of Honshu, Japan, with a Shogun fortress (1610) and a famous Shinto shrine, Atsuta Jingu. Textiles and clocks are made. Pop. (1965) 1,935,000.

NAGPUR (nagpoor'). City in Maharashtra state, India, cap. of N. division and district, seat of N. univ. (1923), with an airport. Close to the cotton-growing area of the Deccan, it is a centre for cotton and silk textiles. Pop. (1961) 643,659.

NAGY (nahzh), **Imre** (1896–1958). Hungarian leader of the revolt against Soviet domination in 1956. He was executed.

NĀ'HUM (7th cent. B.C.). Hebrew prophet, possibly

NAGOYA. Two nude statues frame the 590 ft. high television tower in the beautiful Sakae Park at Nagoya, the largest industrial city of central Japan. Halfway up the tower is an observation room, giving a wonderful view over the city.
Courtesy of Japanese Embassy.

b. in Galilee, and author of a prophecy of the destruction of Nineveh incl. in the O.T.

NĀ'IADS. Water-nymphs of classic mythology.

NAILS. Hard, smooth, elastic appendages to the skin, made of a horny modification of its outer layer, and protecting and strengthening the tips of the fingers and toes. They are related to the claws and hooves of animals. The N. grows from a bed, or matrix, in the lower germinal layer of the skin.

NAIPAUL (nī'pawl), **Vidiadhar Surajprasad** (1932–), British writer. B. in Trinidad of Hindu parents, he was ed. in Port of Spain and at Oxford, then worked as a freelance broadcaster and for the B.B.C. He is best known for his novels *A House for Mr. Biswas* (1961), *Mr. Stone and the Knights Companion* (1963), and *The Mimic Men* (1967).

NAIRN. County town (burgh) of Nairnshire, Scotland, on the Moray Firth. It is a fishing port with a good harbour. Pop. (1961) 4,899.

NAIRNE (närn), **Carolina Oliphant**, baroness (1766–1845). Scottish song-writer, author of 'Land o' the Leal', 'Caller Herrin', and other well-known songs.

NAIRNSHIRE. County of Scotland, bounded on the N. by the Moray Firth. Its principal rivers are the Nairn and Findhorn. Agriculture is carried on, but only a small part is cultivated. The co. town is Nairn. Area 163 sq. m.; pop. (1961) 8,421.

NAIROBI (nirō'bē). Cap. of Kenya, E. Africa, 330 m. by rail N.W. of Mombasa. Founded in 1899, it is well planned; it was granted city status by Royal Charter in 1950. Its elevation (5,450 ft.) gives it a bracing climate. Univ. Coll. (1956) is one of the 3 constituent colls. of the Univ. of E. Africa, and the Lumumba Inst. (1964) is 7 m. to the N. There is an international airport. Pop. (1968) 400,000.

NAMA'QUALAND. Great N. is a desert region N. of the Orange r., S.W. Africa. It is inhabited by the sparsely distributed Namaquas, a Hottentot tribe. Area *c.* 150,000 sq. m. Little N. is the desert region S. of the Orange r., incl. in Cape Prov. Copper and diamonds are mined. Area *c.* 20,000 sq. m.; pop. *c.* 26,000.

NAMIBIA. *See* SOUTH WEST AFRICA.

NAMUR (nahmür'). City and railway junction in Belgium, cap. of the prov. of N., situated at the junction of the Sambre and the Meuse. It has iron and steel foundries, and is famous for cutlery. Pop. (1966) 32,650.

NANAIMO (nahnī'mō). Coal-mining centre of British Columbia, Canada, on the E. coast of Vancouver Is., 60 m. N.W. of Victoria. Pop. (1966) 15,200.

NA'NA SA'HIB (1820–*c.* 1859). Name by which Dandhu Panth, an adopted son of the ex-peshwa of the Mahrattas, was commonly known. He joined the rebels in the Indian Mutiny, and was responsible for the massacre at Cawnpore. After the rebellion he took refuge in Nepal.

NANCHANG. Chinese city, cap. of Kiangsi prov. on the Kan r. 160 m. S.E. of Wuhan. Dating from the 12th cent., it is a road, railway, and air junction, with cotton mills and pottery, glass, match, and soap factories. It is the seat of a univ. Pop. (1957) 398,000.

NANCY (noṅsi'). Cap. of the dept. of Meurthe-et-Moselle, France, on the Meurthe, 175 m. E. of Paris. Dating from the 11th cent., N. has a univ. and contains many fine buildings, incl. the Hôtel de Ville and the cathedral (1742). Pop. (1968) 123,428.

NANKING. Chinese city on the Yangtze-Kiang, 165 m. N.W. of Shanghai, made cap. of Kiangsu prov. in 1952. Dating from the 2nd cent. B.C., and perhaps earlier, it received the name N. (meaning southern cap.) under the Ming dynasty. It was cap. of China under several early dynasties, and from 1368–1403, 1928–37, 1946–9. It is an industrial and communications centre, and has a univ. (1888). On Purple Mountain nearby Sun Yat-Sen is buried. Pop. (1957) 1,419,000.

NANNI'NG. Chinese river port, on the Yü-kiang, a headstream of the Si-kiang (or West River), cap. of Kwengsi-Chuang autonomous region. A former treaty port (1907), it is also a road centre and trades in the fruit and sugar grown in the area. Pop. (1957) 264,000.

NANSEN, Fridtjof (1861–1930). Norwegian explorer, scientist, and statesman. He made his first voyage to Greenland waters in a sealing-ship in 1882, and in 1888-9 attempted to cross the Greenland icefield. He sailed to the Arctic in 1893 in the *Fram*, which was deliberately allowed to drift with an iceflow. Later, N. left the *Fram* and, accompanied by Johansen, continued northwards on foot. They reached 86° 14′ N., the highest latitude then attained, and wintered in Franz Josef Land, returning in 1896. The *Fram* also returned safely. After the F.W.W. N. became League of Nations High Commissioner for refugees, and in 1923 received the Nobel peace prize. The N. inst. for humanist and social research was estab. at Oslo in 1956.

NANTES (nont). Seaport of France, cap. of the dept. of Loire-Atlantique, on the Loire, 35 m. from its mouth. Its buildings incl. the cathedral (1434-1884), built over a 12th cent. crypt, and the castle, founded in 938. Here Henry IV signed the EDICT OF N. (1598), granting religious freedom to the Huguenots. Pop. (1968) 259,208.

NANTEUIL (nontöy'), **Robert** (*c.* 1623–78). French engraver and craftsman, famous for his portraits.

NANTU'CKET. Is. (area 46 sq. m.; pop. 3,600) and pleasure resort 25 m. S. of Cape Cod, Mass, U.S.A. In the 18–19th cents. N. was a famous whaling port.

NA'PALM. Fuel used in flame-throwers and incendiary bombs. Produced from jellied petrol, it is named from *naph*thene and *palm*itic acids.

NAPHTHA (naf'tha). Originally applied to naturally occurring liquid hydrocarbons, the term is now used for the mixtures of hydrocarbons obtained by destructive distillation of petroleum, coal-tar, and shale oil.

NA'PHTHALENE ($C_{10}H_8$). A solid, aromatic hydrocarbon, m.p. 80°C, b.p. 218°C, obtained from the middle oil distillate of coal-tar. A white, shiny, crystalline solid with a penetrating smell, it is used in making indigo and certain azo-dyes; also as a mild disinfectant and insecticide (moth balls have the characteristic smell of N.).

NAPIER, Sir Charles James (1782–1853). British general. After serving in the Peninsular War and capturing a number of vessels in the American War of 1812–14, his great achievement came in his campaigns in Sind 1841-3 which he conquered with a very small force and governed until 1847. He ·seldom agreed with his superiors, but was liked by his men and was the first to mention in despatches men from the ranks who had distinguished themselves. His brother, **Sir William Francis Patrick N.** (1785–1860), wrote a *History of the Peninsular War* (1828–40) in which he had also served.

NAPIER, John (1550–1617). Scottish mathematician. He was the inventor of logarithms, publishing his Tables in 1614, and of 'N.'s Bones' an early type of calculating device for multiplication and division.

NAPIER. Seaport of North Island, New Zealand. Pop. (1967) 39,300.

NAPIER OF MAGDALA, Robert Cornelis Napier, 1st baron (1810–90). British field marshal. Knighted for his services at the siege of Lucknow, and thanked by parliament for his part in the Chinese War of 1855, he crowned his career in the Abyssinian campaign of 1868 by storming Magdala, and was created a baron.

NAPLES. Seaport and cap. of N. prov., situated on the Bay of N., 120 m. S.E. of Rome. Formerly the cap. of the kingdom of N., it is the 3rd town of Italy, and as a port second only in importance to Genoa.

NAPOLEON I. The meeting with Francis II after Austerlitz, a painting by Antoine Jean Gros.

There are shipbuilding yards, factories making locomotives, textiles, paper, etc.; a famous museum and a marine aquarium. To the S. is the Isle of Capri, and behind the city is Mt. Vesuvius, with the ruins of Pompeii at its foot. Outstanding buildings of N. incl. the royal palace, the San Carlo Opera House, and the Castel Nuovo (1283). N. has one of the oldest univs. (1224) in the world. Pop. (1961) 1,179,608.

NAPOLEON I (Bonaparte) (1769–1821). Emperor of the French. B. at Ajaccio, Corsica, he received a commission in the artillery in 1785, and first distinguished himself at the siege of Toulon in 1793. N. m. Josephine de Beauharnais in 1796. Having suppressed a royalist rising in Paris in 1795, he received the command against the Austrians in Italy, and by his victories at Lodi, Arcole, and Rivoli (1796-7), compelled them to make peace. The Directory then accepted his plan to conquer Egypt as a halfway-house to India (1798), but although he overran Egypt and invaded Syria his fleet was destroyed by Nelson. In 1799 he returned to France, overthrew the govt. of the Directory, and estab. his own dictatorship, nominally as First Consul. He then invaded Italy, defeated the Austrians at Marengo (1800), and broke up the coalition which had been formed against France. Peace was restored in 1802.

Soon afterwards a plebiscite confirmed him in his consulship for life, and another in 1804 granted him the title of emperor. While retaining and extending the legal and educational reforms of the Jacobins, he substituted a centralized despotism for the democratic constitution estab. by the Revolution, and by his Concordat conciliated the Church. The war was renewed by Britain in 1803; Austria and Russia joined the coalition against France in 1805, and Prussia in 1806. Prevented by British sea power from invading England, N. drove Austria out of the war by his victories at Ulm and Austerlitz (1805), and Prussia by the victory of Jena (1806), and after the hard-fought battles of Eylau and Friedland formed an alliance with the tsar at Tilsit (1807).

He now attempted to ruin Britain by his 'Continental System' of excluding British goods from Europe, and to enforce its operation sent an army to occupy Portugal, and in 1808 placed his brother Joseph on the Spanish throne. Spain and Portugal revolted, with British assistance, while in 1809 Austria re-entered the war, only to be defeated at Wagram. To assert his equality with the Habsburgs, N. now divorced Josephine and m. the emperor's daughter, Marie Louise. When the tsar failed to enforce the Continental System, N. invaded Russia in 1812, and occupied Moscow, which was set on fire. The disastrous French retreat encouraged Prussia and Austria to declare war in 1813, and N. was defeated at

Leipzig and driven from Germany. After a brilliant campaign on French soil, he abdicated in 1814, and was banished to Elba.

In March 1815 he returned to France and re-assumed power; in June he marched into Belgium to meet the Allies, was defeated at Waterloo, and again abdicated. Having surrendered to the British, he was exiled to St. Helena, where he d. and was buried in 1821. His body was reinterred in the Hôtel des Invalides, Paris, in 1840. For his family, *see* BONAPARTE.

NAPOLEON II (1811–32). Title given by the Bona-partists to the son of Napoleon I and Marie Louise; until 1814 he was known as the king of Rome, and after 1818 as the duke of Reichstadt. After his father's abdication in 1814 he was taken to the Austrian court, where he spent the rest of his life. By Hitler's order his body was removed from Vienna in 1940 and reinterred in the Hôtel des Invalides, Paris.

NAPOLEON III (1808–73). Emperor of the French. The son of Louis Bonaparte and Hortense de Beau-harnais, brother and step-daughter respectively of Napoleon I, he led two unsuccessful revolts, at Strasbourg in 1836 and at Boulogne in 1840, and after the latter was imprisoned. Escaping in 1846, he lived in London until the 1848 revolution. He was elected president of the republic in Dec., and set him-self to secure a following by posing as the champion of order and religion against the revolutionary menace. He secured his re-election by a military coup d'état in 1851, and a year later was proclaimed emperor. Hoping to strengthen his régime by military triumphs, he joined in the Crimean War, waged war with Austria (1859), and attempted unsuccessfully to found a vassal empire in Mexico (1863–7); thereby he aroused the mistrust of Europe and isolated France. At home, his régime was discredited by its notorious corruption; republican and Socialist opposition grew, in spite of severe repression, and forced N., after 1860, to make concessions in the direction of parliamentary govt. Manœuvred by Bismarck in 1870 into war with Prussia, he was forced to surrender at Sedan, where-upon the empire collapsed. After the war he withdrew to England, where he died. *See* illus. p. 824.

His son by the empress Eugénie (q.v.), **Eugène Louis Jean Joseph N., Prince Imperial** (1856–79), was killed fighting with the British Army against the Zulus.

NAPOLI. Italian form of NAPLES.

NARBONNE (nahrbon′). City in Aude dept., France, 8 m. inland from the Mediterranean coast and 34 m. E. of Carcassonne. The former cathedral is of the 13th cent. As Narbo it was the chief town of southern Gaul in Roman times. Pop. (1962) 35,899.

NARCISSUS (nahrsis′us). In Gk. legend, a beauti-ful youth, who rejected the love of the nymph Echo, and as a punishment was made to fall in love with his own reflection in a stream. He eventually pined away for love of himself, and in the place where he d. there sprang up a flower which was named after him. His name is the origin of the psychological term **Narcissism**, meaning an excessive valuation of the self and its attributes, an exaggeration of normal self-respect and pride in oneself into vanity and conceit, which may amount to insanity.

NARCISSUS. Genus of bulbous plants of the family Amaryllidaceae. There are about 35 different species, of which the best-known are the daffodil, jonquil, and poet's N.

NARCOTICS. Drugs

that relieve pain and cause deep sleep. The principal are opium and its derivatives and synthetic modifica-tions (morphine, heroin, etc.); the alcohols (paral-dehyde, ethyl alcohol, avertin, etc.); and the bar-biturates (veronal, luminal, evipan, etc.).

NARES (nārz), **Sir George Strong** (1831–1915). Scottish admiral and explorer. He commanded the *Challenger* during part of her voyage of deep-sea exploration round the world (1872–4), and led the Arctic expedition of 1875–6.

NARSES (nahr′sēz) (c. 478–c. 573). Byzantine statesman and general, originally a eunuch slave, and later an official in the imperial treasury. He was joint commander with Belisarius in Italy 538–9, and in 552 destroyed the Ostrogoths at Taginae.

NARVA (nahr′vah). Seaport of Estonian S.S.R., on the Narva, 70 m. S.W. of Leningrad, founded in 1223 by the Danes. Charles XII of Sweden in 1700 inflicted a severe defeat here on the army of Peter the Great who was besieging N.; but 4 years later Peter captured N. There are tanneries, and textiles and rope are made. Pop. (1967) 25,000.

NARVIK. Seaport in Norway, on Ofot Fjord. It exports iron ore from the Swedish mines. To secure this ore supply the Germans seized N. in April 1940. British, French, Polish, and Norwegian forces re-captured N., but had to abandon it on 10 June owing to the worsening Allied situation elsewhere in Europe; this was the end of fighting in Norway during the S.W.W. Pop. (1967) 13,500.

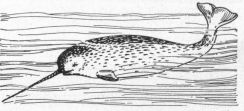

NARWHAL

NARWHAL. A cetacean (*Monodon monoceros*), found only in the Arctic Ocean. The male has a spirally fluted tusk, 6–10 ft. long.

NASEBY (nāz′bi). English village in Northants, 12 m. N.N.W. of Northampton, the scene of the decisive battle of the Civil War (14 June 1645), when the Royalists were defeated by Cromwell and Fairfax.

NASH, John (1752–1835). British architect. He laid out Regent's Park, London, and designed many of the terraces nearby. Between 1813 and 1820 he planned Regent Street (subsequently rebuilt), and later re-paired and enlarged Buckingham Palace for which he designed Marble Arch, intended as the entrance gateway.

NASH, Ogden (1902–71). American poet. B. in Rye, N.Y., he pub. numerous vols. of humorous verse of impeccable technique and quietly puncturing satire, e.g. *Hard Lines* (1931), *The Face is Familiar* (1941), and *Collected Verses* (1961).

NASH, Paul (1889–1946). British artist. B. in London, he became famous for his pictures of the F.F.W., such as 'The Menin Road', in the Imperial War Museum, in which he created strange patterns out of the scorched landscape of the Western Front. During the S.W.W. he was appointed official war artist to the Air Ministry. Two of his most celebrated pictures, depicting the struggle in the air, are *Totes Meer*, and 'The Battle of Britain', reproduced on p. 168. He also illustrated books and designed posters, textiles, stage scenery and costume. His brother, **John Northcote N.** (1893–), is also a painter and engraver. He produced 1916–18 a number

PAUL NASH. One of the leading British artists of the twentieth century.

of pictures for the Imperial War Museum and during the S.W.W. was an official artist to the Admiralty.

NASH, Richard (1674–1762). British dandy, known as Beau Nash. As master of ceremonies at Bath from 1705, he made it the most fashionable watering-place in England, and did much to bring a more polished code of manners into general use.

NASH, Sir Walter (1882–1968). New Zealand statesman. B. at Kidderminster, he emigrated to N. Z. in 1909. In the Labour govt. of 1935 he became Min. of Finance, to which he added the post of Deputy P.M. 1940–9. During the S.W.W. he was a member of the War Cabinet, and Minister to Washington 1942–4. P.M. 1957–60, he led the Opposition 1950–7 and 1960–3: knighted 1965.

NASH(E), Thomas (1567–1601). English poet, dramatist and pamphleteer. B. at Lowestoft, he settled in London *c.* 1588, where he was rapidly drawn into the Martin Marprelate controversy, and wrote at least 3 attacks on the Martinists. Among his later works are the satire *Pierce Pennilesse* (1592); the religious *Christes Teares over Jerusalem* (1593); *Jacke Wilton*, the first English picaresque novel; and the comedy, *Summer's Last Will and Testament.*

NASHUA. City in New Hampshire, U.S.A., founded as Dunstable in 1765, renamed 1836. It makes textiles, hardware, steel goods, etc. Pop. (1960) 39,096.

NASHVILLE. Cap. of Tennessee, U.S.A., on the Cumberland r., 200 m. N.E. of Memphis. An important river port, it is in the fertile area of the Tennessee Valley, with a trade in cotton, tobacco, wheat and livestock; is a banking and commercial complex, and has large printing, recording and music publishing industries. There are 3 univs. and Peabody Coll. was founded by George Peabody (q.v.). N. dates from 1778, and the Confederate army was badly defeated here in 1864. Pop. (1960) 170,874.

NASMYTH, Alexander (1758–1840). Scottish portrait and landscape painter. B. in Edinburgh, he is best remembered for his portrait of Burns in the Scottish National Gallery.

NASMYTH, James (1808–90). Scottish engineering inventor. B. in Edinburgh, the son of Alexander N., he developed a successful foundry at Patricroft and invented his steam-hammer, planing machine, and hydraulic machinery.

NASSAU. Port of New Providence island and cap. of the Bahamas. English settlers founded it in 1629. Pop. (1967) 100,000.

NASSER, Gamal Abdel (1918–70). Egyptian statesman. Son of a postal clerk, he entered the army from Cairo Military Academy, and was wounded in the Palestine War of 1948–9. In 1952 he was the driving power behind the Neguib coup, became P.M. in 1954 and in 1956 pres. of the Rep. of Egypt – of the United Arab Republic from 1958. His appropriation of the Suez Canal (q.v.) and his ambitions for an Egyptian-led Arab union led to disquiet in the area (see under EGYPT, ISRAEL, and YEMEN), but his internal policies were generally sound, although a rapidly increasing population lessened their good effect.

PRESIDENT NASSER
Middle East News Agency.

NASTURTIUM (naster'-shyum). Genus of plants of the family Cruciferae, including *N. officinale*, watercress. The garden species, *Tropaeolum majus*, which has orange- or scarlet-coloured flowers, and *Tropaeolum minus*, which has smaller flowers, belong to the S. American Tropaeolaceae. The leaves and buds are sometimes served in salads.

NATAL. A prov. in the Rep. of S. Africa, to the N.E. of Cape Province, and bounded on the E. by the Indian Ocean; so called because it was discovered by Vasco da Gama on Christmas Day, 1497. From the Drakensberg the country slopes to a fertile sub-tropical coastal plain. There are many plantations of sugar cane. Other products incl. the black wattle (*Acacia mollissima*), maize, fruits, vegetables, tobacco, and coal. The cap. is Pietermaritzburg; the chief port and largest town is Durban. N. was a part of Cape Colony 1844–56, when it was made into a separate colony. Zululand was annexed to N. in 1897, and the districts of Vrijheid,

NASTURTIUM

Utrecht, and part of Wakkerstroom were transferred from the Transvaal to N. in 1903. In 1910 the colony became a part of the Union of South Africa. Area 33,578 sq. m.; pop. (1960) 2,933,447 (340,293 white).

NATAL. Seaport and city of Brazil, cap. of the state of Rio Grande do Norte. It has textile mills and salt refineries. Founded in 1599, N. was made a city in 1822. Pop. (1967) 100,000.

NATIONAL ANTHEM. A patriotic song employed on official occasions. 'God Save the King/Queen' (q.v.), has been accepted as such in Britain since 1745, although both tune and words are of much earlier origin. The music of the Austrian 'Emperor's Hymn' was written by Haydn in 1797, and was retained after the revolution of 1918, with some new words, until 1948. The German *Deutschland über Alles* is sung to the same tune. In 1951 Pres. Heuss selected a new N.A. for the Federal Republic (Germany having been without one 1945–51): this was unpopular and the old one

NATAL. A Kaffir people, the Pondo, live on the south coast of the province, and their women are skilled in coloured beadwork. Their elaborately prepared hair-style takes far longer to arrange to perfection than the European 'permanent wave' *Courtesy of Satour.*

was revived in 1952. The French N.A., the *Marseillaise* (q.v.), dates from the revolution of 1792, and the Belgian *Brabançonne* from that of 1830. The Internationale (q.v.), adopted as the Russian N.A. in 1917, was replaced by the song 'Unbreakable Union of Freeborn Republics' in 1944. The American N.A., 'The Star-spangled Banner', written during the war of 1812, was officially adopted in 1931.

NATIONAL BOOK LEAGUE. British association of authors, publishers, booksellers, librarians, and readers, to encourage the reading and production of better books. Founded as the National Book Council in 1925, it was renamed the N.B.L. in 1944.

NATIONAL DEBT. Debt incurred by the central government of a country. The first issue of government stock in England was made in 1693, to raise a loan of £1,000,000. The main cause of increase in the debt has always been wartime expenditure; thus, after the War of the Spanish Succession, it reached £54,000,000, after the Seven Years War £146,000,000, after the American War £230,000,000 and after the Napoleonic Wars £834,000,000. By 1900 it had been brought down to £610,000,000, but the F.W.W. forced it up, by 1920, to £7,828,000,000, and the S.W.W., by 1945, to £21,870,221,651. By 1968 the figure stood at £33,484,000,000. Stocks were consolidated in 1750–7, the origin of the 3 per cent consols; a further consolidation was carried out by G. J. Goschen (q.v.), in 1888, interest being reduced to 2¾ per cent, and after 1903 to 2½. The U.S. Public Debt (as it is there called), $2,436,453,269 in 1870, was $1,132,357,095 in 1905, but had risen to $24,299,321,467 by 1920 and, although in 1930 it sank to $16,185,309,831, it has since then almost continually risen. In 1968 it was $347,578,406,426.

NATIONAL GALLERY. Art gallery housing the British national collection of pictures, founded in 1824, when parliament voted £57,000 for the purchase of 38 pictures of the Angerstein collection, plus £3,000 for the maintenance of the building in Pall Mall, London, where they were housed. The present building in Trafalgar Square was designed by William Wilkins, and opened in 1838: there have been several extensions. Works of living artists are excluded.

NATIONAL GUARD. *See* MILITIA.

NATIONALISM. A general term for movements aiming at the strengthening of national feeling and tradition, and particularly at the unification of a nation or its liberation from foreign rule. Under the influence of the French Revolution, strong movements arose in the 19th cent. in favour of national unification in Germany and Italy, and of national independence in Italy, Ireland, Belgium, Hungary, Bohemia, Poland, and the Balkan states, and remained a potent factor in European politics until 1918. Since 1900 N. has become a strong force in Asia and Africa. The term N. is also applied to the exaggerated expression of national pride, and to aggressive movements for national aggrandizement, e.g. imperialism and fascism; this represents a perversion of the outlook of the great 19th cent. nationalists.

A revival of interest in the national language, history, traditions, and culture has accompanied and influenced many political movements, e.g. in Ireland, Czechoslovakia, Poland, and Finland. In recent years a strongly national literary movement has developed in Scotland and Wales. N. in music usually takes the form of employing themes and rhythms derived from folk music, as in the works of Dvořák, Sibelius, and Vaughan Williams.

NATIONALIZATION. Policy of bringing essential services and industries under public ownership, pursued by the Labour Govt. which held office in the U.K. 1945–51. Acts were passed nationalizing the Bank of England, coal, and most hospitals (1946); transport and electricity (1947); gas (1948), and iron and steel (1949). In 1953 the succeeding Conser-

NATIONAL PARK. Mixed game, such as these zebra, blue wildebeest and impala, often graze together in big herds, especially at water holes or rivers. It is here that they are most vulnerable to attack, and the methods of defence peculiar to each can be combined for the common good.
Courtesy of The South African Information Service.

vative Govt. provided for the return of road haulage to private enterprise and decentralization of the railways; and denationalization of iron and steel – the last-named re-nationalized by Labour 1967. The term is also used for the taking over of assets in the hands of foreign govts. or cos. in the newly emergent countries, e.g. Abadan, Suez Canal.

NATIONAL LABOUR PARTY. *See* L.P.

NATIONAL LIBERALS. *See* LIBERAL PARTY.

NATIONAL PARKS. Areas set aside and protected from exploitation in order to preserve them for public enjoyment. In England and Wales under the N.P. Act (1949) the Peak District, Lake District, Snowdonia, Dartmoor, Pembrokeshire coast, Yorkshire Dales, Exmoor, and other areas of great natural beauty were designated as N.P. (*See also* NATURE RESERVE.) Port Hacking, N.S.W., Australia, near Sydney, is the chief N.P. in Australia. N.P. in the U.S.A. incl. Crater Lake, Oregon; the Grand Canyon, Arizona; the Mammoth Cave, Kentucky; Mt. McKinley, Alaska; Sequoia and Yosemite, California; and Zion Canyon, Utah. Of the 30 N.P. in Canada, the largest is Jasper (4,200 sq. m.), in the Rockies. Kruger N.P., 8,000 sq. m., established in 1898 as a game reserve (*see* illus.), and Natal N.P. are 2 notable S. African examples.

NATIONAL PHYSICAL LABORATORY. Estab. in 1900 at Teddington, England, the N.P.L. is a research establishment under the control of the Min. of Technology from 1965: the chairman of the visiting committee is the Pres. of the Royal Soc. Subjects studied come under 10 divisions: aerodynamics, applied physics, autonomics, chemical standards, light, mathematics, metallurgy, molecular science, ship, and standards, with special units for advanced instrumentation and inorganic materials.

NATIONAL PORTRAIT GALLERY. Art gallery in St. Martin's Place, Trafalgar Square, London, containing over 3,800 individual portraits of distinguished British men and women of the past, of which about one-third are exhibited in the public galleries. It was founded in 1856: present building opened in 1896.

NATIONAL RESEARCH DEVELOPMENT COUNCIL. Under the Development of Inventions Acts, 1948–65, it exploits inventions deriving from public or private sources, usually acting jointly with industrial firms.

NATIONAL SOCIALISM. *See* GERMANY; HITLER.

NATIONAL TRUST. A non-profit-making organization in Britain incorporated by Act of Parliament in 1895 for the purposes of promoting the permanent preservation of lands and buildings of historic interest or beauty for the people. It administers more than 210,000 acres, with over 1,000 properties.

NATIVITY. Name given to 3 Christian festivals: (1) Christmas; (2) the N. of the Virgin Mary, celebrated by the R.C. and Greek Churches on 8 Sept.; and (3) the N. of John the Baptist, celebrated by the R.C., Greek and Anglican Churches on 24 June.

NATTIER (nahtyā'), **Jean Marc** (1685–1766). French painter. B. in Paris. He painted Tsar Peter the Great in 1715, and is best known for his portraits of the artificial 'Ladies' of Louis XV's court.

NATURAL HISTORY MUSEUM. The 5 natural history departments of the British Museum: zoology, entomology, geology, mineralogy, and botany. The museum is in a building (designed by Waterhouse and erected 1873–80) in S. Kensington.

NATURE RESERVE. Area set aside to preserve its original scenic formation or vegetation, and often to provide a sanctuary and breeding ground for rare birds or animals. The National Parks Act, 1949, gave powers to designate such areas in Britain, to be placed in the charge of the Nature Conservancy estab. 1949.

NAU'CRATIS. Ancient Greek city in Egypt, whose ruins were discovered by Sir Flinders Petrie in 1884, situated in the W. extremity of the Nile delta.

NAURU (now'roo). Pacific island 26 m. S. of the equator in long. 167° E. Discovered in 1798, seized by Germany 1888, it was in 1920 placed under British Empire mandate by the League of Nations, in 1947 under U.N. trusteeship, Australia being the effective administrator except during Japanese occupation 1942–5. N. achieved independence 1968, becoming 'a special member' of the Commonwealth. N.'s importance is due to its phosphate deposits, which will be exhausted *c.* 1990. Area 8 sq. m.; pop. (1968) *c.* 3,000.

NAUSI'CAA. In the *Odyssey*, a daughter of Alcinous, king of Phaeacia, who welcomed Odysseus when he had been cast up by the waves on her island.

NAU'TILUS. Name applied to 2 widely differing cephalopods. The pearly N. (*Nautilus pompilius*), found in the Indo-Pacific Ocean, has a chambered spiral shell and supplies a fine quality mother-of-pearl used in inlay, etc.; the paper N. is also known as the Argonaut (q.v.).

NAVARINO (nahvahrē'nō). Italian and historic name of Pylos Bay, on the W. coast of Peloponnese, Greece, famous for a naval victory, the decisive action in the Greek war of liberation, won here in 1827 by the combined fleets of the English, French, and Russians under Codrington, over the Turkish and Egyptian fleets.

NAVARRE (navahr'). Mountainous prov. of N. Spain, the highest peak being Monte Adi (4,931 ft.). The principal rivers are the Ebro and its tributary the Arga. The cap. is Pamplona; Estella, 51 m. S.W., where Don Carlos was proclaimed king in 1833, is the centre of agitation by Carlists (q.v.) in favour of Don Carlos Hugo (*see* BOURBON TABLE), who m. Princess Irene, dau. of Queen Juliana (q.v.). An annual rally is held on nearby Montejurra mountain. Area 4,092 sq. m.; pop. (1960) 402,000.

This Spanish prov. is part of the old kingdom of N. which incl. also an area in present-day France. N. successfully resisted the Moorish conquerors of Spain and was independent until it became an appanage of the French crown, 1284–1316, by the marriage of Philip IV to the heiress of N. Ferdinand of Aragon annexed Spanish N., 1479, French N. going to Catherine of Foix who kept the royal title. Her grandson became Henry IV of France, and the ancient kingdom of N. was absorbed in the French crownlands in 1620.

NAVARRETE (nahvahrā'tā), **Juan Fernandez** (1526–79), surnamed *El Mudo* (the Mute). Spanish

painter. In 1568 he was appointed painter to Philip II and executed a number of pictures for the Escorial.

NAVE. In architecture, the central part of a church, between the choir and the entrance.

NAVEL. In anatomy, a round scar in the human abdomen, where the umbilical cord was attached until severed after birth.

NAVIGATION ACTS. A series of Acts passed from 1381 onwards, to protect the Eng. shipping industry against foreign competition. The best-known was that of 1651, forbidding the importation of any goods not carried in English ships or the ships of the country where the goods were produced; this was aimed against the Dutch, who controlled most of the carrying trade. The N.A. were repealed in 1849.

NAVY. A nation's warships and the organization to maintain them. Naval power was an important factor in the struggle for supremacy in the Mediterranean in the 5th cent. B.C., e.g. the defeat of Persia by Greece at Salamis, but the first permanent naval organization was estab. by Rome in 311 B.C. with the appointment of navy commissioners to safeguard trade routes from pirates and eliminate the threat of rival sea power. Next came Byzantine dominance until the Turkish invasions of the 12th cent. A.D., and during the Middle Ages the Italian city-states, e.g. Genoa, were influential. From Genoa came the admirals of the first French royal fleet, estab. by Louis IX in the 13th cent., and there was a great deal of cross-Channel raiding during the Hundred Years War (1339–1453) on the part of both sides. The English forces taking part had their origins in the fleet (a few king's ships, plus ships from the shires and a few privileged coastal towns) with which Alfred the Great overcame the Norsemen in 878. Building on the beginnings made by his father, Henry VIII raised a force which incl. a number of proper battleships, created the long-enduring administrative machinery of the Admiralty, and by mounting heavy guns low on a ship's side revolutionized strategy by the use of the 'broadside'. Often compelled to parsimony, Elizabeth yet encouraged Drake, Frobisher, Hawkins, Raleigh and others who were to set the seal on the decline of the great sea power of Spain, which had burgeoned in a great era of exploration and conquest in the early 16th cent., by their defeat of the Armada. In the 17th cent. there was a remarkable development in naval power among the powers of northern Europe, e.g. in the Netherlands, which then founded an empire in the East; in France, where a strong fleet was built up by Richelieu and Louis XIV which maintained the links with possessions in India and Canada; and in England, comparatively briefly under Cromwell. However, effectively reorganized by Pitt in time for the French revolutionary wars, the Royal

NAVY. The *Great Harry*, built by Henry VIII, the first double-decked English warship.

DESTROYER. First ship in the Royal Navy's 'County' class, the dual-purpose *Devonshire* is here seen entering Devonport. She has a displacement of more than 5,000 tons, is 520 ft. long, and is armed with a Seaslug surface-to-air guided-weapons system, two Seacat close-range weapons systems and four radar-controlled 4·5 inch guns in twin mountings. For anti-submarine work she has modern underwater detection equipment and embarks a 'hunter killer' Westland Wessex helicopter. *Crown Copyright.*

Navy under Nelson won a victory over the French at Trafalgar in 1805 which ensured British naval supremacy for the rest of the 19th cent.

In the New World the American navy owes its origin to the need for the more exposed provs. to protect their harbours at the outbreak of the War of Independence, and Washington's need to capture British war supplies. Late in 1775 Washington prepared 5 schooners and a sloop, manned with army personnel, and sent them to prey on inbound supply vessels, and by the time of the Declaration of Independence in 1776 these were augmented by armed brigs and sloops from the various colonies: the hero of the period was John Paul Jones. The fleet earned further distinction in actions against Tripoli 1803–5 and Britain 1812–14, and rapidly expanded during the Civil War and again for the Spanish War of 1898.

In the F.W.W. Britain fought off Germany's bid for naval power, but in the inter-war years the American fleet was developed to protect U.S. trade routes, and also with an eye to the renewed German threat and the new danger from Japan. *See* F.W.W. *and* S.W.W. After the S.W.W. the American fleet emerged as the world's most powerful, although the Soviet Union with the specialization in submarine warfare which its geographical situation renders almost inevitable is a serious contender for equality.

NAVY. U.S.S *Bainbridge*, world's first nuclear-powered guided-missile frigate. *Official U.S. Navy photograph.*

The future development of naval forces is suggested by the plans of the U.K. in 1967 to have Polaris nuclear submarines as the chief strike force; to phase out aircraft carriers and rely instead for support (in the same way as the Army) on R.A.F. land-based aircraft, and to introduce smaller frigates and destroyers, as well as a new class of cruiser, all equipped with surface-to-air guided missiles and helicopters carrying anti-submarine weapons and sonar. But, by 1969, the carrier's role as base seemed likely to be revived.

NAWANAGAR (nownu'gar). Former princely state of India, merged in Saurashtra (q.v.) in 1948. Its cap., Jamnagar (q.v.), is sometimes called N. The famous cricketer Ranjitsinhji (q.v.) was its maharajah.

NAXALITES (nak'salīts). Indian extremist Communists, so-named from the town of Naxalbari, W. Bengal, where a peasant rising was suppressed 1967. Their leader Kanu Sanyal, was released 1969 and terrorist activities continued.

NAXOS (naks'os). An island of Greece, the largest of the Cyclades. Famous since early times for its wine, it was a centre for the worship of Bacchus, who found the deserted Ariadne asleep on its shore. Area 175 sq. m.; pop. 17,000.

NA'ZARETH. A town of Galilee, Israel, famous as the place where Jesus spent his boyhood.

NAZARITE or **Nazirite**. A Hebrew under a vow, who in ancient times observed certain rules until it was fulfilled, e.g. not to cut his hair or to drink wine. Samson and Samuel were Ns. for life.

NAZE, The. Headland on the coast of Essex, England, 5 m. S. of Harwich.

NAZIS (nah'tsēz). German Fascist Party. The name is derived from the first two syllables, as pronounced in German, of the full name, *Nationalsozialistiche Deutsche Arbeiterpartei* (National Socialist German Workers' Party). Related were the movements founded in Britain by Sir Oswald Mosley (q.v.) and Colin Jordan (Nat. Socialist Movement 1962), and in U.S.A. by George Lincoln Rockwell (American Nazi Party 1958) who was assassinated 1967, allegedly by a party 'officer'. *See* FASCISM.

NEAGH (nā), **Lough.** Lake in N. Ireland, the largest in the British Isles (153 sq. m.).

NEAGLE, Dame Anna (1908–   ). Brit. actress. B. at Forest Gate, Essex, she was successful as a dancer and in roles as varied as Nell Gwynn (1934), Victoria the Great (1937), and Odette (1950). D.B.E. 1969.

NEALE (nēl), **Sir John** (1890–   ). British historian. Astor prof. of English history at London 1927–56, he specializes in the Tudor period, e.g. *Queen Elizabeth* (1934) and *Elizabeth I and Her Parliaments* (1953–7).

NEALE, John Mason (1818–66). Anglican churchman, famous as a translator of ancient and medieval hymns, incl. 'Jerusalem, the Golden'.

NEANDERTHAL (-tahl) **MAN.** A species of man of the Palaeolithic period. The name is derived from the locality in the Rhineland where the first skeleton was discovered in 1857. This type of man was much more ape-like than any existing race, though the brain-case was large enough to contain a well-developed brain. It is believed that N.M. became extinct through interbreeding with modern man.

NEAR EAST. Geographical term applied to the regions of Asia and Africa shown on the map opposite. During the S.W.W. the expression Middle East was applied to the same area.

NEATH (nēth). Market town (bor.) in Glamorganshire, S. Wales, situated nr. the mouth of the r. Neath. It contains the remains of a castle, destroyed 1231, and a Cistercian abbey, and has steelworks, foundries and other industries. Nearby is the Roman fort Nidum, discovered 1949. Pop. (1961) 30,884.

NEBRA'SKA. A north-central state of the U.S.A., bounded on the N. by S. Dakota, and on the W. by Wyoming and Colorado. In the W. are the foothills of the Rocky Mountains, rising to over 5,000 ft.; then

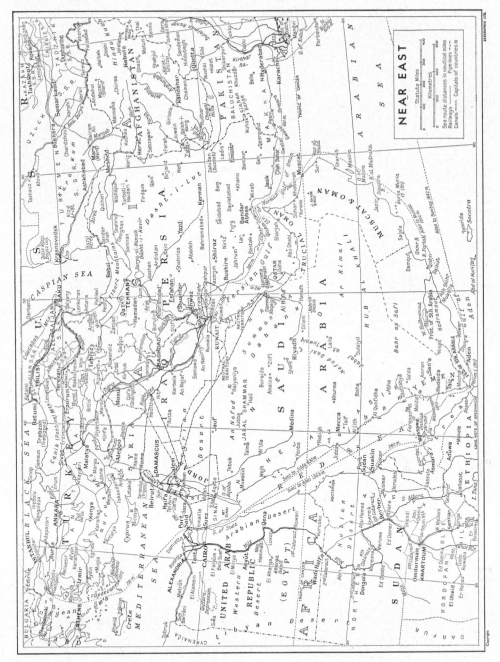

NEAR EAST

Statute Miles
Kilometres
Sea route distances in nautical miles
Railways ——— Pipelines ———
Canals ——— Capitals of countries ⊚

come sandhills now stable and grass-covered; the
prairies, whose fertility is very high, slope to the
Missouri, whose tributaries, White, Platte, and
Niobrara, with the Big Blue, tributary of the Republican, are the chief rivers. The crops incl. maize,
wheat, oats, barley, etc., livestock are important, and
the chief industry is food processing, but fertilizers,

and oil and natural gas are also produced. B. was
purchased by the U.S.A. from France in 1803, and it
became a state of the Union in 1867. Area 77,237
sq. m.; pop. (1970) 1,483,791.

NEBUCHADNEZZAR (nebukadnez'ar) II, or
Nebuchadrezzar (d. 562 B.C.). King of Babylonia.
Shortly before his accession in 604 B.C. he defeated

NEBULA. Hubble's variable nebula, n Monoceros (the Unicorn), is associated with a variable star. Naturally, the appearance of the nebula changes according to the brightness of the star which illuminates it.
Courtesy of Lick Observatory, Univ. of California.

the Egyptians at Carchemish and brought Palestine and Syria into his empire. Judah revolted, with Egyptian assistance, in 596 and 587–586 B.C.; on each occasion N. captured Jerusalem and carried off many of the Jews into captivity. N. largely rebuilt Babylon, constructed the famous Hanging Gardens, and carried out ambitious irrigation schemes.

NE'BULA. A luminous patch in the night sky, composed of thinly spread gas and dust. The most famous N. lies below the Belt of Orion, and is clearly visible to the naked eye; large numbers of similar objects may be seen with the aid of telescopes. It is thought that these nebulae are the birthplaces of the stars, and that fresh stars are being created all the time out of the nebular material. A N. shines because of the stars contained in it; if there are no suitable stars, the N. is *dark*, but may be traced because it blocks out the light of stars lying beyond. The 18th cent. astronomer Messier catalogued over 100 nebular objects, incl. true nebulae; *planetary nebulae*, now known to be stars with extensive gaseous surrounds; and *resolvable* or starry nebulae, now known to be galaxies in their own right, and to lie far beyond the boundaries of our own star-system or galaxy.

NECK. The structures between the head and the trunk. Its bones are the upper 7 (cervical) vertebrae, it comprises many powerful muscles which support and move the head, and in front it contains the pharynx and wind-pipe (trachea), and behind these the gullet (oesophagus). Within it are the large arteries (carotid, temporal, maxillary), and veins (jugular), which supply the brain and head.

NECKER, Jacques (1732–1804). French statesman. B. at Geneva, he made a fortune in Paris as a banker. As Finance Minister, 1776–81, he attempted to introduce certain reforms, and was dismissed through Marie Antoinette's influence. Recalled to office in 1788, he persuaded Louis XVI to summon the States-General; this earned him the hatred of the court, and in July 1789 he was banished. The storming of the Bastille forced Louis to reinstate him, but in Sept. 1790 he resigned and retired to Switzerland. *See* MME DE STAEL.

NE'CTAR. The drink of the Greek gods.

NECTARINE (-ēn or -in). A smooth-skinned peach, usually smaller than other peaches, with firmer flesh.

NEEDLES, The. The name given to a group of rocks lying off the W. extremity of the Isle of Wight, England. On the most westerly, 100 ft. high, is the N. lighthouse. *See* illus., p. 581.

NEFERTITI (-tē'tē) or **Nofretiti** (14th cent. B.C.). Egyptian queen, favourite wife of Ikhnaton (q.v.). She bore 6 daus., and is frequently represented with her husband and children; her name does not appear on monuments later in the reign but it is more probable that she d. than that she was disgraced. The portrait head found at Amarna in 1912 ranks as one of the world's masterpieces, but may be that of one of her daus.

NEGEV. Desert area in S. Israel, lying between Beersheba, where it is *c.* 40 m. wide, and the Gulf of Aqaba, where it tapers to the port of Eilat; *c.* 120 m. long; area *c.* 4,700 sq. m. In ancient times the N. was fertile, and Israel has developed the irrigation begun in the 1930s, notably with a water pipeline (1964) from the Sea of Galilee (Lake Kinnereth). Minerals being exploited incl. oil (1955) at Heletz and copper at Timna, near Eilat. N. is a Hebrew word meaning south or arid.

NEGEV. A giant irrigation pipe.
Courtesy of the Israeli Govt.

NEGLIGENCE. In law, N. consists in doing some act which a prudent and reasonable man would not do, or omitting to do some act which he would do. N. may arise in respect of a person's duty towards an individual or towards his fellow-men in general. In the first class are such duties as arise from parenthood, guardianship, trusteeship, or a contractual relationship. In the second are the duties owed to the community, such as care upon the public highway, the maintenance of structures in a safe condition, etc. Contributory N. is a defence sometimes raised where the defendant to an action for N. claims that the plaintiff by his own N. contributed to the cause of the action.

NEGRI'N, Juan (1889–1956). Spanish Socialist. A one-time prof. of physiology at Madrid, during the Civil War he became Finance Min. in Sept. 1936, and in May 1937 P.M. of the cabinet which conducted the war for the next 2 years. His govt. was overthrown in March 1939 by a military coup d'état, which was shortly followed by the final Republican surrender. N. escaped to France, and thence to England.

NE'GRI SEMBILAN (sembē'lan). State of the Federation of Malaysia, on the W. side of the Malay peninsula. It came under British rule in 1873 and entered the Federated Malay States in 1895. Its cap. is Seremban, its harbour Port Dickson. The chief

NEGRI SEMBILAN. Most of Malaysia's major cities have a botanical garden. This beautiful lake garden at Seremban is a popular weekend attraction for families.
Courtesy Malaysian Govt.

exports are tin, rubber, oil palm, and coconuts. Area 2,550 sq. m.; pop. (1966) 503,323.

NEGRO. A member of the Negroid race: with Caucasoids and Mongoloids one of the 3 main human racial groups. Ns. are mainly found in Africa S. of the Sahara and incl. the S. and Central African pygmies (Negrilloes), but also in the East, e.g., the Indian, S E. Asian and Indonesian pygmies (Negritoes) and the Melanesian Negroids (New Guinea to the Fiji Is.). Ns. of African – espec. W. African – descent are distributed from the 16th cent. as a result of the slave trade in S., Central and N. America.

Characteristic of most Ns. are broad, short nose; high cheek bones; thick, everted lips; black, wiry hair of elliptical section, often short and curly; above average height; and a dark brown skin pigmentation – also shared with some Indian Caucasoids, Australian aborigines, etc. A quadroon is of $\frac{3}{4}$ Caucasoid or Mongoloid blood and $\frac{1}{4}$ Negroid; and an octoroon is $\frac{7}{8}$ Caucasoid or Mongoloid and $\frac{1}{8}$ Negroid: *see also* MULATTO.

The American Ns. comprise the largest single racial group in the U.S.A., *c.* 22,000,000 or approx. 10 per cent of the pop. Of these only 25 per cent – as a result of intermarriage, etc. – are still pure N., and they have adopted the language and usually a non-conformist or revivalist type of Christianity. Formerly almost exclusively employed on cotton and tobacco plantations in the Atlantic and S. Central states, they moved in large numbers to the N. after both world wars to ease the industrial labour shortage, and cities such as N.Y. and Chicago have a large N. population. Particularly after the S.W.W. there have been widespread efforts by Ns. and their supporters to end racial discrimination with some degree of success, e.g. desegregation in schools, buses and restaurants in the S. However, progress is slow and even in the N. educ., housing, employment opportunities, etc., tend to be less for them, with the result that, perhaps inspired by the emergence of the new African states, there are movements such as that of the Black Moslems (q.v.). A report (1968) by Johnson's Nat. Advisory Commission concluded that 'Our nation is moving towards two societies, one Black, one White – separate and unequal', but that it was not too late to reverse the trend, e.g. the Civil Rights Act (1968) protecting the exercise of civil rights by N. in housing, education, employment, jury service, franchise, and use of public facilities. *See* BLACK POWER. For distinctively N. contributions to world culture, *see* AFRICAN NEGRO ART AND JAZZ.

NEHEMI'AH. Jewish statesman, who was appointed governor of Judaea by the king of Persia, rebuilt the walls of Jerusalem, and carried out religious and social reforms. Some scholars date his appointment in 445–444 B.C., others in 384 B.C. His memoirs are incorporated in the O.T. book of N.

NEHRU (nä'rōō), Jawaharlal (1889–1964). Indian statesman. He was b. at Allahabad, the son of Motilal N., a wealthy lawyer who adopted strong Nationalist views. Educ. at Harrow and Cambridge, he practised from 1912 at the Allahabad Bar, and soon became prominent in the Congress Party as the leader of its Socialist left wing, acquiring an influence second only to Gandhi's. During 1921–45 he was imprisoned 9 times for his political activities. He became For. Min. in the interim govt. set up in Sept. 1946, and P.M. on the creation of the Dom. (later

J. NEHRU
Courtesy of the Indian Govt.

Rep.) of India in Aug. 1947. In 1951–4 he was also pres. of the Congress Party (a post in which he had succeeded his father in 1929, and had also held in 1936, 1937, and 1946). N. was the author of several distinguished literary works, notably *Glimpses of World History* (1934), and an autobiography (1936). His influence over the country remained strong as ever until his death. The *J.N.Award for International Understanding* (1966) of 100,000 rupees is awarded annually to individuals not organisations.

His dau. **Indira** (1917–) studied at Oxford, and was imprisoned during the struggle for independence. In 1942 she m. Feroze Gandhi (not related to the Mahatma), and acted as hostess for her father from 1947. In 1966 she succeeded Shastri as P.M. and leader of the Congress Parliamentary Party.

NEILL (nēl), Alexander Sutherland (1883–). British educationist. He worked as a teacher and journalist before founding the International School, Hellerau, Dresden, in 1921, of which his division was later transferred 1st to Austria then to England (Summerhill at Leiston, Suffolk). Famed for his progressive views, he has written *The Problem Child* (1926), *The Problem Parent* (1932), *Summerhill* (1962).

NEISSE (nīs'e). Tributary of the r. Oder in E. Europe, 140 m. long. It rises in the Iser Mountains, Czechoslovakia, and flows generally N. It marks the S. part of the boundary set up in 1945 between E. Germany and Polish-occupied Germany. Another trib. of the Oder, the Glatzer Neisse (Polish Nysa Kluz), lies 110 m. farther E. On its banks is the town of N. (Polish Nysa), from which the German pop. were expelled in 1945; it was cap. of the prince-bishops of Breslau (Wroclaw) from 1198–1810.

NEJD. Region of central Arabia consisting chiefly of desert. It forms part of the kingdom of Saudi Arabia, and is inhabited by Bedouins. The cap. is Riyadh. Area *c.* 800,000 sq. m.; pop. *c.* 4,000,000.

NEKRASOV (nyekrah'sof), Victor (1911–). Ukrainian writer. A journalist, after the S.W.W. he became well known for his book *In the Trenches of Stalingrad* (1946). He later received much hostile criticism for his balanced account of his visits to Italy and the U.S.A. *Both Sides of the Ocean* (1962).

NELSON, Horatio, viscount (1758–1805). British admiral. He was b. at Burnham Thorpe, Norfolk, where his father was rector, and entered the navy in 1770. While serving in the W. Indies he m. Mrs. Frances Nisbet. He was almost continuously on active service in the Mediterranean 1793–1800 and as a result of wounds he lost his right eye in 1794 and his right arm in 1797. His share in the victory off Cape St. Vincent in 1797 made him a national hero, and was rewarded by promotion to rear-admiral.

In 1798 he tracked the French fleet to Aboukir Bay, and almost entirely destroyed it in the Battle of the Nile. He then lingered at Naples for a year, during which he helped to crush a democratic uprising, and fell completely under the influence of Lady Hamilton (q.v.). In 1800 he returned to England, and soon after separated from his wife. He was promoted to vice-admiral in 1801, and sent to the Baltic to operate against the Danes, nominally as second-in-command; in fact, it was N. who was responsible for the victory of Copenhagen, and for negotiating peace with Denmark. On his return to England he was created a visct.

In 1803 he received the Mediterranean command,

HORATIO NELSON
Photo: N.P.G.

and for nearly 2 years blockaded Toulon. When in 1805 Villeneuve eluded him, N. pursued him to the W. Indies and back, and on 21 Oct. totally defeated the combined French and Spanish fleets off Cape Trafalgar, 20 of the enemy ships being captured. N. himself was mortally wounded; his body was brought to England, and buried in St. Paul's.

NELSON. English industrial town (bor.) in Lancs, about 24 m. N. of Manchester. Pop. (1961) 31,950.

NELSON. Town in South Is., New Zealand, situated on Tasman Bay, with an excellent harbour. It has an airport, saw mills, fruit-canning plants, etc. Pop. (1967) 28,100.

NE'MATODA. Phylum covering round or thread worms.

NEME'RTEA. A group of unsegmented worms, allied to the Platyhelminthes. They are ribbon-shaped and mostly marine.

NE'MESIS. Greek goddess of retribution. She punished certain moral faults, esp. *hybris*, the arrogant self-confidence which, more than other crimes, excited the hostility of the gods.

NEMI (nā'mē). Lake occupying an extinct volcanic crater in the Alban Hills, some 18 m. S.E. of Rome, near Aricia. Nearby are the sacred woods and ruins of a famous temple of Diana. Two pleasure barges belonging to Caligula were raised from the bed of the lake, 1930–1; they were burned by the Germans in 1944. A village called N. stands on a hill above the lake, pop. 1,200.

NENNIUS (fl. 796). Welsh chronicler, believed to be the author of a Latin *Historia Britonum*, which contains the earliest reference to King Arthur's wars against the Saxons.

NEOLITHIC or **New Stone Age.** *See* STONE AGE.

NEON (Gk. *neos* new). Chemically inert gas, discovered by Ramsay and Travers in 1898: symbol Ne, at. wt. 20·183, at. no. 10. Present in the atmosphere in the proportion 18 parts per million by volume, it is extracted by liquefaction and fractional distillation. It glows bright orange-red in a discharge tube, e.g. its use in advertisement signs. N. is also used in electronics.

NEO-PLASTICISM. A geometric-abstract movement in painting, sculpture, poster design, and interior decoration, founded by Piet Mondrian.

NEO-PLATONISM. Philosophical system, based on the doctrines of Plato and beliefs adopted from Oriental religions, which developed in the 3rd cent. at Alexandria, and was 1st fully expounded by Plotinus. Its principal doctrine is the attainment of unity with the Deity through purifying ascetic practices. Under Porphyry, N. became the great opponent of Christianity, and its supremacy was almost secured by the advocacy of the emperor Julian. It ceased to exist as an independent system in the 6th cent., but it greatly influenced Augustine, and the whole tradition of Christian mysticism.

NEPAL (nepawl'). An independent kingdom in the Himalayas, bounded on the N. by Tibet, on the E. by Sikkim, and on the S. and W. by India. It is composed of the Tarai, a level strip of land along its S. border, and the Himalayan slopes to the N. culminating in Everest (29,028 ft.), Kanchenjunga (28,146 ft.), and other immense border peaks, which determine the courses of the 4 groups of rivers that divide the country. Katmandu, the cap., stands in the chief valley; it is linked by air with Calcutta. The people are mixed Mongols, Gurkhas (q.v.) being dominant. Sanatan, an ancient form of Hinduism, and Buddhism are the prevailing religions. The effective ruler of N. from 1846 was the hereditary P.M. always a member of the Ráná family; a revolution in 1950 restored power to the king, and a new constitution (1962) provided for a single-chamber national panchayat (council), indirectly elected by local panchayats. All political parties are banned, but under stress of pro-Chinese Communist activities, the Nepali Congress dropped 1968 the demand for democratic govt. Major hydro-electric projects power new industries, e.g. chemicals, leather goods, synthetic textiles, iron and steel, and jute and sugar. India and U.S.A. are aiding construction of a 640 m. E.-W. highway. Area 54,000 sq. m.; pop. (1967) 10,500,000.

NEPHRITIS. Inflammation of the substance of the kidney; Bright's disease. It is sometimes due to cold or pregnancy, but more commonly to infection by a streptococcus, the colon bacillus, or tuberculosis. The 1st symptoms are usually dropsy, an accumulation of fluid under the skin all over the body, back pain, and fever. The degree of illness varies; it may be quickly fatal or not very incapacitating. The principal complication is uraemia (q.v.). Treatment is by rest, purgation, and vapour baths.

NE'PTUNE. Roman god of the sea. Most of his myths are borrowed from the Greek stories of Poseidon. According to these, N., Zeus (Jupiter), and Hades (Pluto), the sons of Cronus, dethroned their father and divided his realms, N. taking the sea.

NEPTUNE. The outermost of the giant planets. It is 2,793,000,000 miles from the Sun, and has a revolution period of 164·8 years. Its diameter is 30,500 miles, and in every respect it seems to be similar to Uranus; it is however considerably fainter, and is not visible to the naked eye. N. was discovered in 1846 by J. Galle and H. d'Arrest at Berlin, after calculations by U. Le Verrier (Fr.) and J. C. Adams (Brit.) indicated its probable position. The surface temperature has been est. at −184°C, and the atmosphere appears turbulent. There is an outer satellite with a very eccentric orbit, and an inner one – Triton – which revolves in a retrograde direction at about the same distance as the Moon from Earth.

NEPTU'NIUM. Transuranic element, symbol Np, at. wt. 237, at. no. 93. It is produced in atomic reactors as an intermediate in making plutonium. U-238 absorbs a neutron to become U-239 which emits a beta-ray from its nucleus thus turning into Np-239 with a half-life of 2·3 days.

NEREIDS (nē'rē-ids). In Greek mythology, minor goddesses of the sea, one of the classes of nymphs. They sometimes mated with mortals, as in the case of Thetis, who bore Achilles.

NE'RGAL. A Babylonian and Assyrian sun-god; he was also the god of war and pestilence, and ruler of the underworld. He was symbolized in sculpture by a winged lion.

NERI, St. Philip (1515–95). Italian ecclesiastic. B. in Florence, in 1533 he went to Rome, where he devoted himself to good works. Ordained a priest in 1551, he organized the Congregation of the Oratory, and built the oratory over the church of St. Jerome, where prayer meetings were held, and scenes from the Bible were performed with music – hence *oratorio*. He was canonized in 1622.

NERINA (nerē'na), **Nadia.** Professional name of S. African dancer Nadine Judd (1927–). With the Royal Ballet 1952–69, she possessed lyric fluency, excelling in roles such as Aurora in *The Sleeping Beauty*

NERO (A.D. 37–68). Roman emperor, whose full name was N. Claudius Caesar Dr sus Germanicus. The son of Domitius Ahenobarbus and Agrippina, he was adopted by his stepfather, Cla udius, and succeeded him as emperor in 54. He has become proverbial for cruelty and debauchery, and is said to have murdered Claudius's son, Britannicus, his mother, his wives, Octavia and Poppaea, and many others. He was a poet and an enthusiast for art, and himself appeared on the public stage as an actor and singer. After the great fire of Rome in 64, he persecuted the Christians, who were suspected of causing it, while an aristocratic conspiracy against him in 65 led to the execution or suicide of Seneca, Lucan, and many others. A military revolt followed in 68; the senate condemned N. to death, whereupon he committed suicide.

NE′RUDA, Jan (1834–91). Czech poet. B. in Prague, the leading Czech writer of his day, he pub. *Cosmic Songs* and *Ballads and Romances* (1883), lyrics of great charm. His *Tales of the Malá Strana* (1878) are stories of Prague life.

NERUDA, Pablo. Pseudonym of Chilean poet Neftalí Ricardo Reyes (1904–). A widely travelled diplomat, he ranges in his verse from the intimate lyric, e.g. *Veinte poemas de amor y una canción desesperada* (1924), to an epic treatment of the history of the American continent *Canto General* (1950).

NERVA, Marcus Cocceius (c. A.D. 35–98). Roman emperor. He was a senator who was proclaimed emperor on Domitian's death in 96, and proved a humane ruler. He introduced state schemes for loans for farmers and family allowances, and an agrarian law for the allotment of land to poor citizens.

NERVAL (nervahl′), **Gérard de.** Adopted name of French Romantic poet Gérard Labrunie (1808–55). He pub. short stories, plays, poems, translations, and the semi-autobiographical romance, *Sylvia* (1848–50). He lived a wandering life, darkened by periodic insanity, and committed suicide.

NERVES. The highly specialized cells with their processes through which all the activities of the body are initiated and controlled. The bodies of the cells form most of the grey matter of the brain and spinal cord (central nervous system); long, fine fibres (axons) run out and branch from these to all parts of the body. One set of Ns. transmits the commands of the will to the muscles (motor), another transmits the sensations from the skin, eyes, ears, digestive system, etc. (peripheral nerves), to the brain (sensory). Much of the work of the Ns. is automatic, and never comes into consciousness at all (autonomic nervous system).

NE′RVI, Pier Luigi (1891–). Italian engineer and architect. Partner in an engineering firm since 1932, he believes in the unity of builder and architect, and was prof. of the technology and technique of construction at Rome (1946–61). Among his most striking works are the National Stadium in Rome (in collaboration with his son Antonio N., 1959) and Field House for Dartmouth College, U.S.A.

NESBIT, Edith (1858–1924). British writer, best remembered for her children's books, e.g. *The Treasure-Seekers* (1899), *The Would-be Goods* (1901) and *Five Children and It* (1902). Her creation of the Bastable family was a notable departure from the conven-

NERVI. One of the most striking examples of modern Italian architecture is the Palace of Labour, Turin, of which the interior is seen here. It was designed jointly by Pier Luigi Nervi and Antonio Nervi, the steel structure being the work of G. Covre. *Courtesy of Studio Nervi.*

NETHERLANDS. Gay national costumes, painted clogs and an ice dance-floor at Marken.
Courtesy of the Netherlands National Tourist Office.

tional, class-conscious mode of the period. She m. the Fabian Hubert Bland (d. 1914), in 1880, her writing being the mainstay of the marriage, and had 4 children.

NESS, Loch. Lake in Inverness-shire, Scotland, 23 m. long, average width 1 m., forming part of the Caledonian Canal. It is surrounded by mountains rising to 2,284 ft. in Mealfourvorie. From 1933 onwards reports of a 'monster' said to have been seen in L.N. were pub.; sceptics offered various suggestions as a possible explanation of the phenomenon.

NESTŌ′RIUS (d. c. 451). Syrian ecclesiastic. Appointed patriarch of Constantinople in 428, he maintained that Mary was the mother of the man Jesus only, and therefore should not be called the 'Mother of God'. This doctrine was condemned by the council of Ephesus in 431, and N. was deposed and banished. His followers, the NESTORIANS, estab. a powerful Church in Syria and Persia, and successfully carried on missionary work in India, N. China, and all over central Asia. They still survive as the Assyrian Church in Syria, Iraq, Persia, etc., and as the Christians of St. Thomas in S. India.

NETHERLANDS. Kingdom of W. Europe, bounded on the N. and W. by the North Sea, on the S. by Belgium, and on the E. by Germany. It is often referred to as Holland, the name of its two wealthiest provs., N. and S. Holland.

PHYSICAL FEATURES. The flatness of the N. is proverbial. Only in S. Gelderland, near the German border, and in Limburg are there any hills, the highest part of the country, rising to c. 1,000 ft., being in S. Limburg. Much land has been wrested from the sea and is below sea-level, esp. in N. and S. Holland; some of the polders, or drained lands, lie 21 ft. below sea-level. A noteworthy feature is the extensive and fertile delta formed by the Rhine and the Maas (Meuse) and their distributaries. Other important rivers are the Ijssel, draining to the Ijsselmeer, and the Scheldt estuary. Off the coast are 2 groups of is.: in the S., Over Flakkee, Schouwen, Tholen, Noord and Zuid Beveland, and Walcheren; in the N. the West Frisian Is. incl. Texel, Vlieland, Terschelling, Ameland, Schiermonnikoog, and Rottumeroog. When plans of reclamation are completed, both groups will form part of the mainland. Reclamation of the former Zuider Zee (q.v.), started in 1920, has already added more than 120,000 acres of cultivable land to the country; and the southern part of the ambitious Delta plan to shut off from the sea the river estuaries of S. Holland and Zeeland – a scheme launched to prevent a repetition of the disastrous sea floods of 1953 which killed

1,800 people and ruined for several years acres of fertile soil—has been completed, linking Walcheren with N. and S. Beveland. The E. Scheldt Bridge (1965) linking Noord-Beveland and Schouwen-Duiveland is Europe's longest, and an integral part of the plan. The whole Delta scheme, with a sea wall linking Walcheren in the S. to a point W. of Rotterdam in the N., was planned for completion by 1978.

ECONOMIC LIFE. Both industry and agriculture are thriving. Agriculture concentrates on cattle breeding and the export of cheese, butter, flower bulbs, and vegetables. The chief crops are rye, potatoes, oats, and sugar beet. Industrial activities incl. shipbuilding; the manufacture of textiles, earthenware, cigars, spirits, paper, electrical equipment, margarine, chemicals; iron and steel goods; the cutting and polishing of diamonds, etc.; refining of petroleum. Coal is mined in Limburg; petroleum (discovered in 1943) is worked; salt is extracted at Hengelo in Overijssel; a huge deposit of natural gas, discovered in 1962, exists in Groningen. Shipping and fishing are of great importance, and there is a large trade with Germany, Belgium, and the U.K. Amsterdam and Rotterdam are among the most important commercial centres of Europe.

The N. is covered by a network of canals, the larger constructed as a means of transport, many others (some very small) used for drainage. The North Sea Canal (linking Amsterdam with the N. Sea), and the New Waterway (running between Rotterdam and the Hook of Holland), can take ocean-going vessels. The state-controlled railways are electrified. Dutch airlines cover the whole world.

AREA AND POPULATION. Area 13,551 sq. m.; incl. gulfs and bays, 15,771 sq. m.: pop. (1968) 12,676,000, incl. some 300,000 Eurasians of Dutch-Indonesian blood, as well as Amboinese soldiers in the Dutch service, who were absorbed 1949–64. The main towns are Amsterdam (the commercial cap.), Rotterdam, The Hague (the admin. cap., chief residence of the royal family, and seat of parliament and the govt.), Utrecht, Haarlem, Eindhoven, Groningen, Tilburg, and Nijmegen. The Roman Catholics form the largest single religious group, and preponderate in the S., but over the whole of the country they are outnumbered by Protestants, the majority of whom are members of the Dutch Reformed Church, to which the royal family belongs; Calvinists are also numerous. The standard of educ. is high. There are 5 public univs., at Leiden (1575), Groningen (1614), Utrecht (1636), Amsterdam (1877), and Rotterdam (1966); 2 religious and 6 technical.

GOVERNMENT. The N. is a constitutional monarchy under the house of Orange. Legislative powers are exercised by the 2 chambers of the States-General, and there is also an advisory Council of State under the presidency of the sovereign. Members of the 1st (upper) chamber (Senators) are elected for 6 years (half retiring every 3 years) by the members of the provincial states; members of the 2nd chamber (Deputies) are directly elected for 4 years by universal suffrage on a system of proportional representation.

For the history and status of the Dutch colonial empire, see INDONESIA; NETHERLANDS ANTILLES; NETHERLANDS EAST INDIES; NEW GUINEA; SURINAM.

History. In Roman times the country S. of the Rhine was brought under Roman rule. The Franks followed, and their kings subdued the Frisians and Saxons N. of the Rhine in the 7th–8th cents., and imposed Christianity on them. After the break-up of the Frankish Empire the local feudal lords, headed by the count of Holland and the bishop of Utrecht, achieved practical independence, although nominally owing allegiance to the Holy Roman Empire. Many Dutch towns during the Middle Ages became prosperous trading centres, usually ruled by a merchant oligarchy. In the 15th cent. the whole of the Low Countries (present-day N. and Belgium) passed to the dukes of Burgundy, and thence to the Habsburgs and Spain.

In the 16th cent. the religious and secular tyranny of Philip II of Spain led to general revolt in the whole of the Netherlands, in which William the Silent, Prince of Orange (1533–84), and his sons Maurice (1567–1625) and Frederick Henry (1584–1647) were the guiding spirits. The south was re-conquered by Spain, but not the north, and at last in 1648 the independence of the north as the Dutch Rep. was recognized under the Treaty of Westphalia (or Munster), The rep., estab. in 1581 as the United Provs., was a confederacy of sovereign provs., and it had become customary to elect the Prince of Orange for the time-being as chief officer (Stadholder) and commander-in-chief for the confederacy. A long struggle took place between the Orangist or popular party, which favoured centralization, and the oligarchical or 'states' rights' party. The oligarchs, headed by De Witt, seized control in 1650, after the death of Frederick Henry, and abolished the stadholderate. Despite the continuing war of independence, during the early 17th cent. the Dutch led the world in trade, in art and in science, and founded an empire in the E. and W. Indies. Commercial and colonial rivalries led to naval wars with England in 1652–4, 1665–7, and 1672–4.

The French invasion of 1672 enabled William of Orange (William III of England) to recover the stadholderate, and thenceforward until 1713 Dutch history was dominated by the struggle with Louis XIV. These wars exhausted the N., which in the 18th cent. ceased to be a great power. The French revolutionary army was welcomed in 1795. In 1806 Napoleon created his brother Louis king of Holland, and in 1810 annexed the country to France. In 1814 the north and south Netherlands were once more united under King William I (son of Prince William V of Orange); but the S. broke away and in 1839 was recognized as independent (see under BELGIUM). A liberal constitution was granted in 1814, and the Crown assumed a constitutional position. The sovereigns have been: William I (reigned 1814–40), William II (1840–9), William III (1849–90), Queen Wilhelmina (1890–1948), and Queen Juliana, who succeeded on her mother's abdication in 1948. Universal suffrage was granted in 1917. The N. were occupied by the Germans 1940–5, while Queen Wilhelmina and her govt. took refuge in London.

Art. With the rise of the Dutch nation in the second half of the 16th cent. came the full emergence of Dutch art with Frans Hals, Pieter Lastman (1585–1633) – the teacher of Rembrandt – and Gerard van Honthorst. Among the many masters of the 17th cent. are Rembrandt and his pupil Gerard Douw; Adriaen van Ostade, who transplanted Flemish peasant scenes; Gerard Ter Borch the Younger, first painter of characteristic Dutch interiors; Albert Cuyp; Jan Steen; Jakob van Ruysdael, greatest of the landscapists; Pieter de Hooch; Jan Vermeer van Delft; Willem van de Velde, sea painter to Charles II of England; Jan van der Heyden; and Meindert Hobbema. The houses, market and town halls of this period were also a consummate expression of the Dutch genius.

In the 18th and 19th cents. there was a marked decline, except for the genre painters Cornelis Troost (1697–1750) and Jozef Israels (1824–1911), and the outstanding genius of Vincent van Gogh.

Language. A branch of the West Germanic, or, more specially, the German division of the Germanic languages (q.v.), and like Flemish (q.v.) an offshoot of Low Franconian, which is known from c. 800. D. is the official language of the Netherlands, whence it spread to the D. colonies; whilst in S. Africa 'Cape Dutch' developed into a language of its own, called Afrikaans (q.v.).

Literature. Earliest known poet to use the Dutch dialect was Henric van Veldeke (12th cent.), but the finest example of early Gothic literature is *Van Den Vos Reinaarde* (About Reynard the Fox) by a poet known only as 'Willem-who-made-the-Madoc'. To the Golden Age belong Pieter C. Hooft (1581–1647), lyricist, playwright and historian; Constantijn Huygens (1596–1687), who was knighted by James I in 1622; Gerbrand A. Bredero (1585–1618), gifted in comedy and light verse; the great lyric, satiric and dramatic poet Joost van den Vondel (1587–1679), and the moralizing poet Father Jacob Cats (1577–1660). As in art, the 18th cent. was generally a period of decline, although the epic poet Willem Bilderdijk (1756–1831) ranks high. The Romantic movement found its fullest expression in the nationalist periodical *De Gids* (The Guide) founded in 1837. Among the best-known writers of the period were Nicolas Beets (1814–1903), with his famous sketches *Camera Obscura*, and Eduard Douwes Dekker (1820–87), who wrote novels under the pseudonym 'Multatuli' and was a forerunner of the movement grouped round a second periodical *De Nieuwe Gids* (The New Guide, estab. 1885) which marked the late 19th cent. revival. Among writers of the period were lyricist Herman Gorter (1864–1927), the staider poet Albert Verwey (1865–1937), the poet, playwright and novelist Frederick van Eeden (1860–1932), the novelists Louis Couperus (1863–1923), Marcellus Emants (1848–1923), and Arthur van Schendel (1874–1946). After the F.W.W. Hendrik Marsman (1899–1940), a rhetorical 'vitalist' influenced by German expressionism, led a school counterbalanced by the more sober *Forum* group led by critic Menno Ter Braak (1902–40). No recent writers have attained international standing.

NETHERLANDS ANTILLES. Overseas part of the kingdom of the Netherlands composed of the islands of Curaçao (q.v.), Aruba, and Bonaire, lying off the coast of Venezuela, together with St. Eustatius, Saba, and the S. part of St. Maarten, *c.* 500 m. to the N.E. Total area 381 sq. m.; pop. (1965) 209,000. Willemstad, on Curaçao, is the cap. Maize, salt, and phosphates are produced, and huge refineries on Curaçao and Aruba treat petroleum from Venezuela. N.A. has full internal autonomy (from 1954) under a gov. assisted by a council of ministers and a single-chamber elected legislature, but oil workers in Curaçao revolted 1969 and demanded the resignation of the N.A. govt. Dutch marines were flown out to restore order.

NETHERLANDS EAST INDIES. Name used for the East Indian Archipelago until those islands achieved independence as Indonesia (q.v.). The Portuguese were the 1st European traders to reach the islands, in the early part of the 16th cent. Before the end of that cent. they had been driven out by the English and the Dutch. But the Dutch soon obtained the monopoly of trade there and in 1602 formed their East India Co., which set up a factory at a spot named Batavia in 1619 (re-named Djakarta in 1949). Gradually the company subdued the warring rulers and brought the islands one after another under its rule until in 1798 (during the French occupation of the Netherlands) the company was abolished. The British seized the N.E.I. to prevent them from falling into French hands, restoring them in 1816 when they came under the control of the Dutch govt. In the 20th cent. various preliminary measures intended to lead to self-govt. were introduced, but this orderly progress was brought to an abrupt end by the Japanese occupation of the N.E.I., 1942–5.

NETTLE. Genus (*Urtica*) of plants, many of which have ovate or lanceolate leaves covered with stinging hairs. When lightly touched these penetrate the skin and release an acrid juice causing inflammation. The common stinging nettle (*U. dioica*), found in

WHITE DEAD NETTLE

waste places in Europe and naturalized in parts of N. America, yields a tough fibre which was made into cloth in ancient Egypt.

NETTLE-RASH. Urticaria; an acute allergic reaction of the skin. In answer to the specific stimulus, whether it be the eating of shellfish, contact with a horse, or an emotional shock, the skin erupts in a rash and weals as though it had been badly stung by nettles, and itches intolerably. Treatment is by removing the cause; by soothing baths and lotions; and by injections of adrenalin. The eruption often disappears as rapidly as it came. *See* ALLERGY.

NEUCHÂTEL (nöshahtel'). Swiss city, cap. of N. canton, nr. the N.E. of N. Lake, 25 m. W. of Berne. It is the seat of a univ. (1909). Pop. (est.) 30,000. The canton lies between N. Lake and the French frontier, in the Jura mts. Area 308 sq. m.; pop. (1960) 147,500.

NEURALGIA (nūral'ja). A severe pain felt along the track of a nerve and not due to inflammation of it (*see* NEURITIS). Some forms are due to exhaustion or illness, others to an unhealthy stimulus, sometimes at a considerable distance – e.g. sciatica – resulting from displacement of one of the discs which lie between the vertebrae. Treatment is by general measures, sometimes by the injection of alcohol into the nerve trunk, and sometimes by cutting or stretching of the nerve.

NEURASTHENIA (nūrasthē'nia). An unscientific term meaning nervous weakness or exhaustion, and used to cover a variety of symptoms of neurosis.

NEURATH (noi'raht), **Constantin von** (1873–1956). German Nazi politician. Ambassador to Britain 1930–2, he then became For. Min., retaining his position under the Hitler régime until 1938, and was 'protector' of Bohemia and Moravia 1939–41. Sentenced at Nuremberg to 15 yrs. imprisonment, he was released on grounds of age and ill-health in 1954.

NEURITIS. Inflammation of a nerve or nerves as a result of poison, infection, or injury. Multiple N., the inflammation of a large number of nerves, results from chronic drunkenness (Korsakow's psychosis), or poisoning by lead, arsenic, etc., or the toxins of diseases such as diphtheria or sleepy sickness.

NEUROSIS. Mental disorder not amounting to insanity, resulting from unrecognized conflict between the patient's primitive and his ethical impulses. It is often classified into anxiety, marked by irrational apprehension; obsession, in which the will is dominated by compulsive 'rituals' such as the need to wash the hands frequently; and hysteria, in which the trouble is chiefly infantile dependence on others and a lack of emotional control.

NEUTRA (noi'trah), **Richard Joseph** (1892–   ). Austrian architect. Ed. at the univs. of Vienna and Zürich, he worked in Switzerland 1919–23, when he went to the U.S.A., where he was naturalized in 1929. His works incl. the Lovell Health House and the Military Academy, both in Los Angeles.

NEUTRALITY. Non-participation in a war between other states. Under international law, neutral states must not supply men, arms, money, or war-supplies to belligerents, or allow the passage of belligerent troops, the establishment of military, naval, or air bases on their territory, or recruiting among their subjects by belligerents. Any favour granted to one belligerent must be extended to the other. Troops entering neutral territory must be interned; belligerent warships may remain in a neutral port for 24 hours, but any prisoners carried must be released. Any violation of N. may be resisted by force. The problem of the rights of neutral goods on belligerent vessels, and vice versa, has been a frequent source of international controversy. An attitude of active sympathy towards a belligerent, known as 'benevolent N.' or 'non-belligerence', is often adopted in practice, although unwarranted by international law; e.g. the attitude of the U.S.A. to Britain 1939–41.

NEUTRINO (nūtrē′nō). A very small uncharged fundamental particle (*see* ATOM) of minute mass, very difficult to detect and of great penetrating power, emitted in all radioactive disintegrations which give rise to beta rays. All reactors emit numbers of Ns.

NEUTRON (nū′tron). A nuclear particle having no electric charge and the approximate mass of a hydrogen nucleus. It is found in the nuclei of atoms and plays a vital part in nuclear fission. Outside a nucleus a N. is radioactive, decaying with a half-life of about 12 min. to give a proton and an electron.

NEVADA (nĕvah′dah). One of the western states of the U.S.A., lying within the Great Basin between

NEVADA. The Comstock Lode, one of the richest-ever deposits of silver, was discovered in 1859, and a U.S. branch mint was established at nearby Carson City in 1866. The building seen here was in use for this purpose 1870–93, but became the Nevada State Museum in 1957.
Courtesy of the Nevada State Museum, Carson City.

the Rockies and Sierra Nevada, forming a plateau (average alt. 5,500 ft.) crossed by mountain ranges and intervening valleys. The climate is arid and the soil barren. The Humboldt and its tributaries provide enough irrigation to permit limited agriculture, but the mining of copper, lead, silver, gold, etc., is more important. Its easy divorce law (only 6 weeks' residence necessary) brought it fame. The cap. is Carson City, but the fastest-growing town is Las Vegas. The Nuclear Rocket Development Station is at Jackass Flats in the N. Desert, c. 70 m. N.W. of Las Vegas. Area 110,540 sq. m.; pop. (1970) 488,738.

NEVERS (nevär′). Cap. of Nièvre dept., France, on the Loire, about 135 m. S.S.E. of Paris. The cathedral was started in the 11th cent., finished c. 1500. Pop. (1962) 41,051.

NEVILLE'S CROSS. Battle fought near Durham between King David Bruce of Scotland and the English under William de la Zouch, archbishop of York, on 17th Oct. 1346. David was taken prisoner.

NEVINS, Allan (1890–1971). American historian. Prof. at Columbia 1931–58, he pub. lives of Frémont, Cleveland, and J. D. Rockefeller.

NEW AMSTERDAM. Town in Guyana, on the Berbice, founded by the Dutch. Pop. (est.) 10,000. *See also* NEW YORK.

NEWARK. Largest city of New Jersey, U.S.A., on the Passaic, 8 m. W. of Manhattan. Its main products are electrical equipment, machinery, fountain pens, chemicals, paints, canned meats. N. dates from 1666, when a settlement called Milford was made on the site. Pop. met. area (1970) 1,845,348.

NEWARK. English market town (bor.) in Notts, on the r. Trent. It contains the ruins of a 12th cent. castle, in which King John d. in 1216. There are engineering industries, and a flourishing trade in corn, cattle, wool, etc. Pop. (1961) 24,610.

NEWBOLT, Sir Henry John (1862–1938). British poet. A barrister 1887–99, he was an authority on naval matters, e.g. *The Year of Trafalgar* (1905) and *A Naval History of the War* (1920) on the F.W.W. His *Songs of the Sea* (1904) and *Songs of the Fleet* (1910) were set to music by Stanford.

NEW BRITAIN. Largest island in the Bismarck Archipelago, W. Pacific, off the N.E. coast of New Guinea (q.v.), and forming part of the Australian New Guinea trust territory. N.B. has a number of active volcanoes, including Father (7,500 ft.), which is the highest peak. The chief town is Rabaul, and the main products are cocoa and copra. Area, incl. the adjacent islands, 14,100 sq. m.; est. pop. (1966) 148,817 (incl. c. 5,000 non-indigenous).

NEW BRUNSWICK. Eastern maritime prov. of Canada, to the N.W. of Nova Scotia. Its sea coast is more than 500 m. long, and there are many bays and harbours. It is undulating country, with hills which rise no higher than 900 ft. above sea-level. Of the many rivers, the most important are the St. John and the St. Croix, both of which flow into the Bay of Fundy. There are also many lakes, the largest being the Grand Lake (67 sq. m.). With large forests in the interior, lumbering is of great importance. The soil is fertile, and wheat, potatoes, oats, and turnips are grown. Fredericton is the cap.; St. John, the chief port, and Moncton are other towns. The chief industries are paper manufacture, saw milling, fishing and fish curing, and mining (lead, zinc, copper), and oil and natural gas.

Discovered by Cartier in 1534, N.B. was first explored by Champlain in 1604 and remained a French colony until, as part of Nova Scotia, it was ceded to England in 1713. It was separated from Nova Scotia in 1784. It is governed by a Lieut.-Gov. with a Legislative Assembly elected for 5 years by adult suffrage. Area 28,335 sq. m. (incl. 519 sq. m. of water); pop. (1966) 616,788.

NEW BUKHARA. *See* BUKHARA.

NEWBURY. English market town (bor.) in Berks, on the Kennet, 16 m. S.W. of Reading. Aircraft, bricks and tiles, chemicals, are made. During the Civil War 2 battles were fought near N., in 1643 and 1644. Pop. (1961) 20,386.

NEWBY, P(ercy) H(oward) (1918–). British novelist. Lecturer in English at Cairo 1942–6, he joined the B.B.C. 1949, and became Controller, Third Programme, 1958. His subtle novels incl. *Something to Answer For* (1968), awarded the first Booker McConnell prize of £5,000 in 1969.

NEW CALEDONIA. French overseas territory in the S. Pacific, situated between Australia and the Fiji Is. Nouméa is the capital. N.C. was discovered by Cook in 1774, and became French in 1853. Area, including dependencies, c. 8,000 sq. m.; pop. (1964) 89,000 (incl. 34,000 Europeans).

NEWCASTLE, Thomas Pelham-Holles, duke of (1693–1768). British Whig politician. He was Sec. of State 1724–54, and then P.M. during the Seven Years War, until 1762, although Pitt was mainly responsible for the conduct of the war.

NEWCASTLE, William Cavendish, duke of (1592–1676). English Royalist. He commanded the king's forces in the N. during the Civil War until 1644, when he was defeated at Marston Moor. He then withdrew to the Netherlands, and lived in exile until the Restoration. His biography was pub. in 1667 by his wife, **Margaret**, duchess of N. (*c.* 1624–74), who also wrote plays, poems, and essays.

NEWCASTLE. City and port of New South Wales, Australia, 70 m. by sea N.N.E. of Sydney. Industries incl. the manufacture of iron, steel, and ships, using coal from nearby mines, discovered 1796. There is a univ. (1965). Pop. (1966) 327,500.

NEWCASTLE-UNDER-LYME. English market town (bor.) in Staffs, 2 m. W. of Stoke-on-Trent. The parish church has a tower dating from the 13th cent. The chief industries are coal mining and the making of clothing, bricks, and tiles. Keele (q.v.) univ. is nearby. Pop. (1961) 76,433.

NEWCASTLE UPON TYNE. English city (co. bor.) and port in Northumberland, on the N. bank of the Tyne, about 8 m. from its mouth. The castle was built by Henry II 1172–7, on the site of an older castle; its keep is still preserved, together with parts of its walls and Black Gate and Watergate. Other noteworthy buildings include St. Nicholas's cathedral, which is (apart from the Perpendicular tower) chiefly

NEWCASTLE UPON TYNE. In the background row upon row of nineteenth-century industrial housing, but in the foreground a pleasing combination of the ancient and the very modern: St. Thomas's church and the new Town Hall.
Courtesy of Tyne Tees Television.

14th cent. work; St. Andrew's church, which dates back to the 12th cent.; and the Guildhall, built in 1658. N. is connected with the neighbouring town of Gateshead by several bridges. Chiefly famous as a coaling centre, it first began to trade in coal in the 13th cent. In 1826 iron works were estab. by George Stephenson, and the first engine used on the Stockton and Darlington railway was made at N. There are good quay and harbour facilities. Major industries incl. coal mining, shipbuilding, marine and electrical engineering, chemical and metal manufactures. The chief exports are coal, iron and steel goods, chemicals, and copper. The H.Q. of the Min. of Social Security is here. Since 1906 N. has had a Lord Mayor. The Univ. of N. (1852) was, until 1963, part of the Univ. of Durham (1832). Pop. (1961) 269,389.

NEW CHURCH. *See* SWEDENBORG.

NEWCHWANG. Town in Liaotung prov., China, the oldest port in the Liao valley, 25 m. N. of Yingkow. Owing to the changing course of the Liao and the silting up of its mouth, the outer port of N. was moved *c.* 1800 to Tienchwang, and in 1836 to Yingkow.

NEWCOMEN, Thomas (1663–1729). British inventor. B. at Dartmouth, he devised an atmospheric steam engine, or 'fire engine', patented in 1705, which was used for pumping water from mines until Watt invented one with a separate condenser.

NEW DEAL. The programme of reforms introduced in U.S.A. by F. D. Roosevelt from 1933 onwards, to counteract the effects of the economic crisis that began in 1929. Immediate relief measures included the provision of employment on public works, and of govt. loans to farmers at low rates of interest, and the raising of agricultural prices by planned restriction of output. Reforms associated with the programme incl. the introduction of old-age and unemployment insurance, measures to prevent the use of sweated labour and child labour, protection of the right to organize against unfair practices by employers, and the provision of loans to local authorities for slum clearance. A notable feature was the Tennessee Valley scheme (q.v.). The N.D. reduced unemployment from 17 million to 8 million, but met with opposition, and many of its provisions were declared unconstitutional by the Supreme Court in 1935–6.

NEW DELHI. *See* DELHI.

NEWDIGATE, Sir Roger (1719–1806). British collector of antique marbles, etc., who founded in 1805 the N. prize for English verse, open to students of Oxford univ.

NEW ENGLAND. The name of a region in the N.E. of the U.S.A., consisting of the states of Maine, New Hampshire, Vermont, Massachusetts, Rhode Is., and Connecticut (qq.v.), which was originally settled in the main by Puritan groups from England. The name was suggested by Capt. John Smith, who explored it in 1614. The original Puritan immigrant developed into the shrewdly witty Yankee (a name which became current in the 18th cent.).

NEW ENGLISH ART CLUB. Society founded in England in 1886 by a group of painters dissatisfied with the administration of the R.A., to secure better representation for younger painters. Its members incl. Sargent, Augustus John, Paul Nash, Rothenstein, and Sickert.

NEW FOREST. Woodland district in Hants, England, W. of Southampton. It was a royal hunting-ground in Saxon times, and was enlarged by William I. Oak trees from the forest were once an important source of timber for the navy. Area 144 sq. m.

NEWFOUNDLAND. Prov. of Canada; it incl. the is. of N., at the entrance of the St. Lawrence r., and the coastal region of Labrador, over which N. was given jurisdiction in 1713; the boundary between the part of Labrador attached to N. and the part attached to the prov. of Quebec was settled in 1927. The island is triangular, with Capes Bauld, Race, and Ray forming the angles. It has a rugged coastline indented with many bays. There are many lakes, of which the largest are Grand Lake (129 sq. m.) and Red Indian Lake (70 sq. m.). The highest mountains, which rise to over 2,500 ft., are in the N.W. Most of the country consists of barren lands and marshes, but the soil is fertile on the borders of the lakes and rivers, and the valleys of the Gander, Humber, and Exploits, the 3 most important rivers, are densely wooded. The chief exports are timber and paper pulp; others incl. iron ore, zinc, lead, and fishery products. St. John's is the cap.

The is. of N. was discovered by Cabot in 1497, and was the first English colony, Sir Humphrey Gilbert formally taking possession in 1583. The French also estab. settlements, and did not recognize British sovereignty until 1713, while disputes over fishing rights continued until 1904. Responsible government was granted to the island in 1855, but in 1934, as N. had fallen into financial difficulties, administration was vested in a governor and a special commission. In 1948 a referendum resulted in favour of federation with Canada, and in 1949 N. became the tenth prov. of Canada. Area 156,185 sq. m.; pop. (1966) 493,396 (of which Labrador formed 110,000 sq. m with pop. 21,157.)

NEWFOUNDLAND. A breed of dog, said to have originated in Newfoundland. There are several varieties, the most important being the black and white, which has a broad muzzle, curly hair and bushy tail.

NEWGATE. A prison in London, England, which stood on the site of the Central Criminal Court. Originally a gatehouse (hence the name), it was estab. in the 12th cent., rebuilt after the Great Fire, and again in 1780, and was demolished in 1903. Public executions were held outside it 1783–1868.

NEW GUINEA. Is. in the S W. Pacific, to the N. of Australia, entirely within the Tropics. It is divided into East, or Australian, N.G. and West N.G. (or W. Irian), formerly Dutch. N.G. is very mountainous, the Nassau Range in the W. reaching 16,000 ft. The chief rivers are the Mamberamo, Sepik, Fly, and Digul. The climate is hot and moist in the coastal dists. Gold, silver, platinum, copper, manganese, and other minerals exist, and oil and natural gas are found both in W. Irian and Papua. Copra, rubber, coffee, kapok are the chief items grown for export; sago, breadfruit, sandalwood are also produced; and there are pearl shell fisheries. The indigenous inhabitants are of Melanesian type; they are divided into many tribes, some in the highlands being pygmies. Area: W. 160,000 sq. m., E. 183,540 sq. m.; pop. W. (1962) 700,000, E. (1966) 1,272,126.

The first Europeans to reach N.G. were the Portuguese, in 1527. In the 17th cent. the Dutch East India Co. laid claim to it, and when the govt. of King William I took over the Indies it estab. regular administration in W. N.G. as part of the Netherlands E. Indies. When the islands to the W. became independent in 1949 as Indonesia, the Dutch retained control of Netherlands N.G. until 1962. It was ceded to Indonesia by the U.N. in 1963, remaining part of Indonesia by an 'Act of Free Choice' 1969.

The annexation of E. N.G. by Queensland in 1883 was not recognized by the home govt. which, however, in 1884 set up a protectorate over S.E. N.G. This was annexed to the Crown 1888, transferred in 1901 to the new govt. of the Commonwealth of Australia, and in 1906 named the Territory of Papua. N.E. N.G. was annexed by Germany in 1884, occupied by Australia 1914, and governed as a mandate from 1921 and trust terr. from 1946 (the whole is. was Japanese-occupied 1942–5). Australia estab. 1949 the combined Trust Terr. of Papua-N.G. (incl. New Britain and adjacent is.), eventually to be independently self-governing. There is an admin. council and house of assembly: the admin. H.Q. is Port Moresby.

NEW HAMPSHIRE. One of the New England states in the N.E. corner of the U.S.A., bounded on the N. by Canada, on the E. by Maine, on the S. by Massachusetts, and on the W. by Vermont. It was one of the original 13 states, and the first colony to declare its independence of Britain, 15 June 1776. Called the 'granite state', it is a mountainous region. The chief rivers are the Connecticut, Androscoggin, Merrimack, Saco, and Piscataqua. Agriculture, formerly the principal occupation, remains important (fruit, poultry, dairy products, etc.); industrial products incl. textiles, paper, leather goods, electrical machinery and apparatus. The state cap. is Concord. Area 9,304 sq. m.; pop. (1970) 737,681.

NEWHAVEN. English seaport (U.D.) in Sussex, on the English Channel, at the mouth of the Ouse, with steamer service to Dieppe. Pop. (1961) 8,325.

NEW HAVEN. Co. seat of New Haven co., Conn., U.S.A., 4 m. from Long Is. Sound and 62 m. E.N.E. of New York. It is the seat of Yale univ. N.H. was founded as Quinnipiac in 1638, renamed in honour of Newhaven, Sussex, 1640. Pop. (1960) 152,048.

NEW HEBRIDES. Group of Pacific is. to the N.W. of Australia under the joint administration (set up 1906) of Britain and France. The principal is. are Espiritu Santo, Malekula, Epi, Ambrym, Efate or Sandwich, Erromanga, Tanna, and Aneityúm. The chief town, Vila, on Efate, was severely damaged by a cyclone 1959. Area 5,700 sq. m.; pop. (1964) 65,800.

NEW JERSEY. One of the 13 original states of the

NEW JERSEY. Built in 1887 to the design of Edison, this combined workshop and laboratory at West Orange saw his development of the motion-picture camera and his work on sound reproduction which led to his evolving the 'modern' long-playing record. *Courtesy of the U.S. National Park Service.*

U.S.A., called the 'garden state', situated on the Atlantic coast between New York and Delaware Bay. The S. half of N.J. is a coastal plain, most of it less than 100 ft. above sea-level. To the N.W. is a triassic lowland, with an irregular surface varying in height up to 900 ft. The N.W. corner of the state is hilly, rising to 1,803 ft. at High Point. The rivers include the Hudson, Passaic, Hackensack, Raritan, and Delaware. Along the coast are a number of pleasure resorts, such as Atlantic City and Cape May. The principal towns incl. Trenton (the cap.), Newark, and Jersey City. Agricultural produce (e.g. asparagus, fruits, potatoes, tomatoes, poultry) is important; industrial products incl. chemicals, electrical machinery, clothing, metal goods. N.J. was perhaps visited by Verrazano in 1524. The Dutch were the first to settle, c. 1620. N.J. became British in 1664. Area 7,836 sq. m.; pop. (1970) 7,168,164.

NEW LONDON. Naval base and yachting centre of S.E. Connecticut, U.S.A., on the r. Thames, 3 m. from Long Island sound. It was founded 1646, and named N.L. 1658. Pop. (1960) 34,182.

NEWLYN. Seaport near Penzance, Cornwall, England, brought within the bor. of Penzance in 1934. It gave its name to a group of artists, 'the N. school', who painted there. The Ordnance Survey relates all heights in the U.K. to the mean sea-level at N.

NEWMAN, Ernest (1868–1959). British music critic. B. in Liverpool, he was music critic to the *Sunday Times* 1920–58, and noted for studies of Gluck, Beethoven, Liszt, and Wagner.

NEWMAN, John Henry (1801–90). British cardinal. B. in London, he was ordained in the C. of E. in 1824, and in 1827 became vicar of St. Mary's, Oxford. There he came under the influence of R. H. Froude and Keble, and in 1833 pub. the first of the *Tracts for the Times*, which gave their name to the 'Tractarian Movement', and culminated in Newman's celebrated *Tract 90* in 1841. He was received into the R.C. Church in 1845, and finally settled as an oratorian at Edgbaston. Appointed rector of Dublin univ. in 1854, he pub. lectures on *The Idea of a University*, and in 1864 pub. his autobiography, *Apologia pro vita sua*, defending himself against Kingsley's attack on the R.C. attitude to truth. His poem, *The Dream of Gerontius*, appeared in 1866, and *The Grammar of Assent*, an analysis of the nature of belief, in 1870. In 1879 he was created a cardinal. His best-known hymn is 'Lead, Kindly Light'. His brother, **Francis William N.** (1805–97), prof. of Latin at Univ. Coll., London, 1846–69, adopted Unitarian views. He wrote the autobiographical *Phases of Faith* (1850).

NEWMARKET. English market town (U.D.) in

Suffolk, 13 m. E.N.E. of Cambridge. Horse-racing has been held here since James I's reign, and the H.Q. of the Jockey Club is at N. Important events are the Two Thousand Guineas, the One Thousand Guineas, the Cambridgeshire, and the Cesarewitch. Pop. (1961) 11,207.

NEW MEXICO. State of the U.S.A., lying between Colorado and the Mexican frontier on a rocky tableland, 2,800 to 6,000 ft. high. In the W. there are extensive forests, and the N.E. region is famous for its beautiful 'parks'. The principal rivers are the Rio Grande and its affluent the Rio Pecos, the Canadian, and San Juan; all are dammed for irrigation. The valleys are fertile, the principal crops being wheat, maize, beans, cotton; cattle are raised. Petroleum and natural gas, potash, copper, uranium, gold, silver are among mineral products. Los Alamos is one of several atomic research centres in N.M. The most characteristic forms of vegetation are the yucca and cactus. N.M. is noted for its mild climate. It was colonized by Spaniards in the 17th cent., was acquired from Mexico by the U.S.A. in 1848, and became a state in 1912, The cap. is Santa Fé, but the largest town is Albuquerque. Area 121,666 sq. m.; pop. (1970) 1,016,000.

NEW ORLEANS (or′le-anz). Chief city of Louisiana, U.S.A., an important commercial centre and port on the Mississippi. At high tide the city is below river-level, and is therefore protected by embankments or levees. It is a market for sugar, rice and cotton; a banking and business centre; has a large oil industry, and produces the Saturn rockets used in *Apollo* spacecraft. There are excellent road, rail and air facilities. Educational institutions incl. Tulane Univ. (1834). N.O. was founded by the French in 1718, and the Vieux Carré or French Quarter with its Mardi Gras celebrations is a tourist attraction. It passed to Spain 1753, was returned to France 1800, and was part of the Louisiana Purchase made by the U.S.A. from France in 1803. In the late 19th cent. it was the birthplace of jazz(q.v.). Pop. met. area (1970) 1,034,316.

NEWPORT. English river-port and market town (bor.) cap. of the Isle of Wight, at the head of the estuary of the Medina. S.W. of the town is Carisbrooke Castle. Pop. (1961) 19,482.

NEWPORT. English seaport (co. bor.) in Monmouthshire, on the r. Usk. It exports iron and coal, has extensive docks and a steelworks at nearby Llanwern. St. Woollos cathedral is partly Norman, and there is a ruined castle. N. was the scene of a Chartist rising in 1839. Pop. (1961) 108,107.

NEWPORT NEWS. City and port of Virginia, U.S.A., on the r. James. It has shipbuilding yards and foundries. Pop. (1960) 113,662.

NEWQUAY (nū′kē). Seaport and holiday resort on the N. coast of Cornwall. Pop. (1961) 11,877.

NEW SOUTH WALES. State of the Australian Commonwealth, at first called New Wales by Capt. Cook, who put in at Botany Bay in 1770, and was struck by the resemblance of the coast to that of Wales. It is situated in the S.E. of Australia. The E. and S.E. coastal district of the country is separated from the inland plains by the Great Dividing Range. In the S.E. are the Australian Alps, of which the highest point is Mt. Kosciusko (7,328 ft.); they extend N. as the Snowy Mts. Behind Sydney the Dividing Range is called the Blue Mts., and to the N. is the New England Range. The coastal dist. is watered by many rivers, incl. the Hunter, Clarence, and Macleay. The W. part of the country is watered by the rivers of the Murray-Darling system, of which the most important are the Murrumbidgee, Lachlan, and Macquarie. The principal towns are Sydney, the most important Australian seaport, in which 60 per cent of the pop. of N.S.W. live, and largest city in the Australian Commonwealth, Newcastle, Wollongong, Broken Hill, Blue Mountains, and Maitland.

N.S.W. is situated in the temperate zone, and has an equable climate. Wheat, rice, maize, oats, sugar cane, tobacco, and fruit are grown. Sheep rearing and forestry are important. There are rich mineral deposits, incl. gold, silver, copper, tin, zinc, and coal. The diversion westward, through the Snowy Mts., of the upper waters of the Snowy r., started in 1949, was planned to provide irrigation and hydro-electric power for large areas of N.S.W. and Victoria.

N.S.W., which was used as a convict settlement 1788–1850, was opened to free immigration 1819, received self-govt. in 1856, and became a state of the Commonwealth of Australia in 1901. Legislative power is vested in a parl. of 2 houses, the legislative council of 60 members, and the legislative assembly of 94 members. Voting is compulsory. Area 309,433 sq. m.; pop. (1966) 4,231,103.

Lord Howe Is., 436 m. N.E. of Sydney, is a dependency. It is volcanic, highest point Mt. Gower 2,840 ft. Area 3,200 acres; pop. 280.

NEWSPAPER. Publication giving news and comments on it. One of the earliest Ns., the Roman *Acta Diurna*, said to have been started by Julius Caesar, contained announcements of marriages, deaths, military appointments, etc., and was posted up in public places. Not until after the invention of printing, however, were news sheets pub. as commercial undertakings, and, following their introduction into Germany (1609) and the Netherlands (1616), the first English N., *The Weekly News*, ed. by N. Bourne and Thos. Archer, appeared in 1622, followed later by the first daily N., *Daily Courant*, in 1702. Despite the stamp duty imposed on Ns. 1713–1855, with the object of restricting them because of their alleged subversive tendencies, by 1776 there were 53 in London alone. The chief British morning daily papers, based on London (1968 circulations in thousands) are: *The Times* (1785) 415, *Guardian* (originally *Manchester Guardian*, 1821–1959) 268, *Daily Telegraph* (1855) 1,378, *Daily Mail* (1896) 2,039, *Daily Express* (1900) 3,786, *Daily Mirror* (1903) 4,948, *Daily Sketch* (1915–71) 885, *The Sun* (*Daily Herald*, 1919–64) 1,009, *Financial Times* (1888) 162; the evening Ns., once 10, now number 2, *Evening News* (1881) 1,094 and *Evening Standard* (1860) 594. Important regional daily papers incl. *Scotsman* (1855) 74 and *Yorkshire Post* (1866) 117.

The chief Sunday Ns. are: *Observer* (1791) 853, *Sunday Times* (1822) 1,440, *News of the World* (1843) 6,131 (largest circulation of any N. in the world), *People* (1881) 5,426, *Sunday Mirror* (formerly *Sunday Pictorial*, 1915) 5,015, *Sunday Express* (1918) 4,206, and *Sunday Telegraph* (1961) 747 – the last 3 are each linked with a daily of the same name.

Owing to the vastness of the U.S.A., no N. there has a national distribution, and none has a circulation comparable with the largest in Britain. The first successful daily N. was the *Pennsylvania Packet and General Advertiser* (1784). In 1968 there were pub. 1,749 daily Ns. in English with a combined circulation of 61,560 thousand; they incl. (circulation in thousands) the *Baltimore Sun* (1837) (morning and evening), 398, *Chicago Tribune* (1847) 805, Sunday edn. 1,124, *Los Angeles Times* (1881) 856, Sunday edn. 1,145, *New York Times* (1851) 840, Sunday edn. 1,494, *Philadelphia Bulletin* (1841) evening 671, Sunday edn. 728, *Philadelphia Inquirer* (1829) 516, Sunday edn. 936, *Wall Street Journal* (1889) 1,079, *Washington Post* (1877) 467. *The Christian Science Monitor* (1908) evening, pub. in Boston, with a circulation of only 202, nevertheless has a world-wide reputation.

Experiments have been made in Japan with photo-telegraphic Ns., for which the original is set in type in the normal way, but the completed pages are then transformed into electronic signals for transmission to sub-stations where facsimiles are made, the ultimate aim being a receiver in every home.

Ns. of world repute pub. outside the U.K. and

U.S.A. incl. *Sydney Bulletin* (1880), Australia; *Times of India* (1838), Bombay; *La Prensa* (1869), Argentina; *Arbeiter-Zeitung* (1889), Vienna; *Le Figaro* (1826) and *Le Monde* (1944), Paris; *Algemeen Handelsblad* (1828) and *De Telegraaf* (1893), Amsterdam; *Die Welt* (1946), Hamburg; and *Frankfurter Allgemeine Zeitung* (1949), Frankfurt-am-Main; *Corriere della Sera* (1875), Milan, and *Avanti* (1896), Rome; *National-Zeitung* (1842), Basle; *Journal de Genève* (1826), Geneva; and *Neue Zürcher Zeitung*, Zürich; *Izvestiya* (1917) and *Pravda* (1912), Russia.

NEWT. Genus of tailed amphibians (*Molge*) in the family Salamandridae, mainly found in Europe. The common N. (*M. vulgaris*) is *c.* 3 in. long.

NEWTON, Sir Isaac (1642–1727). British natural philosopher. B. at Woolsthorpe, Lincs, he was ed. at Grantham grammar school and Trinity Coll., Cambridge, of which he became a fellow in 1667. During 1665–6 he discovered the binomial theorem and the differential and integral calculus, and began to investigate the phenomena of universal gravitation. He was elected F.R.S. in 1672, and soon afterwards published his *New Theory about Light and Colours. De Motu* was written in 1684, and the next year his universal law of gravitation was completely expounded as follows: 'Every particle of matter in the universe attracts every other particle with a force whose direction is that of the line joining the two, and whose magnitude is directly as the product of the masses, and inversely as the square of their distance from each other.' His greatest work, *Philosophiae Naturalis Principia Mathematica*, was pub. in 3 vols. in 1686–7, with the aid of Halley. N. resisted James II's attacks on the liberties of the univ., and sat in the parls. of 1689 and 1701–2 as a Whig. Appointed warden of the mint in 1696, and master in 1699, he carried through a reform of the coinage. He was elected president of the Royal Society in 1703, pub. his *Optics* in 1704, and was knighted in 1705. N. was buried in Westminster Abbey.

N.'s laws of motion are: (1) Every body continues in its state of rest or of uniform motion in a straight line except in so far as it may be compelled to change that state by the action of some external force; (2) change of motion is proportional to the applied force and takes place in the direction of the line of action of the force, and (3) to every action there is an equal and opposite reaction.

NEWTON ABBOT. English market town (U.D.) on r. Teign, Devon, with railway repair shops, pottery and metal works; there are clay mines in the vicinity. Pop. (1961) 18,066.

NEW WESTMINSTER. City and freshwater port of British Columbia, Canada, cap. of British Columbia before it became a prov., on the N. bank of the Fraser r., 12 m. S. of Vancouver. Pop. (1966) 38,013.

NEW YEAR'S DAY. 1 January, the first day of the year; celebrations are held in many parts of the world on this day, and in Scotland, the U.S.A., and other countries it is a public holiday. In England until 1753 the year began for many purposes on 25 March.

NEW YORK CITY. The largest city in the U.S.A., often abbreviated N.Y.C. It is in New York state, on the Atlantic, at the junction of the Hudson and East rivers. N.Y. Bay was discovered by Giovanni da Verrazano, a Florentine, in 1524, and explored by Henry Hudson in 1609. The Dutch estab. a settlement there in 1613, named New Amsterdam in 1626; this was captured by the English in 1664, and renamed N.Y. During the War of Independence, British troops occupied N.Y. from 1776 until evacuation day, 25 Nov. 1784; it was the cap. of the U.S.A., 1785–9. N.Y.C. was formed in 1898 by the creation and linking of the boroughs of the Bronx, Brooklyn, Manhattan, Queens, and Richmond. N.Y.C. is the commercial and financial cap. of the U.S.A., and probably the busiest port in the world. The docks have a total water frontage of over 990 m. The harbour is divided into an outer harbour, called Lower Bay, and an inner harbour, called Upper Bay; these are connected by the Narrows, a channel about 1 m. wide, between Long Is. and Staten Is. The Statue of Liberty stands on Liberty Is. (called Bedloe's Is. until 1956) in the inner harbour. Manhattan Is., the business centre, is 13½ m. long and averages 1½ m. in width. Among the most famous buildings are the H.Q. of the U.N. (1951, *illus.* p. 1058), the Empire State (tallest in the world at 1,250 ft., plus 222 ft. TV tower added 1950), Chrysler (1,046 ft.), 60 Wall Tower (950 ft.) and Chase Manhattan buildings, and Rockefeller Center (850 ft., *illus.* p. 908). The best-known street is Broadway, which is 16 m. long, but 5th Avenue, the main shopping district, is the finest thoroughfare. Greenwich Village, Lower Manhattan, is the artist-writer-Bohemian section. On a 50-acre site between Broadway and the Hudson is the Lincoln Arts Center (opera house, concert hall, theatre, Julliard School of

NEW YORK. By day or night the skyscrapers are breathtaking. The Empire State Building, tallest of all on the far left, has enough floor space to shelter a city of 80,000. *Courtesy of U.S. Travel Service.*

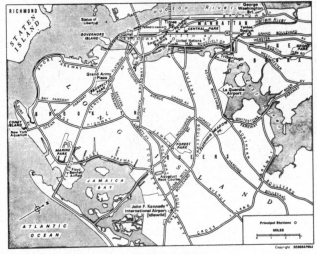

NEW YORK CITY

Music, library, and restaurants). The Metropolitan Museum of Art (1870) has the finest collection in the Western hemisphere (*see* CLOISTERS); the Museum of Modern Art (1929) also covers architectural and industrial design, photography and film; and the Pierpont Morgan Library has a research collection based on that of the millionaire (q.v.). Wall Street is the financial centre of the U.S.A. City Hall is the H.Q. of the Mayor and City Council: *see* TAMMANY HALL. Most famous of the parks, which cover 34,673 acres, is Central Park. The pop. incl. large Negro (*see* HARLEM) and Puerto Rican minorities, as well as large communities of European stock – German, Greek, Hungarian, Irish, Italian, Polish and Russian – and there are *c.* 2,000,000 Jews. The leading newspaper is the *N.Y. Times.* Columbia Univ. (1754) is the most notable of the educational institutions. Largest of the 4 airports is Kennedy International (until 1963 called Idlewild). There are 2 cathedrals: St. John the Divine (1892 Protestant Episcopal: Romanesque and Gothic) and St. Patrick's (1858–79 R.C.: Gothic). Industries incl. printing, publishing, clothing, tobacco, electrical etc. Area 359 sq. m. (incl. 44 sq. m. inland water); pop. (1970) 7,771,730; met. area 11,409,739.

NEW YORK STATE. One of the original 13 states of the U.S.A., the 'Empire State'. The 2nd most populous and wealthiest of the Union, it is situated S. of the r. St. Lawrence, which forms part of the boundary between N.Y. and Canada, and N. of Pennsylvania, and has a coastline on the Atlantic. The central and W. regions are low-lying, but in the E. are the Adirondack and Catskill mts. In the W. there are a number of lakes, of which the largest are Lake Seneca and Lake Cayuga; N.Y. also includes part of Lakes Erie and Ontario. In the E. are the George and Champlain lakes. The most important river is the Hudson, which is connected with the Great Lakes by the Erie canal (1825). The largest cities are New York, Buffalo, Rochester, Syracuse, Yonkers, Albany (the cap.), Niagara Falls, and Utica. N.Y. is the most important manufacturing state in the country, its chief industries being clothing and printing. The administration is in the hands of a Governor, elected for 4 years, and a Senate and Assembly elected for 2.

N.Y. was first explored by Champlain and by Hudson in 1609, was colonized by the Dutch from 1609, and annexed by the English in 1664. The first constitution was adopted in 1777, transforming the colony into a state. Area 49,576 sq. m.; pop. (1970) 18,190,740.

NEW ZEALAND. A country of the British Commonwealth, situated in the S. Pacific between 33° and 53° S. lat. and 167° and 178° E. long., and consisting of a group of islands. The most important are North, South, Stewart (separated from S. Island by Foveaux Strait) and Chatham Islands (Chatham area 347 sq. m. and Pitt area 25 sq. m.), 536 m. E. of N.Z. Outlying is. incl. within N.Z. geographical boundaries are the Kermadec (annexed 1887), Three Kings, Auckland, Campbell, Antipodes, Bounty, Snares and Solander: only the Kermadec and Campbell is. are inhabited. These are grouped with the main is. in 13 statistical areas: *North Island* Auckland (Central and South), East Coast, Hawke's Bay, Northland, Taranaki and Wellington; *South Island* Canterbury, Marlborough, Nelson, Otago, Southland and Westland. The Terrs. Overseas comprise Tokelau Is. (3 atolls transferred 1926 from the former Gilbert and Ellice Is. colony) and Niue Is. (one of the Cook Is., but separately admin. from 1903: chief town Alafi). The Cook Is. (q.v.) are internally self-governing, but share common citizenship with New Zealand. The Ross Dependency (q.v.) is in the Antarctic. *See also* SAMOA.

Physical Features. The coastline of S. Is. is almost unbroken, except in the N. and S.W., but N. Is. has more indentations, and has excellent harbours at Auckland and Wellington.

Except for the N.W. peninsula ending in Cape Maria van Diemen, N. Is. is mountainous and incl. 3 active volcanoes – Ruapehu (9,175 ft.), erupted 1950, highest point in the is., Ngauruhoe (7,515 ft.), erupted 1956, and Tongariro (6,458 ft.), erupted 1950 – as well as the remarkable Rotorua dist. with its geysers and hot springs. In S. Is. the S. Alps stretch almost from one end to the other. The highest peak of this range (and in N.Z.) is Mt. Cook (12,349 ft.), at least 17 other peaks rise above 10,000 ft. In the higher valleys there are huge glaciers.

Most of the rivers are shallow and rapid, and navigable for only a short distance. The Waikato, in N. Is., the largest river in N.Z., rises in the region of Mt. Ruapehu, flows in a northerly direction, and empties into the Tasman Sea; it is navigable for 70 m. In S. Is. the important rivers incl. the Wairau, Mataura, and Waitaki: from the hydro-electric station on the Waitaki at Benmore (1965) power is transmitted by under-sea cable across Cook Strait to N. Island. There are many lakes, of which the largest is Lake Taupo, in N. Is. N.Z. has a temperate climate.

NEW ZEALAND		
	Area in sq. m.	Pop. (1966)
North Island	44,281	1,893,326
South Island	58,093	783,593
Stewart Island	670	(332)*
Chatham Island	372	(520)*
Minor Islands	320	(19)*
	103,736	2,676,919
Island Territories		
Niue Island	100	5,195
Tokelau Islands	4	1,900
Cook Islands	88	19,251
Ross Dependency	175,000	262
* Included in the N. and S. Island totals		

NEW ZEALAND. The signature of the Treaty of Waitangi in 1840. *Courtesy of the High Commissioner for New Zealand.*

Rainfall is moderate, except in the W. of the S. Alps.

The principal cities are Wellington, the cap., Auckland, Hamilton and Palmerston North in N. Is.; Christchurch and Dunedin in S. Is.: all have univs. The majority of the inhabitants of N.Z. are of European (chiefly British) descent. The aboriginal Maori, after decreasing to 42,000 in 1896, numbered 201,159 at the 1966 census, most of them living in N. Is. Area, N.Z. proper, 103,736 sq. m.; island territories, 104 sq. m. Pop. (1966), N.Z. proper 2,676,919 (incl. Maoris); island territories, 7,095.

Economic. The soil is fertile, and the most important industry is agriculture, including sheep and dairy farming. The most important crops are wheat, oats and barley. Fruits and vegetables are also grown. Gold was discovered in 1861 at Tuapeka in Otago, and gold was later exploited in other regions of S. Is. Other minerals incl. silver, silica sand, pumice, limestone and coal, and in the 1960s oil and natural gas were found on and offshore in the Taranaki area of N. Island, near New Plymouth. The chief exports are wool, frozen lamb and dairy produce; production of gold has latterly declined. There are some 3,200 m. of state railway, over 7,000 m. of state highways, and both internal and external air services.

Government. N.Z. is governed by a Gov.-Gen. appointed by the Crown, who is aided by an Executive Council and a General Assembly, or parl., of one house, the House of Representatives, with 80 members including 4 Maoris, popularly elected for 3 years; the former upper chamber or legislative council was abolished from 1 Jan. 1951. Women received the franchise in 1893.

History. N.Z. was occupied by Polynesian tribes before the 14th cent. Its coasts were explored by Tasman in 1642 and by Cook in 1769, 1773, and 1777. British missionaries began to arrive in 1815. By the Treaty of Waitangi (1840) the Maoris accepted British sovereignty; colonization began, and large-scale sheep farming was developed. Self-govt. was granted in 1853. The Maoris resented the loss of their land, and rose in revolt 1845–7 and 1860–72, until concessions were made, incl. representation in parl. Sir George Grey, Gov. 1845–53 and 1861–70, and Radical P.M. 1877–84, was largely responsible for the conciliation of the Maoris and the introduction of manhood suffrage. The Cons. held power 1879–90, and were succeeded by a Lib. govt., which with trade union support ruled until 1912; this govt. introduced women's suffrage (1893) and old-age pensions (1898), and was a pioneer in labour legislation. N.Z. troops served in the S. African War. In 1907 Dominion status was granted. After 1912 the Cons. (Reform) Party regained power, and the trade unions broke with the Libs. to form the Lab. Party. More than 120,000 N.Z. troops fought in the F.W.W., and greatly distinguished themselves at Gallipoli and elsewhere. The Cons. and Libs., who united to form the Nat. Party in 1931,

were defeated in 1935 by the Lab. Party, which introduced a comprehensive social security programme. N.Z. declared war against Germany in 1939 a few minutes after the U.K.; 135,000 New Zealanders served overseas, doing notable work in N. Africa and Italy; 10,000 were killed, and there were some 20,000 other casualties. Since 1949 the Nat. Party has been almost continuously in power. The most vital issue of recent years, owing to N.Z. dependence on the U.K. market, has been the conditions of Britain's entry into the E.E.C.

PRIME MINISTERS OF NEW ZEALAND			
J. Ballance (Lib.)	1891	Sir Joseph Ward	
R. J. Seddon (Lib.)	1893	(United)	1928
W. Hall-Jones (Lib.)	1906	G. W. Forbes	
Sir Joseph Ward (Lib.)		(United)	1930
	1906	M. J. Savage (Lab.)	1935
T. MacKenzie (Lib.)	1912	P. Fraser (Lab.)	1940
W. F. Massey (Reform)		S. G. Holland (Nat.)	1949
	1912	K. J. Holyoake (Nat.)	1957
J. G. Coates (Reform)	1925	Walter Nash (Lab.)	1957
		K. J. Holyoake (Nat.)	1960

Art. N.Z. cannot yet claim to have produced any artist of world-wide fame, except the cartoonist, Sir David Low, but much meritorious work has been done, and there is a lively interest in art, as is evidenced by the many art societies and galleries. The Auckland Society of Arts, founded in 1870, is the oldest art society in N.Z. The N.Z. Academy of Fine Arts and the National Art Gallery are at Wellington. The Maoris are very fine craftsmen, and are noted for their carvings in wood, stone, and bone.

Literature. Among interesting pioneer records are those of Edward Jerningham Wakefield and F. E. Maning (qq.v.); and *A First Year in Canterbury Settlement* by Samuel Butler (q.v.). Earliest of the popular poets was Thomas Bracken, author of the N.Z. national song, followed by native-born Jessie Mackay and W. Pember Reeves (qq.v.), though the latter is better-known as the author of the prose account of N.Z. *The Long White Cloud*, and Ursula Bethell (1874–1945). In the 20th cent. N.Z. literature attained an international appeal with the short stories of Katharine Mansfield (q.v.), produced an excellent exponent of detective fiction in Dame Ngaio Marsh (q.v.), and struck a specifically N.Z. note in *Tutira, the Story of a N.Z. Sheep Station* (1926) by W. H. Guthrie Smith (1861–1940). Poetry of a new quality was written by R. A. K. Mason (1905–71) in the twenties, and in the thirties by a group of which A. R. D. Fairburn (1904–57), with a witty conversational turn, and Allen Curnow (1911–), poet, critic and anthologist, are the most striking. In fiction the thirties were remarkable for the short stories of Frank

NEW ZEALAND. A liner sails out through Wellington's magnificent harbour.
Courtesy of the High Commissioner for New Zealand.

Sargeson (1903–) and Roderick Finlayson (1904–), and the talent of John Mulgan (1911–45), who is remembered both for his novel *Man Alone* (1939), and for his posthumous factual account of the war in which he died, *Report on Experience* (1947). More recently Kendrick Smithyman (1922–) has struck a metaphysical note in poetry, and James K. Baxter (1926–) has pub. fluent lyrics.

NEXO (niks'ö), **Martin Andersen** (1869–1954). Danish novelist. Of humble birth, he was largely self-educated, and produced 2 famous multi-vol. novels *Pelle the Conqueror* (1906–10) and *Ditte, Child of Man* (1917–21). He became a Communist in 1922 after visiting Moscow, where he also fled from the Nazis in the S.W.W., and d. in E. Germany.

NEY, Michel, duke of Elchingen, prince of the Moskowa (1769–1815). Marshal of France. The son of a cooper, he joined the army in 1788, and rose from the ranks to marshal of France. He served throughout the Revolutionary and Napoleonic Wars, commanding the rearguard during the retreat from Moscow, and for his personal courage was called 'the bravest of the brave'. When Napoleon returned from Elba, N. was sent to arrest him, but instead deserted to him and fought at Waterloo. He was subsequently shot for treason.

NGO Dinh Diem (1901–63). Pres. of S. Vietnam. A dedicated nationalist refusing compromise with either the Communist Viet Minh or the French, he became P.M. in 1954, and pres. in 1955 when the country became a rep. The influence exercised by his family, all devout R.Cs., especially his brother Ngo Dinh Nhu and Mme Nhu, led to charges of Buddhist persecution (they form *c.* 70 per cent of the pop.), nepotism, and general intolerance of opposition. Both brothers d., perhaps by suicide, following a military coup in 1963.

NIAGARA FALLS (nī-ag'ara). Two waterfalls on the Niagara r., on the Canadian-U.S.A. border, connecting Lake Erie with Lake Ontario; they are separated by Goat Is. The American Fall, to the N., in U.S.A., is 167 ft. high, 1,080 ft. wide; the Horseshoe Fall, to the S., in Canada, is 160 ft. high, 2,600 ft. across.

On the Niagara r., 2 m. below the falls, lie (1) on the W. bank, N.F., a city of Ontario, Canada, with a large hydro-electric generating plant; pop. (1966) 60,768 (2) on the E. bank, N.F., a city of New York state, U.S.A.. seat of a univ., with hydro-electric

NIAGARA FALLS. The Great Lakes which serve as its reservoir make this the most even-flowing of all waterfalls, 212,000 cubic ft. of water per second passing over it. Besides domestic supplies, the falls provide industrial power economically on a vast scale, for example, they can generate heat for furnaces making calcium cyanamide, which requires a temperature of 3,600°F. *Courtesy of Cyanamid.*

works and a tourist trade; pop. (1960) 102,394.

NIBELUNGENLIED (në'beloongenlëd) (Ger., Song of the Nibelungs). Medieval German epic poem composed from older sources, *c.* 1200, by an unknown author. Siegfried, possessor of the Nibelung treasure, marries Kriemhild, sister of Gunther of Worms, and wins Brunhild as a bride for the latter, and is murdered by Hagen, Gunther's vassal. Kriemhild obtains vengeance for Siegfried's death by marrying Etzel (Attila) of the Huns, at whose court Hagen and Gunther, with their retinue, are slain. Wagner based his *Ring des Nibelungen* mainly on the Norse versions.

NICAEA (nīsē'a). Ancient city of Bithynia, Asia Minor, founded *c.* 316 B.C. Here was held in 325 a famous Council of the Christian Church, convened by the Emperor Constantine I; it promulgated the first version of the Nicene Creed (q.v.). The modern Turkish village of Iznik is on the site.

NICARAGUA (nikarah'gwah). A republic of Central America, N. of Costa Rica, stretching from the Pacific to the Caribbean Sea. Crossing the country from N.W. to S.E. is the main cordillera of Central America. The Caribbean coast is swamp land (*see* MOSQUITIA). The most important towns are Managua (the cap.), León, Matagalpa, and Granada. Corinto, on the Pacific, is the chief port. Products incl. bananas, cotton, coffee, cocoa, sugar, timber, gold, silver, and copper.

The first European to reach N. was Gil Gonzalez de Avila (1522), who brought it under Spanish rule. It remained Spanish until 1821, when it gained its independence. Under the revised constitution of 1960, legislative power is vested in a Congress of two houses of 45 deputies and 18 senators, elected (like the pres.) for 4 years, by popular vote. Area (est.) 57,150 sq. m.; pop. (1967) 1,783,000.

NICE. French resort on the Riviera, 8 m. S.W. of Monte Carlo, on the Bay of the Angels, the cap. of the dept. of Alpes Maritimes. Many festivities are held here, incl. the famous 'Battle of the Flowers', and chocolates and perfume are made. Pop. (1968) 322,442.

NICENE CREED. One of the fundamental creeds of Christianity, promulgated by the Council of Nicaea in 325. It gives the orthodox doctrine of the Trinity as against the Arian heresy. The N.C. was modified by the Council of Constantinople in 381, and the *filioque* clause was added during the 5th and 6th cents. in the western Church.

NICHOLAS, St. (4th cent.). Bishop of Myra in Lycia, and patron saint of Russia, children, merchants, and sailors. His festival is 6 Dec. and the custom of giving presents to children on the eve of this day, still retained in some Continental countries, e.g. Germany and the Netherlands, has been transferred in English-speaking countries to Christmas Day; hence the association of his name, Santa Claus (corruption of San Nicolaas), with the latter festival.

NICHOLAS I (1796–1855). Tsar of Russia from 1825. His ambition to dominate the Balkans involved Russia in war with Turkey in 1827–9, and in the Crimean War.

NICHOLAS II (1868–1918). Last Tsar of Russia. Succeeding Alexander III in 1894, he was dominated by his wife, Princess Alix of Hesse, who, in turn, was under the influence of Rasputin. His mismanagement of the Japanese War led to the revolution of 1905, which he ruthlessly suppressed. He entered the F.W.W. in 1914, and in 1917 was forced to abdicate. N. and his family were shot by the Bolsheviks at Ekaterinburg in July 1918. His recognized heir is the Duchess Christian Ludwig of Mecklenburg, but *see* ANASTASIA.

NICHOLSON, Ben (1894–). British artist. He is the son of the painter, Sir William N. (1872–1949), remembered for the series of striking posters and other works he produced with his brother-in-law, James Pryde, under the signature 'The Beggerstaff

Brothers'. B. at Denham, Bucks, he studied at the Slade, as well as on the Continent and in California. Developing an interest in abstract art, he became known for his geometrical reliefs and as an exponent of Constructivism (q.v.). His work is remarkable for its exquisite control and delicacy. Awarded O.M. 1968.

NICHOLSON, John (1822–57). British soldier. He was administrative officer at Bannu, in the Punjab, 1851–6, and the justice and firmness of his rule led to his being worshipped as a god. Promoted to brig.-gen. on the outbreak of the Mutiny, he crushed resistance in the Punjab, but was killed during the storming of Delhi.

NICKEL. Lustrous white metal discovered by Cronstedt in 1751, the name being an abbreviation of Swedish *kopparnickel* (false copper): symbol Ni, at. wt. 58·71, at. no. 28. It has a high melting point, low electrical and thermal conductivity, and can be magnetized. N. may be readily forged when hot, and is tough, malleable, and ductile when cold. Canada provides the most extensive deposits, which are usually extracted with copper. Smelting precedes separation, after which the N. is purified. It is used in coinage; in chemical and foodstuff industries for its resistance to corrosion; in electronics and for electroplating. The most important use, however, is in alloys with iron, steel, copper, and chromium, incl. N. steel for armourplating and burglar-proof safes, Monel metal, invar, constantan, nichrome permalloy, perminvar, and other magnetic alloys and stainless steels, cupro-N., N.-silver, and others. Finely divided N. is used as a catalyst in the hydrogenation of vegetable oils.

NICOBARS (nikōbahrz′). Group of 19 islands (7 uninhabited) in the Bay of Bengal, S. of the Andamans and forming with the Andamans a territory of the Rep. of India. The Is. were occupied by the Japanese 1942–5. Area 635 sq. m.; pop. (1961) 14,563.

NICOLAI (nik′ōlī), **Otto** (1810–49). German composer. He was a conductor in Vienna and in Berlin, and wrote several operas, of which *The Merry Wives of Windsor* (1849) was an outstanding success.

NICOLSON, Sir Harold (1886–1968). Brit. diplomat and author. Son of Lord Carnock, he entered the Foreign Service, held embassy appointments and served on the British delegation to the Paris Peace Conference of 1919. He was a Nat. Labour M.P. 1935–45, and in 1947 joined the Labour Party. A distinguished biographer, e.g. *Lord Carnock* (1930), *Curzon: the Last Phase* (1934), and *King George V* (1952), he also pub. studies such as *Monarchy* (1962). He m. in 1913 Victoria Sackville-West (q.v.).

NICŌSI′A. Capital of Cyprus, situated 32 m. W. of Famagusta. It has leather, textile, pottery and other industries, and an international airport. N. was the residence of the Lusignan kings of Cyprus 1192–1475. The Venetians, who took Cyprus in 1489, surrounded N. with a high wall which still exists; it fell to the Turks 1571. Pop. (1966) 105,600.

NICOTINE (nik′otēn). An alkaloid obtained from the dried leaves of the tobacco plant (*Nicotiana tabacum* or *N. rustica*). A colourless oil, soluble in water, it turns brown on exposure to the air. Pur N. is poisonous, but, as it is destroyed by burning, it is not present in tobacco smoke.

NIEBUHR (nē′bōōr), **Barthold Georg** (1776–1831). German historian. He was Prussian ambassador at the Holy See 1816–23, and then prof. of Roman history at Bonn until 1831. He wrote a history of Rome (1811–32).

NIEBUHR, Reinhold (1892–1971). American theologian. Prof. of ethics at the Union Theological Seminary, N.Y., 1928–60, he was influential in his books on Christianity and present-day problems, e.g. *Moral Man and Immoral Society* (1932), and *The Structure of Nations and Empires* (1959).

NIEDERSACHSEN. See Lower Saxony.

NIELSEN (nēl′-), **Carl** (1865–1931). Danish composer. At 14 an army bugler, he became director of the Copenhagen Conservatoire in 1915. His reputation extended outside Scandinavia after the S.W.W., and his works are remarkable for their progressive tonality, as in his opera *Saul og David* and 6 symphonies.

NIEMEYER (nē′mīer), **Oscar** (1907–). Brazilian architect. He was one of the architects employed in designing the H.Q. of the U.N. in N.Y., and from 1957 worked on Brasilia (q.v.).

NIEMÖLLER (nē′möller), **Martin** (1892–). German pastor. He led a campaign against the Nazification of the German Church, was dismissed in 1934, and later suffered gaol and the concentration camp, remaining a prisoner throughout the S.W.W. In 1946 he proclaimed Germany's war guilt at the International Missionary Council in Geneva, and 1947–64 was first bp. of the newly formed Evangelical Church of Hesse-Nassau. In 1961 he became a pres. of the World Council of Churches.

NIETZSCHE (nē′tshe), **Friedrich Wilhelm** (1844–1900). German philosopher. B. at Röcken, Saxony, he attended Bonn univ. and was prof. of Greek at Basle 1869–80. He had abandoned theology for philology, and was influenced by the writings of Schopenhauer and the music of Wagner, with whom he became on close terms. Both these attractions passed, however, and ill-health caused his resignation from the univ. He spent his later years in N. Italy, in the Engadine and in S. France. During his mature years till 1889 he pub. *Morgenröte* (1880–1), *Die fröhliche Wissenschaft* (1881–2), *Also sprach Zarathustra* (1883–5), *Jenseits von Gut und Böse* (1885–6), *Genealogie der Moral* (1887), and *Ecce Homo* (1888). He suffered a permanent breakdown in 1889 from overwork and loneliness.

The philosophy of N. is the rejection of the accepted absolute moral values and the 'slave morality' of Christianity. His ideal was the 'Overman' or 'Superman' who would impose his will on those who are too weak and worthless to be anything but slaves. Until this century, his beliefs remained ignored or opposed, by Conservatives and Socialists alike, but support for modern Totalitarianism has often been claimed (possibly wrongly) in Nietzsche's writings.

NIÈVRE (nyävr′). River in central France rising near Varzy and flowing 25 m. S. to join the Loire at Nevers. It gives its name to a dept.

NIGERIA. At work on the blueprint of his concrete sculpture for the Chase Manhattan Bank, Ibadan, Festus Idehen is surrounded by some of his own striking wood carvings.
Courtesy of the Chase Manhattan Bank.

NIGER (nī'jer). Third-longest river in Africa, rising 150 m. from the W. coast, in the highlands bordering Sierra Leone and the rep. of Guinea. It flows N.E., then S.E., and enters the Gulf of Guinea; length 2,600 m. The Benue joins the N. at Lokoja. The N. is a sluggish r., frequently flooding its banks.

NIGER, Republic of. Country in W. Africa, formerly the French colony (later territory) of Niger. It lies N. of Nigeria. Cattle raising and the cultivation of ground-nuts, millet, and cotton are carried on in the S., but the N., where there are uranium deposits, is part of the Sahara desert. The cap. is Niamey (pop. 30,000). Area 459,000 sq. m.; pop. (1965) 3,330,000. The country was occupied by France in 1912, made into a territory 1926. It became independent outside the French Community in 1960, under a president.

NIGERIA, Federation of. A country of the Brit. Commonwealth, in W. Africa on the Gulf of Guinea, with Dahomey to the W., Cameroon to the E., and the rep. of Niger to the N. Since 1967 the former 4 regions have been divided into 12 states: N.-Western, N.-Central, Kano, N.-Eastern, Benue Plateau, W.-Central (former N. region: mainly Moslem); E.-Central, S.-Eastern and Rivers (former E. region: Christian and pagan); Mid-Western, unchanged, and like the Western and Lagos (enlarged from former W. region) Christian and Moslem. The cap. and chief port is Lagos; other large towns are Ibadan, Ogbomosho, Kano, Oshogbo, Abeokuta, and Port Harcourt. Area 356,670 sq. m.; pop. (1967) 61,450,000.

NIGERIA. Girls from Bornu Province in traditional Kanuri costumes. *Courtesy of the Federation of Nigeria.*

Physical Features. To the S. is a coastal strip, a maze of creeks and mangrove swamps, including the delta of the Niger. To the N. of this lies a belt of tropical forest. The rest of the country is savannah, becoming arid and treeless towards the N. The E. strip is rugged and mountainous. The main rivers are the Niger and its tributary the Benue; both are navigable.

The whole country is hot, in the N. the heat is very dry, and in the S. damp and enervating. The dry season is characterized by a dust-laden N.E. wind, the *harmattan*. The annual rainfall, about 72 in. in Lagos, but over 150 in. elsewhere on the coast, is only about 25 in. in the extreme N.

Economic Life. The country is agricultural. The main food-crops are guinea-corn, groundnuts, yams, and cassava, while ground-nuts, palm oil and kernels, and cocoa are exported. There are large herds of cattle in the N. and there is a big export of hides. Minerals incl. oil in the E., tin in the Bauchi plateau, and coal nr. Enugu, and high-grade timber is produced.

NIGERIA. Gelede Society mask from the Yoruba, S. Nigeria, used in funeral dances. *British Museum.*

Inhabitants. The people belong to many different tribes, with widely different languages, social organizations, and customs. In the N. the main tribes are the Hausa and the Fulani; in the W. the Yoruba; in the Mid-W. and E. the Ibo.

Hausa is a *lingua franca*, English the official language. There is a lively literature, e.g. playwrights Wole Soyinka and Hubert Ogunde, and poet Cris Okigbo.

History. Lagos was bought from an African chief by British traders in 1861; in 1886 it became the colony and protectorate of Lagos. Activity in the Niger valley was developed by the National African Co. (later the Royal Niger Co.) which came to an end in 1899; two protectorates, N. Nigeria and S. Nigeria, were set up in 1900: Lagos was joined to S.N. in 1906. In 1954 N. became a federation which in 1960 achieved independence, becoming in 1963 a federal rep. within the Commonwealth. A military *coup d'état* in 1966 led to the death of Tafawa-Balewa (q.v.). After much unrest Maj.-Gen. Jakabu Gowon became head of the Fed. Military Govt. later in 1966, but in 1967 the E. region seceded as the Rep. of Biafra (q.v.) and civil war ensued. Biafran resistance continued in a limited area in the interior until 1970. Elsewhere, the nat. development plan carried on, e.g. the Kainji dam (1969), on the Niger.

NIGHTINGALE, Florence (1820–1910). British hospital reformer. B. in Florence of wealthy parents, in 1854 she took a staff of nurses to Scutari, where inefficiency and insanitary conditions were causing unnecessary loss of life among the British soldiers from the Crimea, and within 6 months reduced the death-rate in the hospitals from 42 to 2 per cent. For the rest of her life, although living in retirement, she worked constantly to raise the status of the nursing profession. She received the O.M. in 1907.

NIGHTINGALE. Songbird (*Luscinia megarhynca*) which winters in Africa, but breeds in S. Europe and S. England in the late spring and early summer. The song of the male has a legendary beauty and though to be heard in the daytime is most striking at night when other birds are silent. Allied species are found in E. Europe.

FLORENCE NIGHTINGALE

NIGHTSHADE. Common name for several plants in the family Solanaceae: best-known are the Black N. (*Solanum nigrum*), bittersweet or woody N. (*S. dulcamara*), and deadly N. or belladonna (q.v.).

NI'HILISTS. Russian revolutionaries of the reign of Alexander II (1855–81). The name, popularized by Turgenev, means those who approve of nothing (Lat. *nihil*) belonging to the existing order. From 1878 they launched a terrorist campaign which culminated in the murder of the Tsar in 1881.

NIJINSKY (nēzhin'ski), **Vaslav** (1890–1950). Russian ballet dancer and choreographer. He made his début in 1908, appeared with the Diaghileff company in Paris in 1909, and later in St. Petersburg. He turned to choreography in 1912, creating *L'après-midi d'un faune, Jeux,* and *Le Sacre du printemps.* After tours of S. and N. America, he retired because of ill-health.

NIJMEGEN (nī'mäkhen). Town in the Netherlands, in the province of Gelderland, on the Waal, about 10 m. S. of Arnhem. The Roman Noviomagus, N. was a free city of the Holy Roman Empire and a member of the Hanseatic

NIGHTSHADE

League. Brewing is carried on and there are leather and tobacco works. Pop. (1967) 144,000.

NIJNI-NOVGOROD. *See* GORKY.

NIKE (nĭ′kē). Greek goddess of victory. One o the most beautiful architectural monuments of Athens was the temple of N. Apteros. N. is shown in sculpture with wings, as in the 'Winged Victory' (Louvre).

NIKOLAYEV (nēkŏlĭ′ef). Seaport in the Ukrainian S.S.R., at the mouth of the S. Bug. on the Black Sea, cap. of N. region. A naval base, it has important shipyards. Pop. (1967) 289,000.

NILE. The longest river in Africa; its remotest head stream is the Luvironzo branch of the r. Kagera flowing from the S.W. into Lake Victoria and thence to the Mediterranean. The N. proper begins where the main stream leaves Lake Victoria 2¼ m. above Owen Falls (q.v.); it is c. 3,500 m. long. From Lake Victoria it flows over rocky country, and there are many cataracts and rapids, including the Murchison Falls, until it enters Lake Albert. From here it flows across flat country and in places spreads out to form lakes. At Lake No it is joined by the Bahr el Ghazal, and from this point to Khartoum it is called the White N. At Khartoum it is joined by the Blue N., which rises in the Ethiopian highlands, and 200 m. below Khartoum it is joined by the Atbara. From Khartoum to Aswan (q.v.) there are 6 cataracts. The N. is navigable to the 2nd cataract, a distance of 960 m. The delta of the N. is 120 m. wide and 105 m. deep.

NILGAI (nēl′gī). Large antelope (*Boselaphus tragocamelus*) found in India. The bull has short conical horns and is bluish-grey.

NÎMES (nēm). City of the S. of France, cap. of the dept. of Gard, 18 m. N.W. of Arles, famous for its Roman remains which incl. an amphitheatre dating from c. 2nd cent. A.D. Pop (1968) 123,292.

NIMITZ (nim′its), **Chester William** (1885–1966). American admiral. He was responsible for the reconquest of the Solomons (1942–3), the Gilbert Is. (1943), and the Marianas and Marshalls (1944), and as U.S. representative signed the Japanese surrender.

NINEVEH (nin′eve). Cap. of the Assyrian Empire from the 8th cent. B.C. until its destruction by the Medes under Cyaxares in 612 B.C. It was situated on the Tigris opposite the modern town of Mosul, and was adorned with splendid palaces. Excavations from 1842 onwards brought to light the ruins of N. under the mounds, or tells, of Kuyunjik and Nebi Yunus.

NINGPO′. Fishing port in Chekiang, China, on the Yung Kiang, 12 m. from its mouth. N. was a centre of foreign trade already under the Tang dynasty (618–907), and was one of the original treaty ports opened to European traders in 1842. It sends fish, tea, cotton, etc., to Shanghai, and makes straw hats and mats, furniture, lace. Pop. (1957) 240,000.

NI′OBE. In Greek legend the daughter of Tantalus and wife of Amphion, king of Thebes. Proud of her 12 children, she showed contempt for the goddess Leto who had only two; whereupon Leto induced her own children, Apollo and Artemis, to slay N.'s. N. d. of grief, and was changed into stone by Zeus.

NIOBIUM. Light grey metal closely allied to tantalum, and known in the U.S. as columbium, which was first prepared by Blomstrand in 1864, though discovered in an ore by Hatchett in 1801: symbol Nb, at. wt. 92·91, at. no. 41. Occurring in a number of rare minerals, it is generally obtained from an African ore, and is a valuable addition to stainless steels, also being used for canning high-temperature nuclear fuel elements, e.g. fast breeder-reactors, espec. when liquid sodium is the coolant.

NIPPON. Transliteration of the native name for Japan.

NIPPUR (nip-poor′). Ancient city of Sumeria, its site now marked by the village of Niffer, Iraq. It lay on the Euphrates (now 25 m. away), 90 m. S.E. of

RICHARD NIXON

Courtesy U.S. Information Service

Baghdad. It was the cult centre of the god Enlil.

NIRENBERG (nē′ren-), **Marshall** (1927–). American biochemist. Working at the Nat. Inst. of Health at Bethesda, Maryland, he was awarded a Nobel prize (with Robert Holley and H. Gobind Khorana) for interpreting the genetic code and its function in protein synthesis in 1968.

NIRVANA (nirvah′na) (lit. 'blowing-out'). In Buddhism, the attainment of perfect serenity by the eradication of all desires. To some Buddhists it means complete annihilation, to others it means the absorption of the self in the infinite.

NITHSDALE, William Maxwell, 5th earl of (1676–1744). Jacobite leader who was captured at Preston, brought to trial in Westminster Hall, and condemned to death on 9 Feb. 1716. With his wife's assistance he escaped from the Tower of London in woman's dress, and fled to Rome.

NITRE (nī′tr) or **Saltpetre.** Potassium nitrate, KNO_3, a mineral found on the ground and in the soil near the surface of the ground at Bihar, India, Persia, and Cape Province, S. Africa. The native salt was formerly used for the manufacture of gunpowder, but the supply of N. for explosives is nowadays largely met by making the salt from nitratine (Chile saltpetre, $NaNO_3$).

NI′TRIC ACID. Mineral acid, HNO_3, also called aqua fortis, first prepared by Raimon Lull (q.v.) by heating nitre and clay: its real nature was demonstrated by Cavendish. Obtained directly from the air by the various processes for fixation of atmospheric nitrogen, it is a strong oxidizing agent, dissolves most metals, and is used for nitration and esterification of organic substances; for explosives, plastics, and dyes; in making sulphuric acid and nitrates.

NI′TROCELLULOSE. Series of esters with 2–6 nitrate groups per molecule, made by the action of concentrated nitric acid on cellulose in the presence of concentrated sulphuric acid: those with 5 or more nitrate groups are explosive (gun cotton), but those with less were used in lacquers, rayon, and plastics, espec. celluloid and photographic film, until replaced by non-inflammable cellulose acetate.

NITROGEN. Colourless, odourless, inert gas isolated by Daniel Rutherford in 1772: symbol N, at. wt. 14·008, at. no. 7. There are an est. 4,000 billion tons of N. in the atmosphere of which it forms c. 78 per cent by vol. (Gk. nitreforming). Many N. compounds, e.g. nitric acid, nitrates, ammonia and the oxides, are of greatest importance in foods, drugs, fertilizers, dyes, and explosives. N. is a constituent of many organic substances, particularly proteins, but is generally obtained from nitrate deposits, e.g. Chile; or from the atmosphere by liquefaction and fractional distillation; or by N. fixation, e.g. the Haber process in which N. and hydrogen are heated under pressure in the presence of a catalyst to form ammonia. In nature atmospheric N. is fixed by certain soil bacteria.

NITROGLYCERINE. Substance produced by the action of nitric and sulphuric acids on glycerol. Very poisonous, it explodes with great violence if heated in a confined space. It is used in the preparation of dynamite, cordite, and other high explosives.

NIXON, Richard Milhous (1913–). American Repub. politician. B. in California, of Quaker family, he became a lawyer, entered Congress in 1947, and in 1948 attracted attention as a member of the Un-American Activities Committee when he pressed for the investigation of Alger Hiss (q.v.). He was senator from California from 1951 until Vice-Pres. of the U.S. under Eisenhower 1953–61. He failed to defeat J. F. Kennedy in the pres. elections of 1961, but in a 'law and order' campaign defeated Vice-Pres. Humphrey in 1968 in one of the most closely contested elections in U.S. history. Abroad he aimed at withdrawal from Vietnam and limitation of future U.S. commitment to repulsion of external aggression rather than combating internal subversion, and aid to Far Eastern countries to stand on their own feet economically and militarily.

NKRUMAH (nkrōō′mah), **Kwame**)–72). Ghanaian statesman. B. in the Gold Coast, he was ed. at a R.C. mission school and Achimota Coll., and was a schoolmaster 1931–4. He studied abroad at Lincoln Coll. and the Univ. ot Pennsylvania, and at the London School of Economics, returning to Africa in 1947 where he formed, in 1949, the Convention People's Party with the aim of immediate self-govt. In 1950 he was imprisoned for incitement of illegal strikes, but was released the same year, becoming P.M. of the Gold Coast (1952–7), of Ghana (1957–60), and first pres. of the rep. 1960. His rule proved increasingly dictatorial. He was deposed while on a visit to Peking 1966, and was appointed joint Head of State of Guinea.

KWAME NKRUMAH

N.K.V.D. *See* M.V.D.

NŌ′AH. Biblical character. The son of Lamech and father of Shem, Ham, and Japheth, he built an ark so that he and his family and specimens of all existing animals might survive the Deluge (Gen. 6–8). In a Babylonian version the hero is Ut-napishtim.

NOAILLES (noh-īy), **Anna Elisabeth Brancovan,** comtesse de (1876–1933). French poet. B. in Paris of a Greek mother and a Rumanian father. Her poetry is of a musical quality; among the best collections are *Le Cœur innombrable* and *L'Ombre des jours.*

NŌ′BEL, Alfred Bernhard (1833–96). Swedish chemist. B. at Stockholm, he invented dynamite in 1867, and ballistite, a smokeless gunpowder, in 1889. He amassed a large fortune from the manufacture of explosives and the exploitation of the Baku oilfields, the bulk of which by his will he left in trust for the endowment of five **Nobel Prizes.** These are awarded internationally each year for outstanding achievement in chemistry, physics, mediciñe, literature, and the promotion of peace: a 6th, for economics and financed by the Swedish Nat. Bank, was first awarded 1969. The prizes have a value of *c.* £30,000.

NOEL-BAKER, Philip John (1889–). British Lab. politician. An ardent supporter of the League of Nations and U.N., he pub. *The Arms Race* (1958), and was in 1959 awarded a Nobel peace prize. In 1950–1 he was Min. of Fuel and Power and was a Lab. M.P. 1929–31 and 1936–70.

NOGINSK (nogēnsk′). City in the R.S.F.S.R., on the Klyazma r., 32 m. E. of Moscow, dating from 1791 and until *c.* 1930 called Bogorodsk. It makes textiles and has saw mills. Pop. (est.) 70,000.

NOGUCHI (nōgoo′chē), **Hideyo** (1876–1928). Japanese bacteriologist, who did much valuable work in connection with syphilitic diseases, and discovered the parasite of yellow fever, a disease from which he died while working in British W. Africa.

NOISE. Unwanted sound, an increasing problem in industrialized societies. Permanent, incurable loss of hearing can be caused by prolonged exposure to high N. levels (above 85 decibels in an octave), and even below this, if the N. is in a narrow frequency band: temporary loss occurs when exposure is for shorter periods. Lower levels of N. form an irritant, but seem not to increase fatigue or affect efficiency to any great extent. Roadside meter tests, introduced by the Min. of Transport in Britain in 1968, allowed 87 decibels as the permitted limit for saloon cars and 92 for lorries.

NŌ′LA. Ancient city of Naples prov., Italy, 17 m. N.E. of Naples, probably of Etruscan origin. The Emperor Augustus d. at N. Pop. (1960) 25,000.

NŌ′LAN, Sidney (1917–). Australian artist. B. in Melbourne, he developed, with little formal training, an individual interpretation of the Australian scene – the explorers and drought landscapes of the outback – but is most famous for his interpretation of the theme of Ned Kelly (q.v.). Created C.B.E. 1963.

NO′LDE, Emil. Name – taken from his native village of N. in Schleswig – adopted by the German Expressionist artist Emil Hansen (1867–1956). Working both in water colour and oil, he excelled in colourful seascapes and such mystic religious works as 'The Last Supper' and 'Joseph tells his Dream'.

NOLLEKENS (nol′ekenz), **Joseph** (1737–1823). British sculptor. B. in Soho, he executed busts of George III, the Prince of Wales (later George IV), Pitt, Fox, Garrick, Sterne, and others.

NOME (nōm). Town on Norton Sound, Alaska. ' Gold was discovered there in 1898–9, and there followed in 1900 a great gold rush, the pop. rising rapidly to 20,000, then declining. Amundsen arrived at N. in 1906 after completing the North-West Passage. The town has become a commercial centre for Seward peninsula. Pop. (est.) 2,000.

NOMINALISM. One of the two main trends in the medieval philosophy of Scholasticism. In opposition to the Realists, who maintained that universals, i.e. the distinctive qualities which enable us to group objects into classes, have a real existence, the Nominalists taught that they are mere names invented to describe the qualities of real things. Controversy on this issue continued at intervals from the 11th to the 15th cent.

NONCONFORMISTS. A term originally applied to the Puritan section of the C. of E. clergy who in the Elizabethan age refused to conform to certain practices of the Church, e.g. the wearing of the surplice and kneeling to receive Holy Communion. After 1662 the term was confined to those who left the Church rather than conform to the Act of Uniformity. It is now applied mainly to members of the Free Churches.

NONJURORS. Clergymen of the Church of England who after the Revolution of 1688 refused to take the oaths of allegiance to William and Mary. They continued to exist as a rival Church for over a century, and consecrated their own bishops, the last of whom d. in 1805. Notable Ns. were Thomas Ken, Jeremy Collier, and William Law.

NORDENSKJÖLD (nor′denshöld), **Nils Adolf Erik,** baron (1832–1901). Swedish explorer. He made voyages to the Arctic with the geologist Torell, and in 1878–9 discovered the North-East Passage. On his return he was made a baron, and pub. the results of his voyage in a series of books, incl. *Voyage of the Vega round Asia and Europe* (Eng. 1881).

NORDIC. A racial type, characterized by tall stature, long (dolichocephalic) head, and fair skin, hair, and eyes, found chiefly in Scandinavia and adjoining parts of Europe. The N. type is present in its purest form among the Swedes and Finns, some what less typically in Norway, Denmark, and the coastal region of Germany, and among the Baltic peoples; it is well represented in Britain, esp. in the north of England and the Western Isles of Scotland.

NORE, The. A sandbank at the mouth of the Thames, England. A lightship – the first of its kind – was placed there in 1732. The 'Mutiny of the Nore' in the British fleet took place in the vicinity in 1797.

NORFOLK, Bernard Marmaduke FitzAlan Howard, 16th duke of (1908–   ). Earl Marshal of England, and premier duke and earl. Succeeding his father in 1917, he was in charge of the Coronation arrangements in 1937 and 1953, and is keenly interested in horses (steward of Jockey Club), agriculture (Joint Parl. Sec. to the Ministry 1941–5), and cricket (manager of the M.C.C. team in Australia 1962–3).

NORFOLK. Co. on the E. coast of England. Its coastline is flat, except at Hunstanton and in the region of Cromer where there are cliffs, and much land has been reclaimed from the Wash near King's Lynn. The chief rivers are the Ouse, Yare, Bure, and Waveney. The series of lakes called the Broads are famous for their wild life, and are favoured for sailing and motor cruises. The soil consists mainly of sand, loam, and chalk. The chief crops incl. oats, wheat, barley, turnips and beet. Turkeys and geese are reared for the London market. Norwich, the co. tn., is the only industrial centre. Other towns incl. Gt. Yarmouth, King's Lynn, Cromer, and Hunstanton. From 1965 large natural gas deposits were located 15–60 m. off the coast, and a terminal was estab. at Bacton. Area 2,054 sq. m.; pop. (1967) 593,990.

NORFOLK. A seaport of Norfolk co., Virginia, U.S.A., on the estuary of the r. James. On the opposite bank is the suburb of Portsmouth, where there is a navy yard. Pop. met. area N.-Portsmouth (1970) 633,142.

NORFOLK ISLAND. Is. in the Pacific, midway between New Zealand and New Caledonia, discovered by Capt. Cook in 1774. N.I. was settled in 1856 by descendants of the mutineers of the *Bounty* from Pitcairn Is., and was under the jurisdiction of New South Wales until 1914, when it became a territory of the Australian Commonwealth. It has fertile soil and an agreeable climate; citrus fruits, bananas, and vegetables are grown, and a whaling station was set up in 1956. Area 13¼ sq. m.; pop. (1968) 1,500.

NORMAN. Style of architecture used in England from the time of Edward the Confessor until about the end of the 12th cent. N. buildings are massive, the semi-circular arch is used (except in the case of small openings for which trefoil arches are sometimes used), buttresses are of slight projection, and vaults are barrel-roofed. Examples are the Keep of the Tower of London, and parts of the cathedrals of Chichester, Gloucester, Oxford, and Ely.

NORMAN ARCH

NORMANDY (Fr. *Normandie*). One of the old provs. of France, on the seaboard of the English Channel; it is covered by the depts. of Seine-Maritime, Eure, Orne, Calvados, and Manche. Its cap. was Rouen, and it incl. also Dieppe, Le Havre, Harfleur, Caen, Falaise, St. Lô, Bayeux, Cherbourg, Coutances, and Alençon.

Part of Roman Gaul and then of the Frankish kingdom of Neustria, the region was occupied by the pagan Norsemen in the early 10th cent., and in 912 Rouen and some neighbouring land was given to their leader Rollo, who after becoming a Christian took the name of Robert. A descendant of Robert was William the Conqueror. During the Anglo-French wars N. changed hands several times, but it was finally conquered by the French under Charles VII in 1450.

N. again became a battleground during the S.W.W. in 1944 after Allied forces had landed on the beaches near Arromanches and Carentan on D-Day (q.v.). There was bitter fighting for weeks, particularly at Caen and Falaise.

NORMAN-FRENCH. The French dialect used by the Norsemen who settled in Normandy in the 10th cent., and subsequently by the Norman ruling class in England. Although generally replaced by English in the 14th cent., it remained the language of the court until the 15th and the official language of the law courts until the 17th, and is still used in the Channel Is. A considerable literature written in England in N.F. exists, including the 12th cent. chronicles of Gaimar and Wace, and the fables of Marie de France.

NORMANS. The Norsemen who were granted Normandy by the king of France in 911, and adopted the French language and culture. During the 11th and 12th cents. they conquered England, parts of Wales and Ireland, S. Italy, Sicily, and Malta, settled in Scotland, and took a prominent part in the Crusades. After the 13th cent. they ceased to exist as a distinct people.

NORRIS, Frank (1870–1902). American novelist. B. in Chicago, he completed only 2 parts of his great projected trilogy, the *Epic of Wheat: Octopus* (1901) dealing with the growing of wheat, and *The Pit* (1903) describing the gamble of the Chicago wheat exchange.

NORSEMEN. The early inhabitants of Norway. The term is used in a more general sense for all the Scandinavian Vikings who during the 8th–11th cents. raided or settled in Britain, Ireland, France, Russia, Iceland, and Greenland.

NORTH, Frederick, 8th lord (1732–92). British statesman. He entered parl. in 1754, became Chancellor of the Exchequer in 1767, and was P.M. in a govt. of Tories and 'King's Friends' in 1770. Throughout his premiership his policy was largely dictated by George III, and it was against his better judgment that he carried on the war with America. He resigned in 1782, returned to office in 1783 in a coalition with Fox, and after its defeat retired from politics.

NORTH, Sir Thomas (*c.* 1535–1601). English translator. His translation of Plutarch's *Lives* (1579), a masterpiece of Elizabethan prose, formed the source of Shakespeare's Roman plays.

NORTH AMERICA. A continent covering 18 per cent of the earth's land area, whose physical bounds reach Panama, Alaska, and Labrador, and divided into N. America proper (Canada, the U.S.A. and Mexico) and CENTRAL AMERICA (q.v.).

N.A. bears marked physical features. The Laurentian region is disordered rock structure in a low-lying ring round Hudson Bay, from Labrador on the E. to the Arctic. Lakes and streams abound amid wild afforestation. The Appalachian area is a mountainous range running from Newfoundland S.W. to Alabama. Called the Appalachians from Nova Scotia to Pennsylvania, and the Allegheny plateau S. to Alabama, the area is occupied by large coal deposits. A coastal plain borders the Gulf of Mexico and the Atlantic. The Western Highlands or Cordilleras are complex ranges forming a vast interior barrier down the W. of the continent from Alaska to Central America. Rising to more than 20,000 ft. in Mt. McKinley, Alaska, the individual ranges are the Alaska range, Brooks range, Mackenzie mts., Rocky mts., Colorado plateau, and Mexican plateau. Parallel to the Rockies are the Coast range, Cascade range, and Sierra Nevadas, which bound narrow, fertile, Pacific-coast plains. The Central Plains are a wide belt stretching from the Arctic to the Gulf of Mexico, averaging 1,500 m. in breadth and including the Canadian and U.S.A. wheat and plantation areas; roughly along the U.S.-Canadian border they slope gently downwards to N. and to S.

The chief river systems are the E.-flowing St.

Lawrence, Missouri, Arkansas, and Rio del Norte; the W.-flowing Yukon, Snake, and Colorado rivers; the S.-flowing Mississippi, and the N.-flowing Mackenzie. Between Canada and U.S.A. lies the unique lake system, comprising Superior, Michigan, Huron, Erie, and Ontario, from which issues the St. Lawrence. The climate varies greatly with latitude.

The American Indians, incl. the Eskimo, are believed to have entered the continent from Asia, to whose people they bear a marked resemblance. They are thought to have numbered c. 1,000,000 when Europeans first arrived, and although some tribes declined into extinction, there has been a general increase in the 20th cent. Today they number c. 200,000 in Canada; 600,000 in U.S.A.; and 3,000,000 in Mexico: their social and economic plight in U.S.A. led to a special federal aid programme being planned 1968. There has been a considerable admixture of White and Negro blood. Negroes, originally introduced as slave labour in the S. of the continent, are now more widely distributed throughout the U.S.A., where they form about 10% of the pop., though only

a quarter have no admixture of White or other blood. There has been continuing immigration into N.A. from Europe since the 17th cent., during the peak period 1880–1930 averaging half a million annually, so that the population is predominantly White. English, with distinctive accents and usages, is the principal language of the U.S.A. and Canada, but French is a strong minority language in Canada, and Spanish is the nat. language of Mexico. The Indian language survives in great diversity.

NORTHAMPTON. Ancient English town (co. bor.), county town of Northants on the r. Nene. It is the centre of the boot and shoe industry. Other industries incl. engineering, leather tanning, iron foundries and the manufacture of leather goods, toys, roller bearings, and women's clothing. There was a settlement at N. before the Norman Conquest, after which a castle was built there. Pop. (1961) 105,361.

NORTHAMPTONSHIRE or Northants. Midland county of England, which incl. the sources of the Cherwell, Avon, Leam, Welland, and Nene. Its churches with broached spires are famous. The N. climate is mild, the soil fertile, and cattle raising and wheat and barley growing are the chief occupations; boots and shoes are widely made. The largest towns

NORTHAMPTONSHIRE. Sulgrave Manor was the ancestral home of the family of George Washington and in 1914 it became a museum. The Stars and Stripes is said to originate in the Washington arms of 3 mullets and two bars seen in the right spandrel of the arch of the main doorway.
Courtesy of Sulgrave Manor Board.

are Northampton (co. town), and Kettering. Area 914 sq. m.; pop. (1967) 433,880.

NORTH ATLANTIC TREATY. Treaty signed in Washington, D.C., on 4 April 1949 by Belgium, Canada, Denmark, France, Iceland, Italy, Luxembourg, Netherlands, Norway, Portugal, U.K., and U.S.A. The signatories agreed that 'an armed attack against one or more of them in Europe or North America shall be considered an attack against them all'. Greece and Turkey acceded in 1952, and Germany in 1955.

The chief body of the N.A.T. Organization is the Council of Foreign Ministers which holds periodic meetings and also functions in permanent session through the appointment of permanent representatives. The unified international secretariat has its H.Q. at Brussels from 1967 (formerly Paris) as does a Military Committee consisting of chiefs of staff (until 1967 in Washington). The military H.Q. is called Supreme Headquarters Allied Powers, Europe (SHAPE) and moved from Rocquencourt, France, to Chièvres-Casteau, nr. Mons, 1967. The Supreme Allied Commanders, Europe and Atlantic, are Americans, but there is also an Allied Commander, Channel – a British admiral. France withdrew from the organisation, but not from the alliance, 1966.

COUNTRIES OF NORTH AMERICA			
	Area in 1,000 sq. m.	Population	Capital
—			
Canada	3,051	20,014,880	Ottawa
St. Pierre and Miquelon (French)	·093	4,614	St. Pierre
United States of America (incl. Hawaii)	3,615	179,323,175	Washington D.C.
Mexico	764	45,671,000	Mexico City
Great Lakes	95	—	—
	7,525	245,013,669	

NORTH CAROLI′NA. State of the U.S.A. on the Atlantic seaboard, one of the original 13. It is fertile and agriculture, incl. the production of tobacco and cotton, is the principal industry. Kaolin, mica, feldspar, tungsten, and granite are worked; timber is important; textiles, cigarettes (about half those produced in the whole Union), furniture, paper, chemicals, and artificial fibres are produced. The fisheries are valuable. The cap. is Raleigh, the largest city Charlotte, and the chief port is Wilmington. Verrazano, 1524, and De Soto, 1540, were the earliest European

NORTH CAROLINA. Erected by George W. Vanderbilt 2 m. south of Asheville, Biltmore is a monumental mansion incorporating French Renaissance elements, and is now preserved as a museum.   *Courtesy of the Biltmore Museum.*

visitors; the first English settlement in America was made on Roanoke Is. in 1585, but it was wiped out. Area 52,712 sq. m.; pop. (1970) 5,082,059.

NORTHCLIFFE, Alfred Charles William Harmsworth, 1st visct. N. (1865–1922). British newspaper proprietor. He founded his publishing business, later the Amalgamated Press, in 1887 and in 1894 took over the *Evening News.* Founding the *Daily Mail* (1896), he revolutionized popular journalism with attractive make-up and writing, and with the *Daily Mirror* (1903) originated the picture paper: in 1908 he also obtained control of *The Times.* He was chairman of the British War Mission in the U.S.A. in 1917. He was created a baron in 1905 and visct. in 1917. His brother Harold Sidney Harmsworth, 1st visct. **Rothermere** (1868–1940), was associated with him in many of his projects, and was founder of the *Sunday Pictorial* in 1915. He was created baron in 1914 (visct. 1919), and was Air Min. 1917–18.

NORTHCOTE, James (1746–1831). British artist. Going to London from his native Plymouth in 1773, he established himself as a portrait painter. He is remembered as the assistant and biographer of Reynolds.

NORTH DAKŌ′TA. West North Central state of the U.S.A., bounded in the N. by Canada, situated in the Great Plain region, and consisting of 3 huge tablelands, viz. the Red River valley in the E., the Pembina mts. in the N.E., and the Missouri plateau which covers the western half of the state. In the S.W. are the Bad Lands, so called because the pioneers had great difficulty in crossing them. The valley of the Red River is very fertile, and grain production is the chief industry of the state. The cap. is Bismarck, the largest town Fargo. Area 70,665 sq. m.; pop. (1970) 617,761.

NORTH-EAST FRONTIER AGENCY. Tribal district geographically in Assam, India, but administered separately by an adviser directly responsible to the Governor of Assam. It lies in the Himalayas on the borders of China (Tibet) and Burma. Disputes over the boundary led to an invasion of the area by

China in 1962. Area 31,438 sq. m.; pop. (1961 est.) 530,000.

NORTH-EAST PASSAGE. The sea route from the Atlantic round the N. of Asia to the Pacific, followed successfully for the first time by A. E. Nordenskjöld (q.v.) in 1878–9. Since 1935 the use of this route has been extensively developed by the Soviet govt., in connection with its colonization of N. Siberia.

NORTHERN IRELAND. A self-governing country within the U.K. estab. in 1920 and comprising the counties of Antrim, Down, Armagh, Tyrone, Londonderry, and Fermanagh, and the co. bors. of Belfast, the cap., and Londonderry, all in the prov. of Ulster. Area 5,242 sq. m.; pop. (1966) 1,484,770. The largest single group, predominant near the border with the Irish Rep., is R.C., but overall the Protestant denominations are in the majority, Presbyterians being the most numerous. There are 2 univs., Queen's (1849) at Belfast and the New Univ. of Ulster at Coleraine (1968).

Physical. Most of N. Ireland occupies a peninsula of Ireland projecting N.E. towards Scotland. Its centre is the fertile basin of Lough Neagh, joined to Belfast Lough by the valley of the Lagan. To the N. are the plateau of Antrim extending to the rugged coast, and the valley of the Bann. Farther W. the Sperrin mts. (Sawel, 2,240 ft.) rise above boggy plateaux, while in the S.E. of the country the Mourne mts. culminate in Slieve Donard (2,796 ft.). A low temperature range and high humidity and precipitation are characteristic of the climate.

Economics. The traditional industries of linen and shipbuilding are maintained, but since the S.W.W. the country has become one of the world's biggest manufacturers of man-made fibres and textiles. There are also chemical, electronics, car component and aircraft industries, and tobacco factories. One quarter of the land surface is mountain and bog – producing peat

NORTHERN IRELAND. The seat of Northern Ireland's Parliament, Stormont was designed by Sir Arnold Thornley in severe classical style and built 1928–32 of Portland stone on a plinth of grey granite from Slieve Donard, the highest peak in the Mountains of Mourne. It is approached by a flight of steps 90 ft. high.   *Courtesy of Northern Ireland Tourist Board.*

and used for rough grazing – but on the remainder a thriving agriculture supports a growing food processing industry. Formerly on a basis of small-holdings, agriculture now moves towards amalgamation in large farms, highly specialized and mechanized. Products include milk, butter, cheese, beef, bacon, eggs and chicken; and the chief crops are barley, oats, hay, potatoes, flax, and – in co. Armagh – fruit.

Government. Since 1920 N.I. has had its own parl. (a House of Commons and a Senate elected by the Commons) at Stormont, near Belfast. It retains the right of sending members to Westminster. A Governor represents the Sovereign, and there is a cabinet consisting of a P.M. and 9 other ministers. The parl. legislates for N.I. except in matters of imperial concern.

History. The recent history of N.I. dates from the early 17th cent. when Protestant Scottish and English 'planters' settled there and gave the region an outlook very different from that of the rest of the island. Separation from the S. came in 1920; the border, which excluded 3 Catholic Ulster counties, was agreed on in 1925. By the 1960s Nationalist agitation for union with the Rep. of Ireland seemed to have faded, but Civil Rights disturbances (espec. in Belfast and Londonderry) from 1968 in protest against alleged discrimination against R.Cs. in employment and housing, and against the restricted franchise in local govt. elections, although met by reform, developed into further rioting and bloodshed which necessitated the despatch of a Brit. military peacekeeping force. By 1972 I.R.A. outrages had disrupted the life of the prov. and direct rule over N.I. by the U.K. Parliament and Govt. was estab., the Stormont Parliament being prorogued. William Whitelaw, as Sec. of State for N.I., made repeated efforts to reach a negotiated peace settlement.

NORTHERN RHODESIA. *See* ZAMBIA.

NORTHERN TERRITORY. A territory of the Commonwealth of Australia, bounded on the N. by the Arafura Sea and lying between Queensland and W. Australia. Darwin is the cap. Most of the N.T. is within the tropics, and the climate is hot, with considerable variations in temperature in the S. There is an insufficient rainfall, but beef cattle are reared, with the help of water from artesian bores; fishing and pearl fishing are carried on on the coast; and gold, copper, tungsten, manganese, bauxite, and uranium are among minerals worked. Area 523,620 sq. m.; pop. (1966) 37,433, plus 21,119 aborigines.

NORTH POLE. *See* ARCTIC.

NORTH RHINE-WESTPHALIA. Land of W. Germany, to the W., in the valley of the Rhine, and including the Ruhr (q.v.) industrial dist. It was formed in 1946 from the N. part of the former Rhine prov. and the prov. of Westphalia (q.v.). Sugar-beet and potatoes are the biggest crops, coal and iron the chief mineral products. All kinds of iron and steel goods, fertilizers, artificial fibres, textiles are made. Düsseldorf is the cap.; other large towns are Cologne, Essen, Dortmund, Duisburg, and Wuppertal. Area 13,110 sq. m.; pop. (1966) 16,835,500.

NORTH SEA. Sea bounded by the E. coast of Britain, and the coasts of Belgium, the Netherlands, Germany, Denmark, and Norway. In the N.E. it joins the Norwegian Sea, and in the S. it meets the Strait of Dover. Its mean depth is about 30 fathoms; greatest depth is 361 fathoms, off Norway. There are a series of banks extending from the coast of Yorkshire to the Skagerrak, the most important being the Dogger Bank. There are rich fisheries, and oil and natural gas resources. Area *c.* 202,000 sq. m.

NORTH SHIELDS. English seaport in Northumberland, at the mouth of the Tyne, opposite South Shields, 7½ m. E.N.E. of Newcastle; it is included in the co. bor. of Tynemouth and exports coal and coke. It has shipbuilding yards, and factories making cables, chemicals, etc.

NORTH UIST. *See* UIST.

NORTHUMBERLAND, John Dudley, duke of (*c.* 1502–53). English statesman. Son of Edmund Dudley, he was created duke of N. in 1551, and was chief minister until Edward VI's death in 1553, when he attempted to place his daughter-in-law Lady Jane Grey on the throne. His misrule had made him so hated that the scheme immediately collapsed, and N. was beheaded.

NORTHUMBERLAND. Co. in the N. of England, separated from Scotland by the Cheviot Hills and the Tweed, and bounded on the S. by Durham, on the W. by Cumberland. The surface in the E. is flat, but it rises to the central moorland region, and in the N.W. there are mountains which culminate in the Cheviot

(2,676 ft.). The chief rivers are the Tyne and Tweed. In the S.W. are the Northumbrian lakes, of which the largest is Greenlee Lough. The chief towns are Newcastle upon Tyne (the co. town), Tynemouth, Blyth, Wallsend, and Whitley Bay. There is a large coalfield in the S.E. and Tyneside is a great industrial area for shipbuilding, engineering, iron, steel, chemicals, etc. Area 2,019 sq. m.; pop. (1967) 828,290.

NORTHUMBRIA. An Anglo-Saxon kingdom covering N.E. England and S.E. Scotland. It originally comprised two independent kingdoms founded in the 6th cent., Bernicia, extending from the Forth to the Tees, and Deira, from the Tees to the Humber, which were united in the 7th cent. During the 7th–8th cents. N., under the influence of Irish missionaries, became a cultural centre of European fame. It accepted the supremacy of Wessex in 827, and during the later 9th cent. was conquered by the Danes.

NORTH-WEST FRONTIER PROVINCE. Prov. of British India, formed in 1901, which lay between Afghanistan and Punjab. Predominantly Moslem, it became part of Pakistan in 1947 and in 1955 was absorbed in W. Pakistan. Containing the Khyber and other passes, this mountainous area was strategically vital to successive Mogul, Sikh and British rulers, who waged constant warfare against the Pathan tribesmen. The cap. was Peshawar.

NORTH-WEST PASSAGE. The sea route from the Atlantic round the N. of Canada to the Pacific. Many attempts were made to discover it from that of Frobisher (1576–8) onwards. Franklin's failure to return in 1847, as planned, from his search for it led to the organization of 39 expeditions in the next 10 years. R. McClure discovered the passage 1850–3, though he did not cover the whole route by sea: this was done for the first time by Amundsen (1903–5). It was first used commercially by the U.S. tanker *Manhattan* 1969 following Alaskan oil discoveries.

NORTHWEST TERRITORIES. The N.W. region of Canada, situated between Yukon on the W. and Baffin Bay on the E., and bounded on the S. by British Columbia, Alberta, Saskatchewan, and Manitoba. In the W. is the r. Mackenzie. There are many lakes, of which the largest are the Great Slave Lake and the Great Bear Lake. The area was the northern part of Rupert's Land, bought by the Canadian govt. from the Hudson's Bay Co. in 1869, and is divided into Mackenzie, Keewatin, and Franklin dists. An Act of 1952 placed the N.W.T. under a commissioner acting at Ottawa under the Min. of Northern Affairs and National Resources. Mining, fur trapping, and fishing are the chief industries. Mineral products incl. gold, silver, pitchblende, and petroleum. The Mackenzie r. and its tributaries are an important means of transport; regular air services operate to and from the main settlements. Area 1,304,903 sq. m.; pop. (1966) 25,995, two-thirds Indian or Eskimo.

NORTHWICH. English market town (U.D.) in Cheshire, on the Weaver, 18 m. N.E. of Chester, long famous for its salt mines and brine springs. It has some beautiful old houses and is an important centre of chemical production. Pop. (1961) 10,454.

NORTON, Caroline Elizabeth Sarah (1808–77). British author. The granddau. of R. B. Sheridan, she m. the Hon. George N. (1800–75) in 1827. In 1836 her husband falsely accused Lord Melbourne of seducing her, and subsequently tried to obtain the profits from her books. In 1877 she m. Sir Maxwell Stirling. Her best works were *Undying One* (1830), dealing with the Wandering Jew; and *Voice from the Factories* (1836), attacking child labour.

NORTON, Charles Eliot (1827–1908). American scholar. B. in Mass., he was prof. of the history of art at Harvard 1873–98, helped to found the *Nation*, and wrote some notable *Letters*.

NORWAY. A kingdom occupying the N. and W. portion of the Scandinavian peninsula, bounded on

1a

the E. by Sweden, Finland, and the U.S.S.R., on the N. by the Arctic Ocean, on the N.W. by the Norwegian Sea, and on the W. by the North Sea.

Physical. The surface is mountainous, the highest part of the country (rising to more than 8,000 ft.) being in the region of the Sogne fjord. There is an

NORWAY. The Church of Our Saviour, Oslo's cathedral, stands in the flower market by the main square. Completed in 1697, it was greatly altered 1850, and the octagonal sacristy dates from 1949–50.
Courtesy of the Norwegian National Tourist Office.

extensive coastline, deeply indented with fjords; and numerous islands lie offshore. Some of the most beautiful fjords are Hardanger, Sogne (largest and deepest), Nord, Trondheim, Vest, and Ofoten. The Midnight Sun (q.v.) is seen in northern N., and at the North Cape part of the sun's disc is continuously above the horizon from mid-May to the end of July, and there is no sunrise for 2 months in winter. During the long winter nights the Northern Lights appear (*see* AURORA).

The only river of any length is the Glomma (350 m.); from the numerous short, rapid rivers with many waterfalls, N. harnesses an ample supply of electric power.

Economic. Forests cover nearly one-quarter of the area; they are one of the principal sources of wealth, and the paper and wood-pulp industries flourish. Although less than one-twenty-fifth of N. is under cultivation, agriculture is an important industry. The principal crops are hay, potatoes, barley, and oats. Cattle and sheep are raised, and there are important fisheries. Whaling is carried on in the Antarctic. The canning industry is growing. The most important mineral products are pyrites and iron ore. The chief towns incl. Oslo (the cap.), Bergen, Trondheim, Stavanger, Drammen, Kristiansand, and Haugesund; there are univs. at Oslo (1811), Bergen (1948), Tromsö, and Trondheim.

The climate, thanks to the Gulf Stream, is not so rigorous as might be expected from the latitude.

Area 125,068 sq. m.; pop. (1967) 3,769,269.

Government. N. is a constitutional monarchy. Under the constitution of 1814 legislative power is vested in the Storting (Parl.), elected every 4 yrs. by men and women over 21. The Storting is then divided by election among its own members into a Lagting (upper committee of one quarter of its members) and Odelsting (lower committee). *See* OLAF V.

History. N. was originally inhabited by a Finnish people, who were gradually conquered by Teutonic invaders from *c.* 1700 B.C. The country remained under local chieftains until Harald Fairhair (reigned 872–*c.* 930), the most powerful of them, unified N. and introduced the feudal system. Christianity was introduced by Olaf II in the 11th cent.; he was defeated

by rebel chiefs backed by Canute in 1030, but his son Magnus I regained the throne 5 years later. Haakon IV (1217–63) estab. the authority of the Crown over the nobles and the Church and made the monarchy hereditary. Denmark and N. were united by marriage in 1380, and in 1397 N., Denmark and Sweden were united under one sovereign; union with Denmark continued after Sweden, following a long struggle, was recognized as independent in 1523. The Reformed religion was introduced in 1536.

Denmark in 1814 ceded N. to Sweden, but the Norwegians declared their independence and adopted a parliamentary constitution. The Swedes then invaded N., and a compromise was reached whereby N. was to remain an independent kingdom, with its own parl., united with Sweden under a common king. Conflict between the Norwegian parl. and the Swedish monarchy continued until 1905, when the parl. declared N. completely independent. This was confirmed by plebiscite, and Prince Charles of Denmark was elected king under the name Haakon VII.

N. was invaded by Germany in April 1940, and in spite of armed resistance by the Norwegian Army, assisted by British and French forces, completely overrun by June. The king and govt. escaped to Britain, while a puppet govt. was set up under Quisling (q.v.). A strong resistance movement was maintained inside N., and 4 million tons of Norwegian merchant shipping rendered good service to the Allies. The Labour Party, which had held office since 1935, except for Aug.–Sept. 1963, were succeeded in 1965 by a 4-party non-socialist coalition.

Language. A member of the Scandinavian branch of the Germanic family of languages. As a consequence of the political union of Norway with Denmark (1380–1814), Danish became the literary medium of Norway, until in the 19th cent. the scholar Aasen (1813–96) produced the *Landsmål*, which he based on the local dialects of Norway; it has been accepted in many dists. of Norway, in schools, in churches, and for speeches in the Storting; but Dano-Norwegian, or the *Riksmål* continues to be used side by side with it.

Literature. The most remarkable production of N. L. before the eclipse which followed the union with Denmark in 1380 are the Skaldic genealogical poems of the 10th cent., the poetic Edda (q.v.) assembled in the 12th, and the prose sagas such as the *Heimskringla* of Snorri Sturlason in the 13th. A revival came in the 17th cent. with the descriptive poetry of Petter Dass (1647–1708), but the work of Ludwig Holberg and Johan Wessel (1742–85) belonged rather to the joint Dano-N. tradition. In the 19th cent. J. S. Welhaven (1807–73) still looked to the Danish connection, but the great national poet Henrik Wergeland turned to Norway's own spiritual resources for inspiration. The national revival became more vigorous through the work of the great folklorists and under the influence of vernacular writers such as Aasmund Vinje (1818–70) and Arne Garborg (1851–1924) who adopted Ivar Aasen's *Landsmål*. The great figures of the later 19th cent. were Björnstjerne Björnson, Henrik Ibsen, and the novelists Jonas Lie and Alexander Kielland. To the earlier 20th cent. belong the novelists Hans Kinck (1865–1926), Knut Hamsun, Sigrid Undset, and Olaf Duun. Later prominent figures are Helge Krog (1889–1962), dramatist and critic; the poets Arnulf Overland (1889–1968) and Olaf Bull (1887–1933); the novelists Johan Falkberget (1879–1967), Cora Sandel (1880–　　　), and Sigurd Hoel (1890–1960); and the poet, playwright, and novelist Nordahl Grieg.

Music. Among well-known names are those of the violinist-composer Ole Bull (1810–80), the nationalist Grieg and the smaller-scale genius of Sinding (qq.v.).

NORWICH (nor′ij). English city (co. bor.), cap. of Norfolk, situated on the Wensum, just above its confluence with the Yare. Notable buildings incl. the cathedral (founded 1096), Norman castle (the keep housing a museum and collection of paintings by the Norwich School), Guildhall (15th cent.), medieval churches, Tudor houses, Georgian Assembly House, City Hall (1938), and Central Library (1963). The Univ. of E. Anglia (1963) is at Earlham to the W. of the city. Industries incl. footwear, engineering, printing, chemicals, clothing, and foodstuffs; and it is a marketing, banking, insurance, and commercial centre. Pop. (1961) 119,904.

NORWICH, Alfred Duff Cooper, 1st visct. N. (1890–1954). British diplomat. Entering parl. as a Unionist (later Cons.) in 1924, he was War Min. 1935–7, and then 1st Lord of the Admiralty, resigning in 1938 in protest against the Munich agreement. Under Churchill he was Min. of Information (1940–1); govt. rep. with the French Committee of National Liberation 1943–4, and ambassador to France 1944–7. Knighted in 1948, he was created a visct. in 1952, and pub. his memoirs, *Old Men Forget*, in 1953. He m. in 1919 Lady Diana Manners (1893–   ), a celebrated beauty, who created a sensation in Max Reinhardt's production of *The Miracle* (1924).

NOSE. The upper orifice of the respiratory tract; the organ of the sense of smell. It is divided down the middle by a septum of cartilage. The nostrils or outer portion contain plates of cartilage which can be moved by muscles and have a growth of stiff hairs at the margin to prevent foreign bodies from entering. The whole nasal cavity is lined with mucous membrane which warms and moistens the air and ejects dirt. Inside the nose 3 wide air spaces, separated by plates of bone, lead back to the nasopharynx at the head of the windpipe. The lining of the lower, or respiratory, part of the cavity is covered with cilia; that of the upper part is furnished with olfactory cells which receive impressions of smell from particles in the entering air and transmit them through special nerves to the brain. The cavity communicates with various sinuses.

NOSTRADA'MUS. Latinized name of Michel de Notredame (1503–66). French astrologer. He was consulted by Catherine de' Medici and was physician-in-ordinary to Charles IX.

NOTTINGHAM. English city (co. bor.), co. tn. of Notts, situated at the confluence of the Leen and the

NOTTINGHAM. To the west of the city is the university, overlooking University Lake. The Trent Building, to the left, is named after Lord Trent (q.v.), and was opened in 1928. Linked to it, on the right, is the Portland Building (1956).
Courtesy of Cecil Howitt & Partners, Architects, Nottingham.

Trent. Situated on an important coalfield, N. is linked by canal with the Atlantic and North Sea, and manufactures lace, hosiery, bicycles and typewriters, tobacco, chemicals, and beer. The castle, erected in the 17th cent. on the site of a Norman fortress, rebuilt 1875, is used as a museum; the R.C. cathedral

(1844) is by Pugin; there is an attractive theatre, and Newstead Abbey, 11 m. N., was the home of Lord Byron. Pop. (1961) 311,645.

NOTTINGHAMSHIRE or Notts. Midland county of England. Most of the county is undulating, rising to a height of 600 ft. in the S.W. Sherwood Forest, famous for its association with Robin Hood, is in the S.W.: what remains of the forest is incl. in the region called the 'Dukeries'. The chief rivers are the Trent and its tributaries, the Idle, Erewash, and Soar. In the W. are Cresswell Crags where remains of pre-historic man have been found. The chief manufactures are lace and hosiery, bicycles, tobacco; and there are also iron foundries and machinery and motor works; coal has been mined since the Middle Ages. The co. tn. is Nottingham. Area 844 sq. m.; pop. (1967) 962,450.

NOUAKCHOTT. Town in W. Africa, cap. of the Islamic rep. of Mauritania. It lies on the Atlantic, 150 m. N.N.E. of St. Louis-de-Sénégal (from which Mauritania was formerly governed). It was built from 1957, with French help. Pop. (1967) 15,000.

NO'VA. A star which suffers an outburst, and flares up for a period which may amount to several weeks – after which it subsides to its former state. In novae such an expansion causes a light increase of 10–15 magnitudes; in supernovae, thought to be the result of the explosion of a complete star, up to 20 magnitudes.

NOVALIS (novah'lēs). Pen-name of Friedrich Leopold, Freiherr von Hardenberg (1772–1801), German poet. The most genuinely inspired poet of the older Romantics, he approached the great problems of God and Nature, life and death, with profound intuition. The death of his fiancée Sophie von Kühn in 1797 called forth the mystical beauty of his *Hymnen an die Nacht* (1800). N. left two unfinished romances, *Die Lehrlinge zu Sais* and *Heinrich von Ofterdingen*.

NO'VA LISBÕ'A. Town of Angola, W. Africa, founded as Huambo in 1912, and intended to replace Luanda as cap. in 1927. It was re-named Nova Lisboa in 1928, but remains only the cap. designate. N.L. is an agricultural trading centre with railway repair shops and an airport. Pop. (est.) 17,000.

NOVA SCOTIA (nōv'ahskōsh'iah). A prov. of Canada, consisting of a long, narrow peninsula and the island of Cape Breton, S. of the Gulf of St. Lawrence. Its E. and S. shores are washed by the Atlantic, and an isthmus, 11½ m. wide, connects the province with New Brunswick. The Cobequid mts. stretch across the interior. The length of the coastline is about 2,000 m.; there are many rivers, most of them under 50 m. long, lakes, and fine harbours. The cap. and chief port is Halifax. Agriculture is the most important industry, particularly dairying, poultry rearing and fruit growing. The fisheries are valuable. Lumbering is carried on, and wood pulp for paper is manufactured. Coal, gypsum, lead, zinc, and copper are mined, and there are iron and steel works, paper mills, food factories, and shipyards. The legislature of N.S. consists of a Lieut.-Gov., who is appointed by the Federal Govt. for a term of 5 years, and a House of Assembly (of 46 members) elected by popular vote every 5 years.

History. N.S. was visited by Cabot in 1497, but it was not until 1604 that a permanent settlement was established by Europeans. In that year the French under De Monts established themselves on the peninsula. In 1613 they were expelled by English colonists from Virginia. The name N.S. was given to the colony, which had hitherto been called Acadia, by Sir William Alexander in 1621. England and France subsequently contended for possession of the territory. In 1713, N.S. (which then incl. present-day New Brunswick and Prince Edward Is.) was ceded to the English; Cape Breton Is. remained French until 1763. N.S. was one of the 4 original provs. of the dominion of Canada, 1867. Area 21,842 sq. m., incl. 1,441 sq. m. of water; pop. (1966) 756,039.

NO'VAYA ZEMLYA'. Group of islands in the Arctic off the N. coast of European Russia. It has few inhabitants, but is visited by seamen and hunters. Whales, seals, walruses, dolphins, and birds are found there in large numbers. Area *c.* 35,000 sq. m.

NOVEL. A full-length fictitious prose narrative. Probably inspired by Oriental story-telling, the European N. originated in Greece in the 2nd cent. B.C. Best-known of the Greek examples is the *Daphnis and Chloë* of Longus, and almost the only surviving specimen of the Latin N. is the *Golden Ass* of Apuleius, based on a Greek model. But the modern N. took its name and inspiration from the Italian *novella*, the short tale of varied character which became popular in the late 13th cent. Most famous of these It. writers were Boccaccio and Bandello, whose works were translated into English in such collections as Painter's *Palace of Pleasure* (1566–7), and inspired the Elizabethan novelists, e.g. Lyly, Sidney, Greene, Nash, and Lodge. In Spain, Cervantes' *Don Quixote* (1604) made an outstanding contribution to the development of the N., but the 17th cent. was largely dominated by the French romances of La Calprenède and Mlle de Scudéry, although Congreve and Aphra Behn continued the English tradition.

In the 18th cent. the realistic novel came to maturity in the work of Defoe, Richardson, Fielding, Sterne, and Smollett. Walpole, and later Mrs. Radcliffe, by their development of Gothic romance, prepared the way for Sir Walter Scott, while Jane Austen perfected the domestic N. of manners. The great representatives of the Victorian Age are Dickens, Thackeray, the Brontës, Kingsley, Charles Reade, George Eliot, Trollope, and Stevenson. The 19th cent. was also a great period for the N. on the Continent, with Hugo, Balzac, the two Dumas, George Sand, and Zola in France; Goethe and Jean Paul in Germany; Gogol, Turgeniev, Dostoievsky, and Tolstoy in Russia; and in America with Cooper, Melville, Hawthorne, Twain, and Howells.

To the transition period from Victorian to modern times belong the rebels Meredith, Butler, Hardy, and Gissing; the slightly alien genius or subject-matter of Henry James, Kipling, Conrad, and George Moore; and the sober realism of Wells, Bennett, and Galsworthy. Slightly later are W. S. Maugham, E. M. Forster, Hugh Walpole, James Joyce, D. H. Lawrence, I. Compton-Burnett, and Virginia Woolf – the last three being particularly influential in the development of N. technique. Among those who began writing in the '20s are J. B. Priestley, Richard Hughes, Aldous Huxley, Christopher Isherwood, Graham Greene, William Plomer, V. S. Pritchett, and Evelyn Waugh; and the women writers E. Bowen, Rose Macaulay, and Rosamund Lehmann. The next decade produced Nigel Balchin, Joyce Cary, Lord Snow, Lawrence Durrell, and George Orwell. Twentieth-cent. novelists abroad incl. (German) Lion Feuchtwanger, Thomas Mann, Franz Kafka, Ernst Wiechert, and Stefan Zweig; (French) André Gide, Marcel Proust, Jules Romains, François Mauriac, and Alain Robbe-Grillet; (Italian) Gabriele d'Annunzio, Ignazio Silone, and Alberto Moravia; (Russian) Maxim Gorky, Mikhail Sholokhov, Aleksei Tolstoi, and Boris Pasternak; (Spanish) Arturo Baréa, Pío Baroja and Ramón Pérez de Ayala; and (American) Edith Wharton, Theodore Dreiser, Ernest Hemingway, Upton Sinclair, Sinclair Lewis, and William Faulkner.

NOVELLO, Ivor. Stage-name of British actor, manager, and composer I. N. Davies (1893–1951). B. in Cardiff, son of the singer Clara Novello Davies, he made his name as a song-writer, e.g. 'Keep the Home Fires Burning', in the F.W.W., and author of straight plays, e.g. *The Truth Game* (1928), but is best remembered for the romantic musical plays in which he often appeared with romantically handsome charm, e.g. *Glamorous Night* (1925), *The Dancing Years* (1939), *Perchance To Dream* (1945–7), *King's Rhapsody* (1949) and *Gay's The Word* (1951).

NO'VGOROD. Town of the R.S.F.S.R., cap. of N. region, on the Volkhov, 2 m. N. of Lake Ilmen. N. dates from the 9th cent. and was an important and prosperous city from the 12th cent. until destroyed by Ivan the Terrible in 1570. It is an agricultural centre and has distilleries, meat-packing works, etc. Pop. (1967) 61,000.

NOVIKOV-PRIBOY, Alexey (1877–1944). Soviet writer. He served in the Tsarist navy, and was a prisoner of war in Japan. He wrote realistic sea stories and novels based on his own experiences, of which the best-known is *Tsushima*.

NOVI PAZAR (nov'e pahzahr'). Town in S. Serbia, Yugoslavia, on the Raska. The original home of the Serbs, it has the ruins of a medieval Serbian castle; the Turks captured it in the 15th cent. Pop. (est.) 12,500.

NOVI SAD. Cap. of the autonomous prov. of Voivodina, Yugoslavia, the seat of a bishopric. Pottery and cotton goods are manufactured. Pop. (1961) 110,877.

NOVOCAINE. A synthetic drug widely used as a local anaesthetic. It has replaced cocaine, being equally strong when injected but only one-third as toxic and not habit-forming. It is, however, not nearly so effective when used as a surface anaesthetic. It is always used with adrenaline.

NOVO KUZNETSK (nov'o kooznyet'sk). Town in Kemerovo region, R.S.F.S.R., on the r. Tom, 225 m. S.S.E. of Tomsk, an important centre of steel and iron manufacture in the Kuzbas. A town of less than 4,000 in 1939, it had a pop. of 484,000 in 1967. It was called Stalinsk 1932–61.

NOVOROSSII'SK. Seaport of the R.S.F.S.R., of the N.E. coast of the Black Sea. Cement. bicycles, furniture, etc., are made. Pop. (1967) 120,000.

NOVOSIBIRSK. Town in the R.S.F.S.R., cap. of N. region. It has flour mills and grain elevators, and factories making textiles, metallurgical goods, plastics, soap, etc.; it is a centre for the distribution of agricultural machinery. Pop. (1967) 1,049,000.

NOVOYA BUKHARA. *See* BUKHARA.

NOYES (noiz), **Alfred** (1880–1958). British poet. B. at Wolverhampton, he was ed. at Oxford, and was prof. of modern English literature at Princeton univ. 1914–23. His 1st vol. of verse, *The Loom of Years* (1902), was followed by many others, equally smooth in versification and traditional in theme, e.g. *Drake, an English Epic* (1906–8) and *The Torch Bearers* (1922–30). His best-known poems incl. 'The Highwayman' and 'Barrel Organ'. Other works incl. the prose *The Unknown God* (1934), telling of his conversion to R. Catholicism, and *The Accusing Ghost* (1957), an attempt to clear the name of Roger Casement.

NOYON (nwah-yoń'). Town in Oise dept., France. Calvin was b. at N. which had a cathedral, destroyed in the F.W.W., founded by Pepin the Short in the 8th cent. Pop. (1962) 9,548.

NU (noo), **U** (1907–). Burmese statesman. He signed the independence treaty in 1947 and became first P.M. of the Rep. of Burma in 1948. He was superseded by General Ne Win in 1958 on the grounds of a state of grave disturbance, returned as P.M. after the 1960 elections, but was arrested (1962–6) following a military coup by the general in 1962.

NU'BIA. A region of N.E. Africa, probably named from *nub*, the ancient Egyptian word for gold. It was one of the chief battlegrounds of the ancient world, where the struggle for supremacy in N. Africa was waged between the black and white peoples, and the great rock-cut temple at Abu Simbel and such forts as Buhen are relics of Egyptian occupation: to the Egyptians northern N. was known as Wawat and

NUBIA. Rameses completed this superb temple, hewn from the living rock and dedicated to the worship of Re-Harmachis, at Abu Simbel (between the Nile's 1st and 2nd cataracts) in 1359 B.C. The 4 seated statues of the king at the entrance are more than 70 ft. high and between the legs of each are large-size statues of Queen Nefertari and some of the royal children. Within (right) there are four 30 ft. statues in the great hall (54 ft. wide and 58 ft. long), again showing the king wearing the Double Crown and holding the crook and flail sceptres. To preserve it from flooding following completion of the High Dam at Aswan, it was cut up and re-erected on higher ground. *Courtesy of the Egyptian State Tourist Administration.*

southern N. as Kush, and of modern N. the north is part of Egypt and the south part of the Rep. of Sudan. Of particular interest are the mysterious X-group, people who occupied the greater part of N. *c.* A.D. 250–550, and whose royal tombs were excavated by W. B. Emery. By the building of the Aswan High Dam the greater part of N. was submerged beneath the extended reservoir (Lake Nasser).

NUCLEAR FISSION. The splitting of a heavy nucleus into 2 (or very rarely more) approximately equal fragments – the fission products. Fission is accompanied by the emission of neutrons (q.v.) and the release of energy. It can be spontaneous, or it can be caused by the impact of a neutron, a fast-charged particle or a photon.

NUCLEAR POWER. *See* ATOMIC ENERGY.

NUCLEAR REACTOR. A structure in which a fission chain reaction can be maintained and controlled. It usually contains a fuel, coolant, and moderator, and is most often surrounded by a concrete biological shield to absorb neutron and gamma-ray emission.

NUCLEAR WARFARE. For the use of nuclear weapons in the S.W.W. *see* BOMB. In a Third World War, with initial concentration on large industrial cities, casualties from blast and fallout (q.v.) have been est. at 120,000,000 if the U.S.S.R. struck first, and 70,000,000 if the U.S.A. began: China might not have sufficient intercontinental ballistic missiles (ICBMs) to strike until the early 1970s and a relatively small no. of bombs could destroy half her own industry and town population since it is concentrated in *c.* 50 cities. Defence would be by anti-ballistic missile (ABM) system, such as the American Nike X, which comprises a radar system, plus 2 types of missile with nuclear warhead, one shorter-range with high acceleration, and one comparatively long-range, able to intercept above the atmosphere. Long-range multiple missiles carrying a number of warheads (MIRV – Multiple Independently Targetable Re-entry Vehicle) were developed by 1968. To avoid the spread of weapon manufacture the U.K., U.S.A., U.S.S.R. and 56 other countries signed a Treaty of Nuclear Non-Proliferation 1968, in force 1970.

NUCLEIC ACIDS. Complex organic acids with long-chain spiralling molecules, some of which like DNA (deoxyribonucleic acid) and RNA (ribonucleic acid) play an important part in protein synthesis and in the transmission of hereditary characteristics.

NUFFIELD, William Richard Morris, visct. N. (1877–1963). British manufacturer and philanthropist. Starting with a small cycle-repairing business, he planned in 1910 a car to run at low cost for the ordinary man, and built up Morris Motors Ltd. at Cowley, Oxford—now merged in British Motor Holdings. His benefactions incl. establishment of the Oxford Medical School Trust, Nuffield Coll., Oxford, and the Nuffield Foundation (1943). He was created baron 1934 and visct. 1938.

NUMA POMPILIUS. Legendary king of Rome, whose reign is traditionally dated 716–679 B.C. He succeeded Romulus and instituted religious rites.

NUMIDIA. Roman name, meaning nomads' land, for a territory of N. Africa, the E. part of modern Algeria.

NUMISMATICS. The study of coins and medals. The invention of coinage is attributed to the Chinese in the 2nd millennium B.C., the earliest types being small-scale bronze reproductions of barter objects – knives, spades, etc. In the W. coinage of stamped,

NUFFIELD. An early 'bullnose' Morris Oxford (1913) driven by Lord Nuffield. He pioneered mass-production and the use of pressed steel for bodies. *British Motor Holdings Ltd.*

guaranteed weight originated with the Lydians of Asia Minor (early 7th cent. B.C.) who used electrum, a local natural mixture of gold and silver: the first to issue gold and silver coins was Croesus of Lydia in the 6th cent. B.C. In modern times the right to make and issue coins is a state monopoly and the great majority are tokens, in that their face value is greater than that of the metal of which they consist. A milled edge, originally used on gold and silver coins for greater security against 'clipping', is retained in some modern token coinage.

NUN (Lat. *nonna*, an elderly woman). Woman devoted to the service of God under the vows of poverty, chastity, and obedience, and living under a certain rule. It is possible that the institution of communities for Ns. preceded the establishment of monasteries (*see* MONASTICISM), and the majority of the male orders have their feminine counterparts. The convent is ruled by a superior (often elected), who is subject to the authority of the bishop of the diocese or sometimes directly to the Pope.

NUNEATON. English market town (bor.) in Warwickshire, 9 m. N.N.E. of Coventry. The principal industry is coal-mining; there are also brickworks and factories making hosiery and other textiles, and hats. Pop. (1961) 56,598.

NUÑEZ DE ARCE (nōōn′yäth dā ahr′thā), **Gaspar** (1832–1903). Spanish poet. B. in Valladolid, he made his reputation with the lyrical and patriotic *Battlecries* (1875); the most famous of his later vols. of verse are *El Vértigo* (1879) and *La Visión de Fray Martín* (1880).

NUREMBERG (Ger. Nürnberg). A city of Bavaria, E. Germany. It lies on the Pegnitz, c. 90 m. N.N.W. of Munich, and was noted for its ancient walls and fine old buildings, incl. the castle; the churches of St. Lorenz, St. Sebald, and Our Lady; the town hall; and the houses of Hans Sachs and Albrecht Dürer, until it suffered some 75 per cent devastation in the S.W.W. Manufactures incl. toys, electrical and other machinery, precision instruments, calculating machines, pencils and fountain pens, textiles, beer. The hop trade is of importance.

A castle was founded on the site in 1050, and in 1219 N. became a free imperial city. During the Middle Ages it attained great importance both as a commercial and a cultural centre, but it decayed after the 30 Years War and was annexed by Bavaria in 1806. Nazi Party rallies were held here from 1933, and in 1945 the N. Trials (q.v.). Pop. (1966) 469,800.

NUREMBERG TRIALS. The trials held in judgment of the leading Nazi war criminals Nov. 1945–Oct. 1946. The International Military Tribunal consisted of 4 judges and 4 prosecutors; 1 of each from U.K., U.S.A., U.S.S.R. and France. The main charges in the indictment were: (1) conspiracy to wage wars of aggression; (2) crimes against peace; (3) war crimes, e.g. murder and ill-treatment of civilians and prisoners of war, deportation of civilians for slave labour, and killing of hostages; (4) crimes against humanity, e.g. mass-murder of Jews and murder and ill-treatment of political opponents. An appendix accused the German Cabinet, General Staff, and High Command, Nazi leadership corps, S.S., S.A., and Gestapo of criminal responsibility. Of the 24 men accused, Krupp was too ill to be tried; Ley committed suicide during the trial, and Bormann, who had fled, was sentenced to death in his absence. Fritsche, Schacht and Papen were acquitted. The other 18 were found guilty on one or more counts. Hess, Funk and Raeder were sentenced to life imprisonment, Shirach and Speer to 20 yrs., Neurath to 15 yrs., and Doenitz to 10 yrs. The remaining 11 men, sentenced to death by hanging, were Goering (committed suicide before execution), Ribbentrop, Kaltenbrunner, Rosenberg, Frank, Frick, Sauckel, Seyss-Inquart, Streicher, Keitel, and Jodl. The leadership corps, S.S., and Gestapo were declared criminal organizations.

NUREYEV (noorā′yef), **Rudolf** (1939–   ). Russian dancer. B. at Ufa, son of a farmer, he was trained at the Kirov Ballet School, then danced with the co. until he sought political asylum in the West while they were appearing in Paris in 1961. He joined Le Grand Ballet du Marquis de Cuevas, and subsequently made a series of appearances with Dame Margot Fonteyn in *Giselle, Marguerite and Armand*, etc.

NURSERY RHYMES. Jingles current among children. Usually limited to a couplet or quatrain with strongly marked rhythm and rhymes, they have often been handed down by oral tradition from remote antiquity. Some of the oldest N.Rs. are connected with a traditional tune and accompanied the ancient ring games, e.g. 'Here we go round the mulberry bush', which were part of the May Day festivities. Others preserve in a mutilated form the memory of incantations and other rites; and yet others, e.g. Jack Sprat, Jack Horner, and Mary with her little lamb, have a factual basis and have commemorated popular figures.

NURSING. The care of the sick, very young or old and disabled. Originally practised by members of religious orders, N. became progressively secularized following the Renaissance and Reformation, but organised training was first instituted in Germany in 1836. The work done there influenced Florence Nightingale (q.v.) who, during the Crimean War, estab. standards of scientific, humanitarian care in military hospitals, which had a beneficial effect throughout the world. In Britain the General Nursing Councils, estab. by the Nurses Registration Act of 1919, register nurses qualified by examination following a 3-year training in a hospital and (since the 1943 Nurses Act) enrol nurses who have completed a less advanced 2-year training. In addition to courses which lead to state registration in special fields of N. (e.g. sick children, mental N., etc.) there are a large number of post-registration programmes for health visiting, midwifery, etc., many organized by the Royal College of Nursing (1916). In the U.S., although registration is the responsibility of individual states, an almost uniform standard has been estab. by the National League for N. (1952). Both 3-year diploma courses in hospital schools and 4–4½-year degree programmes in univs. lead to registration; in addition there is a c. 1-year training for practical nurses. Nursing corps now form an important part of all branches of the services in most countries.

NUSA TENGGARA. Indonesian prov., formed 1954 from the Lesser Sunda Islands. *See* SUNDA ISLANDS.

NUT. A fruit consisting of a kernel with a hard outer shell which decays when ripe, releasing the seed. It may be situated in a whorl of bracts (e.g. filbert), a cupule (e.g. acorn), or fibrous covering (e.g. coconut); embedded in the flesh of a fruit (e.g. almond); or with a bristly outer covering (e.g. chestnut). Most Ns. contain nutritive oils.

NUTHATCH (nut′-). European bird (*Sitta europaea*) about the size of a sparrow, having a blue-grey back and buff breast. It is a climber and feeds chiefly upon nuts. The nest is placed in a hole in a tree, and 5 to 8 white eggs with red spots are laid in early summer.

NUTMEG. Kernel of the seed of the evergreen tree (*Myrista fragrans*), native to the Moluccas. Both the N. and its secondary covering (known as mace) are used as a spice in cookery.

NYASA (nyah′sah). A long, narrow lake in S.E.

NUTMEG

LAKE NYASA. Dhows with lowered sails enter Leopard Bay, near Salima. With one square sail and extremely long yards, these vessels run easily with the monsoons, and once had an evil reputation on the East African coast as slavers.
Courtesy of the Office of the High Commissioner for Malawi.

Africa, discovered by Livingstone from the S. and Roscher from the E. in 1859. The 3rd-largest lake in Africa, it is 350 m. in length, and has a total area of 11,000 sq. m. It was re-named Malawi 1965.

NYA'SALAND. Country of S.E. Africa, known from 1964 as Malawi (q.v.).

NYERERE (nyerär'ē), **Julius Kambarage** (1922–   ). Tanzanian statesman. Ed. at Makerere Univ. Coll. and at Edinburgh, he became a schoolmaster until devoting himself in 1954 to the formation of the Tanganyika African National Union and subsequent campaigning for independence. He became Chief Min. in 1960, was P.M. 1961–2, and was elected 1st pres. of the Tanganyika Rep. 1962 (re-elected 1965, 1970). He introduced one-party govt. in 1963, as more suited to the situation, but is noted for his wisdom and moderation: he is a Christian.

JULIUS NYERERE

NYLON. Name given to a group of synthetic fibre-forming substances which are similar in chemical structure to proteins, and were developed in the U.S.A. by W. H. Carothers and his associates. N. is used in the manufacture of toilet articles, textiles, medical sutures, etc. N. fibres are stronger and more elastic than silk, and relatively insensitive to moisture and mildew. N. is particularly suitable for hosiery

NYLON. The production of nylon yarn begins with the melting of the polymer and its extrusion through spinnerets. It is then cooled and solidified by air currents and wound on to cylinders for cold drawing and processing. Seen here are some of the spinning units at the H.Q. of British Nylon Spinners, Pontypool.
Courtesy of British Nylon Spinners Ltd.

and woven goods simulating other materials such as silks and furs; it is also used in carpets. *See* Du Pont.

NYMPHS (nimfz). In Greek mythology, the guardian spirits of various natural objects. Hamadryads or Dryads were tree Ns., the Naiads were Ns. of springs and pools, the Oreads of hills and rocks, and the Nereids of the sea.

O 15th letter of the Roman alphabet, whose form was derived from the Semitic alphabet. In modern Eng. it represents a wide range of sounds, from the diphthong ō (*so*) to the open sounds in *or*, *on*, etc., and the *oo*-sound in *wolf*, etc.

OAHU (wah'hoo). Chief island in the state of Hawaii, U.S.A., seat of Honolulu, the state cap., of Hawaii univ., and of Pearl Harbor naval base. Pineapples and sugar are grown for export. The island contains several extinct volcanoes, Waikiki and other bathing beaches. Area 589 sq. m.; pop. (1960) 347,529.

OAK. Genus of trees and shrubs (*Quercus*) in the beech family (Fagaceae). Widely distributed in temperate zones, over 300 species are known. They are valuable for their timber, the wood being durable and straight grained. The English oak (*Q. robur*), also found in Europe, grows to a height of 120 ft. and may have a girth of 50 ft. Other European varieties are the evergreen oak (*Q. ilex*), the Turkey oak (*Q. cerris*), and the cork oak (*Q. suber*), of the W. Mediterranean region; valuable American timber Os. are the white O. (*Q. alba*) and the evergreen live O. (*O. virginiana*). *See* illus. p. 802.

OAKHAM. Co. tn. of Rutland, England. An agricultural and hunting centre, it manufactures clothing, boots, and shoes. Pop. (1961) 4,571.

OAKLAND. A seaport and cap. of Alameda co.,

OAK. Tree with leaves, flower, fruit and acorn.

California, U.S.A., on the E. coast of San Francisco Bay. It has shipbuilding yards and fruit-canning, textile and iron and steel factories. An 8 mile double-deck bridge, opened 1936, links O. with San Francisco. Pop. (1960) 367,548.

OAKRIDGE. Town in Tenn., U.S.A., the site of the govt. works set up in 1943 for the manufacture of plutonium for atomic bombs. Pop. in 1945 was 78,000. Pop. (1960) 27,169.

OAKS. Horse-race, run at Epsom by fillies of 3 years old, usually on the Friday of Derby Week.

OASTLER, Richard (1789–1861). British social reformer. B. at Leeds, he opposed child-labour and the Poor Law of 1834, winning the nickname of 'the Factory King', and was largely responsible for securing the Factory Act of 1833 and the Ten Hours' Act of 1847.

OATES, Laurence Edward Grace (1880–1912). British Antarctic explorer who accompanied Scott on his final dash to the South Pole and died, 'a very gallant gentleman', alone in the blizzard. The museum at the home of Gilbert White (q.v.) contains a Captain O. room with relics.

OATES, Titus (1649–1705). British perjurer. A clergyman, he entered the Jesuit colleges at Valladolid and St. Omer as a spy in 1677–8, and on his return to England announced he had discovered a 'popish plot' to murder Charles II and re-estab. Catholicism. Although this story was almost entirely false, many innocent R.Cs. were executed during 1678–80 on O.'s evidence. In 1685 he was flogged, pilloried and imprisoned for perjury. He was pardoned and granted a pension after the revolution of 1688.

OATH. A solemn promise to tell the truth or perform some duty, combined with an appeal to a deity or something held sacred. Primitive peoples often swear on a weapon or the body of a beast of prey, which is appealed to to kill the person swearing if he breaks his word.

In English courts a witness normally swears to tell the truth holding a N.T. in his right hand; in the U.S.A. a witness raises his right hand in taking the O. Sects which object to the taking of Os., e.g. Quakers, and atheists, etc., give a solemn promise to tell the truth. A Jew swears holding the Pentateuch, with his head covered. Mohammedans, Hindus, etc., swear by their respective sacred books; a Chinese witness breaks a saucer before giving evidence. In Scottish courts witnesses swear to tell the truth 'as I shall answer to God at the great day of judgment'.

OATS. Genus of plants (*Avena*); an important cereal food. The plant has long, narrow leaves, and stiff straw stem; the panicles of flowers, and later of grain, hang downwards. The cultivated O. (*A. sativa*) is produced for human food and for feeding horses and domestic animals and birds.

OB. A river of Asiatic Russia, flowing for 2,100 m. from the Altai mts. through the W. Siberian Plain to a delta in the Gulf of Ob in the Arctic Ocean.

O'BAN. Seaport of Argyllshire, Scotland, on the Firth of Lorne. It is a popular tourist centre. Pop. (1961) 6,859.

OBERAMMERGAU (oh'berahm'ergow). Village of Bavaria, Germany, 45 m. S.W. of Munich, noted for the performance approx. each decade since 1634 of a Passion play.

O'BERON. King of the fairies. He figures in the 13th cent. French *Huon of Bordeaux*, was adopted by Shakespeare in *A Midsummer Night's Dream*, and was made the hero of an epic by Wieland and an opera by Weber.

O'BI. A form of witchcraft practised by the Negroes of the W. Indies. It combined Christian elements with pagan ceremonies imported from Africa, such as snake-worship.

OBOE (ō'bō). Musical instrument of the woodwind family. Played vertically, it is a wooden tube with a bell, is double-reeded, and has a yearning, poignant tone. The range is almost 3 octaves. There are O. concertos by E. Goossens and G. Jacob.

OBŌ'TE, (Apollo) Milton (1924–   ). Uganda statesman. A migrant to Kenya in 1950, where he worked as a labourer, salesman and clerk, he was a founder member of the Kenya African Union. Returning home he led the opposition 1961–2, and became P.M. in 1962, taking over in addition For. Affairs and Defence 1963 and the presidency 1966.

OBRE'NOVICH. Name of a Serbian dynasty which ruled 1816–42 and 1859–1903. They were engaged in a feud with the rival house of Karageorgevich. which obtained throne by the murder of the last O. in 1903.

OBERAMMERGAU. In thanksgiving for the cessation of an outbreak of the Black Death (q.v.) in 1632, the villagers vowed to enact a Passion play every ten years, which they have done whenever possible since 1634. With a cast of several hundred, including 62 actors in named roles, an orchestra of 60 and choir of 38 entirely drawn from natives of the village, the play is performed in the open air and lasts for about 8 hours.
Courtesy of the German Tourist Information Bureau.

O'BRIEN, William Smith (1803–64). Irish nationalist. A Limerick landowner, he sat in parliament from 1828, and from 1846 was closely associated with the Young Ireland movement. He led the rebellion of 1848 and was transported to Tasmania. Pardoned, he returned to Ireland in 1856.

OBSERVATORY. A building designed for observation of natural phenomena, especially astronomical. The earliest O. was at Alexandria, built by Ptolemy Soter, c. 300 B.C. The erection of Os. was revived in W. Asia c. A.D. 1000, and extended to Europe. That built on Hveen island, Denmark, in 1576, for Tycho Brahe, was elaborate, but survived only till 1597. It was followed by those at Paris (1667), Greenwich (1675), and Kew (1769).

The number of Os. grew rapidly during the 19th cent., both in Britain and abroad. Development, with more powerful telescopes, has been most marked in the U.S.A., where the principal Os. are at Mount

OCEAN. A mobile undersea powerhouse and diving habitat for use in depths up to 600 ft. in missions of several days' duration. Transfer of personnel would be effected on the bottom by a submersible diving chamber despatched by the support ship. Equipment could include a salvage crane, coring sampler, and trench-digger for laying pipelines.
Courtesy of Cammell Laird & Co. Ltd.

Wilson, California; Flagstaff, Arizona; and Mount Palomar, California. This latter O. is noted for its 200-in. diameter telescope, the largest in use. Radio astronomic Os. – with greater penetration and range – found at Jodrell Bank (q.v.), England; Green Bank, W. Virginia, U.S.A.; are both steerable bowls. Fixed-array types have been constructed in U.S.S.R., Puerto Rico (for U.S. Govt.), and Australia.

O'CASEY, Sean (1884–1964). Irish dramatist. B. in Dublin, he worked as a labourer in early life, and was largely self-educated. His first plays, *The Shadow of a Gunman* (1922), and *Juno and the Paycock* (1925), created a sensation by their realistic picture of Dublin slum life during the 'troubles'; they were followed by *The Plough and the Stars* (1926), an unromantic depiction of the Easter Rebellion, which led to riots when first produced. His later plays, *The Silver Tassie* (1929), *Within the Gates* (1934), *The Star Turns Red* (1940), *Red Roses for Me* (1943), *Oak Leaves and Lavender* (1946) and *The Drums of Father Ned* (1960). O.'s work is unique in its harmonious blending of stark realism with symbolism, tragedy with comedy and Dublin slang with a richly poetic diction. He also pub. a 6-vol. autobiography beginning with *I Knock at the Door* (1939).

OCCAM (oˈkam), or **Ockham, William of** (*c.* 1300–49). English philosopher, known as the Invincible Doctor. B. at Ockham, Surrey, he became a Franciscan monk, defended the doctrine of evangelical poverty against pope John XXII, and was imprisoned at Avignon on charges of heresy in 1328, but escaped to Munich, where he d. In philosophy, he revived the fundamentals of Nominalism.

OCEAN. The continuous water surface of the Earth, covering *c.* 140,000,000 sq. m. or 70.8% of the total area, and having a mean depth of 12,000 ft. There are strictly 3 oceans – Atlantic, Indian, and Pacific (qq.v.) – to which the Arctic (q.v.) is usually added. Their surface temperature varies with latitude; between $-2°C$ and $29°C$; beneath the surface temperature decreases rapidly to 1,200 ft., more slowly to 7,200 ft., and hardly at all deeper still. Changes of temperature are less extreme than those of land, a factor greatly affecting the climate of countries bordering the Os., and prevailing winds and the positioning of land masses affect surface currents which produce further modifications. Salinity averages about $3\frac{1}{2}\%$. Beyond the continental shelves, shallow ledges to 600 ft., the continental slope reaches down the abyssal zone, the largest area, lying between 6,000 and 18,000 ft. Only a small area lies deeper, the greatest recorded depth being 36,198 ft. by the *Vityaz* (U.S.S.R.) in 1957 in the Mariana

Trench in the W. Pacific. Study of the O. floors has provided confirmation, e.g. the extension of the 'break' in the Earth's crust beneath the Atlantic round the Cape of Good Hope, that *c.* 20,000,000 yrs. ago the Earth had a single land mass (Pangea: *see also* WEGENER), with N. America bordering (with Greenland between) on Eurasia; and with Africa's west coast adjoining S. America, and her east coast adjoining India, Antarctica, and Australia.

James Cook (q.v.), the American Matthew Maury (1806–73), and John and James Ross (qq.v.) were pioneers in the study of the Os., known as oceanography or oceanology. Mid-19th cent. submarine cable-laying gave a useful impetus, but the most rapid advances have come since the S.W.W. with the development of new techniques in undersea photography, drilling of cores from the O. floors (*see* MOHOLE), use of sonic sounding devices, and the perfection of manned submersibles – the ships of inner space – able to move about the sea floor at depths of up to 6,000 ft. Besides pure research (*see also* ARCHAEOLOGY), there have been military and commercial incentives, the latter including sea farming (*see* FISHING) and the lure of mineral wealth – under the sea bed (coal, petroleum, natural gas, etc.); in the sediment of its floor and in the natural continuing deposition of valuable metals there (for example, self-forming manganese nodules which are in effect a 'mine' perpetually renewed); and in the waters themselves (bromine, magnesium, potassium, salt, etc. already commercially extracted, and aluminium, calcium, copper, gold, manganese, silver, etc. potentially recoverable). Research centres incl. the British Inst. of Oceanography at Godalming and in the U.S.A. the Naval Oceanographic Office co-operates with the Scripps Inst. (California) and Woods Hole Inst. (New England); international co-operation is assisted by an Oceanographic Commission under UNESCO.

OCEANA'RIUM. Large-size display tank in which aquatic animals and plants live, not separated according to species as in the conventional aquarium

OCEANARIUM. The leaps of the porpoises at feeding-time are enjoyed as much by the performers as by their audience.
Marine Studios, Marineland, Florida

but living together much as they would in their natural environment. The world's first O. was founded by the explorer and naturalist W. Douglas Burden in 1938 at Marine Studios, Marineland, Florida.

OCEANIA (ōsē-ăˈnia). Term embracing the islands of the S. Pacific Ocean. The divisions are Micronesia, Melanesia, and Polynesia; Australasia is sometimes included.

OCEAN ISLAND. Island included within the British colony of Gilbert and Ellice Islands. It became

British in 1900, and is rich in phosphates. Area 2 sq. m.; pop. (1966) 2,300.

OCE'ANUS. In Greek mythology, a river supposed to encircle the earth.

O'CONNELL, Daniel (1775–1847). Irish politician, called 'the Liberator'. B. in Kerry, he was educ. for the priesthood, but adopted a legal career. In 1823 he founded the Catholic Association to press R.C. claims. Although ineligible as an R.C. to take his seat, he was elected M.P. for co. Clare in 1828, and so forced the govt. to grant Catholic emancipation. In parliament he co-operated with the Whigs in the hope of obtaining concessions until 1841, when he launched his campaign for repeal of the union. His timid and vacillating leadership and conservative outlook on social questions alienated his most active supporters, who broke away and formed the 'Young Ireland' movement. He d. at Genoa.

O'CONNOR, Feargus (1794–1855). Irish politician. B. in Ireland, he sat in parliament 1832–5 as a follower of O'Connell, but then, as editor of the *Northern Star* and a powerful speaker, made himself the most influential figure in the English Chartist movement, and its collapse in 1848 helped unsettle his reason and he d. insane.

OCTAVIAN. *See* AUGUSTUS.

O'CTOPUS. Genus of Cephalopoda having a round or oval body, and 8 arms with 2 rows of suckers on each, though the word is sometimes used to cover other members of the order. Occurring in all temperate and tropical seas, where they feed on crabs, etc., they can vary their coloration according to their background and may either swim with their arms or proceed through a type of jet propulsion by means of their funnel. The common O. (*O. vulgaris*), relished as a delicacy in S. Europe, may reach 6 ft. and is sometimes found off Britain. Generally speaking the perils of O. attack are exaggerated, but off the Pacific coast the giant *O. apollyon* may span more than 25 ft.

ODE. Lyric poem containing the spontaneous expression of emotional fervour. Originating in ancient Greece as a chant sung to a musical accompaniment, it was brought to perfection by Sappho and Pindar, and by Horace and Catullus among the Romans. Among the modern writers of Os. are Spenser, Milton, Dryden, Collins, Coleridge, Wordsworth, Shelley, Keats, Tennyson, and Swinburne.

ODENSE (ō'dense). City and port on the island of Fünen, Denmark. Its cathedral was founded in 1086. Hans Andersen was born at O., which has some industry and exports dairy products and hides. Pop. (1965) 107,530.

O'DER. A European river, 550 m. long, rising in Czechoslovakia. It flows generally N.W. past Wroclaw and Frankfort-on-O. to Szczecin, on the Baltic Sea. It was chosen in 1945 as the provisional German-Polish border N. of its confluence with the Neisse.

ODE'SSA. Seaport in the Ukrainian S.S.R. on a bay in the N.W. corner of the Black Sea, cap. of O. region. It is an important commercial air and railway centre, and has excellent harbour facilities. Lying between the Dnieper and Dniester estuaries, O. was founded by Catherine II in 1795 near the site of an ancient Greek settlement. In German occupation 1941–4, O. suffered severe damage under the Russian 'scorched earth' policy and from German destruction. It has a univ. Pop. (1967) 753,000.

ODETS (ōdets'), **Clifford** (1906–63). American playwright. B. in Philadelphia, he was brought up in the Bronx, New York, and went on the stage at 15. He won fame with *Waiting for Lefty* (1935), a one-act play depicting a strike, which was followed by *Awake and Sing* (1935), a play of Jewish life, and *Till the Day I Die* (1935), an anti-Nazi horror play. Later were *Golden Boy* (1937) and *The Country Girl* (1950).

O'DIN. One of the chief gods of the ancient Germanic tribes, called Woden in Anglo-Saxon. The husband of Frigga and father of Baldur and Thor, he lives in Asgard when he is a sky-god, or in Valhalla when he is conceived as a god of the dead and as receiving the ghosts of brave warriors.

ODY'SSEUS. The chief character of the *Odyssey* (*see* HOMER), mentioned also in the *Iliad* as one of the most prominent leaders of the Greek forces at the siege of Troy. He is said to have been the ruler of the island of Ithaca. Among the Greek heroes O. was distinguished for his sagacity.

OEDIPUS (ēd'ipus). Legendary king of Thebes. As his father, King Laius, had been warned by an oracle that his son would kill him, O. was exposed at birth and left to die, but was rescued and brought up by the king of Corinth. When grown to manhood O. killed Laius, whom he did not know, in a quarrel. Having saved Thebes from the Sphinx, he was granted the kingdom, and in ignorance married his mother, Jocasta. After 4 children had been born, the truth came out, whereupon O. blinded himself and Jocasta hanged herself. In his later wanderings O. was led by his dau. Antigone. The story of O. forms the subject of 2 of Sophocles' tragedies.

OEDIPUS COMPLEX. Term invented by Freud for the emotional conflict set up by a young child's relations with his parents. The child develops a sexual passion for his mother, and a feeling of jealousy and hostility towards his father; the unconscious conflicts created by this problem are a major cause of neuroses, and one of the most important factors in the development of character. *Hamlet* has been interpreted as a study in the O.C.

OERSTED (ör'-), **Hans Christian** (1777–1851). Danish scientist. Prof. of physics at Copenhagen from 1806, in 1820 he discovered magnetic fields, thus founding the science of magnetism. The *oersted*, the c.g.s. electromagnetic unit of magnetizing or magnetic force named after him, is equal to the force in dynes on a unit magnetic pole at any point in a vacuum.

OESOPHAGUS (ēso'fagus). The gullet; the passage by which food travels from mouth to stomach. It is about 9 in. long, and its upper end is at the bottom of the pharynx, immediately behind the windpipe.

OESTROGEN. A hormone which produces oestrus, i.e. menstruation in women and heat in the females of the lower mammals. Three principal oestrogens have been isolated – oestrone, oestriol, and oestradiol.

OFFA (d. 796). Anglo-Saxon king of Mercia in 757. He conquered Essex, Kent, Sussex, and Surrey, defeated the Welsh and the West Saxons, and estab. Mercian supremacy over all England S. of the Humber.

O'FFALY. Co. of Rep. of Ireland, in the prov. of Leinster, between Galway on the W. and Kildare on the E. The Shannon flows along its W. boundary; other rivers incl. the Brosna, Clodagh, and Broughill. In the S.E. are the Slieve Bloom mts. Named King's County in honour of Philip II of Spain, husband of Mary I, it was so called until the estab. of the Irish Free State in 1922. The co. town is Tullamore. Area 771 sq. m.; pop. (1966) 51,717.

OFFENBACH (ofenbahk'), **Jacques** (1819–80). French composer. B. at Cologne, he studied at Paris, became a member of the orchestra of the Opéra Comique, and later conductor at the Théâtre Français. He wrote light opera for presentation at the Bouffes Parisiens, of which he held the lease, and afterwards for various theatres. His most widely known works are *Orphée aux enfers* (1858), *La belle Hélène* (1864), and *Les contes d'Hoffmann* (1881).

O'FLAHERTY (ō-flah'herti), **Liam** (1897–). Irish author. B. on the Aran Is., he has written novels of Irish life, notably *Thy Neighbour's Wife, The Informer*, and *Land* (1946), dealing with Fenian activities in co. Mayo, and also short stories, e.g. *Mountain Tavern* and a *Life of Tim Healy*.

O'GAM or **Ogham.** System of alphabetic writing once in use in the British Isles. The name O. is sometimes extended to the oldest-known form of the Gaelic languages. Some 300 funerary inscriptions in O. are known, mainly from the S.W. parts of Ireland, but also from Wales, Scotland, the Isle of Man, and Hampshire. The script developed during the 5th cent. and consists of a system of strokes or notches suited to be carved in rough stones.

OGDEN, Charles Kay (1889–1957). British originator, with I. A. Richards, of Basic English (q.v.). Together they wrote *Foundations of Aesthetics* (1921) and *The Meaning of Meaning* (1923).

OGDON, John (1937–). British pianist. Son of a schoolmaster, he was ed. at Manchester Grammar School and the Manchester Royal Coll. of Music. Appearing on British concert platforms from 1959, he created a sensation in Moscow in 1962 when he won the Tchaikovsky award with Ashkenazy (q.v.). He is noted for his interpretation of Busoni.

O'GILVY, Angus James Bruce (1928–). British business-man. Second son of the earl of Airlie, he was educ. at Eton and Trinity Coll., Oxford, and from 1956 was associated with the Drayton group of investment trusts as a director. In 1963 he m. Princess Alexandra (1936–), sister of the duke of Kent (q.v.), who is styled H.R.H. Princess Alexandra, the Hon. Mrs. Angus O.

OGLETHORPE, James Edward (1696–1785). English soldier. He joined the Guards, and in 1732 obtained a charter for the colony of Georgia, intended as a refuge for debtors and for European Protestants, and administered it himself until 1743.

O'GMORE AND GARW (gar'oo). Coal-mining town (U.D.) in Glamorganshire, S. Wales. Pop. (1961) 20,955.

OGPU. *See* G.P.U.

O'HIGGINS, Bernardo (1776–1842). Chilean soldier and statesman. Of Irish descent, he was foremost among the leaders of the Chilean struggle for independence from Spanish rule 1810–17, and headed the first permanent national govt. 1817–23.

OHIO (ōhī'ō). North-central state of the U.S.A., S. of Lake Erie, between Indiana on the W. and Pennsylvania on the E. It takes its name from the r. Ohio. An important farming state – livestock products, maize, oats, tomatoes, grapes, soya beans, etc. – it is also one of the industrial leaders, producing cars, aircraft, boats, machine tools, industrial and office machinery, electrical goods, hardware and glass, tyres and plastic goods, etc. Minerals incl. bituminous coal, lime, clay, and natural gas. The chief towns are Akron, Cleveland, Cincinnati, Dayton, Toledo, and Columbus, the cap. It became a state 1803. Area 41,222 sq. m.; pop. (1970) 10,652,017.

OHIO. River of the U.S.A., second-largest affluent of the Mississippi. It is formed by the union of the Allegheny and Monongahela at Pittsburgh, Pa., and is 980 m. long. Its name is Indian and means 'beautiful river'.

ÖHLENSCHLÄGER (ö'lenschläger), **Adam Gottob** (1779–1850). Danish Romantic poet and dramatist. B. at Copenhagen, he drew his inspiration from Nordic mythology and history, and estab. his fame with the poem *Guldhornene*. Among his later works are the plays *Hakon Jarl, Baldur hin Gode*, and *Axel og Valborg*; and the verse *Aladdins Lampe*. In 1810 he became prof. of aesthetics at Copenhagen.

OHM, Georg Simon (1787–1854). German physicist.

He was prof. successively at Cologne, Nuremberg, and Munich, and in 1827 promulgated what is known as OHM's LAW: the steady current in a metallic circuit is directly proportional to the constant total electromotive force in the circuit. If a current I flows between two points in a conductor across which the potential difference is E, then by O.'s law E/I is a constant which is known as the *resistance* R between the two points. Hence $E/I = R$. Equations relating E, I and R are often quoted as O.'s law but the term resistance did not enter into the law as originally stated.

OHM. In electricity, the practical unit of resistance, named after G. S. Ohm. A circuit's resistance is 1 ohm when a potential difference of 1 volt is required to produce a current-flow of 1 ampere.

OILS. Three main classes of oils are distinguished: essential oils, mineral oils (*see* PETROLEUM), and fixed or fatty oils. All Os. are composed chiefly of carbon and hydrogen, are inflammable, and usually are insoluble in water. They may be solid at ordinary temperatures, when they are termed fats, or liquid. Most essential oils are liquids and are obtained from vegetable sources. Fixed oils are products of varying consistency, widespread in the animal and vegetable kingdoms. Vegetable oils are generally obtained from the nuts or seeds of plants, and animal oils and fats occur in the fat-containing tissues; fish oils are important in this group. They are widely used as food, in soap manufacture, in paint and varnishes, lubrication and illumination.

OISE (wahz). European river which rises in the Ardennes, Belgium, and flows through France in a generally S.W. direction for 186 m. to fall into the Seine *c*. 40 m. below Paris. It gives its name to the French depts. of O. and Val d'Oise.

OISTRAKH. An informal moment in rehearsal when the two violinists paid a visit to Britain. From left to right, Colin Davis, Igor Oistrakh and David Oistrakh *Photo: Godfrey MacDomnic.*

OI'STRAKH, David Fyodorovich (1908–). Russian violinist. B. at Odessa, he became prof. at the Moscow Conservatory in 1939, and is world-renowned as an executant, often playing with his son **Igor O.** (1931–). Shostakovich has dedicated a violin concerto to him.

OJOS DEL SALADO (okhos' del sahlah'dhō). Peak in the Chilean Andes, *c*. 280 m. S.E. of Antofagasta. Once thought the highest in the Americas, it is 22,539 ft., the 3rd highest.

OKAPI (okan'pi). Animal (*Okapia johnstoni*) of the giraffe family though with much shorter legs and neck, found in central Africa, but very rare and strictly protected. Purplish brown, with creamy face and black and white stripes on the legs, it is beautifully camouflaged.

OKAYAMA (ōkahyahmah). Japanese city in Honshu on the Asahi r. 7 m. from its mouth. It makes textiles and is noted for its fine park and three Buddhist temples. Pop. (1965) 292,000.

OKEHAMPTON. English market town (bor.) in Devon, 22 m. W. of Exeter. It makes shoes, agricultural machinery, and fertilizers; nearby are limestone and slate quarries. Pop. (1961) 3,833.

O'KELLY, Sean Thomas (1882–1966). Irish politician. He collaborated with Griffith in founding Sinn Féin, was Min. for Local Govt. 1932–9, Education Min. 1939, Finance Min. 1939–45, and succeeded Hyde as pres. (1945–59).

ŌKINA'WA. Largest of the Ryukyu Islands (q.v.) in the Pacific Ocean, c. 300 m. S.W. of Japan, of which it was a prefecture until captured by U.S. forces in a violent battle lasting 1 April–21 June 1945, in which there were 47,000 U.S. casualties (12,000 killed and missing) and the Japanese garrison of 60,000 were all killed except for a few hundred taken prisoner. O. and the rest of the Ryukyu Islands continued to be admin. by the U.S.A., but by an agreement 1969 were to revert to Japan 1972. The chief town is Naha (pop. 258,000), cap. of the Ryukyus. Area 485 sq. m.; pop. (1970) 934,000.

OKLAHŌ'MA. South-central state of the U.S.A., deriving its name from an Indian word meaning 'red people'. The surface is for the most part an upland prairie. The principal rivers are the Arkansas, Red, and Canadian. The most important mountains are the Wichita range in the S. and the Ozark range in the E. The climate is continental with considerable extremes between summer and winter temperatures; the O. 'panhandle' is part of the dustbowl area of the U.S.A. Minerals incl. petroleum, natural gas, coal and lead. The chief crop is wheat, and cattle are raised. The principal cities are Oklahoma City (the cap.), and Tulsa. O., part of the Louisiana Purchase of 1803, was admitted to the Union as a state in 1907; it was 'dry' from then until, as the result of a referendum, prohibition was abolished in the state in 1959. Area 69,919 sq. m.; pop. (1970) 2,559,253.

OKLAHOMA CITY. Cap. of Oklahoma, U.S.A., on the North Canadian river, the commercial metropolis of the state. The chief industry is petroleum refining; iron and steel goods, clothing, pottery, paint, flour, and packed meats are other products. O.C. is the seat of a univ. (1904). Pop. (1960) 324,253.

OLAF. Name of 5 kings of Norway. **Olaf I** Tryggvesson (969–1000), elected king in 995, began the conversion of Norway to Christianity, and was killed in a sea battle against the Danes and Swedes. **Olaf II** Haraldsson (995–1030), king from 1015, offended his subjects by his centralizing policy and zeal for Christianity, and was killed in battle by Norwegian rebel chiefs backed by Canute (q.v.) of Denmark. He was declared the patron saint of Norway in 1164. **Olaf V** (1903–) succeeded his father Haakon VII (q.v.) in 1957.

OLD AGE. The progressive degeneration of bodily and mental processes associated with the later years of life. Its cause is still unknown, but every one of the phenomena can occur at almost any age, and the process does not take place throughout the body at an equal speed. Normally, however, ageing begins after about 30. The arteries start to lose their elasticity, so that a greater strain is thrown upon the heart. The resulting gradual impairment of the blood supply is responsible for many of the changes, but between 30 and 60 there is a period of maturity in which, if life is lived sensibly and in accordance with natural law, ageing makes little progress. Research into the causative process of O.A. (gerontology) incl. study of dietary factors, and the mechanisms behind structural changes in arteries and bones.

OLD BAILEY. Properly the name of a street in the City of London, England, leading off Ludgate Hill, but more usually applied to the Central Criminal Court (q.v.) which is there situated.

OLD CATHOLICS. R.Cs. who refused to accept the dogma of papal infallibility, declared in 1870, and set up their own ecclesiastical organization. The movement originated in Bavaria, and still survives in Germany, the Netherlands, Austria, Czechoslovakia, and in Switzerland. Its organization is episcopal. Certain modifications of R.C. practice were adopted, e.g. church services are in the vernacular, not in Lat., and priests are allowed to marry.

OLDENBURG. City in Lower Saxony, W. Germany, 23 m. W. of Bremen on the Hunte, once cap. of O. duchy. It dates from the 9th cent. Pop. (1966) 129,000.

OLDFIELD, Anne (1683–1730). English actress, popularly known as 'Nance O.'. She made her début in 1700, and was successful both in comedy and tragedy.

OLDHAM. English town (co. bor.) in Lancs, 7 m. N.E. of Manchester. It is an important manufacturing centre. There are collieries and foundries in the vicinity. O.'s industries incl. cotton spinning and the manufacture of textile machinery. Pop. (1961) 115,426.

OLD MOORE'S ALMANAC. Annual publication in Britain containing 'prophecies' of the events of the following year. It was first pub. in 1700, under the title *Vox Stellarum*, by Francis Moore (1657–c. 1715), astrologer and quack-doctor, to advertise his pills.

OLD STONE AGE ART. Paintings, engravings, and sculptures of the palaeolithic or O.S.A. – i.e. 20,000 to 10,000 years ago – found in caves and rock shelters in S.W. France and Spain. The usual subjects are animals, such as the mammoth, bison, elephant, and horse, but the human figure is occasionally depicted. The finest examples, distinguished for their great vigour and naturalistic treatment, are the polychrome paintings at Altamira and the paintings in the Lascaux caves (qq.v.). It is supposed that the paintings were in the nature of 'sympathetic magic', designed to increase the food supply.

OLD STYLE. A qualification, often abbreviated as 'O.S.', applied to dates before the year 1752 in England as quoted in later writers. In that year the calendar in use in England was reformed by the omission of 11 days, in order to bring it into line with the more exact Gregorian system, and the beginning of the year was put back from 25 March to 1 Jan. *See* CALENDAR.

OLDUVAI GORGE. Deep cleft in the Serengeti steppe, Tanganyika. In 1958–9 Leakey (q.v.) discovered here Pleistocene remains of gigantic animals – sheep similar in size to a carthorse, pigs as big as a rhinoceros, a gorilla-sized baboon, and a skull (*Zinjanthropus*) with huge teeth that led to the nickname 'Nutcracker Man'. It is thought that conditions in the O.G. enabled creatures of the Pliocene to survive to a comparatively late date.

OLD VIC. Theatre S. of the Thames in Waterloo Rd., London, founded in 1818 as the Coburg. Taken over by Emma Cons in 1880, when it was known as the Royal Victoria Hall, it became a popular centre for opera and drama, and was affectionately dubbed the Old Vic. In 1898 Lilian Baylis, niece of Emma Cons, assumed the management, and in 1914 began the celebrated series of Shakespeare productions, which continued until the S.W.W. The theatre was badly damaged by enemy action in 1940, but the O.V. company continued to appear at the New Theatre, and in 1950 the O.V. was re-opened, becoming in 1963 the temporary home of the National Theatre.

OLEA'NDER. Evergreen shrubs of the genus *Nerium*, native to the Mediterranean region. The pink flowers grow in clusters, and the lance-shaped leaves contain a poisonous juice, oleandrin.

OLGA, St. (d. c. 969). The wife of Igor, the Scandinavian prince of Kiev, her baptism (*c.* 955) was an important step in the Christianization of Russia.

OLIPHANT, **Margaret Oliphant** (1828–97). British novelist. B. in Midlothian, *née* Wilson, she m. her artist cousin, Francis O. (d. 1859) in 1852. Best-known of her numerous books are *The Chronicles of Carlingford,* incl. *Miss Marjoribanks* (1866); and the supernatural *A Beleaguered City* (1880).

OLIVE

OLIPHANT, **Sir Mark** (1901–). Australian physicist. B. in Adelaide, he was Poynting prof. of physics at Birmingham 1937–50, and directed the Research School of Physical Sciences at Canberra 1950–63. He was knighted in 1959.

OLIVE (o'liv). An evergreen tree (*Olea europaea*) of the family Oleaceae. It grows to about 25 ft. high, has spiny branches and opposite, lance-shaped leaves. The white flowers are followed by bluish-black oval fruits, from which O. oil is expressed: pale yellow, it is chiefly composed of glycerides and, besides being edible, is used in soap, ointments, and as a lubricant. It is native to Mediterranean regions, but is now of wide distribution in warm climates.

OLIVENITE (oliv'enīt). Hydrated copper arsenate, occurring as a mineral in olive-green prisms.

OLIVES, **Mount of.** A range of hills E. of Jerusalem. Gethsemane was at its foot, while a chapel (now a mosque), marks the traditional site of the Ascension.

OLI'VIER, **Laurence**, baron (1907–). British actor. B. at Dorking, Surrey, son of a clergyman, he made his début as Katherine in 1922 at Stratford-on-Avon in a boys' performance of *The Taming of the Shrew.* Among his most famous parts are Romeo, Sir Toby Belch, Macbeth, Hamlet, and Archie Rice in *The Entertainer.* His films including *Wuthering Heights* and *Rebecca,* and he has produced, directed and played the leading role in film versions of *Henry V, Hamlet,* and *Richard III.* Knighted in 1947, he was for many years associated with the Old Vic and in 1962 became director of the National Theatre. He m. the actresses Jill Esmond (1930–40), Vivien Leigh (1940–61), with whom he played in *Antony and Cleopatra,* etc., and in 1961

LORD OLIVIER
Photo: Angus McBean.

Joan Plowright. He was created a life peer 1970.

O'LIVINE. A pale green mineral, magnesium iron silicate, $(Mg,Fe)_2SiO_4$. Transparent O. is called chrysolite, and used in jewellery.

OLNEY. English market town in Bucks, on the Ouse, 17 m. N.E. of Buckingham. The house in which Cowper (q.v.) lived is a museum. Women run a 'pancake race' here every Shrove Tuesday (since 1946 in a time contest with Liberal, Kansas). Pop. *c.* 2,500.

OLOMOUC (ōlōmōts'). Town in Czechoslovakia, at the confluence of the Bystrice and Morava. It has a univ. and is an industrial centre. Pop. (1965) 75,000.

OLSZTYN (ol'shtin). Polish form of Allenstein (q.v.), cap. of O. voivodship, in Polish-occupied E. Prussia.

OLYMPIA (olim'pia). An ancient Greek sanctuary, in the W. Peloponnese on the Alpheus, and the scene of the original Olympic Games. It contained temples

of Zeus Olympius, Hera, etc. The events of the Games were contested in the Stadium and Hippodrome; the former for foot-races, boxing, wrestling, etc., the latter for chariot- and horse-races. The Games were held every 4 years (*olympiad* – this method of reckoning time ceased to be used with the abolition of the games in A.D. 394) during a sacred truce and from 776 B.C. continuous records were kept. Religious offerings were followed by the contest, originally only foot-races, but subsequently greatly enlarged. Women were forbidden to be present and contestants were men of Hellenic descent only, until in later years Romans were admitted.

The revival of the Games was initiated by the French Baron Pierre de Coubertin in 1894; an International Olympic Committee organized the meetings which it was intended should be held each 4 years, but they were interrupted by both world wars. The Olympic emblem of 5 interlaced circles represents the 5 continents.

The modern O.G. cover a much wider range of events, e.g. swimming, skating, equestrian events, football, rowing. Similar games on a limited basis are the Commonwealth, European and Asian G.

OLYMPIO, **Sylvanus** (1902–63). Togolese leader. A member of the Ewe tribe, though with some Portuguese blood, O. was interned by Vichy in the S.W.W., and subsequently devoted himself to the struggle for independence. He became P.M. of independent Togo in 1960, and pres. in 1961. He was killed in a military rising.

OLYMPUS (ōlim'pus). Name of a large number of mountains in Greece and in neighbouring countries. The most famous of them, identified with the abode of the gods in the *Iliad,* is a group of hills, the highest point of which reaches 9,570 ft. in the N. of Thessaly.

There is a Mt. Olympus, 7,954 ft., in the Olympic mts., Washington state, U.S.A., which forms Olympic National Park (1938), area 1,390 sq. m.

OMAGH (ō'ma). Co. tn. of Tyrone, N. Ireland, on the r. Strule, 30 m. S. of Londonderry. It grew up round an abbey founded in the 8th cent.; it has ruins of a castle destroyed in 1641. Pop. (1961) 8,109.

O'MAHA. Principal city of Nebraska, U.S.A., and co. seat of Douglas co., on the Missouri. The principal industries incl. lead smelting and meat packing. Pop. (1960) 301,598.

The landing-point in France of the U.S. 5th Corps on 6 June 1944, between Port-en-Bressin and the estuary of the Vire r., Calvados dept., was given the code name O. beach.

OMAN, **Carola Mary Anima** (1897–). British author. She is the dau. of Sir Charles O. (1860–1946), prof. of modern history at Oxford from 1905, who wrote *History of the Peninsular War* (1902–30) and *The Art of War in the 16th Cent.* (1937). Her own books incl. historical novels such as *Miss Barrett's Elopement* and biographies, e.g. *Nelson* (1948), *Sir John Moore* (1953), and *Mary of Modena* (1962).

OMAN. *See* MUSCAT AND OMAN.

O'MAR (*c.* 581–644). Arabian caliph. He was one of Mohammed's ablest advisers, and in 634 succeeded Abu Bekr as the 2nd of the caliphs. During his reign Syria, Palestine, Egypt, and Persia were conquered by the Arabs. He was assassinated. The mosque of O. at Jerusalem is attributed to him.

OMAR KHAYYÁM (khIyahm') (*c.* 1050–1123). Persian astronomer and poet. B. in Nishapur, he founded a school of astronomical research and assisted in reforming the calendar. The result of his observations was the *Jalālī* era, begun in A.D. 1079. In the West, O.K. is chiefly known as a poet through Edward FitzGerald's translation of his *rubā'īs* as *The Rubáiyát,* also trans. by Robert Graves 1967.

OMAYYADS (ōmī'yadz). An Arabic dynasty which held the caliphate 661–750. They were overthrown by Abbasids, but a member of the family escaped to

Spain, and in 756 assumed the title of emir of Cordova. His dynasty, which took the title of caliph in 929, ruled at Cordova until the early 11th cent.

OMBUDSMAN (om'boodsman). Post of Scandinavian origin instituted to safeguard citizen rights against encroachment by the govt. or its employees: introduced in Sweden 1809, Denmark 1954, and Norway 1962. The O. investigates complaints of injustice which would otherwise have no hope of redress. First Commonwealth country to appoint an O. was N.Z. 1962; the U.K. followed 1966 with a Parliamentary Commissioner (Sir Edmund Compton); and Hawaii was the 1st U.S. state to appoint an O. 1967.

OMDURMAN (omdoor'mahn). City in the rep. of Sudan, on the White Nile, opposite Khartoum. It was the residence of the Mahdi, 1884–98, and is an important trading centre. Pop. (1964) 167,000. The Battle of O. (1898) was a victory for Kitchener over the forces of the Mahdi.

OMMANNEY, Francis Downes (1903–). British marine biologist. He has worked in areas as varied as the Arctic and the Seychelles, and lectured 1957–60 at Hong Kong. His books incl. *South Latitude* (1938), *Fragrant Harbour* (1962), dealing with Hong Kong, and *The River Bank* (1966) autobiographical.

OMNIBUS (abbr. bus). A road conveyance for all. Originating in Paris in the reign of Charles X, the first English O. travelled between Paddington and the Bank. The London General O. Co. (founded in 1856)

OMNIBUS. Single-decker Red Arrows are designed to economize in manpower and speed London's rush hour. There is no conductor, fares being inserted into coin boxes, and to increase carrying capacity there is rear seating only, the forward section being for standing passengers.
Courtesy of London Transport.

became the most prominent, and its horse Os. survived until 1911. Since then, the growth of single- and double-decker motor Os. has been universal. Strict safety precautions now govern their usage, and their originally limited journeys extend to transcontinental vehicles usually called motor-coaches.

OMSK. Town in the R.S.F.S.R., cap. of O. region, at the confluence of the Om and the Irtysh. Agricultural and other machinery is made and O. has food-processing factories and saw-mills; also petroleum refineries linked with Tuimazy in Bashkiria by a 1,000 m. pipeline. It developed round a fortress dating from 1716. Pop. (1967) 746,000.

ONASSIS, Aristotle Socrates (1906–). Greek shipowner. B. in Smyrna, he was a refugee to Greece at 16, but revived the family tobacco business in Buenos Aires and became an Argentine citizen. After the S.W.W. he was a pioneer in the construction of supertankers, and his wealth, e.g. the palatial yacht *Christina*, is legendary. He m. Jacqueline Kennedy, widow of J. F. Kennedy in 1968.

ONEGA (on'egah). Second-largest lake in Europe, situated partly in Leningrad region, partly in Karelia A.S.S.R. Area 3,820 sq. m. The O. canal, along its S.

shore, is part of the Mariinsk system linking Leningrad with the r. Volga.

ONEIDA (ōnī'dah). Town in N.Y. state, U.S.A., on O. Creek, 26 m. E. of Syracuse. It makes silverware, fertilizers, paper, etc., but is best known as the site of the O. community, moved here from Vermont in 1848. Members of the community held all things in common, and practised a form of 'complex marriage' much criticized outside the community, which was dissolved in 1879. A co-operative company took over its commercial activities in 1881. Pop. (1960) 11,677.

O'NEILL (ō-nēl'), **Eugene Gladstone** (1888–1953). American playwright. B. in N.Y. City, son of the actor James O., he had varied experience as gold prospector, seaman, actor, etc., and began learning his craft at George Pierce Baker's drama school at Harvard in 1914. His first full-length play *Beyond the Horizon* (1920), an immediate success, was followed by the expressionist study in fear *The Emperor Jones* (1920); the realistic *Anna Christie* (1921); *The Hairy Ape* (1922). *All God's Chillun Got Wings* (1924) dealt with miscegenation, and this, together with the peasant sensuality of *Desire under the Elms* (1924), provoked the censor. Symbolism predominated in *The Great God Brown* (1926) and *Lazarus Laughed* (1927); *Strange Interlude* (1928) used a stream of consciousness method; and the trilogy *Mourning Becomes Electra* (1931) developed the Orestean theme of Greek drama. *Ah, Wilderness!* (1933) approached the norm of New England comedy, *Days Without End* (1934) returned to Catholic inspiration, and *The Iceman Cometh* (1946) struck again a confused note. Events of his own early life, e.g. his mother's mental instability, are portrayed in *Long Day's Journey into Night*. In 1936 he was awarded a Nobel prize and was undoubtedly America's leading dramatist between the wars.

O'NEILL of the Maine, Terence, baron (1914–). Irish statesman. Member for Bannside, co. Antrim, from 1946 he held many posts in the Ulster govt. and was Min. of Finance from 1956 until he succeeded Brookeborough as P.M. (1963–9). Life peer 1970.

ONION (un'yen). Bulbous plant (*Allium cepa*) of the family Liliaceae. Cultivated from ancient times, it probably originated in Asia. The edible part is the bulb, containing an acrid volatile oil, giving a strong flavour. The O. is a biennial, the common species producing a bulb in the 1st season and seeds in the second.

ONSAGER, Lars (1903–). Norwegian-born American chemist. Prof. of theoretical chemistry at Yale from 1945, he was the discoverer in 1931 of the 'reciprocity relations of O.', fundamental to the process of turning heat into energy. He received a Nobel prize in 1968.

ONTARIO. Province of Canada, between the Great Lakes and Hudson Bay. It has an undulating surface, with a range of hills extending towards Lake Huron. The principal rivers are the St. Lawrence and Ottawa. The climate of O. is healthy, the soil in the S. is fertile, and large areas are under cultivation. There are dairy and fruit farms, and cattle and poultry are raised. Tobacco is cultivated. The chief minerals include gold, nickel, copper, and uranium. More than a quarter of the region is covered by forests, and lumbering is one of the most important industries. O. is the most important manufacturing centre in Canada because of its great water-power resources. Railway rolling-stock, agricultural implements, motor-cars, textiles, tannery and rubber products, pulp and paper are among the main manufactures. The chief cities are Toronto (the cap.), Ottawa, Hamilton, Windsor, and London.

O. is administered by its own provincial govt. at the head of which is a Lieut.-Gov., assisted by an executive council and a single-chamber legislature elected for 5 years (117 members in 1969). O. became

British in 1763, and after the War of American Independence many British loyalists settled in the region, from 1791 called Upper Canada until re-named O. in 1867. Area 412,582 sq. m.; pop. (1966) 6,960,870.

O'NYONG-NYONG. Virus disease transmitted by mosquitoes which first appeared in East Africa in 1961. Symptoms: pains in the joints and glands, an itching rash and fever.

ONYX (on'iks). A cryptocrystalline variety of silica having straight parallel bands of different colours; milk-white, black, and red. Sardonyx has layers of sard or red carnelian alternating with lighter layers of O. It can be used for cutting cameos.

OÖLITE (ō'ōlit). A calcareous rock formed of small grains of carbonate of lime, resembling the hard roe of a fish: the name derives from the Gk. for 'egg' and 'stone', coarse-grained Os. are termed pisolites from Gk. for 'pea' and 'stone'. The structure may arise from the accretion of carbonate of lime round grains of sand or particles of shell in moving water. It may also be formed from calcareous algae deposited in hot springs. The term is also used to indicate the middle and upper layers of the Jurassic system.

OOSTENDE. Flemish form, meaning east end, of OSTEND.

OPAL. A non-crystalline form of silica, occurring in stalactites in volcanic rocks. The common O. is opaque, milk-white, yellow, red, blue, or green, and lustrous. The precious O. is colourless, having innumerable cracks from which emanate brilliant colours produced from minute crystals of cristobalite. Os. are found in Hungary, New South Wales (black Os. were 1st discovered here in 1905) and Mexico, noted for fire Os.

OPENCAST MINING. *See* COAL.

OPEN SHOP. A factory or other business employing men not belonging to trade unions, as opposed to the 'closed shop' (q.v.), which employs trade unionists only.

OPERA. A dramatic work in which singing takes the place of speech, and in which the music accompanying the action has paramount importance, although dancing and spectacular staging may also play their part. It originated in late 16th cent. Florence

OPERA. Among the world's most modern opera houses is that of Sydney. The white 'wings' over the auditorium reflect in the harbour like the sails of a yacht.
Courtesy of the N.S.W. Govt. Office.

when a number of young poets and musicians attempted to reproduce in modern form the musical declamation, lyrical monologues, and choruses of classical Greek drama. One of the earliest composers was Jacopo Peri (1561–1633), whose *Euridici* influenced Monteverdi (q.v.). At first solely a court entertainment, O. soon became popular and in 1637 the first public O. house opened in Venice. In the later 17th cent. the elaborately conventional aria, designed to display the virtuosity of the singer, became predominant over the dramatic element, composers of this type of O. incl. Cavalli, Cesti, and Scarlatti. In France O. was developed by Lully and Rameau, and in England by Purcell, but the Italian style retained its ascendancy, as in the career of Handel (q.v.).

Comic O. (*opera buffa*) was developed in Italy by such composers as Pergolesi, while in England *The Beggar's Opera* (1728) started the vogue of the Ballad O., using popular tunes and spoken dialogue, of which *Singspiel* was the German equivalent.

The revolt against artificiality began with Gluck, who insisted on the pre-eminence of the dramatic over the purely vocal element. Mozart learned much from Gluck in his serious operas, but his greatest triumphs were won in the field of Italian *opera buffa*, and in those works, such as *The Magic Flute*, in which, taking the *Singspiel* as a basis, he laid the foundations of a purely German O. This line was continued by Beethoven in *Fidelio*, and in the work of Weber, in which the Romantic style appears for the first time in O. The Italian tradition, which placed the main stress on vocal display and melodic suavity, continued unbroken into the 19th cent. in the Os. of Rossini, Donizetti, and Bellini.

It is in the Romantic O. of Weber and Meyerbeer that the work of Wagner has its roots. Dominating the contemporary operatic scene, he attempted to create, in his 'music-dramas', a new art-form, and completely transformed the 19th cent. conception of O. In Italy, Verdi succeeded in assimilating, in his mature work, much of the Wagnerian technique, without sacrificing the Italian virtues of vocal clarity and melody, and this tradition was continued by Puccini.

French O. in the mid-19th cent., represented by such composers as Delibes, Gounod, Saint-Saëns, and Massenet, tended to be of rather merely importance. More serious artistic ideals were put into practice by Berlioz in *The Trojans*, but the merits of his work were largely neglected in his own time. Bizet's *Carmen* began a fashion for 'realism' in O.; his lead in this respect was followed in Italy by Mascagni, Leoncavallo, and Puccini. Debussy's *Pelléas and Melisande* represented a reaction against the over-emphatic emotionalism of Wagnerian Os. National operatic styles were developed in Russia by Glinka, Rimsky-Korsakov, Mussorgsky, Borodin and Tchaikovsky, and in Bohemia by Smetana, and several notable composers of light O. emerged, incl. Sullivan, Lehar, Offenbach, and Johann Strauss.

In the 20th cent. the atonal school produced an outstanding O. in Berg's *Wozzeck* and the Romanticism of Wagner was revived by Richard Strauss, e.g. *Der Rosenkavalier*. Notable modern composers incl. in Britain Delius, Britten, John Gardner and Phyllis Tate; in the U.S. Gershwin, Menotti, Kurt Weill, and Stravinsky; in Germany Werner Egk; in the U.S.S.R. Prokofiev: and in Italy Mascagni.

OPHTHA'LMIA (of-). Inflammation of the eye. O. neonatorum (newborn) is an acute inflammation of a baby's eyes at birth with the organism of gonorrhoea caught from the mother. Sympathetic O. is the diffuse inflammation of the sound eye which is apt to follow septic inflammation of the other. To prevent it, surgeons remove a damaged eye if there is no hope of its sight being restored.

OPIE, John (1761–1807). British artist. B. in St. Agnes, Cornwall, he became famous as a portrait painter in London from 1780, later painting historical pictures such as 'The Murder of Rizzio'. His 2nd wife, **Amelia O.** (1769–1853), was a popular novelist.

OPIUM. A narcotic drug obtained from the juice of the opium poppy (*Papaver somniferum*). The unripe seed capsules are cut and the milky juice exuded from them is dried and compressed. Most of the O. used for medicinal purposes comes from Turkey. In the Far East a concentrated extract of O. is used for smoking. It is dangerous and habit-forming, containing a high percentage of morphine.

OPO'LE. Town in Poland, cap. of O. voivodship, on the Oder, *c.* 50 m. S.E. of Wroclaw; cap. 1919–45 of the former German prov. of Upper Silesia, O. lies

OPORTO. Built in the form of an amphitheatre on two hills of granite on the left bank of the river Douro, the main part of the city faces the Villa Nova de Gaia where are the red-tiled wine lodges supplied by the vineyards of the Douro district. Spanning the river is the Dom Luiz I bridge (1881–5).
Courtesy of the Portuguese State Office.

in an area placed under Polish admin. in 1945. It dates from the 13th cent. and its many ancient buildings were badly damaged in the S.W.W. Industries incl. cement and textiles. Pop. (1966) 56,000.

OPO'RTO. Second city of Portugal, and cap. of the prov. of Douro Litoral, situated on the r. Douro, near its mouth. It is chiefly famous for the export of port wine. The cathedral dates from the 12th cent., the univ. from 1911. It has an airfield. Pop. (1960) 310,474.

OPO'SSUM. Marsupial of the family Didelphidae. Os. are small arboreal animals, with prehensile tails, hands and feet well adapted for grasping, and yellowish-grey fur. These true Os. are confined to N. and S. America, but the name is popularly applied to the somewhat similar members of Phalangeridae found in Australia, New Zealand, etc.

OPPELN. German form of OPOLE.

OPPENHEIM (op'en-hīm), **Edward Phillips** (1866–1946). British author of some 200 books dealing with high society and the Continental underworld, e.g. *A Prince of Sinners* (1903), *The Moving Finger* (1911) and *The Great Impersonation* (1920).

OPPENHEIMER (op'-enhīmer), **Robert** (1904–67). American physicist. The son of a German immigrant, he worked with Rutherford at Cambridge. As director of the Los Alamos Science Laboratory 1943–5, he was in charge of the development of the 1st atom bomb and director 1947–66 (senior prof. theoretical physics from 1966) Inst. of Advanced Study, Princeton. Objecting to the development of the H-bomb, he was declared a security risk in 1953 by the U.S. Atomic Energy Commission – an incident of the McCarthy era – but was rehabilitated in 1963 when the Commission granted him the Fermi (q.v.) Award.

OPPOSITION, Leader of His/Her Majesty's. In Britain the official title borne since 1937 by the leader of the largest opposition party in the Commons. The post carries a salary of £4,500 p.a.

OPTICS. The scientific study of the phenomena of light and vision, e.g. shadows cast by opaque objects, images formed in mirrors, and lenses, microscopes, telescopes, cameras, etc. Light rays are for all practical purposes straight lines, although Einstein has demon-

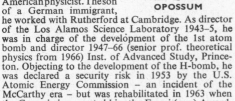

OPOSSUM

strated that they may be 'bent'. On striking a surface they are reflected or refracted with some attendant absorption, and the study of these facts is the subject-matter of geometrical optics. *See* LIGHT.

OPUNTIA. *See* PRICKLY PEAR.

OPUS DEI (ō'pus dā'ē). An R.C. secular institution aiming at the dissemination of the ideals of Christian perfection, particularly in intellectual and influential circles. Founded in Madrid in 1928, and still especially powerful in Spain, it is now international. Its members may be of either sex, lay or clerical.

O'RACLE. In Greek religion, the answer given by a deity to an inquirer, also used of the place where the answer is given. The earliest O. referred to in classical writings is that at Dodona, where priests expounded the meaning of sounds made by the sacred oaks of Zeus; but the best-known is the O. of Apollo at Delphi.

ORADEA (orah'dyah). Ancient town in Rumania, cap. of O. region, 80 m. W.N.W. of Cluj. A railway junction with an airport, it is the centre of a wine-producing area and varied industries incl. agricultural machinery, chemicals, non-ferrous metallurgy, leather goods, printing, glass, textiles, clothing, beer, etc. Made the seat of a bishopric by St. Ladislas in 1083, it was destroyed by the Turks in 1241 and rebuilt. Many of its buildings date from the time of Maria Theresa. It was ceded to Rumania in 1919, held by Hungary 1940–5. Pop. (1966) 122,500.

ORAN (orahn'). Seaport in Algeria, cap. of O. dept. and situated on a hill rising above the Mediterranean, *c.* 230 m. W. of Algiers, with a fine harbour. It was under Spanish rule 1509–1708 and 1732–91, being under Turkish rule in the interval. O. was occupied by France in 1831. After the surrender of France to Germany in 1940, the French warships in the naval base of Mers el-Kebir nearby were put out of action by the R.N. to prevent them from falling into German hands. A univ. was estab. 1967. Pop. (1967) 324,000.

ORANGE, House of. The royal family of the Netherlands. The title is derived from the small principality of O., in S. France, held by the family from the 8th cent. to 1713. They held considerable possessions in the Netherlands, to which, after 1530, was added the German county of Nassau. From the time of William the Silent the family dominated Dutch history, bearing the title of stadholder for the greater part of the 17th and 18th cents. The son of the Stadholder William V was made King William I by the Allies in 1815.

ORANGE (oronzh'). Town in Vaucluse dept., France, 15 m. N. of Avignon. It has remains of a Roman theatre and arch. Pop. (1962) 21,450.

ORANGE. Special species of evergreen tree in the genus *Citrus*, remarkable for bearing blossom and fruit at the same time. They are commercially cultivated in Spain, Israel, Brazil, S. Africa, U.S.A., etc., but seem to have originated in S.E. Asia. Among the principal types are the Jaffa, Maltese blood, tangerine, mandarin, and Seville – the bitter O. used in making marmalade. Os. yield several essential oils.

ORANGE (or'ānj). River of S. Africa, rising on the Mont aux Sources in Basutoland and flowing in a W. direction to the Atlantic. It runs along the S. boundary of the Orange Free State, and was given its name in 1779 in honour of the Dutch stadholder. Length 1,300 m.

ORANGE FREE STATE. Prov. of the Rep. of S. Africa, to the N. of the prov. of the Cape of Good Hope, from which it is separated by the r. Orange. Its surface consists chiefly of plateaux, extending S.W. from the Drakensberg mts. in the E. The principal rivers are the Vaal and Orange. The most important industry is stock farming, and in the E. there is a large area under cultivation. Coal is mined at Vereeniging and at Sasolburg oil fuel is produced from coal; diamonds are found near Jagersfontein and

Koffiefontein, and gold at Odendaalsrust. The chief towns are Bloemfontein (the cap.), Harrismith, Smithfield, Kroonstad, and Jacobsdal. The first Boers settled N. of the r. Orange about 1820. During the Great Trek of 1836 some 10,000 emigrants settled in this region to get away from British rule. The country was annexed by Sir Harry Smith in 1848, but was granted its independence in 1854, when it became the 'Orange Free State'. As the ally of the S. African Republic (Transvaal), it joined in the struggle against the British in the S. African War of 1899–1902. In 1900 it was annexed as a British Crown Colony, named the Orange River Colony. In 1910 it became a prov. of the Union of S. Africa, and reverted to its old name. Area 49,866 sq. m.; pop. (1960) 1,373,790, of whom 274,596 were white.

ORANGEMEN. An Ulster Protestant society founded in 1795 to combat the United Irishmen and the peasant secret societies, a revival of the Orange Institution (1688) formed in support of William (III) of Orange, the anniversary of whose victory over the Irish at the Boyne (1690), is celebrated by O. on 12 July.

O'RANG-UTAN (-oo'-tan). An anthropoid ape (*Simia satyrus*) found solely in Borneo and Sumatra. It stands about 4 ft. high, is covered with red-brown hair, is arboreal in habit, and feeds upon fruits. Sometimes considered the most highly intelligent of the apes, it is being rapidly exterminated.

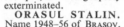

ORANG-UTAN

ORASUL STALIN. Name 1948–56 of BRASOV.

ORATORIANS. An R.C. order of secular priests, called in full Congregation of the Oratory of St. Philip Neri, formally constituted by St. Philip Neri in 1575 at Rome, and characterized by the degree of freedom allowed to individual communities. It was first estab. in England by Cardinal Newman in 1848, and in 1884 Brompton Oratory in London was opened. All churches of the O. are famed for their music.

ORATO'RIO. A musical setting of religious incidents, scored for orchestra, chorus, and solo voices, on a scale more dramatic and larger than a cantata. The term derives from St. Philip Neri's Oratory in Rome, where settings of the *Laudi spirituali* were performed in the 16th cent. The definite form of O. began in the 17th cent. with Cavalieri, Carissimi, Scarlatti, and Schütz, and reached perfection in such works as J. S. Bach's Christmas O. and St. Matthew Passion, and Handel's *The Messiah*, etc. Other famous examples of Os. are Haydn's *Creation* and *Seasons*, Mendelssohn's *Elijah*, and Elgar's *Dream of Gerontius*.

ORCAGNA (orkahn'yah), **Andrea** (c. 1308–68). Italian painter, sculptor, and architect of the Florentine school, whose real name was Andrea di Cione. He studied under Pisano, and was influenced by Giotto.

ORCHESTRA (ōr'kestra). A composite group of instruments combining to play music. The 4 sections into which it is divided are the strings, wood-wind, brass, and percussion. Development of the O. is wrapped up with that of music, particularly with opera and symphony. The bowed strings proved its lasting foundation, and during the 17th and 18th cents. wind, percussion, and plucked instruments were gradually added. The strings have 5 separate subsections, first violins, second violins, violas, violoncellos, and double basses, in strength proportionate to maintain a balance of tone. The wood-wind became standardized by the end of the 18th cent., consisting of a pair each of flutes, oboes, clarinets, and bassoons.

INSTRUMENTS AND ARRANGEMENT OF THE ORCHESTRA					
1st violin	16	Bassoon	2	Tuba	1
2nd violin	16	Piccolo	1	Timpani	3
Viola	12	Cor Anglais	1	Side Drum	1
Violoncello	12	Bass Clarinet	1	Bass Drum	1
Double Bass	8	Double		Triangle	1
Flute	3	Bassoon	1	Cymbals	1
Oboe	2	Horn	4	Gong	1
Clarinet	2	Trumpet	4	Harp	1
		Trombone	3		

PERCUSSION		
BRASS		
WOOD-WIND		
CELLOS	VIOLAS	DOUBLE BASSES
		HARPS
1st VIOLINS	CONDUCTOR	2nd VIOLINS

Later modifications to these were the piccolo, cor anglais, bass clarinet, and double bassoon.

A pair each of trumpets and horns sufficed till the late 18th cent., when trombones began to be specified, appearing in triplicate. Since then 2 extra horns and 1 tuba have been added. Two kettledrums were used during the 17th cent., and their number was later raised to 3. From Turkey came the bass drum, cymbals, side-drum, and triangle.

The harp is the only permanent plucked instrument. Other instruments sometimes incl. are the xylophone, celesta, piano, organ, etc.

ORCHID (or'kid). Family of monocotyledonous plants (Orchidaceae) containing some 5,000 species, distributed throughout the world except in the coldest areas, and most numerous in damp equatorial regions. The flowers have 3 sepals and 3 petals. The lowest petal, the labellum, is usually large, and may be spurred, fringed, pouched, or crested. The flowers are sometimes solitary, but more usually are borne in spikes, racemes or panicles, either erect or drooping. Tropical Os. are epiphytes (attached to trees, etc., although non-parasitic), but temperate Os. commonly grow on the ground, e.g. the spotted orchis (*Orchis maculata*) and other British species. Os. are cultivated under glass for the luxury flower trade, and among private collectors, some specimens commanding very high prices.

PAPHIOPEDELIUM GLAUCOPHYLLUM

ORCZY (ort'si), **Baroness** (1865–1947). Hungarian-born novelist, dau. of baron Felix O., she m. an Englishman, Montague Barstow. Going to London in 1881 to study art, she began to write in 1900, and is best remembered as the author of *The Scarlet Pimpernel* (1905). Sir Percy Blakeney, apparently a foppish weakling but actually bold rescuer of victims of the French Revolution, appeared in many sequels.

ORDEAL. A primitive mode of trial and of testing the guilt of an accused person. It is based on the belief that heaven will protect the innocent, and methods used included walking barefoot over glowing ploughshares, carrying a red-hot iron, and dipping the hand into boiling water. In England such tests were largely superseded after the Norman Conquest by trial by battle. Os. are still used among the Indians, Arabs, and Africans.

ORDER. In classical architecture, the column

ORDERS. L. to r. Doric, Tuscan, Ionic, Corinthian, Composite.

(incl. capital, shaft, and base), and the entablature, considered as an architectural whole. The 5 orders, viz. Doric, Ionic, Corinthian, Tuscan, and Composite, are shown in the illustration above. *See also* COLUMN.

ORDER IN COUNCIL. In Britain an order issued by the sovereign with the advice of the Privy Council; in practice it is issued only on the advice of the cabinet. Acts of parliament often provide for the issue of Os. in C. to regulate the detailed administration of their provisions or they may be used to introduce wartime emergency legislation.

ORDNANCE SURVEY. The official mapping of Britain. Its establishment in 1791 followed the making of military surveys in Scotland and elsewhere. The 1st map – of Kent – was pub. in 1801. Maps of large and small scales have since been produced, and their revision is now the main task of the O.S. Dept., the administration of which is controlled by the Min. of Housing and Local Govt.

OʹREGON. Mountainous N.W. state of the U.S.A. The extensive forests are one of the state's principal sources of wealth. The chief rivers are the Columbia (which flows along most of the N. boundary) and its tributary, the Snake. The chief towns are Portland, Salem (the cap.), and Eugene. The state of O. is the S. part of the much larger O. Country, over the N. boundary of which there was a long-standing dispute with Britain, settled in 1846 when it was agreed that the frontier should be extended to the W. coast along lat. 49° N. O. Country was made a Territory 1848 from which Washington Territory was detached 1853. O. with its present boundaries entered the Union 1859. Spanish explorers visited the coast in the 16th cent. Robert Gray, a U.S. navigator, discovered and named the Columbia r. in 1792. Area 96,981 sq. m.; pop. (1970) 2,091,385.

OʹREL. Town in the R.S.F.S.R., cap. of O. region, situated on the Oka, *c.* 200 m. S.S.W. of Moscow. It is an important grain market and rail centre with engineering industries. Pop. (1967) 202,000.

OʹRENBURG. Town in the R.S.F.S.R., cap. of O. region, on the right bank of the Ural r. *c.* 230 m. E.S.E. of Kuibyshev. It dates from the early 18th

OREGON. Never itself frozen, though more than 6,000 ft. above sea-level, Crater Lake marks the site of an extinct volcano, and the surrounding lava cliffs rise in places to 2,000 ft. Brilliantly blue, it is six miles in diameter and nearly 2,000 ft. deep.   *Courtesy of the U.S. National Parks Service.*

cent. and is an important trading and mining centre. It was called Chkalov 1938–57 in honour of a long-distance flyer. Pop. (1967) 316,000.

ORESTES (ōres'tēz). In Greek legend, the son of Agamemnon, and of his wife, Clytemnestra (qq.v.).

ORFILA (orfēlah'), **Mathieu Joseph Bonaventure** (1787–1853). French scientist of Spanish origin. B. at Mahón, Minorca, he became prof. of medical jurisprudence (1819), and of chemistry (1823) at Paris. His *Traité des poisons* (1813) laid the foundations of the modern toxicology.

ORFORD, Earl of. *See* WALPOLE.

ORGAN. A musical wind instrument of ancient origin, developed from the Pan-pipe and hydraulus, mentioned as early as the 3rd cent. B.C. Leather bags and bellows were added, and the hydraulic type more favoured than the pneumatic O., which has since prevailed. Os. were imported to France from Byzantium in the 8th and 9th cents., after which their manufacture in Europe began. The supersession of the old drawslides by the key system dates from the 11th–13th cent., the first chromatic keyboard from 1361. The more recent designs date from the 1809 composition pedal.

The modern O. produces sound from varying-sized pipes under applied pressure. One note only is sounded by each pipe, but these are grouped into stops, which are ranks or scales of pipes prepared to 'speak' by a knob. These, in turn, form part of a sectional O., one of the tonal divisions comprising the whole O. These separate manuals are the great, swell, choir, solo, echo, and pedal Os., controlled by the player's hands and feet. By this grouping and sub-division extremes of tone and volume are obtained.

Apart from its continued use in churches, the O. has been adapted for entertainment. The electrically controlled O. substitutes electrical impulses and relays for some of the air-pressure controls.

ORGANIC CHEMISTRY. The chemistry of carbon compounds. The great number and diversity of these compounds render it convenient to group them separately. They are built up chiefly through the combination of carbon with hydrogen, oxygen and nitrogen. Compounds containing only carbon and hydrogen are known as hydrocarbons.

O.C. is largely the chemistry of a great variety of homologous series, in which the molecular formulae, when arranged in ascending order, form an arithmetical progression with the common difference CH_2. The physical properties undergo a gradual change from one member to the next.

The chain of carbon atoms forming the backbone of an organic molecule may be built up from beginning to end without branching; or it may throw off branches at one or more points. This division of organic compounds is known as the *Open-Chain*, or *Aliphatic*, compounds. Sometimes, however, the ropes of carbon atoms curl round and form rings. These constitute the second division of organic compounds known as *Closed-Chain*, *Ring*, or *Cyclic*, compounds. Other structural varieties are known. Upon the capacity of carbon atoms to form molecular rings and chains depends the infinite variety of organic nature.

In inorganic chemistry a specific formula usually represents one substance only, but in O.C. it is exceptional for a molecular formula to represent only one substance. Substances having the same molecular formula are called *isomers*, and the relationship is known as *isomerism*. Where substances have the same molecular formula, but differ in their structural formulae, they are called *structural isomers*. Spatial isomers, or stereoisomers, have the same molecular formula, and also the same structural formula, the difference lying in their spatial dispositions. The study of spatial isomers led to the recognition of a new and extensive field of chemistry, known as *stereochemistry*, or 'chemistry in space'.

Hydrocarbons form one of the most prolific of the many organic types. Typical groups containing only carbon, hydrogen, and oxygen are alcohols, aldehydes, ketones, ethers, esters, carbohydrates, etc. Among nitrogenous types are amides, amines, nitro-compounds, amino-acids, proteins, purines, alkaloids, and many others, both natural and artificial. Other organic types contain sulphur, phosphorus, halogens, etc.

The most fundamental of organic chemical reactions are oxidation, reduction, hydrolysis, condensation, polymerization, and molecular rearrangement. In nature, such changes are often brought about through the agency of promoters known as *enzymes*, which act as catalytic agents in promoting specific reactions. The most fundamental of all natural processes is *synthesis*, or building up. In living plant and animal organisms the energy stored in carbohydrate molecules, derived originally from sunlight, is released by slow oxidation and utilized by the organisms. The complex carbohydrates thereby revert to carbon dioxide and water, from whence they were built up with absorption of energy. Thus, a so-called carbon food cycle obtains in nature. In a corresponding nitrogen food cycle, complex proteins are synthesized in nature from carbon dioxide, water, soil nitrates, ammonium salts, etc., and these proteins ultimately revert to the elementary raw materials from whence they sprung, with the discharge of their energy of chemical combination.

Originally it was believed that carbon compounds derived from plant and animal sources could not be artificially prepared in the laboratory, but now many organic compounds can be synthesized, some of which are unknown in nature.

ORGANISATION DE L'ARMÉE SECRÈTE (O.A.S.). French terrorist organization formed in 1961 with the aim of overthrowing the constitutional régime in Algeria and establishing *Algérie française*. It was headed by Gen. Raoul Salan (imprisoned 1962–8) and Bidault (q.v.).

ORGANIZATION FOR ECONOMIC CO-OPERATION AND DEVELOPMENT (OECD). New title of the OEEC from 1961, when the U.S.A. and Canada became full members and its original scope was extended to incl. development aid. Its H.Q. are in Paris.

ORGANIZATION OF AFRICAN UNITY. By its charter, adopted at the Addis Ababa Conference of Heads of African States (30 independent countries were represented) in 1963, it is pledged to eradicate colonialism, emancipate still dependent territories, and improve conditions in the economic, cultural and political spheres throughout Africa and its adjoining islands. The permanent H.Q. is at Addis Ababa.

There is also a French-speaking Joint African, Malagasy and Mauritian Organization (*Organization africaine, malgache et mauritienne:* O.C.A.M.M.), originating in 1962, which works within the framework of the O.A.U. for African solidarity: H.Q. Yaoundé.

ORGANIZATION OF AMERICAN STATES. In 1890 at Washington, under the auspices of U.S. Sec. of State James G. Blaine, the *International Union of the American Republics* was estab. to encourage friendly relations. Its central office at Washington, known from 1910 as the *Pan-American Union*, became in 1948 the central and permanent organ of the more comprehensive O. of A.S.

ORGANIZATION OF CENTRAL AMERICAN STATES (*Organizacion de Estados Centro Americanos:* O.D.E.C.A.). The 1st organization of this name, estab. in 1951, was superseded by a new one in 1962: membership — Costa Rica, El Salvador, Guatemala, Honduras, and Nicaragua, provision being made for Panama to join at a later date. The permanent H.Q. is in Guatemala City.

ORIENTEERING. Sport of pedestrian route-finding, developed in Scandinavia and introduced to Britain *c*. 1960. Competitors start at minute intervals, with a $2\frac{1}{2}$ in. to the mile map marked with the exact location of control points about half a mile apart, where their control cards are stamped.

ORIGEN (ŏ'rijen) (*c*. 185–*c*. 254). A Father of the Christian Church. He was b. probably at Alexandria, and his father was the Christian martyr, Leonidas, beheaded in 202. After teaching at Alexandria 204–32 he was banished and settled in Caesarea, where he founded another school. Under Decius in 250 he was arrested and put to torture at Tyre, where he d.

His writings covered every aspect of Christianity, but he is chiefly remembered for his fanciful method of allegorical exegesis of the Bible.

ORIGINAL SIN. The Christian doctrine that, as a result of Adam's fall, man is by nature corrupt, and can obtain salvation only through divine grace.

ORINŌ'CO. River of northern S. America, flowing for *c*. 1,500 m. through Venezuela, and forming for  *c*. 200 m. the boundary with Colombia in which rise the Guaviare, Meta, Apure, and other left-bank tributaries; right-bank tributaries incl. the Ventuari, Caura, and Caroni. The O. is navigable by large steamers for 700 m. from its Atlantic delta. Rapids obstruct the upper river.

ORIOLES (ŏ'ri-ōlz). Passeriform birds of the Oriolidae family, well known in Europe. They are shy and restless, with brilliant plumage. Other species

GOLDEN ORIOLE

extend to Asia and Africa, while in America the name is applied to the Icteridae family. The golden O. visits Britain.

ORI'SSA. State of the Rep. of India, situated between W. Bengal to the N.E. and the Bay of Bengal and Andhra to the S.W. The Mahanadi flows through the state, and iron is mined. The state of O. includes the former British prov. of O., conquered 1803 and

ORISSA. The great temple of Jagannath, Puri, built in the 12th century A.D.
Photo: Press Information Bureau, Govt. of India.

made an autonomous prov. 1937, and 22 former princely states. Cuttack, the largest city, was replaced as cap. by Bhubaneswar in 1956; Puri is famous for its temple of Jagannath or Juggernaut. Area 60,164 sq. m.; pop. (1961) 17,548,846.

ORIZABA (ōrĕthah'bah). City of Veracruz state, Mexico, 65 m. W.S.W. of Veracruz. It is a popular resort and industries incl. brewing, paper making, and textiles. Pop. (1960) 70,053.

O. peak, over 18,700 ft., a volcano (erupted 1687) 25 m. N. of O. city, is the highest mountain in Mexico. Its Aztec name was Citlalteptl (star mountain).

ORKNEY. A co. of Scotland, consisting of a group of islands situated off the N. coast. It is separated front the mainland by the 6 m. wide Pentland Firth. There are c. 90 islands and islets, of which 28 are inhabited. The most important are Pomona (or 'Mainland'), the largest of the group, N. and S. Ronaldsay, Hoy, Rousay, Stronsay, Westray, Shapinsay, Eday, and Sanday. Kirkwall, on Pomona, is the cap. Owing to the influence of the Gulf Stream, the climate is comparatively mild. The highest point is Ward Hill (1,560 ft.) in Hoy. Fishing and agriculture, incl. rearing of cattle, sheep, and pigs, are the chief occupations. The Os. are the *Orcades* of ancient geographers. They were conquered by Harold I (Fairhair) of Norway in 876, pledged to James III of Scotland for the dowry of Margaret of Denmark 1468, and, the dowry not being paid, annexed by Scotland in 1472. Scapa Flow, used as a base by the R.N. in both world wars, is between Pomona and Hoy. It was here that the surrendered German fleet scuttled itself on 21 June 1919. Area 370 sq. m.; pop. (1961) 18,743.

ORKNEY CAUSEWAY. Construction put up in the F.W.W., completed in 1943 during the S.W.W., joining 4 of the Orkney Is., built to protect the fleet from intrusion through the eastern entrances to Scapa Flow. It has a road surface and serves as a land link between Kirkwall and the islands.

ORKNEYS, South. *See* SOUTH ORKNEYS.

ORLA'NDO, Vittorio Emanuele (1860–1952). Italian politician. As P.M. 1917–19 he attended the Paris Peace Conference, forming one of the 'big four' with Lloyd George, Wilson, and Clemenceau, but dissatisfaction with his handling of the Adriatic settlement led to his resignation. He at first supported Mussolini, but was in retirement 1925–46, when he returned first to the assembly and then the senate.

ORLANDO. City of Florida, U.S.A., named in 1857 after Orlando Reeves, a soldier killed in a clash with Indians. Centrally situated at the hub of communications, it has grown phenomenally industrially. Pop. (1960) 88,135, est. by 1980 c. 800,000.

ORLÉANS (orlā-oñ'). Capital of Loiret dept., France, formerly the cap. of the old prov. of Orléanais, situated on the Loire, 70 m. S.S.W. of Paris. O., of pre-Roman origin, is famous for its association with Joan of Arc (q.v.), who liberated it from the English in 1429, and is an important commercial centre, industries incl. textiles, engineering and processed foods. Pop. (1968) 95,828.

ORMOLU (or'molōō; Fr. *or moulu*, ground gold). A gold-tinted alloy of copper, zinc, and sometimes tin, used for mountings of furniture.

ORMONDE (awr'mond), James Butler, duke of (1610–88). Irish general. He commanded the royalist troops in Ireland 1641–50 during the Irish rebellion and the English revolution, and was Lord-Lieut. 1644–7, 1661–9, and 1677–84. He was created a marquess in 1642 and a duke in 1661. His grandson, James, 2nd duke (1665–1745), succeeded Marlborough as C.-in-C. in 1711, but was impeached in 1715 for Jacobite intrigues, and exiled.

ORMSKIRK. English industrial and market town (U.D.) in Lancs, about 10 m. N.E. of Liverpool. Pop. (1961) 21,815.

ORMUZ (ormooz'). Persian is. in the Persian Gulf with village of O. on its N. coast. O. was formerly the name of a port on the Persian mainland, c. 20 m. E. of the island, visited by Marco Polo in the 13th cent. Trade moved to the island in the 14th cent. and when captured by the Portuguese 1507–14 O. was flourishing. The British took it in 1622, and it gradually lost its importance to Bandar Abbas (q.v.).

ORMUZD. *See* AHURA MAZDA.

ORNE (orn). French river rising E. of Sées and flowing N.W., then N.E. to the English Channel below Caen. A ship canal runs alongside it from Caen to the sea at Ouistreham. The O. is 94 m. long and gives its name to a dept.

ORNITHO'LOGY. The section of zoology concerned with the study of birds (q.v.). It covers not only scientific aspects relating to the structure and classification of birds, but also the activities of the many amateurs in all countries interested primarily in the natural beauty of birds, their habits, song, flight, etc., secondarily in their value to agriculture as destroyers of insect pests. This interest has led to the formation of societies for their protection (developing into their study), of which the Society for the Protection of Birds (1889) in Britain was the first; it received a royal charter in 1904. The Audubon Society (1905) in the U.S.A. has similar aims. France, Canada, Switzerland, the Netherlands are other countries having bird protection societies, and there is an International Council for Bird Preservation. Legislation in various countries to protect wild birds dates from a British Act of 1880.

ORPEN, Sir William Newenham Montague (1878–1931). Irish artist. He studied at Dublin and London, became famous as a portraitist, was knighted in 1918, and was elected R.A. in 1919.

ORPHEUS (-fūs). Mythical Greek poet and musician. He was the son of Apollo and a muse, and m. Eurydice, who d. from the bite of a snake. O. went down to Hades to bring her back, relying on his sweet singing to charm the nether gods. Her return to life was granted on condition that he walked ahead of her without looking back. O. broke this condition, and Eurydice was irretrievably lost. In his grief, he despised the Maenad women of Thrace, and was torn to pieces by them.

The Orphic religion was one of the mystical cults of Greece, its most distinctive feature in doctrine being the belief in a future life in which the condition of O.'s worshippers could be bettered by asceticism and the performance of mystical rites.

ORRIS ROOT. The underground stem of species of iris grown in S. Europe. Violet-scented, it is used in perfumery.

ORSK. Town in Orenburg region, R.S.F.S.R., at the junction of the Or and Ural rivers. Originally a fortress, it has large petroleum refineries fed by a pipeline from Guriev, locomotive and aluminium plants, etc. Pop. (1967) 212,000.

ORTEGA Y GASSET (awrtä'gah-ē-gah'set), José (1883–1955). Spanish philosopher and critic. He considered Communism and Fascism the cause of the downfall of western civilization. His *Toward a Philosophy of History* (1941) contains philosophical reflections on the State, and an interpretation of the meaning of human history.

ORTHOPAEDICS (-pē'diks). The science of correcting deformities. It progressed tremendously during both world wars. Among its most important techniques are the treatment of fractures, bone and nerve grafting, the restoration of function after infantile paralysis, the reconstruction of joints, and especially rehabilitation, in which the patient is treated as a whole and all the resources of surgery, medicine, psychology, physical training and occupational therapy are concentrated on him.

ORTHO'PTERA. Order of terrestrial insects, incl. grasshoppers, crickets, and locusts (qq.v.).

O'RTOLAN. A bird (*Emberiza hortulana*) of the bunting family, common in Europe and W. Asia. Migrating southward or returning, it is netted, then fed and killed for the table. It is variously coloured, with a grey head.

ORTON, Arthur (1834–98). The 'Tichborne Claimant'. B. in Wapping, the son of a butcher, he claimed in 1866 to be Sir Roger Tichborne, bart., who had been lost at sea in 1854, and was accepted as such by Sir Roger's mother. After a sensational trial, he was imprisoned for perjury.

ORVIETO (orvē-ā'tō). City in Terni prov., Italy. It stands on an eminence, 10 m. N.E. of Lake Bolsena. The magnificent 14th cent. cathedral contains sculpture by Orcagna and frescoes by Luca Signorelli and Fra Angelico, and doors (1963) by Emilio Greco (q.v.). It is on the site of Volsinii, one of the 12 Etruscan cities, which was destroyed by the Romans 280 B.C.; it has many Etruscan remains. Pop. (1960) 25,200.

ORWELL, George. Name adopted by British author Eric Blair (1903–50). B. in India, he was ed. at Eton as a scholarship boy, and for 5 yrs. served in the Burmese police force, an experience reflected in the novel *Burmese Days* (1935). Adventures as dishwasher, schoolmaster, and bookshop assistant were related in *Down and Out in Paris and London* (1933) and service for the Republican cause in the Spanish Civil War in *Homage to Catalonia* (1938). His greatest book is the satire *Animal Farm* (1945) which incl. such sayings as 'All animals are equal, but some are more equal than others', but the greatest sensation was made by *1984* (1949) which carries state control of existence to the ultimate.

ORYX

ORYX (or'iks). Genus of large African desert antelope, incl. 6 species, some of which extend to Syria and Arabia, but are almost extinct. Attempts are being made to breed them in captivity. In profile the 2 long horns appear as one and the O. may have given rise to the legend of the unicorn.

OSAKA (ōsah'ka). Second-largest city and a port of Japan. Situated on the island of Honshu, and lying on a plain sheltered by hills and opening on to O. bay, O. is honeycombed with waterways. Oldest city of Japan, it was at times the seat of govt. 4–8th cents., was a mercantile centre in the 18th, and in the 20th set the pace for Japan's revolution based on light industries. Manufactures incl. iron and steel, ships, chemicals, and textiles. It is a tourist centre for Kyoto and the Seto Inland Sea, and linked with Tokyo by fast electric train (124 m.p.h.), and was chosen as the site for the 1970 World Exposition. Pop. (1968) 3,150,000.

OSBORNE, Dorothy (1627–95). English letter-writer. In 1655 she m. Sir William Temple (1628–99), to whom she wrote her letters (1652–4), first pub. in 1888.

OSBORNE, John James (1929–). English dramatist and actor. He became well known as an 'angry young man' when his first play, *Look Back in Anger* (1956), in which the hero satirises middle-class life, was produced. His later plays incl. *The Entertainer* (1957), and *Luther* (1960). He was m. to the actress Mary Ure (1957–63), film critic Penelope Gilliat (1963–8), and actress Jill Bennett from 1968.

OSBORNE HOUSE. A favourite residence of Queen Victoria, for whom it was built in 1845, 1 m. S.E. of Cowes in the Isle of Wight, England. It was presented to the nation by Edward VII.

OSCAR. The name of 2 kings of Sweden and Norway. **Oscar I** (1799–1859) succeeded his father, Charles XIV, in 1844, while his younger son, **Oscar II**

(1829–1907), came to the throne in 1872. He abandoned the title of king of Norway on the separation of the two kingdoms in 1905.

OSCAR. Annual cinema award in various fields (10 in. bronze-gilt statuette) estab. 1927 by the American Academy of Motion Pictures, and nicknamed O. 1931 because a new secretary exclaimed, 'That's like my uncle Oscar!'

OSAKA. In 1585 warlord Toyotomi Hideyoshi, who chose the city as his base for unifying the country, mobilized 30,000 workers for three years to build this giant castle, largely reconstructed. 1931. *Courtesy of Japanese Embassy.*

OSCILLATOR. An O. is a generator producing a desired oscillation. It is an essential part of a radio transmitter, as it generates the high-frequency carrier signal necessary for radio communication. There are many types of O. for different purposes involving various arrangements of valves or transistors, inductors, capacitors, and resistors, and the frequency is often controlled by the vibrations set up in a crystal, e.g. quartz.

O'SCILLOGRAPH. Instrument for producing a graph representing a varying quantity that can be measured electrically as a function of time. The most

OSBORNE HOUSE. In this bedroom, carefully preserved with its original furnishings, Queen Victoria died. Next to the picture of the Prince Consort, to the left of the bedhead, is the pocket in which he placed his watch each night before retiring. *Crown copyright.*

common form now used is the cathode-ray O. *See* CATHODE-RAY TUBE.

OSIER (ō'zhier). A tree or shrub of the willow genus (*Salix*), cultivated for basket making.

OSIPENKO (osype'nkō). Port in the Ukrainian S.S.R., on the N.W. of the Sea of Azov, with ship-building yards, agricultural machinery and aircraft factories, etc. It is a port for petroleum from Baku for refineries in Ukraine. Founded in the 19th cent. as Berdiansk, it was re-named O. in 1940. Pop. (1967) 75,000.

OSI'RIS (Egypt. *Ausar*). Ancient Egyptian god who personified the power of good; he was the enemy of Set, the god of evil. He was united in the sacred triad with his wife Isis, and his son Horus. Slain by Set, he was avenged by Horus, and went to rule over the dead in the underworld.

Ö'SLER, Sir William (1849–1919). British physician. B. in Canada, he was chosen as Regius prof. of medicine at Oxford in 1905, and created a bart. in 1911. He is chiefly remembered for his work on diseases of the blood and the spleen.

OSLO (oz'lō). Cap. of Norway, on the S.E. coast, at the head of Oslo fjord. The first recorded settlement was made by Harald III (Hardrada) *c.* 1050 in Ekeberg, but the modern city lies mainly to the N. and W. of the fortress of Akershus, built by Haakon V in the late 13th cent. This change was due to Christian IV who re-planned the city after the fire of 1624; in his honour it was called Christiania from 1624 to 1924. Important buildings incl. the Royal Palace, the Parl. House, the univ. (1811), the national theatre, and the new town hall (1931–50). O. is a prosperous seaport and has considerable shipbuilding, engineering, and textile industries. Pop. (1967) 485,200.

OSMAN or **Othman I** (1259–1326). Turkish sultan. He began his career in the service of the Seljuk Turks, but in 1299 he set up a kingdom of his own in Bithynia and assumed the title of sultan. He conquered a great part of Asia Minor, so founding the Turkish Empire. His successors were known as 'sons of O.', whence the term 'Ottoman' is derived.

O'SMIUM (Gk. *osme*, odour). Bluish-white, hard, crystalline metal, very heavy and infusible: symbol Os, at. wt. 190·2, at. no. 76. Discovered in 1803 by Tennant in residue left when crude platinum was dissolved in aqua regis (concentrated nitric and hydrochloric acids), it is found in platinum-bearing river sands and with iridium in osmiridium. Heated in air it gives off a pungently irritating poisonous vapour. It is used for lamp filaments, with iridium to form a very hard alloy suitable for pen-nibs and fine machine bearings, and, when finely divided, as a catalyst.

O'SNABRÜCK. City and episcopal see in the Land of Lower Saxony, W. Germany, 70 m. W. of the city of Hanover. Before the S.W.W., when O. was severely damaged, it had fine examples of both Gothic and Renaissance architecture; O. bishopric was founded by Charlemagne, 783. Industries incl. engineering, iron and steel, textiles and clothing, paper, and processed foods. The Treaty of Westphalia was signed at O. and Münster in 1648. Pop. (1966) 141,398.

OSPREY. Bird of prey (*Pandion haliaetus*), known in America from its diet as the fish hawk, and formerly breeding in Scotland. Dark brown above and a striking white below, it measures 2 ft., with a 6 ft. wingspread. The 'O.' plumes of the milliner are those of the egret (q.v.).

OSPREY

OSSA. A mountain in Thessaly, Greece, elevation 6,490 ft. The vale of Tempe separates it from Olympus. Mt. Pelion, to the S., is said to have been piled on O. by the Giants to enable them to scale Olympus.

OSSETIA (osēsh'ia). Area in the Caucasus inhabited chiefly by a fair-haired people called Ossets or Alans. It is divided into **North O.**, an A.S.S.R. of the R.S.F.S.R., cap. Ordzhonikidze; area 3,500 sq. m.; pop. (1967) 518,000 (80 per cent. Ossets); and **South O.**, an autonomous region of Georgian S.S.R.; cap. Tshkinvali; area 1,500 sq. m.; pop. (1967) 102,000 (70 per cent Ossets). N.O. has some industry served by water-power from the r. Terak and grows maize, fruit, and market-garden crops; S.O. is a mountain health resort with lumbering, fruit growing, and livestock rearing.

OSSIAN (osh'ian). Irish hero and poet, properly called Oisin. He is represented as the son of Finn Mac Cumhaill, *c.* A.D. 250, and as having lived to tell the tales of Finn and the Ulster heroes to St. Patrick, *c.* 400. The publication, from 1760 onwards, of the 'Ossianic' poems of J. Macpherson (q.v.), has made O.'s name familiar throughout Europe.

OSSIETZKY (osyets'ki), **Karl von** (1889–1938). German pacifist. A leading figure in Liberal-pacifist circles in republican Germany, he was imprisoned 1931–2 for publishing an article proving that the Reichswehr was secretly rearming, and was sent to a concentration camp 1933–6. The award to him of the Nobel peace prize in 1935 provoked a protest from the German govt.

O'SSORY. Ancient kingdom, lasting until 1110, in Leinster, Ireland; the name is preserved in existent Church of Ireland and R.C. bishoprics.

OSTADE (ostah'de), **Adriaen van** (1610–85). Dutch painter and engraver, famous for his pictures of tavern scenes, village fairs, etc. B. at Haarlem, he studied under F. Hals. His brother, **Isaac van O.** (1621–49), excelled in winter landscapes, and roadside and farmyard scenes.

OSTEND. Seaport and pleasure resort of Belgium, in the prov. of W. Flanders, 67 m. N.W. of Brussels. It has a fine promenade over 3 m. long, and a casino and royal chalet on the sea front. There are large docks, and the Belgian fishing fleet has its headquarters here. Pop. (1966) 57,750.

O'STEO-ARTHRI'TIS. Degenerative disease of the joints in later life, the result of excessive wear or earlier injury, and to which there may be some inherited tendency. The result may be disabling stiffness and wasting of muscles.

OSTEOLOGY. Part of the science of anatomy, dealing with bones and their uses. *See* BONE.

OSTEOMYELITIS (o'stē-ōmī-elī'tis). Infection of bone. The organism may be introduced through an injury or through the blood-stream, especially shortly after an illness. The symptoms are high fever, severe illness, and pain over the limb. If the infection is at the surface of the bone it may quickly form an abscess; if it is deep in the bone marrow it may spread into the circulation and set up fatal blood poisoning.

OSTEOPATHY. A system of unorthodox medical teaching and practice which regards the chief cause of disease as a disorder of structure, a 'lesion' in tissue of any kind, but most commonly a minor displacement of one or more vertebrae. The treatment combines manipulation of the lesion, with other more orthodox remedies. In Great Britain osteopaths have no legal standing.

O'STIA. Ancient Italian town and harbour near the mouth of the Tiber. Dating from *c.* 330 B.C., it was the port of Rome and at one time had a pop. of *c.* 100,000; in modern times a seaside resort (Ostia Mare) has been estab. nearby.

O'STRACISM (-siz-). Political device to preserve order in ancient Athens. As a result of votes written on oyster-shells (Gk. *ostraka*, whence the name), political personages might be exiled for a period of 10 years.

OSTRACO'DA. A sub-class of Crustacea. Found in both salt and fresh water, these minute animals have a bivalve shell enclosing the body and limbs.

O'STRAVA. Town in Czechoslovakia, cap. of N. Moravian region created 1960, 85 m. N.E. of Brno,

OSTRICH. In Victorian and Edwardian times ostrich feathers were the hallmark of feminine fashion, but are now used chiefly in costumes for stage and cabaret productions. These fine specimens are seen in the Mountain Zebra National Park on the Karroo.
Courtesy of the South African Information Service, Pretoria.

in a coal-mining district. It has heavy iron works and furnaces. Pop. (1967) 270,000.

OSTRICH. Genus (*Struthio*) of flightless birds found in Africa and Arabia. The male may be *c.* 8 ft. tall and weigh 300 lb., and is the largest of extant birds. Living in family groups of 1 cock with several hens, the O. has exceptionally strong legs and feet (2-toed) which enable it to run at high speed and are also used in defence. The beautiful tail feathers have commercial value and Os. are bred in farms, especially in S. Africa. *See* RATITAE.

OSTROGOTHS. *See* GOTHS.

OSTRO'VSKY, Alexander Nikolaevich (1823–86). Russian playwright. B. in Moscow, he founded a model theatre and a school of drama at Moscow. His best-known play is *The Storm* (1860), depicting the merchant class.

OSTWALD, Wilhelm (1853–1932). German chemist. B. at Riga, he held professorships at Riga and Leipzig, and in 1909 was awarded the Nobel prize for chemistry. He is remembered for his work on the affinity constants of acids and bases, on the viscosity of solutions, and on oxides of nitrogen.

OSWALD, St. (*c.* 605–42). King of Northumbria. While exiled in Iona, he was converted to Christianity, and in 634 won the Northumbrian crown. With the assistance of St. Aidan he furthered the spread of Christianity until he was defeated and killed by the heathen king Penda of Mercia.

OSWESTRY (oz'estri). English market town (bor.) in Salop, near the Welsh border. There is a church dedicated to St. Oswald, king of Northumbria, who was killed here in 642. Agricultural machinery, plastics, clothing, etc., are made. Pop. (1961) 11,193.

OTAGO (ōtah'go). Statistical area in S. Is., New Zealand, in which sheep are reared, wheat and oats grown, and gold is found. Area 14,070 sq. m.; pop. (1966) 183,477.

O. was formerly the name of a provincial dist., area 25,530 sq. m., with cap. at Dunedin, seat of O. univ.

OTARU (ōtah'roo). Fishing port on W. coast of Hokkaido, Japan, with paper mills; processes fish and makes sake. Pop. (1965) 197,000.

OTHMA'N (*c.* 574–656). Arabian caliph. A son-in-law of Mohammed, he was elected caliph in 644. Under his rule the Arabs became a naval power and captured Cyprus, but his personal weaknesses led to his assassination.

OTHMAN I. *See* OSMAN.

OTRA'NTO. Seaport and archiepiscopal see in Apulia, Italy, on the Strait of O. The cathedral was begun in 1080. Pop. (1960) 4,100.

OTTAWA. Cap. of Canada, in the prov. of Ontario, occupying a hilly region overlooking the r. Ottawa, about 100 m. W. of Montreal. It is divided into 2 parts by the Rideau Canal – to the W. Upper Town, to the E. Lower Town. There are 2 falls providing power for the city, viz. the Chaudière Falls, on the Ottawa, and the Rideau Falls. The principal buildings are the govt. buildings on Parl. Hill, the R.C. cathedral of Notre Dame, Christ Church cathedral, the Nat. Museum, the Nat. Art Gallery, the Observatory, Rideau Hall – the gov.-gen.'s residence – and the Nat. Arts Centre (1969). The chief industry is lumbering, and wood pulp and paper are manufactured. The city was founded when a body of men under John By were building the Rideau Canal, 1826–32, and was named Bytown in By's honour; it was renamed O. (from the Outaouac Indians who traded furs with the French in the 17th cent.) in 1854 and chosen by Queen Victoria as cap. of Canada in 1858. Pop. (1966) 494,535.

OTTAWA AGREEMENTS. The trade agreements concluded at the Imperial Economic Conference, held at Ottawa in 1932, between Britain and the Dominions (except the Irish Free State), India, and S. Rhodesia. The Dominions agreed to lower their preferential tariffs on British manufactures, while Britain admitted almost all Dominion produce free of duty, granted preferences to the rest, and increased duties on foreign imports competing with Dominion produce. The agreements marked the abandonment by Britain of her traditional free-trade policy.

OTTER. Aquatic carnivore of the weasel family. The O. of Europe and Asia (*Lutra vulgaris*) has a broad head, elongated body covered by grey-brown fur, short legs, and webbed feet: including a 1½ ft. tail, it measures *c.* 3½ ft. It lives on fish and in Britain is hunted. There are a no. of American species, e.g. the larger *L. canadensis* of N. America and the commercially valuable fur-bearing sea O. (*Latax lutris*) of the N. Pacific.

OTTO. Name of 4 Holy Roman emperors. **Otto I** (912–73) succeeded in 936, restored the power of the empire, asserted his authority over the Pope and the nobles, ended the Magyar menace by his victory at the Lechfeld in 955, and re-founded the East Mark, or Austria, as a barrier against them. **Otto IV** (*c.* 1182–1218), elected emperor in 1198, engaged in controversy with Innocent III, and was defeated by the Pope's ally, Philip of France, at Bouvines in 1214.

OTTOMAN EMPIRE. Moslem Empire founded in Turkey *c.* A.D. 1300, succeeding the Seljuk Empire. Driven out of central Asia in 1402, the Turks recovered and captured Constantinople in 1453, destroying the remnants of the Byzantine Empire. After various conquests the O.E. by the end of the 16th cent. extended from Hungary to Egypt and parts of Persia. From then a period of disintegration followed until in 1920 the O.E. came to an end, being replaced by the Rep. of Turkey (q.v.).

OTWAY, Thomas (1652–85). British dramatist. B. near Midhurst, Sussex, he wrote for the stage from 1675, his chief plays being *The Orphan* (1680) and *Venice Preserved* (1682). He d. destitute in London.

OUDENAARDE (ow'denahrde). Small town of E. Flanders, Belgium, on the Scheldt, 18 m. S.S.W. of Ghent. O. was the site of Marlborough's victory over the French in 1708.

OUDH (owd). E. part of a former prov. of British India, the United Provs. of Agra and Oudh, 1901–47. O. lay between the Nepal frontier and the Ganges; Lucknow was the cap. Anciently a kingdom, it was under Mogul rule until it regained independence 1732–1856 when the British deposed the king. Area 24,000 sq. m. From 1950 it formed part of the Indian state of Uttar Pradesh.

OUESSANT. French form of USHANT.

OUIDA (oo-ē′da). Pseudonym of British novelist Marie Louise de la Ramée (1839–1908), author of highly coloured romances, e.g. *Under Two Flags* (1867) and *Moths* (1880).

OULU. Port in Finland, cap. of O. dept. It stands on the Gulf of Bothnia at the mouth of the r. O., which drains Lake O. It grew up round a castle built by the Swedes in 1375 (the Swedish name for the town being Uleåborg), and has a cathedral (1830) and univ. (1958). There are saw mills, flour mills, tanneries, shipbuilding yards, etc. Pop. (1967) 81,200.

OUNCE. A unit of weight, the 12th part of a pound troy = 480 grains; in avoirdupois, the 16th part of a pound = 437·5 grains. The fluid O. is a measure of capacity, in the U.K. equivalent to an avoirdupois O. of distilled water at 62°C.

OUNDLE (own′dl). English market town (U.D.) in Northants, 13 m. S.W. of Peterborough. O. grammar school, founded in 1556, developed during the 19th cent. into one of the great public schools. O. dates from before the Norman Conquest. Pop. (1961) 2,546.

OUSE (ōōz). Name of several British rivers. The Great O. rises in Northants, and after a winding course of some 160 m. it enters the Wash N. of King's Lynn. A huge sluice across the Great O., near King's Lynn, part of extensive flood-control works, was opened in 1959. The Yorkshire O. is formed by the junction of the Ure and Swale near Boroughbridge, and joins the Trent to form the Humber. The Sussex O. rises between Horsham and Cuckfield, and flows through the S. Downs to enter the English Channel at Newhaven.

OUSEL or **Ouzel** (ōōzl). Ancient name of the black-bird, now applied to the dipper (or water-O.) and ring-O. Water-Os. occur in Europe and in the Americas.

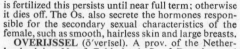

RING OUSEL

OUTLAWRY. Ancient punishment, now virtually obsolete, for felony and mis-demeanour, which meant that the outlaw might be apprehended by any person, and lost al his civil rights, his lands and goods were forfeit to the Crown.

OUTRAM (ōōt′ram), **Sir James** (1803–63). British general. B. in Derbyshire, he entered the Indian Army in 1819, served in the Afghan and Sikh Wars, and commanded in the Persian campaign of 1857. On the outbreak of the Mutiny he co-operated with Havelock to raise the siege of Lucknow, and held the city until relieved by Sir Colin Campbell.

OVAL, The. A cricket ground, dating from 1846, the headquarters of the Surrey County Cricket Club, at Kennington, London, England, The first Test Match between England and Australia was played here in 1880.

OVARIES. The pair of organs which in the female generate the ova, or egg-cells, from which, if they are fertilized, grow the offspring. In woman they are 2 whitish rounded bodies about 1 by 1½ in., situated near the ends of the Fallopian tubes. The ovum develops in the Graafian follicle and bursts out about the 13th day after menstruation starts. In its place grows the 'yellow body' (*corpus luteum*). If the ovum

is fertilized this persists until near full term; otherwise it dies off. The Os. also secrete the hormones responsible for the secondary sexual characteristics of the female, such as smooth, hairless skin and large breasts.

OVERIJSSEL (ō′verīsel). A prov. of the Netherlands, lying N. of Gelderland, S. of Drenthe, and watered by the Ijssel and the Vecht. Zwolle is the cap. Sheep and cattle rearing and dairy farming are the chief occupations. Area 1,300 sq. m.; pop. (1966) 887,300.

OVERTURE. A piece of instrumental music, usually preceding an opera. There are also Os. to suites, plays, etc., and 'concert' overtures such as Elgar's *Cockaigne* and John Ireland's descriptive *London Overture*. The use of an O. in opera came into being during the 17th cent., the 'Italian' O. consisting of 2 quick movements interspersed with a slow one, and the 'French' of a quick movement between 2 in slower tempo.

O'VID (43 B.C.–A.D. 17). Roman poet, whose full name was Publius Ovidius Naso. B. at Sulmo, he studied rhetoric in Rome in preparation for a legal career, but soon turned to literature. In A.D. 8 he was banished by Augustus to Tomi, on the Black Sea, where he d.: this punishment was supposedly for his immoral *Ars amatoria*, but was probably due to some connection with Julia, the profligate dau. of Augustus. Among his works are the youthful *Amores*; the *Heroides*, fictitious love-letters of legendary heroines; the *Metamorphoses*, mythical stories of miraculous transformations; the *Fasti*, forming an incomplete poetic calendar; and the fruits of his exile, the elegiac *Tristia* and *Epistulae ex Ponto*.

OVIEDO (ōvē-ā′dō). An episcopal city, cap. of O. prov., Spain, 16 m. S. of the Bay of Biscay. The cathedral dates from the 14th cent., and there is a univ. (1604). O. makes textiles, matches, chocolate, sugar, etc. Pop. (1960) 127,058.

OVUM. An egg-cell which, if it is fertilized by fusion with a spermatozoon (conception), attaches itself to the rich lining of the womb; there it grows by cell division and differentiation into a child.

OWEN, Alun (Davies) (1926–). British writer. A Bevin boy in the mines during the S.W.W., he gained stage experience in repertory at Perth and Birmingham, spent a year with the Old Vic, and then in 1957 started to write in radio, he became well known for his TV plays, e.g. *No Trams to Lime Street* (1959) and *You Can't Win 'Em All* (1962).

OWEN, Robert (1771–1858). British Socialist and Co-operator. B. at Newtown, Montgomery, he became manager in 1800 of a mill at New Lanark, where by improving working and housing conditions and by providing schools he created a model community. From 1817 he proposed that 'villages of co-operation', self-supporting communities run on Socialist lines, should be founded; these, he believed, would ultimately replace private ownership. After an unsuccessful attempt to run such a community in the U.S.A., he organized the Grand National Consolidated Trades Union in 1833, in order that the unions might take over industry and run it co-operatively. Although this scheme collapsed in 1834, O.'s ideas did much to stimulate the co-operative movement.

OWEN, Wilfred (1893–1918). British poet. B. at Plas Wilmot, Oswestry, in 1913 he went to France as a tutor, returning to England to enlist in 1915, and was killed in action a week before the Armistice. His poetry expresses his hatred of war.

OWEN FALLS. Cataract in Uganda on the White Nile, 2½ m. below the point at which the river leaves Lake Victoria. A dam, built 1949–60, provides hydroelectricity for Uganda and Kenya, and helps to control the flood waters.

OWENS, John (1790–1846). Manchester cotton merchant, who endowed Owens Coll. (1851), nucleus of Manchester Univ.

OWL. Bird of prey in the sub-order Striges, the majority being nocturnal. The Os. are characterized by large eyes encircled by radiating feathers set in a forward position (though the head has a compensating mobility); short, hooked beak; and soft, thick plumage which gives them a soundless flight. The diet consists mainly of rodents consumed whole, the indigestible remains being disgorged in pellets or 'castings'. All species lay white eggs, and, contrary to the habit of most birds, incubation begins as soon as first is laid. Familiar species are the tawny O. (*Strix aluca*) of Europe and the Near East; the large eagle O. (*Bubo ignavus*) of Europe and Asia – both with closely allied species in America – and the long-eared O. (*Asio otus*) and short-eared O. (*A. accipitrinus*) which have a wide range in both the old and new worlds. Also of interest are the little O. (*Athene noctua*), symbol to the Greeks of the goddess of wisdom and naturalized in Britain, and the handsome snowy O. (*Nyctea scandiaca*), which moves south in winter from the Arctic. Generally Os. are sombrely coloured, and have a reputation as birds of ill-omen from the unearthly quality of their cries.

TAWNY OWL

OX. The castrated male of domestic species of cattle (q.v.), used particularly in underdeveloped countries for ploughing and other agricultural purposes, also the extinct wild O. or aurochs of Europe, and extant wild species.

OXA'LIC ACID. One of the oldest known organic acids, $(COOH)_2 \cdot 2H_2O$, it is a white, crystalline, poisonous solid, soluble in water, alcohol, and ether. Salts occur in wood sorrel and other plants. It is used in the leather and textile industries, in dyeing and bleaching, ink manufacture, metal polishes, and for removing rust and ink stains.

OXENSTJERNA (oks'enshärna), **Axel Gustafsson,** count (1583–1654). Swedish statesman. As Chancellor from 1612, he ably seconded Gustavus Adolphus's foreign policy by his organizing and diplomatic ability. He acted as regent for Queen Christina, and conducted the Thirty Years War to a successful conclusion.

OXFORD, Edward de Vere, 17th earl of (1550–1604). English lyric poet, to whom Shakespeare's plays have been attributed by some.

OXFORD. Cathedral city (co. bor.) and co. tn. of Oxfordshire, England, on the Thames, 51 m. W.N.W. of London. The tower of the Saxon church of St. Martin stands close to Carfax, the intersection of the 4 main roads. During the 13th cent. O. was the meeting-place of several parliaments, and during the Civil War was the Royalist headquarters. The city has greatly expanded with the advent of the large Morris motor works at Cowley, developed under Lord Nuffield. O.'s chief magistrate's title was changed from Mayor to Lord Mayor in 1962. Pop. (1961) 106,124. *See* OXFORD UNIVERSITY.

OXFORD AND ASQUITH, Earl of. *See* ASQUITH.

OXFORD GROUP. *See* BUCHMAN, F. N. D.

OXFORD MOVEMENT. Known also as the Tractarian Movement and Catholic Revival, it attempted to revive Catholic religion in the Church of England. Newman dated the movement from Keble's sermon at Oxford in 1833. The O.M. by the turn of the cent. had transformed the face of the Anglican communion, and is represented today by Anglo-Catholicism.

OXFORDSHIRE. A southern midland county of England, bounded on the S. by the Thames. It is

OXFORD COLLEGES			
	Founded in		*Founded in*
University	... 1249	Wadham ...	... 1612
Balliol ...	c. 1263	Pembroke	... 1624
Merton ...	... 1264	Worcester	... 1714
St. Edmund Hall	c. 1278	Hertford ...	... 1740
Exeter ...	... 1314	Keble ...	... 1870
Oriel ...	... 1326	Lady Margaret Hall*	1878
The Queen's	... 1340	Somerville*	... 1879
New ...	... 1379	St. Anne's*	... 1879
Lincoln ...	... 1427	St. Hugh's*	... 1886
All Souls ...	... 1438	St. Hilda's*	... 1893
Magdalen...	... 1458	St. Peter's	... 1928
Brasenose	... 1509	Nuffield**	... 1937
Corpus Christi	... 1517	St. Antony's**	... 1950
Christ Church	... 1546	St. Catherine's	... 1962
Trinity ...	... 1555	Linacre** ...	... 1962
St. John's...	... 1555	St. Cross**	... 1965
Jesus ...	... 1571	Wolfson**	... 1966
	* Women	** Men and women	

for the most part in the Thames basin, but there are the Chiltern Hills in the S.E. and spurs of the Cotswolds in the W. Farming flourishes; bricks, paper, cement, and motor-cars are made. The county town is Oxford; other centres are Banbury and Chipping Norton. Area 749 sq. m.; pop. (1967) 358,690.

OXFORD UNIVERSITY. Oldest of the British univs., it was estab. during the 12th cent., the earliest existing coll. being founded in 1249. After suffering from land confiscation during the Reformation, it was reorganized by Elizabeth in 1571. Besides the colls., notable academic buildings are the Bodleian Library (with the New Bodleian, opened in 1946, with a capacity of 5 million books), the Divinity School, and the Sheldonian Theatre. The U. is governed by the Congregation of the Univ.; Convocation, composed of Masters and Doctors, has a delaying power. Normal business is conducted by the Hebdomadal Council. There are *c.* 10,000 undergraduates.

OXIDE. A binary compound of oxygen and another element. The 3 main classes are: (1) Acidic Os., which combine with basic Os. to form salts; (2) basic Os., reacting with acids to form salts; and (3) neutral Os., possessing neither acid nor basic properties.

OXFORD UNIVERSITY. Magdalen Bridge and College' and, in the foreground, punts moored on the river Cherwell'
Photo: British Travel and Holidays Association'

OXLIP. A wild plant (*Primula elatior*), in character between the primrose and cowslip.

OXUS. Ancient name of AMU DARYA.

OXY-ACETYLENE WELDING. The fusion of metals by burning acetylene in pure oxygen, producing high-temperature flames. In the high-pressure system the gases are delivered to a blowpipe from cylinders in correct proportion.

OXYGEN (Gk. *oxys* acid, and *genes* forming). Colourless, odourless, tasteless, non-toxic gas, slightly soluble in water; symbol O, at. wt. 16·00, at. no. 8. Discovered by Priestley in 1774 by heating mercuric oxide using the sun's rays and a burning glass (and independently in the same year by Scheele), it is the most abundant element, and both free and combined makes up nearly one-half of the total material on the surface of the earth – 21 per cent by volume of the atmosphere, nearly 50 per cent by weight of the rocks, and 89 per cent by weight of the water. The only gas able to support respiration, it is just as essential for almost all combustion, and is used in high-temperature welding, improving blast-furnace working, low-temperature work, and aiding respiration. Liquefied O. is pale blue and magnetic.

O. is obtained by fractional distillation of liquid air, by electrolysis of water, or by heating manganese dioxide with potassium chlorate. It is very reactive, and combines with all other elements except the inert gases and fluorine.

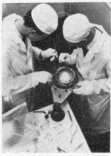

OXYGEN. The liquid-oxygen vacuum insulated container used in high-flying aircraft must be assembled under surgical-clean conditions. To prevent dirt or grease being present while the units are fitted together, surgeon-style gloves are worn and the assembly room at Harlow, Essex, is a fully air-conditioned 'clean area'.
Courtesy of the British Oxygen Co.

OYSTER. Bivalve mollusc of the family Ostreidae, the upper valve being flat, the lower concave, hinged

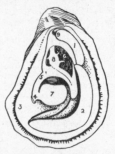

Anatomy of the oyster: I, palps; 2, gills; 3, mantle; 4, vent; 5, intestine; 6, liver; 7, adductor muscle; 8, stomach; 9, mouth.

by an elastic ligament. The mantle, lying against the shell, protects the inner body, which incl. respirative, digestive and reproductive organs. Os. are distinguished by their change of sex, which may alternate annually or more frequently, and by the no. of their eggs – a female may discharge up to a million eggs during a spawning period. Among the species commercially exploited for food are the European O. (*Ostrea edulis*) – there are famous beds at Whitstable, Kent, and Colchester – and the American (*O. virginica*) of the Atlantic coast: the former is larviparous (eggs and larvae remain in the mantle cavity for a period before release) and the latter oviparous (eggs are discharged straight into the water). O. farming is increasingly practised, the beds being specially cleansed for the easy setting of the free-swimming larva (which then as a miniature O. is known as 'spat'), and the Os. later properly spaced for growth and fattened. Pearls (q.v.) are not obtained from members of the true O. family.

OYSTER CATCHER. Wading bird of the plover family. The common O.C. of European coasts (*Haemotopus ostralegus*) is black and white, with a long red beak to open shellfish; the allied American species has an even longer bill and a less musical cry.

O'ZONE. Blue gas O_3 of characteristic odour, a form of oxygen, found in the atmosphere. Slightly soluble in water, it is produced when oxygen or air is subjected to a silent electrical discharge, ultra-violet ray action (e.g. the O. layer in the upper atmosphere is caused by the ultra-violet rays of the sun), or radium emanation. It is a powerful oxidizing agent, and is also used in bleaching and air-conditioning.

P Sixteenth letter of the Roman alphabet. In Semitic languages, in Gk., and in Latin *p* had much of the same sound as it normally has today in English when final, or when following *s* at the beginning of a word, the sound of an unvoiced labial stop. In other positions in English, and especially when initial, *p* is aspirated.

PAARL (pahl). S. African town in Cape Province, the chief centre of the wine industry. P. was settled *c.* 1688 by Huguenots from France who brought the vine with them. The name is Dutch for pearl. Pop. (1960) 38,059 (14,035 white).

PAASIKIVI (pahsikē'vē), **Juho Kusti** (1879–1956). Finnish statesman. A leader of the Coalition Party, he conducted armistice negotiations with Russia in 1944, then becoming premier (1944–6) and succeeding Mannerheim as pres. (1946–56).

PACHMANN (pakh'mahn), **Vladimir de** (1848–1933). Russian pianist. B. at Odessa, he studied at Vienna, made his début in 1869, and was celebrated for his exquisite touch and as an interpreter of Chopin.

PACIFIC ISLANDS, Trust Terr. of. Is. of the Caroline, Marshall and Mariana (except Guam) groups, qq.v., which were formerly mandated to Japan, and became a U.N. Trust Terr. admin. by the U.S.A. in 1947. They consist of over 2,000 atolls and is., area 700 sq. m.; pop. (1967) 91,500.

PACIFIC OCEAN. The largest ocean of the world, extending from Antarctica to the Bering Strait. Area 64,186,300 sq. m.; average depth 13,739 ft.; greatest depth 36,198 ft. in the Mariana Trench.

PACIFIC SECURITY TREATY. See ANZUS.

PACIFISM. The belief that violence should never be resorted to as a means of settling disputes. Among the holders of pacifist views are some Christians, e.g. the Soc. of Friends, Jehovah's Witnesses; some Hindus, e.g. Gandhi and his followers.

PADANG (pahdahng'). Port on the W. coast of Sumatra, Indonesia, seat of a univ. (1951), with an airport. It exports coffee, copra, rubber, tea, resin, etc. The Dutch secured trading rights here in 1663, and built a factory *c.* 1680. Pop. (1961) 325,000.

PADUA. Under the seven domes of the Basilica del Santa the bones of St. Anthony, to whom it is dedicated, rest in a chapel rich in carved marble. Begun soon after his death in 1231, the building was completed in the 14th cent.
Courtesy of the Italian State Tourist Office.

PADERBORN (pah'der-). Town of N. Rhine-Westphalia, W. Germany, already the seat of a bishopric in Charlemagne's time. The 11th–13th cent. cathedral was destroyed in the S.W.W. A former Hanseatic town, it makes textiles, leather goods, precision instruments. Pop. (1960) 52,000.

PADEREWSKI (pahderef'skē), **Ignacz Jean** (1860–1941). Polish pianist, composer and statesman. The son of a Polish patriot, he gained European and American fame after his début in Vienna in 1887 and became a noted exponent of Chopin. After the F.W.W., during which he raised money in America for the relief of Polish war victims and organized the Polish army in France, he became in 1919 P.M. of the newly independent Poland, which he represented at the Peace Conference, but continuing opposition forced him to resign the same year. Having resumed a musical career in 1921, he was Pres. of the Polish National Council in Paris in 1940 and d. in N.Y.

PADUA (pad'ūa) (It. Padova). City of N. Italy,

PAGAN. Close by the river is the Shwezigan pagoda, one of many once belonging to the ancient capital, and now beautifully restored. On its platform are seen votive bowls, a golden dragon, and artificial sacred trees.
Courtesy of the Burmah Oil Co. Ltd.

25 m. W. of Venice. The 13th cent. Palazzo della Ragione, and the basilica of S. Antonio, are notable. The univ., founded in 1222, is famous. Pop. (1961) 198,403.

PAESTUM (pes'tum). Ancient Greek city, near Salerno in S. Italy, founded *c.* 600 B.C. There are a number of temple ruins. *See* illus. under SALERNO.

PAGAN. Village in Burma, S.W. of Mandalay. It lies close to the ruins of a former Burmese cap., founded 847, taken by Kublai Khan 1287.

PAGANINI (pahgahnē'nē), **Nicolo** (1782–1840). Italian violinist. B. at Genoa, he first appeared at 9 years old, and from 1805 took Europe by storm. His appearance, his amours, and his virtuosity, especially his performances on a single string, created the legend of his being in league with the Devil. He composed works for the violin notable rather for their ingenious exploitation of the instrument than intrinsic value.

PAGE, Sir Earle Christmas Grafton (1880–1961). Australian statesman. He led the Country Party 1920–39, was P.M. of a caretaker govt. in April 1939 following Lyons's death, represented Australia in the British War Cabinet 1941–2, and as Min. of Health under Menzies, 1949–55, introduced the Australian health scheme in 1953.

PAGE, Sir Frederick Handley (1885–1962). British aircraft engineer, founder of one of the earliest manufacturing cos. in 1909, and designer of long-range civil aircraft and multi-engined bombers in both wars, e.g. the Halifax in the S.W.W. He was knighted in 1942.

PAGOPAGO (pā'gō-pā'gō). Cap. of American Samoa; a harbour in the island of Tutuila. Formerly a naval coaling station, it was acquired by the U.S.A. under a commercial treaty with the local king in 1872. Pop. (1960) 1,251.

PAHANG (pah-hahng'). State of the Federation of Malaysia, ruled by a sultan. The cap. is Kuantan. Rubber, tin, gold, etc., are exported. Area 13,873 sq. m.; pop. (1966) 418,720.

PAHLA'VI, Riza Khan (1877–1944). Shah of Persia. B. at Savad Kuh, he joined the army. In 1921 he headed a revolt, captured Tehran, and became C.-in-C. He assumed the premiership in 1923, and was crowned shah in 1926. He carried out many reforms, but his attitude towards the Allies in the S.W.W. led to his abdication in 1941.

PAHSIEN (pahsyen'). *See* CHUNGKING.

PAINE, Thomas (1737–1809). British author. B. at Thetford, he went to America in 1774, where he pub. 'Common Sense' (1776), an influential republican pamphlet, and fought for the colonists in the War of Independence. In 1787 P. returned to England, and in 1791 he pub. *The Rights of Man*, an answer to Burke's *Reflections on the Revolution in France*. In 1792 he was indicted for treason but escaped to France, to represent Calais in the Convention. Narrowly escaping the guillotine, he regained his seat after the fall of Robespierre. In 1793 he pub. *The Age of Reason*, opposing Deism to Christianity and Atheism. He returned to America in 1802, and d. in New York.

PAINTING. The chief methods of P. are tempera or distemper, fresco, oil P. (discovered by the Van Eyck brothers in Flanders), and water colour, which evolved from the wash drawings of the 15th–17th cents. and reached its highest development with Turner. The chief kinds of P., apart from those dealing with religious and mythological subjects, are *historical*, as seen in the work of David, Ingres, Delacroix; *portrait*, Van Dyck, Rembrandt, Velasquez, Goya, Reynolds, Gainsborough, Sargent, Sutherland; *landscape*, Claude Lorrain, Corot, Turner, Constable, Cotman; *seascape*, Jan van de Cappelle, van de Velde the Younger, Turner; *genre*, Brueghel, Vermeer, de Hooch; *still life*, Jan and Cornelius van Heem, Chardin, Courbet, Manet, Braque; *abstract*, Picasso, Ernst, Klee, Nicholson.

SCHOOLS OF PAINTING

Italian, 13th–18th cents. *Florence:* Cimabue, Giotto, Orcagna, Taddeo Gaddi, Fra Angelico, Uccello, Masaccio, Filippo and Filippino Lippi, Botticelli, Michelangelo, Sarto. *Siena:* Duccio. *Umbria:* Francesca, Perugino. *Milan:* Leonardo da Vinci, Borgognone, Luini. *Parma:* Correggio. *Venice:* Bellini, Carpaccio, Giorgione, Titian, Palma Vecchio, Tintoretto, Veronese, Tiepolo, Canaletto. *Padua:* Mantegna. *Verona:* Pisano. *Bologna:* The Carracci, Reni, Domenichino. *Rome and Naples:* Raphael, Caravaggio, Sassoferrato, Rosa.

Spanish, 16th–19th cents. El Greco, Ribera, Zurbarán, Velasquez, Murillo, Goya, Picasso.

Flemish, 14th–20th cents. Van Eyck, Weyden, Bouts, Memlinc, Bosch, Brueghel, Mabuse, Patinir, Rubens, Van Dyck, Brouwer, Teniers.

Dutch, 16th–19th cents. Rembrandt, Hobbema, Hooch, Vermeer, Hals, Ostade, Ruisdael, Steen, Hondecoeter, Van Gogh.

German, 15th–20th cents. Lochner, Lucas Cranach, Schongauer, Grünewald, Dürer, Holbein, Elsheimer, Chodowiecki, Kandinsky, Klee, Ernst, Kokoschka.

French, 16th–20th cents. Clouet, Poussin, Claude, Watteau, Chardin, Boucher, Fragonard, David, Ingres, Corot, Géricault, Delacroix, Manet, Monet, Degas, Renoir, Camille Pissarro, Cézanne, Gauguin, Matisse, Rouault, Braque, Utrillo, Vuillard, Vlaminck.

British, 17th–20th cents. Hilliard, Lely, Kneller, Hogarth, Wilson, Reynolds, Stubbs, Gainsborough, Romney, Rowlandson, Raeburn, Blake, Morland, Crome, Lawrence, Girtin, Turner, Constable, Cotman, Cox, Etty, Bonington, Watts, Frith, Hunt, Rossetti, Millais, Burne-Jones, Brangwyn, Sickert, Wilson Steer, Duncan Grant, Augustus John, Paul Nash, Stanley Spencer, Graham Sutherland, Sir Alfred Munnings, Ben Nicolson, John Bratby, Francis Bacon, Victor Pasmore.

American, 18th–20th cents. John S. Copley, Benjamin West, Charles W. Peale, Gilbert Stuart, Washington Allston, John James Audubon, Winslow Homer, Thomas Eakins, J. A. M. Whistler, Mary Cassatt, John S. Sargent, John Marin, Rockwell Kent, Diego Rivera, Lyonel Feininger, Laszlo Moholy-Nagy, Jackson Pollock, Ben Shahn, Edward Giobbi.

PAKISTAN. The massive multi-storeyed Secretariat Buildings housing the offices of the Central Ministries in Islamabad.
Courtesy of the Pakistan Govt.

PAISLEY. Scottish burgh on the White Cart, Renfrewshire, 7 m. W.S.W. of Glasgow; famous for the manufacture of thread, introduced *c.* 1810. There are also distilleries, engineering works, and shipbuilding yards. P. grew up round an abbey founded 1160. Pop. (1961) 95,753.

PAKISTAN (pahkistahn´). Islamic Republic in south Asia. It comprises the provs. of Punjab, Sind, Baluchistan, and N.W. Frontier, and the centrally admin. tribal areas: these were formerly collectively known as West Pakistan 1947–72 to distinguish them from East Pakistan, the prov. lying east of West·Bengal, India, which estab. its independence as Bangladesh (q.v.) in 1972. The cap. (formerly Karachi 1947–59 and Rawalpindi 1959–67) is Islamabad: other important towns are Lahore, Hyderabad, Multan, Peshawar and Quetta.

To the N. and W. are mountain ranges, the remainder of P. is a fertile plain watered by the Indus and its tributaries, aided by complex irrigation systems. The chief crops are wheat, rice, millet and sugar cane, with fruit and dates in the mountainous west. Cattle, sheep, goats, horses and camels are reared. Minerals incl. coal in the N.W., chromite, iron, gypsum, and some oil and natural gas. Industrial growth is being encouraged, and there are cotton and woollen mills, and laquered goods, pottery and embroidered articles are produced.

Area 310,236 sq. m.; pop. (1961) 42,880,378.

History. The name P., for a Moslem division of British India, was put forward at the time of the Round Table Conference of 1930–1; it was made up by Choudhary Rahmat Ali (1897–1951) from the names of the predominantly Moslem parts of the subcontinent: Punjab, N.W. Frontier (inhabited chiefly by Afghans), Kashmir, Sind, and Baluchi*stan* (*stan* in Urdu meaning land; the fact that *pak* means pure in Urdu probably added to the attraction of the name). Moslem fear of domination by the vast Hindu majority in British India brought in 1940 a serious demand for a separate Moslem state which delayed for some years the transformation of India into a dominion. This was at last effected in 1947 by the passing of an Act of the Imperial Parliament in London which divided British India into 2 dominions, predominantly Hindu India and predominantly Moslem P. *See* JINNAH.

In accordance with the distribution of the Moslem population, P. was divided into 2 sections, West Pakistan, which constitutes since 1972 the whole of Pakistan, and East Pakistan, an independent state since 1972 as Bangladesh. The two were separated by a thousand miles of Indian territory. The drawing of the frontiers entailed violent religious disturbances, and the flight of thousands of refugees from India to P. and vice versa, with many deaths and acute distress. These tragic beginnings were overcome, and in 1956 P. became a rep., although choosing to remain within the Commonwealth. However, there was increasing divergence between the eastern and western divisions of the country. Pres. Ayub Khan (q.v.) resigned in 1970, martial law was proclaimed and C-in-C. of the army, Gen. Yahya Khan became president. Plans were announced for a new constitution, but in 1971 E. Pakistan proclaimed secession as Bangladesh, and the forces of W. Pakistan were defeated with Indian aid 3–16 Dec. 1971. West P., now the whole of Pakistan, left the Commonwealth in 1972, under the leadership of the new pres., Zulfiqar Ali Bhutto (1929–), when the independence of Bangladesh was recognised by other Commonwealth members. Under the prov. constitution of 1972 the pres. is elected for 5 years by the combined Nat. and Provincial assemblies. In addition to the official language of Urdu, regional languages may be promoted.

PALAEOCLIMATOLOGY. The determination of climatic conditions on the earth's surface in earlier times. Evidence is drawn from rocks and fossils, by new techniques, e.g. past temperatures may be indicated by the proportions in which certain isotopes of oxygen exist in fossilized materials. Complicating factors are possible changes over the years of the plane of the earth's axis in relation to the sun, and in the pattern of earth's land masses.

PA´LAMAS, Kostes (1859–1943). Greek poet. He enriched the Gk. vernacular as a literary language by his use of it, particularly in his poetry, e.g. *Songs of my Fatherland* (1886) and *The Flute of the King* (1910), expressing vivid awareness of Gk. history.

PALATE. The ceiling of the mouth. The bony front part is the hard, the muscular rear part the soft, P.; this contains in the middle line a short appendage called the uvula. Incomplete fusion of the P. causes interference with speech.

PALA'TINATE. An historic division of W. Germany, dating back before Charlemagne. It was ruled by a county palatine (hence the name) and varied in size. When it was attached to Bavaria in 1815 it consisted of Rhenish (or Lower) P. on the Rhine (cap. Heidelberg), and Upper P. (cap. Amberg on the Vils) some 130 m. to the E. In 1946 Rhenish P. became an administrative division of the Land of Rhineland-Palatinate with cap. at Neustadt; Upper P. remained an administrative div. of Bavaria with cap. at Regensburg.

PALDISKI (pahl'děskē). Small, ice-free port in Estonia, a naval base of the Soviet navy, 25 m. W. of Tallinn at the entrance to the Gulf of Finland.

PALEMBA'NG. Indonesian town, cap. of S. Sumatra prov., centre of petroleum production, with large refineries. Coffee and pepper are important articles of trade. P. was the cap. of a sultanate when the Dutch estab. a trading station there in 1616. The large mosque dates from 1740. Pop. (1961) 500,000.

PALENCIA (pahlen'thē-ah). Ancient walled city, cap. of P. prov., Spain. Pop. (1960) 48,200.

PALE'RMO. Cap. and seaport of Sicily, founded by the Phoenicians. Notable buildings incl. the Capella Palatina built by King Roger II in the 12th cent., univ. (1805) and museum. Pop. (1961) 587,063.

PALESTINE. Historic name of a region in S.W. Asia lying between the Mediterranean and the Jordan-Dead Sea-Araba depression, *the* Holy Land of Jews and Christians, and *a* holy land to Moslems.

Geography. Along the W. coast lies a fertile plain up to 20 m. wide, and to the E. lies the central plateau, which is interrupted only by the plain of Esdraelon. The Jordan runs through a deep rift, which at the

PALESTINE. The bleak and barren Qumran promontory, whose rounded white cliffs overlook the Dead Sea, was once the home of an Essene (q.v.) monastery. In 1947 Bedouin discovered in the caves which honeycomb the upper levels the Dead Sea Scrolls (q.v.). *Courtesy of the Jordan Embassy.*

Dead Sea is 1,292 ft. below sea-level. In the S. is the semi-desert Negev.

The climate varies from the semi-tropical to the sub-alpine. The summer is hot and dry, and most of the heavy winter rains percolate through the limestone rock, so that artificial irrigation is essential for cultivation. Citrus and other fruits, and olives, are grown. Potash and other chemicals come from the Dead Sea area.

History. P.'s position on the main route connecting Egypt with the Euphrates valley, and with Asia Minor,

caused it to come in turn under the domination of Egypt, Assyria, Babylonia, Persia, Macedonia, the Ptolemies, the Seleucids, and Rome. P. formed part of the Roman and later of the Byzantine empire until A.D. 636, when it was conquered by the Arabs. The Crusaders occupied Jerusalem 1099–1187, after which P. came under the rule of the Mamelukes. The Turks conquered the land in 1516, and held it until the F.W.W. when the British conquered it, 1917–18, and estab. a military administration replaced by civil administration in 1920; in 1922 Britain received a League of Nations mandate (which incorporated the BALFOUR DECLARATION, q.v.) to administer an area described as P., but incl. historic P. and lands across the Jordan that were in 1923 recognized by Britain as a separate country (*see* JORDAN, Hashimite Kingdom of). Some 300,000 Jewish immigrants were allowed to enter P. during 1920–39; under the care of the Jewish Agency they developed agriculture and industry. Discontent, in particular over the admission of Jewish settlers to a land that had become Arabic in 636, resulted in serious Arab rebellions in 1929 and 1936–8. Various plans were made, one drawn up in 1939 recommending independence for P. within 10 years, further Jewish immigration after 1944 to be only with Arab consent. The outbreak of the S.W.W. brought the troubles to a temporary end, and both Arab and Jewish Palestinians served as volunteers in the Allied forces. The war over, Jewish terrorist organizations staged a series of outrages. Britain put the problem before the U.N. which proposed partition, accepted by neither Arabs nor Jews; and in 1947 Britain announced its intention to give up the mandate on 15 May 1948. On 14 May, eight hours before the mandate ended, the Jewish Agency broadcast a proclamation of a Jewish state of ISRAEL (q.v.).

The P. Nat. Council, as a Palestinian Arab govt. in exile, is devoted to total liberation of the state of P., on the lines of resistance movements in German-occupied Europe during the S.W.W., the enemy being not the Jews but the Zionists. It co-ordinates activities by Al Fatah, and the P. Liberation Organization (PLO), etc., and is supported by Egypt, Jordan and Syria.

PALESTRINA (pahlestrē'nah), **Giovanni Pierluigi da** (1525–94). Italian composer. B. at Palestrina, he became choirmaster at the Vatican in 1551. A master of contrapuntal composition, P. composed masses, motets, hymns, magnificats, and litanies.

PALEY, William (1743–1805). British latitudinarian theologian, whose *Evidences of Christianity* (1794) and *The Principles of Moral and Political Philosophy* (1795) approach religion from the utilitarian viewpoint.

PALI (pah'lē). The sacred language of the Buddhist canonical texts. Of uncertain origin, it shows the influence of Vedic Sanskrit.

PALISSY (pahlēsē), **Bernard** (*c.* 1510–89). French potter, noted for his richly coloured rustic pottery, e.g. dishes with realistic modelled fish and reptiles or with the network piercing, and a favourite of Catherine de' Medici. Imprisoned in the Bastille as a Huguenot in 1588, he d. there.

PALLADIO (pahlah'dē-ō), **Andrea** (1518–80). Italian architect, whose country houses (e.g. Malcontenta, and the Villa Rotonda nr. Vicenza), designed from 1540 for patrician families of the Venetian Rep. influenced the architecture of Washington's home at Mount Vernon, the palace of Tsarskoe Selo, and in England, Holkham, Prior Park, Stowe, etc.

PALLA'DIUM. White metal of the platinum family, discovered in 1803 by Wollaston, and found in platinum ore in Brazil, California and the Urals, and in nickel ores of Canada: symbol Pd, at. wt. 106·4, at. no. 46. It is also a non-radioactive product of a slow neutron nuclear reactor. P. does not tarnish in air, and when finely divided or spongy absorbs up to 3,000 times its volume of hydrogen and is used as a catalyst. Other uses incl. non-magnetic springs in clocks and watches; parts of delicate balances and surgical instruments; dental fillings; and as alloy with gold to make white gold.

PALLIUM, or Pall. A pure wool vestment worn by the Pope and by Catholic metropolitans, primates, and archbishops. It is in the shape of a Y, falling across the shoulders back and front.

PALM. Plant of the family Palmaceae characterized by a single tall stem carrying a thick cluster of large palmate or pinnate leaves at the top. The majority of the some 1,500 species are tropical or sub-tropical, have products of great economic importance, e.g. the coconut, date, sago, and oil (*Elaeis guineensis*) Ps.

PALMA (pahl′mah). Cap. and port of the Balearic Is., Spain, on Majorca. A Roman colony founded 276 B.C., P. has a cathedral begun in 1229. Products incl. silk and woollen textiles, cement, paper, pottery. There is an airport at Son San Juan. Pop. (1960) 193,862.

PALMA. One of the Canary Islands, Spain, a fertile, wooded island producing wine, fruit, honey, and silk. Area 281 sq. m.; pop. (1960) 76,000. Santa Cruz de la Palma is the principal town.

PALMAS (pahl′mahs), **Las.** Cap. of the Spanish Canary archipelago, on Gran Canaria. The port of La Luz is an important fuelling depot. Pop. (1960) 193,862.

PALM BEACH. Winter resort in Florida, U.S.A., on an island between Lake Worth and the Atlantic. Pop. (1960) 6,055.

PALMER, Sir Frederick (1862–1934). British engineer. The son of a carpenter, he first estab. a reputation as a bridge builder (the Son Bridge at Dehri – India's longest – and the Hooghli and Zambesi bridges), but is now remembered as a port development engineer (Calcutta, London and Southampton), being the first to realize the superiority of long straight quays in dock lay-out for maximum use of space.

PALMER, Samuel (1805–81). British artist, whose landscapes show the influence of Blake.

PALMERSTON, Henry John Temple, 3rd visct. P. (1784–1865). British Whig statesman. He succeeded to an Irish peerage in 1802, and became a Tory M.P. in 1807. He was Secretary-at-War 1809–28, broke with the Tories in 1830, and sat in the Whig cabinets of 1830–4, 1835–41, and 1846–51 as For. Sec. His foreign policy was marked by distrust of France and Russia, against whose designs he upheld the independence of Belgium and Turkey. He became Home Sec. in 1852, and was P.M. from 1855 until 1858. His final period as Premier (1859–65) was marked by the 2nd war with China, and by the American Civil War, in which he nearly involved Britain on the side of the South. Popular with the people, for he made good use of the press, he was a constant source of annoyance to the Queen and other ministers because of his high-handed attitude.

LORD PALMERSTON. A caricature statuette, arm-in-arm with Napoleon III. *Courtesy of Lord Mountbatten of Burma.*

PALMERSTON NORTH. City of N. Island, N. Zealand, centre of a timber-growing and dairy-farming dist. Massey Univ. was estab. in 1963. Pop. (1967) 50,000.

PALMGREN (pahlm′grän), **Selim** (1878–1951). Finnish composer, pianist, and conductor. B. at Bjoerneborg, P. was prof. of composition at Helsinki from 1939. The operas *Daniel Hjort* and *Peter Schlemihl* are 2 of his best-known works.

PALM SUNDAY. The Sunday before Easter, and first day of Holy Week; so called because in the R.C. Church palm branches are carried to commemorate Christ's entry into Jerusalem on that day.

PALMYRA (palmī′ra). Ancient city and oasis in the desert of Syria, lying about 150 m. N.E. of

Damascus. P., the Biblical Tadmor, was flourishing by c. 300 B.C., but was destroyed in A.D. 272 after Queen Zenobia had led a revolt against the Romans. Extensive ruins of the Temple of Bel exist. On the site is a village called Tadmur in Arabic.

PALOMAR, Mount. The location of an observatory, 50 m. N.E. of S. Diego, California, having a 200-in. diam. reflector, when dedicated in 1948 the largest telescope in the world.

PAMIRS (pahmērz). A treeless plateau of C. Asia, most of which is in the U.S.S.R., the rest in China and Afghanistan. The P. are traversed by mountain ranges rising to 24,590 ft.; to the S. lies the Hindu Kush.

PAMPAS. Flat treeless Argentine plains, lying between the Andes and the Atlantic, and rising gradually from the coast to the lower slopes of the mountains. In the E.P. are the great cattle ranches and the flax- and grain-growing area of Argentina; to the W. the P. are arid and unproductive. Characteristic of the P. is P. grass. The prov. of La Pampa is in the E.P. Area 55,100 sq. m.; pop. (1960) 194,200.

PAMPAS GRASS. Genus of S. American grasses (*Gynerium*). *G. argenteum* is grown in gardens and has tall leaves and large panicles of white flowers.

PAMPLONA. Cap. of the Spanish prov. of Navarre and of the old kingdom of Navarre. A pre-Roman town, P. was rebuilt by Pompey in 68 B.C., captured by the Visigoths 476, sacked by Charlemagne 778, and taken by Wellington 1813. It makes wine, leather and shoes, textiles, etc. Pop. (1965) 124,200.

PAN. Greek deity, the patron of flocks and herds, worshipped mainly in Arcadia. He is represented as a man with the horns, ears, and hoofs of a goat, and usually playing upon a shepherd's pipe.

PANAMA (pahnahmah′) **CITY.** Cap. of the rep. of P., situated near the Pacific end of the P. Canal. Founded on the present site in 1673, P. has its port at Balboa, which is in the Canal Zone. An earlier P., 5 m. N.E., founded 1519, was destroyed 1671 by the Welsh buccaneer Morgan. Pop. (1968) 373,200.

PANAMA. A rep. of C. America, forming an isthmus divided at its narrowest point by the P. Canal (q.v.) and the Canal Zone. It is traversed by a chain of mountains running parallel to the coasts. The climate is tropical; products incl. bananas, cacao, pearl shell, etc. P. is governed by a president, and an elected national assembly. Spanish is the official language. The cap. is P. City. Formerly part of Colombia, P. declared its independence in 1903 with the encouragement of the U.S.A., which was interested in the Canal Zone. Area 28,576 sq. m.; pop. (1967) 1,328,700.

PANAMA CANAL. Canal across the Panama isthmus in Central America, connecting the Pacific and Atlantic oceans, and 50 m. long. The original construction company, headed by the French engineer Ferdinand de Lesseps, began construction in 1879, but collapsed in 1889 owing to financial scandals and yellow fever. The work was taken over by the U.S.A. in 1904, and the canal was opened 1914, formally 1920.

The P.C. runs S.E. through the Canal Zone from Cristobal at the Atlantic end to Balboa on the Pacific. It contains 12 locks. In 1968 the canal was used by c. 1,500 ocean-going vessels. Nationalist feeling in Panama and a desire for a greater share in the revenue led to anti-American riots in 1964. In 1967 new treaties were agreed, though not finally ratified, providing for relinquishment of American sovereignty and operation of the P.C. by a binational authority; a larger share of the revenues for Panama; and a U.S. option to build a larger, sea-level canal to the E., so dispensing with the costly lock-system. However, the U.S.A. also has alternative sites in N. Colombia and on the Nicaragua/Costa Rica border under study.

The *Canal Zone* extends for 5 m. on either side of the P.C.; it was leased in perpetuity to the U.S.A. in 1903, ratified 1904. Land area 553 sq. m.; pop. (1967) 55,600.

PAN-AMERICAN HIGHWAY. Roadway, a large part of it suitable for all-weather motoring, linking the U.S.A. with Central and South America. It was suggested at the 5th International Conference of American States, 1923. Starting from Nuevo Laredo, Texas, it runs through Mexico City to Panama City, then down the W. side of S. America to Valparaiso, Chile, where it crosses the Andes and goes to Buenos Aires, Argentina. Total length 15,700 m., most of it completed by 1960.

PAN-AMERICAN UNION. *See* ORGANIZATION OF AMERICAN STATES.

PANAY (pahnī'). One of the Philippine Islands, lying between Mindoro and Negros. The cap. is Iloilo. P. is mountainous, reaching 7,265 ft. in Madiaás. The chief occupation is agriculture; rice, sugar, pineapples bananas, and copra are important products. Copper is mined. The Spaniard Legaspi took P. in 1569; it was occupied by the Japanese 1942–5. Area 4,446 sq. m.; pop. (1960) 1,491,000.

PANCHEN LAMA, 10th Incarnation (1935–). Tibetan spiritual leader, 2nd in importance to the Dalai L. (q.v.). A protégé of the Chinese since childhood, he is not indisputably recognized. On the flight of the Dalai L. in 1959, he was deputed by the Chinese to take over, but stripped of power for subversion 1964, and said to be deported to China 1965.

PANCREAS (pang'krē-as). A gland which secretes ferments necessary for the digestion of starch, protein, and fat. It is about 7 in. long and lies behind and below the stomach. It contains groups of cells called the islets of Langerhans, which secrete insulin. *See* INSULIN and DIABETES.

PANDA. Herbivorous mammal (*Ailurus fulgens*) of the family Ailuridae, found in the region of the Himalayas. Similar to a bear, it is about 1½ ft. long with a bushy tail of equal length. The rich chestnut fur darkens on the underside and the legs are black: there are light-coloured rings on the tail and white markings on the face. The rare giant P. (*Ailuropus melanoleucus*), with striking black and white fur, also a native of N.W. China and Tibet, seldom survives

HIMALAYAN PANDA

in zoos since it needs a diet of special bamboo shoots, etc.

PANDIT, Vijaya Lakshmi (1900–). Indian stateswoman. The sister of J. Nehru, q.v., she m. in 1921 Ranjit S. Pandit, and was India's 1st woman minister (Local Govt. and Health 1937–9). She was ambassador to Russia 1947–9, to U.S.A. 1949–51, High Commissioner in London 1954–61, and Gov. of Maharashtra 1962–4.

PANDO'RA. The first woman, according to Greek mythology. Zeus sent her on earth with a box filled with evils, to counteract the blessings brought to man by Prometheus's gift of fire. When her box was opened the evils flew out, only Hope remaining.

PANGO'LIN or **Scaly Anteater.** Family of scale-covered, toothless mammals (Manidae), resembling large lizards, and up to 3 ft. long. Nocturnal in habit, they are found in Africa and S. Asia.

PANIPA'T. Town in Punjab, Rep. of India. Scene of 3 decisive battles: 1526, when Babar was the victor; 1556, won by Akbar; 1761, when the Mahrattas were defeated by Ahmad Shah of Afghanistan. Pop. (1961) 65,000.

PANKHURST, Emmeline (1858–1928). British suffragette, *née* Goulden. Founder of the Women's Social and Political Union in 1903, she launched in 1906 the militant suffragette campaign, and was several times imprisoned and then released after hunger-strikes. She was supported by her daus. DAME CHRISTABEL P. (1880–1958) the political leader of the movement and SYLVIA P. (1882–1960) who suffered 9 times under the 'Cat and Mouse Act', was a pacifist in the F.W.W., and a staunch supporter of the Ethiopian cause against Italy.

PANSY. Perennial garden flower, also known as heart's ease, derived from the European wild P. (*Viola tricolor*), and known as *V. tricolor hortensis*. The flowers are usually yellow, cream or purple, or a mixture, and there are many highly developed varieties bred for size, colour or special markings.

PANTELLERIA (pahntellerē'ah). Volcanic island in the Mediterranean, 62 m. S.W. of Sicily, part of Trapani prov. P. was inhabited in prehistoric times, colonized by the Phoenicians in the 7th cent. B.C., taken by the Romans 217 B.C., by the Arabs c. A.D. 700. Formerly an Italian naval base, it was demilitarized under the peace treaty of 1947. Pop. (1961) 10,000.

PANTHEISM (pan'thē-izm) (Gk. *pan*, all; *theos*, God). A mode of thought which regards God as a pervading presence immanent in the universe. It is expressed in Egyptian religion and Brahmanism, while Stoicism, Neo-Platonism, Judaism, Christianity, and Islam can be interpreted in pantheistic terms. Modern pantheist philosophers incl. Bruno, Spinoza, Fichte, Schelling, and Hegel. A strong pantheistic element is found in the work of many modern poets.

PA'NTHÉON. A temple for the worship of all the gods. The Roman P., begun in 27 B.C. and rebuilt by Hadrian, is still used as a church. The term P. also denotes a building in which many great men are buried, e.g. the Panthéon at Paris.

PANTHER. Name given in India to the leopard.

PANTOMIME. Among the Romans P. signified a masked actor who performed by means of dumb show, and the tradition continued, notable being the 19th cent. pantomimist Debureau, whose techniques have been revived in the 20th by Marcel Marceau and Jean-Louis Barrault (who played the role of Debureau in the film *Les Enfants du Paradis*). In England P. is a species of dramatic Christmas entertainment, diversified with songs, dances and comedy which, from beginnings connected with the 18th cent. harlequin spectacles, developed in the 19th cent. on fairy-tale and folk-tale themes. After Grimaldi, the clown predominated over the harlequinade. Later in the cent. came the era of music-hall P. with stars such as Dan

Leno, Harriet Vernon, and Vesta Tilley, and magnificent 'transformation' scenes. In the 20th cent. Ps. are fewer, because of the decline of live theatre, but Ps. on ice became popular after the S.W.W. Provincial Ps. are truer to tradition than London productions.

PANZER (pahn'tser). German word meaning 'armour', used in connection with armoured vehicles, regiments, etc. The Nazi P. divisions overwhelmed the French, English, and Belgians in 1940.

PAPACY. The office of the Pope or bishop of Rome, as head of the R.C. Church. According to the R.C. claim, the leadership or 'Keys' of the Church was entrusted by Christ to Peter, who became the first bishop of Rome. For many cents., however, Rome was recognized as only one of the great patriarchates of the Church, and Constantinople never accepted the primacy of Rome, breaking away in 1054. The missions of Gregory I (590–604) marked the P.'s first attempt to extend its authority outside Italy. Its position was strengthened in the 8th–9th cents. by the support of the Frankish kings, and reached its height in the 11th–13th cents. under Gregory VII and Innocent III. In the 14th cent. the P. fell completely under French control; its headquarters were removed to Avignon (1309–78), and this 'Babylonian Captivity' was followed by the Great Schism (1378–1417) between rival popes at Rome and Avignon. The reformation withdrew much of N. and W. Europe from the Roman obedience, and throughout the 17th and 18th cents. the P. lost prestige and political influence. Under Pius IX the Papal States (territory

PAPACY. The inauguration of the 2nd Vatican Council in St. Peter's on 11 October 1962. Enthroned under the canopy of the high altar was Pope John, the Council Fathers sat on either side of the nave, and observers from other Churches were also present.   *Photo: Planet News.*

ruled by the Pope as sovereign) were annexed to Italy in 1870, and the conflict with the Italian monarchy lasted until the Lateran Treaty (1929) recognized papal sovereignty over the Vatican City. The Vatican Council (1870) proclaimed the doctrine that the Pope is infallible when he speaks *ex cathedra.* The Pope is elected by the Sacred College of Cardinals, and his pontificate is dated from his coronation with the tiara,

or triple crown, at St. Peter's. Following the Second Vatican Council (1962–6) an Episcopal Synod (200 bishops elected by the local hierarchies) was estab. 1967 to collaborate with the Pope in the govt. of the Church.

PAPAW'. *See* PAWPAW.

PAPEETE ('little water'). Chief town of Tahiti in the Windward Islands, French Polynesia. It exports

PAPER. Some newsprint is given an additional finishing by being passed rapidly through the rolls of a supercalender stationed beyond the 'dry end' of the machine, as here at Bowater's Kemsley Mills. *Courtesy of the Bowater Organization.*

copra, vanilla, phosphates, mother of pearl. Pop. (1964) 15,220.

PAPEN (pahpen), **Franz von** (1879–1969) German politician. Chancellor in 1932, he negotiated the Nazi-Conservative alliance which put Hitler in power, and was Vice-Chancellor 1933–4, envoy to Austria 1934–8, and ambassador to Turkey 1939–44. At the Nuremberg Trials, 1945–6, he was acquitted, but was imprisoned by a denazification court.

PAPER. Sheet of vegetable fibre, the name deriving from Lat. *papyrus,* a form of writing material made from the water reed and used in ancient Egypt. The invention of true P., made of pulped fishing nets, rags, etc., is credited to Tsai Lun, a Minister of Agriculture under the Han dynasty of China, in A.D. 105. Its use gradually spread from the 8th cent. and the 1st English paper mill was estab. at Stevenage in the 15th cent. The spread of literacy led to the invention by Louis Robert in 1799 of a machine to produce a continuous reel of paper, since production by hand of single sheets could no longer keep pace with demand. Some modern machines have an output of 2,000 ft. per min. or more than 250 tons per day. Apart from its obvious uses in writing, printing and packaging, P. is today also employed in towels and toilet tissues; hardboard, roofing felt, insulating panels and drainpipes; and in electrical work as an insulator.

PAPHOS (pā'fos). Ancient city of Cyprus, originally a Phoenician colony. According to legend Aphrodite landed here after her birth from the sea waves. Pop. (1966) 10,600.

PAPINEAU (pahpěnō'), **Louis Joseph** (1786–1871). Canadian politician. B. in Montreal, he organized the unsuccessful rebellion in Lower Canada in 1837, then fled the country, but returned in 1847 to sit in the United Canadian legislature until 1854.

PAPUA (papoo'a). Name originally given to the island of New Guinea, later particularly to its S.E. section. *See* NEW GUINEA.

PARÁ (pahrah'). State of Brazil containing the lower valley and mouth of the Amazon. Timber, cacao, and Brazil nuts are produced; tyres are made from local rubber. The cap. is Belem. Area 474,770 sq. m.; pop. (1967) 1,914,000.

PARACE′LSUS (1493–1541). Swiss physician and theosophic philosopher, whose real name was Theophrastus Bombastus von Hohenheim. In 1526 he became lecturer in medicine at Basle, and revolutionized the theoretic basis of medicine. From 1529 onwards he wandered Europe, and he d. at Salzburg.

PARACHUTE (par′ashoot). Umbrella-shaped device consisting of some 2 dozen panels of silk or nylon, each with shroud lines to a harness, used to slow down the descent of human being, supplies, etc., from a plane or missile to a safe speed for landing, or sometimes to aid the landing of a plane or missile itself. *See* FREE-FALLING. Leonardo da Vinci sketched a P. design, but the first descent (from a balloon) was made by Garnerin in 1797, and the first drop from an aircraft by Berry in 1912.

PARADISE. Persian word for a park or pleasure garden, and hence applied to the Garden of Eden, the Messianic kingdom, and the heaven of after life.

PARAFFIN. A hydrocarbon (or mixture of hydrocarbons) of the P. series, general formula C_nH_{2n+2}. The lower members are gases, e.g. methane (marsh gas). The middle ones (mainly liquid) form the basis of petrol (gasolene), kerosene (q.v.), lubricating oils, and the higher ones (P. waxes) are used in ointment and cosmetic bases. *See* KEROSENE.

PARAGUAY (pa′ragwī). Inland republic of S. America, bounded by Bolivia to the N., Brazil to the N.E., and Argentina to the S.W. and S. The chief rivers are the Paraná and its tributary, the P., which divides the country in two. The climate is tropical to sub-tropical, with an abundance of summer rain. For the most part, P. lies below 500 ft. a.s.l.; hills in the E. rise to something over 1,500 ft. Much of the land is forested, timber, quebracho (used in tanning), and yerba maté being natural products important commercially. Crops for home consumption incl. maize, mandioca, beans, sugar cane, rice; cotton (for export) and tobacco are also grown, and yerba maté plantations have been estab. Hides and meat are other exports. Minerals found but little worked incl. iron, manganese, and copper.

Under the constitution of 1967 there is a pres. elected for 5 yrs. and a senate and chamber of deputies, also popularly elected. The cap. is Asunción. Both Spanish and Guarani, the language of the Indian inhabitants at the time of the Spanish conquest, are commonly spoken by Paraguayans, the races having mixed. Area 157,000 sq. m.; pop. (1962) 1,819,103.

P. was discovered by Sebastian Cabot in 1526, and Asunción was founded by Spanish settlers in 1537. From *c.* 1600 until 1767, when they were expelled, Jesuit missionaries administered much of the country as a semi-theocratic state. At first a prov. subordinate to the Spanish viceroyalty of Peru, then from 1776 part of the viceroyalty of Buenos Aires, P. in 1811 declared its independence from Spain. J. G. R. Francia, an able lawyer, established himself as despotic president, 1816–40; he was succeeded by his nephew, C. A. López, and he in turn (1862) by his son, F. S. López, who involved P. in a war with Brazil, Argentina, and Uruguay. After 5 years of war P. was invaded and López killed at Aquidaban in 1870. When hostilities ceased the Paraguayan people consisted mainly of women and children. Recovery was slow with many revolutions; and continuing disputes over the frontier with Bolivia in the torrid Chaco zone of the N. flared up into war, 1932–5; arbitration by the U.S.A. and 5 S. American reps. brought a frontier settlement and a peace treaty 1938. Under Pres. Alfredo Stroessner, who achieved power by a military coup in 1954, there was a liberalisation of regime from 1968.

PA′RAKEET. *See* PARROT.

PARALDEHYDE. A colourless liquid $(C_2H_4O)_3$ formed from acetaldehyde. It is soluble in water and is a safe hypnotic.

PARALYSIS. Failure of action of muscle, due to injury or disease of the nerves supplying it. Paresis is partial P. *See* POLIOMYELITIS; and SLEEPY SICKNESS. In hysterical P. the nerves are sound and the disorder is in the emotions and will.

PARAMA′RIBO. Port and cap of Surinam, 15 m. from the sea on the Surinam r., an important trading and commercial centre with an airport at Zanderij 25 m. to the S. Pop. (1967) 123,000.

PARANÁ (pahrahnah′). River of S. America, formed by the confluence of the Rio Grande and Paranaiba. It is joined by the Paraguay at Corrientes, and flows into the Rio de la Plata with the Uruguay. It is about 2,500 m. long.

PARANÁ. River port in Argentina, cap. of Entre Rios prov., 350 m. N.W. of Buenos Aires. It has a handsome cathedral; also flour mills and meat canneries. P. was cap. of Argentina 1853–62. Pop. (1960) 174,000.

PARANOIA. Monomania; a serious form of mental disorder in which the patient believes himself to be an especially superior person menaced by a conspiracy. Around this belief he builds up an elaborate delusional system embracing the whole of his life. Occasionally he will realize that the ideas are false and remain sane, but usually he is possessed by them and may attack one of his 'persecutors'.

PARASITE. A creature depending on another for the necessities of life, e.g. lice, fleas, the acarus that causes scabies, tape-worms, and the microscopic organisms that cause syphilis and malaria. Plants, too, may be parasitic.

PARATHYROIDS (-thī′roid-). Two pairs of small endocrine glands situated in the neck above and beside the thyroid. They control the use of lime (calcium) by the body.

PARATYPHOID (-tī′foid) **FEVER.** An infective fever like typhoid but milder and less dangerous caused by one of three similar paratyphoid bacilli, A, B, and C. These are common in India, western Europe, and the Balkans respectively. These three varieties are known as the enteric group of fevers.

PARENTIS-EN-BORN (pahreñtē′). Lumbertown in Landes dept., France, 40 m. S.S.W. of Bordeaux, centre of an oilfield. Pop. (1962) 2,493.

PARIS Henri d'Orléans, comte de (1909–). Head of the House of Bourbon: *see* BOURBON TABLE. He served in the Foreign Legion under an assumed name 1939–40, and in 1950 on the abrogation of the *loi d'exil* (1886) banning pretenders to the French throne, returned to live in France.

PARIS, Matthew (d. 1259). English chronicler. He entered St. Albans Abbey in 1217, and wrote a valuable history of England down to 1259.

PARIS. Cap. of France in a fertile plain at the confluence of the Marne with the Seine. Formerly it was cap. of Seine dept., but from 1964 the *Ville de Paris* (City of Paris) itself became a dept., and, although Seine-et-Marne was unchanged, the other 2 depts. of the Paris region were reorganised in 7 new depts.: *see* table p. 443.

HISTORY P., the Roman Lutetia, cap. of the Parisii, a Gaulish tribe, was occupied by Julius Caesar, 53 B.C. Clovis made it his cap. *c.* 508, but it attained importance only under the Capetian kings (987–1328). P. was occupied by the English 1420–36, strongly supported the Catholics during the Religious Wars, and was besieged by Henry IV, 1590–4. The Bourbon kings did much to beautify the city. Napoleon adorned it with new boulevards, bridges, and triumphal arches, as did Napoleon III. P. was the centre of the revolutions of 1789–94, 1830, and 1848. It was besieged by the Prussians 1870–1, and during govt. troops under the Commune, and during the F.W.W. suffered from air raids and bombardment. In the S.W.W. it was occupied by the Germans June 1940–Aug. 1944.

2D

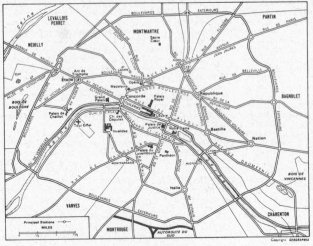

PARIS

MODERN P. The Seine is spanned by 32 bridges, the oldest being the Pont Neuf (1578). On the Ile de la Cité stand Notre-Dame (begun 1163), the seat of the archbishopric, and the Palais de Justice. On the N. bank are the Hôtel de Ville; the former palace of the Louvre, now one of the world's finest art galleries; the Tuileries gardens; and the Place de la Concorde. Thence the Champs Elysées leads to the Place de l'Etoile, in the centre of which is the Arc de Triomphe, with the tomb of the Unknown Warrior under it. Farther W. is the Bois de Boulogne. On the S. bank are the univ. (founded c. 1150); the Panthéon; the Invalides, with the tomb of Napoleon; the Champ de Mars, in which stands the Eiffel Tower; the Luxembourg Palace and Gardens; and the Jardin des Plantes. Montmartre, in the N. of the city, on which stands the 19th cent. basilica of Sacré Cœur, rises to 410 ft. P. is one of France's main industrial centres, producing metal goods, chemicals, leather goods, glass, tobacco, food products, and luxury goods. It is also an important port, being connected by canals with N.E. and N.W. France; besides Orly it also has an airport at Le Bourget 7 m. N.E. Pop. (1968) 2,590,771; conurbation 8,196,746.

PARIS, Treaties of. Name given to a number of peace treaties signed in P., the chief being those concluding the Seven Years War (1763), the American War of Independence, the Napoleonic Wars, and the Crimean War. The peace conference after the F.W.W. which drew up the Treaty of Versailles was held in P. in 1919–20. The P. Peace Conference of 1946 drew up the peace treaties between the Allies and Italy, Rumania, Hungary, Bulgaria, and Finland.

PARISH COUNCILS. Local govt. bodies in English rural districts, estab. by the Local Government Act 1894. Elected triennially, they are empowered to carry out certain public duties, for which purpose they may impose a limited local rate. A P. meeting is an assembly of the electors of a parish, and where there is no P.C. exercises minor responsibilities.

PARIS-PLAGE. See TOUQUET–PARIS PLAGE, LE.

PARK, Mungo (1771–1806). Scottish explorer. B. near Selkirk, he explored the course of the Niger 1795–7, and d. during a 2nd expedition in 1805–6. He pub. Travels in the Interior of Africa (1799).

PARKER, Matthew (1504–75). English churchman. B. at Norwich, he was converted to Protestantism at Cambridge. He received high preferment under Henry VIII and Edward VI, and, as abp. of Canterbury from 1559 was largely responsible for the Elizabethan religious settlement.

PARKER OF WADDINGTON, Hubert Lister P., baron (1900–). British judge. Called to the Bar in 1924, he became a Lord Justice of Appeal in 1954, was noted for his conduct of the bank-rate-leak tribunal in 1957, and succeeded Goddard as Lord Chief Justice (1958–71).

PARKES, Sir Henry (1815–96). Australian statesman. B. in Warwickshire, he emigrated to Australia in 1839, and between 1872 and 1891 was several times P.M. and Colonial Secretary.

PARKINSON, Cyril Northcote (1909–). British historian and satirist. Raffles prof. of history at the Univ. of Malaya, Singapore, 1950–8, he sprang to fame with Parkinson's Law (1958), a study of the world of public and business administration, which laid down that 'work expands to fill the time available for its completion' with its corollary 'subordinates multiply at a fixed rate regardless of the amount of work produced'.

PARKINSON, James (1755–1824). British neurologist and palaeontologist. Parkinson's disease (paralysis agitans) is named after him.

PARLIAMENT. The supreme legislature of Great Britain. P. originated under the Norman kings as the Great Council of royal tenants-in-chief, to which in the 13th cent. representatives of the shires were sometimes summoned. De Montfort's parliament (1265) set a precedent by incl. representatives of the boroughs as well as the shires, which was followed by Edward I from 1275 onwards. Under Edward III the burgesses and knights of the shires began to meet separately from the barons, thus forming the House of Commons. By the 15th cent. P. had acquired the right to legislate, vote and appropriate supplies, examine public accounts, and impeach royal ministers. The powers of P. were much diminished under the Yorkists and Tudors, but under Elizabeth I a new spirit of independence appeared. The revolutions of 1640 and 1688 estab. parliamentary control over the executive and the judiciary, and finally abolished all royal claim to tax or legislate without parliamentary consent. During these struggles the 2 great parties emerged, and after 1688 it became customary for the king to choose his ministers from the party dominant in the Commons.

The English P. was united with the Scottish in 1707, and with the Irish during 1801–1922. The franchise was extended to the middle classes in 1832, to the urban working classes in 1867, to agricultural labourers in 1884, and to women in 1918 and 1928. Payment of members was introduced in 1911. The duration of Ps. was fixed at 3 years in 1694, at 7 in 1716, and at 5 in 1911, but any P. may extend its own life, as happened during both world wars. Constituencies are kept under continuous review by the Parliamentary Boundary Commissions (1944): no. of M.P.s 630.

The House of Lords comprises the temporal peers, i.e. all hereditary peers of England (created to 1707), all hereditary peers of Great Britain (created 1707–1800), and all hereditary peers of the U.K. 1801 onward); all hereditary Scottish peers (under the Peerage Act 1963); all peeresses in their own right (under the same act); all life peers (both the Law Lords and those created under the Life Peerages Act of 1958); and the spiritual peers – the 2 archbps. and

24 of the bps. (London, Durham and Winchester by right, and the rest by date). *See* PEERAGE. Since the P. Act of 1911 the powers of the Lords have been restricted, in that they may delay a bill passed by the Commons for a limited period but not reject it.

Under the Parliament Bill (1968) introduced by Wilson a 2-tier system of voting and non-voting peers would have been estab., salaried, voting members being those *c.* 150 life peers able to attend regularly, supplemented by *c.* 80 newly-created life peers chosen chiefly from existing hereditary peers: the govt. would have been entitled to a 10% majority. The measure gave way to an industrial relations bill.

The Lords are presided over by the Lord Chancellor, and the Commons by the Speaker. A public

PARLIAMENT. The Houses of Parliament look down on the Thames. To the far right is the clock tower containing 'Big Ben' and to the left, high above Westminster Abbey, the Victoria Tower where parliamentary archives are housed.
Photo: J. Allan Cash.

bill is given a preliminary 1st reading and discussed in detail at the 2nd reading; it is then referred to a standing committee, after which it is considered by a committee of the whole House. After the 3rd reading it is sent to the Lords, whose procedure is similar. If it passes both houses, it receives the royal assent and so becomes law.

PARLIAMENT, Houses of. The present H.P. were designed by Sir C. Barry, and built in 1840-60, the previous building having been burnt down in 1834. It incorporates portions of the medieval Palace of Westminster. The Commons debating chamber was destroyed by incendiary bombs in 1941: the rebuilt chamber (opened 1950) is the work of Sir G. G. Scott, and preserves its former character.

PARMA (pahr'mah). Ancient Italian city, cap. of P. prov., Emilia region. It has a 12th cent. Romanesque cathedral and a univ. (1502). Parmesan cheese is exported, and it makes agricultural machinery, shoes, paper, canned goods, etc. On an Etruscan site colonized by the Romans in 183 B.C., P. was the seat of a bishopric by 378. Pop. (1961) 140,844.

PARMIGIANO (pahrmējah'nō). Name assumed by the Italian painter Francesco Mazzola (1504-40). B. at Parma, he was influenced by Correggio and Raphael.

PARNASSIENS (pahrnahsi-eń), **Les.** School of French poets incl. Leconte de Lisle, Mallarmé, and Verlaine, which flourished 1866-76. Named from the review *Parnasse Contemporain*, it advocated 'Art for art's sake' in opposition to the ideas of the Romantics.

PARNASSUS. Mountain in central Greece, 8,062 ft., revered by the ancient Greeks as the abode of Apollo and the Muses. Delphi lies on its S. flank.

PARNELL (pahr'nel), **Charles Stewart** (1846-91).

Irish politician. B. in co. Wicklow, he was elected M.P. for Meath in 1875. P. supported a policy of obstruction and violence, and became the president of the Nationalist Party in 1877. In 1879 he approved the Land League, and his attitude led in 1881 to his imprisonment. He welcomed Gladstone's Home Rule Bill, and continued his agitation after its defeat in 1886. In 1887 *The Times* failed to prove P.'s complicity in the Phoenix Park murders, but in 1889 Captain O'Shea petitioned for divorce on the grounds of his wife's adultery with P.; in 1891 Parnell m. Mrs. O'Shea. For fear of losing the support of Gladstone, his party deposed him in Nov. 1890.

PARR, Catherine (1512-48). 6th wife of Henry VIII. She had already lost 2 husbands when in 1543 she m. Henry VIII. She survived him, and in 1547 m. Lord Seymour of Sudeley.

PARRAMA'TTA. River, W. arm of Port Jackson, New South Wales, Australia. It is 15 m. long and is lined with industrial suburbs of Sydney: Balmain, Drummoyne, Concord on the left bank, P., Ermington and Rydalmere, Ryde, and Hunter's Hill on the right.

PARROT. Order of birds, Psittaci, abundant in the tropics, espec. in Australia and S. America: the smaller species are commonly referred to as parakeets. They are vegetarian, except for the New Zealand kea (*Nestor notabilis*) which has become carnivorous since the settlement of white farmers. Their strong, hooked bills cope easily with fruit and seeds, which they characteristically clasp in their claws while feeding. The plumage is generally very colourful, although the call is commonly a harsh screech: the talent for imitating human speech is most marked in the comparatively sober grey P. (*Psitticus erithacus*) of Africa. The white eggs are usually laid in holes in trees, but the grey-breasted parakeet – though remaining monogamous – combines with the rest of the flock to build enormous nests of twigs in trees, rather like a block of flats. *See* BUDGERIGAR and COCKATOO.

PARRY, Sir Charles Hubert Hastings (1848-1918). British composer. B. at Bournemouth, from 1883 he taught at the R.C.M., becoming director in 1894, and was prof. of music at Oxford 1900-8. He was created a baronet in 1902. His works incl. songs, motets, and the setting of Milton's 'Blest Pair of Sirens'.

PARRY, Sir William Edward (1790-1855). British explorer. In 1819-20 he led an expedition described in his *Journal of a Voyage to Discover a North-West Passage*, and similar explorations in 1821-3 and 1824-5. In 1827 P. attempted to reach the North Pole, attaining a latitude of 82° 45'.

THICK-BILLED PARROT

PARSEES. The followers of Zoroaster (q.v.) who fled from Persia after its conquest by the Arabs, and settled in India in the 8th cent. A.D. They now live mainly in Bombay state, maintaining their cult of the sacred fire and the exposure of their dead. They are proverbial for their business ability and philanthropy. They number about 100,000.

PARSLEY. Biennial herb (*Petroselinum hortense*), cultivated for flavouring: 9-18 in. high, it has bipinnate, aromatic leaves and yellow umbelliferous flowers.

PARSNIP. Biennial plant (*Pastinaca sativa*), 2-4 ft. high, cultivated for its edible tap-root. The leaves are ovate, serrated, and downy beneath, and the flower umbels yellow.

PARSONS, Sir Charles Algernon (1854-1931). British engineer, inventor of the P. steam turbine, who estab. his own firm nr. Newcastle upon Tyne in 1889. He was knighted in 1911 and received the O.M. in 1927.

PARTHENON. The temple of Athena Parthenos (the Virgin) on the Acropolis at Athens. It was built in 447–438 B.C., under the supervision of Phidias, and is considered the most perfect example of Doric architecture. Later it was used as a Christian church and by the Turks as a mosque, then as a powder magazine, as a result of which it was reduced to ruins when the Venetians bombarded the Acropolis in 1687. *See* ELGIN MARBLES.

PARTHIA. Ancient name for a country of W. Asia in what is now N.E. Persia. Originating *c.* 248 B.C., it reached the peak of its power under Mithradates I in the 2nd cent. B.C. Ctesiphon was the cap. of P. which was annexed to Persia in A.D. 226.

PARTNERSHIP. A P. in English law is the relation of 2 or more persons carrying on a common business for profit. It differs from a company in that it may not consist of more than 20 members, and that members (and not only the directors) commonly take part in the conduct of the business. In the U.S.A. the sharing of profits is regarded as the distinctive feature.

PARTRIDGE, Eric (1894–). New Zealand lexicographer. He studied at Oxford after serving in the F.W.W. and settled in England to write with entertaining scholarship *A Dictionary of Slang and Unconventional English, Dictionary of the Underworld, British and American* (1950), and many others.

PARTRIDGE. Game bird, 2 species of which are found in Great Britain. The grey P. (*Perdix cinerea*) is mottled brown above, with grey speckled breast, and patches of chestnut barred on the sides. The French P. (*Caccabis rufa*) is distinguished from the grey P. by red legs, bill, and eyelids. The back is plain brown, with a white throat edged with black. The sides are barred chestnut and black.

PASADENA. City in California, U.S.A., 11 m. N.E. of Los Angeles, originally a Spanish settlement. The annual East-West football game, started here 1902, was held in the Rose Bowl (85,000 seats) from 1923. The Mt. Wilson observatory is 5 m. N.E. Pop. (1960) 116,407.

PASCAL (pahskahl'), **Blaise** (1623–62). French philosopher and mathematician. B. at Clermont-Ferrand, he was a precocious student, and produced a treatise on conic sections in 1640. Coming under Jansenist influence, he took refuge at Port Royal in 1655, and defended the Jansenist doctrines against the Jesuits in the *Lettres Provinciales* (1656). He investigated the laws governing the weight of air, the equilibrium of liquids, the hydraulic press, the infinitesimal calculus, and the mathematical theory of probability. His *Pensées*, a fragmentary apology for the Christian religion, appeared in 1670.

PAS-DE-CALAIS (pah-de-kahlā'). French name for the Strait of Dover; name also of a French dept. bordering the Strait of which Arras is the cap., Calais the chief port.

PASHA. A Turkish title of honour borne originally by military commanders, and later by high civil officials. Abolished in Turkey in 1934, it was in use in other Middle East countries until 1952.

PASK, Gordon (1930–). British electronics engineer and biologist. Ed. at Downing Coll., Cambridge, he has directed research into various cybernetic systems, incl. adaptive teaching machines, and also into self-organizing controllers or chemical and biological computers, and in 1959 worked as assoc. prof. at the Univ. of Illinois.

PASMORE, Victor (1908–). British artist. B. in Surrey, he was in local govt. service with the L.C.C. 1927–37, taught 1949–53 at the Central School of Arts and Crafts, London, where he had once attended evening classes, and was Master of Painting, Durham university, 1954–61. He is noted for abstract com-

GORDON PASK. The inventor in his study at his laboratory in Richmond, Surrey, with Eucrates, his first adaptive teaching machine, built 1954.   *Courtesy of System Research, Ltd.*

positions and as an exponent of the 'classic' tendency in British art.

PASSAU (pahs'sow). Town of Bavaria, W. Germany. at the junction of the Inn and Ilz with the Danube, close to the Austrian frontier. The *Treaty of P.* (1552) between Maurice, Elector of Saxony, and the future Emperor Ferdinand I, allowed the Lutherans full religious liberty, and prepared the way for the Peace of Augsburg: *see* REFORMATION.

PASSCHENDAELE (pa'shendāl). Village in W. Flanders, Belgium, near Ypres. The P. ridge before Ypres was the object of a costly, but unsuccessful, British offensive, July–Nov. 1917; British casualties numbered nearly 400,000 (17,000 officers).

PASSFIELD, Sidney Webb, baron P. (1859–1947). British Socialist theorist. B. in London, he was till 1891 a civil servant, and in 1895 was the principal founder of the London School of Economics, where he was prof. of public administration 1912–27. Among the founders of the Fabian Soc. in 1884, he was a member of the Labour Party executive 1915–25, entered parliament in 1922, and was pres. of the B. of T. 1924, Dominions Sec. 1929–30, and Colonial Sec. 1929–31. He received a peerage in 1929. He m. in 1892 Beatrice Potter (1858–1943), who collaborated with him in a series of books, e.g. *History of Trade Unionism* (1894), *English Local Government* (1906), and *Soviet Communism* (1935), and whose own writing incl. *My Apprenticeship* (1926) and *Our Partnership* (1948).

PASSION FLOWER. Genus of climbing plants (*Passiflora*). The name is derived from the likeness of certain parts of the flower to symbols of the crucifixion of Christ.

PASSIONISTS. R.C. religious order founded in 1720 by St. Paul of the Cross (1694–1775), which combines the active and the contemplative life.

PASSION PLAY.

PASSION FLOWER

A play representing the death and resurrection of a god. In ancient Egypt there were plays in honour of Osiris held at Abydos, and in Greece the mysteries of Dionysus were performed. Christian plays depict the crucifixion and resurrection of Christ, e.g. certain of the medieval miracle plays, and that held at Oberammergau, in Bavaria.

PASSOVER. An ancient Jewish spring festival, which commemorates the Exodus from Egypt. Its

2 main features are a family feast eaten at home on the first evening of the festival, and abstention from leaven throughout the 7 days which it lasts. Formerly a lamb was eaten at the feast, but a shank bone is now substituted.

PASSPORT. Document issued by the foreign office of any country authorizing the bearer to go abroad and guaranteeing him the state's protection. A British P. is generally available for travel to all countries, but some countries require the intending visitor to obtain a special endorsement or *visa*. For the citizen of the U.K. and Colonies a cheaper, simplified travel document is available for short visits to certain countries.

PASTERNAK, Boris Leonidovich (1890–1960). Russian author. B. in Moscow of Jewish parentage, he remained in Russia when his artist father **Leonid P.** (1862–1945) emigrated to Germany, dying in Oxford. His reputation as his country's chief lyric poet mounted from his first vol. *A Twin Cloud* (1914), through *Life is My Sister* (1922), and *On Early Trains* (1941) to the pub. of his selected poems (1945), and he produced excellent translations of Shakespeare's tragedies and Goethe's *Faust*. A Nobel prize followed the pub. in the W. in 1958 of his novel *Dr. Zhivago*, which had been banned in the U.S.S.R. as a 'hostile political act'. His work had previously suffered indirect attack and now, although he refused the prize, he was expelled from the Union of Soviet Writers for his portrayal of the degeneration of a scientist who passes from support of the Revolution to increasing disillusion.

PASTEUR (pahstör'), **Louis** (1822–95). French chemist. B. at Dôle, he became director of scientific studies at the École Normale in 1857, where he announced his discovery of the causes of fermentation in alcohol and milk. His proof that the organisms stimulating it were contained in the atmosphere inspired Lister's work in antiseptic surgery. P. was prof. of chemistry at the Sorbonne 1867–89. Among his later researches were those on silkworm disease, anthrax, and hydrophobia; the Institut Pasteur was founded in 1888. *See* PASTEURIZATION.

PASTEURIZATION. Treatment of milk to reduce the number of micro-organisms it contains, and so protect consumers from disease. A temperature of between 62·8° and 65·5°C is maintained for at least 30 min., then the milk is rapidly cooled to 10°C or lower. The harmful bacteria are killed and the development of the others is delayed.

PASTON LETTERS. A collection of letters and documents, written by or to members of the Norfolk family of P. during 1422–1509.

PASTORAL STAFF. A staff shaped like a shepherd's crook carried by cardinals and bishops on certain formal occasions as a sign of office.

PATAGO'NIA. Geographical area S. of lat. 40° S. and extending westward through Chile to the Pacific. Argentinian P. is divided into the provs. of Chubut, Rio Negro, Santa Cruz, and Tierra del Fuego; Chilean P. into the provs. of Chiloé and Magallanes (which incl. Chilean Tierra del Fuego). Magellan sighted P. in 1520. Both Chile and Argentina claimed the whole area (over 400,000 sq. m.), but agreed to a division in 1881, Chile receiving 72,000 sq. m. Most of Argentinian P. is sterile with a chilly climate and frequent high winds; Chilean P. is cold and damp with dense forest on the lower slopes of the Andes. Sheep rearing is the principal occupation throughout P.; minerals incl. coal and petroleum.

PATCH, Alexander McCarroll (1889–1945). American general. B. in Arizona, he served in the F.W.W., and commanded all Allied Forces in New Caledonia, 1942, later being in charge of operations on Guadalcanal. In 1944 he led the 7th Corps from Italy through France to Germany. He d. of pneumonia.

PA'TEN. Flat dish of gold or silver used for hold-ing the consecrated bread at Holy Communion.

PATENTS. Letters patent, more usually called P., are documents conferring upon a person the exclusive right to make, use, and sell an invention for a limited period, i.e. 16 years. It is not possible to patent an *idea* nor anything which is not *new*. An International Convention (1883) safeguards rights outside the original country of patent, but 16 yrs. is inadequate for inventions arising from modern science and technology and in 1967 the draft patent convention of E.E.C. proposed a term of 20 yrs. The Patent Office in Holborn, London, not only grants patents but registers designs and trade marks.

PATER, Walter Horatio (1839–94). British critic. B. in London, he became a fellow of Brasenose Coll., Oxon., in 1864. A noted stylist and supporter of 'art for art's sake', he pub. *Studies in the History of the Renaissance* (1873); *Marius the Epicurean* (1885); *Imaginary Portraits* (1887), etc.

PA'TERNO'STER. Name for the Lord's Prayer, from the opening words of the Latin version.

PATERSON, Andrew Barton (1864–1941). Australian journalist, known as 'Banjo' P., author of vols. of light verse and the nationally popular 'Waltzing Matilda' adapted from a traditional song.

PATHAN (patahn'). Warrior tribesman of Afghanistan and N.W. Pakistan. *See* N.-W. FRONTIER.

PATMORE, Coventry (1823–96). British poet and critic. He was a librarian at the British Museum 1846–66, and as one of the pre-Raphaelites achieved fame with the poem *The Angel in the House* (1854–63), and the collection of odes *The Unknown Eros* (1877).

PA'TMOS. Greek is. of the Dodecanese. St. John is said to have written Revelation while in exile here. Area 13 sq. m.; pop. (1961) 2,400.

PA'TNA. The cap. of Bihar state, Rep. of India, on the Ganges. It has remains of a hall built by Asoka in the 3rd cent. B.C., and is the seat of a univ. (1917). Pop. (1961) 363,700.

PĀ'TON, Alan (1903–). S. African writer. B. at Pietermaritzburg, he became first a schoolmaster, and in 1935 principal of a reformatory nr. Johannesburg, which he ran on enlightened lines. His novel *Cry, the Beloved Country* (1948) touched the heart of S. Africa's problems: later books incl. the study *Land and People of South Africa* (1956), *The Long View* (1968).

PATRAI (pat're). Port of Greece, on P. Gulf, 45 m. W. of Corinth, cap. of Achaea (Akkaia) nome. The ancient Patrae, it is the only one of the 12 cities of Achaea to survive. Destroyed 1821 during the Greek war of independence, it was rebuilt. It has hydro-electric installations, and textiles and paper are made. Pop. (1961) 95,364.

PATRIARCH (Gk. 'ruler of a family'). The mythical ancestors of the human race and of the Jews, from Adam to the sons of Jacob. In the Orthodox Church the term is used for the primates of 7 of the 10 national Churches.

PATRICIANS. Privileged class in ancient Rome, descended from the original citizens. After the 4th cent. B.C. the rights formerly exercised by the Ps. alone were thrown open to the plebeians, and patrician descent became only a matter of prestige.

PATRICK, St. (c. 389–461 or 493). The patron saint of Ireland. B. in Britain, probably in S. Wales, he was carried off by pirates to 6 years' slavery in Antrim before escaping either to Britain or Gaul – his poor Latinity suggests the former – to train as a missionary. He is variously said to have landed again in Ireland in 432 or 456, and is credited with founding the diocese of Armagh, though this was probably the work of a 'lost apostle' (Palladius or Secundinus), of which he was bp. The later, traditional date of death is probably correct. His work was a vital factor in the spread of Irish Christian influence. Of his writings only his *Confessio* and an *Epistola* survive.

PATTI (pat'ē), **Adelina** (1843–1919). British

soprano. B. at Madrid, she made her debut in America in 1859, and was celebrated in such roles as Lucia and Amina in *La Sonnambula*. She became a British subject in 1898.

PATTON, George Smith (1885–1945). American gen., known for his fiery daring as 'blood and guts' P. He commanded the 2nd Armoured Division in 1940, and in 1942 led the W. Task Force which landed at Casablanca. After commanding the 7th Army, he led the 3rd Army in France, Belgium, and Germany, and in 1945 took over the 15th Army. He d. following a motor accident.

PAU (poh). Town and health resort of S.W. France, cap. of Basses-Pyrénées dept. P. was the birthplace of Henry IV of France and of Marshal Bernadotte, afterwards Charles XIV of Sweden. Pop. (1968) 74,005.

PAUL (c. A.D. 3–c. 64 or 68). Christian saint and apostle, whose real name was Saul. B. in Tarsus, the son of well-to-do Pharisees, he possessed Roman citizenship, and was ed. at Jerusalem at the school of Gamaliel. He took part in the stoning of Stephen, but while on a journey to Damascus was himself converted by a vision. After 3 years' meditation in Arabia, he returned to Damascus to begin his work as an apostle. After some 12 years of preparatory work he set out from Antioch on the first missionary journey among the Gentiles with Barnabas, journeying through Cyprus and Pamphilia. On a 2nd journey he revisited the churches estab. during the 1st, and founded further churches in Greece. The 3rd journey covers similar ground. but is chiefly concerned with his return to Ephesus, which became one of the great centres of Christian teaching. Returning to Jerusalem, he was arrested, appealed to Caesar, and was sent to Rome for trial c. 57 or 59. After 2 years' imprisonment he was possibly released before his final arrest and execution under Nero. Thirteen epistles in the N.T. are attributed to him.

PAUL. Name of 6 popes. Paul VI (Giovanni Battista Montini, 1897–). B. nr. Brescia, the son of

PAUL. Pope Paul VI is seen emerging from the small chapel of the tomb of Christ in Jerusalem, during his pilgrimage to the Holy Land, in 1964.   *Photo: Associated Press.*

a banker and journalist, he spent more than 25 years in the Secretariat of State under Pius XI and Pius XII before becoming archbp. of Milan in 1954. In 1958 he was created a cardinal by Pope John, with whom he was in close accord, and visited the new African states at his request in 1962. In 1963 he succeeded him as pope and was crowned in St. Peter's Square – thought to be the first open-air coronation in the history of the Church – taking the name of Paul as symbolic of ecumenical unity, In 1964 he became the first pope to visit the Holy Land since St. Peter.

PAUL I (1754–1801). Tsar of Russia. The son of Peter III and Catherine II, he succeeded his mother in 1796. His mind was already unhinged, and his foreign policy was capricious. He was assassinated.

PAUL (1901–64). King of the Hellenes. The son of King Constantine, he served in the navy for some years and in 1947 he succeeded his brother George II. He m. in 1938 Princess Frederika (1917–), dau. of the duke of Brunswick, whose political role brought her under attack. He was succeeded by his son Constantine XIII.

PAULING (pawl'-), **Linus Carl** (1901–). American chemist. Professor at the California Institute of Technology 1931–63, he was noted for his fundamental work on the nature of the chemical bond and was awarded the Nobel prize for chemistry in 1954. An outspoken opponent of nuclear testing, he received the Nobel peace prize in 1962.

PAUL.'NUS (d. 644). Missionary. B. in Rome, he joined Augustine in Kent in 601, and converted the Northumbrians in 625, becoming first archbp. of York. He returned to Kent in 633.

PAULUS (pow'lus), **Friedrich** (1890–1957). German field marshal, commander of the forces besieging Stalingrad 1942–3. He gave evidence at Nuremberg, and later lived in E. Germany.

PAUSA'NIAS (2nd cent. A.D.). Greek geographer. B. probably in Lydia, he based his *Description of Greece* on his own travels.

PAVIA (pahvē'ah). Cap. of P. prov., Lombardy, N. Italy. Notable buildings incl. the 11th cent. basilica of S. Michele, the 15th cent. cathedral, and the univ. (1490). In 1525 P. saw the defeat of the French under Francis I by the Emperor Charles V. Pop. (1961) 73,503.

PA'VLOV, Ivan Petrovich (1849–1936). Russian physiologist. B. near Ryazan, he became a director of the Institute of Experimental Medicine at St. Petersburg in 1913. He carried out research on digestion, for which he received a Nobel prize in 1904. His study of conditioned reflexes in animals influenced the behaviourist school of psychology.

PAV'LOVA, Anna (1885–1931). Russian dancer. B. at St. Petersburg, she made her début in 1899, appeared in London in 1910, and subsequently toured the world with outstanding success, espec. in *Le Cygne*, popularizing the Russian ballet everywhere. She d. in Holland.

PAWNBROKER. One who lends money on the security of goods held the traditional sign of the premises being the 3 gold balls which were the symbol used in front of their houses by the medieval Lombard merchants. In Britain, under an Act of 1872 (amended 1960), the sum lent must not exceed £50 and pledges are redeemable within 6 months and 7 days: unredeemed goods pledged for less than £2 become the P.'s property, others are sold by public auction. The trade has much declined in post-war Britain.

PAWPAW or **Papaya**. Tropical tree (*Carica papaya*), originating in S. America and grown in many tropical countries. The edible fruits resemble a melon, with orange-coloured flesh and numerous blackish seeds in the central cavity, and may weigh c. 20 lb. The fruit juice or the tree sap are often used to tenderize meat for the table. In the U.S.A. the name 'pawpaw' is given to *Asimina triloba*, which has an unpleasant odour but carries fleshy edible oval berries c. 3 in. long.

PAXINOU (pak'sin-oo), **Katina** (1904–). Greek actress. Leading lady of the Greek National Theatre from 1932, she excels in the classic roles of Clytemnestra, Electra, Medea, etc., and was awarded an Oscar for her film appearance as Pilar in *For Whom the Bell Tolls*.

PAXTON, Sir Joseph (1801–65). British architect, garden superintendent to the duke of Devonshire from 1826 and designer of the Great Exhibition

PAWPAW. The trees are so rapid in growth that they produce their delicious fruit within a year of the seed being planted. Unfortunately ripe fruit bruises too easily to be transported undamaged and, if packed green, does not ripen properly, so that it is little seen outside the tropics.
Courtesy of the Agent General for Queensland.

building of 1851 (*see* CRYSTAL PALACE), which was revolutionary in its structural use of glass.

P.A.Y.E. (Pay As You Earn). System whereby a proportionate amount of Income Tax is deducted by the employer and handed over to the Inland Revenue before wages are paid, reliefs due being notified to him by a code no. for each employee. Introduced in Britain in 1944 to spread the tax burden over the year for the increasing no. of wage-earners becoming liable, it was devised by Sir Paul Chambers (q.v.).

PAYMASTER-GENERAL. Head of the P.-G.'s Office, the British govt. dept. (estab. 1835) which acts as paying agent for most other depts.

PAYSANDÚ'. Second city of Uruguay, cap. of P. dept., situated on the r. Uruguay *c.* 210 m. N.W. of Montevideo. Tinned meat is the main product. It dates from 1772. Pop. (1968) 65,000.

PAZ (pahth), **Octavio** (1914–). Mexican poet. B. in Mexico City, his *Piedra de Sol* (1957, *Sun Stone*) is a personal statement comparable with Hart Crane's *The Bridge*, and takes as its basic symbol the Aztec Calendar Stone. He has also pub. a study of Mexican culture *The Labyrinth of Solitude* and ed. anthologies.

PEA. Two allied genera in the family Leguminosae, both climbing plants. The garden P. (*Pisum sativum*) has white, lipped flowers, and has been cultivated since ancient times for its seeds, gathered unripe; it grows at its best in England. Cultivated for their flowers are the fragrant sweet P. (*Lathyrus odoratus*), and the scentless everlasting P. (*L. latifolius*).

PEABODY, George (1795–1869). American merchant, banker, and philanthropist. B. in Massachusetts, he came to England in 1837, and in 1862 he founded the P. Trust, to build homes known as P. Buildings for the poor of London.

PEABODY. Town of Mass., U.S.A. Formerly South Danvers, birthplace of George Peabody, it was renamed in his honour in 1868; it is noted for its tanneries, started in the early 18th cent. Pop. (1960) 32,202.

PEACE, Charles (1832–79). British criminal. He carried out many burglaries around Manchester, and in 1876 murdered a policeman during a robbery, another man being sentenced to death, though afterwards reprieved for the crime. After killing Arthur Dyson in a quarrel he removed to London, and continued his burglaries, until he was arrested, tried, and hanged.

PEACE. Canadian river formed in British Columbia by the union at Finlay Forks of the Finlay and Parsnip rivers and flowing through the Rockies and across Alberta to join the Slave r. just N. of Lake Athabasca; length 1,000 m. Discovered *c.* 1780 and explored 1792–3 by Sir Alexander Mackenzie (*c.* 1755–1820), it was used as a means of transport by fur traders. A dam, with 4 times the hydroelectric potential of Hoover Dam, was begun 12 m. E. of Finlay Forks in 1962.

PEACOCK

PEACE CORPS. A body of trained men and women, first estab. in the U.S. by Pres. Kennedy in 1961, providing the necessary skilled manpower required in developing countries, especially in the fields of teaching, agriculture and health. Living among, and at the same level as, the country's inhabitants, volunteers are paid only a small allowance covering their basic needs and maintaining health. The P.C. was inspired by Voluntary Service Overseas (*see* BRITISH VOLUNTEER PROGRAMME), and similar corps have since been formed in other countries.

PEACH. A tree (*Prunus persica*) in the family *Rosaceae*. It has ovate leaves and small white flowers. The yellowish edible fruits have thick velvety skins; the nectarine is a smooth-skinned variety.

PEACOCK, Thomas Love (1785–1866). British satirist. B. at Weymouth, he worked for the East India Company 1819–56. He pub. several books of verse, and the satiric novels *Headlong Hall* (1815), *Melincourt*, *Nightmare Abbey*, and *Crotchet Castle* (1831).

PEACOCK. Genus of gallinaceous birds, native to India and Ceylon. The common P. (*Pavo cristatus*) is rather larger than a pheasant and has a large fan-shaped tail, brightly coloured with blue, green, and purple 'eyes' on a chestnut ground. The female is brown with only a small tail.

PEAK DISTRICT. Tableland of the S. Pennines in N.W. Derbyshire, England. It is a popular tourist region and a National Park. The highest point is Kinder Scout (2,088 ft.).

PEALE, Charles Wilson (1741–1827). American artist. B. in Pennsylvania, and a student with Benjamin West in England 1766–9, he was noted for his portraits of Washington, etc., and also his miniatures.

OCTAVIO PAZ
Courtesy of Grove Press, Inc.

PEANUT. *See* GROUNDNUT.

PEAR. Tree (*Pyrus communis*), closely related to the apple (to which it is second in importance as a fruit producer in

PEALE. During his years in England, in 1766–9, Peale studied under Benjamin West, and the master made this pleasant portrait-study of his pupil.
Courtesy of the New York Historical Society, N.Y. City.

temperate countries), in the family Rosa ceae. Blooming earlier than the apple, it is less hardy.

PEARL. Calcareous substance secreted by many molluscs, which when deposited in thin layers on the inside of the shell forms the mother-of-pearl used in ornamental and inlay work, and when deposited round some irritant body forms Ps. Although commercially valuable Ps. are obtained from freshwater mussels, etc., the precious P. comes from the various species of *Margaritifera* in the family Aviculidae, found in tropical waters off N. and W. Australia, the Californian coast, and in the Indian Ocean. The introduction on a commercial scale by the Japanese *c.* 1920 of cultured Ps., produced by inserting an artificial irritant in the body of the oyster, largely affected the value of natural Ps.

PEARL HARBOR. U.S. Pacific naval base in Oahu, chief of the islands forming Hawaii state, U.S.A., the scene of a Japanese attack on 7 Dec. 1941, during the S.W.W., which took place while Japanese envoys were holding 'peace' talks at Washington. 66 Japanese aircraft operating from aircraft carriers did much serious damage to warships and naval and military aircraft and installations. The local commanders, Admiral Kimmel and Lt.-Gen. Short, were relieved of their commands, and in the report of a final inquiry, made after the war, they were held responsible for the fact that the base, despite warnings, was totally unprepared at the time of the attack.

PEARS, Peter (1910–). British tenor. A co-founder with Britten of the Aldeburgh Festival, he is closely associated with the composer's work and played the title role in *Peter Grimes*: he has also often been the first performer of works by Tippett and Berkeley.

PEARSE, Patrick Henry (1879–1916). Irish poet and republican. B. in Dublin, he was prominent in the Gaelic revival, and led the Easter Rebellion of 1916. He was proclaimed president of the provisional govt., and after its suppression was court-martialled and shot.

PEARSON, Sir Cyril Arthur (1866–1921). British newspaper proprietor. He founded *P.'s Weekly* in 1890 and the *Daily Express* in 1900, and purchased the *Evening Standard* in 1904. Blindness obliged him to retire from business in 1910, and in 1915 he turned his house, St. Dunstan's, Regent's Park, into a hospital for blinded soldiers.

PEARSON, Lester Bowles (1897–). Canadian Liberal statesman, known as 'Mike' P. B. in Toronto, son and grandson of Methodist clergymen, he was ambassador to Washington 1945–6. Appointed For. Min. by St. Laurent (1948–57), he effectively represented Canada at the U.N. and only Soviet opposition prevented his becoming Sec.-Gen.: in 1957 he was awarded a Nobel peace prize principally because of his role in the creation of the U.N. Emergency Force. Leader of the Liberal Party from 1958, he was twice defeated by Diefenbaker at the polls, but in 1963 achieved enough seats to head a minority govt., renewed after a general election (1965–8). In 1968 he became Head of the World Bank Commission on Economic Development.

LESTER PEARSON
Courtesy of the High Commissioner for Canada.

PEARY, Robert Edwin (1856–1920). American Polar explorer. B. in Pennsylvania, at his 7th attempt he was the first man to reach the North Pole, on 6 April 1909. He sailed to Cape Sheridan in the *Roosevelt*, and then made a sledge journey to the Pole.

PEASANTS' REVOLT. The rising of the English peasantry in June 1381. Led by Wat Tyler and John Ball, the rebels occupied London and forced Richard II to abolish serfdom, but after Tyler's murder were compelled to withdraw. The movement was then suppressed, and the king's concessions revoked.

PEAT (pēt). Deposit, which varies from compacted fibre to a type of woody brown coal or lignite, formed by the decomposition of aquatic plants, e.g. sphagnum moss and *Thacomitrum lanuginosum*. It may reach a depth of 30 ft. and extend for miles, Russia, Canada and Finland having large deposits. In Scotland and Ireland, dried P. has been used as fuel from time immemorial and our illus. shows P. being cut in Morayshire for malting the barley used in making Scotch whisky: the peat 'reek' contributes to the flavour.

Courtesy of the Distillers Co. Ltd.

PECAN (pikan′). Nut-producing tree (*Carya illinoensis*), native to southern U.S.A. and possibly N. Mexico, and now widely cultivated. The tree grows to over 150 ft., and the edible nuts are smooth-shelled, the kernel resembling a smoothly ovate walnut. *See* HICKORY.

PECCARY. American genus of pig-like animals (*Dicotyles*), having a gland in the middle of the back which secretes a strong-smelling substance. Blackish in colour, they are covered with bristles, and the skins make a useful leather. Travelling in herds, they are often belligerent.

PECHENGA (pye′chenga). Ice-free fishing port in Murmansk region, R.S.F.S.R., on the Barents Sea, more familiar under its Finnish name Petsamo. Russia ceded P. to Finland in 1920, recovered it under the peace treaty with Finland, 1947. Pop. (est.) 5,000.

PÉCS (pāch). Univ. town of S.W. Hungary, cap. of Baranya county, close to a coalfield. Dating from Roman times, P. was under Turkish rule 1543–1686, and 2 of its churches were originally mosques. Pop. (1966) 130,000.

PEDERSEN (peh′dersen), **Christiern** (1480–1554). Founder of Danish literature. He became a canon of Lund cathedral, and accompanied Christian II into exile in 1525. While in Holland he completed a Danish version of the N.T. and the Psalms (1529–31).

PEDIATRICS. Branch of medicine dealing with diseases of children and the study of childhood.

PEDIMENT. In architecture, the triangular part crowning the fronts of buildings in classic styles. The P. was a distinctive feature of Greek temples.

PEDO′METER. Instrument for measuring the distance covered by a pedestrian from the number of his steps and their average length. It is so arranged that each step moves a swinging weight, which in turn causes a mechanism to rotate and move a pointer step by step over a dial.

PEDRO. Name of 2 emperors of Brazil. **Pedro I** (1798–1834), the son of John VI of Portugal, escaped to Brazil on Napoleon's invasion, and was appointed regent in 1821. He proclaimed Brazil independent in 1822, and was crowned emperor, but abdicated in 1831 and returned to Portugal. His son **Pedro II** (1825–91), who succeeded him, proved an enlightened ruler, but his anti-slavery measures alienated the landowners, who in 1889 compelled him to abdicate.

PEEBLESSHIRE. Pastoral county of S. Scotland. It has several high peaks, such as Broad Law (2,754 ft.) and Hart Fell, and the vales are watered by the Tweed and its tributaries. Coal is mined and woollens manufactured. Peebles is the co. town. Area 347 sq. m.; pop. (1961) 14,117.

PEEL, Sir Robert (1788–1850). British Cons. statesman. B. in Lancs, he entered parliament as a Tory in 1809. As Home Sec. 1822–7 and 1828–30, he founded the modern police force and in 1829 introduced R.C. emancipation. After the passing of the Reform Bill (1832), which he had resisted, he reformed the Tory Party under the name of 'Conservatives', on a basis of accepting necessary reforms and seeking middle-class support. He was Premier 1834–5 and 1841–6; he fell owing to his repeal of the Corn Laws (1846) which was opposed by the majority of his party. He and his followers then formed a 3rd party standing between the Liberals and Conservatives; the majority of the Peelites, including Gladstone, joined the Liberals.

PEEL. Seaport in the Isle of Man, 12 m. W.N.W.

PEEL. On St. Patrick's Isle, at the entrance to the harbour, the saint is said to have founded the first church on Man. The ruined 12–16th cent. castle incorporates (right) St. German's cathedral, of the same period.
Courtesy of the Isle of Man Tourist Board.

of Douglas. The principal occupation is fishing. Pop. (1961) 2,487.

PEELE, George (c. 1558–97). English dramatist. B. in London, he wrote a pastoral, *The Arraignment of Paris*; a fantastic comedy, *The Old Wives' Tale*; and a tragedy, *David and Bethsabe*.

PEEPUL. See BO-TREE.

PEERAGE. In the U.K. the body of nobility holding the hereditary temporal dignities of duke, marquess, earl, viscount and baron: certain hereditary Ps. may be held by a woman in default of a male heir. To these were added in the later 19th cent. the Lords of Appeal in Ordinary, who are life peers, as well as from 1958 a number of specially created life peers of either sex. Since 1963 it has been possible for a peer to disclaim his title (*see* HOME, SIR ALEC DOUGLAS, and HOGG, QUINTIN), usually to enable him to be elected to the Commons, and in 1964 it was ruled that his children need not discontinue use of their courtesy titles. See PARLIAMENT.

PE'GASUS. In Greek mythology, a winged horse which sprang from the blood of Medusa. Hippocrene, the spring of the Muses on Mt. Helicon, is said to have sprung from a blow of his hoof. He was transformed to a constellation.

PEGU (pegōō'). Town of Burma, on the river P., 45 m. N.E. of Rangoon, founded A.D. 573. It is famous for the Shwe-mawdaw pagoda. Pop. c. 47,000.

PÉGUY (pehgwē'), **Charles** (1873–1914). French author and poet. B. at Orléans, he estab. a socialist publishing house in Paris, and from 1900 pub. *Les Cahiers de la Quinzaine*, which aimed at regenerating

French republicanism. His works incl. *Notre Patrie* (1905) and *Mystère de la Charité de Jeanne d'Arc.*

PEIPING. Name, meaning northern peace, 1928–49 of PEKING.

PEKINESE. Toy dog of Oriental origin. Long-haired, they are variously coloured, tan being the most common.

PEKING. Cap. of China, in Hopei prov. It covers the site of Yenking, cap. of the 10th cent. Liao dynasty, and the 13th cent. cap. of Kublai Khan, called by the Mongols Khanbaligh (Marco Polo's Cambaluc), by the Chinese Taitu. The first emperor of the Ming dynasty made Nanking (southern capital) his cap., but in 1421 Peking (northern capital) once more became cap. of the Chinese Empire, and remained so except for 1928–49 when P. was renamed Peiping (northern peace) and the cap. was once more removed to Nanking. P. has iron and steel works, railway repair shops, cotton mills, and factories making agricultural implements and other machinery. It has an airport. Pop. (1968) 7,000,000 in an area of 3,386 sq. m.

PEKING MAN. A skull found near P. in 1927, belonging to the same period as Pithecanthropus (*See* JAVA), but with a more developed brain.

PELAGIUS (pēlāji-us) (c. 360–c. 420). British theologian. He went to Rome c. 400, and there taught that every man possesses free will, denying Augustine's doctrines of pre-destination and original sin. Cleared of heresy by a synod at Jerusalem in 415, he was later condemned by the Pope and the emperor.

PELÉE (pelā'), **Mont.** Volcano in Martinique, French West Indies, famous for the violent eruption of 1902 which destroyed the town of St. Pierre and killed 30,000 people. Eruptions 1929–32 threw up masses of lava which increased the height of the mountain to 4,500 ft.

PELHAM, Henry (1696–1754). British Whig statesman. He held a succession of offices in Walpole's cabinet 1721–42, and was P.M. 1743–54.

PELICAN. Genus of water-fowl, remarkable for the pouch beneath the bill used to store its catches of fish, and incl. the pinkish common P. (*Pelecanus onocrotalus*) of Europe, Asia and Africa; the Australian black-backed P. (*P. constricillatus*); and the American brown P. (*P. occidentalis*), which is marine.

AUSTRALIAN BLACK-BACKED PELICAN

PELLA'GRA. A disease of sub-tropical countries in which the staple food is maize, due to deficiency of nicotinic acid (vitamin B), which is contained in protein foods and yeast.

PELOPONNESE (pel'ŏ̄ponēz). Peninsula forming the S. part of Greece. It is joined to the mainland by the narrow isthmus of Corinth, and is divided into the nomes of Argolis, Arcadia, Achaea (Akkaia), Elia, Corinth, Lakonia, and Massenia, representing its 7 ancient states. Area 8,320 sq. m.; pop. (1961) 1,096,390.

PELOPONNESIAN WAR. See GREEK HISTORY.

PE'MBA. Coral island in the Indian Ocean, 30 m. N.E. of Zanzibar, of which it forms part. Cloves and copra are the chief products; it has a small airfield. Area 380 sq. m.; pop. (1958) 133,858.

PE'MBROKE. Seaport (bor.) and engineering centre in S. Pembrokeshire, Wales. Its castle was begun in 1200; and Henry VII was born at P. Pop. (1961) 12,737.

PEMBROKESHIRE. Extreme S.W. county of

Wales. The Teify and the E. and W. Cleddau are the chief rivers. The main occupations are agriculture and coal-mining. Haverfordwest is the county town; Fishguard, with ferry connections to Ireland, and Milford Haven, with petroleum refineries, are important ports. Most of the coast was made a national park in 1951. Area 614 sq. m.; pop. (1961) 93,980.

PE'MMICAN. A preparation of dried fatless beef or venison pressed into cubes, used as a food by Arctic explorers and N. American Indians.

P.E.N. Literary association estab. in 1921 by C. A. Dawson Scott, to promote international understanding between writers. The initials stand for Poets, Playwrights, Editors, Essayists, Novelists.

PENANCE. Term in theology used for repentance for sin; an R.C. sacrament, involving confession of sins and the reception of absolution; and works performed or punishment self-inflicted in atonement for sin.

PENA'NG. State of W. Malaysia, Fed. of Malaysia under a governor, formed of P. Island (bought by the, British from the ruler of Kedah 1785), Province Wellesley (acquired 1800) and the Dindings on the mainland. Its chief town is George Town. Area 400 sq. m.; pop. (1966) 743,833.

PENARLAG. Welsh name of HAWARDEN.

PENA'RTH. Seaport (U.D.) and resort in Glamor-

PENANG. Malaysia's chief port—the name means 'betel nut' —is built on a promontory running out towards the mainland and lies at the foot of Penang hill (2,428 ft.). There are fine buildings dating from the 19th century as well as modern offices and stores beyond the busy waterfront.
Courtesy of Malaysian Govt.

ganshire, Wales, across the mouth of the Ely from Cardiff. Pop. (1961) 20,897.

PENA'TES. The household gods of a Roman family.

PENDA (d. 655). King of Mercia from 626. He raised Mercia to a powerful kingdom, and defeated and killed 2 Northumbrian kings, Edwin and Oswald. He was killed in battle with the Northumbrians.

PENDLEBURY, John Devitt Stringfellow (1904–41). British archaeologist Working with his wife, he excavated at Tell el Amarna and became the world's leading expert on Crete, pub. in 1939 a survey *Archaeology in Crete*. In the S.W.W. he was deputed to prepare guerrilla resistance on the island, was wounded during the German invasion and shot by his captors.

PÉNE'LOPÉ. Wife of Odysseus. During his absence after the siege of Troy she kept her many suitors at bay by asking them to wait until she had woven a shroud for her father-in-law, but undid her work nightly. When Odysseus returned, he slew her suitors.

PENFIELD, Wilder Graves (1891–). Canadian neurosurgeon. B. in the U.S.A., he has specialized in operations for epilepsy and in the electrical stimulation of the brain. He received the O.M. in 1953.

PENGUIN. Family of flightless seabirds found only in Antarctic regions. Designed for speed in and under the water, they are awkward on land, where they congregate in 'rookeries' to breed. One or 2 eggs are laid in a hole in the ground or 'nest' of stones. Well known among smaller species is the black-footed P.: the largest are the king P. (*Aptenodytes longirostris*) and emperor P. (*A. fosteri*).

BLACK-FOOTED PENGUINS

PENIAKOV, Vladimir. *See* POPSKI'S PRIVATE ARMY.

PENICI'LLIN. An organic acid formed during the growth of the common mould, *Penicillium notatum*. Even in very weak dilutions it prevents the growth of certain bacteria, many of which are harmful to man, e.g. some of the staphylococci and streptococci, and the organisms of pneumonia, gonorrhoea, meningitis, anthrax and tetanus. Extremely valuable in medicine and surgery, it played an important part in the S.W.W. It was discovered by Sir Alexander Fleming, and its practical use was developed by Sir Howard Florey and E. B. Chain at Oxford.

PENINSULAR WAR. The war of 1808–14 caused by Napoleon's invasion of Portugal and Spain. Portugal was occupied by the French in 1807, and in 1808 Napoleon placed his brother Joseph on the Spanish throne. Armed revolts followed all over Spain and Portugal. A British force under Sir Arthur Wellesley was sent to Portugal and defeated the French at Vimeiro; Wellesley was then superseded, and the French were allowed to withdraw. Sir John Moore took command and advanced into Spain, but was forced to retreat to Corunna, when his army was evacuated. Wellesley took a new army to Portugal in 1809, and advanced on Madrid, but after defeating the French at Talavera had to retreat. During 1810–11 Wellesley (now Visct. Wellington) stood on the defensive; in 1812 he won another victory at Salamanca, occupied Madrid, and forced the French to evacuate S. Spain. The victory at Vittoria (1813) drove the French from Spain, and in 1814 Wellington invaded S. France. The war was ended by Napoleon's abdication.

PENIS. The male organ of generation in reptiles, birds, and mammals; it also carries the passage through which urine is discharged from the bladder.

PENKI (pen'chě'). Chinese industrial centre in Liaoning prov., 40 m. S.E. of Mukden. It dates from the 18th cent., but its industrial development began in 1915. It covers nearly 200 sq. m. and produces pig iron, steel, cement, refractories, etc., based on the presence of high-grade coking coal. Pop. (1965) 530,000.

PENN, William (1644–1718). British Quaker and founder of Pennsylvania. B. in London, the son of the Admiral Sir William P. (1621–70), he joined the Quakers in 1667. In 1681 he obtained a grant of land in America, in settlement of a debt owed by the king to his father, on which he estab. the colony of Pennsylvania as a refuge for the persecuted Quakers.

PENNELL, Joseph (1860–1926). American illustrator, etcher, and lithographer. B. in Philadelphia, he settled in London where he came under the influence of J. M. Whistler, whose life he wrote.

PENNEY, William, baron (1909–). Brit. scientist. He worked at Los Alamos (q.v.) 1944–5, and for his design of the first British atom bomb was knighted in 1952. Director of Atomic Weapons Research Establishment 1953–9, he was chairman of U.K.A.E.A. 1964–7: created life peer 1967, awarded O.M. 1969.

PENNINES. System of mountains which has been called 'the backbone of England'. The chain is broken in the centre by a gap through which flow the Aire to the E. and Ribble to the W. The P. stretch from the Scottish border to the Peak in Derbyshire. The section N. of the gap is broader and higher than the S., with Cross Fell (2,930 ft.) the highest of several peaks. Britain s first long-distance footpath was the 250-mile *Pennine Way* (1965: Edale, Derbyshire to Kirk Yetholm, Roxburghshire).

PENNSYLVANIA. One of the original 13 states of the U.S.A. Crossed by the Alleghenies, P. is drained by the Ohio, Susquehanna and Delaware. Lumbering and agriculture are important, but P. has a vast bituminous and anthracite coal output, and is the largest steel-producing state, Pittsburgh being the great centre for its manufacture. Other mineral products incl. petroleum and natural gas. Among agricultural products are cigar leaf tobacco, buckwheat, maize, wheat, potatoes, fruits. P. was founded and named in 1682 by the Quaker William Penn who had been granted land by Charles II in 1681. The chief towns are Philadelphia, Pittsburgh, Erie, Scranton, Allentown and Harrisburg, the cap. Area 45,333 sq. m.; pop. (1970) 11,793,090.

PENNYROYAL. Perennial moorland plant (*Mentha pulegium*). It has ovate leaves, whirls of purplish flowers, and the characteristic scent of mint.

PENNINES. Typical Pennine country: in the distance is Penyghent. *Photo: W. R. Mitchell.*

PENRHYN (pen'rin). Distrjcr of Caenarvonshire, Wales, famous for the P. slate quarjes. P. Castle, formerley seat of the Lord P., became National Ttust property in 1951 and was opened to the public in 1952.

PENRITH. Engljsn market town (U.D.) in Cumberland, 18 m. S.E. of Carlisle. Pop. (1961) 10,931.

PENSACŌ'LA. Seaport of Florida, U.S.A., on the Gulf of Mexico. There is a large naval air-training station. P. was founded by the Spanish in 1696. Pop. (1960) 56,752.

PENTATEUCH (pen'tatūk) (Gk. 5 books). The first 5 books of the O.T., ascribed to Moses.

PE'NTĒCOST (Gk. fiftieth). Jewish festival marking the close of the wheat harvest in Palestine, celebrated on the 50th day after the Passover. It was at P. that the Holy Spirit descended on the Christian Church, an event commemorated on Whit Sunday.

PENTLAND FIRTH. The channel separating the Orkney Islands from N. Scotland, about 14 m. long and 7 m. wide.

PENZA. Town in the R.S.F.S.R., cap. of P. region, 350 m. S.E. of Moscow, at the junction of the P. and Sura rivers. Founded as a fort in 1663, it has saw mills, and factories making bicycles, watches, calculating machines, and textiles; also an airport. Pop. (1967) 324,000.

PENZANCE. English seaport and resort (bor.) in Cornwall, on Mount's Bay, the most westerly town in England. It has a mild climate in which palm trees flourish Pop. (1961) 19,433.

PE'ONY. Genus of perennial plants in the family Ranunculaceae, remarkable for their brilliant and showy flowers. Most popular are the common P. (*Paeonia officinalis*) and the white P. (*P. albiflora*).

BLACK PEPPER

PEORIA (pē-ōr'ia). City in Illinois, U.S.A., on the Illinois r. It is a transport mining, and agricultura centre, seat of Bradley univ. (1897). Fort Crève Cœur was built about here by La Salle in 1680, and became a trading centre; the first American settlers arrived in 1818. Pop. (1960) 103,162.

P.E.P. (Political and Economic Planning). Non-political association publishing reports on aspects of British life, e.g. the press and the health services. Sir Gerald Barry (1899–1968) was one of the founders.

PEPIN (d. 768). King of the Franks. The son of Charles Martel, he acted as mayor of the palace to the last Merovingian king, Childeric III, until in 751 he deposed him and himself assumed the royal title, founding the Carolingian line.

PEPPER. Climbing plant (*Piper nigrum*) native to the E. Indies. When gathered green, the berries are crushed to produce the condiment black P.; when ripening and turning red, the berries produce white P. Cayenne P. is a much hotter variety made from the fruits of *Capsicum fastigatum*, indigenous to tropical America.

PEPPERMINT. Perennial herb (*Mentha piperita*), with ovate aromatic leaves, and purple flowers. Oil of P. is used medicinally and in confectionery.

PEPUSCH (pä'poosh), **Johann Christopher** (1667–1752). German composer. B. in Berlin, he settled in England *c.* 1700 and is best remembered for the anthem 'Rejoice in the Lord', and music for *The Beggar's Opera* and *Polly*.

PEPYS (pēps), **Samuel** (1633–1703). British diarist. B. in London, he entered the navy office in 1660 a few months after beginning his diary. He was appointed secretary to the Admiralty in 1672, imprisoned with loss of office in 1679 on suspicion of being connected with the Popish Plot, reinstated in 1684, and finally deprived at the 1688 Revolution, when he retired to Clapham. His diary, in a personal version of Shelton's shorthand undeciphered until 1825, and discontinued in 1669 owing to failing sight, is unrivalled for its intimacy and the human picture it presents of daily life in the 17th cent.

SAMUEL PEPYS. A lover of music, he is portrayed by John Hayls in the act of studying a piece. *Photo: N.P.G.*

PERAK (pē'ra). State of the Federation of Malaysia

PERAK. The Ubudia Mosque at Kuala Kangsar, was built by the Sultan Idris, regent of Perak, an enlightened ruler and administrator of the late 19th cent. The Italian marble of which the mosque was originally planned to have been built was destroyed by a mad elephant and local stone was substituted. *Courtesy of Malaya House.*

Under British protection from 1874, it is ruled by a sultan. Towns incl. Ipoh the cap. and centre of the Kinta tin-mining fields and Taiping. It exports tin and rubber. Area 7,980 sq. m.; pop. (1966) 1,613,728.

PERCEVAL, Spencer (1762–1812). British Tory statesman. The son of the earl of Egmont, he became Chancellor of the Exchequer in 1807, and P.M. in 1809. He was shot in the lobby of the House of Commons in 1812 by a madman.

PERCH. Genus of spiny-finned fish in the family Percidae. The common freshwater P. (*Perca fluviatilis*), found in Europe, N. Asia, and N. America, is olive-green or yellowish in colour, with 5 or more dark bands across the back.

PERCY, Sir Henry, called **Hotspur** (1364–1403). English soldier. The son of the 1st earl of Northumberland, he defeated the Scots at Homildon Hill in 1402, and was killed at Shrewsbury while in rebellion against Henry IV.

PERCY, Thomas (1729–1811). British scholar and bishop of Dromore from 1782. B. at Bridgnorth, he discovered a MS. collection of songs, ballads, and romances, from which he pub. a selection as *Reliques of Ancient English Poetry* (1765), largely influential in the Romantic revival.

PERCZ (pärtz), **János** (1920–). Hungarian artist. B. in Budapest, he has taught at the Academy of Arts there and since 1948 at an industrial school. At first working mainly in the graphic arts, ceramics and mosaics, from 1950 he specialized in metalwork, and is a leader of the modern Hungarian revival.

PÉREZ GALDOS (pā'reth gahldōs'), **Benito** (1845–1920). Spanish writer, b. at Las Palmas. His novels incl. *La Fontana de oro* (1870), *El Audaz* (1871), the historical series of *Episodios nacionales* (1873–1912), *Gloria* (1877), etc. He also wrote dramas.

PERFUME. Fragrant essence in which more than

PERCZ. 'Female Figure' – filigree figurine in a frame of welded iron. *Courtesy of Corvina Press.*

100 natural aromatic materials may be blended from a range of *c.* 60,000 flowers, leaves, fruits, seeds, woods, barks, resins and roots, linked by natural animal fixatives and various synthetics, the latter increasingly used even in expensive Ps. Favoured ingredients incl. balsam, civet, hyacinth, jasmine, lily of the valley, musk, orange blossom, rose and tuberose.

PERGA. Ruined city of Pamphylia, 10 m. N.E. of Adalia, Turkey, noted for its local cult of Artemis. It was visited by St. Paul.

PERGAMUM. Ancient Greek city in W. Asia Minor, which became the cap. of an independent kingdom in 283 B.C. As the ally of Rome it achieved great political importance in the 2nd cent. B.C., and became a famous centre of art and culture. On its site is the Turkish town of Bergama, pop. (est.) 17,000.

PERI. In Persian mythology, a species of beautiful, harmless beings, between angels and evil spirits, but ruled by Eblis, the greatest of the latter.

PERICLES (*c.* 490–429 B.C.). Athenian statesman. He dominated Athenian politics from 461 as leader of the democratic party. He created a confederation of cities under Athens' leadership, but the disasters of the Peloponnesian War led to his overthrow in 430, and although quickly reinstated he d. soon after. The period of his rule marks the climax of Greek culture.

PÉRIGUEUX (pehrĕgö'). French town, cap. of Dordogne dept., 79 m. E.N.E. of Bordeaux. The Byzantine cathedral dates from 984; there is trade in wine and truffles. Pop. (1962) 41,134.

PERIM (pärēm') Island in the strait of Bab-el-Mandeb, the S. entrance to the Red Sea; part of the Rep. of Southern Yemen. Area 5 sq. m.; pop. 300.

PERIODICAL. Publication brought out at regular intervals, which may be informative, entertaining, religious, etc. One of the earliest Ps. pub. in Britain was the *Compleat Library* (1691/2), which contained articles and reviews of books. Notable later were Steele's *Tatler* (1709), Addison's *Spectator* (1711), the *Gentleman's Magazine* (1731), John Wilkes's *North Briton* (1762), the *Edinburgh Review* (1802–1929), *Quarterly Review* (1806), *Blackwood's Magazine* (1817), *Spectator* (1828), *Punch* (1841), *Economist* (1843), *Contemporary Review* (1866), *New Statesman* (1913), etc. The increasing spread of literacy at the end of the 19th cent. was accompanied by a demand for light reading matter, and there are today a large number of popular P. at various levels.

In the U.S. periodicals, unlike newspapers, circulate all over the country and some achieve vast circulations, e.g. *Reader's Digest* (1922) sold more than 16½ million copies in 1966. Other notable American Ps. are *Saturday Evening Post* (1728–1969), *Nat. Geographic Magazine* (1888), *New Yorker* (1925) – the two latter have a world circulation – *Look* (1937), *Life* (1946).

PERIODIC TABLE OF THE ELEMENTS. A classification following the statement by Mendeleyev (q.v.) in 1869, that 'the properties of elements are in periodic dependence upon their at. wt.'. In each of 9 main groups there are striking similarities among the elements, based on electronic structure and nuclear charge. *See* INORGANIC CHEMISTRY for chart of P.T.

PERISCOPE. An optical instrument designed for observation from a concealed position. The essence of a P. consists of a tube with parallel mirrors at each end inclined at 45° to its axis. It attained prominence in naval (especially in submarines) and military operations of the F.W.W.

PERIWINKLE. Genus of gastropods found between tide-marks in brown seaweed. The common edible species of 'winkle' (*Littorina littorea*), abundant in Britain, has spread to the Atlantic coast of America. Also genus of plants (*Vinca*), of which the lesser P. (*V. minor*), with light blue flowers, is found in Europe.

PERJURY. The offence of deliberately making a false statement on oath when appearing as a witness in legal proceedings, on a point material to the question at issue. In Britain it is punishable by a fine, imprisonment up to 7 years, or both.

PERKIN, Sir William Henry (1838–1907). British chemist. B. in London, he discovered in 1856 the mauve dye which originated the aniline dye industry.

PERLIS. Most northerly state of W. Malaysia, Fed. of Malaysia. Transferred by Siam to Britain in 1909, it is ruled by a raja. Kangar is the cap. Its products are rubber, rice, coconuts, and tin. Area 310 sq. m.; pop. (1966) 116,393.

PERM. Town of the R.S.F.S.R., cap. of P. region, on the Kama near the Urals. It has shipbuilding yards, aircraft and chemical factories, saw mills, etc., and is a centre of petroleum production. It was called Molotov 1940–57. Pop. (1967) 785,000.

PERNAMBUCO (pernahmboo′kō). A N.E. state of Brazil on the Atlantic. The cap. is Recife. Area 37,460 sq. m.; pop. (1967) 4,706,000.

PERNAMBUCO. Another name for RECIFE.

PERO′N, Juan Domingo (1895–). Argentine politician. With a group of pro-Fascist army officers, he seized power in 1943 and was elected pres. in 1946. His popular following fell away, espec. after the death of his wife Eva (1922–52), and he was deposed in 1955. He retired to Spain.

PERPENDICULAR. Name given to a period of English Gothic architecture lasting from the end of the 14th to the middle of the 16th cent. The chief characteristics of the style are: window tracery consisting chiefly of vertical members; arches which are either 'four centred' – i.e. consisting of 4 arcs – or of 2 arcs forming a blunt point; vaults which are lavishly decorated; and wall surfaces covered with traceried panels. Good examples of the style are the choir and cloister of Gloucester cathedral, and King's College chapel, Cambridge.

PERPIGNAN (perpēnyon′). Cap. of the Pyrénées-Orientales dept. of France, on the Têt, 40 m. S. of Narbonne. Overlooking P. is the castle of the counts of Roussillon; the cathedral was founded 1324 by Sancho II, king of Majorca, in whose dominions P. then was. Pop. (1968) 102,191.

PERRAULT (pārō′), **Charles** (1628–1703). French author, chiefly remembered for his prose *Histoires ou Contes du Temps Passé* (1697), which incl. Sleeping Beauty, Red Riding Hood, Blue Beard, Puss in Boots, and Cinderella.

PERRY, Matthew Calbraith (1794–1858). U.S. naval officer, who commanded the expedition which in 1853 reopened communication between Japan and the outside world after 250 years' isolation. In 1854 he negotiated the first U.S.-Japanese treaty.

PERRY. An alcoholic liquor made from pears, mainly in the W. Country of England and Normandy.

PERSE, Saint-John. Pseudonym of the French poet Alexis Saint-Léger Léger (1887–). His 1st book of verse *Éloges* (1911) reflects the colour of the West Indies, where he was b. and raised. Entering the Foreign Service in 1914, he was Sec.-Gen. 1933–40. He then emigrated permanently to the U.S.A., and was deprived of French citizenship by the Vichy govt. His later works incl. *Anabase* (1924), a long poem of epic sweep trans. by T. S. Eliot in 1930; *Exil* (1942), and *Amers* (1957), which celebrates the sea. He was awarded a Nobel prize in 1960.

PERSE′PHONE. Greek goddess, the dau. of Zeus and Demeter. She was carried off to the underworld by Pluto, who later agreed that she should spend 6 months of the year with her mother. The story is a myth for the growth and decay of vegetation.

PERSE′POLIS. Ancient cap. of the Persian Empire, about 40 m. N.E. of Shiraz. It was burned down, by accident or design, after its capture in 331 B.C. by Alexander. Impressive ruins of the royal city have been excavated by the Oriental Institute of Chicago.

PERSEUS (per′sūs). Mythical Greek hero, the son of Zeus and Danae. He slew Medusa. the Gorgon,

PERSEPOLIS. Planned by Darius the Great, and a royal capital, Persepolis is the principal site of Achaemenian Persia and still influences architecture today. The fluted shafts of these tapering 60 ft. columns helped to inspire the design of the modern university of Shiraz.
Courtesy of the Iranian Embassy

saved Andromeda from a sea-monster, and became king of Tiryns.

PERSHING, John Joseph (1860–1948). American gen. B. in Missouri, he served in the Spanish War of 1898, the Philippines 1899–1903, and Mexico 1916–17. He commanded the American Expeditionary Force sent to France 1917–18.

PERSIA. A kingdom of S.W. Asia, lying between the Caspian Sea to the N. and the Persian Gulf to the S. Central Persia is occupied by an extensive plateau crossed by mountain ranges, with semi-desert to the E., but some fertile areas produce cereals, cotton, date, olives, opium and tobacco. Climatic conditions are variable, a general dryness being combined with extremes of heat and cold. The mountain herds of sheep provide wool for the carpets which are P.'s oldest manufacture. P.'s greatest wealth lies in the petroleum wells of the S. developed by British enterprise until the industry was nationalized in 1951. A pipeline links the oilfields with refineries at Abadan at the head of the Persian Gulf. Other industries, much encouraged by the Shah, incl. pharmaceuticals, fertilizers, textiles, cars, and a steelworks nr. Ahwaz estab. 1969. Minerals, not yet fully exploited, also incl. iron, copper, lead, zinc, and chromite. Road and rail networks are rapidly improving, and there is an internat. airport at Tehran. The chief towns are the cap. Tehran, Tabriz, Isfahan, Meshed, Abadan, Shiraz, and Kermanshah.

P. is ruled by a shah and has a parliament of 2

PERSIA. The Shahanshah of Iran and Queen Farah.
Courtesy of the Iranian Embassy.

houses (Majlis, estab. 1906, elected, and Senate, half elected, half nominated by the shah, estab. 1950). Area c. 633,000 sq. m.; pop. (1967) 26,015,000. Most Persians are Shiah Moslems.

History. P. was overrun from c. 1600 B.C. by Aryan tribes, incl. the Persians and the Medes. Cyrus II, who seized the Median throne in 550, formed an empire incl. Babylonia, Syria, and Asia Minor, to which Egypt, Thrace, and Macedonia were later added. During 334–328 it was conquered by Alexander, then passed to Seleucus and his descendants, until overrun in the 3rd cent. B.C. by the Parthians. The Parthian dynasty was overthrown in A.D. 226 by Ardashir, founder of the Sassanid dynasty. During 633–41 P. was conquered for Islam by the Arabs, and then in 1037–55 came under the Seljuk Turks. Their empire broke up in the 12th cent., and was conquered during the 13th cent. by the Mongols. After 1334 P. was again divided until its conquest by Tamerlane in 1380s. A period of anarchy in the later 15th cent. was ended by the accession of the Safavi dynasty, who ruled 1499–1736, but were deposed by the great warrior Nadir Shah (1736–47), after whose death a confused period followed until the accession of the Qajar dynasty (1794–1925). During the 18th cent. P. was threatened by Russian expansion, culminating in the loss of Georgia in 1801 and a large part of Armenia in 1828. Persian claims on Herat, Afghanistan, led to war with Britain in 1856–7. Revolutions in 1905 and 1909 resulted in the establishment of a parliamentary régime. During the F.W.W. P. was occupied by British and Russian forces. An officer, Riza Khan, seized power in 1921, and was proclaimed shah in 1925. P. was occupied by Allied troops during 1941–6, and Riza, who had shown Axis sympathies, abdicated in 1941 in favour of his son Mohammed Riza Shah Pahlavi (1919–). He m. first in 1939 Princess Fawzia of Egypt (div. 1948), secondly in 1951 Soraya Esfandiari (div. 1958) and thirdly in 1959 Farah Diba. Absence of a male heir, only males being eligible to succeed to the Persian throne, led to his divorce from Queen Soraya: a son, Prince Riza, was b. to Queen Farah in 1960. The Shah celebrated the culmination of his 'white revolution' of social and economic reform, incl. distribution of much crown land among the peasants, by his coronation as Shahanshah in 1968.

Art. Persian art dates from the foundation of the Persian nation by Cyrus in 550 B.C. At first the dominant influence was Assyrian art, but throughout its history Persian geographical boundaries have been constantly shifting, and Persian art has been influenced by many different peoples. In pre-Islamic times the Persians were celebrated for their architecture, e.g. the palaces of Darius and Xerxes. Persian carpets, with their beautiful designs based on animal forms, hunting scenes, etc., are the best expression of Persian craftsmanship, but the Persians are also famous for their pottery, especially the ware made at Rhages, probably in the 12th cent. A.D., and their exquisite miniature paintings.

PERSIAN. The earliest language to be used in Persia was the so-called Old Persian (Achaemenian), which used a cuneiform script and appears to date from the period 550–340 B.C. It was followed by Avestic or Zend, the language of the sacred books of Zoroaster. Avestic, which appears to have originated in the N.W. of the country and to have survived until the 3rd cent. A.D., gave way in turn to Pahlavi (3rd–7th cent. A.D.), which shows marked Semitic affinities and incl. much Zoroastrian literature. Parsee or Farsi (A.D. 700–1100) was the immediate predecessor of modern Persian. The latter belongs to the Indoeuropean group of languages, uses the Arabic alphabet with a few additional letters, has many Arabic words, and was once widely used in India.

P. literature prior to the Arab conquest is represented by the sacred books of the Parsees known as the Avesta and later translated into Pahlavi, in which language there also appeared various secular writings. After the conquest the use of Arabic became widespread. The P. language was revived during the 9th cent. and the following cents. saw a succession of brilliant poets incl. the epic writer Firdousi (q.v.), Nizami (1140–1203), who excelled in romance, the didactic S'adi (q.v.), the mystic Rumi (1207–73), the lyrical Hafiz (q.v.), and Jami (q.v.) who combined the gifts of his predecessors and is considered the last of the classical poets. Omar Khayyam (q.v.) whose name is so well known outside Persia is less considered there. In the 16th and 17th cents. many of the best writers worked in India, still using classical forms and themes, and it was not until the revolutionary movements and contact with the West of the present cent. that Persian literature moved forward again. Among modern poets are Adib i Pishavari (d. 1930) and the rebel Lahuti (d. 1957) who spent his later life in the Soviet Union, and prominent after the S.W.W. Parviz Natel Khanlari (1914–) and Mohammed Hussein Shahriyar (1904–).

PERSIAN GULF. A large inlet from the Arabian Sea, running N.W. between Persia and Arabia. Area c. 90,000 sq. m.; average depth 90 ft; length 500 m.; average width is about 150 m.

PERSI'MMON or **Virginian Date Plum.** Tree (*Diospyros virginiana*) of the family Ebenaceae, native to N. America. Some 40 ft. high, the P. has alternate oval leaves, and yellow-green unisexual flowers. The small sweet orange fruits are edible.

PERSPIRATION. Sweat, the secretion of the sweat glands. These microscopic structures are found all over the skin; they secrete all the time and the 'insensible' P. may amount to 3 or 4 pints a day. The sweat consists of water-containing cells and also fatty acids from the sebaceous glands. In a warm atmosphere or on exertion the output is raised to keep the body temperature down by evaporation, and the sweat then becomes visible (sensible). Inflammation of the sweat glands is prickly heat.

PERTH. City, royal burgh, cap. of Perthshire, Scotland. 32 m. N.N.W. of Edinburgh, on the Tay. It

PERTHSHIRE. The river Tay winds gently between wooded banks near Aberfeldy. *Photo: George Outram & Co. Ltd.*

has famous dye-works. Pop. (1961) 41,199. (2) Cap. of W. Australia, 12 m. N.E. of the mouth of the Swan where its port Fremantle lies. P., founded in 1829, is the commercial and cultural hub of the state; it has an airport. Pop. (1966) 558,821.

PERTHSHIRE. Inland county of central Scotland. There are 50 mountains exceeding 3,000 ft., incl. Ben Lawers (3,984 ft.) and Ben More (3,843 ft.). The Grampians lie to the N.W. and the Tay is the chief r. The largest of the narrow lochs are Rannoch and Tay. Crops are raised, but cattle rearing is more important. Perth (the cap.) and Crieff are the chief towns. Area 2,493 sq. m.; pop. (1961) 127,018.

PERU (perōō'). Republic of S. America, bordering the Pacific Ocean and lying wholly within the Tropics.

PERU. The magnificent Baroque façade of the church of San Lorenzo, Lima.
Photo: Mike Andrews (Bell Howarth Ltd.)

It falls into 3 main physical divisions: an infertile coastal belt about 80m. wide; the mountainous Cordillera de los Andes, rising to 20,000 ft., crowned with perpetual snow and ice; and the forested Montaña region in the E. in which rise the headstreams of the Amazon. Lake Titicaca lies partly in P., partly in Bolivia; other Ls. are Junin and Parinacochas. Agriculture is the principal occupation. Cotton, sugar, rice, coffee, wool, hides and skins are the chief products. Sheep, cattle, llamas, alpacas, horses, mules, goats, and swine are raised; the wool of the alpaca and the llama is of importance. The forests of the Montaña supply cedar, mahogany, wild rubber, quinine, and vegetable ivory. Petroleum is worked in the N.W. Cerro de Pasco is famed for its copper mines; and silver, vanadium, bismuth, gold, lead, zinc, antimony and coal are worked. Manufactures incl. cotton, rayon, wool, and other textiles; tyres, cement, soap, fertilizers, and plastics. P. is traversed by the Pan-American Highway. The principal towns are Lima (the cap.), Arequipa, Callao, Cuzco, Trujillo, and Iquitos. There is a univ. at Lima, founded by Charles V in 1551, and 22 other state univs.

The constitution adopted in 1933 and modified in 1936 and 1945 provided for a president elected for 6 years, 2 vice-presidents elected simultaneously, and a Congress consisting of a Chamber of Deputies and a Senate. Area 514,060 sq. m.; pop. (1967) 12,400,000, excl. nomadic Indians and Mestizos in the E. region, c. 1,000,000. Spanish is the official language, but Quechua and Aymara are used by the Indian population.

History. P., together with present-day Bolivia and Ecuador, was the site of the Inca civilization which reached the peak of its power in the early years of the 16th cent. Civil war enabled the Spanish conqueror Francisco Pizarro to seize most of the country before his assassination in 1541, and Spanish rule was firmly estab. An Indian revolt in 1780 failed, and during the successful rebellions in other Spanish possessions in S. America, 1810–22, P. remained the Spanish H.Q., being the last to achieve independence, 1824. Since then the main events in P.'s history have been the abortive union with Bolivia (1836–9), the naval war against Spain (1864–6), the War of the Pacific (1879–83) over the nitrate fields of the Atacama Desert, in which P. was defeated and lost 3 provs. (one, Tacna, was returned in 1929). Other boundary disputes were settled by arbitration in 1902 (with Bolivia), 1927 (with Colombia), 1942 (with Ecuador). P. declared war on Germany and Japan 12 Feb. 1945. American interests predominate in the oil industry and a bloodless military coup followed dissatisfaction with an oil agreement in 1968.

PERU CURRENT. *See* HUMBOLDT CURRENT.

PERUGIA (pehrōō′jah). City of Umbria, Italy, cap.

of P. prov., lying 1,700 ft. above the Tiber, c. 85 m. N. of Rome. A trade centre, it makes silk and woollen textiles and liqueurs. One of the 12 cities of Etruria, it surrendered to Rome 309 B.C. It has a univ. (1276), a 15th cent. cathedral, a municipal palace begun in 1281, and other fine buildings with many art treasures. The Univ. for Foreigners (1925) teaches Italian culture and language. Pop. (1961) 109,596.

PERUGINO (pehrooje̅′nō), **Pietro** (1446–1524). Italian painter whose real name was Vanucci. He worked chiefly in Perugia, and helped to decorate the Sistine Chapel, Rome. Raphael was his pupil.

PESCARA (peskah′rah). Italian town, cap. of P. prov., in Abruzzi e Molise, at the mouth of the P. r. on the Adriatic, the birthplace of d'Annunzio. Hydro-electric installations here supply Rome with electricity. Pop. (1961) 87,076.

PESHAWAR (peshowr′). City in W. Pakistan, 11 m. E. of the Khyber Pass. A place of great strategic value, it has been important since the 2nd cent. It was acquired by the British 1849 and was made cap. of the N.W. Frontier Prov. (abolished 1951). Pop. (1961) 218,691.

PESTALOZZI (pestahlots′e̅), **Johann Heinrich** (1746–1827). Swiss educationist. B. at Zürich, he estab. an experimental school at Burgdorf in 1799, and moved it to Yverdon in 1805. Among his writings are *How Gertrude Teaches her Children*, etc.

PÉTAIN (pehtaṅ′), **Henri Philippe** (1856–1951). French soldier. After studying at St. Cyr, he was commissioned in 1878, and was promoted to general in 1915. His defence of Verdun in 1916 during the F.W.W. made him a national hero, and in 1917 he was created French C.-in-C., although he became subordinate to Foch in 1918. He suppressed a rebellion in Morocco in 1925–6. As a member of the Higher Council of National Defence he advocated a purely defensive military policy, and was strongly cons. in politics. He became P.M. in June 1940, following the disastrous Battle of France, and immediately signed an armistice with Germany. Removing the seat of govt. to Vichy, he estab. a repressive régime on the Fascist model. On the Allied invasion in 1944 he fled to Germany, but returned in 1945 and was sentenced to death for treason, the sentence being commuted to life imprisonment.

JOHANN HEINRICH PESTALOZZI

PETER, St. One of the 12 Apostles. Originally called Simeon or Simon, he was given the nickname of Cephas (a rock; Gk. *petros*) by Jesus. He was a fisherman of Capernaum, and may have been a follower of John the Baptist. It was he who first acknowledged Jesus as the Messiah, and his force of character made him a leader among the Apostles. According to tradition, he settled in Rome in later life, and was crucified there during Nero's persecution in A.D. 64; he is regarded at the first bishop of Rome. Excavations under the Basilica of St. Peter's revealed bones, accepted as those of the Apostle by Pope Paul 1968. Of the Epistles attributed to him, the 1st is probably spurious, and the 2nd certainly is.

PETER I (1672–1725). Tsar of Russia; called the Great. He succeeded to the throne in 1682 on the death of his brother Tsar Feodor, and assumed control of the govt. in 1689. After a successful campaign against the Turks in 1696, he visited Holland and England to study western techniques, and himself worked in Dutch and English shipyards. On his return to Russia he set out to reorganize the country on western lines; the army was modernized, a fleet was built, the admin. and the legal system were remodelled, educ. was encouraged, and the Church was brought under state control. In order to secure an outlet to the Baltic, P. undertook a war with Sweden (1700–21), which resulted in the acquisition of Estonia and part of Latvia and Finland. On the Baltic coast P. built his new capital, St. Petersburg. A war with Persia (1722–3) added Baku to Russia.

Peter's eldest son Alexius (1690–1718) had d. in prison for opposition to his father's reforms, and the son of Alexius later **Peter II** (1715–30) was passed over in the succession to the throne in favour of Peter I's consort Catherine I (q.v.). However, the boy did succeed Catherine in 1727, but d. of smallpox. **Peter III** (1728–62) was the son of Peter I's eldest dau., Anne, wife of the duke of Holstein-Gottorp. In 1741 he was adopted by his aunt, Elizabeth (q.v.), on her succession to the throne and at her behest m. in 1745 the future Catherine II (q.v.). He was deposed in 1762 and d. at the castle of Ropsha, probably murdered by Alexius Orlov.

PETER I (1844–1921). King of Serbia. He was the son of Prince Alexander Karageorgevich, and was elected king when the last Obrenovich king was murdered in 1903. He took part in the retreat of the Serbian Army in 1915, and in 1918 was proclaimed first king of the Serbs, Croats, and Slovenes.

PETRA. Glimpsed through a cleft in the towering rocks, the Khazneh or treasury of the city.
Courtesy of the Jordan Embassy.

PETER II (1923–70). King of Yugoslavia. He succeeded his father, King Alexander, in 1934, and assumed the royal power after the overthrow of the regency in 1941. He escaped to England following the German invasion, and m. Princess Alexandra of Greece in 1944. He was dethroned in 1945.

PETERBOROUGH. Bor. in the co. of Huntingdon and P. on the W. edge of the Fen country. The cathedral is 12–16th cent. Industries incl. engineering. Pop. (1961) 62,031. The *Soke of P.* ceased to be an admin. co. in 1965.

PETERHEAD. Seaport and burgh in E. Aberdeenshire, Scotland, 33 m. N.N.E. of Aberdeen. Industries incl. fishing, shipbuilding, light engineering, whisky distilling, making of woollen textiles. The Old Pretender landed at P. in 1715. Peterhead Bay harbour of refuge, built 1886–1921 by convicts, was extended by convicts 1958. Pop. (1961) 12,497.

PETERLEE. Mining town in Durham, England, founded 1950 and named after Peter Lee, first Labour chairman of a county council. Pop. (1961) 13,792.

PETER LOMBARD (c. 1100–60). Italian theologian. B. at Novara, he lectured on theology in Paris, and became bishop of Paris in 1159. His *Sententiarum libri* considerably influenced Catholic doctrine.

PETERLOO. Name given, in reference to Waterloo, to the 'massacre' in St. Peter's Fields, Manchester, England, on 16 Aug. 1819, when an open-air meeting in support of parliamentary reform was charged by yeomanry and hussars.

PETER'S PENCE. Voluntary annual contribution to the cost of papal administration, originally a compulsory levy of one penny per household.

PETER THE HERMIT (fl. 1095–9). French preacher. He was a priest of Amiens, who by his eloquence in preaching the 1st Crusade induced thousands of peasants to march against the Turks. They were cut to pieces in Asia Minor, but P. escaped and accompanied the main body of crusaders to Jerusalem.

PE'THICK-LAWRENCE, Frederick William, baron (1871–1961). British Labour statesman. Prominent with his first wife Emmeline Pethick (1867–1954, whose name he added to his own) in the woman's suffrage movement, he was imprisoned for his activities in 1912. He stood firm on the pacifist viewpoint in the F.W.W., and having entered parliament in 1923 was created a baron on his appointment by Attlee as Sec. of State for India (1945–7). In 1946 he led the cabinet mission which negotiated Indian independence.

PETITION OF RIGHT. The procedure whereby, before the passing of the Crown Proceedings Act (1947), a subject petitioned for legal relief against the Crown, whether for money due under a contract, or for property of which the Crown had taken possession. Also the petition of parliament accepted by Charles I in 1628, declaring illegal taxation without parliamentary consent, imprisonment without trial, billeting of soldiers on private persons, and use of martial law.

PETÖFI (pet'öfi), **Sándor** (1823–49). Hungarian national poet. B. at Kiskörös, he pub. his first vol. of poems in 1844, and settled in Pest. He expressed his revolutionary ideas in the semi-autobiographical poem 'The Apostle', and fell fighting the Austrians in the battle of Segesvár.

PE'TRA. Ruined city carved out of the red rock at a site in modern Jordan, on the E. slopes of the Wadi el Araba, 56 m. S. of the Dead Sea. An Edomite stronghold, later cap. of the Nabataeans, it was captured by Trajan A.D. 106 and wrecked in the 7th cent. by the Saracens. It was lost to knowledge until re-discovered in 1812 by the Swiss traveller J. L. Burckhardt.

PETRARCH (It. Petrarca), **Francesco** (1304–74). Italian poet and scholar. B. at Arezzo, he was taken to Avignon in 1313, studied law, was ordained in 1326, and entered the service of the Colonnas. In 1341 he was crowned poet in Rome. Later he lived in Milan with the Viscontis, and died at Arqua, near Padua. An ardent patriot, he was inspired by the greatness of ancient Rome. He wrote *Il canzoniere,* sonnets in praise of 'Laura'; *I trionfi,* a moral allegory in *terze rime*; *Africa,* a Lat. epic on Scipio the Elder; and philosophical treatises, etc.

PE'TREL. Two families of seabirds (Procellariidae and Oceanitidae) so called from their skimming the water surface as St. Peter did. Most familiar is the stormy P. of the N. Atlantic (*Hydrobates pelagicus*), also known as Mother Carey's chicken. Seldom coming to land except to breed, the Ps. lay a single egg in holes among the rocks. They are sooty-black with a white patch on the tail.

STORMY PETREL

PE'TRIE, Sir William Matthew Flinders (1853–1942). British Egyptologist. Grandson of Matthew Flinders (q.v.), he surveyed such British sites as Stonehenge, but is remembered for his work in Egypt (Tanis, the Pyramids, Tell el Amarna, Abydos, etc.) 1880–1926 and as 1st Edwards prof. of Egyptology, Univ. Coll., London, where his collections are still used for teaching purposes. He d. at Jerusalem, having spent his later years working in S. Palestine.

PETROGRAD. Name 1914–24 of LENINGRAD.

PETROLEUM or **Mineral Oil.** A thick greenish-brown liquid occurring underground in permeable rocks into which it has probably been forced by pressure, and accumulated in anticlines and other 'traps' below impervious rock layers. Flowing wells are due to gas pressure from above, or water pressure from below the oil, which causes it to rise up the borehole; many wells require artificial aids to bring the oil to the surface. The origin of P. is uncertain, but it is thought to be derived from organic material which has been converted by bacterial action, followed by the effects of heat and pressure.

From the crude P. or rock oil various products are made by distillation and other processes, e.g. fuel oil, gasoline (petrol), kerosine, Diesel or gas oil, lubricating oil, paraffin wax, petroleum jelly. Aviation spirit is a very volatile form of petrol.

The occurrence of mineral oil was known in ancient times, but the exploitation from oil-fields is a modern industry, the first flowing oil-well having been operated in 1859 in Pennsylvania. The earliest oil-fields to be exploited on a large scale were those of the U.S.A., the Caucasus and Mexico, but the pattern of oil production is continually changing. In the 1950s the U.S.A. held the lead, in the 1960s the Near East, and in the next decade fields in Africa, Alaska, Canada, Siberia and Australasia may be among the chief producers. Total world production is c. 2,000,000,000 metric tons annually. From inland fields oil may be carried by pipeline for hundreds of miles, and sea-going tankers may be vessels of more than 200,000 tons. This increase in tanker size in recent years has involved the danger of massive shore pollution and destruction of marine and bird life in case of accidental or deliberate discharge of cargo or residue. Following the loss of the *Torrey Canyon* (1967) off Cornwall, agreement was reached by the major internat. oil cos. in 1968 to pay compensation in such cases.

P. products and chemicals serve as raw materials for widely different industries and are used in large quantities in the manufacture of detergents, man-made fibres, plastics, insecticides, fertilizers, pharmaceuticals, toilet requisites, synthetic rubber, etc. Techniques are also being developed, notably in Japan, whereby micro-organisms, such as bacteria and yeast, are fed on the paraffin contained in petroleum. The protein is then extracted from their cells with the initial aim of producing animal fodder, but eventually human food.

PETRONIUS ARBITER, Gaius (d. A.D. 65). Roman author, the companion of Nero, and supervisor of his licentious pleasures. He committed suicide. His *Satyricon* is a satiric, licentious romance.

PETROPAVLO'VSK. Town in the Kazakh S.S.R., U.S.S.R., on the Ishim, the Trans-Siberian railway,

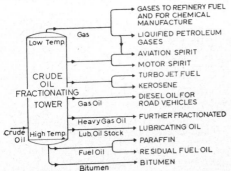

PETROLEUM. A scheme of the basic elements of refining, omitting all the complex mixing and purifying stages. In the fractionating tower a temperature gradient is maintained – highest at the bottom, and lowest at the top. 'Fractions', boiling at various temperatures, are tapped off the column at intervals; from the low-boiling-point gases passing out of the top of the column, to the heavy tar-like substances drained out of the bottom.

and the Transkazakh line, opened 1953. A former caravan station, it was founded as a Russian fortress, 1782: it produces flour, agricultural machinery, leather. Pop. (1967) 162,000.

PETROPAVLOVSK-KAMCHA'TSKI. Russian port and naval base on the S.E. Kamchatka peninsula. Pop. (1967) 119,000.

PETRO'POLIS. Hill resort in Brazil, 27 m. N. of Rio de Janeiro, with textile, chemical, ceramic, and tobacco factories, diamond-cutting works, and a trade in flowers, vegetables, and dairy products. Founded 1845 by immigrants from Bavaria, it was named after Pedro II of Brazil whose favourite summer residence it became. Pop. (1960) 85,000.

PETROSIAN, Tigran (1930–). Russian chess-player. An Armenian, he defeated Botvinnik in the world contest of 1963, and his emergence as champion was symptomatic of modern defensive strategy.

PETROVSK. *See* MAKHACHKALA.

PETROZAVO'DSK. Cap. of Karelia A.S.S.R., R.S.F.S.R., on the W. shore of Lake Onega. It makes metal goods, cement, prefabricated houses, etc., and has saw mills. Peter the Great estab. the township in 1703 as an iron-working centre; it was named P. in 1777. Pop. (1967) 171,000.

PETSAMO. *See* PECHENGA.

PEVENSEY. English village in Sussex, 5 m. N.E. of Eastbourne, the site of William the Conqueror's landing in 1066. The walls remain of the Roman fortress of Anderida.

PEWTER. An alloy of lead and tin, much used formerly for ornaments and domestic utensils.

PFALZ. German name of the PALATINATE.

PFORZHEIM (pforts'hīm). Town of Baden-Württemberg, W. Germany, 16 m. S.E. of Karlsruhe. Gold and silver ware and jewellery are made. It was a Roman settlement, and the residence of margraves of Baden 1300–1565. Pop. (1960) 80,000.

PHA'ETHON. In Greek mythology, the son of Helios, who was allowed for one day to drive the chariot of the sun. Losing control of the horses, he almost set the earth on fire, and was killed by Zeus with a thunderbolt.

PHAGOCYTES (fag'osīts). White blood cells having the property of devouring bacteria. They are lymphocytes and polynuclear cells, and one of the body's chief defences against infection.

PHALARIS (fl. 570–554 B.C.). Tyrant of Agrigentum, Sicily. He is said to have built a brazen bull in which victims were roasted alive. He was killed in a popular revolt. The letters attributed to him were proved by Bentley (q.v.) to be a later forgery.

PHA'LAROPE. Genus of seabirds. Of the 3 species the red-necked (*Phalaropus hyperboreus*) and grey (*P. fulicarius*) visit Britain from the Arctic and *P. wilsoni* is exclusively American. The male is courted by the female and hatches the eggs.

PHALLUS. A model of the male sexual organ, used in fertility rituals in ancient Greece and Asia Minor, in India, and in many other parts of the world.

PHARAOH (fā'rō). Hebrew form of the Egyptian royal title Per-'o. This term, meaning 'great house', was originally applied to the royal household, and after c. 950 B.C. to the king.

PHARISEES (far'izēz) ('separated'). Jewish sect which arose in the 2nd cent. B.C., in protest against all movements towards compromise with Hellenistic culture. Their main emphasis was on strict observance of the law, rather than on ritual; hence they came into conflict with the priestly caste, or Sadducees. Although they believed in a coming Messiah, they rejected political action, and in the 1st cent. A.D. the left wing of their followers, the Zealots, broke away to pursue a revolutionary nationalist policy. After the fall of Jerusalem, P. ideas became the basis of orthodox Judaism.

PHARMACOLOGY (farmakol'ojē). Study of the

origin, application and effect of chemical substances on animals and man. These products of the pharmaceutical industry range from aspirin to anti-cancer agents, and about 3 per cent of gross sales in the U.K. are devoted to research, which in some fields, e.g. chemotherapeutics, is both costly and complex – 4,000 new substances may have to be synthesized to find one or two useful products. Well-proven formulations are listed in the official pharmacopoeia.

PHARYNX (far′ingks). The interior of the throat, the cavity at the back of the mouth. Its walls are made of muscle strengthened with a fibrous layer and lined with mucous membrane. It has an opening into the back of each nostril (choanae) and downwards into the gullet and (through the epiglottis) into the windpipe. On each side the Eustachian tube leads from it to the middle ear. The upper part (nasopharynx) is an airway, but the remainder is a passage for food. Inflammation of the P. is pharyngitis.

PHASMIDA (fas′mida). An order of insects comprising the Stick Insects and Leaf Insects (qq.v.).

PHEASANT (fez′ant). Genus of game birds (*Phasianus*) incl. with the peacock and guinea fowl in the family Phasianidae. The common P. (*P. colchicus*) was introduced from Asia to Europe, according to legend, by the Argonauts who brought it from the banks of the r. Phasis. The plumage of the male is richly tinted with brownish green and yellow and red markings, but the female, like other hens of the genus, is a camouflaged brownish colour: the nest is made in the ground, and the P. is polygamous. In England Ps. are semi-domesticated and the shooting season is Oct. to 31 Jan.: the P. is naturalized in N. America. Among the more exotically beautiful Ps. of other genera, often kept as ornamental birds, are the golden P. (*Chrysolophus pictus*) from China and the argus pheasant of Malaya (*Argusiana argus*) which has metallic spots or 'eyes' on the wings.

PHENOL. *See* Carbolic Acid.

PHIDIAS (fĭd′ias). Greek sculptor. B. at Athens *c.* 500 B.C., he was a friend of Pericles who made him superintendent of public works. He constructed the Propylaea and the Parthenon, and executed the colossal statue of Zeus at Olympia which was one of the seven wonders of the world.

PHILADE′LPHIA. City of the U.S.A., in Pennsylvania, 79 m. S.W. of New York. The Delaware connects it with the Atlantic 100 m. downstream through Delaware Bay. Wm. Penn founded the city in 1682 as a Quaker settlement; its name means brotherly love. Notable buildings incl. the grave of Franklin; Independence Hall (1732–59) in which the Declaration of Independence was adopted, 1776; City Hall (1872) with a tower surmounted by a statue of Penn, total height 548 ft.; and the U.S. Mint, estab. 1792. P. was temporarily capital of the U.S.A. 1790–1800, and attained high eminence in culture. There are the Franklin institute for applied science (1824), and the Univ. of P. (1740); the P. orchestra (1900); the library and the Museum of Art. The port facilities are extensive. The leading products of P. are textiles, chemicals, machinery; other activities are petroleum refining, food processing, printing and publishing. Pop. (1970) 1,926,529; met. area 4,773,804.

PHILAE (fī′lē). Is. in the Nile, Egypt, above the first cataract, with ruins of temples of Isis and Hathor and an unfinished Roman hall. After the completion of the first Aswan dam in 1902 it was

PHILAE. The completion of the High Dam will once more leave the islet permanently above water, and the Temple of Isis (first founded *c.* 350 B.C. and in use till the 6th century) will regain its former beautiful setting of palm trees.
Courtesy of the Egyptian State Tourist Administration.

submerged except during July–Oct. each year; plans for dams to protect it from inundation, to be completed *c.* 1968, were made in connection with the construction, begun in 1960, of the new High Dam. (*See* Aswan.)

PHILATELY. The collection and study of postage stamps. Originating in France *c.* 1860, it became popular throughout the world, London being the world centre. The world's largest collection is in the British Museum, the runner-up being in Smithsonian Institution, Washington: probably the world's finest private collection is that of Queen Elizabeth II. Many countries earn extra revenue and cater for the philatelist by issuing special sets of stamps to commemorate special events, anniversaries, etc., and there are many specialized fields of collection from particular countries to specimens which have some defect, e.g. contemporary issues which are accidentally unperforated.

PHILBY (fil′bi), **Harry St. John Bridger** (1885–1960). British explorer. As chief of the British political mission to central Arabia, 1917–18, he carried out extensive exploration and was the first European to visit the southern provs. of Najd; and in 1932 crossed the Rub 'al Khali desert. He wrote *The Empty Quarter* (1933), *Forty Years in the Wilderness* (1957), etc. His son **Harold P.** (1912–   ), known as Kim P., entered the Foreign Service, but became a Soviet agent and was asked in 1951 to resign: in 1963 he was named as having warned Guy Burgess and Donald Maclean of govt. investigations into their activities in 1951, and took Soviet citizenship.

PHILHARMONIC SOCIETY. The Royal P.S. was founded in London in 1813 by the pianist Johann Baptist Cramer (1771–1858) for the purpose of improving musical standards by means of orchestral concerts organized on a subscription basis. Another P.S. was founded in New York in 1842.

PHILIP. One of the 12 Apostles. He was an inhabitant of Bethsaida, and is said to have worked as a missionary in Asia Minor.

PHILIP (382–336 B.C.). King of Macedonia. After ruling as regent for his nephew, he seized the throne in 359, conquered the Greek cities on the Macedonian coast, Thessaly and Phocis, and defeated the Athenians and Thebans at Chaeronea in 338. He formed the Greek states into a league, and prepared for war with Persia, but was assassinated. He was succeeded by his son, Alexander the Great.

PHILIP. Name of 6 kings of France. **Philip II,** (1165–1223), called Augustus, succeeded in 1180, took part in the 3rd Crusade, conquered Normandy, and defeated a powerful alliance at Bouvines in 1214. **PHILIP IV** (1268–1314). King of France. Called the

H.R.H. THE PRINCE PHILIP, Duke of Edinburgh.
Photo: Baron Studios.

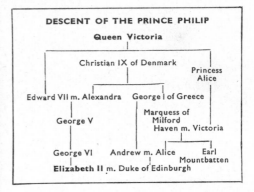

Fair, he engaged in a feud with pope Boniface VIII, whom in 1303 he made a prisoner. Clement V, elected Pope through P.'s influence, transferred his residence to Avignon, and collaborated with P. to suppress the Templars. P. allied with the Scots against England, and attempted to conquer Flanders. **Philip VI** (1293–1350), the first king of the house of Valois, was elected by the barons on the death of his cousin, Charles IV, in 1328. His claim was challenged by Edward III of England, who in 1346 defeated him at Crécy.

PHILIP II (1527–98). King of Spain. The son of the emperor Charles V, he was b. at Valladolid, and in 1554 m. Queen Mary of England. On his father's abdication in 1556 he inherited Spain, the Netherlands, and the Spanish possessions in Italy and America, and in 1580 he annexed Portugal. His intolerance and lack of understanding of the Netherlanders drove them into revolt. Political and religious reasons combined to involve him in war with England, and after 1589 with France. The defeat of the Armada marked the beginning of the decline of Spanish power. P. was buried in the Escorial, which he founded.

PHILIP V (1683–1746). King of Spain. A grandson of Louis XIV of France, he inherited the Spanish crown in 1700, but was not recognized by the Powers until 1713.

PHILIP (1396–1467), known as the Good. Duke of Burgundy from 1419. He engaged in the Hundred Years War as an ally of England and made the Netherlands a centre of art and learning.

PHILIP (1921–). Prince of the U.K. A grandson of George I of Greece and a great-great-grandson of Queen Victoria, he was b. in Corfu but raised in England and ed. at Gordonstoun and Dartmouth Naval Coll. During the S.W.W. he served in the Mediterranean, taking part in the battle of Matapan, and in the Pacific. A naturalized British subject, taking the surname Mountbatten, in March 1947, he m. Princess Elizabeth (from 1952 Elizabeth II) in Westminster Abbey on 20 Nov. 1947, having the previous day received the title Duke of Edinburgh. In 1956 he founded the Duke of Edinburgh's Award Scheme to encourage creative achievement among young people, and is also greatly interested in the Commonwealth. He was created a prince of the U.K. in 1957, and awarded the O.M. in 1968. Vols. of his speeches appeared in 1957 and 1960.

PHILIPPEVILLE (fēlēpvēl'). Town, trade centre, and Mediterranean port of Algeria in the dept. of Constantine, founded by the French 1838, and renamed Skikda after independence. Pop. (1967) 85,000.

PHILIPPI'. Ancient city of Macedonia, founded by Philip of Macedon, 358 B.C. Near P. Antony and Octavius defeated Brutus and Cassius in 42 B.C. It was the first European town where St. Paul preached (c. A.D. 53), founding the congregation to which he addressed the Epistle to the Philippians.

PHILIPPINES, Republic of the. Independent country consisting of more than 7,000 is. lying N. of the equator, between the Pacific Ocean to the E. and the S. China Sea to the W. The main islands are Luzon in the N. and Mindanao in the S.; others incl. Mindoro, Masbate, Samar, Panay, Leyte, Cebu, Negros, Bohol, and Palawan. The is. of the main chain are traversed from N to S by mountain ranges, and there are several volcanoes. Forests cover more than half the land surface and timber, gums and resins, bamboo, vegetable oils, dye woods are important products. The main crops are coconuts (copra and desiccated coconut), cane sugar, rice, maize, tobacco, and hemp. Mineral wealth incl. gold and silver, copper, lead, iron ore, coal, chromite, and quicksilver.

The P. Republic has a president elected for 4 years and eligible to stand for a second term, an elected Senate and House of Representatives.

Area 115,700 sq. m.; pop. (1967) 34,656,000, most of them of Malay stock; aboriginal Negritos number c. 30,000, and Chinese c. 140,000. Eighty per cent are Roman Catholics. The nat. language (from 1946) is Filipino (based on the Malayan dialect, Tagalog), but English (spoken by a third of the people) and Spanish are also official languages. Quezon City, a N.E. suburb of Manila, was proclaimed the cap. in 1948, but many govt. offices remain in Manila, the former cap., pending completion, other towns are Cebu, Davao, and Iloilo.

History. The P. were visited by Magellan in 1521, and Spanish rule and Catholicism were estab. in the 1560s, during the reign of Philip II, in whose honour the islands were named. During the 19th cent. a series of armed revolts occurred. On the conclusion of the Spanish-American War the P. were ceded to the U.S.A. in 1898. In 1935 a semi-independent Commonwealth of the P. was estab., and in 1946 an independent republic was set up; the U.S.A. was in 1947 granted the use of a number of military bases in the is. The Japanese occupied the P. 1942–5 after overcoming a fierce resistance by American and Filipino troops under General MacArthur.

PHILIPPOPOLIS. Greek name of PLOVDIV.

PHILISTINE (fil'istĭn). Originally a contemptuous term applied by German students to non-members of the univ.; hence a person with no interest in intellectual or artistic matters.

PHILISTINES. A people who inhabited the coastal plain of Palestine from the 12th cent. B.C., forming a league of city-states. Coming probably from Asia Minor, they adopted a Semitic language and religion, struggled with the Israelites in the 11th–10th cents. B.C., were temporarily subdued by David, and later passed under Assyrian supremacy.

PHILLIP, Arthur (1738–1814). British founder of New South Wales. He entered the navy in 1755 and rose to vice-admiral. He founded the convict settlement at Sydney in 1788, and was governor until 1792.

PHILLIPS, John Bertram (1906–). British churchman. Ordained in the C. of E. in 1930, he held livings in London and Surrey before becoming prebendary of Chichester Cathedral (1957–60). His colloquial *The New Testament in Modern English* (1958) is outstanding among recent versions: other books incl. *God our Contemporary* (1960).

PHILLPOTTS, Eden (1862–1960). British author. B. in India, son of an army captain, he spent ten years as an insurance clerk before settling in Devon to write. He had a great love of the Dartmoor region, which forms the background of his best work, e.g. the novels *Children of the Mist* (1898), *Sons of the Morning* (1900), *The Secret Woman* (1905: dramatized 1912), and *The Thief of Virtue* (1910); and the plays *The Farmer's Wife* (1917) and *Yellow Sands* (1926), the latter written with his dau. Mary Adelaide Eden P., also a novelist. His prolific output damaged his standing, but at his imaginative best he is a more 'human' Hardy.

PHILO JUDAEUS (fī'lō joodē'-us) (fl. 1st cent. A.D.). Jewish philosopher of Alexandria, who in A.D. 40 undertook a mission to Caligula to protest against the emperor's claim to divine honours. In his writings P. attempts to reconcile Judaism with Platonic and Stoic ideas.

PHILOLOGY. A Greek term, originally meaning 'love of learning and literature'. It is often used in the sense of linguistics (q.v.), but more often defines the critical study of the literary remains of the past, esp. of Gk. and Roman antiquity. In this sense the scholars of Alexandria, who e.g. edited Homer, were philologists. The Renaissance gave great impetus to this kind of study. Dutch scholars took the lead in the 17th cent. whilst Richard Bentley in England held a place of his own. From the study of Sanskrit arose at the beginning of the 19th cent., under Bopp's leadership, what is called comparative P., mainly concerned with the Indo-European (q.v.) family of languages, whilst the Romantic movement greatly inspired the establishment of national Ps. – Germanic and German (Grimm), Romance (Diez), Celtic (Zeuss), etc.

PHILOSOPHY (Gk. love of knowledge). The field of theoretical studies which incl. metaphysics, epistemology (theory of knowledge), ethics and aesthetics, but which continually contracts as specific studies acquire their own estab. disciplines, e.g. mathematics, physics, chemistry, biology and (until this cent.) psychology were formerly incl. in P., and logic is in process of separation. Oldest of all philosophical systems is the Vedic c. 2,500 B.C., but like many other eastern systems it rests on a primarily mystic basis. The first scientific system orginated in Greece in the 6th cent. B.C. with the Milesian school (Thales, Anaximander and Anaximenes). Both they and later pre-Socratics (Pythagoras, Xenophanes, Parmenides, Zeno of Elea, Empedocles, Anaxagoras, Heraclitus and Democritus) were lively theorists, and ideas such as atomism, developed by Democritus, crop up in later schemes of thought. In the 5th cent. among the teachers known as the sophists there emerged in Socrates the apostle of the ideal of reason, and Plato and Aristotle complete the trinity of the golden age of Greek P. Later schools incl. the epicureans (Epicurus), stoics (Zeno) and sceptics (Pyrrho); the eclectics – not a school, but selecting what appealed to them from various systems (Cicero and Seneca) – and the neo-Platonists, infusing a mystic element into the system of Plato (Philo, Plotinus and, as disciple, Julian the Apostate). The close of the Athenian schools of P. by Justinian in A.D. 529 marks the end of ancient P., though many of its teachers moved eastwards and Greek thought emerges in Moslem philosophers such as Avicenna and Averroes, and the Jewish Maimonides. For the West the work of Aristotle was transmitted through Boethius, and the roll of medieval scholastic philosophers, mainly concerned with the reconciliation of ancient P. with Christian belief, begins in the 9th cent. with John Scotus Erigena, and incl. Anselm, Abelard, Albertus Magnus, Thomas Aquinas (greatest of them all), his opponent Duns Scotus, and William of Ockham.

In the 17th cent. Descartes, with his rationalist determination to doubt, and faith in mathematical proof, marks the beginning of modern P., and was followed by Spinoza, Leibniz and Hobbes, but the empiricists, principally an 18th cent. English school (Locke, Berkeley and Hume), turned rather to physics as indicating what can be known and how, and led up to the transcendental criticism of Kant. In the early 19th cent. classical German idealism (Fichte, Schelling, Hegel) repudiated Kant's limitation of human knowledge; and in France Comte developed the positivist thought which attracted Mill and Spencer. Notable also in the cent. are the pessimistic atheism of Schopenhauer; the dialectal materialism of Marx and Engels; the work of Nietzsche and Kierkegaard, which led towards 20th cent. existentialism; the pragmatism of William James and Dewey; and the absolute idealism at the turn of the cent. of the neo-Hegelians (Bradley, Bosanquet, M'Taggart, Royce, Blanshard and Creighton). Among 20th cent. movements are the logical positivism of the Vienna circle (Carnap, Popper, Ayer); the creative evolution of Bergson; neo-Thomism, the revival of the medieval philosophy of Aquinas (Gilson, Maritain); existentialism (Heidegger, Jaspers, Sartre, Marcel); the phenomenology of Husserl, who influenced Ryle; realism (Russell, Moore, Broad and Wittgenstein), and the isolated genius of Whitehead.

PHIZ. Pseudonym of British artist, Hablot Knight Browne (1815–82). B. at Lambeth, he illustrated the greater part of Dickens' *Pickwick Papers*, and others of Dickens' works, as well as novels by Lever and Harrison Ainsworth.

PHLEBITIS (flēbī'tis). Inflammation of the lining of a vein. It causes the blood in the neighbourhood to clot (thrombosis). Simple or non-infective P. may be caused by an injury or pressure, and is common in the main thigh veins of women after childbirth. The blood clots and obstructs the circulation (white leg). Septic P. is caused by infection, e.g. in the lateral sinus and the jugular vein by infection from the middle ear. Fragments of the clot may carry infection to the lungs and cause an abscess.

PHLOX. Genus of plants native to Siberia and N. America. The British varieties are half-hardy annuals cultivated from *Phlox drummondi*. They have lanceolate, opposite leaves, and the flowers, borne in panicles, are red, white or mauve.

PHNÔM-PENH (nompen'). Cap. of Cambodia, on the Mekong, 130 m. W.N.W. of Saigon. It is an important trade centre with handsome buildings in European style, built while Cambodia was under French protection, as well as Buddhist temples, a pagoda, and a Buddhist univ. There is regular stea---

connection with Saigon, and an airport at Pochentong nearby. Pop. (1967) 600,000.

PHOENICIA (fēnish´a). Ancient Greek name for the seaboard of Lebanon and Syria, N. of Mt. Carmel, inhabited in ancient times by a people who called themselves Canaanites. *See* CANAAN. They were seafaring traders and craftsmen, who visited the Scillies (and possibly Cornwall) and are said to have circumnavigated Africa, and their cities (Tyre and Sidon being the chief) were independent states ruled by hereditary kings, but dominated by merchant oligarchies. Documents found at Ugarit in 1929 give much information on their civilization, and their deities incl. El, Baal, Anat, Astarte or Ashtaroth, and Melkart or Moloch. Their colonies were estab. in Cyprus, N. Africa (e.g. Carthage), Malta, Sicily and Spain, and competition from these combined with the attacks of the Sea Peoples, the Assyrians and Greeks, on the cities in P. led to their ultimate decline: the fall of Tyre to Alexander in 332 B.C. ended the separate history of P. Their exports incl. Tyrian purple cloth, furniture (from the timber of Lebanon), and jewellery: Solomon brought workmen from P. to construct and decorate the Temple at Jerusalem.

PHOENIX (fē´niks). Miraculous Egyptian bird which, according to legend, burnt itself to death on a pyre of aromatic woods after 500 years of life, to arise rejuvenated from the ashes.

PHOENIX. City of the U.S.A., cap. of Arizona. It handles dairy products and citrus fruits and because of its dry climate is a popular health resort. Pop. met. area (1970) 963,132.

PHOENIX ISLANDS. Group of 8 is. in the S. Pacific, incl. in the British colony of Gilbert and Ellice Is. in 1937. Hull, Sydney, and Gardner were colonized by Gilbertese 1938–40, until by 1964 droughts had driven them away; Phoenix, Birnie and McKean are also uninhabited; and Canton and Enderbury are claimed by U.S.A., so that in 1939 joint control for aviation and communications was agreed for 50 years, but long-range jets rendered Canton's airport obsolete, and British and Americans left 1967–8. Total land area 11 sq. m.

PHONETICS. The science which deals with the identification, description, and classification of sounds used in articulate speech. P. owes its origin in large measure to A. M. Bell (1819–1905), and much of the pioneer work was done in England. As the letters of the Rom. alphabet are a quite inadequate means of fixing the definite value of speech sound, special phonetic alphabets have been invented of which the International Phonetic Script is best known.

PHONOGRAPH. *See* RADIOGRAM.

PHOSPHATES. Salts of phosphoric acid. They combine with water in 3 proportions to form metaphosphoric acid, pyrophosphoric acid, and ordinary phosphoric acid. Each of these acids gives origin to other series of salts, of which ordinary phosphoric acid is of the greatest importance.

PHOSPHORUS (Gk. *phosphoros*, light-bearing). Element essential to life, discovered by Brand in 1669: symbol P, at. wt. 30·975, at. no. 15. It occurs in several forms, the commonest being white P. (a waxy solid, emitting a greenish glow in air, burning spontaneously to P. pentoxide, and very poisonous) and red P. (neither igniting spontaneously nor poisonous). Production of P. and its compounds has greatly increased since the S.W.W., e.g. the use of soluble phosphates as fertilizers and of other P. compounds in detergents, prevention of scale and corrosion in pipes and boiler tubes, and in certain organic preparations.

PHOTOELECTRIC CELL or **Photocell.** A device for measuring or detecting light. There are 3 main types: in the *photoemissive* cell, radiant light energy causes electrons to be emitted, and a current to flow; in the *photovoltaic* cell, a semiconductor device, it causes an electromotive force to be generated; and in the *photoconductive* cell it causes the resistance to vary.

PHOTOGRAPHY. Modern P. embraces all useful processes for producing images on sensitized materials by radiant energy which may be visible light, ultraviolet, infra-red or X-rays; radiation from radioactive substances, and beams of electrons.

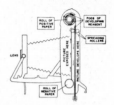

PHOTOGRAPHY. The Polaroid Land Camera produces a finished black and white picture in 10 sec. and a colour picture in approx. 50 sec. Attached to a single paper leader are 2 rolls – one the light sensitive negative film, and the other a non-sensitive positive white paper, for the finished print. After taking a photograph, the paper leader is pulled, and an equal amount of exposed film and positive paper meet precisely to be pulled through 2 s eel rollers, which rupture one of the sealed pods and spread a thin layer of developing reagent between the 2 papers. In a single step the negative is developed, and the positive print formed ready for viewing seconds later.
Courtesy of Polaroid (U.K.) Ltd.

J. N. Niepce produced the first successful photograph in 1822 using silver chloride. Daguerre partnered him in 1829 and discovered that an image could be produced by fuming with mercury vapour an exposed iodized silver plate in a camera (1839), and Fox Talbot independently announced his calotype method also in 1839. From Scott Archer's collodion process (1851) research on emulsions and gelatine reduced the exposure time from 10 sec. to 1/100 sec. by 1900. Panchromatic plates covered the whole spectrum, glass plates were superseded by roll film and box cameras appeared. Colour P. was produced practically in 1891 by Lippman, but Maxwell's tricolour separation process has prevailed as the basis of modern reproduction.

Enormous advances have been made in all branches of P., in equipment, processes and techniques necessitated by the dependence on photography of television, the cinema industry, news pictures, medical, scientific and research requirements, microfilm recording and new processes in the printing industry and for office copying machines.

The most recent developments in cameras incl. the introduction of automatic loading and the production of a colour print inside the camera 50 sec. after exposure.

PHOTOSYNTHESIS. The process in which the energy of sunlight is used by plants to assimilate carbon dioxide and water to form sugars and starches – their basic food. Great insight into this vital process was gained in the 1950s by means of radioisotopes – labelled carbon dioxide and heavy water have been used by M. Calvin (q.v.) et al., and shown to combine within one second of contact – and the pathways through to starches, amino acids, etc., have been followed. *See* LABELLED COMPOUND.

PHRENOLOGY. The theory, now discredited, that by examination of the skull a person's mental development can be measured. It was first propounded by Franz Joseph Gall, a Viennese physician, *c.* 1796.

PHRYGIA (frij´ia). Former kingdom of W. Asia covering the Anatolian tableland, inhabited in ancient times by an Indo-European people; it achieved great prosperity in the 8th cent. B.C. under a line of kings bearing in turn the names Gordius and Midas, but then fell under Lydian rule. From P. the cult of Cybele was introduced into Greece and Rome.

PHRYNE (frī'nē) (4th cent. B.C.). Athenian courtesan famous for her beauty.

PHYLLOXE'RA. Genus of insects in the order Hemiptera similar to aphides. The species *P. vastatrix*, a native of N. America, attacks grape vines, laying its eggs under the bark. European vines are especially susceptible and many French vineyards suffered terribly on the arrival of the pest in Europe in the 19th cent. The insects may be destroyed by spraying with carbon disulphide or petroleum.

PHYSICS. P. (sometimes called 'natural philosophy') is a branch of science which is concerned with the ultimate laws which govern the structure of the universe and forms of matter and energy and their interactions. For convenience P. is often divided into branches such as nuclear or atomic P., solid and liquid state P., electricity, electronics and magnetism, optics, acoustics, heat and thermodynamics. P. is applied on a vast scale, especially in engineering and in measurements. British physicists have included Newton, Cavendish, Faraday, Young, Maxwell, Kelvin, Rutherford and Thomson (qq.v.). In the U.K. the body concerned with the promotion of the advancement and dissemination of a knowledge of P. pure and applied and the elevation of the profession of P. is The Institute of P. and The Physical Society the amalgamation of The Institute and Society having taken place in 1960). There is a British National Committee for P., the secretariat of which is held by The Royal Society, which is the British adhering body for international work in science.

PHYSIOLOGY. That branch of medicine and biology that deals with the functioning of the healthy human body. *See* HUMAN BODY.

PHYSIOTHERAPY. Use of heat (infra-red lamps, hot water, etc.), electrical stimulation (low-voltage currents), massage and exercise to treat patients suffering from rheumatic conditions, leprosy, poliomyelitis, lung complaints, accidental injuries, war wounds, etc. Qualified practitioners are registered with the Chartered Soc. of P. (England and Wales) and Faculty of Physiotherapists (Scotland); in the U.S.A., where they are more commonly called physical therapists, the central body is the American P. Association.

PIACENZA (pē-ahchen'za). City of Emilia, Italy, the cap. of P. province, nr. the Po, 40 m. S.E. of Milan; it has a 12th cent. cathedral and makes iron and brass goods, textiles, pottery; it also has flour mills and printing works. The Roman Placentia, P. dates from 218 B.C. Pop. (1961) 87,930.

PIANOFORTE. A stringed musical instrument, whose keyed hammers make it percussive and capable of soft or strong tones – hence its name. The clavichord and the 16th cent. virginal were forerunners of the design evolved in 1709 by Bartolommeo Cristofori, a Paduan harpsichord-maker. Subsequent improvement has been closely linked with the names of famous P. makers, such as Broadwood and Stodart, Pleyel, Érard, Collard Steinway, Blüthner, and Bechstein. The practice of some designers building the strings vertically has prevailed in the modified form of the upright P. The horizontally strung grand P. is recognized as superior in tone and is used for concert performance. The Player Piano for mechanical reproduction of music was invented in 1842, though much improved in this century.

PICARDY. Former province of France; it covered all the Somme department and parts of Pas de Calais, Aisne, and Oise.

PICA'SSO (RUIZ), Pablo (1881–). Spanish artist. Son of an art teacher José Ruiz Blasco, and an Andalusian mother Maria Picasso López, he discontinued use of the name Ruiz in 1898. B. at Malaga, he was a mature artist at 10, and at 16 was holding

his first exhibition. In 1900 he made an initial visit to Paris, where he was to settle, and during his Blue Period 1901–4 painted mystic distorted figures in blue tones; a brief, more supple, Rose Period 1905–6 followed, but in 1907 he completed the revolutionary 'Les Demoiselles d'Avignon' by which Cubism was fully launched. His subsequent development has been kaleidoscopic, rather than moving along any one path, incl. by turns Classicism, Romanticism, Realism, Expressionism, Abstractionism and Naturalism, and ranging through ceramics, sculpture, sets for ballet (e.g. *Parade* in 1917 for Diaghilev), book illustrations (e.g. Ovid's *Metamorphoses*), portraits (Stravinsky, Valéry, etc.), to his generally acknowledged masterpiece 'Guernica' (1937) a nightmare mural interpretation of the agony of the Civil War in Spain. He is unique in the fertile vigour of his invention, and in his appeal to the amateur as well as the expert, his exhibitions attracting a large popular following.

PICCARD. Launched at Toulon in 1961, the bathyscaphe *L'Archimède* (B-11000) reached depths of more than 31,350 ft. in the Japan Trench in 1962. Built of steel alloy (with nickel and molybden chrome), she weighs 60 tons and can withstand pressures of 180,000 tons. She is the latest development of the original Piccard invention.
Courtesy of Établissement Cinématographique des Armées.

PICCARD, August (1884–1962). Swiss scientist. B. in Basle, he became prof. of physics at the Univ. of Brussels in 1922. In 1931–2 he made record ascents to 55,000 ft. in a balloon of his own design, resulting in important discoveries concerning such stratospheric phenomena as cosmic rays. Subsequently he built and used bathyscaphes for undersea research, notably the *Trieste*, designed in collaboration with his son **Jacques P** (1922–), who in 1960 descended in it to 37,800 ft. in the Challenger Deep, W. Pacific. **Jean P.** (1884–1963), twin brother of August, made a remarkable balloon ascent from Detroit in 1934 with his wife, and was prof. of aeronautical engineering, Univ. of Minnesota. *See* SUBMARINE.

PICKFORD, Mary (1893–). American actress, *née* Smith. B. in Toronto, she became the first star of the silent screen to be known by name, and on her marriage – her second – to Douglas Fairbanks senior in 1920, they were called 'the world's sweethearts'. She later became one of the biggest names in film production, and following her divorce in 1935 m. in 1937 Buddy Rogers.

PICO DELLA MIRANDOLA (pēkō-dellah-mērahn'dōlah), **Giovanni** (1463–94). Italian mystic philosopher. B. at Mirandola, of which his father was prince, he studied Hebrew, Chaldean, and Arabic, showing particular interest in the Kabbala.

PICRIC ACID. Yellow crystalline solid $C_6H_2(NO_2)_3OH$, 2, 4, 6-trinitrophenol. It is a strong acid, dyes wool and silks yellow, is used to treat burns and in the manufacture of explosives.

PICTS. An early people inhabiting Scotland, probably of pre-Celtic origin, and speaking a non-Celtic language. They were united with the Celtic Scots under the rule of Kenneth MacAlpin in 844.

PIDGIN ENGLISH. Business jargon ('pidgin' being the Chinese corruption of the English word business) used in dealing with Chinese and other Oriental and African traders, which utilizes debased English forms arranged according to Chinese idiom.

PIECK (pēk), **Wilhelm** (1876–1960). German Communist. A leader of the 1919 Spartacist revolt, he was a founder of the Socialist Unity Party in 1946 and from 1949 was pres. of the German Democratic Rep.: the office was abolished on his death.

PIEDMONT. A region of N. Italy, bordering Switzerland on the N. and France on the W. and surrounded, except on the E., by the Alps and the Apennines. The most fertile land is near the Po. The main towns are Turin (the capital), Alessandria, Asti, Vercelli, and Novara. From P., under the House of Savoy, the movement for the unification of Italy started in the 19th cent. Area 9,804 sq. m.; pop. (1961) 3,889,962.

PIERNÉ (pē-ārneh´), **Gabriel** (1863–1937). French composer and conductor. In Metz, he succeeded Franck as organist to Ste. Clothilde, Paris, and conducted the Colonne orchestra from 1903. His numerous compositions incl. the 'Entry of the Little Fauns'.

PIETERMARITZBURG (pētermār´itsboorg). Cap. of Natal, S. Africa, 41 m. W.N.W. of Durban, founded in 1838 by Boer trekkers from the Cape, and was named in 1839 in honour of their leaders, Piet Retief and Gert Maritz. Made cap. of Natal 1842, it is an industrial centre with breweries, and factories making boots and shoes, furniture, etc. Pop. (1960) 108,581 (39,770 whites).

PI´ETISM. Movement within the German Lutheran Church originated by Philip Jacob Spener (1635–1705), and intended to revive practical Christianity as against increasing theological dogmatism.

PIEZŌELE´CTRIC EFFECT. The property of some crystals of developing an electromotive force or voltage across opposite faces when subjected to a mechanical strain, and, conversely, of altering in size when subjected to an electromotive force. This effect is utilized in devices used for frequency control and measurement, crystal filters and transducers (q.v.).

PIG. Family of mammals (Suidae) in the order Ungulata. Domesticated Ps. are derived from the European wild boar (*Sus scrofa*), crossed with Asiatic breeds. The chief modification is the concave face, the wild swine having a long snout. The modern housewife's preference for lean meat has led to the development of a hybrid heavy P. combining the good qualities of the Landrace, Saddleback and Large White breeds.

PIGEON. General term for members of the family Columbidae, sometimes also called doves, distinguished by their large crops which, becoming glandular in the breeding season, secrete a milky fluid (so-called 'P.'s milk') which aids digestion of food for the young. There are many species, one of the most important being the blue rock-P. (*Columba livia*) from which the domesticated varieties derive (pouter, fantail, homer, etc.). Similar is the stock-dove (*C. oenas*), but the wood-P. (*C. palumbus*) is much larger and has white patches on the neck. The American species incl. the passenger-P. (*Ectopistes migratorius*), once millions strong but extinct from 1914, and the mourning-doves, which (like the European turtle-doves) live much on the ground. The painted Ps. and fruit Ps. of Australasia and the Malay regions are beautifully coloured.

P.-flying is a popular sport in many Continental countries, as well as Britain (where the National Homing Union has a racing P. manager), and the U.S.A.

PIGOTT (pig´ot), **Richard** (1828–89). Irish forger, who sold *The Times* in 1886 a number of documents

PIGEON. All members of the family are noted for their noisy calls, but the mourning-dove (*Zenaidura carolinensis*) of North and Central America has a peculiarly low and melancholy note. Here the female broods its young on a flimsy nest of twigs and grasses. *Photo: G. Ronald Austing*

purporting to prove the complicity of Parnell and other Irish leaders in political murders. These were proved to be forgeries, and P. committed suicide.

PIGS, Bay of. Inlet on the S. coast of Cuba *c*. 90 m. S.W. of Havana, site of an unsuccessful invasion attempt by 1500 anti-Castro Cuban exiles 17–20 April 1961; 1173 were taken prisoner. The creation of this anti-revolutionary force in the U.S.A. by the C.I.A. had been authorized by the Eisenhower admin. and the project executed under that of J. F. Kennedy.

PIKE. Genus of freshwater fish (*Esox*). Found both in Europe and N. America the common P. (*E. lucius*) has a long body, and broad flattened head with a large mouth studded with backward-pointing teeth; grey-green mottled yellow above, it is white underneath. Sluggish in habit except when pursuing its prey, it is a voracious feeder and mature specimens may reach over 50 lb. Some of the smaller species of American P. are known as 'pickerel'.

PIKE-PERCH. Genus of freshwater fish (*Lucioperca*) of the order Percomorphi. The European P.-P. (*Lucioperca sandra*) reaches a length of 3 or 4 ft., is very voracious, and of some value as a food fish. Related species are found in N. America.

PILATE, Pontius. Roman procurator of Judaea A.D. 26–A.D. 36. Unsympathetic to the Jews, his actions several times provoked riots, and in A.D. 36 he was recalled to Rome to account for disorder in Samaria. Eusebius says he committed suicide.

PILÂTRE DE ROZIER, Jean François (1754–85). French balloonist, who was killed while attempting to fly the English Channel.

PILCHARD. Fish (*Sardina pilchardis*) of the herring family (*Clupeidae*). Bluish-green above and silvery beneath, it grows to *c*. 10 in. long: the chief P. fisheries are off Spain and Portugal.

PILES. Haemorrhoids; varicose veins of the anus. They may be external (covered with skin) or, more commonly, internal (covered with mucous membrane). The cause is increase of pressure in the abdomen, as in childbirth, or constipation. The veins often bleed on defecation; or are extruded from the anus. The remedy is either to remove the piles by cutting or cauterizing, or to harden and close the veins off by injection of a 'sclerosing' fluid.

PILGRIMAGE. Journey to sacred places inspired by religious devotion. For Hindus the holy places incl. Benares and the purifying Ganges; for Buddhists the spots connected with the crises of Buddha's career; for the ancient Greeks the shrines at Delphi, Ephesus, etc.; for the Jews, the sanctuary at Jerusalem; and for Mohammedans, Mecca. Among Christians, Ps. were common by the 2nd cent., and as a direct result of the estab. necessity of making Ps. there arose the numerous hospices catering for pilgrims, the religious orders of knighthood, and the Crusades. The great centres of Christian P. have been, or are, Jerusalem,

Rome, the tomb of St. James of Compostella in Spain, the shrine of Becket at Canterbury, and the holy places at La Salette and Lourdes in France.

PILGRIMAGE OF GRACE. The rebellion of 1536-7 in Lincs and Yorks. In character it was both a movement of the feudal nobility and clergy against the dissolution of the monasteries and Henry VIII's centralizing policy, and a peasant revolt against the enclosure of common lands. The rebels were dispersed by promises, and then executed in large numbers.

PILGRIM FATHERS. Name given to the emigrants who sailed from Plymouth in the *Mayflower* in 1620, and founded the colony of New Plymouth, Mass. Not a quarter of them were Puritan refugees. *See also* DARTMOUTH.

PILGRIMS' WAY. Track running from Winchester to Canterbury, England, which was the route of medieval pilgrims visiting the shrine of Thomas à Becket. Some 120 m. long, the P.W. can still be traced for more than half its length.

PILGRIM TRUST. *See* HARKNESS, EDWARD.

PILLORY. Instrument of punishment consisting of

a wooden frame set on a post, with holes in which the prisoner's head and hands were secured. Its use was abolished in England in 1837.

PILNYAK (pĕlnyahk´), **Boris.** Pseudonym of Russian author Boris Andreyevich Vogau (1894–c. 1937). The somewhat ambiguous tone of his best-known novel *The Volga Falls to the Caspian Sea* (1930), ostensibly supporting the first Five Year Plan but also critical of the Revolution, was received with suspicion. He may have been a victim of the 1936-7 purge.

PILLORY

PILSEN. German form of PLZEN.

PILSUDSKI (pilsood´ski), **Joseph** (1867–1935). Polish statesman. B. in Russian Poland, he founded the Polish Socialist Party in 1892, and was twice imprisoned for anti-Russian activities. During the F.W.W. he commanded a Polish force to fight for Germany, but fell under suspicion of intriguing with the Allies, and in 1917–18 was imprisoned by the Germans. When Poland became independent he was elected Chief of State, and led the unsuccessful Polish attack on Russia in 1920. He retired in 1923, but in 1926 led a military coup which estab. his dictatorship until his death.

PILTDOWN MAN. Fossilized, fragmentary skull which Charles Dawson (d. 1916) 'discovered' at Piltdown in Sussex in 1912. Long believed to represent the oldest human species found in Europe, it was proved a hoax in 1953. The jaw was that of an orangutan, and the cranial bones (though both human and ancient) could not have come from this site.

PIMENTO. Genus of trees found in tropical America. The dried fruits of the species *Pimenta officinalis* are used as spice.

PIMPERNEL. Genus of plants (*Anagallis*) in the family Primulaceae. The Scarlet P. (*A. arvensis*) grows in cornfields and is easy to overlook, since the flowers open only in full sunshine. It is naturalized in N. America.

PINDAR. (*c.* 522 B.C.–442 B.C.). Greek lyric poet. B. near Thebes, he excelled in the choral lyric.

PINDLING, (Lynden) Oscar (1930–). Bahamas statesman. After studying law in London, he returned to the is. to join the newly-formed Progressive Liberal Party, and then became the first Negro Prime

PINEAPPLE. Originally a native of South and Central America, the pineapple is now one of Queensland's most important crops, as at this farm on the coast. Other producing areas are the Philippines, Hawaii, and Malaya.
Courtesy of the Agent-General for Queensland.

Minister of the Bahamas in 1967.

PINE. Genus (*Pinus*) of some 70 species of evergreen coniferous trees, of which the Scots P. (*P. sylvestris*) is grown commercially for soft timber (deal) and its yield of turpentine, tar, pitch, etc. The oldest living thing is probably the bristlecone P. (*P. aristata*), native to California, of which some specimens are said to be *c.* 4,600 years old.

PINEAPPLE. Plant (*Ananas comosus*) native to S. and Central America, now cultivated in many other tropical areas, e.g. Queensland. The mauvish flowers are produced midway in the 2nd year, and subsequently consolidate with their bracts into a fleshy fruit. For export to world markets the fruits are cut unripe and lack the sweet juiciness typical of the tinned P. (usually the smoother-skinned Cayenne variety) which is allowed to mature fully.

PINE'RO, Sir Arthur Wing (1855–1934). British dramatist. B. in London, of Jewish extraction, he became an actor, beginning to write for the stage in 1877. He wrote farces such as *Dandy Dick* (1887), the sentimental *Sweet Lavender*; and the problem plays *The Second Mrs. Tanqueray* (1893), *The Notorious Mrs. Ebbsmith* (1895), and *Mid-Channel* (1909); and *Trelawny of the Wells* (1898).

PINK. *See* CARNATION.

PINKERTON, Allan (1819–84). American detective. B. in Glasgow, he emigrated to the U.S.A. in 1842, where in 1852 he founded P.'s National Detective Agency. In 1861 he prevented a plot to assassinate Lincoln, and from his espionage system, built up in the Civil War, created the Federal secret service.

PINKIANG. Japanese form of HARBIN.

PINKIE. Spot near Musselburgh, Midlothian, Scotland, which was the scene of a defeat of the Scots by the English in 1547.

PINT. Liquid measure of capacity, $\frac{1}{2}$ of a quart, $\frac{1}{8}$ of a gallon; equivalent to 20 fluid oz. in U.K., and 16 fluid oz. in U.S.A.

PI'NTER, Harold (1930–). British dramatist. Of Jewish stock, he had a rigorous training as an actor in provincial repertory 1949–57. *The Caretaker* (1960) brought him success as a playwright, but *The Birthday Party*, produced in 1958, while he was actually working as a caretaker, was a dismal failure. Always concerned with the breakdown of communication between individuals, he essayed a sophisticated sexual level in the acid *The Lover* (1962). He writes also for radio and television.

PINTURICCHIO (pintoorik´kēō) (1454–1513). Italian painter whose real name was Bernardino di Betti. B. at Perugia, he assisted Perugino in decorating the Sistine Chapel, Rome.

PIO'ZZI, Hester Lynch (1741–1821). British author. B. in Caernarvonshire, *née* Salisbury, she m. Henry Thrale in 1763, and in 1765 was introduced to Samuel Johnson, whose friendship she retained until after 3 years' widowhood she m. the musician Gabriele P. in 1784. In 1786 she pub. *Anecdotes of the late S. Johnson*, and in 1788 her correspondence with him.

PIPER, John (1903–). British artist. B. at Epsom, the son of a solicitor, he studied at the R.C.A. and the Slade. From early landscapes of southern England, he went on in the-thirties to two-dimensional abstracts; to pictures of air-raid destruction in the S.W.W., such as the House of Commons and Bath; then to architectural compositions against romantic backgrounds; theatrical settings, e.g. for the operas of Britten; and a window for Coventry Cathedral and panels for the lantern at Liverpool R.C. Cathedral.

PIPIT. Several genera of birds in the family Motacillidae allied to the wagtails, but looking like larks. The European meadow P. (*A. pratensis*) is about the size of a sparrow and streaky brown.

PIRACY. The taking of a ship, or any of its contents, from lawful ownership while on the high seas, punishable under international law by the court of any country where the pirate may be found or taken. Algiers (*see* CORSAIRS), the West Indies (*see* BUCCANEERS), the coast of Trucial Oman (the Pirate Coast), Chinese and Malay waters, and such hideouts as Lundy Is., were long pirate haunts, but modern communications and the complexities of supplying and servicing modern vessels tend to eliminate P. On land similar techniques, known as hijacking, have been applied to long-distance lorries or trucks, and also to aircraft.

PIRAEUS (pīrē'us). Port of both ancient and modern Athens and first port of Greece, on the Gulf of Aegina. Constructed as the port of Athens, *c.* 493 B.C., it was linked with that city by the Long Walls (built *c.* 460 B.C.). After the sack by Sulla in 86 B.C., P. declined. Modern P. is an industrial suburb of Athens, to which it is joined administratively; a fiscal-free zone covering 70 sq. m. was estab. at P. in 1932.

PI'RAN, St. (fl. 500). Patron saint of tinminers, and so of Cornwall and the Cornish nationalist movement. He was sent as a missionary by St. Patrick, and there are remains of his oratory at Perranzabuloe: feast day 5th March.

PIRANDELLO (pērahndel'lō), **Luigi** (1867–1936). Italian writer. B. in Sicily, he settled as a teacher in Rome, and won fame with the novel *The Late Mattia Pascal* (1904) and with numerous short stories. His first venture in the field of drama was *La Morsa* (1912), which was followed by *Six Characters in Search of an Author* (1921), *Henry IV* (1922), etc. In 1934 he received the Nobel prize for literature.

PIRANHA (pirah'nya). S. American fresh-water fish (*Serrasalmo piraya*) found in the Amazon. About 1 ft. long and with razor-edge teeth, they rapidly devour men or animals, espec. if attracted by blood.

PISA (pē'sah). City in Tuscany, Italy, cap. of P. province, on the Arno, 7 m. from the sea. It has an 11th–12th cent. cathedral, the Leaning Tower or campanile, and a univ. (1338). Cotton and silk are manufactured. Founded by Greek colonists, then an Etruscan and a Roman city, P. was in the 11th–14th cents. an independent naval rep. Gombo, off which Shelley was drowned in 1822, is 1½ m. W. Pop. (1961) 91,108.

PISANO (pēzah'nō), **Andrea.** Assumed name of the Italian sculptor Andrea da Pontaderra (1270–1348), whose works incl. one of the doors of the Florentine baptistery and sculptures in the campanile.

PISANO, Niccola (*c.* 1225–*c.* 1278). Italian sculptor who produced pulpits at Siena and Pisa, and the shrine of St. Dominic at Bologna. His son, **Giovanni P.** (1250–1317), was also a sculptor, and designed pulpits.

PISANO, Vittore (1397–1455). Italian artist, called **Pisanello**, chiefly celebrated as a medallist.

PISI'STRATUS (*c.* 605–527 B.C.). Athenian statesman. Although of noble family, he assumed the leadership of the peasant party, and seized power in 561. He was twice expelled, but recovered power from 541 till his death. Ruling as a dictator under constitutional forms, he first had the Homeric poems written down, and founded Greek drama by introducing the Dionysiac peasant festivals into Athens.

PISSARRO, Camille (1830–1903). French painter. B. in the West Indies, he studied under Corot, and became a leader of the Impressionist movement. His son **Lucien P.** (1863–1944), a landscape painter and engraver, came to England in 1890 and in 1916 became a naturalized Englishman.

PISTOIA (pistō'yah). Italian city, cap. of P. prov., 10 m. N.W. of Florence. It is surrounded by walls (1302) and has a cathedral dating from the 12th cent. Steel and small arms, paper, macaroni, and olive oil are produced. P. was the site of Catiline's defeat, 62 c. Pop. (1961) 82,401.

PISTOL. Small firearm (q.v.) designed for one-hand use. Ps. were in use from the early 15th cent. and their evolution closely parallels that of the corresponding shoulder arm. Throughout its history the P. has appealed to the ingenuity of untold numbers of inventors who succeeded in combining it with battle axes, holy-water sprinklers, daggers, bicycle handles, fountain pens, etc. The problem of firing more than once without reloading was tackled by using many combinations of multiple barrels, both stationary and revolving, and although a breech-loading, multi-chambered revolver of 1650 still survives, the first practical solution was Samuel Colt's six-gun (1847). Behind a single barrel, a short 6-chambered cylinder was rotated by cocking the hammer, and a fresh round brought into place. The automatic pistol, operated by gas or recoil, was preferred by the military in many

PISA. On the north-west of the town are the cathedral and famous leaning tower. Weighing 14,000 tons and 179 ft. high, and with foundations only about 10 ft. deep, the tower slopes more each year – about one-eighth of a millimetre – and is nearly 17 ft. from perpendicular, so that the problem of how to prevent it from falling is urgent. Galileo did not make experiments, as legend claims, from the tower's summit.

Photo: A. W. Kerr.

PITCAIRN. The safe arrival of stores is vital, and here oil drums are being carried up the beach after being ferried ashore from the tanker in one of the island 'whale' boats – seen under the thatched roof to the left.
Courtesy of British Petroleum.

countries, but others still favoured the revolver.

PITCAIRN. Island in the Pacific, *c.* 3,300 m. E.N.E. of New Zealand. Discovered in 1767, it was uninhabited until occupied in 1790 by the *Bounty* mutineers, whose presence was discovered in 1808; the present inhabitants are descended from them. Area 2 sq. m.; pop. (1969) 74. The uninhabited islands of Henderson, Ducie, and Oeno, annexed in 1902, were attached to P., which is a British colony.

PITCH (Acoustics). The position of a note in the musical scale; this depends on the frequency of the predominant sound wave. A standard P. was agreed at an international conference in 1939, A above middle C having a frequency of 440.

P. has many other meanings, e.g. the ratio of the rise to the span of a roof, the distance between adjacent turns of a screw thread, the distance an aeroplane advances along its flight path for one revolution of the propeller, the distance between the centre lines of rivets in rows parallel to the seam of a riveted joint, the distance between perforations on the edges of cinema films, etc.

PITCHBLENDE, or **Uranite.** An ore consisting mainly of uranium oxide U_3O_8, but also containing radioactive salt of radium $RaBr_2$, first separated by the Curies in 1898 from P. from N. Bohemia, in which it occurs in about 1 part in 3 million.

PITMAN, Sir Isaac (1813–97). British phonographer. B. in Wilts, he became a teacher, and after studying Samuel Taylor's scheme for shorthand writing, pub. in 1837 his own system, *Stenographic Soundhand*, speedy and accurate, and adapted for use in many languages. A simplified *PitmanScript*, combining letters and signs, was devised 1971 by Emily D. Smith. His grandson **Sir (Isaac) James P.** (1901–   ) devised the 44-letter Initial Teaching Alphabet adopted on a wide scale in the 1960s to help children to read.

PITT, William (1759–1805). British Tory statesman. The son of Lord Chatham (q.v.) he entered parliament

in 1781 as a 'Chathamite' Whig, and took office as Chancellor of the Exchequer in Shelburne's govt. of 1782–3. He became P.M., with the support of the Tories and 'king's friends', in 1783. His main achieve-, ments were his reorganization of the national finances and his commercial treaty with France for reciprocal reduction of tariffs. He allowed the country to drift into war with France in 1793 and had little success in his conduct of the war. After 1792 he conducted a policy of repression of all advocates of reform, which in Ireland provoked a rebellion in 1798. To solve the Irish question he carried through the Act of Union in 1800, but resigned in 1801 when George III refused to accept Catholic emancipation. He returned to office in 1804, and set himself to build up a coalition with Austria and Russia against Napoleon. The news of the defeat of Austerlitz destroyed his hopes; he d. broken-hearted, and was buried in Westminster Abbey.

PITT-RIVERS, Augustus Henry (1827–1900). British archaeologist, *né* Lane-Fox, who assumed the surname P.-R. on succeeding to the estates of his great uncle, the 2nd Lord Rivers. Entering the Grenadiers, he later became a lieut-.gen., and his earliest interests were in firearms, but on his accession to lands rich in archaeological sites he commenced a series of model excavations recorded in *Excavations in Cranbourne Chase* pub. privately from 1887. He was remarkable for his brilliant pioneer recording methods, use of stratification, and recognition of the importance of humble objects. The *P.-R. Museum* at Oxford houses 1,000,000 ethnographic items, and a new extended complex is planned.

PITTSBURGH. Second city of Pennsylvania, U.S.A., at the confluence of the Allegheny and Monongahela to form the Ohio. It is a great port, at the centre of a region producing coal, natural gas, and petroleum. Steel is the main product, but P.'s many industries also incl. shipbuilding; making of glass, aluminium, bricks, pottery; and nuclear energy. P., on the site of Fort Duquesne estab. by the French in 1754, was substantially reconstructed during the 1940s and 1950s. P. univ. (1787) rises to a height of 535 ft. (42 storeys). Pop met. area (1970) 2,382,477.

PITU'ITARY GLAND The most important of the endocrine or ductless glands. About the size of a pea, it is attached to the base of the brain in the 'Turkish saddle', and is divided into 2 distinct lobes. From the

PITTSBURGH. At the point where the Allegheny (left) and Monongahela (right) meet to form the Ohio river is the 'golden triangle', one of the world's most concentrated business centres. Its apex (lower left), formerly a conglomeration of buildings, etc., has been planned as a well-laid-out pleasure ground.
Courtesy of the Chamber of Commerce of Greater Pittsburgh

anterior lobe hormones are obtained which control the activities of other glands (thyroid, gonads and adrenal cortex); and direct-acting hormones affecting milk secretion, and controlling growth. Secretions of the posterior lobe regulate body water balance, contraction of the uterus, etc. A highly complex gland, and 'Master of the Endocrine Orchestra'.

PIUS. Name of 12 popes. **Pius II** (1405–64) achieved fame in early life as an author under the name of Aeneas Silvius. As pope 1458–64 he attempted unsuccessfully to organize a crusade against the Turks. **Pius IV** (1499–1565), a member of the Medici family, became pope in 1559; he reassembled the Council of Trent, and completed its work in 1563. **Pius V** (1504–72), elected in 1566, excommunicated Queen Elizabeth, and organized the expedition against the Turks which won the victory of Lepanto. **Pius VI** (1717–99), elected in 1775, strongly opposed the French Revolution, and d. a prisoner in French hands. His successor in 1800, **Pius VII** (1740–1823), concluded a concordat with France in 1801, and took part in Napoleon's coronation, but was a prisoner 1809–14. After his return to Rome in 1814 he revived the Jesuit order. **Pius IX** (1792–1878) became pope in 1846. He never accepted the incorporation of the Papal States and of Rome in the kingdom of Italy, and proclaimed in 1854 the dogma of the immaculate conception of the Virgin and in 1870 that of papal infallibility. His pontificate was the longest in history. **Pius X** (1835–1914), pope from 1903, canonized 1954, condemned modernism in a manifesto of 1907. **Pius XI** (Achille Ratti, 1857–1939). Nuncio to Poland in 1919 and archbp. of Milan in 1921, he was elected pope in 1922. The Lateran Treaty with Italy was signed in 1929. In his encyclicals he condemned Nazism and anti-Semitism as well as Communism. **Pius XII** (Eugenio Pacelli, 1876–1958). After distinguishing himself as papal nuncio from 1917, he was appointed cardinal in 1929, and Papal Sec. of State in 1930. Elected pope in 1939, he opposed anti-Semitism during the S.W.W. (though his attitude has been the subject of controversy) and made many peace appeals. His proclamation of the new dogma of the bodily assumption of the Virgin Mary (1950) and his restatement of the doctrine that the life of an infant must not be sacrificed to save a mother in labour (1951) roused Protestant criticism. He was subject to visions.

PIZARRO (pĕthahr'rō), **Francisco** (c. 1475–1541). Spanish conqueror of Peru. He took part in the expeditions of Balboa and others. In 1526–7 he explored the N.W. coast of S. America, and in 1530 with 180 followers conquered Peru. The Inca was treacherously seized and murdered. In 1535 P. founded Lima. A feud now began between the Spanish leaders, and P. was assassinated. His half-brother **Gonzalo P.** (c. 1505–48) explored the region E. of Quito 1541–2. He made himself governor in Peru 1544, but was defeated and executed.

PIZZETTI (pĕtset'tē), **Ildebrando** (1880–1968). Italian composer. B. at Parma, he became director of the conservatoire at Milan and in 1936 prof. at the Academy of St. Cecilia, Rome. One of the foremost contemporary Italian composers, he had his operatic version of T. S. Eliot's *Murder in the Cathedral* performed in Milan in 1958.

PLACE, Francis (1771–1854). British Radical. A tailor by trade, he showed great powers as a political organizer and made Westminster a centre of Radicalism. He secured the repeal of the Combination Acts in 1824.

PLAGUE (plāg). Severe infectious disease marked in the classic form by swelling of the buboes or lymphatic glands, hence 'bubonic' P. It is most common in the tropics, India, China, S. America, etc. In medieval Europe it was known as the Black Death (q.v.), but died out when the black rat, through whose fleas it was principally transmitted, was exterminated

by the brown: in the U.S. it has seldom occurred. Incubation is 2–5 days, followed by fever and a state like drunkenness, and death within a week in 25 per cent of cases. Even more virulent are the septicaemic and pneumonic forms, the latter being invariably fatal until the introduction of sulpha drugs and various antibiotics.

PLAICE. Food-fish (*Pleuronectes platessa*) belonging to the flat-fish group, abundant in N. European waters. It is white beneath and brownish with orange spots on the 'eyed' side.

PLANCK (plahnk), **Max** (1858–1947). German phy̆sicist and framer in 1900 of the Quantum Theory. B. at Kiel, he was appointed to the chair of physics at Kiel in 1885, and at Berlin in 1889, and 1930–7 was Pres. of the Kaiser Wilhelm Institute. His writings incl. *Prinzip der Erhaltung der Energie, Einleitung in die theoretische Physik*, and *Where is Science Going?*. An F.R.S. from 1926, he was awarded the Nobel prize for Physics in 1918.

PLANE. Genus of trees (*Platanus*). Species inc. the Oriental P. (*P. orientalis*), a favourite plantation tree of the Greeks and Romans; the London P. (*P. acerifolia*), with palmate 3-lobed (instead of 5-lobed) leaves, which throws off city smog by the smoothness of its foliage and shedding its bark annually in large flakes; and the American P. or buttonwood (*P. occidentalis*). All have pendulous burr-like fruit and are among the handsomest of trees, being capable of growth to 100 ft. high.

PLANETÄRIUM. Optical projection device by means of which the motions of the stars and planets are reproduced for educational purposes on a domed ceiling representing the sky as it appears from Earth.

PLANETARY PROBE. A vehicle sent near, or to, another planet. The guidance and launching techniques are much more complex than with lunar probes, owing to the distances involved; communication problems are also increased. The first really successful vehicle of this type was the U.S. Mariner II, which passed within 25,000 miles of Venus in 1962 (14 Dec.), and sent back information which caused a drastic revision about all previous ideas of Venus as a world. At the present stage of technical development, it seems that only Venus and Mars are within range of such probes.

PLANETARIUM. Three schoolchildren listen to an explanation of the complex mechanism of the Zeiss projector which took the German technicians two months to erect in London. Behind them can be seen a realistic 'skyline'.
Courtesy of The London Planetarium Co. Ltd

TABLE OF THE PLANETS

Name	Mean dist. (millions of m. from Sun)	Period of sidereal revolution in years	Mean diam. in miles	Axial rotation (sidereal)
Mercury	36·0	0·24	3,000	88 days
Venus	67·2	0·62	7,600	243½ ,,
Earth	92·9	1·00	7,927	23 h. 56 m.
Mars	141·6	1·88	4,200	24 h. 37 m. 23 s.
Jupiter	483·3	11·86	88,700	9 h. 55 m.
Saturn	886·0	29·46	74,100	10 h. 14 m.
Uranus	1,782·8	84·02	29,300	c. 11 h.
Neptune	2,793·5	164·8	30,500	c. 16 h.
Pluto	c. 3,666	248	c. 3,650	—

PLANETS. Non-luminous globes revolving around the Sun at various distances and in various periods. Nine Ps. are known; in order of distance from the Sun, they are Mercury, Venus, the Earth, Mars, Jupiter, Saturn, Uranus, Neptune and Pluto. Of these, the first 4, and Pluto, are relatively small, solid bodies; the rest are giants, much larger than the Earth, and with gaseous surfaces. Five planets were known from very ancient times: Uranus was discovered in 1781, Neptune in 1846 and Pluto in 1930.

PLANIMETER. A simple integrating instrument for measuring the area of a plane surface. It consists of 2 hinged arms; one is kept fixed and the other is traced round the boundary of the area. This actuates a small graduated wheel and the area is found from its change in position.

PLANKTON. A term used first by Victor Hensen to denote those small forms of animal and plant life which float or drift in water.

PLANT. Many of the lower plants consist of a single body or thallus upon which the organs of reproduction are borne. Simplest of all are the thread-like waterplants, e.g. *Spirogyra*, which consist of a chain of cells containing chloroplasts, which are responsible for the green colour of the P. and for the provision of its food. The seaweeds and mosses possess a further development of the simple chain of cells in their multi-cellular, simple bodies which have specially modified areas in which the reproductive organs are carried. Higher in the morphological scale are the ferns, which produce leaf-like fronds bearing on their under-surface incrustations in which the spores are carried. The spores are freed and germinate to produce small independent bodies carrying the sexual organs; thus the fern has 2 generations in its life cycle.

The flowering Ps. are by far the largest group, and structurally the most complex. The flowering P. is divided into 3 parts, root, stem, and leaves. Roots may be scattered and fibrous, as in the majority of garden annuals, or developed into a swollen food reserve such as the carrot, turnip, or sugar beet. Stems grow above or below ground. Their cellular structure is designed to carry water and salts in solution from the roots, which have obtained the nourishment from the soil, to the leaves, where they are manufactured into P. food. Underground stems sometimes bear tubers, e.g. potatoes, or fruits, e.g. ground-nuts, while some are prized as economic products, e.g. ginger. Aerial stems occasionally develop food reserves as in the sugar cane, but are more usually merely a means of support for the leaves. The leaves, which are often highly modified, manufacture the food of the P. by means of the chlorophyll which they contain. Flowers are modified leaves arranged in groups and enclosing the reproductive organs from which the fruits and seeds result.

Classification. The classification of Ps. is based on a number of characters. Ps. are grouped by their similarities of constitution into species, within which minor differences are marked as strains and varieties. Species bearing a resemblance to one another are grouped into genera, and similar genera into families. These are classed in the larger divisions cohorts and classes. The principal groups are shown in the Table. *See also* BOTANY; BREEDING; FLOWER.

PLANTA'GENET. Name commonly applied to the royal house of England reigning 1154–1399. It was originally a nickname of Geoffrey, count of Anjou, father of Henry II, who usually wore a sprig of broom (*planta genista*) in his hat, and it was revived *c.* 1450 as a surname by Richard, duke of York, to emphasize the superiority of his claim to the throne to that of Henry VI.

PLANTAIN. Genus of plants (*Plantago*) which are troublesome weeds in lawns, etc., e.g. the great P. (*P. major*) with oval leaves, grooved stalks and a spike of green flowers with purple anthers followed by seeds liked by cage-birds. The name is also given to the genus *Musa* in the tropics: *see* BANANA.

PLANTIN (plontan'), **Christophe** (1514–89). French printer. B. near Tours, he set up his printing house at Antwerp in 1555. The P. type which he designed is still in use.

PLASSEY (plas'ē). Village in W. Bengal, India, on the Bhagirathi r., 31 m. N.N.W. of Krishnagar; it has sugar mills and produces rice, jute, and linseed. It gave its name to Clive's victory in 1757 over Suraj-ud-Dowlah, but the site of the battle had by 1801 been eaten away by the river.

PLASTER OF PARIS. Calcined gypsum which is mixed with water (1 part gypsum, 2¼ parts water) to form a thin paste which later hardens. It is used for taking casts, moulds, etc., and in orthopaedic surgery for setting fractured bones. It is manufactured near Paris: hence the name.

PLASTICS. Synthetic materials which are normally stable, but are plastic at some period during their manufacture. Formerly plastic materials were derived from coal, but since the 1950s the basic materials, espec. for thermoplastics, come from petroleum (q.v.) derivatives. Fast replacing metal and wood in many fields, Ps. (mostly polymers) are used particularly in household equipment, the construction of houses, ships, aircraft (notably the lightweight carbon-fibre-reinforced Ps. developed in the 1960s), and cars, and the electrical industry. They are processed by extrusion, injection moulding, vacuum forming and compression, and can be formed with different consistencies, ranging from hard and rigid, to soft and rubbery. *See* POLYMERIZATION.

PLASTIC SURGERY. The surgical repair of seriously damaged tissues. During the 2 wars a wide variety of methods have been developed whereby surgeons can restore faces that have been almost

CLASSIFICATION OF PLANTS

Class	
Phylum I: **Thallophyta**	
1 **Algae**	Algae, diatoms, etc.
2 **Charophyta**	Stoneworts.
3 **Myxomycetes**	Slime fungi.
4 **Bacteria**	
5 **Fungi**	Moulds toadstools, puff-balls, lichens, etc.
Phylum II: **Archegoniatae**	
1 **Bryophyta**	Liverworts, mosses.
2 **Pteridophyta**	Ferns, fossils, horsetails, club mosses.
Phylum III: **Spermophyta**	
1 **Pteridospermeae**	Fossils.
2 **Gymnospermeae**	Cycads, fossils, maidenhair tree, cone-bearing trees.
3 **Angiosperms**	Flowering plants: (i) Monocotyledons—orchids, grasses, sedges, lilies. (ii) Dicotyledons—families of daisy, pea, coffee, spurge, carrot and sage.

entirely destroyed, replace burnt skin, mend damaged nerves, and perform many other surgical marvels. These operations need careful planning and often take months or years to complete.

PLATA, Rio de la. Spanish name for the river PLATE.

PLATE, River. The estuary into which flow the Parana and Uruguay rivers, on the E. coast of S. America. It is 200 m. long and from 20 to 145 m. wide, and receives the waters draining much of Paraguay, Argentina, Uruguay, Bolivia, and Brazil: all 5 countries agreed 1968 to co-operate in developing the P. basin. Diaz de Solis discovered the estuary *c.* 1515. In Dec. 1939 the German 'pocket-battleship' *Admiral Graf Spee* (14,000 tons) was sunk here by the British cruisers H.M.S. *Exeter, Achilles,* and *Ajax.*

PLATINUM (Span. *platina,* little silver). Greyish-white, ductile and malleable metal, density 21·45, melting point 1773·5°C, untarnishable in air and very resistant to heat and strong acids: symbol Pt., at. wt. 195·09, at. no. 78. P. occurs as the metal, and alloyed with iridium, osmium and other metals of the same group, and with gold and iron, especially in the Urals, S. Africa, Canada and the U.S.A. Both pure and in alloy, it is used extensively in jewellery, dentistry and the chemical industry (in finely divided form, P. acts as a catalyst). It is employed for switch contacts because of its durability; and is valuable in scientific apparatus because P. wires can be sealed gas-tight, through glass.

PLATO (*c.* 428–*c.* 348 B.C.). Athenian philosopher. He early entered politics on the aristocratic side, and in philosophy became a follower of Socrates. He travelled widely, and on his return to Athens, *c.* 387, he founded his Academy, in order to train a new ruling class. He twice visited Syracuse in the hope of playing a part in politics, without success. Of P.'s works *c.* 30 dialogues survive, in which ethical and philosophical problems are discussed. Typical examples are the *Symposium,* on love; the *Ion,* on poetry; the *Phaedo,* on the immortality of the soul; and the *Apology* and *Crito,* on Socrates' trial and death. In many dialogues Socrates is the central figure, and it remains uncertain how far the views attributed to him are his, and how far they are P.'s. P.'s philosophy marks a reaction against the scientific rationalism of the Ionian philosophers. He maintained that mind, not matter, is fundamental, and that

material objects are merely imperfect copies of abstract and eternal 'ideas'; hence he rejected experiment as a scientific method in favour of argument. His political philosophy is expounded in the *Republic* and the *Laws,* both descriptions of ideal states.

PLATYPUS (plat′ipus). Small mammal (*Ornithorhynchus paradoxus*) of the order Monotremata, found in Tasmania and E. Australia. Semi-aquatic, it has naked jaws resembling a duck's beak, small eyes and no trace of an external ear. It lives in long burrows in banks of rivers, where it lays eggs in a rough nest. It feeds on waterworms, insects, etc., and when full-grown is *c.* 18 in. long.

PLAUTUS, Titus Maccius (d. 184 B.C.). Roman dramatist. B. in Umbria, he settled in Rome and worked in a bakery before achieving success as a dramatist. He wrote at least 56 comedies, freely adapted from Greek originals, of which 20 survive. Shakespeare based *The Comedy of Errors* on the *Menoechmi.*

PLAYING CARDS. They originated in China, India, or with the Arabs, and appeared in Europe at the end of the 14th cent. In the 15th cent. the pack was gradually simplified and reduced to the present 52. Among the chief card games are Whist, Bridge, Poker (qq.v.), and Rummy. Canasta, a variant of the last-named, was introduced to the U.S. from Argentina in 1949 and later became very popular in Britain.

PLEASENCE, Donald (1919–). British actor. B. in Yorks., he has been especially successful as Leone Gola in Pirandello's *The Rules of the Game,* Davies in Pinter's *The Caretaker,* and in the film *Dr. Crippen,* conveying the sinister aspect of the outcast from society.

PLEBEIANS. The unprivileged class in ancient Rome, composed of aliens and freedmen, and their descendants. During the 5th–4th cents. B.C. they waged a long struggle with the patricians, until they secured admission to the offices formerly reserved for the patricians.

PLEBISCITE (pleb′isit). A direct vote by all the electors of a country or district on a specific question. Since the 18th cent. it has been employed on many occasions to decide to what country a particular area should belong, e.g. in Upper Silesia and elsewhere after the F.W.W., and in the Saar in 1935.

PLÉIADE (plāyahd′), **La.** Group of 7 poets in 16th cent. France led by Ronsard, who were inspired by classical models to the improvement of French verse. They were so called from the 7 stars of the P. group.

PLEIADES (plī-adēz). The 7 daus. of Atlas, who on being pursued by Orion were changed by the gods at their own request to a cluster of stars. *See* illus. p. 856.

PLEKHANOV (plyekhah′nof), **Georgy Valentinovich** (1857–1918). Russian Socialist. He founded the first Russian Marxist organization in 1883, and pub. theoretical works. He collaborated for some years with Lenin.

PLEURISY (plōō′risi). Inflammation of the pleura – a secreting membrane which covers the lungs and also lines the space in which they rest; the 2 surfaces move easily on one another, being lubricated by small quantities of fluid. When it is inflamed the surfaces may dry up or stick together, making breathing difficult and painful. A large volume of fluid may collect in the 'pleural cavity', the space between the 2 surfaces. Pus in the pleural cavity is called empyema.

PLASTICS. A telephone exchange and offices are housed in plastics at the Bakelite factory, Birmingham. The sections are of sandwich construction with a phenolic foam core between two layers of polyester/glass, deriving their strength from a two-directional curve and sealed together by mastic strip. The steel frame rests on concrete footings, the only other site preparation being provision of a raised slab with a channel to drain off rainwater. Even with timber flooring it weighs one-fifth of a conventional building and is easily dismantled and moved.   *Courtesy of Bakelite Ltd.*

PLEIADES. The stars of the Pleiades cluster (the 'Seven Sisters') together with the nebula in which the stars are immersed. The 'spikes' emanating from the stars are, of course, purely photographic effects, since the bright stars had to be somewhat over-exposed in order to record the excessively faint nebula. The nebula shines purely by reflection. *Courtesy of Lick Observatory, Univ. of California.*

P. occurs in pneumonia and tuberculosis, but may also be a consequence of scarlet fever or rheumatism.

PLE′VEN. Bulgarian town, cap. of P. prov. In the Russo-Turkish war of 1877 Osman Pasha was forced by starvation to surrender P. to the Russians after a siege of 5 months. Pop. (1965) 79,234.

PLEVNA. Russian form of PLEVEN.

PLIMSOLL, Samuel (1824–98). British social reformer. B. in Bristol, he sat in parliament as a Radical 1868–80, and through his efforts the Merchant Shipping Act was passed in 1876, providing for Board of Trade inspection of ships, and the compulsory painting of a load line, or P.'s mark, to show the limit to which a ship may be loaded.

PLINLI′MMON or Plynlimon. Mountain in Montgomery, Wales, with 3 summits, the highest 2,468 ft.

PLINY. Name of 2 Roman writers. GAIUS PLINIUS SECUNDUS, or **P. the Elder** (*c.* A.D. 23–79), b. in N. Italy, held political and military posts, and was killed during the eruption of Vesuvius. Besides histories now lost, he wrote a *Natural History* dealing with astronomy, geography, zoology, and mineralogy. His nephew, GAIUS PLINIUS CAECILIUS SECUNDUS, or **P. the Younger** (*c.* 61–113), was gov. of Bithynia, *c.* 111–13, and carried on a correspondence of great historical interest.

PLISETSKAYA, Maiya (1925–). Russian ballerina. Educ. at the Moscow Choreographic School, she succeeded Ulanova as prima ballerina to the Bolshoi Ballet.

PLOESTI (plŏ′yeshti). Town of Rumania, cap. of P. region, 35 m. N. of Bucharest; it is the centre of the country's petroleum wells. Pop. (1966) 146,973.

PLOMER (plŏŏ′mer), **William** (1903–). S. African author and poet. B. at Pietersburg, N. Transvaal, he joined Roy Campbell in editing the literary journal *Voorslag*. His books incl. the novel *The Invaders*, the verse *The Dorking Thigh* (1945) and *Collected Poems* (1960); and the autobiography *Double Lives* (1943).

PLOTI′NUS (*c.* A.D. 204–70). Greek philosopher. B. in Egypt, he settled in Rome in 244, and opened a school of philosophy. His lectures were ed. by his follower Porphyry, who also wrote his life. P. was the founder of the Neoplatonic system, which profoundly influenced early Christian thought.

PLOUGH. The agricultural implement most normally used in tilling the soil. The hand P. consists essen-

tially of a continuous beam, the front of which is attached to the horse, and the rear branches made into guiding handles. In the central depression are the blades designed to cut the soil, first vertically, and then to turn over the subsoil. The P. is of iron, and cuts to a depth of about 7 in., but there are many variants for special uses. The steam P. was patented in 1855. The 20th cent. has brought tractor and multi-furrow Ps.

PLOVDIV (plov′dif). Second town of Bulgaria, cap. of P. prov., on the Maritsa. It makes textiles and leather goods and has tobacco factories. It was founded by Philip of Macedon, to whom it owes its Greek name of Philippopolis (Philip's city). Pop. (1965) 222,737.

PLOVER. Bird in the family Charadriidae, about 10 in. long and with a short bill. The golden P. (*Charadrius pluvialis*), common on British moorlands, has almost black plumage with yellow spots, the underparts being white in winter and black in summer: there are 2 allied American species. The ringed P. (*Aegialitis hiaticula*) with a black and white face, and black band on the throat, is found on British shores, but largest of the ringed Ps. is the killdeer of N. America (*Oxyechus vociferus*), so called because of its cry.

RINGED PLOVER

PLUM. A tree (*Prunus domestica*), bearing an edible drupe. There are many varieties, including the greengage, damson, and sloe. The dried P. is a prune.

PLUMBAGO. *See* GRAPHITE.

PLUTARCH (ploo′tahrk) (*c.* A.D. 46–120). Greek biographer. B. at Chaeronea, he lectured on philosophy at Rome, and was appointed procurator of Greece by Hadrian. His *Parallel Lives* consist of pairs of biographies of Greek and Roman soldiers and statesmen followed by comparisons between the two. North's translation inspired Shakespeare's Roman plays. P. also wrote essays, known as the *Moralia*.

PLUTO (plōō′tō). In Roman mythology, the lord of Hades. He was the brother of Jupiter and Neptune.

PLUTO. The outermost planet. Its average distance from the Sun is 3,666,000,000 miles, but its orbit is decidedly eccentric, and when at its nearest to the Sun it may be closer in than Neptune. It was discovered in 1930 by C. Tombaugh, at the Flagstaff Observatory, as a result of earlier calculations made by Percival Lowell. P. seems to be a small planet, with a diameter of less than 4,000 miles, and is too faint to be seen except with large telescopes. Very little is known about it, but the surface temperature must be below −200°C, and from P. the Sun would appear only as an intensely bright star.

PLUTO′NIUM. Element discovered in 1940 by Seaborg and his co-workers at the Univ. of Calif. by bombarding uranium with deuterons: symbol Pu, at. wt. 242, at. no. 94. Its most stable isotope Pu-239 (discovered 1941) has a half-life of 24,000 years, is fissile, and usually made in reactors by bombarding U-238 with neutrons. It is used in atom bombs, as a fissionable material in reactors, and for enriching the abundant U-238, but has awkward physical properties, and is very poisonous to animals, being absorbed in bone.

PLYMOUTH. English seaport, city (1928), and co. bor. in Devon, at the mouth of the Plym. Hawkins, Drake and the Pilgrim Fathers sailed from P. Sound. The 'Three Towns' of P., Devonport, and Stonehouse were amalgamated in 1914. The city rises N. from the Hoe headland. Devonport has a dockyard, barracks, and large establishments of the Royal Navy; P. is also an important port for civilian shipping. Its chief magistrate was made lord mayor in 1935.

Following heavy bombing in the S.W.W. the city centre was reconstructed, incl. shopping area, law courts, and municipal offices. The Tamar Bridge now gives P. a direct road link with Cornwall, and there has been major post-war industrial development. Pop. (1961) 204,279. See LADY ASTOR.

PLYMOUTH BRETHREN. Christian Protestant sect characterized by extreme simplicity of belief, founded in Dublin c. 1827 by the Rev. John Nelson Darby (1800–82). The movement gained strength and an assembly was held in Plymouth in 1831 (hence the name P.B.) to celebrate its arrival in England, but by 1848 the movement had split into 'Open' and 'Close' B. The latter refuse communion with all those not of their persuasion, and from 1959, under the leadership of 'Big Jim' Taylor of New York, achieved notoriety through such edicts as those forbidding members to belong to any organised body or to eat with unbelievers. The P.B. are found throughout the world, but notably in the fishing villages of N.E. Scotland: membership 80,000.

PLYNLIMON, PLYNLIMMON. See PLINLIMMON.

PLZEN (pil′sen). Old town in Czechoslovakia, cap. of W. Bohemia region, 52 m. S.W. of Prague. It is famous for its lager beer, and is the site also of the Skoda armament works. Pop. (1968) 144,000.

PNEUMONIA. Term is used to describe inflammation of the lung. Based on cause, Ps. are divided into the Specific Ps., which are caused by a specific pathogenic organism; and the Aspiration Ps., in which some abnormality of the lung respiratory system allows the lung to be attacked by non-specific bacteria of low virulence. Treatment of all forms of P. consists of testing the bacteria in sputum, for sensitivity to antibiotics when an appropriate one is applied. This form of treatment has 'wiped out' P. as a hitherto fatal disease.

PNEUMOTHORAX. Invasion of the pleural cavity by air. Normally this cavity contains only a very slight quantity of lubricating substance, so that a vacuum is complete, and when the chest expands the lungs also expand.

PNOM-PENH. See PHNÔM-PENH.

PO. Longest river in Italy, which rises on the Cottian Alps and flows E. to enter the Adriatic through a wide delta. It irrigates the plains of Piedmont and Lombardy. Length c. 415 m. There are natural gas fields in the Po Valley.

POCAHO′NTAS (c. 1595–1617). Red Indian princess who is said to have saved the life of John Smith when he was captured by her father Powhatan; in fact Smith probably invented the story. P. became a Christian, m. an Englishman, and d. at Gravesend.

PŎ′CHARD. Genus of diving ducks incl. the common P. (*Nyroca ferina*) in which the male has a rich red head, black breast and whitish body and wings with black markings; the canvas-back (*Marila vallisneria*), a related species, is especially prized in America as a table bird.

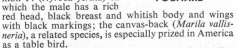

POCHARD

PO CHU-I (772–846). Chinese poet. He held office as president of the Board of War. One of the greatest of the T'ang poets, he cultivated simplicity of style.

PODGORICA. Older name of TITOGRAD.

PODO′LSK. Town in Moscow region, R.S.F.S.R., 25 m. S.W. of Moscow, an industrial centre with petroleum refineries and factories making machinery, sewing machines, cables, cement, ceramics, etc. It received its charter in 1781. Pop. (1967) 160,000.

POE (pō), **Edgar Allan** (1809–49). American author. B. at Boston, he was left an orphan in 1811, and brought up by a Mr. and Mrs. Allan, whose surname

he used as a middle name from 1824. After 3 years in the army 1827–31, he attempted to earn his living by writing, but continued poverty, his addiction to alcohol, and the death of his wife in 1847, seem to have unhinged his mind. His poems have a melancholy lyric beauty and influenced the French symbolist school. His popular reputation rests on his short stories, which specialize either in the creation of horrific atmosphere, e.g. 'The Fall of the House of Usher', or in displays of acute reasoning, e.g. 'The Gold Bug' and 'The Murders in the Rue Morgue', which with their investigators Legrand and Dupin laid the foundation of modern detective fiction.

POET LAUREATE. Poet attached to the royal household. Among the Greeks and Romans the preeminent poet or warrior was awarded a laurel wreath,

POETS LAUREATE

Ben Jonson	1617	Thomas Warton	1785
Sir Wm. Davenant	1638	Henry Pye	1790
John Dryden	1668	Robert Southey	1813
Thomas Shadwell	1689	Wm. Wordsworth	1843
Nahum Tate	1692	Alfred, Lord Tennyson	1850
Nicholas Rowe	1715		
Laurence Eusden	1718	Alfred Austin	1896
Colley Cibber	1730	Robert Bridges	1913
Wm. Whitehead	1757	John Masefield	1930
Cecil Day-Lewis	1968		

hence the modern title of P.L. Among early English poets who had an unofficial status as P.L. were Chaucer, Skelton, Spenser, and Daniel; Jonson had a more definite position, and with Dryden the post was officially estab. There is a stipend of £70 a year, with an extra £27 in lieu of the traditional butt of sack. Although such effusions are no longer obligatory, the P.L. still sometimes produces verses on great national occasions, and is chairman of a committee of 5 poets which awards (usually annually) the King's/Queen's Gold Medal for Poetry, instituted by George V at the suggestion of Masefield.

POETRY. The imaginative expression of emotion or thought, usually in metrical form. In all literatures P. develops to perfection much earlier than prose, largely because it offers greater aids to accurate memorizing before the appearance of writing materials. Most direct in its interpretation of the emotions is lyric P., which incl. such forms as the song, sonnet, ode, elegy, and pastoral. Halfway between lyric and the narrative of the ballad, lay, and epic, is the use of verse in drama. Appealing largely to the intellect on the other hand are moral and didactic P., which incl. satire, parody, and those expositions of philosophical theory, religious doctrine, and practical subjects, which in England have for the most part been confined to prose since the 18th cent.

POGRO M. Russian term, lit. meaning 'devastation', applied to unprovoked attacks on the Jews, especially those carried out with official connivance. The Russian Ps. began in 1881, and were common throughout the country down to the Revolution.

POINCARÉ (pwaṅkahreh′), **Jules Henri** (1854–1912). French mathematician. B. at Nancy, he lectured at Caen and Paris. He developed the fields of pure mathematics, astronomy, and physics.

POINCARÉ, Raymond Nicolas Landry (1860–1934). French statesman, a cousin of Jules Henri P. (q.v.). He became P.M. in 1912, was pres. 1913–20, and again P.M. 1922–4, when he carried out the occupation of the Ruhr, and 1926–9.

POINSE′TTIA. Winter flowering shrub (*Euphorbia pulcherrima*, also known as Mexican Flame-leaf and Christmas-flower), with large red leaves encircling small greenish-yellow flowers. Named after its discoverer, J. R. Poinsett, in 1836, it has recently become a Christmas symbol in the U.S.A. and Canada, although in Mexico it had been known as the Flower of the Holy Night for many years.

POINTILLISM (pwan'tilizm). Technique in oil painting in which dabs of pure colour are applied to the canvas, and arranged in such a way that when viewed from a distance they would blend into harmonious tones. This technique, also known as Neo-Impressionism, was adopted by Seurat, Signac, and others.

POISONS. Substances which when introduced into or applied to the body are capable of injuring health or destroying life, irrespective of temperature or mechanical action. They may be divided into *corrosives*, e.g. sulphuric, nitric, hydrochloric acids, caustic soda, and corrosive sublimate, which burn and destroy the parts with which they come into contact; *irritants* such as arsenic, copper sulphate, zinc chloride, silver nitrate, and green vitriol, which have an irritating effect on the stomach and bowels; *narcotics*, e.g. opium, prussic acid, potassium cyanide, chloroform, carbon monoxide, sewer gases, etc., which affect the brain and spinal cord, inducing a stupor; *narcotico-irritants* which combine intense irritations and finally act as narcotics, e.g. carbolic acid, foxglove, henbane, deadly nightshade (belladonna), tobacco, and many other substances drawn from the vegetable kingdom. In non-corrosive poisoning every effort is made to remove the P. from the system as soon as possible, e.g. usually by vomiting induced by tickling the back of the throat with a feather or administering an emetic. For some corrosive and irritant Ps. there are chemical antidotes. When the P. is unknown, tepid water and an emetic may be administered. In most countries the sale of P. is carefully controlled by law, and, in general, only qualified and registered pharmacists and medical practitioners may dispense them.

POITIERS (pwahtyã'). Town in the Loire basin, cap. of Vienne dept., France. In 507, Alaric II was defeated by Clovis nr. P. and here Charles Martel stemmed the advance of the Saracens in 732. At P. in 1356 Edward the Black Prince defeated the French King John. The cathedral was commenced in 1162. There is a univ. (1431). Pop. (1962) 26,222.

POKER. Universally played card game, originating in 19th cent. America. It has numerous variations. The object is to win stakes, which are almost invariably played for, by obtaining a hand of 5 cards which rank higher than those of opponents. 2 to 8 players participate, bet on their hands, and exchange cards from the pack in turn, until everyone has exactly called the last bet, which is levied for each turn by each player, or has dropped out. The player with the best scoring hand wins the central pool of money. The combinations are as follows: royal flush, ace to ten of one suit; straight flush, 5 of one suit in sequence; 4 of a kind; full house, 3 of a kind, and 2 of a kind; flush, 5 of one suit; straight, 5 cards in sequence; 3 of a kind; 2 pairs; 1 pair.

POLA. Italian form of PULA.

POLAND. A rep. of E. Europe, bounded on the W. by Germany, on the S. by Czechoslovakia, on the N. by the Baltic and Kaliningrad region of the R.S.F.S.R., on the E. by the Lithuanian, White Russian, and Ukrainian S.S.Rs. For the most part undulating, P. is part of the great plain of central Europe, though in the S. it rises, through hills stretching E. from near Wroclaw to the Ukrainian border, into the heights of the Sudeten, Tatra, and Carpathian Mountains on the southern frontier. Of the many rivers, the most important are the Vistula and its chief tributary the W. Bug and the Warta, tributary of the Oder, the lower course of which and its tributary the Neisse form the W. frontier set up in 1945.

ECONOMIC LIFE. P., as it existed before the S.W.W.,

POLAND. In the distance the Vistula flows unchanged, but the Polish parliament building in Warsaw, first built on the country becoming independent in 1918, was completely rebuilt after its destruction in the Second World War.
Courtesy of the Polish Travel Office 'Orbis'

was predominantly agrarian, but changes in its physical structure, particularly the acquisition of almost the whole of the 2 German provs. of Upper and Lower Silesia (a small part of former German Silesia had been allotted to P. after the F.W.W.), and the introduction of govt. planning, enhanced its industrial potential, and by 1960 about one third the pop. was dependent on agriculture. Minerals incl. coal and brown coal, iron, lead, zinc, silver, petroleum and natural gas; cement, fertilizers, steel, textiles, shoes, soap are the chief manufactured products. Potatoes, sugar beet, rye, oats, wheat are the heaviest crops; cattle, pigs, sheep, and horses are reared. Fishing is important.

Chief towns are Warsaw, the cap., Lodz, centre of the textile industry, Krakow (coal and salt mining), Wroclaw, Poznan, Katowice, Lublin, and the ports of Gdansk, Szczecin, and Gdynia.

AREA AND POPULATION. Within the boundaries set up in 1945, the area of P. is 120,330 sq. m.; pop. (1967) 32,065,000. The great majority of those professing a religion are R.C.; the pre-war Jewish pop. of *c*. 3,500,000 has been virtually wiped out, having shrunk to *c*. 30,000.

GOVERNMENT. Under the constitution of 1952 the former pres. was replaced by a 15-member Council of State elected by the Sjem (parliament), itself elected by all citizens over 18. A Council of Ministers is also chosen by the Sjem; but real power rested with the Politbureau (Communist Party Committee).

History. In the 10th cent. the Polish tribes were first united under one ruler, and Christianity was introduced. Under the Jagellon dynasty (1386–1572) P. was united with Lithuania, and became a great power, being the largest and most tolerant country in Europe at the death of Sigismond, last Jagellon, in 1572. Elected kings followed and P.'s strength declined. But Stephen Bathory defeated Ivan the Terrible of Russia in 1581 and in 1683 John III Sobieski vanquished the Turks and forced them to raise their siege of Vienna. In the 18th cent. P. was subjected to pressure by Prussia, Russia, and Austria, ending with the first partition, 1772, which left a much-reduced P. still in existence. A second partition followed in 1793, Prussia and Russia seizing further areas, and, after defeating Tadeusz Kosciuszko who led a patriotic rising, they occupied the rest of the country in 1795 and P. ceased to figure on the map of Europe though it lived on in the spirit of the Polish people. Risings in Russian P. in 1830 and 1863 led to intensified repression and an increased attempt to Russianize the pop.

P. was revived as an independent rep. in 1918, under the leadership of Pilsudski, and was recognized by the Treaty of Versailles, 1919. P. took advantage of Russia's weakness at that time, through war and revolution, to advance into Lithuania and the

Ukraine, the Red Army stopping the Poles before Kiev and driving them back inside P. where in its turn it was defeated by Pilsudski. Russia and P. agreed on a frontier some 150 m. E. of the 'Curzon Line' (q.v.); and Pilsudski remained semi-dictator of P. from 1926 until his death in 1935. In April 1939 the U.K. and France concluded a pact with P. to come to its assistance with military aid if it was attacked. Germany invaded P. from the W. on 1 Sept. and the U.K. and France declared war on Germany on 3 Sept. Russia invaded P. from the E. on 17 Sept.; and by the end of the month Polish resistance was at an end and the country was occupied by Germany and Russia. A govt. in exile was estab. in France, then moved to London in June 1940, and free Polish forces did much to assist the Allied cause.

The Russians drove the Germans from P. 1944–5, and after taking Lublin, 24 July 1944, set up there a national liberation committee which they recognised in Jan. 1945 as the provisional govt. At the Potsdam Conference 1945 the Allies agreed that the part of Germany E. of the Oder-Neisse line and the S. part of E. Prussia should be placed under Polish admin. Nearly half the German pop. of c. $4\frac{1}{2}$ million had fled from these regions before the advancing Russians; the rest were expelled 1946–7. A treaty between Russia and P. in 1945 (ratified 1946) gave P. as E. frontier the Curzon Line with slight modifications in P.'s favour.

By 1947 the Communists, with Russian backing, had gained control of the country, and moderates fled or were imprisoned. Under Gomulka (q.v.) P. took a more liberal independent line after 1956, but nationalist 'Partisans' demonstrated 1968 against low living standards and renewed intellectual restrictions, and attacked 'Zionists' and 'Revisionists'. Pre-war party members (incl. some Jews) had returned from Russian exile in 1945 to fill many high posts, and retained an unpopular Muscovite allegiance. In 1969 Gomulka intervened to halt 'Anti-Zionism', and achieved a compromise allowing increased 'Partisan' influence, but resigned after food price riots in 1970, and was succeeded by Edward Giereck (1913–   ).

POLAR BEAR. *See* BEAR.

PŌLARIZED LIGHT. Ordinary light can be regarded as electromagnetic vibrations at right angles to the line of propagation but in different planes. Light is said to be P. when the vibrations are oriented in a particular direction. Ordinary L. may be plane P. by reflection from a polished surface or by passing it through a Nicol prism or a synthetic polarizing film such as Polaroid, is used to test the strength of sugar solutions, in the measurement of stresses in transparent materials, to prevent glare, etc.

POLDHU (poldū´). Point overlooking Mount's Bay in Cornwall, England, site of Marconi's wireless station (designed by J. A. Fleming, q.v.) from which the first transatlantic signal – 's' in the Morse code – was transmitted to Signal Hill, Newfoundland, on 12 Dec. 1901. A commercial station from 1905, P. maintained vital links with Atlantic convoys during the F.W.W., and its programme broadcasting in 1920 led to the formation of the B.B.C. in 1922. Public transmission ceased in 1922, complete closure following in 1934: the cleared site is now preserved by the National Trust.

POLE, Reginald (1500–58). English churchman. The grandson of the duke of Clarence, brother of Edward IV, he enjoyed the favour of Henry VIII until he opposed his divorce and the royal supremacy. In 1536 he was created a cardinal and settled in Rome. After Mary's accession he returned to England as papal-legate, re-admitted England to the R.C. Church, and succeeded Cranmer as archbp. of Canterbury in 1556.

POLECAT. Species of weasel (*Putorius foetidus*) with light-coloured back and dark belly. The body is about 18 in. long and they have a strong smell.

2E

POLIAKOFF. The perfect balance of his angular forms is enhanced by a use of colour which has invited comparison with that of the early Venetian masters. The artist is seen here at work in his Parisian studio.
Courtesy of the Whitechapel Art Gallery.

POLES. The geographic N. and S. points of penetration of the earth's surface by the axis about which it revolves. The magnetic Ps. are in directions N. and S. at angles of declination to the geographic P. They are the directions towards which a freely suspended magnetic needle will point, and vary continually, both in relation to the geographical poles and according to the point at which the magnetic needle is held.

POLE STAR. The star which is nearest to the celestial N. pole, about 1° distant. It is the brightest of the Ursa Minor constellation, and varies in position slowly. Its position is indicated by the 'pointers' in Ursa Major.

PO′LIAKOFF, Serge (1906–69). Russian artist. B. in Moscow, he was originally a guitarist, settled in France in 1923, and in 1930 took up painting. His work is remarkable for its interlocked shapes and colour harmonies.

POLICE. Force entrusted with the protection of life and property, the preservation of law and order, and the apprehension of offenders. In addition, the P. are responsible for control of traffic. Forces of this type were known in anc. Egypt, Greece, and Rome. In England the first organized P. force was the Bow

POLICE. The Information room at New Scotland Yard: the communications traffic includes almost half a million '999' emergency calls each year.
Photo: Commissioner of Police of the Metropolis.

Street Runners, introduced by Henry Fielding (q.v.) when he was J.P. for Westminster; elsewhere constabulary duties were discharged by individual constables and watchmen commissioned by their local area. In 1829 Peel's govt. passed an act setting up a P. force in London (hence the popular appellation 'peelers'), and an act of 1856 made the provision of P. forces compulsory. Women police were introduced in 1920, motor-cycle patrols 1921, mobile patrols with two-way radio cars 1927, and the 'man on the beat' began to be equipped with radio from 1965 and might use a 'panda' car—named from its stripe marking—from 1967. Special Patrol Groups of experienced men, travelling in their own squad cars and patrol wagons, and concentrating on a specific problem were introduced in 1970; New York has a similar Tactical Patrol Force. Admin. is by the Home Office in England and Wales, except for the City of London police controlled by the City Corporation, and by the Scottish Office in Scotland. There is no central control, Scotland Yard (q.v.) acting only on the invitation of local forces. *See* INTERPOL.

In the U.S.A. there are local, county, and state law-enforcement agencies, plus the F.B.I. (q.v.), subordinate to the Dept. of Justice, which can act directly only in offences against Federal law, though it co-operates with other P. forces when called upon to do so. Some states have no state force, and state governors as a rule have no control over local P.

British P. carry no weapon except a truncheon in normal circumstances, but are armed on occasion; some though not all U.S. police are armed, as are the Royal Canadian Mounted P., the Carabinieri in Italy, the Civil Guards in Spain, some sections of the rather complicated P. forces in France, etc.

POLIGNAC (pōlēnyahk'), **Jules de**, prince (1780–1847). French statesman. He was appointed Pres. of the Council in 1829, and pursued an ultra-royalist policy which provoked the revolution of 1830, after which he was imprisoned until 1836.

POLIOMYELITIS (pol'iomī-elī'tis). Inflammation of the anterior horn cells of the spinal cord, those governing muscle action, producing paralysis. The cause is a filtrable virus carried in the spray of sneezing or coughing and entering the nervous system by the nerve endings in the lining of the upper part of the nose. Infection comes from a carrier, never a patient. Babies are immune up to six months; children of two and three are most susceptible, but no age is free. Incubation is from 10–20 days; then there is a stage of general infection and fever. The second stage might affect the meninges, with pains in the back, neck and limbs. In the third stage paralysis of one or more limbs, or of certain muscle groups, appears. Some of the paralysis is usually permanent. The acute attack is practically never fatal. The methods introduced and developed by Sister Kenny, an Australian nurse, at first excited great opposition by their insistence on active exercises, but are now accepted. In 1954 3 U.S. doctors (J. F. Enders, F. C. Robins, and T. H. Weller) were awarded a Nobel prize for their joint discovery that the P. virus can grow in cultures of various tissues. The injected vaccine developed by Jonas Salk, and the oral vaccine of A. B. Sabin, are widely used in U.S.A. and Europe.

POLISH. A member of the western branch of the Slavonic family of languages. P. literature begins in the 14th cent., but the golden age came in the 16th when Mikolaj Rej of Naglowice developed the language in prose and verse, and the poet Jan Kochanowski flourished. A decline followed until the partial revival under French influence in the 18th cent., and the great Romantic period in the 19th with the poets Adam Mickiewicz, Juljusz Slowacki and Zygmunt Krasinski (1812–59), and the comic dramatist Aleksander Fredro (1795–1876). To the later 19th cent. belong the historical novelist Henryk Sienkiewicz, the

realists Boleslav Prus (1847–1912) and Wladyslav S. Remont (1868–1925), and the dramatist Stanislaw Przybyszewski (1867–1927); and the poets Kazimierz Tetmajer (1865–1940) and Jan Kasprowicz (1860–1926). Among more recent writers are the poets Juljan Tuwim (1894–1954), Kazimierz Wierzynski (1894–   ), Wladyslav Broniewski (1898–1962), and Juljan Przybos (1901–   ); the novelists Juliusz Kaden-Bandrowski (1901–   ) and Ferdynand Goetel (1890–   ); and the poet, novelist and playwright Adam Wazyk.

POLISH CORRIDOR. A strip of territory connecting Poland with the Baltic, and dividing E. Prussia from the rest of Germany, allotted to Poland by the Treaty of Versailles, 1919. With the inclusion of the S. part of E. Prussia in Poland in 1945, the P.C. ceased to exist.

POLITBUREAU. A contraction for 'political bureau', a sub-committee of the Central Committee of the Communist Party of the U.S.S.R., responsible for laying down the lines of party policy. It was known 1952–66 as the presidium, and the gen. sec. was then known as the first sec. *See* R.S.F.S.R.

POLITIAN or **Angelo Poliziano**. Literary name for the Italian poet and scholar Angelo Ambrogini (1454–94). He became tutor to the family of Lorenzo de' Medici and prof. at the Univ. of Florence, and wrote commentaries on classical authors, essays on philology and criticism, and Latin, Greek, and Italian verse.

POLK, James Knox (1795–1849). 11th President of the U.S.A. B. in N. Carolina, he was elected President as a Democrat in 1844, admitted Texas to the Union, and forced the war on Mexico which resulted in the annexation of California and New Mexico.

POLKA. A dance in lively 2/4 time, originating *c.* 1830 in Bohemia.

POLLAIUOLO (pollahyoo-ō'lō), **Antonio** (1429–98). Italian artist. B. at Florence, he produced many objects of art such as crosses, chasubles, etc., and executed frescoes and paintings incl. the 'Martyrdom of St. Sebastian' in the National Gallery, London.

POLLOCK, Jackson (1912–56). American artist. Of Scots-Irish origin, he was the son of a Wyoming farmer. From 1943, following the drive of the unconscious, he adopted increasingly unconventional techniques, e.g. paint thrown or dribbled on to a surface, and became the recognized exponent of 'action painting'. His death – in a Long Is. car crash – echoed the violence of his art, in which he used jewel colours, metal paints, and great abstract freedom.

POLLUTION. The effect on the environment of by-products of all industrial, agricultural and living processes, e.g. noise, smoke, gases, chemical effluents in seas and rivers, indestructible pesticides, sewage and household waste. Natural regeneration counters P. to a degree, but it rapidly escalates to danger level. Complete control would involve drastic reduction of population, and a halt to industrial development.

POLO. Outdoor game played between teams of 4 on horseback. Persia was the home of P. and modern P. was introduced to England in 1869 from India by the military. A code of rules was set out by the Hurlingham club in 1875. The Westchester cup, initiated in 1886, was competed for by repre-

POLO

sentative English and U.S. teams. The present code of rules was adopted in 1939. The ground is not to exceed 300 yds. by 200 yds. or 160 yds. if boarded. The goals are to be at least 250 yds. apart, each 8 yds. wide. The playing time is roughly one hour, divided into suitable periods. The players, whose positions are fairly elastic, use sticks *c*. 52 in. long to hit a ball 3¼ in. diam. and 4¼ to 4¾ oz. The Hurlingham and Ranelagh grounds no longer exist, but those at Roehampton, Cowdray Park, and elsewhere, flourish.

POLO, Marco (*c*. 1254–1324). Venetian traveller. His father and uncle, Nicolo and Maffeo P., travelled overland to China in ˙1260–9, and returned there in 1271–5, taking with them M.P., who entered the imperial service, and was employed on official missions. They returned to Venice in 1292–5. P. was captured while serving against the Genoese in 1298, and while in prison dictated an account of his travels which gives the earliest European description of the Far East.

POLONAISE (polonã′z). A Polish dance, in stately 3/4 time, which dated from the 16th cent. Chopin developed the P. as a musical form.

POLŌ′NIUM. The first radioactive element discovered by the Curies in 1898 (in pitchblende residues) and named after Mme Curie's native Poland: symbol Po, at. wt. 210, at. no. 84. There are some 19 known isotopes, both natural (the most stable being radium F with a half-life of 138·3 days, which emits 5 MeV alpha-particles and is radioactively useful) and man-made.

POLPERRO. Picturesque fishing village and holiday resort in Cornwall, England, 16 m. W. of Plymouth, much frequented by artists.

POLTAVA (poltah′vah). Town in the Ukrainian S.S.R., cap of P. region, on the Vorskla. It is in an agricultural area growing grain, sugar, and fruit. Peter the Great here defeated Charles XII of Sweden in 1709. Pop. (1967) 177,000.

POLTERGEIST (Ger. noisy ghost). In psychic research, name given to the unseen agent, believed by many to be a mischievous spirit or ghost, by means of which objects are moved or hurtled through the air. Famous P. phenomena that occurred at Borley rectory, Suffolk, were described by Harry Price.

POLTORATSK. Old name for ASHKHABAD.

PO′LYANDRY. The system whereby a woman is the wife of several men at the same time. It is found in many parts of the world, e.g. in Madagascar, Malaya, and certain Pacific isles, and among certain Eskimo and S. American Indian tribes. In Tibet and certain parts of India P. takes the form of the marriage of one woman to several brothers.

POLYANTHUS. Garden flower in the family Primulaceae, thought to be a cross between the primrose and cowslip. It occurs in many shades from cream to dark red.

POLYBIUS (polib′ius) (*c*. 201–120 B.C.). Greek historian. B. in Arcadia, he was taken as a prisoner to Rome in 168, but returned to Greece in 151. He was present at the capture of Carthage by his friend Scipio in 146. His history of Rome in 40 books, covering the years 220–146, has largely disappeared.

PO′LYCARP (*c*. A.D. 69–155). Christian martyr. As bishop of Smyrna for over 40 years he carried on a vigorous struggle against various heresies, and was burned alive at a public festival.

POLY′GAMY or **Polygyny.** The system whereby a man may marry several women at the same time. It is found among many primitive hunting, pastoral and agricultural peoples, especially in Africa. Normally it is confined to chiefs and nobles, as in ancient Egypt and among the primitive Teutons, Irish, and Slavs. Among the Hebrews a man could have any number of wives, but Islam limits a man's legal wives to 4. Certain Christian sects, e.g. the Anabaptists of

Münster and the Mormons, have practised polygamy.

PO′LYGON. A plane figure bounded by straight lines. Although incl. a triangle and quadrilateral, it is normally restricted to those figures having more than 4 sides, regular or irregular.

POLYMERIZATION. The chemical union of 2 or more (usually small) molecules to form a new compound of larger molecular wt. There are 3 types: *addition* P., simple multiples of the same compound; *condensation* P. in which molecules are joined together by the elimination of water; and *co*-P. in which the polymer is built up from 2 or more different molecules. There are many important polymers, both natural (e.g. cellulose) and synthetic, e.g. polythene, nylon, etc. *See* PLASTICS.

POLYNĒ′SIA. Easternmost of the 3 ethnic divisions of Pacific Ocean isls., of which the other 2 are Micronesia and Melanesia. It comprises all Oceania lying E. of approx. 170° E. lat., incl. Hawaii and the Gilbert, Ellice, Fiji, Tonga, Phoenix, Tokelau, Samoan, Line, Cook, Society, Tubuai, Marquesas, and Tuamotu Is. The Maori of New Zealand are also Polynesian. Polynesians are probably of Asiatic origin, and distinct from the Negroid Melanesians with whom there has been a degree of mixture. They are tall and possess fine physique. Their skin is brown, and their hair wavy. They are skilled in house- and shipbuilding, carving and fishing.

FRENCH POLYNESIA is an overseas terr. of France, admin. by a governor, but demands for autonomy developed from 1958. It consists of the Society, Tuamotu, and Marquesas Is. (qq.v.). Total land area *c*. 1,500 sq. m.; total pop. 100,000.

POLYPUS. A small benign tumour of the skin due to local overgrowth of cells.

POLYTECHNICS. Institutions providing comprehensive degree and non-degree courses in art and technology, both full and part-time. Most famous is the Regent Street P., London, founded by Quintin Hogg (q.v.) in 1882. In 1966 the Labour Govt. in Britain planned a new 'top tier' in education to rival the univs. with 30 new Ps.: the first 3, at Hatfield, Sheffield and Sunderland, opened 1969.

PO′LYTHEISM. The worship of many gods, as opposed to monotheism. Examples are the religions of ancient Egypt, Babylon, Greece and Rome, modern Mexico, and modern Hinduism.

POMBAL (poñbahl′), **Sebastiao José de Carvalho e Mello,** marquess of (1699–1782). Portuguese statesman. As For. Sec. and War Min. 1749–77 he introduced valuable reforms, but he was dismissed after the death of his patron, King Joseph, in 1777.

POMEGRANATE. The fruit of a deciduous tree (*Punica granatum*) found in W. Asia and N. Africa. The edible seeds of the reddish-yellow fruit can be made into wine.

POMERĀ′NIA. District, formerly a prov. of Germany, along the S. shore of the Baltic Sea. The area of the prov. was 11,680 sq. m. and it stretched W. to E. roughly from just W. of Stralsund to Stolp (Pol. Slupsk): it incl. the is. of Rügen, Usedom (Uznam), and Wollin (Wolin). By the Potsdam agreement, 1945, the part of P. E. of the Oder-Neisse line was placed under Polish administration. The Ger. form of P. is Pommern, the Pol. Pomorze.

POMERANIAN. Breed of dog resembling a small chow. Claimed to be of German origin, it may be black or white or light brown.

POMFRET. Another form of PONTEFRACT.

POMMERN. German form of POMERANIA.

PŌMŌ′NA. Roman goddess of fruit trees.

POMERANIAN

POMORZE. Polish form of POMERANIA.

POMPADOUR, Jeanne Antoinette Poisson, marquise de (1721–64). Mistress of Louis XV. B. in Paris, she became the king's mistress in 1744, and largely dictated the government's policy procuring the

MADAME DE POMPADOUR. By Boucher.
Courtesy of the Trustees of the Wallace Collection.

reversal of France's anti-Austrian for an anti-Prussian policy. She acted as the patroness of Voltaire and the *philosophes.*

POMPEII (pompā′yē). Ancient city in Italy, near Vesuvius, 13 m. E.S.E. of Naples. In A.D. 63 an earthquake destroyed much of the city which had been a Roman port and pleasure resort; it was completely buried beneath lava when Vesuvius erupted in A.D. 79. Over 2,000 people were killed. P. was rediscovered in 1748 and the systematic excavation begun in 1763 still continues. The small modern town of P. lies just to the E.; it makes macaroni and packing boxes, and caters for tourists. Pop. (1960) 6,000.

POMPEY (Gnaeus Pompeius Magnus) (106–48 B.C.). Roman soldier and statesman, known as 'the Great'. In early life he supported Sulla and the aristocratic party, but as consul with Crassus in 70 joined the democrats. He conquered Mithradates of Pontus, and annexed Syria and Palestine. In 60 he formed the 1st Triumvirate with Caesar and Crassus. When it broke down after 53, P. returned to the aristocratic party. On the outbreak of civil war in 49 he withdrew to Greece, was defeated by Caesar at Pharsalia in 48, and was murdered in Egypt.

POMPIDOU (pompēdōō′), **Georges** (1911–). French statesman and scholar. An adviser on De Gaulle's staff 1944–6, he held admin. posts until he became director-general of the French House of Rothschild in 1954, and even then continued in close association with De Gaulle. In 1962 he became P.M., but resigned after the Gaullist victory in the elections of 1968, and was elected to the presidency in 1969 as the Gaullist candidate on De Gaulle's resignation.

PONCE (pōn′thā), **Manuel** (1882–1948). Mexican composer and conductor. Like Chavez he was an ardent nationalist, and made use of folk songs.

PONCE DE LEÓN, Juan (*c.* 1460–1521). Spanish soldier and explorer, discoverer of Florida (1513). He is believed to have sailed with Columbus in 1493, and served 1502–4 in Hispaniola whence in 1508 he conquered Puerto Rico, of which he was made gov. in 1509. He returned to Spain in 1514 to report his discovery of Florida (which he thought was an is.), and was given permission by King Ferdinand to colonize it. In the attempt (1521), he received a severe arrow wound of which he d. in Cuba.

PONDICHE′RRY (Fr. pondĕshārē′). Port on the E. coast of India, 85 m. S. of Madras, cap. of the centrally administered state of P. It was founded by the French in 1674 and changed hands several times between French, Dutch, and British before being returned to France in 1814 at the close of the Napoleonic wars. With Karikal, Yanam, and Mahé it formed a French colony until 1956 when all were transferred to the government of India and made into a centrally administered state pending a decision as to their ultimate fate. French remained the official language. Area 185 sq. m.; pop. (1961) 369,079.

PONDWEED. Genus of aquatic plants (*Potamogeton*) either floating or submerged. The leaves are leathery and elliptical; the flowers grow in green spikes.

PONIATO′WSKI, Joseph Anthony (1763–1813). Polish general. He took part in Kosciuszko's rising of 1794. When in 1807 Napoleon founded the Grand Duchy of Warsaw, P. became War Min. He served in the 1812 campaign, was created a marshal of France, and was killed in action in Germany.

PO′NTA DELGADA (delgah′dah). Resort and port on the S. coast, also cap., of S. Miguel is. in the Azores, Portugal. Pop. (1966) 22,448.

PONTEFRACT. English market town (bor.) in the W. Riding of Yorks, 21 m. S.W. of York. There are remains of a Norman castle where Richard II d. P. liquorice 'cakes' are noted. Pop. (1961) 27,114.

PONTORMO, Jacopo Carucci da (1494–1557). Italian artist. Supreme master of the Florentine Mannerists, he was b. at Pontormo and became apprentice to da Vinci and later worked under Andrea del Sarto. Few of his major works survive, but these incl. 'Joseph and his Kindred in Egypt' in the National Gallery; frescoes for the Certosa di Val d'Erna, now in poor condition, and a 'Madonna and Child with St. John' in the Uffizi. His

PONTORMO. The colouring of this 'Madonna and Child with Two Angels', of which there exist two variants, suggests that it belongs to the period of the Certosa di Val d'Ema frescoes, *c.* 1523.
Courtesy of the M. H. de Young Memorial Museum, San Francisco.

later work is markedly influenced by Michelangelo.

PONTUS. Ancient kingdom of N.E. Asia Minor, bordering the Black Sea, founded *c.* 300 B.C. Under Mithradates VI (120–63 B.C.) it became a great power, but it was conquered by Pompey in 65 B.C.

PONTYPOO'L. English mining and market town (U.D.) in Monmouthshire, 9 m. N. of Newport. Industries besides coal mining incl. manufacture of iron and steel goods, tinplate and glass, and spinning of man-made fibres. Pop. (1961) 39,879.

PONTYPRIDD (pontaprēdh´). Market town (U.D.) in Glamorganshire, Wales, on the Taff, 12 m. N.W. of Cardiff. Industries incl. coal mining, chain and cable works, and the Treforest trading estate (estab. 1937) with light industries. Pop. (1961) 35,536.

PONY. Small horse under 14·2 hands, i.e. 58 in. Although of Celtic origin, all the P. breeds have been crossed with thoroughbred and Arab stock, except for the smallest – the hardy Shetland – which is below 42 in. Other British breeds incl. the small Exmoor and Dartmoor, the slightly larger New Forest, and the large Welsh cob, and similar native breeds are found elsewhere in Europe and the East. Often ridden by adults, e.g. in polo, or used to pull carts, Ps. are favourites with children, and in 1929 the *P. Club* was estab. to encourage good horsemanship among the young. Now spread throughout the world, it holds instructional rallies and inter-branch championships. Since the S.W.W. pony trekking – following routes of scenic beauty, etc. – has been popular for holidays.

POODLE. A highly intelligent breed of dog, incl. the standard (above 15 in. at shoulder); miniature (below 15 in.) and toy (below 11 in.) types.
The P. probably originated in Russia, was naturalized in Germany, where it was used as a sporting dog and gained its name from *Puddler* (one who splashes around in water), and finally became a luxury dog in France, whence it has spread around the world. Their long curly coats, usually cut into elaborate styles, are mostly either black or white (the only colours acceptable in France), although greys and browns are also bred.

POOLE. English seaport (bor.) in Dorset, 5 m. W. of Bournemouth. Pottery is made from local clay; and chemicals, confectionery, agricultural implements are produced. P. harbour, in which is Brownsea Is. where the first Boy Scout camp was held in 1907, was formerly a flying-boat base. Pop. (1961) 88,088.

POONA. Hill city in Maharashtra state, Republic of India, 119 m. S.E. of Bombay. Cotton, paper and jewellery are made, and rice and sugar milled. P. has a univ. and an airport; and at Khadakvasla, 11 m. away, is the National Defence Academy. Pop. (1961) 597,562.

POOR LAW. In England, law for the relief of the destitute poor. The first act for the levy of a compulsory poor rate was passed in 1572, and under the consolidating act of 1601 parish overseers were empowered to provide materials on which to set the unemployed to work, to raise money to relieve the aged, to apprentice pauper children and to build poorhouses. The P.L. of 1834 reorganized the system with boards of guardians elected by the ratepayers, and forbade the relief of the able-bodied except within a workhouse, where conditions were deliberately made repellent: there was violent popular opposition, but the basis of administration remained the same until responsibility was transferred in 1929 to the Min. of Health operating through co. and co. bor. councils. The P.L. system was replaced 1947 by a single relief service admin. by the Nat. Assistance Board, and in 1966 the sharp distinction between contributory and non-contributory benefits was ended by the merger of the board with the Min. of Pensions and Nat. Insurance as the Min. of Social Security.

POPE. *See* PAPACY.

POPE, Alexander (1688–1744). British poet. B. in London, son of an R.C. linen-draper, he was embittered by his personal deformity which made him the butt of his opponents. He attained a rapid reputation with his precocious *Pastorals* (1709), and *Essay on Criticism* (1711), which were followed by the mock-

KARL POPPER

heroic *Rape of the Lock* (1712: enlarged 1714), *Windsor Forest* (1713), and the 'Elegy to the Memory of an Unfortunate Lady' and 'Eloisa to Abelard'. He estab. his financial position for life with the great success of his translation of the *Iliad* (1715–20) and the *Odyssey* (1725–6), and in 1719 settled on his estate at Twickenham which he developed as a miniature compendium of landscape gardening. His edition of Shakespeare (1725) roused the scholarly ridicule of Theobald, and P. revenged himself by making him the hero of his satire on dullness, the *Dunciad* (1728), which was revised in 1743 with Colley Cibber as the chief victim. The *Essay on Man* (1733–4) and *Moral Essays* (1731–5), each consisting of 4 epistles, were shallowly brilliant expositions of philosophy largely influenced by his friend Bolingbroke. The greatest productions of his mature years are the *Imitations of the Satires of Horace* (1733–38). In 1735 also P. manœuvred the publisher Curll into issuing an unauthorized edition of his personal letters, and after denouncing the publication brought out his own version in which the text was judiciously 'improved'. The beloved friend of Swift, Arbuthnot, Gay, and Atterbury, he is outstanding for his workmanship, especially as the creator of the perfectly balanced heroic couplet. *See* illus. p. 394.

PO'PERINGHE. Ancient town in the prov. of W. Flanders, Belgium, 8 m. W. of Ypres. It was British H.Q. on the Flanders front during the F.W.W. The Toc H movement originated here in 1915. Pop. (est.) 17,500.

POPLAR. District of the Greater London bor. of Tower Hamlets, bounded on the S. by the Thames. It contains Blackwall and the Isle of Dogs, and the Millwall and E. and W. India Docks.

POPLAR. Genus of deciduous trees (*Populus*), with broad leaves. The White P. (*P. alba*) has a smooth grey trunk and the leaves are white below. Other varieties are the aspen (*P. tremula*), grey P. (*P. canescens*), Lombardy P. (*P. nigra* var. *italica*).

POPLIN. A fabric with a warp of silk and a weft of worsted giving it a corded surface; it is made chiefly in Dublin.

POPOCATEPETL (pōpōkatā´petl: Aztec, 'smoking mountain'). Volcano, 40 m. S.E. of Mexico City, Mexico. Its 17,520 ft. summit is snow-clad.

POPPER, Sir Karl (1902–). British philosopher. B. in Austria and educ. at Vienna univ., he became prof. of logic and scientific method at London in 1949. His best-known work is *Logik der Forschung* (1934: *The Logic of Scientific Discovery*), maintaining that the growth of science depends on intellectual daring and rational criticism, *The Open Society and Its Enemies* (1944) and *Conjectures and Refutations* (1963).

POPPY. Genus of plants (*Papaver*) having a milky sap, and incl. the crimson field (*P. rhoeas*)

POPPY

and opium Ps. (*see* OPIUM), found in parts of Europe and Asia. Closely related are the California P. (*Eschscholtzia californica*) and the yellow horned or sea P. (*Glaucium flavum*). A large number of cultivated varieties have been developed.

POPSKI'S PRIVATE ARMY. In the S.W.W. a unit of the Long Range Desert Group consisting of 195 picked men under the command of Lt.-Col. Vladimir Peniakov (1897–1951). They worked behind enemy lines in N. Africa and Italy. Peniakov was a naturalized Belgian of Russian parentage, and joined the British Army in Alexandria in 1940.

POPULAR FRONT. A political alliance of Liberals, Socialists, Communists, and other centre and left-wing parties against Fascism. This policy was proposed by the Communist International in 1935, and was adopted in France and Spain, where P.F. governments were elected in 1936; that in France was overthrown in 1938, and in Spain in 1939. In Britain a P.F. policy was advocated by Sir Stafford Cripps and others, but rejected by the Labour Party. The resistance movements in the occupied countries during the S.W.W. represented a revival of the P.F. idea.

PORCELAIN. Derby biscuit-ware dated c. 1780. The secret of producing porcelain of this softly translucent, waxen texture has been lost. *Photo: Lady Lever Collection.*

PORCELAIN (Italian *porcella* small, lustrous seashell). Type of ceramic ware distinguished by its translucence, and traditionally invented in China in the 2nd cent. B.C., but the earliest examples of true P. belong to the late 6th–early 7th cent. A.D., when it may have been discovered by chance in the attempt to copy imported Indian glassware. It was at its finest under the Sung Dynasty, e.g. the blue-green Celadon ware, and the Ming Dynasty, when colouring was particularly brilliant. During the 17th cent., when the Chinese art had begun to lose its inspiration, though technique continued to improve until the 20th, Portuguese trade contacts with Canton led to the 1st importation of P. to western Europe. A 'soft paste P.' – actually a mixture of clay and finely ground glass – was first made in Italy as an imitation, but reached great beauty in its own right in France at St. Cloud and Sèvres. True P. of the Chinese type was first rediscovered by John Böttger of Meissen, nr. Dresden c. 1709, and 'Dresden' as the type of delicacy in china became of world-wide fame: German technicians are still in the forefront of the field. In England, Chelsea, Bow and Derby were noted for their soft paste, but in 1768 true P. was first manufactured at Plymouth; and just as in France P. of Limoges had ousted Sèvres soft paste, so in England the 18th cent. saw the triumphs in P. of the Staffordshire potters Thomas Minton and Josiah Spode (famous for his bone china), and beautiful work at Coalport, Lowestoft, Nantgarw, etc. The individual quality was lost during the 19th cent. to a large extent under the impact of mass-production techniques, but the 20th has seen a fresh approach.

PORCUPINE. Family of large rodents. True Ps., in the family Hystricidae, are found only in the Old World and are terrestrial in habit. They are characterized by long spines in the coat. The colouring is brown with black and white quills. American Ps. constitute the family Erethizontidae and differ from the European varieties in being arboreal, having a prehensile tail, and much shorter spines.

PORDENONE (pōrdānō'ne), Il. Assumed name of the Italian painter Giovanni Antonio de Sacchi (1483–1539). B. near Pordenone, he painted in fresco.

PORI. Town on the Gulf of Bothnia at the mouth of the r. Kokemäki, Finland, kept ice-free all the year. It has saw mills, nickel and copper refineries, and paper, textiles, matches are made. Pop. (1967) 69,885.

PORPHYRIA (porfir'ia). Rare metabolic disorder, known as the 'royal disease' (Gk. *porphyra* purple) found in the houses of Stuart, Hanover and Prussia. Sufferers have incl. Mary Queen of Scots, James I, and George III.

PORPHYRY (por'firi) (A.D. 233–c. 304). Greek Neo-Platonic philosopher. B. at Tyre or in Syria, he settled at Rome in 262, and became a disciple of Plotinus. He wrote numerous philosophical works.

PORPHYRY. A red volcanic rock, of Egyptian origin, much used in Roman ornamentation. It occurs as a thick dyke rediscovered at Jebel Dokhan.

PORPOISE (por'pus). Genus (*Phocaena*) of Cetaceans found in the Atlantic and Pacific. The common P. (*P. communis*) is blue-black above, and whitish below, measures up to 6 ft. and feeds on fish. Schools of Ps. leaping together on the surface often foretell stormy weather. In the U.S.A. the dolphin (q.v.) is commonly referred to as the P.

PORSON, Richard (1759–1808). British scholar. B. in Norfolk of poor parents, he was sent to Cambridge by a patron, and became prof. of Greek there in 1792. His editions of Aeschylus and Euripides are outstanding achievements of Greek scholarship.

PORTAL OF HUNGERFORD, Charles Frederick Algernon, 1st visct. (1893–1971). Brit. airman, Marshal of the R.A.F. He served in the F.W.W., and became director of organization at the Air Ministry 1937–8. A.O.C.-in-C. Bomber Command, March–Oct. 1940, and Chief of Air Staff 1940–5, he received a barony in 1945, and a viscounty in 1946.

PORT ARTHUR. Canadian lake port on Thunder Bay, N.W. shore of Lake Superior, Ontario, a grain and iron shipping centre with saw mills and paper and pulp mills. Pop. (1966) 38,000.

PORT ARTHUR. Deep-water port in Texas, U.S.A., 15 m. S.E. of Beaumont. Founded 1895, it has petroleum refineries, shipyards, brass foundries, chemical factories. It rose to importance with the discovery of petroleum near Beaumont in 1901. Pop. (1960) 66,676.

PORT ARTHUR. Port and naval base in Liaoning prov., China, at the tip of Liaotung peninsula. P.A. was in 1898 leased to Russia, and during the Russo-Japanese War surrendered to the Japanese only after a prolonged siege, June 1904–Jan. 1905. The lease was then transferred to Japan. After the S.W.W., P.A. was occupied by Russian airborne troops 22 Aug. 1945, and by a treaty between the U.S.S.R. and China, 1945, was to be used by them jointly as a naval base for 30 years; a treaty of 1950 provided for its return to China when China and the U.S.S.R. made peace with Japan, but in fact it was returned in 1955. P.A. is important because it is ice-free all the year round. P.A. and Dairen (q.v.), under their Chinese name Lushun-Talien, form the municipality of Lüta: pop. (1965) 3,600,000.

PORT-AU-PRINCE (-ō-prins'). Port and cap. of Haiti, W. Indies. It has an iron foundry, a tannery, a flour mill, and a factory making plastics; also an airport. Pop. (1961) 250,000.

PORT DARWIN. *See* DARWIN.

PORT ELIZABETH. Port in Cape prov., S. Africa,

PORCUPINE

c. 440 m. E. of Capetown on Algoa Bay. It was founded in 1820 by British settlers and named after the wife of Sir Rufane Donkin, then gov. of the Cape. It exports wool, fruit, ostrich feathers, and makes boots, flour, and jam. There is a bilingual univ. (1964). Pop. (1960) 270,815 (94,085 white).

PORTEOUS, John (d. 1736). Captain of the Edinburgh city guard, who was condemned to death for firing on the crowd during a riot, but reprieved. Resenting this, the mob dragged P. from prison and hanged him.

PORTER, Cole (1893–1964). American composer. B. in Indiana, he wrote the music and lyrics for musical comedies, incl. *Gay Divorce, Around the World in Eighty Days* and *Kiss Me, Kate*, and the film *High Society*. 'Night and Day' is his best-known song.

PORTER, Katherine Anne (1890–). American writer. B. at Indian Creek, Texas, she leapt to fame with a vol. of short stories *Flowering Judas* (1930), her reputation for economy and power being maintained in *Pale Horse, Pale Rider* (1939).

PORTLAND, William Bentinck, 1st earl of (*c.* 1649–1709). Dutch statesman. A friend of William of Orange, he took part in the invasion of England in 1688, and received the earldom of P. in 1689. He served in William's campaigns, and negotiated the Treaty of Ryswick and the Partition Treaties.

PORTLAND, William Henry Cavendish Bentinck, 3rd duke of (1738–1809). British statesman. He began his political career as a Whig, and in 1783 became P.M. in the Fox-North coalition govt. During the French Revolution he joined the Tories, becoming P.M. (1807–9).

PORTLAND. (1) Largest city in Oregon, U.S.A., on the Columbia, 108 m. from the sea, at its confluence with the Willamette. Ocean-going vessels can reach P. which has excellent harbour facilities and road, rail and air links. Industries incl. metal processing, espec. aluminium; paper, timber, and lumber machinery; and electronics. Pop. met. area (1970) 992,593 (2) Port and largest city of Maine, U.S.A., on Casco Bay. It has shipbuilding and other industries; the chief export is timber. A first settlement was made on the site in 1633, but wiped out by Indians and French in 1690; re-settlement began in 1718, the place being called Falmouth until 1786. Longfellow was born at P. Pop. (1960) 72,566.

PORTLAND, Isle of. A rocky 'island' off the Dorset coast, England, opposite Weymouth, joined to the mainland by the Chesil Bank (q.v.). It has a 14th cent. castle; a prison, opened 1848, converted into a Borstal 1921; and a naval harbour of refuge. P. stone is quarried. Area 4½ sq. m.

PORT LAOIGHIS (-lē'sh). Co. town of Laoighis Rep. of Ireland, founded 1560 as Maryborough. Pop. (1961) 3,133.

PORT MAHON. See MAHON.

PORTMAN, Eric (1903–69). British film and stage actor. B. in Bradford, he was at his best in modern roles, conveying much by understatement. e.g. Rattigan's *The Browning Version* (1948) and *Separate Tables* (1956); and Fielding in *A Passage to India* (1962).

PORT MORESBY. Port on the S. coast of Papua, administrative centre of the Australian Trust territory of Papua-New Guinea. It dates from 1873. The Univ. of Papua-New Guinea was estab. here 1965. Pop. (1966) 14,000.

PORTO ALEGRE. See RIO GRANDE DO SUL.

PORT-OF-SPAIN. Port and cap. of Trinidad, West Indies. There are 2 cathedrals, and it exports cocoa, sugar, asphalt, copra, rum, petroleum, and angostura bitters. Pop. (1960) 93,954.

PO'RTON DOWN. Site of the Microbiological Research and Chemical Defence Experimental Establishment of the Min. of Defence in Wilts: as a 'germ warfare' centre it came under attack in the 1960s.

PORTO RICO. Another form of PUERTO RICO.

PORT ROYAL. See JAMAICA.

PORT ROYAL DES CHAMPS. A former Cistercian convent, S.W. of Paris, founded in 1204. In 1626 its inmates were moved to Paris, and the buildings were taken over by a male community which became a centre of Jansenist teaching and was in 1638 compelled to vacate the premises; the buildings were destroyed in 1710 by order of Louis XIV.

PORT SAID (sah-ēd'). Port of Egypt, on reclaimed land at the N. end of the Suez Canal. Founded in 1859, it is a fuelling station. Pop. (1960) 244,000.

PORTSMOUTH, Louise de Kérouaille, duchess of (1649–1734). Mistress of Charles II. B. in Brittany, she came to England in 1670. She was acting as Louis XIV's agent, and was generally hated. On Charles's death she returned to France.

PORTSMOUTH. English city and naval port (co. bor.) of Hampshire, 74 m. S.W. of London. It covers Portsea Is., which lies between P. and Langstone harbours, and spreads on to the mainland. The Royal Dockyard and naval station occupy the S.W. area of the is., and the R.N. barracks bear the name of Nelson's flagship, H.M.S. *Victory*, preserved in dry dock nearby. P. harbour opens through a bottleneck with Gosport on its W. side and P. on the E. side. Southsea is a seaside resort with fine views of shipping in the Solent, and the castle is used as a museum of military history. P. was already a port in the days of King Alfred, and in the reign of Henry VIII a French attempt to take it led to the capsize in battle of the warship *Mary Rose* in 1545: in 1969 there were plans to raise the wrecked vessel for preservation. In the S.W.W. German air raids caused heavy damage and P. was an important mounting base for the Allied invasion of France in 1944. Charles Dickens was born in P. and his birthplace in Commercial Road is a museum. Pop. (1961) 215,918.

PORTSMOUTH. (1) Port of New Hampshire, U.S.A., on the estuary of the Piscataqua. Founded in 1623, P. was the state cap. 1679–1775. The treaty which ended the Russo-Japanese war of 1904–5 was signed here. Pop. (1960) 25,833. (2) City in Ohio, at the junction of the Ohio and Scioto rivers. Founded in 1803, it is a mining centre with boot and shoe, furniture, and other factories. Pop. (1960) 33,637. (3) City and port in Virginia, on Elizabeth r., seat of an important U.S. navy yard and training centre, descended from a navy yard set up by the British in 1752. It also makes textiles and raises oysters. Pop. (1960) 114,773.

PORT SUNLIGHT. Garden village on the out-

PORT SUNLIGHT. The Lady Lever Art Gallery, opened in 1922 and designed by William Segar Owen, was given to the nation by Lord Leverhulme in memory of his wife, Lady Elizabeth Ellen Lever, who died in 1913. Items from the collection illustrate entries on Chippendale, Porcelain, Reynolds and Sir Walter Scott.
Courtesy of the Lady Lever Collection.

skirts of Birkenhead. Cheshire, England, founded by 1st Lord Leverhulme in 1888 to include the Lever soap factory and houses for workers in it.

PORT TALBOT. Welsh port (bor.) in Glamorganshire, at the mouth of the Avon, 8 m. E.S.E. of Swansea. The bor. was formed in 1921 by the amalgamation of Aberavon and Margam. The steelworks at Margam were the largest in Europe when opened in 1951; tinplate is made. Pop. (1961) 50,223.

PORTUGAL. Republic of Europe, situated between the Atlantic to the W. and S., and Spain to the E. and N. P. is an elongated area on the W. coast of the Iberian peninsula. It has a maximum length of 360 m. and a maximum breadth of 140 m., and is crossed from N.E. to S.W. by several parallel ranges of mountains between which pass the valleys of the main rivers, viz. the Minho, Douro, Tagus and Guadiana. The Serra da Estrélla incl. the highest ground in P., 6,532 ft. The climate is temperate.

P. is still mainly agricultural. Wheat, maize, potatoes, rye, rice and olives are grown, and P. produces most of the world's cork. Wine, espec. port wine, and sardines are important exports. Minerals incl. coal, copper, iron, wolfram, etc., and the foundry industry, under the impetus of the S.W.W. and assisted by low wages and a disciplined work force, flourishes. Textiles, pottery, glass, leather goods, furniture, and chemicals are also growing manufactures.

The principal towns are Lisbon (the cap.), Oporto, Funchal (Madeira), Coimbra, Setubal, Braga, Evora, and Ponta Delgada (Azores).

Area (incl. the Azores and Madeira, which form an integral part of the country) 35,490 sq. m.; pop. (1966) 9,228,000, mainly R. Catholics. There are univs. at Coimbra (1290), Lisbon, and Oporto (both 1911).

Under the constitution of 1933, as amended 1959, P. is governed by a president elected for 7 years by an electoral college composed of the National Assembly (popularly elected for 4 years) and the Corporative Chamber with representatives of local and overseas authorities.

OVERSEAS POSSESSIONS. These incl. the overseas territories of the Cape Verde Is.; Portuguese Guinea; S. Tomé and Principe; Angola (Portuguese W. Africa); Mozambique (Portuguese E. Africa); Macao; and Portuguese Timor. (For former Portuguese India, *see* GOA.)

History. P. originated in the 11th cent. as a county subject to León, while the S. was ruled by the Moors. Alfonso I (1128–85) captured Lisbon (1147) and made the Tagus the frontier, assuming the title of king in 1140. Alfonso III (1248–79) finally expelled the Moors. During the 13th cent. the Cortes, representing nobles, clergy and cities, began to meet, and secured control of taxation. A commercial treaty with England was signed in 1294, and an alliance estab. in 1373. During the 15th cent. Portuguese mariners explored the African coast, opened the sea route to India, and discovered Brazil; as a result, in the 16th cent. P. founded colonies in Brazil, Africa, India, and the E. Indies. By the 16th cent. the Portuguese kings had become absolute, but when the royal family became extinct in the male line, in 1580, Philip II of Spain seized the crown. The Portuguese rebelled against Spanish rule in 1640, placed the house of Braganza on the throne, and after a long war forced the Spaniards to recognize their independence in 1668. P. fought as the ally of Britain in the War of the Spanish Succession. A period of decadence was ended by the sweeping reforms of Pombal, chief minister 1750–77.

The French invaded P. in 1807, and were not finally expelled by Wellington until 1811. A strong democratic movement developed, and after a civil war (1828–34) constitutional govt. was estab. King Carlos and the Crown Prince were assassinated in 1908; Carlos's younger son Manoel II was driven from the country by a revolution in 1910 and a rep. was pro-

claimed. It successfully faced armed opposition. In 1932 Dr. Salazar became P.M. and estab. a semi-Fascist dictatorship. During the F.W.W. P. declared war on Germany in 1916 and contributed troops in France and Africa; during the S.W.W. P. remained neutral, but under the treaty of 1373 gave the U.K. in 1943–6 facilities for air bases in the Azores. On the incapacity of Salazar in 1968, Caetano took office and the regime tended slightly more to liberalism.

PORTUGUESE. A member of the Romance family of languages, ultimately deriving from Latin, but later subjected to a considerable Arabic influence.

Under Provençal influence, medieval P. literature produced popular ballads and troubadour songs, as well as chronicles, saints' lives, etc., but the Renaissance stimulated the outstanding work of the dramatist Gil Vicente, the lyric poets Sá de Miranda and Antonio Ferreira, the lyric and epic poet Camöens, the historian João de Barros, the romancer Francisco de Moraes, and innumerable travel writers e.g. Fernão M. Pinto. A decline came in the 17th cent. – though poetry is represented by Rodrigues Lobo, religious prose by the Jesuit António Vieira, and drama by Manuel de Melo – and continued in the 18th, despite poets such as António Diniz, Bocage, and Correia Garção. The Romantics incl. the poets Visct. Almeida Garrett and A. F. de Castilho; the historical novelist Alexandre Herculano; and the novelist of passion Camillo Castello Branco. To the Realist reaction belong the poets Antero de Quental, Teófilo Braga, and Guerra Junqueiro; the novelist Eça de Queiroz, and the historian Oliveira Martins. Among more recent writers are the poets Fernando Pessoa, António Nobre, Eugénio de Castro (a leading symbolist), Mário de Sá-Carneiro (a prominent futurist), and the novelists Aquilino Ribeiro and Ferreira de Castro. In Angola there is an interesting school of Portuguese-African poetry.

PORTUGUESE EAST AFRICA. *See* MOZAMBIQUE.

PORTUGUESE GUINEA. Overseas territory of Portugal in W. Africa, bounded N. by Senegal, S. and E. by the Republic of Guinea, W. by the Atlantic. It incl. the Bissagos archipelago and Bolama Is. Products incl. rice, hides, and palm oil. P.G. is ruled by a governor. The principal towns and ports are Bissau (made cap. in 1942) and Bolama. Nationalist guerrillas have been active since 1961. Area 13,948 sq. m.; pop. (1960) 519,229.

PORTUGUESE WEST AFRICA. *See* ANGOLA.

PORT WINE. A rich, sweet, dessert wine, red, tawny, or white, grown in the Douro basin of Portugal and exported from Oporto.

POSEIDON. *See* NEPTUNE.

POSEN. German form of POZNAN.

POSITIVISM. The philosophical system of Auguste Comte (q.v.) based on the idea that man has no knowledge of anything but phenomena, and such knowledge is relative not absolute. In every department of human knowledge 3 stages may be discerned: the theological, in which everything is referred to the gods; the metaphysical, in which abstract ideas are of supreme importance; and the positive, when science takes the place of metaphysics and philosophy. On the basis of P. Comte erected his 'Religion of Humanity', in which the object of adoration was the Great Being, i.e. the personification of humanity as a whole.

POSTGATE, Raymond William (1896–1971). Brit. author. Son of the classical scholar John Percival P. (1853–1926), he was for some years a journalist, mainly on left-wing papers, and wrote the study of working-class history *The Common People* (1946: with G. D. H. Cole) and lives of Wilkes and Lansbury. He was a gourmet and author of books on food and wine.

POST-IMPRESSIONISM. Term applied to various styles of painting which followed Impressionism, and first used by Roger Fry to describe the works of

Cézanne, van Gogh, and Gauguin in 1911. Post-Impressionists often distorted natural appearance for the sake of design or to express their own emotions.

POST OFFICE. Organization originally concerned solely with the conveyance of written communications. Since every centrally organized state depends on a speedy flow of information and instructions, early and efficient systems were devised by the rulers of Assyria, China, Rome, etc. In medieval Europe royal couriers and private messengers were frequently used, but major permanent systems waited on the establishment of the nation state. In England in 1516 Henry VIII appointed Sir Brian Tuke as his Master of the Posts with the task of maintaining not only a constant link between the mobile monarch and his capital, but of maintaining a regular service along the main roads from London: postmasters (usually innkeepers) were appointed, with the duty of passing on mail to the next post and of providing horses for royal couriers. Private persons wishing to send letters (both within the kingdom and across to the Continent) or to travel 'post haste' were permitted to use these services: private posts were consistently discouraged as involving loss of revenue for the state service and facilitating treasonable activities.

In 1635 Charles I briefly appointed Thomas Wither-ings, already a successful 'Postmaster General for Foreign Parts', to improve the domestic services, public correspondence being accepted for the first time for conveyance by messengers at fixed rates. After the Civil War an ordinance of 1654 reaffirmed the repeatedly challenged concept of state monopoly, e.g. the London penny post organized in 1680–2 (when legal action compelled him to desist) by William Dockwra, which was so successful it was continued as part of the official service, Dockwra eventually being appointed comptroller. The uniform penny post advocated by Rowland Hill was instituted in 1840 to replace the former charge varied according to distance – the rate remained unchanged until 1918 – and pre-paid adhesive stamps were instituted.

In the 19th and 20th cents. the P.O. greatly extended its services: money orders (1838), savings bank (1861), telegraphs (1870), postal orders (1881) parcels post (1883), telephone service (1912), overseas telegraph service (1950), transatlantic telephone cable (1956), facilities for data processing by computer (1967), and giro (q.v., 1968). The P.O. acts as agent for government depts. in the collection of certain revenue, disburse-ment of pensions and allowances, issue of some licen-ces, etc., and is responsible for radio and television broadcasting. The 620 ft. London P.O. Tower (1966) is the highest building in Britain, and has micro-wave equipment capable of handling 150,000 simultaneous telephone conversations and 40 television channels. In 1969 the General P.O. ceased to be a govt. dept. and became the P.O., a public corporation headed by a board and chairman: the office of Postmaster General disappeared, but there is a Min. of Posts and Telecommunications.

In America the first postal service was estab. in Massachusetts in 1639, and in 1692 Thomas Neale opened a P.O. at Philadelphia to convey mail to other colonies, but in 1707 his patent was acquired by the govt. and the service gradually expanded. Benjamin Franklin was P.M.G. 1753–74 (deputy 1736–53), becoming in 1775 first P.M.G. of the newly formed P.O. Dept. which was replaced 1970 by a U.S. Postal Service, an independent govt. agency.

International co-operation is ensured through the Universal Postal Union estab. at Berne in 1875.

POTASSIUM (Eng. *potash*, Lat. *kalium*). Soft, silvery-bright, highly reactive metal of the alkali group, symbol K, at. wt. 39·1, at. no. 19. Discovered in 1807 by Sir Humphry Davy by electrolysis of caustic potash (KOH) – the 1st instance of a metal being isolated by an electric current – it reacts violently with water, forming potassium hydroxide and hydro-gen which ignites and burns spontaneously with a violet flame due to the volatilized P. It is, therefore, kept under kerosene or naphtha. Widely distributed in nature in combination with other elements, it is found in salt deposits (carnallite and kainite) and minerals (feldspar, greensand, alunite, leucite), and forms *c*. 2·9 per cent of the earth's solid crust. The salts are important, especially as essential constituents of fertilizers. Alloyed with sodium, it may be used as a coolant in nuclear reactors.

POTATO. Perennial plant (*Solanum tuberosum*) of the Solanaceae, native to S. America, traditionally introduced *c*. 1588 by Sir Walter Raleigh but known rather earlier in Spain. The tuberous roots are used as a vege-table, and are also an im-portant commercial source of alcohol, the residue of the process being useful as cattle food. The sweet P. (*Ipomoea batatas*) of the family Convolvulaceae, is a perennial native to tropical America, difficult of cultivation in adverse conditions. The flesh of the tuberous roots is usually white to orange, and like that of the com-mon P. is used as a source of starch and alcohol, as well as for food. 'Poteen' is an illicit Irish alcoholic liquor made from the common P. or barley and sugar. It is so potent that the drinker may remain drunk after a session for days, though drinking only water.

POTCHEFSTROOM. S. African town, on the r. Mooi, oldest town in Transvaal, founded in 1838 by Boers trekking from the Cape. Pop. (1960) 41,701 (20,520 white).

POTE′MKIN (Russ. potyom′kim) **Grigory Alek-sandrovich, Prince** (1739–91). Russian statesman. B. near Smolensk, he entered the army and attracted the notice of Catherine II, whose favourite he was for some years, never losing her friendship throughout his life. His activities as administrator, army commander (introducing reforms), builder of the Black Sea Fleet, conqueror of the Crimea, developer of S. Russia, founder of the Kherson arsenal. etc., compel admiration

POTO′MAC. River of the U.S.A., rising in the Allegheny mountains, and flowing S.E. through Washington, D.C., into Chesapeake Bay. It is formed by the junction of the N.P. (*c*. 95 m.) and S.P. (*c*. 130 m), and is itself 285 m. long.

POTOSÍ (pōtōsē′). Town in S.W. Bolivia. Standing on the Cerro de P. slopes at 13,189 ft., it is among the highest situated towns in the world. It is famed for its tin and silver mines. Pop. (1965) 65,690.

POTSDAM. Cap. of Potsdam district, East Ger-many, on the Havel, 16 m. S.W. of Berlin. Its notable buildings include the New Palace (1763–70), and Sans Souci, both built by Frederick the Great. The Third Reich (Hitler's régime) was proclaimed in P. garrison church on 21 March 1933. Pop. (1966) 110,693. At P. was held in July 1945 a conference of representatives of Britain, the Soviet Union, and the U.S.A.; which laid down the political and economic principles governing the treatment of Germany in the initial period of Allied control. From the P. conference also went out the ultimatum to Japan demanding uncon-ditional surrender on pain of utter destruction.

POTTER, Beatrix (1866–1943). British writer and illustrator of children's books, beginning with *Peter Rabbit* (1900): her code diaries were pub. 1966. She m. solicitor William Heelis 1913, and bequeathed her Lake District property to the Nat. Trust.

POTTER, Paul (1625–54). Dutch animal painter, the son and pupil of Pieter P., a landscape painter.

POTTER, Stephen (1900–70). British author. A student of Coleridge, e.g. *Coleridge and S.T.C.* (1935), and a literary critic, he was best known for *Gamesmanship* (1947), *Lifemanship* (1950), and *One Upmanship* (1952), humorous studies in how to outwit and outshine the other fellow which have added new words to the language.

POTTERIES, The. The centre of the china and earthenware industry in England, lying in the upper Trent basin of N. Staffordshire. Wedgwood and Minton are famous names associated with the P., which covers the co. bor. of Stoke-on-Trent, formed in 1910 from the separate bors. of Burslem, Hanley, Longton, Fenton, Tunstall, and Stoke-upon-Trent.

POTTERY. Objects fashioned from clay and baked hard: *see also* CERAMICS and PORCELAIN. The earliest known pottery was made by the Egyptians *c.* 5,000 B.C., and they also developed the potter's wheel, but the making of P. is one of the most widespread ancient crafts and its remains are invaluable to the archaeologist, since each culture usually develops its own types which can be dated and so date objects found in association with them, etc. The Greeks were producing P. by the 8th cent. B.C., derived from Egyptian examples, but most typical of their work were the black and red figured vases of *c.* 600–450 B.C. Roman P. was largely imitative of Greek, but particularly notable is their Samian ware, made by a special process involving firing in the moulds. After the fall of Rome there was a hiatus until the conquering Arabs, in their movement westward, brought to Spain in the 8th cent. A.D. the lustrous blue and green glazes used in Persia in the previous cent., but which trace their origin to the brilliant colour oxides developed long before and the skills of Babylon and Nineveh. Especially striking in this period is majolica, ware with an opaque tin-oxide glaze which was exported from Majorca – hence the name. Italy at first merely copied

POTTERY. Scandinavian pottery is famous: these pieces are Finnish.
Courtesy of the Finnish Travel Information Centre.

such exports, but in the Renaissance developed her own style of P., notably the coloured relief work executed by the Della Robbia family. Faience, a glazed porous ware, owes its name to an Italian P. town (**Faenza**), but is peculiarly associated with France, cf. Bernard de Palissy, though later spreading to centres such as Delft in Holland and Nuremberg in Germany. In England there is an honestly utilitarian medieval P. with green and yellow glazes, more highly decorated Cistercian ware in the 16th cent., and attractive slip ware in 17th, but the 18th cent. saw a remarkable flowering with the cream and jasper ware of Wedgwood and the stoneware – a type of P. which had reached its height on the Continent in 15th cent. Germany – of John Dwight of Fulham, continued into the 19th by Sir Henry Doulton. The mass manufacture of porcelain as the 19th cent. continued tended to eclipse P., but in the 20th cent. it has regained artistic standing, e.g. the work of Bernard Leach, Hans Coper, and Lucie Rie.

POULENC (poolonk′), **Francis** (1899–1963). French composer. B. in Paris, he became a member of *Les Six*. His works have a light-hearted vitality and incl. songs, *Rapsodie Nègre* (1916) for piano, wind, strings and voices, and the operas *Les mamelles de Tirésias* and *Les Dialogues des Carmélites* (1937).

POULTRY. 1, Ancona hen; 2, Duckwing game cock; 3, White Wyandotte cock.

POULTRY. Term applied to domestic birds in the order Gallinae, incl. ducks, geese, turkeys (q.v.) and fowls. Good egg-laying breeds of chicken are Leghorns, Minorcas, and Anconas; varieties most suitable for the table are Dorkings and Indian Game; those useful for both purposes are Orpingtons, Rhode Island Reds, Wyandottes and Plymouth Rocks. Since the S.W.W. the development of battery-produced eggs and intensive breeding of broiler fowls for the table introduced into Britain and other countries from the U.S., have roused a public outcry against these 'animal factories'.

POUND, Sir (Alfred) Dudley Pickman Rogers (1877–1943). British admiral of the Fleet. As First Sea Lord and Chief of the British Naval Staff 1939–43, he was responsible for the effective measures taken against the U-boats, and was awarded the O.M. shortly before his death.

POUND, Ezra (1885–). American poet. B. at Hailey, Idaho, he studied the Romance languages and in 1907 was briefly lecturer in French and Spanish at Wabash Coll., Crawfordsville. Going to Europe, he made his home in London for some 13 years, influenced T. S. Eliot, Yeats, and Joyce, and by his first 2 vols. of verse *Personae* and *Exultations* (1909) estab. the lines of the Imagist movement. During 1921–5 he lived in Paris, his friends incl. Gertrude Stein and Hemingway, and then settled in Rapallo. His sympathy with Mussolini's régime and his anti-Semitism aroused resentment in the U.S.A. and U.K., and his broadcasts from Italy in the S.W.W. led to his arrest by American troops in 1945. On the eve of his Washington trial he was found unfit to plead and confined in a mental hospital until, in 1958, the treason charges were dismissed on the ground that he was never likely to be so. On his release, he returned to Italy. His first completely 'modern' poem, and for some his best, was *Hugh Selwyn Mauberley* (1920), but his biggest is the series of *Cantos* intended to reach a 100, which comprise a selective view of history: beginning in 1919 they incl. *The Pisan Cantos* (1949), *Section Rock-Drill* (1956) and *Thrones* (1960). Scholars often disapprove his versions from Old English, Provençal, Chinese, ancient Egyptian, etc., but they have definite value as poetry.

POUND. (1) The standard unit of weight avoirdupois in the U.K., U.S.A. and Canada, composed of 7,000 grains or 16 oz. and equal to 0·45359237 kg. (2) The British standard of currency, equivalent to 240 pence (from 1971 to 100 new pence), formerly

EZRA POUND on his return to Italy in 1958.
Photo: Keystone Press Agency.

issued in gold-sovereign (q.v.) form, but since 1914 as a note. After the abandonment of the gold standard in 1931, its international exchange value has been regulated by the Treasury.

POUSSIN (poosań'), **Nicolas** (1594–1665). French artist. B. at Les Andelys, he went to Rome in 1624, spending the rest of his life there apart from a brief period as court painter to Louis XIII, 1640–3. His landscapes, historical and religious subjects are some of the finest works of the classical tradition and were immensely influential in his native country. His brother-in-law and pupil **Gaspard Dughet** (1613–75), also a landscape painter, adopted the name Gaspard P.

POWELL, Adam Clayton (1908–72). American Democrat politician. Grandson of a Negro slave, he was a min. of the Abyssinian Baptist Church 1937–60. Member of the House of Reps. from 1945, he was excluded 1967 because of alleged misuse of public funds. Re-elected 1968–70, he never regained power.

POWELL, Anthony (1905–). Brit. novelist. His projected 12-vol. Proustian *Music of Time* series, portraying Nicholas Jenkins and his circle of upper class friends began with *A Question of Upbringing* (1951). Its sequels incl. *At Lady Molly's* (1957) and *The Military Philosophers* (1968).

POWELL, Cecil Frank (1903–69). British physicist. In 1948–63 he was prof. at Bristol univ., and in 1950 received a Nobel prize for his development of a new photographic method for the study of nuclear particles. He was chairman scientific policy committee of the European Organization for Nuclear Research (CERN) 1961–3, and director H. H. Wills Physics Laboratory, Bristol, from 1964.

POWELL, Enoch (1912–). Brit. Cons. politician. Prof. of Greek at Sydney 1937–9, he became M.P. for Wolverhampton 1950, was Min. of Health 1960–3, and stood for the party leadership in 1965. His views on defence, nationalisation, and taxation are controversial, and a Birmingham speech on immigration1968 led to his dismissal from the shadow cabinet.

POWER. The rate of doing work or consuming energy expressed in units of work per unit time, e.g. ft. lb./sec. (1 horse power = 550 ft. lb./sec.) or erg./sec. (1 watt = 10^7 erg./sec.).

POWER OF ATTORNEY. A formal instrument, executed under seal, and attested by 2 witnesses, whereby a person gives another authority to act on his behalf, either in a specified number or class of transactions, or generally for a limited period.

POWYS (poo'is), **John Cowper** (1872–1963). British author. B. at Shirley, Derbyshire, he was the brother of the versatile writers Theodore Francis P. (1875–1953) and Llewelyn P. (1884–1939). His verse incl. *Wolfsbane, Mandragora* and *Samphire* – titles which, with those of his critical and philosophical works (e.g. *The Religion of a Sceptic, In Defence of Sensuality,* and *The Meaning of Culture*), and his interest in Rabelais (of whom he pub. a study in 1947), indicate the mystical fantasy and lusty richness of his novels, which incl. *Wolf Solent* (1929) and *A Glastonbury Romance* (1933).

POYNTER, Sir Edward John (1836–1919). British painter. B. in Paris, son of the architect Ambrose P. (1796–1886), he became first head of the Slade School (1871–5), was elected R.A. in 1876 and became principal (1876–81) of the art training schools in S. Kensington (later Royal Coll. of Art). He was director of the National Gallery 1894–1905 and, on Millais' death in 1896, was elected P.R.A. Noted for his decorous nudes, he also designed mosaic panels in Westminster Palace (1870), and painted 'Israel in Egypt', 'The Golden Age' and 'Atlanta's Race'.

POZNAN. Polish city, cap. of P. voivodship, on the Warta, 170 m. W. of Warsaw, the seat of a univ. (1919). Manufactures incl. locomotives and farming machinery, precision instruments, bicycles, aircraft, beer. Settled by German immigrants in 1253, it was a residence of the dukes of Poland from 1296; it passed to Prussia in 1793 and was restored to Poland in 1919. Hindenburg was born at P. Pop. (1966) 441,000.

PRADO. A famous thoroughfare of Madrid, Spain, which gave its name to the picture gallery *Real Museo de Pintura del Prado*, containing the national collection of pictures founded by Charles III in 1785.

PRAETOR (prē'tor). A Roman magistrate, elected annually, who assisted the consuls and presided over the civil courts. The number of Ps. was finally increased to 8, who after a year of office acted as provincial governors for a further year.

PRAGMATISM. Name given to the philosophical doctrine advanced by the American philosopher William James (q.v.) that the truth of a conception may be judged from its bearing upon human conduct. James derived the idea from C. S. Pierce (1839–1914) who introduced the term and the principle into philosophy in 1878.

PRAGUE (prahg). French form of Praha, cap. of Czechoslovakia, on the Vltava. Germans were settled here in the 13th cent. when the kings of Bohemia made it their cap. It was a residence of the Holy Roman Emperors during the 14th to 17th cents. Hitler occupied P. in 1939. The city, which is exceptionally pleasing, rises in terraces from the river. On

PRAGUE. Hradčany Castle, originally the fortified palace of the Bohemian kings, is now the presidential residence and government headquarters. It crowns the Hradcany Hill on the western bank of the r. Vltava, and encloses the cathedral of St. Vitus, founded by King Wenceslas in the 10th cent., rebuilt by Charles IV, and restored in modern times.
Courtesy of the Czechoslovak Travel Bureau.

the left bank is the Hradčany with the castle, and the old town has a profusion of palaces, bridges, and churches. P. is the financial and manufacturing centre of the country, its products incl. flour, sugar, smoked meats, furniture, clothing, gloves, motor-cars, and heavy machinery. Brewing, tanning, and the chemical industries also thrive. The univ. was founded by the Emperor Charles IV in 1348. Pop. (1961) 1,000,000.

PRAIRIE. The central N. American plains, formerly grass-covered, extending over most of the region between the Rockies on the W. and the Great Lakes and Ohio river on the E., and extending northward into Canada.

PRÂKRIT (prah'krit). The popular languages of ancient India, as opposed to Sanskrit. The best-known P. is Māhārastri, used for the later Jain sacred books. The Ps. were also used in lyric poetry and for certain characters in Sanskrit drama.

PRASAD, Rajendra (1884–1963). Indian statesman. Prof. of law at Calcutta univ., he joined Gandhi's non-co-operation movement, later pub. biographies of Gandhi with whom he became closely associated, and was pres. of the Congress Party 1934, 1939 and

1947–8. Several times imprisoned, for his part in the Civil Disobedience Movement incl. 1942–5; he became Pres. of the Constituent Assembly in 1946 and in 1950 1st Pres. of the Rep. of India.

PRAWN

PRAWN. Crustacean in the family Palaemonidae, allied to the shrimp. The common P. (*Leander serratus*), translucently colourless, and 2–3 in. long, is found in shoals in shallow off-shore water in the temperate zone, and is good eating. In tropical rivers, e.g. in the W. Indies and Central America, there are Ps. approaching the size of lobsters.

PRAXI'TELES. Greek sculptor who lived in Athens during the 4th cent. B.C. The works credited to him incl. the statue of Hermes carrying Dionysus and the bas-relief of Aphrodite of Cnidus.

PRAYER. Address to a divine power, whether of supplication, adoration, confession, or thankfulness. Among primitive peoples, P. is often merely a magic formula, compelling the deity to perform the wishes of the worshipper, but with the advance of religion it develops towards disinterested communion with a higher power. The R.C. and Greek churches sanction prayer to the Virgin, angels, and saints, to secure their intercession for the devotee, but Protestant churches limit P. to God alone. Protestant churches also make no provision for prayer for the dead, since this implies belief in Purgatory.

PRAZ (prats), **Mario** (1896–). Italian scholar. Prof. of English language and literature at Rome from 1935, he is known for such studies as *The Romantic Agony* (1930) and *The Flaming Heart* (1958), a study of Anglo-Italian literary relationships, e.g. Crashaw, Machiavelli.

PREDESTINATION. In theology, the doctrine which asserts the foredetermination by God of all events, and of the ultimate election to glory or reprobation to perdition of the individual soul. The theory of P. was elucidated in the controversy between Augustine, who claimed the absolute determination of election by God, and ·Pelagius, who upheld the doctrine of freewill. Luther and Calvin adopted the Augustinian view at the Reformation, although in differing degrees, but Arminius adopted the Pelagian standpoint.

PREEDY, George R. *See* LONG, M. G.

PREFABRICATION. *See* HOUSING.

PREFECT (Fr. *préfet*, präfeh′). In France the govt.'s representative in each dept., the office being first estab. in 1800. In each *commune* (the unit of local govt.) a mayor is elected by the municipal council (themselves elected by universal suffrage), who is head of the local police, and acts with his assistants under the orders of-the P. *See* LOCAL GOVT.

PREGNANCY. The condition in which a child is growing within the womb. It begins at conception and ends at birth, and the normal length is forty weeks, though abortion or premature birth may occur at any time, and the period may be much exceeded. Menstruation stops on conception. After the second month the breasts become tense and tender, the area round the nipple becomes dark brown. Enlargement of the womb can be felt about the end of the third month, and thereafter the abdomen enlarges progressively.

PREMINGER, Otto (Ludwig) (1906–). American producer-director. B. in Vienna, he was associated with the Josefsteater before going to the U.S.A., where he was prof. at Yale 1938–41. His films show a highly developed and intricate technique of story-telling, which clearly presents the issues, without judging

them; and a masterly use of the wide screen and the travelling camera: they incl. *Margin for Error* (1942), *River of No Return* (1953), *Anatomy of a Murder* (1959), *Advise and Consent* (1961), *Hurry Sundown* (1967) and *Skidoo* (1968).

PREMIUM SAVINGS BONDS. *See* LOTTERY and SAVING.

PREMONSTRATENSIANS or **White Canons.** An R.C. monastic order founded by St. Norbert at Prémontré, France, in 1120. Their rule was a stricter version of that of the Augustinian Canons.

PREMPEH I (d. 1931). Ashanti chief. He became king in 1888, and later opposed British rule. He was deported and in 1900 the Ashanti were quelled. Converted to Christianity, he returned to Kumasi in 1924, being made head chief of the people. His nephew, **Prempeh II** (1892–), succeeded him in 1931.

PRE-RAPHAELITE BROTHERHOOD. A group of Victorian artists who abandoned the rules of art developed under Raphael, and painted biblical and literary subjects in a naturalistic style. The Brotherhood, founded in 1848, had only 3 members – Dante Gabriel Rossetti, John Everett Millais, and Holman Hunt – though many other artists came under their influence, notably Ford Madox Brown, Burne-Jones, Frederick Sandys, and Arthur Hughes. The Brotherhood broke up in 1853 when Millais became an A.R.A. and abandoned the Pre-Raphaelite technique.

PRESBYTERIANISM. That system of government of the Christian Church that is based on elders as distinguished from Episcopalianism with its rule by bishops. At the Reformation, P. was expounded by John Calvin, and from his teaching and influence derive the present Presbyterian churches in Scotland (where the estab. Church is Presbyterian), England, the Commonwealth, U.S.A., etc. Each congregation is governed by elders, clerical or lay, who are of equal rank; and congregations are grouped in presbyteries, synods, and general assemblies.

PRESCOTT, William Hickling (1796–1859). American historian. B. in Mass., he was almost completely blinded by an accident, but produced the popular *History of Ferdinand and Isabella, Conquest of Mexico* (1843), and *Conquest of Peru* (1847).

PRESCRIPTION. The legal acquisition of title or right by uninterrupted use or possession from time immemorial.

PRESCRIPTION. An order written in a recognized form by a practitioner of medicine, dentistry, or veterinary surgery to a pharmacist for a preparation of drugs to be used in treatment. By tradition it is written in Latin, except for the directions addressed to the patient. It consists of (1) the superscription *recipe* (take), contracted to ℞; (2) the inscription or body, containing the names and quantities of the drugs to be dispensed; (3) the subscription, or directions to the pharmacist; (4) the signature, consisting of the contraction *Signa*, followed by directions to the patient; and (5) the patient's name, the date and the practitioner's name.

PRESIDENT. The usual title of the head of state in countries without a monarch. The office may range from the equivalent of a constitutional monarch to the actual head of the govt. For presidents of the U.S. *see* UNITED STATES OF AMERICA.

PRESIDENTIAL MEDAL OF FREEDOM. Highest peacetime civilian award in the U.S.A., instituted in 1963, conferred annually on Independence Day by the Pres. on those making significant contributions to the 'quality of American life'. It replaced the Medal of Freedom (1945) awarded for acts and service aiding U.S. security.

PRESS. *See* NEWSPAPERS.

PRESSBURG. German name of BRATISLAVA.

PRESTER JOHN (John the Priest). Fabulous Christian prince who in the 12th–13th cents. was believed to rule a powerful empire in Asia. In the

14th–16th cents. P. J. was identified with the king of Ethiopia.

PRESTON. English seaport (co. bor.) in Lancs, on the Ribble near its mouth, 21 m. S. of Lancaster. At P. in 1648 Cromwell defeated the Royalists. Industries incl. textiles, chemicals, electrical goods, aircraft and shipbuilding. Pop. (1961) 113,208.

PRESTONPANS. A Scottish burgh on the Firth of Forth, E. Lothian, 9 m. E. of Edinburgh. Nearby in 1745 the royal troops were routed by the Jacobites. Pop. (1961) 3,104.

PRESTWICK (prest'wik). Scottish burgh on the Firth of Clyde, Ayrshire, 3 m. N. of Ayr, known for its championship golf course, and as an airport for transatlantic services. Pop. (1961) 12,564.

PRETORIA. Administrative capital of the Rep. of S. Africa, and cap. of Transvaal prov. Founded in 1855, and called after the Boer leader A. Pretorius (1799–1853), it became cap. of Transvaal in 1860, and administrative cap. of the Union in 1910. The government buildings overlook the town, laid out with many parks and gardens. P. univ. was founded in 1930; P. is also the seat of the Univ. of South Africa (1873). Pop. (1960) 415,989 (202,664 white).

PRÉVOST D'EXILES (prävō' degzēl'), **Antoine François** (1697–1763). French author, known as Abbé P. He was a monk, an army officer, lived in England and Holland (1728–33), and in 1754 became prior of St.-Georges-de-Gesnes. Of his sentimental novels, *Manon Lescaut* (1731) is best remembered.

PRIAPUS (prī-ā'pus). Greek god of fertility, usually represented as a grotesquely ugly man with an exaggerated phallus. He was also a god of gardens, where his image was frequently placed as a scarecrow.

PRETORIA. The statue of General Louis Botha, unveiled in 1946, overlooks the beautiful terraced gardens which surround the republic's government buildings (erected 1910–13) on Meintje's Kop. *Courtesy of South Africa Information Service.*

PRI'BILOF ISLANDS. Group of 4 islands in the Bering Sea, of volcanic origin, 200 m. S.W. of Bristol Bay, Alaska, U.S.A.; named after Gerasim Pribilof who discovered them in 1786, they were sold by Russia to the U.S.A. in 1867 with Alaska, of which they form part. They were made a fur-seal reservation in 1868.

PRICES AND INCOMES, Nat. Board for. Estab. in the U.K. 1965 to examine and report on particular cases of rises in prices or wages which would endanger the stability of the economy.

PRICKLY HEAT. Inflammation of the sweat glands; a minor disorder of hot, wet climates, due to excessive sweating. Small vesicles are formed, but quickly dry up and heal.

PRICKLY PEAR. Genus of cacti (*Opuntia*) native to America, especially Mexico and Chile, but naturalized in southern Europe, northern Africa, and Australia, where they are a pest (*see* CACTOBLASTIS). The common P.P. (*O. vulgaris*) is low-growing, with red

or white flowers, and has pleasant-tasting oval fruit. *See also* illus. under CACTUS.

PRIDE, Thomas (d. 1658). A London drayman or brewer, he rose to be a colonel in the Parliamentary Army in the Civil War, and on Cromwell's orders executed in 1648 'Pride's Purge' of the House of Commons of its Presbyterian and Royalist members.

PRIESTLEY, John Boynton (1894–). British author. B. in Bradford, son of a schoolmaster, he was educ. at Trinity Hall, Cambridge, and served in the F.W.W. He estab. his reputation as a novelist with *The Good Companions* (1929), which he dramatized with E. Knoblock in 1931, and reinforced it with *Angel Pavement* (1930) and later books. As a playwright he has often been preoccupied with theories of time, as in *Dangerous Corner* (1932), *Time and the Conways* (1937), *Johnson over Jordan* (1939) and *An Inspector Calls* (1945), but has also a gift for family comedy, e.g. *Laburnum Grove* (1933) and *When We Are Married* (1938), and in 1962 made a stage adaptation with the author of the novel by Iris Murdoch *A Severed Head*. He is also noted for his broadcasts, especially those in wartime, and for his excellent literary criticism, as in *Literature and Western Man* (1960). He m. in 1953 Jacquetta Hawkes (q.v.).

J. B. PRIESTLEY
Photo: Angus McBean

PRIESTLEY, Joseph (1733–1804). British chemist and Nonconformist divine. B. in Leeds, he became a Presbyterian (Unitarian) minister in 1755 and from 1767 was minister of a chapel in Leeds. About 1774 he discovered oxygen, and was elected F.R.S. in 1766. In 1780 he removed to Birmingham, and in 1791 his chapel and house were sacked by the mob because of his support of the French Revolution. In 1794 he emigrated to America.

PRIEST'S HOLE. In Britain, in the time of the penal laws against Roman Catholic priests, a secret room or hiding-place for them. Many still exist in old houses, and a good example is that at Speke Hall. *See* illus. under Liverpool.

PRIMATE. The official title of metropolitans in the Christian Church. The archbishop of Canterbury is the P. of all England, and the archbishop of York the P. of England.

PRIMATES. The highest order of mammals; it includes man, the apes, monkeys, tarsiers, and lemurs.

PRIME MINISTER or **Premier.** In Commonwealth countries, and other states with parliamentary constitutions, the head of the government. The first English P.M. is generally considered to have been Walpole (1721–42), but not until 1905 was the office officially recognized, P.Ms. up to then holding some other office in addition, generally that of First Lord of the Treasury. In the U.K. the P.M. is usually the leader of the largest party in the House of Commons. Since 1902 P.Ms. have invariably been commoners. The salary is £14,000 p.a. In certain Commonwealth countries, e.g. Australia, a distinction is drawn between the Fed. P.M. and the Premier of the individual states.

PRIMO DE RIVERA, Miguel (1870–1930). Spanish soldier and statesman. He was captain-general of Catalonia when in 1923, following the disaster of the Morocco campaign, he became in effect dictator of Spain with the support of Alfonso XIII. In 1925 he became premier, and effected some useful material reforms. He resigned in 1930.

PRIMROSE. Woodland plant (*Primula vulgaris*) common in Britain and Europe, bearing pale yellow

BRITISH PRIME MINISTERS

Sir Robert Walpole	(Whig)	1721	Viscount Palmerston	(Lib.)	1859
Earl of Wilmington	(Whig)	1742	Lord J. Russell	(Lib.)	1865
Henry Pelham	(Whig)	1743	Earl of Derby	(Con.)	1866
Duke of Newcastle	(Whig)	1754	B. Disraeli	(Con.)	1868
Duke of Devonshire	(Whig)	1756	W. E. Gladstone	(Lib.)	1868
Duke of Newcastle	(Whig)	1757	B. Disraeli	(Con.)	1874
Earl of Bute	(Tory)	1762	W. E. Gladstone	(Lib.)	1880
George Grenville	(Whig)	1763	Marquess of Salisbury	(Con.)	1885
Marquess of Rockingham	(Whig)	1765	W. E. Gladstone	(Lib.)	1886
Duke of Grafton	(Whig)	1766	Marquess of Salisbury	(Con.)	1886
Lord North	(Tory)	1770	W. E. Gladstone	(Lib.)	1892
Marquess of Rockingham	(Whig)	1782	Earl of Rosebery	(Lib.)	1894
Earl of Shelburne	(Whig)	1782	Marquess of Salisbury	(Con.)	1895
Duke of Porland	(Coal.)	1783	A. J. Balfour	(Con.)	1902
William Pitt	(Tory)	1783	Sir H. Campbell-		
Henry Addington	(Tory)	1801	Bannerman	(Lib.)	1905
William Pitt	(Tory)	1804	H. H. Asquith	(Lib.)	1908
Lord Grenville	(Whig)	1806	H. H. Asquith	(Coal.)	1915
Duke of Portland	(Tory)	1807	D. Lloyd George	(Coal.)	1916
Spencer Perceval	(Tory)	1809	A Bonar Law	(Con.)	1922
Earl of Liverpool	(Tory)	1812	Stanley Baldwin	(Con.)	1923
George Canning	(Tory)	1827	J. R. MacDonald	(Lab.)	1924
Viscount Goderich	(Tory)	1827	Stanley Baldwin	(Con.)	1924
Duke of Wellington	(Tory)	1828	J. R. MacDonald	(Lab.)	1929
Earl Grey	(Whig)	1830	J. R. MacDonald	(Nat.)	1931
Viscount Melbourne	(Whig)	1834	Stanley Baldwin	(Nat.)	1935
Sir Robert Peel	(Con.)	1834	N. Chamberlain	(Nat.)	1937
Viscount Melbourne	(Whig)	1835	Winston Churchill	(Coal.)	1940
Sir Robert Peel	(Con.)	1841	Clement Attlee	(Lab.)	1945
Lord J. Russell	(Lib.)	1846	Sir W. Churchill	(Con.)	1951
Earl of Derby	(Con.)	1852	Sir Anthony Eden	(Con.)	1955
Lord Aberdeen	(Peelite)	1852	Harold Macmillan	(Con.)	1957
Viscount Palmerston	(Lib.)	1855	Sir Alec Douglas-Home	(Con.)	1963
Earl of Derby	(Con.)	1858	Harold Wilson	(Lab.)	1964
			Edward Heath	(Con.)	1970

flowers in spring. Related to it is the cowslip, and the oxlip may be a hybrid of the two.

PRINCE (Lat. *princeps*, 'first'). A royal or noble title. In Rome and medieval Italy it was used as the title of certain officials, e.g. *princeps senatus*, 'leader of the Senate'. The title was granted to the king's sons in 15th cent. France, and in England from Henry VII's time. The sovereign's eldest son is normally created P. of Wales, and the eldest dau. has often been created Princess Royal: the title is not held by 2 princesses at the same time.

PRINCE ALBERT. Canadian city in Saskatchewan, on the N. Saskatchewan r., 200 m. N. by W. of Regina, h.q. of the Royal Canadian Mounted Police for central and N. Saskatchewan. It has brickyards, flour and timber mills, and breweries. P.A. national park, 1,869 sq. m., opened 1928, lies 35 m. to the N.W. Pop. (1966) 23,560.

PRINCE EDWARD ISLAND. Island prov. of Canada, in a bay of the Gulf of St. Lawrence, separated from New Brunswick and Nova Scotia on the mainland by Northumberland Strait. It is mainly flat with a deeply indented coast. Dairying and fishing are the chief industries; silver-fox breeding is also important, and there are fish-canning factories and timber mills. Charlottetown is the cap. Area 2,184 sq. m.; pop. (1966) 108,535. Discovered by Cabot in 1497, it was claimed in 1603 by the French who called it Île Saint-Jean; taken by the British in 1758 and made a separate colony in 1769, it was re-named P.E.I. in 1798 in honour cf Edward, 4th son of George III, at that time serving as lieut.-general in Canada, duke of Kent 1799 and later father of Queen Victoria. P.E.I. entered the confederation in 1873. In 1965 a 9-m. road and rail tunnel bridge and causeway was projected across Northumberland Strait to link P.E.I. with the New Brunswick coast.

PRINCE IMPERIAL. *See* NAPOLEON III.

PRINCE RUPERT. Canadian port at the mouth of the Skeena r., in Brit. Columbia. on Kaien Island, W. side of Tsimpsean peninsula. A fishing centre with dry dock and cold-storage facilities. Pop. (1966) 14,667.

PRINCESS ROYAL. *See* PRINCE.

PRINCETON. Borough in New Jersey, U.S.A., 50 m. S.W. of New York, the seat of Princeton univ. founded in 1746 at Elizabethtown, moved to Newark 1784, to P. 1756. Pop. (1960) 11,890.

PRINCETOWN. English village on the W. of Dartmoor, Devon, containing Dartmoor prison, opened 1809.

PRINTED CIRCUIT. Method of making electrical contact between electronic components such as resistors, capacitors or transistors without the use of wire. It consists of a pattern of copper foil glued to an insulating board, the terminals of the components being pushed through holes in the board and soldered to the copper foil. The board thus acts as a means of holding the components in place whilst interconnecting them to make an electronic circuit.

PRINTING. The repeated transference of ink or paint from a single surface (the P. surface) to a succession of other surfaces (the printed surfaces), for example, the P. of most works of fiction is carried out by the transference of ink from type (q.v.) and blocks (q.v. under PROCESS ENGRAVING) on to paper. In P. processes the ink is usually laid on the P. surface by rollers; these also cover the non-P. surface, which surrounds the P. surface but does not transfer ink to the paper. The principal techniques are: (1) Letterpress P., in which the P. surface stands up in relief from the non-P. surface; the ink rollers do not touch the non-P. surface, which does not touch the paper. This is the process most widely used for books and newspapers. (2) Lithographic P. in which the P. and non-P. surfaces lie in the same place, e.g. on a single flat plate of zinc, but differ from each other in that the P. surface is covered by a film of greasy ink which rejects water, and the non-P. surface is covered by a film of water which rejects greasy ink. These two films are maintained during P. by alternate applications of ink and water from rollers. Ink and water rollers and both P. and non-P. surfaces touch the whole printed surface. The process is used for some books and magazines and in particular for colour P. (3) Gravure P., in which the ink is contained

PRINTING. Printed by William Caxton (q.v.) c. 1478, this 6-inch wide poster, the first printed advertisement published in Britain, was intended to promote the sales of a service book *The Pyes of Salisbury Use* at the Red Pole in Almonry, Westminster. The Latin tag illustrates the hazards of poster advertising, then as now, and begs that it be not pulled down.
Courtesy of the John Rylands Library.

in cells engraved into a P. plate; the whole plate is inked, the ink is cleaned off the upper or non-P. surface which touches the paper, and on contact between paper and plate the ink is drawn out of the cells on to the paper. This process is used for many magazines and for colour P. in particular. (4) Collotype P., in which the whole surface of the P. plate, which touches the ink rollers and the paper, may contain and transfer ink. As in lithographic P., the process is based on the antipathy of grease and water; that part of the plate which is to print the darkest tones is rendered the least absorbent to water, that part which is to print the lightest tones is rendered the most absorbent, and the tones in between depend on the amount of water absorbed and the extent of its consequent rejection of greasy ink. The process is used only for small editions of illustrations, whether in black only or in colour. (5) Silk-screen P., in which ink or paint is pressed through a stencil, supported by an open-mesh screen, on to the printed surface; the stencil excludes ink from the non-printed area, while over the printed area the ink passes through the screen. This process is used mainly for posters and similar forms of advertising in which bright colours are needed; for example, luminous inks can be used. In letterpress P., P. surfaces are mainly produced by metal casting, but engraving is also used (*see* PROCESS ENGRAVING); in the other processes the P. surfaces are nearly always photographically produced.

P. is believed to have begun in China in the 6th cent. A.D., and it was the Chinese who in the 11th cent. first used movable types. P. did not begin in Europe for another 3 cents.; the European invention of movable types took place in the mid-15th cent., and is usually ascribed to Johann Gutenberg of Mainz. The first book to be printed in Britain was *Dictes and Sayenges of the Phylosophers* by Lord Rivers, printed by William Caxton at Westminster in 1477.

PRIOR. The viceregent of an abbot, who was responsible for monastic discipline, or in certain R.C. monastic orders the principal of a monastery.

PRIOR, Matthew (1664–1721). British poet-diplomat. B. in E. Dorset, he was associated under the Whigs with the negotiation of the treaty of Ryswick and under the Tories with that of Utrecht ('Matt's Peace'), but on the return of the Whigs to power was imprisoned by Walpole 1715–17. His greatest gift as a poet was for light occasional verses.

PRIPET (prē'pet). River of W. Russia, a tributary of the Dnieper which it joins 50 m. above Kiev, Ukrainian S.S.R., after a course *c.* 500 m. The P. marshes near Pinsk were of strategic importance in both world wars.

PRISHVIN (prēsh'vin), **Mikhail Mikhailovich** (1873–1954). Russian writer. A student of agriculture, he was a close student of nature, e.g. *In the Land of Unfrightened Birds* (1907) and his autobiographical novel *Kashchei's Chain* (1924–8).

PRISM. In mathematics, a solid figure (polyhedron) with two equal polygonal faces (bases) in parallel planes; the other faces being parallelograms, of the same number as there are sides to one of the bases. In optics triangular Ps. are widely used in a variety of instruments incl. spectroscopes, binoculars, periscopes, and rangefinders, their properties depending on the refractive index of the material of which they are made and the angles at which they are cut.

PRISON. Place of confinement for those contravening the laws of the state. Until the late 18th cent. criminals were commonly sentenced to death, mutilation or transportation rather than imprisonment, so that the growth of criminal Ps. as opposed to places of detention for those awaiting trial, confined for political reasons, etc., was a late development. One of the greatest reformers in Britain was John Howard (q.v.), whose P. Act of 1778 estab. the principle of separate confinement combined with

work in an attempt at reform, though long a dead letter, was carried out when Pentonville was built in 1842. Penal servitude was introduced in 1857, as an additional deterrent, after the refusal of the colonies to accept transported convicts, but this and hard labour were finally abolished in Britain by the Criminal Justice Act of 1948, so that there is only one form of prison sentence, viz. imprisonment. Under the Criminal Justice Act of 1967 courts may suspend P. sentences of 2 years or less, and, unless the offender has previously been in prison or borstal (q.v.), will normally do so, i.e. sentence only comes into effect if another offence is committed. Persistent offenders may receive an extended sentence for the protection of the public. After serving one-third of their sentence (minimum 12 months), selected prisoners may be released on licence.

It was hoped that the act would relieve the strain on P. services by reducing the large number of short-term prisoners who threatened security, interfered with the treatment of long-term offenders, and formed a 'recruiting ground' for lifelong criminals: the increase in the P. population had been from 11,000 in 1938 to 35,000 in 1968.

All enlightened countries aim at rehabilitation and in Russia, for example, great stress is laid on constructive work and the assimilation of the prisoner to a normal life, e.g. wives may be allowed to live with good-conduct men. Notable experiments have also been made in Britain and elsewhere in 'open Ps.' without bars, release of prisoners to work in ordinary jobs outside the P. in the final stages of their sentence, and after-care on release. *See* PROBATION.

PRISONERS OF WAR. By international convention P.o.W. are entitled to food on the same scale as the captor country's rear-line troops; supply of clothing and footwear; medical attendance; and the right to send and receive letters, and to receive food parcels and reading matter. P.o.W. who are seriously wounded or ill may be repatriated if a medical board, on which 2 doctors out of 3 are neutrals, certifies they are permanently incapacitated as fighting men. These rights are safeguarded by the International Red Cross Committee at Geneva, representatives of which inspect prison-camps.

PRITCHETT, Victor Sawdon (1900–). British novelist, short-story writer and critic. His works incl. *You Make Your Own Life*, and *It May Never Happen*, collections of his short stories, and *The Living Novel* (1946) criticism. As a critic he is associated with the *New Statesman*.

PRIVATE ENTERPRISE. System whereby economic activities are in private hands and are carried on for private profit, as opposed to national, municipal, or co-operative ownership.

PRIVET. Genus of shrubs. The common P. (*Ligustrum vulgare*) hardy, quick-growing and responding well to clipping, is much used for hedges. It has lanceolate leaves and small spikes of white flowers followed by black berries.

PRIVY COUNCIL. A body of royal advisers. It originated in England in Norman times as the council of the chief royal officials, and under the Tudors and early Stuarts became the chief governing body. After 1688 it was replaced by the cabinet, which originated as a committee of the P.C. Its powers are now formal, e.g. royal proclamations and orders-in-council, and membership is an honour granted automatically to Cabinet Ministers—who for the most part comprise the acting council—and to others who have held high political, ecclesiastical or judicial offices in Britain and the Commonwealth. It is presided over by the Lord President of the Council. The *Judicial Committee of the P.C.*, which incl. Commonwealth judges, still acts as a final court of appeal for some members of the Commonwealth, e.g. New Zealand, Ceylon and Malta.

PRIVY PURSE. The amount set apart in the Civil List for the sovereign's personal use. For Queen Elizabeth II it has been fixed at £60,000 a year.

PRIVY SEAL, Lord. An English officer of state, through whose hands all letters-patent had to. pass before the great seal was affixed. The title is now an honorary one, borne by a member of the cabinet entrusted with special non-departmental duties.

PROBATE. Formal proof of a will. If its validity is unquestioned, it is proved in 'common form'; the Executor, in the absence of other interested parties, obtains at a P. Registry a grant upon his own oath. Otherwise, it must be proved in 'solemn form': its validity estab. at a P. Court (in the P., Divorce and Admiralty division), those prejudiced under it being made parties to the action. In the U.S. the 'solemn form' is the more usual, although there may be no question as to validity, and P. is granted generally by courts of special jurisdiction.

PROBATION. A procedure adopted in lieu of prison sentence, in certain cases, e.g., first offenders and children, where the offender is placed under the supervision of a P. Officer appointed by the court, and undergoes certain restrictions. This method is used where it is believed that it will benefit the offender's future behaviour.

PROCESS ENGRAVING. The engraving by photo-mechanical means of a relief surface for the letterpress process of printing (q.v.). A photograph is taken of the image to be reproduced; the image is developed in an acid-resistant coating through the negative on a metal plate; and the non-printing part of the surface, unprotected by acid-resistant, is etched away. The finished plate is known as a block. A line-block can be made from any black and white original, and reproduces the original faithfully; if the original contains shades of grey, they must be reproduced from a half-tone (q.v.) block. A separate block must be made for each colour to be printed; but the full range of colours can be reproduced from a set of 4 half-tone blocks, made from successive photographs of the originals taken through coloured filters, and printed in yellow, cyan (blue-green), magenta (red-blue) and black. The term process engraving is also loosely applied to the photographic preparation of printing surfaces for processes other than letterpress.

PROCRU′STĒS ('the stretcher'). In Greek legend, a robber who tied his victims to a bed, and if they were longer than the bed, cut off their limbs, and if they were shorter, stretched them.

PROCURATOR-FISCAL. An officer attached to the sheriff's court in Scotland charged with the preliminary questioning of witnesses regarding crimes, and also inquiring into the circumstances of suspicious deaths.

PROFIT-SHARING. A system whereby an employer pays his workers a fixed share of his profits. It originated in France in the early 19th cent., and under the influence of the Christian Socialists was widely practised for a time within the co-operative movement.

PROGRESSION. A series of numbers each formed by a specific relationship to its predecessor. An *arithmetical* P. has numbers which increase or decrease by a common sum or difference, e.g. 2, 4, 6, 8 . . . A *geometric* P. has numbers each bearing a fixed ratio to its predecessor, e.g. 3, 6, 12, 24 . . . A *harmonic* P. is a series with numbers whose reciprocals are in arithmetical P., e.g. 1, $\frac{1}{2}$, $\frac{1}{3}$, $\frac{1}{4}$ . . .

PROHIBITION. Laws making illegal the sale of intoxicating liquor, which originated in the U.S.A. Legislation was passed in Maine in 1846, and throughout many states thereafter, but later became a dead letter. Revival of the campaign at the end of the cent. led to a sustained agitation for legislation, which was nourished by the F.W.W. and need for cereals. In 1920 a P. amendment (known as the Volstead Act,

after Congressman V. who introduced it) to the U.S. constitution became operative. Apart from loss of revenue, it led to much smuggling and distilling, and public opinion insisted on its repeal in 1933.

PROKO′VIEV, Serge (1891–1953). Russian composer. B. nr. Ekaterinoslav, he studied at St. Petersburg under Rimsky-Korsakov and achieved fame as a pianist. For some time he lived in London, in the U.S.A., and in Paris, but returned to Moscow in 1934. He composed operas such as *The Love of Three Oranges*; ballets for Diaghileff; symphonies incl. the *Classical Symphony*; the *Scythian Suite*; music for films; piano concertos, of which the 3rd is best known; violin concertos; songs and cantatas, e.g. that for the 29th anniv. of the Oct. Revolution; *Peter and the Wolf*, a fairy tale, etc.

PROLETARIAT. Those classes which possess no property, and therefore depend upon the sale of their labour-power, as opposed to the capitalists or bourgeoisie, who own the means of production, and the petty bourgeoisie, or working small property-owners. They are usually divided into the industrial, the agricultural and the intellectual P. The term is derived from the Lat. *proletarii*, the class possessing no property, who served the state by producing offspring (*proles*).

PROME (prōm). Burmese town and trade centre on the Irrawaddy r. 150 m. N.N.W. of Rangoon, cap. of P. dist. and terminus of a railway from Rangoon. The 180 ft. high Shivesandaw pagoda attracts many pilgrims; silk, lacquer, and paper are among merchandise handled. The E. India Company set up a factory at P. in 1612. In the S.W.W., P. was held by the Japanese 1942–5. Pop. (est.) 30,000.

PROMENADE CONCERTS ('Proms'). Originally, concerts during the performance of which audiences are allowed to walk about. The London P.Cs. (since 1895) are the premier musical activity of England. They were given in the Queen's Hall until it was destroyed by enemy action in 1941, and then in the Royal Albert Hall, and were conducted by Sir Henry Wood until his death. They have fostered the 20th cent. renaissance of music appreciation in England.

PROMETHEUS (promē′thūs). Greek hero, who stole fire from heaven to give to men, and taught them the useful arts. Zeus to punish him chained him to a rock in the Caucasus, where an eagle preyed on his liver, until he was rescued by Hercules.

PROMETHIUM. Element of the rare earth group, of which the existence in nature is unconfirmed: symbol Pm, at. wt. uncertain (probably 147), at. no. 61. Several isotopes, obtained by fission of uranium and by neutron bombardment of neodymium, have been reported by different groups of workers.

PROMISSORY NOTE. A written promise to pay on demand or at a fixed future time a specific sum of money to a named person or bearer. Like a cheque, it may be negotiated by endorsement by the payee.

PRONGBUCK or **Pronghorn.** Only surviving member of a family (Antilocapridae) between deer and cattle. The P. (*Antilocapra americana*) is 3 ft. high, sheds its horns annually, and is a swift runner. It inhabits the N. American plains.

PROPERTIUS (prōper′shius), **Sextus Aurelius** (fl. 30–15 B.C.). Roman poet. B. at Assisi, he settled in Rome, and became a member of the literary circle of Maecenas. The majority of his poems deal with his love for his mistress 'Cynthia'.

PROPHETS. Name given to the succession of Hebrew saints and seers who preached and prophesied in the Hebrew kingdoms in Palestine from the 8th cent. B.C. until the suppression of Jewish independence in 586 B.C. and possibly later. The chief were Elijah, Amos, Hosea, and Isaiah. The prophetic books of the O.T. constitute a division of the Hebrew Bible.

PROPORTIONAL REPRESENTATION. An electoral system designed to ensure that minority votes are not lost, and that the distribution of seats corresponds to that of votes. It should not be confused with (a) the second ballot (used in France from 1928 until the S.W.W.), whereby, if no one candidate receives an absolute majority, a second vote is taken to decide between the top candidates; (b) the alternative vote (widely used in Australia), which achieves the same end in one ballot: the voter numbers the candidates in the order of his preference, the bottom candidates are eliminated in turn, and their votes are transferred to their supporters' next preferences. These methods merely ensure than the majority elects the winner in a particular constituency.

True P.R. requires that constituencies should each return 3 or more members, and has 2 main forms: (a) the party list (common on the Continent), whereby the seats are allotted to each party in proportion to the number of votes cast for it; (b) the single transferable vote (used for example in the Rep. of Ireland since 1922), whereby the voters mark the candidates in order of preference. Votes received by candidates in excess of the number required to win a seat, and those for the bottom candidates who are successively eliminated, are distributed according to the next choice of the voter.

PROPYL ALCOHOL (C_3H_7OH). Two compounds, normal P.A., and isopropyl A. The former is also known as ethyl carbinol. It is a colourless liquid, hygroscopic, has density 0·8, and is miscible with water. P.A. is used in perfumery preparations.

PROSE. The expression of thought in written language without attempt at metrical form. English P. first appeared in the 8th cent., reached a simple perfection under Alfred in the 9th, suffered eclipse following the Conquest, revived by the 14th cent., and attained flexibility and precision with Dryden.

PROSTITUTION. A prostitute is a woman who offers her body in return for payment. Although admitted by civilized societies as an evil ideally to be eradicated, P. is in some countries recognized by the licensing of brothels and the registration of prostitutes – the latter being used as a means of combating the spread of venereal diseases by enforced medical examination and treatment. In England there is a compromise by which, although it is not an offence to be or become a prostitute, fines (with imprisonment for the third offence onwards) are imposed on women convicted of soliciting in a public place: there are also penalties for procuring a woman not a prostitute for purposes of P. and for anyone living on the earnings of a prostitute, and for keeping a brothel.

PROTACTINIUM (Gk. protos first). The 1st element of the actinium series of radioactive elements, symbol Pa, at. wt. 231, at. no. 91: found in nature in all uranium ores, and discovered by Soddy and Cranston (independently by Hahn and Meitner) in 1917. It forms actinium by the loss of an alpha-particle.

PROTECTION. The discouragement by heavy duties of the import of foreign goods likely to compete with home products. The opposite practice is Free Trade (q.v.).

PROTECTORATE. In international law, the relationship between a large state and a small or backward one, over which the former exercises a direct or indirect control. Ps. within the Commonwealth incl. the Solomon Is. P. In English history, the term the P. is applied to the rule of Oliver and Richard Cromwell 1653–9.

PROTEINS (prō'tē-inz). Organic substances containing carbon, hydrogen, oxygen, and nitrogen. They constitute an important part of living cells, and are essential in animal diet. The most common examples are egg-albumen, casein in milk, haemoglobin in blood, and ossein in bone.

PROTESTANTISM. One of the main divisions of Christianity, the others being Roman Catholicism and the Eastern Orthodox Church. Its name is usually derived from the protest made by Luther and his supporters at the Diet of Spires in 1529 against the decision to reaffirm the Edict of the Diet of Worms against the Reformation. The Protestant Churches incl. the Church of England and the Nonconformist or Free Churches in Britain, the Lutheran and Reformed (Calvinist) Churches on the Continent and the great majority of Christians other than Roman Catholics in the Commonwealth, U.S.A., etc.

PROTEUS (prō'tūs). In Gk. mythology an old man, the warden of the sea beasts of Poseidon, who possessed the gift of prophecy, but could transform himself to any form he chose to evade questioning. Also the eel-like, white, eyeless amphibian (P. anguinus) found in the caves of Dalmatia, which has 4 rudimentary legs and external gills; on exposure o light it develops dark pigmentation and becomes fully eyed.

PROTOCOLS OF ZION. An anti-Semitic falsification, purporting to be the notes of a plan for the Jewish world conquest submitted by Herzl in 1897 to the 1st Zionist Congress at Basle, and 1st pub. in Russia in 1905. In 1921 the London Times conclusively proved that the Ps. are a plagiarism of an attack on Napoleon III, pub. in Geneva in 1864.

PROTOPLASM. Greyish, translucent, jelly-like material within and incl. the plasma membrane of a cell, the basis of all living things. Always containing carbon, oxygen, hydrogen, nitrogen and a large proportion of water, it may also comprise sulphur, iron, phosphorus, calcium and iodine, as well as such complex chemical compounds as proteins and fats in colloidal form. Chemical interactions constantly take place in all living matter, and P. is capable of repeatedly reproducing itself.

PROTOZO̅A. Group of unicellular animals. Each cell is capable of individual existence, but many types live in colonies. The body is composed of protoplasm, and in the Foraminifera and Radiolaria a skeleton of calcium carbonate or silica is deposited.

PROUDHON (proodoṅ'), **Pierre Joseph** (1809–65). French anarchist. B. at Besançon, he sat in the Constituent Assembly of 1848, was imprisoned for 3 years, and had to go into exile in Brussels. His ideas, which envisaged a highly decentralized society of small property owners, greatly influenced French Socialist thought. He pub. What is Property? (1840) and Philosophy of Poverty.

PROUST (proost), **Marcel** (1871–1922). French author. B. at Auteuil, son of a wealthy doctor, he was a martyr to asthma from the age of 9. Mixing in society, he gained a reputation as a dilettante, but following the deaths of his father and mother (in 1904 and 1905 respectively) he retired to devote himself to his mammoth autobiographical study, reflecting also the life of his time, which appeared as A la recherche du temps perdu (1913–27: Remembrance of Things Past). A cork-lined workroom for absolute isolation from the world and various other eccentricities, besides his homosexuality, have made him as much written about as writer. A fragmentary early novel Jean Santeuil (written 1899) was pub. in reconstructed form in 1951.

PROUT, Samuel (1783–1852). British water-colour painter. B. at Plymouth, he became famous for his pictures of Continental cities.

PROVENÇAL. A Romance language, also known as langue d'oc, in use in S. France from the early Middle Ages until the 16th cent., when it was replaced by French, although individual dialects survived. P. resembles the Catalan dialect of Spanish, and is closer than French to the original Latin forms.

P. literature originated in the 10th cent., and flowered in the 12th cent. with the work of the troubadours (q.v.), e.g. Bernart de Ventadorn, Arnaut Daniel, Giraud de Borneil, Raimbaut d'Orange, and

Bertran de Born. The Albigensian War in the 13th cent. destroyed the troubadours, and P. disappears as a literary medium from the 14th until the 19th cent. when Jacques Jasmin (1798–1864) and others paved the way for the Félibrige group of poets, of whom the greatest are Joseph Roumanille (1818–91), Frédéric Mistral (1830–1914), and Félix Gras (1844–1901).

PROVENCE (prŏvoṅs'). Ancient prov. of France, on the Mediterranean. Already a Roman *provincia* (hence its name), it varied in size through its history and for a short time *c*. A.D. 900 was a kingdom. Later it was a county held by Alphonso, king of Aragon, Charles of Anjou, king of Naples, and others. The last count bequeathed it in 1482 to Louis XI of France, and his son Charles VIII secured control of it. In 1790 it was divided into the depts. of Basses-Alpes, Var, and Bouches-du-Rhône and part of Vaucluse and Alpes-Maritimes; the name P. is still used for the region, which has its own tongue.

PROVERB. A short familiar expression of a well-estab. ethical or practical truth. The most notable collection of Ps. is in the O.T. book of that name, which forms part of the Wisdom Literature of the ancient Hebrews. Solomon is said (on slender grounds) to have been the author of some of them.

PROVIDENCE. Cap., port and trade centre of Rhode Is. state, U.S.A., on Providence r., 27 m. from the Atlantic. Jewellery, silverware, textiles and textile machinery, watches, chemicals, etc., are manufactured, and meat packing is carried on. P. was settled by Roger Williams in 1636. The 1st Baptist chapel in the American colonies was built in 1638 at P., which is the seat of Brown Univ. (1764). Pop. met. area P.–Pawtucket–Warwick (1970) 900,569.

PROVINCE WELLESLEY. Territory on the W. coast of the Malay peninsula, part of Penang in W. Malaysia. It was settled by the British in 1800. Crops incl. rice, rubber, tobacco and spices. Area 290 sq. m.; pop (est.) 180,000.

PROXY. A person legally authorized to stand in another's place; also the instrument of conferment thereof. The term usually refers to voting at meetings, but there may be marriages by P.

PRU'DHOE BAY. Site on the coast of N. Alaska where oil was struck beneath the frozen tundra in 1968. The field is rich, but the difficulties of working in low temperatures complicate exploitation. *See* NORTH-WEST PASSAGE.

PRUD'HON (prüdoṅ'), **Pierre Paul** (1758–1823). French historical and portrait painter. B. at Cluny, he studied in Paris and later in Rome, where he was so influenced by Correggio, that he became known as the 'French Correggio'. His works incl. 'Vengeance and Justice Pursuing Crime', 'Diana and Jupiter' and a portrait of the Empress Josephine.

PRUNUS. Genus of trees in the family Rosaceae. The white or pink flowers are followed by drupes, often edible. Plums, peaches, apricots, almonds, and cherries all belong to this genus.

PRUSSIA. Former state of Germany, bordering the Baltic, and formed out of a union in 1618 of the Mark of Brandenburg and the Prussian state of the Teutonic Order. The Mark of Brandenburg originated in the 12th cent. under the Ascanians, who were followed by the Wittelsbachs, and in 1415 by the Hohenzollerns. John Sigmund (1608–19) m. Anna, dau. of Albert Frederick, duke of Prussia and last grandmaster of the Teutonic Order, and so united the territories. Frederick William (1640–88), known as the Great Elector, laid the foundations of P.'s military power. Frederick III (1688–1713) assumed the title of King Frederick I of Prussia in 1701. Frederick William I (1713–40) concentrated his energies on the development of P.'s military might and commerce. During the reign of his son Frederick the Great (1740–86) Silesia, E. Frisia, and W. Prussia were annexed. The reign of

Frederick William III (1797–1840) was marked by the disaster of Jena (1806); his possessions were reduced, but after the Congress of Vienna (1815) P. regained its lost territories and also acquired lands in the Rhineland and Saxony. The year 1848 was marked by revolutionary outbreaks. In 1864 war with Denmark, resulted in the acquisition of Schleswig and Holstein, while after the defeat of Austria in 1866 Hanover, Nassau, Frankfurt-am-Main, and Hesse-Cassel were annexed to P. which became the head of the N. German Confederation. In 1871 William I of P. became emperor of all Germany. In 1918 P. became a rep. and a democratic constitution was adopted in 1920. In 1932 the Prussian govt. was removed from office by the Reich govt. of von Papen, and after 1933 P. lost its local independence. The Allies abolished the state of P. in 1946.

PRUSSIC ACID. *See* HYDROCYANIC ACID.

PRYNNE, William (1600–69). English puritan. He pub. in 1632 *Histriomastix*, a work attacking stage-plays, and containing aspersions on the queen for which he was pilloried and lost his ears. In 1637 he was again pilloried and branded for an attack on the bishops. He opposed the execution of Charles I, and actively supported the Restoration.

PRZEMYSL (pzhem'isl). Town of Poland, 60 m. W. of Lvov, on the San. Industrial establishments incl. flour and timber mills, tanneries, distilleries, and factories making ceramics and canning food. Dating according to tradition from the 8th cent., it belonged alternately to Poland and Kiev from the 10th to 14th cents. Austrian 1722–1919, it was a frontier fortress, besieged by the Russians, except for a brief respite, from Sept. 1914 to March 1915. It was in German occupation June 1941 to July 1944. Pop. (1960) 46,000.

PSALMS. Book of the O.T. consisting of 150 poems, the majority of which are songs of praise and were intended to be sung to a musical accompaniment. The Psalter was probably completed in its present form in the 1st cent. B.C., and is divided in 5 books, containing Ps. 1–41, 42–72, 73–89, 90–106, and 107–150. The authorship of many of the Ps. is ascribed to David, but no absolute evidence for this exists.

PSKOV. Town in the R.S.F.S.R., U.S.S.R., on the Velikaya, 9 m. S.E. of Lake P. and 160 m. S.S.W. of Leningrad., cap. of P. region, famous for leather and a trade centre for hemp, flax and timber. It dates from A.D. 965 and was independent 1348–1510, when it became Russian. In the S.W.W. it was in German hands 1941–4. Pop. (1967) 81,000.

PSORIASIS (sorī'asis). An inflammation of the skin marked by raised red patches, usually on the arms and legs, covered with whitish scales. The 1st attack usually takes place in childhood and attacks recur at irregular intervals.

PSYCHE (sī'kē). The personification of the soul in later Gk. literature and art, generally represented as a winged girl. The love story of Cupid and P. is told in Apuleius's 'Golden Ass'.

PSYCHIATRY and PSYCHOTHERAPY. The part of medicine which deals with the diagnosis, treatment and care of the mentally ill. All or any of the disciplines of psychological thought may be involved in treatment, from different viewpoints, and many of the therapists may not be doctors, but highly skilled experts in their particular fields. Many physical methods are available, incl. electric-shock treatment for cases of depression; and an increasing use is made of drugs which produce specific changes in mood and subjective emotional tension. They consist of (1) the tranquillizers (q.v.); (2) anti-excitement and anti-confusional agents; (3) the symptomatic anti-depressants, and (4) the more basic anti-depressants. These physical methods are generally used in conjunction with psychotherapy to achieve long-term and real improvement.

PSYCHIC RESEARCH. The investigation of

phenomena inexplicable by recognized scientific laws. Formerly this was limited to phenomena produced at séances – levitation, ectoplasm, telepathy and supernormal cognition in trance and clairvoyant mediums, activities of apparitions and poltergeists – and useful work was done by the British Society for Psychical Research (1882). Between the wars, however, the study of extra-sensory perception in particular emerged from the séance room to the science laboratory and famous centres are the Parapsychology Laboratory of Duke Univ., N. Carolina (*see* RHINE, J. B.) and the Psychophysical Research Unit at Oxford.

PSYCHOLOGY AND SCHOOLS OF ANALYTIC THOUGHT. The science of the mind (q.v.), and the study of mental life. The mind may be defined as the ñon-material basis of conscious and unconscious thought, functioning in the brain, and an intimate and integral part of the biological entity that is man.

GENERAL P. in which fundamental methods of all sciences are used – observation and experiment – with due allowance for the participation of the observer, in the study of the basic nature of the fundamental processes.

COMPARATIVE P. embraces the similarities and differences between groups such as animals and children; due to race, nationality, sex, class, etc., and between individuals in any group.

APPLIED P. is concerned with the practical application of knowledge to particular problems, incl. child and vocational guidance, intelligence testing, personnel and management selection, efficiency studies, etc.

PATHOLOGICAL P. deals with the classification of mental abnormalities: a necessary prerequisite to treatment. Just as in other aspects of human life, it is seldom possible to place an individual in a 'hard and fast' category, since there is a great deal of overlapping into adjacent groups.

PSYCHOANALYSIS is the school of P. due in origin and development to the work of Sigmund Freud (q.v.). The essential technique involves free association of thoughts, in the waking state, and analysis of the contents of dreams, as a means of revealing the unconscious – ideas and emotions existing beneath the realm of consciousness. There are 4 postulates which are generally accepted by most schools of analytic thought: 1, The existence of psychic determinism; 2, the role of the unconscious; 3, the goal – directed nature of behaviour, and 4, the developmental or historical approach. For a comprehensive account, the reader is referred to Freud's *Introductory Lectures on Psychoanalysis*. The major division between Freudians and those of other schools is concerned with biological orientation and the *libido* theory, which consider that personality is based on biological drives, principally sexual, that are part of the body's heritage, and must pass through certain stages of development during the 1st five years of life; after completion of which they continue to influence behaviour throughout life.

The *non-libido* schools of Horney, Fromm, Adler, Sullivan, *et al*, consider that personality is a social product using biological energy, but suitably modified according to circumstances, strongly influenced but not confined by constitutional or developmental factors, which, in the main, are less important than cultural ones; and possessing needs which arise as much from the individual's society as from his biological make-up.

A difference in outlook exists in the older, more traditional countries, with their emphasis that the source of man's troubles lies deep within himself – biological justifications of original sin and predestination – and the strongly held views of new countries, that men are naturally good, are born free and equal

with nearly infinite potentialities; so that whatever troubles they encounter must be due to social or environmental factors. It is therefore interesting to see that the U.S.A. and the U.S.S.R. shared in the birth of Behaviourism (rejection of the concept of original sin in the form of innate ideas). Arising from the philosophies of John Locke and Rousseau, these ideas spread to the U.S.A. through Jeffersonian democracy; and to the U.S.S.R. by way of Karl Marx.

PTAH (tah). Ancient Egyptian god, one of the Memphis triad; he was the divine potter or artificer, the personification of creative force.

PTARMIGAN (tar'migan). The smallest grouse (*Lagopus mutus*) found in Britain. It also inhabits the Arctic, and its colour changes with its surroundings.

PTERIA. Classical name for BOGHAZKOI.

PTERODACTYL (terōdak'til). An extinct flying lizard, remains of which have been found in rocks of

PTERODACTYL

the Mesozoic age. Somewhat resembling a bat, it had a wing-spread varying from 1 ft. to about 20 ft. The head was bird-like, and the hind legs like those of a lizard, while the fore-legs bore long jointed fingers.

PTOLEMY (tol'emi). Name of a dynasty of Macedonian kings who ruled Egypt. Ptolemy I, one of Alexander's generals, seized Egypt in 323 B.C., and was succeeded by 12 kings of the same name. Ptolemy XIII was put to death in 47 B.C. by his sister Cleopatra, with whose death in 30 B.C. the dynasty ended.

PTOLEMY or **Claudius Ptolemaeus** (2nd cent. A.D.). Astronomer and geographer. A native of Egypt, he carried out observations in Alexandria, and pub. a *Geography*, which was a standard source of information until the 16th cent. The *Ptolemaic system*, which was not superseded by the Copernican until 1543, assumed that the earth was the fixed centre of the universe, with the sun, moon, and stars revolving round it.

PTOMAINE (tō'mā-jn). A class of chemical substances produced by putrefaction. Ps. do not really play a part in food poisoning. 'P. poisoning' is, in fact, usually caused by bacteria of the *Salmonella* group.

PUBERTY (pū'-). The stage of human development in which the secondary sexual characteristics begin to appear and the individual becomes capable of reproduction. In boys it occurs at about 14; in girls usually a little earlier.

PUBES. The lowest part of the front of the trunk, the region where the external generative organs are situated. The underlying bony structure, the pubic arch, is formed by the union in the mid line of the two pubic bones, which are the front portions of the hip bones. In women it is more prominent than in men, to allow more room for the passage of a child's head at birth, and carries a pad of fat and connective tissue, the *mons veneris* (mountain of Venus), for its protection.

PUBLIC HOUSE. In England a house licensed for the consumption of intoxicating liquor, which may be either a 'free' or 'tied' house, according to whether supplies are bought from a particular co. owning the P.H. or whether the landlord has a free choice of suppliers.

PUBLIC SCHOOLS. Term used in a specialized sense in Britain to denote the independent schools which developed principally during the 18th and early 19th cents., although some, such as Eton and Harrow, are ancient foundations originally intended for poor scholars. P.S. are predominantly boarding schools for boys of 12–18 years, which are divided into houses, each in the care of a housemaster. Much of the discipline, incl. sometimes a degree of corporal punishment, is entrusted to senior boys or prefects, though the worst aspects of this system and the once prevalent stress on classical subjects, sports and games, have been modified in recent years. The heads are members of the Headmasters' Conference. The Wilson govt. regarded P.S. as 'socially divisive', and in 1965 estab. a commission to advise on their integration into the State system.

PUBLISHING. The production of books for sale. The publisher arranges for the printing, binding and distribution, to booksellers or through direct mail – the latter being a growing field – but may also share in the creative aspect of book production by commissioning books, by editing otherwise unpublishable work, e.g. Thomas Wolfe, but exercise of this function is controversial, etc. Although all rights in a book may be purchased by the publisher for a single outright fee, it is more usual and generally more fair to publisher and author if a fixed 'royalty' is paid on every copy sold, in return for the exclusive right to pub. in an agreed territory. Rising costs in book production have tended to discourage worthwhile books with a relatively small sale in favour of the best-seller, most markedly in the U.S.A.; other features of modern P. are the growth of non-fiction titles, and the great increase of paper-backs. In Britain most leading publishers are members of the Publishers' Association.

PUCCINI, Giacomo (1858–1924). Italian composer. B. at Lucca, he achieved success with the opera *Manon Lescaut* (1893), which was followed by *La Bohème*, *Madame Butterfly*, *Tosca*, and the unfinished *Turandot*.

PUDOVKIN, Vsevolod Illationovich (1893–1953). Soviet film director. His films incl. *Mother*, *Storm Over Asia*, and *Suvorov*. One of the fathers of Soviet cinema, he wrote *Film Technique* and *Film Acting*.

PUEBLA (pūe'blah). Mexican town, cap. of P. state, on the Pan-American Highway, 65 m. S.E. of Mexico City, noted for cotton weaving, pottery, and sugar refining; it is a market for livestock, fruit, vegetables, etc., and has an airfield. Founded c. 1535 as P. de los Angeles, it was re-named P. de Zaragoza in honour of General Zaragoza who defeated the French there in 1862. There is a univ. (1537) and a cathedral begun in 1552. Nearby are pre-Columbian remains. Pop. (1967) 360,600.

PUEBLO (poo-e'blō), U.S.S. American intelligence vessel captured without resistance by the N. Koreans Jan. 1968, allegedly within their territorial waters: the crew, but not the ship, were released Dec. 1968. A naval court recommended no disciplinary action.

PUERPERAL FEVER. Infection by pus-producing cocci, which enter raw surfaces of the womb and genital tract left by the passage of the child. The mortality used to be severe, but the sulpha drugs and penicillin have made mortality almost negligible.

PUERTO RICO. Is. territory of the U.S.A., in the W. Indies. A mountain range runs E.–W. The chief export crops are sugar, tobacco, pineapples, coffee and coconuts: the chief industries are sugar refining and rum making; textiles, clothing, chemicals, electric and electronic equipment are among manufactures. The cap. is San Juan. Area 3,435 sq. m.; pop. (1967) 2,600,000, mostly white and of Spanish descent, the remainder Negroes and mulattos. Spanish is the official language, but English is widely known. P.R. is administered by a governor (popularly elected for 4 years) and a senate and house of repre-

sentatives. P.R. was discovered by Columbus in 1493, annexed to Spain in 1508, and ceded to the U.S.A. by a treaty of 1898 (ratified 1899), achieving commonwealth status in 1952. A plebiscite 1967 resulted in a majority for retention of this status. There are about 1,000,000 Puerto Ricans in the U.S.A., but greater prosperity means that more return to P.R. than emigrate, in contrast to the depression of the 1940s. For Americans P.R. is a winter holiday resort.

PUFF ADDER. A venomous reptile (*Bitis arietans*) in the family Viperidae. Native to Africa and S. Arabia, it is about 5 ft. long, and yellowish-brown.

PUFFIN. Sea-bird (*Fratercula arctica*), of the auk family, found on the coasts of the northernmost countries of the Atlantic. About 13 in. long, the P. has orange legs, black plumage above and white underparts. In the breeding season the large beak is increased in size, and coloured red, yellow, and blue. One dirty-white egg is laid in a burrow in the soil.

PUFFIN

PUG DOG. Toy dog resembling a small bulldog. Sandy or silvery-fawn in colour, it was introduced into England, from China, by the Dutch East India Co. in the 16th cent.

PUGIN (pū'jin), **Augustus Welby Northmore** (1812 –52). British architect. A convert to R. Catholicism, he was a pioneer of the Gothic revival, assisting Barry (q.v.) with the Houses of Parliament.

PUGLIA. Ital. form of APULIA.

PULA (pōō'lah). Yugoslav city and port with both commercial and naval harbours. Already in Roman days a naval port, Colonia Pietas Julia, it was taken by the Venetians in 1148. It passed to Austria in 1815, to Italy in 1919, to Yugoslavia in 1947. It has a Roman theatre, a temple of Augustus (19 B.C.), and a castle and cathedral constructed under Venetian rule. Pop. (1961) 37,403.

PULITZER, Joseph (1847–1911). American newspaper proprietor. B. in Hungary, he in 1883 became proprietor of the *New York World*. In 1903 he estab. the school of journalism at Columbia Univ. which awards the annual P. prizes in journalism and letters.

PULSAR. Oscillating radio star sending out precisely regular radio pulses, although with wide variation in individual frequency, first discovered by Cambridge astronomers 1967.

PULSE. The impulse transmitted by the heart-beat throughout the arterial system. When the heart muscle contracts it forces blood into the aorta; because the arteries are elastic, the sudden rise of pressure causes a throb or sudden swelling through them all. It can be felt at points where an artery is near the surface of the body, as in the wrist, and is a good indicator of the strength and rate of the heartbeat. The P. is distinct from the actual flow of the blood, which continues more or less uniformly at about 60 cc. a sec. The P. rate is generally about 70 per minute.

PUMA. Carnivorous mammal (*Felis concolor*) of the cat family, found in America. Tawny in colour, the young have black spots and ringed tails. In S. America it is known as the cougar or mountain lion.

PUMA

PUMICE. A volcanic igneous rock. It is very porous and composed mostly of cavities, and has various commercial applications.

PUMPKIN. Genus of annual plants (*Cucurbita*) in the family Cucurbitaceae, probably native to the warmer regions of America and some of which are known in the U.S.A. as squashes, especially the more bushy kinds. The chief species are the common P. (*C. pepo*), of which the vegetable marrow is probably a variety, which has broad, lobed leaves on long trailing stems, and yellow flowers followed by an edible fruit which may weigh up to 100 lb.; the great gourd (*C. maxima*) which may have a fruit double this size; and the musk P. (*C. moschata*) with a musky smell and more elongated fruit: all are commercially important, and are also cultivated in warmer parts of Europe.

PUNCH. Alcoholic liquor compounded of spirits, fruit juice, sugar, spice, and hot water. P. originated in India.

PUNCH. Shortened form of the name Punchinello. The hero of the puppet play 'P. and Judy', in which he overcomes or outwits all opponents, P. has a hooked nose, hunched back, and a squeaky voice. The play is performed by means of glove puppets, manipulated by a single operator concealed in a portable canvas stage frame. P. originated in Italy, and was probably introduced to England at the Restoration.

PUNIC WARS (pū′-). The wars between Rome and Carthage. The 1st (264–241 B.C.) resulted in the cession of Sicily to Rome. During the 2nd (218–201 B.C.) Hannibal invaded Italy, but was finally defeated at Zama. The 3rd (149–146 B.C.) ended in the destruction of Carthage.

PUNJAB (punjahb′). Division of the Indian subcontinent in the N.W. P., meaning 'five rivers', so called from the tributaries of the Indus (Jhelum, Chenab, Ravi, Beas, Sutlej) flowing through it. The chief crops are cotton, sugar, wheat, rice.

Punjab was annexed by Britain in 1849, after the Sikh Wars of 1845–6 and 1848–9, and formed into a prov. with its cap. at Lahore, area 99,000 sq. m. West P., cap. Lahore, area 51,500 sq. m., was a prov. of Pakistan 1947–55 when it was merged in W. Pakistan (re-created a prov. 1970). E.P., later called simply P., was a prov., then a state of the Union of India.

PUNJAB, state of India, was formed in 1956 from the E. part of the former British prov. of P. and a number of princely states within the area. the largest of which was Bahawalpur.

Violent agitation led in 1966 to P. being split on a linguistic basis into 2 new states (joint cap. Chandigarh), known as *Punjab* (Punjabi-speaking) area 29,205 sq. m., pop. 12,000,000, over half being Sikhs; and *Hariana* (Hindi-speaking) area 17,600 sq. m., pop. 7,000,000; with certain hill areas (pop. 1,500,000) being transferred to Himachal Pradesh. After its creation H. remained chronically unstable politically, and in 1968 president's rule was proclaimed.

PUNTA ARENAS (poon′tah ahrā′nahs). Chilean seaport, cap. of Magallanes prov., on Magellan Strait, most southerly town on the American mainland. It is the centre for an area producing coal, copper, gold, timber, wool, meat, and other animal products. The name (Spanish) means sandy point. Pop. (1966) 45,000.

PUPPET. Human, animal, or fantasy figure manipulated on a miniature stage by an unseen operator, although in Japan (*bunraku*) 4 operators, dressed in black to convey invisibility, may combine to manipulate one large puppet, sharing body, head, arms and legs among them. Ps. are of great antiquity (10th cent. B.C. in China) and of world-wide distribution. The main forms are the glove Ps. (*see* PUNCH), string marionettes (q.v.), and rod-operated Ps. which may be seen only as shadows on a screen—the illustrated

shadow plays of Java being of this type.

PURANAS. Religious Sanskrit epics dealing with the mythology of the Hindus, and dating probably from the 8th cent. A.D.

PURBECK, Isle of. A peninsula in Dorset, England, between the English Channel, and Poole Harbour to the N. It is *c.* 8 m. N. to S., 12 m. E. to W. P. marble and china clay are obtained from the 'isle', which incl. Corfe Castle and Swanage.

PURCELL, Henry (1659–95). English composer. B. at Westminster, he became a chorister at the Chape Royal, and subsequently was a pupil of Dr. John Blow. In 1677 he was appointed composer to the Chapel Royal, and in 1679 organist at Westminster Abbey. As composer to the king, P. set to music odes or anthems. *Dido and Aeneas* (1689) was a landmark in the history of opera. P. wrote music for Dryden's *King Arthur* (1691), and for *The Fairy Queen* (1693). The P. Society was formed in 1876.

PURCHAS, Samuel (*c.* 1575–1626). English compiler of travel books, rector of St. Martin's, Ludgate, 1614–26. His collection *P. his Pilgrimage* (1613), was followed by another in 1619, and in 1625 by *Hakluytus Posthumus, or P. his Pilgrimes*, largely based on MSS. left by Hakluyt.

PURGATIVES. Drugs which accelerate or make easier the emptying of the bowel. Laxatives (mild Ps.) incl. bran and agar (bulk laxatives), and liquid paraffin, or agar (lubricants). Saline Ps. incl. Epsom salts and sodium phosphate. Mild irritant Ps. are castor oil, cascara, aloes, rhubarb, and senna.

PURGATORY. Theological term for a state or place of purification of the souls after death. It is held by Roman Catholics, who also believe that its duration may be lessened by the prayers of the faithful.

PURI (poor′ē). Town in Orissa, India, on the Bay of Bengal. The shrine of Juggernaut (q.v.) is there, dating from *c.* A.D. 318; the annual festival attracts thousands of pilgrims. Pop. (est.) 50,000.

PURITANS. Term applied after 1564 to those members of the C. of E. who wished to eliminate Catholic survivals in its ritual, or who wished to substitute a presbyterian for the episcopal form of church govt. The term is used to cover also the Separatists, who withdrew from the Church altogether. Under James I and Charles I the Ps. came to be identified with the parliamentary opposition. After the Restoration they were driven out of the Church, and the term P. was replaced in general use by 'Dissenter' or 'Nonconformist'.

PURPLE HEART, Order of the. The earliest

PUPPET. Made of paper-thin leather, the puppets of this Wayang shadow play are manipulated against a white screen: women are allowed only on the darkened further side, but men and boys are permitted to watch the puppeteer at work. The traditional stories of the Hindu epics are still popular today. *Courtesy of Indonesian Embassy.*

American military award for distinguished service beyond the call of duty, estab. by Washington in 1782, when it was the equivalent of the modern Congressional Medal of Honour. Of purple cloth bound at the edges and measuring 2½ in. from top to bottom, it was worn on the facings over the left breast: our illus. shows the only extant P.H. of this period, awarded to Sgt. Elijah Churchill of the 2nd Regt. Light Dragoons (Connecticut) in 1783. After the American Revolution it lapsed until revived by Pres. Hoover in 1932, when it was issued to those wounded in the F.W.W. and subsequently; the modern P.H. is of bronze and enamel.

PURPLE HEART
Courtesy of Washington's H.Q. and Museum, N.Y.

Also current slang parlance for a stimulant P.H.-shaped pill, widely sought after by junior drug-addicts.

PURPURA (per′pūra). Spontaneous bleeding below the skin. The condition is like bruising, but the blood is localized in spots which may be as large as a coin. They occur in smallpox and kidney disease, but are also the main symptoms of certain recognized ailments.

PUS. Thick, yellowish fluid formed by the bodies of white blood cells killed in conflict with invading bacteria, and of superficial cells of granulation or mucous membrane which die and are shed off. P. is formed wherever infection exists, and an enclosed collection of P. is an abscess.

PUSA′N. The chief port of S. Korea, nearest point to Japan on the Asiatic mainland, a railway and industrial centre (textiles, rubber, salt and, at nearby Pohang, iron and steel); fishing also is important. P. was invaded by the Japanese in 1592, opened to foreign trade in 1883. It was a U.N. supply port during the Korean War of 1950–2. Pop. (1966) 1,429,726.

PUSEY, Edward Bouverie (1800–82). British churchman. Ed. at Eton and Christ Church, Oxford, he was ordained in 1828 when he became Regius prof. of Hebrew at the univ., and in 1835 joined J. H. Newman (q.v.) in issuing the *Tracts for the Times*. After Newman's secession to Rome, P. became leader of the High Church Party or Puseyites, striving until his death to keep them from final conversion. His work is continued through P. House at Oxford, founded in his memory, which contains his library.

PUSHKIN (poosh′-), **Alexander Sergeievich** (1799–1837). Russian poet. B. at Moscow, he held administrative posts, was exiled several times for his liberal views, and d. of wounds he received in a duel. At first influenced by Byron, the study of Shakespeare later led him towards realism. The great national poet of Russia, P. was a supreme lyricist, and wrote verse novels such as *Robber Brothers*, *The Gypsies*, etc., and the great verse romance *Eugene Onegin* (1822–33); the novel *The Captain's Daughter* (1836), and the tragedy *Boris Godunov* (1825).

PUSHKIN. Town in Leningrad region, R.S.F.S.R., 16 m. S. of Leningrad. P. was founded by Peter the Great as Tsarskoe Selo (tsar's village); it became the imperial summer residence under Elizabeth and Catherine the Great, and both Catherine and Alexander I (1792–6) built palaces there. The 1st railway in Russia linked Tsarskoe Selo with St. Petersburg (Leningrad), 1837. In the 1920s the place was re-named Detskoe Selo (children's village), in 1937 Pushkin in honour of the poet; there are large parks, the P. literature research institute; paper, clothing, and chemicals are made. P. was held 1941–4 by the Germans who devastated it before retreating; it was subsequently restored. Pop. (est.) 55,000.

PUSHTU. The language of the Afghans, belonging to the E. Iranian group.

PUTREFACTION (pū-). Decomposition of organic matter through the action of a large variety of micro-organisms. The P. in a human corpse will often give reliable information on the time and cause of death.

PUTTING THE WEIGHT. An ancient sport which has survived in the form of putting a 16 lb. shot from a 7 ft. circle boarded 4 in. high.

PUVIS DE CHAVANNES (püvès′ de shahvahn′), **Pierre Cécile** (1824–98). French painter. B. at Lyons, he first exhibited in the Salon in 1850, and subsequently estab. a reputation as a decorative painter.

PUY, Le or **Le-Puy-en-Velay** (le-pü-ē′-oñ-velā′). Cap. of Haute-Loire dept., S.E. France, 90 m. S.W. of Lyons. It lies on a plateau of Mt. Anis, pinnacles of rock rising abruptly from which make it unique. The cathedral, 11th–12th cents., stands on one of these. Le P. was a place of pilgrimage in the Middle Ages. It is noted for its hand-made lace. Pop. (1962) 28,007.

PUY-DE-DÔME (pü-ē′-de-dōm′). Extinct volcano in the Auvergne Mountains, central France, 4,806 ft. high. It lies 6 m. W. of Clermont-Ferrand and on its slopes are ruins of a temple of Mercury. Pascal carried out experiments on air pressure in 1648 on the P.-de-D., which gives its name to a dept. of France.

PU YI, Henry (1906–67). Emperor of China and Manchukuo. He succeeded to the Chinese throne in 1908 under the name Hsuan Tung, and was deposed in 1912, but restored for a week in 1917. In 1932 he became pres. of the Japanese puppet state of Manchukuo, assumed the title of emperor in 1934 and was captured by the Russians in 1945 and taken to Siberia. In 1949 he was handed over to Mao Tse-tung, was freed in 1959, and became in 1964 a deputy in the Chinese Parliament.

PYELITIS (pī-elī′tis). Inflammation of the pelvis of the kidney, a hollow chamber in which the urine is collected before discharge.

PYGMALION (pigma′lion). In Greek legend, a king of Cyprus who fell in love with an ivory statue he had made. Aphrodite breathed life into the statue, which he married.

PYGMY (pig′mi). A member of a race of diminutive humans. There are African and Asiatic Ps., Negrillos and Negritos respectively.

PYLOS. Greek name of NAVARINO.

PYM, John (1584–1643). English statesman. B. in Som., he first entered parliament in 1614, and was largely responsible for the Petition of Right. As leader of the Puritan opposition in the Long Parliament, he moved the impeachment of Strafford and Laud, and drew up the Grand Remonstrance. He was the chief of the 5 members whom Charles I attempted to arrest in 1642. Shortly before his death he negotiated the alliance between parliament and the Scots.

PYONGYANG. Chief city of N. Korea, on the Taedong with ancient walls. Pop. (1967) 653,100.

PYORRHOEA (pī-orē′a). Discharge of pus from tissues between the tooth substance and the gum.

PYRAMID. A massive building of pyramidal shape erected as a royal tomb to protect the body and thereby to preserve the spirit. Such Ps. are found only in Egypt and the most famous at Gizeh, nr. Cairo, incl. the Great P. of Khufu (Gk. Cheops), the P. of Khafra (Gk. Chephren, *see* EGYPT illus.) and that of Menkaura (Gk. Mycerinus). As ritual centres of worship, Ps. were erected by the Aztecs and Mayas, e.g. Chichen Itza (q.v.) and Cholula, 70 m. from Mexico City, where in 1967 the world's largest P. in ground area (990 ft. base with a height of 195 ft.) was discovered, in the midst of 4 smaller Ps. and many other buildings.

PYRAMIDS. A game played on a billiard table, in which 15 coloured balls are arranged pyramidally, the apex-ball resting on the 'pyramid-spot'. The object of the game is to pocket more balls than one's opponent.

PY′RAMUS AND THI′SBE. Babylonian lovers whose story is told by Ovid. T. lost her veil when pursued by a lion, which tore it to pieces. It was found covered with blood by P., who believing her to be dead stabbed himself. On finding his body she killed herself.

PYRENEES (pir′enēz). Mountain range of S.W. Europe, separating the Iberian peninsula from France. The Ps. extend *c.* 270 m. from the Bay of Biscay to the Mediterranean and vary in width from 25 m. to 90 m. The central P. incl. Aneto, Fr. Néthon (11,168 ft.), Posets (11,047 ft.), and Mont Perdu (Span. Perdido, 10,997 ft.), The range gives its name to 3 Fr. depts., P.-Atlantiques, Hautes-P., and P.-Orientales.

Agreement was reached in 1962 between France and Spain for the construction of a tunnel nearly 2 m. long to link Aragnouet, S.E. of Tarbes, France, with Bielsa, Spain.

PYRETHRUM (pīrē′thrum). Sub-division of the genus Chrysanthemum in the family Compositae. The ornamental species *C. coccineum* is commonly grown in gardens, and feverfew (*C. parthenium*) is a British wild flower. P. powder is a powerful contact insecticide for aphis, mosquitoes, etc.

PYRIDINE (pir′idīn). A liquid base (C_5H_5N) occurring in coal tar and bone oil. It has a sickly odour, is soluble in water, and is used as a solvent.

PYRITES. *See* IRON PYRITES.

PYROGA′LLIC ACID or **Pyrogallol.** An acid ($C_6H_3(OH)_3$) prepared from gallic acid. It is used in photographic developers and for the estimation of oxygen in gas analysis.

PYROMETER. Instrument for measuring high temperatures: 3 typical types are thermoelectric, optical, and radiation. Resistance thermometers are sometimes used as Ps.

PYROXENE (pī′roksēn). An important group of minerals, occurring as brown, green, or black rocks. They are silicates of calcium, magnesium, iron, etc.

PYRRHO (pir′ō) (*c.* 360–270 B.C.). Greek philosopher. B. at Elis, he maintained that as it was impossible to attain certainty, man should seek peace of mind by renouncing all claims to knowledge.

PYRRHUS (pir′us) (*c.* 318–272 B.C.). King of Epirus, who in 280 invaded Italy as the ally of the Tarentines against the Romans. Although he twice defeated them, he suffered heavy losses (hence 'a

Pyrrhic victory'). Defeated at Beneventum in 275, he returned to Greece.

PYTHAGORAS (pīthag′ōras) (*c.* 570–500 B.C.). Greek philosopher. B. in Samos, he settled in Croton in S. Italy, and there founded a religious brotherhood which exercised great influence in politics until it was suppressed in the 5th cent. Their doctrines incl. the immortality of the soul and its transmigration. They devoted much attention to mathematics, and anticipated much of Euclid's work in geometry. *P.'s theorem* states that in a right-angled triangle the square on the hypotenuse is equal to the sum of the squares on the other 2 sides.

PYTHAGORAS OF RHEGIUM (rē′ji-um). Greek sculptor of the 5th cent. B.C. B. at Samos, he settled in Rhegium, Italy, and estab. a reputation for his statues of athletes.

PYTHEAS (pith′e-as) (4th cent. B.C.). Greek navigator of Marseilles, who explored the W. coasts of Europe at least as far as Denmark, travelled through Britain, and visited 'Thule', probably the Shetlands.

PYTHIAN GAMES (pith′ian). Ancient Greek festival in honour of Apollo, celebrated near Delphi every 4 years.

PYTHIAS. In Greek story, a Pythagorean whose friend Damon offered his own life as security when P. was condemned to death by a tyrant.

PYTHON (pī′thon). Genus of tropical snakes in the Boa family. They are non-poisonous, but kill

PYTHON

their prey by constriction. They grow to 30 ft. in length.

PYX. Vessel used in R.C. churches for the reservation of the blessed sacrament. The Trial of the P. is the test of the coinage by a goldsmith, at the hall of the Goldsmiths' Company, London, and is so called from the P. or box, in which specimens of each variety of coin minted are preserved.

Q 17th letter of the alphabet, representing *koppa* of the earliest Greek alphabet. In Latin, as in English, it is always followed by *u*: *qu*, pron. *kw*.

QATAR (kah′tahr). Sheikdom occupying Q. peninsula in eastern Arabia which stretches *c.* 130 m. into the Persian Gulf. Q. is in exclusive treaty relations with the U.K., agreed 1916. The discoveries of rich petroleum deposits soon after the S.W.W. gave its ruler great wealth: production is about 10,000,000 tons annually. The cap. is Doha (pop. 50,000) and the oil terminal at Umm Said is being developed as a port. Area *c.* 8,000 sq. m.; pop. (1967) 75,000.

QATTARA (kahtah′rah). A tract of the W. Desert, Egypt. It lies up to 400 ft. below sea-level and consists of very soft sand and, being virtually impassable to vehicles, it afforded protection to the left flank of the Allied armies before and at the battle of Alamein in 1942. Area 7,500 sq. m.

QISARAYA. Small port in Israel, on the Mediterranean coast 32 m. N. of Tel Aviv-Jaffa. It is on the site of ancient Caesarea, founded by Herod 13 B.C., where Paul was imprisoned for two years.

QUAESTOR (kwē′-). A Roman magistrate whose duties were mainly concerned with public finances. The Qs. originated as assistants to the consuls. Both urban and military Qs. existed, the latter being attached to the commanding generals in the provinces.

QUAGGA. Extinct species of wild horse (*Equus quagga*), resembling the

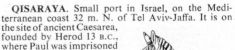

QUAGGA

zebra. Excessive hunting caused its dying out after 1858, when the last one was sent to the London Zoo from Cape Colony. Reddish-brown, with darker stripes on the fore-parts, it was whitish beneath.

QUAI D'ORSAY (kā-dorsā'). Part of the left bank of the Seine in Paris, where the French Foreign Office and other government buildings are situated.

QUAIL. Smallest species of the partridge family. The common Q. (*Coturnix coturnix*) is reddish brown, and is found in Europe, Asia, and Africa. They are highly valued as food, and are netted while migrating to and from N. Africa.

QUAKERS. Popular name for the Religious Society of Friends; the name Q. was applied to the Society's founder George Fox when he was before the magistrates at Derby in 1650, because he bade Judge Bennet to quake at the name of the Lord. In practical Christian living Qs. broke with many conventions and suffered fierce persecution. They dressed simply, refused to take oaths and to take off their hats in the presence of social superiors, and abandoned all titles. They still refuse to take any part in war. They have no professional ministry, and are guided by the 'inner light'. The meetings for worship begin with a period of silence, which continues until a member (of either sex) is guided to utter a word of exhortation or teaching, of prayer or praise. The Qs. are organized in 'meetings' composed of representatives of the congregations; the Yearly Meeting carries greatest weight. H.Q. is Friends' House, Euston Road, London.

QUANTRILL (kwon'tril), **William Clarke** (1837–65). American guerrilla. B. in Ohio, he had been a teacher, gambler and horse thief before commanding a unit on the Confederate side in the Civil War, said to have incl. Jesse and Frank James. He assisted in the capture of Independence, Mo., in 1862 and in Kansas in 1863 led the sack of Lawrence and put to death 17 captives after defeating a Union cavalry force at Baxter Springs. Wounded in a skirmish with Union troops in Kentucky in 1865, he probably d. there shortly after, but ballad legend (which also converts him to a kindly hero) maintains he returned to teach school in Texas.

QUANTUM THEORY. In physics, a theory advanced by Max Planck (q.v.) in 1900 to account for the phenomena of the distribution of the radiant energy from a 'black body' (one whose surface absorbs all the radiation of any wavelength that falls upon it) between the various wavelengths in the spectrum of the radiation. Planck assumed that the energy emitted consisted of separate multiples of a fundamental unit or *quantum* of energy. The theory was eventually supported by research into X-rays and the theory of spectra, and was applied in photoelectricity. Attention was then directed to its reconciliation with the wave-theory of light. The development of modern physics and its applications particularly in nuclear power and electronics is largely based on the Q.T. and developments from it.

QUARANTINE (kwo'rantēn). A term derived from the Fr. *quarantaine* (40 days), and applied to any period during which persons, animals, and vessels suspected of carrying disease are detained and isolated.

QUARRYING. The commercial exploitation of rock deposits, e.g. marble, slate, granite. Machine cutting is used to minimize damage when dimension stone, i.e. blocks or slabs of definite size, is required for ornamental or specialized uses (paving, wall finishes, roofing, etc.); for the broken or crushed stone used in concrete, road beds, etc., and which in modern times forms the greater part of the Q. industry, explosives are the most frequent method.

QUART. A capacity measure consisting of 2 pints, or a $\frac{1}{4}$ of a gallon.

QUARTER. A measure of avoirdupois weight, named for its proportion of a cwt., equivalent to 28 lb. As a grain measure it contains 8 bushels.

QUARTER DAYS. The appointed dates on which quarterly rents, etc., become due. These are 25 March, 24 June, 29 Sept., and 25 Dec., or Lady, Midsummer, Michaelmas, and Christmas Days respectively.

QUARTZ. Rock occurring most frequently in the oldest geological strata. As a mineral it is one of the most common of the earth's crust and consists of silica (SiO_2), sometimes with oxides. There are numerous different forms and colours incl. rock crystal, amethyst, rose Q., yellow Q., smoky Q., etc., tourmaline, agate, bloodstone, cornelian, jasper, onyx, sard, chalcedony, calcite, fluorite, granites, granite porphyries, felsites, gneisses, schists, quartzite and sand. Generally hard and crystalline, it is used for jewellery and ornamental purposes, and extensively in the ceramic arts, in optical and scientific instruments, and electronics in which Q. crystals are used for frequency standards.

QUASAR (kwā'zar). Very brilliant, very distant, astronomical object (quasi-stellar radio source), emitting an enormous quantity of energy in light and radio waves. Qs. are thinly scattered in the universe, and light from the most distant will have taken 10,000,000 years to reach us, so that its life may well have ended in the interval. Qs. were first discovered 1964–5, and their existence supports the 'big bang' theory of the universe (q.v.) Similar in appearance to Qs., but radio quiet, are the quasi-stellar objects (QSOs): apparently small, many show light variation. More than 100 Qs are known and c. 50 QSOs.

QUASIMODO (kwahsimō'dō), **Salvatore** (1901–68). Italian poet. He first became known with *Acque e terre* (1930), and his later books, e.g. *Nuove Poesie* (1942) and *Il falso e vero verde* (1956), reflect a growing preoccupation with contemporary political and social problems. He won a Nobel prize 1959.

QUASSIA (kwas'ia). Tree (*Picrasma excelsa*) of the W. Indies: an infusion of the wood supplies a bitter tonic and a hop substitute.

QUATERNIONS. A form of calculus devised by Sir William Rowan Hamilton (1805–65), of Dublin. As a geometry it is primarily concerned with the operations whereby one quantity or vector is changed into another, direction being taken into account as well as magnitude. The method is of great use in geometrical and dynamical problems.

QUATHLAMBA. A name for the DRAKENSBERG.

QUATRE BRAS (kahtr-brah'). A hamlet in Brabant, Belgium, situated 20 m. S.E. of Brussels, where Wellington defeated Ney on 16 June 1815.

QUEBEC (kwebek'). Port of Canada, cap. of Q. province. It is situated on the N. bank of the St. Lawrence, c. 300 m. from its mouth, and is important as a railway terminus and manufacturing city (pulp and paper, machinery, steel, rope, musical instruments, textiles, etc.). Points of interest incl. Dufferin Terrace, the Château Frontenac hotel, the citadel, Roman Catholic and Anglican cathedrals, the church of Notre Dame des Victoires, Laval Univ., the provincial parliament buildings, and the Quebec bridge. There are excellent harbour facilities. Q. was founded in 1608 by Samuel de Champlain, and in 1759 was captured from the French, under Montcalm, by the British, under Wolfe, after a battle on the Plains of Abraham nearby in which both commanders were killed. Q. was cap. of Canada 1763–1841. It remains a chief centre of French-Canadian culture. At the *Q. Conference* (1943) Roosevelt, Churchill, Mackenzie King and Tse-ven Soong approved Mountbatten as supreme Allied commander S.E. Asia and plans for the invasion of France. Pop. of met. area (1966) 413,397.

QUEBEC. Eastern province of Canada, bounded by the U.S.A. to the S., Ontario to the S.W., Hudson Bay and Strait to the W. and N., and Newfoundland (Labrador) to the N.E. The lowlands of the St. Lawrence, which flows N.E. to the Gulf of St. Lawrence, are bounded to the S. by the Notre Dame

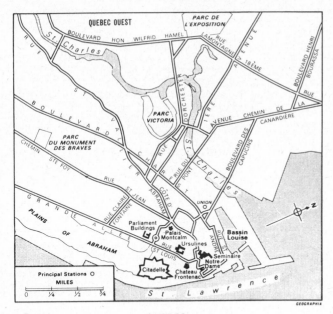

QUEBEC

Montreal, Q. (the cap.), Verdun, Three Rivers, Sherbrooke, and Hull. There are 4 R.C. univs., Laval (1852), Montreal (1920), Sherbrooke (1954) and Quebec (1969), and 3 Protestant, McGill (1821), Bishop's (1845) and Sir George Williams Univ. (1929). The educational system is organized throughout on a denominational basis. The Lieut.-Gov. is assisted by a Legislative Council, members appointed for life, and a Legislative Assembly, elected for 5 years. In the 1960s there was a resurgence of nationalism in Q., a renewal of cultural links with France, and a call for greater powers for member states under a revised Canadian constitution.

Area 594,860 sq. m.; pop. (1966) 5,780,845 (the majority Roman Catholics of French stock).

QUEBRACHO (kebrah'cho). The name of several S. American trees with very hard wood. The bark of the White Q. (*Aspidosperma Q.*) is used medicinally; the Red Q. (*Quebrachia Lorentzii*) is used in tanning.

QUEEN CHARLOTTE ISLANDS. Canadian group of is. lying *c.* 100 m. off the coast of British Columbia, to which it belongs politically. Graham and Moresby are the largest is. Lumbering, fishing, and cattle raising are the chief industries. The Q.C.I. were visited by Juan Perez in 1774, by Cook in 1778.

Area 3,780 sq. m.; pop. (est.) 3,000.

QUEEN'S AWARD TO INDUSTRY, The. Award made (from 1966) to organizations, not individuals, to recognize export and technological achievement: holders are entitled to display the special emblem for 5 yrs. Limited in no., they are granted annually on the birthday of Queen Elizabeth II (21st April).

QUEENSBERRY, John Sholto Douglas, 8th marquess of (1844–1900). British administrator and sportsman. He succeeded to the title in 1858, and 1872–80 served as a Scottish representative peer. In 1867 he drew up the Q. rules which govern boxing.

QUEEN'S COUNSEL. *See* KING'S COUNSEL.

QUEEN'S COUNTY. *See* LAOIGHIS.

QUEENSLAND. A state of the Commonwealth of Australia, comprising the whole N.E. portion of the continent. The Great Dividing Range runs parallel to the E. coast for 1,000 m. to the frontier with New South Wales in the S., the greatest height being Mt. Bartle Frere (5,438 ft.). The Great Barrier Reef (q.v.) lies off the N.E. coast. The main rivers are the Burdekin, Fitzroy, Flinders, and Mitchell. The climate of most of Q. is tropical but not unhealthy. Almost all land is state owned and leased. Cattle and sheep are reared; cereals, fruit, cotton, sugar and tobacco grown; and dairying and forestry are important. Minerals incl. bauxite, coal, gold, copper, lead, zinc, and oil and natural gas W. of Brisbane. Tourism is increasingly important. *See* illus. p. 884. There are factories for processing the primary products. The chief towns are Brisbane (the cap.), Townsville, Rockhampton, Toowoomba and Ipswich. Q. has a Gov., assisted by an Executive Council, and a single-chamber Legislative Assembly. Until 1859 Q. formed part of New South Wales. A no. of scattered is. beyond the Barrier Reef were created a Fed. Terr. 1969. Area 670,500 sq. m.; pop. (1966) 1,663,685.

QUEEN'S PROCTOR. *See* KING'S PROCTOR.

QUEENSTOWN. Former name of COBH.

mountains, an extension of the Appalachians, and to the N. by the Laurentian plateau, much of which is densely forested, and which forms the major portion of the province. The chief natural resources are abundant timber and water power, provided by the many rivers and lakes, vast iron deposits in Ungava region, asbestos, mica, copper, lead-graphite, and other mineral deposits. The climate is severe but healthy. Growing industries incl. pulp and paper, chemicals, non-ferrous metals, textiles, electrical goods, aircraft, railway rolling stock, and food processing. Agriculture remains important, with oats and other grain, fodder crops, dairy produce, maple sugar and fruit; and forestry, fishing, fur-trapping and fur-ranching are also carried on. The largest cities are

QUEBEC. Industrial development is rapidly dispelling the conception of the province as merely picturesque. The Arvida aluminium smelter, with a capacity of 373,000 short tons, is the world's largest and with ancillary buildings covers an area 1¾ miles long by ¾ mile wide. In the background is the Saguenay river and the town of Chicoutimi.

Courtesy of the Aluminium Company of Canada Ltd.

QUEMOY (kimoi'). Group of isls. off Fukien prov., China, held by the Nationalist Govt. in Formosa. Area 60 sq. m.; pop. (est.) 40,000. Though not specifically committed to their protection, after they had been shelled from the mainland the U.S. govt. announced in 1960 that it would defend them in the event of an actual attack.

QUENEAU (kenoh'), **Raymond** (1903–). French author. His poetry bears the enduring impress of his early Surrealist associations, and he is most accessible to the English reader in his humorous novels, e.g. *Zazie dans le Métro* (1959), portraying a precocious little Parisienne.

QUENNE'LL, Peter (1905–). British author. Son of Marjorie and C. H. B. Quennell, joint authors of the historical series incl. *Everyday Things in England*, he has edited *History Today* since its foundation in 1951. He is an authority on the 18th cent., e.g. his edition of *The Memoirs of William Hickey* (1960), and Byron, e.g. *Byron, the Years of Fame*.

QUESNAY (kānā), **François** (1694–1774). French economist and physician. B. near Paris, he became physician to Louis XV, and *c.* 1750 founded the group of *Économistes* with Jean de Gournay. His chief work *Tableau Économique* (1758) advocated physiocracy, government according to natural order.

QUETTA (kwet'tah). Town of Baluchistan, Pakistan, near the Afghanistan border, cap. of Q. division. There is a military staff college (1907). Coal is mined nearby. Pop. (1961) 106,633.

QUETZALCOATL (kātzahlkōwahtl'). Mexican god. He was said to have reigned on earth during a golden age and to have disappeared after promising to return. Cortez was thought by the Mexican Indians to have been Q. when he invaded their land.

QUEVEDO Y VILLEGAS (kāvā'dō-ē-vēlyā'-gahs), **Francisco Gomez de** (1580–1645). Spanish satirical writer. B. at Madrid, he fled to Sicily in 1611 after killing his opponent in a duel, was recalled to Spain in 1621, and imprisoned 1639–43 for his political writings. Q. wrote much of passing brilliance, such as *Vida del Buscon Pablos* (1626), and *Las Visiones* (1627).

QUEZON CITY (kāz'on). City in the Philippine Republic, built on a site 10 m. N.E. of Manila chosen by Pres. Quezon, in whose honour it was named. It became the formal cap. of the rep. in 1948, though pending completion Manila was still the seat of much of the administration. Pop. (1967) 482,400.

QUIBERON (kēbroṅ'). Coast town in the Morbihan dept., France. In 1759 Q. Bay saw the defeat of the French fleet under Conflans by Hawke. Pop. (1960) 4,540.

QUICKSILVER. See MERCURY.

QUIETISM (kwī-etism). A religious attitude, displayed periodically in the history of Christianity, consisting of passive contemplation and meditation to achieve union with the Divine. The founder of modern Q. was the Spanish priest Molinos who pub. a *Guida Spirituale* in 1675.

QUILIMANE (kēlēmah'nā) or **Quelimane**. Port of Mozambique on the Q. river. Pop. *c.* 10,000.

QUILLER-COUCH (-kooch), **Sir Arthur Thomas** (1863–1944). British author. B. at Bodmin, he was prof. of English literature at Cambridge from 1912, and besides editing *The Oxford Book of English Verse* (1900), etc., made a name as a novelist, e.g. *The Splendid Spur* (1889) under the pseudonym 'Q'.

QUILTER, Roger (1877–1953). British composer. B. at Brighton, he was educ. at Eton, and studied under Knorr at Frankfurt Conservatoire. He is best known for song settings from Dowson, Shakespeare, etc., incl. 'Now Sleeps the Crimson Petal' and 'To Daisies', and for his 'Children's Overture' and music for *Where the Rainbow Ends*.

QUIMPER (kaṅpār'). Cap. and port of Finistère dept., France. The cathedral dating from the 15th cent. is a fine example of Gothic architecture. Pop. (1962) 50,670.

QUINCE. A spreading tree (*Cydonia vulgaris*), bearing a bitter, yellow, pear-shaped fruit, used as a preserve, either individually or with apples.

QUINCEY, de. See DE QUINCEY.

QUININE (kwinēn'). Chief alkaloid in cinchona bark, introduced to Europe from Peru (1639) for treating the ague. Later it was used to kill the blood parasites causing malaria, but has been supplanted by the

QUINCE

less toxic and more powerful synthetics.

QUINQUAGESIMA (kwinkwajes'ima). The Sunday before Lent. The name is probably due to Q. being 50 days before Easter.

QUINSY. Old name for acute tonsillitis, particularly the type where a tonsillar abscess forms.

QUINTERO (kintār'o), **Serafin Alvarez** (1871–1938) and **Joaquin Alvarez** (1873–1945). Spanish dramatists. B. near Seville, these brothers always worked together and from 1897 they produced some 200 successful plays, principally dealing with Andalusia. Among them are *Papá Juan: Centenario* (1909) and *Los Mosquitos* (1928).

QUINTI'LIAN (Marcus Fabius Quintilianus) (*c.* A.D. 35–95). Roman rhetorician. B. at Calagurris, Spain, he taught rhetoric in Rome from 68 and later composed the *Institutio Oratoria*, in which he advocated a simple and sincere style of public speaking.

QUI'PUS. A system of knotted cords of one or several colours used by the Incas of ancient Peru for conveying messages and making computations. The art of interpreting it has been lost.

QUI'RINAL. One of the 7 hills on which ancient Rome was built. Its summit is occupied by a palace built in 1574 as a summer residence for the Pope and occupied 1870–1946 by the kings of Italy. The name Q. is derived from that of the god Quirinus.

QUI'SLING, Vidkun (1887–1945). Norwegian politician. Leader from 1933 of the Norwegian Fascist Party, he aided the Nazi invasion in 1940 by delaying mobilization and urging non-resistance. Made premier by Hitler in 1942, he was arrested and shot as a traitor by his countrymen in 1945. His name became used to stigmatize all guilty of his type of treason.

QUITO (kē'tō). Cap. of Ecuador, already a town before the Incas took it *c.* 1470. The Spaniards captured it in 1534. It lies at an altitude of 9,350 ft. in

QUEENSLAND. Coconut palms, hibiscus, frangipani, jacaranda, etc., grow to the sea's edge in this holiday paradise on the beautiful coast near Proserpine.
Courtesy of Dr. F. J. Giles.

the Cordillera, and although only 14′ S. of the equator, has a climate of perpetual spring owing to its height. Notable are the cathedral, univ. (1787) and Jesuits' church. Q. is the principal textile centre of Ecuador; it also makes beer, flour, leather, ceramics, chemicals, soap; gold, silver and other metal articles. It is the seat of an archbishopric. Pop. (1966) 462,860.

QUIXOTE, Don. *See* CERVANTES.

QUMRAN (koomrahn′), **Khirbet.** Ruined site, excavated from 1951, in the foothills on the N.W. shores of the Dead Sea. Originally an iron age fort (6th cent. B.C.) it was occupied in the late 2nd cent. B.C. by a monastic community, the Essenes (q.v.), until the buildings were burnt down in A.D. 68. The Dead Sea Scrolls (q.v.) comprise their library, hidden for safekeeping and never reclaimed.

QUOITS (koits). Game in which a heavy, sharp-edged, iron ring or quoit is thrown, over or near to an iron 'hob' from 18 yards distance, where is placed a second hob. A circular clay area surrounds each hob, and play proceeds as in bowls, from end to end, 2 points being awarded for a 'ringer' and 1 for the quoit nearest the hob. The quoit weighs 7–9 lb., and has an 8 in. diameter.

QUORUM (kwō′rum). A minimum number of members required for the validity of the proceedings of any assembly.

R Eighteenth letter of the alphabet, corresponding to the Semitic *resh* and Greek *rho*. A liquid, pronounced with the tip of the tongue on the palate, it is sometimes 'trilled' by vibration of the tongue, especially in Scotland, but in S. England is often weak when used medially and silent finally.

RA. Ancient Egyptian sun-god and king of the gods, later identified with the Theban sun-god Ammon. He was depicted with a hawk's head.

RAAB (rahb), **Julius** (1891–1964). Austrian statesman. A building contractor, he withdrew from political life when Hitler took over Austria, but in 1945 was a founder of the cons. Austrian People's Party, and as Chancellor (1953–61) negotiated the Peace Treaty (1955) which ended the occupation of Austria by the 4 powers.

RABA′T. Seaport on the Atlantic coast of Morocco, of which it is one of the caps. It is 110 m. W. of Fez. Textiles and carpets are manufactured and there is a univ. (1957). Pop. (1965) 261,450.

RABAUL (rahbowl′). Sea- and airport of New Britain, cap. of Australian-mandated New Guinea until 1937 when it was destroyed by an earthquake. It was restored, but was again destroyed by the R.A.F. after its occupation by the Japanese in 1942. Again rebuilt after the S.W.W., R. became a port handling chiefly copra. Pop. (est.) 4,000.

RABBI (ra′bī). Jewish doctor of the law, particularly one dealing with ecclesiastical affairs.

RABBIT. Rodent (*Oryctolagus cuniculus*) of the family Leporidae. Widely distributed in Europe and America, it has become a pest because of its destructive feeding and prolific breeding (several litters in a season), man having destroyed its natural enemies or introduced it to a country such as Australia where these are largely non-existent. Until the advent of myxomatosis (q.v.) the flesh was commonly eaten in Britain: the disease also modified the mode of life of surviving Rs. which tended to move from the ramified underground burrows or 'warrens', where they formed large colonies, to living and breeding in the open. The natural coat is grey, but this is treated and dyed commercially to imitate more costly furs. Many specialized forms are bred for show purposes, etc., e.g. the English lop-eared, and the long-haired Angora.

RABELAIS (rahbelä′), **François** (c. 1495–1553). French author. B. at Chinon, Touraine, he became a monk, and, having studied medicine, lectured on anatomy. His great works are *La Vie inestimable de Gargantua* (1535) and *Faits et dits héroiques du grand Pantagruel* (1533), satiric allegories laced with coarseness, broad humour, and philosophy, which tell the adventures of the 2 giants, Gargantua and Pantagruel, father and son.

RABI (rahbē), **Isidore Isaac** (1898–   ). American physicist. B. in Vienna, he was prof. at Columbia Univ. 1937–50. and Higgins prof. of physics, Columbia 1950–64. In 1940 he organized the Radiation Laboratory at the Mass. Institute of Technology for the development of radar for military purposes. He has written on electron spin resonance, and electrical and magnetic properties of the nucleus, and was awarded a Nobel prize in 1944 for precision measurements on neutrons.

RABIES (rā′bi-ēz). *See* HYDROPHOBIA.

RÃ′CHEL. Character of the O.T. A dau. of Laban, she was the favoured wife of Jacob, by whom she was the mother of Joseph and Benjamin.

RACHEL (rahshel′). Stage-name of the French tragedienne Elizabeth Félix (1821–58). B. in Switzerland, of Jewish extraction, she achieved success in Racine's *Phèdre* in 1843, and won a European reputation.

RACHMAN (rakh′man), **Peter** (1920–62). Polish immigrant to Britain. Buying up cheaply rented houses in London controlled under the 1957 Rent Act, he used blackmail and physical violence to evict the tenants, and sold the then decontrolled property at great profit, let it at exorbitant rates to prostitutes, etc. These tactics became known as Rachmanism.

RACHMANINOV (rakhmahn′ēnof), **Sergei Vassilievich** (1873–1943). Russian composer. B. at Oneg, Novgorod, he studied at the St. Petersburg and Moscow conservatoires, and toured as a concert pianist. At the Revolution he went to the U.S.A. His dramatically emotional music has a strong melodic basis and incl. operas, e.g. *Francesca da Rimini* (1906) based on Pushkin's play; 3 symphonies; piano pieces and songs. Among his most familiar works are the 'Prelude in C sharp minor', the 2nd piano concerto in C minor, and 'Rhapsody on a Theme by Paganini' for piano and orchestra.

RACIAL DISCRIMINATION. National or personal prejudice due to differences of religion, colour or blood, or to historical enmity, and leading to unfavourable distinctions socially, politically, economically, or legally. R.D. on religious or intellectual grounds is found in e.g. anti-Semitism (q.v.); in the traditional Chinese contempt for European barbarism; in the Moslem wars against the infidel, etc. R.D. is usually automatically practised by stronger against weaker races, e.g. Indian Hindu *caste* ('*varna*' means 'colour') system probably developed from the conquest of the (darker) aborigines by the advancing Aryan peoples; the Untouchables are the darkest Indians. Discrimination against the Negro is largely the aftermath of the European slave trade, but is also practised by Indians and others; and American light-skinned Negroes tend to look down on the darker. On the other hand, anti-White feelings are manifested by the Black Muslims in the U.S., and by some newly emergent African nations. Even within Israel there are complaints of discrimination by the European Jews against the darker-skinned, less-educated Jews of the Middle Eastern countries.

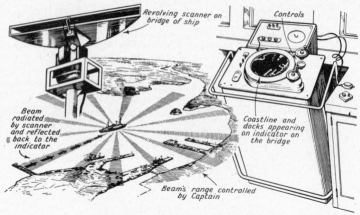

RADAR. A ship makes her way into harbour.

As a result of the 'Yellow Peril' scare of the late 19th and early 20th cents. there is general prejudice by Caucasian peoples against Mongolian as well as Negroid peoples. Traditional race hatred between many countries is the result of wars, occupation, etc., for example in the U.K. there is still prejudice against Irish, Welsh, etc., and vice versa. Expression of R.D. may range from complete segregation of races as in e.g. S. Africa, through unofficial but effective discrimination, which defies the law, to the hard-to-isolate, mainly social disabilities. As a rule, R.D., where recognized, is generally regarded as harmful on practical as well as on moral grounds and may be combated by legislation, e.g. in the U.K. the Race Relations Acts of 1965, prohibiting R.D. in places of public resort and creating the new offence of incitement to R.D. in a public meeting, and 1968, prohibiting D. in employment, housing, and provision of goods and services; and in the U.S.A. the Civil Rights Acts of 1964 and 1968, and the Voting Rights Act of 1965. A United Nations convention on the elimination of R.D. came into force 1969.

RACINE (rahsĕn'), **Jean** (1639–99). French dramatist. B. at La Ferté-Milon, he became the friend of Boileau, La Fontaine, and Molière. His earlier tragedies incl. *Andromaque* (1667), *Britannicus* (1669), *Bajazet* (1672), *Mithridate* (1673), *Iphigénie* (1674), and *Phèdre* (1677). After the failure of the last-named he no longer wrote for the secular stage, but influenced by Mme de Maintenon produced the 2 religious dramas, *Esther* (1689) and *Athalie* (1691).

RACKETS or **Racquets.** A game played in an enclosed court usually 60 ft. long and 30 ft. wide, by 2 or 4 persons each with a racket about 2½ ft. long weighing 9 oz. The ball has a diameter of 1 in. and weighs 1 oz. Play begins from a service box, one of which is marked at each side of mid-court, and the ball must be hit above a 9 ft. line on the endwall. After service it may be played anywhere above a 27 in. high line on the end-wall, the general rules of tennis applying thereafter. Scoring is similar to badminton. Squash R. is played on a smaller court.

RACOON or **Raccoon.** American carnivorous mammal (*Procyon lotor*) of the family Procyonidae. Some 2 ft. long, with a grey-

RACOON

ish brown body, and black and white ringed tail, the R. is an omnivorous feeder, and is nocturnal in habit.

RADAR. A process of locating the position of an object in space, of direction finding and navigation by short radio waves. The name 'radar', standing for the phrase *Radio Direction and Range*, was adopted from U.S.A. All solids and liquids reflect radio waves, which are uninfluenced by darkness, clouds or fog. To detect any reflecting object it is necessary to send out a beam of small-wavelength (1 cm.–100 cm.) short-pulse radio waves and to use receivers to pick up the reflected beam. It is then possible to determine the direction of arrival of the reflected waves and thus the direction of the object with respect to the receiving station. The distance (range) may be determined by timing the journey of the radio waves to the reflecting object and back. Radio waves travel with a speed of approximately 186,000 m./sec.; they therefore travel to and from an object 100 m. away in about 1/1,000 sec. Accurate and speedy measurements of time intervals of this order is the second basic principle of R.

Some of the first experiments on distance measurement by radio location were carried out by E. V. (later Sir Edward) Appleton who located the Heaviside layer 60 m. up in the sky, as did Breit and Tuve (1928) in the U.S.A.

The application of radio location to military purposes was begun in 1935 by a group of British scientists led by R. A. Watson Watt (later Sir Robert), and when war broke out in 1939, Britain was already provided with radio-location sentinels for the detection of aircraft. During S.W.W. the technique was considerably developed and new apparatus was constantly evolved. Apart from military uses, R. is now fitted to numerous ships and aircraft to increase safety of navigation in darkness, cloud and fog; and is also used for air traffic control, the production of aerial maps, the study of meteorological conditions, and complete marine and aerial navigation systems.

RADAR ASTRONOMY. The application of radar principles to astronomical research. The Moon was contacted by radar more than 20 years ago, and echoes have also been obtained from the Sun, Mars, Venus and Mercury. Timing the delay in receiving echoes from Venus has led to an improved determination for the distance of that planet, and has hence enabled astronomers to measure the 'astronomical unit', or Earth-Sun distance, with greater precision.

RADCLIFFE, Anne (1764–1823). British novelist (*née* Ward), the chief exponent of the Gothic novel, or romance of terror. Her best-known work is *The Mysteries of Udolpho* (1794).

RADHAKRISHNAN, Sir Sarvepalli (1888–). Indian scholar. After holding univ. posts in India, he was Spalding prof. of eastern religions and ethics at Oxford 1936–52. was ambassador to Moscow 1949–52, and pres. of India 1962–7.

RADIC (rah'dich), **Stjepan** (1871–1928). Yugoslav politician. B. near Fiume, he led the Croat national movement within the Austro-Hungarian Empire, and supported union with Serbia in 1919. His opposition to Serbian supremacy within Yugoslavia led to his murder in the parliament house.

RADICAL. A chemical structure, formed by 2 or more elements, which partakes in reactions without disintegration, yet often cannot exist alone. The behaviour of compound Rs. forms a vital part of organic chemistry.

RADICALS. Before 1832 in Britain the supporters of parliamentary reform, and subsequently the advanced wing of the Liberal Party. During the 1860s the Rs., led by Cobden, Bright, and J. S. Mill, stood for extension of the franchise, free trade, and laissez-faire, but after 1870, under the leadership of J. Chamberlain, Dilke, and Bradlaugh, they adopted a republican and semi-Socialist programme. With the growth of Socialism in the later 19th cent. Radicalism lost its popular basis, and ceased to exist as an organized movement. In the U.S.A. the term R. is applied to any holder of left-wing opinion.

RADIGUET (rahdigeh'), **Raymond** (1903–23). French author. An infant prodigy of poetry, he is best remembered for his novels *Le Diable au corps* (1923) and *Le Bal du Comte d'Orgel* (1924), sophisticated in their treatment of love and human relationships generally.

RADIO. The transmission and reception of radio waves. James Clerk Maxwell first developed the theory of electromagnetic waves in 1864, confirmed practically in the laboratory in 1888 by Heinrich Hertz. Marconi developed the work, in 1896 succeeding in establishing communication between Penarth and Weston-super-Mare; 5 years later he received a signal in Newfoundland transmitted from Poldhu in Cornwall. The phenomenon of waves moving round the curvature of the earth was simultaneously explained by Heaviside and Kennelly in their theories of a layer of upper atmosphere which acts as an electrical conductor instead of an insulator. The invention of the radio valve by Fleming (1904) laid open the way for broadcasting, which began in Britain in 1920. Later evolution has produced television in 1934, and radar (qq.v.).

When an electric charge is made to surge up and down a transmitting aerial, electric and magnetic 'strains' or waves are produced, which travel outwards at 186,000 m. (300,000,000 metres) per sec. One such wave is emitted for each oscillation of the charge, whose frequency is expressed by the number of these 'cycles' completed per sec. The wavelength is thus equal to the velocity (metres per sec.) divided by frequency (cycles per sec.), in terms of metres. Radio waves range in wavelength from 20 kilometres to less than a centimetre.

The ground waves radiated are weakened by loss of energy over the land. The sky waves (those which travel upward) traverse greater distances by rebounding from the ionosphere in 'hops'. Medium and long waves are used for restricted ranges, and short waves, which suffer greatest loss over ground, for long-distance telephony and broadcasting.

In modern transmitters the electrical oscillations are generated by means of a thermionic valve set in a circuit consisting of an inductance (usually a wire coil) and capacitance (usually a capacitor of sheets of metal with air between). To prevent the dying away of the oscillations when the energy is expended, a valve is coupled which maintains them by injections of energy. They are then amplified further until powerful enough to transmit. The oscillations alone, however, are merely carrier waves and must be 'modulated' by the impression of the desired intelligence which is conveyed forth as part of the radiated wave. The aerial transmits the high-frequency oscillations into a relatively great volume of space; short waves are suited to 'beaming' or directive transmission. (*See* BROADCASTING.)

The receiving aerial intercepts some of the transmitted waves, which set up a minute current, conducted to the receiver, whose purpose is to separate from these high frequencies the low frequencies containing the transmitted intelligence, and reconvert them through a loud-speaker into sound. The receiver must be adjusted so that its electrical characteristics are similar to those of the transmitting circuits. It is set at the desired, or resonant, frequency, when it receives these oscillations much more violently than any others. As in transmission, the circuit consists of inductance coils and air or mica capacitors. Tuned circuits are devised to allow a small band only of frequencies to be received. The currents set up by the incoming wave are oscillating at high frequency, and to modulate the oscillations so that only low frequencies are applied to the loud-speaker, a detector – a one-way device – is used, consisting of one or more valves or transistors. The simple 'diode' suppresses the requisite frequencies, conveying the remainder on for conversion. To boost the current to the strength to enter the speaker, audio frequency amplifying valves or transistors are used.

The low-frequency impulses are finally applied to the loud-speaker, consisting of a coil of thin wire mounted on a 'former' rigidly attached to a paper cone. The coil is suspended in a powerful magnetic field and the whole left free to move. The currents fed to the coil produce a magnetic field which interacts with the permanent magnetic field to cause coil movement and vibrations in the cone. These are identical with the vibrations produced by the original sounds, and as they occur also in air are reproduced identically by the receiver.

RADIOACTIVITY. The phenomena exhibited by a small class of substances, e.g. uranium, thorium, radium, and actinium, which spontaneously emit radiations that penetrate substances opaque to normal light, affect a photographic plate in the dark, produce phosphorescence in certain minerals, and ionize gases. These same properties are exhibited by other radiations such as X-rays, but only when the exciting agent is external. The spontaneous emission is due to the disintegration of the actual atoms of the radioactive element, and may be accompanied by explosive violence which produces new atoms differing in properties from the parent element.

Röntgen discovered X-rays in 1895, and in 1896 Becquerel found that uranium radiations affected a photographic plate in darkness. The next year Mme Curie separated radium, beginning the search for the elements subsequently discovered. Rutherford investigated these radiations, and classified them into alpha, beta, and gamma rays. In atomic-bomb research great strides were made in the study of R. Since 1940 elements up to 103 have been produced from uranium, in addition to hundreds of artificial radioactive isotopes: *See* ATOM; ISOTOPE.

RADIOASTRONOMY. A new branch of astronomical science, dating from the pioneer work of K. Jansky in the 1930s. Celestial objects send out radiations of all kinds; the long-wavelength radiations ('radio waves') do not affect the human eye, and so cannot be seen, but they may be focused and studied by means of special instruments known as radio telescopes. These telescopes are of various designs; a very famous one is the 250-foot metal paraboloid erected at Jodrell Bank, in Cheshire. *See* illus. p. 599.

Radio sources incl. the Sun; various objects inside our Galaxy, thought to be the gas-clouds produced by old supernovae; and certain external galaxies. It is believed that some of the remote sources represent collisions between galaxies, so that the 2 systems concerned are passing through each other; the individual stars seldom or never collide, but the interstellar material spread between the stars is violently agitated, and produces the radio waves picked up on Earth. It must be added, however, that some Russian authorities reject this explanation, and believe that the radio emission is produced by a galaxy which is in the process of separating into 2 systems.

R.A. has become one of the most important branches of A., and a *radio-heliograph* (specialized radiotelescope for sun research invented by Englishman Paul Wild) was built 1966 at Narrabri, 310 m. N. of Sydney, Australia; it will forecast for American astronauts on moon flights when dangerous solar and cosmic radiation is to be expected. *See* GALAXY illus. p. 457.

RADIO BEACON. A radio transmitter whose radiations enable a craft to determine its direction or position relative to the beacon by means of a communications receiver or direction finder.

RADIO FREQUENCIES AND WAVELENGTHS, Classification of. In order to name them it is convenient to group frequencies and wavelengths together in bands, each band referring to waves having similar propagation characteristics, and for which similar techniques are used in the radio terminal equipment. According to the British Standards Institution the arbitrary verbal classification is:

Very low frequency (v.l.f.)		below 30 kc/s
Low frequency (l.f.)	30 to	300 kc/s
Medium frequency (m.f.	300 to	3,000 kc/s
High frequency (h.f.)	3 to	30 Mc/s
Very high frequency (v.h.f.)	30 to	300 Mc/s
Ultra-high frequency (u.h.f.)	300 to	3,000 Mc/s
Super-high frequency (s.h.f.)	3,000 to	30,000 Mc/s
Extra-high frequency (e.h.f.)	30,000 to	300,000 Mc/s

RADIOGRAM. The 'stereogram', devised to give the special effects of space and depth which can be achieved by the stereophonic records developed in the 1950s, has a special pick-up (1), radio and twin amplifiers (2), and loud-speakers (3 and 4), and is two radiograms in one. Controls (5) are placed well forward and there is space for record storage (6).
Courtesy of Ultra Radio and Television Ltd.

RADIOGRAM. Combined unit containing a radio receiver and sound amplifier, single or automatic gramophone turntable and pick-up, loudspeaker and record storage; housed in a single cabinet. Provision is often made for the use of an extension loud-speaker, and feeding in the output from a tape recorder. The name 'phonograph', obsolete in British usage, is still preferred in the U.S.

RADIO'GRAPHY. The production of shadows on sensitized film by X-rays. They are produced when a high unidirectional voltage is applied to the electrodes in a vacuum tube – giving rise to a stream of electrons from the cathode – which when stopped at the anode produce X-rays. These penetrate matter according to its atomic weight, density and thickness. In doing so they cast shadows on the film and are used to examine the internal parts of the body, or in industry to examine solid materials, e.g. weld seams, pipelines, etc.

RADIOTHE'RAPY. The treatment of disease by radiation obtained from X-ray machines or radioactive sources. The effect of the radiation is to reduce the activity of dividing cells and is of especial value for its effect on certain malignant tissues, certain non-malignant tumours and some diseases of the skin. Generally speaking the rays of the ordinary diagnostic X-ray machine are not penetrating enough to be very efficient in treatment, and for this purpose more powerful machines are required operating from 10,000 to over 30 million volts. The lower-voltage machines are similar to conventional X-ray machines, the higher-voltage ones may be of special design, e.g. linear accelerators and betatrons.

Much R. is now given using artificially produced radio isotopes (q.v.). Radioactive cobalt (symbol Co) is the most useful, as this produces gamma rays (very penetrating), and machines with sources of this material are used instead of very high-energy X-ray machines. Similarly certain radioactive substances may be used by actual administration to patients, e.g. radioactive iodine for thyroid disease.

In the past much use was made of radium, but this has now been largely supplanted by artificially produced radioactive substances, which are more easily obtainable. Small sources may actually be implanted into the tissue being treated, in an attempt to localize the irradiation.

RADISH. Cultivated biennial herbs (*Raphanus sativus*) of the Cruciferae family, with fleshy, edible roots. The latter may vary in colour through white, red, and black, and have a pungent taste.

RA'DIUM (Lat. *radius* ray). A brilliant white radioactive metal, symbol Ra, at. wt. 226, at. no. 88. The salt R. bromide was first separated by M. and Mme Curie in 1898 from Bohemian pitchblende, but R. itself was not isolated until 1911 (by Mme Curie and Debierne). More volatile than barium, which it resembles chemically, its m.p. is 700°C. It is obtained commercially as bromide or chloride from pitchblende (q.v.), which occurs in Czechoslovakia, E. Africa and Colorado. R. disintegrates spontaneously with the emission of alpha particles and forms the radioactive chemically inert gas radon (q.v.). Both were used for cancer therapy, but have been replaced by radioactive Co. 60. Both R. and Co. 60 are used extensively in industrial radiography.

RADNORSHIRE. Border co. of Wales. Part of the high central plateau of Wales, R. is famed for its sheep breeding, and rises to its greatest height in the wild Forest of Radnor. The chief rivers are the Wye and Teme. Presteigne is the co. town. Area 471 sq. m.; pop. (1961) 18,431.

RADOM (rah'dōm). Town of Poland, 60 m. S. of Warsaw. There are iron works and tanneries, and bicycles, machinery, boots and shoes, beer, flour, and tobacco are manufactured. R.'s first church was begun in 1187. R. went to Austria in 1795, to Russia in 1825, and was returned to Poland in 1919. Pop. (1966) 145,000.

RA'DON. Radioactive gas formed by the disintegration of radium (q.v.), formerly called radium emanation, then niton (Lat. *nitens* shining) and from 1923 radon: symbol Rn, at. wt. 222, at. no. 86. Discovered in 1900 by Dorn, it was isolated by Ramsay and Gray 8 years later.

RAEBURN (rā'-), **Sir Henry** (1756–1823). Scottish

artist. B. in Edinburgh, he travelled in Italy, returning to his native city in 1787 as a portrait painter. In 1815 he was elected R.A., and in 1822 was knighted.

RAEDER (rā′der), **Erich** (1876–1960). German Admiral. Chief of Staff to Hipper in the F.W.W.,

he became head of the navy in 1928, but was dismissed by Hitler in 1943 because of his failure to prevent Allied Arctic convoys reaching Russia. Sentenced to life imprisonment at Nuremberg, he was released on grounds of ill-health in 1955.

RAFFLES, Sir Thomas Stamford (1781–1826). British administrator. He entered the E. India Co.'s service in early life, took part in the capture of Java from the Dutch in 1811, and while gov. of Sumatra 1818–23 was responsible for the acquisition and foundation of Singapore in 1819. He was a founder and first pres. of the Zoological Society.

SIR THOMAS RAFFLES.
By G. F. Joseph.
Photo: N.P.G.

RAGLAN, FitzRoy James Henry Somerset, 1st baron R. (1788–1855). British general. In the Peninsular War under Wellington, he was foremost in the storming of Badajoz, and at Waterloo lost his right arm. He commanded the British forces in the Crimea, being created field marshal after Inkerman, but the later losses and privations of his troops were said to have accelerated his death from dysentery. The R. sleeve, with no shoulder seam but cut right up to the neckline, is named after him. **FitzRoy Richard Somerset,** 4th baron R. (1885–1964), pub. anthropological works written from a diffusionist standpoint, e.g. *Jocasta's Crime* (1933) and *The Origins of Religion* (1949).

RAGTIME. The syncopation originated by American Negroes at the beginning of the cent. which came into fashion about 1910 and merged into jazz. It was characterized by a fast, ragged, rhythm.

RAGUSA (rahgōō′zah). Italian town in Sicily, cap. of R. prov., 34 m. W.S.W. of Syracuse. It stands over 1,500 ft. above the r. R. It makes cotton and woollen textiles, but chief interest is in the ancient tombs in caves nearby. Pop. (1961) 55,724; prov. 247,198. Also the Italian name of DUBROVNIK. The word argosy comes from this R. famed under Turkish rule in the 16th cent. for its trading fleets: at that time, R. was called in England Arrogosa.

RAGWORT. Perennial plant (*Senecio jacobaea*), of the Compositae. Some 3 or 4 ft. high, it produces brilliant yellow flowers, and is an abundant weed.

RAHERE (d. 1144). Minstrel and favourite of Henry I, who in 1123 founded St. Bartholomew's priory, Smithfield, and St. Bartholomew's hospital, London.

RAH′MAN PUTRA, Tunku (meaning 'prince') **Abdul** (1903–). Malayan statesman. A younger son of a former sultan of Kedah, he was ed. both in Malaya and at Cambridge and studied law at the

TUNKU ABDUL RAHMAN
Courtesy of High Commissioner for Malaya.

Inner Temple. As leader of the Alliance Party he took part in the independence negotiations in 1955, became P.M. of Malaya in 1957, was returned to power in 1959, and was the prime mover in the creation of Malaysia 1963. In 1964 he was again returned to power by an overwhelming majority as P.M. of Malaysia, in face of the threat to the existence of the new federation from Sukarno; resigned 1970. His successful play *Mahsuri* (1941) was filmed 1958.

RAIKES, Robert (1735–1811). British educationist. B. at Gloucester, where he ran a printing business, he started a Sunday school in 1780, the beginning of the Sunday-school movement.

WATER RAIL

RAIL. A general name for birds of the Rallidae family. The corncrake or Land-R. (*Crex crex*) has a grating cry, and is brown above and whitish below. Others are the coot, moorhen, and water R.

RAILWAYS. Track laid for the passage of trains conveying passengers and goods. The use of rails to reduce friction was recognized early, iron rails being utilized at collieries in the 18th cent. The imaginative abilities of the English steam pioneers, Newcomen, Watt, *et al.*, led to the realization of self-propelled steam rail vehicles, by Trevithick (1804), Hedley (1813) and Stephenson (1825), whose 'Rocket' drew a coach along part of the Manchester-Liverpool line at 30 m.p.h. in 1829. The widespread and haphazard building which followed – at enormous cost in money and engineering skill – resulted in 250 separate companies; which resolved into 4 systems in 1921, and became the nationalized 'British Railways' in 1948, known as 'British Rail' from 1965, which has *c.* 14,000 m. of route. European Rs. developed quickly during the 19th cent., and in the U.S.A. and Canada the growth of Rs. was intimately tied to westward expansion, and made full exploitation of the central and western territories possible. With their present mileages of 225,000 (U.S.A.) and 43,000 (Canadian National and Canadian Pacific), they are vital for freight transport.

After the S.W.W. the Rs. suffered increasing competition from other forms of transport. In the U.S.A. the growth of internal air services cut the demand for passenger transport, and in the U.K. freight carriage passed increasingly to road haulage. Rationalizat on and adjustments are taking place in both countries, and recommendations of the controversial Beeching Renort (1963) are being implemented on British Rail.

The era of steam supremacy is ending. In countries where electricity is cheap, e.g. Switzerland, the R. are totally electrified, since it is more efficient to centralize the power source than carry it around. Elsewhere diesel power is replacing steam as more efficient (lower fuel costs) and running more hours in the day. There are, however, many technical problems, varying according to operating conditions in different countries, still to be resolved. *See* illus. p. 890.

RAIMU (rāmü′) (1883–1946). Stage-name of the French actor and comedian Jules Muraire. His films incl. *Marius* and *Un Carnet de Bal*.

RAINBOW. An arch formed in the sky showing the prismatic colours in their order. It is caused by the refraction of rays of light by rain globules. The colours of the R. are the same, and in the same order, as in the spectrum.

RAINE, Kathleen (1908–). British poet. Dau. of a schoolmaster, she was educ. at Girton Coll., Cambridge, and took her degree in Natural Sciences. Her vols. of poetry incl. *Stone and Flower* (1943) and

The Pythoness (1949) and reflect both the Northumberland landscape of her upbringing and the religious feeling which led her to the Roman Catholic Church in 1944. She was formerly m. to the poet and sociologist Charles Madge.

RAINIER III, Prince. *See* MONACO.

RAINIER. Mountain in the Cascade Range, Washington state, U.S.A., 14,408 ft., crowned by 14 glaciers and carrying dense forests on its slopes. It is a quiescent volcano. Mount R. national park, 377 sq. m., was dedicated in 1899.

RAIS (räs), or **Retz, Gilles de** (1404–40). French soldier. He played a distinguished part in the struggle for the expulsion of the English from France, and was closely associated with Joan of Arc. In 1440 he was accused of practising witchcraft and the sacrifice of children, and was hanged.

RAISIN. Dried grape; the chief kinds are the common R., the sultana or seedless R., and the currant. They are produced in the Mediterranean area, California, Australia, etc.

RAJAGOPALACHA'RYA, Chakravarti (1878–   ), Indian statesman. Prominent in the Congress Party leadership from 1919, he broke with them during the S.W.W. to advocate a peaceful settlement with Britain and recognition of the Moslem League's claim to separation. He succeeded Lord Mountbatten as Gov. Gen. (1948–50), was Home Minister for India (1950–1) and Chief Min., Govt. of Madras (1952–4).

RAJASTHAN (rah'jastahn). Union of princely states of Rajputana formed in 1948 and subsequently enlarged; one of the states of the Union of India. It incl. the famous former princely states of Jodhpur, Bikaner, Jaipur, and Udaipur. The cap. is Jaipur. Work on a 425 m. irrigation canal began in 1958. Area 132,150 sq. m.; pop. (1961) 20,155,602.

RAJPUT. High-caste Hindus of India, predominantly soldiers and landowners. They are widespread over N. India. The Rajput states of W. India are now merged in Rajasthan. The Rana family (ruling aristocracy of Nepal until 1951) is also Rajput.

RALEIGH or **Ralegh** (raw'li), **Sir Walter** (*c.* 1552–1618). English adventurer. B. in Devon, he served in early life in France and Ireland, and at sea against the Spaniards. He won Elizabeth I's favour, and in 1584 was knighted. He made several unsuccessful attempts 1584–7 to establish a colony in 'Virginia' (now N. Carolina). He led an exploring expedition to S. America in 1595, which he described in his

Discovery of Guiana, and distinguished himself in the expeditions to Cadiz in 1596 and the Azores in 1597. After James I's accession in 1603 he was condemned to death on a charge of conspiracy, but reprieved and imprisoned in the Tower, where he wrote his unfinished *History of the World.* Released in 1616, he led a gold-seeking expedition to the Orinoco, which failed disastrously, and on his return was beheaded under his former sentence.

RALEIGH, Sir Walter (1861–1922). British scholar. Prof. of English literature at Oxford from 1904,

he was a gifted teacher: his books incl. *The English Novel* (1894) and studies of Milton, Wordsworth, and Shakespeare.

RAMADA'N or **Ramazan.** The 9th month of the Moslem year, throughout which a strict fast is observed during the hours of daylight.

RAMADIER (rahmah-dyā'), **Paul** (1888–1961). French Socialist. Entering the Chamber in 1928, he subsequently held many ministerial posts and was premier Jan.–Nov. 1947. It was during these months that Communist participation in post-war govts. ended.

RAMAN (rah'man), **Sir Venkata** (1888–1970). Indian physicist. Awarded a Nobel prize in 1930 for his discovery in 1928 of the *R. Effect*: the scattering of monochromatic light when passed through a transparent substance. He became in 1948 director of the R. Research Institute and national research prof. of physics.

RAMAYANA (rahmah'yana). A Sanskrit epic poem of the 6th–4th cents. B.C. Consisting of 48,000 lines, it describes the adventures of the hero Rama, later identified with the god Vishnu, and incorporates both mythical and historical elements.

RAMBERT (ronbār'), **Dame Marie** (1888–   ). British ballet dancer and teacher. B. in Warsaw, she danced with the Diaghileff ballet 1912–13, opened the R. School in 1920, and in 1926 founded the *Ballet R.* which she directs. She m. in 1918 Ashley Dukes

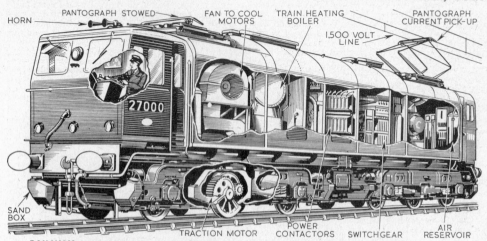

RAILWAY. Sectional drawing of an express electric passenger locomotive on the Manchester-Sheffield-Wath line, the first all-electric main line in Britain, which was inaugurated in January 1955.

(1885–1959), playwright and producer, and was created D.B.E. in 1962.

RAMÉE, Louise de la. See OUIDA.

RAMESES (ram′esēz). Name of 11 ancient Egyptian kings. **Rameses II** (reigned c. 1300–1225 B.C.), the son of Seti I, successfully waged war on the Hittites, and carried out colossal works of art such as the rock temple at Abu Simbel. **Rameses III** (reigned c. 1200–1168 B.C.) won a naval victory over the Philistines and other barbarian peoples, and asserted his suzerainty over Palestine.

RAMILLIES (ram′ilēz, F. rahmēyē′). Village in Brabant, Belgium, 13 m. N. of Namur, scene of Marlborough's victory over the French on 23 May 1706, during the War of the Spanish Succession.

RAM MOHUN ROY. See BRAHMA SAMAJ.

RAMSAY, Allan (1686–1758). Scottish poet. B. in Lanarkshire, he became a wig-maker and then a bookseller in Edinburgh. He pub. *The Tea-Table Miscellany*, and *The Evergreen*, collections of ancient and modern Scottish song.

RAMSAY, Sir William (1852–1916). British chemist. B. at Glasgow, he became prof. of chemistry at Bristol in 1880, and London (1887–1913). He became an F.R.S. in 1888, was knighted in 1902, and received a Nobel prize in 1904. Together with Lord Rayleigh he discovered argon in 1894. In 1895 R. manufactured helium, and in 1898, in co-operation with M. Travers, identified neon, krypton, and xenon. With F. Soddy he noted the transmutation of radium into helium in 1903. This discovery led in 1910 to that of the density and atomic weight of radium.

RAMSEY, Michael (1904–). Archbishop of Canterbury. Educ. at Repton and Cambridge, he was ordained in 1928. In 1940 he became prof. of divinity at the Univ. of Durham and in 1950 Regius prof. of divinity at Cambridge, until his appointment as bishop of Durham in 1952. He became archbishop of York in 1956 and in 1961 succeeded Dr. Fisher (q.v.), becoming the 100th archbishop of Canterbury and Primate of All England.

RAMSGATE. English port (bor.) and seaside resort in the Isle of Thanet, Kent. The 'royal harbour' (1795) was named by George IV. Pop. (1961) 36,906.

RAMUZ (rahmü′), **Charles Ferdinand** (1878–1947). Swiss novelist. B. nr. Lausanne, he lived largely in Paris until 1914, when he returned to Switzerland to inspire the new review *Les Cahiers Vaudois*. His works incl. the verse *Chansons* (1914); the lyric prose *Chant de Notre Rhône* (1920), *Passage du poète*, *La Beauté sur la terre* (1928), and a *Journal*.

RANCE (raṅs). River in Brittany, France, flowing into the Channel between Dinard and St. Malo, where a dam built 1960–7 (with a lock for ships) uses the 44 ft. tides to feed the world's first successful tidal power station.

RAND. Dutch word for edge or brink. It is used as an abbreviation for the Witwatersrand, a gold-bearing ridge in Transvaal, S. Africa, extending for c. 40 m. W. and E. of Johannesburg. Gold was first found here in 1854; mining began in 1874: the average annual output is c. 16 million oz. The R. became the basic unit of S. Africa's new decimal currency in 1961.

RANGOON. Cap. of Burma on the R. river, 20 m. from the sea. It is a great commercial centre, exporting rice, teak, and petroleum. There is a univ. (1920). The golden Shwe Dagôn pagoda, founded according to tradition in 585 B.C., is a centre of pilgrimage for Burmese Buddhists. A city called Dagôn was founded on the site in 746; the name R. (meaning end of conflict) was given to it by Alaungpaya in 1755 when he made it his cap. The E. India Co. set up a factory in 1790 at R., which was captured by the British in 1852. Pop. (1967) 1,616,948.

RANJITSI′NHJI, Kumar Shri (1872–1933). Maharajah of Nawanagar. A brilliant batsman, he

played cricket for Sussex, and in 1896, 1897–8, 1899, and 1902 played for England against Australia.

RANK, Joseph Arthur, baron (1888–1972). British business man. B. at Hull, he became chairman of Joseph R. Ltd., the flour-milling firm founded by his father, but through the R. Organization Ltd. (chairman 1941–62 and pres. from 1962) extended his interests to film exhibition and production, television, tenpin bowling, xerography, etc. In 1957 he was raised to the peerage.

RANKE (rahn′ke), **Leopold von** (1795–1886). German historian. For 50 years a prof. at Berlin Univ. he laid the basis of modern historical research. His works incl. histories of *The Popes during the 16th and 17th cents.* (1834–6), *Prussia during the 17th and 18th cents.* (1847–8), and *England, principally in 17th cent.* (1859–68).

RANSOM, John Crowe (1888–). American poet. B. in Tennessee, he was a Rhodes scholar, and was prof. of English at Vanderbilt Univ. 1927–37 and then Carnegie prof. of poetry at Kenyon Coll. His vols. of romantic but anti-rhetorical verse incl. *Poems about God* (1919), and *Two Gentlemen in Bonds* (1926).

RANSOME, Arthur (1884–1967). British author. Once a journalist – he was correspondent in Russia for the *Daily News* during the F.W.W. and the Revolution – he was best known for his books for children, beginning with *Swallows and Amazons* (1930), and incl. in the series *Peter Duck* (1932) and *Great Northern?* (1947). These are marked by depth of characterization and technical accuracy, and for many of them the author was his own illustrator.

RANUNCULA′CEAE. A family of dicotyledonous plants, with distinctive flowers and divided leaves, which incl. the clematis, anemone, buttercup (Ranunculus), delphinium, and peony.

RAPALLO (rahpahl′lō). A port and winter resort of Liguria, Italy, situated 15 m. E.S.E. of Genoa on the Gulf of R. A treaty signed here by Italy and Yugoslavia in 1920 settled their common frontier; and a treaty signed by Germany and Russia at R. in 1922 cancelled their claims on one another for war indemnities.

RAPANUI. Another name for EASTER ISLAND.

RAPE. Two plant species, *Brassica campestris* and *Brassica napus*, grown for their seeds, which yield the pungent mustard R. oil. The common turnip is a variety of the former, and the swede turnip of the latter.

RAPHAEL SANZIO (ra′fä-el sahn′zē-ō) (1483–1520). Italian painter. B. at Urbino, the son of Giovanni Santi, a court painter, he at first studied under his father, and in 1499 went to Perugia, where he entered the studio of Perugino. The influence of the latter is shown in R.'s paintings of St. Michael, St.

RANGOON. The Shwe Dagôn pagoda, plated with pure gold and rising to 368 ft. *Courtesy of Burmah Oil Co.*

George, the Three Hesperides, and the Coronation of the Virgin. In 1504–8 he was in Florence, where he studied the works of Leonardo da Vinci, Michelangelo, Massaccio, and Fra Bartolommeo. Paintings of this period incl. the 'St. Catherine' and the 'Ansidei Madonna' in the National Gallery. In 1508 he went to Rome where he was employed by pope Julius II to redecorate a number of rooms in the Vatican. Thenceforward he painted a great many works – frescoes, easel pictures, etc. – of which some of the most famous incl. 'St. Cecilia', the 'Disputa', 'School of Athens', and the 'Sistine Madonna' at Dresden. His works are distinguished for their beauty of form and colour, and he ranks as one of the greatest figures in the history of art.

RARE EARTHS. The oxides of metals found in certain rare minerals. The elements incl. under the heading of R.E. are those nos. 21, 39, and 57–71: see table under Inorganic Chemistry.

RARE GASES. The name applied to the elements helium, neon, argon, krypton, xenon, and radon, characterized by their lack of chemical affinity.

RASMUSSEN (rahs'moosen), **Knud Johan Victor** (1879–1933). Danish explorer, of Eskimo descent. He travelled in Lapland, Greenland, Baffin Island, and Siberia, and estab. that the Eskimoes are of Red Indian origin.

RASPBERRY. A prickly cane-plant (*Rubus idaeus*) of the Rosaceae family with white flowers followed by white or red fruits. These are used for jam and wine.

RASPUTIN, Gregory Efimovich (1871–1916). Russian monk. The illiterate son of a poor peasant, he claimed divine powers, and in 1907 was presented at court, where he acquired great influence over the Tsarina because of her belief that he could cure her son, the Tsarevitch, of haemophilia. The control he exercised through her over political and ecclesiastical appointments, and his notorious debauchery, created a scandal which did much to discredit the monarchy. He was murdered by a group of nobles.

RAT. Name given to the larger members of the family Muridae. The Brown R. (*Mus norvegicus*) is about 8 in. long with a tail of almost equal length. It frequents sewers, docks, and warehouses, and in the country hedges, ricks, granaries, and other food stores. Brown Rs. also infest ships, by which they have been spread over the world. The Black or Long-tailed R. (*Mus rattus*) is smaller than the Brown R., by which it has largely been replaced. Some Black Rs. are still found in docks and on ships. They do not interbreed with the Brown Rs. See PLAGUE.

RATES and **RATING.** Rates are a form of local taxation imposed by local authorities to finance their various activities. In England and Wales a 'General Rate' is levied to cover expenditure on all purposes in urban districts, and in rural districts is supplemented by 'Special Rates' to cover expenditure on activities not common to the whole of the area. Water Rates are in the nature of a specific charge for the supply of water, and are usually based on local rating assessments. General and Special Rates are levied at an appropriate figure in the £ on the assessment of all rateable property, agricultural land and buildings being exempt. Increased expenditure on education, etc. has led to mounting R., and in 1966 rebates were introduced for lower income groups.

RATHBONE, Eleanor (1873–1946). British politician. B. in Liverpool, she became a member of the Liverpool City Council (1909–34), and Independent M.P. for the Combined English Univs., 1929–46. She was an ardent advocate of women's suffrage, widows' pensions, and in particular family allowances.

RATHENAU (rah tenow), **Walter** (1867–1922). German statesman. A leading industrialist, he was appointed economic director during the F.W.W. After the war he founded the Democratic Party, and became For. Min., 1922. He signed the Rapallo

Treaty of friendship with Russia n 1922, and soon after was murdered by right-wing fanatics.

RATHLIN. An is. 4 m. off the N. coast of N. Ireland and included in the county of Antrim. St. Columba founded a church on R. in the 6th cent.; and

Sir Terence RATTIGAN
Photo: Angus McBean

Robert Bruce went into hiding there after his defeat by the English at Methven in 1306.

RATIBOR (rah'tēbōr). German form of RACIBORZ.

RATIONALISM. In the history of human thought, the belief that reason is the most important, if not the only, means of ascertaining truth. The name is usually applied to the system of thought which interprets religious doctrines by the light of reason, questioning traditional and rejecting supernatural authority. The Rationalist movement arose in Germany in the 18th cent., and in the 19th it extended to Britain and U.S.A.

RA'TISBON. French name of REGENSBURG.

RATITAE (rāti'tē). One of the 2 main divisions of birds. It is represented by the ostrich, rhea, emu, cassowary, and kiwi. See BIRDS.

RATTIGAN, Sir Terence (1911–). Brit. playwright. B. in London, he writes naturalistic plays of the English middle class, believing that a play stands or falls artistically as well as commercially by the judgement of the wider audience. They incl. the comedy *French Without Tears* (1936); *The Winslow Boy* (1945) based on a real-life incident of a naval cadet wrongly accused of theft; *The Browning Version* (1948), study of a schoolmaster; *Separate Tables* (1954), set in a Bournemouth hotel; and *Ross* (1960) dealing with T.E. Lawrence.

RATTLESNAKE

RATTLESNAKE. A snake of the N. American genus *Crotalus*, distinguished by the horny flat rings of the tail, which 'rattle' when vibrated. The venom injected by the R. is fatal.

RAVEL (rahvel'), **Maurice** (1875–1937). French composer. B. at Ciboure, he achieved a reputation with the piano pieces *Pavane pour une Infante défunte* (1899), and *Jeux d'eau* (1901). Among his later works are the sensational *Boléro*; the ballet *Daphnis et Chloé*; the operas *L'Heure espagnole* and *L'Enfant et les sortilèges*; and the piano compositions *Gaspard de la nuit, Miroirs*, etc.

RAVEN

RAVEN. Bird (*Corvus corax*) in the crow family. About 2 ft. long, the R. has black and lustrous plumage. Found only in the northern hemisphere, it is rare in Britain, breeding chiefly in N. Scotland.

RAVE'NNA. City of Emilia, Italy, cap. of R. prov. It lies in a marshy plain and is famous for its Byzantine churches. R. was a Roman port and naval station, and 404–93 was the cap. of the W. Roman emperors, 493–526 of Theodoric, and later of the Byzantine exarchs 539–750. Byron lived for some months at R., home of the Countess Guiccioli, during the years 1819–21. Pop. (1961) 115,205.

RAVI (rah'vē). River in the Indian sub-continent, a tributary of the Chenab which it joins 35 m. above Multan. It rises in India, forms the boundary between India and Pakistan for some 70 m., and enters Pakistan about 15 m. above Lahore, the chief town on its course of 450 m. It is an important source of water for the Punjab irrigation canal system.

RAWALPINDI. City of W. Pakistan, in the foothills of the Himalayas. It is a great military, road, and rail

RAWALPINDI. As well as irrigation water, the Rawal Dam on the Kurang river (capacity 47,500 cu. ft.) supplies some 14 million gallons of drinking water to Islamabad and nearby Rawalpindi. *Courtesy of the Pakistan High Commission.*

centre and 1959–67 was cap. of Pakistan pending the construction of Islamabad immediately to the N.W. Pop. (1961) 340,175.

RAWLINSON, Sir Henry Creswicke (1810–95). British orientalist. B. in Oxfordshire, he became political agent in Baghdad in 1844, and translated Darius' cuneiform inscription at Behistun. He continued the work of excavation begun by Layard, and pub. a *History of Assyria*, etc.

RAWSTHORNE, Alan (1905–71). British composer. B. in Lancs., he first became known by his 'Theme and Variations for Two Violins' (1938), which was followed by other tersely virile works incl. 'Symphonic Studies', the cantata *Kubla Khan*, the 'Concerto for String Orchestra', and a vigorously inventive 'Sonata for Violin and Piano' (1959).

RAY or **Wray, John** (1627–1705). British botanist, whose *Methodus plantarum* (1682) was the first to divide flowering plants into monocotyledons and dicotyledons, etc. The R. Society, founded in 1844, perpetuates his memory.

RAY, Satyajit (1921–). Indian film director. B. in Bengal, and a commercial artist before he turned to films, he is well known for his trilogy of Bengali life, *Pather Panchali*, 1955, *Aparajito* (1956: *The Unvanquished*), and *Apur Sansar* (1959: *The World of Apu*).

RAY. Name given to fish of the order Hypotremata, which incl. the electric Rs., saw-fish, sting Rs., devil-fish, and the 2 most common British species, the common skate and the thornback R.

Also the path along which a wave may be considered to travel, i.e. perpendicular to the wave front.

RAYLEIGH (rā'li), **John W. Strutt, 3rd baron R.** (1842–1919). British physicist. He was prof. of experimental physics at Cambridge 1879–84, and of

THORNBACK RAY

natural philosophy at the Royal Institution 1887–1905. He wrote the standard *Treatise on Sound* and experimented in optics and microscopy. With Sir William Ramsay, R. discovered argon. He was awarded the O.M., and was president of the Royal Society 1905–8, when he became chancellor of Cambridge Univ. In 1904 he received a Nobel prize.

RAYON. The name which has superseded artificial silk for the filaments made from the solidification of solutions of modified cellulose. The 3 types of commercial importance are viscose, acetate, and copper R.

RAZORBILL. A resident British seabird (*Alca torda*), of the auk family, which breeds on cliffs. It has a curved beak, and is black above and white below.

RAZOR-SHELL or **Razor-Fish.** A genus (*Solen*) of bivalve molluscs, with narrow elongated shells, resembling a razor handle and delicately coloured. They are found in sand among rocks.

READ, Sir Herbert (1893–1968). British writer. Prof. of fine arts at Edinburgh 1931–3, he wrote widely on art, e.g. *The Meaning of Art* (1931) and *The Philosophy of Modern Art* (1952); pub. much verse, e.g. his *Collected Poems* (1946); and was a leading exponent of anarchist thought.

READE, Charles (1814–84). British author. B. in Oxfordshire, he was called to the Bar in 1843, but devoted himself to writing in London. As a dramatist his great successes were *Masks and Faces* (1852: pub. in novel form as *Peg Woffington* in 1853), and *The Lyons Mail* (1854). Among his novels are *It's Never too Late to Mend* (1856); his historical masterpiece *The Cloister and the Hearth* (1861); and *Hard Cash* (1863). His nephew **William Winwood R.** (1838–75) wrote the extremely popular *Martyrdom of Man* (1872), a rationalistic survey of history.

READING, Rufus Daniel Isaacs, 1st marquess of (1860–1935). Liberal statesman. Son of a Jewish merchant, he was called to the Bar and entered parliament in 1904. He became Attorney-Gen. in 1910 and Lord Chief Justice in 1913. Raised to the peerage in 1914, he was Viceroy of India 1921–6. On his return to England he was made a marquess, and in the National govt. he was For. Sec. in 1931. His widow, **Stella** (1894–1971), dowager marchioness of R., was created a baroness (life peerage) in her own right in 1958, and was the founder (1938) of the Women's Voluntary Services for Civil Defence.

READING. English town (co. bor.), co. town of Berks, on the Thames at its junction with the Kennet. An important railway junction and agricultural centre, it is noted for biscuit manufacture. The univ. (1926), founded as a univ. coll. in 1892, specializes in agriculture and horticulture, but has also faculties in arts, science, music, etc. Oscar Wilde passed his 2 years' imprisonment at R. Pop. (1961) 119,870.

READING. City of Pa., U.S.A., important as a manufacturing centre. It was founded in 1748 by two sons of Wm Penn. Pop. (1960) 98.177.

REAGAN, Ronald (1911–). American actor and politician. Star from the thirties of 50 films and later also in television, he became Rep. gov. of California in 1967, his term being noted for battles against insurgent students of the Univ. of California. In 1968 he made a bid for the Rep. presidential nomination.

REALISM. In the medieval philosophy known as Scholasticism, the theory that the only truly real things are 'universals'; it is thus opposed both to Nominalism and to Conceptualism. In modern philosophy the term stands for the doctrine that there is an intuitively appreciated reality apart from what is presented to consciousness, that what is experienced through the senses has an independent existence. As such it is opposed to Idealism. Modern realists incl. C. D. Broad and (although their views were later modified) Russell and G. E. Moore: Wittgenstein has been an important later influence.

REAL PRESENCE. The belief that there are present in the properly consecrated Eucharist the body and blood of Jesus Christ. It is held by Roman Catholics, and in some sense by Anglo-Catholics.

RÉAUMUR (rā-ōmür′), **René Antoine Ferchault de** (1683–1757). French scientist. B. at La Rochelle, his researches assisted the development of French industry, and included a method of tinning iron. He invented the R. thermometer scale, in which freezing point is 0° and boiling point 80°.

RECALL. A political device providing for the immediate recall of an elected delegate if he acts contrary to the wishes of his constituents. It originated in Switzerland, and since 1903 has been adopted in a number of states of U.S.A. A certain percentage of the electorate must sign an application for a fresh election.

RÉCAMIER (rehkahmyā′), **Jeanne Françoise** (1777–1849). French leader of society. B. at Lyons, *née* Bernard, she m. at 15 Jacques R., an elderly banker. She was the 'queen' of a salon of literary and political celebrities.

RECIFE (resē′fe). Seaport of Brazil, cap. of Pernambuco state, at the mouth of the r. Capibaribe. Its proximity to Europe and good harbour give it great commercial importance. It has an airport. Founded in 1504, R. is intersected by waterways. It is the seat of a univ. (1946) and is a naval base. Industries incl. sugar refining, fruit canning, and the making of cotton textiles and flour. Pop. (1960) 797,234.

RECKLINGHAUSEN (-howsen). Town in North Rhine-Westphalia, W. Germany, 15 m. N.W. of Dortmund. Coal mines and iron foundries are nearby and it has iron foundries, chemical and textile factories, engineering works, etc. R. is said to have been founded by Charlemagne. Pop. (1966) 127,578.

RECORDER. Chief legal officer of an English city or borough having a court of quarter sessions. He must be a barrister of 5 years' standing, and sits as sole judge of the court of quarter sessions in his district. The Recorder of the City of London is the chief judge in the Mayor's Court, but elsewhere the post is often an honorary distinction.

Also, name applied generally to the flute family and in particular to the true Rs. of English origin.

RECORD OFFICE, Public. Estab. in 1838 in Chancery Lane, London, the P.R.O. contains the English national records since the Norman Conquest, brought together from Courts of Law and Govt. Depts., incl. Domesday Book, the Gunpowder Plot papers, and the log of H.M.S. *Victory* at Trafalgar. *See* ARCHIVES.

RECTIFIER. Device for obtaining unidirectional current from an alternating source of supply, either by inversion of or suppression of alternate half-waves. Rs. are necessary in the conversion of a.c. supply to d.c. The many different types all depend on being able to pass current in one direction and unable to pass it in the reverse direction.

RECTOR. Term applied to an Anglican clergyman who receives the whole of the tithes levied in his parish, as against a vicar who draws only part; also to the head of certain universities and colleges.

RED. Slang term for a revolutionary, Anarchist or Communist, which originated in the 19th cent. in the form 'red republican', meaning a republican who favoured a social as well as a political revolution, generally by armed violence.

RED ARMY. Title formerly borne by the army of the U.S.S.R. It developed from the Red Guards, or volunteers who carried out the Bolshevik revolution, and received its name because it fought under the red flag. The name R.A. was abolished in 1946, 'Soviet Army' being substituted.

REDCAR. English seaside resort in the N. Riding of Yorks, from 1968 a district of the C.B. of Teesside.

RED CROSS, The. International agency founded to assist wounded and prisoners in war. Prompted by war horrors described by the Swiss, Henri Dunant, the Geneva Convention of 1864 laid down the principles ensuring the safety of ambulances, hospitals, stores, and personnel distinguished by the emblem of the red Geneva Cross on a white ground. The British R.C. Society was founded in 1870, and incorporated in 1908. In addition to dealing with associated problems of war, e.g. refugees, and the care of the disabled, the R.C. is increasingly concerned with the disasters of peace – epidemics, floods, earthquakes, accidents, etc. The R.C. also works in close association with the St. John Ambulance Association. The American National R.C. was founded 1881.

RED DEER. Woodland deer (*Cervus elaphus*) of Europe and W. Asia which in Britain is kept ornamentally in parks, but is also hunted on Exmoor and 'stalked' in Scotland as 'sport'. The male is antlered, and reaches 4½ ft. at the shoulder: in the rutting season in autumn its 'bell' or roar is formidable. The young are spotted, but adults commonly lose these markings.

REDDITCH. English town in Worcs, 12 m. S. of Birmingham, famous for needles; fishing tackle, cycles and motor-cycles, motor and aeroplane parts, and electrical equipment are other products. Pop. (1961) 34,077.

RED DUSTER. Popular name for the Red Ensign, flag of the British mercantile marine. First used in 1674, it was shared with the R.N. until 1864, when it became the exclusive symbol of merchant ships.

RED FLAG. The international symbol of Socialism. In France it was used as a revolutionary emblem from 1792 onward, and was adopted officially as its flag by the Paris Commune of 1871. Since the revolution of Nov. 1917, it has been the national flag of the U.S.S.R.; as such it bears a golden hammer and sickle crossed (*see* frontispiece), symbolizing the unity of the industrial workers and peasants, under a gold-rimmed 5-pointed star, signifying peace between the 5 continents. 'The Red Flag', the Labour Party anthem, was written by Jim Connell during the 1889 London strike.

REDGRAVE, Sir Michael (Scudamore) (1908–). British actor. B. in Bristol, the son of an actor, he made a reputation for sensitive playing in *Thunder Rock* (1941: filmed 1942), is noted for his stylish, well-balanced Shakespearian performances, and has appeared with special distinction in his own stage adaptation of James's *The Aspern Papers* (1959) and in Chekhov's *Uncle Vanya* (1962–3). He was knighted in 1959. His dau. **Vanessa R.** (1937–), with whom he has sometimes appeared, became famous for her interpretation of Ophelia, and subsequently appeared as Nina in Chekhov's *The Seagull*, etc.

RED GUARDS. In the U.S.S.R. the armed workers who took part in the Bolshevik revolution 1917: in China from 1966 the school and college students with red armbands who furthered the Cultural Revolution by attacking old ideas, culture, habits and customs.

RED INDIANS. *See* INDIANS, AMERICAN.

REDL, Alfred. *See* SECRET SERVICE.

REDMOND, John Edward (1856–1918). Irish statesman, leader of the Nationalist Party from the death of Parnell until after the Easter Rebellion in 1916. He was elected an M.P. in 1881, and from 1900 was the acknowledged head of the Irish parliamentary party. After the general elections of 1910 he held the balance of power in the House of Commons, and was able to secure the introduction of a Home Rule bill. Strong opposition was encountered in Ulster, and in 1914 the Ulster Covenanters and R.'s Nationalist Volunteers seemed likely to come to open war. When the F.W.W. broke out, however, R. flung all his influence into the country's war effort, and in recognition of his patriotism the Home Rule bill was passed, although its operation was to be suspended until the end of the war. The rise of Sinn Féin and the Easter Rebellion were bitter blows, and R. d. a disappointed man. His brother, **William R.** (1861–1917), also a prominent Nationalist M.P., joined the army in 1914, and d. of wounds in France.

REDOUTÉ (redootā'), **Pierre Joseph** (1759–1840). French artist, the 'Raphael of Flowers'. Patronized by the Empress Josephine and the Bourbon court, he produced superb volumes of flower paintings, the finest being *Les Roses* (1817–24). To delicacy of touch, he added a profound knowledge of plant structure.

RED RIVER SETTLEMENT. Colony of Scottish settlers founded in 1811–12 by Lord Selkirk in the basin of the Red river, near the site on which Winnipeg was later built. The Hudson's Bay Co. had acquired control by 1836; when its rights were transferred to the Dominion of Canada in 1869, Louis Riel (q.v.) raised a short-lived rebellion.

REDRUTH (-rooth). English market town, 17 m. N.E. of Penzance, Cornwall. Principal centre of the county's tin-mining industry. *See* CAMBORNE.

RED SEA. A strip of water, about 1,200 m. long, and varying in width from 100 to 200 m., running S.E. from Suez to the straits of Bab-el-Mandeb. Occupying part of the Great Rift Valley, it separates Egypt, the Sudan Republic, and Ethiopia in Africa from Arabia in Asia. The R.S. is referred to in the O.T., notably in Exodus, chap. 14, which relates the story of the escape of the Israelites across the R.S. from Pharaoh and his chariots. The sludge of its floor is said to be mineral-rich.

REDSHANK. Bird (*Tringa totanus*) of N. Europe and Asia, where it nests in swampy areas, although wintering farther south. Named from its long red legs, it is greyish, speckled black and *c*. 1 ft. long.

REDSTART. Bird (*Phoenicurus phoenicurus*) which winters in Africa and spends the summer in Europe. Named from its red tail, it has a dark grey head (with white mark on the forehead) and back, and brown wings with lighter underparts. The American R. (*Setophaga ruticilla*) belongs to a different family.

RED TAPE. Phrase descriptive of bureaucratic methods, derived from the 'pink' fastening for departmental bundles of documents in Britain.

REDWING. Member of the thrush species (*Turdus musica*), rather smaller than the song thrush, and with reddish wing and body markings. It breeds in the north of Europe and Asia, moving south in winter.

REDWOOD. *See* SEQUOIA.

REED, Sir Carol (1906–). British film producer and director. He worked in the theatre before going into film production in 1930, and his films incl. *Odd Man Out* (1947); *The Fallen Idol* (1950) and *The Third Man* (1950), both written for him by Graham Greene; *Outcast of the Islands* (1953), and *The Running Man* (1962).

REED. Perennial aquatic grasses. The common R. (*Phragmites communis*) attains a height of 12 ft. or more, having stiff erect leaves, and straight stems bearing a plume of purplish flowers.

REED. In music, the sound-producing medium of various families of instruments, so called because it is made from the outer layer of the R. (*Arundo donax*). The 'beating' R., which vibrates against the side of the instrument tube, is used in the organ (the R. in this

COMMON REED

case being metal), clarinet, etc., and the 'free' R. which vibrates from side to side within the tube, in the mouth organ, harmonium, accordion, etc.

REEVES, William Pember (1857–1932). New Zealand statesman and writer. He was Minister of Education in N.Z. (1891–6), and director of the London School of Economics (1908–19). He wrote poetry and the classic description of his native country, *Long White Cloud* (1898).

REFEREE. An arbitrator. The term is most commonly used of the official in charge of a game, such as football, but may also be applied in law to members of the court of Rs. appointed by the House of Commons to give judgment on petitions against private bills, etc., and to the 3 official Rs. to whom cases before the High Court may be submitted.

REFERENDUM. The procedure whereby a decision on proposed legislation is referred to the electorate for settlement by direct popular vote. It is most frequently employed in Switzerland, but has also been used in Canada, Australia, New Zealand, and certain states of the U.S.A.

REFORMATION, The. The movement which in the 16th cent. ended the religious unity of W. Europe, and resulted in the establishment of the Protestant Churches. Reforming movements akin to Protestantism had existed since the 12th cent., e.g. the Waldenses in France and Germany, the Lollards in England, and the Hussites in Bohemia, but these had all been driven underground. The success of the R. in the 16th cent. was due partly to the rise of centralized absolute monarchies, which resented the political power of the papacy, and partly to the price revolution, which impelled kings and nobles to confiscate the Church's enormous wealth.

The R. began in Germany in 1517 with Luther's (q.v.) protest against the sale of indulgences; the title of 'Protestants' came into general use in 1529. The Peace of Augsburg (1555) left N. and W. Germany Protestant, and E. and S. Germany R.C. An offshoot of German Protestantism was the Anabaptist movement. Lutheranism was officially adopted by Sweden in 1527 and by Denmark in 1536. In Switzerland the R. was begun by Zwingli (q.v.) in 1518; it later came under the leadership of Calvin (q.v.). Calvinism found many followers in France, where the Huguenots (q.v.), although a minority, were strong enough to carry on a religious war, 1562–98. Both Calvinism and Anabaptism were strong in Holland, where resentment of religious persecution was a main cause of the war of independence (1568–1609). The English R. was begun under Henry VIII, who repudiated papal authority in 1534, and dissolved the monasteries. Under Edward VI Protestantism was established, and after a reaction under Mary, the process was completed by Elizabeth. The Scottish R., led by Knox (q.v.), triumphed in 1560. In Italy, Spain, and Portugal Protestantism was crushed by the Inquisition; in Bohemia, Poland, and Hungary it won considerable support, but was almost stamped out in the 17th cent.

REFRIGERATION. The process of absorbing heat at a low temperature and rejecting it at a higher temperature. R. is used in the food industries for the preservation of foodstuffs by chilling or freezing, the storage time which can be tolerated varying with the character of the foodstuff and, in general, increasing as the storage temperature is lowered. R. is also used in industrial processes and in air-conditioning (comfort cooling). *See also* DEEP FREEZING.

The R. process may be effected by gas expansion, by absorption cycles or most commonly by the vapour compression cycle. This is based on the fact that a fluid will absorb heat in changing from the liquid to the gaseous state, and reject heat when changed from gaseous to liquid state: absorption can take place at a low temperature and heat rejection can take place at a higher temperature. Fluids used as refrigerants in the vapour compression cycle incl. carbon dioxide (used most in R. plants on ships), ammonia (generally in industrial and marine equipment), and Refrigerant-12 (dichlorodifluoromethane), the most useful fluid in domestic and small commercial plants such as are used in shops and markets.

REFUGEES. See DISPLACED PERSONS.

REGALIA or **Crown Jewels.** The symbols of royal authority. The British R. were broken up during the Commonwealth, with the exception of the ampulla and anointing spoon, and the present set mainly dates from after the Restoration. A daring attempt to steal them was made in 1671 by Colonel Blood, who was subsequently pardoned and pensioned by Charles II. Formerly kept in the Wakefield Tower, they were moved 1967 to the newly-built Crown Jewel House, in the Tower of London, and are elaborately guarded. Among the chief items are St. Edward's Crown; the Imperial State Crown; the jewelled Sword of State used only at the Coronation; the Sword of State used at the opening of Parliament and on other State occasions; the Curtana (Sword of Mercy); the Swords of Temporal and Spiritual Justice; the Orb; the Royal Sceptre or Sceptre with the Cross (containing the great Star of Africa, cut from the Cullinan diamond); the Rod with the Dove; St. Edward's Staff; the Spurs; the Coronation Ring (the 'Wedding Ring of England'); the Armills (gold bracelets, given by the Commonwealth countries in 1953); the Ampulla (which contains the holy oil for the anointing); and the Anointing Spoon.

REGENCY STYLE. Style of architecture which prevailed in England during the latter part of the 18th cent. and the early part of the 19th cent. The style is characterized by its restrained simplicity, and its imitation of ancient classic architecture, especially Greek. The most famous architects of the period were Henry Holland, who designed many domestic buildings, John Nash (q.v.), and Decimus Burton, who designed the screen at Hyde Park Corner.

REGENSBURG (reh'gensboorg). City of Bavaria, W. Germany, on the Danube at its confluence with the Regen, 63 m. N.N.E. of Munich. Many fine medieval buildings remain. It is on the site of a Celtic settlement going back to 500 B.C., became the Roman Castra Regina in A.D. 179, a free city in 1245, and seat of the German Diet from the 16th cent. to 1806. It was incl. in Bavaria in 1810. Pop. (1966) 125,412.

REGENT. One who discharges the royal functions during the king's minority or incapacity. Since Henry VIII's reign a R. or council of regency has always been appointed by act of Parliament. The Prince of Wales, later George IV, acted as R. during George III's insanity, 1811–20; hence this period is usually referred to as 'the Regency'.

REGER (reh'ger), **Max** (1873–1916). German composer and pianist. He was b. in Bavaria, and became organist at Weiden. He taught at Munich, 1905–7, was professor at the Leipzig Conservatoire from 1907, and conductor of the Meiningen ducal orchestra 1911–13. He composed prolifically, but alcoholic excess led to his early death. His works incl. fine organ and piano music, chamber music and songs.

REGGIO (rej'ō). Port of Calabria, Italy, on the Straits of Messina, producing wine, oil, silk and perfumery. Pop. (1966) 161,270. Also, a town of Emilia, at the foot of the Apennines. Pop. (1966) 124,950.

REGINA (reji'na). Cap. of Saskatchewan prov., Canada, 357 m. W. of Winnipeg. It is the heart of a grain and oil producing region, and growth has been stimulated by the development of potash resources of the prov.; industries incl. oil refining, cement, steel, farm machinery, fertilizers, and flour. It was founded 1882 on a site where Indians had piled the bones of slain buffalo, hence nicknames such as Bone Creek, but was called Regina in honour of Victoria, and is known as Queen City of the Plains. The Mounties'

museum is a tourist attraction. Pop. (1966) 131,127.

RÉGNIER (rehnyā'), **Henri François Joseph de** (1864–1936). French symbolist writer. He won fame as a poet with Les Médailles d'argile, etc., but his realistic novels, such as La Double Maîtresse were also successful.

REICH (rīkh). The German state. The Nazi régime was known as the 3rd R., the 1st generally being identified with the Holy Roman Empire, and the 2nd with the German Empire of 1871–1918.

REICHSTADT, Duke of. See NAPOLEON II.

REICHSTAG (rīkhs'tahg) **FIRE.** The burning of the Reichstag building at Berlin on 27 Feb. 1933, which was probably organized by Nazis, led by Goering, and by them attributed to the Communists. Van der Lubbe, a half-witted Dutchman who was probably a Nazi tool, Torgler, a Communist deputy, and Dimitrov (q.v.), Popov, and Tanev, Bulgarian Communists, were tried at Leipzig. Dimitrov's defence forced the court to acquit all the prisoners except Van der Lubbe, who was executed.

REID, Sir George Houston (1845–1918). Australian statesman. B. in Renfrewshire, he was taken to Australia in 1852, and became Prime Minister of the Commonwealth 1904–5. After serving as High Commissioner in London 1910–16, he was elected a Cons. member of the English House of Commons.

REID, Thomas (1710–96). Scottish philosopher. B. in Kincardineshire, he became a Presbyterian minister, and in 1764 succeeded Adam Smith as prof. of moral philosophy at Glasgow. He wrote an Enquiry into the Human Mind on the Principles of Common Sense (1764), and other works in which he elaborated his 'common-sense philosophy'. There are certain self-evident things, he maintained, such as the material external world and the human soul, which are believed to exist by 'the consent of ages and nations, of the learned and unlearned'.

REID, Thomas Mayne (1818–83). Irish novelist, b. in co. Down, Ireland. After a dozen years of adventure in America, including active service in the Mexican War of 1846, he settled in England in 1850, and wrote books for boys, e.g. The Rifle Rangers (1850).

REIGATE (rī'gāt). English market town (bor.) in Surrey, 20 m. S. of London, at the foot of the N. Downs. R. grew up round a Norman castle, built by the Warenne family and destroyed during the Civil War. Pop. (1961) 53,710.

REIMARUS (rīmah'roos), **Hermann Samuel** (1694–1768). German philosopher and scholar. B. at Hamburg, he was prof. of Hebrew there from 1727. In writings published posthumously by Lessing, he adopted an attitude towards Christianity that won him the title of the first of the biblical higher critics.

REIMS (rēmz; Fr. raṅs). City in Marne dept., N.E. France, 80 m. E.N.E. of Paris on the Vesle, the Roman Durocorturum; from 987 all but six French kings were crowned at R. Ceded to England by the 1420 treaty of Troyes, the city was retaken by Joan of Arc, who in 1429 had Charles VII consecrated in the cathedral built during the 13th cent. The Mars Gate dates from the 4th cent. R. is the seat of an archbishopric, and the centre of the great champagne industry. Woollen and other textiles are manufactured. Pop. (1968) 152,967.

REINACH (rī'nahkh), **Joseph** (1856–1921). French politician. He sat in the Chamber of Deputies 1889–98 and 1906–14, championed many social reforms, and strongly opposed Gen. Boulanger. Himself a Jew, he was among Dreyfus' (q.v.) most active supporters. His brother **Salomon R.** (1858–1932), a distinguished archaeologist, was appointed keeper of the national museums in 1902.

REINCARNATION. The doctrine that the soul after death may enter another human body or that of an animal. It has appeared in the teachings of many religions and philosophies, e.g. Buddhism, Hinduism,

Jainism, the philosophies of Pythagoras and Plato, certain Christian heresies, and Theosophy.

REINDEER. Deer of the Arctic and sub-Arctic, common to both E. and W. hemispheres. About 4 ft. high at the shoulder, it has a very thick, brownish coat and broad hoofs well adapted to travel over snow. It is the only deer in which antlers are also present in the female: these are 4–5 ft. long and are shed in winter. The Scandinavian form (*Rangifer tarandus*) has been domesticated by the Lapps for cents., and has been introduced to Alaska and the Canadian Arctic. The American form (*R. caribou*), known as caribou, occurs in 2 forms – the large woodland caribou of the more southerly region and the barren-ground caribou of the north. R. migrate southward in winter, moving in large herds, and it is in Dec.–March that the Lapps round them up for sorting by their owners: a frilly greyish lichen (*Cladonia rangiferina*), popularly known as R. moss, is their main food.

REINHARDT (rīn′hahrt), **Max** (1873–1943). German theatrical producer. He acted and then produced at the Deutsches Theater, Berlin, 1895–1932, and the Kammerspielhaus, 1906–32. He produced Shakespeare, Molière, Ibsen, Shaw, etc., and 1911–12 *The Miracle* and *Oedipus Rex* in London. He initiated the Salzburg Festival where he produced *Everyman*. After 1933 he went to the U.S.A., becoming an American citizen in 1940, and produced films such as *A Midsummer Night's Dream*.

REITH, John Charles Walsham, 1st baron (1889–1971). Brit. public servant. As 1st general manager (1922–7) and 1st director-general (1927–38) of the B.B.C., he supervised the creation and development of British radio services and of the world's first regular TV service (1936): the annual series of broadcast R. Lectures (1947), given by outstanding leaders of contemporary thought, were named in his honour. He was 1st chairman of B.O.A.C. 1939–40; headed the board reorganizing the Commonwealth cable and wireless system 1946–50, and the Colonial Development Corporation 1950–9. He was a pioneer advocate of the publicly owned but independently operated utility corporation.

RÉJANE (rāzhahn′), **Gabrielle.** Stage-name of the French actress G. Réju (1857–1920). B. in Paris, she scored her first success in 1883 in *Ma Camarade*. Later vehicles for her vital, emotional ability were *Madame Sans Gêne* (1893), *Zaza,* and *La Passerelle*.

RELATIVITY. Theory of physics, associated with the name of Albert Einstein (q.v.), based on the requirement that the laws of physics should be unaffected by the uniform motion of the observer. The need for such a theory became apparent in 1887, when Michelson and Morley performed an experiment to determine the velocity with which the earth moved through the hypothetical ether. No such velocity was, however, detected; and Lorenz and Fitzgerald suggested that this was because a measuring rod or body in motion suffers a contraction in length in the direction of its motion – a correction just sufficient to account for the negative result of the Michelson–Morley experiment. This suggestion was given rational justification by Einstein in the Special Theory of R. in 1905. It may be impossible to determine absolute motion by any experiment whatever, he said; the phenomena of nature will be the same to 2 unaccelerated observers moving with any uniform velocity relative to one another.

Ten years later Einstein advanced his General Theory of R., which was even more revolutionary in its impact on the world of physics. Newton's theory of gravitation had to be abandoned because it was incompatible with the Special Theory of R. Einstein now explained gravitation in terms of the properties of space and time, and not by the idea of a gravitational force of attraction. The idea of 'force of gravitation' is abandoned. The planets, stars, etc., move as they do, not because they are influenced by forces coming from other bodies in the universe, but because of the special nature of the world of space and time in the neighbourhood of matter. Einstein's theory, furthermore, led to the remarkable conclusion that light-rays are 'bent'. In the vast interstellar spaces unaffected by gravitating masses, light-rays travel in straight lines; but when they come within the field of influence of a star or other massive body they are deflected by the latter's gravitational field by an amount directly proportional to the body's mass.

The Einstein theory was carefully tested by expeditions despatched by the observatories of Greenwich and Cambridge to observe the eclipse of the sun of 1919, and the results were conclusively in its favour. The theory also predicts the 'shift' of certain lines in the solar spectrum, the precession in the orbit of Mercury, and the bending of light-rays in the neighbourhood of the sun, and these results admit of experimental verification.

RELAY, Electrical. Switching device operated by an electric current, causing abrupt changes, e.g. making or breaking the circuit, changing of the circuit connections, or variation in the circuit characteristics.

RELICS. Objects associated with Christ or a saint, or parts of a saint's body, preserved as objects of religious veneration. The cult of R. gave rise to many abuses in the Middle Ages, and it was condemned by the Protestant reformers but upheld by the Council of Trent. Relic-worship is widely practised in Lamaism, Mahayana Buddhism, etc.

RELIEF. In architecture, a term applied to carved figures and other forms which project from the background. The Italian terms *basso-rilievo* (low relief), *mezzo-rilievo* (middle relief), and *alto-rilievo* (high relief) are used according to the thickness of the sculpture from the background. The French term *bas-relief* is commonly used for low relief.

RELIGION. Term usually derived from the Latin *religāre*, to bind, that is used to describe man's attitude towards the gods or God. In original Buddhism, there is no Deity; yet Buddhism, like atheistic Jainism, and Confucianism, which is primarily a code of good behaviour, is always included in the list of the world's religions. E. B. Tylor gave as 'the minimum definition of religion, the belief in spiritual beings'. Matthew Arnold defined it as 'morality touched with emotion', but, as Prof. W. K. Clifford pointed out, some religious facts are immoral, e.g. human sacrifices to the gods, sacred prostitution, suttee, and thuggery. Prof. J. E. M'Taggart thought of R. as a feeling of harmony between oneself and the universe. Some modern theologians find the essence of R. to lie in a feeling of awe or reverence for the Unseen Power who or which is believed to be making for righteousness.

The chief religions are: (a) the Oriental faiths: Hinduism, Buddhism, Jainism, Sikhism, Parseeism, Confucianism and Taoism in China, Japanese Shinto; and (b) Judaism, Christianity, and Islam (Mohammedanism) – 'religions of a book'. Of Christianity the principal divisions are the Roman Catholic, the Eastern Orthodox, and the Protestant.

RELIGION, Comparative. The impartial study of the various religions of the world. The first-known surviving attempt at a kind of philosophy of religious beliefs is contained in fragments of the Greek thinker Xenophanes (6th cent. B.C.). Herodotus and Aristotle contributed to the study. The Middle Ages provided nothing but naive tales and observations, and the Reformation had a narrowing influence. Really serious comparative work did not begin until the 17th cent., when the Jesuits in China produced some interesting studies. Towards the end of the 18th cent. a little body of English missionary scholars in Calcutta began to study the sacred books of India. An immense stimulus was given to the investigation of religious beliefs by the Darwinian theory of Evolution. Notable workers in the field incl. Max Müller, Sir James Frazer, Sir E. B. Tylor, Andrew Lang and R. C. Zaehner. Much of the raw material of the science has been provided by Christian missionaries. The more recent observers have been field anthropologists.

REMARQUE (rehmahrk´), **Erich Maria** (1898–1970). German novelist. B. at Osnabrück, he was a soldier in the F.W.W., and his anti-war sentiments, expressed in his most famous book *All Quiet on the Western Front* (1929), led to his being deprived of his German nationality in 1938; he eventually settled in the U.S.A. in 1939, and later became an American citizen. Later books incl. *The Arch of Triumph* (1946) and *A Time to Live and a Time to Die* (1954).

REMBRANDT, Harmensz van Rijn (1606–69). Dutch painter and etcher. B. in Leyden, the son of a wealthy miller, he studied under Swanenburch, an architectural painter of Leyden, and for a short

time under Peter Lastman in Amsterdam. The greatest painter of the Dutch school, he is famous for his masterly treatment of light and shade, his portraits of old people, and his great gift for depicting objects which are commonly regarded as ugly – e.g. 'Sirloin of Beef', and 'Slaughtered Ox' – as things of beauty. He is also the greatest of etchers. His earliest pictures – e.g. 'St. Paul in Prison' and 'St. Jerome' – were painted in Leyden, but most of his work was executed in Amsterdam, where he settled in 1631. He is said to have visited England about

REMBRANDT. One of more than 60 known self-portraits.
Courtesy of the Walker Art Gallery.

1661–2. In 1656 he was declared bankrupt, and a collection of his etchings and drawings were sold for a fraction of their value. But he continued to work diligently, and in the closing years of his life he produced some of his best works. Besides those mentioned, his most famous works incl. 'Presentation in the Temple', the 'Anatomy Lesson', 'The Night Watch', 'Woman Taken in Adultery', 'The Good Samaritan', and a number of self-portraits.

REMEMBRANCE SUNDAY. National Day of Remembrance for both world wars. A 'two-minute silence' is observed at the actual time of the signature of the Armistice with Germany on 11 Nov. 1918 in the F.W.W., and services of commemoration are held, with wreaths of 'Flanders poppies' being laid at the Whitehall Cenotaph and elsewhere. The poppies are also worn by individuals and are made and sold by disabled members of the British Legion in aid of war invalids and their dependants. Observed 1919–45 as Armistice Day (always on 11 Nov.), it was then renamed R.S. and observed on the 1st or 2nd Sunday of the month: since 1956 it has been fixed as the 2nd Sunday.

REMINGTON, Philo (1816–89). American inventor. B. at Litchfield, New York, he is chiefly remembered as the inventor of the R. typewriter.

REMIZOV (remēz´of), **Aleksei Mikhailovich** (1877–

1957). Russian writer. B. n Moscow, he was expelled from the univ. there for political activities, and from 1921 lived in exile. His works are varied in form and remarkable for their verbal artistry which has influenced later writers: they incl. *Chasy* (1904: *The Clock*), *Pyataya yazva* (1912: *The Fifth Pestilence*) – both novels – and an autobiography which appeared in 1951.

RENAISSANCE (Fr. rebirth). The intellectual movement, which originated in 14th–16th cent. Italy, and spread over W. Europe in the 16th cent. Among its outstanding characteristics were an emphasis on the potentialities of the individual and this life; the belief in the power of education to produce the 'complete man', the man of action who is also master of all the culture of his age; the desire to enlarge the bounds of learning; the growth of scepticism and free thought; and the acceptance of Greek and Latin literature and art as models.

The beginning of the Italian R. is usually dated in the 14th cent. with the work of Dante, Petrarch, and Boccaccio; in the 16th it was almost extinguished by the Counter-Reformation. From Italy the humanists, such as Erasmus, spread the enthusiasm for classical learning through W. Europe, and during the 16th cent. the ideals of the R. came gradually to dominate French, Spanish, and English culture. The invention of printing and the geographical discoveries gave a further impetus to the new

spirit. Biblical criticism of Erasmus and others contributed to the Reformation, and although the 2 movements often came into conflict, such writers as Spenser and Milton successfully reconciled their ideas. Apart from those named, typical figures of the R. were Machiavelli, Ariosto, da Vinci, Michelangelo, Tasso, Bruno, Galileo and Campanella in Italy; Rabelais and Montaigne in France; Cervantes in Spain; Camoens in Portugal; Copernicus in Poland; and More, Sidney, Marlowe, Shakespeare and Bacon in England.

RENAISSANCE. Incarnation of the ideal, many-gifted man, Leonardo da Vinci – a self-portrait drawn in chalk.

RENAN (renoń´), **Joseph Ernest** (1823–92). French philosopher and religious historian. B. at Tréguier, he at first studied for the priesthood, but devoted himself to independent researches into biblical history. His *Life of Jesus* (1863) was strongly criticized for its rationalizing tendencies. Later works are on Paul, Marcus Aurelius, and the history of Israel. *Souvenirs d'Enfance* (1883) is autobiographical.

RENAULT, Mary. Pseudonym of novelist Mary Challans (1905–). Originally a nurse, she has made her name with her re-creations of the myths and history of ancient Greece, e.g. the trilogy dealing with Theseus: *The Last of the Wine* (1956), *The King Must Die* (1958), and *The Bull From the Sea* (1962).

RENFREW (-froo). Royal burgh and co. town of Renfrewshire, Scotland, near the Clyde, 5 m. W.N.W. of Glasgow. It has a shipbuilding industry. Pop. (1961) 17,946.

RENFREWSHIRE. W. country of central Scotland bordering the Firth of Clyde, Undulating country is drained by the Gryfe, White and Black Cart, and provides good pasture. Coal, iron, and ironclay are mined, granite quarried, and thread produced at Paisley. Cotton and flax spinning and woollen manufacturing are other staple occupations. Renfrew is the cap.; other towns incl. Paisley, Greenock, and Port Glasgow. Area 240 sq. m.; pop. (1961) 338,815.

RENI (rā'nē), **Guido** (1575–1642). Italian painter of the Bolognese school. B. at Calvenzano, he was influenced by Caravaggio, and in *c.* 1602 settled in Rome where he painted his masterpiece, 'Phoebus and the Hours preceded by Aurora'. He eventually returned to Bologna where he founded a school.

RENNES (ren). Capital of Ille-et-Vilaine dept., W. France, at the confluence of the Ille and Vilaine, 35 m. S.S.E. of St. Malo. It has a univ. which pays particular attention to Breton culture, and is the seat of an archbishopric. It was originally the cap. of the Armorican tribe of the Redones. The 2nd Dreyfus trial, 1899, was held at R. Pop. (1968) 180,943.

RENNIE, John (1761–1821). Scottish engineer, b. at Phantassie, whose best-known structures were Southwark, Waterloo (q.v.), and London bridges.

RE'NO. City of Nevada, U.S.A., on the Truckee. It dates from 1868 and is best known as a place of temporary residence in order to take advantage of the state divorce laws, which require only 6 weeks' residence and provide extensive grounds on which to sue. R. is also the seat of the state univ. (1874), and has some industry, e.g. meat packing. Pop. (1960) 51,470.

RENOIR (renwahr'), **Pierre Auguste** (1841–1919). French painter. B. at Limoges, after serving as an apprentice to a porcelain manufacturer, he studied under Gleyre and was friendly with Sisley and Monet. He became one of the leading painters of the French Impressionist movement. His paintings show a sensitive touch, and a fine sense of colour; he is particularly noted for his nudes. Among his best-known works are Les Parapluies', 'The Bathers', and 'La Loge'. His son, **Jean R.** (1894–), is a film director. His films include *La Grande Illusion* (1936), *La Marseillaise,* and *La Bête Humaine. See* illus. p. 562.

REPARATIONS. Indemnities paid by countries defeated in war, as by Germany in both world wars.

REPRIEVE. The legal temporary suspension of the execution of a sentence pronounced after conviction of a capital offence. It is usually associated with the death penalty. In Britain it is made by the Crown on the advice of the Home Sec., and in the U.S.A. it is the prerogative of state govs.: the Pres. having this power in the case of federal offences, e.g. treason.

REPTILES. Class of vertebrates (Reptilia) including the snakes, lizards, crocodiles, turtles and tortoises. They are distinguished from the Amphibia by the absence of gills, breathing by means of lungs. They are cold-blooded, produced from eggs, and the skin is usually covered with scales. Many extinct forms are known, including the orders Pterosauria, Rhynchocephalia (containing one living form, the tuatara), Plesiosauria, Ichthyosauria, and Dinosauria. The chief living orders are the Chelonia (tortoises and turtles), Crocodilia (alligators and crocodiles), and Squamata, divided into 3 sub-orders, Lacertilia (lizards); Rhiptoglossa (chameleons); Ophidia (snakes).

REPTILE. An extinct species – Icthyosaurus.

REPTON. English village in Derbyshire known for its public school, founded 1557, under the will of Sir John Port. Cap. of the kings of Mercia, R. has a 14th cent. church of St. Wystan which incorporates remains of a Saxon church. Pop. (est.) 2,000.

REPUBLICAN PARTY. One of America's 2 leading political parties, formed in 1854 by a coalition of opponents to slavery, who elected their 1st president, Abraham Lincoln in 1860. In the early years, the R.P. supported protective tariffs; and preference for genuine settlers (homesteaders) over speculators for unsettled public land. Coupled with these liberal measures were conservative tendencies and an antagonism of the legislature to the executive, which were markedly expressed after Lincoln's assassination in the impeachment of Andrew Johnson, his Democratic and southern successor, and the election of Gen. Grant to the presidency in 1868 and 1872, which were both residues of civil-war bitterness – the party being divided into those who considered the South a beaten nation, and those who did not recognize the secession, and wished to reintegrate the South into the country as a whole. Towards the end of the century the R.P. was identified with U.S. imperialism, and industrial expansion. The era of President Theodore Roosevelt saw attempts at regulation and control of big business, and in forming the Progressive Party in 1912 he effectively removed the liberal influence from the R.P. until the 1940s. With few intermissions, the R.P. controlled the legislature from the 1860s until defeated by the 'New Deal' Democrats in 1932. The R.P. remained in eclipse until the election of Eisenhower in 1952, rather a personal triumph than that of the party which only narrowly managed to secure an initial control of Congress, soon lost and not regained even by the next R. pres., Richard Nixon, in 1968. After an isolationist period before the S.W.W., the R.P. became committed to an active foreign policy and Democratic and R. party platforms in 1968 were very close.

REREDOS (rēr'dos). An ornamental screen or wall-facing at the back of the altar of a church. *See* illus. under GOTHIC ARCHITECTURE for the R. at Winchester.

RESIN. A substance exuded from pines, firs, and other trees, in gummy drops which harden in air. Varnishes are the commonest products of the hard resins, and ointments those of the soft resins. Rosin is the solid residue of distilled turpentine, a soft R.

RESISTANCE, Electrical. The property of a substance which restricts the flow of electricity through it, associated with conversion of electrical energy to heat; also the magnitude of this property. A *resistor* is an element whose principal characteristic is R., which depends on many factors which may include any or all of the following: the nature of the material, its temperature, dimensions, and thermal properties; degree of impurity, the nature and state of illumination of the surface and the frequency and magnitude of the current. The practical unit of R. is the ohm.

RESISTANCE MOVEMENTS. The opposition movements in Axis-occupied countries during the S.W.W. In E. Europe these took the form of guerrilla warfare, among the most successful being the partisan movement led by Tito in Yugoslavia, the guerrillas in Greece and Poland, and the partisan band behind the German lines in Russia. In more industrialized countries, such as France, Belgium, and Czechoslovakia, sabotage in war factories and on the railways, combined with underground propaganda and the assassination of particularly obnoxious Germans and collaborators, was more important. In these countries also, however, guerrilla activity was maintained, the groups affording a refuge for men resisting conscription for forced labour. Specialized forms of resistance were devised by particular sections of the community, such as the Norwegian clergy, who boycotted the Quisling-controlled State Church. Most of the R.Ms. were based on an alliance of all anti-Fascist parties, but in some countries, such as Yugoslavia and Greece, serious conflict arose between left- and right-wing movements.

RESPIGHI (respē'gē), **Ottorino** (1879–1936). Italian composer. B. at Bologna, he studied under Rimsky-Korsakov, and in 1913 became prof. of composition at the Accademia di Santa Cecilia in Rome. He composed operas, and orchestral works of a descriptive nature, e.g. *Fontane di Roma*, etc.

RESPIRATION. The process by which the blood gives up carbon dioxide and is charged with oxygen. Used blood is forced into the lungs by the contraction of the right ventricle of the heart; there it passes through fine capillary vessels with very thin walls in contact with the air cells. From these the blood takes up oxygen (about 4 per cent of the total volume of the air), giving up the same quantity of carbon dioxide, together with water and small quantities of ammonia and waste matter. The rate of R. at rest in the adult is about 18 to the minute; during sleep it becomes slower, and during exertion, emotion, or fever it may be much increased.

RESTIF DE LA BRETONNE (rātǔf' de lah breton'), **Nicolas Edmé** (1734–1806). French author. B. at Sacy, he led an adventurous life and is remembered for the licentious novel *Le Paysan perverti* and the autobiography *Monsieur Nicolas*. His *Les Nuits de Paris*, an intimate record of the lower depths of the city 1786–93, is invaluable to the social historian.

RETRIEVER. Breed of sporting dog. The flat or wavy-coated R. was derived from the Labrador R. and the setter or collie. The head and neck are long, the body rather short, and the coat black or liver-coloured. The curly-coated R. is partly derived from the poodle and is usually black.

RETZ, Gilles de. *See* RAIS.

RETZ (räs), **Jean François Paul de Gondi,** Cardinal de (1614–79). French politician. A churchman with political ambitions, he stirred up and largely led the insurrection of the Fronde (q.v.). After a period of imprisonment and exile he was restored to favour in 1662 and created abbot of St. Denis. His *Memoirs* are of great historical interest.

RÉUNION (rä-ünyoṅ'). French is. in the Indian Ocean, 420 m. E. of Madagascar. In Piton des Neiges it rises to over 10,000 ft. The climate is fairly good; sugar, rum, and manioc are produced. St. Denis is the cap. R. was discovered by a Portuguese navigator Pedro de Mascarenhas in 1513, annexed by Louis XIII (who named it Bourbon) in 1642, and remained French except for 1810–15 when it was in English hands. Area 970 sq. m.; pop. (1966) 408,541.

REUTER (roi'ter), **Paul Julius,** baron de (1816–99). Founder of Reuters international news agency. B. at Cassel, Germany, he began a continental pigeon post in 1849, and, with improved telegraphic communications, he planned to estab. a news agency in Paris. Govt. restrictions there prevented this, and in 1851 he set up his office in London. Not until 1858, however, did he persuade the Press to use his news telegrams from the Continent, in which year the service also became world-wide. Under Sir Roderick Jones (1877–1962), Reuters became a private trust in 1916, and was taken over by the Newspaper Proprietors' Association 1926–41.

REVAL, REVEL. *See* TALLIN.

REVERE, Paul. *See* LEXINGTON.

REVOLVER. *See* FIREARMS.

REVUE. A stage presentation originating as a loosely constructed satire on current events. Although in some measure retaining this form the R. often implies merely a variety of scenes.

REYKJAVÍK (rä'kyahvik). Cap. and chief port of Iceland, on its S.W. coast. It has a univ. founded in 1911, and a cathedral. Many of the houses are wood. It is a modern city, heated by underground mains fed by the volcanic springs to the E. Pop. (1966) 79,202.

REYNOLDS. A study, dated 1765, of the wife and daughters of James Paine (1725–89), architect of Kedleston Hall and other country houses, in the grand manner of Vanbrugh. Polly, the younger daughter, later married Tilly Kettle (c. 1740–86), an artist whose portraits are so similar to those of Reynolds as to be mistaken for the work of the master. *See* portrait of Warren Hastings.
Courtesy of the Lady Lever Collection.

REYNAUD (rānō'), **Paul** (1878–1966). French politician. He entered the Chamber of Deputies in 1928, and was Finance Min. 1938–40. He succeeded Daladier as P.M. in March 1940, but resigned in June, after the German break-through. He was held a prisoner until 1945, first in France, and later in Germany. In 1953–4 he was a deputy premier in the Laniel govt.

REYNOLDS, Sir Joshua (1723–92). British artist. B. near Plymouth, he went to London at the age of 17, and was apprenticed to Thomas Hudson, a mediocre portrait painter. From 1743 he was active as a portrait painter in London and Plymouth, but in 1749 went abroad to complete his studies. He spent over 2 years in Rome, visited other Italian cities, and settling in London in 1752 he became the most famous portrait painter of his day and the first president of the R.A. (1768). He was a life-long friend of Dr. Johnson, and at R.'s suggestion the 'Literary Club' was founded in 1764. He painted portraits of Johnson, Goldsmith, Garrick, and other famous people of his day, in a style synthesized from that of the old masters, but overlaid with his own inventiveness. He was knighted in 1768. His artistic theories are propounded in his *Discourses*.

RHE'A. Genus of birds, found only in S. America. They are incapable of flight, and differ from the ostrich in having a feathered neck and head and three-toed feet, and in their smaller size. There are 3 species, *R. americana, R. darwini,* and *R. macrorhyncha*.

RHEE, Syngman (1875–1965). Korean politician. A rebel under Chinese rule, he was imprisoned 1897–1904, during which time he became a Christian convert. After some years in America he went back to Korea in 1910 to agitate against the now prevailing Japanese control, and was expelled until his return in 1945. Pres. of the Korean Rep. from 1948 until riots forced him to resign and leave the country in

1960, he estab. a repressive dictatorship and was an embarrassing ally for the U.S.A.

RHEIMS. *See* REIMS.

RHENIUM (Lat. *Rhenus*, Rhine). Hard grey metal; symbol Re, at. wt. 186·22, at. no. 75. Discovered in 1925 by Noddack, Tacke and Berg in the minerals columbite, tantalite and wolframite, it is used in thermocouples and as a catalyst for dehydrogenation.

RHE'SUS MONKEY. A species of macaque (*Macacus rhesus*), also known as the bandar, found in N. India. Brown, tinged with grey, the hair is long and straight; the face and buttocks are bare and red. The Rh factor is a substance found in the red blood cells of 85 per cent of human beings; is presumed similar to a substance found in the red blood cells of R.Ms.

RHEUMATISM. A term loosely applied to a large variety of ailments associated with inflammation of joints and muscles. Acute R., or rheumatic fever, is, however, a definite disease probably caused by a certain type of coccus. It is commonest between 15 and 30 and in cold, damp weather. It is marked by illness, high temperature, and inflammation of joints, which is apt to pass rapidly from one to another. It lasts about 2 weeks, and its chief danger is the damage it does to the heart muscle. There is a form of infective R. which attacks elderly patients, and may develop into osteo-arthritis, or severe muscular stiffness with signs of chronic infection.

RHINE, Joseph Banks (1895–   ). American expert on extra-sensory perception. He was director of the Parapsychology Laboratory, Duke Univ. from 1935, and of the Parapsychology Institute, Durham, N.C., from 1964. His controlled experiments in telepathy, clairvoyance, precognition and psychokinesis have estab. a scientific basis for belief in these phenomena.

RHINE. River of Europe. It rises in Switzerland, and forms the frontier between Switzerland and (i) Liechtenstein, (ii) Austria from Liechtenstein to Lake Constance, (iii) Germany from Lake Constance to Basle, and the Franco-German frontier from Basle to near Karlsruhe, where it enters Germany. It receives the Neckar, Main, Moselle, Ruhr. Crossing the Dutch border, it becomes a wide delta covering the S.W. of the Netherlands, and with many branches which link and divide and link again. One branch, the Ijssel, runs N. from just E. of Arnhem to the Ijsselmeer; the others, of which the chief are the Lek and the Waal, link eventually with the Maas (Meuse) and Scheldt (Escaut) to fall into the North Sea by a number of mouths, the most important being the canalized New Waterway and the Scheldt estuary. It is navigable for vessels up to 1,300 tons as far as Basle. Length *c.* 800 m.

RHINELAND-PALATINATE. Land of Germany formed in 1946 of the Rhenish Palatinate (*see* PALATINATE) and parts of Hessen, Rhine prov. and Hessen-Nassau. Much of it is wooded mountain country, and forestry is carried on; cattle, pigs and poultry are reared; wheat, rye, barley, oats and potatoes are grown; and wine and tobacco are produced. The chief industries are chemicals, leather goods and machinery. The cap. is Mainz. Area 7,656 sq. m.; pop. (1966) 3,612,700.

RHINE PROVINCE. Former prov. of Prussia, in S.W. Germany. It incl. the Saar area (Saarland), part of the Ruhr, and the famous vineyards of the Rhine and Moselle valleys; Cologne was its chief city. It was divided in 1945 between the British and French occupation zones, and in 1946 the N. (British-occupied) part was incl. in the Land of North Rhine-Westphalia; the S. (French-occupied) part in the Land of Rhineland-Palatinate.

RHINOCEROS (rīno'seros). Ungulate mammal of the family Rhinocerotidae. Best-known are the one-horned Indian R. (*Rhinoceros unicornis*), 5 ft. at the shoulder and with a thick, tubercled skin, folded into shield-like pieces; the African black R. (*Diceros bicornis*), bad-tempered and with a prehensile upper lip for feeding on shrubs; and the docile broad-lipped or 'white' R. (*Ceratotherium simus*), actually slaty-grey and with a squarish mouth for browsing grass. Both the latter are smooth-skinned and two-horned, but the white is rare and at 6 ft. the largest living R.: an extinct species reached 15 ft.

AFRICAN RHINOCEROS

RHODE ISLAND. Smallest state of the U.S.A., on the Atlantic coast. One of the original 13 states, R.I. was founded in 1636 by Roger Williams, who had been exiled from Massachusetts Bay Colony for religious dissent. The coastline is indented by Narragansett Bay, running 28 m. inland. Industries incl. textiles, formerly most important but declining after the S.W.W. and overtaken by varied manufactures, jewellery, silverware, machinery, rubber and plastics. Poultry (espec. R.I. reds) and dairying flourish; apples and potatoes are grown; and there are valuable fish and shellfish resources. The cap. is Providence, and Newport has been a noted seaside resort from the mid-19th cent. Area 1,214 sq. m.; pop. (1970) 949,723.

RHODES, Cecil John (1853–1902). S. African statesman. B. at Bishop's Stortford, Herts, he went to Natal in 1870. As head of De Beers Consolidated Mines and Goldfields of S. Africa, Ltd., he amassed a large fortune. He entered the Cape legislature in 1881, and became Prime Minister in 1890. Aiming at the formation of a S. African federation and of a block of British territory from the Cape to Cairo, he was largely responsible for the annexation of Bechuanaland in 1885, and formed the British S. Africa Co. in 1889, which occupied Mashonaland and Matabeleland, thus forming Rhodesia. The discovery of his complicity in the Jameson Raid forced him to resign the premiership in 1896. The R. Scholarships were founded at Oxford under his will, for students from the Commonwealth, U.S.A., and Germany.

RHODES. Largest of the Dodecanese, in the E Aegean Sea. It was first settled by Greeks *c.* 1000 B.C., held by the Knights Hospitallers of St. John 1306–1522, taken from Turkish rule by the Italian occupation in 1912, and ceded to Greece in 1947. Grapes and olives are grown. R. is the cap., pop. (1961) 27,393. Area 545 sq. m.; pop. (est.) 60,000.

RHODESIA. Country of S. central Africa bounded by Zambia to the N., Mozambique to the W., and the Rep. of S. Africa to the S. It incl. the Great Dyke, a ridge of high veld 4–6,000 ft. high running for 350 m. S.W.–N.E. between Bulawayo and Salisbury (the cap.) and elsewhere slopes down to low veld, 1–2,000 ft. high; the climate of R. is modified by its altitude and is healthy for Europeans. Incl. in R. are the Matopo Hills, where Rhodes is buried, Victoria Falls, and Zimbabwe. Products incl. maize, groundnuts, kaffir corn, cotton and tobacco; cattle (except in the tse-tse belt along the Zambesi) and goats; and a wealth of minerals—asbestos, chromite, coal, copper, diamonds, gold, emeralds, nickel and platinum. Other towns beside Bulawayo and Salisbury, incl. Umtali, Gwelo, Wankie, and Que Que. Area 150,333 sq. m.; pop. (1967) 4,530,000, incl. 228,000 whites.

The combined area occupied by Zambia (q.v.) and R. was incl. in the cession made to the Brit. S. Africa Co. in 1889, and the whole was named R. in 1895 in honour of Cecil Rhodes (q.v.). The portion S. of the Zambesi, then known as Southern R., was granted

RHODESIA. One of the country's most important products, tobacco is still reaped mainly by hand, as on this farm near Salisbury.   *Courtesy of the High Commissioner for Rhodesia.*

responsible govt. in 1923, was a member of the Federation of R. and Nyasaland 1953–63, and under the new constitution of 1961 incl. Africans for the first time in the enlarged Legislative Assembly. Southern R. became known as R. in 1964, after the creation of Zambia, and pressure mounted for full independence. The British govt. stipulated that the terms must be acceptable to all R.'s citizens, and 11 Nov. 1965 R. made a Unilateral Declaration of Independence (U.D.I.). The U.K. imposed trade restrictions and an oil embargo, and in 1966 (following a Commonwealth Conference) an attempted negotiated settlement on board H.M.S. *Tiger* with the Rhodesian Front regime, led by Ian Smith (q.v.), failed and mandatory sanctions were imposed by the U.N. Further discussions 1968 between Smith and Harold Wilson in H.M.S. *Fearless*, again off Gibraltar, were also abortive. After a referendum held by Ian Smith, R. became a rep. 1970. Under the constitution there is a pres., senate, and house of assembly of 66 members (50 European and 16 African): the voters' rolls are racially separate.

See ZIMBABWE.

RHO′DIUM (Gk. *rhodon*, rose). Silvery-white metal of the platinum family, symbol Rh, at. wt. 102·91, at. no. 45, discovered in 1803 by Wollaston. Its salts form red solutions, and it is found native with platinum in river sands in the Urals and the Americas. Used in thermocouples and in electro-plating, it gives a corrosion-free highly polished surface, superior to that of chromium.

RHODODENDRON

RHODODE′NDRON. A genus of evergreen and deciduous shrubs in the family Ericaceae. The ovate leaves are often dark and leathery, and the large racemes of flowers occur in all colours except blue.

RHONDDA (ron′dha). Welsh coal-mining town (bor.) in Glamorganshire, comprising 2 main valleys in the E. of the S. Wales coal area; it also has many light industries. Pop. (1961) 100,314.

RHÔNE (rōn). Large river of S. Europe. It rises in Switzerland, flows through the Lake of Geneva to Lyons in France, where at its confluence with the Saône the upper limit of navigation is reached. The river turns due S., passes Vienne and Avignon, and takes in the Isère and other tributaries. Near Arles it divides into the Grand and Petit R., flowing respectively S.E. and S.W. into the Mediterranean W. of Marseilles, and forming a two-armed delta; the area between the distributories is the Camargue, a desolate, mosquito-plagued marsh *c.* 300 sq. m. in extent, the haunt of flamingo and other birds. Drainage has brought parts of the Camargue under cultivation, especially for rice. The Rhône is harnessed for hydro-electricity, the chief dam being at Genissiat in the dept. of Ain, constructed 1938–48.

RHUBARB (rōō′-). Perennial plant (*Rheum hybridum*) grown for its edible leaf stalks. The leaves are poisonous. The roots of *R. palmatum* are used medicinally.

RHYME or **Rime.** A feature of verse which arises from identity in sound of the endings of certain words. Although avoided in Japanese verse as a blemish, it exists in most Asiatic and modern European languages. It was, however, unknown in classical Greek and Latin verse, and in Anglo-Saxon and other old Teutonic poetry its place was taken by alliteration. R. first appeared in W. Europe in late Latin poetry.

RHYS (rēs), **Jean** (1894–   ). British novelist. Dau. of a Creole (Dominica) mother and a Welshman, she pub. *Voyage in the Dark* (1934) and other books before the S.W.W., but made a wide reputation with *Wide Sargasso Sea* (1966), recreating the early life of the mad Creole wife of Rochester in *Jane Eyre*.

RIBBENTROP, Joachim von (1893–1946). German Nazi leader. B. in the Rhineland, he served in the F.W.W., and subsequently became a champagne-salesman. He joined the Nazi Party in 1932, acted as Hitler's adviser on foreign affairs, and was German ambassador to Britain 1936–8. As For. Min. 1938–45, he was largely responsible for Germany's aggressive foreign policy. He was tried at Nuremberg as a war criminal in 1946, and hanged.

RIBERA (rēbă′rah), **Jusepe** (1591–1656). Spanish painter and etcher. B. near Valencia, he went to Italy where he was known as *Spagnoletto* ('Little Spaniard'). He was a realistic painter, and was fond of depicting gruesome subjects, e.g. the 'Martyrdom of St. Bartholomew'. His etchings show great originality.

RIBS. Twelve curved bones with cartilage on each side of the chest. At the rear each pair is joined to one of the vertebrae of the spine. The upper 7 are 'true' ribs, because they are joined by cartilage directly to the breast bone (sternum); the 8th, 9th and 10th are each joined by cartilage to the rib above; the 11th and 12th ('floating ribs') are not attached in front at all. The Rs. protect the lungs and heart and at the same time allow the chest to expand and contract easily.

RICE. A crop that grows best on low river flats subject to frequent flooding, rice can also be planted – as is being done here in Java – on terraced hillsides which are specially irrigated.   *Courtesy of Indonesian Embassy.*

RICARDO, David (1772–1823). British economist. After making a fortune on the London Stock Exchange, he pub. in 1817 *Principles of Political Economy*, in which 'laws' of rent, value, and wages, long generally accepted, were clearly enunciated.

RICE, Elmer (1892–1967). American playwright. B in New York City, he was best known for the Expressionist *The Adding Machine* (1923) and *Street Scene* (1929), which was made into an opera by Kurt Weill.

RICE. The principal cereal of the wet regions of the tropics; the yield is very large, and R. is said to be the staple food of one-third of mankind. It is derived from grass of the genus *Oryza*, which is probably native to India and S.E. Asia. It has been cultivated since prehistoric days in the East, and has now been introduced into suitable lands in other parts of the world. It is a crop that matures quickly, taking 150–200 days in warm, very wet conditions. During its growing period it needs to be flooded either by the heavy monsoon rains or by adequate irrigation. This restricts the cultivation of swamp rice, the usual kind, to level land and terraces. A poorer variety, known as hill rice, is grown on hillsides. Paddy, or unhusked R., has valuable vitamins which are lost in husking or polishing, but it is only in the polished state that R. enters into European trade. Outside Asia there is some R. production in the Po valley of Italy, and in the United States in Louisiana, Carolina, and in California. New varieties with greatly increased protein content are being developed by gamma radiation for commercial cultivation from 1975.

RICHARD I, called **Coeur-de-Lion** (1157–99). King of England. The 3rd son of Henry II, against whom he twice rebelled, he succeeded to the crown in 1189. In the 3rd Crusade 1191–2 he showed courage and generalship, although he failed to recover Jerusalem. While returning overland he was captured by the duke of Austria, who handed him over to the Emperor Henry VI, and he was held prisoner until a large ransom was raised. His later years were spent in warfare in France, and he was killed while besieging Châlus. Himself a poet, he became a hero of romances after his death.

RICHARD II (1367–1400). King of England. B. at Bordeaux, the son of Edward the Black Prince, he succeeded his grandfather Edward III in 1377, the govt. being in the hands of a council of regency. During the Peasants' Revolt in 1381 he showed much courage. His fondness for favourites resulted in conflicts with parliament, and in 1388 the baronial party headed by the duke of Gloucester had many of his friends executed. R. recovered control in 1389, and ruled moderately until 1397, when he had Gloucester murdered, and his leading opponents executed or banished, and made himself absolute. In 1399 his cousin the duke of Hereford (later Henry IV) returned from exile to lead a revolt; R. was deposed by parliament and imprisoned in Pontefract Castle, where he d. mysteriously.

RICHARD III (1452–85). King of England. The son of Richard, duke of York, he was created duke of Gloucester by his brother Edward IV, and distinguished himself in the Wars of the Roses. On Edward's death in 1483 he was created protector to his nephew Edward V, and soon secured the crown on the plea that Edward IV's sons were illegitimate. He proved a capable ruler, but the suspicion that he had murdered Edward V and his brother undermined his popularity. In 1485 Henry, earl of Richmond, raised a rebellion, and R. was defeated and killed at Bosworth. Modern scholars tend to minimize the evidence for his crimes as Tudor propaganda.

RICHARDS, Frank. Pseudonym of British author Charles Hamilton (1875–1961). Writing for the boys' papers *Magnet* and *Gem*, he invented the Greyfriars public school at which the most famous pupil was the immortal fat boy, always in trouble, Billy Bunter.

RICHARDS, Sir Gordon (1905–). British jockey. First riding in 1920, he had 21,834 mounts and 4,870 winners before his retirement in 1954. He was 26 times champion jockey, and was knighted in 1953, the year he won the Derby with Pinza.

RICHARDSON, Henry Handel. Pseudonym of Australian author Ethel Henrietta R. (1880–1946). B. in Melbourne, she left Australia at the age of 18, and never returned, although her books have a predominantly Australian outlook. Her best-known books are *Maurice Guest* (1908), *The Fortunes of Richard Mahony* (1917–29), and the *Young Cosima* (1939).

RICHARDSON, Sir Ralph David (1902–). British actor. In an extensive career on stage from 1921 and in films from 1933, he achieved success as actor-director of the Old Vic 1944–7, with plays incl. *Peer Gynt* and *Cyrano de Bergerac*. Some later performances were in *Flowering Cherry* (1958) and *The Rivals* (1966). His films incl. *Anna Karenina* (1948) and *The Looking-Glass War* (1968).

RICHARDSON, Samuel (1689–1761). British novelist. B. in Derbyshire, he was apprenticed to a printer, setting up his own business in London in 1719, and becoming printer to the House of Commons. His *Pamela* (1740–1), written in letter form, achieved a sensational vogue both in England and on the Continent, and was followed by *Clarissa* (1747–8), and *Sir Charles Grandison* (1753–4). Remarkable for his analysis of the feminine mind, R. exercised great influence on the development of the novel.

RICHARDSON, Tony (1928–). British director and producer. With George Devine he estab. the 'English Stage Co.' in 1955 at the Royal Court Theatre, London, and has been artistic dir. there since 1956; his productions incl. *Look Back in Anger* (1956). In 1958, he founded with John Osborne (q.v.) Woodfall Films, and has produced or directed *A Taste of Honey* (1961), *Saturday Night and Sunday Morning* (1960), and *The Charge of the Light Brigade* (1968). He was m. to actress Vanessa Redgrave 1962–7.

RICHBOROUGH. English seaport in Kent, at the mouth of the Stour r. The Roman Rutupiae, it was in Roman times and for some centuries after an important port and military base, H.Q. of the count of the Saxon Shore. The retreat of the sea left R. in the midst of salt marshes, but during the world wars it was brought into use again as a military port.

RICHELIEU (rēshlyö´), **Armand Jean du Plessis de** (1585–1642). French cardinal and statesman. B. at Paris of a noble family, he entered the Church, and was created bishop of Luçon in 1606, and a cardinal in 1622. Through the influence of Marie de' Medici he became Louis XIII's chief minister in 1624, a position he retained until his death. At home he aimed to make the monarchy absolute; he ruthlessly crushed opposition by the nobility, and destroyed the political power of the Huguenots, while leaving them religious freedom. Abroad he sought to establish French supremacy by breaking the power of the Habsburgs; he therefore supported Gustavus Adolphus and the German Protestant princes against Austria, and in 1635 brought France into the 30 Years War. *See illus. p. 449.*

RICHMOND. (1) English town (bor.) in the N. Riding of Yorks, 12 m. S.W. of Darlington, on the Swale. The castle remains date from 1071, and there is a restored Georgian theatre. Henry VII took his earlier title, earl of R., from this town. Pop. (1961) 5,764. (2) Cap of Virginia, U.S.A., on the r. James, *c.* 70 m. from the Atlantic. R. is the centre of the vast Virginian tobacco trade and manufactures immense quantities of cigarettes. It was the Confederate cap. 1861–5; a museum commemorates Edgar Allan Poe's association with R. Pop. (1960) 219,158.

RICHMOND-UPON-THAMES. Bor. in the S.W. of Greater London. Little remains in Richmond of the 14th cent. palace where Elizabeth I died, but the riverside gardens and Richmond hill and park make it a favourite resort of Londoners. The bor. incl. Barnes and Twickenham (q.v.). Pop. (1967) 179,040.

RICHTER (rikh'ter), **Johann Paul Friedrich** (1763–1825). German author, commonly known as Jean Paul. B. in Bavaria, he created a series of comic eccentrics only rivalled by Dickens. His books incl. *Hesperus* (1794), a fictitious biography which estab. his fame; *Quintus Fixlein* (1796); *Siebenkäs* (1796–7); *Titan* (1800–3); *Die Flegeljahre* (1804–5: *The Awkward Age*); and *Dr. Katzenbergers Badereise* (1809: *Dr. Katzenberger's Journey to the Watering-place*).

SVIATOSLAV RICHTER
Photo: Godfrey MacDomnic.

RICHTER, Sviatoslav (1915–). Russian pianist. He is noted for his remote detached approach, and is an outstanding interpreter of Schumann.

RICHTHOFEN (rikht'-höfen), **Manfred**, freiherr von (1892–1918). German airman. B. at Schweidnitz, Silesia, he commanded in the F.W.W. a crack fighter squadron known as the R. circus, and shot down 80 aircraft before being killed in action.

RICKETS. A vitamin D deficiency disease of young children, marked by softening of the bones. Formerly frequent in British slum children, it is sometimes seen in the children of Negro immigrants, since pigmentation of the skin lessens ability to make best use of the limited sunlight, which acts on fats to produce the vitamin D necessary to enable lime to be deposited in the bones, so hardening them.

RIDGEWAY, The. Grassy track dating from prehistoric times which runs along the Berkshire Downs in England from White Horse Hill to near Streatley.

RIDGWAY, Matthew Bunker (1895–). American gen. He served with distinction during the S.W.W. in the Sicilian, Italian, Normandy, and German campaigns. In April 1951 he succeeded MacArthur as commander of the U.N. and U.S. forces in the Far Eastern theatre, incl. Korea. He was Supreme Allied Commander, Europe, 1952–3, and U.S. Chief of Staff 1953–5.

RIDING, Laura (1901–). American poet. A member of the Fugitive Group of poets, which flourished in the Southern U.S. 1915–28, she went to England in 1926, remaining abroad until 1939, during which time she collaborated with Robert Graves (q.v.) on *A Survey of Modernist Poetry* (1927). She pub. her *Collected Poems* in 1938.

RIDLEY, Nicholas (*c.* 1500–55). English Protestant bishop. He became chaplain to Henry VIII in 1541, and bishop of London in 1550. He took an active part in the Reformation and supported Lady Jane Grey's claim to the throne. After Mary's accession he was arrested and burned as a heretic.

RIEL (rē-el'), **Louis** (1844–85). French-Canadian rebel. B. at St. Boniface, he championed the cause of the Métis (half-breeds), and in 1869–70 led an unsuccessful revolt and set up a provisional govt. at Winnipeg. After leading a second rising in Saskatchewan in 1885 he was hanged for treason.

RIEMANN (rē'mahn), **Georg Friedrich Bernhard** (1826–66). German mathematician. B. in Hanover prov., he studied theology at Göttingen, but soon turned to mathematics. He was prof. at Göttingen from 1857, and originated what is called Riemannian geometry – a non-Euclidean system.

RIENZI (rē-en'zē), **Cola di** (*c.* 1313–54). Roman political reformer. At a time when the Papacy was estab. at Avignon, he proclaimed in 1347 the restoration of the ancient Roman republic. In a few months he was expelled from the city, and a second attempt was ended by his assassination.

RIESMAN (rēz'man), **David** (1909–). American sociologist. Educ. at Harvard, he was prof. of law at Buffalo 1937–41, of social sciences at Chicago 1946–58 and at Harvard from 1958. His best-known book is *The Lonely Crowd: A Study of the Changing American Character* (1950).

RIF, Er. Mountain range about 180 m. long on the Mediterranean seaboard of Morocco. The Riffs, under Abdel Krim (q.v.), put up a prolonged resistance to Spaniards and French.

RIGA (rē'gah). Cap. and seaport of the Latvian S.S.R., U.S.S.R., on the Daugava (W. Dvina), 8 m. from the Gulf of R. It has Hanseatic League remains. There is a univ. (1919). A member of the Hanseatic League from 1282, R. has belonged in turn to Poland, 1582, Sweden 1621, and Russia, 1710. The name means 'tortuous'. Pop. (1967) 680,000.

RIGHT OF WAY. A public R. of W. is a right exercisable by any member of the public to pass over land. Such rights arise from the dedication of the land (e.g. a road) to public use. Also relevant to motorists approaching an intersection. There is rarely any clear-cut ruling as to who has priority, but in France, with certain exceptions, a motorist must give way to traffic entering the road from his right.

RIGHTS OF MAN AND THE CITIZEN, Declaration of the. Statement issued by the French National Assembly in 1789. It lists as fundamental rights: representation in the legislature; equality before the law, and of opportunity; freedom from arbitrary imprisonment; religious freedom, and freedom of speech and the Press; taxation in proportion to ability to pay; and security of property. The preamble to the French constitution of 1946 reaffirms these rights, and adds others, e.g. equal rights for women; the right to work, to join a trade union, to strike, and to social security, leisure, support in old age, and free education.

RIJEKA (riyāk'a). Yugoslav city and port on the E. coast of the peninsula of Istra, at the mouth of the Rečina r. It has petroleum refineries, distilleries, paper mills, chemical and tobacco factories, etc. Acquired by the Habsburg rulers of Austria in 1465, it was given to Croatia in 1776, incorporated in Hungary 1807, re-united with Croatia in 1848, seized by Gabriele d'Annunzio (q.v.) in 1919, annexed by Italy in 1924, ceded to Yugoslavia in 1947. Its Italian and historic name Fiume is derived from its original

RIJEKA. Behind the waterfront is one of the new blocks of flats and offices that rise on the heights, and in the foreground lies one of the many ships that crowd the deep-water quays of this ancient port. *Courtesy Yugoslav National Tourist Office.*

name, St. Vitus in Flumine. Pop. (1961), with the suburb of Sušak on the other side of the river, 100,339.

RILKE (rēl'ke), **Rainer Maria** (1875–1926). Austrian poet. B. at Prague of Carinthian stock, he was intended for a military career, but soon turned to literature. He travelled widely, especially in Russia, and was for a time Rodin's secretary. His prose works incl. the semi-autobiographical *Notebook of Malte Laurids Brigge*, and his poetical works the *Sonnets to Orpheus* and the *Duino Elegies*. His verse is characterized by a form of mystic pantheism which seeks to achieve a state of ecstasy in which existence can be apprehended as a whole. He d. in Switzerland.

RIMBAUD (raṅbō'), **Jean Nicolas Arthur** (1854–91). French Symbolist poet. B. at Charleville, he went to Paris where he became the friend of Verlaine, who tried to murder him when they quarrelled. He then wandered Europe, travelled to the E. Indies and Abyssinia, and d. at Marseilles. His verse is often obscure, but it has exerted an enormous influence on 20th cent. poets. His best-known vol. is *Illuminations* (1886).

RIMINI (rē'mēnē). Seaport and popular bathing resort of Emilia, Italy, on the Adriatic 69 m. S.E. of Bologna. Macaroni, shoes, furniture, textiles, ships are made. As the Roman Ariminum, it was the terminus of the Flaminian and Aemilian Ways. Francesca da Rimini was assassinated there in 1285. R. was very badly damaged in Sept. 1944: it formed the eastern strongpoint of the German 'Gothic' defence line, and was taken by the Allies only after severe fighting. Pop. (1966) 109,000.

RIMSKY-KORSAKOV (rimz'ki korsahkof'), **Nikolai Andreievich** (1844–1908). Russian composer. B. at Tikhvin, Novgorod, he served in the navy some years. In 1872 he finished his first opera, but previously he had written the symphonic poem *Sadko* (1867) and the programme symphony *Antar* (1868). He often utilized Russian folk idioms and rhythms, and may be regarded as a nationalist composer. His operas incl. *The Maid of Pskov*, *The Snow Maiden*, and *The Golden Cockerel*.

RINEANNA. *See* SHANNON AIRPORT.

RING. A circlet, usually of precious metal, sometimes set with gems, worn on a finger as a decoration or token. The origin of the wedding R. is uncertain, but in Roman times betrothal Rs. were bestowed. Rs. were used for money in ancient Egypt and elsewhere, and their connection with the Church still survives in instances such as the English Coronation.

RINGWORM or **Tinea.** The results of infestation by one of a group of parasitic microscopic fungi. In R. of the scalp the fungus (trichophyton) produces round patches of slight inflammation from which the hair falls out or breaks off. The treatment is by X-rays and drugs aimed at destroying the fungus. R. of the skin, commonly called athlete's foot, starts in the cracks between the little and the 4th toes, and may spread over the foot and other parts of the body, to produce a weeping eczema and an intolerable itch.

RINTELEN, Fritz von (d. 1949). German spy. He led a spy ring in U.S.A. during the F.W.W., sabotaging the shipment of Allied munitions until captured in 1915. He later settled in England and pub. the reminiscent *Dark Invader*.

RIO DE JANEIRO (rē'ō de zhahnā'rō). City and seaport of Brazil, cap. of Guanabara state, situated on the W. of a fine natural harbour. The name commemorates its discovery on 1 Jan. 1502, though there is in fact no river. Portuguese and French settlers strove for supremacy in the 16th cent., the former prevailing. R. de J. became cap. of independent Brazil in 1822, and remained cap. until replaced by Brasilia (q.v.) in 1960. The harbour, with the impressive Sugar Loaf mt. at its entrance, is ringed by a 20 m. boulevard. The older parts of the city contain the commercial section, modern development pro-

ducing such spacious thoroughfares as the Avenida Rio Branco. Some buildings of the colonial period and some 17th cent. Jesuit churches survive. The docks deal with the produce of large parts of Brazil including coffee, sugar, hides, etc. The city's own products are of the domestic-consumer type. It has 3 univs. and an airport, and is a naval base. Pop. (1960) 3,307,163.

RIO DE LA PLATA. Spanish name for the r. PLATE.

RIO DE ORO. District of the overseas prov. of Spanish Sahara (q.v.) on the Atlantic coast of N. Africa from Cape Blanco to Cape Bojador. It is mainly desert. The cap. is Villa Cisneros (pop. 6,000). The people are almost entirely nomadic, regularly crossing the frontiers with Morocco, Algeria and Mauretania. Area *c.* 73,000 sq. m.; pop. *c.* 50,000.

RIO GRANDE (rē'ō gran'di *or* grand). River (1,800 m.) flowing from the Rockies in S. Colorado to the Gulf of Mexico, and forming along the last 1,500 m. of its length the Texas-Mexico border. Changes in the course of the river led to disputes between U.S.A. and Mexico, settled 1970.

RIO GRANDE DO SUL (rē'ō grahn'dā doo sool). South-east state of Brazil. Its cap. is Pôrto Alegre (pop. 640,000), also formerly known as Rio Grande do Sul, which lies at the head of the Lagoa dos Patos, a tidewater lake. The city's industries incl. meat-packing, tanning, and textiles, and there are 2 univs. founded in 1934 and 1948. Area 105,088 sq. m.; pop. (1967) 6,500,000.

RIOM (ryoṅ'). Town in the Puy-de-Dôme dept. of central France on the Ambène. A pleasant town with many handsome 15th and 16th cent. houses, it was the scene in 1942 of a 'war guilt' trial of several prominent Frenchmen, incl. Blum, Daladier, and Gamelin (qq.v.), organized by the Vichy govt. at the instigation of Hitler. Instead of a trial of the accused men, the proceedings developed into an argument as to the reasons for France's unprepared-ness, and, again at Hitler's instigation, the court was adjourned, then dissolved. The defendants were kept in prison until released by the Allies in 1945. Pop. (1962) 15,416.

RIO MUNI. Another name for SPANISH GUINEA.

RIOT ACT. Act passed in 1714 to suppress Jacobite disorders. Under it, if 12 or more persons assemble unlawfully to the disturbance of the public peace, a magistrate may read a proclamation ordering them to disperse; if the rioters nevertheless continue together for an hour after the reading of the proclamation they are guilty of felony, and may be dispersed by force.

RIPON (rip'on), **George Frederick Samuel Robinson,** 1st marquess of (1827–1909). British Liberal statesman. After some years as an M.P., he succeeded to the title of earl of R. in 1859, and received a marquessate in 1871. He was War Minister 1863–6 Sec. for India 1866–8, viceroy of India 1880–4, Col. Sec. 1892–5, and Lord Privy Seal 1905–8.

RIPON. English cathedral city and market town (bor.) in the W. Riding of Yorks, 25 m. N. of Leeds, on the Ure. The cathedral was built 1154 to 1520. Pop. (1961) 10,490.

RISORGIMENTO (rēsōrjēmen'tō) (Ital. resur-rection). The movement for Italian national unity and independence which began after 1815. The risings of 1848–9 failed, but the Austrian War of 1859 was followed by the foundation of the Italian kingdom in 1861. The addition of Venetia to Italy in 1866, and of Rome in 1870, completed the R.

RITCHIE-CALDER, baron. *See* CALDER.

RIVERA (rēvär'ah), **Diego** (1886–1957). Mexican artist. A convinced Communist, he expressed his ideas in the vast and vivid fresco murals he executed in Mexico and the U.S.A., making this form widely popular.

RIVERA, Primo de. *See* PRIMO DE RIVERA.

RIVERINA. District of New South Wales, Australia, between the Lachlan and Murray rivers, through which runs the Murrumbidgee. On fertile land, artificially irrigated from the 3 rivers, wool, wheat, and fruit are produced.

RIVER PLATE. *See* PLATE.

RIVERS, William Halse Rivers (1864–1922). Anthropologist and psychologist. He founded the Cambridge school of experimental psychology, and made expeditions to the Torres Straits and the Todas of India from which proceeded his *Kinship* (1914) and *History of Melanesian Society* (1915). Influenced by Freud, he also wrote *Instinct and the Unconscious* and *Conflict and Dream* (1923).

RIVERSIDE. City in California, U.S.A., on the Santa Ana r. 58 m. E. by S. of Los Angeles. Founded in 1870, it is the centre of a citrus-growing district and has a citrus research station. The seedless orange was developed at R. in 1873. Pop. met. area (1970) San-Bernadino–R.–Ontario 1,121,074.

RIVIERA (rēvē-ā′rah). The Mediterranean coast of France and Italy, from about Toulon to Spezia. The Maritime Alps and the Apennines protect it from N. winds, and contribute to its subtropical aspect. The usually mild winter climate makes it a popular resort for the wealthy or invalid. The main towns are Toulon, Cannes, Nice, Monte Carlo, Menton, San Remo, Savona, Genoa, Rapallo, and Spezia.

RIYADH. One of the caps. of Saudi Arabia, cap. also of Nejd, connected by rail with Damman on the Persian Gulf and by road with Kuwait and Hail. It is surrounded by a high wall with six fortified gates, outside which are date gardens irrigated from deep wells. There is a large royal palace. Pop. (est.) 300,000.

RIZZIO (rēt′sē-ō), **David** (1533–66). Italian adventurer at the court of Mary Queen of Scots. After the queen's marriage to Darnley in 1565, his influence increased so as to arouse jealousies that ended in his murder by certain nobles.

R.N.A. *See* NUCLEIC ACID.

ROACH. Freshwater fish (*Rutilus rutilus*) of N. Europe, dark green above, whitish below, and with reddish lower fins.

ROANOKE (rōnōke). City in Virginia, U.S.A., on the R. r. 55 m. W. of Lynchburg. Founded in 1834 as Big Lick, it was a small village until 1881 when the repair shops of the Virginia Railway were set up

ROACH

there, after which it developed rapidly. Besides doing railway repairs, it produces chemicals, steel goods, furniture, and textiles. The name is Indian and means shell money. Pop. (1960) 97,110.

ROBBERY. In English law, a variety of theft: stealing from the person, with force used to intimidate the victim: maximum penalty, life imprisonment.

ROBBE-GRILLET (rōb grēyeh′), **Alain** (1922–). French author. B. at Brest, he qualified as an agronomist and worked in Africa and the West Indies as a research biologist before turning to writing. He is the leading theorist of *le nouveau roman*, e.g. his own *Les Gommes* (1953: *The Erasers*) and *Dans le Labyrinthe* (1959), which concentrates on detailed description of physical objects, etc. Other members of the school (for whom, as literary director of *Les Editions de Minuit*, he is publisher) incl. Butor and Sarraute. He also wrote the script for the film *L'Année Dernière à Marienbad* (1961).

ROBBIA (rob′bē-ah), **Della.** Family of Florentine architects and sculptors. **Luca della R.** (1400–82) executed a number of important works of sculpture in Florence, and produced some beautiful sculptured

ANDREA DELLA ROBBIA. 'The Madonna adoring the Child'.
Courtesy of Courtauld Institute Galleries, London.

work in terracotta, now known as D.R. ware. **Andrea della R.** (1435–1525), the nephew and pupil of Luca, also produced enamelled reliefs. Five of Andrea's sons carried on the family tradition; the most famous were **Giovanni della R.** (1469–1529), who equalled his father, and **Girolamo della R.** (1488–1566), also an architect and sculptor.

ROBBINS, Frederick C(hapman) (1916–). American physician. B. in Alabama, he was prof. of pediatrics at Western Reserve Univ. Medical School from 1952, and with John F. Enders and Thomas H. Weller was awarded a Nobel prize in 1954 for their discovery of the ability of a polio virus to grow in cultures of different tissues.

ROBBINS, Jerome (1918–). American dancer and choreographer. A chorus-boy on Broadway, and then soloist with the newly formed American Ballet Theatre 1941–6, he became in 1949 associate artistic director of the N.Y. City Ballet. Among his ballets are *Fancy Free* (1944; with Leonard Bernstein), *Facsimile* (1946), *The Age of Anxiety* (1950; again with Bernstein and based on Auden's poem). He also choreographed *The King and I* and *West Side Story* for both stage and screen.

ROBBINS, Lionel Charles, baron (1898–). British economist. Prof. at the London School of Economics 1929–61, and author of books on many aspects of his subject, he was chairman of a govt. committee on higher education, which in 1963 produced the *R. Report* recommending an emergency programme to increase the number of higher educ. places from 216,000 in 1963 to 560,000 in 1980.

ROBERT. Name of 3 kings of Scotland. For Robert I *see* BRUCE, ROBERT. **Robert II** (1316–90), the son of Walter, steward of Scotland, and Marjory, daughter of Robert I, became king in 1371. He was the founder of the house of Stuart. **Robert III** (*c.* 1340–1406) succeeded his father Robert II in 1390.

ROBERT. Name of 2 dukes of Normandy. **Robert I,** called the Devil (d. 1035), became duke in 1028, and was the father of William the Conqueror. He is the hero of several romances. **Robert II** (*c.* 1054–1134), eldest son of William the Conqueror, succeeded him as duke of Normandy, but not as king of England, in 1087, and took part in the 1st Crusade. He was deposed by his brother Henry I in 1106.

ROBERTI (robār′ti), **Ercole** (*c.* 1450–96). Italian painter, who worked in Bologna in his middle years and later at Ferrara where he was in the service of the Este family. His works incl. 'A Concert' in the Nat. Gallery, London, and an altar-piece 'Madonna and Saints' in the Brera, Milan.

ROBERTS, Sir Charles George Douglas (1860–1943). Canadian poet and author. B. near Fredericton, he was prof. at King's College, Nova Scotia, 1885–95. He pub. books of lyric verse incl. *Orion* (1880), but was best known for his stories of animal life.

ROBERTS, Frederick Sleigh, 1st earl (1832–1914). British field marshal, known as 'Bobs'. B. at Cawnpore, he joined the Bengal Artillery in 1851, and served through the Indian Mutiny, receiving the V.C., and the Abyssinian campaign of 1867–8. During the Afghan War of 1878–80 he occupied Kabul, and subsequently made a famous march to Kandahar, where he won a complete victory. After serving as C.-in-C.

in India 1885–93, and Ireland 1895–9, he received the command in S. Africa, where during 1900 he forced Cronje to surrender at Paardeberg, and by his occupation of Bloemfontein and Pretoria made possible the annexation of the Transvaal and Orange Free State. On returning to England he received an earldom, and was C.-in-C. 1900–5. In later life he strongly advocated conscription. Early in the F.W.W. he d. at St. Omer while visiting the trenches.

ROBERTS, Tom (Thomas William) (1856–1931). Australian artist, introducer to Australia of plein-air impressionism. B. in England, he arrived in Australia in 1869, returning to Europe to study in 1881 (see RUSSELL, J.P.). He painted the official picture of the opening of the first Federal parliament.

ROBERTSON OF OAKRIDGE, Brian Hubert Robertson, 1st baron (1896–). British general. The son of **Sir William R.** (1860–1933), who rose from private in 1877 to field marshal in 1920. Active in the F.W.W. he also served during the S.W.W. in the Middle East and Italy. After being Military Gov. British zone of Germany 1947–9 (U.K. High Commissioner 1949–50), he was C.-in-C. Middle East 1950–3. On retirement from the army he became chairman of the British Transport Commission (1953–61).

ROBERTSON, Thomas William (1829–71). British dramatist. At first an actor, in his family tradition, he had his first success as a dramatist with *David Garrick* (1864), which set a new, realistic trend in English drama of the time: later plays, in many of which the Bancrofts acted, incl. *Society* (1865) and *Caste* (1867).

ROBESON, Paul (1898–). American Negro bass singer and actor. Admitted to the Bar in New York, he turned to acting in 1921; his N.Y. stage successes incl. *All God's Chillun Got Wings* (1924) and *Othello* (1944), and he has also appeared in stage and film versions of *The Emperor Jones* and *Show Boat*. His career has been in eclipse, and he was denied a U.S. passport 1950–8, because of his association with left-wing movements; he is an advocate of Negro rights.

ROBESPIERRE (rōbe-spyār'), **Maximilien François Marie Isidore de** (1758–94). French statesman. B. at Arras, he had a distinguished legal career, and was elected to the National Assembly of 1789–91. His defence of democratic principles made him widely popular in Paris, while his disinterestedness won him the nickname of 'the Incorruptible'. As leader of the Jacobins in the National Convention he supported the execution of Louis XVI and the overthrow of the Girondins, and in July 1793 was elected to the Committee of Public Safety. His zeal for social reform, his attacks on the anti-religious and other excesses of the terrorists, made him enemies on both right and left; a conspiracy was formed against him, and in July 1794 he was overthrown and guillotined.

ROBERTI. This 'Pieta' shows excellently the artist's use of linear modelling and powerful exploitation of light and detail to convey a realistic effect.
Photo: Walker Art Gallery, Liverpool.

RÕBEY, Sir George. Stage-name of British comedian George Edward Wade (1869–1954), the 'Prime Minister of Mirth'. Dressed in close-buttoned frock coat and semi-clerical bowler, he sang such songs as 'Tempt Me Not!' and – in the F.W.W. Bing Boys show – 'In Other Words' and was a master of significant gesture and voice inflection. He was also renowned as an amateur violin maker, and was knighted in 1954.

ROBIN. Song-bird (*Erithacus rubecula*) in the thrush family. It is found in Europe, W. Asia, Africa, and the Azores. Both sexes are olive-brown, with a red breast. The nest is constructed in a sheltered place, and from 5 to 7 white freckled eggs are laid.

ROBIN HOOD. Legendary outlaw, who from the 14th cent. on became the hero of many popular ballads. It is doubtful whether his story has any historical basis; in their anti-clericalism and defiance of authority the ballads reflect the revolutionary spirit of the peasantry in the years preceding the rebellion of 1381. R.H. was also the hero of folk-plays, customarily performed on May Day, and was sometimes identified with the May King.

ROBINSON, Edwin Arlington (1869–1935). American poet. B. in Maine, he dealt mainly with psychological themes in the manner of Browning. Among his publications are *The Children of the Night* (1897), which estab. his reputation, *The Man Against the Sky*, *Tristram*, *The Man Who Died Twice*, and *King Jasper* (1935).

ROBINSON, Henry Crabb (1775–1867). British writer, whose diaries, journals, and letters are a valuable source of information on his friends Lamb, Coleridge, Wordsworth, and Southey.

ROBINSON, John Arthur Thomas (1919–), British Anglican churchman. Son of a clergyman, he was bp. of Woolwich 1959–69 and lecturer in theology, Trinity Coll., Cambridge, from 1969. A Modernist, he has written several books incl. the controversial *Honest to God* (1963), which was interpreted as denying a personal God.

ROBINSON, Lennox (1886–1958). Irish playwright. B. nr. Cork, he became manager of the Abbey Theatre n 1910 and made it the home of realism rather than poetic folklore. His own plays incl. *The Whiteheaded Boy* (1916) and *The White Blackbird* (1925).

ROBINSON, Sir Robert (1886–). British scientist. Waynflete prof. of chemistry at Oxford in 1939–55, he was pres. of the Royal Society 1945–50, and won a Nobel prize for researches in plant biology, especially in the structure of alkaloids (1947), receiving the O.M. in 1949. He was knighted in 1939.

ROBINSON, W(illiam) Heath (1872–1944). British black-and-white artist, famous for his humorous drawings of fantastically complex machinery for performing simple operations, e.g. raising one's hat.

RÕBOT. Term derived from the Czech word meaning 'work', and signifying an automaton in human form. It was first coined by Karel Čapek (q.v.) in his play *R.U.R.* (1921).

ROB ROY MACGREGOR (1671–1734). Scottish Highland outlaw, nominally a grazier who lived for years by cattle-lifting and blackmail.

ROBSART, Amy (c. 1532–60). The 1st wife of Robert Dudley, earl of Leicester (q.v.), whom she m. in 1550. She d. mysteriously at Cumnor Hall, Oxon. It was widely believed Leicester had had her murdered because he hoped to marry Elizabeth I.

ROBSON, Dame Flora (1902–). British actress. B. at S. Shields, she made her début in 1921, and her many deeply sensitive interpretations incl. Miss Tina in *The Aspern Papers* (1959). She was created D.B.E. in 1960.

ROCHDALE. English industrial town (co. bor.) in Lancashire on the Roch 10 m. N.E. of Manchester. The 'R. Pioneers' founded the first Co-operative Society in England, in Toad Lane, Rochdale, in 1844.

Textiles, machinery, asbestos, etc., are manufactured. Pop. (1961) 85,785.

ROCHEFORT. Port in Charente-Maritime dept., W. France, 20 m. S.E. of La Rochelle and 9 m. from the mouth of the Charente. Metal goods and machinery are made; grain, wine, dairy produce are exported. The port, at which Napoleon embarked for England in 1815, dates from 1666. Pop. (1962) 33,584.

ROCHELLE (rōshel'), **La.** Seaport and cap. of Charente-Maritime dept., W. France. The cathedral, completed 1762, and episcopal palaces are of note, and industries incl. shipbuilding and saw-milling. It was a stronghold of the Huguenots, who defended it unsuccessfully against Richelieu in 1627–8. Pop. (1962) 68,445.

ROCHESTER, John Wilmot, 2nd earl of (1647–80). British poet. Although he showed gallantry at sea in the 2nd Dutch War, he spent most of his time at court, where he became notorious for debauchery. His poems incl. many graceful lyrics and some powerful satires, the best of which, *A Satire against Mankind*, shows a spirit akin to Swift's.

ROCHESTER. City of Kent, England, on the Medway, just W. of Chatham. The castle keep (12th cent.) is one of the finest specimens of Norman architecture in England. The cathedral was built in the 12th–15th cents. The nearby Borstal prison gave its name to a system of treatment of juvenile delinquents introduced in 1908. The site was already a port in pre-Roman days. R. has many associations with Dickens. Pop. (1961) 50,121.

ROCHESTER. City of New York state, U.S.A., on the Genesee 6 m. S. of Lake Ontario. There are flour mills, and Kodak films and cameras are manufactured. R. has a univ. (1850). Pop. met. area (1970) 875,636.

RO'CHET. A vestment worn mainly by R.C. and Anglican bishops and abbots. The R.C. type reaches to the knee, while the Anglican is nearly to the feet.

ROCK'ALL. Rock islet in the Atlantic, about 83 ft. wide and 300 ft. in circumference, lying 230 m. W. of N. Uist in the Hebrides. It was annexed by Britain in 1955. R. gives its name to a sea area off the British Isles used in weather forecasts for shipping.

ROCKEFELLER, John D(avison) (1839–1937). American millionaire, pres. of Standard Oil, which by 1878 controlled 90 per cent of U.S. refineries. His son John D(avison) R., Jnr. (1874–1960), devoted himself to the management of the philanthropic R. Foundation (1913), until 1952 when the chairmanship was taken over by his son John D(avison) R., 3rd (1906–　). The last-named's younger brother Nelson (Aldrich) R. (1908–　) entered politics as a Republican and became governor of N.Y. state in 1958: his political career survived his divorce in 1962, but he failed in his attempt to win the Republican presidential nomination 1964 and 1968.

The **R. Center** in Manhattan, N.Y., is the largest privately owned business and entertainment centre in the world, covering 14½ acres and incl. Radio City Music Hall (the world's largest indoor theatre, seating 6,200), the RCA Building (world's largest privately owned office building). Planned by J.D.R., Jnr., and begun in 1931, the Center is a 'city within a city' comprising gardens, shops, restaurants (The Rainbow Room, etc.), and a celebrated skating rink.

ROCKEFELLER CENTER. Facing on to the west side of the Avenue of the Americas is the 48-storey Time and Life Building completed in 1959.
Courtesy of Rockefeller Center Inc.

ROCKET and **ROCKET WARFARE.** Projectile driven through space by the reaction on the rocket of the fast-burning fuel within. Rs. have been valued for their pleasing effect as fireworks, over the last 7 cents., but their intensive development as a means of propulsion to high altitudes – carrying payloads – started only in the inter-war years, e.g. the state-supported work in Germany (*see* VON BRAUN, WERNHER), and of Prof. R. H. Goddard (1882–1945) in the U.S.A.

In warfare the head of the R. carries an explosive device. First reported as used by the Chinese against the Tartars in the 13th cent., such Rs. were only sporadically employed as offensive weapons, until the S.W.W. when they were used to good effect by aircraft, and latterly by the Germans in their V2 attacks on the London area (1944–5) – the V2 (50 ft. long, and carrying 1 ton of high explosive in its warhead) was the 1st guided missile.

Since the S.W.W., the devastating combination of refined, precise guidance systems with atomic warheads has produced missiles which are the key to international power politics. They are designed for short, medium and long range; and may be for surface to surface, air to surface, or surface to air use.

The only form of propulsion available which can function in a vacuum, Rs. are essential to research in outer space, e.g. the giant 3-stage Saturn 5 rocket used to launch the *Apollo* space craft (363 ft. high). Incomparably more efficient than such a chemical R. engine as Saturn are the nuclear R. engines being developed from 1960 for planetary exploration.

ROCKHAMPTON. Port of Queensland, Australia, on the Fitzroy estuary. It is in a region producing dairy products and coal, gold and copper; it has meat-canning factories. Pop. (1966) 46,052.

ROCKINGHAM, Charles Watson Wentworth, 2nd marquess of (1730–82). British Whig statesman. He succeeded his father as marquess in 1750. As P.M. 1765–6 he repealed the Stamp Act, and subsequently supported the Americans' claim to independence. He again became P.M. in 1782, but d. in office.

ROCKY MOUNTAINS. The Canadian Pacific Railway provides one of the best means of seeing the glorious scenery of the area. *Courtesy of the Canadian Pacific Railway.*

ROCKY MOUNTAINS. The dominating section of the N. American mountain system. They extend from the junction with the Mexican plateau, northward through the W. central states of the U.S.A., through Canada to the Alaskan border. Many large rivers rise in the R.M. incl. the Missouri. The main peaks are Mt. Elbert, 14,431 ft., in Colorado; Fremont's Peak, 13,781 ft., in Wyoming; and Mt. Logan, 19,850 ft., on the Canadian-Alaskan border.

ROCOCO (rokō'ko). Style of architecture and decoration which prevailed in France at the time of the Regency and the reign of Louis XV. It is characterized by bizarre ornamentation, and complete lack of restraint. It is a degenerate form of Baroque (q.v.).

RODENTS. Order of gnawing mammals (Rodentia). There are 2 Sub-orders, the Simplicidentata (single-toothed Rs.) incl. the squirrels, dormice, mice, voles and guinea-pigs, and the Duplicidentata (double-toothed Rs.) having only one family, the hares and rabbits. Most species are burrowers and are vegetarian in habit. Hibernation is common.

RODEO (rōdā′-ō). Originally a round-up of cattle on the western ranges of America, it has developed into a cowboy tournament, in which challenges are thrown out by the men of various herds at round-ups.

RODGERS, Richard (1902–). American composer. His scores for musicals incl. *Boys from Syracuse* (1938), *Oklahoma* (1943), *The King and I* (1951) and *The Sound of Music* (1959). He collaborated with Oscar Hammerstein.

RODIN (rōdaṅ′), **Auguste** (1840–1917). French sculptor. B. in Paris, he studied under Barye and Carrier-Belleuse, and visited Italy in 1875, where he studied the works of Donatello and Michelangelo. In 1877 he made a tour of the French cathedrals, and was much influenced by Gothic sculpture. He settled near Paris. His best-known works incl. 'The Thinker', 'The Kiss' and 'The Burghers of Calais' (copy in Embankment Gardens at Westminster). Many of his works are in the R. Museum, Paris.

RODIN. 'The Kiss'.

RODNEY, George Brydges Rodney, baron (1718–92). British admiral. His first action was under Hawke against the French off Ushant in 1747. In 1762 he captured Martinique, St. Lucia, and Grenada, and received a baronetcy in 1764. In 1780 he relieved Gibraltar by defeating a Spanish squadron off Cape St. Vincent. In 1782 he crushed the French fleet under count de Grasse off Dominica, for which brilliant victory he was raised to the peerage.

RODO′STO. Gr. name of TEKIRDAG.

ROEBUCK. Species of deer (*Capreolus capreolus*). found in Europe and Asia. Still occurring wild in Scotland, it stands about 2 ft. in height, has short three-pronged antlers which are shed in December, and in summer is reddish, in winter greyish-brown.

ROESELAERE. Flem. form of ROULERS.

ROGATION DAYS. The 3 days before Ascension Day in the Christian calendar. The processions marking the occasion in England have mostly lapsed.

ROGERS, Bruce (1870–1957). American typographer and book designer, largely responsible for the importance now given to book design in this country as well as the U.S.A. His own finest work was the lectern Bible for O.U.P. (1935).

ROGERS, Samuel (1763–1855). British poet. He succeeded his father as head of a banking firm in 1793, and having estab. his poetical reputation with *The Pleasures of Memory* (1792), retired from business in 1803, and devoted himself to literary and social life, giving celebrated 'breakfasts' at his home near Green

WILLIAM ROGERS
U.S. Information Service

Park. His poetry is correct but cold, and he now lives mainly in his *Table Talk* and *Recollections*.

ROGERS, William Pierce (1913–). American lawyer. A Republican, and a strong advocate of Civil Rights, he was Attorney-Gen. under Eisenhower 1957–61, and became Sec. of State 1969.

ROGET (rozhā′), **Peter Mark** (1779–1869). British physician, one of the founders of the Univ. of London, and author of a *Thesaurus of English Words and Phrases* (1852: latest rev. 1964).

ROHMER, Sax. Pseudonym of British crime writer Arthur Sarsfield Ward (1886–1959), creator of the sinister Chinese Dr. Fu Manchu (1913).

ROKOSSO′VSKY, Konstantin (1896–1968). Polish-born soldier, prominent in the battles of Moscow, Stalingrad and Orel, and the liberation of Poland in the S.W.W. Though created a marshal of the Soviet Union, he assumed Polish citizenship in 1949 and was Polish C.-in-C. and War Min. until 1956. He subsequently served again in the Russian defence ministry.

ROLAND (d. 778). French soldier, killed by the Basques during Charlemagne's invasion of Spain. He subsequently became the hero of the 11th cent. *Chanson de Roland*, Ariosto's *Orlando Furioso*, and many other romances.

ROLAND DE LA PLATIÈRE (rōloṅ′ de la plahtyār′), **Manon Jeanne** (1754–93). French politician. *Née* Phlipon, she m. JEAN MARIE R. (1734–93), a leader of the Girondins during the French Revolution, and set up a salon which became the party's centre. She was guillotined in 1793, and on hearing of her death her husband, who had escaped from Paris, committed suicide. Her memoirs, written in prison, are of interest.

ROLFE, Frederick (1860–1913). British writer, known under his assumed style of Baron Corvo. In early life he studied for the R.C. priesthood, but was diverted into a literary career. Not until the publication in 1934 of A. J. A. Symons's *The Quest for Corvo* was there any general appreciation of Rolfe's *Hadrian VII, Desire and Pursuit of the Whole, Weird of the Wanderer*, strange creations of a tortured mind.

ROLLAND (roloṅ′), **Romain** (1866–1944). French novelist and dramatist. B. at Clamecy, he was prof. of the history of music at the Sorbonne 1904–10. He wrote works on Beethoven and Handel, novels such as the voluminous *Jean-Christophe* (1904–12), for which he received the Nobel prize in 1915, and the plays *Danton* and *Le 14 juillet*.

ROLLER. Group of birds in the family Coraciidae, resembling crows. They are found in the Old World, and the species *Coracias garrulus* is an occasional British visitor. The name is derived from their habit of rolling over in flight.

ROLLER-SKATING. See SKATING.

ROLLS, Charles Stewart (1877–1910). British motor pioneer. He participated in many motor races, and in 1906 founded, with the car-designer Henry Royce, Rolls-Royce Ltd.

ROMAINS (rōmaṅ′), **Jules.** Pseudonym of French novelist, playwright and poet Louis Farigoule (1885–). B. in the Cévennes, he lectured in philosophy in Paris and the provs. (1909–19), and developed the theory of Unanimisme, i.e. that every group has a communal existence greater than that of the individual, which intensifies their perceptions and emotions. He expressed this in the verse *La Vie unanime* (1908), the novel *Mort de quelqu'un* (1911: *Death of a Nobody*), etc. Of his plays, the farce *Knock, ou le Triomphe de la médecine* (1923: *Dr. Knock*) is best known. His later work is contained in the cycle of *c*. 30 novels *Les Hommes de bonne volonté* (1932 onward: *Men of Good Will*).

ROMAN ART. The development of R.A. dates from about the 4th cent. B.C. Before that time the art of Rome was chiefly Etruscan or Graeco-Etruscan. The Romans learnt a great deal from their Etruscan neighbours, e.g. realistic portraiture, and in architecture

ROMAN ART. On his return rom Jerusalem, Titus and his father celebrated a triumph. The Arch of Titus, in the Roman Forum, has fine bas-reliefs of the procession.

the characteristic form of Roman temples, which was based on Etruscan models. Later, Greek influence dominated R.A.; after the conquests of the later Republic, Roman generals returned with examples of Greek art, and Greek craftsmen were employed in the decoration of Roman palaces. At the time of Augustus Greek influence was still dominant, but art was enlisted in the service of the State, and sculpture and other forms of art of this period show great technical skill. Roman painting was confined to interior decoration, e.g. the wall paintings of Pompeii and of the houses and tombs of Rome. The Romans were skilful mosaic artists, and mosaics were produced in most places in the Empire, especially in Africa, Gaul, and Antioch.

ARCHITECTURE. Architecture was the dominant Roman art. It had its rise in the last decades of the Republic; it developed during the Empire and attained ostentatious magnificence at the time of Augustus and Hadrian. The Romans derived the principle of arched construction from the Etruscans. From Greek art they acquired the classic orders, the generic type of circular buildings, the portico, the theatre, the monumental gateways, the circus, and the public place. In Rome the chief feature of planning was the variety of the Fora. These were the market places and were surrounded by shops, temples, and public buildings. Every provincial city had its forum, that at Pompeii being famous. Roman temples were of two types, rectangular and circular, the latter deriving from Etruscan and Greek precedent. The chief circular temple is the Pantheon of Agrippa in Rome. The basilica, which was adapted from Greek examples, became the most important of the Roman public buildings. It served as a general place of assembly for purposes of law and of exchange. The Roman theatre also followed Greek models, though there were certain modifications such as the more monumental treatment of the stage, and the use of a pit with seats reserved for senators in place of the ancient orchestra. The amphitheatre is essentially a Roman creation – the most famous example is the Colosseum in Rome. The triumphal arch was built to commemorate great victories – those erected in honour of Trajan and Marcus Aurelius are exceptionally fine. Among the Roman works of utility, which are great feats of engineering skill, are the aqueducts. Palaces, residences, and villas were highly developed, and attained to a splendour hitherto unknown.

, ROMAN BRITAIN. Roman relations with Britain began with Caesar's invasions of 55 and 54 B.C., but the actual conquest was not begun until A.D. 43.

England was rapidly Romanized, but N. of York few remains of Roman civilization have been found. After several unsuccessful attempts to conquer Scotland the N. frontier was fixed at Hadrian's Wall (q.v.). During the 4th cent. Britain suffered from raids by the Saxons, Picts, and Scots. The Roman armies were withdrawn in 407 but there were partial re-occupations 417–c. 427 and c. 450. Roman towns incl. London, York, Chester, Caerleon, St. Albans, Colchester, Lincoln, Gloucester, and Bath. The most permanent remains of the occupation were the system of military roads radiating from London.

ROMAN CATHOLICISM. The largest Christian denomination; it is estimated that there are about 585 million Roman Catholics in the world today. They describe themselves not as Roman Catholics, but as Catholics, i.e. members of the Universal, One, Holy, Catholic, and Apostolic Church, founded by Jesus Christ. The doctrinal basis of the Church is the 3 creeds, the Bible (the officially approved version is the Vulgate in Latin made by St. Jerome), and Christian tradition. The Church claims to preach a set of doctrines that were revealed in the lifetime of the Apostles and have been preserved by continuous tradition ever since; but doctrine has developed in the sense that beliefs that were once implicit have been made explicit, e.g. the doctrine of the Immaculate Conception of the Virgin Mary, (1854) and of her Assumption (1950). The characteristic function of the Church is the offering of public prayer; the clergy are bound to recite certain prayers at fixed times daily. The central act of worship is the Mass – the representation to God of the Sacrifice made on the Cross. It is believed that when the priest repeats Christ's words spoken at the Last Supper, the bread and wine on the altar become Christ's body and blood, although no change takes place in their outward appearance. The Host, or Sacred Bread, is referred to as the Blessed Sacrament. There are 6 other sacraments, viz., baptism, confirmation, confession and penance, matrimony, holy orders, and the anointing of the sick, formerly extreme unction. The Church is intimately concerned with the preservation of the moral law; it is opposed to the remarriage of divorced persons, and certain forms of birth control. Great emphasis is laid on the ascetic tradition and on the religious life of retirement from the world; there are more than 300 different Orders of men, e.g. the Benedictine monks, the Franciscan and Dominican friars, the Jesuits, and many more Orders of women. From the earliest times high honours have been paid to those Christians who have proved themselves worthy of the name of saint; the process of official canonization was simplified in 1969. It is believed that miracles constitute one of the hallmarks of sanctity; and public prayers may be addressed to the saints asking them to intercede with God on the behalf of men. It is held that at death the soul passes into the intermediate state of Purgatory, where it is cleansed from the stain of sin. The eternal home of the blessed is Heaven, while the incorrigibly wicked are doomed to Hell. The head of the Church is the Pope, who is primarily the bishop of Rome; for many cents. he has been an Italian. Since 1870 it has been a Catholic dogma that the Pope as Christ's Vicar is infallible when he makes solemn pronouncements on matters of faith and morals. However, since the S.W.W. there has been a tendency to widen the source of authority (*see* PAPACY), and to co-operation in the oecumenical movement which has assisted a review of the tenets of R.C.: issues under discussion have incl. the form of church govt. and services, the rules and dress of monastic orders, the role of 'worker' priests, clerical celibacy, birth control and divorce. *See* VATICAN CITY.

ROMANCE. Term applied in modern usage to any highly coloured prose fiction remote from the conditions of everyday life, and in medieval times to the lengthy stories in verse and prose which became popular in France c. 1200, and spread throughout Europe. The Rs. usually dealt with the adventures of Charlemagne and his heroes, King Arthur and his knights, or the classical themes of Troy, Thebes, etc.

ROMANCE LANGUAGES. A group of languages all of which descend directly from Popular (Vulgar) Latin, the spoken language of the Roman Empire. They incl. Italian, Spanish, Portuguese, Provençal (and Catalan), French, Rumanian, and Romansh (Rhaeto-Romanic).

ROMANESQUE. Style of architecture which prevailed in western Europe from the 9th to the 13th cent. The style varied in different countries, but everywhere the round arch was employed. In planning, different methods of subdivision were favoured to accord with experiments in vaulting. Arches were introduced to spring directly from the capitals of columns, and a system of arcading was devised. The basilican plan was in general use for the early buildings, but in the 12th cent. the cruciform found acceptance. For towers square, octagonal, and circular plans were followed.

ROMAN HISTORY. According to tradition Rome was founded in 753 B.C., and was ruled in succession by 7 kings. The Etruscan dynasty of the Tarquins was expelled in 510, and a republic was estab., governed by 2 chief magistrates, or consuls, who were elected annually by the popular assembly, and a council of elders, or Senate. The concentration of power in the hands of the patrician aristocracy, who monopolized the magistracies and membership of the Senate, aroused the opposition of the plebeian masses. By a long struggle they secured the right to elect tribunes to defend their interests, the codification of the laws, and the right to marry patricians; in 367 it was enacted that one consul must be a plebeian, and by 300 all the magistracies were thrown open to them.

Meanwhile Rome was extending her power over her neighbours. The cities of Latium were formed into a league, under Roman suzerainty. The temporary occupation of Rome by the Gauls in 390 failed to check her advance. The Etruscans to the N. were subdued during the 5th-4th cents., and the Samnites to the S.E. during 343–290. The Greek cities of the S., in spite of the assistance granted them by King Pyrrhus of Epirus, were conquered in 280–272. With the conquest of Cisalpine Gaul (Lombardy) in 226–222, Rome became mistress of Italy.

Inevitably she now came into conflict with Carthage, which was attempting to conquer Sicily. The 1st Punic War (264–241), during which the Roman navy was founded, ended in a Roman victory and the annexation of Sicily, to which in 238 Sardinia was added. These new possessions were treated, not as self-governing 'allies', but as provinces ruled by Roman governors. The Carthaginian attempt to found a new empire in S.E. Spain aroused Roman suspicions, and in 218 war was renewed. Hannibal invaded Italy and won a brilliant series of victories, until a Roman invasion of Africa forced him to withdraw. The victory of Zama in 202 was followed by Carthage's surrender and the cession of her Spanish colonies. By 133 most of Spain had been subdued. Rome now became drawn into Greek and Asiatic politics. Three wars with Macedon were followed by its conversion into a province in 148, while after a revolt in 146 Greece also became in effect a Roman province. In the same year Carthage was destroyed and its territory annexed. On the death of the king of Pergamum in 133, Rome succeeded to his kingdom, which incl. half Asia Minor.

The continual wars had ruined the Italian farmer class while enriching the aristocracy, who built up huge estates cultivated by slave labour. In 133 Tiberius Gracchus, to meet this evil, put forward proposals for agrarian reforms, and was murdered by the senatorial party. His policy was taken up in 123 by his brother Gaius Gracchus, who added proposals for limiting the powers of the senatorial oligarchy, and was likewise murdered. The leadership of the democrats passed to Marius, who had conquered Numidia in 109–106 and saved Italy from a German invasion in 102, while the senate found a champion in Sulla. A revolt of the Italian cities in 91–88 compelled Rome to grant them the franchise. While Sulla was repelling an invasion of Greece by Mithradates of Pontus (87–84) Marius seized power; on his return in 82 Sulla launched a reign of terror and revised the constitution in the Senate's interests.

His changes were reversed in 70 by Pompey and Crassus, but the social struggle continued; Spartacus led a dangerous slave revolt in 73–71, and the democratic extremists, led by Catiline, rebelled in 63. Having crushed Mithradates and annexed Syria and the rest of Asia Minor during 66–62, Pompey returned to form an alliance in 60 with the democratic leaders Crassus and Caesar. The latter received the command in S.E. Gaul, annexed in 121, and by 51 had conquered Gaul as far as the Rhine. During his absence, Pompey drifted into the senatorial party, and Caesar's return to Italy in 49 was the signal for civil war, from which Caesar emerged as master of Rome. His programme of social and political reform was interrupted by his assassination in 44. The empire was now divided between his nephew Octavian, who ruled the W., and Antony, who as Cleopatra's lover ruled the E. from Egypt; war between them began in 32, and with the deaths of Antony and Cleopatra in 30 Egypt was annexed.

Octavian, henceforward known as Augustus, was now absolute, although in theory he was only *princeps* (first citizen), and republican forms were retained. The establishment of an efficient centralized govt., in place of that of the corrupt senatorial oligarchy, proved an immense gain to the empire. Augustus made the Rhine and the Danube its frontiers; Claudius in A.D. 43 added Britain. The dynasty founded by Augustus held power until A.D. 68, and was succeeded by the Flavian house (69–96). Under Nerva, Trajan, Hadrian, Antoninus Pius, and Marcus Aurelius (96–180) the empire enjoyed a golden age of peace and prosperity. Trajan added Dacia and Mesopotamia to the empire, the latter was abandoned by Hadrian, and thereafter expansion ceased.

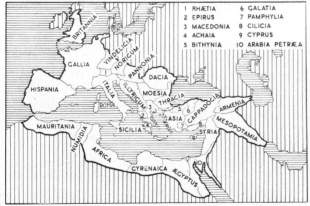

1 RHÆTIA	6 GALATIA
2 EPIRUS	7 PAMPHYLIA
3 MACEDONIA	8 CILICIA
4 ACHAIA	9 CYPRUS
5 BITHYNIA	10 ARABIA PETRÆA

The Roman Empire in A.D. 117, the time of its greatest expansion.

A cent. of war and disorder followed Marcus Aurelius's death, during which a succession of generals were placed on the throne by their armies. A deep-rooted economic crisis sapped the empire's vitality, while the frontiers were threatened by Franks, Goths, and Parthians. Diocletian (284–305) reorganized the empire as a centralized autocracy ruling through an ubiquitous bureaucracy. Constantine I (324–37) recognized the political value of Christianity, which Diocletian had persecuted as subversive, and himself became a convert. He removed the capital to Constantinople, and from 364 the empire, as too large to administer, was divided between emperors at Constantinople and Rome. Reforms failed to check inner decay or aggression from without. The Goths overran Greece and Italy, sacked Rome in 410, and finally settled in Spain. The Vandals conquered Italy. Britain was abandoned in 407. The Huns raided Gaul and Italy in 451–2. When the last emperor was deposed, in 476, the western empire ceased to exist even in name.

ROMAN LAW. One of the 2 great European legal systems, English law being the other. It originated under the republic, was developed under the empire, and continued in use in the Byzantine Empire until 1453. The first codification was that of the 12 Tables (450 B.C.), of which only fragments survive. R.L. assumed its final form in the codification of Justinian (A.D. 528–34). An outstanding feature of R.L. was its system of international law (*jus gentium*), applied in disputes between Romans and foreigners or provincials, or between provincials of different states. During the Middle Ages R.L. was adopted, with local modifications, all over Europe, mainly through the Church's influence; its later diffusion was largely due to the influence of the French *Code Napoléon*, based on R.L., which was adopted in the 19th cent. by several states of E. Europe and Asia, and in Egypt. Inside the Commonwealth, R.L. forms the basis of the legal systems of Scotland and Quebec, and is also the basis of that of S. Africa, the 2 latter being of French and Dutch origin respectively.

ROMANOV (rōmahn′of). Name of the dynasty which ruled Russia from 1613 to the revolution of March 1917.

ROMAN RELIGION. In the religion of the ancient Romans, traces are found of fetishism, e.g. reverence paid to stones and trees, and totemism, e.g. the wolf-cult. Its strongest element was the domestic cults, e.g. of Janus, Vesta, and the Penates, deities of the threshold, hearth, and store-cupboard respectively. Agricultural elements were the spring fertility rites, the harvest and sowing festivals, and the worship of Jupiter, Mars, and Ceres, who were originally agricultural deities. Other cults were introduced from Etruria (Minerva, Juno), Latium (Diana), and Greece (Apollo), and native gods became identified with those of Greece. Under the empire the state religion was a purely political instrument, typified by the deification of dead emperors. While the educated classes turned to Stoicism or scepticism, the masses found solace in such Oriental mystery cults as that of Isis, in Mithraism, and in Christianity, which made their appeal to the senses, the mind, and conscience.

ROMANSH. A Romance language (q.v.), which in 1937 was added to French, German, and Italian, to become the 4th national language of Switzerland. It is spoken by some 50,000 people in the eastern cantons.

ROMANTICISM. Term applied in all arts to the tendency which puts imagination before reason, and abandons the classical ideals of absolute clarity and perfection of form. In literature R. emerged with increasing strength during the later 18th cent., reaching an open declaration with the publication of the *Lyrical Ballads* by Wordsworth and Coleridge in 1798, and inspired the work of Byron, Shelley, and Keats. In prose R. is represented by the 'terror'

romances of the Radcliffe school, and the historical novels of Scott. Among the great representatives of R. abroad are Arnim, Brentano, Novalis, Eichendorff, and Tieck in Germany; Chateaubriand, Lamartine, Musset, de Vigny, and Hugo in France; and Manzoni and Foscolo in Italy. In music R. may be found in Schubert, but is generally considered to begin with Weber, to incl. Schumann, Wagner, and Brahms, and to close with Mahler. In art R. especially denotes the movement which began in France in 1830 as a reaction against the classicism of David and his followers. Its chief exponents were Delacroix and Géricault.

ROMANY. *See* GYPSIES.

ROME (*Roma*). Cap. of the Italian Republic and R. prov. and Latium region, situated on the Tiber, 17 m. from the Tyrrhenian Sea. To the E. of the river lies the main part of the city, incl. the 7 hills (Quirinal, Aventine, Caelian, Esquiline, Viminal, Palatine, and Capitol) on which the ancient city stood; to the W. the popular quarter of Trastevere, the more modern residential quarters of the Prati, and the Vatican (q.v.). The Forum, Colosseum, Pantheon (at present a church), Castel Sant' Angelo (the mausoleum of the Emperor Hadrian), and baths of Caracalla are among the remains of ancient R., while the Lateran, Quirinal, Colonna, Borghese, Barberini, Doria Pamfili, and Farnese palaces date from the Renaissance period. Notable buildings of more recent times incl. the monument to Victor Emmanuel II on the Capitol hill, University City, Policlinico, Palace of Justice, Parliament, and Italian Forum. Apart from St. Peter's the main ecclesiastical edifices incl. St. John Lateran, St. Paul's, S. Lorenzo, S. Maria Maggiore, and S. Maria degli Angeli. Via dei Fori Imperiali (which traverses the Forum), Via Nazionale, Corso Vittorio Emmanuele, and Corso Umberto are fine thoroughfares. Piazza Venezia (where is situated the Palazzo Venezia, c. 1455), Piazza del Popolo, Piazza Navona, Campo dei Fiori, Piazza Barberine, Piazza di Spagna, and Piazza Colonna are among the fine squares, many of which are adorned with beautiful fountains. The main open spaces are the Villa Borghese, which adjoins the Pincio terrace from which there is a good view of the Vatican and the heights of Monte Mario, and the Janiculum, which is the site of an immense statue of Garibaldi. Academic institutions incl. the univ. and British and French schools of art. R. has few industries but is an important road, rail and air centre. An underground railway 7 m. long, built 1938–55, runs from the central railway station, which was constructed 1938–50, to Laurentina, S.W.

ROME. The Castel Sant' Angelo, built as a mausoleum for the Emperor Hadrian, and for centuries the fortress of the city. In the foreground the bridge of Sant' Angelo spans the Tiber.
Courtesy of the Italian State Tourist Office.

of the city. A new international airport was opened at Fiumicino in 1961. A large section of the pop. finds employment in govt. offices. Pop. (1961) 2,160,773.

History. For the early history of R. *see* ROMAN HISTORY. After the deposition of the last emperor, Romulus Augustulus, in 476 the papacy (q.v.) became the real ruler of R., and from the 8th cent. was recognized as such, although attempts were made, e.g. by Arnold of Brescia (1143–55) and Rienzi (1347–54), to revive the rep. As a result of the French Revolution R. temporarily became a republic in 1798–9, and was annexed to the French Empire 1808–14, until the Pope returned on Napoleon's fall. During the 1848–9 revolution, a republic was estab. under Mazzini's leadership, but in spite of Garibaldi's defence was overthrown by French troops. In 1870 R. became the cap. of Italy, the Pope retiring into the Vatican until 1929 when the Vatican City was recognized as a sovereign state. The occupation of R. by the Fascists in 1922 marked the beginning of Mussolini's rule. After his fall in 1943 R. was occupied by the Germans, but was captured by the Allies in 1944.

ROME, Treaties of. After discussions at Messina, Sicily, in 1955, two treaties were signed at Rome in March, 1957 which estab. the European Economic and Atomic Energy Communities. *See* EUROPEAN UNION.

ROMILLY (rom'ili), **Sir Samuel** (1757–1818). British reformer. B. in London, the son of a watch-maker, he became a barrister, and in 1806 was appointed Solicitor-General and knighted. As an M.P. he devoted himself to the reform of the criminal law.

ROMMEL, Erwin (1891–1944). German field marshal. B. in Swabia, he served in the F.W.W., later joining the Nazi Party. He was prominent in the annexations of central Europe, the fall of France, the N. African war (when he earned the nickname 'desert fox'), and the 1944 operations.

ROMNEY, George (1734–1802). British artist. B. near Dalton-in-Furness, Lancs, the son of a carpenter and cabinet-maker, he was practically self-taught. He set up as a portrait painter in 1757, and deserting his wife and children in 1762 he went to London where he became one of the most successful portrait painters of his day. His most famous sitter was Lady Hamilton.

ROMNEY MARSH. A stretch of drained marsh-land on the Kent coast, England, between Hythe and Rye, used for sheep pasture. The seaward point is Dungeness. R.M. was reclaimed in Roman times, and is famed for its churches. **New Romney**, a borough formed by the amalgamation of R., one of the Cinque Ports (q.v.), with Littlestone and Greatstone, is now more than a mile from the sea. Pop. (1961) 2,556.

ROMSEY (rum'zi). English market town (bor.) in Hampshire, on the Test, 8 m. N.W. of Southampton. R. Abbey was founded by Edward the elder; the main surviving feature is the fine Norman church. The mansion of Broadlands nearby, seat of Earl Mountbatten, was formerly the seat of Lord Palmerston. Pop. (1961) 6,229.

RO'MULUS. The legendary founder and first king of Rome, the son of Mars by Rhea Silvia. R. and his twin brother Remus were exposed by their great-uncle Amulius, but were suckled by a she-wolf and rescued by a shepherd. On reaching manhood they killed Amulius and founded Rome. Having murdered Remus, R. reigned alone until he disappeared in a storm, and thereafter was worshipped as a god under the name of Quirinus.

ROMULUS AUGUSTUS (c. A.D. 461–?). Last Roman emperor in the West. When about 14 he was made emperor by his soldier father Orestes in 475, but compelled to abdicate in 476 by Odoacer, leader of the barbarian mercenaries, who nicknamed him Augustulus. Orestes was executed and R. confined to a Neapolitan villa where he d. at an unknown date.

RONCESVALLES (ronthesvahl'yes). Village of N.

Spain, in the Pyrenees 5 m. S. of the French frontier, celebrated as the scene of the defeat of the rearguard of Charlemagne's army under Roland, who with the 12 peers was slain.

RONSARD (ronsahr'), **Pierre de** (1524–85). French poet. B. near Couture, he was a page at the French court and spent some years in Britain. His intended diplomatic career was cut short by deafness, and he retired to study the classical writers, emerging in 1550 as the leader of the Pléiade (q.v.). An original and lightly sensitive stylist, he pub. *Odes* (1550), *Amours*, and *Abrégé de l'art poétique français.* He was patronized by Charles IX, but was bitterly opposed by the followers of Marot.

RÖNTGEN, Wilhelm Konrad (1845–1923). German physicist. B. at Lennep, he became in 1879 director of the Physical Institute at Giessen, and in 1885 at Würzburg, where he conducted his experiments which resulted in the discovery of the rays named after him, in 1895. While investigating the passage of electricity through gases, he noticed the fluorescence of a barium-platinocyanide screen. This radiation R. found would pass through some substances opaque to light, and affect a photographic plate. As the X-ray, the development of this invention has revolutionized surgery. He received the Nobel prize in 1901, and the international unit for the measurement of X or gamma radiation, is named after him.

ROOD. Alternative name for the Cross of Christ specially applied to the large crucifix which was placed above the R.-screen in medieval churches. Also a surface measure, denoting a quarter of an acre.

ROODEPOORT-MARAISBURG (rürdepürt-marit'zbörkh). Town in Transvaal, South Africa, 9 m. W. of Johannesburg. It lies at a height of 5,725 ft. and is a gold-mining and residential place. Leander Starr Jameson (q.v.) and his followers surrendered here in 1896. Pop. (1960) 94,740 (40,711 white).

ROOK. Bird (*Corvus frugilegus*) of the crow family. The plumage is black and lustrous, and the face bare. Rs. live in colonies at the tops of trees, usually near human habitation.

ROOKE, Sir George (1650–1709). British admiral. He took part in the actions off Beachy Head, 1690, and La Hogue, 1692, and in 1702 destroyed the French and Spanish fleet at Vigo. Together with Sir Clowdisley Shovell, he captured Gibraltar and defeated the French at Malaga in 1704.

ROON (rōn), **Albrecht Theodor Emil,** count von (1803–79). Prussian field marshal. B. near Kolberg, he was War Minister from 1859 and reorganized the army so thoroughly that the 1866 and 1870–1 victories were made possible.

ROOSEVELT, Franklin Delano (1882–1945). 32nd president of the U.S.A. B. at Hyde Park, New York, of a landowning family, he was educ. in Europe and at Harvard and Columbia univs. In 1905 he m. Anna Eleanor R. In 1907 R. was admitted to the Bar and began practising in New York. He entered politics in 1910, when he was elected to the state senate as a Democrat. He held the Assistant Secretaryship of the navy in Wilson's govts. 1913–21, and did much to increase the efficiency of the navy during the F.W.W. He was nominated for the vice-presidency in 1920, but with the Democratic defeat returned to his legal practice. The infantile paralysis from which he suffered till his death afflicted him in 1921, but extensive treatment lessened its effect. He served as Governor of New York 1929–33.

He was nominated as Democratic candidate for the presidency in 1932, and won a decisive victory. Amid a grave economic depression he took office in 1933, and at once displayed determined leadership. Surrounding himself by a 'brains trust' of experts, he launched a carefully spaced legislative programme, which Congress had to accept. Banks, which he closed during the crisis, were reopened; Federal credit was

THE ROOSEVELTS. Eleanor Roosevelt was a distant cousin of F.D.R., as well as being his wife, and was his staunch supporter in all his campaigns. This photo was taken just before his re-election for a fourth term. *Courtesy of U.S.I.S.*

restored, and when the New Deal got under way, the gold standard was abandoned, and the dollar devalued. In 1935 R. introduced the Utilities Act, directed against abuses in the large holding companies, and the Social Security Act, providing for unemployment and old-age insurance.

The presidential election of 1936 was fought entirely on the record of the New Deal, and resulted in a sweeping victory for R. During 1935-6 he was involved in a long conflict with the Supreme Court, who declared several of his measures unconstitutional, until the retirement or death of certain of its members enabled him to secure the support of a liberal majority. In 1938 R. introduced measures for farm relief and the improvement of working conditions. In his foreign policy he endeavoured to use his influence to restrain Axis aggression, and to establish 'Good Neighbour' relations with the American countries.

Soon after the outbreak of war he launched a vast rearmament programme, introduced conscription, and provided for the supply of armaments to the Allies on a 'cash-and-carry' basis. In spite of strong isolationist opposition, and the fact that he was breaking a long-standing precedent in standing for a 3rd term, he was re-elected in 1940. He then introduced his 'lease-lend' plan for the supply of war materials to the Allies, announced that the U.S. would become the 'arsenal of democracy', and in 1941 drew up with Mr. Churchill the Atlantic Charter as a statement of Allied war aims. In that year he defined the 'Four Freedoms' (q.v.). From the Japanese attack on Pearl Harbor in Dec. 1941, he devoted himself solely to the conduct of the war. He participated in the Washington (1942) and Casablanca conferences (1943), to plan the Mediterranean assault, and in those at Quebec, Cairo, Tehran (1943), and Yalta (1945), at which the final preparations were made for the Allied victory. He was re-elected for a 4th term in 1944. His sudden death on 12 April 1945 was the cause of worldwide mourning. *See also* NEW DEAL.

His wife **Eleanor R.** (1884–1962) whom he m. in 1905, actively furthered his political career. A prominent social worker and lecturer, her newspaper column 'My Day' was widely syndicated, and she was a U.S. delegate to the U.N. general assembly, and later chairman of the U.N. commission on human rights 1946-51. Within the Democratic Party she formed the left-wing Americans for Democratic Action group in 1947. Her books incl. *This I Remember* (1950), and *You Learn By Living* (1960).

ROOSEVELT, Theodore (1858–1919). 26th President of the U.S.A. B. in New York, he was elected to the state legislature as a Republican in 1881. He was Assistant Secretary of the Navy 1897-8, and during the Spanish War of 1898 commanded a volunteer force of 'rough riders'. After serving as Governor of N.Y. 1898–1900 he was elected Vice-President in 1900 to McKinley, whom he succeeded as President on his assassination in 1901, and was re-elected in 1904. In office he campaigned against the great trusts, and initiated measures for the conservation of national resources, while carrying on a jingoist foreign policy designed to enforce U.S. supremacy over Latin America. Alienated after his retirement in 1909 by the conservatism of his successor Taft, he formed the Progressive or 'Bull Moose' Party, as whose candidate he unsuccessfully ran for the presidency in 1912 against Taft and Wilson. During the F.W.W. he strongly advocated American intervention. He wrote historical and other works, incl. *The Naval War of 1812* (1882) and *The Winning of the West* (1889–96).

ROOT, Elihu (1845–1937). American statesman. After a successful legal career, he became War Minister 1899–1904, and Secretary of State 1905–9. He assisted in 1920 in drawing up the plan for the Permanent Cour: of International Justice.

ROOT. The underground extremities of plants. Rs. often form the storehouse of nutritious food substances, as well as absorbing moisture, etc., from the soil. The main R. is known as the tap-root, and has various qualifying names according to the form it assumes, e.g. conical, napiform (turnip-shaped), fusiform (spindle-shaped). The subsidiary Rs. are known as fibrous Rs. and may be divided as follows: (a) nontuberous and (b) tuberous, including moniliform (necklace-shaped), nodulose (bearing knobs towards the extremities), and annulated (divided into rings).

ROPE. Stout cordage, or twisted fibres, over 1 in. diameter. It is made similarly to thread or twine, by twisting yarns together to form strands, which are then in turn twisted round each other in the direction opposite to that of the yarns. To form a hawser-laid R., three of these strands are twisted, while for a cable-laid R. three hawsers are used. A shroud-laid R. consists of a central strand surrounded by several others twisted. Although hemp is the commonest material used to make R., increasing use of nylon is made for specialized purposes.

ROPS, Félicien (1833–98). Belgian artist. B. at Namur, he painted in the manner of Courbet and executed many engravings, being particularly adept in the use of dry paint and soft varnish.

RORAIMA (rorī′ma), **Mount.** Plateau (Indian 'Mother of Rivers') some 20 m. sq. and 8,625 ft. above sea-level at the conjunction of British Guiana, Brazil and Venezuela. It is thought to have taken its present form 300 million years ago, and the isolation due to its sheer 1,000 ft. cliffs has ensured a largely unique fauna and flora. However, the inhospitable, eroded rock supports only some grasses, bushes, flowers, insects and small amphibians. Conan Doyle's *The Lost World*, inspired by reports of its strange character, was entirely fanciful in envisaging it still as it was in the palaeozoic period, with prehistoric monsters roaming primeval forest. *See* illus. p. 163.

RORQUAL (rōr′kwawl). A species of *Balaenoptera* – large, long, fin-whales. The blue whale (*B. sibbaldi*) is the largest of all animals, measuring 100 ft. and more. The common R. (*B. physalas*) is slate-colour and not quite so long.

RORSCHACH (ror′shakh), **Hermann** (1884–1922). Swiss psychiatrist, influenced by Freud and Jung, whose methods of diagnosis incl. the *Formdeutversuch* or R. test consisting of 10 bilaterally symmetrical, amorphous, ink-blot patterns (5 black and white, 5 coloured) which the subject is asked to interpret, his answers revealing personality type, degree of intelligence and emotional stability.

ROSA, Carl August Nikolaus (1842–89). German musician. A successful violinist and conductor, he founded with his wife, the singer Parepa (d. 1874), an opera co., with which they came to England in 1871. The **C.R. Opera Co.** was formed after a London season in 1875, and became well known for its presentation of opera in English, in London and the provinces, and for its encouragement of English operatic composers and singers. In 1958 the co. dissolved, and the majority of its members were eventually incorporated (1959) into the Sadler's Wells Opera Co., which was then able to maintain 2 cos. of equal status, one constantly on tour.

ROSA, Salvator (1615–73). Italian painter. B. near Naples, he spent much of his time when a youth travelling in southern Italy, where he copied from nature. He went to Rome in 1635, and estab. a great reputation as a landscape painter. He also wrote verse satires.

ROSACEAE (rōzā′sē-ē). A large family of seed-bearing plants which produce many temperate fruits e.g. the apple, pear, plum, cherry, peach, and almond, as well as the rose and other flowers.

ROSARIO (rōsah′rē-ō). River port of Argentina, Santa Fé prov., 175 m. N.W. of Buenos Aires, on the Parana. Founded in 1725, it has sugar refineries, meat-packing and maté-processing factories, etc. Wheat, flour, meat, etc., are exported. Pop. (1960) 672,000.

ROSARY. Form of prayer used by R.Cs. consisting of 150 Aves and 15 Paternosters and Glorias; also a string of 165 beads for keeping counts of the prayers.

ROSAY (rōsā′), **Françoise.** French actress. B. in Paris, she m. Jacques Feyder, film director. Her films incl. *La kermesse héroïque* (1936), *Un carnet de bal* (1938), *Johnny Frenchman* (1945), *Une femme disparait*, and *The Naked Heart.*

ROSCELLINUS (roselī′nus), **Johannes** (*c.* 1050–*c.* 1122). Medieval thinker; regarded as the founder of the Scholastic philosophy because of his defence of Nominalism against Anselm.

ROSCIUS (rosh′ius) **GALLUS, Quintus** (*c.* 126–62 B.C.). Roman actor, originally a slave, who achieved fame and fortune by his acting ability. His name has become proverbial for a great actor.

ROSCOMMON. County of Rep. of Ireland in the prov. of Connacht, bounded on the E. by the Shannon. A number of lakes (e.g. Gara, Key, Allen) lie partly or wholly in R., which is noted for its pastures. The co. town, also R., has remains of a castle put up in the 13th cent. by English settlers. The name, originally Ros-Comain, means wood round a monastery. Pop. (1966) 56,228.

ROSE. Genus of flowering plants (family Rosaceae). Many cultivated forms have been derived from the sweet briar (*Rosa rubiginosa*) and the dog-rose (*R. canina*). There are many climbing varieties, but the more cultivated forms are bush roses and standards. These are cultivated roses grafted on to a briar stem.

ROSEBERY, Archibald Philip Primrose, 5th earl of (1847–1929). Liberal statesman. Educ. at Eton and Oxford, he succeeded to the title in 1868, and was appointed Commissioner of Works 1885, and For. Sec. 1886 and 1892–4. He succeeded Gladstone as P.M. in 1894, but his govt. survived less than a year. After 1896 his imperialist views gradually estranged him from the Liberal Party. He pub. several historical works, incl. *Napoleon: the Last Phase* (1900) and lives of Pitt, Chatham, Peel, and Cromwell. He was also a noted racehorse-owner, winning the Derby 3 times. His son **Albert Edward,** 6th earl of R. (1882–), was Regional Commissioner for Scotland 1941–5, and Sec. of State for Scotland in the 'caretaker' govt., 1945, and Pres. National Liberal Party 1945–7.

ROSEMARY. Evergreen shrub (*Rosmarinus officinalis*) bearing small scented leaves. An aromatic oil is extracted from the clusters of pale purple flowers.

ROSENBERG (rōzenberg), **Alfred** (1893–1946). German politician. B. at Tallinn, he became the chief Nazi ideologist. He supervised the training of the party, and 1941–4 was Reich Minister for eastern occupied territories. He was tried at Nuremberg in 1946 as a war criminal and hanged.

ROSENBERG, Julius and Ethel. See SECRET SERVICE.

ROSES, Wars of the. The civil wars fought between the adherents of the House of Lancaster, which ruled England 1399–1461, and the House of York, which claimed the throne. The two parties used the red and the white rose respectively as their badges. The first battle was fought at St. Albans in 1455. War was renewed in 1459–61, ending in the Yorkist claimant's accession as Edward IV, and the destruction of the Lancastrians at Towton. A Lancastrian rising in 1464 was crushed at Hexham. A temporary Lancastrian restoration took place in 1470–1, ended by the Yorkist victories at Barnet and Tewkesbury. Peace reigned until Henry of Richmond's victory at Bosworth in 1485 restored a branch of the House of Lancaster; as Henry VII he m. Elizabeth of York, and so united the two Houses. Yorkist rebellions continued, however, until 1497.

ROSETTA (Arab. Rashid). Town in Egypt, on the main W. arm (to which it gives its name) of the Nile delta, 110 m. N.W. of Cairo. Pop. (est.) 30,000. The Rosetta Stone with a trilingual inscription was found here in 1799 by one of Napoleon's officers, captured by the British in 1801, and in 1802 placed in the British Museum. See HIEROGLYPHIC.

ROSEWOOD. The name of several kinds of ornamental timber, produced and exported in large quantities from Rio de Janeiro, Bahia, Jamaica, and Honduras. It is a rich brown, and polishes well.

ROSICRUCIANS (rōzikroo′shianz). Name adopted by certain early 17th cent. philosophers, who claimed occult powers, and employed the terminology of alchemy to expound their mystical doctrines. The alleged founder was Christian Rosencreutz who flourished *c.* 1460. Several societies have been founded in Britain and the U.S.A. which claim to be their successors.

ROSS. English market town (U.D.) in Herefordshire, 12 m. S.E. of Hereford. Agricultural implements are manufactured. The philanthropist John Kyrle (1637–1724), who made his home at R. and was chosen sheriff in 1683, is called the Man of R. Pop. (1961) 5,643.

ROSS, Sir John (1777–1856). Scottish rear-admiral and explorer. He served in the wars with France and made voyages of Arctic exploration in 1818, 1829–33 and 1850. His nephew **Sir James R.** (1800–62) made several Arctic voyages with his uncle and with Parry (1819–27), determined the position of the magnetic north pole in 1831, and in 1839–43 commanded an Antarctic expedition. See ROSS ISLAND AND DEPENDENCY, named after him.

ROSS, Sir Ronald (1857–1932). British physician and bacteriologist. B. in India, he served 1881–99 in the Indian Medical Service, and 1895–8 discovered the malaria parasite and studied its life-history. He became prof. of tropical medicine at Liverpool, received a Nobel prize in 1902, and wrote poems, essays, memoirs, as well as scientific papers.

ROSS AND CRO′MARTY. Highland co. of Scotland which incl. Lewis in the Outer Hebrides and many small islands. The coast is indented by many sea-lochs. Several high peaks rise in the S. to more than 3,800 ft., and Ben Wyvis in the N.E. is 3,429 ft. There are extensive deer forests. The Glomach Falls (370 ft.) are the deepest in Britain, and Loch Maree is a renowned beauty spot. Sheep and cattle grazing are the main industries; oats are the chief crop. Dingwall is the co. town. R. and C., originally 2 earldoms, became cos., R. in 1661, C. in 1685; C.

was made up of areas scattered over R., and the 2 were made one co. in 1899. Area 3,089 sq. m.; pop. (1961) 57,607.

ROSS DEPENDENCY. All the islands and territories between 160° E. and 150° W. long. S. of 60° S. lat.; it incl. Edward VII Land, Ross Sea and its islands, and parts of Victoria Land. It was placed under New Zealand jurisdiction by an Order in Council of 1923. Whaling is carried on, and there are a few scientific bases with c. 250 staff. Area 175,000 sq. m.

ROSSETTI, Christina Georgina (1830–94). British poet. The sister of Dante R., and a devout Anglican, she produced much popular lyric and religious verse, e.g. *Goblin Market* and other poems (1862).

ROSSETTI, Dante Gabriel (1828–82). British poet and artist whose full name was Gabriel Charles Dante R. B. in London, the son of the Italian patriot Gabriele R. (1783–1854), who settled in England in 1824, he studied at the R.A. schools and under Madox Brown, and in 1848 formed the Pre-Raphaelite brotherhood together with Millais and Hunt. He early began writing verse, and pub. *The Blessed Damozel* in 1850, but on the death in 1862 of the beautiful Elizabeth Siddal (whom he had m. in 1860) he buried his verse MSS. with her. These were recovered in 1869, and when pub. as *Poems* (1870) were attacked on the grounds of morality as belonging to the 'fleshly school of poetry'. *Ballads and Sonnets* appeared in 1881, and he also pub. translations from Dante, Villon, and others. His best-known paintings incl. 'Beata Beatrix', 'Monna Vanna', 'The Beloved', and 'Dante's Dream'. His brother, **William Michael R.** (1829–1919), was one of the later members of the Pre-Raphaelite Brotherhood, and pub. art and literary criticism.

ROSSINI (rossē'nē), **Gioachino Antonio** (1792–1868). Italian composer. B. at Pesaro, his first success was the opera *Tancredi* (1813). In 1816 his *Il Barbiere di Siviglia* was produced at Rome, and was at first a failure. During his fertile composition period, 1815–23, he produced 20 operas, but after *Guillaume Tell* (1829) gave up writing opera. His later years were spent in Bologna and Paris. Among the works of this period are the *Stabat Mater* (1831–41), and the piano music first pub. in 1919 and arranged for ballet by Respighi as *La Boutique fantasque.*

ROSS ISLAND. Name of 2 islands in Antarctica, one in Weddell Sea, discovered 1903 by Nordenskjöld, area c. 1,500 sq. m.; the other in Ross Sea discovered 1841 by Ross, area c. 2,500 sq. m. and incl. the volcanoes Mt. Erebus (13,202 ft.), active, and Mt. Terror (10,750 ft.), extinct.

ROSSLARE. Port of co. Wexford, Republic of Ireland, 9 m. S.E. of Wexford. Founded by the English in 1210, it was made the Irish terminus of the steamer route from Fishguard in 1906. Pop. (1961) 550.

ROSTAND (rostahn'), **Edmond** (1869–1918). French dramatist. B. at Marseilles, he achieved immediate success with *Les romanesques* (1894), which was followed by *La Princesse lointaine* (1895); *La Samaritaine* (1897); *Cyrano de Bergerac* (1897), his greatest triumph; *L'Aiglon* (1900), which provided Bernhardt with one of her greatest roles; and *Chantecler* (1910), in which Lucien Guitry appeared.

ROSTOCK (ro'stok). Port in E. Germany, on the Warnow, 8 m. S. of the Baltic. Founded in 1189 on a long-inhabited site, it became in the 14th cent. a powerful member of the Hanseatic League. It has a univ. (1419). Pop. (1966) 186,450.

ROSTOV-ON-DON (rostov'-). Seaport in the Russian S.F.S.R., cap. of R. region, on the Don, 14 m. E. of the Sea of Azov. R. has shipyards; tobacco, motor-car and locomotive, and textile factories. It dates from 1761, and is linked by river and canal with Volgograd on the Volga. Part of R. region is within the Donbas (q.v.). Pop. (1967) 737,000.

ROSTROPŌ'VICH, Mstislav Leopoldovich (1927–). Russian cellist. B. at Baku, he was first taught by his father. A soloist with the Moscow Philharmonia Orchestra from 1946, he became prof. in 1957 at the Moscow Conservatoire where he was once a student. His mastery of his instrument has prompted a number of composers to write for him, incl. Prokoviev (his unfinished 'Concerto for Cello' was completed by R.), Shostakovich, Khachaturian and Benjamin Britten.

ROSYTH (rōsīth'). A naval base and dockyard in Scotland, built 1909, on the N. shore of the Firth of Forth, 2 m. S. of Dunfermline in which it was incorporated in 1911.

ROTARY CLUB. Society founded to foster the ideal of service to others and composed of business and professional men. The first R.C. (so called because the meetings were held at the offices of each member in rotation) was estab. by Paul Harris in 1905 in Chicago; the first British R.C. was founded in 1911. The R. International had in 1963 some 535,000 members in 8,405 clubs throughout the world.

ROTHAMSTED. English agricultural experimental station 4 m. N.W. of St. Albans, Herts, founded by Sir James Bennet Lawes (1816–1900) to carry out soil research. Its records go back to 1843. Lawes endowed the station in 1889, and in 1899 formed the Lawes Agricultural Trust to continue the work. When the Executive Council of Commonwealth Agricultural Bureaux was set up in 1929, the bureau dealing with soils was attached to R.

ROTHENBURG (rō'tenboorg) **OB DER TAUBER** (tow'ber). Town in Bavaria, W. Germany, 40 m. W. of Nuremberg, famous for its medieval buildings, churches, and walls. *See* illus. p. 472.

RŌ'THENSTEIN, Sir William (1872–1945). British artist, son of a German immigrant who settled in Bradford. His work, now out of favour, incl. decorations for St. Stephen's Hall, Westminster, and portrait drawings. He was Principal of the Royal College of Art 1920–35, and helped Epstein, Paul Nash, and Henry Moore. His elder son **Sir John R.** (1901–) was Director of the Tate Gallery 1938–64, his younger son **Michael R.** (1908–) is an artist, noted as a printmaker.

ROTHERHAM. English market town (co. bor.) in the W.R. of Yorkshire, 5 m. N.E. of Sheffield, on the Don and Rother. Industries incl. iron and steel, pottery, glassworks, brewing. Pop. (1961) 85,346.

ROTHERHITHE. District in Southwark, London, England. On the S. bank of the Thames, it contains a considerable dock area, and is linked with the N. bank by R. Tunnel (1908), pedestrians and vehicles, to Stepney, and Thames Tunnel (1843), railway, to Wapping.

ROTHERMERE. *See* under NORTHCLIFFE.

ROTHESAY (roth'si). Royal burgh (1400) and co. town of Buteshire, on the Isle of Bute, W. Scotland. It is a popular resort. Pop. (1961) 7,656.

ROTHSCHILD (roths'-child). The name of a Jewish family, famed for its activity in the financial world for 2 cents. Mayer Anselm (1744–1812) set up as a moneylender in Frankfurt-am-Main, and important houses were estab. throughout Europe by his 10 children. Nathan Mayer (1777–1836) settled in England, and his grandson Nathaniel (1840–1915) was created a baron in 1885. Lionel Walter (1868–1937) succeeded his father as 2nd baron R. and was a noted naturalist: his nephew Nathaniel (1910–), 3rd baron R., is a scientist and headed the central policy review staff in the Cabinet Office from 1970. James de R. (1878–1957), originally a member of the French branch, but who became a naturalized Briton, bequeathed to the nation Waddesdon Manor, near Aylesbury.

ROTORUA. Town in North Island, New Zealand, in the Hot Spring District, near Lake R. There are medicinal springs, and active volcanoes, which, with hills and lakes, form a vast scenic attraction for many visitors. Pop. (1967) 27,000.

ROTTERDAM. Second city and chief port of the Netherlands, on the Rotte and the Maas mouth of the Rhine-Maas delta; the Nieuwe Waterweg (new waterway), constructed 1866–90, links R. with the North Sea for shipping. R. dates from the 12th cent. or earlier, and developed as a port threaded with waterways. There is a statue of Erasmus, who was born at R., in the market place; the Groote Kerk (great church) or Church of St. Lawrence, begun early in the 15th cent., was gutted in the German air attack of 14 May 1940, and subsequently restored. R.'s museums and art collections are notable. Industries incl. brewing, distilling, shipbuilding, sugar and petroleum refining, and the manufacture of margarine and tobacco. The city centre was destroyed by German

ROTTERDAM. Built in the city's yards, a newly completed nitric-acid tanker sails down the New Meuse. The acid is carried in eight separate tanks for greater safety,
Courtesy of G. & J. Weir Holding Ltd., Glasgow.

air attack in 1940, but has been completely rebuilt, and an underground railway system constructed (opened 1968). The dockyards have been greatly extended, with modern container and bulk cargo handling facilities, and the R.-Europort complex is one of the premier ocean cargo ports of the world. Pop. (1967) 723,958.

ROUAULT (roo-ō), **Georges** (1871–1958). French artist. B. in Paris, the son of a cabinet-maker, he was apprenticed to a stained-glass maker – the influence of this craft being obvious in his later paintings – and studied under Gustave Moreau. His works incl. 'Aunt Sallies' and 'The Three Judges', both in the Tate, and moving religious subjects, e.g. 'The Holy Face' as imprinted on the veil of St. Veronica.

ROUBAIX (roobā'). Town in Nord dept., N. France, 6 m. N.E. of Lille, important centre of French woollen textile production. Pop. (1962) 113,163.

ROUBILLAC (roobēyahk'), **Louis François** (1695–1762). French sculptor. B. at Lyons, he went to England where he was patronized by Walpole, becoming the most popular sculptor of his day. His principal works incl. statues of Handel, Newton, and George I, and busts of Shakespeare and Pope (*see* illus. p. 394). His name is sometimes less correctly spelled Roubiliac.

ROUEN (roo-oñ'). French port, cap. of Seine-Maritime dept., on the Seine, 87 m. N.W. of Paris. It was also cap. of Normandy from 912. Lost by King John 1204, it was in English possession 1419–49; Joan of Arc was burned in the market place 1431. The cathedral (13th–16th cent.) is famous (its right-hand tower, Tour de Beurre, was paid for by the sale of indulgences to eat butter during Lent), and there are other notable buildings. R. is a centre of the wine trade. Industries incl. cotton spinning and weaving, distilling, and petroleum refining. Pop. (1968) 120,471.

ROUGET DE LISLE (roozhā' de lēl), **Claude Joseph** (1760–1836). French author and army officer. B. at Lons-le-Saunier, he composed, at Strasbourg, *La Marseillaise*, the French national anthem and song of the revolution.

ROULERS (roolā'). Town in W. Flanders prov., Belgium, 13 m. N.W. of Courtrai. Linen, jute, and other textiles are made. R. was an important German base during the F.W.W. Pop. (1966) 40,000.

ROULETTE (roolet'). A gambling game, associated with Monte Carlo, consisting of betting on the numbered divisions of a turning wheel into which an ivory ball will fall. They are coloured alternately black and red, with numbers from 0–36. The table, on which bets are laid, is designed in 3 columns of numbers corresponding to those of the wheel, and many methods of betting exist, with the odds appropriate to the chances against the number appearing. The play is under the control of a croupier.

ROUMANIA. *See* RUMANIA.

ROUNDHEADS. Nickname applied to the parliamentary party during the revolution of 1640–60. It had a sneering implication, since at the time only the lower classes wore their hair short.

ROUP. A contagious disease of poultry and game. Caused by unhealthy conditions, it is characterized by swelling of the face and purulent catarrh.

ROUSE, William Henry Denham (1863–1950). British educationist and classical scholar. He taught at Rugby 1896–1901, was headmaster of Perse School, Cambridge, 1902–28, and univ. teacher of Sanskrit 1903–39. His publications incl. *Greek Votive Offerings* (1902), and the renowned *Latin on the Direct Method* (1925).

ROUSSEAU (roosō'), **Henri** (1844–1910). French artist known as *Le Douanier* (customs official) because this was for a time his profession. B. in Laval, he exhibited at the *Salon des Indépendants* from 1886 to 1910, and was associated with the group which was led by Apollinaire and Picasso. He painted landscapes, animals and jungle scenes.

ROUSSEAU, Jean Jacques (1712–78). French philosopher. B. in Geneva, he was apprenticed in turn to a lawyer and engraver, but ran away and from 1728 led the wandering life described in his *Confessions*. The first of many ill-repaid patrons was Mme Warens, whose lover he became. On the breakdown of this relationship he went to Paris, where he took as his mistress the servant girl, Thérèse le Vasseur: their 5 children were deposited in the foundling hospital. In 1754 he pub. a *Discourse on the Origin of Inequality*, denouncing civilized society, which made him famous, but retired to country seclusion to produce the sentimental romance *La Nouvelle Héloïse* (1760); the revolutionary *Du Contrat social* (1762); and the educational treatise *Émile* (1762). The democratic political implications and the deistic viewpoint of the latter caused it to be condemned by Church and State, and R. fled abroad, living for a time in England under the patronage of Hume. He later returned to France, but suffered from an increasing persecution mania until his death. R. was buried in the Panthéon.

ROUSSEAU, Pierre Étienne Théodore (1812–67). French landscape painter of the Barbizon School. B. in Paris, he studied under Rémond and Guyon Lethière. He came under the influence of Constable and Bonington, sketched from nature in many parts of France, and settling in Barbizon in 1848 he became one of the pioneers of Romanticism.

ROUSSEL (roosel'), **Albert** (1869–1937). French composer. B. at Tourcoing, he entered upon a naval career, studied under d'Indy, and later was influenced by Stravinsky. He composed symphonies, operas, etc.

ROUSSEL, Raymond (1877–1933). French poet, novelist and playwright. A wealthy amateur of literature, he wrote his surrealist fictio n in prose and verse the most notable being *La Doublure* (1897) in alexandrine couplets; and *Impressions d'Afrique* (1910): he adapted the latter for the stage and *L'Étoile au front* and *La Poussière de soleils* were written as plays – all having a hostile reception.' A neurotic, he was treated by Janet (q.v.) who detailed his case history in *De l'Angoisse à l'extase*. In the posthumous *Comment j'ai écrit certains de mes livres* (1935) he explains his theory of writing, and is regarded as a precursor of the *nouveau roman*.

ROWAN. *See* MOUNTAIN ASH.

ROWE (rō), **Nicholas** (1674–1718). English dramatist and poet. He entered the Middle Temple in 1691, and inherited a fortune from his father. His most famous dramas are *The Fair Penitent* (1703), and *Jane Shore* (1714), in which Mrs. Siddons played. He ed. Shakespeare, and was Poet Laureate from 1715.

ROWING. Propulsion of a boat by successive strokes of oars. A rower may handle either 2 oars (sculling) or more commonly 1 oar, especially in racing boats, consisting of 2-, 4- or 8- man crews, with or without coxswain (steersman). The first recorded English race, still surviving, was Doggett's Coat and Badge, initiated in 1715 between Thames watermen: there were similar races between ferrymen of the Hudson river, New York, in 1811 and 1823. Amateur rowing as a sport, developing early in England (Leander club 1817) and later in the U.S.A. (Detroit boat club 1839), has become internationally popular. In the U.K. the chief annual events incl., the Oxford and Cambridge boat race, the Thames head of the river race, and the Henley Royal regatta, also a major international event. In the U.S.A. the Harvard-Yale boat race, held on the Thames at New London, and the Poughkeepsie regatta, are the premier events, while international contests in all classes are held during the Olympic Games.

ROWLANDSON, Thomas (1756–1827). British caricaturist. B. in London, he studied at the R.A. Schools and in Paris. Impoverished by gambling, he turned from portrait painting to caricature. His *Tour of Dr. Syntax in Search of the Picturesque*, and its 2 sequels, proved very popular. Other works incl. 'The Dance of Death', and illustrations for Smollett, Goldsmith, and Sterne.

ROWLEY, William (c. 1585–c. 1642). English dramatist. He became an actor, wrote *All's Lost by Lust*, and collaborated with Thomas Middleton in *The Changeling* and *The Spanish Gypsie*.

ROWSE, Alfred Leslie (1903–). British historian. A fellow of All Souls Coll., Oxford, he has made a popular as well as a scholarly reputation with *Sir Richard Grenville* (1937), *Tudor Cornwall* (1941) – he is himself a native of the co. – *The Use of History* (1946), *The England of Elizabeth* (1950) and a biography *William Shakespeare* (1963).

ROXBURGH (-buro). Border co. of Scotland. It is mainly upland, and incl. the fringes of the Cheviots. The Tweed enters R. for a few miles in the N., and its tributary the Teviot forms the largest dale of the co. Liddel Water in the S. drains to the Esk. There are numerous ancient remains, incl. Roman stations, the castles of Hermitage and Branxholm, and the monastic ruins at Melrose. Jedburgh is the co. town. R. is primarily a sheep-raising county, and tweed and hosiery are manufactured. Area 666 sq. m.; pop. (1961) 43,171.

ROY, Jamini (1887–). Indian artist. B. in W. Bengal, he was early influenced by European painting, but his later style is based on folk art – colourful, rhythmic, clearly outlined – with traditional themes used in a seemingly naive but instantly appealing manner.

ROYAL ACADEMY OF ARTS. An institution founded in London in 1768 by George III to encourage painting, sculpture, and architecture, the 1st pres. being Sir Joshua Reynolds. In 1771 the academy was granted quarters in Somerset House, but in 1836 it moved to the National Gallery, and in 1867 was granted a lease of Old Burlington House. An annual summer exhibition is held at the academy for the works of contemporary artists. The R.A. Schools give instruction in painting, sculpture, and architecture free of charge.

ROYAL ACADEMY OF DRAMATIC ART. Founded by Herbert Beerbohm Tree in 1904, it is the foremost academy of its kind in Britain. Its headquarters have been in Gower Street, London, since 1905, and a Royal Charter was granted in 1920.

ROYAL ACADEMY OF MUSIC. The senior music school in the British Commonwealth (1822). It provides a full-time complete musical education, holds examinations (open) for the L.R.A.M Diploma and offers scholarships for competition. Admission is by competitive entrance examination.

ROYAL AERONAUTICAL SOCIETY. The oldest aviation body, formed in 1866. Its members discussed and explored the possibilities of flight long before its successful achievement. Among members have been Lord Brabazon, Sir A. Verdon Roe, Sir F. Handley Page, and Sir G. de Havilland.

ROYAL AIR FORCE. *See* AIR FORCE.

ROYAL BALLET. Title under which the Sadler's Wells Ballet (the senior co. estab. at Covent Garden), Sadler's Wells Theatre Ballet (the junior co. at Sadler's Wells), and the Sadler's Wells School (Richmond, Surrey) were incorporated in 1957.

ROYAL COLLEGE OF MUSIC. A London college, opened in 1883, which combines with the Royal Academy of Music for local examinations.

ROYAL HORTICULTURAL SOCIETY. Instituted in 1804 for the improvement of horticulture, it holds a series of flower shows at Vincent Square, London, the great annual show at Chelsea being a social event, and has 300 acres of gardens, orchards and trial grounds at Wisley in Surrey. The Lindley Library is probably the world's finest horticultural collection, and the soc. itself pub. many books.

ROYAL HOUSEHOLD. Name given to those persons who are in the personal service of the sovereign. The chief officers of the R.H. are the Lord Chamberlain, the Lord Steward, and the Master of the Horse. Separate Hs. are maintained by other principal members of the Royal Family.

ROYAL INSTITUTION OF GREAT BRITAIN. An organization for the 'promotion, diffusion, and extension of science and useful knowledge', founded in London in 1799. Faraday and Davy are among distinguished scientists who have used the laboratories.

ROYAL MARINES. *See* MARINES.

ROYAL MILITARY ACADEMY. *See* SANDHURST.

ROYAL OPERA HOUSE. The leading English opera house, in Covent Garden, London. The original theatre was opened in 1732, a second in 1809, and the present one in 1858.

ROYAL SOCIETY. The oldest and premier scientific society of Britain. It originated in 1645 and its charter dates from 1660. The Copley and other medals are awarded periodically, and scientific papers are read at Burlington House, London. The Scottish counterpart is the R.S. of Edinburgh.

ROYAL SOCIETY FOR THE PREVENTION OF CRUELTY TO ANIMALS (R.S.P.C.A.). A society formed in 1824 to improve the conditions under which animals were kept and to abolish the gross cruelties which flourished on all sides. Since then further legislation has been initiated by the R.S.P.C.A. to strengthen the efforts of its inspectors and clinic workers.

ROYAL WARRANT HOLDERS. An association of business firms authorized to display the royal crest, signifying royal patronage by appointment.

ROYAN (rwahyoṅ'). French resort, yachting and fishing port in Charente-Maritime dept., at the mouth of the Gironde, with fine sands. Devastated during the S.W.W., it was subsequently rebuilt in contemporary style under the direction of a group of architects incl. Simon, Ursault, and Gillet and the engineer-designer Sarger. Pop. (1962) 17,232.

ROYAT (rwahyah′). French spa in Puy-de-Dôme dept., 2 m. S.W. of Clermont-Ferrand. Nearly 1,500 ft. above the Tiretaine, it has a fine fortress-church dating from the 10th cent. Its alkaline and arsenical warm springs, used in treating heart conditions, were known to the Romans. Pop. (1962) 4,210.

SIR HENRY ROYCE
Courtesy of Rolls-Royce.

ROYCE, Sir Frederick Henry (1863–1933). British self-styled 'mechanic'. Originally a manufacturer of electric dynamos and cranes, he so impressed C. S. Rolls (q.v.) by the car he built for his own personal use in 1904 that the Rolls-Royce partnership was formed. Suffering in later life from ill-health he designed his most famous car the Phantom II Continental – remarkable for silence, speed and refinement – without ever visiting the factory, but his greatest achievement was the R.-type engine which powered the Schneider Trophy-winning seaplane in 1929 and 1931, and was later developed into the Merlin engine which enabled the R.A.F. Hurricanes and Spitfires to defeat the Luftwaffe in the S.W.W.

ROYCE, Josiah (1855–1916). American philosopher. B. at Grass Valley, California, he became professor of philosophy at Harvard in 1892, and Alford professor in 1914. His writings reveal a deep consideration of human nature and its varied ideals.

RUANDA (rooan′da). Republic in central Africa, part of the former Belgian trust territory of Ruanda-Urundi. It became independent on 1 July 1962, and was admitted to membership of the United Nations on 26 July. R. lies between Tanganyika and Congo Republic (cap. Léopoldville), and produces coffee, cotton, and cattle. Following independence there was bitter conflict between the 2 chief ethnic groups, the Watutsi (the former feudal overlords) and the now predominant Bahutu. It is industrially undeveloped, but has reserves of tin, gold, and wolframite, and under Lake Kivu there is methane gas. Kagera Nat. Park has a wealth of untouched flora and fauna. The cap. is Kigali. Area 10,169 sq. m.; pop. (1968) 3,300,000.

RUANDA-URUNDI (-ooroon′di). Area which before the F.W.W. was part of German E. Africa. It was administered by Belgium under League of Nations mandate from 1920, under U.N. trusteeship from 1946. From 1925 it was linked administratively with the Belgian Congo (Congo Republic). The territory became independent in 1962 in two parts, Ruanda as a republic, and Urundi as the kingdom of Burundi.

RUB‛ AL KHALI (roob-al-kha′lē). Vast sandy desert in S. Arabia. Bertram Thomas was the first European to cross it, 1930–1. The name (Arabic) means empty quarter. Area 250,000 sq. m.

RUBBER. The coagulated latex of a great range of plants, mainly from the New World. Most important is Para R. (so called from its original place of export) which derives from the tree *Hevea brasiliensis*. It was introduced from Brazil to S.E. Asia, where most of the world supply is now produced, the chief exporting countries being Malaya, Indonesia, Ceylon, Cambodia, Siam, Sarawak, and Brunei. At about 7 years the tree, which may grow to 60 ft., is ready for 'tapping', small incisions being made in the trunk and the latex dropped into collecting cups. Other sources of R. are: *Manihot glaziovii*, another Brazilian tree, which supplies Ceara R., and *Koksagyz*, or Russian dandelion, which grows in temperate climates and can yield about 100 lb. of R. per ton of roots. In the 20th cent. world production of R. has increased a hundredfold, and the S.W.W. stimulated the production of synthetic R. to replace the supplies from Malayan sources overrun by the Japanese.

There are an infinite variety of synthetic Rs. adapted to special purposes, but overwhelmingly the most important economically is S.B.R. (styrene-butadene rubber). Cheaper than natural R., it is preferable for some purposes (e.g. car tyre treads, where its higher abrasion-resistance is useful), and is either blended with natural R. or used alone for industrial moulding and extrusions, shoe soles, hosepipes, latex foam, etc.

EDMUND RUBBRA

RUBBRA, Edmund Duncan (1901–   ). British composer. B. at Northampton, he studied under Holst and is a master of contrapuntal writing, cf. his study

RUBBER. Smuggled from Brazil by Sir Henry Wickham (q.v.) some thousands of seeds of *Hevea brasiliensis* were carefully cultivated at Kew and sent out as seedlings to estab. the rubber plantations of the Far East. Malaya, whose plantations date from 1877, is the world's foremost producer of natural rubber, and on the left latex is seen being collected in the traditional way. Preliminary processing produces either sheet or crêpe rubber, and on the right crêpe is seen being machined through heavy rollers, after which the lengths are dried on racks.
Courtesy of Malaya House.

RUBENS. In the house at Antwerp (left), built to his own design, Rubens lived from 1610 to 1644. Restoration was completed in 1946, and it now contains some of the best work of the master and his students, notably Jordaens. The vigorously natural treatment and delicate flesh tints in 'The Virgin and Child with St. Elizabeth and the Child Baptist' are typical.
Courtesy of Belgian National Tourist Office and the Walker Art Gallery

Counterpoint (1960). His compositions incl. 7 symphonies, the opera *Bee-bee-bei*, chamber music, songs, etc.

RUBENS (roobenz), **Peter Paul** (1577–1640). Flemish painter. B. at Siegen, Westphalia, he was taken to Antwerp in 1587, and after studying under Verhaecht, Adam van Noort, and O. van Veen went to Italy in 1600. In 1605 he visited Spain, and at Madrid painted many portraits of the Spanish nobility. He settled in Antwerp in 1609, and became court painter to the Archduke Albert and his wife Isabella. His masterpiece, the 'Descent from the Cross', in the Antwerp cathedral, was painted in 1611–14. In 1620 he went to France at the invitation of Marie de' Medici, and painted a number of pictures commemorating her marriage to Henry IV. In 1628 he again went to Madrid where he met Velasquez. In 1629–30 he was in London as envoy to Charles I, and painted a portrait of the king and his queen, and the 'War and Peace', now in the National Gallery. He is noted as a fine colourist, and excelled in the use of the pencil.

RUBIACEAE (roobi-ā'sē-ē). Large family of plants mainly found in the tropics; its typical genus is *Rubia*, or madder.

RUBICON (roo'bikon). Ancient name of the small river flowing into the Adriatic which, under the Roman republic, marked the boundary between Italy proper and Cisalpine Gaul. When Caesar led his army across it in 49 B.C. he therefore declared war on the republic; hence to 'cross the R.' means to take an irrevocable step. Its identity is not certain, but the Fiumicino is officially recognized as the R.; it rises in the Etruscan Apennines 10 m. W.N.W. of San Marino and enters the Adriatic 10 m. N.W. of Rimini.

RUBIDIUM (Lat. *rubidius*, dark red). Soft white metal of the alkali group which tarnishes instantly in air and ignites spontaneously: symbol Rb, at. wt. 85·48, at. no. 37. Discovered spectroscopically by Bunsen and Kirchoff in the mineral lepidolite, it is slightly radioactive, and is used as a photo-sensitor, having the closest colour response to that of the eye.

RUBINSTEIN, Artur (1888–). Polish pianist, domiciled in U.S.A. He studied in Warsaw and Berlin,

and has appeared with the world's major symphony orchestras.

RUBUS (rōō'bus). Genus of shrubs or herbs, whose white or pink flowers are followed by edible fruits. It includes *R. idaeus*, the raspberry, and *R. fruticosus*, brambles and blackberries.

RUBY. With the emerald (q.v.) probably the most precious of gem stones, of red transparent corundum, crystallizing in the hexagonal system; it is without true cleavage. The true R. is found mainly in Burma, but Rs. have been produced artificially and are widely used in lasers (q.v.).

RUDD or **Red-Eye.** Freshwater fish, *Scardinius erythrophthalmus*, common in lakes and slow rivers of England and N. Europe. Coppery-coloured with red fins and eyes, it reaches a length of 18 in.

RUDOLPH. Name of 2 Holy Roman Emperors. **Rudolph I** (1218–91), originally count of Habsburg, was elected emperor in 1273. He was the first Habsburg emperor, and founded the greatness of his House by investing his sons with the duchies of Austria and Styria. **Rudolph II** (1552–1612) succeeded his father Maximilian II in 1576. His intolerant policy led to unrest in Hungary and Bohemia, which compelled R. to surrender Hungary to his brother Matthias in 1608, and to grant the Bohemians religious freedom.

RUDOLPH (1858–89). Crown Prince of Austria. The only son of the emperor Francis Joseph, he early showed progressive views which brought him into conflict with his father. In 1889 he and his mistress, Marie Vetsera, were found shot in his hunting lodge at Mayerling. The official verdict was suicide.

RUE. A shrubby herb (*Ruta*), of the family Rutaceae, native to S. Europe and temperate Asia. Common R., *R. graveolens*, formerly called Herb of Grace, was much used in medieval medicine.

RUFF. Bird (*Machetes pugnax*) of the snipe family (Scolopacidae). The name is taken from the frill of erectile feathers developed in breeding-time round the neck of the male. The R. no longer breeds in Britain, but is found across N. Europe and Asia, and migrates S. in winter.

RUGBY. English market town (bor.) in Warwickshire, near the Avon, 10 m. S.S.E. of Coventry. It is an important rail junction and has engineering works. R. School, founded in 1567 under the will of Lawrence Sheriff, attained fame during the headmastership, 1828–52, of Thomas Arnold (q.v.); R. football originated at the school. Pop. (1961) 51,651.

RUHR (rōōr). River of Germany, a right-bank tributary of the Rhine. It rises N. of Winterberg and flows N.W. then W. to Arnsberg and Neheim. Entering the R. coalfield about Hagen, it passes near Essen and through Mülheim to join the Rhine at Duisburg-Hamborn. The R. valley is famous as the centre of the German iron and steel industry. Length 142 m. The area was occupied by French and Belgian troops 1923–5 in an unsuccessful attempt to force Germany to pay reparations laid down in the Treaty of Versailles. During the S.W.W. the R. district was severely bombed from the air and was conquered by the Allies 1–18 April 1945, 325,000 German troops being taken prisoner. Allied control of the area came to an end with the setting up of the European Coal and Steel Community in 1952.

RUIZ (rōō-ēth′), **Juan** (*c.* 1283–*c.*1350). Spanish poet, archpriest of Hita. His *Libro de buen amor* has made him the most outstanding of medieval Spanish poets. The work contains parodies, satires, and an autobiography.

RULE OF THE ROAD. In Britain, this states that vehicles should be kept to the left of the road or be liable for any ensuing damage. The reverse procedure applies nearly everywhere else in the world, all traffic keeping to the right. This latter is the rule at sea, and for 2 ships crossing, the one having the other on her starboard must give way.

RUM. A mountainous island of the Inner Hebrides, Inverness-shire, Scotland, 15 m. N. of Ardnamurchan Point. Haskeval is 2,659 ft. high. It was made a nature reserve in 1957. Area, 42 sq. m.

RUM. Spirit fermented and distilled from sugar cane. Scummings from the sugar-pans produce the best R., molasses the lowest grade.

RUMANIA (rōōmä′nia). A republic of S.E. Europe, bounded by Bulgaria, the Black Sea, the U.S.S.R., Hungary, and Yugoslavia.

PHYSICAL FEATURES. R. is traversed from N. to S. by the Carpathians and from E. to W. by the Transylvanian Alps, the 2 ranges forming a great arc separating Transylvania to the N.W. from the plains of Wallachia and Moldavia. The main rivers are the Danube, which reaches the Black Sea through an extensive delta; its tributaries the Prut (which forms the boundary with the U.S.S.R.), Siret, Ialomita, Arges, Olt, and Jiu; and the Mures and Somesul in

RUMANIA. Voronet Church near Suceava, the former capital of Moldavia, has exterior murals nearly five hundred years old.
Courtesy of the Rumanian Embassy.

Transylvania. There are numerous lakes in the vicinity of the lower Danube. The plains of the E. and S. are exposed to great extremes of climate.

ECONOMIC LIFE. Since the S.W.W. industry has rapidly overtaken agriculture in importance, with large-scale electrification; extension of iron and steel manufacture, and of light and heavy industry, aided by R.'s reserves of coal, lignite, manganese, copper, lead and zinc. Oil, formerly exploited only at Ploesti, and natural gas, have been discovered elsewhere, notably gas in Transylvania; and the chemical industry has a large output of fertilizers, synthetic yarns, and plastics. Following sweeping agrarian reforms, cattle, pigs and sheep are increasingly raised; wheat, maize, sunflower, sugar beet, and grapes are important crops; and forests (covering ¼ of the country) supply a large timber industry. There is a road and rail network, and an international airport at Bucharest, and river and maritime transport developed via the Danube and Black Sea, which also support a fishing industry. Tourism is encouraged by the scenery, and rich remains of earlier cultures: resorts incl. Mamaia and the spa Eforie, both on the Black Sea, and winter sports centres such as Sinaia.

AREA AND POPULATION. R. covers 61,700 sq. m.; pop. (1967) 19,287,245 (incl. Hungarian, German, Jewish, Russian, Turkish and other minorities). The main towns are Bucharest (the cap.), Cluj, Iasi, Timisoara, Ploesti, Braila, Galati Oradea, Brasov, Arad and Constanta. Univs. exist at Bucharest, Iasi, Cluj, Timisoara, and Craiova. The majority of the pop. belong to the Rumanian Orthodox Church.

GOVERNMENT. Under the Constitution of 1965 (more liberal than the Soviet model of 1952) the Grand Nat. Assembly is elected for 4 yrs. by workers over 18, and the P.M. and other members of the Council of State are responsible to the assembly: there is a pres.

History. The Romans conquered Dacia, now R., in A.D. 101–7, and introduced colonists (who incl. Ovid); many of these inter-married with the native population. After the withdrawal of the Romans in 275, R. was occupied by the Goths, and during the 6th–12th cents. was overrun by Huns, Bulgars, Slavs, and other invaders. In the 14th cent. the principalities of Wallachia, in the S., and Moldavia, in the E., were founded. Wallachia fell under Turkish suzerainty in the course of the 15th cent., Moldavia early in the 16th. From 1829–56 Turkish suzerainty was exchanged for Russian protection. In 1859 both principalities elected as prince Alexander Cuza who proclaimed their union; he was deposed in 1866, and Prince Charles of Hohenzollern-Sigmaringen elected. After the Russo-Turkish War (1877–8), in which R. sided with Russia, the great powers recognized R.'s independence, and in 1881 Prince Charles assumed the royal title as Carol I.

R. fought against Bulgaria in the 2nd Balkan War (1913) and annexed S. Dobruja. It entered the F.W.W. on the Allied side in 1916, was occupied by the Germans 1917–18, and received Bessarabia and Transylvania under the peace settlement. During the 1930s the pro-Fascist Iron Guard became prominent; to counter them Carol II in 1938 estab. his own dictatorship, but when in 1940 he had to surrender Bessarabia, N. Transylvania, and S. Dobruja to Russia, Hungary, and Bulgaria respectively, the Iron Guard seized power, and forced him to abdicate in favour of his son Michael. R. was occupied by the Germans in 1940, and declared war on Russia in 1941. When the Germans were expelled by the Red Army in 1944 a coalition of left and centre parties took power, and R. declared war on Germany. By the peace treaty of 1947 between R. and the Allies, R. recovered Transylvania; Bessarabia and N. Bukhovina went to Russia, S. Dobruja to Bulgaria. Michael abdicated later that year, and a rep. was estab., of which the Communists rapidly gained control,

Russian occupation forces remained in R. until 1958, but thereafter R. took a more independent attitude, e.g. condemnation of the Soviet invasion of Czechoslovakia, and forged closer trading links with the West, e.g. the 1960 agreement with U.K.

RUMANIAN. One of the Romance languages, it developed from the Popular Latin spoken by the Roman settlers of Dacia, but later was strongly influenced by Slav languages. Only in the 19th cent. was the Cyrillic alphabet abandoned in favour of the Roman. The most important dialect is Daco-R., spoken in Wallachia, Moldavia, Bessarabia, Transylvania, Bukhovina, and the Dobruja; Macedo-R. is spoken in Macedonia, Albania, Thessaly, and Epirus.

Rumanian Literature. It was not until the 16th cent. that Church Slavonic was replaced by R. in the translation of the Gospels (1560) issued by Diakonus Koresi: a complete Bible appeared in 1688. Of the chronicle writers and translators the best is Dmitrie Cantemir (1673–1723). The greater part of the 18th and early 19th cents. was dominated by Greek influences, and was a period of decline. Ion Radulescu (1802–72) brought the new 'romantic' inspiration to R.L., and a new interest in R. folk songs arose. Other writers of the time were Vasile Cârlova (1809–31), the lyric poet; the historical novelist Dimitrie Bolintineanu (1826–73); and the versatile Vasile Alecsandri (1819–90). Typical of the new period following the achievement of national union was the critic Tito Maiorescu (1840–1917), who influenced the greatest R. poet Mihail Eminescu (1850–89). Other popular writers are the dramatist Ion Caragiale (1852–1912); the novelists Carmen Sylva (1843–1916), Duiliu Zamfirescu (1858–1922), and Mihail Sadoveanu; and the poets S. Josif (1877–1913) and P. Cerna (1881–1913).

RUMFORD, Benjamin Thompson, count R. (1753–1814). Scientist and administrator. B. in Mass., he served on the English side in the War of American Independence, and later was an official of the duke of Bavaria, for whom he effected civil and military reforms. He became a count of the Holy Roman Empire in 1791. Returning to England in 1798 he announced his theory that heat is a mode of motion and not a substance, and in 1799 helped found the Royal Institution. From 1804 he lived in France.

RUNCIMAN, Walter, 1st viscount (1870–1949). Liberal politician. The son of the 1st baron R., a prominent shipowner, he entered parliament in 1899, and was President of the Board of Education 1908–11; of Agriculture 1911–14; and of Trade 1914–16. He returned to the Board of Trade in 1931–7, and was Lord President of the Council 1938–9. In 1938 he undertook a mission to Czechoslovakia to persuade the Czechs to make concessions to Germany.

RUNCORN. English river port (U.D.) in Cheshire, on the Mersey, 12 m. S.E. of Liverpool. It is also on the Manchester Ship Canal, and has leather, chemical, and shipbuilding industries. Pop. (1961) 26,035.

RUNDSTEDT (roond'stet), Karl Rudolf Gerd von (1875–1953). German field marshal. He took part in the Polish campaign in 1939, and was largely responsible for the German break-through in France in 1940. Defeated on the Ukrainian front in 1941, he was appointed C.-in-C. in France in 1942. He stubbornly resisted the Allied invasion in 1944 and in Dec. launched a temporarily successful offensive in the Ardennes. He was captured, but in 1949 war-crime charges were dropped owing to his ill-health.

RUNEBERG (roo'neberg), Johan Ludwig (1804–77). Finnish poet who wrote in Swedish. B. at Jakobstad, Finland, his verse romance, Grafven i Perrho (1831), won the gold medal of the Swedish Academy. Although living in Finland he remains the most popular of Swedish poets. His works incl. Nadeschda (1841), the patriotic poems Fänrik Ståls Sägner (1848 and 1860), and the legend cycle King Fjalar.

RUNES. The oldest Germanic script, chiefly adapted from the Lat. alphabet. Rs. were scratched in wood, metal, stone, or bones. The earliest runic inscriptions date from the 3rd cent. and were found in Denmark. Rs. were used in England in Anglo-Saxon times, and the Bewcastle and Ruthwell crosses are among the most notable runic monuments. Several 11th cent. Norse runestones are claimed to have been found in the U.S.A.

RUNNYMEDE. A meadow on the S. bank of the Thames near Egham, Surrey, England, where on 15 June 1215 King John put his seal to Magna Carta. An acre of land at R. was dedicated as memorial to J. F. Kennedy in 1964, in combination with a scholarship scheme for sending students to American univs. Overlooking R., on Cooper's Hill, is a memorial to 20,455 men and women of Commonwealth air forces who died during the S.W.W and have no known grave. A new bridge across the Thames was completed at R. in 1961.

RUNYON, Damon (1884–1946). American writer. B. in Manhattan, Kansas, he was a war correspondent in Mexico and Europe, and a sports and crime reporter in New York. His collection of short stories, Guys and Dolls (1932), was an immediate success, and was followed by others. Dealing with the seamier side of New York life, the stories are told with wry humour in the racy, specialized argot developed by R. for the purpose.

RUPERT, Prince (1619–82). English general and admiral. Son of the Elector Palatine and James I's dau. Elizabeth, he came to England in 1642, to fight for his uncle Charles I, and proved a dashing cavalry leader. Defeated by Cromwell at Marston Moor and Naseby, he commanded a royalist privateering fleet 1649–52 until driven from the seas by Blake. He returned to England in 1660, and distinguished himself as an admiral in the Dutch Wars.

RUPERT'S LAND Name given in honour of Prince Rupert (q.v.), to a large area of N. Canada granted to the Hudson's Bay Company in 1670, sold by the company to the Dominion of Canada in 1869, and subsequently divided between Quebec, Ontario, Manitoba, and the Northwest Territories, when the name disappeared, except as the territorial title of one of Canada's Protestant archbps.

RUPTURE. See HERNIA.

RUSE (roo'se). Bulgarian river port on the right bank of the Danube, cap. of R. prov. It is familiar historically by its Anglicized Turkish name, Rustchuk. The Turks built a great fortress here. R. has an airport and is linked with Giurgiu, Rumania, on the opposite bank of the Danube by a railway and road bridge opened in 1954. Pop. (1965) 128,400.

RUSH. Genus of plants (Juncus) in the family Juncaceae (q.v.), found in wet places in cold and temperate regions. The common R. has hollow stems which have been used for mat-making and basket work since ancient times.

RUSK, Dean (1909–   ). American statesman. B. in Georgia, the s. of a post-office worker, he was ed. at Davidson College, N. Carolina, and the univs. of Oxford and Berlin. During the S.W.W. he fought in the U.S. Army in the Burma-China area and became Deputy Chief of Staff of U.S. Forces. After the war he was Sec. of State for U.N. affairs until 1950 when, as Asst. Sec. of State for Far Eastern Affairs, he played a prominent part in dealing with the Korean War problems. In 1952 he became Pres. of the Rockefeller (q.v.) Foundation and 1961–8, as a Democrat, was Sec. of State.

RUSKIN, John (1819–1900). British writer. B. in London, only child of a prosperous wine-merchant, he was able to travel widely and was ed. at Oxford. The first vol. of his Modern Painters appeared in 1843. Many works followed, incl. The Seven Lamps of Architecture (1849) in which he stated his philosophy of art, and *The Stones of Venice* (1851–3). His writings hastened the appreciation of unorthodox painters such as Turner and the Pre-Raphaelites. In 1848 he m. Euphemia Chalmers Gray, but the marriage proved a failure; 6 years later Mrs. R. secured a decree of nullity and later m. Millais. The 5th and final vol. of *Modern Painters* appeared in 1860, and the remaining years of R.'s life were devoted to social and economic problems, in which he adopted a radical outlook. To this period belong a huge series of lectures, pamphlets, *Unto this Last* (1862), *Sesame and Lilies* (1865), *The Crown of Wild Olive* (1866), etc. From 1869 to 1879 R. was Slade prof. of Art at Oxford, and he made a number of social experiments, such as 'St. George's Guild', to which he contributed £7,000, for the establishment of an industry on socialist lines. His last years were spent at Brantwood, Coniston.

JOHN RUSKIN. Chalk drawing by George Richmond. *Photo: N.P.G.*

Ruskin College was founded in Oxford in 1899 by an American, Walter Vrooman, to provide education in the social sciences for working men. It is supported by contributions from trade unions, etc.

RUSSELL, Bertrand Arthur William, 3rd earl (1872–1970). Brit. philosopher and mathematician. B. at Trelleck, the grandson of the 1st earl, he was ed. at Trinity College, Cambridge, where he specialized in mathematics and became a lecturer. R.'s pacifist attitude in the F.W.W. lost him the lectureship, and he served 6 months' imprisonment for an article he wrote in a pacifist journal. His *Introduction to Mathematical Philosophy* (1919), was written in prison. After visits to U.S.S.R. and China, he went to U.S.A. in 1938 and taught at many univs. He later returned to England, and is a fellow of Trinity College, Cambridge. Among his most important works are *Principles of Mathematics* (1903); *Principia Mathematica* (1910: with A. Whitehead); *Problems of Philosophy* (1911); *Principles of Social Reconstruction* (1917); *Marriage and Morals* (1929); *An Enquiry into Meaning and Truth* (1940); *History of Western Philosophy* (1946), and *New Hopes for a Changing World* (1951). He succeeded his brother in the earldom in 1931, and was awarded the O.M. in 1949 and the Nobel literary prize for 1950. From 1949 he advocated nuclear disarmament, and until 1963 was on the Committee of 100, a militant branch of the Campaign for Nuclear Disarmament.

RUSSELL, Charles Taze. *See* JEHOVAH'S WITNESSES.

RUSSELL, Countess. *See* ARNIM, Countess von.

RUSSELL, George William (1867–1935). Irish poet and essayist. Editor of *The Irish Homestead* 1904–23, and *The Irish Statesman* 1923–30, he was an ardent nationalist and agricultural organizer. He helped found the Irish national theatre, and his poetry, pub. under the pseudonym 'AE', incl. *Gods of War* (1915) and reflects his interest in mysticism and theosophy.

RUSSELL, John, 1st earl (1792–1878). British Liberal statesman, known as Lord John Russell. The son of the 6th duke of Bedford, he entered the Commons in 1813, and supported Catholic Emancipation and the Reform Bill. He was Paymaster-General 1830–4, Home Sec. 1835–9, Colonial Sec. 1839–41, and P.M. 1846–52. He entered Aberdeen's cabinet as For. Sec. in 1852, and was Colonial Sec. in 1855. In Palmerston's 2nd govt. of 1859–65 he was For. Sec. and gave valuable assistance to Italy's struggle for unity, although his policies on Poland, Denmark and the American Civil War provoked much criticism. He succeeded Palmerston as P.M. in 1865, but on the defeat of his Reform Bill in 1866 retired. He received an earldom in 1861.

RUSSELL, John Peter (1858–1931). Australian artist. B. in Sydney, he met Tom Roberts (q.v.) in 1881 on the voyage to England, and became a member of the French post-impressionist group. His portrait of Van Gogh is in the Stedelijk Museum, Amsterdam.

RUSSELL, Lord William (1639–83). British Whig statesman. The son of the 1st duke of Bedford he was among the founders of the Whig Party, and actively supported the Exclusion Bill in parliament. He was accused of complicity in the Rye House Plot, on dubious evidence, in 1683, and executed.

RUSSELL, Sir William Howard (1821–1907). British journalist. B. in Ireland, he acted as *The Times* correspondent during the Crimean War, and created a sensation by his exposure of the mismanagement of the campaign. He was knighted in 1895.

RUSSELL OF KILLOWEN, Charles, 1st baron (1832–1900). Lord Chief Justice of England. B. in Ireland, he was called to the Bar in 1859 and became a Liberal M.P. in 1880. He was Attorney-General in 1886 and 1892–4. In 1887 he appeared for Parnell before the commission investigating *The Times* allegations against the Irish leader, and in 1893 he represented Britain before the Behring Sea Commission. He was raised to the peerage in 1894 and in the same year appointed Lord Chief Justice.

RUSSELL OF LIVERPOOL, Edward Frederick Langley Russell, 2nd baron (.895–   ). British barrister. As Deputy Judge Advocate-General B.A.O.R. 1946–7 and 1948–51, he was responsible for all war-crime trials in the British Zone of Germany 1946–50, and has pub. *The Scourge of the Swastika* (1954), *The Trial of Adolf Eichmann* (1962), etc.

RUSSIA. Historic name for the European territories of the Union of Soviet Socialist Republics. *See* SOVIET UNION.

RUSSIAN. A member of the Slavonic branch of the Indo-European family of languages. It represents the eastern group of Slavonic, and incl. Great Russian, the general literary idiom; Little R. or Ukrainian; and White R., centring round Vilna, Minsk, Vitebsk, and Smolensk.

RUSSIAN ART. From the 10th cent., when Russia was organized as an independent state, until the time of Peter the Great, Russian architecture and painting followed

RUSSIAN ART. 'London – Beer is Good for You', an example of modern style by decorative artist Oscar Yitsakevitch Rabin (1930–   ). *Courtesy of the Grosvenor Gallery.*

the Byzantine style, and was dominated by the Greek Orthodox Church. Sculpture did not flourish because it was not allowed in churches. The Russians, however, displayed good taste in the art of icon-painting, for which they are famous, and the greatest master of this art was Andrea Rublyov (1370–1430). In the 17th cent. Peter the Great introduced western ideals into Russia, and foreign architects were employed to build his new cap. of

St. Petersburg. For 2 cents. the art of Russia reflected tendencies in Italy, France, Germany, and England. In the Soviet Union art has been enlisted in the service of the State. Extreme forms of modern art are not encouraged, though they were in the early days of the Soviet régime, when the Russians sought to free art from all traditional slavery, and replaced the Imperial Academy by a Free College of Art.

RUSSIAN HISTORY. The southern steppes of R. were originally inhabited by nomadic peoples, and the northern forests by Slavonic tribes, who slowly spread southward. Viking chieftains in the 9th–10th cents. estab. their own rule in Novgorod, Kiev, and other cities, and in the 10th–12th Kiev temporarily united the Russian tribes into an empire. Christianity was introduced from Constantinople in 988. In the 13th cent. the Mongols (the Golden Horde) overran the southern steppes, compelling the Russian princes to pay tribute, while in the 14th Byelorussia and the Ukraine came under Polish rule. Ivan III, prince of Moscow (1462–1505), threw off the Mongol yoke, and united the N.W., while Ivan IV (1547–84) assumed the title of tsar and conquered Kazan and Astrakhan. During his reign the colonization of Siberia began, and by 1700 it had reached the Pacific. A period of anarchy succeeded Ivan's death, until the first Romanov tsar was elected in 1613. Following a Cossack revolt, the E. Ukraine was reunited with R. in 1667.

Peter I (1682–1725) modernized the administration and army, founded a navy, introduced western education, and wrested the Baltic seaboard from Sweden. Catherine II (1762–96) annexed the Crimea and part of Poland, and recovered the W. Ukraine and White Russia. Russia intervened in the Revolutionary and Napoleonic Wars (1798–1801, 1805–7), and after repelling Napoleon's invasion took part in his overthrow (1812–14). During the 19th cent. revolutionary ideas steadily spread, in spite of harsh repression. A rapid development of industry followed the abolition of serfdom (1861); a working-class movement developed, and in 1898 the Social Democratic Party was founded. A revolution in 1905, although suppressed, compelled the tsar to accept a parliament with limited powers. Abroad, Russian attempts to dominate the Balkans led to wars with Turkey in 1827–9, 1853–6, and 1877–8, and provoked the hostility of Britain, France, and Austria. Russian expansion in central Asia also aroused British suspicions, while in the Far East the treaties of Aigun (1858) and Peking (1860) were imposed on China, annexing territories N. of the Amur and E. of the Ussuri rivers, and the occupation of Manchuria resulted in war with Japan in 1904–5. Russo-German rivalries in the Balkans nevertheless brought Russia into an alliance with France (1895) and Britain (1907), and were a main cause of the F.W.W. in 1914.

A revolution in March 1917 estab. a republic, but the provisional govt.'s failure to make peace rallied popular support to the Bolsheviks, led by Lenin, who in Nov. seized power. Peace was concluded with Germany at Brest-Litovsk in March, 1918. During 1918–21 British, French, U.S., and Japanese forces invaded Russia, while 'White' armies carried on civil war; Poland, Lithuania, Latvia, Estonia, and Finland became independent, Rumania occupied Bessarabia, and Poland seized the W. Ukraine and White Russia. A federal constitution was adopted in 1923. The 'war communism' policy was replaced in 1921 by the 'New Economic Policy' (N.E.P.) of tolerating some private business. Inner party controversies followed Lenin's death, ending with the adoption of Stalin's policy of 'Socialism in one country' and the inauguration of the 1st 5-year plan. During 1928–39 heavy and light industries were developed, and agriculture collectivized.

From 1933 Russia put forward a policy of collective resistance to aggression. In 1939 she concluded a

ALEXEI KOSYGIN
Photo: Novosti Press Agency.

non-aggression pact with Germany, and after the German conquest of Poland reoccupied the W. Ukraine and White Russia. There was a short Russo-Finnish War in 1939–40. During 1940 Bessarabia, Lithuania, Latvia and Estonia entered the Soviet Union. For events 1941–5, *see* SECOND WORLD WAR.

Russia was startled by the Hungarian Revolution of 1956 into savage repression that antagonized the West and embittered relations with Yugoslavia until 1961, but on becoming P.M., in 1958, Khrushchev extended his de-Stalinization campaign, begun in 1956. His policy of 'peaceful co-existence in competition with capitalism' led to the Sino-Soviet ideological rift, which from 1960 worsened, with Russian opposition to China's Cultural Revolution and bloodshed on the frontier (notably on the Ussuri, q.v.) accompanied by demands for revision of the Aigun/Peking treaties. Relations with the West remained uneasy, e.g. the Cuban crisis of 1962, but the nuclear test-ban agreement of 1963 marked some amelioration. At home there were splendid achievements in space research (q.v.), and improvement in supplies of consumer goods. Khrushchev's fall in 1964 marked a return to Cold War attitudes under Brezhnev and Kosygin (qq.v.). The naked military expediency of the invasion of Czechoslovakia in 1968 was strongly condemned even by many Communist parties abroad, Soviet ideological leadership being particularly assailed by the Italian party, and emergent Africa alienated.

RUSSIAN LITERATURE. The earliest productions of R.L. are the sermons and chronicles and the unique prose poem 'Tale of the Armament of Igor', belonging to the period in 11th and 12th cents. when the centre of literary culture was Kiev. By the close of the 14th cent. leadership had passed to Moscow, which was completely divorced from developments in the West until the 18th century: most noteworthy in this period are the political letters of Ivan the Terrible, the religious writings of the priest Avvakum (1620–81), who was the first to use vernacular Slavonic in literature, and the traditional oral folk-poems dealing with legendary and historical heroes which were collected in the 18th and 19th cents. Modern Russian literature begins with Mikhail Lomonosov (c. 1711–65), who fused

RUSSIA. In the heart of one of the world's loveliest holiday regions, Sochi on the Black Sea.   *Photo: Novosti Press Agency.*

elements of the elaborate Church Slavonic with colloquial Russian to create an effective written medium. Greatest of these earlier writers, working directly under French influence, were the fabulist Ivan Krylov (1768–1844) and the historian Nikolai Karamzin (1765–1826). Poetry reached its greatest height with Alexander Pushkin, and the tempestuously Byronic Mikhail Lermontov, while prose was dominated by Nikolai Gogol. Typical of the intellectual unrest of the mid-19th cent. is the prose writer Alexander Herzen, but to this generation also belong the great realist novelists Ivan Turgenev, Ivan Goncharov, Fyodor Dostoievsky, and Leo Tolstoy. Among their followers are the humorous Nikolai Leskov (1831–95), the morbid Vsevolod Garshin (1855–88), and Vladimir Korolenko (1853–1921), and in drama the isolated genius of Anton Chekhov. Rising from the pervading pessimism of the '80s came Maxim Gorky, and his followers Alexander Kuprin and Ivan Bunin; in contrast are the depressingly negative Leonid Andreyev and Mikhail Artsybashev. To the more mystic school of thought belong the novelist Dmitri Merezhkovsky and the poet philosopher Vladimir Soloviev, who moulded the thought of the greatest of the Symbolist poets, Alexander Blok.

Many writers left the country at the Revolution, but in the 1920s two groups emerged – the militantly Socialist L.E.F. led by the Futurist Mayakovsky (q.v.) and the fellow-travellers of N.E.P. incl. Pilnyak, Pasternak, Alexei Tolstoy, and Ehrenburg (qq.v.). Literary standards sank to a very low ebb during the first 5-year plan 1928–32, when facts were compulsorily falsified to present a rosy view of contemporary life in the effort to fortify Socialism, but the novelist Sholokhov and poets O. E. Mandelshtam Anna Akhmatova (1888–1966) and Nikolai Tikhonov (1896–) were notable. More freedom was allowed by the subsequent Realism, e.g. Simonov (q.v.) and the work of the poet Tvardovsky (1910–71) during the S.W.W. Censorship closed down again from 1946 until the thaw after Stalin's death, when the work of Dudintsev illustrates the new atmosphere of liberty, but political considerations still affect the official attitude to literature, e.g. the incident of Pasternak's Nobel prize and the public disclaimers made by such a writer as Yevtushenko. The situation deteriorated further from the mid-1960s, e.g. the imprisonment in 1966 of novelists Andrei Sinyavsky (1926–) and Yuli Daniel (1926–) for smuggling their works abroad for publication, and the request in 1969 of Anatoly Kuznetsov (1929–) to settle in Britain after attacks on his novel *The Fire* (1969), which obliquely criticized the regime. Beloved by all Russians, partly perhaps because so apart from politics, is the nonsens verse of Kornei Chukovsky. *See* SOLZHENITSYN.

RUSSIAN SOVIET FEDERAL SOCIALIST REPUBLIC (R.S.F.S.R.). A constituent republic of the U.S.S.R. It is by far the largest of the Soviet states, and reaches from the Gulf of Finland to the Pacific and from the Arctic to the Black and Caspian Seas. Its area accounts for about three-quarters of that of the U.S.S.R. Most of its surface is occupied by the great plain of E. Europe and Siberia. In Europe the Black Earth district to the S. and S.E. of Moscow is famed for its rich soil and is of great agricultural importance. Farther N. extensive forests provide the main economic resource of the area, though there are extensive mineral deposits, espec. in the Urals. The Volga rises in the Valdai Hills between Leningrad and Moscow, and later flows through a steppe-like area which incl. many manufacturing centres. Farther S., in the Kuban and the foothills of the Caucasus, is a warm temperate region of great fertility. The Caucasus rise to heights of over 16,000 ft.; the Urals, which form the geographical boundary between Europe and Asia and seldom exceed 5,000 ft., are the nucleus of a region of immense mineral wealth and industrial

RUSSIAN SOVIET FEDERAL SOCIALIST REPUBLIC

	Area in sq. m.	Pop. in 1,000s	Capital
Autonomous Soviet Socialist Republics			
Bashkir	55,400	3,757	Ufa
*Buriat	135,600	780	Ulan Ude
Chechen-Ingush	7,350	1,033	Grozny
Chuvash	7,100	1,192	Cheboksary
Daghestan	19,400	1,361	Makhachkala
Kabardino-Balkar	4,800	530	Nalchik
Kalmuck	29,300	248	Elista
Karelian	66,500	707	Petrozavodsk
Komi	160,500	974	Syktyvkar
Mari	8,900	653	Yoshkar-Ola
Mordvinian	10,100	1,010	Saransk
N. Ossetian	3,100	518	Dzaudzhikau
Tatar	26.200	3,127	Kazan
*Tuva	65,800	217	Kyzyl
Udmurt	16,200	1,379	Izhevsk
*Yakut	1,197,800	646	Yakutsk
Autonomous Regions			
Adyge	1,700	366	Maikop
Karachai-Cherkess	5,440	330	Cherkesk
Gorno-Altai	35,700	169	Gorno-Altaisk
*Jewish	13,900	174	Birobidjan
*Khakass	24,000	462	Abakan
National Districts			
*Aga-Buriat	9,400	34	Aginskoye
*Chukchi	274,500	23	Anadyr
*Evenki	285,900	28	Tura
*Khanty-Mansi	215,500	124	Khanty-Mansiisk
Komi-Permyak	12,000	226	Kudymkar
*Koryak	151,700	23	Palana
Nenets	67,300	34	Naryan-Mar
*Taimyr	316 700	28	Dudinka
*Ust-Orda Buriat	135.700	680	Ust-Ordynsky
*Yamal-Nenets	258,800	45	Salekhard
R.S.F.S.R.	2,968,800	107,667	Moscow
	6,591,090	127,300	

* In Asia

activity. The Siberian portion of the R.S.F.S.R. has been much developed since the Revolution, especially during the S.W.W. and after, and has become of exceptional industrial importance. Agriculture and stock raising thrive in the S. half of the region; to the N. of this are forests, although the area under cultivation is extending every year; the far N. lies within the Arctic Circle. In the far east forestry, fishing and trapping are carried on; in the peninsula of Kamchatka fishing, and in the S. some agriculture. The Altai, Abakan, Tannu, Baikal, Yablonoi, Kolyma, and Anadyr ranges are the loftiest in Asiatic R.S.F.S.R. The main rivers are, in Europe: the Don, Volga, Moskva (or Moscow), N. Dvina, and Pechora; in Asia: the Ural, Kama, Ob, Tobol, Irtish, Yenisei, Angara, Lena (famous for its goldfields), and Amur. A number of the rivers, in both Europe and Asia, have been harnessed for irrigation and power. The Gulf of Finland is linked by river and canal with the White Sea and the Volga and Don rivers.

The largest towns incl. Moscow, the cap. (cap. also of the U.S.S.R.), Kaliningrad, Leningrad, Gorki, Rostov-on-Don, Volgograd, Sverdlovsk, Novosibirsk, Kazan, Kuibyshev, Saratov, Voronezh, Yaroslavl, Ivanovo, Archangel, Omsk, Chelyabinsk, Tula, Perm, Astrakhan, Ufa, and Irkutsk.

POLITICAL STRUCTURE. The R.S.F.S.R. proper is made up of 6 territories and 49 regions; within it also are the A.S.S.Rs., autonomous regions, and national dists. shown in the table.

Govt. is by the presidium of the elected Supreme Soviet; the pres. of the presidium is pres. also of the R.S.F.S.R.; there is also a council of ministers and a political bureau of the central committee of a Communist Party.

AREA AND POPULATION. The R.S.F.S.R. covers 6,570,400 sq. m.; pop. at the census of 1959 was 117,500,000; (1967 est.) 127,300,000, the great majority Russians but incl. Tartars, Mordovians, Chuvashis, Bashkirs, Poles, Chechens, and others. In spite of strong official discouragement of religion, a number of Russians still profess the Russian Orthodox faith, and there are many Moslems in N. Caucasia and parts of Asia. The Jewish pop., considerable before the S.W.W., was much reduced during the German occupation of W. European Russia.

EDUCATION. This is free and compulsory from 7 to 15 or 16, and in large towns up to 17. Of the many univs. those of Moscow, Leningrad, Odessa, Gorki, and Sverdlovsk are notable; there are also numerous institutes of higher technical and scientific instruction.

HISTORY. The All-Russian Congress of Soviets was set up by a coup d'état of the Bolsheviks on 7 Nov. 1917 (25 Oct. O.S. – hence the 'October Revolution'), and a govt. consisting of a council of people's commissars was formed, led by Lenin. In elections held later in Nov. the Bolsheviks were defeated – only 215 Bolsheviks and supporters were returned out of 707 deputies; but the Bolsheviks knew their own minds and early in 1918 they dispersed the constituent assembly, made peace with Germany, and proceeded, in the face of famine, civil war, and foreign attack, to estab. a strong Communist govt. With the agreement for the formation of the U.S.S.R., reached in 1922, ratified 1924, the history of the R.S.F.S.R. becomes part of that of the U.S.S.R. *See* SOVIET UNION.

RUSSO-JAPANESE WAR. This struggle was brought about by Russian penetration in Manchuria, culminating in the lease of Port Arthur in 1896, and the occupation of the Amur prov. in 1900. In 1904 diplomatic relations were broken off by the Japanese, who then without warning attacked the Russian fleet at Port Arthur. The outstanding events of the subsequent fighting were the siege and surrender of the Russian garrison in Port Arthur (May 1904–Jan. 1905) and the destruction of the Russian Baltic fleet in the Tsushima Straits (May 1905). Peace was concluded at Portsmouth, U.S.A., in 1905. Russian rights in Port Arthur passed to Japan, together with the Manchurian railway; Korea became a Japanese sphere of influence, and Sakhalin was divided between Russia and Japan.

RUST. Common name for the minute parasitic plants of the order Uredineae, which appear on the leaves of their hosts as orange-red spots, later becoming darker, when they are known as mildew. The best-known is the Wheat R. (*Puccinia graminis*).

RUST. Reddish deposit formed on iron by the action of water, oxygen, and 'impurities', i.e. carbon dioxide in the air, or carbon, sulphur, etc., in the metal. The impurity forms a conducting solution with the water; causing an electrolytic effect by which salts of iron are formed and then decomposed by the oxygen. Oil painting provides protection.

RUTH, George Herman 1895–1948). American

BABE RUTH. In the uniform of the New York Yankees.
Courtesy of The U.S. National Baseball Hall of Fame.

baseball player, known as 'Babe' R. B. at Baltimore, he joined the Boston Braves in 1914, becoming one of the best left-hand pitchers of all time, and in 1920 was sold to the N.Y. Yankees. He returned to Boston in 1934 but left the team the same year. A baseball 'idol', he played in 10 world series and made 714 home runs (60 in one season in 1927).

RUTH. Character of the O.T. whose story is told in the Book of R. The daughter-in-law of Naomi, she m. Boaz, and became the ancestress of David.

RUTHÉNIA. Region in central Europe, home of the Ruthenes or Russniaks. Before the F.W.W. it was within Austria-Hungary. After the dual monarchy split up in 1918, part of R. was incl. in Czechoslovakia (as the autonomous prov. of R.), part in Poland, part in Rumania. All 3 were ceded to Russia after the S.W.W., Czech and Polish R. in 1945, Rumanian R. in 1947, and were incorporated in the Ukrainian S.S.R.; Czech R. (sometimes called Transcarpathian R.) became Zakarpatskay (= transcarpathian) region, cap. Uzhgorod. The Ruthenian (Uniat) Church, to which most Ruthenes belonged, was suppressed in Russian Poland in 1873; abolished in 1948.

RUTHÉNIUM. Metallic element discovered in 1843 in platinum ore. Its symbol is Ru, atomic no. 44, atomic weight 101·1.

RUTHERFORD, Ernest, 1st baron (1871–1937). N. Zealand physicist. He was prof. at Montreal 1898–1907, at Manchester 1907–19, and at Cambridge 1919–37, where he was also director of the Cavendish Laboratory. He was awarded the Nobel prize in 1908 and knighted in 1914, and became a fellow of Trinity College, Cambridge, in 1919. In 1925 he received the O.M., and became pres. of the Royal Society, of which he had been a fellow since 1903, and in 1931 was created Baron R. of Nelson, N.Z. A pioneer of modern atomic science, his main researches were in the field of radioactivity, and he was the first to recognize the nuclear nature of the atom.

RUTHERFORD, Dame Margaret (1892–1972). Brit. actress. Specializing in formidable yet jovially eccentric females, she incl. among her best roles Mme Arcati (1941) in *Blithe Spirit,* Miss Prism (1939) and Lady Bracknell (1947) in *The Importance of Being Earnest,* and was at home on stage or screen.

RUTHERFORD, Mark. Pen-name of British novelist William Hale White (1831–1913). B. at Bedford, he was ed. for the Congregationalist ministry, which he abandoned for conscientious reasons. His spiritual struggle is described in *The Autobiography of M.R.* (1881) and *M.R.'s Deliverance* (1885). His novels incl. *Catherine Furze* (1893).

RUTILE (rōōt'il). Mineral, a native form of titanium dioxide, TiO_2. Formerly of little economic value, it is now greatly sought after for producing white pigments used to give brilliant whiteness to paint, paper, and plastics, and for making titanium (q.v.). The sands of Australia's E. and W. coasts are a major world source.

RUTLAND. The smallest county of England, lying between Leicestershire and Northants. The centre is occupied by the Vale of Catmose, and elsewhere low hills are found. The Welland, which marks the S.E. boundary of the county, is the main river. Part of the area is under grass and sheep and cattle are raised, and barley, wheat, oats, and root crops are cultivated. Stilton cheese is made. Oakham is the co. town, and Uppingham is known for its school. Plans put forward in 1960 for the abolition of R. as a separate co. were strongly opposed by its inhabitants. Area 152 sq. m.; pop. (1967) 29,110.

RUWENZORI (roo-). Mountain mass near the equator in central Africa; it is 65 m. long and upwards of 30 m. wide. The highest peak is Marghanita (16,763 ft.) in the Stanley group. R. was discovered by Stanley in his 1887–9 journey of exploration. The name means cloud king.

SAGAN (sahgaṅ'), **Françoise** (1935–). French novelist, author of femininely psychological studies of love relationships incl. *Bonjour Tristesse* (1954). *Aimez-vous Brahms?* (1959). She has also ventured into ballet (*Le Rendezvous manqué*) and the drama (*Château en Suède*).

SAGE. Perennial herb (*Salvia officinalis*). The grey-green aromatic leaves are used in cookery as a seasoning: 2–4 ft. high, it has blue flowers.

SĀ'GO. The starchy material obtained from the pith of the S. palm, which forms a nutritious food, and is used for manufacturing glucose.

SAHARA (sahah'rah). The largest desert in the world, covering 3½ million sq. m. of N. Africa, from the Atlantic to the Nile. Small tracts are below sea-level, but the Tibesti mountains rise to over 11,000 ft. Oases of natural springs from underground reservoirs punctuate and determine the beaten tracks. It covers the south of Morocco, Algeria, Tunisia, and Libya, W. Egypt, much of Mauritania, Mali, Niger, and Chad, and part of W. Sudan Republic. Discovery in the 1950s in the Algerian S. of considerable reserves of petroleum and natural gas greatly altered the economic aspect of the S. and its nomadic people.

SAHARA. 'The Great Martian God', a painting 18 ft. high.
Courtesy of Henri Lhote.

In prehistoric times the S. was fertile, supporting rich animal and human life as illustrated by the rock paintings of the Tassili-n-Ajjer in the central S. discovered (1956) and recorded by Henri Lhote, pupil of the Abbé Breuil, in *The Tassili Frescoes*.

SAIDA. *See* SIDON.

SAIGON (sīgon'). Cap. of S. Vietnam, on the S. river 34 m. from the sea. An important port and commercial centre, its industries incl. shipbuilding, textiles, rice, sugar, soap and rubber. There is a univ. With its mainly Chinese twin city of Cholon it has a pop. (1966) of 2,000,000. The *Battle of S.* 29 Jan.–23 Feb. 1968 involved the expulsion of 5,000 infiltrating Viet Cong by S. Vietnamese and U.S. forces.

SAINT. A man or woman eminent for piety, usually one who has been canonized by the Catholic Church. The lives of many thousands of Ss. have been collected by the Bollandists, and the number is added to by the process of canonization (q.v.). A new Calendar of Ss.' days was approved by Paul VI from 1970: among those excluded as probably never existing were Ss. Barbara, Catherine, Christopher and Ursula; Ss. George, Januarius, Nicholas (Santa Claus) and Vitus were among those listed only for optional veneration; and among new Ss. for obligatory veneration were St. Thomas More and the Uganda martyrs.

ST. ALBANS. English city (bor.) and seat of a bishopric in Herts, 20 m. N.W. of London; it grew up round an abbey founded by King Offa II in 793 in honour of St. Alban (q.v.). Near by are remains of the Roman city of Verulamium on Watling St. The battle of St. A. in 1455 opened the Wars of the Roses. Pop. (1961) 50,276.

ST. ANDREWS. Royal burgh and univ. town on the Fifeshire coast of Scotland, 12 m. S.E. of Dundee. Ruins exist of the 12th cent. cathedral and 13th cent. castle. The city is the headquarters of golf and of the Royal and Ancient Club, founded in 1754. The univ., founded in 1411, is the oldest in Scotland. Pop. (1961) 9,888.

ST. ASAPH (az'af). Cathedral city of Flintshire, N. Wales, on the Elwy, 5 m. S.S.E. of Rhyl. The

ST. AUGUSTINE. The Castillo de San Marcos, outpost of the vast Spanish empire in the New World, was built 1672–96. The walls are 30 ft. high and up to 12 ft. thick, and it successfully withstood a 50-day siege by James Moore, Governor of S. Carolina, in 1702 and another in 1740 by James Oglethorpe, founder of Georgia. It was used as a prison in the 19th century, and it was from here that Wildcat led an escape in 1837 during the Seminole War.
Courtesy of Castillo de San Marcos National Monument.

cathedral dates from the 14th cent. Its Welsh name is Llanelwy. Pop. (est.) 1,800.

ST. AUGUSTINE. City in Florida, U.S.A., 37 m. S.S.E. of Jacksonville. A port and a holiday resort, it is the oldest town in the U.S.A., having been founded in 1565 by Pedro Menendez de Aviles near the site of Juan Ponce de Leon's landing place (1513). Drake burned it in 1586, Capt. John Davis burned it in 1665. It was ceded to the U.S.A., in 1821. St. A. incl. the oldest house (probably late 16th cent.) and the oldest masonry fort (1672) in the U.S.A. Pop. (1960) 14,734.

ST. AU'STELL. English market town (U.D.) in Cornwall, 14 m. N.E. of Truro, the centre of the china clay area which supplies the Staffordshire potteries. Pop. (1961) 25,027.

ST. BARTHOLOMEW, Massacre of. *See* BARTHOLOMEW.

ST. BERNARD. Name of 2 passes in the Alps. (1) Great St. B. Pass (8,110 ft.) is situated in the Pennine Alps between Piedmont, Italy, and Valais, Switzerland. Near the crest is the famous hospice founded in the 10th cent. for pilgrims. A road usable by pack-horses crossed it by A.D. 69; Napoleon I marched across the pass into Italy in 1800. A road tunnel 3·6 m. long under the Great St. B. was opened 1964. (2) Little St. B. Pass (7,179 ft.) crosses the Graian Alps, between Piedmont and Savoie, France. Hannibal is said to have invaded Italy by this route.

ST. BERNARD DOG. Large mastiff named after the monks of St. Bernard, who kept them for finding lost travellers and to act as guides. They are squarely built, with pendulous ears and lips and large feet.

ST. CHRISTOPHER. Another name for St. Kitts. *See under* LEEWARD ISLANDS.

ST. CLOUD (saṅ klōō'). Town 2 m. W. of Paris on the Seine. The 17th cent. palace was the favourite residence of Napoleon, and he here m. Marie Louise: it was destroyed during the Siege of Paris in 1870. Within the beautiful park is the nat. Sèvres porcelain factory. Pop. (1962) 26,746.

ST. CYR (saṅ sēr). The military coll., founded by Napoleon in 1808 at the village of St. Cyr, nr. Versailles, was destroyed by bombing from the air during the S.W.W.; it was transferred to Coëtquidon in Morbihan dept. in 1946.

ST. DAVID'S. Cathedral city in Pemb., S. Wales. The cathedral, founded by St. David, the patron saint of Wales, was rebuilt between 1180 and 1522. It is the largest church in Wales. Pop. (est.) 1,580.

ST. DENIS. Town in Seine–St. Denis dept., France, 4 m. N. of Paris. The abbey church, founded in 626, is Gothic and contains the tombs of many of the kings of France. Abelard was a monk in the abbey of St. D. Pop. (1962) 95,072.

ST. DUNSTAN'S. Welfare organization, founded in 1915 by Sir Arthur Pearson, for British servicemen blinded through the F.W.W. or subsequent military operations. It is dependent upon voluntary aid, and trains men in occupations, besides providing pensions and allowances.

SAINTE-BEUVE (san-böv'), **Charles Augustin** (1804–69). French critic. B. at Boulogne-sur-Mer, he contributed to the *Revue des deux mondes* from 1831. In 1840 he was appointed a keeper of the Mazarin library, and was elected to the French Academy in 1844. His chief work was *L'Histoire de Port Royal* (1840–8); his *Causeries du lundi* are masterpieces of criticism.

ST. ETIENNE (sant-atyen'). Cap. town of the Loire dept., France. It has an important silk industry; coal and iron-ore are mined, and there are heavy manufactures. Pop. (1968) 213,468.

SAINT-EXUPERY (sant-äksüperē'), **Antoine de** (1900–44). French airman and author. He served in the S.W.W. with the French Air Force, and disappeared on a mission over France from Corsica. His works incl. the autobiographical *Vol de Nuit*, and *Lettre à un Otage*.

ST. GALL. Cap. of St. G. canton, Switzerland. It grew up about a Benedictine abbey built round a cell inhabited by an Irish hermit, Gall, 614–640, and was famous as a centre of learning in the 8th–10th cents. The library of its ancient abbey is renowned for early MSS. Pop. (1966) 78,000.

SAINT-GAUDENS, Augustus (1848–1907). American sculptor. B. in Dublin, Ireland, he was taken to America when a child. His principal works incl. statues of Lincoln (Chicago), and R. L. Stevenson (Edinburgh).

ST. GERMAIN-EN-LAYE (san-zherman'-on-lā). Town 13 m. W. of Paris, France. Pop. (1962) 37,391. The Treaty of St. G. (1919) concluded the war between Austria and the Allies. Representatives of the U.S.A. (an associated power) signed it, but after the Senate failed to ratify the Treaty of Versailles, the Treaty of St. G. was not submitted to it. The U.S.A. made a separate peace with Austria in 1921.

ST. GOTTHARD PASS. A famous road and rail route from N. Europe to Italy, connecting the lakes Lucerne and Maggiore. The hospice on the pass (6,929 ft.) dates from 1331. The rail tunnel (1872–82) rises to 3,786 ft. and is 9¼ m. long; a road tunnel at an average height of 3,760 ft. was begun 1970.

ST. HELE'NA. An is. in the S. Atlantic, 1,200 m. W. of Africa. It became a British possession in 1673. Napoleon d. in exile there in 1821; his body was taken to France in 1840. The cap. is Jamestown. Area 47 sq. m.; pop. (1966) 4,650. Ascension and Tristan da Cunha are dependencies.

ST. HELENS. English industrial town (co. bor.) in Lancs, 12 m. N.E. of Liverpool, connected to the Mersey by canal. It is the chief English centre of crown, plate, and sheet glass manufacture. Pop. (1961) 108,348.

ST. HELIER (hel'yer). Seaside resort and cap. of Jersey, Channel Islands. The Jersey legislature sits in the *salle des états* here. Pop. (est.) 28,000.

ST. IVES. (1) English fishing port and holiday resort (bor.) with an artists' colony, in Cornwall, on St. I. Bay. It took its name from an Irish princess called Ia (5th cent.). Pop. (1961) 9,337. (2) English market town (bor.) in Hunts on the Ouse, 5 m. E. of Huntingdon. Cromwell lived at St. I. 1631–6; it took its name from a 6th cent. missionary. Pop. (1961) 15,361.

ST. JAMES'S PALACE. Situated in Pall Mall,

London, this was a royal residence from 1698 to 1837, and royal levées are still held there. Foreign ambassadors are accredited to the Court of St. James's.

SAINT JOHN. Largest city of New Brunswick, Canada, on the St. J. r. It is an important fishing centre and port for an agricultural and lumbering area. Founded by the French as Saint-Jean in 1635, it was taken by the British in 1758. Pop. (1966) 90,000.

ST. JOHN OF JERUSALEM, Knights Hospitallers of. An Order of Christian chivalry named after the hospital founded at Jerusalem about 1048 for the benefit of pilgrims. In 1291, the knights were forced to leave Palestine, and went first to Cyprus and then to Rhodes, when secular matters, military and economic, were added to their activities. From 1530 they were estab. at Malta until their virtual dissolution in 1798. The Order still continues in Rome. A Protestant English offshoot, chartered in 1888, works mainly through the St. John Ambulance Association (instruction in first-aid, etc.), and Brigade (hospital work and first aid), whose numbers in 1962 were 150,900 adults and 98,000 cadets.

ST. JOHN'S. Cap. city and chief port of Newfoundland, on the E. coast, in the peninsula of Avalon. Its main industries depend on the whale, seal, and cod fisheries. Sir Humphrey Gilbert founded St. J. in 1582. Pop. (1966) 100,851.

SAINT-JUST (san-zhüst), **Louis Antoine Léon Florelle de** (1767–94). French revolutionary. A close associate of Robespierre, he became a member of the Committee of Public Safety in 1793, and was guillotined with Robespierre.

ST. KILDA. Group of small islands 50 m. W. of Harris and westernmost of the Outer Hebrides, Scotland. The last 35 inhabitants were moved to the mainland in 1930, but in 1957 a missile tracking station was established here in connection with the S. Uist rocket range; the same year, under the will of the 5th Marquess of Bute (1907–56), St. K. was acquired by the National Trust for Scotland, under whose auspices summer working parties visit the is.

ST. KITTS. *See under* LEEWARD ISLANDS.

ST. LAURENT (lōron'), **Louis Stephen** (1882–). Canadian Liberal politician. Called to the Quebec Bar in 1905, he became Min. of Justice in 1941, took over the additional post of For. Min. in 1946, and was P.M. from 1948 to his defeat in 1957, when he was succeeded in the party leadership in 1958 by Lester Pearson.

ST. LAWRENCE. River of N. America which, with the Great Lakes at its head, forms one of the world's great river highways. Leaving Lake Ontario, it marks the U.S.A.-Canadian frontier for nearly 100 m.; the rest of its course to the Gulf of St. L. lies in Canada. Montreal is built on a large island near the confluence of the Ottawa r. The St. L. is ice-bound for 5 months of the year. Length *c.* 650 m. The St. L. Seaway, 135 m. long, constructed 1954–9, made it possible for sea-going ships to reach the ports on the Great Lakes; it also added immensely to the hydroelectric capacity of the r. The cost of the works, est. at $600 million, was met as to two-thirds by Canada one-third by the U.S.A. It was formally opened by Elizabeth II and Pres. Eisenhower 26 June 1959, but the first ships – *c.* 40 – had passed up it behind the Canadian govt. ice-breaker *D'Iberville* on 25 April.

ST. LEGER (le'jer). One of the 5 classic British horse races. It was instituted by Colonel St. Leger in 1776, and is run at Doncaster in Sept. The distance is 1¾ m. 132 yds.

ST. LEONARDS. *See* HASTINGS.

ST. LÔ (san loh). Cap. of Manche dept., France, on the Vire. An important agricultural and road centre, it was destroyed 10–18 July 1944, when U.S. forces captured it from the Germans in the S.W.W. The

MONT ST.-MICHEL. From its dangerous quicksands Earl Harold rescued two Norman soldiers, as the future William the Conqueror watched, and in 1091 the future Henry I was besieged here by his brothers Robert and William Rufus. *Courtesy of French National Tourist Office.*

name comes from a bishop of Coutances who built a church on the site. Pop. (1962) 16,072.

ST. LOUIS (loo′-is). Chief city and river port of Missouri, U.S.A., on the Mississippi about 10 m. below its confluence with the Missouri. Founded as a trading post by the French in 1764, it passed to the U.S.A. in 1803 by the Louisiana Purchase, and has many important industries. The 630 ft. Gateway Arch (1965) is a memorial by Saarinen to the pioneers of the W. Industries incl. cars, steel, aerospace equipment, electrical goods, shoes, brewing and food processing. Pop. met. area (1970) 2,331,371.

ST. LUCIA (loo′sha). One of the Windward Islands, West Indies. Discovered by Columbus 1502, settled by the French 1635, it became British 1803 and an assoc. state of the U.K. 1967. It produces bananas and other fruits, lime juice, sugar, coconuts. Castries is the cap. Area 233 sq. m.; pop. (1966) 110,142.

ST. MALO (san mahlō′). Seaport in the Ille-et-Vilaine dept., W. France, on the Rance estuary. The town is noted as a tourist resort. It took its name from a Welshman who was bishop there in the 6th cent. Pop. (1962) 17,800.

ST. MICHAEL AND ST. GEORGE. A British order of knighthood founded in 1818, and usually awarded for services rendered in the British Commonwealth countries overseas. The 3 grades are: Knight Grand Cross (G.C.M.G.), Knight Commander (K.C.M.G.), and Companion (C.M.G.).

ST. MICHAEL'S MOUNT. Is. in Mount's Bay, Cornwall, connected at low tide by a causeway to the mainland. A castle stands on the summit. It was presented by Lord St. Levan to the National Trust in 1954. Area 21 acres. Also, Mont St.-Michel (q.v.), off the N.W. coast of France, illus. above.

ST. MORITZ. Village and winter-sports centre in Grisons canton, Switzerland, on the St. M. lake. The Cresta Run dates from 1885. Pop. (est.) 2,500.

ST. NAZAIRE (san nahzār′). Seaport in Loire-Atlantique dept., France, at the mouth of the Loire on the Bay of Biscay. Used as a submarine base by the Germans during the S.W.W., it suffered heavily from air raids; it was the scene of a British Commando raid, 28 March 1942, in which 212 out of 353 taking part were lost (killed or missing). Pop. (1968) 63,289.

ST. OMER (sant-ōmār′). A town in Pas-de-Calais dept., France, on the Aa, 26 m. S.E. of Calais. From 1914–16 the British G.H.Q. was located at St. O. Pop. (1962) 20,911.

ST. PAUL. Cap. city of Minnesota, U.S.A., on the Mississippi adjoining Minneapolis. A road, rail

and air centre, its industries incl. electronics, publishing and printing, petrochemicals, cosmetics, and meat-packing. Pop. (1960) 313,411.

ST. PAUL'S CATHEDRAL. The cathedral church of the City of London, and the largest Protestant church in England. A Saxon church on the site was replaced by a Norman by 1240, which was destroyed by the Great Fire in 1666. The present building was designed by Wren and built 1675–1710. Its length is 513 ft. Interior features are the whispering gallery, the Wellington monument, and the tombs of Wellington and Nelson in the crypt.

ST. PETER PORT. The chief town and port of Guernsey, Channel Is. Victor Hugo lived here 1855–70. Pop. (1961) 15,706.

ST. PETERSBURG. *See* LENINGRAD.

ST. PETERSBURG. Coast town of Florida, U.S.A. Nicknamed Sunshine City, it is a flourishing resort, and mushroomed industrially with the development of space industry in the 1950s. Pop. (1960) 181,298.

SAINT-PIERRE (san-pyar′), **Jacques Henri Bernardin de** (1737–1814). French writer. He is best known for his romantic *Paul et Virginie* (1789).

ST. PIERRE. Group of small barren is. off S.W. Newfoundland. Cod-fishing and cod-salting, drying, and canning are the main occupations. Area 10 sq. m.; pop. (1967) 4,614. With Miquelon (q.v.) it forms an overseas territory of France.

ST. QUENTIN (san kontan′). Town in Aisne dept., N. France, on the Somme 21 m. S. of Cambrai. The Prussians defeated the French in 1871 at St. Q. which suffered badly during the F.W.W. Pop. (1962) 62,579.

SAINT-SAËNS (san-sahns′), **Camille** (1835–1921). French composer. B. in Paris, he studied at the Conservatoire and under Gounod, and in 1857 became organist at the Madeleine. He achieved success as a pianist, and estab. his reputation as a composer with the 4 symphonic poems *Le Rouet d'Omphale, La Danse Macabre, Phaéton,* and *La Jeunesse d'Hercule.* Among his other works are 3 symphonies, 5 piano concertos, and the opera *Samson et Dalila.*

SAINTSBURY, George Edward Bateman (1845–1933). British man of letters. B. at Southampton, he was prof. of rhetoric and English literature at Edinburgh, 1895–1915. He wrote *A Short History of English Literature* (1898), *The English Novel* (1913), etc.

SAINT-SIMON (san-sēmon′), **Claude Henri**, comte de (1760–1825). French Socialist. B. in Paris, he fought in the American War of Independence, and was imprisoned during the French Revolution. He wrote prolifically, e.g. *Du système industriel* (1821) and *Nouveau christianisme* (1825), advocating a state of society ruled by technicians and industrialists.

ST. SIMON, Louis de Rouvroy, duc de (1675–1755). French writer. B. in Paris, he served with the Household Corps, and in his *Mémoires* (1691–1723) gives an acute portrayal of the French court.

ST. VINCENT. *See* JERVIS, JOHN.

ST. VINCENT. One of the Windward Is., West Indies. It became a British possession in 1783 and, after some internal disagreements, became an assoc. state of the U.K. 1969. The cap. is Kingstown. Bananas, arrowroot, copra, sugar, rum, spices are produced. Area 150 sq. m.; pop. (1966) 87,000.

ST. VITUS' DANCE. Chorea; a disease of the nervous system associated with rheumatic fever. The chief symptoms are involuntary movements of the face and limbs, sometimes so violent as to interfere with sleep and feeding.

SAKE (sak′ā). Japanese rice-wine; yellowish-tinted, with 15% alcohol content, it is drunk hot.

SAKI. Pseudonym of British author Hugh Hector Munro (1870–1916). B. in Burma, where he served an unhappy year with the Military Police, he became a journalist, was foreign correspondent to the *Morning Post* 1902–8, and was killed in action on the Western

Front. He produced a number of ingeniously witty short stories set in the Edwardian fashionable world and the brilliant novel *The Unbearable Bassington* (1912), with its playboy hero Comus Bassington.

SAKHALI'N. Island in the N. Pacific, 600 m. long from N.–S. Two parallel mountain ranges, rising to over 5,000 ft., extend throughout its length. The N. is much colder than the S., where dairy farming is carried on and leguminous crops, oats, barley, sugar beet, etc. are grown, with rice and wheat in the central valley. Fishing is very important. S. also produces timber, petroleum in the N.E., coal in the W. centre. Area 29,000 sq. m.; pop. (est.) 500,000, incl. aboriginal Ainus and Gilyaks.

A Russian explorer Poyarkov visited S. in 1644 and subsequently it was colonized by Russians and Japanese. South S. was in 1875 ceded by Japan to Russia, which used the is. as a political convict settlement. Japan regained S.S. in 1905, but again ceded it to Russia in 1945. In 1947 the isl. together with the Kuriles (q.v.) was formed into the S. region of the R.S.F.S.R., cap. Yuzhno-Sakhalinsk (Jap. Toyohara).

SAKKA'RA. A village of Egypt, 10 m. S. of Cairo, with 20 pyramids of which the oldest (3rd dynasty) is the 'Step Pyramid' designed by Imhotep (q.v.), whose own tomb here was the nucleus of the Aesklepieion, a famed centre of healing in the ancient world.

SA'LADIN or **Sala-ud-din** (1138–93). Sultan of Egypt. He entered the service of the atabeg of Mosul, on whose behalf he conquered Egypt in 1164–74, and after his death was proclaimed sultan in 1175. He conquered Syria in 1174–87, and in 1187 recovered Jerusalem from the Christians. The 3rd Crusade followed, led by Richard I of England, but it failed to capture Jerusalem, and in 1192 S. and Richard made peace.

SALAMA'NCA. Cap. of S. prov., W. Spain, on the Tormes, 160 m. N.W. of Madrid. It has a univ. (founded *c.* 1230) and a 12th cent. cruciform cathedral. Pop. (1965) 105,780. Wellington's most important victory against the French in the Peninsular campaign was won here on 22 July 1812.

SPOTTED SALAMANDER

SALAMANDER. Genus of old-world amphibians. Best-known is the spotted or fire S. (*Salamandra maculosa*), black with bright yellow markings: the old legend that Ss. are unharmed by fire, or even extinguish it, is unfounded. Among the related species of America is the Axolotl (q.v.).

SA'LAMIS. Greek is. in the Gulf of Aegina. It was the scene in 480 B.C. of a naval battle in which the Persians were defeated by the Greeks. The town of S., on the W. coast, is a modern naval station. Area of is. 39 sq. m.; pop. (est.) 18,000.

SAL AMMO'NIAC. Another name for ammonium chloride (NH₄Cl). It occurs in mineral form as a white sublimation round the crater of a volcano and may be prepared synthetically. Its chief use is in 'dry-cell' batteries.

SALAZAR (-thahr'), **Antonio de Oliveira** (1889–1970). Portuguese dictator. He was P.M. 1932–68, exercising a virtual dictatorship. A corporative constitution on the Italian model was introduced in 1933, and until 1945 S.'s National Union, which he founded in 1930, remained the only legal party. S. was also For. Min. 1936–47, and during the S.W.W. maintained Portuguese neutrality. He was incapacitated 1968 by a cerebral stroke.

SA'LEM. City of Mass., U.S.A., 15 m. N.E. of Boston. It is an important manufacturing centre. Dating from 1626, in 1692 it was the scene of famous

SALEM. Cursed by Hawthorne's great-grandfather, a judge at the witchcraft trials, the House of Seven Gables (built in 1668) was used by the novelist as the setting for his great romance. *Courtesy of House of Seven Gables.*

witchcraft trials. Roger Williams (q.v.) was pastor here 1631 until expelled 1636. Hawthorne was b. at S. Pop. (1960) 39,211.

Another SALEM, in Oregon, U.S.A., was settled *c.* 1840, made state cap. 1860. It is a lumbering and fruit-packing centre, and has flourmills and woollen textile factories. Pop. (1960) 49,142.

SALE'RNO. Seaport of Campania, Italy, cap. of S. prov., 30 m. S.E. of Naples. Founded by the Romans *c.* 194 B.C., S. was destroyed by Charlemagne, and sacked by the Emperor Henry VI in 1194. Both its school of medicine and its univ. (1150–1817, revived 1944) were famous in medieval times. On 9 Sept. 1943, the Allies made an important landing in the Gulf of S. To the S.E. are the ruins of Paestum (q.v.). Pop. (1961) 118,171.

SALFORD. English city (co. bor.) in Lancs., on the Irwell, adjoining Manchester. It forms part of the port of Manchester and the ship canal's largest docks are in S. Textiles and chemicals are manufactured and coal is mined. S. was given a charter in 1231, created a city 1926. Salford Univ. (1966) was founded 1896 as the Royal Tech. Inst. Pop. (1961) 154,963.

SALICY'LIC ACID (Orthohydroxybenzoic acid, HO.C₆H₄.COOH). White solid, crystallizing into prismatic needles at 159°C. It is used as an antiseptic, in food preparation, dyestuffs and in the preparation of aspirin.

SALINGER (sǎl'injer), **J(erome) D(avid)** (1919–   ). American writer. B. in New York he contributed to

SALERNO. The temples of Paestum form the greatest surviving gallery of Doric architecture. Largest of them – 79 ft. wide and 196 ft. long – and finely preserved, is the temple, originally dedicated to Hera *c.* 450 B.C., but later known as the temple of Poseidon. *Courtesy of the Italian Cultural Institute.*

SALISBURY. Sketch in oils by Constable of the cathedral from the river meadows.
Courtesy of the National Gallery.

the *New Yorker* and estab. his reputation with the novel *The Catcher in the Rye* (1951), which was followed by a vol. of short stories, and *Franny & Zooey* which deals in 2 stories with members of the Jewish Glass family already introduced in earlier work. His key characters are often children and his adults psychologically complex.

SALISBURY, Robert Arthur Talbot Gascoyne-Cecil, 3rd marquess of (1830–1903). British cons. statesman. B. at Hatfield, he entered the Commons in 1853, and succeeded to the title in 1868. He was Indian Sec. 1866–7 and 1874–8; and as For. Sec. 1878–80 took part in the Congress of Berlin. As P.M. 1885–6, 1886–92, and 1895–1902 he gave his main attention to foreign policy and for most of the time was For. Sec. His son, **James Edward Hubert Gascoyne-Cecil,** 4th marquess (1861–1947) entered the Commons in 1885, and was Lord Privy Seal 1903–5 and Pres. of the B. of T. 1905–6. After the F.W.W. he was Pres. of the Council 1922–4 and Lord Privy Seal 1924–9. The latter's son **Robert Arthur James Gascoyne-Cecil,** 5th marquess (1893–1972) sat in the Commons 1929–41, when he was created Baron Cecil. He was Dominions Sec. 1940–2 and 1943–5, Colonial Sec. 1942, and Lord Privy Seal 1942–3 and 1951–2, and Lord Pres. of the Council 1952–7.

SALISBURY, Robert Cecil, 1st earl of. *See* CECIL, ROBERT.

SALISBURY. English cathedral city, co. town of Wilts, on the Avon, 84 m. S.W. of London. The cathedral of St. Mary, built 1220–66, is one of the finest specimens of Early English architecture; its decorated spire (404 ft.) is the highest in England. S. grew up round the cathedral and has many old and interesting buildings. It makes beer, hardware, carpets, etc., and is an agricultural centre. Another name for it is New Sarum, Sarum being a medieval Latin corruption of the ancient Romano-British name Sorbiodonum. Old Sarum, on a 300 ft. hill to the N., was deserted when New Sarum was founded in 1220, but was later again inhabited; it was brought within the city boundary in 1953. Pop. (1961) 35,471.

SALISBURY. Capital of Rhodesia, on the Mashonaland plateau nearly 5,000 ft. above sea-level. It is the centre of a rich farming area (tobacco and maize) with tobacco and other manufactures, and is a hub of communications. In 1953 a multiracial univ. was founded on a site overlooking the city. An international airport called New Sarum lies 7 m. from the city. The British occupied the site in 1890 and named it Fort S. in honour of Lord Salisbury, then P.M. of the U.K. It was made a city 1935, and was cap. of the Fed. of Rhodesia and Nyasaland 1953–63. Pop. (1967) 358,000, incl. 91,000 Europeans.

SALISBURY PLAIN. A 300 sq. m. area of open downs in Wiltshire, England, between Salisbury and Devizes. For many years it has been a military training area. It rises to 770 ft. in Westbury Down, and incl. Stonehenge (q.v.).

SALK, Jonas Edward (1914–). American physician. B. and ed. in New York, he in 1963 became director of the S. Institute for Biological Studies, California. A specialist in poliomyelitis (q.v.), he developed the S. vaccine in 1954.

SA'LLUST, or **Gaius Sallustius Crispus** (86–34 B.C.). Roman historian. He had an active political career as a supporter of Caesar, and his histories of Catiline's conspiracy and the Jugurthine War are written in a condensed and epigrammatic style.

SALMON. Genus of food-fishes in the family Salmonidae. The normal colour is silvery, blue-grey above with a few dark spots, but the colour changes at the spawning season. S. spawn up rivers in fresh water where the eggs hatch, but most of their life is spent in the sea. The spawning season is between Sept. and Jan., although they occasionally spawn at other times. The orange-coloured eggs are about ¼ in. in diameter, are laid on the river bed, fertilized by the male, and then covered with gravel by the female. The incubation period is from 5 weeks to 5 months. On hatching from the egg the young fish are known as *alevins*, and when they begin feeding they are called *parr*. At about 2 years old the coat becomes silvery, and the young parr are then *smolts*. When the young fish return to the river to spawn between 3 and 3½ years of age they are *grilse*.

SALO'NIKA. Form often used in English for THESSALONIKA.

SALT. Sodium chloride (NaCl), found in sea water, as rock salt, in brine deposits, etc. In chemistry, salts are compounds comprised of an acid and a base united in definite proportions, e.g. hydrochloric acid and caustic soda unite to form the salt sodium chloride, and water.

SALTCOATS. A burgh, holiday resort, and fishing port of Ayrshire, Scotland, on the Firth of Clyde, 25 m. S.W. of Glasgow. It was a centre of the salt industry 1600–1800. Pop. (1961) 14,187.

SALT LAKE CITY. Cap. of Utah, U.S.A., and H.Q. of the Mormons (q.v.), on the Jordan, 11 m. S.E. of the Great Salt Lake. In 1847 Brigham Young laid out the city as a Mormon settlement, and the great granite temple was built 1853–93. To the W. is a vast open pit copper mine and the city has smelters and refineries, meat-packing and printing plants, and salt and oil refineries. Pop. (1960) 189,454.

SALUKI (saloo'ki). Breed of dog, also called the Gazelle Hound, descended from the hound of the Bedouins of the African deserts. As bred today it resembles the greyhound, is from 24–28 in. high, and coloured fawn, cream, or white.

SALVADO'R. Seaport in Brazil, cap. of Bahia state. Founded in 1510, it was cap. of Brazil 1549–1763. It is the seat of an archbishopric and of a univ. (1946), and is also a naval base. Pop. (1960) 655,735.

SALVADO'R, EL. The smallest and most thickly populated Central American republic, bounded by Guatemala on the W., Honduras on the N., and the Pacific on the S. Inland from a narrow coast plain is a high, fertile plateau, with active volcanoes. El S. lies within the Tropics, but alt. moderates temps. over a large part of the country. Coffee, cotton, sugar and sisal are grown, and there are sugar refineries and textile factories. About one third of El S. is forested.

Chief towns are the cap. San Salvador and Santa Ana; on the coast are the ports of La Union, La Libertad and Acajutla. The constitution of 1950 provided for the election by universal suffrage of a pres. for 6 years with a single chamber legislative assembly elected for 2 years. El S., part of the Central American Federation from 1821, became independent in 1839. The prevailing religion is R.C. Educ. is in theory free and compulsory, but more than half the pop. over 10 is illiterate. The language is Spanish and the people are of Spanish-Indian extraction, few pure-bred Indians surviving. Area 8,260 sq. m., pop. (1966) 3,036,500.

There is long-standing tension between El S. and Honduras, many Salvadoreans having emigrated to their less densely populated neighbour. In 1969, following defeat of H. by El S. in a soccer match, open warfare with heavy casualties lasted some weeks.

SALVAGE. Saving for re-use, either as a whole or in part, of any property threatened with destruction, especially important at sea and against fire. Also the compensation payable to those who by voluntary effort have saved a ship and/or its cargo and passengers from complete loss through shipwreck, fire, or enemy action: in the U.K. this comes under the jurisdiction of the Admiralty Division of the High Court.

The fire insurance companies of Britain maintain S. Corps in London, Liverpool, and Glasgow which co-operate with the fire-fighting services in the salvaging of goods, etc., threatened by fire. The London S. Corps dates from 1866, before which date firefighting also was organized by fire insurance companies for those insured by them.

SALVARSAN. An organic compound; the first specific anti-bacterial agent, discovered by Paul Ehrlich in 1909; chemical formula $C_{12}H_{12}N_2O_2As_2 \cdot 2Hcc2H_2O$ 3, 3′-diamino 4, 4′-dihydroxy-arseno-benzene dihydrochloride. Because of its destructive effect on *Spirochaeta pallida*, it was widely used in the treatment of syphilis, prior to the development of antibiotics (q.v.). Another name for it is 606, referring to the number of experiments performed by Ehrlich in its discovery.

SALVATION ARMY. Christian evangelical, social service, and social reform organization, originally British but later worldwide. It began with revivalist services in a tent in Whitechapel, London, in 1865 conducted by William Booth who, with his wife and other helpers, formed the Christian Revival Association, renamed the East London Christian Mission, extended to cover all London in 1870. Booth used the expression 'salvation army' in a leaflet pub. in 1878, and it was soon accepted as the name of the body, which adopted military titles for its officials, and called its weekly journal the *War Cry*. The organization is now world-wide.

SAL VOLATILE (volat′ilē). A mixture of ammonium carbonate, bicarbonate and carbamate; smelling salts. It is a strong reflex stimulant, and is of value in restoring consciousness after a fainting attack or narcotic poisoning.

SALZBURG (sahlts′-boorg). City in Austria, cap.

SALZBURG. The Getriedegasse and the still narrower passages running from it take the visitor straight back to the Middle Ages. At its end the early-gothic Blasiuskirche can be glimpsed, and above rise the massive ramparts built by Santino Solari in the days of Prince-Archbishop Paris Lodron.
Courtesy of Austrian State Tourist Department.

of S. prov. on the Salzach, seat of an archbishopric founded *c.* 700. There is a 17th cent. cathedral. As Mozart's birthplace, S. is the scene of an annual music festival. Pop. (1961) 106,892. The prov. of S. contains some beautiful mountain scenery and lakes. Pop. (1961) 345,713.

SAMA′RA. Name until 1935 of KUIBYSHEV.

SAMA′RIA. Cap. of the kingdom of Israel during the 10th–8th cents. B.C., renamed Sebaste by Herod the Great. Excavations by Harvard Univ., 1908–10, and a joint Anglo-U.S. expedition, 1931–5, revealed extensive remains.

SAMA′RITANS. The descendants of the colonists settled by the Assyrians in Samaria, after the destruction of the Israelite kingdom in 722 B.C. They adopted Judaism, but rejected all sacred books except the Pentateuch, and regarded their temple on Mt. Gerizim, not that at Jerusalem, as God's true sanctuary; hence much ill-feeling existed between Ss. and Jews. A very small community still exists at Nablus.

SAMARITANS, The. Voluntary organization to help those tempted to suicide or despair, founded in 1953 at St. Stephen's Church, Walbrook, London, by the Rector, Chad Varah (1911–), and subsequently extended throughout Britain and overseas. The S. consist of groups of trained lay people, each directed by a professional (usually a clergyman) in consultation with psychiatrists, psychotherapists and doctors. They offer friendship and counselling to 'clients' who may use their emergency telephone numbers by day or night.

SAMA′RIUM. A rare earth element, symbol Sm, at. no. 62, at. wt. 150·35. It is a hard, grey, brittle metal, found in cerite, samarskite, and gadolinite, and is slightly radioactive.

SAMARKA′ND. City of the Uzbek S.S.R., U.S.S.R., cap. of S. region, nr. the r. Zerafshan, 135 m. E. of Bukhara. From 1369 it was the cap. of the empire of Tamerlaine (Timur) whose mausoleum and summer palace still exist, and it was then ruled by the Chinese and the emirs of Bukhara before the Russians occupied it in 1868. It remained a centre of Moslem culture until the Revolution. Cotton-ginning and silk manufacture are carried on. Pop. (1967) 240,000.

SAMA′RRA. Ancient town in Iraq, on the Tigris, 65 m. N.N.W. of Baghdad. Founded in 836 by the Abbasid Caliph Motassim, it was the Abbasid cap. until 876, and is a place of pilgrimage for Shiah Moslems. A barrage built at S. 1951–5 controls the water of the Tigris and prevents the former annual flooding of Baghdad.

SAMO′A. Group of volcanic islands in the S.W. Pacific, *c.* 500 m. N.N.E. of Fiji. They are in 2 groups. (1) the rep. of S. to the W. which incl. Savaii and Upolu. The cap. is Apia, on Upolu. Copra, bananas, and cocoa are exported. The people are Christians. The islands were German before the F.W.W., after it under New Zealand League of Nations mandate, then U.N. trusteeship. It was given independence 1 Jan. 1962, and was treated as a continuing member of the Commonwealth until admitted to full membership 1970. Area 1,133 sq. m.; pop. (1961) 113,567, of whom 101,288 were Samoans.

(2) U.S. Samoa to the E., incl. Tutuila, Tau, and (200 m. N.N.W. of Samoa) Swain's Island. It was acquired by the U.S.A. in 1899 by agreement with Britain and Germany. Pago Pago on Tutuila is the cap. Area 76 sq. m.; pop. (1960) 20,040, of U.S. nationality.

SĂ′MOS. Greek island in the Aegean Sea, lying *c.* 1 m. off the W. coast of Asiatic Turkey. Mountainous but fertile, S. produces wine, olive oil, etc. Vathi is the cap., and Teganion is on the site of the ancient city of S. destroyed by Darius. Area 180 sq. m.; pop. (1961) 52,034.

SA'MOYED. Arctic breed of dog, similar to a chow, but with more pointed face and a white coat.

SAMPHIRE (sam'fir). Perennial plant (*Crithmum maritimum*) found on sea cliffs of Europe. The aromatic leaves are fleshy and sharply pointed; the flowers grow in yellow-green umbels. It is used in salads, etc.

SAMSON. A hero of the ancient Hebrews, one of the 'judges' who ruled Israel in Palestine before the establishment of the monarchy. His story is told in the O.T. book of Judges.

SA'MUEL. The last of the 'judges' who ruled the Israelites before the establishment of the Hebrew kingdom in Palestine, and the first of the line of prophets. His story is told in the first book of the O.T. that bears his name; this, and 2 Sam., cover the reigns of Saul and David.

SAMUEL, Herbert Louis, 1st visct. (1870–1963). British Liberal statesman. Son of a Liverpool banker, he became High Commissioner of Palestine 1920–5 and was the 1st Jew to govern the Holy Land for c. 2,000 years. He suggested the formation of the National Govt. set up in 1931, but resigned as a Free Trader in 1932, leading the Liberal Opposition until 1935. Created a visct. in 1937, he was awarded the O.M. in 1958.

SAMUELSON, Paul (1915–). American economist. He became prof. at the Massachusetts Inst. of Technology in 1940, and was awarded a Nobel prize 1970 for his application of scientific analysis to theory. His books incl. *Economics* (1948) and *Linear Programming and Economic Analysis* (1958).

SAN'A (sahnah'). Cap. of Yemen, S.W. Arabia, 200 m. N. of Aden. A walled city, it has a fine mosque Pop. about 50,000.

SAN ANDREAS FAULT. Vertical break in the Earth's surface 20 m. deep and 600 m. long: Los Angeles rests on the W. half (moving N.W.) and San Francisco on the E. half (moving S.E.): in 50 million yrs. the two will meet. Meanwhile built-up pressure causes earthquakes.

SAN ANTONIO. Town of S. Texas, U.S.A., a commercial and financial centre. Industries incl. aircraft maintenance, oil refining, and meat packing, and the U.S. Air Force has a base and School of Aerospace Medicine here. The city grew up around the Alamo (q.v.). Pop. met. area (1970) 863,669.

SANCTIONS. In international law, measures used to enforce the fulfilment of treaty obligations. The Covenant of the League of Nations provided for the use of the economic boycott against aggressors, but attempts to apply it against Italy during the Abyssinian War of 1935–6 proved ineffective. The U.N. Charter similarly provides for the application of economic and military S.

SAND (sond), **George.** Pseudonym of French authoress Armandine Lucile Aurore Dupin (1804–76), adopted from the name of Jules Sandeau, one of her early companions in Paris. She m. in 1822 Casimir Dudevant, but separated from him after 9 years and henceforth lived in Paris as a writer. Among her early liaisons were those with Alfred de Musset and Chopin. From 1848 she lived at the château of Nohant. Her novels reflect her own marital and intellectual experiences, and incl. *Valentine* (1832), *Consuelo* (1842), *Le Péché de M. Antoine* (1847), and *La Mare au diable* (1846). She also pub. *Histoire de ma vie, Elle et lui* (which describes her love affair with de Musset) and 'Letters'.

SAND. The accumulation of fine-grained fragmentary mineral matter chiefly composed of quartz grains (impure silica SiO_2). It is derived from the rocks of the land surfaces, and is especially characteristic of shallow water and land deposits, to which it is carried by running water, wind or ice. The origin of the grains may be detected by their shape, e.g. sand deposited by running water has a sub-angular nature, while wind-blown Ss. are well-rounded. Ss. are classi-

fied into marine, freshwater glacial. and terrestrial.

SANDBURG, Carl August (1878–1967). American poet. B. in Illinois, he served an apprenticeship to realism as farm labourer, bricklayer, etc., and the open, factual construction of his poetry bears its lasting impress from *Chicago Poems* (1916) onward to *Complete Poems* (1950). He wrote an interesting autobiography *Always the Young Stranger* (1953).

SANDHURST. Small English town in Berks., lying c. 4½ m. S.S.E. of Wokingham. In the vicinity are the Royal Military Academy (for which S. is often used as a synonym) and Wellington Coll., a public school.

SAN DIEGO (dē-ā'gō). City of California, U.S.A., near the Mexican border. It has a fine natural harbour exporting the produce of Imperial Valley. It has fish canneries and a notable zoo, and is an important military and naval base with large aircraft missile plants. Pop. (1970) 675,788.

SAND PAINTING 'Water Chant' shows the 4 water monsters. In the centre are water and moisture clouds, with four holy plants radiating from the circular pool of water. Rainbow Girl surrounds and protects the painting. *Courtesy of the Museum of Navajo Ceremonial Art, Santa Fé, N.M.*

SAND PAINTING. A picture made by preparing an adhesive ground on which coloured sands are laid. In Japan, from at least the 18th cent., natural and artificially coloured sands have been used to depict all types of scene, and the technique has also been used by European artists. Very striking are the S.Ps. used as temporary altars during certain phases of Navajo Indian ceremonial.

SANDPIPER. Group of birds in the snipe family Scolopacidae. The common S. (*Tringa hypoleucus*) is a small graceful bird with long slender bill and short tail, drab above and white below. In summer it breeds in Britain and most of the rest of Europe nr. water, and winters far south.

SANDRINGHAM. English village in Norfolk, 6 m. N.E. of King's Lynn. S. House, a private residence of the British sovereign, was built by the Prince of Wales (afterwards Edward VII) 1869–71 on the estate which he had bought in 1863. George V died at S.; George VI, b. at York Cottage, S., died at S. House.

SANDSTONE. Rocks formed of the consolidation of former sands. The principal component is quartz, and Ss. are classified according to the materials that cement together the grains of quartz, etc., e.g. ferruginous, siliceous, calcareous, barytic, gypseous, and pyritic.

COMMON SANDPIPER

SANDU'SKY. City and resort in Ohio, U.S.A., on S. Bay, Lake Erie. It is an important grain-shipping port and makes chemicals, paper, agricultural machinery, etc. Founded as a trading post early in the 18th cent., S. was later made a fort destroyed by Indians 1763, but re-built. The present town was founded as Portland 1817, re-named 1844. Pop. (1960) 31,989.

SANDWICH, John Montagu, 4th earl of (1718–92). British politician. He was 1st Lord of the Admiralty 1771–82, and the Sandwich Is. are named after him, as are sandwiches, which he invented in order to eat without leaving the gaming-table.

Victor Montagu (1906–　), known as Visct. Hinchingbrooke till he succeeded his father as 10th earl of S. in 1962, disclaimed his peerages 1964. He was chairman of the Tory Reform Committee 1943–4, and has opposed U.K. entry to the Common Market.

SANDWICH. English market town (bor.) in Kent, one of the Cinque ports, on the r. Stour. An important port for cents. before the Norman Conquest, it lost its usefulness through the silting up of the harbour in the 16th cent. It has a number of medieval buildings. Pop. (1961) 4,234.

SANDWICH ISLANDS. Another name for HAWAII.

SANDYS (sands), **Duncan** (1908–　). British Cons. politician. Entering Parliament in 1935, he was Min. of Works 1944–5, Min. of Supply 1951–4, Min. of Housing and Local Govt. 1954–7, Min. of Defence 1957–9, Min. of Aviation 1959–60, and was Sec. of State for Commonwealth Relations 1960–4 and also for the Colonies (1962), negotiating, amongst other things, the agreement (1963) on the Malaysian Federation. His first marriage in 1935 was to Diana, dau. of Sir Winston Churchill.

SANDYS, Oliver. Pseudonym of British novelist Mrs. Marguerite Evans (1894–1964), neé Jervis. She was first m. to Count Barcynska, and as Countess B. became known as the author of *Love Never Dies, We Lost Our Way*, etc. Her 2nd husband was Caradoc Evans, whose biography she pub. in 1948. Besides novels, she has also pub. her autobiography *Full and Frank* under the pseudonym S.

SAN FRANCISCO. Principal port on the Pacific coast of the U.S.A., in California, on S.F. Bay. The city stands on a peninsula S. of the Golden Gate, a strait 1 m. wide, 5 m. long, giving access to the Bay and crossed by the 2nd longest single-span bridge (4,200 ft.) in the world, completed 1937. In the bay is Alcatraz (q.v.) island. Industries incl. meat-packing, fruit canning, printing and publishing, and the manufacture of metal goods. There is a large international airport. S.F. dates from 1776; it was a trading post when captured by the U.S.A. in 1846 during the war with Mexico. An earthquake in 1906 almost completely destroyed the city and killed 452 people. Pop. met. area S.F.–Oakland (1970) 3,068,403.

The international conference which drew up the United Nations Charter was held at S.F. in 1945; and the peace treaty between the Western Allies and Japan, in force from 1952, was signed there in 1951.

SANGER, Frederick (1918–　). British biochemist. He was Beit Memorial Fellow at Cambridge 1944–51, when he became a staff member of the Medical Research Council. He was made F.R.S. in 1954, and awarded a Nobel Prize in chemistry 1958 for his elucidation of the molecular structure of insulin – at that time the largest protein and most complex enzyme to be so investigated.

SANGER, John (1816–89). British circus proprietor. B. in Somerset, he and his brother 'Lord' George (1825–1911) toured the country with their circus, and in 1871 began to produce annual equestrian pantomimes at Astley's. The brothers later produced their own separate shows. 'Lord' George was shot by an employee at Finchley.

SANHEDRIN (san′ēdrin). The supreme Jewish court at Jerusalem during the 2nd cent. B.C.,–1st cent. A.D. It consisted of members of the priestly aristocracy, and was presided over by the high priest.

SAN JOSÉ (san hōzā). A city of California, U.S.A., 50 m. S.S.E. of San Francisco; it has important fruit canneries, and after the S.W.W. grew industrially, notably as a centre for aerospace research and development. Pop. met. area (1970) 1,057,023.

SAN JOSÉ. Cap. of Costa Rica; the main trade is in coffee. cacao, and sugar cane. The univ. of Costa Rica (1843) is near by. Pop. (1966) 185,640.

SAN JUAN (san hwan′). Cap. of S.J. prov.,

Argentina, on the S.J. r., 97 m. N. of Mendoza. It is a centre of the wine industry, gold and copper are mined in the vicinity. S.J. was virtually destroyed by an earthquake in 1944. Pop. (1960) 82,000.

SAN JUAN. Cap. of the Commonwealth of Puerto Rico, on an is. off the N. coast. The fortresses of El Morro and San Cristóbal, the governor's palace Fortaleza, and the cathedral are of interest. Pop. (1960) 432,508.

SANKEY, Ira David (1840–1908). American evangelist, who toured Britain and America with D. L. Moody (q.v.). He compiled *Sacred Songs and Solos* (1873).

SANKT GALLEN. German form of ST. GALL.

SAN MARINO (mahrē′nō). Independent republic bounded by Italian territory, lying some 12 m. S.W. of Rimini. It claims to be the oldest state in Europe, having been founded in the 4th cent. A.D., and is one of the world's smallest states (area 22½ sq. m.). S.M., the cap., stands on Mt. Titano (2,650 ft.), a spur of the Apennines. Govt. is by a Great and General Council of 60 elected members, two of whom are appointed biannually to act as regents (*Capitani reggenti*). Women may vote (from 1960) but not be elected. S.M., which entered into a customs union with Italy in 1862, is under Italian protection. Pop. (1967) 18,181.

SAN MARTÍN (mahrtēn′), **José de** (1778–1850). S. American soldier. B. in Argentina, he served in the Spanish army during the Peninsular War, but after 1812 devoted himself to the S. American struggle for independence, playing a large part in the liberation of Argentina, Chile, and Peru.

SAN REMO (rä′mō). Seaport and popular winter resort on the Gulf of Genoa, Liguria, N. Italy. There is a casino; perfumes and mosaics are made. Pop. (1960) 55,000.

SAN SALVADOR. Cap. of the republic of El Salvador in Central America, 30 m. inland from the Pacific at the foot of the S.S. volcano (8,360 ft.) S.S. was founded in 1525; it has several times suffered badly from earthquakes. Pop. (1961) 255,744.

SANSCULOTTES (French, without knee-breeches). Term applied during the French Revolution to the working classes, who wore trousers, as opposed to the aristocracy and bourgeoisie, who wore knee-breeches.

SAN SEBASTIÁN. Seaport and bathing resort, cap. of the prov. of Guipúzcoa, on the Bay of Biscay, Spain. It became fashionable after Queen Maria Christina, mother of the posthumous Alfonso XIII, made it the summer residence of the court in 1886. S.S., formerly a walled town, was besieged by Wellington in 1813; its walls were removed in 1863. Pop. (1965) 153,660.

SANSKRIT. The literary language of ancient India, belonging to the Indo-Iranian or Aryan branch of the Indo-European family of languages. The oldest form of S. is Vedic (*c.* 1500 B.C.), the medium in which the 4 Vedas (q.v.) and the associated Brahmanas, Aranyakas, and Upanishads were written. Classical S., with its fixed vocabulary and grammar, was the creation of the grammarians, notably Panini in the 4th cent. B.C., but Vedic also continued to be used for several cents. Works written in Classical S. incl. the national epics, the *Mahabharata* and *Ramayana* (qq.v.), and the later artificial epics, of which Kalidasa's *Family of Rama* and *Birth of the War God* are the most famous. In lyric poetry the names of Jayadeva and Bhartrihari, and in drama that of Bhavabhuti, are noteworthy, but in both fields Kalidasa is again considered to excel all others. Other interesting literary forms are the prose romance, represented by Dandin's *Adventures of the Ten Princes*; the beast fables of the *Panchatantra*; and Somadeva's collection of verse fairy tales in the *Kathasaritsagara*. There is practically no historical writing in S., but there are many works dealing with philosophy, law, grammar, astronomy, algebra, and medicine.

SANSOM, William (1912–). English writer. *The Stories of W.S.* (1963) illustrate his development from the Kafkaesque *Fireman Flower* (1944) to a superb command of atmosphere and a genius for the tale of terror which reflects his admiration for Poe. Besides short stories, he has written novels such as *The Body* (1949), a study in jealousy, *The Cautious Heart* (1958) and *The Last Hours of Sandra Lee* (1961).

SANTA CLAUS. *See* NICHOLAS, ST.

SANTA CRUZ DE LA SIERRA (sahnta krooth de lah sie′rah). Cap. of S.C. dept. in E. Bolivia. Sugar cane and cattle were the chief base of local industry until newly discovered oil and natural gas led to phenomenal growth. Pop. (1966) 99,000.

SANTA CRUZ DE TENERIFE (sahnta krooth de ten′erif). Cap. of Tenerife and of the Canary Isls., it is a fuelling port and cable centre. S.C. was bombarded by Blake in 1657; by Nelson in 1797 – the action in which he lost his arm. Pop. (1965) 163,540.

SANTA FÉ (fā). Cap. of New Mexico, U.S.A. on the r. Santa Fé, about 40 m. W. of Las Vegas. It has a number of buildings from the Spanish period, incl. a palace (1609–10); the cathedral (1869) is on the site of a monastery built 1622. S.F. is noted for its

SANTA FÉ. New Mexico was ruled successively by Spanish, Indian, Mexican and American Governors, who occupied this Palace of the Governors, Santa Fé, continuously from 1610 until 1909. The Palace – the oldest government building in the U.S.A. – now houses the Museum of New Mexico.
Courtesy of the Museum of New Mexico, Santa Fé.

Indian jewellery and textiles; tourism is its chief industry. Pop. (1960) 34,676, many Spanish-speaking.

SANTA FÉ (fā). Cap. of S.F. prov., Argentina, on the Salado 95 m. N. of Rosario. Founded in 1573, it has shipyards and exports timber, cattle, and wool. Pop. (1960) 260,000.

SANTANDER (-dār′). Spanish city on the Bay of Biscay, cap of S. prov., which is traversed by the Cantabrian Mts. It is a port with shipyards, breweries, etc. S. was sacked by Soult in 1808. Hundreds died when a vessel carrying dynamite blew up in 1893; and a fire in 1941 swept away many old buildings and led to the re-planning of the town. Pop. (1965) 130,430.

SANTAYANA (-yah′na), **George** (1863–1952). Spanish philosopher. B. at Madrid, he graduated at Harvard, where he taught the history of philosophy, 1889–1911. His books incl. *The Life of Reason* (1905–6), *The Realm of Truth* (1937), *Background of my Life* (1945), vols. of poems, and the novel *The Last Puritan*.

SANTIAGO (santē-ah′gō). Cap. of Chile and of S. prov., about 60 m. S.E. of Valparaiso. Founded in 1541, it is a handsome city, well laid out with broad avenues, e.g. the Alameda, or Avenida de las Delicias, and fine public buildings and a cathedral. There are 2 univs. Pop of Greater S. (1965) 2,450,000.

SANTIAGO. The city is built on the plain between the Andes mountains and the heights of Cuesta del Prado, around the rocky hill of Santa Lucía, once its citadel. Here is the residential district, looking towards San Cristóbal Hill, one of three hills to the north, and in the distance the Andes.
Courtesy of Anglo-Chilean Society.

SANTIAGO DE COMPOSTELA (kompostāl′ah). Spanish city in Galicia, 33 m. S.S.W. of Corunna. It has a univ. and is an archiepiscopal see. The cathedral begun 1078) was built above the reputed grave of Sant Iago el Mayor (St. James the elder), patron saint of Spain. Pop. (1965) 64,780.

SANTO DOMINGO. Cap. city and chief seaport of the Dominican Republic, also formerly called S.D. It stands on the S. coast of the is., and was founded in 1496 by Bartholomew Columbus. Its cathedral was built 1514–40. It was called Ciudad Trujillo 1936–61. Pop. (1964) 529,400.

SANTOS. Seaport of Brazil, 200 m. S.E. of Rio de Janeiro. It is the world's greatest coffee port, and is free to Bolivia and Paraguay. Pop. (1960) 265,753.

SAÔNE (sōn). French r., 268 m. long, which rises in the Vosges and joins the Rhône at Lyons.

SAO PAULO (sowṅ pow′lō). Brazilian city, 3,000 ft. a.s.l., 2′ S. of the Tropic of Capricorn and 45 m. N.W. of its port Santos, on the Atlantic, cap. of S.P. prov. Originating as a Jesuit mission in 1554, it is the centre of the coffee trade of Brazil and has meat-packing plants. Pop. (1960) 3,776,581.

SAPPER. Pseudonym of British author Cyril McNeile (1888–1937). Entering the Royal Engineers in 1907, he retired with the rank of lieut.-col. in 1919. In 1920 he pub. *Bulldog Drummond*, and continued the adventures of the hero in numerous sequels.

SAPPHIRE (saf′īr). Transparent blue precious stone, a variety of corundum, the less valuable forms being yellow, green and colourless. Ceylon and Burma provide the best stones, usually found in alluvial soil. Ss. are made artificially on a large scale for industry and used almost universally as points in gramophone record reproducing heads (pick-ups).

SAPPHO (b. *c.* 600 B.C.). Greek lyric poet. B. at Mytilene or Lesbos, she was the centre of a feminine literary coterie at Mytilene, and was the friend of Alcaeus. She is said to have thrown herself from the

SÃO PAULO. As the centre of a rich coffee-growing district of the state, Campinas was the natural site for the foundation in 1887 of this beautifully set Agricultural Institute.
Courtesy of the Brazilian Information Service.

Leucadian rock, owing to her love for Phaon being unrequited. Her poems survive only fragmentarily.

SAPPŌRŌ. Cap. city of Hokkaido, Japan, nr. the E. coast. Industries incl. rubber manufacture and food processing, its beer being famous. It is also a winter sports centre, with a snow festival remarkable for giant figures sculptured in ice. There is a univ. (1918). Pop. (1965) 821,000.

SAPROPHYTE (sap′rŏfīt). Plant feeding on organic compounds in solution, and wholly or partly lacking in chlorophyll. Ss. are generally fungi and live upon dead plants and animals. The moulds on foodstuffs and the dry-rot of timber are caused by saprophytic fungi. Ss. are useful scavengers, and in sewage farms and refuse dumps break down organic matter into nutrients easily assimilable by green plants. Many orchids, also, are incl. among Ss.

SA′RACENS (-s-). Greek and Roman term for the Arabs, hence used in medieval Europe for all Moslems.

SARAGO′SSA. City in N. Spain, on the Ebro, cap. of S. prov. It has 2 cathedrals, one dating from the 12th cent., and a univ. It makes leather and leather goods, textiles, machinery, glass, porcelain, beer, etc. Founded as Salduba in pre-Roman days, it was named S. after the Roman conqueror Caesar Augustus; later it was captured by Suebi, Visigoths, and Moors, and was taken in 1118 by Alfonso the Warrior, King of Navarre and Aragon, after a nine months' siege; it remained cap. of Aragon until the end of the 15th cent. S. held out against the French 1808–9 when Agustina (d. 1859) became a national heroine: her story is told in Byron's *Childe Harold*. Pop. (1965) 393,425.

SARAJEVO (-yā′vō). City of Yugoslavia, cap. of Bosnia-Herçegovina federal republic, on the Miljačka. The assassination at S. of Archduke Francis Ferdinand, heir apparent to the throne of Austria-Hungary, by Gavrilo Princip, a Bosnian, on 28 June 1914, precipitated the F.W.W. Pop. (1961) 142,423.

SARATŌ′GA SPRINGS. City and spa in New York State, U.S.A., 38 m. N. of Albany. Pop. (1960) 16,630.

Near by in 1777 Gen. John Burgoyne (q.v.) was defeated in 2 engagements by Horatio Gates to whom he surrendered. He and some 6,000 men remained prisoners until the end of the War of American Independence.

SARATOV (sahrah′tof). City of the R.S.F.S.R., on the Volga, cap. of S. region, 230 m. N.N.E. of Volgograd. The centre of a petroleum field with a pipe-line supplying Moscow 500 m. W., it has also shipbuilding, engineering, and printing industries; and a univ. (1909). Pop. (1967) 699,000.

SARAWAK (sarah′wak). State of the Fed. of Malaysia, occupying the N.W. sector of Borneo and forming (with Sabah) E. Malaysia. The coast is backed by a broad plain, but inland is broken, mountainous country. The climate is hot and wet. S. was ceded to Sir James ('Rajah') Brooke by the Sultan of Brunei in 1841 in return for his aid in a campaign against the Dayaks (q.v.), and was placed by his nephew Sir Charles under British protection in 1888. The Japanese occupied S. 1941–5 during a period of military rule the Rajah, H.H. Sir Charles Vyner Brooke, was reinstated in 1946; five weeks later he ceded S. to the Crown. It was a Crown colony 1946–63, when it acceded to Malaysia. The cap. is Kuching, on the S. r.; Sibu is a port on the Rejang. The principal product is petroleum from the Miri oilfield: others are rubber, timber, bauxite, sago and pepper. Area *c*. 47,000 sq. m.; pop. (1966) 862,000 incl. 323,000 Dyaks, 282,000 Chinese, 2,000 Europeans.

SARD. and **SA′RDONYX.** *See* ONYX.

SARDINE. Term applied to various types of small fish (*Sardina pilchardus*) in the herring family, which are packed in oil in sealed tins. The name comes from Sardinia, as many of the fish are caught in the neigh-

bourhood of that is. There are also extensive S. fisheries off the coast of Brittany. In the U.K. the term is legally restricted to the young of the pilchard (q.v.) by a court ruling of 1915.

SARDINIA. Island in the Mediterranean to the S. of Corsica, made an autonomous region of Italy in 1948; the Italian form of the name is Sardegna. S. is mountainous and for the most part barren, but in the S.W. cereals, olives, and the vine are grown; cork is an important export; lead, zinc, coal, and lignite are mined. S. was inhabited already in the Bronze Age, from which remain many *nuraghi* (fortified dwellings). Ruled from the 15th cent. successively by Spain, Austria, and Savoy, S. was absorbed in Italy when Victor Emmanuel II became King of Italy in 1861. Area 9,298 sq. m.; pop. (1961) 1,413,289.

SARDOU (sahrdōō′), **Victorien** (1831–1908). French dramatist. His plays, many of which were written for such stars as Bernhardt and Irving, incl. *Fédora* (1882), *La Tosca* (1887) and *Robespierre* (1902).

SARGASSO SEA. That part of the N. Atlantic lying between 40° and 80°W. and 25° and 30°N. which is notorious for its floating seaweed (*Sargassum bacciferum*). Ocean currents sweep round the area clockwise leaving the centre virtually still.

SIR MALCOLM SARGENT. A night at the Proms: the soloist is Amy Shuard.   *Photo: Godfrey MacDomnic.*

SARGENT, Sir (Harold) Malcolm (Watts) (1895–1967). British conductor. From 1923 he was prof. at the R.C.M., was chief conductor of the B.B.C. Symphony Orchestra 1950–7, and then continued as chief guest conductor and conductor-in-chief of the 'Proms'. He had an easy, polished style.

SARGENT, John Singer (1856–1925). American artist. B. in Florence of American parents, he studied there and in Paris. He settled in London, and was elected R.A. in 1897. His principal works incl. intimately perceptive portraits of the Wertheimer family, Lord Ribblesdale, T. Roosevelt, Rockefeller, and others and the F.W.W. picture 'Gassed'.

SA′RGON. Name of 2 Mesopotamian kings. **Sargon I** (*c*. 2700 B.C.), king of Akkad, founded the first Babylonian empire. **Sargon II** (reigned 722–705 B.C.), king of Assyria, carried the Israelites into captivity.

SARK. One of the Channel Islands, 6 m. E. of Guernsey. It is divided into Great S. and Little S. connected by an isthmus called the Coupée, and is of great natural beauty. The Seignurie of S. was estab. by Elizabeth I, the ruler being known as Seigneur or Dame, and there is a parliament, the Chief Pleas. There is no income tax and cars are forbidden. Area 2 sq. m.; pop. (1961) 560.

SARO′YAN, William (1908–   ). American author.

B. in California, he told of his childhood there in *The Bicycle Rider in Beverly Hills* (1950), and made his name as a short-story writer, e.g. *The Daring Young Man on the Flying Trapeze* (1934), idealizing the hopes and sentiments of the 'little man', and later collections. His work as a playwright incl. *The Time of Your Life* (1939) and *Talking to You* (1962).

SARRAUTE (sahrōt,), **Nathalie** (1902–). French novelist. B. in Ivanovo, N. of Moscow, she was taken to France when 2 yrs. old, and her education incl. a yr. at Oxford in 1922. Married to a French barrister, Raymond S., she lives in Paris. Her books try to give the live, half-conscious interactions of minds in contact with one another, and she is comparatively uninterested in plot, character and style: they incl. *Portrait of a Man Unknown*, *The Planetarium* and *The Golden Fruits* (1964). *See* illus. p. 450.

SARRELOUIS. French form of SAARLAUTERN.

SARSAPARI'LLA. A drink prepared from the long twisted roots of plants in the genus *Smilax*, native to Central America.

SARTHE (sahrt). French r. which rises in the E. of Orne dept. and flows generally S.S.W. for 175 m. to join the Mayenne nr. Angers and form the Maine.

SARTRE (sahrtr), **Jean-Paul** (1905–). French author and philosopher. B. in Paris, he became a teacher, publishing his 1st novel *La Nausée* in 1937. In the S.W.W. he was taken prisoner for 9 months, but returned from Germany to work for the resistance. Founder of the philosophical school of Existentialism (q.v.), he edits its journal *Les Temps Modernes*, and its tenets are expressed in the novels – a trilogy – of *Les Chemins de la Liberté* (1944–5) and in his strongly dramatic plays, e.g. *Les Mouches* (1947: *The Flies*); *Huis Clos* (1945: *In Camera*), 2 women and 1 man confined in the hell they make for each other; *Le Putain respectueuse* (1947: *The Respectful Prostitute*), attacking racial discrimination in the South of the U.S.A.; *Crime Passionnel* (1948), an attack on certain aspects of Communism with which S. yet retains its general sympathy; and *Nekrassov* (1957). Awarded the Nobel prize for literature in 1964, he refused it in advance for 'personal reasons'.

SĀ'RUM. *See under* SALISBURY, Wilts, England.

SASKATCHEWAN (saskach'e-wan). Prairie prov. of Canada, between Alberta and Manitoba. The N. is an area of forest, lakes, and sub-arctic tundra. Minerals incl. oil, potash, cadmium, copper, gold silver, zinc, uranium, coal and salt, and there is natural gas incl. helium. Southern S. is Canada's greatest wheat-growing area: other crops are oats, barley, rye and flax. The Gardiner Dam (1967) on the South S. river, 60 m. S. of Saskatoon, provides irrigation and hydroelectricity. The towns incl. Regina (the cap.), Saskatoon, and Moose Jaw. The name comes from the Indian name Kis-is-ska-tche-wan (fast flowing) of the S. r. formed by the junction nr. Prince Albert of the North S. and South S., which rise in the Rockies, to flow into Lake Winnipeg. Area 251,700 sq. m.; pop. (1966) 955,344.

SASKATOO'N. City in Saskatchewan, Canada, on the S. Saskatchewan r., 150 m. N.W. of Regina. An important railway junction, it is the seat of the univ. of Saskatchewan (1907) and makes cement, chemicals, and metal goods. Pop. (1966) 113,074.

SASSOON, Siegfried (1886–1967). British poet. Ed. at Cambridge, he enlisted in 1915, serving in France and Palestine, and expressed in his *War Poems* (1919) the disillusion of his generation. He pub. his *Collected Poems 1908–56* (1961), and as a prose writer is known for his *Memoirs of a Foxhunting Man* (1928).

SATIE (sahtē'), **Erik** (1866–1925). French composer. B. at Honfleur, he became a member of *Les Six*. His compositions incl. 'Limp preludes for a dog' and 'Pieces in the shape of a pear'.

SATO, Eisaku (1901–). Japanese statesman. Son of a brewer of saké, he opposed the policies of Ikeda in the Liberal-Democratic Party, and in 1964 succeeded him as P.M., pledged to a more independent foreign policy and avoidance of 'poverty within prosperity'. His brother **Nobosuke Kishi** (1896–), who changed his name from S. on adoption into the Kishi family when young, was P.M. 1957–60, being forced to resign after public demonstration against the revised security treaty he negotiated with the U.S.A.

SATURN. Roman god of agriculure, later identified with the Greek god Cronus. He was believed to be the father of Jupiter, Neptune, and Pluto, who dethroned him, and his reign was identified with the Golden Age of equality and plenty. At his festival, the Saturnalia, in Dec., gifts were exchanged, and slaves were treated as their masters' equals.

SATURN. The second of the giant planets. It has a mean distance from the Sun of 886,100,000 miles, and a revolution period of 29½ years. In size it is second only to Jupiter; the equatorial diameter is 74,100 m., and the mass 95 times that of the Earth. Like Jupiter, S. is appreciably flattened at the poles. This is a result of its rapid axial rotation period, which amounts to only 10¼ hours.

SATURN. Taken with a 36-inch refractor, this photograph shows Saturn's ring system, together with the dark Cassini Division between the two bright rings.
Courtesy of Lick Observatory, Univ. of California.

Basically, S. resembles Jupiter; its surface is gaseous, and the temperature is extremely low (about −240°F.). Belts may be seen crossing its disk, and there are occasional short-lived spots, the best example of modern times being the conspicuous white spot discovered by the British amateur astronomer W. T. Hay in 1933. However, S. is unique in possessing a system of rings, composed of numerous small particles moving round the planet in the manner of dwarf satellites, and giving the impression of solid sheets. There are 3 rings, 2 of which are bright and the third (the Crêpe Ring) semi-transparent; between the 2 bright rings is a prominent gap, known as the Cassini Division in honour of its discoverer. It is possible that the ring system was produced as the result of the break-up of a former satellite.

Of S.'s 9 surviving satellites, one – Titan, discovered by C. Huygens in 1655 – is visible with a small telescope; it is over 3,000 miles in diameter, and has a tenuous atmosphere composed of methane. The remaining satellites are considerably smaller.

SATYAGRAHA. Term applied in India to non-violent resistance. It was first employed by Gandhi in 1918, and the idea owes much to Tolstoy.

SATYR. In Greek mythology, woodland beings characterized by pointed ears, 2 horns on the forehead, and a tail, who were supposed to attend Dionysus. In Roman writers they are confused with the goat-footed fauns.

SAUDI ARABIA (sow'di). Kingdom of S.W. Asia occupying the greater part of the Arabian peninsula. Most of the area is desert. Nejd in the interior and Hejaz on the Red Sea coast were in 1927 united under Ibn Saud, former Sultan of Nejd, who proclaimed himself king of both. His son Saud Ibn Abdul-Aziz (1902–69) succeeded him in 1953. The joint capitals are Mecca and Riyadh. Slavery was abolished 1963. Petroleum is worked at Damman, on the Persian Gulf, where it was discovered in 1936, Abqaiq,-Ain Dar, and elsewhere. A railway, opened 1951, links Riyadh with the oilfields and the coast at Damman; there are airports at Jedda, Dhahran, and Riyadh. A good road joins Jedda with Mecca and Medina, and several others radiate from Riyadh. The unrest in the Arab world was reflected in S.A., and reactionary King Saud ibn Abdul-Aziz was replaced in 1964 by his brother Faisal (q.v.). Area *c.* 800,000 sq. m.; pop. *c.* 6,000,000, the majority nomads.

SAUL. First king of Israel (d. about 1010 B.C.). The son of Kish, he was anointed by Samuel, and after his victory against the Ammonites was made king by the people at Gilgal. He lost the favour of God and committed suicide.

SAULT STE. MARIE (soo sānt mahrē′). Twin cities on the U.S.-Canadian frontier, at the falls in St. Mary's river joining lakes Superior and Huron. S. Ste. M., Ontario, manufactures steel and paper. Pop. (1966) 74,594. S. Ste. M., Michigan, had a pop. of 18,722 in 1960. Two international canals bypass the falls, which were discovered by Etienne Brulé in 1612, *sault* (modern Fr. *saut*) meaning falls.

SAUMUR (sōmür′). Town in Maine-et-Loire dept., France, on the Loire, famous for its cavalry school (1768) and sparkling wines. Pop. (1962) 22,876.

SAUNA (saw′na). Finnish bath. Known for a thousand years and once a sacred cult, the S. bath is

SAUNA. Although modern fire regulations prohibit the use of wood in towns, the traditional bathhouse is built of wood. The majority of Finland's half million saunas are on the shores of her lakes, which provide the essential cold plunge.
Courtesy of the Finnish Travel Information Centre.

traditionally still taken on Saturday. Above a wood fire specially selected black cobblestones, about the size of a man's fist, are heated on an iron grate and water is thrown on them to produce a steam bath at *c.* 90°C (200°F). Perspiration begins in *c.* 10 mins. and, after a beating with whisks made of birch twigs, the bather cools off with a plunge into cold water.

SAUTERNES (sōtärn′). A village of Gironde dept., S.W. France, which has given its name to the sweet white table wines of the district. Pop. (1962) 640.

SAVAGE, Michael Joseph (1872–1940). New Zealand statesman. B. in Australia, he settled in New Zealand in 1907, and worked as a miner. He entered parliament in 1919, became leader of the Labour Party in 1933, and formed a govt. in 1935 in which he was P.M. and Min. for External Affairs and Native Affairs. His govt. introduced much social security legislation. He d. in office.

SAVANNAH. City of Georgia, U.S.A., on the S. river 18 m. from its mouth. Founded in 1733, it

exports cotton, and makes cottonseed oil, fertilizers, machinery, etc. The *Savannah*, first ship fitted with steam power to cross the Atlantic, was built at S.; she made most of the journey (1819), which took 25 days, under sail. Pop. (1960) 149,245.

SAVA′NNAH or **Savanna.** Term, perhaps of Carib origin, applied by the Spaniards to treeless plains of tropical American prairies, now denoting any extensive tropical grassland.

SAVING. The reservation of a portion of income for future needs, seldom in modern times the massing of a money hoard, because of dangers of fire and theft, but tending to be synonymous with investment. The purchase of precious stones, antiques, works of art, property, etc., for appreciation of value was hit 1965 by a capital gains tax (for values over £1,000) levied on realized gains at disposal or at death. Small-scale savers have an increasingly large field opening to them. Very frequent is the acquisition of a home by regular payments on a mortgage obtained through a building society or bank, the house passing to the mortgagor when the purchase price plus interest is paid off. Popular also are life insurance policies producing at the end of a specified time a lump sum or annuity; the majority now issued are 'with profits', i.e. the people insured benefit through profits from the investments of the company. Steady inflation has also led to the linking of policies and also of private enterprise pensions schemes, with unit trusts. These trusts offer the small saver an opportunity, formerly limited to the more wealthy man operating through a stockbroker, to invest in stocks and shares. The managers of the trusts spread their funds over a large number of these, and by his purchase of a 'unit' the saver gains a fractional share in each, so being safeguarded against substantial loss by the failure of any particular share. Apart from the costs of management, all profits are distributed: this is not usually the case with the similarly spread investment trusts.

For small savers who wish to have their money at ready call, but also to secure a modest interest, the most usual recourse is the Trustee Savings Banks (regulated by acts of Parliament) which date from the early 19th cent.; the Post Office Savings Bank (1861); or the Building Societies (q.v.). The govt., which makes certain tax concessions to people investing in these and in home ownership and insurance policies, also offers the small saver Premium Savings Bonds (1956) repayable at par, earning no interest, but eligible for prizes awarded monthly to holders in a draw made by ERNIE (q.v.). Nat. Savings Certificates (1916) which earn graduated tax-free interest payable only on ultimate encashment; British Savings Bonds, carrying in addition to regular interest a tax-free bonus after a given number of years; and, introduced by Chancellor Roy Jenkins in the 1969 budget, a contractual Save As You Earn scheme with tax-free terminal bonuses after five years' subscription and again after seven years without withdrawal, early withdrawals being penalized by very low payment of interest.

Similar methods of saving are available in other countries incl. the U.S.A., where the govt. has issued a number of series of savings bonds.

SAVOIE (sahvwah′), **Combe de.** Glacial valley *c.* 20 m. long through which the Isère r. runs, Savoie dept., France. It lies between the Bauges and Belledame ranges of the Alps. The road to Mont Cenis and the Little St. Bernard passes runs through it; and the depts. of Savoie and Haute-Savoie take their names from it.

SAVONARŌ′LA, Girolamo (1452–98). Italian reformer. B. at Ferrara, he became a Dominican friar in 1474, and was elected prior of St. Mark's Convent at Florence in 1491. His eloquent preaching, and his reputation as a visionary and prophet won him immense popular influence, and in 1494 he led a revolt which expelled the Medicis and estab. a democratic republic. But his denunciations of Pope Alexander VI led to his excommunication in 1497, and in 1498 he was arrested, tortured, hanged, and burned for heresy.

SAVOY. Area, formerly a prov. of the kingdom of Sardinia which, with Nice, was ceded to France in 1860 by Victor Emmanuel II (king of Italy from 1861) in return for French assistance in driving the Austrians from Italy. It lies between the Alps, the Lake of Geneva, and the r. Rhône, and was formed into the depts. of Savoie and Haute-Savoie. *See also* Savoie, Combe de.

Turnip sawfly and larva.

SAWFLY. Family of insects in the order Hymenoptera. The name is derived from the saw-like edge of the female's ovipositor. There are about 2,000 species which damage plants either by feeding on them or by the larvae burrowing in the tissues.

SAXE, Maurice, comte de (1696–1750). Soldier. The natural son of the elector of Saxony, he served under Marlborough and Eugène, and for his brilliant exploits in the War of the Austrian Succession was created a marshal of France in 1743.

SAXE. French form of Saxony.

SAXE COBURG-GOTHA (gōta). A ducal title held by members of the Wettin family. Albert the Prince Consort was the son of Ernest, the 1st duke; and Alfred the duke of Edinburgh, succeeded his uncle in 1893. On his death in 1900, the title passed to his nephew, the duke of Albany, who abdicated in 1918.

SA′XIFRAGE. Genus of plants (*Saxifraga*) in the family Saxifragaceae. They occur in rocky, mountainous, and alpine situations. London Pride (*S. umbrosa*) is a familiar example.

SAXONY. English form of Sachsen, a former kingdom, later state, of Germany. It lay between Prussia, Bavaria, and Bohemia; Dresden was the cap. It got its name from its Saxon inhabitants and originally reached as far W. as the Rhine, covering most of the Land of W. Germany formed in 1946 and named Lower Saxony. S. was conquered by Charlemagne, but when his empire broke up after his death became a dukedom. This itself was broken up in the 12th cent., and the area called S. subsequently underwent many fluctuations. The Reformation originated in S., Luther being a native. In the 16th cent. the ruler of S. became an Elector and later a king. S. supported Napoleon I and half the kingdom was given to Prussia by the Congress of Vienna, 1815, becoming the Prussian prov. of S. The remaining kingdom joined the German Empire, founded 1871. At the end of the F.W.W. the king abdicated and S. became one of the federal states of the German Republic. After the S.W.W., S. lay in E. Germany and in 1946 was, with part of Silesia, made a new Land of S., abolished in 1952.

SAXONY, Lower. *See* Lower Saxony.

SAXONY-ANHALT. Land of E. Germany, 1946–52. It consisted of Anhalt, a former duchy and state, and most of the former Prussian prov. of Saxony.

SAXOPHONE. A wind instrument made of brass and possessing

SAXOPHONE

woodwind characteristics. It was invented by Adolphe Sax (1814–94) as one of a series of such instruments which also included the saxhorn. Several varieties of S. exist, all having a conical brass tube, curved at each end and with 20 keys controlling notes.

SAYERS, Dorothy Leigh (1893–1957). British author. Ed. at Somerville Coll., Oxford, where she read history, she made her name with her creation of Lord Peter Wimsey, the dilettante detective with a taste in wines and 1st editions, who appeared initially in *Whose Body?* (1923); other crime stories incl. *The Nine Tailors* (1934) and *Busman's Honeymoon* (1937). She also wrote books on religious subjects and the radio series on the life of Christ *The Man Born to be King*.

SCA′BIOUS. Genus of European plants (*Scabiosa*) in the family Dipsacaceae. The field S. (*S. arvensis*) has lilac flowers and a bristly calyx; other species are the sea S. and the Devil's bit S.

SCAFELL (scawfell′) **PIKE.** Highest mountain in England (3,210 ft.). It is in Cumberland, in the Lake District, and is separated from Scafell (3,162 ft.) by a scree-covered ridge called Mickledore. The summit of the pike is National Trust property, presented as a war memorial by the 3rd Lord Leconfield in 1919.

SCALAR QUANTITY. *See* Vector.

SCALLOP. Genus of bi-valve molluscs (*Pecten*) in the family Pectinidae found in all seas. The shell is fan-shaped with 2 ear-like projections near the hinge. The edible S. (*P. opercularis*) is sedentary but not fixed; *P. jacobaeus* was used as a badge by pilgrims from Compostela.

SCANDINA′VIA. Peninsula of N.W. Europe, comprising the kingdoms of Norway and Sweden. Politically and culturally it also includes Denmark and is sometimes considered to include Finland.

SCALLOP

SCA′NDIUM. A scarce metal element of the rare metallic earth group; symbol Sc, at. wt. 44·96; at. no. 21. It was discovered in 1879 in the Scandinavian mineral euxenite.

SCAPA FLOW. Expanse of sea in the Orkney Islands, Scotland, formerly a base of the R.N. The main base of the Grand Fleet during the F.W.W., in 1919 it was the scene of the scuttling of 71 surrendered German warships. It remained the principal base of the home fleet until 1957.

SCARBOROUGH. English spa and seaside resort (bor.) in N. Riding of Yorks. Edith and Sacheverell Sitwell were b. at S. The remains of S. castle overlook the town, which was shelled by German submarines during the F.W.W. Pop. (1961) 42,587.

SCARLATTI (skahrlaht′tē), **Alessandro** (1659–1752). Italian musician. B. at Trapani, he became master of the chapel at the court of Naples and founded the Neapolitan school of opera, writing more than 100 operas himself and other notable church music. His eldest son, **Domenico S.** (1685–1757), was also a composer and is best remembered for his harpsichord sonatas.

SCARLET FEVER. Scarlatina; an infective fever caused by a haemolytic streptococcus. It is transmitted usually by direct infection in spray from speaking or coughing. The incubation period is under a week. The rash is a uniform redness, with small bright red points. Earache due to inflammation is a common complication. Peeling of the skin occurs in convalescence. The disease is currently much less severe, and treatment is often assisted by antibiotics, e.g. penicillin.

SCHACHT (shahkht), **Hjalmar** (1877–1970). Ger. financier and politician. As Economics Min. from

1934, he co-operated in Hitler's rearmament plans. Differences on policy led to his resignation in 1937, although he remained Min. without Portfolio until 1943. Imprisoned in 1944, he was acquitted at Nuremberg, and successfully appealed against sentence by a German de-nazification court.

SCHAFFHAUSEN (shahf'howzen). A Swiss canton adjoining Germany and divided into three parts by German territory (area 115 sq. m.; pop. (1960) 65,981). Its cap., also S., pop. (est.) 27,000, lies near the falls in the Rhine and manufactures watches, chemicals and textiles; it was bombed in error by U.S. planes, 1 April 1944, when 37 people were killed.

SCHEER (shehr), **Reinhard** (1863–1928). German admiral. B. in Hesse-Nassau, he was appointed commander of the High Sea Fleet in 1916, and was in command at the battle of Jutland.

SCHELDT (skelt). English name for the European r. called in Dutch Schelde, in French Escaut. It rises in Aisne dept., N. France, and flows for 250 m. N., N.E., then W., through Belgium and the Netherlands to enter the North Sea by the W. Scheldt S. of Walcheren, a wide estuary of great importance to shipping. Antwerp is the most important town on the S.

The East S., to the N. of Walcheren Island, was formerly an arm of the S., but was cut off from it in 1862 when S Beveland was linked with the mainland by dykes to carry the railway to Flushing; it will eventually be cut off from the North Sea. (*See under* NETHERLANDS.)

SCHENECTADY (skenek'tadi). Cap. of S. county, New York, U.S.A., on the r. Mohawk. It dates from 1662 and is an industrial centre with well-known scientific research laboratories. Pop. (1960) 81,682.

SCHICK TEST. A means of ascertaining by the injection of a small dose of diphtheria toxin whether a person is immune to diphtheria or not. In a susceptible person a local flush appears.

SCHIEDAM (skhēdahm'). Town of S. Holland, Netherlands, 3 m. W. of Rotterdam, and famous for its gin. It received its charter in 1273 and about the turn of the 18th–19th cents. sent much gin to the U.S.A. Pop. (1967) 82,200.

SCHILLER (shil'ler), **Johann Christoph Friedrich von** (1759–1805). German author. B. at Marbach (Württemberg), he qualified as a doctor but, after the success of his drama *The Robbers*, devoted himself to literature and became theatrical director at Mannheim, where he produced his tragedies *Fiesco* and *Love and Intrigue*, and began the more mature drama *Don Carlos*. In 1789 he settled at Jena, where he was prof. of history and completed *The History of the Thirty Years War*, and in 1799 at Weimar, where he developed his close friendship with Goethe. His later works incl. the classical dramas *Wallenstein* (a trilogy), *Maria Stuart*, *The Maid of Orleans*, and *William Tell*, and *Naive and Sentimental Poetry*, an outstanding work of literary criticism. S., a high-minded idealist and lover of freedom, also attained great popularity with his shorter poems.

SCHIPPERKE (shi'perke). A tailless watchdog, bred in Belgium. It has black fur and erect ears.

SCHIPPERKE

SCHIRACH (shē'rakh), **Baldur von** (1907–). German Nazi leader. He acted as youth leader of Germany 1936–40, and as gauleiter of Vienna 1940–5, where he carried out the policy of deporting all Jews. He was tried at Nuremberg in 1945–6, and sentenced to 20 years' imprisonment; released 1966.

SCHIST (shist). Foliated rock, crystalline in nature, which presents layers of various minerals easily divisible into thin lenticular plates. The dominant mineral normally names each variety.

SCHIZOPHRE'NIA (sk-). 'Split personality', a psychological disorder which may be due to some biochemical abnormality in a brain structurally normal, and involves a fundamental inability to face life. Tranquillizers, such as reserpine, are used to relieve the symptoms (social withdrawal, delusions, hallucinations).

SCHLEGEL (shleh'gel), **August Wilhelm von** (1767–1845). German author. B. at Hanover, he was an important figure in the Romantic movement. His Vienna lectures on *Dramatic Art and Literature* were epoch-making, and he is also remembered for his translations of Shakespeare. His brother, **Friedrich von S.** (1772–1892), studied Greek and Sanskrit literature, and wrote extensively on literary history.

SCHLESWIG-HOLSTEIN (shlesvig hol'stīn). Land of W. Germany, bounded by Denmark to the N. and traversed by the Kiel Canal. Cereals, potatoes and sugar-beet are grown, but S.-H. is predominantly industrial with most of her pop. engaged in shipbuilding, mechanical and electrical engineering and textiles. The largest towns are Kiel (the cap.), Lübeck, Flensburg, and Schleswig; the last has a fine cathedral. Area 6,054 sq. m.; pop. (1966) 2,473,000.

History. Schleswig (Danish Slesvig) and Holstein were 2 duchies held by the kings of Denmark from 1460, but were not part of the kingdom; a number of the inhabitants were German, and Holstein was a member of the German Confederation formed in 1815. Possession of the duchies had long been disputed by Prussia, and when Frederick VII of Denmark died without an heir in 1863, Prussia, supported by Austria, fought and defeated the Danes in 1864, and in 1866 annexed the two duchies. A plebiscite held in 1920 gave the N. part of Schleswig to Denmark which made it into the provs. of Haderslev and Aabenraa; the rest, with Holstein, remained part of Germany.

SCHLIEMANN (shlē'mahn), **Heinrich** (1822–90). German archaeologist. Fascinated from an early age by the Homeric epics, he retired from business in 1863 to study archaeology, and in 1871 began excavating at Hissarlik, which he estab. as the site of Troy, although the 'palace and treasure of Priam' which he discovered belong to an earlier settlement on the site than the one which Homer describes. His most important later excavations were at Mycenae, where he thought he had discovered the grave of Agamemnon, though again the find was of an earlier period.

SCHNABEL (shnah'bel), **Artur** (1882–1951). American pianist. B. in Austria. he taught music at the Berlin State Academy 1926–31, but settled in the U.S.A. in 1939, and composed symphonies and other works. He excelled in Beethoven.

SCHNEIDER TROPHY (shni'der). An aviation trophy presented by Jacques Schneider in 1913 for competition between seaplanes of any nation. From the first holder, M. Prévost in 1913. who averaged 45·75 m.p.h. the trophy changed hands several times before being won outright by Britain, a.ter victories in 1927, 1929, and 1931, the last creating a world's record of 340·08 m.p.h.

SCHOENBERG (shön'bärg), **Arnold** (1874–1951). Austro-American composer of Jewish descent. B. in Vienna, he developed the twelve-note system (*see* ATONALITY), and taught at the Berlin State Academy 1924–33. Driven from Germany by the Nazis, he settled in the U.S.A. in 1933. Among his works are the *Gurrelieder*, the opera *Moses and Aaron* and *Pierrot Lunaire* for voice and chamber orchestra.

SCHOLASTICISM (sk-). Name given to the theological and philosophical system of Christian Europe in the Middle Ages. John Scotus (Erigena) is sometimes regarded as the founder, but the succession of 'Schoolmen' definitely opened with Roscellinus at the end of the 11th cent., when in his advocacy of Nominalism he was countered by Anselm, the champion of Realism. The controversy over 'Universals' thus begun continued for several cents. William of Champeaux, Abélard, Alexander of Hales, Albertus Magnus, and Peter Lombard played prominent parts, but the greatest names are those of Thomas Aquinas, whose writings became the classical textbooks of Catholic doctrine, and the Franciscan Duns Scotus. The last of the Schoolmen is usually reckoned to have been William of Occam, who, in the first half of the 14th cent., restated Nominalism. In the present cent. there has been a revival of interest in Scholasticism, as seen in the writings of Jacques Maritain and other Catholic scholars.

SCHOLES (skōlz), **Percy Alfred** (1877–1958). British musicologist, remembered as the editor of the *Oxford Companion to Music.*

SCHOOL. A place in which instruction is given to the young in preparation for life. Schooling is compulsory in the U.K. from 5–15 years (14 until 1947; 16 from 1972–3). In England and Wales under the Education (Butler) Act of 1944, Ss. run by local authorities with govt. aid, in which the majority of children are educated, are divided into (1) primary Ss., incl. nursery (below 5), infant (5–7), and junior Ss. (7–11); and (2) secondary Ss. for those over 11, incl. in 1971 grammar, technical, modern and comprehensive – some of the former reorganized as comprehensive, catering for all pupils, and incl. Direct Grant and state-aided Ss. There are about 200 semi-independent non-profit-making Direct Grant grammar or secondary technical who take mainly fee-paying pupils and over 25 per cent nominated by local authorities, and over 10,000 state-aided Ss. (mainly religious). Most independent Ss. (some 4,000) charge fees and incl. public Ss. (e.g. Eton, Harrow, Winchester, Rugby and Repton), many of which are old foundations set up originally for poor scholars, and private Ss. of varying excellence. All Ss. are subject to govt. inspection and inefficient independent Ss. may be closed. State Ss., except some specialized Ss. and a few others, are provided only for day pupils, but public and private Ss. may be day or boarding establishments, or both. In Scotland there are public Ss. managed by the L.E.A., grant-aided Ss. conducted by voluntary managers and a small no. of independent Ss. which receive no state grant.

In France S. attendance is compulsory 6–16 (as from 1967), and Ss. are divided at primary level into infant (*écoles maternelles*), primary (*écoles primaires élémentaires*) and secondary modern (*collèges d'enseignement général*) and at secondary level generally into 4 yr. technical colleges (*collèges d'enseignement technique*) and the academic *lycées* (7 yr. course in preparation for the *baccalauréat*). In W. Germany full-time S. attendance is compulsory from 6–14, as is part-time vocational study to 18 for those not attending the intermediate (*Mittelschule*) or grammar S. (*Gymnasium*). In the U.S.S.R. education is free and compulsory from 7–15 or 16, in the larger towns to 17; co-education, introduced after the 1917 revolution and abolished in 1943, was re-introduced in 1954. In China, following the Cultural Revolution of 1967, the period of S. has been shortened: 4 yrs. primary, 5 secondary and 2–4 at univ., with all senior students giving half their time to work in farm or factory.

In the U.S.A. S. attendance is compulsory from 6 until 16–18, but in larger centres kindergartens and nursery Ss. are provided for the under-6s. There is free access to the public Ss., i.e. those supported by public money and which are attended by 80 per cent of the pop., in all 50 states at 3 levels: elementary (6 grades or years), junior high (3 grades) and senior high (3 grades). The 6 grades of secondary education are comprehensive, and it is only at the 13th and 14th grades in the junior colleges which are being in-

creasingly provided for the group 18–20 that education is biased as general, vocational or as supplying 2 years of undergraduate college work.

SCHOPENHAUER (shō´penhow-er), **Arthur** (1788–1860). German philosopher. B. at Danzig, he graduated at Jena and pub. in 1813 his *Fourfold Root of the Principle of Sufficient Reason*; and in 1818 his chief work, *The World as Will and Idea*, in which his pessimistic philosophy is expounded.

SCHREINER (shrī´ner), **Olive** (1862–1920). S. African writer. B. in Basutoland, the dau. of a missionary, she was the sister of **William Philip S.** (1857–1910), who was P.M. of Cape Colony 1898–1900, and m. in 1894 S. C. Cronwright. In 1883 she pub. *The Story of an African Farm*, a powerful novel describing life on the S. African veldt.

SCHRÖDINGER (shrö´dinger), **Erwin** (1887–1961). Austrian physicist. B. at Vienna, he became in 1940 senior prof. at the Dublin Institute for Advanced Studies. He greatly advanced the study of wave mechanics, and was awarded a Nobel prize in 1933.

SCHUBERT (shōō´bärt), **Franz Peter** (1797–1828). Austrian musician. B. at Vienna, the son of a school-

SCHUBERT. A water colour, dated 1825, by W. A. Rieder in the Historical Museum, Vienna, the city where Franz Schubert composed the majority of his works.
Courtesy of the Historical Museum, Vienna.

teacher, he himself was a school-teacher for 3 years, but composed busily in his spare time. In 1816 he gave up teaching to compose, and in 1818 was appointed music teacher to the Esterházy family on their estate in W. Hungary. Very shortly he was back in Vienna, where he lived henceforth a Bohemian existence. He was only 31 when he died, but his musical output was prodigious. Greatest of the 9 known symphonies are the incomplete B minor and the C major. He contributed much to chamber and pianoforte music, including sonatas and fantasias, but his most treasured works are his songs, of which he wrote nearly 300, including 3 great cycles.

SCHUMAN (shooman´), **Robert** (1886–1963). French statesman. He was P.M. 1947–8, and as Foreign Min. 1948–53 created the Coal and Steel Pool (the 'S. Plan' treaty of 1951) and prepared the basis of the Common Market.

SCHUMANN, Maurice (1911–). French politician. A war-time broadcaster from London, he was For. Min. 1951–4 and again from 1969 under Pompidou: he favoured Britain's entry to the Common Market.

SCHUMANN (shōō´mahn), **Robert Alexander** (1810–56). German musician. B. at Zwickau, Saxony, he taught at Leipzig conservatoire and was musical director at Düsseldorf 1850–3. As a composer he excelled in pianoforte compositions and in *Lieder*; his piano concerto Op. 54 and sonatas Opp. 11 and 22 are particularly famous. He wrote also much chamber music. His musical-criticisms were pub. in his *Neue Zeitschrift für Musik*. From 1854 he was confined in an asylum near Bonn, following a suicide attempt, and there he died. His wife, the pianist **Clara Josephine Wieck** (1819–96), whom he m. in 1841, devoted herself to the popularization of his work, and appeared frequently in London 1865–88.

SCHUSCHNIGG (shoosh'nig), **Kurt von** (1897–). Austrian statesman. A lawyer, he was elected a Christian Social deputy in 1927, and succeeded Dollfuss as Chancellor in 1934, when he was confronted with the Nazi menace from within and without. In Feb. 1938 he was forced to accept a Nazi Min. of the Interior, and a month later Austria was invaded and annexed. S. was imprisoned in Germany until 1945, when he went to U.S.A.

SCHWARZKOPF shvah'rtskopf), **Elisabeth** (1915–). German soprano. Educated at the Berlin High School of music, she is noted for her dramatic interpretation of operatic roles, such as Elvira in *Don Giovanni* and Marschallin in *Der Rosenkavalier*, and is also a concert singer.

ELISABETH SCHWARZKOPF
Photo: Godfrey MacDomnic.

SCHWARZWALD (shvah'rtsvahlt) (Ger., black forest. *See* BLACK FOREST.

SCHWEITZER (shvīt'ser), **Albert** (1875–1965). French theologian, organist and missionary surgeon. He founded a hospital in 1913 at Lambaréné, Rep. of Gabon, where he afterwards remained, except for brief intervals spent giving recitals of organ music, mainly Bach, to raise funds for his medical work. His many books incl. a standard life of Bach (1905), *The Quest of the Historical Jesus* (1906), *On the Edge of the Primeval Forest* (1921), *My Life and Thought* (1931). He was awarded the Nobel peace prize in 1952. His nephew **Pierre-Paul S.** (1912–) became in 1963 managing director of the International Monetary fund.

SCHWERIN (shvärēn'). Cap. of S. dist., E. Germany, situated on Lake S., 32 m. S.E. of Lübeck. S. received its charter from Henry the Lion in 1161; once the cap. of Mecklenburg-S., it has the former grand-ducal palace and a 15th cent. cathedral. Pop. (1966) 94,000.

SCHWYZ (shvits). A canton of Switzerland, bordering lakes Lucerne, Zürich, and Zug. It is mountainous and forested. One of the 3 original cantons of the Swiss Confederation, it gave its name from *c.* 1450 to the whole country. Area 351 sq. m.; pop. (1960) 78,048. The cap. is S. Pop (est.) 11,000.

SCIATICA. Persistent pain felt along the course of the sciatic nerve. It is sometimes due to inflammation of the nerve itself (neuritis), but often to the effects of pressure or inflammation (rheumatism, gout, fibrositis, etc.) on one of the nerves leading out of the lower spine.

SCIENCE RESEARCH. In the U.K. there are 4 research councils: *Medical* (1913), *Agricultural* (1931), and (replacing the Dept. of Scientific and Industrial R. under the S. and Technology Act 1965) *Science Research* and *Natural Environment*. The S.R.C. deals with fundamental R. not allocated to the others and, like them, supports R. at the univs. and its own establishments, incl. Atlas Computer Laboratory and Rutherford High Energy Laboratory (Berks), Daresbury Nuclear Physics Laboratory (Lancs), Radio and Space R. Station (Bucks), and the Royal Observatories (Hurstmonceux and Edinburgh): N.E.R.C. deals with ecology and the earth sciences. The *Nat. R. Development Corporation* (1948) secures exploitation of inventions derived from publicly supported

research. In the U.S.A. a *Nat. R. Council* (1916) estab. by the privately organized Nat. Academy of Ss. is drawn from the univs., industry and govt.

SCIENTOLOGY (sī-ent-). An 'applied religious philosophy', its name derived from Lat. *scire* 'to know' and Gk. *logos* 'branch of learning', founded in California in 1954 by Lafayette Ronald Hubbard (1911–) as the *Church of S.*, its H.Q. from 1959 being at Saint Hill Manor, East Grinstead, Sussex. It claims to 'increase man's spiritual awareness', but the movement has met with criticism, and in 1968 a govt. inquiry was set up into the practice of S. in Britain.

SCILLA (sil'a). Genus of bulbous plants of the Liliaceae family, bearing blue, pink, or white flowers; it incl. the wild hyacinth or bluebell.

SCILLY ISLANDS (sil'i). Group of islands, forming a rural dist. of Cornwall, England; they lie 25 m. S.W. of Land's End. Only 5 of the 140 islands and islets are inhabited, viz. St. Mary's, Tresco, St. Martin, Bryher, and St. Agnes. Hugh Town on St. Mary's is the cap. The mild climate and rich soil enable early vegetables and spring flowers to be produced in abundance. Area 6·3 sq. m.; pop. (1961) 2,273.

SCIPIO (sip'io), **Publius Cornelius** (d. 211 B.C.). Roman general. Elected consul in 218, during the 2nd Punic War, he was defeated by Hannibal at Ticinus and killed by the Carthaginians in Spain.

SCIPIO, Publius Cornelius, known as Scipio Africanus Major (237–*c*. 183 B.C.). Roman general, who destroyed the Carthaginian armies in Spain during 210–206. He invaded Carthage in 204, and defeated Hannibal at Zama (202).

SCIPIO, Publius Cornelius (*c*. 185–129 B.C.), known as Scipio Africanus Minor. Roman general. Appointed supreme commander during the 3rd Punic War, he took Carthage in 146, and razed it to the ground. As Governor of Spain he subdued that country in 134.

SCONE (skoon). Scottish village in Perthshire, on the Tay 2 m. N. of Perth. In its ancient abbey and royal palace most of the Scottish kings were crowned on the 'stone of destiny', now in the Coronation Chair at Westminster. A modern palace now occupies the site. Pop. (1961) 2,977.

SCOPOLAMINE. *See* HYOSCINE.

SCORPION (skōr'-). Order (Scorpiones) in the class Arachnida. Common in tropical and subtropical regions, they vary in size from ½ in. to 6 in. in length, and are viviparous and nocturnal. The sting is poisonous, but not usually fatal to healthy persons.

SCOTLAND. That part of Great Britain lying N. of the border with England. In addition to the mainland, it comprises numerous islands, incl. Arran, Bute, in the Firth of Clyde, the Inner and Outer Hebrides off the W. coast; and the Orkneys and Shetlands to the N. The W. coast is very broken, with numerous sea lochs, but the E. coast is comparatively regular. Among the main rivers are the Spey, Don, Dee, Esk, Tay, Forth, and Tweed, flowing into the North Sea; the Annan, Nith, Cree, and Esk into Solway Firth; and the Ayr, Clyde, Carron, etc., flowing into the Atlantic. The largest inland lochs are the Lomond, Maree, Ericht, Awe, Katrine, Tay, Rannoch, and Ness.

PHYSICAL. Most of the surface is highland except in the centre and extreme N.E. The Cheviot Hills lie on the border with England, and farther N. are the Lammermuir and other ranges of the Southern Uplands. These are bounded on the N. by the central Lowlands watered by the Clyde and Forth, and containing most of the country's population and industries. Farther N. still, rise the Ochill and Sidlaw Hills, and the Campsie Fells, while to the N.W. of a line running from the mouth of the Clyde to the mouth of the S. Esk lie the Highlands, a mountainous area which in turn is divided into S.E. and N.W. portions by Glen More traversed by the Caledonian Canal and

COUNTIES OF SCOTLAND

County	Area in sq. m. (exclusive of inland water)	Pop. (1961 census)	County town
Aberdeen...	... 1,971	298,503	Aberdeen
Angus (Forfar)	... 873	278,370	Forfar
Argyll ...	... 3,124	59,345	Inverary
Ayr ...	... 1,132	342,855	Ayr
Banff ...	... 630	46,400	Banff
Berwick ...	... 457	22,441	Duns
Bute ...	... 218	15,129	Rothesay
Caithness...	... 686	27,345	Wick
Clackmannan	... 54½	41,391	Alloa
Dumfries ...	... 1,072	88,423	Dumfries
Dunbarton	... 246	184,546	Dumbarton
East Lothian	... 267	52,653	Haddington
Fife ...	... 504	320,541	Cupar
Inverness...	... 4,211	83,425	Inverness
Kincardine	... 382	48,810	Stonehaven
Kinross ...	... 82	6,704	Kinross
Kirkcudbright	... 900	28,877	Kirkcubbright
Lanark ...	... 879	1,626,317	Lanark
Midlothian	... 366	580,332	Edinburgh
Moray ...	... 476	49,156	Elgin
Nairn ...	... 163	8,421	Nairn
Orkney ...	... 370	18,743	Kirkwall
Peebles ...	... 347	14,117	Peebles
Perth ...	... 2,493	127,018	Perth
Renfrew ...	... 240	338,815	Paisley
Ross and Cromarty	3,089	57,607	Dingwall
Roxburgh...	... 666	43,171	Jedburgh
Selkirk ...	... 267	21,055	Selkirk
Shetland (Zetland)	550	17,809	Lerwick
Stirling ...	... 451	194,858	Stirling
Sutherland	... 2,028	13,442	Dornoch
West Lothian	... 120	92,764	Linlithgow
Wigtown ...	... 487¼	29,107	Wigtown
Total	... 29,802	5,178,490	

Scale of Miles
0   25   50   75   100

ATLANTIC OCEAN
NORTH SEA
Orkney Islands
Cape Wrath
The Minch
Outer Hebrides
Moray Firth
Grampians
R. Don
R. Dee
Ben Nevis
Green More
Inner Hebrides
Mull
Firth of Tay
Firth of Forth
Jura
R. Clyde
Islay
R. Tay
R. Ayr
R. Tweed
Firth of Clyde
Cheviot Hills
Mull of Galloway

Below 300 feet
300-1000 feet
1000-2000 feet
Over 2000 feet

Lochs Ness and Lochy. The Grampians, in the S.E. portion, incl. Ben Nevis (4,406 ft.), highest mountain in the British Isles, and Ben Lomond, Ben Lawers, Ben Macdhui, ·Cairngorm, and other heights.

ECONOMIC. The narrow, diagonal central belt between the Firths of Clyde and Forth contains some 4 out of the 5 million population, and it was here that prosperity arose in the Industrial Revolution with shipbuilding, and the iron and coal fields that supported Scotland's heavy industry. Since the S.W.W. and particularly from the 1960s there has been a rationalization and modernization of the traditional industries, and an attempt to stem the continuing pop. decline through emigration by bringing in new industries such as aluminium smelting, petrochemicals and plastics, and – largely through American investment – electronics and business machines. Development of Tayside has been undertaken, and also promotion of a linear city from Tain to Inverness in the Moray Firth area. A break has been made with the tradition of cheap rented tenements (originally built by 19th-cent. employers and now a millstone round the necks of local authorities), and a remarkable series of new towns has sprung up along the central belt – Cumbernauld (q.v.), East Kilbride, Glenrothes, Irvine and Livingston.

The Highlands, besides their commercial value as a source of hydroelectric power, are one of Europe's greatest tourist attractions for their scenery; their grouse, deer and salmon; and their winter sport facilities. Here, and in Aberdeenshire and Ayrshire, fine cattle are raised; miniature ponies come from the Shetlands; and sheep are widely grazed. The chief crops are oats, barley, wheat and roots, and there is a dairy farming in the S.W. Forestry and fishing are important. Among specialized products which are valued exports are the tweeds of Harris and Scottish whisky. The road and rail systems are good – the bridges over the Forth and Tay being remarkable

feats of engineering – and there is a major airport at Prestwick. The chief towns are Edinburgh, the cap., and Glasgow (each with 2 univs.), and St. Andrews, Aberdeen, Dundee and Stirling are also univ. cities: the general standard of education is traditionally high.

POPULATION. Descendants of the original Celtic inhabitants form the majority of the population, though in the extreme N. and the Orkneys and Shetlands the Norse strain is marked. In 1961, 76,587 persons in the Highlands spoke Gaelic (see SCOTTISH GAELIC) of whom 1,079 spoke Gaelic only. During the 19th and 20th cents. there has been a strong current of emigration to England and other parts of the Commonwealth and to the U.S.A. At the same time many Irish settled in the industrial areas of the Lowlands. The majority of the people belong to the (Presbyterian) Church of S. (q.v.). Area (incl. 609 sq. m. of inland water) 30,411 sq. m.; pop. (1967) 5,186,600.

History. Before the Roman conquest of South Britain in the 1st cent. A.D., what is now S. was inhabited by Goidelic Celts, later called Picts. The Romans made some attempts at conquest, and during the 2nd cent. temporarily occupied the Lowlands. In the 6th cent. the Angles overran the S.E. up to the Firth of Forth; the Britons, driven northward, occupied the S.W., while Scots from Ireland settled in Argyllshire. Christianity was introduced from Ireland during the 5th–6th cents. The Picts and Scots were united by Kenneth MacAlpin in c. 844; the S.E. was conquered by Malcolm II in 1015, and in 1034 the Britons were brought into the Scottish kingdom. S. suffered during the 9th cent. from raids by the Norsemen, who held the Hebrides until the 13th cent., and the Orkneys and Shetlands until the 15th. From the 11th cent. many Englishmen and Normans settled in S.; the English language spread over the Lowlands, and the feudal system was estab. in the 12th cent.

Edward I's attempt to annex S led to a series of revolts led by Wallace and Bruce (1296-1314), ending in the Scottish victory at Bannockburn, although

SCOTLAND. Rising 340 ft. above the plain, Castle Hill at Stirling is a natural citadel and has been fortified since time out of mind. In the castle's Douglas Room James II stabbed the Earl of Douglas in 1452. *Photo: George Outram & Co. Ltd.*

England did not recognize Scottish independence until 1328. Anglo-Scottish relations continued unfriendly until the Reformation; Scottish foreign policy was based on a French alliance, which sometimes, as at Flodden (1513), resulted in disaster. The Scottish parliament, of one house, originating as a council of barons and clergy, assumed its final form with the admission of burgess representatives in the 14th cent. The Stuart dynasty, founded by Robert II who came to the throne in 1371 (N.S.), attempted with little success to control the turbulent nobles; several met violent deaths, and a succession of regencies weakened the monarchy. James IV (reigned 1488–1513) m. Margaret, dau. of Henry VII of England, in 1503.

Under Knox's leadership Calvinism was estab. as the national religion in 1560, and its victory was consolidated by Queen Mary's deposition in 1567. James VI, who, as a great-great-grandson of Henry VII inherited the English crown in 1603 from the childless Elizabeth I, and Charles I sought to bring the democratic Presbyterian Church under royal control by remodelling it on Anglican lines. The Scots

rebelled in 1638, and during the Civil War were allied with the English parliamentarians; after Charles's execution, however, they supported his son Charles II, and were conquered by Cromwell, who brought them under English rule 1651–60. Throughout the Restoration period the Presbyterians were persecuted, until the revolution of 1688 brought relief. The Scottish parliament was united with the English in 1707.

Dislike of the union was largely responsible for the Jacobite risings of 1715 and 1745. The latter was followed by the destruction of the clan system, and the eviction of many Highland farmers to make way for sheep-runs. The Union stimulated trade with America, while the coal, iron, shipbuilding and textile industries all expanded greatly during and after the Industrial Revolution. During the 18th cent. S.'s political representation was notoriously corrupt, and S. was prominent in the Radical movement from 1792 to the Reform Bill.

The later 19th cent. saw a new wave of 'clearances' in the Highlands, as sheep-farms gave way to deer forests. There has been a strong working-class movement in the industrial districts of S. since Chartist days; Glasgow in particular long remained an I.L.P. stronghold. During the 20th cent. a nationalist movement demanding the re-establishment of the Scottish parliament has developed. The first Scottish Nationalist M.P. was elected 1945, but it was not until the 1960s that the party gained strength.

SCOTLAND, Church of. The body of Christians recognized by the State as the established and national C. of S. Protestant in theology and presbyterian in organization, it was estab. in 1560 at the Reformation and after attempts to impose episcopacy, re-estab. in 1690. In 1929 the United Free C. of S., which was the result of a large secession in 1843, was re-united with the original body. The country is divided into some 2,400 parishes, in each of which there is a kirk session consisting of the minister and of several laymen called elders. Parishes are grouped into presbyteries; and these again into synods. The supreme court is the General Assembly of clergymen and laymen chosen by the presbyteries; it meets in May under a Moderator, and a Lord High Commissioner attends as the Queen's representative. The Bible is the supreme rule of faith and life, and a subordinate standard is the Westminster Confession of Faith. Worship is based on the Directory issued in 1645 and the Book of Common Order 1940. There are 1¼ million members, and in 1968 the Gen. Assembly voted that women be admitted to the Ministry.

SOVEREIGNS OF SCOTLAND

(From the unification of Scotland to the union of the crowns of Scotland and England.)

Celtic Kings

Malcolm II	... ...	1005	Edgar	1097
Duncan I	...	1034	Alexander I ...	1107
Macbeth	... ...	1040	David I	1124
Malcolm III Canmore		1057	Malcolm IV ...	1153
Donald Ban...	...	1093	William the Lion	1165
Duncan II	... ...	1094	Alexander II ...	1214
Donald Ban			Alexander III ...	1249
(restored)	...	1095		
Margaret of Norway 1286–90				

English Domination

John Balliol	...1292–6	Annexed to		
		England	1296–1306	

House of Bruce

Robert I Bruce	...	1306	David II... ...	1329

House of Stuart

Robert II	... ...	1371	James IV ...	1488
Robert III	...	1390	James V ...	1513
James I	...	1406	Mary	1542
James II	...	1437	James VI ...	1567
James III	...	1460	Union of Crowns	1603

SCOTLAND. This detail from Stanley Cursiter's painting 'The Conversation Piece' shows four of Scotland's literary figures, left to right, Edwin Muir, James Bridie, Neil Gunn and Eric Linklater. *Photo: George Outram & Co.*

SCOTLAND YARD. Headquarters of the Metropolitan Police, at Broadway, Westminster, London. Originally in S.Y. off Whitehall, it was removed to New S.Y. on the Embankment, close to the Houses of Parliament, in 1890, and in 1967 to the 21-storey building at Victoria which retained the same name. As the seat of the Criminal Investigation Dept., S.Y. is a synonym for the force of detectives.

SCOTS LAW. As compared with English law, Scottish law differs in particular in the extent to which actions involving large sums are initiated in the lower courts, and the absence of the separate system of Equity. In criminal law the principal distinguishing feature is the all-pervading system of public prosecution. The supreme civil court of Scotland is the House of Lords. Below this comes the Court of Session, possessing an original and an appellate jurisdiction; its judges have the honorary title of Lord, and a division of the Inner House, as the appeal court is called, is presided over by the Lord President, or by the Lord Justice-Clerk. Below the Court of Session is the Sheriff Court, one of which is found in every county. The supreme criminal court is the High Court of Justiciary. Other courts are the Burgh courts (criminal) where the bailies preside, and there are also justices' courts (civil and criminal). There are considerable differences in court procedure. The jury consists of 15 and may arrive at its verdict by a majority. A verdict of 'not proven' is competent. There is no coroner: the Procurator-Fiscal inquires into all suspicious deaths.

SCOTS PINE. see PINE.

SCOTT, Elizabeth Whitworth (1898–1972). British architect. She designed (after winning an international competition) the Royal Shakespeare Theatre at Stratford.

SCOTT, Sir (George) Gilbert (1811–78). British architect. Largely responsible for the mid-19th-cent. Gothic revival in England, he renovated many churches incl. Ely cathedral and Westminster Abbey with debateable results; and designed the Albert Memorial, the Foreign Office and St. Pancras Station. His grandson **Sir Giles Gilbert S.** (1880–1960), also an architect, received as his first commission Liverpool Anglican cathedral, and besides many other churches, designed Cambridge Univ. Library, Waterloo Bridge, and with his brother **Adrian Gilbert S.** (1882–1963) rebuilt the House of Commons after the S.W.W. He was awarded the O.M. in 1944.

SCOTT, Robert Falcon (1868–1912). British Antarctic explorer. B. at Devonport, he entered the navy in 1882. He commanded 2 Antarctic expeditions, in the *Discovery*, 1901–4, and in the *Terra Nova*, 1910–12. On 18 Jan. 1912 he reached the S. Pole, shortly after Amundsen, but on the return journey he and his companions, Wilson, Oates, Bowers, and Evans, perished. His journal was recovered and pub. in 1913. His widow **Kathleen** (d. 1947), given rank as widow of a K.C.B. in recognition of his work, was herself a sculptor, e.g. her statue of her husband in Waterloo Place, London; in 1922 she m. the Cons. politician Edward Hilton Young, later Lord Kennet.

His son **Peter S.** (1909–) is well known as a naturalist, e.g. his television programme *Look*, his paintings of birds (especially geese), his position as founder director of the Wildfowl Trust, and his books which incl. the autobiography *The Eye of the Wind* (1961). He has also undertaken exploratory expeditions to the Canadian Arctic, Iceland, etc., often in pursuit of ornithological interests, is a keen yacht racer, and in 1963 became British national gliding champion.

SCOTT, Sir Walter (1771–1832). Scottish poet and novelist. B. in Edinburgh, the son of a lawyer, he was educ. at the high school and univ., and in 1792 qualified as an advocate. An early attack of infantile

SIR WALTER SCOTT
By Chantrey, with his favourite dog, Maida.
Photo:
Lady Lever Collection.

paralysis lamed him slightly for life. His first literary works were translations of German ballads, and in 1797 he m. Charlotte Charpentier or Carpenter, of French origin. His *Minstrelsy of the Scottish Border* appeared in 1802, and henceforth he combined the practice of literature with legal appointments. *The Lay of the Last Minstrel* (1805) was an immediate success, and so too were *Marmion* (1808), *The Lady of the Lake* (1810), *Rokeby* (1813), and *Lord of the Isles* (1815). Out of the proceeds he purchased and rebuilt the house of Abbotsford on the Tweed, but Byron had to some extent now captured the lead with a newer style of verse romance, and S. turned to prose fiction. *Waverley* was issued in 1814, and gave its name to a long series of historical novels, incl. *Guy Mannering, The Antiquary, Old Mortality, Rob Roy, The Heart of Midlothian* and *The Bride of Lammermoor. Ivanhoe* (1819) transferred the scene to England; *Kenilworth, Peveril of the Peak, The Talisman* (1825), and *The Fair Maid of Perth* (1828) followed. In 1820 S. was created a baronet, but in 1826 he was involved in financial ruin through the bankruptcy of Constable his chief publisher, with whom fell Ballantyne & Co., the firm of printers and publishers in which S. had been for many years a sleeping partner. Refusing to accept bankruptcy, he set himself to pay off the combined debts of over £120,000. *Woodstock* (1826), a life of Napoleon, and *Tales of a Grandfather*, are among the chief products of these last painful years. The last outstanding liabilities were cleared after his death on the security of copyrights. Continuous overwork ended in a nervous breakdown. He d. at Abbotsford on 21 Sept 1832. His *Journal* was issued in 1890, and his life by J. G. Lockhart, his son-in-law, in 1837. His finest works were the books dealing with the troubled times of the Covenanters, still in living memory in his boyhood, and he excels in depicting the speech and character of ordinary, fundamentally good, people.

SCOTTISH GAELIC. This forms with Irish Gaelic and Manx the Gaelic branch of the Celtic languages, and often agrees with Manx where it differs from Irish. S.G. was introduced to Scotland by warriors from Ireland at the end of the 5th cent. It attained its widest extent in the 11th cent. It has continuously declined until by 1961 the Gaelic-speaking population numbered 76,587, and was restricted to the Western Isles and the fringes of the N. and W.

LITERATURE. The earliest examples of S.G. prose belong to 1000–1150, but the most important early original composition is the history of the MacDonalds in the Red and Black Books at Clanranald. The first printed book in S.G. was a translation of Knox's Prayer Book in 1567. Prose Gaelic is at its best in the folk-tales, proverbs, and essays by writers such as Norman MacLeod in the 19th cent. and Donald Lamont at the present day.

S.G. poetry falls into 2 main categories. The older syllabic verse was composed by professional bards. The chief sources of our knowledge of this are the Book of the Dean of Lismore (16th cent.), which is also the main early source for the Ossianic ballads; the panegyrics in the Books of Clanranald; and the Fernaig MS. Modern S.G. stressed poetry began in the 17th cent. but reached its zenith during the Jacobite period with Alexander MacDonald, Duncan Macintyre, Rob Donn, and Dugald Buchanan. Only

SCOTTISH TERRIER

William Livingstone (1808–70) kept alive the old nationalistic spirit in the 19th cent. Emergent during and after the S.W.W. was a new school impatient of tradition, incl. Somhairle MacGilleathain, George Campbell-Hay and Ruaraidh MacThómais.

SCOTTISH TERRIER. Breed of dog, known also as Aberdeen terrier. A small rough-haired terrier, either black or white, it is a good hunter.

SCRAMBLING CIRCUIT. A transmitting circuit which renders signals unintelligible unless received by the corresponding unscrambling circuit.

SCREAMERS. Birds in family Palamedeidae so named because of their harsh cries. The horned S. (*Palamedea cornuta*) has a horn-like growth on the head and black and grey plumage; *Chauna chavaria*, the crested S., also found in S. America, is often domesticated.

CRESTED SCREAMER

SCRIABIN (skrē-ahbin′), **Alexander Nicolas** (1871–1915). Russian composer. B. at Moscow, he wrote *Prometheus* and other tone-poems, employing a revolutionary system of harmony. He profoundly affected Russian music, and was also a pianist.

SCRIBE (skrēb), **Augustin Eugène** (1791–1861). French dramatist. B. in Paris, he achieved fame with the *Nuit de la Garde nationale*, and with numerous assistants produced many plays of technical merit but little profundity, incl. *Verre d'eau*, *Adrienne Lecouvreur*, and *Bertrand et Raton*.

SCRIBES. A Jewish group, incl. both priests and laymen, who devoted themselves to the study of the law of Moses, and who sat in the Sanhedrin. In the N.T. they are associated with the Pharisees.

SCULLIN, James Henry (1876–1953). Australian Labour statesman. B. at Ballarat, he sat in the House of Representatives 1910–13, and was re-elected in 1922. He was leader of the Federal Parliamentary Labour Party 1928–35, and P.M. and Min. of Industry 1929–31.

SCULPTURE. Traditionally the artistic shaping in relief or in the round of static materials such as wood, stone, metal and plastic. All the ancient civilizations – Assyrian, Egyptian, Indian, Chinese, Maya, etc. – have left examples of great sculpture, for the most part by unknown artists, and even in the case of the more recent masterpieces of European Gothic the craftsmen are un-named. Traditional European S. descends through that of Greece, Rome and Renaissance Italy, but particularly influential in the development of modern S. in the W. has been the work of Negroes of E. Africa, the natives of the South Sea Islands, and other 'primitive' peoples. An unusual departure in

SCULPTURE. In front of Helsinki Stadium Wäinö Aaltonen's statue of the runner Paavo Nurmi, holder in 1928 of 24 world records for distances varying from the mile to the marathon.
Courtesy of the Finnish Travel Information Centre

the 20th cent. has been the invention by Alexander Calder (q.v.) of the *mobile* in which the suspended components move spontaneously with the currents of air. An extension is the *structure vivante*, of which the leading exponents are Bury, Soto and Takis. In this motion is achieved by some mechanism which follows a set pattern devised by the artist, the materials used incl. such unusual items as magnets, lenses and bubbles, and the artistic impression created incl. also a certain element of sound.

SEA HORSE

Among the world's most famous sculptors are: *Classical Greek*: Phidias, Praxiteles, and Scopas; *Renaissance*: Donatello, Verrocchio, Della Robbia, and Michelangelo; *Baroque*: Bernini, Girardon, and Houdon; *Neo-Classic*: Canova, Thorwaldsen, and Flaxman; and *20th cent.*: Rodin, Maillol, Gill, Epstein, Meštrović, Dobson, Reid Dick, Henry Moore, Hepworth, Ayrton, Brancusi, Lipchitz, Butler, Borglum, and Milles.

SCUNTHORPE. English industrial town (bor.) in Lincs, 24 m. W. of Grimsby. It has one of Europe's largest iron and steel works. Pop. (1961) 67,257.

SCURVY. A disease due to lack of vitamin C that is contained in fresh vegetables, fruit and milk. The symptoms are bleeding into the skin, swelling of the gums, and drying up of the skin and hair. Treatment is by giving the vitamin.

SCUTARI (skōō′tahrē). (1) Italian form of Üsküdar, Turkey; (2) Shkodër, Albania.

SCYLLA (sil′a) and **CHARYBDIS** (karib′dis). In classical mythology a sea-monster and a whirlpool, between which Odysseus had to sail. Later writers located them in the Straits of Messina.

SCYPHOZOA. Large group of jelly-fish in the phylum Coelenterata, some measuring over 6 ft. across.

SCYTHIA (sith′i-a). Regions N. of the Black Sea varying in extent from time to time, and between the Carpathians and the Don, inhabited by the Scythians from the 7th–1st cents. B.C. Darius I made an unsuccessful attempt to conquer the Scythians in the 6th cent. B.C.; from the middle of the 4th they were slowly superseded by the Sarmatians.

SEA-ANEMONE. A section of the class Anthozoa in the phylum Coelenterata. Tube-like, they are attached at one end to some substratum, the other end being open and fringed with tentacles. They feed on crustaceans and other minute organisms. S.-As. occur in many beautiful colours, especially in tropical waters.

SEABORG, Glenn T(heodore) (1912–). American nuclear chemist. While director of nuclear chemistry research at Berkeley (1946–58), he was awarded with E. M. McMillan (also of the Univ. of California) a Nobel prize in 1951 for discoveries of 3 transuranium elements; and the production of radio-isotope U-233. In 1961 he became chairman of the U.S. Atomic Energy Commission.

SEA CUCUMBER. Slug-like echinoderm of the class Holothuroidea. The cylindrical body may be several feet in length, and dried S.Cs. from N. Australia and the Pacific seaboard of the U.S.A. are esteemed for the table by the Chinese.

SEAGULL. *See* GULL.

SEAHAM. English seaport (U.D.) in Durham, 5 m. S. of Sunderland. A village until the opening of coal-mines in the vicinity in the early 19th cent., it grew rapidly thereafter. It gave its name to the parl. constituency of Seaham Harbour which J. R. MacDonald, the sitting member and former P.M., lost to Emanuel

Shinwell in 1935 by more than 20,000 votes. Byron married Anne Isabella Milbanke at S. Hall nearby, 1815. Pop. (1961) 26,048.

SEA-HORSE. Several genera of fishes of which *Hippocampus* is typical. They range from the Atlantic through the Mediterranean to Australia. The body is compressed and covered with bony plates raised into tubercles or spines. There is a crest on the head, and the tail is prehensile. *See* illus. p. 948.

SEA KALE. Perennial plant (*Crambe maritima*) of the family Cruciferae cultivated in Europe as a vegetable. The young shoots are forced and blanched.

COMMON SEAL. Possibly origin of mermaid legends.
Photo: Ben Darby.

SEAL. Group of carnivorous marine mammals which are subdivided into the eared fur Ss. or Otariidae, and the earless hair or true Ss., the Phocidae. The fur Ss. or sea lions are found chiefly in the N. Pacific and the Behring Sea, and have been ruthlessly persecuted for the sake of their skins. They have sharper muzzles than the true Ss., and use their hind limbs in moving on land. The hair or true Ss. belong to the N. Atlantic and the Arctic Oceans, and incl. the 2 species known in Britain, the intelligent common S. (*Phoca vitulina*), and the grey S. (*Halichoerus grypus*); and the valuable Greenland S. (*Phoca groenlandica*). The streamlined body has the limbs converted to flippers, and in the hair Ss. the posterior limbs are joined with the tail. The rare elephant-S. or sea-elephant (*Mirunga*), so-named because of its enlarged proboscis, is the largest of all Ss., and is found in the S. Atlantic and Pacific. The male grows much larger than the female and may reach over 20 ft.

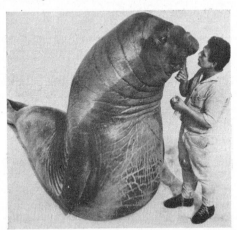

ELEPHANT SEAL. Tristan, so named because captured off Tristan da Cunha, is a popular inmate of Stuttgart Zoo. He is more than 12 ft. long, weighs about 1½ tons and has an appetite for fish in proportion.
Courtesy of Wilhelma, Stuttgart.

SEA LILY. Class (Crinoidea) of deep water echinoderms. Their rayed bodies are often borne on a stalk.

SEA LION. *See* SEAL.

SEALYHAM. Breed of terrier dog, named after the place in Pembrokeshire where it originated as a cross of the Welsh and Jack Russell terriers.

SEAMAN, Sir Owen (1861–1936). British journalist and humorous poet. Ed. at Cambridge, he joined the staff of *Punch* in 1897, and was editor 1906–32. He was made a baronet in 1933. He pub. *The Battle of the Bays* (1896), *In Cap and Bells*, etc.

SEAPLANE. An aeroplane capable of taking off from, and alighting on, water. There are 2 classes, viz. float-planes and flying-boats. The float-plane is similar to a landplane but has floats in place of wheels; the flying-boat has a hull shaped like a boat, and may also have floats attached to the wing tips. Although Ss. have the advantage of needing no airfield, they depend on smooth water for a good landing and since the S.W.W. have not often been built.

SEARLE (serl), **Ronald** (1920–). British artist. A skilled draughtsman and cartoonist, he is well known for his sketches of places and people, e.g. *Paris Sketch Book* (1950), *Rake's Progress* (1955); and for the creation of the schoolgirls of St. Trinian's in 1941, whom he abandoned in 1953.

SEATTLE (sē-atl'). Port of the state of Washington, U.S.A., situated between Puget Sound and Lake Washington. First settled 1851, as the nearest port for Alaska, S. grew in the late 19th cent. under the impetus of the Gold Rush. In the 20th it has become a major centre for the manufacture of jet aircraft (Boeing), and also has shipbuilding, timber and paper industries. There are 2 univs., Washington (1861) and Seattle (1891). Pop. (1970) 524,263.

SEA URCHINS. Popular name for a class of Echinoderms, marine animals in which the rays are not free as in star fishes and brittle stars, but united to form a globular, heart-shaped, or shield-shaped and flattened body, enclosed with plates of lime and covered with spines. Sometimes the spines are holding organs, and they also assist in locomotion. S.Us. feed on seaweed and the animals frequenting them, and are edible.

SEAWEED. General name for a vast collection of lower plant-forms that belong to the Algae (q.v.) division of the Thallophyta. They grow from about high-water mark to a depth of 50 to 100 fathoms, and are green, blue-green, red or brown. Many species are used as human food, e.g. Purple Laver (*Porphyra vulgaris*), Green Laver (*Ulva latissima*), and Caragheen Moss (*Chondrus crispus*). Ss. also enter into the production of iodine, soap, and glass, and some provide a valuable manure. *See* illus. p. 28.

SEBASTIAN, St. Christian martyr, first shot with arrows and then beaten to death *c.* 288.

SEBA'STOPOL. *See* SEVASTOPOL.

SEBENKO. Ital. name of SIBENIK.

SECOND WORLD WAR. The war of 1939–45 between the United Nations, headed by Britain, the U.S.A., the U.S.S.R., France, and China, on the one side, and the Axis powers, Nazi Germany under Hitler, Fascist Italy under Mussolini, and Japan under Hirohito, with their satellites, on the other. The war was preceded by a long series of acts of aggression by the Axis powers: the Japanese conquest of Manchuria (1931), the Italian conquest of Ethiopia (1935–6), German and Italian intervention in the Spanish Civil War (1936–9), the Japanese invasion of China (1937), the German annexation of Austria (March 1938), Sudetenland (Sept. 1938), and Czechoslovakia (March 1939), and the Italian conquest of Albania (April 1939). Britain and France attempted to meet this menace with an 'appeasement' policy, culminating in the Munich agreement (Sept. 1938). The reaction of public opinion to the annexation of Czechoslovakia forced the British and French govts. to open negotiations with the U.S.S.R. for a peace bloc; these broke down in Aug. 1939, when the U.S.S.R. concluded a non-aggression pact with Germany. On 1 Sept. Germany invaded Poland and,

2 days later Britain and France declared war. By 10 Sept. all the Dominions, except Eire, had also declared war.

The Conquest of Poland and the West 1939-40. Polish resistance speedily collapsed before the German blitzkrieg, although Warsaw held out gallantly until 27 Sept. After the Polish débâcle Russian forces reoccupied the W. Ukraine and Byelorussia, which had been annexed by Poland from Russia in 1920. On the W. front both sides remained almost completely inactive behind the Maginot and Siegfried lines until May 1940.

A new stage opened on 9 April 1940, with the German invasion of Denmark, which capitulated without resistance, and of Norway. British and French forces were landed to support Norway's resistance, but in June the invasion of France compelled their withdrawal. British dissatisfaction at the conduct of the campaign caused the fall of the Chamberlain govt., which was succeeded on 10 May by a coalition headed by Winston Churchill.

On the same day the Germans invaded the Netherlands, which surrendered on 15 May, and Belgium. German panzer divisions broke through the French line at Sedan and raced to the Channel, thus cutting off the Allied forces which had entered Belgium from the main French forces. The surrender of King Leopold of Belgium on 28 May compelled them to fall back on Dunkirk (q.v.), whence they were evacuated by a hurriedly collected rescue fleet. The French position was rendered hopeless by Italy's declaration of war on 10 June, and an armistice was signed on 22 June, whereby the Germans occupied N. France and the W. coast. Meanwhile in London the Free French movement was founded by Gen. de Gaulle.

Britain fights alone 1940-1. From Aug.-Oct. the Battle of Britain (q.v.) raged, as the Luftwaffe launched their mass daylight raids; when it ended they had lost nearly 2,000 aircraft destroyed in daylight. Night raids followed, directed first against London, and then against such provincial cities as Coventry, Birmingham, Bristol, Manchester, Liverpool, Plymouth, Glasgow and Hull. In May 1941 the attack subsided, having completely failed to break the resistance of the British people.

The Italians invaded Greece in Oct. 1940, only to be driven back far into Albania. Germany, in order to complete her control of the Balkans, attacked both Greece and Yugoslavia on 6 April 1941, and by 1 May had overrun both and compelled the British forces sent to the assistance of Greece to withdraw. A month later Crete had been invaded and occupied by German parachutists in spite of stubborn resistance by British and Commonwealth troops.

Russia and the U.S.A. enter the War 1941-2. A new stage opened on 22 June 1941 when Germany, in alliance with Finland, Hungary, and Rumania, attacked Russia. By Dec. the invaders, standing on a line from Lake Ladoga to the mouth of the Don, were within 25 m. of Moscow, and Leningrad was besieged. A Russian counter-offensive in Dec. 1941-March 1942 forced the Germans to retreat along their whole line, but in June they launched a new offensive designed to secure control of the Caucasian oilfields. Sevastopol was stormed, and by Aug. they had reached the Caucasus and were attacking Stalingrad.

Since the Battle of Britain American opinion had inclined ever more strongly, in spite of isolationist opposition, towards Roosevelt's policy of making the U.S.A. 'the arsenal of democracy', which was put into operation with the passage of the Lease-Lend Act in March 1941. On 7 Dec. Japan attacked the U.S. naval base at Pearl Harbor, and declared war on Britain and the U.S.A., and 4 days later Germany and Italy declared war on the U.S.A. The war in Europe, and the Sino-Japanese War which had been in progress since 1937, now became 2 aspects of a single world-wide struggle.

Africa and the Near East, 1940-3. The long campaign in N. Africa opened in Sept. 1940, with an Italian drive from Libya into Egypt, which reached Sidi Barrāni. Gen. Wavell counter-attacked during Dec. 1940-Feb. 1941, and advanced into Cyrenaica. The withdrawal of troops for the Balkan campaign then weakened his army, while German forces under Rommel were poured into Africa, and during March-April pushed the British back into Egypt. A new offensive by the 8th Army in Nov. 1941-Jan. 1942 drove into Libya, but was halted at Gazala, whence during May-July Rommel launched a counter-offensive which ended 70 m. from Alexandria. In

In July 1942, the Afrika Korps were at the frontier of Egypt; disaster was averted by Montgomery's great victory at Alamein in Oct. This remarkable photograph shows Australians advancing through a smoke-screen during the battle.

Oct.-Nov. Gen. Montgomery, commanding the 8th Army, won a resounding victory at El Alamein, and began a rapid advance westward, while on 8 Nov. large British and U.S. forces under Gen. Eisenhower landed in Morocco and Algeria. Caught between converging armies, the last Axis forces in Africa surrendered in May 1943.

In E. Africa the Italians had occupied British Somaliland in Aug. 1940. Forces from Kenya entered Italian Somaliland in Feb. 1941, while Eritrea was invaded from the Sudan. By May the Italian empire in E. Africa, incl. Ethiopia, was in British hands, and British Somaliland had been recovered.

The control of the Middle East was of vital importance to the British position in the Mediterranean, and vigorous measures proved necessary to counteract German intrigues in that area. Following the seizure of power by a pro-Axis premier in April 1941 British forces occupied Iraq, and in June Syria, where a pro-Vichy administration held power, was also occupied. In Aug. British and Russian troops entered Persia, where the shah was under German influence, and converted it into an important supply-line to Russia.

Italy 1943-5. Allied forces from N. Africa overran Sicily in July-Aug. 1943, and invaded the Italian mainland on 3 Sept. On 25 July Mussolini was overthrown; the new govt. signed an armistice on 8 Sept., and declared war on Germany on 13 Oct. Large German forces entered Italy, and put up a stubborn resistance, first on the Gustav Line, S. of Rome, and after it was broken in May 1944 on the Gothic Line, from Pisa to Rimini. This in turn was breached in Sept., and after a final Allied offensive in April 1945 the Germans surrendered on 29 April.

Victory in the East 1943-5. The failure of the

Germans to capture Stalingrad, together with the victory of El Alamein and the landings in N. Africa, marked the turning-point of the war. A Russian offensive in Nov. 1942–March 1943 cleared the Caucasus and drove the Germans back to the Donetz, while at Stalingrad 330,000 of the invaders were killed or captured. A new German drive in July was halted within a week; the Russians then opened an offensive which continued until Nov., and recaptured Kiev and Zhitomir. During Jan.–April 1944 they liberated the Ukraine and entered Rumania. A general offensive in June–Oct. expelled the invaders from Russian soil, forced Finland, Rumania, and Bulgaria out of the war, and entered E. Prussia, Poland and Yugoslavia. British forces entered Greece in Oct., and by the end of 1944 the Germans had been expelled from the greater part of the Balkans. Valuable assistance was rendered to the Allies by Tito's partisans, and by the Greek and Albanian resistance movements. A last Russian offensive in Jan.–May 1945 liberated Poland and Austria, entered Czechoslovakia, and reached Berlin.

Victory in the West 1944-5. The way had been prepared for the opening of the 'second front' in the W. by Allied mass bombing raids on Germany, which since 1940 had steadily increased in number and size. On 6 June 1944 the invasion was launched, under the supreme command of Gen. Eisenhower. A bridgehead was estab. in N.W. France between Cherbourg and Le Havre, and after much hard fighting the Americans broke through the German lines at St. Lô, and the British at Caen. On 15 Aug. U.S. and Free French troops landed on the Mediterranean coast and advanced rapidly northwards. The people of Paris rose, and compelled the Germans to surrender on 25 Aug. By the end of Sept. the Allies had liberated most of France, and entered Belgium and the Netherlands, but the airborne operation at Arnhem (q.v.) was a failure, and on the German frontier they were halted by the Siegfried Line. After a temporary set-back caused by Rundstedt's counter-offensive in the Ardennes in Dec., they launched a new offensive in Feb. 1945 which broke the Siegfried Line. In March the Rhine was crossed; the Canadians advanced through the Netherlands; the British into N. Germany, the Americans and French into Central and S. Germany. On 24 April the Russians entered Berlin, which surrendered on 2 May. On 7 May Germany surrendered unconditionally.

The War at Sea. In the Atlantic British merchant ships had to contend with German submarines and surface raiders, who from 1940 controlled the coastline from Norway to France. Shipping losses reached their height in 1942; thereafter they declined, as more escort vessels and aircraft became available for convoys. Outstanding engagements in the Atlantic were the battle of the river Plate (13 Dec. 1939), when 3 cruisers badly damaged the *Admiral Graf Spee*; the engagements in Narvik harbour (10 and 13 April 1940); and the sinking of the *Hood* by the *Bismarck* (24 May 1941) and of the *Bismarck* by the *Dorsetshire* (27 May). Italy's entry into the war created a dangerous situation in the Mediterranean until 1943, and Malta, the chief British naval base, suffered continual bombing. A spectacular victory over the Italian fleet was won off Cape Matapan on 28 March 1941. The delivery of

'Loading tanks for Russia', by Leslie Cole.
Courtesy of the Imperial War Museum.

vital supplies to Russia via the Arctic Ocean and the Barents Sea was maintained in face of heavy opposition and natural difficulty.

The Japanese War 1941-5. The attack on Pearl Harbor, which put the U.S. Pacific fleet out of action, air raids on the Philippines, and the sinking

In spite of tremendous difficulties in terrain and transportation the 14th army in Burma engaged and defeated the bulk of the Japanese land forces in the Far East. This painting by Leslie Cole shows an armed patrol of the Queen's Own (R.W.K.) in the flooded Sittang Bend. *Courtesy of Imperial War Museum.*

of the *Prince of Wales* and the *Repulse* on 10 Dec. 1941 temporarily gave the Japanese naval and air supremacy in the Pacific. They immediately overran Malaya from Thailand, where they had estab. bases, and captured Singapore with 60,000 British troops in Feb. 1942. Hong Kong had surrendered on 25 Dec. The conquest of the Philippines was completed by 6 May, when Corregidor fell, although guerrilla resistance continued, and that of the Dutch E. Indies by 10 March. Burma was also invaded from Thailand, and after the fall of Mandalay in May the British forces there were withdrawn to India. During Jan.-March Japanese troops were landed in New Britain, the Solomons, and New Guinea.

The first Allied successes against the Japanese were the naval victories in the Coral Sea (4–7 May) and off Midway (4–7 June), when U.S. aircraft inflicted heavy losses on Japanese fleets. Another victory followed on 2–5 March 1943, when a Japanese convoy was destroyed in the Bismarck Sea. A successful offensive was launched in New Guinea in Sept. 1942–Jan. 1943, while during Aug. 1942–Feb. 1943 U.S. marines expelled the Japanese from Guadalcanal, in the Solomons. After occupying certain of the Aleutian Is. in June 1942, the Japanese were forced to withdraw in May–Aug. 1943.

From 1943 the command against Japan was divided between Lord Mountbatten in Burma, Admiral Nimitz in the Central Pacific, and Gen. MacArthur in the S.W. Pacific. A threatened invasion of India was averted in March–June 1944; the reconquest of Burma was begun in Jan. 1945, and was practically completed with the fall of Rangoon in May. In the Central Pacific, the Gilbert, Marshall, and Mariana Islands were seized by the Allies in 1943-4, and in the S.W. New Guinea was slowly reconquered. In Oct. 1944 the reconquest of the Philippines began, and was completed by July 1945. The seizure of Iwo-Jima in Feb.–March 1945, and of Okinawa in April–June, supplied the necessary bases for the final attack on Japan.

The end came suddenly. An atom bomb was dropped on Hiroshima on 6 Aug., and another on Nagasaki on 9 Aug. Russia declared war on Japan, and invaded Manchuria on 8 Aug. Hirohito announced his acceptance of the Allied terms on 14 Aug., and the formal surrender was signed on 2 Sept.

SECRET AGENT. *See* SECRET SERVICE.

SECRETARIES. Officials of public companies and societies, etc., whose chief professional organizations in Britain are the Chartered Institute of Ss. and the Corporation of Ss.

SECRETARY BIRD. Bird of prey (*Serpentarius secretarius*), native to S. Africa, whose erectile crest of feathers bears some fancied resemblance to a pen behind a clerk's ear – hence the name. Mainly grey, with black and white tail feathers, it stands about 4 ft. high, and is officially protected on account of the deadly way in which it hunts poisonous snakes.

SECRETARY BIRD

SECRETARY OF STATE. Originally the title given under Elizabeth I to 2 officials conducting the royal correspondence. It is now borne by a number of the more important ministries, e.g. the S. of S. for Foreign Affairs, etc. In the U.S. the Foreign Minister is called the Secretary of State.

SECRET SERVICE. Govt. organization maintained by most countries to keep a check on the activities of foreign agents (counter-espionage) and to secure information from foreign countries relating to activities considered likely to endanger the safety of the state (espionage). In the U.K. the service is divided into defence intelligence and political intelligence – working for the Foreign Office. This service is paid for by secret funds – until 1945 a nominal figure of £100 was incl. in the estimates to cover the S.S., but in 1946 parliament began to make an annual vote of £2,500,000 (£10,500,000 by 1969) in the U.S.A. the F.B.I. (q.v.) deals with espionage, treason, and other matters relating to security. *See* STEPHENSON, SIR WILLIAM.

Spies may be (i) citizens sent abroad to work in the interests of their own country; (ii) citizens spying on their own country for the benefit of another; (iii) double spies working simultaneously for their own and another country. The first kind are usually persons of integrity (T. E. Lawrence was a famous British example who worked against the Turks in the Near East during the F.W.W.; another was the German naval capt. Franz von Rintelen (q.v.) who carried out sabotage in the U.S.A. on behalf of Germany and against the Allies in the same war); the second kind are traitors to their own country and often work for money but, especially in the 20th cent., may be actuated by a misplaced idealism (e.g. Karl Fuchs, a German refugee and brilliant scientist who became a British subject and gave the Russians the secret of the atom bomb, receiving only £100 for information which only he could have given); the third kind usually work for money, though not always for substantial amounts: the most notorious double spy was probably Colonel Alfred Redl, who while head of espionage in the Austro-Hungarian secret service before the F.W.W. (and very successful in his job) also spied on his own country for Russia, among other things passing to the Russians the Austro-Hungarian mobilization plans in the event of war.

In war-time spies are normally executed, generally after civil or military trial, though in the actual battle area they are likely to be shot out of hand. Among the most notorious war-time spies was Mata Hari, a woman of Dutch origin who had spent a number of years in Java and posed as a Javanese: she spied for the Germans and was caught and shot by the French in 1917. In peace-time the punishment of a convicted spy may vary from imprisonment (Fuchs was con-

demned to 14 years) to expulsion. Among the few spies executed in peace-time were Julius Rosenberg and his wife Ethel, who were executed at Sing Sing, N.Y., in 1953 for passing atom bomb secrets to Russia.

The operations of the S.S. depend on codes (in which groups of letters or numbers represent words, sentences, or a definite combination of word sequences) and ciphers, in which a letter (or number) represents another letter. The easier a cipher or code is to use, the easier it is to break, and vice versa. At the time of the Japanese attack on Pearl Harbor, the Americans had broken the code used by the Japanese who, because of the extreme difficulty of basing a code on the Japanese language, were in fact using one based on English. Invisible ink, microfilm records, secretly installed listening and recording apparatus are other adjuncts of the S.S. One method of counter-espionage is to plant false information on known agents of another country – and this false information, having gone the rounds, has been known to deceive the originator on its return home, at least momentarily.

Espionage in England and France dates from the 17th cent., in Germany from the mid-19th cent. Russia had an elaborate system of internal espionage long before the 1917 Revolution, and under the Soviet govt. both internal and external espionage services have been elaborated and made more effective.

SECUNDERABA′D. N. suburb of Hyderabad city, Andhra, India, formerly a separate town. It was founded as a British army cantonment, with a parade ground where 7,000 troops could be exercised. The Indian army took it over after independence, 1947. It was by experiments at S. that Sir Ronald Ross estab. that malaria is carried by the anopheles mosquito.

SEDAN (sedoń′). Frontier town on the Meuse, in Ardennes dept., France. In 1870 S. was the scene of Napoleon III's surrender to the Germans; in the S.W.W. S. was in German occupation 1940–4. It has textile mills, dyestuffs, and other industrial plants. Its prosperity dates from the days when it was a Huguenot centre. Turenne was b. at S. Pop. (1962) 21,766.

SEDAN CHAIR (sedan′). Portable vehicle accommodating one person, and carried on 2 poles by 2 bearers. It is said to have been invented at Sedan, was introduced into England during the reign of James I, and was in general use in the 18th cent.

SEDATIVES. Drugs and other measures which depress the function of the nerves and produce a soothing effect, e.g. bromides, aspirin, paraldehyde, barbital and its derivatives. Since the S.W.W. many new drugs have come into use to replace and reinforce the older ones. Important among the *tranquillizers* are chlorpromazine, reserpine and meprobamate and among the *anti-depressants* Nardil and Marplan. These can act in some cases as very efficient Ss.

SEDDON, Richard John (1845–1906). New Zealand Liberal statesman. B. in Lancs, he emigrated to Australia, and in 1866 to New Zealand. He entered the legislature in 1879 and was P.M. 1893–1906.

SEDGE. Genus (*Carex*) of perennial grasslike plants, of the Cyperaceae family, that grow for the most part in wet and swampy ground, fens and marshes. Some are used in paper-making.

SEDGEMOOR. Tract of country, formerly marshy, 3 m. S.E. of Bridgwater, in Somerset, England, where in 1685 Monmouth's rebellion was crushed.

SEDITION. In the U.K., S. is an offence against the Crown and govt., differing from treason (q.v.) in that it is not capital. Attempts to bring into contempt or hatred the person of the reigning monarch, the govt. as lawfully estab., or either house of parl.; or to incite the sovereign's subjects to bring about a change of govt. other than by lawful means are Ss. The raising of discontent between different sections of those subjects is also S. In the 18th and 19th cents it was eld by the courts that any criticism of the govt. was editious, and in 1758 John Shebbeare was imprisoned or libelling William III (d. 1702) and George I (d. 1727); this attitude has entirely changed, and it is accepted that any criticism of the govt. aimed at reform is allowable. In the U.S.A., under a wartime act of 1917, reinstated 1950, S. is (i) making a false report intended to interfere with the operations of U.S. armed forces or to assist the enemy; (ii) attempting to seduce the armed forces from their allegiance or to obstruct recruiting.

SEELAND. The main island of Denmark on which Copenhagen is situated. It is low-lying with an irregular coastline. Dairy farming is the main occupation. Area 2,700 sq. m.; pop. (1960 est.) 1,893,163.

SEELEY, Sir John Robert (1834–95). British historian. B. in London, he was ed. at Cambridge, where he became prof. of modern history in 1869. His *The Expansion of England* (1883) was a masterly study of the growth of the British Empire.

SEFERIS (sefā'ris), **George.** Pseudonym of the Greek poet and diplomat George Seferiades (1900–71). B. in Smyrna, he was ed. at Athens Univ. and at the Sorbonne, and entered the diplomatic service, becoming ambassador to the Lebanon (1953–7) and then to the U.K. (1957–62), when he did much to help resolve the Cyprus crisis. He pub. his first vol. of lyrics in 1931 and his *Collected Poems* in 1950, his work having a deep feeling for the Hellenic world and showing the influence of the French symbolists and of T. S. Eliot, whose *The Waste Land* he trans. into modern Greek. He received a Nobel prize 1963.

SÉGAL, Arthur (1875–1944). Rumanian artist. Born in Rumania, he later worked in various Continental countries and in England. His art is an extension of Cubism, though he returned in his last period to naturalism, and was a remarkable pioneering force in modern art.

SEGŌ'VIA, Andrès (1894–). Spanish guitarist. Performing at concerts throughout the world from 1914, he has estab. the guitar as a serious instrument by his arrangements for it of classical works by Bach, Handel, Scarlatti, etc.

SEGŌ'VIA. Town of central Spain, cap. of S. prov., c. 40 m. N.W. of Madrid, and famous for its Moorish alcázar, 16th cent. cathedral, and Roman aqueduct. Textiles are made. Isabella of Castile was crowned at S. in 1474. Pop. (1960) 31,000.

SÉGUR (sehgür'), **Louis Philippe,** comte de (1753–1830). French diplomat. B. in Paris, he was ambassador to St. Petersburg for 5 years, and served in the American War of Independence. He pub. historical works, and *Mémoires*.

SEINE (sān). River of France which rises N.W. of Dijon on the plateau of Langres and flows for 481 m., generally in a N.W. direction, to the English Channel near Le Havre, passing through Paris and Rouen and receiving the Yonne, Marne, Oise, etc.

SEISMO'LOGY (sīz-). Study of earthquake phenomena. See EARTHQUAKE.

SEISMOGRAPH. Instrument for recording earth tremors.

SEKHMET. Egyptian goddess of heat and fire. She was represented with the head of a lioness, and worshipped at Memphis as the wife of Ptah.

SEKONDI (sek'undē). Port in Ghana, W. Africa, with a boatbuilding yard. Pop. (1960) 34,513

SELA'NGOR. State of the Fed. of Malaysia. it was under British protection from 1874, and a Federated State 1895–1946. Kuala Lumpur, on the Klang r., is the cap. of S. and of the Federation. Klang is the seat of the Sultan and a centre for rubber-growing and tin-mining. Port Swettenham exports tin. Area 3,167 sq. m.; pop. (1966) 1,386,251.

SELBORNE, Roundell Palmer, 1st earl of (1812–95). British lawyer and statesman. He was Lord Chancellor in Gladstone's govts. of 1872–4 and 1880–5, and carried through the Judicature Act of 1873, which reorganized the law courts.

SELBORNE. English village in Hampshire, 5 m. S.S.E. of Alton, made famous by *The Natural History of S.* (1789) of Gilbert White (1720–93) who was b. here. The S. Society (founded 1885) promotes the study of wild life.

SELDEN, John (1584–1654). English jurist and statesman. B. in Sussex, he was an ardent Parliamentarian and opponent of Divine Right, and wrote legal works. His *Table Talk* (1689) consists of short essays on political and religious questions.

SELE'NE. Greek moon-goddess, in later times identified with Artemis.

SELE'NIUM (Gk. *Selene* Moon). Element discovered in 1817 by Berzelius, associated with tellurium and the sulphur family, and existing in several allotropic forms, the grey being a conductor of electricity when illuminated and its conductivity increasing markedly with the brightness of the incident light: symbol Se, at. wt. 78·96, at. no. 34. It occurs as selenides and in many sulphide ores, and is used in making red glasses and enamels, and as a semi-conductor used extensively in photocells and rectifiers.

SELFRIDGE, Harry Gordon (1857–1947). American business man. B. in Wisconsin, U.S.A., he became a member of the firm of Marshall Field & Co. of Chicago. Retiring in 1903, he then went to London, and in 1909 founded the Selfridge Store, the first mammoth department store in Britain.

SELKIRK, Alexander (1676–1721). Scottish sailor. While serving in 1704 as a privateer under Dampier he was marooned on Juan Fernandez island, where he remained until rescued in 1709. This episode suggested Defoe's *Robinson Crusoe*.

SELKIRK. Scottish market town (burgh), cap. of Selkirkshire, on the Ettrick, c. 5 m. S.W. of Galashiels It manufactures woollens. Pop. (1961) 5,634.

SELKIRKSHIRE. Inland county of Scotland. The main rivers are the Tweed, Yarrow, and Ettrick. The county is mainly hilly and sheep are grazed extensively. Wool manufacture and tanning are the main industries. Selkirk is the cap. and Galashiels the largest town. Area 267 sq. m.; pop. (1961) 21,055.

SELOUS (selōō), **Frederick Courtney** (1851–1917). British explorer and big-game hunter. B. in London, he went to S. Africa in 1871, and led the British S. Africa Company's pioneer expedition to Mashonaland (1890–2), later fighting in the Matabele wars. He was killed in action at Beho Beho, E. Africa.

SELWYN, George Augustus (1809–78). British churchman. Appointed bp. of New Zealand and Melanesia in 1841, he preached in Maori and travelled throughout his enormous diocese. He reluctantly became bp. of Lichfield in 1868. In 1882 S. Coll., Cambridge, was founded in his memory.

SELZNICK, David Oliver (1902–1965). American film producer. B. at Pittsburgh, he produced for various companies before himself organizing Vanguard Films Inc., Selznick Studio, etc. His productions incl. *King Kong* and *Gone with the Wind*.

SEMA'NTICS. Branch of philology dealing with the changing meaning of words, also known as semasiology.

SEMAPHORE (sem'afor). A signalling apparatus consisting of a post with movable arms, the position of which conveys the message. By night lights are employed. In the army and navy signallers convey messages by their arms with or without the aid of flags.

SEMARA'NG. Indonesian town in Java, cap. of Central Java prov., 270 m. E.S.E. of Djakarta. Its exposed harbour is not safe in the time of the monsoon. There are shipbuilding yards; exports incl. coffee, teak, sugar, tobacco, kapok, and petroleum from nearby oilfields. Pop. (1967) 503,153.

SE'MELE. In Greek mythology, the daughter of

Cadmus and mother of Dionysus by Zeus. At Hera's suggestion she demanded that Zeus should appear to her in all his glory, but when he did so she was consumed by lightning.

SEMICONDUCTOR. Crystalline material whose electrical conductivity lies between that of metals and insulators and increases with temperature over a certain range, and in some cases upon illumination. Some common Ss. are germanium, silicon, selenium, cuprous oxide, cadmium sulphide, boron, lead telluride; their most important applications are in transistors and light-sensitive cells.

SEMIPALATI′NSK (semē-). Town in Kazakh S.S.R., cap. of S. region, on the Irtysh r. Founded 1718 as a Russian frontier post, it has meat packing factories, tanneries, and flourmills. The region produces nickel and chromium and includes the Kvzyl Kum atomic testing ground. Pop. (1967) 197,000.

SEMI′RAMIS (*c.* 800 B.C.). Assyrian queen, who was later identified with the goddess Ishtar.

SE′MITES. Traditionally, the descendants of Shem, one of the sons of Noah, but in ethnology the name of a number of Caucasian peoples of the Near and Middle East. Most widely distributed are the Jews; closely related to them were the Ammonites, Moabites, and Edomites; also in the ancient world were the Babylonians, Assyrians, Chaldaeans, Carthaginians, Phoenicians, and Canaanites, and in the modern world are the Arabs, Ethiopians, Syrians, etc. Typical features are a whitish skin, black hair, prominent nose, full lips, and dolichocephalic skull. From the Ss. have sprung the great world religions of Judaism, Christianity and Islam.

SEMITIC LANGUAGES. A family of languages consisting of 4 chief divisions: (1) the eastern, including Babylonian and Assyrian; (2) the northern, including Aramaic and its offsprings Palmyrene, Nabataean, Samaritan, etc.; (3) the western, mainly represented by Hebrew and Phoenician (whence Punic); and (4) the southern, with Arabic and its offsprings, also Ethiopic whence Amharic, Tigré, etc., and Sabaean and Minaean.

SEMOLINA (-lē′na). Hard grains of wheat, too coarse to be sieved in the bolting of flour. The food is used in the form of puddings, and also is an integral part of macaroni, etc.

SENANA′YAKE, Don Stephen (1884–1952). Ceylonese statesman. He was first P.M. of the Dominion 1947–52, and was succeeded in the office by his son **Dudley Shelton S.** (1911–) 1952–3, 1960, and 1965–70.

SENATE (sen′at). The Roman 'council of elders'. Originally consisting of the heads of patrician families, it was recruited from ex-magistrates and persons who had rendered notable public service, but was periodically purged by the censors. Although nominally advisory, it controlled finance and foreign policy. Under the empire it lost all real power.

The U.S. Senate consists of 100 members, 2 from each state, elected for a 6-year term. The Italian upper chamber is also known as the S., as is that of France under the 5th Republic. The name is also given to the governing bodies in the univs. of Cambridge and London.

SE′NECA, Lucius Annaeus (*c.* 4 B.C.–A.D. 65). Roman philosopher. B. at Cordova, he was the son of Seneca the Elder (d. A.D. 39), author of books on rhetoric. S. was Nero's tutor but after his accession fell into disfavour and committed suicide at Nero's order. He wrote essays on ethical subjects from the Stoic standpoint, and 9 tragedies which in 16th cent. England were accepted as classical models.

SENEFELDER (sā′ne-), **Alois** (1771–1834). German engraver. B. at Prague, he is famous for his discovery in 1796 of the art of lithography.

SENEGAL (senegawl′). River of W. Africa, formed by the confluence of the Bafing and the Bakhoy and flowing for 700 m. in a N.W. and W. direction to reach the Atlantic near St. Louis. In 1968 the Organization of Riparian States of the River S. (Guinea, Mali, Mauretania and S.) was formed to develop the river valley, incl. a dam for hydroelectric power and irrigation at Joina Falls in Mali: its H.Q. is in Dakar. The river gives its name to the **Republic of Senegal** which lies S. of the r. with a coastline on the Atlantic. Except on the coast, it surrounds Gambia. Cattle, sheep, goats, pigs, camels and horses are reared; groundnuts, millet, maize are grown. Minerals incl. phosphates, titanium, bauxite and iron ore. The cap. is Dakar. Area 76,000 sq. m.; pop. (1965) 3,500,000.

The French estab. themselves on the coast of S. early in the 17th cent. and gradually extended their authority inland. Made a colony 1895 and a territory 1946, S. became independent within the Fr. Community 1960: a Treaty of Assocn. was signed with Gambia 1967. The pres. is Léopold Senghor (1906–), also a poet and essayist, elected 1960; and there is a P.M. and cabinet responsible to a nat. assembly, elected by universal suffrage.

SENNA. *See* CASSIA.

SENNACHERIB (sena′kerib) (reigned 705–681 B.C.). King of Assyria. He crushed revolts in Tyre, Sidon and Babylon, but failed to capture Jerusalem, and was murdered by his sons.

SENNA′R. Town of Sudan Republic on the Blue Nile, 160 m. S.E. of Khartoum. It is a railway junction, and nearby is the Sennar dam (1926), part of the Gezira irrigation scheme. Pop. *c.* 8,000.

SENS (soṅs). Cathedral town in Yonne dept., France, on the Yonne, famous for its cathedral and old walls. Manufactures incl. chemicals and cutlery. Pop. (1962) 21,742.

SENUSSI (senoo′sē), **Sidi Mohammed ben Ali es** (*c.* 1796–1860). Moslem religious reformer. B. in Algeria, he preached a return to the puritanism of early Islam and met with much success in Libya, where he made Jaghbub his centre and founded the sect called after him. The S., who attacked the British during the F.W.W., were subdued by the Italians in 1931, and in the S.W.W. they joined a Libyan Arab Force formed by Britain.

SEOUL (se-ool′). Cap. of S. Korea, nr. the Han r., and with its port at Inchon. There is a 14th cent. palace, univ., and engineering, textile, and food processing industries. Pop. (1967) 3,800,000.

SEPTICAEMIA (-sē′-). Blood poisoning; the invasion of the circulating blood by bacteria, as may occur in bacterial endocarditis. The condition is serious, but made less so by the advent of antibiotics.

SEPT-ÎLES. Town in Quebec, Canada, on 6 islands and a spur of the mainland in a bay on the N. shore of the St. Lawrence, 350 m. E.N.E. of Quebec city. A trading post since 1650, it became the port for the iron ore deposits discovered in 1950 near Schefferville, Labrador, with which it is linked by a railway, completed 1954, 358 m. long. Pop. (1961) 14,196.

SEPTUAGESIMA. The 3rd Sunday before Lent; the 70th day before Easter.

SEPTUAGINT (Lat. *septuaginta*, seventy). Oldest Greek version of the O.T., traditionally made by 70 scholars.

SEQUOIA (sēkwoi′a). Genus of conifers in the family Taxodiaceae. There are 2 species, the redwood (*S. sempervirens*) of the Californian coast, and the bigtree (*S. gigantea*), also evergreen, which is the largest of living trees and, except for the bristlecone pine, the oldest, e.g. the General Sherman tree in the S. National Park (estab. in California in 1890) is 272 ft. high, has a diameter of 30 ft., and is more than 3,000 years old.

SERAING (seraṅ′). Belgian town on the Meuse, 4 m. S.W. of Liège, famed for the locomotive and engineering works founded in 1817 by John Cockerill, an Englishman. Pop. (1966) 40,937.

SERAJEVO. See SARAJEVO.

SERAMPU'R. Town of W. Bengal, Republic of India, on the Hooghli, *c.* 10 m. N.N.W. of Calcutta. A Danish settlement, it was bought by the British in 1845. Pop. (1961) 91,521.

SERANG. Alternative form of CERAM.

SERAPHIM (ser'afim). Celestial beings, of a high order of angelic hierarchy, mentioned in Isaiah.

SERĀ'PIS. Graeco-Egyptian god, a combination of Hades and Osiris, invented by the Ptolemies; his finest temple was the Serapeum at Alexandria.

SERBIA. Federal republic of Yugoslavia, including the autonomous areas of Vojvodina and Kostovo-Metohija. It includes the federal cap., Belgrade. In the N. are fertile plains watered by the Danube but the S. is mountainous. Wheat, maize, fruit, flax, tobacco, and vines are cultivated. Mineral resources are being developed. Area 34,080 sq. m.; pop. (1961) 7,629,113.

History. The Serbs settled in the Balkans in the 7th cent., and accepted Christianity in the 9th. They were united into one kingdom *c.* 1169, and under Stephen Dushan (1331–55) founded an empire covering most of the Balkans. After their defeat at Kossovo (1389) they became tributary to the Turks, who in 1459 annexed S. Uprisings in 1804–16, led by Kara George and Milosh Obrenovich, forced the Turks to recognize S. as an autonomous principality under Milosh. The assassination of Kara George by his orders gave rise to a long feud between the 2 houses. After a war with Turkey in 1876–8 S. became an independent kingdom. On the assassination of the last Obrenovich in 1903 the Karageorgevich dynasty came to the throne. The Balkan Wars of 1912–13 greatly enlarged S.'s territory at the expense of Turkey and Bulgaria. S.'s designs on Bosnia and Herzegovina, backed by Russia, led to friction with Austria, culminating in the outbreak of war in 1914. S. was completely overrun in 1915–16, and was occupied until 1918, when it became the nucleus of the new kingdom of the Serbs, Croats and Slovenes, later Yugoslavia (q.v.).

SERFDOM. The legal and economic status of peasants under feudalism (q.v.). The serf was normally bound to the soil; while he could not be sold like a slave, he was not free to leave his lord's estate. He had to give a certain number of days' unpaid labour every week on his lord's land, in addition to extra labour at harvest time and other busy seasons, and to pay tribute in kind; in return he was allowed to cultivate a portion of the estate for his own benefit. In England S. died out during the 14th–17th cents., but it lingered on in France until 1789, in Russia until 1861, and in most European countries until the early 19th cent.

SERGIUS OF RADO-NEZH, St. (1314/19–1392). Russian saint, founder of the monastery of the Blessed Trinity in the forest near Radonezh. Prior from 1334, he personified the Russian monastic ideal, and besides acting as mediator among Russian feudal princes, inspired Dmitri's victory over the Tartars at Kulikovo.

SERIALISM. See DUNNE, JOHN WILLIAM.

SERINGAPATA'M. Town of Mysore state, Republic of India, 10 m. N. of Mysore city. It was the cap. of the state 1610–1799, when it was taken from

ST. SERGIUS. Even under the Soviet régime many thousands of pilgrims still visit the saint's tomb in the small Church of the Trinity and St. Sergius built at Zagorsk in 1422, some 40 miles from Moscow. The silver shrine containing the relics of the saint was the gift of Ivan the Terrible.
Courtesy of Constantin de Grunwald.

SERVICE TREE

Tippoo Sahib (who d. of wounds) by Cornwallis. Pop. *c.* 12,000.

SEROWE (serō'wā) Capital town of the Bamangwato tribe, numbering about 200,000, in Botswana. Pop. (1964) 34,182.

SERPENT. See SNAKE.

SERPENTINE. A mineral, hydrated magnesium silicate, occurring usually in soft rocks. The green mottled appearance resembles that of a serpent. The rare precious S. is used for ornamentation. Fibrous varieties are known as asbestos (q.v.) and chrysotile.

SĒ'RUM. (1) The clear part of the blood left after clotting and removal of blood corpuscles and fibrin; and the exudate in blisters. It contains the substances which protect against disease (antibodies), and also other proteins; as well as the fats and sugars of the blood. (2) The fluid which lubricates the peritoneum, pleura and other body cavities not open to the air.

SERVĒ'TUS, Michael (1511–53). Spanish theologian. B. in Navarre, he practised medicine at Vienne. In his theological writings he put forward unitarian and Anabaptist views, for which he was persecuted by the Inquisition at Lyons, and burned alive by Calvin at Geneva.

SERVICE, Robert William (1874–1938). Anglo-Canadian author. B. in Preston, he emigrated to Canada at 20, and achieved great popularity with ballads of the Yukon in gold-rush days, e.g. 'The Shooting of Dan McGrew'.

SERVICE TREE. Tree *Sorbus domestica* of the Rosaceae, found in Europe and Asia. It has pinnate leaves and small oval fruit. The wild S.T. (*Pyrus sorbus*) is a native of Britain.

SERVO SYSTEM. An automatic control system in which the output follows the input in a desired way, and incorporating a feedback to the input derived from the difference between the actual and the desired output.

SESAME (ses'amē). Annual plant (*Sesamum indicum*) of the family Pedaliaceae, which originated in the East. The Indian variety (*S. orientale*) produces oily seeds used for food and soap making.

SESSION, Court of. See COURT OF SESSION.

SET. Egyptian god of night, the desert, and of all evils; he was the murderer of Osiris, and is portrayed as a grotesque animal.

SÈTE (set). Seaport on the Mediterranean coast of France, in Hérault dept., 18 m. S.W. of Montpellier. A fishing centre, it has sardine canneries and trades in wine, brandy, chemicals, etc. It was founded in 1666 as an outlet to the Canal du Midi. Pop. (1962) 36,816.

SETON, Ernest Thompson (1860–1946). British author, whose name was originally Ernest S. Thompson. B. in England, he was brought up in Canada, became noted for his animal drawings and books.

SETON-WATSON, Robert William (1879–1951). British historian. B. in Perthshire, he made a detailed study of central European problems, was prof. of Czechoslovak studies at Oxford 1945–9, and wrote

ERNEST THOMPSON SETON. A male ruffed grouse 'ready to drum' with outspread wings against the air in courtship display.
Courtesy of New York State Museum and Science Service.

2B

The Rise of Nationality in the Balkans, Britain and the Dictators, etc. His son **George S.-W.** (1916–), became prof. of Russian history at London in 1951, and has pub. *The New Imperialism* (1961), etc.

SETTER

SETTER. Breed of dogs, so called because they are trained in crouching or 'setting' on the sight of game to be pursued. The English S. may be black, tan, or liver and white; the Scottish S. is of a much heavier type; and the Irish S. is usually a rich red.

SETTLEMENT, Act of. Act passed in 1701 confining the succession to the throne of Great Britain to Protestants, and settling the succession, after William III and Anne, on the house of Hanover.

SEURAT (sörah'), **Georges** (1859–91). French artist. B. in Paris, he introduced with Signac the technique of Pointillism (q.v.), an outstanding example of his work being 'La Baignarde' (Tate Gallery). In our illus. 'A Young Woman holding a powder-puff' – the girl is the artist's mistress Mlle Madeleine Knobloch. The mirror on the wall once showed a self-portrait of Seurat – still visible under X-ray – but this was painted out for the sake of decorum before the work was exhibited and the pot of flowers substituted.

Courtesy of Courtauld Institute Galleries, London.

SEVASTOPOL (sěvast'opol). Port and fortress in the Crimea, Ukraine S.S.R., base of the Russian Black Sea fleet and a seaside resort, with shipbuilding yards and a wine-making industry. S. was founded by Catherine II in 1784. The fortress was besieged by the English and French Oct. 1854–Sept. 1855 before S. fell; the Germans took it after a siege from Nov. 1941–4 July 1942; the Russians re-took it in 1944. Pop. (1967) 200,000.

SEVENOAKS. English market town (U.D.) in Kent, 20 m. S.S.E. of London. Nearby are the 17th cent. houses Knole, given to the Nat. Trust by 4th baron Sackville 1946, and Chevening, given to the nation by 7th earl Stanhope 1959, either as a home for the P.M. of the day or a member of the royal family. Pop. (1961) 17,604.

SEVENTH DAY ADVENTISTS. Religious sect having its main following in America, whose distinctive tenet is that Saturday is the Sabbath.

SEVEN WONDERS OF THE WORLD. In antiquity, the pyramids of Egypt; the hanging gardens at Babylon; the temple of Artemis at Ephesus; the statue of Zeus at Olympia; the mausoleum at Halicarnassus; the Colossus of Rhodes; and the Pharos (lighthouse) at Alexandria.

SEVEN YEARS WAR. The war of 1756–63 between Britain and Prussia on the one hand, and France, Austria, and Russia on the other. Its military interest centres on the successful struggle of Frederick II of Prussia against great odds. Britain's part in the war, under the direction of Chatham, was mainly confined to operations at sea, notably the victory of Quiberon Bay (1759), and in the colonies. The victories of Wolfe and Clive resulted in the conquest of Canada and the foundation of the Indian empire.

SEVERN. River of Wales and England, 210 m. long. It rises in N. Wales on the N.E. side of Plynlimmon, and flows through Shrewsbury, Worcester and Gloucester to the Bristol Channel. It is famous for its high bore (6 ft. tidal wave): S. England and S. Wales are linked nr. Chepstow by a rail tunnel (1873–85) and road bridge (1966). A barrage has been proposed (seaward of Cardiff and Weston-super-Mare) which would provide electric power, improve dock developments in Cardiff, Bristol, etc., and provide sailing facilities.

SEVE'RUS, Lucius Septimius (146–211). Roman emperor. B. in N. Africa, he held a command on the Danube when in 193 the emperor Pertinax was murdered. Proclaimed emperor by his troops, S. proved an able administrator. He d. at York while campaigning against the Caledonians.

SÉVIGNÉ (sāvēnyā'), **Marie de Rabutin-Chantal, marquise de** (1626–96), French letter-writer. B. in Paris, in her letters to her dau., the comtesse de Grignan, she gives a vivid picture of contemporary customs and events.

SEVILLE (sev'il). City of Spain, on the Guadalquivir 60 m. N. of Cadiz. Once the centre of a Moorish kingdom, it is famous for the Alcázar, 15th–16th cent. cathedral, church of La Caridad, univ. (1502), and museum. Machinery, spirits, porcelain, silk, and tobacco are manufactured. Pop. (1960) 442,890.

SÈVRE. Name of 2 French rivers from which the dept. of Deux Sèvres takes its name. The S. Nantaise rises 10 m. W. of Parthenay and flows 85 m. to join the Loire at Nantes; the S. Niortaise rises 5 m. N.E. of Melle and flows 95 m. in a westerly direction to the Bay of Biscay. Niort, cap. of the dept., stands on the S. Niortaise.

SÈVRES (sāvr). *See* ST. CLOUD.

SEWAGE DISPOSAL. Sewage – the waste products and refuse from houses, factories, establishments of every kind, streets, etc. – is conveyed through sewers and subjected to purification before being discharged into rivers or the sea. S. works are the responsibility of local authorities. The sludge may be spread over fields attached to the works, or it may be processed and sold as a fertilizer. In places near the coast, raw S. may be flowed or dumped into the sea. In some countries, China in particular, S. is carefully conserved as manure.

SEWELL, Anna (1820–78). British author, known for her story of a horse, *Black Beauty* (1877).

SEWING MACHINE. Apparatus for the mechanical sewing of cloth, leather, etc., by a needle, powered by hand, treadle, or belted electric motor. Among early inventors was the Englishman Thomas Saint in 1790. The popular modern lockstitch machine, using a double thread, was invented independently in America by both Walter Hunt (1834) and Elias Howe (1846). Howe's machine was the basis of the machine patented in 1851 by the American Isaac Singer (1811–75). *See also* ULTRASONICS.

SEX and REPRODUCTION. S. may be defined as the distinction between male and female that forms the basis of sexual reproduction. Amongst the more lowly

SEVEN YEARS WAR. Built originally by the French in 1755, and in 1758 captured by the English and renamed Fort Ticonderoga ('place between two lakes'), this fort was on the line of water communication from Canada to the British colonies and hence of great strategic importance in the Seven Years War, and later in the War of American Independence. Restoration was begun in 1909.　*Courtesy of Fort Ticonderoga.*

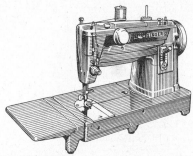

SEWING MACHINE. A masterpiece in versatility, the Singer 431 can blind hem, darn, embroider in two colours, pleat, gather, buttonhole and even sew on the buttons. And – the latest development – can be switched from normal lock-titch to easily pulled-out chain-stitch in half a minute, so that hand tacking is dispensed with.
Courtesy of the Singer Sewing Machine Co.

organisms, and even in some insects, reproduction is a process in which S. may have no part. S. only appears as an essential to reproduction much higher up in the evolutionary scale, and sexual union may be looked upon as being a method of pooling the germ plasm of 2 different lines of descent, thus providing a far greater number of useful mutations. In the higher animals the sexual union of male and female is necessary for the appearance of new life.

Amongst mammals the ova, or egg-cells, are all alike, but the sperms are of 2 kinds, and the sex of the offspring will depend on which kind of sperm has fused with the egg-cell. Sexual characteristics may be divided into primary, i.e. the genital organs and the primary sexual glands, and secondary, which incl. in the woman the more roomy pelvis and the more even distribution of the subcutaneous fat, and differences in the quality and distribution of the hair. The development of the larynx is also greater in the male. At puberty there are marked physical and psychological changes in the body. The emotion of sexual love is aroused or accompanied by visual, auditory, olfactory, and tactile impressions.

Reproduction. The end to which the sexual act is directed is the production of a new individual through the union of an ovum and a spermatozoon. A spermatozoon is about $\frac{1}{500}$ in. long and consists of a rounded head, a tail by means of which it propels itself, and a middle or connecting piece. In a cubic centimetre of fertile human semen more than a hundred million spermatozoa may be present. The female gamete, or ovum, very much larger than the spermatozoon, is a spherical nucleated cell surrounded by a transparent capsule. The ova are developed in round collections of cells, known as Graffian follicles, which are scattered throughout the substance of the ovary. As these follicles become mature they slowly approach the surface of the ovary and each month one ruptures, discharging its contained ovum into the trumpet-shaped end of the Fallopian tube. This act of ovulation usually occurs about midway between 2 successive menstruations. If intercourse has taken place about the time of ovulation, one of the spermatozoa may succeed in reaching the ovum during its passage along the Fallopian tube. It burrows into the capsule of the ovum and its nucleus unites with that of the ovum. A single nucleus is thus formed, half of the chromosomes being derived from the mother and half from the father. The oosperm (the product of this fusion) then begins rapidly to divide, and by the end of the 5th week the rudiments of all the more important organs of the embryo have been laid down. When pregnancy has lasted approximately 280 days the act of parturition begins. *See* CHILDBIRTH.

The beginning of the reproductive life of a woman is marked by the first appearance of the menstrual flow, and its end by the menopause and the cessation of this flow between the ages of 35 and 55. A man may be able to beget children to a very advanced age.

SE'XTANT. An instrument, invented by John Hadley in 1730, used in navigating and surveying, to measure the sun's altitude at noon and the angular distances between objects. It has 2 mirrors, one half-silvered, the other rotatable, to coincide the direct vision of an object with a reflected image, the angle being read on to a graduated vernier scale.

SEYCHELLES (sāshel'). Group of *c.* 100 islands in the Indian Ocean to the N.E. of Madagascar. Colonized by the French in mid-17th cent., it was seized by the British in 1794, made a dependency of Mauritius 1810, and a separate crown colony 1903. Under the constitution of 1970 there is a gov., council of ministers and legislative assembly with an elected majority. The chief products are copra, vanilla, cinnamon, patchouli and guano. The cap. is Victoria, on the largest is. Mahé (pop. 12,000), which is used by the U.S.A. for tracking and telemetry facilities; the second largest is. is Praslin, famous for its double coconuts. English is the official language; Creole and French are also spoken. Area 89 sq. m. (over half being the is. of Mahé); pop. (1967) 48,730. *See* BRITISH INDIAN OCEAN TERRITORY.

SEYMOUR, Jane (*c.* 1509–37). Third wife of Henry VIII, whom she m. in 1536. She d. soon after the birth of her son (Edward VI).

SEYSS-INQUART (sīs-in'kvahrt), **Arthur** (1892–1946). Austrian Nazi leader. He conspired against Austrian independence, and became governor of Austria in 1938. As commissioner for the Netherlands 1940–4 he ruthlessly suppressed all opposition. He was tried at Nuremberg as a war criminal and hanged.

SEYCHELLES. Peculiar to the islands is the coco de mer palm (*Lodoicea Maldivica*). The great double kernel, which takes 10 years to ripen, is the largest known fruit.
Courtesy of the Seychelles Government

SFAX (sfahks). A port of Tunisia, N. Africa, cap. of S. dist., situated on the Gulf of Gabès, *c.* 150 m. S.S.E. of Tunis. S. exports phosphates, olive oil, dates, almonds, esparto grass, and sponges. It has an airfield, and makes leather, soap, carpets, etc.; there are also salt works. A Phoenician and later a Roman colony, S. was occupied by French in 1881. It was taken by the British from the German and Italian occupiers in 1943 during the N. African campaign of the S.W.W. Pop. (1966) 250,000.

SFORZA. Name of a famous Italian family who held the duchy of Milan 1450–99 and 1522–35. Their court was a centre of Renaissance culture, **Ludovico S.** (1451–1508) being famous as the patron of Leonardo da Vinci and other artists. *See* illus. p. 733.

's GRAVENHAGE. *See* HAGUE, THE.

SHACKLETON, Sir Ernest (1874–1922). British Antarctic explorer. B. in co. Clare, Ireland, he was a member of Scott's Antarctic expedition of 1901–4. In 1907–9 he commanded an expedition which reached 88° 23' S. lat., and next commanded the expedition of 1914–16 when he had to abandon his ship, the *Endurance*, in the Weddell Sea. He d. on board the *Quest* on another expedition to the Antarctic.

SHAD. A food-fish (*Alosa*) of the herring family. *A. alosa*, the allice, and *A. finta*, the twaite, are the Brit. species.

SHADWELL, Thomas (1642–92). English dramatist and poet. His plays incl. *Epsom Wells* and *Bury Fair*,

He was involved in a violent feud with Dryden whom he attacked in 'The Medal of John Bayes' (1682) and succeeded as poet laureate.

S.H.A.E.F. Abbreviated form of the Supreme Headquarters Allied Expeditionary Force which came into being on 15 Feb. 1944, at Norfolk House, St. James's Square, London. In March 1944 it was moved to Bushy Park, near Kingston-on-Thames, where the final plans for the Allied invasion of Europe were worked out. The Supreme Commander was General Dwight D. Eisenhower.

SHAFI'I (shahfē-ē) or **ASH-SHAFI'I** (767-820). Moslem jurist, founder of one of the 4 great schools of Islamic law, named Shafiites after him.

SHAFTESBURY, Anthony Ashley Cooper, 1st earl of (1621–83). English Whig statesman. B. in Dorset, he served in the Civil War first on the royalist and later on the parliamentary side, supported the Restoration, and received a barony in 1661 and an earldom in 1672, when he became Lord Chancellor. In 1673, he went into opposition, and began to organize the Whig Party. He led the agitation for the exclusion of the duke of York from the succession, and in 1679 secured the passage of the Habeas Corpus Act. Accused of treason in 1681, he fled to Amsterdam, where he d.

SHAFTESBURY, Anthony Ashley Cooper, 3rd earl of (1671–1713). English philosopher, author of *Characteristics* (1711) and other ethical speculations.

SHAFTESBURY, Anthony Ashley Cooper, 7th earl of (1801–85). British philanthropical statesman. He entered parliament as a Tory in 1826, and succeeded to the title in 1851. He strongly supported the Ten-Hours' Act of 1847 and other factory legislation, and was largely responsible for the Act of 1842 forbidding the employment of women and children underground in mines. He was associated with the movement for the establishment of 'ragged' schools for the poor.

SHAFTESBURY. English market town (bor.) in Dorset, 19 m. S.W. of Salisbury. Alfred is said to have founded an abbey on the site in 880; Canute d. at S. in 1035. It is an important agricultural centre. Pop. (1961) 3,366.

SHAG. *See* CORMORANT.

SHAH (Persian, 'ruler'). Title borne by the king of Persia.

SHAH-JEHA'N (1592–1666). Mogul emperor of India from 1627, when he succeeded his father Jehangir. He warred successfully in the Deccan, but was not so fortunate in his campaigns against the Persians. From 1658 he was a prisoner of his son Aurungzebe.

SHAHN, Ben (1898–1969). American artist. B. in Lithuania, he was taken to the U.S. as a child and became a commercial lithographer. His work has a sharp photographic realism, and shows an interest in social issues e.g. his series on Dreyfus, Sacco and Vanzetti and Prohibition; and as a mural artist he worked at Radio City (with Diego Rivera) and the Federal Security Building 1940–2.

SHAKESPEARE. A Portrait engraved by Martin Droeshout for the First folio, 1623.

SHAKERS. Popular name for the Christian sect of the United Society of Believers in Christ's Second Appearing, founded by James and Jane Wardley in England about 1747, and carried into N. America in 1774 by Ann Lee (1736–84), the wife of a Manchester blacksmith. The name was applied because of the ecstatic shakings of the sectaries in their worship. The sect still exists in U.S.A.

SHAKESPEARE, William (1564–1616). English dramatist and poet. B. at Stratford-on-Avon, he was the son of John S., a prosperous wool-dealer, and after an education at Stratford grammar school may have become a schoolmaster. In 1582 he m. Anne Hathaway, who bore him 3 children. Having joined a company of players, probably Leicester's, by 1589 he was estab. in London as a playwright. His earliest plays, written *c*. 1589–93, were the tragedy *Titus Andronicus*, the comedies *The Comedy of Errors*, *The Taming of the Shrew*, and *Two Gentlemen of Verona*, the 3 parts of *Henry VI*, and *Richard III*. The earl of Southampton became his patron *c*. 1593; S. dedicated to him his poems *Venus and Adonis* (1593) and *Lucrece* (1594), and wrote *Love's Labour's Lost*, satirizing Raleigh's circle, for his amusement. Southampton seems to be the man addressed in S.'s sonnets (written *c*. 1593–6).

SHAMYL
Courtesy of Col. C. H. Ellis.

From 1594 onwards S. was a member of the Chamberlain's (later the King's) company of players. During 1593–8 he had no serious rival as a dramatist, and prospered sufficiently to buy a coat of arms in 1596, and New Place, Stratford, in 1597. Three plays containing a strong lyrical element – *Romeo and Juliet*, *Midsummer Night's Dream*, and *Richard II* – appeared 1594–5, and were followed by *King John* and *The Merchant of Venice* in 1596. The Falstaff plays of 1597–9 – *Henry IV* (parts I and II), *Henry V*, and *The Merry Wives of Windsor* – brought his popularity to its height. About the same time he collaborated in *Sir Thomas More*, and wrote *Julius Caesar* (1599). Three romantic comedies, unparalleled in their combination of wit and lyricism – *Much Ado about Nothing*, *As You Like It*, and *Twelfth Night* (*c*. 1598–1601) – brought this predominantly comic period to an end.

The plays which followed, beginning in 1601 with *Hamlet*, show an obsession with the darker side of human nature. The 'dark' comedies *Troilus and Cressida*, *All's Well that Ends Well*, and *Measure for Measure* (*c*. 1601–4) are bitter and cynical. *Othello*, *Macbeth*, and *King Lear* followed 1604–6, together with *Timon of Athens*, in which S.'s pessimism reaches its depths. The last 2 tragedies, *Antony and Cleopatra* and *Coriolanus* (*c*. 1607–8), show a striking reaction towards a calmer acceptance of life.

The final group of plays, *Pericles* (which is only partly S.'s), *Cymbeline*, *The Winter's Tale*, and *The Tempest* (*c*. 1608–11), have many features in common; all but the first are in Fletcher's manner, and were written for an aristocratic audience. During 1613 S. collaborated with Fletcher in *Henry VIII*, and probably in *Two Noble Kinsmen* and the lost *Cardenio*. His last years were spent in Stratford, where he d. on 23 April 1616, and was buried in the parish church. A collected edition of his plays (the 1st Folio) was pub. by 2 of his fellow-actors, Heminge and Condell, in 1623. The only authentic portraits are that in the 1st Folio and the bust on his tomb.

SHAKHTY (shah'khti). Town in the R.S.F.S.R., 50 m. N.E. of Rostov, centre of an important anthracite coal-mining area. It makes textiles, leather, metal goods, etc.; nearby are stone quarries. Pop. (1967) 208,000.

SHALLO'T. A plant (*Allium asca.onicum*) allied to the onion. Its bulbous roots are used in pickles.

SHALMANE'SER. Name of 5 Assyrian kings. **Shalmaneser III** (reigned 859–824 B.C.) pursued an aggressive policy, and made Babylon and Israel tributary to Assyria.

SHAMANISM (shah'manizm). Name (possibly

derived from the Hindustani *shaman*, an idolater) applied to the religious beliefs and practices of the aboriginal tribes of N. Asia, and by extension to the very similar systems prevailing among the N. American Indians. The outstanding figure is the *shaman*, or medicine-man, a seer and sorcerer, who is believed to make contact with spirits of good and evil.

SHAMROCK. Name given to several trifoliate plants of family Leguminosae. One is said to have been used by St. Patrick to illustrate the doctrine of the Holy Trinity, and it was made the national badge of Ireland.

SHAMYL (shahmil') (*c.* 1797–1871). Caucasian soldier. He led the tribesmen of Daghestan in a fight for independence from Russia from 1834 until, when the Russians were able to deploy greater forces after the Crimean War, he was taken in 1859. His not-too-rigorous captivity in Russia ended with his death at Medina on pilgrimage to Mecca. The official Russian attitude to his campaigns varies according to whether local nationalism is at the moment being encouraged or repressed.

SHANGHAI. Great Western Road in the former International Settlement which reverted to the Chinese Government after the Second World War. Peasants bring in their farm produce for the street market. *Photo: Camera Press.*

SHANGHAI (shanghī'). Great port and city in Kiangsu prov., China, on the Hwang-pu 15 m. from its entry into the Yangtze-kiang estuary. A city from 1360, it became important only after 1842 when the treaty of Nanking opened it to foreign trade and an important international settlement developed which remained the commercial centre of the city after extra-territorial powers were given up by the powers, 1943–6. Industries incl. manufacture of textiles, paper, chemicals, steel, agricultural implements, precision instruments; shipbuilding, flour and vegetable-oil milling, petroleum refining. The port handles *c.* 50 per cent of China's imports and exports. S., 350 sq. m. in area, is the largest city in Asia and a 'special municipality'. Pop. (1966) 10,000,000.

SHANNON. Longest river in Ireland. Rising in co. Cavan, it flows through Loughs Allen and Ree and past Athlone, and reaches the Atlantic through an extensive estuary below Limerick. Famous for salmon, it is also the major source of electric power in the rep., works for which were constructed 1924–30 at and above Ardnacrusha, 3 m. N. of Limerick.

SHANNON AIRPORT. Transatlantic airport on the r. Shannon in co. Clare, Irish Republic. Its Irish name is Rineanna.

SHANS. Name given to tribesfolk who live in the mountainous borderlands between China, Siam, and Burma. They are akin to the Laos and the Siamese.

41 semi-dependent states in the N. of Burma are called the Shan States; they were annexed by Britain in 1885 and now form part of the Burmese Union. Area 57,816 sq. m.

SHANSI (shahnsē'). Inland prov. of China, partially surrounded by the older part of the Great Wall (246–209 B.C.). A loess-covered plateau rising in the N. to 5,000 ft., it grows cotton, tobacco, wheat, barley, and the vine; anthracite and bituminous coal, iron, and salt are produced. The cap. is Taiyuan. Area 60,700 sq. m. Pop. (1968) 18,000,000 many of them Moslems.

SHANTUNG (shantoong'). Maritime prov. of N. China, incl. S. peninsula. Winter wheat, soya beans, ground-nuts, cotton, tobacco, and fruits are grown. S. silk, from wild silkworms, is spun and woven; minerals incl. coal, iron-ore, gold and kaolin. S. is traversed by the Hwang-ho and the Grand Canal. Tsinan is the cap. Area 59,200 sq. m.; pop. (1968) 56,000,000.

SHAPI'RŌ, Karl (1913–). American poet. B. at Baltimore, he first attracted attention in 1934 with 5 poems under the title 'Noun', and after service in the S.W.W. wrote the striking *V Letter* (1945). He taught at Johns Hopkins 1947–50 and became prof. of writing at Nebraska 1956, and ed. *Poetry* (1950–5) and *Prairie Schooner* 1956–63.

SHARE. In finance, that part of the capital of a company held by a member (shareholder). Shares may be numbered and are issued as units of definite face value; shareholders are not always called on to pay the full face value of their shares, though they bind themselves to do so if called upon. Preference shares carry a fixed rate of dividend and have first claim on the profits of the company; ordinary shares have second claim, and if profits have been good may attract a higher dividend than the preference shares; deferred shares rank for dividend only after the rights of preference and ordinary shareholders have been satisfied. Fully paid-up shares can be converted by the company into stock (q.v.).

SHARKS. Name given to the bigger members of the order Pleurotremata, a large group of marine fish with cartilaginous skeletons. Distributed over the whole world, although more common in tropical seas, they vary from the 'smooth hound' (*Mustelus laevis*) of British waters, 4–6 ft. long, to the swift voracious man-eater (*Carcharodon rondeletti*), often 40 ft. long, found in warmer waters. They have an acute sense of smell, and eyes which, although

SHANNON. At Limerick the river flows past King John's castle, a Norman fortress with walls ten feet thick and magnificent drum towers, and under Thomond Bridge. St. Munchin's church, in the background, was founded in the 7th century. *Courtesy of the Irish Tourist Board.*

SHARK. Common in the Pacific, the grey shark (*Carcharhinus menisorrah*) grows to about 7 ft. and will attack man without provocation. Fortunately for the photographer, these specimens in a Marshall Island lagoon are merely inquisitive.
Courtesy of Edmund S. Hobson.

having no acuity of vision or sense of colour, are highly sensitive to light. Centres for shark study are the Lerner Marine Laboratory in the Bahamas, the Univ. of Hawaii, and the Oceanographic Research Institute, Durban. Ss. have potential importance as a source of leather, oil and protein.

SHARP, Cecil (1859–1924). British collector of folk song. B. in London, he travelled the country to record and so save from extinction the folk-song tradition, e.g. *English Folk Song* (1921: 2 vols.), and when in the U.S.A. tracked down survivals of English song in the Appalachians, etc. Cecil Sharp House, the H.Q. in London of the English Folk Song and Folk Dance Society, commemorates his work.

SHARP, Granville (1735–1813). British philanthropist. B. at Durham, he was prominent in the anti-slavery movement, and in 1772 secured a legal decision 'that as soon as any slave sets foot on English territory he becomes free'.

SHARP, William (1855–1905). Scottish author. B. in Paisley, he wrote literary criticism, poetry, and novels under his own name, but is best remembered for his mystic romances, e.g. *The Mountain Lovers* (1895); and plays, e.g. *The Immortal Hour* (1900), written under the pseudonym Fiona Macleod.

SHARPEVILLE. Town of the Rep. of S. Africa, 5 m. N. of Vereeniging. On 21 March 1960 a crowd of black S. Africans, variously est. at 5–20,000, was fired upon by police during a campaign launched by the Pan-Africanist Congress (P.A.C.) against the Pass Laws (first intro. in the 19th cent. to aid identification of Africans moving into settled areas: 'passes' are carried by all African males over 16 and incl. residential permit, employer's certificate, tax receipt, etc.). Casualties were 67 dead and 186 wounded.

SHASTON. See SHAFTESBURY.

SHA'STRI, Lal Bahadur (1904–66). Indian politician. Several times imprisoned for civil disobedience before independence, he later held various ministerial posts, and in 1964 succeeded Nehru as P.M. He d. of a heart attack in Tashkent, following signature of a peace agreement with Pakistan. Small of stature, he was known as the 'Sparrow'.

SHATT-EL-ARAB (river of Arabia). Estuary, *c.* 120 m. long, formed below Kurna, Iraq, by the junction of the Euphrates and the Tigris, and flowing into the Persian Gulf. It is *c.* 600 yds. wide, and for the last 50 m. forms the Iraqi boundary with Persia. Basra in Iraq, Abadan and Khorramshahr in Persia are on its banks.

SHAW, George Bernard (1856–1950). Irish dramatist. B. in Dublin, the son of a civil servant, he came to London in 1876, where he became a brilliant debater

among the Fabians. Of the 5 novels he wrote 1879–83, the least unsuccessful was *Cashel Byron's Profession* (1886). His alliance with the new thought in the theatre was illustrated by his *Quintessence of Ibsenism* (1891), and in 1892 his first play *Widowers' Houses* was produced. It was the first of the *Plays: Pleasant and Unpleasant* (1898), which incl. *The Philanderer*; *Mrs. Warren's Profession*, dealing with prostitution; and the pleasant comedies *Arms and the Man*, *Candida*, *You Never Can Tell*, and *Man of Destiny*, a Napoleonic incident. The *Three Plays for Puritans* of 1901 contained the witty *Devil's Disciple*; *Caesar and Cleopatra*; and *Captain Brassbound's Conversion*, written for Ellen Terry. The epic *Man and Superman* (1903), expanding his theme of Creative Evolution, was followed by *John Bull's Other Island* (1904), and *Major Barbara* (1905). *The Doctor's Dilemma*, *Getting Married*, and *The Shewing-up of Blanco Posnet* were pub. in 1911. His next vol. (1914) contained *The Dark Lady of the Sonnets*, touching the Shakespeare problem; *Misalliance*, and *Fanny's First Play*.

Androcles and the Lion was pub. in 1916 with the comedy *Pygmalion*, written for Mrs. Patrick Campbell. *Heartbreak House* (1917) symbolizes the breakdown of European civilization, and in *Back to Methuselah* (1921) S. once more faced the problems of social evolution. Latest of his great dramas is *St. Joan* (1924). Among the plays of the last years are *The Apple Cart* (1929), *Village Wooing*, *Geneva*, *In Good King Charles's Golden Days*, *Buoyant Billions*, and *Far-Fetched Fables*.

Important for the understanding of S.'s thought are the voluminous prefaces to the plays; *The Intelligent Woman's Guide to Socialism and Capitalism* (1928); *Adventures of a Black Girl in Search of God* (1932); *Sixty Years of Fabianism* (1947); and the vol. of music criticism *The Perfect Wagnerite* (1898). His letters to the actress Ellen Terry (pub. 1931) are also of great interest. In 1925 he received a Nobel prize. *See* illus. p. 395.

SHAWCROSS, Hartley William, baron (1902–). British Labour politician and lawyer. He was called to the Bar in 1925, entered parliament in 1945, and while Attorney-General 1945–51 was chief prosecutor for the U.K. at Nuremberg. He was pres. of the Board of Trade in 1951, and in 1959 was created a life peer, following his resignation in 1958 as M.P. for St. Helens from 1945, partly because of disagreement with Labour policy, e.g. the extension of nationalization of industry.

SHAZA'R, Zalman (1889–). Israeli statesman. B. in Russia (*né* Rubashov), he settled in Palestine in 1924, and as Israeli's 1st Min. of Education (1949–50) introduced free education. In 1963 he succeeded Ben-Zvi as president.

SHCHERBAKO'V. See RYBINSK.

SHEARWATER. Genus of birds related to the petrels. The Manx S. (*Puffinus anglorum*) is the only species which breeds in Britain.

SHE'BA. Biblical name for Sabaea, in modern Yemen, S.W. Arabia, formerly famous as a source of gold and spices. According to 1 Kings 10, its queen visited Solomon; Ethiopian tradition traces the royal house of Ethiopia to their union.

SHECHEM (shĕ'kem). Ancient town of Palestine, near Samaria, the traditional burial place of Joseph nearby is Jacob's well. S. was destroyed *c.* A.D. 67 by Vespasian; on its site stands Nablus (a corruption of Neapolis, built by Hadrian), pop. (est.) 25,000. Allenby's defeat of the Turks in 1918 in the battle of S. completed the conquest of Palestine.

SHEEN, Fulton (John) (1895–). American R.C. prelate. Aux. bp. of New York 1951–66, and bp. of Rochester, N.Y. 1966–9, he achieved widespread influence by his radio Catholic Hour, and television programmes.

SHEEP. Ungulate mammals of the genus *Ovis*. Domesticated S. are derived from wild species native to the drier uplands of central Asia. They can be reared on many lands unfit for arable agriculture, and their use in rotation on arable land also helps to maintain its fertility. They do well in most temperate regions, especially on hilly land. Several well-known cheeses, such as Roquefort and Parmesan, are made from sheep's milk. Breeds are specialized either for wool or flesh production: most of these are of British origin, except the Merino of the Mediterranean, now raised in Australia, New Zealand, S. Africa, and the U.S.A. In Great Britain the best S. lands are in the

SHEEP. Left: top, Hampshire Down ewe; bottom, Suffolk ram. Right: top, Wiltshire Horn ram; bottom, Cheviot tup.

southern uplands, the Cheviots, the Welsh uplands, the Pennines, and the Cotswolds. Other S.-raising lands are the U.S.S.R., Argentine, and Spain.

SHEEPDOG. A rough-coated, tailless breed of dog, formerly much used by shepherds, farmers, and drovers in the S. of England and in Wales, but now mainly a show dog. In colour it is grey or blue-grey.

SHEERNESS. English seaport and holiday resort on the Isle of Sheppey, Kent, at the confluence of the Thames and the Medway. Originally a fortress (1660), captured and held for a brief while by the Dutch under Admiral Reuter in 1667, it was until 1960 the site of a royal dockyard. Pop. (1961) 14,123.

SHEFFIELD. English industrial city (co. bor.) in the W. Riding of Yorks, 18 m. S.W. of Doncaster. Iron smelting has been carried on since the 12th cent., and by the 14th cent. S. cutlery was famous. During the Industrial Revolution its iron and steel manufactures developed rapidly. Cutlery of all kinds, permanent magnets, drills, precision tools are among S.'s products. Other industries incl. electro-plating, typefounding, and the manufacture of optical glass. The parish church of SS. Peter and Paul (14th–15th cents.) is the cathedral of S. bishopric (1914). The fine City Hall was opened in 1932. Mary Queen of Scots was imprisoned at S. 1570–84, part of the time in the Norman castle, which was captured by the Parliamentarians 1644 and subsequently destroyed. Incorporated in 1843, S. was created a city in 1893, and has had a Lord Mayor since 1897. The univ. was chartered in 1905, and the colls. of art and technology were amalgamated to form Yorkshire's polytechnic (q.v.) 1969. Pop. (1961) 493,954.

SHEFFIELD PLATE. Articles produced by fusing copper with silver, giving a beautiful surface like that of standard silver. The process, invented by Thomas Boulsover (1704–88), a Sheffield cutler, in 1742–3, was displaced by electro-plating in the 1840s.

SHELBURNE, William Petty FitzMaurice, 2nd earl of (1737–1805). British Whig statesman. B. at Dublin, he entered the House of Lords in 1761 and became a follower of Chatham. He opposed George III's American policy, and as P.M. 1783 concluded peace with the U.S.A. He was created marquess of Lansdowne in 1784.

SHELDRAKE. Duck (*Tadorna tadorna*) with dark green head and red bill and the rest of the plumage strikingly marked in black, white and chestnut. Of widespread distribution in the Old World, it lays its eggs in rabbit burrows in sandy coasts and may be protected for the sake of these and its down by the local people.

SHELLAC. See LAC.

SHELLEY, Mary Wollstonecraft (1797–1851). British author; dau. of William Godwin and his wife Mary Wollstonecraft, and 2nd wife of P. B. Shelley. She eloped with him in 1814 and was m. in 1816. Her *Frankenstein*, the story of a man who created a monster and gave it life, was pub. in 1818. She wrote other novels and ed. the poet's works.

SHELLEY, Percy Bysshe (1792–1822). British lyric poet. B. at Warnham, he was ed. at Eton and University Coll., Oxford, where his collaboration in a pamphlet on *The Necessity of Atheism* (1811) caused his expulsion. While living in London he fell in love with 16-year-old Harriet Westbrook whom he m. in 1811. He visited Ireland and Wales writing pamphlets defending vegetarianism and political freedom, and in 1813 pub. privately the revolutionary poem *Queen Mab*. Meanwhile he had become estranged from his wife and in 1814 left England with Mary Wollstonecraft Godwin, whom he m. in 1816 after Harriet had drowned herself. *Alastor*, written in 1815, was followed by the epic *The Revolt of Islam*, and by 1818 S. was living in Italy. Here he produced the tragedy *The Cenci;* the satire on Wordsworth, *Peter Bell the Third* (1819); and the lyric drama *Prometheus Unbound* (1820). Other works of the period are 'Ode to the West Wind', 'The Cloud', and 'The Skylark'; 'The Sensitive Plant' and 'The Witch of Atlas'; 'Epipsychidion'; 'Adonais' (1821) and the lyric drama *Hellas* (1822); and the prose *Defence of Poetry* (1821). In July 1822 S. was drowned while sailing near Spezia, and his ashes were buried in Rome. *See* illus. p. 394.

SHELLFISH. Popular name for edible molluscs and crustaceans, incl. the whelk and periwinkle, mussel, oyster, lobster, crab, shrimp, etc.

SHELL-SHOCK. An obsolete name for various forms of nervous disorder, chiefly hysterical (*see* HYSTERIA), seen in soldiers exposed to heavy explosions or buried, but not confined to them. Such 'war neuroses' are often an aggravation of a previous neurotic conflict. Skilled psychotherapy has been effective in their cure.

SHENANDO'AH. River in Virginia, U.S.A., a trib. of the Potomac which it joins at Harper's Ferry. The S. valley was the site, 1862–4, of important operations in the American Civil War.

SHENSI (shensē′). A northern prov. of China, S. of the Great Wall. It is mountainous, and the Hwang-ho r. valley, forming the N.E. boundary of the prov., is an important commercial route; its trib. the Wei-ho crosses S. Coal, iron, salt, gold, nickel, and petroleum are found; grain, cotton are grown, livestock reared. Yen-an was the Communists' cap. 1936–47. An earthquake in 1556 is said to have killed 830,000 people. Sian is the cap. Area 75,600 sq. m.; pop. (1968) 21,000,000, many of them Moslems.

SHENSTONE, William (1714–63). British poet. B. in Worcestershire, his most popular poem was the Spenserian *Schoolmistress* (1742). His country estate at the Leasowes was a famous example of landscape gardening.

SHENYANG. City in N.E. China, cap. of Liaoning prov., cradle of the Manchu dynasty whose members are buried in the vicinity. S. is a centre of heavy industry. S. (then called Mukden) was opened to foreign trade in 1903, and was the scene, 20 Feb.–10

March 1905, of a terrible battle in which the Russians suffered defeat by the Japanese (Russian losses, 26,500 killed, 40,000 prisoners; Japanese, 41,000 killed and wounded). Pop. (1957 est.) 2,411,000.

SHEPHERD'S PURSE. Annual plant (*Capsella bursa-pastoris*) of the Cruciferae family, interesting for its world-wide distribution in the temperate zones. It is a persistent weed with white flowers followed by 2-valved seed pouches from which the name derives.

SHEPPARD, Hugh Richard Lawrie ('Dick') (1880–1937). British Anglican clergyman. He was vicar of St. Martin-in-the-Fields, 1914–27, and by his broadcast services made that church one of the most famous in London. He was dean of Canterbury 1929–31 and a canon of St. Paul's 1934–7, and founded the Peace Pledge Union in 1934.

SHEPPARD, Jack (1702–24). British criminal. B. in Stepney, he was an apprentice carpenter, but turned early to theft and by 4 escapes from prison became a popular hero. He was finally caught and hanged.

SHEPPEY. English island off the N. coast of Kent, at the mouth of the Medway. It is linked with the mainland by Kingsferry road and rail bridge over the Swale, completed 1960. *See* SHEERNESS.

SHEPSTONE, Sir Theophilus (1817–93). S. African statesman. B. near Bristol, he was appointed secretary for native affairs in Natal in 1856, and in 1877 carried out the annexation of the Transvaal.

SHERATON, Thomas (*c.* 1751–1806). English furniture designer. B. at Stockton-on-Tees, he went to London and pub. his *Cabinet-maker's and Upholsterer's Drawing Book* in 1791, and *The Cabinet Dictionary* in 1802. He was influenced by Hepplewhite and Chippendale and his work has grace and simplicity.

SHERBORNE. English market town (U.D.) in Dorset, on the Yeo, 19 m. N. of Dorchester. It has a 12th cent. castle, 15th cent. abbey church, and a public school, founded 1550. Pop. (1961) 6,062.

SHERIDAN, Philip Henry (1831–88). American general. B. at Albany, N.Y., of Irish parentage, he achieved distinction in the Civil War as a Federal cavalry leader. Grant gave him command of the cavalry in 1864, and soon after of the army in the Shenandoah valley, which he cleared of Confederates. He was appointed C.-in-C. in 1883.

SHERIDAN, Richard Brinsley (1751–1816). British dramatist. B. in Dublin, he was ed. at Harrow, and m. Elizabeth Linley, dau. of the composer, in 1773. Turning to the stage he wrote the brilliant social comedy *The Rivals* in 1775, and in 1776 became lessee of Drury Lane theatre, where he produced *The School for Scandal* (1777) and *The Critic* (1779). In 1780 he entered Parliament as an adherent of Fox, directed the impeachment of Warren Hastings, and was treasurer to the navy 1806–7. His last years were clouded by the burning down of his theatre in 1809, the loss of his parliamentary seat in 1812, and by complete financial ruin and mental breakdown.

SHERIFF ('shire-reeve'). The chief administrative officer of an English co.; in Scotland the judicial duties of the office have survived with greater importance. The office (elective until Edward II) and name are of pre-Conquest origin. The S., who is appointed annually by royal patent, and is chosen from the leading landowners, acts as returning officer for parliamentary elections, and attends the judges on circuit. His duties of keeping prisoners in safe custody, preparing panels of jurors for assizes, executing writs and death sentences, are supervised by the Under-S. The City of London has 2 Ss. elected by the Liverymen. In the U.S.A. the S. of the co. is generally elected and combines some judicial authority with administrative duties.

SHERMAN, William Tecumseh (1820–91). American general. B. in Ohio, he received a command in the Federal army on the Mississippi front early in the Civil War, and collaborated with Grant in the

Vicksburg campaign. In 1864 he captured Atlanta, whence he marched to the sea, laying Georgia waste, and then drove the Confederates northwards. He was C.-in-C. 1869–83.

SHERRIFF, R(obert) C(edric) (1896–). British playwright. B. at Kingston-on-Thames, he achieved fame with the anti-heroic war play *Journey's End* (1929). A later success was *Home at Seven* (1950).

SHERRINGTON, Sir Charles Scott (1857–1952). British physiologist. B. in London, he was prof. at Liverpool 1895–1913 and Waynflete prof. of physiology at Oxford 1913–35. He wrote *The Integrative Action of the Nervous System* (1906), which formulated the principles of reflex action. He was also a poet. He received the O.M. in 1924, and was made G.B.E. in 1922.

SHERRY. A dry, white wine from the vineyards of S. Spain between the Guadalquivir and Guadelete. The name derives from the town of Xeres, or Jerez de la Frontera, the centre of the region.

'sHERTOGENBOSCH. *See* 's HERTOGENBOSH.

SHERWOOD, Mrs. Mary Martha (1775–1851). British writer for children, *née* Butt. Her *History of the Fairchild Family* (1818–47) combined moral piety with sound characterization.

SHERWOOD, Robert (1896–1955). American dramatist. After fighting with the Canadian forces in France in the F.W.W., he became a journalist in New York, and achieved his first great success with *The Petrified Forest* (1934). Later plays incl. *Idiot's Delight* (1936), *Abe Lincoln in Illinois* (1938) and *There Shall Be No Night* (1940) – for each of which he received a Pulitzer prize. In the S.W.W. he did much to promote Britain's cause, and pub. the serious historical study *Roosevelt and Hopkins* (1949).

SHERWOOD FOREST. A hilly stretch of parkland in W. Nottinghamshire, England, formerly a royal forest, area *c.* 200 sq. m. It is associated with Robin Hood.

SHETLAND PONY

SHETLAND ISLES. A group of more than 100 islands, lying N.E. of the Orkneys and forming the most northerly Scottish county, officially called ZETLAND. Of the 19 inhabited, Mainland (378 sq. m.) and Yell (83 sq. m.) are the largest; Fair Isle and Unst are espec. famous for coloured hand-knit woollens, and Muckle Flugga (60° 51′ 30″ N. lat.) is the northernmost of the Brit. Isles. They were under Scandinavian rule 875–1468, and still have many affinities with Scandinavia. Lerwick (pop. 6,000), on Mainland, is the capital. Area 550 sq. m.; pop. (1961) 17,809.

SHIAHS (shē′ahz) or **SHIITES.** One of the 2 great sects into which the Moslem world is divided, the other being the Sunnites. Their distinctive tenet is belief in Ali as the first true successor or caliph of Mohammed, whereas their rivals hold that Ali's 3 predecessors were legitimate caliphs. The Shiahs also reject the Sunna, or verbal utterances of the Prophet. The Shiah stronghold is Persia.

SHIELD. Any material used to reduce the amount of radiation (electrostatic, electromagnetic, heat, nuclear, etc.) reaching from one region of space to another, or any material used as a protection against falling debris, as in tunnelling, etc. Electrical conductors are used for electrostatic Ss., soft iron for electromagnetic Ss., and poor conductors of heat for heat Ss. Heavy materials such as lead and concrete are used for protection against X-ray and nuclear radiation. *See* BIOLOGICAL S.

SHIKOKU. One of the 4 main islands of Japan, S. of Honshu, E. of Kyushu. With a mild climate and rainfall up to 105 in. a year in the S., it rises in Mt.

Ishizuchi to 6,497 ft. Much of it is forested; rice, wheat, tobacco, soya beans, orchard fruits are grown; salt, copper, tobacco, lumber, and fruit exported. Area 6,869 sq. m.; pop. *c.* 4,500,000.

SHIMONOSEKI (shimōnōsek'ē). Japanese seaport in the extreme S.W. of Honshu, opened to foreign trade 1890. A treaty concluded at S. between China and Japan 1895 gave Japan Formosa and the Pescadores (lost 1935). Pop. (1965) 254,000.

SHINGLES. *See* HERPES.

SHINTO. The Chinese transliteration of the Japanese for Kami-no-Michi, the Way or Doctrine of

SHINTO. Shrine of the Sun-goddess at Ise, Japan.

the Gods, the indigenous religion of Japan. This is a mixture of nature-worship and loyalty to the reigning dynasty as descendants of the Sun-goddess, Amaterasu-Omikami. State S. is the national faith of Japan; its holiest shrine is at Ise, where in the temple of the Sun-goddess is preserved the mirror that she is supposed to have given to Jimmu, the 1st emperor, in the 7th cent. B.C. Sect S. consists of 130 sects, each founded by an historical character; the sects are officially recognized, but are not State-supported, as was State S. until its disestablishment by Gen. MacArthur's decree after the S.W.W. Un-questioning obedience and devotion to the emperor is inculcated, but there is also an exemplary ethic.

SHINTY. A winter game popular in the Scottish Highlands, played between teams of 12 players with sticks and a ball. It resembles hockey and lacrosse.

SHINWELL, Emanuel, baron (1884–   ). British Labour politician. B in London, he spent his youth in Glasgow, and became national organizer of the Marine Workers' Union. He sat in parliament 1922–4 and 1928–31, was Sec. for Mines 1924 and 1930–1, and in 1935 won Seaham from Ramsay McDonald. As Min. of Fuel and Power 1945–7 he carried through the nationalization of the mines. He was War Min. 1947–50, and Defence Min. 1950–1. Created Life Peer 1970.

SHIP. Sea-going vessel of considerable size. Greeks and Phoenicians built wooden Ss., propelled by oar or sail. The Romans and Carthaginians fought in galleys equipped with rams and rowed by tiers of oarsmen. The oaken Ss. of the Norsemen were for rough seas, and the fleet of Richard Cœur de Lion was largely of sail. The compass was invented in the 14th cent. and the 15th cent. saw the beginnings of Britain's Royal Navy; Henry VIII built the *Great Harry*, the first double-decked English warship. In the 16th cent. Ss. were short and high-sterned, and despite Pett's 3-decker in the 17th cent. English Ss. did not bear comparison with Spanish and Dutch until the era of Sir Robert Seppings, a shipbuilding pioneer in the early 19th cent. By 1840 iron had largely replaced wood, but fast-sailing clippers survived, built with wooden planks on iron frames. America and Britain made steam experiments as the 19th cent. opened. The *Comet* appeared in 1812, the Canadian *Royal William* crossed the Atlantic in 1833, and the English *Great Western* steamed from Bristol to New York in 1838. Pettit Smith applied the screw to the *Archimedes* in 1839, and after 1850 the paddle-wheel became obsolete. The introduction of the compound engine and turbine, the latter in 1902, completed the revolution in pro-

pulsion until the advent of nuclear-powered vessels after the S.W.W., chiefly submarines, but incl. the merchant ship N.S. *Savannah* (U.S.A.) launched 1959. *See* NAVY.

SHIP MONEY. Tax for support of the navy, levied on the coastal districts of England in the Middle Ages. Charles I's attempts to levy it on the whole country in 1634–6, without parliamentary consent and in time of peace, aroused strong opposition, J. Hampden and others refusing to pay. S.M. was declared illegal by parliament in 1641.

SHIRAZ (shē'rahz). Ancient walled city of S. Persia, the cap. of Fars prov. It is noted for its wines, carpets, and silverwork, and for its many beautiful mosques. There is a univ. It has suffered from earthquakes. Pop. (1964) 206,000.

SHKODËR (shkō'drah). Albanian town, on the Bojana, S.E. of Lake S., 12 m. from the Adriatic. It makes woollens and cement, and trades in hides, salt, tobacco, etc. During the F.W.W. it was occupied by the Austrians

SHIRAZ. A silversmith at work: such skills have been handed down through countless generations.
Courtesy of the Iranian Govt.

1916–18; during the Second by the Italians. Its Italian name is Scutari. Pop. (1967) 47,000.

SHOCK. A dangerous condition due to over-stimulation of the sensory nerves by severe injury or operation, or to loss of blood or plasma (as in burning), or to overpowering emotion. The blood-vessels dilate and the pressure falls below that necessary to supply the tissues of the body, especially the vital nerve-centres of the brain. Treatment is by rest, and, in the case of blood loss, by restoration of the normal circulating volume.

SHOEBURYNESS. Promontory on the Essex coast, England, N. of the Thames estuary, occupied by a school of gunnery.

SHOGUN. Formerly, the hereditary C.-in-C. of the Japanese Army. Though nominally subject to the emperor, he was the real ruler of Japan. In 1867 the emperor re-assumed power.

SHŌLAPU'R. Town in Maharashtra state, India, on the Deccan. It makes textiles, leather goods, chemicals, etc. Nearby is a large reservoir used for irrigation. Pop. (1961) 337,544.

SHOL'OKHOV, Mikhail Aleksandrovich (1905–   ). Russian novelist. B. at Kruzhilin, he had a variety of experience during the Civil War in various jobs, pub. a vol. of short stories in 1926, and then the great book that made his name, *Tikhi Don* (4 vols. 1928–40: *And Quiet Flows the Don* and *The Don Flows Home to the Sea*), telling realistically of the Don Cossacks he had known in his boyhood in the Kuban and how their lives were affected by the Revolution and Civil War. His other famous work is *Podnyataya Tselina* (1932: *Virgin Soil Upturned*): 2nd vol. 1959. He was awarded a Nobel prize 1965. *See* illus. p. 976.

SHOP. Building for the retail sale of goods. Until the later 19th cent. S. development had been almost static since ancient times, but with the growth of manufactured goods and the concentration of population in big towns came the development of the department store, in effect a number of small specialist shops under one roof, and of the chain store, with many Ss. scattered in different towns or counties and able to buy wholesale in such quantities that prices could be lowered below those of smaller competitors. As a development of wholesale purchase came direct links with factories producing goods, often under the same ownership, which further cut costs and even the elimination of the S. itself by direct mail or mail order (q.v.). It was also unusual until the 20th cent. to enter a S. without a particular purchase in mind, then came the invitation to walk round 'without obligation', then the notion of self-service (made more general by shortage of staff after the S.W.W.) from a selection of goods on the shelves, and – on the way – press-button shopping, in which buttons are pressed beneath display samples of the goods required and the various requirements of the customer are delivered already packaged together with a bill at the shop exit. The leader in the development of most of these ideas has been the U.S.A., where such gimmicks as trading stamps (long known in Britain) have grown to a large-scale business and then been re-exported.

SHOP STEWARD. A trade union representative in a 'shop' or department of a factory, who recruits for the union, inspects contribution cards and reports grievances to the district committee. Originating in the engineering industry, this form of organization has spread to all large industrial undertakings.

SHOREHAM BY SEA. English seaport (U.D.) in Sussex, 6 m. W. of Brighton, near the mouth of the Adur. Pop. (1961) 17,391.

SHORTHAND. System of rapid writing specially adapted to recording the spoken word. The Greeks and Romans practised systems of abbreviated writing, but the earliest S. system to be based on the alphabet and to follow the spelling of words was that of John Willis pub. in 1602. Later orthographic systems were those of Thomas Shelton (pub. 1630), which was used by Pepys, and that of Thomas Gurney (pub. 1750), which was used by Dickens. Phonetic systems, based entirely on the sound of words, began to appear in the 18th cent., and were perfected by Isaac Pitman. The system of John Gregg rejects the geometric forms of Pitman S. for cursive forms based on those of ordinary script. Speeds of 280 words a minute are attainable by either system. Another well-known system is Dutton's.

SHOSTAKÓ'VICH, Dmitry Dmitrievich (1906–   ). Russian composer. B. in Leningrad, where he studied the piano and composition at the Conservatoire, he has written 13 symphonies, the 1st in 1926 and the most famous of the others being the 5th (with its sub-title 'A Soviet Artist's Reply to Just Criticism') in 1937, the patriotic 7th or *Leningrad* (1941) which marked a temporary return to favour; and the moving 10th (1955). He has also written ballets and operas, most famous of the latter being *The Nose* and *A Lady Macbeth of Mtensk* (1936) which was found by authority too divorced from the proletariat, but after years of suppression was revived in 1963 as *Katerina Ismailova*. His appointment as First Sec. of the Soviet Union of Composers in 1960 illustrated reconciliation with officialdom.

SHOVELL (shuv'-), **Sir Cloudesley** (c. 1650–1707). English admiral. He took part with Rooke (q.v.) in the capture of Gibraltar in 1704, and as admiral and C.-in-C. of the fleet shared

SHOSTAKOVICH
Photo: Godfrey MacDomnic.

in the destruction of the French Mediterranean naval forces. His flagship *Association*, with 4 other ships of the homeward bound fleet (some 2,000 men), was lost off the Scillies in 1707, the admiral himself coming safely ashore, where he was strangled by a woman of the is. for his rings. Cannon and treasure from *Association* were recovered 1967–8.

SHOVELLER. Fresh-water duck (*Spatula clypeata*), so named from its broad flattened beak, with green head and white and brown body plumage. Spending the summer in N. Europe or America, it winters farther S. and visits Britain.

SHOW JUMPING. Competitive horse jumping over a course of fences. In the post-S.W.W. years S.J. has become an important part of most horse shows, the winner usually being the competitor with fewest 'faults', i.e. penalty marks given for knocking down or refusing fences, etc., but in time competitions is the competitor completing the course most quickly, additional seconds being added for such mistakes. Important international competitions are held in London, Dublin, Rotterdam, Aachen, Lucerne and Geneva (alternate years), Madrid, Lisbon, Rome, New York and Toronto. Notable riders incl. the British Col. Harry Llewellyn, Wilf White, Peter Robeson Pat Smythe, David Broome, David Barker, Harvey Smith and Anneli Drummond Hay; the German H. Winkler and Alwin Schockemöhle; the Italian Capt. P. d'Inzeo and Graziano Mancinelli; and the American Bill Steinkraus, Frank Chapot and George Morris.

SHOVELLER

SHRAPNEL, Henry (1761–1842). Inventor of the S. shell. He served in the R.A. and became a lieut.-gen. in 1837. His shell was first used in 1804.

SHREW. Insectivorous mammal of the family Soricidae, resembling a mouse and renowned for its insatiable appetite. The common S. (*Sorex araneus*) is *c.* 3 in. long. The pigmy shrewmouse (*S. minutus*) is the smallest British mammal. There are many other species in the N. hemisphere and some are aquatic.

SHREW

SHREWSBURY (shrōz'buri), **earl of.** Title in the peerage of England, held by the family of Talbot since 1442. It is the premier earldom of England.

SHREWSBURY. Co. town (bor.) of Salop, England, on the Severn. A modernized Norman castle is used as council offices, and the abbey church has a Norman nave. S. School, founded by Edward VI in 1552, is a leading public school. As Pengwern, S. was *c.* the 5th cent. cap. of the kingdom of Powis, later part of Mercia. At the battle of S., 1403, Henry IV defeated the rebels led by Hotspur (Harry Percy, son of the earl of Northumberland), who was killed. Pop. (1961) 49,726.

SHRIKE. Family of birds (Laniidae), distinguished by a long-toothed bill, and incl. many species, e.g. the Great Grey S. (*Lanius excubitor*) and Lesser Grey S. (*L. minor*), the Woodchat S. (*L. senator*), the Red-backed S. (*L. collurio*), etc. They feed on insects, small birds, and other small animals which they impale on thorns – whence their popular name of butcher-birds.

SHRIMP. A salt-water crustacean of the family Crangonidae, closely allied to the prawns, and hunting for food at night. The edible Common S. of N.

SIR CLOUDESLEY SHOVELL. Among the treasure recovered from the *Association* wreck site off the treacherous Gilstone Ledges was this solid silver plate bearing Sir Cloudesley's coat of arms, seen here filled with silver pieces of eight also found by Roland Morris and his team of divers.
Courtesy of Roland Morris.

Europe (*Crangon vulgaris*) is grey, changes its colour to brown when boiled, and is *c.* 2 in. long. In Japan and on the Atlantic coast of southern U.S.A. they form the basis of a large industry.

SHRI′VER, Robert Sargent (1915–). American Democratic politician. Son of a Wall Street banker, he was ed. at Yale, was called to the N.Y. Bar in 1941, and in 1953 m. Eunice Mary, sister of J. F. Kennedy. In 1961–66 he was director of the Peace Corps, of the Office of Opportunity (anti-poverty agency) 1964–8, and ambassador in Paris from 1968.

SHROPSHIRE or **Salop**. An English county bordering Wales to the E. of Montgomery, and bisected N.W. to S.E. by the Severn. The N. is generally flat, but to the S.W. the Clee Hills rise to 1,796 ft. (formerly to 1,805 ft., reduced by quarrying). Ellesmere is the largest of several lakes in the N.W. Coal and iron-ore are mined, but agriculture is the main occupation; cattle and sheep are reared, and cheese and other dairy produce made. Shrewsbury is the co. town. Area 1,348 sq. m.; pop. (1967) 326,010.

SHROVE TUESDAY. The day before Ash Wednesday. The name comes from the Anglo-Saxon *scrifan*, to shrive, and in olden days it was the time for confession before Lent. Another name for it is Pancake Tuesday; the pancakes are a survival of merrymaking in anticipation of Lenten abstinence.

SHRUB. Woody plant smaller than a tree and usually divided into separate stems near the ground.

SHUTE, Nevil. Pseudonym of British novelist N. S. Norway (1899–1960). B. in Ealing, son of a civil servant, he was ed. at Shrewsbury and Balliol and became an aircraft technician. He pub. his 1st novel in 1926, but it was not until during the S.W.W., in which he served in the R.N.V.R., that he became a best-seller. His always technically accurate books incl. *Pied Piper* (1942), *No Highway* (1948) and *A Town Like Alice* (1949). In 1950 he settled in Australia.

SIALKOT (sē-ahlkōt′). Town and trade centre of W. Pakistan, near the Chenab. Surgical and sports goods are produced on a large scale; also metal goods, leather goods, carpets, textiles. Pop. (1961) 164,346.

SIAN (sē-an′). Chinese city, cap. of Shensi prov., a great trade centre with cotton mills. S. was cap. of China under the Chou dynasty (*c.* 1100 B.C.); under the Han dynasty (206 B.C. to A.D. 220), when it was called Changan (long peace); under the Tang dynasty (618–906), as Siking (western cap.). The Manchus named it Sian (western peace); it reverted to the name Changan 1913–32; Siking 1932–43; Sian in 1943. The imperial court retired to S. following the Boxer rising, 1900. Pop. (1957 est.) 1,310,000.

SIBELIUS (sēbā′le-us), **Jean Christian** (1865–1957). Finnish composer. Intended by his father for the law, he studied the violin and composition at Helsingfors and went on to Berlin and Vienna. Recognized as a major composer only in Britain and the U.S.A., he has a simple austerity in his work which incl. the orchestral *En Saga* and *Karelia*; the tone-poems *Finlandia* and *Night Ride and Sunrise*; the appealing *Valse Triste*; *Voces Intimae*, a string quartet; and 7 symphonies.

SIBERIA. Geographical name for Asiatic R.S.F.S.R., bordered on the N. by the Arctic Ocean; S. by China, the Mongolian People's Republic, and Kazakh S.S.R.; W. by the Urals; E. by the Pacific. Much of it is within the Arctic Circle. Overrun by Russia in the 17th cent., from the 18th it was used as a place of exile for both political and criminal prisoners. The building of the Trans-Siberian railway (1892–1905) led to considerable voluntary settlement. Under Soviet rule, many prisoners continued to be sent to S., but colonization, with industrial and agricultural development, was undertaken on a considerable scale, and in W. Siberia there are large nat. gas deposits. Novosibirsk (q.v.) is the largest city in S. Area *c.* 5,000,000 sq. m.; pop. *c.* 30,000,000.

SIBLEY, Antoinette (1939–). British dancer. Joining the Royal Ballet in 1956, she became senior soloist in 1960. Her roles incl. Odette/Odile, Giselle, the betrayed girl in *The Rake's Progress*, and in 1964 she appeared in the première of Ashton's *The Dream*. In 1964 she m. Michael Somes (q.v.).

ANTOINETTE SIBLEY. As Titania in Ashton's *The Dream*.
Photo: Houston Rogers.

SIBYL. In classical mythology, a priestess of Apollo, who was supposed to prophesy under his inspiration. One Sibyl in particular, the Cumaean Sibyl, appears in Roman story as offering to sell to King Tarquin the Proud nine books of prophecies; the price was too high, but at length the king bought the three books that she had not destroyed for the price originally demanded for the set. These **Sibylline Books**, kept at Rome, were consulted in state emergencies. The alleged cave of the Cumaean S. was discovered in 1932 on Monte Cuma, nr. Naples.

SICILY. The largest island in the Mediterranean, forming with Lipari, Egadi, Ustica, and Pantelleria islands an autonomous region (1946) of Italy. Separated from the mainland by the Strait of Messina, S. is roughly triangular, tapering towards the W. The N. and centre are mountainous incl. Etna (10,755 ft., but est. at 11,000 after recent eruptions); elsewhere undulating hills and river valleys are found. The Simeto, Platani, and Salso are the main rivers. Low rainfall, a hot climate and extensive deforestation have led to water shortage, but supplies have recently been improved by harnessing mtn. streams, etc. Cereal (wheat, barley, oats, maize) and citrus fruit production has improved, and olives, vines and almonds are grown. Industrial development doubled 1960–70 based on the island's sulphur, and oil and natural gas resources nr. Ragusa which are among the richest in Europe. Other industries incl. cars, heavy vehicles, cement, hosiery, knitwear, shipbuilding, vegetable canning and wine making. Tunny fishing is of importance. The road and rail networks are adequate between Palermo, the cap., and the ports of Catania, Messina, Syracuse, and Marsala. Area 9,923 sq. m.; pop. (1961) 4,711,783.

The earliest recorded inhabitants of S. were the Sicans and Sicels. The Greeks first arrived in the 8th cent. B.C. and estab. a number of independent city states, among which Agrigentum, Gela, and Syracuse were of great importance. After 400 B.C. the Carthaginians occupied the W. part of the island and 210 B.C.–A.D. 440 S. was a Roman prov. and an important granary for Rome. Goths and Byzantines conquered S. in turn; the period of Saracen rule 878–c. 1090 was one of great prosperity, maintained under subsequent Norman and Hohenstaufen rulers. From 1302 the Aragonese, then Spain, later the Bourbons of Naples, ruled S. which in 1815 was formed with Naples into the Kingdom of the Two Sicilies. In 1860 Garibaldi drove the Bourbons out of S. and in 1861 it became part of the new Kingdom of Italy. There was extensive emigration in the 19th and early 20th cents. owing to under-employment and over-population, and under the Fascist régime land-reclamation schemes were carried out. Invaded and conquered by the Allies 10 July to 8 Aug. 1943, S. was still faced with chronic unemployment after the S.W.W. since its resources, e.g. sulphur, could not be exploited without capital investment, and development projects such as the Bruca dam were impeded by the Mafia (q.v.), resurgent after being driven underground by Mussolini, and the strength of the separatist movement led to a measure of autonomy being granted by the Italian govt. in the new constitution of 1947. Social worker Danilo Dolci (1924–) has done much since the 1950s to combat the Mafia stranglehold and ameliorate the employment position.

SICKERT, Walter Richard (1860–1942). British artist. B. in Munich, the son of a Danish painter, he was taken to London and studied at the Slade School and under Whistler. He estab. a reputation as a painter of Impressionistic pictures, his works incl. 'Mamma Mia Poareta', 'The Area Steps', 'The Evening Primrose', and 'Bath'. He became president of the Royal Society of British Artists, and was elected R.A. in 1934.

SIDDONS, Sarah (1755–1831). English actress. B. at Brecon, Wales, the dau. of Roger Kemble, she m. in 1773 William Siddons. Her first success in Otway's *Venice Preserved* in 1774 led to her engagement in 1775 to appear with Garrick at Drury Lane. The majesty of her presence made her a superb Lady Macbeth, and her other parts incl. Desdemona, Ophelia and Volumnia. She appeared with acclaim until her retirement in 1812, her admirers incl. Johnson and Walpole: Reynolds painted her as 'The Tragic Muse'.

SIDGWICK, Henry (1838–1900). British philosopher. Knightsbridge prof. of moral philosophy at Cambridge from 1883, he is remembered for his utilitarian *Methods of Ethics* (1874), a comparison of various schools, and *The Principles of Political Economy* (1883). He was a founder and 1st pres. of the Soc. for Pyschical Research.

SIDI BARRÂNI (sid'i barah'nē). Coastal settlement of Egypt, about 230 m. W. of Alexandria, the scene of much fighting 1940–2, during the S.W.W.

SIDI-BEL ABBÈS. Town and trade centre in Algeria, 35 m. S. of Oran. When Algeria was French, it was the H.Q. of the Foreign Legion. Pop. (1967) 101,000.

SIDNEY, Algernon (1622–83). English Republican. The son of the 2nd earl of Leicester, he served in the parliamentary army during the Civil War, and after the Restoration lived in exile until 1677, when he returned to England and was a prominent Whig. Accused of complicity in the Rye House Plot, he was beheaded.

SIDNEY, Sir Philip (1554–86). English poet and soldier. B. at Penshurst, Kent, he entered Parliament in 1581, and in 1583 was knighted. In 1585 he was made governor of Flushing, and was mortally wounded at Zutphen, fighting the Spaniards. Among his works are the sonnet sequence *Astrophel and Stella* (1591); the romance *Arcadia* (1590); and the *Apologie for Poetrie* (1595), the earliest work of English literary criticism.

SI'DON. Chief city of ancient Phoenicia, bitter rival of Tyre from c. 1400 B.C. until conquered by Sennacherib, 701 B.C. Later a Roman city, taken by the Arabs A.D. 637, fought over during the Crusades. On the W. part of it stands Saida, Lebanon.

SIEGFRIED (sēg'frēd). Germanic hero. It is uncertain whether his story has a historical basis, but it was current about 700. In the poems of the Norse Elder Edda and in the prose Völsunga Saga S. appears under the name of Sigurd. The best-known version is in the German *Nibelungenlied*.

SIEMENS (sē'mens). Family of 4 brothers, creators of a vast industrial empire: most famous were the eldest, **Ernst Werner von S.** (1818–92), who founded in 1847 the original electrical firm of Siemens und Halske and made many inventions in telegraphy; and **Wilhelm** (1823–83), who became in 1859 a British subject and was knighted in 1883 as Sir William S. He was manager of the firm S. Brothers, and was concerned with the development of the dynamo, etc.

SIENA (sē-ā'nah). City of Tuscany, Italy, cap. of S. prov., 31 m. S. of Florence. The city, which dates back to Roman times, is famous for its architecture, and for a school of painting which flourished from the 13th to the 16th cent. There is a univ. (1300), and a Gothic cathedral, completed 1243. Straw plaiting is carried on, chemicals, cork articles, sausage, etc., are made, and there is trade in wine and olive oil. An annual race on horseback, the Palio, has been held in the main square since the Middle Ages. Pop (1961) 62,215.

SIENKIEWICZ (syenkye'vich), **Henryk** (1846–1916). Polish author. His books incl. the 17th cent. historical trilogy *With Fire and Sword*, *The Deluge* and *Pan Michael* (1890–3); *Quo Vadis?* (1895), set in Rome in the time of Nero, and *Without Dogma* (1891).

SIERRA LEONE (sē-er'ra lēōn' or lā-ōnā). Country of W. Africa, between Rep. of Guinea in the N. and Liberia in the S.E. It has a very hot and moist climate. Agriculture supports more than half the pop., main products being palm-kernels, ground-nuts, kolanuts, rice, cocoa, coffee, ginger, and cassava. There are vegetable-oil mills, furniture workshops, and various village industries incl. fishing and weaving. Diamonds (about half of gem quality), the most valuable export, iron-ore, and chromite are mined. S.L. is the former British colony, a small area acquired 1788 for repatriating homeless Africans from London and, later, rescued from slave ships, and protectorate (1896) over the hinterland, which achieved self-govt. 1958, and independence within the British Commonwealth 1961. After military govt. 1967–8, parliamentary rule was restored, but a state of emergency again ensued by the end of 1968. The cap. is Freetown. Area 27,925 sq. m.; pop. (1963) 2,183,000.

SIEYÈS (sē-āyās'), **Emmanuel-Joseph** (1748–1836). French statesman. Born at Fréjus, he entered the Church, and in 1788 achieved fame with his pamphlet *What is the Third Estate?* He sat in the National Assembly and the National Convention. Elected a Director in 1799, he supported Napoleon's coup d'état, and sat in the senate. He lived in exile 1815–30.

SIGNAC (sēnyahk'), **Paul** (1863–1935). French artist. Parisian-born, he was influenced by Monet, and in 1884 joined with Seurat in founding the Société des Artistes Indépendants. Fond of sailing, he expanded his brilliant water-colours made on the spot into large canvases instinct with colour and light, often composed of squarish 'mosaic' blobs.

SIGNALS. Method of communication using flags, light, radio telephony, radio telegraphy, etc. The International Code of S. used by shipping was drawn up by an international committee and pub. in 1931. The codes and abbreviations used by aircraft are dealt with by the International Civil Aviation Organization (1944). *See* MORSE CODE and SEMAPHORE.

SIKHISM (sē'kizm). The religion of between 4 and 5 million Indians living for the most part in the Punjab. It was founded by Nanak (1469–c.1539). Its basis is the Unity of God and the Brotherhood of Man, and in it caste plays a comparatively small part. On Nanak's death he was followed as Guru – chief priest – by a succession of rulers who converted the Sikhs – the word means disciple – into a military confraternity which established itself as a political power. Guru Gobind Singh instituted the Khanda-di-Pahul, the Baptism of the Sword, and established the Khalsa ('the pure'), the Brotherhood of the faithful, the Singhs. The Singhs wear the 5 Ks: *kes*, long hair; *kangha*, a comb; *kirpan*, a sword; *kachh*, long drawers; and *kara*, a steel bracelet. The last of the Gurus, Gobind Singh, was assassinated by a Moslem in 1708, and since then the Granth Sahib, the holy book of the Sikhs, has taken the place of a leader. On the partition of India many Sikhs migrated from W. to E. Punjab, and in 1966 the efforts of Sant Fateh Singh (c. 1911–) led to the creation of a separate Sikh state by partition of Punjab (q.v.).

SI-KIANG ('West River'). River of China, rising in Yunnan and flowing into the South China Sea. Canton lies on the N. arm of its delta. Hong Kong island lies off the mouth.

SIKKIM (sik'im). Small state in the Himalayas, bordering Nepal, Bhutan, and Tibet (China). Maize and rice are grown. S. is under the protection of the Rep. of India. The cap. is Gangtok. King (*Chogyal*) Palden Thondup Namgyal (1924–) succeeded his father as maharajah in 1963, but was crowned under the title of king in 1965: his wife, née Hope Cooke, is American-born. Area 2,745 sq. m.; pop. (1961) 162,189.

SIKO'RSKI, Wladyslaw (1881–1943). Polish gen. and statesman. B. in Galicia, he organized in 1909 the nationalist military organization, which during the F.W.W. fought for the central powers. He served in the Russian war of 1920, and was P.M. 1922–3 and War Min. 1923–5. He became P.M. in Sept. 1939 of the exiled Polish govt., which transferred to London in 1940. He was killed in an air crash.

SI'LAGE. Fodder preserved in a silo, an airtight structure for pressing green crops. It is now extended to refer to stacked crops which may be preserved indefinitely.

SILCHESTER. Archaeological site in Hants., England, 6 m. N. of Basingstoke. One of the most important towns in Britain in the Roman period. S. is the only town in the prov. known in such detail.

SILE'NUS. In Greek mythology, the son of Hermes, or Pan, and companion of Dionysus. He is portrayed as a jovial old man, usually drunk.

SILE'SIA. Region of central Europe. Before the F.W.W. all except a small part of S. had belonged to Germany since it was wrested from Austria (which had held it since 1675) by Frederick II of Prussia in 1745. In 1919, c. 1,700 sq. m. (most of the part in Austria) went to newly formed Czechoslovakia; c. 1,600 sq. m. to revived Poland; the rest, 13,000 sq. m., remained part of Germany. Following the S.W.W. all German S. lying E. of the Oder–W. Neisse line was transferred to Polish administration, 1945, and most of its German inhabitants were expelled, as were those of German origin in Czechoslovak S. The largest towns are Wroclaw (Breslau), Katowice, Zabrze (Hindenburg), Chorzow (Königshütte), Gliwice (Gleiwitz), and Bytom (Beuthen) in Poland and Opava (Troppau) in Czechoslovakia.

SILHOUETTE (siloo-et'). A profile or shadow portrait filled in in black or a dark colour, named after Étienne de Silhouette (1709–67), a French finance minister whose economy led to his name being applied to cheap things. *See* illus. p. 482.

SI'LICON. A non-metallic chemical element, symbol Si (Lat. *silex*, flint), at. wt., 28·09, and at. no. 14. It is used in the making of glass and as a hardener in steel alloys.

Silicones are synthetic chemical products, characterized by their chemical inertness, good electrical properties, and ability to repel water. They are based on a chain of oxygen and silicon atoms, the latter having organic groups attached to them. These groups and the basic silicone structure can be varied to produce silicone rubber, longer-lasting electrical material, paints, industrial grease, domestic polishes, water-repellent fluids for treating masonry, stain-resistant fabric finishes, etc.

SILICO'SIS. A condition affecting workers who inhale flint dust, e.g. anthracite miners and stone cutters. The lung tissue becomes fibrous through constant small injury and repair, less capable of aerating the blood and less resistant to tuberculosis.

SILK. Fine, soft thread produced by the larva of

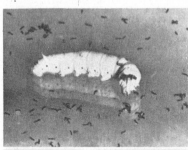

SILK. A fully grown silkworm (*top left*) surrounded by newly hatched worms: at maturity, the silkworm is 8,000 times heavier and 23 times larger than when first hatched. Just emerged from the cocoon (*bottom left*) a silkmoth waits for its wings to dry and expand: in forcing its way out – the aperture is seen to the right – it broke the continuous filament of which the cocoon is composed. The leading threads of each cocoon are unravelled (*right*) and are ready for passing to the reeling-machine operator.
Courtesy of the Silk Centre.

SILVER. The chalice on the left, depicting the life of Moses, is of German origin and dates from 1600 – it once belonged to the Rothschilds: the jug on the right was given to Nelson in 1795 by 'his friend Spencer [First Lord of the Admiralty] in recognition of services rendered at Leghorn and Genoa'.
Courtesy of Miss A. Mitchell-Hedges.

the silkworm moth, the most commonly cultivated species being *Bombyx mori*, and used in the manufacture of textiles. The 'worm' or larva attains maturity within a month of hatching from the egg, feeding on the leaves of white mulberry trees, and then 'spins' a protective cocoon of fine silk thread. Before it can emerge as the perfect insect, when it would in the natural state live for a few days (mating and egg-laying then taking place), the silk maker ensures its death by plunging the cocoon in hot water or in a hot oven. To allow it to emerge would damage the thread: from such damaged cocoons the inferior spun S. is made. The thread from a number of cocoons is then reeled together to form a strong filament of raw S.: one cocoon contains *c.* 300 yds. of thread. The introduction of synthetics originally harmed the S. industry, but S. has properties synthetics do not possess and rising standards of living have produced an increased demand for real S. Japan produces just over half the world's S. (mostly for domestic use in kimonos, etc.) followed by China (23 per cent) and the Soviet Union (9 per cent): Italy and France, as having climates best suited to the trees on which the larvae must feed and to the requirements of the insect's own development, are European producers.

SILLITOE, Alan (1928–). English novelist. Raised in Nottingham, he set there his first book, *Saturday Night and Sunday Morning* (1958), which reflected in its hero, Arthur Seaton, the complete transformation of working-class status in England since the S.W.W. Later books incl. *The Key to the Door* (1961), also set in Nottingham, and *The Rats* (1960) – poetry.

SILONE (sēlōn'ā), **Ignazio** (1900–). Italian novelist. Once Communist, he is a non-party socialist. His best-known novel, *Fontamara* (1933) – a simple, moving description of the hopes and disillusionment of a peasant village – was followed by others e.g. *A Handful of Blackberries* (1952), dealing with the problem of the individual in politics.

SILSOE, Arthur Malcolm Trustram Eve, baron S. (1894–). British lawyer. Chairman of the War Damage (1941–9) and Local Govt. Boundary (1945–9) commissions, he became First Church Estates Commissioner in 1954 and was First Crown Estate Commissioner 1955–62. He was created a baron in 1963.

SILVA, Antonio José da (1705–39). Portuguese dramatist. B. at Rio de Janeiro, he settled in Lisbon where he was burnt by the Inquisition. His comedies, such as *Don Quixote* (1733) and *Amphitriao* (1736), ridiculed 18th cent. society.

SILVĀ'NUS. A Roman woodland deity, identified in later times with Pan.

SILVER. A lustrous silvery metal extremely malleable and ductile: symbol Ag (Lat. *argentum*), at. wt. 107·873, at. no. 47. Known since prehistoric times, S. occurs native in Peru, but the chief ores are sulphides, from which the metal is extracted by smelting with lead. It is the best metallic conductor of both heat and electricity, and its most important compounds are the chloride and bromide which darken on exposure to light, the basis of photographic emulsions. S. is used for tableware, jewellery, coinage, electrical contacts and electro-plating, and as a solder it makes good metallic joints at 720°C. The world's greatest producer of silver is Mexico (*c.* 40,000,000 troy oz. p.a.), followed by the U.S.A., Canada, Peru, the U.S.S.R., Australia and Japan.

SIMENON (sēmenoṅ'), **Georges** (1903–). Belgian author. B. in Liège, of Dutch and Breton blood, he is the son of an insurance salesman. On his father's death he had to cut short his education, but rebelled against being apprenticed to a baker, and became a bookstore assistant for a time before joining the staff of a local newspaper. At 20 he went to Paris and started writing pulp fiction, then at 30 began the realistic and psychologically sound series of detective novels built round the character of Inspector Maigret of the Paris Sûreté, and his loyal assistants. These have been translated, filmed, and televised the world over. He has also written numerous 'plain novels', as he terms them, without the prop of police detection, such as *A Wife at Sea*, *The Stain on the Snow*, and *The Woman in the Grey House.*

SIMEON STYLITES, St. (*c.* 390–459). Syrian Christian ascetic, who lived for 37 years on a pillar.

SIMFEROPOL (simferō'poly). Town in the Crimea, Ukrainian S.S.R., 40 m. N.E. of Sevastopol, cap. of Crimea region. Soap, tobacco, etc., are manufactured. S. was occupied by the Germans Nov. 1941–April 1944. It is on the site of the Tartar town of Ak-Mechet, conquered by the Russians 1783 and renamed. Pop. (1967) 217,000.

GEORGES SIMENON

SI'MLA. Cap. of Himachal Pradesh, Rep. of India, 7,500 ft. a.s.l., in the Himalayan foothills, 170 m. N. of Delhi. The summer seat of govt. of British India, 1864–1947, it was made cap. of Himachal Pradesh on its formation in 1948. Pop. (1961) 42,597.

SIMON, John Allsebrook, visct. (1873–1954). British Liberal politician and lawyer. As Home Sec. in 1915 he resigned in protest against conscription in 1916 and served in the R.F.C. Entering the Nat. Govt. in 1931 as For. Sec., he was Home Sec. 1935–7, and Chancellor of the Exchequer 1937–40. His chief mark was made by his judgments as Lord Chancellor 1940–5.

SIMONOV (sēm'ōnof), **Konstantin** (1915–). Russian writer. Belonging to the generation which has grown up devoted to the interests of the Soviet State, he originally made his name as a playwright, and in the S.W.W. served as correspondent at the front for *Red Star*. His novel *Days and Nights* (1944) deals with the defence of Stalingrad on a purely military level, and his play *The Russian Question* (1946) is strongly anti-western on Stalinist lines, but *Victims and Heroes* (1959, U.S., *The Living and the Dead*) takes advantage of the new freedom under Khrushchev to make bold criticisms of the handling of the Soviet-German conflict.

SIMONSTOWN. Naval base in S. Africa, estab. 1814. It lies on False Bay, 23 m. S. of Capetown. The site was settled by the Dutch in 1741, taken by the British 1795. Britain withdrew the C.-in-C. South Atlantic from S. 1967, but continues to use facilities there. Pop. *c.* 10,000.

SI'MONY. Name given to the buying and selling of presentation to an ecclesiastical benefice, preferment, etc. It is derived from Simon Magnus, who (as told in Acts viii) offered the Apostles money in return for the power of the Holy Ghost.

SIMPLON (sanplon'). Pass on the borders of Switzerland and Italy. It runs in a S.E. direction from Brig to Domodossola, rises to a height of 6,582 ft., and is followed by a road built by Napoleon I, 1800–5. Under it runs the S. tunnel, 1906–22, 12·3 m.

SIMPSON, Sir James Young (1811–70). British physician. He took his M.D. at Edinburgh in 1832, became pres. of the Royal Medical Soc. 1835, and prof. of midwifery 1839. He was largely instrumental in the introduction of chloroform as an anaesthetic in 1847. He was created a baronet in 1866.

SIMPSON, Norman Frederick (1919–). British dramatist. A lecturer in history and English for adult education, his plays *A Resounding Tinkle* (1957), *The Hole* (1958), and *One Way Pendulum* (1959) show the logical development of an abnormal situation, and belong to the 'Theatre of the Absurd'.

SINAI (sī'nī). Egyptian peninsula between the gulfs of Suez and Aqaba, at the head of the Red Sea. The Mount Sinai, on which Moses received from Jehovah the tables of the Law, has been variously identified. In St. Catherine's monastery Tischendorf discovered in 1844 the Codex Sinaiticus, purchased from Russia in 1923 and placed in the British Museum. It was occupied by Israel from 1967.

SINA'TRA, Frank (1917–). American singer. B. in Hoboken, N.J., the son of a former prizefighter, he achieved fame as a heart-throb singer – 'Night and Day', 'You'd Be So Nice to Come Home To', etc., and then estab. himself as an actor, as in *From Here to Eternity* (1953) which won him an Oscar.

SINCLAIR, Archibald. *See* LORD THURSO.

SINCLAIR, Upton (1878–1968). American novelist. B. in Baltimore, he attracted attention with *The Jungle* (1906), dealing with the Chicago stockyards. Among his later works are *Boston* (1928), and the Lanny Budd series, incl. *Presidential Agent* (1944).

SIND. Prov. of Pakistan and former prov. of Brit. India, annexed by Britain in 1843: it was merged in the prov. of W. Pakistan 1955–70. Area 47,000 sq. m.; mainly in the Indus delta.

SIMONOV. He became chairman of the Soviet Writers' Union during the period when writers were being ruthlessly forced to toe the Stalinist line, and even in 1956, as editor of *Novy Mir*, was strongly criticised for his publication of Dudintsev's *Not by Bread Alone*.

SI'NDING, Christian (1856–1941). Norwegian composer. His works incl. 3 symphonies, piano pieces and songs. **Otto** (1842–1909) and **Stephan** (1846–1922),

SINGAPORE. Greeting the arrival of a ship in the traditional way, Chinese dancers perform the Lion Dance on the quay at Singapore for the passengers of the *Oriana*. Music is provided by a percussion band. *Courtesy of P. & O. Orient Lines.*

his brothers, were painter and sculptor respectively.

SINGAPORE. Island state of Asia, lying off the southern tip of Malaya and joined to the mainland by a causeway carrying road and railway across the Strait of Johore. Area 220 sq. m.; pop. (1967) 1,955,600, of whom 1,454,500 were Chinese, 18,900 European, 159,400 Indian and Pakistani, and 283,500 Malay. The cap., also S., lies on the S. coast; the airport is at Paya Lebar, 6½ m. from the city.

S. island, then a swampy jungle, was leased from the sultan of Johore, on the advice of Stamford Raffles, by the East India Co. in 1819, ceded to the Co. in 1824, and passed to the Crown in 1858. It was detached from India in 1867 and placed under the Colonial Office as part of the Straits Settlement crown colony, dissolved in 1946, S. then becoming a separate crown colony. Given independence 1959, S. was incl. in Malaysia, but seceded 1965, becoming a rep. within the Commonwealth.

During the S.W.W., S. was in Japanese occupation 15 Feb. 1942–12 Sept. 1945; the great naval base, constructed on the N. coast 1923–4 and 1934–8 at a cost of more than £11,000,000, proving useless in defence since its great guns were directed only southwards, its designers never having contemplated invasion from the N., which in the event happened.

S., the cap., founded by Raffles in 1819 on the site of an old town destroyed by the Javanese *c.* 1377, developed into a very important entrepôt and port, serving the whole of Malaya and exporting rubber, tin, copra, etc., in quantity. It is also a major international airport. Made a city in 1951, it has fine buildings, incl. Anglican and R.C. cathedrals, the Raffles museum, and S. univ. (1949). The naval dockyard was handed over to S. govt. for conversion to commercial use in 1968.

SING SING. Name until 1901 of the U.S. village of Ossining, New York, famous as the site of a state prison (1825, rebuilt 1930).

SINKIANG-UIGHUR (sin'kyang' wē'goor). Auton. region of China, bordering Kazakh S.S.R. and the Mongolian People's Republic; Tibet lies to the S. The semi-desert depressions of Dzungaria and Tarim are separated by the Tien Shan mountain system. The people and army resisted the Maoist Cultural Revolution and in 1967 there were Sino-Soviet frontier clashes – China's nuclear testing ground is at Lop-Nor (q.v.). Urumchi is the cap. Area 635,800 sq. m.; pop. (1968) 8,000,000.

SINN FEIN (shin fān) (Gaelic, 'We ourselves'). Irish nationalist party, founded by Arthur Griffith in 1905, with a policy of resistance to British rule. After 1917 it became under De Valera the centre of the republican movement, and ousted the old Home Rule Party in the 1918 elections. It survived only as a small extremist group after the creation of Fianna Fáil.

SINO-JAPANESE WARS. The first war between China and Japan, in 1894–5, ended in a Japanese victory and the annexation of Formosa and the Pescadores. In 1931–2 the Japanese occupied Manchuria, which they formed into the puppet state of Manchukuo, and attacked Shanghai. War was renewed in 1937, when the Japanese overran N.E. China and seized Shanghai and Nanking. In 1938 they captured Hankow and Canton, and the Chinese cap. was transferred to Chungking. A period of stalemate followed. The Japanese attack on Britain and the U.S.A. in 1941 was followed by the extension of lease-lend aid to China, but the loss of Burma cut off a valuable source of supplies. A Japanese offensive in 1944 seriously threatened Chungking. The Chinese shared in the final offensive in 1945, and received the Japanese surrender at Nanking in Sept.

SIOUX (soo) **CITY.** City of Iowa, U.S.A., on the Missouri near its junction with the Big Sioux r. Founded 1849, it is an important livestock and dairy-products centre. Pop. (1960) 89,159.

SIOUX FALLS. Largest city in S. Dakota, U.S.A., on the Big Sioux r., near the 100 ft. high Sioux Falls which supply power for its industry. Pop. (1960) 65,466.

SIOUX INDIANS. Principal tribe of the Dakota family of N. American Indians, now confined to S. Dakota and Nebraska. Gen. George Custer (1839–76) was killed with 250 men when he moved against a S. camp at Little Bighorn, Montana (under chiefs Crazy Horse and Sitting Bull): the site of Custer's 'Last Stand' is a nat. monument.

SIRENS. In Greek mythology, sea nymphs who lured sailors on to the rocks by their singing. When Odysseus passed them he tied himself to the mast and stuffed his companions' ears with wax, while the Argonauts escaped them because Orpheus' singing surpassed theirs.

SIRO'CCO. A hot, normally dry and dust-laden wind which blows from the highland of Africa to N. Africa, Malta, Sicily, and Italy. It occurs mainly in the spring. The name S. has been applied to southerly winds in the E. of the U.S.A.

SISAL HEMP. *See* HEMP.

SI'SKIN. Bird (*Carduelis spinus*) in the finch family Fringillidae, found in the Old World from Britain to Japan: it is greenish yellow with an attractive song. The American S. is more accurately the pine-finch (*Spinus pinus*).

SISKIN

SISLEY (sis'li), **Alfred** (1840–99). French artist. B. in Paris, of English parents, he studied under Gleyre, and became associated with Monet and Renoir. He met with little success in his lifetime, but he is now regarded as among the best of the Impressionists. A landscape painter, he painted the effects of light at different times of the day.

SISYPHUS (sis'ifus). A mythical king of Corinth, who was condemned in the underworld to roll uphill a huge stone which always rolled down again when it reached the top.

SITWELL, Sir Osbert (1892–1969). Brit. poet and author. B. in London, the son of Sir George S. (1860–1943), he went to Eton, and served in the Grenadier Guards 1912–19. He pub. his *Selected Poems* in 1943, and wrote art criticism, novels, e.g. *A Place of One's Own* (1941); and a series of autobiographical vols.: *Left Hand! Right Hand!*, *The Scarlet Tree*, *Great Morning, Laughter in the Next Room, Noble Essences* and *Tales My Father Taught Me* (1945–62). His brother, **Sacheverell S.** (1897–　), was b. at

THE SITWELLS. Dame Edith, a magnificent romantic in her dress as in her poetry, and Sir Osbert.

Scarborough, and has pub. art criticism, e.g. *Southern Baroque Art* (1924), and *British Architects and Craftsmen* (1945); poetry; and prose miscellanies such as *Sacred and Profane Love*, and *Splendours and Miseries*. His sister **Dame Edith S.** (1887–1964), also b. in Scarborough, pub. *Collected Poems* (1930), and *Shadow of Cain* (1948); the prose *Life of Alexander Pope* (1930), and *Aspects of Modern Poetry* (1934); and the autobiography *Taken Care Of* (1965).

SIVA (sē'vah) or **SHIVA** (Skr. for 'propitious'). The 3rd person in the Hindu triad. As Mahadeva (great lord), he is the creator, symbolized by the phallic *linga*, who restores what as Mahakala he destroys. He is often sculptured as Nataraja, performing his fruitful cosmic dance. His consort or female principle (*sakti*), is Parvati, otherwise known as Durga or Kali.

SIXTUS. Name of 5 popes. **Sixtus IV** (1414–84), who became pope in 1471, built the Sistine Chapel, which is named after him. **Sixtus V** (1521–90), who became pope in 1585, supported the Spanish Armada and the Catholic League against Henry IV.

SJAELLAND. *See* SEELAND.

SKA'GERRAK. Arm of the North Sea between the S. coast of Norway and the N. coast of Denmark. In May 1916 it was the scene of a naval action called in Britain the battle of Jutland.

SKANE (skaw'ne). Densely peopled prov. of S. Sweden. A fertile agricultural region, Danish until ceded to Sweden in 1658, it comprises the counties of Malmöhus and Kristianstad; Malmö and Hälsingborg are important centres.

SKATE. The name of several species of flat fish of the ray family. The common S. (*Raia batis*) is from 2 to 4 ft. long, greyish in colour, with black specks. Found off the British coasts, it is eaten. The egg-cases ('mermaids' purses') are often thrown up by the tide.

SKATING. Self-propulsion on ice by means of bladed skates, or on some prepared surface (usually a poilite or masonite rink) by means of skates with 4 small wooden (usually maple) rollers. Ice S. probably originated in Scandinavia, the first skates being animal bones, was popular on the canals of medieval Holland, and in the 17th and 18th cents. in England and on the Continent. The 1st English S. club was founded in London in 1842, followed in 1849 by one in Philadelphia, where the 1st all-iron skate was invented in

SKATE

1850 by E. W. Bushnell: the 1st artificial ice rink was opened in London in 1876. National bodies incl. the National S. Assocn. of Gt. Britain (1879), U.S. Figure S. Assocn. (1886) and the Canadian Figure S. Assocn. (1888), all subject to the International S. Union. Competitive S. events incl. figure (comprising compulsory figures and free S.) for men, women and pairs; dance – for pairs; speed – for men and women. Roller S. 1st developed in the 18th cent., but the modern 4-wheel skate was the invention of the American James L. Plympton who also opened the 1st rink at Newport, Rhode Island, in 1866. Events are as for ice S., and in Britain the N.S.A. is the governing body: international control is exercised by the Fédération Internationale de Patinage à Roulettes. *See also* ICE HOCKEY.

SKEGNESS. English holiday resort (U.D.) on the Lincolnshire coast. The first Butlin (q.v.) holiday camp was at S., 1936. Pop. (1961) 12,843.

SKELTON, John (c. 1460–1529). English poet. He became tutor to Prince Henry, later Henry VIII, and took orders in 1498. Among his poems are *Colyn Cloute, Phylyp Sparowe*, and *The Tunning of Elynour Rumming*.

SKI'DDAW. Mountain (3,054 ft.) of Cumberland, England, in the Lake District, c. 7 m. N. of Keswick.

SKIING. Self-propulsion on snow by means of elongated wooden or metal skis, 3–5 in. wide, c. 7 ft. long and bent upward at the tip; usually with the assistance of ski poles held in the hands. Prehistoric types of ski date in Sweden to c. 3,000 B.C., but they were primarily a means of civil or military transport

SKIING. Ideal for the learner or the expert limbering up for winter sports is the plastic slope now installed in large stores or (as here) in the open air. *Courtesy of Bakelite Ltd.*

until the sport developed in Norway c. 1860. Competition events incl. slalom, in which flags (placed to make the turns as difficult as possible) mark out a course of varying gradient; cross-country racing; and ski jumping – over 300 ft. being achieved. The Fédération Internationale des Skieurs (1924) is linked with the Ski Club of Great Britain (1924), the Canadian Amateur Ski Assocn. (1920), the Nat. Ski Assocn. of America (1904), etc. Allied to the ski is the N. American Indian snow shoe, a broad framework covered with a thong web, and useful for travel in thick forest. In water S. the skis are wider and shorter than snow skis, and the skier is towed by a motorboat.

SKIKDA. *See* PHILIPPEVILLE.

SKIN. The covering of the body. Its outer layer, the epidermis, is insensitive and protective, and the cells of this are constantly being rubbed away and replaced from below; the lower layer, the true skin or corium, is full of blood-vessels and nerves of sensation, touch and temperature control. It contains the hair roots, and the sweat and sebaceous glands, and is supported by a network of fibrous and elastic cells. Skin diseases may be the result of infection, e.g. impetigo, herpes or rarely tuberculosis; tumours, e.g.

SKIPTON. The castle, of which the gateway is seen here, was built partly in the reign of Edward II and partly in that of Henry VIII, and was once the chief seat of the Cliffords. John, the 9th baron, was the murderer of the earl of Rutland in the battle of Wakefield in 1460. *Photo: W. R. Mitchell*

cancer; fungus invasion, e.g. ringworm; rashes from a multiplicity of common drugs, or contact or allergic dermatitis from furs, hair dyes and some detergents. Skin-grafting is the repair of injured skin by placing pieces of skin taken from elsewhere on the body so that the cells may multiply and cover it.

SKIPTON. English market town (U.D.) in the W. Riding, Yorks, about 22 m. N.W. of Leeds. It has a ruined castle and textile factories. Pop. (1961) 12,988.

SKITTLES. A game with the object of knocking down 9 wooden S. forming a square at one end of an alley by means of a ball hurled from the other. An angle of the square faces the alley. The game resembles tenpin bowling (q.v.).

SKOPJE (skop'yä). Cap. of Macedonia, Yugoslavia, on the Vardar. On the site of an ancient town destroyed by earthquake in the 5th cent., it was taken by the Serbian king Milutin in the 13th cent.; he made it his cap. Again destroyed by earthquake 1963, S. was rebuilt on a safer nearby site. There are chromium mines, iron and steelworks, and an airport. S. is a Moslem centre. Pop. (1970) 380,000

SKUA (skioo'a). Genus of seabirds, of which the largest is the great S. (*Stercorarius skua*) of the N. Atlantic, 2 ft. long and dark brown on the upper parts. Very aggressive, the Ss. seldom fish for themselves and rely on forcing gulls to disgorge their catch.

SKULL. The collection of flat and irregularly shaped bones (22 in all) which enclose and protect the brain and form the face. The brain case (cranium) consists of plates of bone joined by sutures. The bones of the face carry the upper teeth and enclose some air spaces (sinuses) and form the framework for the eyes, nose and mouth. The lower jaw is hinged to the middle of the cranium at its lower edge. Inside, the cranium is hollowed into various shallow cavities into which fit different parts of the brain; the plate corresponding to the back of the head (occipital) is jointed at its lower edge with the upper section of the spine (atlas and axis). The floor of the skull is pierced by a great hole for the spinal cord and a number of apertures through which pass other nerves and blood-vessels.

SKUNK. N. American mammal of the family *Mustelidae*. The common S. (*Mephitis mephitica*) has a long, arched body, short legs, a bushy tail, and a black fur with white streaks on the back In self-defence it discharges a foul-smelling fluid.

SKYDIVING. *See* FREEFALLING.

SKYE (skī). Largest island of the Inner Hebrides, part of Inverness-shire, Scotland, separated from the mainland by the Sound of Sleat. The principal port is Portree. Area 643 sq. m.; pop. (1961) 7,400. *See* illus. p. 520.

SKYE TERRIER. Variety of Scotch terrier. It is rather small with a long coat, varying from dark blue to light grey in colour.

SKYLARK. *See* LARK.

SKYROS (skī'ros). Greek island, one of the N. Sporades, in the Aegean Sea, rising to 2,608 ft. Wheat, figs, olive oil, fish, and cheese are produced, and there are deposits of marble, chromite, and iron. Rupert Brooke (1888–1915) is buried on S. Area 79 sq. m.; pop. (est.) 4,000. The cap. is also S., pop. 3,000.

SKYSCRAPER. *See* UNITED STATES: ARCHITECTURE.

SLADE, Felix (1790–1868). British art collector. B. in London, he bequeathed most of his art collection to the British Museum, and endowed Slade art professorships at Oxford, Cambridge, and University College, London. The Slade School is a branch of University College.

SLADEK (slah'dek), **Josev Vaclav** (1845–1912). Czech poet. He spent some time as a trapper in America and later became a lecturer at Prague. He produced lyrics and translations of English poets.

SLANDER. One variety of defamation, the other being libel (q.v.). Defamatory spoken words or gestures constitute S., but if broadcast, constitute a libel. Such Ss. as imputing incapacity to a person in his profession, or unchastity to a woman, are actionable without proof of pecuniary loss. As in the case of libel, the S. must be pub. to some person other than the person defamed for it to be actionable.

SLATE. Kind of fine-grained, bluish-purple rock which splits readily into thin slabs suitable for roofing. It is highly resistant to atmospheric conditions, and is also used for writing purposes with chalk. The N. Welsh kind is finest.

SLAVERY. The legal and economic status of being another's property. S. probably originated in early agricultural societies, the slaves being recruited from prisoners of war. In Greece and Rome S. formed the economic basis of society. From the 2nd cent. B.C. conquest flooded Rome with slaves, who in the 1st cent. A.D. outnumbered free men in Italy, and several slave revolts occurred. The economic crisis of the 2nd cent. A.D. onwards led to alleviation of the slaves' lot, and serfdom replaced S. It nevertheless died out slowly, surviving in England until the 11th cent. The colonization of America led to a revival of S. in the 16th cent., and to the establishment of a traffic in Negro slaves. Humanitarian agitation led to the prohibition of the slave trade in the British dominions in 1807 and of slave-holding itself in 1833. Leaders of the movement were Granville Sharp, Thomas Clarkson and Wilberforce. In the U.S.A. the Civil War turned largely on slavery, which was declared illegal by Lincoln in 1865. Although officially abolished, S. tends to linger in remoter areas of Africa.

SLAVKOV. Czech name of AUSTERLITZ.

SLAVS (slahvz). Indo-European race. They appear to have originated in the Carpathian regions, and by the 7th cent. had occupied an area lying between the Baltic, Elbe, Adriatic, and Black Sea. During the 9th cent. they embraced Christianity, and in the course of the Middle Ages they were expelled from what is now E. Germany. After the 16th cent. S. settled in Siberia on an increasingly large scale. The S. have for long been divided into well-defined national groups, among which the Russians (E. Slavs) are by far the largest. Others incl. the Poles, Czechs, Slovaks, and Wends (W. Slavs), and Serbo-Croats, Slovenes, and Bulgars (S. Slavs).

SLEEP. A state in which the whole organism is at rest. Very little is known about its nature, but it is marked by unconsciousness, relaxation of muscles, slow pulse, and quiet breathing. The amount of sleep required by individuals varies; children and the sick require most and the aged least. The average is seven hours a day. Sleeplessness is largely due to anxiety.

SLEEPING SICKNESS. Trypanosomiasis; acute disease caused by blood parasites carried by the tsetse fly, etc. When the parasites enter the cerebrospinal fluid, the patient becomes apathetic, and sleeps continually until he dies. The chief symptoms are fever, rash, illness, and sensitivity of the bones to blows. Early cases may be cured with antimony, arsenic and more recently suramin.

SLEEPY SICKNESS. Encephalitis lethargica; acutely infectious disease chiefly affecting the central nervous system. Inflammation of the brain, caused by an unidentified virus, is followed by death in 40 per cent of cases and invalidism in a large proportion of others.

SLIDE RULE. A mathematical instrument used for rapid calculations; incl. multiplication, division, and the extraction of square-roots.

SLI'GŌ. Maritime county of Connacht, Republic of Ireland. The Darty mountains in the N.E. rise to 2,113 ft., in Ben Bulben. Loughs Arrow, Gill, and Gara are of striking beauty. Dairying and stock raising are the main occupations, but coal, lead, copper and iron are found. Area 694 sq. m.; pop. (1961) 53,558. The cap. is S., on the Garrogue, which is famous for its cathedral (1870) and the abbey ruins. Pop. (1966) 51,263.

SLIM, William Joseph, 1st visct. (1891–1970). Brit. field marshal. As commander of the 14th Army 1943–5, he was largely responsible for the victory in Burma, and was C.I.G.S. 1948–52. He was Gov.-Gen. of Australia from 1953 until 1960 when he was also created visct.

SLOANE (slōn), **Sir Hans** (1660–1753). British physician. B. in Co. Down, he settled in London, and in 1721 founded the Chelsea Physic Garden. He was president of the Royal College of Physicians 1719–35, and in 1727 succeeded Newton as president of the Royal Society. His library, etc., which he bequeathed to the nation, formed the nucleus of the British Museum.

SLOE. *See* BLACKTHORN.

SLOTH. Family (Bradypodidae) of mammals of the order Edentata, confined to S. America. They have small rounded heads, rudimentary tails, and prolonged forelimbs: each foot has long curved claws adapted to clinging upside down from trees. The fur is greyish-brown, and the diet vegetarian. The chief species are the 3-toed S. or aï (*Bradypus tridactylus*), and the 2-toed S. (*Choloepus didactylus*) of Brazil.

SLOUGH (slow). English industrial town (bor.) in Bucks, near Windsor. There is a large trading estate with numerous engineering and other factories. Sir William Herschel (q.v.) and his sister carried out much of their astronomical research at S. Pop. (1961) 80,503.

SLOVAKIA. Region in the E. of Czechoslovakia settled in the 5th–6th cents. by Slavonic tribes; occupied by the Magyars in the 10th cent.; part of the kingdom of Hungary until 1918 when it became a prov. of Czechoslovakia (q.v.). S. was a puppet state under German domination 1939–45, and was abolished as an administrative division in 1949. Its cap. and chief town was Bratislava.

SLOVENES (slōvēnz'). Slav people, inhabiting Slovenia and parts of Styria, and Carinthia. They speak a language akin to Serbo-Croat, and number c. 1,600,000.

SLOVE'NIA. Federal rep. of Yugoslavia, lying between Austria to the N., and Croatia to the S. The surface is mountainous, and agriculture and forestry are important. Ljubljana is the cap. Before 1918 S. was the Austrian prov. of Carniola. Area 7,719 sq. m.; pop. (1961) 1,584,368.

SLOWACKI (slō'vaki), **Juljusz** (1809–49). Polish poet and dramatist. B. at Krzemieniec, he obtained a govt. post in Warsaw in 1829, but after 1831 lived mainly in France.

SLOW-WORM. See BLINDWORM.

SLUG. An air-breathing gastropod of the families Limacidae and Arionidae, and related families. The grey field S. (*Agriolimax agrestis*) is the commonest British species, and a pest to crops and garden plants.

SLUIS or **Sluys.** Town of Zeeland, Netherlands, 10 m. N.E. of Bruges, with which it is connected by canal. A naval battle in which the English defeated the French was fought here in 1340, but since then the sea has receded. Pop. (est.) 2,000.

SMALL ARMS. One of the 2 main divisions of firearms (q.v.), S.A. came into use in the late 14th cent. as portable hand-guns, supported on the ground and ignited by hand. The matchlock, evolved during the 15th cent., used a match of tow and saltpetre gripped by an S-shaped lever which was rocked towards the touch hole with one finger, enabling the gun to be held, aimed and fired in much the same way as today. Front and back sights, followed by a curved stock which could be held against the shoulder (in the hackbut or Hookgun), gave increased precision. The inherent difficulty involved in keeping a match alight in wet weather was overcome by the introduction of the wheel lock, c. 1515, in which a shower of sparks was produced by a spring-drawn steel wheel struck by iron pyrites. This cumbrous and expensive mechanism evolved into the simpler flintlock c. 1625, operated by flint striking steel and in general use for 200 years until a dramatic advance, the 'percussion cap', invented in 1810 by a sport-loving Scottish clergyman, Alexander Forsyth, removed the need for external igniters. Henceforth, weapons were fired by a small explosive detonator placed behind or within the base of the bullet, struck by a built-in hammer. The principles of rifling, breech loading and the repeater, although known since the 16th cent. were not successfully exploited until the 19th cent. It was known that imparting a spin made the bullet's flight truer, but the difficulty of making the bullet bite the grooves had until then prevented the use of rifling. The Baker rifle, issued to the Rifle Brigade in 1800, was loaded from the front of the barrel (muzzle), and had a mallet for hammering the bullets into the grooves. The first breech loader was Von Dreyse's 'needle gun', issued to the Prussian army in 1842, in which the detonator was incorporated with the cartridge. By 1870 breech loading was in general use, being quicker, and sweeping the barrel out after each firing. An early rifle with bolt action was the Lee-Metford (1888) followed by the Lee-Enfield, both having a 'magazine' beneath the breech, containing a number of cartridges. With modifications this model is still used by the British army. U.S. developments favoured the repeater (Winchester *et al.*) in which the fired case was extracted and ejected, the hammer cocked, and a new charge inserted into the chamber, all by one reciprocation of a finger lever. In the semi-automatic, part of the explosion energy performs the same operations: the Garand, used by the U.S. army, is of this type. Completely automatic weapons were increasingly adopted during the S.W.W. From 1954 the British army standardized upon the Belgian F.N.

30 which is gas operated and can fire shots singly or automatically at 650–700 rounds per min.

SMALLPOX. Variola; a specific infective fever, probably caused by a filtrable virus. It is highly infectious and contagious. Incubation is from 12 to 14 days. The first symptoms are headache, pain in the back, and fever; on the second day a preliminary rash appears, and on the third a thick eruption, mostly on the arms, legs, and face. Blisters form and become purulent, and begin to break and dry up about the 12th day. Permanent pitting and scarring result. The type of the disease marked by bleeding under the skin is usually fatal, and in cases where the pustules coalesce about half the patients die. The other types are less dangerous. Complications incl. broncho-pneumonia, blindness due to inflammation of the eyes, middle-ear disease, and paralysis. Vaccination is a reliable preventive, at least of the severer types, and in civilized countries, S. is now rare.

SMART, Christopher (1722–71). British poet. He became a fellow of Pembroke Coll., Cambridge, but settled in London as a hack writer. He was confined in 1756 to an asylum, where he wrote his greatest poems, 'A Song to David' and 'Rejoice in the Lamb'.

SMELT. Small fish of the family Osmeridae and the genus *Osmerus*. The most common European S. is the sparling (*Osmerus eperlanus*), which is noted for its delicate flavour: related species occur on the coasts of the U.S.A.

SMELTING. The extraction of metal from ore by melting. The blast furnace is the commonest appliance for this process, consisting of a tall shaft which receives coke, flux, and ore at the top, and discharges the molten products at the bottom. The hot blast is about 500–800°C.

SMETANA (smet'ahnah), **Friedrich** (1824–84). Czech composer. B. at Litomyšl, he was largely ed. in Germany, and became conductor of the Gothenburg Philharmonic Society in 1856. He settled in Prague in 1863, where in 1866 he became conductor at the national theatre, and his music developed a national character. He became deaf in 1874, lost his reason in 1883, and d. in an asylum. His finest works are the operas *The Bartered Bride* (1866) and *Dalibor*, and the symphonic suite *My Country*.

SMETHWICK (smedh'ik). English industrial town part of the co. bor. of Warley, Worcs. Iron, glass, chemical products, and machinery are made. West Indian and Asian immigration was a controversial election issue in 1964. Pop. (1961) 68,372.

SMILES, Samuel (1812–1904). Scottish author. B. at Haddington, he became in turn a doctor, journalist, and sec. to railway companies. He achieved fame with a life of Stephenson (1857), and the popular didactic work, *Self Help* (1859).

SMIRKE (smerk), **Sir Robert** (1781–1867). British architect. B. in London, he designed the British Museum and Covent Garden Theatre. He was elected R.A. in 1811, and knighted in 1831.

SMITH, Adam (1723–90). Scottish economist. B. at Kirkcaldy, he was prof. of moral philosophy at Glasgow 1752–63, publishing his *Theory of Moral Sentiments* in 1759. In *The Wealth of Nations* (1776), the basic idea is of annual labour being the source of a nation's necessaries, and the case is put for free trade in opposition to mercantilist theories; this originated the classical British school of political economy, and largely estab. economics as a separate science.

SMITH, Dodie. British dramatist, she wrote until 1935 under the pseudonym C. L. Anthony. B. in Lancs, she made her reputation with plays of middle-class life, e.g. *Autumn Crocus* (1931), *Call it a Day* (1935), and *Dear Octopus* (1938); she has also written novels and the children's book *The Hundred and One Dalmatians* (1956).

SMITH, Lady Eleanor (1902–45). British novelist. The elder dau. of the 1st earl of Birkenhead, she was an authority on gypsy and circus life, and on ballet. Her books incl. *Red Wagon, Ballerina, The Man in Grey* and *Magic Lantern*.

SMITH, Sir Henry George Wakelyn (1787–1860). British gen. He served in the Peninsular War, and m. a Spanish lady. Subsequently he fought in S. Africa and India, and was governor of Cape Colony 1847–52. Ladysmith is named after his wife and Harrismith after himself.

SMITH, Ian Douglas (1919–   ). Rhodesian statesman. A farmer, b. at Selukwe, Rhodesia, he served in the R.A.F. during the S.W.W. In 1948 he became a member of the S. Rhodesia legislative assembly, was a foundation member of the Rhodesian Front 1962, and Min. of the Treasury under Winston Field (1962–4), whom he succeeded as P.M. In 1965 he made a unilateral declaration of Rhodesia s independence.

SMITH, John (1580–1631). English colonizer. After an adventurous early life, he took part in the colonization of Virginia, acting as president of the colony 1608–9. During an expedition among the Indians his life is said to have been saved by Pocahontas (q.v.). He explored New England in 1614, and pub. pamphlets on America and an autobiography.

SMITH, Joseph. *See* MORMONS.

SMITH, Sir Matthew (1879–1960). British artist, known for his exuberant treatment of nudes, luscious fruits and flowers, and landscapes.

SMITH, Sir Ross Macpherson (1892–1922), and **Sir Keith Macpherson S.** (1890–1955). Australian airmen. Brothers, they were the first to fly from England to Australia in 1919, and for this exploit were knighted.

SMITH, Sydney (1771–1845). British clergyman and author. B. in Essex, he took orders in 1794. While a tutor at Edinburgh, he was among the founders of the *Edinburgh Review* in 1802, and moved to London in 1803, where his brilliant conversational powers made him a leading figure in Whig society, and in 1831 became a canon of St. Paul's. The *Plymley Letters* (1807–8), a plea for Catholic emancipation, is his best-known work.

SMITH, William (1769–1839). British geologist. B. in Oxfordshire, he became a surveyor, and pub. a *Geological Map of England* (1815). He estab. the identification of strata by their fossils, and was often known as Strata S.

SMITH, William Robertson (1846–94). Scots theologian. The articles on the Bible which he contributed to the *Encyclopaedia Britannica* resulted in an unsuccessful prosecution for heresy. In 1883 he was appointed prof. of Arabic at Cambridge. His *Religion of the Semites* (1889) is a classic.

SMITHFIELD. Site of a meat market (1868) and poultry and provision market (1889), covering nearly 10 acres in the City of London, England. Formerly an open space, it was the scene of the execution of many Protestant martyrs in the 16th cent., and of the murder of Wat Tyler in 1381, while the annual Bartholomew Fair was held here from 1614 to 1855. A rocket bomb nearby on 8 March 1945 severely damaged the buildings which were occupied by the military during the S.W.W. The poultry section was destroyed by fire, 1958, re-opened 1963.

SMITHSON, James (1765–1829). British chemist and mineralogist. The Smithsonian Institution in Washington, D.C., was estab. in 1846, following his bequest of £100,000 for this purpose, and incl. a museum, art gallery, zoo park, and astrophysical observatory.

SMOG. Natural fog plus impurities (unburned carbon and sulphur dioxide) from domestic fires, industrial furnaces and internal combustion engines (petrol or diesel). The use of smokeless fuels, the treatment of effluent and penalties for excessive smoke from poorly maintained and operated vehicles have had some effect, but the great cities, notably London and Los Angeles, still frequently suffer and there is even substantial loss of life, e.g. among chronic bronchitics.

SMOLENSK. City of the R.S.F.S.R., cap. of S. region, on the Dnieper, 230 m. W.S.W. of Moscow. Dating from 882, Russian from 1667, it is an educational centre with a 17th–18th cent. cathedral. Its many industries incl. textile and clothing factories, distilleries, and flour mills. Napoleon defeated the Russians at S. in 1812; and fierce fighting centred on the city in 1941 and 1943. Pop. (1967) 189,000.

SMOLLETT, Tobias George (1721–71). British novelist. B. in Dunbartonshire, he was apprenticed to a Glasgow surgeon, and sailed to the W. Indies in 1740 as a naval surgeon. Returning in 1744, he made his name by the picaresque novels *Roderick Random* (1748), *Peregrine Pickle* (1751), *Ferdinand Count Fathom* (1753), *Sir Lancelot Greaves* (1760–2), and *Humphrey Clinker* (1771). His methods and vivid characterization greatly influenced Dickens. Among his other works are a *History of England*; a translation of *Don Quixote*; *Travels through France and Italy* (1766), utilizing his experiences in search of health in 1763; and the satire, *Adventures of an Atom* (1769). He d. near Leghorn.

SMUGGLING. The illegal import or export of prohibited goods, or the evasion of customs duties on dutiable goods. Restrictions on imports, originally a means of preventing debasement of coinage (e.g. in 14th cent. England), were later used for raising revenue, mainly on luxury goods, and led to a flourishing period of S. during the 18th cent., in spirits, tobacco, lace, etc. Certain regions were famed for their activities – until the mid-19th cent. the islanders of Scilly, England, poor in natural resources, thought little of the 80-mile round trip to France in their long boats to bring back a half-ton of contraband – and even today the state of Andorra exists on its 2 principal industries of tourism and S. Modern S., on both the national and international scale, is concerned with such items as watches, diamonds, gold, and narcotics; and is punishable by fines, and in some cases by imprisonment. *See* COASTGUARD.

SMUT and BUNT. Parasitic fungi, of the order Ustilaginales, which infect flowering plants, especially cereals.

SMUTS, Jan Christian (1870–1950). S. African statesman and soldier. B. in Cape Colony, he studied at Cambridge, and was admitted to the Bar. Having settled in the Transvaal, he was appointed state attorney in 1898, and during the S. African War commanded the Boer forces in Cape Colony. He subsequently worked for reconciliation between Boers and British and became Min. of the Interior 1910–12 and Defence Min. 1910–20, on the establishment of the Union. He commanded the S. African forces in E. Africa 1916–17, and entered the imperial war cabinet in 1917. He was P.M. 1919–24, and Min. of Justice 1933–9, and on the outbreak of war succeeded Gen. Hertzog as Premier. He held office until defeated at the general election in 1948. He was created a field marshal in 1941, received the O.M. in 1947, and became chancellor of Cambridge univ. in 1948. His philosophical work *Holism and Evolution* was pub. in 1926.

SMYRNA (smer'nah). *See* IZMIR.

SMYTH (smīdh), **Dame Ethel** (1858–1944). British composer. B. in London, she studied in Leipzig, and in 1893 her Mass in D was performed in London. Her works incl. the operas *Fantasio, The Wreckers, The Boatswain's Mate, Fête Galante,* and *Entente Cordiale*. She suffered imprisonment as an ardent suffragette. In 1922 she was made D.B.E. She wrote the autobiographical *Female Pipings in Eden* and *What Happened Next* (1940).

SMYTHE (smīth), **Francis Sydney** (1900–49). British mountaineer. B. in Maidstone, he took part in the Kangchenjunga (1930), Kamet (1931), and Everest

(1933, 1936, and 1938) expeditions, and also wrote *Kamet Conquered* (1932), and *Adventures of a Mountaineer* (1940).

SNAEFELL (snā-). Highest mountain in the Isle of Man, 2,034 ft. high.

SNAIL. Species of air-breathing gastropods, with spiral shells. The more typical Ss. of the genus *Helix*, and family Helicidae, embrace over 1,600 species. The common garden S. (*Helix aspersa*), is very destructive to plants; the Roman S. (*Helix pomatia*) is bred for food on the Continent.

SNAKE. A member of the reptilian order Ophidia, characterized by an elongated limbless body possibly evolved because it is advantageous in progression through dense vegetation: one of the most striking internal modifications is the absence or greatly reduced size of the left lung. There are some 3,000 species found in the tropic and temperate zones, but none in New Zealand, Ireland, Iceland, and near the poles. The skin is covered in scales which are markedly wider underneath where they form, in all except a few species, an essential aid to locomotion, e.g. a S. is helpless on glass where these scales can effect no 'grip' on the surface: progression may be undulant, 'concertina' or creeping, or a combination. Detailed vision is limited at a distance, though movement is immediately seen; hearing is restricted to ground vibrations (sound waves are not perceived); the sense of touch is acute; besides the sense of smell through the nasal passages, the flickering tongue picks up airborne particles which are then passed to special organs in the mouth for investigation; and some, e.g. rattlesnakes, have a cavity between eye and nostril which is sensitive to infra-red rays (useful in locating warm-blooded prey in the dark). All Ss. are carnivorous, and often camouflaged for better concealment in hunting as well as their own protection. Some are oviparous and others ovoviviparous, i.e. the eggs are retained in the oviducts until development is complete; in both cases the young are immediately self-sufficient.

The majority of Ss. belong to the Colubridae, chiefly harmless, e.g. the common grass snake of Europe, but incl. the deadly African boomslang

SNAKE. A king brown snake being 'milked' at the Commonwealth Serum Laboratories, Victoria. The venom – the clear fluid at the bottom of the glass – is used in making antivenins.
Courtesy of Gary C. Lewis.

Dispholidus typus. The venomous families incl. the Elapidae comprising the true cobras (q.v.), the New World coral Ss., and the Australian taipan, copperhead and death adder; the Viperidae (*see* VIPER), and the Hydrophidae, aquatic sea Ss. Stocks of antivenins are maintained for emergency use by the Institut

Pasteur (Paris), Wyeth Laboratories (Philadelphia), Haffkine Institute (Bombay), etc. Among the more primitive Ss. are the Boidae, which still show links with the lizards and incl. the boa constrictor, anaconda and python: these kill by constriction but only comparatively small animals.

SNAPDRAGON *See* ANTIRRHINUM.

SNIPE. Seen here in its usual habitat among the tallish grasses of low, wet meadows, the snipe is marked by black bars on the tail and sides; the bill and legs are greenish-grey.
Photo: G. Ronald Austing.

SNIPE. Marsh bird (*Capella gallinago*) distinguished by its long straight bill, found throughout Europe and valued for the table. Wilson's S. (*C. delicata*) of N. America is almost identical. Other species are the rare great S. (*C. media*) and the small jack S. (*Lymneryptes minimus*).

SNOEK (snōōk). Fish (*Thyrsites atun*) of the family Trichiuridae, found at the Cape of Good Hope and in New Zealand and S. Australia, and used as food.

SNOOKER. Game played on a billiards table, a combination of billiards, pool, and pyramids. The game is played with 22 coloured balls.

SNORING. A loud rattling noise during sleep made by vibration of the soft palate caused by streams of air entering the nose and mouth at the same time.

SNORRI STURLASON (snor'rē stoor lāson) (1179–1241). Icelandic author of the *Heimskringla*, a saga chronicle of Norwegian kings until 1177, and the Prose Edda.

SNOW, Charles Percy, baron (1905–). British novelist. B. at Leicester, he was a fellow of Christ's Coll., Cambridge, 1930–5 (tutor 1935–45), and was chief of scientific personnel at the Min of Labour in the S.W.W. His sequence of books under the title of 'Strangers and Brothers' ranges the English social scale from provincial lower-middle class to the aristocracy, from the 1920s. The 1st-person narrator in all of them is 'Lewis Eliot' who 'learns to know himself through other people, and other people through himself'; they incl. *Time of Hope* (1949); *The Masters* (1951), an analysis of the conflict over the election of the master of a Cambridge college, successfully dramatized in 1963; *The New Men* (1954), scientists facing the problems of nuclear fission; and *Corridors of Power* (1964). In 1957 he was knighted. In 1959 his Rede Lecture at Cambridge (pub. 1960 as *The Two Cultures and the Scientific Revolution*) added a phrase to the language and created something of a sensation by its discussion of the lack of communication in the West between literary and scientific intellectuals. In 1964–6 he was parliamentary sec. to the Min. of Technology and

LORD SNOW. On a visit to Russia he shares an uproarious joke with Mikhail Sholokhov (left).

Courtesy of Lord Snow.

received a life peerage. He m. in 1950 **Pamela Hansford Johnson** (1912–), also a fine novelist. B. in London she has a gift for subtly delineated character, as in *Too Dear for my Possessing* (1940), *An Avenue of Stone* (1947), *A Summer to Decide* (1948), and *The Impossible Marriage* (1954), and has also pub. studies of I. Compton Burnett and Proust, and the play *Corinth House* (1948).

SNOW. Flaked particles formed by the condensation in air of excess vapour below freezing point. Light reflecting in the crystals of the flake gives S. a white appearance.

SNOWDEN, Philip, 1st visct. (1864–1937). British Labour statesman. B. in Yorks, he worked as a civil servant, and entered parliament in 1906. He stood on the extreme right of the Labour Party, and as Chancellor of the Exchequer, 1924 and 1929–31, pursued a strongly orthodox financial policy. He entered the National Govt. in 1931 as Lord Privy Seal, but resigned in 1932. He received a viscounty in 1931. His wife, **Ethel,** viscountess S. (1881–1951), *née* Annakin, was prominent in the women's suffrage and temperance movements.

SNOWDON, Anthony Armstrong-Jones, earl of (1930–). British designer. The son of Ronald Armstrong-Jones, Q.C., and his 1st wife, later countess of Rosse, he was ed. at Eton and Cambridge. Becoming a professional photographer, he held a one-man exhibition in London in 1956, and achieved great success with his studies of the children of Queen Elizabeth II. In 1960 he m. H.R.H. Princess Margaret (q.v.), and was created earl of S. a few weeks before the birth of their son, visct. Linley, in 1961.

SNOWDON. Highest mountain in Wales, 3,560 ft. above sea-level. It consists of a cluster of five peaks. At the foot of S. are the Llanberis, Aberglaslyn, and

SNOWDONIA. Beyond Llyn Padarn lies Snowdonia, now a National Park, and visited every year by thousands of tourists.

Photo: Roy J. Westlake.

Rhyd-ddu passes. A rack railway ascends to the summit from Llanberis. Snowdonia the surrounding mountain system, is a Nat. Park (1951).

SNOWDROP. Plant (*Galanthus nivalis*) of the Amaryllidaceae. A spring-blooming bulb, it bears single, white, bell-shaped flowers.

SNOWY. Australian river, 265 m. long, rising near Mt. Kosciusko in N.S.W. and flowing across Victoria to Bass Strait. A project sanctioned by an act of the Commonwealth parliament in 1949 for diverting its upper waters through the S. mts. into the Murrumbidgee began to produce power in 1955. Its purpose was to provide irrigation water as well as electricity to Victoria and N.S.W.

SNUFF. Powdered tobacco inhaled as a stimulant or sedative. It was common in 17th cent. England, and became universal in the 18th.

SNYDERS (snī-), **Frans** (1579–1657). Flemish painter. B. at Antwerp, he studied under Breughel. At first he painted still-life, but turned to animal painting, his principal works incl. hunting subjects.

SOAMES (sōmz), **Sir Christopher** (1920–). British Cons. politician. He served in the S.W.W. before entering parliament in 1950. He became Sec. of State For War (1958–60), and Min. of Agriculture, Fisheries and Food (1960–4), and in 1968 ambassador to Paris. He m. in 1947 Mary, dau. of Sir Winston Churchill.

SOANE (sōn), **Sir John** (1753–1837). British architect. B. near Reading, he rebuilt the Bank of England, and was elected R.A. in 1802. He presented his house in Lincoln's Inn Fields – now the Soane Museum – and his art treasures to the nation.

SOAP. A chemical compound, yielding a lather used in washing; a mixture of the sodium salts of palmitic, stearic, and oleic acids. Made by the action of caustic soda or caustic potash on fats, of animal and vegetable origin. Household Ss. are variously shaped coloured and usually perfumed.

SOAPSTONE. *See* STEATITE.

SOBIESKI, John. *See* JOHN III, king of Poland.

SOCIAL CONTRACT. Term in political philosophy for the theory that civil society originated when men agreed to surrender the complete freedom they enjoyed in the state of nature. Hobbes used this theory to justify absolute monarchy, whereas Locke and Rousseau derived from it the inference that all government rests on the support of the governed.

SOCIAL CREDIT. Economic theory put forward by Major C. H. Douglas, which finds the cause of crises in the control of money by the banks, leading to a shortage of purchasing power. Suggested remedies are the payment of a 'national dividend', or that the retailer should sell his goods below cost, his losses, plus a commission, being credited to him by the bank. The British S.C. Party (founded in 1920, at first under the name Kibbo Kift, by John G. Hargrave) had little success, but in Canada, Alberta (since 1935) and Br. Columbia (since 1952) have had S.C. govts., though carrying out of S.C theory has been vetoed by higher authority.

SOCIALISM. A movement aiming at the establishment of a classless society through the substitution of common for private ownership of the means of production, distribution, and exchange. The term is used both to cover all movements with this aim, e.g. Communism, Anarchism, Syndicalism, etc., and more narrowly for Evolutionary S., or Social Democracy.

Anticipations of S. can be found in the ideas of many religious sects, e.g. the Anabaptists and Diggers, and in such Utopias as those of Plato and More. Modern S. originated 1789–1848, in the revolutionary Communism of Babeuf, and the 'Utopian S.' of Owen, Saint-Simon, and Fourier, to which the term was first applied *c.* 1830. Marx and Engels placed S. on a scientific basis, and formed the 1st Socialist International (1864–72). The Paris Commune (1871) estab. a Socialist govt. for a few weeks.

In the later 19th cent. Socialist parties arose in most European countries, the strongest being the German Social Democratic Party; in Britain the Social Democratic Federation was founded in 1881, and the I.L.P. in 1893. This period witnessed a reaction against Marxism, typified by the Fabians and the German Revisionists, at the time when in Russia the Bolsheviks were reviving the original revolutionary significance of Marx's teachings. Weakened by these divisions, the 2nd International (founded in 1889) collapsed in 1914, right-wing Socialists in all countries supporting participation in the F.W.W while the left opposed it. The Russian revolution removed S. from the sphere of theory to that of practice, and was followed in 1919 by the foundation of the 3rd International, which completed the division between right and left. This lack of unity, in spite of the temporary successes of the Popular Fronts in France and Spain in 1936–8, facilitated the rise of Fascism.

After the S.W.W. Socialist and Communist parties tended to formal union in E. Europe, subsequent Communist control later being modified, e.g. Poland and Rumania. Elsewhere in Europe there was no uniform pattern, e.g. the break in Labour rule in the U.K. (1945–61, 1964–70), and the reverse to S. in Norway 1965. In Asia S. is very powerful.

SOCIAL SECURITY. Term for freedom from want through state provision, first used officially in the S.S. Act of the U.S. Congress (1935), passed to enable the Federal govt. to cope with the effects of the Great Depression of 1929. The principle involved is, however, a good deal older than that: in Germany compulsory social insurance was estab. in 1883; in Britain compulsory health and unemployment insurance in 1911, non-contributory old-age pensions in 1909.

The S.S. Act of 1935 dealt with old age, survivor's and unemployment insurance, maternal and child welfare, public assistance, and assistance to those suffering from economic distress; unemployment is dealt with by the Dept. of Labor, other S.S. services by the Dept. of Health, Education and Welfare. Increased social benefits and a 'medicare' scheme for the elderly were provided under the S.S. Act 1965.

The term S.S. was first used officially in Britain in 1944, and following the Beveridge (q.v.) Report in 1942, a series of acts was passed from 1945 to widen the scope of S.S. in covering unemployment, industrial injury, sickness, death (provision for widows and orphans), retirement, family allowances, and medical attention. The cost is partly covered by compulsory insurance paid by employers and employees, but to avoid the sharp distinction between contributory and non-contributory benefits the Nat. Assistance Board was merged in 1966 with the Min. of Pensions and Nat. Insurance as the Min. of S.S., and in 1968 with the Min. of Health as Dept. of Health and S. S.

SOCIETY ISLANDS. French archipelago in the S. Pacific, incl. the Leeward (Huahiné, Raiatéa, Tahaa, Borabora, and Maupiti) and Windward (Tahiti and Moorea) groups. Papeete on Tahiti is the cap. Discovered by the British 1767, the S.I. became a Fr. protectorate 1843 and were annexed by France 1880; they form part of Fr. Polynesia. Area 650 sq. m.; pop. (1962) 61,600.

SOCINUS (sōsi'nus). Latinized name of **Lelio Francesco Maria Sozini** (1525–62), Italian Protestant theologian. He adopted Unitarian views on the nature of Christ, which were developed by his nephew, **Fausto Paolo Sozzini** (1539–1604). The latter taught pacifist and anarchist doctrines akin to Tolstoy's; his beliefs are known as Socinianism.

SOCIOLOGY. The study of society, which is the network of human interactions and interrelations. Morris Ginsberg, prof. at London 1929–54, has listed the main areas as: (1) *Social morphology*, which incl. 'the investigation of the quantity and quality of the population' and 'the description and classification of the principal types of social groups and institutions'. (2) *Social control*, 'the study of law, morals, religion, convention, fashion and other sustaining and regulating agencies'. (3) *Social processes*, meaning 'the study of the various modes of interaction between individuals or groups, incl. cooperation and conflict, social differentiation and integration, development, arrest and decay'. (4) *Social pathology*, 'the study of social maladjustments and disturbances'. S. (term invented by Comte in 1873) is closely related to economics, anthropology, psychology and statistics.

Some sociologists take a wide range, and try by deriving the present from the past, to discover general principles of development, e.g. Toynbee's *A Study of History*, in which are shown the same principles of rise and decline of civilization throughout the whole of human history; the concept of historicism, strongly challenged by K. Popper *et al.* Some consider large societies, e.g. G. D. H. Cole's *The Condition of Britain*, and Margaret Mead's *The American Character*; whereas others discuss communities, e.g. *A Chinese Village* by M. C. Yang and *Plainsville, U.S.A.* by James West; and some studies concentrate on the intimate detail of a single society either primitive or modern.

SOCOTRA (sŏkō'trah). Island in the Indian Ocean 600 m. E. of Aden, formerly part of the Mahri sultanate of Qishn and S., but from 1967 merged in the rep. of Southern Yemen; the sultanate came under British protection in 1886. Livestock are reared. Area 1,400 sq. m.; pop. (est.) 8,000.

SOCRATES (sok'ratēz) (*c.* 469–399 B.C.). Athenian philosopher. He is said to have been a sculptor, and served as a soldier, but the greater part of his life he devoted to philosophical discussion. Our main sources of biographical information are Plato's dialogues, Xenophon's *Memorabilia*, and Aristophanes' satirical picture in *The Clouds*; it is uncertain how far Plato attributed his own opinions to S. In philosophy he rejected the search for scientific knowledge, and set himself to guide men to clear thought on ethics and politics; his method was by pretending ignorance to encourage others to talk, and then by cross-examination to expose their inconsistencies. He was accused in 399 of impiety and corrupting the young, and in spite of an eloquent defence condemned to die by drinking hemlock. His trial and death are movingly described by Plato.

SOCRATES. A satyr-type portrait in the British Museum.

SŌ'DA. Common name for sodium carbonate. S.-water is made effervescent by an infusion of carbonic acid under pressure.

SODDY, Frederick (1877–1956). British physical chemist. After working for Rutherford and Ramsay, he was prof. of chemistry at Aberdeen 1914–19 and at Oxford 1919–36. A pioneer of research into atomic disintegration – he coined the term 'isotopes' – he did classic work on radioactivity (*Chemistry of the Radio-Elements*, 1912–14), and was awarded a Nobel prize in 1921. Other scientific books incl. *The Interpretation of the Atom* (1932), and *The Story of Atomic Energy* (1949). Having strong views on education, economics and finance, he also pub. *Cartesian Economics* (1922) and *The Arch Enemy of Economic Freedom* (1943).

SÖ'DERBLOOM, Nathan (1866–1931). Swedish churchman. He became archbp. of Uppsala and primate of Sweden in 1914. He organized the Stockholm Oecumenical Congress in 1925, and was awarded the Nobel peace prize in 1930.

SŌ′DIUM. A soft bright silvery reactive metal tarnishing quickly on exposure to air and reacting violently with water to form S. hydroxide: symbol Na (Lat. *natrium*), at. wt. 22·991, at. no. 11. First isolated by Sir Humphry Davy in 1807, it is found abundantly in combination, the commonest form being S. chloride (NaCl – common salt). S. metal is used to a limited extent as a spectroscopic reference, in discharge lamps, and alloyed with potassium as a heat-transfer medium in nuclear reactors.

S. compounds are of the widest industrial importance and thousands of tons are manufactured annually. Among the more important are common salt, S. carbonate (Na_2CO_9 – washing soda), and bicarbonate ($NaHCO_3$ – baking powder), S. hydroxide or caustic soda (NaOH), S. nitrate or Chile saltpetre ($NaNO_3$ – fertilizer), S. thiosulphate or hypo ($Na_2S_2O_3.5H_2O$ – photographic fixer).

An artificial isotope of S., with a half-life of 15 hr. is a valuable tracer in the human body.

SO′DOM and GOMO′RRAH. 2 of the 5 'cities of the plain' in the Dead Sea area, which according to Genesis were destroyed by fire and brimstone for their wickedness.

SO′DOR AND MAN. Bishopric of the Church of England, at present comprising the Isle of Man only, but incl. 1154–1334 the Hebrides and other islands W. of Scotland. The bishop has an honorary seat in the House of Lords, and is a member of the Manx House of Keys. Peel is the centre of the diocese.

SOFIA (sōfē′ah). Cap. of Bulgaria since 1878. It lies at the foot of Vitosha Mts., about 80 m. N.W. of Plovdiv, and has many fine modern buildings, incl. the univ. (1880) and the 19th cent. cathedral. Industries incl. textile, rubber, leather, machinery, and electric-equipment making and food processing. There are 2 airports. Pop. (1967) 858,876.

SOHO (sō′hō). Quarter of W. London, between Charing Cross Rd. and Regent St. There are many foreign restaurants, night clubs, film co. offices (Wardour Street) and teenage fashion (Carnaby Street).

SOISSONS (swah′soñ). French town, in Aisne dept., 65 m. N.E. of Paris. It has a 12–13th cent. cathedral and markets agricultural produce. Clovis defeated the Romans at S., 486, ending Roman rule in France. Pop. (1962) 24,359.

SO′KOL ('falcon'). Czech educational and athletic organization founded in 1862, which plays an important part in public life. The movement also flourishes in Poland, Bulgaria, Yugoslavia, and other Slav countries. Until 1948 it was non-political.

SŌ′KŌTO. Division of the N.-Western state of Nigeria; from early in the 19th cent. until 1903, when it was occupied by the British, S. was a Fula sultanate, with a cap. town also S., and an area of 40,000 sq. m.

SOLANACEAE. Family of dicotyledonous plants of the tropical and temperate zones, many being natives of the Americas, e.g. the potato, tobacco and tomato; best-known of the British species is deadly nightshade.

SOLAN-GOOSE. See GANNET.

SOLAR ENERGY, Direct Utilization of. Solar furnaces concentrate the sun's rays at the focus of a parabolic mirror, thus providing a small area of intense heat. In this way temperatures of up to 4,000°C. have been produced with a 60 in. parabolic mirror. S. cells which produce electric current directly from the sun's rays have been developed particularly for satellites and space research, and utilize semiconductor materials such as cadmium sulphide and silicon and boron interfaces. Storage of S.E. may have enormous potential for domestic heating, power for under-developed countries and for sea-water-distillation plant in arid countries.

SOLAR SYSTEM. See PLANETS.

SOLAR WIND. Continuous outward projection from the inner corona of the sun of high-speed streams of low-density hot ionized gas or plasma. The velocity, temperature and density of the S.W. appear to be much higher when solar flares occur, and it is thought to be the cause of radio blackouts, geomagnetic storms, and auroral displays. First detailed information on the structure of the S.W. was obtained during the flight of the U.S. spacecraft *Mariner 2* in 1962.

SOLE. Genus (*Solea*) of flat fish in the family Pleuronectidae. The Common S. (*S. vulgaris*) is up to 2 ft. long, feeds at night on worms etc., and is a valued European food-dish, as is the rarer lemon S. (*S. lascaris*); the little American Ss., in the genus *Achirus*, have no food value.

SOLENT, The. Strait between the Isle of Wight and the mainland of Hampshire, England. It is a famous yachting centre.

SOL-FA (-fah), **Tonic.** System of musical notation, invented by John Spencer Curwen, *c.* 1840, and utilized by many choral singers as a simpler alternative to staff-notation. Both in its restriction to single parts and in its limited interpretation of the composer's intentions, the system possesses drawbacks. The notes are named *doh, ray, me, fah, soh, lah, te*, and the key is indicated so that the singers know how their keynote *doh* is to be interpreted. Time divisions are indicated by bar-lines.

SOLFERINO (-rē′nō). Village in Verona, N. Italy, 5 m. S. of Lake Garda, site of the battle in which Napoleon III defeated the Austrians in 1859.

SOLICITOR. A member of one of the 2 branches of the English legal profession, the other being barristers (q.v.). A S. conducts legal work on behalf of clients, but until the Courts Act (1971) had a right to represent him only in the inferior courts. He may now appear in and conduct cases in the Crown Courts, and is eligible, in the same way as a barrister of 10 yrs standing, to be appointed a Recorder, and eventually a Circuit judge. See LAW COURTS. The **Solicitor-Gen.** is a law officer of the Crown, acting as deputy to the Attorney-Gen.: he is a political appointee with ministerial rank. In the U.S.A. the term S. may be used for practitioners in the courts of equity, and, as in England, some public offices have special Ss., and there has been since 1870 a S.-Gen.

SOLID CIRCUIT. Normally an electronic circuit is made by joining together by wire separately made electronic components. In a S.C. all the components (resistors, capacitors, transistors and diodes) and interconnections are made at the same time and by the same processes in or on one piece of single crystal silicon. The small size of this construction (an amplifier could have dimensions of $4 \times 80 \times 80$ thousandths of an inch) accounts for its use in the electronics for space vehicles and aircraft.

SOLINGEN (zō′lingen). Town of North Rhine-Westphalia, Germany, 13 m. E. of Düsseldorf, noted in the Middle Ages for its sword blades and still famous for its high-quality steel used for razor blades, cutlery, etc. Pop. (1961) 170,917.

SOLOGUB (sol′ogoob), **Fyodor.** Pseudonym of Russian author Fyodor Kuzmich Teternikov (1863–1927). B. in St. Petersburg, where he was a schoolmaster 1887–1927, he was the earliest symbolist poet to gain recognition, pub. his 1st vol. of verse in 1897. In his satiric novel *Melki bes* (1907: *The Little Demon*) the chief character, Peredonov, has become proverbial for the meanly evil.

SO′LOMON (reigned *c.* 974–*c.* 937 B.C.). King of Israel. The son of David by Bathsheba, he acquired great wealth by trade, which he employed in building the temple at Jerusalem. His heavy taxation and use of forced labour aroused discontent, and his kingdom disintegrated. He became proverbial for wisdom, as is shown by the attribution of the much later *Proverbs*, *Ecclesiastes*, and *Song of Songs* to him. King S.'s Mines were at Aqaba (anc. Ezion-geber): copper and iron ore was smelted.

SOLOMON. Pseudonym of the British pianist S. Cuttner (1902–). B. in London, and first appearing at the age of 8, he is internationally known as an interpreter of the classical composers.

SOLOMON ISLANDS. Archipelago in the W. Pacific, lying E. of New Guinea. The northern members of the group, incl. Bougainville, Buka, and adjacent islands, which belonged to Germany 1899–1918, form part of Australian New Guinea (q.v.). They are very mountainous, with several volcanoes: and produce bananas, coconuts, taros, and sweet potatoes. Kieta, Rawa, and Tinputs (on Bougainville), are the main harbours. Area 4,100 sq. m.; pop. (1966) 71,762.

The southern members – Guadalcanal (q.v.), Malaita, San Cristobal, New Georgia, etc. – came under British protection 1893–9. The physical features and products resemble those of the Australian group. Area 11,500 sq. m.; pop. (1967) 145,630, nearly all Melanesians.

In 1942–5 the S.I. witnessed fierce fighting between Japanese and Allied forces (U.S. and later Australian).

SOLON (*c.* 638–558 B.C.). Athenian statesman. Elected archon *c.* 594, he carried out a revision of the constitution which laid the foundations of Athenian democracy.

SOLOVIEV, Vladimir Sergevich (1853–1900). Russian poet, philosopher, and theologian. B. in Moscow, he travelled to England and the East 1875–7, and was dismissed from univ. posts at Moscow and St. Petersburg owing to his unorthodox beliefs. In his writings, e.g. *History of Ethics, The Justification of the Good*, and *War, Progress, and the End of History* (1900), he stresses the unity of mankind.

SOLSTICE (sol'stis). Either of the 2 points reached by the sun, when its declination is greatest N. or S. It has also come to imply the time at which each of these occur, namely 21 June and 21 Dec.

SOLTI (shol'ti), Georg (1912–). Hungarian conductor. B. in Budapest, he was musical director of the Munich (1946–52) and Frankfurt (1952–61) operas, before being appointed to Covent Garden, where he infused fresh life by a series of glittering new productions and revivals.

SOLWAY FIRTH. Arm of the sea more than a mile long formed by the estuary of the Esk, and dividing England from Scotland at the W. end of the border. It also receives the Dee, Eden, Annan, and Nith, and merges into the Irish Sea.

GEORG SOLTI
Photo: Godfrey MacDomnic.

SOLYMAN II (sōōlāmahn'), called the **Magnificent** (1494–1566). Sultan of Turkey. Succeeding his father in 1520, he greatly extended the Turkish Empire. Belgrade was captured in 1521, and Rhodes in 1522: the victory of Mohacs (1526) brought much of Hungary under Turkish rule, and in 1529 Vienna was unsuccessfully besieged. Baghdad and Armenia were captured from the Persians in 1534.

SOLZHENITSYN (solzhenit'sin), **Alexander,** (1919–). Russian novelist. He was in a forced labour camp 1945–53 and sent to Siberia 1953–7, but Khrushchev ensured publication of *One Day in the Life of Ivan Denisovich* (1962) dealing with Stalin's prison camps. *Cancer Ward* (1968) again attacks restrictions on freedom. Nobel prize 1970.

SOMA. Indian intoxicating drink obtained from the fermented sap of *Asclepias acida* plant. In ancient times it was worshipped as a deity and used in sacrifices to Indra.

SOMALILAND, FRENCH. Territory in E. Africa, on the coast of the Gulf of Aden. The climate is hot and dry. Salt is worked; cattle reared, and fishing is a main occupation. The French estab. themselves at Obock in 1862. Djibouti, the cap. and chief port, was created by them in 1888; it is linked with Addis Ababa by rail. Following a referendum 1967 resulting in a majority for continued association with France, S. was re-named Terr. of the Afars and Issas. A liberation movement is supported by the O.A.U. Area 8,500 sq. m.; pop. (1966) 108,000.

SOMALI (sōmah'lē) **REPUBLIC.** Country of E. Africa, extending along the coast of the Gulf of Aden and the Indian Ocean, occupying the 'horn' of Africa. The climate is hot and dry, but where water is available the soil is productive. The interior is barren and mountainous, rising to 6,000 ft. The Juba and its trib. the Shebelli are the chief rivers. Rearing of cattle, camels, sheep, and donkeys is the principal occupation; rice, dates, and sugar are grown; gums and resins, hides and skins are exported. Mogadishu is the cap. and chief port; other towns are Berbera Obbia, and Kismayu on the coast, Hargeisa in the N. inland. Area 246,000 sq. m.; pop. (1968) 2,500,000.

The S.R. was formed in 1960 by the union of former British and Italian Somaliland. Br. Somaliland (68,000 sq. m.) was made a protectorate 1885–7. Ital. Somaliland was estab. as a colony 1927, incorporated 1936 in Ital. E. Africa, conquered 1941 by the British who administered it until 1950 when it was again administered by Italy under U.N. trusteeship until it became independent as the S.R. in 1960. Brit. Somaliland, accorded independence in the same year, elected to join the S.R. The presence across the border of 50,000 Somalis in Ethiopia and 100,000 in Kenya led to disputes with both countries, but agreement was reached 1967.

SOMERSET (sum'-), Edward Seymour, duke of (*c.* 1506–52). English statesman. The son of a Wilts gentleman, he was created earl of Hertford after Henry VIII's marriage to his sister Jane, and in 1547 became regent for Edward VI, with the title of Protector, and duke of S. A liberal and tolerant ruler, he offended the landowners by his attempts to check enclosure, and the Protestants by his moderate religious policy. He was overthrown in 1549, and beheaded in 1552 on a trumped-up charge of treason. The duchy was restored in 1660 to his descendants.

SOMERSET. County in S.W. England, washed on its N. and N.W. shores by the Bristol Channel. Its coastline consists of low cliffs and marshy tracts of land, whence the sea is kept out by a system of dykes and sluices. The principal rivers are the Avon, Parret, and Exe. In the N. are the Mendip Hills (in which are the Cheddar caves) and in the W. the Quantock Hills and Exmoor, with Dunkery Beacon (1,707 ft.) the highest point. Dairy farming and cider making are distinctive. In the Exmoor district ponies thrive. Principal towns are Bath, Wells, and Taunton (the co. town): part of Bristol is in S. Area 1,613 sq. m.; pop. (1967) 644,460.

SOMERSET HOUSE. Government offices in the Strand, London, built in 1775. It contains the audit, inland revenue, and Registrar-General's offices, and the probate registry, where wills are kept. The E. wing is occupied by King's College.

SOMERVILLE, Edith Oenone (1861–1949). Irish novelist, best known for her stories of Irish life written jointly with her cousin, Violet Martin (q.v.).

SOMES, Michael (1917–). British dancer and choreographer. Making his début with the Sadler's Wells co. in 1934, he became the leading male dancer of the Royal Ballet, of which he is also asst. director.

He has often partnered Fonteyn (q.v.). In 1964 he m. ballerina Antoinette Sibley (q.v.).

SOMME (som). River of N. France 150 m. long, which rises in Aisne dept. near St. Quentin, flows in a N. and W. direction past Amiens and Abbeville, and reaches the English Channel through a road estuary. It gives its name to a dept.

SOMME, Battle of the. Allied offensive in the F.W.W., on the western front, between Beaumont-Hamel and Chaulnes, in July–Nov. 1916, during which tanks were used for the first time. Comparatively slight gains were made, at very heavy cost. The German offensive around St. Quentin in March–April 1918 is sometimes called the 2nd battle of the S.

SONAR. In the F.W.W. an Allied Submarine Detection Investigation Committee was estab. and the apparatus perfected c. 1920 for detecting the presence of enemy U-boats beneath the sea-surface by the use of ultrasonic echoes was named from its initials ASDIC. In 1963 the name was changed, to accord with NATO practice, to S. See ECHO SOUNDING.

SONATA (sonah′ta). Term originally used to describe a composition for instruments, as opposed to the cantata, which is a composition for voices. The S. is usually played on one or two instruments, and consists of a series of related movements.

SONG. Musical setting of a poem for accompanied or unaccompanied single voice. Among the composers of Ss. are, English: Dowland, Lawes, Purcell, Arne, Sterndale-Bennett, Parry, Stanford, Quilter, Vaughan Williams, Delius, Moeran, Warlock, Ireland, Britten, Tippett, and Phyllis Tate; German: Mozart, Beethoven, Schubert, Schumann, Brahms, Wolf, Richard Strauss, Mahler, Hindemith and Webern; French: Gounod, Debussy, Duparc, Fauré, Poulenc and Ravel; Hungarian: Liszt; Russian: Moussorgsky, Tchaikovsky, Rachmaninoff, Glinka and A. S. Dargomïzhsky (1813–69); and American: Edward MacDowell, Sidney Homer (1864–1953), Charles Ives, Ernst Bacon (1898–   ), Paul Nordoff (1909–   ), Theodore Chanler (1902–   ), David Diamond (1915–   ) and George Gershwin.

SONNET. Poetic form introduced from Italy to England by Sir Thomas Wyatt, who followed in principle the Petrarchan mode, which, strictly interpreted, has the rhyme scheme abba abba, cdcdcd, with a turn of thought at the close of the octave; Milton and Wordsworth are exponents of this type. The Elizabethan form, as used by Shakespeare, has the rhyme scheme abab, cdcd efef gg.

SOOCHOW. City of Kiangsu prov., China, on the Grand Canal 50 m. W. of Shanghai. The seat of a univ., it makes cotton and silk textiles, jade carvings and embroidery, and trades in rice. S. dates from c. 1000 B.C., the name S. from 7th cent. A.D. Marco Polo visited S. which was made a treaty port 1896. It was called Wuhsien 1912–49. Pop. (est.) 450,000.

SOONG, T. V. or **Sung Tsu-wen** (1891–   ). Chinese statesman. He was For. Min 1941–4, and P.M. 1944–7. He is a brother of Mme. Chiang Kai-shek and of Mme Sun Yat-sen.

SOPER, Donald, baron (1903–   ). British Methodist Minister to the Central London Mission 1929–36, and supt. of the West London Mission, Kingsway Hall, from 1936, he is well known for his ready sincerity in debate and through television appearances. His books incl. *All His Grace* (1957) and *Aflame with Faith*, and as a speaker at Hyde Park Corner he has influenced many. In 1965 he became a life peer.

SOPHI′A (1630–1714). Electress of Hanover. The dau. of the Elector Palatine and Elizabeth, dau. of James I of England, she m. the elector of Hanover. She was recognized as in the succession to the English throne in 1701. Her son, George I, founded the Hanoverian dynasty.

SOPHISTS (sof′ists). Greek teachers of the 5th cent. B.C. who lectured on culture, rhetoric, and politics. Owing to the picture of them drawn by Plato, 'sophistry' now means dishonest reasoning.

SOPHOCLES (sof′ōklēz) (495–406 B.C.). Athenian tragic poet. He produced his first plays in 468, when he won the prize in competition with Aeschylus, and wrote over 120 plays, of which only 7 survive; these are *Ajax, Electra, The Trachinian Maidens, Philoctetes,* and the Theban tragedies *Antigone, King Oedipus,* and *Oedipus at Colonus.* He modified the form of tragedy by the introduction of a 3rd actor and speeded the action by lessening the role of the chorus. Whereas he said of Euripides 'He paints men as they are', he said of himself 'I paint men as they ought to be' and is noted for his noble grandeur and preservation of traditional values.

SOPWITH, Sir Thomas Octave Murdoch (1888–   ). British aviator. In 1910 he won a £4,000 prize for a flight from England to the Continent, and in 1912 founded the Sopwith Aviation Co. of which he was chairman 1925–7. He was chairman of the Hawker Siddeley Group 1935–63 and subsequently pres.: he was knighted in 1953.

SORBONNE (sorbon′). Alternative name for the Univ. of Paris. The S. was founded in 1253 by Robert de Sorbon, chaplain to Louis IX, as an institution for theological studies. Richelieu reconstructed the buildings in 1626, which were again rebuilt in 1885. In 1808 the S. became the seat of the Académie of Paris and of the Univ. of Paris.

SOREL, Albert (1842–1906). French historian. B. at Honfleur, he was at the Foreign Office 1866–75. His great work is *L'Europe et la Révolution Française.*

SOREL, Georges (1847–1922). French philosopher. B. at Cherbourg, he glorified violence in his writings, notably *Reflections on Violence* (1908), and taught that an élite must lead the people by means of myths. He championed the Syndicalist movement before 1914, and in later life showed Fascist sympathies.

SORGHUM (sor′gum). A genus of grasses – also called Indian millet, guinea-corn, or durra – grown in Africa, India, China, U.S.A., and S. Europe.

SORO′RITIES. See FRATERNITIES.

SORREL. Several species of plants in the genus *Rumex*, especially the garden S. (*R. acetosa*) native to N. Europe and Asia, and cultivated for its leaves, used in salads, etc.

SORRE′NTO. Coast resort on the Gulf of Naples, Italy, noted for its climate, scenery, and wine. Pop. (est.) 12,000.

S.O.S. International Morse distress signal, transmitted by any available means, e.g. flags, semaphore, radio: chosen because '3 short, 3 long, 3 short' is the most distinctive and easiest signal to transmit, it is popularly regarded in English as representing 'Save our Souls'. 'Mayday', corresponding to Fr. m'aider, is the distress code by radio telephone.

SŌTŌ, Ferdinando de (c. 1496–1542). Spanish explorer, who in 1539 led an expedition which explored Florida, Georgia, and the Mississippi.

SOULT (sōōlt), **Nicolas Jean de Dieu** (1769–1851). Marshal of France. He entered the army in 1785, served in the Revolutionary Wars, and was created a marshal in 1804 and duke of Dalmatia in 1808. He held high commands in Spain throughout the Peninsular War, and was chief of staff at Waterloo. He was War Minister 1830–4 and 1840–4.

SOUND. A physiological sensation received by the ear, which originates in a vibration which communicates itself to the air, and travels in every direction, spreading out as an expanding sphere. All S. waves travel with a speed which depends on the temperature of the atmosphere, and is about 1,120 ft. per second under ordinary conditions. The pitch of the S. depends on the number of vibrations imposed on the air per second, but the speed is unaffected. The loudness of a S. is dependent primarily on the extent

SOUND. For comfortable living and working it is increasingly recognized that acoustics are vitally important. This anechoic (echo-less) chamber, lined with sponge wedges, is for the detailed study of the processes of sound transmission and general acoustic research and forms part of the new physics laboratories of the Building Research Station of the Department of Scientific and Industrial Research opened at Watford in 1963.
Courtesy of the Dept. of Scientific and Industrial Research.

of the to and fro vibration of the air – what is known as the amplitude of the waves. In man, the lowest audible note has a frequency of about 26 vibrations per second, and the highest one of about 18,000: the lower limit of this range varies little with age, but the upper range falls steadily from adolescence onward. *See* ACOUSTICS and NOISE.

SOUND, The. Arm of the sea which runs from the Kattegat in the N. to the Baltic in the S., and separates Denmark from Sweden. It is 30 m. long, 3–37 m. wide.

SOUSA (sōō′zah), **John Philip** (1854–1932). American composer. B. in Washington, he became bandmaster of the U.S. Marines in 1880, and of his own band in 1892. He is best known for his many marches, e.g. 'Washington Post' and 'Stars and Stripes'.

SOUTH AFRICA, Rep. of (Afrikaans *Republiek van Suid Afrika*). Country occupying the S. extremity of the African continent.

PHYSICAL FEATURES. Most of S. Africa is occupied by the plateau of the High Veld, 3–4,000 ft. In the S. the lesser plateaux of the Little and Great Karroo step down from the Veld. On the S. and E. these plateaux are rimmed by mountain ranges variously named (from S. to N.) the Swarteberg, Sneeuwberg, Stormberg, Drakensberg (incl. Mont aux Sources, 10,822 ft., the highest point in the Republic), and Zoutpansberg. In Transvaal the Veld is crossed by the long ridge of Witwatersrand, on which stands Johannesburg. Close to Capetown stands Table Mountain, 3,550 ft. The main rivers are, from N. to S., the Limpopo, Vaal, and Orange. Over much of the country the climate is temperate, though N. Natal is semitropical. Big game is common in many districts, and is preserved in national parks. The Veld is a natural grassland.

ECONOMIC. A world leader in trade and industrial growth, S.A. produces cereals (maize and wheat), fruit (citrus, pears, peaches, apples, grapes, etc.), sugar and tea (in Natal), and excellent wines, the vine having been introduced to the Cape by 17th cent. Huguenot settlers. Cattle and sheep are bred on a large scale, wool being important. Enormous mineral resources incl. gold (q.v.), mainly from the Witwatersrand mines of Transvaal, diamonds, from the Kimberley district, and platinum; and antimony, asbestos, chromite, coal, copper, corundum, graphite, iron ore, lead, magnesite, manganese, nickel, phosphates, tin, titanium, tungsten, and uranium. S.A. has the world's largest oil-from-coal project, and natural gas and oil

SOUTH AFRICA. The Voortrekkers' monument, Pretoria, commemorating the Great Trek.
Courtesy of the South African Information Service.

were discovered 1969 off the Cape Coast. Industries incl. iron and steel, tobacco, textiles and clothing, jams and fruit canning, fertilizers, pharmaceuticals, synthetic rubber, plastics, leather, furniture, and explosives (the world's largest plant is at Modderfontein). Railways, airways, and harbours are govt.-operated. The chief towns are Johannesburg, Capetown (the seat of the legislature), Durban, Pretoria (the administrative cap.), Port Elizabeth, Bloemfontein, East London, and Pietermaritzburg.

GOVERNMENT. S.A. is a republic with a state pres. elected for 7 years by an electoral coll. consisting of the members of both houses of parliament, the Senate, partly elected and partly appointed by the govt., for 5 years, and the House of Assembly, elected by white citizens from among their number, also for 5 years. In 1970 Coloured representation in parliament ceased, but the Coloured Persons' Representative Council, with limited jurisdiction in Coloured affairs, was enlarged from 1969 and the franchise extended to all men and women over 21. The National Party has been in power since 1948.

POPULATION. A rigid policy of *apartheid* (racial segregation) of white from all Coloured peoples is maintained. Afrikaans and English are both official languages. There are 11 univs. restricted to the white pop.; they incl. Capetown (1918), Witwatersrand (1921) at Johannesburg, Stellenbosch (1916). The univ. of S.A. (1873), centred at Pretoria, is an examin-

DIVISIONS OF THE REPUBLIC OF SOUTH AFRICA

	Area in sq. m.	Population (1960 census)	Capital
Provinces			
Cape of Good Hope	278,465	5,342,720	Cape Town
Natal	33,578	2,979,920	Pietermaritzburg
Transvaal	110,450	6,273,477	Pretoria
Orange Free State	49,866	1,386,547	Bloemfontein
	472,359	15,982,664*	
Administered territory			
S.W. Africa	317,887 ⎱	525,959‡	Windhoek
Walvis Bay†	374 ⎰		
	790,620	16,508,623	

* 3,088,492 white.
† Part of Cape of Good Hope province, but administered with S.W. Africa.
‡ 73,154 white.

ing body with courses for external students only: the 5 non-white univ. colls. (3 African, 1 Coloured and 1 Asian) were given univ. status 1969. The churches (the largest is the Nederduits Gereformeerde Kerk, Dutch Reformed Church) separate their congregations into white and non-white.

Area (excl. S.W. Africa, q.v.) 472,733 sq. m. (incl. Walvis Bay, 434 sq. m., which is administered with S.W. Africa); pop. (1968) 19,167,000 (Whites 3,639,000; Coloured 1,912,000; Asian 574,000; Africans 13,042,000).

History. S.A. was discovered by Diaz who rounded the Cape in 1488. The Dutch E. India Co. occupied the site of Capetown in 1652 as a port of call on the way to the Indies. Occupied by the British 1795 when the Netherlands was occupied by French, restored 1802–6, Capetown and the hinterland were acquired by Britain in 1814 for a sum of £6,000,000. The first European settlers in Natal, on the coast near Durban, were British, 1824. In 1836 some 10,000 Dutch, wishing to escape from British rule, set out on the 'Great Trek' and founded the rep. of Transvaal and the Orange Free State; they also settled in N. Natal, which became part of Cape Colony in 1844, and a separate colony in 1856. The discovery of diamonds at Kimberley, in Cape Colony, and of gold in Transvaal, attracted numerous prospectors, between whom and the Dutch farmers (Boers), who had no interest in this mineral wealth, conflict developed. Britain attempted to occupy Transvaal, 1877–81, but withdrew after a severe defeat at Majuba (1881). Denial of citizenship rights to the temporary mining settlers (Uitlanders) in Transvaal, and the imperialist ambitions of Cecil Rhodes and others, led to the Jameson Raid (see L. S. JAMESON) and the S. African War (1899–1902). This opened with a series of British defeats, but in 1900 Lord Roberts forced Cronje to surrender at Paardeberg; Bloemfontein, Johannesburg, and Pretoria were captured; and Kimberley, Ladysmith, and Mafeking were relieved after long sieges. The Boers, led by Smuts and Botha, continued guerrilla resistance until 1902 when peace was made at Vereeniging, and Transvaal and the Orange Free State acknowledged British sovereignty. In 1910 the Union of S.A. was formed to incl. the provinces of Cape of Good Hope, Natal, Orange Free State, and Transvaal. The outbreak of the F.W.W. was marked by a Boer rebellion, speedily crushed by Smuts. German S.W. Africa was occupied, and Union forces served with distinction in E. Africa and in France. Between the wars the political life of the Union was marked by the alternating terms of office of the republican nationalists under Hertzog and the S. African Party under Smuts, who wished to maintain the Commonwealth connection.

On the outbreak of the S.W.W. in 1939, Smuts, having secured the defeat in the S.A. parl. of a motion for neutrality put forward by the P.M., Hertzog, took over the premiership. S.A. troops played a major part in the conquest of Ital. E. Africa and served with distinction in N. Africa and in Italy. The Nationalist Party (led by Dr. Malan, q.v.) returned to office in 1948 with a small majority, later increased. In 1959 the National Party, formed in 1951 by the union of the Nationalist and Afrikaner parties, secured 103 seats (out of 160). A referendum in 1960 resulted in a vote of 849,958 for, 775,878 against, S.A.'s becoming a republic; and in 1961 the govt., led by Dr. Hendrik Verwoerd, unable to accept Commonwealth opposition to *apartheid*, took S.A. out of the British Commonwealth. On Verwoerd's assassination 1966, his successor B. J. Vorster followed the same policy.

Art. S.A. can boast of a number of accomplished artists, incl. Gwelo Goodman, Rowarth, Naude, Volschenk, Neville Lewis, and Pieter Wenning, though no distinctive S. African school of painting has developed. There are fine collections of Euro-

pean paintings, e.g. at Capetown and Johannesburg.

The architecture of S.A. has remained under Dutch influence, early domestic buildings were similar in style to buildings in Amsterdam. After 1815 a sort of classic Renaissance took place, but architecture deteriorated in style after the discovery of diamonds in 1867, when many buildings were erected hastily and haphazardly. The most noteworthy individual contribution to the architecture of S.A. was made by Sir Herbert Baker, who was commissioned by Rhodes to reconstruct *Groote Schuur* (originally built in the 17th cent.), Dutch in style, and later designed Government House and Capital Buildings at Pretoria, the Rhodes Memorial on Table Mountain, and the cathedrals at Capetown and Johannesburg.

SOUTH AFRICA. Largest Christian denomination of the Republic, the Dutch Reformed Church is enterprisingly original in the design of new buildings for worship, as in this church at Vanderbijl Park.
Courtesy of the South African Information Service.

Literature. Founder of S. African literature in English was Thomas Pringle (1789–1834), who pub. lyric poetry and the prose *Narrative of a Residence in S. Africa.* The missionary, Arthur S. Cripps, and the Scot, Charles Murray, also produced excellent verse, but the finest of the more recent poets, Roy Campbell and Francis C. Slater, are S. African-born. The 1st work of S. African fiction to achieve fame outside the country was Olive Schreiner's *Story of an African Farm* (1883), later writers in English of international repute incl. Sara G. Millin, Pauline Smith (author of *The Little Karroo*), William Plomer, and Laurens van der Post. *See also* AFRIKAANS.

SOUTH AMERICA. Continent covering 14 per cent of the earth's land area, joined to Central and N. America by the Panama isthmus; it is almost entirely to the E. of the northern continent. The relief is divided into 3 longitudinal areas. The Andes in the W. run parallel to the Pacific coastline, and rise to more than 20,000 ft.; the great central plains, the Llanos, Selvas, Chaco, and Pampas, stretch from the Orinoco basin to Patagonia; and the Brazilian and Guiana highlands.

S. of the Orinoco basin the Amazon river system,

COUNTRIES OF SOUTH AMERICA

	Area in 1,000s sq. m.	Population (in 1000s)	Capital
Argentina	1,073	22,520	Buenos Aires
Bolivia	424	4,334	La Paz
Brazil	3,287	87,209	Brasilia
Chile	286	7,400	Santiago
Colombia	440	19,300	Bogotá
Ecuador	116	5,586	Quito
Guiana:			
Guiana, incl.			
Inini (French)	34	34	Cayenne
Guyana (Brit.)	83	692	Georgetown
Surinam			
(Netherlands)	55	350	Paramaribo
Paraguay	157	2,161	Asunción
Peru	514	12,400	Lima
Uruguay	72	2,783	Montevideo
Venezuela	352	9,169	Caracas
	6,893	173,938	

SOUTH AMERICA. Mountain and river systems.

flowing through dense forest land to the Atlantic, dominates the N. of the continent. In Brazil deep valleys are cut in the highland by many rivers flowing E. and N.; thence, too, the Parana, Paraguay, and Uruguay flow S. to form the La Plata estuary, draining the fertile central plains. S. of the Colorado and Negro is the Patagonian desert, covering the tapering strip of S.A. to Tierra del Fuego.

The Amazon belt has an equatorial type of climate with a heavy rainfall. The rainfall generally is heavy, except in the narrow coastal strips of Peru and N. Chile which, with most of Patagonia, are virtually desert.

Although many pure Indians exist, mainly in Bolivia, Peru, and Ecuador, the introduction of Negroes and Europeans has brought about a thorough racial mixture. Except in Brazil, where Portuguese is spoken, Spanish is the common tongue. The Indian language origins remain obscure; Chibcha, Kichua, and Araukan are the main groups of the W., in Colombia, Peru, and Chile, and other distinct groups exist in the E. Ethnologically and linguistically there are slight affinities with Melanesia and aboriginal Australia.

SOUTHA'MPTON, Henry Wriothesley, 3rd earl of (1573–1624). English courtier and patron of Shake-speare, who dedicated 'Venus and Adonis' and 'Lucrece' to him, and possibly addressed him in the sonnets.

SOUTHAMPTON. City and seaport in Hants, England, 79 m. S.W. of London, on S. Water, between the estuaries of the Itchen and Test. The King George V graving dock, constructed 1927–34, is one of the largest in the world, and S. is the chief port for trans-atlantic routes. The major passenger port – Gateway to Britain – S. is also being developed as a great cargo port. It is also an airport, and has engineering works, flour mills, chemical, plastics, tobacco and other fac-tories. S. univ., founded 1862 as a univ. coll., received

a royal charter in 1952. S. was founded before the Norman Conquest, created a city 1964. Pop. (1961) 204,707.

SOUTH ARABIA, Federation of. Federation formed in 1959 by 6 Arab chiefs in the Western Aden Protectorate; 5 other chiefs had joined when in 1963 the colony of Aden became a member, at which time the Aden Protectorates (E. and W.) were renamed the Protectorate of S. Arabia. Following independence 1967, S.A. became the Democratic Rep. of Southern Yemen (q.v.).

SOUTH AUSTRALIA. State of the Commonwealth of Australia. Dairying and wheat and fruit growing are carried on, especially in the irrigated area in the Murray Valley, but 80 per cent of the state is given to cattle and sheep grazing. S.A. produces 75 per cent of Australia's wine, and 90 per cent of its brandy. Fruit canning is important, and there are also factories making textiles and clothing, metal goods and machines, paper, chemicals, etc. Whyalla exports iron ore and is an industrial centre; uranium is found at Radium Hill and natural gas in the N.E.; and there is an experimental rocket range at Woomera. Govt. is by a legislative council and house of assembly. The cap. is Adelaide. Area 380,070 sq. m.; pop. (1961) 969,258.

SOUTH CAROLI'NA. A southern, Atlantic state of the U.S.A., one of the original 13. Tobacco, cotton, and soya beans are the principal crops. Industries incl. manufacture of textiles and clothing, paper and wood pulp, furniture, bricks, meat products. The first settlers (1526) were Spaniards; as Carolina, the area was given by Charles I to Robert Heath in 1629. Columbia, the cap., Greenville, and Charleston are the largest towns. Area 31,055 sq. m.; pop. (1970) 2,590,576.

SOUTHCOTT, Joanna (1750–1814). British religionist. B. in Devon, she prophesied the end of the world from 1792 onwards, and shortly before her death from brain disease announced she was about to give birth to a new Messiah. A mysterious box left by her to be opened in time of national crisis proved valueless in 1928, but the claim is still revived.

SOUTH DAKO'TA. A northern-central state of the U.S.A. It is for the most part broad prairie, and W. of the 'Bad Lands' rise the Black Hills. The state is drained by the Missouri. Wheat, Indian corn, and oats form the leading crops. Gold, mica and uranium are mined, and the main industries are connected with agriculture. Sioux Falls is the largest town, and Pierre (pop. 10,088) is the cap. Area 77,047 sq. m.; pop. (1970) 666,257.

SOUTH-EAST ASIA TREATY ORGANIZA-TION (SEATO). Collective defensive system created under a treaty signed 8 Sept. 1954, in Manila, by Australia, France, N.Z., Pakistan, the Philippines, Thailand, the U.K. and the U.S.A. S. Vietnam, Cam-bodia and Laos are protocol states; France no longer attends meetings.

SOUTHEND-ON-SEA. Seaside resort (co. bor.) in Essex, England, 35 m. E. of London, at the mouth of the Thames. The famous pier, more than 1¼ m. long, was built to accommodate pleasure-steamers at low tide. In addition to catering for visitors, S.-on-S. has light engineering and radio industries, furniture and textile factories, brickyards, boatbuilding yards, etc. Pop. (1961) 164,976.

SOUTHERN CROSS. A constellation in the southern hemisphere of the heavens, consisting of four principal stars arranged in the shape of a cross.

SOUTHEY (sow'dhi), Robert (1774–1843). British poet and author. B. at Bristol, he settled at Keswick, to be near Coleridge. He abandoned his early revolu-tionary views, and from 1808 contributed regularly to the Tory Quarterly Review. In 1813 he became poet laureate, but his verse is forgotten, and he is better known for his life of Nelson, and his Letters.

SOUTH GEORGIA. A British whaling island in the S. Atlantic, 800 m. E. by S. of the Falkland Islands, of which it is a dependency. It was discovered by Cook in 1775. Area 1,600 sq. m.; pop. (1961) 561.

SOUTH ORKNEYS. A British island group (uninhabited) in the Southern Ocean, a dependency of the Falkland Islands, discovered in 1821 by George Powell. The 2 main islands are Laurie and Coronation.

SOUTHSEA. A district of Portsmouth (q.v.).

SOUTH SEA BUBBLE. The financial crisis of 1720. The South Sea Co., founded in 1711, which enjoyed a monopoly of trade with S. America, offered in 1719 to take over the national debt in return for further concessions. Its £100 shares rapidly rose to £1,000, and an orgy of speculation followed. When the 'bubble' burst, thousands were ruined. The discovery that cabinet ministers had been guilty of corruption led to a political crisis; Walpole became P.M., and restored financial confidence.

SOUTH SHETLANDS. A British archipelago of 12 uninhabited islands in the Southern Ocean, a dependency of the Falkland Islands (q.v.). Area 1,800 sq. m.

SOUTH SHIELDS. Seaport (co. bor.) in co. Durham, England, on the Tyne. Manufactures incl. cables and chemicals. Pop. (1961) 109,533.

SOUTH UIST. See under UIST.

SOUTHWARK (suth'ark). Inner bor. of Greater London – commonly called The Borough – and incorporating from 1965 Bermondsey and Camberwell. It is on the S. of the Thames opposite the City: St. Saviour's cathedral dates from the 12th cent. and the George Inn (1677) is London's last galleried inn. See GLOBE THEATRE. Pop. (1967) 300,720.

SOUTH WEST AFRICA. Territory of S. Africa, on the Atlantic S. of Angola, from which it is separated in the W. by the r. Kunene, N. of the Cape of Good Hope prov., from which it is separated by the Orange r. Most of the area is barren upland, and in the E. is the Kalahari Desert, but there is some good grazing. Cattle, sheep, and goats are raised, and there is an important trade in skins. Mineral wealth incl. diamonds, vanadium, tin, and copper. Windhoek is the cap., and the chief ports are Lüderitz and Walvis Bay (admin. with S.W.A. though part of Cape Prov.). Area 317,825 sq. m. (excl. Walvis Bay, 434 sq. m.); pop. (1960) 525,959 (73,460 white).

S.W.A. was annexed by Germany in 1884, and in 1904–7 it was the scene of the Herero rebellion, which was put down with great harshness. In the F.W.W. South African forces under Botha occupied all S.W.A. 1914–15. The terr. was mandated by the League of Nations to South Africa in 1920, and a declaration by the U.N. in 1966 that the mandate was terminated was rejected by South Africa: the U.N. declared 1968 that S.W.A. would in future be known as Namibia. Under a South African govt. act of 1968 legislative councils were to be estab. in 6 areas as a step to self-governing Bantu homelands, largest being Ovamboland, pop. 270,000, with cap. at Oshakati.

SOVEREIGN. British gold coin, introduced by Henry VII, worth £1 (100p). It became the standard monetary unit in 1817, but minting ceased for currency purposes in 1914. Although it is illegal for residents in the U.K. to hold gold coin, otherwise than in coin collections, the S. is still current in the Middle East and large quantities are struck.

SOVIET (Russian, council). The original Ss. were strike committees elected by the Russian workers during the 1905 revolution. After the deposition of the tsar in 1917 local Ss. were set up by peasants, soldiers, and industrial workers, and they selected delegates to an All-Russian Congress of Ss., which in Nov., under Bolshevik leadership, took over the govt. (See SOVIET UNION.) Ss. have been set up in many other countries during periods of crisis, e.g. in Germany in 1918 and Hungary in 1919, and the

Councils of Action during the British general strike in 1926. And at the present day similar systems exist in other Communist states.

SOVIET FAR EAST. Geographical (not admin. division of Asiatic R.S.F.S.R., on the Pacific coast. It covers the Amur, Lower Amur, Kamchatka, and Sakhalin regions, and Khabarovsk and Maritime terrs.

SOVIETSK (sovyetsk'). Town in Kaliningrad region, R.S.F.S.R., 60 m. N.E. of Kaliningrad city. Saw milling, paper and wood-pulp making, distilling, cheese making are among its industries. The former Tilsit (renamed S. in 1946), it was the site of a meeting in 1807 at which Napoleon made peace with Russia and Prussia. Pop. (est.) 60,000. See KALININGRAD.

SOVIET UNION. Abbreviation for the Union of Soviet Socialist Republics (U.S.S.R.). The Russian Soviet Federated Socialist Republic (R.S.F.S.R.; q.v.), was formed after the 1917 revolution, and in

UNION OF SOVIET SOCIALIST REPUBLICS

	Area in sq. m.	Population in 1,000s)	Capital
R.S.F.S.R.	6,570,400	127,911	Moscow
Armenia	11,500	2,306	Yerivan
Azerbaijan	33,100	4,917	Baku
Estonia	18,300	1,304	Tallinn
Georgia	29,400	4,659	Tbilisi
Kazakh S.S.R.	1,061,600	12,678	Alma-Ata
Kirghiz S.S.R.	76,100	2,836	Frunze
Latvia	25,000	2,298	Riga
Lithuania	25,300	3,064	Vilnius
Moldavia	13,100	3,484	Kishinev
Tadzhik S.S.R.	55,000	2,736	Dushambe
Turkmen S.S.R.	187,000	2,029	Ashkhabad
Ukraine	222,600	46,381	Kiev
Uzbek S.S.R.	157,400	11,266	Tashkent
White Russia	80,500	8,820	Minsk
U.S.S.R.	8,566,300	236,689	Moscow

1924 the union with the Ukrainian and White Russian Republics and the Transcaucasian Soviet Federal Socialist Republic to form the U.S.S.R. was ratified. In 1963 there were 15 constituent republics (see table), and the est. pop. was 225,000,000. Under the 1936 constitution the central govt. at Moscow is responsible for defence, foreign policy, foreign trade, communications, and heavy industries, while the govts. of the constituent republics deal with all other subjects. National groups within several of the constituent republics have a measure of self-govt., the R.S.F.S.R. incl. the largest number of such autonomous units.

The highest organ of govt. is the Supreme Soviet of 2 chambers elected for 4 years – the Soviet of the Union (elected on a basis of 1 deputy for every 300,000 of the pop.) and the Soviet of Nationalities consisting of 25 deputies from each constituent rep., 11 from each autonomous rep., 5 from each autonomous region, and 1 from each national area. The Supreme Soviet elects its Presidium, which acts as an executive committee between its sessions, and the Council of Ministers, or Cabinet. Each constituent republic and autonomous republic has its own Supreme Soviet, of one chamber, and Council of Ministers. All citizens over 18 may vote by ballot. Deputies may be recalled by a majority of their constituents. Local govt. is in the hands of district, town, and village soviets.

All industries and means of communication are State-owned, and are normally organized under either an all-Union ministry or a ministry of a constituent republic. Local authorities often run industrial

SPACE RESEARCH. Lunar module pilot, Edwin Aldrin, descends the steps of the module ladder to walk on the Moon. This picture was taken by the commander of the *Apollo XI* mission, Neil Armstrong, with a 70 mm lunar surface camera. On the right, a Saturn vehicle is rolled out for the *Apollo IX* preliminary mission to evaluate the spacecraft lunar module system's performance during a manned Earth orbital flight.

Courtesy of NASA.

military purposes. Europe's chief organizations for space research are Eurospace (non-profit-making assocn. of cos. of 9 countries); European Launcher Development Organization (ELDO, 1962); European Space Research Organization (ESRO, estab. 1962) and the International Committee on Space Research (COSPAR, estab. 1958) – all with H.Q. in Paris.

Space Research earth satellites and S. probes incl.: *Sputnik I* (U.S.S.R.) 4 Oct. 1957 measured temperatures and atmospheric density and orbited at 142–558 m. in 96·2 min.; *Explorer I* (U.S.A.) 31 Jan. 1958 discovered Van Allen radiation belt and orbited at 217–1,100 m. in 106·2 min.; *Vostok I* (U.S.S.R.: Gagarin; q.v.) 12 April 1961, first manned space ship, recovered after single orbit in 89·1 min. at 109–88 m.; *Friendship 7* (U.S.A.: Lieut-Col. Glenn) 20 Feb. 1962, 3 orbits in 4 hr. 40 min. at 100–160 m.; *Telstar* (U.S.A.) 10 July 1962, communications satellite which later transmitted the first live television pictures between U.S. and Europe, circling the earth at 158 min. intervals at 593–3,502 m.; *Vostok 6* (U.S.S.R.) 16–19 June 1963, the first woman space traveller, Lt. Valentina Tereshkova, 48 orbits of Earth; *Voskhod I* (U.S.S.R.) 12–13 Oct. 1964, first space ship with more than one person aboard (3 men), 16 orbits in just over 24 hr.; *Voskhod II* (U.S.S.R.) 18 March, 1965, Pavel Belyaev and Alexei Leonov (first man to walk in space; *Luna 9* (U.S.S.R.) 3 Feb. 1966, first unmanned soft landing on the Moon; *Gemini X* (U.S.A.) 18–21 July, 1966, docking of space ship and target vehicle; Cape Kennedy, U.S.A., 27 Jan. 1967 three astronauts burned to death testing a spacecraft on the ground; *Soyuz 1* (U.S.S.R.) 24 April 1967, cosmonaut Vladimir Komarov, first man to be killed in space when his ship crashlanded; *Cosmos 186 and 188* (U.S.S.R.) 30 Oct. 1967, unmanned spacecraft achieved automatic link-up, separation and departure in different orbits; *Zond 5* (U.S.S.R.) 15–21 Sept. 1968, first unmanned craft to go round Moon and back to Earth; *Apollo VIII* (U.S.A.) 21–27 Dec. 1968 first manned craft to go round Moon and return – Frank Borman, James A. Lovell and William A. Anders; *Soyuz 4 and 5* (U.S.S.R.) 14–18 Jan, 1969, formed first orbiting space station; *Apollo XI* (U.S.A.) achieved manned landing on the Moon: see LUNAR PROBE and MODULE. *See* also MARS and VENUS.

and trading enterprises. Agriculture is carried on mainly in collective farms (q.v.), but some farms are State-owned. Peasants and craftsmen may work on their own account, provided they do not employ the labour of others. Trade in the countryside is largely in the hands of co-operative societies. Industry and agriculture are run in accordance with a plan, usually covering 5 years, drawn up by the State Planning Commission. *See also* articles on the constituent republics.

SOYA (soi′ah) **BEAN.** Leguminous plant (*Glycine hispida*), native to E. Asia, particularly to Japan and China. It is grown as a seed or forage crop, and is used as hay or in oil-form for human consumption. A more recent product has been soya flour.

SPA. Town in Liège prov., Belgium, famous since the 14th cent. for its mineral springs. It has given its name to similar centres elsewhere. Pop. (1962) 9,040.

SPAAK (spahk), **Paul-Henri** (1899–1972). Belgian Socialist. From before the S.W.W. he consistently held high office, being For. Min. 1936–8, P.M. 1938–9, For. Min. 1939–46, P.M. and For. Min. 1947–9, For. Min. 1954–7, and assistant P.M. and For. Min. 1961–6. An ardent advocate of international peace, he was awarded the Charlemagne prize in 1957.

SPACE. The continuum which incl. the galaxies. It used to be thought that S. must be empty, but this is now known not to be the case. In the Solar System, there is a great deal of thinly spread matter; there is also a vast amount of gas and dust between the stars of our Galaxy, and probably there is also appreciable matter in intergalactic space. The absorption of light by this tenuous material has to be taken into account in any astronomical investigation involving large distances.

Air S. is the volume of space between the surface of the earth and an altitude of 80,000 metres. Beyond is *Outer S.*, and in 1967 Britain, Russia and the U.S.A. signed a treaty banning nuclear weapons there, and the use of the Moon and other celestial bodies for

SPAIN (Estado Español, Spanish State). State of S.W. Europe, occupying most of the Iberian peninsula, from the Pyrenees to the Strait of Gibraltar. Most of its area is occupied by the Meseta, a plateau sloping to the S.W. and crossed by several mountain ranges, incl. the Sierra de Guadarrama, the Sierra de Toledo, and the Sierra Morena. This plateau is bounded on the S. by the Sierra Nevada, where the Mulhacen (11,411 ft.) is the highest mountain in Spain; and to the N. by the Pyrenees and by the Cantabrian mountains. The Guadalquivir, Guadiana, Tagus, Douro, and Mino flow to the Atlantic; and the Ebro and its tributaries to the Mediterranean. The Balearic and Canary

Islands are incl. in S. The interior has extremes of temperature in summer and winter. The main plateau is very dry, but the N.W. enjoys an equable climate with much rain, while Andalusia is sub-tropical.

ECONOMIC. Two-thirds of the pop. depend on agriculture. Many fruits are cultivated, incl. grapes, oranges, dates, olives, and pomegranates; as well as wheat, barley, potatoes, and sugar beet. Sheep and cattle are raised. Lead and silver are found in Murcia in the S.E., and the Rio Tinto mines near Huelva have one of the largest copper deposits in the world. Mercury is obtained near Almaden, and iron ore in the Basque country. Coal is worked in the Asturias. Industry is little developed, though Barcelona has important metallurgical, textile, and paper industries and Oviedo and Bilbao specialize in the manufacture of metal goods. Madrid is the cap.; other large towns are Barcelona, Valencia, Seville, Malaga, Saragossa, Murcia, and Bilbao.

GOVERNMENT. Dictator of S. from 1939, Franco embodied in an Organic Law of 1966 his announcement of 1947 that S. was once more a monarchy, with himself acting as regent and Head of State (*Caudillo*) till death or incapacity. In 1969 he nominated Juan Carlos (*see* BOURBON TABLE) as the future King of Spain, formally declaring him Prince of Spain, as opposed to the traditional monarchist title for the heir to the throne, Prince of the Asturias: Juan Carlos had m. in 1962 Princess Sophia of Greece, dau. of King Paul of the Hellenes and Queen Frederika. The single party (Falange Española) is headed by Franco, though the 1966 law provided for delegation to a P.M. chosen by himself. The Cortes (re-estab. 1942) is composed on corporative lines (though from 1966 with 100 of its *c.* 500 members elected by heads of families and their wives), and approves of laws put before it.

AREA AND POPULATION. The area (incl. the Balearic and Canary Islands) is 194,232 sq. m. The inhabitants are mainly of Iberian stock, with a strong Moorish admixture in the S. Elementary education is free and compulsory. The country forms 12 educational regions, each with its own univ. Roman Catholicism is the official religion. The total pop. (incl. the Balearics and the Canaries) was 32,275,434 in 1968.

OVERSEAS POSSESSIONS. Of the once vast overseas empire little remains – the towns of Ceuta and Melilla, and Spanish Sahara; *see* also EQUATORIAL GUINEA and IFNI.

History. Pre-Roman S. was inhabited by Iberians, Celts, and Celtiberians. The Phoenicians and Greeks early estab. colonies on the coast, and the Carthaginians attempted to found an empire in the S.E. This fell into Roman hands in *c.* 200 and after a long struggle all S. was absorbed into the Roman Empire. At the invitation of Rome the Visigoths entered S. in A.D. 414 and set up a kingdom there, *c.* 530–700. In 711 the country was overrun by the Moors. The Christians maintained their resistance from the northern mountains, and by 1250 had reconquered all S. except the kingdom of Granada. During this struggle a number of small Christian kingdoms were founded, all of which by the 13th cent. had been absorbed by Castile and Aragon. The marriage of Ferdinand of Aragon to Isabella of Castile, 1469, brought their domains together on their accession, 1479; and the conquest of Granada in 1492 completed the unification of S.

Under Ferdinand and Isabella, Charles I (*see* CHARLES V, Holy Roman Emperor), and Philip II, S. became the greatest power in Europe, and the mistress of a world-wide empire. Columbus's discoveries made on behalf of S. were followed by the conquest of most of Central and S. America; Naples and Sicily were annexed in 1503, Milan in 1535, and Portugal in 1580, while Charles I inherited the Netherlands. But with the revolt in the Netherlands and the defeat of the Armada (1588), S.'s power began

to decline; the loss of civil and religious freedom, constant wars, inflation, a corrupt bureaucracy, and the expulsion of the Jews and Moors undermined her economic life, and in the 17th cent. she ceased to be a great power. By the peace of Utrecht (1713) S. lost the S. Netherlands (the N. had been recognized as independent in 1648), Naples, Sicily, Milan, and Gibraltar. During the 18th cent. reforms were undertaken, and considerable economic progress was made. S. became involved in the Revolutionary and Napoleonic Wars, first as the ally, later as the opponent, of France; the French occupied S. in 1808, and it was not until 1814 that they were expelled, with British assistance.

Throughout the 19th cent. conflict raged between monarchists and Liberals; revolutions and civil wars occurred in 1820–3, 1833–9, and 1868, besides many minor revolts, and a republic was temporarily estab. in 1873–4. S. lost her American colonies during 1810–30, and after the war with the U.S.A. of 1898 ceded Cuba and the Philippines to the U.S.A. Republicanism, Socialism, and anarchism grew after 1900; Primo de Rivera's dictatorship (1923–30) failed to save the monarchy under Alfonso XIII, and in 1931 a republic was estab.

In 1936 the Popular Front, an alliance of centre and left parties, took office, and introduced agrarian and other reforms which aroused the opposition of the landlords and the Church. A military revolt followed, headed by Gen. Franco (q.v.); the insurgents or Nationalists seized power in the S. and N.W., but revolts in Madrid, Barcelona, and elsewhere were suppressed by the workers' militia. Madrid held out for 2½ years. Italian troops and German air forces fought on the Nationalist side, while the Republicans or loyalists received minimal assistance from Russia, and volunteers from many countries formed the International Brigade to fight for the govt. Bilbao and the Basque country were bombed into submission by the Nationalists in 1937, and in 1938 they cut off Catalonia from the main Republican territory. Barcelona fell in Jan. 1939, and the war ended with the surrender of Madrid in April. A Fascist dictatorship was estab., the only authorized party being the Falange. During the S.W.W., S. was nominally neutral, but inclined to the Axis. In the 1960s there was friction with Britain over Gibraltar.

SPALATO. Ital. form of SPLIT.

SPALDING (spawld'-). English market town (U.D.) in Holland, Lincs, 14 m. S.S.W. of Boston. The neighbourhood is famous for its bulb farming. Pop. (1961) 14,821.

SPANIEL. A group of dogs, characterized by large, drooping ears and a long, silky coat. The Clumber S. takes its name from the estate of the duke of Newcastle, who imported them from France; it is lemon and white, and very silent when hunting. The Sussex S., believed to be the oldest variety, is a golden liver colour. The cocker is a small S., which varies in colour from liver or liver and white to black. Toy Ss., kept as pets, are divided into the black-and-tan King Charles, and the red and white Blenheim.

SUSSEX SPANIEL

SPANISH. The S. language is of Latin origin, and also borrowed much from the Moors during their occupation of the peninsula. The dialect of Castile was adopted as the official language towards the end of the 13th cent., but it has never supplanted the other regional idioms, among which Catalan has achieved the status of an independent language, while Galician is very close to Portuguese. Basque, which is spoken in the extreme N.E. of Spain, is unrelated

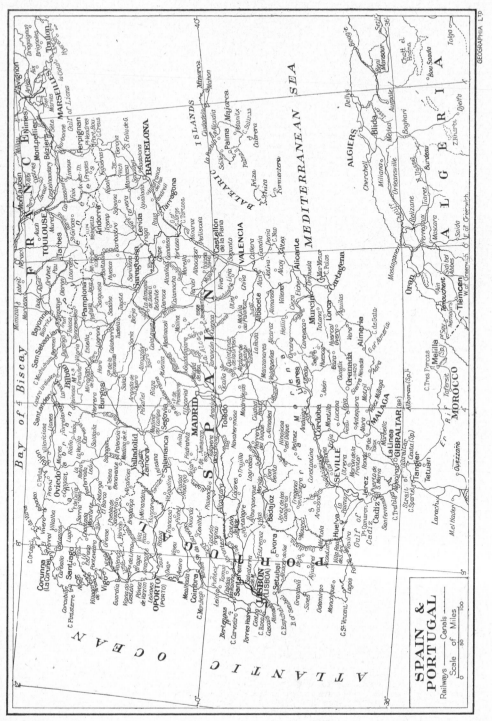

SPAIN & PORTUGAL

Railways ____ Canals ____

Scale of Miles

to any other European language. S. is the official
language of all the Latin American republics except
Brazil, and is also spoken in the Philippines and
among Sephardic Jews in N. Africa, the Middle East,
and the Balkans. An official language of the United
Nations, S. is spoken by about 90 million persons.

Literature. Of the classical epics, the 12th cent.
El Cantar de Mio Cid is the only complete example.
The founder of Castilian prose was King Alfonso X,
the Wise, who also wrote lyric poetry in the Galician
dialect. The first true poet was the 14th cent. satirist,
Juan Ruiz, archpriest of Hita. To the 15th cent.
belong the marquis of Santillana (Iñigo López de
Mendoza), poet, critic, and collector of proverbs; the
chivalric romances, e.g. the *Amadis de Gaula*; the
ballads dealing with the struggle against the Moors;
and the *Celestina*, a novel in dramatic form. The
flowering of the verse drama began with Lope de
Rueda (d. 1565), and reached its height with Lope de
Vega and Calderon de la Barca. In poetry the Golden
Age of the 15th–16th cents. produced the lyrical
Garcilaso de la Vega; the patriotic Fernando de
Herrera (1534–97); the mystics Santa Teresa and Luis
de Léon; Luis de Gongora (1561–1627), whose
elaborate style popularized the decadent 'gongorism';
and the biting satire of Francisco de Quevedo. In
fiction there developed the pastoral romance, e.g.
Jorge de Montemayor's *Diana*; the picaresque novel,
estab. by the anonymous *Lazarillo de Tormes*; and the
work of Cervantes. In the 18th cent. the Benedictine
Benito J. Feijóo introduced scientific thought to
Spain, and French influence emerged in the comedies
of Leandro F. de Moratín (1760–1828), etc. Typical of
the romantic era were the poet-dramatists Ángel de
Saavedra (duque de Rivas) (1791–1865), and José
Zorrilla; and the lyricist José de Espronceda (1810–42).
Among 19th cent. novelists are Fernán Caballero,
Pedro de Alarcón, Juan Valera (1824–1905), Emilia
condesa de Pardo Bazán (1852–1921), José de Pereda,
and Armando Palacio Valdés; a 19th cent. dramatist is
José Echegaray.

The 'Generation of 1898' incl. the philosophers
Miguel de Unamuno and José Ortega y Gasset; the
novelists Pío Baroja, Benito Pérez Galdós (1843–1920),
Ramón Pérez de Ayala (1880–1960), Ramón del
Valle-Inclán, and Gabriel Miró; the prose writers
'Azorín' and Angel Ganivet (1865–98); and the poets
Juan Ramón Jiménez, and the Nicaraguan Rubén
Darío, who went to Europe and did much to revolu-
tionize 20th cent. S. poetry, introducing new rhythms,
vers libre, etc. The next generation of writers incl.
the prose writers Salvador da Madariaga, Arturo
Barea, and C. J. Cela (1916–); and the poets
Miguel Hernández (1910–51), Antonio Machado,
F. García Lorca, Jorge Guillén, Rafael Alberti,
Pedro Salinas (1892–1951), Vicente Aleixandre
(1898–), and Luis Cernuda (1904–); dramatists
were Jacinto Benavente, the brothers Quintero, and
– the most striking – F. García Lorca. The Civil War
and the strict censorship of the Franco govt. to some
extent disrupted the mid-cent. literary life, but
writers of the younger generation, occasionally writing
in exile, incl. the novelists Rafael Sánchez Ferlosio
(1927–), Ana María Matute, Juan Goytisolo
(1931–) and José Maria Gironella (1917–), and
the poets Blas de Otero (1916–) and José Hierro
(1922–).

In Central and S. America there is vigorous life
and the growth of a new tradition, especially in
poetry. Mexico has been particularly fertile in poetic
talent, e.g. Salvador Díaz Mirón (1858–1928) who
influenced Darío, Ramón López Verlarde (1888–
1921), Alfonso Reyes (1889–), Xavier Villaurrutia
(1904–42), Alberto Quintero Álvarez (1914–44) and
Octavio Paz. Other notable names incl. the Nobel
prizewinner Gabriela Mistral and Pablo Neruda –
both of Chile; the Argentinian Ricardo E. Molinari

(1898–); Julio Herrera y Reissig (1875–1910) of
Uruguay; César Vallejo (1895–1937) of Peru; Jorge
Carrera Andrade (1903–) of Ecuador; and Nicolás
Guillén, a Cuban of Spanish and African descent.

SPANISH ARMADA. The fleet sent by Philip II
of Spain against England in 1588. Consisting of 130
ships, it sailed from Lisbon, and carried on a running
fight up-Channel with the English fleet of 197 small
ships under Howard of Effingham and Drake. The
A. anchored off Calais, but was forced to put to sea
by fireships, and a general action followed off Gravelines. What remained of the A. escaped round the N.
of Scotland and W. of Ireland, suffering many losses
by storm and shipwreck on the way. Only about half
the original fleet returned to Spain: *see* illus. p. 382.

SPANISH ART. Painting. Little pre-10th cent.
painting still exists, but many examples of Romanesque art (10th–13th cent.), mainly brilliantly coloured

SPANISH ART. To the left, El Greco's 'Man with his hand on
his breast' in the Prado, and, to the right, 'Magdalena' by
Pedro de Mena (d. 1693) in the Museo de San Gregorio at
Valladolid.   *Courtesy of the Spanish Ministry of Information.*

church murals, survive. Gothic murals and altar
panels (13th–15th cent.) are more freely natural.

Italian and Flemish influences contributed to
Spanish Renaissance painting, and the great masters
of this period (end of 15th–16th cent.) incl. Bartolomé
Bermejo (*c.* 1440–95), Alonzo Sánchez Coello
(1515–90), Luis de Vargas (1502–68), Francisco de
Herrera the Elder, Juan de Juanes (1523–79), Ribalta,
Navarrette (1526–79), Luis de Morales (1509–86), and
the greatest of all, El Greco.

Whereas previously there had been regional distinctions in style, in the 17th cent. a national school
developed, of which the greatest names were Ribera,
Zurbaran, Velasquez and Murillo.

The greatest Spanish artist of the 18th cent. was
Goya, who exerted a great influence on European art
of the following cent. Painters of the 20th cent. incl.
the cubist Juan Gris (1887–1927), the surrealists Joan
Miró and Salvador Dali (qq.v.), the impressionist
Joaquín Sorolla y Bastida (1863–1923) and, most
notably, Pablo Picasso (q.v.). In Spanish America an
important school of mural painting emerged in
Mexico with the work of the 'Big Four' – José Orozco
(1883–1949), Diego Rivera (q.v.), David Siqueiros
(1898–), and Rufino Tamayo (1899–).

Architecture. The various styles of Spanish architecture are: *Roman* (3rd–5th cent., the period of
Roman rule); *Asturian* (9th cent.), which takes its
name from the district in N.W. Spain which was
unconquered by the Moors; *Mozarabic* (9th–11th
cent.), a style of Spanish Christian architecture,
which shows the influence of Mohammedan architecture; *Romanesque* (11th and 12th cents.); *Gothic*
(13th–16th cent.); *Renaissance* (15th–17th cent.),
which is uninspired though based on Italian models;
Baroque (17th–18th cent.), a style which the Spaniards
delighted in, but carried to excess in the fantastic
designs of Churriguera and his followers; *Neo-Classic*

(18th and 19th cents.); *Modern* Oscar Niemeyer (q.v.) and Antonio Gaudi.

Sculpture. The most outstanding sculptors incl. Borgoña (d. *c.* 1543), Berruguete (*c.* 1486–1561), Gregorio Fernandez (1566–1636), Montañes (1564–1649), and Alonso de los Rios.

SPANISH GUINEA. The Spanish overseas provs. of Fernando Po and Rio Muni, which in 1968 became the independent unitary state of Equatorial Guinea (q.v.).

SPANISH SAHARA. Spanish overseas prov. on the Atlantic coast of W. Africa, The cap. is El Aaiún. Morocco and Mauretania lay claim to the area, which is rich in phosphates. Area 102,680 sq. m.; pop. (1967) 48,000.

SPANISH SUCCESSION. Name given to the war of 1701–14 between Britain, Austria, the Netherlands, Portugal, and Denmark on the one side, and France, Spain, and Bavaria on the other, that was caused by Louis XIV's acceptance of the Spanish throne on behalf of his grandson, Philip, in defiance of the Partition Treaty of 1700, whereby it was to pass to the archduke Charles of Austria. The French attempted in 1704 to end the war by a march on Vienna, but were defeated at Blenheim by Marlborough and Eugène of Savoy. The main campaigns were fought in Belgium, where Marlborough won victories at Ramillies (1706), Oudenarde (1708), and Malplaquet (1709). The Allies invaded Spain in 1705, and twice occupied Madrid, but failed to hold it. By the Treaties of Utrecht (1713), and Rastatt (1714), the Allies recognized Philip as king of Spain; Gibraltar, Minorca, and Nova Scotia were ceded to Britain, and Belgium, Milan, and Naples to Austria.

SPANISH TOWN. Town in Jamaica, 15 m. W.N.W. of Kingston. Founded by Diego Columbus *c.* 1525, it was the cap. of Jamaica 1535–1871. Pop. (est.) 12,000.

SPARK, Muriel. Scottish novelist. B. in Edinburgh, she is a convert to Catholicism, and exercises a stylish gift of enigmatic satire in *Memento Mori* (1959), and *The Prime of Miss Jean Brodie* (1961), the story of an Edinburgh school mistress.

SPARROW. Bird of the genus *Passer* in the family Fringillidae. The house S. (*P. domesticus*) is numerous in N. Europe and Asia, and is naturalized in N. America, Australia and New Zealand. The tree S. (*P. montanus*), less common in Britain, is the prevalent species in parts of Europe and in China. Rearing several families a year, the S. rapidly becomes a pest when natural enemies are few. The American Ss. are buntings.

SPARROW-HAWK. Genus (*Accipiter*) of birds in the family Falconidae. The common S. (*A. nisus*) is a woodland bird, preying on smaller birds and mammals, and so much persecuted by gamekeepers.

SPARROW-HAWK

SPARTA. Ancient Greek city state in Peloponnese, on the r. Eurotas *c.* 20 m. from the sea. The Dorians formed the ruling race, the original inhabitants being divided into perioeci, tributaries without political rights, and helots or serfs. The state was ruled by 2 hereditary kings, and under the constitution attributed to Lycurgus all citizens were trained for war from boyhood; hence the Spartans became proverbial for their indifference to pain or death, their contempt for luxury and the arts, and their harsh treatment of the helots. They distinguished themselves in the Persian and Peloponnesian wars, but in the 2nd cent. B.C. sank into insignificance.

S., the modern town founded in 1834, is cap. of Laconia nome. Pop. (1961) 7,900.

SPARTACUS (d. 71 B.C.). A Thracian gladiator, who in 73 B.C. led a revolt of gladiators and slaves at Capua. After defeating several Roman armies, he was himself defeated and killed by Crassus, and thousands of his followers were crucified. The *Spartacus League*, a German Socialist organization founded by Liebnecht in 1916 to carry on anti-war activity, in 1919 became the German Communist Party.

SPARTE. Another form of mod. SPARTA.

SPASTICS. Those suffering from cerebral palsy and who consequently have difficulty in moving their arms and legs, and sometimes in speech and swallowing, too. The condition is caused by interference with the development of the brain while it is actively growing before birth, at birth, or in the first year or so of life. It is not progressive, and good training helps to combat the extent of damage. It is more common in cases of premature birth.

SPEAKER. The title applied to the presiding officer charged with the preservation of order in the legislatures of various countries. In the U.K. the Lord Chancellor fills the office in the House of Lords; in the House of Commons Mr. Speaker is elected each parliament, usually occupying the position for considerable periods. The original appointment dates from 1377.

SPECIFIC GRAVITY. The ratio of the weight of a given volume of a substance at a given temperature to an equal volume of some standard substance, usually at the same temperature. The standard substance for liquids and solids is water, normally at 4°C or 20°C, and is therefore an abstract number independent of units. For scientific work *density*, the mass of unit volume, is preferred.

SPECIFIC HEAT. The quantity of heat required to raise unit mass of a substance by one degree. It is usually expressed in calories per deg. C per gram.

SPECTACLES. A pair of lenses fitted in a frame and worn in front of the eyes to correct or assist defective vision. They are said to have been invented in the 13th cent. by a Florentine monk. Few people found the need for S. until printing was invented, when the demand for them increased rapidly. It is not known when S. was introduced into England, but in 1629 Charles I granted a charter to the Spectacle Makers' Guild. Common defects of the eye corrected by spectacle lenses are short sight or myopia by concave (spherical) lenses, long sight or hypermetropia by convex (spherical) lenses, and astigmatism by cylindrical lenses, the direction of the axes of the cylinders being specified. Spherical and cylindrical lenses may be combined in one lens. For convenience bi-focal S. provide for correction both at a distance and for reading by combining 2 lenses of different curvatures in one piece of glass. See CONTACT LENS.

SPECTROSCOPY. A branch of physics dealing with methods of excitation, detection and study of spectra (*see* SPECTRUM), covering the complete range of electromagnetic wavelengths from radio through infra-red, visible light, ultra-violet and X-rays to gamma rays (*see* FREQUENCY SPECTRUM OF ELECTROMAGNETIC WAVES), and of arrangements in order of the energies of collections of atomic particles (electrons, neutrons, etc.). S. is of fundamental importance and wide application in academic research, industry, medicine and forensic science. It provides a rapid and accurate method of detecting, analysing and identifying minute quantities of materials non-destructively, yielding valuable information on the structure of atoms and molecules and the composition and motions of heavenly bodies.

SPECTRUM. An arrangement in order of magnitude of radiated frequencies of electromagnetic waves, or of the energies of atomic particles. The visible S. was first studied by Newton who showed in 1672 that a band of white light (sunlight) passing through a glass prism could be broken into a band of coloured light, ranging from violet through indigo, blue, green, yellow, and orange to red. Light can be regarded as electromagnetic waves and most sources emit waves of complex shape which can be broken up or 'dispersed' by suitable means, such as by a spectroscope, an instrument containing a collimator, a prism or diffraction grating, and a telescope, into a succession of individual waves arranged in order of wavelength.

There are many types of S., both emission and absorption, for radiation and particles. A few common examples may be cited: an incandescent body gives rise to a *continuous S.* where the dispersed radiation is distributed uninterruptedly over a range of wavelengths. An element gives a *line S.* - one or more bright discrete lines at characteristic intervals. Molecular gases give *band S.* in which there are groups of close-packed lines shaded in one direction of wavelength. In an *absorption* S. dark lines or spaces replace the characteristic bright lines of the absorbing medium. The *mass* S. of an element is obtained from a mass spectrograph and shows the relative proportions of its isotopes. (*See also* SPECTROSCOPY.)

SPEE (shpā), **Maximilian,** count von (1861–1914). German admiral. B. in Copenhagen, he held North Sea and Far Eastern commands before the F.W.W. S. went down with his flagship in the 1914 battle of the Falkland Islands, and the *Graf Spee* battleship was named after him.

SPEEDO'METER. Indicating instrument attached to the gear-box of a vehicle by a flexible drive to give the speed of the vehicle in miles or kilometres per hour on a dial easily visible to the driver.

SPEED RECORDS. Among human beings, the 'fastest men alive', at 17,550 m.p.h., are astronauts Yuri N. Gagarin (1961) and Walter M. Schirra (1962). On the ground, Lt.-Col. Stapp engaged in medical tests achieved 632 m.p.h. on a rocket sled, at Alamogordo, U.S.A., in 1954. By human effort alone, iceskater. Eugeniy Grischin (U.S.S.R.) has reached 28·23 m.p.h.: on foot over 100 yds. R. Hays (U.S.A., 1963), 22·47 m.p.h.; and over one mile, P. G. Snell (N.Z., 1962), 15·36 m.p.h. Among animals, the swift – fastest creature in the world – is able to fly at 70–100 m.p.h., the cheetah can attain 65 m.p.h. for short periods; the Sei whale 35 knots on the surface of the water, and other species of whale can cruise at 20 m.p.h. for up to 1,000 m.

On rail: the steam-locomotive S.R. is held by Sir Nigel Gressley's Mallard at 126 m.p.h. in 1938, but the absolute S.R. belongs to 2 French (S.N.C.F.) electric locomotives (BB 9004 and CC 7107) which on successive days in 1955 attained 205·6 m.p.h. over 1¼ m. at Morceur. Man's preoccupation with speed in motor-cars has shown itself from earliest times; Count Gaston de Chasseloup-Lanbat registering the first successful Land S.R. in 1898 near Paris, with his electric brougham, at 39·24 m.p.h. Many makes – notably Stanley, Ford, Napier, Sunbeam, Delage, Fiat – and many drivers, incl. Oldfield, Marriott, Segrave, the Campbells, Cobb and Eyston, have progressively raised speeds in the 20th cent. Until 1964, when the official world land S.R. rested with Donald Campbell at 403.1 m.p.h., conventional wheel-driven cars had to be used, but the Fédération Internationale de l'Automobile then decided to accept jet-propelled cars (though these must be steered by a driver through their wheels): Craig Breedlove (U.S.A.) reached 600.6 m.p.h. in Nov. 1965 at Bonneville, Utah, in his aircraft-shaped, three-wheeled *Spirit of America,* but Gary Gabelich raised the record to 622.4 in his *Blue Flame* 23 Oct. 1970.

Speed on water has claimed the lives of 3 eminent car drivers, Segrave, Cobb and Donald Campbell, and the record 285.2 m.p.h. was achieved on Lake Guntersville, Alabama, by Lee Taylor, jr. (U.S.A.) in 1967. Although earthbound vehicles and conventional aircraft rely mainly on jet engines to reach highest speeds, fixed-wing aircraft have progressed to rocket power, and William Knight in the North American Aviation X-15 (illus. p. 431) wrested the absolute record for winged aircraft with 4,534 m.p.h in 1967 nr. Edwards Air Force Base, Calif.

SPEENHAMLAND SYSTEM. Method of poor relief in England started by Berkshire magistrates in 1795, whereby wages were supplemented from the poor-rates. It encouraged farmers to pay low wages, however, and was superseded by the 1834 Poor Law.

SPEKE (spēk), **John Hanning** (1827–64). British explorer. B. in Somerset, he served with the Indian army and in the Crimea, and in 1856 joined Burton (whom he had previously accompanied to Somaliland) in an expedition to the African lakes. When Burton became ill, S. went on to discover the Victoria Nyanza, but his claim that it was the source of the Nile was disputed by Burton even after Speke and Grant made a 2nd expedition 1860–3 to confirm the point. He accidentally shot himself while shooting near Bath, where he was to have disputed publicly with Burton the next day.

SPELEOLOGY (Gr. *spēlaion* cave). The scientific study of caves, incl. their origin, development, physical structure, flora, fauna, folk-lore, exploration,

SPELEOLOGY. Adventuring underground sometimes has its glimpses of beauty as well as the spice of danger. This formation of stalactites and stalagmites is in the East Passage of the Gaping Gill system, Yorkshire. *Photo: W. R. Mitchell.*

surveying, photography, cave-diving, rescue work, etc. It first developed in France in the late 19th cent., where the Société de Spéléologie was founded in 1895, and in the form of 'pot-holing' – which involves following the course of underground rivers or streams – has in the 20th cent. become a popular sport. In 1963 a world underground depth record of 3,723 ft. was achieved by a British team exploring the Berger cave nr. Grenoble.

SPELLMAN, Francis Joseph (1889–1967). American R.C. churchman. B. in Mass., he was the 1st American priest to be called to service in the secretariat of state at the Vatican. In 1939 he became abp. of New York and U.S. military vicar, and cardinal 1946.

SPENBOROUGH. English manufacturing town (bor.) in the W. Riding of Yorks, 5 m. S.E. of Bradford. It makes textiles of all kinds, leather, chemicals machinery. Pop. (1961) 36,412.

SPENCE, Sir Basil (1907–). British architect. He was prof. of architecture at the Royal Academy 1961–68, and his works incl. the Univ. of Sussex, Coventry Cathedral, the British embassy in Rome, and buildings for the Festival of Britain in 1951. He was knighted in 1960 and received the O.M. in 1962.

SPENCER, Herbert (1820–1903). British philosopher. B. at Derby, he was an engineer before entering journalism. While sub-editor on *The Economist,* he wrote *Social Statics* (1851), expounding his *laissez-*

faire views on social and political problems. and in 1855 *Principles of Psychology* appeared. His *Education* (1861) is still of practical value. In the same year he began his *System of Synthetic Philosophy*, in which he applied the evolutionary principle of 'the change from homogeneity to heterogeneity' to the whole field of human knowledge. The chief of the 10 vols. are: *First Principles* (1862), and *Principles* of biology, psychology, sociology, and ethics. Other works are *The Study of Sociology*, *Man v. the State*, *Essays*, and an autobiography.

SPENCER, Sir Stanley (1891–1959). British artist. B. at Cookham-on-Thames, where he spent most of his life apart from his service in the F.W.W., he made village life there his means of interpreting the Christian faith to which he held, e.g. 'Christ Carrying the Cross' and 'Resurrection' (both in the Tate Gallery).

SIR STANLEY SPENCER
A self-portrait.

His major work is the series of mural paintings for the oratory of All Souls' at Burghclere in Berks, completed 1933. His work combines regard for detail with disregard for reality, achieving a sense of innocence. He was knighted in 1959. In 1962 the *S.P. Gallery*, devoted to his work, was opened at Cookham. His brother **Gilbert S.** (1892–) is a landscape artist.

SPENDER, Stephen (1909–). British poet, the nephew of John Alfred S. (1862–1942), editor of the Liberal *Westminster Gazette* 1896–1922. Ed. at Univ. Coll., Oxford, he founded with Cyril Connolly the magazine *Horizon* (of which he was co-editor 1939–41) and 1953–67 was co-editor of *Encounter*. His vols. of verse, characterized by introspective sensitivity, incl. *Twenty Poems* (1930), *Vienna* (1934), *The Still Centre* (1939) and *Poems of Dedication* (1946). Other works incl. the verse drama *Trial of a Judge* (1938), the autobiography *World Within World* (1951), and his joint editorship of *English and American Poets and Poetry* (1963).

SPENGLER (shpeng'ler), **Oswald** (1880–1936). German philosopher. In his *Decline of the West* (1918), and his political writings, he maintained civilization was doomed, and glorified primitive man. He was much admired by the Nazis.

SPENSER, Edmund (1552–99). English poet. B. in London, he was ed. at Cambridge, entered the service of the earl of Leicester, and in 1579 pub. *The Shepheard's Calendar*. In 1580 he became secretary to the Lord Deputy in Ireland, and at Kilcolman Castle completed the first 3 books of the great moral allegory *The Faerie Queene* (1590). He twice visited England in the vain hope of preferment at court. In 1598 Kilcolman Castle was burnt down by rebels, and S. with his family narrowly escaped. Three further books of *The Faerie Queene* were pub. in 1596, but the remaining 6 were probably lost in the fire. He d. in London, and was buried in Westminster Abbey. S.'s other works incl. the elegy on Sidney, *Astrophel* (1586); the love sonnets or *Amoretti* and the *Epithalamion* (1595); and a prose *View of the Present State of Ireland*. The modern reader is often deterred by the element of allegory, but S. remains the 'poet's poet' in his versification, richness of language, and fertile imagery.

SPERMACETI. Glistening wax-like substance, not a true oil, which is contained in the numerous cells of the huge, almost rectangular, S. 'case' in the head of the sperm whale. It was once much in demand for candles and is today used in ointments. *Sperm oil*, a mixture of sperm whale oil and S., is readily absorbed by the skin and is used in lipsticks and kin creams, and also as a lubricant for submarine

and aeroplane engines, and in the manufacture of detergents. For Sperm Whale *see* CACHALOT.

SPEYER (shpīr). Ancient city in Rhineland-Palatinate, Germany, on the Rhine, 16 m. S. of Mannheim. The name Protestant originated here, from the protests of the Lutherans to the diet of Spires, 1529. Pop. (est.) 34,000.

SPEZIA (spet'sē-ah), **La**. City of Liguria, from 1861 Italy's leading naval harbour. Shelley was drowned in the Gulf of S., 1822. Pop. (1961) 121,191.

SPHINX (sfinks). A fabulous monster, represented in Egyptian art as a lion with a man's head. It also figures in the art of Greece, Assyria, Persia, etc. The best-known example is the Great S. at Gizeh, Egypt, 189 ft. long, built *c.* 2900–2750 B.C.

SPICE ISLANDS. Old name for the MOLUCCAS.

SPICES. Aromatic vegetable substances used as condiments and for flavouring food. They are obtained from tropical plants, and include pepper, cayenne pepper, nutmeg, ginger, and cinnamon.

SPIDER. Animal of the order Arachnida – not an insect – in which the head and breast are merged to form the cephalothorax, connected to the abdomen by a characteristic narrow waist. On the under-surface of the abdomen are the spinnerets from which a viscid fluid is exuded which hardens on exposure to the air to form silky threads, used to spin webs – in which the S. nests and catches its prey – and as a safeguard against falling. Species of particular interest incl. the common garden S. (*Aranea diadema*) which spins webs of remarkable beauty; the zebra S. (*Salticus scenicus*), a longer-sighted species which stalks its prey and has pads on its feet which enable it to walk even on glass; the poisonous tarantula and black widow (qq.v.); the water S. (*Argyroneta aquatica*) which fills a 'diving bell' home with air trapped on the hairs of the body; and the largest members of the group, the bird-eating Ss. of S. America (*Mygale*),

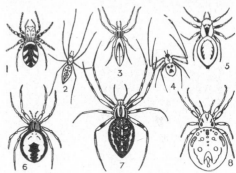

SPIDERS. 1, Salticus scenicus (zebra spider); 2, Tetragnatha solandrii; 3, Tibellus oblongus; 4, Ero theoracica; 5, Evarcha falcata; 6, Araneus pyramidatus; 7, Araneus diadematus (garden spider); 8, Araneus quadratus.

with bodies *c.* 2 in. long and a leg-span of a foot. Ss. are generally useful to man in their destruction of harmful insects and an acre of English grassland may contain *c.* 2¼ million.

SPI'KENARD. Perennial herb (*Nardostachys jatamansi*), of the family Valerianaceae, also called nard, the source of a famous perfume used in ointments by eastern peoples and the Romans.

SPILLANE, Mickey (1918–). American writer. B. in Brooklyn, N.J., he began by writing for pulp magazines and became known for violent crime novels featuring Mike Hammer, the 'one-man police force', e.g. *Vengeance is Mine* and *The Long Wait*.

SPILSBURY, Sir Bernard Henry (1877–1947). British authority on forensic medicine. Home Office pathologist for 25 years, he was remarkable for his success in using modern scientific methods for the solution of murders, especially in poisoning cases.

SPINACH (spin'ej). Annual plant (*Spinacia oleracea*) in the family Chenopodiaceae. A native of Asia, it is cultivated for its leaves which are used as a vegetable, especially in the U.S.A.

SPINE. The backbone. It contains 26 bones called vertebrae, including the sacrum and coccyx. The vertebra has a semicircular, thick rounded body at the front to take weight, a bony ring behind through which passes the spinal cord, and 3 projections of bone (processes), one on each side and one to the rear. The lowest part of the S. is the sacrum, a broad triangular structure consisting of 5 rudimentary vertebrae fused together, jointed to the hip bones and ending in the tail bone (coccyx), which consists of 4 fused vertebrae. The S. in man has four curves (front to rear), which allow for increased size of chest and pelvic cavities; also permit springing, to minimize jolting of internal organs.

SPI'NEL. A group of minerals possessing cubic symmetry and consisting chiefly of magnesia and alumina. The alumina S. contain the gem varieties, such as the ruby, and occur in Ceylon and Burma.

SPINET. A keyboard instrument, smaller than a harpsichord, and distinguished from the larger instrument by having only one string for each note.

SPINNING. The art of drawing out and twisting fibres into threads, by hand or machinery. The simplest method of S. is by distaff (a stick holding the raw wool), and spindle (the wooden implement used in drawing out the thread): the S. wheel was a later

SPINNING. Traditionally spinning is women's work, but men cope very satisfactorily with the new ring frames installed at the Bee Hive Spinning Co. works at Bolton as part of the cotton industry's post-war modernization.
Courtesy of The Cotton Board, Manchester.

device which revolved the spindle, often by means of a treadle-operated flywheel. In the late 18th cent. mechanization of S. was effected. Hargreaves' S. jenny allowed many threads to be drawn at the same time; Arkwright used Lewis Paul's device for superseding the human hand by rollers in drawing out the thread; and Crompton combined the principles of Hargreaves and Arkwright in his mule-spinner.

SPINOZA (spinō'zah), **Benedict** (or **Baruch**) (1632–77). Dutch philosopher. B. at Amsterdam of Portuguese-Jewish stock, he abandoned Judaism for a rationalistic pantheism that owed much to Descartes. He taught that all that we know, mind and matter, is a manifestation of the all-embracing substance that is God. Persecuted by the Jews, he had to leave Amsterdam and finally settled at The Hague, where he made a living by polishing optical glasses. An

exposition of the Cartesian philosophy and *Tractatus Theologico-Politicus*, the first rationalist critique of the Bible, were pub. during his life, but his greatest work, the *Ethics*, appeared in 1677.

SPIRAEA. Genus of herbaceous plants and shrubs in the family Rosaceae which incl. meadow sweet (*S. salicifolia*): there are many cultivated species with ornamental cymes of flowers.

SPIRES. French form of SPEYER.

SPIRITS OF SALTS. *See* HYDROCHLORIC ACID.

SPIRITUALISM. A belief in the survival of the human personality and in communication between the living and those who have 'passed on'. The spiritualist movement originated in America in 1848. In England the Society for Psychical Research was founded in 1882 by W. H. Myers and Henry Sidgwick to investigate the claims of S. Famous spiritualists incl. D. D. Home, Sir William Crookes, Sir Oliver Lodge, Sir A. Conan Doyle, and Lord Dowding.

SPITHEAD. An anchorage in the Solent, off Portsmouth, England. The name is often applied to the whole of the eastern arm of the Solent (q.v.).

SPITSBERGEN. Group of Norwegian islands in the Arctic Ocean 300 m. E. of Greenland. The 4 main islands are West S., North East Land, Edge Island, and Barents Island; Hope Island and Bear Island are attached to S., which is heavily glaciated. Coal is mined by Norway and Russia. A telemetry station for tracking artificial satelites was estab. 1965. Area 24,000 sq. m.; pop. (1966) 3,000.

SPITTELER (shpit'eler), **Carl Friedrich Georg** (1845–1924). Swiss author. B. near Basle, he was a private tutor in Russia 1871–9, becoming a journalist on returning to Switzerland. In 1919 he was awarded the Nobel prize. His works incl. the prose epic *Prometheus und Epimetheus*, the epic poem *Der Olympische Frühling*, and the autobiography *Meine frühesten Erlebnisse*.

SPITZ DOG. *See* POMERANIAN.

SPLEEN. An organ about 5 in. by 3 in., situated under the diaphragm on the left of the body. Its function is not well known, but is in part concerned with the production and destruction of blood cells.

SPLIT. Yugoslav port and tourist centre, on the Adriatic, founded by Diocletian *c.* A.D. 300. It manufactures cement. Pop. (1961) 99,614.

SPOCK, Benjamin McLane (1903–). American child-care expert, prof. of child development at Western Reserve univ. 1955–67. Himself a father of 2 sons, he writes, as in *Problems of Parents* (1963) of the family as a balanced whole.

SPODE (spōd), **Josiah** (1754–1827). British potter. Son of Josiah S., who had been an apprentice of Thomas Whieldon, and started his own works at Stoke-on-Trent in 1770, he succeeded him in 1797. He was responsible for developing bone porcelain (bone ash, china stone and china clay) *c.* 1800, which was produced at all English factories in the 19th cent., and became potter to George III in 1806.

SPOHR (shpohr), **Ludwig** (1784–1859). German composer and violinist. B. at Brunswick, he was court choirmaster at Cassel 1822–57. His works incl. operas, symphonies, the oratorios *Calvary* and *The Last Judgment*, and chamber music.

SPOKANE (spōkan'). City of Washington, U.S.A., at the falls of the S. river, which are harnessed for its many industries. It is the centre of a lumbering and mining region and the seat of Gonzaga univ. Pop. (1960) 181,608.

SPOLETO. Ancient town in Perugia, Umbria, Italy, of great architectural interest, a papal possession 1220–1860. Pop. (est.) 38,000.

SPONGES. Many-celled animals forming the subkingdom Porifera. A simple sponge is vase-shaped, supported by three-rayed spicules. There is a constant flow of water through the pores of the sponge, leaving again by the oscule, or opening at the top. The more complex Ss. are colonized, the body cavity being lined with cells which absorb nutritious material in the water, or have reproductive functions. Ss. are classified according to the chemical nature and arrangement of the spicules into Calcareous Ss., Glass Ss., Common Ss., Four-rayed Ss., Fleshy Ss., Single-rayed Ss., and Horny Ss. Most Ss., are marine, but some are found in fresh water. The toilet S. is the prepared skeleton of a colony.

SPONTI'NI, Gasparo Luigi Pacifico (1774–1851). Italian composer. B. in Ancona, he spent many years in Paris and Berlin and is best known for his operas, *La Vestale* and *Agnes von Hohenstaufen.*

SPOONBILL. A family of birds, Plataleidae, characterized by their long, flat bills, dilated at the tip in the shape of a spoon.

SPOONER, William Archibald (1844–1930). British scholar. Warden of New Coll., Oxon, 1903–24, he was famed for lapses of the tongue, e.g. 'Kinquering congs their titles take'. These were exaggerated by repute, and similar errors became known as Spoonerisms.

SPORADES (spor'adēz). Alternative name for the Dodecanese (q.v.).

SPORE. The one-celled reproductive body of Cryptogams or flowerless plants. They are generally light enough to be carried by the wind. Under certain conditions they are produced by bacteria.

SPOROZOA. A large division of unicellular parasitic protozoa. They readily produce reproductive spores which are transmitted from one host to another. Many of them cause serious diseases, such as malaria and sleeping sickness.

SPRAIN. An injury to ligaments or tendons round a joint without dislocation. Its usual cause is a wrench or twist.

SPRAT. European fish (*Clupea sprattus*) of the herring family. The full-grown S. is about 4 in. long, and occurs in large numbers in British seas.

SPRING, Howard (1889–1965). British author. B. in Cardiff, he became a journalist and critic, and estab. his reputation as a novelist with *Shabby Tiger* (1934), *My Son, My Son!* (1938), *Fame is the Spur* (1940), *The Houses in Between* (1951), and *I Met a Lady* (1961). His autobiographical vols. incl. *Heaven Lies About Us* (1939).

SPRINGBOK. Species of S. African antelope (*Gazella euchore*), about 30 in. high and with black, lyrate horns. The coat is tawny, but a stripe of white, erectile hair runs down the middle of the back and the underparts are also white. The name derives from the animal's sudden leaps in the air. It is the national emblem of S. Africa, and her national football team and her soldiers are known as Ss.

SPRINGBOK. Remarkable for its periodic migrations, the springbok formerly occurred in such numbers that the herds might be half a mile across and take several hours to pass a given point. This specimen is in the Etosha Pan Game Reserve in S.W. Africa.
Courtesy of Satour.

SPRINGFIELD. Name of a number of places in the U.S.A., the chief of which are: (1) Cap. of Ill., on the Sangamon, 17 m. S.W. of Chicago. It was the home of Abraham Lincoln 1837–61, and is a manufacturing and agricultural centre, with bituminous coal mines in the vicinity. Pop. (1960) 83,271. (2) City of Mass., on the Connecticut; settled in 1636, it has many industries. Pop. (1960) 174,463. (3) City of Mo., an agricultural centre founded 1830. Pop. (1960) 95,865. (4) City of Ohio, 22 m. E.N.E. of Dayton. Founded 1799, it has heavy industry, and

makes leather goods, paper products, measuring instruments, etc. Pop. (1960) 82,723.

SPRING-TAILS or **Collembola.** Order of wingless insects, belonging to the section Apterygota, commonly known as Ss., from their having the cerci on the abdomen modified into a forked organ which enables the insect to jump. Widely distributed, they may feed on decaying vegetable matter or (in some species) on the living plant.

SPRUCE. Coniferous trees in the genera *Picea* and *Tsuga.* The Norway S. (*P. excelsa*) and the hemlock S. (*T. canadensis*) are important timber-trees.

SPURGE. Genus of trees and shrubs in the family Euphorbiaceae. Many have fleshy leaves and a milky juice.

SPURGEON, Charles Haddon (1834–92). British Nonconformist. A pastor at 18, he was renowned as a preacher, and was minister of the Metropolitan (S.'s) Tabernacle, specially built for him in London, from 1861: his sermons sold in enormous quantities.

SPRUCE

SPURN HEAD. Promontory on the Yorkshire coast, England, forming the N. shore of the Humber estuary.

SPURS, Battle of the. Victory won by Henry VIII at Guinegate, N.W. France, in 1513; the name recalls the speed of the French retreat.

SPY. *See* SECRET SERVICE.

SQUASH. *See* PUMPKIN.

SQUASH RACKETS. *See* RACKETS.

SQUID. Group of marine cephalopod molluscs. The common S. (*Loligo vulgaris*) of the Mediterranean extends in the Atlantic to British waters: the 2 long tentacles are used to seize its prey and the 8 smaller to hold it while feeding. Origin of many tales of sea monsters in the N. Atlantic is the giant S. (*Architeuthis princeps*) which may reach a total length of 50 ft. The flying S. (*Ommastrephes bartrami*) leaps on the surface rather than flies. A number of species carry light organs at certain points on the body and produce striking phosphorescent effects.

SQUIRE, Sir John Collings (1884–1958). British poet. Founder-editor of the *London Mercury* 1919–34, he was knighted in 1933, and as one of the Georgian poets pub. vols. of pleasing verse, incl. such excellent parodies as *Steps to Parnassus* (1913).

SQUIRE or **Esquire.** Originally a young man training for knighthood, who acted as attendant on a knight. From the later Middle Ages the term was loosely applied to a rank between those of knight and gentleman; hence, 'esquire' is used in England after the surname on letters, etc., purely as a courtesy title.

SQUIRREL. Family of rodents (Sciuridae). The common or red S. (*Sciurus vulgaris*) occurs throughout Europe and northern Asia: the fur is a rich red, and the tail handsomely bushy. Omnivorous, it rears its young in nests or 'dreys', and although less active in winter, when it relies for food mainly on stores of nuts, etc., made in the summer, does not hibernate. In Britain the red S. has been almost entirely superseded by the larger

FLYING SQUID

grey S. (*S. carolinensis*) introduced from N. Amer.

SRI LANKA. *See* CEYLON.

SRINAGAR (srinug´-ger). Cap. of Jammu and Kashmir, on the Jhelum, a beautiful city and resort intersected by waterways. It makes carpets, papier mâché, leather goods, etc. Pop. (1961) 285,257.

S.S. (Ger. *Schutz-Staffel*, 'protective squadron'). Nazi élite corps, organized in 1928. Under Himmler's command it reached 500,000, incl. both full-time members (*Waffen-S.S.*, 'armed S.S.'), who fought in the S.W.W., and spare-time members. It carried out police duties, and became infamous for its share in the persecution of the Jews, the brutalities of the concentration camps, and the administration of occupied territories. The Nuremberg court condemned it in 1946.

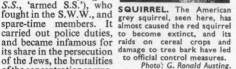

SQUIRREL. The American grey squirrel, seen here, has almost caused the red squirrel to become extinct, and its raids on cereal crops and damage to tree bark have led to official control measures.
Photo: G. Ronald Austing.

STABILIZERS. Fins fitted to the sides of a ship and governed automatically by gyro mechanism, which can reduce a 30° side-to-side roll to 3°.

STABROEK. Dutch name of Georgetown, Brit. Guiana.

STAËL (stahl), **Anne Louise Germaine de** (1766–1817). French author. B. in Paris, the dau. of the financier Jacques Necker, she m. the baron de S. in 1786. An ardent advocate of political freedom, she was banished from Paris by Napoleon, but gathered round her at Coppet on Lake Geneva men such as A. W. von Schlegel, Byron, and Benjamin Constant. Her relationship with the last-named inspired her novels *Delphine* and *Corinne*. Her most influential work was *De l'Allemagne* (1810), which revealed to France the richness of German literature.

STAFFA. Uninhabited island of the Inner Hebrides, Argyllshire, Scotland, 54 m. W. of Oban, with remarkable caves.

STAFFORD. Co. town (bor.) of Staffs, England, 23 m. N.W. of Birmingham. Boots and shoes are manufactured. Pop. (1961) 47,814.

STAFFORDSHIRE. Midland county of England. Apart from hills in the extreme N. and S. it is flat, being the vale of the Trent and its tributaries. The North and South S. coalfields support 2 important industrial areas: in the S. the Black Country between Birmingham and Wolverhampton, with a variety of industries including iron and steel works; and in the N. the Potteries round Stoke-on-Trent. Stafford is the co. town. Area 1,157 sq. m.; pop. (1967) 1,820,890.

STAGHOUND. Breed of dog used for hunting stags. The old English S. was a type of bloodhound, but now a large foxhound is given the name.

STAINED GLASS. Term applied to the coloured transparent glass which is cut into various shapes and joined by lead strips to form a pictorial window design. The art is said to have originated in the Near East. At first it was usual for only one monumental figure to be represented on each window, but by the middle of the 12th cent. incidents in the life of Christ or of one of the saints were commonly depicted. Some of the most beautiful examples of medieval S.G. are to be found in the cathedrals of Canterbury, Lincoln, Chartres, Cologne, and Rouen. Modern designers incl. Morris, Burne-Jones, and James Hogan. Since the S.W.W. the 6th cent. use of thick, faceted glass joined by cement has been revived. *See* illus. p. 2.

STAINER, Sir John (1840–1901). British organist and composer. B. in London, he became organist of St. Paul's in 1872, receiving a knighthood on his resignation in 1888, was a prof. from 1876 (principal from 1881) at the National Training School for Music (now Royal College of Music), and prof. of music at Oxford 1889–99. Most notable among his religious choral works are *The Crucifixion*, an oratorio, and *The Daughter of Jairus*, a cantata.

STAIR, James Dalrymple, 1st visct. S. (1619–95). Scottish statesman. As president of the Court of Session his moderation brought him into disfavour, and in 1682 he fled to Holland, but returned to office with William of Orange, who created him visct. S. His *Institutions of the Law of Scotland* (1681) is a classic on jurisprudence.

STALACTITE and **STALAGMITE.** A deposit of lime formed in caves by the downward trickling of water containing carbonate of lime. Stalactites are those hanging from the roof, and stalagmites those accumulated on the floor. *See* illus. p. 990.

STALIN ('steel'). Adopted name of Soviet statesman **Joseph Vissarionovich Djugashvili** (1879–1953). B. at Gori, near Tiflis, the son of a Georgian shoemaker, he was ed. for the priesthood, but was expelled from his seminary for carrying on Marxist propaganda. He joined the Social Democratic Party in 1898, and was exiled to Siberia 5 times 1903–12, but on each occasion escaped and resumed his revolutionary activities. By 1913 he was editing *Pravda* and directing the Bolshevik group in the Duma, while his book, *The National and Colonial Question*, attracted Lenin's attention. From 1913 until the revolution of March 1917 he was an exile in Siberia. He then became a member of the Communist Party's political bureau, and sat on the committee which directed the Nov. revolution. Appointed Commissar for Nationalities in the Soviet govt. he was responsible for the decree granting equal rights to all peoples of the Russian Empire. During the civil wars he held various commands, and distinguished himself by his defence of Tsaritsin (now Volgograd) against the 'Whites'. He was appointed gen. sec. of the Communist Party in 1922. Lenin's death in 1924 was followed by prolonged controversies within the party between S., who advocated the industrialization of Russia and the construction of a fully Socialist society, and Trotsky, who denied the possibility of Socialism inside Russia until revolution had occurred in western Europe. S.'s policy was finally accepted in 1927, and was put into operation from 1928 onwards in the five-year plans. The constitution of 1936 was largely his work. S. held no govt. post until 1941, when he became chairman of the Council of People's

STAINED GLASS. A section of the concreted stained-glass panel designed by Pierre Fourmaintraux for the church of St. Raphael, Stalybridge. Tobias sets out on his journey (left), with his little dog, and under the guidance of a strange youth (the angel Raphael) catches the fish which brings him a bride and cures his father's blindness.
Courtesy of Whitefriars Stained Glass Studios.

Commissars, a position equivalent to P.M. He was largely responsible for Soviet strategy during the S.W.W., and received the rank of marshal of the Soviet Union in 1943, and that of generalissimo in 1945. He met Churchill and Roosevelt at Tehran in 1943 and at Yalta in 1945, and took part in the Potsdam conference. His writings incl. *Foundations of Leninism* and *Dialectical and Historical Materialism*. After his death his 'cult of personality' and the harshness of his one-man rule were condemned. By his 2nd wife, Nadezhda Alliluyeva, S. had a dau. **Svetlana** (1925–), who left Russia 1967 and pub. memories of her father in *Twenty Letters to a Friend* (1967).

STALINGRAD. See VOLGOGRAD.

STAMBOUL. See ISTANBUL.

STAMP. See PHILATELY and POST OFFICE.

STANDARD. See FLAG.

STANFORD, Sir Charles Villiers (1852–1924). Irish composer. As prof. of composition and orchestral playing at the R.C.M. from 1882 and of music at Cambridge from 1887, he taught John Ireland, Eugene Goossens, Vaughan Williams, Gustav Holst, etc. His own works are little performed.

STANHOPE (stan'op), **Lady Hester** (1776–1839). British traveller. Niece to William Pitt, she acted as his private sec., but on his death left England and eventually settled in the Lebanon nr. Sidon, where she held sway over the local tribes: Kinglake (q.v.) was entertained by her, as described in *Eothen*.

STANISLAVSKY, Constantine (1863–1938). Stagename of the Russian actor-producer Constantine Alexeev. B. in Moscow, he was a founder of the Moscow Art Theatre and excelled as the interpreter of Chekhov and Gorky. His 'method', expressed in *My Life in Art* (1934) and other books, has had an immense influence on modern acting.

STANLEY. See DERBY, EARL OF.

STANLEY, Arthur Penrhyn (1815–81). British Anglican churchman. B. in Cheshire, he was a leader of the Broad Church movement, and was prof. of ecclesiastical history at Oxford 1856–63, when he became dean of Westminster.

STANLEY, Sir Henry Morton (1841–1904). British explorer. B. at Denbigh, reared in a workhouse, and adopted by a cotton broker named S.; he went to New Orleans in 1859, was appointed correspondent for the *New York Herald* in 1867, and was commissioned by Gordon Bennett to go to Africa to find Livingstone. He arrived at Zanzibar in 1871, met Livingstone at Ujiji, and together they explored the N. end of Lake Tanganyika. His book, *How I Found Livingstone* (1872), was a best-seller. He later traced the course of the Congo to the sea, and in 1879 founded the Congo Free State.

STANLEY. Cap. of the Falkland Islands, S. Atlantic, at the extreme E. of the group. Pop. (1962) 1,074.

STAR. A globe of extremely hot gas, radiating because of nuclear processes taking place inside it. The Sun, which is an average star, has a surface temperature of 6,000°C., and a central temperature of between 12,000,000° and 15,000,000°C.; it is at least 6,000 million years old, and will continue radiating in its present form for several thousands of millions of years to come. However, many Ss. are known to be much more luminous than the Sun: S. Doradûs, in the southern hemisphere, is equal to at least one million Suns, and yet is so remote that it cannot be seen without a telescope. Even the nearest S., Proxima Centauri, is more than 4 light-years (roughly 25 million million miles) away. The Ss. are of different types, and are divided broadly into Giant and Dwarf branches; the Sun is classed as a dwarf. No telescope yet constructed will show a S. as anything but a point of light, and our knowledge of them is gained from studies carried out with instruments based upon the principle of the spectroscope. It is thought that many Ss. may well have planetary systems essentially similar to our own Solar System, though direct proof is lacking at present. *See* charts pp. 996–8.

STARFISH

STARCH. A widely distributed carbohydrate, that occurs in granular form in cereals and pulses, fruits of leguminous plants, and potato tubers. Separation is achieved by macerating potatoes, and fermenting grains. The white powder is then subjected to chemical processes which suit it for use as a stiffener in the textile, paper, and laundering industries.

STAR CHAMBER. Tribunal consisting of members of the king's council which met in an apartment of Westminster Palace, which had a starred ceiling. Under the Tudors it dealt with offenders strong enough to defy the ordinary courts, and was generally respected for its speedy administration of justice. Its harsh persecution of Puritans under Charles I made it unpopular, and in 1641 it was abolished.

STAR CLUSTER. A group of stars, much more closely crowded than is usual in the Galaxy. Cs. may be 'loose' or 'open', such as the Pleiades (Seven Sisters), or 'globular', such as Omega Centauri. Among famous naked-eye open clusters are the Pleiades (q.v.), the Hyades, and Praesepe. Large numbers of telescopic clusters are known.

STAR-FISHES. Class of echinoderms, Asteroidea. The body is extended into 5 arms, and is covered with spines and small pincer-like organs. There are also a number of small tubular processes on the skin surface which assist in respiration, and small tube-feet sometimes with suckers at the end. The poisonous and predatory 'crown of thorns' S. of the Pacific, once rare, multiplied disastrously from 1960, destroying large areas of coral reef, e.g. 100 sq. m. of Australia's Great Barrier Reef in less than 10 years and a large section off the coast of Guam.

STARK, Dame Freya (1893–). Brit. traveller, author of many notable books on Arab countries and their people incl. *Baghdad Sketches* (1933), and the autobiographical *Travellers' Prelude* (1950) and *Dust in the Lion's Paw* (1961). She m. in 1947 the orientalist and historian Stewart Perowne.

STARLING. Bird (*Sturnus vulgaris*) common in N. Europe and Asia and naturalized in N. America from the late 19th cent. The black, speckled plumage is

STARLING. The short square tail, large feet and pointed wings of the starling make it easily recognizable in the air.   *Photo: G. Ronald Austing.*

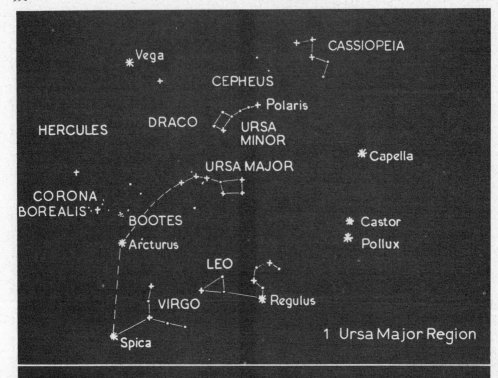

1 Ursa Major Region

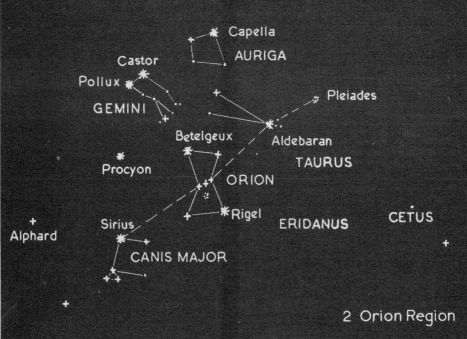

2 Orion Region

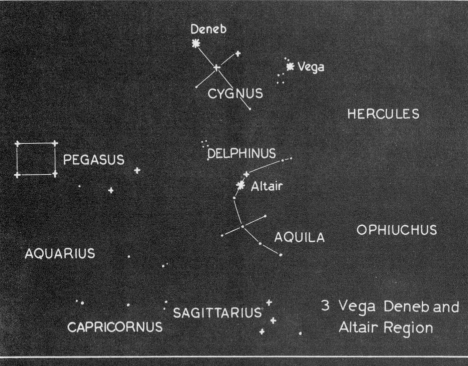

Deneb

Vega

CYGNUS

HERCULES

PEGASUS

DELPHINUS

Altair

AQUILA

OPHIUCHUS

AQUARIUS

SAGITTARIUS

CAPRICORNUS

3 Vega Deneb and Altair Region

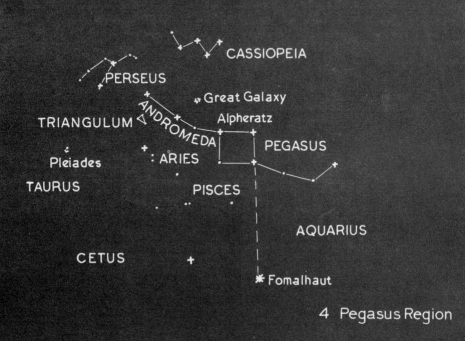

CASSIOPEIA

PERSEUS

Great Galaxy

TRIANGULUM

ANDROMEDA

Alpheratz

PEGASUS

Pleiades

ARIES

TAURUS

PISCES

AQUARIUS

CETUS

Fomalhaut

4 Pegasus Region

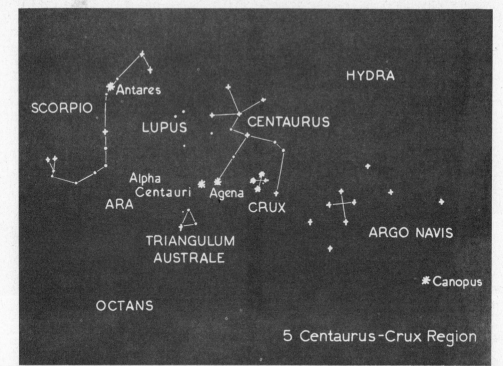

SCORPIO

HYDRA

Antares

LUPUS

CENTAURUS

Alpha
Centauri

Agena

ARA

CRUX

ARGO NAVIS

TRIANGULUM
AUSTRALE

Canopus

OCTANS

5 Centaurus-Crux Region

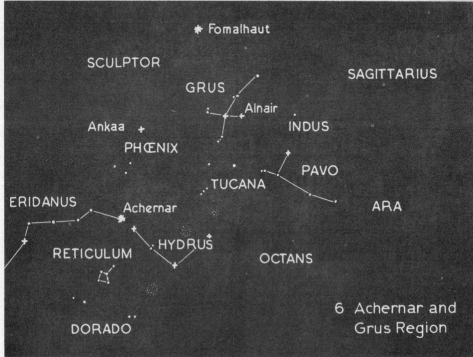

Fomalhaut

SCULPTOR

SAGITTARIUS

GRUS

Alnair

INDUS

Ankaa

PHŒNIX

PAVO

TUCANA

ERIDANUS

Achernar

ARA

RETICULUM

HYDRUS

OCTANS

DORADO

6 Achernar and
Grus Region

glossed with green and purple. Its own call is a bright whistle, but it is a mimic of the songs of other birds. Strikingly gregarious in feeding, flight and roosting, it often becomes a pest in large cities, e.g. London, where it becomes attached to certain buildings as 'dormitories', returning each night from omnivorous foraging in the countryside.

STASSEN, Harold Edward (1907–). American Republican politician. B. in Minnesota, he was admitted to the Bar there in 1929, and was governor 1939–43. In 1948 and 1952 he was candidate for the Republican nomination for the presidency, was director Foreign Operations Admin. 1953–5, and special assistant to Eisenhower for disarmament 1955–8.

STASSFURT (shtahs'foort). Town of Magdeburg dist., E. Germany, 18 m. S. of Magdeburg, famous for its salt beds. Pop. (est.) 29,000.

STATE DEPARTMENT. *See* FOREIGN RELATIONS.

STATEN (stat'n) **ISLAND.** Island in New York harbour, U.S.A., constituting the bor. of Richmond. Pop. (1960) 221,991.

STATIC ELECTRICITY. Electric charge acquired by a body by means of electrostatic induction or friction. Its effects are due to the electrostatic forces produced by the charge. Separation of electric charge is often brought about in everyday life by rubbing different materials together, and this is rendered visible by the sparks produced on combing one's hair in the dark or removing a nylon vest. S.E. produces serious effects in many industries, e.g. in printing works where measures have to be taken to discharge the S.E. to prevent papers sticking together. In other processes S.E. is useful as in paint spraying where the parts to be sprayed are charged with electricity of opposite sign to that on the paint droplets, and in xerography (q.v.).

STATICS. The branch of mechanics concerned with the behaviour of bodies at rest and forces in equilibrium, and distinguished from dynamics.

STATIONERY OFFICE, H.M. An office estab. in 1786 to supply books, stationery, etc., to British govt. depts., and to superintend the printing of govt. reports, etc., and books and pamphlets in an increasingly wide field from national works of art to industrial and agricultural processes. The corresponding estab. in the U.S.A. is the Govt. Printing Office.

STATIONS OF THE CROSS. A series of pictures or images, usually 14, depicting the closing scenes of the Passion of Christ.

STAUDINGER (stow'dinge), **Hermann** (1881–1965). German scientist. Prof. of organic chemistry at Freiburg 1926–51, he founded macro-molecular chemistry by researches into the structure of albumen, cellulose, and rubber, and was awarded a Nobel prize 1953.

STAVA'NGER. Fishing port of S.W. Norway, with shipbuilding, fish canning, soap making, and other industries. Pop. (1967) 79,700.

STAVISKY CASE. French financial scandal. Alexandre S. (1866–1934), made a large fortune by floating fraudulent companies and selling forged bonds, and became owner of several newspapers. When in 1933 his activities were revealed he committed suicide. The discovery that a member of the Chautemps govt. was involved led to the govt.'s fall and the Fascist riots of Feb. 1934.

STEAM. A dry, invisible gas formed by vaporizing water. The visible cloud which normally forms in the air when water is vaporized is due to minute suspended water particles. In this state it is called wet S. The 'saturation temperature' is the temperature at which droplets begin to form from water vapour. S. is widely used in chemical and other industrial processes and for the generation of power.

STEAM ENGINE. A machine which uses steam as the working agent in order to convert heat energy into mechanical work. An account of a S.E. was pub.

by the marquis of Worcester in 1663, and a Frenchman, Papin, described what was unquestionably the first cylinder and piston engine in 1690. Captain Savery patented an engine in 1698. The S.E. was later improved by Newcomen, Beighton, and others, but it remained imperfect until James Watt introduced the separate condenser and air-pump, patented in 1769, and made various other improvements. Richard Trevithick invented the first steam-propelled vehicle in 1801. George Stephenson successfully applied the S.E. to locomotives in 1829 and in 1802 William Symington built the first steamboat, a pioneer attempt which was followed up by Robert Fulton and Henry Bell.

STEA'RIC ACID ($C_{17}H_{35}COOH$). A saturated fatty acid, soluble in alcohol and ether, but not water. When pure, it is colourless and waxy.

STE'ARIN ($C_{17}H_{35}COO$)$_3$.C_3H_5. The name given to the solid first separated on the cooling of many liquid fats or oils; to a mixture of stearic and palmitic acid; and to glycerides of stearic acid.

STE'ATITE. A hydrous magnesium silicate, usually occurring in beds of metamorphosed serpentine. A massive form of talc, it has a greasy feeling, accounting for its other name, soapstone.

STEBARK. Polish name of TANNENBERG.

STEED (sted), **Henry Wickham** (1871–1956). British journalist. Foreign correspondent for *The Times* in Vienna 1902–13, he was then foreign editor 1914–19 and editor 1919–22. Owner-editor of the *Review of Reviews* 1923–30, he lectured on central European history at King's Coll., London, 1925–38, and pub. *The Hapsburg Monarchy* (1913), studies of Baldwin and Hitler, *The Press* (1938), etc.

STEEL. Iron containing from 0·1 per cent–1·5 per cent carbon. Mild S., which is used for general structural work, and medium carbon S., used for rails, axles, etc., were formerly made by the Bessemer process (invented in 1856), and subsequently by the open-hearth process of Siemens and Martin (perfected 1864–7). The most recent development in steel making is the expanding use of pneumatic processes for the production of low and medium carbon Ss., mainly the Austrian L.D. and the Swedish Kaldo processes. High carbon Ss., used in cutting tools, etc., are made by electric-arc processes which allow precise control during the refining period, whilst the exceptionally high-alloy Ss. such as high-speed Ss. are melted by induction furnaces.

The mechanical properties of S. can be varied enormously by heat treatment and alloy additions. When special properties such as corrosion resistance (stainless Ss.), wear resistance, high tensile properties, etc., are required, suitable quantities of nickel, chromium, molybdenum, manganese, tungsten, vanadium, etc., are added. *See* illus. p. 1000.

STEELE, Sir Richard (1672–1729). Irish essayist. B. in Dublin, he entered the guards, and then settled in London, and originated *The Tatler* (1709–11), in which Addison collaborated. They continued their joint work in *The Spectator* (1711–12), and *The Guardian* (1713). He also wrote plays, e.g. *The Conscious Lovers* (1722). He was knighted in 1715.

STEEN (stän), **Jan** (1626–79). Dutch painter. B. at Leiden, he painted genre pictures from all walks of life e.g. 'The Music Master', and 'Tavern Company'.

STEEN, Marguerite (1894–). British author. She taught dancing, then acted for 3 years with Fred Terry, an experience which paved the way for her biographical *A Pride of Terrys* (1962). Her novels incl. *Matador* (1934: dramatized in collaboration with Matheson Lang in 1936), *The Sun is My Undoing* (1941), and *The Woman in the Back Seat* (1959).

STEEPLECHASE. *See* HORSE-RACING.

STEER, Philip Wilson (1860–1942). British artist. B. at Birkenhead, he studied in Paris, and was influenced by the Impressionists, becoming a leader (with Sickert) of the English movement A founder

STEEL. One of the largest integrated iron and steel works in Europe, the Spencer Works on the marshland at Llanwern, Monmouthshire, was opened in 1962. Features to be noted are: 1, coal stocks; 2, coal-blending bunkers; 3, coke ovens; 4, gasholders; 5, sinter plant; 6, limestone, breeze and boiler coal stocks; 7, cooling towers (a medieval waterway runs at their feet); 8, power plant; 9, blast furnaces; 10, steel plant; 11, hot mill; 12, oxygen plant; 13, hot sheet finishing; 14, central engineering workshop; 15, cold mill.

Courtesy of Richard Thomas and Baldwins.

member of the New English Art Club, he had a delicately sharp individualized style in his landscapes and portraits, e.g. 'The Beach at Walberswick' (Tate Gallery). In 1931 he was awarded the O.M.

STEIN (shtīn), **Sir Aurel** (1862–1943). British archaeologist. B. in Budapest, he carried out archaeological explorations in central Asia, China, India, and the Middle East. In 1910 he was appointed superintendent of the Indian Archaeological Survey. He became a British subject, and was knighted in 1912.

STEIN (stīn), **Gertrude** (1874–1946). American author. B. in Pennsylvania, she studied medicine, and in 1904 went to Paris, where she became acquainted with Picasso. In her work she adopted a cinematic technique, using repetition, absence of punctuation, etc., to convey instantaneous continuity. Her works incl. the self-portrait, *Autobiography of Alice B. Toklas* (1933), *Paris France* (1940), and *Wars I Have Seen* (1946).

STEIN (shtīn), **Heinrich Friedrich Karl**, baron vom (1757–1831). Prussian statesman and patriot, who as chief minister 1807–8 introduced sweeping reforms, was exiled by Napoleon in 1808, helped to establish the Russo-Prussian alliance against Napoleon, and founded the *Monumenta Germaniae Historica*.

STEINBECK, **John Ernst** (1902–68). American novelist. B. in California, he first achieved success with *Tortilla Flat* (1935), a humorous study of the lives of Monterey *paisanos*, following this with *In Dubious Battle* (1936), dealing with the brutal development of a strike by migrant fruit pickers; *Of Mice and*

Men (1937), a compassionate vignette of 2 migrant farm labourers, one a feeble-minded giant, which was dramatized by the author and also filmed; and *The Grapes of Wrath* (1939), the saga of a farming family, refugees from the Oklahoma 'dust bowl', who struggle vainly against the inequitable conditions of the California they once regarded as their 'Promised Land'. Later books incl. *Cannery Row* (1944), *East of Eden* (1952), and *Winter of our Discontent* (1961). In 1962 S. was awarded a Nobel prize.

STEINER (shtīner), **Rudolf** (1861–1925). Austrian philosopher. B. in Austria, he became leader of the German theosophists, but broke with them and developed his own teaching, known as 'Anthroposophy'. His school, the Goetheanum, near Basle, was destroyed by fire in 1922, but has since been rebuilt.

STEINWAY (shtīnwā), **Henry Engelhard** (1797–1871). German piano manufacturer. He founded a factory in Germany, emigrated to U.S. in 1849 and estab. a firm there (1853).

STELLENBOSCH (-bos). Town of Cape Prov., S. Africa, 31 m. E. of Capetown, centre of a wine-producing dist., seat of a univ. (1918), and, next to Capetown, oldest European settlement in S.A. (1679). Pop. (1960) 22,233 (10,673 white).

STENDHAL (stoṅdahl'). Pseudonym of French novelist Marie Henri Beyle (1783–1842). B. in Grenoble, he served in Napoleon's armies, taking part in the ill-fated Russian campaign, and, failing in his hopes of becoming a prefect, lived in Italy from 1814 until suspicion of espionage drove him back to Paris in 1821, where he lived by literary hackwork. The reputation of his novels *Le Rouge et le Noir* (1830) and *La Chartreuse de Parme* (1839), pioneer in their psychological subtlety, began with a review of the latter by Balzac in 1840. From 1830 he was a member of the consular service, spending his leaves in Paris.

STEPHEN (*c.* 1097–1154). King of England. A grandson of William I, he was elected king in 1135, although he had previously recognized Henry I's dau. Matilda as heiress to the throne. When in 1139 Matilda landed in England, a war began which reduced England to anarchy. It ended in 1153, when S. acknowledged Matilda's son, Henry, as his heir.

STEPHEN I (975?–1038). Hungarian king. He succeeded his father in 997, completed the conversion of Hungary to Christianity, and was canonized in 1083.

STEPHEN, **Sir Leslie** (1832–1904). British man-of-letters. Editor of the *Cornhill Magazine* 1871–82, and author of *English Thought in the 18th Century* (1876), etc., he is best remembered as editor of the *Dictionary of National Biography* 1885–91. He was knighted in 1902.

STEPHENS, **James** (1882–1950). Irish author. B.

at Dublin, he is best known for his prose fantasies, *The Crock of Gold* (1912) and *The Demi-Gods*; and vols. of poems beginning with *Insurrections* (1909).

STEPHENSON, George (1781–1848). British engineer. B. near Newcastle, he became engine-wright at Killingworth Colliery, and here built his 1st locomotive in 1814. He also invented a safety lamp in 1815. He was appointed engineer of the Stockton and Darlington Railway, the world's 1st public railway, in 1821, and of the Liverpool and Manchester Railway in 1826. In 1829 he won a £500 prize with his famous 'Rocket'. His son, **Robert S.** (1803–59), achieved distinction as a civil engineer, constructing railway bridges, notably the high-level bridge at Newcastle, and the Menai and Conway tubular bridges.

STEPHENSON, Sir William (1896–). Canadian industrialist and intelligence expert. B. near Winnipeg, he was an ace fighter in the F.W.W., and in 1922 patented a device for transmitting photos by wireless which made him a millionaire. His business contacts allowed him to keep Churchill informed on Hitler's re-armament programme, and he was invited in 1940 to head British Security Coordination (B.S.C.) with its H.Q. in N.Y. Co-operating with Hoover (q.v.) and Donovan, he also helped them to build up the American intelligence service, and was awarded by Truman the Medal of Merit, the 1st foreigner to be so honoured.

SIR WILLIAM
STEPHENSON
Courtesy of C. H. Ellis.

STEPNEY. District of the Greater London bor. of Tower Hamlets, on the N. of the Thames, E. of the City. It incl. the Tower, and large docks.

STE'PNIAK. Pseudonym of the Russian writer, Sergius Mikhailovitch Kravchinsky (1852–95). He became a revolutionary, and after 1880 lived in exile. His books incl. *Underground Russia* (1883), and the novel *The Career of a Nihilist* (1889).

STEREOPHONIC SOUND. *See* RADIOGRAM.

STERILIZATION. Destruction of the power of reproduction. A man may be sterilized by tying off the tubes carrying seed from the testicles to the seminal vesicles, a woman by tying the Fallopian tubes. Fertility can be restored by removal of the ligatures, if the tubes are still open. Either sex may be permanently sterilized by cutting out a portion of each tube, or by removing the testicles or ovaries (castration), or by giving them a sufficiently powerful dose of X-rays. Male sterilisation is much used as a birth control measure in India. The word S. is also applied to the killing of bacteria by heat (asepsis) or disinfectants.

STERLING, John (1806–44). Scottish writer, the centre of a literary group incl. Tennyson, J. S. Mill, and Carlyle, who wrote his life.

STERN, G(ladys) B(ertha) (1890–). British author. B. in London, she began writing as a child and estab. her reputation with a trilogy of Jewish life, *Tents of Israel*, *A Deputy was King*, and *Mosaic*, collected as *The Rakonitz Chronicles* (1932): the 1st was dramatized 1931 as *The Matriarch*. Later books incl. *Dolphin Cottage* (1962).

STERNE, Laurence (1713–68). Irish writer. B. at Clonmel, Ireland, he took orders in 1737 and became vicar of Sutton-in-the-Forest, Yorks, in the next year. In 1741 he m. Elizabeth Lumley, an unhappy union largely because of his wandering amorous propensities, e.g. his sentimental love affair with Eliza Draper, of which the *Letters of Yorick to Eliza* (1775) is a record. His chief work is *The Life and Opinions of*

Tristram Shandy, Gent. (1760–7), an eccentrically whimsical and bawdy novel which made him a London 'lion'. Also very popular was his *A Sentimental Journey through France and Italy* (1768), born of his journeys abroad in 1762 and 1765 in search of a cure for his tuberculosis.

STE'THOSCOPE. Instrument used to ascertain the condition of the heart and lungs by listening to their action. It was invented by R. T. Laënnec (1781–1826), in 1819, and as now used consists of a small plate to be placed against the body and connected by flexible tubes with 2 ear-pieces.

STETTIN (shtetēn'). Ger. form of SZCZECIN.

STETTI'NIUS, Edward (1900–49). U.S. industrialist and administrator. B. at Chicago, he was lend-lease administrator and special assistant to Roosevelt 1941–3. He was Sec. of State 1944–5, and U.S. representative on the U.N. Security Council 1945–6.

STEVENAGE. English town (U.D.) in Herts, 28 m. N. of London. Dating from medieval times, S. was chosen in 1946 for development as a 'new town'. Pop. (1961) 42,964.

STEVENS, Wallace (1879–1955). American poet. B. in Reading, Penn., and ed. at Harvard and the N.Y. Law School, he became a lawyer, eventually specializing in insurance. His vols. of poems incl. *Harmonium* (1923) – his first and very badly received – *The Man with the Blue Guitar* (1937) and *The Necessary Angel* (1951). A sensuous technician, he had an obscurity that yielded to intimate study.

STEVENSON, Adlai (1900–65). American statesman. B. in Los Angeles, he was ed. at Princeton, and from Northwestern Univ. Law School went on to be admitted to the Bar in 1926. As gov. of Illinois 1949–53 he campaigned vigorously against corruption in public life, and as Democratic candidate for the presidency in 1952 and 1956 was twice beaten by Eisenhower. In 1945 he had been chief U.S. delegate at the founding conference of the U.N.

STEVENSON, Robert (1772–1850). Scottish engineer. B. in Glasgow, he built many lighthouses, incl. that on Bell Rock, 1807–11.

STEVENSON, Robert Louis (1850–94). Scottish author and poet. B. in Edinburgh, he studied at the univ., and became an advocate, but never practised. He travelled on the Continent to improve his health, as recounted in *An Inland Voyage* (1878), and *Travels with a Donkey* (1879). In 1879 he went to the U.S.A., m. Mrs. Osbourne, and returning to Britain in 1880, pub. the vol. of stories, *The New Arabian Nights* (1882), and essays, e.g. *Virginibus Puerisque* (1881), and *Familiar Studies of Men and Books* (1882). Fame came to him with *Treasure Island* (1883), which was followed by *Kidnapped* (1886; with its sequel *Catriona* in 1893), *The Black Arrow* (1888), *The Master of Ballantrae* (1889), *Dr. Jekyll and Mr. Hyde* (1886); and the incomplete *Weir of Hermiston* (1896) and *St. Ives* (1897). The humorous *Wrong Box* and the novels *The Wrecker* and *Ebb-tide* were written in collaboration with his stepson, Lloyd Osbourne (1868–1920). In 1890 he settled at Vailima, in Samoa, where he d. His *A Child's Garden of Verses* appeared in 1885, and his Letters in 1899.

STEWART, James (1908–). American actor. B. in Indiana, Pa., he served in the American air force during the S.W.W., and then resumed a career in which his usual film role was the gangly, stubbornly honest, ordinary American, e.g. *Mr. Smith Goes to Washington*.

STEWART, Michael (1906–). British Labour politician. Entering parliament in 1945, he was Under-Sec. of State for War in the Attlee govt. 1947–51, Min. for Education and Science 1964–5, and succeeded Gordon Walker as Foreign Sec. (1965–6), when he followed George Brown as First Sec. of State (1966–8) and Min. for Economic Affairs (1966–7), and as Sec. for Foreign Affairs in 1968–70.

STICK INSECTS. Family of insects (Phasmidae) of the order Phasmida, closely resembling sticks, twigs, etc. Many species are wingless.

STICKLEBACKS. Fishes in the family Gastrosteidae; the popular name is derived from the spines which take the place of the dorsal fin.

STI'GMATA. Impressions of marks corresponding to the 5 wounds of Christ received at His crucifixion, which are said to have been received by St. Francis and other saints.

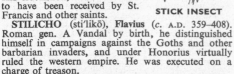

STICK INSECT

STILICHO (sti'likō), **Flavius** (c. A.D. 359–408). Roman gen. A Vandal by birth, he distinguished himself in campaigns against the Goths and other barbarian invaders, and under Honorius virtually ruled the western empire. He was executed on a charge of treason.

STILLINGFLEET, Edward (1635–99). Anglican churchman, dean of St. Paul's from 1678, and bp. of Worcester from 1689. He wrote in defence of C. of E.

STILTON. English village in Hunts, on the Great North Road, 6 m. S.W. of Peterborough. It gave its name to a cheese brought here in coaching days from surrounding farms for transport to London. S. cheese is made in Hunts, Leics, and Rutland.

STILWELL, Joseph Warren (1883–1946). American gen., nicknamed 'Vinegar Joe'. B. in Florida, he became in 1942 U.S. military representative in China, led the Chinese armies operating with the British in Burma, and later commanded all U.S. forces in the Chinese, Burmese and Indian theatres. Recalled to U.S.A. in 1944 because of differences with Chiang Kai-shek, he commanded the U.S. 10th Army on Okinawa, so sharing in Japan's final defeat.

STIMSON, Henry Lewis (1867–1950). American statesman. B. in New York, he was War Sec. in Taft's cabinet 1911–13, and 1929–33 Hoover's Sec. of State. In 1940–5 he was War Sec.

STINKHORN. Species of fungus (*Ithyphallus impudicus*). It first appears as a white ball, which breaks, and a cylindrical column of white spongy substance shoots from it. The upper cells are filled with an olive jelly which gives off a penetrating odour attracting blowflies, which assist in its propagation.

STINKWOOD. South African tree (*Ocotea bullata*). The timber smells unpleasant when first felled, but is fine-grained and durable, so that much early S. African furniture was made from it.

STINNES, Hugo (1870–1924). German industrialist and financier. He entered the family business in 1890, and later founded his own firm. He built up a huge industrial 'empire', and was chief contractor of war material during the F.W.W.

STIRLING. Royal burgh and co. town of Stirlingshire, Scotland, 29 m. N.E. of Glasgow, on the Forth. It makes concrete, linoleum, agricultural implements, etc. S. castle, dating from before 1124, when Alexander I died in it, was long a residence of the kings of Scotland. A univ. was estab. in 1964. Pop. (1961) 27,553. *See* illus. p. 946.

STIRLINGSHIRE. A central county of Scotland, lying between the Firth of Forth and Loch Lomond. Besides the outlying Lennox hills, the northern boundary incl. a fringe of the Highlands. The main rivers are the Forth and Carron. Ben Lomond reaches 3,192 ft. The county contains 3 famous battlefields, Stirling Bridge, Falkirk, and Bannockburn. Near the Forth cereals and potatoes are grown, and sheep are bred; coal is mined, petroleum refined, and aluminium worked. Area 451 sq. m.; pop. (1961) 194,858.

STIRNER (shtěr'ner), **Max.** Pseudonym of Kaspar Schmidt (1805–56), German philosopher. In his *Der Einzige und sein Eigentum* he advocated an extreme individualism akin to anarchism.

STOAT. *See* ERMINE.

STOCK. Popular garden flower, whose species have been derived from the wild genus *Matthiola*. The chief varieties are simple-stemmed, queen's, and ten-week; night-scented S. is *M. tristis*.

STOCK. In finance, the fully paid-up capital of a company. It is bought and sold by subscribers not in units or shares (*see* SHARE), but in terms of its current cash value.

STOCK EXCHANGE. Institution for the buying and selling of stocks and shares. There are S.Es. in London, Glasgow, Cardiff, and other cities of the U.K.; in Montreal, Sydney, and other British Commonwealth cities; in N.Y. (usually referred to as Wall Street, from its location) and other U.S. cities; in Paris (Bourse), Amsterdam (Beurs), and other Continental caps. and big towns. The London S.E. opened 1801, is the oldest; before 1801 securities were bought and sold in the coffeehouses in Change Alley. The London S.E. is owned by a private company and controlled by a council, elected annually, which is responsible for the rules governing business transactions. Members, totalling some 4,000, pay heavy fees and must provide sureties; they are re-elected annually and are divided rigidly into brokers (who buy and sell stocks and shares for the public on commission) and jobbers (who as a rule deal only with brokers). Strangers are not allowed on the floor of the house. The *S.E. Official List*, pub. daily, is made up from the day's transactions. Stamp duties are payable on the transfer of securities and on the contract notes. There are 2 settlement days in each month, when settlement of accounts must be made.

In S.E. terms a *bear* is a speculator who has sold securities he does not as yet possess in the expectation of buying them back at a lower price before Settling Day; a *bull* buys securities he does not intend to 'take up', i.e. pay for, but hopes to sell at a higher price and pocket the difference; and a *stag* applies for shares in new issues to sell them at a profit as soon as possible to members of the investing public.

STOCKHOLM (stok'hōlm). Cap., important port, and cultural centre of Sweden, on the mainland and island fringe where Lake Mälar discharges into the Baltic. Staden island, the original settlement, contains the market place, the royal palace (1697–1754), a church dedicated to St. Nicholas (1264), and the imposing town hall (1923). On Norrmalm are the houses

STOCKHOLM. A rich treasure house for the archaeologist, the Swedish warship *Vasa* was raised in 1961 from the harbour where she sank at the outset of her maiden voyage in 1628. Built for Gustavus II Adolphus, she was rediscovered by a Swedish oil technologist, Anders Franzén, in 1956, and has been preserved with most of her original fittings and contents in a special museum. *Courtesy of the Vasa Museum, Stockholm.*

of parl. and the bank of Sweden. A network of bridges links the islands and the mainland; an underground railway was completed in 1957; there is an airport at Bromma. S. is the usual residence of the king, the seat of most of Sweden's educational institutions and of the Nobel Institute. Industries incl. iron and steel manufacture, engineering, shipbuilding, textile and paper making, sugar refining, printing. Pop. (1966) 781,118.

STOCKPORT. English town (co. bor.) in Cheshire, on the Lancs border, near the Mersey. Cotton goods are manufactured. Pop. (1962) 142,469.

STOCKS. This seven-holed stocks at Winchcomb is said to have been made to give special accommodation for a regular customer – a one-legged drunkard. *Photo: George H. Haines.*

STOCKS. Wooden device used until the 19th cent. to confine the legs or arms of minor offenders, who were exposed to public ridicule.

STOCKTON-ON-TEES. Former bor. of Durham, England, 5 m. above the mouth of the Tees, which in 1968 was merged in Teesside (q.v.). It has shipbuilding, steel, chemical and other industries.

STOCKWOOD, Arthur Mervyn (1913–). British Anglican churchman. Vicar of the univ. church, Cambridge, from 1955 till he became bp. of Southwark in 1959, he is a prominent modernist. Some of his views have caused much controversy.

STOICS (stō'iks). Greek school of philosophy, founded c. 300 B.C. by Zeno; it derived its name from the Stoa, or porch, at Athens in which he taught. The Ss. were pantheistic materialists who believed that happiness lies in accepting the law of the universe. In ethics they emphasized human brotherhood; their outlook was internationalist, and they denounced slavery. In the 3rd and 2nd cents. B.C. Ss. took a prominent part in Greek and Roman revolutionary movements. After the 1st cent. B.C. Stoicism became the philosophy of the Roman ruling class, and lost its revolutionary significance; outstanding Ss. of this period were Seneca, Epictetus, and Marcus Aurelius.

STOKE-ON-TRENT. English industrial city (co. bor.) in Staffs, formed in 1910 by the amalgamation of Burslem, Hanley, Longton Stoke-upon-Trent, Fenton, and Tunstall. It is the chief centre of pottery making in Britain, the 'Five Towns' of Arnold Bennett's novels. Pop. (1961) 265,506.

STOKE POGES. English village in Bucks, 2 m. N. of Slough. The poet Gray is buried in the churchyard, probably the scene of his 'Elegy'.

STOKER, Bram (i.e. Abraham) (1847–1912). British novelist. He studied pure mathematics at Trinity College, Dublin, qualified as a barrister, and worked in the Irish Civil Service – the Registrar of Petty Sessions Clerk's Department – from 1866 until 1878.

In the latter year he became business manager to Henry Irving, remaining with him for 27 years. His most famous book is *Dracula* (1897), a tale of werewolves and vampires, but he pub. a number of other novels as well as personal *Reminiscences of Henry Irving.*

STOKES, Sir George Gabriel (1819–1903). Irish physicist and mathematician, prof. of mathematics at Cambridge from 1849, and renowned for his researches in the theory of light. He formulated a law for the force opposing a small sphere falling through a viscous liquid, and the c.g.s. unit of kinematic viscosity is named after him.

STOKOWSKI (stokof'ski), **Leopold** (1887–). American conductor. B. in London of British and Polish parentage, he studied at the R.C.M. and was conductor of the Cincinnati Symphony Orchestra (1909–12) and of the Philadelphia Orchestra (1913–36), becoming an American citizen in 1915. An outstanding experimentalist, he has introduced much contemporary music into the U.S. (notably Mahler's 8th Symphony) and has appeared in several films (e.g. Walt Disney's *Fantasia*, 1940). He conducted the Houston Symphony Orchestra 1955–60 and from 1962 the American Symphony Orchestra.

STOLE. Ecclesiastical vestment of the R.C. Church. It is a narrow strip worn over the shoulders during Mass.

STOMACH. The first receptacle of food after swallowing. It is a bag of muscle situated just below the diaphragm and pear-shaped. Food enters it by the gullet (oesophagus), is digested by the acid juice secreted by the S. lining, and then passes through the pylorus into the duodenum.

STONE AGE. Name given to the period in prehistory before the discovery of the use of metals, i.e. when man's tools and weapons were made chiefly of flint. It is divided into the Old S.A. or Palaeolithic and the New S.A. or Neolithic; in the latter the flint implements were more finely chipped. Sometimes an Eolithic or Dawn Stone Age is distinguished. The

STOKOWSKI. Against a tapestry background of the faces of young 'promenaders', Stokowski makes his first appearance at a Promenade Concert in 1963 at the Albert Hall. *Photo: Godfrey MacDomnic.*

men of the Old S.A. were hunters, and their few remains have been found in the deposits of caves, river gravel, and so on. The period is divided into Upper, Middle, and Lower, each of which is subdivided into stages whose names are usually derived from the sites where the characteristic implements were first discovered, viz. *Upper*: Magdalenian, Solutrean, and Aurignacian; *Middle*: Mousterian; *Lower*: Acheulean and Chellean. Palaeolithic men lived in caves, and the most striking survivals of their culture are their wall paintings, e.g. at Altamira and Lascaux. They were contemporary with the mammoth, woolly rhinoceros, reindeer, and cave bear, and lived before and during the ice ages. Neolithic man lived in a milder climate, and made the first steps in agriculture, domestication of animals, weaving, and pottery making. In Europe the S.A. merged into the Bronze Age about 2000 B.C.

STONECHAT. Small bird (*Saxicola rubicola*) of the thrush family (Turdidae) frequently found in Europe and Asia. The male has a black head and throat, tawny breast, and dark back; the female has a brown head and a speckled throat.

STONEHENGE. Prehistoric megalithic monument on Salisbury Plain, near Amesbury, Wilts. Several

STONEHENGE. The local sandstone, or 'sarsen', was used for the 18 ft. by 7 ft. uprights which each weigh 26 tons, and were skilfully made slightly convex to give 'true' perspective. A secondary circle and horseshoe within the sarsens was built of bluestones, originally brought from Pembrokeshire.
Photo: A. W. Kerr.

different monuments of differing date have been erected on the site from *c*. 1900 B.C., and the structure illustrated belongs to the third period *c*. 1500–1400 B.C. Its main feature consisted originally of a circle of 30 upright stones, their tops linked by lintel stones to form a continuous circle about 100 ft. across. Within the circle was a horseshoe arrangement of 5 trilithons (each of 2 uprights plus a lintel, but set as separate entities), a so-called 'altar stone' – an upright pillar – on the axis of the horseshoe which was open to the north-east, etc. Though probably having a religious purpose, S. was not a Druid temple; the stones are so arranged that they could have been used to make astronomical calculations.

STOOLBALL. An ancient game, considered the ancestor of cricket, the main differences being that in S. bowling is underhand, and the ball is soft.

STOPES, Marie Carmichael (1880–1958). British advocate of birth control. B. in Edinburgh, she m. in 1918 H. V. Roe and in 1921 founded in London the mothers' clinic for birth control. Her publications incl. plays and verse as well as such best-sellers as *Married Love* (1918).

STORK. Bird, of which the best-known species is the white S. (*Ciconia alba*), which is encouraged to nest on roofs as a symbol of good luck and fertility, hence the popular association with childbirth. About 3 ft. high, it has striking black and white plumage and red bill and legs. It winters in Africa, returning to Europe (not to Britain) in spring. The black S. (*C. nigra*) nests in trees and though white beneath, is

HOUSE STORK

bronze-black above and is also found throughout most of Europe. The New World has a single S. American species.

STORM, Theodor (1817–88). German author. A lawyer, he devoted himself to literature from 1880, and wrote lyric verse and stories such as the idyllic *Immensee* (1851) and the tragic *Der Schimmelreiter* (1888: *The Rider of the White Horse*).

STORNOWAY. Fishing port and chief town of the Outer Hebrides, a burgh on the E. coast of Lewis, Ross and Cromarty, Scotland. S. was founded by James VI (I of England). Pop. (1961) 5,221.

STOTHARD (stodh'ahrd), **Thomas** (1755–1834). British artist. His subject pictures, e.g. 'The Canterbury Pilgrims' were colourful and popular.

STOURBRIDGE. English industrial town (bor.) in Worcs, 14 m. W. of Birmingham. Glass and fire bricks are manufactured. Pop. (1961) 43,917.

STOUT, Sir Robert (1844–1930). New Zealand Liberal statesman. B. in the Shetlands, he emigrated to New Zealand in 1863, was P.M. 1884–7, and Chief Justice 1899–1926.

STOW, John (*c*. 1525–1605). English antiquary. B. in London, he wrote chronicles and a detailed and interesting *Survey of London* (1598).

STOWE, Harriet Beecher (1811–96). American author of the anti-slavery novel, *Uncle Tom's Cabin*, first pub. as a serial 1851–2. She was a dau. of Lyman Beecher (q.v.), and m. in 1836 C. E. Stowe, a theological prof.

STOWE. English public school, founded 1923 in S. House (*c*. 1660), 3 m. N. of Buckingham, until 1889 the seat of the dukes of Buckingham and Chandos.

STRA'BO (*c*. 63 B.C.–A.D. 24). Greek geographer. B. in Pontus, he travelled widely to collect material for his *Geography*, which has survived almost entire.

STRACHEY, Giles Lytton (1880–1932). British author. Ed. at Trinity Coll., Oxford, he wrote the attractive *Landmarks in French Literature* (1912), but won fame and set a vogue by his graceful denigration in *Eminent Victorians* (1918) of Cardinal Manning, Florence Nightingale, Thomas Arnold, and Gen. Gordon. In *Queen Victoria* (1921), however, he was almost conquered by his subject.

STRADIVARI (strahdēvah'rē), **Antonio** (1644–1737). Italian violin-maker, who set up his workshop at Cremona during the 1660s. His sons carried on his work, but the secret of his soft varnish was never revealed.

STRAFFORD, Thomas Wentworth, earl of (1593–1641). English statesman. He sat in James I's and Charles I's parliaments, and was among the leaders of the opposition. In 1628 he went over to the king's side and was created visct. Wentworth. As Lord Deputy of Ireland from 1632 he pursued a despotic policy. On returning to England in 1639 he became Charles's chief adviser, pressed him to take repressive measures, and in 1640 received an earldom. When the Long Parliament met he was impeached and beheaded.

STRAITS SETTLEMENTS. Former British crown colony, 1867–1946, a prov. of the East India Co., 1826–58, consisting of Singapore, Malacca, Penang, Cocos Is., Christmas Is., and Labuan (qq.v.).

STRALSUND (strahl'soond). Baltic port of Rostock dist., E. Germany, opposite the island of Rügen. Founded 1209, it was a Hanse town. Pop. (est.) 50,000.

STRANG, William (1859–1921). Scottish artist. He is remembered for his realistic portrait etchings of Hardy, Kipling and others. He settled in London in 1875 and became R.A. in 1921.

STRANG, William, 1st baron (1893–). British diplomat. Entering the Foreign Office in 1919, he was adviser to the C.-in-C. of the British forces of occupation in Germany 1945–7, permanent Under-Sec. of the German section at the Foreign Office 1947–9, and then until his retirement in 1953 permanent Under-Sec. of

State. His books incl. *The Foreign Office* (1955) and *The Diplomatic Career* (1962).

STRANRAER (stranrahr'). Scottish seaport (burgh) in Wigtownshire, at the head of Loch Ryan. There are regular sailings to and from Larne, N. Ireland. Pop. (1961) 9,249.

STRASBOURG (straz'boorg; Ger. Strassburg). Cap. of Bas-Rhin dept., France, on the Rhine, historic cap. of Alsace. There is a Gothic cathedral, and the House of Europe (1950) is the meeting-place of the Council of Europe. Seized by France in 1681, it was surrendered to Germany 1870–1919 and 1940–4. It is noted for preserves and has motor-car and tobacco factories, printing and publishing works, etc. Pop. (1968) 249,390.

STRATFORD-UPON-AVON. English market town (bor.) in Warwicks, the birthplace of Shakespeare whose grave is in the parish church. The Royal Shakespeare Theatre (1932) replaced an earlier

STRATFORD-UPON-AVON. The Royal Shakespeare Theatre, designed by Elizabeth Scott. The Royal Shakespeare Company, in its annual season, attracts tourists from all over the world. *Courtesy The Royal Shakespeare Theatre.*

building (1877–9) burnt down in 1926. Shakespeare's birthplace, purchased 1847, contains relics of his life and times. Pop. (1961) 16,847. **Stratford**, city and port of Ontario, Canada, also has a Shakespeare festival.

STRATHCONA AND MOUNT ROYAL, Donald Alexander Smith, 1st baron (1820–1914). Canadian statesman. B. in Scotland, he joined the Hudson's Bay Company in 1838, and in 1868 became governor of Hudson Bay. He played a prominent part in railway development, and 1896–1911 was High Commissioner for Canada.

STRATOSPHERE. That part of the atmosphere beyond 6 m. from the earth, wherein the temperature is constant. After the minimum −55°C. is reached, there is even a slight rise up to 25 m. in the extremely rarefied air. Piccard made famous ascents in 1931–2, and important discoveries were made in 1935, when the U.S.A.S. balloon Explorer II reached 72,395 ft. (13½ m.). Exploration now is by rocket.

STRAUS (strows), **Oscar** (1870–1954). Austrian composer. B. at Vienna, he composed operettas, e.g. *The Chocolate Soldier*.

STRAUSS, Johann (1825–99). Austrian composer. B. in Vienna, he was the son of Johann Strauss (1804–49), a composer of waltz music. In 1862 he relinquished conducting for composition, and wrote operettas, such as *Die Fledermaus*, and numerous waltzes, e.g. 'The Blue Danube', 'Tales from the Vienna Woods', etc., which gained him the title 'The Waltz King'.

STRAUSS, Richard (1864–1949). German composer. B. at Munich, he wrote the symphonic tone

STRAVINSKY. On a visit to Britain, the composer conducts the B.B.C. Symphony Orchestra. *Photo: Godfrey MacDomnic.*

poems *Don Juan, Death and Transfiguration*, and *Till Eulenspiegel* (1895), and many songs. His operas incl. *Salome, Elektra, Der Rosenkavalier, Ariadne auf Naxos*, and *Arabella*. He became president of the Reichsmusikkammer, but resigned in 1935 when his opera *Die schweigsame Frau* was boycotted because the libretto was written by S. Zweig (q.v.).

STRAVINSKY, Igor (1882–1971). Russo-American composer. B. near St. Petersburg, he studied under Rimsky-Korsakov and, for the Diaghilev ballet, wrote *The Firebird* (1910), *Petrushka* (1911) and *The Rite of Spring* (1913), which aroused controversy on account of their unorthodox rhythm and harmony. Having lived in Paris from 1920, he went to the U.S. in 1939 and in 1945 took American citizenship. His works incl. symphonies, concertos (for violin and piano), chamber music, a mass (1948) and operas, e.g. *The Rake's Progress* (1951) and *The Flood* (1962).

STRAWBERRY. Genus (*Fragaria*) of fruiting plants of the Rosaceae family which incl. the wild S. of Europe (*F. vesca*), and the N. American meadow S. (*F. virginiana*) and the Chilean (*F. chiloensis*) from which the modern cultivated hybrids derive. Although naturally a dwarf perennial, in commercial cultivation the S. is allowed to produce only 2 or 3 crops before being replaced by new stock or 'runners' allowed to develop from selected plants.

STREICHER (stri'kher), **Julius** (1885–1946). Nazi politician. He began anti-Semitic agitations after the F.W.W., took part in the 1923 *putsch*, and founded and edited *Der Stürmer*. He was tried and hanged.

STREIT (strit), **Clarence Kirshman** (1896–). American author. He became pres. in 1939 of Federal Union, Inc., a society formed to further his proposals for a union of America and the democracies of western Europe and the British Commonwealth, contained in his book *Union Now* (1939), and in 1958 pres. of the International Movement for Atlantic Union.

STREPTOMYCIN. Antibiotic (q.v.). Discovered in 1944 by Dr. Selman Waksman at New Jersey, it is prepared from micro-organisms in earth-mould, and is used in the treatment of tuberculosis, influenzal meningitis, and other infections, some of which are unaffected by penicillin.

STRESEMANN (strā'semahn), **Gustav** (1878–1929). German statesman. B. in Berlin, he became leader of the National Liberal Party in 1917. He was Chancellor in 1923 and 1924, and several times For. Min. S. concluded the Locarno Pact in 1925, and in 1926 shared the Nobel peace prize with Briand.

STRETFORD. English industrial town (bor.) in Lancs, 4 m. S.W. of Manchester. Old Trafford, the Lancs county cricket ground, is in S. Pop. (1961) 60,331.

STRIKES and **Lock-outs.** A S. is a stoppage of work by workpeople in order to obtain or to resist a change in their wages, hours, or conditions; a L. occurs when employers shut out their employees to force them to accept such a change, e.g. the L. of the

HOUSES OF STUART, HANOVER, AND WINDSOR

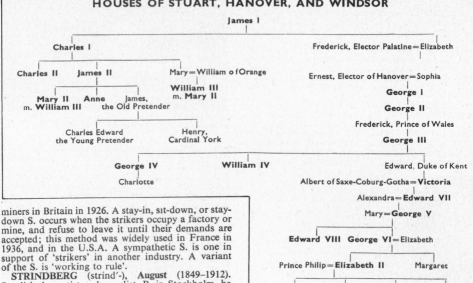

James I

Charles I — Frederick, Elector Palatine = Elizabeth

Charles II — James II — Mary = William o f Orange — Ernest, Elector of Hanover = Sophia

William III m. Mary II

George I

Mary II m. William III — Anne — James, the Old Pretender

George II

Charles Edward the Young Pretender — Henry, Cardinal York

Frederick, Prince of Wales

George III

George IV — William IV — Edward, Duke of Kent

Charlotte — Albert of Saxe-Coburg-Gotha = Victoria

Alexandra = Edward VII

Mary = George V

Edward VIII — George VI = Elizabeth

Prince Philip = Elizabeth II — Margaret

Charles — Anne — Andrew — Edward

miners in Britain in 1926. A stay-in, sit-down, or stay-down S. occurs when the strikers occupy a factory or mine, and refuse to leave it until their demands are accepted; this method was widely used in France in 1936, and in the U.S.A. A sympathetic S. is one in support of 'strikers' in another industry. A variant of the S. is 'working to rule'.

STRINDBERG (strind'-), **August** (1849–1912). Swedish dramatist and novelist. B. in Stockholm, he held a post in the Royal Library there 1874–82, but after 1883 he lived as a writer, mainly abroad. He was a strong critic of contemporary Swedish society, and (although thrice married) a woman-hater and a deep pessimist. He wrote historical dramas, e.g. *Gustavus Adolphus* (1900); pseudo-autobiographies, e.g. *The Son of a Servant* and *The Confessions of a Fool*; satirical comedies – *Bengt's Wife*; and tragedies – *The Father* (1887).

STRINGFELLOW, John (1799–1883). British inventor of the first model power-driven aeroplane (1848).

STROMBOLI (strom'bōlē). Italian island, one of the Lipari Islands, on which is an active volcano, 3,038 ft. high. The island produces Malmsey wine and capers. Area 4·7 sq. m.; pop. 1,200.

STRONTIUM (Strontian, town in Scotland). A silver-white ductile metal, symbol Sr, at. wt. 87·63, at. no. 38. Discovered by a Scot named Crawford in 1790, and isolated electrolytically by Davy in 1808, it is widely distributed in small quantities as the sulphate and carbonate. The metal resembles calcium and its salts give a brilliant red colour to a flame, are used for fireworks, and the oxide is used in sugar refining.

A long-lived radioactive isotope Sr-90 is produced in the fission of uranium and is a dangerous component of fallout since it is taken up by plants and ingested by cattle which pass it to their milk. When ingested by humans it accumulates in bones causing tumours. An underwater sound beacon drawing energy from Sr-90 is being developed as a navigational aid in the U.S.A. It will be used by ships in a similar way to a radio beacon.

STROUD. English market town (U.D.) in Glos, 10 m. S. of Gloucester, in the Cotswolds. Cloth making is the oldest industry. Pop. (1961) 17,461.

STRUTT, Jedediah (1726–97). British inventor, an associate of Sir Richard Arkwright. He invented *c.* 1755 a machine to produce ribbed hosiery.

STRYCHNINE (strik'nin). A bitter-tasting alkaloid ($C_{21}H_{22}O_2N_2$), usually obtained by powdering the seeds of plants of the genus *Strychnos*, e.g. *S. nux vomica*. It is a violent tetanizing poison. *See* also the related drug CURARE.

STRYDOM (strā'dom), **Johannes** (1893–1958). S.

African National statesman, P.M. 1954–8, he furthered apartheid.

STUART or **Stewart, House of.** Royal family who inherited the Scottish throne in 1371, and the English in 1603. *See* Table above.

STUBBS, George (1724–1806). British artist. B. in Liverpool, son of a currier, he was originally a portrait painter, but in 1758 rented a farm and carried out a long series of dissections which resulted in his book of engravings *The Anatomy of the Horse* (1766). Henceforward he had no lack of commissions, and his paintings are a record of the turf, the hunting field and the golden age of English country life, e.g. 'Phaeton and Pair', 'Gimcrack on Newmarket Heath', 'Haymakers' and 'Reapers'.

STUBBS, William (1825–1901). British churchman and historian. He took orders in 1850, and was prof. of modern history at Oxford 1866–84. His great work is the *Constitutional History of England* (1873–8). He was bp. of Chester 1884–9, and of Oxford 1889–1901.

STUD, National. Estab. at Gillingham, Dorset, and West Grinstead, Sussex, England, maintained by the Horserace Betting Levy Board (until 1963 by the Min. of Agriculture). Founded in Dec. 1915 when Lord Wavertree presented to the nation his stud at Kildare, it removed to England in 1943, and produced thoroughbreds, mainly for export, incl. many notable racehorses, esp. for the sovereign, but since 1964 only stallions have been kept for visiting mares.

STURGEON. Genus (*Acipenser*) of fish incl. the common European S. (*A. sturio*) which reaches *c.*

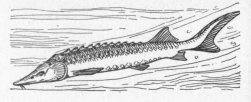

SUBMARINE. Britain's first nuclear submarine H.M.S. *Dreadnought*: (1) reactor compartment, (2) reactor control compartment, (3) auxiliary machinery, (4) diesel generator, (5) escape hatch, (6) main condenser, (7) main turbines, (8) electric propulsion motor (alternative drive), (9) rudders, (10) after hydroplane, (11) surface navigating bridge, (12) periscope, (13) radar and radio aerials, (14) snort, (15) control room, (16) electric batteries, (17) crew's quarters, (18) mess, (19) electrical space, (20) forward hydroplane, (21) torpedo space, (22) torpedo tubes, (23) stowed anchor, (24) galley.   *Courtesy of Rolls-Royce and Associates Ltd.*

10 ft. and in England is a royal fish, traditionally belonging to the Crown, but actually poor eating. The most valuable species, of which the roe is made into caviare, are those of the rivers of the Black and Caspian seas, more especially *A. stellatus*, which is only 5 ft. long, but the S. of the Great Lakes of N. America (*A. rubicundus*) is also used.

STUTTGART (shtoot'gahrt). Capital of Baden-Württemberg, Germany, on the river Neckar. There is a publishing trade, and important factories and rail yards. Pop. (1966) 625,258.

STYLE, Old and **New**. See CALENDAR; OLD STYLE.

STYRIA (stir'ia). Prov. of Austria, in the eastern Alps. S. is mainly mountainous. Forestry is important, iron ore, lignite, and graphite are mined, and there are blast furnaces and steel works. Graz is the cap. Area 6,326 sq. m.; pop. (1961) 1,137,460.

STYX (stiks). In Greek mythology the river surrounding the underworld. See CHARON.

SUAKIN (swah'kin). Seaport in Sudan Republic, partly on an islet in the Red Sea, partly on the mainland. It cannot take vessels of more than 20 ft. draught, is much used by pilgrims going to Mecca. Pop. (est.) 6,000.

SUBMARINE. Submersible boat, operating down to 1,000 ft. and relying on gas or liquid ballast tanks to achieve buoyancy. An early attempt was the S. constructed for James I by the Dutchman Cornelius van Drebel in 1620, but serious development began with attempted use of the S. in warfare in the 18th cent. The 1st naval S. or submersible torpedo boat, the *Gymnote*, was launched by France in 1888 and John P. Holland, an Irish emigrant to the U.S.A., designed a S. c. 1875 which was adopted by both the U.S. and British navies for their 1st warships of this kind at the turn of the cent. In both the world wars the S., from the ocean-going to the midget type, played a vital role and after the S.W.W. came the atomic S. and in the 1960s developments in oceanography (q.v.) and commercial pipe-laying of less wide-ranging 'submersibles', usually carrying pilot and observer, and divers released to undertake high dexterity tasks – some operate with external manipulators down to 6,000 ft. See PICCARD and WARSHIP.

SUBOTICA. Largest town of Vojvodina, Yugo-

slavia. It is an agricultural centre with many manufactures. Pop. (1961) 75,036.

SUBPOENA (-pē'na) (Lat. 'under penalty'). A writ issued early in litigation requiring a person to be present at a specified time and place to give evidence before a court or a judicial officer.

SUBWAY. See UNDERGROUND.

SUCEAVA. See under BUKOVINA.

SUCKING FISH. Several genera of fishes having an adhesive disc on the head by means of which they attach themselves to ships, sharks, or turtles.

SUCKLING, Sir John (1609–42). English poet. B. at Whitton, he was an ardent Royalist. His chief lyrics appeared in *Fragmenta Aurea* (1646).

SUCRE (sōō'krā). Nominal cap. of Bolivia, commercial and road centre, seat of the supreme court and of the Univ. of San Francisco Xavier (1624), probably the oldest univ. in S. America. S. was founded 1538; the cathedral dates from 1553. Brewing, distilling, petroleum refining are industries. Pop. (1965) 57,608.

SUDAN (soodahn'). Geographical term used to describe N. Africa, S. of Algeria, Tunis, Libya, from the Atlantic to the Red Sea.

Sudan Republic lies S. of Egypt, N. of Uganda, with a coastline on the Red Sea. The climate is tropical, hot, and dry. Desert in the N., it is fertile in the S., producing dura, maize, ground-nuts, cotton, etc. Gum arabic is gathered from a species of acacia. The Nile traverses the rep. from S. to N. and is important both for irrigation and as a means of transport; there are 2,800 m. of railways and a govt. air service. Port Sudan is the chief port; the cap. is Khartoum. Area 967,500 sq. m.; pop. (1964 est.) 13,000,000. Subdued by an Anglo-Egyptian army under Kitchener 1896–8, S. was admin. as an Anglo-Egyptian condominium 1899–1956, when it became a rep. The S. (Negroid and pagan) aims at secession from the N. (Arab and Moslem) as Anzania; revolt began in 1963 in the 3 most southerly of the 9 provs., and despite promised autonomy the rebel Anya Nya continued guerrilla warfare in 1971: the govt. forces received Soviet aid. See also MALI, REPUBLIC OF.

SUDBURY. English market town (bor.) on the Stour, Suffolk. Silk, matting, flour, marine engines are produced; woollens, introduced in the 14th cent. by Flemings, were formerly made: Pop. (1961) 6,643.

SUDBURY. City in Ontario, Canada, 38 m. N. of Lake Huron; most of the world's nickel is mined here. Pop. (1966) 84,888.

SUDERMANN (zōō'dermahn), **Hermann** (1857–1928). German dramatist and novelist. B. in E. Prussia, he wrote the novels *Frau Sorge, Der Katzensteg*, etc.; and such plays as *Die Ehre* and *Heimat*.

SUDETENLAND (soodeh'ten-). Term applied to an area of Czechoslovakia close to the Sudeten mts., many of whose inhabitants before the S.W.W. were of German origin, settled in the district for generations. Nazi agitation among them led to the Munich crisis in Sept. 1938, following which the S. was ceded to Germany which annexed all Czechoslovakia in 1939. After the S.W.W., S. was returned to Czechoslovakia and more than 2 million of its German-speaking inhabitants were expelled.

SUE (sü), **Eugène** (1804–57). French novelist. B. in Paris, he served as naval surgeon 1824–30. His novels incl. *The Mysteries of Paris* and *The Wandering Jew*. Elected a member of the National Assembly in 1850, he retired to Annecy after Napoleon III's coup d'état.

SUETONIUS TRANQUILLUS (swētō'nius), **Gaius** (fl. 2nd cent. A.D.). Latin historian, whose *Lives of the Caesars* gives much personal information.

SUEZ (soo'ez). Port of the U.A.R. (Egypt) at the Red Sea terminus of the S. Canal. Pop. (1963) 203,000.

SUEZ CANAL. Artificial waterway from Port Said to Suez, linking the Mediterranean and Red seas, separating Africa from Asia, and providing the shortest sea route from Europe to the East, to Australasia, and to the E. coast of Africa. The French S.C. Company was formed in 1858 to execute the scheme of Ferdinand de Lesseps. The canal was opened in 1869, and in 1875 Disraeli acquired for Britain from the khedive of Egypt 177,642 (out of 400,000) shares for £4 million. The 1888 Convention of Constantinople opened it to all nations. The S.C. was admin. by a co. with offices in Paris controlled by a council of 33 (10 of them British) until 1956 when it was forcibly nationalized by Pres. Nasser. It was blocked by Egypt during the Arab-Israeli war (1967) and subsequently kept closed. Length (incl. dredged approach channels) 103 m.; minimum width 197 ft., average depth 34 ft.

SUFFOLK. An eastern county of England. It has a low undulating surface, and a flat coastline. Most is under plough, producing barley, wheat, and sugar

SUFFOLK. The garden of the birthplace of artist Thomas Gainsborough at Sudbury, now preserved as a museum and containing a number of his landscapes and portraits.
Courtesy of Gainsborough's House Society

beet. It is noted for its horses (S. Punches), formerly much used in agriculture. The principal rivers are the Waveney, **Alde, Deben, Orwell**, and **Stour**; part of the Broads (q.v.) is in S., which is divided admin. into East S. (cap. Ipswich) and West S. (cap. Bury St. Edmunds). Ipswich is the co. town. Area 1,482 sq. m.; pop. (1967) 531,430.

SUFISM (sōō'fizm). Mohammedan religious movement which rejected ritual and sought a return to primitive simplicity. It originated in Persia, was influenced by Neoplatonism, and coloured the thought of Hafiz, Sadi, Omar, and other Persian writers. Sufi doctrines are a kind of mystical pantheism.

SUGAR. A substance that, in one or another form, occurs in many plants as they approach maturity. It most commonly occurs in fruits, but the sugar of commerce is derived chiefly from the stems of the sugar cane or the roots of the S. beet. S. cane (*Saccharum*) is native to S.E. Asia, but is now cultivated in many tropical and sub-tropical lands. It grows to 6 or 12 ft. in height and 1½ in. in thickness. **S. beet** (*Beta*) is a root crop of temperate regions, and was first cultivated in England about 1909.

SUHARTO (1921–   ). Indonesian general. Anti-Communist, he became army commander 1965, and in 1966 ousted Sukarno, himself becoming chairman of the presidium. He ended confrontation with Malaysia.

SUICIDE. Self-murder. In English law it was until 1960 a criminal offence if committed while of sound mind: technically a felony (*felonia de se*) it was at one time punished by confiscation of the S.'s goods and until 1823 burial was at night, without burial service, and with a stake through the heart. Hence the frequency with which the coroners' juries often found a verdict that the S. committed the act while insane.

SUKARNO (soo'-), **Achmed** (1901–70). Indonesian statesman. B. nr. Surabaja, son of a schoolmaster, he took part in the nationalist movement before the S.W.W., co-operated in the native administration set up by the Japanese during their occupation, and became pres. of the Indonesian Rep. set up in 1945. He became P.M. 1959 and was created head of state for life 1963, but was deprived of the premiership 1966 and of the life presidency 1967 by Suharto (q.v.).

SUKKUR (sookoor'). Town and river port in W. Pakistan, on the lower Indus, with railway workshops. The Lloyd Barrage (1923–32), sometimes called the S. Barrage, lies 2 m. W. Pop. (1961) 103,216.

SULAWESI. Another form of CELEBES.

SULGRAVE. English village in Northants, 2½ m. N.W. of Helmdon. S. Manor, ancestral home 1539–1610 of George Washington's family, was presented in 1914 to the S. Institute and opened as a Washington Museum. *See* illus. p. 793.

SU'LLA, Lucius Cornelius (138–78 B.C.). Roman soldier and statesman. He distinguished himself in the Jugurthine, Teuton, and Social wars, and became the leading figure in the senatorial party. After forcibly suppressing the democrats in 88, he successfully waged war on Mithradates of Pontus. During his absence the democrats seized power, but on his return in 82 he captured Rome and massacred his opponents. Declared dictator, he carried out constitutional reforms, strengthening the senate.

SULLIVAN, Sir Arthur Seymour (1842–1900). British composer. B. in London, he became a choirboy at the Chapel Royal, and studied at Leipzig. He composed oratorios, but became famous for the light operas written in collaboration with Sir W. S. Gilbert (q.v.). These incl. *H.M.S. Pinafore* (1878), *The Pirates of Penzance* (1879), *Patience* (1881), *The Mikado* (1885), *The Yeoman of the Guard* (1888), and *The Gondoliers* (1889), and have achieved a deservedly lasting popularity. The partnership broke down owing to temperamental incompatibility. S. also wrote the serious opera *Ivanhoe*, the ballad 'The Lost Chord', etc.

SULLY (sülē'), **Maximilien de Béthune**, duc de

(1560–1641). French statesman. He served on the Huguenot side during the Wars of Religion, and as Henry IV's superintendent of finances 1598–1611 contributed greatly to France's recovery.

SULLY-PRUDHOMME (-prüdom'), **Armand** (1839–1907). French poet. B. in Paris, he wrote philosophical verse showing psychological insight. *Les Solitudes, Les Vaines Tendresses, La Justice,* and *Le Bonheur* are outstanding.

SULPHA DRUGS. Sulphonamides; synthetic Ds. allied to the aniline dyes, which prevent certain bacteria from multiplying, used in the prevention and treatment of childbirth fever, pneumonia, and wound infection.

SULPHUR. Known from ancient times, it is a pale yellow, odourless, brittle solid; insoluble in water, soluble in carbon disulphide and a good electrical insulator; symbol S, at. wt. 32·066, at. no. 16. Widely distributed as the element in volcanic regions, and as sulphides of many metals. There are two crystalline forms and an allotropic plastic form. It is essential to life, resembles oxygen chemically and can replace this element to form innumerable organic and inorganic compounds. It is widely used in the manufacture of sulphuric acid and in chemicals and explosives, matches, fireworks, dyes, fungicides, drugs, etc., and in vulcanizing rubber, particularly for tyres.

SULPHU'RIC ACID (H_2SO_4) or **Oil of Vitriol.** A colourless, oily liquid, used in the manufacture of hydrochloric acid, nitric acid, explosives, coal-tar derivatives, and in many industrial processes.

SULPI'CIANS. Order of R.C. priests founded *c.* 1645 by the Abbé·Olier to train aspirants to the Church, and named after the parish of St. Sulpice, Paris, where they originated.

SUMATRA (soomah'tra). Largest island of Indonesia. E. of a longitudinal mountain range is a

SUMATRA. Largest of Sumatra's numerous mountain lakes is Lake Toba, 15 m. wide and 45 m. long, with its island Pulau Samosir. Beautiful gardens, such as those seen here, lie along its shores. *Courtesy of Indonesian Embassy.*

wide plain; both are heavily forested. The chief products are rubber, rice, tobacco, tea, timber, tin, and petroleum. Important towns are Palembang, Padang, Benkulen. In the late 16th cent. the Dutch estab. trading posts. Area 165,000 sq. m.; pop. (1967) 18,300,000.

SUME'RIANS. A people possibly akin to the Dravidians of India. who inhabited S. Babylonia from ·c. 4000 B.C., and founded Babylonian culture.

SUMMERSKILL, Edith, baroness (1901–). British Labour politician. B. in London, she was ed. at King's Coll., London, and Charing Cross Hospital, qualifying as a doctor in 1924, and m. the next year Jeffrey Samuel, a general practitioner. Entering parliament in 1938, she was Min. of National Insurance 1950–1, and became known as a redoubtable fighter for women's rights and an opponent of boxing, e.g. *The Ignoble Art* (1956). Her *Letters to my Daughter*

(1957) were to Shirley S. (1931–), who took her mother's surname, also a doctor and from 1964 Labour M.P. In 1961 she was created a life peeress.

SUMMER TIME. The practice introduced in the U.K. in 1916, whereby legal time from spring to autumn is an hour in advance of Greenwich mean time. It was permanently in force Feb. 1940–Oct. 1945 and Feb. 1968–Oct. 1971. Double S.T. (2 hours in advance), was in force 1941–5 and 1947. *See* TIME.

SUMMONS. Legal term denoting the citation to appear in court on a certain date, which is served on a person by an official, and which states the claim made by the plaintiff.

SUN. The star around which the Earth revolves. It is 864,000 miles in diameter, and lies at a distance of

just under 93,000,000 miles. Like all stars, it is composed of intensely hot gas; hydrogen is a major constituent. The surface temperature is 6,000°C., and the central temperature between 12,000,000° and 15,000,000°C. It produces its energy by nuclear reactions, resulting in the conversion of hydrogen into helium with a steady loss of mass amounting to 4,000,000 tons per second.

Telescopically, the S. is seen to show various dark patches, known as sunspots. These are cooler areas (around 4,000° C.), and are relatively short-lived, though they may become very large. Associated with spot-groups are the bright patches termed *faculae*. The S. shows semi-regular cycles of activity, with maxima occurring about every 11 years. At solar maxima, spot-groups are very frequent, whereas at solar minima the disc may be entirely clear for several days consecutively.

With spectroscopic equipment it is possible to examine the *prominences*, masses of glowing hydrogen rising from the S.'s bright surface or *photosphere*, as well as the short-lived but violent outbreaks known as *flares*, usually associated with spot-groups. Only during a total eclipse may prominences be seen with the naked eye. This also applies to the outer surround or *corona*, composed of highly tenuous gas at a remarkably high temperature.

Modern astronomers regard the S. as a dwarf star and certainly it is in no way exceptional in the Galaxy. Since it possesses a system of planets, there is no reason to doubt that other stars have planetary systems of their own.

SUNBURY-ON-THAMES. English market town and boating centre (U.D.) in Surrey. 17 m. S.W. of London, with petroleum-research laboratories opened 1962. Formerly in the admin. co. of

SUN. These solar prominences were photographed during the total solar eclipse of 1932. Spectroscopic instruments enable the prominences to be studied at any time, but only during a total eclipse are they visible to the naked eye. *Courtesy of Lick Observatory Univ. of California*

Middlesex, it was excluded from Greater London and transferred to Surrey 1964–5. Pop. (1961) 33,403.

SUNDA ISLANDS. Name given to the islands of Indonesia W. of the Moluccas. The Great S.I. incl.

Sumatra, Java, Borneo, Celebes, and Billiton; the Lesser S.I., Bali, Lombok, Sumbawa, Flores, Sumba, Timor.

SUNDAY. The first day of the week and, in the Christian world, the day set apart for divine worship (in memory of Christ's resurrection), thus replacing the Jewish sabbath. In the U.K. labour, the sale of certain goods, and other activities were regulated by law from medieval times, most notably the Sunday Observance Acts of 1625 and 1780 – infringements continuing to be opposed in the 20th cent. by the Lord's Day Observance Society – but under the Sunday Entertainments Bill (1969) curbs on sports, theatres and dancing were to be lifted, introducing the 'Continental Sunday'. In the U.S.A. similar laws to those of England were general in colonial times, but subsequent enforcement has been lax.

Sunday Schools, of which the 1st was estab. at Gloucester, England, by Robert Raikes in 1780, were valuable originally, not merely as sources of religious instruction, but as enabling the poorest children to learn to read and write before the introduction of free day schools. The movement passed to the U.S.A. early in the 19th cent. and still continues, although the tendency is to replace them by special services for the young or combined family worship.

SUNDERLAND, Robert Spencer, 2nd earl of (1640–1702). British politician. He became James II's Sec. of State, and embraced Catholicism. He fled to Holland in 1688, but returned in 1691 and re-entered politics as a Whig. On his advice William III adopted the system of choosing the govt. from the dominant party in the Commons.

SUNDERLAND. English seaport and industrial town (co. bor.) in co. Durham, at the mouth of the Wear, 14 m. N.E. of Durham. Although shipbuilding is a long-established industry, S. owes its growth to coal-mining. There is a polytechnic (1969) and civic theatre – the S. Empire. Pop. (1961) 189,629.

SUNDEW. *See* INSECTIVOROUS PLANTS.

SUNDIAL. An instrument for measuring time by means of a shadow cast by the sun. It consists of a dial-plane marked with the hours, and a style or gnomon from which the shadow is cast. The style is parallel to the earth's axis, and points to the N.

SUNDSVALL (soonds'vahl). Seaport with timber and wood-pulp industries in the Västernorrland district of Sweden on the Gulf of Bothnia, 260 m. N. of Stockholm. Pop. (1960) 29,355.

SUN-FISH. Large fishes (*Orthagoriscus* and *Ranzania*) distributed throughout temperate and tropical seas. The body is compressed and almost circular. The rough S. (*O. mola*) is about 7 ft. long and sometimes appears in British waters.

SUNFLOWER. Genus of plants (*Helianthus*) in the family Compositae. The common S. (*H. annus*) is a native of N. America, grows to *c.* 15 ft. in favourable conditions, and is commercially cultivated in central Europe and the U.S.S.R. for the oil-bearing seeds which follow the yellow-petalled flowers.

SU'NNIS. Followers of the Sunni rite, the more orthodox of the 2 main divisions of Islam (q.v.) and predominant in most Islamic countries except Persia. The name derives from the *Sunna*, a book of rules inspired by Mohammed.

SUNSPOT. *See* SUN.

SUNSTROKE. Illness resulting from the action of strong sunlight on brain cells, partly through the scalp and back of the neck, but chiefly through the eyes. It is therefore preventable by the wearing of tinted glasses and a thick hat, even in the tropics.

SUN YAT-SEN (1867–1925). Chinese statesman. The son of a Christian farmer, he founded the Kuomintang party in 1894. After many years in exile he returned to China during the 1911 revolution, and was provisional pres. of the rep. in 1912. When the reactionaries obtained control he estab. a republican govt. at Canton in 1921, in which he was proclaimed pres. His '3 people's principles' of nationalism, democracy, and social reform are accepted by both the Kuomintang and the Chinese Communists. His widow Soong Ching-ling (1890–), ed. in U.S.A., remained influential in Chinese politics, being Vice-Chairman of the Rep. from 1959, but was under attack in 1967 in the Cultural Revolution.

SUPERCONDUCTIVITY. The phenomenon of S., discovered by Kamerlingh Onnes in 1911, is exhibited by some metals and metallic compounds whose resistance decreases uniformly with decreasing temperature until at a critical temperature (the superconducting point), within a few degrees of the absolute zero, the resistance suddenly falls to zero. In this superconducting state an electric current induced by a magnetic field in a closed circuit or ring of the material will continue after the magnetic field has been removed, so long as the material remains below the superconducting point. Important industrial applications of this phenomenon are being actively explored. *See* CRYOGENICS.

SUPERIOR, Lake. The largest freshwater lake in the world, one of the Great Lakes of N. America. Two-thirds lie in the U.S.A., the rest in Canada. It discharges via the St. Mary into Lake Huron. Area 31,820 sq. m.: greatest depth 1,333 ft.

SUPERNOVA. A stellar explosion on a vast scale, when a formerly obscure star suffers a cataclysmic outburst during which it blows most of its material away into space. For a brief period, perhaps a few weeks, the S. emits millions of times as much radiation as the Sun. Only 3 supernovae have been observed in our Galaxy since the year A.D. 1000, though supernovae have been frequently detected in external galaxies.

SUPERSONIC SPEED. Speed greater than that of sound, which at sea-level is about 760 m.p.h. and decreases with altitude until at 40,000 ft. it is only 660 m.p.h.; above that it remains constant. The first airman to achieve S.S. was Englishman Squadron Leader John Derry in a De Havilland 108 research aeroplane on 6 Sept. 1948, in a 35 min. flight; at 30,000–40,000 ft. he dived steeply and reached a speed of about 675 m.p.h.

When an aircraft exceeds the speed of sound (passes the sound barrier) shock waves are built up round the aircraft giving rise to a sonic boom, often heard at ground-level. Supersonic flight with its attendant complexities developed from the 1960s. *See* SPEED RECORDS.

SUPRARE'NAL GLANDS. *See* ADRENAL GLANDS.

SUPRE'MATISM. Abstract-art movement founded in 1913 by the Russian painter Malevich, who expressed its aim as 'the supremacy of pure feeling or perception in the pictorial arts – the experience of non-objectivity'.

SUPREME COURT. The highest judicial tribunal in the U.S.A., composed of a chief justice (Warren Burger from 1969), and 8 associate justices. Vacancies are filled by the pres. and members can be removed only by impeachment. *See* LAW COURTS.

SUR. Arabic name of TYRE.

SURABAYA (soorabah'ya). Chief port of Indonesia, cap. of E. Java prov., on the N. coast of Java. It is an important naval and military base, with shipbuilding yards; also a centre of the petroleum industry. Pop. (1967) 1,007,945.

SURAJ-UD-DOWLAH (soorahj ood dow'lah). *See* BLACK HOLE OF CALCUTTA and PLASSEY.

SURAT (sooraht'). City in Gujarat state, India, 167 m. N. of Bombay, at the mouth of the Tapti, site of the 1st E. India Co. factory in India (1612). Cotton and silk are woven. Pop. (1961) 288,026.

SURGERY. The art of treating bodily injuries or disorders by manual means – traditionally the knife. During the S.W.W. plastic surgery was greatly advanced, and more recent developments incl. operations on heart, lung and kidney, using artificial equipment as substitute organs and, increasingly during the 1960s, using organs from live or dead donors – transplant S.: *see* HEART. Instruments are more varied – in addition to the scalpel and electric cautery, beamed high-energy ultrasonic waves may be used, and the intense light energy of the laser may prove surgically useful.

SURINAM. Country in the N. of S. America, between Guyana and French Guiana, also chief r. of the country at the mouth of which stands the cap. Paramaribo. Sugar, coffee, rice, bananas, and other tropical crops are grown; bauxite is the chief mineral product. Founded as a colony by the English (1650), S. became Dutch in 1667, and under the constitution of 1954 became an autonomous part of the kingdom of the Netherlands; the sovereign is represented by a gov. who is assisted by a ministry, an advisory council, and an elected legislative council. Area 55,143 sq. m.; pop. (1967) 350,000.

SUPERNOVA IN NGC 7331. In the upper picture a supernova is shown; in the lower picture it is not. This supernova, in a remote galaxy, shone millions of times more brightly than the Sun when at its maximum. The surrounding stars are foreground stars belonging to our own galaxy.
Courtesy of Lick Observatory, Univ. of California.

SURRE'ALISM. Art movement which developed from Dadaism, and was founded *c.* 1924, when André Breton issued its first manifesto. It repudiated all aesthetic values, and derived a great deal from Freudian theories. The movement spread to poetry and had an influence on photography, the film, commercial art, and stage scenery. Its leading exponents incl. Salvador Dali, Hans Arp, Georgio de Chirico, and others – e.g. Picasso, Henry Moore, and Edward Burra – were influenced by it.

SURREY, Henry Howard, earl of (*c.* 1517–47). English poet. The son of the 3rd duke of Norfolk, he served in France 1544–6, and was executed on a poorly based charge of high treason. He shared with Wyatt the honour of introducing the sonnet to England, and through his translation of the *Aeneid* pioneered the use of blank verse.

SURREY. A southern co. of England. The chalk North Downs span the county from Farnham in the W. to Caterham in the E., the Wey and Mole flowing N. through 2 gaps into the Thames. Market-gardening and agriculture are carried on. Guildford is the co. town, although co. hall and the assizes are at Kingston upon Thames. Under the reorganization of the London Govt. Act (1963) S. lost considerably both in pop. and rateable value by the incorporation of its metropolitan areas in the new Greater London. Area 650 sq. m.; pop. (1967) 985,930.

SURTEES, Robert Smith (1803–64). British sporting novelist. He created Jorrocks, a sporting grocer, and in 1838 pub. *Jorrocks's Jaunts and Jollities.*

SURVEYING. The art of determining the value of all descriptions of landed and house property and of the various interests therein; the practice of managing and developing estates and the science of admeasuring and delineating the physical features of the earth; the valuation, management, development and survey of mineral property and the measuring and estimating of artificer's work.

SURYA (soor'ya). In Hindu mythology the personification of the Sun.

SUSA (soo'sah). Port and commercial centre (French Sousse) on the E. coast of Tunisia. It has Roman remains. Pop. (1966) 82,666.

SUSLOV (soos'lof), **Mikhail** (1902–). Soviet politician. Joining the Communist Party in 1921, he headed the Cominform conference in 1948 which led to Yugoslavia's expulsion, was chief editor of *Pravda* 1949–50, and in 1956 was in charge of the suppression of the Hungarian revolt and in 1963 of the abortive negotiations with China. He is a member of the Presidium of the Supreme Soviet (1947) and of the Central Committee of the C.P.S.U., and as Party Sec. in 1964 indicted the Chinese leadership for offences against international Communism.

SUSSEX. A south-coast co. of England. The chalk South Downs extend eastward to Beachy Head, rising at Duncton Beacon to 837 ft. The rivers incl. the Arun, Adur, Ouse, and Rother. According to tradition, a Saxon chief Ella landed in what is now S. in 477, defeated the inhabitants, and founded the kingdom of the South Saxons which was absorbed by Wessex in 825. Among the historic remains are the earthwork at Cissbury; castles at Arundel, Pevensey, Hurstmonceux, Lewes, etc. S. is well wooded; root and cereal crops are grown; and cattle and sheep reared. Coast resorts, Brighton being the largest, range from Bognor Regis to Hastings. S. is divided administratively into E. and W., with their centres at Lewes and Chichester respectively; Lewes is cap. of the co. S. univ. (1961) is at Brighton. Area 1,457 sq. m.; pop. (1967) 1,173,730.

SUTHERLAND, Graham Vivian (1903–). British artist. B. in London, he studied at the Goldsmiths' School of Art, and in his early work was influenced by Blake and the Surrealists. After 1936 his style suddenly matured and broadened; and the detailed presentation of some unusually coloured insect, vegetable or mineral form assumed symbolic force. In his portraits, e.g. Maugham, Beaverbrook, Helena Rubinstein, he has usually achieved popular as well as artistic success, but his study of Churchill was controversial. In 1960 he was awarded the O.M. and his tapestry design for Coventry (q.v.) Cathedral was acclaimed in 1962.

SUTHERLAND, Joan (1926–). Australian soprano. Going to England in 1951, she made her début the next year as First Lady in *The Magic Flute*: other successes incl. *Lucia di Lammermoor*, Donna Anna in *Don Giovanni*, and Desdemona in *Otello*.

SUTHERLANDSHIRE. Extreme N. maritime co. of Scotland. There are deep sea-lochs, and the W. is mountainous, Ben More Assynt rising to 3,278 ft. The Oykell flows S.E. to Dornoch Firth. Sheep are raised, and tweeds manufactured. Dornoch is the co. town. Area 2,028 sq. m.; pop. (1961) 13,442.

SU'TLEJ. One of the 'Five Rivers' of the Punjab, flowing through India and Pakistan. It rises in Tibet at 15,200 ft., traverses the Punjab plains, and joins the Chenab nr. Madwala. Length 900 m.

SUTTEE (sutě'). Custom whereby a Hindu widow throws herself alive on her husband's funeral pyre. Forbidden under British rule in 1829, it enjoys sporadic illegal revivals in modern India.

SUTTNER (soot'ner), **Bertha,** baroness von (1843–1914). Austrian pacifist writer, author of the novel *Die Waffen nieder* (1889). She worked for a time with Alfred Nobel, and won the Nobel peace prize in 1905.

SUTTON COLDFIELD. English town (bor.) in Warwicks, with TV transmitter built 1949. Pop. (1961) 72,143.

SUTTON HOO. Village nr. Woodbridge, Suffolk, England, where in 1939 an E. Anglian ship-burial of c. A.D. 650 was excavated. The objects discovered – jewellery, armour, weapons – were placed in the B.M.

SUTTON IN ASHFIELD. English industrial town in Notts, 13 m. N. by W. of Nottingham; hosiery is the chief product; plastics are made and coal is worked. Pop. (1961) 40,438.

SUVA. City, seaport, and cap. of Fiji on S. coast of Viti Levu. Pop. (1966) 54,150.

SVALBARD. Norwegian name of SPITSBERGEN.

SVERDLO'VSK. Town of the Russian S.F.S.R., E. of the Urals. Copper, iron, platinum, etc., are mined, and there are heavy industries. S. has a univ. Formerly called Ekaterinburg, it was the site of the murder of Nicholas II and his family (1918). Pop. (1967) 940,000.

Another, S., in Ukraine S.S.R., 35 m. S.S.W. of Lugansk, is a coal-mining centre.

SVEVO (zvā'vō), **Italo.** Pseudonym of Italian writer Ettore Schmitz (1861–1928). His 2 major works, *Senilita* (1898: *A Man Grows Older*), and *La Coscienza di Zeno* (1924: *Confessions of Zeno*), describe, with a dispassionate irony, the bourgeois world of his native Trieste.

SWABIA. Historic region, a duchy 1079–1268, in S.W. Germany, covering parts of S.W. Bavaria, Württemberg-Hohenzollern, and S. Baden. The part in Bavaria is an admin. div. of that Land, cap. Augsburg. Area 3,818 sq. m.; pop. (est.) 1,300,000. Industries incl. making of textiles, cattle raising, dairy farming; much of it is covered by the Black Forest where tourism is important.

SWAHILI (swahě'li). Mohammedan people of mixed Bantu and Arab descent, numbering about a million, and inhabiting the coastal areas of S. Kenya and N. Tanganyika. Their language is of Bantu origin, and has official status throughout both countries.

SWALLOW. Genus (*Hirundo*) of birds incl. the common S. (*H. rustica*) which winters in Africa and visits Europe April–Sept. Steel-blue above and creamy white beneath, it has a red-brown throat and deeply forked tail. Two broods a year are reared in nests of

mud and straw shaped like a half-saucer and built on ledges of rock, etc. In N. America the barn S. (*H. erythrogastra*), which winters in Brazil, is the prevalent species.

SWAN, Sir Joseph Wilson (1828–1914). British inventor (in the U.K.) of the incandescent filament electric lamp. B. at Sunderland, he also made discoveries in photographic development and printing.

SWAN. Genus of birds (*Cygnus*) in the duck family, of which they are the largest members. The mute S. (*C. olor*) is up to 5 ft. long, has white plumage, an orange bill with a black knob surmounting it, and black legs; the voice is limited to a harsh hiss. Mating is generally for life and the young (cygnets) are at first grey, later brownish. Wild in eastern Europe, it is half tame in the west and in England is a royal bird, since it was once highly valued for the table. On the Thames, at the annual swan-upping, the cygnets are still marked on the beak as either the property of the Crown or of the 2 privileged City cos., the Dyers and Vintners. Other species incl. the whooper (*C. musicus*) of N. Europe and Asia, and Bewick's S. (*C. bewicki*) both rare in Britain; the black S. of Australia (*C. atratus*); and N. American trumpeter S. (*C. buccinator*).

SWANAGE. English holiday resort (U.D.) in Dorset, on the Isle of Purbeck, with stone quarries nearby. Pop. (1961) 8,112. *See* illus. under DINOSAUR.

SWANSEA. Welsh port (co. bor.) in Glam, 45 m. W.N.W. of Cardiff, port for the S. Wales coalfield. S. is the tinplate centre for the country, and copper, zinc, etc., are smelted. Pop. (1961) 166,740.

SWASTIKA. A symbolic ornament of ancient origin. It consists of a cross, at the end of whose lines perpendiculars extend all in the same clockwise or anti-clockwise direction. The S. was used by the Aryans and by Buddhists as a mystic symbol. Hitler decreed that it should become the German flag in 1935, it having previously only represented the Nazi Party. For this purpose the cross was also represented upright.

SWATOW'. Port in Kwangtung prov., China, at the mouth of the Han r. Opened to foreign trade in 1858, S. became the chief port for Chinese emigration to Malaya and other parts of S.E. Asia; it exports sugar, tropical fruit, etc., produced locally. Pop. (est.) 200,000.

SWAZILAND (swah'zě-). Kingdom in S.E. Africa, bounded N., W., and S. by Transvaal prov. of S. Africa, E. by Mozambique. Mountainous in the W., veld country in the E., it has a good climate, except for great heat in the lower-lying areas, and is free of malaria. The cap. is Mbabane. The Swazi King, Sobhuza II (1904–), was victorious in the first general election in 1964, as leader of the Imbokodvo Nat. Movement, internal self-govt. followed in 1966, and independence as a sovereign kingdom within the Commonwealth in 1968. Sugar, cotton, rice and citrus fruit are grown, and cattle and sheep raised; minerals incl. anthracite, tin, asbestos, iron ore, calcite and barytes. The iron deposits at Ngwenya were linked by rail 1964 with Lourenço Marques. Area 6,704 sq. m.; pop. (1966) 389,492.

SWEDEN. A kingdom occupying the E. part of the peninsula of Scandinavia in N. Europe with a coastline c. 4,700 m. long on the Baltic Sea.

PHYSICAL FEATURES. A mountain range runs along most of the Norwegian border, and the main regions are the mountainous two-thirds in the N., culminating in Sarjektjåkko (6,971 ft.); the central lowlands; the Småland highlands; and the fertile Skane in the extreme south. Lakes are numerous, the largest being Väner, Vätter, Mälar, and Hjälmar, all in the central region. The main river is the Göta. Öland and Götland are S.'s largest islands. The climate varies greatly. An almost treeless region in the extreme N. gives place to a zone of birch forests, while much of the centre of the country is covered by dense coniferous

SWEDEN. From the theoretical viewpoint the sphere is the most economical form to heat – one reason for its choice by architect Ralph Erskine for this all-season residence on Lisö Island off the Baltic coast. The house is based on the three main areas of the Swedish home – comfy winter area, semi-enclosed area with windscreening for spring and autumn, and the forest and water for summer use. *Courtesy of Ralph Erskine.*

forests. Bears, wolves, and elks haunt the remoter forests, and reindeer are numerous in Lapland.

ECONOMIC. N. Sweden is chiefly important for its minerals and forests, while the central region combines mining and agriculture, and the S. specializes in raising wheat and sugar beet and stock. Timber, pulp and paper milling industries give valuable exports. Huge iron deposits are worked in Lapland and other minerals incl. lead, zinc, sulphur, copper, silver and uranium. Hydroelectricity supplies power for engineering, shipbuilding, vehicle, electrical equipment, tool, petrochemical and plastics industries. The chief towns are Stockholm (the cap.), Göteborg, Malmö, Norrköping, Hälsingborg, Orebro, and Uppsala.

AREA AND POPULATION. Of mainly Nordic stock, the Swedes have a good educational system, with univs. at Uppsala, Lund, Göteborg, Stockholm, and Umeå. Most of the pop. belong to the State Lutheran Church. Area 173,629 sq. m.; pop. (1968) 7,893,704.

History. S. was divided in early times between 2 peoples, the Swedes in the N. and the Goths in the S., who were united under one king by Sverker (1134–55). Christianity became generally accepted about the same time, and a series of crusades in the 12th–14th cents. brought Finland under Swedish rule. The Riksdag, incl. representatives of the nobles, clergy, and burgesses, was founded in 1359; peasant representatives were added in 1435. The Union of Kalmar (1397) united Denmark, Norway, and S. under a Danish dynasty, but Swedish national feeling led to several revolts, the last of which, in 1520–3, ended the union, and placed Gustavus Vasa on the throne. Lutheranism became the national religion in 1527.

S.'s ambitions to dominate the Baltic coastline involved her in the 16th–18th cents. in many wars with Denmark, Poland, Russia, and Brandenburg, which in spite of the victories of Gustavus Adolphus (1611–32), Charles X (1654–60), and Charles XII (1697–1718), left her exhausted and impoverished. Ruled by a corrupt oligarchy, S. sank into insignificance until Gustavus III (1771–92) estab. an enlightened despotism. When in 1818 the Vasa line became extinct the crown passed to the French marshal Bernadotte, who reigned as Charles XIV (1818–44) and estab. a dynasty whose sixth member, Gustaf VI Adolph (1882–), ascended the throne in 1950.

S. lost Finland to Russia in 1809, but seized Norway in 1814, a union dissolved in 1905. Since 1814 S. has pursued a policy of neutrality. A new constitution adopted in 1809 ended the period of absolutism; this was amended in 1866, when a Riksdag of 2 chambers replaced the 4 estates; in 1971, when the Riksdag became unicameral; and in 1907, when universal suffrage was adopted. The Social Democrats, founded in 1889, are the strongest party, and have contributed to S.'s record as a pioneer in social-security legislation.

SWE'DENBORG, Emanuel (1688–1772). Swedish philosopher. B. at Stockholm, son of an unorthodox bp., he distinguished himself as a scientist – in geology, magnetic theory, functions of the brain, etc. – being much ahead of his time, and then from 1747 devoted himself to scriptural study, living much in London. His writing (in Latin) incl. *Divine Love and Wisdom*, in which he taught that the Last Judgment having taken place in 1757 there had succeeded The New Church signified by the New Jerusalem in the Revelation of which he was the prophet. An actual sect., for which his writings are the scriptures (Swedenborgians), was not estab. until 1788 by a Clerkenwell printer Robert Hindmarsh.

SWEDISH. A member of the northern or Scandinavian division of the Germanic languages. By the 14th cent. there were a number of rhymed chronicles, ballads and folk songs, but modern literature begins in the 17th cent. with the epic poet Georg Stjernhjelm (1598–1672). In the 18th cent. the names of Linnaeus, Celsius and Swedenborg typify the country's intellectual ferment, and the poet-historian Olof von Dalin was an outstanding literary figure. The period 1771–1809, covering the reigns of Gustavus III (himself a playwright) and Gustavus IV, saw much literary activity, e.g. the song lyrics of Karl Michael Bellman (1740–95), and the dramas of Gudmund Jöran Adlerbeth (1751–1818) and Henrik Kellgren (1751–95), who assisted the king in the royal theatre. Outstanding names of the Romantic era are those of poet-playwright Per Daniel Amadeus Atterbom (1790–1855), the poets Esaias Tegnér and Eric G. Geier (1783–1847) who sought inspiration in the legendary heroic past, and Afzelius, editor of national folk songs. To the period of romantic transition belong the novelist and poet Viktor Rydberg, the classic poet Carl Snoilsky (1841–1903), and the Finnish epic poet Johan Ludwig Runeberg (1804–77), but realism emerged in the novels of Carl Almqvist and Frederika Bremer (1801–65), and broke through in tortured agony in the work of Strindberg. A new romantic idealism followed, e.g. the poets Gustaf Fröding (1860–1911), Erik Axel Karlfeldt and Verner von Heidenstam (1859–1940), and the novelist Selma Lagerlöf – the last 3 all Nobel prizewinners. Among more recent writers are the novelists Hjalmar Söderberg (1869–1941), Sigfrid Siwertz (1882–), Gustaf Hellström (1882–1953), Elin Wagner (1882–1949), Hjalmar Bergman (1883–1930), Agnes von Krusenstjerna (1894–1940), and Vilhelm Moberg (1898–); the poet Hjalmar Gullberg (1898–), and those equally at home in both mediums – Birger Sjöberg (1885–1929), Karin Boye (1900–41), Harry Martinson (1904–), Artur Lundqvist (1906–), and Pär Lagerkvist, another Nobel prizewinner.

SWEDISH ART. The rise of Sweden in the 17th cent. ushered in a great cultural era. In the environs of Stockholm are the royal residences of Ulriksdal (1660), Karlsborg (1696–1718), and Drottningholm. Renaissance churches of Stockholm incl. Maria Magdalen (1650), St. Catherina (1725), and the church of Adolphus Frederick (1751–71). Towards the end of the 18th cent. French influence is apparent. From 1830 to 1880 Swedish architecture reflected various tendencies in fashion in Germany and Denmark, but from 1890 the teachings of William Morris were influential on Swedish arts and crafts, and in the 20th cent. Sweden became a world leader in industrial art. Contemporary Swedish architecture has also attracted much attention, the tendency is towards austerity.

SWEET, Henry (1845–1912). British philologist,

author of works on Old and Middle English, who transplanted to England German scientific techniques of study. He was said to be the original of Prof. Higgins in *Pygmalion*.

SWEET WILLIAM. Garden plant (*Dianthus barbatus*), also called bearded pink because of its bearded petals. The clusters of small flowers are pink, red or white, the leaves elliptical and dark green. The S.W. is named after William, duke of Cumberland, also known as 'Butcher' Cumberland.

SWEYN (swān) (d. 1014). King of Denmark. Succeeding to the throne c. 986, he repeatedly raided England, and conquered it in 1013, being accepted as king. His early death led to the recall of Ethelred to the throne.

SWIFT, Jonathan (1667–1745). Irish writer and churchman. B. in Dublin, he became sec. to Sir William Temple at Moor Park, Surrey, where began his friendship with 'Stella' – Hester Johnson (1681–1728). Returning to Ireland, he was ordained in the English Church (1694), and in 1699 was made a prebendary of St. Patrick's, Dublin. His satirical *Battle of the Books* and *Tale of a Tub* were pub. in 1804. In 1710 he became a Tory pamphleteer, and obtained the deanery of St. Patrick in 1713. His *Journal to Stella* is a series of letters, 1710–13, in which he described his life in London. In 1714 he returned to Ireland, where he wrote *The Drapier's Letters*, opposing the introduction of inferior copper coins into Ireland. In 1726 appeared his best-known work, *Gulliver's Travels*. For some years before his death he was insane. He may have m. Stella, but was deeply involved 1708–23 with Esther Vanhomrigh (1690–1723), whom he called 'Vanessa'.

SWIFT. Family of birds (Micropodidae), the fastest creatures alive, with a flying speed of 70–100 m.p.h. The common S. (*Apus apus*) migrates from Africa to Europe in summer: drab-coloured, it has a short forked tail, poorly developed feet and legs, and curved wings longer than the body. The nests of the closely related genus *Collocalia* are used in China for birdsnest soup.

SWIMMING. The self-propulsion of the body through water. The dog paddle is probably the original 'instinctive' stroke, but the first to be developed in Europe as a skilled technique was the breast stroke in the 16th cent., still used in competitive S., as is the faster but exhausting variant originating in the U.S.A. in the 1930s, the butterfly breast stroke, although the other developments from it – the side and overarm strokes – are out of fashion. Fastest known stroke is the crawl (developed by the Australians at the beginning of this cent. from a method in use by the South Sea Islanders), from which in turn came the back crawl in the 1920s, especially popular in competition S. because it allows the swimmer to breathe freely throughout. The water is entered by the 'racing plunge' or by diving, the latter being divided for competition purposes into springboard and firmboard events. Earliest of competitive S. bodies was the English Amateur S. Assocn. (1869), and the Fédération Internationale de Natation Amateur (1908) was founded in London. With the invention of frogman equipment – flippers for the feet, breathing apparatus, and even mechanical propulsion, underwater S. has developed special techniques of its own. *See also* CHANNEL SWIMMING.

SWINBURNE, Algernon Charles (1837–1909). British poet. B. in London, he was ed. at Eton and Balliol Coll., Oxford, and attained fame with the tragedy *Atalanta in Calydon* (1865). *Poems and Ballads* (1866) was also acclaimed for its lyric fire, but in both Britain and the U.S.A. its pagan spirit brought unfavourable comment. In a wrangling controversy that lasted some years he and Rossetti were attacked in 1871 by Robert W. Buchanan, as leaders of 'the fleshly school of poetry'. Among the best of later verse are *Songs Before Sunrise* (1871), revolutionary in its political attitude, and 2 further vols. of *Poems and Ballads* (1878 and 1889). In 1879 he moved to the home of Watts-Dunton (q.v.) at Putney, where he lived in retirement after a career of excess.

SWINDON. Town (bor.) in Wilts, 77 m. W. of London. The railway works (1841) to which it owed its growth declined in the 1950s, and varied new industries moved in. Pop. (1961) 91,736.

SWINE FEVER. Name given to 3 infectious diseases of swine, viz. swine plague, infectious pneumonia, and hog cholera, which are compulsorily notifiable.

SWING MUSIC. An offshoot of jazz (q.v.) which flourished from c. 1930 to the late 1940s; characterized by a simple harmonic base (of varying tempo) supplied by the rhythm section (percussion, guitar, piano), with a superimposed melodic line carried usually by a solo instrument, e.g. trumpet, clarinet or saxophone.

SWINNERTON, Frank Arthur (1884–). British novelist and critic. He estab. his reputation during many years as a publisher's reader (1900–25). A friend of Hugh Walpole, E. V. Lucas, Kathleen Mansfield, etc., between the wars, his histories *The Georgian Literary Scene* (1935), *Background with Chorus* (1956), and *Figures in the Foreground* (1963), intimately surveyed the literary scene 1900–40 and his prodigious output of novels, noted for their speed,

FRANK
SWINNERTON

sagacity and compassion, incl. *Nocturne* (1917), *A Woman in Sunshine* (1944) and *Death of a Highbrow* (1961). He is an attractive essayist.

SWINTON, Sir Ernest (1868–1951). British soldier and historian. Entering the army in 1888, he served in S. Africa and the F.W.W., rising to the rank of major-gen., and was the inventor of the tank in 1916. Knighted in 1923, he was Chichele prof. of military history at Oxford, 1925–39.

SWITHIN or **SWITHUN, St.** (d. 862). A chancellor of King Ethelwolf, he was bp. of Winchester 852–62. In 971 his body was to be reburied, but the day chosen, 15 July, now St. S.'s Day, was so wet that the translation was delayed. This gave rise to the superstition that if it rains on that day it will be rainy for 40 days.

SWITZERLAND. Confederate republic of W. Europe, bounded by Germany on the N., Austria on the E., Italy on the S., and France on the N.W.

PHYSICAL FEATURES. S. is extremely mountainous; a central plain traversed by the Aar is shut in by the Alps to the S. and by the Jura to the N. The Upper Rhine and Rhône lie between the Bernese Oberland and the main chain of the Alps. The Swiss Alps culminate in Monte Rosa (15,217 ft.). The Rhine, its tributary the Aar, the Rhône, and the Ticino, are the main rivers. There is a large number of lakes: Lake Geneva, through which flows the Rhône, lies partly in France; Lake Constance, which is traversed by the Rhine, is shared with Germany and Austria, and Lakes Maggiore and Lugano with Italy.

The climate shows considerable variations. The

föhn is a warm, dry southerly wind, while the *bise* is cold and northerly.

ECONOMIC LIFE. Lakes, rivers and mountains, forests and areas suitable only for pasturage take up three-quarters of the country, but the remainder serves to render S. agriculturally almost self-sufficient. Wheat, barley, potatoes, tobacco and vines are grown, and dairy farming is highly developed.

There are almost no industrial raw materials or fuel resources, but hydro-electric power is cheap and industry relies on processing raw materials and semi-manufactured goods, and specialized sophisticated products. The chief industries are machinery, metal-working, chemicals, watches and textiles, with smaller specialities incl. chocolates and perfumery. Some 90% of goods are for export and one third of the labour force is foreign, mainly Italian. Also very important are tourism, foreign investment, banking and insurance. Communications are excellent.

AREA AND POPULATION. The pop. in 1969 was 6,100,000 in an area of 15,941 sq. m. Over 3,000,000 persons speak German, *c.* 1,000,000 French, 280,000 Italian, and 50,000 Romansch: 58 per cent of the pop. are Protestants, 41 per cent Catholics.

The principal towns incl. Berne (the cap.), Zürich, Basle, Geneva, Lausanne, Fribourg, and Neuchâtel, each of which is the seat of a univ.

CONSTITUTION. Two chambers, a national council, elected directly, and a Council of States, with members chosen by the cantons, together form the Federal Assembly, which elects the executive Federal Council for 4 years and the President of the Confederation for 1 year. Extensive powers are reserved for the cantons and the communes. Women were enfranchised 1971.

History. S. originated politically in 1291, when the 'forest cantons' of Schwyz, Uri, and Lower Unter-walden formed the Everlasting League for the defence of their liberties against their Habsburg overlords; practical freedom from Habsburg control was secured in 1389, and from the suzerainty of the emperor in 1499. The entry of new towns and districts, incl. Lucerne, Zürich, and Berne, brought the number of cantons to 8 by 1353 and to 13 by 1513. The Reformation was accepted during 1523–9 by Zürich, Berne, and Basle, but the rural cantons remained R.C. S.'s complete independence was recognized by the Treaty of Westphalia, 1648.

After the suppression of the Peasant War (1653), the cantonal govts. fell increasingly into the hands of small oligarchies. A French invasion in 1798 estab. a centralized govt.; this was modified by Napoleon's Act of Mediation (1803), which made S. a democratic federation. Under the 1815 peace settlement S. received Geneva and other territories, increas-

SWITZERLAND. The first Cook's Tour to Switzerland in 1863 opened up the Continent to the middle-class tourist, and was re-enacted in 1963 by a party in 19th century dress.
Courtesy of Thomas Cook & Son, Ltd.

CANTONS OF THE SWISS REPUBLIC

	Area in sq .m.	Pop. (1960 census)	Capital
*Aargau/Argovie	542	360,940	Aarau
*Appenzell:			
A.Ausser Rhoden/ A.Rhodes Extérieures	94	48,920	Herisau
A.Inner Rhoden/ A.Rhodes Intérieures	66	12,943	Appenzell
*Basel-Stadt/Bâle-Ville	14	225,588	Basel/Bâle
*Basel-Land/Bâle-Campagne	165	148,282	Liestal
*Bern/Berne	2,659	889,523	Bern/Berne
‡Freiburg/Fribourg	645	159,194	Freiburg/ Fribourg
‡Genf/Genève	109	259,234	Genf/ Genève
*Glarus/Glaris	264	40,148	Glarus/ Glaris
*†§Graubünden/ Grisons/Grigioni/ Grishun	2,745	147,458	Chur/Coire
*Luzern/Lucerne	577	253,446	Luzern/ Lucerne
‡Neuenberg/ Neuchâtel	308	147,633	Neuenberg/ Neuchâtel
*Sankt Gallen/ St. Gall	778	339,489	Sankt Gallen/St. Gall
*Schaffhausen/ Schaffhouse	115	65,981	Schaffhausen/ Schaffhouse
*Schwyz	351	78,048	Schwyz
*Solothurn/Soleure	305	200,816	Solothurn/ Soleure
*Thurgau/Thurgovie	388	166,420	Frauenfeld
†Ticino (Ital.; F. & G. Tessin)	1,085	195,566	Bellinzona
*Unterwalden: Obwalden/ Obwald	190	23,135	Sarnen
Nidwalden/ Nidwald	106	22,188	Stanz/Stans
*Uri	415	32,021	Altdorf
‡Wallis/Valais	2,020	177,783	Sitten/Sion
‡Waadt/Vaud	1,240	429,512	Lausanne
*Zug/Zoug	92	52,489	Zug/Zoug
*Zürich	668	952,304	Zürich
	15,941	5,429,061	

NOTE: Switzerland has 4 national languages, German, French, Italian, and Romansch. Most of the cantons and capitals have German and French forms of their name: here the German is given first, the French second. Grisons also has an Italian (shown third) and a Romansch (shown fourth) form. The prevailing language in each canton is indicated: * German, ‡ French, † Italian, § Romansch.

ing the number of cantons to 22, a new constitution was adopted whereby S. again became a confederation, and the powers guaranteed Swiss neutrality. Following a struggle between the Liberals and Catholics a revised federal constitution, giving the central govt. wide powers, was introduced in 1848; a further revision in 1874 increased its powers, and introduced the principle of the referendum. S. maintained its neutrality during both world wars.

SWORD-FISH. Family of fishes (Xiphiidae). They are characterized by the long sword-like weapon protruding from the upper jaw. The common S. (*Xiphias gladius*) sometimes reaches Britain. The sail-fishes and spear-fishes are of the closely related family Istiophoridae. *See* illus. p. 1016.

SYCAMORE (sik′amor). Species of tree (*Acer*

pseudoplatanus). The leaves are five-lobed, and the hanging racemes of flowers are followed by winged fruits. The timber is used for furniture making.

SYDNEY (sid'ni). Seaport and cap. of N.S.W., largest city of Australia. It lies on Port Jackson, 4 m. W. of the Pacific Ocean. From Darling Harbour is shipped a large proportion of Australia's exports.

SWORD-FISH

Bligh House survives from the Regency city; S. Bridge (1923–32) has a single span of 1,652 ft., and the Opera House (*see* illus. p. 809) was begun 1959. S. is Australia's prime internat. airport, has engineering and metal processing industries, and is a wool mart and major financial and educational centre with 3 univs.– Sydney (1850), N.S.W. (1958) and Macquarie (1967). Pop. (1966) 2,539,630.

SYENITE (sī'enīt). A group of grey, crystalline, plutonic rocks, composed of feldspar and hornblende, distinguished from granite by the absence of quartz.

SYKTYVKAR (siktifkahr'). Russian city, cap. of Komi A.S.S.R., on the Vychegda r., a lumbering centre with saw mills, paper factories, tanneries, etc. It was founded 1740 as a Russian colony. Pop. (1967) 102,000.

SYLHET (sil-het'). Dist. in E. Pakistan, the valley of the Surma, formerly in Assam. The cap. is also called S. Rice, tea, jute, sugar, etc., are cultivated. Pop. (1961) 3,489,589.

SYMBOLISTS. School of French poets, represented by Verlaine, Mallarmé, and Rimbaud, who used words for their symbolic rather than their concrete meaning: the intimate, personal interpretations employed tended to produce obscurity.

SYMINGTON, William (1763–1831). British inventor. B. in Lanarks, he invented the road locomotive, and in 1788 a steamboat engine, building in 1802 at Grangemouth the first successful steamboat.

SYMONDS (si'mondz), **John Addington** (1840–93). British writer. B. at Bristol, he spent much of his life in Italy and Switzerland, and pub. *The History of the Renaissance in Italy* (1875–86), literary criticism, and a translation of Cellini's autobiography.

SYMONS (si'monz), **Arthur** (1865–1945). British writer. Son of a Methodist minister, he developed a precocious literary gift, and wide friendships with Toulouse-Lautrec, Mallarmé, Beardsley, Yeats and Conrad. He introduced Eliot to the work of Laforgue and, of his numerous books, *The Symbolist Movement in Literature* (1900) is best known. In 1908 he suffered a severe mental breakdown, but partially recovered.

SYMPHONY (sim'foni). A musical composition for orchestra, traditionally in 4 contrasted but closely related movements. It developed from the smaller sonata form, the Italian overture, and the dance suite of the 18th cent. Haydn estab. a mature form of S. in his later works, written in allegro, slow, scherzo, and allegro movements. Mozart in lyrical mood, and Beethoven with dramatic tones, expanded the classical form, which has been developed further by successive composers, such as Brahms, Tchaikovsky, Brückner, Dvořák, Mahler, Sibelius, Vaughan Williams, Rubbra, Piston, Prokoviev, Shostakovich, Stravinsky, Copland.

SYNAGOGUE (sin'agog). The building used by Jews for their religious worship. As an institution it dates from the destruction of the temple in Jerusalem in A.D. 70, though it had been in course of development from the time of the Exile.

SYNCLINE (sing'klīn). *See* ANTICLINE.

SYNCOPE (sin'kopi). Name for FAINTING (q.v.).

SYNDICALISM (sin'dikalizm). Revolutionary labour movement advocating the ownership and control of each industry by the workers in it, organized in their trade union. It rejects parliamentary activity in favour of 'direct action' by means of strikes, culminating in a revolutionary general strike. S. originated in England under Robert Owen's influence in the 1830s, but first became widespread in France after 1900. It exercised considerable influence in England *c.* 1910–24, Tom Mann being its principal spokesman, and was preached in the U.S. by the Industrial Workers of the World. After 1918 S. was absorbed by Communism or Anarchism.

SYNGE (sing), **John Millington** (1871–1909). Irish playwright. B. nr. Dublin, he was ed. at Trinity Coll., Dublin, and when living in Paris in 1898 was persuaded by Yeats to go to the W. of Ireland and the Aran Is. Absorbing the characteristic poetic turns of speech of the local people, he wrote plays incl. *The Shadow of the Glen* (1903), *Riders to the Sea* (1904), *The Well of the Saints* (1907), *The Playboy of the Western World*, and the unfinished *Deidre of the Sorrows*. His presentation of the Irish tended to upset his compatriots, and when *Playboy* (1907) was first presented at the Abbey Theatre there were riots.

SYNOVITIS (sinovī'tis). Inflammation of the lining of a joint, caused by injury or infection.

SYPHILIS (si'filis). The principal venereal disease, due to infection of the blood by the parasite *treponema pallidum*. It is communicated almost entirely by sexual intercourse. The first sign is a nodule, sometimes ulcerated (chancre); some weeks afterwards a rash appears all over the body, with ulcers in the mouth and throat. Later, swellings occur under the skin and in the internal organs, and destroy the surrounding tissues, incl. bone. The brain cells may be affected (general paralysis of the insane, *locomotor ataxia*). Treatment must be sought early; and in Britain is offered free by all large local authorities.

SYRACUSE (sī'rakūz). Port of Sicily, Italy, on the E. coast, 81 m. S.W. of Messina. Chemicals, salt and wine are produced. It has a cathedral and remains of temples, aqueducts, catacombs, and an amphitheatre. S. was founded in 734 B.C. and became a centre of Greek culture and power, especially under the elder and younger Dionysius (406–343 B.C.). S. was taken by the Romans in 212 B.C., and was destroyed by Saracens in 878. The rebuilt town was taken by the Normans in the 11th cent. Pop. (1961) 90,333.

SYRACUSE (sir'akūz). City in New York state, U.S.A., 147 m. W. of Albany at the S. end of Lake Onondaga, and connected with the Great Lakes, the Hudson, and the St. Lawrence by canals. Manufactures incl. typewriters, agricultural implements, clothing, furniture. S. was founded 1805 on the site of an Iroquois cap. Pop. met. area (1970) 629,190.

SYRIA (sir'ia). Asian republic in the Near East. Most of S. consists of a desert plateau. Mt. Hermon and the Anti-Lebanon, both on the Lebanese border, are the main elevations. The country is drained by the Euphrates and its tributaries. Damascus is the cap.: other towns are Aleppo, Homs, and Hama. S. has a coastline of about 120 m. on the Mediterranean, Latakia being its chief port.

Wheat, barley, sorghum, olives, tobacco, cotton, and grapes are cultivated and cattle, sheep, goats, camels, donkeys, and horses are reared. S. is traversed by 3 oil pipelines from Arabia. Silk, soap, tobacco, leather, and brassware are manufactured.

There have been frequent military coups, but under the provisional constitution of 1969 there is an elected People's Assembly which elects a pres., but only the Baath political party (split between more dominant 'nationalists' favouring war with Israel and 'progressives', favouring concentration on the economy) is permitted. Area 72,000 sq. m.; pop. (1970) 6,294,000, the majority Moslem Arabs. Arabic is the main language. The Syrian univ. (1924) is at Damascus.

History. S. was originally divided between various small kingdoms which fought against Israel, and were subdued by the Assyrians. It was subsequently occupied, by the Babylonians, Persians, and Macedonians, but gained importance under Seleucus Nicator (301 B.C.), founder of Antioch, and Antiochus the Great. After forming part of the Roman and Byzantine empires, it was conquered by the Saracens in 636. During the Middle Ages it was the scene of many of the Crusaders' exploits. The area forming S. belonged to Turkey 1516–1918. It was occupied by Brit. and Fr. troops 1918–19, and in 1920, with Lebanon, was placed under Fr. mandate (confirmed 1922). The 2 terrs. were separated in 1925, S. gaining full independence in 1946. Union with Egypt, proclaimed in 1958 and abandoned 1961, was again under discussion later.

SYRINGA

SYRIAC (sir'iak). One of the Semitic languages, originally the Aramaic dialect of Edessa. From *c.* 700 B.C.–*c.* A.D. 700, it was spoken over a large area of C. Asia. The alphabet was similar to that of Hebrew. S. survives as the ritual language of the Nestorian Church. S. literature was mainly theological in character.

SYRINGA (siring'ga). Genus of shrubs. Lilac (*S. vulgaris*) is the best-known, but the name is given to a number of other plants, notably mock orange, which is in the family Saxifragaceae.

SZCZECIN (sche'chin). Baltic port of Poland, on the Oder, 17 m. above its entrance into the Zalew Szczecinska (Stettiner Haff) and 84 m. N.E. of Berlin. Under the Ger. form of its name, Stettin, it was Germany's chief port on the Baltic until after the S.W.W. when it came under Polish admin. A member of the Hanseatic League from 1278, it was Swedish 1648–1720 when it was occupied by Prussia. The Russians captured it, 1945. Catherine the Great was b. at S. Pop. (1966) 315,000.

SZECHWAN (sechwahn'). Prov. of W. China, lies high; it is surrounded by mts., well forested, and drained by the Yangtze Kiang and its tributaries. The Red Basin forms the heart of the prov. Chengtu (cap.) and Chungking are the main towns. Chief products incl. timber, rice, winter wheat, millet, ground-nuts, cotton, sugar cane, coal, iron, copper, salt, petroleum. Sikang prov. was merged in S. in 1955; combined area 219,700 sq. m.; pop. (1968) 70,000,000.

SZEGED (seg'ed). City and co. bor. in Hungary, near the confluence of the Maros and Tisa, 100 m. S.E.

SZEGED. The Tisa, seen here flowing across the centre of the picture, almost completely destroyed Szeged by floods in 1879 and little of the ancient town survives.
Courtesy of the Hungarian News and Information Service.

of Budapest. S. is an industrial and commercial centre, with a univ. It was held by the Turks 1528–1688. Pop. (1967) 118,000.

SZYMANOWSKI (shimanov'ski), **Karol** (1883–1937). Polish composer. B. in the Ukraine, he became director of the Conservatoire at Warsaw in 1922. S. composed orchestral works, operas, and piano music.

T The 20th letter of the alphabet, whose sound is the unvoiced dental stop. The earliest form was X, which the Phoenicians called *tau*, a cross or sign, but in the Gk. alphabet its form was T.

TABLE BAY. Inlet in the S.W. coast of the Cape of Good Hope, S.A., on which stands Capetown. It is overlooked by Table Mountain (3,550 ft.).

TABLE TENNIS. Indoor game developed in Britain *c.* 1880, possibly from real T., which was known until the adoption of the present name by the International T.T. Assocn. in 1926 as ping pong. It is played by 2 or 4 players using solid-headed wooden bats and celluloid balls on a rectangular table (9 ft. by 5 ft. wide, and 2 ft. 6 in. above the floor), with a net 6 in. high dividing the table into 2 equal courts. Points are scored if the opponent makes a fault (fails to return a ball, strikes into the net, etc.), and 21 points make a game, a match being 2 out of 3 games. The blade may be bare wood or covered with sand-

paper, but in competition additional speed is gained with rubber-covered (first used 1903) or sponge-covered bats. In the 1950s the Japanese, and in the 1960s the Chinese, estab. world supremacy in the game.

TABORA. Cap. of Western prov., Tanganyika. Road and rail centre. Founded by the Arabs *c.* 1820 as a trading base for slaves and ivory. Pop. (est.) 15,000.

TABRIZ (tahbrēz). Persian commercial city, cap. of prov. 3 (part of Azerbaijan). It has a univ. and makes carpets, textiles, soap, matches, alcohol. Pop. (1964) 387,803. *See* illus. p. 1018.

TABU or **Taboo.** Polynesian word meaning 'forbidden', applied to magical and religious objects and practices which are generally prohibited.

TACITUS (tas'itus), **Cornelius** (*c.* 55–120?). Roman historian. An eminent lawyer, he m. a dau. of Julius Agricola, and in 97 was consul under Nerva. He wrote a life of Agricola; the *Germania*, describing the German

TABRIZ. The Shah Goli Lake.   *Courtesy of the Iranian Govt.*

tribes; the *Historiae*, a history of the empire from Galba to Domitian (69–97), and the *Annales*, reaching from Tiberius to Nero. He is famed for the succinct compression of his style.

TA'CNA. City of S. Peru, cap. of T. dept. Near T., Chile in 1880 defeated a combined Peruvian–Bolivian army and occupied T. until 1929. Pop. (est.) 17,000.

TACO'MA. Port of Washington state, U.S.A. Founded 1868, it became important through its choice as the terminus of the N.P.R. (1873). Pop. (1960) 147,979. T. is also another name for Mt. Rainier.

TADEMA. *See* ALMA TADEMA.

TADZHIK (tahjik′) **S.S.R.** Asiatic rep. of the U.S.S.R., separated on the S. from Afghanistan and China by the Amu-Darya r. The cap. is Dushambe. T. incls. the highest peak in the U.S.S.R. (24,000 ft.), in the Pamir Plateau. With the help of artificial irrigation, cotton, fruits, and other crops are grown; lead, zinc, radium, mica, sulphur are among minerals worked. T. was admitted to the Union in 1929. Area 55,000 sq. m.; pop (1967) 2,654,000.

TAFA'WA-BALE'WA, Alhaji Sir Abubakar (1912–66). Nigerian statesman. Entering the House of Representatives in 1952, he was Min. of Works (1952–4) and of Transport (1954–7). In 1957 he became P.M. of the Fed. of Nigeria, but was abducted and assassinated in the *coup d'état* of Jan. 1966.

TA'FFETA (Persian *tafta*, twisted). Light plainly woven silk fabric with a high lustre; the term may be applied to silk and wool mixtures, etc.

TAFFRAIL. *See* DORLING, H. T.

TAFT, William Howard (1857–1930). 27th President of the U.S.A. B. at Cincinnati, he was Secretary of War 1904–8, and was elected president in 1908 as a Republican. He was defeated in the election of 1912, and served as chief justice of the Supreme Court, 1921–30. His son, **Robert T.** (1889–1953), a Republican senator from 1939, was a candidate for the presidential nomination in 1940, 1944, 1948, and 1952, and was sponsor of the T.-Hartley Labor Act of 1947 (bitterly opposed by organized labour).

TAGANRO'G. Port of the R.S.F.S.R., on T. Gulf, an arm of the Sea of Azov. T. is icebound in the winter. It makes metal goods, aircraft, machinery, shoes. Russia annexed it 1769. There is a museum devoted to Chekhov who was b. at T. Pop. (1967) 238,000.

TAGLIONI (tahlyō′nē), **Maria** (1804–84). Italian dancer. She was particularly successful in *La Sylphide*, composed by her father, and was noted for her ethereal grace.

TAGORE (tagōr′), **Sir Rabindranath** (1861–1941). Indian writer. B. in Calcutta, in 1901 he estab. the 'Abode of Peace', a school which developed into an international univ. His translations of his collection of lyrics *Gitanjali* and his verse play *Chitra* brought him world fame, and in 1913 he received a Nobel prize. An ardent social reformer and nationalist, in 1919 he resigned the knighthood he had received in 1915 in protest against British repression. His nephew **Abanindranath T.** (1871–1951) was the father of modern Indian painting. He drew his subjects from Indian history and mythology. Abanindranath's elder brother **Gaganendranath T.** (1867–1938) was also a gifted artist.

TĀ'GUS. River which rises in Spain, in the mountains of Albarracin, and flows through Portugal to the Atlantic at Lisbon: it is 566 m. long, longest river in the Iberian peninsula. The Salazar Bridge (1966) linking Lisbon and Almada is the longest suspension bridge in Europe. The T.-Segura Project (1968) is planned to channel water *c.* 150 m. to the Murcia/Alicante region in the rainless south, where *c.* 500,000 acres will be irrigated to produce early fruit and vegetables for the European market.

TAHITI (tahē′ti). Largest of the Society Islands, part of Fr. Polynesia. T. was visited by Captain Cook (1769) and by Bligh of the *Bounty* (1788). T. came under French protection in 1843, becoming a colony in 1880. Papeete is the cap. Area 402 sq. m.; pop. (1962) 45,430.

TAINE (tān), **Hippolyte Adolphe** (1828–93). French critic and historian. He was appointed prof. at the École des Beaux Arts, in 1864. In his critical writings, e.g. *History of English Literature* (1863) and *Philosophy of Art* (1865–9), he analyses literary works as the products of period, race, and environment. He also pub. *Origins of Contemporary France*.

TAIT, Archibald Campbell (1811–82). British churchman. B. in Edinburgh, he was headmaster of Rugby 1842–8, and became bp. of London in 1856, and archbp. of Canterbury in 1868. His attempt to suppress ritualism through the Public Worship Act (1874) aroused much opposition.

TAIWAN (tiwahn′). Chinese name of FORMOSA.

TAIYUAN (tīyoo-ahn′). Walled cap. of Shansi prov., China, on the Fen-ho, seat of Shansi univ. It makes iron and steel goods, cotton textiles, agricultural implements, etc. Pop. (1957) 1,020,000.

TAJ MAHAL (tahzh mahahl′). *See* AGRA.

TAKAO (tahkow′). Japanese name of KAOHSIUNG.

TAKORA'DI. Port in Ghana, W. Africa. The harbour, opened in 1928, is the only deep harbour between Sierra Leone and Nigeria. Pop. (1960) 41,000.

TALAVERA DE LA REINA (tahlahvā′rah dā lah rā′ēnah). Town of central Spain, on the Tagus, 75 m. S.W. of Madrid. In 1809 Wellesley defeated the French here. Pop. (est.) 24,000.

TALBOT, William Henry Fox (1800–77). British photographic pioneer. His development of the talbotype method (1839–41) – contemporary with Daguerre's experiments – laid the foundation of modern photography; he also made instantaneous photographs in 1851 and photo engravings in 1852.

TALC. A magnesium silicate, $3MgO.4SiO_2.H_2O$, occurring in crystals, but the massive form known as steatite or soapstone is more common. French chalk and potstone are varieties of T. It is used in cosmetics, for lubricants, and as a filler in paper manufacture.

TALIEN. Another form of DAREN.

TALLAHA'SSEE. Cap. of Florida, U.S.A., *c.* 160 m. W. of Jacksonville, centre of an agricultural and lumbering area, seat of Florida state univ. It dates from 1824; De Soto discovered an Indian settlement on the site in 1539. Pop. (1960) 48,174.

TALLCHIEF, Maria (1929–). American dancer. Dau. of an Osage Indian chief and a mother of Scots-Irish descent, she trained as a concert pianist as well as a dancer. A pupil of Nijinska, she was m. 1946–51 to Balanchine, appearing in his ballet *Firebird*. In 1957 she became première danseuse étoile at the Paris Opéra.

TALLEYRAND-PÉRIGORD (tahlāroň′-pārēgōr′),

Charles Maurice de (1754–1838). French statesman. B. in Paris, he was bp. of Autun, 1789–91. He was a supporter of moderate reform, but fled to the U.S.A. during the Terror. Returning to France in 1796, he served as For. Min. under the Directory 1797–9, and under Napoleon 1799–1807. He represented France at the Congress of Vienna 1814–15, and was ambassador to London 1830–4.

TA'LLIN. Seaport and cap. of the Estonian S.S.R. on the Gulf of Finland, with a fine harbour closed by ice for 3 months every year. It has a univ., and a castle dating from the 13th cent. Founded 1219 as Reval, it was a Hansa town, passed to Sweden 1561, to Russia 1750. Pop. (1967) 340,000.

TALLIS, Thomas (*c.* 1505–85). English organist and composer. He was organist at Waltham Abbey until 1540, and with his pupil Byrd was joint organist at the Chapel Royal from 1572. T. wrote masses, anthems, and much other church music.

TALMA (tahlmah′), **François Joseph** (1763–1826). French tragic actor. He made his début in 1787, and advocated realism in scenery and costume.

TA'LMUD (late Heb. for 'teaching'). Chief work of Jewish post-Biblical literature, based on the *Mishnah*. To this was added the *Gemara*, discussions centring on its texts, during the 3rd and 4th cents.

TA'MARIND. Species of tropical tree (*Tamarindus indica*) in the family Leguminosae. An evergreen, it has pinnate leaves, reddish-yellow flowers, followed by pods, the pulp of which is used medicinally.

TAMARISK. Genus of shrubs (*Tamarix*), which flourish in warm, salty, desert regions where no other vegetation is found. The common T. or salt cedar (*T. gallica*) has evergreen, scale-like leaves and spikes of very small, pink or white flowers. *See* MANNA.

TAMATAVE (tahmahtahv′). Chief port of Madagascar, on its E. coast. Pop. (1965) 49,400.

TAMBOURINE (tam′boorēn). Musical instrument of ancient origin, almost unchanged since Roman times. A shallow drum with a single skin and loosely set jingles which increase its effect.

TAMBO'V. Cap. of T. region, R.S.F.S.R., on the Tsna in the black-earth area, with flour mills, distilleries, railway workshops, artificial-rubber factories, etc. Pop. (1967)206,000.

TAMERLA′NE or **Timur i Leng** (1336–1405). Mongol conqueror. B. in Turkestan, he made himself ruler of Samarkand in 1369, conquered Persia, Azerbaijan, Armenia, and Georgia, and broke the power of the Golden Horde. In 1398–9 he invaded the Punjab and sacked Delhi; he then invaded Syria and Asia Minor, and captured the sultan at Angora.

TA'MIL. Chief of the Dravidian languages; spoken by *c.* 18 million in S. India and Ceylon.

TAMIL NADU. *See* MADRAS.

TA'MMANY HALL. Democratic Party organization in New York. It originated in 1789 as the Society of St. Tammany, named after a Red Indian chief. Dominant from 1800 till the 1930s, it gained a reputation for gangsterism and corruption: La Guardia (q.v.) and John Lindsay (1965) were the only Rep. mayors

TA'MMUZ. Sumerian vegetation deity, who died at midsummer and was brought back from the underworld in spring by his lover Ishtar. His cult spread over Babylonia, Syria, Phoenicia, and Palestine. In Greek mythology T. appears as Adonis.

TAMPA, City, port, and resort on the W. coast of Florida, U.S.A., famous for its cigars; it also has fruit and vegetable canneries, shipyards, and factories making boxes, fertilizers, clothing, etc. Pop. met. area T.–St. Petersburg (1970) 999,613.

TAMPERE (tahm′pārā). City of Finland between Lakes Näsi and Pyhä, important industrially (textiles, paper, shoes, turbines, etc.). Pop. (1967) 147,340.

TAMPICO (tahmpē′kō). Port and air port of Mexico, on the Pánuco, 6 m. from the Gulf of Mexico. It is surrounded by oilfields. Pop. (1967) 147,700.

TAMWORTH. English market town (bor.) in Staffs on the Tame, 15 m. N.E. of Birmingham. Clothing and paper are manufactured. It was once the cap. of Mercia. Pop. (1961) 13,555. Another T. is a township of N.S.W., Australia, a railway and dairying centre. Pop. (1966) 21,682.

TANA (tah′na). Lake of Ethiopia, the source of the Blue Nile, at a height of *c.* 6,000 ft. Area *c.* 1,400 sq. m.

TANABA'TA. The Japanese 'star festival' celebrated annually on the night of 7 July. It is dedicated to Altair and Vega, 2 stars in the constellation Aquila, who are united once yearly in the Milky Way, according to legend, and represent 2 star-crossed lovers allowed by the gods to meet on that night. Of Chinese origin, T. was introduced to Japan in the 8th cent.

TANAGER (tan′ajer). Family of birds (*Tanagridae*) similar to finches. Found in Central and S. America, they all have brilliant plumage.

TA'NAGRA. City of ancient Greece, in E. Boetia, where Spain defeated Athens, 457 B.C. Many terracotta statues and statuettes were excavated towards the end of the 19th cent.

TAN'ANARIVE. Fr. form of ANTANANARIVO.

TANGA. Seaport in Tanganyika, E. Africa, on T. Bay, 75 m. N. of Zanzibar. Pop. (1968) 61,000.

TANGANYIKA (-yē′ka). *See* TANZANIA.

TANGERINE (-nj-). A type of orange (*Citrus nobilis*) similar to a mandarin.

TANGIER (tanjēr′). Seaport and largest commercial city in Morocco, on the Straits of Gibraltar. Taken by the Portuguese in 1471, it passed to England in 1662 as part of the dowry of Catherine of Braganza, but was abandoned in 1684, becoming later a centre of Barbary pirates. A convention signed 1923, effective 1925, made T. and *c.* 225 sq. m. behind it an international zone. Spain administered it 1940–5; in 1956 it was restored to independent Morocco. Pop. (1965) 166,290.

TANGIER. The old Casbah.
Courtesy of British European Airways.

TANGO. A slow dance of African origin, in 2-4 time, resembling the Spanish Habanera.

TANGSHA'N. Industrial city in Hopei prov. 65 m. N.E. of Tientsin. It makes steel, pottery, cement, etc., and has a power plant based on local coal. Pop. (1957) 800,000.

TANIZA'KI, Junichirô (1886–1965). Japanese novelist. B. in Tokyo, son of a family of printers, he was ed. at Tokyo Imperial Univ. His earlier work has a melodramatic and lurid quality, but after the earthquake of 1923 he moved to the Kyoto-Osaka region where ancient tradition is stronger, and his genius flowered. His books incl. a modernized version of *The Tale of Genji* (1939–41), *The Makioka Sisters* (3 vols., 1943–8), and *The Key* (1956). *See illus. p. 593.*

TANK. Originally a code name given to the first successful tracked armoured fighting vehicle used in the battle of the Somme in 1916. A T. consists of a body or hull of thick steel, on which are mounted machine guns and a larger gun. The hull contains the crew (usually consisting of a commander, driver, and 2 or 3 men), engine, wireless, fuel tanks, ammunition, etc. The T. travels on endless bands, or 'tracks', to traverse rough terrain. *See* SWINTON, SIR ERNEST.

TANKER. Ship with a tank for carrying mineral oil, liquefied gas, molasses, etc. in bulk. They may be of great size, the largest having a gross tonnage of over 300,000, and being more than 1,100 ft. long.

TANNENBERG (tahn'nenberg). Village in Polish-occupied E. Germany where in 1410 the Poles and Lithuanians defeated the Teutonic Knights, and in 1914 Hindenburg defeated the Russians.

TANNIC ACID or **Tannin** ($C_{14}H_{10}O_9$). Astringent substance occurring in gall nuts, tree barks, and roots, fruits, etc. Its most important property is that of precipitating gelatin to give an insoluble compound, used in the manufacture of leather from hides.

TANNU-TUVA. *See* TUVA.

TANSY. Perennial plant (*Tanacetum vulgare*) in the family Compositae, found in Europe and naturalized in N. America. The heads of yellow flowers grow in clusters, and the deeply indented leaves are used in cooking for their bitter flavour.

TA'NTALUM. Bluish-white metal, ductile and malleable, and resembling platinum when polished: symbol Ta, at. wt. 180·95, at. no. 73. Discovered in 1802 by Ekeberg, it occurs chiefly in the mineral tantalite. T. can be drawn into wire with a very high melting point and great tenacity (useful for filament lamps subject to vibration), and is used in alloys; for corrosion-resistant laboratory apparatus and chemical equipment; as a catalyst in the manufacture of synthetic rubber; in tools and instruments; as a getter in vacuum technique; and in rectifiers and capacitors. T. carbide is an important abrasive.

TA'NTALUS. In Greek mythology, a king who was punished in the underworld for his crimes by being tormented with hunger and thirst.

TANZA'NIA, United Rep. of. Country in E. Africa, formed in 1964 by the union of Tanganyika and Zanzibar (q.v.).

The narrow coastal plain of Tanganyika rises to an extensive plateau, with Kilima-njaro to the N. and the Livingstone Mts. (over 9,000 ft.) to the S.W.; parts of Lakes Victoria and Tanganyika are also incl. The climate is equatorial, and sisal, coffee, cotton and timber are produced: minerals incl. diamonds, gold, tin and mica. The Tanzam Highway (1,000 m.) links the Zambian copperbelt with Dar-es-Salaam, which is the cap of both T. and Tanganyika: other important towns in the latter are Tanga and Tabora. During the F.W.W. Tanganyika (formerly part of Ger. E. Africa) was conquered by Britain, under whom it became a League of Nations mandate 1921, changed to U.N. trusteeship 1946. Given independence 1961, it remained as a rep. within the Brit. Commonwealth 1962, as did T. on its formation 1964. Area of T. 363,700 sq. m. (of Tanganyika 362,680); pop. (1967) 12,231,342 (of Tanganyika 11,876,982).

TAOISM (tow'-izm or tah'-ō-izm). Chinese philosophical system and religion, said to have been founded by Lâo Tze probably in the 4th cent. B.C. Tao, meaning 'road' or 'way', denotes the hidden Principle of the Universe. Less stress is laid on doing good deeds than on the avoidance of all positive action. Later Lâo Tze was deified, forming one of the trinity of the Three Pure Ones, and many other spiritual beings were worshipped. The chief text is the *Tao Tê Ching*, attributed to Lâo Tze. Present-day T. is largely a popular system of magic.

TAPE RECORDER. Instrument for recording electrical signals on a layer of iron oxide, coated on to thin plastic tape. The electrical impulses are fed to the electromagnetic recording head, which magnetizes the tape in proportion to the frequency and amplitude of the original signal.

TAPE RECORDER. General view of the Ampex VR 2000 video tape installation at the B.B.C. Television Centre, which records both sound and vision. *Courtesy of the B.B.C.*

For playback, the tape is passed over (the same or) another head to convert magnetic into electrical impulses, which are then amplified for reproduction. The higher the frequency to be recorded the faster the tape must be passed over the heads. Typical speeds are: 1⅞ in./sec. (speech); 3¾ and 7½ in./sec. (domestic music recording); 15 and 30 in./sec. (professional music recording); and up to 400 in./sec. for radio frequencies.

TAPESTRY. Ornamental textile used for wall-hangings, furniture, and curtains. The T. design is threaded into the warp, and various shades of wool are used. Many ancient peoples made Ts., and during the Dark Ages the art was practised in the monasteries. European Ts. of the 13th cent. were frequently ornamented with oriental designs brought back by the Crusaders. The great European centres of T. weaving were at Arras, Brussels, Aubusson, Beauvais, and Mortlake. The Gobelin T. factory of Paris was made a royal establishment in the 17th cent. In England, William Morris estab. the Merton Abbey looms in 1877. Many fine Ts. are still made in France. *See* illus. of Coventry Cathedral.

TAPE-WORM or **Cestode.** Flat parasitic worm with no digestive organs. They have a complicated life-history, and usually reach man within imperfectly

TAPESTRY. Detail of the three figures of the Trinity from 'The Seven Days of Creation', one of a set of 16th century tapestries in silk and wool on the Redemption of Man. Once in the treasury of the cathedral of Toledo, they were given to the M. H. de Young Museum by the William R. Hearst Foundation. *Courtesy of the M. H. de Young Memorial Museum, San Francisco.*

cooked meat or fish, causing anaemia and intestinal disorders.

TAPIO'CA. Perennial plant (*Manihot utilissima*) of tropical S. America. It contains a poisonous juice which is drawn off before the spindle-shaped root is prepared to make T.

TA'PIR. Genus of ungulate mammals (*Tapirus*), having a short trunk, thick hairy skin, and 4 toes on the front and 3 on the hind feet. The 4 S. American species are black; the Malayan T. has white hindquarters.

MALAYAN TAPIR

TAR. A dark brown or black viscous liquid, obtained by the destructive distillation of coal, shale, wood, etc. From wood T., creosote and paraffin are produced. Ts. consist of hydrocarbons, acids, and bases. *See* COAL TAR.

TARA (tah'rah) **HILL.** Site in co. Meath, Rep. of Ireland, 507 ft., of a palace and coronation place of many kings of Ireland, abandoned in the 6th cent. St. Patrick preached at T.

TARA'NTO. Seaport and naval base of Apulia, S. Italy, on the Gulf of T., site of the ancient Greek Tarentum, founded by Sparta in the 8th cent. B.C. In 1940 the Brit. Fleet Air Arm sank or severely damaged 6 Italian naval vessels during a night air-torpedo attack. Its steelworks is part of the new industrial complex of S. Italy. Pop. (1961) 191,515.

TARANTULA. Poisonous spider (*Lycosa tarantula*) with a body 1 in. long, so named from its occurrence nr. Taranto in Apulia, Italy. It spins no web, relying on its speed in hunting. In the Middle Ages its bite was thought to cause hysterical ailments for which dancing was the cure, hence the dance named tarantella.

TARBES (tahrb). Cap. of Hautes-Pyrénées dept., S.W. France, a tourist centre for the Pyrénées. It belonged to England 1360–1406. Théophile Gautier and Marshal Foch were b. at T. Pop. (1962) 50,715.

TARE. Another name for VETCH (q.v.).

TARGUM (tahr'gum). Collection of Aramaic translations, interpretations, and paraphrases of the O.T. The T. was not written down until *c.* A.D. 100.

TARIM (tahrēm). A region of internal drainage in the Sinkiang prov. of China, between the Tien-shan and Kunlun mountains, watered by the Yarkand-Darya. Area 350,000 sq. m.

TARKINGTON, Booth (1869–1946). American novelist. B. in Indiana, he won popularity with his romantic *Monsieur Beaucaire* (1900), and realistic novels of the Middle West, *The Magnificent Ambersons* (1918) and *Alice Adams* (1921).

TARN (tahrn). Fr. river, rising in the Cévennes and flowing 220 m. to the Garonne.

TARO (tah'rō), **Cocco** or **Eddoes.** Names given to a plant (*Colocasia antiquorum*) of the family Araceae, native to the South Seas: the tubers are eaten.

TA'RPON. Large fish (*Megalops atlanticus*) found in the S. Atlantic. It grows to about 6 ft. long.

TARQUINIUS (tahrkwin'ius) **SUPE'RBUS.** The last king of Rome, who according to legend reigned 534–510 B.C., and was expelled following the violation of Lucretia by his son Sextus.

TARRAGO'NA. Port in Catalonia, Spain, 55 m. S.W. of Barcelona, cap. of T. prov., noted for its wine. T. has a cathedral and Roman remains, incl. a fine aqueduct. Pop. (1960) 44,000.

TA'RSHISH. A city mentioned in the O.T., prob-

ably the Phoenician settlement of Tartessus in Spain.

TA'RSIER. Small primate (*Tarsius spectrum*) intermediate on the evolutionary scale between lemurs and anthropoids. About the size of a rat, it has thick. light brown fur, very large eyes, and long feet and hands. Nocturnal and arboreal, it moves by leaping. It is found in the Malayan islands.

TARSIER

TARSU'S. Town of Turkey, on the T. r., *c.* 10 m. from the sea. Cap. of the ancient Roman prov. of Cilicia, and famous as St. Paul's birthplace, it was a meeting place for Greek and Asiatic culture. Pop. (1965) 51,000.

TARTAN. A worsted cloth woven in a chequered pattern, consisting of stripes of different colours and widths crossing one another. T. kilts and plaids were worn by the Scottish highlanders from the 15th cent., clans having distinctive patterns. After the 1745 rebellion the use of the T. was illegal until 1782.

TARTA'RIC ACID ($C_4H_6O_6$). Commonly occurring vegetable acid, present in fruit juices in the form of salts of potassium, calcium, and magnesium, and used in effervescent drinks and baking powders.

TARTARS. *See* TATARS.

TA'RTARUS. In Greek mythology, a part of the underworld where the wicked are punished.

TARTU (tahr'tōō). Town in Estonian S.S.R., on the Emback, said to date from 1030. It belonged to the Teutonic Knights until taken by Russia 1558; Poland and Sweden held it for periods, Russia recovering it in 1704. It has a univ. (1632) founded by Gustavus Adolphus of Sweden. Pop. (1967) 80,000.

TASHKE'NT. Cap. of Uzbek S.S.R., and of T. region, 160 m. N. of Samarkand. Dating from the 7th cent., it became Russian in 1865. It has a univ., manufactures textiles, metal and leather goods, etc. Largely destroyed by earthquake 1966, it was rebuilt. Pop. (1967) 1,241,000. *Declaration of T.*: see KASHMIR.

TASMAN (tahs'mahn), **Abel Janszoon** (*c.* 1603–59). Dutch navigator. In 1642–3 he discovered Tasmania (which he called Van Diemen's Land in honour of the Gov.-Gen. of the Netherlands Indies, but was renamed Tasmania in 1853 in T.'s honour), New Zealand, and the Tonga and Fiji Islands.

TASMA'NIA. State of the Commonwealth of Australia, consisting of a large island (T.) and various small islands which lie 140 m. off the S.E. of the mainland, from which T. is separated by Bass Strait. T. is triangular in shape; the interior is mountainous, rising in Cradle Mt. to 5,069 ft. The rivers (among which are the Derwent, Huon, Gordon, and Tamar) have been harnessed for electricity. Numerous lakes incl. Great Lake and Lake Sorell. The climate is mild with moderate rainfall except in the mts. of the W. where the rainfall is heavy.

Wheat, oats, peas, fruit, and potatoes are grown, and there are apple orchards in the S. Sheep, cattle, horses, and pigs thrive, and wool, cheese, and butter are exported. Mineral wealth incl. silver, coal, and zinc. Hobart is the cap. and the seat of T. univ. (1890); Launceston the only other town of importance. Area (incl. Macquarie and King Islands and the Furneaux Group) 26,215 sq. m.; pop. (1966) 371,416. T., discovered by Tasman 1642, was settled in 1803, and formed part of N.S.W. until 1825. Responsible govt. was introduced in 1856 and in 1901 T. joined the Commonwealth of Australia.

TASMANIAN DEVIL. Marsupial (*Sarcophilus ursinus*) found in Tasmania. Similar to a bear, it has dark brown fur with white patches on the chest and hind parts, and is nocturnal and carnivorous.

TASSO (tahs′so), **Torquato** (1544–95). Italian poet. At first a law student at Padua, he was enabled to overcome his father's opposition to a literary career by the success of his romantic poem *Rinaldo* (1562), dedicated to Cardinal Luigi d'Este, who took him to Paris, where he met the members of the Pléiade (q.v.). Later he was under the patronage of the cardinal's brother, Duke Alfonso d'Este of Ferrara, for whose court theatre he wrote his pastoral play *Aminta* in 1573. His great work is his romantic epic of the First Crusade *La Gerusalemme Liberata* (1574: *Jerusalem Delivered*), much superior to the *Gerusalemme Conquistata*, written in the stress of mental instability and delusion which set in from 1576.

TATARS (tah′tahrz). Although sometimes loosely used to incl. other Turkic and Mongol peoples, the name applies more accurately to those speaking a language of the N.W. branch of Turkic. Mainly Moslem, they represent in the U.S.S.R., where they live mainly in the Tatar A.S.S.R. (cap. Kazan), but also in the Uzbek S.S.R. (whence they were deported from the Crimea, q.v., in 1945) and S.W. Siberia, the remnant of the 'Mongol' invasion of the 13th cent. The Crimean Ts. (*c.* 500,000) agitated 1968–9 for their return from Uzbekistan and the restoration of the Crimean A.S.S.R.

TATE, Harry (1873–1940). British music-hall comedian, famous for his sketches, 'Motoring', etc. He was one of the first comedians to broadcast.

TATE, Nahum (1652–1715). Irish poet. B. in Dublin, he wrote an adaptation of *King Lear*, to which he gave a happy ending, a version of the psalms, and hymns; his best-known poem is 'While shepherds watched'. He became poet laureate in 1692.

TATE, Phyllis (1911–). British composer. B. nr. London, she studied at the Royal Academy of Music. Her principal works incl. *Concerto for Saxophone and Strings* (1944), *The Lady of Shalott*, for tenor and instruments (1956), the operas *The Lodger* (1957–8), based on the story of Jack the Ripper, and *Dark Pilgrimage* (for television, 1962), and *Duo Concertante* for trumpet, bassoon and small orchestra (1962).

PHYLLIS TATE

TATE GALLERY. Art gallery at Millbank, London. It contains national collections of pictures and sculpture, those of the British school from the late 16th cent., and of modern foreign art from 1800. Built by the generosity of Sir Henry Tate (1819–99), sugar merchant and philanthropist, it was opened in 1897, and was greatly enlarged by Sir J. Duveen and his son Lord Duveen of Millbank (the wings to house the Turner Bequest, and Modern Foreign Art, and the Sculpture Hall).

TATIAN (tāshian) (2nd cent. A.D.). Christian apologist. B. in Assyria, he compiled a *Diatesseron*, or harmony of the gospels.

TATTERSALL'S. Bloodstock auctioneers estab. at Knightsbridge Green, S.W. London, since 1864. It is named after Richard T. (1724–95), who founded T. at Hyde Park Corner in 1766.

TATUM, E(dward) L(awrie) (1909–). American microbiologist, prof. at the Rockefeller Inst., New York from 1957. *See* BEADLE, GEORGE WELLS.

TAUNTON. Co. town (bor.) of Somerset, England, 30 m. N.E. of Exeter. Historic buildings incl. the Elizabethan hall in which Jeffreys conducted his 'Bloody Assize' (1685). T. makes gloves, shirts, agricultural-implements, etc. Pop. (1961) 35,178.

TAUPO (taw′pō). The largest lake in New Zealand, in N. Island, area 238 sq. m., depth 534 ft.

TAURUS. Mt. range in S. Asia Minor, forming the S. edge of the Anatolian plateau, and rising to over 12,000 ft.

TAVENER, John (1944–). British composer. Greatly influenced by Messiaen and Stravinsky, his works incl. *In Alium, The Whale, Celtic Requiem*, and an opera based on Genet's *Notre dame des Fleurs*.

TAVISTOCK. English market town (U.D.) in Devon, on the r. Tavy, 15 m. N. of Plymouth. It has a ruined 10th cent. abbey whose lands were given to John Russell, ancestor of the dukes of Bedford, when the monasteries were dissolved by Henry VIII; the eldest son of the duke uses the title marquess of Tavistock. Pop. (1961) 6,086.

TAWNEY, Richard Henry (1880–1962). British historian. An ardent socialist, he was prof. of economic history, Univ. of London, 1931–49, and produced the major *Agrarian Problem in the 16th Cent.* (1912) and *Religion and the Rise of Capitalism* (1926).

TAXATION. The part of the national revenue raised by compulsory dues and charges, as distinct from that derived from public property. From the 19th cent. when govts. came into existence based on a wide electorate and broadened the scope of legislation needing to be supported by T. (education, transport, defence, health, pensions and allowances) the scheme of T. became increasingly comprehensive, and in the mid-20th cent. T. is used by govts. as a means of stimulating or restraining the national economy, or to modify the national life in any desired direction, e.g. the encouragement by reduction of T. of any type of manufacture or discouragement by heavy T. of consumption of any commodity. In newly emergent countries T., therefore, tends to be very light, e.g. India and Pakistan, because incomes, are low and services, etc., undeveloped; midway in the T. scale come countries such as Brazil and the Argentine; and at the top the U.K. with 30 per cent of the gross national product, France and W. Germany 28 per cent, U.S.A. 25 per cent, the Netherlands 23 per cent and Italy 22 per cent.

Direct taxes, which are for the most part graduated according to income, etc., are increasingly used in the West; more expensive to collect because individually assessed, they compensate by being the most productive. Most important is *income tax*, collected by the Inland Revenue in Britain, as are the other direct taxes, i.e. *surtax*, a tax paid in addition to income tax and designed to bear heavily on large unearned incomes; *corporation tax* on co. profits (replacing 1966–7 income and profits tax); *capital gains tax*, aimed from 1961 at preventing the use of capital as untaxed income; and *selective employment tax*, intended from 1966 to redress the balance between manufacturing industry (liable to purchase tax) and the service industries which had no such burden, and to direct labour from the latter to the former; and *death duties*. Another form of direct T. is the *rates* (q.v.) collected by local authorities which are based on the value of buildings on a site: it has been suggested that these be replaced by a local (state) income tax as in the U.S.A.

Indirect taxes, the most favoured method of T. in the U.S.S.R., incl. in Britain the taxes on tobacco, spirits, wine, beer, petrol (*see* CUSTOMS AND EXCISE); and betting and purchase tax. The last-named, introduced in 1940, is charged when goods are delivered from a registered trader to the retailer: this system is less complicated than a sales tax (as in U.S.A.) where the tax is deducted by the retailer at the moment of sale to the customer, but results in loss or gain to the retailer when tax changes are made on goods already purchased from the registered trader. Generally speaking, unless limited to luxury goods, indirect tax bears more heavily on the poorer classes. The European Common Market adopted 1967 plans for a value-added tax system based on the French T.V.A. (Taxe sur la Valeur Ajoutée), which is charged at each stage in production and distribution on the value added to the product.

TAXŌ'DIUM. Genus of trees in the family Taxodiaceae. The American deciduous cypress, *Taxodium distichum*, grows in or near water, and is a timber tree.

TAYLOR, Alan John Percivale (1906–). British historian. Lecturer in international history at Oxford 1953–63, he has made a popular as well as a scholarly reputation by such books as *From Napoleon to Stalin* (1956) and *The Origins of the Second World War* (1961), and by his lectures on TV.

TAYLOR, Elizabeth (1932–). British actress. Going to Hollywood, where she finished her education, she estab. her position as the world's most highly paid actress with *A Place in the Sun* (1950), *Giant* (1956), *Butterfield 8* (1960), for which she gained an Academy Award, and *Cleopatra* (1963). She m. (1) Conrad Hilton, Jnr., (2) actor Michael Wilding – both being divorced – (3) impresario Mike Todd, killed in an air crash, (4) singer Eddie Fisher, and (5) actor Richard Burton.

TAYLOR, Sir Geoffrey (1886–). British scientist. In 1944 he was awarded the Copley Medal for work in aerodynamics, hydrodynamics and structure of metals, and worked 1944–5 at Los Alamos on the first atom bomb. In 1969 he received the O.M.

TAYLOR, Jeremy (1613–67). Anglican divine. B. at Cambridge, he was deprived of his living by the Puritans in 1644, and thrice imprisoned as a royalist under the Commonwealth. His books incl. *Liberty of Prophesying* (1646), a defence of toleration, and *Holy Living* (1650) and *Holy Dying* (1651). He became bp. of Down in 1661.

TAYLOR, Zachary (1784–1850). 12th President of the U.S.A. B. in Virginia, he commanded the invasion of Mexico in 1846–7, and was elected president as a Whig in 1848.

TBILISI (tbilyĕ′sē). Cap. of Georgian S.S.R., on the Kura, close to the foothills of the Caucasus. It dates back to the 5th cent. The seat of a univ., it manufactures textiles, machinery, ceramics, tobacco, etc. Pop. (1967) 842,000.

TCHAIKOVSKY (chĭkov′ski), **Peter Ilyich** (1840–93). Russian composer. B. at Kamsko-Votinsk, he became a prof. of harmony at Moscow in 1865, and later met Balakirev and the nationalist circle. The 2nd symphony was performed in 1873, and the piano concerto in B flat minor in 1875. T. wrote several operas, incl. *Eugene Onegin*; ballet music, *The Swan Lake*, *The Sleeping Beauty*, and *The Nutcracker*; orchestral fantasies, *Romeo and Juliet*, *Francesca da Rimini*, and *Hamlet*; 3 piano concertos and a violin concerto; and chamber and vocal music. All these enjoy wide popularity, as do the 4th, 5th and 6th symphonies.

TEA. Leaves, flowers and fruit.
Courtesy of the Tea Bureau.

TEA. Plant (*Thea sinensis*) from the leaves of which the beverage of the same name is made. Left to itself it develops into a 40 ft. tree, but is restricted in cultivation to bushes 3–5 ft. high, from which at *c.* 5 yrs. the young shoots and leaves are picked. After 24 hrs. spread on shelves in the 'withering' lofts, the leaves are broken up by rolling machines, which release the essential oils, and allowed to ferment. This process is then halted by passing the leaves through ovens where moisture is removed and the blackish-brown T. emerges ready for sifting into the various grades.

Known in China as early as 2737 B.C., T. was first brought to Europe in A.D. 1610, but was not in use in England until 1657. It rapidly became a fashionable drink but remained expensive because cargoes had to be brought from China in the specially fast T. clippers. In 1823, however, T. was found growing wild in northern India, and some 10 years later plantations were estab. in Assam and then in Ceylon: other modern producers incl. Africa, S. America, Russia, Indonesia and Persia. Methods of consumption vary: in Japan special T. houses and an elaborate T. ceremony have evolved; in England 'afternoon' T. had its own ritual; and in Tibet hard slabs of compressed T. are used as money before being finally brewed.

TEAK. Timber tree (*Tectona grandis*) grown in India, Burma, and Java. The wood is very hard and is used for shipbuilding.

TEAL. Small duck (*Anas crecca*). The drake has a reddish-brown head with green and buff markings on either side, and a black and white line on the wing. The female is buff and brown.

TEASEL. Species of plant (*Dipsacus fullonum*). It grows in waste places to a height of 6 ft. The purple flowers grow in an egg-shaped head, divided by hooked bracts. T. brushes are made from the heads.

TEASEL

TEBA′LDI, Renata (1922–). Italian soprano, remarkable for the controlled purity of her voice and excelling in roles from Puccini.

TECHNETIUM. The first artificially made element (Gk. *technetos*, artificial), symbol Tc, at. wt. 99, at. no. 43. Originally produced by Perrier and Segré (California) in 1937 by bombarding molybdenum with deuterons or neutrons, it was later isolated in large amounts from the fission products of uranium and may have importance in alloys.

TECHNO′CRACY. Govt. by technical experts. Certain contemporary writers, e.g. J. Burnham in *The Managerial Revolution*, have maintained that modern society is tending towards T.

TECHNOLOGY. The practical application of the arts and sciences in industry and commerce. Britain's industrial revolution preceded that of Europe by half a century, and her prosperity stimulated Continental countries to encourage technological education in order to emulate her. France estab. the École Polytechnique, the 1st technological univ., in 1794 and Germany founded the remarkable series of Technische Hochschulen with one in Berlin in 1799. In Britain education in T. was catered for by the mechanics institutes, notably the Univ. of Manchester Inst. of Science and T. (founded 1824, created univ. 1966) which, together with the Imperial College of Science and T. (estab. 1907), still form the focus of technological work. America was quick to grasp the importance of T., most of her univs. having schools of engineering and T., and also estab. a number of institutes on European lines of which the most famous are the Massachusetts (1861) and California Institutes of T. and the Rensselaer Polytechnic Institute (founded at Troy, N.Y., in 1824). The mass production of technologists, exceeding the pace of both western

Europe and the U.S.A., has been concentrated upon by the Soviet Union and increasingly by China.

In 1950 an *International Vocational Training Competition* was inaugurated by Spain and is held each year in a different country.

TECUMSEH (tekum′se) (1768–1813). Shawnee Indian chief. He attempted to unite all the Red Indian tribes into a confederation, and was killed while fighting the Americans as an ally of the British.

TEDDER, Arthur William, 1st baron (1890–1967). Marshal of the Royal Air Force. He was Air Officer Commanding R.A.F. Far East 1936–8, and Middle East 1941–3, where his method of pattern bombing known as 'Tedder's carpet' became famous. As Deputy Supreme Commander under Eisenhower 1943–5, he was largely responsible for the initial success of the 1944 Normandy landings.

TEDDINGTON. Part of Twickenham, in the Greater London bor. of Richmond upon Thames. T. Lock, 74 m. upstream, is the highest point reached by the tide. The National Physical Laboratory (1900) is at T.

TEESSIDE. Co. bor. in N. Riding, Yorks, created 1968 by amalgamation of Middlesbrough, Stockton on Tees, Redcar (qq.v.), etc. There are oil refineries, petrochemical works, a reorganized steel industry, an airport and modern port facilities. Pop. (1968) 400,000.

TEETH. Hard structures within the mouth, growing from each jaw in 2 semicircular rows and meeting (occlusion) in the act of biting. The first set, the milk teeth, appear from age 6 months to 2½ yrs., and number 20. The permanent dentition replaces these from the 6th year onwards, the wisdom teeth (3rd molars) sometimes not appearing until the age 25 or 30. It consists of 32 teeth: 2 incisors, 1 canine (eye tooth), 2 premolars, and 3 molars on each side of each jaw. A tooth is made of bony substance called dentine. It has a root or roots set in a socket of fine bone (alveolus), a neck covered by gum, and a crown covered with hard white enamel. It is hollow and filled with a highly sensitive pulp made of nerves and blood vessels. The chief diseases of teeth are misplacements resulting from defect or disturbance of the tooth-germs before birth; eruption out of the proper places; caries (decay), and pyorrhoea.

TEHRAN (tärahn′). Cap. of Persia, 60 m. S. of the Caspian Sea, hub of road and rail communications; with an airport. Cotton, tobacco, soap, and sugar are manufactured. In 1943 T. was the scene of the first meeting between Stalin, Roosevelt, and Churchill. Pop. (1966) 2,803,130.

TEHRAN. Rapidly expanding as a centre of commerce and finance – the Markazi Bank is seen to the left – the capital has trebled its population since the S.W.W.
Courtesy of Imperial Iranian Embassy.

TEL AVIV. A view of the waterfront.
Courtesy of the Israel Government Tourist Office.

TEIGNMOUTH (tin′muth). English port, resort, and market town (U.D.) on the S. coast of Devon, 15 m. S. of Exeter. Pop. (1961) 11,576.

TEILHARD DE CHARDIN (tāyahr de zhahrdiń′), **Pierre** (1881–1955). French mystic and palaeontologist. B. in the Puy-de-Dôme, of well-to-do parents, he entered the Society of Jesus in 1899, was ordained in 1911, and during the F.W.W. was a stretcher bearer, taking his final vows in 1918. His *Letters from a Traveller* describes his travels in little-explored China, in Europe and America, as a palaeontologist. His books on philosophical themes were not allowed to be pub. by his superiors as they seemed to tend to pan-psychism. He attempted to relate psychic and physical energy, and evolved his concept of the *noosphere* – the union of thought of human beings. His other books incl. *The Phenomenon of Man* and *Le Milieu divin.* From 1951 he lived in the U.S.

TEJO. Port. form of TAGUS.

TEKIRDAG (tekir′dah). Turkish port on the European shore of the Sea of Marmara, cap. of T. il. It is said to have been founded by the Samians. Pop. (est.) 20,000.

TEL AVIV-JAFFA (avĕv′). City in Israel, on the Mediterranean, 33 m. N.W. of Jerusalem. Textiles, sugar, chemicals are made; printing and publishing are important. T.A. (founded 1909) was combined with Jaffa (q.v.) 1949: their sister ports were superseded by Ashdod 1965. Pop. (1967) 389,700.

TELECOMMUNICATIONS (Gk. *tele*, afar). The 1st apparatus used for communication over a distance, apart from such devices as semaphore, heliograph, etc., was the *telegraph*. The earliest practicable instrument was invented by Cooke and Wheatstone in 1837, and used by railway cos., the 1st public line being laid between Paddington and Slough in 1843. Morse invented a signalling code (still used), and a recording telegraph, 1st used commercially between England and France in 1851. As a result of Hertz's discoveries using electromagnetic waves, Marconi estab. wireless communication between England and France (1899) and across the Atlantic (1901). On the principal telegraph routes *teleprinters* (keyboard-operated telegraph machines in which the transmitted baudot code – 5 unit, with start and stop – automatically prints the received message) are used in conjunction with voice-frequency carrier apparatus. This enables a large number i.e. 36 telegrams to be signalled simultaneously on the same circuit.

The *telephone* was invented in 1876 by Alexander Graham Bell, as a result of Faraday's discovery of electromagnetism, and today it is possible to communicate with most countries by telephone cable,

TELECOMMUNICATIONS. An artist's conception of the *Intelsat III* satellite off the east coast of Brazil. The 41-in. high cylinder is covered by 10,000 solar cells which convert sunlight to electrical energy to power the many electrical and electronic components. Surmounting it is the antenna system, making the satellite's overall height 78 in.
Courtesy of the American Telephone and Telegraph Co.

e.g. a submarine cable between Britain and Belgium can carry 216 simultaneous conversations. However, the chief method of speeding long-distance calls on land is microwave radio transmission, the drawback to this being that the transmissions follow a straight line from tower to tower, so that over the sea the system becomes impracticable.

The solution was found in the suggestion in 1954 by John R. Pierce of the Bell Telephone Laboratories that space satellites be used for overseas communications, and on 10 July 1962 Telstar (developed by Bell) was launched from Cape Kennedy. Such early types were fast-moving and low-orbiting, but the 1969 series of four *Intelsat III* commercial communications satellites are placed in synchronous orbit *c.* 22,300 miles from Earth and appear to be almost stationary. Two are over the heavy traffic area of the Atlantic, and one each over the Indian Ocean and Pacific. Telephony and television transmissions are carried simultaneously, and as the satellite spins clockwise to maintain stability, the antenna (which enables the satellite to receive and transmit signals) spins anti-clockwise at the same speed, so keeping it always pointed towards Earth in the correct communications position. The number of Earth stations is rapidly increasing (Etam, U.S.A. and Goonhilly, q.v., being noted for research), and by 1971 *Intelsat IV* satellites, with capacities exceeding 5,000 telephone circuits are contracted for service.

TELEGRAPH. *See* TELECOMMUNICATIONS.

TEL EL AMARNA. *See* AMARNA TABLETS.

TEL-EL-KEBIR (-kebĕr′). Village of Lower Egypt. Here Arabi Pasha was defeated by Sir Garnet Wolseley in 1882.

TELE′PATHY (Gk. for 'feeling from afar'). The term was coined by F. W. H. Myers who defined it as 'the communication of impressions of any kind from one mind to another, independently of the recognized channels of sense'. The card experiments of Prof. J. B. Rhine of Duke univ., N. Carolina, and of Dr. S. G. Soal of London univ. have tended to prove the reality of the phenomenon. In the U.S.S.R., experiments have been made with T. as a means of communication between astronauts.

TE′LESCOPE. An instrument for magnifying distant objects. The 2 essential components are an object-glass – i.e. a lens or concave mirror – which collects and focuses light, and an eyepiece for magnifying this image. Lippershey is credited with the 1st T. in 1608, but Galileo constructed several famous instruments from 1609. Newton designed the 1st reflecting T. The T. at the Mount Palomar Observatory, 130 m. S.E. of Pasadena, California, which was installed in 1948, has a 200in. lens, and enables 'island universes' 2,000,000,000 light years distant to be seen. The world's largest T. is in the Caucasus, U.S.S.R., and has a 236in. lens. *See also* RADIO TELESCOPE.

TELEVISION. Name given to the reproduction by radio of scenes enacted at a distance. In 1873 it was realized that since the electrical properties of selenium vary according to the amount of light to which it is exposed, light could be converted into electrical impulses, making it possible to transmit such impulses over a distance and then re-convert them into light. The chief difficulty was seen to be the 'splitting of the picture' so that the infinite variety of light and shade values might be transmitted and reproduced. In 1908 Campbell-Swinton pointed out that the transmission and reception would be better done by the use of cathode-ray tubes. Mechanical devices were used at the first practical demonstration of actual television, given by J. L. Baird in London on 27 Jan. 1926, and cathode-ray tubes used experimentally by the B.B.C. from 1934. The world's first public T. service was started from the B.B.C. station at the Alexandra Palace, in N. London, on 2 Nov. 1936. Both sound and vision programmes are received on the same aerial. The vision programme is taken to the vision receiver, at whose output end is a cathode-ray tube whose flattened end constitutes the viewing screen. The minute currents set up by the incoming vision signals are magnified in order to bring them up to a workable strength. The end of the tube, upon which the scene is to appear, has its inside surface coated with a fluorescent material which is bombarded by a stream of electrons emitted by a gun in the neck; light is thereby produced; a separate signal being used to control brightness. The resulting light and shade patterns give an effective reproduction of the original scene. Twenty-five pictures are built up each second with interlaced scanning (30 in U.S.), with a total of

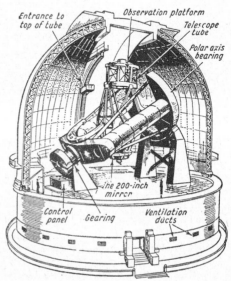

TELESCOPE. Inside the dome of the telescope at Mt. Palomar. U.S.A.

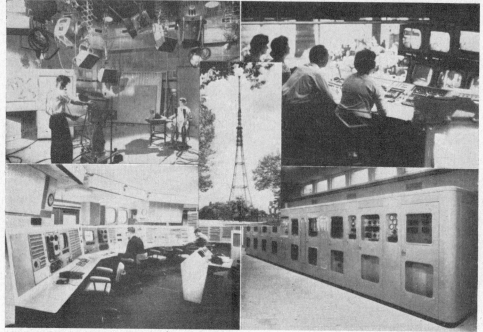

TELEVISION. The complex 'chain' that brings the programme to the viewer: (*top left*) a studio used for announcements, interviews, weather forecasts, etc.; (*top right*) the production gallery during a variety show, with (left to right) secretary, assistant to the producer, producer, vision mixer and – far right – the monitor screens; (*bottom left*) the main control desk in the central apparatus room; (*bottom right*) the vision transmitter – the final radio-frequency stage is grid-modulated and is capable of a peak power output of approx. 40 kw; (*centre*) the tower and transmitting aerial system at the Crystal Palace station.
Courtesy of the British Broadcasting Corporation.

405 lines. From 1964 the B.B.C. effected a change to a system using 625 lines, in common with the rest of Europe, in order to facilitate trans-continental programmes (Eurovision).

For colour T. the scene to be transmitted is similarly analysed by the T. camera into a large number, 625, of horizontal lines and the information along each line is transmitted in sequence. In black and white T. it is only the brightness of each part of the line which is important. In colour T. it is necessary to measure the characteristics of the colour at every point along each scanning line, to transmit signals which are a measure of these characteristics, and at the receiver to build up a colour picture based on these signals.

Baird gave a demonstration of colour T. in London in 1928, but it was not until Dec. 1953 that the first successful system was adopted for broadcasting, in the U.S.A. This is called the N.T.S.C. system, since it was developed by the National Television System Committee, and variations of it have been developed in Europe, e.g. SECAM (sequential and memory) system in France and the PAL (phase alternation by line) in W. Germany. All 3 differ only in the way colour signals are prepared for transmission. Agreement on a universal European system failing in 1964, the U.K. in 1967 adopted PAL (as did W. Germany, Netherlands and Switzerland) and France and the U.S.S.R. adopted SECAM.

The method of colour reproduction is related to that used in painting, colour photography and printing. Just as the artist uses a palette with only a few basic colours which he combines to form a full range of hues in his picture, so in colour T. the receiver reproduces only three basic colours: red, green and blue. The effect of yellow, for example, is reproduced by combining equal amounts of red and green lights, while white is imitated by a mixture of all 3 basic colours. It is then possible to specify the colour which it is required to transmit by sending signals which indicate the amounts of red, green and blue lights which are to be generated at the receiver.

To transmit each of these 3 signals in the same way as the single brightness signal in black and white T. would need 3 times the normal bandwidth, and reduce the number of possible stations and programmes to one third of that possible with monochrome T. The 3 signals are therefore coded into one complex signal which is transmitted as a more or less normal black and white signal, and which produces a satisfactory – or compatible – picture on ordinary black and white receivers. A fraction of each primary red, green and blue signal is added together to produce the normal brightness, or luminance signal. The minimum of extra colouring information is then sent by a special subcarrier signal which is superimposed on the brightness signal. This extra colouring information corresponds to the hue and saturation (*see* COLOUR) of the transmitted colour, but without any of the fine detail of the picture. The impression of sharpness is conveyed only by the brightness signal, the colouring being added as a broad colour wash. The various colour systems differ only in the way in which the colouring signals are sent on the subcarrier signal.

The colour receiver has to amplify the complex signal and decode it back to the basic red, green and blue signals; these primary signals are then applied to a colour cathode-ray tube. The colour display tube is the heart of any colour receiver. Many designs of colour picture tube have been invented and the most successful of these is known as the shadow mask tube. It operates on similar electronic principles to the black and white T. picture tube, but the screen is composed

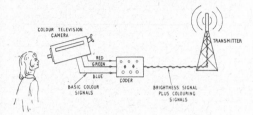

of a fine mosaic of over one million dots arranged in an orderly fashion. One-third of the dots glow red when bombarded by electrons, one-third glow green and one-third blue. There are 3 sources of electrons,

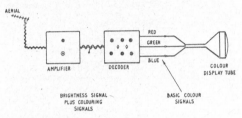

respectively modulated by the red, green and blue signals. The tube is so arranged that the shadow mask itself shadows the green and blue glowing dots from the red electrons, and so on. The glowing dots are

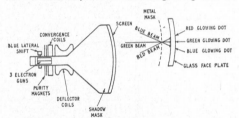

so small that from a normal viewing distance the colours merge into one another and a picture with a full range of apparent colours is seen.

TELFORD, Thomas (1757–1834). Scottish civil engineer. A shepherd's son, and erstwhile poet, mason and surveyor, he opened up N. Scotland by building 920 m. of new roads; constructed many aqueducts and canals incl. the famed Caledonian (1803–23); and erected the Menai bridge on the suspension principle, scarcely tried previously in England.

TELL, William. Swiss hero, who is said to have been sentenced, for refusing to salute the Habsburg badge, to shoot an apple off his son's head. Having accomplished this, he shot the tyrannical Austrian ruler. This story has no historical basis.

TELLU′RIUM. Silver-white, brittle, semi-metallic element of the sulphur group, discovered by Müller von Richtenstein in 1782 and named by Klaproth in 1798 from Lat. *tellus*, earth; symbol Te, at. wt. 127·61, at. no. 52. It is used in colouring glass (blue to brown) and in the electrolytic refining of zinc. Its strength and hardness are greatly increased by addition of 0·1 per cent lead, when it is used for pipes and cable sheaths.

TE′MA. Port of Ghana, 17 m. E. of Accra. Opened 1962 it superseded the 'surf' ports at Accra, Cape Coast, etc.

TEMESVAR. Hungarian form of 'TIMISOARA.

TEMPERA. A method of painting in which a gelatinous substance is employed. A form of T. was used in ancient Egypt, and by many Italian masters.

TEMPERATURE. The state of hotness or coldness of a body (measured in degrees Centigrade or Fahrenheit) and the condition which determines whether or not it will transfer heat to, or receive heat from, another body according to the laws of thermodynamics (q.v.). The normal temperature of the human body taken in the mouth is 98·4°F. Variation by more than a degree or so indicates ill-health, a rise signifying excessive activity (usually due to infection), and a decrease signifying deficient heat production (usually due to lessened vitality). To convert °C to °F multiply by ⅑ and add 32; °F to °C subtract 32 then multiply by ⅝.

TEMPEST, Dame Mary (Marie) Susan (1866–1942). British actress, noted for her stylish playing in such comedies as Somerset Maugham's *Penelope*.

TEMPLARS. A religious order, founded in 1119, of knights who took vows of poverty, chastity, and obedience and devoted themselves to the recovery of Palestine from the Saracens. They played a distinguished part in the Crusades of the 12th and 13th cents. The enormous wealth of the order aroused the envy of Philip IV of France, who arranged for charges of heresy to be brought against its members in 1307, and the order was suppressed.

TEMPLE, William (1881–1944). British churchman. Son of Frederick T. (1821–1902), liberal theologian and abp. of Canterbury 1896–1902, he became headmaster of Repton (1910–14), rector of St. James's, Piccadilly (1914–18), and as bp. of Manchester (1921–9) won a high reputation for his application of Christian beliefs to social matters. He was abp. of York 1929–42 and of Canterbury 1942–4, and wrote *Christianity and the State* (1928) and *Nature, Man and God* (1934), more influential than intellectually sound.

TEMPLE, Sir William (1628–99). English statesman. He had a distinguished diplomatic career, and negotiated the Triple Alliance with Holland and Sweden in 1668, and the marriage of Princess Mary to William of Orange in 1677. After 1681, disapproving of Charles II's policy, he retired to Moor Park, Surrey, where he wrote his attractive essays.

TEMPLE. A group of buildings S. of Fleet St., London, which formed the English headquarters of the Templars 1185–1313, and since the 14th cent. has been occupied by 2 of the Inns of Court, the Inner T. and the Middle T. The round church built by the Templars and consecrated 1185, severely damaged by air raids 1941, was restored by 1958.

TEMPLE. The centre of Jewish national worship at Jerusalem. Three Ts. occupied the site: Solomon's

TEMPERATURE. The industrial use of extremely low temperatures is illustrated by the liquefaction plant at Arzew, where natural gas from the Saharan field is reduced to −258°F. In the background are the 6,000 ton storage tanks, and a tanker *Methane Progress*. See Gas. *Courtesy of the Gas Council.*

T., which was destroyed by Nebuchadrezzar; Zerubbabel's T., built after the return from Babylon; and Herod's T., which was destroyed by the Romans in A.D. 70. The Mosque of Omar occupies the site. The Wailing Wall is the surviving part of the western wall of the platform of the enclosure of the T. of Herod, so-called by tourists because of the oriental chanting style of the Jews in their prayers there. Under Jordanian rule Jews had no access to the spot, but took this part of the city in the 1967 campaign.

TEMPLE BAR. Western gateway of the City of London, England, standing between Fleet St. and the Strand. Rebuilt by Wren in 1672, it was removed in 1878 to Theobald's Park, Herts, but in 1967 it was proposed to return it to the City. The heads of traitors were formerly displayed on spikes on T.B. A figure of a griffin marks the site.

TEMPLER, Sir Gerald (1898–　). British field marshal. He served in both world wars, but is especially remembered for his work as High Commissioner in Malaya 1952–4, following the assassination of his predecessor, Sir Henry Gurney. He was C.I.G.S. 1955–8.

TEMPLEWOOD, Samuel John Gurney Hoare, 1st visct. T. (1880–1959). British Cons. statesman. When For. Sec. in 1935, public indignation at the Hoare-Laval agreement for the cession of Ethiopian territory to Italy forced his resignation, but his later offices incl. Home Sec. 1937–9, Air Min. 1940, and ambassador to Spain 1940–4.

TENBY, Lord. See LLOYD GEORGE.

TENCH. Freshwater fish (*Tinca vulgaris*). A member of the carp family, it is about 18 in. long, olive-green above and grey beneath. The scales are small, and there is a barbel at each side of the mouth.

TENERIFE (tenerif'). The largest of the Canary Islands, Spain. Santa Cruz de T., the main town, is the cap. of one of the 2 provs. of the group. The chief feature of the island is the active volcano of T. 12,815 ft. high. Area 795 sq. m.; pop. (1960) 387,000.

TENIERS (tenẽrs'), **David** (1582–1649), the Elder. Flemish painter. B. at Antwerp, he studied under Rubens and Elsheimer, and painted scenes of everyday life in Flanders. His son, **David T.** (1610–90) the Younger, was influenced by Rubens and Brouwer, became court painter to Archduke Leopold William, and is considered the finest of Flemish genre painters.

TENNESSEE (tenesē'). S. central state of the U.S.A., having the Unaka and Great Smoky mountains (part of the Appalachians) as its E. boundary, and the Mississippi as the W. The T. river waters the valley between the Appalachians and the Cumberland plateau, and re-enters the W. of the state, joining the Ohio in Kentucky. In the N., the Cumberland is the main river. Lumbering is important, and maize, wheat, cotton, tobacco are grown. Coal, zinc, pyrites and phosphate are among minerals worked. Research centres incl. Oak Ridge (q.v.) and the Arnold Engineering Development Centre for aircraft. The cap. is Nashville, the largest town Memphis. T. entered the Union in 1796. Pop. (1970) 3,924,164.

TENNESSEE VALLEY AUTHORITY. An organization in the U.S.A. created by an Act of Congress, 1933, to develop the Tennessee river system for navigation, flood control, and generation of hydroelectric power. A system of publicly owned dams was constructed to utilize the waters to improve land-management practices, and experiments in agricultural chemistry and biology were carried out.

TENNIEL (ten'i-el), **Sir John** (1820–1914). British humorous artist. B. in London, he joined *Punch* in 1850, and for over 50 years he was a leading cartoonist on that magazine. He illustrated *Alice in Wonderland* and other books.

TENNIS. An ancient game played by the English and French aristocracy from the 14th cent. It is now called Royal, Court, Lord's, or Real T. It is played indoors on a court bisected by a net. Inlet into each end and one side of the court is a sloping roof, against which the ball may be hit. See LAWN TENNIS.

TENNYSON, Alfred, 1st baron (1809–92). British poet. B. at Somersby, Lincs, he was ed. at Trinity Coll., Cambridge, where he became the friend of A. H. Hallam. In 1827 he pub. *Poems, by Two Brothers*, written with Charles T. (1808–79), and in 1830 *Poems, chiefly Lyrical*. His full power emerged in the *Poems* of 1832. The death of Hallam in 1833 inspired the *In Memoriam*, not published until 1850. A further vol. of *Poems* appeared in 1842, and the less successful *Princess* in 1847. In 1850 T. m. Emily Sellwood, and succeeded Wordsworth as poet laureate. *Maud* followed in 1855, and the series of Arthurian legends *The Idylls of the King* appeared 1857–85. Among the later vols. are *Enoch Arden* (1864), *Lucretius* (1868), *The Revenge* (1878), *Ballads and other Poems* (1880), *Tiresias* (1885), *Demeter* (1889), and *The Death of Oenone* (1892). He also wrote verse dramas, the most successful being *Becket* (1884). In 1884 T. was raised to the peerage. He was buried in Westminster Abbey. His poetry is characterized by craftsmanship and musical utterance. His brother **Charles T.** adopted the additional surname of Turner in 1830, and is remembered for his fine sonnets.

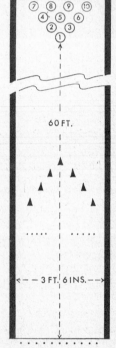

TENPIN BOWLING. A game of very early origin, said to have been taken to the U.S.A. by Dutch settlers in the 17th cent. Modern bowling lanes measure 60 ft. to the nearest pin and have an extra 15 ft. approach area; they are 3 ft. 6 in. wide. Balls weighing from 10 to 16 lb. are made of rubber composition and drilled with holes for thumb and two fingers. Pins made of maple are 15 in. high. The game is usually between two players or teams of 3, 4, or 5 players a side. A game of tenpins is made up of 10 'frames'. The frame is the bowler's turn to play and in each frame he may bowl twice. He scores one point for each pin knocked down, with bonus points for knocking all ten pins down in either one ball or two. The player or team making the greater score wins.

The U.S. National Bowling Association was formed in 1875. The game, in its modern form, is now finding considerable popularity in Britain.

TEPLICE. Industrial city and spa in Czechoslovakia 10 m. W. of Usti. Peat and lignite are mined, glass, porcelain, cement, paper, etc., made. Its springs give warm radioactive water. Goethe and Beethoven met at T. in 1812. Pop. (1967) 52,000.

TERBIUM. A metallic element, symbol Tb, at. wt. 158·93, at. no. 65. It is one of the group of rare earths.

TER BORCH (ter borkh), **Gerard** (1617–81). Dutch painter. B. at Zwolle, the son of a painter, he came under the influence of Frans Hals, visited England, and painted studies of refined Dutch life, e.g. 'A Lady at Her Toilet' in the Wallace Collection. 'The Peace of Munster' (1648) in the National Gallery is one of his principal works.

TEREBINTH or **Turpentine Tree**. Small tree (*Pistacia terebinthus*) which yields Cyprus turpentine from the bark.

TERENCE (Publius Terentius Afer) (*c.* 190–159 B.C.). Roman dramatist. B. at Carthage, he was brought to Rome as a slave. After receiving his freedom he devoted himself to literature, and enjoyed the patronage of Scipio. His surviving 6 comedies, mostly imitated from Greek models, are distinguished for their subtle characterization and purity of style.

TERESA, St. (1515–82). Spanish mystic. B. at Avila, she entered a Carmelite nunnery, and in 1562 founded a new and stricter order. She was subject to fainting fits, during which she claimed to see visions. She wrote *The Way to Perfection*, and an autobiography. In 1622 she was canonized and became the first woman 'Doctor of the Church' in 1970.

TERMITES. Soft-bodied insects forming the order Isoptera, also known as white ants. They are different in structure and metamorphosis from ants, but are social in habit, often building huge nests or *termitaria*. There are 5 chief castes or types, comprising 2 sterile forms and 3 reproductive forms. In the chief reproductive caste both males and females are winged; other reproductive members are short-winged or wingless. The sterile castes are wingless and are divided into *soldiers* which defend the colony, and *workers* which construct the termitarium and provide food. Ts. feed largely on wood and do much damage in tropical and sub-tropical countries.

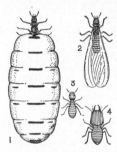

TERMITES. I, queen; 2, winged male; 3, worker; 4, soldier.

TERMS. Periods of the year during which law courts, univs., or schools are open. In England the law courts sit usually from a date in Jan. to one in March (Hilary T.); April to May (Easter T.): May to July (Trinity T.); and Oct. to Dec. (Michaelmas T.). At Oxford the full Ts. are Hilary or Lent, Trinity, and Michaelmas T. At Cambridge the corresponding Ts. are Lent, Easter, and Michaelmas.

TERN. Genus of sea-birds (*Sterna*). Of the 8 species, 5 breed in Britain. They are characterized by long wings and a forked tail. The underparts are white or grey and the crown of the head black.

TERRA COTTA. A form of baked clay used in building, sculpture, and pottery. It was first employed in ancient countries where there was no stone available. The term is specifically applied to small figures or figurines, e.g. those found at Tanagra (q.v.).

TERRAPIN. Name commonly given to freshwater members of the tortoise order. The diamond back T., a N. American coastal species, is considered a delicacy.

SCULPTURED TERRAPIN

TERRIER. Group of dogs formerly used in hunting rabbits and game. Small and fleet-footed, they are highly intelligent. They incl. the Fox Ts., Aberdeen T., Irish T., Sealyham T., and Bull T.

TERRITORIAL ARMY. Created in Britain as the T. Force (1908) from volunteer regiments formally incorporated in 1872, it was raised and admin. by County Associations and intended primarily for home defence: it was renamed T.A. in 1922. Merged with the Regular Army in the S.W.W., it was revived 1947, but replaced 1967 by a smaller, more highly trained Territorial and Army Volunteer Reserve.

TERRY, Dame Ellen (1847–1928). British actress. She made her début in 1856, and from 1878 was Irving's leading lady, portraying Shakespearian roles. In 1864 she m. G. F. Watts (q.v.), but separation and divorce followed. While she lived with E. W. Godwin 1868–74, 2 children were born to her (*see* CRAIG, E. G.); and she subsequently made 2 further unsuccessful marriages. Later she appeared in plays by her friend, G. B. Shaw, with whom she had a delightful correspondence.

TERTIARIES. Associations of R.C. laymen who, without abandoning their family life or their usual callings, attempt to live in accordance with the teachings of the friars. The first such order was founded by St. Francis in 1221.

TERTULLIAN (*c.* 155–222). Christian father. B. at Carthage, he was converted *c.* 192. His theological works are the earliest important Christian writings in Latin. In later life T. became a Montanist.

TERZA RIMA. Italian metre used in Dante's *Divine Comedy*, consisting of 3-line stanzas in which the 2nd line rhymes with the 1st and 3rd of the following stanza. The best-known English example is Shelley's 'Ode to the West Wind'.

TEST ACT. Act passed in England in 1673 requiring all holders of public office to renounce transubstantiation and take the sacrament in an Anglican church, thus excluding R.Cs. and Nonconformists from office. Its clauses were repealed in 1828–9.

TETANUS. Lockjaw; an acute infectious disease caused by a bacillus chiefly found in richly manured soil. Its toxins affect the central nervous system, producing violent and painful spasm of the muscles.

TETRAZZINI (tetrahtsē'nē), **Luisa** (1871–1940). Italian coloratura soprano. B. at Florence, she made her début in 1895, and toured Europe and America.

TETUAN (tetoo-ahn'). Town in N.E. Morocco, near the Mediterranean coast, 40 m. S.E. of Tangier. Pop. (1961) 101,000.

TEUTONIC KNIGHTS. German military order, founded in 1190, which from 1228 devoted itself to crusading against the pagan Prussians and Lithuanians. They ruled Prussia until the 15th cent.

TEXAS. Southern state of the U.S.A., on the Mexican border and the Gulf of Mexico, until Alaska became a state (1959) largest in the Union. The Rio Grande del Norte and Red river form the S.W. and N.E. boundaries respectively. Other large rivers are the Canadian, Colorado, and Brazos. In the extreme W. is the barren Llano Estacado plateau which falls rapidly to the Great Plains and prairies. Texas leads all states in cotton, cattle, and petroleum production. Maize, oats, wheat, and fruit are cultivated. There are petroleum refineries, flour-mills, lumber-mills, and meat-packing factories. Austin is the cap., Houston the largest town, and both have univ. Area 267,339 sq. m.; pop. (1970) 11,196,730.

TEXEL (tek'sel). Dutch is., largest and most westerly of the Frisian islands, separated from N. Holland by the Marsdiep. Off T., Blake defeated Tromp and de Ruyter in 1654. Area 64 sq. m.

TEXTILES. Materials woven from spun thread. The art of weaving textiles is one of the earliest developed by man. Sheep's wool, linen, and silk were used in the Old World, cotton and animal fibres (from e.g. the llama) in the New. Spinning and weaving (qq.v.) remain essentially what they have always been, but the adaptation of machinery to both processes from the 18th cent. onwards not only made possible much quicker production, but also added greatly to fineness and variety of texture. The basic materials – wool from various animals, silk, linen, cotton – continue to be used, but from the invention in 1883 of artificial silk (rayon) thread by Hilaire de Chardonnet, man has developed a number of synthetic

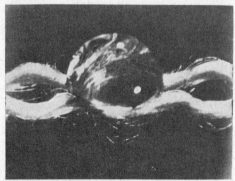

TEXTILES. A drop of oil balances on two strands of a fabric treated with Scotchguard rain and stain repeller: untreated fibres would at once absorb the oil.
Courtesy of Minnesota Mining and Manufacturing Co.

threads, most of them derived chemically from coal or mineral oil, and marketed under trade names, e.g. nylon, terylene, and orlon; these are sometimes used alone, often together with natural fibres. Fabrics made by hand or machine knitting, though not strictly textiles (from Lat. *texere*, to weave) are much used in a similar way, especially for women's suits and dresses. Among the most welcome advances in 20th cent. T. manufacture have been the development of flame resistant and easy-care fabrics – crease resisting, permanently pleated, easily washable, and 'drip-dry', and treated with water and once stain repeller.

TEYTE (tāt), **Dame Maggie** (1888–). British lyric soprano. Having studied under Jean de Reszke in Paris, she made an inimitable reputation in Mozartian roles, e.g. Cherubino in *The Marriage of Figaro*, and was coached as Mélisande by Debussy himself. In 1958 she was created D.B.E.

THACKERAY, William Makepeace (1811–63). British novelist. Son of an E. India Co. official, he was b. in Calcutta, and ed. at Charterhouse and Trinity Coll., Cambridge. After a brief essay at the law in the Middle Temple, he went to study art in Paris, and ultimately settled to journalism in London. For *Fraser's Magazine* he wrote 'The Yellowplush Correspondence' (1837–8), and 'The Great Hoggarty Diamond' (1841), and for *Punch* 'Mr. Punch's Prize Novelists' (1847) and 'The Snobs of England' (1847), using such pseudonyms as Michael Angelo Titmarsh. In 1836 he had m., but in 1840 his wife became insane in childbed, leaving him with 2 daus. for whom he wrote the fairy tale *The Rose and the Ring* (1855). The 1st and greatest work to appear under his own name was *Vanity Fair* (1847–8), with its splendidly vixenish heroine Becky Sharp; later novels are *Pendennis* (1848), *Esmond* (1852: with a sequel *The Virginians* 1857–9), and *The Newcomes* (1853–5), in which T.'s tendency to sentimentality is most marked. In 1857 T. unsuccessfully attempted to enter Parliament, and 1860–2 was editor of the *Cornhill Magazine*, in which his last 2 novels, *The Adventures of Philip* and *Denis Duval* were pub.

THAILAND (tī'-). Independent kingdom in S.E. Asia, long familiar in the W. as Siam. It is bordered W. by Burma; S. by the Federation of Malaya, the Gulf of Siam, and Cambodia; E. by Laos. The name Muang T'ai, meaning Land of the Free People and translated Thailand, was adopted in 1939. T. is mountainous in the N., barren in the E., has a central fertile alluvial plain, and a narrow hilly strip in S. which is part of the Malay peninsula. The main rivers are the Menam (r.) Chao Phraya (important for transport) and its tribs.; the Mekong marks about 600 m. of the E. frontier, the Salveen c. 200 m. of the W. The climate is tropical.

Rice is by far the most important crop; others incl. sugar, tobacco, cotton, peanuts; oxen, buffaloes, and pigs are reared. The forests of the N. produce teak; mineral deposits incl. tin, wolfram, rubies, sapphires. There is an inland waterway system, a rail system linked with that of Malaysia, and good modern roads. Bangkok is the capital and chief port, with a modern airport at Don Muang: other important towns are Thonburi and Chiengmai. Area 198,247 sq. m.; pop. (1967) 32,000,000. The people are predominantly Buddhist.

The Siamese monarchy, which until 1932 was absolute, originated c. 1350; the present dynasty dates from 1782. The Portuguese reached Siam in 1511, the Dutch followed in the 17th cent., in which cent. the (Eng.) East India Co. had a factory at Ayuthia for some years. A treaty of friendship and trade between Britain and Siam was signed in 1826; treaties with other European powers followed. After the F.W.W. increasing national consciousness led in 1932 to the promulgation of a constitution restricting the absolute power of the king. Siam was occupied in Dec. 1941 by the Japanese and declared war on Britain and the U.S.A. a few weeks later. Peace was signed in 1946, Siam having taken no active part in operations except to occupy parts of Burma and Malaya (subsequently voluntarily restored). King Ananda Mahidol was assassinated in 1946 and was succeeded by his brother Phumibol Adulyadij. A series of coups d'état, generally bloodless, led to rule by a military junta. Under a new constitution in 1968 there was provision for the King (who must be Buddhist) to appoint a Council of Ministers, who must be neither members of the Senate nor the House of Representatives. Communist guerrillas have been active from 1965, mainly in the N. and E. on the Laotian border, and in the far S. on the Malaysian border, and the U.S.A. has supplied military advisers and aid.

THAIS (thā-is) (4th cent. B.C.). Greek courtesan, mistress of Alexander the Great and later wife of Ptolemy, king of Egypt. She was supposed to have instigated the burning of Persepolis.

THALES (thā'lēz) (640–546 B.C.). Greek philosophic scientist who fl. at Miletus in Asia Minor, made important advances in geometry, and as a materialist in philosophy put forward a theory that all matter and life originated from water.

THALI'A. The muse of comedy in ancient Greece.

THALI'DOMIDE. Tranquillizer developed by a W. German pharmaceutical firm in 1957: more than 5,000 expectant mothers gave birth to malformed children as a result of taking it, and the drug was withdrawn in 1961.

THALLIUM (Gk. *thallos* budding twig). Bluish-grey metal which tarnishes in air, is soft like lead, malleable but of low tenacity: symbol Tl, at. wt. 204·39, at. no. 81. Discovered spectroscopically and isolated by Crookes in 1861 (by Lamy 1862), it is a poor conductor of electricity and its compounds are poisonous, being used as rat poison and insecticide. Tl-104, a strong beta emitter, is used to gauge thickness of materials which absorb beta rays.

THAMES (temz). English river on which London stands. Its headstreams rise in the Cotswold hills above Cirencester and unite above Lechlade. Its chief tributaries from the N. are the Windrush Evenlode, Cherwell, Thame, Colne, Lea, and Roding; and from the S., Kennet, Loddon, Wey, Mole, Darent, and

Medway.' From Gravesend the Thames estuary extends to the Nore. There are many bridges across the river, the lowest being Tower Bridge; there are road, underground railway, and pedestrian tunnels underneath the river at various points in the London area; and ferries at Woolwich and Gravesend. Below London Bridge is the Pool, and below again the great London docks. The T. is controlled by the Port of London Authority (1909) from its mouth to Teddington (where a lock prevents the tide from going farther upstream) and thence upstream by the T. Conservancy Board (1857). Length from Lechlade to the Nore, 210 m. To prevent flooding under freak weather conditions, as in 1953, 1956, a fixed barrage has been suggested at Woolwich making the T. non-tidal.

THA′NET, Isle of. N.E. corner of Kent, England, bounded by the North Sea and the r. Stour. It was an island until the 16th cent. On it stand Margate, Ramsgate, and Broadstairs.

THANKSGIVING DAY. In U.S.A., a national holiday observed on the 4th Thursday in Nov. It was first celebrated in 1621 by the Pilgrim Fathers.

THANT, U (1909–   ). Burmese diplomat. B. in the Irrawaddy Delta, he became a schoolmaster and, together with his close friend U Nu (q.v.), worked for his country's independence. In 1952 he joined the Burmese mission at the U.N., succeeded Hammarskjold as Sec.-General in 1961: term renewed 1966.

THEATRE. The place or building in which dramatic performances are given. The first European Ts. were in Greece and were originally open spaces round the altar of Dionysus. The great stone theatre at Athens was begun c. 500 B.C., and its semicircular plan provided for an audience of 20,000 or 30,000 people sitting in tiers on the surrounding slopes; it served as a model for the Ts. that were erected in all the important cities of the Graeco-Roman world. After the collapse of the Roman Empire the Ts. were

THEATRE. An Elizabethan playhouse designed and made by Dr. Richard Southern, with C. Walter Hodges. Not intended to represent any one Elizabethan theatre in particular, it combines all the information we have about any of them.
Courtesy of the British Council.

deserted, but extant Roman Ts. are at, e.g., Orange, France, and near St. Albans, England. In medieval times, several stages of wood and canvas, one for each scene, were set up side by side in fairgrounds and market squares for the performance of mimes and miracle plays. Small enclosed Ts. were built in the

16th cent.. and that at Vicenza, built by Palladio (1518–80), still exists. The first London T. was the 'Theatre' in Shoreditch built in 1576 by James Burbage (d. 1597), who also opened the first covered T in London, the Blackfriars (1596). Famous London Ts. incl. the Haymarket (1720, rebuilt 1821), Drury Lane (1663), and Her Majesty's (1705), both several times rebuilt. In the U.S.A. the centre of the theatrical world is N.Y. City, with numerous Ts. on Broadway, e.g. the Biltmore, Booth, Lunt-Fontanne, Helen Hayes, and Lyceum, although Williamsburg, Va. (1716), and Philadelphia (1766) had Ts. earlier.

In the 20th cent. the large commercial theatres have been affected by the cinema and TV, but there have also been developments resulting in a new infusion of life. These incl. the 'little Ts.' off Broadway, which often give a dramatist his first production, and of which the first was the Theatre Guild (1919), others being the Gate, Phoenix, Greenwich, Mews, and Bouwerie Lane; in Britain the work of the repertory theatres, e.g. Birmingham, and of the Old Vic (q.v.); and in Ireland the Abbey (q.v.). Since the S.W.W. in Britain Ts. have often been built as a symbol of civic pride, e.g. at Chichester, Coventry and Guildford; and since c. 1925 the U.S.A. has acquired a number of community, regional and univ. Ts., e.g. the Alley Playhouse, Houston; Margot Jones's T., Dallas; the Actors Workshop, San Francisco; Penthouse T., Univ. of Washington, Seattle. Ts. are also often incl. as part of larger cultural centres, e.g. the Lincoln Center, N.Y.; Place des Arts, Montreal; and the National T. planned for London's South Bank as a home for the National T. co. launched in 1963. National Ts., of which the Comédie Française (founded by Louis XIV in 1680 and with a permanent home from 1792) was the first, exist in Stockholm, Moscow, Athens, Copenhagen, Vienna and elsewhere. *See* illus. pp. 37, 355, 749.

THEBAINE (thē′bā-in) ($C_{19}H_{21}NO_3$). A highly poisonous alkaloid contained in opium.

THEBES (thēbz). Ancient city of Upper Egypt on both banks of the Nile, probably founded under the 1st dynasty. About 1600 B.C. it became the capital of all Egypt. The present villages of Luxor and Karnak mark its site, and contain magnificent ruins.

THEBES. Capital of Boeotia in ancient Greece. In the Peloponnesian War it was allied with Sparta against Athens, and for a short time after 371 B.C. it was the most powerful state in Greece. Alexander the Great destroyed it in 336 B.C. and although it was restored it was never again important. Pindar (q.v. lived at T.

THEFT. *See* LARCENY.

THEISM (thē′izm). Belief in the existence of a God, usually conceived of as a personal being, who has revealed Himself to the world in a special revelation. In its widest use the term means belief in the existence of gods. *See* DEISM.

THE′MIS. In Greek mythology, personification of law and order. She was the dau. of Uranus and Ge.

THEMI′STOCLES (c. 514–449 B.C.). Athenian soldier and statesman. In 483 he was largely responsible for the ostracizing of Aristides, and for 10 years he exercised almost supreme power in the state. In the Persian War he played a distinguished part in the battle of Salamis (480) and then rebuilt and strengthened the walls of Athens. About 470 Spartan influence secured his banishment, and he fled into Asia, where Artaxerxes, the Persian king, received him with favour. Henceforth he lived at Magnesia.

THEO′CRITUS (fl. c. 270 B.C.). Greek poet. B. probably at Syracuse, he spent much of his life at Alexandria. His *Idylls*, truthful pictures of rustic life distinguished by deep feeling for nature, have served as a model for all subsequent pastoral poetry.

THEODOLITE (thē-o′dolīt). Instrument used in surveying for the measurement of horizontal and vertical angles. It consists of a small telescope mounted so as to move on 2 graduated circles, one horizontal and the other vertical, while its axes pass through the centres of the circles.

THEODORA (thē-ōdō′ra) (*c.* A.D. 508–548). Byzantine empress, consort of Justinian, whom she m. *c.* 523; earlier she had been his mistress and a common courtesan. As queen she earned a high reputation for courage and charity.

THEODORA′KIS, Mikis (1925–). Greek composer. He gained an internat. reputation by 'Zorba's dance', etc. Active in left-wing politics, he was imprisoned in 1967 for attempting to overthrow the military régime; released 1970.

THEO′DORIC I. King of the Visigoths, 418–51. He was a grandson of Alaric, warred successfully against the Romans, but united with them against the Huns under Attila and fell at Châlons.

THEODORIC (455–526). Founder of the Ostrogothic monarchy in Italy; called Theodoric the Great. Succeeding his father as king about 474, he warred intermittently against the Romans and was given permission by the Emperor Zeno to secure Italy from Odoacer. With 250,000 Ostrogoths he overran the peninsula, and on Odoacer's murder was accepted as king. For 33 years he ruled with ability.

THEODOSIUS (thē-ōdō′shius) I (*c.* 346–395). Roman emperor of the East, called the Great. B. in Spain, he served under his father, a Roman general, in Britain and the Balkans, and in 379 was called to become emperor of the East as the colleague of Gratian, the emperor of the West. In 4 years T. completely dispersed the Goths, concluding peace with them in 382. In 394 T. became sole emperor. The chief blot on his fame is his massacre of 7,000 citizens of Thessalonica in 390 after there had been rioting in the circus.

THEO′LOGY. The science of religion, concerned chiefly with God and with man's relationship to Him. Natural T. deals with what may be discovered by reason and a study of the natural world; Revealed T. has for its subject the specific doctrines of Christianity, Islam, and the other world faiths.

THEORBO (thē-ôr′bo) or **Archlute.** Musical instrument, a large member of the lute (q.v.) family.

THEO′SOPHY. Name applied to various systems of 'divine wisdom', but in particular to the doctrines of the Theosophical Society founded in 1875 by Mme. Blavatsky (q.v.) and Col. H. S. Olcott. These are based on the Hindu principles of karma and reincarnation, with Nirvana as the goal of the aspiring soul.

THEOTOCOPULI. *See* GRECO, EL.

THÉRÈSE OF LISIEUX (1873–97). French saint. B. at Alençon, dau. of a watchmaker, she entered a Carmelite convent at L. at 15, where her holy life induced her superior to ask her to write her spiritual autobiography. She advocated the Little Way of goodness in small things in everyday life, and is known as Little Flower of Jesus. She d. of tuberculosis and was canonized in 1925.

THERM. Unit of heat used in the measurement of domestic and industrial gas, and equal to 100,000 Btu (British thermal unit, q.v.).

THERMIC LANCE. Tube of mild steel, enclosing tightly-packed small steel rods and fed with oxygen. On ignition temperatures above 3000°C are produced and the T.L. becomes its own sustaining fuel. It rapidly penetrates walls and steel plate, e.g. a 9-in. steel door can be cut through in less than 30 sec. Criminals have used T.Ls. but alarm systems can detect the radiation emitted by a T.L. in operation.

THERMIO′NICS. That branch of science that deals with the emission of electrons from matter under the influence of heat. A thermionic valve, largely used in telegraphy and telephony and still more so in radio and radar, is a device using space conduction by thermionically emitted electrons.

Classification is into diode, triode, and multi-electrode valves, but in many applications valves are now being replaced by transistors (q.v.).

THERMODYNAMICS. The science of the transfer of heat into other forms of energy, on which is based the study of the efficient working of engines, e.g. the steam and internal combustion. The 3 laws of T. are: (1) energy can be neither created nor destroyed: heat and mechanical work being mutually convertible; (2) it is impossible for an unaided self-acting machine to convey heat from one body to another at a higher temperature; (3) it is impossible by any procedure, no matter how idealized, to reduce any system to the absolute zero of temperature in a finite number of operations. Put into mathematical form these have widespread applications in physics and chemistry.

THERMOMETER. An instrument for measuring temperature (q.v.) depending on the nearly uniform change in physical properties, of expansion in a solid liquid or gas; or the change in electrical properties such as resistance with temperature. The commonest form used at ordinary temperatures is the mercury or alcohol-in-glass T. reading directly against a scale marked in degrees Centigrade (Celsius) or Fahrenheit. (*See* p. 1027 for conversion factor.) Other instruments incl. *thermocouples* depending on the voltage generated between the junctions of 2 dissimilar metals; *resistance thermometers* depending on the change of electrical resistance of a conductor with temperature; *pyrometers* (q.v.) *thermistors* depending on the change of electrical resistance of a semiconductor with temperature; *bimetallic strips* depending on dissimilar rates of expansion of 2 metals, and *gas thermometers* depending on the gas laws.

THERMOMETER

THERMOPYLAE (thermo′pilē). A narrow pass in Greece from Thessaly to Locris, famous for its heroic defence against the Persians in 480 B.C. by Leonidas, King of Sparta, and *c.* 1,000 men, who fought to the death.

THESSALONI′KI. Port in Greek Macedonia at the head of the Gulf of T. with some industry – textile making, shipbuilding, brewing, tanning, etc. It is on the site of Thessalonica, the Roman city to whose inhabitants St. Paul addressed 2 famous epistles. Founded from Corinth 315 B.C., captured by Saracens A.D. 904, by the Turks 1430. it was restored to Greece 1912. It was an Allied base in the F.W.W., and was occupied by the Germans 1941–44. Pop. (1961) 377,026.

THE′SSALY. Prov. in Greece, bordering the Aegean, a fertile plain enclosed by mts. and comprising the towns of Kardhitsa, Larisa, Magnesia, and Trikkala. Area 5,907 sq. m.; pop. (1961) 694,461.

THIBAULT, J. A. *See* FRANCE, ANATOLE.

THIERS (tyär′), **Louis Adolphe** (1797–1877). French statesman and historian. B. at Marseilles, he achieved fame with his *History of the French Revolution* (1823–7) and *History of the Consulate and Empire* (1845–60). He held cabinet posts under Louis Philippe, and from 1863 led the parliamentary opposition to Napoleon III. As head of the provisional govt. in 1871 he negotiated peace with Prussia and suppressed the Paris Commune. He was 1st President of the 3rd Republic 1871–3.

THIRKELL, Angela. *See* MACKAIL, J. W.

THIRTY-NINE ARTICLES. *See* ANGLICAN COMMUNION.

THIRTY YEARS WAR. The war fought in Germany 1618–48. Nominally a religious war, it originated in the ambition of the Habsburgs to obtain political control of all Germany. The war began with the revolt of the Bohemians against Austrian rule in 1618–20, and after their defeat was continued by certain Protestant princes, who were aided during 1625–7 by Denmark. Gustavus Adolphus of Sweden intervened on the Protestant side in 1630, and overran N. Germany before he was killed in 1632. After the Swedish defeat at Nördlingen (1634) France entered the war in 1635, and inflicted several defeats on the emperor's Spanish allies. By the Treaty of Westphalia (1648) France received S. Alsace, and Sweden certain provinces on the Baltic, while the emperor's authority over Germany became purely nominal. The war was largely fought by armies of mercenaries, such as those of Wallenstein, Tilly, and Mansfeld, which devastated Germany.

THISTLE, Several genera of plants in the family Compositae, the best-known being *Carduus* and *Cirsium*, found in the N. hemisphere. The flower heads are purple and cottony, the leaves are deeply indented and spiny: a T. is the Scottish national emblem.

DYLAN THOMAS. By A. E. John, in Cardiff Museum.
Photo: British Travel and Holidays Association.

THISTLE, Most Ancient and Most Noble Order of the. Scottish order of knighthood (K.T.) founded in 1687. There are sixteen knights, and the Queen is sovereign of the order. Its motto is *Nemo me impune lacessit* (No one provokes me with impunity).

THISTLEWOOD, Arthur (1770–1820). English Radical. A follower of Thomas Spence, he was active in the Radical movement and was executed as the chief leader of the Cato St. conspiracy.

THOMAS, St. One of the 12 apostles. He is said to have preached Christianity in Parthia or India; hence the ancient S. Indian churches are called 'the Christians of St. T.'. He is not the author of the so-called Gospel of St. T. *See* BIBLE.

THOMAS, Dylan Marlais (1914–53). Welsh poet. B. in Swansea, son of the English master at the local grammar school where he was ed., he worked as a reporter on the *South Wales Evening Post*, then settled as a journalist in London and pub. his 1st vol. *Eighteen Poems* in 1934. He reached a lilting mastery of his medium in *Deaths and Entrances* (1946) and the radio 'play' *Under Milk Wood* (1954): the short stories of *Portrait of the Artist as a Young Dog* (1940) are autobiographical. A dipsomaniac, he d. in N.Y. where he had made a no. of reading and lecture tours. Repeatedly anthologized, e.g. his celebration of his 30th birthday 'Poem in October' and 'Fern Hill', an evocation of his youth, he has become a legend.

THOMAS, (Philip) Edward (1878–1917). British poet and author of books on the English countryside. In 1916 he pub. *Six Poems* under the pseudonym of Edward Eastaway; vols. under his own name were *Poems* (1917) and *Last Poems* (1918), dealing with nature idealistically. T. was killed in action in the F.W.W. at Arras. His wife Helen T. (1877–1967) pub. the biographical vols. *As it was*, and *World without End.*

THOMAS, Ronald Stuart (*c.* 1914–). Welsh poet. Rector of Managon 1942–54 and vicar of St. Michael's Eglwysfach from 1954, he has made a reputation with such vols. as *Song at the Year's Turning* (1955), which illustrate the conflict between traditional Welsh values and 'English' sterilely encroaching civilization.

THOMAS À KEMPIS. Alternative name of THOMAS HAMMERKEN (*c.* 1380–1471), German monk. B. at Kempen, near Düsseldorf, he entered the Augustinian monastery of Zwolle. His *Imitation of Christ* is perhaps the best-known devotional work ever written.

THOMPSON, Francis (1859–1907). British poet. B. at Preston, he settled in London, where he fell into poverty and ill health. Wilfrid and Alice Meynell procured the publication of his poems in 1893, incl. 'The Hound of Heaven'. In this and later vols. (*Sister Songs* and *New Poems*) T., who was a Roman Catholic, expressed a mystic view of life.

THOMPSON, John Taliaferro (1860–1940). American colonel, and inventor of the T. sub-machine-gun, predecessor of the tommy-gun. B. in Kentucky, he retired from the army in 1914.

THOMSON, Elihu (1853–1937). American inventor. B. in England, he lived in U.S.A. from 1858, and was prof. of chemistry and mechanics at Philadelphia (1876–80). He founded, with E. J. Houston, the Thomson-Houston Electric Co. in 1882, later merging with the Edison Co. to form the General Electric Co. As director of the research laboratory, he made important advances into the nature of the electric arc, invented the first high-frequency dynamos and transformers. He also contributed to improvements on many aspects of incandescent lighting and radiology.

THOMSON, James (1700–48). British poet. B. in Roxburghshire, he wrote the influential descriptive poem *The Seasons* (1726–30) in blank verse, and the song, 'Rule, Britannia'.

THOMSON, James (1834–82). Scottish poet, who wrote as 'B.V.' (Bysshe Vanolis). B. in Renfrewshire, he became an army schoolmaster and a journalist. His poem 'The City of Dreadful Night' (1880) reflects deep despair.

THOMSON, Sir Joseph John (1856–1940). British physicist. Ed. at Manchester and Cambridge, where he became Cavendish prof. of experimental physics (1884–1918), he organized the Cavendish research laboratory which became a world-famous centre of atomic research. His work resulted in the discovery of the electron which inaugurated the electrical theory of the atom, and his elucidation of positive rays and their application to an analysis of neon led to Aston's discovery of isotopes. He is regarded as the founder of modern physics, and was awarded a Nobel prize in 1906 and the O.M. in 1913. His son **Sir George Paget T.** (1892–), ed. at Cambridge, was prof. of physics at the Imperial Coll. of Science 1930–52, where he carried out aeronautical and atomic research, and in 1937 received (with C. J. Davisson) a Nobel prize for work on interference phenomena in the irridation of crystals by electrons. He was master of Corpus Christi Coll., Cambridge, 1952–62.

THOMSON OF FLEET, Roy Herbert (1894–), 1st baron. British newspaper proprietor. B. in Toronto of Scottish descent, he bought his first newspaper in 1934 and came to control many groups in Britain (incl. Kemsley Newspapers 1959 and Times Newspapers Ltd. 1966, producing both *The Times* and *Sunday Times*), Canada and the U.S.A., in addition to several radio and TV stations. In 1962 he set up the T. Foundation, a £5,000,000 trust, to train developing countries in the techniques of mass media. Created a baron in 1964, he lost his Canadian citizenship.

THOR. The Norse god of thunder. He was represented as a man of enormous strength, who defended mankind against demons.

THOREAU (thō'rō), **Henry David** (1817–62). American author and naturalist. B. at Concord, Mass., he is best known for his *Walden, or Life in the Woods* (1854). Some 30 vols. of later works are based on his daily journals of walks and nature observations.

THŌ'RIUM. Dark grey, naturally radioactive metal, widely distributed throughout the world in minerals, particularly monazite beach sands: symbol Th, at. wt. 232·05, at. no. 90. Discovered by Berzelius (1828), it has a half-life $1\cdot39 \times 10^{10}$ years, and its greatest potential use is breeding from it uranium-233, an excellent fuel for power reactors.

THORNDIKE, Dame Sybil (1882–). British actress. She made her early reputation as a splendid *St. Joan* (1924) and has subsequently played in Shakespeare, Ibsen, Eliot, and several of N. C. Hunter's plays, e.g. *A Day by the Sea*. Created D.B.E. in 1931. She often appeared with her husband Sir Lewis Casson (1875–1969), and her brother **Russell T.** (1885–) is also an actor and author of novels featuring 18th cent. parson crook 'Dr. Syn'. The T. Theatre, Leatherhead (1969), is named after her, and the theatre workshop after her husband.

THORNEYCROFT, Peter, baron (1909–). British Cons. politician. Pres. of the Board of Trade (1951–7), Chancellor of the Exchequer (1957–8), Min. of Aviation (1960–2), and Min. of Defence (1962–4). He was created a life peer 1967.

THORNHILL, Sir James (1676–1734). English historical painter. He decorated the dome of St. Paul's, and executed paintings for Hampton Court and Greenwich Hospital. Hogarth was his pupil and son-in-law.

THORWALDSEN (tŏr'-), **Bertel** (1770–1844). Danish sculptor. B. at sea, he studied in Rome where he became friendly with Canova. His output was enormous, and he excelled in classical and mythological subjects, e.g. 'The Triumph of Alexander'.

THOTH (tōt). The Egyptian god of wisdom and learning. He was represented as a scribe with the head of an ibis, the bird sacred to him.

THOTHMES (tŏtmes). Name of 4 Egyptian kings of the 18th dynasty. Thothmes I (reigned 1540–1501 B.C.) founded the Egyptian empire in Syria. His grandson, Thothmes III, reigned *c.* 1500–1446, extended the empire to the Euphrates, and conquered Nubia.

THRACE. Region in S.E. Europe, on the N. shore of the Aegean where the anc. Greeks estab. a number of colonies. It was ruled in turn by Persia, Macedon, Rome, and Byzantium. The Turks held it from the 15th cent. until 1878 when Bulgaria secured the N., Greece the S. After the F.W.W. T. was divided between Greece, of which it forms a prov. (3,315 sq. m.; pop., 1961, 356,708), and Turkey (9,065 sq. m.).

THREE RIVERS. *See* Trois Rivières.

THRIFT. Genus of plants (*Statice*) in the family Plumbaginaceae. Sea T. (*S. armeria*) occurs on seashores and cliffs in Europe. The leaves are small and linear. The pink flowers rise on straight stems.

THROAT. The structures in front of the neck, incl. the wind pipe (trachea), the gullet (oesophagus), the blood vessels passing to the head from the heart, the thyroid gland, and the tissues at the back of the mouth.

THROMBŌ'SIS. Development during life of a blood-clot within a vessel or the heart, causing restriction of blood flow.

THRUSH. Family of birds (Turdidae). The song T. (*Turdus musicus*) is about 8 in. long, brown above. and with a paler throat and breast speckled with dark

SONG THRUSH

brown: it is one of Britain's finest songbirds. Slightly larger is the missel T. (*T. viscivorous*), nicknamed the storm cock because it often sings before and during wild, wet weather. N. American species incl. the hermit T. (*Hylocichla guttata*), a beautiful songster, and the wood T. (*T. mustelina*).

THUCYDIDES (thūsid'idēz) (*c.* 460–400 B.C.). Athenian historian. He held a command in the Peloponnesian War in 424, but met so little success that he was banished until 404. In his *History of the Peloponnesian War* he attempted a scientific and impartial history of his own time.

THUGS. Hindu sect who sacrificed travellers to Kali, the goddess of destruction, by strangling them. They were suppressed *c.* 1830.

THŪ'LE. Greek and Roman name for the most northerly land known. It was applied to the Shetlands, the Orkneys and Iceland, and by later writers to Scandinavia.

THULIUM. A metallic element, symbol Tm, at. wt. 168·94, at. no. 69. It is one of the rare-earth metals.

THURBER, James Grover (1894–1961). American humorist. B. in Columbus, Ohio, he made his name with short stories in the *New Yorker*, perhaps the most famous of these being 'The Secret Life of Walter Mitty'. His doodle drawings also first appeared in this magazine, and incl. preposterous impressions of dogs whom T. placed above the human species. Blind in one eye from boyhood he was totally blind in the last decade but continued his work.

THURINGIA (tooring'ia). A German Free State, 1919–34, a gau under the Nazis, it was enlarged and made a Land, 1946–52, of E. Germany; then its historic boundaries were obliterated in the new dists. of Erfurt, Gera, and Suhl. It contained the fertile Saale plain and, in the S., the beautiful Thüringer Wald: the cap. was Weimar.

THURLOW, Edward, 1st baron (1731–1806). British lawyer. He entered parliament as a Tory in 1768. As Lord Chancellor 1778–83 and 1783–92 he was notorious for his violent opposition to all reform.

THURSO, Archibald Sinclair, visct. T. (1890–1970). British Liberal statesman. After some years in the army, he entered parliament in 1922, and, appointed Sec. for Scotland in the Nat. Govt. of 1931, resigned as a Free Trader in 1932. He led the parliamentary Liberal party 1935–45, was Air Min. 1940–5, and in 1952 was created visct. T.

THURSO. Seaport (burgh) in Caithness on T. bay, the Scottish mainland terminus of the steamer service to the Orkneys. (Pop. 1961) 8,038.

THYME (tīm). Genus of plants (*Thymus*) in the Labiatae family. Garden T. (*T. vulgaris*), a native of the Mediterranean, has aromatic leaves used for seasoning, white or reddish flowers, and a slightly woody growth under a foot high.

THYMUS (thī'mus). A ductless gland near the root of the neck. It develops early in embryonic life, continues to grow after birth, but atrophies before adult life. Its function is not known.

THYROID (thī'roid). One of the principal endocrine glands, situated in front of the throat. It secretes thyroxin, a hormone containing iodine. This stimulates growth, metabolism, and other functions of the body. Abnormal action produces Graves' disease, deficient action produces myxoedema and cretinism.

TIARA (ti-ah'ra). The triple crown worn by the Pope. The term was originally applied to a head-dress worn by the ancient Persians.

TI'BER. River of Italy on which Rome stands. It rises in the Apennines and flows for 250 m. in a S. direction before reaching the Tyrrhenian Sea by 2 mouths, the chief 17 m. S.E. of Rome.

TĪBE'RIAS. Town in Israel on the W. shore of the Sea of Galilee (sometimes called Lake T.); there are medicinal springs in the vicinity. Herod Antipas founded T. *c.* 20 B.C. Pop. (1967) 19,000.

TIBE'RIUS, Claudius Nero (42 B.C.–A.D. 37). Roman emperor. The stepson and adopted son of Augustus, he had a distinguished military career, and on Augustus's death in A.D. 14 succeeded to the empire. He was a conscientious ruler under whom the empire prospered. In later life he retired to Capri.

TIBESTI (tēbestē'). Mountainous region, rising to 11,000 ft., of the Sahara, in N. Chad, not far from the S. Libyan border. It is famed for its camels.

TIBET. Country of central Asia, occupying a lofty barren plateau bounded by the Himalayas to the S.

TIBET. A case of Buddhas with silver holy water bowls before it which formed the wall of the private sitting room of the Dalai Lama (q.v.) at Potala Palace, Lhasa.
Courtesy of Stuart Gelder

and S.W. and the Kunlun Mts. to the N., traversed from W. to E. by the Bukamagna, Karakoram, and other ranges, and having an average elevation of 13,000–15,000 ft. The Sutlej, Brahmaputra, and Indus rise in T., which has numerous lakes, many salty. The yak is the main domestic animal. Wool is exported, and other products incl. borax, salt, horn, musk, herbs, and furs. Gold, iron pyrites, lapis lazuli, and mercury are mined. Lamaism (q.v.), introduced in A.D. 640, is the prevailing religion. Polyandry is common. Lhasa is the cap.

T. was an independent kingdom from the 5th cent. A.D. From c. 1700 to 1912 it was under nominal Chinese suzerainty, a claim made effective in 1951 when the historic ruler, the Dalai Lama, was driven from the country and the monks (perhaps a quarter of the pop.) were forced out of the monasteries. T. became an autonomous region of China 1965. The Maoist Cultural Revolution was resisted by people and army. Area c. 471,700 sq. m.; pop. (1968) 1,000,000.

TIBU'LLUS, Albius (c. 54–19 B.C.). Roman poet, author of bucolic elegies and love poems.

TICHBORNE CASE. *See* ORTON.

TICKS. Two families of Acari in the Arachnida. Allied to the mites T. are blood-sucking disease-carrying parasites on men, animals, and birds.

TIDES. Rise and fall of waters due to the gravitational forces of the moon and sun. High water occurs at an average interval of 12 hours 24½ min. The highest or spring tides are at or near new and full moon, and the lowest or neap tides when the moon is in the 1st or 3rd quarter. Some seas, e.g. the Mediterranean,

have very small tides. Gravitational T. – the pull of nearby groups of stars – have also been observed to affect the galaxies.

TIECK (tēk), **Johann Ludwig** (1773–1853). German writer. One of the leaders of the Romantic movement, he wrote much poetry, and collected folk-tales, some of which he dramatized, e.g. *Puss in Boots.*

TIEN-SHAN. One of the great mountain systems of central Asia, on the borders of the U.S.S.R. and China, and extending eastwards across Sinkiang-Uighur into Mongolia. Pobeda (victory) Peak rises to 24,406 ft.

TIENTSIN (tyentsi'n). Chinese port, formerly the cap of Hopei prov., it was created a special municipality, and is sit. where the Pei-ho joins the Grand Canal, 75 m. S.E. of Peking. Opened to foreign trade 1860, T. suffered badly in the Boxer rising, 1900. Its name means ford of heaven. Pop. (1968) 4,000,000.

TIEPOLO (tē-ā'pōlō), **Giovanni Battista** (1692–1769). Italian artist. B. at Venice, he was a master of colour and executed delightful decorations in churches and palaces, with transparent atmospheric effects, e.g. the episcopal palace Würzburg.

TIERRA DEL FUEGO (tē-er'rah del fwā'gō). Group of is. separated from the S. tip of S. America by Magellan Strait. The W., 10,460 sq. m., is part of the Chilean prov. of Magallanes; the E. is a prov. of Argentina (area 8,072 sq. m., pop. (1965) 8,000; cap. Ushuaia). The name (Span.) means land of fire. The southernmost point of the group is Cape Horn.

TIFLIS. Russian form of TBILISI.

TIGER. Largest of the great cats (*Felis tigris*), formerly found in much of Central Asia but increasingly rare. The striped markings – black on reddish fawn – are present from birth, though rare cream or black specimens have been known. The T. reaches a length of 10–12 ft., may be either solitary or one of a family party, is a good swimmer, and feeds for preference on deer or cattle, man-eating being the result of weakened powers or shortage of other game.

TI'GRIS. River of Turkey and Iraq, one of the two great rivers of Mesopotamia (q.v.). The T. rises in the Anti-Taurus and flows for more than 1,000 m. to join the Euphrates c. 45 m. above Basra. Mosul and Baghdad stand on it.

TILBURY. English port in Essex on the N. bank of the Thames, with important docks serving London. It dates from Roman times.

TILLEY, Vesta. Stage-name of British music-hall and pantomime artist Matilda Alice Powles (1864–1952), celebrated as a male impersonator.

TILLOTSON, John Robert (1630–94). English churchman, abp. of Canterbury from 1691. Dean of St. Paul's 1689–91, he was renowned as a preacher, and m. a niece of Oliver Cromwell.

TILLY, Jan Tserklaes, count (1559–1632). Imperialist general in the Thirty Years War. Notorious for his storming of Magdeburg in 1631, he was defeated by Gustavus Adolphus at Breitenfeld, and at the Lech, in which latter battle he was mortally wounded.

TILSIT. *See* SOVIETSK.

TIMARU (timaroo'). Port and airport on Canterbury Bight, S. Island, New Zealand, with an artificial harbour, freezing plants, flour mills, pottery works, breweries, etc. The name, from the Maori, means place of shelter. Pop. (1967) 27,600.

TIMBER. Name given to woods used for building, furniture making, pulp making, etc. It is divided into 3 groups: 1. Tropical hard woods, e.g. mahogany, teak, ebony, and rosewood, obtained from Central

America, W. Indies, W. Africa, and Asia. 2. Hardwoods of temperate regions in Europe and N. America, include oak, elm, beech, and the hard eucalyptus woods of Australia, known as jarrah and karri. 3. Timber of coniferous trees – pine, fir, spruce, larch, etc., which are the easiest of all trees to work. Sawdust and shavings compacted into sheets with synthetic resins, and often veneered on both sides, are used for their strength and stability. *See also* FORESTRY.

TIMBU'KTU. Town in Mali Rep., 9 m. N. of the Niger on the S. edge of the Sahara. Founded in the 11th cent., it is an important caravan centre. Pop. (1967) 9,000.

TIME. For the purposes of everyday life, the alternation of day and night consequent upon the rotation of the earth on its axis. The natural unit of time is the true or apparent solar day, the period in which the earth makes a complete rotation relative to the sun. Apparent solar time suffers from the disadvantage that the days are not of equal length; a fundamental unit of time is adopted, therefore, the mean solar day, equal to the average length of the apparent solar day. Since the sun crosses different meridians at different moments there is a local apparent time and a local mean time, the local noon being defined as the passage of the sun across the meridian passing through that place. Since 1884 Greenwich meridian has been adopted as the prime meridian, from which all longitudes are measured. The local mean time of places W. of Greenwich is earlier than that of Greenwich, and vice versa (*see* Map I in Atlas). A system of standard or zone times has been adopted by most countries, the standard of time differing from Greenwich mean time by an integral number of hours. Each hour corresponds to 15° longitude. The meridian of 180° longitude more or less – the date line – separates the half-zone in which the time is 12 hours fast on Greenwich mean time from that in which it is 12 hours slow. The interval of time taken by the earth to make one complete rotation relative to the stars is called the sidereal day. *See* ATOMIC T.

TIMISOARA (tēmēshwah'rah). Town in W. Rumania, cap. of T. region. It has a univ. (1962), flour mills, breweries, and factories making tobacco, leather, cloth, paper, etc. Pop. (1966) 174,388.

TI'MOR. Largest and most easterly island of the lesser Sunda group of the Malay archipelago. The N.E. portion is an overseas prov. of Portugal, area 7,330 sq. m.; pop. (1960) 517,079; cap. Dili. The Portuguese estab. themselves on T. in the 16th cent. The remainder is part of Indonesia (E. Nusa Tenggara), area 24,500 sq. m.; pop. (est.) 1,700,000; cap. Kupang (occupied by the Dutch in 1618). Sandalwood, pearl shell, bêche-de-mer, coffee, copra, etc., are exported.

TIMOSHENKO, Semyon Konstantinovich (1895–1970). Marshal of the Soviet Union. B. in Bessarabia, of peasant parents, he served in the F.W.W., and distinguished himself in the Civil War 1918–21. In 1940 he was made a marshal, and during the S.W.W. held high commands. He was a member of the C.C.C.P. 1939–52.

TI'MOTHY. The companion of St. Paul on his missionary journeys, and in his imprisonment, to whom 2 of the Pauline epistles are addressed.

TIN. The most usual of the several varieties of T., is a silver-white, crystalline metal, malleable and somewhat ductile, which crumbles to a greyish powder at low temperatures: symbol Sn (Lat. *stannum*), at. wt. 118·70, at. no. 50. It is found chiefly in the mineral cassiterite SnO_2 in Malaysia, Indonesia and Bolivia, and is chiefly used as a protective coating to resist corrosion on iron and steel, i.e. the 'tin can' food container. Its use was known in the ancient world and the mines in Cornwall, where working was renewed in the 1960s, were being worked in the Bronze Age. Other important alloys, besides bronze, incl. solder, type metal, pewter, and metals for bearings.

TI'NBERGEN, Nikolaas (1907–). Dutch zoologist. Professor in Animal Behaviour, Oxford Univ., from 1966, he has pub. *The Study of Instinct* (1951).

TINDOUF (tēndōōf'). Oasis and village, with an airfield, in the extreme W. of Algeria, *c.* 80 m. S. of the Moroccan border. Deposits of iron have been found in the neighbourhood, and there are plans for joint Moroccan – Algerian exploitation.

TINTAGEL (tinta'jel). English village on the Atlantic coast near Camelford, Cornwall. Its castle is associated with the Arthurian legends.

TINTORE'TTO. Name given to the Venetian painter Jacopo Robusti (1518–94) because his father was a dyer (*Tintore*). Chief painter of the later Venetian school, he did many portraits and biblical scenes. 'The Paradise', in the Ducal palace at Venice, is the largest picture on canvas by any great master (34 × 74 ft.).

TIPPERA'RY. An inland county of Munster, Rep. of Ireland, watered by the Shannon and Suir. Some parts are mountainous; in the S.W. is the Golden Vale, one of Ireland's most fertile regions. Dairying is the chief industry. Clonmel is the co. town; other towns are Tipperary, Cashel Carrick-on-Suir, and Nenagh. Area 1,643 sq. m.; pop. (1966) 122,812.

TIPPET1, Sir Michael (1905–). Brit. composer. Ed. at the R.C.M., he was director of music at Morley College 1940–51, and the same sensitive concern for humanity which led to his brief imprisonment as a conscientious objector in 1943 appears in his oratorio *A Child of Our Time* (1941). Later works incl. operas, notably *King Priam* (1961), two piano sonatas, a Magnificat and Nunc Dimittis written for St. John's Coll., Cambridge (1961), and incidental music for *The Tempest* (1962). He was knighted 1966.

TIPPOO' SAHIB (1753–99). Sultan of Mysore, India, from 1782, when he succeeded his father Hyder Ali. He was killed in a war with the British.

TIRANA (tērah'na). Cap. of Albania, 20 m. E. of Durrës. Founded in the 17th cent., T. makes cotton textiles, soap, cigarettes, etc., and is the seat of a univ. Pop. (1966) 152,500.

TIROL. Alpine prov. of Austria, lying between Bavaria and Italy. It is watered by the Inn and its tributaries. Cap., Innsbruck. Area, 4,883 sq. m.; pop. (1961) 462,476.

TIRPITZ (tir'pits), **Alfred von** (1849–1930). German admiral. As Sec. for the Navy 1897–1916 he was largely responsible for the F.W.W. U-boat campaign.

TIRSO DE MOLINA (tērsō de mōlē'nah). Name taken by Gabriel Tellez (1571–1648), Spanish dramatist, who wrote some 400 comedies.

TIROL. The mountains surrounding Innsbruck are a winter sports paradise. Ski tracks lead down between the trees to the valley, and the Glungezer (8,837 ft.) rises in the distance.
Courtesy of Austrian State Tourist Department.

TIRUCHIRAPALLI (tiroochirapa'li). Indian city in Madras state, on the Cauvery, cap. of T. dist. It makes cotton textiles, cigars, gold and silver filigree. A place of pilgrimage, it was cap. of Tamil kingdoms from the 10th–17th cent. The name means three-headed demon. Pop. (1961) 249,862.

TIRYNS. Site of Greek city in Argolis, with massive remains of the Mycenean culture.

TISCHENDORF, Konstantin von (1815–74). German biblical scholar, who discovered in the monastery on Mt. Sinai the 4th cent. Codex Sinaiticus of the N.T.

TISSOT (tēsō'), **James Joseph Jacques** (1836–1902). French artist. Serving in the Franco-Prussian War, he subsequently went to London and produced a number of highly detailed and attractive renderings of the Victorian social scene.

TIT or **Titmouse.** Name given to members of the Passerine family Paradae, of birds. Six species, all insect eaters, are found in Britain, viz. the crested, blue, cole, great, marsh and long-tailed.

'TĪTA'NIC'. The supposedly unsinkable British White Star liner that struck an iceberg in 1912. More than 1,500 people were drowned.

TĪTA'NIUM. Lustrous, steel-like white metal resembling iron, burning in air, and the only metal to burn in nitrogen: symbol Ti, at. wt. 47·90, at. no. 22. Discovered by Gregor (1791), it was named by Klaproth in 1795 and obtained pure by Hunter in 1910. Its compounds occur in practically all igneous rocks and their sedimentary deposits. The oxide is used in high-grade white pigments, and some barium compounds are used in high value capacitors. Of great strength and corrosion-resistance, it is used in Concorde and spacecraft, and was found on the Moon in the Sea of Tranquillity.

TĪTANS. In Greek mythology, the sons and daus. of Uranus and Ge, who warred against Zeus, but were thrust into the underworld.

TITHES (literally, tenths). In England payment exacted from the inhabitants of a parish for the maintenance of the church and its incumbent. Originally it was payable in kind, and was levied on all yearly profits, but in the 19th cent. a rent charge was substituted. By the Tithe Act, 1936, rent charge was replaced by 'redemption annuities' payable to the Crown, govt. stock being issued to T.-owners.

TITHWA. Chinese name for URUMCHI.

TITIAN (tish'an). Anglicized form of the name of Italian artist Tiziano (Vecellio) (c. 1477–1576). He studied under the Bellinis, and was strongly influenced by Giorgione. In 1548 he painted the equestrian portrait of Charles V, and later executed many pictures for Philip II of Spain. His most important works incl. 'Bacchus and Ariadne', 'Venus and Adonis', and the 'Entombment of Christ'.

TITICACA (tētēkah'kah). Mountain lake in the Andes, part in Bolivia and part in Peru, over 12,500 ft. above the sea. It is 130 m. long; area 3,200 sq. m. Its waters are harnessed for hydro-electric power and irrigation. See illus. p. 148.

TITO (tē'tō). Assumed name of the Yugoslav soldier and statesman Josip Broz (1892–   ). B. in Croatia, he served in the Austrian army during the F.W.W., was captured by the Russians, and fought in the Red Army during the Civil Wars. Returning to Yugoslavia in 1923, he became prominent as a Communist. After the German invasion of 1941, he organized the National Liberation Army which carried on guerrilla warfare against the occupying forces. He received the title of marshal in 1943. In 1946 he became P.M. of the Federal Rep. and C.-in-C. of the armed forces, and was largely responsible for the settlement of the Yugoslav minority question on a federal basis. Under a new constitution in 1953 he became Pres., and was re-elected in 1954, 1958 and 1963. Denounced by the Cominform, particularly the U.S.S.R., in 1948 for his (successful) system of decentralized, profit-sharing workers' councils, very popular with the peasantry, his belief that there are different national roads to socialism, and his subsequent foreign policy of 'positive neutralism', Tito became one of the principal leaders of the uncommitted nations in world politics. Subsequently relations with the U.S.S.R. improved.

TITOGRAD (tē'tograd). Yugoslav town, cap. of Montenegro, on the Moracha. A commercial centre with tobacco factories and sawmills. it is on the site of Diocletian's birthplace. Until the S.W.W., when it was badly damaged, it was called Podgorica; it was rebuilt, and renamed in 1948 in honour of Marshal Tito. Pop. (1961) 30,657.

TITUS, Flavius Sabinus Vespasianus (A.D. 40–81). Roman emperor. Eldest son of Vespasian, he was a distinguished soldier and stormed Jerusalem in A.D. 70. He became emperor in 79.

TIVERTON (tiv'-). English town (bor.) in Devon on the Exe, 13 m. N. of Exeter. Here is Blundell's School (1604); the original building was given to the National Trust in 1954. Pop. (1961) 12,296.

TIVOLI (tē'vōlē). Ancient town of Italy, 20 m. E.N.E. of Rome, with ruins of Hadrian's villa and other Roman remains; also the Villa d'Este (1549) with its gardens.

T.N.T. ($C_6H_2(NO_2)_3CH_3$). Short for trinitrotoluene, a powerful high explosive; a yellow crystalline solid, prepared from toluene acted upon by sulphuric and nitric acids.

TOAD. Genus of amphibians, of world-wide distribution, except in Australia and Madagascar. The common T. (*Bufo vulgaris*) of Europe and Asia has a rough, usually dark brown skin in which there are glands secreting a poisonous fluid which makes it unattractive as food for other animals: it needs this protection as its usual progress is a slow, ungainly crawl. The eggs are laid, not in a mass as with frogs, but in long strings. The common T. of N. America, *B. lentiginosa*, is very similar.

TOADSTOOLS. See FUNGI.

TOBACCO. A narcotic plant of the genus *Nicotiana*, family Solanaceae, whose dried leaves are prepared for smoking, chewing, and as snuff. The generally cultivated species is *N. tabacum*, a native of America: it was introduced to Europe as a medicinal plant in the 16th cent. and the habit of smoking T. was probably brought to England c. 1556 by Hawkins. See CIGAR; CIGARETTE. The best-known Ts. are grown in U.S.A. (Virginia, N. and S. Carolina, Georgia, Kentucky, Tennessee); the Commonwealth (Ontario, Rhodesia, Malawi); and Turkey, Greece, and Bulgaria. By 'topping' the plants about a dozen large leaves are produced which are cured by exposure to the sun, air currents, or artificial heat, and subsequently mature for 2 or 3 years in the warehouse.

TOBA'GO. See under TRINIDAD.

TOBATA. See under KITAKYUSHU.

TOBOGGAN. Flat-bottomed vehicle with curved-up tip, carrying runners, which is used in coasting down snow slopes or on artificial curved courses or 'chutes' of high-banked snow and ice, e.g. the Cresta run. As incl. in the Winter Olympics, tobogganing consists of two-man or four-man 'car' events in which steering is by a pivoting front section, and the action of the 'brakeman' from behind; the 2 single-man events are in fixed Ts., in which the competitor either sits (steering by leaning), or lies on his stomach (steering by footwork).

TOBO'LSK. Town in Tyumen region, R.S.F.S.R., where the Tobol joins the Irtysh. It dates from 1587. Formerly engaged in the fur trade, it is a general trade centre with shipyards, sawmills, etc., and a theatre founded 1797. Pop. (est.) 46,000.

TOBRUK (tobrook'). Port in Libya, the anc. Antipyrgos, 60 m. W. of Bardia, with the best harbour in Cyrenaica. Occupied by the Italians in 1911, during the S.W.W. it was taken by the Brit. in 1941, and was the site of a memorable unsuccessful siege by Axis forces April-Dec. 1941. In June 1942 the Brit. 8th Army retreated to Egypt, leaving a garrison at T. which was captured by the Germans later the same month, an event that led to changes in the N. African Brit. command. Pop. (est.) 5,000.

TOC H. Organization for Christian fellowship, founded at Poperinghe in 1915 by the Rev. Neville Talbot and the Rev. P. T. B. Clayton; it was named Talbot House in memory of Gilbert Talbot who was killed in action in July 1915. Toc H is the army signaller's designation of the initials.

TOCQUEVILLE (tokvēl'), **Aléxis Charles Henri Clérel de** (1805–59). French historian, author of *Démocratie en Amérique* (1835) and *L' Ancien Régime et la Révolution* (1856).

TOKYO. Seen here from the Imperial Palace grounds is Japan's most famous bridge, the Nijubashi, or Double Bridge, which crosses one of the several surrounding moats and leads to the main gate. It is used only on official occasions, such as when a foreign envoy presents his credentials to the Emperor.
Courtesy of Japanese Embassy.

TODD, Alexander Robertus, baron (1907–). British organic chemist. B. in Glasgow, he was prof. at Manchester 1938–44, and Cambridge from 1944. Elected F.R.S. in 1942, he was awarded a Nobel prize in 1957 for his work on the nucleic acids: important in inherited characteristics – for transmitting and putting them into effect.

TODMORDEN. English industrial and market town (bor.) in Yorks W. Riding, 19 m. N.E. of Manchester. It is a cotton spinning and weaving town. Pop. (1961) 17,416.

TODT (tōt), **Fritz** (1891–1942). German engineer. He w as responsible for the Siegfried Line and the great auto-bahn roads, and as Min. for Arma-ments 1940–2 built the Atlantic Wall.

TO'GŌ. Rep. in W. Africa, between Ghana and Dahomey, with a short coastline on the Gulf of Guinea. Area 20,000 sq. m.; pop. (1965) 1,650,000, cap. Lomé. Cocoa, coffee, palm kernels, bauxite, chromite, and phosphates are among its products. The rep. is part of the German colony of T. which in 1922 was divided between France and Britain under League of Nations mandate, transferred in 1946 to U.N. trusteeship. In 1956 British Togoland voted for integration with Ghana (q.v.); French T. chose to become an independent rep. outside the Fr. Community. Independent T. suffered much unrest (*see* OLYMPIO) and in 1967 the army assumed power by a bloodless coup.

TO'JŌ, Hideki (1884–1948). Japanese politician. As P.M. 1941–4 he was mainly responsible for the attack on Pearl Harbor. He was tried and hanged as a war criminal.

TOKAJ (tō'koi). Hungarian town at the confluence of the Bodrog and the Tisa, famous for its wine. Pop. (est.) 6,000.

TO'KYŌ. Cap. of Japan, on T. Bay on the island of Honshu. The delta of the Sumida r. separates the city proper from the suburb of Honjo. Formerly

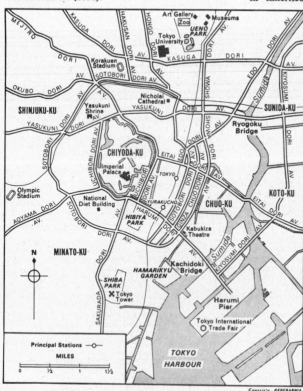

TOKYO

called Yedo and founded in the 16th cent., it was named T. (eastern city) in 1868 when the emperor removed his court there from Kyoto. T., badly damaged by an earthquake in 1923 when some 58,000 people were killed, was 80 per cent destroyed from the air in the S.W.W. Rebuilding was rapid, and in the 1960s there has been a movement of pop. to the perimeter, and the growth of Shinjuku to rival the central Ginza shopping area. Within T. are the Imperial Palace, National Diet, Nat. Theatre, T. Univ. (1877) and many others, museums, the Nat. Athletic Stadium, and it is the H.Q. of broadcasting, publishing and economic life. T. Internat. Airport is at Haneda. Pop. (1969) 11,000,000.

TOLEDO (tōlā′dō). (1) Spanish city on the Tagus, 42 m. S.W. of Madrid; capital of T. prov. Its cathedral was built 1227–1493, and there are Moorish remains. For centuries T. sword blades were famous; cloth and steel cutlery are manufactured. Pop. (est.) 35,000.

(2) City and port in Ohio, U.S.A., on Maumee Bay at the W. end of lake Erie. Very important industrially (motor vehicles, electrical appliances, glass, food processing, etc.). Pop. met. area (1970) 685,387.

TOLKIEN (tol′kēn), **John Ronald Reuel** (1892–   ). British scholar. Merton prof. of English at Oxford 1945–59, he is celebrated for his creation of a world – Middle-Earth – peopled with Hobbits, Dwarfs, Men, etc., with their own language, history and myth, as described espec. in the 3 vols. of his epic story *The Fellowship of the Ring* (1954–5).

TOLLER, Ernst (1893–1939). German playwright. Taking part in the abortive Socialist revolt in Bavaria in 1919, he was imprisoned for 5 years, was an exile under Hitler, and committed suicide in New York. His Expressionist plays incl. *Massemensch* (1921: *Masses and Man*) and *Feuer aus den Kesseln* (1930: *Draw the Fires*).

TOLPUDDLE MARTYRS. Six farm labourers of Tolpuddle, nr. Dorchester, who in 1834 were transported to Australia for forming a Trade Union. After a nation-wide agitation they were pardoned 2 years later.

TOLSTOY (tol′stoi), **Alexei Nikolaievich** (1882–1945). Russian author. B. at Kuibyshev, he trained as an engineer, and in 1907 pub. a vol. of symbolist lyrics. After being a soldier in the White army, he went to Paris, and before returning to Russia in 1922 wrote the 1st part of his trilogy *Khozhdeniye po mukam* (*Road to Calvary*), awarded a Stalin prize in 1942. Other works are the historical novel *Peter the Great* (1929–34) and the play *Ivan the Terrible*.

TOLSTOY, Leo Nikolaievich (1828–1910). Russian novelist. B. of noble family at Yasnaya Polyana in Tula, he fought in the Crimean War. A series of *Tales from Sebastopol* made him famous. His masterpieces are *War and Peace*, dealing with the Napoleonic struggle (1866), and *Anna Karenina* (1877). Later he devoted himself to preaching a gospel of brotherhood and love. Such books as *What is Religion?* and the *Kreutzer Sonata* had a didactic and religious purpose *Resurrection*, his last novel, appeared in 1900. Excommunicated for his heretical views, he gave up the use of his property, lived as a peasant, and d. a fugitive from his home at Astapovo.

TOLTECS. Ancient people of Central America whose culture preceded that of the Aztecs and Mayas.

TOLUENE (tōl′ū-ēn). A colourless, inflammable liquid, $C_6H_5CH_3$, b.p. 110°C, and insoluble in water. Obtained as a by-product in the distillation of coaltar, it is used as a solvent, and as a starting point in the manufacture of many substances incl. explosives (*see* T.N.T.), dyes, perfumes and sulphonic acids.

TOMASI (tōmah′si), **Giuseppe, Prince of Lampedusa** (1896–1957). Italian writer. He became famous for his novel *Il Gattopardo* (1958: *The Leopard*), pub. posthumously, which describes the Bourbon regime,

Garibaldi's victory, and the dawn of modern Italy, in his native Sicily, as experienced by the vividly portrayed character of Prince Fabrizio and his family.

TOMATO. Annual plant (*Lycopersicon esculentum*) of the Solanaceae family, native to S. America, sometimes also known as the 'love-apple' although any aphrodisiac quality of the globose red or yellow fruits is imaginary. As a salad crop Ts. are grown in N. America and Europe under glass.

TOMLINSON, H(enry) M(ajor) (1873–1958). British author. B. in London, he was a war correspondent in the F.W.W. and literary editor of the *Nation* and *Athenaeum* 1917–23. His books, which have the tang of the sea he loved in their writing, incl. *The Sea and the Jungle* (1912), *Gallions Reach* (1927), and *Morning Light* (1946).

TOMMY-GUN. Name for any light automatic carbine or rifle fired from hip or shoulder, derived from the U.S. Thompson sub-machine-gun.

TOMSK. Russian city, cap. of T. region, on the Tom r. and on a branch of the Trans-Siberian railway. It has a univ. (1888); sawmills, distilleries, factories making electric motors, plastics, etc. Pop. (1967) 311,000.

TOM THUMB. Name from an English folk tale frequently given to dwarfs, in particular Charles Sherwood Stratton (1838–83), known as General T.T.

TON. The English or long T. is 2,240 lb., the American or short T. is 2,000 lb. and the metric T. is 1,000 kg. or 2,204·6 lb.

TONE, Theobald Wolfe (1763–98). Irish nationalist. Called to the Bar in 1789, he was prominent in the revolutionary society of the United Irishmen. In 1798 he accompanied the French invasion of Ireland, was captured and condemned to death, but cut his throat in prison.

TO′NGA. Polynesian kingdom in the S. Pacific consisting of 3 groups of islands; cap. Nukualofa on Tongatapu. They were visited by Captain Cook in 1773, who called them the Friendly Islands, and came under British Protection in 1900 and became a sovereign member of the Commonwealth in 1970. King Tungi (1918–   ) succeeded his mother, Queen Salote, in 1965. He is assisted by a cabinet, privy council, and legislative assembly of 21. The state religion is Wesleyanism. Area 270 sq. m.; pop. (1970) 80,000.

TONGKING. *See* TONKIN.

TONGUE. Muscular organ in the floor of the mouth. It has a thick root attached to a U-shaped bone (hyoid) behind; a thin fold of mucous membrane

TOLTECS. These recently excavated monolithic figures 30 ft. high dominate the dusty plain at Tula, a Toltec site in the state of Hidalgo, Mexico.
Courtesy of the Mexican Government Tourism Dept.

connects its lower middle line with the floor of the mouth. It is covered with mucous membrane containing many nerves and also the 'taste buds', which distinguish the qualities called salt, sweet, sour and bitter. It directs food to the teeth, presses food and drink back into the throat in the act of swallowing and by modifying the voice forms articulate speech.

TONKA. Tree (*Dypteryx odorata*) of the family Leguminosae, native to Guiana. Its fruit, a dry, fibrous pod, contains a single aromatic seed used in perfumery.

TONKIN. Name of a former Fr. protectorate, from 1950 part of Vietnam (q.v.). It was in the **T. Gulf**, after a minor engagement on 2 Aug. 1964, that the U.S. destroyers *Maddox* and *Turner Joy* reported a night attack on 4 Aug. by N. Vietnamese torpedo boats. It has been suggested that radar and sonar effects were misinterpreted, but a retaliatory air attack was made on N. Vietnam which led to the eventual despatch of over 1,000,000 U.S. troops to battle in S. Vietnam.

TONSILS. A pair of gland-like bodies between the 2 arches (fauces) of the soft palate at the back of the mouth. Their function is not understood, but they hold disease germs and are often removed by surgery.

TONSURE. Ritual shaving or cutting of the hair as a symbol of dedication to the clerical state in the R.C. and Eastern Orthodox churches. In the former, where it is now used only by certain orders, the crown is shaved, leaving a fringe all round to resemble Christ's crown of thorns; in the latter the hair is now merely shorn close.

TOOKE, John Horne (1736–1812). British politician and philologist. B. in London, he was in holy orders 1760–3. He was a supporter of Wilkes (q.v) 1765–71, and his radical opinions led to his trial and acquittal on a charge of treason in 1794. He wrote the philological *Diversions of Purley.*

TOOLS, Machine. Strictly the term incl. woodworking M. Ts., but is generally used for all tools operated by power. They are the basis of industrial production, and their most important use is in the manufacture of engines and machines. The chief M.T. is the lathe, from which the others have developed. The industrial potential of a country is often calculated by the number of M.Ts. available. Automatic control of M.Ts. is an important modern development. *See* AUTOMATION.

TOOWOO´MBA. City, agricultural centre, and health resort in S.E. Queensland, 65 m. W. of Brisbane. Pop. (1966) 55,774.

TO´PAZ. Mineral valued as a gemstone. It crystallizes in the rhombic system and has a perfect basal cleavage. It varies from yellow to white, blue or pink, and is found in Brazil, Peru, Ceylon, and Siberia.

TOPE. Small shark (*Galeus canis*) ranging through temperate and tropical seas. Dark grey above and white beneath, it reaches *c.* 7 ft.: the young are born alive, sometimes 50 at a time.

TOPE. Kind of tumulus found in India and S.E. Asia; a Buddhist monument usually built over a relic of Buddha or his disciples. They date from 300 B.C.–A.D. 400, and the most famous are at Sanchi, near Bhilsa, C. India.

TOPE´KA. Cap. of Kansas, U.S.A., on the r. Kansas, 55 m. W. of Kansas City. Laid out in 1854, T. became state cap. in 1861. It has woollen mills, machine shops, foundries, etc. Pop. (1960) 119,484.

TOPLADY, Augustus Montague (1740–78). British Anglican clergyman. B. at Farnham, he pub. his famous hymn 'Rock of Ages' in 1775.

TOPOLSKI, Feliks (1907–). Polish artist. Settling in England in 1935 and becoming naturalized in 1947, he has a versatile gift for war pictures, theatrical settings and costumes, murals and portraits.

TOR BAY. Co. bor. in S. Devon, England, created 1968 from the bor. of Torquay and the U.Ds. of Brixham and Paignton. Pop. (1968) 96,980.

TORGAU (tor´gow). Town in Leipzig dist., E. Germany. Here Frederick the Great defeated the Austrians in 1760, and U.S. and Russian forces first made contact in the S.W.W. Pop. (est.) 18,000.

TORINO. Ital. form of TURIN.

TORNA´DO. Extremely violent revolving storm, caused by a rising column of warm air propelled by strong wind. The diameter may be a few hundred yards or less, but the T. rises to a great height, and is marked by swirling funnel-shaped clouds. Moving at a speed of *c.* 30 m.p.h., Ts. are common in the Mississippi basin and cause great destruction.

TORONTO. Canadian city, cap. of Ontario (1797), on the N. shore of Lake Ontario. It is an important

TORONTO. The waterfront has excellent modern facilities, the marine terminal development and the increased number of vessels calling being a direct result of the construction of the St. Lawrence Seaway. *Courtesy of the Port of Toronto.*

port, and industries incl. making of farm machinery, motor cars, meat packing and other food processing. Cheap power is drawn from Niagara Falls. It is also a great commercial, banking, and publishing centre. Central T. is being re-developed, with underground shopping streets linking the giant complex, of which T.-Dominion Centre and New City Hall form part. It has theatres (O'Keefe Centre, Massey Hall and Royal Alexander Theatre), is the nat. television centre, and mounts an annual Canadian Nat. Exhibition. There is a univ. (1827). T. dates from 1794, built on the site of a French fort (1749); it was constituted a city 1834. Pop. (1966) 664,584; Greater T. 2,158,496.

TORPEDO. Self-propelled submarine projectile used in naval warfare. Invented in 1805 by R. Fulton, the 1st T. consisted of an explosive charge only, and propulsion mechanism was added in 1862 by R. Whitehead. The modern T. is cigar-shaped, 21 in. by *c.* 20 ft., powered by compressed air, with a warhead of 500 lb. of T.N.T. In the S.W.W. 'human Ts. were piloted by suicide crews. From the 1960s Ts were used by atomic-powered submarines (q.v.), pickets and destroyers.

TORPEDO FISH or **Electric Ray.** Family of fishes, the Torpedinidae, whose electric organs between the pectoral fin and the head can give a powerful shock. *T. hebetans* is found off England.

TORQUAY (torke´). English seaside resort and residential town in S. Devon on Tor Bay. Once a fishing village, T. dates from the 12th cent., and in 1968 became part of the co. bor. of Tor Bay (q.v.).

TORQUEMADA (tōrkämah´dah), **Tomás de** (1420–98). Spanish inquisitor. B. at Valladolid, he became a Dominican, revived the Inquisition, and is said to have been responsible for the burning of 10,000 persons. T. also expelled the Jews from Spain.

TORRES STRAIT. An 80 m. wide channel separating New Guinea from Australia, scattered with reefs, discovered by Torres in 1606.

TORRES VEDRAS. Town of Portugal, 25 m. N. of Lisbon. The 'lines of T. V.' were built by Wellington in the Peninsular War. Pop. (est.) 5,000.

TORRICELLI (tor-rēchel'lē), **Evangelista** (1608–47). Italian physicist. B. at Faenza, he discovered the principle of the barometer, inventing the T. tube and the T. vacuum in 1643.

TORSION. The state of strain set up in a material by virtue of being twisted, e.g. when a thread wire or rod is twisted, the T. which is set up in the material returns or tends to return it to its original state. An instrument which makes use of this is the T. balance, a sensitive device for measuring small gravitational or magnetic forces, or electric charges, by balancing these against the restoring force set up by them in a suspended fibre.

TORTOISE. Reptile of the order Chelonia, of which the marine and freshwater forms are known as turtles. It has a characteristic 'shell' consisting of a curved upper carapace and flattened lower plastron which are joined at the sides, and the head and limbs may be retracted within it, to a greater or lesser extent, in time of danger. Herbivorous it has no teeth but the mouth forms a sharp edged 'beak': eggs are laid in mud and hatched by the sun. Best-known species are the small N. African T. (*Testudo graeca*), also found in Asia Minor, often imported to languish in British gardens, and the giant species of the Galapagos and Seychelles which reach a great age, maybe 4 ft. long, and yield c. 200 pounds of meat – hence their almost complete extermination by passing ships.

N. AFRICAN TORTOISE

TORTOISE ISLANDS. Eng. name of the GALAPAGOS IS.

TORTO'SA. Fortified town in Tarragona prov., Spain, on the Ebro, with a cathedral founded 1158. T. was a Roman colony. Pop. (est.) 15,000.

TORTURE. The infliction of bodily pain, esp. to extort evidence or confession. At one time a feature of most judicial systems, it was abolished in England c. 1640, in Scotland in 1708, and in France in 1789, but was revived by the Nazis and Japanese during the S.W.W. The usual instruments of T. in Europe were the rack, wheel, thumbscrew, and boot.

TORUN (to'rōōny). Town in Poland on the Vistula, 30 m. E.S.E. of Bydgoszcz, founded by the Teutonic Knights (13th cent.). It has a univ. Copernicus was b. at T. Pop. (1966) 115,000.

TORY PARTY. Name applied c. 1680–1830 to the forerunner of the present Conservative Party. The original Tories were Irish guerrillas who warred on the English; hence the name was transferred, at first in a derogatory sense, to the Royalists who opposed the Exclusion Bill. The T.P. largely supported the revolution of 1688, but fell under suspicion of Jacobite sympathies and were excluded from office 1714–60. Under George III they regained power, which they held almost continuously until 1830. They were traditionally the party of squire and parson, as opposed to the Whigs, who drew their support largely from the trading classes and Nonconformists. Of late years the name has been revived as an alternative to Conservative.

TOSCANINI (toskahnē'ni), **Arturo** (1867–1957). Italian conductor. B. in Parma, he made La Scala, Milan – where he conducted 1898–1903, 1906–8, and 1920–9 – the world's leading opera house. However, he was opposed to the Fascist régime, and in 1936 returned to America, where he had conducted at the Metropolitan 1908–15, the N.B.C. Symphony Orchestra being formed for him in 1937. He retired in 1954.

TOSTI (tos'tē), **Sir Francesco Paolo** (1846–1916). Italian song writer, who went to England in 1875, and was appointed singing-master to the royal family. His best-known song is 'Good-Bye'.

TOTALIZATOR or **Tote.** Device on horse-racing courses and greyhound tracks to record bets and pay winnings without the intervention of a bookmaker.

TOTEMISM. System of belief common among primitive peoples, whereby the members of a clan believe themselves to be descended from an animal or plant: this totem (Algonquin Indian, 'my guardian spirit') is sacred to them, and they are forbidden to eat it. T. is usually associated with exogamy, i.e. members of the same clan are forbidden to intermarry. It still exists among the Australian aborigines and the Red Indians, and formerly prevailed over most of Europe and Asia.

TO'TILA (d. 552). King of the Ostrogoths, who warred with Justinian for Italy, and was killed by Narses at the battle of Taginae.

TOTTENHAM. District of the Greater London bor. of Haringey. Settled in Danish times, it has a church (All Hallows) dating in part from the 12th cent. Bruce Castle (16th cent.) was built on a site belonging to Robert Bruce's father. T. Hotspurs are a famous football team.

TOUCAN (tookahn'). Bird of the family Ramphastidae with very large, often brilliantly coloured beak, espec. in the genus *Rhamphastes*. Living in small flocks in S. America forests, Ts. often have handsome plumage, are omnivorous, and lay their eggs in holes in trees.

TOUCAN

TOULON (toolon'). Seaport in Var dept., France, on the Mediterranean, 30 m. S.E. of Marseilles. It is the chief Mediterranean naval station of France, with defences commanding the sea and large dockyards. Petroleum refining, and the making of chemicals, furniture, and clothing are among its industries. The Roman Telo Martius, T. was made a port by Henry IV. Occupied by the Brit. in 1793; Napoleon first distinguished himself in driving them out. Pop. (1968) 174,746.

TOULOUSE (toolōōs'). Cap. of Haute-Garonne dept., S. France, on the Garonne 140 m. S.E. of Bordeaux, T. was an important place before the Roman conquest. Cap. of the Visigoths and later (781–843) of Aquitaine, it has a medieval cathedral and a univ. (c. 1230). Woollens and silks are manufactured. Wellington repulsed Soult at T. in 1814. Pop. (1968) 370,796.

TOULOUSE-LAUTREC (-lawtrek'), **Henri Raymonde de** (1864–1901). B. at Albi, where a L. Museum commemorates him, he was dwarfed and crippled by both his thighs having been broken in boyhood. Of noble descent – the counts of T. – he now preferred to plunge himself into the unquestioning and convivial life of Montmartre and produced posters and colour lithographs of striking linear dexterity showing can-can dancers, circus acrobats, brothel scenes, etc. His life was shortened by his heavy drinking. *See* illus. p. 1042.

TOUQUET-PARIS-PLAGE (tookā'), **Le.** Fashionable resort of France, Pas-de-Calais dept., on the Channel coast with fine sands and pinewoods. Pop. (1962) 4,064.

TOURAINE (toorān'). Ancient prov. of France

TOULOUSE-LAUTREC. Dated 1899, 'The tête-à-tête supper' was probably set in the Parisian restaurant Le Rat Mort. It is said that the man was the artist Charles Conder.
Courtauld Institute Galleries, London.

whose cap. was Tours. It is covered by Indre-et-Loire dept. and part of Indre.

TOURCOING (toorkwan'). Town in Nord dept., France, near the Belgian border, an important textile centre since the 12th cent. Pop. (1962) 90,105.

TOURMALINE. Hard, brittle mineral, a complex of various metal silicates, and containing aluminium and boron. Small Ts. are generally found in granites and gneisses. The common varieties are opaque, ranging from black (schorl) to pink, and the transparent gemstones may be colourless (achroit), rose pink (rubellite), green (Brazilian emerald), blue (indicolite, Brazilian sapphire), or brown (dravite).

TOURNAI (tōōrnā') (Flem. Doornik). Town in Hainaut prov., Belgium, on the Scheldt. On the site of a Roman relay post, it has a Romanesque cathedral dating from the 11th cent. Carpets, cement, leather are made. Pop. (1966) 33,309.

TOURNAMENT or **Tourney.** Martial sports popular in the Middle Ages. Events incl. mounted combats and mock fights with sword, spear or dagger. The T. was introduced into England from France in the 11th cent., and flourished until the 16th cent.

TOURNEUR (tur'ner), **Cyril** (c. 1575–1626). English dramatist. His *Revenger's Tragedy* (pub. 1607) and *Atheist's Tragedy* (pub. 1611) are among the most powerful of Stuart dramas.

TOURS (toor). Cap. of Indre-et-Loire dept., France, in the Loire valley, historic cap. of Touraine. The cathedral (12th-16th cent.) was badly damaged in the S.W.W. Iron and steel goods, boots and shoes are made. Balzac was b. at T. Pop. (1968) 128,120.

TOUSSAINT L'OUVERTURE (toosan'loovertür'), **Pierre Dominique** (c. 1746–1803). Negro soldier. B. at Haiti, he was a slave and joined the insurrection of 1791. He helped the French when they abolished slavery, became C.-in-C. of St. Domingo in 1796, and turned against the French when they re-imposed slavery. He was captured and d. in prison in France.

TOVEY (tō'vi), **Sir Donald Francis** (1875–1940). British composer. He studied under Parry, was appointed Reid prof. at Edinburgh in 1914, and was knighted in 1935. He wrote an opera, *The Bride of Dionysus*, and chamber music.

TOWER OF LONDON. Fortress on the Thames bank to the E. of the City. The keep, or White Tower, was built c. 1078 by Bishop Gundulf on the site of British and Roman fortifications. It is surrounded by 2 strong walls and a moat (now dry), and was for cents. a royal residence and the principal state prison. The T.o.L. is today a barracks, an armoury, and a museum. Among prisoners executed there were More, Anne Boleyn, Katherine Howard, Lady Jane Grey, Essex, Strafford, Laud, and Monmouth. *See* REGALIA.

TOWN PLANNING. System of land use in the best interests of the community, with especial stress on aesthetic as well as practical considerations, such as the separation of traffic and pedestrians, provision of easily accessible shops, schools, cinemas, theatres, etc.

TOWNSVILLE. City in N. Queensland, Australia, on the E. coast, founded 1868, port for sugar and meat. Japanese aircraft attacked T. in 1942. Pop. (1966) 58,760.

TOXAEMIA (toksē'mia). Invasion of the blood by poison, especially that generated within the body.

TOYNBEE, Arnold (1852–83). British economist and reformer. At Oxford he devoted himself to economics and history, and lectured widely in industrial districts on social problems. He went to Whitechapel in 1875, and was associated with the work of Canon Barnett. TOYNBEE HALL, the first of many social and educational settlements in E. London, was named after him in 1885. His nephew **Arnold Joseph T.** (1889–) was director of studies at the Royal Institute of International Affairs 1925–55. In his *A Study of History* (10 vols 1934–54) he attempts, as a metaphysician, to discover the laws governing the rise and fall of civilizations. The latter's son **Philip T.** (1916–) is a novelist and became in 1950 foreign correspondent of the *Observer*. *Pantaloon* and *Two Brothers* (1964) are instalments of a verse autobiography.

TRABLUS. Arabic form of TRIPOLI Libya.

TRABZON (trahbzon'). Turkish city, cap. of T. il,

TOWN PLANNING. Rebuilding the 62 acre Barbican area in the City of London, devastated by bombing in the Second World War, presents in miniature all the problems of town planning. In the centre are St. Giles's Church, Cripplegate, City of London School for Girls and the Guildhall School of Music and Drama. Besides three 36 storey residential towers, there are residential quadrangles in the immediate foreground and centre background, and the remaining high blocks contain offices. A podium 20 ft. above the street connects the various buildings, shops and tube stations, and separates pedestrians from the traffic, car parks and warehouses below.
Courtesy of Chamberlin, Powell and Bon

a port exporting fruit, tobacco. hides and skins, and other local produce, on the Black Sea 220 m. S.W. of Batum. T. is on the site of a Greek colony. The Black Sea Univ. was estab. 1963. Pop. (1965) 65,600.

TRACTARIANISM. *See* OXFORD MOVEMENT.

TRADE MARK. Distinctive indication (either a name or 'mark') attached to the product of a particular proprietor who must register a legal claim: in Britain it must conform to the T.Ms. Act, 1905.

TRADES UNION CONGRESS. Voluntary organization of trade unions, founded in Britain in 1868, in which delegates of affiliated unions meet annually to consider matters affecting their members. Today there are some 150 affiliated unions, with an aggregate membership of 9,000,000. The Annual Congress elects a General Council which functions for the T.U.C. in all matters concerned with trade unions.

TRADE UNIONS. Organizations of employed workers, formed primarily for the purpose of collec-

TRADE UNIONS. Jack Jones of the T.G.W.U. at the Trades Union Congress 1969, and (*below*) the General Council at the centenary congress of 1968.

Photo: Syndication International

tive bargaining, and also to provide trade and friendly benefits for members. Trade unions of a kind existed in the Middle Ages as journeymen guilds, and combinations of wage earners were formed in the 18th cent., but modern trade unionism is a product of the Industrial Revolution. Five cents. of repressive legislation in Britain culminated in the passing of the Combination Acts (q.v.), but on the repeal of these in 1824–5, organizations of workpeople were permitted to engage in collective bargaining although still subject to legal restrictions and with no legal protection for their funds until the enactment of a series of Trade Union Acts, 1871–6. Successive Acts of Parliament broadened the unions' field of action, e.g. the 1913 Act which allowed the Unions to engage in political activities. The T.U.C. was for many years mainly representative of unions of craftsmen but in the last decade of the 19th cent. the organization of unskilled labour, beginning with the London dock strike of 1899, spread rapidly. Industrial Unionism, meaning the organization of all workers in one industry or trade began about this time; but the characteristic feature of the so-called New Unionism a' the time of the 1899 dock strike was the rise of the general labour unions (e.g. the Dock Workers and General Labourers in the gas industry, etc.). In more recent years trade unionism has spread to professional workers, technicians, farm workers, administrative and clerical workers, as well as women.

The restrictive Trade Disputes and T.U. Act (1927), passed after the general strike of 1926, was repealed in 1946. The Wilson govt. abandoned plans for legislative reform of T.U. in 1969, and the Industrial Relations Act (1971) of the Heath govt. (incl. registration of T.U., legal enforcement of collective agreements, compulsory 'cooling off' periods, and strike ballots) was controversial.

The great growth of American T.U., apart from the abortive Knights of Labor 1869–86 (*see also* A.F.L./C.I.O.) came in the post-Depression years. The movement has a record of greater bitterness and violence than in Britain, but at the present-day has the reputation of being more open to the acceptance of new techniques, taking a broader view of these as conducive to eventual greater prosperity. Probably the most advanced T.U. system is that of Sweden where conflicts of Us. within an industry – frequent in Britain – are largely eliminated, and where employers and Us. co-operate more freely. *See* INTERNAT. T.U.

TRAFALGAR, Cape. Low headland in S.W. Spain off which Nelson defeated a Franco-Spanish fleet on 21 Oct. 1805, near the W. entrance to the Straits of Gibraltar. Nelson was mortally wounded in the battle.

TRAHER'NE, Thomas (*c.* 1637–74). English metaphysical writer. B. at Hereford, he was vicar of Teddington 1667–74. His moving lyric poetry and his prose *Centuries of Meditations* (1908), were undiscovered until the late 19th cent.

TRAIL. Canadian city in British Columbia on the Columbia r. At Tadenac, *c.* 2 m. away, is one of the largest non-ferrous smelters in the Brit. Commonwealth. Pop. (1966) 11,600.

TRA'JAN or **Marcus Ulpius Trajanus** (*c.* A.D. 52–117). Roman emperor. B. near Seville, he distinguished himself as a soldier, and was adopted as heir by the emperor Nerva, whom he succeeded in A.D. 98. A just and conscientious ruler, he carried on a correspondence with Pliny on the Christians. He conquered Dacia 101–106, and much of Parthia 114–117. T.'s column at Rome commemorates his victories.

TRAMWAYS. The conveyance system, characterized by the running of wheeled vehicles along parallel rails laid on or alongside public highways. It originated in the colliery vehicles which ran on iron rails from 1776. The earliest passenger T. system was in 1832, in New York, and in the 1860s horse-drawn trams plied in London and Liverpool. The first electric trams, between Portrush and Giant's Causeway, were opened in 1883. Ts. are now powered either by conductor rails below ground or conductor arms connected to overhead wires. Their lack of manœuvrability in traffic has led to their supersession by buses.

TRANQUILLIZERS. *See* SEDATIVES.

TRANSCAUCASIA. Area of the U.S.S.R. to the S. of the Caucasus. Here lie Armenia, Azerbaijan (qq.v.), and Georgia which in 1922 formed the Transcaucasian S.F.S.R., broken up in 1936 when each of its members became a separate rep. of the U.S.S.R.

TRANSCENDENTALISM. A mode of thought, originating with Kant, 'concerned not with objects, but with our mode of knowing objects'. From Germany T. was introduced into England, and influenced Coleridge and Carlyle. In New England T. developed *c.* 1840–60 into a mystical doctrine which saw God as immanent in nature and the human soul. Outstanding American transcendentalists are Thoreau and Emerson.

TRANSDUCER. A power-transforming device which enables energy in any form (electrical, acoustical, mechanical) to flow from one transmission system to another. The energy flowing to and from a T. may be of the same or of different forms, e.g. an electrical motor receives electrical energy and delivers it to a mechanical system; a gramophone pick-up crystal receives mechanical energy from the needle and delivers it as electrical energy; and a loudspeaker receives an electrical input and delivers an acoustical output.

TRANSFER ORBIT. The orbit followed by a planetary probe. To send such a vehicle by the shortest route would mean continuous expenditure of fuel, which is clearly impossible; it is therefore necessary for the vehicle to move, for most of the journey, in free fall. A probe aimed at Venus has to be 'slowed down' relative to the Earth, so that it enters an elliptical transfer orbit with its perigee (point of closest approach to the Sun) at the same distance as the orbit of Venus; with Mars, the vehicle has to be 'speeded up' relative to the Earth, so that it reaches its apogee (furthest point from the Sun) at the same distance as the orbit of Mars. The need for moving in a transfer orbit, in free fall, means that journeys to the planets are somewhat protracted, but the only way to overcome this difficulty will be to develop nuclear fuels – which will not be an easy matter.

TRANSFORMER. Piece of apparatus without moving parts in which by electromagnetic induction an alternating or intermittent current of one voltage is transformed to another voltage, without change of frequency. A T. has 2 coils, a primary for the input, and a secondary for the output. The ratio of the primary to the secondary voltages (and currents) is directly (and inversely) proportional to the number of turns in the primary and secondary coils. Ts. are widely used in electrical apparatus of all kinds and in particular in power transmission where high voltages and low currents are utilized.

TRANSISTOR. A semiconductor device with 3 or more electrodes. It can act as an amplifier, oscillator photoelectric cell or switch, and usually operates on a very small amount of power. The T. was invented at Bell Telephone Laboratories in America by John Bardeen and Walter Brittain, developing the work of William Shockley. Present-day Ts. commonly consist of a tiny sandwich of semiconductor material, usually germanium or silicon, specially prepared so that the alternate layers have different electrical properties.

A crystal of pure germanium or silicon would act as an insulator. By introducing impurities in the form of atoms of other materials (e.g. boron, arsenic or indium in minute amounts of the order of 1 part in 100 million) the layers may be made either n-type, having an excess of electrons, or p-type, having a deficiency of electrons. This enables electrons to flow from one layer to another in one direction only.

Ts. have had a tremendous impact on the electronics industry and although only invented in 1948 are now made in thousands of millions each year. They perform many of the same functions as the thermionic valve, but have the advantages of greater reliability, long life, compactness and instantaneous action, no warming-up period being necessary. They are widely used in most electronic equipment, but especially for portable radios and television computers, satellites, space research and in microminiaturization.

TRANSJORDAN. Name 1923–46 of the Hashimite kingdom of JORDAN.

TRANSKEI (trans'ki). Part of Cape prov., S. Africa, extending N.E. from Great Kei r. to the border of Natal and incl. Tembuland, Pondoland, and Griqualand E. The area is inhabited by Xhosa, most advanced of the Bantu tribes in the rep., and in 1963 became the self-governing terr. of T. within the rep. of S. Africa, with its own elected parl. and separate T. citizenship for all Xhosa (whether living in T. or not). Whites were given no political rights within the terr. in which the main towns are Umtata (cap.), Kokstad, and Port St. Johns. The univ. coll. at Fort Hare is the oldest African univ. in S. Africa. Area 16,544 sq. m.; pop. (1960) 1,407,815 Bantu; 17,514 whites; 13,840 coloured.

TRANSMIGRATION OF SOULS or **Metem-**

psychosis. The belief that after death the soul may pass into another human being, an animal or a plant, and that it has so passed on innumerable earlier occasions. The belief was held by the ancient Egyptians, by Pythagoras, Plato, and their followers, and by the Cathars and other heretical Christian sects, and is an integral part of the teachings of Hinduism and Buddhism, and of the Theosophists.

TRANSPORT AND GENERAL WORKERS UNION. Trade union founded in 1921 by the amalgamation of a number of dockers' and road transport workers' unions, previously associated in the Transport Workers' Federation. The largest T. union in Britain, its gen secs. have incl. Bevin, Cousins, and from 1969 Jack Jones (1913–   ).   *See* illus. p. 1043.

TRANSPORTATION. Punishment which involved the sending of convicted persons to overseas possessions either for life or for shorter periods. It was introduced in England towards the end of the 17th cent. and was abolished in 1864 after many thousands had been transported, especially to Australia.

TRANS-SIBERIAN RAILWAY. Line connecting the cities of European Russia with Omsk, Novosibirsk, Irkutsk, and Khabarovsk, and terminating at Vladivostok on the Pacific. It took 1891–1905 to build; from St. Petersburg (Leningrad) to Vladivostok is c. 5,400 m.

TRANSUBSTANTIATION. The R.C. doctrine that the bread and wine at the Eucharist are transformed into the body and blood of Christ. This doctrine, which evolved during the 9th–13th cents., is rejected by Protestant Churches.

TRANSURANIUM ELEMENTS. Family of synthetic elements following the last naturally occurring element, uranium (at. no. 92). Produced by bombarding uranium or other T.Es. with various atomic particles. *See* Table p. 1045.

TRANSVAAL. N. prov. of the rep. of South Africa bordering S. Rhodesia on the N. The S. and S.W. are occupied by the high veld, rising to Witwatersrand, then sinking northward to the low veld. The main rivers are the Vaal and Limpopo with their tributaries. The economic life is dominated by the gold fields of the 'Rand'. Near Pretoria are diamond mines, discovered 1886; coal, iron ore, copper, lead, tin, manganese are among other minerals worked. Cattle and sheep are reared; maize, tobacco, and fruit are grown. There are iron and steel works at Pretoria, brick, tile, and pottery factories, etc.

The prov. is governed by an administrator, who is assisted by a provincial council and an executive committee. English and Afrikaans are the official languages. The largest towns are Pretoria (the cap.), Johannesburg, Germiston, Brakpan, Springs, Benoni, Krugersdorp, and Rondepoort. There are univs. at Pretoria and Johannesburg (Witwatersrand).

The T. was settled from 1836 by Boers from Cape Colony. After subduing the Zulus they set up a rep. recognized by Britain as independent in 1852. Owing to troubles with the Zulu inhabitants, T. was in 1877 annexed by Britain at the request of some of the settlers; but in 1880 the T. rebelled, inflicting a severe defeat on the Brit. at Majuba Hill (1881), and republican rule was restored, though subject to British suzerainty. After the S.A. War of 1899–1902, T. became a British colony, and in 1910 a prov. of the Union of S.A. Area 110,450 sq. m.; pop. (1960) 6,273,477 (1,468,305 white).

TRANSYLVĀ́NIA. Area of Rumania, once a prov., bounded S. by the Transylvanian Alps and E. and N.E. by the Carpathians. The Bihar Mountains rise in the centre of T., the surface of which is hilly except in the extreme W. Agriculture, stock-breeding, and forestry thrive, and wine and brandy are produced. Exploitation of mineral wealth, natural gas, lignite, gold, silver, copper, iron, etc. has been rapid since the S.W.W.

TABLE OF TRANSURANIUM ELEMENTS

At. No.	Name	Symbol	Year discovered	Source of first preparation	Isotope identified	Half Life of first isotope identified
93	NEPTUNIUM	Np	1940	Irradiation of uranium 238 with neutrons	Np^{239}	2·35 days
94	PLUTONIUM	Pu	1941	Bombardment of uranium 238 with deuterons	Pu^{238}	86·4 years
95	AMERICIUM	Am	1944	Irradiation of plutonium 239 with neutrons	Am^{241}	458 years
96	CURIUM	Cm	1944	Bombardment of plutonium 239 with helium ions	Cm^{242}	162·5 days
97	BERKELIUM	Bk	1949	Bombardment of americium 241 with helium ions	Bk^{243}	4·5 hours
98	CALIFORNIUM	Cf	1950	Bombardment of curium 242 with helium ions	Cf^{245}	44 minutes
99	EINSTEINIUM	Es	1952	Irradiation of uranium 238 with neutrons in first thermonuclear explosion	Es^{253}	20 days
100	FERMIUM	Fm	1953	Irradiation of uranium 238 with neutrons in first thermonuclear explosion	Fm^{255}	16 hours
101	MENDELEVIUM	Mv	1955	Bombardment of einsteinium 253 with helium ions	Mv^{256}	1·5 hours
102	NOBELIUM	No	1958	Bombardment of curium 246 with carbon ions	102^{255}	3 seconds
103	LAWRENCIUM	Lw	1961	Bombardment of californium 252 with boron ions	Lw^{257}	8 seconds

Courtesy of 'Scientific American'

Cluj is the chief town. Area 24,000 sq. m. T., which had been part of Hungary from c. 1000–1526, 1691–1848, 1868–1918, was united with Rumania in 1918 by the vote of its inhabitants. The Vienna Award of 1940, made by Ribbentrop and Ciano, gave most of T. back to Hungary, a gift cancelled in the peace treaty with Hungary, 1947.

TRAPANI (trah'pahnē). Port and naval base in N.W. Sicily, Italy, c. 30 m. N. of Marsala. Settled originally by the Carthaginians, it is the cap. of T. prov. It was badly damaged in the S.W.W. Pop. (1961) 75,537.

TRAPPISTS. R.C. order of monks and nuns, renowned for the strictness of their rule, which incl. the maintenance of silence. It originated in 1664 at La Trappe, in Normandy, as a reformed version of the Cistercian rule, and is now absorbed again in the latter.

TRAVEL SICKNESS. Nausea and vomiting caused by travelling in trains, buses, aeroplanes, cars, and ships. The constant vibrations and movements are thought to stimulate changes in the semicircular canals forming the labyrinth of the middle ear, and failure of the individual to adapt to this stimulation, which may be reinforced by visual stimulation as well as psychological factors, is thought to be the cause of T.S., although the exact mechanisms involved remain obscure. There are many proprietary cures on the market, some of which contain anti-histamine drugs.

TRAVERS, Benjamin (1886–). British dramatist. B. in London, he wrote farces for Tom Walls, Ralph Lynn and Robertson Hare, incl. *A Cuckoo in the Nest* (1925), *Rookery Nook* (1926), and *Thark* (1927), known from the theatre at which they were played as the 'Aldwych' farces.

TREACLE. Brown viscid syrup obtained during sugar refining: the paler 'golden syrup' is obtained at a later stage. See MOLASSES.

TREADMILL. Penal appliance devised in 1818 by Sir William Cubitt (1785–1861), and long disused. It consisted of a large hollow cylinder around which were steps; by treading on these the prisoner caused the cylinder to revolve and thus pump water, grind corn, etc.

TREASON. An act of betrayal, generally used only of acts against the sovereign or the state to which the perpetrator owes allegiance. In this sense T. was defined in England by the Statute of Treasons, 1352, the principal Ts. being (1) compassing the wounding, imprisonment, or death of the sovereign; (2) seducing the king's wife or eldest dau. or the wife of the heir; (3) levying war against the sovereign in his (her) realm; (4) being adherent to the sovereign's enemies within the realm, giving them aid or comfort in the realm or elsewhere. The punishment on conviction of

T. is death. The Treachery Act, 1940, supplemented the law of T. by making it an offence punishable by death for any person, whether owing allegiance to the British crown or not, to assist the naval, military, or air operations of the enemy, or to impede the forces of the Crown: 16 spies (not normally capable of T., though liable to be shot in the field) were convicted under this act, which expired in 1946. During the 20th cent., persons hanged for T. in the U.K. have incl. Casement (1916), John Amery (1945), and William Joyce (1946) who, though he claimed to be a U.S. citizen by birth, carried a British passport valid until 1940 at the time he went to Germany in August 1939.

In the U.S.A., T. is defined in Article III, Section 3, of the Constitution: 'T. against the United States shall consist only in levying war against them, or in adhering to their enemies, giving them aid and comfort. No person shall be convicted of treason unless on the testimony of 2 witnesses to the same overt act, or on confession in open court. The Congress shall have power to declare the punishment of treason.'

TREASURE TROVE. In England, any gold or silver, plate or bullion found concealed in a house or the ground, the owner being unknown. Normally, treasure originally hidden, and not abandoned, belongs to the Crown, but if the treasure was casually lost or intentionally abandoned, the first finder is entitled to it against all but the true owner. Objects buried with no intention of recovering them, e.g. in a burial mound, do not rank as T.T., and belong to the owner of the ground.

TREASURY. Govt. dept. constituted in 1612 to collect and manage public revenue. The P.M. is generally the First Lord of the T., the Chancellor of the Exchequer is the financial head; with 5 junior lords these form the Lords Commissioners of the T. One of the 2 joint Permanent Secs. to the T. is the official head of the Civil Service.

TREBIZOND. Another form of TRABZON.

TREE, Sir Herbert Beerbohm (1853–1917). British actor-manager. B. in London, the half-brother of Max Beerbohm (q.v.), he managed the Haymarket theatre 1887–96, and Her Majesty's 1897–1917, building the latter entirely from the profits of *Trilby*. He appeared both in Shakespeare and modern roles, often with his wife, **Lady T.**, *née* Maud Holt.

TREE. Name given to perennial plants characterized by a woody stem and branches, and larger than shrubs. Gymnosperm Ts. are classified in 4 divisions: cycads or sago-palms; the maidenhair tree; gnetums; and conifers. Angiosperm Ts. are divided into monocotyledons, incl. palms, bamboos, etc., and dicotyledons, comprising the largest group.

Trees as symbols of fertility play a large part in primitive religion; thus the carrying of green boughs round the village, as a fertility rite, and the maypole dance, originally performed round the sacred T., figured in the English May Day festival. Trees or groves were the scene of festivals or the home of oracles, e.g. at the oak of Dodona, in Epirus. The oak was the sacred T. of Jupiter, and was also venerated by the Druids. Many peoples believe that Ts. are inhabited by spirits, who die with them, e.g. the Dryads of the Greeks.

TREE CREEPER. *See* CREEPER.

TREITSCHKE (trītsh′ke), **Heinrich von** (1834–96). German historian. At first a Liberal, he later adopted a Pan-German standpoint. His best-known work is the *History of Germany in the 19th Cent.*

TREMATODES. *See* FLUKE.

TRENCH, Anthony Chenevix (1919–). British educationist. A distant connection of Richard Chenevix T., he was headmaster of Bradfield Coll. 1955–63 and of Eton Coll. 1964–9, where he banished boxing from the curriculum.

TRENCH, Richard Chenevix (1807–86). Irish Anglican churchman. B. in Dublin, he was dean of Westminster and (1864–84) archbp. of Dublin. A poet and philologist, he planned the Oxford *New English Dictionary*

TRENCHARD, Hugh Montague, 1st visct. (1873–1956). British airman and administrator, nicknamed 'Boom', because of his loud voice. As G.O.C. of the R.F.C. 1915–17 he was responsible for air operations in the F.W W., and as Chief of Air Staff 1918–29 organized the R.A.F. in preparation for its role in the S.W.W. In 1927 he was created 1st Marshal of the R.A.F. and in 1930 received a viscounty. As Commissioner of the Metropolitan Police, he carried out the 'T. Reforms' incl. the estab. of the Police Coll. at Hendon and the application of more scientific methods in detection. In 1951 he was awarded the O.M.

TRENGGANU. Traditionally seafarers, the Malays are believed to have reached the country by sea, not infiltrating beyond the coastal areas until encouraged by the British to develop the hinterland. Here on the east coast, where the population is chiefly Malay, fishing is still the most important industry, although the catches are often poor.
Courtesy of Malaya House.

TRENGGANU (-gah′noo). State of W. Malaysia, Fed. of Malaysia, on the E. coast. The cap. is Kuala T. Copra, black pepper, tin and wolfram are exported. Area 5,050 sq. m.; pop. (1966) 371,370.

TRENT, Jesse Boot, 1st baron T. (1850–1931).

British industrialist. B. in Nottingham, he worked in his mother's herbalist shop at 13, had a shop of his own by 1877, and in 1883 estab. J. Boot & Co. Ltd. (from 1888 the Boot Pure Drug Co.) probably the earliest modern 'chain store'. In 1881 he gave £500,000 to build Univ. Coll., Nottingham.

TRENT, Council of. A council of the R.C. Church held at Trento, N. Italy, Dec. 1545 to Dec. 1563, incl. adjournments. It defined many Catholic doctrines, and reformed abuses within the Church.

TRENT. Third longest river of England. It rises in the S. Pennines and flows first S. and then generally N.E. through the Midlands to enter the Humber. Length 170 m. It is navigable by barges for nearly 100 m.

TRENTI′NO-ALTO ADIGE (ade′zhä). Autonomous region in N. Italy, once part of the old rep. of Venice, then part of Austria until ceded to Italy under the Treaty of Saint-Germain-en-Laye, 1919. It consists of the provs. of Bolzano and Trento. Bolzano (S. Tirol) remained German-speaking in spite of attempts at forcible Italianization by the fascist govt. and the migration to Germany in 1939 of some 70 per cent of the pop.; Trento has always been Italian-speaking. The peace treaty between Italy and the Allies, 1947, provided that the German-speaking inhabitants of the region should have equal rights, and in 1948 the region was made autonomous. Continued agitation by the German-speaking pop. led in 1969 to further autonomy for the northern prov. of Bolzano. The cap. is Trento. Area 5,256 sq. m.; pop. (1961) 785,491.

TRE′NTO. Cap. of Trentino-Alto Adige autonomous region, Italy, and of T. prov., on the Adige, a city famous in history for the Council of Trent (Ger. form of its name), 1545–1563, which issued decrees, confirmed by Pope Pius IV in 1564, settling many points of R.C. dogma as part of the so-called Counter-Reformation. Pop. (1961) 74,766.

TRENTON. Cap. of New Jersey, U.S.A., on the Delaware, 30 m. N.E. of Philadelphia. Pottery and steel cable are manufactured. Washington defeated the British at T., 1776. Pop. (1960) 114,167.

TRESPASSER. Technically, a trespass is an unlawful interference with the person or property of another. but in general speech a T. is a person who goes on the land of another without lawful authority. A landowner has the right to eject a T. by the use of reasonable force. Alternatively, he may sue him for trespass. If a T. is injured whilst on the land of another, he cannot recover damages from the landowner, unless the landowner has done some positive act of injury to him. In English law, a trespass to land is not a crime.

TREVELYAN (trevil′yan), **Sir George Otto** (1838–1928). British liberal statesman. A nephew of Lord Macaulay, whose biography he wrote (1876), he was a M.P. 1865–97, and Chief Sec. for Ireland 1882–4, Chancellor of the Duchy of Lancaster 1884–5, and Sec. for Scotland 1892–5. His other books incl. *The Early History of C. J. Fox* (1880) and *The American Revolution* (1909). His eldest son **Sir Charles Philips** (1870–1958) was a Liberal M.P. 1899–1918 and (Labour) 1922–31. The 2nd son **Robert Calverley** (1872–1951) wrote creditable poetry, e.g. *The Bride of Dionysus* (1912), and the 3rd son **George Macaulay** (1876–1962), Regius prof. of history at Cambridge 1927–40, wrote *England in the Age of Wycliffe, England under Queen Anne* (1930–4), and an illuminating *English Social History* (1944): he was awarded the O.M. in 1930.

TRÈVES. Fr. form of TRIER.

TREVISO (trāvē′sō). Town in Veneto region, Italy, 18 m. N. of Venice, cap. of T. prov. It dates from Roman times. The cathedral, founded 1141, was enlarged in the 15th cent. Pop. (1961) 75,217.

TREVITHICK, Richard (1771–1833). British engineer. B. in Cornwall, he constructed in 1801 a road locomotive run by steam, which carried passengers, and in 1804 the first steam-engine to be run on rails.

TREVOR-ROPER, Hugh Redwald (1914–). British historian. Regius prof. of modern history at Oxford from 1957, he has interests in the Tudor/Stuart period, e.g. *Archbishop Laud* and *The Gentry, 1540–1640*, but he attracted widespread attention by *The Last Days of Hitler* (1947), written after he had been sent to Berlin to probe the facts.

TRIANON (trĕ'anoṅ), **Treaty of.** The peace treaty between Hungary and the Allies signed at the Trianon Palace, Versailles, in 1920.

TRIBUNE (tri'būn). Roman magistrate of plebeian family, elected annually to defend the interests of the plebeians. When the office was instituted in 494 B.C. there were 2 Ts.; the number was later increased to 10. They could veto the decisions of any other magistrate.

TRICHINA (tri'kina). Parasitic nematode which breeds in rats, pigs, and man. If the larvae enter the intestine they will spread through the bloodstream into the muscles, remaining for long periods, and causing the disease called trichinosis.

TRICHINO'POLY, another form of TIRUCHIRAPALLI.

TRIER (trēr). City in Rhineland-Palatinate, W. Germany, on the Moselle near the Luxembourg frontier. It has notable Roman remains. Its cathedral, founded in the 11th cent., was destroyed in the S.W.W. Pop. (1966) 86,000.

TRIESTE (trē-est'; Ital. trē-e'stā). Italian city and free port on the Adriatic, in Friuli-Venezia Giulia region. The Roman Tergeste, T. became Austrian in 1382 and, except for occupation by Napoleon 1809–14, remained so until 1918 when the Allies occupied it and it was transferred to Italy under the treaty of Saint-Germain-en-Laye. Yugoslavia claimed T. and after S.W.W. T., with its surroundings (298 sq. m. in all), was made a demilitarized free zone under a gov. to be appointed by the U.N. which failed to agree on the gov. to be chosen; and in 1954 the U.K., U.S.A., Italy, and Yugoslavia agreed that 81½ sq. m. of the enclave (incl. the port) should go to Italy, the rest to Yugoslavia. Pop. (1961) 273,390.

TRIGONO'METRY. Branch of mathematics which solves problems relating to plane and spherical triangles. Its principles are based on the fixed proportions of angles and sides in a right-angled triangle. It is of importance in surveying. Invented by Hipparchus (q.v.), it was developed by Ptolemy of Alexandria (q.v.) and was known to Hindu and Arab mathematicians.

TRILLING, Lionel (1905–). American literary critic. B. in N.Y. city, he was ed. at Columbia univ., where he became prof. of literature 1965. Appreciative of the sociological background to literature, he helped to make E. M. Forster known in the U.S. by his study in 1944. Other books incl. *The Liberal Imagination* (1950) and *Freud and the Crisis in our Culture* (1955).

TRILOBITE (trī'lobīt) Extinct marine arthropod (class Trilobita) of the Palaeozoic period. The Ts. had segmented bodies and ranged from a fraction of an inch to over a foot in length.

TRIMURTI (trimoor'ti). The Hindu triad, representing the Absolute Spirit in its 3 aspects: Brahma, personifying creation; Vishnu, preservation; Siva, destruction.

TRILOBITE

TRINCŌMALEE'. Seaport on the N.E. coast of Ceylon, with a fine natural harbour, an early Tamil settlement. T. was a British naval base until 1957. Pop. (1963) 33,000.

TRINIDAD AND TOBĀ'GŌ. Independent state within the Brit. Commonwealth comprising Trinidad, second largest and most southerly of the W. Indian Islands, Tobago, 19 m. N.E. of Trinidad, and some smaller islands. Trinidad lies 7 m. N. of the nearest point of Venezuela and rises to 3,085 ft. in Mt. Aripo. The climate is tropical with cool nights. Agriculture is the main occupation; sugar, cocoa, coffee, citrus fruits are produced. Petroleum and asphalt are the chief mineral products. Discovered by Columbus 1498, colonized by the Spaniards 1532, Trinidad was taken by the Brit. 1797, ceded to them 1802. Area 1,864 sq. m.; pop. (1960) 794,624 (43 per cent of African origin, 36 per cent of E. Indian). Tobago was ceded to Britain in 1814 by the Fr. It produces copra, cocoa, fresh vegetables, poultry and other livestock, etc. Area 116 sq. m.; pop. (1960) 33,333.

The cap. of T. and T. is Port of Spain, Trinidad. T. and T., a member of the Federation of the West Indies, 1956, was given independence when that projected federation came to an end in 1962. It has a gov.-gen. and a parl. with an elected house of representatives and an appointed senate.

TRINITY. In Christian theology, the doctrine that while God is one in nature, He is three distinct persons, the Father, the Son, and the Holy Ghost. It became Catholic doctrine in the Nicene Creed (q.v.).

TRI'POLI. Port of the Lebanon, 40 m. N.N.E. of Beirut, the terminus of an oil pipe-line from Kirkuk. It stands on the site of a Phoenician city. Pop. (1966) 175,000.

TRIPOLI. Chief seaport· airport, and one of the 2 caps. of Libya, also cap of T. division, on the Mediterranean. There are Roman remains. Developed by the Italians after 1911, T. became their chief N. African port. Pop. (1964) 245,000.

TRIPOLITA'NIA. Former prov. of Libya, N. Africa, stretching from Cyrenaica in the E. to Tunisia in the W. Tripoli was the cap. Italy captured T. from Turkey in 1912. The Brit. 8th Army made a rapid advance through T. Dec. 1942 – Jan. 1943 during the N. African campaign. Area *c.* 136,000 sq. m. In 1963 T. was subdivided into admin. divisions.

TRIPURA (trepoo'ra). State of the Rep. of India (union terr. 1956–71), formerly a princely state, between E. Pakistan and Assam. It grows rice, cotton, tea, sugar cane, etc. The cap. is Agartala. Area 4,036 sq. m.; pop. (1961) 1,142,005.

TRISTAN or **Tristram.** Legendary Celtic hero. His story is laid mainly at the court of King Mark of Cornwall. His love for Iseult of Ireland has inspired many medieval and modern versions, especially Wagner's opera *Tristan und Isolde.*

TRISTEARIN. *See* STEARIN.

TRI'STAN DA CUNHA (koon'ya). Group of 4 small islands in the Atlantic, midway between S. Africa and S. America, a dependency (1938) of St. Helena (q.v.). T. da C. proper is a volcano (7,164 ft.), long thought to be extinct, which erupted violently in 1961. Evacuated to Britain, the people returned in 1963. Area 40 sq. m.; pop. (1967) 269. T. da C., then uninhabited, was occupied by the Brit. in 1814.

TRI'TON. In Greek mythology, a merman, son of Poseidon and Amphitrite.

TRIU'MVIRS. Two groups of 3 magistrates governing the Roman republic. The first T. (60 B.C.) were Julius Caesar, Pompey, and Crassus, the 2nd (43 B.C.), Augustus, Antony, and Lepidus.

TRIVA'NDRUM. Indian city, cap. of Kerala state and of T. dist., 50 m. N.W. of Cape Comorin. Once cap. of the former princely state of Travancore, it has a univ. (1937), an old fort, and a famous shrine. It is noted for ivory and wood carving. Pop. (1961) 302,214.

TROGLODYTES (trog'lōdīts). Greek term for cave-dwellers, designating certain tribes in the ancient world. The best-known were those of S. Egypt and Ethiopia, a primitive pastoral people.

TROGONS. Beautiful tropical birds of the New and Old World in the family Trogonidae. The Central

American Quetzal (*Pharomacrus mocinno*) has golden-green tail plumes 3 ft. in length.

TROIS RIVIÉRES (trwah rēvyär). City in Quebec, Canada, a lumber port 86 m. N.E. of Montreal with pulp, paper, and cotton mills and iron foundries. Champlain founded it 1634. Pop. (1961) 53,477.

TROLLEYBUS. Type of bus driven by electric power collected from overhead wires, and having the advantage over a tram of rather greater manœuvrability. However, modern traffic conditions render them still obstructive, and they are decreasingly used.

TROLLOPE, Anthony (1815–82). British novelist. B. in London, he entered the Post Office as a clerk in

1834, invented the pillar box, and rose to a responsible position as surveyor before retiring in 1867. His 1st successful novel was *The Warden* (1855), which began the series set in the imaginary co. of Barsetshire: *Barchester Towers* (1857), *Doctor Thorne*, *Framley Parsonage*, *The Small House at Allington*, and *The Last Chronicle of Barset* (1867) – his masterpiece. Other books incl. *The Three Clerks, Orley Farm, The Belton Estate, The Claverings, The Eustace Diamonds*, and *Dr. Wortle's School*; and a political group including *Phineas Finn* and *The Prime Minister*. He delineated the English middle classes with mellowed insight in an easy pleasant style. His *Autobiography*, pub. in 1883, shocked the public by its workmanlike attitude to his art. His mother **Frances Milton T.** (1780–1863) was also a novelist and wrote a caustic account of the *Domestic Manners of the Americans* (1832).

TROMBONE. A brass wind musical instrument, developed from the sackbut. It consists of a tube bent double, varied notes being obtained by an inner sliding tube. The 4 sizes are alto, tenor, bass, and contra-bass.

TROMP, Maarten Harpertszoon (1597–1653). Dutch admiral. B. at Brielle, he twice defeated the Spaniards in 1639. He was defeated by Blake in May 1652, but in Nov. triumphed over Blake in the Strait of Dover. In Feb.–June 1653 he was defeated by Blake, Monk, and Deane, and was killed off the Dutch coast. His son, **Cornelius T.** (1629–91), also an admiral, won fame in 1673 for his battle against the English and French fleets.

TROMSÖ. Fishing port in N.W. Norway, situated on T. island off the mainland. The battleship *Tirpitz* was sunk by British bombers in 1944 when at anchor in T. fjord. There is a univ. (1968). Pop. (1961) 12,363.

TRONDHEIM (tron'dhīm). Fishing port with fish canneries; textile, margarine, soap factories, etc., at the mouth of the Nid, on T. fjord. It was cap. of Norway in the 10–11th cent. and has a univ. (1968). Pop. (1963) 57,453.

TROPICS. The Ts. of Cancer and Capricorn (parallels of latitude 23° 28′ N. and S. of the equator) prescribe the northernmost and southernmost limits of the area of the earth's surface in which the sun can be directly overhead.

TROPINE (trōpīn). ($C_8H_{15}ON$). A white crystalline solid formed by the hydrolysis of alkaloid atropine.

TROPISMS. Automatic movements of plants in reaction to certain influences. Two common T. are the growth toward water (hydrotropism) and toward light (heliotropism).

TROPOSPHERE (trōp'ōsfēr). The lower part of the earth's atmosphere extending about 6½ m. upwards from the earth's surface, in which temperature decreases with height except in local layers of temperature inversion. The *tropopause* is the upper boundary of the

TRONDHEIM. The cathedral, where Norwegian kings are crowned, was begun in the 11th century. Often burned, it has always been restored, and is the country's finest church.
Courtesy of the Norwegian National Tourist Office

T. above which the temperature is constant or even increases slightly with respect to height.

TROSSACHS. Woodland glen between Lochs Katrine and Achray in Perthshire, Scotland, 2 m. long, a favourite tourist spot. *See* illus. p. 530.

TROTSKY, Leon Davidovitch. Assumed name of Russian revolutionary Lev D. Bronstein (1879–1940). B. nr. Elizavetgrad, of Jewish parentage, he was twice exiled to Siberia for Marxist activities, and with Lenin organized the revolution of Nov. 1917, and conducted the peace negotiations with Germany. As Commissar for War he was responsible for the raising of the Red Army. T. differed with the Communist Party on policy, and was expelled from the Council of People's Commissars in 1925, and from the party in 1927. Exiled in 1929, he settled in Mexico, where he was assassinated possibly at Stalin's instigation. He wrote many works criticising the Soviet régime, notably his *History of the Russian Revolution*.

TROUBADOURS (troo'badoorz). Class of poets of Provence and S. France, who fl. in the 11th–13th cents., and included both nobles and inferior minstrels. The Ts. originated a type of lyric poetry, devoted mainly to themes of exalted love and the idealization of women, and to the glorifying of the deeds of their patrons. Contemporary with the Ts. were the *Trouvères*, the epic poets of N. France.

TROUT. Fish closely related to the salmon. The common T. (*Salmo fario*) is widely distributed in Europe, occurring in British fresh and coastal waters. Sea T. are generally silvery and river T. olive-brown, both having spotted fins and sides. In the U.S.A. the name T. is given to various species, notably to the rainbow T. (*Salmo gairdneri irideus*) which has been naturalized in many other countries.

COMMON TROUT

TROUVILLE (troovēl')-**SUR-MER.** Summer resort and fishing port in Calvados dept., France, on the estuary of the Seine. Pop. (1962) 6,822.

TROY or **Ilium.** Ancient city of Asia Minor, in the district called the Troad. Homer's Iliad tells of the siege and destruction of T. by the Greeks. After a 10 years' investment it fell to the Greeks through the stratagem of the wooden horse, c. 1184 B.C. Excavations by H. Schliemann revealed 9 different cities buried one beneath the other, of which the 7th, a post-Mycenaean fortress, was probably the Homeric T.

TROYES (trwah). French city, cap. of Aube dept., on the Seine, wealthiest city of the anc. prov. of Champagne. The treaty of T. (1420) granted the French crown to Henry V of England. Pop. (1968) 74,898.

TRUCIAL STATES. Seven small sheikdoms (Fujairah, Ras al Khaimah, Umm al Qaiwain, Ajman, Sharjah and Kalba, Dubai, and Abu Dhabi) on the former 'pirate' coast of the Persian Gulf N. of Muscat and Oman. They derive the name T.S. from the agreements made in 1820 and later renewed with Britain to ensure a condition of truce in the area, and suppression of piracy and of the slave trade. Oil discoveries in the 1960s gave them unforeseen importance, notably Abu Dhabi (q.v.) ruled by Sheikh Zaid: area 26,000 sq. m.; pop. (1969) 50,000 and Dubai ruled by Sheikh Rashid: area 1,500 sq. m.; pop. (1969) 70,000 – both incl. large foreign populations. The twin towns of Dubai–Deira form the largest commercial centre of the area, and nearby Port Rashid (1967–73) will on completion be the region's chief port: there is also an internat. airport. Total area of T.S. 32,000 sq. m.: pop. (1968) 180,200. *See* ARAB EMIRATES, Fed. of.

TRUDEAU (troodoh'), **Pierre Elliott** (1919–). Canadian Liberal statesman. Called to the Quebec Bar in 1943, he became Min. of Justice and Attorney-General in 1967, and in 1968 succeeded Pearson as P.M. In the General Election of 1968 he was returned with an overall majority. He strongly opposes Quebec separatism, and favours negotiations with Red China and the U.S.S.R.

TRUFFLE. Subterranean fungus, highly valued in cookery and confectionery. The finest (*Tuber melanosporum*) comes from Périgord, generally growing under oak trees: it is rounded, blackish brown and covered with warts externally, and with blackish flesh. Pigs like Ts. and are used to locate them, as are dogs.

TRUJILLO. City and port, founded 1535, in Peru, 320 m. N.W. of Lima. Exports incl. sugar and copper. Pop. (1965) 123,500.

TRUJILLO MOLINA (trōōhē'yō mōlē'nah), **Rafael Leonidas** (1891–1961). Dominican dictator. Pres. of the rep. 1930–8 and 1942–52, he was also generalissimo of the armed forces from 1933, and retained control behind the scenes even after handing over the presidency to his brother in 1952. Although under his regime the island was transformed to a modern state by the erection of schools and hospitals and by public works programmes, his suppression of political opponents led to his assassination.

TRUMAN, Harry S. (Shippe) (1884–). 33rd President of U.S.A. B. in Lamar, Missouri, he practised law, rose to rank of major in the F.W.W. and entered the senate as a Democrat in 1935. In Jan. 1945 he became Vice-President, and on Roosevelt's death in April succeeded to the presidency. In 1948 he was elected for a second term, but in April 1952 declined to stand again. During his term of office he took the responsibility for dropping the atom bombs on Japan at the close of the S.W.W., when he attempted to stem the rise of Communism by the extension of economic and military aid to friendly countries, and by armed intervention in S. Korea, on behalf of U.N.

TRUMPET. Brass wind musical instrument; a doubled tube with valves.

TRUMPETER. A genus of crane-like birds. *Psophia crepitans* is found in British Guiana.

TRURO. English city (bor.) in Cornwall, at the head of Fal estuary. Its cathedral was built 1880–1910. Pop. (1961) 13,328.

TRUST. (1) Legal term for an arrangement by which A is empowered to act property belonging to B for the benefit of C. A and B may be the same person; B and C may not be. (2) In business, the link-

ing of several companies either by transferring shares of the separate cos. to trustees or by the creation of a holding co. whose shares are exchanged for those of the separate cos. Either method prevents the competition that would exist if the cos. involved had remained independent, and in the U.S.A. both were made illegal by the Sherman Anti-T. Act, 1890, enforced with vigour for the first time by 'T. buster' Pres. Theodore Roosevelt. A notable application of the act was the dissolution into its component cos. of the Standard Oil Co. of N.J. by the Supreme Court, 1911. (3) A unit T. holds and manages a number of marketable securities; by buying a 'unit' in such a trust, the purchaser has a proportionate interest in each of the securities so that his risk is spread. (4) An investment T. is not in modern times a T., but a public co. which invests in marketable securities money subscribed by its shareholders who receive dividends from the income earned by the T. (5) A body formed with some special, usually charitable, object: e.g. the National T. (q.v.); the Carnegie U.K. T. (1913), whose chief object is the provision of free libraries. Similar bodies in the U.S.A. are the Rockefeller (1913) and Ford (1936) Foundations.

The PUBLIC TRUSTEE (1908, under an act of 1906) is an English official empowered to act as executor and trustee, either alone or with others, of the estate of anyone who appoints him.

TRUST TERRITORY. Non-self-governing territory, either held under mandate (q.v.); or detached from an enemy state after the S.W.W.; or voluntarily placed under the U.N. trusteeship system by the state responsible for its administration, on terms agreed between the latter and the U.N. The T.Ts. are progressively prepared for independence, and supervision by the U.N. involves the sending of regular missions to, and the hearing of oral petitions from them. T.Ts. not yet self-governing incl. the Pacific Islands T.T.

TSANA. Another form of TANA.

TSANGPU. Name 1913–46 of WUCHOW.

TSAR. Title of the Russian emperors. It derives from the Lat. *Caesar.*

TSARITSYN. Old name of VOLGOGRAD.

TSCHAIKOVSKY. *See* TCHAIKOVSKY.

TSETSE. Fly of the genus *Glossina*, related to the house fly, species of which transmit the disease nagana to cattle and sleeping sickness to man.

TSETSE FLY

TSINA'N. Anc. Chinese walled city on the Hwang Ho, cap. of Shantung prov., a commercial and food processing centre with a textile industry. Pop (1953) 680,000.

TSINGTAO (-tow'). Good Chinese port on Kiaochow Bay in Shantung prov. with cotton and flour mills, engineering and locomotive works, etc. T., chief town in Kiaochow terr. ceded to Germany in 1898, was captured in 1914 by Brit. and Japanese forces and restored to China. Pop. (1957) 1,121,000.

TSUSHIMA (tsoo'shimah). Island of Japan, S.E. of Korea. It is mountainous and consists of 2 halves, united at low tide. In the T. Strait the Russian fleet was destroyed by the Japanese in 1905. Area 271 sq. m.

TUAMOTU (tōō'ahmō'tōō) **ISLANDS.** Group of c. 80 atolls stretching 1,300 m. in the central Pacific, part of French Polynesia. Discovered 1606 by Span. explorers, they were annexed by France in 1881. They produce pearls and copra. Area 411 sq. m.; pop. (1962) 7,000.

TUBERCULOSIS (T.B.). Disease caused by different species of tubercle bacillus affecting birds, cattle and man. Bovine T., carried in milk, affects bones, joints and glands, chiefly of young people, and has largely been eradicated in highly developed countries by efficient control of dairying and pasteurization. Human T., an airborne infection, attacks mainly the lungs; also intestines, skin, brain, etc., of persons of any age. Highly successful treatment is available by a combination of the drugs *Isoniazid* (INH), *Streptomycin* and *para amino sulphonic acid* (PAS), and lengthy bed rest is seldom necessary.

Diagnostic methods incl. regular chest X-ray; and the tuberculin test, in which an extract of a tubercle bacillus is implanted under the skin, causing a reaction in men or animals suffering from T.

TÜBINGEN. Town in Baden-Württemberg, W. Germany, on the Neckar 22 m. S. of Stuttgart. It has factories making paper, textiles, surgical instruments, etc. T. dates from the 11th cent. and has a univ. (1477). It was cap. of the French zone of occupation after the S.W.W. Pop. (1967) 50,000.

TUBMAN, William V. S. (1895–1971). Liberian statesman. A descendant of American slaves, he was called to the Bar in 1917, and was a senator 1923–31 and 1934–7 and Associate Justice of the Supreme Court 1937–44. From his election as pres. in 1944, he concentrated on uniting the varied races. His assassination had often been plotted, but he was re-elected 1951, 1955, 1959, 1963, 1967, 1971. *See* illus. p. 402.

TUCUMAN (tookooman'). Cap. of T. prov., Argentina, on the Sali, in the foothills of the Andes.

TUBERCULOSIS. Complete eradication is now possible and this Viet-Namese child in a refugee camp near Saigon is being treated under his government's overall BCG vaccination programme. The harmless bacillus used was produced by Calmette and Guerin in 1906, hence the initials used to describe it.
Courtesy of W.H.O.

It has sugar mills, distilleries, etc. Founded 1565, T. was the site in 1816 of the signing of the Argentine declaration of independence from Spain. Pop. (1960) 287,000.

TUDOR. English dynasty descended from the Welshman Owen T., the 2nd husband of Catherine of France, the widow of Henry V. Their son Edmund m. Margaret Beaufort, the great-granddau. of John of Gaunt, and was the father of Henry VII, who ascended the throne in 1485. *See* table p. 392.

TULA (tōō′lah). Cap. of T. region, R.S.F.S.R., 100 m. S. of Moscow. It has a govt. ordnance factory founded 1712 by Peter the Great. Pop. (1967) 371.000.

TULIP. Genus of plants (*Tulipa*) in the family liliaceae. The garden T. (*T. Gesneriana*) probably originated in the Near East, and, quickly adopted in Europe during the 16th cent., became a craze in the 17th cent. Holland (*cf.* Dumas *The Black Tulip*) when extravagant prices were paid for rarely coloured bulbs. It is today commercially cultivated on a large scale in the Netherlands and E. Anglia. The T. tree (*Liriodendron tulipifera*) is a member of the magnolia family, with large tulip-shaped blooms.

TULL, Jethro (1674–1741). British agriculturalist. Farming in his native Berkshire, he developed *c.* 1701 a drill enabling seeds to be sown mechanically, and so spaced that cultivation between was possible in the growth period. He pub. *Horse-hoeing Husbandry* (1731).

TU′LSA. Town in Oklahoma, U.S.A., founded 1880, which grew rapidly after the discovery of petroleum in the vicinity in 1901. T. is a major centre of petroleum refining and the hub of a great complex of oil pipe-lines. Pop. (1960) 261,685.

TUNBRIDGE WELLS, Royal. English spa (bor.) in Kent, with chalybeate spring discovered in 1606. Pop. (1961) 39,855.

TUNDRA (toon′dra). A region of high latitude almost devoid of trees. The term, formerly applied to part of N. Russia, is now used for all such regions.

TUNGSTEN. *See* WOLFRAM.

PROFILE OF CHESAPEAKE BAY BRIDGE-TUNNEL

CHESAPEAKE BEACH   Thimble Shoal Tunnel—5,738 feet   Chesapeake Channel Tunnel—5,450 feet   North Channel Bridge   Fisherman Inlet Bridge   WISE POINT

TUNNEL. Most famous of trench-type are the two-mile long tunnels of the 17·6 m. bridge-tunnel crossing the mouth of the Chesapeake Bay, Virginia, and linking Wise Point and Chesapeake Beach (see profile), opened 1964. They are built of 300 ft. long prefabricated sections of water-tight, double-walled steel casing launched like ships (left); these are sunk into an open trench and when they have been joined by divers and the end plates removed are given a thick protective covering of sand. The 3 sections of roadway trestle (12·2 m.) supported by pre-stressed concrete piles link the

tunnels, access to the latter being gained by 4 man-made islands (right). Built in 35–40 ft. of water, these are each ¼ m. long and rise 30 ft. above the surface.
Courtesy of the Project Information Office, Chesapeake Bay Bridge & Tunnel District.

TUNICATA. A class of marine animals, of a low order of vertebrates, who exist on the sea-bed or rocks. *Ascidia mentuala*, or sea-squirt, is grey-green.

TŪ'NIS. Cap. of Tunisia, on T. bay, linked by a 7-m. canal (1893) with La Goulette on the Mediterranean. An old Arab city, T. was occupied by the Fr. in 1881 and developed by them. In Axis occupation 1942–3, it was captured without serious damage by the Allies. Carthage (q.v.), 9 m. N.E., has become a residential suburb of T. Pop. (1966) 642,384.

TUNI'SIA. Independent rep. in N. Africa, situated between Algeria to the W., Libya to the S.E., and the Mediterranean to the E. and N. The N. is traversed by mountain ranges and incl. fertile areas near the coast, while to the S. of the Shott el Jerid salt lakes most of the land is desert. T. was once heavily forested, and a re-afforestation programme is sponsored by the U.N. Wheat, barley, oats, and esparto grass are cultivated, and wine and olive oil are produced. Dates, almonds, oranges, and lemons are of importance. Sheep, goats, cattle, donkeys, and camels thrive. Mineral wealth incl. phosphates, iron, and lead. Woollen goods, carpets, pottery, and copper ware are manufactured. Tunis is the cap., other centres incl. Sfax, Bizerta, Sousse, Kairouan and Gabès. Area 48,000 sq. m.; pop. (1966) 4,457,862.

TUNNEL. Tunnelling is an increasingly important branch of civil engineering in mining, transport, etc. In the 19th cent. there were 2 major advances: the use of compressed air within the T. to balance the external pressure of water and of the T. shield to support the face and assist excavation. In recent years there have been notable developments in linings, e.g. concrete segments and steel liner plates, and in the use of rotary diggers and cutters, and of explosives. Famous Ts. incl.: Chesapeake Bay Bridge-Tunnel (1963), at 17½ m. the longest in the world (*See* illus. p. 1050); the Simplon (1922: 12·3 m.) and Mont Blanc (1962: 7 m.) under the Alps; and the Seikan (1975: 22¾ m.) which will link Honshu and Hokkaido and be the world's longest.

TUNNY. Fish of the mackerel family (*Thunnus thynnus*), also known as tuna, which may reach 14 ft. and weigh c. 1800 lb. It has been fished since ancient times in the Mediterranean as food, and in the 20th cent. fishing for T. with rod and line from a motor-boat has become fashionable on the Pacific coast of N. America and elsewhere.

TUPAC AMARU (tōō'pahk ahmahrōō') (1743–81). Name assumed by the Peruvian Indian leader Jose Gabriel Condorcanqui, who revolted against Spanish rule in 1780 and was executed in Cuzco: he claimed to be a descendant of the last of the Incas. The name *Tupamaros* was adopted by the urban left-wing guerrilla organization founded c. 1960 by Raul Sendic, operating in Montevideo.

TURBINE. A rotary steam engine in which the kinetic energy of steam or water is converted into work. Essentially it consists of a shaft, wheel, or rotor, carrying a number of vanes or blades; against the latter are directed jets of steam which cause the shaft to rotate at a high speed. Ts. are classified as impulse or reaction. The former, e.g. the de Laval T. patented in 1882, works purely by impulse; steam is expanded in a nozzle or nozzles from the initial steam pressure to a certain back-pressure, thereby converting its heat and pressure energy into kinetic energy of flow. Some part of this kinetic energy is then absorbed by the moving blades attached to the wheel or rotor, which is mounted on a shaft supported within a casing. In reaction Ts. there is a combination of impulse and

reaction effects. Fixed and moving blades are attached alternately to the casing and the rotors, and the steam suffers a gradual fall in pressure as it flows through the blade channels, when the corresponding heat drop results in an increase in its velocity. The steam engine of Hero of Alexandria (130 B.C.) was the prototype of the reaction T. Modern development is largely due to Sir C. Parsons (q.v.). Ts. are used in steamships, electricity generation, etc.

Later is the *gas-turbine* in which a compressed mixture of air and gas, or vaporized fuel, is ignited and, in expanding through the T., generates mechanical power; the compression is effected by a turbo-blower on the same shaft. Developed for aircraft, these Ts. have a future in power stations, and for land and water locomotion.

TURBOT. Flat-fish (*Rhombus maximus*) found in the Mediterranean and especially in the North Sea. Some 2 ft. long and weighing more than 30 lb., it is an epicure's dish.

TURE'NNE, Henri de la Tour d'Auvergne, vicomte de (1611–75). French marshal, one of the ablest of Louis XIV's generals.

TURGENEV (toorgān'yef), Ivan Sergeievich (1818–83). Russian author. B. in Orel prov., son of an army officer, he studied at Moscow, St. Petersburg, and Berlin, and worked for 2 yrs. in the Ministry of the Interior before finally devoting himself to literature. Among his works are the play *A Month in the Country* (1849); the series *A Sportsman's Sketches* collected 1852 which helped to bring about the abolition of serfdom; and the novels *A Nest of Gentlefolk* (1858), *Fathers and Sons* (1862), and *Virgin Soil* (1877). His poetic realism has a pessimism which did not accord with the optimism of the coming revolutionary era and he left the country in 1856, returning only for visits. His characterization, especially of women, is excellent.

TURIN. A photograph of the Holy Shroud.
Photo: G. Enrie, Turin.

TURGOT (tūrgō'), Anne Robert Jacques (1727–81). French statesman. B. in Paris, he was appointed Comptroller-General of Finance in 1774, but his drastic economies led to his dismissal in 1776.

TŪRI'N. Chief city of Piedmont, Italy, on the Po, in a fertile plain at the foot of the Alps. It has a univ. (1404) and a cathedral (15th cent.) It was cap. of the kingdom of Sardinia from 1720, of Italy 1861–4. Motor-cars, silk and other textiles, iron and steel goods, are manufactured. Pop. (1961) 1,019,230.

The *Holy Shroud of T.* is an ancient piece of linen, long revered as the 'clean linen' in which Christ's body was wrapped. Brown and reddish stains suggest the imprint of a crucified body, and photographs (1898–1931) show the perfect form of a man with the traditional face of Christ. Tests suggest chemical action might produce such an image in the circumstances of the crucifixion.

TURKESTAN. Geographical name for a large area in central Asia divided between the U.S.S.R. (Kazakh, Kirghiz, Tadzhik, Turkmen, and Uzbek S.S.Rs.), Afghanistan (anc. Bactria), and China (part of Sinkiang-Uighur).

TURKEY. Genus of birds (*Meleagris*) in the pheasant family. The domesticated T. (*M. gallopavo*) derives from the American wild species, introduced to Europe in the 16th cent., and the name may have been adopted from its cry. It is the traditional bird eaten at American Thanksgiving and in Britain at Christmas, but since the S.W.W. has been intensively bred, in the same way as chicken, as an all-year-round table bird. *See* illus. p. 82.

TURKEY

TURKEY. Republic of Europe and Asia, occupying Asia Minor and Turkish Thrace in Europe. European T. is separated from Asia Minor by the Bosporus, the Sea of Marmara, and the Dardanelles. The interior of Asia Minor is an extensive plateau. The Taurus and Anti-taurus mts. lie in the S., rising to over 12,000 ft., the Egri Dagh range to the E., and the mts. of Pontus to the N. along the Black Sea. The main rivers are in Europe the Maritsa and in Asia the Euphrates and Tigris, Kizil, Irmak Buyuk and Menderes (Maeandes). There are numerous lakes. Ankara, in the central plateau, is the cap.; Istanbul (Constantinople) in Europe, the largest city.

Most of T. is fertile, and cereals, cotton, tobacco, sugar and many kinds of fruit are grown. Tobacco and dried fruits are exported. Sheep, goats, cattle, donkeys, and horses thrive. Coal, lignite, chrome, and copper are mined; iron and steel, textiles, paper, glass, sugar, and cement are among manufactures.

GOVERNMENT. The 1961 constitution laid down the election of the pres. for 7 years by the Grand National Assembly and the Senate (both popularly elected) in joint session. Area 296,108 sq. m. (9,065 sq. m. in Europe); pop. (1969) 34,400,000 (c. 2½ million in Europe); 98 per cent of the pop. is Moslem.

History. The Turks originated in Mongolia, whence in the 6th cent. they spread into Turkestan. During the 7th cent. they adopted Islam. The Seljuk Turks in 1055 secured political control of the caliphate, and estab. an empire in Asia Minor. The Ottoman Turks. driven from Central Asia by the Mongols, entered the service of the Seljuks, and Osman I in 1299 founded a kingdom of his own. Having overrun Asia Minor, the Ottomans began their European conquests by seizing Gallipoli in 1354, captured Constantinople in 1453, and by 1480 were masters of the Balkans. By 1550 they had conquered Egypt, Syria, Arabia, Mesopotamia, Tripoli, and most of Hungary; thereafter the empire ceased to expand, although Cyprus was taken in 1571 and Crete in 1669.

The Christian counter-offensive opened in 1683 with the defeat of the Turks before Vienna; in 1699 the Turks lost Hungary, and in 1774 Russia ousted T. from Moldavia, Wallachia, and the Crimea. In the Balkans there was an unsuccessful revolt in Serbia in 1804, but in 1821–9 Greece threw off Turkish rule. Russia's attempts to exploit this situation were resisted by Britain and France, which in the Crimean War (1854–6) fought on T.'s side. The Bulgarian rising of 1876 led to a new war between T. and Russia, and by the Treaty of Berlin (1878) T. lost Bulgaria, Bosnia, and Herzegovina. A militant nationalist group, the Young Turks, secured the grant of a constitution in 1908; Italy took advantage of the ensuing crisis to seize Tripoli in 1911–12, while the Balkan states in 1912–13 expelled the Turks from Albania and Macedonia. T. entered the F.W.W. on the German side in 1914, only to lose Syria, Arabia, Mesopotamia, and its nominal suzerainty in Egypt.

The Greek occupation of Smyrna (Izmir) in 1919 provoked a patriotic reaction; Mustapha Kemal (Atatürk) estab. a provisional govt. at Angora (Ankara) in 1920, expelled the Greeks, and in 1923 a national assembly proclaimed T. a rep., with Kemal as first pres. The new republic carried out a sweeping policy of westernization: Islam ceased to be the state

religion, polygamy was abolished, and a new legal code was introduced. Kemal's People's Party ruled until 1950, the Democratic Party till the military episode of 1960–1 (*see* MENDERES), then coalitions till the Justice Party (a continuation of the Democratic) returned to power 1965. Neutral, but friendly to the Allies, in the S.W.W., T. developed links with Russia as well as the West in the 1960s.

Archaeological sites incl. Troy (Hissarlik) and Catal Hüyük, fortified city of *c.* 6,000 B.C. discovered with painted temples and objets d'art in 1961.

TURKISH. A member of the Altaic family of languages, agglutinative in character. Originally it was written in Arabic script, but in 1928 the Latin alphabet became compulsory. For cents. T. literature was based on Turkish models, but under Suleiman the Great began the Golden Age of which the poet Fuzuli (d. 1563) is the great exemplar, and which continued in the following cent. with the great poet satirist Nef'i of Erzerum (d. 1635) and others. During the 19th cent. westernization overtook T.L., e.g. the following of French models by Ibrahim Shinasi Effendi (1826–71), poet and prose writer. Joined with him as a founder of the New School was Mehmed Namik Kemal (1840–80), poet and author of the revolutionary play *Vatan* (*The Fatherland*), which caused his exile by the sultan. Unlike these in turning rather to Persian and Arabic than native sources for his vocabulary was the poet Tevfik Fikret (1867–1915). Among more recent names are those of the poet Mehmed Akif (1873–1936), author of the words of the Turkish national anthem; and the poet and novelist Yasher Kemal.

TURKMEN S.S.R. Republic of the U.S.S.R. formed (1924) from part of Russian Turkestan; admitted to the Union in 1925. It lies E. of the Caspian Sea. Its Turkmen inhabitants, the majority nomadic before the F.W.W., have been settled under Soviet rule; many are Moslems. The Kara Kum desert covers a great part of the rep., but artificial irrigation is increasing the area under cultivation. Cotton, wool, Astrakhan fur, etc., are produced, and carpets made. The cap. is Ashkhabad. Area 187,000 sq. m.; pop. (1967) 1,971,000.

TURKS AND CAICOS ISLANDS. Group of small W. Indian islands forming a Brit. colony; they lie *c.* 450 m. N.E. of Jamaica, of which they were a dependency 1873–1962. Their administrator is assisted by a legislative assembly (the majority elected) and an executive council. They produce salt, sisal, and crawfish. Grand Turk, largest of the group, is the seat of govt. Area 166 sq. m.; pop. (1966) 6,000.

TURK-SIB RAILWAY. Branch of the Trans-Siberian railway (q.v.) linking Novosibirsk in Siberia with Tashkent (Uzbek S.S.R., part of Russian Turkestan). It was opened in 1930.

TURKU (toor'koo). Finnish port on the r. Aurajoki, near its mouth. It has a castle, cathedral, and 2 univs. (Swedish, 1919, and Finnish, 1922). Pop. (1967) 145,689.

TU'RMERIC. The tuberous rhizomes of *Curcuma longa*, a perennial plant cultivated in India. It is used in curries and as a dyestuff.

TURKU. Built on an island at the mouth of the River Aura, the castle has guarded this waterway to the town since 1280, though it did not take until the 16th century the form to which it was carefully restored in 1961.
Courtesy of the Finnish Tourist Information Centre.

TURNER, Dame Eva (1899–). British soprano. B. in Lancs, she was prima donna of the Carl Rosa Opera Co. 1916–24, and has appeared throughout the

J. M. W. TURNER.
Pencil sketch by Charles
Martin.   *Photo: N.P.G.*

world in *Turandot, Aïda*, etc. She was created D.B.E. in 1962.

TURNER, Joseph Mallord William (1775–1851). British landscape artist. B. in London, son of a barber, he studied at the Academy School, was elected R.A. in 1802, and in 1809 became prof. of perspective at the Academy. He travelled widely on the Continent, the effect of his time in Italy can be seen in 'Crossing the Brook' (Nat. Gallery), and beautiful Venetian scenes, but in later life he developed an increasing freedom in capturing effects of weather and light in sea and sky with breathtaking grandeur e.g. 'Rain, Steam and Speed', 'Snow Storm'. Always solitary – he never m. – he was not greatly appreciated in his lifetime, though championed by Ruskin, but greatly influenced the development of English art and the work of the Impressionists. He worked with equal effect in oil and water colour, and bequeathed many of his pictures to the nation.

TURNER, Merfyn (1915–). British social worker, founder of the first 'Norman House' for homeless, discharged prisoners in London in 1955, described in *Safe Lodging* (1961). A number of other such houses were estab. in various parts of Britain with the help of the Margery Fry Memorial Fund (1959).

TURNIP. Biennial plant (*Brassica rapa*) cultivated in temperate climates for its edible white or yellow-fleshed 'root' and the young leaves, which are used as a green vegetable: closely allied is the swede-T. or rutabaga (*Brassica napobrassica*), of greater food value, firmer-fleshed and longer-keeping. Both types are valuable both for human food and livestock fodder.

TURNPIKE. *See* HIGHWAY.

TURPENTINE. A solution of resins obtained by distillation from the sap of conifers. Its chief uses are as a diluent of paint and in varnish.

TURPIN, Dick (1706–39). English highwayman. B. at Hempstead, Essex, the son of an innkeeper, he turned to highway robbery, cattle-thieving, and smuggling, and was hanged at York. His legendary ride from London to York on his mare Black Bess, described by W. H. Ainsworth in *Rookwood*, is probably based on one of *c.* 190 m. from Gad's Hill to York completed in 15 hr. in 1676 by the highwayman John Nevison (1639–84).

TURQUOISE (tur'kwoiz). A precious stone: hydrous phosphate of aluminium and copper, bluish green in colour, found in Persia, Turkestan, Mexico, etc.

TURTLE. Name for marine and freshwater species of tortoise (q.v.). The legs are modified to oar-like flippers for swimming, and the 'shell' is a more streamlined heart shape than that of the tortoise. Many are carnivorous: the eggs are laid in the sand of the sea shore. Well-known species are the green T. (*Chelonia mydas*), source of T. soup; the hawksbill (*Eretmochelys imbricata*), source of 'tortoise-shell'; the loggerhead (*Caretta caretta*); the snapper (*Chelydra serpentina*)

HAWKSBILL TURTLE

which lives up to its name; and the giant leathery T. (*Sphargis coriacea*) which reaches 6-8 ft. and weighs half a ton.

TU'SCANY. An Italian region, a former grand duchy, in the N.W. of the peninsula. It corresponds in large part to anc. Etruria. The Apennines reach into it; the Arno is the chief river. Tuscan was adopted as standard, literary Italian. Towns incl. Florence, Pisa, Leghorn, and Siena. Area 8,877 sq. m.; pop. (1961) 3,267,374.

TUSSAUD, Madame (1760–1850). French wax-modeller. B. Anne Marie Grosholtz in Berne, she went in 1766 to Paris to live with her famous wax-modeller uncle, Phillipe Curtius, whom she soon outshone, and during the French Revolution they were forced to take death masks of many victims and leaders (some still exist in the modern Chamber of Horrors). In 1794 she m. François Tussaud, but they separated, and in 1802 she estab. her exhibition in the Strand, London. It was transferred to Baker St. in 1833 and to Marylebone Rd. in 1884 (destroyed by fire 1925, but reopened 1928).

MARIE TUSSAUD. By her son.   *Photo: N.P.G.*

TUTANKHAMEN (tootankah'men) (reigned 1360–1350 B.C.). King of Egypt. A member of the royal house of the 18th dynasty, and a son of Ikhnaton or of Amenhotep III, he may have succeeded to the throne when 11 yrs. old and was aged approx. 20 at his death. Little is known of his reign, but in 1922 his tomb was discovered by Lord Carnarvon and Howard Carter in the Valley of the Kings at Luxor. Although robbers had entered it shortly after the funeral, it had been then resealed by his officials and escaped further rifling – the only ancient royal tomb to have done so. The richness of the find, incl. the solid gold coffin, captured the imagination of the world.

TUTUŌ'LA, Amos (1920–). Nigerian novelist. Writing in English, he works through the traditional background stories of his people in *The Palm-Wine Drunkard* (1952), *The Brave Huntress* (1958), and *The Feather Woman of The Jungle* (1962), and uses an individual African idiom.

TUVA (tōo'va). A.S.S.R. of the R.S.F.S.R. It lies N.W. of Mongolia (Mongolian People's Rep.) of which it was part until 1911. It was declared a Russian protectorate 1914. After the 1917 revolution it was the independent Tannu-Tuva rep. 1920 until incorporated in the R.S.F.S.R. as an autonomous region in 1944. It was made the T. A.S.S.R. in 1961. There is good pasture; gold and asbestos are worked, and there are hydro-electric installations. The cap. is Kyzyl. Area 65,800 sq. m.; pop. (1967) 217,000.

TVER. Old name of KALININ.

TWAIN, Mark. Pseudonym (a call used for depth sounding by Mississippi pilots) of the American writer Samuel Langhorne Clemens (1835–1910). B. at Florida, Missouri, he was a printer, Mississippi pilot, and goldminer before turning to writing. After a tour

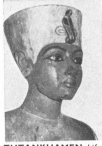

TUTANKHAMEN. Life-size bust of stuccoed and painted wood from the tomb.   *Cairo Museum.*

of Europe he wrote *The Innocents Abroad* (1869), establishing his reputation as a humorist. He subsequently wrote *The Adventures of Tom Sawyer* (1876), *The Adventures of Huckleberry Finn* (1885), and *A Connecticut Yankee at King Arthur's Court* (1889).

TWEED. A river in the S. of Scotland rising in Peeblesshire and entering the North Sea at Berwick, in Northumberland. Length 97 m.

TWEED. Cloth made of woollen yarn, usually of several shades, but in its original form without regular pattern and woven on a hand-loom in the remoter parts of Ireland, Wales and Scotland, the most famous being Harris T.; it is highly durable and largely weather-proof. In modern times it is often machine woven, patterned, and processed. *See* illus. p. 513.

TWEEDDALE. Another name for PEEBLESSHIRE.

TWEEDSMUIR, Lord. *See* BUCHAN, JOHN.

TWELFTH DAY. In the Christian calendar the feast of the Epiphany kept on the 12th day after Christmas, 6 Jan. In olden times many convivial ceremonies were connected with Twelfth Night.

TWICKENHAM. District in the Greater London bor. of Richmond-upon-Thames. Famous residents have incl. Alexander Pope, J. M. W. Turner, Horace Walpole at Strawberry Hill, and Clarendon at York House. T. incl. Hampton Court and a famous ground of the Rugby Union.

TWILIGHT SLEEP. A method of anaesthesia used in childbirth, involving the hypodermic injection of analgesics and narcotics.

TWINS. Two individuals produced at one birth. Strictly speaking, two animals developed and born at the same time are T. only if they are the products of the division of a single fertilized ovum or egg cell. Human T. resulting from the simultaneous development of two fertilized eggs are not true T. The latter are always of the same sex.

TYBURN (tī'-). An English stream running underground from Hampstead to the Thames at Westminster; T. gallows stood near the present junction of Oxford St. and Edgware Rd., from the 12th cent. until 1783.

TYLER, John (1790–1862). 10th Pres. of the U.S.A. B. in Virginia, he was elected Vice-Pres. in 1840 and became Pres. in 1841. In 1845 Texas was annexed. In the Civil War he adhered to the Confederates.

TYLER, Wat (d. 1381). English leader of the peasants in the revolt of 1381. B. in Kent or Essex, he served in the French wars. After taking Canterbury he led the peasants to Blackheath and occupied London. At Mile End Richard II met the rebels and promised to redress their grievances. At a further conference at Smithfield, Tyler was murdered by the Lord Mayor, Sir William Walworth.

TYNDALE (tin'dal), **William** (*c.* 1492–1536). English translator of the Bible. B. probably in Glos, he studied at Oxford and Cambridge and was ordained. In 1525 he began to print his English N.T. at Cologne and had to flee to Worms, where the work was completed. In 1530 was pub. his Pentateuch at Antwerp. The first vol. of Holy Scripture printed in England was his revised N.T. in 1536. He was seized at Antwerp, and imprisoned at Vilvorde, where he was tried as a heretic, and strangled and burnt.

TYNE (tīn). River, navigable to Newcastle, which flows 30 m. across E. Northumberland to the North Sea. The T. (1967) road tunnel is at Jarrow.

TYNEMOUTH (tin'muth). English port (co. bor.) and pleasure resort in Northumberland on the N. bank of the Tyne. Pop. (1961) 70,112.

TYNWALD (tin'wold). The parliament of the Isle of Man, consisting of the governor, a legislative council and the House of Keys.

TYPE. Piece of metal cast in rectangular shape for printing (q.v.) by the letterpress process. The sign to be printed, e.g. a letter or punctuation mark, is cast in relief on the face of the T., which in Britain is ·918 in.

high overall. The width of the T. across the letter varies according to the design of the letter: the depth of the T. up and down the letter varies according to the size of the alphabet used, and is measured in points (almost exactly 72 to the inch); this encyclopaedia is set in 7-point. One particular style of alphabet, together with its appropriate marks of punctuation etc., is a fount; a set of alphabets of the same style, in sizes varying from say 6-point to 72-point, is a series of founts. The style of alphabet is the type-face; this type-face is Times roman, *this is Times italic* and **this is Times bold roman.** The T. of books is mechanically composed or set (arranged in order) and cast at the same time, and is later melted for re-use.

When a page has been set and cast, a cardboard or plastic mould can be taken from the printing-surface, and a stereotype or duplicate plate of the whole page cast from the mould in type-metal. An electrically conductive mould of the T. can have a copper coating deposited on it by electrolysis; this shell when removed from the mould is an electrotype. Stereotypes and electrotypes are used in place of the original T. for letterpress printing. For other printing processes, metal T. is unnecessary, as photographic images of the characters can be set by photo-composition.

TYPEWRITER. A hand-operated machine for producing characters similar to those of printing. The

TYPEWRITER. In the I.B.M. 72 (left), produced in 1962, typebars are replaced by a travelling spherical plastic typehead the size of a golf ball (right), which has the 88 characters of the standard keyboard in relief on its surface, and glides along a cylindrical metal rod. Typeheads are instantly interchangeable to enable the operator to switch from one style of type to another, or to a different series of characters, e.g. Greek or Russian. Speeds of 186 words per minute can be reached.   *Courtesy of Rowse Muir Publications Ltd.*

1st practicable T. was built at Milwaukee, Wisconsin, by C. L. Sholes, C. Glidden and S. W. Soulé in 1867, and by 1874 E. Remington and Sons, the gun makers whose name was soon given to the Ts., produced under contract the 1st machines for sale. Later developments incl. tabulators from *c.* 1898, portable machines *c.* 1912, gradual introduction of electrical operation (allowing increased speed, since the keys are touched not depressed), proportional spacing in 1940, and rotating typehead with stationary platen in 1962.

TYPHOID FEVER (tī'foid). An infectious disease contracted by swallowing the specific bacillus. This may be present in the urine or faeces of a patient or a carrier, or may be conveyed by flies. Ulcers form in the small intestine and may bleed internally or perforate with great danger to life.

TYPHOON (tīfōōn'). A violent revolving storm that occurs, chiefly in autumn, along the eastern seaboard of Asia between the Philippines and Japan.

TYPHUS (tī'fus). An infectious disease, often fatal, caused by a microbe carried in the excreta of lice. It enters the body usually by abrasions in the feet, and is epidemic among overcrowded human beings.

TYR (tir). The Scandinavian god of battles. The Anglo-Saxons called him Týw, hence 'Tuesday'.

TYRE (tīr). English name of a town in Lebanon (Arabic Sûr), *c.* 50 m. S. of Beirut, formerly a port until its harbour silted up. Pop. (est.) 12,000. T. stands on the site of anc. T., a seaport of Phoenicia. Built partly on the mainland and partly on 2 small islands, the city was a great commercial centre and famous for its purple dye. Besieged by Alexander the Great 333-332 B.C. and captured, it came under Roman rule 64 B.C. and was taken by the Arabs A.D. 638. The Crusaders captured it 1124, and it never recovered from the destruction it suffered when the Arabs recaptured it, 1291.

TYRE. The rubber hoop fitted round the rims of bicycle, motor-car and road vehicle wheels. The first pneumatic rubber T. was patented by R. W. Thompson in 1845, but it was John Boyd Dunlop of Belfast who independently re-invented pneumatic Ts. for use with bicycles 1888-9.

TYROL. *See* TIROL.

TYRONE (tirōn'). Co. of Northern Ireland. Chief rivers are the Derg, Blackwater, and Foyle. Agriculture is the principal industry; linens, woollens, soap, etc., are manufactured. Omagh is the co. town. Area 1,218 sq. m.; pop. (1966) 135,634.

TZU-HSI (tsoo-shē') (1836-1908). Dowager empress of China. Of humble birth, she was sold as a slave to a general who presented her to the emperor Hsien-Feng as a concubine. On his death in 1861 she became regent for her son; he d. in 1875 and she became regent for her nephew Kwang-hsu. She was held responsible for the Boxer rebellion in 1900.

U The 21st letter of the English alphabet, and the 20th in the ancient Roman, in which it was identical with *V*. Not until the 19th cent. were *U* and *V* definitely separated in English dictionaries. It has various sounds, e.g. as in *truth* (ōō), *bull* (oo), *but* (u), *duke* (yū), short *i* (*busy*), short *e* (*bury*).

UBANGI-SHARI. *See* CENTRAL AFRICAN REP.

U-BOAT. Name given to the German submarine (*Unterseeboot*) in both world wars, because they were named U followed by a number.

UCCELLO (oochel'lō), **Paolo.** Name used by Italian artist Paolo di Dono (1397-1475). Apprenticed to Ghiberti, he is celebrated for his decorative use of perspective, and his works incl. the 'Nativity' fresco (Florence) and 3 battle pictures for the Palazzo Medici, one of which is in the National Gallery.

UDAIPUR (oodipoor'). Indian city in Rajasthan, once cap. of the former princely state of U., incorporated in Rajasthan 1948. A handsome city with several palaces (2 on islands in a lake), and the Jagannath temple (*c.* 1640), it was founded 1568. Most of its buildings are cream or white. Pop. (1961) 111,139.

U'DALL, Nicholas (1504-56). English schoolmaster and playwright, author of *Ralph Roister Doister* (*c.* 1553), the first known English comedy.

UDINE (oodē'nā). Italian city, cap. of U. prov., 80 m. N.E. of Venice. U. was the cap. of Friuli in the 13th cent., passed to Venice 1420. It makes textiles, leather goods, paper, sugar. Pop. (1961) 85,205.

UDMURT (oodmoort'). A.S.S.R. of the R.S.F.S.R., in the W. Ural foothills. Its products incl. timber, flax, potatoes, peat, quartz; there is some industry, e.g. metallurgy at Izhevsk (the cap.). Area 16,200 sq. m.; pop. (1969 est.) 1,377,000.

UFA (oo'fah). Cap. of Bashkir A.S.S.R., R.S.F.S.R., in the W. Urals on the r. Bielaia, founded by the Russians 1574. It has railway workshops, shipyards, distilleries, sawmills. Pop. (1967) 704,000.

UGA'NDA. Independent rep. in central Africa, lying between the Sudan Rep. and Tanganyika. It has an average alt. of 4,000 ft. a.s.l., and is drained by the White Nile; parts of Lakes Victoria, Edward, and Albert are within the rep., which incl. also Lakes George and Kioga. Cotton, coffee, sugar, tobacco are among important crops; tin is mined in the W., and there are deposits of iron, copper, manganese and other minerals. The cap. is Kampala, other towns incl. Entebbe, Jinja, and Mbale. The Owen Falls (q.v.) dam serves industrial development which incl. smelting of copper from Kilembe. Area 93,981 sq. m.; pop. (1967) 7,750,000 (*c.* 9,000 Europeans).

Made a Brit. protectorate 1894, U. became independent 1962, and a rep. within the Commonwealth

1963. In 1967 Milton Obote (q.v.) estab. a unitary rep. with himself as pres., elected for 5 years as both Head of State and Head of Govt. by the Nat. Assembly (one-third nominated by the pres.): the hereditary kingdoms were subdivided into admin. districts (*see* BUGANDA).

U'GARIT. Small kingdom (modern Ras Shamra) on the coast of Syria *c.* 10 m. N. of Latakia, excavated by Claude Schaeffer from 1929. It was a commercial centre, and in the palace numerous documents in cuneiform have been discovered, as well as an early Ugaritic alphabet of 22 letters – the earliest alphabet known - closely related to the Phoenician from which our own ultimately derives. Most of the discoveries are 15-13th cent. B.C., but some *c.* 7000 B.C.

UHLAND (ōō'lahnt), **Johann Ludwig** (1787-1862). German poet, author of ballads and lyrics in the Romantic tradition.

UIST (ū'-ist). Two small Scottish islands in the Outer Hebrides, Inverness-shire, N. U. with pop. (1961) 1,921 and S. U., pop. (1961) 3,983. A guided missile range was opened on S. U. in 1959; Loch Druidibeg is a nature reserve.

UJIJI (oojē'jē). Town in Tanganyika, on Lake Tanganyika, a commercial centre originally an Arab trading post for slaves and ivory. It is linked by rail with Dar-es-Salaam. Pop. (1965) 15,000.

UKRAINE (ūkrān'). A constituent republic of the

UGANDA. Rapidly expanding Mbale, the country's third largest town, acquired a cathedral in 1963. Built of reinforced concrete, it was made twelve-sided to allow as many as possible of the congregation to have a close uninterrupted view of the altar.   *Courtesy of Edward D. Mills and Partners architects.*

U.S.S.R., lying in the S.W., reaching from the Black Sea to Poland. The U. is the grea cereal-growing area of Russia, and sugar-beet and other crops flourish. The Donetz coalfield is the richest in the Soviet Union; iron ore is also mined, and steel and pig-iron are important products. Chief rivers are the Dnieper, which is harnessed at the Dnieper dam (1932) to supply hydro-electric power, the Donetz and the Bug. Natural gas is exported to Austria. The cap. Kiev is the historic centre of Ukrainian culture. Other cities are Kharkhov, Odessa, Dnepropetrovsk, Donetsk, and Nikolayev. Area 222,600 sq. m.; pop. (1968) 46,381,000.

The majority of the people are Ukrainians, or Little Russians; the official language is Ukrainian, a Slavonic dialect. Ukrainian literature goes back to the Middle Ages. The first modern Ukrainian writer was Ivan Kotlyarevsky (1769–1838); the great national writer is Taras Shevchenko (1841–61).

U. was a state already in the 9th cent. Russia absorbed E. U. in 1667, the rest in 1793. U. proclaimed itself a people's rep. in 1917, a soviet rep. in 1919; from 1923 it formed one of the reps. of the U.S.S.R. The Germans overran it in the S.W.W. For additions to U. after the S.W.W., see BESSARABIA, BUKHOVINA, RUTHENIA; see also CRIMEA.

ŪKULELE (-ä′li). A small guitar used by Hawaiian islanders, and introduced into Britain and America.

ULAN BATOR. Cap. of the Mongolian People's Rep. Linked with Ulan Ude by rail, it is the seat of a univ. (1942); it is also a trading centre and has an airport. Pop. (1962 est.) 196,000.

ULA′NOVA, Galina (1910–). Russian dancer. Both her father and mother danced at the Mariinsky Theatre, and s he herself trained at the state school of her native Leningrad. She was 1944–61 prima ballerina of the Bolshoi theatre ballet, and continued as ballet master to the company. Her roles incl. Odette-Odile, Giselle and Juliet. See BALLET.

ULAN UDE. Cap. of Buriat A.S.S.R., R.S.F.S.R., on the r. Ud., and the Trans-Siberian rly. It has industrial plants incl. sawmills and factories making motor-cars and glass. Pop. (1967) 227,000.

ULCER. Sloughing of skin or mucous membrane. It is caused either by infection (e.g. syphilitic ulcer), inadequate blood supply (e.g. varicose ulcer), or irritation (e.g. gastric ulcer).

ULEÅBORG. Swedish name of OULU.

ULM (oolm). German city and fortress in Baden-Württemberg, on the Danube. A free imperial city from the 14th cent. to 1802, it has a fine Gothic cathedral (1377) which escaped damage in the S.W.W. when two-thirds of U. was destroyed. It makes vehicles, agricultural machinery, precision instruments, textiles, etc. Pop. (1966) 92,000.

ULSTER. Northernmost of the Irish provinces, divided into 9 counties, of which 6 (Antrim, Armagh, Down, Fermanagh, Londonderry, and Tyrone) constitute Northern Ireland, while 3 (Cavan, Donegal, and Monaghan) are in the Republic. From Jacobean times it was a centre of English, later Scottish, settlement; it incl. Belfast and the chief industrial centres of the island (linen and synthetic textiles, chemicals, shipbuilding, etc.) and agriculture is highly developed. Total area 8,335 sq. m. Pop. (1966) 1,693,073.

ULTRAMONTANISM ('beyond the mountains', i.e. the Alps). Term applied to the Italian party in the R.C. Church who lay great stress on papal claims.

ULTRASONICS. Ultrasonic rays are physical vibrations in matter ocurring at frequencies above 20,000 cycles per second which is the approximate limit of human hearing. Propagation of U. in air or other gas is very poor and nearly all practical applications are in liquids or solids. The earliest practical application was to detect submarines during the F.W.W. but recently the field has greatly expanded.

The lower frequencies of 20,000 – 80,000 cycles are mainly used for cleaning n industry and in hospitals. Higher frequencies have been used in the form of pulses to produce echoes as a means of measuring the depth of the sea, to detect flaws in metal and to show displacements of the brain in surgery. Recently it has become possible to make photographic records of cross-sections by U. using the ultrasonic tomograph. First used in the U.S.A., it was invented by British radiologist Douglas Gordon: the part of the patient's

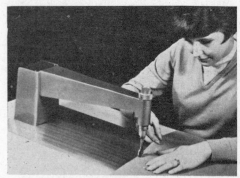

ULTRASONICS. When a number of layers of fabrics are subjected to intense high frequency vibrations they interlock or bond together so intimately that it would be easier to tear the main fabric rather than rip the seam apart. The threadless stitcher illustrated is an ultrasonic bonder mainly designed for use with medium and lightweight man-made fabrics.
Courtesy of Omega Laboratories Ltd.

body to be diagnosed is immersed in a water tank, a probe being passed round in the water and a picture being built up by a camera inside the machine.

High power U. has been used with focussing arrangements to destroy tissue at a depth in the body, and using extremely high frequencies of 1,000 megacycles or more it has been possible to make an ultrasonic microscope.

ULTRA-VIOLET RADIATION. Light rays invisible to the naked eye, of a wavelength less than 3,900 Angström units, the lower limit being about 10 Å when the X-ray range begins. Physiologically they are extremely powerful, producing sunburn and causing the formation of vitamin D; they are strongly germicidal and may be produced artifically by mercury vapour and arc lamps for therapeutic use. U.V.R. may be detected with ordinary photographic plates or films down to 2,000 Å. Below this Schumann plates and special vacuum apparatus must be used. It can also be studied by its fluorescent effect on suitable materials.

ULYSSES. See ODYSSEUS.

UMBA′LLA. Indian city in Punjab, an important military cantonment, and a commercial and trading centre with some manufactures and an airport. Pop. (1961) 105,543.

UMBELLI′FERAE. Plant family of dicotyledons containing about 200 genera and 2,700 species, characterized by an inflorescence in which all the foot stalks of a flower cluster radiate from a common point at the top of the stem. They include hemlock, celery, fool's parsley, and carrot.

UMBERTO II (Humbert) (1904–). Last king of Italy. He succeeded on the abdication of his father, Victor Emmanuel III, on 9 May 1946, and abdicated on 13 June and left the country. From 1944 he had been Lieut.-Gen. of the realm. He subsequently settled in Portugal as the Count di Sarre.

UMBRELLA. Portable protection against the rain – when used against the sun usually called a parasol or sunshade. They were used by the Chinese more than

1,000 yrs. B.C. and also by the rulers of ancient Egypt and Assyria, when they were also a symbol of power, as they are still regarded in parts of Africa, etc. Revived in clerical use in 16th cent. Italy, Us. were first carried as an everyday protection in England by Jonas Hanway (1712–86), and are still part of 'regulation City uniform'. *See* illus. p. 674.

UMBRIA. A region of Italy in the central Apennines, drained by the Tiber. Perugia and Terni are the chief towns. Area 3,265 sq. m.; pop. (1961) 788,546.

UNAMUNO (oonahmoo′nō), **Miguel de** (1864–1936). Spanish writer. B. at Bilbao and proud of his Basque origin, he was prof. of Greek at Salamanca from 1892 and rector of the univ. from 1900, but was exiled 1924–30 for criticism of the military directorate of Primo de Rivera. His works incl. a mystic poem on survival of death *El Cristo de Velazquez* (1920: *The Velazquez Christ*); the key philosophical study *Del Sentimiento Trágico de la Vida* (1913: *The Tragic Sense of Life*); an interpretation of Cervantes, travel books, plays, stories and novels (e.g. *Niebla*). He is widely influential in the Spanish-speaking world, but an individualistic style has made translation difficult.

UNCLE SAM. Nickname for the U.S.A. It originated during the war of 1812, probably from the initials U.S. placed on government property.

UNDERGROUND. Name for London's city and suburban rail services, operated from 1933 by the London Passenger Transport Board (re-named L.T. Executive 1948–62, L.T. Board from 1963), which cover a network of over 240 m. – 90 m. of it below ground – more than 2 million passenger journeys being made per week. The world's first U. (1863), 4 m. in length, was the conception of a London solicitor to relieve traffic congestion; the latest extension, the Victoria Line (1963–9), runs to Walthamstow in the N.W. and is being extended S. of the Thames. The major cities of the world have Us. and each system reflects some characteristics of its people, from the frenetic activity of the N.Y. 'subway' to the ordered calm of the Tokyo U. and monumental Moscow U.

UNDERWOOD, Leon (1890–). British artist and sculptor. B. in London, he has travelled widely to

LEON UNDERWOOD. A skilled craftsman, as well as a forceful artist, he is seen here at work in his studio on the maquette for his bronze 'Ideas', which was commissioned by the L.C.C. for their Hillgrove Estate, near Swiss Cottage.
Courtesy of the Kaplan Gallery: Photo by J. S. Lewinski.

Iceland, the U.S., Mexico and W. Africa, devoting several books to the masks, wood carvings and bronzes of the last-named. His rhythmic figures are powerful symbols of human myth.

UNDSET (oond′set), **Sigrid** (1882–1949). Norwegian novelist. B. in Denmark, she was a clerk in Oslo 1899–1909, and first won fame with *Jenny* (1912). Her masterpiece is *Kristin Lavransdatter* (1920–2), set in the 14th cent., which is strongly Catholic – she was in 1925 received into the R.C. Church. In 1928 she was awarded a Nobel prize.

UNEMPLOYMENT. Lack of employment on a large scale. A certain proportion of U. is 'frictional', i.e. due to the flow of labour from a depressed to a prosperous industry, but the term as used today relates to U. of a different character, i.e. long-term mass U., such as became a permanent feature of economic life in all industrial countries between the two world wars, e.g. in the U.S.A. there were 3–4 million unemployed even during the 1929 boom. In Britain, for at least 150 years before 1939, the supply of labour always exceeded the demand except in war-time, and economic crises accompanied by mass U. were recurrent from 1785. The percentage of unemployed (in trade unions) averaged 6 during 1883–1913 and 14·2 (of those covered by the old U. Insurance Acts) 1921–38. The S.W.W. and the rebuilding and expansion that followed meant shortage of labour rather than U. in Britain and on the Continent, but how far control of the economy could maintain this position became conjectural in the subsequent years as the figures began to fluctuate; during 1945–60 the average was 1·7 per cent of all workers. In the U.S.A. certain areas, especially those with a large Negro population, still have chronic U. problems, the total ranging from c. 3½ to 5 million. In some countries, e.g. Latin America and parts of Italy, there is chronic 'underemployment' because the territories are under-developed, and in others, e.g. the newly emergent African states and India, there tends to be lack of employment in the higher grades for which students may have been educated, leading in both cases to governmental instability. *See* SOCIAL SECURITY.

UNGARE′TTI, Guiseppe (1888–1970). Italian poet. B. in Alexandria, and later living in Paris and São Paulo, he shows in his lyrics a cosmopolitan independence of Italian poetic tradition, and they are noted for their spare simplicity, esp. the poems (pervaded by a horror of war), in his best-known collection *Allegria di naufragi* (1919: *L'Allegria*).

UNGULA′TA. Large order of mammals including all the hoofed forms, ranging from pigs to elephants.

UNIATE (i.e. united Greek or Eastern Orthodox and R.C. Church). Name given to those Christian Churches which accept the full Catholic faith and the supremacy of the Pope, and are in full communion with the R.C. Church, but retain their own liturgy and separate organization.

U′NICORN. Fabulous animal referred to by classical writers, said to live in India and to be like a horse but with one straight horn. *See* ORYX.

UNIFORMITY. Name given to 2 acts of parliament. The 1st (1559) imposed the Prayer Book on the whole English kingdom; the 2nd (1662) required the Prayer Book to be used in all churches, and some 2,000 ministers who refused to comply were ejected.

UNION. The Act of Union of 1707 effected the union of England and Scotland, and that of 1801 of England and Ireland. The latter was abrogated when the Irish Free State was constituted in 1922.

UNION FLAG. The British national flag, popularly called the *U. Jack*, although this is accurate only when it is flown on the jackstaff of a warship. *See* FLAG.

UNION MOVEMENT. Political group in Britain. Originating with the New Party founded by Sir Oswald Mosley (q.v.) and a number of Labour M.Ps. in 1931, it later developed into the British Union of Fascists (1932). An attempt by the 'blackshirts' to march through the East End of London in 1936 led to the Public Order Act, forbidding the wearing of such political uniforms. In 1940 the organization was declared illegal and its leaders interned, but at the end of the S.W.W. it was revived as the U.M., its anti-Jewish and anti-colour doctrines leading to disordet at its meetings.

UNION OF SOVIET SOCIALIST REPUBLICS (U.S.S.R.). *See* Soviet Union; Russia.

UNITARIANS. A Christian denomination which rejects the orthodox doctrine of the Trinity, asserts the Fatherhood of God and the Brotherhood of Man, and gives a pre-eminent position to Jesus Christ as a religious teacher, while denying his Deity. Us. also reject the doctrines of original sin, the atonement, and eternal punishment, and they have no creeds. The various congregations are linked in the General Assembly of Unitarian and Free Christian Churches.

UNITED ARAB REPUBLIC. Union formed 1958, broken 1961, between Egypt and Syria. Egypt continued to use the name after the breach.

UNITED KINGDOM. Name for England and Scotland together from the accession of James VI of Scotland as James I of England, 1603, confirmed by the Act of Union, 1707, and extended to incl. Ireland, 1801, the full title being U.K. of England, Scotland, and Ireland; from 1927 the form U.K. of England, Scotland and N. Ireland was used.

UNITED KINGDOM ATOMIC ENERGY AUTHORITY. Estab. by the U.K.A.E. Act of 1954, it controls atomic-energy research and development, the Min. for Science being responsible for general policy and for funds provided for the authority. It has a five-fold organization: 1, *Research Group* at Harwell (q.v.); 2, *Weapons Group* at Aldermaston (q.v.); 3, *Reactor Group* responsible for the Dounreay and Windscale nuclear power reactors and the Winfrith (Dorset) A.E. Establishment; 4, *Production Group*, responsible for managing uranium and plutonium factories at Springfields (Lancs), Windscale, and Capenhurst (Cheshire), and for the Chapelcross and Calder Hall nuclear reactors; and 5, *Engineering Group*, responsible for the design and construction of U.K.A.E. plants, etc. – H.Q. for the 3 last-named are at Risley, Lancs.

UNITED NATIONS. An association of states pledged to maintain international peace and security, and to promote international co-operation. Its charter, which was drawn up by the San Francisco Conference in 1945, is based on proposals drafted at the Dumbarton Oaks Conference. It succeeded the League of Nations (q.v.).

The 6 principal organs of the U.N are (1) the *General Assembly* of representatives of all member states, which meets regularly once a year, and may discuss any matter within the scope of the charter, but may not make recommendations on anything already being dealt with by the Security

UNITED NATIONS. The permanent headquarters of the U.N. in New York occupies an 18-acre site on Manhattan Island between First Avenue and the East River. To the right is the 39-storey Secretariat, with the General Assembly beyond, and the Library in the foreground.
Courtesy of the United Nations.

Council. Decisions on important questions are made by a two-third majority of members voting, and on other questions by a simple majority, each member having one vote. (2) the *Security Council* consisting of 5 permanent members (U.K., U.S.A., U.S.S.R., France and Communist China), and 6 others elected for 2 years by the General Assembly. Its decisions must be supported by at least 7 of its members, incl. all permanent members, who thus exercise the right of veto. Taking cognizance of disputes, it may undertake investigations into the circumstances and make recommendations to the parties concerned, and may call on all members to take economic or military measures to enforce its decisions. (3) the *Economic and Social Council*, consisting of representatives of 18 member states, elected for 3 years by the General Assembly, which initiates studies of international economic, social, cultural, educational, health and related matters, and may make recommendations to the General Assembly. It operates largely through specialized commissions of international experts on economics, transport and communications, human rights, status of women, etc. It also co-ordinates the activities of such specialized intergovernmental agencies as the U.N. Educational, Scientific and Cultural Organization (UNESCO 1946) to combat illiteracy, raise living standards through education, etc.; International Labour Organization (q.v.); Food and Agriculture Organization (FAO 1945), to help the nations improve food production and distribution, raise nutritional standards, etc.; International Atomic Energy Agency (IAEA 1957) to develop the peaceful uses of atomic energy; World Health Organization (WHO 1946), to prevent the spread of, and eliminate, such diseases as malaria and tuberculosis; International Monetary Fund and International Bank for Reconstruction and Development, which promote international economic co-operation, etc. (4) the *Trusteeship Council*, consisting of members administering Trust Territories (q.v.), other permanent members of the Security Council, plus sufficient other elected members to balance the administering powers. (5) the *International Court of Justice* (q.v.) at The Hague which is U.N.'s principal judicial organ: the 15 judges are elected by the General Assembly and the Security Council, and U.N. members are pledged by the charter to comply with the decisions of the court in cases to which they are a party. (6) the *Secretariat*, the administrative body, consisting of the Secretary General, appointed by the General Assembly on the recommendation of the Security Council for 5 years, and an international staff.

Members contribute according to their resources, an apportionment being made by the General Assembly, with the addition of voluntary contributions from some govts. – to the funds of the U.N. which finance the programme of assistance carried out by the U.N., intergovernmental agencies, the U.N. Children's Fund (UNICEF), the U.N. refugee organizations, and the U.N. Special Fund for undeveloped countries.

The preponderance of influence in the U.N., originally with the Allied States of the S.W.W., is now more widely spread. Although part of the value of the U.N. lies in recognition of member states as sovereign and equal, the rapid increase in membership of minor —in some cases minute—states was causing concern by 1972 (132 members) as lessening the weight of voting decisions. Taiwan (Nationalist China), formerly a permanent member of the Security Council, was expelled 1971 on the admission of Communist China. The U.N. also suffers from the lack of adequate and independent funds and forces, and the intrusion of the Cold War which divides members into adherents of the E. or W. and the uncommitted.

UNITED PROVINCES OF AGRA AND OUDH. Prov. of British India which formed the major part of the state of Uttar Pradesh

UNITED STATES OF AMERICA (U.S.A.).

Federal republic in North America, extending from the Atlantic to the Pacific and from Canada to Mexico, plus the outlying states of Alaska and Hawaii.

Physical. The U.S.A. proper, occupying the central part of the N. American land mass, is about 2,700 m. long from E. to W., and has a greatest width from N. to S. of about 1,600 m. The surface consists of vast central plains, bounded by great mountain ranges, the Rockies in the W. and the Appalachians in the E. To the E. of the Appalachians are the Atlantic coast lowlands. W. of the Appalachians is the 'Central Valley', extending from the Great Lakes to the Gulf of Mexico and taking up about half the entire area of the country; here are the Prairies and the Great Plains, constituting one of the most important agricultural areas on the globe. The only considerable exception to its level uniformity is the Ozark mts. in Arkansas and Oklahoma. W. of the plains rises the great system of mountains, to the E. the Rockies, to the W. the Sierra Nevada and the Cascade mts. and Coast ranges, with a great plateau, much of it desert, in between. The highest point in the U.S.A. (and in N. America) is Mt. McKinley (20,270 ft.) in Alaska; the lowest, Death Valley (280 ft. below sea-level) in Calif. Mt. Whitney, Calif., reaches 14,495 ft.; Mt. Elbert, Col., highest point in the Rockies, 14,420 ft. In the W. is a narrow, fertile strip bordering the Pacific. The main river system is the Missouri-Mississippi basin, flowing through the central plains; the chief rivers flowing into the Pacific are the Columbia (which rises in Canada) in the N. and the Colorado in the S. The many rivers of the Atlantic slope are comparatively short, though of great importance. In the N. are the Great Lakes, of which Michigan is wholly in the U.S.A., the others being partly in Canada; there are many smaller lakes.

CLIMATE. In the centre and the mountains of the Cordillera (Rockies, Sierra Nevada, etc.) the climate is one of extreme cold and heat. The Pacific coastal area has a more uniform climate than the Atlantic seaboard, where the winters are severe. California is renowned for its geniality. Tropical conditions prevail in the S. states. In the E. rainfall is abundant, and conditions for urban and agricultural life are excellent. The Plains are liable to drought, and areas in the mtns. and plateaux are almost rainless.

REGIONS. There are traditionally some ten great regions. (1) New England, the historic core of the Union. Maine, Vermont, New Hampshire, Massachusetts, Rhode Island, and Connecticut cover most of the area of original settlement, and are today one of the chief centres of population and industry. (2) New York, the 'Empire State', has nearly 10 per cent of the pop. and about a quarter of the country's wealth. (3) The Middle Atlantic States consist of Pennsylvania, New Jersey, and Delaware, and include the vast coal, iron and steel area of Pittsburgh as well as much farm land. (4) The Middle West is the industrial centre, and the most typically American; it includes Ohio, Indiana, Illinois, Michigan, and Wisconsin; agriculture is important, but more so are the industries based on the iron-ore of Michigan. (5) The Prairie States (Minnesota, Iowa, N. Dakota, S. Dakota, Nebraska, and Kansas) are one huge granary, producing spring wheat in the N. and winter wheat or maize farther south. (6) The Mountain States (Montana, Wyoming, Colorado, New Mexico, Utah, Arizona, Nevada, and Idaho) comprise the pastureland to the E. of the Rockies, the Rockies with sheep and cattle ranches and mineral mines, and the desert region on the plateaux. (7) The Pacific States, California, famed for fruit and films, Oregon, Washington, Alaska and Hawaii. (8) The South consists of Virginia, N. Carolina, S. Carolina, Georgia, Alabama, Mississippi, Louisiana, and Florida. Tobacco, rice, and cotton are the chief crops. (9) The S.W. contains Texas and

PRESIDENTS OF U.S.A.

	Name	Party	Inaugurated
1.	George Washington	Federalist	1789
2.	John Adams	,,	1797
3.	Thomas Jefferson	Democrat Rep.	1801
4.	James Madison	,,	1809
5.	James Monroe	,, ,,	1817
6.	John Quincy Adams	,, ,,	1825
7.	Andrew Jackson	Democrat	1829
8.	Martin Van Buren	,,	1837
9.	William Henry Harrison	Whig	1841
10.	John Tyler		1841
11.	James Knox Polk	Democrat	1845
12.	Zachary Taylor	Whig	1849
13.	Millard Fillmore	,,	1850
14.	Franklin Pierce	Democrat	1853
15.	James Buchanan	,,	1857
16.	Abraham Lincoln	Republican	1861
17.	Andrew Johnson	Democrat	1865
18.	Ulysses Simpson Grant	Republican	1869
19.	Rutherford Birchard Hayes	,,	1877
20.	James Abram Garfield	,,	1881
21.	Chester Alan Arthur	,,	1881
22.	Grover Cleveland	Democrat	1885
23.	Benjamin Harrison	Republican	1889
24.	Grover Cleveland	Democrat	1893
25.	William McKinley	Republican	1897
26.	Theodore Roosevelt	,,	1901
27.	William Howard Taft	,,	1909
28.	Woodrow Wilson	Democrat	1913
29.	Warren Gamaliel Harding	Republican	1921
30.	Calvin Coolidge	,,	1923
31.	Herbert C. Hoover	,,	1929
32.	Franklin Delano Roosevelt	Democrat	1933
33.	Harry S. Truman	,,	1945
34.	Dwight D. Eisenhower	Republican	1953
35.	John F. Kennedy	Democrat	1961
36.	Lyndon B. Johnson	,,	1963
37.	Richard M. Nixon	Republican	1969

Oklahoma, home of the cowboy, but nowadays more remarkable for its vast output of petroleum. (10) The Border States (i.e. states separating different economic areas): Maryland, West Virginia, Arkansas, Kentucky, Tennessee, Missouri. Modifying these divisions are new industries divorced from local resources, new mineral discoveries, the rapid industrialisation of the South, and the pop. attraction of sunshine, California in the 1950s and Florida in the 1960s.

Government. The U.S.A. comprises 50 states, and the District of Columbia. Each state is self-governing in local matters, but confides to the central government at Washington the control of foreign affairs and the army and navy. Police, education, public health, etc. remain within the scope of the individual states, but since the Roosevelt 'New Deal' in the 1930s the federal govt. has concerned itself with social provisions of one kind and another. The cap. is Washington, D.C., which belongs to no state, being administered directly by the Federal govt. Executive power is vested in the President, elected by popular vote every 4 years, and by the 22nd amendment (1951) eligible to stand for 2 terms only; he chooses the members of the Cabinet, who may not be (as in Britain) members of the legislature. Legislative power is vested in Congress, composed of 2 houses: the Senate, with 2 members from each state, elected to serve 6 years, one-third re-elected every 2 years; and the House of Representatives of 435 members, distributed according to pop. among the states, and elected for 2 years. For U.S.A. territories, see Table page 1060.

POPULATION. The original settlers in New England and Virginia were mainly of British stock, but immigration over the past 150 years has made the U.S.A. the world's melting-pot of races. In 1970 the Negroes (descendants of Africans imported as slaves) numbered 22,700,000; the (Red) Indian pop. 791,800. The largest religious denomination is the Roman Catholic, followed by Baptists and Methodists. There were 5½ million professing Jews in 1960.

History. Spaniards made (in Florida), in 1565, the first white settlements in what became the U.S.A. The first English settlement was at Jamestown, Virginia, in 1607. In 1620 the 'Pilgrim Fathers' landed at Plymouth, and eventually founded Massachusetts. English R.Cs. founded Maryland in 1634, English Quakers founded Pennsylvania in 1682. A Dutch settlement (1611) on Manhattan Is., named New Amsterdam 1626, was re-named New York after it was taken by the English in 1664. Throughout most of the 18th cent. the English colonies were threatened by French expansion from the Great Lakes in Canada to Louisiana, but the threat from the French ended with the Seven Years War (1756–63). In 1775 the 13 colonies (N.H., Mass., R.I., Conn., N.Y., N.J., Pa., Del., Va., N.C., S.C., Md., and Ga.) rose against the home govt., declaring themselves in 1776 to be 'free and independent states'. Led by George Washington, they defeated George III's armies in the War of American Independence (called by U.S. citizens the War of the Revolution). By the Treaty of Paris, 1783, Britain recognized the independence of the 13 colonies. A constitution drawn up in 1787 came into force in 1789 and, with amendments, remains in force. Washington was chosen first pres. In 1803 Louisiana (q.v.) was bought from Napoleon and in 1819 Florida from Spain. In 1812–14 a war was fought with England because of commercial disputes arising out of the conflict with Napoleon in Europe, and the British captured and burnt Washington. Later expansion westward carried the terrs. of the U.S.A. to the Pacific and the war with Mexico, 1846–8, secured from that country the vast lands eventually organized as (U.S.) California, Utah, New Mexico, and Texas. Alaska was purchased from Russia in 1867. *See* also HAWAII.

In 1861–5 was fought the Civil War, or the War between the States, between 11 of the Southern States (S.C., Miss., Fla., Ala., Ga., La., Tex., joined later by Va., Ark., Tenn., and N.C.), the Confederate States,

UNITED STATES. In 1585 Raleigh (q.v.) sent out 108 colonists from Plymouth to America under the command of his cousin, Sir Richard Grenville. Round the strongpoint now known as 'Fort Raleigh' (seen restored above) the first English settlement was established, at the north end of Roanoke Island, North Carolina, but in 1586 Drake took the dissatisfied survivors back to England.
Courtesy of U.S. National Park Service.

which wished to maintain their 'states' rights', in particular the peculiar institution of Negro slavery, and claimed the right to secede from the Union; and the Northern or Federal States which fought to maintain the Union. The Confederate States chose Jefferson Davis as President; the leader of the North was President Lincoln. For 4 years the conflict went on. At first the Confederates were successful under Lee at the battles

UNITED STATES OF AMERICA

State with date of admission to Union	Area	Pop. (1970 census)	Capital
Alabama (1819)	51,609	3,444,165	Montgomery
Alaska (1959)	586,400	302,173	Juneau
Arizona (1912)	113,909	1,772,482	Phoenix
Arkansas (1836)	53,104	1,923,295	Little Rock
California (1850)	158,693	19,953,134	Sacramento
Colorado (1876)	104,247	2,207,259	Denver
Connecticut (1788)	5,009	3,032,217	Hartford
Delaware (1787)	2,057	548,104	Dover
Florida (1845)	58,560	6,789,443	Tallahassee
Georgia (1788)	58,876	4,589,575	Atlanta
Hawaii (1959)	6,423	769,913	Honolulu
Idaho (1890)	83,557	713,008	Boise
Illinois (1818)	56,400	11,113,976	Springfield
Indiana (1816)	36,291	5,193,669	Indianapolis
Iowa (1846)	56,290	2,825,041	Des Moines
Kansas (1861)	82,276	2,249,071	Topeka
Kentucky (1792)	40,395	3,219,311	Frankfort
Louisiana (1812)	48,523	3,643,180	Baton Rouge
Maine (1820)	33,215	993,663	Augusta
Maryland (1788)	10,577	3,922,399	Annapolis
Massachusetts (1788)	8,257	5,689,170	Boston
Michigan (1837)	58,216	8,875,083	Lansing
Minnesota (1858)	84,068	3,805,069	St. Paul
Mississippi (1817)	47,716	2,216,912	Jackson
Missouri (1821)	69,674	4,677,399	Jefferson City
Montana (1889)	141,138	694,409	Helena
Nebraska (1867)	77,227	1,483,791	Lincoln
Nevada (1864)	110,540	488,738	Carson City
New Hampshire (1788)	9,304	737,681	Concord
New Jersey (1787)	7,836	7,168,164	Trenton
New Mexico (1912)	121,666	1,016,000	Sante Fé
New York (1788)	49,576	18,190,740	Albany
North Carolina (1789)	52,712	5,082,059	Raleigh
North Dakota (1889)	70,665	617,761	Bismarck
Ohio (1803)	41,222	10,652,017	Columbus
Oklahoma (1907)	69,919	2,559,253	Oklahoma City
Oregon (1859)	96,981	2,019,385	Salem
Pennsylvania (1787)	45,333	11,793,909	Harrisburg
Rhode Island (1790)	1,214	949,723	Providence
South Carolina (1788)	31,055	2,590,516	Columbia
South Dakota (1889)	77,047	666,257	Pierre
Tennessee (1796)	42,244	3,924,164	Nashville
Texas (1845)	267,339	11,196,730	Austin
Utah (1896)	84,916	1,059,273	Salt Lake City
Vermont (1791)	9,609	444,732	Montpelier
Virginia (1788)	40,815	4,648,494	Richmond
Washington (1889)	68,192	3,409,169	Olympia
West Virginia (1863)	24,181	1,744,237	Charleston
Wisconsin (1848)	56,154	4,417,933	Madison
Wyoming (1890)	97,914	332,416	Cheyenne
District of Columbia	69	756,510	
	3,615,210†	204,765,770	
Dependencies**			
Panama Canal Zone	553	42,122	Balboa Heights
Puerto Rico	3,435	2,349,544	San Juan
Virgin Islands	135	32,099	Charlotte Amalie
American Samoa	76	20,051	Pago Pago
Guam	206	67,044	Agaña
	3,619,615	207,276,630	

*Non-white 20,491,443.   **1960 census.
†Does not include the part of the Great Lakes in U.S.A. (60,760 sq. m.), but does include other inland water.

of Bull Run (1861 and 1862), but Lee suffered a repulse at Gettysburg in 1863; Grant overran the Mississippi states and Sherman marched through Georgia to the sea. On 9 April 1865, Lee surrendered to Grant at Appomattox Court House.

THOMAS JEFFERSON.
Author of the Declaration of Independence.
Courtesy of USIS

and a month later the war was over. Casualties on both sides incl. *c.* 600,000 dead. Slavery was ended, but the war, and in particular its aftermath when the S. was occupied by the N. as if it had been a foreign conquered country, left behind bitterness that had not entirely evaporated a hundred years later.

The war had immensely stimulated the industrial development of the N. and had led to the construction of roads and railways. With its end, a great outburst of economic activity began. The country's vast natural resources were exploited. Thousands more miles of railway were laid. The prairies were peopled. Americans referred with pride to 'God's own country', and extolled the virtues of private enterprise. Occasional depressions broke the tide of prosperity, but progress was vast and rapid until 1929 when the greatest of slumps engulfed America. When F. D. Roosevelt became President in 1933 he embarked on a 'New Deal' which broke with American tradition.

The U.S.A. had come into the F.W.W. in 1917, and a majority of the Senate voted for the Treaty of Versailles (which incl. Pres. Wilson's League of Nations), but not the two-thirds majority required by the Constitution for the making of a treaty, and a period of isolationism followed. Peace was made with the Central Powers by separate treaties in 1921. Brought into the S.W.W. by the Japanese attack on Pearl Harbor in 1941, the U.S.A. played a major part in the winning of that war, and in the peace-making (*see* MARSHALL, G. C.). Direct military action on behalf of the U.N. was taken in Korea (q.v.), but resources were strained by Vietnam (q.v.) and continued overseas aid. Kennedy and Johnson had moved to alleviate poverty at home and the Negro problem, and with Nixon came greater stress on military withdrawal and elimination of internal disruption.

Art. The first American-born artist was the portraitist Robert Feke (*c.* 1705–50), but best-known of early masters is Benjamin West – working mainly in England – who encouraged the portraitist John Singleton Copley, and whose pupils incl. Gilbert Stuart, Thomas Sully, and Charles Willson Peale. To the 19th cent. belong the dramatic landscapes of Washington Allston, the nature pictures of Audubon, the seascapes of Winslow Homer, the realism of Thomas Eakins, and the romantic landscapes of the Hudson River school, e.g. English-born Thomas Cole (1801–48) and later George Inness (1825–94). Appreciated abroad were the markedly individual gifts of Whistler, Mary Cassat and John Singer Sargent towards the end of the cent., and the mysticism of the recluse Albert Pinkham Ryder (1847–1917). Notable in the early 20th cent. was the Ashcan school, so nicknamed because of its concern with slum squalor e.g. George B. Luks (1867–1933) which influenced the work of George W. Bellows (1882–1925) and Rockwell Kent. A pioneer of European movements such as Expressionism was Max Weber (1881–1961) and more recent artists who blend such influences in their work incl. John Marin; Grant Wood (1892–1942), whose realistic American Gothic was the sensation of the 1930s; the Mexican Diego Rivera, who worked

in the States; Lyonel Feininger; the apostle of Action painting, Jackson Pollock; and the politically concerned Ben Shahn. In sculpture the best-known names incl. Hiram Powers (1805–73), Horatio Greenough (1805–52), Thomas Crawford (1814–57), Augustus St. Gaudens, Lorado Taft (1860–1936), George Grey Barnard (1863–1938), Gutzon Borglum, Carl Milles, Lipchitz, Archipenko, and Calder, inventor of mobiles.

Architecture. Early influences derived from England, e.g. early buildings at Harvard and William and Mary resemble Oxford and Cambridge; the Georgian-type houses of Virginia and Pennsylvania; and the churches in the style of Wren. The purely classic phase was introduced by Thomas Jefferson towards the end of the 18th cent., e.g. the Federal Capitol at Washington by William Thornton (1761–1828). After the Civil War came a generation of French-trained architects, e.g. H. H. Richardson, chief exponent of a modified Romanesque. A revival of 'Queen Anne' style followed, and then towards the end of the 19th cent. a 2nd classical revival, e.g. Columbia Univ., N.Y. and Pennsylvania Terminal Station. Most characteristic of the U.S. is the skyscraper (the word was 1st used in 1891) which owed its origin to the development of a method of building in which walls are carried on a framework of steel combined with the high cost of land in city centres. The most individual of modern U.S. architects was Frank Lloyd Wright, but impressive work has also been produced by Richard Buckminster Fuller, Gropius and Van der Rohe, successive directors of the Bauhaus, the Saarinens (father and son), and Richard Neutra. *See* illus. pp. 57, 908, 1058, 1073.

Literature. American literature of the colonial period (1607–1765) includes travel books and religious verse, but was mainly theological: Roger Williams, Cotton Mather, and Jonathan Edwards were typical Puritan writers. Franklin's *Autobiography* is the first work of more than historical interest. The revolutionary period (1765–1800) produced much political writing, e.g. by Paine, Jefferson, and Hamilton, and one noteworthy poet, Philip Freneau. In the early 19th cent. the influence of the English Romantics became evident, notably in Washington Irving's tales and Fenimore Cooper's novels of Redskin life.

During 1830–60 intellectual life centred on New England, which produced the essayists Emerson,

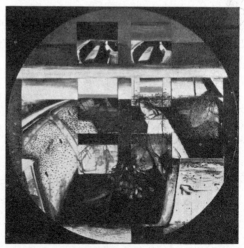

UNITED STATES ART. 'November 22nd' by Edward Giobbi was inspired by the assassination of President Kennedy. *Courtesy of the Trustees of the Tate Gallery, London.*

Thoreau, and Holmes; the poets Bryant, Longfellow, Lowell, and Whittier; the historians Parkman, Prescott, and Motley; and the novelist Hawthorne. Outside the New England circle stood Poe, Melville, and Whitman.

The disillusionment of the post-Civil War period (1865–1900) found expression in the realistic or psychological novel. Ambrose Bierce and Stephen Crane wrote realistic war stories; Mark Twain and Bret Harte dealt with western life; and the growth of industrialism led to the rise of the sociological novel, notably in the work of W. D. Howells, while Henry James, and his disciple Edith Wharton, developed the novel of psychological analysis. A major poet of this period was Emily Dickinson.

WALT WHITMAN
Courtesy of Walt Whitman House.

Since 1900 the main trend in the novel has been realistic, and American writers have exerted a growing influence in Europe, e.g. Jack London, Upton Sinclair, and Theodore Dreiser, and after the F.W.W. by Sherwood Anderson, Sinclair Lewis, and Ernest Hemingway; the southern writers Erskine Caldwell and William Faulkner; and the proletarian James T. Farrell, John Dos Passos, and John Steinbeck. Aside from the main tradition is the romantic or subjective fiction of Thornton Wilder, J. B. Cabell, and Henry Miller. Among the more important writers emerging since the S.W.W. are Truman Capote, J. D. Salinger, John Updike, Norman Mailer, Nelson Algren, Saul Bellow, Bernard Malamud and Jack Kerouac, apostle of the Beat generation. The short story has attracted many of the major novelists from James onward, and was popularized as a form by O. Henry; writers specializing in it incl. Ring Lardner, Katharine Anne Porter, William Saroyan, and James Thurber.

In drama the U.S.A. produced a powerful group of dramatists between the wars, incl. Eugene O'Neill, Maxwell Anderson, Elmer Rice and Clifford Odets; and the work of Wilder led towards the post-war work of Tennessee Williams and Arthur Miller, and the younger generation of which Edward Albee is representative. Traditional poets

JOHN UPDIKE
Courtesy of Andre Deutsch.

incl. E. A. Robinson, R. Frost, Elinor Wylie, E. St. Vincent Millay, with more experimental work being done by E. L. Masters, Carl Sandburg, Ezra Pound, T. S. Eliot and Amy Lowell, and attempts at the great American epic in Hart Crane's *The Bridge* and S. V. Benet's *John Brown's Body*. Among the most striking of later writers are Conrad Aiken, Archibald MacLeish, Karl Shapiro, Robinson Jeffers, Wallace Stevens, Marianne Moore, Robert Lowell, and Theodore Roethke (1908–63). In the field of literary criticism Irving Babbitt, George Santayana, H. L. Mencken and Edmund Wilson did useful work; more recent names incl. Cleanth Brooks and Lionel Trilling.

UNIVERSE. The overall celestial system, containing thousands of millions of star-systems or *galaxies*. Each galaxy is composed of thousands of millions of stars, together with interstellar material. It may be assumed that our own Galaxy is typical, and that our Sun is an average star. It has been found that galaxies tend to congregate in groups, and that each group is receding from each other group, so that the whole universe is expanding. The distances involved are, of course, very great, and modern techniques can probe out to approximately 5,000 million light-years.

The origin of the universe is still a matter for debate. On the various 'evolutionary' theories, all matter was created at one moment, in the remote past: the universe is evolving, and will eventually die. According to the 'steady-state' theory, supported by H. Bondi and others, the universe has always existed, and will exist for ever; as old galaxies die, new ones are formed out of matter which is being steadily created out of nothingness. In 1966 R. H. Dicke of Princeton Univ. envisaged a 'pulsating' U., without beginning or end, but alternately contracting and expanding.

UNIVERSITY. A community or corporation of men and women devoted to higher learning. The first European university was Salerno (9th cent.), followed by Bologna, Paris, Oxford, and Cambridge in the 12th cent. St. Andrews, the first Scottish U., was founded in 1411, and Trinity Coll., Dublin, in 1591. London U. dates from 1836, Manchester from 1851, the U. of Wales from 1893. The oldest Us. in U.S.A. are: Harvard (1636), William and Mary (1693), Yale (1701), and Princeton (1746). Recent innovations incl. Us. serving international areas, e.g. the Middle East Technical U. (1961) at Ankara, supported by the U.N., and the British Open U. (1969) combining correspondence packages, radio, television and brief residence periods for young and old excl. from conventional Us. by pressure on resources.

UNKNOWN WARRIOR. Name given to a fallen soldier who was taken as representative of all those killed in the F.W.W., and was given a national funeral. The British U.W. or Soldier was buried in Westminster Abbey in 1920. France, Belgium, U.S.A., and other countries each have their U.Ws.

UNRUH, Fritz von (1885–). German dramatist, novelist, and poet. Resigning his commission in the Prussian Guards in 1912, he wrote anti-militaristic plays. *Opfergang* (1916: *The Way of Sacrifice*) describes the battle of Verdun. A leading Expressionist, he lived in France and the U.S.A. 1933–52: later books incl. *Der nie verlor* (1945: *The End is Not Yet*).

UNTOUCHABLES. See CASTE.

UPANISHADS. The most spiritual division of the Vedic texts which form the scriptures of Hinduism. They number nearly 200.

UPAS TREE. A tree (*Antiaris toxicaria*) of the fig family, whose gum is very poisonous and was used by the E. Indian natives to tip their arrows.

UPDIKE, John (1932–). American author. Ed. at Harvard and the Ruskin School of Drawing and Fine Art at Oxford, he was on the *New Yorker* staff 1955–7, and besides the novels (*Rabbit, Run*, 1961, *Couples*, 1968, etc.) and short stories (*The Same Door*, 1962 and *Pigeon Feathers*, 1963) which have estab. his reputation for polished overtones, has written poetry, e.g. *Telephone Poles* (1964).

UPPER VOLTA. See VOLTAIC REPUBLIC.

UPPSALA (up′sah′la). Swedish city, 40 m. W.N.W. of Stockholm, with a univ. (1477) and a 13th cent. cathedral long used in the crowning of kings of

UPAS TREE

Sweden; Linnaeus, who lived at U., is commemorated in the cathedral. U. is the seat of the Lutheran primate of Sweden. Pop. (1966) 94,587.

UR. Ancient city of Mesopotamia, the Ur of the Chaldees of the Bible; *c.* 140 m. S.E. of Babylon and 6 m. from the Euphrates. Excavations by Sir Leonard Woolley show that it was inhabited 3,500 B.C. Chief ruin is a ziggurat or temple tower.

URAE′MIA. Condition due to the retention in the blood of substances usually eliminated by the kidneys.

U′RALS. Mountain system running from the Arctic to the Caspian Sea and separating Europe from Asia. The highest peak is Naradnaya (6,182 ft.). The middle Urals is one of the most important industrial regions of the U.S.S.R., owing to its vast mineral wealth. Perm, Chelyabinsk, Sverdlovsk, Magnitogorsk and Zlatoust are important industrial centres.

URA′NIUM. Lustrous white metal, malleable and ductile, tarnishing in air: symbol U, at. wt. 238·07, at. no. 92. It was discovered by Klaproth in 1789 in pitchblende and first prepared by Peligot in 1842. The chief ore is uranite (pitchblende U_3O_8), and recent technological advances have made possible its extraction from low-grade ores. Small amounts of its compounds are used in the ceramics industry to give yellow glazes, and as a mordant in dyeing.

U. isotopes have been of vital importance in the production of atomic energy. Although U-238 is most abundant (99 per cent), U-235 is the only naturally occurring readily fissible isotope (1 part in 140) and U-233 is a fissile material that can be produced by the neutron irradiation of thorium-232.

URANIUM. Before leaving the mill each drum of uranium concentrate, known as 'yellow cake' because of its bright colour, is sampled and analysed to provide the user with a precise record of the oxide content. Wearing a protective mask and gloves, this worker at Rio Algom's Nordic mill in Ontario, prepares a sample.
Courtesy of the Rio Algom Mines Ltd.

U′RANUS. In Gk. mythology, the sky-god, responsible for rain and warming sun. He was the husband of Ge and father of Cronus and the Titans.

URANUS. The seventh planet of the Solar System. It is 1,783,000,000 miles from the Sun, and has a revolution period of 84 years. Though it is a giant, with a diameter of 29,300 miles, it is barely visible to the naked eye, and was not known in ancient times: it was discovered by W. Herschel in 1781. In constitution it seems to be similar to the larger giants, Jupiter and Saturn. It has 5 satellites, named Miranda, Ariel, Umbriel, Titania and Oberon.

URBAN II. Pope 1088–99; he launched the 1st Crusade at Clermont in 1095.

URDU (oor′doo). Indian language, a variety of Hindustani that has borrowed largely from Persian and Arabic and is spoken mostly by Moslems.

U′REA. A crystalline substance found in urine and the other body fluids. It is the chief material by means of which the body excretes waste nitrogen. Produced synthetically, it forms a valuable nitrogenous fertilizer, and is used in the production of drugs, explosives, etc.

UREY (u′rē), **Harold Clayton** (1893–). American chemist. In 1932 he isolated heavy water and discovered deuterium (q.v.), receiving a Nobel prize in 1934; and was director of the War Research Atomic Bomb Project, Columbia, 1940–5. In 1958 he became prof. of chemistry-at-large, Univ. of California, and his books incl. studies of nuclear and atomic structure, and the origin of the planets.

URFÉ (ürf′ā), **Honoré d'** (1568–1625). French writer. B. at Marseilles, he is remembered for his romantic novel *Astrée* (1610), with incidents based on the life of Henry IV, which set a vogue. He was killed by a fall from his horse on military service against Spain.

URGA. Another name for ULAN BATOR.

URIAL (oo′rial). The wild sheep (*Ovis vignei*), about 3 ft. high, of the Himalayan countries.

URIAL

U′RIC ACID. A substance formed from the breakdown of food and body protein. It is a normal constituent of urine, but if formed in excess and not excreted it is deposited in sharp crystals in the joints and other tissues, causing symptoms of gout; or it may form stones in the kidneys or bladder (calculi).

U′RIM and **THU′MMIM.** Two mysterious objects in the breastplate of the High Priest of the ancient Hebrews, whereby they exercised divination.

U′RINE. An amber-coloured fluid made by the kidneys from the blood. It contains excess water, salts, protein, waste products, a pigment and some acid. The kidneys pass it through 2 fine tubes (ureters) to the bladder, which may act as a reservoir for up to 20 oz. at a time. It then passes into the urethra, which opens to the outside by a sphincter (constricting) muscle under voluntary control.

URSA MAJOR and **MINOR.** The Great and the Little Bear; 2 constellations of the N. hemisphere. The former consists of 7 bright stars, and a line joining the 2 outermost (the pointers), if produced, passes close to the Pole Star (q.v.) which is in U. Minor.

URSULA, St. A British virgin saint and martyr supposed to have been martyred with her maidens by the Huns in the Rhineland, in 238 or about 451.

U′RSULINES. A R.C. religious order founded at Brescia, by St. Angela Merici in 1537, and renowned for its educational work among girls.

URUGUAY (oorugwī). Smallest of the South American republics, lying between Brazil and the estuary of the River Plate, and separated from Argentina by the r. Uruguay. The chief river is the Negro. Hilly in the N., U. is mainly an extension of the Pampas, and cattle-breeding and sheep-farming are the chief occupations, wool, leather, and meat (incl. canned meat) being the chief exports. The cap. is Montevideo; other towns are Salto, Paysandu, and Rivera. U. is divided admin. into 19 depts. Area 72,180 sq. m.; pop. (1967) 2,783,000.

Spanish is the official language, and Roman Catholicism the prevailing religion. Under the constitution of 1967 a presidential regime was reintroduced, executive power being placed in the hands of a pres. and vice-pres. elected for 5 yrs.: congress comprises an elected senate of 30, plus the vice-pres., and a house of deputies. In recent years U. has suffered chronic inflation and social unrest: *see* TUPAC AMARU.

The oldest town in U. is Colonia, founded by the Portuguese in 1680; the Spanish founded Montevideo in 1726, captured Colonia 1777 and secured authority over the area now forming U. In 1814 Spanish rule was thrown off under the leadership of José Artigas who ruled as a dictator until driven out by Brazil in 1820. From 1825–8 Argentina and Brazil fought to secure the area, declared independent 1828; but it was 1853 before its independence was recognized by its neighbours.

URUMCHI (oorumchē'). Cap. of Sinkiang-Uighur autonomous region, China. At the N. foot of the Tien-Shan, it is close to a coalfield and makes cotton textiles. cement, chemicals, iron and steel goods, etc. Pop. (1967) 180,000.

URUNDI. *See* BURUNDI.

USHANT. French island 11 m. W. of Brittany off which Howe defeated the French, 1794 ('the glorious First of June').

USKÜB. Turkish name of SKOPJE.

USKÜDAR. Suburb of Istanbul, Turkey, formerly a separate town which became well known under the form Scutari as the site of the hospital set up by Florence Nightingale in the Crimean War.

USSHER, James (1581–1656). Irish churchman. B. in Dublin, he became archbp. of Armagh in 1625, but after 1641 was forced by the Irish rebellion to live in England. He devised the system of chronology still printed in some Bibles.

U.S.S.R. Abbreviation for the Union of Soviet Socialist Republics. *See* SOVIET UNION.

USSU'RI RIVER. Tributary of the Amur, rising N. of Vladivostock, which joins it S. of Khabarovsk, and forms part of the border between the Chinese prov. of Heilungkiang and the U.S.S.R. There were military clashes 1968–9 over the sovereignty of Damansky Is. (Chenpao) in mid-river.

USTINOV (oost'inof), **Peter** (1921–). British actor-dramatist. B. in London, he has ventured into almost every aspect of film and theatre life. His plays incl. *House of Regrets* (1942) and *The Love of Four Colonels* (1951), in which latter he appeared, and he was author, director, producer and principal actor in the film *Private Angelo* (1949). In 1963 he became joint director of the Nottingham Playhouse.

UST-KAMENOGORSK. Chief centre of the atomic industry in the U.S.S.R. in the Altai Mtns. Pop. (1967) 207,000.

UTAGAWA, Kuniyoshi (1798–1861). Japanese artist of the Ukiyoye or Popular school of painting and print designing. He produced some 8–10,000 prints concerning figures of history and legend, and was in trouble for lampooning the govt. His studies of cats are excellent.

UTAH (ū'taw). A Rocky Mountain state of U.S.A. In the W. is the Great Basin which incl. the Great Salt Lake and the Great American Desert. E. of the Wasatch range lies the plateau at *c.* 10,000 ft., deeply dissected by the Colorado river system. Only about 2·5 per cent of the land is under crops (wheat, oats, alfalfa, sugar beet, etc.), and most of that is made productive by artificial irrigation; cattle and sheep are raised, wool being important. Minerals incl. gold, silver, uranium, coal, and salt; steel is among manufactures. Salt Lake City is the cap., Ogden the only other large town. Area 84,916 sq. m.; pop. (1970) 1,059,273.

U. is part of the area ceded by Mexico in 1848; it was colonized and developed by the Mormons (Latter-day Saints) who first entered Salt Lake valley in 1847, and remain the largest religious body in the state. Organized as a terr. 1850, it was not admitted to the Union as a state until 1896 because of the long refusal of the Mormons to give up plural marriage.

UTAMARO, Kitagawa (1753–1806). Japanese artist, famed for his designs of colour-prints.

U'TICA. City in N. York state, U.S.A., cap. of Oneida co. on Mohawk r. Incorporated as a village 1798, a city 1836, U. makes textiles, firearms, etc. The pop. (100;410 in 1960) incl. a large Welsh group who hold an annual eisteddfod.

UTILITARIANISM. *See* BENTHAM, J.

UTŌ'PIA (Gk., nowhere). Name given by Sir Thomas More to the imaginary commonwealth described in his *Utopia* (1516), and hence applied to similar dream-countries of other writers, e.g. Plato's *Republic*, Bacon's *Atlantis*, and Campanella's *City of the Sun. See also* WELLS, H. G.

UTRECHT (ū'trekt). Capital of U. province, Netherlands, on the Kromme Rijn (crooked Rhine) 22 m. S.E. of Amsterdam. Dating from Roman times, U. is the seat of a univ. (1636) and of a R.C. and an Old Catholic archbishopric. The 14th cent. cathedral tower has stood isolated since the nave was blown down in 1674. Textiles. carpets, motor-cars, chemicals pottery are among U.'s products. Pop. (1967) 274,485. The Peace of U. in 1713 concluded the War of the Spanish Succession.

UTRILLO (ootrēl'yō), **Maurice** (1883–1955). French artist. Son of a trapeze-performer who became

UTRILLO. A corner of Montmartre takes on new magic.
Courtesy of the Trustees of the Tate Gallery.

an artist's model after she suffered a fall, and later an artist herself, he was born following an assault on her by a drunken man, and was himself a drug addict and dipsomaniac from an early age. He is most celebrated for his townscapes of his native Paris, especially Montmartre, often painted from postcard photographs, but intensely and individually realized, e.g. 'Au Lapin Agile', 'Moulin de la Galette', and 'Nôtre-Dame de Paris'.

UTTAR PRADESH. State of the Republic of India formed in 1950 from the United Prov. of Agra and Oudh and neighbouring small princely states. It lies in central N. India and comprises the upper plain of the Ganges. Agriculture, helped in the W. by artificial irrigation, is the main occupation. Lucknow is the capital, Kanpur the largest city, followed by Agra, Varanesi, Allahabad, Bareilly, and Meerut. Area 113,654 sq. m.; pop. (1961) 73,746,401.

UZBEK S.S.R. Constituent republics of the U.S.S.R. in central Asia, lying between Kazakh S.S.R. to the N. and Turkmen S.S.R. to the S. Much of it is desert, but artificial irrigation is highly developed and more than 60 per cent of the Soviet Union's cotton is grown in U., as well as much rice and lucerne. A pipeline carries natural gas from U. to Chelyabinsk in the Urals. Tashkent is the cap.; it also incl. Bukhara, Samarkand, Khiva, and Kokand. About 60 per cent of the inhabitants are Uzbeks, a Turkic people; many are Sunni Mohammedans. Area 157,400 sq. m.; pop. (1967) 10,890,000.

V Twenty-second letter of the alphabet. It was not differentiated from U until about the 16th cent. In sound it is the voiced dentilabial spirant. In the Roman notation V equals 5.

VAAL (vahl). S. African river, the chief tributary of the Orange. It rises in the Drakensberg and for much of its course of *c.* 750 m. it separates Transvaal from Orange Free State. Harnessed to produce electric power, it joins with the coalfields alongside to make the valley the equivalent of the Ruhr.

VACCINATION. The insertion beneath the skin of a small quantity of lymph from a calf immune to cowpox, with a view to producing a general reaction by which the subject develops immunity to smallpox. The practice dates from an experiment by Edward Jenner (q.v.) in 1796. V. of children was compulsory in Britain 1853–1948, unless parents made a declaration of objection.

VACUUM (vak′u-um). Strictly speaking, a region completely empty of matter; in physics the term means any enclosure in which the gas pressure is considerably less than the atmospheric. The V. CLEANER was invented by the Scotsman Hubert Cecil Booth (1871–1955) who was prompted by seeing an American dust-blowing machine in 1901 to reverse the process and invent a device for the extraction of dust from carpets and upholstery by suction: his first machine was on wheels and operated from the street, tubes being taken into the house. V. FLASKS, originally known as Dewar vessels after Sir James Dewar, their inventor, are glass vessels with double walls, the space between which is a V.

VADUZ (vah′doots′). Capital of the European principality of Liechtenstein; pop. (1968) 4,000.

VAIHINGER (fī′inger), **Hans** (1852–1933). German philosopher, author of the *Philosophy of As If* (1911). He maintained that the human mind can never attain to certainty on ultimate issues, and that all knowledge must inevitably consist only of fictions and hypotheses.

VAISHNAVAS. A Hindu sect, chiefly in Bengal, founded by Chaitanya (q.v.) in the 16th cent.

VALDIVIA (vahldē′vē-ah). Chilean port, industrial town, and resort, cap. of V. prov. It has shipyards, tanneries, breweries, soap factories, etc. It was founded 1552 by Spanish conquistador Pedro de V. (*c.* 1500–54), conqueror of Chile. Pop. (1966) 73,000.

VALENCE (vahloṅs′) French town and river port on the Rhône, cap. of Drôme dept. It is of pre-Roman origin, and has a Romanesque cathedral consecrated 1095. Pop. (1968) 62,358.

VALENCIA (valen′sya). (1) Third city of Spain, cap. of V. prov., near the mouth of the Guadalaviar. It is the seat of an archbishopric and a univ. (1411). Pop. (1965) 584,670. (2) Cap. of Carabobo state, Venezuela, standing 1,568 ft. a.s.l. Founded 1555, V. is a tourist and trading centre and makes textiles, leather, sugar, etc. Pop. (1964) 204,270.

VALENCIENNES (vahloṅsyen′). French town in Nord dept. on the Escaut (Schelde) in the centre of a rich coalfield. It has many industries, and was formerly famous for its lace. It became French in 1678. Pop. (1968) 46,626.

VALENCY. In chemistry, a measure of the atom-binding capacity of the atoms in an element; or the number of atoms of hydrogen or of any other standard univalent element capable of uniting with one atom of the element. The elements are described as uni-, di-, tri, and tetra-valent when they unite with 1, 2, 3, and 4 univalent atoms respectively.

VALENTINE (d. 270). Christian saint and martyr, supposed to have perished at Rome. The custom of sending 'valentines' on 14 Feb., his festival, seems unconnected with the saint, deriving from the Roman Lupercalia, a festival celebrated in mid-Feb.

VALENTINO (valentē′nō), **Rudolf** (1895–1926). Italian film actor in U.S.A., who was famed for his

VALERIAN

'handsome lover' parts in *The Four Horsemen, The Sheik,* and *Blood and Sand.*

VALERA. See DE VALERA.

VALERA (vahlā′rah), **Juan** (1824–1905). Spanish novelist who was also a diplomat and politician. His romances include *Pepita Jiménez, El comendador Mendoza,* and *Doña Luz.*

VALE′RIAN. Genus of perennial plants found in temperate northern hemisphere. The root of common V. (*Valeriana officinalis*) is used medicinally as a carminative and sedative.

VALÉRY (vahlārē′), **Paul** (1871–1945). French poet. B. at Cette, he became a member of the circle of symbolists of which Mallarmé was the centre, but for many years abandoned poetry and turned to mathematics and philosophy. In 1917 he pub. the poem *La Jeune Parque,* followed by *Charmes, Le Cimetière Marin,* etc., and by critical studies and philosophical dialogues. V.'s poetry became of the greatest importance for its intellectual content.

VALHA′LLA. In Scandinavian mythology, the 'Hall of the Slain' in Odin's palace, to which were conducted the souls of those who fell in battle. At doomsday (Ragnarök) they will fight with Odin against the giants.

VALKYRIES (val′kirēz). In northern mythology, divine maidens who transport to Odin the souls of heroes who have died in battle.

VALLADOLID (vahl′ahdōlid′). Spanish city, cap. of V. prov. It has a cathedral (1595) and univ. (1346). It was cap. of Castile and Leon in the 14th–15th cents., then of Spain until 1560. Ferdinand and Isabella were married at V. (1469); Columbus died there. V. is a centre of agricultural trade. Pop. (1965) 181,765.

VALLE D'AOSTA (vahl′e dah-os′tah). Autonomous region in N.W. Italy; most of its inhabitants are French-speaking. Area 1,260 sq. m.; pop. (1961) 99,754.

VALLE-INCLÁN (vahl′yä ēnklahn′), **Ramón del** (1866–1936). Spanish writer. A brilliant stylist, he is remembered for his poetic prose *Sonatas* (1902–5), telling the story of the amorous marquis of Bradomín and *Tirano Banderas* (1926), a novel set in S. America.

VALLE′TTA. Cap. of Malta and port of call for Far Eastern liners. The former palace (16th cent.) of the Grand Master of the Knights Hospitallers is the

VALLETTA. The Grand Harbour.   *Courtesy of B.E.A.*

governor's residence. V., founded 1566, suffered severe damage from air bombardment during the S.W.W. Pop. (1967) 15,362.

VALLEY FORGE. Site some 20 m. N.W. of Philadelphia, U.S.A., where Washington's army spent the winter of 1777–8 in terrible hardship during the American War of Independence.

VALLEY OF TEN THOUSAND SMOKES. Valley in Alaska, U.S.A., where in 1912 the eruption of Mt. Katmai, one of the largest volcanic explosions ever known, took place, though without loss of life since the area was uninhabited. It was dedicated in 1918 as the Katmai Nat. Monument; the many fissures on the valley floor still emit steam jets.

VALMY (vahlmē'). French village in the Marne dept. where the army of the French Revolution under Dumouriez defeated the Prussians in 1792. Pop. (1962) 354.

VALOIS (vahlwah'). French family, originally counts of V. in the Oise dept., members of which occupied the French throne, 1328–1589.

VALONA. Italian form of VLONË.

VALPARAISO (vahlpahrī'zō). Second city of Chile, capital of V. prov., on the Pacific. It has many factories, and is the busiest commercial port on the W. coast of S. America. Founded in 1536, it was occupied by Drake 1578, by Hawkins 1595, pillaged by the Dutch 1600, bombarded by Spain 1866; it has also suffered much from earthquakes. Pop. (1966) 261,684.

VAMPIRE. In the demonology of the Slavonic peoples, a ghost or spirit who emerges from the grave at night and sucks the blood of sleeping men. The name was transferred to the V. bats of S. and Central America which suck the blood of sleeping cattle or human beings: the most common species is the Central American *Desmodus rufus*, about 3 in. long. The effect of their attacks has been much exaggerated.

VAN (vahn). Turkish city on Lake V., cap. of V. il. On a site that has been inhabited for more than 3,000 years, it was the scene of Armenian massacres 1895–6. It makes cotton textiles. Pop. (est.) 15,000.

VANADIUM (Scandinavian goddess Vanadis). Silver-white hard metal, discovered by Del Rio in 1801, and isolated by Roscoe in 1869: symbol V, at wt. 50·95, at. no. 23. It occurs in the rare minerals vanadinite and patronite, and its chief use is in alloying steel to which it imparts toughness, elasticity and tensile strength. V. compounds (vanadates) are used in the preparation of aniline black for colouring glass.

VAN ALLEN, James Alfred (1914–). American physicist, a pioneer in high-altitude research with rockets, and prof. of physics at the State Univ. of Iowa since 1951. In 1958, following examination of data obtained by 2 *Explorer* earth satellites, he discovered the V.A. belts (of particles from the sun trapped by the earth's field). These were 2 zones of intense radiation; one of altitude between 1,400–3,400 m., and the other between 8,000–12,000 m. In 1962 an American high altitude nuclear test resulted in the creation of a temporary artificial 'little' V.A. belt of trapped electrons, prejudicial to astrophysical and geophysical research and space flight.

VANBRUGH (van'bra), **Dame Irene** (1872–1949). British actress, *née* Barnes, whose roles incl. Gwendolen in *The Importance of Being Earnest* and Mary Lasenby in *The Admirable Crichton*. She m. in 1901 Dion Boucicault, Irish playwright and actor, and was created D.B.E. in 1941. She is commemorated by the *V. Theatre* at R.A.D.A. Her sister **Violet V.** (1867–1942) was also an accomplished actress.

VANBRUGH, Sir John (1664–1726). English dramatist and architect. B. in London, he designed Blenheim Palace and the 1st Haymarket Theatre, London. Of his many comedies the most notable are *The Relapse* (1696) and *The Provok'd Wife* (1697).

VAN BUREN, Martin (1782–1862). 8th President

of the U.S.A. Secretary of State (1829–31) and then Minister to England, he was elected President on the Democratic ticket in 1835 and held office until 1840.

VANCOUVER (vankōō'ver), **George** (c. 1758–98). British navigator. Entering the navy at 13, he accompanied Cook on his 2nd and 3rd voyages of discovery, and 1791–4 voyaged about the Pacific. He circumnavigated V. Island, which is named after him.

VANCOUVER. Canadian is. off the Pacific coast, part of Brit. Columbia, the cap. of which, Victoria, is sit. on V. Coal is mined and timber is produced; fishing is important. V. was first visited by Capt. Cook, 1778, and was surveyed, 1792, by Capt. George Vancouver, after whom it is named. Area 12,408 sq. m.

VANCOUVER. Third city of Canada and its chief Pacific seaport, on the mainland of Brit. Columbia, Pacific terminus of the Canadian Pacific rly.; it has an airport and is the seat of a univ. Industries incl. refining of petroleum brought by pipeline (1953) from Alberta, engineering, shipbuilding, aircraft, lumbering, fishing, textiles, pulp and paper. V. was founded 1825 by the Hudson's Bay Co. Pop. (1966) 410,375; Greater V. 892,286.

VANDALS. A Teutonic people akin to the Goths, who early in the 5th cent. A.D. moved from N. Germany to invade the Roman provinces in Gaul and Spain. Many settled in Andalusia (*Vandalitia*), and others moved on to N. Africa in 429. In the next cent. they acknowledged Roman overlordship.

VANDERBILT, Cornelius (1794–1877). American millionaire. B. at Staten Island, N.Y., he made his fortune in steamships and railways. His eldest son **William Henry V.** (1821–85) and grandson **Cornelius V.** (1843–99) expanded the family's businesses.

VAN DER POST, Laurens Jan (1906–). S. African writer. His books are concerned with the duality of man's existence, which is symbolized in Africa by the tension between black and white, Boer and Briton, city and veld, as in *Flamingo Feather* (1955), in which the hero is a Boer whose best friend is a Briton. Later books incl. studies of Russia (1967) and Japan (1968).

VAN DER WAALS (van dur wah'ls), **Johannes Diderik** (1837–1923). Dutch physicist. He made considerable contributions to physical properties of matter, especially intermolecular attractions, and the relation between the pressure and volume of a gas in the transition between liquid and gas phases. He received a Nobel prize in 1910. His *equation of state* $(P + \frac{a}{b})(v - b) = RT$, (where p = pressure, v = volume, T = absolute temperature, R = gas constant; a and b are corrections for the particular gas), gives a close approximation to the behaviour of ordinary gases.

VAN DE VELDE. Family of artists. Both **William V.** the elder (1611–93) and his son **William V.** the younger (1633–1707) painted sea battles for Charles II and James II. Another son **Adriaen V.** (1636–72) executed landscapes, and figures in works by Ruysdael, and others.

VAN DIEMEN. See DIEMEN.

VAN DONGEN (don'gen), **Kees** (1877–1968). Dutch artist. Living in Paris from the age of 20, he was linked with German avant-garde Expressionism, as well as being a fashionable portrait painter of women.

VAN DRUTEN, John William (1901–57). British playwright. B. in London, he qualified as a solicitor before beginning to write, his greatest success being *Young Woodley* (1928), treating the once-daring theme of love between a pupil and a schoolmaster's wife.

VAN DYCK (dīk), **Sir Anthony** (1599–1641). Flemish painter. B. at Antwerp, he was for 4 years an assistant to Rubens. He visited England 1620–1, and was painter to James I. He then worked for a time in Italy, but in 1628 returned to Antwerp where he painted many religious works and portraits. In 1632 he was invited to England by Charles I, became court painter, and was knighted.

VANE, Sir Henry (1613–62). English statesman. In 1640 elected a member of the Long Parliament, he was prominent in the impeachment of Laud, and 1643–53 was in effect the civilian head of the Parliamentary government. At the Restoration he was executed as a chief of the Republican Party.

VAN EYCK. *See* EYCK.

VAN GOGH. *See* GOGH.

VANILLA. Genus of orchids, several of which bear pods which when dried are the source of V. flavouring, used in confectionery, etc. The finest V. comes from *V. planifolia*, a native of Mexico, now cultivated elsewhere.

VANINI (vahnē'nē), **Lucilio** (1585–1619). Italian pantheistic thinker. B. near Naples, he took orders in the R.C. Church, but developed freethinking views. He was burnt at the stake as an atheist at Toulouse.

VANNES (vahn). French town and small port in Brittany, cap. of Morbihan dept. It is of pre-Roman origin and has remarkable megalithic monuments in the vicinity. Pop. (1962) 34,107.

VANSI'TTART, Robert Gilbert, 1st baron (1881–1957). British diplomat. Entering the diplomatic service in 1902, he was Permanent Under Sec. of State for Foreign Affairs 1930–8 and Chief Diplomatic Adviser to the For. Sec. 1938–41. He was noted for his anti-German polemic. He was created baron 1941.

VAN T'HOFF, Jacobus Henricus (1852–1911). Dutch physical chemist. He explained the 'asymmetric' carbon atom occurring in optically active compounds, and his greatest work – the concept of chemical affinity as the maximum work obtainable which results from a reaction – was shown with measurements of osmotic and gas pressures, and reversible electric batteries. He was the 1st recipient of the Nobel prize in 1901.

VAR (vahr). River in S. France, rising in the Maritime Alps and flowing generally S.S.E. for 84 m. into the Mediterranean near Nice. It gives its name to a dept.

VARANESI. Indian city on the Ganges r. in Uttar Pradesh, more familiar in the W. under the form Benares. It is a city holy to Hindus with a 3 m. water frontage of stairways (ghats), leading up from the river to innumerable streets, temples, and the 1,500 golden shrines. The ritual of purification is daily practised by thousands of devout Hindus, who bathe from the ghats in the sacred river. At the burning ghats, the ashes, following cremation, are scattered on the river, a ritual supposed to ensure a favourable reincarnation. Pop. (1961) 573,558.

VARGAS (vahr'gahs), **Getulio** (1883–1954). Brazilian lawyer and statesman. He led the revolution of 1930, and was president 1930–45 and from 1951 till his suicide following a political crisis.

VARIABLE STAR. A star whose brightness changes, either regularly or irregularly, over a short period. Apart from the eclipsing Ss., where the light-change is due to the periodical eclipse of the S. by a binary companion, variables do actually change in luminosity and in radius. Particularly interesting are the *Cepheids*, whose periods are perfectly regular, and range from a few hours up to a few weeks. There are also the less precise long-period variables, such as Mira Ceti (period about 331 days) and the irregular variables such as Betelgeux in Orion.

VARICOSE VEINS. Veins that have become dilated or stretched, especially those on the inner side of the leg, knee, and thigh. The complaint is usually caused by prolonged standing.

VARLEY, John (1778–1842). British water-colourist, known for his Thames-side scenes, and, from the time of his first visit to N. Wales in 1799, for mountain landscapes.

VARNA. Bulgarian fortress, and seaport, on an inlet of the Black Sea. Pop. (1965) 180,000.

VARNISH. Name given to resins or resinous gums

VATICAN. Almost all this tiny walled state is shown here. At its heart is St. Peter's, approached through the Piazza San Pietro with its magnificent quadruple colonnade designed by Bernini. Built 1506–1626 on the supposed site of the tomb of the apostle, it is the largest church in Christendom. Immediately behind it are the Vatican Gardens, and to the right is the Vatican palace which includes the Pope's private apartments, the Vatican museums and the Sistine Chapel with its Michelangelo frescoes. *Photo: Courtesy of Italian State Tourist Office.*

dissolved in linseed oil, turpentine, etc., that are used in house decoration, furniture making, automobile and carriage work, etc.

VASARI (vahsah'rē), **Giorgio** (1511–74). Italian painter and architect, remembered for his *Lives of the Painters, Sculptors, and Architects* (1550).

VASCO DA GAMA. *See* GAMA.

VATICAN CITY STATE, The. Independent sovereign state, created by the Lateran Treaty, 1929, of which the Pope is the head. The Holy See covers the V. palace (the Pope's official residence) and the basilica and square of St. Peter's in the heart of Rome, several other basilicas in and near Rome, and the Pope's summer residence at Castel Gandolfo. The Sovereign Pontiff appoints a layman as governor. Area 109 acres; pop. *c.* 1,000.

VAUBAN (vōbon'), **Sébastien le Prestre de** (1633–1707). French marshal and military engineer. In Louis XIV's wars he conducted many sieges, and rebuilt many of the fortresses on France's E. frontier.

VAUCLUSE (vōklüz'). Mt. range in S.E. France, *c.* 25 m. long, part of the Provence Alps, to the E. of Avignon, rising to 4,075 ft. It gives its name to a dept.

VAUD (voh). Canton of S.W. Switzerland adjoining Lake Geneva. Lausanne is the cap., and it incl. Montreux, Vevey and other tourist resorts. Area 1,240 sq. m.; pop. (1960) 377,585.

VAUGHAN (vawn), **Henry** (1622–95). Welsh poet, called the Silurist, because he was a native of the land of the ancient Silures. B. in Brecknockshire, he was a physician, and pub. several vols. of religious verse and prose devotions. A disciple of Donne, V. is ranked as a metaphysical poet, and his mystical outlook on nature influenced Wordsworth and others.

VAUGHAN WILLIAMS, Ralph (1872–1958). British composer. B. at Down Ampney, Glos, he studied at Cambridge and the R.C.M., and also learnt from Max Bruch in Berlin and Ravel in Paris. Early works incl. the choral and orchestral settings of Whitman 'Towards the Unknown Region' (1907) and 'A Sea Symphony' (1910); and 'A London Symphony' (1914). After the F.W.W. came the 'Pastoral' symphony; the Mass in G minor for unaccompanied choir; the ballad opera *Hugh the Drover* (1924) and several symphonies. In 1951 his operatic morality *The Pilgrim's Progress* which incl. the earlier cantata 'The Shepherds of the Delectable Mountains' was performed for the Festival of Britain. Later works incl. 'Sinfonia Antartica', developed from his film score – one of several – for *Scott of the Antarctic* and a Ninth Symphony. His genius was very English, owing much to folk song, and music of the Tudor period and Purcell; he received the O.M. in 1935.

VECTOR. Any physical quantity that has both magnitude and direction, such as the velocity or acceleration of a body, as distinct from a scalar quantity which has magnitude and no direction, such as speed, density, or mass. The direction of a V. is often indicated by an arrow on a line of length equal to its magnitude and in technical writing it is denoted by heavy (Clarendon) type.

VEDA (vā'da) (Sanskrit, divine knowledge). The most sacred of the Hindu scriptures, hymns written in an old form of Sanskrit; the oldest may date from 1500 or 2000 B.C. The 4 main collections are: the Rigveda (hymns and praises); Yajurveda (prayers and sacrificial formulae); Sâmaveda (tunes and chants); and Atharvaveda, or V. of the Atharvans, the officiating priests at the sacrifices.

VEGA (vā'gah), **Garcilaso de la** (c. 1540–c. 1616). Spanish writer. Son of a Spanish conquistador and an Inca princess, he wrote an account of the conquest of Florida and *Commentarios* on the history of Peru.

VEGA CARPIO (kahr'pē-ō), **Lope Felix de** (1562–1635). Spanish poet and dramatist. B. at Madrid, he served with the Armada in 1588, and in 1613 took orders. He wrote epics, pastorals, odes, sonnets, and novels, and over 1,500 plays.

VEGETARIANISM. The practice of restricting diet to foods of vegetable origin, for humanitarian or health reasons. The stricter vegetarians abstain from all food which comes from animals, incl. eggs, milk, butter, and cheese.

VEINS. Thin-walled muscular tubes which carry blood from all parts of the body to the heart. They contain valves which prevent the blood from running back when moving against gravity. With the exception of the Vs. leading from the lungs to the heart, they always carry blood which has lost oxygen and is therefore dark.

VELAZQUEZ (velath'keth or velas'kwiz), **Don Diego de Silva y** (1599–1660). Spanish painter. B. in Seville, he became in 1623 court painter to Philip IV, whom he painted repeatedly, and in 1652 was appointed court-marshal. He owed much to Titian, Rubens, and Tintoretto. *See* illus. p. 712.

VELVET. A plain silk fabric with a short thick pile, largely used for rich draperies, hangings, etc. Utrecht and Genoa are famed centres of manufacture.

VENDÉE (voñdā'). R. of W. France which rises near the village of La Châtaigneraie and flows 45 m. to join the Sèvre Niortaise 7 m. E. of the Bay of Biscay. It gives its name to a dept. where a peasant rising against the revolutionary govt. (the War of the Vendée) began in 1793 and spread to other parts of France, lasting until 1795.

VENDE'TTA. Name given to a survival of the blood feud that existed until recently in Corsica and parts of Sardinia and Sicily.

VENDÔME (voñdōm'), **Louis Joseph,** duc de (1654–1712). Marshal of France. In the war of the Spanish Succession he was defeated by Marlborough at Oudenarde in 1708, but was successful later in Spain.

VENEREAL DISEASE. *See* SYPHILIS; GONORRHOEA.

VENETIA (venē'shia). Roman name of that part of N.E. Italy which later became the rep. of Venice and covers approx. the 'three Venices' – in Ital. Venezia-Tridentina (Trentino-Alto-Adige, q.v.); Veneto (called Venezia Euganea 1919–47) which incl. the delta of the Po, a fertile territory at the foot of the mountains, and portions of the Dolomites, Carnic and Julian alps. Its cities incl. Venice, Padua, Verona, and Vicenza. Area 7,095 sq. m.; pop. (1961) 3,833,837; and Venezia Giulia (*see* FRIULI-VENEZIA GIULIA).

VENEZIA. Ital. form of VENICE.

VENEZUELA (venizwā'la). Federal rep. of S. America on the Caribbean coast, between Brazil and Colombia, occupying the whole of the lower basin of the Orinoco and the coastal plain bordering the gulf of Maracaibo. Coffee, cocoa, cotton, sugar cane, etc., are produced, and sheep, cattle, etc., are raised; in the forest region rubber and timber are obtained. V. is rich in minerals, incl. iron-ore and petroleum. 70 per cent of the people are Mestizos. Caracas is the cap., other important cities are Maracaibo, Barquisimeto, Valencia, Maracay, San Cristobal and Ciudad Bolivar.

Government is by a president and a congress of 2 chambers. The country is divided into a federal district, 20 states, and 2 territories. Spanish is the official language, and the prevailing religion R.C. Left-wing extremist activity is supported by Castro from Cuba. Area 352,150 sq. m.; pop. (1967) 9,189,000.

Columbus visited V. in 1498; it was the Spanish captaincy-general of Caracas 1550–1822 when, led by Simon Bolivar (q.v.), it rebelled and, as part of Colombia, was freed from Spain. V. became an independent rep. in 1830.

VENICE (ven'is). Italian city, seaport, and naval base. It stands on a group of low-lying islands at the head of the Adriatic, built for the most part on piles,

and is connected with the mainland by a rail and road viaduct. The Grand Canal divides V. into 2; the 'streets' are canals, and motor boats and gondolas are the means of conveyance. It is possible to walk all over the city whose quietness is one of its great charms. In the Piazza of St. Mark are situated the campanile, the Doge's palace, and the cathedral of St. Mark,

VENICE. One of Venice's more than 400 bridges, the Bridge of Sighs, built by Contino in the 16th cent., joins the ducal palace to the state prison.
Photo: A. W. Kerr.

dating from the 4th cent. There are Byzantine palaces, Gothic churches, and gems of Renaissance architecture. The Lido, c. 2 m. S.E. of V., is a popular bathing resort. Among V.'s oldest industries are the making of glass and fine textiles. The gradual flooding of the city is being caused by the slow sinking of the plain and the consequent rising sea-level. In addition, overbuilding and ill-considered filling-in of canals in the 19th cent. has led to an urgent need for a town-planning scheme. Pop. (1961) 336,184.

V. was founded by refugees from mainland cities sacked by the Huns in the 5th cent. For many cents. V. was an independent rep., stretching at one time to the Alps (*see* VENETIA) and governed by an aristocratic oligarchy and dependent upon Mediterranean commerce for its prosperity. At the head of the rep. was the Council of Ten and the Senate, which appointed the Doge. The rep. was overthrown by Napoleon in 1797. In 1815 V. became Austrian, and in 1866 part of the kingdom of Italy.

VENIZELOS (venizā'los), **Eleutherios** (1864–1936). Greek statesman. B. in Crete, he entered politics, becoming Premier of Greece in 1911. He resigned in 1915 when King Constantine refused to join the Allies in the F.W.W., but became Premier under Alexander in 1917, and brought Greece into the war.

Defeated in 1920, he was again Prime Minister in 1924, 1928–32, and 1933. He was exiled in 1935.

VENT, Îles du. Fr. name for the SOCIETY Is.

VENTRIS, Michael George Francis (1922–56). British architect and archaeologist, remembered for his decipherment of Minoan Linear B., the language of the tablets found at Knossos and Pylos. He showed that it was a very early form of Greek and so led the way to a revision of existing views on early Greek history. He was killed in a road accident.

VENTSPILS. Port of Latvian S.S.R., U.S.S.R., on the Baltic, a lumbering centre. It was founded 1314, annexed by Russia 1795. Pop. (est.) 20,000.

VENUS. The 2nd planet in order of distance from the Sun. It has a mean distance from the Sun of 67,000,000 miles, and a revolution period of $243\frac{1}{2}$ days; it may approach the Earth to within 24,000,000 miles, and is then nearer than any important celestial body apart from the Moon. Its diameter is 7,600 miles, and its mass 0·83 of that of the Earth. Probe *Venus III* (U.S.S.R.) in 1966 was the first man-made object to land on another planet. V. rotates more slowly than any other planet, and also in the opposite direction to all except Uranus, possibly because a moon travelling counter to its original rotation may have been drawn into a narrowing orbit round V., first retarding, then reversing its spin. Tidal movements involved would have caused heat by friction, with volcanic eruptions giving rise to the brilliantly coloured clouds of mercury compounds still surrounding V., and eventually the moon would have crashed into the planet. The surface temperature is *c.* 470°C, and the misty atmosphere permanently veiling V. is 15 times as dense as that of Earth and mainly carbon dioxide.

VENUS. Roman goddess of beauty, growth, and love, identified with the Greek Aphrodite.

VENUS' FLY TRAP. *See* INSECTIVOROUS PLANTS.

VERACRUZ (ve'rakrooz). City and seaport of Mexico, on the Gulf of Mexico. Cortez founded Villa Nueva de la Vera Cruz (Span., New Town of the True Cross) nearby in 1519; it was transferred to its present site 1599. Pop. (1967) 185,900.

VERBÉNA. Genus of plants of the Verbenaceae family, having tubular flowers arranged in close spikes. Colours range from white to rose, violet, and purple. There are about 100 species, mostly in the American tropics. The garden V. (*Lippia citriodora*) belongs to the same family.

VERCORS (vārkōr'). Pseudonym adopted by French writer and artist Jean Bruller (1902–) while a member of the French resistance during the S.W.W. Under the occupation he estab. in 1941 a clandestine publishing house, Les Editions de Minuit, from which appeared his novel *Le Silence de la mer* (1942), of the resistance, smuggled abroad.

VERCORS
Photo: Ergy Landau.

VERDI (vār'dē), **Guiseppe (Fortunino Francesco)** (1813–1901). Italian composer. B. near Busseto, the son of a village innkeeper, he wrote his first symphony at 15 and then studied in Milan. His first opera *Oberto* was given at La Scala in 1839, and was followed by *Ernani* (Venice, 1844). After visiting London and Paris he returned to Italy and wrote *Rigoletto* (1851), *Il Trovatore* (1853), *La Traviata* (1853), *Don Carlos* (1867), *Aïda* (1871), *Otello* (1877), *Falstaff* (1893), and other operas, as well as religious music, e.g. the *Requiem*.

VERDIGRIS. A basic copper acetate, used as a wood preservative, in anti-fouling compositions, and

formerly in green paint. It is an irritant poison.

VERDUN (verdun'). Fortress town of N.E. France on the Meuse. During the F.W.W. it became the symbol of French resistance, withstanding a terrific German onslaught in 1916. Pop. (1962) 25,238.

VERHAEREN (verhah'ren), **Emile** (1855–1916). Belgian poet. B. near Antwerp, he was a leader in the Belgian literary revival of the 1880s.

VERLAINE (verlān'), **Paul** (1844–96). French poet. B. at Metz, he became an insurance clerk in Paris. His first vol. of poems, *Poèmes saturniens*, appeared in 1866, followed by *La bonne chanson* (1870) and *Sagesse* (1881). Other works are *Romances sans paroles* (1874), *Amour* (1888), and *Bonheur* (1891). From 1871 he wandered about France, Belgium, and England with Rimbaud until an attempt to shoot his fellow-traveller brought V. 2 years' imprisonment.

VERMEER (vermār'), **Jan** (1632–75). Dutch artist. B. at Delft, he spent most of his life and d. there. His paintings are distinguished by their harmonious colouring and technical excellence. 'Lady at the Virginals' is in the National Gallery. *See* MEEGEREN, HANS VAN.

VERMONT. A N. Atlantic state of U.S.A., traversed by the Green Mts. (from which it derives its name). Lake Champlain lies on the W. Dairy products are important; china clay, asbestos, and granite, marble and slate are worked; and business machines, furniture and paper made. V. entered the Union in 1791. Montpelier is the cap. Area 9,609 sq. m.; pop. (1970) 444,732.

VERMOUTH (ver'muth). A white wine flavoured by the masceration of bitter herbs and fortified by alcohol. It is prepared in France and Italy.

VERNE (vārn), **Jules** (1828–1905). French author. B. at Nantes, he went to Paris and estab. a reputation as a writer of travellers' tales which show scientific prevision: *Five Weeks in a Balloon* (1862), *Journey to the Centre of the Earth*, *Twenty Thousand Leagues under the Sea*, *Around the World in Eighty Days* (1872), etc.

VERNEY, Sir Edmund (1590–1642). English courtier, knight-marshal to Charles I from 1626. He sat as an M.P. in both the Short and Long parliaments, and though sympathizing with the Parliamentary position remained true to his allegiance: he d. at his post as royal standard bearer at Edgehill. His son Ralph (1613–96) adhered to the opposing party, and his industry was responsible for the preservation at Claydon, the family home in Bucks, of the Verney Papers, a valuable record of this and later periods.

VERNIER. A device for taking readings on a graduated scale to a fraction of division: a short divided scale which slides along the main scale and carries the index or pointer. It was invented by Pierre V. (*c.* 1580–1637), who lived at Ornans in Burgundy.

VERNON, Edward (1684–1757). English admiral, captured Portobello in 1739, with a loss of only 7 men.

VERONA. Cap. of V. prov., Veneto, Italy, on the Adige. It has a 12th cent. cathedral and fine Roman remains. It is an agricultural market town with printing and paper works and makes plastics, furniture, macaroni, etc. A school of painting flourished at V. in the 15th and 16th cents. Pop. (1961) 221,138.

VERONESE (vārōnā'ze), **Paolo** (1528–88). Italian painter. B. in Verona, he delighted in painting gorgeous banquets, pageantry, and material splendour. His 'Family of Darius at the feet of Alexander' is in the National Gallery, London. He d. at Venice. *See* illus. p. 1070.

VERONICA. Christian saint, a woman of Jerusalem who lent her veil or kerchief to Jesus to wipe the sweat from his brow on the road to Calvary; whereupon the image of the Lord's face was printed upon it. What is alleged to be the actual veil is preserved in St. Peter's, Rome.

VERROCCHIO (vārok'kē-ō), **Andrea del** (1435–88). Italian artist, whose real name was Cioni. His only

VERONESE. Probably a *modello* for a late altar-piece, 'The Baptism of Christ' has its closest parallels in the Redentore at Venice which was completed by Veronese's heirs.
Courtauld Institute Galleries, London.

surviving painting is the 'Baptism of Christ' at Florence; his sculptures incl. the equestrian statue of Colleoni at Venice.

VERSAILLES (vārsī'). French town, cap. of the Les Yvelines dept., 12 m. S.W. of Paris. Its great palace was built mainly by Louis XIV; here the German Empire was proclaimed in 1871 and the Peace Conference was held after the F.W.W. The Grand and Petit Trianon are smaller palaces. Pop. (1962) 95,149.

The TREATY OF V. was signed on 28 June 1919, between the Allies and Associated Powers (the U.S.A. being an Associated Power) on the one hand and Germany on the other. In the forefront of the treaty were the clauses to establish the League of Nations. Germany surrendered Alsace-Lorraine (q.v.) to France, large areas to Poland, and smaller areas to Czechoslovakia, Lithuania, Belgium, and Denmark. The Rhineland was demilitarized, and restrictions were put on German armaments. Germany accepted responsibility for war damage, and provision was made for the payment of reparations. The U.S.A. never ratified the treaty, but made a separate peace with Germany and Austria, 1921.

VERSE. The arrangement of words in a rhythmical pattern. Besides metre (q.v.) an important element in verse is provided by *rhyme* which arises from identity in sound of the endings of certain words. Rhyme first made its appearance in western Europe in late Latin poetry, and from thence passed into use in the modern European languages. The binding together of lines into groups by means of a unified rhyme-scheme leads to the creation of the *stanza*.

Classical Greek verse depended upon quantity, a long syllable (indicated thus —) being regarded as occupying twice the time taken up by a short syllable (⌣). Long and short syllables were combined in *feet*, such as:

(1) Dactyl: — ⌣ ⌣; (2) Spondee: — —;
(3) Anapaest: ⌣ ⌣ —; (4) Iamb: ⌣ —;
5) Trochee: — ⌣.

Blank verse consists of unrhymed five-stress lines. It was introduced by Surrey, and later became, as perfected by Marlowe, Shakespeare, and Milton, the standard metre for English dramatic and epic poetry. The *Spenserian Stanza*, rhyming ababbcbcc – the last line being of 12 syllables, was used by Spenser in *The Faerie Queen*. The *Shakespearean Sonnet* consisted of 4 quatrains and a couplet, thus: abab, cdcd, efef, gg. It was first devised by Surrey. The *Pindaric Ode* was modelled on the ancient Greek form with its structure of *strophe*, *antistrophe*, and *epode*. Gray's 'The Bard' and 'The Progress of Poesy' are the best-known examples. *Free Verse* is applied to any verse the rhythmical basis of which is not obvious. *See* also BALLAD; ODE; POETRY, SONNET, etc.

VERTEBRATA. A main sub-division of the animal kingdom, incl. all the backboned animals – mammals (incl. man), birds, reptiles, amphibians, fish.

VERULĀ'MIUM. Roman-British town whose remains have been excavated close to St. Albans. Boadicea burnt it in A.D. 61, but it was rebuilt.

VERWOERD (fervoort'), **Hendrik Frensch** (1901–66). S. African statesman. B. in Amsterdam, the son of missionary parents, he was ed. at the univs. of Leipzig, Hamburg and Berlin. He held chairs of applied psychology and sociology at Stellenbosch (1927–37), before devoting himself to building up the Nationalist paper *Die Transvaler* (1938–48). Elected to the Senate in 1948, he was Min. of Native Affairs 1950–8, and although he did much to improve African housing in the cities, he was chief promoter of apartheid legislation. As P.M. in 1958 he pledged himself to estab. a rep., achieving this in 1961, *see* BRITISH COMMONWEALTH. He was assassinated in the House of Assembly by a parliamentary messenger Dimitri Tsafendas, a Portuguese b. in Mozambique.

VESPĀ'SIAN (Titus Flavius Vespasianus) (A.D. 9–79). Roman emperor. Son of a moneylender, he had a distinguished military career and was proclaimed emperor by his soldiers in A.D. 69 when he was campaigning in Palestine. He reorganized the eastern provinces, and was a capable administrator.

VESPERS. The 7th of the 8 canonical hours in the Catholic Church. The *Sicilian V.* is the name given to a massacre of the French rulers in Sicily in 1282.

VESPUCCI (vespoo'chē), **Amerigo** (1454–1512). Florentine navigator, who in 1497 sailed for the New World, and claimed to have reached the mainland of N. America a few days before John Cabot. America is named after A.V.

VESTA. Roman hearth goddess, identified with the Greek Hestia. In Rome her shrine stood in the Forum where was the sacred hearth, whose fire was never allowed to go out. The tenders of the flame were the 6 Vestal Virgins.

VESŪ'VIUS. Active volcano in Italy, about 10 m. E.S.E. of Naples, and *c.* 3,890 ft. high. It caused the destruction of Pompeii in A.D. 79, and has often erupted.

VETCH or **Tare.** A leguminous annual plant (*Vicia sativa*) with trailing or climbing stems and reddish-purple flowers. Winter V. produces spring fodder, and spring V. is cut for hay.

VETERINARY SCIENCE. The science that treats the diseases of domestic animals; more generally it covers their anatomy, breeding, and relations to man. The Royal College of V. Surgeons (1844) maintains a statutory register of qualified practitioners and the American V. Medical Assocn. was estab. in 1883. World V congresses were held in 1863 and 1963.

VETO. Name given to the right of a sovereign, branch of the legislature, or other political power, to prevent the enactment or the operation of a law. In Britain the House of Lords has a suspensory V. over all legislation with the exception of finance measures; in theory the sovereign may V. any Act, but the right has not been exercised since the 18th cent. The V. is used in the Security Council of the U.N.

VI'AN, Sir Philip (1894–1968). Brit. Admiral of the Fleet. In 1940 he was the hero of the *Altmark* (q.v.) incident, and in 1941 commanded the destroyers which chased the *Bismarck*.

VIANNEY, Jean. *See* CURÉ D'ARS.

VIBORG (vē'-). (1) Town in Jutland, Denmark, on V. lake, with breweries, textile and tobacco factories, etc. Pop. (est.) 25,000. (2) Swedish form of VYBORG.

VIBU'RNUM. Genus of shrubs of the honeysuckle family. *V. lantana* is the wayfaring tree and *V. opulus* the cranberry tree.

VICAR. In the C. of E. a parish priest. *See* RECTOR.

VICENTE (visen'tä), **Gil** (*c.* 1465–1536?). Portuguese poet and dramatist. He was a goldsmith and from 1502 wrote plays for the Port. court. They range from religious dramas to romantic comedies.

VICENZA (vēchen'tzah). Italian city and episcopal see in Veneto, cap. of V. prov. It has a 13th cent. cathedral and makes textiles and musical instruments. It was the Roman Vicetia. Pop. (1961) 97,617.

VICHY (vē'shē). Health resort with thermal springs already known to the Romans, in Allier dept., France. In 1940–4 it was the seat of Marshal Pétain's govt. – whence the phrase Vichy France, i.e. that part of France not occupied by German troops until Nov. 1942. Pop. (1962) 31,322.

VICO (vē'kō), **Giovanni Battista** (1668–1744). Italian philosopher. B. at Naples, he became prof. of rhetoric there in 1697 and in 1735 historiographer royal. His *Scienza Nuova* (1725) originated the philosophy of history.

VICTOR EMMANUEL II (1820–78). First king of united Italy. B. in Turin, he became king of Sardinia on the abdication of his father Charles Albert, following defeat in war with the Austrians in 1849. In 1855 he allied Sardinia with France and Britain in the Crimean War. In 1859 in alliance with the French he defeated the Austrians and annexed Lombardy. By 1860 most of Italy had come under his rule, and in 1861 he was proclaimed king of Italy. In 1870 he made Rome his capital.

VICTOR EMMANUEL III (1869–1947). King of Italy. B. at Naples, he became king in 1900 on the assassination of his father, King Humbert I. He acquiesced in the Fascist régime, but co-operated with the Allies from 1943, and in 1946 abdicated.

QUEEN VICTORIA. As she nurses the future Edward VIII, Edward VII (then Prince of Wales) and George V (then Duke of York) stand behind her.
Photo: Radio Times Hulton Picture Library.

VICTORIA (1819 – 1901)- Queen of the U.K. and Empress of India. Only child of Edward, duke of Kent, 4th son of George III, she was b. 24 May 1819 at Kensington Palace, and became queen in 1837 on the death of her uncle William IV. In 1840 she m. Prince Albert of Saxe-Coburg and Gotha, and had 4 sons and 5 daus., viz. Victoria, Princess Royal (1840–1901), wife of Frederick III, German

emperor; Edward VII; Alice, Grand-duchess of Hesse; Alfred, Duke of Edinburgh and Saxe-Coburg-Gotha; Helena, Princess Christian; Louise, Duchess of Argyll; Arthur, Duke of Connaught; Leopold, Duke of Albany; and Beatrice, Princess Henry of Battenberg. The Prince Consort d. in 1861, and for many years the Queen was in retirement – a fact which led to the growth of republican sentiment. Of all her Prime Ministers, Disraeli (Lord Beaconsfield) proved himself the most agreeable, and in 1876 he proclaimed her Empress of India. From 1848 she regularly visited the Scottish highlands, where she had her seat at Balmoral, built to Prince Albert's designs; another favourite home was Osborne House in the Isle of Wight. By 1887 the year of her jubilee, she had regained the public's affection, and something more than affection was shown at the diamond jubilee in 1897. A detailed picture of her life is given in her *Letters* and in her *Journal of Our Life in the Highlands*, etc. She d. at Osborne, 22 Jan. 1901, and was buried at Windsor. *See* illus. p. 815.

VICTORIA. A state of the Australian Commonwealth, in the S.E. of the continent. It is traversed from E. to W. by a chain of mountains, part of the Great Dividing Range; for the rest the surface is fertile lowland. Sheep grazing and agriculture are principal occupations; large areas are under orchards, vegetables and vineyards. Minerals incl. coal and gold, and oil and natural gas in the Bass Strait. Manufactures are mainly those connected with agriculture and forestry. The pop. is mainly concentrated in Melbourne (the cap.), Ballarat, Bendigo, and Geelong. Area 87,884 sq. m.; pop. (1967) 3,271,993.

V. was discovered by Capt. Cook in 1770 and was settled in the 1830s. In 1851 it was made a separate colony, after being part of N.S.W., and was named after Queen Victoria. In 1901 it became one of the states of the Commonwealth of Australia. The state legislature consists of a Governor, a Legislative Council, and a Legislative Assembly.

VICTORIA. Cap. of British Columbia, Canada, on Vancouver Is. It is a great port, an industrial centre, and a railway junction with factories making furniture, clothing, chemicals, etc., and shipyards. V. was founded as Fort V. in 1843 by the Hudson's Bay Co. and has a univ. (1963). Pop. (1966) 57,453.

VICTORIA. Cap. of Hong Kong (q.v.), commonly itself called Hong Kong.

VICTORIA, Lake. Africa's largest lake, on the equator at an altitude of 3,726 ft.; area, over 26,800 sq. m.; 255 m. long. Most important of its affluents is the Kagera, the Nile's remotest headstream; the Nile issues from it. The lake was discovered by Speke in 1858, who named it after Queen Victoria. It is partly in Uganda, in Kenya, and in Tanganyika. *See* OWEN FALLS.

VICTORIA CROSS. British decoration for conspicuous bravery instituted by Queen Victoria in 1856. It is bronze, 1½ in. in diameter, and has a crimson ribbon. Until the supply was exhausted in 1942 all V.Cs. were struck from the metal of cannon captured from the Russians at Sevastopol: they are now made from gunmetal supplied by the Royal Mint. Those eligible incl. members of the army, navy, and air force; members of the nursing services; and civilians under the direction of the 3 fighting services.

VICTORIA FALLS. Falls on the r. Zambesi on the border of N. and S. Rhodesia, S. Africa. The river is some 1,860 yds. wide, and drops over a chasm some 400 ft. deep to flow through a 100 ft. wide gorge. The Falls were discovered by Livingstone in 1855, and named after Queen Victoria.

VICTORIA ORDER, Royal. A British order of chivalry instituted in 1896 by Queen Victoria as a reward for personal services to the sovereign. It comprises Knight or Dame Grand Cross (G.C.V.O.), Knight Commander (K.C.V.O.), Dame Commander

(D.C.V.O.), Commander (C.V.O.), Member (M.V.O.).

'**VICTORY.**' British battleship, 2,164 tons, launched in 1765, and now in dry dock in Portsmouth harbour. She was the flagship of Nelson at Trafalgar.

VICUÑA (vikoon′ya). A small ruminant (*Lama vicugna*) which lives in herds on the Andean plateaux. Its soft brown wool is used in textile manufacture.

VIDOCQ (vēdok′), **François Eugène** (1775–1857). French detective. B. at Arras, he was a criminal, but in 1809 enlisted as a spy in the Paris police. He rose to be chief of the detective dept.

VIENNA. Capital of the Austrian republic, on the Danube at the foot of the Wiener Wald. It consists of an old city, nearly circular, whose former fortifications were replaced (1860) by the Ringstrasse. The cathedral of St. Stephen dates from the 13th cent. The Hofburg, the former imperial palace, contains the national library. Among the notable buildings are the houses of parliament (1883), the royal palace of Schönbrunn (started 1696); the Rathaus (1873–83); the univ., founded 1365; the Burgtheater, many museums, etc. V. was until 1918 the cap. of the Austro-Hungarian Empire and the commercial centre of eastern Europe. It became the Habsburg capital in 1278. In 1934 it was the scene of a Socialist and of a Fascist rising. V. suffered much destruction during fighting in the S.W.W., after which it was divided into

VIENNA. Across the Helden Platz, looking from the roof of the Neue Hofburg, and beyond the trees of the Ring, are the Parliament Building (1883) and (to the right) the towering pinnacles of the City Hall (1873).
Courtesy of Austrian State Tourist Department.

U.S., Brit., Fr., and Russian zones of occupation 1945–55. Pop. (1962 est.) 1,627,600.

The CONGRESS OF V. 1814–15 effected the settlement of Europe after the Napoleonic Wars.

VIENNE (vē-en′). French river which rises in Corrèze and flows 223 m. N. and N.W. to the Loire above Saumur. The town of V. in Isère dept. has engineering and textile industries. Pop. (1962) 28,162.

VIETNAM (vē-et′-). Country of S.E. Asia, comprising the former French colonies of Tonkin, Annam, and Cochin-China which were occupied by the Japanese 1941–5, and accorded independence by France 1950. Fighting between Communist forces under Ho Chi-minh and French units followed until in 1954, following a conference in Geneva, V. was divided along the 17th parallel of lat. into N.V. (Communist), cap. Hanoi, area 63,000 sq. m., pop. (1967) 17,800,000; and S.V. (democratic), cap. Saigon, area 66,281 sq. m., pop. (1967) 15,300,000. In S.V. the rule of Ngo Dinh Diem (q.v.) was followed from 1963 by a series of crisis cabinets and in 1967 a new constitution was adopted with a popularly elected pres. (Nguyen Van Thieu), senate and house of reps. The guerrilla National Liberation Front (estab. by the

Communists 1960, hence known as Viet Cong) gained strength: leaders incl. Vietminh veterans who went to N.V. in 1954, later returning, and the rank and file were variously described as ordinary S. Vietnamese or predominantly N. Vietnamese infiltrators. Increasing military aid to the guerrillas by China via N.V. and to the S.V. govt. by the U.S.A. led to dangerous international tension from 1964: *see* TONKIN GULF. Pres. Johnson offered to negotiate 1968, and Nixon followed up the offer.

VIGNY (vēnyē′), **Alfred de** (1797–1863). French poet. B. at Loches, he joined the army at 16 and had 12 years′ service. His first vol. of poems appeared in

VIKINGS. Normally sailing under one large square sail, for easy manœuvrability, particularly in battle, the Vikings relied on the high prow and stern, shown in the Oseberg ship seen here, pointed fore and aft, and on rowing power – usually about 10 oarsmen a side.
Photo: Universitets Oldsaksamling, Oslo.

1822, his prose romance *Cinq-Mars* in 1826, and his drama *Chatterton* in 1835. The title of the latter illustrates his interest in England, where he lived some years, and in 1828 he m. an Englishwoman. Some of his best poems are in *Les Destinées* (1864).

VIGO (vē′gō). Spanish seaport and naval station on V. bay in Galicia with petroleum refineries, tanneries, paper mills, distilleries, etc. Pop. (1961) 165,000.

VIIPURI. Finnish name of VYBORG.

VIKINGS. Name given to the Scandinavian 'seawarriors' who in the 8th–10th cents. raided and settled the coasts of G. Britain and W. Europe, later extending their attacks to include Spain and Italy, going as far south as Constantinople and N. Africa and as far east as Russia. *See* NORSEMEN.

VILLA-LOBOS (vē′lah lō′bōs), **Heitor** (1881–1959). Brazilian composer. By travelling widely in his native country he became familiar with its folk music, and developed a nationalistic style, particularly using orchestras of hundreds and choirs of thousands. Artur Rubenstein discovered him 1918.

VILLARS (vēlahr′), **Claude Louis Hector de,** duc de (1653–1734). Marshal of France, who was defeated by Marlborough at Malplaquet in 1709.

VILLEHARDOUIN (vēlahrdoo-aṅ′), **Geoffroy de** (*c.* 1160–*c.* 1213). The first historian to write in the French language. He was b. near Troyes and wrote a chronicle of the 4th crusade.

VILLEINAGE. The system of serfdom that prevailed in Europe in the Middle Ages. At the time of the Domesday Book, the villeins were the most numerous element in the English population, providing the labour force for the manors. By the 15th cent. V. had been supplanted by a system of free tenure and labour, but it continued in France until 1789.

VILLIERS DE L'ISLE ADAM (vēyā′ de lēl

ahdoń'), **Philippe Auguste Mathias,** comte de (1838–89). French poet, the inaugurator of the Symbolist movement. He wrote the drama *Axel; Isis,* a romance of the supernatural; verse, and short stories.

VILLON (vēyoń'), **François** (1431–85). French poet. B. at Paris of apparently humble parentage, he dropped his own surname (Montcorbier or de Logos) to assume that of a canon – a relative who sent him to study at the Sorbonne, where he graduated in 1449 and took his M.A. in 1452. In 1455 he stabbed a priest in a street fight and had to flee the city. About this time he was a member of the Brotherhood of the Coquille, using their argot in some half dozen of his ballades. Pardoned the next year he returned to Paris – the *Petit Testament* belonging to this time – but was soon in flight again after robbing the Collège of Navarre, and was briefly at rest at the court of the duke of Orléans until sentenced to death for an unknown offence from which he was saved by the amnesty of a public holiday. Theft and public brawling continued to occupy his time, in addition to the production of the *Grand Testament* (1461), but in 1463 a sentence of death in Paris, which he managed to have commuted to 10 yr. banishment, is the last that is really known of him. His satiric humour, matchless pathos, and fertile lyric power make him a world poet.

VILNIUS. Cap. of Lithuanian S.S.R. An important fortress already in the 12th cent., cap. of Lithuania from 1323, Polish 1447–1795 (when Russia annexed it) and a centre of Polish and Jewish culture, it was claimed by both Poland and Lithuania after the F.W.W. V. was given to Poland 1921, occupied by Russia 1939, and immediately transferred to Lithuania. Pop. (1967) 317,000. The Russian form Vilna is often used.

VIMY. Small French town in Pas-de-Calais dept. Pop. (1962) 3,009. V. Ridge nearby, a spur of the ridge of Notre Dame de Lorette, 5 m. N. by E. of Arras, was taken by Canadian troops during the battle of Arras, April 1917: 11,285 Canadians were lost.

VINCENT DE PAUL (1576–1660). French R.C. saint. B. in Gascony, he was ordained in 1600, was captured by Barbary pirates and was a slave in Tunis until 1607. He founded the Lazarists (q.v.) and a sisterhood of charity. He was canonized in 1737.

VINE. A climbing plant (*Vitis vinifera*) of the family Viticeae, a native of Asia Minor, cultivated from antiquity for its fruit, which is eaten or made into wine (q.v.) or other fermented drinks; dried fruits of certain varieties are raisins and currants.

VINEGAR. A weak solution of acetic acid containing salts and colouring matter. White V. is obtained from inferior wines, malt V. from beer.

VINLAND. Norse name for the Hudson Straits/Gulf of St. Lawrence area of N. America, which Lief Ericsson (q.v.) believed an 'island-continent .

VIOL. Family of bowed musical instruments, resembling the violin, but with a flatter back.

VIOLET (*Viola*). Large genus of plants which includes the sweet V. (*V. odorata*), dog V. (*V. canina*), wild pansy (*V. tricolor*), and the viola (*V. cornuta*).

VIOLIN. A stringed musical instrument played with a bow. It superseded the viol from the 17th cent.; famous early makers were the Amati family in Cremona, Stradivari, and G. A. Guarnieri. It consists of a resonant body comprising belly and back, a neck with fingerboard attached and 4 catgut strings carried

VIOLIN and CELLO

from a tailpiece over a bridge to tuning-pegs on the neck. The **Viola** is slightly larger and thicker than the violin; like the violin it is tuned in 5ths, but is a 5th below. The **Violoncello** is much larger than either of the above and is held between the player's knees. The **Double Bass** is the largest of the family.

VIPER. Family of poisonous snakes. The true Vs. (*Viperinae*), abundant in Africa and S.W. Asia, incl. the adder (*Vipera berus*), Britain's only poisonous snake; the African puff adder (*Bitis arietans*) and the horned V. of N. Africa (*Cerastes cornutus*). The second sub-family (*Crotalinae*) incl. the pit vipers and rattlesnakes of the Americas, which have a pit between the eye and nostril.

COMMON VIPER

VIRCHOW (vēr'khō), **Rudolf** (1821–1902). German pathologist. B. in Pomerania, he was a prof. at Berlin and from 1880 leader of the opposition to Bismarck in the Reichstag. His *Cellular Pathology* (1858) opened a new chapter in pathology.

VIRGIL (Publius Vergilius Maro) (70–19 B.C.). Roman poet. B. near Mantua, he belonged to the yeoman class whose life he eulogized in his poems. His *Eclogues,* 10 pastoral poems, appeared in 37 B.C. The *Georgics* or 'Art of Husbandry' followed in 30 B.C. and confirmed his position as the chief poet of the age. The last years of his life were spent in composing the *Aeneid,* an epic poem in 12 books intended to glorify the Julian dynasty whose head was Augustus, V.'s imperial patron. Horace was his friend. His superbly musical and moving gift of language ensured his acceptance as the voice of imperial Rome for succeeding cents., and by the 3rd cent. his works were used for divination – the Sortes Virgilianae. The apparent forecast of the birth of Christ in the 4th ecologue led to his acceptance as an 'honorary' Christian by the medieval Church and hence as approved reading, and in popular legend he became a powerful magician.

VIRGINIA. One of the 13 original states of the U.S.A., in the S. Atlantic group. It comprises a coastal plain, the Piedmont plateau, and the Allegheny Mts. Chief rivers are the Potomac, Rappahannock, York,

VIRGINIA. Washington's home at Mount Vernon, where he lived from 1759 until his death, is now a national shrine.
Courtesy of United States Information Service.

and James. The chief crops are sweet potatoes, corn, tobacco, apples, peaches and peanuts. Coal is mined, and growing industries incl. furniture, paper, chemicals, processed food, textiles and cigarettes. There are also shipyards and a fishing industry. The cap. is Richmond; other towns are Norfolk, Roanoke, Portsmouth, and Newport News. Area 40,815 sq. m.; pop. (1970) 4,648,494.

V. was named in honour of Elizabeth I; it was settled in 1607, the first permanent English settlement in N. America. It took a leading part in the revolutionary struggle against England, and was a Confederate state in the American Civil War.

VIRGIN ISLANDS. Group of *c.* 50 islands in the West Indies, of which St. Thomas, St. Croix, and St. John were bought by U.S.A. from Denmark in 1917. The cap. is Charlotte Amalie on St. Thomas. Area 133 sq. m.; pop. (1960) 32,099. The other V.Is. are a Brit. colony, cap. Road Town on Tortola. Under the 1967 constitution govt. is exercised through the Chief Minister, advised by an Executive Council, and there is a Legislative Council with elected majority. Area 59 sq. m.; pop. (1967) 8,895.

VIRUS, or **Filter-passing Viruses.** Organisms so small that they pass through the bacterial filter. They were first discovered in 1898. Diseases carried by them are foot-and-mouth, rabies, yellow-fever, canine distemper, smallpox, typhus, mumps, &c.

VISBY. Swedish town, capital of Gotland (q.v.), and in the Middle Ages a Hansa town. It lies 115 m. S. of Stockholm. Pop. (est.) 16,000.

VISCONTI, Luchino (1906–). Italian film and theatrical director. B. in Milan, of an aristocratic family, his 1st film *Ossessione* (1942), the 1st Italian 'neo-realist' film, was followed by *La Terra Trema* (1948), a documentary about Sicilian fishermen, *Senso* (1954), and *Rocco and his Brothers* (1961); their powerful social comment has led to violent controversy with the Italian govt. and the R.C. Church. Other films incl. *The Leopard* (1963). He is also famous for his theatrical and opera productions at Milan.

VISCOSITY. The internal friction or resistance to relative motion of the parts of a fluid. Fluids like pitch, treacle and heavy oils are highly viscous, but a perfect fluid would be non-viscous.

VISCOUNT. In the peerage of the United Kingdom, the 4th degree of nobility, between earl and baron.

VISHNU (vish′noo). Second of the 3 gods constituting the Hindu triad. He is the Preserver, and is believed to have assumed human form on a number of occasions; 10 of such avataras or incarnations are described, the most famous being as Rama and as Krishna. His worshippers are the Vaishnavas (q.v.).

VISIGOTHS. *See* GOTHS.

VISTULA. Polish river which rises in the Carpathians and runs S.E., across Poland to the Baltic at Gdansk. Length 678 m.

VITAMINS. Organic substances normally present n small and variable amounts in different foods and of which the absence or partial deficiency in the diet leads to various characteristic diseases and disturbances. Although in 1662 Admiral Hawkins was aware of the value of 'sower oranges and lemmons' against scurvy, it was not fully estab. until about 1915 that several deficiency diseases were preventable and curable by extracts from certain foods. By then it was known that two groups of factors were involved, one being water-soluble and present, for example, in yeast, rice-polishings and wheat-germ, and the other fat-soluble and present in egg-yolk, butter, fish-liver oils and so on. The water-soluble substance, known to be effective against beri-beri, was named vitamine B. (The name 'vitamine' later changed to 'vitamin' was chosen to indicate it was an amine and essential to life.) The fat-soluble vitamin complex was at first called vitamine A. With improving analytical techniques these have been subsequently separated into their various components, and others have been discovered. Not all are amines, but the term V. remains.

Of some 20 known Vs., the majority are found in different related forms, and are prepared industrially either by extraction from natural sources, or artificially by chemical synthesis. As their structures have been identified, most of them are now known by their chemical names; thus vitamin C (anti-scurvy) is ascorbic acid, vitamin B_1 (anti beri-beri) is thiamine, vitamin D_2 (anti-rickets) is calciferol, and so on.

Vitamin B_{12}, (cobalamine), active against pernicious anaemia, and vitamin K (phylloquinone), effective in a particular haemorrhagic disease, are further examples.

VITEBSK (vétebsk′). Town, dating from the 10th cent., in White Russian S.S.R., on the Dvina. It manufactures glass, boots and shoes, etc. It has been Lithuanian, Russian, and Polish. Pop. (1967) 194,000.

VITORIA. City in N. Spain, cap. of Alava prov. Here in 1813 Wellington defeated the French. Pop. (1965) 105.358.

VITRIOL. Oil of V. is sulphuric acid; blue, green, and white Vs. are copper, ferrous, and zinc suplhate respectively.

VITTORIO VENETO (ven′etō). Italian town in Veneto which gives its name to the final victory of the Italians and British over the Austrians in Oct. 1918. It makes motor-cycles, agricultural machinery, furniture, paper, textiles, etc. Pop. (est.) 14,000.

VITUS. Christian saint, supposed to have been a Sicilian who was martyred at Rome early in the 4th cent. His aid is invoked in Catholic lands against the nervous complaint called St. Vitus' Dance (q.v.).

VIVISECTION. *See* ANTI-VIVISECTION.

VIZCAYA. Basque form of BISCAY.

VLADIMIR (*c.* 956–1015). Russian saint. As grandduke of Kiev, he was converted to Christianity in 988, m. a Christian princess, and Christianized his subjects.

VLADIVOSTOK. City and port of the R.S.F.S.R. in the Far East, on Amur Bay; it is the most important naval and commercial centre on the Russian Pacific coast, and is kept open by icebreakers throughout the year. Pop. (1967) 379,000.

VLAMINCK (vlamink′), **Maurice de** (1878–1958). French artist. B. in Paris, he was persuaded to take up painting as a career by Derain, and became famous for his landscapes, often scenes in snow. He also wrote poetry, novels and essays.

VLISSINGEN. Dutch form of FLUSHING.

VLONÉ (vlon′a). Albanian town and port, site of the declaration of independence by Albania in 1912. It had been Turkish since 1464. Pop. (1960) 45,350.

VODKA. The Russian national drink; a strong colourless liquor distilled from rye, potatoes, maize, and barley.

VOICE. Sound produced by the passage of air between the vocal cords, 2 folds of mucous membrane stretched across the larynx. The sound is much amplified by the hollow sinuses of the face, and is articulated by the muscles of the tongue and cheek. The use of the V. is controlled by the brain, and it will be lost or impaired if the speech centres are damaged.

VOLCANO. A vent in the earth's crust from which

VOLCANO. White Island in the Bay of Plenty, off North Island, New Zealand. The crater formation, fringe vegetation and thermal activities are clearly seen.
Courtesy of the High Commissioner for New Zealand.

are ejected molten rock, lava, ashes, gases, etc. Usually it is cone-shaped with a pit-like opening at the top called the crater. Some Vs., e.g. Stromboli and Vesuvius, eject the material with explosive violence; others are a quiet type in which the lava rises up into the crater and flows over the brim. Many Vs. are submarine. The chief V. regions are the Pacific (Cape Horn to Alaska); central Andes (world's highest, Guallatiri 19,882 ft., Chile); North Island, N.Z.; Hawaii; Japan and Antarctica.

VOLE. Sub-family of mice (Microtinae), widely distributed over Europe, Asia, and N. America. They are brownish or greyish above, the underside is white. The chief British types are the water V. (*Microtus amphibius*); the short-tailed field mouse (*M. agrestis*); and the bank V. (*M. glareolus*).

BANK VOLE

VOLGA (vol'gah). Longest river of Europe: 2,290 m. (2,200 m. navigable). It drains most of middle and E. European Russia, rising in the Valdai plateau and flowing into the Caspian through *c.* 200 mouths 55 m. below Astrakhan.

VOLGOGRAD. Town in the R.S.F.S.R., on the r. Volga. Metal goods and machinery are manufactured, and there are saw mills, petroleum refineries, etc. Pop. (1967) 720,000. V. was called Stalingrad 1925–61; its successful defence, 1942–3, against the Germans was a turning point of the S.W.W.

VOLLEYBALL. Team game invented in the U.S.A. in 1895, played on a court 60 ft. long by 30 ft. wide, divided into two by an 8 ft. high net. The 6 players of each team rotate in position through the 6 subsections 15 ft. by 10 ft. into which each half of the court is divided. The ball, slightly smaller than a basketball, is hit with palm or fist, the aim being to ground it in the opponents' court.

VOLT. The practical unit of electromotive force (e.m.f.) and potential difference (p.d.). It is defined as the e.m.f. or p.d. which, when steadily applied to a conductor of resistance one ohm, produces a current of one ampere.

VOLTA, Alessandro (1745–1827). Italian physicist and pioneer of electrical science. B. at Como, he was a professor there and at Pavia. He invented the voltaic pile, the electrophorus and an electroscope. The volt (q.v.) is named after him.

VOLTA. The site chosen for the implementation of the Volta River Project is Akosombo, 58 m. from Accra. The diver shown here is helping to lay the foundations of the dam.
Courtesy of Ghana Information Services.

VOLTA. The principal river of Ghana, with a length of *c.* 1,000 m., and 2 main upper branches, the Black and White V. Under the V. River Project, first envisaged 1924, it will be dammed to provide power for general purposes and for the manufacture of aluminium from the country's bauxite deposits.

VOLTAÏC REPUBLIC. Inland state of W. Africa, lying N. of Ghana. Cattle and sheep are reared, ground-nuts and cotton grown. Some mineral deposits (gold, manganese, copper, etc.) have been found. V.R., formerly called Upper Volta, was annexed by France in 1896. Given independence in 1958, it chose in 1960 to become a rep. outside the Fr. Community. Cap. Ouagadougou. Area 106,000 sq. m.; pop. (1967) 5,000,000.

VOLTAIRE (voltăr'). Pseudonym of Fr. writer François-Marie Arouet (1694–1778). B. at Paris, son of a notary, he adopted his pseudonym, probably an anagram of Arouet l(e) j(eune), in 1718. He had already started writing poetry at his Jesuit seminary in Paris, and having left school in 1711 was twice imprisoned in the Bastille and thrice exiled from the capital between 1716 and 1726 for libellous political verse: *Oedipe* his first essay in tragedy was staged in 1718. While in England 1726–9 he dedicated an epic poem on Henry IV, *La Henriade*, to Queen Caroline, and on returning to France pub. the successful *Histoire de Charles XII* (1731), and produced the play *Zaïre* (1732). His *Lettres philosophiques sur les Anglais* 1733, a panegyric of English ways, thought and political practice, led to his taking refuge with his mistress, the marquise de Chatelet (d. 1749) at Cirey in Champagne – where he wrote his best play *Mérope*, 1743, and much of *Le Siècle de Louis XIV*. In 1751–3 he was at the court of Frederick the Great, who had long admired him, but the association ended in deep enmity, and from 1754 he estab. himself near Geneva – after 1758 at Ferney, 4 m. away over the French border, hence the nickname 'patriarch of Ferney'. Among his other works are *La Pucelle*, a verse libel of Joan of Arc; the satirical tale *Zadig*; *Candide* (1759), a parody on Leibniz's 'best of all possible worlds'; and the tragedy *Irène* (1778), for which his visit to Paris to attend its production was a popular but exhausting triumph which accelerated his death there. In religion a Deist, V. devoted himself to crushing the spirit of intolerance: *see* CALAS. His remains were transferred in 1791 to the Panthéon in Paris.

VON BRAUN (brown), **Wernher** (1912–). German scientist. Technical director of the liquid-fuel-rocket and guided-missile centre at Peenemünde 1937–45, he developed the V-2 rocket used against England. After the S.W.W. he went to America to work on guided missiles and in 1960 became director of the George C. Marshall Space Flight Center in Alabama for the National Aeronautics and Space Administration, working on the Apollo project. *See* MOON.

VOODOO. Among the Negroes of the West Indies, Haiti in particular, a cult of serpent worship, phallicism, magical practices, etc.

VORONEZH. Cap. of V. region of the R.S.F.S.R., and administrative centre of the Black Earth area. It stands on the V., near where it joins the Don and has many industries, and a univ. founded at Dorpat (Tartu) in 1803 moved to V. during the F.W.W. There has been a town on the site since the 11th cent. Pop. (1967) 592,000.

VOROSHILOV, Klementiy Efremovich (1881–1969) Marshal of the Soviet Union. He joined the Bolsheviks in 1903, and was many times arrested, exiled, but escaped. Commander N.W. front in 1941, he failed to deal with the German blitzkrieg. In 1953–60 he was pres. of the Presidium of the U.S.S.R.

VOROSHILOVGRAD. See LUGANSK.

VORSTER (först'-), **Balthazar Johannes** (1915–). South African statesman. B. in Jamestown, Cape Prov., he was interned during the S.W.W. as a member of the militant Afrikaner nationalist organization Ossewabrandwag. A Nationalist M.P. from 1953, he was Min. of Justice 1961-6 (being responsible for indefinite detention of political offenders, etc.), when he succeeded as P.M. on the assassination of Verwoerd.

VORTICISM. A movement (1913-22) in English painting, with aims similar to those of Futurism (q.v.). Its exponents, of whom Wyndham Lewis was the leader, believed that painting should reflect the complexity of the modern industrial world.

VOSGES (vōzh). Mt. range in E. France, rising in the Ballon de Guebwiller to 4,667 ft. and forming the W. edge of the Rhine rift valley.

VOTE. Expression of opinion by ballot, show of hands, etc. All British subjects over 18 (21 until 1969), except peers, lunatics, and felons, are entitled to vote, a register being prepared annually, and since 1872 voting has been by secret ballot. In parliamentary elections the ballot boxes are opened by the returning officer, who counts the Vs. in the presence of the candidates or their agents. Under the Corrupt and Illegal Practices Act (1883) any candidate attempting to influence voters by gifts, loans or promises, or by intimidation, is liable to fine or imprisonment. Since 1945 the franchise in local govt. has in effect been assimilated to the parliamentary.

In the U.S.A. the voting age was reduced from 21 to 18 by legislation from 1971 (the age limit already being 18 in Georgia and Kentucky, 19 in Alaska, and 20 in Hawaii), but there may be conditions as to previous residence (varying according to state), and until declared illegal in 1965, literacy tests or payment of a poll tax were often used to decrease the Negro vote in the South. In local govt. similar rules apply.

Voting in newly emergent states, as in Africa, often raises problems of literacy or differing local languages and instead of the names of candidates being written on the ballot paper, the colourful pictorial emblems of their party may be used. Absence of accurate registers might also encourage plural voting, so that the voter (having once voted) may be marked on the hand with temporarily 'indelible ink'.

VOTIAK (votyahk´). Name 1920-32 of an autonomous region of the R.S.F.S.R. which became UDMURT A.S.S.R.

VRIES (vrēs), **Hugo de** (1848-1935). Dutch botanist, a pioneer in the study of plant evolution.

VUILLARD (vüēyahr´), **Edouard** (1886-1940). French artist. B. at Cuiseaux, he lived most of his life in Montmartre, and excels in portraits and homely interior scenes in which his mother - manager of a dressmaker's shop - often features.

VUILLARD. 'Mlle Natanson in the Artist's Studio' painted c. 1918.
Photo: Leeds Art Gallery and Temple Newsam House.

VULCAN. See HEPHAESTUS.

VULGATE. The Latin translation of the Bible made mainly by St. Jerome in the 4th cent., and so called because of its vulgar (general) use in the R.C. Church.

VULTURE. Group of birds of prey. The head and neck are bare, the plumage shaggy, and the beak and claws are hooked. True Vs. occur only in the Old World; the American forms include the condor (q.v.), turkey buzzard, and black buzzard or carrion crow.

VYBORG (vē´borg). Port and naval base in the R.S.F.S.R., on the Gulf of Finland, 70 m. N.W. of Leningrad. Founded by the Swedes 1293, annexed by Russia 1721, it was Finnish until ceded to the U.S.S.R. in 1940. Pop. (est.) 60,000.

VULTURE

VYSHINSKY, Andrei (1883-1954). Soviet statesman. B. at Odessa, he joined the Mensheviks in 1902, fought in the Civil Wars, and became a Bolshevik in 1920. As Commissar for Justice he acted as prosecutor at the treason trials of 1936-8. He was For. Min. 1949-53 (deputy 1940-9 and from 1953), and having often represented the U.S.S.R. at the U.N., was appointed permanent Soviet representative by Malenkov in 1953.

W The 23rd letter of the English alphabet, representing a semi-vowel, viz. a *u* in consonantic function. It is called double *u* because it was written *uu* or *vv* which in ligature resulted in *w*. It is not pronounced before *r* (*write, wren*) and in cases such as *two* and *sword*.

WADI HALFA (wah´dē hal´fa). Frontier town in Sudan Rep., on the Nile, the N. terminus of the Sudan railway. Pop. *c.* 14,000.

WAGGA WAGGA (wo´ga wo´ga). Town in N.S. Wales, Australia, on the Murrumbidgee, 70 m. N.N.E. of Albury, centre of an agricultural area. Pop. (1966) 22,092.

WAGNER (vahg´ner), **Richard** (1813-83). German composer. B. at Leipzig, he became director of the Magdeburg theatre, where he produced, unsuccessfully, his first opera, *Das Liebesverbot*. He lived in Paris, 1839-42. His opera *Rienzi* was produced at Dresden in 1842, followed by *The Flying Dutchman* in 1843. As conductor at the Dresden opera house he composed *Tannhäuser* and *Lohengrin*. In 1849 he fled to Paris to escape arrest for taking part in the 1848 revolutionary riots. Liszt befriended him, and produced *Lohengrin* at Weimar in 1850. W. was later allowed to return to Germany, and in 1864 won the favour of Ludwig II of Bavaria. In 1866-72 W. lived in Switzerland near Lucerne. His *Tristan und Isolde* was produced at Munich in 1865, and W. founded the festival theatre at Bayreuth, where in 1876 *The Ring of the Nibelung* was given its first performance. His last work, *Parsifal*, was produced in 1882. W. d. at Venice.

W. revolutionized the 19th cent. conception of opera, envisaging it as a wholly new art-form, in which musical, poetic, and scenic elements should be unified; and by such devices as the use of *leitmotif* he gave to opera thematic unity and coherence.

The Bayreuth tradition was carried on by W.'s wife

Cosima (1837–1930), Liszt's daughter, whom he had m. in 1870 after her first husband, Hans von Bülow, had divorced her; by her son **Siegfried W.** (1869–1930), himself a composer of operas such as *Der Bärenhäuter*, *Der Kobold*, etc.; and by Siegfried's wife **Winifred** (1897–   ), who was fined in 1947 for actively supporting the Nazi régime. R.W.'s daughter Eva m. H. S. Chamberlain (q.v.). In 1950 the festival was taken over by **Wieland** (1917–66) and **Wolfgang W.** (1919–   ), the sons of Siegfried and Winifred.

WAGNER-JAUREGG (-yow′rek), **Julius** (1857–1940). Austrian neurologist. He received a Nobel prize in 1927 for his work on the use of induced fevers in treating mental illness, e.g. malaria in cases of general paralysis of the insane.

WAGRAM (vahg′rahm). Austrian village, 10 m. N.N.E. of Vienna, the scene in July 1809 of Napoleon's victory over the Austrians under Archduke Charles. Pop. *c.* 4,000.

WAGTAIL. Genus of birds (*Motacilla*). Found mostly in N. Europe and Asia, they are small, with a slender bill and long tail. Three species breed in the British Isles: the pied W. (*M. lugubris*), the grey W. (*M. melanope*), and the blue-headed W.

PIED WAGTAIL

WAHHABIS (wah-hah′-bēz). Mohammedan sect founded by Mohammed ibn Abdul Wahab (1691–1787), whose doctrines call for a strict observance of the precepts of the Koran. They predominate in Saudi Arabia today.

WAIN, John Barrington (1925–   ). British author. Ed. at St. John's Coll., Oxford, he lectured in English literature at the Univ. of Reading 1947–55. His books incl. the novels *Hurry on Down* (1953), and *The Smaller Sky* (1967); vols. of poetry and criticism and the autobiography *Sprightly Running* (1962).

WAKAMATSU. *See* KITAKYUSHU.

WAKEFIELD, Edward Gibbon (1796–1862). British colonial statesman. B. in London, he was imprisoned for abducting an heiress 1826–9, and became manager of the S. Australian Association which founded a colony in 1836. He was an agent for the New Zealand Land Co. 1839–46, and emigrated there in 1853. His son, **Edward Jerningham W.** (1820–79), wrote *Adventure in New Zealand* (1845).

WAKEFIELD. English industrial city (co. bor.), cap. of the W. Riding of Yorks., 6 m. S. of Leeds. The Lancastrians defeated the Yorkists here in 1460. Worsteds, chemicals, machine tools, etc., are made, and there are collieries. Pop. (1961) 61,591.

WAKE ISLAND. A small Pacific island between the Philippines and Hawaii. Annexed by the U.S.A. in 1898, it was uninhabited until in 1935 it was made an air staging point, with a garrison; it was occupied by the Japanese 1941–5. Area 3 sq. m.; pop. (1960) 1,097.

WALACHIA. *See* WALLACHIA.

WALCHEREN (wahl′kheren). Island of Zeeland, Netherlands, in the estuary of the Scheldt. The surface is flat and for the most part below sea-level. Dairy farming forms the main activity. The chief towns are Flushing and Middelburg, the cap. Its motto is *Luctor et emergo* (I struggle and emerge). A Brit. force seized W. in 1809; after 7,000 of the garrison of 15,000 had died of malaria, the remainder were withdrawn. It was flooded by deliberate breaching of the dykes to drive out the Germans 1944–5, and in 1953 by abnormally high tides. Area 80 sq. m.

WALDE′NSĒS. Christian Church, founded *c.* 1170 by Peter Waldo, a merchant of Lyons. They lived in voluntary poverty, refused to take oaths or take part in war, and later rejected the doctrines of transubstantiation, purgatory, and the invocation of saints. Although subjected to persecution until the 17th cent., they spread in France, Germany, and Italy, and still survive in Piedmont.

WALES. Principality of Great Britain, lying between England to the E., the Bristol Channel to the S., and the Irish Channel to the W. and N. Off the N.W. of the mainland lies Anglesey.

PHYSICAL FEATURES. With the exception of the island of Anglesey, and of areas near the coast and in the valleys of the larger rivers, the surface is mountainous. The main massif of the Cambrian mountains runs from N. to S. and includes Snowdon (3,560 ft.), the highest point in England and Wales, Cader Idris, Plinlimon, the Black Mountains, and the Brecon Beacons. Among the rivers are the Dee, Conway, Dovey, Ystwyth, Teifi, Towy, Loughor, Neath, and Taff. The Usk, Wye, and Severn rise in Wales. The Alwen, Vyrnwy and Trawsfynydd Reservoirs are in N. Wales, and the Birmingham Corporation Reservoirs are in Radnor. *See* map p. 387.

WALES. Caerphilly Castle, in Glamorgan, built late in the reign of Henry III, is the earliest and finest example in Britain of the concentric type which exploits a flat situation by use of successive lines of defence.
Photo: British Travel and Holidays Association.

ECONOMIC. Agriculture is important in N. Wales, but the S. is one of the greatest industrial areas of Great Britain. Throughout W. sheep are grazed, and on the more level ground cattle are bred, and oats, barley, wheat, and roots cultivated. Coal is mined in the valleys of the S.E. and, on a smaller scale, near Wrexham in the N.E. Slate is quarried in the N., where lead is also mined. Abundant supplies of coal encouraged the growth of the iron and steel, tin-plate, and copper-smelting industries; export of coal, reviving in the 1960s, built up the ports of Cardiff, Penarth, Barry and Port Talbot. Nickel and oil are refined. Shipbuilding and engineering are also carried on. Hydroelectric power has been harnessed, and is used for the manufacture of aluminium. In the N. and S.W. there is a flourishing tourist traffic. The largest towns are Cardiff (the capital), Swansea, Rhondda and Merthyr Tydfil. Rhyl, Colwyn Bay, and Llandudno are seaside resorts. From Holyhead (Anglesey) and Fishguard (Pembrokeshire) steamship services ply to Ireland.

POLITICAL STRUCTURE. Administratively W. is joined with England, though certain legislation is applicable only to the principality, which is divided into 12 counties, to which is added Monmouthshire, incl. in England for some purposes until 1970.

POPULATION. The Welsh are a Celtic people. The majority belong to various Nonconformist denominations, e.g. the Calvinistic Methodists or Presbyterian Church of Wales, Methodists, Baptists, Independents, and Congregationalists. There are cathedrals at

PRINCE OF WALES.
H.R.H. Prince Charles robed for his Investiture.

Photo: Camera Press.

St. David's, Bangor, St. Asaph, Llandaff, and Brecon. The Anglican Church in Wales has been disestablished since 1914. The University of W., founded in 1893, comprises the colleges of Aberystwyth, Bangor, Cardiff, and Swansea. At Aberystwyth there is also a national library, and at Cardiff a national museum. The general system of education is similar to that of England, but Welsh is used as an additional medium. Welsh is spoken most widely in the N. Excl. Mon. Area 8,030 sq. m.; pop. (est. 1967) 2,709,930. *See* WELSH LANGUAGE AND LITERATURE.

History. Welsh history, as distinct from English, begins with the Anglo-Saxon conquest of the 5th–7th cents. The Anglo-Saxon victories at Deorham (577) and Chester (613) cut off W. from the other areas still held by the Britons, while in the 8th cent. the Mercian frontier was pushed forward to Offa's Dyke. During the 9th–11th cents. the Vikings raided the coasts. At this time W. was divided into small states organized on a tribal basis, although princes such as Rhodri (844–78), Howel the Good (*c.* 904–49) and Griffith ap Llewelyn (1039–63) temporarily united the country. The Norman marcher barons gradually conquered much of the S., but in the N. Llewelyn I (1194–1240) and Llewelyn II (1246–82) maintained a stout resistance, until the conquest of W. was completed by Edward I in 1283. A last rising was led by Owen Glendower in 1400–13.

Henry VIII in 1536 incorporated W. politically into England, and gave it parliamentary representation. Although the Reformation and Puritanism aroused little response, and in the 17th cent. W. was mainly Royalist and Jacobite, since the Evangelical Revival of the 18th cent. nonconformity has become a powerful factor in Welsh life. During the 18th cent. a strong coal and iron industry developed in the S.; in the 19th cent. the miners and ironworkers were militant supporters of Chartism, and W. has long been a stronghold of trade unionism and Socialism. Between the world wars W. suffered greatly from industrial depression; unemployment reached 21 per cent in 1937,

COUNTIES OF WALES

	Area in sq. m.	Pop. (1961 census)	County Town
Anglesey	276	51,700	Beaumaris
Brecknockshire	733	55,544	Brecon
Caernarvonshire	569	121,194	Caernarvon
Cardiganshire	692	53,564	Cardigan
Carmarthenshire	919	167,736	Carmarthen
Denbighshire	669	173,843	Denbigh
Flintshire	256	149,888	Mold
Glamorganshire	818	1,227,828	Cardiff
Merionethshire	660	39,007	Dolgellau
Monmouthshire	542	443,689	Monmouth
Montgomeryshire	811	44,228	Welshpool
Pembrokeshire	614	93,980	Haverfordwest (Welsh Hwlffordd)
Radnor	471	18,431	Presteigne
	8,030	2,640,632	

and a considerable exodus of population took place. It recovered during and after the S.W.W., but agitation for 'home rule' grew and the Welsh Nationalist Party (Plaid Cymru) returned its first member to Westminster 1966.

WALES, Prince of. Title granted to Prince Edward, afterwards Edward II, in 1301, since when it has normally be conferred on the sovereign's eldest son. Prince Charles (q.v.) was invested as 21st P. of W. at Caernarvon in 1969 by Elizabeth II.

WALEY, Arthur (1889–1966). British orientalist. He served in the Department of Prints and Drawings, British Museum, and trans. both from the Japanese and Chinese, being particularly famous for his renderings of Chinese verse in rhymeless *vers libre*.

WALKER, Patrick (Chrestien) Gordon (1902–). British Labour statesman. Entering Parliament as M.P. for Smethwick in 1945, he was P.P.S. to Herbert Morrison in 1946, and Sec. of State for Commonwealth Relations 1950–1. In 1964 he lost his seat at Smethwick, where immigration became an issue. Defeated also at Leyton, he resigned as Foreign Sec. (Oct. 1964–Jan. 1965), but regained this seat 1966. He was Min. for Education and Science 1967–8.

WALLABY. Member of the kangaroo family (q.v.). The group includes the true Ws. or 'brush' kangaroos of the scrub jungle, and the rock Ws.

WALLACE, Alfred Russel (1823–1913). British naturalist. B. in Usk, he travelled on the Amazon, and in 1858 a joint paper on the theory of evolution by W. and Darwin was read to the Linnean Society. Awarded the O.M. 1910.

ROCK WALLABY

WALLACE, Edgar (1875–1932). British author. B. at Greenwich, he was the illegitimate son of an actress who placed him with a Billingsgate fish porter. After a varied series of jobs, incl. newsboy, and a spell in the army, he was a war correspondent 1899–1902, and in 1905 pub. his 1st full-length novel *The Four Just Men*. Later books, written on copious supplies of weak tea, incl. the African stories *Sanders of the River* (1911); crime thrillers, e.g. *A King by Night* (1926) and a series built round the elderly detective Mr. J. G. Reeder; and books with a race-course setting, e.g. *The Flying Fifty-Five*. He was also a brilliantly successful writer of melodramas, e.g. *The Ringer* (1926), *The Squeaker* (1928), and *On the Spot* (1931), inspired by the career of Al Capone.

WALLACE, Henry Agard (1888–1965). American statesman. B. in Iowa, he was Secretary of Agriculture 1933–40. In Roosevelt's 3rd term, W. was vice-pres., and was Progressive pres. candidate 1948.

WALLACE, Lewis (1827–1905). U.S. general and novelist. He served in the Mexican and Civil Wars, and subsequently became governor of New Mexico and minister to Turkey. He wrote the historical novels *The Fair God* (1873) and *Ben-Hur* (1880).

WALLACE, Sir Richard (1818–90). British art connoisseur. He inherited a valuable art collection from his father, the marquis of Hertford. His widow bequeathed it to the nation and it is on view at Hertford House, London, which was acquired by the govt. The **Wallace Collection**, as it is called, contains many works by the 18th cent. French masters. *See* illus. pp. 198, 205, 679.

WALLACE, Sir William (*c.* 1272–1305). Scottish patriot. B. near Paisley, he led a revolt against English rule in 1297, won a victory at Stirling, and assumed the title of governor of Scotland. He was defeated by Edward I at Falkirk in 1298, and in 1305 was captured and executed.

WALLACHIA (woläk′iah). Former prov. of Rumania, in the S. of that country. An agricultural area of *c*. 30,000 sq. m., it was an independent principality in the Middle Ages, paying tribute to the Turks from 1343, under Turkish rule 1387 until united with Moldavia in 1861 to form Rumania.

WALLASEY. English seaside resort (co. bor.) in Cheshire at the mouth of the Mersey opposite Liverpool. Pop. (1961) 103,213.

WALLENSTEIN (vahl′lenstīn), **Albrecht von** (1583–1634). German general. B. in Bohemia, he commanded the Imperial armies with great success in the 30 Years War, but was dismissed in 1630 by the emperor, who feared his ambition. He was recalled in 1631 to face Gustavus Adolphus, and plotted for a principality of his own. In 1634 he was assassinated by his officers.

WALLER, Edmund (1606–87). English poet. He sat in the Long Parliament, and later eulogized both Cromwell and Charles II. He is remembered mainly for such lyrics as 'Go, lovely rose'.

WALLFLOWER. Perennial plant (*Cheiranthus cheiri*) in the family Cruciferae, cultivated for its fragrant red, yellow, or brown flowers.

WALLIS, Sir Barnes Neville (1887–). British aeronautical engineer. He designed the airship R 100, the bombs used against the Möhne and Eder dams in 1943, assisted development of the Anglo-French Concorde supersonic airliner, and was the inventor of the swing-wing aircraft. He was knighted 1968.

WALLOONS. A Romanized Celtic people of S.E. Belgium, numbering *c*. 3 million and speaking a French dialect. Against W. predominance the Flemish movement arose in the 19th century.

WALLSEND. English industrial town (bor.) in Northumberland, on the Tyne at the E. end of Hadrian's Wall. Shipbuilding, engineering, and coal mining are the chief occupations. Pop. (1961) 49,785.

WALL STREET. Thoroughfare in New York, so called from a stockade erected 1653. The stock exchange is on it, and it has come to be used as a synonym for stock dealing in the U.S.A.

WALNUT. Tree (*Juglans regia*) probably originating in S.E. Europe, which may have been introduced to England by Roman times and to N. America by the early colonists. It may reach 100 ft., and produces a full crop of nuts about a dozen years from planting: the timber is a favourite in furniture making.

WALPOLE, Horace, 4th earl of Orford (1717–97). English author. The son of Sir Robert Walpole, he sat in parliament as a Whig 1741–67, and succeeded to the peerage in 1791. He converted his house at Strawberry Hill into a Gothic castle, and by his novel, *The Castle of Otranto* (1765), set a fashion for 'tales of terror'. His letters are of interest.

WALPOLE, Sir Hugh (1884–1941). British novelist. B. in New Zealand, he was brought to England when 5, and in the F.W.W. served with the Red Cross in Russia, an experience reflected in *The Dark Forest* (1916). Best-known of his books are *The Cathedral* (1922) and *The Old Ladies* (1924), both set in the imaginary cathedral city of Polchester, and marked by a creation of atmosphere and hint of sadism peculiar to him. Less happy is the historical epic series the *Herries Chronicle* (1930–3) set in the Lake District.

WALPOLE, Sir Robert, 1st earl of Orford (1676–1745). British Whig Prime Minister. B. at Houghton, Norfolk, he entered parliament in 1701, and became Secretary at War 1708–10, Treasurer of the Navy 1710, and First Lord of the Treasury and Chancellor of the Exchequer 1715–17 and 1721–42. He is reckoned as the 1st P.M. His rule has become proverbial for corruption. He encouraged trade by pursuing a pacific foreign policy, but in 1739 he was forced into war with Spain. On his resignation in 1742 he received an earldom. *See* illus. p. 391.

WALPURGIS (val-), **St.** (d. 779). English nun who preached Christianity in Germany. **W. Night,** the night before 1 May, her feast day, was associated with witches' sabbaths, and particularly with that held on the Brocken in the Harz mts.

WALRUS. Carnivorous marine mammal (*Odobenus rosmarus*) of the Arctic. It reaches a dozen feet in length, has webbed flippers, a bristly moustache, and large tusks from which ivory carvings are made.

WALRUS

WALSALL (wawl′sel). English industrial town (co. bor.) in Staffs, 8 m. N.W. of Birmingham. Leather goods, castings and tubes, and electrical equipment are produced. It already had a mayor in the 15th cent. Pop. (1961) 117,836.

WALSINGHAM, Sir Francis (*c*. 1530–90). English politician. As Sec. of State from 1573, he advocated a strong anti-Spanish policy, and ran the govt.'s spy system.

WALTER, Hubert (d. 1205). Archbishop of Canterbury 1193–1205. As justiciar 1193–8 he ruled England during Richard I's absence and introduced the offices of coroner and justice of the peace.

WALTER, John (1739–1812). British newspaper editor, founder of *The Times*. Outstanding contributors to the development of the paper were his son JOHN W. II (1776–1847) and grandson JOHN W. III (1818–94). His great-great-grandson JOHN W (1873–1968) was chairman of the directors of the paper 1910–23.

WALTER, Lucy (*c*. 1630–58). Englishwoman, mistress of Charles II, whom she met while a Royalist refugee at The Hague in 1648. Her son was the duke of Monmouth.

WALTHER VON DER VOGELWEIDE (vah′lter fon der fōg′elvīde) (*c*. 1170–*c*. 1230). German poet, greatest of the Minnesinger. Of noble birth, he lived in his youth at the Austrian ducal court in Vienna, adopting a wandering life after the death of his patron in 1198. His lyrics deal esp. with love, but also with religion and politics.

WALTON, Izaak (1593–1683). English author. B. at Stafford, he settled in London as an ironmonger, and wrote short biographies of Donne, Hooker, George Herbert, etc., and the classic *Compleat Angler* (1653).

WALTON, Sir William Turner (1902–). British composer. B. in Oldham, he was ed. at the Cathedral Choir School and Christ Church, Oxford. Among his works are *Façade* (1923) to words by Edith Sitwell, later produced as a ballet; a viola concerto; the oratorio *Belshazzar's Feast*; 2 symphonies (1935 and 1960); a violin concerto (1939); a sonata for violin and pianoforte (1949) and variations on a theme by Hindemith (1963). He also composed film music for *Henry V, Hamlet* and *Richard III*. O.M. 1967.

WALVIS BAY. Chief port of S.W. Africa, a detached part of Cape Prov. from 1878, but admin. with S.W. Africa from 1922. Area 434 sq. m.; pop. (1961) 16,490 (5,067 white).

WAND, John William Charles (1885–). British Anglican churchman. Chaplain to the Forces 1915–19, he was bp. of Bath and Wells 1943–5, and bp. of London 1945–55. He has pub. *What St. Paul said* (1952), etc.

WANDERING JEW. A Jew who, according to legend, insulted Christ on His way to Calvary, and was condemned to wander about the world until His second coming. Sometimes he is called Ahasuerus.

WANGANUI (wong-ganoo′-i). City, port and airport in North Island, New Zealand, on the W. river. It makes textiles and clothing. Pop. (1967) 36,200.

WANTAGE. English market town (U.D.) in Berks,

WAPITI

in the Vale of the White Horse, *c.* 15 m. S.W. of Oxford, the birthplace of King Alfred. Pop. (1961) 5,940.

WAPITI. Species of deer (*Cervus canadensis*), native to N. America. It is reddish-brown in colour and may stand over 5 ft. in height.

WARATAH. Australian genus of trees and shrubs of the Proteaceae family, *Telopea speciosissima* bears large heads of crimson flowers in crimson bracts.

WARBLER. Family of song birds, Sylviidae. Small, insectivorous birds, generally with plain plumage, they are found mostly in the E. hemisphere. Species found in Britain incl. the white-throat, black-cap, garden W. (genus *Sylvia*); the chiff-chaff, wood and willow wrens (*Phylloscopus*); the reed and sedge Ws. (*Acrocephalus*); and the goldcrest (*Regulus*). The American Ws. are brighter and more closely allied to the Tanagers.

WAR CRIMES. The United Nations War Crimes Commission was set up in 1943 to investigate German atrocities against Allied nationals, and at the Foreign Ministers' conference in Moscow it was agreed that criminals should be tried at the place of their crimes. For the trial of major criminals *see* NUREMBERG TRIALS. Major Japanese criminals were tried before the International Military Tribunal in Tokyo, and others by the legal section of the Allied supreme command.

WARD, Artemus. Pseudonym of American humorist Charles Farrar Browne (1834–67). B. at Waterford (Maine), he achieved great popularity with comic writings such as *Artemus Ward: His Book*, *Artemus Ward: His Book of Goaks*, etc.

WARATAH

WARD, Barbara (1914–). British economist. She became in 1968 Schweitzer prof. of internat. economic development at Columbia. She m. in 1950 (Sir) Robert Jackson. Her books incl. *Policy for the West* (1951) and *The Rich Nations and the Poor Nations* (1962).

WARD, Mrs. Humphrey (1851–1920). British novelist, *née* Arnold, who became well known under her married name for serious didactic books, e.g. *Robert Elsmere* (1888), a study of religious doubt. She was a niece of M. Arnold (q.v.) and an opponent of women's emancipation.

WARD, Sir Leslie (1851–1922). British caricaturist, famous under the pseudonym 'Spy' for his caricatures in *Vanity Fair*.

WARE. English market town (U.D.) in Herts, on the Lea, 20 m. N. of London, best known for the 'Great Bed of W.' (mentioned by Shakespeare and preserved in the V. and A. Museum) and for the ride of John Gilpin there and back from Islington, related by William Cowper. Surgical goods, drugs, plastics, etc., are manufactured. Pop. (1961) 9,980.

WARHOL, Andy (1929–). American artist. B. in Pittsburgh, of Czech immigrant parents, he studied at the Carnegie Inst. of Technology, and worked as a commercial artist 1950–60. He then led the Pop Art movement with stylised reproductions of Campbell's soup tins, stills of Marilyn Monroe, etc. and

from 1963 made films such as *Flesh*, which came under the censor.

WARLOCK, Peter. Pseudonym of British composer Philip Heseltine (1894–1930). B. at London, he composed about 100 exquisite songs, a few orchestral pieces, and 'The Curlew' for tenor and chamber orchestra, and under his own name wrote books on musical subjects and ed. old English music.

WARM SPRINGS. U.S. health resort in Georgia, *c.* 40 m. N.N.E. of Columbus. F. D. Roosevelt, a victim of poliomyelitis, went to W.S. to recover in 1921, revisited it a number of times, and died there.

WARNER, Rex (1905–). British author. Making his début with *Poems* (1937), he has produced translations – Euripides, Aeschylus, Xenophon, Plutarch and St. Augustine – and a varied original output incl. novels *The Young Caeser* and *Imperial Caeser* (1958–60) and *Pericles the Athenian* (1963). He became Univ. Prof. at the Univ. of Connecticut in 1964.

WAR OFFICE. Govt. dept. formerly controlling British military affairs. The Board of Ordnance, which existed in the 14th cent., was absorbed into the War Dept. after the Crimean War and the whole named the W.O. In 1964 its essential core became a subordinate branch of the newly estab. Min. of Defence.

WARRANT OFFICER. Rank between commissioned and non-commissioned officers in the British Army, and the highest non-commissioned rank in ground trades of the R.A.F. and the R.A.F. regiment.

WARREN, Earl (1891–). American lawyer. Attorney-Gen. of California 1939–43 and gov. of the state 1949–53, he was Chief Justice of the Supreme Court 1953–69. Under him a body of liberal legal rulings, notably in civil rights, was handed down.

WARRINGTON. English industrial town (co. bor.) in Lancs, on the Mersey, 14 m. E. of Liverpool. Industries incl. soap, tanning, engineering, metal working. Pop. (1961) 75,533.

WARSAW. Cap. of Poland on the Vistula, 325 m. E. of Berlin. It is terraced above the river. The anc. city was virtually destroyed during the S.W.W., but with the help of old paintings, etc., was reconstructed on the same lines. W. dates from the 13th cent.; it replaced Cracow as cap. in 1595. It has suffered a number of sieges; in the S.W.W. it fell to the Germans 27 Sept. 1939; there was an heroic but abortive rising of its citizens against the German occupiers on 1 Aug. 1944. W. was not liberated until 17 Jan. 1945. Pop. (1966) 1,261,000. The *Warsaw Treaty* (1955) signed by U.S.S.R., Albania (excl. 1962), Bulgaria, Czechoslovakia, E. Germany, Hungary, Poland and Rumania, estab. a 20-yr. alliance on the lines of NATO.

WARSAW. The Church of the Congregation of the Blessed Sacrament was originally built by King John III Sobieski to commemorate his victory over the Turks at Vienna in 1683. After their destruction in the S.W.W. both the church and the buildings on market place in which it stands were reconstructed in the old style.   *Courtesy of the Polish Travel Office, 'Orbis'.*

WARSHIP. The cruiser H.M.S. *Lion*, seen leaving Malta, is 555 ft. long, with a beam measurement of 64 ft., and is crewed by some 720 officers and men. Her 6 inch and 3 inch guns have radar-controlled turrets and an extremely high rate of fire.
Crown Copyright.

WARSHIP. A fighting ship armed and manned for war. Between the world wars the battleship (q.v.) was regarded as supreme, but became increasingly vulnerable to air attack and by 1958 the last of America's battleships, the U.S.S. *Wisconsin*, had joined the 'mothball fleet'.

The *aircraft carrier* (q.v.) has assumed the role of flagship, because of the superior striking power and range of its aircraft, but in the R.N. is itself being phased out by 1972. To replace it in giving naval squadrons air support economical 'mini-carriers' using vertical take-off Harrier aircraft were under consideration 1969: the Soviet *Moskva* helicopter assault carrier is on allied lines. Heaviest W. afloat, although retaining high mobility, is the U.S.S. *Enterprise* (1961) at 75,000 tons, first of its class to be nuclear-powered and with a flight-deck over 1,000 ft. long, maximum width 252 ft., and a capacity of *c.* 100 aircraft. The maximum speed is 35 knots: range 140,000 m.

Next in size (8–10,000 tons) is the *cruiser*, self-contained, self-sufficient and able to sail half across the world without refuelling. Sufficiently protected not to reduce their (33 knots) speed too greatly, they carry a substantial armament, and are intended to patrol the ocean highways for the defence of sea-borne trade, to search out and destroy enemy surface raiders, act as scouts for the battle fleet at sea, and maintain communication between the fleet and its base or destination. Guided-missile ships are increasingly used and are rapidly replacing conventional cruisers. During and after the S.W.W. the smaller (*c.* 2,000–5,000 tons) *destroyer* (intended for the destruction of torpedo-boats and submarines) and *frigate* (q.v.) have tended to merge to one group of very fast (*c.* 36 knots), well-armed but unarmoured escort vessels, the majority equipped for anti-aircraft and anti-submarine work.

The *submarine* (q.v.) may well be the major W. of the future, cf. its numerical preponderance in the fleet of the U.S.S.R. Conventionally powered vessels have greatly increased underwater speed and range by the 'snort' air intake, or by use of hydrogen peroxide to burn the fuel, and the world's 1st nuclear-powered sub. U.S.S. *Nautilus* (1955) has a range of 40,000 m., sufficient to encircle the globe without surfacing. In addition to torpedoes, nuclear-powered submarines are armed with 'Polaris' atomic missiles which may be fired below surface and have a range of *c.* 3,000 m.

WART HOG. Two species of African wild swine (*Phacochoerus aethiopicus* and *P. africanus*) which have enormous heads with a bristly mane, fleshy pads beneath the eyes, and 4 large tusks.

WARTON, Joseph (1722–1800). English poet, headmaster of Winchester 1766–93, whose verse and

Essay on the Writings and Genius of Pope (1756–82) marked an 'anti-classical' reaction. His brother, Thomas W. (1728–90), was prof. of poetry at Oxford 1757–67 and pub. the 1st *History of English Poetry* (1774–81).

WARTS. Verrucae; unsightly protuberances commonly caused by local overgrowth of skin. Ordinary warts on the hands may be removed by caustics. Another type, found on the feet, is infectious.

WARWICK, Richard Neville, earl of, called the King-maker (1428–71). English statesman. During the Wars of the Roses he fought at first on the Yorkist side, and was largely responsible for placing Edward IV on the throne. Having quarrelled with him, he restored Henry VI in 1470, but was defeated and killed by Edward at Barnet.

WARWICK. Co. town (bor.) of Warwickshire, England, on the Avon, 20 m. S.E. of Birmingham. The 14th cent. castle has a collection of paintings: the Univ. of W. was estab. 1965. Pop. (1961) 16,032.

WARWICKSHIRE. Midland county of England, whose main rivers are the Avon and Tame. In the north lies the Forest of Arden. The county is much cultivated and possesses rich coalfields. Its industrial towns incl. Birmingham and Coventry. Warwick is the co. town; other centres are Stratford-on-Avon and Leamington Spa. 983 sq. m.: pop. (1967) 2,110,360.

WARWICKSHIRE. On the Avon above Stratford, Charlecote Park provides a beautiful setting for a fine herd of deer. Tradition has it that Shakespeare left for London as a result of a poaching incident on the estate and satirized its owner, Sir Thomas Lucy, as Justice Shallow.
Courtesy of the National Trust.

WASH, The. Rectangular bay of the North Sea in England between Norfolk and Lincoln. The coast is marshy. King John lost his baggage and treasure in the W., 1216.

WASHINGTON, Booker Taliaferro (*c.* 1859–1915). American Negro educationist, who founded in 1881 Tuskegee Institute, a Negro co-educational college in Alabama. He wrote *Up from Slavery* (1901).

WASHINGTON, George (1732–99). 1st President of the U.S.A. B. in Virginia, he distinguished himself as a soldier in campaigns against the French and Indians 1753–7, and was elected to the Virginia House of Burgesses. As a strong opponent of the British govt.'s policy, he sat in the Continental Congresses of 1774 and 1775, and on the outbreak of war was chosen C.-in-C. For the course of the war *see* AMERICAN INDEPENDENCE, WAR OF. After the war he retired to his estate, Mount Vernon, but in 1787 he re-entered politics as president of the Constitutional Convention. He was elected President of the U.S.A. in 1789, and re-elected in 1793, but refused to serve a

GEORGE WASHINGTON. A commanding portrait by Gilbert Stuart of the 6 ft. 3 in. president.
Courtesy of the New York Historical Society, N.Y. City.

3rd term, setting a precedent that was followed until 1940. Although he attempted to draw his ministers from all factions, his aristocratic outlook alienated Jefferson, with whose resignation in 1793 the 2-party system originated. In his farewell address (1796) W. maintained that the U.S.A. should avoid European quarrels and entangling alliances. He d. and was buried at Mount Vernon, Virginia.

WASHINGTON. Pacific state of the U.S.A., watered by the Columbia and its tributaries. Except for the S.W. and for the Great Plain of the Columbia r. to the E., nearly all W. is mountainous. The Cascade Range runs parallel to the coast, and between Puget Sound and the Pacific are the Olympic Mts. The chief agricultural products are apples and other fruit, wheat, oats, etc. Cattle and sheep are bred. Industries incl. aircraft, ships, road transport vehicles; lumber and paper from extensive forests; processed food, chemicals, cement, and exploitation of zinc, uranium, lead, gold and silver. The cap. is Olympia; the largest towns are Seattle, Spokane, and Tacoma. W., which incl. Mt. Rainier and Olympia National Parks, was admitted to the Union in 1889. Area 68,192 sq. m.; pop. (1970) 3,409,169.

WASHINGTON. Cap. of the U.S.A., on the Potomac, coterminous with the Dist. of Columbia. The city is laid out according to a uniform plan made by Pierre L'Enfant, a French engineer officer – the 1st modern cap. city to be designed as such. Its many fine buildings incl. the Capitol, Lincoln Memorial, Washington Monument, White House, Supreme Court, Library of Congress, Department of Commerce, Pentagon (housing the War Department), Corcoran and National Galleries, and Folger Shakespeare Library. W. was founded in 1790, and has been the federal cap. since 1800. In 1814 it was burnt by the British. Most of the permanent population consists of govt. employees. Pop. (1970) 764,000; met. area 2,856,809.

WASP. Name of certain stinging insects in the order Hymenoptera. Of the 290 British species, only a

few are true Ws. (*Vespidae*); the rest are digger Ws. There are 7 British species of social Ws. in the genus *Vespa*, some nesting below ground, others in trees or bushes, and the largest being the hornet: all the others are solitary. Among social Ws. the queens devote themselves to egg-laying, the fertilized eggs producing female workers; the males arise from unfertilized eggs and have no sting. The larvae are fed on insects, but the mature insects feed mainly on fruit and sugar. In winter the fecundated queens hibernate, but the other Ws die.

WASPS. 1, Red-banded sand wasp; 2, common wasp; 3, greater horntail.

WASSERMANN (vahs′sermahn), **August von** (1866–1925). German prof. of medicine. B. at Bamberg, he became head of the department of experimental therapy and serum research at the Robert Koch Institute in Berlin in 1906 and, in 1913, director of the Kaiser Wilhelm Inst. there. In 1907 he discovered a sero-diagnosis of syphilis (W. reaction).

WATCH. See CLOCKS.

WATER (H_2O). A liquid, without colour, taste, or odour; an oxide of hydrogen. W. begins to freeze solid at 0°C and 32°F, and to boil at 100°C and 212°F. Liquid, it is virtually incompressible; frozen, it expands by 1/11th of its volume. 1 cu. cm. weighs 1 gramme at 4°C, forming the unit of specific gravity. It has the highest known specific heat, and acts as an efficient solvent, particularly when hot. It

WATER. Reservoirs in the West, although often beautiful because of their surroundings, tend to be strictly functional in design. In the East, as here at Penang, a different tradition prevails.   *Photo: Deane.*

takes the form of sea, rain, and vapour, and tempers and distributes the sun's heat, and supports all forms of land and marine life. W. covers 70 per cent of the earth's surface. Water supply in sparsely populated regions comes usually from natural springs, supplemented by pumps and wells. Urban sources are deep artesian wells, rivers and reservoirs, usually formed from enlarged lakes or dammed and flooded valleys, from which W. is conveyed by pipes, conduits and aqueducts (q.v.) to filter beds. By seeping through layers of shingle, gravel and sand, harmful organisms are removed, and the W. is then distributed (sometimes with such additions as chlorine or fluorine, qq.v.) by pumping or gravitation through mains and pipes. In towns, besides industrial demands, domestic and municipal (road-washing, sewage, etc.) needs account for *c.* 30 gals per head each day, and supplies are a pressing problem in dry, fast-developing areas such as California.

WATER-BUGS. Several families of aquatic hemipterous insects. They incl. the Hydrometridae (pond-skaters) and Notonectidae, of which the waterboatman is the chief member.

WATERBURY. City of Connecticut, U.S.A., on the Naugatuck, dating from 1674. Clocks, watches, and brass and copper ware are manufactured. Pop. (1960) 107,130.

WATER-COLOUR PAINTING. Method of painting with pigments mixed with water. Known in China as early as the 3rd cent., the art as practised today developed in England, where it was the ideal medium for the expression of shifting vagaries of weather, in the 18th cent. Artists excelling in W.C.P. incl. Sandby, Cozens, Cotman, de Wirt, Turner, Constable, Cox, Varley, Sargent, Marin, Steer, Cezanne, Signac, Dufy, Nolde, Klee, Paul and John Nash. The Royal Soc. of Painters in Water Colours was founded 1804.

WATERCRESS. Perennial aquatic plant (*Nasturtium officinale*), found in Europe and Asia, and cultivated as a salad crop.

WATERFLEA. Aquatic crustaceans in the order Cladocera. The commonest species is *Daphnia pulex*.

WATERFORD. (1) Co. town (co. bor.) and port of W. county, Rep. of Ireland, on the Suir. Pop. (1966) 29,842. (2) County of Munster, Rep. of Ireland watered by the Suir and Blackwater. The Comeragh and Monavallagh ranges rise in the N. and centre.

WATERFORD. Nearly 100 ft. high, the 12th century round tower of ruined St. Declan's church on Ram Head at Ardmore is an almost perfect specimen among these detached campaniles which served as watchtowers and keeps in the times of the Norse raiders. For security's sake the entrance door was placed 13 ft. from the ground.
Courtesy of the Irish Tourist Board.

Cattle raising, brewing and distilling are the chief occupations. Area 710 sq. m.; pop. (1966) 73,080.

WATER LILY. Aquatic plants in the family Nymphaeaceae. The fleshy roots are embedded in the mud and the large round leaves float on the water. The beautiful flowers may be white, pink, yellow or blue: the white *Nymphaea alba* and yellow *Nuphar luteum* are common in Great Britain, and the *Victoria regia*, with leaves about 6 ft. in diameter, occurs in the Amazon. *See* LOTUS.

WATERLOO. Village 8 m. S. of Brussels. Nearby, on 18 June 1815, Wellington defeated Napoleon. Wellington had 68,000 men, of whom 24,000 were British, the remainder being German, Dutch, and Belgian, and Napoleon 72,000. During the last stage of the battle Wellington was supported by the Prussians under Blücher.

WATERLOO CUP. The most important greyhound race in England, known as 'the courser's Derby', and named after the Waterloo Hotel, Liverpool, whose proprietor originated the race in 1836. It is held annually, usually in Feb.

WATER POWER. *See* HYDRO-ELECTRIC POWER.

WATFORD. English market town (bor.) in Herts, on the Colne and the Grand Union Canal. Printing, brewing, malting, corn milling and iron founding are important industries. The church of St. Mary dates from 1230. Pop. (1961) 75,630.

WATSON, John Broadus. *See* BEHAVIOURISM.

WATSON-WATT, Sir Robert (Alexander) (1892–). British physicist. During a long career in govt. service (1915–52), he proposed in 1935 a method of radiolocation of aircraft – later developed into radar – a key contribution to the S.W.W. He was deputy chairman of the Radio Board of the War Cabinet 1943–6, and subsequently was a scientific consultant in the U.S.A. and U.K. He was knighted in 1942.

WATT, James (1736–1819). Scottish engineer. B. at Greenock, he became mathematical instrument maker to Glasgow univ. in 1757. While repairing a model of Newcomen's steam engine in 1764, he devised an exterior condenser to eliminate the loss of power involved in the engine. Patented in 1769, the invention was applied to engines which W. and Boulton manufactured near Birmingham.

WATT. Electrical unit of power. In the c.g.s.
2M

system, it is work done at the rate of 1 joule or 10^7 erg per second, or the amount of energy expended per second by a current of 1 ampere under a p.d. of 1 volt. The power in Ws. is found by multiplying the current in amperes by the p.d. in volts.

WATTEAU (vahtō′), **Antoine** (1684–1721). French painter. B. in Valenciennes, he went to Paris in 1702, and under the influence of the Flemish genre painters painted scenes of tavern and of military life. He later became famous as a painter of the *fête galante*. He was admitted to the French Academy in 1717 and visited London in 1719.

WATTLE. Name given in Australia, where the fluffy golden flowers are the national emblem, to certain species of Acacia (q.v.). Wonderfully adapted to drought conditions, the specially tough leaves further avoid loss of water through transpiration by turning their edges only to the direct rays of the sun. The Ws. are used for tannin and fencing.

WATTS, George Frederick (1817–1904). British artist. B. in London, he studied in the R.A. Schools. In 1864 he m. Ellen Terry: later the marriage was dissolved. In 1867 he was elected R.A. He painted allegorical, biblical, and classical subjects, and portraits, many of which are in the National Portrait Gallery, and others in the Watts art gallery at Compton, nr. Guildford. As a sculptor he executed 'Physical Energy' for Rhodes' grave in S. Africa, and a replica in Kensington Gardens.

WATTS, Isaac (1674–1748). British Nonconformist churchman and hymn-writer. He wrote 'O God, our help in ages past', and other hymns.

WATTS-DUNTON, Walter Theodore (1832–1914). British writer, author of *Aylwin* (1898) a novel of gypsy life, poems and critical work. He was a close friend of Swinburne, who shared his house at Putney for many years, Rossetti and Borrow, cf. *Old Familiar Faces* (1915).

WAUGH, Evelyn Arthur St. John (1903–66). British novelist. Ed. at Oxford, he later became an R.C. and pub. studies of Edmund Campion and Ronald Knox. During the S.W.W. he served with distinction. His novels incl. satirical studies such as *Decline and Fall* (1928), *Vile Bodies*, *Put Out More Flags*, and *The Loved One* (1948); also *Brideshead Revisited* (1945), a serious work. His brother, **Alec W.** (1898–), was ed. at Sherborne and Sandhurst. He served in the army 1917–18 and also 1939–45. Among his works are *The Loom of Youth* (1917), *No Truce with Time*, and *Island in the Sun* (1956). **Auberon W.** (1940–), son of Evelyn, is a Tory and R.C., and has written witty novels incl. *Consider the Lilies* (1968).

WAVELL, Archibald, 1st earl (1883–1950). British field marshal. He served in the F.W.W. and was appointed C.-in-C. Middle East in July 1939. He conducted the N. African war against Italy 1940–1, and achieved notable successes there as well as in Ethiopia. W. was transferred to C.-in-C. India in July 1941, and succeeded Lord Linlithgow as viceroy (1943–7), being created visct. in 1943.

WAVERLEY, John Anderson, 1st visct. W. (1882–1958). British administrator. B. in Edinburgh, he had a distinguished Civil Service career, was Gov. of Bengal 1932–7, and in 1938 was elected 'National' M.P. for the Scottish Univs. A few months later, as Lord Privy Seal, he organized Civil Defence and in 1939 became Home Sec. and Min. for Home Security (the nationally distributed home outdoor – Anderson – air-raid shelters were named after him). He became Lord Pres. of the Council in 1940 and was Chancellor of the Exchequer 1943–5. He was knighted in 1919 and created a visct. in 1952.

WAXWING. Family of birds (*Ampelidae*) found in the northern hemisphere. The Bohemian W. (*Ampelis garrulus*) is greyish-brown above with a reddish-chestnut crest, black streak at the eye, and variegated wings with 'wax tips'. *See* illus. p. 1084.

WAXWING. The cedar waxwing (*A. cedrorum*) is purplish-cinnamon above, with grey wings tipped with the red horny appendages which give its name. It feeds on berries, particularly those of the red cedar. *Photo: G. Ronald Austing.*

WAZIRISTAN. Tribal territory of W. Pakistan, on the border with Afghanistan. The inhabitants, Waziris and Mahsuds, are warlike, and are a source of trouble to Pakistan, as formerly to British India. Area 5,700 sq. m.

WA'ZYK (vazik), **Adam** (1905–). Polish writer. B. in Warsaw, he made his name with *Poem for Adults* (1955), a protest against the régime which preceded the fall of the Stalinists in 1956. In 1957 he resigned with others from the party, disappointed in Gomulka's illiberalism. He is also a novelist and playwright.

WEALD (wēld). District of S.E. England between the N. and S. Downs, comprising parts of Kent, Sussex, and Surrey. Its name is from an Anglo-Saxon word meaning wooded tract, but most of the trees which once covered the W. were cut down as fuel for the olden Sussex ironworks. It is occupied by grazing land, hop gardens, and orchards.

WEASEL. Carnivorous mammal in the family Mustelidae, feeding mainly on mice, voles and rats. The common W. (*Mustela nivalis*) of Europe and Asia has an elongated body, short legs and tail. The fur is red-brown above and white beneath, but in winter in cold climates is wholly white, acting as camouflage against snow. There are several American species.

WEATHER. See METEOROLOGY.

WEATHERHEAD, Leslie D. (1893–). British Methodist minister. Minister of the City Temple, London, 1936–60, he is noted for his interest in psychology as a practical help to living and the interpretation of religion. His books incl. *A Plain Man Looks at the Cross* and *The Resurrection of Christ in the Light of Modern Science and Psychical Research*.

WEAVING. The production of fabric by means of a loom. It is a craft of world-wide distribution since ancient times, and the products of Egypt and Assyria can compare with modern output. The basic process is the interlacing at right angles of longitudinal threads (the warp) and crosswise threads (the weft), the latter being carried across from one side of the loom to the other by the shuttle. Hand-looms may be horizontal or vertical – the latter being the type which has developed industrially in the West – and are still used, e.g. in the manufacture of tweeds in the British Isles. Of great importance in the hand-loom era was the Jacquard machine, the last in a series of inventions

for producing complicated designs, which was perfected in the early 19th cent. The power-loom (1786) was essentially the invention of the English clergyman, Edmund Cartwright. There have been many subsequent improvements, but one of the hindrances to yet further increased speed has been the time taken by the passage of the shuttle: in the 1960s there were experiments in Japan with the propulsion of the weft by water-jet.

WEBB, Sir Aston (1849–1930). British architect, designer of the new front of Buckingham Palace; Admiralty Arch; the chief section of the Victoria and Albert Mus.; and Britannia Royal Naval College. He was pres. of the R.A. 1919–25.

WEBB, Mary (1882–1927). British novelist. B. in Shropshire, she wrote of country life and characters, e.g. *Precious Bane*, which became known through a recommendation by Earl (Stanley) Baldwin.

WEBB, Matthew (1848–83). English swimmer. B. in Shropshire, he was the first to swim the English Channel, in 21¾ hours, in 1875. He was drowned in trying to negotiate the Niagara rapids.

WEBB, Sidney. See PASSFIELD, LORD.

WEBER (veh'ber), **Carl Maria von** (1786–1826). German composer. B. in Eutin, he became kapellmeister at Breslau (1804–6), Prague (1813–16), and Dresden, (1816). The originator of the romantic opera, he composed *Abu Hassan* (1811), *Der Freischütz* (1820), *Euryanthe* (1823), as well as instrumental and pianoforte works. He d. during a visit to London where he produced his opera *Oberon*, written for the Covent Garden theatre.

WEBSTER, Daniel (1782–1852). American statesman and orator. B. in New Hampshire, he sat in the House of Representatives from 1813, and in the Senate from 1827, at first as a Federalist and later as a Whig. He became Sec. of State 1841–3 and 1850–2, and negotiated the Ashburton Treaty (1842) which fixed the Maine-Canada boundary.

WEBSTER, John (*c.* 1580–*c.* 1625). English dramatist. He wrote *The White Devil* and *The Duchess of Malfi*, usually considered the greatest English tragedies outside Shakespeare, and the tragicomedy *The Devil's Law Case*.

WEBSTER, Noah (1758–1843). American lexicographer, b. in Connecticut. His *American Dictionary of the English Language* (1828) standardized American deviations from English spelling.

WEBSTER, Thomas (1800–86). British artist. With J. C. Horsley (q.v.) a leader of the Victorian domestic school of painting, specializing in such subjects as 'The Dame's School' and 'Village Gossips'.

WEDDELL, James (1787–1834). British Antarctic explorer. In 1823 he reached 75° S. lat. and 35° W. long. The W. Sea is named after him.

WEDEKIND (veh'dekint), **Frank** (1864–1918). German dramatist. B. at Hanover, he became in succession journalist, advertising agent, book-keeper to a circus, and actor and producer. He achieved fame with *Frühlings Erwachen*, *Der Marquis von Keith*, *Die Büchse der Pandora*, etc. Many of his writings gave offence on account of alleged pornographic tendencies.

WEDGWOOD, Dame Cicely Veronica (1910–). British historian. Dau. of Sir Ralph W. (1874–1956), the railway administrator, she is an authority on the 17th cent. and has pub. fine studies of *Strafford* (1935), *Cromwell* (1939), *William the Silent* (1944), *Richelieu and the French Monarchy* (1949), *Montrose* (1952), *The King's Peace* (1955), and *The King's War* (1958). Created D.B.E. 1968, she was awarded the O.M. 1969.

WEDGWOOD, Josiah (1730–95). British potter. B. at Burslem, Staffs, where he estab. his factory (Etruria) in 1759, he is most celebrated for his jasper ware, a type of unglazed porcelain with the general properties of basalt, capable of being coloured throughout (blue, green or black), with the design in bas-relief in white. From 1775 he employed Flaxman as a designer, but many fine portrait medallions were the work of his chief modeller William Hackwood. Very famous is his copy of the Portland Vase. Modern W. ware is an important British export. *See* also illus. p. 125.

WEDNESBURY (wenz-). English industrial town in Staffs, from 1965 divided between the co. bors. of Walsall and W. Bromwich, built on the site of a temple to Woden. Steel tubes and castings, etc., are produced. Pop. (1961) 34,511.

WEEVER. Genus of fish (*Trachinus*) found off European coasts, the greater W. (*T. draco*) and lesser W. (*T. vipera*) off Britain. They bury themselves in sand, and bathers may be wounded by treading on their poison-charged dorsal spines.

WEEVIL. Division of beetles (Rhynchophora) in the order Coleoptera. The head has a prolonged rostrum, which in the female is used to bore a hole in which to place the eggs. The larvae are white; the adult beetles of *Phyllobius* and *Polydrusus*, the common British genera, are bright green. They feed on vegetable matter. In America the granary W. (*Calandra granaria*) attacks grain, the cotton-boll W. (*Anthonomus grandis*) damages cotton crops.

WEGENER (vāg'-), **Alfred** (1880–1930). German polar explorer and geophysicist. He made 3 expeditions to Greenland and d. on a fourth, but is chiefly remembered for 'W.'s Hypothesis', expounded in *Origin of Continents and Oceans* (1915). *See* CONTINENT.

WEIGHTLESSNESS. The condition whereby there is no gravitational force acting on a body, either because gravitational force is cancelled out by equal and opposite acceleration, or the body is so far outside a planet's gravitational field that it exerts no force upon it.

WEIGHTS AND MEASURES. *See* p. 1118.

WEIHAI (wā'hī). Port in Shantung, China; also a commercial centre. It produces textiles, rubber articles, matches, soap, vegetable oils. It was leased to Britain 1898–1930, during which time it was a naval and coaling station. It was occupied by the Japanese 1938–45. Weihaiwei, its name until 1949, means awe-inspiring seafort. Pop. (1957) 222,000.

WEIL (vīl), **Simone** (1909–43). French author. Of well-to-do Jewish Parisian family, she was for a time a schoolmistress, then plunged into working-class life, tried to help the Republicans in Spain and during the S.W.W. worked briefly for de Gaulle in London. She d. in an English sanatorium. Apart from essays, her works (advocating political quietism) were posthumously pub. incl. *The Need for Roots* (1952), *Waiting on God* (1951) and her notebooks in 1956.

WEILL (vīl), **Kurt** (1900–50). American composer. B. in Germany, he wrote chamber and orchestral music, but is best known for the operas in which he collaborated with Brecht (q.v.), e.g. *The Threepenny Opera* (1928) (an adaptation of John Gay's *The Beggar's Opera*), with its song 'Mack the Knife', and *The Rise and Fall of the City of Mahagonny* (1930), which attacks social corruption and caused a riot at its première in Leipzig. He tried to evolve a new form of musical theatre, using subjects with a contemporary relevance and the simplest possible musical means. With the rise of the Nazis he left Germany for the U.S., where he wrote a number of successful scores for Broadway. Other important works incl. the opera *Die Burgschaft* (1931). He was m. to the singer Lotte Lenya (q.v.).

WEIMAR (vī'mahr). Town of Erfurt district, E. Germany, on the Ilm 13 m. E. of Erfurt. Before 1918 it was cap. of the grand-duchy of Saxe-Weimar, and was subsequently cap. of Thuringia. In the late 18th and early 19th cents. it was a great cultural centre and the residence of Goethe, Schiller, and Herder. Pop. (1965) 67,000.

WEIMAR REPUBLIC. Name for the republican

régime in Germany 1918–33. which was destroyed by Hitler and his followers. It took its name from the city where in Feb. 1919 a constituent assembly met to draw up a democratic constitution.

WEINBERGER (vīn'berger), **Jaromir** (1896–1967). Czech composer. B. at Prague he taught composition in New York and Europe. His *Schwanda the Bagpiper* is the most successful of several operas.

WEIZMANN (vīts'-). **Chaim** (1874–1952). Zionist leader – he was Pres. of Israel 1948–52 – and chemist. B. in Russia, he became a naturalized British subject, and as director of the Admiralty laboratories 1916–19 discovered a process for the manufacture of acetone. He conducted the negotiations leading up to the Balfour Declaration.

WELDING. The making of a union between pieces of metal or non-metal, at faces rendered plastic or liquid by heat or by pressure or both. Forge W., employed by blacksmiths since early times, was the only method available until near the end of the 19th

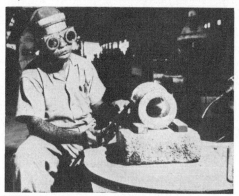

WELDING. Using a welding torch to prepare a casting in the workshops of 'Demba' at Mackenzie, 65 miles south of Georgetown in British Guiana.
Courtesy of the Demerara Bauxite Company Ltd.

cent. The principal modern processes are gas and electric-arc W., in which the heat from a gas flame or an arc melts the faces to be joined and additional 'filler metal' is usually added; and resistance W. in which the weld is formed by a combination of resistance heating from an electric current, and pressure. Recent developments incl. electric-slag and electron-beam W. processes.

WELE'NSKY, Sir Roy (1907–). Rhodesian statesman. B. in Salisbury, S. Rhodesia, he became a noted trade union worker among the railwaymen, and was heavyweight boxing champion of the Rhodesias. He succeeded Malvern as P.M. (1956–63).

WELHAVEN (vel'hahven), **Johan Sebastian Cammermeyer** (1807–73). Norwegian poet. B. at Bergen, he was prof. of philosophy at Christiania 1839–68. A supporter of the Dano-Norwegian culture, he is one of the greatest Norwegian masters of poetic form. His works incl. the satiric *Norges Daemring* (1834), songs based on folklore, etc.

WELLAND SHIP CANAL. Waterway, 25 m. long, cut through the Niagara peninsula to join Lakes Erie and Ontario, completed 1932. It is in Canadian territory. It replaced an earlier canal opened in 1832.

WELLES, Orson (1915–). American actor, producer and director. In 193. he collaborated in founding the Mercury Theatre, N.Y., where his productions incl. a modern dress version of *Julius Caesar*. In 1938 his realistic broadcast presentation of H. G. Wells' *The War of the Worlds* caused panic among listeners. In 1940 he wrote, produced, directed and starred in *Citizen Kane*, his 1st film, and other

2M*

film roles incl. the character of Harry Lime in *The Third Man* (1950); his film of Kafka's book *The Trial* appeared in 1963.

WELLESLEY, Richard Colley, marquess (1760–1842). British statesman. The brother of the duke of Wellington, he was Gov.-Gen. of India 1798–1805, and by his victories over the Mahrattas greatly extended the territory under British rule. He was For. Sec. 1809–12, and Lord Lieutenant of Ireland 1821–8 and 1833–4.

WELLESZ (vel'ess), **Egon** (1885–). Austrian composer and musicologist. As prof. of music at Vienna from 1913, he specialized in the history of Byzantine, Renaissance and modern music, and on leaving Austria settled in Oxford, where he was reader in Byzantine music 1948–56. His compositions incl. operas such as *Alkestis*; symphonies, notably the 5th (1956), ballet music, and a series of string quartets; and his writings incl. a biography of Schoenberg, and several studies of Byzantine music.

WELLINGTON, Arthur Wellesley, 1st duke of (1769–1852). British soldier and Tory statesman. B. either in Meath or Dublin, Ireland, he was ed. at Eton, and in 1787 entered the army. Going to India in 1796, he was a major-general by 1802, and achieved victories over the Mahrattas at Assaye and Argaum in 1803. These victories and his negotiation of the peace of 1803 earned him a knighthood, and he returned to England in 1805, but it was as lt.-general and commander of the forces in the Iberian Peninsula (*see* PENINSULAR WAR) that he estab. his reputation. He defeated the French at Vimeiro, but was superseded and recalled, although he again received the command in 1809. He was made visct. W. in 1809, earl and marquess of W. in 1812, and having expelled the French from Spain in 1814 was made duke of W. He was appointed ambassador to Paris (1814–15), took part in the Congress of Vienna, and, following Napoleon's escape from Elba, defeated him at Quatre-Bras and at Waterloo (1815). This last victory made him the most influential man in Europe; he again took part in the Vienna Congress, where he opposed the dismemberment of France, and supported the restoration of the Bourbons. He commanded the army of occupation until 1818. As Tory P.M. 1828–30 he was not a success: he was forced against his will to concede Catholic emancipation, while his opposition to parliamentary reform made him extremely unpopular for a time. He was For. Sec. 1834–5, and was a member of the cabinet 1841–6. He held the office of C.-in-C. of the forces at various times from 1827, and held it for life from 1842. *See* APSLEY HOUSE.

WELLINGTON. Capital of New Zealand, in N. Island, on Cook Strait. It was founded in 1840 by Col. Gibbon Wakefield, as the first settlement of the New Zealand Co., and rises on hills in a fertile volcanic region. The residence of the Governor-General and the seat of govt. since 1865, it possesses the Houses of Parliament, Victoria univ., the national museum, and – as the seat of an Anglican bp. and an R.C. archbp. – 2 cathedrals. There is an excellent harbour, an airport, and good railway communications. Among its manufactures are woollen goods, soap, shoes, meat, and bricks. Pop. Greater W. (1967) 170,500.

WELLS, Herbert George (1866–1946). British author. B. at Bromley, Kent, son of a professional cricketer, he took his degree at the Royal College of Science, S. Kensington, taught for some years, and then made his name in science fiction with *The Time Machine* (1895), *The Invisible Man* (1897), *The War of the Worlds* (1898), etc. Next he turned to psychological and sociological novels, lively and human – *Kipps* (1905), *Tono-Bungay* (1909), *Ann Veronica* (1909) – in which sexual relationships were frankly treated and which aroused much protest – *The History of Mr. Polly* (1910), and *Mr. Britling sees it Through* (1916).

Of his many other books, *The Outline of History* (1920) and *The Shape of Things to Come* (1933), from which a number of his prophecies were fulfilled, are notable. He exerted a vitalizing, releasing effect on his contemporaries, providing them with a new ideology.

WELLS. English city (bor.) in Somerset, 19 m. S. of Bristol. The 12th–13th cent. cathedral was built

WELLS. The cathedral, seen across the moat of the bishop's palace, is one of the loveliest in England. It was begun in the 12th century and the 160 ft. high central tower was completed early in the 14th, but the two western towers have remained incomplete.

near the site of a Saxon church. W. was made the seat of a bishopric *c*. 900, changed to Bath and Wells in 1244. Pop. (1961) 6,691.

WELSH. A member of the Brythonic group of the Celtic (q.v.) family of languages, known from *c*. 800. In 1961 about 26,223 people in Wales and Monmouthshire spoke W. only; another 656,000 W. and Eng.

The chief remains of early W. literature are contained in the Four Ancient Books of Wales – the Black Book of Carmarthen, the Book of Taliessin, the Book of Aneirin, and the Red Book of Hergest – anthologies of prose and verse of the 6th–14th cents. Characteristic of W. poetry is the bardic system of ensuring the continuance of traditional conventions: most celebrated of the 12th cent. bards was Cynddelw. The English conquest of 1282 involved the fall of the princes who supported them, but after a period of decline a new school arose in S. Wales with a new freedom in form and sentiment, the most famous poet being the 14th cent. Davydd ap Gwilym, and in the next cent. the classical metrist Davydd ab Edmwnd. With the Reformation biblical translations were undertaken, and Morgan Llwyd and Ellis Wynn o Lasynys wrote religious prose. Popular metres resembling those of England developed, e.g. the poems of Huw Morys. In the 18th cent. the classical poetic forms revived with Gronwy Owen, and the Eisteddfod movement began: popular measures were used by the hymn-writer William Williams. The 19th cent. saw few notable figures save the novelist Daniel Owen, but the foundation of a Welsh univ. and the work there of Sir John Morris Jones produced a 20th cent. revival with the poets T. Gwynn Jones, S. Roberts, W. J. Gruffydd, etc.

WELSH CORGI. Breed of dog, with a fox-like head, and pricked ears. The coat is dense and any colour except pure white. There are 2 types, the Pembrokeshire and the heavier Cardiganshire.

WELWYN GARDEN CITY. English town (U.D.) in Herts, 20 m. N. of London, founded in 1919–20 by Ebenezer Howard. The principal industries are chemicals, electrical engineering, metal goods, clothing, and food preparation. Pop. (1961) 34,944.

WEMBLEY. District of the Greater London bor. of Brent. W. Stadium, opened in 1924, has been the scene of the British Empire Exhibition, the annual F.A. cup final, and in 1948 of the Olympic Games.

WENCESLAS (wen'seslas), **St.** (d. c. 929). Duke of Bohemia, who attempted to spread Christianity among his people, and was murdered by his brother. He is the patron saint of Czechoslovakia, and the 'good king W.' of the carol.

WENCHOW. Port and industrial town in Chekiang, China, at the mouth of the Wu-kiang. It was opened to foreign trade in 1877 and became prosperous, but has declined in importance. Pop. (1957) 201,600.

WENTWORTH, William Charles (1793–1872). Australian lawyer and statesman. B. in New South Wales, he led a movement which secured partial self-govt. in 1842, and responsible govt. in 1856. He founded Sydney univ. in 1852, and worked for the estab. of Australian federation.

WERFEL (ver'-), **Franz** (1890–1945). Austrian poet, dramatist, and novelist. B. in Prague, he lived in Germany, Austria, and France, and in 1940 escaped from a French concentration camp to the U.S.A., where he d. His works incl. the poems *Der Weltfreund, Wir sind, Der Gerichtstag*, etc.; the plays *Juarez und Maximilian, Paulus unter den Juden*, and *Das Reich Gottes in Böhmen*; and the novels *Verdi* and *The Song of Bernadette*.

WERGELAND (vär'gelahnd), **Henrik** (1808–45). Norwegian lyric poet. B. at Christiansand, he was the greatest leader of the Norwegian revival.

WERTH, Alexander (1901–69). British journalist. B. in St. Petersburg, he was ed. at Glasgow univ., and became foreign correspondent in Paris and Moscow for the *Guardian, Sunday Times*, etc., excelling in pungent comment also in his books, e.g. *America in Doubt* (1959) and *The Khrushchev Phase* (1961).

WE'SKER, Arnold (1932–). British playwright. Brought up in Hackney, London, he made his name with the trilogy *Chicken Soup with Barley, Roots* and *I'm Talking about Jerusalem* (1959–60), which has an earthy socialist realism derived from his own breadth of human experience as carpenter's mate, farm hand, pastry cook, etc. A later success, *Chips with Everything* (1962), is directed against a prevalent soggy lack of standards. In 1961 he became director of Centre 42.

WESLEY, John (1703–91). British founder of Methodism (q.v.). B. at Epworth, Lincs, where his father was the rector, he went to Christ Church, Oxford, and was ordained in the C. of E. in 1728. Returning to the college in 1729 as a tutor, he was one of the original band of Methodists. In 1735 he went to Georgia as a missionary. On his return he experienced 'conversion' at a service at the Moravian church in Aldersgate Street, London, on 24 May 1738, and from being a rigid High Churchman developed into an ardent Evangelical. When the pulpits of the Established Church were closed to him and his followers, he took the Gospel to the masses. For 50 years he rode about the country on horseback, preaching daily, largely in the open air, and often several times a day. He is said to have travelled 250,000 m. and preached 40,000 sermons. His literary output was great, and his sermons became the doctrinal standard of the Wesleyan Methodist Church. His *Journal* gives an intimate picture of the man and his work. His brother **Charles W.** (1707–88) was one of the original Methodists at Oxford and became a principal preacher and theologian of the Wesleyan Methodists. He wrote some 6,500 hymns, incl. 'Jesu, lover of my soul'. Charles's son, **Samuel W.** (1766–1837), was a celebrated organist, and composer of oratorios, church and chamber music.

WESSEX. The kingdom of the West Saxons, said to have been founded by Cerdic c. 500, which comprised Hants, Dorset, Wilts, Berks, Som., and Devon. Egbert in 829 estab. West Saxon supremacy over all England. Thomas Hardy popularized the use of the term W. for the S.W. counties.

WEST, Benjamin (1738–1820). American artist. B. in Pennsylvania, he settled in London in 1763, and became pres. of the R.A. in 1792. He painted historical pictures, incl. 'The Death of Wolfe', and many early American artists studied with him: *see* UNITED STATES: ART.

WEST, Mae (1892–). American actress. She made her début in 1897, was popular in vaudeville, and appeared in plays, such as *Diamond Lil*, and films.

WEST, Dame Rebecca. Pseudonym of British author Cicily Isabel Fairfield (1892–). A perceptive writer- on political matters, she has pub. the Yugoslav study *Black Lamb and Grey Falcon* (1942), *The Meaning of Treason* (1949), *The Vassall Affair* (1963), etc. She was created D.B.E. in 1959.

WEST BROMWICH. English industrial town (co. bor.) in Staffs, 6 m. N.W. of Birmingham. Industries incl. springs, tubes, foundries, and rolling mills. Pop. (1961) 95,909.

WESTERMARCK, Edward Alexander (1862–1939). Finnish anthropologist, noted for his studies *The History of Marriage* (1891) and *The Origin and Development of the Moral Ideas* (1906–8).

WESTERN AUSTRALIA. The largest state of the Australian Commonwealth, covering all of the continent W. of long. 129° E. Towns incl. Perth, the cap., and Fremantle, the chief port, on the W. coast, Bunbury, Kalgoorlie, Geraldton, and Albany. The chief rivers are the Fitzroy, Fortescue, Gascoyne, Murchison, and Swan. Most of the interior is desert. In 1826 a convicts' settlement was estab. at King George Sound, and in 1829 the Swan River Settlement was estab. Development came with gold strikes at Kimberley 1885 and Kalgoorlie 1893: and the state has many other minerals – iron, copper, nickel, silver, coal and oil (Barrow Island) – particularly rich discoveries being made in the 1960s. Wheat and other cereals, fruit, tobacco, and wool are produced. Large areas are irrigated for dairying and stockraising in the N. and along the S.W. coast. Responsible govt. was achieved in 1890, and in 1901 W.A. was one of the states federated in the Commonwealth of Australia. The govt. is vested in the Gov., the Legislative Council, and the Legislative Assembly. Area 975,920 sq. m.; pop. (1966) 848,100.

WESTERN ISLES. Another name for the HEBRIDES.

WEST HARTLEPOOL. *See* HARTLEPOOL.

WEST INDIES. An archipelago lying between the

WEST INDIES. The Caribbean is a world of its own and to meet its special conditions a cross-bred herd of Indian Brahman and Aberdeen Angus cattle have been built up on Jamaica for beef production by Alcan. *Courtesy of Alcan Jamaica Ltd.*

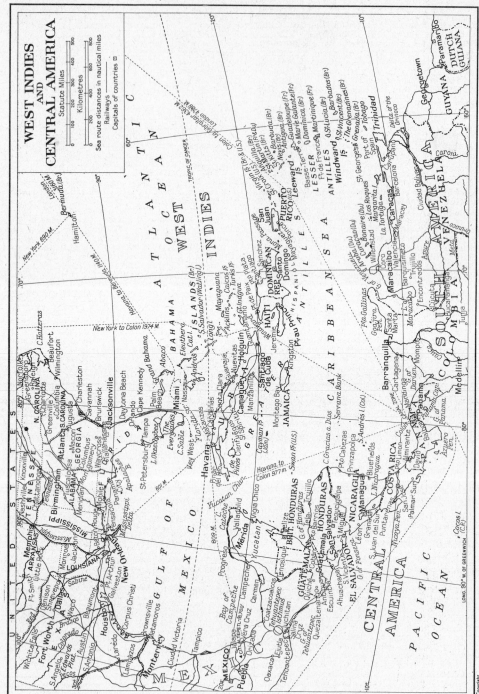

WEST INDIES
AND
CENTRAL AMERICA

Statute Miles

Kilometres

See route distances in nautical miles
Railways
Capitals of countries ⊡

GEOGRAPHIA LTD.

Copyright

coasts of Florida and Venezuela, and dividing the Atlantic Ocean from the Gulf of Mexico and the Caribbean Sea. They consist of the British W.I.; Curaçao, belonging to the Netherlands; Guadeloupe and Martinique, belonging to France; Puerto Rico, belonging to the U.S.A.; the Virgin Islands, belonging to the U.S.A. and Britain; and the independent Cuba, Dominican Republic, and Haiti (qq.v.).

The Federation of the WEST INDIES, comprising Antigua, Barbados, Dominica, Grenada, Jamaica, Montserrat, St. Kitts with Nevis and Anguilla, St. Lucia, St. Vincent, and Trinidad and Tobago (qq.v.), came into existence in 1958. This federation, of which the federal parliament was at Port-of-Spain, Trinidad, came to an end in 1962 when first Jamaica and then Trinidad and Tobago withdrew. Attempts at a new federation were abandoned in 1965, and individual solutions sought. The difficulties of the smaller dependencies in assuming the burden of full independence were met by the creation of the new non-colonial status of Associated State (q.v.), assumed in 1967 by Antigua, Dominica, Grenada, St. Christopher-Nevis-Anguilla and St. Lucia. There is a built-in option for independence on a two-thirds vote of the local legislature plus a referendum, and association with another Caribbean country within the Commonwealth may be voted without a referendum.

WEST LOTHIAN. Central county of Scotland, bordering the S. shore of the Firth of Forth. The Almond is the chief river, with its tributary the Avon. Agriculture and dairy farming are carried on. Coal is mined and iron worked. Linlithgow is the co. town; other towns are Bathgate and Bo'ness. Area 120 sq. m.; pop. (1961) 92,764.

WE'STMACOTT, Sir Richard (1775–1856). British sculptor. He studied under Canova in Rome, was elected R.A. in 1811, and became a prof. at the Academy. He executed monuments in Westminster Abbey and in St. Paul's, and the 'Achilles' in Hyde Park, etc.

WESTMEATH. Inland co. of Leinster, Republic of Ireland. It is drained by the Shannon, Inny, and Brosna, and noted for the Loughs Ree, Sheelin, Ennell, etc. Agriculture and dairy farming are the main occupations; there are limestone quarries; some textiles are manufactured. Mullingar is the co. town. Area 681 sq. m.; pop. (1966) 52,900.

WESTMINSTER. City, most famous of the Greater London boroughs, on the N. bank of the Thames between Kensington and the City of London. It contains the London palaces of the sovereign (Buckingham and St. James's), Houses of Parliament, Westminster Abbey (see below), Whitehall with its many govt. offices, and the Cenotaph; Westminster (R.C.) Cathedral, the Methodist Central Hall, Victoria and Charing Cross stations, the National Gallery, and Trafalgar Square; Westminster, Charing Cross, and St. George's hospitals; theatres and clubs, and many other important buildings. It also incl. Hyde, Green, and St. James's Parks and part of Kensington Gardens. From 1965 W. has had a Lord Mayor. Pop. (1967) 258,930.

WESTMINSTER BRIDGE, crossing the Thames from the Houses of Parliament to St. Thomas's hospital, was rebuilt 1856–62. WESTMINSTER HALL is a relic of the old palace of the English kings; it was originally built by William II in 1097; its magnificent oak roof was erected by Richard II, 1394–9. The hall was the seat of the English law courts until 1882. WESTMINSTER CATHEDRAL, the seat of the R.C. archbishopric of W., was begun in 1895 and consecrated in 1910; it is in the Byzantine style. WESTMINSTER SCHOOL, one of the great English public schools, was originally a school attached to the abbey, whence its name of St. Peter's College. Elizabeth I refounded it in 1560. WESTMINSTER HOSPITAL (1719) was opened on its present site in 1939.

WESTMINSTER ABBEY. Built on a marshy site that was once Thorney Island, W.A. was traditionally founded by Sebert, king of the East Saxons, early in the 7th cent.; its official title is the Collegiate Church of St. Peter. The Norman church and monastery were consecrated under Edward the Confessor in 1065, but rebuilding was begun by Henry III in 1245 and was finished in 1528 shortly before the monastery was dissolved. Later additions to what is a fine example of pointed Gothic incl. Henry VII's chapel and the west towers, completed in 1740 to a design by Nicholas Hawksmoor. All the English sovereigns (save Edward V) have been crowned in the abbey since William I, and many of them, incl. Edward the Confessor, Henry III, Edward I, Henry VII, Elizabeth I, Charles II, William III, Anne, and George II, are buried there. The Coronation Chair contains the 'stone of destiny' (traditionally Jacob's pillow at Bethel) on which the Scottish kings were crowned; it was brought to London by Edward I. The abbey is crowded with memorials (incl. the Battle of Britain Memorial Chapel dedicated 1947) and tombs of statesmen, writers, and others, incl. the 'Unknown Warrior', who have left their mark on English history.

WESTMORLAND. N.W. county of England, S. of Cumberland with a coastal outlet on Morecambe Bay. It is part of the Fell country and Lake District. The highest peaks are Helvellyn (3,118 ft.) and Bow Fell (2,960 ft.); the lakes incl. Windermere, part of Ullswater, Grasmere, Rydal Water, and Hawes Water. Cattle and sheep are pastured, and there are small manufacturing and mining activities. Appleby, the co. town, and Kendal are the chief towns. W. has been a county since c. 1100. Area 789 sq. m.; pop. (1967) 68,030.

WESTON-SUPER-MARE. English seaside resort (bor.) in Somerset, on the Bristol Channel 21 m. W.S.W. of Bristol, a fishing village until the early 19th cent. Pop. (1961) 43,923.

WESTPHALIA (–fāl'ia). Former prov. of Prussia, from 1946 part of the Land of North Rhine-Westphalia (q.v.). An independent duchy from the Middle Ages, W. was incorporated in Prussia by the Congress of Vienna, 1815, and made a prov. 1816 with Münster as its cap. W. incl. the Ruhr (q.v.), chief industrial area of Germany, and was the scene of violent fighting during the last stages of the S.W.W.

The kingdom of W., 1807–13, created by Napoleon, did not incl. the duchy, but consisted of Prussian lands W. of the Elbe, Hessen, Brunswick, and Hanover.

WEST POINT. Location in N.Y. state, on the Hudson, 50 m. N. of N.Y.C., site of the U.S. Military Academy (commonly referred to as W.P.), estab. in 1802. W.P. has been a military post since 1778. The majority of the cadetships are awarded on the recommendation of a Senator or Representative; candidates must be U.S. citizens 17–22.

WEST VIRGINIA. Mountainous E. state of the U.S.A. The Ohio, Monongahela, and the 2 Kanawhas are the chief rivers, while the Alleghenies run S.W. through the state. This hilly country provides fruit, poultry and dairy products, and is rich in hardwood forests. Resources incl. coal, natural gas and petroleum, which support a chemical industry incl. manmade fibres and plastics, and steel, glass and pottery are manufactured; petroleum refined; and meat packed. Charleston is the cap. W.V. was part of Virginia until 1861 when the western cos. of Va. voted against secession and formed themselves into a separate state, admitted to the Union 1863. Area 24,181 sq. m.; pop. (1970) 1,744,237.

WEXFORD. Seaport and co. town (U.D.) of Wexford, Rep. of Ireland, on the Slaney. Shipbuilding and fishing are carried on. Founded by the Danes in the 9th cent., W. was devastated by Cromwell in 1649. Pop. (1961) 10,002.

WEXFORD. Co. of the Rep. of Ireland, in the prov. of Leinster, on the S.E. coast. There are hills in the N.W., and the co. is watered by the Barrow and Slaney. The co. town is Wexford. Fishing and the production of oats, barley, potatoes, etc., sheep, pigs and poultry are the chief industries. Area 908 sq. m.; pop. (1966) 33,437.

WEYDEN (vīden), **Rogier van der** (*c.* 1399–1464). Flemish painter. B. at Tournai, he settled at Brussels after 1429. His 'Descent from the Cross' is in Madrid.

WEYGAND (vāgon'), **Maxime** (1867–1965). French general. Chief of staff to Foch and chief of the Allied general staff in 1918, he successfully defended Warsaw against the Red Army in 1920, and was appointed C.-in-C. in May 1940. He advised surrender to Germany, and was subsequently Defence Min. in Pétain's govt., and High Commissioner of N. Africa 1940–1. He was a prisoner in Germany 1942–5, and after his return to France was arrested, released in 1946, and in 1949 the sentence of national infamy was quashed.

WEYMOUTH (wā'muth) and **Melcombe Regis** (mel'kum rē'jis). English seaport and resort (bor.) in Dorset, at the mouth of the Wey. W. bay is a fleet anchorage. W., which dates from the 10th cent., was the 1st place in England to suffer from the Black Death, 1348. M.R. was incorporated with W. in 1571. George III made W. popular as a seabathing resort. Pop. (1961) 40,962.

WHALES. Member of a large group of mammals in the order Cetacea (q.v.), adapted for marine life. They swim chiefly by using the fin-tail, the fore-limbs or flippers maintaining balance, and when rising to the surface to breathe eject a column of exhausted air and water from the blowhole, i.e. nostril. The Mysta-coceti feed on plankton, strained through their whale-bone plates, but the Odontoceti use their teeth to capture their prey, though not to eat it, since they swallow it whole. Especially ferocious is the killer W., of which one captured specimen had 32 adult seals

WHALES. 1, Killer whale; 2, bottle-nose; 3, rorqual.

in its stomach. The milk on which the young are suckled resembles condensed milk, having a water content of only 40–50 per cent. The most important whaling product is oil (used principally in making soap and margarine), and catches are restricted by inter-national agreement to conserve supplies: the high intelligence of Ws. means that their slaughter, usually by shell harpoon guns, involves great cruelty. The herd instinct is strongly developed, some species keeping in touch by emitting sounds, and some are migrant from the polar regions to warmer waters in winter. The blue W. is the biggest living animal, averaging 85 ft. in length and weighing 106 tons.

WHARTON, Edith (1862–1937). American author, *née* Jones. Her work was greatly influenced by her friend Henry James, and her psychological novels incl. *The House of Mirth*, the tragic *Ethan Frome*, *The Custom of the Country*, and *The Age of Innocence*.

WHEAT. Cereal plant derived from the wild *Triticum*, a grass native to the Middle East. It has been cultivated since Neolithic times, and is the chief cereal used in bread making in temperate climates which suit its growth. W. is killed by frost, and damp renders the grain soft: warm dry regions

DENNIS WHEATLEY

produce the most valuable grain. The chief wheat-producing areas of the world are the Ukraine, central and N.W. United States, the Punjab, the prairie provinces of Canada, parts of France and S. Germany, Italy, Argentina, and S.E. Australia. Flour is milled from the endo-sperm, the coatings of the grain producing bran and pollard. Semolina is also prepared from W.

WHEATEAR. Small mi-gratory bird (*Saxicola oenanthe*) found throughout the Old World and also in parts of N. America. The plumage is light grey above and white below, with a white patch on the back, a black face-patch, and black and white wings and tail.

WHEATLEY, Dennis Yates (1897–). British novelist. B. in London, he served in the F.W.W., and in 1932 sold the family wine business to take up writing. With a gift of narrative that recalls Dumas, he has written a 'saga' of the adventures of Roger Brook, secret agent in the French Revolutionary period; a series dealing with black magic and occult-ism and another on wartime espionage – *They Used Dark Forces* (1964) combines both these last themes.

WHEATSTONE, Sir Charles (1802–75). British physicist. B. in Gloucester, he was originally a musical-instrument maker, but became in 1834 prof. of experimental philosophy at King's Coll., London. His inventions incl. the concertina, harmonica, and stereoscope, and he took out the first patent for the electric telegraph with W. F. Cooke in 1837. He measured the speed of electric discharge in conductors, and also devised the *W. bridge* (a special electrical network for measuring resistance) from an idea of S. Hunter Christie's.

WHEELER, Sir Charles (1892–). British sculptor. He has executed sculptures for India House, and the Bank of England; and the bust of Jellicoe in Trafalgar Sq. He was P.R.A. 1956-66.

WHEELER, Sir (Robert Eric) Mortimer (1890–). British archaeologist. He was keeper and sec. of the London Museum 1926–44, director-gen. of archaeo-logy in India 1944–8, and prof. of the archaeology of the Roman provs. at the Univ. of London 1948–55: these posts reflect the breadth of his interests and his attractive presentation of his striking work at Maiden Castle and in revealing the Indus Valley civilization, as well as his TV appearances, has made him one of the best-known of modern archaeologists.

WHELDON, Huw (1916–). British television producer. Joining the B.B.C. in 1952, he produced such programmes as Portraits of Power and Monitor; headed Music and Documentaries 1963–5, was pro-gramme controller 1965–8, and in 1969 became managing director B.B.C. television.

WHELK. Family of marine gastropods. The com-mon W. (*Buccinum undatum*) is widely distributed round the N. Sea and Atlantic. It is fished for bait and food, and has a thick spiral shell.

WHIG PARTY. The predecessor of the present Liberal Party. The name, first applied to the rebel Covenanters in Scotland, came into use in 1679 for supporters of the Exclusion Bill. The W.P. strongly supported the 1688 revolution, and was in power con-tinuously 1714–60. Led by a group of great land-owning families, it drew its support mainly from the business classes and the Nonconformists; it advocated the development of industry and commerce, a vigorous foreign policy, and religious toleration. During the

French Revolution the W.P. adopted a policy of parliamentary reform. After the triumph of this policy in 1832 the name 'Liberal' replaced that of Whig. In U.S. history the name W.P. was used during 1836 –54 by one of the 2 major parties, which opposed the radical policy of Andrew Jackson and defended commercial interests.

WHIP. In Britain an M.P. employed by his party to secure attendance of members of the party at important debates. The govt. chief W., and the 3 junior Ws., are salaried officials; the Ws. of opposition parties are unpaid. The term, which is derived from the whipper-in of a hunt, is also applied to the summons to attend sent to members.

WHIPPET. Breed of dog resembling a small (15–20 lb.) greyhound. The W. was developed, as a cross between the greyhound and fox terrier, by the colliers of northern England, who race them along a straight track, at the end of which their owners stand calling them.

WHIPSNADE. English locality in Beds, 3 m. S. of Dunstable, site of a zoological park covering 500 acres belonging to the London Zoological Society, where wild animals, and birds, are bred and exhibited in their natural state. It was opened to the public in 1931.

WHISKY. An ardent spirit containing a large percentage of alcohol, distilled chiefly from cereals. For many years Scotland has been the centre of the whisky-distilling industry. W. is obtained from malt in Scotland and Ireland, and from Indian corn or rye in the U.S.A. In Ireland and the U.S. it is spelt 'whiskey'.

WHISKY. Scottish crofters of two hundred years ago used copper kettles to distil their whisky. The modern still, with a capacity of 4,000 gallons and taking 6 smiths a month to hammer into shape, is also made of copper since this will not corrode or impart any alien flavour.
Courtesy of Johnnie Walker Scotch Whisky.

WHIST. A card game played by 2 sides of 2 partners each. Each player is dealt 13 cards. The object of the game is to score tricks, a trick being gained by the partners who play the highest card of a suit, or the highest trump card, the trump suit being determined before the start of the game. Each trick over 6 counts one point to the partners, who score 5 points for a game, and 2 games for a rubber.

WHISTLER, James Abbott McNeill (1834–1903). American artist. B. in Mass., he abandoned a military career for painting, and in 1855 went to Paris where he was associated with the Impressionists. He settled in Chelsea, executed etchings of the Thames, and painted 'Old Battersea Bridge', 'The Symphony in White', and portraits. His 'Nocturnes', 1877, were adversely criticized by Ruskin, and led to the libel trial of 1878 in which W. was awarded a farthing damages. W. retaliated in 1890 with *The Gentle Art of Making Enemies*.

WHISTLER, Rex John (1905–44). British artist, celebrated for fanciful murals, e.g. Tate Gallery Restaurant and Haddon Hall. He was killed in Normandy in the S.W.W. His brother **Laurence W.** (1912–), a poet and diamond-point engraver on glass, uses the stippling process invented by the Dutch in the 17th

cent., in which the design is composed of small dots hammered into the glass.

WHITBY. English fishing port (U.D.) in the N. Riding of Yorks, at the mouth of the Esk. Ruins remain of the Benedictine abbey (1078) built on the site of an abbey founded by St. Hilda 657, destroyed by the Danes 867. Capt. Cook's ship *Resolution* was built at W., where he had served his apprenticeship. There are large reserves of potash, running out under the sea, in the area. Pop. (1961) 11,662.

WHITBY, Synod of. Ecclesiastical council held in 664, which marks the triumph of the Roman over the Irish form of Christianity in England.

WHITE, Byron Raymond (1917–). American lawyer. A leading footballer he was awarded a Rhodes Scholarship to Oxford in 1939, while studying at the Univ. of Colorado, and later worked his way through Yale law school by playing professional football. He became an associate justice of the Supreme Court in 1962.

WHITE, Elwyn Brooks (1899–). American essayist. B. at Mount Vernon, N.Y., he was ed. at Cornell univ., where his tutor Will Strunk helped to mould his jauntily precise style. Entering journalism as a reporter, he has been greatly influential in American writing as contributing editor to the *New Yorker*: collections of his pieces incl. *The Points of My Compass* (1963), and he collaborated with Thurber in *Is Sex Necessary?* (1929).

WHITE, Gilbert (1720–93). English naturalist. B. at Selborne, Hants, he took orders in 1747, and in 1751 retired to his birthplace. His *Natural History and Antiquities of Selborne* (1789) is a classic, and his home 'The Wakes' was opened as a museum and library in 1955.

WHITE, Patrick (1912–). Australian novelist and playwright. Ed. at Cheltenham College and Cambridge, he pub. his 1st book *Happy Valley*, portraying suffering as a condition of existence, in 1939. Similar allegorical overtones occur in the more mature *The Aunt's Story* (1946), *Voss* (1957) and *Riders in the Chariot* (1961), which also draw strongly on the resources of his native Australia. His most important play is *The Ham Funeral*.

WHITE, T(erence) H(anbury) (1906–64). British writer, best known for his retelling in 4 vols. of the Arthurian legend, beginning with *The Sword in the Stone* (1938), and pub. collectively as *The Once and Future King* (1958).

WHITE, William Hale. *See* RUTHERFORD, MARK.

WHITEFIELD, George (1714–70). British evangelist. B. at Gloucester, he came under Methodist influence while at Oxford. He took orders in 1738, but was suspended for his unorthodox doctrines and methods. For many years he travelled through Britain and America, and by his preaching contributed greatly to the evangelical revival. W.'s Tabernacle was built for him in Tottenham Court Rd., London (1756: bombed 1945 but rebuilt). He d. while visiting New England.

WHITEFISH. Name applied to freshwater fishes of the salmon family, belonging to the genus *Coregonus*. Abundant in N. American lakes, they also occur in Europe and Asia; 3 species are found in Britain.

WHITEHAVEN. English seaport (bor.) in Cumberland, with large docks. There are coal mines extending beneath the sea which have suffered several bad accidents, e.g. 136 men killed in 1910, 104 in 1947. Pop. (1961) 17,541.

WHITEHEAD, Alfred North (1861–1947). British philosopher and mathematician. He was prof of applied mathematics at London 1914–24, and 1924–37 prof. of philosophy at Harvard, U.S.A. In his 'theory of organism' he attempted a synthesis of metaphysics and science. Among his works are *Principia Mathematica* (1910–13; with Bertrand Russell), *Concept of*

Nature, and *Adventures of Ideas* (1933). W. received the O.M. in 1945.

WHITEHORSE. Cap. of Yukon Territory, Canada, on Lewes r., centre of a mining and fur-trapping region. W. is the terminus of a railway to Skagway, Alaska, U.S.A., and on the N.W. Highway; it also has an airport. It replaced Dawson as cap. in 1953. Pop. (1966) 4,771.

WHITE HORSE, Vale of the. Valley of the Ock, which flows into the Thames at Abingdon, England. It takes its name from the figure of a horse, 374 ft. long, cut in the chalk at Uffington, Berks. Similar figures are found at Bratton, Wilts, and elsewhere in England; some are probably prehistoric, and of totemic origin. *See* illus. p. 233.

WHITE HOUSE. Official residence of the president of U.S.A., in Washington, D.C. It is a plain edifice of sandstone painted white, built in the Italian renaissance style, 1792–9, to the designs of Hoban, who also restored it after it was fired by the British in 1814. The interior was completely rebuilt 1948–52 and the décor remodelled by Jacqueline Kennedy (q.v.). The name is first recorded in 1811.

WHITEMAN, Paul (1891–1967). American dance-band leader specializing in 'symphonic' jazz. He wrote an autobiography, *Jazz.*

WHITE RUSSIA. S.S.R. of the U.S.S.R. bordering on Poland. It is low-lying, and is drained by the W. Dvina, Dnieper and its tribs., incl. the Pripet and Beresina. The Pripet Marshes lie in the E.; forest covers more than a quarter of its area. The climate is mild and damp. Products incl. potatoes, flax, pigs, cattle, sheep in the agricultural area; chemicals, matches, timber, paper, textiles, lorries, cement, leather are industrial products. Power stations operate on peat from the extensive peat bogs. The rep. suffered severely under German invasion and occupation during the S.W.W. Minsk is the cap.; other large towns are Vitebsk and Gomel. Area 80,500 sq. m.; pop. (1968) 8,820,000.

WHITES. Term applied to the counter-revolutionary party during the French Revolution, when the royalists used the white lily of the French monarchy as their badge, and also during the Russian Civil Wars of 1917–21.

WHITE SEA. Gulf of the Arctic Ocean, on which stands the N. Russian port of Archangel. The N. Dvina and Onega flow into the W.S. which is frozen in the winter. The W.S. is linked by canal with the Baltic, the Black, and the Caspian Seas.

WHITING. Food-fish (*Gadus merlangus*) common in N. European waters. It differs from the haddock by the absence of a barbel on the chin.

WHITLAM, Edward Gough (1916–). Australian Labour statesman. A lawyer, he entered the Fed. Parliament in 1952, became leader of the Opposition in 1967, and in 1972 P.M. and Foreign Minister.

WHITMAN, Walt(er) (1819–92). American poet. B. on Long Island, he worked in printing offices, as a schoolteacher, and as a journalist. In 1855 he pub. his most influential vol., later much enlarged, *Leaves of Grass.* He preached an American vision of freedom in union, expressed in verse stripped of the conventional ornaments of rhyme and regular metre. In 1865 he pub. *Drum-Taps*, a vol. inspired by his work as an army nurse during the Civil War. *See* illus. p. 1062.

WHITSTABLE. English resort (U.D.) in Kent at the mouth of the Swale. 6 m. N.W. of Canterbury. W. oysters are celebrated. Pop. (1961) 19,534.

WHITSUNDAY. Church festival held 7 weeks after Easter, corresponding to the Jewish Pentecost and commemorating the descent of the Holy Spirit on the apostles. The name is probably derived from the white garments worn by candidates for baptism at the festival.

WHITTEN-BROWN, Sir Arthur (1886–1948). British airman. After serving in the F.W.W., he took part in the first non-stop flight across the Atlantic as navigator to Capt. John Alcock (q.v.) in 1919.

WHITTIER, John Greenleaf (1807–92). American poet. B. in Mass, of a Quaker family, he entered politics and journalism, and became a powerful opponent of slavery, as in the verse *Voices of Freedom* (1846). Among his other works are *Legends of New England in Prose and Verse, Songs of Labor* and the New England narrative *Snow-Bound* (1866).

WHITTINGTON, Richard (d. 1423). English merchant. B. in Glos, he made a large fortune as a mercer, and was mayor of London 1397–8, 1406–7, and 1419–20. His cat first appears in a play of 1605.

WHITTLE, Sir Frank (1907–). British engineer. He was on the special-duty list working on jet propulsion 1937–46. In 1941, the Gloster aircraft flew with the Whittle jet engine, and in 1948 his pioneer work in this field was recognized by a govt. award of £100,000.

WHOOPING COUGH. Pertussis; a specific infectious fever probably due to a bacillus and conveyed by droplets from the nose and throat. It is marked by a peculiar and obstinate cough ending in a long crowing inspiration. The patient should be isolated for 5 weeks, and the cough may persist for months.

WHORTLEBERRY. *See* BILBERRY.

WHYMPER, Edward (1840–1911). British mountaineer. He made the first ascents of many alpine peaks incl. the Matterhorn (1865), and in the Andes scaled Chimborazo and other mountains. He was a capable wood-engraver, and wrote *Scrambles amongst the Alps* (1871), and *Zermatt and the Matterhorn* (1897).

WICHITA (wē'chēta). Largest city of Kansas, U.S.A., on the Arkansas, a milling centre with petroleum refineries, stockyards, foundries, and factories making aircraft, motor-vehicles, etc. W. has a municipal airport. Pop. (1960) 254,698.

WICK. Scottish seaport (royal burgh), co. town of Caithness, founded 1808 by the British Fisheries Association, an important fishing port (formerly chiefly herring) with shipyards, distilleries, etc., and an airport. Pop. (1961) 7,397.

WICKHAM, Sir Henry (1846–1928). British planter, who collected rubber seeds in Brazil, which then had a monopoly in rubber production, and so founded the plantations of Ceylon, Malaya, etc.

WICKLOW. Maritime co. of Leinster, Rep. of Ireland, S. of Dublin. The centre is occupied by W. mountains which reach 3,039 ft. in Lugnaquilla. The Slaney and Liffey are the main rivers. The co. town is the seaport (U.D.) of W.; pop. (1961) 3,117. Cattle are bred and lead and copper mined. Area 782 sq. m.; pop. (1966) 60,428.

WIDECOMBE-IN-THE-MOOR (wid'icum). English village on Dartmoor, Devon, 5 m. N.W. of Ashburton, made famous by the song 'Widecombe Fair'. Pop. (est.) 700.

WIDGEON. Wild duck (*Anas penelope*). Smaller than the common wild duck, it has a red-brown head with cream crown greyish-pink breast and white beneath. The bill is blue-grey. In winter it frequents British coasts, but breeds farther south.

WID'NES. English industrial town (bor.) in Lancs, on the Mersey, 12 m. S.E. of Liverpool, with soap and chemical manufactures. Pop. (1961) 52,168.

WIECHERT (vē'khert), **Ernst** (1887–1950). German novelist. B. in East Prussia, he wrote melancholy novels of great beauty of diction, of which *The Baroness* (1934), *The Girl and the Ferryman* (1932) and others were trans. into Eng. *The Forest of the Dead* (1947) is an account of his experiences in Buchenwald concentration camp.

WIELAND (vē'lahnt), **Christoph Martin** (1733–1813). German poet and novelist. After attempts at religious poetry, he came under the influence of Voltaire and Rousseau, and wrote graceful novels such as *Agathon*, the satirical *Abderiten*, etc., and tales in verse such as *Oberon, Musarion,* and others, W. was prof. at Erfurt 1769–72, and subsequently became tutor at the court of Weimar. He first trans. Shakespeare into German (1762–6).

WIEN. Ger. form of VIENNA.

WIESBADEN (vēs'bahden). Cap. of the Land of Hessen, W. Germany. W. was the cap. of the former duchy of Nassau from the 12th cent. to 1866. Pop. (1967) 258,178.

WIG. Artificial head of hair, worn as an adornment, disguise, or to conceal baldness. Ws. were known in the ancient world, and have been found on Egyptian mummies. The 16th cent. periwig imitated real hair, and developed into the elaborate peruke which became part of dress, and under Queen Anne Ws. covering the back and shoulders became fashionable. Ws. are worn in England and some Commonwealth countries as part of the costume of judges, barristers, and some parliamentary officials, and in the 1960s were fashionable (either in real hair or synthetics) for women.

WIGAN (wi'gan). English market and industrial town (co. bor.) in Lancs, on the Douglas, 12 m. N. of

WIESBADEN. Its hot springs with temperatures up to 150°F were known to the Romans. The modern Kurhaus, built 1904–7, replaced the structure of 1810 and now contains a casino, several restaurants, a concert hall and a nightclub. In the foreground is part of the fountain colonnade.
Courtesy of the German Tourist Information Bureau.

Warrington. Coal is worked, textiles, boots and shoes, bricks, pipes, and many other goods are manufactured. An old town, W. was captured by the Parliamentarians during the Civil War in 1643 and 1651. The W. 'alps', an area of industrial dereliction incl. colliery spoil heaps, is being re-shaped and developed with ski-slopes, boating facilities, etc., and is an outstanding example of reclamation after industrial blight. Pop. (1961) 100,158.

WIGGIN, Kate Douglas (1856–1923). American author. B. in Philadelphia, she was a pioneer in the running of kindergartens in America, and wrote *Rebecca of Sunnybrook Farm* (1903), etc.

WIGHT, Isle of. *See* ISLE OF WIGHT.

WIGTOWN. County of S.W. Scotland extending to the Rhinns of Galloway double peninsula, in the Irish Sea. The N.E. of the county is moorland. Dairying is the staple occupation. Stranraer is the chief port. W. the co. town. Area 487½ sq. m.; pop. (1961) 29,107.

WILBERFORCE, William (1759–1833). British reformer. B. at Hull, he began his attacks on slavery while at school, and from 1788 devoted himself to its abolition. He entered parliament in 1780, in 1807 his bill for the abolition of the slave-trade was passed,

OSCAR WILDE. 'The name of Dante Gabriel Rossetti is heard for the first time in the Western States of America. Time: 1882. Lecturer: Mr. Oscar Wilde', a cartoon by Sir Max Beerbohm. *Courtesy of the Trustees of the Tate Gallery.*

and in 1833, largely due to his efforts, slavery was abolished throughout the British Empire. His son Samuel W. (1805–73) was bp. of Oxford 1845–69, and then of Winchester, and was a noted defender of Anglican orthodoxy against the Tractarians.

WILBUR, Richard (1921–). American poet. B. in N.Y., he is a university teacher and his verse has an appropriate polish and substance, e.g. *The Beautiful Changes* (1947) and *Things of This World* (1957).

WILD, Jonathan (c. 1682–1725). English criminal, who organized the thieves of London and ran an office which for a payment returned stolen goods to their owners. He was hanged at Tyburn.

WILDE, Oscar Fingal O'Flahertie Wills (1854–1900). Irish writer. B. in Dublin, he was ed. there and at Magdalen Coll., Oxford, where he was a leader of the aesthetic circle burlesqued in Gilbert's *Patience*. His first *Poems* appeared in 1881, the novel *The Picture of Dorian Gray* in 1891, and the series of brilliantly witty comedies *Lady Windermere's Fan* (1892), *A Woman of No Importance* (1893), *An Ideal Husband* (1895), and *The Importance of Being Earnest*, (1895). After his conviction in 1895 for homosexuality he was imprisoned for 2 years. This experience prompted his *Ballad of Reading Gaol* (1898) and *De Profundis*, written in prison, and pub. in full for the first time in 1949. He latterly lived on the Continent.

WILDEBEEST. Two species of S. African antelope. The blue W. or brindled gnu (*Gorgon taurinus*) is grey or slaty brown; the black W. or white-tailed gnu (*Connochaeles gnu*) is smaller.

WILDER, Billy (1905–). Austrian-American film director. B. in Vienna, he was a journalist before writing and directing such German films as *People on Sunday*. In Hollywood from 1934, where he collaborated with Charles Brackett on film scripts, e.g. *Ninotchka* (1939), he directed, as well as collaborating on the

BLUE WILDEBEEST

script of *Lost Weekend* (1945) and *Sunset Boulevard* (1950), and such sophisticated comedies as *Some Like it Hot* (1959) and *The Apartment* (1960).

WILDER, Thornton Niven (1897–). American playwright and novelist. B. at Madison, Wisconsin, he made his name with the novel *The Bridge of San Luis Rey* (1927), tracing the lives of those involved in a disaster, which had many imitators: best of later books was *The Ides of March* (1942), set in ancient Rome. His plays *Our Town* (1938) and *The Skin of Our Teeth* (1942) were attempts to deepen the content of contemporary drama on lines later taken up by Miller and Williams.

THORNTON WILDER

WILFRID, St. (634–709). B. in Northumbria, he became bp. of York in 665, after defending the Roman cause at the Synod of Whitby.

WILHELMSHAVEN (vil′hehmshahfen). Seaport of Lower Saxony, on Jade Bay. W. Germany's chief naval station, it has many small industries and is a holiday resort. Pop. (1966) 101,370.

WILKES, John (1727–97). British Radical politician. B. in Clerkenwell, he entered parliament as a Whig in 1757. His attacks on Bute in his paper, *The North Briton*, led to his outlawry in 1764; he fled to France, and on his return in 1768 was imprisoned. He was 4 times elected M.P. for Middlesex, but the Commons refused to admit him, and finally declared his opponent elected. This secured him strong working- and middle-class support, and in 1774 he was allowed to take his seat in parliament, where he championed parliamentary reform, religious toleration, and American independence.

WILKIE, Sir David (1785–1841). Scottish genre painter. B. in Fifeshire, he studied at the R.A. schools, and estab. his popularity with 'Village Politicians' in 1806. Other works incl. 'The Blind Fiddler', 'Village Festival', and 'The Parish Beadle'. He was elected R.A. in 1811, and became painter-in-ordinary to the king in 1830.

WILKINS, Sir Hubert (1888–1958). Australian explorer. B. in S. Australia, he studied engineering, learnt to fly in 1910 and visited both polar regions. In 1928 he flew from Barrow (Alaska) to Green Harbour (Spitsbergen), for which he was knighted, and in 1928–9 made an Antarctic flight which proved that Graham Land is an island: Ben Eielson was his pilot on both flights. He also planned to reach the N. pole by submarine.

WILL. An instrument executed by a person (being neither an infant nor lunatic) as a disposition of his property on death. The rules governing the execution of Ws. are mainly contained in the Ws. Act, 1837. A soldier or sailor on active service may make a W. in any clear form, but otherwise the W. must be in writing or print. It must be signed by the testator in the presence of 2 witnesses who also sign, and may not be beneficiaries under the W. Practice in the U.S.A. is based on similar lines.

WILLIAM I, called the Conqueror (c. 1027–87). King of England and duke of Normandy. B. at Falaise, the illegitimate son of duke Robert the Devil, he succeeded his father in the duchy in 1035. Claiming that he had been bequeathed the English throne by his kinsman Edward the Confessor, he invaded England in 1066, defeated and killed Harold at Hastings, and was crowned king. His reign marks the complete establishment of feudalism in England, although W. kept the barons firmly under Crown con-

trol. He d. at Rouen after a fall from his horse, and was buried at Caen. *See* illus. p. 512.

WILLIAM II, called Rufus (the Red), (c. 1056–1100). King of England. The 3rd son of William I, he inherited England in 1087, and spent much of his reign attempting to conquer Normandy from his brother Robert. His exactions led to baronial revolts, while his methods of extorting money from the Church brought him into conflict with archbishop Anselm. He was killed while hunting in the New Forest, and was buried in Winchester cathedral.

WILLIAM III, called W. of Orange (1650–1702). King of Gt. Britain and Ireland. B. at The Hague, the son of William II of Orange, and Mary, dau. of Charles I, the French invasion of the Netherlands in 1672 led to his installation as stadholder. His stubborn resistance forced Louis XIV to make peace in 1678, and from that time he devoted himself to building up a European alliance to resist French aggression. In 1677 he m. his cousin Mary, dau. of James, duke of York. Invited by the opposition, he invaded England in 1688, and accepted the crown, as joint sovereign with Mary, in 1689. He accepted a constitutional settlement whereby parliament secured the main control of policy, although he attempted to safeguard his power by playing off the 2 parties against each other. Much of his reign he spent campaigning, first in Ireland, where in 1690 he defeated James II at the Boyne, and later against the French in Flanders.

WILLIAM IV (1765–1837). King of the United Kingdom. B. at Buckingham Palace, the 3rd son of George III, he was cr. duke of Clarence in 1789, and m. Adelaide of Saxe-Meiningen in 1818. He succeeded George IV in 1830, and during the Reform Bill crisis secured its passage by agreeing to create new peers.

WILLIAM I (1797–1888). King of Prussia and German emperor. B. at Berlin, the son of Frederick William III, he served in the Napoleonic campaigns of 1814–15, and helped to crush the 1848 revolution. He succeeded his brother Frederick William IV in 1861. His policy was largely dictated by Bismarck (q.v.), who secured his proclamation as German emperor in 1871.

WILLIAM II (1859–1941). German emperor. The son of Frederick III and of Victoria, dau. of Queen Victoria, he succeeded his father in 1888. He began his reign by forcing Bismarck to resign in 1890, and his blundering interventions in the field of foreign policy were usually disastrous. During the 1914 crisis, he at first approved Austria's ultimatum to Serbia; then, realizing war was imminent, strove to prevent it when it was too late. On the outbreak of revolution in 1918 he fled to Holland, and spent the rest of his life at the castle of Doorn.

WILLIAM. Name of 3 kings of the Netherlands. **William I** (1772–1844), the son of Prince William V of Orange, lived in exile during the French occupation of 1795–1813, and fought against Napoleon at Jena and Wagram. In 1814 he assumed the title of king; the Austrian Netherlands was added to his kingdom by the Allies in 1815, but secured independence (recognized by the Powers 1839) by the revolution of 1830. W.'s unpopularity led to his abdication in 1840. His son **William II** (1792–1849) served with the British Army in the Peninsular War and at Waterloo. He succeeded his father in 1840, and by conceding a liberal constitution in 1848 averted revolution. William II's son, **William III** (1817–90), reigned 1849–90.

WILLIAM, called the Lion (1143–1214). King of Scotland. He became king in 1165. While invading England in 1174 he was captured and forced to do homage for his kingdom to Henry II, but the English claim to suzerainty was abandoned by Richard I in 1189 for a money payment.

WILLIAM. Ger. Crown Prince. *See* FREDERICK W

WILLIAM, called the Silent (1533–84). Prince of

Orange. The son of the count of Nassau, he inherited the principality of Orange in 1544. He was brought up as a Catholic, and was appointed governor of Holland by Philip II of Spain in 1559. He opposed Philip's tyranny and intolerance, and in 1572 joined the revolt of Holland and Zeeland against Spanish rule; he accepted Protestantism in 1573, and from that time was accepted as the Dutch national leader. His policy of uniting the Protestant and Catholic provinces by religious toleration failed; the S. provinces submitted to Spain, while the N. formed a federation in 1579, and repudiated Spanish suzerainty in 1581. W. was assassinated at Delft by a Spanish agent. Though talkative, he knew how to hold his tongue on matters of importance – hence his nickname.

WILLIAM OF MALMESBURY (c. 1080–c. 1143). English historian. A monk of Malmesbury Abbey, Wilts, he compiled the *Gesta regum* and *Historia novella*, together formed a history of England to 1142.

WILLIAM OF WYKEHAM (c. 1323–1404). English churchman. B. at Wickham, Hants, he entered the royal service c. 1347. He was bp. of Winchester from 1367, Lord Chancellor 1367–72 and 1389–91. He founded New Coll., Oxford, in 1379, and Winchester Coll. in 1378.

WILLIAMS, Emlyn (1905–). Welsh actor, playwright, and producer. B. in Mostyn, Flintshire, he made his stage début in 1927, and has since appeared in many plays, including his own *Night Must Fall*, and *The Corn is Green*, and gave a remarkable solo performance as Dickens in readings from the novelist (1951–2) and similarly as Dylan Thomas (1955 and 1957–8). He pub. his autobiography *George* – his own unused first Christian name – in 1961.

WILLIAMS, Sir George. See YOUNG MEN'S CHRISTIAN ASSOCIATION.

WILLIAMS, Roger (c. 1604–84). English colonizer. B. in London, he emigrated to Massachusetts, but was banished in 1635 for advocating religious toleration. He founded the colony of Rhode Island, on a basis of democracy and complete religious freedom, in 1636.

WILLIAMS, Tennessee. Pseudonym of American playwright Thomas Lanier W. (1911–). B. in Missouri, his work is heavy with the frustrations of life in the Deep South. among his women characters, e.g. *The Glass Menagerie* (1945), *A Streetcar named Desire* (1947), *Cat on a Hot Tin Roof* (1955) and *The Night of the Iguana* (1961). He has also written a number of screen plays, e.g. *The Rose Tattoo*, and the novel *The Roman Spring of Mrs. Stone*.

WILLIAMS, William Carlos (1883–1963). Am. poet. B. in Rutherford, New Jersey, he used spare images and language, and advanced forms of verse in intellectual patterns. His earlier and later poems were collected 1950–1, and in the latter year he also pub. his *Autobiography*.

WILLIAMSBURG. City of Va., U.S.A., on a peninsula between York and James rivers, 45 m. E.S.E. of Richmond. It is the seat of William and Mary College (1693). Dating from 1632, W. was the cap. of the colony of Va. 1699–1779. Beginning 1927, it has been restored, chiefly at the expense of John D. Rockefeller Jr., to its 18th cent. appearance, incl. the costume worn by its inhabitants, and is a great show place. Pop. (1960) 6,832.

WILLIAMSON, Henry (1895–). British author, known for such stories of animal life as *Tarka The Otter* (1927).

WILLINGDON, Freeman Freeman-Thomas, 1st marquess of (1866–1941). British Liberal statesman. He entered parliament in 1900, and was raised to the peerage in 1910. He was Governor of Bombay 1913–18 and of Madras 1918–24; Governor-General of Canada 1926–30 and Viceroy of India 1931–6.

WILLIS, Ted, baron (1914–). British playwright. B. in London, he became known for his television

scripts for the police series *Dixon of Dock Green* (1955–63) and plays of working-class life such as *Woman in a Dressing Gown*, which won the Berlin Award as a film (1958). Active in socialist fields, he was in 1963 created a life peer.

WILL-O'-THE-WISP or **Ignis Fatuus.** Hovering light seen above marshy ground, possibly due to the spontaneous ignition of methane (q.v.).

WILLOW. Genus (*Salix*) of trees and shrubs in the family Salicaceae, which flourish in damp places. The leaves are lance-shaped, and the flowers appear as catkins. Among species found in Britain are the crack W. (*S. fragilis*), the white W. (*S. alba*), the goat W. (*S. caprea*), the weeping W. (*S. babylonica*; a native of China), and the common osier (*S. viminalis*). Cricket bats are made from the white W. (*var. caerulea*).

WILLOW-HERB. Genus of plants (*Epilobium*). The best-known is rose-bay W. or fireweed W. (*E. angustifolium*), common in woods and waste places. It grows to a considerable height, with long terminal racemes of red or purplish flowers.

WILLOW WREN. Small bird (*Phylloscopus rochilus*) of the Warbler group.

WILMINGTON. City and port of Delaware, U.S.A., on r. Delaware. Principal industries incl. shipbuilding, and the manufacture of chemicals, leather, iron and steel goods, textiles. The Swedes built Fort Cristina on the site (1638); it passed to the Dutch (1655), the English (1664). Services are still held in the church of Holy Trinity (1698). W. is the H.Q. of Du Pont enterprises, which started with the foundation of a powder mill (1802) by E. J. du Pont de Nemours. Pop. (1960) 95,827.

WILSON, Angus (1913–). British author. Attached to the Foreign Office during the S.W.W., he was deputy to the superintendent of the B.M. Reading Room 1949–55, and became professor at East Anglia Univ. in 1966. His acidly humorous books incl. *Hemlock and After* (1952), *Anglo-Saxon Attitudes* (1956) and *The Old Men at the Zoo* (1961).

WILSON, Charles Thomson Rees (1869–1959). British physicist. Jacksonian prof. of natural philosophy at Cambridge 1925–34, he was in 1911 the inventor of the W. cloud chamber which enabled the path of an atom to be visibly tracked. In 1927 he shared with A. H. Compton a Nobel prize. See CLOUD CHAMBER.

WILSON, Colin (1931–). British author. Leaving school in his native Leicester at 16, he worked as a labourer, in a plastics factory, etc., and then caused a sensation with *The Outsider* (1956). Later he made a reputation with thrillers, e.g. *Necessary Doubt* (1964).

WILSON, Edmund (1895–1972). American author. B. in New Jersey, he is known for his critical works *Axel's Castle*, *The Wound and the Bow* and *Classics and Commercials* (1951).

WILSON, Sir Henry Hughes (1864–1922). British soldier. He served in Burma, S. Africa, and the F.W.W., became C.I.G.S. in 1918 and was created field marshal. He was murdered in London by Irish terrorists.

WILSON, Henry Maitland, 1st baron (1881–1964). British field marshal. He served in the S. African and F.W.W., and in 1939 became G.O.C. in C. Egypt. In 1941 he took command of the 9th Army in the Near East, became C.-in-C., Middle East in 1943, and in 1944 was Supreme Allied Commander in the Mediterranean theatre. In 1945–7 he was head of the British Joint Staff Mission in Washington. He was created a baron in 1946.

WILSON, (James) Harold (1916–). British Labour statesman. B. in Huddersfield, son of a works chemist, he lectured in economics at Oxford in 1937, became a Fellow of Univ. College in 1938, and was elected M.P. in 1945. He succeeded Sir Stafford Cripps as Pres. of the Board of Trade, but in protest against cuts in social-service spending he resigned in 1951.

HAROLD WILSON

In 1960 he had a crushing defeat when he challenged Gaitskell's party leadership, but on the latter's death succeeded him. Victorious in the general election of 1964 (increased majority 1966), he encountered opposition to his 'productivity, prices and incomes policy' within his party, but by 1969–70 had consolidated his position. His defeat at the general election June 1970 contradicted the majority of public opinion polls: he remained Leader of the Opposition His memoirs of his premiership were controversial.

WILSON, Thomas Woodrow (1856–1924). 28th President of the U.S.A. B. at Staunton, Virginia, he became president of Princeton univ. in 1902. In 1910 he was elected Democratic governor of New Jersey, and in 1912 and again in 1916 he was elected President of the U.S.A. He initiated measures against the Trusts and secured valuable social legislation. He strove to keep the U.S.A. neutral during the F.W.W. but the German U-boat campaign forced him to declare war in 1917. In Jan. 1918 he issued his 'Fourteen Points' as a basis for a just peace settlement. At the peace conference in Paris he was successful in securing the inclusion of the League of Nations in the Treaty of Versailles. But on his return to America the treaty, though accepted by a majority of the Senate, failed to secure the two-thirds majority necessary, under the Constitution, for ratification.

WILTON. English market town (bor.) in Wilts, 2½ m. W. of Salisbury. W. House, the seat of the earl of Pembroke, was built from designs by Holbein and Inigo Jones, and is associated with Sir Philip Sidney and Shakespeare. W. has been famous for its carpets from the 16th cent. Pop. (1961) 3,404.

WILTSHIRE. S.W. co. of England, N. of Hants and Dorset. In the S. is Salisbury Plain; to the N.E. are Marlborough Downs and Savernake Forest. The principal rivers are the Kennet, Bristol Avon, and

WILTSHIRE. Longleat, seat of the marquess of Bath, was built 1566–80 on the site of an ancient priory. Its library contains the earliest Shakespeare folios, its pictures include works by Titian and Raphael, and its Great Hall looks just as it did when Queen Elizabeth was entertained at the house in 1574.
Courtesy of the marquess of Bath.

Salisbury Avon. The chief crop is wheat, and much of the county is under pasture. Salisbury is the co. town; other centres are Trowbridge (admin. centre), Swindon, Devizes, and Westbury. Stonehenge and Avebury are famous prehistoric monuments. Area 1,344 sq. m.; pop. (1967) 479,080.

WIMBLEDON. District of the Greater London

bor. of Merton, H.Q. of the All-England Lawn Tennis Club where world-famous international matches have been held since 1877.

WINCHELL, Walter (1897–1972). American journalist. B. in N.Y. City, he was a columnist on the *New York Mirror* 1929–69, his bitingly satiric writings being syndicated throughout the U.S.A.

WINCHESTER. English cathedral city (bor.) in Hants on the Itchen, 12 m. N. of Southampton. It was fortified by the Romans, and became the capital of Wessex. Its cathedral (Gothic and Norman) contains the remains of Saxon kings: buit on marshland it was in danger of collapse in 1905 but was saved largely by the efforts of the diver William Walker (d. 1918) who is commemorated by a bronze statue, erected 1964. Little of the Norman castle remains, but in the hall King Arthur's Round Table (so-called) is shown. W. College (1394) developed from a 7th cent. grammar school. Pop. (1961) 28,643. *See* illus. p. 486.

WINCKELMANN (vin'kelmahn), **Johann Joachim** (1717–68). German critic and archaeologist. His *History of the Art of Antiquity* (1764) estab. a new standard of aesthetic appreciation of classical art.

WINDAU. Ger. name of VENTSPILS.

WINDERMERE. Largest lake in England, in Westmorland, 10½ m. long, 1 m. wide, a tourist and fishing attraction. The town of W. (U.D.), formerly called Birtwaite, is on the E. shore. Pop. (1961) 6,556.

WINDHOEK (-hook). Capital of S.W. Africa, 180 m. E. of Walvis Bay, centre of a dairying region with cold-storage plants and an airport; there are hot springs nearby. Pop. (1960) 36,049 (19,382 white).

WINDMILL. A mill with sails or vanes which by the action of wind upon them drive machinery for grinding corn, pumping water, etc. Ws. were used in the E. in ancient times, and in Europe they were first used in Germany and the Netherlands in the 12th cent. The main types of W. are the 'post' mill, which is turned round a post when the direction of the wind changes, and the 'tower' mill which has a revolving construction at the top. In the U.S.A. a light type of W. with steel sails supported on a long steel girder shaft was introduced for use on farms.

WINDS. Name given to lateral movements of the earth's atmosphere. Along the equator there is a belt of low pressure, the Doldrums, and towards this belt the Trade Winds blow from the Horse Latitudes – high-pressure areas about 30° N. and 30° S. of the equator. In the northern hemisphere the Trade Winds blow from the N.E., and in the southern from the S.E. Also from the Horse Latitudes blow the westerlies towards the poles – N. of the equator these are S.W. winds, and S. of the equator they blow from the N.W. This theoretical arrangement is affected by the distribution of land and water. There are many local Ws., while on the margin of equatorial calms there may be developed the violent storms known as tornadoes, typhoons, etc. The force of wind is expressed by the Beaufort Scale (q.v.).

WINDSOR, Duke of. *See* EDWARD VIII.

WINDSOR, House of. Official name of the British royal family, adopted in place of 'the house of Saxe-Coburg-Gotha' in 1917. In 1960 Elizabeth II decided that certain of her descendants i.e. those not entitled to the prefix H.R.H., would in future use the surname Mountbatten-Windsor. *See* Table, p.1006.

WINDSOR. City and lake port in Ontario, Canada, on the Detroit r., opposite Detroit, U.S.A. It is a great rail and agricultural centre and makes motor-car engines, iron and steel goods, bricks, etc. Pop. (1966) 192,544.

WINDSOR, New. English town (royal bor.) in Berks, on the Thames. It is dominated by W. Castle (q.v.), and has a 17th cent. guildhall of Wren's design. The Treaty of W., 1373, estab. a permanent alliance between England and Portugal. Pop. (1961) 27,126.

WINDSOR CASTLE. The British royal residence in the municipal borough of Windsor, Berks. It was founded by William the Conqueror on the site of an even earlier stronghold. In the Lower Ward are St. George's Chapel, a fine example of Perpendicular architecture and the chapel of the Order of the Garter; and the Albert Memorial Chapel, below which are buried George III, George IV, William IV, George V and George VI. Beyond the Round Tower or Keep is the Upper Ward containing the state apartments and the Queen's private apartments. In the Home Park adjoining the castle is Frogmore House and the Royal Mausoleum where Queen Victoria and the Prince Consort rest. Windsor Great Park, with its artificial lake, Virginia Water, lies to the south.

WINDWARD ISLANDS. Group of British islands in the W. Indies. All 4 colonies, Grenada, St. Vincent, St. Lucia and Dominica (qq.v.), with the Grenadines, divided between Grenada and St. Vincent, were to have become Associated States in 1967, but internal political disagreement prevented the change of status in St. Vincent until 1969. Total area 811 sq. m.; pop. (1966) 364,000.

Other islands called W.I. are the N. group of the Cape Verde Is.; St. Martin (St. Marten), St. Eustatius, and Saba in the Lesser Antilles; Tahiti, Moorea, and Makatea in French Polynesia. The name indicates that they are in the path of the prevailing wind.

WINE. The fermented juice of ripe grapes. The yeast *Saccharomyces ellipsoideus*, which normally lives on the skin of the grape, turns the sugar into ethyl alcohol. For a dry W., fermentation is allowed to go on until the sugar is all or nearly all converted; for a sweet or medium W. the change is arrested at the appropriate time by drawing off the liquor from the grape pulp (*marc*). The quality of W. depends on the type of grape used, the soil, and the climate. The traditional treading of the grapes has been almost entirely replaced by pressing machines. *See* illus. p. 441.

Red W. is produced from the whole grape, white W. from the juice only. Natural sparkling (actually bubbling) Ws. have been bottled while still fermenting; sparkling champagne is artifically carbonated (natural champagne, rarely met with outside France, is still). Many palatable Ws. do not travel well, and can be found only in the place of origin. France is outstanding as a producer of W.: the finest and the widest variety come from there. Other countries producing excellent Ws. incl. Germany, Hungary, Yugoslavia, Italy, Switzerland, South Africa (where the vine was introduced by Huguenot settlers in 1688), and the U.S.A., where 90% of production is in California.

W. of a kind can be made from a great many fruits, vegetables, and flowers, and in country districts elderflower, elderberry, parsnip, dandelion, rhubarb, gooseberry, etc., Ws. are regularly made.

WINGATE, Orde Charles (1903–44). British soldier. In 1936 he estab. a reputation for his unorthodox tactics against the ex-Mufti of Jerusalem in Palestine and in the S.W.W. served under Wavell in the Middle East, and later led the 'Chindits' (q.v.) in guerrilla operations against the Japanese in Burma. He was killed in an aeroplane accident in Burma.

A village on Mt. Carmel in Israel, inaugurated 1953, was called W. after him.

WINNIPEG. Cap. of Manitoba prov., Canada, at the confluence of the Assiniboine and Red rivers. 45 m. S. of Lake W., 60 m. N. of the U.S. border. It is an important railway and financial centre. W. is a great grain market with flour mills, saw mills, foundries, meat-packing works; factories making boxes, bricks, confectionery etc.; printing and bookbinding works. It began as a fur-trading post (1763), and fur auctions are still held. Pop. (1966) 257,000.

Lake W. area 9,400 sq. m., a popular holiday resort.

WINTERGREEN. Genus of plants (*Pyrola*) in the heath family. *P. minor*, with rounded white flowers, is a woodland plant. From the leaves of the N. American *Gaultheria procumbens* is extracted oil of W. used in treating rheumatism.

WINTERHALTER (vin'terhahlter), **Franz Xavier** (1806–73). German artist. B. in the Black Forest, he studied at Munich Academy, and was court painter to the Grand Duke Leopold at Karlsruhe. He painted portraits of Queen Victoria, Napoleon III, etc.

WINTERTHUR (vin'tertoor). Swiss town and spa in the canton of Zürich, 13 m. N.E. of Zürich, manufacturing rly. engines and textiles. Pop. (1961) 84,300.

WIREWORM. See CLICK-BEETLE.

WISBECH (wis'bĕch). English market town and port (bor.) on the Nene, in the Isle of Ely, centre of a bulb-growing area, with fruit- and vegetable-canning factories, printing works, etc. William the Conqueror built a castle at W., which dates from the 7th cent. Pop. (1961) 17,512.

WISCO′NSIN. N. Central state of the U.S.A., a high plain sloping from the Great Lakes in the E. to the Mississippi. There are dense forests, esp. in the N.; and in the S. there is prairie land. W. is the premier dairying state of the U.S.A., and much of the grain produced is fed to livestock; wheat growing and milling are also important. Manufactures, based on local supplies of coal, iron, zinc and lead, incl. agricultural machinery, pumps, metal furniture, precision instruments, plumbing equipment. The chief cities are Madison, the capital, and Milwaukee. Area 56,154 sq. m.; pop. (1970) 4,417,933.

WISE, Thomas James (1859–1937). British bibliographer. He collected the Ashley Library of first editions, chiefly English poets and dramatists 1890–1930, acquired by the B.M. at his death, but is chiefly remembered for his forgeries of supposed privately printed first editions of Browning, Tennyson, Swinburne, etc. His activities were revealed by J. Carter and G. Pollard in 1934 and in 1956 it was found that he had perfected his own copies of 17th cent. plays by abstracting leaves from B.M. copies.

WISEMAN, Nicholas Patrick Stephen (1802–65). British cardinal. B. in Seville, he was rector of the English college at Rome, and became the first abp. of Westminster in 1850.

WI′SHART, George (*c.* 1513–46). Scottish Protestant reformer, burned for heresy at St. Andrews. He was closely associated with Knox.

WISTA′RIA. A climbing shrub (*Wistaria chinensis*) in the family Leguminoseae, native to China. It has racemes of pale mauve flowers, and pinnate leaves.

WISTER, Owen (1860–1938). American novelist. B. in Philadelphia, a grandson of Fanny Kemble, he was famous for stories of cowboys in the American west, e.g. *The Virginian* (1902).

WITAN or **Witenagemot.** The council of the Anglo-Saxon kings, which was composed of officers of the household, the greater landowners, the bishops, and the abbots of important monasteries. *See* illus. p. 390.

WISTARIA

WITCHCRAFT. The supposed power of working magic with the aid of the devil. Witches were persecuted all over W. Europe during the 15th–17th cents., among the best-known cases being those of Joan of Arc and Gilles de Rais. 'White' witches who use 'supernatural' powers for good purposes, e.g. in charming warts, may still be found in England, and after the S.W.W. there was a revival of interest in W. or 'black magic'.

WITCH HAZEL. Flowering shrub (*Hamamelis virginiana*). An astringent extract prepared from the bark and leaves is used in medicine.

WITNESS. One who supplies the testimony in courts of law, on which cases are decided. The rules as to when evidence is admissible are complex, but direct oral testimony of relevant facts, given by Ws. who were present, is required whenever possible.

WITNEY. English market town (U.D.) in Oxfordshire, on the Windrush. Blankets and other woollen goods are manufactured. Pop. (1961) 9,217.

WITT, John de (1625–72). Dutch statesman. B. at Dort, he became Grand Pensionary of Holland, and virtual Prime Minister, in 1653. By his skilful diplomacy he conducted the English Wars of 1652–4 and 1665–7 to an honourable conclusion, and in 1668 formed the Triple Alliance with England and Sweden against Louis XIV. His brother **Cornelius de W.** (1623–72) distinguished himself as a naval commander in the English Wars. After the Orangist reaction of 1672 Cornelius was imprisoned; John resigned, and while he was visiting his brother both were murdered by the mob.

WITTELSBACH (vit'telsbakh). Bavarian dynasty, who ruled Bavaria as dukes from 1180, electors from 1623, and kings 1806–1918. Prince Rupprecht (1869–1955), son of King Ludwig III and descended from Elizabeth, dau. of James I of England, was technically a claimant to the British throne and the claim descends to his son Prince Albrecht (1905–).

WITTENBERG. Town of Halle district, E. Germany, 40 m. N.E. of Halle, on the Elbe, associated with Martin Luther. There is a Luther museum in the Augustinian monastery. Luther preached in the Stadtkirche (in which he is buried), nailed his 95 theses to the door of the Schlosskirche in 1517, and was prof. of philosophy in the univ. of W. (1502) transferred to Halle in 1815. The painters Lucas Cranach (father and son) lived at W. Pop. (1966) 46,000.

WITTGENSTEIN (vit'genshtīn), **Ludwig** (1889–1951). German philosopher. Arriving from Berlin at Cambridge in 1912, he pub. in 1922 – aided by Bertrand Russell – his influential *Tractatus Logico-Philosophicus*; and in 1953 *Philosophical Investigations*.

WOAD. Species of plant (*Isatis tinctoria*) in the family Cruciferae. It has arrow-shaped leaves and clusters of yellow flowers. A blue dye, made from the fermented leaves, was used by the ancient Britons to stain their bodies when going into battle.

WODEHOUSE (wood'-), **Pelham Grenville** (1881–). British humorist, who became a U.S. citizen in 1955. He is author of a long series of novels, featuring Bertie Wooster and his impeccable manservant Jeeves, who live in a world of scatty aristocrats and fossilized, upper-class slang.

WODEN. *See* ODIN.

WOFFINGTON, Margaret (*c.* 1714–60). Irish actress, better known as Peg W. She played in Dublin as a child and made her début at Covent Garden in 1740. She often played male roles.

WOLF (vōlf), **Friedrich August** (1759–1824). German classical scholar, prof. at Halle (1783–1807), who in his *Prolegomena ad Homerum* (1797) put forth the theory that the *Odyssey* and *Iliad* are based on original lays which were later joined.

WOLF, Hugo (1860–1903). Austrian composer. B. at Windischgraz, in Styria, he studied at Vienna conservatoire, became a critic on a Viennese paper, and d. in a Vienna lunatic asylum. His songs belong to the greatest achievements of the Ger. *Lieder* tradition. He also composed the opera *Der Corregidor* and orchestral works, such as 'Italian Serenade'.

WOLF. Wild member of the dog family. The common W. of Europe and Asia (*Canis lupus*) has thick greyish fur. The larger timber W. (*C. nubilus*), and the small coyote (q.v.) occur in N. America. Ws. inhabit both open and wooded country, and commonly hunt in packs.

WOLFE, Charles (1791–1823). Irish curate, author of one great poem, 'The Burial of Sir John Moore'.

WOLFE, James (1727–59). British soldier. B. at Westerham, Kent, he entered the army in 1741 and served at the battles of Dettingen, Falkirk, Culloden, and Laffeldt. In 1758 he served under Amherst in Canada, and played a conspicuous part in the siege of Louisburg. In 1759 he was promoted major-general, and commanded the victorious expedition against Quebec, in which he lost his life.

WOLFE, Thomas (1900–38). American novelist. B. in N. Carolina, he was ed. at the univ. and at Harvard, and travelled to Europe. He believed that good writing was the work of the unconscious, and poured out an enormous quantity of wordage which was cut and shaped by his publisher/editor Maxwell Perkins. His 4 books are *Look Homeward, Angel* (1929), *Of Time and the River* (1935) and the posthumous *The Web and the Rock* (1939) and *You Can't go Home Again* (1940).

WOLFENDEN, Sir John (1906–). British educationist. Headmaster of Shrewsbury 1944–50, he is noted for his balanced chairmanship of the committee on homosexual offences and prostitution 1954–7, family service units 1957–63, etc., and in 1969 became director and principal librarian, British Museum. He was knighted in 1956.

WOLF-FERRARI (vŏlf-ferah'rē), **Ermanno** (1876–1948). Italian-German composer, b. at Venice, whose operas incl. *Il segreto di Susanna, I gioielli della Madonna*, and many others.

WOLFIT, Sir Donald (1902–68). British actor-manager. B. at Newark-on-Trent, he formed his own Shakesperian company in 1937, and excelled in the larger-than-life roles of Shylock, Lear, Volpone, etc.

WOLFRAM. Grey, hard metal, ductile and malleable, formerly (until 1949) officially known as tungsten: symbol W, at. wt. 183·86, at. no. 74. Recognized and named by Scheele in 1781, and discovered by the d'Elhujar brothers in 1783, it occurs as wolframite ($FeWO_4$), scheelite ($CaWO_4$) and huberite ($MnWO_4$). Non-magnetic, it is insoluble except in a mixture of nitric and hydrofluoric acids, and has the highest melting point (3370°C) of any metal. W. is used in alloy steels for armour plate, projectiles, high-speed cutting tools, etc., for lamp filaments and thermionic valves. Its salts are used in the paint and tanning industries.

WOLFSBURG. Town 16 m. N.E. of Brunswick in W. Germany, chosen 1938 as the Volkswagen (Hitler's 'People's Car') factory site. Pop. *c.* 25,000.

WOLFSON, Sir Isaac (1897–). British merchant. Chairman of Great Universal Stores Ltd. from 1946, he estab. the W. Foundation 1955 to advance health, education and youth activities, and endowed 1966 (jointly with Ford Foundation) W. College, Oxford, concentrating on science and technology.

WOLLONGONG (wool'lengong). Town and seaport of N.S.W., Australia, 40 m. S. of Sydney. Coal is mined nearby, and there are iron and steel works. Pop. Greater W. (1966) 178,100.

WOLLSTONECRAFT, Mary. *See* under GODWIN, WILLIAM.

WOLSELEY (wool'zli), **Garnet Joseph, 1st visct.** (1833–1913). British field marshal. He entered the army in 1852, and his victory at the battle of Tel-el-Kebir, 1882, was raised to the peerage. After leading the Gordon relief expedition of 1884–5 he was created a visct. He was C.-in-C. 1895–1900.

THOMAS WOLSEY

WOLSEY, Thomas (*c.* 1475–1530). English cardinal

and statesman. B. at Ipswich, the son of a butcher, he was ed. at Magdalen College, Oxford, and took holy orders. Under Henry VIII he had rapid advancement, being made bp. of Lincoln and archbp. of York in 1514. Several other sees were conferred on him, and in 1515 he was created a cardinal and became Lord Chancellor of England. During the next 10 years he was one of the most powerful men in Europe. Under him the smaller English monasteries were dissolved, and zeal for the New Learning found expression in Cardinal College (later Christ Church) at Oxford. But his reluctance to further Henry's divorce from Catherine of Aragon led to his downfall in 1529, and in 1530 he was charged with high treason and arrested. He d. at Leicester Abbey.

WOLVERHAMPTON. English industrial town (co. bor.) in Staffs, 13 m. N.W. of Birmingham. Among the numerous manufactures are locks and safes, tyres, commercial vehicles, aircraft, artificial fibres, diesel engines. Nearby are collieries and iron-works. The cruciform church of St. Peter was refounded on the site of an earlier monastery in 994. Pop. (1961) 150,385.

WOMBAT. Marsupial of the family Vombatidae, e.g. *Vombatus ursinus* of Tasmania and *V. platyrhinus* of S. Australia. They have coarse brownish fur, live in burrows, and are nocturnal and vegetarian.

WOMBAT

WOMEN'S INSTITUTES. Local organizations of women in country districts for the purpose of mutual fellowship and practice of useful crafts. The first was founded in 1897 at Stoney Creek, Ontario, under the presidency of Mrs. Adelaide Hoodless. The movement is non-class, non-sectarian, and non-party political, and was taken to Britain by Mrs. Alfred Watt, the 1st W.I. being opened in Anglesey.

WOMEN'S SERVICES. The organized use on a large scale of the services of women to assist the prosecution of warfare is of comparatively recent development. They may be used to replace men called to serve in the armed forces in their peacetime occupations, e.g. in factories or agriculture, as with the *Women's Land Army* in Britain 1917–20; to act as volunteer part-time auxiliaries for new tasks created by war, e.g. the *Women's Voluntary Services* (W.V.S.), an amalgamation in Britain in 1938 of already existing bodies which cared for evacuees, gave service in hospitals, assisted air-raid victims, etc., and was continued after the S.W.W. (created W. Royal V.S. 1966); or to enlist as auxiliaries to the armed services. Use of women in actual combat is regarded with repugnance by most civilized states, except in such dire emergency as the desperate Russian stand against the German invaders in the S.W.W., but may be accepted as routine in such newly emergent states as Cuba and Israel. In Britain there are separate corps for all 3 services: *Women's Royal Army Corps* (W.R.A.C.) created in 1949 to take over the functions of the Auxiliary Territorial Service, estab. in 1938 but with a F.W.W. equivalent in the Women's Army Auxiliary Corps (W.A.A.C.); *Women's Royal Naval Service* (W.R.N.S.) 1917–19 and 1939 onwards; and the *Women's Royal Air Force* (W.R.A.F.) estab. in 1918 but known 1939–48 as the Women's Auxiliary Air Force (W.A.A.F.); and also nursing services, i.e. Queen Alexandra's Army Nursing Corps and Naval Nursing Service, and for the R.A.F. Princess Mary's Nursing Service. In the U.S.A. there is a separate Women's Army Corps (W.A.C.), estab. in 1948, which developed from the Women's Army Auxiliary Corps (W.A.A.C.), in turn originating in F.W.W. organization on the British model; but although there are nurse corps for the 3 services, there are no separate auxiliary corps for the navy and air force, women being integrated into the general structure.

WOOD, Haydn (1882–1950). British composer. A violinist, he wrote a violin concerto among other works, but is best known for his songs which incl. 'Roses of Picardy'.

WOOD, Mrs. Henry (1814–87). British novelist, *née* Ellen Price. Dau. of a glove manufacturer, she m. a merchant, but was widowed and settled in London to write. She won early fame with *East Lynne* (1861), later books incl. *The Channings* (1862) and the Johnny Ludlow series of detective stories.

WOOD, Sir Henry (1869–1944). British conductor. B. in London, he studied at the R.A.M., had experience as an organist and operatic conductor, and from 1895 until his death conducted the London Promenade Concerts, now named after him. He greatly promoted a new national interest in music, and encouraged many young British composers. As a composer he is remembered by the 'Fantasia of Sea Songs' which ends each Promenade season.

WOOD, John (*c.* 1705–54). British architect, known as 'Wood of Bath' because he did his best work for that city. He designed the Royal Crescent.

WOODCOCK, George (1904–). British trade union official. Gen. Sec. of the T.U.C. 1960–69, he then became chairman of the Industrial Relations Commission.

WOOD-CARVING. The art of carving wood figures in relief or in the round, decorative forms, etc. It was practised in the earliest times, and is practised today by civilized and primitive peoples in most parts of the world. Works of the Negroes of West Africa and of the natives of the South Sea islands are noteworthy. In India, China, and other eastern countries images of deities, etc., have been executed in wood throughout many cents. In Mohammedan countries interior decoration in mosques and other buildings is executed in wood. In Europe, Gothic craftsmen produced much beautiful work such as carved doors, effigies, mouldings, misericords, and reredoses, and many of the great craftsmen of the Renaissance worked in wood, as do many leading modern sculptors.

WOODCUTS and **WOOD ENGRAVINGS.** In making a woodcut a block of smooth-grained wood is used, the most suitable kinds being lime, cherry, American whitewood, and maple. The block is cut along the grain, and the areas and lines of the design are left in relief. This is probably the oldest printing process, dating from the 15th cent., and it was commonly used by early printers for book-illustration.

Wood engravings have not the coarseness of wood-cuts; they are usually made in boxwood, though apple and pear are sometimes used. The block is cut across the grain, and it is possible to obtain subtle tonal effects. In the 18th cent. Thomas Bewick developed the medium to perfection. Later wood engravers incl. Eric Gill, Clare Leighton, Rockwell Kent, and Eric Daglish.

WOODFORDE, James (1740–1803). British clergyman. He was a fellow and sub-warden of New College, Oxon., and held livings in Somerset and Norfolk. His diary covering 1758–1802 is remarkable for its presentation of rural England.

WOODLOUSE. Name given to certain Isopoda (Crustacea) of the family Oniscidae. Unlike all other Isopoda they live on land and breathe air, but damp is necessary to their existence. The eggs are carried by the female in a pouch beneath the thorax.

WOODPECKER. Birds allied to the wrynecks, with whom they form the family Picidae. They live on insects obtained from crevices in the bark of trees. The British green W. or yaffle (*Picus viridis*) is green with red crown and yellow rump, and about the size of a jay. The greater and lesser spotted Ws. (*Dryobates major* and *D. minor*), also British species, have black,

**GREAT SPOTTED
WOODPECKER**

red, and white plumage. There are numerous species in N. America.

WOODSTOCK. English town (bor.) in Oxon, 8 m. N.W. of Oxford, dating back to the 11th cent. It has many associations with the sovereigns of England: Henry I built a palace at W.; Fair Rosamund, mistress of Henry II, is supposed to have lived there; the Black Prince was b. there; and Elizabeth I was imprisoned at W. by Mary I in 1554. Pop. (1961) 1,808.

WOODWORM. The common name for the larval stage of certain wood-boring beetles. Dead or injured trees are their natural target, but they become a serious menace when they attack structural timber and furniture. Most common in Britain are the furniture beetle (*Anobium punctatum*), generally attacking older timber and est. to be present in half the country's buildings; the powder-post beetle (*Lyctus* sp.), attacking newer timber; the death-watch beetle (q.v.), whose presence always coincides with fungal decay; and the wood-boring weevils. Special wood preservatives have been developed to combat W., which has markedly increased since the S.W.W. In warmer countries the greatest danger to timber is from termites (q.v.).

WOOKEY HOLE. Natural cave near Wells, Som., England, in which flint implements of Old Stone Age man with bones of extinct animals have been found.

WOOL. The natural fibrous covering of the sheep, and also of the llama, angora goat, etc. The domestic sheep, *Ovis aries*, provides the great bulk of the fibres used in commerce. In Britain there are some 26 breeds, and the wool is classified as lustre (incl. Lincoln, Leicester, S. Devon, Cotswold, Dartmoor), demi-lustre (Cheviot, Exmoor Horn, and Romney Marsh), down (Dorset, Oxford, Suffolk, Hampshire, Southdown, etc.), and mountain (Blackface, Swaledale, Welsh White, Welsh Black, etc.). Lustre Ws. are used for making worsted dress fabrics, linings, braids, and so on. Demi-lustre Ws. are rather finer in quality, and are used for suitings, overcoats, and costumes, and worsted serge fabrics. First of English-grown Ws. are the down; they are used for hosiery yarns, and some for woollen cloths. Mountain Ws. are coarse and poor in quality, often comprising wool and hair mixed; they are useful for making carpets, homespun tweeds, and low-quality woollen suitings and hosiery.

Most of the world's finest W. comes from the merino sheep, which is not successfully acclimatized in Britain. In 1797 it was introduced into Australia, which has become the world's largest producer of Merino Ws.: S. Africa and S. America are also large producers. Ws. from cross-bred sheep (usually a cross

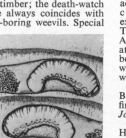

WOODWORM. Two burrowing larvae of the common furniture beetle, which attacks soft wood, and reveals its presence by circular flight holes and wood dust or 'frass' on the surface.
Courtesy of N. E. Hickin, Scientific Director, Rentokil Laboratories.

of one of the lustre class with a merino) are produced in New Zealand. Since the S.W.W. blendings of W. with synthetic fibres have been developed.

WOOLF, Virginia (1882–1941). British author. B. in London, a dau. of Sir Leslie Stephen, she pub. her 1st novel *The Voyage Out* in 1915. In *Mrs. Dalloway* (1925) she perfected her 'stream of consciousness' technique. Among her later books are *To the Lighthouse*, *The Waves*, *The Years*, and the unrevised *Between the Acts* (1941). She also pub. biographies *Flush* and *Roger Fry*; and criticism and essays as *The Common Reader*, *A Room of One's Own*, and *The Moment* (1948). She m. in 1912 **Leonard Sidney W.** (1880–1969), literary editor of the *Nation* 1923–30, and joint-editor of the *Political Quarterly* 1931–59. They jointly founded the Hogarth Press in 1917. He pub. a remarkable 4-vol. autobiography 1960–7.

WOOLLETT, William (1735–85). British engraver. One of the greatest masters of the art, in 1775 he was appointed engraver to George III.

WOOLLEY, Sir Leonard (1880–1960). British archaeologist. Although he carried out valuable excavation at Carchemish, Tell El-Amarna, and Atchana (Hatay), he is best remembered for his work at Ur where he discovered evidence of what may have been the biblical flood, and remains of the ziggurats which inspired the story of the Tower of Babel, as well as relics of rich social and cultural life.

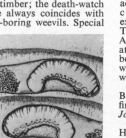

VIRGINIA WOOLF. Chalk drawing by Francis Dodd. *Photo: N.P.G.*

WOOLMAN, John (1720–72). American Quaker. B. in Northampton, N.J., he was one of the first anti-slavery agitators, and left an important *Journal*.

WOOLSACK. Name given to the seat of the Lord High Chancellor in the House of Lords; it is a large square bag of wool and is a reminder of the principal source of English wealth in the Middle Ages.

WOOLWICH. District, on both sides of the Thames, divided from 1964 between the Greater London bors. of Newham (the part N. of the Thames), and Greenwich. The Royal Military Academy was moved from W. to Sandhurst in 1946. An ordnance depot was set up at W. in 1518, a foundry in 1716, and George III gave it the name Royal Arsenal in 1805: it was closed down 1967.

WOOLWORTH, Frank Winfield (1852–1919). American business man. He opened his 1st successful 'five and ten cent' store at Lancaster, Pa., in 1879, and, together with his brother **C. S. Woolworth** (1856–1947), built up a chain of similar shops throughout the U.S.A., Canada, Great Britain, Ireland, and the Continent. The headquarters are in the Woolworth Building, a New York skyscraper, built 1912. *See* HUTTON, BARBARA.

WOOMERA. Small town in S. Australia, 110 m. N.W. of Port Augusta, from which W. draws its water supply; centre of a rocket and atomic-weapon proving range estab. 1946 and covering 3,000 sq. m. to which public access is forbidden. The name (aboriginal) means weapon thrower. There are 3 airfields. Pop. (est.) 3,000.

WOOTTON OF ABINGER, Barbara Frances Wootton, baroness (1897–). British educationist and economist. Prof. of social studies at London 1948–52, she has pub. *Freedom under Planning* (1945), *Social Science and Social Pathology* (1959), etc., and was created a life peer in 1958.

WORCESTER. (1) English episcopal city (co. bor.),

co. town of Worcs, on the Severn. The bishopric was founded c. 679, the cathedral, much restored, in the 11th cent. The cathedral school dates from 1541 and the Royal W. porcelain works from 1751. W. sauce, gloves, boots and shoes, are manufactured. At W. in 1651 Cromwell defeated Charles II. Pop. (1961) 65,865.

(2) Port and 2nd-largest city of Mass., U.S.A., on the Blackstone river. Dating from 1713, it makes textiles and textile looms, abrasives, carpets, clothing, etc. Pop. (1960) 186,587.

WORCESTERSHIRE. Midland county of England. In the S. are the Cotswold hills and in the S.W. the Malverns. The chief river is the Severn, which, with its tributaries the Teme, Stour, and Avon, forms the vales of W., Teme, and Evesham. The county is famous for its orchards and market gardens, and coal and ironstone are mined. Droitwich is noted for its lime springs and radio station, Kidderminster for carpets, and the towns to the N.E. are incl. in the Black Country. Worcester is the county town. Area 703 sq. m.; pop. (1967) 669,400.

WORDSWORTH, William (1770–1850). British poet. B. at Cockermouth, in Cumberland, he was ed. at Hawkshead School and St. John's Coll., Cantab. Going to France in 1791, he sympathized deeply with the revolutionaries, and fell in love with Marie-Anne Vallon, by whom he had an illegitimate dau. Returning to England just before the Terror he pub. *The Evening Walk* and *Descriptive Sketches* in 1793. In 1797 he settled with his sister Dorothy W. (1771–1855) in Som., in order to be near Coleridge. The 2 friends collaborated in the *Lyrical Ballads* (1798). After visiting Germany 1798–9 he settled at Grasmere in 1799. In 1802 he m. Mary Hutchinson, and in 1805 finished the autobiographical *Prelude*, unpub. till 1850. The *Poems* of 1807 mark the close of his early inspiration. His later vols. incl. *The Excursion* (1814), which together with the *Prelude* was intended to form part of a great poem *The Recluse*; *The White Doe oj Rylstone* (1815), *The River Duddon* (1820), *Ecclesiastical Sketches* (1822), and *Yarrow Revisited* (1835). In 1842 W. received a govt. pension, and in 1843 succeeded Southey as poet laureate.

WORKSOP. English market and industrial town (bor.) in Notts, on the Notts coalfield. Mary Queen of Scots was imprisoned at W. Manor (burned 1761). Pop. (1961) 34,237.

WORLD WARS. See FIRST and SECOND W.W.

WORM. Term popularly used for various elongated limbless creatures. Zoologically Ws. incl. the flat worms such as flukes and tapeworms (qq.v.); the roundworms or Nematoda, e.g. the potato eelworm and the hookworm, an animal parasite; the marine worms or Nemertea (q.v.); and the segmented Ws. or Annelida (q.v.).

WORMS (vŏrms). Historical town, Rhineland Palatinate, W. Germany (formerly in Hessen). It is situated on the Rhine, 13 m. N. of Ludwigshafen. There is a Romanesque cathedral which escaped damage in the S.W.W. when the town suffered badly. W. began as a Celtic settlement, was the Barbetomagus of the Romans, Burgundian cap. in the 5th cent., seat of a bishopric from Roman times to 1797. Luther appeared before a Diet held at W. in 1521 and, with his followers, was outlawed by the emperor. Leather,

WORMS. The 12th cent. Romanesque cathedral originally founded in the 8th cent.

Courtesy of the German Tourist Information Bureau.

chemicals, sugar, furniture, etc., are made; and the wines of the dist. are famous. Pop. (1966) 61,000.

WORMWOOD. Name given to aromatic herbs of the genus *Artemisia*, Compositae family. *A. absinthium*, an ingredient of absinth, grows wild in Britain.

WORRELL, Sir Frank (1924–67). W. Indian cricketer. B. in Barbados, he was ed. at the univs. of Jamaica and Manchester, and 1st captained a W. Indian test team in the Australian tour of 1960–1. He was equally good as a bowler and batsman. He was knighted 1964.

WORTHING. English seaside resort (bor.) in Sussex at the foot of the S. Downs. There are traces of prehistoric and Roman occupation in the vicinity. It is famous for tomatoes. Pop. (1961) 80,143.

WOTTON, Sir Henry (1568–1639). English writer. B. in Kent, he was employed on diplomatic missions under James I, and was provost of Eton from 1624. The *Reliquiae Wottonianae* (1651) contains the lyric 'You meaner beauties of the night'.

WOUVERMAN (wow'vermahn), **Philip** (1619–68). Dutch painter. B. at Haarlem, he painted landscapes and battle pieces. His brothers **Pieter** (1623–82) and **Jan** (1629–66) painted similar scenes.

WRANGEL, Ferdinand Petrovich, baron von (1794–1870). Russian vice-admiral and Arctic explorer, after whom W. Island is named.

WRANGEL, Peter Nicholaievich, baron (1878–1928). Russian general. B. at St. Petersburg, he commanded a division of Cossacks in the F.W.W., and in 1920 became C.-in-C. of the 'White' army in the Crimea operating against the Bolsheviks. Later he became a mining engineer in Brussels.

WRASSE. Fish of the family Labridae, found in temperate and tropical seas. The most common British species is the ballan W. (*Labrus maculatus*).

WREN (ren), **Sir Christopher** (1632–1723). English architect. B. at East Knoyle, Wilts, he studied mathematics, and in 1660 became a prof. of astronomy at Oxford. His opportunity as an architect came after the Great Fire of London (1666). He prepared a plan for rebuilding the city, but it was not adopted. W.'s greatest achievement was St. Paul's Cathedral, built 1675–1710. The most noteworthy of his City churches are St. Michael's, Cornhill; St. Bride's, Fleet St.; and St. Mary-le-Bow, Cheapside. His other buildings incl. the Royal Exchange, Marlborough House—the W. towers of Westminster Abbey, often attributed to him, were the design of his pupil Hawksmoor—and buildings at Oxford, incl. the Sheldonian Theatre and the Ashmolean Museum. *See* illus. p. 1102.

WREN, Percival Christopher (1885–1941). British novelist. Out of his experiences in the French and Indian armies he wrote such martial novels as *Beau Geste* (1924), dealing with the Foreign Legion.

WREN. Name given to birds of the Passerine family, in particular *Troglodytes troglodytes*, a small brown bird, about 4 in. long, with a cocked-up tail.

WRESTLING. Sport in which 2 contestants strive to throw one another to the ground. It was very popular among the ancient Egyptians and Greeks, and was first incl. in the Olympiad about 704 B.C. The Romans adopted it from the Greeks, and in the Middle Ages it was a favourite English sport. It is widely practised in the Orient, particularly in Japan.

In Britain there are several styles. In N. England and S. Scotland wrestlers adopt the Cumberland style in which there is no ground play – the wrestler who first touches the ground loses the match. In the West Country (Cornwall and Devon) style, the wrestlers wear a short-strong jacket and before one is vanquished 2 shoulders and one hip or 2 hips and one shoulder must touch the ground. 'Catch as catch can', or the Lancashire style, allows ground struggling, and the aim is to force both the opponent's shoulders to the ground. Of recent years 'all-in' W. which

SIR CHRISTOPHER WREN. Portrait by Sir Godfrey Kneller, dated 1711, showing the architect with the plans for St. Paul's. A tablet within the north doorway gives his epitaph: Si monumentum requiris, circumspice – If you seek his monument, look about you. *Photo: N.P.G.*

recognizes no fouls has enjoyed a considerable vogue in Britain and U.S.A. In Japanese *sumo*, a bout is won by downing an opponent within the circle in the arena, or throwing him outside.

WREXHAM. Welsh market town (bor.) in Denbighshire, 12 m. S.W. of Chester, the seat of the R.C. bishopric of Menevia (Wales). Elihu Yale, benefactor of Yale univ., d. at W. and is buried in the 15th cent. church of St. Giles. Pop. (1961) 35,427.

WRIGHT, Frank Lloyd (1869–1959). American architect. B. at Richland Center, Wisconsin, the son of a minister and a schoolmistress of Welsh descent, he studied as a civil engineer, but turned to architecture on seeing the newly erected wing of the Wisconsin State Capitol collapse. One of the outstanding architects of the 20th cent., he has influenced design all over the world by his freedom from convention and rule. Among his works are his Wisconsin home Taliesin; and the Guggenheim Museum, N.Y.C. (1959).

WRIGHT, Joseph (1855–1930). British philologist. Prof. of comparative philology at Oxford 1901–25, he saved English local speech from oblivion by his 6-vol. *English Dialect Dictionary* (1896–1905).

WRIGHT, Judith (1915–). Australian poet. B. at Armidale, N.S.W., and m. to the philosopher J. P. McKinney, she has produced vols. of direct verse rooted in the Australian background, e.g. *The Moving Image* (1946) and *The Two Fires* (1955).

WRIGHT, Orville (1871–1948) and **Wilbur** (1867–1912). American flying pioneers. Orville was b. at Dayton, Ohio, and Wilbur in Indiana. Interested in gliding by Lilienthal's experiments in Germany, they made aeronautical researches and experiments while running a bicycle-repair business at Dayton. Eventually they built an aeroplane, driven by a 4-cylinder petrol motor of 12 h.p., which was successfully flown by Orville at Kitty Hawk, N.C., on 17 Dec. 1903 – the first controlled flight made by a heavier-than-air machine. The original machine (now in Washington) was exhibited at the Science Mus., S. Ken. 1928–48, and has been replaced by an exact replica. *See* illus. p. 431.

WRIGHT, Richard (1908–60). American Negro author. B. at Natchez, Mississippi, he went to New York in 1937 and in 1940 attracted attention with his portrayal of a Negro murderer as a creature of circumstance in *Native Son*. Later books incl. the autobiographical *Black Boy* (1945) and *The Outsider* (1953). Disillusioned with Communism (cf. his contribution to *The God That Failed*), he d. in Paris where he had settled in 1946 in protest against treatment of his race in the U.S.A.

WRIT. In English law, a precept under seal issued in the name of some executive officer of the Crown, e.g. the Lord Chancellor or a judge, and directed to some public officer such as a county sheriff, or to some private person, commanding him to take certain action in relation to a suit. Thus a W. constitutes the first step in legal proceedings, whether civil or criminal.

WRITERS TO THE SIGNET. A Scottish equivalent of English solicitors: a society of law agents whose predecessors were originally clerks in the Sec. of State's office entrusted with the preparation of documents requiring the signet or seal. The preparation of Crown writs, charters, etc., is the exclusive privilege of the society.

WRITING. The first stage in the development of W., leading to the true alphabet (q.v.) is the picture-W. on wood, rock, etc., examples of which date from *c.* 20,000 B.C. Primitive peoples of America, Africa, Polynesia, and Australia combine conventionalized picture-characters to represent simple ideas; Egyptian hieroglyphics, Babylonian and Assyrian cuneiform and Chinese writing use both these ideographs and phonetic word symbols side by side. Syllabic writing, found in the 2 Japanese developments of Chinese writing, grows up by the continued use of a symbol to represent the sound of a short word. Following the phonetic decay of their language the Egyptians evolved single consonant signs, but continued to combine them with ideographs, etc. A more advanced phonetic form of W. than the alphabet, in which each sign theoretically represents one sound, is shorthand.

WROCLAW (vros'lav). Town in Polish-admin. Germany, at the junction of the Oder and the Ohle, formerly cap. of German Silesia. Better known under its Ger. name Breslau, it grew up round the cathedral (1148), was in succession Polish, cap. of an independent duchy, Bohemian, Hungarian until Frederick the Great captured it (1742), then part of Prussia until Prussia was abolished in 1945. It suffered badly during the S.W.W. but was subsequently restored. It has a univ. (1811), originally a Jesuit college (1702). Pop. (1966) 477,000.

WRYNECK. Small bird (*Iynx torquilla*), a British summer visitant, which has a peculiar habit of twisting its head and neck – whence its name – and a distinctive call. It is generally grey, spotted and barred with brown.

WUCHANG. *See* under WUHAN.

WUCHOW. Chinese port and trade centre, on the Kwei r. in Kwangsi prov., making silk and cotton textiles, sulphuric acid, etc. It is *c.* 120 m. above Canton and was opened to foreign trade in 1897. It has a univ. Pop. (est.) 300,000.

WUHAN (three cities). Chinese city, cap. of Hupei prov., formed by the amalgamation of the anc. cities of Hankow, Hanyang, and Wuchang. It is at the junction of the Yangtze and the Han rivers and is a great centre and one of the chief industrial areas of China, with iron and steel and armaments works, cotton and silk textile factories, paper mills, etc. The three cities were in Japanese occupation 1938–45. There was a serious anti-Mao revolt in 1967 during the Cultural Revolution. Pop. (1957) 2,146,000.

WUHING (woo'hing'). Chinese city in Chekiang prov., on Tai Lake. It is an important agricultural centre and makes silk textiles. Pop. (est.) 50,000.

WUPPERTAL (voop'pertahl). Industrial town of N. Rhine-Westphalia, Germany, *c.* 20 m. E. of Düsseldorf, formed 1929 (named 1931) by uniting Elberfield (13th cent.) and Barmen (11th cent.). Pop. (1966) 420,500.

WÜRTTEMBERG (vür'temberg). Former kingdom in S.W. Germany, 1805–1918, which joined the Ger. Reich in 1870. Its cap. was Stuttgart. Divided in 1946 between the Lander of W.-Baden and W.-Hohenzollern, from 1952 it was part of the Land of Baden-Württemberg (q.v.).

WÜRZBURG (vürts'boorg). Town in Bavaria, W. Germany, on the Main, 55 m. N.W. of Nuremberg. W. became the seat of a bishopric in 1417 and has an 11th cent. cathedral, an episcopal palace, a univ. (1402–34, refounded 1582). Furniture, leather goods, etc., are made and there are printing and engineering works, breweries and trade in wine. Pop. (1966) 120,890.

WYATT, Sir Thomas (*c.* 1503–42). English poet. He was employed on diplomatic missions by Henry VIII, and in 1536 was imprisoned for a time in the Tower, since he was thought to have been the lover of Anne Boleyn. In 1541 W. was again imprisoned on charges of treason. With the earl of Surrey, he pioneered the use of the sonnet in England. His son **Sir Thomas W. the Younger** (d. 1554) was one of the leaders in the revolt of 1554 intended to prevent the marriage of Queen Mary with Philip of Spain. After attacking the City of London, he was captured and executed.

WYCHERLEY, William (1640–1710). English dramatist. B. near Shrewsbury, he was ed. in France, and his 1st comedy *Love in a Wood* won him court favour in 1671. His modern reputation rests on the licentious *The Country Wife* and *The Plain Dealer* (1674).

WYCLIFFE, John (*c.* 1320–84). English reformer. B. probably nr. Richmond, Yorks, he went to Oxford and about 1360 was Master of Balliol Coll. From

1374 he was rector of Lutterworth. Allying himself with the party of John of Gaunt, who were opposed to ecclesiastical influence at court, he attacked abuses in the Church and about 1378 moved on to criticize such fundamental doctrines as priestly absolution, confession, and indulgences. He sent out bands of travelling preachers, and set disciples to work on translating the Bible into English. Although denounced as a heretic, he d. peacefully at Lutterworth.

SIR THOMAS WYATT, son of the poet.
Photo: N.P.G.

WYNNE, David (1926–). British artist. B. in Hants, he was ed. at Stowe School and Trinity Coll., Cambridge. His works incl. portraits of Beecham, Gielgud, Menuhin and The Beatles; the marble 'Breath of Life' and bronze 'Christ and Mary Magdalen'. *See illus.* p. 485.

WYOMING (wī-ō'ming). One of the Rocky Mountain states of the U.S.A. It is semi-arid, and agriculture is possible only by irrigation and by 'dry-farming'. Mineral wealth is immense; petroleum, tin, natural gas, sodium salts, coal, phosphates, sulphur and uranium. Sheep and beef cattle are raised in large numbers. The state contains the Yellowstone national park, opened in 1872, and the Teton national park; and the tourist industry is next in importance to petroleum. The cap. is Cheyenne (pop. 1960, 43,505). W., admitted to the Union in 1890, gave women the franchise 1869. first representative body to do so. Pop. (1970) 332,416.

WYSS (vis), **Johann Rudolf** (1781–1830). Swiss author. B. at Berne, where he became prof. He is remembered for his *Swiss Family Robinson* (1813).

X The 24th letter in the English alphabet, having the sound which can be well represented medially by ks, and initially by z. It is derived through the Latin from the alphabet of western Greece, and was the last letter in the earlier Latin alphabet.

XAVIER (zav'i-er), **St. Francis** (1506–52). Jesuit missionary, known as the 'Apostle of the Indies'. B. at his mother's castle of Xavier in the Basque country of Spain, he became a lecturer at the univ. of Paris, and there was one of the first 7 members of the Order of Jesus (1534). Ordained priest in 1537, he went as a Catholic missionary to the Portuguese colonies in the Indies, arriving at Goa in 1542. In 1549–51 he was in Japan, establishing a Christian mission which lasted for 100 years. Returning to Goa in 1552, he sailed for China, and died of fever near Canton. He was canonized in 1621.

XENON (zen'on) (Gk. *xenon*, stranger). A heavy inert gas of the argon family, discovered in 1898 by Ramsay and Travers in the residue from liquid air: symbol Xe, at. wt. 131·30, at. no. 54. It occurs in the atmosphere to the extent of about one part in 20 million, and is used in incandescent lamps, in electronic flash lamps, and to give a beautiful blue glow in a discharge tube. It is a fission product of uranium nuclear reactors. Radioactive X. has recently been used in a new technique to measure the flow of blood

to the brain during acceleration on a centrifuge in connection with the effects of supersonic speeds on humans.

XENOPHANES (zenof'anēz) (fl. 6th cent. B.C.). Greek poet of Ionia, formerly thought to be the founder of the Eleatic school of philosophy. He was a scathing critic of anthropomorphism.

XENOPHON (zen'ofōn) (*c.* 430–*c.* 354 B.C.). Greek historian, philosopher, and soldier. B. in Athens, in his youth he was a friend and ardent disciple of Socrates. In 401 B.C. he accompanied a body of Greek mercenaries employed by the Persian prince Cyrus in an expedition against Cyrus's brother, the king of Persia. Cyrus was killed in the battle of Cunaxa, and the Greeks were left stranded in the heart of the Persian Empire. X. succeeded to the command, and led them across more than 1,000 m. of enemy-infested country to the Bosphorus. This 'march of the 10,000 Greeks' is the subject of his amous historical work, the *Anabasis*. Subsequently he served in the Spartan Army, and lived on his estate at Scillus in Elis. Among his other works are the *Memorabilia*, *Apology*, and *Symposium*, consisting of recollections of Socrates.

XEROGRAPHY. A dry, non-chemical method of producing images without the use of negatives or sensitized paper. An electrostatically charged photoconductive plate (1 and 2)is exposed in a camera to

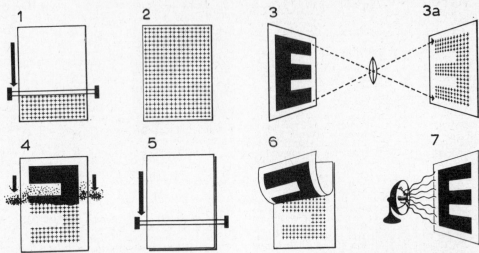

the object to be copied (3), allowing the charge to remain only in the area corresponding to the object (3A). The latent image thus formed on the plate is developed by contact with powder which adheres only to the image (4); this powder image is then usually transferred on to ordinary paper or some other flat surface (5 and 6), and heated quickly to form a permanent print (7). Applications incl. document copying, enlarging from microfilm, preparing printing masters for offset litho and dyeline machines, making X-ray pictures and printing high-speed computer output.

XERXES I (zerk′sez). King of Persia, 485–465 B.C. The son of Darius, he became king on his father's death, and continued with the project of invading Greece. At the head of an army of perhaps 400,000 men, supported by a fleet of 800 ships, X. in 480 B.C. crossed the Hellespont over a bridge of boats. The Greek fleet was beaten at Artemisium, the pass of Thermopylae was stormed, Athens was taken and burnt. But at Salamis the Persian fleet was annihilated by the Greeks under Themistocles and X. returned to Persia. where he was murdered.

XHOSA (kŏ′sah). *See* KAFFIR and TRANSKEI.

XOCHIMILCO (khŏchēmēl′kō). Lake about 7 m. S.S.E. of Mexico City, Mexico, famous for its floating gardens.

X-RAYS, or Röntgen rays after their discoverer in 1895, are those radiations in the electromagnetic spectrum which are next to ultra-violet rays in the direction of the shorter wavelengths. They are identical in character with wireless and light waves, but very much shorter. They can penetrate bodies opaque to ordinary light, even a thin sheet of lead or several feet of wood; this property is made use of in radiography, when the bones of the human body are clearly revealed in an X-ray photograph. Even more valuable is their use in radiotherapy; living cells are more resistant to X-rays than malignant ones, so that deep-seated growths may be successfully attacked and often dispersed or destroyed. Generally speaking they are emitted when high-speed electrons

suffer an abrupt loss of energy. Whilst invisible they may be detected by photographic plates, fluorescent screens and by the ionization they produce in gases.

X-ray astronomy has developed since the S.W.W. The Sun and other sources in the universe emit X-rays which are prevented by the atmosphere, which acts as if it were a yard-thick lead shield, from reaching us. The first rocket used to take X-ray photographs was a German V-2, which was captured and used at White Sands, New Mexico, in 1948, but in the 1960s Britain made great advances using the triaxially stabilised Skylark rocket fired in experiments at Woomera.

XYLOPHONE (zī′lōfōn). Musical instrument consisting of a number of wooden bars, arranged in rows over resonators, and struck with hammers.

XOCHIMILCO. Hired pleasure boats beautifully decorated with fresh-cut flowers navigate the canals between the gardens on the lake. Some carry singers and guitarists to provide entertainment for the citizens of Mexico City, for whom it is a favourite leisure haunt.

Y The 25th letter in the English alphabet, derived through the later Latin alphabet from the Greek letter *upsilon*. In modern English it represents the sound of long and short *i*, when used as a vowel, and when used as a consonant in such words as yoke, yacht, etc., is a palatal spirant.

YACHT (yot). A small and light vessel, whether sailing or power-driven, used for pleasure-cruising or for racing. Most prominent of English yacht clubs is the Royal Y. Squadron, estab. at Cowes in 1812, and the Y. Racing Assocn. was founded in 1875 to regulate the sport. *See* AMERICA'S CUP. The royal yacht *Britannia* (1953) has a displacement of 4,000 tons, and overall length of 413 ft.

YAK. The wild ox (*Bos grunniens*) of Tibet, related to the bisons. When wild it is black, but in domestication it is often black and white. It stands nearly 6 ft. at the shoulder, and has characteristic long shaggy hair on the underparts.

YAKUT (yakōōt') **A.S.S.R.** An Asian autonomous rep. of the R.S.F.S.R., in the valley of the Lena r. Much of its surface is barren tundra, and the climate is severe, but there is some agriculture in the S. Gold, silver, diamonds, tin, mica, coal, etc., are mined; fur-bearing animals (sable, silver fox, etc.) are both trapped and bred; reindeer are reared. Roads total *c.* 6,000 m.; there are internal air services and an external service to Irkutsk. Y. became an autonomous rep. in 1922. The Yakuts, a people of Turkic stock and formerly nomadic, were subdued by Russia in the 17th cent. The cap is Yakutsk (pop. 1967, 95,000) on the Lena. Area 1,197,800 sq. m.; pop. (1967) 646,000.

YALE. Third-oldest (1701) and one of the most important univs. of U.S.A. It is at New Haven, Conn., and was named after Elihu Yale (1648–1721), b. at Boston, Mass., one-time governor of Fort St. George, Madras, who in 1718 sent a cargo of books, pictures, etc., which realized £562 12s. for the benefit of the then college (univ. 1887).

YA'LTA. Russian holiday resort with a pleasant climate in the Crimea, Ukrainian S.S.R., 32 m. E.S.E. of Sevastopol. Livadia, summer palace built by Nicholas II 1910–11, was the site of the Y. conference, 1945, at which Churchill, Roosevelt, and Stalin completed plans for the defeat of Germany and the foundation of the U.N.

YAM. The thick tuberous roots of plants of the genus *Dioscorea*, which in tropical countries, e.g. the S. Sea islands, are eaten in the place of potatoes.

YANG-KÜ. Name 1912–47 of TAIYUAN.

YANGTZE-KIANG (yang'tsa kyang'). The reatest river of China, rising in Tibet, and flowing into the Yellow Sea. Length *c.* 3,400 m. A road-rail bridge (22,000 ft. long) was opened at Nanking 1968.

YANKEE. Name often applied by Europeans to the people of the U.S.A. in general, although more properly confined to those of the New England states.

YARD. A measure of length, equal to 3 ft. or 36 in. It is supposed to have been the length of the arm of King Henry I.

YARKAND (yahrkand') (Chinese *Soche*). A walled city of Sinkiang-Uighur in an oasis of the Tarim basin. Irrigation ensures agriculture and pastoral activity. It is a centre of Islamic culture. Pop. *c.* 80,000.

YARMOUTH, or Great Yarmouth. English fishing port and seaside resort (co. bor.) in Norfolk, at the mouth of the Yare. It has a good harbour, and claims to be the largest herring port in the world. Other industries incl. shipbuilding, marine engineering, and textiles. Pop. (1961) 52,860. Another YARMOUTH, a

small port in the Isle of Wight, is a yachting centre. The French burned it in 1377 and 1544.

YAROSLAVL (yahrōslahvl'). Town in the R.S.F.S.R., cap. of Y. region, on the Volga 155 m. N.E. of Moscow. It takes its name from Yaroslav the Wise who founded it in 1024, and has a number of old buildings. Y. makes textiles synthetic rubber, paints, motor-lorries, etc. Pop. (1967) 486,000.

YARROW, or Milfoil. A common wayside plant (*Achillea millefolium*) of the Compositae family, found throughout the northern hemisphere usually with flat-topped clusters of white flowers.

YARROW. A Scottish river, 14 m. long, in Selkirkshire, flowing into the Tweed, and famous in poetry.

YAWATA (yahwah'ta). *See* KITAKYUSHU.

YAWS. A contagious disease common in the West Indies, characterized by red, raspberry-like eruptions upon the face, toes, and other parts of the body. A very similar disease is found in W. Africa.

YAWS. Five-year-old Ede Nwaebgo of Nigeria (left), disfigured by the disease, and (right) after 10 days' penicillin treatment. *Courtesy of W.H.O.*

YAZD. Alternative form of YEZD.

YEAR. A unit of time measurement. The calendar Y. consists of 365 days, but leap Y. – a Y. the date of which is divisible by 4 without remainder – consists of 366 days, an extra day being added to Feb. The last of a cent. is not leap Y., however, unless it is divisible by 400. The tropical, solar, or equinoctial Y. is the time taken by the earth to revolve round the sun from equinox to equinox, i.e. 365·2422 mean solar days (365 days, 5 hrs. 48 mins. 46 secs.). The sidereal Y. in which the observation is made on a star is 365 days, 6 hrs. 9 mins. 9 secs. An historical Y. begins on 1 Jan. but up to 1752 the civil or legal Y. began on 25 March. The regnal Y. begins on the anniversary of the sovereign's accession; it is used in the dating of Acts of Parliament.

YEAST. A mass of minute circular or oval vegetable cells about 1/3000th in. in diameter, each of which is a complete plant capable under suitable conditions of reproducing new cells by budding. When placed in a sugar solution they multiply and convert the sugar into alcohol and carbon dioxide. Ys. are used in leavening bread, fermenting beer, etc.

YEATS (yāts), **William Butler** (1865–1939). Irish poet. Of Anglo-Irish stock, he was b. in Dublin, son of a lawyer turned painter. He became the leading figure of the Celtic revival, helping to found the Abbey Theatre, and as a believer in Irish nationalism sitting in the Irish senate 1922–8. His early poetry e.g. *The Wind Among the Reeds* (1899) is romantically and exotically lyrical, and he drew on Irish legend for his poetic plays e.g. *The Countess Kathleen* (1892) and *Deidre* (1907), but broke through to a new sharply resilient style with *Responsibilities* (1914). In his personal life there was also a break: the beautiful Maude Gonne to whom many of his poems had been addressed finally refused to marry him, and in 1917 he m. Georgic Hyde-Lees, whose gifts as a medium reinforced his leanings towards mystic symbolism, cf. the prose *A Vision* (1925 and 1937). His later vols. of verse, of astonishing maturity and lyric inspiration, incl. *The Wild Swans at Coole* (1919), *The Tower* (1927), *The Winding Stair* (1933) and *Last Poems* (1939). His prose works incl. *Autobiographies* (1926), *Dramatis Personae* (1936), *Letters* (1954) and *My Theologies* (1959).

His younger brother, **Jack Butler Y.** (1871–1957), was a well-known artist, using black-and-white to illustrate his own stories, and oil to depict scenes of Irish life, e.g. 'Back from the Races' in the Tate, and later legendary themes.

YEDO. Name until 1868 of TOKYO.

'YELLOW BOOK.' An illustrated quarterly magazine pub. in London 1894–7, in which appeared literary and artistic contributions from Aubrey Beardsley, Max Beerbohm, Henry James, etc.

YELLOW FEVER. Sometimes called yellow jack. An endemic infective F. of the tropics, particularly prevalent in the Caribbean area, Brazil, and the W. Coast of Africa. One of the symptoms is a yellowish skin. It has been brought under control following the discovery that it is carried by a mosquito. The 1st effective vaccines were produced by Max Theiler of N.Y. (Nobel prize 1951).

YELLOWKNIFE. Cap. of N.W. Territories, Canada from 1967, centre of a gold-mining area discovered in 1934. It is on the N. shore of Great Slave Lake and was founded 1935. It has an airport. Pop. (1966) 3,741.

YELLOW RIVER. *See* HWANG-HO.

YELLOWSTONE NATIONAL PARK. A national American reserve, estab. 1872 and maintained by the U.S. govt. in N.W. Wyoming, on a broad plateau in the Rocky Mts. It incl. more than 3,000 geysers and hot springs, and very fine scenery. Area 3,458 sq. m.

YEMEN (yem'en). Country in S.W. Arabia, the *Arabia Felix* of the ancients, bounded on the N. by Saudi Arabia and on the S. by Democratic Rep. of Y. It is the most fertile region of Arabia and exports coffee, grain, etc. The king was killed in a revolt 1962 and a rep. estab., but royalists (with Saudi aid) resisted the new govt. (aided by Egypt): there was a compromise peace 1970. There are 2 caps., San'a and Taiz: other towns are the ports Mocha and Hodeida. Area 75,000 sq. m.; pop. *c.* 4,500,000.

YEMEN, People's Democratic Rep. of. State of S.W. Arabia from 1967: for earlier history *see* ADEN. Cotton is the chief export crop, and modern irrigation is being adopted. The cap. is Madinet al-Shaab. In 1969 the pres. was overthrown and a 5-man presidential council set up. Area 61,890 sq. m.; pop. (1969) 1,500,000. Also part of Y. are the is. of Perim and Socotra (q.v.) and Kamaran (area 70 sq. m.).

YENISEI (yenēsā'-ē). Great river of Asiatic Russia, rising in Tuva region and flowing across the Siberian plain into the Arctic Ocean. Its length is about 2,360 m.; its chief tributary is the Angara.

YEOMAN (yō'-). In England, between the break-up of the feudal system and the agricultural revolution of the 18th–19th cents., a small landowner who farmed his own fields.

YEOMANRY. Volunteer cavalry organized 1794, and incl. in the Territorial Army (q.v.) 1907.

YEOMEN OF THE GUARD. A military corps which was founded by Henry VII in 1485 and since then has constituted the bodyguard of the English sovereign. Its duties are purely ceremonial, and the uniform and weapons are much as they were in Tudor times. The nickname of 'Beefeaters' is supposed to have originated in 1669 when the grand-duke of Tuscany ascribed their fine appearance to beef.

YEREVAN (yerevahn'). Cap. of Armenian S.S.R., in the valley of the Zanga, a few m. N. of the Turkish border. It makes tractor parts, machine tools,

chemicals, bricks, bicycles, wine, and cans fruit and vegetables. The Armenian state univ. (1921) is at Y. Founded in the 7th cent., Y. was alternately Turkish and Persian from the 15th cent. until ceded to Russia, 1828. Pop. (1962 est.) 583,000.

YERSIN (yärsaň'), **Alexandre Émile John** (1863–1943). Swiss bacteriologist, who discovered the plague bacillus in Hong Kong in 1894 and prepared a serum.

YEVTUSHE'NKO, Yevgeny (1933–). Russian poet. B. in Siberia, he aroused controversy by his anti-Stalinist 'Stalin's Heirs' (1936), pub. with Khrushchev's support. He pub. his *Autobiography* (1963).

YEW

YEW. An evergreen tree (*Taxus baccata*) belonging to the Taxaceae family. It has densely spreading branches with very dark, linear, leathery leaves. The seeds are set in a fleshy, rose-red cup. Both leaves and seeds are poisonous.

YEZD. Town of central Persia, in a fertile oasis *c.* 170 m. E.S.E. of Isfahan. It is on an important trade route, and is renowned for its woven silks. Pop. (1956) 63,502.

YEZIDIS (yezē'dēz). A religious sect of Iraq, whose chief centre is near Mosul. Their religion is a mixture of Christianity and Islam; they practise baptism and circumcision, but regard the devil as God's agent and endeavour to keep in his favour.

YEZO (yez'ō). Another name for HOKKAIDO.

Y-FACTOR. All men inherit from their fathers one Y chromosome (q.v.) which gives them their male characteristics, and some (probably 1 in 300) inherit 2, which gives added height, greater emotional instability, inability to bear frustration, and great aggressiveness. Crimes of violence are frequently committed by such men and possession of the Y-factor, immediately detectable under the microscope, has in France and Australia (1968) been successfully pleaded in mitigation in murder cases.

YIDDISH (Ger. *Jüdisch*, Jewish). The language spoken by Polish and Russian Jews that is based on the German spoken by their ancestors in the Rhineland and has absorbed many Hebrew, Russian, Polish, etc., words. Its literature arose out of the folk songs of eastern Europe and assumed importance in the latter half of the 19th cent., when Russian Jewish writers such as Spektor, Frug, Abramovich, Peretz, and Sholem Alechem wrote in Yiddish.

YŌ'GA (Sanskrit, union). A system of Hindu philosophy, characterized by belief in a personal deity with whom it is possible to attain mystical and ecstatic union by the practice of hypnosis and a complicated and prolonged system of mortification of the senses, e.g. by abstract meditation, induced apathy, rigidity of posture, ascetic practices, concentration of mind on one particular point, etc. Siva is the Great Yogi. The system is attributed to Patanjali, a Hindu seer who is supposed to have flourished about 150 B.C. at Gonda, Oudh.

YOKOHAMA (yŏkohah'ma). Japanese seaport on Tokyo Bay, 18 m. S.W. of Tokyo. Commodore Perry (q.v.) landed at Y. in 1854, and in 1859 it was the 1st Japanese port opened to foreign trade, growing rapidly from a small fishing village to the chief centre of trade with Europe and America. Almost destroyed in an earthquake (1923) it was also rebuilt after S.W.W. air raids. Pop. (1965) 1,789,000.

YOKOSUKA. Japanese seaport and naval base (1884) on Tokyo Bay, S. of Yokohama. Pop. (1965) 317,000.

YONGE (yung), **Charlotte Mary** (1823–1901).

British author of some 120 novels, biographies, and educational works, marked by strong religious views of a High Church character. *The Heir of Redclyffe* (1853) was her 1st highly successful novel.

YONI. *See* LINGAM.

YONKERS (yung'-). City adjoining New York, U.S.A., on the Hudson. Originally a Dutch settlement dating from *c.* 1650, it is a busy manufacturing centre, and a residential district. Pop. (1960) 190,634.

YONNE (yon). French river, 180 m. long, rising in the Morvan Mts. and flowing generally N. into the Seine near Montereau. It gives its name to a dept.

YORK. A royal dynasty of England, founded by Richard duke of Y. (1411–60), who during the reign of Henry VI (of the House of Lancaster) claimed the throne as the descendant of Lionel duke of Clarence, 3rd son of Edward III, Henry being descended from the 4th son. The Yorkists and the Lancastrians fought out the issue in the Wars of the Roses. Y. was slain at the battle of Wakefield in 1460, but in the next year his son became king as Edward IV, and was followed by his son Edward V and his brother Richard III. The last-named fell at Bosworth in 1485, and the Lancastrian victor became king as Henry VII. To consolidate his claim, Henry m. the eldest dau. of Edward IV.

YORK, Frederick Augustus, duke of (1763–1827). Second son of George III, he was an unsuccessful commander against the French in the Netherlands 1793–9. From 1798 to 1809 he' was British C.-in-C. He founded the Duke of Y.'s School for soldiers' sons at Chelsea; and the Duke of Y.'s column in Waterloo Place, London, commemorates him.

YORK, Archbishop of. Metropolitan of the northern prov., and Primate of England, the abp. of Y. ranks next to the Lord High Chancellor. The Most Rev. **Frederick Donald Coggan** (1909–), appointed 1961, was 93rd of the line.

YORK, Duke of. A title often borne by the second or later son of an English king, e.g. George, later George V, 2nd son of Edward VII; and Albert Frederick, 2nd son of George V, later King George VI.

YORK. City (co. bor.) of England, cap. of Yorkshire and seat of an archbishopric. It is on the Ouse, 188 m. N.W. of London. It was a British city before

YORK. The walls of the city are mainly 14th century, but parts are Norman, and Bootham Bar, the main gateway to the north, has a Norman arch. In the background is the cathedral of St. Peter, known as York Minster, completed in the 15th century. *Courtesy of the City of York Information Service.*

YORKSHIRE. Kilnsey Crag, which dominates the upper valley of the river Wharfe in the West Riding.
Photo: W. R. Mitchell.

it became the Roman Eboracum, military cap. of the Roman garrison. Paulinus, 1st bp. of Y., was consecrated there in 627; the see was raised to an archbishopric 732. From the early Middle Ages it has been the cap. of the N., and is a residential and ecclesiastical centre with many important manufacturing firms. York Minster is built on the site of the wooden church in which Paulinus baptized King Edwin in 627. The present structure was begun *c.* 1230 and building continued until 1474, when the W. tower was finished. It was seriously damaged by fire in 1829. Its stained glass is famous. Much of the 14th cent. city wall remains, with 4 principal gates or bars. The 15th cent. guildhall (bombed 1942) was reconstructed 1962. The Theatre Royal, site of a theatre since 1765, was renovated 1965. The Univ. of Y. received its charter 1963. Pop. (1961) 104,468.

YORKSHIRE. Largest county of England, in the N.E. of the country, lying between the Tees and the Humber estuary, and fronting the North Sea. The geographical county (cap. York) is divided into Ridings (i.e. thirds), N., E., and W. The surface is upland in the E. (Y. Moors and Y. Wolds), while in the centre is the great plain of York. The Pennine Range in the W. is penetrated by beautiful valleys, or dales, the principal being Teesdale, Wensleydale, Swaledale, Nidderdale, Wharfedale, and Airedale. The chief peaks are Mickle Fell (2,591 ft.), Whernside, and Ingleborough. The Aire Gap is a convenient link between Yorks and Lancs. The Cleveland Hills provide large quantities of iron ore as well as building stone, and the potash deposits near Staithes are the richest in Europe. In the West Riding there are valuable coalfields, and here too are Leeds, Bradford, Halifax, and Huddersfield, centres of the textile industry. Sheffield is a centre for iron and steel goods. The East Riding is a great agricultural district.

The Industrial Revolution achieved here some of its greatest transformations, yet in the moors and dales agricultural and pastoral life proceeds very much as it has done for cents. Area 6,254 sq. m.; pop. (1967) 4,916,910.

YOSEMITE (yōse'mitē) **NATIONAL PARK.** Area of 1,175 sq. m. in central E. California, U.S.A., dedicated 1890, in the Sierra Nevada. Mountainous and of great beauty, it incl. Y. and other gorges, Y. Falls, 2,500 ft. high in 3 leaps, and many other waterfalls, and 3 groves of giant sequoias.

YOUGHAL (yawl). Irish seaport and resort (U.D.) on the Blackwater estuary, co. Cork, originally settled by Norsemen: it is a centre of salmon fishing and makes pottery and silks. Pop. (1961) 5,136.

YOUNG, Arthur (1741–1820). British writer on agriculture. His *Travels in France* (1792) gives a vivid picture of the *ancien régime* in decline, and he began

BRIGHAM YOUNG
Courtesy of the Church of Jesus Christ of Latter-Day Saints.

the pub. of 45 *Annals o, Agriculture* from 1784. In 1793 he was appointed sec. of the Board of Agriculture.

YOUNG, Brigham (1801–77). American religious leader. B. in Vermont, he joined the Mormon Church in 1832, and 3 years later was appointed an apostle. After a successful recruiting mission in Liverpool, he returned to U.S.A., and as successor of Joseph Smith, recently murdered, led the Mormon migration to the Great Salt Lake in Utah (1846), founded Salt Lake City, and ruled the colony well until his death.

YOUNG, Edward (1683–1765). British poet, author of *Night Thoughts on Li, e, Death, and Immortality*, once universally popular.

YOUNG, Francis Brett (1884–1954). British novelist. B. in Worcs, he became a doctor and practised in Brixham, Devon, then lived in Capri before settling in the Midlands. Beginning with a study of Robert Bridges, and *Marching on Tanga* (1918; an account of life with the British forces in E. Africa), he produced a series of detailed novels of middle-class life, incl. *The Young Physician* (1919), *Portrait of Clare* (1927), *A Man about the House* (1942).

YOUNGHUSBAND, Sir Francis (1863–1942). British soldier and explorer. B. in India, he entered the army in 1882 and 20 years later accompanied the mission that opened up Tibet. He wrote travel books and works on comparative religion.

YOUNG MEN'S CHRISTIAN ASSOCIATION (Y.M.C.A.). Founded in London in 1844 by (Sir) George Williams (1821–1905) in the drapery firm in St. Paul's churchyard in which he was a clerk, the Y.M.C.A. is an association of young men, without distinction of race or colour, who seek to improve themselves spiritually, intellectually, and physically.

YOUNGSTOWN. City of Ohio, U.S.A., in a rich mining area, with iron and steel plants. Pop. (1960) 166,689.

YOUNG WOMEN'S CHRISTIAN ASSOCIATION (Y.W.C.A.). Organization for women and girls, formed in 1887 when 2 organizations, both founded in 1855 – the one by Miss Emma Robarts and the other by Lady Kinnaird – combined their work.

YPRES (ēpr), **John Denton Pinkstone French**, 1st earl of (1852–1925). British field marshal. He entered the army in 1874, and in the South African War of 1899 defeated the Boers at Elandslaagte, relieved Kimberley, and captured Bloemfontein. In 1912 he became Chief of the General Staff, but resigned in 1914. Later in the year he was appointed C.-in-C. of the B.E.F. to France, and held the command until the end of 1915. Lord-Lieut. of Ireland 1918–21, he was created an earl on his resignation.

YPRES. French ēpr; or 'wipers' in British Army pron.; Flem. **Ieper.** Belgian town in W. Flanders, 25 m. S. of Ostend. Its old cloth hall and the cathedral were among the casualties of the F.W.W. The Menin Gate (1927) is a memorial to British soldiers lost in the great battles fought round the town 1914–18. Pop. (1966) 18,000.

YSSELMEER. Alt. spelling of IJSSELMEER.

YTTERBIUM (iter'-). Chemical element. Symbol Yb; at. wt. 173·04; at. no. 70. It is a rare metal occurring in rare earths that contain yttrium.

YTTRIUM (it'-). Chemical element. Symbol Y.; at. wt. 88·91; at. no. 39. It is the most basic of the rare earth metals.

YUCATAN (yookahtahn'). A peninsula in Central America, most of it in Mexico but extending into British Honduras and Guatemala. Tropical crops are grown. It is inhabited by Indians of Maya stock, and there are remains of the civilization which the Spanish conquerors found in decline. Area *c.* 70,000 sq. m.

YUCCA (yuk'a). In botany, a genus of the Liliaceae, with some 30 species occurring in Mexico and the S.W. of U.S.A. The leaves are stiff and sword-shaped and the flowers white and campanulate.

YUCCA

YUGOSLAVIA. A federal rep. (see table for units) of S.E. Europe in the Balkan peninsula. It has a much indented Adriatic coastline, and mountainous surface save in the N. and N.E., where are the fertile lowlands of the middle Danube and its tributaries, Drava, Tagiss (Tisa), Sava, and Morava. The climate is continental. The cap. is Belgrade. Most of the people are members of the Eastern Orthodox Church, though there are many Roman Catholics in the N.W.; 12·5 per cent of the pop. are Mohammedan. The Slovene, Macedonian, and Serbo-Croat languages are officially recognized, the last being in general use. Agriculture supports *c.* 50 per cent of the pop., wheat and maize being the main crops. Minerals worked incl. coal, copper, lead, iron, aluminium, mercury, petroleum. Iron and steel, cement, fertilizers, and textiles are among industrial products. Horses, cattle, sheep, pigs, and poultry are raised.

CONSTITUTION. The constitution of 1963 gave Y. the name of the Socialist Federal Rep. of Y. The Fed. Assembly is subdivided into 5 chambers – Federal, Economic, Education and Culture, Social Welfare and Health, and Organisational-Political – with an additional chamber of Nationalities within the Federal chamber. The Assembly elects the pres. and fed. executive council.

Area 98,740 sq. m.; pop. (1967) 19,958,000.

HISTORY. Y. came into existence in 1918 as the kingdom of the Serbs, Croats, and Slovenes with the Serbian Peter (I) Karageorgevich as king. Peter I died in 1921 and was succeeded by his son Alexander

YUGOSLAVIA. Rab is built on a steep ridge on the west coast of the island of the same name in the Gulf of Kvarner, northern Yugoslavia. Its houses are closely packed and the belfries of three of its four churches rise almost side by side along the shore. *Courtesy of the Yugoslav National Tourist Office.*

FEDERAL REPUBLIC OF YUGOSLAVIA			
	Area in sq. m.	Population (1961 census)	Capita
Serbia	34,107	7,642,227	Belgrade
Croatia	21,824	4,159,696	Zagreb
Slovenia	7,817	1,591,523	Ljubluana
Bosnia-Hercegovina	19,736	3,277,948	Sarajevo
Macedonia	9,925	1,406,003	Skopje
Montenegro	5,331	471,894	Titograd
	98,740	18,549,291	

who, faced with difficulties at home and abroad (espec. with Italy), estab. a military dictatorship in 1929. He was assassinated in Marseilles, during an official visit to France, 1934. His young son Peter II (1923–70) succeeded and a regency under his uncle Paul was set up until Peter assumed power early in 1941. German invasion followed, and the whole country was overrun; the king took refuge in England, and Y. became an area of grim guerrilla warfare until the Germans were expelled with the help in the last months of Russian forces. The guerrilla leader Josip Broz (Marshal Tito) estab. a Communist govt., and following an election in 1945 a new constitution organizing the country into a republican federation of 6 reps. was proclaimed. Y. subsequently developed her internal and external policies independently of Soviet Communism.

Literature. The Yugoslav or Serbo-Croat language belongs to the southern branch of the Slavonic languages. Y. literature begins in the 9th cent. with the translation into Slavonic of the church service books. Its great glory is the folk poetry, particularly the song cycles dealing with the battle of Kosovo and the hero Marko Kraljevič. After the cents. of national repression a revival came, notably under Dositej Obradovič (1739–1811). Poets of the earlier 19th cent. incl. the prince-bishop Petar Njegoš (1813–51), France Prešern (1800–49), and Ivan Mazuranič (1814–90). Later, Russian influence predominated. More modern writers incl. the novelist Ivan Cankar (1876–1918), dramatist Ivo Vojnovič (1857–1929), and poet Oton Zupančič (1878–1949).

YUKON (yōō′kon). Terr. of N.W. Canada, named after its chief r. the Y. It incl. the highest point in Canada, Mt. Logan (19,539 ft.), in the Mt. Elias range of the Rockies on the border of Alaska, U.S.A., to the W. Settlement dates from the discovery of gold in the Klondike valley in 1896, and Y. was organized as a political unit in 1898 with Dawson as cap., replaced 1953 by Whitehorse (q.v.). The N.W. Highway and branches link much of the terr. Petroleum and natural gas, gold and silver are worked; also coal. Fur trapping is important. Area 207,076 sq. m.; pop. (1966) 14,382.

YUNGNING. Name 1913–45 of NANNING.

YUNNAN (yün′ahn′). Prov. of S.W. China adjoining Burma and N. Vietnam. It is mountainous and well forested. Tin, copper, lead, zinc, coal, salt and other minerals are worked; tea, tobacco, rice, wheat are grown. The Salween and Mekong flow through it, and the Yangtze in the N. It is traversed by the Burma Road. The cap. is Kunming, also called Y. Area 162,000 sq. m.; pop. (1968) 23,000,000.

YUZOVKA (yōōz′ofka). See DONETSK.

Z The 26th and last letter in the English and other modern alphabets. It was the 6th in the classical Greek alphabet, but it was found only in the later Roman alphabet. It is used initially and medially in many words of Greek or Oriental origin, and the modern tendency is to employ it in preference to *s* in such words as *baptize*, *organize*, derived ultimately from the Greek.

ZAANDAM (zahndahm). Dutch town in N. Holland prov. on the Zaan, 5½ m. N.W. of Amsterdam. Peter the Great stayed at Z. in 1697 to study shipbuilding, then an important industry at Z. It has flour, timber, and paper mills. Pop. (1967) 117,240.

ZABALETA (thubalā′tah), **Nicanor** (1907–). Spanish harpist, noted for his efforts to enlarge the repertoire of original harp music by commissioning new works from e.g. Milhaud (q.v.) and Joaquín Rodrigo, and by reviving interest in classical harp music, particularly that of the 15th and 16th cents. in Spain and Portugal.

ZABRZE (zah′bzhe). Silesian town in Polish-admin. Germany, formed in 1905 by the amalgamation of several towns. It has collieries, foundries, etc. Pop. (1966) 198,000.

ZADAR (zah′dah). Yugoslav port and holiday resort on the Adriatic Sea. The Roman Jadera, it was alternately held and lost by the Venetian Rep. from the 12th cent. until seized by Austria in 1813 and made cap. of Dalmatia, 1815–1918. It belonged to Italy 1920–47 and was severely damaged in the S.W.W. Pop. (1961) 25,000.

ZADKINE (zad′kēn), **Ossip** (1890–1967). French cubist sculptor. Russian-born, he became French by service in the Foreign Legion, and spent most of his life in Paris, though often exhibiting in London, where he had also studied. Working in varied materials, he represented the human form in abstract terms, e.g. Laocoon and his variations on an Orpheus theme.

ZAGREB (zahg′reb). Yugoslav city, cap. of Croatia, on the Sava. It has a Gothic cathedral and a univ., and was a Roman city. Manufactures incl. leather, linen, carpets, rly. wagons. Pop. (1961) 430,802. *See* illus. p. 1110.

ZAHAROFF, Sir Basil (1849–1936). International financier and armaments 'king'. B. in Anatolia of Greek parents, he was very much a man of mystery. For his aid to the Allies during the F.W.W. he received a British knighthood. He was a munificent patron of univs. in England, France, and Russia.

ZAÏRE. See CONGO, Rep. of.

ZAKYNTHOS (zan′kēnthos). Most southerly of the Ionian Is., Greece. Olives, currants, and the vine are grown; carpets are made. Area 157 sq. m.; pop. (1961) 35,451.

ZA′MA. Site of battle fought in 202 B.C. in Numidia (now Algeria) in which the Carthaginians under Hannibal were defeated by the Romans under Scipio, so ending the Second Punic War.

ZAMBE′ZI. River of Africa, c. 1,600 m. long, with headstreams in Zambia, Angola, and Congo (cap. Leopoldville). It flows generally E. to the Indian Ocean which it enters through a wide delta near Chinde, Mozambique. Though broken by the Victoria

Falls (harnessed for power, 1938) and many rapids, the Z. is important as a highway. *See* KARIBA.

ZA'MBIA. Rep. of S. central Africa, formerly known as Northern Rhodesia (*see* RHODESIA). It has an altitude of 3,000–5,000 ft., except in river valleys, and incl. Lake Bangweulu and part of Lake Mweru, and the Kariba Dam (q.v.). Maize, ground-nuts, cassava, Kaffir corn and tobacco are produced, and cattle reared. By far the most valuable mineral is the copper from the Copperbelt adjoining Katanga, Congo: others are zinc, lead, and vanadium. Lusaka replaced Livingstone as cap. in 1935; Kitwe, Ndola, Broken Hill and Fort Jameson are other towns. Area *c.* 288,130 sq. m.; pop. (1966) 3,894,400.

N.R. was visited by the Portuguese in the late 18th cent., and by Livingstone for the first time in 1851. Made a British protectorate in 1924, it was a member of the Federation of Rhodesia and Nyasaland 1953–63, was granted self-govt. in 1963 and in 1964 the name Zambia was adopted. Under Pres. Kenneth Kaunda (q.v.) there has been increased govt. control of the economy, e.g. the taking over by the state of all mineral rights in 1969.

ZAMENHOF (tsah'men-), **Lazarus Ludovik** (1859–1917). Polish-Jewish oculist of Warsaw, who invented the international language, Esperanto.

ZAMORA Y TORRES. *See* ALCALA ZAMORA.

ZAGREB. Built on a neighbouring hill to its rival for many centuries, the Kaptol, is the Upper Town. To the right is St. Mark's church, the roof bearing the coats of arms of Crotia, Slavonia and Dalmatia, and of Zagreb. Slightly in front and to the right is the vast parliament building.
Courtesy Yugoslav National Tourist Office.

ZANTE (zahn'te). Ital. form of ZAKYNTHOS.

ZANZIBAR (zanzibahr'). Country in E. Africa, consisting of the island of Z. (50 m. long; area 640 sq. m.), and 25 m. N. the island of Pemba (42 m. long; area 380 sq. m.), and some adjacent islets. The soil is fertile, but the climate is oppressively humid. Cloves are the principal product, followed by copra. The cap. also Z., is on the W. coast of Z. Is. Pop. (1967) 354,360; Pemba 164,243.

Formerly a sultanate, Z. was placed by its ruler under Brit. protection in 1890, and remained a protectorate until accorded independence in 1963. The sultan immediately handed over to Kenya the coastal strip of that country which had been part of Z. for *c.* 500 years. In 1964 an army revolt drove the sultan into exile and estab. a rep., and shortly after-wards Z. was linked in a rep. with Tanganyika (q.v.).

ZAPOROZHE (zahporozh'ye). City in Ukrainian S.S.R. on the Dnieper, cap. of Z. region, and site of the Dnieper Dam (q.v.). Z. manufactures steel, chemicals, aluminium goods, etc., and is an important

centre for pig-iron and magnesium. The Russians did not defend it in 1941, but re-took it from the Germans in 1943. Pop. (1967) 571,000.

ZARA. Ital. form of ZADAR.

ZARAGOZA. Span. spelling of SARAGOSSA.

ZEALAND. *See* SEELAND, Denmark; ZEELAND, Netherlands.

ZE'BRA. Name given to striped equine species; the stripes serve as camouflage against the desert and mountainous background. The true or mountain Z. (*Equus zebra*) was once common in Cape Colony and Natal and still sur-vives in parts of S. Africa and Angola. It has short legs and long ears and is silvery-white with black or dark brown markings. Grevy's Z. (*E. grevyi*) is much larger, and has finer and clearer markings; it inhabits Ethiopia and Somaliland; Burchell's Z. (*E. burchelli*), which is intermediate in

size, has white ears, a long mane, and full tail; it roams the plains N. of the Orange river.

ZE'BU. Indian ox (*Bos indicus*), light-coloured with a large fatty hump near the shoulders. It is used for draught, and is held to be sacred.

ZEDEKIAH (zedekI'-ah). Last of the kings of the Hebrew kingdom of Judah. Nebuchadrezzar gave him the throne in 597 B.C., but in 586 he was taken away to Babylon as a blinded captive.

ZEEBRUGGE (zābroog'ge). Small Belgian port on the North Sea. The harbour and 9 m. canal to Bruges were built 1896–1907. In the F.W.W., when it was a German submarine base, it was attacked on 23 April 1918 by a British force under Admiral Keyes (q.v.) and the canal entrance was blocked.

ZEELAND (zē'-). Prov. of the Netherlands, incl. the estuary of the Scheldt and the is. of Walcheren and N. and S. Beveland, adjoining Belgium on the S. Most of its surface is below sea-level. Cap. Middel-burg. Area 660 sq. m.; pop. (1966) 295,374.

ZEFFIRE'LLI, G. Franco (1923–). Italian theatrical director and designer, famous for his beautiful and lavish designs and production of plays, e.g. *Romeo and Juliet* at the Old Vic (1960), of operas, e.g. *Tosca* (1964), and of films, e.g. *The Taming of the Shrew* (1967).

ZEISS (tsIs), **Carl** (1816–88). German optician. He opened his 1st workshop at Jena in 1846 and in 1866 joined forces with Ernst Abbe (1840–1905), producing microscopes, field glasses, etc.

ZENDAVE'STA. The sacred scriptures of the Zoroastrians, represented by the modern Parsees. The Avesta consists of liturgical books for the use of the Parsee priests, and the *Gathas* contain the dis-courses and revelations of Zoroaster. The Zend portion is the commentary thereon.

ZE'NITH. Opposite of nadir; the upper pole of the celestial horizon or the point in the sky immediately above the observer.

ZE'NO (fl. *c.* 460 B.C.). Greek philosopher, one of the Eleatic school. He was a disciple of Parmenides and controverted current views on space and time by such paradoxes as that of Achilles and the tortoise.

ZENO (*c.* 340–265 B.C.). Greek philosopher, b. at Citium in Cyprus and probably a Phoenician, who founded the Stoic school of philosophy at Athens.

ZENŌ'BIA. Queen of Palmyra in the Syrian desert from A.D. 266, when on her husband's death she assumed the crown as regent for her sons, until 272 when she was defeated by the Roman emperor Aurelain and taken as a captive to Rome.

ZEPPELIN (tse'pelēn), **Ferdinand,** count von (1838–1917). German airship pioneer. On his retirement from the army in 1891 he devoted himself to the study of aeronautics. His 1st airship was built in 1900 after many failures; it remained aloft for 20 minutes and then crashed on landing. But during the F.W.W. Germany employed a number of Zeppelins in bombing London and other parts of England. In the 1960s Japan and the U.S.S.R. experimented with nuclear-powered craft.

ZERMATT (tsermaht'). Swiss tourist and winter-sports centre in the Valais canton at the foot of the Matterhorn. Pop. (1960) 2,700.

ZETLAND. Official form of SHETLAND.

ZEUS (zūs). The supreme god in the Greek pantheon, corresponding to the Roman Jupiter. He was the son of Kronos, and his chief spouse was Hera. As the supreme god he dispensed good and evil and was the father and saviour of all mankind. He is frequently represented holding the thunderbolt and the aegis or shield of fringed goatskin.

ZHDANOV (zhdah'nof). Port of the Ukraine, U.S.S.R., on the Sea of Azov. Formerly Mariupol, it was renamed 1944 in honour of Andrei Zhdanov (1896–1948), statesman and defender of Leningrad, who was born at Mariupol. It has iron and steel industries. Pop. (1967) 373,000.

ZHITO'MIR. Town in Ukrainian S.S.R., cap. oɪ Z. region, on the Teterev, a trib. of the Dnieper. Dating from the 13th cent., it is a timber and grain centre with furniture factories, etc. Pop. (1967) 133,000.

ZHUKOV (zhŏŏk'of), **Grigory Konstantinovich** (1896–). Marshal of the Soviet Union. Early in 1941 he became Chief of Staff, commanded the armies defending Moscow in 1941, directed the counter-offensive at Stalingrad in 1942–3, and organized the relief of Leningrad in 1943. Appointed commander on the Ukrainian front in March 1944, he led the offensive which ended with the fall of Berlin, headed the Allied delegation which received the German surrender, and subsequently commanded the Russian occupation forces inside Germany, 1945–6. He succeeded Bulganin as Min. of Defence (1955–7).

ZIEGLER (zēg'ler), **Karl** (1898–). German organic chemist. After studying at Marburg univ. he was prof. at Heidelberg and Halle univs., and from 1943 was director of the Max Planck Inst. for Carbon Research at Mulheim. In 1963 he was awarded a Nobel prize for his work on the chemistry and technology of high polymers, e.g. the combination of many molecules of the simple gas ethylene, into the plastic, polythene.

ZIGGURAT. In ancient Babylonia and Assyria, a stepped pyramid of sun-baked brick faced with glazed bricks or tiles on which stood a shrine to a deity. The Tower of Babel may have been a Z.

ZIMBABWE (zēmbabh'wē). Bantu word meaning stone house, used esp. for extensive ruins near Victoria, in Mashonaland, Rhodesia. They incl. a massive fortress, a temple, and 2 conical towers, one 34 ft., the other 6½ ft. high. Discovered 1868 by Adam Renders, they were judged to date from c. A.D. 600 following radio-carbon tests in 1952 on timber taken from the building. Their origin remains uncertain. The Z. bird, derived from soapstone sculptures of fish eagles found in the ruins, is the national emblem of Rhodesia. The name has been adopted by black Rhodesian nation-alists and the Z. African Nat. Union (Z.A.N.U.) is led by the Rev. Ndabaningi Sithole, detained from 1964 and sentenced to 6 yrs. imprisonment 1969 for alleged incitement to the attempted murder of Ian Smith and 2 of his ministers.

ZINC. Bluish-white metal, symbol Zn, at. wt. 65·38, at. no. 30. From very early times it has been used as a component of brass but it was not recognized as a separate metal until 1746 by Marggraf, by heating calamine with charcoal. Ores occur in many parts of the world, but the principal source of supply is U.S.A. Its chief modern uses are in the production of galvanized iron and in alloys, especially brass. Its

compounds are used in medicine, and in paints, Z. oxide being an important white pigment.

ZINO'VIEV, Grigory (1883–1936). Russian politi-cian. A prominent Bolshevik, he returned to Russia in 1917 with Lenin and played a leading part in the Revolution. As head of the Communist International (1919) his name was linked with the forged letter in-citing Britain's Communists to rise, which helped to topple the Labour govt. in 1924. As one of the 'Old Bolsheviks', he was accused of high treason and shot.

ZI'ON. Name of the Jebusite stronghold in Jeru-salem that was captured by King David. On the same hill was built the temple and in due course Z. became a synonym for Jerusalem, and the City of God.

ZIONISM. A Jewish movement aiming at the establishment in Palestine of a Jewish state with its cap. at Jerusalem, the 'city of Zion'. As a modern movement it dates from 1896, when Theodor Herzl pub. his *Jewish State*, outlining a scheme for erecting an autonomous Jewish commonwealth under Turkish suzerainty. The Zionist Organization was estab. at Basle in 1897. During the F.W.W. Weizmann was instrumental in securing the Balfour Declaration (q.v.), and in 1948 the Jews in Palestine proclaimed the state of Israel.

ZIRCO'NIUM (Arabic *zargun*, gold colour). A rare metal of the titanium family, symbol Zr, at. wt. 91·22, at. no. 40. Discovered in zircon by Klaproth in 1789, and isolated by Berzelius in 1824, it is used in alloys.

ZLATOUST (zlahto-ōōst'). Town in Chelyabinsk region, R.S.F.S.R., in the S. Urals, founded in 1754 as an iron- and copper-working settlement, destroyed 1774 by a peasant rising, but developed as an arma-ments centre from the time of Napoleon's invasion of Russia. Since the Revolution, Z. has become one of the chief metallurgical centres of the R.S.F.S.R. Pop. (1967) 176,000.

ZO'DIAC. Name given by the ancient Greeks to that zone of the heavens containing the paths of the sun, moon and the 5 planets then known. It was about 16° in width, and the stars contained in it were grouped into 12 constellations to each of which was given a symbol, viz. Aries, ♈; Taurus, ♉; Gemini, ♊; Cancer, ♋; Leo, ♌; Virgo, ♍; Libra, ♎; Scorpio, ♏; Sagittarius, ♐; Capricornus, ♑; Aquarius, ♒; Pisces, ♓.

ZODIACAL LIGHT. A cone-shaped light some-times seen extending from the sun along the ecliptic, visible after sunset or before sunrise. It is due to thinly spread material in the central plane of the Solar System. From Britain it is never bright, but it may be conspicuous when observed from countries with clearer atmosphere.

ZO'FFANY, Johann (1733–1810). German portrait painter. Settling in England in 1758, he became R.A. in 1769, executing many conversation pieces.

ZOG (1895–1961). King of Albania. A member of an important Albanian family, he became P.M. of Albania in 1922, pres. of the rep. in 1925, and king in 1928. He was driven out by the Italians in 1939.

ZOLA, Émile Édouard Charles Antoine (1840–1902). French novelist. B. in Paris, he was a journalist and clerk in Paris until his *Contes à Ninon* (1864) enabled him to devote himself to literature. In 1867 he pub. the masterly study in remorse *Thérèse Raquin*, and in 1871 *La Fortune des Rougon* began the series of some 20 novels portraying the fortunes of a French family under the 2nd Empire, incl. *Le Ventre de Paris* (1874), *La Faute de l'Abbé Mouret* (1875), *L'Assommoir* (1878), *Nana* (1880), *Germinal* (1885), *La Terre* (1888), and *La Débâcle* (1892). Among later novels are the trilogy *Trois Villes* (1894–8), and *Fécondité* (1899). In 1898 he pub. *J'accuse*, indicting the persecutors of Dreyfus.

ZO'MBA. Cap. of Malawi, 20 m. E. of Lake Shirwa, until a new cap. is built at Lilongwe: Z. will become a univ. town. Pop. (1966) 19,616.

ZOO. Short for zoological gardens, i.e. places where wild animals are kept in captivity, whether as an interesting spectacle or in pursuit of scientific knowledge. Henry I started a royal menagerie at Woodstock, Oxon, later transferred to the Tower of London, and in 1831 the king presented the collection in the Tower menagerie to the Zoological Society in Regent's Park, London. *See* HAGENBECK; WHIPSNADE.

ZOOLOGY (zō-o'loji) (Gk. *zōon*, animal). That branch of biology that is concerned with the study of animals. The popular name for it is Natural History, but it comprises not only a description of present-day animals, but the evolution of animal forms, anatomy and physiology, embryology and morphology, geographical distribution, and ecology, etc.

ZORN (tsörn), **Anders** (1860–1920). Swedish impressionist painter of Dalecarlian peasants and nudes.

ZOROASTER (zörö-as'ter), or more correctly **Zarathustra** (600 or 1000 B.C. ?). Persian seer, founder of the religion known after him as Zoroastrianism. He was a Mede or a Persian, and was popularly supposed to be the first of the Magi or Wise Men. In the Zendavesta he features as a religious prophet, the author of hymns (the Gathas) in honour of Ormuzd the Good God. He is said to have found a powerful patron in a prince of eastern Iran, and to have married into the court circle. His date is uncertain.

ZOROASTRIANISM. The religion founded by Zoroaster (q.v.), represented today by the Parsees. Its theology is dualistic, the Good God Ahura Mazda or Ormuzd being opposed by the Evil God, Angra Mainyu or Ahriman. These are represented in the Avesta (*see* ZENDAVESTA) as being perpetually in conflict, but ultimately the victory will be Ormuzd's. A ceremonial was devised for purifying and keeping clean both soul and body. Worship was at altars on which burnt the sacred fire. A priestly caste was instituted. The dead were exposed to vultures.

ZORRILLA (thör-rēl'yah), **José** (1817–93). Spanish poet and playwright. B. at Valladolid, he based his plays chiefly on national legends.

ZOSHCHE'NKO, Mikhail Mikhailovich (1895–1958). Russian short-story writer. His best work – richly satirical – was done in the 1920s and early 1930s, e.g. *Respected Citizens* (1926) and *Private Life* (1933). His autobiography in 1943 reflected the pressure exercised by the C.P., and was not allowed to be completed.

ZOUAVES (zoo-ahvz'). Corps of French infantry soldiers, first raised in Algeria in 1831 from the Berber Kabyle tribe of Z. Before long, however, the native element was eliminated, and only a half-Arab dress was retained as a characteristic.

ZUCKERMAN (zook'-), **Solly**, baron (1904–   ). British scientist. B. in Cape Town, he originally specialized in anatomy, but after the S.W.W. was concerned with the wider range of policy, espec. defence, as Chief Scientific Adviser to the govt. 1960–71. He was awarded the O.M. 1968, and on his retirement in 1971 was created a life peer.

ZUIDER ZEE (zoi'der zā; Dutch, south sea). Former gulf of the N. Sea in the Netherlands, area 2,027 sq. m.; *See* IJSSELMEER.

ZULOAGA (thoo-lo-ah'ga), **Ignacio** (1870–1945). Spanish painter, b. in Vizcaya; he favoured bullfighters and other Spanish types.

ZULULAND (zoo'loo-). Region in the N.E. of Natal prov., S. Africa. It was annexed by Britain in 1887, and incorporated in Natal in 1897: the major part forms the Zulu *bantustan*, sugar, cotton and coffee plantations occupying the rest. The St. Lucia coalfield is connected by rail with Durban.

The Zulus probably reached the country early in

ZULULAND. The huts of a Zulu *kraal* are constructed with the same deft skill needed to fashion basketwork, such as that on the left, and the bead ornamentation these women are proudly displaying. *Courtesy of Satour.*

the 17th cent. and under Chaka (1810–28) became a formidable military power. His half brother Dingaan (q.v.) estab. an even more bloodthirsty régime. Subsequent rulers were Dingaan's half-brother Panda (1840–73), and Panda's son Cetewayo (q.v.) and grandson Dinizulu, who d. in 1913 exiled to the Transvaal. The Zulu *bantustan* was estab. 1970, the Chief Executive Officer or P.M. of the Zulu Territorial Authority being Chief Gatsha Buthelezi, a great-grandson of Cetewayo. The cap. is Nongoma, the traditional cap. of Eshowe having been taken over by white investment.

Area 10,425 sq. m.; pop. (est.) 400,000.

ZURBARÁN (thoorbahrahn'), **Francisco de** (1598–?1669). Spanish painter, sometimes called the Spanish Caravaggio. He painted subjects from Church history, e.g. a series (with Herrera) on the life of St. Bonaventura.

ZÜRICH (tsü'rikh). Swiss city, cap. of Z. canton, most populous and economically important in the country. It stands beside the lake of Z. It has a univ. (refounded 1833) and is the intellectual cap. of German-speaking Switzerland. Industries incl. machinery, electrical goods, cotton spinning, silk, etc. Pop. (1960) 439,600.

ZUTPHEN (züt'fen). Town in Gelderland prov., Netherlands. near which Sir Philip Sidney was fatally wounded. Pop. (1967) 27,017.

ZWEIG (zvīg), **Arnold** (1887–1968). German novelist, playwright and poet. B. in Silesia, he was Jewish and left Germany on the Nazis coming to power. He is best-remembered for his realistic novel of a Russian peasant in the German army *The Case of Sergeant Grischa* (1927).

ZWEIG (zvīg), **Stefan** (1881–1942). Austrian writer. A Viennese Jew, he found the world of Nazidom too much and committed suicide with his wife in Rio de Janeiro. He wrote poems and novels, but is best remembered for literary studies, e.g. Balzac, Dickens, Dostoyevsky, Stendhal.

ZWICKAU (tsvik'ow). Town in Karlmarxstadt district. E. Germany, on an important coalfield. Pop. (1966) 128, 184.

ZWINGLI (tsving'lē), **Ulrich** (1484–1531). Swiss Protestant. B. at St. Gall, he was ordained an R.C. priest in 1506, but by 1519 was a Reformer, and led the movement in Switzerland. In a war against the cantons which had not accepted the Reformation he was killed in a skirmish at Kappel.

ZWO'LLE. Cap. of Overijssel prov., Netherlands, a market town with brewing, distilling, butter making and other industries. Pop. (1967) 59,900.

Abbreviations

A Angström, answer. **A1**, first class (of ships). **A.A.**, Anti-Aircraft, Automobile Association. **A.A.A.**, Amateur Athletic Association, American Automobile Association. **A. and M.**, Ancient and Modern (hymnal). **A.A.U.**, Amateur Athletic Union (U.S.). **A.B.**, Able-bodied seaman. **A.B.A.**, Amateur Boxing Association. **Ab. init.**, *ab initio* (L., from the beginning). **Abl.**, ablative. **Abp.**, archbishop. **A.C.**, Aircraftman, alternating current, *ante Christum* (L., before Christ). **A/c**, account. **Acc.**, accusative. **A. Cdre**, Air Commodore. **A.C.F.**, Army Cadet Force. **ACTH**, Adrenocorticotrophic hormone. **A.D.**, *anno domini* (L., in the year of the Lord). **Ad.**, advertisement. **A.D.C.**, aide-de-camp. **Add.**, addenda. **Adj.**, adjective. **Ad. lib.**, *ad libitum* (L., as much as desired). **Adm.**, Admiral(ty). **Admin.**, administer(ed), administration. **Adv.**, Advent, adverb. **A.E.A.**, Atomic Energy Authority. **A.E.C.**, Atomic Energy Commission (U.S.). **A.E.I.**, Associated Electrical Industries. **Aet.**, *aetatis* (L., of the age). **A.E.U.**, Amalgamated Engineering Union. **A.F.**, audiofrequency. **A.F.L.–C.I.O.**, American Federation of Labor-Congress of Industrial Organizations (U.S.). **A.G.**, airgunner. **A.H.**, *anno hegirae* (L., in the year of the Hegira – Mohammedan calendar). **A.I.D.**, Agency for International Development. **Ala.**, Alabama. **Alas.**, Alaska. **alt.**, altitude. **Alta.**, Alberta. **a.m.**, *ante meridiem* (L., before noon). **amp.**, ampere. **Anniv.**, anniversary. **anon.**, anonymous. **A.O.C.** (in-C), Air Officer Commanding (in-Chief). **A.P.**, Associated Press. **approx.**, approximate(ly). **Aq.**, *aqua* (L., water). **arch.**, archaic, architecture, **archbp.**, archbishop. **Ariz.**, Arizona. **Ark.**, Arkansas. **A.R.P.**, Air Raid Precautions. **Arr.**, arranged, arrive(s). **A.S.**, Anglo-Saxon, anti-submarine. **a.s.l.**, above sea-level. **A.S.P.C.A.**, American Society for the Prevention of Cruelty to Animals. **assist.**, assistant. **assoc.**, associate(d). **assn.**, association. **A.S.S.R.**, Autonomous Soviet Socialist Republic. **asst.**, assistant. **A.T.C.**, Air Transport Command (U.S.), Air Training Corps. **A/T**, anti-tank. **at. no.**, atomic number. **A.T.S.**, Auxiliary Territorial Service. **at. wt.**, atomic weight. **A.U.C.**, *anno urbis conditae* (L., 'in the year of the founding of the city' [Rome], 753 B.C.). **Aug.**, August. **aux.**, auxiliary. **A.V.**, Authorized Version (of the Bible). **avdp.**, avoirdupois. **A.W.O.L.**, absent without leave.

B Born, brother. **B.A.**, Bachelor of Arts, British Academy, British Association (for the Advancement of Science), Buenos Aires. **Bac.**, *baccalaureus* (L., bachelor). **b. and b.**, bed and breakfast. **B.A.O.R.**, British Army of the Rhine. **Bart.**, baronet. **Bart's**, St. Bartholomew's Hospital, London. **B.B.C.**, British Broadcasting Corporation (originally Company). **B.C.**, Before Christ, borough council, British Columbia, British Council. **B.Ch.**, Bachelor of Surgery (L., *chirurgiae*). **B.C.L.**, Bachelor of Civil Law. **B.Com.**, Bachelor of Commerce. **B.D.**, Bachelor of Divinity. **Bde.**, brigade. **b.e.**, bill of exchange. **B.E.A.**, British European Airways. **Beds**, Bedfordshire. **B.E.F.**, British Expeditionary Force. **B.F.M.**, British Empire Medal. **B.Eng.**, Bachelor of Engineering. **Berks**, Berkshire. **b.f.**, brought forward. **B.I.S.**, Bank for International Settlements. **bk.**, book, bank. **b.l.**, bill of lading. **B.Litt.**,

Bachelor of Letters (L., *Litterarum*). **B.LL.**, Bachelor of Laws (L., *Legum*). **B.M.**, Bachelor of Medicine, British Museum. **B.M.A.**, British Medical Association. **B.M.H.**, British Motor Holdings (Ltd.). **Bn.**, battalion. **B.O.A.C.**, British Overseas Airways Corporation. **B. of E.**, Bank of England. **bor.**, borough. **bos'n**, boatswain. **B.O.T.**, Board of Trade. **bot.**, botany(ical). **B.P.**, British Pharmacopoeia. **b.p.**, boiling point. **Bp.**, bishop. **B.R.**, British Rail. **Brec**, Breconshire. **Brit.**, British. **Bros.**, brothers. **B.R.S.**, British Road Services. **B.S.A.**, Birmingham Small Arms (Company). **B.Sc.**, Bachelor of Science. **B.S.I.**, British Standards Institution. **B.S.T.**, British standard time (known internationally as C.E.T., q.v.). **Bt.**, baronet. **B.T.U.**, Board of Trade Unit. **Bucks**, Buckinghamshire. **bus**, omnibus (L., for all). **B.V.M.**, Blessed Virgin Mary. **Byz.**, Byzantine.

C *Centum* (L., hundred). **C.** capacitance, Centigrade, Central, coulomb. **c.**, centimetre, chapter, cubic, *circa* (L., about). **C.A.**, Consumers' Association. **cal.**, calorie. **Calif.**, California. **Cambs**, Cambridgeshire. **Can.**, canon. **Cantab.**, *Cantabrigiensis* (L., member of Cambridge University). **cap.**, capital, chapter. **Capt.**, captain. **car.**, carat. **cat.**, catalogue. **C.B.**, confined to barracks, county borough. **C.C.**, Coastal Command, county council(lor), cricket club. **c.c.**, cubic centimetre, cubic contents. **C.C.C.**, Central Criminal Court, Commodity Credit Corporation (U.S.). **C.D.**, Civil Defence, Contagious Diseases (Acts), *Corps Diplomatique* (Fr., diplomatic body). **C.D.C.**, Commonwealth Development Corporation. **Cdre.**, Commodore. **C.E.**, Chancellor of the Exchequer. **C.E.G.B.**, Central Electricity Generating Board. **C.E.M.A.**, Council for the Encouragement of Music and the Arts. **cent.**, century. **C.E.R.N.**, European Organization (formerly Council) for Nuclear Research (*Conseil Européen de la Recherche Nucléaire*). **C.E.T.**, Central European Time. **cet. par.**, *ceteris paribus* (L., other things being equal). **C.F.**, Chaplain to the Forces. **c.f.**, carried forward. **cf.**, *confer* (L., compare). **C.G.**, centre of gravity. **cg.**, centigramme. **C.G.S.**, Chief of the General Staff. **C.G.T.**, Confédération Générale du Travail (Fr., general confederation of work; equivalent of British T.U.C.). **C.H.**, Companion of Honour. **c.h.**, central heating. **Ch.**, chaplain, church. **Ches.**, Cheshire. **C.I.**, Channel Islands. **C.I.A.**, Central Intelligence Agency (U.S.). **C.I.D.**, Criminal Investigation Department. **C.I.G.S.**, Chief of the Imperial General Staff. **C.-in-C.**, Commander-in-Chief. **C.I.O.**: see A.F.L.–C.I.O. **Cl.**, classical. **cm.**, centimetre. **C.M.G.**, Companion of the Order of St. Michael and St. George, Congressional Medal for Gallantry (U.S.). **C.M.S.**, Church Missionary Society. **C.N.D.**, Campaign for Nuclear Disarmament. **C.O.**, Colonial (or Commonwealth) Office, commanding officer, conscientious objector, Crown Office. **Co.**, company, county. **c/o**, care of. **C.O.D.**, cash on delivery. **C. of E.**, Church of England. **C.O.I.**, Central Office of Information. **C.o.I.D.**, Council of Industrial Design. **Col.**, colonel, colonial, Colorado. **Col-Gen.**, colonel-general. **Coll.**, college. **Com.**, Communist, commissioner. **Comdt.**, commandant. **Comecon**, council for mutual economic aid (Communist).

con., *contra* (L., against). **conf.**, conference. **conj.**, conjugation, conjunction. **Conn.**, Connacht, Connecticut. **Cons.**, Conservative. **contd.**, continued. **Co-op.**, Co-operative. **Cor.**, Corinthian(s), coroner. **C.O.R.E.**, Congress of Racial Equality (U.S.). **Corpn.**, corporation. **cos.**, cosine. **cox**, coxswain. **C.P.**, Common Prayer, Communist Party. **c.p.**, carriage paid, candle-power. **Cpl.**, Corporal. **cr.**, created, credit. **C.R.C.**, Civil Rights Commission (U.S.). **cresc.**, *crescendo* (Ital., becoming louder), crescent. **c/s**, cycles per second. **C.S.C.**, Conspicuous Service Cross (U.S.). **C.S.E.**, Certificate of Secondary Education. **cts.**, cents, centimes. **cttee.**, committee. **cu.**, **cub.**, cubic. **C.U.P.**, Cambridge University Press. **C.V.O.**, Commander of the Royal Victorian Order. **C.W.S.**, Co-operative Wholesale Society. **cwt.**, hundredweight.

D Five hundred (Roman). **d.**, daughter, *denarius* (L., penny), died. **D.A.**, District Attorney (U.S.). **dam**, dekametre. **dat.**, dative. **dau.**, daughter. **dB**, decibel. **D.B.E.**, Dame Commander of the Order of the British Empire. **D.C.**, *da capo* (Ital., from the beginning), direct current, District of Columbia (U.S.). **D.C.L.**, Doctor of Civil Law. **D.D.**, Doctor of Divinity. **deb.**, debenture. **dec.**, deceased. **Del.**, Delaware. **del.**, *delineavit* (L., he drew). **dele.**, delete. **Dept.**, department. **Deut.**, Deuteronomy. **D.F.**, Defender of the Faith. **D.F.C.**, Distinguished Flying Cross. **D.F.M.**, Distinguished Flying Medal. **D.G.**, *Dei Gratia* (L., by the grace of God), Director General, Dragoon Guards. **D.I.**, Defence Intelligence. **diam.**, diameter. **dim.**, *diminuendo* (Ital., becoming quieter). **dip.**, diploma. **dir.**, director. **dist.**, district. **div.**, division, divorced. **divi.**, dividend. **dl.**, decilitre. **D. Litt.**, Doctor of Letters (L., *Litterarum*). **D.M.**, Doctor of Medicine. **D. Mus.**, Doctor of Music. **D.N.A.**, deoxy-ribonucleic acid. **D.N.B.**, Dictionary of National Biography. **do.**, ditto. **D.O.M.**, *Deo Optimo Maximo* (L., to God the best and greatest). **Dom.**, Dominican, Dominion, *Dominus* (L. lord, master). **D.O.R.A.**, Defence of the Realm Act. **doz.**, dozen. **D.P.**, displaced person(s). **D.R.**, dead reckoning. **Dr.**, debtor, doctor. **dr.**, dram, drawer (of a cheque). **D.S.**, *dal segno* (Ital., [repeat] from the mark). **D.Sc.**, Doctor of Science. **D.S.O.**, Distinguished Service Order. **d.s.p.**, *decessit sine prole* (L., died without issue). **D.T.**, delirium tremens. **Duo.**, duodecimo (12). **D.V.**, *deo volente* (L., God willing).

E Earl, east, eastern, English, second class (of ships). **e.**, eldest. **E. & O.E.**, errors and omissions excepted. **Ebor**, *Eboracensis* (L., of York). **Eccl.**, (Book of) Ecclesiastes. **Econ.**, economics. **E.C.S.C.**, European Coal and Steel Community. **Ed.**, editor, edited, educated, Edward. **E.D.C.**, European Defence Community. **Edin.**, Edinburgh. **educ.**, educated, education. **E.E.C.**, European Economic Community. **E.F.T.A.**, European Free Trade Association. **e.g.**, *exempli gratia* (L., for the sake of example). **e.h.f.**, extra high frequency. **el.**, electric, element. **eld.**, eldest. **E.L.D.O.**, European Space Vehicle Launcher Development Organization. **E.M.F.**, electro-motive force. **E.M.U.**, electro-magnetic unit. **E.N.E.A.**, European Nuclear Energy Agency. **Eng.**, English. **E.N.S.A.**, Entertainments National Service Association. E.O.K.A., Ethniki Organosis Kyprion Agoniston (Gk., Organization for the Cyprus struggle). E.R., Elisabetha Regina (L., Queen Elizabeth), Eduardus Rex (L., King Edward), East Riding (of Yorks), Eastern Region (British Rail). E.R.N.I.E., Electronic random number indicating equipment. esp., espec., especial(ly). Esq., esquire. E.S.R.O., European Space Research Organization. est., estimated. estab., established. E.S.U., electrostatic unit. et al., et alii (L., and others). etc., et cetera (L., and the rest). et seq., et sequens (L., and the following one), and et seqq., et sequentes – more than one. E.T.U., Electrical Trades Union. Euc., Euclid. Euratom, European Atomic Energy Community. Exch. Exchange, Exchequer. excl., excluding. exec., executive, executed. ex lib., ex libris (L., from the books). exor., executor.

F Fahrenheit. f., farad, father, foot or feet, feminine, forte (Ital., loud), frequency. F.A., Football Association. F.A.A., Federal Aviation Agency (U.S.), Fleet Air Arm. fam., familiar(ly), family. F.A.O., Food and Agriculture Organization (of the United Nations). F.B.I., Federal Bureau of Investigation (U.S.), Federation of British Industries. F.C., football club. F.C.C., Federal Communications Commission (U.S.). F.C.O., Foreign and Commonwealth Office. fcp., foolscap. F.D.A., Food and Drug Administration (U.S.). F.D.R., Franklin Delano Roosevelt. Fed., federal, federated. Fedn., federation. fem., feminine. ff., folios, fortissimo (Ital., loudest). F.H., fire hydrant. F.H.A., Federal Housing Administration (U.S.). Fid. Def., fidei defensor (L., defender of the faith). fig., figurative(ly). fl., floruit (L., he flourished), fluid. Fla., Florida. Flt. Lt., Flight Lieutenant. F.M., Field Marshal, frequency modulation. F.O., Foreign Office. F/O., Flying Officer. f.o.b., free on board. foll., following. f.o.r., free on rail. For., foreign. f.p., freezing point. F.P.S., foot-pound-second (system of units). Fr., Father, franc(s), French. Fra., frater (L., brother). freq., frequency. Fri., Friday. F.R.S., Federal Reserve System (U.S.), Fellow of the Royal Society. f.s., foot seconds. ft., foot or feet, fort. fur., furlong. fwd., forward. F.W.W., First World War.

G Grain(s), gramme(s). Ga., Georgia. Gael., Gaelic. gal., gallon. Gall., gallery. G.A.T.T., General Agreement on Tariffs and Trade. G.B., Great Britain. G.C., George Cross. G.C.B., Knight Grand Cross of the Order of the Bath. G.C.F., greatest common factor. G.C.M., greatest common measure. Gdns., gardens. Gen., General, Genesis. gen., gender, genitive, genus. Geog., geography. Geol., geology. Geom., geometry. Ger., German. Gestapo, Geheime Staatspolizei (Ger., state secret police). G.H.Q., general headquarters. G.I., Government (or General) Issue (U.S.), colloquially a U.S. soldier. Gib., Gibraltar. Gk., Greek. Glam, Glamorganshire. G.L.C., Greater London Council. Glos, Gloucestershire. G.M., George Medal. gm., gramme(s). G.M.C., General Medical Council. G.M.T., Greenwich Mean Time. G.O.C. (-in-C.), General Officer Commanding (-in-Chief). G.O.M., Grand Old Man (W. E. Gladstone, nickname given originally by Labouchere). G.O.P., Grand Old Party – i.e. the Republicans (U.S.). Gov., Governor Gov.-Gen., Governor-General. govt., government. G.P., general practitioner (medical). G.P.O., General Post Office. Gr.,

Greek. gr., grain(s). gravity. granddau., granddaughter. G.R.I., Georgius Rex Imperator (L., George, King and Emperor). g.s., grandson. gt., great.

H Henry (unit of inductance). ha, hectare. hab., habitat (L., he lives). h. & c., hot and cold (water). Hants, Hampshire. H.C., House of Common. h.c. honoris causa (L., as a way of honouring). H.C.F., highest common factor. H. Com., High Commissioner. H.E., high explosive, His Excellency. Herts, Hertfordshire. H.F., high frequency. H.G., Home Guard. hg., hectogramme(s). H.H., His (Her) Highness. hist., history. H.J.S., hic jacet sepultus (L., here lies buried). hl., hectolitre(s). H.M., His (Her) Majesty. hm., hectometre(s). H.M.A.S., His (Her) Majesty's Australian Ship. H.M.C.S., His (Her) Majesty's Canadian Ship. H.M.F., His (Her) Majesty's Forces. H.M.S., His (Her) Majesty's Service, His (Her) Majesty's Ship. H.M.S.O., His (Her) Majesty's Stationery Office. H.O., head office, hold over, Home Office. Hon., Honorary, Honourable. Hon. Sec., honorary secretary. H.P., half-pay, high pressure, hire purchase, horse-power. H.Q., headquarters. hr., hour. H.R.H., His (Her) Royal Highness. H.T., high tension. ht., height. Hunts, Huntingdonshire. H.W.M., high water mark.

I One (Roman). I., island. Ia., Iowa. I.A.E.A., International Atomic Energy Agency. ibid., ibidem (L., in the same place). I.B.R.D., International Bank for Reconstruction and Development (World Bank). I.C., internal combustion. I.C.A., International Co-operation Administration (U.S.). I.C.A.O., International Civil Aviation Organization. I.C.B.M., inter-continental ballistic missile. I.C.C., Interstate Commerce Commission (U.S.). I.C.F.T.U., International Confederation of Free Trade Unions. I.C.I., Imperial Chemical Industries. I.C.S.U., International Council of Scientific Unions. id., idem (L., the same). I.D.B., illicit diamond buyer, Inter-American Development Bank. i.e., id est (L., that is). I.F.S., Irish Free State. I.F.T.U., International Federation of Trade Unions. I.G.Y., International Geophysical Year. I.H.S., popularly Jesus Hominum Salvator (L., Jesus, Saviour of mankind), but properly the first three letters of the name Jesus in Greek. Ill., Illinois. illus., illustrated, illustration. I.L.O., International Labour Organization (of the U.N.). I.L.P., Independent Labour Party. I.M.F., International Monetary Fund. Imp., imperator (L., emperor). imp., imprimatur (L., let it be printed). in., inch. Inc., incorporated. incl., includes, including, inclusive. incog., incognito (Ital., unknown). Ind., Indiana. inf., infantry, infra (L., below). init., initio (L., at the beginning). in loc., in loco (L., in place). inns., innings. I.N.R.I., Jesus Nazarenus Rex Judaeorum (L., Jesus the Nazarene, King of the Jews). inst., instant (the present month), institute. int., interest. inter., intermediate. intercom., inter-communication(s). intr., intransitive. intro., introduction. introd., introduced. Io., Idaho. I.O.M., Isle of Man. I.O.U., I owe you. I.O.W., Isle of Wight. I.Q., intelligence quotient. I.R.A., Irish Republican Army. I.R.B.M., intermediate-range ballistic missile. I.R.C., International Red Cross. I.R.S., Internal Revenue Service (U.S.). Is., Isl(s), island(s). isot., isotope, isotopic. It., Italian. I.T.A., Independent Television Authority, Initial Teaching Alphabet.

Ital., Italian. tal. italic(s). I.T.U., International Telecommunication Union. I.T.V., Independent Television.

J Joule, judge, justice. J.A., Judge Advocate. Jeep, general purposes (g.p.) (car). j.g., junior grade (U.S.). Jnr., junior. J.P., justice of the peace, jet propulsion. jr., junior. Jun., junior.

K Kilogramme(s), king, knight. Kan., Kansas. K.A.N.U., Kenya African National Union. K.B., King's Bench. K.B.D., King's Bench Division. K.B.E., Knight Commander Order of the British Empire. K.C., King's Counsel. kc., kilocycle(s). kcs., kilocycles per second. K.C.B., Knight Commander of the Bath. K.C.V.O., Knight Commander of the Victorian Order. K.G., Knight of the Garter. kg., kilogramme(s). kg./cal., kilogramme-calorie. kin., kinetic K.K.K., Ku-Klux-Klan. kl., kilolitre. km., kilometre(s). kn., knot. k.-o., knock-out. K.R., King's Regulations. K.T., Knight of the Order of the Thistle. Kt., knight bachelor. kV., kilovolt. kVA., kilovolt-ampere. kW., kilowatt. kWh., kilowatt-hour. Ky., Kentucky.

L Fifty (Roman). L. lake, Lancers (in regimental names), Latin, left, Liberal, licentiate (in, e.g., L.R.A.M., Licentiate of the Royal Academy of Music), litre. £, libra (L., pound(s) – money). £A, Australian pound. L.A., local authority. La., Lousiana. Lab., Labour, Labrador. L.A.F.T.A., Latin American Free Trade Association. Lancs, Lancashire. Lat., Latin. lat., latitude. lat. ht., latent heat. lb., libra (L., pound(s) – weight). l.b.w., leg before wicket. l.c., lower case (i.e. small letter). L.C.C., London County Council. L.C.J., Lord Chief Justice. L.C.M., lowest common multiple. L./Cpl., Lance-Corporal. Ld., Lord. ld., load. Ldg., leading. L.E.A., local education authority. Leics., Leicestershire. l.f., low frequency. L.H., left hand. L.I., Long Island. Lib., Liberal. lib., library. Lieut., Lieutenant. Lim., (County) Limerick. lin., linear. Lincs, Lincolnshire. Lit., literature. lit., literally, literary. Lit. Hum., Literae Humaniores (L., humane letters, name of a School in the University of Oxford). Litt. D., Doctor of Letters (Literae). L.J., Lord Justice. Lk., Luke. LL.B., Bachelor of Laws. LL.D., Doctor of Laws. L.M.R., London Midland Region (British Rail). loc.cit., loco citato (L., in the place cited). L. of N., League of Nations. log(s)., logarithm(s). Londin., Londinienis (L., of London). long., longitude. loq., loquitur (L., he speaks). L.P., liquid petroleum, long-playing (record). L.P.O., London Philharmonic Orchestra. L.P.T.B., London Passenger Transport Board. Lr., lower. L.S., locus sigilli (L., place of the seal). L. s. d., librae solidi denarii (L., pounds, shillings, pence). L.S.E., London School of Economics (and Political Science). L.S.O., London Symphony Orchestra. Lt., Lieutenant. lt., light. L.T.A., Lawn Tennis Association. Ltd., limited (liability). L.W., long wave. L.W.L., load water line. L.W.M., low water mark.

M Mille (thousand, Roman). M. Mach number, marquess, Monsieur (Fr., mister). m., married, masculine, metre(s), mile(s), million, minute(s), mother. M.A., Maritime Administration (U.S.), Master of Arts. ma., major. mag., magazine, magneto, magnitude. Magd, Magdalen College, Oxford; Magdalene College, Cambridge. Maj., Major. Maj.-Gen., Major-General. Man., Manitoba.

Mar., March. mar., married. March., Marchioness. marg., margarine, marginal. Marq., Marquess. Maser, Microwave Amplification by Stimulated Emission of Radiation. Mass., Massachusetts. mat., matinée. maths., mathematics. Matric., matriculation. Matt., Matthew. Max., maximum. M.B., Bachelor of Medicine, motor-boat. M.B.E., Member of the Order of the British Empire. M.C., Military Cross, Master of Ceremonies, motor-cycle. M/C., Manchester. M.C.C., Marylebone Cricket Club, Middlesex County Council. M.D., Doctor of Medicine, mentally deficient. Md., Maryland. M.E., Middle English, marine engineer, mechanical engineer (R.N.). Me., Maine. Mech., mechanics. Med., medical, medieval, medium, Mediterranean. memo., memorandum. Mer., Merionethshire. mer., meridian. Met., metallurgy, meteorology, Metropolitan. meth., methylated spirit. m.f., medium frequency, mezzo forte (Ital., moderately loud), more follows. mfd., manufactured. mfg., manufacturing. M.F.H., Master of Foxhounds. Mg, magnesium. mg., milligram(s). M.G.M., Metro-Goldwyn-Mayer. Mgr., Monsignor. M.H.D., magnetohydrodynamics. M.I., Military Intelligence. mi., minor. Mich., Michigan. Middx, Middlesex. mil., military. Min., mineral(ogy), minimum, Minister, Ministry, minute. Minn., Minnesota. Min Plenip., Minister Plenipotentiary. misc., miscellaneous. Miss., Mississippi. M.I.T., Massachusetts Institute of Technology. m.k.s., metre-kilogramme-second (system of units). mkt., market. ml., millilitre(s). Mlle., mademoiselle (Fr., miss). M.M., Military Medal. mm., millimetre(s). Mme., madame. M.N., Merchant Navy. Mo., Missouri, month. mod., moderate, moderato (Ital., at a moderate pace), modern. M.O.H., medical officer of health; M.O.I., Ministry of Information. mol., molecule. Mon., Monday, Monmouthshire. Mont., Montana. Montgom, Montgomeryshire. M.P., Member of Parliament; Metropolitan Police, military police. m.p., melting point, mezzo piano (Ital., moderately soft). m.p.g., miles per gallon. m.p.h., miles per hour. M.R., Master of the Rolls. Mr., Mister. M.R.A., Moral Rearmament. M.R.C., Medical Research Council. M.R.P., Mouvement Républicain Populaire (Fr., political party; people's republican movement). Mrs., mistress. M.S., minesweeper, motor ship. MS(S), manuscript(s). M.Sc., Master of Science. m.s.l., mean sea-level. Mt(s)., mount, mountain(s). M.T.B., motor torpedoboat. mth., month. mun., municipal. mus., museum, music(al). M.V., merchant vessel, motor vessel. MVA, 1,000 kVA. M.V.O., Member of the Victorian Order. M.W., molecular weight. M.Y., motor yacht.

N Nitrogen. N., Nationalist, north, northern. n., name, nephew, neuter, noun. N.A.A.C.P., National Association for the Advancement of Colored People (U.S.). N.A.A.F.I., Navy, Army and Air Force Institutes. nat., national. N.A.T.O., North Atlantic Treaty Organization. N.B., New Brunswick, nota bene (L., note well). N.B.C., National Broadcasting Company (U.S.). N.B.S., National Bureau of Standards (U.S.). N.C., North Carolina. N.C.B., National Coal Board. n.c.o., non-commissioned officer. N.D(ak)., North Dakota. n.d., no date. Neb., Nebraska. N.E.D.O., National Economic Development Office ('Neddy'). neg., negative. nem. con., nemine contradicente (L., with no one opposing). N.E.P., New Economic Policy (U.S.S.R.). Nev., Nevada. N.F., Newfoundland,

Norman French. N.G., nitro-glycerin. N.H., New Hampshire. N.H.S., National Health Service. N.I., Northern Ireland. N.I.H., National Institutes of Health (U.S.). N.J., New Jersey. nit., nitrate, nitric. N.L.R.B., National Labor Relations Board (U.S.). N.M., New Mexico. n.o., not out (cricket). no., numero (L., in number). nom., nominative. non seq., non sequitur (L., it does not follow). Norf, Norfolk. Northants, Northamptonshire. Notts, Nottinghamshire. Nov., November. N.P., notary public. n.p., new paragraph. N.P.A., Newspaper Proprietors' Association. N.P.G., National Portrait Gallery. N.P.L., National Physical Laboratory. N.P.R., Northern Pacific Railroad. N.R., North Riding (of Yorkshire). nr., near. N.R.A., National Rifle Association. N.R.D.C., National Research Development Corporation. N.S., new style (calendar), Nova Scotia. N.S.B., National Savings Bank (former P.O.S.B.). N.S.C., National Security Council (U.S.). N.S.F., National Science Foundation (U.S.). N.S.P.C.C., National Society for the Prevention of Cruelty to Children. N.S.W., New South Wales. N.T., New Testament, Northern Territory (Australia). n.u., name unknown. N.U.J., National Union of Journalists. N.U.M., National Union of Mineworkers. N.U.R., National Union of Railwaymen. N.U.T., National Union of Teachers. N.W.I., Netherlands West Indies. N.W.M.P., North-West Mounted Police. N.Y., New York. N.Y.C., New York City. N.Z., New Zealand.

O Ohio. o/a, on account. O.A.S., on active service, Organisation de l'Armée Secrète, Organization of American States. O.A.U., Organization of African Unity. ob., obiit (L., he died). O.B.E., (Officer of the) Order of the British Empire. obj., objective. obs., observation, obsolete. O.C., Officer Commanding. O.C.A.M., Joint African and Malagasy Organization (Organisation commune africaine et malgache). O.C.A.S., Organization of Central American States (also O.D.E.C.A., q.v.). oct., octavo. O.D.E.C.A., Organizacion de Estados Centroamericanos (Span., organization of Central American states). O.E., Old English. O.E.C.D., Organization for Economic Co-operation and Development. O.E.D., Oxford English Dictionary. O.F., Old French. off., official. O.H.M.S., on Her (His) Majesty's Service. O.K.—correct or approved (no actual meaning). Okla., Oklahoma. O.M., (Member of the) Order of Merit. Ont., Ontario. O.P., observation post, out of print, Order of Preachers (Dominicans). op., opus (L., work), used for a musical composition. op. cit., opere citato (L., in the work quoted). opp., opposite. Ops., operations (military). opt., optical, optional. O.R., other ranks. Ore., Oregon. orig., original. Ork., Orkney Islands. ornith., ornithology. O.R.R., owner's risk rates. O.S., Old Saxon, Old Style (calendar), outsize. o.s., only son. O.S.A., Official Secrets Act. o.s.p., obiit sine prole (L., died without issue). O.T., Old Testament. O.U.D.S., Oxford University Dramatic Society. O.U.P., Oxford University Press. ox., oxalate, oxide. Oxfam., Oxford Committee for Famine Relief. Oxon., Oxfordshire, Oxoniensis (L., of Oxford). Oz, ozone. oz., ounce(s).

P (car) park, passed, port. p., page, past, pawn, new pence (U.K. decimal currency), piano (Ital., soft). P.A., Press Association. p.a., per annum (L., yearly). Pa., Pennsylvania. P.A.A.,

Pan-American Airways. P. & O., Peninsular and Oriental (Steamship Company). par., paragraph, parallel, parish. para., paragraph. parl., parliament(ary). part., participle, particular. P.A.S., para-aminosulphonic acid. P.A.Y.E., pay as you earn. P.B., prayer book. P.B.I., 'poor bloody infantry'. P.C., parish council, police constable, Privy Council(lor). p.c., per centum (L., by the hundred), postcard. P.D.S.A., People's Dispensary for Sick Animals. P.E.I., Prince Edward Island. Pemb., Pembrokeshire. pen., peninsula. per cent., per centum (L., by the hundred). per pro, per procurationem (L., by proxy). Pfc., Private first-class (U.S.). P.G., paying guest. P.H., Purple Heart (decoration, U.S.). Ph.D., Doctor of Philosophy. Phil., Philadelphia, philosophy. phot., photograph(ic). P.H.S., Public Health Service (U.S.). Phys., physics. pinx., pinxit (L., he painted). pizz., pizzicato (Ital., plucked). pl., place, platoon, plural. P.L.A., Port of London Authority. P.M., paymaster, Prime Minister. p.m., post meridiem (L., after noon), post mortem (L., after death). P.M.G., Postmaster General. P.O., post office, postal order, Pilot Officer, Petty Officer. Pol., Polish. Poly, Polytechnic. pop., population, popular(ly). Port., Portuguese. P.O.S.B., Post Office Savings Bank. pot., potential. P.O.W., prisoner of war. P.P., parish priest. pp., per procurationem (L., by proxy). pp., pages, pianissimo (Ital., very soft). P.P.S., parliamentary (or principal) private secretary, post-postscript. P.Q., Province of Quebec. P.R., Proportional Representation. pr., proton. prec., preceding. prelim., preliminary. prep., preparation, preposition. pres., president. prin., principal. P.R.O., Public Record Office, public relations officer. prof., professor. prom., promenade (concert), promontory. pron., pronoun, pronounced. pro tem., pro tempore (L., for the time being). Prov., (Book of) Proverbs. prov., province, provisional, provost. provs., provinces. prox., proximo (mense) (L., in the next month). P.S., postscript, private secretary. Ps., Psalm(s). pseud., pseudonym. P.T., physical training. pt., pint, past, point, port. Pte., private (soldier). P.T.O., please turn over, Public Trustee Office. pub., public house, published. publ., published, publisher.

Q Queen, question, the Quarto Shakespeare. q., quart, quire. Q.B., Queen's Bench. Q.C., Queen's Counsel. Q.E.D., quod erat demonstrandum (L., which was to be proved). Q.E.F., quod erat faciendum (L., which was to be done). Qld., Queensland. Q.M., quartermaster, Queen's Messenger. Q.M.G., Quartermaster General. Q.M.S., Quartermaster Sergeant. Q.R., Queen's Regulations. qr., quarter, quire. Q.S., quarter sessions. qt., quart. qto., quarto. Que., Quebec. quot., quotation, quotient. q.v., quod vide (L., which see: plural, qq.v.).

R Regiment, Rex (king), Regina (queen) right, Réaumur, resistance. r., radius, river, rod(s), rood(s). R.A., Rear Admiral, Royal Academician, Royal Academy, Royal Artillery. R.A.A.F., Royal Australian Air Force. R.A.C., Royal Armoured Corps, Royal Automobile Club. rad., radiation, radius, root. R.A.D.A., Royal Academy of Dramatic Art. radar, radio direction and range. R.Ae.S., Royal Aeronautical Society. R.A.F., Royal Air Force. R.A.F.V.R., Royal Air Force Volunteer Reserve. rall., rallentando (Ital., slowing down). R.A.M., Royal Academy of Music. R.A.M.C., Royal Army Medical Corps. R.A.N., Royal Australian Navy. R.A.S.C., Royal Army Service Corps. R.C., Red Cross

Roman Catholic(ism). **R.C.A.,** Royal Canadian Academy *or* Army, Royal College of Art. **R.C.A.F.,** Royal Canadian Air Force. **R.C.M.,** Royal College of Music. **R.C.M.P.,** Royal Canadian Mounted Police. **R.C.N.,** Royal Canadian Navy, Royal College of Nursing. **R.C.S.,** Royal College of Surgeons, Royal Corps of Signals. **R.C.V.S.,** Royal College of Veterinary Surgeons. **R./D.,** refer to drawer (of an overdrawn cheque). **Rd.,** road. **R.D.C.,** Rural District Council. **R.E.,** Royal Engineers, Royal Exchange. **Recce.,** reconnaissance. **recd.,** received. **ref.,** referred, reference. **reg.,** region(al), registered, regular(ly). **Reg. Prof.,** Regius Professor. **regt.,** regiment. **R.E.M.E.,** Royal Electrical and Mechanical Engineers. **Ren.,** Renaissance. **rep.,** republic(an), representative, repertory (theatre). **repub.,** republic. **Rev.,** Reverend, Revenue, Revolution (political). **rev.,** reverse(d), revise(d), revolution (mechanical). **R.F.,** radio-frequency, République Française (French Republic). **R.F.C.,** Royal Flying Corps, Rugby Football Club. **R.G.S.,** Royal Geographical Society. **Rh.** (in Rh. negative, Rh. positive), Rhesus. **R.H.S.,** Royal Horticultural Society, Royal Humane Society. **R.I.,** *Rex Imperator* (L., king emperor), Rhode Island, Royal Institution. **R.I.B.A.,** Royal Institute of British Architects. **R.I.I.A.,** Royal Institute of International Affairs. **R.I.P.,** *requiescat in pace* (L., may he rest in peace). **rit.,** *ritardando* (Ital., becoming slower). **riv.,** river. **R./L.,** radio-location. **R.L.S.,** Robert Louis Stevenson. **rly.,** railway. **R.M.,** Royal Mail, Royal Marines. **R.M.A.,** Royal Military Academy. **R.M.C.,** Royal Military College. **R.Met.S.,** Royal Meteorological Society. **R.N.,** Royal Navy. **R.N.A.,** ribonucleic acid. **R.N.I.B.,** Royal National Institute for the Blind. **R.N.L.I.,** Royal National Lifeboat Institution. **R.N.V.R.,** Royal Naval Volunteer Reserve. **R.N.Z.A.F.,** Royal New Zealand Air Force. **R.N.Z.N.,** Royal New Zealand Navy. **R.O.,** Royal Observatory. **Ro.,** *recto* (L., on the right-[hand page]). **R.O.C.,** Royal Observer Corps. **R.O.S.P.A.,** Royal Society for the Prevention of Accidents. **R.P.,** Regius Professor. **R.P.C.,** Royal Pioneer Corps. **R.P.M.,** retail price maintenance. **r.p.m.,** revolutions per minute. **R.P.S.,** Royal Photographic Society. **R.S.,** Royal Society. **R.S.A.,** Royal Scottish Academy, Royal Society of Arts. **R.S.F.S.R.,** Russian Soviet Federal (*or* Federative) Socialist Republic. **R.S.M.,** Royal School of Medicine *or* of Mines. **R.S.P.C.A.,** Royal Society for the Prevention of Cruelty to Animals. **R.S.V.P.,** *répondez, s'il vous plait* (Fr., reply, if you please). **R./T.,** radio-telephony. **R.T.C.,** Royal Tank Corps. **Rt. Hon.,** Right Honourable. **Rt. Rev.,** Right Reverend. **R.U.,** Rugby Union. **Russ.,** Russian.

S Saint, socialist, *socius* (L., fellow), south, southern. **s.,** son, second(s), shilling(s), singular, succeeded. **S.A.,** Salvation Army, Society of Antiquaries, South Africa, Sturm-Abteilung (Ger., storm troops). **Salop,** Shropshire. **S.A.S.,** Scandinavian Air Lines. **Sask.,** Saskatchewan. **Sax.,** Saxon, saxophone. **S.A.Y.E.,** Save As You Earn. **S.B.R.,** styrene butadiene rubber. **S.C.,** South Carolina. **sc.,** small capitals. **sc.,** scene, science, *scilicet* (L., let it be understood). **scr.,** scruple. **sculp(s).,** *sculpsit* (L., he carved it). **S.D(ak).,** South Dakota. **s.d.,** semi-detached, *sine die* (L., without a day, indefinitely). **sd.,** signed, sewed. **S.E.,** stock exchange, south-east(ern). **S.E.A.T.O.,** South East Asia Treaty Organization. **S.E.C.,** Securities and Exchange Commission (U.S.). **sec.,** secant, second(ary), secretary. **S.E.T.,** Selective Employment Tax. **sf.,** *sforzando* (Ital., with sudden emphasis). **S.F.S.R.,** Soviet Federal (*or* Federated) Socialist Republic. **s.g.,** specific gravity. **Sgt.,** Sergeant. **S.H.A.E.F.,** Supreme Headquarters Allied Expeditionary Force. **S.H.A.P.E.,** Supreme Headquarters Allied Powers Europe. **s.h.f,** super high frequency. **S.I.,** International System (*Système International*, metric). **sic** (L., thus), so written. **sing.,** singular. **sit.,** situated. **S.J.,** Society of Jesus (Jesuits). **Skt.,** Sanskrit. **Slav.,** Slavonic. **S/Ldr.,** Squadron Leader. **S./Lt.,** Sub-Lieutenant. **S.N.C.F.,** Societé Nationale des Chemins de Fer (national railway system of France). **S.O.,** Scottish Office. **Soc.,** society, socialist. **Som.,** Somerset. **S.P.,** starting price (betting), *sine prole* (L., without issue). **Span.,** Spanish. **S.P.C.K.,** Society for Promoting Christian Knowledge. **spec.,** special(ly). species, speculation. **sp.gr.,** specific gravity. **S.P.Q.R.,** *Senatus Populusque Romanus* (L., the Roman senate and people). **S.P.R.,** Society for Psychical Research. **sq.,** square. **sqn.,** squadron. **S.R.,** Southern Region (British Rail). **S.R.N.,** state registered nurse. **S.S.,** steamship, Schutz-Staffel (Ger., protective squadron). **S.S.A.F.A.,** Soldiers', Sailors', and Airmen's Families Association. **S.S.R.,** Soviet Socialist Republic. **S.S.S.,** Selective Service System (U.S.). **St.,** saint, street, strait. **Sta.,** *santa* (Ital., female saint). **Staffs,** Staffordshire. **S.T.D.,** subscriber trunk dialling. **Ste.,** *sainte* (Fr., female saint). **stet** (L., let it stand). **stg.,** sterling. **stn.,** station. **sub.,** submarine, subscription. substitute. **subj.,** subject(ive), subjunctive. **Suff.,**Suffolk. **sup.,** *supra* (L., above). **S.W.W.,** Second World War. **Sx,** Sussex. **Sy,** Surrey. **syn.,** synonym.

T Ton(s), temperature, telephone. **T.A.,** Territorial Army, telegraphic address. **tan.,** tangent, tannin. **T.A.N.U.,** Tanganyika African National Union. **T.B.,** tuberculosis. **tech.,** technical. **temp.,** temporary, temperature, *tempore* (L., in the time of). **ten.,** tenor, *tenuto* (Ital., sustained). **Tenn.,** Tennessee. **terr.,** territory. **Tex.,** Texas. **T.G.W.U.,** Transport and General Workers' Union. **tn.,** town, transportation (U.S.). **T.N.T.,** trinitrotoluene. **tote,** totalisator. **trans.,** transitive, transitional, translated, translation. **treas.,** treasurer. **trib.,** tributary. **trig.,** trigonometry. **trs.,** transfer, transpose. **T.T.,** Tourist Trophy, teetotal, tuberculin tested. **T.U.C.,** Trades Union Congress. **T.V.,** television. **T.V.A.,** value-added tax (*Taxe sur la Valeur Ajoutée*), Tennessee Valley Authority (U.S.). **T.W.A.,** Trans-World Airlines.

U Unionist, Utah, universal (exhibition, in cinema). **u.,** uncle. **U.A.P.,** United Australia Party. **U.A.R.,** United Arab Republic. **U-boat,** Unterseeboot (Ger., submarine). **u.c.,** upper case (capital letters). **U.C.H.,** University College Hospital (London). **U.C.L.,** University College, London. **U.D.,** urban district. **U.D.C.,** urban district council. **u.h.f.,** ultra high frequency. **U.K.,** United Kingdom. **ult.,** ultimate, *ultimo (mense)* (L., in the last month). **U.N.,** United Nations. **U.N.A.,** U.N. Association. **U.N.C.T.A.D.,** U.N. Conference on Trade and Development. **U.N.D.P.,** U.N. Development Programme. **U.N.E.S.C.O.,** U.N. Educational, Scientific, and Cultural Organization. **U.N.I.C.E.F.,** U.N. Children's Fund. **univ.,** university. **unm.,** unmarried. **unpub.,** unpublished. **U.N.R.R.A.,** U.N. Relief and Rehabilitation Administration. **U.N.R.W.A.,** U.N. Relief and Works Agency (for Palestine Refugees). **U.P.,** United Press. **U.P.U.,** Universal Postal Union. **U.S.,** under-secretary, United Services, United States. **U.S.A.,** United States of [North] America. **U.S.A.F.,** United States Air Force. **U.S.I.A.,** United States Information Agency. **U.S.M.C.,** United States Marine Corps. **U.S.N.,** United States Navy. **U.S.S.,** United States ship. **U.S.S.R.,** Union of Soviet Socialist Republics. **ux.,** *uxor* (L., wife).

V Five (Roman). **V.,** viscount, Vice-*Vergeltungswaffe* (Ger., reprisal weapon). **v.,** *versus* (L., against), *vice* (L., in place of), *vide* (L., see), verb, verse, very, volt. **V. and A.,** Victoria and Albert (Museum). **Va.,** Virginia. **vac.,** vacation. **V.A.D.,** Voluntary Aid Detachment. **van.,** advantage (tennis). **var.,** various. **Vat.,** Vatican. **V.C.,** Victoria Cross. **V.D.,** venereal disease(s). **V.E. Day,** Victory in Europe day. **Ven.,** venerable. **verb. sap.,** *verbum sapienti (satis)* (L., a word is enough to the wise). **vet.,** veterinary (surgeon). **v.h.f.,** very high frequency. **V.I.P.,** very important person. **visct.,** viscount. **viz.,** *videlicet* (L., that is to say, namely). **V.J. Day,** Victory over Japan day. **v.l.f.,** very low frequency. **V.M.,** Victory Medal. **vol.,** volume, volcanic. **V.R.,** *Victoria Regina* (L., Queen Victoria). **v.s.,** *vide supra* (L., see above). **Vt.,** Vermont. **V.T.O.,** vertical take-off. **Vulg.,** Vulgate. **v.v.,** *vice versa* (L., the other way round). **vv.,** verses.

W Welsh, west(ern), Warden. **w.,** watt, week, wife, with. **W.A.,** Western Australia. **W.A.A.C.,** Women's Army Auxiliary Corps (in F.W.W.). **W.A.A.F.,** Women's Auxiliary Air Force. **W.A.C.,** Women's Army Corps (U.S.). **Warwicks,** Warwickshire. **Wash.,** Washington (state). **W.A.V.E.S.,** Women Accepted for Volunteer Emergency Service (U.S. Navy). **W.C.,** water closet. **W.C.C.,** World Council of Churches. **W./Cdr.,** Wing-Commander. **W.D.,** War Department. **W.E.A.,** Workers' Educational Association. **W.E.U.,** Western European Union. **w.f.,** wrong fount (of type). **W.F.T.U.,** World Federation of Trade Unions. **Wh,** watt-hour. **wh.,** which. **W.H.O.,** World Health Organization. **W.I.,** West Indies, Women's Institute. **Wilts,** Wiltshire. **Wisc.,** Wisconsin. **W/L,** wavelength. **W.L.A.,** Women's Land Army. **W.M.O.,** World Meteorological Organization. **W.O.,** War Office, Warrant Officer. **Worcs.,** Worcestershire. **W.P.A.,** Works Progress Administration (U.S.). **W.R.,** Western Region (British Rail), West Riding (of Yorkshire). **W.R.A.C.,** Women's Royal Army Corps. **W.R.A.F.,** Women's Royal Air Force. **W.R.N.S.,** Women's Royal Naval Service. **W.R.V.S.,** Women's Royal Voluntary Services. **W.S.,** writer to the signet. **wt.,** weight. **W.Va.,** West Virginia. **Wyo.,** Wyoming.

X Ten (Roman), Christ. **Xmas,** Christmas. **XX,** double strength (of beer). **XXX,** triple strength.

Y yd(s)., yard(s). **Y.H.A.,** Youth Hostels Association. **Y.M.C.A.,** Young Men's Christian Association. **Yorks,** Yorkshire. **yr.,** year, your, younger. **yrs.,** years, yours. **Y.W.C.A.,** Young Women's Christian Association.

Z Impedance, zero. **Z.A.N.U.,** Zimbabwe African National Union. **Zoo,** zoological garden. **zool.,** zoological.

Customary Forms of Address

Ambassador. 'To His Excellency' followed by customary title of the individual. *Begin*, 'Sir' or 'My Lord' (according to rank); *end*, 'I have the honour to be, sir (or My Lord), Your Excellency's most humble and obedient servant.

Archbishop. 'The Most Rev. His Grace the Lord Archbishop of ——.' *Begin*, 'My Lord Archbishop', or 'Your Grace'; *end*, 'I remain, My Lord Archbishop, Your Grace's obedient servant.' The wife of an Archbishop is simply 'Mrs. ——.'

An R.C. **Archbishop** is addressed : 'The Most Rev. the Archbishop of ——.'

Baron. 'To the Rt. Hon. Lord ——.' *Begin*, 'My Lord'; *end*, 'I have the honour to be, My Lord, Your Lordship's obedient servant.' **Baroness.** 'The Rt. Hon. Lady ——.' *Begin*, 'Madam'; *end*, 'I have the honour to be, Madam, Your Ladyship's obedient servant.' Refer to 'Your Ladyship'. **Baroness in her own right:** as for the wife of a Baron.

Baronet. 'Sir John ——, Bt.' *Begin*, 'Sir'; *end*, 'I have the honour to remain, Sir, Your obedient servant.' **Baronet's wife.** 'Lady ——' (omit Christian name). *Begin*, 'Madam'; *end*, 'I have the honour to remain, Madam, Your obedient servant.' Refer to 'Your Ladyship'.

Bishop. 'To the Right Rev. the Lord Bishop of ——.' *Begin*, 'My Lord'; *end*, 'I remain, My Lord, Your Lordship's obedient servant.' Refer to 'My Lord', or 'Your Lordship'. The wife of a Bishop is simply 'Mrs. ——.'

An R.C. **Bishop** is addressed : 'The Rt. Rev. the Bishop of ——.'

Bishop Suffragan. 'To the Rt. Rev. the Lord Bishop Suffragan of ——'; otherwise as for a Bishop.

Cabinet, Members of U.S.: 'To Mr. (or the Hon.) ——, Secretary of State.' *Begin*, 'Dear Sir' or 'Dear Mr. Secretary'; *end*, 'Yours faithfully'

Cardinal. 'To His Eminence Cardinal ——.' *Begin*, 'My Lord Cardinal' or 'My Lord'; *end*, 'I have the honour to remain, My Lord, Your Eminence's obedient child.'

Clergy. 'The Rev. (Christian name and surname).' *Begin*, 'Rev. Sir'; less formally, 'Sir'.

R.C. Clergy. 'To the Rev. Father ——.' *Begin*, 'Dear Rev. Father'; *end*, 'I beg to remain, dear Rev. Father, Your devoted and obedient child.'

Countess. 'The Right Hon. the Countess of ——.' *Begin*, 'Madam'; refer to as 'Your Ladyship'; *end*, 'I have the honour to be, Madam, Your Ladyship's obedient servant.' **Countess in her own right:** as for an Earl's wife.

Dame. 'To Dame Jane ——,' followed by G.C.V.O., D.C.V.O., G.B.E., D.B.E., as appropriate. *Begin*, 'Madam'; *end*, 'I beg to remain, dear Madam, Your obedient servant.'

N.B. Correctly the wife of a Bt. or a Knight is referred to as 'Dame ——' (husband's surname), but this form has fallen into disuse except in legal documents. *See* under Baronet; Knight.

Daughters of Peers. Daus. of Dukes, Marquesses, and Earls are styled 'Lady Jane ——' (family name); daus. of Viscounts and Barons: 'The Hon. Jane ——' (family name). On marriage to a man without title, a Knight, or a Bt., Lady Jane retains her style, substituting her husband's for her father's family name; The Hon. Jane becomes The Hon. Mrs. —— or The Hon. Lady ——, according to whether her husband has no title or is a Knight or Bt. (The title Hon. is never

used in speaking.) On marriage to a peer, the dau. of a peer uses the customary form appropriate to her rank.

Dean (of a cathedral). 'The Very Rev. the Dean of ——.' *Begin*, 'Very Rev. Sir'; *end*, 'I have the honour to remain, Reverend Sir, Your obedient servant.'

Doctor. The letters M.D., LL.D., etc., are appended to the ordinary form of address, e.g., 'J. —— (initial and surname), Esq., M.D.' Alternatively, 'Dr. J. ——,' never 'Dr. J. ——, Esq.'

Duke. 'To His Grace the Duke of ——.' *Begin*, 'My Lord Duke' or 'Your Grace'; *end*, 'I have the honour to be, My Lord Duke, Your Grace's obedient servant.' Refer to 'Your Grace'. **Royal Duke.** 'To His Royal Highness the Duke of ——.' *Begin*, 'Sir'; *end*, 'I remain, Sir, Your Royal Highness's obedient servant.' *See* Daughters, Son of Peers.

Earl. 'The Rt. Hon. the Earl of ——.' *Begin*, 'My Lord'; refer to 'Your Lordship'; *end*, 'I have the honour to be, my Lord, Your Lordship's obedient servant.' An Earl's wife is a Countess (q.v.). *See also* Daughters, Sons of Peers.

Governor of a U.S. State. 'To the Hon. —— or 'To Governor ——.' *Begin*, 'Sir'; *end*, 'Yours faithfully'

Judge. 'The Hon. Mr. Justice ——'; or 'The Hon. Sir (Christian name and surname).' *Begin*, 'Sir'. Only when on the bench is he referred to as 'My Lord' and 'His Lordship'. **In the U.S.A.:** 'The Hon.' followed by the title of office (e.g. Chief Justice of the U.S.A., Associate Justice of the Supreme Court of the U.S.A.). *Begin*, 'Dear Sir', 'Dear Mr. Chief Justice', 'Dear Judge Smith', as appropriate.

Judge of County Court. 'His Honour Judge ——.' When on the bench refer to 'Your Honour'.

Justice of Peace. 'To the Rt. Worshipful ——, J.P.' Refer to, when on the bench, as 'Your Worship'.

King. 'To the King's Most Excellent Majesty.' *Begin*, 'Sire', or 'May it please Your Majesty'; *end*, 'I have the honour to remain, Your Majesty's most humble and obedient subject'; refer to as 'Your Majesty'.

Knight Bachelor. As for Baronet, but omitting the abbreviation 'Bt.'

Knight of the Bath, of the Garter, etc. As for Knight Bachelor, but adding the letters K.C.B., K.G., etc.

Knight's wife. As for Baronet's wife.

Lord Chancellor. 'To the Rt. Hon. the Lord Chancellor.' Otherwise according to rank in the peerage.

Lord Chief Justice. 'The Rt. Hon. the Lord Chief Justice of England.' Otherwise according to rank in the peerage.

Lord Provost. 'The Rt. Hon. the Lord Provost of (Edinburgh, Glasgow)'; or 'The Lord Provost of (Aberdeen, Dundee, Elgin and Perth).' *Begin*, 'My Lord Provost', or 'My Lord'; refer to 'Your Lordship'. His wife is sometimes addressed 'The Lady Provost .

Marchioness. 'The Most Hon. the Marchioness of ——.' *Begin*, 'Madam'; refer to 'Your Ladyship'; *end*, 'I have the honour to be, Madam, Your Ladyship's obedient servant.'

Marquess. 'The Most Hon. the Marquess of ——.' *Begin*, 'My Lord Marquess'; refer to 'Your Lordship'; *end*, 'I have the honour to be, My Lord Marquess, Your Lordship's obedient servant.'

Mayor. 'The Worshipful the Mayor of ——'; or (if the Mayor of a City) 'The Right Worshipful the Mayor of ——.' *Begin*, 'Sir'; refer to 'Your Worship';

in speaking one refers usually to 'Mr. Mayor'; *end*, 'I remain, Sir, Your most obedient servant.'

Member of Parliament. The letters M.P. are added to the ordinary form of address.

Moderator of the Assembly of the Church of Scotland. 'To the Right Rev. the Moderator ——.' *Begin*, 'Right Rev. Sir'; *end*, 'I remain, Right Rev. Sir, Your most obedient servant.'

Officers in the Navy, Army, and Air Force. If a title is held this is added after the military rank, e.g., 'Admiral the Rt. Hon. the Viscount ——,' or 'Air Marshal Sir ——, K.C.B.'

The Pope. 'To His Holiness the Pope.' *Begin*, 'Your Holiness'; *end*, 'I have the honour to remain Your Holiness's most humble child.'

President of the U.S.A. 'To the President, The White House, Washington, D.C., U.S.A.' *Begin*, 'Dear Sir', 'Mr. President', or 'Dear Mr. President'; *end*, 'Yours faithfully'

Prime Minister. 'The Rt. Hon. ——, M.P.' or his personal title if any.

Prince of the British Royal House. 'His Royal Highness Prince (Christian name)'; or if a Duke, 'H.R.H. the Duke of ——.' In either case begin 'Sir'; refer to 'Your Royal Highness'; *end*, 'I remain, Sir, Your Royal Highness's most humble and obedient servant.'

Princess of the British Royal House. 'To H.R.H. Princess (Christian name)'; or if a Duchess, 'H.R.H. the Duchess of ——.' *Begin*, 'Madam'; refer to 'Your Royal Highness'; *end*, 'I have the honour to be, Madam, Your Royal Highness's most humble and obedient servant.'

Queen. 'To the Queen's Most Excellent Majesty.' *Begin*, 'Madam', or 'May it please Your Majesty'; refer to 'Your Majesty'; *end*, 'I remain, Madam, Your Majesty's most humble and obedient subject.

Representatives of the U.S. Congress. 'To the Hon. ——.' *Begin*, 'Dear Mr. Representative'.

Secretary of State. 'His Majesty's Principal Secretary of State for the (War) Department' or 'The Secretary of State for (War).'

Senators of the U.S. Congress. 'To the Hon. ——.' *Begin*, 'Dear Mr. Senator'.

Sons of Peers. The eldest son of a Duke, Marquess, or Earl uses, by courtesy, his father's second title and is addressed as though he actually held the peerage; where there is no second title in the family, he is called Lord —— (family name); younger sons of Dukes and Marquesses are styled Lord John —— (family name), their wives become Lady John ——. Younger sons of Earls and all sons of Viscounts and Barons are styled The Hon. John —— (family name), their wives The Hon. Mrs. ——. (The title Hon. is never used in speaking.)

Viscount. 'The Rt. Hon. the Viscount ——.' *Begin*, 'My Lord'; refer to 'Your Lordship'; *end*, 'I have the honour to be, my Lord, Your Lordship's obedient servant.'

Viscountess. 'The Rt. Hon. the Viscountess ——.' *Begin*, 'Madam'; refer to 'Your Ladyship'; *end*, as Countess.

Widow of a Peer. If the mother, stepmother or grandmother of the actual peer, she is formally 'The Dowager Duchess of ——', etc., when the actual peer is married. But it has become much more usual to use the style 'Jane, Duchess of ——,' etc. Similar usage applies to the **widow of a Baronet.**

Weights and Measures

METRIC SYSTEM

(base units indicated by **bold type**)

BRITISH SYSTEM

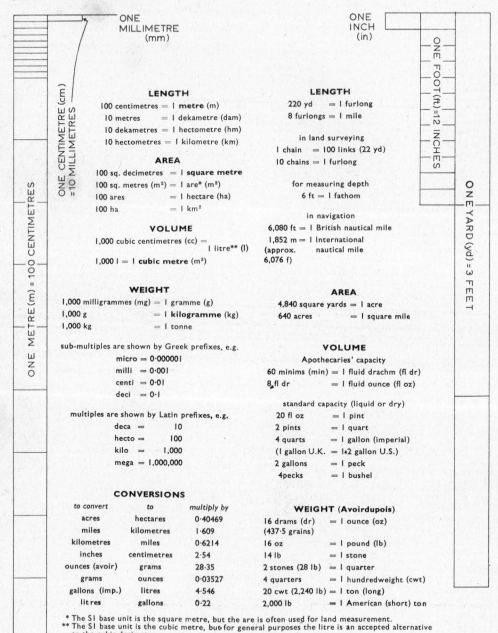

ONE
MILLIMETRE
(mm)

ONE
INCH
(in)

ONE CENTIMETRE (cm)
=10 MILLIMETRES

ONE METRE (m) = 100 CENTIMETRES

ONE FOOT (ft) =12 INCHES

ONE YARD (yd) = 3 FEET

LENGTH

100 centimetres	= 1 **metre** (m)
10 metres	= 1 dekametre (dam)
10 dekametres	= 1 hectometre (hm)
10 hectometres	= 1 kilometre (km)

AREA

100 sq. decimetres	= 1 **square metre**
100 sq. metres (m²)	= 1 are* (m²)
100 ares	= 1 hectare (ha)
100 ha	= 1 km²

VOLUME

1,000 cubic centimetres (cc) =
1 litre** (l)

1,000 l = 1 **cubic metre** (m³)

WEIGHT

1,000 milligrammes (mg)	= 1 gramme (g)
1,000 g	= 1 **kilogramme** (kg)
1,000 kg	= 1 tonne

sub-multiples are shown by Greek prefixes, e.g.

micro	= 0·000001
milli	= 0·001
centi	= 0·01
deci	= 0·1

multiples are shown by Latin prefixes, e.g.

deca	=	10
hecto	=	100
kilo	=	1,000
mega	=	1,000,000

CONVERSIONS

to convert	to	multiply by
acres	hectares	0·40469
miles	kilometres	1·609
kilometres	miles	0·6214
inches	centimetres	2·54
ounces (avoir)	grams	28·35
grams	ounces	0·03527
gallons (imp.)	litres	4·546
litres	gallons	0·22

LENGTH

| 220 yd | = 1 furlong |
| 8 furlongs | = 1 mile |

in land surveying

| 1 chain | = 100 links (22 yd) |
| 10 chains | = 1 furlong |

for measuring depth

6 ft = 1 fathom

in navigation

6,080 ft	= 1 British nautical mile
1,852 m	= 1 International
(approx.	nautical mile
6,076 f)	

AREA

| 4,840 square yards | = 1 acre |
| 640 acres | = 1 square mile |

VOLUME

Apothecaries' capacity

| 60 minims (min) | = 1 fluid drachm (fl dr) |
| 8 fl dr | = 1 fluid ounce (fl oz) |

standard capacity (liquid or dry)

20 fl oz	= 1 pint
2 pints	= 1 quart
4 quarts	= 1 gallon (imperial)
(1 gallon U.K.	= 1·2 gallon U.S.)
2 gallons	= 1 peck
4 pecks	= 1 bushel

WEIGHT (Avoirdupois)

16 drams (dr)	= 1 ounce (oz)
(437·5 grains)	
16 oz	= 1 pound (lb)
14 lb	= 1 stone
2 stones (28 lb)	= 1 quarter
4 quarters	= 1 hundredweight (cwt)
20 cwt (2,240 lb)	= 1 ton (long)
2,000 lb	= 1 American (short) ton

* The SI base unit is the square metre, but the are is often used for land measurement.
** The SI base unit is the cubic metre, but for general purposes the litre is an accepted alternative
    to the cubic decimetre.

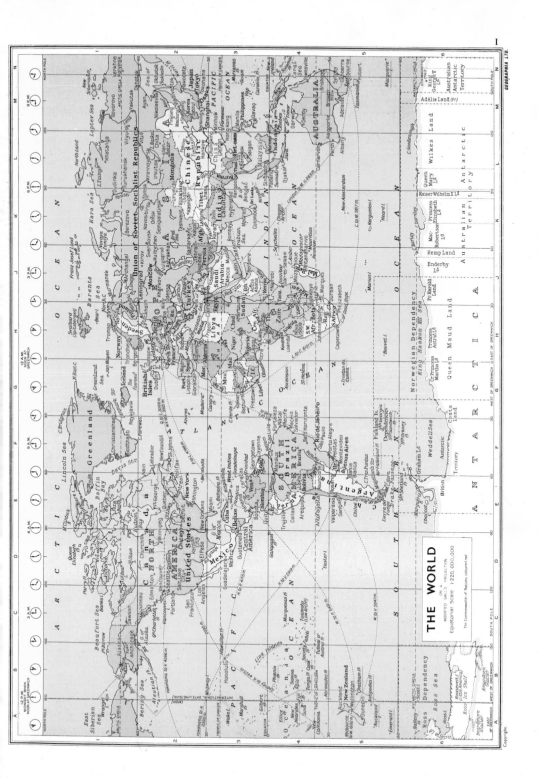

I

GEOGRAPHIA LTD.

THE WORLD

ON A
MODIFIED GALL'S PROJECTION
Equatorial Scale 1:220,000,000
The Commonwealth of Nations coloured red

Copyright

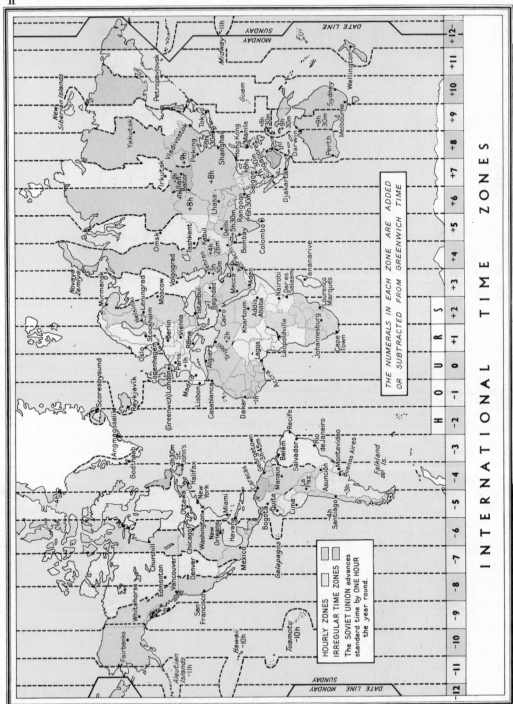

INTERNATIONAL TIME ZONES

THE NUMERALS IN EACH ZONE ARE ADDED
OR SUBTRACTED FROM GREENWICH TIME

HOURS

HOURLY ZONES
IRREGULAR TIME ZONES
The SOVIET UNION advances
standard time by ONE HOUR
the year round.

ENGLAND & WALES

Scale 1 : 4,080,000

Statute Miles

Kilometres

Sea route distances in nautical miles
Principal railways ——— Canals

GEOGRAPHIA LTD.

SCOTLAND

Scale 1 : 3,300,000
Statute Miles
Kilometres
Sea route distances in nautical miles
Railways ——— Canals ———

SHETLAND ISLANDS

ON SAME SCALE

GEOGRAPHIA LTD.

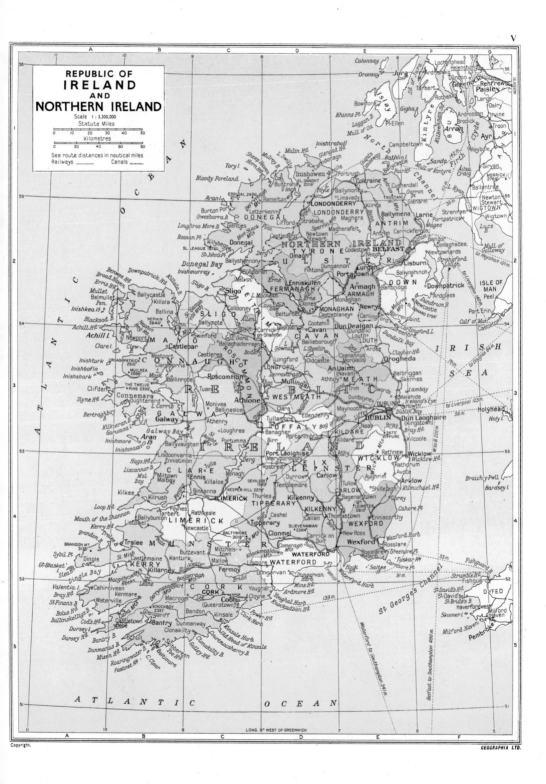

V

REPUBLIC OF
IRELAND
AND
NORTHERN IRELAND

Scale 1 : 3,300,000
Statute Miles

Kilometres

Sea route distances in nautical miles
Railways   Canals

GEOGRAPHIA LTD.

LONG. 8° WEST OF GREENWICH

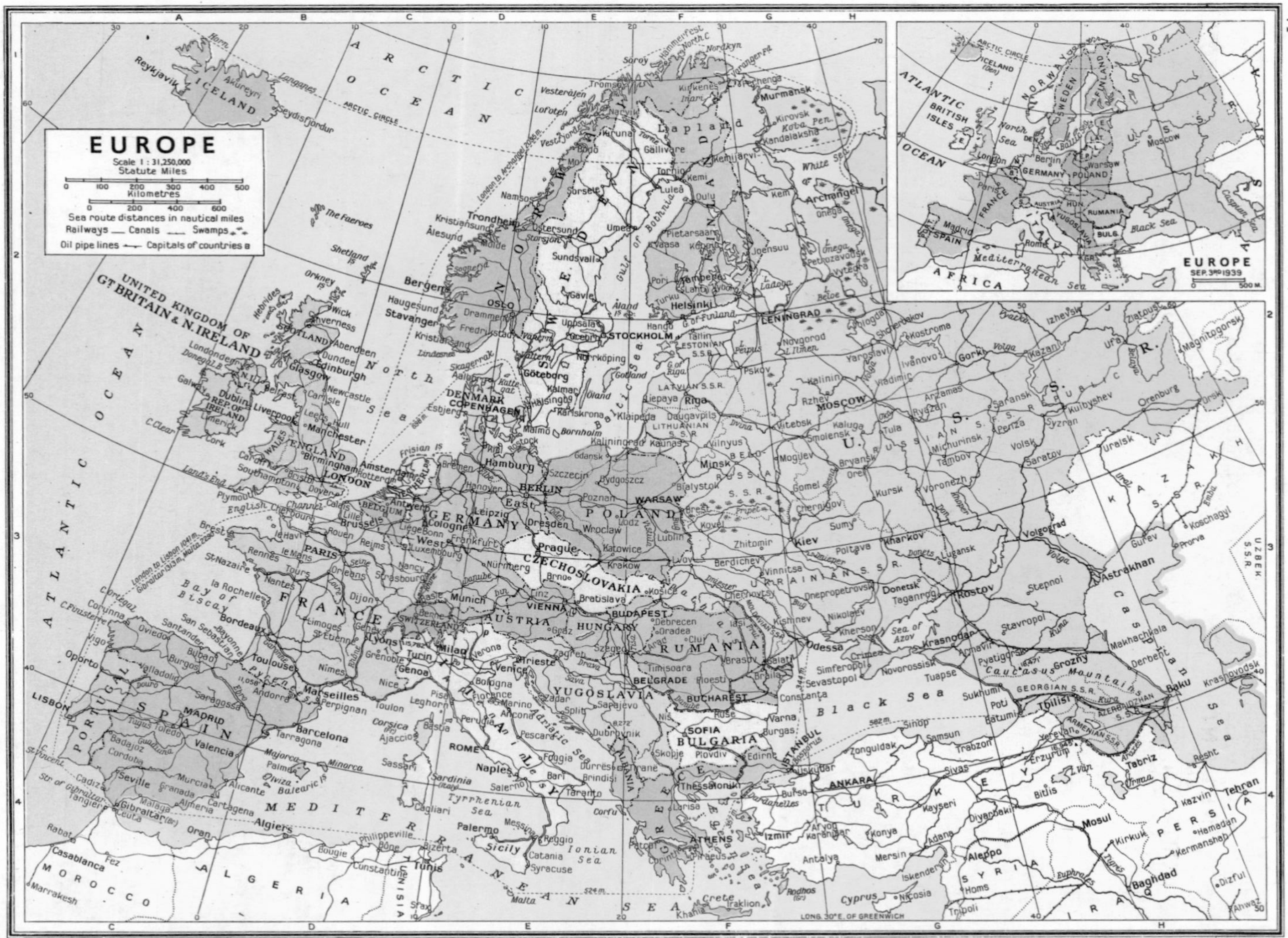

EUROPE

Scale 1 : 31,250,000
Statute Miles

Kilometers

Sea route distances in nautical miles
Railways — Canals — Swamps
Oil pipe lines — Capitals of countries ▣

UNITED KINGDOM OF
GT. BRITAIN & N. IRELAND

EUROPE

GEOGRAPHIA LTD.

Copyright

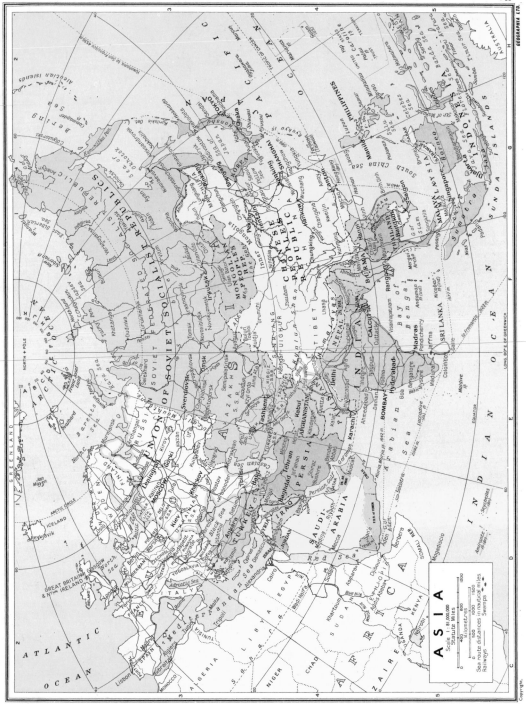

GEOGRAPHIA LTD.

A S I A

Scale 1:81,000,000
Statute Miles

Kilometres

Sea route distances in nautical miles
Railways
Swamps

Copyright.

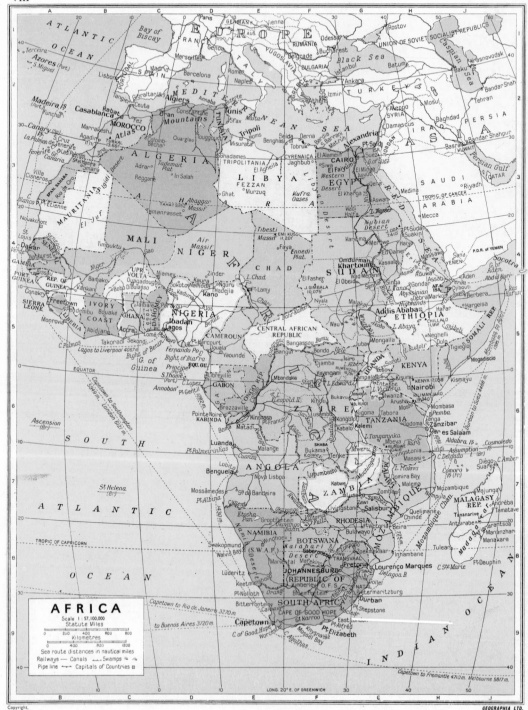

AFRICA

Scale 1 : 57,100,000
Statute Miles
0 200 400 600 800
Kilometres
0 400 800 1200

Sea route distances in nautical miles
Railways — Canals — Swamps
Pipe line — Capitals of Countries ⊡

LONG. 20° E. OF GREENWICH

Copyright.

GEOGRAPHIA LTD.

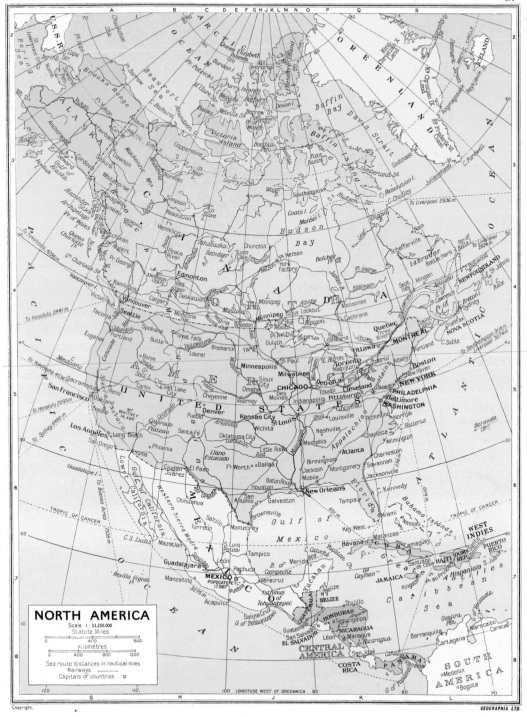

NORTH AMERICA

Scale 1 : 53,250,000

Statute Miles

0   400   800

Kilometres

0   400   800

Sea route distances in nautical miles
Railways
Capitals of countries

GEOGRAPHIA LTD.

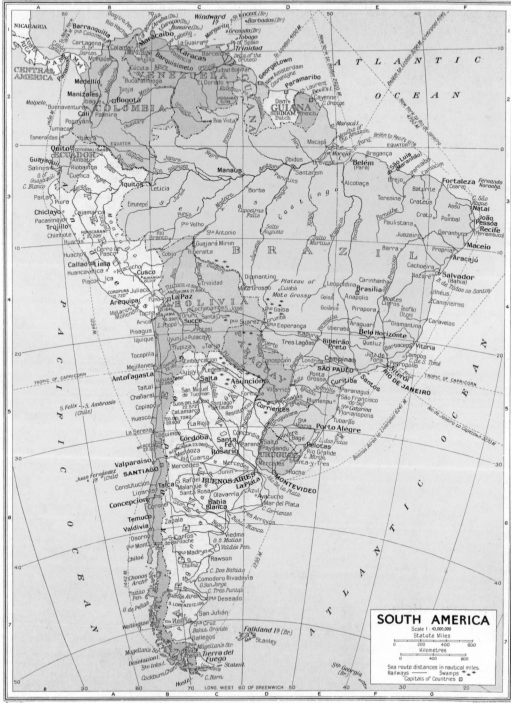

SOUTH AMERICA

Scale 1 : 43,000,000

Statute Miles

Kilometres

Sea route distances in nautical miles.
Railways   Swamps
Capitals of Countries ⊞

GEOGRAPHIA LTD.

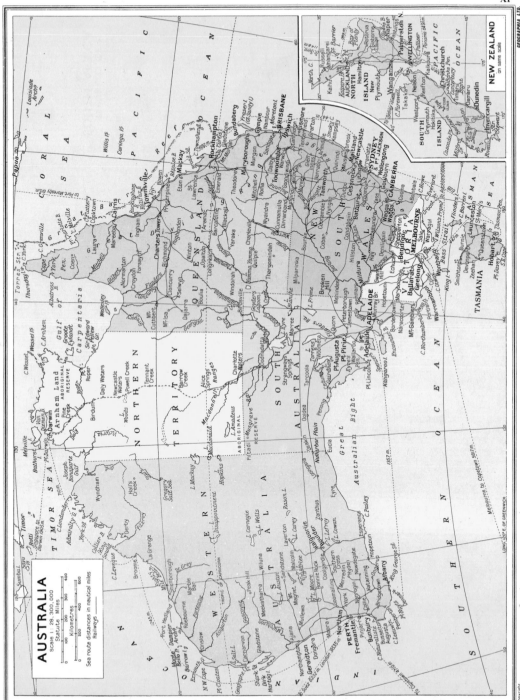

AUSTRALIA
Scale 1 : 28,300,000
Statute Miles
Kilometres
Sea route distances in nautical miles
Railways

NEW ZEALAND
on same scale

LONG. 133° E. OF GREENWICH

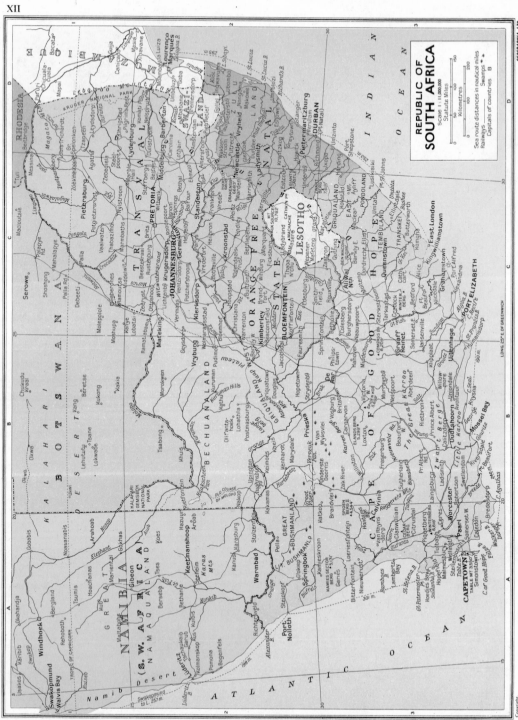

REPUBLIC OF
SOUTH AFRICA
Scale 1 : 11,000,000

Statute Miles

Kilometres

Sea route distances in nautical miles
Railways .... Swamps
Capitals of countries B

GEOGRAPHIA LTD